THE WORLD ALMANAC®

AND BOOK OF FACTS

2024

WORLD ALMANAC BOOKS

THE WORLD ALMANAC
AND BOOK OF FACTS
2024

Executive Editor: Sarah Janssen

Contributors: Emily Dolbear, Robert Famighetti, Matt Friedlander, Marshall Gerometta, Jacqueline Laks Gorman, Richard Hantula, M. L. Liu, Laurence A. Marschall, William A. McGeveran Jr., Jessica A. Newport, Janet M. Olson, John Rosenthal, Stevonnie Ross, Peter J. Schmidtke, Matthew Silverman, George W. Smith IV, Edward A. Thomas, Lori P. Wiesenfeld

Production: Newgen North America
Design and Production, Year in Pictures: Chris Schultz, Skyhorse Publishing
Design, Cover: Takeshi Takahashi
Photo Research: Edward A. Thomas
Index Editor: Nan Badgett

The World Almanac®
An imprint of Skyhorse Publishing, Inc.
Visit our website at www.skyhorsepublishing.com.
Please follow our publisher Tony Lyons on Instagram @tonylyonsisuncertain.

Hardcover	Ebook	Paperback
ISBN-13: 978-1-5107-7761-3	ISBN-13: 978-1-5107-7762-0	ISBN-13: 978-1-5107-7760-6
ISBN-10: 1-5107-7761-X	ISBN-10: 1-5107-7762-8	ISBN-10: 1-5107-7760-1

International Standard Serial Number
0084-1382

The World Almanac® and Book of Facts 2024
Book printed and bound in the United States of America
Date printed: November 2023
10 9 8 7 6 5 4 3 2 1

CONTENTS

2023: SPECIAL FEATURES AND YEAR IN REVIEW

THE WORLD ALMANAC AND BOOK OF FACTS 2024

Top 10 News Topics of 2023

1. Thousands Die in Unprecedented Hamas Attack on Israel, Ferocious Counterattack. The Palestinian militant group Hamas on Oct. 7 launched a surprise, coordinated assault on Israel. A Gaza-based rocket barrage was joined by a major ground assault, as militants overwhelmed border checkpoints, killed 1,400 Israeli soldiers and civilians, and took 240 hostages. Israel declared war on Hamas and responded with heavy and repeated air strikes against Gaza throughout the rest of Oct. An Oct. 17 rocket strike on or near a Gaza hospital killed almost 500 there, but the cause was being investigated. Gaza officials said more than 8,500 mostly civilian Palestinians—including over 3,500 children—had been killed as of Oct. 31. Israel cut off food, electricity, and fuel supplies to the enclave before allowing in limited humanitarian aid; more than 60% of Gaza's 2.3 mil residents were displaced by the end of Oct. Israeli ground incursions into Gaza began Oct. 27.

2. Russian Invasion of Ukraine Lingers. Russia's ongoing bloody invasion of Ukraine passed its 20th month in late Oct. with neither force showing signs of conceding. Aided by increasingly advanced weaponry from the U.S. and other allies, Ukraine ramped up air assaults throughout Sept. on the Crimean Peninsula—illegally annexed by Russia in 2014—including a missile attack that destroyed the headquarters of Russia's Black Sea naval fleet in Sevastopol. Extensive Russian minefields appeared to mostly stall Ukraine's counteroffensive—launched in early June—on multiple fronts. According to the UN, over 9,600 civilians were confirmed killed in the invasion as of Sept. 10, though the actual number was likely much higher. The U.S. in Aug. 2023 estimated Ukraine's combat casualties as perhaps 70,000 killed and 100,000-120,000 wounded and Russia's at around 300,000 (incl. 120,000 dead and at least 170,000 injured).

3. House Leadership in Chaos Amid Government Shutdown Threat. An ongoing fracture within the House's majority Republican caucus detonated Oct. 3 as far-right lawmakers initiated the ousting of House Speaker Kevin McCarthy (R, CA) from his leadership post, resulting in a 216-210 vote for the first removal of a speaker in U.S. history. The ouster followed McCarthy's decision to compromise with Democrats to pass an emergency 45-day funding bill—without spending cuts demanded by the far-right—to avoid a government shutdown at the end of Sept. When the GOP took narrow control (222-212) of the House in Jan. 2023, McCarthy was only able to secure the speakership on the 15th round of voting, after ultraconservatives forced major concessions, including the rule that made the vote to oust him easier. After 22 chaotic days, the House Oct. 25 elected as speaker far-right relative unknown Mike Johnson (R, LA), the fourth Republican nominated for the post since McCarthy's dismissal, as a Nov. 2023 shutdown threat loomed.

4. Former Pres. Trump Faces Scores of Charges in Four Criminal Indictments. Former Pres. Donald Trump by Aug. 14 faced 91 criminal felony charges—incl. 47 state counts—across four separate cases, at least three of which were scheduled to go to trial in 2024 as he campaigned as the Republican front-runner for the nation's top office. Trump, the first former or sitting president to be formally charged, pleaded not guilty to all counts. The first set of charges, unsealed in New York in early Apr., stemmed from a $130,000 "hush-money" payment made ahead of the 2016 election to cover up an alleged affair. A second state indictment, anti-racketeering (RICO) charges in Georgia issued in mid-Aug., concerned Trump's alleged attempt to conspire to alter the state's 2020 election outcome. The U.S. Justice Dept. charged Trump in June with mishandling classified government documents at his Mar-a-Lago, FL, estate, and again in June over his efforts to overturn the 2020 election results.

5. Inflation Ebbs Amid "Summer of Strikes," Other Economic Uncertainty. The annual U.S. inflation rate continued to decline from its 40-year-high 9.1% in June 2022 to 3.0% a year later—before creeping up to 3.7% in both Aug. and Sept.—as the Federal Reserve maintained its program of interest rate hikes to reach their highest levels since 2001. Average interest rates on 30-year fixed mortgages rose above 7.9% by Oct., their highest level since 2000. Annual wage growth beginning in May outpaced inflation for the first time in more than two years. A number of labor strikes—over 300 by mid-Oct.—included high-profile work stoppages by Hollywood screenwriters and actors, "Big Three" auto workers represented by the UAW, and Kaiser Permanente employees in what constituted the largest strike by health care workers in American history. But GDP growth remained high (4.9% annualized rate in the third quarter of 2023), and unemployment was at or near historic lows (under 4%).

6. Extreme Weather Events Wreak Havoc Around the World. The UN in a Sept. 2023 report again warned that nations continued to fall far short on reducing carbon emissions as needed to limit the rise of average global temperatures and avoid severe climate disorder. Numerous events and metrics were at least partially attributed to climate change, including flooding that killed thousands of people in eastern Libya and West Africa and Canada's worst wildfire season on record. Wildfires in Hawaii that killed 99 people in Aug. and severe flooding in California Jan.-Mar. were among a record 24 U.S. weather events in 2023 (as of Oct. 10) that caused estimated damages of $1 bil or more. Extreme heat waves gripped multiple Northern Hemisphere regions in July, contributing to that month's designation by NOAA as Earth's hottest on record.

7. Deadly Earthquakes Devastate Turkey, Syria, Morocco, and Afghanistan. A 7.8 magnitude earthquake struck south-central Turkey Feb. 6, killing more than 50,000 people there and over 8,400 in neighboring Syria, and displacing more than 5.9 mil people. In Turkey, police arrested more than 275 people accused of lax adherence to building codes, said to have contributed to the staggering death toll. Syrian Pres. Bashar al-Assad was accused of preventing aid from reaching areas held by groups he opposed. In Sept., a magnitude 6.8 earthquake in western Morocco killed at least 2,960 people, the month before two magnitude 6.3 quakes and numerous aftershocks killed more than 1,480 people in western Afghanistan.

8. WHO Ends Coronavirus Public Health Emergency as Pandemic Recedes. The World Health Org. May 5 ended its global health emergency designation for COVID-19, citing a more than yearlong decrease in cases globally. According to WHO data as of May 4, authorities had tallied over 6.9 mil cumulative confirmed deaths from the virus globally, including over 1.1 mil in the U.S., where the public health emergency formally ended on May 11. More than 13.4 bil vaccine doses had been administered globally at that time, with 5.1 bil persons fully vaccinated. In late Jan., officials in China said the massive wave of infections that struck the country after it abandoned its stringent "zero COVID" policy the month prior had peaked; some outside experts said up to 1.5 mil may have died in China amid the outbreak, far more than officially reported.

9. LGBTQ Rights, Race, and Abortion Dominate U.S. "Culture Wars." Republican-controlled states enacted a wave of anti-LGBTQ legislation in 2023, including a record number of measures restricting the rights of trans persons. Though at least 20 states approved bans on gender-affirming care for minors, a federal judge in June struck down Arkansas's first-in-the-nation ban. By Apr., the ACLU reported more than 60 bills restricting public school discussion of gender or sexuality, which corresponded with a surge in challenges of books with LGBTQ characters or by or about persons of color in schools and libraries. Abortion access after the 2022 overturning of *Roe v. Wade* remained contentious. Court challenges on access and new regulations played out nationwide; as of Oct. 24, abortion was banned or restricted in 21 states, according to the *NY Times*. In June, the U.S. Supreme Court, 6-3, ruled in favor of a designer who refused to create wedding websites for same-sex couples; the same majority also effectively outlawed race-conscious, or "affirmative action," admission programs at colleges and universities.

10. Biden Embraces Strict Border Rule as Migrant Surge Continues. Immigrant rights groups and some Democratic lawmakers condemned the Biden administration's new southern border policy requiring migrants to apply for asylum en route in another country before seeking refuge in the U.S. Mirroring a Trump-era restriction, it went into effect May 11 upon the expiration of the temporary COVID-era Title 42, which allowed border authorities to summarily turn away migrants entering illegally rather than allow them to remain in the U.S. while seeking asylum. Agents' daily encounters with migrants at the southern border reached a monthly record of nearly 270,000 in Sept., according to U.S. Customs and Border Protection, contributing to a record FY2023 total of 2.47 mil, above 2022's record 2.38 mil.

THE WORLD
AT A GLANCE

ELECTION PREVIEW, 2024

Key Election Dates by State, 2024

Source: National Conference of State Legislatures; The Green Papers

Political parties use primaries and caucuses to determine which candidates will run in the Nov. 5, 2024, general election.

Dates are subject to change by legislative action. The dates here are based on state election resources or statutory requirements as of July 2023, supplemented with additional research as of Oct. 2023. Some states schedule runoffs, which are not shown here, to be held after state primary voting.

Republican National Convention: July 15-18, 2024, Milwaukee, WI
Democratic National Convention: Aug. 19-22, 2024, Chicago, IL

State	Presidential primary or caucus	State primary	State	Presidential primary or caucus	State primary
Alabama	Mar. 5	Mar. 5	Montana	June 4	June 4
Alaska	Mar. 5 (R) | Apr. 6 (D)	Aug. 20	Nebraska	May 14	May 14
Arizona	Mar. 19	Aug. 6	Nevada	Feb. 6, Feb. 8 (R)[2]	June 11
Arkansas	Mar. 5	Mar. 5	New Hampshire	Jan. 23 (R)[3] | Feb. 6 (D)	Sept. 10
California	Mar. 5	Mar. 5	New Jersey	June 4	June 4
Colorado	Mar. 5	June 25	New Mexico	June 4	June 4
Connecticut	Apr. 2	Aug. 13	New York	Apr. 2	June 25
Delaware	Apr. 2	Sept. 3	North Carolina	Mar. 5	Mar. 5
Florida	Mar. 19	Aug. 20	North Dakota	Mar. 4 (R) | Apr. 6 (D)	June 11
Georgia	Mar. 12	May 21	Ohio	Mar. 19	Mar. 19
Hawaii	Mar. 12 (R) | Apr. 6 (D)	Aug. 10	Oklahoma	Mar. 5	June 18
Idaho	Mar. 2 (R) | May 23 (D)	May 21	Oregon	May 21	May 21
Illinois	Mar. 19	Mar. 19	Pennsylvania	Apr. 23	Apr. 23
Indiana	May 7	May 7	Rhode Island	Apr. 2	Sept. 10
Iowa	Jan. 15	June 4	South Carolina	Feb. 24 (R) | Feb. 3 (D)	June 11
Kansas	Mar. 19	Aug. 6	South Dakota	June 4	June 4
Kentucky	May 21	May 21	Tennessee	Mar. 5	Aug. 1
Louisiana	Mar. 23	Mar. 23	Texas	Mar. 5	Mar. 5
Maine	Mar. 5	June 11	Utah	Mar. 5	June 25
Maryland	May 14	Apr. 23	Vermont	Mar. 5	Aug. 13
Massachusetts	Mar. 5	Sept. 17	Virginia	Mar. 5	June 18
Michigan	Feb. 27	Aug. 6	Washington	Mar. 12	Aug. 6
Minnesota	Mar. 5	Aug. 13	West Virginia	May 14	May 14
Mississippi	Mar. 12	Mar. 12	Wisconsin	Apr. 2	Aug. 13
Missouri	Mar. 2 (R) | Mar. 23 (D)	Aug. 6	Wyoming	TBD (R) | Apr. 13 (D)	Aug. 20

TBD = To be determined as of Oct. 2023. (1) The Dem. Natl. Committee granted Iowa "conditional approval" to hold an in-person, Democratic presidential caucus Jan. 15, with results not released until Super Tuesday, Mar. 5. (2) Nevada scheduled a state-run presidential primary Feb. 6, two days before the Republican Party-run caucus Feb. 8. The Nevada GOP barred candidates from participating in both and said it would award delegates based on the results of the caucus. (3) The New Hampshire secretary of state is authorized by statute to pick a presidential primary date seven days earlier than any other state's presidential primary.

Presidential Candidate Fundraising Leaders, 2023

Source: Federal Election Commission
Reflects filings as of Sept. 30, 2023, unless noted.

Candidate	Total receipts	Total disbursements	Cash on hand
Donald Trump (R)	$60,523,078	$22,981,118	$37,541,961
Joe Biden (D)	56,760,363	24,840,472	32,180,366
Ron DeSantis (R)	31,647,462	19,320,557	12,326,905
Vivek Ramaswamy (R)	26,609,180	22,361,303	4,247,877
Nikki Haley (R)	18,709,236	7,157,544	11,551,692
Doug Burgum (R)	15,179,666	12,857,090	2,322,576
Robert F. Kennedy Jr. (Ind.)	15,078,528	8,906,488	6,172,041
Perry Johnson (R)	14,572,964	13,445,215	1,127,750
Tim Scott (R)	12,178,315	20,626,614	13,330,124
Ryan Binkley (R)	7,086,371	7,074,934	11,437
Chris Christie (R)	5,439,033	1,523,814	3,915,219
Mike Pence (R)[1]	4,525,729	3,344,277	1,181,452
Marianne Williamson (D)	2,676,034	2,621,842	104,005
William Hurd (R)[2]	1,452,538	1,229,464	223,074
Larry Elder (R)	1,437,945	1,193,444	244,501
Francis X. Suarez (R)[3]	1,425,517	1,365,124	60,393
Rollan Roberts II (R)	1,280,956	38,307	1,252,245
Asa Hutchinson (R)	1,249,302	924,015	325,287

(1) Suspended campaign, Oct. 30, 2023. (2) Withdrew from race, Oct. 9, 2023. (3) Withdrew from race, Aug. 29, 2023.

Presidential Candidates, 2024

Source: Federal Election Commission (FEC); candidate campaign websites; World Almanac research. Net worth, *Forbes*, Aug. 2023, unless noted. Opinion polls are averages for specified period, Real Clear Politics; some candidates did not have a presence in the site's polling averages.

Democratic Candidates

Joe Biden

Full name: Joseph Robinette Biden Jr.
Born: Nov. 20, 1942, in Scranton, PA
Inauguration Day age: 82 years old
Home state: Delaware
Education: BA, Univ. of Delaware, 1965; JD, Syracuse Univ., 1968
Religion: Roman Catholic
Military service: none
Family: married Neilia Hunter (1942-72), 1966; children: Beau (1969-2015), Hunter (b. 1970), Naomi (1971-72); married Jill Tracy Biden (née Jacobs) (b. 1951), 1977; children: Ashley (b. 1981).
Net worth: $10 mil
Career highlights: attorney/public defender, Wilmington, DE, 1969-72; member, New Castle County Council, 1970-72; U.S. senator (DE), 1973-2009; chair, Senate Judiciary Committee, 1987-95; chair, Foreign Relations Committee, 2001-03, 2007-09; contender for Dem. presidential nomination, 1988, 2008; U.S. vice president, 2009-17; president, 2021- .
Announced candidacy: Apr. 25, 2023
Opinion polls: Party support, Oct. 1, 2023: 64.9%; highest rating, Sept. 14, 2023: 67.8%.
Website: joebiden.com

Dean Phillips

Full name: Dean Benson Phillips
Born: Jan. 20, 1969, in St. Paul, MN, as Dean Benson Pfefer
Inauguration Day age: 56 years old
Home state: Minnesota
Education: BA, Brown Univ., 1991; MBA, Univ. of Minnesota, 2000.
Religion: Jewish
Military service: none (birth father, a U.S. Army captain, was killed in Vietnam War helicopter crash, 1969)
Family: married Karin Einisman, 1995; two children; div. 2015; married Annalise Glick, 2019.
Net worth: $124 mil (OpenSecrets.org, 2020)
Career highlights: Pres./CEO, Phillips Distilling Co., 2000-12; CEO, Talenti, 2012-14; founder, Penny's Coffee, 2016-22; U.S. representative (D, MN), 2019-present.
Announced candidacy: Oct. 26, 2023
Website: www.dean24.com

Cenk Uygur

Full name: Cenk Kadir Uygur
Born: Mar. 21, 1970
Inauguration Day age: 54 years old
Home state: California
Education: BS, Wharton School of Business, Univ. of Pennsylvania; JD, Columbia Univ.
Religion: Agnostic
Military service: none
Family: Married Wendy Lang; two children.
Career highlights: host/cofounder of *The Young Turks* show, 2002; cofounder, Justice Democrats PAC, 2017; primary candidate for U.S. representative (CA), 2020.
Announced candidacy: Oct. 12, 2023
Website: www.cenkforamerica.com

Marianne Williamson

Full name: Marianne Deborah Williamson
Born: July 8, 1952, in Houston, TX
Inauguration Day age: 72 years old
Home state: California
Education: coursework, Pomona Coll.
Religion: Jewish
Military service: none
Family: briefly married, 1979; one child.
Net worth: $2.5 mil (*Forbes* est., Oct. 2023)
Career highlights: author of 15 self-help/spirituality books; founder, Project Angel Food, 1989; pastor, Unity Church, 1998-2002; cofounder, The Peace Alliance, 2004; contender for Dem. presidential nomination, 2020.
Announced candidacy: Feb. 23, 2023
Opinion polls. Party support, Oct. 1, 2023: 4.8%; highest rating, Apr. 27-May 8, 2023: 8.5%.
Website: marianne2024.com

Republican Candidates

Donald J. Trump

Full name: Donald John Trump
Born: June 14, 1946, in Queens, NY
Inauguration Day age: 78 years old
Home state: New York
Education: Fordham Univ., 1964-66; BS, Wharton School of Finance, Univ. of Pennsylvania, 1968
Religion: Nondenominational Christian
Military service: none
Family: married Ivana Marie Trump (née Zelnícková) (1949-2022), 1977; children: Donald Jr. (b. 1977), Ivanka (b. 1981), Eric (b. 1984); div. 1992; married Marla Maples (b. 1963), 1993; daughter: Tiffany (b. 1993); div. 1999; married Melania Trump (née Knauss) (b. 1970), 2005; son: Barron (b. 2006).
Net worth: $2.6 bil (*Forbes* est., Oct. 2023)
Career highlights: assumed control of family business, 1971; star and coproducer, NBC's *The Apprentice* and *Celebrity Apprentice*, 2004-15; president of the U.S., 2017-21.
Announced candidacy: Nov. 15, 2022
Opinion polls. Party support, Oct. 1, 2023: 56.9%; highest rating, Sept. 20, 2023: 58.8%.
Website: www.donaldjtrump.com

Ryan Binkley

Born: Nov. 19, 1967, in Columbus, GA
Inauguration Day age: 57 years old
Home state: Texas
Education: BBA, Univ. of Texas; MBA, Southern Methodist Univ.
Religion: Nondenominational Christian
Military service: none
Family: married Ellie Binkley, 1999; five children.
Net worth: $75 mil (spokesperson's claim, unaudited, July 2023)
Career highlights: pres./CEO, Generational Group, 2006-present; cofounder/pastor of Create Church, 2013-present.
Announced candidacy: Apr. 23, 2023
Website: binkley2024.com

Doug Burgum

Full name: Douglas James Burgum
Born: Aug. 1, 1956, in Arthur, ND
Inauguration Day age: 68 years old
Home state: North Dakota
Education: BA, North Dakota State Univ., 1978; MBA, Stanford Univ., 1980
Military service: none
Family: married Karen Stoker, 1991; three children; div. 2003; married Kathryn Helgaas, 2016.
Net worth: $1.1 bil (Yahoo! Finance, Sept. 2022)

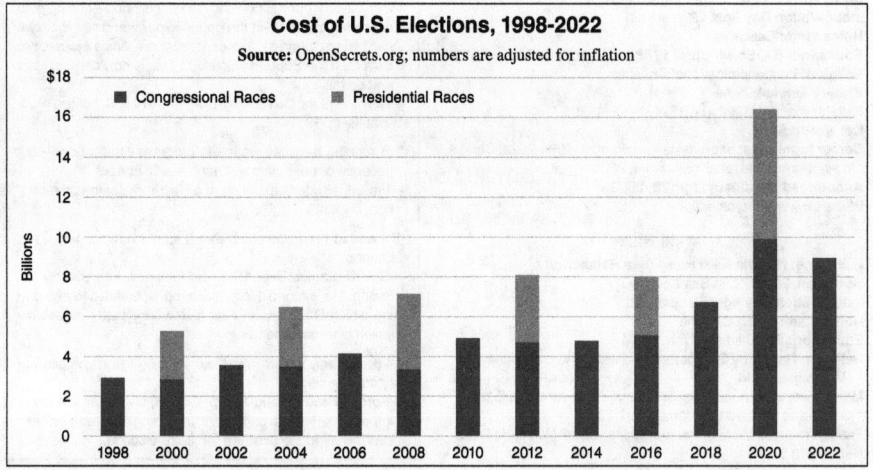

Cost of U.S. Elections, 1998-2022

Source: OpenSecrets.org; numbers are adjusted for inflation

Career highlights: CEO/chair, Great Plains Software, 1983-2001 (sold co. to Microsoft); senior vice pres., Microsoft, 2001-07; venture capitalist, 2008-16; North Dakota governor, 2016-present.
Announced candidacy: June 7, 2023
Opinion polls. Party support, Oct. 1, 2023: 0.9%; highest rating, Oct. 4, 2023: 1.1%.
Website: www.dougburgum.com

Chris Christie

Full name: Christopher James Christie
Born: Sept. 6, 1962, in Newark, NJ
Inauguration Day age: 62 years old
Home state: New Jersey
Education: BS, Univ. of Delaware, 1984; JD, Seton Hall Univ., 1987
Religion: Roman Catholic
Military service: none
Family: married Mary Pat Foster, 1986; four children.
Net worth: $15 mil (Forbes est., Oct. 2023)
Career highlights: attorney, 1987-present; lobbyist, 1999-2001; U.S. attorney, 2002-08; New Jersey governor, 2010-18; contender for Rep. presidential nomination, 2016.
Announced candidacy: June 6, 2023
Opinion polls. Party support, Oct. 1, 2023: 2.9%; highest rating, Sept. 11, 2023: 3.6%.
Website: chrischristie.com

Ron DeSantis

Full name: Ronald Dion DeSantis
Born: September 14, 1978, in Jacksonville, FL
Inauguration Day age: 46 years old
Home state: Florida
Education: BA, Yale Univ., 2001; JD, Harvard Law School, 2005
Religion: Roman Catholic
Military service: U.S. Navy, 2004-10 (active), 2010-19 (reserve); retired rank: lt. commander
Family: married Casey DeSantis (née Black), 2009; three children.
Net worth: $1.5 mil (Forbes est., Sept. 2023)
Career highlights: Navy Judge Advocate General's Corps (JAG), 2004-08; special assistant U.S. attorney, 2008-10; U.S. representative (FL), 2013-18; Florida governor, 2019-present.
Announced candidacy: May 24, 2023
Opinion polls. Party support, Oct. 1, 2023: 13.5%; highest rating, Jan. 20-23, 2023: 31.3%.
Website: rondesantis.com

Larry Elder

Full name: Laurence Allen Elder
Born: Apr. 27, 1952, in Los Angeles, CA
Inauguration Day age: 72 years old
Home state: California
Education: BA, Brown Univ., 1974; JD, Univ. of Michigan, 1977
Religion: nondenominational Christian
Military service: none
Family: married, 1992; div. 1994.
Net worth: $4 mil
Career highlights: attorney; talk-radio host, 1994-2022; California gubernatorial recall contender, 2021.
Announced candidacy: Apr. 20, 2023
Website: www.larryelder.com

Nikki Haley

Full name: Nimrata Nikki Haley (née Randhawa)
Born: Jan. 20, 1972, in Bamberg, SC
Inauguration Day age: 53 years old
Home state: South Carolina
Education: BS, Clemson Univ., 1994
Religion: Raised by Sikh parents; converted to Christianity (Methodist), 1996
Military service: none (husband served with Army National Guard and deployed to Afghanistan, 2013).
Family: married Michael Haley, 1996; children: Nalin and Rena.
Net worth: $8 mil

Campaign Trail Quotes, 2023

"Wokeness is a virus more dangerous than any pandemic, hands down."
—Fmr. UN Ambassador Nikki Haley (R), Mar. 3, at the Conservative Political Action Conference (CPAC).

"I'm living proof that America is the land of opportunity and not a land of oppression."
—Sen. Tim Scott (R, SC) May 22 in event in North Charleston, SC, launching his 2024 Republican presidential campaign.

"I will do what I need to do to be up on that stage to try to save my party and save my country."
—Fmr. New Jersey Gov. Chris Christie (R), on CNN June 18, regarding his pledge to support the eventual Republican nominee as a condition the party required to be debate eligible.

"COVID-19 is targeted to attack Caucasians and Black people. The people who are most immune are Ashkenazi Jews and Chinese. We don't know if it was deliberately targeted or not."
—Robert F. Kennedy Jr., attorney and then-contender for the Democratic presidential nomination, July 11, in video first published by NY Post; the false remarks drew strong criticism and Kennedy later declared he was neither a racist nor an anti-Semite.

"We're going to have all these deep state people, you know, we're going to start slitting throats on day one."
—Florida Gov. Ron DeSantis (R) in remarks at a Rye, NH, campaign event July 30.

"I'm a wrestling fan. I'm imagining a royal rumble on the debate stage."
—Jaime Harrison, chair of the Democratic National Committee, Aug. 21, in anticipation of the first Republican presidential debate.

"If you have a broken car, you don't turn over the keys to the people who broke it again."
—Vivek Ramaswamy (R), at first Republican debate Aug. 23, in Milwaukee, WI.

"It would be a great thing if both President Biden and former President Trump would stand aside."
—Sen. Mitt Romney (R, UT), in remarks to reporters after announcing Sept. 13 he would not run for reelection in part due to his age; the former presidential nominee urged other candidates to do the same.

"Both sides of our nation—they're very divided—can point to examples of people in the opposite party and say, look, we can't trust Congress. We can't trust the White House. We can't trust the Supreme Court. ... This is how democracies end up failing."
—North Dakota Gov. Doug Burgum, to NPR Politics Podcast, Sept. 19

"I'm running because we made progress—that's good—but because our democracy, I think, is still at risk."
—Pres. Joe Biden, speaking at a New York campaign reception, Sept. 20.

"If I was at home watching that, I would have changed the channel."
—Gov. DeSantis, Sept. 27, in an interview immediately following the second Republican presidential debate, during which DeSantis and six fellow candidates repeatedly yelled over one another.

"I'll be the only politician in history where I won't be allowed to criticize people."
—Former Pres. Donald Trump, Oct. 16, shortly after a judge imposed a limited gag order regarding the federal case over his efforts to overturn the 2020 election.

Career highlights: South Carolina state representative, 2005-11; South Carolina governor, 2011-17; UN ambassador, 2017-18.
Announced candidacy: Feb. 14, 2023
Opinion polls. Party support, Oct. 1, 2023: 6.5%; highest rating, Oct. 17, 2023: 7.8%.
Website: nikkihaley.com

Asa Hutchinson

Full name: William Asa Hutchinson II
Born: Dec. 3, 1950, in Bentonville, AR
Inauguration Day age: 74 years old
Home state: Arkansas
Education: BA, Bob Jones Univ., 1972; JD, Univ. of Arkansas, 1975
Religion: Baptist
Military service: none
Family: married Susan Burrell Hutchinson, 1973; children: Asa III, John, Seth, and Sarah
Net worth: $1.5 mil
Career highlights: U.S. attorney, 1982-85; U.S. representative (AR), 1997-2001; director, Drug Enforcement Admin., 2001-03; Arkansas governor, 2015-23
Announced candidacy: Apr. 2, 2023
Opinion polls. Party support, Oct. 1, 2023: 0.9%; highest rating, May 21-22, 2023: 1.3%.
Website: www.asa2024.com

Perry Johnson

Full name: Perry Lawrence Johnson
Inauguration Day age: 76 years old
Home state: Michigan
Education: BS, Univ. of Illinois at Urbana-Champaign; grad. coursework, Univ. of Detroit
Military service: none
Family: married Diana Johnson, 2008; three children.
Career highlights: international quality-control standards expert, author, and entrepreneur; Michigan gubernatorial contender, 2022 (did not appear on ballot).
Announced candidacy: Mar. 2, 2023
Website: www.perryjohnson.com

Mike Pence

Full name: Michael Richard Pence
Born: June 7, 1959, in Columbus, IN
Inauguration Day age: 65 years old
Home state: Indiana
Education: BA, Hanover Coll., 1981; JD, Indiana Univ. School of Law, 1986
Religion: Evangelical Christian
Military service: none
Family: married Karen Pence (neé Batten) (b. 1957), 1985; children: Michael, Charlotte, Audrey.
Net worth: $4 mil (*Forbes* est., July 2023)
Career highlights: attorney in private practice, 1986-91; pres., Indiana Policy Review Foundation, 1991-93; host, syndicated radio talk show, 1992-99, and morning TV talk show, 1995-99; U.S. representative (IN), 2001-13; chair, House Republican Conference, 2009-11; Indiana governor, 2013-17; U.S. vice president, 2017-21.
Announced candidacy: June 7, 2023
Opinion polls. Party support, Oct. 1, 2023: 3.9%; highest rating, July 1-11, 2022: 9.3%.
Website: mikepence2024.com

Vivek Ramaswamy

Full name: Vivek Ganapathy Ramaswamy
Born: Aug. 9, 1985, in Cincinnati, OH
Inauguration Day age: 39 years old
Home state: Ohio
Education: BA, Harvard Univ., 2007; JD, Yale Univ., 2013
Religion: Hindu
Military service: none
Family: married Dr. Apoorva Ramaswamy (née Tewari), 2015; two children.

Net worth: $950 mil
Career highlights: author; partner, QVT Financial, 2007-14; founder/CEO, Roivant Sciences drug co., 2014-21; founder, Strive Asset Management, 2022.
Announced candidacy: Feb. 21, 2023
Opinion polls. Party support, Oct. 1, 2023: 5.2%; highest rating, Sept. 21, 2023: 8.1%.
Website: www.vivek2024.com

Tim Scott

Full name: Timothy Eugene Scott
Born: Sept. 19, 1965, in North Charleston, SC
Inauguration Day age: 59 years old
Home state: South Carolina
Education: coursework, Presbyterian Coll.; BS, Charleston Southern Univ., 1988
Religion: Evangelical Christian
Military service: none
Family: Never married; no children.
Net worth: $1 mil
Career highlights: insurance agent/financial advisor; member, Charleston County Council, 1995-2008; South Carolina representative, 2009-11; U.S. representative (SC), 2011-13; U.S. senator (SC), 2013-present.
Announced candidacy: May 22, 2023
Opinion polls. Party support, Oct. 1, 2023: 2.6%; highest rating, July 2-5, 2023: 3.6%.
Website: votetimscott.com

Independent Candidates
Robert F. Kennedy Jr.

Party: Independent (originally filed to run as Democrat)
Full name: Robert Francis Kennedy Jr.
Born: Jan. 17, 1954, in Washington, DC
Inauguration Day age: 71 years old
Home state: New York
Education: BA, Harvard Univ., 1976; London School of Economics; JD, Univ. of Virginia School of Law, 1982; LLM, Pace Law School, 1987
Religion: Roman Catholic
Military service: none
Family: married Emily Ruth Black (b. 1957), 1982; children: Robert (b. 1984), Kathleen (b. 1988); div. 1994; married Mary Kathleen Richardson (1959-2012), 1994; children: Conor (b. 1994), Kyra (b. 1995), William (b. 1997), Aidan (b. 2001); married Cheryl Hines (b. 1965), 2014.
Net worth: $15 mil
Career highlights: environmental lawyer, 1985-present; Riverkeeper, 1985-2017; cofounder/pres., Waterkeeper Alliance, 1999-2020; founder/chair, Children's Health Defense, 2018-present.
Announced candidacy: Apr. 5, 2023
Opinion polls. Party support, Oct. 1, 2023: 14.9%; highest rating, Apr. 27-May 8, 2023: 20.0%.
Website: www.kennedy24.com

Cornel West

Party: Independent (originally intended to run for nomination of People's Party, then of Green Party)
Full name: Cornel Ronald West
Born: June 2, 1953, in Tulsa, OK
Inauguration Day age: 72 years old
Home state: California
Education: BA, Harvard Univ., 1973; MA, PhD, Princeton Univ., 1980
Religion: Christian
Military service: none
Family: Four previous marriages; married Dr. Annahita Mahdavi West, 2021; two children
Net worth:
Career highlights: author of 20 books, incl. *Race Matters* (1993), *Democracy Matters* (2004); philosophy, African American Studies, and American Studies professor, Union Theological Seminary, Yale Univ., Princeton Univ., Harvard Univ.
Announced candidacy: June 5, 2023
Website: www.cornelwest2024.com

STATE GOVERNMENT

Governors of States and Territories

Source: National Governors Assn.; Council of State Governments; World Almanac research
As of Oct. 2023, of the 50 state governors, 26 were Republicans and 24 were Democrats. Salary information is as of Jan. 2023 unless noted. Some governors forego or donate their salary.

State/territory	Governor	Term began	Term ends	Previous terms served	Maximum consecutive terms	Salary
Alabama	Kay Ivey (R)	Jan. 2023	Jan. 2027	1+	2	$124,563
Alaska	Mike Dunleavy (R)	Dec. 2022	Dec. 2026	1	2	145,000
American Samoa	Lemanu P.S. Mauga (D)	Jan. 2021	Jan. 2025	—	2	90,000[1]
Arizona	Katie Hobbs (D)	Jan. 2023	Jan. 2027	—	2	95,000
Arkansas	Sarah Huckabee Sanders (R)	Jan. 2023	Jan. 2027	—	2	158,739
California	Gavin Newsom (D)	Jan. 2023	Jan. 2027	1	2	218,556
Colorado	Jared Polis (D)	Jan. 2023	Jan. 2027	1	2	90,000
Connecticut	Ned Lamont (D)	Jan. 2023	Jan. 2027	1	—	150,000
Delaware	John Carney (D)	Jan. 2021	Jan. 2025	1	2	171,000
Florida	Ron DeSantis (R)	Jan. 2023	Jan. 2027	1	2	134,181
Georgia	Brian Kemp (R)	Jan. 2023	Jan. 2027	1	2	175,000
Guam	Lou Leon Guerrero (D)	Jan. 2023	Jan. 2027	1	2	130,000[1]
Hawaii	Josh Green (D)	Dec. 2022	Dec. 2026	—	2	165,048
Idaho	Brad Little (R)	Jan. 2023	Jan. 2027	1	—	138,302
Illinois	JB Pritzker (D)	Jan. 2023	Jan. 2027	1	—	184,758
Indiana	Eric Holcomb (R)	Jan. 2021	Jan. 2025	1	2	134,051
Iowa	Kim Reynolds (R)	Jan. 2023	Jan. 2027	1+	—	130,000
Kansas	Laura Kelly (D)	Jan. 2023	Jan. 2027	1	2	110,707
Kentucky	Andy Beshear (D)	Dec. 2019	Dec. 2023	—	2	152,181
Louisiana[2]	John Bel Edwards (D)	Jan. 2020	Jan. 2024	1	2	130,000
Maine	Janet Mills (D)	Jan. 2023	Jan. 2027	1	2	70,000
Maryland	Wes Moore (D)	Jan. 2023	Jan. 2027	—	2	180,000
Massachusetts	Maura Healey (D)	Jan. 2023	Jan. 2027	—	—	185,000
Michigan	Gretchen Whitmer (D)	Jan. 2023	Jan. 2027	1	2	159,300
Minnesota	Tim Walz (D)	Jan. 2023	Jan. 2027	1	—	127,629
Mississippi	Tate Reeves (R)	Jan. 2020	Jan. 2024	—	2	122,160
Missouri	Mike Parson (R)	Jan. 2021	Jan. 2025	1+	2	137,167
Montana	Greg Gianforte (R)	Jan. 2021	Jan. 2025	—	2	118,397
Nebraska	Jim Pillen (R)	Jan. 2023	Jan. 2027	—	2	105,000
Nevada	Joe Lombardo (R)	Jan. 2023	Jan. 2027	—	2	163,474
New Hampshire	Chris Sununu (R)	Jan. 2023	Jan. 2025	3	—	144,483
New Jersey	Phil Murphy (D)	Jan. 2022	Jan. 2026	1	2	175,000
New Mexico	Michelle Lujan Grisham (D)	Jan. 2023	Jan. 2027	1	2	110,000
New York	Kathy Hochul (D)	Jan. 2023	Jan. 2027	—+	2	250,000
North Carolina	Roy Cooper (D)	Jan. 2021	Jan. 2025	1	2	165,750
North Dakota	Doug Burgum (R)	Dec. 2020	Dec. 2024	—	—	140,830
Northern Mariana Islands	Arnold Palacios (I)	Jan. 2023	Jan. 2027	—	2	70,000[1]
Ohio	Mike DeWine (R)	Jan. 2023	Jan. 2027	1	2	168,106
Oklahoma	Kevin Stitt (R)	Jan. 2023	Jan. 2027	1	2	147,000
Oregon	Tina Kotek (D)	Jan. 2023	Jan. 2027	—	2	98,600
Pennsylvania	Josh Shapiro (D)	Jan. 2023	Jan. 2027	—	2	213,026
Puerto Rico	Pedro Pierluisi (D)	Jan. 2021	Jan. 2025	—	2	70,000[1]
Rhode Island	Dan McKee (D)	Jan. 2023	Jan. 2027	—+	2	145,755
South Carolina	Henry McMaster (R)	Jan. 2023	Jan. 2027	1+	2	106,078
South Dakota	Kristi Noem (R)	Jan. 2023	Jan. 2027	1	2	121,578
Tennessee	Bill Lee (R)	Jan. 2023	Jan. 2027	1	2	204,336
Texas	Greg Abbott (R)	Jan. 2023	Jan. 2027	2	—	153,750
Utah	Spencer Cox (R)	Jan. 2021	Jan. 2025	—	—	165,600
Vermont	Phil Scott (R)	Jan. 2023	Jan. 2025	2	—	191,734
Virgin Islands	Albert Bryan (D)	Jan. 2023	Jan. 2027	1	2	150,000[1]
Virginia	Glenn Youngkin (R)	Jan. 2022	Jan. 2026	—	1	175,000
Washington	Jay Inslee (D)	Jan. 2021	Jan. 2025	2	—	187,353
West Virginia	Jim Justice (R)	Jan. 2021	Jan. 2025	1	2	150,000
Wisconsin	Tony Evers (D)	Jan. 2023	Jan. 2027	1	—	152,756
Wyoming	Mark Gordon (R)	Jan. 2023	Jan. 2027	—	2	105,000

— = Not applicable. + = Served an additional partial term, most often due to prior governor leaving office following resignation or appointment to another post. (1) As of 2021. (2) Louisiana Atty. Gen. Jeff Landry (R) won 51.6% of the vote in the state's first-round voting Oct. 14, 2023, forestalling a runoff, to become governor-elect.

CHRONOLOGY OF EVENTS

Nov. 1, 2022, to Oct. 31, 2023

The Chronology of Events reports the top National, International, and General news stories, month by month.

November 2022

National

Republicans Make Gains in House; Democrats Hold Senate—Republicans achieved a muted victory in general election voting Nov. 8, gaining control of the House of Representatives by a slim margin and adding a check on the Democratic Party, which had controlled both the legislative and executive branches of the federal government since Pres. Joe Biden took office in Jan. 2021. Falling short of a decisive "red wave" House takeover, the GOP added a net total of 10 seats (for a 222-213 majority) after close races were decided. Rep. Kevin McCarthy (R, CA), entering his ninth term, was widely expected to serve as House Speaker when the 118th Congress convened in Jan. 2023, though several far-right members of the party publicly said they would not support him. On Nov. 30, House Democrats elected Rep. Hakeem Jeffries (NY) to lead the party in place of Rep. Nancy Pelosi (CA), who stepped down from her leadership role after 20 years; Jeffries became the first Black representative to lead a party delegation in Congress.

Democrats maintained control of the Senate without any losses and picked up a highly contested open seat in Pennsylvania, previously held by a Republican, after the state's lieutenant governor John Fetterman defeated GOP nominee Mehmet Oz by nearly five points. Incumbent Democrats prevailed in tight races against challengers in Arizona and Nevada. The race in Georgia between former football star Herschel Walker (R) and incumbent Sen. Raphael Warnock went to a Dec. 6 runoff after neither candidate drew the state-required 50% threshold; Warnock prevailed, 51.4% to 48.6%, securing the Democrats' 51-49 majority.

Democratic and GOP gubernatorial candidates each won 18 races from among the 36 seats at stake, with Republicans flipping one seat (Nevada) and Democrats three (Arizona, Maryland, Massachusetts). Arizona secretary of state Katie Hobbs edged Trump-backed election denier Kari Lake in arguably the country's most closely watched governor's race.

According to the U.S. Elections Project, more than 115.5 mil Americans (46.6% of eligible voters) participated in the 2022 elections, down from 50.0% in 2018.

FTX Digital Currency Platform Collapses; Turbulent Twitter Takeover Commences; More Tech Layoffs; Other Business, Economic News—The Bahamas-based cryptocurrency exchange FTX—valued at $32 bil in early 2022 and reportedly the world's second-largest crypto market by trading volume—declared bankruptcy and its CEO Sam Bankman-Fried resigned Nov. 11. A Nov. 2 report by news site CoinDesk had revealed a large portion of the assets of FTX's trading arm, Alameda Research, consisted of FTX-issued cryptocurrency.

In early Nov., a little over a week after acquiring social media company Twitter, billionaire owner Elon Musk fired via email about half of its 7,500 employees, followed by approximately 4,400 contract employees on Nov. 13. Some advertisers announced they would stop marketing on the platform, reportedly over concerns of Twitter loosening its content moderation policies.

Reflecting tech industry fears of a looming recession, Facebook Nov. 9 laid off more than 11,000 employees. Five days later, the *NY Times* reported plans by Amazon to cut 10,000 jobs.

The Federal Reserve amid stubbornly elevated inflation levels raised its benchmark interest rate on Nov. 2 by 0.75%, to 3.75%-4%, the highest rate since 2008, marking its fourth straight three-quarters point hike among six increases in 2022. Annual U.S. inflation decreased slightly in Oct. to 7.7%, from 8.2% in Sept., according to the Bureau of Labor Statistics (BLS) Consumer Price Index report released Nov. 10. The U.S. economy added 261,000 jobs in Oct., the BLS reported Nov. 4, as the unemployment rate rose 0.2 points to 3.7%. The Dow Jones Industrial Average closed Nov. at 34,589.77, up almost 5.7% from Oct., as the S&P 500 finished the month at 4,080.11,

a 5.4% increase; the Nasdaq Composite Index gained 4.4% to close at 11,468.00.

Attorney General Announces Special Counsel to Lead Trump Probes; Other Developments—U.S. Atty. Gen. Merrick Garland, appointed by Pres. Biden in 2021, named a special counsel—Jack Smith, a former war crimes prosecutor—Nov. 18 to oversee investigations into the holding of highly classified documents at former Pres. Donald Trump's Mar-a-Lago, Florida estate, and Trump's alleged role in the Jan. 6, 2021, Capitol insurrection. Garland's announcement came three days after Trump declared he would run in the 2024 presidential race. On Nov. 19, social media company Twitter's new owner, Elon Musk, restored Trump's user account—suspended two days after the Jan. 6 attack following tweets the company said glorified violence.

Stewart Rhodes, leader of the Oath Keepers far-right militia group, was found guilty Nov. 29 of the seldom utilized Civil War-era charge of seditious conspiracy for his role in the Jan. 6 events. The 58-year-old was sentenced May 25, 2023, to 18 years in prison.

International

Netanyahu Reelected to Lead Far-Right Israeli Government—Former Israeli prime minister Benjamin Netanyahu's return to power was sealed after his right-wing, Likud-led coalition won a majority of Knesset (parliamentary) seats in voting held Nov. 1, Israel's fifth general election in four years. (Of 120 seats, Likud won 32, and ultra-Orthodox parties and a far-right alliance received 18 and 14, respectively.) Taking the reins from a centrist caretaker government, Netanyahu, already Israel's longest-serving PM (1996-99, 2009-21), was sworn in to a record sixth term on Dec. 29 even as he faced an ongoing corruption trial. The coalition had pledged to annex the Israeli-occupied West Bank, legalize currently illegitimate Israeli settlements, and maintain extensive subsidies to ultra-Orthodox supporters.

Ethiopian Government, Tigray Rebels Sign Peace Deal—Aiming to end a brutal two-year-long civil war in northern Ethiopia, officials from the country's federal government and the breakaway region of Tigray agreed on a permanent ceasefire Nov. 2 at African Union-negotiated peace talks in Pretoria, South Africa. The fragile agreement called for the disarmament and reintegration of Tigray fighters and full humanitarian access to the region, which federal forces blockaded throughout the war. The Ethiopian government also agreed to restore vital services such as banking and electricity and to work to rebuild infrastructure in neighboring Amhara and Afar regions. Forces from neighboring Eritrea—allied with Ethiopian government forces though not part of the peace deal—were alleged to have slaughtered more than 300 civilians in roughly 10 villages in the week before the agreement was signed; the Tigray Emergency Center accused them of killing more than 110 later in the month. Rights groups throughout the conflict had accused both sides of war crimes. Eritrean troops began withdrawing from Tigray in late Jan. 2023.

Though reliable totals varied, a Univ. of Ghent, Belgium, team estimated up to 600,000 civilians died in Tigray Nov. 2020-Aug. 2022 due to war, the majority from starvation. According to the UN World Food Programme, 13.6 mil people in Tigray, Afar, and Amhara were dependent on aid as the country simultaneously faced its most severe drought in four decades.

Ukraine Retakes Kherson; Other Russian Invasion News—Ukrainian troops on Nov. 11 moved into the southern Black Sea port city of Kherson a day after Russian forces withdrew, marking a major victory for Ukraine's counteroffensive against Russia's ongoing invasion. Kherson, a regional capital, had been occupied for more than eight months. As with other previously liberated areas, Ukrainian officials reported evidence of alleged atrocities by Russian troops. Upon Kherson's liberation, less than a third of its 300,000 pre-war residents remained, and many lacked heat, electricity, and running water. Widespread waves of Russian cruise missile attacks continued throughout the month against energy infrastructure, and Ukrainian Pres. Volodymyr Zelenskyy said Nov. 17 that missile strikes had left at least 10 mil residents, mostly in the Kyiv, Odessa, Sumy, and Vinnytsia regions, without electricity shortly before the arrival of winter.

The European Parliament on Nov. 23 identified Russia as a "state sponsor of terrorism," citing human rights violations and attacks on energy and civilian targets, including hospitals, schools, and bomb shelters. U.S. Pres. Joe Biden that same day announced the third round of U.S. military assistance to Ukraine, bringing the Biden administration total to $19.7 bil. Russia on Nov. 2 agreed to rejoin a UN-brokered agreement that guaranteed safe passage for ships carrying grain from Ukraine.

Biden and Xi Meet Amid Tense U.S.-China Relations—U.S. Pres. Joe Biden met with Chinese Pres. Xi Jinping Nov. 14 on the sidelines of the G20 Conference in Bali, Indonesia, in the pair's first in-person encounter since Biden was elected. According to a White House statement following the 3.5-hour-long talks, Biden reiterated the U.S.'s commitment to its one-China policy, which allows it to maintain unofficial relations with Taiwan, but raised objections over China's "coercive and increasingly aggressive" military actions off Taiwan's coast and airspace. The White House said both presidents voiced their opposition to the use and threat of nuclear weapons by Russia in Ukraine, and Biden warned Xi that the U.S. would increase its military presence on the Korean Peninsula if China failed to check North Korea's own nuclear weapons development. Biden and Xi also reportedly agreed to restart climate negotiations, stalled since U.S. House Speaker Nancy Pelosi's Taiwan trip in Aug. 2022.

Historic Agreement Compensates Developing Countries for Climate Impacts; Other Climate News—Diplomats from almost 200 countries at the 2022 UN Climate Change Conference in Sharm El Sheikh, Egypt, reached a historic agreement Nov. 20 for so-called developed nations, including the U.S., to establish a "loss and damage" fund to financially compensate poorer countries for the economic effects of climate change. The fund, details of which remained to be determined, was negotiated against the backdrop of recent climate-related disasters, including intensifying drought in Somalia, Ethiopia, and Kenya, and flooding in Pakistan that killed more than 1,700 people and caused an estimated $40 bil in damages. In late Oct., the UN's environmental arm released a report warning that current government policies leave the world on track to reach an average 2.8°C (5°F) warming above preindustrial levels by 2100, which would induce a "climate catastrophe" according to UN Sec.-Gen. António Guterres.

Anti-Lockdown Protests Erupt in China; Other COVID-19 Pandemic News—Rare, large-scale demonstrations protesting the country's zero-tolerance COVID-19 measures broke out in mid-Nov. in China's industrial port city of Guangzhou and spread to at least 15 other cities and a number of universities. Police clashed with protesters in multiple cities including Shanghai and Guangzhou; Guangzhou and Chongqing authorities on Nov. 30 announced an easing of COVID measures. The deaths of 10 people in a Nov. 24 high-rise apartment fire in Urumqi, Xinjiang, were blamed on the building's COVID-19 lockdown rules.

The World Health Org. reported 639 mil confirmed cumulative global cases as of Nov. 30, with over 6.6 mil deaths; the U.S. reached 97.3 mil cumulative cases (1.1 mil deaths). A continuing fall surge among children of respiratory viruses, including coronavirus, flu, and RSV (respiratory syncytial virus) left about three-quarters of pediatric hospital beds full nationwide, according to the Dept. of Health and Human Services. According to Our World in Data, 68.9% of the U.S. population was fully vaccinated, compared to 63% worldwide.

General

Houston Astros Win World Series—The Houston Astros won the World Series over the wild card Philadelphia Phillies, in a 4-1 Game 6 victory on Nov. 5 at Minute Maid Park in Houston, TX. Clinching their first championship since the franchise's sign stealing scandal-tainted title in 2017, Houston's Series highlights included a 5-0 victory in Game 4 that saw four Astros

hurlers combine to pull off the first no-hitter in a World Series game since 1956. Astros shortstop Jeremy Peña, who hit 10 for 25 with a home run in Game 5, was named World Series MVP. Houston's 73-year-old manager Dusty Baker became the oldest manager to win a World Series, over 40 years after winning a title as an outfielder with the L.A. Dodgers.

Los Angeles FC Takes MLS Cup—Los Angeles FC bested the Philadelphia Union 3-0 on penalty kicks following a 3-3 draw, at Banc of California Stadium in Los Angeles, Nov. 5, to win their first MLS Cup since joining the league in 2018. Tied 2-2 after 90 min. of regulation play, the teams deadlocked again after LAFC forward Gareth Bale scored on a dramatic header in the 128th minute, forcing a penalty shootout during which backup LAFC goalkeeper John McCarthy pulled off two saves that earned him Cup MVP designation. Starting LAFC goalie Maxime Crépeau broke his right leg in the 110th minute after colliding with Union forward Cory Burke, earning Crépeau a red card. With its MLS Cup and World Series losses, Philadelphia became the first city to lose two major sports championships on the same day.

Mass Shootings Kill in Colorado, Virginia; Other Mass Violence News—A body armor-clad gunman shot and killed five people late Nov. 19 at LGBTQ bar Club Q in Colorado Springs, CO. A 22-year-old suspect, who reportedly ran a neo-Nazi website and was identified as Anderson Lee Aldrich, was taken into custody after being disarmed and subdued by patrons. Media reported authorities had failed to invoke the state's "red flag" law allowing temporary seizure of a suspect's guns after Aldrich was arrested in 2021 for an alleged bomb threat.

On Nov. 22, a 31-year-old Walmart manager opened fire on coworkers in Chesapeake, VA, killing six before dying by suicide. Nine days earlier, three Univ. of Virginia football players were shot and killed on a bus, allegedly by a fellow student and former player as they returned to campus from a school field trip. Four Univ. of Idaho students were discovered stabbed to death that same day in an off-campus residence in Moscow, Idaho; the suspect, 28-year-old Washington State Univ. graduate student Bryan Kohberger, was arrested in Pennsylvania Dec. 30.

Nikolas Cruz, convicted of killing 17 students and staff at Marjory Stoneman Douglas High School in Parkland, FL, in 2018, was sentenced Nov. 2 to 34 consecutive life terms.

Quake Kills Hundreds in Indonesia—A magnitude 5.6 earthquake struck Indonesia's most populated province of West Java Nov. 21, killing more than 330 people, according to national officials. With an epicenter near Cianjur and tremors felt in Jakarta about 65 mi north, the quake displaced more than 73,000 people.

NASA Craft Achieves Lunar Orbit—NASA's unmanned *Orion* spacecraft Nov. 25 entered orbit around the moon, passing about 81 mi above its surface, marking an early milestone in the agency's Artemis program to land astronauts on the moon by 2025. Launched Nov. 16, *Orion* returned with a splashdown in the Pacific Ocean off the coast of Mexico, Dec. 11.

Mauna Loa Erupts for First Time in 38 Years—Hawaii's Mauna Loa, the world's largest active volcano, erupted Nov. 27 for the first time since 1984. South-centrally located on the state's largest island, Mauna Loa ("long mountain" in Hawaiian), spewed molten lava across 16.5 sq mi before scientists Dec. 13 declared it was no longer erupting. No injuries/fatalities or major damage occurred.

December 2022
National

Trump Organization Found Guilty of Tax Fraud, Other Crimes; House Committee Releases Trump's Tax Returns—The Trump Organization was found guilty by a Manhattan jury Dec. 6 on all 17 charges against the real estate business of former Pres. Donald Trump and his family, including tax fraud, conspiracy, falsifying business records, and other financial crimes. For over 15 years beginning in 2005, the company had regularly provided executives with substantial off-the-books (and untaxed) compensation, including luxury cars, private school tuition, and free apartments. Trump Org. in Jan. 2023 was ordered to pay the maximum criminal penalty of $1.6 mil. Former Trump Org. CFO Allen H. Weisselberg, who had pleaded guilty and testified against the company, was sentenced to five months in jail.

The House Ways and Means Committee on Dec. 30 publicly released six years (2015-20) of Trump's tax returns after the U.S. Supreme Court Nov. 22 rejected a last attempt by Trump to shield them from Congress. The court's action capped a three-year legal fight between Trump and the committee. The tax records showed that Trump paid just $750 in federal income taxes for each of 2016 and 2017—confirming a 2020 *NY Times* report Trump had disputed—and nothing at all in 2020 due to business losses. The returns further revealed that the IRS did not carry out mandatory audits of Trump during his first two years as president, debunking Trump's assertions that he could not publicly release his tax returns—as every president since Richard Nixon had done while campaigning for office—due to ongoing IRS reviews.

Biden Signs Bipartisan Respect for Marriage Act—Pres. Biden Dec. 13 signed the Respect for Marriage Act, guaranteeing federal protections to same-sex and interracial couples. Passed by the Senate, 61-36, in late Nov. as amended with "religious liberty protections," the bill was approved in the House Dec. 8, 258-169. The legislation was introduced in apparent response to U.S. Supreme Court Justice Clarence Thomas's concurring opinion in *Dobbs v. Jackson Women's Health Org.*, the decision that overturned the federal constitutional right to an abortion in June 2022, that the Court "should reconsider" its 2015 ruling legalizing same-sex marriage throughout the U.S. According to a Gallup poll conducted in May 2022, 71% of Americans support same-sex marriage, up from 27% in 1996.

Federal Reserve Imposes Seventh Rate Increase of 2022 as Wall Street Finishes Down for Year; Freight Rail Strike Averted; Other Business, Economic News—The Federal Reserve continued efforts to ease inflation using its only available tool, raising benchmark interest rates Dec. 14 by a half-point—the seventh increase in 2022—to 4.25%-4.5%. The Fed's announcement came the day after the Bureau of Labor Statistics (BLS) reported that annual U.S. inflation rose 7.1% in Nov., down from 7.7% in Oct. Capping a year of volatile oil prices, national average gas prices dropped to $3.06/gal in late Dec. The U.S. added 263,000 jobs in Nov. as unemployment held at 3.7%, according to a BLS report released Dec. 2. In its third and final estimate for the third quarter of 2022, the Bureau of Economic Analysis said that U.S. GDP grew at an annualized rate of 3.2%, compared to a 0.6% decrease in the previous three months.

Averting a nationwide freight rail workers' strike, Pres. Joe Biden signed a measure Dec. 2 that included a 24% pay increase over five years, retroactive to 2020. Citing antitrust concerns, the Federal Trade Commission on Dec. 8 sued to block Microsoft's $69-bil acquisition of video game giant Activision Blizzard. Drawing ire from air travelers as hundreds were left stranded for days, Southwest Airlines canceled some 16,700 flights over 10 days due to severe weather, staffing issues, and outdated technology.

The Dow Jones Industrial Average closed Dec. at 33,147.25, down almost 4.2% from Nov. as the S&P 500 finished the month at 3,839.50, a 5.9% decrease; the Nasdaq Composite Index, meanwhile, lost over 8.7% to close at 10,466.48. The three indices logged their worst year overall since 2008, with the Dow down nearly 8.8%; tech-heavy Nasdaq, down 33.1%; and the S&P 500, down 19.4% in 2022.

January 6 House Committee Recommends Criminal Charges Against Trump, Releases Final Report; Other Developments—Finalizing an 18-month investigation, the House select committee investigating the Jan. 6, 2021, attack on the U.S. Capitol released its final report Dec. 22, in which it faulted then-Pres. Donald Trump as the "central cause" of the attack and recommended the Justice Dept. bring charges against him. The criminal allegations included obstructing an official proceeding (Congress's electoral vote count), conspiracy to defraud the U.S., conspiracy to make a false statement (relating to the Trump team's "fake electors" scheme), and inciting/assisting/aiding or

comforting an insurrection. Containing citations from more than 1,000 interviews, the report also included new evidence, notably a text message from Trump's former aide Hope Hicks noting that he twice refused her suggestion to call on attendees of his rally speech preceding the insurrection to act peacefully; she testified that a White House lawyer made the same request to Trump. At its 10th and final public hearing Dec. 19, the committee unanimously recommended the charges against Trump and referred four GOP House representatives to the House's ethics committee for disobeying subpoenas to testify before the committee. By early Jan. 2023, the Justice Dept. had charged more than 950 people for their roles in the Jan. 6 riot.

On Dec. 1, the Atlanta-based 11th U.S. Circuit Court of Appeals unanimously overturned the appointment by a federal judge of a special master to review more than 100 classified documents the FBI seized from Trump's Mar-a-Lago estate in Aug. 2022. The panel rejected Trump's lawyer's claim that the case necessitated outside intervention.

Biden Approves $1.7-Trillion Spending Measure—Pres. Biden signed a $1.7-tril spending bill Dec. 29, averting a partial government shutdown. Funding the government through Sept. 2023, it provided $772.5 bil in domestic spending, a roughly 6% increase, along with a 10% hike for military/defense programs, to $858 bil. In their last major act in control of both chambers, Democrats touted boosts in funding for Pell grants for low-income college students, substance abuse prevention/treatment, veterans' medical care, disaster aid, and food assistance, among other programs. The measure also provided nearly $45 bil to support Ukraine and NATO allies and amended the Electoral Count Act to specify that the U.S. vice president cannot unilaterally overturn election results, as former Pres. Donald Trump had requested then-Vice Pres. Mike Pence do in Jan. 2021. The House passed the bill Dec. 23, 225-201, primarily along party lines, a day after the Senate approved it, 68-29.

International

Peruvian President Arrested, Ousted After Attempted Coup—Peruvian Pres. Pedro Castillo (a leftist elected in June 2021) was arrested Dec. 7, shortly after he failed in his attempt to dissolve the national congress and install an emergency government ahead of a third impeachment vote by lawmakers over Castillo's alleged corruption. Multiple cabinet members resigned over what Peru's high court branded a coup, and an overwhelming majority of the congress voted to remove Castillo from office. First Vice Pres. Dina Boluarte was sworn in to replace Castillo, making her Peru's first female president. A judge in mid-Dec. ordered that Castillo, considered a flight risk, remain in pretrial detention for 18 months.

Pro-Castillo demonstrators immediately gathered in the capital and called for early elections in 2023, to which Boluarte agreed but Congress repeatedly rejected. Protests spread widely, particularly in northern towns and rural southern and central Andes communities heavily supportive of Castillo. Boluarte Dec. 14 declared a nationwide 30-day state of emergency in response. Amnesty Intl. and other rights groups accused Peruvian authorities of responding with disproportionate force; 25 people were killed by Dec. 18, including 10 protesters Dec. 15 in the south-central city of Ayacucho. (At least 60 people were reportedly killed by mid-Feb.)

China Rolls Back "Zero-Covid," Faces National Wave; U.S. Life Expectancy Declines; Other Pandemic News—COVID-19 infections skyrocketed after China announced Dec. 7 it was ending some of its harshest zero-COVID restrictions—including mandatory public testing, mass lockdowns, and centralized quarantines—that had been the focus of rare major street protests in Nov. According to the World Health Org., China surpassed 84.9 mil confirmed total cases (including 45,888 deaths, which WHO called underreported) by the close of Dec., a more than 776% monthly increase. Both figures were widely viewed as unreliable, given discontinued testing measures (a growing concern for establishing accurate COVID tallies worldwide) and China's national health commission announcement on Dec. 14 that it was no longer tracking asymptomatic case numbers. Bloomberg News reported that a Chinese health commission internal report said that 248 mil people—close to 18% of China's total population—were probably infected by COVID-19 in the first 20 days of Dec. alone. According to Our World in Data, 89.5% of residents in China were fully vaccinated as of Dec. 31, compared with 69.1% in the U.S. and 63.3% worldwide.

U.S. confirmed cases trended mostly upward over the month, reaching over a half-million for the week ending Dec. 19, according to WHO, the most since late Aug. Cumulatively, the U.S. surpassed 99.4 mil documented cases and over 1.08 mil deaths by Dec. 31, according to WHO, which reported over 730 mil cases globally (with nearly 6.7 mil deaths).

U.S. average life expectancy according to CDC reports released Dec. 22 decreased seven months to 76.4 years in 2021. The decline, which followed a 1.8 year drop in 2020 due primarily to COVID-19, was also attributed to drug overdoses, particularly from synthetic opioids.

German Coup Plot Thwarted—Foiling a right-wing plot aimed at taking over Germany, some 3,000 police carried out coordinated raids Dec. 7 in 11 of the country's 16 states and arrested 25 alleged conspirators, 2 of them in Austria and Italy. Those arrested—including a minor prince, a former member of parliament, and ex-military personnel—belonged to a group of about 50 people with ideological ties to far-right fringe groups such as QAnon and the Reichsbürger (Citizens of the Reich) movement; they had reportedly planned to attack parliament and execute Germany's chancellor. The developments highlighted the rise in right-wing extremism in the country, including a failed attempt in Apr. 2022 to kidnap Germany's health minister and a 2020 shooting attack in Hanau that had killed nine.

WNBA Star Griner Released in Russia-U.S. Prisoner Swap—Russia released American WNBA star Brittney Griner Dec. 8 in exchange for Russian arms dealer Viktor Bout, held in the U.S. since 2010 and convicted the following year of conspiring to kill U.S. citizens. Two-time Olympic gold medalist Griner, in Russian detention since mid-Feb., had been sentenced in early Aug. to nine years in a penal colony after she pleaded guilty to bringing cannabis vape cartridges into the country. Pres. Biden vowed to continue to work for the release of 52-year-old former Marine Paul Whelan, detained in Russia since 2018. Amid strained relations with Russia, the U.S. State Dept. had designated both Whelan and Griner wrongfully detained.

Ukraine's President Meets With Biden, Addresses U.S. Congress; Other Invasion News—Aiming to strengthen U.S. support for Ukraine, Ukrainian Pres. Volodymyr Zelenskyy met Dec. 21 with U.S. Pres. Biden in a surprise White House visit; it was believed to be Zelenskyy's first trip outside Ukraine since Russia launched its invasion roughly 10 months earlier. Zelenskyy addressed a joint session of Congress that evening and requested more U.S. aid, asserting that Ukraine would "never surrender"; U.S. military support allocated since the invasion began totaled about $21.2 bil as of Dec. 21. Within Ukraine, Russia continued to launch waves of drone and missile attacks on multiple cities and key energy sector targets as winter set in and Ukrainian troops maintained their counteroffensive. Russia in early Dec. accused Ukraine of drone attacks on two air bases 300-450 mi northeast of Ukraine that killed three officers and damaged aircraft and which, if verified, constituted Ukraine's deepest attacks yet in Russia.

General

Danish Researchers Report Discovery of Oldest DNA—Danish scientists in *Nature* Dec. 7 announced they had found 2-mil-year-old DNA—by far the oldest yet identified—in a sediment deposit in Greenland's northern tip. While the area now is largely barren Arctic desert, the DNA samples showed genetic material from more than 100 types of flora and fauna including mastodons, reindeer, geese, and poplar and birch trees. The previous oldest-known DNA, an estimated 1.2-1.65 mil years old, was extracted from a mammoth tooth found in Siberia.

Flooding, Landslides Prove Deadly in Kinshasa—The death toll from flooding and landslides triggered by a night of torrential rains Dec. 12-13 in Kinshasa, Dem. Rep. of the Congo, neared 170 people by Dec. 16, according to the UN and local authorities. Officials blamed poor flood management in the sprawling capital, the country's largest city with some 16 mil residents, as well as climate change.

U.S. Scientists Report Nuclear Fusion Breakthrough—Researchers achieved the long-awaited scientific milestone of producing a nuclear fusion reaction with a net gain of energy, according to a U.S. Dept. of Energy announcement Dec. 13. The historic experiment—carried out using over 190 laser beams at Lawrence Livermore National Laboratory, near San Francisco, CA—created enough energy to boil only 15-20 kettles of water, but government scientists heralded the endeavor for its proof of concept of eventual use in nuclear power stations. Fusion has the potential to create more energy than current fission technology without generating the latter's long-lasting radioactive byproducts.

Argentina Triumphs in Men's World Cup—Argentina's national soccer team won its third FIFA men's World Cup title in a nail-biter Dec. 18, defeating defending champion France 4-2 on penalty kicks after a 3-3 draw in front of a nearly 89,000-person crowd at Lusail Stadium in Lusail, Qatar. Tied 2-2 at the end of regulation play, the teams were deadlocked again after extra time; Argentina scored in the 109th minute, France nine minutes later. Argentina's veteran superstar Lionel Messi earned the Golden Ball award for best player of tournament, making him the first player in history to earn the award twice.

Argentina's victory capped the month-long, 64-game tournament hosted by Qatar, which had drawn criticism for the country's legal prohibition of homosexuality, reported mistreatment of migrant workers employed to construct World Cup venues, and other corruption allegations. Among tournament matchups, Morocco defeated Portugal, 1-0, on Dec. 10 to become the first African team to reach a World Cup semifinal. The U.S. was eliminated by the Netherlands, 3-1, in the round of 16 a week earlier.

Winter Storm Kills Dozens in U.S.—A major storm impacted roughly the eastern two-thirds of the U.S. beginning Dec. 23, delivering bitter temperatures, heavy winds, and drifting snow and killing at least 65 people in more than a dozen states. About two-thirds of the deaths were in Erie County, NY, where snowfall in Buffalo reached almost 52 inches over five days.

Pope Emeritus Benedict XVI Dies—Retired Pope Benedict XVI, born Joseph Aloisius Ratzinger in Germany, died Dec. 31 at the age of 95. Elected pope in 2005 following the death of Pope John Paul II, Benedict was viewed as an intellectual and a traditionalist, though his tenure was overshadowed by his handling of widespread allegations of sexual abuse in the church. A Munich archdiocese-commissioned report released in early 2022 found Benedict as an archbishop in Germany had failed to take adequate action against four priests accused of abuse. Citing ill health and age, Benedict had resigned in 2013, becoming the first Catholic Pope to abdicate in more than 600 years.

January 2023
National

Biden Administration Introduces New Border Enforcement Measures—Pres. Joe Biden announced Jan. 5 the U.S. would begin turning away up to 30,000 migrants per month from Cuba, Haiti, Nicaragua, and Venezuela who cross into the U.S. without authorization from Mexico in an expansion of the court-challenged, COVID-era Title 42 rule that allowed migrants to be immediately deported. Biden also called for the U.S. to accept up to 30,000 migrants per month from those four countries to stay for a two-year period via the Dept. of Homeland Security's humanitarian parole program, provided they arrived legally and passed background checks. Three days later, Biden visited El Paso, TX, in his first trip to the U.S.-Mexico border since becoming president. El Paso's mayor in Dec. 2022 had declared a state of emergency with the increase of migrants at the border.

Migrant encounters with Customs and Border Protection at the southwest border reached a monthly record 251,487 in Dec.; it hit an all-time high 2.38 mil in FY2022, up 37% from the year prior.

The White House on Feb. 21 proposed a temporary, two-year rule barring asylum eligibility to migrants who do not first seek protection in another country through which they traveled en route to the U.S.; those not crossing through legal ports of entry would also be disqualified. Criticized by migrant advocates, the restrictions were set to take effect upon Title 42's expiration May 11.

McCarthy Wins Speakership on 15th Vote; Divided 118th Congress Convenes—With Republicans taking control of the House (222-213) after four years in the minority, Congress's members-elect were not sworn in until Jan. 7—four days after the chamber was scheduled to convene—after Rep. Kevin McCarthy (R, CA) was elected speaker with the minimum 216 votes required (six GOP members voted present) after 15 floor votes, the most required to elect a speaker since 1855. To secure his leadership, McCarthy—the minority leader, 2019-23, and majority leader, 2014-19—agreed to major concessions to far-right members, including passing a rule that would make it easier to force out the speaker. Hakeem Jeffries (D, NY) became the first Black representative to lead a major political party in Congress, replacing outgoing Speaker Nancy Pelosi (D, CA; Pelosi maintained her seat but resigned from party leadership). At the end of the month, newly elected Rep. George Santos (R, NY) stepped down from two committees after admitting to campaigning on a heavily fabricated background. (He also faced campaign finance investigations.)

In the Senate, where Democrats maintained control (51—including 3 independents—to 49), Chuck Schumer (D, NY) and Mitch McConnell (R, KY) retained their majority and minority leader positions, respectively. The month prior, Sen. Kyrsten Sinema (AZ, elected in 2018), changed her affiliation from Democrat to independent but continued to caucus with Democrats. The new Congress included a record number of women (128 in the House, including nonvoting members; 25 in the Senate). Sen. Patty Murray (D, WA) became the chamber's first female president pro tempore.

Classified Documents Found at President Biden's Home, Office; Other Documents Found at Ex-VP Pence's Home—CBS News Jan. 9 reported that Pres. Joe Biden's personal lawyers in early Nov. found 10 classified documents from Biden's tenure as vice president stored illegally at the Penn Biden Center in Washington, DC. Two days later, NBC News reported another batch of classified documents were discovered Dec. 20 in what was later revealed to be the garage of Biden's Wilmington, DE, private residence. Additional classified documents were also detected on the same property in Jan. by Biden and White House lawyers as well as FBI agents invited by the president. Atty. Gen. Merrick Garland on Jan. 12 named a special counsel to investigate.

The discoveries drew criticism from Republican lawmakers who claimed former Pres. Donald Trump, who faced an ongoing Justice Dept. probe into possible mishandling of classified White House records, had been treated unfairly. Democrats, in turn, contrasted Biden's cooperation with Trump's apparent resistance to turning over documents—eventually numbering more than 300 classified files—as legally required, necessitating a DOJ warrant.

On Jan. 18, staff for former Vice Pres. Mike Pence alerted the National Archives that Pence, too, had discovered confidential files—reportedly about a dozen—at his Indiana home.

U.S. Hits Debt Ceiling, Risking Default; Other Business, Economic News—The U.S. on Jan. 19 reached its statutory debt limit of $31.4 tril, forcing the Treasury Dept. to take "extraordinary measures" to prevent a default crisis, according to a letter Treasure Sec. Janet Yellen sent to Congress. Stopgap accounting steps taken, including postponing Civil Service Retirement and Disability Fund investments, would allow the U.S. to pay its bills only through early June. Some House Republicans had vowed to tie any increase in the nation's debt ceiling to spending cuts. On Jan. 12, the Bureau of Labor Statistics (BLS) reported that annualized U.S. inflation was 6.5% as of Dec., marking the sixth straight month of declining rates. The BLS reported Jan. 6 that the U.S. added 223,000 jobs in Dec. with a 3.5% unemployment rate for the 24th straight month of growth, bringing the total number of jobs created in 2022 to roughly 4.5 mil. The strong job growth report came amid continuing tech-sector layoff announcements, which persisted through Jan., including Microsoft (10,000 jobs cut), Google parent co. Alphabet (about 12,000), and streaming music service Spotify (600).

The European Union Jan. 4 fined Facebook parent Meta more than $400 mil after claiming its collection of user data for targeted ads violated EU privacy laws. On Jan. 24, the Justice Dept. filed its second antitrust suit against Google, alleging it unlawfully pushed to dominate the digital ads market. The Dow Jones Industrial Average closed Jan. at 34,086.04, up over 2.8% from Dec., and the S&P 500 finished the month at 4,076.60, a nearly 6.2% increase. The Nasdaq Composite Index gained close to 10.7% to close at 11,584.55.

Memphis Police Release Video of Deadly Beating by Officers—Memphis, TN, police released graphic footage Jan. 27 showing five of its officers repeatedly assaulting 29-year-old Black man Tyre Nichols, who died Jan. 10, three days after what began with a traffic stop. The officers, all five of whom were Black, were fired and indicted on second-degree murder charges. Memphis police chief Cerelyn Davis called the incident a "failing of basic humanity." Emergency medical personnel, who did not aid Nichols for at least 19 minutes after arriving on the scene, were also fired. The police dept. announced it had disbanded the specialized Scorpion unit involved.

International

Ukrainian Missile Strike Kills Dozens of Russian Troops; Western Countries Send Tanks; Other Invasion News—A Ukrainian missile strike on temporary military barracks in Makiivka in the Russian-occupied Donetsk region in eastern Ukraine Dec. 31-Jan. 1 killed at least 89 Russian troops according to Russia (Ukrainian authorities said roughly 400 were killed) in the deadliest single attack on Russian personnel since Russia's invasion more than 10 months earlier. Though Ukrainian forces by the close of 2022 had retaken some territory seized earlier by Russia, intense fighting continued as invading troops sought to breach Ukrainian defenses in the provinces of Kharkiv, Luhansk, Zaporizhzhia, and Donetsk in particular. Among the casualties from waves of missile attacks on key cities and infrastructure across Ukraine were more than 40 people killed by a strike on a high-rise civilian residence in east-centrally located Dnipro.

A Ukrainian official in late Jan. confirmed that Western nations, including the U.S., Germany, and the UK, had agreed to supply Ukraine with over 320 heavy tanks, a major boost to Ukraine's limited arsenal. The White House on Jan. 6 announced the U.S. would send an additional $3.75 bil in military aid to Ukraine and affected neighboring countries, bringing the total to $24.2 bil.

Al-Shabab Attacks Kill Scores of Somali Civilians—The al-Qaeda-linked group al-Shabab claimed responsibility for two car bombings Jan. 4 in Mahas, Somalia, that killed 35 people, including at least 8 from a single family. Reportedly targeting the homes of a local official and a national lawmaker, the violence was said to be in retaliation for a U.S.-backed offensive Somalia launched in Aug. 2022. Dozens more were killed in al-Shabab-claimed attacks in Jan., adding to roughly 3,850 fatalities resulting from 1,200 occurrences of political violence by al-Shabab in Aug.-Dec. 2022, according to the U.S.-based Armed Conflict Location & Event Data Project (ACLED). In late Jan., a U.S. raid in northern Somalia killed a senior Islamic State leader and 10 associates.

Bolsonaro Followers Stage Failed Coup in Brasília—Hundreds of supporters of Brazil's former Pres. Jair Bolsonaro stormed the presidential palace, national congress, and supreme court in the capital, Brasília, Jan. 8, one week after the inauguration of his opponent, leftist Pres. Luiz Inácio Lula da Silva. Security personnel spent more than five hours clearing the buildings and detained around 1,500 people. The chaos left dozens in need of medical treatment and lawmakers' offices severely vandalized. The incident drew prompt comparisons to the Jan. 6, 2021, insurrection by supporters of then-U.S. Pres. Donald Trump, himself a Bolsonaro ally, at the U.S. Capitol; Bolsonaro had similarly made unfounded assertions of election fraud. Brazilian government officials accused the military (in which Bolsonaro was a longtime officer and a key foundation of his political support) of shielding rioters, reportedly allowing many to escape. By the end of Jan., Lula had fired dozens of officers, including the army chief and roughly 50 working in presidential security.

China's Coronavirus Surge on Downswing; Other Pandemic News—The ferocious wave of COVID-19 that gripped China in Dec. peaked and declined in Jan., according to China's Center for Disease Control, which on Jan. 25 reported a 72% drop in monthly critical cases, and a 79% fall in hospital-recorded daily deaths. Several days earlier, a senior Chinese government scientist said 80% of China's population had been infected with coronavirus. On Jan. 8, for the first time since 2020, mainland China had reopened its border with Hong Kong and rescinded most quarantine requirements for arriving travelers. By the end of Jan., World Health Org. reported 98.5 mil cumulative confirmed COVID-19 cases in China (incl. 113,873 deaths); 100.9 mil cases in the U.S. (nearly 1.1 mil deaths); and 753.5 mil worldwide cases (over 6.8 mil deaths).

According to Our World in Data, 89.5% of residents in China were fully vaccinated by late Jan., compared with 69.3% in the U.S., and 63.6% worldwide. Africa (28.0%) and the European Union (72.8%) remained the regions with the lowest and highest portions fully inoculated, respectively.

Former NATO General Wins Czech Presidency—Former NATO Military Committee Chair Gen. Petr Pavel Jan. 28 easily defeated billionaire right-wing populist and former (2017-21) prime minister Andrej Babis in runoff voting for the presidency of Czechia, seen by many analysts as an early test of populism's hold on Europe ahead of multiple key elections in 2023. Winning by a 58.3% to 42.7% margin as turnout reached a record 70.2%, Pavel had drawn the support of the ruling center-right government and pledged to continue to support Ukraine against Russia's invasion. Term-limited, divisive outgoing Pres. Milos Zeman had endorsed Babis. Though largely symbolic, the president's role includes choosing the prime minister and chief of the country's national bank.

Pakistan Mosque Blast Kills Scores of Police—A suicide bombing Jan. 30 killed at least 100 people, nearly all law enforcement, in a mosque within a walled police compound in Peshawar, Pakistan. Officials blamed a Pakistan offshoot of the Taliban for the attack (which they denied), which occurred amid a recent increase in violence targeting Pakistani police and security forces. In Dec., the ruling Taliban regime in neighboring Afghanistan had announced an immediate ban on women studying at universities, further restricting female education; the fundamentalist group effectively barred girls from attending secondary school soon after the U.S. military's Aug. 2021 withdrawal. In late Dec., the Taliban also prohibited Afghan women from working for national and international NGOs.

General

Georgia Wins Back-to-Back College Football Championships With Lopsided Win Over TCU—The Univ. of Georgia Bulldogs walloped the Texas Christian Univ. Horned Frogs, 65-7, at SoFi Stadium in Inglewood, CA, Jan. 9, securing their second-straight College Football Playoff title. The 58-point margin of victory for Georgia, which went 40 seasons (1981-2020) without a championship, was the widest in any college bowl game in history, according to ESPN. Bulldogs quarterback Stetson Bennett IV was named the game's offensive MVP after completing 18 of 25 passes for 304 yards and four touchdowns and running for two more.

***The Banshees of Inisherin, The Fabelmans* Big Winners at Golden Globes**—The Hollywood Foreign Press Assn. (HFPA) awarded best drama film to *The Fabelmans* at the 80th Golden Globe Awards ceremony in Beverly Hills, CA, Jan. 10. *The Banshees of Inisherin* won best musical/comedy, and the movie's co-star Colin Farrell won best actor in that category. Austin Butler was awarded best actor in a drama film for *Elvis*, while Cate Blanchett nabbed the corresponding best actress trophy for *Tár*. HBO's *House of the Dragon* won best TV drama, while ABC's *Abbott Elementary* earned best musical/comedy series. Hosted by Jerrod Carmichael, the awards were televised on NBC, a year

after the network dropped the show over the HFPA's financial improprieties and lack of diversity.

U.S. Investigates Hundreds of New UFO Sightings—According to a Pentagon report released Jan. 12, the agency logged 366 new instances of unidentified aerial phenomena (UAP)—informally but more commonly referred to as UFOs—since issuing its last report in June 2021, covering incidents from Nov. 2004 to Mar. 2021. (Of the new sightings, 119 were observed prior to Mar. 2021 but submitted after the previous report's release.) Though Pentagon officials stressed their findings did not provide evidence of extraterrestrial life, they were unable to explain over 170 of the sightings; 163 were attributed to "balloon or balloon-entities" and 26 to drones. By Apr. 2023, the Pentagon said it was probing 650 potential sightings.

Mass Shootings Leave 18 Dead in Three Days in California; Six-Year-Old Shoots Virginia Teacher—A gunman carried out an attack on a crowd of mostly elderly Asian American dancers at the Star Ballroom in Monterey Park, CA, Jan. 21, killing 11. The shooter, 72-year-old Chinese immigrant Huu Can Tran, a regular attendee at the dance hall years earlier, then attempted to enter another dance venue several miles away but was disarmed by a worker. He died by suicide as police approached his van Jan. 22. Two days later, 66-year-old Chunli Zhao, also from China, killed seven coworkers at two mushroom farms where the shooter had worked in Half Moon Bay, CA. In Jan. alone, almost 90 people were killed in U.S. mass shootings (defined as four or more people killed/injured), according to the Gun Violence Archive.

On Jan. 6, a six-year-old student in Newport News, VA, shot his first-grade teacher, injuring her; she sued the school district, accusing officials of ignoring warnings that he possessed a gun.

Baseball Hall of Fame Inducts Rolen, McGriff—The Baseball Writers' Assn. of America elected third baseman Scott Rolen to the National Baseball Hall of Fame Jan. 24 with 76.3% of the vote in his sixth year on the ballot. An eight-time Gold Glove winner and seven-time All-Star, Rolen racked up 316 home runs and 1,287 RBIs over 17 seasons, mostly with the Philadelphia Phillies and St. Louis Cardinals. On Dec. 4, first baseman Fred McGriff, with 493 home runs, was unanimously elected by the Contemporary Baseball Era Players Committee.

Sabalenka, Djokovic Take Australian Open Titles—No. 5-seed Aryna Sabalenka of Belarus defeated Kazakhstan's Elena Rybakina, the No. 22 seed, (4-6, 6-3, 6-4) in the Australian Open women's singles final at Rod Laver Arena in Melbourne, Jan. 28. The win gave Sabalenka her first Grand Slam singles title. The following night, No. 4-seed Novak Djokovic of Serbia bested No. 3-seed Stefanos Tsitsipas of Greece in straight sets (6-3, 7-6, 7-6), extending his tournament title record to 10 and tying Rafael Nadal's men's career record of 22 Grand Slam singles titles.

February 2023
National

Freight Train Spills Toxic Chemicals in Ohio Small Town—A Norfolk Southern freight train carrying hazardous industrial chemicals derailed Feb. 3 in the northeastern Ohio town of East Palestine, resulting in a massive fire and the mandatory evacuation of hundreds of residents. Federal personnel began monitoring for airborne contaminants from 11 of the 38 derailed train cars, and Ohio Gov. Mike DeWine (R) on Feb. 5 activated the National Guard to assist efforts. After expanding the evacuation zone to roughly half the town's 4,700 residents, local officials the following day set fire to more than 115,000 gallons of vented vinyl chloride in a controlled burn intended to forestall a potential explosion. Residents were allowed to return to their homes Feb. 8 after state testing found that air and municipal water supplies were safe. However, many residents remained concerned, and some reported headaches, rashes, and nausea. Though a federal disaster was not declared, the Federal Emergency Management Agency (FEMA) on Feb. 18 sent staff, and the Environmental Protection Agency (EPA) ordered Norfolk Southern to pay for cleanup and safety testing. The EPA reported as of Mar. 17 that more than 6.8 mil gallons of liquid waste and over 5,400 tons of solid waste had been removed and cautioned that remediation would likely span three more months.

Some lawmakers and local officials and residents criticized the federal response as inadequate, in particular that of Transportation Sec. Pete Buttigieg, who did not visit until Feb. 23. Another Norfolk Southern train derailed in early Mar., northeast of Dayton, OH, but it was not carrying toxic materials.

U.S. Adds Jobs as Inflation Continues to Cool; Other Business, Economic News—Despite widespread severe winter weather and continuing tech sector layoffs, the U.S. economy added 517,000 jobs in Jan. as the unemployment rate dipped a tenth of a point to 3.4%, the lowest level since 1969, according to a Bureau of Labor Statistics (BLS) report released Feb. 3. A separate BLS report issued Feb. 14 showed annual U.S. inflation easing for the seventh-straight month in Jan., to 6.4%. Citing concerns over data privacy and misinformation, the White House on Feb. 27 directed government agencies to remove the Chinese-owned social media app TikTok from all government devices, with limited exceptions. Canada and the EU Commission in Feb. also banned TikTok from official devices; UK, New Zealand, and France followed suit for government devices in Mar., with France also banning Instagram and Twitter. Bracing for potentially more interest rate hikes from the Federal Reserve, the Dow Jones Industrial Average finished Feb. at 32,656.70, down 4.2% from Jan., as the S&P 500 closed the month at 3,970.15, a 2.6% decrease. The Nasdaq Composite Index lost 1.1% to close at 11,455.54.

Biden Hails Economy, Bipartisanship in State of the Union—Pres. Joe Biden delivered his first State of the Union address Feb. 7 to a newly divided Congress, focusing most of his nearly 73-min. address on domestic issues. Biden touted the U.S.'s current 50-year-low unemployment rate and declining inflation, and implored lawmakers to "finish the job" and further stimulate the economy with additional legislation. Biden also praised Congress's bipartisan support of Ukraine, federal protections for same-sex marriage, and electoral reforms, as well as record enrollment in Obamacare and a new out-of-pocket cap on prescription drug costs for Medicare recipients, set to take effect in 2025 through last year's Inflation Reduction Act. Though he lauded specific bipartisan policies, the president received audible pushback from the other side of the aisle after he referenced conservative efforts to slash social security and Medicare spending; he also drew loud protest in reference to his immigration policies and to the increase in national debt under former Pres. Donald Trump.

International

U.S. Increases Military Footprint in Philippines—The U.S. and Philippines on Feb. 1 announced an agreement to boost U.S. military presence in the Southeast Asian country to four additional bases—bringing the total to nine. Analysts said the pact was intended to counter recent Chinese aggression against Taiwan and elsewhere in the South China Sea. One of the new locations, Naval Base Camilo Osias in Luzon, was just a few hundred miles' south of Taiwan; another on Balabac Island was in proximity to key maritime routes along which the Philippines and China claimed disputed territory, including islands fortified with Chinese military installations. Among other U.S. regional defense agreements, the U.S. in Jan. said it would deploy a Marine Corps unit to Okinawa, Japan, to help defend outer islands; open a new Marine base on Guam; and boost military technology cooperation with India.

U.S. Downs Chinese Balloon in U.S. Airspace—A U.S. Air Force jet Feb. 4 shot down a large Chinese spy balloon flying at an altitude of about 60,000 ft off the coast of South Carolina, one week after the balloon was first detected in U.S. airspace above Alaska's Aleutian Islands. Though Pres. Biden drew criticism from some lawmakers over his delay in ordering the balloon's downing, homeland security officials said doing so over Alaska and its deeper waters would likely have complicated recovery efforts while acting after it reentered U.S. airspace over Idaho could endanger civilians. U.S. officials also said they took measures to prevent the balloon from accessing vital information, though China continued to insist the craft, reportedly the size of

three school buses, was an offtrack weather balloon. Amid the resulting diplomatic standoff, U.S. sec. of state Antony Blinken canceled a planned China visit.

U.S. military aircraft shot down three more unidentified airborne objects Feb. 10-12, over Alaskan waters, in Canada's central Yukon (with the cooperation of Canada), and over Lake Huron.

Earthquake Kills Over 58,000 in Turkey and Syria—A devastating 7.8 magnitude earthquake struck south-central Turkey near the Syrian border early Feb. 6, killing more than 50,000 people in Turkey and over 8,400 in Syria, and displacing more than 5.9 mil people. Though Turkey's response was criticized as uncoordinated and lacking equipment and personnel, more than 141,000 people from 94 countries assisted in rescue efforts, which successfully freed some survivors trapped in rubble for more than 11 days. The quake and its numerous aftershocks—including a 7.5 magnitude tremor about 60 mi north that same day—leveled or greatly damaged an estimated 160,000 buildings in Turkey, drawing accusations of lax adherence to building safety codes. By Mar. 13, police had reportedly arrested more than 275 people on such code violations.

International sanctions and damage to infrastructure slowed aid to Syria, already overwhelmed by 12 years of civil war. Syrian Pres. Bashar al-Assad was accused of preventing humanitarian shipments from reaching areas held by opposition groups. Amnesty Intl. said at least 100 trucks were prevented from entering Kurdish-controlled neighborhoods in the hard-hit city of Aleppo Feb. 9-22. Assad on Feb. 13 agreed to allow UN aid to enter rebel-held territory from two additional border crossings, up from just one controlled crossing with Turkey.

The U.S. as of Mar. 20 had committed $235 mil to support relief efforts in both countries. The UN in early Mar. estimated that damages would exceed $100 bil in Turkey alone.

Suspected Islamic State Attack in Syria Kills 68—The UK-based Syrian Observatory for Human Rights accused the Sunni extremist group Islamic State (IS) of killing at least 68 people near Al-Sukhnah, Homs province, Syria, Feb. 17. The attack was perpetrated by gunmen on motorcycles firing on the mostly civilian victims as they foraged for desert truffles; on Feb. 11, IS militants killed at least 16 truffle hunters and security personnel outside Palmyra, in the same province. A joint U.S.-Syrian Democratic Forces helicopter raid in northeastern Syria Feb. 16 killed senior IS leader Hamza al-Homsi.

Burkina Faso Attacks Kill Dozens of Government Troops—Suspected jihadists killed more than 50 soldiers Feb. 17 in an ambush near Déou, Oudalan province, Burkina Faso. Three days later, at least 15 soldiers were killed in another ambush in Tin-Akoff. In a statement Feb. 24, IS claimed responsibility for the attack near Déou. Attacks by al-Qaeda- and IS-linked militants had killed more than than 10,000 people in Burkina Faso since 2015 and displaced roughly 2 mil, according to aid organizations. At the same time, human rights groups alleged multiple episodes of violence by Burkinabè government forces against civilians. Human Rights Watch said soldiers had killed more than 150 civilians Apr. 20 in Karma, Yatenga province.

Burkina Faso's army on Feb. 19 announced the official end of French anti-insurgent military operations in the country; its postcoup military government had suspended a 2018 accord with France the month before. After nine years, French forces fully withdrew from neighboring Mali in Aug. 2022.

Ukraine War Enters Second Year; Other Invasion News—The one year-anniversary of Russia's ongoing bloody invasion of Ukraine passed on Feb. 24, with neither Russian Pres. Vladimir Putin nor his Ukrainian counterpart, Volodymyr Zelenskyy, showing signs of capitulating. The UN on Feb. 21 said at least 8,000 civilians were confirmed killed in the conflict, but cautioned the actual number was likely much higher. Official casualty figures had been unreliable since fighting began, but U.S. officials estimated some 100,000 Ukrainian troops and 200,000 Russian forces had been killed or wounded by early Feb. Fierce fighting persisted around Bakhmut, viewed as a key strategic city along the roughly 600-mi-long front line in the east and south of Ukraine. About 5.4 mil Ukrainians were internally displaced by the invasion as of Jan. 23, according to the UN's Intl.

Organization for Migration, and the UN High Commissioner for Refugees recorded 8.1 mil Ukrainian refugees in other countries as of Feb. 28.

U.S. Pres. Joe Biden met with Zelenskyy in a surprise visit to Kyiv on Feb. 20. Though Biden Feb. 24 announced an additional $2 bil in military assistance, bringing the total over the past 12 months to $32 bil, public support in the U.S. was on the decline. An Associated Press-NORC Ctr. for Public Affairs Research poll released in mid-Feb. showed 48% of Americans favoring the U.S. send weapons to Ukraine, compared to 60% surveyed in May 2022. Citing American support for Ukraine, Putin on Feb. 21 halted Russia's participation in the New START treaty, its last active nuclear weapons reduction pact with the U.S.

Nigeria's Ruling Party Wins Heavily Disputed Presidential Election—Bola Tinubu, candidate for Nigeria's ruling centrist All Progressives Congress, was elected president in Feb. 25 voting that was questioned by opposition candidates. Nigeria's national election commission Mar. 1 declared Tinubu, a former two-term governor of Lagos State, the winner with about 36.6% of the vote, making him the first president to win less than 50% support; the runner-up, former Vice Pres. Atiku Abubakar, received about 29.1%, followed by the Labour Party's Peter Obi, with 25.4%. Amid the commission's slow release of results online, the opposition alleged vote manipulation and noted delayed openings for many polling stations and voter intimidation, including sporadic violence. Abubakar in early Mar. led mass protests in the capital. Civil society groups demanding a review of the Feb. vote, as well as Mar. 18 polling for gubernatorial and state roles, held daily protests. By late Mar., police had arrested more than 780 people for disrupting polling. Tinubu was sworn in May 29.

Facing economic stagnation and surging inflation, Africa's largest economy and most populous country was also confronting an extremist uprising in the northeast and separatist violence in the southeast.

U.S. Government Report Supports Lab Leak Theory With "Low Confidence"; Other COVID News—A U.S. Dept. of Energy report found that the global COVID-19 pandemic likely resulted from an accidental leak of the virus from a lab in China, according to a Feb. 26 *Wall Street Journal* report. The *WSJ* stressed, however, that the report's conclusion was made with "low confidence." Rather than validate prior claims that the virus originated in a lab in Wuhan, China, the report instead added to debate among agencies.

By the end of Feb., the World Health Org. reported more than 102.0 mil cases (with 1.1 mil deaths) in the U.S., and approx. 758.1 mil cumulative cases (with 6.9 mil deaths) worldwide. According to Our World in Data, 69.4% of the U.S. population was fully vaccinated at the close of Feb., compared with 63.9% worldwide.

General

Beyoncé Breaks Grammy Record; Harry Styles Wins Big—R&B superstar Beyoncé won four awards, including best dance/electronic recording for "Break My Soul" at the 65th Grammy Awards ceremony held Feb. 5 at Crypto.com Arena in Los Angeles, bringing her to a record 32 career awards. Lizzo won record of the year for "About Damn Time," Harry Styles claimed album of the year as well as best pop vocal album for *Harry's House*, and Bonnie Raitt brought home song of the year for "Just Like That."

Kansas City Defeats Philadelphia in Super Bowl LVII; Other NFL News—The Kansas City Chiefs edged the Philadelphia Eagles, 38-35, at State Farm Stadium in Glendale, AZ, to win Super Bowl LVII, on Feb. 12. The Chiefs at halftime faced a 10-point deficit, which they erased early in the fourth quarter. Harrison Butker kicked the game-winning field goal with less than .08 sec. remaining. Chiefs QB Patrick Mahomes was named Super Bowl MVP, having completed 21 of 27 passes for 182 yards and 3 touchdowns. The broadcast, which included a halftime show headlined by Rihanna, was the most watched Super Bowl ever, drawing an average 115.1 mil viewers, above the previous high of 114.4 mil set in 2015.

Buffalo Bills 24-year-old safety Damar Hamlin suffered a cardiac arrest on the field Jan. 2 during a Week 17 game against the Cincinnati Bengals; the game was suspended and then canceled. Hamlin was medically cleared to return to play less than four months later. In Feb., 10 former NFL players sued the league's benefits program, claiming it wrongfully denied their disability claims.

Stenhouse Jr. Wins Longest-Ever Daytona 500—Ricky Stenhouse Jr. won the 65th Daytona 500 Feb. 19 in Daytona, FL, holding off Joey Logano under a caution flag due to a multicar wreck behind the leaders on the race's final lap. Stenhouse's win, the third of his Cup Series career, came in double overtime on lap 212 (530 miles), making it the longest Daytona 500 in race history. Of 40 drivers who started the race, accidents sidelined 16, including 2022 winner Austin Cindric.

Webb Telescope Finds Six Massive Early Galaxies—Based on data from NASA and the European Space Agency's James Webb Space Telescope, astronomers in a study published Feb. 22 in *Nature* reported they had detected light emitted from six large candidate galaxies (meaning that further data is needed to confirm they are galaxies) roughly 500-700 mil years after the big bang created the universe 13.8 bil years ago. Though older galaxies were discovered after the Webb telescope first achieved solar orbit in early 2022, researchers said these six objects are far larger, challenging scientists' established notions about the formation of galaxies.

Dozens Killed in Greek Rail Collision—Greece's deadliest ever rail accident occurred Feb. 28 when a passenger train traveling on the wrong track at over 100 mph collided head-on with a freight train near Larissa, killing at least 57 among more than 350 people on board. A reportedly inexperienced stationmaster was charged with homicide in the wake of the wreck, which left multiple derailed cars in flames. The country's transportation minister and other officials also resigned amid accusations that the country's rail network—privatized in 2017—was not properly maintained.

March 2023

National

States Pass Wave of Anti-LGBTQ Legislation—Tennessee Gov. Bill Lee (R) Mar. 2 signed the country's first ban on drag shows and limits on health care for transgender minors amid an unprecedented flurry of legislation targeting LGBTQ persons, especially trans individuals, in GOP strongholds. Tennessee was one of close to 20 states in 2023, including Florida, Georgia, and Texas, to enact a partial or complete ban on gender-affirming care for minors, in opposition to the American Medical Assn.'s recommendations to health care providers. Montana lawmakers drew national attention in Apr. when they barred transgender Rep. Zooey Zephyr from the floor after she criticized the state's newly enacted ban on gender affirming care. In late Apr., Missouri became the first state to limit gender-affirming treatment for adults in addition to minors.

According to the ACLU, as of the end of June, Republican lawmakers in nearly every state had introduced more than 490 anti-LGBTQ bills in 2023. Of those, 77 were signed into law. As of Apr., the ACLU reported more than 60 bills restricting gender or sexuality instruction in public schools, in the manner of Florida's controversial 2022 "Don't Say Gay" law. Among other measures, bills barring transgender students from gender-segregated school sports passed in at least eight states.

A federal judge June 2 struck down Tennessee's anti-drag law, citing First Amendment infringement, but legal wrangling was expected to continue.

Regulators Move to Limit Damages of Major Bank Failures; Federal Reserve Raises Rates; Other Business, Economic News—California-based Silicon Valley Bank (SVB) collapsed Mar. 10 following a bank run triggered in part by its Mar. 8 announcement that it had sold over $20 bil in long-term bonds at a loss. Regulators in a joint statement Mar. 12 said the federal government would guarantee all customers' deposits made to SVB as well as to New York-headquartered Signature Bank, which folded that day due to "poor management," according to an FDIC report. On Mar. 8, cryptocurrency-focused Silvergate Bank, headquartered in California, had also collapsed amid the stagnant crypto market. In Switzerland, UBS agreed Mar. 19 to acquire nearly insolvent rival Credit Suisse for more than $3.2 bil.

Despite the banking turmoil, the Federal Reserve on Mar. 22 raised its benchmark interest rate—the ninth time in 12 months—another quarter point, to a 4.75%-5.0% range. According to a Bureau of Labor Statistics (BLS) report issued Mar. 14, the annual U.S. inflation rate was 6.0%, continuing its downward trajectory compared to a year earlier.

The U.S. economy added a better-than-expected 311,000 jobs in Feb. as the unemployment rate ticked up to 3.6%, according to a separate BLS report released Mar. 10. Facebook parent company Meta on Mar. 14 announced another 10,000 jobs would be cut as tech sector layoffs continued. On Mar. 30 the Bureau of Economic Analysis reported that U.S. real gross domestic product in the fourth quarter of 2022 increased at an annual rate of 2.6%, down from 3.2% the previous quarter, which analysis attributed in part to a decline in consumer spending. The Dow Jones Industrial Average finished Mar. at 33,274.15, up 1.9% from Feb.; the S&P 500 closed the month at 4,109.31, a 3.5% increase. The Nasdaq Composite Index gained 6.7% to close at 12,221.91.

Arctic Ocean Closed to New Drilling as Alaska Oil Project Gets Go-Ahead; EPA Announces Plan to Cut Smog Emissions—The White House on Mar. 12 declared future oil and gas drilling would be restricted in the entire Arctic Ocean and separately moved to set aside more than half of the 23-mil-acre National Petroleum Reserve-Alaska. The move was seen by some critics as an attempt by Pres. Joe Biden to temper criticism from climate activists and some Democratic lawmakers and Alaska Natives over the administration's approval Mar. 13 of a controversial $8-bil drilling operation in the Alaska reserve known as Willow that will potentially produce more than 600 mil barrels of crude oil—in tandem with a host of potential environmental effects—over three decades.

The federal Environment Protection Agency Mar. 15 announced measures to reinforce its "good neighbor" rule, mandating coal-burning utilities and industrial facilities meet current caps for nitrogen oxide emissions that impact communities downwind of noncompliant states. Criticized by coal and manufacturing interests, the revised rule directly applied to 23 states not yet in adherence in the Midwest and West.

Former Student Kills Six at Nashville Private School—A shooter at the Covenant School, a private Christian school in Nashville, TN, Mar. 27, killed three 9-year-olds and three staff members. The 28-year-old suspect, Aiden Hale, was shot dead by responding police. Reportedly under treatment for an emotional disorder, Hale, who had previously attended the school, owned seven legally purchased firearms—including three used in the attack—that his parents told investigators Hale had hidden from them in the home they shared. According to the Gun Violence Archive, the Covenant shooting was the 132nd mass shooting of 2023, bringing the yearly totals to 506 people injured and 189 killed.

Students at roughly 300 schools across 41 states and DC held walkouts Apr. 5 demanding gun reform. Citing the Covenant School attack among others nationally, Tennessee Gov. Lee signed an executive order Apr. 11 expanding background checks for gun purchases and called on his GOP-controlled legislature to pass a red flag law, allowing temporary seizure of guns from those a judge finds to be a risk. Nineteen states (including GOP-controlled Florida and Indiana) and DC already have red flag laws in effect.

Amid record overall U.S. gun deaths and renewed calls for gun regulation, some states had loosened their gun regulations in the past decade. At least 30 states now allow teachers to carry guns in classrooms; South Dakota was the first, in 2013, to permit school employees to bring guns to schools. Florida in early Apr. became the 26th state (up from 10 in 2020) to allow permitless carry of concealed handguns and North Carolina, Mar. 29, legalized purchase of a handgun without a permit.

International

World's Nations Agree to Protect High Seas—Capping close to two decades of talks, representatives from all UN member countries on Mar. 4 signed a landmark agreement that provided for the creation of marine sanctuaries in international waters—which make up about two-thirds of the world's oceans—to achieve the goal of conserving 30% of the planet's land and oceans by 2030, up from the roughly 17% of land and 8% of oceans currently under protection. The so-called high seas treaty established an oversight body and set protocols for impact assessments of fishing and other ocean-based commercial ventures. At least 60 UN member countries need to ratify the agreement for it to take effect.

Chinese Pres. Xi Secures Unprecedented Third Term—Pres. Xi Jinping of China was appointed to a third five-year term Mar. 10 as the 2,952 delegates of the National People's Congress voted unanimously to reelect the 69-year-old, who did not face any official challengers. Longtime Xi ally Li Qiang was appointed China's premier, effectively second in rank under Xi, on Mar. 11. China's longest-serving head of state since the People's Republic of China was established in 1949, Xi took office as general sec. of the Chinese Communist Party (CCP) in 2012 and president in 2013. He consolidated control over the CCP, markedly increased media censorship, and reasserted the party's authority over policymaking before eliminating the two-term limit on presidential leadership in 2018. Major challenges facing Xi and China in 2023 and beyond included diffusing international trade tensions and reinvigorating its domestic economy; at 3%, China's 2022 GDP growth rate was its second lowest in 40 years.

On Mar. 27, former Taiwanese Pres. Ma Ying-jeou met with a Chinese official in Shanghai, making him the first leader of Taiwan to travel to mainland China since the revolution in 1949.

ICC Charges Putin With War Crimes; Fighting Ramps Up in Bakhmut; U.S. Journalist Detained in Russia—The International Criminal Court (ICC) in The Hague, Netherlands, issued an arrest warrant Mar. 18 for Russian Pres. Vladimir Putin, alleging he played a direct role in the unlawful deportation of Ukrainian children to Russia during the ongoing invasion. Though the ICC lacked jurisdiction in Russia (which is not an ICC signatory), the warrant would impact Putin's ability to travel internationally without risking arrest. Chinese Pres. Xi Mar. 20-22 made his first state visit to Russia since the invasion began in Feb. 2022; China had pledged to remain neutral in the conflict. Poland Mar. 16 announced it was sending four MiG-29s to Ukraine, making it the first NATO country to pledge fighter aircraft against Russia's aggression; Slovakia the next day said it would supply 13 MiGs.

Despite reportedly heavy troop casualties, Russia continued its six-month-long assault on the eastern Ukrainian city of Bakhmut in the Donetsk region, with its mercenary Wagner Group Mar. 8 claiming control of the eastern portion. The next day, Russia launched its largest air assault on major Ukrainian cities in weeks; at least six people were killed, and hundreds of thousands were left without heat or electricity.

Wall Street Journal reporter Evan Gershkovich was detained in central Russia Mar. 29 and charged with espionage. He was the first American journalist to be arrested there on spying charges since the Cold War.

Netanyahu Delays Israeli Judicial Overhaul After Paralyzing Strike, Protests—Israeli Prime Min. Benjamin Netanyahu on Mar. 27 announced he was pausing his government's far-reaching plan to give Israel's parliament, the Knesset, greater control over the judicial system. A day earlier, ongoing protests crescendoed as an estimated 600,000 protesters took to Israel's streets within hours of Netanyahu's firing of Defense Min. Yoav Gallant, who had criticized the proposed changes and called for their renegotiation. Demonstrators in Tel Aviv set fires blocking a major roadway; outside Netanyahu's Jerusalem residence, thousands were fired upon by police water cannons. A general strike declared by Israel's largest trade union alongside mass protests the next morning, Mar. 27, effectively shut down the country ahead of Netanyahu's retreat that evening.

The proposed judicial overhaul would, most significantly, allow the Knesset to invalidate Supreme Court decisions with a simple majority, eliminate judicial review of laws, and increase the ruling government's power to appoint judges.

COVID-19 Pandemic Declaration Passes Three-Year Mark—More than three years after the World Health Org. declared COVID-19 a pandemic, the agency reported over 761.2 mil cumulative confirmed cases (with 6.9 mil deaths) as of the end of Mar. WHO continued to caution, as in previous months, that its totals underestimated the true number of infections due to dramatic reductions in testing and reporting at the local, national, and international level.

The U.S. case tally had reached nearly 102.7 mil (with 1.1 mil deaths) according to WHO. The CDC reported 69.4% of the U.S. pop. (and over 94% of those 65 years and older) fully vaccinated as of Mar. 29, with just 16.5% having received the updated (bivalent) booster (42.1% of those 65 years and older). According to World in Data, 64.2% of the world's pop. was fully vaccinated as of Mar. 30.

General

Prominent South Carolina Attorney Convicted of Killing Wife, Son—A South Carolina jury on Mar. 2 swiftly found attorney Alex Murdaugh guilty of murdering wife Margaret and his 22-year-old son, Paul, capping a highly publicized six-week trial. Prosecutors said the 54-year-old Murdaugh, scion of a prominent South Carolina legal dynasty, carried out the double murder in June 2021 to divert scrutiny from alleged financial crimes with which he was later charged, including money laundering, tax evasion, and fraud. Murdaugh was sentenced Mar. 3 to two consecutive life terms without the possibility of parole.

Everything Everywhere All at Once **Wins Big at Oscars**—The multiverse family epic *Everything Everywhere All at Once* picked up seven Academy Awards, including best picture, and best director and best original screenplay for filmmakers Daniel Kwan and Daniel Scheinert, at the 95th Academy Awards ceremony held Mar. 12 at the Dolby Theatre in Los Angeles. *Everything's* Michelle Yeoh, Ke Huy Quan, and Jamie Lee Curtis won the best actress, supporting actor, and supporting actress awards, respectively. Brendan Fraser claimed best actor for *The Whale*.

Cyclone Freddy Kills Hundreds in Malawi, Mozambique—Cyclone Freddy lashed southern Africa's Malawi Mar. 12 with heavy rains, causing flooding and mudslides that killed more than 1,000; at least 165 people were killed in neighboring Mozambique and 17 in Madagascar. Malawian Pres. Lazarus Chakwera issued a disaster declaration for the 10 districts most heavily affected by the storm—including the hardhit commercial center of Blantyre—which also displaced some half million Malawians. Considered the longest-duration tropical cyclone on record at 34 days, Freddy first formed Feb. 6 off Australia's northwest coast before traveling 5,000 mi across the Indian Ocean.

Japan Outplays U.S. in World Baseball Classic—Japan captured its third World Baseball Classic title, edging the U.S. squad, 3-2, in the final matchup Mar. 21 at LoanDepot Park in Miami, FL. Japan's star pitcher Shohei Ohtani, who claimed the tournament's MVP award with a 1.86 ERA and a .435 batting avg. (including a home run), earned the final out by striking out his L.A. Angels teammate Mike Trout.

Deadly Tornadoes Strike Mississippi, Alabama—Mississippi's Delta region was hit Mar. 24 by tornadoes and severe weather that killed at least 25 people, in addition to 1 fatality in Alabama. An EF-4 twister with winds up to 170 mph—the most destructive of more than 20 reported tornadoes in the two states that day, according to the Natl. Weather Service—roared for nearly 60 mi and leveled much of the small town of Rolling Fork, MS. Pres. Biden issued a major disaster declaration for the four most heavily affected counties in the state.

"Atmospheric River" Brings Severe Flooding to California—California was lashed by intermittent heavy rainfall from so-called atmospheric rivers—narrow corridors of water vapor in the atmosphere—Dec. 2022 through late Mar. 2023 that caused major flooding, numerous landslides, heavy winds, and significant snowfall at higher elevations in parts of the state's northern,

Central Coast, Central Valley, and southern regions (incl. Los Angeles), where weaker storms had hit starting in late Oct. The weather events were collectively blamed for the deaths of more than 25 people and damages of at least $3.5 bil, according to an early NOAA estimate.

Meteorologists noted that while the state experiences over 40 atmospheric rivers on average annually, five of nine that made landfall Dec. 26-Jan. 17 were rated strong or extreme. (Climate change allows atmospheric river systems to hold more moisture and thus deliver more rain.) By Jan. 12, Pres. Biden's disaster declaration covered 41 of California's 58 counties. During that three-week period, San Francisco received a 161-year-high 17.6 in. of rain, Oakland drew a record 18.3 in., and Honeydew (Humboldt County) recorded over 47.4 in. Additional strong-rated storms on Mar. 10 and Mar. 14 drenched northern and central cities yet again. Among other atmospheric river-related phenomena the same month, a bomb cyclone (or bombogenesis, officially) struck the Bay Area Mar. 21 with 60 mph winds before dumping more rain on L.A. and generating two rare tornadoes; at least five people were killed by the storm system.

Despite inflicting widespread damage, the storms also replenished 12 of the state's 17 key reservoirs severely diminished by three years of intense drought, officials said in early Apr. State data also showed the northern, central, and southern Sierra snowpack levels recharged to 192%, 237%, and 300% of their Apr. 1 averages, respectively, causing concern over more flooding.

April 2023
National

Trump Charged Over "Hush-Money" Bribe—Former Pres. Donald Trump was formally arraigned Apr. 4 in a Manhattan criminal court on 34 counts of falsifying business records stemming from a $130,000 "hush-money" payment Trump fixer Michael Cohen made ahead of the 2016 election to cover up an affair Trump allegedly had. Indicted by a grand jury the week prior, Trump, the first former or sitting president charged with a crime, pleaded not guilty. The presiding judge later set a date of Mar. 2024 for the trial. Though an NPR/PBS NewsHour/Marist College poll released Mar. 27 found 56% of Americans believed the investigation into Trump to be fair, 80% of Republicans surveyed believed it was a "witch hunt."

The current front-runner in polls for the GOP's 2024 presidential nomination, Trump continued to face multiple ongoing investigations, including by the U.S. Dept. of Justice into his handling of classified materials after leaving office and his role in the Jan. 6 Capitol riots (and efforts to overturn the election), and by the Georgia district attorney's office into election interference there.

Tennessee Assembly Ejects Two Black Lawmakers Over Gun Control Protest—Tennessee's GOP-controlled state assembly took the extraordinary move Apr. 6 of expelling two Black freshman Democratic lawmakers, Reps. Justin Jones (by a 72-25 vote) and Justin J. Pearson (68-26), for breaking the chamber's decorum rules a week earlier. In the wake of a Nashville school shooting that killed six people Mar. 27, the two representatives, along with a third lawmaker, Rep. Gloria Johnson (D), had led a gun control demonstration at the capitol that interrupted a legislative session. Lawmakers failed by 1 vote to oust Johnson, who is white. Jones and Pearson were each unanimously reinstated by their respective local governing body: Jones by Nashville's city council, Apr. 10, and Pearson by the Shelby County (Memphis) Commission, Apr. 12.

COVID-19 Emergency Ends in U.S.; Other COVID-19 News—Pres. Joe Biden signed a bill Apr. 10 immediately ending the 37-month-old COVID-19 pandemic national emergency. The measure most immediately affected programs such as mortgage forbearance and veteran assistance but did not sunset the separate federal public health emergency order set to end in May. The development came as new confirmed cases in the U.S. continued to decline, to less than 86,500 for the week ending Apr. 24 according to the World Health Org., though testing coverage and reporting also continued to drop precipitously in 2023. WHO recorded around 103.3 mil cumulative confirmed cases (incl. 1.1 mil deaths) in the U.S. by May 1, and 765.0 mil globally (incl. 6.9 mil deaths).

The CDC Apr. 19 recommended a second bivalent COVID-19 vaccine dose for older (65+ years) and immunocompromised adults. As of Apr. 26, the CDC reported just 42.6% in that age group in the U.S. had received one bivalent booster, and just 20.3% of those 18 and older; 69.4% of the U.S. population had completed the primary vaccine series (compared to 64.3% of the world population, as reported by Our World in Data).

U.S. Inflation Continues to Cool; Bud Light Ad Triggers Backlash; Other Business, Economic News—Annual U.S. inflation fell in Mar. for the ninth straight month, down a full point to 5%, its lowest level since May 2021, according to a Bureau of Labor Statistics (BLS) report released Apr. 12. The U.S. added 236,000 jobs in Mar. as the unemployment rate dipped a tenth of a point to 3.5%, according to a separate report issued Apr. 7 by the BLS. The weakest monthly jobs gain since Dec. 2020 was still interpreted favorably by economists following nine consecutive interest rate hikes by the Federal Reserve and tech sector layoffs totaling more than 158,000 over the first three months of 2023.

Transgender influencer and actor Dylan Mulvaney posted a sponsored video Apr. 1 to Instagram promoting Anheuser-Busch's top-selling Bud Light brand, quickly sparking a conservative-led boycott that markedly affected profits; Bud Light sales fell 24.6% over the four weeks ending June 3 compared to a year ago, according to NielsenIQ data. Anheuser-Busch also drew criticism from many LGBTQ advocates who accused the beer giant of backpedaling support for the trans community in response to the protest.

On Apr. 3, U.S. crude oil prices jumped more than 5.5% after OPEC+ (responsible for roughly 40% of global production) announced it was cutting production by 1.66 mil barrels daily. Struggling home goods retailer Bed Bath & Beyond filed for bankruptcy Apr. 23. The UK Apr. 26 blocked Microsoft's $68.7-bil acquisition of gaming giant Activision Blizzard, citing decreased competition. The Dow Jones Industrial Average closed Apr. at 34,098.16, up 2.5% from Mar.; the S&P 500 increased 1.5% to finish the month at 4,169.48; and the Nasdaq Composite Index closed at 12,226.58, gaining just 0.04%.

National Guardsman Arrested in Major Classified Documents Leak—FBI agents Apr. 13 arrested 21-year-old Massachusetts Air National Guardsman Jack Teixeira for allegedly posting hundreds of highly classified U.S. military documents pertaining to Russia's ongoing invasion of Ukraine to a semi-public Discord community as early as Dec. 2022. Disclosing assessments of the Ukrainian military's weaponry and battalion strength, the documents also revealed U.S. interception of Russian defense ministry communications and details on Russia's military capability in Ukraine and strategic plans, some of which had been obtained through sources put at risk by the leak. Said to be the largest known breach of U.S. intelligence since Edward Snowden's leak of global surveillance programs in 2013, the documents exposed U.S. spying on allies, including Israel and South Korea. Teixeira was indicted in mid-June on federal charges.

Fox News Settles Dominion Election Defamation Suit—Averting a lengthy defamation trial, Fox News agreed Apr. 18 to pay Dominion Voting Systems $787.5 mil to settle accusations that the network knowingly promoted false claims that Dominion manipulated its electronic voting machines during the 2020 election to take votes from Pres. Trump. Documents related to the case—including subpoenaed text messages and deposition testimony—revealed that popular Fox News hosts Tucker Carlson, Sean Hannity, and Laura Ingraham had privately rejected Trump's vote-rigging claims against Dominion even as they repeated them on air, and that the hosts had mocked and denigrated Trump attorney Sidney Powell and even Trump himself.

Carlson, perhaps the network's most popular host in its sought-after 8 PM slot, was fired for unspecified reasons less than a week after the settlement was reached. In early Mar., Carlson had aired selected clips from among more than 40,000 hours of security footage from the Jan. 6, 2021, Capitol attack—provided to him directly by House Speaker Kevin McCarthy (R, CA)—and concluded the pro-Trump mob to be largely peaceful "sightseers." Capitol Police Chief Thomas Manger publicly disputed Carlson's commentary, as did a number of Republican senators including Senate Minority Leader Mitch McConnell. According to the Justice Dept., about 140 police officers were assaulted in the attack.

Supreme Court Protects Access to Abortion Drug as Appeals Proceed; Other Abortion Access News—In the Supreme Court's most significant abortion-related ruling since it struck down *Roe v. Wade* 10 months earlier, the Court (7-2) Apr. 21 upheld nationwide access to mifepristone, a drug used in roughly half of all U.S. abortions, when it halted a Texas federal judge's two-week-old preliminary ruling revoking FDA approval for the drug while a case against its use proceeded. (At nearly the same time, a Washington State federal judge had barred the FDA from limiting mifepristone in 18 Democrat-led states that filed suit to preserve its use, setting up a legal battle.) The injunction drew immediate criticism from the White House, which disputed both the judge's claim that the FDA improperly approved mifepristone in 2000 and the characterization of the drug as unsafe. Subsequent reports cited data showing fewer deaths from the drug than from either penicillin or Viagra.

Idaho in early Apr. become the first state to criminalize helping a minor travel to another state to receive an abortion without parental consent. Florida Gov. Ron DeSantis (R) on Apr. 13 signed a bill banning abortions after six weeks of pregnancy; it was set to go into effect July 1 pending legal challenges. Three female Republican state lawmakers thwarted a bill in South Carolina in late Apr. that would outlaw nearly all abortions from conception; a six-week ban was signed into law there on May 25 over their filibuster efforts. The next day, a state circuit judge temporarily blocked the ban pending higher court review. The outcome was viewed as pivotal given South Carolina's status as the last state in the Southeast that had not significantly limited abortion access. According to an NBC News poll conducted in mid-Apr., 58% of Americans said abortion should be legal in all/most cases.

International

Finland Joins NATO in Defiance of Russia; Other Ukraine Invasion Developments—Finland Apr. 4 became the 31st member of NATO, doubling the alliance's border with Russia to nearly 1,600 mi as Russia continued to wage unprovoked war in Ukraine. Russian Pres. Vladimir Putin had repeatedly warned against NATO expansion and threatened military consequences, but fear of further aggression by Russia appeared to drive both Finland and Sweden to apply for membership in May 2022. (Sweden's accession had been blocked by Hungary and Turkey.)

Heavy fighting continued in the eastern Ukrainian city of Bakhmut, with Russia's mercenary Wagner Group declaring "legal control" after planting a flag in the central district, though Ukrainian forces continued to contest its western sections. On Apr. 28, at least 25 civilians were reportedly killed in Russian missile strikes on multiple Ukrainian cities including Kyiv. Russian officials alleged two Ukrainian drones hit a large oil depot in Sevastopol in Russian-occupied Crimea Apr. 29, causing a major fire.

Civil War Flares in Sudan—Heavy fighting erupted Apr. 15 in the Sudanese capital of Khartoum between the once-aligned Sudanese Armed Forces and paramilitary Rapid Support Forces (RSF), killing more than 50 civilians that day. The two factions had shared power since a 2019 military coup but disagreed on the integration of RSF forces into the military; each blamed the other for initiating the latest attacks. Fighting also ignited in the western region of Darfur, wracked by conflict in 2003-20. Though the RSF claimed to have seized both Khartoum's international airport and the presidential palace, the army reportedly retook the latter the following day. As hostilities continued, U.S. and other countries' officials urged their citizens in Sudan to shelter in place or evacuate. U.S. diplomats were airlifted out of Sudan on Apr. 22 upon the embassy's temporary closure.

The combatants broke multiple cease-fires in Apr., including a three-day truce negotiated by the U.S. and Saudi Arabia. According to the UN, by May 23, almost 1.4 mil people were displaced, including 345,000 who fled to neighboring Egypt, Chad, and Ethiopia. The U.S.-based Armed Conflict Location and Event Data Project reported more than 1,800 deaths in the fighting, including 700 in West Darfur's capital, El Geneina, by May 19.

France's Macron Signs Contentious Retirement Age Increase—French Pres. Emmanuel Macron signed a measure Apr. 15 raising the country's minimum retirement age by two years, to 64, following three months of mass protests over the deeply unpopular measure. Macron insisted the change was needed to financially stabilize France's pension system. Government officials reported more than 1.1 mil demonstrators participated Jan. 19 in the first national union-backed protest over the matter, and organized protests continued, with strikes targeting the public transit, power, and education sectors. Up to 3.5 mil protesters participated in each of nine national demonstrations throughout Mar., according to unions; other strikes affected garbage collection, loading docks, and oil refining.

Macron Mar. 16 invoked special executive powers to enact the overhaul, bypassing parliament even after the Senate approved the measure, 195-112, in anticipation of its rejection in the National Assembly. Police in Paris that night used tear gas and water cannons against protesters and arrested more than 200, nearly all of whom were released without charges. Macron's govt., Mar. 20, narrowly survived crucial no-confidence votes. France's Constitutional Council on Apr. 14 upheld the age hike.

General

Nearly 150 Tornadoes Touch Down in U.S., Killing Dozens—A total of 145 confirmed tornadoes—135 of which occurred within a 24-hour span—struck 16 states Mar. 31-Apr. 1 in the Southeast, Mid-Atlantic, and Midwest, killing at least 32 people. It was the third-largest recorded outbreak in U.S. history. The outbreak's strongest tornado was rated EF-4 with winds up to 170 mph, in Iowa; 11 EF-3 funnel clouds were also confirmed. A tornado early Apr. 5 killed five people in a mobile home in Bollinger County, MO. Those deaths brought the total killed in the U.S. from tornadoes in 2023 to at least 63, approaching the normal 12-month average in just the first 4 months of 2023.

LSU Women, UConn Men Win NCAA Basketball Titles—The Louisiana State Univ. Tigers overwhelmed the Iowa Hawkeyes, 102-85, to win the school's first women's NCAA basketball championship at American Airlines Center in Dallas, TX, Apr. 2. Up 17 points at halftime, the Tigers held off a comeback rally by Iowa that stalled amid multiple fouls. Forward Angel Reese, with 15 points, 10 rebounds, and 5 assists in the final and averaging 21.3 points and 15.2 rebounds across all six tournament games, was named the most outstanding player of the Final Four.

The Univ. of Connecticut Huskies defeated the San Diego State Univ. Aztecs, 76-59, at NRG Stadium in Houston, TX, Apr. 3, giving the school its fifth men's NCAA tournament title. Racking up 17 points and 10 rebounds in the final and averaging 19.7 points and 9.8 rebounds in the tournament, Huskies forward Adama Sanogo was named the Final Four's most outstanding player.

Rahm Claims Masters—Spaniard Jon Rahm bested American golfers Phil Mickelson and Brooks Koepka by four strokes at Augusta Natl. Golf Club in Augusta, GA, Apr. 9, to win his first Masters tournament and second career major. The 28-year-old entered the final round two shots behind Koepka before sinking two birdie putts on the back nine to finish 12-under 276. Appearing in his 25th Masters, injury-addled, five-time green-jacket winner Tiger Woods withdrew before the close of the third round after visibly limping.

Mass Shootings Kill 14 in Kentucky, Alabama, Texas—An employee carried out a shooting at Old National Bank in downtown Louisville, KY, Apr. 10, killing five people and injuring two police officers and six others; police then killed the 25-year-old shooter. In an emotional press conference, Kentucky Gov. Andy Beshear (D) said he lost "one of his closest friends" in the shooting. Six days later, four celebrants were shot and killed at a sweet 16 birthday party in Dadeville, AL. On Apr. 28, a man outside Cleveland, TX, allegedly shot and killed five people in a neighboring house, including a 9-year-old boy, after one of the residents asked him to stop shooting a gun in his yard. After a four-day search, the 38-year-old suspect was arrested.

Other shootings also drew media attention: two high-school cheerleaders were shot near Austin, TX, after one of them

opened the door of a car she mistakenly thought was hers; an upstate New York homeowner fatally shot a 20-year-old woman when the car she was in turned into the wrong driveway; and a Black teen in Kansas City, MO, was injured by the homeowner after he rang the doorbell at the wrong address.

***Phantom* Ends 35-Year Broadway Run**—Broadway's longest-running musical, *The Phantom of the Opera*, wrapped up its last show Apr. 16 at New York City's Majestic Theatre, marking 13,981 total performances since Jan. 1988. Created by British composer Andrew Lloyd Webber, *Phantom*, which debuted in London in 1986, claimed seven Tony Awards, including best musical. Its closure left *Chicago* (1996 revival) as the current longest-running Broadway show.

May 2023

National

First Republic Bank Collapses; Hollywood Writers Strike; EU Fines Meta; Other Economic News—Federal regulators May 1 seized San Francisco-based First Republic Bank after a so-called bank run induced the second-largest bank collapse in U.S. history (behind Washington Mutual, 2008); nearly all assets were acquired by JP Morgan Chase. The third midsize bank to fail within two months, First Republic's credit rating had been downgraded in Mar. over its large balance of uninsured deposits.

On May 2, the Writers Guild of America, representing some 11,500 TV and film screenwriters, went on strike for the first time in 15 years. At issue were compensation—including downward-trending pay and staffing levels for streaming projects—and the eventual, probable use of artificial intelligence in scriptwriting.

The European Union May 22 fined Meta approx. $1.3 bil for transferring the personal data of European Facebook users to its U.S. servers, a violation of EU privacy regulations. The fine was the largest imposed under the five-year-old policies. On May 24, Meta terminated 5,100 more employees, bringing its total layoffs since Nov. 2022 to over 21,000. Montana Gov. Greg Gianforte (R) signed a bill May 17 banning the popular Chinese-owned app TikTok over data privacy concerns. The ban, set to take effect in Jan. 2024, was expected to draw legal challenges.

The Federal Reserve on May 3 boosted its benchmark interest rate another quarter point—the 10th hike in 14 months. According to a Bureau of Labor Statistics (BLS) report issued May 10, the annual U.S. inflation rate was 4.9% in Apr., its lowest level in two years. In a separate BLS report released May 5, the U.S. economy added a better-than-expected 253,000 jobs in Apr. as the unemployment rate ticked down to 3.4%, the lowest rate since 1969. The Dow Jones Industrial Average closed May at 32,908.27, down 3.5% from Apr.; the S&P 500 was nearly flat, up just 0.2% to finish the month at 4,179.83; and the Nasdaq Composite Index closed at 12,935.29, gaining 5.8%.

Supreme Court Justice Thomas Under Scrutiny Amid Financial Disclosure Violations—ProPublica on May 4 reported that U.S. Supreme Court Justice Clarence Thomas had failed to disclose up to $150,000 in boarding school tuition payments made in the late 2000s by Republican donor Harlan Crow on behalf of Thomas's grandnephew. A month earlier, ProPublica was first to report that Thomas did not disclose multiple vacations paid for by Crow, including rides in his private jet and on his superyacht, or that Crow in 2014 bought three properties from Thomas and his family members. The disclosure revelations about the court's longest-serving justice came roughly a year after ethics questions were raised regarding his wife, Virginia Thomas, over her participation in 2020 election result denialism. Supreme Court justices are required to file annual financial disclosures. Stricter rules regarding gifts were introduced in Mar. 2023.

DeSantis Escalates Disney Feud—Florida Gov. Ron DeSantis (R) signed a bill May 5 that effectively empowered a board to invalidate the state's development agreements with Walt Disney Co. regarding its control of roughly 25,000 acres in two counties, escalating a 14-month-long public dispute. Disney had criticized a 2022 law—dubbed the "Don't Say Gay" law by opponents—restricting "instruction" and "classroom discussion about sexual orientation or gender identity" in the state's public schools. The May 5 legislation retroactively nullified actions by Disney-allied board members to override DeSantis's efforts to take over the Reedy Creek Improvement District; the 55-year-old special taxing authority had effectively empowered Disney with self-governing status. Disney in Apr. had filed suit against DeSantis for "unconstitutional" and "retaliatory" acts; DeSantis's "replacement" board in turn sued Disney, setting up a legal fight.

A declared 2024 GOP presidential candidate before the end of the month, DeSantis's clash with Disney was part of a wider package of "anti-woke" policies. Other new legislation supported by DeSantis prohibited critical race theory in schools and workplaces and banned state funding for diversity, equity, and inclusion programs in public colleges/universities.

Jury Finds Trump Liable in Sexual Assault Case—A nine-member federal civil jury in New York City May 9 unanimously determined former Pres. Donald Trump sexually assaulted writer E. Jean Carroll in the mid-1990s and defamed her in the lead-up to the trial; the jury awarded Carroll $5 mil. Carroll alleged Trump raped her in a department store dressing room, then defamed her by claiming that she fabricated the incident to boost book sales. (Carroll made the accusation public in 2019 in a *New York* magazine excerpt of her memoir.) Two other women testified during the proceedings, which began Apr. 25, that Trump had similarly assaulted them. On June 29, a federal judge in Manhattan denied Trump's presidential immunity argument seeking to dismiss a second (initial) defamation suit by Carroll.

Pandemic Southern Border Rules Expire—U.S. southern border enforcement policy changed significantly upon the termination May 11 of the COVID-19 public health emergency and corresponding 38-month-old Title 42 order. The temporary regulation had allowed border authorities to summarily turn away some 2.8 million migrants entering illegally rather than allow them to remain in the U.S. while seeking asylum. Following a 10% increase in monthly encounters with migrants by agents along the border in Apr., the White House May 2 announced it was boosting the number of National Guard troops assisting border patrol with administrative tasks from 2,500 to 4,000. Local and state officials anticipated a large influx post-Title 42 as daily migrant encounters at the border in the days leading up to the policy's expiration reached an unprecedented 10,000. Nevertheless, by May 14, Homeland Security Sec. Alejandro Mayorkas said apprehensions had dropped by half; by June 2 the number was down 70% from record highs.

Immediately upon the expiration of Title 42, the ACLU and other rights groups sued the Biden administration after a new restriction mirroring a Trump-era policy went into effect that required migrants to apply for (and be denied asylum) in another country en route before they could seek refuge in the U.S.

Key States Agree on Colorado River Drought Plan—Arizona, California, and Nevada agreed to reduce their usage of water from the drought-stricken Colorado River by a combined 13% through 2026 in a tentative plan announced May 22. Equivalent to 3 mil acre-feet, or the capacity of 6 mil Olympic-sized swimming pools, the reduction forestalled federal emergency measures after a yearlong impasse. Though the river's basin states saw an unusually wet and snowy winter that assisted reservoirs in rebounding from dangerously low levels, experts said the influx did not ameliorate long-term effects of an ongoing 20-year-old "megadrought," including groundwater depletion. Supplying drinking water to some 40 million people in seven states, the Colorado River also irrigates 5.5-6 mil acres of farmland and generates electricity through its hydroelectric dams.

International

WHO Ends COVID-19 Global Health Emergency; U.S. Ends Its Equivalent—The World Health Org. May 5 declared an end to the global health emergency designation for COVID-19, citing the more than yearlong downward trajectory in cases globally. According to the agency, weekly worldwide deaths from the virus had fallen from more than 41,000 at the beginning of Jan. 2023 to around 4,702 by Apr. 24. WHO first declared coronavirus a Public Health Emergency of International Concern (PHEIC) in Jan. 2020, six weeks before it was labeled a pandemic. According to WHO data, authorities as of May 3 tallied roughly 765 mil cumulative confirmed COVID-19 cases

(and 6.9 mil deaths) globally. Europe led in WHO's regional case tally, with more than 275 mil, while the Americas posted the greatest number of deaths: over 2.9 mil, including over 1.1 mil in the U.S. More than 13.4 bil vaccine doses had been administered globally, with 5.1 bil persons fully vaccinated. Pres. Joe Biden ended the COVID-19 public health emergency for the U.S. as anticipated on May 11.

Pakistan's Ex-PM Arrested, Sparking Deadly Unrest—Former Pakistani Prime Min. Imran Khan was arrested on corruption charges in Islamabad, May 9, setting off violent mass street protests in support of the still-popular politician in multiple cities. Demonstrators blocked roadways, threw rocks and Molotov cocktails, and set fires; by May 10, at least eight people had been killed in clashes that also injured more than 150 police officers, who responded to the protesters in force with rubber bullets and tear gas. Khan—the country's first prime minister removed from office through a parliamentary no-confidence vote—accused the military of playing a role in his arrest, just as he had done after his ouster in Apr. 2022. Within hours, protesters stormed the army's headquarters in nearby Rawalpindi; they also ransacked the army corps commander's residence in Lahore. On May 11, Pakistan's supreme court invalidated Khan's arrest and ordered his release. Security forces reportedly arrested over 4,000 people in the aftermath of the protests, including at least 10 senior members of Khan's opposition political party. The country was struggling with soaring inflation and stagnating economic growth, exacerbated by political unrest.

Troops Kill Hundreds of Unarmed Mali Villagers—Malian and foreign forces killed over 500 civilians during an anti-jihadist operation in Mali's south-central village of Moura over five days in late Mar. 2022, according to a report released May 12 by the UN's Office of the United Nations High Commissioner for Human Rights. Based on satellite imagery and interviews with witnesses and victims, the assessment significantly raised the death toll from a previous Human Rights Watch estimate. Rights groups, media, and others accused Russia-based Wagner Group mercenaries—not explicitly accused in the report—of also contributing to the atrocities.

Russian Mercenaries Claim Bakhmut Takeover; Other Ukraine News—Russia's Wagner Group mercenary chief Yevgeny Prigozhin said May 20 that his fighters had taken complete control of the mostly leveled eastern Ukrainian city of Bakhmut after more than eight months of fierce fighting. In contrast, Ukraine's military said it still held a small area in the southwestern outskirts and was continuing to contest parts of its suburbs. By the end of May, Prigozhin said his forces had started transferring control to the Russian army. With more than 20,000 Wagner mercenaries killed there, according to Prigozhin, and an unknown number of Ukrainian troops also slain, Bakhmut (prewar pop. approx. 70,000) was said to be the site of the bloodiest fighting in Russia's ongoing 15-month-old invasion.

In early May, Russia accused Ukraine of attempting to assassinate Russian Pres. Vladimir Putin after air defenses shot down two drones over the Kremlin in Moscow; though Ukraine denied the incursion, U.S. intelligence officials speaking anonymously to the *NY Times* said Ukrainians were likely responsible. Ukraine also officially denied responsibility for an attack on Moscow May 30 that Russian officials said consisted of eight drones, all intercepted, that injured at least two people and damaged buildings. In a shift, Pres. Biden at the G7 Summit in Hiroshima, Japan, backed a plan by allies to train Ukrainian pilots on U.S.-made F-16 fighter aircraft and to help Ukraine acquire the fighters.

Turkey's Erdogan Reelected in Presidential Runoff—Turkey's increasingly autocratic Pres. Recep Tayyip Erdogan won a third five-year term in runoff voting May 28, besting opposition leader Kemal Kilicdaroglu, 52%-48%. The highly contested race followed criticism over the Erdogan government's response to a devastating Feb. 2023 earthquake that killed over 50,000 Turkish people; analysts said the death toll was exacerbated by lax building codes under the ruling right-wing Justice and Development Party (AKP). The country's sky-high inflation was blamed partially on Erdogan's economic policy, which oversaw Turkey's central bank cutting interest rates even as inflation spiked to mid-double-digits.

International observers assessed the election as free but not fair, with the Organization for Security and Co-operation in Europe (OSCE) citing heavily biased media. Erdogan's AKP retained its parliamentary majority in first-round voting May 14.

General

Flooding, Landslides Kill 500 in Central Africa—Flooding and landslides brought on by torrential rains May 2-4 in Democratic Republic of the Congo killed over 400 people in the villages of Bushushu and Nyamukubi, South Kivu province. At least 5,000 people were still missing as of May 10; the flooding destroyed some 1,200 houses.

In neighboring Rwanda, heavy rains May 2-3 induced flooding in northern and western regions, killing over 125 people.

Mage Wins Kentucky Derby, National Treasure Clinches Preakness—After a slow start, 15-to-1 long shot Mage overtook Two Phil's down the backstretch to win the 149th Kentucky Derby by a length in 2:01.57 at Churchill Downs in Louisville May 6. It was the first Derby win for jockey Javier Castellano in his 16th attempt. The Derby was overshadowed to a degree by the deaths of seven horses at the track over 10 days prior to the race; five more horses died at Churchill Downs by the end of May, prompting track officials June 2 to suspend races to investigate safety protocols.

At the 148th Preakness Stakes at Pimlico Race Course in Baltimore, May 20, National Treasure (at 5-2 odds) claimed an early lead and held off late-charging Blazing Sevens by a neck in 1:55.12. Mage placed third.

King Charles III Crowned in London Ceremony—The UK's King Charles III and Queen Camilla were formally crowned in a historic ceremony scaled down due to rain at London's Westminster Abbey, May 6. In the UK, 18.8 mil viewers watched the ceremony on TV (26.2 mil watched the funeral of his mother, Queen Elizabeth II, in Sept. 2022), joined by 10.3 mil viewers in the U.S. Previously known as the Prince of Wales, 74-year-old Charles, who had been heir-apparent for seven decades, immediately acceded to the throne upon Elizabeth's death.

Cyclone Mocha Ravages Myanmar—Powerful Cyclone Mocha made landfall in Rakhine state, Myanmar, May 7, as a Category 5 storm with winds up to 130 mph. The storm unleashed flash flooding and destructive winds, killing at least 145 people in Rakhine, according to the country's military government, before weakening inland. (The exiled National Unity Govt. of Myanmar cited a death toll of over 400.) The majority of those killed were members of the internally displaced Rohingya minority group. Mocha reportedly caused roughly $1.5 bil in damages, including the destruction of more than 215,000 homes.

U.S. Overdose Deaths Plateau at Grim Height—Fatal drug overdoses in the U.S. stabilized in 2022 at the record levels achieved in each of the previous two years, according to preliminary data released May 17 by the CDC. The agency's provisional number of 109,680 fatal overdoses narrowly passed the 109,179 in 2021 to be the highest annual tally ever, with more than two-thirds (68%) of deaths again attributed to synthetic opioids, primarily fentanyl.

Koepka Prevails at PGA Championship—Brooks Koepka won the 105th PGA championship—his third tournament title and fifth major victory—at Oak Hill Country Club in Pittsford, NY, May 21. Koepka scored birdies on holes two through four and pulled off four more on the back nine to finish with a 9-under-271, two shots ahead of fellow American Scottie Scheffler and Norway's Viktor Hovland.

Man Regains Walking Ability With Brain and Spine Implants—A Dutch man paralyzed below the waist by a spinal cord injury more than a decade ago regained the ability to walk via thought-controlled implants, according to a study published May 24 in *Nature*. Two digital implants—developed by the Swiss Federal Institute of Technology—revived communication between the man's brain and injured spinal cord, allowing him to walk 330-660 ft per day and stand unassisted for 2-3 mins. The breakthrough was hailed by researchers and further trials were planned.

Newgarden Triumphant at Indianapolis 500—American Josef Newgarden clinched the 107th Indianapolis 500 at Indianapolis Motor Speedway May 28 in dramatic fashion, overtaking defending champion Marcus Ericsson of Sweden before the third turn of a final-lap restart and holding him off by just 0.0974 seconds, the fourth-closest finish in race history.

June 2023
National

Biden Signs Debt Ceiling Deal, Averting Historic Default—Pres. Joe Biden June 3 signed into law a contentiously negotiated bill that suspended the U.S.'s $31.4 tril debt limit through Jan. 1, 2025. Known as the Bipartisan Budget Agreement, the deal brokered by Biden and House Speaker Kevin McCarthy (R, CA) capped nondefense discretionary spending in FY2024 to 2023 levels and increased it by just 1% the next fiscal year, reduced IRS funding, rescinded some $28 bil in unallocated pandemic funds, and raised the work requirement age ceiling for able-bodied persons receiving federal food assistance to 55 years old from 49. The bill easily passed the Senate (63-36) June 1; the House approved it (314-117) the next day. Republican opponents to the bill's passage called for additional spending cuts; Democratic nay votes particularly opposed the new food assistance requirements.

Biden delivered his first live, televised Oval Office address June 2, during which he praised Democrats and Republicans for their negotiation efforts that forestalled "economic collapse."

Trump Indicted in Federal Classified Documents Case—Former Pres. Donald Trump was indicted by a federal grand jury in Miami, FL, June 8, on criminal charges related to alleged mishandling of classified government documents at his Mar-a-Lago estate. In addition to illegally retaining and refusing to return more than two dozen "secret" or "top secret" documents to the FBI and National Archives, the charges included one count of obstruction and multiple counts of making false statements and concealing documents from a federal probe. On July 27, special counsel Jack Smith brought additional charges, two linked to a claim Trump had asked a Mar-a-Lago employee to delete surveillance video, and a third accusing him of retaining a classified national defense document, which he allegedly showed to visitors at his Bedminster, NJ, golf course. The first former president indicted on federal charges, Trump was said to have improperly kept possession of about 300 classified documents, including about 100 the FBI seized in a raid on Mar-a-Lago in Aug. 2022.

On June 13, Trump pleaded not guilty to all charges and continued to dismiss the investigation as a "witch hunt" via social media. The indictment appeared to decrease his support among Republicans only slightly, with 60% reporting a favorable view of him in an Associated Press-NORC Center for Public Affairs Research poll June 22-26, down from 68% in Apr. The trial was given an anticipated start date in May 2024.

Federal Reserve Pauses Rate Increases; Other Business, Economic News—The Federal Reserve June 14 said it was not increasing the benchmark interest rate—as it had done to target stubbornly high inflation at an unprecedented 10 consecutive meetings over the past 12 months—but signaled two more rate increases were likely before the end of 2023 to achieve the Fed's 2% inflation target. The Bureau of Labor Statistics (BLS) reported June 13 that annual U.S. inflation was at 4.0% in May. According to a separate BLS report released June 2, the U.S. economy added a better-than-predicted 253,000 jobs in May as the unemployment rate ticked up to 3.7%. The Bureau of Economic Analysis's revised figures, released June 29, showed that in the first quarter of 2023, real GDP increased at an annual rate of 2.0% compared to 2.6% over the previous quarter.

The Dow Jones Industrial Average closed June at 34,407.60, up 4.6% from May, as the S&P 500 rose 6.5% to finish the month at 4,450.38; the Nasdaq Composite Index closed at 13,787.92, up 6.6%.

Pres. Biden Launches 2024 Campaign; Field of Republican Presidential Candidates Takes Shape—Touting "Bidenomics" and low unemployment, Pres. Joe Biden (D) held his first 2024 reelection campaign rally June 17, hosted by the AFL-CIO at the Pennsylvania Convention Center in Philadelphia, after his official reelection announcement in Apr. 2023. Author Marianne Williamson, also a 2020 primary candidate, and attorney, political scion, and vaccine skeptic Robert F. Kennedy Jr., were challenging Biden for the Democratic nomination; on June 5, left-wing activist and academic Cornel West declared a third-party bid.

At least 13 candidates were vying for the Republican nomination by the end of June, with former Montana sec. of state Corey Stapleton the first to formally enter the race, in Nov. 2022, followed days later by former Pres. Donald Trump. Trump's UN Ambassador, former South Carolina Gov. Nikki Haley, and entrepreneur Vivek Ramaswamy entered in Feb. 2023, followed in Apr. by former Arkansas Gov. Asa Hutchinson and radio host Larry Elder. Sen. Tim Scott (SC) and Florida Gov. Ron DeSantis announced their bids in May, ahead of former New Jersey Gov. Chris Christie (June 6), North Dakota Gov. Doug Burgum and former Vice Pres. Mike Pence (June 7), Miami Mayor Francis Suarez (June 15), and former U.S. Rep. Will Hurd (TX) (June 22). Trump held a commanding lead in polls of Republican voters, with 52.4% support according to the RealClearPolitics June 30 polling average, trailed by DeSantis, with 21.5%, and 5.7% for Pence; the rest of the field failed to register above 4%.

Supreme Court Concludes Term With Key Rulings on Student Loans, Affirmative Action, Elections—The U.S. Supreme Court ended its 2022-23 term June 30 with a much-anticipated ruling in *Biden v. Nebraska* that blocked the Biden administration's plan to cancel as much as $20,000 in outstanding student loan debt per borrower. Writing for the majority in a 6-3 decision, Chief Justice John Roberts asserted that such sweeping action could only be carried out with the approval of Congress; the Court's three liberal associate justices dissented. That day, the same majority overrode a Colorado anti-discrimination law when they concluded in *303 Creative LLC v. Elenis* that the First Amendment allows a web designer to refuse to create sites for same-sex weddings. In a landmark decision June 29 that effectively upended 40 years of legal precedent, the same six-justice majority also ruled that race-conscious admissions policies—commonly known as affirmative action—used at both the public Univ. of North Carolina and elite, private Harvard Univ. violated the equal protection clause of the 14th Amendment and Title VI of the Civil Rights Act of 1964.

On June 27, Roberts and Associate Justices Brett Kavanaugh and Amy Coney Barrett sided with the three-justice liberal bloc in *Moore v. Harper*, in rejecting a controversial legal theory that would have allowed state lawmakers to regulate federal elections without state court oversight or interference. In a 5-4 ruling June 8, the same majority minus Barrett concluded in *Allen v. Milligan* that Alabama lawmakers violated Black residents' voting rights by drawing a congressional map with white majorities in six of seven districts despite the Black population comprising more than a quarter of the state's population.

International

White House Hosts Indian Prime Minister—Pres. Joe Biden hosted Indian Prime Min. Narendra Modi for a formal White House state dinner June 22 after he addressed a joint session of Congress, marking the first official state visit to the U.S. by an Indian prime minister in 14 years. Seen by observers as an opportunity for Biden to solidify relations with India—the world's most populous nation as of Apr. 2023—amid increasing Chinese aggression in the Indo-Pacific region, the highly watched visit drew criticism from some in the Indian American community over rights abuses by Modi. In 2005-14, the U.S. State Dept. had barred Modi from entry into the U.S. over alleged religious freedom violations during riots that killed more than 1,000 mostly Muslims in 2002 in Gujarat state, where he served as chief minister.

Police Killing of Unarmed Teen Ignites Protests in France—Violent protests and rioting erupted throughout France after police shot and killed unarmed 17-year-old Nahel Merzouk during a traffic stop June 27 in Nanterre, a Paris suburb. Though police initially said Merzouk, of Moroccan and Algerian descent, drove his vehicle toward them, bystander video made widely available appeared to contradict that claim.

Protests decrying police racism started that evening in Nanterre, with some demonstrators setting cars on fire and erecting barricades. Though some protests remained peaceful, unrest in numerous cities continued for at least four nights; the mayor of another Paris suburb had his home set on fire July 2, injuring his wife and a child. France's interior minister June 30 announced the nationwide deployment of 45,000 officers supported by light armored vehicles. Police—of whom 700 officers were injured—arrested around 3,400 people in connection with the riots; fire crews attended thousands of fires (including vehicle and trash can fires) before rioting eased in early July. The officer who shot Merzouk was charged with voluntary manslaughter.

Fighting Escalates Between Rival Sudanese Forces—Fighting in Sudan between the once-aligned Sudanese Armed Forces (SAF) and paramilitary Rapid Support Forces (RSF) intensified, marked by the abduction and execution June 14 of West Darfur state governor Khamis Abakar, who had accused the RSF of genocide. (Civilian testimonies in West Darfur's capital of Geneina alleged both arbitrary killings and mass rapes; the RSF was also accused of killing hundreds of civilians in North Darfur.) Citing repeated cease-fire violations since revived fighting broke out in the capital, Khartoum, in mid-Apr., U.S. and Saudi Arabian negotiators June 1 suspended peace talks in Jeddah, Saudi Arabia, a day after rocket fire—apparently launched from an area under SAF control—killed at least 18 people at a market in Khartoum. Another Khartoum strike blamed on SAF forces killed at least 17 people, including 5 children, June 17. According to the Armed Conflict Location and Event Data Project (ACLED), more than 1,020 people were killed in the conflict's second full month, May 20-June 16; by July 21, some 2.6 mil Sudanese were internally displaced, according to the UN's refugee agency, with 738,000 others fled abroad, mostly to Egypt, Chad, and South Sudan.

Wagner Group Launches Short-Lived Revolt Against Moscow; Other Russian Invasion Developments—Posing an unexpected threat to Russian Pres. Vladimir Putin, Yevgeny Prigozhin—head of the Wagner Group of mostly Russian mercenaries—staged a rebellion lasting less than 24 hours June 23-24, demanding the ousting of certain leadership, including defense minister Sergei Shoigu and Russia's top general, Valery Gerasimov. After an armed Wagner Group convoy took control of the Russian city of Rostov-on-Don and its military facilities, Wagner forces and tanks made their way to within 125 mi of Moscow, fending off defensive attacks by Russian aircraft and helicopters. Prigozhin ordered the convoy back to Ukraine—where Wagner had been fighting in Putin's 16-month-old invasion—only after Belarus Pres. Aleksandr Lukashenko reportedly negotiated a settlement that included exile in Belarus for Prigozhin and Kremlin assurances that Wagner troops would not be prosecuted.

A consensus of military experts and Ukrainian officials blamed Russian forces for an explosion that breached southern Ukraine's Kakhovka Dam near Kherson June 6, causing massive flooding. Russia continued air strikes on cities including Kyiv, Odesa, and Kherson. Ukrainian forces June 8 launched a counteroffensive in southeastern areas of the war's 600-mi-long front.

General

India Train Collision Kills Nearly 300—At least 290 people were killed in a three-train accident in India 170 mi south of Kolkata, June 2. The deadliest rail incident in the country in more than 20 years occurred after a passenger train diverted onto a track where it slammed into a stationary freight train at nearly 80 mph. On an adjacent track, a second passenger train traveling in the opposite direction collided with several of the derailed passenger cars. Government officials said a signaling error was likely responsible for the diversion.

Swiatek, Djokovic Take French Open Titles—Top-seeded defending champion Iga Swiatek of Poland outlasted Czechia's unseeded Karolína Muchová (6-2, 5-7, 6-4) to win her third French Open women's singles title in four years and her fourth Grand Slam June 10 at Roland Garros in Paris, France. The next night, No. 3-ranked Novak Djokovic of Serbia overcame No. 4-ranked Casper Ruud of Norway (7-6, 6-3, 7-5), earning the 36-year-old star his record 23rd Grand Slam men's singles title.

Denver Nuggets Win NBA Championship—The Denver Nuggets clinched closely contested Game 5, 94-89, over the Miami Heat at Ball Arena in Denver, CO, June 12, for the 47-year-old franchise's first NBA championship. After missing 20 of their 22 first 3-point shots and 7 of their first 13 free throws, the Nuggets bounced back from a 51-44 deficit at the half to claim the title. Denver center Nikola Jokić earned Finals MVP designation, averaging 30.2 points, 14 rebounds, and 7.2 assists over the five matchups.

Vegas Golden Knights Take Home Stanley Cup—The Vegas Golden Knights dominated the Florida Panthers, 9-3, June 13 in Game 5 at T-Mobile Arena in Las Vegas, NV, to win the team's first Stanley Cup since its debut season in 2017-18. Golden Knights forward Jonathan Marchessault won the Conn Smythe Trophy as playoff MVP, with 13 goals and 12 assists in 22 games.

Mediterranean Migrant Boat Capsizes, Killing Hundreds; 100+ Die in Nigerian Ferry Boat Accident—A fishing trawler packed with up to 750 migrants overturned and sank off the coast of Pylos, Greece, June 14, after departing Libya, leaving at least 82 people confirmed dead and up to 500 missing, the UN said. At least 104 people were rescued, but multiple survivors questioned rescue and recovery efforts or said the Greek coast guard caused the capsizing when they attempted to tow the boat, an allegation the coast guard denied but was supported by a joint investigation by *The Guardian* and other media. The wreck highlighted the ongoing danger of seeking refuge in Europe via sea routes—since 2014, the UN's Intl. Org. for Migration has documented close to 28,000 deaths and missing persons in the Mediterranean.

On June 12, at least 106 people drowned in north-central Nigeria after a boat carrying 250 wedding guests overturned on the Niger River.

Titanic-Bound Submersible Implodes, Killing All Passengers—Commercial submersible *Titan* June 18 lost contact with support personnel just 1 hour, 45 minutes after commencing its dive to the wreckage of the *Titanic*, located about 12,500 ft below the surface off the coast of Newfoundland, Canada. The U.S. Coast Guard led an extensive search for the 22-ft-long vessel operated by OceanGate Expeditions, whose American CEO Stockton Rush was among the five passengers onboard. Coast Guard officials June 22 said the submersible had experienced a "catastrophic implosion" that killed all onboard and announced that human remains and at least five pieces of *Titan* were found on the ocean floor, about 1,600 ft from the *Titanic* wreckage. Numerous experts had reportedly raised safety concerns over the uncertified craft.

Underdog Wins U.S. Open; PGA-LIV Golf Merger Stuns—Wyndham Clark won the 123rd U.S. Open and his first major title June 18 at the Los Angeles Country Club in Los Angeles despite never having finished above 75th in a major championship. Starting the final round tied with fellow American Rickie Fowler, the 29-year-old Clark seized the lead after birdying the fourth hole and finished with a 10-under-270, one shot ahead of Rory McIlroy.

In a surprise announcement June 6, the PGA tour agreed to merge with upstart Saudi-funded rival LIV Golf, ending nearly two years of litigation and disputes, including PGA's suspension of players choosing to compete in LIV tournaments. The tentative deal also folded in the DP (European) World Tour. Human rights advocates and other LIV Golf critics—who primarily oppose the league due to its Saudi ownership—condemned the development.

Forest Fires Across Canada Force Evacuations, Tank Air Quality—Canada was experiencing its worst wildfire season on record, the Canadian Interagency Forest Fire Centre declared June 26, reporting more than 490 active fires at the end of the month, mostly in Québec, Alberta, British Columbia, and Ontario. By July 6, fires had burned some 27.7 mil acres and forced evacuations of more than 155,000 residents. Resulting heavy smoke caused intermittently severe air quality issues in Canada and the U.S., and blanketed major cities including Chicago,

New York, Philadelphia, and Toronto in thick haze. More than 100 mil Americans were affected June 30 alone.

July 2023
National

U.S. Destroys Last Known Chemical Weapons—Pres. Joe Biden announced July 7 that the U.S. had fully eliminated the last of its chemical weapons stockpile, capping a decades-long effort to rid itself of some 30,000+ tons stored at the end of the Cold War. Signed by 193 countries, the Chemical Weapons Convention, which took effect in 1997, required all signatories to destroy their remaining supplies. The U.S. was believed to be the last state party to do so, delayed in part due to environmental challenges. According to the United Nations, chemical weapons killed more than 100,000 people in World War I and had killed or injured at least 1 million more in global conflicts since.

Hollywood on Strike; UPS Averts Strike; L.A.-Area Hotel Workers Walk Off Job—SAG-AFTRA, the labor union representing about 160,000 TV and movie actors, went on strike July 13 for the first time in 43 years. The union was advocating for higher base pay, a greater share of streaming revenues, and clearer regulations on the use of artificial intelligence, including actors' likenesses. The actors joined the 11,500 WGA screenwriters on the picket line since May 2 over similar demands, making it the first time both unions were simultaneously on strike since 1960.

On July 25, shipping giant UPS and the Teamsters union representing more than 340,000 of the company's workers nationwide agreed on a tentative contract, forestalling what would have reportedly been the largest single-employer strike in U.S. history. In early July, hotel workers in southern California began striking in waves over pay and benefits.

Another Fed Interest Rate Increase; Microsoft-Activision Blizzard Deal Cleared; FDA Approves First Over-the-Counter Birth Control Pill; Other Economic, Business News—The Federal Reserve July 24 raised its key interest rate by another quarter-point to its highest level in 22 years; it was the 11th such increase since Mar. 2022. The annual inflation rate reached a 27-month-low 3.0%, according to a Bureau of Labor Statistics (BLS) report released July 13, but the Federal Reserve had repeatedly signaled that it hoped to limit year-over-year inflation to 2.0%. The BLS in a separate report issued July 7 announced that the U.S. economy added a lower-than-expected 209,000 jobs in June, as the unemployment rate dipped a tenth of a point to 3.6%.

A San Francisco federal judge July 11 approved Microsoft's $69-bil acquisition of video game maker Activision Blizzard, reportedly the largest-ever tech industry acquisition, dismissing a Federal Trade Commission challenge. The FDA July 13 approved Perrigo's Opill as the first non-prescription birth control pill available in the U.S. Earlier in the month, the agency fully approved Leqembi, the first drug shown to slow Alzheimer's disease progression despite it carrying an elevated risk of potentially fatal brain swelling. On July 21, defense contractor Booz Allen Hamilton agreed to pay $377 mil to settle Justice Dept. allegations that it overcharged the federal government to make up for business losses.

The Dow Jones Industrial Average closed July at 35,559.53 up 3.3% from June; the S&P 500 rose 3.1% to finish the month at 4,588.96; the Nasdaq Composite Index closed at 14,346.02, up 4.0%.

International

Israel Launches Major Offensive in West Bank; Israeli Parliament Votes to Limit Supreme Court—Israeli forces July 3-4 carried out the largest assault on the Palestinian-occupied West Bank in almost two decades, killing at least 12 Palestinians and injuring over 100 more civilians in the Jenin refugee camp. The offensive action, which targeted alleged militant factions with drone-fired missiles and ground operations involving roughly a thousand ground troops, displaced more than 4,000 people and damaged or destroyed 800+ houses, according to

Jenin officials. UN Sec.-Gen. António Guterres publicly condemned the operation as an excessive use of force.

Israel's parliament, the Knesset, July 24 voted to restrict the Israeli supreme court's ability to invalidate government decisions, disregarding more than six months of mass protests against the judicial overhaul plan. Opposition lawmakers boycotted the vote, saying that the measure removed an important check on the government. Multiple polls showed most Israelis opposed the plan, and more than 10,000 military reservists said they would no longer serve if the overhaul proceeded.

U.S. Sends Ukraine Controversial Cluster Bomb Aid; Russia Pulls Out of Grain Deal; Other Developments—The Biden administration announced July 7 it would provide an additional $800-mil weapons package to Ukraine to resist Russia's ongoing invasion. The aid package notably included cluster bombs, which are banned by more than 100 countries due to the bombs' likelihood of detonating long after impact, posing a greater risk to civilians. Despite repeated requests from Ukrainian Pres. Volodymyr Zelenskyy, Biden continued to refuse to provide long-range missiles.

Russia July 17 ended its participation in a deal pledging safe passage of Ukraine's grain exports from blockaded Black Sea ports, hours after Ukraine damaged a key bridge linking Russian-occupied Crimea with southern Ukraine. Further jeopardizing the global food supply, Russia carried out targeted attacks on Ukrainian grain silos and ports in July and Aug. On July 30 and Aug. 1, Ukrainian drone attacks reportedly destroyed small sections of high-rise buildings in Moscow, causing no casualties.

NATO Sec.-Gen. Jens Stoltenberg July 11 said NATO leaders would invite Ukraine to join the alliance when they agree on conditions, as Pres. Biden publicly said the ongoing war between Russia and Ukraine would need to end before the alliance would consider Ukraine's membership.

American Soldier Flees to North Korea; U.S. Docks Nuclear Sub in South Korea; Other Related News—U.S. military officials reported that a 23-year-old Army private stationed in South Korea "willfully and without authorization" ran across the demilitarized zone (DMZ) into North Korea, July 18. Recently released from a South Korean prison after serving a 50-day sentence on an assault charge, Pvt. Travis King was scheduled to fly to the U.S. to face further disciplinary action when he evaded his escorts and joined a civilian group touring the DMZ. North Korean state media Aug. 16 reported King sought entry due to "mistreatment and racial discrimination" in the Army; the country later announced it was expelling King, who arrived back at a U.S. military base in late Sept. King was thought to be the first U.S. soldier to cross into North Korea since 1982.

The U.S. Navy's nuclear-powered, ballistic missile submarine USS *Kentucky* arrived in South Korea July 18; a second, unarmed U.S. sub docked in South Korea July 24. Both were part of an enhanced defense cooperation agreement negotiated between the nations' presidents at the White House in Apr. 2023. On July 12, North Korea test-launched another intercontinental ballistic missile, which reportedly landed in waters roughly 155 mi west of Japan's Okushiri Island.

Niger Military Faction Ousts President—Niger's presidential guard carried out an apparent coup d'état July 26, as U.S.-backed Pres. Mohamed Bazoum and his family were detained in their home indefinitely, and military leaders announced via state television that the president had been removed from power. The military also closed the borders, suspended national institutions, and launched a nationwide curfew. Gen. Abdourahamane Tchiani made a televised appearance July 28 as the de facto leader of the new military junta and claimed Bazoum was ousted over the landlocked West African nation's "deteriorating security situation." A key Western ally in the fight against Islamic jihadist insurgencies in the Sahel region over the past decade, Niger had in fact experienced decreasing casualties from such violence in 2022. But the alliance with the West, including the presence of roughly 1,100 U.S. and 1,500 French troops in Niger, may have fueled internal tensions. (Both the U.S. and France suspended military cooperation with Niger by early Aug.)

In power since 2021, Bazoum's tenure marked Niger's first peaceful, democratic transition since its independence in 1960, despite military elements unsuccessfully attempting a takeover days before his swearing-in. Since 2020, military coups had removed the elected leadership in at least three other West African nations.

U.S. Orders Staff Out of Haiti Amid Spiraling Violence—The State Dept. July 28 ordered non-emergency U.S. staff and their families to vacate Haiti due to soaring violence and an elevated risk of kidnapping. According to a UN official, as of Aug. 15, more than 2,400 people had been killed in escalating gang violence there in 2023; more than 950 people were kidnapped over the same period. The UN's migration agency reported more than 200,000 Haitians displaced thus far in 2023. Observers linked the unrest to the power vacuum generated by the July 2021 assassination of Haiti's then-Pres. Jovenel Moïse. Criminal gangs now reportedly control approx. 80% of the capital, Port-au-Prince, and surging violence has led to the closure of schools and medical clinics.

ISIS Blast Kills Over 50 in Pakistan—An ISIS affiliate claimed responsibility for a suicide bombing in northwest Pakistan, near the border with Afghanistan, that killed at least 54 people July 30 at an election rally held by Jamiat Ulema-e-Islam-Fazl, a government-allied Islamist political party. In a statement, Islamic State-Khorasan (ISIS-K) said it carried out the attack against democracy "as a regime hostile to true Islam"; parliamentary elections were expected to be held in Oct. or Nov. Pakistan had experienced a rebound in militant violence following the breakdown in late Nov. 2022 of a five-month-old ceasefire between the government and the Pakistani Taliban (TTP). On July 12, an attack in the southwestern province of Baluchistan claimed by a likely TTP-affiliated group killed at least nine soldiers and one civilian.

General

European Space Telescope Blasts Off to Observe "Dark Universe"—The European Space Agency July 1 launched Euclid, its new wide-angle space telescope, via SpaceX Falcon 9 rocket from Cape Canaveral, FL. Designed in cooperation with NASA to scan more than a third of the sky and detect galaxies as distant as 10 bil light-years away, the 15-ft-long Euclid would allow ESA scientists to develop research on the still-little-known phenomena of dark energy and dark matter theorized to constitute some 95% of the universe. Euclid reached its solar orbit, which it shares with NASA's James Webb Space Telescope, about one month later.

Corpuz Clinches U.S. Women's Open—Claiming both her first major title and first LPGA Tour win, Hawaiian native Allisen Corpuz clinched the 78th U.S. Women's Open at Pebble Beach Golf Links in Pebble Beach, CA, July 9. The 25-year-old Corpuz, who started the final day one shot behind the lead, pulled off six birdies to finish at 9-under 279, three shots ahead of Charley Hull of England and South Korea's Jiyai Shin.

Arrest Made in Gilgo Beach Murders—Manhattan architect Rex Heuermann was arrested July 13 and charged with the 2009-10 killings of three women whose bodies were discovered along Long Island's Gilgo Beach. (The 59-year-old was also suspected in the death of a fourth woman found in the same area in late 2010.) Investigators relied heavily on analysis of phone location data and DNA samples to link Heuermann to the women—all sex workers who appeared to have died by strangulation.

Vondrousová, Alcaraz Take Wimbledon Titles—In a shocking upset, Czech Republic's Markéta Vondrousová overcame No. 6-seed Ons Jabeur of Tunisia in straight sets (6-4, 6-4) in just 1 hr., 20 min., to capture the Wimbledon women's singles championship at London's All-England Club, July 15, and her first career Grand Slam. Ranked 42nd in the world going into the tournament, Vondrousová became the first unseeded player to win the Wimbledon singles title in the Open era, as well as the lowest ranked ever to do so. The next day, No. 1-seed Carlos Alcaraz of Spain pulled off a stunning comeback after a first-set loss to No. 2-seed, defending champion Novak Djokovic of Serbia, rallying to defeat the veteran superstar (1-6, 7-6, 6-1, 3-6, 6-4) over a match spanning 4 hr., 42 min.

Kenyan Starvation Cult Kills Hundreds—Twelve bodies were exhumed July 17 in Kenya's southern coastal region, reportedly pushing the death toll among followers of an anti-Western doomsday cult to more than 400. Pastor Paul Mackenzie, head of the Good News International Church, was arrested in mid-Apr. after authorities began uncovering bodies from shallow graves in a forested area near the town of Malindi; Mackenzie had allegedly instructed the majority of the victims to starve themselves to death in order to "meet Jesus." More than 35 other suspects were also in custody, though none were yet charged.

Harman Wins Golf's British Open—American Brian Harman won the 151st Open Championship and his first major title at Royal Liverpool Golf Club in Hoylake, Wirral, England, July 23. Holding a five-shot lead going into the final round, Harman on the last day countered three bogeys with three birdies amid pouring rain to finish at 13-under 271, six shots ahead of four rivals tied for second.

Vingegaard Wins Second Tour de France—Defending champion Jonas Vingegaard won the 110th Tour de France July 23 in Paris, finishing the grueling 2,116-mi, 21-stage course in 82 hr., 5 min., 42 sec. The 26-year-old Dane retained the yellow jersey as overall race leader from the mountainous sixth stage on, holding off 2020-21 champ Tadej Pogacar of Slovenia at the close of the Tour by 7 min., 31 sec., and third place rider Adam Yates (UK) by 10 min., 56 sec. Belgium's Jasper Philipsen claimed his first green sprinter's jersey after winning four stages. Pogacar won the white jersey (best young rider) for the fourth straight year.

Record-High Heat on Several Continents; Catastrophic Flooding in Vermont; Other Climate-Related Developments—Extreme heat waves in July gripped multiple Northern Hemisphere regions, including Asia, southern Europe, Mexico, and the U.S. Phoenix, Arizona's largest city, saw 31 straight days with temperatures exceeding 110°F through July 30, smashing the previous streak of 18 days set in 1974. NOAA reported that both Arizona and New Mexico had their hottest Julys on record, each by almost 2°F. According to the National Weather Service, more than 170 mil Americans were under heat alerts in late July as the heat wave expanded to the Great Plains, Midwest, and Northeast. Researchers also noted unprecedented ocean water temperatures in southern Florida.

China's arid northwest recorded a national all-time high of 126°F on July 16, the same day U.S. climate envoy John Kerry arrived there to revive climate talks between the world's two largest greenhouse gas emitters. Heat-attributed deaths mounted; in Mexico, officials cited 250 deaths during the four months ending July 22. In Aug., NOAA reported that July 2023 was Earth's hottest month on record, with combined global land and ocean surface temperatures 2.02°F higher than the 20th-century average of 60.4°F.

Hundreds of blazes continued to burn in Canada, which was battling its worst fire season on record. Numerous fires stoked by dry conditions also raged in North Africa and southern Europe, including in Algeria, Italy, Greece, and Spain's Canary Islands. Wildfires forced the evacuation of roughly 19,000 people from the Greek tourist island of Rhodes. Flash flooding triggered by sudden and heavy rainfall associated with warmer, moister air also affected multiple U.S. states, particularly Vermont, wide swaths of which were devastated by flooding July 10-11 that killed at least two people. AccuWeather estimated $3-$5 bil in damage in the Northeast. July downpours also led to the deaths of at least five people in southeastern Pennsylvania, and four in Canada's Nova Scotia. Within Asia, more than 40 people were killed in South Korea after torrential rains impacted central and southern parts of the country.

August 2023
National

Trump Legal Issues Mount With New Federal, State Charges—A federal grand jury in Washington, DC, indicted former Pres. Donald Trump Aug. 1 on four conspiracy and obstruction charges related to his efforts to overturn the 2020

election results. In the indictment, prosecutors alleged Trump knew his election fraud assertions were false and sought to undermine the results, by leaning on state officials to ignore vote totals, setting up "fake electors" to falsely certify Trump victories, and pressuring then-Vice Pres. Mike Pence to reject the Electoral College results during Congress's election certification process. Special counsel Jack Smith, in a post-indictment statement, said that the Capitol insurrection of Jan. 6 was incited by Trump's lies "targeted at obstructing a bedrock function of the U.S. government." Trump, whose attorneys dismissed the case as an attack on his free speech rights, pleaded not guilty Aug. 3.

A Fulton County, GA, special grand jury Aug. 14 indicted Trump and 18 co-defendants over their attempts to overturn his election loss in that state specifically. Trump was charged with 13 counts, including violating Georgia's anti-racketeering (RICO) law, for having "unlawfully conspired" to alter the election outcome while engaging in a "criminal enterprise." Other defendants included former prominent Trump staffers Mark Meadows, Rudy Giuliani, John Eastman, and Sidney Powell. Key evidence in the case included a series of recorded phone calls between Trump and election officials, including Georgia Sec. of State Brad Raffensperger (R), during which Trump invoked multiple false claims of voting irregularities and the need to "find 11,780 votes." All 19 defendants pleaded not guilty; Trump, who was processed Aug. 24 at Fulton County Jail—including having a mug shot taken—before posting bail, discounted the investigation as a "witch hunt." By the end of Aug., Trump faced 91 criminal charges in four separate cases.

On July 18, Michigan Atty. Gen. Dana Nessel announced criminal charges against all of the state's 16 "fake electors" for Trump, and by Aug. 3, prosecutors had filed charges against three Michigan Republicans for attempting to tamper with voting machines in the state during the 2020 election. Joe Biggs, a former leader of the neofascist Proud Boys, was sentenced Aug. 31 to 17 years in federal prison for his role in the Jan. 6 riot at the Capitol. Another former Proud Boys leader, Enrique Tarrio, received a 22-year sentence on Sept. 5.

Trucking Giant Yellow Folds; Purdue Pharma Settlement Is Rejected; Other Business, Economic News—Facing massive debt and slowing business, the Nashville-based trucking company Yellow filed for Chapter 11 bankruptcy protection Aug. 6, one week after it shut down operations and laid off all of its 30,000 employees. The 99-year-old company, which specialized in "less-than-truckload" shipping, faced increasing competition in recent decades that helped push its debt load to about $1.5 bil as of late Mar., despite having received $700 mil in federal pandemic relief funds.

On Aug. 10, the U.S. Supreme Court paused a bankruptcy plan by OxyContin maker Purdue Pharma that would have paid up to $6 bil to help mitigate the opioid epidemic but protected the company's owners, the Sackler family, from financial liability. A federal judge in Manhattan Aug. 11 revoked bail for FTX co-founder Sam Bankman-Fried after alleging he had attempted to influence witnesses ahead of his upcoming fraud trial.

According to a Bureau of Labor Statistics (BLS) report released Aug. 4, the U.S. added a lower-than-expected 187,000 jobs in July, and the unemployment rate ticked down from 3.6% to 3.5%. In a separate report Aug. 10, the BLS said that the annual U.S. inflation rate as of July was 3.2%. At the beginning of Aug., the credit rating agency Fitch lowered the U.S. rating to AA+ from AAA, citing an "erosion of governance," including Congress's recent debt ceiling deadlock. The Dow Jones Industrial Average closed Aug. at 34,721.91, down 2.4%, and the S&P 500 dropped 1.8% to finish the month at 4,507.66; the Nasdaq Composite Index ended Aug. at 14,034.97, a 2.2% decline from July.

Select Republican Candidates Spar at First Debate—Eight Republican presidential candidates appeared Aug. 23 in Milwaukee, WI, at the first GOP primary debate of the 2024 election cycle. Trump, the overwhelming frontrunner in national polling, skipped the two-hour event hosted by Fox News after declaring via social media that he would not participate in primary debates because voters knew "what a successful presidency I had." Trump instead appeared that evening in a pretaped interview with former Fox News host Tucker Carlson that streamed on X (formerly Twitter); candidates at the debate were asked whether Trump would have their support. Entrepreneur and first-time candidate for public office Vivek Ramaswamy said he would pardon Trump and that the U.S. should encourage Ukraine to cede territory to Russia; he was bluntly criticized by former New Jersey Gov. Chris Christie, former Vice Pres. Mike Pence, and former UN Ambassador Nikki Haley. Highlighting the party's differences over abortion, Haley quarreled with Pence, who advocated a national abortion ban; North Dakota Gov. Doug Burgum also came out against a federal prohibition, while Sen. Tim Scott (SC) appeared to back Pence.

International

Sudanese Refugees Exceed 1 Million as Factional Hostilities Continue; Other Conflict News—More than 1 mil people had fled Sudan to nearby countries to escape violence between Sudan's army and the paramilitary Rapid Support Forces (RSF), as of Aug. 15, according to the UN's Intl. Org. for Migration. The agency also estimated more than 3.4 mil Sudanese had been internally displaced. The head of the RSF Aug. 27 released a 10-point peace plan that was immediately dismissed by the Sudanese military. The UN has accused the RSF of committing extrajudicial killings, torture, and rape; an official in West Darfur said the group was responsible for 30 mass graves with at least 1,000 bodies discovered in and around El Geneina. (Rights groups have also accused Sudan's army of abuses.) Among other developments, the RSF by Aug. 4. claimed full control of Central Darfur state. Intensifying fighting in South Darfur state later in the month killed at least 39 civilians in Nyala; more than 7,500 people had been killed since Apr., according to a Sept. 8 report by the UK-based Armed Conflict Location and Event Data Project.

Thai Parliament Elects Compromise Candidate—Thailand's parliament on Aug. 22 chose 60-year-old real estate tycoon Srettha Thavisin as prime minister after his populist Pheu Thai party cobbled together an 11-party coalition, ending three months of deadlock. The progressive Move Forward party, blocked from power by the country's military-appointed Senate, was not included in the ruling coalition despite its upset victory in general elections May 14, in which Move Forward won 151 out of 500 seats vs. 141 by Pheu Thai. Though Thavisin previously said he would not align himself with military leadership, his ruling coalition included two military-backed parties linked to outgoing Prime Min. Prayut Chan-ocha, a former army officer who came to power in a 2014 coup.

Former Prime Min. Thaksin Shinawatra, removed from power by a 2006 coup, returned to Thailand Aug. 22 after more than 15 years in exile; that same day, the country's high court sentenced the 74-year-old to eight years in prison (commuted to one year by Thailand's king) over multiple corruption charges.

Progressive Upstart Wins Guatemalan Presidency—Anticorruption champion Bernardo Arévalo from the progressive Movimiento Semilla (Seed Movement) party won Guatemala's presidency in runoff voting, 58.0%-37.2%, Aug. 20 over conservative party candidate Sandra Torres, a former first lady. Multiple attempts by the political establishment failed to disqualify Arévalo; rights groups had denounced the barring of at least three other left- and right-leaning presidential candidates from the general election on what they claimed were insufficient grounds.

Military Ousts Gabon's President—Military officers in Gabon seized power Aug. 30 from Pres. Ali Bongo Ondimba after it was declared he had won a third term in the Aug. 26 general election, which international observers questioned. President since 2009, Bongo had been accused of corruption and election fraud offenses and had endured a failed coup in 2019. Though cheered by crowds in Libreville, the coup—the seventh in two years in Central and West Africa—was condemned by the UN and the African Union; the latter suspended Gabon's membership. Promising elections, coup leader Gen. Brice Oligui Nguema was sworn in Sept. 4 as interim president; Bongo remained under house arrest. Despite Gabon's vast oil reserves,

about one third of its residents live in poverty, according to the World Bank.

Ukraine Escalates Drone Attacks on Crimea; Mercenary Leader Known for Challenging Kremlin Is Killed in Plane Crash—Ukraine's military Aug. 30 carried out what was thought to be its largest drone assault on Russian-held territory, including Moscow, since the start of the invasion of Ukraine 18 months earlier. At the same time, Russia launched its heaviest air attack in months on Ukraine's capitol, Kyiv, killing at least two people. Continuing to strike bridges linking Ukraine and Crimea, Ukrainian drones in early Aug. also damaged a large, empty Russian oil tanker and a Russian warship. Though opposing forces remained largely deadlocked in Ukraine's nearly three-month-old counteroffensive, Ukrainian troops in late Aug. retook the village of Robotyne, near the southern city of Zaporizhzhia.

On Aug. 23, a private jet carrying Yevgeny Prigozhin—head of Wagner mercenary group who in June staged a brief revolt against the Kremlin and Russian forces—crashed in Russia, killing Prigozhin and all nine others onboard. U.S. intelligence officials reported preliminarily that a deliberate explosion caused the crash, furthering immediate speculation that Russian Pres. Vladimir Putin had targeted Prigozhin for assassination.

General

Lahaina Wildfire Kills 97 in Maui; Official Response Questioned—A fast-moving wildfire tore through the historic city of Lahaina on Hawaii's island of Maui Aug. 8, killing at least 97 people (with 31 missing) as of Sept. 15 and reducing much of Lahaina to charred ruins. The wildfire was the deadliest in the U.S since 1918, exceeding California's 2018 Camp Fire (85 deaths). The blaze was initially reported at dawn as a small brush fire and considered fully contained less than three hours later. But it flared midafternoon, wind gusts spreading the flames quickly amid extremely dry conditions through large tracts of unmanaged, nonnative grasses previously deemed a fire risk. Residents attempting to evacuate encountered gridlocked traffic, forcing them to abandon their vehicles and seek safety in the ocean. Pres. Joe Biden Aug. 10 issued a major disaster declaration for Maui, which he visited Aug. 21.

Questions mounted over the response by local and state government officials, especially their decision to not activate an extensive emergency siren system. The head of Maui's emergency management agency, who resigned Aug. 17, said the alarms could have caused residents to flee inland toward fire. Though some residents reported receiving text alerts on their mobile devices, others did not; warnings on radio/TV or cable were limited due to power outages from the earlier blaze. Hawaiian Electric Co., the local power utility, acknowledged its power lines caused the initial fire after they were downed by high winds, but said it de-energized them hours before the fire flared after containment.

Spain Triumphs in Women's World Cup Soccer Tournament—Spain's national soccer team won its first FIFA women's World Cup title Aug. 20, edging England, the reigning European champs, 1-0, in front of more than 75,000 fans at a packed Stadium Australia in Sydney, Australia. Spain's captain Olga Carmona scored the only goal in the 29th minute against England goalie Mary Earps, who allowed only four goals during the tournament and earned the tournament's Golden Glove award for best goalkeeper despite her team's loss. Spain midfielder Aitana Bonmatí was awarded the Golden Ball as the tournament's top player, racking up three goals and two assists over seven games.

Overshadowing Spain's triumph, its soccer federation president, Luis Rubiales, kissed player Jennifer Hermoso—without her consent, she said—on the field following the game. Rubiales was suspended by FIFA and ultimately resigned his post after several weeks of criticism.

Spain's victory capped the monthlong, 64-game tournament hosted by Australia and New Zealand that saw the debut of eight new teams. The U.S. squad, aiming to become the first team ever to win three consecutive titles, was eliminated by Sweden

Aug. 6 in an overtime shootout (5-4), and failed to reach the semifinal round for the first time.

Rare West Coast Tropical Storm Batters Southern California—Tropical storm Hilary Aug. 20 unleashed torrential rain and winds on Southern California and Nevada Aug. 20. The storm system, which had strengthened over ocean waters to a Category 4 hurricane before being downgraded and making landfall in Mexico's Baja California peninsula, dumped record rainfall in the region, including 13.5 in. in San Bernardino and 11.74 in. in San Jacinto. Hilary was the first tropical storm in 84 years to cross directly over the Los Angeles Basin.

India Achieves Historic Landing Near Lunar South Pole; Russian Moon Mission Fails—The Indian space agency's unmanned *Chandrayaan-3* spacecraft carried out a controlled landing on the moon Aug. 23, making history as the first to achieve a soft landing near the lunar south pole. Scientists have hypothesized that the location may have frozen water deposits. The mission's solar-powered, SUV-sized lander and rover operated on the surface for under two weeks.

Russia's first attempted lunar mission since 1976 ended in disaster Aug. 19, when its unmanned craft crashed into the surface during landing preparations.

Florida Gunman Kills Three in Racist Attack—A white gunman whom police said authored racist screeds carried out an attack at a Dollar General store, Aug. 26, in Jacksonville, FL, killing three Black people, before fatally shooting himself. Police said the presence of security officers at another discount store and at a nearby historically Black college may have deterred the 21-year-old shooter, Ryan Christopher Palmeter, from attacks in those locations.

Biles Claims Record Eighth U.S. Gymnastics Title—At SAP Center in San Jose, CA, Aug. 27, Olympic gold medalist Simone Biles won her eighth national championship, the most ever by any U.S. gymnast, male or female. (She was previously tied with Alfred Jochim who claimed a then-record seventh title 90 years earlier.) The 26-year-old Biles, who also became the oldest all-around U.S. women's champ, set new marks in just her second competition after a two-year hiatus.

On Oct. 6 in Antwerp, Belgium, Biles claimed her 34th gold medal (world championships and Olympics combined), surpassing Vitaly Scherbo of Belarus to become the most decorated gymnast in history; by Oct. 8, she won her 37th.

Hurricane Idalia Strikes Florida's Big Bend—Idalia made landfall Aug. 30 near Keaton Beach, FL, in the state's Big Bend region, as a Category 3 storm with sustained winds up to 125 mph. Due to the region's sparse population and a reportedly high rate of evacuation, few deaths were reported. Property damage on the Gulf Coast from Florida to Georgia was still extensive, with high winds, storm surge (measured at up to 8.9 ft. in Cedar Key, FL, and thought to be higher elsewhere), and torrential rains (9.4 in. in Clearwater Beach, FL; 8.2 in. near Valdosta, GA; and 11.57 in. in Mullins, NC). As of Sept. 5, Pres. Joe Biden had approved a major disaster declaration for 13 Florida counties. According to early estimates, Idalia caused up to $20 bil in damages.

Deadly Blaze in Unmaintained South African Residential Building Kills Dozens—More than 75 people were killed after an early morning fire Aug. 31 tore through a derelict five-story building in central Johannesburg. Though owned by the city and occupied by around 200 people according to some estimates, the city no longer maintained the building. It also lacked functioning fire escapes, and according to authorities, its security gates were locked. Like other so-called hijacked buildings in downtown Johannesburg, it had reportedly been taken over by criminal gangs, who charged rent to those unable to afford other housing, such as undocumented migrants.

September 2023
National

House Republicans Launch Presidential Impeachment Inquiry; Justice Dept. Indicts New Jersey Senator—Under pressure from far-right Republicans, House Speaker Kevin McCarthy (R, CA) Sept. 12 announced he was directing three House committees to open an impeachment inquiry into Pres. Joe Biden. House Republicans had not offered proof Biden, while serving in public office, had ever benefited from or was influenced by his son Hunter's business dealings while serving in public office but said opening an inquiry would allow them to access additional records and evidence, including banking documents. Numerous legislators, including Republican Senators, objected to the inquiry, and the White House called it "extreme politics at its worst."

The next week, a House Judiciary Committee hearing accused Atty. Gen. Merrick Garland of overseeing a politically biased "two-tiered" Justice Dept. that targeted former Pres. Donald Trump for prosecution—Trump currently faced 44 federal counts—while providing preferential treatment to Hunter Biden. A federal prosecutor Sept. 22 indicted Sen. Bob Menendez (D, NJ) and his wife on corruption charges. The 69-year-old three-term senator was accused of accepting hundreds of thousands of dollars in cash and over $100,000 in gold bars in exchange for improperly using his office's influence. Menendez's 2017 trial on unrelated bribery charges had ended in a mistrial after the jury deadlocked.

President's Son Indicted on Gun Charges—Special counsel David Weiss Sept. 14 indicted 53-year-old Hunter Biden on three federal gun charges stemming from a gun purchase Hunter made in 2018 while addicted to illegal drugs. The charges were apparently the first in U.S. history levied against a sitting president's child. Hunter Biden pleaded not guilty in early Oct. In June 2023, he had agreed with Weiss, the Trump-appointed Delaware U.S. attorney, to plead guilty on tax charges to avoid prosecution on the gun charges, but the deal collapsed July 26 after a judge refused to approve it. In July, two IRS whistleblowers had alleged in congressional testimony that Pres. Biden's Justice Dept. had impeded a tax investigation into Hunter, a claim Weiss rejected. Trump and Republican lawmakers have accused Hunter of a range of malfeasance in his business dealings.

Autoworkers Union Rolls Out Strike; Hollywood Writers Reach Tentative Deal—Adding to an active year of U.S. labor stoppages, the United Auto Workers (UAW) union on Sept. 15 initiated strikes against the U.S.'s largest automakers—Ford, General Motors, and Stellantis (parent company of Chrysler, Dodge, and Jeep)—marking the first time it targeted work stoppages at all three simultaneously. The walkouts initially involved 12,700 workers (more than 8% of UAW's members) at three plants in Missouri, Ohio, and Michigan but were expanded Sept. 22 to 38 parts-distribution centers in 20 states that employed approx. 5,600 more UAW members. (Ford, which reportedly met some of the strikers' requirements in negotiations, was spared the distribution center strikes.) Pres. Biden Sept. 26 became the first sitting U.S. president to participate in a union picket line when he joined striking UAW workers near Detroit. Along with pay increases and cost-of-living adjustments, the UAW's contract demands included eliminating tiered wages, transitioning to a four-day workweek, and gaining the right to represent workers at 10 electric-vehicle battery factories.

On Sept. 26, film and TV writers ended their nearly five-month-old strike after a tentative agreement between major studios and the Writers Guild of America. The new three-year contract, ratified by members Oct. 9, included increased pay and health and pension contributions, as well as new foreign streaming residuals, viewership-based streaming bonuses, and assurances against use of artificial intelligence. Actors represented by SAG-AFTRA, who began striking in mid-July, remained on strike.

U.S. Grants Temporary Legal Status to Venezuelan Migrants; Other Immigration News—Dept. of Homeland Security (DHS) Sec. Alejandro Mayorkas announced Sept. 20 that the U.S. was giving Temporary Protected Status (TPS) to approx. 472,000 Venezuelans in the U.S., referencing unsafe conditions and political instability that blocked their safe return to Venezuela. TPS, which includes temporary protection from removal as well as work authorization, was extended only to those Venezuelans in the U.S. as of July 31, 2023, by any means of entry. Critics denounced the move as incentivizing more undocumented migrants.

DHS that same day announced 800 more military personnel would be sent to the southern border, among several other measures. According to preliminary data, U.S. agents apprehended migrants there more than 232,000 times in Aug. 2023.

FTC Sues Amazon on Antitrust Charges; Other Business, Economic News—The Federal Trade Commission (FTC) and 17 states filed an antitrust suit against tech giant Amazon Sept. 26, alleging the retail tech giant had abused its position—dominating some 40% of e-commerce by some estimates—to improperly force its logistics and fulfillment services on third-party sellers, resulting in artificially increased prices and decreased quality for consumers. The FTC under Biden appointee Lina Khan had been more active in efforts to rein in tech companies but was notably unsuccessful in its effort to block Microsoft's acquisition of video game giant Activision Blizzard.

The Dow Jones Industrial Average closed Sept. at 33,507.50, down 3.5% from Aug. The S&P 500 dropped 4.9% to finish the month at 4,288.05, and the Nasdaq Composite Index ended Sept. at 13,219.32, a 5.8% decline. According to a Bureau of Labor Statistics (BLS) report released Sept. 13, high housing costs and accelerating gas prices—up 10.6% from the month prior—pushed the annual inflation rate to 3.7%. A separate BLS report released Sept. 1 showed the U.S. economy added 187,000 jobs in Aug., up 30,000 from July's revised total, as unemployment ticked up to 3.8%, the highest rate since Feb. 2022. The Bureau of Economic Analysis Sept. 28 in its third and final estimate for the second quarter of 2023 said that U.S. GDP grew at an annualized rate of 2.1%, nearly even with 2.2% the previous quarter. U.S. Census data released Sept. 14 showed the national rate of remote work declined 2.7% in 2022, to a still-high 15.2%. Before the COVID-19 pandemic spurred telecommuting's adoption in 2020, just 5.7% (2019) worked remotely.

Congress Avoids Government Shutdown Amid Speaker's Freedom Caucus Feud—Pres. Biden late Sept. 30 signed into law a temporary measure that maintained federal funding at current levels for 45 days, narrowly averting a government shutdown set to begin at midnight. The shutdown had appeared all but inevitable after the GOP-led House Sept. 29 voted down a 30-day funding bill backed by House Speaker Kevin McCarthy (R, CA). A bloc of 21 far-right House conservatives, led by Rep. Matt Gaetz (R, FL), joined all Democrats in opposition to the bill, which included 30% spending cuts for most federal agencies and stringent border security provisions. After McCarthy dropped the spending cuts, the House Sept. 30 overwhelmingly passed the short-term bill (335-91), with the support of 126 Republicans and most Democrats. The Senate passed it (88-9) with about 3 hr. to spare before the shutdown deadline.

Six-term Sen. Dianne Feinstein (D, CA) died in Washington, DC, Sept. 29, the morning after casting her last vote. The 90-year-old was best known for her roles in the passage of the 1994 assault weapons ban as well as for the release, against bipartisan opposition, of a report on post-9/11 CIA interrogation techniques. But media and constituents alike had more recently questioned her ability to fulfill the responsibilities of the office due to declining health.

International

Iran Prisoner Swap Frees Five U.S. Citizens, Unfreezes Some Oil Revenue—Five Americans in Iran whom the U.S. had designated "wrongfully detained" were released Sept. 18 in exchange for five freed Iranians, who'd been charged with violating U.S. sanctions, and the unfreezing of $6 bil in Iranian oil revenue. Though some of the deal's critics said the money was equivalent to a ransom payment that would encourage arbitrary detainment of more Americans, the White House committed to stringent monitoring and sanctions to ensure the funds' use for humanitarian purposes.

Canada Expels Indian Diplomat, Alleging Assassination Link—Canadian Prime Min. Justin Trudeau Sept. 18 informed lawmakers that security officials were tracking "credible allegations" of Indian involvement in the June 2023 assassination of Sikh community leader Hardeep Singh Nijjar in Surrey, BC, a suburb of Vancouver. That same day, Canada expelled the head

of Indian intelligence in Canada; in early Oct., India in retaliation ordered the expulsion of more than 40 Canadian diplomats. Indian officials forcefully denied responsibility for the assassination but had previously designated Nijjar a terrorist and alleged he had sponsored violent attacks in India aimed at establishing an independent Sikh Khalistan state.

Azerbaijan Offensive Sparks Exodus of Ethnic Armenians—Azerbaijan carried out a large-scale military operation Sept. 19-20 against the ethnic-Armenian-majority breakaway state of Nagorno-Karabakh (or Artsakh, in Armenian), giving it full control of the South Caucasus region for the first time since 1994. By early Oct., more than 80% of the disputed territory's population (more than 100,000 people) had fled to neighboring Armenia. Separatist regime Pres. Samvel Shahramanyan signed a decree in late Sept. dissolving the self-declared republic and its institutions by Jan. 1, 2024.

The offensive's death toll was disputed, with some claiming more than 400 people died, including more than 190 Azerbaijani troops. At least 170 ethnic Armenians were killed by a massive explosion at a fuel depot where they had assembled in preparation to flee. (In late 2020, some 7,000 military troops and 170 civilians were killed in fighting over 44 days, during which Azerbaijan recaptured territory.) Azerbaijan justified the attack as a response to recent "provocations," but Armenian Prime Min. Nikol Pashinyan branded it "ethnic cleansing" and the U.S. and EU, among others, condemned it.

Ukraine Accelerates Attacks on Russian-Occupied Crimea as Counteroffensive Grinds On, Other Invasion News—Ukraine increased air assaults throughout the month on the Crimean Peninsula—illegally annexed by Russia in 2014—including a missile attack Sept. 22 that destroyed the headquarters of Russia's Black Sea naval fleet in Sevastopol. Earlier in the month, Ukraine's military took credit for damaging a submarine and a landing ship and claimed to have retaken four strategic drilling platforms. The country's slow-moving counteroffensive made labored micro-gains in the face of extensive Russian minefields. The Biden administration in early Sept. announced another $175 mil in security assistance, including the provision of armor-piercing tank rounds for the first time. The pledge brought total U.S. security assistance to more than $43 bil since the start of Russia's invasion in Feb. 2022.

Ukrainian Pres. Volodymyr Zelenskyy Sept. 21 addressed the U.S. Congress, urging lawmakers, including some skeptical Republicans, to maintain or increase aid; he also met with Pres. Biden. On Sept. 13, Russian Pres. Vladimir Putin held a summit with North Korean counterpart Kim Jong Un in Russia's Far East, sparking fears of an agreement by Kim to supply weapons to Putin for the ongoing invasion.

General

Strong Quake Kills 2,900 in Morocco—A magnitude 6.8 earthquake devastated western Morocco's Marrakesh-Safi region Sept. 8, killing at least 2,960 people—mostly outside Marrakesh—and damaging at least 50,000 homes. The relatively shallow earthquake, with its epicenter in the Atlas Mountains roughly 45 mi southwest of Marrakesh, was the country's deadliest since 1960. In the days following the disaster, Morocco was criticized for accepting rescue teams from just four countries—Qatar, Spain, UAE, and UK—while rejecting offers of help from others, including the U.S. and France.

Gauff, Djokovic Claim U.S. Open Titles—Rallying from a set down, No. 6-seed Coco Gauff overcame No. 2-seed Aryna Sabalenka of Belarus (2-6, 6-3, 6-2) to win the U.S. Open women's singles championship and her first Grand Slam title Sept. 9 at Arthur Ashe Stadium in Flushing, NY. The 19-year-old American was the first teen to triumph at the U.S. Open since Serena Williams in 1999.

No. 2-seed Novak Djokovic of Serbia defeated No. 3-seed Daniil Medvedev of Russia in straight sets (6-3, 7-6, 6-3) Sept. 10 to notch his fourth Open championship and 24th career Grand Slam singles title, the most by any player—male or female—in the Open Era.

Storm-Related Flood Deaths Exceed 4,000 in Eastern Libya—At least 4,000 people in the eastern Libyan port city of Derna died after heavy rains from Tropical Storm Daniel led to the collapse Sept. 11 of two dams. According to state media, a 23-ft wave was unleashed by the burst dams, inundating a quarter of the city. The UN confirmed Libya's rival governments were cooperating on relief efforts. By Sept. 19, the rebel government in control of much of eastern Libya had divided the city into four sections to protect against disease outbreaks, though many residents lacked clean drinking water. Hundreds of demonstrators massed outside Derna's Al Sahabah Mosque Sept. 18 demanding accountability for the dams' failure, as the rival governments had ignored repeated warnings about neglected maintenance. On Sept. 25, eight current and former officials, including Derna's mayor, were indicted on related charges. Some 8,500 people were still missing as of the end of the month.

Structure Fires in Iraq, Vietnam Kill 150—More than 100 people were killed Sept. 26 in a fast-moving fire at a crowded wedding hall in Qaraqosh, Iraq. Fireworks were said to have ignited highly flammable ceiling panels. Some 900 people were reportedly present and most, including the bride and groom, escaped. The venue owner and 13 others were arrested over alleged safety violations.

At least 56 people were killed in Hanoi, Vietnam, after a fire broke out late Sept. 12 in a nine-story apartment building that housed about 150 people. The building's location at the end of a narrow alley challenged firefighting and rescue efforts; its owner was charged with violating regulations.

NASA Astronaut Sets U.S. Space-Duration Record—NASA astronaut Frank Rubio touched down in Kazakhstan Sept. 27 after 371 consecutive days in space, eclipsing by 16 days the previous U.S. record held by Mark Vande Hei. Rubio arrived at the International Space Station (ISS) with two Russian cosmonauts in Sept. 2022 for a 180-day mission. They were unable to return to Earth as scheduled after the spacecraft on which they arrived was damaged; an uncrewed Russian Soyuz capsule was launched to retrieve them. Russia's Valeri Polyakov holds the world record of 437 consecutive days in space, set in 1995.

October 2023
National

Hard-Right Ousts Speaker McCarthy; Fractious GOP Caucus Elects Replacement After 22-Day Gridlock—A contingent of far-right Republicans proposed a vote that removed House Speaker Kevin McCarthy (R, CA) from his post, 216-210, on Oct. 3, marking the first time in history the chamber ousted a sitting speaker. The development followed McCarthy's decision to pass an emergency 45-day funding bill—without deep spending cuts demanded by the hard-right, informally led by Rep. Matt Gaetz (R, FL)—to avert a partial federal government shutdown at the end of Sept. Gaetz also voiced his deep opposition to the debt-limit compromise reached by McCarthy and Pres. Joe Biden in May-June. McCarthy gained the speakership in Jan. 2023 only after far-right representatives forced major concessions from him, including lowering the threshold of lawmakers required to trigger a "motion to vacate," which ultimately cost him the post.

After 22 chaotic days, House Republicans Oct. 25 elected relatively unknown ultraconservative Rep. Mike Johnson (R, LA) as the new speaker. Johnson's selection alarmed Democrats due to his key role in efforts to overturn the 2020 presidential election results for Trump. Three prior nominees—Majority Leader Steve Scalise (R, LA), Rep. Jim Jordan (R, OH), and Majority Whip Tom Emmer (R, MN)—failed to gather adequate support.

Trump Advisers Plead Guilty in Georgia Election Case; Other Trump Legal Developments—Ongoing legal proceedings against former Pres. Donald Trump yielded several noteworthy developments, most significantly guilty pleas by three former legal advisers charged in Georgia's anti-racketeering (RICO) case arising from Trump's alleged efforts to overturn the state's 2020 election results. All three—Kenneth Chesebro, Sidney Powell, and Jenna Ellis—pleaded guilty by Oct. 24 to misdemeanor charges and agreed to testify for the prosecution.

On Oct. 25, a New York judge in the state's civil fraud case against Trump fined him $10,000 for comments to reporters about a "very partisan" person in the court, five days after he was

fined half that amount over a Truth Social post that the judge said disparaged his clerk. In the federal election interference case Oct. 29, a federal judge reimposed a limited gag order on Trump that had been temporarily lifted after being put in place Oct. 16.

Devastating Mass Shooting Forces Lockdown in Maine—A gunman Oct. 25 killed 18 people and injured 13 others in two separate attacks in Lewiston, ME. The suspected shooter, a 40-year-old Army reservist identified as Robert Card, opened fire at a bowling alley and then at a bar about 4 mi away 12 min. later. A citywide lockdown and extensive hunt ensued; the shooter was found dead Oct. 27 from an apparent self-inflicted gunshot. In the aftermath, questions were raised about law enforcement's apparent awareness of his declining mental health—including a two-week psychiatric hospitalization following violent threats made against his Army Reserve unit—and why they did not invoke Maine's "yellow-flag" law, under which someone deemed a threat to themselves or others may be detained and their weapons confiscated.

Auto Workers Union Ends Strikes Targeting "Big Three" After Major Contract Gains; Other Business, Economic News—The United Auto Workers (UAW) union reached a tentative deal Oct. 25 with Ford, its members' largest employer, that provided employees with at least a 25% pay increase through Apr. 2028 and the right to strike over future plant closures, among other benefits. Though it still required ratification by UAW's 57,000 members employed at Ford, about 16,600 of those on the picket line were immediately back to work. UAW reached similar terms with Stellantis (parent company of Chrysler, Dodge, and Jeep), Oct. 28, and General Motors, Oct. 30, ending targeted work stoppages that UAW had rolled out since mid-Sept.

About 75,000 unionized Kaiser Permanente employees walked off the job Oct. 4-6 in four Western states, mostly in California, in what was reportedly the largest health care sector strike in U.S. history; a tentative agreement was reached Oct. 13. That same day, Microsoft completed its $68.7-bil takeover of game maker Activision Blizzard after overcoming 20 months of UK and U.S. regulatory hurdles.

According to a Bureau of Labor Statistics (BLS) report released Oct. 12, the annual U.S. inflation rate was 3.7% in Sept., mostly flat from Aug. The BLS reported Oct. 6 the U.S. economy added 336,000 jobs in Sept. as the unemployment rate held at 3.8%; GDP growth, reported by the Commerce Dept. Oct. 26, also remained high, with a 4.9% annualized pace in the third quarter of 2023. The Dow Jones Industrial Average closed Oct. at 33,052.87, down 1.4% from Sept., as the S&P 500 dropped 2.2% to close the month at 4,193.80; the Nasdaq Composite Index finished Oct. at 12,851.24, a 2.8% decline.

International

Brutal Hamas Assault Kills 1,400 in Israel, Triggering Counterattack on Gaza That Kills Thousands More—In the deadliest attack on Israel since the Yom Kippur War 50 years earlier, the Islamist militant group Hamas on Oct. 7 launched a coordinated, multipronged surprise attack from the Gaza Strip, the Palestinian territory under its control in southwestern Israel, killing more than 1,400 in Israel, including 315 soldiers and at least 32 Americans. The assault began around 6:30 AM with Hamas firing barrages of rockets—2,200 over the first six hours, according to Israeli officials—a number of which penetrated Israel's Iron Dome defense system. Hamas militants on foot and motorcycle stormed Gaza blockades, joined by others arriving by motorboat and paraglider, and attacked small towns, kibbutzim communities, and military bases; at least 260 were killed at a music festival near Re'im. Hamas also reportedly took about 240 hostages back to Gaza. Israel formally declared war on Hamas on Oct. 8 and said it had largely regained control, Oct. 10, of the areas that had been attacked.

Israel launched immediate, massive retaliatory air strikes on Gaza, killing more than 230 people the same day it came under attack; the Israeli Defense Force (IDF) activated 300,000 reservists. By Oct. 31, the death toll in Gaza had passed 8,500—mostly civilians including at least 3,500 children according to the UN and the Gaza Ministry of Health. Hamas condemned an Oct. 17 attack on a Gaza hospital that it claimed killed almost 500, blaming IDF airstrikes; U.S. and IDF officials said the cause was an errant rocket from another militant group. Palestinian officials Oct. 24 said overnight strikes by Israel killed at least 700 in Gaza, the highest 24-hour death toll since the start of the conflict. Israeli forces through late Oct. had carried out several brief incursions, though a full-scale ground offensive remained possible. On Oct. 31-Nov. 1—in what the UN human rights office said may have constituted war crimes—Israeli air strikes hit Gaza's largest refugee camp, Jabalia, bringing down residential buildings and killing at least 195 people according to the Gaza Government Media Office. Israel said it had successfully targeted and killed a senior Hamas commander there. About 130 Palestinians were also reportedly killed in the West Bank by the end of the month.

UN Sec.-Gen. António Guterres, in an address to the Security Council Oct. 24, said the Hamas attacks cannot justify the "collective punishment of the Palestinian people" and called on Israel to permit faster delivery of humanitarian aid into the territory, little of which had reached residents since Israel on Oct. 9 closed Gaza off from food, fuel, and other necessary supplies. A U.S. official, quoted in the *Times of Israel* Oct. 30 said that Israel had agreed to allow 100 aid trucks into Gaza daily, through the Rafah, Egypt, crossing. (Prior to the siege, some 500 trucks carrying aid and other goods would enter Gaza every day.) By the end of the month, more than 60% of Gaza's 2.3 mil residents were displaced. The U.S. and most Western governments publicly expressed strong support for Israel, though Pres. Biden, during a rare televised Oval Office address Oct. 19, said he had warned Israel's government "not to be blinded by rage"; the Biden administration Oct. 18 pledged $100 mil in humanitarian assistance to Palestinians in Gaza and the West Bank.

New Zealand Election Swings Country Right—New Zealand's conservative National Party handily defeated the ruling center-left Labour Party in general elections Oct. 14 following campaigns focused on cost-of-living and a struggling national economy. Led by former airline executive Christopher Luxon, the National Party won almost 39% of votes to secure 50 of 121 parliamentary seats; the Labour Party won 27% of votes to finish with just 34 seats, down 31 seats from 2020 voting. Luxon was expected to form a governing alliance with the libertarian ACT party. In power for six years, Labour suffered a setback in Jan. after Prime Min. Jacinda Ardern unexpectedly resigned amid increasing frustration over rising inflation and her government's strict COVID-19 policies.

Poland Voters Eject Right-Wing Government—Poland's voters dealt a blow Oct. 15 to the country's ruling right-wing Law and Justice (PiS) party, erasing its outright majority in the lower house (Sejm) of parliament with a 74.4% voter turnout, the highest for a national election in Poland since communism fell in 1989. Though PiS received the largest share of votes, at 35.4%, three opposition parties were expected to form a governing pro-EU alliance with a collective 53.7%—including the leftist Civic Coalition, with 30.7%—enough to take 248 out of 460 seats. The three opposition parties had all vowed to restore judicial independence, which PiS had eroded during its eight years in power, costing Poland billions in EU funding.

Business Heir Elected Ecuador President Amid Soaring Violence—Conservative lawmaker and banana empire heir Daniel Noboa won a tight runoff election for Ecuador's presidency Oct. 15, defeating leftist attorney Luisa González, 51.8%-48.2%, with 82.3% turnout. Noboa was elected to serve the remainder of the term of center-right Pres. Guillermo Lasso, who in May had dissolved the opposition-led parliament to forestall impeachment proceedings against him over corruption allegations. Voting followed a wave of political violence, including the assassination in Aug. of anti-corruption presidential candidate Fernando Villavicencio as he left a rally. An unprecedented spike in violent crime over the past three years was said to be driven largely by fighting between drug-trafficking gangs. The youngest president in Ecuadorian history, 35-year-old Noboa pledged to reinvigorate Ecuador's struggling economy and generate employment for younger people, as well as beef up security to address violent crime.

Ukraine Deploys U.S.-Supplied Long-Range Missiles; Other Russian Invasion Developments—Ukrainian Pres. Volodymyr Zelenskyy Oct. 17 in his nightly address said that his country's military had utilized U.S.-supplied long-range Army Tactical Missile System ballistic missiles (ATACMS) for the first time. The announcement followed claims by Ukraine's forces that it had struck two airfields in Luhansk and Berdyansk in Russian-occupied eastern and southern Ukraine, respectively, causing deep damages and casualties. The Biden administration had previously hesitated to arm Ukraine with ATACMS over fears they could widen the conflict to Russia itself; the models sent were reportedly limited in range to 100 mi.

Ukrainian officials said a missile strike on a café and shop in the village of Hroza, Kharkiv, Oct. 5 killed 59 people; if confirmed, it would be one of Russia's deadliest attacks on civilians in the 20-month invasion. Foreign ministers or other representatives of all 27 European Union member countries met Oct. 2 in Kyiv to reaffirm support for Ukraine; Poland's government in Sept. had halted weapons shipments as a result of a grain dispute between the two countries. Slovakia's new pro-Russia prime minister halted military aid to Ukraine later in Oct. Concerns also centered on apparently flagging support for Ukraine funding among some Republican members of U.S. Congress.

General

Pope Expresses Willingness to Bless Same-Sex Couples—Responding to five conservative cardinals in an Oct. 2 letter, Pope Francis for the first time signaled his openness to Catholic priests blessing same-sex unions. Though his latest remarks were viewed by progressive Catholics as a meaningful step, the Pope also stated that the Church only recognizes officially marriage between a man and a woman. Ahead of a UN climate summit set to begin in late Nov. in Dubai, United Arab Emirates, the Pope in a statement released Oct. 4 leveled climate criticism in multiple directions, including at climate-change deniers, "irresponsible" Western excesses, inaction by businesses and leaders, and indifference within the Catholic Church itself.

New Mexico Footprints Offer Changes to Human Timeline in North America—Research published Oct. 5 in the journal *Science* appeared to bolster scientists' claims that fossil footprints in New Mexico's White Sands National Park, first reported in 2021, date to between 21,000 and 23,000 years ago, much earlier than humans were previously thought to have been in North America. The new research scrutinized the age of both ancient pollen grains and quartz sand in a sediment layer containing the footprints. The development upends the broadly accepted theory that the first humans in North America arrived 13,000-15,000 years ago, when the-lower sea levels exposed a land bridge between Russia and Alaska.

Deadly Quakes Strike Western Afghanistan—A pair of magnitude 6.3 earthquakes wreaked destruction in western Afghanistan's Herat province on Oct. 7, killing more than 1,480 people according to the UN, and leaving at least 114,000 people in urgent need of humanitarian aid. UNICEF said over 90% of those killed were women and children. The initial quakes were followed by numerous aftershocks and other quakes, including one of magnitude 6.3 and another of magnitude 5.4 on Oct. 15. The UN said the earthquakes damaged at least 40 health care facilities along with thousands of homes.

Aces Claim Back-to-Back WNBA Championships—The Las Vegas Aces edged the New York Liberty, 70-69, in Game 4, Oct. 18 at Barclays Center in Brooklyn, NY, to claim their second straight Women's National Basketball Association championship. The first repeat winners in 21 years, the Aces overcame two injured starters and a nine-point deficit at the half with the help of A'ja Wilson, who was named Finals MVP with 24 points and 16 rebounds in Game 4.

Surprise Category 5 Hurricane Slams Mexico—Hurricane Otis killed at least 48 people after making landfall near the Mexican resort city of Acapulco in the early morning hours of Oct. 25 as a Category 5 storm, with sustained winds of 165 mph that extensively damaged high-rise hotels and buildings. Otis, the strongest hurricane on record to impact Mexico's Pacific coast, defied forecasters when it unexpectedly and rapidly grew in intensity from tropical storm status to Category 5 over the course of 24 hours, just three hours ahead of landfall.

OBITUARIES

For those whose deaths occurred Nov. 1, 2022 to Oct. 31, 2023.

A

Abourezk, James, 92, U.S. sen. (D, SD, 1973-79) and rep. (1971-73) who advocated for Native Americans; Sioux Falls, SD, Feb. 24, 2023.

Ahtisaari, Martti, 86, Finnish president (1994-2000) honored with the Nobel Peace Prize for international conflict resolution efforts; Helsinki, Finland, Oct. 16, 2023.

Alley, Kirstie, 71, Emmy Award-winning actress best known for *Cheers* (1987-93); Clearwater, FL, Dec. 5, 2022.

Amis, Martin, 73, British author known for his satirical novels, including *Money* (1984) and *London Fields* (1989); Lake Worth, FL, May 19, 2023.

Anger, Kenneth, 96, filmmaker whose book *Hollywood Babylon* (1965) documented purported scandals of showbiz history; Yucca Valley, CA, May 11, 2023.

Aniston, John, 89, Greek-American actor who appeared on soap opera *Days of Our Lives* for decades; Nov. 11, 2022.

Arkin, Alan, 89, Oscar and Tony Award-winning actor known for *Glengarry Glen Ross* (1992) and *Little Miss Sunshine* (2006); San Marcos, CA, June 29, 2023.

Armstrong, Heather, 47, blogger who wrote under the pseudonym Dooce about motherhood and mental health; Salt Lake City, UT, May 9, 2023.

B

Bacharach, Burt, 94, Oscar and Grammy Award-winning composer whose hits included "Raindrops Keep Fallin' on My Head" (1969) and "Close to You" (1970); Los Angeles, CA, Feb. 8, 2023.

Badalamenti, Angelo, 85, Grammy Award-winning composer known for scoring David Lynch's *Blue Velvet* (1986) and *Twin Peaks* (1990-92); Lincoln Park, NJ, Dec. 11, 2022.

Banks, Russell, 82, novelist whose work about domestic conflicts included *Continental Drift* (1985) and *Cloudsplitter* (1998); Saratoga Springs, NY, Jan. 7, 2023.

Barker, Bob, 99, Emmy Award-winning game show host known for *Truth or Consequences* (1956-75) and *The Price Is Right* (1972-2007); Los Angeles, CA, Aug. 26, 2023.

Beck, Jeff, 78, 8-time Grammy Award-winning British blues-rock guitarist with the Yardbirds and his own ensembles; Riverhall, Eng., UK, Jan. 10, 2023.

Belafonte, Harry, 96, Emmy, Grammy, and Tony Award-winning singer, actor, and activist; calypso hits included "Day-O (The Banana Boat Song)" (1956); also helped organize the 1963 March on Washington, DC; New York, NY, Apr. 25, 2023.

Belzer, Richard, 78, comedian and actor who portrayed cynical detective John Munch in *Homicide: Life on the Street* (1993-99) and *Law & Order: Special Victims Unit* (1999-2016); Beaulieu-sur-Mer, France, Feb. 19, 2023.

Benedict XVI (Joseph Ratzinger), 95, German Roman Catholic leader; first pope (2005-13) to resign in nearly 600 years; he was separately faulted for his response to the church's sex abuse scandals; Vatican City, Dec. 31, 2022.

Bennett, Tony, 96, Grammy Award-winning singer whose 7-decade career included the signature song "I Left My Heart in San Francisco" (1962); New York, NY, July 21, 2023.

Berg, Paul, 96, Nobel Prize-winning biochemist who in 1971 combined DNA from two organisms, pioneering the field of genetic engineering; Stanford, CA, Feb. 15, 2023.

Birkin, Jane, 76, British-born actress, singer, and fashion icon who collaborated with Serge Gainsbourg on "Je t'aime ... moi non plus" (1969); Paris, France, July 16, 2023.

Blake, Robert, 89, Emmy Award-winning actor known for *In Cold Blood* (1967) and *Baretta* (1975-78); acquitted in 2005 of killing his wife but found liable in the related civil case; Los Angeles, CA, Mar. 9, 2023.

Born, Ira "Bob", 98, businessman known as "Father of Peeps"; he modernized production of the popular marshmallow candies; Conshohocken, PA, Jan. 29, 2023.

Boss, Stephen "tWitch", 40, dancer and choreographer most famous as the DJ on *The Ellen DeGeneres Show* (2014-22); Encino, CA, Dec. 13, 2022.

Botero, Fernando, 91, Colombian artist known for creating rotund and whimsical figures, both human and animal; Monaco, Sept. 15, 2023.

Brathwaite, Kwame, 85, photographer and activist who chronicled Black lives in the 1960s and popularized the phrase "Black Is Beautiful"; New York, NY, Apr. 1, 2023.

Brooks, Frederick, Jr., 91, computer scientist who documented the process of creating an early IBM operating system in *The Mythical Man-Month: Essays on Software Engineering* (1975); Chapel Hill, NC, Nov. 17, 2022.

Brown, Jim, 87, Hall of Fame NFL running back, activist, and actor; his films included *The Dirty Dozen* (1967) and *Mars Attacks!* (1996); Los Angeles, CA, May 18, 2023.

Brown, John Y., Jr., 88, Kentucky governor (D, 1979-83) and businessman who built Kentucky Fried Chicken into a multimillion-dollar empire; Lexington, KY, Nov. 22, 2022.

Bryant Donham, Carolyn, 88, white woman who accused Emmett Till, a Black 14-year-old, of offending her, leading to his 1955 murder, for which her husband and friend were acquitted; Westlake, LA, Apr. 25, 2023.

Buffett, Jimmy, 76, singer-songwriter known for escapist beach rock and devoted "Parrothead" fans who helped parlay the hit "Margaritaville" (1977) into a business empire; Sag Harbor, NY, Sept. 1, 2023.

Bumbry, Grace, 86, mezzo-soprano opera singer who was the first Black diva to appear at the Bayreuth Festival (1961); Vienna, Austria, May 7, 2023.

Burks-Brooks, Catherine, 83, Black college student made famous as one of the Freedom Riders in 1961; Birmingham, AL, July 3, 2023.

Butkus, Dick, 80, Hall of Fame Chicago Bears linebacker who later acted in *Brian's Song* (1971); Malibu, CA, Oct. 5, 2023.

C

Cara, Irene, 63, Academy and Grammy Award-winning singer and actress known for film themes "Fame" (1980) and "Flashdance ... What a Feeling" (1983); Largo, FL, Nov. 25, 2022.

Carter, Aaron, 34, child actor and singer whose first album was released when he was 9; Lancaster, CA, Nov. 5, 2022.

Casterline, Dorothy, 95, Deaf linguist who co-wrote the first major dictionary of what became known as American Sign Language; Irmo, SC, Aug. 8, 2023.

Christopher, Don, 88, farmer who founded Christopher Ranch (1956), the leading producer of garlic in the U.S.; Gilroy, CA, Dec. 12, 2022.

Cloud, Angus, 25, actor best known for HBO's *Euphoria* (2019-22); Oakland, CA, July 31, 2023.

Conroy, Kevin, 66, actor who voiced Batman for three decades in animated films, TV series, and video games; New York, NY, Nov. 10, 2022.

Constantine II, 82, monarch (1964-73) who was Greece's last king and an Olympic gold medal-winning sailor (1960); Athens, Greece, Jan. 10, 2023.

Conway, Eddie, 76, Black Panther activist wrongly convicted of murder in 1971 and imprisoned for almost 44 years; Long Beach, CA, Feb. 13, 2023.

Crosby, David, 81, Rock & Roll Hall of Fame singer-songwriter who was a founding member of both the Byrds and Crosby, Stills, Nash & Young; Santa Ynez, CA, Jan. 18, 2023.

Curtis, Lois, 55, lead plaintiff in the 1999 Supreme Court case that affirmed the rights of people with developmental disabilities to live outside institutions; Clarkston, GA, Nov. 3, 2022.

D

Darcelle XV (Walter Cole), 92, entertainer crowned the world's oldest working drag performer in 2016 by *Guinness World Records*; Portland, OR, Mar. 23, 2023.

Deer, Ada, 88, Native American rights advocate who served as asst. sec. of the interior for Indian affairs (1993-97); Fitchburg, WI, Aug. 15, 2023.

Diener, Theodor, 102, Swiss-born pathologist who discovered viroids, the smallest known agents of infectious disease; Beltsville, MD, Mar. 28, 2023.

Dillon, Melinda, 83, actress known for *Close Encounters of the Third Kind* (1977) and *A Christmas Story* (1983); Los Angeles, CA, Jan. 9, 2023.

Doshi, Balkrishna, 95, Pritzker Prize-winning Indian architect known for modernist, brutalist buildings; Ahmedabad, India, Jan. 24, 2023.

Duncan, Arthur, 97, tap dancer who was the first Black regular performer on a TV variety show (*The Betty White Show*, 1954); Moreno Valley, CA, Jan. 4, 2023.

E

Ellsberg, Daniel, 92, military contractor who leaked the Pentagon Papers (1971), a damning classified study about U.S.-Vietnam policy; Kensington, CA, June 16, 2023.

F

Falconer, Ian, 63, children's author best known for the bestselling Olivia series; Norwalk, CT, Mar. 7, 2023.

al-Fayed, Mohamed, 94, Egyptian businessman who for years owned Harrod's in London; son Dodi was killed with Princess Diana in a 1997 car crash; London, Eng., UK, Aug. 30, 2023.

Feeney, Chuck, 92, businessman who built a duty-free empire and made billions, then quietly gave his entire fortune away; San Francisco, CA, Oct. 9, 2023.

Feinstein, Dianne, 90, U.S. sen. (D, CA, 1992-2023) known for Federal Assault Weapons Ban (1994) and leading Senate investigation of CIA techniques post-9/11; Washington, DC, Sept. 29, 2023.

Ferencz, Ben, 103, Hungarian-born U.S. Army lawyer who was chief prosecutor of Nazi war crimes at the Nuremberg Trials; Boynton Beach, FL, Apr. 7, 2023.

Fischer, Carl, 98, photographer known for provocative magazine covers, including Muhammad Ali as a martyred St. Sebastian for Esquire (1968); New York, NY, Apr. 7, 2023.

Fosbury, Dick, 76, Olympic gold medalwinning high jumper (1968) whose backwards form became known as the "Fosbury Flop"; Salt Lake City, UT, Mar. 12, 2023.

Friedkin, William, 87, Academy Awardwinning director known for The French Connection (1971) and The Exorcist (1973); Los Angeles, CA, Aug. 7, 2023.

G

Gallagher (Leo Anthony Gallagher), 76, comedian known for props, like using a sledgehammer to smash watermelons; Palm Springs, CA, Nov. 11, 2022.

Gambon, Michael, 82, British stage actor also known as Prof. Dumbledore in six Harry Potter films; Witham, Eng., UK, Sept. 27, 2023.

Geddie, Bill, 68, TV producer who in 1997 co-created Emmy Award-winning daytime show The View with Barbara Walters; Rancho Mirage, CA, July 20, 2023.

Georgelin, Jean-Louis, 74, former French Army general overseeing restoration of Notre-Dame after devastating 2019 fire; Bordes-Uchentein, France, Aug. 18, 2023.

Gilberto, Astrud, 83, Grammy Awardwinning Brazilian samba and bossa nova singer known for "The Girl from Ipanema" (1964); Philadelphia, PA, June 5, 2023.

Gilot, Françoise, 101, French artist who was the muse and lover of Pablo Picasso; became an accomplished painter in her own right; New York, NY, June 6, 2023.

Glück, Louise, 80, Nobel Prize-winning poet whose work explored grief and trauma in austere verse; Cambridge, MA, Oct. 13, 2023.

Goldman, Bo, 90, Academy Awardwinning screenwriter of One Flew Over the Cuckoo's Nest (1975) and Scent of a Woman (1992); Helendale, CA, July 25, 2023.

Goodenough, John B., 100, Nobel Prize-winning scientist who helped create the rechargeable lithium-ion battery; Austin, TX, June 25, 2023.

Goodman, Len, 78, British ballroom dancer; head judge on Dancing With the Stars (2005-22) and the UK TV show it was based on; Kent, Eng., UK, Apr. 22, 2023.

Gottlieb, Robert, 92, writer-editor who served as editor-in-chief at publishers Simon & Schuster and Alfred A. Knopf, and at The New Yorker magazine; New York, NY, June 14, 2023.

Graham, "Superstar" Billy, 79, pro wrestler known for his superhero physique; Phoenix, AZ, May 17, 2023.

Grant, Bud, 95, Hall of Fame football coach who took the Minnesota Vikings to four Super Bowls in 18 years but lost each game; Bloomington, MN, Mar. 11, 2023.

Gray, Nicholas, 86, founder of Gray's Papaya (1973), a chain of New York City hot dog and papaya juice stands; New York, NY, May 19, 2023.

Greene, Gael, 88, restaurant critic; cofounder of Citymeals on Wheels in New York City; New York, NY, Nov. 1, 2022.

H

Hagge, Marlene, 89, Hall of Fame golfer who won 26 pro tournaments and co-founded the LPGA (1950); Rancho Mirage, CA, May 16, 2023.

Hanssen, Robert, 79, FBI agent convicted of espionage for Russia; Fremont County, CO, June 5, 2023.

Harnick, Sheldon, 99, Tony Awardwinning lyricist known for Fiorello! (1959) and Fiddler on the Roof (1964); New York, NY, June 23, 2023.

Harris, Franco, 72, Hall of Fame Pittsburgh Steelers running back who won four Super Bowls and whose 1972 "Immaculate Reception" became iconic; Sewickley, PA, Dec. 20, 2022.

Harwell, Steve, 56, lead singer for Smash Mouth; known for hits "Walkin' on the Sun" (1997) and "All Star" (1999); Boise, ID, Sept. 4, 2023.

Hébras, Robert, 97, last living French survivor of the Nazis' Oradour-sur-Glane civilian massacre, June 10, 1944; Saint-Junien, France, Feb. 11, 2023.

Heumann, Judy, 75, activist widely acclaimed as the mother of the disability rights movement; Washington, DC, Mar. 4, 2023.

Howe, Tina, 85, playwright known for Painting Churches (1983) and Coastal Disturbances (1986); New York, NY, Aug. 28, 2023.

Hull, Bobby, 84, Canadian Hall of Fame hockey player known as "the Golden Jet"; led the Chicago Blackhawks to the 1961 Stanley Cup; Wheaton, IL, Jan. 30, 2023.

Humphries, Barry, 89, Australian comedian who performed as Dame Edna, known for her lilac wig, rhinestone eyeglasses, and insults; Sydney, NSW, Australia, Apr. 22, 2023.

I

The Iron Sheik (Khosrow Vaziri), 81, Iranian-born Hall of Fame pro wrestler who used his Middle Eastern background in his ring character; Fayetteville, GA, June 7, 2023.

Isley, Rudolph, 84, singer-songwriter with The Isley Brothers who cowrote hits "Shout" (1959) and "It's Your Thing" (1969); Chicago, IL, Oct. 11, 2023.

Isozaki, Arata, 91, Pritzker Prize-winning Japanese architect whose works included the Museum of Contemporary Art (1986), in Los Angeles; Naha, Okinawa, Japan, Dec. 28, 2022.

J

Jackson, Glenda, 87, Academy, Tony, and Emmy Award-winning English actress and member of UK Parliament (1992-2015); London, Eng., UK, June 15, 2023.

Jaffee, Al, 102, cartoonist for Mad magazine for 65 years; credited with creating its signature fold-in feature; New York, NY, Apr. 10, 2023.

Jakes, John, 90, bestselling historical novelist known for North and South trilogy and the eight-volume Kent Family Chronicles; Sarasota, FL, Mar. 11, 2023.

Jamal, Ahmad, 92, jazz pianist known for his innovation and influence on other musicians, including Miles Davis; Ashley Falls, MA, Apr. 16, 2023.

Jenrette, John, 86, U.S. rep. (D, SC, 1975-80) convicted of bribery in the Abscam corruption scandal (1980); Conway, SC, Mar. 17, 2023.

Jiang Zemin, 96, Chinese Communist Party gen. sec. (1989-2002) and president (1993-2003) who modernized the military amid economic growth; Shanghai, China, Nov. 30, 2022.

Jolicoeur, David, 54, Grammy Awardwinning rapper and songwriter who was a member of hip-hop trio De La Soul (1988-2023); Feb. 12, 2023.

Jones, Elayne, 94, percussionist who in 1949 was the first Black musician to play with a U.S. opera orchestra; Walnut Creek, CA, Dec. 17, 2022.

Jones, Ron Cephas, 66, Emmy Award-winning actor known for This Is Us (2016-22) and Mr. Robot (2015-16); Aug. 19, 2023.

K

Kaczynski, Ted, 81, mathematician arrested in 1996 as the Unabomber, who over 17 years sent mail bombs that killed 3 and injured 23; Durham County, NC, June 10, 2023.

Karpatkin, Rhoda, 93, Consumers Union leader who published the influential Consumer Reports magazine (1974-2001); New York, NY, Aug. 4, 2023.

Keller, Evelyn Fox, 87, physicist, biologist, and philosopher who critiqued science through a feminist lens; Cambridge, MA, Sept. 22, 2023.

Kessler, Gladys, 85, federal judge who issued a landmark 2006 ruling against the tobacco industry; Washington, DC, Mar. 16, 2023.

Kirkman, Terry, 83, musician and songwriter who as a founding member of the Association wrote "Cherish" (1966); Montclair, CA, Sept. 23, 2023.

Knievel, Robbie, 60, daredevil known for motorcycle jumps; Reno, NV, Jan. 13, 2023.

Kundera, Milan, 94, Czech-born writer known for The Unbearable Lightness of Being (1984); Paris, France, July 11, 2023.

Kushner, Harold, 88, rabbi and author of the bestselling When Bad Things Happen to Good People (1981); Canton, MA, Apr. 28, 2023.

L

Laurie, Piper, 91, Emmy Award-winning actress best known for Carrie (1976) and Children of a Lesser God (1986); Los Angeles, CA, Oct. 14, 2023.

Lee, Bill, 94, bassist and composer known for scoring Spike Lee films including She's Gotta Have It (1986) and

Do the Right Thing (1989); Brooklyn, NY, May 24, 2023.

Levine, Leon, 85, founder of Family Dollar; Charlotte, NC, Apr. 5, 2023.

Li Keqiang, 68, Chinese premier (2013-23) known for economic pragmatism; Shanghai, China, Oct. 27, 2023.

Lightfoot, Gordon, 84, Canadian singer-songwriter whose hits included "The Wreck of the Edmund Fitzgerald" (1976); Toronto, ON, Can., May 1, 2023.

Lo, Eileen Yin-Fei, 85, Chinese-born chef who wrote eleven cookbooks; Montclair, NJ, Nov. 13, 2022.

Lollobrigida, Gina, 95, Italian actress known for sex appeal in films such as *The Hunchback of Notre Dame* (1956) and *Come September* (1961); Rome, Italy, Jan. 16. 2023.

Loring, Lisa, 64, actress who played Wednesday Addams on *The Addams Family* (1964-66); Burbank, CA, Jan. 28, 2023.

Love, Barbara, 85, feminist activist and writer who co-founded Identity House, a counseling center for LGBTQ adults; Bronx, NY, Nov. 13, 2022.

Lujack, Johnny, 98, Heisman Trophy-winning Notre Dame quarterback (1947); Naples, FL, July 25, 2023.

M

Mahan, Larry, 79, rodeo champion who was the subject of Oscar-winning documentary *The Great American Cowboy* (1973); Valley View, TX, May 7, 2023.

Maharis, George, 94, actor and singer known for *Route 66* (1960-63); Beverly Hills, CA, May 24, 2023.

Mahindra, Keshub, 99, Indian chair of Mahindra Group tech conglomerate; convicted in 2010 of death by negligence in the 1984 Bhopal gas disaster's 15,000 deaths; Mumbai, India, Apr. 12, 2023.

McCallum, David, 90, Scottish actor known for roles in *The Man From U.N.C.L.E.* (1964-68) and *NCIS* (2003-23); New York, NY, Sept. 25, 2023.

McCarthy, Cormac, 89, Pulitzer Prize-winning novelist known for apocalyptic westerns such as *Blood Meridian* (1985) and *All the Pretty Horses* (1992); Santa Fe, NM, June 13, 2023.

McCarver, Tim, 81, Emmy Award-winning catcher whose 21-year MLB tenure was followed by a three-decade broadcasting career; Memphis, TN, Feb. 16, 2023.

McCombs, Red, 95, executive who co-founded iHeartMedia (1972); one-time owner of San Antonio Spurs, Minnesota Vikings, and Denver Nuggets; San Antonio, TX, Feb. 19, 2023.

McGrath, Bob, 90, actor best known for portraying Bob on *Sesame Street* (1969-2016); Norwood, NJ, Dec. 4, 2022.

McVie, Christine, 79, British singer-songwriter with Fleetwood Mac who wrote hits such as "Don't Stop" and "You Make Loving Fun" (both 1977); London, Eng., UK, Nov. 30, 2022.

Meaker, Marijane, 95, writer who helped launch the lesbian pulp fiction genre; East Hampton, NY, Nov. 21, 2022.

Meggett, Emily, 90, chef and author who helped preserve recipes of the coastal Geechee-Gullah community; Edisto Island, SC, Apr. 21, 2023.

Meisner, Randy, 77, Grammy Award-winning bassist and singer-songwriter with the Eagles who wrote the hit song "Take It to the Limit" (1975); Los Angeles, CA, July 26, 2023.

Meyers, Gerald, 94, CEO of automaker AMC who oversaw the development of the Jeep Cherokee and the unusually shaped Pacer; West Bloomfield, MI, June 19, 2023.

Minow, Newton, 97, FCC chairman (1961-63), who criticized TV programming then as "a vast wasteland"; Chicago, IL, May 6, 2023.

Mirsch, Walter, 101, producer whose company was credited with Oscar winners *The Apartment* (1960), *West Side Story* (1961), and *In the Heat of the Night* (1967); Los Angeles, CA, Feb. 24, 2023.

Mitchell, Charlene, 92, activist who was the first Black woman to run for president (1968); New York, NY, Dec. 14, 2022.

Mitnick, Kevin, 59, computer security consultant and convicted hacker; Pittsburgh, PA, July 16, 2023.

Miyamura, Hiroshi, 97, first living Japanese American soldier to receive the Medal of Honor; Phoenix, AZ, Nov. 29, 2022.

Moll, Richard, 80, actor known for the sitcom *Night Court* (1984-92); Big Bear Lake, CA, Oct. 26, 2023.

Moore, Billie, 79, Hall of Fame basketball coach who won national college titles with two women's teams; Fullerton, CA, Dec. 14, 2022.

Moore, Gordon, 94, engineer and co-founder of Intel Corp. (1968) known for "Moore's law," which observed that the number of transistors per silicon chip doubles every year; Waimea, HI, Mar. 24, 2023.

Morrissett, Lloyd, 93, psychologist who co-created *Sesame Street* (1969); San Diego, CA, Jan. 15, 2023.

Mozilo, Angelo, 84, CEO of Countrywide Financial (1969-2008) who paid $22.5 mil in fines after the SEC accused him of fraud and insider trading; Montecito, CA, July 16, 2023.

Müller, K. Alex, 95, Nobel Prize-winning Swiss physicist; Zurich, Switzerland, Jan. 9, 2023.

Musharraf, Pervez, 79, Pakistani military leader who served as president (2001-08); Dubai, UAE, Feb. 5, 2023.

N

Napolitano, Giorgio, 98, Italian president (2006-15) who pursued stability; Rome, Italy, Sept. 22, 2023.

Nasseri, Mehran Karimi, 77, Iranian refugee who lived in a Paris airport for decades, Charles de Gaulle Airport, Paris, France, Nov. 11, 2022.

Nero, Peter, 89, Grammy Award-winning pianist and conductor who directed the Philly Pops (1979-2013); Eustis, FL, July 6, 2023.

O

O'Connor, Sinéad, 56, Grammy Award-winning Irish singer-songwriter known for "Nothing Compares 2 U" (1990) and for drawing ire after condemning the Catholic Church response to clerical sexual abuse; London, Eng., UK, July 26, 2023.

P

Pedott, Joseph, 91, advertising executive who popularized Chia Pets through TV campaigns; San Francisco, CA, June 22, 2023.

Pelé (Edson Arantes do Nascimento), 82, Brazilian soccer forward considered one of the all-time best players and the sport's first international star; São Paulo, Brazil, Dec. 29, 2022.

Perry, Anne, 84, British detective novelist who as a teenager served five years in prison for helping a friend kill her mother; Los Angeles, CA, Apr. 10, 2023.

Perry, Gaylord, 84, Hall of Fame pitcher who struck out 3,534 batters and won the Cy Young Award in both leagues; Gaffney, SC, Dec. 1, 2022.

Perry, Matthew, 54, actor best known as Chandler Bing on sitcom *Friends* (1994-2004); Los Angeles, CA, Oct. 28, 2023.

Phantom of the Opera, 35, Broadway run of the acclaimed musical, after a record-breaking 13,981 performances; New York, NY, Apr. 16, 2023.

Pointer, Anita, 74, Grammy Award-winning singer-songwriter with the Pointer Sisters, whose hits included "I'm So Excited" (1982) and "Jump" (1984); Beverly Hills, CA, Dec. 31, 2022

Prescott, Edward, 81, Nobel Prize-winning economist who challenged the idea of short-term remedies to boost the economy; Paradise Valley, AZ, Nov. 6, 2022.

Presley, Lisa Marie, 54, singer-songwriter and only child of Elvis Presley; also known for brief marriage to pop superstar Michael Jackson; Los Angeles, CA, Jan. 12, 2023.

Prigozhin, Yevgeny, 62, oligarch who co-founded Wagner Group, a paramilitary force; launched a short-lived rebellion against Russian military leadership and was killed in a plane explosion two months later; Russia, Aug. 23, 2023.

Q

Quant, Mary, 93, British fashion designer who popularized miniskirts and hot pants; Surrey, Eng., UK, Apr. 13, 2023.

R

Rabanne, Paco, 88, Spanish fashion designer who incorporated metal and plastic into forward thinking designs; Portsall, France, Feb. 3, 2023.

Rawls, Betsy, 95, Hall of Fame golfer who won 55 LPGA tour events, including 8 Majors; Lewes, DE, Oct. 21, 2023.

Reddick, Lance, 60, actor known for roles in *The Wire* (2002-08) and *Fringe* (2008-13), and in four John Wick films; Los Angeles, CA, Mar. 17, 2023.

Reed, Willis, 80, Hall of Fame MVP-winning basketball player who led NY Knicks to two titles; Houston, TX, Mar. 21, 2023.

Reichert, Julia, 76, Academy Award-winning documentarian who focused on the working class; Yellow Springs, OH, Dec. 1, 2022.

Reubens, Paul, 70, Emmy Award-winning actor best known for creating and performing the iconic character Pee-wee Herman in TV and film; Los Angeles, CA, July 30, 2023.

Rich, Adam, 54, child actor best known for *Eight Is Enough* (1977-81); Los Angeles, CA, Jan. 7, 2023.

Richardson, Bill, 75, U.S. rep. (D, NM, 1983-97), energy sec. (1998-2001), and New Mexico gov. (2003-11); Chatham, MA, Sept. 1, 2023.

Riordan, Richard, 92, Los Angeles mayor (R, 1993-2001) who oversaw rebuilding after the tumultuous riots of 1992 and the 1994 Northridge earthquake; Brentwood, CA, Apr. 19, 2023.

Robertson, Pat, 93, televangelist best known for hosting *The 700 Club* since 1966 and for his opinions on LGBTQ rights, 9/11, and Hurricane Katrina; Virginia Beach, VA, June 8, 2023.

Robertson, Robbie, 80, Canadian guitarist and songwriter known for rock group the Band and his Martin Scorsese film scores, from *Raging Bull* (1980) to *Killers of the Flower Moon* (2023); Los Angeles, CA, Aug. 9, 2023.

Robinson, Brooks, 86, Hall of Fame Baltimore Orioles third baseman (1955-77) known for defense who helped win two World Series (1966, 1970); Owings Mills, MD, Sept. 26, 2023.

Rorem, Ned, 99, Pulitzer Prize-winning composer and writer best known for his art-songs and his explicit diaries; New York, NY, Nov. 18, 2022.

Roundtree, Richard, 81, actor best known as title character in blaxploitation classic *Shaft* (1971) and its four sequels; Los Angeles, CA, Oct. 24, 2023.

Rush, Stockton, 61, OceanGate CEO who died, along with four passengers, in his *Titan* submersible on a dive to the *Titanic* wreck; North Atlantic Ocean, June 22, 2023.

S

Safir, Howard, 81, New York City police commissioner (1996-2000); Annapolis, MD, Sept. 11, 2023.

Sakamoto, Ryuichi, 71, Academy Award-winning Japanese film composer best known for *The Last Emperor* (1987); Tokyo, Japan, Mar. 28, 2023.

Saltman, Roy, 90, computer scientist who warned about hanging chads on punch-card ballots a decade before they became the focus of the 2000 presidential election; Rockville, MD, Apr. 21, 2023.

Sands, Julian, 65, British actor known for *A Room with a View* (1985); San Gabriel Mountains, Mount Baldy, CA, Jan. 2023.

Saura, Carlos, 91, Spanish film director whose works, including *Cría Cuervos* (1976), were often allegories of life under Francisco Franco; Madrid, Spain, Feb. 10, 2023.

Schroeder, Pat, 82, U.S. rep. (D, CO, 1973-97) who fought for women's rights and for passage of the Family and Medical Leave Act; Celebration, FL, Mar. 13, 2023.

Scotto, Renata, 89, Italian soprano known for her acting ability over a nearly 50-year opera career; Savona, Italy, Aug. 16, 2023.

Serrano, Lupe, 92, Chilean-born American ballerina who was the first Hispanic principal dancer with American Ballet Theatre; Syosset, NY, Jan. 16, 2023.

Shorter, Wayne, 89, 12-time Grammy Award-winning saxophonist and composer known for work with Miles Davis and Art Blakey and founding the jazz fusion band Weather Report; Los Angeles, CA, Mar. 2, 2023.

Silverstein, Charles, 87, psychologist who in 1973 helped persuade the American Psychiatric Association to stop classifying homosexuality as a mental disorder and later co-wrote *The Joy of Gay Sex* (1997); New York, NY, Jan. 30, 2023.

Simic, Charles, 84, Pulitzer Prize-winning Serbian-born American poet whose work often focused on his childhood during World War II; Dover, NH, Jan. 9, 2023.

Sizemore, Tom, 61, actor known for *Saving Private Ryan* (1998) and *Black Hawk Down* (2001); Burbank, CA, Mar. 3, 2023.

Somers, Suzanne, 76, actress and wellness entrepreneur known for the sitcom *Three's Company* (1977-81) and her ubiquitous ThighMaster ads; Palm Springs, CA, Oct. 15, 2023.

Springer, Jerry, 79, British-born TV host known for his provocative eponymous talk show (1991-2018); also Cincinnati mayor (1977-78); Evanston, IL, Apr. 27, 2023.

Stein, Seymour, 80, executive who co-founded Sire Records (1966) and known for identifying new talent, including Madonna and the Ramones; Los Angeles, CA, Apr. 2, 2023.

Straub, Jean-Marie, 89, French director known for radical films; Rolle, Switzerland, Nov. 20, 2022.

Strong, Barrett, 81, R&B singer-songwriter who co-wrote "I Heard It Through the Grapevine" (1967); Jan. 29, 2023.

T

Takeoff (Kirsnick Khari Ball), 28, rapper in hip-hop trio Migos; Houston, TX, Nov. 1, 2022.

Teuber, Klaus, 70, German designer known for board game *Settlers of Catan* (1995); Apr. 1, 2023.

Topol, Chaim, 87, Israeli actor known for starring in *Fiddler on the Roof* in film (1971) and on stage; Tel Aviv, Israel, Mar. 9, 2023.

Toyoda, Shoichiro, 97, Japanese president (1982-92) and chair (1992-99) of Toyota Motor Corp. who expanded the company into a true global entity; Feb. 14, 2023.

Triplett, Donald, 89, first person diagnosed with autism (1943); Forest, MS, June 15, 2023.

Turner, Tina, 83, Grammy Award-winning singer and actress known for exuberant performances of hits "Proud Mary" (1971) and "What's Love Got to Do With It" (1984); Küsnacht, Switzerland, May 24, 2023.

V

Van Ellis, Hughes, 102, one of three known remaining survivors of the 1921 Tulsa massacre; Denver, CO, Oct. 9, 2023.

Verlaine, Tom, 73, singer-songwriter and guitarist known for indie-rock group Television and their debut album *Marquee Moon* (1977); New York, NY, Jan. 28, 2023.

Vincenz, Lilli, 85, German-born American activist who was one of the first lesbians to join the gay rights organization Mattachine Society of Washington; Oakton, VA, June 27, 2023.

W

Wagner, Robin, 89, Tony Award-winning set designer whose Broadway sets included *Dreamgirls* (1981) and *The Producers* (2001); New York, NY, May 29, 2023.

Wahl, Grant, 49, sports journalist, best known for soccer, who died while covering the World Cup in Qatar; Lusail, Qatar, Dec. 9, 2022.

Wakefield, Tim, 57, Boston Red Sox knuckleballer (1995-2011) and TV analyst; MA, Oct. 1, 2023.

Walters, Barbara, 93, pioneering TV journalist who was the first woman co-anchor of a network evening news program and co-created *The View* (1997-); also known for interviews of high-profile subjects; New York, NY, Dec. 30, 2022.

Warnock, John, 82, co-founder of Adobe Systems Inc. who helped develop the PDF file format; Los Altos, CA, Aug. 19, 2023.

Watts, André, 77, Grammy Award-winning pianist who was one of the first Black concert pianists to achieve international acclaim; Bloomington, IN, July 12, 2023.

Weil, Cynthia, 82, Grammy Award-winning songwriter who collaborated with husband Barry Mann on hit songs like "You've Lost That Lovin' Feelin'" (1964); Beverly Hills, CA, June 1, 2023.

Welch, Raquel, 82, actress, model, and sex symbol known for *One Million Years B.C.* (1966) and *The Three Musketeers* (1973); Los Angeles, CA, Feb. 15, 2023.

Weldon, Fay, 91, British author known for *The Life and Loves of a She-Devil* (1983); Northampton, Eng., UK, Jan. 4, 2023.

Westwood, Vivienne, 81, British fashion designer known as the "godmother of punk"; London, Eng., UK, Dec. 29, 2022.

Whitlock, Tom, 68, Academy Award-winning songwriter who co-wrote "Take My Breath Away" and "Danger Zone" for *Top Gun* (1986); Gallatin, TN, Feb. 18, 2023.

Whitworth, Kathy, 83 Hall of Fame pro golfer who won a record 88 LGPA tournaments; Flower Mound, TX, Dec. 24, 2022.

Williams, Cindy, 75, actress known for *American Graffiti* (1973) and *Laverne & Shirley* (1976-82); Los Angeles, CA, Jan. 25, 2023.

Williams, Treat, 71, actor known for films *Hair* (1979) and *Prince of the City* (1981), as well as the TV series *Everwood* (2002-06); Albany, NY, June 12, 2023.

Willis, Beverly, 95, architect best known for the San Francisco Ballet Building; Branford, CT, Oct. 1, 2023.

Wilmut, Ian, 79, British embryologist who led the project that cloned a mammal for the first time (Dolly the sheep, in 1996); Midlothian, Scotland, Sept. 10, 2023.

Winston, George, 74, Grammy Award-winning pianist and composer; Williamsport, PA, June 4, 2023.

Witkin, Evelyn M., 102, geneticist who discovered how DNA can be damaged and repaired; Plainsboro Township, NJ, July 8, 2023.

Wirtz, Rocky, 70, Chicago Blackhawks owner (2007-23); Evanston, IL, July 25, 2023.

Wright, Gary, 80, singer-songwriter known for 1976 hit "Dream Weaver"; Palos Verdes Estates, CA, Sept. 4, 2023.

Y

Yellin, Jean Fagan, 92, historian who discovered that *Incidents in the Life of a Slave Girl* (1861), long thought to be fiction, was written by former enslaved woman Harriet Jacobs; Sarasota, FL, July 19, 2023.

Z

Zah, Peterson, 85, chair (1983-87) and first president of the Navajo Nation (1991-95); helped create the Navajo Nation's Permanent Trust Fund; Fort Defiance, AZ, Mar. 7, 2023.

Zeman, Jacklyn, 70, actress who portrayed Bobbie Spencer on *General Hospital* (1977-2010, 2013-23); Thousand Oaks, CA, May 9, 2023.

The U.S. Supreme Court's 2022-23 term began Oct. 3, 2022. The justices decided 56 cases, not including those decided without oral argument, or one case argued in Jan. 2023 then dismissed as improvidently granted. Chief Justice John G. Roberts Jr., nominated by Pres. George W. Bush in 2005, presided over his 18th full term. The eight associate justices, in order of seniority, were Clarence Thomas, Samuel A. Alito Jr., Sonia Sotomayor, Elena Kagan, Neil M. Gorsuch, Brett M. Kavanaugh, Amy Coney Barrett, and Ketanji Brown Jackson.

Notable Supreme Court Decisions, 2022-23

Note: Gray shading in the columns on the right indicate justices who voted with the majority; unshaded boxes indicate justices who dissented. MO = wrote majority opinion; DO = wrote or co-wrote dissenting opinion; CO = wrote concurring opinion; COJ = wrote opinion concurring in judgment; CO = wrote opinion concurring in judgment but not in its reasoning; COP = wrote opinion concurring in part of the judgment; CDO = wrote opinion concurring in part of the judgment and dissenting in part of the judgment. In some cases a majority opinion was issued *per curiam* ("by the Court"), with no justice signing it.

Column headers (left to right): Jackson, Kagan, Sotomayor, Roberts, Thomas, Alito, Gorsuch, Kavanaugh, Barrett

Affirmative Action

The Court, 6-3, June 29 ruled that race-conscious admissions policies at colleges and universities were unlawful, effectively rejecting precedent that held race could be considered among a range of factors. The joint decision, in *Students for Fair Admissions v. Harvard* and *Students for Fair Admissions v. University of North Carolina* applied to both public and private institutions but not to the nation's military academies.

Copyright Law

The Court May 18 ruled, 7-2, that the licensing of a portrait of Prince, derived from a photograph, for the cover of a magazine about the singer, exceeded the bounds of "fair use" and infringed the photographer's copyright. The case was *Andy Warhol Foundation for the Visual Arts v. Goldsmith*.

Environment

In *Sackett v. Environmental Protection Agency*, May 25, the Court unanimously decided that the EPA had overstepped its authority, and a 5-4 majority held that the 1972 Clean Water Act did not permit the EPA to regulate discharges into wetlands with no "continuous surface connection" with a body of water. It was the second decision in as many years to significantly limit the EPA's administrative powers.

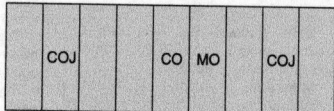

First Amendment

In *303 Creative LLC v. Elenis*, the justices held June 30, 6-3, that First Amendment protections prevented Colorado from requiring a designer to create wedding websites for same-sex couples, contradicting a state law that prohibited discrimination based on sexual orientation.

In a unanimous decision in *Groff v. DeJoy* June 29, the Court expanded the religious accommodations required of employers. The ruling, in favor of a mail carrier whose Christian faith did not allow him to work Sundays, held that employers needed to show that granting the accommodation would create substantial increased costs.

Interstate Commerce

In *National Pork Producers Council v. Ross*, the Court May 11 upheld a California law intended to prevent animal cruelty, dismissing a claim by out-of-state pork producers that it impermissibly burdened interstate commerce. The 5-4 majority differed on the basis for the decision.

Native American Rights

In *Haaland v. Brackeen*, the Court upheld the 1978 Indian Child Welfare Act in a 7-2 decision June 15, arguing that Congress had the power to make laws regarding tribes and child welfare. The ruling did not resolve whether the law amounted to racial discrimination against non-Native families—and a violation of the equal protection clause—as the original suit had argued.

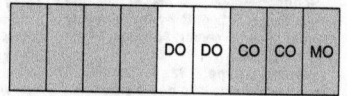

Student Loans

The Court in a 6-3 ruling June 30 said that the Biden administration's education secretary did not have the authority to establish a forgiveness program that would have canceled approx. $430 bil in federal student loan debt. The case was *Biden v. Nebraska*.

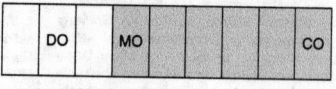

Voting Rights and Elections

In the *Allen v. Milligan* ruling announced June 8, the Court decided, 5-4, an Alabama congressional redistricting map had minimized the power of Black voters and likely violated Section 2 of the Voting Rights Act of 1965, which some civil rights advocates had feared would be overturned altogether.

The Court in *Moore v. Harper*, June 27, decided that state legislatures could not set rules for federal elections unchecked. The 6-3 decision dismissed the "independent state legislature" theory that had the potential to permanently transform the conduct of federal elections.

NOTABLE QUOTES, 2023

National News

"I never claimed to be Jewish, I am Catholic. Because I learned my maternal family had a Jewish background I said I was 'Jew-ish.'"
—**Rep. George Santos** (R, NY), Dec. 26, 2022, on one of the lies he told about his background.

"From the outside, it looks like chaos … From the inside, it is."
—**Rep. Ryan Zinke** (R, MT), Jan. 6, 2023, on the 15-ballot process that elected Kevin McCarthy (R, CA) Speaker of the House.

"People introducing and passing these laws underestimate how much a child knows about their own body and about their own brain."
—**Ash Homan**, a 12-year-old transgender boy from Omaha, NE, Feb. 8, 2023, in Nebraska statehouse testimony as lawmakers considered a ban on gender-affirming care for minors.

"The Biden administration had a chance to shoot it down over Alaska and they chose to let it spy all across America."
—**Sen. Tom Cotton** (R, AR), Feb. 9, 2023, on the handling of the Chinese spy balloon that traversed U.S. airspace.

"President Trump is joining some of the most incredible people in history being arrested today. Nelson Mandela was arrested; served time in prison. Jesus. Jesus was arrested and murdered by the Roman government."
—**Rep. Marjorie Taylor Greene** (R, GA), Apr. 4, 2023.

"I think my conservative colleagues … don't feel like we should negotiate with our hostage."
—**Rep. Matt Gaetz** (R, FL), May 23, 2023, on negotiating an agreement on the debt limit.

"If even half of it is true, he's toast. It is a very detailed indictment and it's very, very damning."
—**Former Atty. Gen. William Barr**, one-time Trump appointee, June 11, 2023, on the federal indictment of former Pres. Trump concerning his handling of classified documents.

"Threatening me with 400 years in prison for possessing my own presidential papers, which just about every other president has done, is one of the most outrageous and vicious legal theories ever put forward in an American court of law."
—**Former Pres. Donald Trump**, June 13, 2023, after pleading not guilty to 37 federal charges related to his handling of classified documents.

"…the tragic failure of this Court was its misinterpretation of the Reconstruction Amendments, as Justice Harlan predicted in *Plessy*. We should not repeat this mistake merely because we think, as our predecessors thought, that the present arrangements are superior to the Constitution."
—**U.S. Supreme Court Justice Clarence Thomas**, June 29, 2023, in 6-3 majority opinion striking down use of affirmative action in college admissions.

"With let-them-eat-cake obliviousness, today, the majority pulls the ripcord and announces 'colorblindness for all' by legal fiat. But deeming race irrelevant in law does not make it so in life."
—**U.S. Supreme Court Justice Ketanji Brown Jackson**, June 29, 2023, in her dissent to the Court's affirmative action-ending ruling.

"The president specifically asked me, and his gaggle of crackpot lawyers asked me, to literally reject votes, which would have resulted in the issue being turned over to the House of Representatives, and literally chaos would have ensued."
—**Former Vice Pres. Mike Pence** (R), in an Aug. 2, 2023, Fox News interview.

"They're basically treating these asylum seekers, these human beings like animals… You see clothing of people, including kids—it's stuck to the wire, literally stuck to the razor wire."
—**Rep. Joaquin Castro** (D, TX), Aug. 8, 2023, on the Eagle Pass area where Texas installed razor wire and a weaponized floating buoy to prevent border crossings.

"I don't see an ending to this … This issue will destroy New York City."
—**New York City Mayor Eric Adams** (D), Sept. 6, 2023, on the migrant crisis and need for federal relief.

"If the Republicans had a smoking gun or even a dripping water pistol, they would be presenting it today."
—**Rep. Jamie Raskin** (D, MD), Sept. 28, 2023, during the first hearing of the House's Biden impeachment inquiry.

"They don't get to say they're conservative when they're angry and they're chaotic."
—**Rep. Kevin McCarthy** (R, CA), after being removed as Speaker of the House, Oct. 3, 2023.

"It is now the responsibility of the GOP members to end the House Republican Civil War."
—**Rep. Hakeem Jeffries** (D, NY), the House minority leader, Oct. 3, 2023.

Around the World

"…it wasn't only an attack on the Capitol like in the U.S. It was kind of a message that they don't believe in any of the democratic institutions that control our country."
—**Laís Martins**, Brazilian freelance journalist, on the country's Jan. 8, 2023, insurrection.

"The overhaul is an assassination of the Declaration of Independence, which will turn Israel into a dictatorship."
—**Former Israel Prime Minister Ehud Barak**, Feb. 25, 2023, on the proposed changes to Israel's judiciary.

"Geographically, their addition to the alliance adds a huge, difficult-to-defend board that complicates Putin's calculus."
—**Adm. James G. Stavridis** (ret.), former NATO commander, on Finland joining NATO, as reported in *NY Times* Apr. 4, 2023.

"Everything dear to me, everything I loved, worked for, and dreamed about was shattered in an instant."
—**Ruslan**, a Ukrainian salt miner-turned-soldier fighting near Bakhmut when the Russians took control of his nearby hometown and its mine in Apr. 2023.

"He made some serious mistakes in life, but he also achieved necessary results, for himself and, when I asked him about it, for our common cause."
—**Russia Pres. Vladimir Putin**, Aug. 24, 2023, on the death of Wagner mercenary boss Yevgeny Prigozhin.

"I would recommend all critics to shut up, come to Ukraine, and try to liberate one square centimeter by themselves."
—**Ukraine Foreign Min. Dmytro Kuleba**, Aug. 31, 2023, on criticism of his country's slow counteroffensive progress.

"The dog days of summer are not just barking, they are biting."
—**UN Sec.-Gen. António Guterres** in a statement Sept. 6, 2023, on the season's record-setting heat.

"We are at war and we will win it."
—**Israel Prime Min. Benjamin Netanyahu**, Oct. 7, 2023, immediately after Hamas mounted a shocking attack on Israel.

"I believe deeply that the majority of people of all kinds do not want to see Gaza leveled and innocents killed, & that they feel and hold the pain of Israeli families destroyed."
—**Rep. Alexandria Ocasio-Cortez** (D, NY), Oct. 12, 2023, in reaction to Israel's counteroffensive in Gaza and the Oct. 7 Hamas attack.

People and Culture

"Lionel Messi has conquered his final peak. Lionel Messi has shaken hands with paradise. … He has his crowning moment and, of course, he is not alone."
—**Sportscaster Peter Drury**, on the soccer legend who led Argentina to the title in his fifth FIFA World Cup tournament appearance, Dec. 18, 2022.

"The only thing I can compare it to is the phenomenon of Beatlemania."
—**Billy Joel**, legendary singer-songwriter, on attending a Taylor Swift Eras Tour show in Tampa, FL, Apr. 15, 2023.

"I come not to be served but to serve."
—**King Charles III**, May 6, 2023, at his formal coronation as UK monarch.

"*Titanic*'s captain was handed multiple warnings about ice ahead, and steamed full ahead into a known ice field … You have the people that were designing and operating this sub who were warned."
—**James Cameron**, *Titanic* film director and underwater exploration enthusiast, June 23, 2023, discussing the *Titan* submersible's implosion, which killed all five passengers.

"They plead poverty, that they're losing money left and right when giving hundreds of millions of dollars to their CEOs. It is disgusting. Shame on them!"
—**SAG-AFTRA Pres. Fran Drescher**, July 13, 2023, in impassioned announcement that the actors' union would go on strike.

"Simply put, I was not respected."
—**Jennifer Hermoso**, a member of Spain's World Cup-winning soccer team, Aug. 25, 2023, on an unwanted kiss from soccer boss Luis Rubiales that sparked a "Me Too" moment in Spain.

"Honestly, to those who thought they were putting water on my fire, you really were adding gas to it."
—**Coco Gauff**, on winning the U.S. Open, her first Grand Slam tennis singles title, Sept. 9, 2023.

"If you ask me, do I believe there's life in a universe that is so vast that it's hard for me to comprehend how big it is, my personal answer is yes."
—**NASA Admin. Bill Nelson** on the release of a study of unidentified aerial (or anomalous) phenomena, more commonly known as UFOs, Sept. 14, 2023.

"He told me he has been successful at everything in life, but he can't figure out how to die."
—**James Earl "Chip" Carter III**, son of former Pres. Jimmy Carter, in *Washington Post* Sept. 30, 2023, the eve of his father's 99th birthday, seven months after starting hospice care.

Last Will and Testament

An anonymous Brazilian soccer fan made headlines in late June 2023, when he announced he was leaving everything he owned to Neymar, the star striker on the Brazilian national soccer team, who had an estimated 2023 income of $85 million, according to *Forbes*. The fan was only 30 years old, he told the Brazilian news site *Metrópoles*, but "I am not in very good health, and… I don't have anyone to leave my things to. I wouldn't want the government or relatives I don't get along with to take my things." He said he identified with Neymar because of the star's relationship with his father, which reminded him of his own father-son bond. He had previously tried to gift his assets to his idol; when that failed, he wrote the will, stipulating that all his possessions "go to Neymar da Silva Santos Júnior" and had the document notarized to make it official.

"I know that, above all, he is not greedy," the fan said, "something a bit rare these days." Neymar did not comment.

The Conductor Seemed a Bit Robotic

Add one more job to the list of professions threatened by artificial intelligence (AI): orchestra conductor. On June 30, EveR 6, a two-armed robot designed by the Korea Institute of Industrial Technology, took the stage with South Korea's National Orchestra for the first time. EveR 6—the R is for *robot*—uses motion capture technology to replicate a human conductor's baton movements. The performance, titled <absence>, was an experiment to probe the relationship between art and science when a human conductor is not present. Ironically, though, on this evening, a human conductor *was* present, because even the most advanced robot conductor can't listen to or make eye contact with musicians (yet).

Choi Soo-yeoul, artistic director of the Busan Philharmonic Orchestra, shared the podium with EveR 6's animatronic head and shoulders. Each conductor led the orchestra for two pieces, and they collaborated on a fifth work. Initial reactions to the performance were mixed. Some audience members were impressed with EveR 6's precise baton movements. But Kim Bo-deul-saem, a flautist with the orchestra that night, told the *Korea Times* it was hard to follow the robot conductor, "because it did not consider the players' breathing."

Flag on the Play

Because of its ubiquity, minor mistakes on Wikipedia can have a lasting impact. Reports in 2023 noted that the online encyclopedia had been showing an incorrect version of the Vatican City (Holy See) flag from 2017 to 2022. The differences between the official flag and the Wikipedia version weren't as obvious as, say, reversing the colors of the Stars and Stripes. On the official flag, a white-and-gold papal tiara floats above a pair of crossed keys. On the Wikipedia image, uploaded by an anonymous editor who thought the site's previous flag image had a yellow stripe that needed color-correcting, the base of the tiara was erroneously red. Because Wikipedia is a go-to source of high-resolution, copyright-free images, the incorrect version was then replicated so often that it became more common than the official flag, sold not only on Amazon but outside the United Nations headquarters in New York and in Italian souvenir shops. The wrong flag even flew outside some buildings owned by the Vatican. In June 2023, a doorman at a Vatican-owned office building told Catholic News Service that the building bought its flag online or "from one of the shops around the building" rather than from the Floreria Apostolica Vaticana, the official agency.

The Wikipedia page was amended with a corrected image in 2023. In hopes of preventing further flag errors, Father William Becker, a pastor from Blooming Prairie, MN, wrote a book about the Vatican flag and created a website to make quality, reproducible images of the correct version available to download. Unlike Wikipedia, Becker's site can only be edited by him.

Dog Days of Summer

Every five years or so, golden retrievers and their owners make a pilgrimage to Guisachan House, an abandoned estate in the Scottish Highlands where the breed was originally developed in 1868. Activities include dog-training sessions, a haggis-hurling competition, an afternoon tea, and a mile-long torchlight parade to the castle ruins, where participants raise a toast to Sir Dudley Marjoribanks (later Lord Tweedmouth), who was credited with being the first to breed a wavy-coated retriever with a tweed water spaniel 155 years earlier. The July 2023 event was the largest-ever gathering: 488 canines, from more than a dozen countries, braved intermittent rain (no thunderstorms, thankfully) to pose for a group photo and attended the five-day-long event.

The Golden Retriever Club of Scotland met in Guisachan informally in 2001; some 50 people and about 40 dogs attended that first meeting. Five years later, the club organized a more formal gathering and a photographer to commemorate the 188 dogs that made the trip. The number of pooch participants has increased with every reunion since. The next Guisachan House reunion is expected to be held in 2028.

No Such Thing as a Free Lunch

A Canadian government surplus sale in Aug. 2023 made world headlines unexpectedly when one of its items went viral, all over a controversial sandwich garnish. A mascot costume of a donair—the Canadian equivalent of a gyro or doner kebab sandwich, with a sweeter, condensed milk-based sauce—sparked a bidding war. (Introduced by Greek immigrants in Nova Scotia during the 1970s, donairs were proclaimed the official food of Halifax, Nova Scotia, in 2015, but Alberta claims the highest per-capita consumption levels in all of Canada.) The provincial government of Alberta, which had commissioned the original costume for a public service campaign against distracted driving, first listed the price at $50 (about $37, in U.S. dollars). The costume is accessorized with lettuce, a common topping in Alberta's version of the sandwich, but as forbidden as ketchup on a Chicago dog elsewhere, including in Nova Scotia. When Halifax-based shops swore to remove the lettuce if they won the auction, bidding surged. Adil Asim, owner of an Alberta-based donair chain, ended up taking the prize, paying a whopping C$16,025 (U.S. $11,900). His closest competition came from Steve Wallis, who planned to use the costume to raise money for local food banks, so they planned to team up to showcase the costume at a charity event.

You Can't Walk on Water

If nothing else, Reza Baluchi is resolute. No matter how many times the U.S. Coast Guard tries to stop him, the 51-year old Iranian refugee is undeterred in his quest to prove the seaworthiness of his "hydro pod," a giant floating hamster wheel he propels by running. In Aug. 2023, Coast Guard officials spotted him and his unorthodox wire-and-buoy vessel about 70 nautical miles east of Tybee Island, GA. He told the officers he planned to "run" all the way to London, over 4,000 miles away, and refused to abandon the voyage even though Hurricane Franklin was bearing down. The Coast Guard decreed Baluchi's journey in the hydro pod "manifestly unsafe," but he resisted several attempts to take him into custody before finally submitting. The latest saga echoed several earlier attempts, all of which ended in Coast Guard intervention. In 2014 and 2016, Baluchi endeavored to travel 1,000 miles from Boca Raton, FL, to Bermuda. And in 2021, he abandoned a journey from St. Augustine, FL, to New York when he couldn't find his backup GPS device and charging cables.

Baluchi's odysseys on land have been more successful. In 2003, the former cyclist for Iran's national team made a charity run from Los Angeles to New York, timing his arrival in NYC to coincide with the second anniversary of the Sept. 11, 2001, attacks. And in 2007, he spent 202 days running the perimeter of the United States, a journey of 11,720 miles, to raise money for Children's Hospital of Denver.

HISTORICAL ANNIVERSARIES

1924 — 100 Years Ago

Joseph Stalin struggles against other potential successors to consolidate control of the Soviet Union following Vladimir Lenin's death Jan. 21.

British Empire Exposition, with participation by 56 of 58 territories, opens Apr. 23 in London, England, and receives at least 17 million visitors by Nov. 1.

Wheeling Steel mine explosion in Benwood, WV, kills 119 miners on Apr. 28.

Pres. Calvin Coolidge May 24 signs the Immigration Act of 1924; the law bans immigration from Asia, limits immigrants from Southern and Eastern Europe, and establishes U.S. Border Patrol.

The Indian Citizenship Act, enacted June 2, confers U.S. citizenship on all Native Americans born in the U.S.

The Dawes Plan, intended to resolve the crisis over Germany's World War I reparation payments and occupation of the Ruhr Valley by French and Belgian troops, is signed in Paris Aug. 16.

Nathan Leopold Jr. and Richard Loeb are sentenced to life in prison Sept. 10 for murder of 14-year-old Bobby Franks in infamous "thrill killing."

Incumbent Calvin Coolidge (R) is elected U.S. president, Nov. 4, defeating former Rep. John W. Davis (D, WV) and Sen. Robert M. La Follette Sr. (Progressive Party, WI). Wyoming's Nellie Tayloe Ross is first woman ever elected governor.

Adolf Hitler receives a five-year sentence for treason over his role in the Beer Hall Putsch; he is released Dec. 20 after less than nine months, having used the time to dictate the first volume of *Mein Kampf*.

Art. George Bellows's *Dempsey and Firpo*, Edward Hopper's *New York Pavements*, Georgia O'Keeffe's *From the Lake*, Yasuo Kuniyoshi's *Landscape*.

Film. Buster Keaton's *The Navigator* and *Sherlock Jr.*, *He Who Gets Slapped* starring Lon Chaney, John Ford's *The Iron Horse*, *The Thief of Bagdad* starring Douglas Fairbanks, Erich von Stroheim's *Greed*. MGM forms from merger of Metro Pictures, Goldwyn Pictures, and Louis B. Mayer Pictures.

Health and medicine. First tetanus and scarlet fever vaccines are discovered. Hans Berger records first electroencephalogram (EEG) of human brain activity.

Literature. Thomas Mann's *Buddenbrooks* is published in English translation; E. M. Forster's *A Passage to India*; Pablo Neruda's *Twenty Love Poems and a Song of Despair*.

Music. Composer George Gershwin writes *Rhapsody in Blue*, premiering it in Feb. with Paul Whiteman's orchestra in a concert called "An Experiment in Modern Music."

Nonfiction. *The Cross Word Puzzle Book*, first collection of crossword puzzles, is published by Simon & Schuster. Yvan Goll and André Breton publish dueling Surrealist manifestos.

Pop music. "California, Here I Come," recorded by Al Jolson; "Hard Hearted Hannah"; "It Had to Be You," written by Isham Jones and Gus Kahn. "Tea for Two" debuts in the pre-Broadway tour of *No, No, Nanette* and goes on to become a major pop hit.

Radio. BBC broadcasts the world's first play written especially for radio. Pres. Coolidge makes first presidential political speech broadcast by radio.

Science and technology. "Taung Child," the first known fossil remains of *Australopithecus*, is discovered in South Africa. Louis de Broglie proposes that electrons sometimes behave as waves and that all matter has wave properties, a central part of quantum mechanics theory. Edwin Hubble announces his discovery that the Milky Way is only one of many galaxies.

Sports. First Winter Olympics is held in Chamonix, France; Boston Bruins are the first NHL team based in U.S.

Theater. George and Ira Gershwin's *Lady, Be Good* debuts on Broadway starring Fred and Adele Astaire.

Miscellaneous. Pres. Coolidge appoints J. Edgar Hoover to lead the Bureau of Investigation, predecessor to the FBI.

1974 — 50 Years Ago

Israeli Prime Min. Golda Meir resigns Apr. 11 and is replaced June 3 by Yitzhak Rabin.

A left-wing military junta Apr. 25 overthrows Portugal's government in Carnation Revolution.

West German Chancellor Willy Brandt resigns May 6 in wake of the "Guillaume Affair," in which one of Brandt's assistants was identified as an East German spy.

India successfully detonates its first nuclear weapon May 18.

The Cypriot National Guard, led by Greek army officers, seizes control of Cyprus's government July 15. Turkey invades the island July 20, and by Aug. 16, occupies the northeastern 40%.

Supreme Court rules, 8-0 on July 24, that Pres. Richard Nixon must turn over 64 audiotapes of White House conversations.

House Judiciary Committee, in televised hearings July 24-30, recommends articles of impeachment against Pres. Nixon.

Pres. Nixon announces his resignation, Aug. 8, and steps down Aug. 9; Vice Pres. Gerald Ford, himself named to replace Vice Pres. Spiro Agnew and sworn in just eight months earlier, becomes 38th U.S. president.

Citing the country's need to move on, Pres. Ford, Sept. 8, issues pardon to Nixon for any federal crimes he committed while president.

Ethiopian emperor Haile Selassie is deposed Sept. 12 after decades in power.

NY Times publishes seismic article Dec. 22 on CIA engagement in illegal domestic surveillance.

Art. Whitney Museum of American Art hosts a major retrospective of Jacob Lawrence's work. Marina Abramović's *Rhythm 0*, Judy Chicago's *Rejection Drawings*, Sylvia Plimack Mangold's *Floor With Horizontal Mirror*.

Film. Mel Brooks's *Blazing Saddles* and *Young Frankenstein*; Roman Polanski's *Chinatown* starring Jack Nicholson; Francis Ford Coppola's *The Conversation* and *The Godfather Part II*; *The Towering Inferno* starring Paul Newman and Steve McQueen; John Cassavetes's *A Woman Under the Influence* starring Gena Rowlands and Peter Falk.

Health and medicine. First "Tommy John" surgery is performed on the MLB pitcher who gave the procedure its name. Henry Heimlich describes the abdominal thrust method to address choking now known as the Heimlich maneuver.

Literature. John le Carré's *Tinker, Tailor, Soldier, Spy*; James A. Michener's *Centennial*; Robert M. Pirsig's *Zen and the Art of Motorcycle Maintenance*; Michael Shaara's *The Killer Angels*.

Music. Philip Glass's *Music in Twelve Parts*, Dmitri Shostakovich's *String Quartet No. 15*, Karlheinz Stockhausen's *Inori*.

Nonfiction. Robert A. Caro's *The Power Broker*; Annie Dillard's *Pilgrim at Tinker Creek*; Shelby Foote's *The Civil War: A Narrative: Volume 3: Red River to Appomattox*; Studs Terkel's *Working*; Bob Woodward and Carl Bernstein's *All the President's Men*.

Pop music. ABBA wins Eurovision song contest with "Waterloo." Carl Douglas's "Kung Fu Fighting," Terry Jacks's "Seasons in the Sun," Steve Miller Band's "The Joker," Joni Mitchell's *Court and Spark*.

Science and technology. U.S. paleontologist Donald Johanson and graduate student Tom Gray discover "Lucy"—a partial skeleton of *Australopithecus afarensis*—in Ethiopia.

Sports. Hank Aaron of the Atlanta Braves hits his 715th home run Apr. 8 to break Babe Ruth's career record. Host country West Germany wins men's FIFA World Cup soccer tournament. Muhammad Ali knocks out George Foreman in fight for heavyweight title in "Rumble in the Jungle."

Television. Marlo Thomas's *Free to Be... You and Me* special airs; *Little House on the Prairie* and spinoff sitcoms *Happy Days*, *Good Times*, and *Rhoda* debut.

Theater. *Gypsy* revival starring Angela Lansbury and *Equus* starring Anthony Hopkins open on Broadway.

Miscellaneous. Terracotta Army, thousands of warrior sculptures dating to 200 BCE in Shaanxi, China, is discovered. Scannable barcodes are introduced in U.S. shops. Hungarian professor Erno Rubik invents the Rubik's Cube puzzle toy.

1999 — 25 Years Ago

The euro currency is established Jan. 1.

Pres. Bill Clinton is acquitted, Feb. 12, in Senate impeachment trial on perjury and obstruction of justice charges.

Euthanasia activist Dr. Jack Kevorkian is convicted of second-degree murder Mar. 26 for his role in the death of terminally ill man.

In mass shooting at Columbine High School in Littleton, CO, two teens kill 12 fellow students and a teacher Apr. 20, then die by suicide.

Ehud Barak is elected Israeli prime minister May 17.

Yugoslavia and NATO sign a peace treaty June 9, and a NATO-led peacekeeping force deploys to Kosovo.

Pakistani Prime Minister Nawaz Sharif is ousted in a coup led by Gen. Pervez Musharraf Oct. 12.

EgyptAir Flight 990 crashes into the Atlantic Ocean south of Nantucket, MA, Oct. 31, killing all 217 aboard.

Russian Pres. Boris Yeltsin resigns Dec. 31, leaving Prime Min. Vladimir Putin as acting president.

Art. British art collector Charles Saatchi's controversial *Sensation* exhibit opens at the Brooklyn Museum and is challenged by New York City Mayor Rudolph Giuliani. Louise Bourgeois's *Maman*, Andreas Gursky's *99 Cent*, Barbara Kruger's *Don't Make Me Angry* and *Untitled (Thinking of You)*, Olafur Eliasson's *Spiral Pavilion*.

Film. Sam Mendes's *American Beauty* starring Annette Bening and Kevin Spacey; *Being John Malkovich*; Wim Wenders's *Buena Vista Social Club*; *Boys Don't Cry* starring Hilary Swank; *Girl, Interrupted* starring Angelina Jolie and Winona Ryder; David Fincher's *Fight Club* starring Brad Pitt and Edward Norton; *The Green Mile* starring Tom Hanks; Paul Thomas Anderson's *Magnolia* starring Tom Cruise; Lana and Lilly Wachowski's *The Matrix* starring Keanu Reeves; M. Night Shyamalan's *The Sixth Sense*; *Star Wars: Episode I—The Phantom Menace*; *Toy Story 2*.

Literature. Seamus Heaney publishes his translation of *Beowulf*. Isabel Allende's *Daughter of Fortune*, Laurie Halse Anderson's *Speak*, J. M. Coetzee's *Disgrace*, Ha Jin's *Waiting*, Jhumpa Lahiri's *Interpreter of Maladies*, Jonathan Lethem's *Motherless Brooklyn*, Susan Sontag's *In America*, Neal Stephenson's *Cryptonomicon*.

Music. Karl Jenkins's *The Armed Man*.

Nonfiction. Samuel R. Delany's *Times Square Red, Times Square Blue*; E. J. Graff's *What Is Marriage For?*; Brian Greene's *The Elegant Universe*; John McCain's *Faith of My Fathers*.

Pop music. Christina Aguilera's "Genie in a Bottle," Fiona Apple's *When the Pawn...*, Destiny's Child's *The Writing's on the Wall*, Dr. Dre's *2001*, Eminem's *The Slim Shady LP*, Magnetic Fields' *69 Love Songs*, Ricky Martin's "Livin' la Vida Loca," Red Hot Chili Peppers' *Californication*, The Roots' *Things Fall Apart*, "Smooth" by Santana feat. Rob Thomas, TLC's "No Scrubs."

Science and technology. Napster peer-to-peer file-sharing site launches. First BlackBerry "email pager" mobile device is released.

Sports. Denver Broncos win second straight Super Bowl; NY Yankees win second straight World Series. Host country U.S. wins women's FIFA World Cup soccer tournament.

Television. HBO introduces *The Sopranos*; Jon Stewart debuts as host of Comedy Central's *The Daily Show*. *Family Guy*, *Law & Order: SVU*, *SmackDown!*, *The West Wing*, and *Who Wants to Be a Millionaire?* air first episodes.

Theater. Revivals of *Death of a Salesman*, starring Brian Dennehy, and *Annie Get Your Gun*, starring Bernadette Peters, open on Broadway.

Miscellaneous. John F. Kennedy Jr., the 38-year-old son of the 35th president, dies in private plane crash. Appearing on CNN's *Larry King Live*, NYC real estate magnate Donald Trump announces his run for the 2000 Reform Party presidential nomination.

WORLD ALMANAC EDITORS' PICKS
2023 Time Capsule

The editors of *The World Almanac* have selected the following items as representative of the year 2023.

- The House Speaker's gavel, which Rep. Kevin McCarthy (R, CA) won Jan. 7, 2023, after a record 15 ballots, and held for only nine months.
- A basketball, symbolically passed from L.A. Lakers legend Kareem Abdul-Jabbar to LeBron James, as James became the NBA's all-time leading scorer Feb. 7, 2023.
- A fan-created friendship bracelet from Taylor Swift's Eras Tour and the iconic Loewe "hands" bodysuit Beyoncé wore as a costume during her Renaissance World Tour, souvenirs of 2023's two biggest-selling live concert tours.
- The titular phantom's mask prop from the 13,981st and final performance of Broadway's *Phantom of the Opera* on Apr. 16, 2023.
- King Charles III's crown from his formal coronation ceremony at Westminster Abbey in London May 6.
- Picket signs from 2023's many high-profile labor strikes, including the writers' and actors' union strikes that began in May and July, respectively, as well as the United Auto Workers' work stoppages launched in Sept. 2023.

- A legacy blue checkmark and abandoned bird logo from Twitter, known as X since July 23, 2023, when chair Elon Musk decided to rebrand the social network.
- A sapling from the 150-year-old landmark banyan tree in Lahaina, HI, which appeared to have mostly survived the devastating Aug. 8, 2023, Maui wildfire.
- Indictment paperwork for Sen. Bob Menendez (D, NJ), Rep. George Santos (R, NY), and former Pres. Donald Trump, along with Trump's Aug. 24, 2023, Georgia mugshot, the first ever taken of a former or sitting president.
- Samples of the asteroid Bennu, returned to Earth by the OSIRIS-REx mission Sept. 24, 2023. (Early studies of the samples show evidence of high-carbon content and water, which together might indicate the building blocks of life on Earth.)
- The final red Netflix DVD envelope sent out on Sept. 29, 2023, the last of the on-demand DVDs that launched the now-streaming tech giant's business 25 years ago.

U.S. Gross Domestic Product, 1930-2022
Source: Bureau of Economic Analysis, U.S. Dept. of Commerce
(in billions of current dollars)

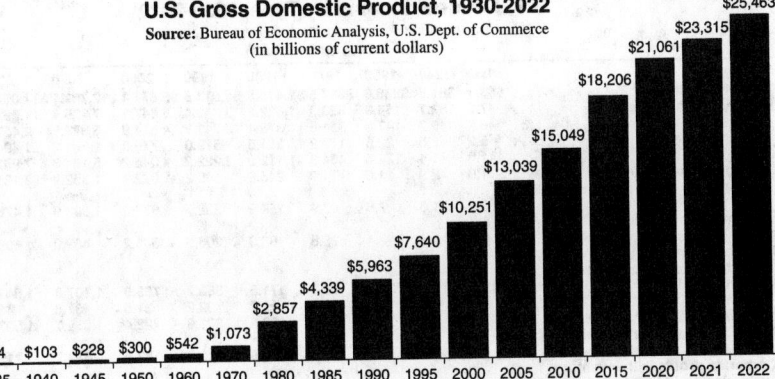

Tracking the U.S. Economy, 1970-2022
Source: Bureau of Economic Analysis, U.S. Dept. of Commerce
(in billions of current dollars, revised)

	1970	1980	1990	2000	2010	2020	2021	2022
Gross domestic product	$1,073.3	$2,857.3	$5,963.1	$10,251.0	$15,049.0	$21,060.5	$23,315.1	$25,462.7
Gross national product	1,079.7	2,891.5	5,997.8	10,289.4	15,254.6	21,257.4	23,488.2	25,640.1
Less: Consumption of fixed capital	136.8	428.4	888.5	1,511.2	2,390.9	3,577.8	3,831.6	4,284.7
Equals: Net national product	942.9	2,463.1	5,109.3	8,778.2	12,863.7	17,679.7	19,656.6	21,355.4
Less: Statistical discrepancy	5.3	44.4	95.5	–94.2	82.5	–214.9	–128.9	–162.6
Equals: National income	937.5	2,418.6	5,013.8	8,872.4	12,781.1	17,894.6	19,785.5	21,518.0
Less: Corporate profits with inventory valuation and capital consumption adjustments	86.2	223.6	417.7	786.6	1,728.7	2,260.1	2,771.1	2,952.6
Less: Taxes on production and imports less subsidies[1]	86.6	190.5	398.0	662.7	1,007.3	869.0	1,181.5	1,648.7
Less: Contributions for government social insurance, domestic	46.4	166.2	410.1	705.8	983.7	1,450.0	1,540.8	1,672.1
Less: Net interest and miscellaneous payments on assets	39.5	182.2	433.4	542.1	471.0	665.8	644.1	542.1
Less: Business current transfer payments (net)	4.4	14.0	39.2	85.2	127.9	144.1	171.0	183.3
Less: Current surplus of government enterprises	–1.0	–4.5	3.7	11.5	–20.1	–0.1	2.1	–3.4
Plus: Personal income receipts on assets	114.9	396.9	1,005.3	1,490.0	1,786.8	3,095.4	3,202.4	3,343.9
Plus: Personal current transfer receipts	74.7	280.1	596.9	1,087.3	2,325.2	4,231.2	4,617.3	3,910.7
Equals: Personal income	865.0	2,323.6	4,913.8	8,655.9	12,594.5	19,832.3	21,294.8	21,777.2
Addenda:								
Gross domestic income	1,068.0	2,812.9	5,867.6	10,345.2	14,966.4	21,275.4	23,444.0	25,625.4
Gross national income	1,074.4	2,847.1	5,902.3	10,383.7	15,172.1	21,472.4	23,617.1	25,802.8

Note: Numbers may not add up to totals due to rounding. (1) Subsidies are included net of the current surplus of government enterprises.

U.S. Gross Domestic Product, 2005-22
Source: Bureau of Economic Analysis, U.S. Dept. of Commerce

	Billions of current dollars				Billions of constant (2012) dollars			
	2005	2010	2020	2022	2005	2010	2020	2022
Gross domestic product	$13,039.2	$15,049.0	$21,060.5	$25,462.7	$14,901.3	$15,649.0	$18,509.1	$20,014.1
Personal consumption expenditures	8,769.1	10,260.3	14,116.2	17,357.2	10,093.8	10,716.0	12,700.7	14,130.3
Goods	3,082.9	3,317.8	4,670.1	5,941.3	3,384.7	3,485.7	4,955.7	5,535.9
Durable goods	1,128.6	1,049.0	1,646.8	2,185.5	1,004.9	1,027.3	1,914.2	2,259.0
Nondurable goods	1,954.3	2,268.9	3,023.3	3,755.9	2,383.4	2,461.3	3,066.7	3,319.6
Services	5,686.1	6,942.4	9,446.0	11,415.8	6,707.4	7,230.4	7,863.6	8,733.5
Gross private domestic investment	2,534.7	2,165.5	3,642.9	4,632.5	2,670.6	2,216.5	3,306.5	3,746.9
Fixed investment	2,477.2	2,111.6	3,698.7	4,473.6	2,618.7	2,164.2	3,326.8	3,569.2
Nonresidential	1,621.0	1,735.0	2,797.9	3,347.0	1,716.4	1,781.0	2,666.0	2,944.8
Structures	353.0	379.8	614.4	651.2	466.1	412.8	510.4	446.2
Equipment	794.9	777.0	1,077.8	1,322.3	760.0	781.2	1,107.3	1,274.0
Intellectual property products	473.1	578.2	1,105.7	1,373.4	493.1	588.1	1,051.2	1,254.5
Residential	856.2	376.6	900.8	1,126.6	885.4	383.0	649.8	643.1
Change in inventories	57.5	53.9	–55.8	158.9	63.7	57.3	–54.6	125.0
Net exports of goods and services	–739.9	–532.3	–627.5	–975.0	–915.4	–589.4	–922.6	–1,356.7
Exports	1,301.6	1,857.2	2,148.6	2,975.8	1,526.1	1,989.5	2,231.7	2,534.4
Goods	919.3	1,272.9	1,420.0	2,064.2	1,082.6	1,369.4	1,609.7	1,837.7
Services	382.2	584.3	728.6	911.6	443.6	620.1	635.8	714.1
Imports	2,041.5	2,389.6	2,776.1	3,950.9	2,441.4	2,578.9	3,154.3	3,891.0
Goods	1,722.8	1,947.0	2,304.5	3,277.2	2,075.8	2,117.3	2,744.6	3,359.6
Services	318.7	442.5	471.6	673.7	366.6	461.5	431.3	553.0
Government consumption expenditures and gross investment	2,475.3	3,155.6	3,928.9	4,448.1	3,013.8	3,308.0	3,406.7	3,406.5
Federal	947.8	1,300.2	1,520.6	1,646.7	1,099.2	1,348.4	1,358.9	1,355.3
National defense	609.4	828.0	882.4	924.9	708.6	861.3	801.1	769.3
Nondefense	338.4	472.2	638.1	721.7	390.8	487.0	556.6	583.8
State and local	1,527.5	1,855.4	2,408.3	2,801.4	1,918.3	1,959.8	2,048.5	2,051.2

U.S. National Income by Type, 1930-2022

Source: Bureau of Economic Analysis, U.S. Dept. of Commerce
(in billions of current dollars)

	1930	1940	1950	1970	1980	1990	2000	2010	2020	2022
NATIONAL INCOME[1]	$83.1	$91.5	$266.6	$937.5	$2,418.6	$5,013.8	$8,872.4	$12,781.1	$17,894.6	$21,518.0
Employee compensation	47.2	52.7	158.3	623.3	1,622.2	3,340.4	5,847.1	7,925.4	11,592.7	13,564.5
Wages and salaries	46.2	49.9	147.3	551.6	1,373.4	2,741.2	4,824.9	6,372.5	9,457.4	11,189.6
Government	5.2	8.5	22.6	117.2	261.5	519.0	779.8	1,191.2	1,494.5	1,613.8
Other	41.0	41.4	124.6	434.3	1,112.0	2,222.2	4,045.2	5,181.3	7,962.9	9,575.8
Supplements to wages and salaries	1.0	2.9	11.0	71.8	248.8	599.2	1,022.2	1,552.9	2,135.4	2,374.9
Employer contributions for employee pension and insurance funds	0.9	1.5	7.6	47.9	159.9	392.7	677.0	1,083.9	1,476.2	1,612.5
Employer contributions for government social insurance	0.0	1.4	3.4	23.8	88.9	206.5	345.2	469.0	659.1	762.4
Proprietors' income with inventory valuation and capital consumption adjustments	10.9	12.2	37.5	77.8	171.6	353.2	753.9	1,107.3	1,643.1	1,848.3
Farm	3.9	4.1	12.9	12.9	11.7	32.2	31.5	37.6	45.2	91.7
Nonfarm	7.0	8.2	24.6	64.9	159.9	321.0	722.4	1,069.7	1,597.9	1,756.6
Rental income of persons with capital consumption adjustments	5.4	3.8	8.8	20.7	19.0	28.2	183.5	433.7	719.8	781.9
Corporate profits with inventory valuation and capital consumption adjustments	7.5	9.9	36.1	86.2	223.6	417.7	786.6	1,728.7	2,260.1	2,952.6
Taxes on corporate income	0.8	2.8	17.7	31.3	75.5	121.8	233.4	272.3	288.9	473.8
Profits after tax with inventory valuation and capital consumption adjustments	6.7	7.0	18.3	55.0	148.1	295.9	553.1	1,456.5	1,971.2	2,478.8
Net dividends	5.5	4.0	9.0	27.8	75.8	192.7	410.2	643.2	1,541.3	1,705.4
Undistributed profits with inventory valuation and capital consumption adjustments	1.2	3.0	9.3	27.2	72.3	103.2	142.9	813.3	429.9	773.4
Net interest and miscellaneous payments	4.8	3.3	3.1	39.5	182.2	433.4	542.1	471.0	665.8	542.1

Note: Numbers may not add up to totals because of rounding and incomplete enumeration. (1) National income is the aggregate of labor and property earnings that arise in the production of goods and services. It is the sum of employee compensation, proprietors' income, rental income, adjusted corporate profits, and net interest. It measures the total factor costs of goods and services produced by the economy. Income is measured before deduction of taxes. Total national income figures include adjustments not itemized.

U.S. National Income by Industry, 2000-22

Source: Bureau of Economic Analysis, U.S. Dept. of Commerce
(in billions of current dollars)

	2000	2005	2010	2015	2020	2021	2022
National income without capital consumption adjustment	$8,780.9	$11,292.5	$12,712.4	$15,670.7	$17,622.7	$19,490.2	$21,433.9
Domestic industries	8,742.5	11,217.7	12,506.7	15,450.3	17,425.7	19,317.1	21,256.5
Private industries	7,699.2	9,855.8	10,855.9	13,633.8	15,331.4	17,151.3	19,012.6
Agriculture, forestry, fishing, and hunting	74.4	97.1	112.2	147.1	111.6	138.8	209.7
Mining	90.6	176.1	183.9	156.1	87.7	200.7	375.0
Utilities	135.3	162.1	183.1	177.3	208.6	210.4	225.4
Construction	474.9	651.1	533.7	749.9	938.2	1,021.2	1,129.1
Manufacturing	1,243.4	1,335.0	1,346.9	1,696.0	1,636.7	1,849.3	2,144.9
Durable goods	758.8	762.8	750.3	983.1	1,001.0	1,131.9	1,298.4
Nondurable goods	484.5	572.2	596.6	713.0	635.7	717.4	846.5
Wholesale trade	570.0	684.6	727.4	939.1	1,003.6	1,116.7	1,274.7
Retail trade	666.3	857.3	863.2	1,072.0	1,243.7	1,453.0	1,525.9
Transportation and warehousing	272.2	335.2	383.9	504.7	525.6	630.3	747.5
Information	316.8	439.3	458.0	598.1	691.1	793.8	824.4
Finance, insurance, real estate, rental, and leasing	1,456.7	1,912.5	2,162.4	2,666.4	3,215.2	3,391.3	3,463.9
Professional and business services[1]	1,087.1	1,441.9	1,729.4	2,225.6	2,711.3	3,077.4	3,431.9
Educational services, health care, and social assistance	688.1	987.3	1,303.2	1,559.4	1,855.6	2,001.7	2,140.7
Arts, entertainment, recreation, accommodation, and food services	340.2	439.7	495.0	680.6	612.4	747.7	942.7
Other services, except government	283.3	336.7	373.7	461.5	489.9	519.1	576.9
Government	1,043.2	1,361.9	1,650.8	1,816.5	2,094.3	2,165.8	2,243.9
Rest of the world	38.5	74.8	205.6	220.4	197.0	173.1	177.4

Note: Estimates based on the 2012 North American Industry Classification System (NAICS). (1) Consists of professional, scientific, and technical services; management of companies and enterprises; and administrative and waste management services.

Measuring Inflation: Consumer Price Index

The Consumer Price Index (CPI) is a measure of the change in prices over time of one or more kinds of basic consumer goods and services. The overall CPI is based on the price of food, clothing, shelter, and fuels; transportation fares; charges for doctors' and dentists' services; drug prices; and the cost of other goods and services bought for day-to-day living. Since Jan. 1988, the base period for comparison has been 1982-84, which equals 100.0. The price of apparel, entertainment and recreation, and education and communication have not risen significantly, while the cost of medical care has more than quadrupled since 1982-84. The Consumer Price Index for all urban consumers (CPI-U) covers about 93% of the total U.S. population. The Bureau of Labor Statistics also publishes a separate Consumer Price Index for urban wage earners and clerical workers (CPI-W), which covers about 29% of the total U.S. population.

Distribution of U.S. Total Personal Income, 1930-2022

Source: Bureau of Economic Analysis, U.S. Dept. of Commerce
(in billions of current dollars, except for per capita figures)

Year	Personal income	Personal current taxes	Disposable personal income	Personal outlays	Personal savings	Savings as % of income[1]	Disposable personal income per capita Current dollars	Disposable personal income per capita Constant (2012) dollars
1930	$76.5	$1.6	$75.0	$71.6	$3.3	4.5%	$609.0	$6,836.0
1940	79.4	1.7	77.7	72.4	5.3	6.8	588.0	7,957.0
1950	233.7	18.9	214.8	194.8	20.0	9.3	1,416.0	10,687.0
1960	422.1	46.1	376.1	338.2	37.9	10.1	2,080.0	12,654.0
1970	865.0	103.1	762.0	664.4	97.6	12.8	3,715.0	17,768.0
1980	2,323.6	299.5	2,024.1	1,800.1	224.1	11.1	8,888.0	21,584.0
1990	4,913.8	594.7	4,319.1	3,958.0	361.1	8.4	17,264.0	27,303.0
2000	8,655.9	1,236.3	7,419.6	7,068.1	351.4	4.7	26,274.0	33,645.0
2005	10,604.9	1,212.5	9,392.5	9,124.5	268.0	2.9	31,732.0	36,526.0
2010	12,594.5	1,237.6	11,356.9	10,647.6	709.3	6.2	36,654.0	38,282.0
2015	15,685.2	1,939.9	13,745.3	12,710.4	1,034.9	7.5	42,672.0	41,383.0
2019	18,424.4	2,205.1	16,219.3	14,981.5	1,237.8	7.6	49,073.0	44,644.0
2020	19,832.3	2,236.4	17,595.9	14,603.6	2,992.3	17.0	53,034.0	47,716.0
2021	21,294.8	2,661.7	18,633.1	16,389.8	2,243.4	12.0	56,065.0	48,490.0
2022	21,777.2	3,196.6	18,580.6	17,922.5	658.1	3.5	55,698.0	45,343.0

Note: Personal income minus current taxes equals disposable income; disposable income minus outlays equals savings. Figures may not add up to totals because of rounding. (1) Personal savings as a percentage of disposable personal income.

Inflation: U.S. Consumer Price Index, 1915-2022

Source: Bureau of Labor Statistics, U.S. Dept. of Labor

In general, prices as measured by the U.S. Consumer Price Index have risen steadily since World War II. What cost $1.00 in 1982-84 cost about $0.10 in 1915, $0.18 in 1945, and $2.93 in 2022.

(Annual averages of monthly figures, for all urban consumers. 1982-84 = 100.)

Inflation: U.S. Consumer Price Index by Major Group, 1915-2022

Source: Bureau of Labor Statistics, U.S. Dept. of Labor
For all urban consumers. 1982-84 = 100, unless otherwise noted.

Year	All items	Apparel	Energy	Food & beverages	Housing	Transportation	Medical care	Entertainment & recreation[1,2]	Educ. & communication[1]	Other goods & services
1915	10.1	15.3	—	—	—	—	—	—	—	—
1920	20.0	43.1	—	—	—	—	—	—	—	—
1930	16.7	24.2	—	—	—	—	—	—	—	—
1940	14.0	21.8	—	—	—	14.2	10.4	—	—	—
1945	18.0	31.4	—	—	—	15.9	11.9	—	—	—
1950	24.1	40.3	—	—	—	22.7	15.1	—	—	—
1955	26.8	42.9	—	—	—	25.8	18.2	—	—	—
1960	29.6	45.7	22.4	—	—	29.8	22.3	—	—	—
1965	31.5	47.8	22.9	—	—	31.9	25.2	—	—	40.9
1970	38.8	59.2	25.5	40.1	36.4	37.5	34.0	—	—	53.9
1975	53.8	72.5	42.1	60.2	50.7	50.1	47.5	—	—	75.2
1980	82.4	90.9	86.0	86.7	81.1	83.1	74.9	—	—	114.5
1985	107.6	105.0	101.6	105.6	107.7	106.4	113.5	—	—	159.0
1990	130.7	124.1	102.1	132.1	128.5	120.5	162.8	—	—	206.9
1995	152.4	132.0	105.2	148.9	148.5	139.1	220.5	94.5	92.2	271.1
2000	172.2	129.6	124.6	168.4	169.6	153.3	260.8	103.3	102.5	271.1
2005	195.3	119.5	177.1	191.2	195.7	173.9	323.2	109.4	113.7	313.4
2010	218.1	119.5	211.4	220.0	216.3	193.4	388.4	113.3	129.9	381.3
2015	237.0	125.9	202.9	246.8	238.1	199.1	446.8	115.9	138.2	414.9
2019	255.7	124.1	215.3	258.0	266.0	210.1	498.4	120.6	137.8	451.3
2020	258.8	118.1	196.9	266.6	271.8	201.3	518.9	122.2	140.3	462.4
2021	271.0	121.0	238.3	276.8	280.7	230.7	525.3	125.2	142.6	476.8
2022	292.7	127.1	298.3	303.3	300.8	266.3	546.6	130.8	143.8	506.4

— = Comparable data not available. Note: Data is not seasonally adjusted. (1) Dec. 1997 = 100. (2) Entertainment was reclassified as Recreation in 1997.

Inflation Rate by Selected Categories, 2021-23

Source: Bureau of Labor Statistics, U.S. Dept. of Labor

For all urban consumers. 1982-84 = 100; change in the Consumer Price Index for selected categories in the 12 months ending June 2022 and June 2023.

Category	2022	2023	Category	2022	2023	Category	2022	2023
All items	9.1%	3.0%	Food	10.4%	5.7%	Used cars and trucks	7.1%	–5.2%
Energy	41.6	–16.7	Food at home	12.2	4.7	Apparel	5.2	3.1
Fuel oil	98.5	–36.6	Food away from home	7.7	7.7	Medical care commodities	3.2	4.2
Gasoline (all types)	59.9	–26.5	All items less food and			Transportation services	8.8	8.2
Electricity	13.7	5.4	energy	5.9	4.8	Shelter	5.6	7.8
Utility (piped) gas service	38.4	–18.6	New vehicles	11.4	4.1	Medical care services	4.8	–0.8

U.S. Inflation Rate, 1915-2023

Source: Bureau of Labor Statistics, U.S. Dept. of Labor

Inflation is the rate at which the Consumer Price Index increases year over year. If the CPI decreases, as it did during the Great Depression, that is known as deflation.

* = Estimate based on the change in the CPI from second quarter 2022 to second quarter 2023.

World's Wealthiest Individuals, 2023

Source: *Forbes* magazine, Apr. 4, 2023

Rank Name, country	Source of wealth	Net worth (bil)
1. Bernard Arnault*, France	LVMH	$211.0
2. Elon Musk, U.S.	Tesla, SpaceX	180.0
3. Jeff Bezos, U.S.	Amazon	114.0
4. Larry Ellison, U.S.	Oracle	107.0
5. Warren Buffett, U.S.	Berkshire Hathaway	106.0
6. Bill Gates, U.S.	Microsoft	104.0
7. Michael Bloomberg, U.S.	Bloomberg LP	94.5
8. Carlos Slim Helu*, Mexico	Telecom	93.0
9. Mukesh Ambani, India	Diversified	83.4
10. Steve Ballmer, U.S.	Microsoft	80.7
11. Francoise Bettencourt Meyers*, France	L'Oréal	80.5
12. Larry Page, U.S.	Google	79.2
13. Amancio Ortega, Spain	Zara	77.3
14. Sergey Brin, U.S.	Google	76.0
15. Zhong Shanshan, China	Beverages, pharmaceuticals	68.0
16. Mark Zuckerberg, U.S.	Facebook	64.4
17. Charles Koch, U.S.	Koch Industries	59.0
Julia Koch*, U.S.	Koch Industries	59.0
19. Jim Walton, U.S.	Walmart	58.8
20. Rob Walton, U.S.	Walmart	57.6
21. Alice Walton, U.S.	Walmart	56.7
22. David Thomson*, Canada	Media	54.4
23. Michael Dell, U.S.	Dell Technologies	50.1
24. Gautam Adani, India	Infrastructure, commodities	47.2
25. Phil Knight*, U.S.	Nike	45.1
26. Zhang Yiming, China	TikTok	45.0
27. Dieter Schwarz, Germany	Retail	42.9
28. François Pinault*, France	Luxury goods	40.1
29. Klaus-Michael Kuehne, Germany	Shipping	39.1
30. Giovanni Ferrero, Italy	Nutella, chocolates	38.9
31. Jacqueline Mars, U.S.	Candy, pet food	38.3
John Mars, U.S.	Candy, pet food	38.3
33. Li Ka-shing, Hong Kong	Diversified	38.0
34. Ma Huateng, China	Internet media	35.3
35. Miriam Adelson*, U.S.	Casinos	35.0
Ken Griffin, U.S.	Hedge funds	35.0
37. Mark Mateschitz, Austria	Red Bull	34.7
38. Robin Zeng, Hong Kong	Batteries	33.4
39. Tadashi Yanai*, Japan	Fashion retail	32.6

Rank Name, country	Source of wealth	Net worth (bil)
40. Len Blavatnik, U.S.	Music, chemicals	$32.1
41. Alain Wertheimer, France	Chanel	31.6
Gerard Wertheimer, France	Chanel	31.6
43. Gianluigi Aponte, Switzerland	Shipping	31.2
Rafaela Aponte-Diamant, Switzerland	Shipping	31.2
45. Colin Zheng Huang, China	E-commerce	30.2
46. Reinhold Wuerth*, Germany	Fasteners	29.7
47. Lee Shau Kee, Hong Kong	Real estate	29.5
48. Jeff Yass, U.S.	Trading, investments	28.5
49. Jim Simons, U.S.	Hedge funds	28.1
50. Stephen Schwarzman, U.S.	Investments	27.8
51. Susanne Klatten, Germany	BMW, pharmaceuticals	27.4
52. Gina Rinehart, Australia	Mining	27.0
53. William Lei Ding, China	Online games	26.7
54. Germán Larrea Mota Velasco*, Mexico	Mining	26.6
55. Shiv Nadar, India	Software services	25.6
56. Low Tuck Kwong, Indonesia	Coal	25.5
57. Thomas Peterffy, U.S.	Discount brokerage	25.3
58. Andrey Melnichenko*, Russia	Fertilizers, coal	25.2
59. Stefan Quandt, Germany	BMW	24.6
60. MacKenzie Scott, U.S.	Amazon	24.4
61. R. Budi Hartono, Indonesia	Banking, tobacco	24.2
62. Vladimir Potanin, Russia	Metals	23.7
63. Jack Ma, China	E-commerce	23.5
64. He Xiangjian*, China	Home appliances	23.4
65. Iris Fontbona*, Chile	Mining	23.1
Michael Hartono, Indonesia	Banking, tobacco	23.1
67. James Ratcliffe, U.K.	Chemicals	22.9
68. Cyrus Poonawalla, India	Vaccines	22.6
69. Masayoshi Son, Japan	Internet, telecom	22.4
70. Vladimir Lisin, Russia	Steel, transport	22.1
71. Emmanuel Besnier, France	Cheese	22.0
72. Abigail Johnson*, U.S.	Fidelity	21.6
Leonid Mikhelson*, Russia	Gas, chemicals	21.6
74. Lukas Walton, U.S.	Walmart	21.2
Wang Wei, China	Package delivery	21.2
76. Jensen Huang, U.S.	Semiconductors	21.1

* = Represents wealth held by individual and family members.

Median Income by Race, Hispanic Origin, and Sex, 1948-2022

Source: Current Population Survey, U.S. Census Bureau, U.S. Dept. of Commerce

Race, Hispanic origin, and year		Male			Female		
		Number with income (thous.)	Median income Current dollars	2022 dollars	Number with income (thous.)	Median income Current dollars	2022 dollars
All races	1948	47,370	$2,396	$23,950	22,730	$1,009	$10,080
	1950	47,590	2,570	25,680	24,650	953	9,524
	1960	55,170	4,080	33,270	36,530	1,261	10,280
	1970	65,010	6,670	42,370	51,650	2,237	14,210
	1980	78,660	12,530	40,030	80,830	4,920	15,720
	1990	88,220	20,290	41,680	92,250	10,070	20,680
	2000	98,500	28,340	45,540	101,700	16,060	25,810
	2010	105,200	32,210	42,030	107,200	20,780	27,110
	2020	117,900	42,700	48,130	118,400	29,410	33,150
	2022	119,400	48,450	48,450	119,700	32,790	32,790
White	1948	NA	2,510	25,090	NA	1,133	11,320
	1950	NA	2,709	27,070	NA	1,060	10,590
	1960	49,790	4,296	35,030	32,000	1,352	11,030
	1970	58,450	7,011	44,540	45,290	2,266	14,400
	1980	69,420	13,330	42,580	70,570	4,947	15,810
	1990	76,480	21,170	43,480	78,570	10,320	21,190
	2000	83,370	29,800	47,880	84,120	16,080	25,840
	2010	86,370	34,370	44,860	85,490	20,900	27,270
	2020	93,390	45,520	51,310	91,220	29,930	33,740
	2022	93,730	50,240	50,240	91,560	32,600	32,600
White, not Hispanic	1980	65,560	13,680	43,710	67,080	4,980	15,910
	1990	69,990	21,960	45,100	72,940	10,580	21,730
	2000	72,530	31,510	50,630	75,210	16,670	26,780
	2010	72,720	37,150	48,480	74,000	21,720	28,340
	2020	75,690	50,190	56,570	75,880	31,490	35,500
	2022	75,200	52,720	52,720	75,490	35,180	35,180
Black	1948	NA	1,363	13,620	NA	492	4,917
	1950	NA	1,471	14,700	NA	474	4,737
	1960	5,384	2,260	18,430	4,525	837	6,825
	1970	5,844	4,157	26,410	5,844	2,063	13,110
	1980	7,387	8,009	25,590	8,596	4,580	14,630
	1990	8,820	12,870	26,430	10,690	8,328	17,110
	2000	9,905	21,340	34,300	12,460	15,880	25,520
	2010	11,430	23,090	30,130	14,210	19,550	25,510
	2020	14,630	31,150	35,110	16,980	26,670	30,060
	2022	14,880	37,080	37,080	17,260	32,170	32,170
Asian	1990	2,235	19,390	39,830	2,333	11,090	22,770
	2000	4,303	30,830	49,540	4,192	17,360	27,890
	2010	5,406	35,120	45,830	5,604	23,550	30,730
	2020	7,548	51,330	57,860	7,930	33,540	37,810
	2022	8,254	60,970	60,970	8,351	40,660	40,660
Hispanic	1980	3,996	9,659	30,860	3,617	4,405	14,070
	1990	6,767	13,470	27,670	5,903	7,532	15,470
	2000	11,340	19,500	31,330	9,431	12,250	19,680
	2010	15,110	22,420	29,260	12,950	16,290	21,260
	2020	19,940	32,080	36,160	17,450	22,910	25,820
	2022	20,810	37,260	37,260	18,360	26,800	26,800

NA = Not available. **Note:** Income for persons 15 years of age and over beginning in Mar. 1980; 14 years of age and over as of Mar. of the following year for previous years. Beginning in 2010, totals for Black and Asian include those who identified themselves as being that race in combination with some other race; totals for white are for those who identified as white alone. Before 2010, Asian category includes Pacific Islanders. Hispanic persons may be of any race.

Consumer Credit Outstanding, 2010-22

Source: Federal Reserve System

(in billions of dollars, not seasonally adjusted)

	2010	2020	2022		2010	2020	2022
TOTAL	$2,647.2	$4,184.9	$4,895.0	Finance companies	$81.5	$17.1	$22.3
Major holders				Credit unions	36.3	62.3	74.7
Depository institutions	1,185.5	1,687.5	2,032.2	Nonfinancial business	25.5	20.0	20.0
Finance companies	705.0	551.4	682.7	**Nonrevolving**	1,807.8	3,210.3	3,682.4
Credit unions	226.5	505.1	636.7	Depository institutions	520.8	812.2	936.6
Federal government[1]	363.8	1,381.0	1,487.3	Finance companies	623.5	534.3	660.5
Nonprofit and				Credit unions	190.1	442.8	562.0
educational institutions[2]	71.3	24.1	20.3	Federal government[1]	363.8	1,381.0	1,487.3
Nonfinancial business	44.8	35.8	35.8	Nonprofit and			
Major types of credit, by holder				educational institutions[2]	71.3	24.1	20.3
Revolving	839.4	974.6	1,212.6	Nonfinancial business	19.3	15.8	15.8
Depository institutions	664.7	875.3	1,095.7				

(1) Includes student loans originated by the Dept. of Education under the Federal Direct Loan Program and the Perkins Loan Program, as well as Federal Family Education Program loans that the government purchased under the Ensuring Continued Access to Student Loans Act. (2) Includes student loans originated under the Federal Family Education Loan Program and held by educational institutions and nonprofit organizations.

Poverty Thresholds by Family Size, 1980-2022
Source: U.S. Census Bureau, U.S. Dept. of Commerce

	1980	1990	2000	2010	2022		1980	1990	2000	2010	2022
1 person	$4,190	$6,652	$8,791	$11,140	$14,880	3 people	$6,565	$10,420	$13,740	$17,370	$23,280
Under age 65....	4,290	6,800	8,959	11,340	15,230	4 people	8,414	13,360	17,600	22,320	29,950
Age 65 or older ..	3,949	6,268	8,259	10,460	14,040	5 people	9,966	15,790	20,820	26,440	35,510
2 people	5,363	8,509	11,240	14,220	18,900	6 people	11,270	17,840	23,530	29,900	40,160
Householder						7 people	12,760	20,240	26,750	34,020	45,690
under age 65 ..	5,537	8,794	11,590	14,680	19,690	8 people	14,200	22,580	29,700	37,950	51,010
Householder age						9 or more people ..	16,900	26,850	35,150	45,220	60,300
65 or older.....	4,983	7,905	10,420	13,190	17,710						

Note: Weighted averages; not used for computing poverty data.

Persons Below Poverty Level by Race and Hispanic Origin, 1960-2022
Source: U.S. Census Bureau, U.S. Dept. of Commerce

	Number below poverty level (mil)					% of subgroup below poverty level					Avg. income cutoff, family of 4 at poverty level[4]
Year	All races[1]	Asian[2]	White	Black[2]	Hispanic[3]	All races[1]	Asian[2]	White	Black[2]	Hispanic[3]	
1960	39.9	NA	28.3	NA	NA	22.2%	NA	17.8%	NA	NA	$3,022
1970	25.4	NA	17.5	7.5	NA	12.6	NA	9.9	33.5%	NA	3,968
1980	29.3	NA	19.7	8.6	3.5	13.0	NA	10.2	32.5	25.7%	8,414
1990	33.6	0.9	22.3	9.8	6.0	13.5	12.2%	10.7	31.9	28.1	13,360
2000	31.6	1.3	21.7	8.0	7.7	11.3	9.9	9.5	22.5	21.5	17,600
2005	37.0	1.5	24.9	9.5	9.4	12.6	10.9	10.6	24.7	21.8	19,970
2010	46.3	2.1	31.1	11.6	13.5	15.1	12.0	13.0	27.4	26.5	22,320
2015	43.1	2.2	28.6	10.8	12.1	13.5	11.1	11.6	23.9	21.4	24,260
2020	37.6	1.8	25.2	9.3	10.5	11.5	8.0	10.1	19.3	17.0	26,500
2021	37.9	2.1	24.9	9.3	10.7	11.6	9.0	10.0	19.3	17.1	27,740
2022	37.9	2.0	26.1	8.4	10.8	11.5	8.2	10.5	17.0	16.9	29,950

NA = Not available. **Note:** Because of a change in the definition of poverty, data prior to 1980 are not directly comparable to data since 1980. (1) Includes other races not shown separately. (2) Beginning in 2002, numbers include those who identified themselves as being Asian or Black in combination with some other race. For 1990-2000, Asian includes Pacific Islanders. (3) Persons of Hispanic origin may be of any race. (4) Figures for 1960-80 for nonfarm families only.

Families Below Poverty Level by Status, Race, and Sex, 1980-2022
Source: U.S. Census Bureau, U.S. Dept. of Commerce
(numbers in thousands)

	All families			Married-couple families			Male householder, no spouse present			Female householder, no spouse present		
		Below poverty level			Below poverty level			Below poverty level			Below poverty level	
Year and race	Total	Number	Percent	Total	Number	Percent	Total	Number	Percent	Total	Number	Percent
All races												
1980	60,310	6,217	10.3%	49,290	3,032	6.2%	1,933	213	11.0%	9,082	2,972	32.7%
1990	66,320	7,098	10.7	52,150	2,981	5.7	2,907	349	12.0	11,270	3,768	33.4
2000	73,780	6,400	8.7	56,600	2,637	4.7	4,277	485	11.3	12,900	3,278	25.4
2010	79,560	9,400	11.8	58,670	3,681	6.3	5,649	892	15.8	15,240	4,827	31.7
2020	83,720	7,284	8.7	61,300	2,853	4.7	6,964	797	11.4	15,460	3,634	23.5
2022	84,350	7,400	8.8	62,180	3,117	5.0	7,130	821	11.5	15,040	3,462	23.0
White[1]												
1980	52,710	4,195	8.0	44,860	2,437	5.4	1,584	149	9.4	6,266	1,609	25.7
1990	56,800	4,622	8.1	47,010	2,386	5.1	2,277	226	9.9	7,512	2,010	26.8
2000	61,330	4,333	7.1	49,470	2,181	4.4	3,283	332	10.1	8,574	1,820	21.2
2010	63,980	6,305	9.9	50,020	2,921	5.8	4,176	563	13.5	9,784	2,822	28.8
2020	65,710	4,910	7.5	50,740	2,263	4.5	5,009	481	9.6	9,958	2,166	21.8
2022	65,670	5,136	7.8	51,050	2,480	4.9	5,092	542	10.6	9,522	2,114	22.2
Black[1]												
1980	6,317	1,826	28.9	3,392	474	14.0	291	52	17.7	2,634	1,301	49.4
1990	7,471	2,193	29.3	3,569	448	12.6	472	97	20.6	3,430	1,648	48.1
2000	8,731	1,686	19.3	4,214	266	6.3	732	120	16.3	3,785	1,300	34.3
2010	9,982	2,403	24.1	4,473	407	9.1	979	257	26.3	4,531	1,738	38.4
2020	10,820	1,795	16.6	5,059	306	6.0	1,314	241	18.4	4,446	1,248	28.1
2022	11,080	1,583	14.3	5,407	305	5.6	1,299	200	15.4	4,374	1,078	24.6
Asian[1]												
2002	2,939	218	7.4	2,344	137	5.9	241	30	12.6	354	51	14.3
2010	4,094	379	9.2	3,210	232	7.2	328	32	9.7	556	115	20.7
2020	5,509	347	6.3	4,475	218	4.9	394	30	7.7	641	99	15.4
2022	5,800	363	6.3	4,662	228	4.9	465	30	6.6	673	105	15.6
Hispanic[2]												
1980	3,235	751	23.2	2,365	363	15.3	164	26	16.0	706	362	51.3
1990	4,981	1,244	25.0	3,454	605	17.5	341	66	19.4	1,186	573	48.3
2000	8,017	1,540	19.2	5,426	772	14.2	765	104	13.6	1,826	664	36.4
2010	11,280	2,739	24.3	7,065	1,221	17.3	1,241	248	20.0	2,978	1,270	42.6
2020	13,700	2,028	14.8	8,597	848	9.9	1,686	203	12.1	3,412	976	28.6
2022	14,240	2,169	15.2	8,960	900	10.0	1,895	266	14.0	3,386	1,002	29.6

Note: The Census Bureau revised race categories in 2002, so data after 2002 are not directly comparable with data for previous years. (1) Beginning in 2010, totals for white include only those who identified themselves as white alone; totals for Black and Asian include those who identified themselves as that race alone or in combination with some other race. (2) Persons of Hispanic origin may be of any race.

Poverty Rates by State, 1990-2022

Source: U.S. Census Bureau, U.S. Dept. of Commerce

The poverty rate is the proportion of the population with income below the government's official poverty level, which is the same nationwide but is adjusted each year for inflation.

State	1990	2000	2010	2020	2022	State	1990	2000	2010	2020	2022
Alabama	19.2%	13.3%	17.2%	14.9%	13.6%	Montana	16.3%	14.1%	14.5%	10.9%	10.4%
Alaska	11.4	7.6	12.5	13.4	9.6	Nebraska	10.3	8.6	10.2	8.3	7.9
Arizona	13.7	11.7	18.8	10.9	12.7	Nevada	9.8	8.8	16.6	12.9	12.0
Arkansas	19.6	16.5	15.3	14.1	16.6	New Hampshire	6.3	4.5	6.5	6.2	8.3
California	13.9	12.7	16.3	11.1	11.2	New Jersey	9.2	7.3	11.1	8.2	8.7
Colorado	13.7	9.8	12.3	9.5	8.1	New Mexico	20.9	17.5	18.3	16.6	20.2
Connecticut	6.0	7.7	8.6	11.2	10.2	New York	14.3	13.9	16.0	11.8	12.7
Delaware	6.9	8.4	12.2	10.5	9.3	North Carolina	13.0	12.5	17.4	13.8	14.2
Dist. of Columbia	21.1	15.2	19.5	16.8	13.4	North Dakota	13.7	10.4	12.6	10.7	9.7
Florida	14.4	11.0	16.0	13.3	13.5	Ohio	11.5	10.0	15.4	12.7	9.9
Georgia	15.8	12.1	18.8	13.3	11.7	Oklahoma	15.6	14.9	16.3	15.5	16.9
Hawaii	11.0	8.9	12.4	10.9	8.8	Oregon	9.2	10.9	14.3	9.4	9.9
Idaho	14.9	12.5	13.8	9.1	8.2	Pennsylvania	11.0	8.6	12.2	10.7	10.9
Illinois	13.7	10.7	14.1	8.0	9.5	Rhode Island	7.5	10.2	14.0	8.5	8.4
Indiana	13.0	8.5	16.3	12.1	10.4	South Carolina	16.2	11.1	16.9	13.4	12.9
Iowa	10.4	8.3	10.3	9.2	9.4	South Dakota	13.3	10.7	13.6	11.6	9.1
Kansas	10.3	8.0	14.5	9.3	10.5	Tennessee	16.9	13.5	16.7	13.1	10.5
Kentucky	17.3	12.6	17.7	13.9	17.1	Texas	15.9	15.5	18.4	14.0	13.5
Louisiana	23.6	17.2	21.5	15.5	16.9	Utah	8.2	7.6	10.0	7.4	6.0
Maine	13.1	10.1	12.6	8.0	9.6	Vermont	10.9	10.0	10.8	8.6	9.0
Maryland	9.9	7.4	10.9	9.4	8.6	Virginia	11.1	8.3	10.7	7.8	8.3
Massachusetts	10.7	9.8	10.9	8.4	9.6	Washington	8.9	10.8	11.6	8.2	9.0
Michigan	14.3	9.9	15.7	11.2	12.1	West Virginia	18.1	14.7	16.8	14.2	15.5
Minnesota	12.0	5.7	10.8	8.5	7.6	Wisconsin	9.3	9.3	10.1	8.0	6.6
Mississippi	25.7	14.9	22.5	17.6	18.4	Wyoming	11.0	10.8	9.6	9.7	7.1
Missouri	13.4	9.2	15.0	10.7	11.4	**United States**	13.5	11.3	15.1	11.5	11.5

Income Inequality in the U.S., 1970-2022

Source: U.S. Census Bureau, U.S. Dept. of Commerce

Top earners' share of income has grown considerably over the past half century. In 1970, the richest 5% of Americans earned 16.6% percent of all income while the share earned by the poorest 20% was 4.1%. By 2022, the top 5% took home 23.5% of income and the poorest 20% earned just 3.0% of the total. The middle quintile's share declined from 17.4% to 14.0% over the same period.

Income group	Mean income in 2022	Percentage of income earned by each quintile										
		1970	1980	1990	1995	2000	2005	2010	2015	2020	2021	2022
Lowest 20%	$16,120	4.1%	4.2%	3.8%	3.7%	3.6%	3.4%	3.3%	3.1%	3.0%	2.9%	3.0%
Second quintile	43,850	10.8	10.2	9.6	9.1	8.9	8.6	8.5	8.2	8.2	8.0	8.2
Middle 20%	74,730	17.4	16.8	15.9	15.2	14.8	14.6	14.6	14.3	14.0	13.9	14.0
Fourth quintile	119,900	24.5	24.7	24.0	23.3	23.0	23.0	23.4	23.2	22.6	22.6	22.5
Highest 20%	277,300	43.3	44.1	46.6	48.7	49.8	50.4	50.3	51.1	52.2	52.7	52.1
Top 5%	499,900	16.6	16.5	18.5	21.0	22.1	22.2	21.3	22.1	23.0	23.5	23.5

Temporary Assistance for Needy Families (TANF), 1997-2021

Source: Office of Family Assistance, Admin. for Children and Families, U.S. Dept. of Health and Human Services

Year	Total TANF expenditures (mil)	Average number of monthly cash beneficiaries			Year	Total TANF expenditures (mil)	Average number of monthly cash beneficiaries		
		Families	Recipients	Children			Families	Recipients	Children
1997	$19,010.2	3,936,610	10,935,125	NA	2011	$30,264.1	1,921,243	4,599,846	3,435,218
2000	24,780.7	2,229,315	5,833,043	4,303,943	2012	28,867.3	1,876,426	4,476,476	3,351,971
2002	25,414.4	2,038,373	5,067,963	3,791,560	2013	29,147.1	1,751,067	4,102,491	3,091,076
2003	26,340.0	2,009,666	4,900,889	3,693,056	2014	29,350.9	1,652,996	3,894,213	2,934,582
2004	25,821.2	1,965,960	4,722,588	3,581,448	2015	29,295.9	1,333,707	4,176,387	2,370,198
2005	25,580.1	1,901,810	4,495,175	3,428,885	2016	28,321.2	1,206,820	3,886,868	2,144,955
2006	25,593.8	1,789,460	4,179,295	3,207,216	2017	28,701.0	1,095,368	3,650,293	1,943,028
2007	26,922.0	1,697,432	3,957,330	3,047,043	2018	28,719.7	1,004,923	3,234,514	1,785,278
2008	28,129.7	1,726,799	4,041,292	3,084,413	2019	28,483.0	916,614	2,940,845	1,640,805
2009	30,577.8	1,847,152	4,364,979	3,280,150	2020	28,984.0	885,522	2,027,980	1,573,156
2010	33,255.5	1,847,152	4,364,979	3,280,150	2021	28,037.9	804,117	1,847,644	1,424,759

NA = Not available.

Adults Receiving TANF Funds by Employment Status, 2021

Source: Office of Family Assistance, Admin. for Children and Families, U.S. Dept. of Health and Human Services

State	Adults	Employed	State	Adults	Employed	State	Adults	Employed	State	Adults	Employed
AL	2,377	31.5%	IL	2,216	82.4%	NE	1,026	53.8%	SC	2,761	14.3%
AK	1,445	28.0	IN	3,892	17.3	NV	3,541	29.8	SD	371	11.9
AZ	2,010	11.8	IA	3,493	21.0	NH	1,248	26.3	TN	5,367	23.0
AR	846	12.7	KS	1,744	32.7	NJ	5,667	5.0	TX	5,923	5.0
CA	141,087	19.3	KY	3,361	26.4	NM	8,321	5.4	UT	958	14.1
CO	7,091	48.7	LA	1,102	9.3	NY	46,761	16.4	VT	679	11.3
CT	2,741	17.2	ME	2,269	21.2	NC	2,749	7.8	VA	7,416	17.9
DE	531	23.7	MD	18,712	20.5	ND	588	22.7	WA	18,627	10.3
DC	4,585	9.1	MA	15,367	12.1	OH	8,136	21.6	WV	1,364	14.5
FL	14,576	4.2	MI	3,855	20.3	OK	1,642	8.8	WI	5,679	20.5
GA	1,394	15.7	MN	12,256	24.4	OR	9,006	2.3	WY	261	23.8
Guam	221	1.2	MS	213	3.2	PA	14,876	15.3	U.S. total	417,256	17.5
HI	7,300	19.6	MO	3,194	12.9	Puerto Rico	4,147	1.0			
ID	30	7.3	MT	891	33.4	RI	1,285	10.9			
						Virgin Isls.	59	2.4			

TANF = Temporary Assistance for Needy Families.

Selected Personal Consumption Expenditures in the U.S., 1980-2022

Source: Bureau of Economic Analysis, U.S. Dept. of Commerce
(in billions of dollars)

	1980	1990	2000	2010	2020	2021	2022
Personal consumption expenditures	$1,750.7	$3,809.0	$6,767.2	$10,260.3	$14,116.2	$15,902.6	$17,357.2
GOODS	799.8	1,491.3	2,453.2	3,317.8	4,670.1	5,496.5	5,941.3
Durable goods	226.4	497.1	912.6	1,049.0	1,646.8	2,060.2	2,185.5
Motor vehicles and parts	84.4	205.1	363.2	344.5	533.9	688.7	723.2
New motor vehicles	54.3	134.7	210.7	182.3	292.8	351.2	372.4
Net purchases of used motor vehicles	12.2	42.2	110.7	105.6	161.4	243.0	248.4
Motor vehicle parts and accessories	17.9	28.3	41.8	56.6	79.7	94.4	102.3
Furnishings, durable household equipment	67.8	120.9	208.1	240.9	411.9	495.0	527.7
Furniture and furnishings	36.9	69.2	121.7	140.5	265.7	323.6	344.8
Household appliances	15.1	23.7	34.1	44.1	63.6	74.8	78.2
Glassware, tableware, and household utensils	10.6	18.4	35.3	36.4	44.9	53.7	57.0
Recreational goods and vehicles	46.5	105.6	230.9	298.6	494.5	603.9	645.5
Video, audio, photo, and info-processing equip.	21.9	56.1	127.7	182.8	297.0	356.0	376.3
Sporting equipment, guns, ammunition	8.9	19.9	39.1	52.8	98.1	120.7	130.8
Sports and recreational vehicles	9.8	16.6	34.9	35.8	73.5	95.0	103.9
Recreational books	4.7	10.9	24.4	22.6	19.4	24.0	25.9
Other durable goods	27.6	65.5	110.4	165.0	206.4	272.6	291.1
Jewelry and watches	15.0	30.3	49.1	60.9	72.7	106.0	112.2
Therapeutic appliances and equipment	5.1	18.4	32.2	52.4	70.7	86.2	93.3
Nondurable goods	573.4	994.2	1,540.6	2,268.9	3,023.3	3,436.3	3,755.9
Food and beverages purchased for off-premises consumption	239.2	391.2	540.6	786.9	1,126.1	1,205.0	1,277.6
Food and nonalcoholic beverages	208.0	341.2	463.1	678.6	960.7	1,028.2	1,093.8
Alcoholic beverages	30.0	49.3	77.1	107.9	164.9	176.2	183.1
Clothing and footwear	103.0	195.2	280.8	316.6	358.4	461.3	491.4
Women's and girls' clothing	48.5	94.5	132.7	149.2	163.5	211.5	225.5
Men's and boys' clothing	30.9	57.4	85.9	83.7	95.2	122.8	133.2
Children's and infants' clothing	3.9	8.1	11.4	18.0	17.5	21.3	22.5
Other clothing materials and footwear	19.7	35.3	50.8	65.8	82.2	105.7	110.2
Gasoline and other energy goods	101.9	124.2	184.5	336.7	247.8	369.4	492.8
Other nondurable goods	129.3	283.6	534.7	828.7	1,291.1	1,400.5	1,494.1
Pharmaceutical and other medical products	18.7	59.1	159.0	326.1	576.4	585.1	629.3
Recreational items	22.0	50.9	91.9	129.9	196.6	236.0	255.6
Household supplies	29.1	54.2	86.7	108.2	162.5	181.3	192.5
Personal care products	18.7	39.3	68.5	106.0	145.5	167.1	176.6
Tobacco	20.9	41.0	68.5	97.9	103.5	107.1	105.6
Magazines, newspapers, and stationery	18.1	36.5	56.6	52.2	95.5	112.8	123.0
SERVICES	950.9	2,317.7	4,314.0	6,942.4	9,446.0	10,406.1	11,415.8
Housing and utilities	312.5	696.5	1,198.6	1,947.9	2,666.6	2,775.4	2,996.6
Housing	246.6	570.6	1,010.5	1,648.1	2,315.7	2,400.8	2,568.0
Rental of tenant-occupied nonfarm housing	62.5	150.8	227.9	361.1	559.0	576.3	616.5
Imputed rental of owner-occupied nonfarm housing	178.4	412.8	768.9	1,267.6	1,731.7	1,798.9	1,924.4
Household utilities	65.9	125.9	188.1	299.9	351.0	374.6	428.6
Water supply and sanitation	9.4	27.1	50.4	78.5	110.2	115.8	124.3
Electricity	37.2	71.8	98.4	166.8	190.0	199.8	227.4
Natural gas	19.3	27.0	39.3	54.6	50.7	59.0	76.9
Health care	171.7	506.2	918.4	1,699.6	2,339.2	2,583.5	2,725.9
Outpatient services	70.6	232.1	436.6	774.6	1,074.0	1,181.4	1,250.9
Physician services	43.3	134.8	229.2	410.5	559.8	611.0	638.1
Dental services	13.7	32.4	63.6	104.5	117.1	134.0	147.1
Paramedical services	13.6	64.9	143.8	259.6	397.1	436.4	465.7
Hospitals	84.7	228.8	393.9	769.9	1,079.5	1,217.1	1,272.4
Nursing homes	16.4	45.3	87.9	155.1	185.7	184.9	202.6
Transportation services	55.4	126.4	261.3	305.2	367.7	444.1	547.3
Motor vehicle services	35.1	87.2	174.4	201.0	285.0	305.5	333.0
Motor vehicle maintenance and repair	31.2	73.9	112.5	136.7	183.4	195.1	214.4
Public transportation	20.2	39.2	86.9	104.2	82.7	138.5	214.4
Recreation services	40.8	121.8	254.4	403.7	439.6	528.5	615.4
Membership clubs, sports centers, parks, theaters, museums	20.1	49.7	91.9	146.1	115.2	142.7	195.3
Audio-video, photographic, and information-processing equipment services	10.7	37.9	70.1	106.4	148.9	161.3	170.9
Gambling	6.7	23.7	67.6	109.4	111.1	152.6	162.7
Food services and accommodations	121.7	262.7	408.8	635.7	813.5	1,060.9	1,253.6
Purchased meals and beverages	105.9	228.3	344.9	521.8	711.2	907.5	1,041.1
Accommodations	10.3	27.6	55.0	98.6	82.0	131.6	187.3
Financial services and insurance	91.7	230.8	541.9	768.0	1,170.6	1,275.0	1,316.9
Financial services	47.8	119.0	335.7	479.0	750.3	837.2	859.8
Insurance	43.9	111.7	206.3	289.0	420.3	437.7	457.1
Other services	127.1	297.5	572.6	887.9	1,145.6	1,273.2	1,433.0
Telecommunication services	27.6	60.7	126.4	147.6	158.8	169.3	178.5
Internet access	—	0.1	12.0	40.5	76.4	81.5	85.1
Higher education	12.9	34.7	76.8	155.0	184.7	185.2	193.2
Nursery, elementary, and secondary schools	6.7	14.8	24.1	35.6	48.9	52.0	56.9
Commercial and vocational schools	4.2	11.1	24.3	39.9	52.2	56.2	64.6
Professional and other services	24.8	67.7	113.0	158.9	208.6	226.4	243.2
Personal care and clothing services	17.9	44.5	80.4	115.8	117.1	140.4	171.6
Social services and religious activities	14.0	41.2	81.1	139.0	213.0	232.1	255.5
Household maintenance	13.8	25.4	49.2	61.6	94.1	98.5	104.8

Note: Subtotals may not add up to totals due to rounding or incomplete enumeration.

Leading U.S. Businesses, 2022

Source: *Fortune* magazine, June 2023

(ranked by 2022 revenues, in millions of dollars)

Industry/company (rank)	Revenues
Advertising	
Omnicom Group (290)	$14,289
Interpublic Group (371)	10,928
Aerospace	
RTX (57)	$67,074
Boeing (58)	66,608
Lockheed Martin (60)	65,984
General Dynamics (105)	39,407
Northrop Grumman (113)	36,602
L3Harris Technologies (246)	17,062
Textron (318)	12,869
Huntington Ingalls Industries (375)	10,676
Airlines	
Delta Air Lines (85)	$50,582
American Airlines Group (89)	48,971
United Airlines Holdings (96)	44,955
Southwest Airlines (165)	23,814
Alaska Air Group (398)	9,646
JetBlue Airways (417)	9,158
Apparel	
Nike (93)	$46,710
VF (349)	11,842
PVH (422)	9,024
Skechers U.S.A. (488)	7,445
Automotive Retailing, Services	
CarMax (124)	$33,197
Lithia Motors (145)	28,188
Penske Automotive Group (147)	27,815
AutoNation (151)	26,985
Group 1 Automotive (252)	16,412
Asbury Automotive Group (268)	15,434
Sonic Automotive (299)	14,001
Carvana (308)	13,604
Avis Budget Group (346)	11,994
Hertz Global Holdings (435)	8,685
Beverages	
Coca-Cola (100)	$43,004
Keurig Dr Pepper (296)	14,057
Molson Coors Beverage (374)	10,701
Constellation Brands (430)	8,821
Building Materials, Glass	
Builders FirstSource (172)	$22,726
Owens Corning (395)	9,761
UFP Industries (403)	9,627
Fortune Brands Innovations (469)	7,923
Vulcan Materials (494)	7,315
Chemicals	
Dow (75)	$56,902
3M (116)	34,229
Sherwin-Williams (178)	22,149
Mosaic (217)	19,125
PPG Industries (232)	17,652
DuPont (250)	16,549
Westlake (263)	15,794
Ecolab (293)	14,188
Air Products & Chemicals (322)	12,699
International Flavors & Fragrances (332)	12,440
CF Industries Holdings (365)	11,186
Eastman Chemical (377)	10,580
Celanese (396)	9,673
Olin (410)	9,376
Huntsman (433)	8,715
Albemarle (493)	7,320
Commercial Banks	
JPMorgan Chase (23)	$154,792
Bank of America (32)	115,053
Citigroup (36)	101,078
Wells Fargo (47)	82,859
Goldman Sachs Group (55)	68,711
Morgan Stanley (61)	65,936
Capital One Financial (106)	38,373
U.S. Bancorp (149)	27,401
Truist Financial (157)	25,356
PNC Financial Services Group (168)	23,542
Bank of New York Mellon (201)	19,991
Discover Financial Services (273)	15,202
State Street (305)	13,692
Fifth Third Bancorp (411)	9,353
Citizens Financial Group (419)	9,069
M&T Bank (439)	8,604

Industry/company (rank)	Revenues
KeyCorp (459)	$8,130
Huntington Bancshares (466)	7,950
Northern Trust (477)	7,752
Regions Financial (483)	7,531
SVB Financial Group (491)	7,401
Computer Software	
Microsoft (13)	$198,270
Oracle (101)	42,440
Salesforce (133)	31,352
Adobe (233)	17,606
VMware (313)	13,350
Intuit (321)	12,726
ServiceNow (499)	7,245
Computers, Office Equipment	
Apple (4)	$394,328
Dell Technologies (34)	102,301
HP (63)	62,983
Hewlett Packard Enterprise (143)	28,496
Western Digital (221)	18,793
NCR (474)	7,844
Construction, Farm Machinery	
Caterpillar (68)	$59,427
Deere (81)	52,577
AGCO (324)	12,651
Oshkosh (455)	8,282
Diversified Financials	
Fannie Mae (28)	$121,596
Freddie Mac (45)	86,717
StoneX Group (59)	66,036
American Express (77)	55,625
Marsh & McLennan (193)	20,720
Synchrony Financial (235)	17,526
Ameriprise Financial (289)	14,347
Icahn Enterprises (294)	14,101
Ally Financial (338)	12,199
Arthur J. Gallagher (443)	8,551
Blackstone (444)	8,518
Diversified Outsourcing Services	
Automatic Data Processing (251)	$16,498
Aramark (253)	16,327
Cintas (473)	7,855
ABM Industries (475)	7,807
Electronics, Electrical Equipment	
Honeywell International (115)	$35,466
Whirlpool (203)	19,724
Corning (292)	14,189
Rockwell Automation (476)	7,760
Energy	
World Kinect (70)	$59,043
NRG Energy (130)	31,543
Constellation Energy (162)	24,440
Vistra (304)	13,728
EQT (487)	7,498
Engineering & Construction	
Quanta Services (244)	$17,074
Jacobs Solutions (277)	14,923
Fluor (303)	13,744
Peter Kiewit Sons' (307)	13,663
AECOM (310)	13,496
EMCOR Group (369)	11,076
MasTec (394)	9,778
Entertainment	
Walt Disney (48)	$82,722
Warner Bros. Discovery (118)	33,817
Netflix (129)	31,616
Paramount Global (134)	31,331
Live Nation Entertainment (248)	16,681
Fox (300)	13,974
Liberty Media (340)	12,164
Activision Blizzard (484)	7,528
Equipment Leasing	
United Rentals (376)	$11,642
Financial Data Services	
Visa (137)	$29,310
PayPal Holdings (148)	27,518
Mastercard (177)	22,237
Fiserv (230)	17,737
Block (234)	17,532
Fidelity National Information Services (283)	14,528
S&P Global (366)	11,181
Global Payments (425)	8,976

Industry/company (rank)	Revenues
Food Consumer Products	
PepsiCo (46)	$86,392
Mondelez International (131)	31,496
Kraft Heinz (153)	26,485
Land O'Lakes (213)	19,226
General Mills (219)	18,993
Kellogg (270)	15,315
Hormel Foods (330)	12,459
Conagra Brands (360)	11,536
Hershey (347)	10,419
Campbell Soup (442)	8,562
J.M. Smucker (465)	7,999
Food Production	
Archer Daniels Midland (35)	$101,556
Tyson Foods (80)	53,282
CHS (90)	47,792
Corteva (283)	17,455
Andersons (239)	17,351
Seaboard (364)	11,243
Ingredion (468)	7,946
Food Services	
Starbucks (125)	$32,250
McDonald's (169)	23,183
Darden Restaurants (402)	9,630
Yum China Holdings (405)	9,569
Chipotle Mexican Grill (438)	8,635
Food & Drug Stores	
Kroger (24)	$148,258
Walgreens Boots Alliance (27)	132,703
Albertsons (53)	71,887
Publix Super Markets (78)	54,942
Rite Aid (161)	24,568
Forest & Paper Products	
Weyerhaeuser (385)	$10,184
General Merchandisers	
Walmart (1)	$611,289
Costco Wholesale (12)	226,954
Target (33)	109,120
Macy's (158)	25,305
BJ's Wholesale Club (210)	19,315
Kohl's (226)	18,098
Nordstrom (267)	15,530
Health Care: Insurance & Managed Care	
UnitedHealth Group (5)	$324,162
Elevance Health (22)	156,595
Centene (25)	144,547
Humana (42)	92,870
Molina Healthcare (126)	31,974
Health Care: Medical Facilities	
HCA Healthcare (66)	$60,233
Tenet Healthcare (215)	19,174
Universal Health Services (311)	13,399
Community Health Systems (337)	12,211
DaVita (357)	11,610
Health Care: Pharmacy & Other Services	
CVS Health (6)	$322,467
Cigna (15)	180,516
Laboratory Corp. of America (278)	14,877
IQVIA Holdings (286)	14,410
Quest Diagnostics (391)	9,883
Home Equipment & Furnishings	
Stanley Black & Decker (227)	$18,004
Mohawk Industries (351)	11,737
Newell Brands (408)	9,459
Masco (436)	8,680
Homebuilders	
Lennar (119)	$33,671
D.R. Horton (120)	33,480
PulteGroup (259)	16,229
NVR (376)	10,580
Toll Brothers (382)	10,276
Taylor Morrison Home (457)	8,225
Hotels, Casinos, Resorts	
Marriott International (192)	$20,773
MGM Resorts International (315)	13,128
Caesars Entertainment (354)	11,647
Hilton Worldwide Holdings (431)	8,773
Household & Personal Products	
Procter & Gamble (51)	$80,187
Kimberly-Clark (199)	20,175

Industry/company (rank)	Revenues
Colgate-Palmolive (228)	$17,967
Estée Lauder (230)	17,737
Industrial Machinery	
General Electric (52)	$76,555
Cummins (146)	28,074
Carrier Global (196)	20,421
Emerson Electric (206)	19,629
Illinois Tool Works (260)	15,932
Parker-Hannifin (261)	15,862
Otis Worldwide (306)	13,685
Dover (445)	8,508
Westinghouse Air Brake Technologies (453)	8,362
Information Technology Services	
IBM (65)	$60,530
CDW (166)	23,749
Cognizant Technology Solutions (208)	19,428
Kyndryl Holdings (225)	18,317
DXC Technology (255)	16,265
Leidos Holdings (288)	14,396
Insight Enterprises (379)	10,431
Booz Allen Hamilton Holding (452)	8,364
Science Applications International (479)	7,704
Insurance, Life, Health (Mutual)	
New York Life Insurance (71)	$58,445
TIAA (103)	40,911
Massachusetts Mutual Life Insurance (104)	40,281
Northwestern Mutual (111)	36,921
Guardian Life Ins. Co. of America (281)	14,653
Western & Southern Financial Group (314)	13,156
Mutual of Omaha (328)	12,531
Thrivent Financial for Lutherans (412)	9,347
Insurance, Life, Health (Stock)	
MetLife (54)	$69,898
Prudential Financial (67)	60,050
Aflac (207)	19,502
Lincoln National (222)	18,766
Principal Financial (236)	17,492
Reinsurance Group of America (257)	16,258
Jackson Financial (282)	14,551
Equitable Holdings (298)	14,017
Pacific Life (312)	13,360
Unum Group (347)	11,991
Brighthouse Financial (448)	8,473
Genworth Financial (486)	7,507
Insurance: Property & Casualty (Mutual)	
State Farm Insurance (44)	$89,328
Nationwide (83)	51,450
Farmers Insurance Exchange (295)	14,092
Auto-Owners Insurance (362)	11,407
Erie Insurance Group (414)	9,296
Insurance: Property & Casualty (Stock)	
Berkshire Hathaway (7)	$302,089
American International Group (76)	56,437
Allstate (84)	51,412
Liberty Mutual Insurance Group (86)	49,956
Progressive (88)	49,611
Travelers (112)	36,884
USAA (114)	36,297
Hartford Financial Services Group (174)	22,362
Loews (297)	14,044
American Family Insurance Group (301)	13,814
Markel (352)	11,675
Fidelity National Financial (359)	11,556
W.R. Berkley (367)	11,167
Assurant (481)	10,193
Old Republic International (462)	8,084
First American Financial (481)	7,605
Internet Services & Retailing	
Amazon (2)	$513,983
Alphabet (8)	282,836
Meta Platforms (31)	116,609
Uber Technologies (127)	31,877
Coupang (195)	20,583

Industry/company (rank)	Revenues
Booking Holdings (243)	$17,090
Opendoor Technologies (266)	15,567
Wayfair (336)	12,218
Qurate Retail (342)	12,106
Expedia Group (353)	11,667
Chewy (389)	10,099
eBay (393)	9,795
Airbnb (450)	8,399
Mail, Package & Freight Delivery	
United Parcel Service (37)	$100,338
FedEx (41)	93,512
Medical Products & Equipment	
Abbott Laboratories (99)	$43,653
Danaher (132)	31,471
Becton Dickinson (209)	19,408
Stryker (224)	18,449
Baxter International (274)	15,113
Boston Scientific (323)	12,682
Metals	
Nucor (102)	$41,513
Cleveland-Cliffs (170)	22,989
Steel Dynamics (176)	22,261
United States Steel (186)	21,065
Reliance Steel & Aluminum (247)	17,025
Alcoa (331)	12,451
Arconic (426)	8,961
Commercial Metals (428)	8,914
Mining, Crude Oil Production	
ConocoPhillips (49)	$82,156
Occidental Petroleum (110)	37,095
EOG Resources (156)	25,702
Pioneer Natural Resources (164)	24,294
Freeport-McMoRan (171)	22,780
Devon Energy (216)	19,169
Southwestern Energy (275)	15,002
Ovintiv (329)	12,464
APA (341)	12,132
Newmont (348)	11,915
Chesapeake Energy (350)	11,743
Hess (358)	11,570
Diamondback Energy (400)	9,643
Continental Resources (407)	9,474
Coterra Energy (420)	9,051
Marathon Oil (464)	8,036
Motor Vehicles & Parts	
Ford Motor (19)	$158,057
General Motors (21)	156,735
Tesla (50)	81,462
Paccar (140)	28,820
Lear (189)	20,892
Goodyear Tire & Rubber (191)	20,805
Thor Industries (254)	16,313
BorgWarner (262)	15,801
Dana (387)	10,156
Autoliv (429)	8,842
Network & Other Communications Equipment	
Cisco Systems (82)	$51,557
Amphenol (326)	12,623
CommScope Holding (415)	9,228
Motorola Solutions (418)	9,112
Oil & Gas Equipment, Services	
Baker Hughes (185)	$21,156
Halliburton (197)	20,297
Packaging, Containers	
WestRock (183)	$21,257
International Paper (184)	21,161
Ball (269)	15,349
Berry Global Group (284)	14,495
Crown Holdings (317)	12,943
Graphic Packaging Holding (409)	9,440
Avery Dennison (421)	9,039
Packaging Corp. of America (447)	8,478
Sonoco Products (498)	7,251
Petroleum Refining	
Exxon Mobil (3)	$413,680
Chevron (10)	246,252
Marathon Petroleum (16)	180,012
Phillips 66 (17)	175,702
Valero Energy (18)	171,189
PBF Energy (92)	46,830
HF Sinclair (107)	38,205
Delek US Holdings (198)	20,246
Par Pacific Holdings (492)	7,322
Pharmaceuticals	
Pfizer (38)	$100,330
Johnson & Johnson (40)	94,943

Industry/company (rank)	Revenues
Merck (69)	$59,283
AbbVie (73)	58,054
Bristol-Myers Squibb (95)	46,159
Eli Lilly (142)	28,541
Gilead Sciences (150)	27,281
Amgen (154)	26,323
Moderna (211)	19,263
Viatris (256)	16,263
Regeneron Pharmaceuticals (339)	12,173
Biogen (386)	10,173
Vertex Pharmaceuticals (427)	8,931
Zoetis (463)	8,080
Pipelines	
Energy Transfer (43)	$89,876
Enterprise Products Partners (72)	58,186
Plains GP Holdings (74)	57,342
Cheniere Energy (122)	33,428
Oneok (173)	22,387
Targa Resources (188)	20,930
Kinder Morgan (214)	19,200
DCP Midstream (276)	14,993
Williams (370)	10,965
EnLink Midstream (406)	9,542
NGL Energy Partners (467)	7,948
Publishing, Printing	
News Corp. (381)	$10,385
Railroads	
Union Pacific (159)	$24,875
CSX (279)	14,853
Norfolk Southern (320)	12,745
Real Estate	
CBRE Group (135)	$30,828
Jones Lang LaSalle (190)	20,862
American Tower (373)	10,711
Equinix (497)	7,263
Scientific, Photographic, & Control Equipment	
Thermo Fisher Scientific (97)	$44,915
Avantor (485)	7,512
Securities	
Charles Schwab (175)	$22,307
BlackRock (229)	17,873
Jones Financial (Edward Jones) (333)	12,411
Apollo Global Management (356)	11,627
Raymond James Financial (363)	11,308
Intercontinental Exchange (401)	9,636
LPL Financial Holdings (440)	8,601
Franklin Resources (456)	8,275
KKR (492)	7,273
Semiconductors & Other Electronic Components	
Intel (62)	$63,054
Qualcomm (98)	44,200
Jabil (121)	33,478
Broadcom (123)	33,203
Micron Technology (136)	30,758
Nvidia (152)	26,974
Applied Materials (155)	25,785
Advanced Micro Devices (167)	23,601
Texas Instruments (200)	20,028
Lam Research (240)	17,227
Analog Devices (344)	12,014
KLA (416)	9,212
ON Semiconductor (454)	8,326
Sanmina (471)	7,891
Specialty Retailers: Apparel	
TJX (87)	$49,936
Ross Stores (223)	18,696
Gap (265)	15,616
Foot Locker (432)	8,759
Burlington Stores (434)	8,703
Lululemon athletica (461)	8,111
Specialty Retailers: Other	
Home Depot (20)	$157,403
Lowe's (39)	97,059
Best Buy (94)	46,298
Dollar General (108)	37,845
Dollar Tree (144)	28,332
Murphy USA (182)	21,266
AutoZone (258)	16,252
O'Reilly Automotive (287)	14,410
Tractor Supply (291)	14,205
Casey's General Stores (316)	12,953
Dick's Sporting Goods (334)	12,368
Advance Auto Parts (368)	11,155
TravelCenters of America (372)	10,845

Industry/company (rank)	Revenues
Ulta Beauty (383)	$10,209
Williams-Sonoma (437)	8,674
ODP (446)	8,491
ARKO (460)	8,128
Bed Bath & Beyond (472)	7,868
Bath & Body Works (482)	7,560
Telecommunications	
Verizon Communications (26)	$136,835
Comcast (29)	121,427
AT&T (30)	120,741
Charter Communications (79)	54,022
Lumen Technologies (237)	17,478
DISH Network (249)	16,679
Altice USA (397)	9,648
Temporary Help	
ManpowerGroup (202)	$19,828
Robert Half (500)	7,238
Tobacco	
Philip Morris International (128)	$31,762
Altria Group (194)	20,688
Transportation Equipment	
Polaris (424)	$8,987
Transportation & Logistics	
C.H. Robinson Worldwide (160)	$24,697
Expeditors Intl. of Washington (245)	17,071
Ryder System (345)	12,011
GXO Logistics (423)	8,993
XPO (478)	7,718
Trucking, Truck Leasing	
J.B. Hunt Transport Services (280)	$14,814

Industry/company (rank)	Revenues
Landstar System (489)	$7,440
Knight-Swift Transportation Holdings (490)	7,429
Utilities: Gas & Electric	
Southern (138)	$29,279
Duke Energy (141)	28,784
PG&E (141)	21,680
NextEra Energy (187)	20,956
American Electric Power (205)	19,640
DTE Energy (212)	19,228
Exelon (218)	19,078
Edison International (241)	17,220
Dominion Energy (242)	17,174
Consolidated Edison (264)	15,670
Xcel Energy (271)	15,310
Sempra (285)	14,439
Entergy (302)	13,764
AES (327)	12,617
Eversource Energy (335)	12,289
FirstEnergy (343)	12,053
UGI (388)	10,106
Public Service Enterprise Group (392)	9,800
WEC Energy Group (404)	9,597
CenterPoint Energy (413)	9,321
CMS Energy (441)	8,596
PPL (470)	7,902
Ameren (480)	7,662
Waste Management	
Waste Management (204)	$19,698

Industry/company (rank)	Revenues
Republic Services (309)	$13,511
Wholesalers: Diversified	
Genuine Parts (179)	$22,096
WESCO International (181)	21,420
W.W. Grainger (272)	15,228
LKQ (319)	12,794
Univar Solutions (361)	11,475
Graybar Electric (378)	10,534
Beacon Roofing Supply (449)	8,430
Boise Cascade (451)	8,387
A-Mark Precious Metals (458)	8,159
Watsco (495)	7,274
Wholesalers: Electronics & Office Equipment	
TD Synnex (64)	$62,344
Arrow Electronics (109)	37,124
Avnet (163)	24,311
Wholesalers: Food & Grocery	
Sysco (56)	$68,636
Performance Food Group (91)	47,194
US Foods Holding (117)	34,057
United Natural Foods (139)	28,928
SpartanNash (399)	9,643
Wholesalers: Health Care	
McKesson (9)	$263,966
AmerisourceBergen (11)	238,587
Cardinal Health (14)	181,364
Henry Schein (325)	12,647
Owens & Minor (390)	9,956

World's Largest Companies, 2022

Source: *Fortune* magazine, July 2023
(ranked by 2022 revenues, in millions of dollars)

Rank	Company (2021 rank), country	Revenue
1.	Walmart (1), U.S.	$611,289
2.	Saudi Aramco (6), Saudi Arabia	603,651
3.	State Grid (3), China	530,009
4.	Amazon (2), U.S.	513,983
5.	China National Petroleum (4), China	483,019
6.	Sinopec Group (5), China	471,154
7.	Exxon Mobil (12), U.S.	413,680
8.	Apple (7), U.S.	394,328
9.	Shell (15), UK	386,201
10.	UnitedHealth Group (11), U.S.	324,162
11.	CVS Health (10), U.S.	322,467
12.	Trafigura Group (19), Singapore	318,476
13.	China State Construction Engineering (9), China	305,885
14.	Berkshire Hathaway (14), U.S.	302,089
15.	Volkswagen (8), Germany	293,685
16.	Uniper (NA), Germany	288,309
17.	Alphabet (17), U.S.	282,836
18.	McKesson (16), U.S.	276,711
19.	Toyota Motor (13), Japan	274,491
20.	TotalEnergies (27), France	263,310
21.	Glencore (23), Switzerland	255,984
22.	BP (35), UK	248,891
23.	Chevron (37), U.S.	246,252
24.	AmerisourceBergen (21), U.S.	238,587
25.	Samsung Electronics (18), South Korea	234,129
26.	Costco Wholesale (26), U.S.	226,954
27.	Hon Hai Precision Industry (20), Taiwan	222,535
28.	Industrial & Commercial Bank of China (22), China	214,766
29.	China Construction Bank (24), China	202,753
30.	Microsoft (33), U.S.	198,270
31.	Stellantis (29), Netherlands	188,888
32.	Agricultural Bank of China (28), China	187,061
33.	Ping An Insurance (25), China	181,566
34.	Cardinal Health (36), U.S.	181,364
35.	Cigna (30), U.S.	180,516
36.	Marathon Petroleum (49), U.S.	180,012
37.	Phillips 66 (74), U.S.	175,702
38.	Sinochem Holdings (31), China	173,834
39.	China Railway Engineering Group (34), China	171,669
40.	Valero Energy (82), U.S.	171,189
41.	Gazprom (52), Russia	167,832
42.	China National Offshore Oil (65), China	164,762
43.	China Railway Construction (39), China	163,037
44.	China Baowu Steel Group (44), China	161,698
45.	Mitsubishi (41), Japan	159,371
46.	Ford Motor (53), U.S.	158,057
47.	Mercedes-Benz Group (38), Germany	157,782
48.	Home Depot (43), U.S.	157,403
49.	Bank of China (42), China	156,924
50.	General Motors (64), U.S.	156,735

Rank	Company (2021 rank), country	Revenue
51.	Elevance Health (50), U.S. (formerly Anthem)	$156,595
52.	JD.com (46), China	155,533
53.	JPMorgan Chase (63), U.S.	154,792
54.	China Life Insurance (40), China	151,487
55.	Électricité de France (95), France	150,902
56.	Equinor (114), Norway	150,806
57.	BMW Group (59), Germany	149,991
58.	Kroger (51), U.S.	148,258
59.	Enel (90), Italy	147,790
60.	Centene (66), U.S.	144,547
61.	ENI (111), Italy	140,667
62.	China Mobile Communications (57), China	139,597
63.	China Communications Construction (60), China	138,270
64.	Verizon Communications (54), U.S.	136,835
65.	China Minmetals (58), China	133,541
66.	Walgreens Boots Alliance (45), U.S.	132,703
67.	Allianz (47), Germany	129,059
68.	Alibaba Group Holding (55), China	126,813
69.	Xiamen C&D (77), China	125,971
70.	Honda Motor (61), Japan	124,912
71.	Petrobras (128), Brazil	124,474
72.	Shandong Energy Group (69), China	124,089
73.	E.ON (112), Germany	121,646
74.	China Resources (70), China	121,643
75.	Fannie Mae (93), U.S.	121,596
76.	China Energy Investment (85), China	121,584
77.	Comcast (73), U.S.	121,427
78.	AT&T (32), U.S.	120,741
79.	Deutsche Telekom (62), Germany	120,108
80.	Pemex (128), Mexico	118,537
81.	Meta Platforms (71), U.S.	116,609
82.	Bank of America (105), U.S.	115,053
83.	China Southern Power Grid (89), China	113,674
84.	SAIC Motor (68), China	110,612
85.	Hyundai Motor (92), South Korea	110,412
86.	China Post Group (81), China	110,271
87.	COFCO (91), China	110,222
88.	Reliance industries (104), India	109,523
89.	Engie (130), France	109,175
90.	Target (87), U.S.	109,120
91.	AXA (48), France	109,067
92.	SK (117), South Korea	105,959
93.	Mitsui (88), Japan	105,694
94.	Indian Oil (142), India	105,349
95.	Xiamen ITG Holding Group (106), China	103,090
96.	Itochu (78), Japan	103,029
97.	Dell Technologies (86), U.S.	102,301
98.	Archer Daniels Midland (124), U.S.	101,556
99.	Citigroup (141), U.S.	101,078
100.	CITIC Group (102), China	100,769

NA = Not available.

Top U.S. Franchises, 2023

Source: *Entrepreneur* magazine; as of Aug. 2023, unless otherwise noted

Rank	Company (2022 rank)	Type of business	U.S. locations[1]	Startup costs[2]
1.	Taco Bell (1)	Mexican-inspired food	6,768	$576,000-3.4 mil
2.	Popeyes Louisiana Kitchen (3)	Fried chicken, seafood, biscuits	2,904	$384,000-3.5 mil
3.	Jersey Mike's Subs (4)	Subs, Philly cheesesteaks	2,535	$194,000-955,000
4.	The UPS Store (2)	Shipping, packing, mailboxes, printing, faxing	5,195	$122,000-508,000
5.	Dunkin' (11)	Coffee, doughnuts, baked goods	9,339	$438,000-1.8 mil
6.	Kumon (6)	Supplemental education	1,620	$68,000-147,000
7.	Ace Hardware (12)	Hardware and home improvement stores	4,695	$292,000-2.1 mil
8.	Culver's (5)	Frozen custard, specialty burgers	911	$2.3 mil-5.8 mil
9.	Hampton by Hilton (17)	Upper midscale hotels	2,345	$12.3 mil-22.8 mil
10.	Wingstop (16)	Chicken wings, fries, sides	1,749	$315,000-948,000
11.	Tropical Smoothie Cafe (10)	Smoothies, salads, wraps, sandwiches	1,311	$277,000-584,000
12.	Arby's (18)	Sandwiches, fries, shakes	2,305	$629,000-2.3 mil
13.	KFC (26)	Chicken	3,842	$1.4 mil-3.2 mil
14.	McDonald's (14)	Burgers, chicken, salads, beverages	12,759	$1.4 mil-2.5 mil
15.	Wendy's (NA)	Burgers; chicken, breakfast sandwiches	5,589	$330,000-3.7 mil
16.	Servpro (8)	Fire, water, and other damage cleanup	2,176	$236,000-297,000
17.	Smoothie King (13)	Smoothies, smoothie bowls	1,074	$264,000-1.2 mil
18.	7-Eleven (9)	Convenience stores	7,202	$125,000-1.3 mil
19.	Budget Blinds (15)	Window coverings, window film, rugs	1,350	$141,000-212,000
20.	Snap-on Tools (21)	Professional tools and equipment	3,267	$201,000-465,000
21.	Valvoline Instant Oil Change (39)	Oil changes and preventive maintenance	858	$178,000-3.3 mil
22.	Pet Supplies Plus (20)	Pet food, supplies; bathing and grooming	468	$493,000-1.8 mil
23.	Burger King (NA)	Burgers, fries, breakfast	6,993	$1.8 mil-4.2 mil
24.	Great Clips (23)	Hair salons	4,268	$178,000-377,000
25.	DoubleTree by Hilton (44)	Upscale hotels and resorts	349	$27.6 mil-97.4 mil

NA = Not available. **Note:** Franchises are ranked by a combination of factors, including financial strength and stability, growth rate, number of locations, startup costs, and whether the company provides financing. (1) As of Oct. 8, 2023. Does not include company-owned franchises. (2) Includes franchise fees, which vary, and other startup expenses.

Small Businesses in the U.S. Economy, 1978-2021

Source: Business Dynamics Statistics, U.S. Census Bureau; Small Business Administration

Year	Total businesses	Small businesses	Small businesses as % of GDP	Total employed	Small business employees	% employed by small business
1978	3,558,378	3,547,996	NA	70,141,112	37,953,978	54.1%
1980	3,739,076	3,727,927	51.0%	74,985,039	39,956,592	53.3
1985	4,072,907	4,060,582	50.0	81,691,290	44,746,190	54.8
1990	4,445,237	4,430,179	51.0	93,670,458	50,735,621	54.2
1995	4,673,760	4,657,842	50.0	99,010,719	52,998,057	53.5
2000	4,902,684	4,884,940	46.9	113,580,997	58,007,291	51.1
2005	5,167,221	5,149,273	45.5	115,436,979	59,451,624	51.5
2006	5,256,390	5,238,178	45.4	119,274,051	61,127,462	51.2
2007	5,293,170	5,274,020	45.4	119,789,950	60,699,984	50.7
2008	5,232,176	5,212,159	45.0	119,579,986	59,905,485	50.1
2009	5,090,273	5,071,186	44.7	113,690,727	56,192,412	49.4
2010	5,018,827	5,000,479	44.4	111,311,896	55,243,563	49.6
2011	4,995,833	4,978,026	44.3	112,880,615	55,708,620	49.4
2012	5,042,668	5,024,309	44.2	115,350,389	56,930,174	49.4
2013	5,067,524	5,048,509	43.6	117,601,993	57,447,338	48.8
2014	5,104,517	5,085,184	43.5	120,123,275	58,492,221	48.7
2015	5,151,172	5,131,464	NA	123,230,544	59,650,817	48.4
2016	5,218,382	5,198,268	NA	125,752,970	60,654,649	48.2
2017	5,251,898	5,231,314	NA	127,487,795	61,620,952	48.3
2018	5,287,859	5,267,368	NA	129,708,103	61,780,732	47.6
2019	5,337,016	5,315,822	NA	131,929,507	62,399,926	47.3
2020	5,341,601	5,320,108	NA	132,733,734	62,264,729	46.9
2021	5,377,307	5,355,741	NA	126,864,765	59,092,171	46.6

NA = Not available. **Note:** Small businesses are firms employing fewer than 500 people. Figures include only businesses with paid employees.

Denominations of U.S. Currency

Since 1969 the largest denomination of U.S. currency that has been issued is the $100 bill. As larger-denomination bills reach the Federal Reserve Bank, they are removed from circulation. Because some discontinued currency is expected to be in the hands of holders for many years, the description of the various denominations below is continued.

Note	Portrait	Embellishment on back	Note	Portrait	Embellishment on back
$1	George Washington	Great Seal of U.S.	$500[1]	William McKinley	Ornate denominational marking
2	Thomas Jefferson	Signers of Declaration	1,000[2]	Grover Cleveland	Ornate denominational marking
5	Abraham Lincoln	Lincoln Memorial	5,000	James Madison	Washington resigning as Army commander
10	Alexander Hamilton	U.S. Treasury			
20	Andrew Jackson	White House	10,000	Salmon Chase	Embarkation of the Pilgrims
50	Ulysses S. Grant	U.S. Capitol	100,000[3]	Woodrow Wilson	Ornate denominational marking
100	Benjamin Franklin	Independence Hall			

(1) John Marshall appeared on the earliest version of the $500 bill. (2) Alexander Hamilton appeared on the earliest version of the $1,000 bill, but these were discontinued to avoid confusion with the $10 bill. (3) For use only in transactions between Federal Reserve System and Treasury Department.

The U.S. $1 Bill

Plate position: Shows where on the 32-note plate this bill was printed.

Serial number: Each bill has its own.

Federal Reserve Bank number: Shows which district issued the bill.

Federal Reserve seal: The name of the Federal Reserve Bank that issued the bill is printed in the seal. The letter also tells you which bank distributed the bill. Here are the number and letter codes for the 12 Federal Reserve Banks:

1/A: Boston
2/B: New York
3/C: Philadelphia
4/D: Cleveland
5/E: Richmond
6/F: Atlanta
7/G: Chicago
8/H: St. Louis
9/I: Minneapolis
10/J: Kansas City
11/K: Dallas
12/L: San Francisco

Treasury Department seal: The balancing scales represent justice. The pointed stripe across the middle has 13 stars for the original 13 colonies. The key represents authority.

Plate serial number: Shows which printing plate was used for the face of the bill.

Treasurer of the U.S. signature

Series indicator: Year note's design was first used.

Secretary of the Treasury signature

Plate serial number: Shows which plate was used for the back.

Front of the Great Seal of the United States: The bald eagle is the national bird. The shield has 13 stripes for the 13 original colonies. The eagle holds 13 arrows (symbol of war) and an olive branch with 13 olives and leaves (symbol of peace). Above the eagle is the motto "E Pluribus Unum," Latin for "out of many, one," and a constellation of 13 stars.

Reverse of the Great Seal of the United States: The pyramid symbolizes something that endures for ages. The eye, known as the Eye of Providence, probably comes from an ancient Egyptian symbol. The pyramid has 13 levels; at its base are the Roman numerals for 1776, the year of American independence. "Annuit Coeptis" is Latin for "God has favored our undertaking." "Novus Ordo Seclorum" is Latin for "a new order of the ages." Both phrases are from the works of the Roman poet Virgil.

U.S. Currency and Coin

Source: Bureau of the Fiscal Service, U.S. Dept. of the Treasury

Total Money in Circulation, 1955-2023

Date	Dollars (mil)	Per capita[1]	Date	Dollars (mil)	Per capita[1]	Date	Dollars (mil)	Per capita[1]
June 30, 1955	$30,229	$183	Sept. 30, 1990	$278,903	$1,105	June 30, 2017	$1,561,808	$4,800
June 30, 1960	32,064	177	Sept. 30, 1995	409,272	1,553	June 30, 2018	1,666,817	5,081
June 30, 1965	39,719	204	Sept. 30, 2000	568,614	2,061	June 30, 2019	1,742,978	5,294
June 30, 1970	54,351	265	Sept. 30, 2005	766,487	2,578	June 30, 2020	1,969,957	5,970
June 30, 1975	81,196	380	June 30, 2010	945,138	3,051	June 30, 2021	2,183,379	6,565
Sept. 30, 1980	129,916	581	June 30, 2015	1,368,622	4,260	June 30, 2022	2,281,465	6,853
Sept. 30, 1985	187,337	782	June 30, 2016	1,463,923	4,520	June 30, 2023	2,345,428	6,998

(1) Based on U.S. Census Bureau population estimates.

Money in Circulation by Denomination, 2023

Denomination	Amount in circulation	Denomination	Amount in circulation	Denomination	Amount in circulation
$1	$14,448,320,528	$50	$124,684,431,750	$10,000	$3,450,000
$2	3,072,820,762	$100	1,883,835,292,700	Partial notes[1]	600
$5	17,587,980,575	$500	141,716,500	Total currency	$ 2,295,080,259,665
$10	23,322,877,150	$1,000	165,124,000	Total coins	$50,347,410,029
$20	227,816,480,100	$5,000	1,765,000	Total currency and coins	$2,345,427,669,694

(1) Represents the value of certain partial denominations not presented for redemption.

U.S. Budget Receipts and Outlays, 1789-1940

Source: U.S. Dept. of the Treasury

(in thousands of dollars; annual statements for years ending June 30, unless otherwise noted)

Yearly average	Receipts	Outlays	Yearly average	Receipts	Outlays	Yearly average	Receipts	Outlays
1789-1800[1]	$5,717	$5,776	1866-1870	$447,301	$377,642	1906-1910	$628,507	$639,178
1801-1810[2]	13,056	9,086	1871-1875	336,830	287,460	1911-1915	710,227	720,252
1811-1820[2]	21,032	23,943	1876-1880	288,124	255,598	1916-1920	3,483,652	8,065,333
1821-1830[2]	21,928	16,162	1881-1885	366,961	257,691	1921-1925	4,306,673	3,578,989
1831-1840[2]	30,461	24,495	1886-1890	375,448	279,134	1926-1930	4,069,138	3,182,807
1841-1850[2]	28,545	34,097	1891-1895	352,891	363,599	1931-1935	2,770,973	5,214,874
1851-1860	60,237	60,163	1896-1900	434,877	457,451	1936-1940	4,960,614	10,192,367
1861-1865	160,907	683,785	1901-1905	559,481	535,500			

(1) Average for period Mar. 4, 1789, to Dec. 31, 1800. (2) Years 1801-42 end Dec. 31; average for 1841-50 is for the period Jan. 1, 1841, to June 30, 1850.

U.S. Budget Receipts and Outlays, Fiscal Years 2000-22

Source: Congressional Budget Office; *Budget of the U.S. Government*, Office of Mgmt. and Budget, Exec. Office of the President

A $236-bil government surplus in 2000 ballooned into a $1.4-tril deficit by 2009. The deficit was reduced by nearly $1 tril, 2009-15, but it began rising again in 2016 and was close to $1 tril again by 2019. In 2020, the deficit soared past $3 tril, in large part because of COVID-19, but by 2022, the shortfall had been cut by more than half.

(in millions of current dollars; numbers may not add up to totals because of independent rounding or omitted subcategories, including some subcategories with negative values)

Function and subfunction	2000	2010	2015	2020	2021	2022
NET RECEIPTS	**$2,025,191**	**$2,162,706**	**$3,249,890**	**$3,421,164**	**$4,047,111**	**$4,897,399**
Individual income taxes	1,004,462	898,549	1,540,802	1,608,663	2,044,377	2,632,146
Corporation income taxes	207,289	191,437	343,797	211,845	371,831	424,865
Social insurance and retirement receipts	652,852	864,814	1,065,257	1,309,955	1,314,088	1,483,527
Employment and general retirement	**620,451**	**815,894**	**1,010,427**	**1,261,651**	**1,251,858**	**1,410,735**
Old-age and survivors insurance (off-budget)	411,677	539,996	658,543	825,307	814,034	911,191
Disability insurance (off-budget)	68,907	91,691	111,829	140,121	138,289	154,784
Hospital insurance	135,529	180,068	234,189	291,778	294,818	339,145
Railroad retirement/pension fund (trust funds)	2,688	2,285	3,336	2,717	2,875	3,249
Railroad social security equivalent account	1,650	1,854	2,530	1,728	1,842	2,366
Unemployment insurance	**27,640**	**44,823**	**51,178**	**43,104**	**56,602**	**66,498**
Other retirement	**4,761**	**4,097**	**3,652**	**5,200**	**5,628**	**6,294**
Excise taxes	68,865	66,909	98,279	86,780	75,274	87,728
Federal funds	**22,692**	**18,256**	**37,759**	**29,579**	**18,387**	**24,064**
Alcohol	8,140	9,229	9,639	9,490	10,274	10,196
Tobacco	7,221	17,160	14,453	12,354	12,136	11,259
Telephone	5,670	993	607	370	321	316
Transportation fuels	819	−11,030	−3,394	−6,525	−6,036	−5,126
Trust funds	**46,173**	**48,653**	**60,520**	**57,201**	**56,887**	**63,664**
Transportation	34,972	34,992	40,813	42,764	43,464	46,631
Airport and airway	9,739	10,612	14,268	9,016	8,184	11,377
Black lung disability	518	595	552	301	286	180
Inland waterway	101	74	98	112	128	124
Oil spill liability	182	476	496	400	552	562
Aquatic resources	342	580	574	646	599	634
Leaking underground storage tank	184	169	179	219	242	245
Tobacco assessments	—	937	49	—	2	1
Vaccine injury compensation	133	218	275	310	313	333
Other receipts	91,723	140,997	201,755	203,921	241,541	269,133
OUTLAYS	**1,788,950**	**3,457,079**	**3,691,850**	**6,553,621**	**6,822,470**	**6,273,324**
National defense	**294,363**	**693,485**	**589,659**	**724,645**	**753,901**	**765,823**
Department of Defense—Military	281,029	666,703	562,499	690,420	717,581	726,632
Military personnel	75,950	155,690	145,206	161,416	172,580	180,774
Operation and maintenance	105,812	275,988	247,239	278,865	286,184	291,069
Procurement	51,696	133,603	101,342	139,055	141,440	136,176
Research, development, test, and evaluation	37,602	76,990	64,124	99,875	105,663	107,059
Military construction	5,109	21,169	8,132	8,882	9,146	9,726
Family housing	3,413	3,173	1,198	1,293	1,450	1,423
Atomic energy defense activities	12,138	19,308	18,692	24,479	25,800	28,291
Defense-related activities	1,196	7,474	8,468	9,746	10,520	10,900
International affairs	**17,213**	**45,195**	**52,040**	**67,666**	**46,947**	**71,699**
International development and humanitarian assistance	6,516	19,014	24,087	28,226	33,428	34,163
International security assistance	6,387	11,363	12,907	12,080	9,152	26,104
Conduct of foreign affairs	4,708	13,557	13,246	16,621	15,270	14,400
Foreign information and exchange activities	817	1,485	1,531	1,621	1,633	1,969
International financial programs	−1,215	−224	269	9,118	−12,536	−4,937
General science, space, and technology	**18,594**	**30,100**	**29,412**	**34,022**	**35,534**	**37,404**
General science and basic research	6,167	11,730	11,719	13,301	14,045	15,205
Space flight, research, and supporting activities	12,427	18,370	17,693	20,721	21,489	22,199
Energy	**−761**	**11,618**	**6,841**	**7,083**	**5,977**	**−9,132**
Energy supply	−1,818	5,801	4,710	5,498	4,779	4,063
Energy conservation	666	4,997	1,187	1,241	1,352	32
Emergency energy preparedness	162	199	449	−246	−750	−13,844
Energy information, policy, and regulation	229	621	495	590	596	617
Natural resources and environment	**25,003**	**43,667**	**36,033**	**42,450**	**44,160**	**41,389**
Water resources	5,078	11,662	7,760	8,910	9,652	1,045
Conservation and land management	6,762	10,783	10,519	13,539	14,811	10,144
Recreational resources	2,540	3,911	3,501	4,195	4,204	4,480
Pollution control and abatement	7,395	10,841	7,240	8,731	8,383	9,174
Agriculture	**36,458**	**21,356**	**18,500**	**47,298**	**47,398**	**33,065**
Farm income stabilization	33,442	16,478	13,424	26,403	16,663	16,437
Agricultural research and services	3,016	4,878	5,076	20,895	30,735	16,628
Commerce and housing credit	**3,207**	**−82,316**	**−37,905**	**572,071**	**307,847**	**−19,075**
Mortgage credit	−3,335	35,804	−35,658	−26,494	−31,758	−43,386
Postal service	2,129	−682	−1,610	−2,346	−2,679	2,636
Deposit insurance	−3,053	−32,033	−12,812	−7,238	−9,025	−11,525
Transportation	**46,853**	**91,972**	**89,533**	**145,623**	**154,291**	**131,084**
Ground transportation	31,697	60,784	59,126	78,945	81,631	89,961
Air transportation	10,571	21,431	20,033	55,075	59,890	28,397
Water transportation	4,394	9,351	9,994	11,151	12,255	12,260
Community and regional development	**10,623**	**23,894**	**20,669**	**81,878**	**44,655**	**69,963**
Community development	5,480	9,901	7,817	6,368	9,039	17,040
Area and regional development	2,538	3,249	3,861	4,193	3,354	6,001
Disaster relief and insurance	2,605	10,744	8,991	71,317	32,262	46,922
Education, training, employment, and social services	**53,766**	**128,595**	**122,035**	**237,754**	**298,406**	**677,305**
Elementary, secondary, and vocational education	20,578	73,261	40,022	51,352	90,530	153,955
Higher education	10,117	20,905	51,315	152,971	172,679	518,089
Research and general education aids	2,543	3,631	3,493	3,909	4,098	4,261

Function and subfunction	2000	2010	2015	2020	2021	2022
Training and employment	$6,777	$9,854	$7,103	$6,594	$7,293	$7,550
Social services	12,557	19,179	18,303	20,974	21,924	22,733
Health	154,502	369,081	482,257	747,582	796,450	914,081
Health care services	136,201	330,710	446,368	703,791	750,008	864,578
Health research and training	15,977	34,227	31,426	38,766	41,007	42,642
Consumer and occupational health and safety	2,324	4,144	4,463	5,025	5,435	6,861
Medicare	197,113	451,636	546,202	776,225	696,458	755,094
Income security	253,673	622,106	508,800	1,263,639	1,647,729	866,097
General retirement and disability insurance (excl. social security)	5,189	6,564	7,805	2,106	6,215	12,078
Federal employee retirement and disability	77,101	119,763	139,123	153,822	156,095	168,692
Unemployment compensation	23,012	160,145	34,978	475,124	396,185	36,802
Housing assistance	28,949	58,651	47,823	52,997	89,810	76,463
Food and nutrition assistance	32,483	95,110	104,797	115,389	168,392	193,932
Social security	409,423	706,737	887,753	1,095,816	1,134,586	1,218,663
Veterans benefits and services	47,040	108,478	159,781	218,655	234,282	274,404
Income security for veterans	24,958	49,257	76,403	110,055	115,828	139,926
Veterans education, training, and rehabilitation	1,285	8,089	13,383	12,847	12,044	11,936
Hospital and medical care for veterans	19,516	45,714	61,893	90,594	99,864	110,706
Veterans housing	364	540	743	−3,420	−3,416	1,591
Administration of justice	28,499	54,383	51,906	71,997	71,430	71,323
Federal law enforcement activities	12,121	28,713	26,937	37,839	38,296	38,203
Federal litigative and judicial activities	7,762	14,494	14,717	17,865	18,380	18,462
Federal correctional activities	3,707	6,327	7,049	7,764	7,670	7,540
Criminal justice assistance	4,909	4,849	3,203	8,529	7,084	7,118
General government	13,013	23,014	20,956	180,109	273,941	133,214
Legislative functions	2,227	4,100	3,751	4,659	4,695	5,058
Executive direction and management	456	528	510	478	586	609
Central fiscal operations	8,285	11,906	11,096	12,140	13,692	14,496
General property and records management	−32	1,194	−490	76	−1,151	−991
Central personnel management	184	338	81	231	231	318
General purpose fiscal assistance	2,084	5,082	7,266	155,206	250,693	114,902
Deductions for offsetting receipts	−2,383	−2,154	−4,786	−2,154	−3,366	−4,312
Net interest	222,949	196,194	223,181	345,470	352,338	475,887
Undistributed offsetting receipts	−42,581	−82,116	−115,803	−106,362	−123,860	−234,964
TOTAL SURPLUS/DEFICIT	236,241	−1,294,373	−441,960	−3,132,457	−2,775,359	−1,375,925

— = Not available.

Federal Receipts, Outlays, and Surpluses or Deficits, 1901-2023

Source: *Budget of the U.S. Government, Fiscal Year 2023*, Office of Management and Budget, Exec. Office of the President
(in millions of current dollars)

Fiscal year	Receipts	Outlays	Surplus or deficit (−)	Fiscal year	Receipts	Outlays	Surplus or deficit (−)	Fiscal year	Receipts	Outlays	Surplus or deficit (−)
1901	$588	$525	$63	1942	$14,634	$35,137	−$20,503	1983	$600,562	$808,364	−$207,802
1902	562	485	77	1943	24,001	78,555	−54,554	1984	666,438	851,805	−185,367
1903	562	517	45	1944	43,747	91,304	−47,557	1985	734,037	946,344	−212,308
1904	541	584	−43	1945	45,159	92,712	−47,553	1986	769,155	990,382	−221,227
1905	544	567	−23	1946	39,296	55,232	−15,936	1987	854,287	1,004,017	−149,730
1906	595	570	25	1947	38,514	34,496	4,018	1988	909,238	1,064,416	−155,178
1907	666	579	87	1948	41,560	29,764	11,796	1989	991,104	1,143,743	−152,639
1908	602	659	−57	1949	39,415	38,835	580	1990	1,031,958	1,252,993	−221,036
1909	604	694	−89	1950	39,443	42,562	−3,119	1991	1,054,988	1,324,226	−269,238
1910	676	694	−18	1951	51,616	45,514	6,102	1992	1,091,208	1,381,529	−290,321
1911	702	691	11	1952	66,167	67,686	−1,519	1993	1,154,334	1,409,386	−255,051
1912	693	690	3	1953	69,608	76,101	−6,493	1994	1,258,566	1,461,752	−203,186
1913	714	715	—	1954	69,701	70,855	−1,154	1995	1,351,790	1,515,742	−163,952
1914	725	726	−1	1955	65,451	68,444	−2,993	1996	1,453,053	1,560,484	−107,431
1915	683	746	−63	1956	74,587	70,640	3,947	1997	1,579,232	1,601,116	−21,884
1916	761	713	48	1957	79,990	76,578	3,412	1998	1,721,728	1,652,458	69,270
1917	1,101	1,954	−853	1958	79,636	82,405	−2,769	1999	1,827,452	1,701,842	125,610
1918	3,645	12,677	−9,032	1959	79,249	92,098	−12,849	2000	2,025,191	1,788,950	236,241
1919	5,130	18,493	−13,363	1960	92,492	92,191	301	2001	1,991,082	1,862,846	128,236
1920	6,649	6,358	291	1961	94,388	97,723	−3,335	2002	1,853,136	2,010,894	−157,758
1921	5,571	5,062	509	1962	99,676	106,821	−7,146	2003	1,782,314	2,159,899	−377,585
1922	4,026	3,289	736	1963	106,560	111,316	−4,756	2004	1,880,114	2,292,841	−412,727
1923	3,853	3,140	713	1964	112,613	118,528	−5,915	2005	2,153,611	2,471,957	−318,346
1924	3,871	2,908	963	1965	116,817	118,228	−1,411	2006	2,406,869	2,655,050	−248,181
1925	3,641	2,924	717	1966	130,835	134,532	−3,698	2007	2,567,985	2,728,686	−160,701
1926	3,795	2,930	865	1967	148,822	157,464	−8,643	2008	2,523,991	2,982,544	−458,553
1927	4,013	2,857	1,155	1968	152,973	178,134	−25,161	2009	2,104,989	3,517,677	−1,412,688
1928	3,900	2,961	939	1969	186,882	183,640	3,242	2010	2,162,706	3,457,079	−1,294,373
1929	3,862	3,127	734	1970	192,807	195,649	−2,842	2011	2,303,466	3,603,065	−1,299,599
1930	4,058	3,320	738	1971	187,139	210,172	−23,033	2012	2,449,990	3,526,563	−1,076,573
1931	3,116	3,577	−462	1972	207,309	230,681	−23,373	2013	2,775,106	3,454,881	−679,775
1932	1,924	4,659	−2,735	1973	230,799	245,707	−14,908	2014	3,021,491	3,506,284	−484,793
1933	1,997	4,598	−2,602	1974	263,224	269,359	−6,135	2015	3,249,890	3,691,850	−441,960
1934	2,955	6,541	−3,586	1975	279,090	332,332	−53,242	2016	3,267,965	3,852,615	−584,650
1935	3,609	6,412	−2,803	1976	298,060	371,792	−73,732	2017	3,316,184	3,981,634	−665,450
1936	3,923	8,228	−4,304	1977	355,559	409,218	−53,659	2018	3,329,907	4,109,047	−779,140
1937	5,387	7,580	−2,193	1978	399,561	458,746	−59,185	2019	3,463,364	4,446,960	−983,596
1938	6,751	6,840	−89	1979	463,302	504,028	−40,726	2020	3,421,164	6,553,621	−3,132,457
1939	6,295	9,141	−2,846	1980	517,112	590,941	−73,830	2021	4,047,111	6,822,470	−2,775,359
1940	6,548	9,468	−2,920	1981	599,272	678,241	−78,968	2022	4,897,399	6,273,324	−1,375,925
1941	8,712	13,653	−4,941	1982	617,766	745,743	−127,977	2023[1]	4,802,483	6,371,827	−1,569,344

— = $500,000 or less. Figures in **bold** denote annual surplus. **Note:** Budget figures prior to 1933 are based on administrative budget concepts rather than unified budget concepts. Through 1976, fiscal year ends June 30; after 1976, fiscal year ends Sept. 30. Surplus or deficit column may not equal difference between figures because of rounding. (1) Estimate as of Mar. 2023.

Public Debt of the U.S., 1946-2027

Source: *Budget of the U.S. Government, Fiscal Year 2024*, Office of Management and Budget, Exec. Office of the President

Year	Debt held by public			Interest on public debt as % of—		Year	Debt held by public			Interest on public debt as % of—	
	Current dollars (bil)	FY2022 dollars (bil)	As % of GDP	Total federal outlays	GDP		Current dollars (bil)	FY2022 dollars (bil)	As % of GDP	Total federal outlays	GDP
1946	$241.9	$2,916.7	106.1%	7.6%	1.8%	2010	$9,018.9	$11,799.1	60.6%	6.6%	1.5%
1950	219.0	2,133.8	78.6	11.4	1.7	2015	13,116.7	15,733.0	72.5	7.1	1.4
1955	226.6	1,940.5	55.8	7.6	1.3	2017	14,665.4	17,140.0	76.2	7.8	1.6
1960	236.8	1,797.3	44.3	8.5	1.5	2018	15,749.6	17,985.2	77.6	9.0	1.8
1965	260.8	1,854.6	36.8	8.1	1.4	2019	16,800.7	18,817.0	79.4	9.5	2.0
1970	283.2	1,678.5	27.1	7.9	1.5	2020	21,016.7	23,229.2	99.8	5.9	1.8
1975	394.7	1,723.2	24.6	7.5	1.6	2021	22,282.8	23,826.9	98.4	6.1	1.8
1980	711.9	2,161.0	25.5	10.6	2.2	2022	24,252.4	24,252.4	97.0	8.5	2.1
1985	1,507.3	3,487.1	35.3	16.2	3.6	2023[1]	25,909.8	24,718.1	98.4	11.3	2.7
1990	2,411.6	4,793.5	40.9	16.2	3.4	2024[1]	27,782.7	25,892.9	102.0	12.3	3.1
1995	3,604.4	6,319.0	47.7	15.8	3.2	2025[1]	29,591.7	27,005.0	104.1	12.5	3.1
2000	3,409.8	5,509.3	33.7	13.0	2.3	2026[1]	31,232.8	27,919.0	105.2	12.8	3.1
2005	4,592.2	6,629.5	35.8	7.7	1.5	2027[1]	32,850.6	28,760.7	106.3	12.9	3.2

Note: As of end of fiscal year. Through 1976, the fiscal year ended June 30. From 1977 on, the fiscal year ended Sept. 30. (1) Estimate.

State Finances: Revenues, Taxes, Expenditures, and Debt, 2021

Source: U.S. Census Bureau, U.S. Dept. of Commerce

(in thousands of dollars)

State	Total revenue	General revenue	Revenues Intergovernmental revenue	Taxes	Total expenditure	Debt at end of fiscal year
Alabama	$42,744,424	$38,326,661	$15,878,493	$14,251,329	$39,430,705	$9,118,128
Alaska	10,389,233	9,178,114	5,260,485	1,053,400	13,281,202	5,652,311
Arizona	57,705,881	52,047,873	25,561,976	20,817,605	53,245,525	8,969,733
Arkansas	28,213,820	26,644,503	10,746,792	11,726,678	27,542,132	7,868,953
California	504,381,850	410,636,676	116,803,579	248,188,154	468,457,717	144,313,743
Colorado	46,751,819	40,076,190	14,384,700	18,817,848	46,270,243	22,328,511
Connecticut	47,470,892	40,117,376	12,777,730	22,066,648	36,900,207	41,965,429
Delaware	13,932,880	13,045,792	5,315,164	5,395,712	12,839,920	5,370,040
Florida	126,292,984	114,029,559	42,721,773	49,314,384	121,129,290	21,437,107
Georgia	68,300,546	60,932,942	26,262,760	27,850,996	71,193,683	14,627,512
Hawaii	23,277,323	20,506,030	9,018,177	8,046,691	17,817,850	11,521,014
Idaho	15,246,700	13,265,103	5,152,842	6,472,467	13,394,246	3,422,989
Illinois	118,117,046	97,479,077	31,262,939	55,531,962	123,261,594	64,743,158
Indiana	70,059,871	66,391,645	31,122,742	26,645,852	52,188,949	21,781,589
Iowa	29,114,357	26,132,201	8,452,676	11,816,502	28,838,245	6,379,930
Kansas	26,575,714	24,485,238	6,617,130	11,615,757	24,713,773	6,706,015
Kentucky	44,566,408	39,004,301	18,058,670	14,617,202	43,747,754	15,362,300
Louisiana	43,362,871	37,907,510	20,913,908	12,257,234	44,147,286	16,982,504
Maine	12,826,585	11,776,444	4,914,655	5,452,250	12,584,585	5,627,663
Maryland	58,049,343	51,031,162	19,392,050	25,220,541	59,400,461	30,652,002
Massachusetts	86,120,499	74,528,984	27,578,584	36,336,125	85,007,834	79,692,181
Michigan	88,194,407	78,992,870	29,459,635	34,431,625	89,748,230	33,621,791
Minnesota	61,465,272	53,128,580	15,732,974	31,793,412	59,990,344	16,497,365
Mississippi	26,705,382	23,358,365	10,601,280	9,353,158	25,271,477	7,465,082
Missouri	42,145,677	37,442,085	15,389,965	15,091,423	41,341,575	19,143,395
Montana	11,032,106	9,977,337	5,140,433	3,880,366	9,307,013	2,622,550
Nebraska	15,206,074	14,524,893	5,527,373	6,960,988	14,350,526	2,578,278
Nevada	21,876,113	18,677,128	6,589,132	10,416,344	22,844,761	3,593,979
New Hampshire	10,904,056	9,087,504	4,100,526	3,213,039	10,919,342	7,225,623
New Jersey	95,472,433	81,223,527	24,884,158	43,683,029	88,176,004	70,952,710
New Mexico	28,013,443	25,398,916	12,146,268	7,471,575	27,742,123	7,434,683
New York	233,384,146	200,232,890	83,883,457	93,503,736	241,779,293	170,355,214
North Carolina	98,872,610	73,865,856	28,099,181	34,711,694	76,023,189	15,073,723
North Dakota	10,419,472	9,331,669	3,750,161	3,908,672	9,295,476	2,683,267
Ohio	105,906,603	87,270,553	35,943,796	34,909,388	104,296,674	34,849,903
Oklahoma	30,978,736	27,683,745	10,355,355	11,299,244	30,002,030	8,151,947
Oregon	49,042,830	41,602,320	13,775,775	17,799,808	46,209,080	14,424,636
Pennsylvania	136,016,605	117,866,834	46,255,973	49,571,347	126,801,633	53,216,521
Rhode Island	13,969,218	12,681,272	6,476,654	4,344,340	12,276,862	9,437,805
South Carolina	40,393,477	34,997,242	13,037,780	13,286,248	40,269,096	12,856,658
South Dakota	5,828,436	5,205,080	2,037,206	2,149,543	7,276,327	3,902,400
Tennessee	43,381,352	41,714,603	17,340,564	19,977,968	42,796,545	6,919,362
Texas	214,868,203	193,789,786	88,753,054	65,377,430	201,786,634	52,664,275
Utah	29,984,752	27,404,644	7,403,999	12,631,617	28,056,050	7,030,825
Vermont	8,419,220	7,838,219	2,694,118	4,102,929	10,455,844	3,426,102
Virginia	77,518,291	72,187,671	24,111,868	32,328,105	70,951,130	31,041,855
Washington	74,134,158	63,376,345	21,113,014	32,614,091	76,187,889	30,206,602
West Virginia	17,735,301	16,194,098	6,899,273	6,046,197	18,546,551	13,368,743
Wisconsin	50,260,813	45,328,576	14,225,073	22,300,918	50,903,217	21,978,336
Wyoming	7,505,301	6,375,373	3,103,070	1,874,876	7,555,184	924,246
United States	**$3,123,135,533**	**$2,704,301,362**	**$1,017,028,940**	**$1,262,528,447**	**$2,986,553,300**	**$1,208,170,688**

Note: Figures may not add up to totals because of rounding.

State and Local Government Receipts and Current Expenditures, 1960-2022

Source: Bureau of Economic Analysis, U.S. Dept. of Commerce
(in billions of current dollars; as of Aug. 2023)

	1960	1970	1980	1990	2000	2010	2020	2021	2022
Current receipts	**$44.2**	**$119.1**	**$335.9**	**$730.1**	**$1,304.3**	**$1,993.1**	**$3,095.6**	**$3,525.0**	**$3,526.7**
Current tax receipts	37.0	91.3	230.0	519.1	893.2	1,306.4	1,951.0	2,138.5	2,281.1
Personal current taxes	4.2	14.2	48.9	122.6	236.7	294.1	506.0	553.8	587.0
Income taxes	2.5	10.9	42.6	109.6	217.4	265.8	466.3	512.2	544.5
Other	1.7	3.3	6.3	13.0	19.4	28.3	39.7	41.7	42.6
Taxes on production and imports	31.5	73.3	166.7	374.1	621.3	966.3	1,370.5	1,488.8	1,570.7
Sales taxes	5.3	17.0	53.6	125.6	221.4	295.1	446.7	499.5	535.2
Excise taxes	6.8	14.7	29.2	58.7	95.5	154.8	207.4	223.9	232.8
Property taxes	16.2	36.7	68.8	161.5	254.7	438.6	608.4	645.5	675.1
Other	3.1	5.0	15.0	28.2	49.8	77.8	107.9	119.9	127.6
Taxes on corporate income	1.2	3.7	14.5	22.5	35.2	46.1	74.6	95.8	123.4
Contributions for government social insurance	0.5	1.1	3.6	10.0	10.8	17.8	20.6	22.8	23.9
Income receipts on assets	1.3	5.2	26.3	68.5	94.4	82.2	104.5	106.7	109.1
Interest receipts	1.0	4.3	23.1	64.1	86.8	67.8	86.9	89.0	90.8
Dividends	—	—	0.1	0.2	1.4	3.0	6.2	6.2	6.4
Rents and royalties	0.3	0.8	3.1	4.2	6.3	11.4	11.4	11.6	11.8
Current transfer receipts	4.3	20.1	76.9	126.4	299.7	604.4	1,020.8	1,256.3	1,113.1
Federal grants-in-aid	3.8	18.3	69.7	104.4	233.1	505.2	878.9	1,112.1	951.8
From business (net)	0.2	0.6	2.5	7.1	28.6	40.3	55.4	56.8	62.7
From persons	0.3	1.2	4.7	14.9	38.0	58.8	86.3	86.9	91.6
Current surplus of government enterprises	1.2	1.4	-0.8	6.1	6.1	-17.7	-1.3	0.5	-0.3
Current expenditures	**41.7**	**117.6**	**341.8**	**766.3**	**1,345.0**	**2,300.6**	**3,082.3**	**3,300.1**	**3,574.6**
Consumption expenditures	33.5	90.4	249.0	544.0	961.9	1,508.1	1,968.8	2,106.9	2,322.1
Government social benefit payments to persons	4.6	16.1	51.2	127.7	271.4	523.9	817.0	902.8	981.6
Interest payments	3.6	11.1	41.2	94.3	111.1	267.0	295.9	287.2	270.3
Subsidies	0.0	0.0	0.4	0.4	0.5	1.6	0.6	3.1	0.7
Net state and local government saving	**2.5**	**1.4**	**-5.9**	**-36.2**	**-40.6**	**-307.5**	**13.3**	**224.9**	**-47.8**
Social insurance funds	0.0	0.2	1.3	2.0	2.0	0.9	3.4	5.8	5.7
Other	2.5	1.3	-7.2	-38.2	-42.6	-308.4	9.9	219.1	-53.5
Addenda:									
Total receipts	**47.2**	**125.3**	**354.5**	**755.1**	**1,348.5**	**2,070.0**	**3,179.3**	**3,608.0**	**3,757.8**
Current receipts	44.2	119.1	335.9	730.1	1,304.3	1,993.1	3,095.6	3,525.0	3,526.7
Capital transfer receipts	3.0	6.2	18.6	25.0	44.2	76.9	83.7	83.1	231.0
Total expenditures	**52.1**	**137.1**	**376.6**	**837.6**	**1,468.4**	**2,446.4**	**3,237.3**	**3,437.3**	**3,705.2**
Current expenditures	41.7	117.6	341.8	766.3	1,345.0	2,300.6	3,082.3	3,300.1	3,574.6
Gross government investment	14.1	29.3	65.7	132.2	231.5	347.3	439.6	444.6	479.4
Net purchases of nonproduced assets	0.9	1.1	2.2	5.7	8.6	12.0	16.6	17.0	17.6
Less: Consumption of fixed capital	4.5	10.9	33.1	66.6	116.6	213.4	301.2	324.4	368.9
Net lending or net borrowing (–)	**-4.9**	**-11.8**	**-22.1**	**-82.5**	**-119.9**	**-376.4**	**-57.9**	**170.8**	**52.6**

— = Not applicable.

Federal Deposit Insurance Corporation (FDIC)

The Federal Deposit Insurance Corporation (FDIC) was created by Congress during the height of the Depression to maintain stability and public confidence in the nation's banking system. It covered depositors for up to $2,500 in case of bank failure in 1934; the limit today is 100 times that much, or $250,000. In its unique role as deposit insurer of banks and savings associations, and in cooperation with other federal and state regulatory agencies, the FDIC seeks to promote the safety and soundness of insured depository institutions in the U.S. financial system.

The quarterly premiums on deposit insurance are paid by the banks rather than by consumers. The amount of the premium is based on the institution's balance of insured deposits for the preceding quarter and the institution's risk to the insurance fund. In 2009, Congress permanently increased the limit that the FDIC may borrow from the U.S. Treasury from $30 bil to $100 bil.

U.S. Banks, 1935-2023

Source: *Summary of Deposits*, Federal Deposit Insurance Corp. (FDIC)
Comprises all FDIC-insured commercial and savings banks, including savings and loan institutions (S&Ls).

	Number of banks					Deposits (in mil dollars)				
		Commercial banks[2]			Savings banks, total		Commercial banks[2]			Savings banks, total
Year	All banks[1]	National charter	State charter	Non-members		All deposits[1]	National charter	State charter	Non-members	
1935[3]	15,295	5,386	1,001	7,735	1,173	$45,102	$24,802	$13,653	$5,669	$978
1940	15,772	5,144	1,342	6,956	2,330	67,494	35,787	20,642	7,040	4,025
1950	16,500	4,958	1,912	6,576	3,054	171,963	84,941	41,602	19,726	25,694
1960	17,549	4,530	1,641	6,955	4,423	310,262	120,242	65,487	34,369	90,164
1970	18,205	4,621	1,147	7,743	4,694	686,901	285,436	101,512	95,566	204,367
1980	18,763	4,425	997	9,013	4,328	1,832,716	656,752	191,183	344,311	640,470
1990	15,158	3,979	1,009	7,355	2,815	3,637,292	1,558,915	397,797	693,438	987,142
1995	12,289	2,941	995	6,230	2,082	3,214,678	1,337,105	439,430	696,108	735,856
2000	10,119	2,302	996	5,180	1,622	4,003,744	1,792,773	707,562	793,275	706,461
2005	8,856	1,864	906	4,779	1,294	5,933,763	2,946,589	765,673	1,191,977	1,023,641
2010	7,821	1,427	836	4,413	1,135	7,676,878	4,305,697	1,002,425	1,464,022	891,159
2015	6,358	1,027	816	3,629	876	10,657,721	6,393,433	1,573,880	1,823,558	823,906
2019	5,313	798	746	3,086	673	12,813,120	7,688,213	2,038,002	2,121,386	924,329
2020	5,076	779	702	2,949	636	15,590,139	9,616,766	2,179,212	2,696,151	1,054,195
2021	4,960	755	693	2,887	615	17,235,467	10,350,965	2,595,643	3,055,213	1,194,327
2022	4,781	733	662	2,784	592	18,141,022	10,763,034	2,732,220	3,375,272	1,220,165
2023	4,655	712	662	2,697	574	17,269,424	10,607,385	2,493,974	3,096,490	1,018,763

Note: Figures are for the end of the year shown through 1990 and for June 30 thereafter. (1) Includes U.S. branches of foreign banks not listed separately. (2) Nonmembers are banks that are not members of the Federal Reserve System; national charter and state charter institutions are Federal Reserve members. (3) Figures for 1935 do not include S&Ls, the data for which are not available.

U.S. Bank Failures, 1934-2023

Source: Federal Deposit Insurance Corp. (FDIC)

Covers all FDIC-insured commercial and savings banks, including savings and loan institutions (S&Ls) 1980 and after. As of Oct. 11, 2023.

Year	Closed or assisted	Year	Closed or assisted	Year	Closed or assisted	Year	Closed or assisted	Year	Closed or assisted
1934	9	1970-79	79	1991	271	2003	3	2015	8
1935	25	1980	22	1992	181	2004	4	2016	5
1936	69	1981	40	1993	50	2005	0	2017	8
1937	75	1982	119	1994	15	2006	0	2018	0
1938	74	1983	99	1995	8	2007	3	2019	4
1939	60	1984	106	1996	6	2008	30	2020	4
1940	43	1985	180	1997	1	2009	148	2021	0
1941	15	1986	204	1998	3	2010	157	2022	0
1942	20	1987	262	1999	8	2011	92	2023	3
1943-49	21	1988	470	2000	7	2012	51	**Total,**	
1950-59	28	1989	534	2001	4	2013	24	**1934-2023**	**4,107**
1960-69	44	1990	382	2002	11	2014	18		

Largest U.S. Bank Holding Companies, 2023

Source: National Information Center, Federal Financial Institutions Examination Council
(ranked by total assets, in millions of dollars; as of Mar. 31, 2023)

Rank	Institution, location	Assets	Rank	Institution, location	Assets
1.	JPMorgan Chase & Co., New York, NY	$3,744,305	24.	UBS Americas Holding LLC, New York, NY	$197,394
2.	Bank of America Corp., Charlotte, NC	3,194,657	25.	Ally Financial Inc., Detroit, MI	196,165
3.	Citigroup Inc., New York, NY	2,455,113	26.	Huntington Bancshares inc., Columbus, OH	189,070
4.	Wells Fargo & Company, San Francisco, CA	1,886,400	27.	Barclays U.S. LLC, New York, NY	182,263
5.	Goldman Sachs Group, Inc., New York, NY	1,538,349	28.	Santander Holdings USA, Inc., Boston, MA	177,558
6.	Morgan Stanley, New York, NY	1,199,904	29.	Ameriprise Financial, Inc. Minneapolis, MN	166,648
7.	U.S. Bancorp, Minneapolis, MN	682,377	30.	RBC US Group Holdings LLC, Toronto, Canada	165,401
8.	Truist Financial Corp., Charlotte, NC	574,354	31.	Regions Financial Corp., Birmingham, AL	154,296
9.	PNC Financial Services Group, Inc., Pittsburgh, PA	561,825	32.	Northern Trust Corp., Chicago, IL	151,108
10.	Charles Schwab Corp., Westlake, TX	535,552	33.	Discover Financial Services, Riverwoods, IL	133,061
11.	TD Group U.S. Holdings LLC, Wilmington, DE	514,340	34.	DB USA (Deutsche Bank), New York, NY	128,005
12.	Capital One Financial Corp., McLean, VA.	471,660	35.	New York Community Bancorp., Hicksville, NY	123,706
13.	Bank of New York Mellon Corp., New York, NY	425,112	36.	Synchrony Financial, Stamford, CT	107,853
14.	BMO Financial Corp., Chicago, IL	295,194	37.	Comerica Inc., Dallas TX	91,327
15.	State Street Corp., Boston, MA	290,816	38.	First Horizon Corp., Memphis, TN.	80,731
16.	American Express Co., New York, NY	235,842	39.	Raymond James Financial, Inc.,	
17.	Citizens Financial Group, Inc., Providence, RI	222,656		St. Petersburg, FL	79,180
18.	HSBC North America Holdings Inc., New York, NY	217,027	40.	Webster Financial Corp., Stamford, CT.	74,844
19.	First Citizens Bancshares Inc., Raleigh, NC	214,711	41.	BNP Paribas USA, Inc., New York, NY	72,077
20.	Fifth Third Bancorp, Cincinnati, OH	208,657	42.	Western Alliance Bancorporation, Phoenix, AZ	71,047
21.	United Services Automobile Association, San Antonio, TX	204,720	43.	Mizuho Americas LLC, New York, NY.	68,212
22.	M&T Bank Corp., Buffalo, NY	202,956	44.	Popular, Inc., San Juan, PR	67,676
23.	KeyCorp, Cleveland, OH.	197,622	45.	CIBC Bancorp USA Inc., Chicago, IL	67,442
			46.	East West Bancorp. Inc., Pasadena, CA.	67,245

Note: Includes foreign-owned banks with a strong presence in the U.S.

Status of Top Recipients of Treasury Department "Bailout" Funds, 2022

Source: ProPublica

Since Oct. 2008, the federal government has spent $635 bil to bail out 987 institutions severely affected by that year's financial crisis. As of Aug. 18, 2022, the government had recouped $390 bil in loans and $353 bil in dividends, interest, and other returns, leading to an overall profit of more than $109 bil. Disbursements to some companies currently appear as losses but may ultimately turn a profit; those investments are listed in *italics*. Companies that failed to repay the government and never will are listed in ***bold italics***.
(in billions of dollars, ranked by amount disbursed)

Recipient	Disbursed	Repaid[1]	Net profit or amount outstanding	Recipient	Disbursed	Repaid[1]	Net profit or amount outstanding
Fannie Mae	$119.8	$181.3	$61.5	BB&T	$3.1	$3.3	$0.2
Freddie Mac	71.6	119.7	48.0	Bank of New York Mellon	3.0	3.2	0.2
AIG	67.8	72.9	5.0	KeyCorp	2.5	2.9	0.4
General Motors	50.7	39.4	−11.3	CalHFA Mortgage Assistance Corp.	2.4	0.0	−2.4
Bank of America	45.0	49.6	4.6	*CIT Group*	2.3	—	−2.3
Citigroup	45.0	58.4	13.4	*Bank of America subsidiaries (incl. Countrywide)*	2.3	0.0	−2.3
JPMorgan Chase	25.0	26.7	1.7	Comerica Incorporated	2.3	2.6	0.3
Wells Fargo	25.0	27.3	2.3	State Street	2.0	2.1	0.1
GMAC (now Ally Financial)	16.3	19.3	3.1	RLJ Western Asset Public/ Private Master Fund, L.P.	1.9	2.3	0.5
Chrysler	10.7	9.5	−1.2	*Select Portfolio Servicing*	1.8	0.0	−1.8
Goldman Sachs	10.0	11.4	1.4	Invesco Legacy Securities Master Fund, L.P.	1.7	2.3	0.6
Morgan Stanley	10.0	11.3	1.3	Marshall & Ilsley	1.7	1.9	0.2
PNC Financial Services	7.6	8.3	0.7	*Oaktree PPIP Fund, L.P.*	1.7	2.0	0.3
U.S. Bancorp	6.6	6.9	0.3	Nationstar Mortgage, LLC dba Mr. Cooper	1.6	0.0	−1.6
PHH Mortgage, subsidiary of Ocwen Financial Corp.	5.0	0.0	−5.0	Blackrock PPIF, L.P.	1.6	2.0	0.4
SunTrust	4.9	5.4	0.5	*Northern Trust*	1.6	1.7	0.1
Capital One Financial Corp.	3.6	3.8	0.3	Chrysler Financial Services	1.5	1.5	—
Regions Financial Corp.	3.5	4.1	0.6	Marathon Legacy Securities Public–Private Investment Partnership, L.P.	1.4	1.8	0.4
Wellington Management Legacy Securities PPIF Master Fund, LP	3.4	4.2	0.7	Zions Bancorp	1.4	1.7	0.3
Fifth Third Bancorp	3.4	4.0	0.6	Huntington Bancshares	1.4	1.6	0.2
Hartford Financial Services.	3.4	4.2	0.8	Discover Financial Services	1.2	1.5	0.2
Wells Fargo Bank, NA.	3.4	0.0	−3.4	*Florida Housing Finance Corp.*	1.1	0.0	−1.1
American Express	3.4	3.8	0.4				
AG GECC PPIF Master Fund, L.P.	3.4	4.3	0.9				
JPMorgan Chase subsidiaries	3.2	0.0	−3.2				
AllianceBernstein Legacy Securities Master Fund, L.P.	3.2	3.8	0.6				

— = Less than $0.1 bil. **Note:** Total includes other disbursements not shown. Figures may not add up to totals due to rounding. (1) Amounts repaid include principal, dividends, interest, warrants, and other proceeds.

Federal Reserve System

The Federal Reserve System is the central bank for the U.S. The system was established on Dec. 23, 1913, originally to give the country an elastic currency, provide facilities for discounting commercial paper, and improve the supervision of banking. Since then, the system's responsibilities have been broadened. Over the years, stability and growth of the economy, a high level of employment, stability in the purchasing power of the dollar, and reasonable balance in transactions with other countries have come to be recognized as primary objectives of governmental economic policy.

The Federal Reserve System consists of three key entities: the Board of Governors, 12 District Reserve Banks and their branches, and the Federal Open Market Committee. Several advisory councils help the board meet its varied responsibilities.

The hub of the system is the seven-member **Board of Governors** in Washington, DC. The members of the board are appointed by the president and confirmed by the Senate to 14-year terms. The president also appoints the chair and vice chair of the board from among the board members for four-year terms. As of Oct. 2023, the board members were Jerome H. Powell, chair; Philip N. Jefferson, vice chair; Michael S. Barr, vice chair for supervision; Michelle W. Bowman; Lisa D. Cook; Adriana D. Kugler; and Christopher J. Waller.

The 12 **Federal Reserve Banks** and their branch offices serve as the decentralized portion of the system, carrying out day-to-day operations such as circulating currency and coin and providing fiscal agency functions and payments mechanism services. The 12 Reserve Banks are located in Boston, New York, Philadelphia, Cleveland, Richmond, Atlanta, Chicago, St. Louis, Minneapolis, Kansas City, Dallas, and San Francisco.

The system's principal function is monetary policy, which it controls using three tools: reserve requirements, the discount rate, and open market operations.

Uniform **reserve requirements**, set by the board, are applied to the transaction accounts and nonpersonal time deposits of all depository institutions. Responsibility for setting the **discount rate** (the interest rate at which depository institutions can borrow money from the Reserve Banks) is shared by the Board of Governors and the Reserve Banks. Changes in the discount rate are recommended by the individual boards of directors of the Reserve Banks and are subject to approval by the Board of Governors.

The most important tool of monetary policy is **open market operations**, or the purchase and sale of government securities. Responsibility for influencing the cost and availability of money and credit through the purchase and sale of government securities lies with the **Federal Open Market Committee** (FOMC), which comprises the seven members of the Board of Governors, the president of the Federal Reserve Bank of New York, and four other Federal Reserve Bank presidents, who each serve one-year terms on a rotating basis. The committee bases its decisions on economic and financial developments and outlook, setting yearly growth objectives for key measures of money supply and credit. The decisions of the committee are carried out by the domestic trading desk of the Federal Reserve Bank of New York.

A Federal Advisory Council of banking industry representatives meets with the Federal Reserve Board four times a year to discuss business and financial conditions, as well as to make recommendations.

Website: www.federalreserve.gov

Federal Reserve Board Benchmark Interest Rates, 1955-2023

The interest rate that the Federal Reserve charges its member banks to borrow money overnight, the discount rate, was divided into two categories in 2003: primary credit, for banks in sound financial condition, and secondary credit, for banks that do not qualify for primary credit. The secondary credit rate is ½ a percentage point higher than the primary credit rate shown here for Jan. 9, 2003, and thereafter. Banks typically raise or lower the rates they extend to customers in accordance with changes in these rates.

Effective date	Rate	Effective date	Rate	Effective date	Rate	Effective date	Rate	Effective date	Rate
1955		**1971 (cont.)**		**1981**		**1999**		**2008**	
Jan. 3	1½	July 16	5	May 5	14	Aug. 24	4¾	Jan. 22	4
Apr. 15	1¾	Nov. 19	4¾	Nov. 2	13	Nov. 16	5	Jan. 30	3½
Aug. 5	2	Dec. 17	4½	Dec. 4	12	**2000**		Mar. 17	3¼
Sept. 9	2¼	**1973**		**1982**		Feb. 2	5¼	Mar. 18	2½
Nov. 18	2½	Jan. 15	5	July 20	11½	Mar. 21	5½	Apr. 30	2¼
1956		Feb. 26	5½	Aug. 2	11	May 16	6	Oct. 8	1¾
Apr. 13	2¾	May 4	5¾	Aug. 16	10	**2001**		Oct. 29	1¼
Aug. 24	3	May 11	6	Aug. 27	10	Jan. 3	5¾	Dec. 16	½
1957		June 11	6½	Oct. 12	9½	Jan. 31	5	**2010**	
Aug. 23	3½	July 2	7	Dec. 15	8½	Mar. 20	4½	Feb. 19	¾
Nov. 15	3	Aug. 14	7½	**1984**		Apr. 18	4	**2015**	
1958		**1974**		Apr. 9	9	May 15	3½	Dec. 17	1
Jan. 24	2¾	Apr. 25	8	Nov. 21	8½	June 27	3¼	**2016**	
Mar. 7	2¼	Dec. 9	7¾	Dec. 24	8	Aug. 21	3	Dec. 15	1¼
Apr. 18	1¾	**1975**		**1985**		Sept. 17	2½	**2017**	
Sept. 12	2	Jan. 10	7¼	May 20	7½	Oct. 2	2	Mar. 16	1½
Nov. 7	2½	Feb. 5	6¾	**1986**		Dec. 11	1¼	June 15	1¾
1959		Mar. 19	6¼	Mar. 7	7	**2002**		Dec. 14	2
Mar. 6	3	May 16	6	Apr. 21	6½	Nov. 6	¾	**2018**	
May 29	3½	**1976**		July 11	6	**2003**		Mar. 22	2¼
Sept. 11	4	Jan. 19	5½	Aug. 21	5½	Jan. 9	2¼	June 14	2½
1960		Nov. 22	5¼	**1987**		June 25	2	Sept. 27	2¾
June 10	3½	**1977**		Sept. 4	6	**2004**		Dec. 20	3
Aug. 12	3	Aug. 31	5¾	**1988**		June 30	2¼	**2019**	
1963		Oct. 26	6	Aug. 9	6½	Aug. 10	2½	Aug. 1	2¾
July 17	3½	**1978**		**1989**		Sept. 21	2¾	Sept. 19	2½
1964		Jan. 9	6½	Feb. 24	7	Nov. 10	3	Oct. 31	2¼
Nov. 24	4	May 11	7	**1990**		Dec. 14	3¼	**2020**	
1965		July 3	7¼	Dec. 18	6½	**2005**		Mar. 4	1¾
Dec. 6	4½	Aug. 21	7¾	**1991**		Feb. 2	3½	Mar. 16	¼
1967		Sept. 22	8	Apr. 30	5½	Mar. 22	3¾	**2022**	
Apr. 7	4	Oct. 16	8½	Sept. 13	5	May 3	4	Mar. 17	½
Nov. 20	4½	Nov. 1	9½	Nov. 6	4½	June 30	4¼	May 5	1
1968		**1979**		Dec. 20	3½	Aug. 9	4½	June 16	1¾
Mar. 22	5	July 20	10	**1992**		Sept. 20	4¾	July 28	2½
Apr. 19	5½	Aug. 17	10½	July 2	3	Nov. 1	5	Sept. 22	3¼
Aug. 30	5¼	Sept. 19	11	**1994**		Dec. 13	5¼	Nov. 3	4
Dec. 18	5½	Oct. 8	12	May 17	3½	**2006**		Dec. 15	4½
1969		**1980**		Aug. 16	4	Jan. 31	5½	**2023**	
Apr. 4	6	Feb. 15	13	Nov. 15	4¾	Mar. 28	5¾	Feb. 2	4¾
1970		May 30	12	**1995**		May 10	6	Mar. 23	5
Nov. 13	5¾	June 13	11	Feb. 1	5	June 29	6¼	May 4	5¼
Dec. 4	5½	July 28	10	**1996**		**2007**		July 27	5½
1971		Sept. 26	11	Jan. 31	5	Aug. 17	5¾		
Jan. 8	5¼	Nov. 17	12	**1998**		Sept. 18	5¼		
Jan. 22	5	Dec. 5	13	Oct. 15	4¾	Nov. 1	5		
Feb. 19	4¾			Nov. 17	4½	Dec. 12	4¾		

U.S. Holdings of Foreign Securities, 2005-21

Source: *U.S. Portfolio Holdings of Foreign Securities*, U.S. Dept. of the Treasury
(in billions of dollars; countries ranked by 2021 holdings)

Country	2005	2010	2015	2020	2021	Country	2005	2010	2015	2020	2021
Cayman Islands[1]	$249	$366	$1,216	$2,565	$2,804	Spain	$70	$87	$115	$163	$172
United Kingdom	815	1,001	1,239	1,395	1,615	Jersey[1]	19	42	92	138	170
Canada	419	695	705	1,168	1,472	Mexico	86	109	148	153	165
Japan	531	519	822	1,296	1,283	Italy	79	66	107	148	162
Ireland	75	132	498	698	926	Brazil	90	235	116	168	151
France	274	366	474	698	801	Hong Kong	46	135	134	166	149
Netherlands	192	233	404	628	752	Singapore	36	64	99	92	120
Switzerland	196	327	420	632	742	Israel	44	64	80	94	118
Germany	217	299	378	535	564	Norway	36	56	58	72	86
Australia	128	323	296	378	460	British Virgin					
Taiwan	58	95	108	304	371	Islands[1]	8	16	63	65	85
India	33	91	130	234	306	Russia	29	62	40	74	84
China	28	102	108	287	303	Indonesia	9	35	47	69	71
Bermuda	187	160	217	283	299	Finland	49	41	38	60	70
South Korea	119	148	171	300	282	South Africa	34	78	63	79	70
Sweden	75	122	138	196	264	Belgium	25	35	68	64	69
Luxembourg	46	100	128	198	222	Guernsey[1]	6	15	38	53	65
Denmark	25	49	90	158	181	Total[2]	4,609	6,763	9,451	14,387	16,319

(1) Not included in UK totals though it is a territory/dependency. (2) Includes countries not shown.

S&P 500 Index, 1965-2023

Source: S&P Dow Jones Indices
(as of Oct. 12, 2023)

Year	Highest close		Lowest close		Year	Highest close		Lowest close	
1965	Nov. 15	92.63	June 28	81.60	2013	Dec. 31	1,848.36	Jan. 8	1,457.15
1970	Jan. 5	93.46	May 26	69.29	2014	Dec. 29	2,090.57	Feb. 3	1,741.89
1975	July 15	95.61	Jan. 8	70.04	2015	May 21	2,130.82	Aug. 25	1,867.61
1980	Nov. 28	140.52	Mar. 27	98.22	2016	Dec. 13	2,271.72	Feb. 11	1,829.08
1985	Dec. 16	212.02	Jan. 4	163.68	2017	Dec. 18	2,690.16	Jan. 3	2,257.83
1990	July 16	368.95	Oct. 11	295.46	2018	Sept. 20	2,930.75	Dec. 24	2,351.10
1995	Dec. 13	621.69	Jan. 3	459.11	2019	Dec. 27	3,240.02	Jan. 3	2,447.89
2000	Mar. 24	1,527.46	Dec. 20	1,264.74	2020	Dec. 31	3,756.07	Mar. 23	2,237.40
2005	Dec. 14	1,272.74	Apr. 20	1,137.50	2021	Dec. 29	4,793.06	Jan. 4	3,700.65
2010	Dec. 29	1,259.78	July 2	1,022.58	2022	Jan. 3	4,796.56	Oct. 12	3,577.03
2011	Apr. 29	1,363.61	Oct. 3	1,099.23	2023	July 31	4,588.96	Jan. 5	3,808.10
2012	Sept. 14	1,465.77	Jan. 3	1,277.06					

Record One-Day Gains and Losses of the Dow Jones Industrial Average

Source: S&P Dow Jones Indices
(ranked by largest one-day losses and gains for two terms; as of Oct. 12, 2023)

		Greatest % gains					Greatest point gains		
Rank	Date	Close	Net chg.	% chg.	Rank	Date	Close	Net chg.	% chg.
1.	3/15/1933	62.10	8.26	15.34%	1.	3/24/2020	20,704.91	2,112.98	11.37%
2.	10/6/1931	99.34	12.86	14.87	2.	3/13/2020	23,185.62	1,985.00	9.36
3.	10/30/1929	258.47	28.40	12.34	3.	4/6/2020	22,679.99	1,627.46	7.73
4.	3/24/2020	20,704.91	2,112.98	11.37	4.	3/26/2020	22,552.17	1,351.62	6.38
5.	9/21/1932	75.16	7.67	11.36	5.	3/2/2020	26,703.32	1,293.97	5.09

		Greatest % losses					Greatest point losses		
Rank	Date	Close	Net chg.	% chg.	Rank	Date	Close	Net chg.	% chg.
1.	12/12/1914	54.62	−16.80	−23.52%	1.	3/16/2020	20,188.52	−2,997.10	−12.93%
2.	10/19/1987	1,738.74	−508.00	−22.61	2.	3/12/2020	21,200.62	−2,352.60	−9.99
3.	3/16/2020	20,188.52	−2,997.10	−12.93	3.	3/9/2020	23,851.02	−2,013.76	−7.79
4.	10/28/1929	260.64	−38.33	−12.82	4.	6/11/2020	25,128.17	−1,861.82	−6.90
5.	10/29/1929	230.07	−30.57	−11.73	5.	3/11/2020	23,553.22	−1,464.95	−5.86

Dow Jones Industrial Average, 1965-2023

Source: S&P Dow Jones Indices
(as of Oct. 12, 2023)

Year	Highest close		Lowest close		Year	Highest close		Lowest close	
1965	Dec. 31	969.26	June 28	840.59	2007	Oct. 9	14,164.53	Mar. 5	12,050.41
1970	Dec. 29	842.00	May 6	631.16	2008	Jan. 3	13,056.72	Nov. 20	7,552.29
1975	July 15	881.81	Jan. 2	632.04	2009	Dec. 30	10,548.51	Mar. 9	6,547.05
1980	Nov. 20	1,000.17	Apr. 21	759.13	2010	Dec. 29	11,585.38	July 2	9,686.48
1985	Dec. 16	1,553.10	Jan. 4	1,184.96	2011	Apr. 29	12,810.54	Oct. 3	10,655.30
1990	July 16	2,999.75	Oct. 11	2,365.10	2012	Oct. 5	13,610.15	June 4	12,101.46
1995	Dec. 13	5,216.47	Jan. 30	3,832.08	2013	Dec. 31	16,576.66	Jan. 8	13,328.85
1996	Dec. 27	6,560.91	Jan. 10	5,032.94	2014	Dec. 26	18,053.71	Feb. 3	15,372.80
1997	Aug. 6	8,259.31	Apr. 11	6,391.69	2015	May 19	18,312.39	Aug. 25	15,666.44
1998	Nov. 23	9,374.27	Aug. 31	7,539.07	2016	Dec. 20	19,974.62	Feb. 11	15,660.18
1999	Dec. 31	11,497.12	Jan. 22	9,120.67	2017	Dec. 28	24,837.51	Jan. 19	19,732.40
2000	Jan. 14	11,722.98	Mar. 7	9,796.03	2018	Oct. 3	26,828.39	Dec. 24	21,792.20
2001	May 21	11,337.92	Sept. 21	8,235.81	2019	Dec. 27	28,645.26	Jan. 3	22,686.22
2002	Mar. 19	10,635.25	Oct. 9	7,286.27	2020	Feb. 12	29,551.42	Mar. 23	18,591.93
2003	Dec. 31	10,453.90	Mar. 11	7,524.06	2021	Dec. 29	36,488.63	Jan. 29	29,982.62
2004	Dec. 28	10,854.54	Oct. 25	9,749.99	2022	Jan. 4	36,799.65	Sept. 30	28,725.51
2005	Mar. 4	10,940.50	Apr. 20	10,012.36	2023	Aug. 1	35,630.68	Mar. 13	31,819.14
2006	Dec. 27	12,510.57	Jan. 20	10,667.39					

Milestones of the Dow Jones Industrial Average

(as of Oct. 12, 2023)

First close over—		First close over—		First close over—		First close over—		First close over—	
100	Jan. 12, 1906	4,500	June 16, 1995	13,000	Apr. 25, 2007	21,000	Mar. 1, 2017	29,000	Jan. 15, 2020
500	Mar. 12, 1956	5,000	Nov. 21, 1995	14,000	July 19, 2007	22,000	Aug. 2, 2017	30,000	Nov. 24, 2020
1,000	Nov. 14, 1972	6,000	Oct. 14, 1996	15,000	June 27, 2013	23,000	Oct. 17, 2017	31,000	Jan. 7, 2021
1,500	Dec. 11, 1985	7,000	Feb. 13, 1997	16,000	Nov. 21, 2013	24,000	Nov. 30, 2017	32,000	Mar. 10, 2021
2,000	Jan. 8, 1987	8,000	July 16, 1997	17,000	July 3, 2014	25,000	Jan. 4, 2018	33,000	Mar. 17, 2021
2,500	July 17, 1987	9,000	Apr. 6, 1998	18,000	Dec. 23, 2014	26,000	Jan. 16, 2018	34,000	Apr. 15, 2021
3,000	Apr. 17, 1991	10,000	Mar. 29, 1999	19,000	Nov. 22, 2016	27,000	July 11, 2019	35,000	July 23, 2021
3,500	May 19, 1993	11,000	May 3, 1999	20,000	Jan. 25, 2017	28,000	Nov. 15, 2019	36,000	Nov. 2, 2021
4,000	Feb. 23, 1995	12,000	Oct. 19, 2006						

Components of the Dow Jones Averages

(as of Oct. 12, 2023)

Dow Jones Industrial Average

- 3M Co. (MMM)
- American Express Co. (AXP)
- Amgen Inc. (AMGN)
- Apple Inc. (AAPL)
- Boeing Co. (BA)
- Caterpillar Inc. (CAT)
- Chevron Corp. (CVX)
- Cisco Systems Inc. (CSCO)
- Coca-Cola Co. (KO)
- Dow Inc. (DOW)
- Goldman Sachs Group Inc. (GS)

- Home Depot Inc. (HD)
- Honeywell International Inc. (HON)
- Intel Corp. (INTC)
- International Business Machines Corp. (IBM)
- Johnson & Johnson (JNJ)
- JPMorgan Chase & Co. (JPM)
- McDonald's Corp. (MCD)
- Merck & Co. Inc. (MRK)
- Microsoft Corp. (MSFT)

- Nike Inc. (NKE)
- Procter & Gamble Co. (PG)
- Salesforce Inc. (CRM)
- Travelers Companies Inc. (TRV)
- UnitedHealth Group Inc. (UNH)
- Verizon Communications Inc. (VZ)
- Visa Inc. (V)
- Walgreens Boots Alliance Inc. (WBA)
- Walmart Inc. (WMT)
- Walt Disney Co. (DIS)

Dow Jones Utility Average

- AES Corp. (AES)
- American Electric Power Co. Inc. (AEP)
- American Water Works Co. (AWK)
- Atmos Energy Corp. (ATO)
- Consolidated Edison Inc. (ED)

- Dominion Energy Inc. (D)
- Duke Energy Corp. (DUK)
- Edison International (EIX)
- Exelon Corp. (EXC)
- FirstEnergy Corp. (FE)
- NextEra Energy Inc. (NEE)

- Public Service Enterprise Group Inc. (PEG)
- Sempra (SRE)
- Southern Co. (SO)
- Xcel Energy Inc. (XEL)

Dow Jones Transportation Average

- Alaska Air Group Inc. (ALK)
- American Airlines Group Inc. (AAL)
- Avis Budget Group Inc. (CAR)
- C.H. Robinson Worldwide Inc. (CHRW)
- CSX Corp. (CSX)
- Delta Air Lines Inc. (DAL)
- Expeditors International of Washington Inc. (EXPD)

- FedEx Corp. (FDX)
- J.B. Hunt Transport Services Inc. (JBHT)
- JetBlue Airways Corp. (JBLU)
- Kirby Corp. (KEX)
- Landstar System Inc. (LSTR)
- Matson Inc. (MATX)

- Norfolk Southern Corp. (NSC)
- Old Dominion Freight Line Inc. (ODFL)
- Ryder System Inc. (R)
- Southwest Airlines Co. (LUV)
- Union Pacific Corp. (UNP)
- United Airlines Holdings Inc. (UAL)
- United Parcel Service Inc. (UPS)

Record One-Day Gains and Losses of the Nasdaq Composite Index

Source: Nasdaq, Inc.

(ranked by largest one-day losses and gains for two terms; as of Oct. 12, 2023)

	Greatest point gains			Greatest % gains			Greatest point losses			Greatest % losses	
Rank	Date	Change	Rank	Date	% change	Rank	Date	Change	Rank	Date	% change
1.	11/10/2022	760.97	1.	1/3/2001	14.17%	1.	3/16/2020	−970.28	1.	3/16/2020	−12.32%
2.	3/13/2020	673.07	2.	10/13/2008	11.81	2.	3/12/2020	−750.25	2.	10/19/1987	−11.35
3.	3/24/2020	557.18	3.	12/5/2000	10.48	3.	5/5/2022	−647.16	3.	4/14/2000	−9.67
4.	4/6/2020	540.15	4.	10/28/2008	9.53	4.	9/13/2022	−632.84	4.	3/12/2020	−9.43
5.	3/16/2020	487.93	5.	3/13/2020	9.35	5.	3/9/2020	−624.94	5.	9/29/2008	−9.14
6.	11/30/2022	484.22	6.	4/5/2001	8.92	6.	9/3/2020	−598.34	6.	10/20/1987	−9.00
7.	7/27/2022	469.85	7.	4/18/2001	8.12	7.	5/18/2022	−566.37	7.	10/26/1987	−9.00
8.	1/31/2022	469.31	8.	3/24/2020	8.12	8.	2/3/2022	−538.73	8.	12/1/2008	−8.95
9.	3/9/2021	464.66	9.	5/30/2000	7.94	9.	4/29/2022	−536.89	9.	8/31/1998	−8.56
10.	12/7/2021	461.76	10.	10/13/2000	7.87	10.	6/13/2022	−530.80	10.	10/15/2008	−8.47

Nasdaq Composite Index Closing Prices, 1971-2023

Source: Nasdaq, Inc.; as of Oct. 12, 2023

Year	High	Low	Year	High	Low	Year	High	Low	Year	High	Low
1971	114.12	99.68	1987	456.27	288.49	2000	5,048.62	2,332.78	2012	3,183.95	2,648.36
1975	88.00	60.70	1988	397.54	329.00	2001	2,892.36	1,387.06	2013	4,176.59	3,091.81
1976	97.88	78.06	1989	487.60	376.87	2002	2,059.38	1,114.11	2014	4,806.91	3,996.96
1977	105.05	93.66	1990	470.30	322.93	2003	2,009.88	1,271.47	2015	5,218.86	4,506.49
1978	139.25	99.09	1991	586.35	352.85	2004	2,178.00	1,752.00	2016	5,487.44	4,266.84
1979	152.29	117.84	1992	676.95	545.85	2005	2,273.37	1,904.18	2017	6,965.36	5,429.09
1980	208.29	124.09	1993	790.56	645.02	2006	2,465.98	2,020.39	2018	8,109.69	6,192.92
1981	223.96	170.80	1994	803.93	691.23	2007	2,811.61	2,340.68	2019	9,022.39	6,463.50
1982	241.63	158.92	1995	1,072.82	740.53	2008	2,609.63	1,505.90	2020	12,899.42	6,860.67
1983	329.11	229.88	1996	1,328.45	978.17	2009	2,167.70	1,265.52	2021	16,057.44	12,609.16
1984	288.41	223.91	1997	1,748.62	1,194.39	2010	2,671.48	2,091.79	2022	15,832.80	10,213.29
1985	325.53	245.82	1998	2,200.63	1,357.09	2011	2,873.54	2,335.83	2023	14,358.02	10,305.24
1986	411.21	322.14	1999	4,090.61	2,193.13						

Average Yields of Treasury, Corporate, and State and Local Bonds, 1977-2023

Source: Office of Market Finance, U.S. Dept. of the Treasury; Federal Reserve System

Year	Treasury 30-year bonds[1]	New Aa corporate bonds[2]	State and local bonds[3]	Year	Treasury 30-year bonds[1]	New Aa corporate bonds[2]	State and local bonds[3]	Year	Treasury 30-year bonds[1]	New Aa corporate bonds[2]	State and local bonds[3]
1977	7.75%	8.02%	5.68%	1993	6.59%	7.22%	5.59%	2009	4.08%	5.31%	4.62%
1978	8.49	8.73	6.03	1994	7.37	7.96	6.19	2010	4.25	4.94	4.30
1979	9.28	9.63	6.52	1995	6.88	7.59	5.95	2011	3.91	4.64	4.50
1980	11.27	11.94	8.55	1996	6.71	7.37	5.76	2012	2.92	3.67	3.73
1981	13.45	14.17	11.34	1997	6.61	7.26	5.52	2013	3.45	4.24	4.26
1982	12.76	13.79	11.64	1998	5.58	6.53	5.09	2014	3.34	4.16	4.24
1983	11.18	12.04	9.51	1999	5.87	7.04	5.43	2015	2.84	3.89	3.65
1984	12.41	12.71	10.10	2000	5.94	7.62	5.71	2016	2.59	3.67	3.14
1985	10.79	11.37	9.11	2001	5.49	7.08	5.15	2017	2.89	3.74	NA
1986	7.78	9.02	7.34	2002	5.43	6.49	5.04	2018	3.11	3.93	NA
1987	8.59	9.38	7.65	2003	4.96	5.67	4.75	2019	2.58	3.39	NA
1988	8.96	9.71	7.68	2004	5.04	5.63	4.68	2020	1.56	2.48	NA
1989	8.45	9.26	7.23	2005	4.64	5.24	4.40	2021	2.06	2.70	NA
1990	8.61	9.32	7.27	2006	4.91	5.59	4.40	2022	3.11	4.07	NA
1991	8.14	8.77	6.92	2007	4.84	5.56	4.40	2023[4]	4.47	5.13	NA
1992	7.67	8.14	6.44	2008	4.28	5.63	4.85				

NA = Not available. (1) On Feb. 18, 2002, the U.S. Treasury discontinued the 30-year constant maturity yield and reintroduced it on Feb. 9, 2006; rates in the interim are for 20-year yields. (2) Treasury series based on 3-week moving average of reoffering yields of new corporate bonds rated Aa by Moody's Investors Service with an original maturity of at least 20 years. Treasury discontinued yield index after Jan. 31, 2003. Rates thereafter are for Moody's seasoned Aaa corporate bonds as listed by Federal Reserve. (3) Index of new reoffering yields on 20-year general obligations rated Aa by Moody's Investors Service; discontinued by Treasury Jan. 31, 2003; rates thereafter are from Bond Buyer Index of general obligation, 20 years to maturity, mixed quality state and local bonds. (4) Rates are for Sept. 2023.

Ownership of U.S. Treasury Securities, 1990-2022

Source: *Treasury Bulletin, Sept. 2023,* Financial Management Service, U.S. Dept. of the Treasury

In 1990, just over 14% of U.S. treasury securities were held by foreign and international investors. By 2022, the total public debt had grown nearly tenfold, while the portion held by investors outside the U.S. had grown to 23%.

(in billions of dollars)

	1990	1995	2000	2005	2010	2015	2020	2021	2022
Total public debt	$3,365	$4,989	$5,662	$8,170	$14,025	$18,922	$27,748	$29,617	$31,420
Federal Reserve and intra-governmental holdings	1,060	1,681	2,782	4,200	5,656	7,711	10,809	12,126	12,401
Total privately held	2,305	3,308	2,880	3,971	8,369	11,211	16,939	17,491	19,019
Depository institutions	207	315	261	129	319	547	1,265	1,734	1,715
U.S. savings bonds	126	185	185	205	188	172	147	146	174
Private pension funds[1]	130	142	182	184	207	505	772	771	755
Pension funds of state and local governments	145	192	206	154	154	175	354	415	313
Insurance companies	138	242	117	202	248	310	398	419	391
Mutual funds	163	287	338	254	722	1,318	3,785	3,412	2,417
State and local governments	411	290	246	512	596	681	1,112	1,441	1,563
Foreign and international	487	835	1,201	2,034	4,436	6,146	7,071	7,741	7,303
Other investors[2]	500	821	145	295	1,500	1,357	2,035	1,413	4,388

(1) Includes securities held by the Federal Employees Retirement System Thrift Savings Plan "G Fund." (2) Includes individuals, government-sponsored enterprises, brokers and dealers, bank personal trusts and estates, corporate and noncorporate businesses, and other investors.

Financial Assets of U.S. Families, 1989-2019

Source: Survey of Consumer Finances (triennial), Federal Reserve System

Category	1989	1992	1995	1998	2001	2004	2007	2010	2013	2016	2019
Median net worth (thous.)	$47.2	$61.3	$66.4	$78.0	$106.1	$107.2	$126.4	$77.3	$83.7	$103.5	$121.7
Average net worth (thous.)	183.7	230.5	244.8	307.4	487.0	517.1	584.6	498.8	551.3	736.0	748.8
Percent of families holding asset											
Any asset	NA	NA	96.3	96.8	96.7	97.9	97.7	97.4	97.9	99.4	99.6
Any financial asset	88.4	90.7	91.0	92.9	93.1	93.8	93.9	94.0	94.5	98.5	98.7
Transaction accounts	85.1	87.5	87.0	90.5	90.9	91.3	92.1	92.5	93.2	98.0	98.2
Certificates of deposit	19.4	16.6	14.3	15.3	15.7	12.7	16.1	12.2	7.8	6.5	7.7
Savings bonds	23.8	22.7	22.8	19.3	16.7	17.6	14.9	12.0	10.0	8.6	7.5
Bonds	5.3	4.7	3.1	3.0	3.0	1.8	1.6	1.6	1.4	1.2	1.1
Stocks	16.2	17.8	15.2	19.2	21.3	20.7	17.9	15.1	13.8	13.9	15.2
Pooled investment funds (mutual funds)	7.1	11.2	12.3	16.5	17.7	15.0	11.4	8.7	8.2	10.0	9.0
Retirement accounts	35.4	39.3	45.2	48.8	52.2	49.7	52.6	50.4	49.2	52.1	50.5
Cash value life insurance	34.7	35.3	32.0	29.6	28.0	24.2	23.0	19.7	19.2	19.4	19.0
Other managed assets	3.5	4.3	3.9	5.9	6.6	7.3	5.8	5.7	5.2	5.5	5.9
Other	13.4	11.4	11.1	9.4	9.3	10.0	9.3	8.0	6.9	8.1	7.4
Any nonfinancial asset	89.1	91.3	90.9	89.9	90.7	92.5	92.0	91.3	91.0	90.8	91.4
Vehicles	83.6	86.4	84.1	82.8	84.8	86.3	87.0	86.7	86.3	85.2	85.4
Primary residence	63.8	63.8	64.7	66.2	67.7	69.1	68.6	67.3	65.2	63.7	64.9
Other residential property	20.0	20.0	11.8	12.8	11.3	12.5	13.7	14.3	13.2	13.8	13.1
Equity in nonresidential property	NA	NA	9.4	8.6	8.3	8.3	8.1	7.7	7.2	6.2	6.7
Business equity	13.2	14.9	11.1	11.5	11.8	11.5	12.0	13.3	11.7	13.0	13.4
Other	11.9	8.5	9.0	8.5	7.6	7.8	7.2	7.0	7.3	6.5	7.9

NA = Not available.

Characteristics of Mutual Fund Investors, 2022

Source: *Investment Company Fact Book 2023,* Investment Company Institute

Median age of head of household	54	Married or living with a partner	71%
Median annual household income	$100,000	College graduates	54%
Median household financial assets	$250,000	Hold more than half their financial assets in mutual funds	66%
Median mutual fund assets	$125,000		
Median number of funds owned	3	Own Individual Retirement Accounts (IRAs)	67%
Employed (full- or part-time)	64%	Own defined contribution retirement plan accounts	81%

Total Assets and New Cash Flow of Mutual Funds by Type, 2000-22

Source: Investment Company Fact Book 2023, Investment Company Institute

Sector	2000	2005	2010	2015	2018	2020	2021	2022
				Total net assets (year-end, in mil)				
Consumer	$1,042	$1,405	$3,113	$9,514	$7,925	$11,230	$12,944	$9,505
Financial	16,087	11,837	6,286	10,222	10,600	8,692	13,568	10,664
Health	45,921	45,398	32,507	124,538	101,961	135,174	141,862	120,763
Natural resources	2,885	11,972	22,714	28,988	29,472	17,651	22,179	26,659
Precious metals	1,143	7,003	23,065	4,487	3,780	7,242	6,194	5,480
Real estate	11,675	59,158	55,120	101,459	94,209	105,174	149,549	99,372
Tech./telecom.	103,853	34,366	30,738	47,088	57,421	115,462	133,585	77,903
Utilities	22,908	28,390	33,332	32,516	29,000	26,535	30,519	36,075
Other sectors	3,917	3,189	4,597	7,006	6,633	7,134	8,995	6,867
				New net cash flow[1] (annual, in mil)				
Consumer	−$122	−$209	$101	$2,235	−$429	−$588	−$291	−$307
Financial	−534	−1,586	−626	978	−1,311	−1,532	2,209	−1,049
Health	9,256	836	−2,407	11,007	−4,071	−3,743	−6,168	−7,926
Natural resources	248	3,471	1,493	−688	−2,972	−4,349	−1,464	1,465
Precious metals	−214	1,027	2,330	−37	−505	581	−313	47
Real estate	339	3,000	1,746	−4,552	−11,439	−4,182	2,500	−12,614
Tech./telecom.	43,837	−8,541	−1,391	288	−2,858	−1,326	−5,443	−10,796
Utilities	1,201	3,311	−848	−2,585	−4,043	−2,580	−1,434	1,643
Other sectors	−187	121	724	−1,510	−1,411	−867	360	−927

(1) Dollar value of new sales minus redemptions combined with net exchanges.

Mutual Fund Ownership, 1940-2022

Source: Investment Company Fact Book 2023, Investment Company Institute

Year	Mutual funds	Mutual fund accounts (thous.)	Total net assets (bil)	Households owning mutual funds Number (thous.)	Households owning mutual funds Percent of all households	Exchange-traded funds (ETFs) Number of funds	Exchange-traded funds (ETFs) Total net assets (bil)
1940	68	296	$0.45	NA	NA	NA	NA
1950	98	939	2.53	NA	NA	NA	NA
1960	161	4,898	17.03	NA	NA	NA	NA
1970	361	10,690	47.62	NA	NA	NA	NA
1980	564	12,088	134.76	4,600	5.7%	NA	NA
1990	3,078	61,948	1,064.34	23,400	25.1	NA	NA
2000	8,134	244,705	6,955.94	48,600	45.7	80	$65.59
2010	7,540	291,299	11,830.53	53,200	45.3	923	991.99
2011	7,575	279,715	11,629.77	52,900	44.1	1,135	1,048.14
2012	7,590	257,074	13,052.84	53,800	44.4	1,195	1,337.12
2013	7,715	264,848	15,048.04	56,700	46.3	1,295	1,674.71
2014	7,927	NA	15,867.05	53,200	43.3	1,412	1,974.55
2015	8,115	NA	15,647.73	53,600	43.0	1,597	2,100.68
2016	8,067	NA	16,342.28	54,900	43.6	1,717	2,524.54
2017	7,958	NA	18,749.91	56,200	44.5	1,836	3,401.02
2018	8,097	NA	17,697.29	56,000	43.9	1,989	3,371.15
2019	7,947	NA	21,276.56	58,500	45.5	2,096	4,396.21
2020	7,627	NA	23,833.94	58,700	45.7	2,203	5,449.36
2021	7,478	NA	26,903.44	59,000	45.4	2,570	7,190.51
2022	7,393	NA	22,110.09	68,600	52.0	2,844	6,476.77

NA = Not available. **Note:** Does not include data for funds that invest primarily in other mutual funds. Mutual fund accounts data include both individual and omnibus accounts.

World's Leading Gold Producers, 1980-2022

Source: Mineral Commodity Summaries 2023, U.S. Geological Survey, U.S. Dept. of the Interior
(ranked by 2022 production; in thousands of troy ounces)

Country	1980	1990	2000	2005	2010	2015	2018	2019	2020	2022[1]
China	225	3,215	5,787	7,234	11,092	14,468	12,892	12,217	11,735	10,610
Australia	548	7,845	9,530	8,423	8,391	8,938	10,127	10,449	10,545	10,288
Russia[2]	8,300	9,710	4,598	5,279	6,173	8,102	9,999	9,806	9,806	10,288
Canada	1,627	5,433	5,022	3,844	2,926	4,919	5,884	5,626	5,466	7,073
United States	970	9,452	11,349	8,231	7,427	6,880	7,266	6,430	6,205	5,466
Mexico	196	311	848	976	2,347	4,340	3,762	3,569	3,279	3,858
Kazakhstan	NA	NA	NA	NA	NA	NA	3,215	3,440	2,025	3,858
South Africa	21,669	19,451	13,767	9,474	6,076	4,662	3,762	3,376	3,086	3,537
Uzbekistan	NA	NA	2,733	2,894	2,894	3,279	3,344	2,990	3,247	3,215
Peru	134	293	4,263	6,682	5,273	4,662	4,598	4,115	2,797	3,215
Ghana	353	540	2,318	2,149	2,637	2,829	4,083	4,565	4,019	2,894
Indonesia	60	360	4,006	4,200	3,858	3,119	4,340	4,469	2,765	2,251
Burkina Faso	NA	NA	NA	NA	NA	NA	NA	NA	1,865	2,251
Brazil	NA	NA	NA	NA	1,865	2,604	2,733	2,894	2,508	1,929
Colombia	NA	NA	NA	NA	NA	NA	NA	NA	1,543	1,929
Tanzania	NA	NA	NA	NA	NA	NA	NA	NA	1,511	1,929
World[3]	39,197	70,089	82,949	79,412	82,306	99,667	106,097	106,097	97,417	99,667

NA = Not available. **Note:** One metric ton is equal to 32,150.7 troy ounces. (1) Estimated. (2) Figures for 1980-90 refer to the former USSR. Includes gold recovered as a byproduct but excludes secondary production. (3) Includes countries not shown here.

Gold Owned by the U.S., 2023

Source: *Status Report of U.S. Treasury-Owned Gold*, Bureau of the Fiscal Service, U.S. Dept. of the Treasury

(as of Aug. 31, 2023; numbers may not add to totals due to rounding)

	Fine troy ounces	Book value		Fine troy ounces	Book value
Total Treasury-owned gold	261,498,926	$11,041,059,958	**Held by the Federal Reserve**		
Gold bullion..................	258,641,878	10,920,429,099	Bank..................	13,452,811	$568,007,257
Gold coins, blanks,			Gold bullion..................	13,378,981	564,890,013
miscellaneous..............	2,857,048	120,630,859	Federal Reserve Banks–		
Held by the U.S. Mint	248,046,116	10,473,052,701	NY vault.................	13,376,988	564,805,851
Denver, CO, deep storage	43,853,707	1,851,599,996	Federal Reserve Banks–display	1,993	84,162
Fort Knox, KY, deep storage	147,341,858	6,221,097,413	Gold coins..................	73,830	3,117,244
West Point, NY, deep storage ...	54,067,331	2,282,841,677	Federal Reserve Banks–		
Gold coins, blanks,			NY vault.................	73,452	3,101,308
miscellaneous..............	2,783,219	117,513,615	Federal Reserve Banks–display	377	15,936

Prices of Precious Metals, 1990-2022

Source: *Mineral Commodity Summaries 2023*, U.S. Geological Survey, U.S. Dept. of the Interior

	Dollars per troy ounce					Dollars per pound			
Year	Platinum[1]	Palladium[1]	Rhodium[1]	Gold	Silver	Copper[2]	Lead[3]	Tin[4]	Zinc[5]
1990	$467	NA	NA	$385	$4.82	$1.23	$0.46	$3.86	$0.75
1995	425	$153	$463	386	5.15	1.38	0.42	4.16	0.56
2000	549	692	1,990	280	5.00	0.88	0.44	3.70	0.56
2005	900	204	2,060	446	7.34	1.74	0.61	4.83	0.67
2010	1,616	531	2,459	1,228	20.20	3.48	1.09	12.40	1.02
2011	1,725	739	2,204	1,572	35.28	4.06	1.22	15.75	1.06
2012	1,555	649	1,275	1,673	31.22	3.67	1.14	12.83	0.96
2013	1,490	730	1,069	1,415	23.87	3.40	1.10	13.52	0.96
2014	1,388	810	1,174	1,269	19.09	3.18	1.06	10.23	1.07
2015	1,056	695	955	1,163	15.72	2.56	0.91	7.56	0.96
2016	990	617	697	1,252	17.20	2.25	0.94	8.39	1.01
2017	951	874	1,113	1,261	17.08	2.85	1.15	9.37	1.39
2018	883	1,036	2,225	1,272	15.73	2.99	1.11	9.36	1.41
2019	867	1,544	3,919	1,395	16.24	2.80	1.00	8.68	1.24
2020	886	2,205	11,205	1,774	20.58	2.87	0.91	7.99	1.11
2021	1,094	2,419	20,254	1,801	25.23	4.32	1.13	15.80	1.46
2022[E]	980	2,200	17,000	1,800	21.00	4.10	1.15	16.00	1.90

NA = Not available. E = Estimated. (1) Average annual dealer prices. (2) U.S. producer price for cathode copper. (3) North American producer price through 2012; North American market price thereafter. (4) *Platts Metals Week* composite price through 2013; New York dealer prices thereafter. (5) *Platts Metals Week* price for North American special high grade zinc except for 1990, which shows average price for high grade zinc.

Who Owns What: Familiar Consumer Products and Services

The following is a partial list of well-known consumer brands with their (U.S.) parent companies as of Sept. 2023. Among brands not listed are many whose parent companies have the same or a similar name (e.g., Colgate is owned by Colgate-Palmolive Co.).

ABC broadcasting: Walt Disney
Ace bandages: 3M
Advil: Haleon
Ajax cleanser: Colgate-Palmolive
Amana appliances: Whirlpool
American Girl: Mattel
Aquafina water: PepsiCo
Arm & Hammer: Church & Dwight
Band-Aid bandages: Kenvue
Barbie dolls: Mattel
Ben & Jerry's ice cream: Unilever
Benadryl: Kenvue
Ben's Original Rice: Mars
Betty Crocker products: General Mills
Bounty paper towels: Procter & Gamble
Braun appliances: Procter & Gamble
Brita water systems: Clorox
Cadbury chocolates: Mondelēz International
Calphalon cookware: Newell Rubbermaid
Canada Dry ginger ale: Keurig Dr Pepper
Cap'n Crunch cereal: PepsiCo
Cascade dishwasher detergent: Procter & Gamble
Charmin toilet tissue: Procter & Gamble
Cheer detergent: Procter & Gamble
Chips Ahoy!: Mondelēz International
Claritin allergy products: Bayer
Contadina tomatoes: Del Monte
Crest toothpaste: Procter & Gamble
Crisco shortening: B&G Foods
Dairy Queen: Berkshire Hathaway
Dasani water: Coca-Cola
Depends adult diapers: Kimberly-Clark
Dove soap: Unilever
Dreyer's ice cream: Nestlé
Elmer's glue: Newell Rubbermaid
ESPN networks: Walt Disney
Febreze: Procter & Gamble
Fisher-Price toys: Mattel
Folgers coffee: J.M. Smucker

Frito-Lay's snacks: PepsiCo
Fruit of the Loom apparel: Berkshire Hathaway
Gatorade sports drinks: PepsiCo
GEICO auto insurance: Berkshire Hathaway
Gerber baby food: Nestlé
Gillette: Procter & Gamble
Glad products: Clorox
Glade air fresheners: S.C. Johnson
Green Giant vegetables: B&G Foods
Grey Poupon mustard: Kraft Heinz
Halls cough drops: Mondelēz International
HBO: Warner Bros. Discovery
Head & Shoulders shampoo: Procter & Gamble
Healthy Choice meals: ConAgra
Hebrew National meats: ConAgra
Hellmann's mayonnaise: Unilever
Hidden Valley Salad dressings: Clorox
Hill's Pet Nutrition: Colgate-Palmolive
Hillshire Farm: Tyson Foods
Hot Pockets: Nestlé
Hot Wheels/Matchbox cars: Mattel
Huggies diapers: Kimberly-Clark
Hulu: Walt Disney
Hunt's tomatoes: ConAgra
Iams pet food: Mars
Irish Spring soap: Colgate-Palmolive
Ivory soap: Procter & Gamble
Jell-O: Kraft Heinz
Jennie-O turkey: Hormel
Jif peanut butter: J.M. Smucker
Jimmy Dean sausages: Tyson Foods
Jolly Rancher candy: Hershey
Keebler cookies: Ferrero
KFC restaurants: Yum! Brands
Kingsford charcoal: Clorox
KitchenAid appliances: Whirlpool
Kiwi shoe products: S.C. Johnson
Kleenex: Kimberly-Clark
Knorr soups: Unilever

Kool-Aid: Kraft Heinz
Lipton tea: Ekaterra
Listerine mouthwash: Kenvue
Maxwell House coffee: Kraft Heinz
Maytag appliances: Whirlpool
Meow Mix pet food: J.M. Smucker
Milk-Bone dog snacks: J.M. Smucker
Minute Maid juices: Coca-Cola
Mr. Clean: Procter & Gamble
Mr. Coffee: Newell Rubbermaid
National Geographic: Walt Disney
Mott's applesauce: Keurig Dr Pepper
Neosporin: Kenvue
Neutrogena soap: Kenvue
9Lives cat food: Post Holdings
o.b. tampons: Edgewell Personal Care
OFF! insect repellents: S.C. Johnson
Olay: Procter & Gamble
Old Navy clothing: Gap
Old Spice: Procter & Gamble
Oral-B toothbrushes: Procter & Gamble
Ore-Ida potatoes: Kraft Heinz
Oreo cookies: Mondelēz International
Oscar Mayer meats: Kraft Heinz
Pampers diapers: Procter & Gamble
Pantene shampoo: Procter & Gamble
Paper Mate pens: Newell Rubbermaid
Pepto-Bismol: Procter & Gamble
Perrier water: Nestlé
Pine-Sol cleaner: Clorox
Pirates' Booty: Hershey
Pizza Hut restaurants: Yum! Brands
Planters nuts: Hormel
Popsicle frozen treats: Unilever
Post-it notes: 3M
Prego pasta sauce: Campbell Soup
Pringles snacks: Kellogg Co.
Purina pet food: Nestlé
Q-tips: Unilever
Quaker Oats: PepsiCo
Raid insecticide: S.C. Johnson

Reese's candy: Hershey
Rice-A-Roni: PepsiCo
Right Guard deodorant: Thriving Brands
Ritz crackers: Mondelēz International
Rogaine hair treatment: Kenvue
Roundup herbicide: Bayer
Saran wrap: S.C. Johnson
Schick razors: Edgewell Personal Care
Scope mouthwash: Procter & Gamble
Scotch tape: 3M
Showtime: Paramount
Skippy peanut butter: Hormel

Splenda artificial sweetener: Heartland
   Food Products Group
Taco Bell restaurants: Yum! Brands
Tampax tampons: Procter & Gamble
Tide detergent: Procter & Gamble
Timberland apparel: VF Corp.
Topo Chico water & seltzers: Coca-Cola
Trident gum: Mondelēz International
Trojan condoms: Church & Dwight
Tropicana juice: PAI Partners
Tubi: Fox
Tums antacids: Haleon

Twitch: Amazon
Tylenol: Kenvue
Vaseline: Unilever
VCA animal hospitals: Mars
V8 vegetable juice: Campbell Soup
Velveeta cheese products: Kraft Heinz
Vicks cold medicines: Procter & Gamble
Visine eye drops: Kenvue
Windex cleaning products: S.C. Johnson
Wrigley's candy and gum: Mars
Yoplait yogurt: General Mills
Ziploc storage bags: S.C. Johnson

U.S. Home Ownership Rates by Selected Characteristics 1970-2023
Source: U.S. Census Bureau, U.S. Dept. of Commerce

	1970	1980	1990	1995	2000	2010	2015	2020	2021	2022	2023
Region											
Northeast	58.2%	60.8%	62.2%	62.3%	63.4%	64.2%	60.2%	62.4%	61.8%	62.1%	62.5%
Midwest	69.3	69.4	67.4	68.5	72.2	70.8	68.4	69.2	70.7	70.1	70.2
South	66.3	68.6	65.8	66.5	69.2	69.1	64.9	67.6	67.1	67.8	67.5
West	59.4	60.2	57.3	59.8	61.9	61.4	58.5	60.1	60.1	60.9	61.7
Age											
Under 35 years	—	—	—	38.7	40.2	39.0	34.8	37.3	37.8	39.1	38.5
35-44 years	—	—	—	65.1	67.5	65.6	58.0	61.5	61.3	61.9	63.1
45-54 years	—	—	—	75.2	76.7	73.6	69.9	70.3	69.4	70.6	70.8
55-64 years	—	—	—	79.9	80.3	78.7	75.4	76.3	75.4	75.1	75.5
65+ years	—	—	—	78.1	80.3	80.4	78.5	78.7	79.6	79.3	78.9
Race/ethnicity[1]											
White	—	—	—	70.2	73.7	74.4	71.6	73.7	74.2	74.6	74.5
Black	—	—	—	42.6	46.7	46.2	43.0	44.0	44.6	45.3	45.7
Hispanic	—	—	—	42.2	45.4	47.8	45.4	48.9	47.5	48.3	49.0
Other	—	—	—	47.6	54.4	55.7	52.6	56.0	56.2	57.3	58.0
Income[2]											
Median family income or greater	—	—	—	79.5	81.8	81.9	78.3	78.8	78.9	79.0	78.8
Less than median family income	—	—	—	48.6	50.8	51.9	48.6	51.8	51.9	52.6	53.0
Total U.S.	64.0	65.5	63.7	64.7	67.2	66.9	63.4	65.3	65.4	65.8	65.9

Note: Figures are for 2nd quarter of year shown, except in 2020, which shows 1st-quarter data (COVID-19 impaired completion of the survey for 2nd quarter). Not seasonally adjusted. (1) Hispanic householders may be of any race. "Other" includes householders self-identifying as Asian, Native Hawaiian/Pacific Islander, and American Indian/Alaska Native, as well as combinations of two or more races/ethnicities. (2) Due to a change in survey methodology, data from 2010 and later are not directly comparable with prior years.

U.S. Housing Affordability, 1990-2023
Source: National Association of REALTORS®

Year[1]	Median-priced existing home	Average mortgage rate[2]	Monthly principal & interest payment	Payment as % of median monthly income	Year[1]	Median-priced existing home	Average mortgage rate[2]	Monthly principal & interest payment	Payment as % of median monthly income
1990	$92,000	10.04%	$648	22.0%	2017	$248,800	4.20%	$973	15.8%
1995	110,500	7.85	639	18.9	2018	261,600	4.72	1,088	17.1
2000	139,000	8.03	818	19.3	2019	274,600	4.04	1,054	15.7
2005	219,000	5.91	1,040	22.4	2020	300,200	3.17	1,035	14.7
2010	173,100	4.89	734	14.5	2021	357,100	3.01	1,206	16.9
2015	223,900	4.03	858	15.1	2022	392,800	5.40	1,765	24.1
2016	235,500	3.88	886	15.0	2023	416,000	6.79	2,167	28.5

(1) 2023 figures are for June, the latest available. All other figures are annual averages. (2) All figures assume a down payment of 20% of the home price. Based on effective rate on loans closed on existing homes for the period shown.

S&P/Case-Shiller National Home Price Index, 1975-2023
Source: S&P Dow Jones Indices

This index compares the median price of existing U.S. homes over time. The baseline for comparison is Jan. 2000; all numbers before or after reflect home prices in relation to it. For example, the June 2023 index of 308.3 means that home prices were more than triple what they were 23 years earlier, while the Jan. 1975 index of 25.2 means prices then were 25.2% of what they were in 2000.

Median Price of Existing Single-Family Homes, by Metropolitan Area, 2010-23

Source: National Association of REALTORS®

Median prices are in thousands of dollars and based on all transactions within time period shown.

Metropolitan area	2010	2020	2023[1]
Akron, OH	$108.9	$168.1	$206.0
Albany-Schenectady-Troy, NY	195.7	232.5	296.3
Albuquerque, NM	178.7	248.1	361.4
Allentown-Bethlehem-Easton, PA-NJ	224.0	234.9	330.7
Anaheim-Santa Ana-Irvine, CA	546.4	900.0	1,250.0
Atlanta-Sandy Springs-Marietta, GA	114.8	260.8	376.5
Atlantic City-Hammonton, NJ	226.4	247.2	317.5
Austin-Round Rock, TX	193.6	367.1	496.3
Baltimore-Columbia-Towson, MD	246.1	328.5	399.8
Baton Rouge, LA	169.6	229.7	268.6
Beaumont-Port Arthur, TX	125.1	180.3	214.8
Birmingham-Hoover, AL	143.0	246.2	315.8
Boise City-Nampa, ID	136.2	353.9	480.8
Boston-Cambridge-Newton, MA-NH	357.3	563.7	734.2
Boulder, CO	358.1	645.9	871.2
Bridgeport-Stamford-Norwalk, CT	408.6	544.0	722.4
Buffalo-Cheektowaga-Niagara Falls, NY	121.2	178.5	236.8
Burlington-South Burlington, VT	261.2	342.9	486.5
Canton-Massillon, OH	90.9	155.4	188.8
Cape Coral-Fort Myers, FL	88.9	289.0	439.0
Champaign-Urbana, IL	141.9	168.6	211.9
Charleston-North Charleston, SC	200.5	324.4	430.2
Charleston, WV	129.1	147.5	173.5
Charlotte-Concord-Gastonia, NC-SC	143.3	296.2	403.1
Chattanooga, TN-GA	121.4	220.1	297.4
Chicago-Naperville-Elgin, IL-IN-WI	191.4	287.6	362.6
Cincinnati, OH-KY-IN	128.0	208.9	294.2
Cleveland-Elyria, OH	114.5	179.5	228.7
Colorado Springs, CO	195.5	361.7	467.1
Columbia, SC	142.6	202.9	277.6
Columbus, OH	136.4	240.8	327.5
Corpus Christi, TX	135.1	225.4	274.9
Crestview-Fort Walton Beach-Destin, FL	NA	339.9	432.0
Cumberland, MD-WV	100.3	120.9	145.4
Dallas-Fort Worth-Arlington, TX	143.8	287.2	389.8
Davenport-Moline-Rock Island, IA-IL	112.2	142.8	179.8
Dayton, OH	103.6	175.8	234.8
Deltona-Daytona Beach-Ormond Beach, FL	115.6	244.9	355.0
Denver-Aurora-Lakewood, CO	232.4	492.7	674.5
Des Moines-West Des Moines, IA	150.9	229.6	296.6
Detroit-Warren-Dearborn, MI	NA	221.3	265.3
Dover, DE	193.3	241.2	323.3
Durham-Chapel Hill, NC	158.3	326.3	495.5
Elmira, NY	101.0	120.4	144.5
El Paso, TX	134.3	177.8	221.8
Erie, PA	107.7	135.1	169.0
Eugene, OR	196.3	354.9	475.4
Fargo, ND-MN	146.4	233.5	300.8
Fayetteville, NC	152.5	163.2	239.8
Fayetteville-Springdale-Rogers, AR-MO	NA	226.3	356.0
Fort Collins, CO	NA	446.0	628.9
Fort Wayne, IN	97.4	169.3	236.6
Fresno, CA	NA	314.0	420.0
Gainesville, FL	161.6	255.0	366.0
Gary-Hammond, IN	122.9	203.4	260.9
Grand Rapids-Wyoming, MI	91.5	230.1	330.3
Green Bay, WI	130.4	204.2	296.4
Greensboro-High Point, NC	129.8	199.2	287.0
Greenville-Anderson-Mauldin, SC	145.3	240.9	333.9
Gulfport-Biloxi-Pascagoulia, MS	125.0	171.3	229.2
Harrisburg-Carlisle, PA	NA	195.8	250.7
Hartford-West Hartford-East Hartford, CT	235.8	264.5	357.8
Honolulu, HI	607.6	851.5	1,060.7
Houston-The Woodlands-Sugar Land, TX	155.0	263.8	348.3
Huntsville, AL	NA	248.0	324.3
Indianapolis-Carmel-Anderson, IN	123.3	227.6	311.2
Jackson, MS	133.2	198.8	240.8
Jacksonville, FL	137.7	279.0	390.9
Kansas City, MO-KS	141.6	237.4	333.9
Knoxville, TN	140.9	229.8	342.4
Lakeland-Winter Haven, FL	NA	230.0	335.9
Lansing-East Lansing, MI	84.4	173.3	226.1

Metropolitan area	2010	2020	2023[1]
Las Vegas-Henderson-Paradise, NV	$138.0	$331.0	$449.6
Lexington-Fayette, KY	143.2	201.2	261.3
Lincoln, NE	133.6	219.8	292.7
Little Rock-North Little Rock-Conway, AR	132.5	166.9	212.6
Los Angeles-Long Beach-Glendale, CA	323.3	673.1	789.4
Louisville/Jefferson County, KY-IN	134.6	212.1	270.9
Madison, WI	217.7	326.4	429.2
Manchester-Nashua, NH	232.0	357.8	489.5
Memphis, TN-MS-AR	120.2	221.2	287.9
Miami-Fort Lauderdale-West Palm Beach, FL	201.9	398.0	605.0
Milwaukee-Waukesha-West Allis, WI	205.9	291.3	387.4
Minneapolis-St. Paul-Bloomington, MN-WI	170.6	315.2	386.7
Mobile, AL	121.0	167.1	228.7
Montgomery, AL	129.0	171.0	214.2
Myrtle Beach-Conway-North Myrtle Beach, SC-NC	NA	250.2	368.3
Nashville-Davidson--Murfreesboro--Franklin, TN	153.8	298.9	401.3
New Haven-Milford, CT	231.0	265.9	365.8
New Orleans-Metairie, LA	159.7	240.5	287.1
New York-Newark-Jersey City, NY-NJ-PA	393.7	469.1	629.0
North Port-Sarasota-Bradenton, FL	164.6	334.9	525.0
Oklahoma City, OK	145.7	174.9	247.6
Omaha-Council Bluffs, NE-IA	137.3	220.6	297.5
Orlando-Kissimmee-Sanford, FL	134.7	301.6	435.0
Palm Bay-Melbourne-Titusville, FL	103.0	260.4	360.0
Pensacola-Ferry Pass-Brent, FL	141.0	240.0	330.0
Peoria, IL	116.9	128.1	156.6
Philadelphia-Camden-Wilmington, PA-NJ-DE-MD	214.9	272.9	352.9
Phoenix-Mesa-Scottsdale, AZ	139.2	333.0	464.2
Pittsburgh, PA	NA	182.3	225.9
Portland-South Portland, ME	NA	356.2	538.7
Portland-Vancouver-Hillsboro, OR-WA	237.3	451.0	599.4
Providence-Warwick, RI-MA	228.5	347.3	462.3
Raleigh, NC	190.4	325.2	471.6
Reading, PA	153.3	190.8	267.5
Reno, NV	179.5	440.8	585.8
Richmond, VA	NA	303.4	395.0
Riverside-San Bernardino-Ontario, CA	179.3	422.6	570.0
Rochester, NY	118.9	170.4	240.6
Rockford, IL	106.9	141.3	176.3
Sacramento--Roseville--Arden-Arcade, CA	184.2	421.0	530.0
St. Louis, MO-IL	131.1	205.8	266.2
Salem, OR	173.5	353.6	451.0
Salt Lake City, UT	206.5	391.0	546.9
San Antonio-New Braunfels, TX	151.0	254.3	334.1
San Diego-Carlsbad, CA	385.7	710.0	942.4
San Francisco-Oakland-Hayward, CA	525.6	1,100.0	1,335.0
San Jose-Sunnyvale-Santa Clara, CA	595.0	1,385.0	1,800.0
Seattle-Tacoma-Bellevue, WA	295.7	596.9	793.3
Shreveport-Bossier City, LA	156.6	179.5	224.8
Spokane-Spokane Valley, WA	172.2	307.4	424.4
Springfield, IL	124.0	148.0	162.6
Springfield, MA	190.0	249.0	336.0
Springfield, MO	109.1	172.1	247.0
Syracuse, NY	125.1	161.4	211.6
Tallahassee, FL	152.8	248.0	332.0
Tampa-St. Petersburg-Clearwater, FL	134.2	272.0	409.9
Toledo, OH	81.5	145.2	177.2
Trenton, NJ	250.7	300.0	409.4
Tucson, AZ	156.6	265.1	383.3
Tulsa, OK	132.3	195.9	262.0
Virginia Beach-Norfolk-Newport News, VA-NC	205.0	275.0	339.7
Washington-Arlington-Alexandria, DC-VA-MD-WV	325.3	475.4	629.0
Wichita, KS	118.7	175.0	220.7
Winston-Salem, NC	134.7	202.4	292.2
Worcester, MA-CT	223.3	325.2	452.0
York-Hanover, PA	158.6	199.3	265.8
Youngstown-Warren-Boardman, OH-PA	67.2	119.0	157.3

NA = Not available. (1) Preliminary figures for second quarter, 2023.

Characteristics of American Housing Units, 2011-21
Source: *American Housing Survey, 2011-21*, U.S. Census Bureau, U.S. Dept. of Commerce

Characteristic	2011	2015	2019	2021
Total housing units ..	114,833	118,290	124,135	128,504
Percentage of all homes				
Units in structure				
1, detached	64.3%	63.1%	63.9%	63.6%
1, attached	5.8	7.3	5.2	6.3
2-4	7.8	7.5	7.3	6.6
5-9	4.8	4.4	4.8	4.3
10-19	4.4	4.0	4.2	5.4
20-49	3.2	3.3	3.8	3.5
50 or more	3.6	4.5	5.2	4.9
Manufactured/mobile home or trailer......	6.1	5.8	5.4	5.2
Condominiums	6.4	5.2	6.0	6.0
Year built				
2020-21............	NA	NA	NA	0.8
2015-19............	NA	NA	2.8	4.6
2010-14............	NA	3.2	4.4	3.9
2005-09............	6.1	6.5	6.4	6.0
2000-04............	7.1	7.4	7.6	8.0
1995-99............	6.9	7.1	7.6	7.1
1990-94............	5.3	6.1	5.3	5.3
1985-89............	6.8	6.8	7.2	6.8
1980-84............	5.8	7.1	6.1	6.3
1970-79............	18.7	14.8	14.5	14.4
1960-69............	11.8	11.0	10.6	10.3
1950-59............	10.3	10.9	10.3	9.6
1940-49............	5.8	5.0	4.5	4.5
1930-39............	4.2	3.2	2.8	2.5
1920-29............	4.0	3.9	3.8	3.8
1919 or earlier......	6.7	6.9	6.2	6.0
Median year built ...	1974	1976	1978	1979
Lot size (single-family homes only)				
Less than 1/8 acre ..	15.6	15.8	10.1	14.4
1/8-1/4 acre........	25.8	33.2	23.8	33.5
1/4-1/2 acre........	18.8	20.2	14.0	19.5
1/2-1 acre	12.0	9.1	6.9	9.3
1-5 acres	20.0	14.7	11.3	15.1
5-10 acres	3.2	2.9	2.4	3.2
10+ acres	4.7	4.3	3.7	4.9
Square footage of unit				
Less than 500	2.7	1.9	2.4	2.3
500-749...........	6.7	5.4	6.5	6.4
750-999...........	11.1	9.6	11.8	11.8

Characteristic	2011	2015	2019	2021
1,000-1,499.......	23.0%	19.7%	23.6%	23.6%
1,500-1,999.......	18.6	16.6	18.5	18.6
2,000-2,499.......	12.4	11.0	12.3	12.3
2,500-2,999.......	6.4	5.7	6.6	6.5
3,000-3,999.......	6.1	5.6	6.2	6.2
4,000 or more	3.9	2.8	3.2	3.1
Number of bedrooms				
None	0.8	0.8	0.7	0.8
1	10.4	10.9	11.1	10.9
2	24.9	25.3	24.5	24.5
3	42.4	40.7	39.9	40.1
4 or more	21.4	22.3	23.8	23.7
Number of complete bathrooms				
1	34.2	33.4	31.6	31.0
1-1/2	13.2	12.0	11.4	11.0
2	52.2[1]	30.3	31.0	31.5
2-1/2	NA	13.2	13.5	13.6
3 or more	NA	11.0	12.4	13.0
Mortgage characteristics				
None, owned free and clear	34.0	40.8	26.6	41.9
One regular mortgage only	56.6	50.9	33.2	51.6
Two or more regular mortgages	8.8	2.8	1.2	1.3
Median outstanding loan amount......	$120,000	$120,000	$136,500	$150,000
Equipment				
Washing machine ...	83.2	82.5	85.8	85.9
Clothes dryer......	81.0	80.9	84.5	84.8
Dishwasher........	67.0	68.2	73.9	74.6
Central air conditioning	65.7	67.6	71.4	72.4
Main heating fuel[2]				
Piped gas	50.6	46.6	45.1	45.1
Electricity	35.0	41.1	43.2	44.0
Fuel oil............	7.0	5.2	4.6	4.5
Bottled gas	4.8	4.0	4.3	4.3

NA = Not applicable/not available. (1) Figure is for 2 or more bathrooms. (2) Not all heating fuels are shown here.

Fair Market Rents for Select Metropolitan Areas, 2024
Source: *Fair Market Rents FY 2024*, U.S. Dept. of Housing and Urban Development (HUD)

Metropolitan area	0	1	2	3	4
Atlanta, GA	$1,599	$1,643	$1,844	$2,230	$2,707
Austin, TX	1,519	1,635	1,924	2,470	2,840
Baltimore, MD.......	1,379	1,582	1,943	2,519	2,849
Birmingham, AL	983	1,109	1,245	1,570	1,752
Boston, MA..........	2,212	2,377	2,827	3,418	3,765
Buffalo, NY	951	992	1,163	1,424	1,604
Charlotte, NC	1,347	1,384	1,554	1,936	2,481
Chicago, IL	1,399	1,507	1,714	2,182	2,583
Cincinnati, OH	810	919	1,195	1,588	1,766
Cleveland, OH	811	913	1,108	1,434	1,527
Columbus, OH	970	1,065	1,302	1,574	1,745
Dallas, TX..........	1,426	1,500	1,758	2,212	2,847
Denver, CO..........	1,658	1,835	2,201	2,874	3,225
Detroit, MI..........	920	1,019	1,291	1,595	1,719
Hartford, CT	1,121	1,319	1,654	2,000	2,425
Honolulu, HI	1,573	1,720	2,252	3,174	3,822
Houston, TX	1,073	1,135	1,357	1,792	2,303
Indianapolis, IN.....	982	1,145	1,349	1,758	2,126
Jacksonville, FL	1,240	1,354	1,604	2,027	2,579
Kansas City, MO.....	985	1,098	1,258	1,645	1,931
Las Vegas, NV	1,214	1,377	1,643	2,315	2,731
Los Angeles, CA......	1,777	2,006	2,544	3,263	3,600
Louisville, KY	976	1,077	1,301	1,701	1,955
Memphis, TN	1,031	1,146	1,298	1,711	1,995
Miami, FL	1,683	1,884	2,324	3,027	3,589
Milwaukee, WI.	$845	$979	$1,170	$1,460	$1,592
Minneapolis, MN......	1,174	1,327	1,622	2,188	2,478
Nashville, TN	1,404	1,442	1,619	2,035	2,482
New Orleans, LA	986	1,149	1,362	1,750	2,039
New York, NY	2,386	2,451	2,752	3,434	3,700
Oklahoma City, OK....	824	884	1,091	1,454	1,605
Orlando, FL..........	1,558	1,638	1,857	2,362	2,849
Philadelphia, PA	1,303	1,451	1,737	2,100	2,422
Phoenix, AZ	1,460	1,599	1,877	2,541	2,890
Pittsburgh, PA	917	965	1,161	1,474	1,605
Portland, OR........	1,650	1,776	2,024	2,809	3,254
Providence, RI	1,289	1,398	1,693	2,047	2,536
Richmond, VA.......	1,328	1,365	1,532	1,959	2,393
Riverside, CA	1,517	1,611	2,010	2,707	3,304
Sacramento, CA	1,543	1,666	2,072	2,884	3,321
St. Louis, MO	928	972	1,209	1,565	1,818
Salt Lake City, UT....	1,121	1,338	1,606	2,168	2,452
San Antonio, TX	1,067	1,197	1,458	1,846	2,206
San Diego, CA	2,062	2,248	2,833	3,819	4,638
San Francisco, CA ...	2,292	2,818	3,359	4,112	4,473
San Jose, CA	2,383	2,694	3,132	4,011	4,425
San Juan, PR	556	583	668	882	1,056
Seattle, WA	2,211	2,269	2,645	3,510	4,080
Tampa, FL..........	1,449	1,562	1,851	2,367	2,888
Washington, DC	1,772	1,803	2,045	2,544	3,015

Number of bedrooms column headers: 0, 1, 2, 3, 4 for both sides.

Note: Figures are projections made in the previous fiscal year. Metropolitan areas include adjacent cities not shown here. Fair market rents are primarily used by HUD to determine payment standard amounts for the Housing Choice Voucher program.

Rental Vacancy Rates in U.S. Metropolitan Areas, 1990-2022
Source: *Housing Vacancies and Homeownership, 2023*, U.S. Census Bureau, U.S. Dept. of Commerce

MSA	1990	2000	2010	2020	2022	MSA	1990	2000	2010	2020	2022
Akron, OH	NA	8.1%	12.5%	6.1%	4.2%	Milwaukee, WI	11.3%	3.5%	7.4%	4.6%	5.9%
Albany, NY	7.2%	9.3	8.0	9.5	9.2	Minneapolis-St. Paul, MN-WI	6.5	2.7	8.2	4.0	6.7
Albuquerque, NM	11.6	9.3	5.0	5.4	5.5	Nashville, TN	13.8	15.5	11.1	7.3	6.4
Allentown, PA-NJ	NA	4.6	9.1	3.9	6.1	New Haven, CT	4.7	4.0	15.2	7.8	2.6
Atlanta, GA	5.2	5.4	13.8	6.4	6.7	New Orleans, LA	4.1	6.2	6.6	6.1	6.6
Austin, TX	6.6	1.9	11.8	6.6	5.6	New York, NY-NJ-PA	9.2	6.8	9.6	4.5	3.5
Baltimore, MD	5.2	23.3	6.3	7.0	5.3	Oklahoma City, OK	22.6	16.0	19.0	6.4	10.6
Baton Rouge, LA	6.0	2.7	11.8	7.4	5.1	Omaha, NE-IA	NA	7.6	6.4	6.5	4.2
Birmingham, AL	3.4	17.5	9.4	18.5	12.7	Orlando, FL	4.8	2.2	11.6	8.6	6.5
Boston, MA-NH	5.9	8.8	8.8	4.7	2.5	Philadelphia, PA-NJ-DE-MD	10.1	7.4	16.3	5.4	4.2
Bridgeport, CT	6.6	6.9	6.2	3.4	2.4	Phoenix, AZ	9.6	8.3	7.8	4.9	6.4
Buffalo, NY	6.3	10.6	8.7	5.0	7.1	Pittsburgh, PA	10.3	9.6	4.2	9.3	8.3
Charleston, SC	5.0	10.5	11.2	27.7	8.8	Portland, OR-WA	8.3	10.3	9.5	4.3	4.0
Charlotte, NC-SC	12.3	9.2	12.1	5.6	5.9	Providence, RI-MA	3.3	6.4	7.5	3.5	4.5
Chicago, IL-IN-WI	5.0	8.2	12.0	7.4	6.1	Raleigh, NC	9.4	4.8	11.4	2.3	7.1
Cincinnati, OH-KY-IN	8.9	4.6	11.3	7.9	6.3	Richmond, VA	NA	13.8	13.5	2.7	3.0
Cleveland, OH	7.6	8.7	9.4	5.5	3.2	Riverside-San Bernardino, CA	5.3	6.1	12.3	4.4	3.5
Columbia, SC	NA	8.7	8.0	4.5	6.1	Rochester, NY	5.6	11.6	6.3	2.0	5.0
Columbus, OH	8.0	6.2	13.5	5.9	3.8	Sacramento, CA	7.4	5.6	8.4	4.2	2.3
Dallas-Ft. Worth, TX	8.9	6.9	18.6	7.2	6.8	St. Louis, MO-IL	7.8	6.5	11.2	5.3	6.8
Dayton, OH	NA	6.9	8.2	4.1	5.6	Salt Lake City, UT	11.7	7.5	6.0	6.2	4.6
Denver, CO	7.9	8.9	16.4	4.8	5.1	San Antonio, TX	9.9	7.5	14.0	7.2	8.1
Detroit, MI	NA	7.6	5.8	5.7	4.5	San Diego-Carlsbad, CA	6.9	4.0	7.8	3.9	3.6
Fort Myers, FL	7.8	8.4	11.1	15.5	11.6	San Francisco, CA	4.2	3.1	6.0	5.3	5.4
Fresno, CA	11.2	10.9	10.1	0.8	2.5	San Jose, CA	4.6	3.0	8.2	4.4	4.7
Grand Rapids, MI	3.8	4.9	6.9	4.6	2.4	Sarasota, FL	6.3	4.2	10.1	10.3	5.7
Greensboro NC	9.6	13.4	12.8	7.2	10.2	Seattle, WA	NA	3.0	7.4	3.6	4.9
Hartford, CT	6.1	12.3	11.6	8.1	4.4	Syracuse, NY	3.1	5.4	7.3	11.8	7.4
Honolulu, HI	NA	10.8	15.9	5.5	5.7	Tampa, FL	10.7	16.4	10.6	8.9	8.1
Houston, TX	9.5	9.9	7.2	9.7	8.9	Toledo, OH	NA	10.7	12.6	6.2	9.2
Indianapolis, IN	9.9	8.8	16.2	10.4	11.0	Tucson, AZ	10.4	9.5	14.4	8.6	8.0
Jacksonville, FL	NA	10.7	14.1	7.5	6.2	Tulsa, OK	NA	9.1	11.1	8.6	5.6
Kansas City, MO-KS	6.2	4.7	13.9	9.4	7.8	Virginia Beach, VA-NC	NA	3.0	8.8	5.5	6.3
Knoxville, TN	7.5	7.2	14.0	4.5	6.7	Washington, DC-VA-MD-WV	6.7	7.0	8.8	5.5	5.3
Las Vegas, NV	10.2	7.1	13.8	5.0	5.7	Worcester, MA	NA	22.9	7.5	1.3	1.6
Little Rock, AR	6.3	8.8	6.7	9.1	11.4						
Los Angeles, CA	5.2	4.0	9.6	3.6	4.1						
Louisville, KY-IN	3.6	5.9	18.5	6.4	5.3						
Memphis, TN-AR-MS	6.5	3.9	10.1	6.6	6.4						
Miami, FL	8.3	4.0	7.6	5.4	6.3						

MSA = Metropolitan statistical area.

Affordable Housing Shortages in U.S. Metropolitan Areas, 2022
Source: *The Gap: A Shortage of Affordable Homes, 2023*, National Low Income Housing Coalition

Affordable housing is in short supply in every state in the U.S. and in all of the 50 largest metropolitan areas. The table below shows the number of affordable and available homes per 100 households at two income levels: very low income, defined as earning 20-50% of the area median income, and extremely low income, those households earning 20% or less of the area median income.

MSA	Very low income AAH per 100 households	Deficit of AAH	Extremely low income AAH per 100 households	Deficit of AAH	MSA	Very low income AAH per 100 households	Deficit of AAH	Extremely low income AAH per 100 households	Deficit of AAH
Atlanta, GA	44	157,482	25	121,163	New Orleans, LA	41	47,431	27	40,087
Austin, TX	42	87,953	16	70,364	New York, NY	43	824,689	31	653,160
Baltimore, MD	56	70,480	31	67,217	Oklahoma City, OK	68	26,944	30	35,052
Boston, MA	57	139,874	44	122,820	Orlando, FL	21	92,108	15	55,860
Buffalo, NY	76	18,941	34	33,942	Philadelphia, PA	58	153,794	29	162,931
Charlotte, NC	64	44,000	32	49,395	Phoenix, AZ	35	132,321	19	87,234
Chicago, IL	58	227,215	28	234,668	Pittsburgh, PA	80	28,433	48	44,754
Cincinnati, OH	82	25,736	38	54,415	Portland, OR	38	89,475	22	68,217
Cleveland, OH	75	34,526	38	56,663	Providence, RI	70	37,010	48	41,828
Columbus, OH	68	39,631	30	51,479	Raleigh, NC	70	23,567	29	34,025
Dallas, TX	37	256,485	16	182,184	Richmond, VA	59	31,809	27	33,236
Denver, CO	38	100,832	23	71,515	Riverside, CA	33	113,707	20	79,084
Detroit, MI	60	88,746	31	95,995	Rochester, NY	68	21,330	27	31,215
Hartford, CT	64	27,813	35	31,719	Sacramento, CA	40	80,954	27	62,300
Houston, TX	40	231,780	19	174,827	St. Louis, MO	81	29,132	37	57,338
Indianapolis, IN	71	29,197	32	39,004	San Antonio, TX	41	77,618	33	51,831
Jacksonville, FL	42	43,235	21	35,956	San Diego, CA	24	132,524	19	82,893
Kansas City, MO	74	33,169	39	42,772	San Francisco, CA	46	155,017	34	124,089
Las Vegas, NV	24	98,486	14	67,338	San Jose, CA	46	54,630	30	44,093
Los Angeles, CA	24	627,606	20	392,156	Seattle, WA	41	135,833	25	102,187
Louisville, KY	63	26,821	35	27,798	Tampa, FL	36	97,846	21	71,786
Memphis, TN	46	39,452	28	34,951	Tucson, AZ	50	29,703	24	26,085
Miami, FL	22	236,232	22	143,528	Virginia Beach, VA	43	57,328	25	43,311
Milwaukee, WI	78	23,671	28	46,420	Washington, DC	49	167,417	27	148,945
Minneapolis, MN	67	63,113	36	71,491	**United States**	**55**	**8,009,313**	**33**	**7,337,216**
Nashville, TN	56	46,461	33	40,389					

MSA = Metropolitan statistical area. AAH = Affordable and available homes.

TRADE

U.S. Trade in Goods With Selected Countries and Major Areas, 2022

Source: U.S. Census Bureau and U.S. Bureau of Economic Analysis, U.S. Dept. of Commerce; *World Development Indicators 2022*, The World Bank

Weighted mean tariff rate is the average of tariffs applied to all products weighted by the product's share of the country's imports. A low tariff on a heavily imported product, therefore, has more impact on the weighted mean tariff rate than a high tariff on a product that is rarely imported. Weighted mean tariff rates in 2021 were generally based on 2020 trade data.

(trade in millions of dollars; top 25 countries as ranked by amount of total trade in goods with U.S.)

Rank	Country	Total trade with U.S.	U.S. exports to (rank)	U.S. imports from (rank)	U.S. trade balance with (rank[1])	Weighted mean tariff rate, 2020
1.	Canada	$793,014	$356,453 (1)	$436,562 (3)	−$80,109 (4)	1.5%
2.	Mexico	779,084	324,310 (2)	454,775 (2)	−130,465 (2)	1.2
3.	China[2]	690,319	154,012 (3)	536,307 (1)	−382,295 (1)	2.5
4.	Japan	228,244	80,180 (4)	148,064 (4)	−67,884 (6)	2.2
5.	Germany	219,184	72,553 (7)	146,630 (5)	−74,077 (5)	1.5
6.	South Korea	187,510	72,116 (8)	115,394 (7)	−43,278 (9)	5.5
7.	United Kingdom	140,160	76,208 (5)	63,952 (12)	12,256 (227)	1.3
8.	Vietnam	138,837	11,356 (34)	127,481 (6)	−116,125 (3)	NA
9.	Taiwan	135,967	44,242 (13)	91,725 (8)	−47,483 (8)	6.2
10.	India	132,697	47,160 (10)	85,537 (9)	−38,377 (12)	1.3
11.	Netherlands	107,756	73,207 (6)	34,549 (18)	38,659 (233)	1.5
12.	France	103,328	46,025 (12)	57,304 (15)	−11,279 (20)	1.5
13.	Ireland	98,580	16,011 (24)	82,569 (10)	−66,558 (7)	1.4
14.	Italy	96,788	27,713 (17)	69,075 (11)	−41,362 (11)	1.5
15.	Switzerland	96,131	36,727 (14)	59,404 (13)	−22,677 (15)	1.5
16.	Brazil	92,756	53,841 (9)	38,915 (17)	14,926 (231)	8.4
17.	Singapore	77,783	46,177 (11)	31,606 (20)	14,571 (230)	3.6
18.	Thailand	74,473	15,818 (25)	58,654 (14)	−42,836 (10)	0.1
19.	Malaysia	72,396	18,195 (23)	54,201 (16)	−36,006 (13)	3.5
20.	Belgium	62,428	35,810 (15)	26,618 (21)	9,192 (225)	1.5
21.	Spain	49,687	26,695 (18)	22,992 (23)	3,704 (218)	0.7
22.	Australia	46,722	30,552 (16)	16,171 (29)	14,381 (229)	2.0
23.	Indonesia	44,346	9,802 (36)	34,545 (19)	−24,743 (14)	4.1
24.	Colombia	39,304	20,819 (22)	18,485 (26)	2,335 (216)	1.5
25.	Chile	37,825	22,257 (20)	15,568 (31)	6,689 (223)	0.0

Major area/group

North America	$1,572,098	$680,762	$891,336	−$210,574
Europe	1,216,256	491,578	724,679	−233,101
Euro Area	806,954	316,981	489,973	−172,992
EU	904,057	350,791	553,266	−202,475
Africa	72,492	30,677	41,816	−11,139
OECD	3,288,026	1,381,641	1,906,385	−524,744
Pacific Rim Countries	1,549,625	495,077	1,054,547	−559,470
Asia-Near East	134,110	59,627	74,482	−14,855
Asia-South	160,149	53,897	106,252	−52,354
ASEAN	447,688	111,409	336,280	−224,871
APEC	3,410,783	1,240,296	2,170,487	−930,191
South/Central America	373,934	224,723	149,211	75,512
Twenty Latin Amer. Reps.	1,118,585	525,444	593,141	−67,696
Latin Amer. Free Trade Association	1,019,337	463,421	555,917	−92,496
CAFTA-DR	83,957	48,308	35,650	12,658
Central Amer. Common Market	63,027	34,285	28,742	5,543
NATO Allies	1,723,537	770,866	952,672	−181,806
WORLD TOTAL	5,307,687	2,065,157	3,242,530	−1,177,373

NA = Not available. **Note:** Figures shown are on Census Bureau basis and are not seasonally adjusted. Figures may not equal totals due to rounding. Country grouping data reflect groups at the time of reporting. Rankings include territories as well as nations. (1) Rank by size of U.S. trade deficit. (2) Not incl. Hong Kong and Macau.

Countries With Highest and Lowest Mean Tariff Rates, 2020

Source: *World Development Indicators 2022*, The World Bank

	HIGHEST TARIFF RATES	Weighted mean tariff rate[1]		LOWEST TARIFF RATES	Weighted mean tariff rate[1]
Rank	Country		Rank	Country	
1.	Bermuda	24.07%	1.	Hong Kong	0.00%
2.	Belize	18.69		Macau	0.00
3.	The Gambia	17.82		Sudan	0.00
4.	Djibouti	17.56[2]	4.	Brunei	0.02
5.	The Bahamas	17.05[3]	5.	Singapore	0.05
6.	Cayman Islands	16.72[4]	6.	Georgia	0.21
7.	Fiji	16.62	7.	Chile	0.43
8.	Central African Republic	16.44[5]	8.	Peru	0.66
9.	Chad	16.36[4]	9.	Australia	0.71
10.	Equatorial Guinea	15.63[6]	10.	Botswana	0.80
11.	Cameroon	15.46[7]	11.	New Zealand	0.85
12.	Gabon	14.50[7]	12.	Mauritius	0.92
13.	Nauru	14.39	13.	Laos	0.97
14.	Venezuela	14.06	14.	Albania	1.10
15.	Sierra Leone	14.05	15.	Mexico	1.21[3]
16.	Solomon Islands	13.62	16.	Moldova	1.26
17.	Antigua and Barbuda	13.07		Namibia	1.26
18.	Vanuatu	12.66	18.	United Kingdom	1.28
19.	Nigeria	12.37	19.	Vietnam	1.34
20.	Guinea	12.23	20.	Switzerland	1.36

(1) 2020 unless otherwise noted. (2) 2014. (3) 2018. (4) 2016. (5) 2017. (6) 2007. (7) 2019.

U.S. Exports and Imports by Principal Commodities, 2022

Source: U.S. Census Bureau and U.S. Bureau of Economic Analysis, U.S. Dept. of Commerce

(in millions of dollars)

Item[1]	Exports	Imports	Item	Exports	Imports
Total[1]	**$2,065,157**	**$3,242,530**	Fertilizers	$6,543	$12,442
Manufactured goods	**1,293,928**	**2,793,141**	Plastics in primary forms	46,890	23,991
Agricultural commodities	**195,856**	**199,323**	Plastics in nonprimary forms	15,892	16,626
			Chemical materials and products	45,471	33,869
Food and live animals	**131,991**	**160,712**	**Manufactured goods by material**	**119,685**	**366,531**
Live animals other than fish	1,135	3,635	Leather and leather manufactures	707	1,570
Meat and preparations	25,435	14,303	Rubber manufactures	9,736	28,979
Dairy products and birds	8,165	3,214	Cork and wood manufactures	2,532	18,861
Fish and preparations	4,982	29,586	Paper and paperboard	16,565	21,590
Cereals and preparations	36,090	16,276	Textile yarn, fabrics	12,271	36,293
Vegetables and fruits	22,741	48,849	Nonmetallic mineral manufactures	13,479	55,221
Sugar, preparations, and honey	2,384	6,917	Iron and steel	16,767	54,825
Coffee, tea, cocoa, and spices	3,301	19,058	Nonferrous metals	18,779	70,640
Feeding stuff for animals	16,690	5,440	Manufactures of metals	28,849	78,554
Miscellaneous edible products	11,068	13,433	**Machinery and transport**		
Beverages and tobacco	**6,580**	**33,811**	**equipment**	**502,161**	**1,272,481**
Beverages	5,497	31,437	Power-generating machinery	37,380	77,946
Tobacco and manufactures	1,083	2,374	Specialized industrial machinery	54,581	75,889
Crude materials except fuels	**108,267**	**51,012**	Metalworking machinery	4,885	11,992
Hides, skins, and furskins (raw)	1,112	36	General industrial machinery	65,620	134,649
Oil seeds and oleaginous fruits	36,355	1,715	Office machinery	19,299	172,861
Crude rubber	2,899	4,019	Telecommunications equipment	18,650	187,169
Cork and wood	7,585	15,021	Electrical machinery	86,090	265,523
Pulp and waste paper	10,627	4,976	Road vehicles	122,751	314,010
Textile fibers including waste	11,051	1,571	Transport equipment	92,907	32,442
Crude fertilizers	3,327	3,724	**Miscellaneous manufactured**		
Metalliferous ores and metal scrap	31,833	11,900	**articles**	**131,884**	**530,413**
Crude animal and vegetable materials	3,477	8,050	Prefabricated buildings	2,416	15,352
Mineral fuels and lubricants	**373,924**	**309,198**	Furniture	5,519	63,886
Coal, coke, and briquettes	18,571	1,281	Travel goods	700	13,641
Petroleum products and preparations	258,342	283,306	Apparel and clothing accessories	3,740	110,382
Gas, natural and manufactured	96,280	20,184	Footwear	899	35,894
Electric current	732	4,428	Scientific and controlling equipment	54,891	76,962
Animal and vegetable oils	**3,371**	**13,802**	Photographic equipment	6,313	18,295
Animal oil and fat	787	1,286	Miscellaneous manufactured		
Fixed vegetable fats and oil, crude	1,929	11,632	articles	57,405	196,002
Animal or vegetable fats, processed	655	884	**Miscellaneous commodities**	**87,691**	**131,356**
Chemicals and related products	**279,295**	**373,214**	Special transactions	8,624	94,461
Organic chemicals	51,081	66,454	Coin, including gold coin	236	3,042
Inorganic chemicals	15,946	17,686	Coin, other than gold	90	2,161
Dyeing, tanning, and coloring			Gold, nonmonetary	27,850	10,022
materials	8,345	5,662	Low value estimate	50,890	21,670
Medicinal and pharmaceutical			**Re-exports**	**320,306**	**NA**
products	70,946	174,124	Agricultural commodities	6,410	NA
Essential oil and retinoids	18,180	22,359	Manufactured goods	305,354	NA

NA = Not applicable. **Note:** Numbers may not add up to totals due to rounding. (1) Total on Census Bureau basis; includes re-exports.

Trends in U.S. Foreign Trade, 1790–2022

Source: U.S. Census Bureau and U.S. Bureau of Economic Analysis, U.S. Dept. of Commerce

In 1790, U.S. exports and imports combined came to $43 mil, and there was a $3 mil trade deficit. The trade balance was positive for much of the 20th century, but the U.S. has had a trade deficit every year starting in 1976.

(in millions of dollars)

Year	Exports	Imports	Trade balance	Year	Exports	Imports	Trade balance	Year	Exports	Imports	Trade balance
1790	$20	$23	–$3	1905	$1,519	$1,118	$401	2002	$986,096	$1,406,762	–$420,665
1800	71	91	–20	1910	1,745	1,557	188	2003	1,028,136	1,524,428	–496,242
1810	67	85	–19	1915	2,769	1,674	1,094	2004	1,168,120	1,778,957	–610,837
1815	53	113	–60	1920	8,228	5,278	2,950	2005	1,291,503	2,008,046	–716,543
1820	70	74	–5	1925	4,910	4,227	683	2006	1,463,992	2,227,524	–763,532
1825	91	90	1	1930	3,843	3,061	782	2007	1,660,813	2,371,812	–710,998
1830	72	63	9	1935	2,283	2,047	235	2008	1,849,585	2,561,937	–712,351
1835	115	137	–22	1940	4,021	2,625	1,396	2009	1,592,791	1,987,563	–394,772
1840	124	98	25	1945	9,806	4,159	5,646	2010	1,872,318	2,375,408	–503,090
1845	106	113	–7	1950	9,997	8,954	1,043	2011	2,143,551	2,698,074	–554,522
1850	144	174	–29	1955	14,298	11,566	2,732	2012	2,247,453	2,773,359	–525,906
1855	219	258	–39	1960	25,939	22,433	3,508	2013	2,313,121	2,759,982	–446,861
1860	334	354	–20	1965	35,285	30,621	4,664	2014	2,392,615	2,876,566	–483,952
1865	166	239	–73	1970	56,640	54,385	2,255	2015	2,280,778	2,771,554	–490,776
1870	393	436	–43	1975	132,585	120,181	12,403	2016	2,240,823	2,720,281	–479,459
1875	513	533	–20	1980	271,835	291,242	–19,407	2017	2,394,476	2,911,415	–516,939
1880	836	668	168	1985	289,071	410,951	–121,879	2018	2,542,462	3,121,057	–578,594
1885	742	578	165	1990	535,234	616,098	–80,865	2019	2,546,276	3,105,670	–559,395
1890	858	789	69	1995	794,387	890,771	–96,384	2020	2,160,147	2,813,028	–652,881
1895	808	732	76	2000	1,082,963	1,452,648	–369,685	2021	2,567,027	3,408,600	–841,573
1900	1,394	850	545	2001	1,015,306	1,375,739	–360,373	2022	3,018,455	3,969,643	–951,188

Note: Figures shown using balance of payments basis.

World Trade Organization (WTO)

The World Trade Organization is an international body that seeks to promote free trade by eliminating barriers to trade. Founded in 1995, the WTO had grown to 164 member countries as of Oct. 2023, with 25 others, including Belarus, Iran, Iraq, and Vatican City, granted observer status. International intergovernmental organizations, such as the International Monetary Fund and the World Bank, have also been granted observer status. With the exception of Vatican City, observers must start accession negotiations within five years of becoming observers.

U.S. Trade in Goods and Services, 2022

Source: U.S. Census Bureau and U.S. Bureau of Economic Analysis, U.S. Dept. of Commerce
(top countries as ranked by amount of total trade with U.S.; in millions of dollars)

Country and category	Food and live animals	Beverages and tobacco	Crude materials, except fuels	Mineral fuels, lubricants	Chemicals	Manu-factured goods	Machinery and transport equip-ment	Misc. manu-factured articles	Commodities and transac-tions[1]	Total[2]
Canada										
U.S. exports to	$27,280	$1,838	$8,676	$34,960	$46,198	$43,035	$140,142	$32,770	$19,140	$352,994
U.S. imports from	33,418	1,347	19,635	164,425	37,346	57,137	87,011	20,003	23,107	448,335
Trade balance	−6,138	491	−10,959	−129,466	8,852	−14,102	53,132	12,767	−3,967	−93,342
Mexico										
U.S. exports to	22,158	324	11,751	55,979	39,935	37,754	121,237	24,799	9,791	324,378
U.S. imports from	32,542	11,717	2,835	26,665	11,100	35,422	279,480	46,128	12,956	459,205
Trade balance	−10,385	−11,393	8,916	29,314	28,835	2,332	−158,243	−21,329	−3,164	−134,827
China										
U.S. exports to	16,667	266	29,476	13,472	27,459	7,076	44,672	13,023	1,689	153,837
U.S. imports from	6,061	68	2,083	247	39,491	66,198	279,078	172,395	10,019	575,710
Trade balance	10,606	198	27,393	13,225	−12,032	−59,122	−234,406	−159,372	−8,330	−421,873
Japan										
U.S. exports to	12,492	300	6,201	13,393	16,164	3,908	16,938	9,436	1,455	80,317
U.S. imports from	1,304	338	957	1,239	17,072	11,135	106,290	12,333	3,700	154,446
Trade balance	11,188	−37	5,243	12,154	−908	−7,227	−89,353	−2,897	−2,245	−74,129
Germany										
U.S. exports to	1,112	151	4,586	4,798	13,567	5,333	32,173	8,255	2,892	72,922
U.S. imports from	2,231	360	1,875	636	32,227	15,679	74,785	14,472	8,169	150,462
Trade balance	−1,118	−209	2,711	4,162	−18,660	−10,346	−42,612	−6,217	−5,278	−77,539
South Korea										
U.S. exports to	8,181	182	3,042	19,833	9,717	2,213	21,045	6,010	1,064	71,470
U.S. imports from	1,324	217	663	5,676	13,148	14,979	71,287	11,909	1,660	120,872
Trade balance	6,857	−35	2,379	14,156	−3,431	−12,766	−50,242	−5,899	−596	−49,402
Vietnam										
U.S. exports to	1,739	109	2,926	251	1,958	568	3,140	612	94	11,398
U.S. imports from	4,990	67	388	525	771	10,384	61,246	57,111	897	135,877
Trade balance	−3,251	42	2,537	250	1,187	−9,816	−58,106	−56,499	−803	−124,478

Note: Figures for exports are "free alongside ship" values; figures for imports are "cost, insurance, and freight" values. Neither is directly comparable with the Census Bureau basis shown in other tables in this section. Trade balance is with U.S.; subtracting imports from exports may not equal trade balance due to rounding. Total includes categories not shown here. (1) Not classified elsewhere. (2) Total includes animal and vegetable oils, fats, and waxes, not shown separately.

Exchange Rates for Foreign Currencies, 1970-2022

Source: Federal Reserve Board
One U.S. dollar was worth the following amounts in each country's national currency; exchange rates are annual averages.

Country (currency)	1970	1980	1990	2000	2010	2015	2018	2020	2021	2022
Australia (dollar)	0.90	0.88	1.28	1.72	1.09	1.33	1.34	1.45	1.33	1.44
Austria (schilling; euro)	25.88	12.95	11.37	1.08	0.75	0.90	0.85	0.88	0.85	0.95
Belgium (franc; euro)	49.68	29.24	33.42	1.08	0.75	0.90	0.85	0.88	0.85	0.95
Brazil (real)	NA	NA	NA	1.83	1.76	3.34	3.65	5.16	5.40	5.16
Canada (dollar)	1.01	1.17	1.17	1.49	1.03	1.28	1.30	1.34	1.25	1.30
China (yuan)	NA	NA	4.79	8.28	6.77	6.28	6.61	6.90	6.45	6.73
Denmark (krone)	7.49	5.63	6.19	8.10	5.63	6.73	6.31	6.54	6.29	7.08
France (franc; euro)	5.52	4.22	5.45	1.08	0.75	0.90	0.85	0.88	0.85	0.95
Germany[1] (mark; euro)	3.65	1.82	1.62	1.08	0.75	0.90	0.85	0.88	0.85	0.95
Greece (drachma; euro)	30.00	42.62	158.51	365.92	0.75	0.90	0.85	0.88	0.85	0.95
Hong Kong (dollar)	NA	NA	7.79	7.79	7.77	7.75	7.84	7.76	7.77	7.83
India (rupee)	7.58	7.89	17.50	45.00	45.65	64.11	68.37	74.14	73.94	78.58
Ireland (pound; euro)	2.40	2.06	1.66	1.08	0.75	0.90	0.85	0.88	0.85	0.95
Italy (lira; euro)	623.00	856.00	1,198.00	1.08	0.75	0.90	0.85	0.88	0.85	0.95
Japan (yen)	357.60	226.63	144.79	107.80	87.78	121.05	110.40	106.78	109.84	131.46
Malaysia (ringgit)	3.09	2.18	2.71	3.80	3.22	3.90	4.03	4.20	4.14	4.40
Mexico (peso[2])	NA	NA	NA	9.46	12.62	15.87	19.22	21.55	20.28	20.12
Netherlands (guilder; euro)	3.60	2.0	1.82	1.08	0.75	0.90	0.85	0.88	0.85	0.95
Norway (krone)	7.14	4.94	6.26	8.81	6.05	8.07	8.13	9.43	8.60	9.61
Portugal (escudo; euro)	28.75	50.08	142.55	1.08	0.75	0.90	0.85	0.88	0.85	0.95
Singapore (dollar)	3.08	2.14	1.81	1.73	1.36	1.37	1.35	1.38	1.34	1.38
South Korea (won)	310.57	607.43	707.76	1,130.90	1,155.74	1,130.96	1,099.29	1,180.56	1,144.89	1,291.78
Spain (peseta; euro)	69.72	71.76	101.93	1.08	0.75	0.90	0.85	0.88	0.85	0.95
Sweden (krona)	5.17	4.23	5.92	9.17	7.20	8.44	8.69	9.22	8.58	10.12
Switzerland (franc)	4.32	1.68	1.39	1.69	1.04	0.96	0.98	0.94	0.91	0.96
Taiwan (dollar)	NA	NA	26.92	31.26	31.50	31.74	30.13	29.46	27.94	29.80
Thailand (baht)	21.00	20.48	25.58	40.21	31.70	34.24	32.30	31.31	32.01	35.05
United Kingdom (pound)	0.42	0.43	0.56	0.66	0.65	0.65	0.75	0.78	0.73	0.81

NA = Not available. **Note:** The euro, the European Union's single currency, replaced the national currencies in the EU nations shown above. Since 1999 (or 2001 in the case of Greece), the euro has been fixed at the following conversion rates: 13.7603 Austrian schillings, 40.3399 Belgian francs, 6.55957 French francs, 1.95583 German marks, 340.750 Greek drachmas, 0.787564 Irish pounds, 1,936.27 Italian lire, 2.20371 Netherlands guilders, 200.482 Portuguese escudos, and 166.386 Spanish pesetas. (1) West Germany before 1991. (2) Mexico re-based its currency in 1993; earlier values are not comparable.

Top U.S. Trading Partners, 1985-2022

Source: U.S. Census Bureau, U.S. Dept. of Commerce

(in millions of dollars; top five countries as ranked by amount of total trade with U.S. in 2022)

Country/category	1985	1990	1995	2000	2005	2010	2015	2020	2021	2022
Canada										
U.S. exports to	$47,251	$83,674	$127,226	$178,941	$211,899	$249,257	$280,855	$256,212	$309,604	$356,453
U.S. imports from	69,006	91,380	144,370	230,838	290,384	277,637	296,305	270,026	357,280	436,562
Trade balance......	–21,755	–7,706	–17,144	–51,897	–78,486	–28,380	–15,450	–13,813	–47,675	–80,109
Mexico										
U.S. exports to	13,635	28,279	46,292	111,349	120,248	163,665	236,460	212,513	277,078	324,310
U.S. imports from	19,132	30,157	62,100	135,926	170,109	229,986	296,433	323,477	382,589	454,775
Trade balance......	–5,497	–1,878	–15,808	–24,577	–49,861	–66,321	–59,973	–110,964	–105,511	–130,465
China										
U.S. exports	3,856	4,806	11,754	16,185	41,192	91,911	115,873	124,582	151,432	154,012
U.S. imports from ...	3,862	15,237	45,543	100,018	243,470	364,953	483,202	432,548	504,286	536,307
Trade balance......	–6	–10,431	–33,790	–83,833	–202,278	–273,042	–367,328	–307,967	–352,854	–382,295
Japan										
U.S. exports to	22,631	48,580	64,343	64,924	54,681	60,472	62,388	64,030	74,736	80,180
U.S. imports from ...	68,783	89,684	123,479	146,479	138,004	120,552	131,446	119,507	134,833	148,064
Trade balance......	–46,152	–41,105	–59,137	–81,555	–83,323	–60,080	–69,058	–55,476	–60,097	–67,884
Germany										
U.S. exports to	9,050	18,760	22,394	29,448	34,184	48,155	49,979	58,002	65,308	72,553
U.S. imports from ...	20,239	28,162	36,844	58,513	84,751	82,450	124,888	114,897	134,847	146,630
Trade balance......	–11,189	–9,402	–14,450	–29,065	–50,567	–34,295	–74,909	–56,895	–69,539	–74,077

Note: Figures shown are on Census Bureau basis.

Busiest U.S. Ports, 2021

Source: U.S. Army Corps of Engineers, Dept. of the Army, U.S. Dept. of Defense

(figures in millions of short tons; ranked by total tonnage handled)

Rank	Port	Domestic	Foreign	Total	Rank	Port	Domestic	Foreign	Total
1.	Houston, TX	75.9	190.7	266.5	26.	Indiana (Southern District), IN	24.2	0.0	24.2
2.	South Louisiana, LA	115.7	109.0	224.7	27.	Pascagoula, MS	9.7	14.0	23.8
3.	Corpus Christi, TX	22.6	141.8	164.4	28.	Everglades, FL	11.6	12.2	23.7
4.	New York, NY-NJ.	40.7	101.6	142.3	29.	Tacoma, WA	4.5	18.9	23.4
5.	Long Beach, CA	14.8	76.7	91.5	30.	Seattle, WA...........	4.6	18.4	22.9
6.	New Orleans, LA	45.3	44.3	89.5	31.	Richmond, CA	4.1	16.8	20.9
7.	Beaumont, TX.	18.2	56.3	74.6	32.	South Jersey, NJ	8.4	11.8	20.2
8.	Baton Rouge, LA	44.5	26.8	71.2	33.	Oakland, CA	0.8	18.1	18.9
9.	Virginia, VA	5.3	59.2	64.5	34.	Kalama, WA	1.5	16.9	18.4
10.	Los Angeles, CA.......	3.1	61.1	64.3	35.	Jacksonville, FL	8.6	8.8	17.4
11.	Plaquemines, LA	28.6	24.1	52.7	36.	Pittsburgh, PA	16.4	0.0	16.4
12.	Mobile, AL.	17.5	32.8	50.3	37.	Two Harbors, MN	11.5	4.3	15.8
13.	Lake Charles, LA	21.9	26.4	48.3	38.	Honolulu, HI	13.4	1.3	14.8
14.	Savannah, GA	0.8	46.8	47.7	39.	Mid-America, IL-IA-MO ...	13.5	0.0	13.5
15.	Freeport, TX	4.8	37.5	42.2	40.	Boston, MA	3.1	10.2	13.3
16.	Port Arthur, TX	17.3	23.0	40.2	41.	Longview, WA	0.9	11.5	12.4
17.	Baltimore, MD.	4.5	33.0	37.4	42.	Cleveland-Cuyahoga, OH	10.3	2.0	12.4
18.	Duluth-Superior, MN-WI ...	25.9	6.5	32.5	43.	Galveston, TX	5.4	6.6	12.0
19.	Philadelphia, PA	10.1	20.6	30.7	44.	Toledo-Lucas County, OH	7.5	4.5	12.0
20.	Indiana (Northern District), IN	29.6	0.7	30.3	45.	New Bourbon, MO	11.6	0.0	11.6
21.	Tampa, FL............	18.6	11.4	30.0	46.	San Juan, PR	5.1	6.1	11.2
22.	Charleston, SC........	1.6	26.8	28.4	47.	Illinois International, IL	7.9	2.4	10.3
23.	Texas City, TX	11.6	16.4	28.0	48.	Vancouver, WA	2.2	7.6	9.8
24.	Valdez, AK	24.0	1.5	25.5	49.	Detroit-Wayne County, MI	7.3	2.4	9.7
25.	Portland, OR.	9.5	14.9	24.5	50.	Anacortes, WA	7.1	2.5	9.6

World's Busiest Ports, 2017-21

Source: Lloyd's List

(ranked by throughput volume in 2021 as measured in thousands of twenty-ft equivalent units (TEUs))

Rank	Port	Volume (TEUs)					Percent change			
		2017	2018	2019	2020	2021	2017-18	2018-19	2019-20	2020-21
1.	Shanghai, China...........	40,233	42,010	43,303	43,503	47,030	4.4%	3.1%	0.5%	8.1%
2.	Singapore...............	33,667	36,599	37,196	36,871	37,470	8.7	1.6	–0.9	1.6
3.	Ningbo-Zhoushan, China....	24,607	26,351	27,530	28,720	31,070	7.1	4.5	4.3	8.2
4.	Shenzhen, China	25,209	25,740	25,770	26,550	28,768	2.1	0.1	3.0	8.4
5.	Guangzhou, China	20,370	21,922	23,236	23,505	24,180	7.6	6.0	1.2	2.9
6.	Qingdao, China.	18,262	19,315	21,010	22,010	23,710	5.8	8.8	4.8	7.7
7.	Busan, South Korea	20,493	21,663	21,992	21,824	22,706	5.7	1.5	–0.8	4.0
8.	Tianjin, China	15,040	15,972	17,264	18,353	20,269	6.2	8.1	6.3	10.4
9.	Hong Kong, China	20,770	19,596	18,361	17,953	17,798	–5.7	–6.3	–2.2	–0.9
10.	Rotterdam, Netherlands ...	13,734	14,513	14,811	14,349	15,300	5.7	2.1	–3.1	6.6
11.	Dubai, United Arab Emirates ..	15,368	14,954	14,111	13,488	13,742	–2.7	–5.6	–4.4	1.9
12.	Port Klang, Malaysia	11,978	12,316	13,581	13,244	13,724	2.8	10.3	–2.5	3.6
13.	Xiamen, China	10,380	10,702	11,122	11,410	12,046	3.1	3.9	2.6	5.6
14.	Antwerp, Belgium	10,451	11,100	11,860	12,031	12,020	6.2	6.8	1.4	–0.1
15.	Tanjung Pelepas, Malaysia ...	8,261	8,961	9,100	9,800	11,200	8.5	1.6	7.7	14.3
16.	Los Angeles, CA, U.S.	9,343	9,459	9,338	9,213	10,678	1.2	–1.3	–1.3	15.9
17.	Kaohsiung, Taiwan	10,271	10,446	10,429	9,622	9,864	1.7	–0.2	–7.7	2.5
18.	Long Beach, CA, U.S.	7,545	8,091	7,632	8,113	9,384	7.2	–5.7	6.3	15.7
19.	New York & New Jersey, U.S.	6,711	7,180	7,471	7,586	8,986	7.0	4.1	1.5	18.5
20.	Hamburg, Germany	8,860	8,730	9,274	8,540	8,715	–1.5	6.2	–7.9	2.0

Note: A TEU is the size of a typical shipping container.

Value of Freight Shipments by Transportation Mode, 2017-22
Source: Freight Analysis Framework, U.S. Dept. of Transportation
(value in billions of 2017 dollars)

Mode of transportation	2017				2022			
	Total	Domestic	Exports	Imports	Total	Domestic	Exports	Imports
Truck	$12,017	$11,297	$368	$353	$12,626	$11,897	$365	$363
Rail	404	227	64	113	394	230	60	104
Water	360	184	55	121	345	179	58	108
Air[1]	1,226	159	496	571	1,255	165	502	588
Multiple modes and mail	3,926	2,362	527	1,037	4,251	2,555	577	1,119
Pipeline	928	851	14	63	955	865	29	62
Other and unknown	45	2	31	12	44	2	31	11
Total	18,907	15,082	1,555	2,270	19,869	15,892	1,623	2,355

Note: Imports and exports that pass through the U.S. from a foreign origin to a foreign destination by any mode not included. All truck, rail, water, and pipeline movements that involve more than one mode, including exports and imports that change mode at international gateways, are included in multiple modes and mail to avoid double counting. (1) Including truck-air.

Merchant Fleets of the World, 2022
Source: *Review of Maritime Transport, 2022*, United Nations Conference on Trade and Development
(ranked by dead-weight tonnage under flag of registration as of Jan. 1, 2022)

Flag of registration	Number of ships	Percent of total world ships	Dead-weight tonnage (thous.)	Percent of total world tonnage	Average vessel size (dead-weight tons)	Tonnage change, 2020-21
1. Panama	8,025	7.8%	350,401	15.9%	43,664	1.7%
2. Liberia	4,311	4.2	335,114	15.2	77,735	11.9
3. Marshall Islands	4,042	3.9	289,781	13.2	71,693	5.7
4. Hong Kong (China)	2,661	2.6	207,816	9.5	78,097	1.4
5. Singapore	3,227	3.1	131,369	6.0	40,709	−3.6
6. China	7,309	7.1	114,952	5.2	15,727	6.0
7. Malta	2,047	2.0	114,910	5.2	56,136	−0.9
8. The Bahamas	1,307	1.3	72,998	3.3	55,851	−1.8
9. Greece	1,234	1.2	61,817	2.8	50,095	−4.3
10. Japan	5,590	5.4	40,263	1.8	7,203	2.4
11. Cyprus	1,030	1.0	33,461	1.5	32,487	−1.7
12. Indonesia	11,015	10.7	29,332	1.3	2,663	1.1
13. Denmark	612	0.6	26,061	1.2	42,583	5.6
14. Madeira	672	0.7	25,863	1.2	38,486	13.7
15. Norway	695	0.7	21,300	1.0	30,648	−3.1
16. Isle of Man	291	0.3	20,661	0.9	71,002	−6.1
17. Iran	942	0.9	20,195	0.9	21,439	−2.6
18. India	1,810	1.8	16,934	0.8	9,356	−1.1
19. South Korea	2,063	2.0	15,635	0.7	7,579	−0.6
20. Saudi Arabia	413	0.4	13,887	0.6	33,625	1.6
21. United States	3,636	3.5	12,526	0.6	3,445	−0.1
22. Vietnam	1,975	1.9	12,331	0.6	6,244	19.4
23. United Kingdom	881	0.9	11,292	0.5	12,817	−3.8
24. Russia	2,917	2.8	11,039	0.5	3,784	1.1
25. Italy	1,266	1.2	9,969	0.5	7,875	−11.4
26. Belgium	199	0.2	9,791	0.4	49,200	1.6
27. Malaysia	1,790	1.7	9,269	0.4	5,178	−9.6
28. Bermuda	135	0.1	7,888	0.4	58,430	−2.0
29. Germany	591	0.6	7,096	0.3	12,007	−9.8
30. Taiwan	450	0.4	6,755	0.3	15,011	−5.4
World total	102,899	100.0	2,199,107	100.0	21,372	2.9

Note: World total includes flags of registration not shown.

U.S. International Transactions, 1970-2022
Source: U.S. Bureau of Economic Analysis, U.S. Dept. of Commerce
(in millions of dollars)

CURRENT ACCOUNT	1970	1980	1990	2000	2010	2020	2021	2022
Exports of goods and services and income receipts (credits)	$68,388	$344,440	$712,128	$1,469,648	$2,623,991	$3,260,095	$3,819,231	$4,424,636
Goods	42,469	224,250	387,401	784,940	1,290,279	1,432,218	1,765,884	2,089,925
Services	14,171	47,585	147,833	290,381	562,759	726,433	801,143	928,530
Primary income receipts	11,748	72,605	176,894	356,706	680,169	936,236	1,077,227	1,217,853
Imports of goods and services and income payments (debits)	66,055	342,124	791,097	1,873,098	3,055,256	3,879,793	4,650,676	5,396,231
Goods	39,866	249,750	498,438	1,231,722	1,938,950	2,346,103	2,849,395	3,272,935
Services	14,519	41,492	117,660	216,115	409,313	466,521	559,205	696,707
Primary income payments	5,514	42,533	148,345	338,637	511,948	773,146	927,297	1,069,300
Secondary income payments (current transfers)[1]	6,156	8,349	26,654	86,624	195,045	294,008	314,778	357,289
CAPITAL ACCOUNT								
Capital transfer receipts, other credits	NA	NA	0	35	0	372	3,864	8,400
Capital transfer payments, other debits	NA	NA	7,220	36	157	5,903	6,375	13,003
Net U.S. acquisition of financial assets[2]	9,336	86,968	103,985	587,682	958,703	943,091	1,242,954	840,582
Net U.S. incurrence of liabilities[2]	7,226	62,036	162,109	1,066,074	1,391,042	1,634,965	1,992,760	1,564,676
Balance on current account	2,331	2,318	−78,969	−403,450	−431,265	−619,698	−831,445	−971,595
Balance on capital account	NA	NA	−7,221	−1	−157	−5,532	−2,511	−4,603
Net lending (+) or net borrowing (−) from financial-acct. transactions[3]	2,331	2,318	−86,190	−403,451	−431,422	−696,980	−788,834	−804,792

NA = Not available or applicable. (1) Includes U.S. government and private transfers, such as U.S. government grants and pensions, fines and penalties, withholding taxes, personal transfers (remittances), insurance-related transfers, and other current transfers. (2) Excludes financial derivatives. (3) Net lending means that U.S. residents are net suppliers of funds to foreign residents, and net borrowing means the opposite. Net lending or net borrowing can be computed from current- and capital-account transactions or from financial-account transactions.

U.S. International Direct Investments, 1990-2022
Source: U.S. Bureau of Economic Analysis, U.S. Dept. of Commerce
(in millions of dollars)

	U.S. direct investment abroad					Foreign direct investment in U.S.				
	1990	2000	2010	2020	2022	1990	2000	2010	2020	2022
All countries[1]	$430,521	$1,316,247	$3,741,910	$6,063,288	$6,581,044	$394,911	$1,256,867	$2,280,044	$4,613,481	$5,254,816
Canada	69,508	132,472	295,206	366,880	438,766	29,544	114,309	192,463	487,449	589,288
Europe[1]	214,739	687,320	2,034,559	3,606,804	4,026,811	247,320	887,014	1,659,774	2,980,117	3,396,499
Austria	1,113	2,872	11,485	4,296	4,051	625	3,007	4,532	15,346	17,641
Belgium	9,464	17,973	43,975	65,733	61,456	3,900	14,787	69,565	66,093	71,257
Czechia	NA	1,228	5,268	5,025	5,386	NA	NA	65	NA	NA
Denmark	1,726	5,270	11,802	15,376	14,016	819	4,025	7,772	30,173	39,428
Finland	544	1,342	1,597	3,617	4,429	1,504	8,875	4,943	8,082	9,868
France	19,164	42,628	78,320	106,517	112,017	18,650	125,740	189,763	282,257	297,637
Germany	27,609	55,508	103,319	152,278	190,237	28,232	122,412	203,077	347,509	431,449
Greece	282	795	1,775	481	2,245	94	659	–41	NA	NA
Hungary	NA	1,920	4,237	13,866	14,354	NA	5,287	39,266	NA	NA
Ireland	5,894	35,903	158,851	379,886	574,323	1,340	25,523	24,097	249,295	295,001
Italy	14,063	23,484	27,137	27,459	26,107	1,524	6,576	20,142	31,294	39,752
Luxembourg	1,697	27,849	272,206	654,941	605,304	2,195	58,930	170,309	316,922	323,661
Netherlands	19,120	115,429	514,689	827,419	944,604	64,671	138,894	234,408	554,720	617,076
Norway	4,209	4,379	28,541	13,627	13,484	773	2,665	10,478	30,362	36,872
Poland	NA	3,884	13,152	11,956	11,960	29	57	4,386	NA	NA
Portugal	897	2,664	2,612	1,905	3,830	–19	–68	204	NA	NA
Russia	NA	1,147	10,040	12,874	9,637	NA	118	5,689	NA	NA
Spain	7,868	21,236	52,390	37,238	35,625	792	5,068	43,095	84,571	75,712
Sweden	1,787	25,959	23,275	55,608	60,280	5,484	21,991	38,780	59,964	94,146
Switzerland	25,099	55,377	119,891	236,767	212,235	17,674	64,719	180,642	293,461	307,231
Turkey	522	1,826	4,155	6,223	5,761	20	188	749	NA	NA
UK	72,707	230,762	501,247	944,908	1,077,519	98,676	277,613	400,435	535,715	663,369
Latin America[1]	71,413	266,576	752,788	1,024,534	1,037,998	20,168	53,691	62,130	209,774	211,876
Argentina	2,531	17,488	11,747	13,325	12,645	420	364	464	NA	NA
The Bahamas	4,004	NA	NA	NA	NA	1,535	1,254	1,753	1,897	2,187
Barbados	252	2,141	7,524	57,819	28,332	191	1,560	706	NA	NA
Bermuda	20,169	60,114	265,524	288,011	206,389	1,550	18,336	365	52,021	35,008
Brazil	14,384	36,717	66,963	69,086	80,963	377	882	1,357	4,480	4,198
Chile	1,896	10,052	30,747	27,152	29,160	5	24	391	NA	NA
Colombia	1,677	3,693	6,181	6,452	7,074	55	2	382	NA	NA
Costa Rica	251	1,716	1,827	3,066	2,906	–2	2	–48	NA	NA
Curaçao[2]	–4,501	NA	NA	NA	NA	12,974	3,807	2,819	1,193	967
Dom. Rep.	529	1,143	1,432	2,567	2,531	0	79	–142	NA	NA
Ecuador	280	832	1,283	929	1,000	6	29	77	NA	NA
Honduras	262	399	936	894	1,371	8	–3	7	NA	NA
Mexico	10,313	39,352	85,751	110,753	130,274	575	7,462	10,970	20,646	33,787
Panama	9,289	30,758	5,156	3,500	3,775	4,188	3,819	952	1,796	1,928
Peru	599	3,130	7,196	7,222	9,125	NA	–13	182	NA	NA
UK isls. in Caribbean[3]	5,929	33,451	191,680	350,988	430,395	–2,979	15,191	38,477	99,194	97,739
Venezuela	1,087	10,531	10,255	3,106	3,246	496	792	3,122	1,381	3,008
Africa[1]	3,650	11,891	54,816	43,808	46,169	505	2,700	2,265	9,875	11,160
Egypt	1,231	1,998	12,599	10,665	12,708	1	–4	–277	NA	NA
Nigeria	–401	470	5,058	6,786	5,621	–17	NA	23	NA	NA
South Africa	775	3,562	6,017	6,748	7,394	10	704	699	3,552	4,533
Middle East[1]	3,959	10,863	34,431	80,790	80,148	4,425	6,506	16,808	41,336	43,907
Israel	746	3,735	9,464	41,329	42,521	640	3,012	8,714	10,487	10,554
Kuwait	NA	NA	NA	NA	NA	NA	NA	NA	1,423	1,400
Lebanon	NA	NA	NA	NA	NA	NA	NA	NA	2	–2
Saudi Arabia	1,899	3,661	7,436	11,188	12,212	1,811	NA	NA	6,395	6,795
UAE	409	683	4,935	16,054	16,862	99	64	747	20,409	22,625
Asia and Pacific[1]	64,718	207,125	570,111	940,473	951,153	92,948	192,647	346,605	884,928	1,002,087
Australia	15,110	34,838	125,421	178,223	173,653	6,542	18,775	35,632	85,809	106,519
China	354	11,140	58,996	116,508	126,104	NA	277	3,300	36,738	28,659
Hong Kong	6,055	27,447	41,264	94,495	89,437	1,511	1,493	4,440	14,212	14,174
India	372	2,379	24,666	42,291	51,553	NA	96	4,102	1,658	3,749
Indonesia	3,207	8,904	10,558	12,158	11,913	25	16	138	NA	NA
Japan	22,599	57,091	113,523	118,453	77,489	83,091	159,690	255,012	632,079	711,963
Korea, South	2,695	8,968	26,233	37,550	36,655	–1,009	3,110	15,746	60,548	74,696
Malaysia	1,466	7,910	11,791	13,788	13,165	56	310	338	1,034	1,060
New Zealand	3,156	4,271	6,724	11,701	10,630	157	395	584	2,396	3,246
Philippines	1,355	3,638	5,399	5,037	6,163	77	47	103	NA	NA
Singapore	3,975	24,133	102,778	264,188	309,441	1,289	5,087	21,517	28,486	36,880
Taiwan	2,226	7,836	22,188	18,569	16,653	836	3,174	4,642	17,974	16,101
Thailand	1,790	5,824	12,999	15,484	15,755	150	132	158	NA	NA

NA = Not available. **Note:** On a historical cost basis. Direct investment is a category of cross-border investment associated with a resident in one economy having control or a significant degree of influence on the management of an enterprise resident in another economy. Ownership or control of 10% or more of the voting securities of an entity in another economy is the threshold for separating direct investment from other types of investment. (1) Totals and subtotals include countries or territories not shown in table. (2) Curaçao figures before 2010 are for the entire Netherlands Antilles, a confederation that ended in 2010. (3) Incl. British Virgin Islands, Cayman Islands, Montserrat, and Turks and Caicos Islands.

Top Motor Vehicle Producing Nations, 2022

Source: International Organization of Motor Vehicle Manufacturers (OICA)
(in thousands of units; ranked by total production)

Nation	Total motor vehicles	Cars	Commercial vehicles[1]	% change, 2021-22[2]	Nation	Total motor vehicles	Cars	Commercial vehicles[1]	% change, 2021-22[2]
China[3]	27,021	23,836	3,185	3%	South Africa	556	309	246	11%
U.S.	10,060	1,752	8,309	10	Argentina	537	258	279	24
Japan	7,836	6,566	1,269	0	Romania	509	509	0	21
India	5,457	4,439	1,018	24	Poland	484	255	229	10
South Korea	3,757	3,438	319	9	Morocco	465	405	60	15
Germany	3,678	3,480	197	11	Hungary	442	442	0	6
Mexico	3,509	658	2,851	10	Uzbekistan	334	328	5	38
Brazil	2,370	1,825	545	5	Portugal	322	256	66	11
Spain	2,219	1,785	434	6	Belgium	277	232	44	6
Thailand	1,884	594	1,289	12	Taiwan	261	191	70	-2
Indonesia	1,470	1,214	256	31	Kazakhstan	113	103	9	22
France	1,383	1,010	373	2	Austria	108	108	0	-21
Türkiye	1,353	811	542	6	Finland	73	73	0	-15
Canada	1,229	289	939	10	Slovenia	68	68	0	-29
Czechia	1,224	1,218	7	10	Serbia	4	4	0	-79
Slovakia	1,000	1,000	0	-3	Ukraine	1	1	0	-82
UK	877	775	102	-6	Others	2,030	1,791	239	NA
Italy	796	473	323	0	**NAFTA**	**14,798**	**2,699**	**12,099**	**10**
Malaysia	702	650	52	46	**Total**	**85,017**	**61,599**	**23,418**	**6**
Russia	608	449	160	-61					

NA = Not applicable. NAFTA = North American Free Trade Agreement. **Note:** Numbers may not add up to totals due to rounding. (1) Includes light commercial vehicles, heavy trucks, coaches, and buses. (2) Percent change in number of total motor vehicles. (3) Not including Taiwan.

World Motor Vehicle Production, 1950-2022

Source: For 1950-90, American Automobile Manufacturers Assn.; 2000-12, Automotive News Data Center and R.L. Polk; 2013-22, OICA
(in thousands of units)

Year	U.S.	Canada	Europe[1]	Japan	Other	World total	U.S. % of world total
1950	8,006	388	1,991	32	160	10,577	75.7%
1960	7,905	398	6,837	482	866	16,488	47.9
1970	8,284	1,160	13,049	5,289	1,637	29,419	28.2
1980	8,010	1,324	15,496	11,043	2,692	38,565	20.8
1990	9,783	1,928	18,866	13,487	4,496	48,554	20.1
2000	12,832	2,952	17,678	10,145	16,098	59,704	21.5
2005	12,018	2,665	20,855	10,800	20,691	67,892	17.7
2010	7,632	2,074	19,371	9,197	35,036	73,311	10.4
2011	8,462	2,127	20,709	7,901	36,828	76,027	11.1
2012	10,142	2,454	22,324	9,448	36,714	81,082	12.5
2013	11,066	2,380	19,923	9,630	44,508	87,507	12.6
2014	11,661	2,394	20,430	9,775	45,536	89,776	12.9
2015	12,100	2,283	21,096	9,278	46,024	90,781	13.3
2016	12,198	2,370	21,700	9,205	49,504	94,977	12.8
2017	11,190	2,200	22,161	9,694	52,058	97,303	11.5
2018	10,986	2,000	21,273	9,201	48,079	91,539	12.0
2019	10,893	1,917	21,531	9,685	48,095	92,121	11.8
2020	8,821	1,376	16,904	8,068	42,481	77,650	11.4
2021	9,157	1,115	16,338	7,837	45,758	80,205	11.4
2022	10,060	1,229	16,217	7,836	49,675	85,017	11.8

Note: Data may not be fully comparable across all years because they are derived from different sources. Number of units may not add up to totals due to rounding. (1) Prior to 2004, numbers exclude Eastern European production.

Passenger Cars Imported Into the U.S. by Country of Origin, 1970-2022

Source: U.S. Census Bureau, U.S. Dept. of Commerce
(in number of units)

Year	Mexico	Japan	Canada	S. Korea	Germany[1]	UK	Sweden	Italy	France	Total[2]
1970	NA	381,338	692,783	NA	674,945	76,257	57,844	42,523	37,114	2,013,420
1975	0	695,573	733,766	NA	370,012	67,106	51,993	102,344	15,647	2,074,653
1980	1	1,991,502	594,770	NA	338,711	32,517	61,496	46,899	47,386	3,116,448
1985	13,647	2,527,467	1,144,805	NA	473,110	24,474	142,640	8,689	42,882	4,397,679
1990	215,986	1,867,794	1,220,221	201,475	245,286	27,271	93,084	11,045	1,976	3,944,602
1995	462,800	1,114,360	1,552,691	131,718	204,932	42,450	82,593	1,031	14	3,624,428
2000	933,948	1,837,631	2,138,825	568,153	491,704	81,079	86,707	3,129	28,024	6,326,013
2005	693,149	1,832,534	1,967,985	730,500	547,191	184,716	93,736	5,377	412	6,564,844
2010	902,565	1,569,220	1,741,493	515,601	506,053	96,689	38,749	4,298	4,153	5,668,111
2015	1,438,840	1,609,709	1,969,502	1,065,972	639,879	134,413	37,789	132,340	28,034	7,420,613
2016	1,417,616	1,714,368	2,010,907	1,001,021	555,577	199,611	47,769	133,002	16,497	7,482,316
2017	1,724,526	1,731,889	1,850,765	929,530	502,059	217,341	58,492	159,802	9,801	7,660,401
2018	1,934,412	1,729,301	1,641,534	831,164	458,829	235,133	43,359	153,426	5,091	7,551,409
2019	2,018,770	1,734,743	1,558,959	916,610	413,528	213,528	60,147	102,641	2,413	7,478,857
2020	1,528,214	1,402,501	1,190,967	874,236	286,410	138,742	69,719	91,693	656	5,972,315
2021	1,388,925	1,351,459	952,147	826,761	294,936	134,262	78,756	57,848	453	5,516,956
2022	1,495,341	1,300,232	963,032	872,017	280,493	82,617	74,036	54,974	618	5,539,857

NA = Not available. **Note:** Includes new and used cars. Excludes cars assembled in U.S. foreign trade zones. (1) Figures prior to 1991 are for West Germany. (2) Includes units imported from countries not shown in table.

Passenger Car Production in U.S. Plants, 2020-22

Source: Wards Intelligence
(in number of units; only 2022 models with at least 10,000 produced included)

	2022	2021	2020
FORD TOTAL	65,480	65,590	72,793
Ford Mustang	65,480	65,590	65,668
GENERAL MOTORS TOTAL	233,349	97,916	208,826
Cadillac CT4	12,351	5,116	10,858
Cadillac CT5	20,079	7,510	20,443
Chevrolet Camaro	29,332	22,399	27,797
Chevrolet Corvette	38,686	36,010	22,076
Chevrolet Malibu	132,360	26,860	110,192
HONDA TOTAL	282,878	258,489	363,420
Acura Integra	17,605	—	—
Acura TLX	15,344	17,435	29,749
Honda Accord	193,428	174,549	209,459
Honda Civic	42,744	40,352	91,009
HYUNDAI TOTAL	35,748	92,590	163,114
Hyundai Elantra	34,040	49,785	77,028
KIA TOTAL	64,547	80,061	72,549
Kia K5	64,547	80,061	53,755
NISSAN TOTAL	166,974	129,210	147,908
Nissan Altima	144,622	101,732	118,258
Nissan Leaf	13,150	12,262	12,575
SUBARU TOTAL	55,097	54,830	75,558
Subaru Impreza	32,333	33,176	48,416
Subaru Legacy	22,764	21,654	27,142
TESLA TOTAL	340,898	245,632	267,680
Tesla Model 3	297,174	235,538	244,271
Tesla Model S	43,724	10,094	23,409
TOYOTA TOTAL	500,587	489,630	495,690
Lexus ES	43,187	44,523	38,637
Toyota Avalon	17,246	19,874	23,220
Toyota Camry	307,470	296,936	292,239
Toyota Corolla	132,684	128,297	141,586
VOLVO TOTAL	13,743	22,940	30,020
Volvo 60	13,743	22,940	30,020
TOTAL CARS	1,766,495	1,562,717	1,924,398

— = No production. **Note:** Totals may include models not shown.

Light Truck Production in U.S. Plants, 2020-22

Source: Wards Intelligence
(in number of units; only 2022 models with at least 10,000 produced included)

	2022	2021	2020
BMW TOTAL	416,301	433,748	361,361
BMW X3	101,323	118,249	100,815
BMW X4	56,212	55,490	43,745
BMW X5	159,144	170,680	139,029
BMW X6	42,509	38,605	36,668
BMW X7	56,826	50,724	41,104
FORD TOTAL	1,768,047	1,560,582	1,599,642
Ford Bronco	139,062	54,562	128
Ford Econoline	38,830	40,575	37,572
Ford Escape	187,761	141,385	195,611
Ford Expedition	70,102	82,649	80,117
Ford Explorer	253,370	228,002	240,711
Ford F-Series	807,302	753,853	731,013
Ford Ranger	60,750	98,592	91,660
Ford Transit	129,937	98,536	147,849
Lincoln Aviator	27,008	21,765	25,510
Lincoln Corsair	35,779	20,854	29,110
Lincoln Navigator	18,146	19,809	20,361
GENERAL MOTORS TOTAL	1,493,768	1,360,989	1,296,062
Buick Enclave	41,672	40,836	38,506
Cadillac Escalade	29,664	33,294	14,131
Cadillac Escalade ESV	17,748	18,021	7,686
Cadillac XT4	33,303	8,073	28,497
Cadillac XT5	37,849	25,397	44,785
Cadillac XT6	24,141	18,994	23,355
Chevrolet Bolt	15,365	19,515	30,218
Chevrolet Bolt EUV	29,097	14,911	—
Chevrolet Colorado	103,756	85,193	94,569
Chevrolet Express	51,458	29,343	52,083
Chevrolet Silverado	357,566	393,367	331,498
Chevrolet Suburban	60,059	50,741	36,304
Chevrolet Tahoe	130,885	121,863	98,645
Chevrolet Traverse	119,353	114,573	140,119
GMC Acadia	65,888	51,024	76,038
GMC Canyon	36,407	28,620	27,211
GMC Savana	24,285	10,967	18,184
GMC Sierra	207,894	189,935	166,914
GMC Yukon	65,240	65,633	45,252
GMC Yukon XL	40,102	40,560	21,852
HONDA TOTAL	549,030	597,835	603,028
Acura MDX	59,322	50,885	56,567
Acura RDX	31,504	53,792	63,115
Honda CR-V	188,098	209,974	207,259
Honda Odyssey	57,861	59,990	81,980
Honda Passport	47,462	51,014	37,900
Honda Pilot	114,349	130,358	122,062
Honda Ridgeline	50,434	41,822	34,055
HYUNDAI TOTAL	297,084	198,816	105,521
Hyundai Santa Cruz	41,965	15,025	—
Hyundai Santa Fe	121,164	102,084	105,521
Hyundai Tucson	133,955	81,707	—
KIA TOTAL	275,453	175,039	149,725
Kia Sorento	79,384	76,587	67,411
Kia Sportage	89,209	—	—
Kia Telluride	106,860	98,452	82,314
MERCEDES TOTAL	316,939	294,789	239,957
Mercedes EQS CUV	10,752	—	—
Mercedes GLE	195,433	198,362	164,480
Mercedes GLS	55,507	54,569	44,777
Mercedes Sprinter	55,247	41,858	30,700
NAVISTAR TOTAL	18,564	10,713	14,521
Chevrolet Express	11,046	7,558	11,209
NISSAN TOTAL	371,776	322,578	283,161
Infiniti QX60	27,164	3,255	17,616
Nissan Frontier	86,316	65,526	28,352
Nissan Murano	35,268	50,791	55,874
Nissan Pathfinder	80,630	32,250	51,960
Nissan Rogue	127,256	138,479	90,180
Nissan Titan	15,142	23,153	26,143
RIVIAN TOTAL	24,338	1,015	—
Rivian R1T	12,880	987	—
STELLANTIS TOTAL	1,169,830	1,171,025	1,061,424
Dodge Durango	68,651	67,775	60,266
Jeep Cherokee	58,392	58,542	139,847
Jeep Gladiator	99,454	91,755	78,845
Jeep Grand Cherokee	266,967	301,181	221,177
Jeep Wagoneer	47,452	21,042	—
Jeep Wrangler	254,797	249,542	220,154
Ram Pickup	374,117	381,188	341,135
SUBARU TOTAL	231,308	214,816	238,900
Subaru Ascent	68,511	60,522	69,292
Subaru Outback	162,797	154,294	169,608
TESLA TOTAL	301,975	195,524	89,100
Tesla Model X	27,453	14,326	31,396
Tesla Model Y	274,522	181,198	57,704
TOYOTA TOTAL	554,494	641,239	508,237
Toyota Highlander	271,386	292,479	241,962
Toyota RAV4	77,233	76,869	36,254
Toyota Sienna	79,686	127,270	52,173
Toyota Tundra	120,056	86,546	97,136
TOYOTA MAZDA TOTAL	104,074	12,303	
Mazda CX-50	29,539	—	—
Toyota Corolla Cross	74,535	12,303	
VOLKSWAGEN TOTAL	121,062	114,232	104,063
Volkswagen Atlas/ Atlas Cross Sport	112,236	114,232	104,063
LIGHT TRUCK TOTAL	8,016,968	7,307,551	6,656,326

— = No production. **Note:** Totals may include models not shown.

Domestic and Imported Retail Vehicle Sales in the U.S., 1980-2022

Source: Wards Intelligence

(in number of units)

Year	Cars Domestic[2]	Cars Imports	Total cars	Light trucks Domestic[2]	Light trucks Imports	Total light trucks	All vehicles[1] Domestic[2]	All vehicles[1] Imports	Total vehicles
1980	6,579,778	2,369,457	8,949,235	1,750,735	478,887	2,229,622	8,330,513	2,848,344	11,178,857
1985	8,204,670	2,774,517	10,979,187	3,629,080	832,186	4,461,266	12,109,999	3,615,292	15,725,291
1990	6,916,860	2,384,346	9,301,206	3,956,756	611,941	4,568,697	11,133,504	3,013,865	14,147,369
1995	7,113,902	1,506,257	8,620,159	5,705,708	402,181	6,107,889	13,192,861	1,923,464	15,116,325
2000	6,761,603	2,016,120	8,777,723	7,719,707	852,325	8,572,032	14,922,648	2,889,025	17,811,673
2002	5,816,671	2,225,584	8,042,255	7,707,738	1,066,375	8,774,113	13,829,568	3,309,084	17,138,652
2003	5,472,500	2,083,051	7,555,551	7,856,322	1,227,180	9,083,502	13,638,351	3,329,091	16,967,442
2004	5,333,496	2,149,059	7,482,555	8,138,107	1,246,258	9,384,365	13,880,251	3,418,322	17,298,573
2005	5,473,450	2,186,533	7,659,983	8,072,456	1,215,315	9,287,771	14,020,528	3,423,801	17,444,329
2006	5,416,828	2,344,764	7,761,592	7,396,058	1,346,750	8,742,808	13,334,843	3,714,138	17,048,981
2007	5,197,271	2,365,063	7,562,334	7,138,803	1,388,085	8,526,888	12,687,016	3,773,299	16,460,315
2008	4,490,863	2,278,271	6,769,134	5,329,165	1,096,469	6,425,634	10,107,753	3,385,439	13,493,192
2009	3,558,283	1,843,282	5,401,565	4,116,550	884,242	5,000,792	7,867,766	2,734,277	10,602,043
2010	3,791,499	1,844,240	5,635,739	5,020,441	898,644	5,919,085	9,020,088	2,752,438	11,772,526
2011	4,145,964	1,946,897	6,092,861	5,666,512	982,443	6,648,955	10,108,762	2,939,624	13,048,386
2012	5,119,844	2,125,325	7,245,169	6,127,314	1,060,720	7,188,034	11,581,776	3,197,708	14,779,484
2013	5,433,158	2,153,176	7,586,334	6,704,449	1,239,268	7,943,767	12,479,306	3,403,406	15,882,712
2014	5,609,878	2,098,122	7,708,000	7,384,280	1,359,910	8,744,190	13,388,628	3,471,215	16,859,843
2015	5,595,123	1,933,403	7,528,526	8,097,387	1,782,078	9,879,465	14,127,526	3,729,798	17,857,324
2016	5,145,575	1,737,771	6,883,346	8,436,243	2,157,722	10,593,965	13,969,117	3,909,190	17,878,307
2017	4,592,965	1,496,238	6,089,203	8,651,782	2,409,100	11,060,882	13,644,445	3,920,682	17,565,127
2018	4,086,889	1,223,388	5,310,277	9,153,418	2,761,253	11,914,671	13,711,080	4,001,724	17,712,804
2019	3,543,923	1,175,787	4,719,710	9,621,675	2,619,677	12,241,352	13,676,873	3,811,281	17,488,154
2020	2,559,778	842,060	3,401,838	8,614,605	2,455,405	11,070,010	11,571,020	3,310,336	14,881,356
2021	2,375,728	974,322	3,350,050	9,006,441	2,590,432	11,596,873	11,830,596	3,577,919	15,408,515
2022	2,043,341	815,234	2,858,575	8,815,654	2,080,110	10,895,764	11,325,637	2,904,687	14,230,324

Note: Vehicles are cars and light trucks belonging to gross vehicle weight (GVW) classes 1-3 (under 14,001 lbs). (1) Except for 1980, "All vehicles" includes medium and heavy trucks. (2) Includes the U.S., Canada, and Mexico.

U.S. Sales of Hybrid, Electric, and Fuel Cell Vehicles, 2000-22

Source: Wards Intelligence; in number of units sold

Power type	2000	2005	2010	2015	2016	2017	2019	2020	2021	2022
Hybrid car	9,350	151,253	231,819	350,753	276,995	252,366	230,676	161,078	215,041	186,247
Hybrid light truck	0	54,575	42,286	22,606	64,797	111,363	168,768	293,989	584,005	580,165
Total hybrid	**9,350**	**205,828**	**274,105**	**373,359**	**341,792**	**363,729**	**399,444**	**455,067**	**799,046**	**766,412**
Electric car	463	0	326	72,313	64,307	62,208	184,728	119,552	191,006	270,677
Electric light truck	0	0	0	61	16,067	40,172	49,094	118,988	268,418	477,305
Total electric	**463**	**0**	**326**	**72,374**	**80,374**	**102,380**	**233,822**	**238,540**	**459,424**	**747,982**
Fuel cell car	0	6	17	74	1,042	2,285	1,822	730	2,911	2,299
Fuel cell light truck	0	0	0	34	40	28	267	208	430	408
Total fuel cell	**0**	**6**	**17**	**108**	**1,082**	**2,313**	**2,089**	**938**	**3,341**	**2,707**
Plug-in hybrid car	0	0	326	41,739	60,972	76,420	58,576	30,860	41,125	24,179
Plug-in hybrid light truck	0	0	0	2,076	10,357	14,607	27,215	38,189	134,992	159,153
Total plug-in hybrid	**0**	**0**	**326**	**43,815**	**71,329**	**91,027**	**85,791**	**69,049**	**176,117**	**183,332**

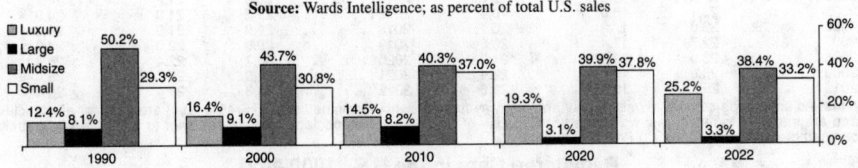

U.S. Retail Car Sales by Vehicle Size, 1990-2022
Source: Wards Intelligence; as percent of total U.S. sales

Legend: ☐ Luxury ■ Large ■ Midsize ☐ Small

- 1990: 12.4%, 8.1%, 50.2%, 29.3%
- 2000: 16.4%, 9.1%, 43.7%, 30.8%
- 2010: 14.5%, 8.2%, 40.3%, 37.0%
- 2020: 19.3%, 3.1%, 39.9%, 37.8%
- 2022: 25.2%, 3.3%, 38.4%, 33.2%

U.S. Light Truck Sales by Type, 1990-2022
Source: Wards Intelligence; as percent of total U.S. sales

Legend: ☐ Cross utility ■ Sport utility ■ Van ☐ Pickup

- 1990: 20.3%, 28.7%, 50.2% (NA for Cross utility)
- 2000: 7.1%, 34.7%, 20.8%, 37.1%
- 2010: 13.5%, 11.5%, 27.0%, 47.9%
- 2020: 11.4%, 6.2%, 25.8%, 56.6%
- 2022: 12.9%, 5.6%, 24.3%, 57.1%

NA = Not applicable. **Note:** Comm. chassis sales (not shown) were 0.8% (for 1990), 0.2% (2000), 0.1% (2010), 0.02% (2020), 0.01% (2022).

Top-Selling Passenger Cars in the U.S., 2020-22

Source: Wards Intelligence; ranked by number of vehicles sold

Car	2022 sales	Car	2021 sales	Car	2020 sales
1. Toyota Camry	295,201	1. Toyota Camry	313,795	1. Toyota Camry	294,348
2. Toyota Corolla	222,216	2. Honda Civic	263,787	2. Honda Civic	261,225
3. Tesla Model 3	188,500	3. Toyota Corolla	248,993	3. Toyota Corolla	237,178
4. Honda Accord	154,612	4. Honda Accord	202,676	4. Honda Accord	199,458
5. Nissan Altima	139,955	5. Tesla Model 3	139,503	5. Nissan Altima	137,988
6. Honda Civic	133,932	6. Nissan Sentra	127,861	6. Ford Fusion	110,665
7. Hyundai Elantra	117,177	7. Hyundai Elantra	124,422	7. Hyundai Elantra	105,475
8. Chevrolet Malibu	115,467	8. Kia Forte	115,929	8. Chevrolet Malibu	102,651
9. Kia Forte	108,424	9. Nissan Altima	103,777	9. Nissan Sentra	94,646
10. Dodge Charger	80,074	10. Hyundai Sonata	93,142	10. Tesla Model 3	86,759

Top-Selling Light Trucks in the U.S., 2020-22

Source: Wards Intelligence; ranked by number of vehicles sold

Truck	2022 sales	Truck	2021 sales	Truck	2020 sales
1. Ford F-Series	597,020	1. Ford F-Series	656,039	1. Ford F-Series	721,132
2. Chevrolet Silverado	513,354	2. Ram Pickup	544,458	2. Chevrolet Silverado	586,675
3. Ram Pickup	448,205	3. Chevrolet Silverado	519,774	3. Ram Pickup	547,881
4. Toyota RAV4	399,941	4. Toyota RAV4	407,739	4. Toyota RAV4	430,387
5. GMC Sierra	241,522	5. Honda CR-V	361,271	5. Honda CR-V	333,502
6. Honda CR-V	238,155	6. Nissan Rogue	285,602	6. Chevrolet Equinox	270,994
7. Toyota Tacoma	237,323	7. Jeep Grand Cherokee	264,444	7. GMC Sierra	253,016
8. Jeep Grand Cherokee	223,345	8. Toyota Highlander	264,128	8. Toyota Tacoma	238,806
9. Toyota Highlander	222,805	9. Toyota Tacoma	252,520	9. Nissan Rogue	227,935
10. Tesla Model Y	212,600	10. GMC Sierra	248,924	10. Ford Explorer	226,217

Most Popular Colors by Vehicle Type, 2022

Source: Axalta Coating Systems; for 2022 model year in North America

Luxury cars/SUVs		Intermediate cars/CUVs		Compact/sports cars		Trucks/SUVs	
Color	Percent	Color	Percent	Color	Percent	Color	Percent
White/pearl white	27%	White/pearl white	34%	White/pearl white	24%	White/pearl white	30%
Black/effect black	21	Gray	23	Black/effect black	20	Black/effect black	21
Gray	19	Black/effect black	15	Gray	17	Gray	19
Blue	12	Silver	11	Blue	15	Blue	10
Silver	10	Blue	9	Silver	9	Red	8
Red	6	Red	6	Red	9	Silver	7
Brown/beige	3	Brown/beige	2	Brown/beige	1	Brown/beige	2
Yellow/gold	1	Green	<1	Yellow/gold	1	Green	2
Green	<1	Yellow/gold	<1	Green	1	Yellow/gold	<1
Other	1	Other	<1	Other	2	Other	<1

U.S. Light-Duty Vehicle Fuel Efficiency, 1975-2022

Source: Natl. Vehicle and Fuel Emissions Laboratory, Office of Transportation and Air Quality, U.S. Environmental Protection Agency

Cars and light-duty trucks (SUVs, minivans, passenger vans, and pickup trucks) showed significant fuel-efficiency improvements from 1975 through 1987, when the fuel economy for both combined reached a high of 22 miles per gallon (mpg). The fuel economy value mainly declined, 1988-2004, but since 2005, fuel economy has generally increased, reaching a new all-time high of 26.4 mpg in 2022.

Year[1]	Cars (mpg)	Light-duty trucks (mpg)	All light-duty vehicles (mpg)	Year[1]	Cars (mpg)	Light-duty trucks (mpg)	All light-duty vehicles (mpg)
1975	13.5	11.6	13.1	2011	25.4	19.1	22.3
1980	20.0	15.8	19.2	2012	26.9	19.3	23.6
1985	23.0	17.5	21.3	2013	27.6	19.8	24.2
1990	23.3	17.4	21.2	2014	27.6	20.3	24.1
1995	23.3	17.0	20.5	2015	28.2	21.1	24.6
2000	22.5	16.8	19.8	2016	28.5	21.2	24.7
2005	23.1	16.9	19.9	2017	29.2	21.3	24.9
2006	23.0	17.2	20.1	2018	29.9	21.9	25.1
2007	23.7	17.4	20.6	2019	29.9	22.0	24.9
2008	23.9	17.8	21.0	2020	30.7	22.4	25.4
2009	25.0	18.5	22.4	2021	31.8	22.7	25.4
2010	25.7	18.8	22.6	2022[2]	33.3	23.4	26.4

Note: Adjusted mpg composite values (city and highway fuel efficiency combined in a 55%/45% ratio) are used for all vehicles and are intended to reflect real-world use. (1) Because of changes in methodology, mpg figures prior to 1986 are not entirely comparable with later values. (2) Preliminary.

Registered Cars in the U.S., 1900-2021

Source: Office of Highway Policy Information, Federal Highway Administration, U.S. Dept. of Transportation

(number of automobiles for public and private use)

Year	Reg. cars	Year	Reg. cars	Year	Reg. cars	Year	Reg. cars	Year	Reg. cars
1900	8,000	1945	25,796,985	1990	133,700,497	2006	135,399,945	2014	113,898,845
1905	77,400	1950	40,339,077	1995	128,386,775	2007	135,932,930	2015	112,864,228
1910	458,377	1955	52,144,739	2000	133,621,420	2008	137,079,843	2016	112,961,266
1915	2,332,426	1960	61,671,390	2001	137,633,467	2009	134,879,600	2017	111,177,029
1920	8,131,522	1965	75,257,588	2002	135,920,677	2010	130,892,240	2018	111,242,132
1925	17,481,001	1970	89,243,557	2003	135,669,897	2011	125,656,528	2019	108,547,710
1930	23,034,753	1975	106,705,934	2004	136,430,651	2012	111,289,906	2020	105,143,990
1935	22,567,827	1980	121,600,843	2005	136,568,083	2013	113,676,345	2021	102,973,881
1940	27,465,826	1985	127,885,193						

Note: There were no publicly owned vehicles before 1925; statistics also exclude military vehicles for all years. Alaska and Hawaii data included since 1960.

Licensed Drivers by Age and Sex, 1980-2021

Source: Office of Highway Policy Information, Federal Highway Administration, U.S. Dept. of Transportation
(numbers in thousands)

Age (years)	1980 Total	1990 Total	2000 Total	2010 Male	2010 Female	2010 Total	2021 Male	2021 Female	2021 Total	% total drivers
Under 16	93	43	27	199	198	398	55	56	111	0.0%
16	1,823	1,443	1,470	608	605	1,213	537	554	1,091	0.5
17	2,790	2,132	2,331	1,025	1,004	2,028	918	908	1,826	0.8
18	3,247	2,595	2,839	1,408	1,323	2,731	1,319	1,243	2,561	1.1
19	3,542	3,037	3,077	1,641	1,546	3,187	1,490	1,428	2,918	1.3
19 and under	11,496	9,249	9,744	4,880	4,676	9,556	4,318	4,189	8,508	3.7
20	3,636	3,229	3,140	1,744	1,682	3,426	1,658	1,576	3,234	1.4
21	3,733	3,249	3,172	1,756	1,717	3,474	1,772	1,679	3,450	1.5
22	3,811	3,262	3,182	1,757	1,725	3,483	1,769	1,687	3,457	1.5
23	3,938	3,398	3,247	1,767	1,748	3,515	1,829	1,756	3,585	1.5
24	3,915	3,758	3,225	1,792	1,779	3,571	1,886	1,824	3,709	1.6
20-24	19,032	16,897	15,966	8,817	8,651	17,469	8,914	8,522	17,436	7.5
25-29	18,925	19,895	17,586	9,179	9,253	18,431	9,984	9,812	19,796	8.5
30-34	17,369	20,578	19,155	8,934	8,915	17,849	10,419	10,439	20,859	9.0
35-39	13,696	19,055	21,059	9,079	9,082	18,161	10,118	10,186	20,304	8.7
40-44	11,134	16,905	21,093	9,613	9,565	19,178	9,558	9,681	19,239	8.3
45-49	10,076	13,020	19,154	10,381	10,433	20,814	9,001	9,107	18,108	7.8
50-54	10,090	10,484	16,868	10,241	10,388	20,628	9,617	9,719	19,336	8.3
55-59	9,770	9,438	12,760	9,127	9,313	18,440	9,851	10,065	19,916	8.6
60-64	8,232	9,235	9,915	7,847	8,011	15,858	9,657	10,040	19,697	8.5
65-69	6,580	8,375	8,386	5,652	5,816	11,468	8,295	8,811	17,105	7.3
70-74	NA	NA	7,468	4,029	4,202	8,231	6,704	7,223	13,927	6.0
75-79	NA	NA	5,911	2,966	3,192	6,158	4,324	4,717	9,041	3.9
80-84	NA	NA	3,511	2,090	2,373	4,464	2,537	2,842	5,380	2.3
85 and over	NA	NA	2,050	1,541	1,870	3,411	1,917	2,213	4,130	1.8
Total................	145,295	167,015	190,625	104,374	105,740	210,115	115,215	117,567	232,782	100.0

NA = Not available. **Note:** Numbers may not add up to totals due to rounding.

Mobile Device Handheld Phone and Texting Laws for Drivers, 2023

Source: Insurance Institute for Highway Safety; as of Aug. 2023

State	Handheld ban	Texting ban	Enforcement	State	Handheld ban	Texting ban	Enforcement	State	Handheld ban	Texting ban	Enforcement
AL	Yes	Yes	S[1]	KY	No[5]	Yes	P	ND	No[5]	Yes	P
AK	No	Yes	P	LA	No[5,6,7]	Yes	P[8]	OH	No[5]	Yes	P
AZ	Yes	Yes	P[2]	ME	Yes	Yes	P	OK	No[6]	Yes	P
AR	No[3]	Yes	P	MD	Yes	Yes	P	OR	Yes	Yes	P
CA	Yes	Yes	P[4]	MA	Yes	Yes	P	PA	No	Yes	P
CO	No[5]	Yes	P	MI	Yes[6]	Yes	P	RI	Yes	Yes	P
CT	Yes	Yes	P	MN	Yes	Yes	P	SC	No	Yes	P
DE	Yes	Yes	P	MS	No	Yes	P	SD	No[6]	Yes	P[12]
DC	Yes	Yes	P	MO	Yes	Yes	S[9]	TN	Yes	Yes	P
FL	No	Yes	S	MT	No	No	NA	TX	No[5]	Yes	P[4]
GA	Yes	Yes	P	NE	No[10]	Yes	S	UT	No[5]	Yes	P
HI	Yes	Yes	P	NV	Yes	Yes	P	VT	Yes	Yes	P
ID	Yes	Yes	P	NH	Yes	Yes	P	VA	Yes	Yes	P
IL	Yes	Yes	P	NJ	Yes	Yes	P	WA	Yes	Yes	P
IN	Yes	Yes	P	NM	No[6]	Yes	P	WV	Yes	Yes	P
IA	No[6]	Yes	P	NY	Yes	Yes	P	WI	No[6]	Yes	P
KS	No[6]	Yes	P	NC	No[5]	Yes	P	WY	No	Yes	P

NA = Not applicable. P = Officer may stop vehicle for violation (primary); S = Officer may issue citation only when vehicle is stopped for another moving violation (secondary). **Note:** Laws shown for licensed passenger car drivers. Different laws and regulations apply to school bus, municipal transit, and other mass transit operators. Different laws may apply in school zones, construction zones, or other such areas. (1) Primary for 16-year-old drivers and for 17-year-old drivers who have held an intermediate license for fewer than 6 months. (2) Secondary for learner's permit holders and intermediate license holders during the first 6 months after licensing. (3) Yes for drivers under 21 years of age. (4) Secondary for cellphone use by young drivers. (5) Yes for drivers under 18. (6) Yes for learner's permit and intermediate license holders. (7) Yes for drivers in the year after getting their first license. (8) Secondary for cellphone use by novice drivers age 18 and older. (9) An officer may only issue a warning. (10) Yes for learner's permit and intermediate license holders under 18. (11) Primary for drivers younger than 18. (12) Secondary for learner's permit and intermediate license holders.

Selected Motor Vehicle Statistics

Source: Federal Highway Admin., U.S. Dept. of Transportation; Insurance Inst. for Highway Safety; U.S. Energy Information Admin. Driver's license age requirements, state gas tax, and safety belt use laws (incl. laws passed, but not in effect) as of 2023. Other figures are for 2021.

STATE	Driver's license age requirements		Gas taxes (cents/ gal)[5]	Safety belt use law[6]	Licensed drivers		Reg. motor vehicles per 1,000 pop.	Fuel use per reg. motor vehicle (gal)	Annual miles driven		
	Learner's permit	Regular[1]			Per 1,000 resident pop.	Per reg. motor vehicle			Per gal used	Per reg. vehicle	Per lic. driver
Alabama	15	17	47.60	P(a)	806	0.74	1,084	798	16.49	13,157	17,699
Alaska	14	16y, 6m	27.35	P	709	0.77	936	604	13.87	8,383	11,077
Arizona	15y, 6m	16y, 6m	37.40	S	796	0.97	833	677	17.97	12,162	12,728
Arkansas	14	18	43.30	P	762	0.66	1,175	646	16.72	10,809	16,657
California	15y, 6m	17	86.52	P	691	0.88	799	549	18.07	9,915	11,464
Colorado	15	17	44.34	S	759	0.88	877	599	17.63	10,564	12,204
Connecticut	16	18[2,3,4]	43.40	P(a)	723	0.95	765	616	17.08	10,516	11,122
Delaware	16	17[2]	41.40	P	846	1.83	471	1,237	17.38	21,501	11,965
Dist. of Columbia	16	18[4]	52.60	P	763	1.53	542	337	26.51	8,940	6,356
Florida	15	18	55.70	P	741	0.85	881	582	19.50	11,343	13,476
Georgia	15	18[2]	50.35	P	710	0.85	847	691	19.10	13,200	15,747
Hawaii	15y, 6m	17[2]	36.90	P	636	0.75	857	380	21.24	8,071	10,869
Idaho	14y, 6m	16[2]	51.40	S	707	0.68	1,040	644	15.17	9,770	14,372
Illinois	15	18[2]	84.90	P	660	0.76	868	534	16.60	8,863	11,659
Indiana	15	18	73.90	P	681	0.74	917	724	17.40	12,600	16,963
Iowa	14	17[2]	48.40	P	735	0.62	1,202	631	13.64	8,606	14,087
Kansas	14	16y, 6m	43.43	P(a)	712	0.81	888	704	17.27	12,160	15,166
Kentucky	16	17[2]	48.50	P	661	0.69	978	695	15.69	10,913	16,143
Louisiana	15	17[4]	39.33	P	743	0.92	835	785	18.05	14,169	15,920
Maine	15	16y, 9m[2]	49.80	P	770	0.76	1,011	622	16.88	10,492	13,781
Maryland	15y, 9m	18[2]	65.59	P(a)	720	0.92	797	628	18.36	11,526	12,749
Massachusetts	16	18[2]	45.60	S	702	0.95	745	572	19.85	11,353	12,064
Michigan	14y, 9m	17[2]	66.10	P	794	0.85	951	580	17.45	10,123	12,120
Minnesota	15	17[2]	49.00	P	726	0.75	966	591	17.54	10,372	13,799
Mississippi	15	16y, 6m	36.80	P	689	0.86	809	1,044	16.40	17,124	20,097
Missouri	15	17y, 11m	43.37	S(b)	693	0.76	909	774	18.39	14,238	18,664
Montana	14y, 6m	16[2]	52.15	S	776	0.40	1,938	414	15.23	6,300	15,737
Nebraska	15	17	48.30	P	733	0.76	985	752	14.59	10,969	14,741
Nevada	15y, 6m	18[2]	42.21	S	684	0.80	851	614	16.47	10,118	12,590
New Hampshire	15y, 6m	18[2]	42.23	None	846	0.84	1,021	579	15.99	9,260	11,176
New Jersey	16	18	59.85	P	697	1.05	674	694	16.97	11,788	11,401
New Mexico	15	16y, 6m[2]	37.28	P	698	0.82	880	955	15.08	14,400	18,158
New York	16	17[2]	36.88	P	599	1.27	474	723	15.72	11,358	8,996
North Carolina	15	16y, 6m[2]	59.15	P(a)	736	0.91	825	724	18.68	13,521	15,162
North Dakota	14	16[2]	41.43	P	709	0.61	1,194	759	13.18	10,004	16,837
Ohio	15y, 6m	18[2]	56.90	S	703	0.77	925	600	17.29	10,367	13,632
Oklahoma	15y, 6m	16y, 6m	38.40	P	652	0.78	841	870	15.34	13,349	17,232
Oregon	15	17[2,3]	56.40	P	714	0.77	945	547	16.81	9,186	12,159
Pennsylvania	16	17	80.60	S(b)	702	0.84	843	572	16.44	9,397	11,286
Rhode Island	16	17y, 6m[2]	56.52	P	689	0.96	732	543	17.29	9,388	9,975
South Carolina	15	16y, 6m	47.15	P	769	0.85	981	742	15.23	11,291	14,406
South Dakota	14	16	48.40	S	750	0.48	1,600	538	12.97	6,974	14,891
Tennessee	15	17	45.80	P	718	0.76	962	687	17.92	12,304	16,487
Texas	15[2]	18	38.40	P	620	0.81	779	884	14.02	12,386	15,577
Utah	15	17[2]	53.55	P	675	0.81	850	632	18.74	11,851	15,240
Vermont	15	16y, 6m[2]	50.92	S	727	0.78	952	568	18.98	10,784	14,107
Virginia	15y, 6m	18[2]	57.50	S	684	0.79	885	687	15.24	10,468	13,548
Washington	15	17[2]	71.22	P	758	0.76	1,029	424	17.10	7,255	9,849
West Virginia	15	17	55.60	P	638	0.95	684	1,086	12.15	13,190	14,126
Wisconsin	15[2]	16y, 9m[2]	51.30	P	736	0.77	978	616	18.29	11,264	14,970
Wyoming	15	16y, 6m[2]	42.40	S	744	0.50	1,505	846	15.06	12,740	25,778
U.S. AVERAGE			**50.66**		**702**	**0.84**	**851**	**656**	**16.91**	**11,094**	**13,456**

Note: Most states have graduated licensing systems that phase in full driving privileges. During the learner's stage, driving generally is not permitted without adult supervision. In an intermediate stage, young licensees may be allowed to drive unsupervised under certain conditions. (1) Min. age at which all restrictions may be lifted on private passenger car operation. (2) Applicants under a specified age (typically between 17 and 19) must complete driver education. (3) Home training (CT) or more hours of supervised driving (OR) may be substituted for driver ed. (4) Learner's stage mandatory for all license applicants regardless of age. (5) Includes 18.4 cents per gallon in federal excise taxes. (6) P = Officer may stop vehicle for violation (primary); S = Officer may issue seat belt citation only when vehicle is stopped for another moving violation (secondary). (a) Secondary enforcement for rear seat occupants; (b) Primary enforcement for children under a specified age.

International Tourism Receipts, 2000-22

Source: World Tourism Organization (UNWTO), © UNWTO; as of Aug. 2023
(in billions of U.S. dollars; ranked by 2022 figures)

Rank	Country	2000	2010	2019	2020	2021	2022
1.	U.S.	$100.2	$130.3	$199.0	$72.5	$70.2	$135.2
2.	Spain	30.9	58.8	79.7	18.5	34.5	72.9
3.	Italy	22.2	38.6	58.6	26.6	33.1	68.2
4.	France	33.0	57.1	63.5	32.6	40.8	59.7
5.	Italy	27.5	38.8	49.6	19.8	25.2	44.3
6.	Türkiye	7.6	22.6	34.3	13.3	26.6	41.2
7.	United Arab Emirates	1.1	31.5	38.4	24.6	34.4	NA
8.	Germany	18.7	34.7	41.8	22.1	22.3	31.5
9.	Mexico	8.3	12.0	24.6	11.0	19.8	28.0
10.	Canada	10.8	17.6	29.8	13.6	14.5	24.0
11.	Saudi Arabia	NA	6.7	16.4	4.0	3.8	23.5
12.	Australia	9.4	32.6	45.5	25.8	17.0	23.4
13.	Portugal	5.2	10.1	20.5	8.8	11.9	22.2
14.	Austria	9.8	18.6	22.9	13.8	9.9	19.2
15.	Greece	9.2	12.7	20.4	4.9	12.4	18.6
16.	Switzerland	6.6	14.8	18.1	10.2	11.0	16.2
17.	Netherlands	7.2	11.7	18.6	9.7	9.4	16.1
18.	Poland	5.7	9.4	14.0	8.2	9.1	14.4
19.	Croatia	2.8	7.2	11.8	5.5	10.8	13.4
20.	South Korea	6.8	10.3	20.9	10.3	10.8	12.0
21.	Singapore	5.1	14.2	20.3	5.4	4.1	11.8
22.	China[1]	16.2	45.8	35.8	10.0	11.3	9.6
23.	Japan	3.4	13.2	46.1	10.7	4.9	9.2
24.	Sweden	4.1	8.3	9.2	4.3	6.1	9.0
25.	Morocco	2.0	6.7	8.2	3.8	3.8	9.0
26.	Egypt	NA	$12.5	$13.0	$4.4	$8.9	NA
27.	Macau	$3.2	22.3	40.1	9.2	15.3	$8.7
28.	Denmark	3.7	5.9	8.7	4.0	4.5	8.7
29.	India	3.5	14.5	30.7	13.0	8.7	NA
30.	Dom. Rep.	2.9	4.2	7.5	2.7	5.7	8.4
31.	Qatar	0.1	0.6	5.4	3.6	4.3	7.3
32.	Belgium	6.6	11.4	8.8	6.4	6.3	6.9
33.	Indonesia	5.0	7.0	16.9	3.4	0.5	6.7
34.	Malaysia	5.0	18.1	19.8	3.0	0.1	6.3
35.	Colombia	1.0	2.8	5.7	1.6	2.7	6.3
36.	Ireland	2.6	4.1	6.5	2.4	2.7	6.2
37.	Jordan	NA	3.6	5.8	1.4	2.8	5.8
38.	Hungary	3.8	5.7	7.3	3.2	4.2	5.6
39.	Russia	3.4	8.8	11.0	3.9	4.0	5.5
40.	Israel	4.4	4.9	7.6	2.5	2.2	5.5
41.	Norway	2.2	4.7	5.9	1.8	1.9	5.5
42.	Luxembourg	NA	5.7	5.3	4.4	5.5	5.3
43.	Czechia	3.0	7.2	7.3	3.6	3.1	5.1
44.	Thailand	7.5	20.1	59.8	13.4	5.1	NA
45.	Brazil	1.8	5.3	6.0	3.0	2.9	5.0
46.	Romania	NA	1.1	3.6	1.4	3.3	4.8
47.	South Africa	2.7	9.1	8.4	2.5	2.1	4.8
48.	Philippines	2.2	2.6	9.8	1.8	0.6	4.2
49.	New Zealand	2.9	6.5	10.5	5.8	2.9	4.2
50.	Vietnam	NA	4.5	11.8	2.5	0.1	3.8
	World[2]	495	983	1,467	550	627	1,012

NA = Not available. (1) Not including Hong Kong and Macau. (2) Includes countries not shown.

International Tourist Arrivals by Country of Destination, 2000-22

Source: World Tourism Organization (UNWTO), © UNWTO; as of Aug. 2023
(visitors in millions; ranked by 2022 figures)

Rank	Country	2000	2010	2019	2020	2021	2022	% change, 2000-22
1.	Spain	46.4	52.7	83.5	18.9	31.2	71.7	54.4%
2.	U.S.	51.2	60.0	79.4	19.2	22.1	50.9	-0.6
3.	Türkiye	9.6	31.4	51.2	15.9	29.9	50.5	425.5
4.	Italy	41.2	43.6	64.5	25.2	26.9	49.8	20.9
5.	France	77.2	77.7	90.9	41.7	48.4	NA	NA
6.	Mexico	20.6	23.3	45.0	24.3	31.9	38.3	86.1
7.	UK	23.2	28.9	39.4	11.1	5.9	30.5	31.6
8.	Germany	19.0	23.9	35.2	10.9	10.3	28.5	49.8
9.	Greece	13.1	15.0	31.4	7.4	14.7	27.8	112.5
10.	Austria	18.0	16.2	22.7	9.6	8.4	26.2	45.6
11.	United Arab Emirates	3.1[2]	7.4[2]	21.6	7.2	11.5	22.7	626.0
12.	Denmark	3.5	26.7	32.1	16.1	18.4	NA	NA
13.	Saudi Arabia	6.6	10.9	17.5	4.1	3.5	16.5	150.2
14.	Netherlands	10.0	10.8	17.5	5.1	4.3	15.9	59.4
15.	Croatia	5.3	9.0	17.4	5.6	10.6	15.3	189.1
16.	Canada	19.6	16.2	22.2	3.0	3.1	12.8	-34.6
17.	Romania	NA	7.5	12.8	5.0	6.8	12.7	NA
18.	Hungary	3.0	9.5	16.9	7.4	7.9	12.7	321.7
19.	Thailand	9.6	15.9	39.9	6.7	0.4	11.2	16.1
20.	Bulgaria	2.8	6.1	12.6	5.0	7.2	10.9	288.9
21.	Morocco	4.3	9.3	12.9	2.8	3.7	10.9	152.8
22.	Malaysia	10.2	24.6	26.1	4.3	0.1	10.1	-1.3
23.	Poland	17.4	58.3	21.2	8.4	9.7	NA	NA
24.	Portugal	5.7	6.8	24.6	6.5	9.6	NA	NA
25.	Belgium	6.5	7.2	9.3	2.6	3.2	8.2	26.6
26.	Dom. Rep.	3.0	4.1	6.5	2.4	5.0	7.2	138.7%
27.	India	2.6	5.8	17.9	6.3	7.0	NA	NA
28.	Albania	NA	2.4	6.4	2.7	5.7	6.7	NA
29.	Tunisia	5.1	7.8	9.4	2.0	2.5	6.4	26.3
30.	Singapore	6.1	11.6	19.1	2.7	0.3	6.3	3.4
31.	South Africa	5.9	8.1	10.2	2.8	2.3	5.7	-3.4
32.	China	31.2	55.7	65.7	8.0	5.7	NA	NA
33.	Indonesia	5.0	7.0	16.1	4.1	1.6	5.5	NA
34.	Uzbekistan	NA	1.0	6.8	1.6	1.9	5.2	NA
35.	Kazakhstan	NA	4.1	8.5	2.0	1.3	4.7	NA
36.	Colombia	NA	2.4	4.2	1.3	2.2	4.4	NA
37.	Jordan	NA	4.2	4.5	1.1	2.0	4.3	NA
38.	Ukraine	6.4	21.2	13.4	3.4	4.3	NA	NA
39.	Iran	NA	2.9	9.1	1.6	1.0	4.1	NA
40.	Slovenia	NA	2.1	4.7	1.2	1.8	3.9	NA
41.	Argentina	2.9	6.7	7.4	2.1	0.3	3.9	34.1
42.	Japan	4.8	8.6	31.9	4.1	0.3	3.8	-20.2
43.	Bahrain	NA	12.0	11.1	1.9	2.2	3.7	NA
44.	Australia	4.9	5.9	9.5	1.8	0.3	3.7	-24.7
45.	Vietnam	2.1	5.1	18.0	3.8	0.2	3.7	74.3
46.	Georgia	NA	1.1	5.1	1.1	1.6	3.7	NA
47.	Brazil	5.3	5.2	6.4	2.2	0.8	3.6	-31.5
48.	Andorra	NA	1.8	3.1	1.9	2.0	3.6	NA
49.	Cyprus	NA	2.2	4.0	0.6	1.9	3.2	NA
50.	South Korea	5.3	8.8	17.5	2.5	1.0	3.2	-39.6
	World	674	963	1,465	407	456	963	42.9

NA = Not available. (1) Not including Hong Kong and Macau. (2) Dubai only. (3) Includes countries not shown.

World Tourism Receipts, 1990-2022

Source: World Tourism Organization (UNWTO), © UNWTO; as of Aug. 2023
(in billions of U.S. dollars)

Year	Receipts[1]	Year	Receipts[1]	Year	Receipts[1]	Year	Receipts[1]	Year	Receipts[1]	Year	Receipts[1]
1990	$271	1999	$475	2004	$652	2009	$901	2014	$1,294	2019	$1,467
1995	415	2000	495	2005	704	2010	983	2015	1,201	2020	550
1996	449	2001	481	2006	766	2011	1,099	2016	1,230	2021	627
1997	449	2002	501	2007	883	2012	1,142	2017	1,324	2022	1,012
1998	457	2003	549	2008	968	2013	1,236	2018	1,438		

(1) Total of all transactions made by or on behalf of visitors for the duration of their visit. Does not include receipts from international passenger transport contracted from companies outside a traveler's country of residence.

International Travel to the U.S., 1990-2022

Source: National Travel and Tourism Office, Intl. Trade Admin., U.S. Dept. of Commerce
(number of visitors in millions)

U.S. Domestic Leisure Travel Volume, 2000-22

Source: U.S. Travel Assn.
(in billions of person-trips of 50 mi or more, one-way)

Note: Method of collecting travel data has been revised; data for earlier years have been adjusted to maintain comparability.

Top 10 U.S. States by Traveler Spending, 2021

Source: U.S. Travel Assn.
(domestic and international traveler spending within state, in billions of dollars)

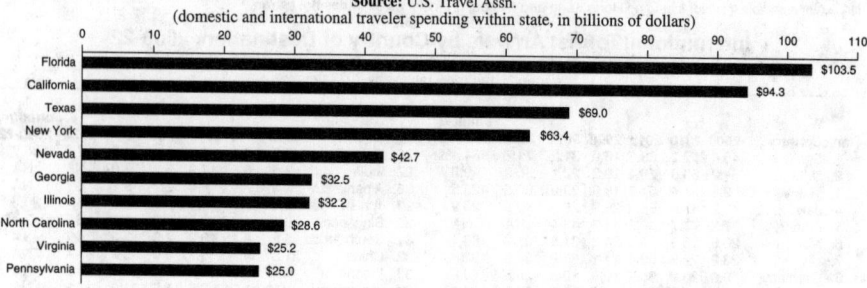

State	Spending
Florida	$103.5
California	$94.3
Texas	$69.0
New York	$63.4
Nevada	$42.7
Georgia	$32.5
Illinois	$32.2
North Carolina	$28.6
Virginia	$25.2
Pennsylvania	$25.0

International Visitors to the U.S. by Top Countries of Origin, 2022

Source: National Travel and Tourism Office, Intl. Trade Admin., U.S. Dept. of Commerce
(ranked by number of visitors)

Country of origin	Visitors	Expenditures (mil)	Expenditures per visitor	Country of origin	Visitors	Expenditures (mil)	Expenditures per visitor
1. Canada	14,382,227	$14,678	$1,021	12. Australia	641,772	$4,508	$7,024
2. Mexico	12,534,501	17,946	1,432	13. Japan	597,330	3,136	5,250
3. United Kingdom	3,466,107	12,232	3,529	14. Argentina	524,841	2,446	4,660
4. Germany	1,481,008	5,964	4,027	15. Netherlands	473,009	1,801	3,808
5. France	1,317,882	4,849	3,679	16. Dominican Republic	431,672	1,744	4,040
6. India	1,256,915	13,228	10,524	17. Chile	411,931	1,604	3,894
7. Brazil	1,224,974	6,329	5,167	18. Ireland	402,619	1,525	3,788
8. Colombia	943,819	3,291	3,487	19. Ecuador	369,927	NA	NA
9. South Korea	919,796	5,480	5,958	20. China	368,111	13,963	37,931
10. Spain	773,421	2,967	3,836	All countries	50,869,685	164,534	3,234
11. Italy	717,593	3,064	4,270				

NA = Not available. **Note:** Expenditures include passenger fares.

Traveler Spending in the U.S., 1987-2022

Source: National Travel and Tourism Office, Intl. Trade Admin., U.S. Dept. of Commerce; U.S. Travel Assn.
(in billions of dollars by origin of traveler)

Year	Domestic	International	Year	Domestic	International	Year	Domestic	International
1987	$235	$31	2003	$496	$65	2013	$751	$135
1990	291	43	2004	532	75	2014	792	136
1995	360	63	2005	572	82	2015	814	157
1996	385	70	2006	610	86	2016	837	156
1997	406	73	2007	641	97	2017	882	156
1998	425	71	2008	662	110	2018	933	156
1999	458	75	2009	606	94	2019	992	181
2000	503	82	2010	644	104	2020	682	41
2001	484	72	2011	694	119	2021	868	41
2002	478	67	2012	728	127	2022	918	99

Characteristics of U.S. Travelers Visiting Overseas Destinations, 2021

Source: Survey of Intl. Air Travelers, National Travel and Tourism Office, Intl. Trade Admin., U.S. Dept. of Commerce

Total U.S. resident travelers	18,214,000
Males	47.5%
Females	52.5%
Avg. age of males (yrs.)	43.5
Avg. age of females (yrs.)	42.0
Median annual household income	$100,000
Used prepaid package	7.6%
Visited only one country	92.8%
Advanced trip decision (median days)	45
Mean number of persons in travel party	1.5
Median number of nights	10

Main purpose of trip	% of travelers
Vacation/holiday	53.7%
Visit friends/relatives	36.8
Business	3.9
Education	2.1
Health treatment	1.1
Convention/conference/trade show	0.8
Religion/pilgrimage	0.7

Leisure/recreational activities[1]	% of travelers
Sightseeing	72.5%
Shopping	64.3
Small towns/countryside	40.6
Experience fine dining	32.6
Historical locations	29.2
Guided tours	28.5
Water sports	25.1
National parks/monuments	24.0
Cultural/ethnic heritage sites	22.7
Art galleries/museums	20.9
Nightclubbing	18.3
Environmental/ecological excursions	9.8
Amusement/theme parks	8.3
Casino/gamble	8.2
Camping/hiking	7.9
Concert/play/musical	6.5
Sporting event	4.6
Hunting/fishing	3.9
Golfing/tennis	3.4
Snow sports	1.3

(1) Percentages based on multiple responses.

U.S. Resident Travel Abroad, 1996-2022

Source: National Travel and Tourism Office, Intl. Trade Admin., U.S. Dept. of Commerce
(numbers in thousands)

Year	Canada	Mexico	Europe	Caribbean	Asia	S. Amer.	Cent. Amer.	Oceania	Middle East	Africa	Total
1996	3,047	3,992	8,946	4,021	3,155[1]	1,456	1,046	592	434	138	26,826
2000	3,836	4,949	12,963	4,664	3,931	1,878	1,598	877	445	230	35,371
2005	3,912	5,673	12,553	5,397	4,816	2,181	2,300	783	554	204	38,372
2010	11,749	20,015	11,104	5,716	4,861	2,129	2,263	687	1,339	408	37,355
2012	11,854	20,367	11,245	6,435	4,313	1,703	2,394	547	1,500	365	60,723
2013	12,008	20,546	11,408	6,546	4,327	1,735	2,496	572	1,579	352	61,570
2014	11,515	25,882	11,892	7,172	4,509	1,772	2,697	601	1,780	358	68,176
2015	12,669	28,733	12,599	7,648	4,843	1,869	2,791	643	2,045	351	74,191
2016	13,895	31,194	13,614	7,879	5,383	2,010	2,984	725	2,176	365	80,226
2017	14,326	35,050	15,793	8,321	5,771	1,925	3,032	776	2,306	403	87,703
2018	14,341	36,923	17,742	8,702	6,253	2,104	3,237	861	2,443	432	93,038
2019	14,994	39,942	19,049	9,368	6,546	2,338	3,451	958	2,545	552	99,745
2020	1,929	21,729	2,582	3,098	1,114	772	1,104	247	737	187	33,499
2021	2,093	28,789	5,238	6,399	626	1,401	2,585	63	1,516	385	49,097
2022	9,088	33,540	15,822	9,208	2,653	2,506	3,702	461	3,120	630	80,730

Note: 2010-22 estimates for Canada and Mexico incl. all modes of transportation used. Estimates for Canada and Mexico (1996-2005) and for all other regions for all years are available only for air travel to countries in that region. (1) Region called Far East.

U.S. Commercial Airline Safety, 1985-2021

Source: National Transportation Safety Board; Federal Aviation Administration, U.S. Dept. of Transportation

Year	Departures (mil)	Fatal accidents	Fatalities[1]	Rate of fatal accidents[2]	Year	Departures (mil)	Fatal accidents	Fatalities[1]	Rate of fatal accidents[2]
1985	6.1	4	197	0.066	2011	9.4	0	0	—
1990	7.8	4	11	0.051	2012	9.2	0	0	—
1995	8.1	1	160	0.012	2013	9.3	0	0	—
2000	11.1	2	89	0.018	2014	9.0	0	0	—
2001[3]	10.6	6	531	0.019	2015	9.0	0	0	—
2005	10.9	3	22	0.027	2016	9.1	0	0	—
2006	10.6	2	50	0.019	2017	9.1	0	0	—
2007	10.7	0	0	—	2018	9.4	1	1	0.011
2008	10.3	0	0	—	2019	9.6	1	1	0.010
2009	9.6	1	50	0.010	2020	5.8	0	0	—
2010	9.5	0	0	—	2021	7.6	0	0	—

— = Not applicable. Note: Statistics are for scheduled commercial carriers. (1) Includes deaths that occurred on the ground as a result of an accident, except for fatalities resulting from the Sept. 11, 2001, terrorist attacks. (2) Per 100,000 departures. (3) The Sept. 11, 2001, terrorist attacks have been included among the number of fatal accidents but have been excluded when calculating the fatal accident rate.

U.S. Airline Statistics, 1995-2022

Source: Airlines for America

	1995	2000	2005	2010	2015	2018	2020	2021	2022
Passengers enplaned (mil)[1]	547.8	666.1	738.6	720.5	798.2	889.0	369.4	666.2	852.5
Revenue passenger miles (bil)[1,2]	540.7	692.8	779.0	798.0	902.2	1,011.5	378.0	687.9	947.9
Available seat miles (bil)[1,3]	807.1	957.0	1,003.4	972.6	1,077.0	1,208.2	643.2	932.9	1,141.2
Cargo revenue ton miles (mil)[1,2]	16,921	23,888	28,039	27,885	27,062	30,638	28,742	32,421	32,339
% of seating utilized[1]	67.0%	72.4%	77.6%	82.1%	83.8%	83.7%	58.8%	73.7%	83.1%
Passenger revenue (mil)[4] . . .	$70,132	$94,307	$94,340	$104,431	$126,880	$139,005	$49,888	$86,705	$155,155
Net profit (mil)[4]	$2,001	$2,238	−$28,647	$2,245	$24,794	$11,775	−$35,047	−$2,801	$1,630
Total employment (thous.)[5]	595.6	739.6	619.6	564.4	605.3	719.2	707.9	715.9	765.1

(1) Scheduled service only. (2) One fare-paying passenger or one ton of revenue cargo transported one mile. (3) One seat transported one mile. (4) Passenger carriers only. (5) Figures are of the sum of full-time and part-time employees.

Top 25 U.S. Passenger Airlines, 2022

Source: Airlines for America

In 2022, 99.7% of all passengers enplaned flew on the top 25 U.S. passenger airlines.
(in millions; ranked by number of passengers enplaned in scheduled service in 2022)

#	Airline	Passengers	#	Airline	Passengers	#	Airline	Passengers	#	Airline	Passengers
1.	Southwest Airlines	157.0	8.	Alaska Airlines	31.7	15.	Hawaiian Airlines	10.0	21.	Air Wisconsin Airlines	2.9
2.	American Airlines	150.8	9.	Frontier Airlines	25.5	16.	Mesa Airlines	7.8	22.	GoJet Airlines	2.0
3.	Delta Air Lines	141.6	10.	Allegiant Air	16.7	17.	Horizon Air	5.6	23.	Avelo Airlines	1.2
4.	United Air Lines	112.6	11.	Republic Airline	16.1	18.	Piedmont Airlines	3.7	24.	Breeze Airways	1.0
5.	SkyWest Airlines	39.9	12.	Envoy Air	14.0	19.	Sun Country Airlines	3.6	25.	Silver Airways	0.6
6.	JetBlue Airways	36.6	13.	Endeavor Air	12.3	20.	Commutair	3.2			
7.	Spirit Air Lines	38.4	14.	PSA Airlines	12.2						

Note: Includes domestic and international passengers on U.S. airlines.

Top North American Airports by Passenger Traffic, 2022

Top World Airports by Passenger Traffic, 2022

Source: Annual World Airport Traffic Report, 2023 Edition, Airports Council Intl.

City/airport name (airport code)	Total passengers[1]	City/airport name (country; airport code)	Total passengers[1]
1. Hartsfield-Jackson Atlanta Intl. (ATL)	93,699,630	1. Dubai Intl. (United Arab Emirates; DXB)	66,069,981
2. Dallas/Ft. Worth Intl. (DFW)	73,362,946	2. Istanbul Intl. (Turkey [Türkiye]; IST)	64,289,107
3. Denver Intl. (DEN)	69,286,461	3. London Heathrow (UK; LHR)	61,614,230
4. Chicago O'Hare Intl. (ORD)	68,340,619	4. Delhi Indira Gandhi Intl. (India; DEL)	59,490,074
5. Los Angeles Intl. (LAX)	65,924,298	5. Paris Charles de Gaulle (France; CDG)	57,474,033
6. New York John F. Kennedy Intl. (JFK)	55,287,711	6. Amsterdam Schiphol (Netherlands; AMS)	52,472,188
7. Las Vegas McCarran Intl. (LAS)	52,694,312	7. Adolfo Suárez Madrid-Barajas (Spain; MAD)	50,602,864
8. Miami Intl. (MIA)	50,684,396	8. Tokyo Haneda Intl. (Japan; HND)	50,334,354
9. Orlando Intl. (MCO)	50,178,499	9. Flughafen Frankfurt/Main (Germany; FRA)	48,918,482
10. Charlotte Douglas Intl. (CLT)	47,758,605	10. Barcelona-El Prat (Spain; BCN)	41,616,302
11. Mexico City Benito Juárez Intl. (MEX)	46,258,521	11. Jakarta Soekarno-Hatta Intl. (Indonesia; CGK)	39,603,449
12. Seattle-Tacoma Intl. (SEA)	45,964,321	12. Mumbai Chhatrapati Shivaji Intl. (India; BOM)	38,332,106
13. Phoenix Sky Harbor Intl. (PHX)	44,397,854	13. Doha Hamad Intl. (Qatar; DOH)	35,730,482
14. Newark Liberty Intl. (EWR)	43,565,254	14. Bogotá El Dorado Intl. (Colombia; BOG)	35,362,529
15. San Francisco Intl. (SFO)	42,281,641	15. São Paulo Guarulhos Intl. (Brazil; GRU)	34,481,318
16. Houston George Bush Intercontinental (IAH)	40,974,831	16. Ho Chi Minh City Tan Son Nhat Intl. (Vietnam; SGN)	34,278,320
17. Boston Logan Intl. (BOS)	36,112,473	17. London Gatwick (UK; LGW)	32,848,088
18. Toronto Pearson Intl. (YYZ)	35,627,429	18. Singapore Changi (Singapore; SIN)	32,202,000
19. Ft. Lauderdale-Hollywood Intl. (FLL)	31,686,404	19. Jeddah King Abulaziz Intl. (Saudi Arabia; JED)	31,649,459
20. Minneapolis/St. Paul Intl. (MSP)	31,241,822	20. Munich (Germany; MUC)	31,642,738

Note: World list excludes North American airports and airports that do not participate in Airports Council Intl.'s Airport Traffic Statistics collection. (1) Arriving and departing passengers and direct transit passengers counted once.

Busiest Amtrak Stations, 2022

Source: Amtrak

(in thous.; ranked by total ridership)

Station	Tickets from	Tickets to	Total ridership	Station	Tickets from	Tickets to	Total ridership
New York (Penn. Sta.), NY	3,963	4,046	8,009	Sacramento, CA	245	212	457
Washington, DC	1,821	1,811	3,632	San Diego (Downtown), CA	228	215	443
Philadelphia (30th Street Sta.), PA	1,524	1,534	3,058	Wilmington, DE	219	215	434
Chicago (Union Sta.), IL	1,173	1,187	2,359	Seattle (King Street Sta.), WA	194	190	385
Boston (South Sta.), MA	606	611	1,217	Milwaukee (Downtown), WI	196	184	380
Los Angeles, CA	464	464	929	Portland (Union Sta.), OR	188	187	375
Baltimore (Penn Sta.), MD	425	414	839	Boston (North Sta.), MA	168	179	347
Albany-Rensselaer, NY	323	318	640	Bakersfield, CA	156	159	315
New Haven (Union Sta.), CT	312	306	617	Lancaster, PA	163	142	306
Boston (Back Bay Sta.), MA	299	308	607	Route 128 (Westwood), MA	151	152	304
Providence (Amtrak), RI	279	290	569	Richmond (Staples Mill Rd.), VA	155	148	303
BWI Airport Sta., MD	260	262	522	St. Louis, MO	146	147	293
Newark (Penn Sta.), NJ	246	249	495				

U.S. Public Transportation Usage, 1996-2021

Source: Federal Transit Administration, U.S. Dept. of Transportation

Public transportation usage is measured in unlinked passenger trips (UPT), which counts the number of passengers who board public transportation vehicles each time they board.

(UPT in millions)

Number of passengers by year						Number of passengers by mode of transportation		
Year	UPT	Year	UPT	Year	UPT	Mode	2012 UPT	2021 UPT	% change, 2012-21
1996	7,565	2006	9,379	2014	10,633	Bus	5,212	2,234	−57.1%
1997	7,982	2007	10,054	2015	10,496	Heavy rail[1]	3,743	1,607	−57.1
1998	8,115	2008	10,367	2016	10,369	Commuter rail[2]	469	148	−68.4
1999	8,522	2009	10,252	2017	10,063	Light rail[3]	449	177	−60.6
2000	8,720	2010	10,082	2018	9,863	Other	347	156	−55.0
2002	9,018	2011	10,209	2019	9,880	Demand response[4]	102	63	−38.3
2004	8,937	2012	10,472	2020	5,938	Vanpool	36	16	−55.5
2005	9,175	2013	10,528	2021	4,469				

(1) An electric railway with the ability to carry a heavy volume of passengers and characterized by high-speed and rapid-acceleration passenger rail cars operating singly or in multi-car trains on fixed rails. (2) An electric- or diesel-propelled railway for urban passenger travel that operates between a central city and outlying areas. (3) An electric railway that operates singly on fixed rails and is powered by overhead electric lines. (4) Includes passenger cars, vans, or small buses dispatched by request to pick up passengers and transport them to their destinations.

Public Spending on Transportation Infrastructure, 1960-2017
Source: *Public Spending on Transportation and Water Infrastructure, 1956 to 2017*, Congressional Budget Office

Year	Federal spending[1]			State and local spending[2]		
	Highways	Mass transit and rail	Aviation	Highways	Mass transit and rail	Aviation
1960	60.33%	0.20%	11.59%	61.45%	6.47%	2.70%
1970	55.81	1.89	17.30	59.98	7.47	4.42
1980	32.83	19.45	12.68	51.99	9.84	4.20
1990	42.17	12.69	20.92	43.15	13.25	4.92
2000	46.61	11.38	19.16	41.84	13.77	6.55
2005	45.03	14.00	20.42	40.27	14.86	6.30
2010	45.13	15.79	16.69	37.09	15.10	6.68
2015	46.73	15.71	17.36	38.10	71.01	5.86
2016	47.32	16.94	17.00	38.40	16.84	5.71
2017	46.59	17.30	17.05	38.31	16.83	5.94
PERCENT CHANGE						
1960-2017	−22.77	8,550.00	47.11	−37.66	160.12	120.00
2000-17	−0.04	52.02	−11.01	−8.44	22.22	−9.31

Note: State and local spending is net of federal grants and loan subsidies. (1) Figures represent percentage of total federal infrastructure spending for the year, including categories not shown. (2) Figures represent percentage of total state and local infrastructure spending for the year, including categories not shown.

Record-Breaking Roller Coasters
Source: Roller Coaster DataBase; World Almanac research; as of Aug. 2023

Steel-Tracked Roller Coasters

Fastest	Roller coaster	Theme park, location
149.1 mph	Formula Rossa	Ferrari World Abu Dhabi, United Arab Emirates
128.0	Kingda Ka	Six Flags Great Adventure, Jackson, NJ
111.8	Red Force	Ferrari Land, Salou, Spain
100.0	SUPERMAN: Escape from Krypton	Six Flags Magic Mountain, Valencia, CA
95.0	Steel Dragon 2000	Nagashima Spa Land, Kuwana, Japan
95.0	Fury 325	Carowinds, Charlotte, NC

Tallest
456 ft	Kingda Ka	Six Flags Great Adventure, Jackson, NJ
415	SUPERMAN: Escape from Krypton	Six Flags Magic Mountain, Valencia, CA
367.3	Red Force	Ferrari Land, Salou, Spain
325	Fury 325	Carowinds, Charlotte, NC
318.3	Steel Dragon 2000	Nagashima Spa Land, Kuwana, Japan

Largest drop
418 ft	Kingda Ka	Six Flags Great Adventure, Jackson, NJ
328.1	SUPERMAN: Escape from Krypton	Six Flags Magic Mountain, Valencia, CA
320	Fury 325	Carowinds, Charlotte, NC
306.8	Steel Dragon 2000	Nagashima Spa Land, Kuwana, Japan
306	Leviathan	Canada's Wonderland, Vaughan, ON, Canada

Longest
8,133.2 ft.	Steel Dragon 2000	Nagashima Spa Land, Kuwana, Japan
6,804.5	Formula Rossa	Ferrari World Abu Dhabi, United Arab Emirates
6,708.7	Fujiyama	Fuji-Q Highland, Fujiyoshida, Japan
6,602	Fury 325	Carowinds, Charlotte, NC
6,595	Millennium Force	Cedar Point, Sandusky, OH

Inversions
14	Smiler	Alton Towers, Alton, UK
10	Colossus	Thorpe Park, Chertsey, UK
10	10 Inversion Roller Coaster	Chimelong Paradise, Panyu, China
10	Crazy Coaster	Loca Joy Holiday Theme Park, Yongchuan, China
10	Altair	Cinecittà World, Rome, Italy
10	Velikolukskiy Myasokombinat-2	Wonder Island, St. Petersburg, Russia
10	Sik	Flamingo Land, Malton, UK

Wood-Tracked Roller Coasters

Fastest	Roller coaster	Theme park, location
72.0	Goliath	Six Flags Great America, Gurnee, IL
71.5	Wildfire	Kolmården Wildlife Park, Norrköping, Sweden
70.0	El Toro	Six Flags Great Adventure, Jackson, NJ
68.4	Colossos - Kampf der Giganten	Heide Park Resort, Soltau, Germany
68.0	Outlaw Run	Silver Dollar City, Branson, MO

Tallest
183.8 ft.	Wildfire	Kolmården Wildlife Park, Norrköping, Sweden
183.8	T Express	Everland, Yongin-si, S. Korea
181	El Toro	Six Flags Great Adventure, Jackson, NJ
165	Goliath	Six Flags Great America, Gurnee, IL
164	Colossos - Kampf der Giganten	Heide Park Resort, Soltau, Germany

Largest drop
180 ft	Goliath	Six Flags Great America, Gurnee, IL
176	El Toro	Six Flags Great Adventure, Jackson, NJ
162	Outlaw Run	Silver Dollar City, Branson, MO
160.8	Wildfire	Kolmården Wildlife Park, Norrköping, Sweden
159.1	Colossos - Kampf der Giganten	Heide Park Resort, Soltau, Germany

Longest
7,361 ft.	The Beast	Kings Island, Mason, OH
6,442	The Voyage	Holiday World, Santa Claus, IN
5,383.8	T Express	Everland, Yongin-si, S. Korea
5,383	Shivering Timbers	Michigan's Adventure, Muskegon, MI
5,249.3	Jupiter	Kijima Kogen, Beppu, Japan

Inversions
3	Outlaw Run	Silver Dollar City, Branson, MO
3	Wildfire	Kolmården Wildlife Park, Norrköping, Sweden
2	Goliath	Six Flags Great America, Gurnee, IL
1	Hades 360	Mt. Olympus Water & Theme Park, Wisconsin Dells, WI
1	Jungle Trailblazer	Oriental Heritage, Jiujiang, China
1	Jungle Trailblazer	Oriental Heritage, Huaiyin, China
1	Jungle Trailblazer	Oriental Heritage, Cixi, China
1	Mine Blower	Fun Spot America, Kissimmee, FL

Most Visited Amusement/Theme Parks, 2019-22

Source: Themed Entertainment Association
(visitors in thousands; ranked by 2019 figures)

	North America					**World**		
Rank	**Park, location**	**2019 visitors**	**2022 visitors**		**Rank**	**Park, location**	**2019 visitors**	**2022 visitors**
1.	Magic Kingdom[1], FL.........	20,963	17,133		1.	Tokyo Disneyland, Tokyo, Japan.........	17,910	12,000
2.	Disneyland, CA.............	18,666	16,881		2.	Tokyo DisneySea, Tokyo, Japan.........	14,650	10,100
3.	Disney's Animal Kingdom[1], FL ..	13,888	9,027		3.	Universal Studios Japan, Osaka, Japan....	14,500	12,350
4.	Epcot[1], FL.................	12,444	10,000		4.	Chimelong Ocean Kingdom, Hengqin, China	11,736	4,400
5.	Disney's Hollywood Studios[1], FL	11,483	10,900		5.	Shanghai Disneyland, Shanghai, China....	11,210	5,300
6.	Universal Studios Florida[2], FL ..	10,922	10,750		6.	Disneyland Park at Disneyland Paris,		
7.	Islands of Adventure[2], FL......	10,375	11,025			Marne-La-Vallée, France.............	9,745	9,930
8.	Disney California Adventure, CA	9,861	9,000		7.	Everland, Gyeonggi-do, South Korea.....	6,606	5,770
9.	Universal Studios Hollywood, CA	9,147	8,400		8.	Lotte World, Seoul, South Korea.........	5,953	4,520
10.	SeaWorld Orlando, FL	4,640	4,454		9.	Nagashima Spa Land, Kuwana, Japan....	5,950	4,200
					10.	Europa-Park, Rust, Germany............	5,750	6,000

Note: Ranked by 2019 figures because 2022 attendance trends continued to be impacted by the COVID-19 pandemic. World list excludes North American parks. (1) Located at Walt Disney World. (2) Located at Universal Orlando.

Passports, Foreign Travel, and Regulations for Air Travel

Source: Bureau of Consular Affairs, U.S. Dept. of State; Centers for Disease Control and Prevention (CDC), U.S. Dept. of Health and Human Services; Transportation Security Administration (TSA), U.S. Dept. of Homeland Security

Passports, Visas

Passports are issued by the Dept. of State to U.S. citizens and nationals to provide documentation for foreign travel. As of Oct. 2023, the fees for a new passport book and passport card for persons ages 16 and over total $195; provided certain criteria are met, these can be renewed for $160. For a passport book alone, fees are $165 for a new passport and $130 for passport renewal.

In 2008, the U.S. government began issuing passport cards. Travelers arriving by land or sea from Canada, Mexico, the Caribbean, and Bermuda may present a passport card to enter the U.S. Passport cards may not be used for air travel, however. The fees for a new passport card for persons ages 16 and over total $65 ($30 to renew).

As of Oct. 2023, the processing time for passport applications was 8-11 weeks, and expedited processing time was 5-7 weeks (at an additional $60 fee).

A U.S. passport is often sufficient for U.S. citizens to gain admission for a limited stay in another country. Some countries also require an entry visa. Each country has its own specific guidelines concerning length and purpose of visit, among other considerations. Visitors may need to provide proof of sufficient funds for their intended stay, onward/return tickets, and/or at least six months remaining validity on their U.S. passports.

All persons traveling by air outside of the U.S. (excluding direct travel to and from a U.S. territory) are required to present a passport or other valid document upon reentering the U.S.

For up-to-date passport and international travel information, visit the State Dept.'s Consular Affairs website (travel.state.gov) or call U.S. Passports at 1-877-487-2778.

COVID-19 Impact on Foreign Travel

The COVID-19 pandemic had a devastating effect on international travel in 2020, although travel began to increase in early 2021 and had returned to pre-pandemic levels by 2023. In May 2023, the CDC said that noncitizen, nonimmigrant air passengers no longer need to show proof of being fully vaccinated with a COVID-19 vaccine to board a flight to the U.S.

As of Oct. 2023, travelers were recommended to follow safety precautions related to the COVID-19 pandemic while traveling, including not traveling when sick, wearing face masks in crowded areas, and taking additional precautions if recently exposed to someone with COVID-19.

Summary of TSA Regulations

Airplane carry-ons. TSA promotes the liquids (or "3-1-1") rule regarding carry-on items. Containers with liquids, gels, aerosols, creams, or pastes must hold **3.4 oz**

(100 mL) or less; these containers should be packed inside a single **1**-quart, clear plastic, resealable bag; and this **1** bag must go through checkpoint security. Exceptions to the liquids rule include medication, baby formula and food, and breast milk; these items must be removed and screened separately.

Security checkpoint identification. Adult travelers (18 years of age and over) must present a photo ID. Acceptable documents include a U.S. passport or passport card; foreign government-issued passport; state-issued driver's license; permanent resident card; or U.S. Dept. of Defense ID, among others. Starting May 7, 2025, travelers using a state-issued driver's license must have the enhanced version or one that is compliant with the REAL ID Act.

Screening process. Travelers may wear loose fitting or religious garments (incl. head coverings) through security. They may be subject to additional screening if clothing could conceal prohibited items. Travelers may request a private area if selected for personal screening. Travelers will be screened by someone of the same gender.

In Dec. 2011, the TSA began the TSA PreCheck program, allowing expedited screening at airport security for preapproved passengers; the 5-year membership cost $85. As of Oct. 2023, this was available at more than 200 U.S. airports and by more than 90 participating airlines.

Disability-related permitted carry-on items:

- Wheelchairs, mobility scooters
- Crutches, canes, and walkers
- Portable oxygen concentrators (if they meet specific FAA criteria)
- Medications and associated supplies
- Service animals

Permitted carry-on items:

- Disposable and electric razors (blades not allowed)
- Eye drops and contact lens solution (3.4 oz or less)
- Strollers, baby carriers, child car seats
- Beverages (any size) purchased after security screening

Prohibited carry-on items:

- Knives (except plastic or round-bladed butter knives), incl. pocket knives and knives that are religious objects
- Firearms or realistic firearm replicas, ammunition
- Screwdrivers, wrenches, pliers, and other tools more than 7 in. in length; hammers
- Self-defense sprays

For complete travel information, visit www.tsa.gov/travel

EMPLOYMENT

Employment and Unemployment in the U.S., 1900-2022

Source: Bureau of Labor Statistics, U.S. Dept. of Labor

(civilian labor force, persons 16 years of age and older unless otherwise noted; annual averages, in thousands)

Year	Employed	Unemployed Number	Rate	Year	Employed	Unemployed Number	Rate	Year	Employed	Unemployed Number	Rate
1900[1]	26,956	1,420	5.0%	1995	124,900	7,404	5.6%	2009	139,877	14,265	9.3%
1910[1]	34,599	2,150	5.9	1996	126,708	7,236	5.4	2010	139,064	14,825	9.6
1920[1]	39,208	2,132	5.2	1997	129,558	6,739	4.9	2011	139,869	13,747	8.9
1930[1]	44,183	4,340	8.9	1998	131,463	6,210	4.5	2012	142,469	12,506	8.1
1940[1]	47,520	8,120	14.6	1999	133,488	5,880	4.2	2013	143,929	11,460	7.4
1950	58,918	3,288	5.3	2000	136,891	5,692	4.0	2014	146,305	9,617	6.2
1960	65,778	3,852	5.5	2001	136,933	6,801	4.7	2015	148,834	8,296	5.3
1965	71,088	3,366	4.5	2002	136,485	8,378	5.8	2016	151,436	7,751	4.9
1970	78,678	4,093	4.9	2003	137,736	8,774	6.0	2017	153,337	6,982	4.4
1975	85,846	7,929	8.5	2004	139,252	8,149	5.5	2018	155,761	6,314	3.9
1980	99,303	7,637	7.1	2005	141,730	7,591	5.1	2019	157,538	6,001	3.7
1985	107,150	8,312	7.2	2006	144,427	7,001	4.6	2020	147,795	12,947	8.1
1990	118,793	7,047	5.6	2007	146,047	7,078	4.6	2021	152,581	8,623	5.3
1994	123,060	7,996	6.1	2008	145,362	8,924	5.8	2022	158,291	5,996	3.6

Note: Because of revisions in population controls, data for a given year may not be strictly comparable to other years. **Other unemployment rates (1905-55),** persons 14 years of age and older: 1905, 4.3%; 1915, 8.5%; 1925, 3.2%; 1935, 20.3%; 1936, 16.9%; 1937, 14.3%; 1938, 19.0%; 1939, 17.2%; 1945, 1.9%; 1955, 4.4%. (1) Persons 14 years of age and older.

Unemployment Rate and Benefits Data by State, 2022

Source: Employment and Training Admin., U.S. Dept. of Labor; state programs only

State/terr.	Unemployment rate	Monetarily eligible claimants	Number of first payments	Number of final payments	Initial claims	Benefits paid	Average weekly benefit	Employers subject to state law
AL	2.6%	83,592	30,919	12,697	140,756	$59,698,190	$248.60	111,729
AK	4.0	24,492	12,653	4,033	44,009	55,693,889	285.54	20,246
AZ	3.8	93,416	52,258	17,583	144,236	157,882,817	256.73	161,651
AR	3.3	49,344	25,583	6,673	73,875	55,468,958	279.98	79,867
CA	4.2	883,138	889,890	433,854	2,250,854	4,559,243,016	341.90	1,589,067
CO	3.0	106,724	68,192	18,105	150,071	374,781,488	483.04	218,504
CT	4.2	153,577	80,456	16,167	201,884	371,538,613	430.74	118,494
DE	4.5	20,751	9,319	2,160	31,454	34,888,774	303.34	38,590
DC	4.7	23,896	9,165	3,261	34,777	46,801,742	395.04	40,932
FL	2.9	177,107	140,389	73,734	320,027	310,966,623	251.72	677,202
GA	3.0	163,839	92,214	26,043	280,472	123,924,982	322.56	293,548
HI	3.5	27,968	19,711	6,199	66,789	141,581,044	541.24	38,497
ID	2.7	33,664	23,823	6,209	56,673	69,411,517	391.96	75,612
IL	4.6	296,400	227,926	70,684	505,527	1,379,886,697	441.16	340,921
IN	3.0	121,571	62,540	11,805	249,946	177,302,230	296.27	144,140
IA	2.7	56,104	51,596	8,393	98,161	234,089,601	475.56	86,501
KS	2.7	56,362	23,501	7,963	87,483	80,498,251	434.82	82,509
KY	3.9	67,491	27,028	5,783	154,854	179,714,920	397.84	106,480
LA	3.7	56,115	27,309	11,683	90,853	109,580,144	222.47	110,033
ME	3.0	21,818	15,623	4,006	30,554	82,313,478	406.13	52,983
MD	3.2	152,455	52,003	16,891	152,204	334,779,568	360.12	145,075
MA	3.8	195,570	156,835	44,501	308,424	1,136,801,766	603.49	252,349
MI	4.2	235,342	172,009	47,702	435,458	629,259,169	354.30	235,827
MN	2.7	164,188	106,590	40,188	225,436	793,869,240	521.06	153,841
MS	3.9	36,867	16,981	2,945	63,205	23,562,601	216.51	62,872
MO	2.5	101,179	53,243	15,433	204,508	157,791,415	276.12	185,344
MT	2.6	23,049	16,473	4,395	34,817	64,027,668	462.67	51,400
NE	2.3	22,778	12,570	2,517	35,249	53,038,500	385.02	64,452
NV	5.4	71,529	46,424	14,977	112,023	208,024,256	401.02	93,152
NH	2.5	14,646	8,224	814	20,355	25,311,332	335.47	51,736
NJ	3.7	265,376	207,046	82,232	423,614	1,689,306,839	535.00	271,631
NM	4.0	34,142	23,007	8,573	52,578	119,424,768	385.34	54,567
NY	4.3	493,435	352,788	127,099	840,151	1,878,010,400	395.35	539,864
NC	3.7	123,535	57,090	30,155	178,374	133,651,221	279.33	278,492
ND	2.1	14,029	10,470	4,300	18,361	57,331,038	498.41	27,058
OH	4.0	305,711	117,628	19,287	519,279	562,054,293	427.33	244,240
OK	3.0	90,571	34,722	13,858	152,422	149,308,613	363.74	96,912
OR	4.2	113,226	63,611	20,916	201,100	451,689,379	473.40	141,991
PA	4.4	286,374	210,171	40,372	481,221	1,141,953,507	432.67	326,637
PR	6.0	47,522	46,221	14,508	79,819	24,321,447	201.58	57,824
RI	3.2	30,867	24,220	5,849	50,112	121,870,857	418.56	42,216
SC	3.2	74,444	38,870	10,682	107,155	100,059,771	283.40	135,752
SD	2.1	7,496	4,058	513	10,420	21,918,871	409.11	33,136
TN	3.4	90,684	44,095	9,978	140,929	125,829,543	242.55	154,825
TX	3.9	499,586	299,274	113,032	744,749	1,653,132,126	448.41	639,066
UT	2.3	60,564	27,497	6,415	85,173	130,107,462	490.75	104,298
VT	2.6	13,665	10,519	1,264	21,750	42,596,227	441.33	27,134
VA	2.9	116,317	19,955	19,674	165,937	120,055,048	338.43	252,632
VI	NA	652	822	2,334	1,786	8,752,897	474.90	4,294
WA	4.2	178,241	123,336	31,114	322,084	873,138,853	602.68	252,849
WV	3.9	35,430	25,035	5,331	44,168	87,744,934	315.75	40,016
WI	2.9	130,175	83,206	12,011	252,696	273,676,442	329.88	164,865
WY	3.6	10,665	7,633	1,593	16,615	39,441,448	435.76	25,777
U.S.	3.6	6,557,679	4,362,721	1,518,488	11,515,427	21,837,108,478	401.44	9,599,630

NA = Not available.

Weekly Unemployment Insurance Claims, 2000-23
Source: Employment and Training Admin., U.S. Dept. of Labor

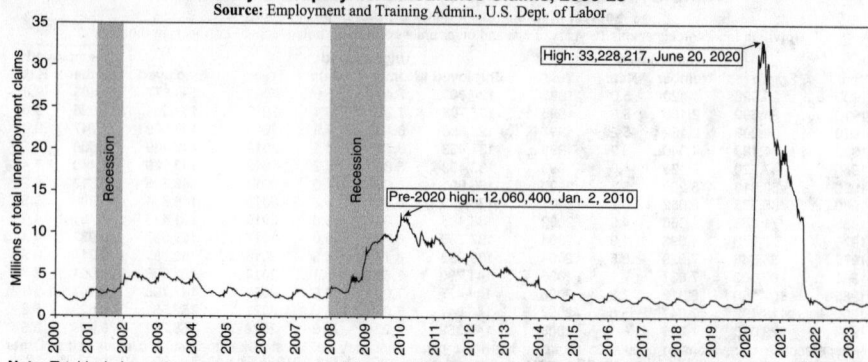

High: 33,228,217, June 20, 2020

Pre-2020 high: 12,060,400, Jan. 2, 2010

Note: Total includes state programs, programs for federal employees and ex-service members, extended and emergency programs, short-time compensation, Pandemic Unemployment Assistance, and Pandemic Emergency Unemployment Compensation.

U.S. Unemployment Duration by Industry and Occupation, 2022
Source: Bureau of Labor Statistics, U.S. Dept. of Labor

Occupation	Total	Less than 5 weeks	5 to 14 weeks	15 to 26 weeks	27 weeks and over	Average (mean) duration	Median duration
Management, professional, and related	1,355	473	402	170	310	24.2	9.0
Management, business, and financial operations	530	170	159	74	128	25.9	9.9
Professional and related	825	303	243	97	183	23.2	8.4
Service	1,281	487	346	157	290	22.3	8.4
Sales and office	1,176	412	342	171	252	22.2	9.3
Sales and related	579	211	163	82	123	22.0	9.0
Office and administrative support	598	200	179	89	129	22.4	9.4
Natural resources, construction, and maintenance	658	277	176	73	132	19.9	7.3
Farming, fishing, and forestry	71	28	22	9	11	17.7	7.6
Construction and extraction	477	206	126	52	93	19.6	6.8
Installation, maintenance, and repair	110	43	27	12	28	22.6	9.0
Production, transportation, and material moving	1,027	379	292	130	226	23.1	8.7
Production	332	127	92	41	72	22.8	8.6
Transportation and material moving	695	252	200	89	154	23.3	8.8
Industry[1]							
Agriculture and related industries	89	31	29	13	16	18.4	8.7
Mining, quarrying, and oil and gas extraction	18	5	4	3	6	—	—
Construction	474	203	129	49	92	19.3	7.0
Manufacturing	459	162	125	68	104	24.0	9.6
Durable goods	283	96	79	42	66	25.8	9.8
Nondurable goods	177	66	47	26	38	21.1	9.3
Wholesale and retail trade	806	279	232	118	177	22.7	9.2
Transportation and utilities	371	135	108	48	80	22.3	8.9
Information	81	26	25	11	19	23.7	9.7
Financial activities	206	68	61	29	47	24.7	9.9
Professional and business services	683	238	212	84	149	22.5	9.0
Education and health services	866	323	254	103	185	21.6	8.3
Leisure and hospitality	789	317	221	94	157	20.8	7.7
Other services	203	74	49	28	52	25.6	9.8
Public administration	127	40	36	16	34	23.9	9.8
No previous work experience	482	183	148	53	98	22.6	8.3
Total unemployed[2]	**5,996**	**2,216**	**1,711**	**756**	**1,314**	**22.6**	**8.7**

Note: Persons 16 years of age and older. (1) Includes wage and salary workers only. (2) Includes persons whose last job was in the U.S. Armed Forces.

U.S. Displaced Workers, 2022
Source: Bureau of Labor Statistics, U.S. Dept. of Labor

	Number (thous.)	Plant or company closed down or moved	Insufficient work	Position or shift abolished
		Reason for job loss (% distrib.)		
Total displaced workers	**3,596**	**38.1%**	**30.9%**	**31.0%**
Age: 20 to 24 years	119	39.1	39.2	21.7
25 to 54 years	2,227	37.9	31.2	30.8
55 to 64 years	852	35.7	32.8	31.5
65 years and over	398	43.5	23.0	33.5
Sex: Men	1,889	35.2	33.3	31.5
Women	1,708	41.3	28.3	30.4
Race: White	2,819	37.1	30.2	32.7
Black	357	44.4	28.4	27.2
Asian	278	29.7	42.0	28.3
Hispanic or Latino	597	46.3	35.2	18.5

NA = Not available. Note: As of Jan. 2022. Displaced workers are persons age 20 or older who lost or left jobs they had held for at least three years. Workers in this table were displaced between Jan. 2019 and Dec. 2021. Hispanic or Latino persons may be of any race.

U.S. Unemployment Rates by Selected Characteristics, 1995-2023

Source: Bureau of Labor Statistics, U.S. Dept. of Labor

	1995	2000	2005	2010	2015	2020	2021	2022 Jan.	2022 June	2022 Yr.	2023 Jan.	2023 June
Total (all civilian workers)	5.6%	4.0%	5.1%	9.6%	5.3%	8.1%	5.3%	4.4%	3.8%	3.6%	3.9%	3.8%
Men, 20 years and older	4.8	3.3	4.4	9.8	4.9	7.4	5.2	4.5	3.3	3.4	3.9	3.3
Women, 20 years and older	4.9	3.6	4.6	8.0	4.8	8.0	5.0	3.8	3.6	3.3	3.2	3.4
Both sexes, 16 to 19 years	17.3	13.1	16.6	25.9	16.9	17.9	11.7	11.6	13.1	10.8	10.9	13.3
White	4.9	3.5	4.4	8.7	4.6	7.3	4.7	3.9	3.5	3.2	3.5	3.3
Black	10.4	7.6	10.0	16.0	9.6	11.4	8.6	7.3	6.1	6.1	5.6	6.4
Asian	—	3.6	4.0	7.5	3.8	8.7	5.0	3.7	3.2	2.8	3.0	3.4
Hispanic or Latino (any race)	9.3	5.7	6.0	12.5	6.6	10.4	6.8	5.5	4.4	4.3	5.5	4.3
Married men, spouse present[1]	3.3	—	—	6.8	2.8	4.9	3.2	2.0	2.0	1.9	1.8	1.8
Married women, spouse present[1]	3.9	—	—	5.9	3.1	6.3	3.4	2.4	2.3	2.2	1.9	2.2
Women who maintain families, spouse absent	8.0	5.9	7.8	12.3	7.4	9.6	7.1	5.0	4.5	4.8	3.8	4.8
Occupation												
Management, professional, and related	2.4	1.8	2.3	4.7	2.5	4.5	2.8	2.3	3.8	2.0	2.1	2.2
Service	7.5	5.2	6.4	10.3	6.7	13.0	7.8	6.7	4.5	4.8	5.3	4.3
Sales and office	5.0	3.8	4.8	9.0	5.1	8.0	5.3	4.1	3.9	3.7	3.8	3.5
Natural resources, constr., and maintenance	—	5.3	6.5	16.1	7.2	8.9	6.6	6.2	4.0	4.4	6.0	3.3
Production, transp., and material moving	—	5.1	6.5	12.8	6.3	10.2	7.1	6.0	4.7	4.9	4.7	5.2
Industry												
Nonagricultural private wage and salary workers	5.8	4.1	5.2	9.9	5.1	8.4	5.4	4.5	3.5	3.6	3.9	3.3
Mining	5.2	4.4	3.1	9.4	8.6	11.3	11.2	8.4	1.6	3.0	0.3	1.3
Construction	11.5	6.2	7.4	20.6	7.3	8.7	6.5	7.1	3.7	4.6	6.9	3.6
Manufacturing	4.9	3.5	4.9	10.6	4.3	6.8	4.3	3.6	3.0	3.0	2.6	2.6
Durable goods	4.4	3.2	4.6	11.2	4.1	6.7	4.1	3.1	2.9	2.9	2.3	2.4
Nondurable goods	5.7	4.0	5.3	9.6	4.6	6.8	4.7	4.4	3.2	3.1	3.1	2.9
Wholesale and retail trade	6.5	4.3	5.4	9.5	5.5	8.3	5.9	4.8	4.1	4.1	5.1	4.4
Transportation and utilities	4.5	3.4	4.1	8.4	4.4	9.3	6.3	4.5	3.8	4.1	4.2	3.1
Information	—	3.2	5.0	9.7	3.9	7.5	5.4	4.2	3.1	2.9	3.9	3.1
Financial activities	3.3	2.4	2.9	6.9	2.6	3.8	2.9	1.9	2.1	1.9	2.3	2.2
Professional and business services	—	4.8	6.2	10.8	5.6	6.7	5.2	4.5	3.4	3.5	3.5	3.3
Education and health services	—	2.5	3.4	5.8	3.6	5.7	3.5	2.9	3.3	2.7	2.4	2.8
Leisure and hospitality	—	6.6	7.8	12.2	7.9	19.4	10.1	8.2	5.2	5.8	6.0	5.1
Other services	8.4	3.9	4.8	8.5	5.2	9.8	5.4	4.9	2.5	3.1	3.3	2.1
Agriculture and related private wage and salary workers	11.1	9.0	8.3	13.9	9.4	8.1	7.6	8.5	4.4	5.6	4.9	5.1
Government workers	2.9	2.1	2.6	4.4	2.7	4.8	2.7	2.2	3.1	2.1	1.9	3.0
Self-employed and unpaid family workers	—	2.1	2.7	5.9	3.9	6.4	4.9	4.1	2.7	3.2	3.5	3.3

— = Not available. **Note:** All monthly rates are unadjusted, except for married men and women, which are seasonally adjusted.
(1) Beginning in Jan. 2020, data refers to persons in both opposite-sex and same-sex married couples. Data for prior years refers to persons in opposite-sex married couples only.

U.S. Workers by Industry and Type, 2012, 2022

Source: Bureau of Labor Statistics, U.S. Dept. of Labor

(in thousands)

Industry	2012 Total employed	2012 Private industry workers	2012 Govt. workers	2012 Self-employed workers	2022 Total employed	2022 Private industry workers[1]	2022 Govt. workers	2022 Self-employed workers[2]
Mining[3]	957	932	5	20	601	583	4	14
Construction	8,964	7,025	414	1,518	11,790	9,682	404	1,696
Manufacturing	14,686	14,269	103	308	15,231	14,786	120	323
Durable goods	9,244	8,970	86	183	9,619	9,340	97	180
Nondurable goods	5,443	5,299	16	125	5,612	5,446	23	143
Wholesale and retail trade	19,876	18,860	126	872	19,462	18,637	83	734
Wholesale trade	3,694	3,542	13	138	3,166	3,070	6	90
Retail trade	16,182	15,317	113	734	16,295	15,568	77	645
Transportation and utilities	7,271	5,512	1,403	355	10,079	8,031	1,346	696
Transportation and warehousing	6,082	4,660	1,065	355	8,699	7,019	987	687
Utilities	1,190	851	338	—	1,380	1,013	359	—
Information	2,971	2,643	186	141	2,867	2,536	180	150
Financial activities	9,590	8,710	227	651	11,033	10,052	190	788
Finance and insurance	6,786	6,412	135	237	7,786	7,444	119	222
Real estate and rental and leasing	2,804	2,297	92	413	3,248	2,608	71	566
Professional and business services	16,539	13,971	443	2,109	20,628	18,214	473	1,927
Professional and technical services	9,913	8,508	250	1,145	13,662	12,299	282	1,078
Management, administrative, and waste services	6,626	5,463	193	964	6,967	5,915	191	849
Education and health services	32,350	20,973	10,271	1,101	35,377	24,171	10,235	966
Educational services	12,945	4,254	8,472	218	13,860	5,029	8,628	202
Health care and social assistance	19,405	16,719	1,798	883	21,517	19,142	1,607	764
Hospitals	6,113	5,333	769	11	7,329	6,558	752	18
Health services, except hospitals	10,009	9,128	476	403	10,724	9,951	368	401
Social assistance	3,283	2,258	553	469	3,465	2,633	487	344
Leisure and hospitality	13,193	12,098	426	659	13,728	12,600	400	724
Arts, entertainment, and recreation	3,022	2,264	348	408	3,380	2,555	323	502
Accommodation and food services	10,171	9,834	78	251	10,347	10,045	77	222
Other services	7,168	6,100	38	1,016	7,530	6,371	39	1,112
Other services, except private households	6,430	5,362	38	1,016	6,875	5,716	39	1,112
Private households	738	738	—	—	655	655	—	—
Public administration	6,717	—	6,717	—	7,674	—	7,674	—

— = No data or data that do not meet publication criteria. (1) Includes self-employed workers whose businesses are incorporated.
(2) Unincorporated. (3) Includes quarrying and oil and gas extraction.

Persons Not in the U.S. Labor Force, 2022

Source: Bureau of Labor Statistics, U.S. Dept. of Labor

The Labor Dept.'s unemployment rate, based on its household survey, shows the number of people out of work as a percentage of adults age 16 and older in the labor force. That rate excludes the millions of adults considered to be not in the labor force.

(in thousands)

	Number	Age in years			Sex	
		16 to 24	25 to 54	55 and over	Men	Women
Total not in the labor force	99,686	16,864	22,325	60,497	41,197	58,490
Do not want a job now[1]...............	94,047	15,292	19,865	58,891	38,506	55,541
Want a job[1]............................	5,639	1,573	2,460	1,606	2,691	2,948
Did not search for work in previous year	3,500	929	1,405	1,166	1,636	1,864
Searched in previous year but not previous four weeks[2]	2,139	644	1,055	440	1,055	1,084
Not available to work now	656	239	320	97	273	382
Available to work now	1,484	405	735	343	782	702
Reason not currently looking[3]						
Discouraged over job prospects[4]........	407	97	204	106	254	153
Reasons other than discouragement.....	1,077	308	531	237	528	549
Family responsibilities	171	23	112	36	58	114
In school or training	132	106	23	3	66	66
Ill health or disability..............	140	17	67	56	66	73
Other[5]...........................	633	161	329	143	337	296

(1) Includes some persons who are not asked if they want a job. (2) Persons who had a job in the prior 12 months must have searched since the end of that job to be considered unemployed. (3) Of those available to work now. (4) Includes believing no work is available, not being able to find work, lacking necessary schooling or training, thought of as too young or old by employers, and other types of discrimination. (5) Includes those who did not actively look for work in the prior four weeks for such reasons as child-care and transportation problems, as well as a small number for which reason for nonparticipation was not ascertained.

U.S. Small Business Employment by Industry, 2020

Source: U.S Census Bureau, U.S. Dept. of Commerce

Industry	Small business employment	Total private employment	% small business employment
Health care and social assistance	9,220,370	21,216,569	43.5%
Accommodation and food services...................	8,626,069	14,377,016	60.0
Construction	5,804,811	7,182,071	80.8
Professional, scientific, and technical services......	5,419,235	9,554,479	56.7
Other services (excl. public administration)	4,722,015	5,601,688	84.3
Administrative, support, waste management, and remediation services..	3,812,491	12,718,021	30.0
Wholesale trade	3,304,404	6,145,378	53.8
Finance and insurance	1,888,303	6,682,343	28.3
Educational services	1,728,879	3,832,033	45.1
Real estate, rental and leasing	1,510,739	2,280,633	66.2
Arts, entertainment, and recreation	1,485,876	2,504,959	59.3
Information	974,236	3,577,460	27.2
Management of companies and enterprises	371,998	3,571,149	10.4
Mining, quarrying, and oil and gas extraction	258,462	577,921	44.7
Agriculture, forestry, fishing and hunting...........	137,511	167,204	82.2
Utilities	113,729	637,058	17.9
Industries not classified	17,170	17,170	100.0
Total employed	**61,608,985**	**134,163,349**	**45.9**

Note: A small business is defined here as a firm employing fewer than 500 employees.

U.S. Occupations Projected to Grow Most, 2022-32

Source: Employment Projections Program, Bureau of Labor Statistics, U.S. Dept. of Labor

(ranked by greatest positive change in number of jobs; numbers in thousands)

Occupation	Employment		Change, 2022-32		Median annual wage, 2022[1]
	2022	2032	Number	Percent	
Total, all occupations	164,482.6	169,148.1	4,665.5	2.8%	$46,310
Home health and personal care aides	3,715.5	4,520.1	804.6	21.7	30,180
Software developers	1,594.5	2,004.9	410.4	25.7	127,260
Cooks, restaurant	1,361.2	1,638.9	277.6	20.4	34,110
Stockers and order fillers	2,851.6	3,030.3	178.6	6.3	34,220
Registered nurses..............................	3,172.5	3,349.9	177.4	5.6	81,220
Laborers and freight, stock, and material movers, hand.	2,988.5	3,147.3	158.8	5.3	36,110
General and operations managers................	3,507.8	3,655.1	147.3	4.2	98,100
Medical and health services managers	509.5	654.2	144.7	28.4	104,830
Light truck drivers..............................	1,164.6	1,298.4	133.8	11.5	40,410
Financial managers	792.6	919.2	126.6	16.0	139,790
Nurse practitioners	266.3	384.9	118.6	44.5	121,610
Market research analysts and marketing specialists ...	868.6	985.2	116.6	13.4	68,230
Medical assistants	764.4	870.2	105.9	13.9	38,270
Management analysts	987.6	1,083.3	95.7	9.7	95,290
Heavy and tractor-trailer truck drivers............	2,192.3	2,281.5	89.3	4.1	49,920
Computer and information systems managers	557.4	643.3	86.0	15.4	164,070
Substance abuse, behavioral disorder, and mental health counselors	388.2	459.6	71.5	18.4	49,710
Accountants and auditors	1,538.4	1,605.8	67.4	4.4	78,000
Lawyers	826.3	888.7	62.4	7.5	135,740
Construction laborers	1,418.6	1,480.5	61.9	4.4	40,750
First-line supervisors of food preparation and serving workers ...	1,221.7	1,281.8	60.0	4.9	37,050
Industrial machinery mechanics..................	402.2	462.1	59.9	14.9	59,830
Data scientists	168.9	228.2	59.4	35.2	103,500
Maintenance and repair workers, general..........	1,607.2	1,664.4	57.2	3.6	44,980
Nursing assistants	1,361.3	1,417.8	56.5	4.1	35,760
Project management specialists..................	881.3	936.0	54.7	6.2	95,370

(1) Wage data cover nonfarm wage and salary workers and do not cover the self-employed, owners and partners in unincorporated firms, or household workers.

U.S. Occupations Projected to Decline Most, 2021-32

Source: Employment Projections Program, Bureau of Labor Statistics, U.S. Dept. of Labor
(ranked by greatest negative change in number of jobs; numbers in thousands)

Occupation	Employment 2022	Employment 2032	Change, 2022-32 Number	Change, 2022-32 Percent	Median annual wage, 2022[1]
Total, all occupations	164,482.6	169,148.1	4,665.5	2.8%	$46,310
Cashiers	3,345.8	2,997.7	–348.1	–10.4	28,240
Secretaries and administrative assistants[2]	2,030.2	1,794.3	–235.9	–11.6	41,000
Office clerks, general	2,668.2	2,492.8	–175.4	–6.6	38,040
Customer service representatives	2,982.9	2,820.2	–162.7	–5.5	37,780
Miscellaneous assemblers and fabricators	1,500.4	1,388.6	–111.8	–7.5	37,280
Bookkeeping, accounting, and auditing clerks	1,735.8	1,627.5	–108.3	–6.2	45,860
Executive secretaries and executive administrative assistants. . .	511.1	403.0	–108.1	–21.1	65,980
Cooks, fast food	742.0	640.4	–101.6	–13.7	27,640
First-line supervisors of retail sales workers	1,405.8	1,311.8	–94.0	–6.7	45,250
First-line supervisors of office and administrative support workers	1,567.2	1,486.4	–80.7	–5.2	61,370
Retail salespersons	3,765.6	3,686.4	–79.1	–2.1	30,600
Shipping, receiving, and inventory clerks	862.9	790.6	–72.2	–8.4	37,760
Waiters and waitresses.	2,194.1	2,125.5	–68.6	–3.1	29,120
Tellers	364.1	311.1	–52.9	–14.5	36,380
Food preparation workers	931.8	887.0	–44.8	–4.8	29,790

(1) Wage data cover nonfarm wage and salary workers and do not cover the self-employed, owners and partners in unincorporated firms, or household workers. (2) Excl. legal, medical, executive.

Projected Employment by Typical Entry-Level Education, 2022-32

Source: Employment Projections Program, Bureau of Labor Statistics, U.S. Dept. of Labor

Typical entry-level education	Employment, 2022 Number (thous.)	Employment, 2022 Percent distribution	% change in employment, 2022-32	Median annual wage, 2022[1]
Total, all occupations	164,482.6	100.0%	2.8%	$46,310
Doctoral or professional degree	4,368.7	2.7	7.0	114,020
Master's degree	3,099.0	1.9	11.3	80,180
Bachelor's degree.	40,373.7	24.5	6.7	81,570
Associate's degree	3,422.7	2.1	5.7	60,170
Postsecondary nondegree award	10,113.3	6.1	5.5	45,790
Some college, no degree	4,301.8	2.6	–2.2	40,580
High school diploma or equivalent	62,532.5	38.0	0.9	41,850
No formal educational credential	36,271.0	22.1	0.2	31,380

Note: The occupational employment and growth rates shown include projected growth in all jobs, not just entry-level jobs. (1) Wage data cover nonfarm wage and salary workers and do not cover the self-employed, owners and partners in unincorporated firms, or household workers.

Highest Average Weekly Wages by County, 2022

Source: Bureau of Labor Statistics, U.S. Dept. of Labor

County	Avg. weekly wage	% change, 2021-22	County	Avg. weekly wage	% change, 2021-22
Santa Clara, CA	$3,329	–15.0%	Fairfax, VA.	$2,051	–1.6%
San Francisco, CA	2,962	–22.6	Middlesex, MA	2,040	–5.5
San Mateo, CA	2,939	–20.7	Fairfield, CT	2,033	–4.3
New York, NY	2,936	–9.4	Morris, NJ	1,882	–2.6
Suffolk, MA	2,497	–4.2	Somerset, NJ	1,847	–0.4
Washington, DC	2,291	–1.1	Alexandria City, VA	1,844	0.3
King, WA	2,195	–5.4	Denver, CO	1,794	–1.4
Arlington, VA	2,181	–3.5	Alameda, CA	1,791	–3.8

Note: Figures shown are for the 4th quarter, from among the 355 largest U.S. counties, which comprise 72.9% of total covered workers. Hidalgo County, TX, recorded the lowest average weekly earnings among the largest counties, with an average of $827. It was followed by Cameron, TX ($838); Horry, SC ($886); Harrison, MS ($886); Webb, TX ($888); Washington, UT ($909); El Paso, TX ($935); Cleveland, OK ($937); Yakima, WA ($945); and Mahoning, OH ($956). Data include all workers covered by state and federal unemployment insurance programs.

Fatal Occupational Injuries, 2021

Source: Census of Fatal Occupational Injuries, Bureau of Labor Statistics, U.S. Dept. of Labor

Event or exposure	Fatalities Number	%	Event or exposure	Fatalities Number	%
Total.	5,190	100%	Nonroadway incident involving motorized land vehicle	201	4%
Violence and other injuries by persons or animals	**761**	**15**	Nonroadway noncollision incident . . .	153	3
Intentional injury by person	718	14	Jack-knifed or overturned, nonroadway. . .	100	2
Homicides	481	9	**Fire or explosion. . . . .**	**76**	**1**
Shooting by other person—intentional. . . .	387	7	**Fall, slip, trip . . . .**	**850**	**16**
Stabbing, cutting, slashing, piercing . . .	45	1	Fall on same level	145	3
Suicides	236	5	Fall to lower level	680	13
Transportation incidents	**1,982**	**38**	Fall from collapsing structure or equipment	51	1
Aircraft incidents	100	2	Fall through surface or existing opening	77	1
Rail vehicle incidents	33	1	**Exposure to harmful substances or environments**	**798**	**15**
Pedestrian vehicular incident	337	6	Exposure to electricity.	152	3
Pedestrian struck by vehicle in work zone . .	49	1	Exposure to temperature extremes. . .	43	1
Water vehicle incident.	39	1	Exposure to other harmful substances	551	11
Roadway incident involving motorized land vehicle	1,253	24	Inhalation of harmful substance . . .	72	1
Roadway collision with other vehicle	649	13	**Contact with objects and equipment**	**705**	**14**
Roadway collision moving in same direction	184	4	Struck by object or equipment	473	9
Roadway collision moving in opposite directions, oncoming	218	4	Struck by powered vehicle, nontransport . . .	169	3
Roadway collision moving perpendicularly	129	2	Struck by falling object or equipment	227	4
Roadway collision with object other than vehicle	319	6	Struck by discharged or flying object	24	0
Vehicle struck object or animal on side of roadway.	283	5	Caught in or compressed by equipment or objects.	143	3
Roadway noncollision incident	279	5	Caught in running equipment or machinery	93	2
Jack-knifed or overturned, roadway.	207	4	Struck, caught, or crushed in collapsing structure, equipment, or material	79	2

Note: Percentages show incidence rate per total fatalities.

U.S. Occupational Injuries and Illnesses Involving Days Away From Work, 2020

Source: Bureau of Labor Statistics, U.S. Dept. of Labor

Characteristic	Total cases[2]	Percent of days-away-from-work cases[1] involving—							Median days away from work
		1 day	2 days	3-5 days	6-10 days	11-20 days	21-30 days	31 days or more	
Total	1,176,340	8.5%	6.9%	12.9%	18.3%	22.6%	7.6%	23.2%	12
Male	577,990	10.1	7.6	14.5	14.9	18.2	7.4	27.4	12
Female	585,540	7.1	6.2	11.5	21.8	26.6	7.8	19.0	12
Age									
14-15 years	180	11.1	—	33.3	22.2	11.1	16.7	—	6
16-19 years	32,790	17.4	11.4	18.2	18.3	20.5	4.6	9.8	7
20-24 years	108,800	10.5	8.9	16.6	21.7	23.1	5.8	13.4	10
25-34 years	250,050	9.6	7.2	14.3	20.0	24.0	6.7	18.3	10
35-44 years	232,790	8.1	6.6	13.0	18.7	23.1	7.8	22.6	12
45-54 years	241,620	7.1	6.5	11.7	17.3	21.1	8.5	27.9	14
55-64 years	217,100	7.4	6.0	11.3	16.5	20.9	8.3	29.7	14
65 years and over	53,480	6.2	5.5	11.7	14.3	21.4	8.5	32.4	14
Age group not reported	39,540	9.5	5.8	7.5	17.9	31.3	9.5	18.5	14
Occupation(s)									
Management, business, financial	49,930	8.8	7.1	11.5	22.2	29.1	6.4	14.9	11
Computer, engineering, science	6,860	8.9	5.8	17.9	15.2	27.3	7.0	17.8	11
Education, legal, community service, arts, media	21,610	13.5	6.2	15.2	21.9	20.7	8.1	14.4	10
Health-care practitioners, technical	177,650	4.5	3.9	9.3	25.5	32.5	8.9	15.4	12
Service	328,020	7.9	6.5	12.8	21.0	25.6	7.7	18.5	11
Sales and related	60,130	9.0	9.2	16.2	14.6	20.7	6.4	23.9	11
Office and administrative support	49,770	7.6	7.3	11.3	23.9	24.5	7.0	18.5	10
Farming, fishing, forestry	15,990	14.2	9.3	17.3	15.0	16.4	6.1	21.8	8
Construction, extraction	69,790	12.5	9.9	14.6	11.3	12.4	7.6	31.8	12
Installation, maintenance, repair	77,770	12.3	7.3	14.5	12.7	15.6	7.3	30.4	12
Production	111,150	11.5	8.3	14.2	15.2	20.6	7.3	22.9	11
Transportation, material moving	205,580	7.7	7.1	13.6	12.7	15.2	7.5	36.2	15

— = Data do not meet publication guidelines or may be too small to be displayed. **Note:** Because of rounding and data exclusion of nonclassifiable responses, data may not sum to the totals. (1) Cases include those that resulted in days away from work, some of which also included job transfer or restriction. (2) Number of nonfatal occupational injuries and illnesses involving days away from work for private industry workers.

Federal Minimum Hourly Wage Rates

Source: Bureau of Labor Statistics, U.S. Dept. of Labor; as of May 2023

Effective date	Minimum wage	% avg. earnings[1]	In 2023 dollars	Effective date	Minimum wage	% avg. earnings[1]	In 2023 dollars
Oct. 24, 1938	$0.25	40%	$5.43	Jan. 1, 1978	$2.65	43%	$12.89
Oct. 24, 1939	0.30	48	6.52	Jan. 1, 1979	2.90	43	12.91
Oct. 24, 1945	0.40	39	6.72	Jan. 1, 1980	3.10	43	12.12
Jan. 25, 1950	0.75	52	9.71	Jan. 1, 1981	3.35	42	11.71
Mar. 1, 1956	1.00	51	11.35	Apr. 1, 1990	3.80	35	8.97
Sept. 3, 1961	1.15	50	11.66	Apr. 1, 1991	4.25	38	9.56
Sept. 3, 1963	1.25	51	12.38	Oct. 1, 1996	4.75	37	9.13
Feb. 1, 1967	1.40	49	12.94	Sept. 1, 1997	5.15	39	9.72
Feb. 1, 1968	1.60	53	14.23	July 24, 2007	5.85	34	8.54
May 1, 1974	2.00	45	12.52	July 24, 2008	6.55	37	9.06
Jan. 1, 1975	2.10	43	12.26	July 24, 2009	7.25	40	10.24
Jan. 1, 1976	2.30	44	12.58				

Note: Before 1961, the minimum wage applied primarily to employees engaged in, or producing goods for, interstate commerce. The 1961 amendments extended coverage primarily to employees in large retail and service enterprises and to local transit, construction, and gas station employees. The 1966 and subsequent amendments extended coverage to farm workers; government employees; workers in various retail and service trades; and certain domestic workers. Starting in 1978, minimum wage applied equally to all covered, nonexempt workers. Exceptions apply to certain workers with disabilities, full-time students, persons under age 20 in their first 90 days of employment, and tipped employees. (1) Percent of gross hourly earnings of production workers in manufacturing.

Civilian Employment of the Federal Government, 1940-2024

Source: U.S. Office of Personnel Management; Office of Management and Budget
(numbers in thousands)

Year	Total executive branch	Dept. of Defense	Total employees	Agriculture	HHS, Education, Social Sec.[1]	Homeland Sec.	Interior	Justice	Transportation	Treasury	Veterans Affairs	Other
1940	699	256	443	98	9	18	46	11	NA	45	40	176
1945	3,370	2,635	736	82	11	20	45	19	NA	84	65	409
1950	1,439	753	686	84	13	20	66	20	NA	76	188	219
1955	1,860	1,187	673	86	40	21	54	24	NA	65	178	206
1960	1,808	1,047	761	99	62	21	56	24	NA	62	172	265
1965	1,901	1,034	867	113	87	21	71	27	NA	74	167	307
1970	2,203	1,219	983	118	112	23	75	33	62	84	169	308
1975	2,149	1,042	1,107	121	147	31	80	47	69	101	213	297
1980	2,161	960	1,201	129	163	40	77	48	66	102	228	346
1985	2,112	1,029	1,084	107	137	39	72	51	55	106	221	294
1990	2,174	1,006	1,168	111	122	48	71	66	59	130	214	347
1995	1,970	822	1,148	104	129	54	72	82	57	129	228	292
2000	1,814	660	1,153	95	128		67	95	57	113	203	328
2005	1,830	653	1,177	100	128	143	70	103	56	110	222	244
2010	2,128	741	1,386	96	137	173	71	113	57	112	285	342
2015	2,042	725	1,317	86	139	179	64	114	54	95	335	251
2020	2,180	777	1,403	79	139	198	61	114	53	91	389	279
2022	2,186	772	1,413	85	142	203	62	115	53	94	412	248
2024[2]	2,356	795	1,561	102	154	216	68	116	54	114	454	270

NA = Not available. HHS = Health and Human Services. **Note:** End-of-fiscal-year count; U.S. Postal Service excluded. All years are not directly comparable, as 1940-80 is civilian employment of full-time permanent, temporary, part-time, and intermittent employees; 1985-2024 is full-time equivalent employees. (1) Estimated, 1940-50. (2) Estimated.

Unemployment Rates and Earnings by Education, 2022
Source: Bureau of Labor Statistics, U.S. Dept. of Labor

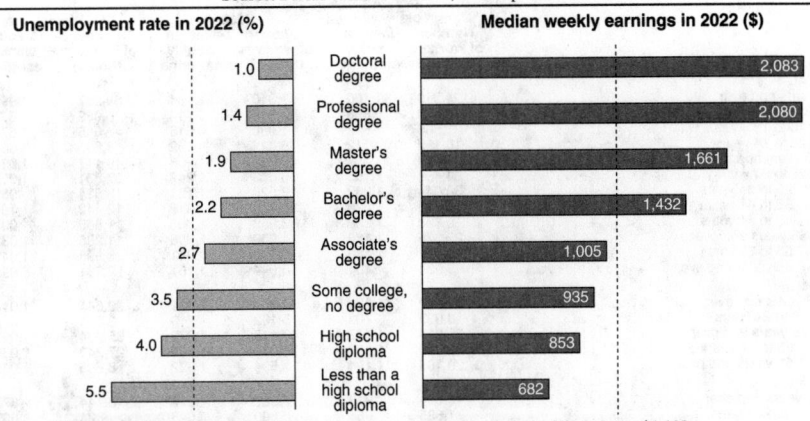

Unemployment rate in 2022 (%)

1.0	Doctoral degree
1.4	Professional degree
1.9	Master's degree
2.2	Bachelor's degree
2.7	Associate's degree
3.5	Some college, no degree
4.0	High school diploma
5.5	Less than a high school diploma

Median weekly earnings in 2022 ($)

Doctoral degree	2,083
Professional degree	2,080
Master's degree	1,661
Bachelor's degree	1,432
Associate's degree	1,005
Some college, no degree	935
High school diploma	853
Less than a high school diploma	682

All workers: 3.0%   **All workers: $1,123**

Note: Data for persons age 25 and over. Earnings are for full-time wage and salary workers.

Median Earnings by Industry and Sex, 2021
Source: American Community Survey (ACS), U.S. Census Bureau, U.S. Dept. of Commerce

	Employed			Median earnings			
Industry	**Total**	**% men**	**% women**	**Total**	**Men**	**Women**	**Women's as % of men's**
Total	156,380,433	52.6%	47.4%	$42,358	$50,391	$36,726	72.9%
Agriculture, forestry, fishing and hunting, and mining . . .	2,445,458	78.3	21.7	40,065	42,681	26,605	62.3
Construction	10,773,757	89.2	10.8	45,307	45,815	41,094	89.7
Manufacturing	15,738,828	70.4	29.6	51,521	56,119	41,492	73.9
Wholesale trade	3,616,410	69.7	30.3	51,340	54,476	44,170	81.1
Retail trade	17,307,114	52.2	47.8	27,385	32,013	23,256	72.6
Transportation and warehousing, and utilities.	9,237,812	74.3	25.7	45,701	50,379	35,857	71.2
Information	2,908,107	60.6	39.4	63,926	73,964	51,436	69.5
Finance and insurance, and real estate and rental and leasing	10,659,331	46.4	53.6	61,669	77,486	51,946	67.0
Professional, scientific, and management, administrative, and waste management services. . . .	19,360,141	57.3	42.7	55,596	65,862	45,224	68.7
Educational services, and health care and social assistance.	36,749,102	26.3	73.7	43,502	53,793	40,888	76.0
Arts, entertainment, and recreation, and accommodation and food services.	12,892,907	48.4	51.6	18,526	21,851	15,902	72.8
Other services, except public administration	7,170,404	46.9	53.1	30,628	38,782	23,927	61.7
Public administration	7,521,062	54.4	45.6	62,488	71,491	52,516	73.5

Note: For the civilian employed population 16 years of age and over including workers not employed full-time.

Net Productivity and Workers' Hourly Compensation, 1948-2021
Source: Economic Policy Institute (EPI), based on U.S. Bureau of Economic Analysis and U.S. Bureau of Labor Statistics data
This graph shows the cumulative percent change since 1948 in net productivity and hourly compensation in the U.S. Net productivity is the growth of goods and services produced minus depreciation per hour worked. Hourly compensation is average wages and benefits for private sector production and nonsupervisory workers, who make up around 80% of private payroll employment.

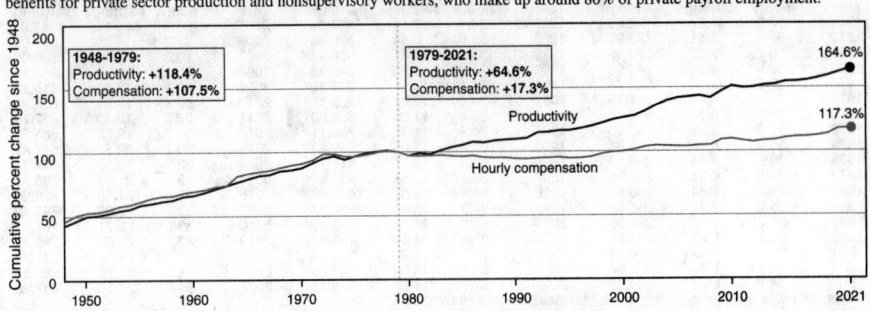

1948-1979:
Productivity: +118.4%
Compensation: +107.5%

1979-2021:
Productivity: +64.6%
Compensation: +17.3%

Productivity — 164.6%
Hourly compensation — 117.3%

U.S. Median Weekly Earnings, 2023
Source: Bureau of Labor Statistics, U.S. Dept. of Labor

AGE, RACE, AND ETHNICITY	Total		Men		Women	
	Number of workers (thous.)	Median weekly earnings	Number of workers (thous.)	Median weekly earnings	Number of workers (thous.)	Median weekly earnings
TOTAL						
16 years and over	121,516	$1,100	67,310	$1,181	54,207	$993
16 to 24 years	11,697	698	6,608	714	5,089	672
16 to 19 years	1,565	603	980	618	585	579
20 to 24 years	10,132	712	5,627	732	4,505	687
25 years and over	109,819	1,157	60,702	1,255	49,117	1,050
25 to 54 years	84,494	1,155	46,663	1,247	37,831	1,055
25 to 34 years	30,044	1,042	16,520	1,121	13,524	966
35 to 44 years	28,628	1,229	16,186	1,319	12,442	1,134
45 to 54 years	25,822	1,233	13,958	1,385	11,865	1,095
55 years and over	25,325	1,166	14,039	1,296	11,286	1,032
55 to 64 years	19,991	1,186	10,995	1,341	8,995	1,043
65 years and over	5,334	1,101	3,044	1,161	2,291	999
White						
16 years and over	91,952	1,126	52,307	1,201	39,645	1,016
16 to 24 years	8,933	703	5,192	719	3,741	674
25 years and over	83,019	1,177	47,115	1,272	35,904	1,082
25 to 54 years	62,850	1,172	35,611	1,263	27,240	1,086
55 years and over	20,169	1,194	11,504	1,322	8,665	1,065
Black						
16 years and over	16,631	913	7,887	975	8,744	877
16 to 24 years	1,625	654	800	648	824	657
25 years and over	15,007	952	7,087	1,026	7,920	898
25 to 54 years	11,854	944	5,627	1,014	6,226	895
55 years and over	3,153	985	1,460	1,128	1,693	925
Asian						
16 years and over	8,440	1,449	4,684	1,617	3,756	1,310
16 to 24 years	522	936	307	854	215	983
25 years and over	7,918	1,491	4,377	1,729	3,541	1,328
25 to 54 years	6,476	1,528	3,600	1,744	2,876	1,399
55 years and over	1,442	1,293	777	1,572	665	997
Hispanic[1]						
16 years and over	22,846	851	13,533	892	9,313	788
16 to 24 years	3,035	663	1,775	678	1,260	638
25 years and over	19,811	904	11,758	948	8,053	842
25 to 54 years	16,301	910	9,707	949	6,594	870
55 years and over	3,510	874	2,052	947	1,459	742
OCCUPATION						
Management, professional, and related	55,929	1,501	26,835	1,751	29,093	1,312
Management, business, and financial operations	23,892	1,588	12,423	1,805	11,470	1,403
Professional and related	32,037	1,443	14,413	1,724	17,624	1,249
Service	16,080	718	7,881	777	8,199	675
Sales and office	21,843	914	8,863	1,058	12,980	845
Sales and related	9,287	1,022	5,077	1,187	4,211	825
Office and administrative support	12,555	878	3,786	947	8,769	849
Natural resources, construction, and maintenance	11,741	995	11,165	1,005	576	747
Farming, fishing, and forestry	601	711	467	743	134	637
Construction and extraction	7,000	982	6,713	987	287	807
Installation, maintenance, and repair	4,139	1,040	3,984	1,049	155	837
Production, transportation, and material moving	15,924	846	12,566	894	3,359	725
Production	7,180	897	5,407	949	1,773	749
Transportation and material moving	8,744	814	7,158	854	1,586	710

Note: Not seasonally adjusted; figures are median usual weekly earnings of full-time wage and salary workers for second quarter 2023. Total includes races not shown here. (1) May be of any race.

Average Hours and Earnings of U.S. Production Workers, 1969-2022
Source: Bureau of Labor Statistics, U.S. Dept. of Labor
(annual averages)

Year	Weekly hours	Hourly earnings	Weekly earnings	Year	Weekly hours	Hourly earnings	Weekly earnings	Year	Weekly hours	Hourly earnings	Weekly earnings
1969	37.5	$3.22	$120.80	1987	34.7	$9.14	$317.33	2005	33.8	$16.11	$543.91
1970	37.0	3.41	125.91	1988	34.6	9.44	326.50	2006	33.9	16.75	567.00
1971	36.7	3.63	133.35	1989	34.5	9.81	338.42	2007	33.8	17.41	589.09
1972	36.9	3.91	143.99	1990	34.3	10.20	349.63	2008	33.6	18.06	607.10
1973	36.9	4.14	152.71	1991	34.1	10.51	358.46	2009	33.1	18.60	615.82
1974	36.4	4.44	161.76	1992	34.2	10.77	368.17	2010	33.4	19.04	635.86
1975	36.0	4.74	170.45	1993	34.3	11.04	378.80	2011	33.6	19.43	652.75
1976	36.0	5.06	182.36	1994	34.5	11.33	391.11	2012	33.7	19.73	665.56
1977	35.9	5.44	195.34	1995	34.3	11.65	399.93	2013	33.7	20.13	677.62
1978	35.8	5.88	210.17	1996	34.3	12.04	413.17	2014	33.7	20.60	694.74
1979	35.6	6.34	225.46	1997	34.5	12.51	431.67	2015	33.7	21.03	708.73
1980	35.2	6.84	240.83	1998	34.5	13.01	448.47	2016	33.6	21.53	723.20
1981	35.2	7.43	261.29	1999	34.3	13.48	463.07	2017	33.7	22.05	742.42
1982	34.7	7.86	272.98	2000	34.3	14.01	480.90	2018	33.8	22.71	767.01
1983	34.9	8.20	286.34	2001	33.9	14.54	493.53	2019	33.6	23.51	790.64
1984	35.1	8.49	298.00	2002	33.9	14.96	506.48	2020	33.9	24.68	837.39
1985	34.9	8.73	304.37	2003	33.7	15.36	517.65	2021	34.2	25.90	886.54
1986	34.7	8.92	309.69	2004	33.7	15.68	528.65	2022	34.0	27.56	937.25

Note: Data refer to production workers and nonsupervisory employees.

Elderly in U.S. Labor Force, 1900-2022

Source: U.S. Census Bureau, U.S. Dept. of Commerce

(percent of persons age 65 and older who participated in the labor force; 1910 figures not available)

Year	Men	Women
1900	63.1	8.3
1920	55.6	7.3
1930	54.0	7.3
1940	41.8	6.1
1950	45.8	9.7
1960	33.1	10.8
1970	26.8	9.7
1980	19.0	8.1
1990	16.3	8.6
2000	17.7	9.4
2010	20.5	12.9
2020	23.9	15.8
2022	23.7	15.5

U.S. Union Membership, 1930-2022

Source: Bureau of Labor Statistics, U.S. Dept. of Labor

(numbers in thousands)

Year	Total employed[1]	% in union	Union members[2]	Year	Total employed[1]	% in union	Union members[2]	Year	Total employed[1]	% in union	Union members[2]
1930	29,424	11.6%	3,401	1975	76,945	25.5%	19,611	2014	131,431	11.1%	14,576
1935	27,053	13.2	3,584	1980	90,564	21.9	19,843	2015	133,743	11.1	14,795
1940	32,376	26.9	8,717	1985	94,521	18.0	16,996	2016	136,101	10.7	14,555
1945	40,394	35.5	14,322	1990	103,905	16.1	16,740	2017	137,890	10.7	14,817
1950	45,222	31.5	14,267	1995	110,038	14.9	16,360	2018	140,099	10.5	14,744
1955	50,675	33.2	16,802	2000	120,786	13.5	16,258	2019	141,737	10.3	14,574
1960	54,234	31.4	17,049	2005	125,889	12.5	15,685	2020	132,174	10.8	14,253
1965	60,815	28.4	17,299	2010	124,073	11.9	14,715	2021	136,393	10.3	14,012
1970	70,920	27.3	19,381	2012	127,577	11.3	14,366	2022	141,673	10.1	14,285

(1) Prior to 1985, total labor force figure, which includes unemployed persons. From 1985 on, does not include self-employed workers. (2) From 1930 to 1980, includes dues-paying members of traditional trade unions, regardless of employment status; after 1980, includes employed only. From 1985 on, includes members of employee associations similar to a union.

Median Weekly Earnings of U.S. Workers by Union Affiliation, 2000, 2022

Source: Bureau of Labor Statistics, U.S. Dept. of Labor

Sex and age	2000				2022			
	Total	Union members[1]	Represented by unions[2]	Non-union	Total	Union members[1]	Represented by unions[2]	Non-union
Total, 16 years and older	**$576**	**$696**	**$691**	**$542**	**$1,059**	**$1,216**	**$1,203**	**$1,029**
16 to 24 years	361	437	436	355	691	795	798	685
25 years and older	611	709	705	592	1,123	1,242	1,233	1,100
25 to 34 years	550	627	624	529	992	1,115	1,104	979
35 to 44 years	631	716	712	614	1,181	1,329	1,320	1,161
45 to 54 years	671	755	752	639	1,194	1,350	1,327	1,167
55 to 64 years	617	727	723	592	1,154	1,225	1,223	1,144
65 years and older	442	577	565	422	1,031	1,157	1,179	1,010
Men, 16 years and older	**646**	**739**	**737**	**620**	**1,154**	**1,273**	**1,266**	**1,137**
16 to 24 years	376	458	457	370	713	801	805	707
25 years and older	700	753	752	682	1,219	1,314	1,305	1,201
25 to 34 years	603	678	675	591	1,040	1,147	1,144	1,023
35 to 44 years	731	776	774	718	1,297	1,409	1,397	1,270
45 to 54 years	777	801	799	769	1,336	1,405	1,378	1,324
55 to 64 years	738	755	757	729	1,294	1,303	1,301	1,293
65 years and older	537	613	613	514	1,196	1,234	1,264	1,179
Women, 16 years and older	**491**	**616**	**613**	**472**	**958**	**1,146**	**1,135**	**932**
16 to 24 years	342	406	405	339	656	778	779	649
25 years and older	515	627	623	497	1,002	1,160	1,151	979
25 to 34 years	493	579	578	483	938	1,069	1,049	923
35 to 44 years	520	605	604	506	1,065	1,202	1,192	1,036
45 to 54 years	565	697	692	522	1,058	1,262	1,238	1,018
55 to 64 years	505	659	647	481	1,007	1,146	1,145	987
65 years and older	378	485	484	365	874	968	973	857

Note: Data refer to the sole or principal job of full-time wage and salary workers. Excludes self-employed workers regardless of whether or not their businesses are incorporated. (1) Includes members of an employee association similar to a union. (2) Includes members of a labor union as well as those whose jobs are covered by a union or an employee-association contract.

Work Stoppages (Strikes and Lockouts) in the U.S., 1950-2022

Source: Bureau of Labor Statistics, U.S. Dept. of Labor; involving 1,000 workers or more

Year	No.	Workers (thous.)	Days idle (thous.)	Year	No.	Workers (thous.)	Days idle (thous.)	Year	No.	Workers (thous.)	Days idle (thous.)
1950	424	1,698	30,390	1991	40	392	4,584	2007	21	189	1,265
1955	363	2,055	21,180	1992	35	364	3,989	2008	15	72	1,954
1960	222	896	13,260	1993	35	182	3,981	2009	5	13	124
1965	268	999	15,140	1994	45	322	5,021	2010	11	45	302
1970	381	2,468	52,761	1995	31	192	5,771	2011	19	113	1,020
1975	235	965	17,563	1996	37	273	4,889	2012	19	148	1,131
1980	187	795	20,844	1997	29	339	4,497	2013	15	55	290
1982	96	656	9,061	1998	34	387	5,116	2014	11	34	200
1983	81	909	17,461	1999	17	73	1,996	2015	12	47	740
1984	62	376	8,499	2000	39	394	20,419	2016	15	99	1,543
1985	54	324	7,079	2001	29	99	1,151	2017	7	25	440
1986	69	533	11,861	2002	19	46	660	2018	20	485	2,815
1987	46	174	4,481	2003	14	129	4,091	2019	25	426	3,244
1988	40	118	4,381	2004	17	171	3,344	2020	8	27	966
1989	51	452	16,996	2005	22	100	1,736	2021	16	81	1,552
1990	44	185	5,926	2006	20	70	2,688	2022	23	121	2,313

Note: Numbers cover stoppages that began in the year indicated. Workers are counted more than once if they are involved in more than one stoppage during the year. For work stoppages ongoing at the end of a calendar year, days idle include only the days for the calendar year.

ENERGY

U.S. Energy Overview, 1960-2022

Source: *Monthly Energy Review*, July 2023, Energy Information Administration (EIA), U.S. Dept. of Energy; in quadrillion Btu

	1960	1970	1980	1990	2000	2005	2010	2015	2020	2021	2022
Production	42.79	63.46	67.15	70.67	71.27	69.38	74.91	88.29	95.65	98.20	102.83
Fossil fuels	39.86	59.15	58.98	58.52	57.31	55.00	58.16	70.19	75.81	77.86	81.49
Coal[1]	10.82	14.61	18.60	22.49	22.74	23.19	22.04	17.95	10.70	11.60	12.05
Natural gas (dry)	12.66	21.67	19.91	18.33	19.66	18.56	21.81	28.07	34.73	35.80	37.11E
Crude oil[2]	14.94	20.40	18.25	15.57	12.36	10.97	11.61	19.70	23.57	23.37	24.66E
Natural gas plant liquids (NGPL)	1.45	2.48	2.23	2.14	2.55	2.28	2.71	4.48	6.81	7.10	7.67
Nuclear electric power	0.01	0.24	2.74	6.10	7.86	8.16	8.43	8.34	8.25	8.13	8.05
Renewable energy	2.93	4.07	5.43	6.04	6.10	6.22	8.31	9.77	11.59	12.21	13.29
Conventional hydroelectric power[3]	1.61	2.63	2.90	3.05	2.81	2.70	2.54	2.32	2.50	2.23	2.32
Biomass[4]	1.32	1.43	2.48	2.74	3.01	3.10	4.55	5.03	4.71	4.91	5.04
Geothermal energy	(s)	0.01	0.05	0.17	0.16	0.18	0.21	0.21	0.20	0.21	0.21
Solar	NA	NA	NA	0.06	0.06	0.06	0.09	0.43	1.21	1.52	1.87
Wind	NA	NA	NA	0.03	0.06	0.18	0.92	1.78	2.96	3.35	3.85
Imports	4.19	8.34	15.80	18.82	28.87	34.66	29.87	23.79	19.99	21.46	21.48
Coal	0.01	—	0.03	0.07	0.31	0.76	0.48	0.26	0.11	0.11	0.14
Natural gas	0.16	0.85	1.01	1.55	3.87	4.45	3.83	2.79	2.62	2.88	3.10
Petroleum[5]	4.00	7.47	14.66	17.12	24.42	29.20	25.36	20.41	16.98	18.20	17.97
Crude oil[2]	2.20	2.81	11.20	12.77	19.78	22.09	20.14	16.30	13.04	13.54	13.93
Petroleum products[6]	1.80	4.66	3.46	4.35	4.64	7.11	5.22	4.11	3.94	4.66	4.04
Biomass[7]	NA	NA	NA	NA	(s)	0.01	(s)	0.08	0.07	0.08	0.07
Electricity	0.02	0.02	0.09	0.06	0.17	0.15	0.15	0.26	0.21	0.18	0.19
Exports	1.48	2.63	3.70	4.75	3.96	4.46	8.18	12.90	23.46	25.07	27.45
Coal	1.02	1.94	2.42	2.77	1.53	1.27	2.10	1.85	1.73	2.06	2.10
Natural gas	0.01	0.07	0.05	0.09	0.25	0.74	1.15	1.80	5.33	6.71	6.97
Petroleum	0.43	0.55	1.16	1.82	2.11	2.34	4.78	9.12	16.11	15.95	17.98
Crude oil[2]	0.02	0.03	0.61	0.23	0.11	0.07	0.09	0.96	6.70	6.19	7.52
Petroleum products[6]	0.41	0.52	0.55	1.59	2.00	2.28	4.69	8.15	9.41	9.76	10.46
Biomass[8]	NA	NA	NA	NA	NA	(s)	0.05	0.08	0.23	0.25	0.29
Electricity	—	0.01	0.01	0.06	0.05	0.07	0.07	0.03	0.05	0.05	0.05
Consumption	45.04	67.82	78.02	84.43	98.70	100.10	97.51	97.40	92.91	97.74	100.29
Fossil fuels	42.09	63.50	69.78	72.28	84.62	85.62	80.72	79.09	73.08	77.43	79.05
Coal	9.84	12.27	15.42	19.17	22.58	22.80	20.83	15.55	9.18	10.55	9.85
Natural gas[9]	12.39	21.80	20.24	19.60	23.82	22.57	24.58	28.19	31.58	31.69	33.41
Petroleum[10]	19.87	29.50	34.16	33.50	38.15	40.22	35.32	35.37	32.33	35.24	35.85
Nuclear electric power	0.01	0.24	2.74	6.10	7.86	8.16	8.43	8.34	8.25	8.13	8.05
Renewable energy	2.93	4.07	5.43	6.04	6.10	6.23	8.27	9.75	11.42	12.05	13.06
Conventional hydroelectric power[3]	1.61	2.63	2.90	3.05	2.81	2.70	2.54	2.32	2.50	2.23	2.32
Biomass[4]	1.32	1.43	2.48	2.74	3.01	3.11	4.51	5.02	4.55	4.75	4.81
Geothermal energy	(s)	0.01	0.05	0.17	0.16	0.18	0.21	0.21	0.20	0.21	0.21
Solar	NA	NA	NA	0.06	0.06	0.06	0.09	0.43	1.21	1.52	1.87
Wind	NA	NA	NA	0.03	0.06	0.18	0.92	1.78	2.96	3.35	3.85

NA = Not available. — = Less than 0.005 quadrillion Btu. (s) = Less than 0.5 trillion Btu. E = Estimate. **Note:** Numbers may not add up to totals because of rounding. (1) Incl. waste coal supplied beginning in 1989 and refuse recovery beginning in 2001. (2) Incl. lease condensate. Imports incl. crude oil for the Strategic Petroleum Reserve, which began in 1977. (3) Starting in 1990, pumped storage was removed and expanded coverage of industrial use of hydroelectric power was included. (4) Category known as "wood, waste, and alcohol" for years prior to 2000. Includes wood, waste, and alcohol fuels (ethanol blended into motor gasoline). Ethanol is included in both Petroleum and Biomass categories but is only counted once in totals. (5) Imports incl. crude oil for the Strategic Petroleum Reserve, which began in 1977. Imports/exports excl. biofuels. (6) Incl. unfinished oils, natural gasoline, and gasoline blending components; excl. biofuels. (7) Beginning in 1993, incl. fuel ethanol (minus denaturant); also incl. biodiesel (beginning in 2001), renewable diesel fuel (beginning in 2011), and other biofuels (beginning in 2021). (8) Beginning in 2001, incl. biodiesel; beginning in 2010, also incl. fuel ethanol (minus denaturant); beginning in 2016, also incl. wood and wood-derived fuels. (9) Excl. supplemental gaseous fuels. (10) Petroleum products supplied; excl. biofuels.

U.S. Energy Consumption by Source, 1950-2022

Source: *Monthly Energy Review*, July 2023, Energy Information Administration (EIA), U.S. Dept. of Energy

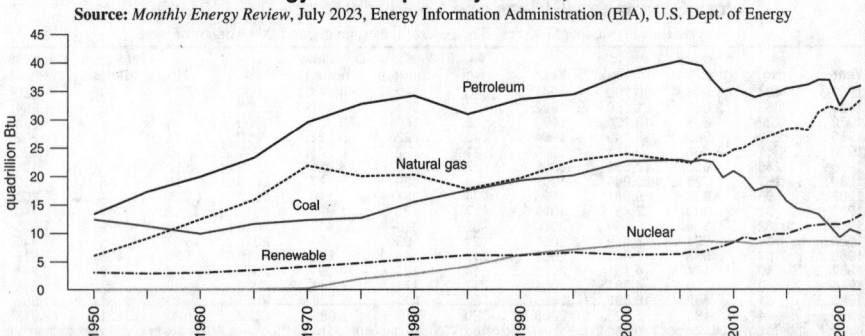

World's Largest Energy Producers and Consumers, 1980-2021

Source: Energy Information Administration (EIA), U.S. Dept. of Energy

(primary energy in quadrillion Btu; ranked by 2021 data as of June 5, 2023)

Production	1980	1990	2000	2010	2015	2017	2018	2019	2020	2021
1. China	19.54	31.88	41.26	97.06	114.40	112.07	118.05	123.84	127.00	134.96
2. United States	67.15	70.67	71.27	74.91	88.30	88.13	95.81	101.49	95.75	98.34
3. Russia	NA	NA	42.60	54.16	57.68	61.43	63.48	64.30	60.18	64.10
4. Saudi Arabia	22.43	15.92	21.59	23.33	28.15	28.49	29.18	27.86	26.65	26.59
5. Canada	10.16	13.16	17.74	18.23	20.91	22.70	23.61	23.46	22.64	23.41
6. India	2.83	6.36	8.60	14.02	15.47	16.84	17.85	18.32	17.97	18.99
7. Australia	3.72	6.59	9.64	13.22	15.65	16.87	17.36	18.92	18.68	18.01
8. Iran	3.94	7.65	10.40	14.65	14.57	18.33	18.37	15.93	15.62	16.70
9. Indonesia	4.22	5.27	7.50	12.86	14.38	14.25	16.07	17.05	15.37	16.27
10. Brazil	1.98	4.03	6.62	10.15	11.19	11.97	12.17	12.75	12.11	11.88
11. United Arab Emirates	3.89	5.51	6.77	7.71	9.73	9.85	9.76	10.73	10.05	10.09
12. Qatar	1.20	1.14	2.83	7.78	9.78	9.77	9.74	9.65	9.72	9.88
13. Norway	2.93	5.80	10.30	9.46	9.53	9.84	9.47	8.87	9.49	9.70
14. Iraq	5.45	4.54	5.62	5.27	8.75	9.97	10.33	10.59	9.18	9.24
15. Kazakhstan	NA	NA	3.95	7.13	7.55	7.73	8.13	8.03	7.71	7.26
16. Algeria	2.80	4.75	6.19	6.93	6.70	6.83	6.76	6.47	5.97	6.66
17. Kuwait	3.99	2.79	5.04	5.63	7.12	7.05	7.16	7.13	6.61	6.54
18. Mexico	5.71	7.64	9.38	8.86	7.69	6.67	6.25	5.79	5.83	5.87
19. South Africa	2.54	3.87	5.20	5.78	5.85	5.91	5.84	5.92	5.67	5.30
20. Nigeria	4.49	4.07	5.18	6.38	6.45	5.97	5.94	6.04	5.72	5.15
21. France	2.35	4.27	5.04	5.18	5.35	4.95	5.29	5.10	4.61	4.84
22. United Kingdom	8.71	9.00	11.16	6.35	5.17	5.33	5.51	5.47	5.34	4.50
23. Egypt	1.45	2.36	2.55	3.90	3.33	3.54	3.92	4.17	3.83	4.16
24. Kazakhstan	0.66	1.87	3.17	3.85	4.00	4.25	4.37	4.42	4.04	4.11
25. Germany	NA	NA	5.46	5.07	4.97	4.90	4.79	4.48	4.05	4.08

Consumption	1980	1990	2000	2010	2015	2017	2018	2019	2020	2021
1. China	19.11	28.37	42.47	112.00	137.01	142.12	147.21	151.81	156.03	165.16
2. United States	78.02	84.43	98.70	97.51	97.41	97.66	101.24	100.48	93.01	97.91
3. Russia	NA	NA	26.78	30.30	30.97	31.27	32.39	32.60	32.81	34.21
4. India	3.75	7.42	12.21	22.20	27.16	29.36	31.21	31.75	29.96	31.96
5. Japan	15.81	19.26	22.27	21.50	19.38	19.47	19.27	18.95	17.72	18.13
6. Canada	9.59	10.71	12.56	13.70	14.72	14.96	15.16	14.75	13.85	14.17
7. South Korea	1.88	4.06	8.10	10.87	11.91	12.33	12.42	12.39	12.14	12.71
8. Germany	NA	NA	14.39	14.14	13.64	14.20	13.81	13.36	12.18	12.50
9. Brazil	3.90	5.86	8.48	11.46	12.59	12.54	12.48	12.60	11.77	12.09
10. Iran	1.60	3.01	5.14	9.03	10.66	11.38	11.88	11.92	11.70	12.05
11. France	8.64	9.24	10.89	10.98	10.40	10.27	10.32	10.14	9.09	9.73
12. Saudi Arabia	1.65	3.34	5.10	9.86	9.86	11.91	11.66	11.36	9.08	9.18
13. Indonesia	1.16	2.31	4.15	6.19	6.78	7.11	7.70	8.04	7.44	8.14
14. United Kingdom	8.99	9.29	9.90	9.19	8.36	8.26	8.23	7.98	7.16	7.14
15. Mexico	3.80	4.72	6.49	7.53	7.80	7.95	7.81	7.91	7.00	7.05
16. Türkiye	1.00	1.94	3.17	4.50	5.76	6.46	6.39	6.61	6.39	6.81
17. Italy	6.20	6.73	7.58	7.68	6.77	6.78	6.82	6.54	6.06	6.57
18. Australia	2.99	3.85	4.80	5.65	5.78	6.20	6.17	6.21	5.83	5.92
19. Spain	3.18	4.01	5.51	6.21	5.60	5.77	5.86	5.77	5.17	5.43
20. South Africa	2.62	3.82	4.61	5.62	5.60	5.73	5.52	5.81	5.60	5.42
21. Thailand	0.50	1.25	2.57	4.41	5.15	5.41	5.52	5.39	5.02	5.24
22. United Arab Emirates	0.28	1.23	2.09	3.64	4.70	4.65	4.35	4.61	4.61	4.64
23. Vietnam	0.12	0.22	0.67	1.89	2.84	3.37	3.66	4.05	4.10	4.27
24. Poland	4.76	4.27	3.71	4.11	4.10	4.43	4.38	4.28	4.10	4.25
25. Taiwan	1.09	2.03	3.60	4.66	4.70	4.48	4.73	3.80	3.77	3.93

NA = Not applicable or not available.

Average U.S. Gasoline Prices, 1976-2023

Source: *Monthly Energy Review*, July 2023; *Short-Term Energy Outlook*, July 2023; Energy Information Administration (EIA), U.S. Dept. of Energy

(in dollars per gallon, including taxes; constant dollars is price in July 2023 dollars)

Year	Current dollars Unleaded regular	Diesel	Constant dollars, unleaded regular[1]	Year	Current dollars Unleaded regular	Diesel	Constant dollars, unleaded regular[1]
1976	$0.61	NA	$3.28	2010	$2.79	$2.99	$3.88
1980	1.25	NA	4.60	2011	3.53	3.84	4.77
1985	1.20	NA	3.30	2012	3.64	3.97	4.81
1990	1.16	NA	2.63	2013	3.53	3.92	4.58
1995	1.15	$1.11	2.22	2014	3.37	3.83	4.33
1996	1.23	1.24	2.33	2015	2.45	2.71	3.12
1997	1.23	1.20	2.27	2016	2.14	2.30	2.73
1998	1.06	1.04	1.92	2017	2.41	2.65	3.00
1999	1.17	1.12	2.08	2018	2.74	3.18	3.31
2000	1.51	1.49	2.63	2019	2.64	3.06	3.10
2005	2.30	2.40	3.54	2020	2.17	2.55	2.57
2006	2.59	2.71	3.89	2021	3.05	3.29	3.39
2007	2.80	2.89	4.12	2022	4.09	4.99	4.13
2008	3.27	3.80	4.61	2023	3.71[2]	3.80[2]	3.40[3]
2009	2.35	2.47	3.33				

NA = Not applicable. (1) Base prices vary slightly from unleaded regular column at left. (2) June 2023 figure. (3) Forecast.

Energy Consumption by State, 2021

Source: State Energy Data System, Energy Information Administration (EIA), U.S. Dept. of Energy

Total Consumption					Consumption per Capita				
Rank, state	Btu (tril)	Rank, state	Btu (tril)		Rank, state	Btu (mil)	Rank, state	Btu (mil)	
1. Texas	14,358.7	27. Massachusetts	1,343.7		1. Alaska	931.9	27. Missouri	285.3	
2. California	7,387.9	28. Maryland	1,269.2		2. Louisiana	925.4	28. Virginia	281.9	
3. Florida	4,313.2	29. Mississippi	1,085.0		3. North Dakota	904.9	29. Pennsylvania	279.2	
4. Louisiana	4,282.1	30. Arkansas	1,079.1		4. Wyoming	869.9	30. Maine	270.1	
5. Illinois	3,723.6	31. Kansas	1,073.7		5. Iowa	490.1	31. Michigan	270.0	
6. Pennsylvania	3,633.6	32. Oregon	1,047.8		6. Texas	485.8	32. Georgia	262.7	
7. New York	3,542.3	33. Nebraska	898.0		7. West Virginia	477.8	33. Colorado	259.7	
8. Ohio	3,542.0	34. West Virginia	853.1		8. South Dakota	457.7	34. Utah	253.7	
9. Georgia	2,833.5	35. Utah	847.2		9. Nebraska	457.3	35. North Carolina	248.7	
10. Indiana	2,726.8	36. Nevada	761.3		10. Oklahoma	413.8	36. Oregon	246.2	
11. Michigan	2,710.2	37. New Mexico	739.0		11. Indiana	400.2	37. Washington	245.0	
12. North Carolina	2,627.6	38. Connecticut	704.4		12. Montana	391.9	38. Nevada	242.0	
13. Virginia	2,440.4	39. North Dakota	703.9		13. Alabama	389.2	39. District of Columbia	225.3	
14. Tennessee	2,196.1	40. Alaska	684.2		14. Kentucky	374.7	40. New Hampshire	217.3	
15. New Jersey	1,999.8	41. Idaho	573.0		15. Mississippi	367.8	41. New Jersey	215.8	
16. Alabama	1,965.2	42. Wyoming	504.1		16. Kansas	365.5	42. Arizona	215.2	
17. Washington	1,896.8	43. Montana	433.5		17. Arkansas	356.4	43. Maryland	205.6	
18. Minnesota	1,820.6	44. South Dakota	410.2		18. New Mexico	349.1	44. Vermont	199.0	
19. Wisconsin	1,763.2	45. Maine	372.0		19. Minnesota	318.8	45. Florida	197.6	
20. Missouri	1,760.0	46. New Hampshire	301.6		20. Tennessee	315.1	46. Connecticut	194.4	
21. Kentucky	1,688.5	47. Delaware	295.5		21. South Carolina	313.8	47. Massachusetts	192.2	
22. Oklahoma	1,651.7	48. Hawaii	270.8		22. Ohio	301.1	48. California	188.7	
23. South Carolina	1,629.8	49. Rhode Island	186.0		23. Idaho	300.9	49. Hawaii	187.1	
24. Iowa	1,567.3	50. District of Columbia	150.7		24. Wisconsin	299.9	50. New York	178.4	
25. Arizona	1,563.1	51. Vermont	128.8		25. Delaware	294.1	51. Rhode Island	169.5	
26. Colorado	1,509.2	**United States**	97,810.0[1]		26. Illinois	293.5	**United States**	294.6	

(1) Includes −48.7 trillion Btu of net imports of coal coke that are not allocated to the states.

U.S. Production of Crude Oil by State, 1990-2022

Source: Energy Information Administration (EIA), U.S. Dept. of Energy

Oil production in North Dakota more than tripled between 2010 and 2022 through the use of hydraulic fracturing, or fracking, a process by which water, sand, and chemicals are injected at high pressure to create fractures in shale rock, releasing the oil or natural gas within. Fracking accounted for just 2% of U.S. oil production in 2000 but grew to 66% by 2022.

(in thousands of barrels; ranked by 2022 production)

Rank, state	1990	2000	2010	2020	2022	Rank, state	1990	2000	2010	2020	2022
1. TX	678,478	443,397	426,767	1,773,050	1,841,754	18. MI	19,676	7,907	6,980	4,132	4,528
2. NM	67,250	67,198	65,569	375,419	574,327	19. AR	10,386	7,154	5,733	4,143	4,401
3. ND	36,717	32,719	112,555	433,564	386,041	20. AL	18,538	10,457	7,155	4,294	3,817
4. AK	647,309	355,199	218,904	163,852	159,611	21. KY	5,409	3,465	2,519	2,265	2,252
5. CO	30,453	18,481	33,068	171,635	157,532	22. IN	3,000	2,098	1,835	1,402	1,710
6. OK	112,273	69,976	70,196	173,217	151,537	23. NE	5,889	2,957	2,331	1,674	1,607
7. CA	320,868	271,132	200,370	142,221	122,421	24. FL	5,675	4,626	1,777	1,488	1,214
8. WY	103,856	60,726	53,890	89,056	90,939	25. SD	1,648	1,170	1,607	1,047	960
9. UT	27,604	15,636	24,663	31,001	46,429	26. NY	415	210	381	147	236
10. LA	147,582	105,425	67,590	36,697	36,447	27. NV	4,011	621	426	196	229
11. KS	55,428	34,463	40,470	28,261	28,328	28. TN	506	346	257	152	146
12. OH	10,008	6,575	4,772	23,864	21,963	29. MO	146	94	146	62	67
13. MT	19,810	15,428	25,332	19,085	20,576	30. ID	NA	NA	0	1	37
14. WV	2,143	1,400	1,842	19,059	16,283	31. AZ	121	59	37	5	6
15. MS	27,034	19,844	23,981	14,166	12,656	32. VA	16	9	12	5	5
16. IL	19,954	12,206	9,067	7,150	6,925	**Federal offshore**	299,835	558,242	588,335	614,434	638,874
17. PA	2,641	1,500	3,238	5,532	4,907	**U.S. total**	2,684,687	2,130,707	2,001,805	4,142,277	4,338,766

NA = Not available. **Note:** One barrel is equal to 42 U.S. gallons.

Dry Shale Gas Production in the U.S., 2000-23

Source: Energy Information Administration (EIA), U.S. Dept. of Energy

(production in billions of cubic ft per day; ranked by 2023 production)

Site name (primary location)	2000	2005	2010	2015	2017	2019	2020	2021	2022	2023
Marcellus (PA, WV, OH, NY)	—	—	0.45	15.09	17.10	21.70	23.40	25.41	25.44	25.36
Permian (TX, NM)	0.64	0.64	0.94	2.85	4.37	8.81	11.47	12.37	14.05	16.46
Haynesville (LA, TX)	0.14	0.10	2.44	3.86	3.78	8.06	9.48	10.24	12.39	14.19
Utica (OH, PA, WV)	—	—	—	2.03	4.28	7.04	6.98	6.61	5.69	4.65
Eagle Ford (TX)	—	—	0.12	4.76	3.95	4.37	4.65	3.77	3.99	4.12
Woodford (OK)	0.01	0.02	0.97	1.97	2.46	2.97	2.91	2.62	2.68	2.91
Niobrara-Codell (CO, WY)	0.26	0.36	0.54	1.23	1.63	2.31	2.80	2.49	2.50	2.58
Mississippian (OK)	0.68	0.76	0.65	1.28	1.43	2.73	2.77	2.17	2.14	2.38
Bakken (ND, MT)	0.01	0.02	0.11	0.89	1.02	1.73	2.17	2.10	2.09	2.25
Barnett (TX)	0.13	0.97	4.13	3.93	2.89	2.46	2.19	2.00	1.89	1.83
Fayetteville (AR)	—	—	1.81	2.64	1.76	1.32	1.18	1.09	0.99	0.82
Other U.S. shale locations	1.13	1.09	3.13	4.40	3.29	3.14	2.84	2.53	2.38	2.24
Total	3.01	3.96	15.30	44.94	47.97	66.65	72.85	73.38	76.24	79.80

— = Less than 0.01 billions of cubic ft per day. **Note:** Figures are monthly averages of production per day estimates as of Jan. 31 of year shown. Numbers may not add up to totals because of rounding.

U.S. Petroleum Trade, 1950-2022

Source: *Monthly Energy Review*, July 2023, Energy Information Administration (EIA), U.S. Dept. of Energy
(in thousands of barrels per day; average for the year)

Year	Imports from Persian Gulf[1]	Total imports	Total exports	Net imports[2]	Petroleum products supplied[3]	Year	Imports from Persian Gulf[1]	Total imports	Total exports	Net imports[2]	Petroleum products supplied[3]
1950	NA	850	305	545	6,458	2005	2,334	13,714	1,165	12,549	20,802
1955	NA	1,248	368	880	8,455	2010	1,711	11,793	2,353	9,441	19,178
1960	326	1,815	202	1,613	9,797	2015	1,507	9,449	4,738	4,711	19,532
1965	359	2,468	187	2,281	11,512	2016	1,766	10,055	5,261	4,795	19,692
1970	184	3,419	259	3,161	14,697	2017	1,746	10,144	6,376	3,768	19,952
1975	1,165	6,056	209	5,846	16,322	2018	1,578	9,943	7,601	2,341	20,512
1980	1,519	6,909	544	6,365	17,056	2019	963	9,141	8,471	670	20,543
1985	311	5,067	781	4,286	15,726	2020	766	7,863	8,498	-635	18,186
1990	1,966	8,018	857	7,161	16,988	2021	691	8,474	8,536	-62	19,890
1995	1,573	8,835	949	7,886	17,725	2022	980	8,318	9,577	-1,260	20,280
2000	2,488	11,459	1,040	10,419	19,701						

NA = Not available. **Note:** U.S. exports include shipments to U.S. territories; imports include receipts from U.S. territories. Numbers may not add up to totals because of rounding. (1) Bahrain, Iran, Iraq, Kuwait, Qatar, Saudi Arabia, United Arab Emirates, and the Neutral Zone between Kuwait and Saudi Arabia. (2) Total imports minus total exports. (3) Includes field production, refinery production, imports, and unaccounted-for crude oil minus change in stocks, crude oil losses, refinery inputs, and exports.

World Fossil Fuel Reserves

Source: International Energy Statistics Database, Energy Information Administration (EIA), U.S. Dept. of Energy

	Crude oil (bil barrels), 2021	Natural gas (tril cu ft), 2021	Coal (mil short tons), 2021		Crude oil (bil barrels), 2021	Natural gas (tril cu ft), 2021	Coal (mil short tons), 2021
North America	222.8[1]	543.0[1]	260,331	**Middle East**	847.8	2,843.1	1,326
Canada	170.3	73.0	7,255	Bahrain	0.2	2.9	0
Greenland	0.0	0.0	202	Iran	208.6	1,200.3	1,326
Mexico	5.8	6.4	1,335	Iraq	145.0	131.7	0
United States	47.1[1]	465.4[1]	251,539	Israel	0.0	6.2	0
Central & South America	331.1	268.5	15,090	Kuwait	101.5	63.0	0
Argentina	2.5	14.0	551	Oman	5.4	23.0	0
Bolivia	0.2	10.7	1	Qatar	25.2	842.6	0
Brazil	12.7	12.9	7,271	Saudi Arabia	258.6	332.8	0
Chile	0.2	3.5	1,302	Syria	2.5	8.5	0
Colombia	2.0	3.1	5,020	UAE	97.8	215.1	0
Cuba	0.1	2.5	0	Yemen	3.0	16.9	0
Ecuador	8.3	0.4	26	**Africa**	125.3	624.1[1]	16,355
Peru	0.9	10.6	112	Algeria	12.2	159.1	65
Trinidad & Tobago	0.2	10.5	0	Angola	7.8	12.1	0
Venezuela	303.8	200.4	806	Botswana	0.0	0.0	1,830
Europe	13.5	80.9	113,116	Congo, Dem. Rep. of	0.2	0.0	97
Albania	0.2	0.2	575	Congo Rep.	2.9	10.0	0
Bosnia & Herz.	0.0	0.0	2,496	Egypt	3.3	63.0	18
Bulgaria	0.0	0.2	2,608	Eswatini	0.0	0.0	159
Czechia	0.0	0.1	3,963	Libya	48.4	53.1	0
Germany	0.1	0.8	39,573	Mozambique	0.0	100.0	1,975
Greece	0.0	0.0	3,170	Nigeria	36.9	203.4	379
Hungary	0.0	0.1	3,207	South Africa	0.0	NA	10,905
Kosovo	0.0	0.0	1,724	Sudan	5.0	3.0	0
Montenegro	0.0	0.0	157	Tanzania	0.0	0.2	297
Netherlands	0.1	4.7	548	Zambia	0.0	0.0	50
North Macedonia	0.0	0.0	366	Zimbabwe	0.0	0.0	553
Norway	8.1	54.5	2	**Asia & Oceania**	46.7[1]	590.2	506,690
Poland	0.1	3.2	31,450	Afghanistan	0.0	1.8	73
Romania	0.6	3.7	321	Australia	2.4	114.0	165,597
Serbia	0.1	1.7	8,283	Bangladesh	0.0	4.5	323
Slovakia	0.0	0.5	149	Brunei	1.1	9.2	0
Slovenia	0.0	0.0	409	China	26.0	235.0	157,847
Spain	0.2	0.1	1,308	India	4.6	48.8	122,414
Turkey	0.4	0.1	12,704	Indonesia	2.5	49.7	38,436
United Kingdom	2.5	6.4	29	Japan	0.0	0.7	386
Eurasia	118.9	2,338.0	248,274	Korea, North	0.0	0.0	661
Armenia	0.0	0.0	180	Korea, South	NA	0.3	359
Azerbaijan	7.0	60.0	0	Laos	0.0	0.0	554
Belarus	0.2	0.1	0	Malaysia	3.6	42.0	249
Georgia	0.0	0.3	222	Mongolia	NA	0.0	2,778
Kazakhstan	30.0	85.0	28,225	Myanmar	0.1	22.5	7
Kyrgyzstan	0.0	0.2	1,070	New Zealand	0.0	1.1	8,350
Russia	80.0	1,688.2	178,757	Pakistan	0.5	20.9	3,377
Tajikistan	0.0	0.2	413	Philippines	0.1	3.5	398
Turkmenistan	0.6	400.0	0	Thailand	0.3	4.9	1,172
Ukraine	0.4	39.0	37,892	Vietnam	4.4	24.7	3,704
Uzbekistan	0.6	65.0	1,516	**World**	1,661.9[1]	7,257.2[1]	1,161,182

NA = Not available. **Note:** Regional and world totals may include countries not shown. Proved reserves only. Some countries omitted for lack of appreciable reserves. (1) As of 2020, the latest year available.

U.S. Crude Oil Imports by Selected Countries, 1975-2022

Source: Energy Information Administration (EIA), U.S. Dept. of Energy

The United States' dependence on foreign oil continued to decline as a consequence of increased U.S. production of crude oil, natural gas, and domestic biofuels like ethanol and biodiesel. Imports stood at just 6.3 mil barrels a day in 2022, down from more than 10.1 mil barrels per day in 2005. Since 2004, Canada has been the largest foreign supplier of U.S. oil. In 2022, it was responsible for about 60% of all U.S. oil imports, nearly four times as much as those from all OPEC countries combined.

(in thousands of barrels per day; ranked by 2022 imports)

Country	1975	1980	1985	1990	1995	2000	2005	2010	2015	2020	2022
Canada............	600	199	468	643	1,040	1,348	1,633	1,970	3,169	3,596	3,794
Mexico.............	70	507	715	689	1,027	1,313	1,556	1,152	688	656	637
*Saudi Arabia......	701	1,250	132	1,195	1,260	1,523	1,445	1,082	1,052	498	456
*Iraq..............	2	28	46	514	0	620	527	415	229	176	244
Colombia..........	0	0	0	140	.207	318	156	338	373	248	223
Brazil.............	0	1	0	0	0	5	94	255	190	77	146
Ecuador[1].........	0	0	0	0	96	125	276	210	225	169	142
*Nigeria...........	746	841	280	784	621	875	1,077	983	54	67	94
*Libya.............	223	548	0	0	0	0	44	43	3	9	79
Guyana...........	NA	NA	NA	NA	NA	NA	NA	NA	NA	27	77
Argentina.........	NA	NA	NA	NA	44	53	56	29	18	34	62
Ghana............	NA	NA	NA	NA	NA	NA	NA	NA	NA	24	56
Trinidad and Tobago......	115	115	98	76	62	56	64	45	7	38	44
*Angola[2].........	71	37	104	236	360	295	456	383	124	28	43
United Kingdom.........	0	173	278	155	341	291	224	120	11	28	39
*Kuwait...........	4	27	4	79	213	263	227	195	204	21	27
Kazakhstan...........	NA	NA	NA	NA	NA	NA	12	18		17	23
Russia[3]...........	0	0	0	1	14	7	199	269	38	76	20
Norway...........	12	144	31	96	258	302	119	25	9	14	19
*Algeria...........	264	456	84	63	27	1	228	328	3	7	16
*United Arab Emirates....	117	172	35	9	5	3	9	2	2	5	12
Peru..............	NA	NA	NA	NA	21	4	4	14	6	6	7
*Congo Republic[4].......	NA	NA	NA	NA	20	42	25	70	9	5	5
Indonesia[5]...........	379	314	292	98	64	36	19	33	36	NA	3
*Gabon[6]............	NA	NA	NA	NA	229	143	127	47	10	NA	2
Australia...........	0	0	21	47	16	49	10	10	10	NA	2
Guatemala.........	NA	NA	NA	NA	8	18	11	11	8	4	2
Tunisia...........	NA	NA	NA	NA	NA	NA	NA	NA	NA	NA	2
*Iran.............	278	8	27	0	0	0	NA	NA	NA	NA	1
Non-OPEC countries....	NA	NA	NA	NA	3,660	4,526	5,310	4,661	4,690	5,060	5,299
OPEC countries........	3,211	3,864	1,312	3,514	3,570	4,544	4,816	4,553	2,673	815	979
Persian Gulf countries[7]..	1,121	1,508	244	1,801	1,479	2,409	2,207	1,694	1,487	700	740
TOTAL.........	**4,105**	**5,263**	**3,201**	**5,894**	**7,230**	**9,071**	**10,126**	**9,213**	**7,363**	**5,875**	**6,278**

* = OPEC member, as of 2022. NA = Not available. **Note:** Subtotals and totals include countries not shown here. For years of OPEC membership, see footnotes on individual countries. (1) Suspended its OPEC membership in Dec. 1992, rejoined in Oct. 2007, and again withdrew in Jan. 2020. Imports in 1995-2005 and 2020-22 appear in non-OPEC totals, and imports in 2010-15 appear in OPEC totals. (2) Became a member of OPEC as of 2007 and is not included in OPEC totals from before that year. (3) May include oil from USSR states before 1992. (4) Member of OPEC as of 2018; not included in OPEC totals before that year. (5) Suspended OPEC membership in Jan. 2009, rejoined in Jan. 2016, and again withdrew in Nov. 2016. Imports in 1975-2005 appear in OPEC totals, and imports in 2010-22 appear in non-OPEC totals. (6) Withdrew from OPEC in Jan. 1995 and rejoined in July 2016. Imports for 1995-2015 appear in non-OPEC totals. (7) Bahrain, Iran, Iraq, Kuwait, Qatar, Saudi Arabia, and United Arab Emirates.

U.S. Coal Production and Consumption, 1950-2022

Source: *Monthly Energy Review*, July 2023; *Annual Coal Report 2021*; Energy Information Administration (EIA); U.S. Dept. of Energy

(in thousand short tons)

Year	Coal production[1]			Coal consumption				
	Surface mining	Underground mining	Total production	Residential[2]	Commercial	Industrial	Electric power[3]	Total consumption
1950	139,388	421,000	560,388	51,562	63,021	224,637	91,871	494,102
1960	141,745	292,584	434,329	24,159	16,789	177,402	176,685	398,081
1970	272,131	340,530	612,661	9,024	7,090	186,637	320,182	523,231
1975	361,174	293,467	654,641	2,823	6,587	147,244	405,962	562,640
1980	492,192	337,508	829,700	1,355	5,097	127,004	569,274	702,730
1985	532,838	350,800	883,638	1,711	6,068	116,429	693,841	818,049
1990	604,529	424,546	1,029,076	1,345	5,379	115,207	782,567	904,498
1995	636,725	396,249	1,032,974	755	5,052	106,067	850,230	962,104
2000	699,953	373,659	1,073,612	454	3,673	94,147	985,821	1,084,095
2005	762,887	368,612	1,131,498	378	4,342	83,774	1,037,485	1,125,978
2010	747,214	337,155	1,084,368	NA	3,081	70,381	975,052	1,048,514
2015	590,119	306,821	896,941	NA	1,503	58,167	738,444	798,115
2018	480,806	275,361	756,167	NA	972	49,917	637,217	688,105
2020	339,905	195,530	535,434	NA	793	40,073	435,827	476,693
2021	356,834	220,597	577,431	NA	811	43,434	501,435	545,679
2022	NA	NA	594,915	NA	800	41,900	469,938	512,638

NA = Not available. (1) A small amount of refuse recovery has been included in coal production figures since 2001. (2) Beginning in 2008, residential coal consumption data no longer collected by the EIA. (3) Electricity-only and combined-heat-and-power (CHP) plants whose primary business is to sell electricity or electricity and heat to the public. Through 1988, data are for electric utilities only; beginning in 1989, data are for electric utilities and independent power producers.

World Nuclear Power Summary, 2022

Source: *Nuclear Power Reactors in the World*, International Atomic Energy Agency (IAEA); as of Dec. 31, 2022

Country	Reactors in operation No. of units	Reactors in operation Total MW(e)	Reactors under construction[1] No. of units	Reactors under construction[1] Total MW(e)	Nuclear electricity supplied in 2022 TW(e).h[2]	Nuclear electricity supplied in 2022 % of nation's total	Total operating experience[3] Years	Total operating experience[3] Months
Argentina	3	1,641	1	25	7.5	5.4%	97	2
Armenia	1	416	0	—	2.6	31.0	55	3
Belarus	1	1,110	1	1,110	4.4	11.9	2	2
Belgium	6	4,936	0	—	41.7	46.4	324	4
Brazil	2	1,884	1	1,340	13.7	2.5	63	3
Bulgaria	2	2,006	0	—	15.8	32.5	173	3
Canada	19	13,624	0	—	81.7	12.9	903	0
China	54	52,181	20	20,284	395.4	5.0	513	2
Czechia	6	3,934	0	—	29.3	36.7	188	10
Finland	5	4,394	0	—	24.2	35.0	176	2
France	56	61,370	1	1,630	282.1	62.6	2,449	0
Germany	3	4,055	0	—	31.9	5.8	834	8
Hungary	4	1,916	0	—	15.0	47.0	150	2
India	19	6,290	8	6,028	42.0	3.1	594	11
Iran	1	915	1	974	6.0	1.7	11	4
Japan	10	9,486	2	2,653	51.9	6.1	2,020	6
Korea, South	25	24,489	3	4,020	167.5	30.4	644	9
Mexico	2	1,552	0	—	10.5	4.5	61	11
Netherlands	1	482	0	—	3.9	3.3	78	0
Pakistan	6	3,262	0	—	22.2	16.2	98	9
Romania	2	1,300	0	—	10.2	19.3	41	11
Russia	37	27,727	3	2,700	209.5	19.6	1,447	7
Slovakia	4	1,868	2	880	14.8	59.2	184	7
Slovenia	1	688	0	—	5.3	42.8	41	3
South Africa	2	1,854	0	—	10.1	4.9	76	3
Spain	7	7,123	0	—	56.2	20.3	368	2
Sweden	6	6,937	0	—	50.0	29.5	486	0
Switzerland	4	2,973	0	—	23.2	36.4	236	11
Taiwan	3	2,859	NA	NA	22.9	9.1	239	8
Ukraine	15	13,107	2	2,070	NA	NA	563	0
United Arab Emirates	3	4,011	1	1,310	19.3	12.3	4	0
United Kingdom	9	5,883	2	3,260	43.6	14.2	1,658	9
United States	92	94,718	2	2,234	772.2	18.2	4,825	9
TOTAL	**411**	**370,991**	**58**	**59,334**	**2,486.6**	**—**	**19,764**	**11**

— = Not applicable. NA = Not available. MW(e) = Megawatt electricity. (1) Bangladesh, Egypt and Türkiye have reactors under construction, which are included in totals but not listed separately. (2) 1 terawatt-hour [TW(e).h] = 10⁶ megawatt-hour [MW(e).h]. For an average power plant, 1 TW(e).h = 0.39 megaton of coal equivalent (input) and 0.23 megaton of oil equivalent (input). (3) Total includes shutdown plants for countries not listed here: Italy (80 years, 8 months), Kazakhstan (25 years, 10 months), and Lithuania (43 years, 6 months).

Nuclear Reliance by Nation, 2022

Source: *Nuclear Power Reactors in the World*, International Atomic Energy Agency (IAEA)

(nuclear electricity generation as % of total electricity generated within country; as of Dec. 31, 2022)

Rank	Country	Nuclear share	Rank	Country	Nuclear share	Rank	Country	Nuclear share	Rank	Country	Nuclear share
1.	France	62.6%	9.	Bulgaria	32.6%	17.	Pakistan	16.2%	25.	Argentina	5.4%
2.	Slovakia	59.2	10.	Armenia	31.0	18.	United Kingdom	14.2	26.	China	5.0
3.	Hungary	47.0	11.	South Korea	30.4	19.	Canada	12.9	27.	South Africa	4.9
4.	Belgium	46.4	12.	Sweden	29.4	20.	Belarus	11.9	28.	Mexico	4.5
5.	Slovenia	42.8	13.	Spain	20.3	21.	Taiwan	9.1	29.	Netherlands	3.3
6.	Czechia	36.7	14.	Russia	19.6	22.	UAE	6.8	30.	India	3.1
7.	Switzerland	36.4	15.	Romania	19.4	23.	Japan	6.1	31.	Brazil	2.5
8.	Finland	35.0	16.	United States	18.2	24.	Germany	5.8	32.	Iran	1.7

U.S. Nuclear Generation, 1957-2022

Source: *Monthly Energy Review*, July 2023, Energy Information Administration (EIA), U.S. Dept. of Energy

Years	Total operable units[1]	Net summer capacity (mil kW)[2]	Nuclear electricity generation (mil kW) kWh	Nuclear share of electricity net generation	Capacity factor[3]	Years	Total operable units[1]	Net summer capacity (mil kW)[2]	Nuclear electricity generation (mil kW) kWh	Nuclear share of electricity net generation	Capacity factor[3]
1957	1	0.055	10	—	NA	2008	104	100.755	806,208	19.6%	91.1%
1958	1	0.055	165	—	NA	2009	104	101.004	798,855	20.2	90.3
1959	2	0.055	188	—	NA	2010	104	101.167	806,968	19.6	91.1
1960	3	0.411	518	0.1%	NA	2011	104	101.419	790,204	19.3	89.1
1965	13	0.793	3,657	0.3	NA	2012	104	101.885	769,331	19.0	86.1
1970	20	7.004	21,804	1.4	NA	2013	100	99.240	789,016	19.4	89.9
1975	57	37.267	172,505	9.0	55.9%	2014	99	98.569	797,166	19.5	91.7
1980	71	51.810	251,116	11.0	56.3	2015	99	98.672	797,178	19.5	92.3
1985	96	79.397	383,691	15.5	58.0	2016	99	99.565	805,694	19.8	92.3
1990	112	99.624	576,862	19.0	66.0	2017	99	99.629	804,950	19.9	92.3
1995	109	99.515	673,402	20.1	77.4	2018	98	99.433	807,084	19.3	92.5
2000	104	97.860	753,893	19.8	88.1	2019	96	98.119	809,409	19.6	93.4
2005	104	99.988	781,986	19.3	89.3	2020	94	96.501	789,879	19.7	92.4
2006	104	100.334	787,219	19.4	89.6	2021	93	95.546	779,645	19.0	92.8
2007	104	100.266	806,425	19.4	91.8	2022	92	94.765E	771,537	18.2	92.6E

NA = Not available. — = Less than 0.05%. E = Estimate. (1) Total of nuclear generating units holding full-power licenses, or equivalent permission to operate. (2) The maximum output that generating equipment can supply to system load, as demonstrated by a multi-hour test, at the time of summer peak demand (June 1 through Sept. 30). (3) Beginning in 2008, capacity factor data calculated using a new methodology.

U.S. Nuclear Reactors Generating the Most Electricity, 2022

Source: Energy Information Administration (EIA), U.S. Dept. of Energy
(in megawatt hours)

Rank	Reactor, location	Electricity generated	Capacity[1]	Rank	Reactor, location	Electricity generated	Capacity[1]
1.	South Texas-1, Bay City, TX	11,582,852	101.7%	13.	Palo Verde-3, Wintersburg, AZ ..	10,331,463	89.9%
2.	Peach Bottom-3, Delta, PA	11,532,538	102.5	14.	Catawba-1, York, SC.	10,277,595	101.1
3.	Palo Verde-2, Wintersburg, AZ ..	11,192,853	97.2	15.	Braidwood-2, Braceville, IL.	10,257,345	101.5
4.	Browns Ferry-2, Athens, AL	10,981,475	103.8	16.	McGuire-2, Huntersville, NC	10,228,639	100.9
5.	Seabrook-1, Seabrook, NH.	10,921,528	99.9	17.	Vogtle-1, Waynesboro, GA	10,141,460	100.7
6.	Peach Bottom-2, Delta, PA	10,651,265	96.1	18.	Salem-2, Hancocks Bridge, NJ. .	10,059,949	100.8
7.	Susquehanna-2, Salem Township, PA	10,601,890	97.1	19.	Limerick-2, Limerick, PA.	10,049,366	102.2
				20.	Watts Bar-1, Spring City, TN	10,016,728	101.8
8.	Byron-1, Byron, IL.	10,425,578	102.2	21.	LaSalle-2, Marseilles, IL.	9,941,967	100.1
9.	Palo Verde-1, Wintersburg, AZ ..	10,418,477	90.7	22.	Braidwood-1, Braceville, IL.	9,898,285	95.5
10.	Comanche Peak-2, Glen Rose, TX.	10,361,446	99.0	23.	Columbia-1, Richland, WA	9,851,535	97.7
				24.	Nine Mile Point-2, Scriba, NY . . .	9,804,697	87.1
11.	South Texas-2, Bay City, TX	10,337,033	92.2	25.	Sequoyah-2, Soddy-Daisy, TN ..	9,777,315	99.2
12.	Perry-1, Perry, OH	10,334,454	95.1				

Note: Data is preliminary. (1) The ratio of power generated to the maximum potential generation expressed as a percentage.

Renewable Energy Sources

Source: U.S. Dept. of Energy

Concern over the environmental impact of burning fossil fuels has helped spur interest in alternative fuels that are less polluting. And because the supply of fossil fuels is finite and diminishing, there is interest in "renewable" sources that do not deplete existing supplies. However, renewable energy sources still make up only a small share of U.S. domestic energy production (about 12.9% in 2022). The main reason for this is their relatively higher cost (in some cases two to four times that of power obtained from traditional fuels). The following are the major renewable energy sources available.

Biomass is plant- and animal-derived material usable as an energy source. It includes wood and wood processing waste; agricultural crops and waste materials; food, yard, and wood waste in garbage; and animal manure and human sewage. As of July 2023, biomass was the most common renewable energy source in the U.S. Biomass such as wood can be burned to produce heat and generate electricity. Agricultural crops can be burned as a fuel or converted to liquid biofuels such as ethanol and biodiesel; these are usually blended with petroleum fuels but can also be used on their own. Second-generation biofuels are made from non-food crops. While biomass fuels provide some benefits to the environment, such as reduced waste in landfills, they still produce carbon dioxide and other pollutants.

Geothermal energy is generated from heat inside the Earth. This form of energy is both clean and renewable. The technology has caught on in countries with substantial geothermal activity such as Iceland, where it accounts for approximately two-thirds of primary energy use. In the U.S., the best sources for geothermal power are in the West, Alaska, and in Hawaii, where geothermal energy resources are close to the Earth's surface. Drilling wells and testing the temperature deep underground is the most reliable method for locating geothermal reservoirs, which are largely undetectable above ground.

Hydrogen is the most abundant element in the universe. It does not naturally occur on Earth as a pure gas or liquid but is always combined with other elements (such as oxygen, to form water, or carbon, to form methane). If hydrogen is to be used for energy, it must be separated from these other elements. The two most common methods for producing hydrogen are steam reforming and electrolysis (water splitting).

NASA began using liquid hydrogen in the 1950s as a rocket fuel and used hydrogen fuel cells to power electrical systems on spacecraft. Fuel cells produce electricity by combining hydrogen and oxygen atoms. Hydrogen use in vehicles is a major focus of fuel cell research and development, and several vehicle manufacturers have begun making light-duty hydrogen fuel cell electric vehicles available in regions where hydrogen fueling stations have been built.

Hydropower, or hydroelectric power, is generated by water flowing through turbines. Along with biomass fuels and wind power, it is one of the most common renewable energy sources in the U.S. today by amount of energy produced. A dam on a river is a common hydropower producer. No harmful air pollutants are produced, but the dams needed to generate power can harm river ecosystems. Researchers are working on technologies to maximize use of hydropower and reduce adverse environmental effects.

Ocean energy can be generated in two ways. Ocean thermal energy conversion uses heat that the ocean absorbs from the sun to power generators, sometimes producing drinkable desalinated water as a byproduct. Mechanical ocean energy is generated by the movement of tides and waves through turbines. In both cases, power generation is not very efficient with current technology. New methods of capturing this energy are under development. Mechanical ocean energy requires the building of large dams or breakwater-type structures called tidal barrages, which could harm coastal ecosystems.

Solar energy is generated using light from the sun. Solar energy is increasingly used to generate electricity. Photovoltaic (PV) cells, also called solar cells, are made of semiconducting materials that can directly convert sunlight to electricity without producing any harmful waste. Arrays of mirrors can concentrate the sun's rays onto PV panels, making solar collectors more efficient. Solar thermal systems can use sunlight to heat water. According to the Dept. of Energy, homes incorporating solar heating designs can save 50%-80% on water heating bills. Solar energy is limited by its dependence on a range of factors, including location, time of day, time of year, and weather conditions.

Wind energy uses wind turbines to produce energy. It is one of the most common renewable energy sources in the U.S. today. Wind turbines typically are perched on towers 100 ft tall or higher; they are often placed in large groups ("farms"), which are sometimes located offshore. Farmers and homeowners sometimes use stand-alone turbines to generate supplemental electricity. Tax credits for wind energy producers and government incentives for homeowners have lowered the price of wind power. But some object to wind farms because of their appearance or the noise the turbines make. Wind power raises few other environmental problems, but the turbines can pose a danger to birds. In addition, because weather is involved, consistent energy generation can be a challenge.

CRIME

Crime in the U.S., 2020-21

Source: *The Transition to the National Incident-Based Reporting System (NIBRS)*, Uniform Crime Reporting (UCR) Program, FBI, USDOJ

Because law enforcement agencies participating in the UCR program are undergoing transition to a newer reporting system, the FBI received insufficient data for 2021 to release its annual report showing long-term trends. The numbers of crime offenses in this table are rounded to the nearest 100. **Violent crimes** involve force or the threat of force: murder and nonnegligent manslaughter, rape, aggravated assault, and robbery. **Property crimes** include burglary, larceny-theft, motor vehicle theft, and arson.

Region	Offense	Number			Rate per 100,000 pop.		
		2021	2020	% change, 2020-21	2021	2020	% change, 2020-21
Total U.S.	All violent crime	1,313,200	1,326,600	−1.0%	395.7	402.6	−1.7%
	Murder and nonnegligent manslaughter	22,900	22,000	4.3	6.9	6.7	3.5
	Rape (revised definition)	144,300	139,500	3.4	43.5	42.3	2.7
	Rape	107,500	103,500	3.9	32.4	31.4	3.1
	Sodomy	26,100	25,700	1.7	7.9	7.8	1.0
	Sexual assault with an object	10,700	10,400	3.2	3.2	3.2	2.5
	Aggravated assault[1]	943,800	944,800	−0.1	284.4	286.7	−0.8
	Robbery	202,200	220,200	−8.2	60.9	66.8	−8.9
Northeast	All violent crime	152,700	144,100	6.0	267.2	258.0	3.6
	Murder and nonnegligent manslaughter	2,800	2,200	27.9	4.9	3.9	25.0
	Rape (revised definition)	17,400	17,600	−0.8	30.5	31.4	−3.1
	Rape	13,000	14,700	−11.1	22.8	26.3	−13.1
	Sodomy	3,600	2,200	60.1	6.2	4.0	56.4
	Sexual assault with an object	—	700	—	—	1.2	—
	Aggravated assault[1]	102,400	99,700	2.8	179.2	178.4	0.4
	Robbery	30,100	24,700	21.9	52.6	44.2	19.1
Midwest	All violent crime	250,600	260,600	−3.8	364.1	381.6	−4.6
	Murder and nonnegligent manslaughter	4,500	4,200	8.5	6.6	6.1	7.7
	Rape (revised definition)	33,800	32,400	4.4	49.2	47.4	3.7
	Rape	26,300	25,000	4.9	38.2	36.7	4.1
	Sodomy	5,900	5,700	3.9	8.6	8.3	3.1
	Sexual assault with an object	1,700	1,700	0.1	2.4	2.4	−0.7
	Aggravated assault[1]	176,300	187,000	−5.7	256.2	273.7	−6.4
	Robbery	35,900	37,100	−3.2	52.2	54.3	−3.9
South	All violent crime	560,500	564,600	−0.7	440.5	445.6	−1.2
	Murder and nonnegligent manslaughter	10,800	10,100	7.2	8.5	7.9	6.7
	Rape (revised definition)	55,900	55,600	0.5	43.9	43.9	0.1
	Rape	40,000	40,100	−0.2	31.4	31.6	−0.6
	Sodomy	10,900	10,500	3.5	8.5	8.3	3.1
	Sexual assault with an object	5,100	5,100	0.1	4.0	4.0	−0.4
	Aggravated assault[1]	418,500	407,200	2.8	328.9	321.4	2.3
	Robbery	75,300	91,700	−17.9	59.2	72.4	−18.2
West	All violent crime	—	—	—	—	—	—
	Murder and nonnegligent manslaughter	—	—	—	—	—	—
	Rape (revised definition)	38,800	37,000	4.9	49.4	47.1	4.9
	Rape	29,000	27,200	6.6	36.9	34.6	6.6
	Sodomy	6,000	5,800	3.7	7.6	7.3	3.7
	Sexual assault with an object	3,800	—	—	4.9	—	—
	Aggravated assault[1]	—	—	—	—	—	—
	Robbery	62,500	56,100	11.4	79.5	71.3	11.4
Total U.S.	All property crime[2]	6,416,800	6,672,500	−3.8	1,933.4	2,025.0	−4.5
	Burglary/breaking and entering	899,700	1,015,000	−11.4	271.1	308.0	−12.0
	Larceny/theft offenses[3]	4,627,000	4,865,100	−4.9	1,394.1	1,476.5	−5.6
	Motor vehicle theft	890,200	792,400	12.3	268.2	240.5	11.5
	Arson[2]	40,900	42,200	−3.2	12.3	12.8	−3.9

— = Data suppressed based on NIBRS estimation suppression rules. (1) An unlawful attack upon another involving the use or threatening display of a weapon to produce severe bodily injury. (2) Arson does not count in the overall property crime measure. (3) The unlawful taking of another's property not involving force or fraud (pocket-picking, shoplifting, theft of motor vehicle parts, etc.).

Violent Crime Rates in the U.S., 1970-2020

Source: *Crime in the United States, 2020*, Uniform Crime Reporting (UCR) Program, Federal Bureau of Investigation (FBI), U.S. Dept. of Justice

After rising throughout the 1970s and 1980s, the violent crime rate dropped sharply, from a historic high of 758.2 reported offenses per 100,000 population in 1991 to nearly half that in 2020 (387.8). The rates of aggravated assault and robbery decreased even more precipitously over that same time period.

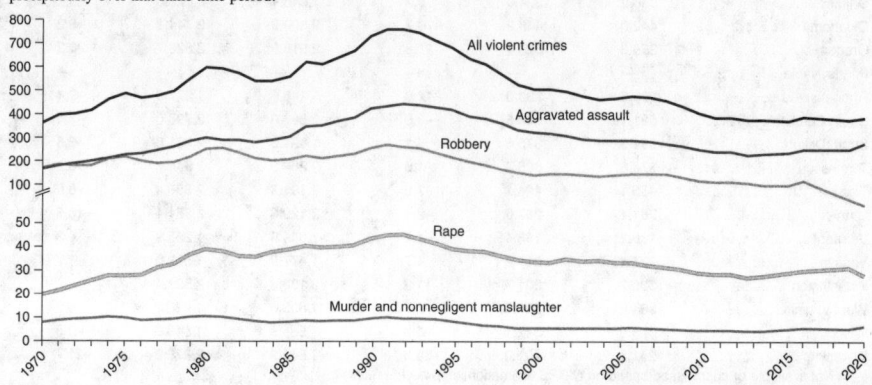

U.S. Crime Rates by State, 2020-21

Source: *The Transition to the National Incident-Based Reporting System (NIBRS): A Comparison of 2020 and 2021 NIBRS Estimates,* Uniform Crime Reporting (UCR) Program, Federal Bureau of Investigation (FBI), U.S. Dept. of Justice

(per 100,000 inhabitants)

State	Violent crime			Property crime		
	2021	2020	Percent change, 2020-21	2021	2020	Percent change, 2020-21
Alabama	596.3	—	—	2,585.3	—	—
Alaska	551.2	—	—	1,151.1	—	—
Arizona	262.0	—	—	1,435.4	—	—
Arkansas	708.5	684.9	3.5%	2,646.6	2,737.5	–3.3%
California	—	—	—	—	—	—
Colorado	481.0	435.9	10.4	3,135.4	2,904.2	8.0
Connecticut	162.1	169.6	–4.4	1,509.9	1,580.0	–4.4
Delaware	420.2	451.1	–6.8	1,943.6	2,038.8	–4.7
Dist. of Columbia	968.6	—	—	4,109.4	—	—
Florida	—	—	—	—	—	—
Georgia	393.9	388.1	1.5	1,749.2	1,895.8	–7.7
Hawaii	—	—	—	—	—	—
Idaho	249.5	261.4	–4.6	1,045.3	1,205.7	–13.3
Illinois	—	—	—	—	—	—
Indiana	313.9	439.6	–28.6	1,658.3	1,935.3	–14.3
Iowa	301.0	312.0	–3.5	1,568.3	1,769.5	–11.4
Kansas	419.1	441.1	–5.0	2,079.6	2,228.0	–6.7
Kentucky	284.7	295.2	–3.5	1,734.2	1,971.7	–12.0
Louisiana	661.0	498.2	32.7	2,672.5	2,195.3	21.7
Maine	113.1	123.4	–8.4	1,165.7	1,154.3	1.0
Maryland	—	—	—	—	—	—
Massachusetts	304.7	315.9	–3.5	1,044.4	1,118.0	–6.6
Michigan	495.1	495.7	–0.1	1,380.5	1,422.4	–2.9
Minnesota	315.7	256.1	23.3	2,064.1	1,693.1	21.9
Mississippi	241.3	246.9	–2.3	1,786.7	2,100.7	–14.9
Missouri	534.9	617.4	–13.4	2,378.4	2,774.6	–14.3
Montana	474.2	424.3	11.8	2,152.4	2,284.4	–5.8
Nebraska	246.8	154.3	60.0	1,546.6	976.4	58.4
Nevada	429.7	521.0	–17.5	2,301.1	2,198.6	4.7
New Hampshire	137.3	145.4	–5.6	1,063.1	1,101.0	–3.4
New Jersey	—	—	—	—	—	—
New Mexico	—	—	—	—	—	—
New York	101.9	—	—	710.1		
North Carolina	430.4	449.5	–4.3	2,240.3	2,417.3	–7.3
North Dakota	261.5	259.0	1.0	2,191.0	2,114.4	3.6
Ohio	336.2	334.0	0.7	1,846.1	2,023.0	–8.7
Oklahoma	442.0	445.2	–0.7	2,600.9	2,744.2	–5.2
Oregon	358.8	320.9	11.8	2,818.3	2,823.7	–0.2
Pennsylvania	—	—	—	—	—	—
Rhode Island	203.6	233.0	–12.6	1,246.6	1,277.0	–2.4
South Carolina	521.1	540.5	–3.6	2,588.0	2,796.0	–7.4
South Dakota	394.9	375.6	5.1	1,891.0	2,021.6	–6.5
Tennessee	674.6	685.7	–1.6	2,284.3	2,544.7	–10.2
Texas	455.1	494.1	–7.9	2,191.5	2,396.4	–8.6
Utah	261.1	267.6	–2.4	2,129.8	2,551.1	–16.5
Vermont	186.2	188.4	–1.1	1,344.0	1,288.9	4.3
Virginia	227.4	217.2	4.7	1,477.9	1,503.0	–1.7
Washington	335.7	301.7	11.2	3,133.6	2,897.4	8.2
West Virginia	364.2	399.0	–8.7	1,803.6	1,936.9	–6.9
Wisconsin	323.8	342.1	–5.3	1,534.9	1,546.6	–0.8
Wyoming	241.1	401.0	–39.9	1,862.2	2,378.2	–21.7

— = Not available or suppressed based on NIBRS estimation suppression rules.

Incidents, Offenses, Victims, and Known Offenders by Offense Category, 2021

Source: *NIBRS, 2021*, Uniform Crime Reporting (UCR) Program, Federal Bureau of Investigation (FBI), U.S. Dept. of Justice

Offense category	Incidents[1]	Offenses	Victims[2]	Known offenders[3]
Total	9,436,674	11,091,951	11,649,379	8,536,946
Crimes against persons	**2,552,446**	**2,939,412**	**2,939,412**	**2,704,042**
Assault offenses	2,335,159	2,706,772	2,706,772	2,485,302
Homicide offenses	15,249	16,537	16,537	16,977
Human trafficking offenses	1,827	2,141	2,141	1,992
Kidnapping/abduction	33,429	36,919	36,919	36,578
Sex offenses	166,782	177,043	177,043	163,193
Crimes against property	**6,531,976**	**6,531,976**	**7,089,310**	**3,915,790**
Arson	26,491	26,491	32,192	18,780
Bribery	739	739	776	766
Burglary/breaking and entering	584,913	584,913	679,055	366,221
Counterfeiting/forgery	107,047	107,047	117,524	84,402
Destruction/damage/vandalism of property	1,283,633	1,283,633	1,396,060	789,704
Embezzlement	22,610	22,610	23,627	22,880
Extortion/blackmail	12,270	12,270	12,674	6,812
Fraud offenses	761,698	761,698	819,614	375,292
Larceny/theft offenses	2,967,229	2,967,229	3,162,752	1,677,135
Motor vehicle theft	554,618	554,618	580,156	308,208
Robbery	121,103	121,103	159,013	160,276
Stolen property offenses	89,625	89,625	105,867	105,314
Crimes against society	**1,620,563**	**1,620,563**	**1,620,657**	**1,917,114**
Animal cruelty	16,497	16,497	16,498	14,890
Drug/narcotic offenses	1,290,858	1,290,858	1,290,905	1,568,259
Gambling offenses	1,815	1,815	1,815	2,765
Pornography/obscene material	31,873	31,873	31,876	26,348
Prostitution offenses	11,565	11,565	11,566	13,184
Weapon law violations	267,955	267,955	267,997	291,668

(1) Column figures do not add up to total. If multiple offenses were committed in an incident, the incident was counted under each offense category but only once in the total. (2) The number of victims associated with each offense type. (3) The identity of a suspect may not be necessarily known, but an attribute of the suspect has been identified that distinguishes them from an unknown offender. Column figures do not account for the 3,525,952 incidents with unknown offenders.

Criminal Victimization, 2017-21

Source: National Crime Victimization Survey, Bureau of Justice Statistics (BJS), U.S. Dept. of Justice

A crime committed against an individual or single household—whether threatened, attempted, or completed—counts as one **victimization.** Because more than one person may be victimized during a criminal incident, the number of victimizations may be greater than the number of personal crime incidents. **Victimization rates** measure the frequency with which victimizations occurred per 1,000 persons age 12 or older or per 1,000 households.

	Number				Rate			
Crime type	2017	2018	2020	2021	2017	2018	2020	2021
Violent crime[1]	5,612,670	6,385,520	4,558,150	4,598,310	20.6	23.2	16.4	16.5
Rape/sexual assault	393,980	734,630	319,950	324,500	1.4	2.7	1.2	1.2
Robbery	613,840	573,100	437,260	464,280	2.3	2.1	1.6	1.7
Assault	4,604,850	5,077,790	3,800,950	3,809,530	16.9	18.4	13.7	13.6
Aggravated assault	993,170	1,058,040	812,180	766,330	3.6	3.8	2.9	2.7
Simple assault	3,611,680	4,019,750	2,988,770	3,043,190	13.3	14.6	10.7	10.9
Violent crime excl. simple assault[2]	2,000,990	2,365,770	1,569,390	1,555,110	7.3	8.6	5.6	5.6
Selected characteristics of violent crime								
Domestic violence[3]	1,237,960	1,333,050	856,750	910,880	4.5	4.8	3.1	3.3
Intimate partner violence[4]	666,310	847,230	484,830	473,730	2.4	3.1	1.7	1.7
Stranger violence	2,034,100	2,493,750	1,973,200	2,056,150	7.5	9.1	7.1	7.4
Violent crime with an injury	1,248,480	1,449,530	1,160,920	975,340	4.6	5.3	4.2	3.5
Violent crime with a weapon	1,260,810	1,329,700	938,740	895,560	4.6	4.8	3.4	3.2
Property crime	**13,340,220**	**13,502,840**	**12,085,170**	**11,682,060**	**108.4**	**108.2**	**94.5**	**90.3**
Burglary/trespassing[5]	2,538,170	2,639,620	1,741,250	1,800,350	20.6	21.1	13.6	13.9
Burglary[6]	1,688,890	1,867,620	1,210,640	1,142,900	13.7	15.0	9.5	8.8
Trespassing[7]	849,280	772,000	530,610	657,440	6.9	6.2	4.1	5.1
Motor vehicle theft	516,810	534,010	545,810	558,670	4.2	4.3	4.3	4.3
Other theft[8]	10,285,240	10,329,210	9,798,110	9,323,040	83.6	82.7	76.6	72.1

Note: Details may not add up to totals due to rounding. (1) Excl. homicide because survey is based on interviews with victims. (2) Incl. rape or sexual assault, robbery, and aggravated assault. (3) Committed by current or former intimate partners or family members. (4) Committed by current or former spouses, boyfriends, or girlfriends. (5) Incl. unlawful, forcible, or attempted entry of places, incl. a permanent residence, other residence (e.g., hotel room), or other structure (e.g., garage). Excl. trespassing on land. (6) Incl. only crimes where the offender committed or attempted a theft. (7) Incl. crimes where the offender did not commit or attempt a theft. Excl. trespassing on land. (8) Incl. other unlawful or attempted unlawful taking of property or cash without personal contact with victim.

Prison Population by State, 2000-21

Source: National Prisoner Statistics Program, Bureau of Justice Statistics (BJS), U.S. Dept. of Justice

As of Dec. 31, 2021, 1,204,322 prisoners were under the jurisdiction, or legal authority, of state (86.9%) or federal (13.1%) correctional authorities, a 25.5% decrease from a peak U.S. prison population of 1,615,487 in 2009. Prison populations in many states continued to decline after large changes in 2019-20 due to the COVID-19 pandemic. Jails, which are locally operated, typically hold persons awaiting trial or sentencing as well as those sentenced to one year or less.

Jurisdiction	2000	2020	2021	% change, 2020-21	Jurisdiction	2000	2020	2021	% change, 2020-21
U.S. total	1,394,231	1,221,164	1,204,322	−1.4%	Mississippi	20,241	17,577	17,332	−1.4%
Federal[1,2]	145,416	152,156	157,314	3.4	Missouri[4]	27,543	23,062	23,422	1.6
State	1,248,815	1,069,008	1,047,008	−2.1	Montana	3,105	3,927	4,313	9.8
Alabama	26,406	25,328	25,032	−1.2	Nebraska	3,895	5,306	5,600	5.5
Alaska[3]	4,173	4,578	4,639	1.3	Nevada	10,063	11,249	10,202	−9.3
Arizona	26,510	37,794	33,914	−10.3	New Hampshire	2,257	2,352	2,127	−9.6
Arkansas	11,915	16,094	17,022	5.8	New Jersey	29,784	12,830	12,506	−2.5
California	163,001	100,396	101,441	1.0	New Mexico	5,342	5,500	5,154	−6.3
Colorado	16,833	16,259	15,865	−2.4	New York	70,199	34,128	30,338	−11.1
Connecticut[3]	18,355	9,559	9,889	3.5	North Carolina	31,266	29,461	28,995	−1.6
Delaware[3]	6,921	4,710	4,810	2.1	North Dakota	1,076	1,401	1,689	20.6
Dist. of Columbia[2]	10,352	—	—		Ohio	45,833	45,036	45,029	0.0
Florida	71,319	81,027	80,417	−0.8	Oklahoma[5]	23,181	22,462	22,391	−0.3
Georgia	44,232	47,141	47,010	−0.3	Oregon	10,580	12,753	13,198	3.5
Hawaii[3]	5,053	4,171	4,102	−1.7	Pennsylvania	36,847	39,357	37,194	−5.5
Idaho[4]	5,535	8,356	8,907	6.6	Rhode Island[3]	3,286	2,227	2,238	0.5
Illinois	45,281	29,729	28,475	−4.2	South Carolina	21,778	16,157	15,759	−2.5
Indiana	20,125	26,051	24,716	−5.1	South Dakota	2,616	3,250	3,353	3.2
Iowa	7,955	8,307	8,562	3.1	Tennessee	22,166	22,685	21,995	−3.0
Kansas	8,344	8,779	8,521	−2.9	Texas	166,719	135,906	133,772	−1.6
Kentucky	14,919	18,552	18,560	0.0	Utah	5,637	5,448	5,907	8.4
Louisiana	35,207	26,964	26,074	−3.3	Vermont[3]	1,697	1,284	1,287	0.2
Maine	1,679	1,714	1,577	−8.0	Virginia	30,168	31,838	30,357	−4.7
Maryland	23,538	15,623	15,134	−3.1	Washington	14,915	15,724	13,674	−13.0
Massachusetts	10,722	6,762	6,148	−9.1	West Virginia	3,856	6,044	5,847	−3.3
Michigan	47,718	33,617	32,186	−4.3	Wisconsin	20,754	20,298	20,202	−0.5
Minnesota	6,238	8,148	8,003	−1.8	Wyoming	1,680	2,087	2,123	1.7

— = Not calculated because counts for 2020 and 2021 are not comparable, not applicable, or not available. (1) Incl. adult prisoners held in nonsecure community-corrections facilities and adults and persons age 17 or younger held in privately operated facilities. (2) DC has not operated a prison system since year-end 2001. 2000 figure incl. jail and prison population. Felons sentenced under DC's criminal code are currently housed in federal facilities. (3) Prisons and jails form one integrated system. Data incl. total jail and prison populations. (4) State does not incl. persons held in federal or other state prisons in its jurisdiction count. (5) Incl. persons in county jails waiting to be moved to state prison.

Death Penalty by State, 1930-2023

Source: *Capital Punishment*, Natl. Prisoner Statistics Program, BJS, USDOJ; Death Penalty Information Center (DPIC)

In 2021, five states executed 8 inmates while 2,469 prisoners remained under sentence of death at the end of 2020, according to the most recent data available from the Bureau of Justice Statistics (BJS). The death row population has decreased every year since 2000.

As of mid-2023, 27 states and the federal government authorized the death penalty. According to the DPIC, six states executed 18 inmates in 2022; 17 executions took place in five states Jan.-Sept. 2023. Of the 23 states without the death penalty, 8 states that did not execute anyone after 1930 are not shown here (Alaska, Hawaii, Maine, Michigan, Minnesota, North Dakota, Rhode Island, and Wisconsin). More recently, capital punishment was abolished in New Mexico (2009), Illinois (2011), Connecticut (2012), Maryland (2013), New Hampshire (2019; one person remains on state's death row as repeal was not retroactive), Colorado (2020), and Virginia (2021). State supreme courts struck down the death penalty as unconstitutional in Delaware (2016) and Washington (2018). Governors issued moratoriums on executions in Oregon (2011), Pennsylvania (2015), and California (2019). Nebraska voters, in a 2016 referendum, overturned their state's ban on capital punishment. The federal government resumed executions in 2020, after a nearly 17-year hiatus, but the Biden administration imposed a moratorium July 1, 2021.

All death penalty states authorized lethal injection as their primary method of execution. Some states also permitted execution by electrocution, lethal gas, hanging, firing squad, and nitrogen hypoxia.

Jurisdiction	Prisoners under death sentence, 2020[1]	Executions 2021[3]	Executions 2020	Executions 1977-2021	Executions 1930-2021	Jurisdiction	Prisoners under death sentence, 2020[1]	Executions 2021[3]	Executions 2020	Executions 1977-2021	Executions 1930-2021
U.S. total	2,469	11	17	1,540	5,399	Missouri	20	1	1	91	153
Federal[1]	51	3	10	16	49	Montana	2	0	0	3	9
State	2,418	8	7	1,524	5,350	Nebraska	12	0	0	4	8
Alabama	170	1	1	68	203	Nevada	67	0	0	12	41
Arizona	116	0	0	37	75	New Hampshire	1	0	0	0	1
Arkansas	29	0	0	31	149	New Jersey	—	—	0	0	74
California	703	0	0	13	305	New Mexico[3]	0	0	0	1	9
Colorado	0	0	0	1	48	New York	0	0	0	0	329
Connecticut	—	—	0	1	22	North Carolina	137	0	0	43	306
Delaware[3]	0	—	0	16	28	Ohio	137	0	0	56	228
Dist. of Columbia	—	—	0	0	40	Oklahoma	45	2	0	114	174
Florida	337	0	0	99	269	Oregon	24	0	0	2	21
Georgia	40	0	1	76	442	Pennsylvania	118	0	0	3	155
Idaho	8	0	0	3	6	South Carolina	36	0	0	43	205
Illinois	—	—	0	12	102	South Dakota	1	0	0	5	6
Indiana	8	0	0	20	61	Tennessee	50	0	1	13	106
Iowa	—	—	0	0	18	Texas	206	3	3	573	870
Kansas	10	0	0	0	15	Utah	7	0	0	7	20
Kentucky	26	0	0	3	106	Vermont	—	—	0	0	4
Louisiana	66	0	0	28	161	Virginia	2	0	0	113	205
Maryland	—	—	0	5	73	Washington	0	0	0	5	52
Massachusetts	—	—	0	0	27	West Virginia	—	—	0	0	40
Mississippi	40	1	0	22	176	Wyoming	0	0	0	0	8

— = Not available or applicable. (1) As of year end. Excludes persons held under Armed Forces jurisdiction with a military death sentence for murder. (2) Excludes 160 executions carried out by military authorities between 1930 and 1961. (3) BJS advance count.

U.S. Prison Population, 1925-2021

Source: National Prisoner Statistics Program, Bureau of Justice Statistics (BJS), U.S. Dept. of Justice

As recently as 1970, the U.S. had fewer than 200,000 people behind bars nationwide, or less than 1 in 1,000 residents. That number rose steadily from the 1970s on, reaching an all-time high of 1.62 mil prisoners in 2009. The imprisonment rate has declined since its high of 506 prisoners per 100,000 residents in both 2007 and 2008.

Year	Prisoners	Imprison-ment rate	Year	Prisoners	Imprison-ment rate	Year	Prisoners	Imprison-ment rate
1925	91,669	79	1980	329,821	138	2013	1,576,950	479
1930	129,453	104	1990	773,919	295	2015	1,526,603	459
1940	173,706	131	1995	1,125,874	411	2017	1,489,189	442
1950	166,165	109	2000	1,394,231	470	2019	1,430,165	419
1960	212,953	117	2005	1,525,910	492	2020	1,221,164	357
1970	196,441	96	2010	1,613,803	500	2021	1,204,322	350

Note: Imprisonment rate is per 100,000 U.S. residents of all ages at year end based on U.S. Census Bureau pop. ests. Since 1971, the rate is of prisoners sentenced to more than one year. Data for 1940-70 include all adult felons serving sentences in state and federal institutions. In 1977, the BJS began to include persons under state jurisdiction but not in a state's physical custody, such as persons in private prisons, local jails, and other facilities. Figures may not be directly comparable over time.

Prison Situation Under Correctional Authorities' Jurisdiction, 2021

Source: *Prisoners in 2021*, National Prisoner Statistics Program, Bureau of Justice Statistics (BJS), U.S. Dept. of Justice

Largest prison populations		% change in prison population, 2020-21		Imprisonment rate of sentenced prisoners		Prison population as % of maximum estimated capacity	
Jurisdiction	Number	Jurisdiction	% change[1]	Jurisdiction	Rate[2]	Jurisdiction	% max. capacity[3]
U.S. total	1,204,322	U.S. total	−1.38%	U.S. total	350	U.S. total	NA
Federal[4]	157,314	Federal[4]	3.39	Federal[4]	43	Federal	100.05%
State	1,047,008	State	−2.06	State	307	State	NA
1. Texas	133,772	1. North Dakota	20.56	1. Mississippi	575	1. Nebraska	121.01
2. California	101,441	2. Montana	9.83	2. Louisiana	564	2. Idaho	108.28
3. Florida	80,417	3. Utah	8.43	3. Arkansas	559	3. Iowa	100.42
4. Georgia	47,010	4. Arkansas	5.77	4. Oklahoma[6]	555	4. Colorado	94.63
5. Ohio	45,029	5. Nebraska	5.54	5. Arizona	453	5. North Dakota	93.44
6. Pennsylvania	37,194	6. Oregon	3.49	6. Idaho[5]	449	6. Virginia	92.57
7. Arizona	33,914	7. Connecticut[7]	3.45	7. Texas	443	7. Arkansas	91.08
8. Michigan	32,186	8. South Dakota	3.17	8. Georgia	427	8. Alaska	90.02
9. Virginia	30,357	9. Iowa	3.07	9. Kentucky	411	9. Michigan	90.00
10. New York	30,338	10. Delaware[7]	2.12	10. Montana	387	10. Texas	88.38
11. North Carolina	28,995	11. Wyoming	1.72	11. Alabama	384	11. Alabama	87.63
12. Illinois	28,475	12. Missouri[5]	1.56	12. Ohio	382	12. Indiana[8]	87.44
13. Louisiana	26,074	13. Alaska[7]	1.33	13. Missouri[5]	374	13. Wisconsin	86.54
14. Alabama	25,032	14. California	1.04	14. South Dakota[2]	371	14. Florida	85.06
15. Indiana	24,716	15. Rhode Island[7]	0.49	15. Florida	367	15. Oklahoma	84.62
16. Missouri[5]	23,422	16. Vermont[7]	0.23	16. Wyoming	366	16. South Dakota[9]	83.18
17. Oklahoma[6]	22,391	17. Kentucky	0.04	17. Virginia	351	17. Hawaii	82.87
18. Tennessee	21,995	18. Ohio	−0.02	18. Indiana	335	18. Missouri	82.69
19. Wisconsin	20,202	19. Georgia	−0.28	19. West Virginia	328	19. Washington	82.68
20. Kentucky	18,560	20. Oklahoma[6]	−0.32	20. Nevada	323	20. California	82.60

NA = Not applicable. **Note:** Jurisdiction refers to the legal authority of state or federal correctional officials over a prisoner, regardless of where the prisoner is held, at year end. Sentenced felons from DC were the responsibility of the Federal Bureau of Prisons. BJS-imputed counts are included in U.S. and state totals. (1) Rankings do not incl. ID. (2) Prisoners sentenced to more than one year per 100,000 U.S. residents based on Census Bureau pop. figures except SD, which incl. a small number of prisoners sentenced to one year or less. (3) Based on custody counts, not jurisdiction population, excl. inmates held in local jails, other states, or private facilities unless otherwise noted. As % of rated, operational, or design capacity. Some states define capacity differently from BJS. CT and OH do not report capacity data. (4) Incl. adult prisoners held in nonsecure community-corrections facilities and adults and persons age 17 or younger held in privately operated facilities. (5) State does not incl. persons held in federal or other state prisons in its jurisdiction count. (6) Incl. persons in county jails waiting to be moved to state prison. (7) Prisons and jails form integrated system. Data incl. total jail and prison pops. (8) Incl. state-owned facilities staffed with private correctional company employees. (9) Incl. persons in private facilities.

Imprisonment Rates by Gender, Race, Hispanic Origin, and Age, 2021

Source: *Prisoners in 2021*, Bureau of Justice Statistics (BJS), U.S. Dept. of Justice

(number of prisoners sentenced to more than one year under the jurisdiction of state or federal correctional officials per 100,000 U.S. residents in a given category at year end)

Age	All prisoners[2]	Male					Female				
		All male	White	Black	Hispanic	Other[1]	All female	White	Black	Hispanic	Other[1]
Total[2]	350	659	327	1,807	810	4,391	47	38	62	49	430
18-19	55	103	33	381	84	305	5	2	13	6	14
20-24	357	657	247	1,985	725	2,690	45	31	74	50	425
25-29	699	1,272	531	3,379	1,541	6,271	106	82	144	111	781
30-34	811	1,478	714	3,692	1,793	9,281	131	111	145	135	969
35-39	815	1,484	780	3,831	1,774	11,611	131	117	138	129	1,183
40-44	755	1,397	731	3,693	1,643	11,366	107	94	123	103	888
45-49	607	1,138	607	3,035	1,347	12,771	78	70	96	66	885
50-54	471	887	483	2,413	1,051	9,897	56	47	75	49	800
55-59	372	716	392	1,946	869	9,072	38	29	56	37	746
60-64	242	476	253	1,328	657	6,553	21	15	33	21	474
65 or older	83	178	101	488	317	3,183	5	4	8	6	131
Total no. (thous.)[2]	**1,163.7**	**1,084.7**	**318.8**	**364.5**	**258.6**	**142.7**	**78.9**	**37.2**	**13.5**	**15.2**	**13.1**

Note: Resident population estimates are from the U.S. Census Bureau. Includes imputed counts for any states that did not submit prisoner data. Hispanics may be of any race. White, Black, and "other" exclude persons of Hispanic origin. (1) Includes Asians, Native Hawaiians, other Pacific Islanders, American Indians, Alaska Natives, and persons of two or more races. (2) Persons of all ages, including those age 17 or younger.

Prisoners and Incarceration Rates in Selected Countries, 2005-22

Source: UN Crime Trends Survey, United Nations (UN) Office on Drugs and Crime; World Prison Brief, Inst. for Crime & Justice Policy Research

Incarceration rates are per 100,000 population. For years given unless otherwise noted.

Country	Number of prisoners 2022	2015	2010	2005	Country	Incarceration rates 2021	2015	2010	2005
Argentina	102,150[2]	72,693	59,227	55,423	Antigua and Barbuda	514.8[3]	409.7[5]	344.2	242.9
Azerbaijan....	22,334	23,311[5]	21,971	17,845	Bahamas, The	468.7	—	342.4	832.9
Brazil.......	835,643[2]	698,618	513,954	361,402	Barbados	302.3	343.1	331.3	370.0
China.......	—	1,604,394	1,630,000	—	Belize........	481.6[3]	—	720.9	492.2
Colombia	98,242	120,444	86,028	66,829	Brazil............	389.9	340.5	261.7	193.5
Dominican Rep.	26,238	24,602	20,743	12,657	Costa Rica........	301.1	286.0	229.3	204.3
El Salvador ...	39,538	33,258	26,214	12,901	Dominica..........	508.4[3]	258.5	429.1	410.6
Ethiopia.....	110,000[3]	—	104,467	72,211[7]	El Salvador.......	636.3[4]	533.7	428.8	213.7
India.......	554,034[2]	419,623	368,998	358,368	Eswatini..........	282.0	318.4	340.5[6]	248.8
Indonesia....	275,518	173,572	117,863	97,691	Fiji...............	257.3	169.5	121.2	127.2
Kazakhstan...	35,228	42,114	55,140	52,203	Grenada..........	473.5	421.9	384.1	215.0
Malaysia.....	67,038[2]	51,109	38,387	35,644	Iran..............	216.5[3]	267.7[5]	327.5[6]	191.5
Mexico.....	230,000	221,439	188,013	208,272	Palau............	427.2	404.6	504.4[6]	489.1
Morocco.....	88,941[2]	74,039	64,877	50,933	Panama..........	457.9	449.6	346.1	370.9
Myanmar (Burma)....	100,324[3]	79,668[5]	66,000[6]	—	Peru.............	266.1	257.8	155.5	117.3
Panama.......	21,113	17,790	12,542	12,262	Russia...........	321.1	446.6	572.0	572.6
Peru........	90,293	79,185	45,464	33,010	Rwanda..........	565.3	466.2	533.5	—
Philippines....	166,912[2]	139,469	95,390	91,200[7]	St. Kitts and Nevis....	281.5	460.4[5]	594.9	505.6[7]
Poland......	71,866	72,695	82,372	84,875	St. Vincent and the Grenadines.......	369.0	937.1[5]	950.5	973.7[7]
Russia.......	439,453	646,085	819,280	823,444	Seychelles........	—	695.5[5]	467.5	188.6
South Africa ..	144,938	159,771	163,312	157,402	Thailand	412.4	460.2	308.9	246.6
Thailand.....	295,250[2]	323,473	210,855	162,293	Trinidad and Tobago ..	249.2	—	261.7	275.4
Turkey (Türkiye)	297,863[2]	177,262	120,194	55,966	Turkey (Türkiye).....	351.4	222.6	164.2	81.5
UK[1]........	78,324[2]	86,193	85,002	75,121	U.S..............	524.4	669.4	732.4	741.3
U.S.......	1,767,300[2]	2,172,800	2,279,100	2,200,400	Uruguay..........	336.2[4]	293.8	259.5	187.2
Venezuela...	67,200	49,664	40,825	19,257[7]					

— = Not available. **Note:** Use caution when making comparisons because of differences in each country's legal definitions and methods of offense counting and reporting. (1) England and Wales. (2) For 2021. (3) 2020. (4) 2019. (5) 2016. (6) 2011. (7) 2006.

Law Enforcement Officers and Civilian Employees, 2021-22

Source: *Crime in the United States, Law Enforcement Officers Killed and Assaulted*; FBI; U.S. Dept. of Justice

As of Oct. 31, 2022, city, county, state, college and university, and tribal agencies around the country collectively employed 1,018,345 full-time law enforcement workers. About 69.5% of these employees were sworn officers. The FBI defines a law enforcement officer as a person who ordinarily carries a firearm and badge, has full arrest powers, and is paid from specific dedicated government funds. Civilians (e.g., clerks, radio dispatchers, correctional officers) made up the remainder.

Altogether, they provided service to an estimated 306.0 mil people around the country, meaning there were 3.3 full-time law enforcement employees and 2.3 sworn officers per 1,000 residents.

The great majority of officers (86.5%) were men, while women made up 60.3% of civilian employees. The most populous state, California, employed the greatest number of full-time law enforcement workers (116,036). Washington, DC, had the highest rate, with 6.9 full-time law enforcement employees per 1,000 residents, followed by New Jersey (5.4) and Wyoming (4.7). Washington state had the lowest, with 2.0 per 1,000 residents.

Nationwide, 60 law enforcement officers were killed feloniously (that is, willfully and intentionally by the offender) in the line of duty in 2022, compared to 73 officers in 2021. Of the 60 officers, 49 were killed with firearms. Twelve were ambushed, and six were killed in unprovoked attacks. On average, the officers were 39 years of age and had served in law enforcement for seven years when killed. An additional 58 officers were killed accidentally in 2022 while on the job, 34 of them in motor vehicle crashes. In 2021, 43,649 officers were reported to have been assaulted in the line of duty. The highest percentage (28.6%) were assaulted while responding to disturbance calls such as family quarrels or bar fights.

Sentenced State Prisoners by Offense and Selected Characteristics, 2020

Source: *Prisoners in 2021*, Bureau of Justice Statistics (BJS), U.S. Dept. of Justice

Most serious offense	All prisoners[1]	Male	Female	White[2]	Black[2]	Hispanic
Total number of sentenced prisoners........	1,043,705	973,343	70,362	327,300	345,500	226,800
	Percent of total or subset of prisoners by most serious offense					
Violent..................................	62.4%	63.9%	45.0%	54.6%	67.9%	79.2%
Murder/nonnegligent manslaughter	15.0	15.2	14.3	11.5	18.2	17.2
Negligent manslaughter	1.8	1.6	3.8	1.6	1.0	1.3
Rape/sexual assault	15.5	16.4	3.1	19.6	9.7	15.9
Robbery	12.5	12.9	7.7	6.7	19.3	11.7
Aggravated/simple assault	13.9	14.1	11.5	11.5	15.4	28.8
Other................................	3.8	3.7	4.7	3.7	4.1	4.3
Property.................................	13.5	13.1	19.3	18.5	10.9	8.0
Burglary................................	7.6	7.8	6.0	9.3	7.0	5.4
Larceny/theft	2.5	2.3	6.0	4.2	2.0	1.0
Motor vehicle theft.......................	0.7	0.7	0.9	0.8	0.4	0.4
Fraud.................................	1.2	1.0	4.5	2.1	0.8	0.4
Other.................................	1.4	1.4	2.0	2.1	0.8	0.8
Drug[3]...................................	12.6	11.8	24.7	15.1	10.8	6.4
Public order[4]..............................	10.5	10.5	9.9	11.0	10.0	6.1
Other/unspecified[5].........................	0.7	0.6	1.1	0.8	0.4	0.3

Note: Year-end estimates based on prisoners with a sentence of more than one year under the jurisdiction, or legal authority, of state correctional officials. Ests. for race or Hispanic origin are rounded to the nearest 100. Details may not add up to totals due to rounding and missing offense data. Hispanics may be of any race. (1) Includes race categories not shown here and persons of two or more races. (2) Excludes persons of Hispanic origin. (3) Incl. possession, trafficking, and other and unspecified drug offenses. (4) Incl. weapons, driving under the influence or while intoxicated, and court offenses; commercialized vice, morals, and decency offenses; liquor law violations; probation and parole violations; and other public order offenses. (5) Incl. juvenile offenses and other unspecified offense categories.

Arrestees by Race and Arrest Offense, 2021

Source: *NIBRS, 2021*, Uniform Crime Reporting (UCR) Program, Federal Bureau of Investigation (FBI), U.S. Dept. of Justice

Law enforcement agencies report all persons processed by arrest, citation, or summons for committing an offense. Because reporting is done through an incident report or an arrest report, a person arrested on more than one charge in connection with an incident would be counted only once. This table also does not duplicate data for arrestees reported to have been involved in more than one incident.

Arrest offense category	Total arrestees	White	Black/ Afr. Amer.	Amer. Indian/ AK Native	Asian	Native Hawaiian/ other Pac. Isl.	Unknown race
Total	**4,538,284**	**66.4%**	**27.4%**	**2.5%**	**1.1%**	**0.3%**	**2.2%**
Group A offenses							
Crimes against persons	**816,942**	**60.3**	**34.0**	**2.3**	**1.3**	**0.4**	**1.7**
Assault offenses	773,342	60.2	34.1	2.3	1.3	0.4	1.7
Homicide offenses	8,365	39.3	57.3	1.4	0.8	0.1	1.1
Human trafficking offenses	378	61.6	32.0	1.1	2.4	0.3	2.6
Kidnapping/abduction	11,134	60.4	35.1	1.6	1.1	0.3	1.5
Sex offenses	23,723	68.8	24.3	1.8	1.6	0.4	3.1
Crimes against property	**700,947**	**64.3**	**30.7**	**2.0**	**1.0**	**0.3**	**1.8**
Arson	5,083	70.6	23.7	2.5	1.4	0.4	1.4
Bribery	278	72.3	22.7	2.5	1.1	0.7	0.7
Burglary/breaking and entering	68,440	67.3	28.1	2.0	0.9	0.3	1.4
Counterfeiting/forgery	15,499	66.5	28.5	1.2	1.4	0.3	2.1
Destruction/damage/vandalism of property	99,309	65.1	29.4	2.3	1.1	0.2	1.8
Embezzlement	5,117	57.5	38.1	0.6	1.5	0.04	2.3
Extortion/blackmail	322	72.7	23.6	1.2	0.6	0.0	1.9
Fraud offenses	47,326	62.8	31.7	2.1	1.0	0.2	2.2
Larceny/theft offenses	340,053	66.7	28.4	1.9	1.0	0.2	1.8
Motor vehicle theft	44,435	64.5	30.8	2.2	0.9	0.3	1.3
Robbery	28,962	39.8	57.4	1.4	0.7	0.5	1.2
Stolen property offenses	46,123	56.4	37.8	1.9	1.3	0.7	1.9
Crimes against society	**824,494**	**65.1**	**30.1**	**1.8**	**0.9**	**0.2**	**2.0**
Animal cruelty	2,750	71.6	22.3	1.5	1.7	0.3	2.6
Drug/narcotic offenses	707,971	68.6	26.5	1.9	0.8	0.2	2.1
Gambling offenses	649	42.7	38.1	0.9	13.4	0.6	4.3
Pornography/obscene material	4,443	77.4	17.7	0.5	1.8	0.2	2.4
Prostitution offenses	7,928	51.7	38.9	0.5	7.5	0.3	1.1
Weapon law violations	100,753	41.0	55.5	1.0	0.8	0.2	1.5
Group B offenses	**2,195,901**	**69.8**	**22.9**	**3.1**	**1.2**	**0.4**	**2.6**
Curfew/loitering/vagrancy violations	14,659	63.2	23.9	3.7	2.5	0.9	5.7
Disorderly conduct	151,136	62.2	28.7	5.6	0.9	0.3	2.3
Driving under the influence	463,100	75.5	16.0	2.6	1.6	0.3	3.9
Family offenses, nonviolent	34,251	66.6	24.9	5.7	0.9	0.2	1.7
Liquor law violations	72,753	73.6	14.2	4.4	1.5	0.7	5.7
Trespass of real property	149,769	63.6	29.3	2.8	1.5	0.7	2.1
All other offenses	1,310,233	69.3	24.3	2.9	1.0	0.4	2.1

(1) Percentages may not add up to 100 because of rounding.

Foreign Nationals Removed From the U.S. by Criminal Status and Nationality, 2012-21

Source: *Immigration Enforcement Actions*, Office of Immigration Statistics, U.S. Dept. of Homeland Security
(countries ranked by total foreign nationals removed in 2021)

	2012		2014		2016		2018		2020		2021	
Country of nationality	Total removed	% criminal[1]	Total removed	% criminal[1]	Total removed	% criminal[1]	Total removed	% criminal[1]	Total removed	% criminal[1]	Total removed	% criminal[1]
Total	415,579	48.1%	405,026	42.6%	332,263	35.1%	327,861	45.2%	237,861	50.1%	89,191	70.9%
Mexico	300,469	50.4	265,022	47.6	236,593	35.1	208,123	43.3	149,309	52.6	54,138	74.2
Guatemala	38,885	34.7	54,405	25.2	33,863	31.3	49,132	40.3	28,337	36.2	7,701	57.0
Honduras	31,724	43.6	40,877	34.4	22,073	39.1	28,384	44.7	20,557	46.7	5,038	63.3
Colombia	1,607	65.8	1,375	62.3	2,097	36.5	2,666	86.5	1,947	82.1	3,024	90.0
El Salvador	18,910	45.8	26,671	33.6	20,341	33.2	14,921	47.2	12,162	41.4	2,778	72.9
Brazil	2,738	15.6	980	28.7	1,507	22.2	2,131	55.5	2,286	58.0	1,962	22.7
Ecuador	1,766	40.1	1,569	36.4	1,432	32.5	1,427	62.2	3,117	48.3	1,857	42.4
Dominican Rep.	2,896	75.5	2,072	79.2	1,981	75.1	1,870	80.2	1,919	77.5	1,726	79.3
Jamaica	1,327	87.2	1,043	80.0	1,084	57.5	1,085	91.4	1,243	94.2	1,295	94.4
Nicaragua	1,426	51.1	1,318	48.8	883	44.4	962	58.9	1,456	42.9	1,033	39.1
All other countries[2]	13,831	46.6	9,694	48.2	10,409	34.5	16,853	65.2	15,528	51.7	8,639	75.8

Note: Fiscal year (Oct. 1-Sept. 30) data. Excludes persons removed by Customs and Border Protection, which does not identify whether foreign nationals are criminals. (1) Of total removed by country, persons with a prior criminal conviction. (2) Incl. unknown.

Gun Violence Incidents and Deaths, 2015-23

Source: Gun Violence Archive

The Gun Violence Archive is an independent data collection and research group with no affiliation with any advocacy organization. Since 2013, it has maintained an online archive of gun violence incidents, which it collects daily from more than 7,500 media, law enforcement, government, and commercial sources.

(number of actual deaths, injuries, or gun violence [GV] incidents verified as of Aug. 18, 2023; 2023 data are for partial year)

	2015	2017	2019	2021	2023		2015	2017	2019	2021	2023
Total GV incidents	48,113	58,116	NA	NA	NA	Mass shootings[3]	333	347	414	688	452
Total GV deaths, all causes	NA	NA	40,609	45,110	27,453	Mass murders[3]	NA	NA	31	28	29
						Home invasion	2,330	2,567	NA	NA	NA
Deaths[1]	13,582	15,751	15,519	21,020	12,141	Defensive use	1,397	2,117	1,621	1,313	763
Suicides[2]	NA	NA	25,090	24,090	15,312	Unintentional shooting	1,997	2,065	1,911	2,026	1,036
Injuries	26,892	31,362	30,205	40,532	24,136	**Officer-involved incidents[4]**					
Children killed/injured	679	721	696	1,058	646	Officer killed/injured	279	302	364	440	281
Teens (age 12-17) killed/injured	2,699	3,261	3,129	4,647	3,607	Subject-suspect killed/injured	2,044	2,148	2,085	2,214	1,441
Murder/suicide incidents	NA	NA	632	593	442						

NA = Not available. **Note:** All numbers are subject to change or incidents recategorized. (1) From 2019 on, includes homicide, murder, unintentional shootings, and defensive gun use. (2) Calculation based on Centers for Disease Control and Prevention suicide data. (3) Four or more people shot and/or killed in a single event, at the same general time and location, not including the shooter. (4) Numbers for 2015 and 2017 are of reported and verified incidents. Numbers for 2019, 2021, and 2023 are of source verified deaths and injuries.

Hate Crimes by Offense Type and Bias Motivation, 2021

Source: *Supplemental Hate Crime Statistics, 2021,* Uniform Crime Reporting (UCR) Program, FBI, U.S. Dept. of Justice

Hate crimes are defined as crimes motivated in whole or in part by the offender's bias against a characteristic such as race, ethnicity, or religion. The Hate Crime Statistics Act of 1990 led to the collection of hate crime data as part of the FBI's UCR program. Not all law enforcement agencies that participate in the UCR program submit hate crime data, so the data presented is not representative of the nation as a whole. In 2021, 14,859 agencies, representing 302.3 mil inhabitants, participated in the Hate Crime Statistics Program.

Bias motivation	Total offenses	Crimes against persons				Crimes against property					Crimes against society[3]
		Aggravated assault	Simple assault	Intimidation	Other[1]	Robbery	Burglary	Larceny-theft	Destruction/damage/vandalism	Other[2]	
Total	12,411	1,670	2,955	3,595	107	177	152	500	2,718	270	267
Single-bias incidents	12,020	1,651	2,881	3,423	98	175	146	494	2,620	268	264
Race/ethnicity/ancestry	7,736	1,182	1,912	2,382	38	109	86	236	1,475	137	179
Anti-white	1,303	195	393	289	17	22	28	108	128	61	62
Anti-Black or African American	3,790	565	826	1,344	7	27	21	59	848	29	64
Anti-American Indian or Alaska Native	148	15	33	19	3	0	5	22	16	14	21
Anti-Asian	820	109	270	227	4	28	14	8	149	8	3
Anti-Native Hawaiian or other Pacific Isl.	48	3	10	4	0	0	1	11	3	8	8
Anti-multiple races, group	216	9	33	51	0	1	1	6	107	2	6
Anti-Arab	131	26	26	54	0	0	1	4	17	2	1
Anti-Hispanic or Latino	886	213	244	279	5	26	8	8	90	4	9
Anti-other race/ethnicity/ancestry	394	47	77	115	2	5	7	10	117	9	5
Religion	1,690	80	196	341	15	9	36	125	762	69	57
Anti-Jewish	851	30	79	175	5	8	9	16	518	8	3
Anti-Catholic	99	4	6	10	1	0	1	2	61	5	9
Anti-Islamic (Muslim)	177	17	47	67	2	0	2	4	32	4	2
Anti-Sikh	187	11	20	9	6	0	9	52	29	29	22
Anti-other religion[4]	308	17	41	64	1	1	11	44	92	20	17
Anti-multiple religions, group	49	1	2	16	0	0	2	2	20	3	3
Anti-atheism/agnosticism/etc.	19	0	1	0	0	0	2	5	10	0	1
Sexual orientation	1,929	298	569	560	20	42	9	83	301	39	8
Anti-gay (male)	1,034	213	337	273	6	35	3	21	127	13	6
Anti-lesbian	225	27	75	82	1	0	1	6	31	2	0
Anti-lesbian, gay, bisexual, or transgender (mixed group)	610	56	139	183	11	7	4	52	137	19	2
Anti-heterosexual	14	1	1	3	2	0	0	2	1	4	0
Anti-bisexual	46	1	17	19	0	0	1	2	5	1	0
Gender	112	12	34	29	5	3	4	4	15	4	2
Anti-male	19	1	7	3	0	0	1	1	5	0	1
Anti-female	93	11	27	26	5	3	3	3	10	4	1
Gender identity	385	61	126	85	12	10	5	21	47	9	9
Anti-transgender	271	48	87	70	8	8	1	10	33	5	1
Anti-gender non-conforming	114	13	39	15	4	2	4	11	14	4	8
Disability	168	18	44	26	8	2	6	25	20	10	9
Anti-physical disability	60	4	18	10	0	1	3	11	8	2	3
Anti-mental disability	108	14	26	16	8	1	3	14	12	8	6
Multiple-bias incidents[5]	391	19	74	172	9	2	6	6	98	2	3

(1) Incl. murder/nonnegligent manslaughter, rape (revised definition only), human trafficking, commercial sex acts, and additional offenses not shown. (2) Incl. arson, motor vehicle theft, and additional offenses not shown. (3) Incl. animal cruelty, drug/narcotic offenses, gambling offenses, prostitution offenses, and weapon law violations, where society as a whole is considered the victim. (4) Incl. offenses against religions not shown. (5) Incidents in which one or more offense types are motivated by two or more biases.

Federal Sentence Length by Type of Crime, 2022

Source: *Sourcebook of Federal Sentencing Statistics,* U.S. Sentencing Commission

Data based on court documentation for federal cases involving felonies and misdemeanors (excluding petty misdemeanors) in which the offender was sentenced in fiscal year 2022 (Oct. 1-Sept. 30). Excl. cases where data was missing or indeterminate.

Type of crime[1]	Mean months	Median months	Number of cases	Type of crime[1]	Mean months	Median months	Number of cases
Total	52	27	63,763	Fraud/theft/embezzlement	22	12	5,456
Administration of justice	12	8	647	Immigration	12	8	17,615
Antitrust	5	0	8	Individual rights[2]	41	18	91
Arson	45	42	106	Kidnapping	182	160	127
Assault	65	43	833	Manslaughter	86	68	80
Bribery/corruption	19	12	360	Money laundering	61	33	1,191
Burglary/trespass	19	11	111	Murder	260	240	408
Child pornography	110	96	1,435	National defense	37	17	174
Commercialized vice	24	16	73	Obscenity/other sex offenses	22	18	342
Drug possession	3	0	260	Prison offenses	12	9	499
Drug trafficking	78	60	19,930	Robbery	106	96	1,443
Environmental	4	0	145	Sexual abuse	207	180	1,499
Extortion/racketeering	44	24	112	Stalking/harassing	27	18	265
Firearms	49	37	9,240	Tax	14	9	496
Food and drug	12	4	37	Other[3]	3	0	669
Forgery/counterfeiting/copyright	16	12	111				

Note: Sentences of 470 months or greater (including life) and probation were incl. in avg. computations as 470 months and 0 months, respectively. (1) As detailed in presentence report or determined by the applicable offense with the highest statutory sentencing range. (2) For example, obstructing an election or registration or intercepting communications or eavesdropping, among other offenses. (3) Incl. interference with a flight crew or the unlawful sale, transportation, possession, etc., of drug paraphernalia, among other felony and misc. offenses not in any of the other categories.

American Deaths in Terrorist Attacks, 1995-2020

Source: Global Terrorism Database, National Consortium for the Study of Terrorism and Responses to Terrorism (START)

Year	Total attacks in U.S.	Total deaths in U.S.	U.S. deaths in U.S.	U.S. deaths worldwide	Year	Total attacks in U.S.	Total deaths in U.S.	U.S. deaths in U.S.	U.S. deaths worldwide
1995	60	178	177	195	2009	12	22	22	23
1996	35	2	2	36	2010	17	4	4	6
1997	42	2	1	14	2011	10	0	0	3
1998	31	4	3	135	2012	20	7	6	12
1999	53	20	20	25	2013	20	23	21	29
2000	42	8	7	43	2014	29	26	26	41
2001	47	3,014	2,916	2,918	2015	39	54	53	68
2002	33	4	0	30	2016	68	68	59	79
2003	33	0	0	17	2017	66	98	87	102
2004	9	0	0	5	2018	73	45	45	50
2005	21	0	0	3	2019	64	51	40	52
2006	6	1	1	4	2020	103	NA	NA	NA
2007	8	0	0	1	**Total**	**959**	**3,633**	**3,492**	**3,905**
2008	18	2	2	14					

NA = Not yet available. **Note:** Number of deaths includes perpetrators. Deaths worldwide exclude deaths in Afghanistan and Iraq.

Notable Terrorist Incidents Worldwide Since 1971

Source: U.S. Dept. of State; *Facts On File World News Digest*; World Almanac research

Selected noteworthy incidents, excluding most assassinations, kidnappings, and military targets. Does not include all incidents in Iraq or Afghanistan, 2001-present; see also Chronology of the Year's Events.

1971—Mar. 1: Senate wing of U.S. Capitol Building in Wash., DC, bombed by Weather Underground; no deaths.

1972—July 21: "Bloody Friday." Provisional IRA exploded 20+ bombs across Belfast, N. Ireland; 9 killed, hundreds injured. **Sept. 5:** Palestinian group Black September killed 2 Israeli athletes and seized 9 others at Olympic Village in Munich, W. Germany, during Summer Olympics; 9 hostages, 5 militants, 1 Ger. officer died in botched rescue.

1973—Dec. 17: Palestinian gunmen attacked Rome airport and bombed plane on tarmac; hijacked Lufthansa plane with 5 Italian hostages to Athens, Greece, then to Kuwait; 31 killed.

1974—June 17: Houses of Parliament in London, England, bombed by Provisional IRA; 11 injured.

1975—Jan. 27: Puerto Rican FALN nationalists bombed Fraunces Tavern in New York City; 4 killed, 53 injured. **Jan. 29:** U.S. State Dept. building in Wash., DC, bombed by Weather Underground; no deaths.

1976—June 27: Palestinian and Baader-Meinhof militants forced Air France jet to land in Entebbe, Uganda. Israeli army rescued 103 hostages from airport terminal in battle with terrorists and Ugandan troops, July 3-4; 32 killed in all.

1978—Mar. 11: Palestinian militants shot civilians and hijacked bus with hostages from Haifa to Tel Aviv, Israel. Bus exploded during firefight with police at a roadblock; 38 killed.

1979—Nov. 4: Iranian radicals seized U.S. embassy in Tehran, taking 66 Americans hostage. 52 were held until Jan. 20, 1981. **Nov. 20:** Around 200 Islamic fundamentalists opposed to the Saudi monarchy seized Grand Mosque in Mecca, Saudi Arabia, and held hundreds of pilgrims hostage. Saudi forces retook mosque Dec. 4; about 270 died.

1980—Feb. 27: Members of leftist guerrilla group April 19 Movement (M-19) seized Dominican Republic embassy in Bogota, Colombia; 80 hostages taken, 18 held until Apr. 27.

1983—Apr. 18: Hezbollah suicide truck bomb at U.S. embassy in Beirut, Lebanon, killed 63. **Oct. 9:** N. Korean agents ambushed a S. Korean govt. delegation in Rangoon, Burma, killing 21. **Oct. 23:** Hezbollah suicide truck bombings of U.S. and French military bases, Beirut, Lebanon; 242 Americans, 58 French killed.

1984—Sept. 20: U.S. embassy annex nr. Beirut, Lebanon, bombed, killing approx. 20. **Sept. 20:** In worst bioterrorism attack in U.S. history, members of Rajneesh cult contaminated an Oregon salad bar with salmonella, sickening 751.

1985—Apr. 12: Bomb blast at restaurant nr. U.S. air base in Torrejon, Spain; 18 killed. **June 14:** Hezbollah members hijacked TWA Flight 847 with 153 passengers and crew to Beirut, Lebanon; 39 held for 17 days, 1 U.S. Navy sailor killed. **June 23:** Air India Flight 182 destroyed by bomb off coast of Ireland; 329 killed. Blamed on Sikh terrorists. **Oct. 7:** Four Palestinians hijacked Italian cruise ship *Achille Lauro*; 1 passenger killed. **Nov. 23:** EgyptAir Flight 648 from Athens, Greece, to Cairo hijacked to Malta by Palestinian group Abu Nidal; 60 killed in rescue. **Dec. 27:** Palestinian militants opened fire at El-Al (Isr.) airline counters at Rome and Vienna airports; 19 killed.

1986—Apr. 5: Nightclub in Berlin, W. Germany, bombed; 3 killed, incl. 2 U.S. service personnel, 200+ hurt. 3 Libyan embassy workers in Germany convicted.

1987—Apr. 17: Bomb in Sri Lankan capital killed 100+; blamed on Tamil rebels who, 4 days later, attacked Sinhalese travelers on highway, killing 127. **June 19:** Basque group ETA bombed supermarket garage in Barcelona, Spain; 21 killed. **Nov. 29:** Bomb planted by N. Korean agents exploded on Korean Air Lines Flight 858 over Indian Ocean; 115 killed.

1988—Dec. 21: Pan Am Flight 103 exploded over Lockerbie, Scotland, killing all 259 aboard and 11 on ground; Libya took responsibility for bombing in Aug. 2003.

1989—Sept. 19: French UTA Flight 722 from Congo Republic to Paris destroyed by bomb in midair over Niger; 170 killed.

1992—Mar. 17: Israeli embassy in Buenos Aires, Argentina, bombed; 28 killed, 200+ injured. Hezbollah suspected.

1993—Feb. 26: Truck bomb exploded in World Trade Center garage in New York City; 6 killed. Blast later linked to al-Qaeda. **Mar. 12-19:** At least 11 bombs ripped through Bombay and Calcutta, India; 300+ killed.

1994—Feb. 25: U.S.-born Israeli settler Baruch Goldstein opened fire in mosque in Hebron, West Bank; about 30 Muslim worshippers killed. **July 18:** Buenos Aires, Argentina, Jewish center bombed; 87 killed. Blamed on Hezbollah.

1995—Mar. 20: Twelve killed and over 5,000 injured when Japanese cult members released sarin nerve gas in Tokyo subway cars. **Apr. 19:** Murrah Federal Building in Oklahoma City bombed, killing 168. Timothy McVeigh and Terry Nichols convicted. McVeigh executed in 2001; Nichols sentenced to life in prison. **Nov. 13:** U.S. military compound in Riyadh, Saudi Arabia, bombed by Islamic Movement of Change; 7 killed.

1996—Jan. 31: Tamil Tigers drove explosives-laden truck into Central Bank in Colombo, Sri Lanka; 90 killed. **June 25:** Fuel truck exploded outside Khobar Towers, U.S. military complex in Dhahran, Saudi Arabia; killed 19. **July 27:** Bomb exploded in Atlanta, GA, during Olympic Games; killed 2, injured 100+. Extremist Eric Robert Rudolph sentenced to life in prison, 2005. **Dec. 3:** Bomb exploded on subway in Paris; 4 killed, 86 injured. Algerian Islamic extremist group suspected.

1997—Nov. 17: Gamaa al-Islamiya militants killed 58 tourists and 4 Egyptians in Valley of the Kings nr. Luxor, Egypt.

1998—Aug. 7: U.S. embassies in Nairobi, Kenya, and Dar-es-Salaam, Tanzania, bombed; 257 people killed. Al-Qaeda claimed responsibility. **Aug. 15:** IRA car bomb outside courthouse in Omagh, N. Ireland, killed 29. **Oct. 18:** National Liberation Army of Colombia blew up Ocensa oil pipeline; about 71 killed.

1999—Sept. 9-16: Three buildings bombed in Moscow and Volgodonsk, Russia; about 300 killed. Chechen rebels blamed.

2000—Oct. 12: Small boat assisting in docking of USS *Cole* exploded alongside it in Aden, Yemen; 17 U.S. sailors killed. Blamed on al-Qaeda.

2001—Sept. 11: 19 al-Qaeda terrorists hijacked 4 U.S. domestic flights, including 2 planes that crashed into New York City's World Trade Center towers and 1 into Pentagon. Total dead minus hijackers: 2,977; deadliest terrorist attack yet on U.S. soil. **Sept.-Nov. 7:** Letters tainted with deadly anthrax bacteria mailed through U.S. postal system killed 5, sickened 17; investigation concluded in 2010 that government-employed microbiologist Bruce Ivins, who died by suicide in 2008, was responsible.

2002—Mar. 27: Suicide bombing at hotel in Netanya, Israel, during Passover celebration; 27 killed. **Oct. 12:** Resort in Bali, Indonesia, bombed; 202 dead. Jemaah Islamiah blamed. **Oct. 23:** Chechen guerrillas seized theater in Moscow, held 700+ hostages. Russian authorities gassed theater; most guerrillas and about 128 hostages killed. **Dec. 27:** Chechen rebels plowed truck bomb into pro-Russian govt. headquarters in Grozny, Chechnya; 80 killed, 152 injured.

2003—May 12-13: Al-Qaeda militants detonated car bombs at 3 residential complexes used by Westerners in Riyadh, Saudi Arabia; 34 killed. **May 16:** Five explosions in Casablanca, Morocco; 44 killed. Blamed on al-Qaeda. **Aug. 19:** UN headquarters in Baghdad bombed by truck; 22 killed, incl. UN envoy to Iraq. **Aug. 25:** 2 bombs exploded in taxis in Mumbai, India; 46 killed. Islamic militants suspected. **Nov. 15:** Two synagogues in Istanbul, Turkey, bombed; 25 killed. **Nov. 20:** British consulate and offices of HSBC bombed in Istanbul, Turkey; 27 killed. Blamed on al-Qaeda. **Dec. 5:** Suicide bombing on commuter train in Yessentuki, Russia; 44 killed. Blamed on Chechen rebels.

2004—Feb. 6: Bomb exploded in Moscow subway; 39 killed, 130 injured. Chechen rebels blamed. **Mar. 11:** Al-Qaeda cell bombed 4 commuter trains during morning rush hour in Madrid, Spain; 191 killed, about 1,200 injured. **May 29:** Al-Qaeda militants stormed foreigner compound in Khobar, Saudi Arabia, taking hostages; 22 killed. **Aug. 24:** Chechen suicide bombers caused crash of two Russian passenger planes in diff. parts of Russia; 90 killed. **Sept. 1:** Chechen militants seized school in Beslan, in North Ossetia, Russia; held 1,000+ hostage for 3 days before Russian troops stormed school. About 330 killed, incl. 27 hostage-takers.

2005—July 7: Four bombs exploded on 3 separate subways and 1 bus in London, Eng.; 52 killed, about 700 injured. **July 23:** Three car bombs exploded in Sharm el-Sheik, Egypt, resorts; about 90 killed. **Nov. 9:** 3 suicide bombings targeted hotels in Amman, Jordan; killed 56. Al-Qaeda in Iraq took responsibility.

2006—July 11: 8 explosions struck 7 different trains and 1 station of public commuter rail system in Mumbai, India; 207 killed. Lashkar-e-Qahhar (Army of Terror) claimed responsibility.

2007—Feb. 19: Train traveling between New Delhi and border with Pakistan caught fire, 68 killed; Indian ministers blamed Muslim militants for trying to disrupt peace talks between India and Pakistan. **Dec. 11:** Two coordinated car bombs went off outside govt. building and UN office building in Algiers, Algeria; 41 killed, incl. 17 UN employees, 170 wounded.

2008—Sept. 20: Suicide bomber in truck set off explosion outside of Marriott Hotel in Islamabad, Pakistan; 53 killed, 271 wounded. **Nov. 26-29:** Series of attacks and bombings on luxury hotels and high-profile targets in Mumbai, India; 171 killed, 300 injured.

2009—Feb. 20: Suicide bomber targeted Shiite funeral in Dera Ismail Khan, Pakistan; 30 killed. **Nov. 5:** U.S. Army major opened fire on Fort Hood (TX) military base, killing 13 and wounding 30+. **Dec. 25:** A Nigerian man failed to blow up a flight from Amsterdam to Detroit with bomb hidden in his underpants.

2010—Jan. 1: Taliban suicide bomber killed more than 100 on playground in NW Pakistan. **Mar. 29:** Two female Chechen separatists detonated suicide bombs at two landmark Moscow subway stations, killing at least 40. **July 9:** Suicide bombers targeted tribal elders in Mohmand, Pakistan, killing more than 100. **July 11:** Several bombs claimed by al-Shabab exploded simultaneously in Kampala, Uganda, killing more than 70 people who had gathered to watch the World Cup final broadcast.

2011—Jan. 24: Suicide bomber killed 35 in Moscow's Domodedovo Airport, location chosen to maximize deaths of foreigners. **July 22:** Anders Behring Breivik, right-wing Norwegian extremist, set off a bomb in van outside govt. buildings in Oslo, then massacred dozens of young people at a summer camp on Tyrifjorden Lake, bringing death toll to 77.

2012—Jan. 21: Series of attacks by Islamist extremist group Boko Haram killed more than 185 in Kano, Nigeria. **May 21:** Suicide bomber claimed by al-Qaeda in the Arabian Peninsula (AQAP) killed more than 100 soldiers during military parade rehearsal in Yemeni presidential palace. **Aug. 5:** White supremacist fatally shot 6 worshippers at a Sikh temple before killing himself, Oak Creek, WI. **Sept. 11:** Terrorists stormed U.S. embassy in Benghazi, Libya, killing 4 Americans, including U.S. Amb. J. Christopher Stevens.

2013—Apr. 15: Two bombs exploded nr. Boston Marathon finish line, killing 3 and injuring 264; 4-day search ended in death of suspect Tamerlan Tsarnaev and capture of his brother, Dzhokhar, a naturalized Chechen immigrant. **Sept. 21:** Al-Shabab, a Somali militant group, killed up to 70 people and wounded at least 175 at a Nairobi, Kenya, shopping mall.

2014—Apr.-May: Islamist extremist group Boko Haram kidnapped more than 250 girls from schools in Nigeria; killed more than 150 villagers in Gamboru. **Dec. 15:** Nine Taliban gunmen attacked military-affiliated school in Peshawar, Pakistan, executing about 150, including 132 children.

2015—Jan. 7: Gunmen stormed Paris offices of *Charlie Hebdo*, a satirical newspaper, killing 12. Two days later, French police killed suspects, brothers who identified themselves as belonging to AQAP. **Mar. 18:** Gunmen killed 21 tourists and a police officer at Tunisia's National Bardo Museum. Several terrorist groups claimed credit. **Apr. 2:** Al-Shabab militants killed 147 students at Kenya's Garissa Univ. after separating Christian and Muslim students. **June 17:** Lone white-supremacist gunman killed 9, incl. a state senator, in a historically Black church in Charleston, SC. **Oct. 31:** Terrorists downed a Russian charter flight shortly after takeoff from Egyptian resort, killing all 224 onboard. Egyptian affiliate of the Sunni extremist group the Islamic State in Iraq and Syria (ISIS) said it smuggled a soda-can bomb onto plane. **Nov. 13:** Series of coordinated suicide bombings and other attacks by ISIS on Paris cafes, a soccer stadium, and a concert hall killed 137 (incl. 7 attackers); wounded 350+. **Dec. 2:** A heavily armed married couple opened fire on the husband's coworkers at a holiday party for San Bernardino (CA) County Health Dept., killing 14, wounding 21.

2016—Mar. 22: Three explosions in Brussels, two at the airport and one at a busy subway station, killed 35 people (incl. 3 bombers) and injured 300+. ISIS claimed credit; investigators linked perpetrators to 2015 Paris attacks. **June 12:** Lone gunman killed 49 people and wounded 53 at a gay nightclub in Orlando, FL. **July 7:** A heavily armed man shot and killed five police officers and wounded seven other officers and two civilians in downtown Dallas, TX, during peaceful protest. **July 14:** Tunisian-born man drove rented truck into Bastille Day crowds in Nice, France, killing 86 and injuring 400+. **Dec. 19:** Tunisian man on Germany's terror watch list drove hijacked truck through outdoor market in Berlin, killing 12; 56+ injured.

2017—May 22: Suicide bomber detonated in entrance hall of Manchester, England, arena as fans left a concert by U.S. singer Ariana Grande, killing 22; 800 injured. **June 3:** Three assailants in a van hit pedestrians on London Bridge before exiting vehicle and attacking people with knives; 8 killed and 48+ injured. **Aug. 18:** A Moroccan man killed 2 and injured 8 with a knife in Turku, Finland; country's first terror attack. **Oct. 14:** Two truck bombs detonated in Mogadishu, Somalia, leaving 512 dead, 300+ injured. Blamed on al-Shabab. **Nov. 24:** Attack on Sufi mosque in Bir al-Abed, Egypt, by extremists affiliated with ISIS, killed 311 people and injured 100+ others.

2018—Oct. 27: Man opened fire inside Tree of Life Congregation synagogue in Pittsburgh, PA, killing 11 worshippers.

2019—Mar. 15: Australian gunman attacked two mosques in Christchurch, New Zealand, killing 51. **Apr. 21:** Nine Muslim extremists with alleged links to Islamic State staged suicide bombings in churches and hotels on Easter Sunday in Sri Lanka, killing more than 250. **Aug. 3:** White nationalist targeting Hispanic immigrants killed 23, injured 20+ at Walmart store in El Paso, TX. **Aug. 18:** Suicide bomber killed at least 80 people and injured 180+ at a wedding party in Kabul, Afghanistan. ISIS claimed responsibility. **Dec. 28:** Al-Shabab claimed credit for truck bombing at a Mogadishu, Somalia, police checkpoint that killed 85.

2021—Aug. 26: ISIS-K claimed responsibility for attack outside Kabul, Afghanistan, airport that killed at least 170 Afghans and 13 U.S. service personnel.

2022—Mar. 4: ISIS-K claimed suicide bombing at Shiite mosque that killed at least 65 in Peshawar, Pakistan. **May 14:** White supremacist fatally shot 10 Black people in predominantly Black neighborhood of Buffalo, NY.

Notable Assassinations Since 1865

1865—Apr. 14: U.S. Pres. Abraham Lincoln shot by John Wilkes Booth, well-known actor with Confederate sympathies, at Ford's Theater in Washington, DC; died Apr. 15.

1881—Mar. 13: Alexander II of Russia. **July 2:** U.S. Pres. James A. Garfield shot by Charles J. Guiteau, disappointed office seeker, in Washington, DC; died Sept. 19.

1894—June 24: French Pres. Sadi Carnot by Sante Caserio, Italian anarchist, in Lyon.

1898—Sept. 10: Empress Elizabeth of Austria stabbed by Luigi Lucchesi, Italian anarchist.

1900—July 29: Umberto I, king of Italy, shot by an anarchist.

1901—Sept. 6: U.S. Pres. William McKinley shot by Leon Czolgosz, anarchist, in Buffalo, NY; died Sept. 14.

1908—Feb. 1: King Carlos I of Portugal and his son Luís Filipe, in Lisbon.

1913—Feb. 23: Mexican Pres. Francisco I. Madero and Vice Pres. José María Pino Suárez. **Mar. 18:** King George of Greece, by an anarchist.

1914—June 28: Archduke Franz Ferdinand of Austria-Hungary and his wife shot by Gavrilo Princip, Serb nationalist, in Sarajevo, Bosnia.

1916—Dec. 30: Grigory Rasputin, Russian mystic and court figure, by group of aristocrats.

1918—July 12: Grand Duke Michael of Russia, at Perm. **July 16:** Nicholas II, former (abdicated) czar of Russia; his wife, Czarina Alexandra; their son, Czarevitch Alexis; their daughters, Grand Duchesses Olga, Tatiana, Marie, Anastasia; and 4 members of household executed by Bolsheviks at Ekaterinburg.

1920—May 20: Mexican Pres. Gen. Venustiano Carranza, in Tlaxcalantongo.

1922—Aug. 22: Michael Collins, Irish revolutionary, in West Cork. **Dec. 16:** Polish Pres. Gabriel Narutowicz in Warsaw.

1923—July 20: Gen. Francisco "Pancho" Villa, ex-rebel leader, in Parral, Mexico.

1928—July 17: Gen. Alvaro Obregon, president-elect of Mexico, in San Angel.

1932—May 6: French Pres. Paul Doumer shot by Russian émigré, Pavel Gorgulov, in Paris.

1934—July 25: Austrian Chancellor Engelbert Dollfuss by Nazis, in Vienna.

1935—Sept. 8: Sen. Huey P. Long, former Louisiana governor, shot by Dr. Carl Austin Weiss, son-in-law of political opponent, in Baton Rouge; died Sept. 10.

1940—Aug. 20: Leon Trotsky (Lev Bronstein), exiled Soviet commissar of war, fatally wounded with ice ax by Soviet agent nr. Mexico City.

1948—Jan. 30: Leader of movement for Indian independence Mohandas K. Gandhi (Mahatma) shot by Hindu fanatic in New Delhi. **Sept. 17:** Count Folke Bernadotte, UN mediator for Palestine, by Jewish extremists in Jerusalem.

1951—July 20: Jordanian King Abdullah ibn Hussein. **Oct. 16:** Prime Min. Liaquat Ali Khan of Pakistan shot, in Rawalpindi.

1956—Sept. 21: Pres. Anastasio Somoza of Nicaragua shot in León by a young of his guards.

1957—July 26: Guatemalan Pres. Carlos Castillo Armas, in Guatemala City by one of his guards.

1958—July 14: King Faisal of Iraq, Crown Prince Abdullah, and **July 15,** Prem. Nuri as-Said, by rebels in Baghdad.

1959—Sept. 25: Prime Min. Solomon Bandaranaike of Ceylon (Sri Lanka), by Buddhist monk in Colombo.

1961—Jan. 17: First elected prime min. of dem. Rep. of the Congo, Patrice Lumumba, in Katanga Prov. by political rivals. **May 30:** Dominican dictator Rafael Trujillo, nr. Ciudad Trujillo.

1963—June 12: Medgar Evers, NAACP's Mississippi field secretary, shot by Byron De La Beckwith in Jackson, MS. **Nov. 2:** Pres. Ngo Dinh Diem of South Vietnam and his brother, Ngo Dinh Nhu, in military coup. **Nov. 22:** U.S. Pres. John F. Kennedy shot while riding in motorcade through downtown Dallas, TX; accused gunman Lee Harvey Oswald murdered by nightclub owner Jack Ruby while awaiting trial.

1965—Jan. 21: Iranian Prem. Hassan Ali Mansour, in Tehran. **Feb. 21:** Malcolm X, Black nationalist leader, shot by 3 men linked to Nation of Islam at New York City rally.

1966—Sept. 6: Prime Min. Hendrik F. Verwoerd of South Africa stabbed to death in parliament at Cape Town.

1968—Apr. 4: Rev. Martin Luther King Jr. fatally shot in Memphis, TN; James Earl Ray convicted of crime. **June 5:** Sen. Robert F. Kennedy (D, NY) shot in Los Angeles; died June 6. Sirhan Sirhan convicted of crime.

1971—Nov. 28: Jordanian Prime Min. Wasfi Tal by Palestinian guerrillas, in Cairo, Egypt.

1973—Mar. 2: U.S. Amb. Cleo A. Noel Jr., U.S. Charge d'Affaires George C. Moore, and Belgian Charge d'Affaires Guy Eid by Palestinian guerrillas, in Khartoum, Sudan. **Dec. 20:** Spanish Prem. Luis Carrero Blanco in car bombing by Basque separatist group ETA, in Madrid.

1974—Aug. 19: U.S. Amb. to Cyprus, Rodger P. Davies, by sniper's bullet in Nicosia.

1975—Feb. 11: Pres. Richard Ratsimandrava of Madagascar shot in Antananarivo. **Mar. 25:** Saudi Arabian King Faisal shot by nephew Prince Musad Abdel Aziz, in Riyadh. **Aug. 15:** Bangladesh Pres. Sheik Mujibur Rahman killed in coup.

1976—Feb. 13: Nigerian head of state, Gen. Murtala Ramat Mohammed, by self-styled young revolutionaries.

1977—Mar. 16: Kamal Jumblatt, Lebanese Druze chieftain, shot nr. Beirut. **Mar. 18:** Rep. of the Congo Pres. Marien Ngouabi shot in Brazzaville.

1978—May 9: Former Italian Prem. Aldo Moro killed by Red Brigades terrorists who had abducted him Mar. 16 in Rome and held him hostage. **July 9:** Former Iraqi Prem. Abdul Razzak al-Naif shot in London.

1979—Aug. 27: Lord Mountbatten and 3 others died from an IRA bomb on his boat off coast of Co. Sligo, Ireland. **Oct. 26:** S. Korean Pres. Park Chung Hee and 6 bodyguards fatally shot by Kim Jae Kyu, head of S. Korean intelligence agency.

1980—Apr. 12: Liberian Pres. William R. Tolbert, in military coup. **Sept. 17:** Former Nicaraguan Pres. Anastasio Somoza Debayle shot in Paraguay.

1981—Oct. 6: Egyptian Pres. Anwar al-Sadat shot by commandos while reviewing military parade in Cairo; 7 others killed.

1982—Sept. 14: Lebanese Pres.-elect Bashir Gemayel killed by bomb in east Beirut.

1983—Aug. 21: Philippine opposition leader Benigno Aquino Jr. shot at Manila Intl. Airport.

1984—Oct. 31: Indian Prime Min. Indira Gandhi shot by 2 Sikh bodyguards in New Delhi.

1986—Feb. 28: Swedish Prime Min. Olof Palme shot on Stockholm street; case officially closed in 2020 when a prosecutor identified the assassin as Stig Engström (by suicide, 2000).

1987—June 1: Lebanese Prem. Rashid Karami killed when bomb exploded aboard helicopter.

1988—Apr. 16: PLO military chief Khalil Wazir (Abu Jihad) gunned down by Israeli commandos in Tunisia.

1989—Aug. 18: Colombian pres. candidate Luis Carlos Galán killed by Medellín cartel drug traffickers at campaign rally in Bogotá. **Nov. 22:** Lebanese Pres. Rene Moawad killed when bomb exploded next to his motorcade.

1990—Mar. 22: Colombian pres. candidate Bernardo Jaramillo Ossa shot at airport in Bogotá.

1991—May 21: Former Indian Prime Min. Rajiv Gandhi killed by bomb during election rally in Madras.

1992—June 29: Algerian Pres. Mohamed Boudiaf shot in Annaba.

1993—May 1: Sri Lankan Pres. Ranasinghe Premadasa killed by suicide bomber in Colombo.

1994—Apr. 6: Burundian Pres. Cyprien Ntaryamira and Rwandan Pres. Juvénal Habyarimana killed with 8 others when their plane was shot down, precipitating Rwandan genocide.

1995—Nov. 4: Israeli Prime Min. Yitzhak Rabin shot by Jewish extremist at peace rally in Tel Aviv.

1996—Oct. 2: Andrei Lukanov, former Bulgarian prime min., shot outside of Sofia home.

1998—Apr. 26: Guatemalan Roman Catholic Bishop Juan José Gerardi Conedera, human rights champion, beaten to death in Guatemala City.

1999—Apr. 9: Niger Pres. Ibrahim Bare Mainassara killed by dissident soldiers. **Oct. 27:** Armenian Prime Min. Vazgen Sarkissian, with 7 others, shot during session of parliament.

2001—Jan. 16: Dem. Rep. of Congo Pres. Laurent Kabila shot to death by bodyguard at pres. palace in Kinshasa. **June 1:** Nepal's King Birendra, Queen Aiswarya, and 7 other royals fatally shot by Crown Prince Dipendra, who then killed self.

2002—July 6: Afghan Vice Pres. Haji Abdul Qadir shot outside his office in Kabul.

2003—Mar. 12: Serbian Prime Min. Zoran Djindjic shot by para-military snipers outside govt. headquarters in Belgrade.

2004—Feb. 13: Former Chechen Pres. Zelimkhan Yandarbiyev killed after car exploded in Qatar. **Mar. 22:** Sheik Ahmed Yassin, spiritual leader of Hamas, by Israeli missile attack in Gaza City. **May 9:** Chechen Pres. Akhmad Kadyrov by bomb at WWII memorial service in Grozny. **Nov. 2:** Filmmaker Theo van Gogh, critic of Islam and great-grandnephew of painter Vincent van Gogh, shot and stabbed by Muslim militant in Amsterdam.

2005—Jan. 4: Baghdad Gov. Ali al-Haidari gunned down by insurgents in Baghdad, Iraq.

2007—Aug. 2: *Oakland Post* editor Chauncey Bailey, who was investigating financial status of Your Black Muslim Bakery, shot in Oakland, CA. **Dec. 27:** Benazir Bhutto, former Pakistani prime min. and first female elected leader of a Muslim state, by bomb and gunman later linked to then-Pres. Pervez Musharraf.

2008—Feb. 12: Imad Mughniyeh, top Hezbollah commander and reputed mastermind of the 1983 bombing of U.S. embassy in Beirut, by car bomb in Damascus, Syria. **Oct. 23:** Ivo Pukanic, editor-in-chief of Croatian political newspaper *Nacional*, killed in Zagreb when bomb exploded nr. his car.

2009—Mar. 2: Guinea-Bissau's longtime Pres. João Bernardo Vieira shot by army troops outside his home in Bissau. **May 31:** Dr. George Tiller, one of the few doctors in the U.S. to perform abortions late in pregnancy, shot to death in his Wichita, KS, church by anti-abortion extremist.

2011—Sept. 20: Burhanuddin Rabbani, leader of Afghanistan's High Peace Council and a former pres., killed in his Kabul home by assassin with explosives hidden in his turban.

2012—Jan. 11: Iranian nuclear scientist Mostafa Ahmadi Roshan killed by car bomb.

2014—Sept. 1: U.S. airstrikes killed Ahmed Abdi Godane, leader of Somalia-based Islamist militant group al-Shabab.

2015—Feb. 27: Boris Y. Nemtsov, Russian opposition leader and former first deputy prime minister, shot near Red Square.

2016—June 16: UK Labour MP Jo Cox shot and stabbed in West Yorkshire by far-right assailant. **Dec. 20:** Turkish police officer shot Russian ambassador to Turkey, Andrei Karlov, in Ankara.

2017—Feb. 13: Kim Jong Nam, half-brother to N. Korean leader Kim Jong Un, killed in chemical nerve agent attack at Kuala Lumpur airport. Two women, charged in attack by Malaysian authorities, blamed coercion by N. Korean agents. **Oct. 16:** Maltese investigative journalist Daphne Caruana Galizia killed in a car bombing.

2018—Feb. 21: Slovak journalist Ján Kuciak and fiancée shot dead in their home. **Oct. 2:** Saudi journalist Jamal Khashoggi, a U.S. resident, murdered inside Saudi consulate in Istanbul, Turkey; U.S., other intelligence agencies pointed to Saudi crown prince Mohammed bin Salman's involvement.

2020—Jan. 3: Iranian Gen. Qassem Soleimani killed by U.S. airstrike in Baghdad.

2021—July 7: Haitian Pres. Jovenel Moïse killed by mercenaries in his home.

2022—July 8: Japanese former prime min. Shinzo Abe fatally shot while campaigning for his party. **July 31:** Egyptian Ayman al-Zawahiri, al-Qaeda cofounder and successor to Osama bin Laden, killed in U.S. drone strike in Kabul, Afghanistan.

2023—Aug. 9: Ecuadorian anticorruption pres. candidate Fernando Villavicencio shot after campaign event in Quito. **Aug. 23:** Russian Yevgeny Prigozhin, chief of Wagner mercenary group and one-time Putin ally, in a plane crash caused by an intentional explosion/sabotage.

MILITARY AFFAIRS

Chairmen of the Joint Chiefs of Staff, 1949-2023

Chairman	Service	Chairman	Service
Gen. of the Army Omar N. Bradley, USA	8/16/1949-8/15/1953	Gen. Colin L. Powell, USA	10/1/1989-9/30/1993
Adm. Arthur W. Radford, USN	8/15/1953-8/15/1957	Gen. John M. Shalikashvili, USA	10/25/1993-9/30/1997
Gen. Nathan F. Twining, USAF	8/15/1957-9/30/1960	Gen. Henry H. Shelton, USA	10/1/1997-9/30/2001
Gen. Lyman L. Lemnitzer, USA	10/1/1960-9/30/1962	Gen. Richard B. Myers, USAF	10/1/2001-9/30/2005
Gen. Maxwell D. Taylor, USA	10/1/1962-7/1/1964	Gen. Peter Pace, USMC	10/1/2005-9/30/2007
Gen. Earle G. Wheeler, USA	7/3/1964-7/2/1970	Adm. Michael G. Mullen, USN	10/1/2007-9/30/2011
Adm. Thomas H. Moorer, USN	7/2/1970-7/1/1974	Gen. Martin E. Dempsey, USA	10/1/2011-9/30/2015
Gen. George S. Brown, USAF	7/1/1974-6/20/1978	Gen. Joseph F. Dunford Jr., USMC	10/1/2015-9/30/2019
Gen. David C. Jones, USAF	6/21/1978-6/18/1982	Gen. Mark A. Milley, USA	10/1/2019-9/30/2023
Gen. John W. Vessey Jr., USA	6/18/1982-9/30/1985	Gen. Charles Q. Brown Jr., USAF	10/1/2023-
Adm. William J. Crowe Jr., USN	10/1/1985-9/30/1989		

Chief Commanding Officers of the U.S. Military

Chairman, Joint Chiefs of Staff: Gen. Charles Q. Brown Jr. (USAF). **Vice Chairman:** Adm. Christopher W. Grady (USN)

Date of rank is date when the individual achieved his or her current rank. While serving in any of these positions, or as commander of a unified or specified combatant command, basic pay is $17,675.10 per month. Officers below hold positions listed as of Oct. 1, 2023.

Army

Chief of Staff (CSA)	Date of rank
George, Randy A.	Aug. 5, 2022
Other Generals	
Brito, Gary M.	Sept. 8, 2022
Cavoli, Christopher G.	Oct. 1, 2020
Dickinson, James H.	Aug. 20, 2020
Fenton, Bryan P.	Aug. 30, 2022
Flynn, Charles A.	June 4, 2021
Hamilton, Charles R.	Mar. 16, 2023
Hokanson, Daniel R.	Aug. 3, 2020
Kurilla, Michael E.	Apr. 1, 2022
LaCamera, Paul J.	Nov. 18, 2019
Nakasone, Paul M.	May 4, 2018
Poppas, Andrew P.	July 8, 2022
Rainey, James E.	Oct. 4, 2022
Richardson, Laura J.	Oct. 29, 2021
Williams, Darryl A.	June 27, 2022

Marine Corps

Commandant of the Marine Corps (CMC)	Date of rank
Smith, Eric M.	Oct. 8, 2021
Other Generals	
Langley, Michael E.	Aug. 6, 2022

Coast Guard

Commandant, with rank of Admiral	Date of rank
Fagan, Linda L.	June 18, 2021
Vice Commandant, with rank of Admiral	
Poulin, Steven D.	May 31, 2022

Air Force

Acting Chief of Staff (CSAF or AF/CC)	Date of rank
Allvin, David W.	Nov. 12, 2020
Other Generals	
Bussiere, Thomas A.	Dec. 7, 2022
Cotton, Anthony J.	Aug. 27, 2021
Hecker, James B.	June 27, 2022
Kelly, Mark D.	Aug. 28, 2020
Minihan, Michael A.	Oct. 5, 2021
Richardson, Duke Z.	June 13, 2022
Van Ovost, Jacqueline D.	Aug. 20, 2020
VanHerck, Glen D.	Aug. 20, 2020
Wilsbach, Kenneth S.	July 8, 2020

Space Force

	Date of rank
Saltzman, B. Chance	Nov. 2, 2022
Thompson, David D.	Oct. 1, 2020

Navy

Acting Chief of Naval Operations (CNO)	Date of rank
Franchetti, Lisa M. (surface warfare)	Sept. 2, 2022
Other Admirals	
Aquilino, John C. (aviator)	May 17, 2018
Caldwell, James F., Jr. (submariner)	Aug. 14, 2015
Caudle, Daryl L. (submariner)	Dec. 7, 2021
Grady, Christopher W. (surface warfare)	May 4, 2018
Munsch, Stuart B. (submariner)	June 27, 2022
Paparo, Samuel J., Jr. (aviator)	May 5, 2021

Commanders of the Unified Combatant Commands

U.S. European Command, Stuttgart-Vaihingen, Germany:
Gen. Christopher G. Cavoli (U.S. Army)
U.S. Indo-Pacific Command, Honolulu, Hawaii:
Adm. John C. Aquilino (USN)
U.S. Special Operations Command, MacDill AFB, Florida:
Gen. Bryan P. Fenton (U.S. Army)
U.S. Transportation Command, Scott AFB, Illinois:
Gen. Jacqueline Van Ovost (USAF)
U.S. Central Command, MacDill AFB, Florida:
Gen. Michael E. Kurilla (U.S. Army)
U.S. Southern Command, Doral, Florida:
Gen. Laura J. Richardson (U.S. Army)

U.S. Northern Command, Peterson AFB, Colorado:
Gen. Glen D. VanHerck (USAF)
U.S. Strategic Command, Offutt AFB, Nebraska:
Gen. Anthony J. Cotton (USAF)
U.S. Africa Command, Kelley Barracks, Stuttgart, Germany:
Gen. Michael E. Langley (USMC)
U.S. Cyber Command, Fort George G. Meade, Maryland:
Gen. Paul M. Nakasone (USAF)
U.S. Space Command, Peterson AFB, Colorado:
Gen. James H. Dickinson (U.S. Army)

North Atlantic Treaty Organization (NATO) International Commands

NATO Headquarters: Chairman, NATO Military Committee: Admiral Rob Bauer (Royal Netherlands Navy)
Strategic Commands:
Allied Command Operations (ACO): Gen. Christopher G. Cavoli (U.S. Army), Supreme Allied Commander Europe
Allied Command Transformation (ACT): Gen. Philippe Lavigne (French Air Force), Supreme Allied Commander Transformation

ACO Operational Level Commands:
Joint Force Command Brunssum (JFC Brunssum):
Gen. Guglielmo Luigi Miglietta (Italian Army), Commander
Joint Force Command Naples (JFC Naples):
Adm. Stuart B. Munsch (USN), Commander
Joint Force Command Norfolk (JFC Norfolk):
Vice Adm. Daniel Dwyer (USN), Commander

Directors of the Central Intelligence Agency, 1946-2023

In 1942, Pres. Franklin D. Roosevelt established the Office of Strategic Services (OSS); it was disbanded in 1945. In 1946, Pres. Harry Truman established the Central Intelligence Group (CIG) to operate under the National Intelligence Authority (NIA). A 1947 law replaced the NIA with the National Security Council (NSC) and the CIG with the Central Intelligence Agency (CIA).

Director	Served	Appointed by President	Director	Served	Appointed by President
Adm. Sidney W. Souers	1946	Truman	William H. Webster	1987-1991	Reagan
Gen. Hoyt S. Vandenberg	1946-1947	Truman	Robert M. Gates	1991-1993	Bush, G. H. W.
Adm. Roscoe H. Hillenkoetter	1947-1950	Truman	R. James Woolsey	1993-1995	Clinton
Gen. Walter Bedell Smith	1950-1953	Truman	John M. Deutch	1995-1996	Clinton
Allen W. Dulles	1953-1961	Eisenhower	George J. Tenet	1997-2004	Clinton
John A. McCone	1961-1965	Kennedy	Porter Goss	2004-2006	Bush, G. W.
Adm. William F. Raborn Jr.	1965-1966	Johnson, L. B.	Gen. Michael V. Hayden	2006-2009	Bush, G. W.
Richard Helms	1966-1973	Johnson, L. B.	Leon E. Panetta	2009-2011	Obama
James R. Schlesinger	1973	Nixon	Gen. David H. Petraeus	2011-2012	Obama
William E. Colby	1973-1976	Nixon	John O. Brennan	2013-2017	Obama
George H. W. Bush	1976-1977	Ford	Michael R. Pompeo	2017-2018	Trump
Adm. Stansfield Turner	1977-1981	Carter	Gina Haspel	2018-2021	Trump
William J. Casey	1981-1987	Reagan	William J. Burns	2021-	Biden

U.S. Military Personnel Strength on Active Duty Worldwide, 2022

Source: U.S. Dept. of Defense
(as of Sept. 30, 2022)

Area	Personnel	Area	Personnel	Area	Personnel
TOTAL WORLDWIDE[1]	1,343,794	EAST ASIA AND PACIFIC		FORMER SOVIET UNION	
U.S., TERRITORIES, AND		Australia	1,580	Regional total	194
SPEC. LOCATIONS		British Indian Ocean Territory . . .	222	EUROPE	
Regional total	1,178,928	China	59	Belgium	1,143
OTHER WESTERN		Japan	53,973	France	75
HEMISPHERE		South Korea	25,372	Germany	35,781
The Bahamas	61	Philippines	211	Greece	387
Brazil	57	Singapore	218	Greenland	135
Canada	155	Thailand	110	Hungary	78
Colombia	66	Regional total	81,990	Italy	12,432
Cuba (Guantánamo)	596	NORTH AFRICA, NEAR EAST, AND		Lithuania	121
El Salvador	52	SOUTH ASIA		Netherlands	434
Honduras	342	Bahrain	3,698	Norway	90
Mexico	83	Egypt	199	Poland	264
Regional total	1,755	Iraq	149	Portugal	251
SUB-SAHARAN AFRICA		Israel	113	Romania	138
Djibouti	509	Jordan	112	Spain	3,164
Kenya	49	Kuwait	714	Turkey (Türkiye)	1,735
South Africa	46	Qatar	397	United Kingdom	9,840
Regional total	1,113	Saudi Arabia	320	Regional total	66,450
		United Arab Emirates	362		
		Regional total	6,333		

Note: Most countries and areas with fewer than 100 assigned U.S. military members not listed; regional totals include personnel stationed in countries and areas not shown. (1) Includes undistributed/other personnel.

U.S. Military Personnel on Active Duty in U.S. States and Territories, 2022

Source: U.S. Dept. of Defense
(as of Sept. 30, 2022)

State/area	Active personnel	Reserve personnel	State/area	Active personnel	Reserve personnel	State/area	Active personnel	Reserve personnel
Alabama	8,244	18,671	Maryland	29,599	18,213	South Carolina . .	38,322	17,388
Alaska	20,206	4,607	Massachusetts . .	3,350	13,764	South Dakota . . .	3,388	4,527
Arizona	17,482	14,834	Michigan	1,900	14,523	Tennessee	2,378	17,302
Arkansas	3,740	10,703	Minnesota	580	17,375	Texas	114,245	55,124
California	163,393	53,482	Mississippi	11,067	14,422	Utah	4,503	11,389
Colorado	37,990	13,793	Missouri	14,409	17,928	Vermont	141	3,127
Connecticut	6,224	6,701	Montana	3,253	4,037	Virginia	129,492	25,119
Delaware	3,490	4,916	Nebraska	6,499	5,940	Washington	62,130	17,027
Dist. of Columbia	11,024	3,730	Nevada	12,275	7,954	West Virginia	177	7,569
Florida	66,971	37,444	New Hampshire	1,115	3,953	Wisconsin	993	13,213
Georgia	63,873	26,512	New Jersey	7,954	16,858	Wyoming	3,148	2,942
Hawaii	40,485	9,546	New Mexico	13,437	4,694	Unknown[1]	7,851	71
Idaho	3,511	5,249	New York	19,364	28,280	U.S. total	1,172,058	749,568
Illinois	22,679	23,362	North Carolina . .	95,999	20,416	American Samoa	2	234
Indiana	1,043	17,009	North Dakota . . .	7,272	4,460	Guam	6,667	2,473
Iowa	246	10,923	Ohio	6,846	26,085	N. Mariana Isls . . .	13	63
Kansas	20,566	9,879	Oklahoma	21,114	12,843	Puerto Rico	176	11,578
Kentucky	34,608	12,008	Oregon	1,514	8,762	U.S. Virgin Isls . . .	10	654
Louisiana	14,910	16,341	Pennsylvania . . .	2,468	26,756	Wake Island	2	0
Maine	797	3,424	Rhode Island . . .	3,793	4,373	Territorial total	6,870	15,002

Note: Armed Forces (AF) Europe, AF the Americas, and AF Pacific—deployed primarily at sea or not at fixed-duty stations (1,611 reserve)—are not shown. (1) Includes undistributed/other personnel.

U.S. Army Personnel on Active Duty, 1940-2022

Source: Dept. of the Army, U.S. Dept. of Defense
(as of midyear, except where noted)

Date	Total strength[1]	Commissioned officers			Warrant officers[3]		Enlisted personnel		
		Total	Male	Female[2]	Male	Female	Total	Male	Female
1940	267,767	17,563	16,624	939	763	—	249,441	249,441	—
1942	3,074,184	203,137	190,662	12,475	3,285	—	2,867,762	2,867,762	—
1943	6,993,102	557,657	521,435	36,222	21,919	—	6,413,526	6,358,200	55,325
1944	7,992,868	740,077	692,351	47,726	36,893	10	7,215,888	7,144,601	71,287
1945	8,266,373	835,403	772,511	62,892	56,216	44	7,374,710	7,283,930	90,780
1946	1,889,690	257,300	240,658	16,642	9,826	18	1,622,546	1,605,847	16,699
1950	591,487	67,784	63,375	4,409	4,760	22	518,921	512,370	6,551
1960	871,348	91,056	86,832	4,224	10,141	39	770,112	761,833	8,279
1965	967,049	101,812	98,029	3,783	10,285	23	854,929	846,409	8,520
1970	1,319,735	143,704	138,469	5,235	23,005	13	1,153,013	1,141,537	11,476
1975	781,316	89,756	85,184	4,572	13,214	22	678,324	640,621	37,703
1980 (Sept. 30)	772,661	85,339	77,843	7,496	13,265	113	673,944	612,593	61,351
1990 (Mar. 31)	746,220	91,330	79,520	11,810	15,177	470	639,713	567,015	72,698
2000	471,633	66,344	56,391	9,953	10,608	781	393,900	333,947	59,953
2005 (Sept. 30)	492,728	69,174	57,675	11,499	11,506	976	406,923	346,194	57,354
2010 (Sept. 30)	566,045	78,588	64,952	13,636	14,106	1,434	467,248	406,871	60,377
2015 (Dec. 31)	482,264	78,586	64,223	14,363	13,577	1,421	384,301	331,620	52,681
2018	468,331	77,850	63,184	14,666	12,987	1,378	372,667	319,270	53,397
2019	472,209	78,883	63,733	15,150	12,905	1,395	375,600	321,500	54,100
2020	476,306	78,739	63,388	15,351	12,818	1,433	379,993	323,683	56,310
2021	486,141	79,795	63,878	15,917	13,171	1,457	387,170	329,761	57,409
2022 (Sept. 30)	465,625	78,620	62,537	16,083	13,538	1,503	367,585	313,391	54,194

— = Not applicable. **Note:** Represents strength of active Army, including Philippine Scouts (1940-46), ret. Regular Army personnel on extended active duty, and National Guard and Reserve personnel on extended active duty; excl. those (e.g., U.S. Military Academy cadets, contract surgeons, and National Guard and Reserve personnel) not on extended active duty. (1) Includes categories not listed, e.g., West Point cadets. Data for 1940-46 include personnel in the Army Air Forces and its predecessors (Air Service and Air Corps). (2) Includes Army Nurse Corps for all years, Women's Army Corps (1942-78), and Medical Specialists Corps (1949 and after). (3) Act of Congress approved Apr. 27, 1926, directed the appointment as warrant officers of field clerks still in active service. Includes flight officers as follows: 1943, 5,700; 1944, 13,615; 1945, 31,117; 1946, 2,580.

U.S. Navy Personnel on Active Duty, 1940-2023
Source: U.S. Dept. of Defense
(as of midyear, except where noted)

Year	Officers	Nurses[1]	Enlisted	Officer candidates[1]	Total[2]	Year	Officers	Nurses[1]	Enlisted	Officer candidates[1]	Total[2]
1940	13,162	442	144,824	2,569	160,997	2012	53,799	—	262,975	—	321,300
1945	320,293	11,086	2,988,207	61,231	3,380,817	2013	54,062	—	263,647	—	322,242
1950	42,687	1,964	331,860	5,037	381,538	2014	54,852	—	265,622	—	323,792
1960	67,456	2,103	544,040	4,385	617,984	2015	54,770	—	268,408	—	326,504
1970	78,488	2,273	605,899	6,000	692,660	2016	54,973	—	271,100	—	330,556
1980	63,100	—	464,100	—	527,200	2017	55,047	—	264,404	—	323,938
1990 (Sept.)	74,429	—	530,133	—	604,562	2018	55,401	—	268,340	—	328,244
1995 (May)	61,075	—	402,626	—	463,701	2019	55,475	—	275,474	—	335,444
2000 (Oct.)	53,698	—	320,212	—	373,910	2020	56,248	—	279,147	—	339,782
2005	54,039	—	305,368	—	363,858	2021	56,698	—	288,547	—	349,769
2010	53,071	—	273,609	—	330,065	2022	57,105	—	282,481	—	344,022
2011	53,620	—	270,425	—	328,648	2023 (May)	56,406	—	272,147	—	331,856

— = Not applicable. (1) Starting in 1980, "Nurses" are included with "Officers," and "Officer candidates" are included with "Enlisted." (2) May include categories not shown, e.g., midshipmen.

U.S. Air Force Personnel on Active Duty, 1918-2023
Source: U.S. Dept. of Defense
(as of midyear, except where noted)

Year	Total	Year	Total	Year	Total	Year	Total	Year	Total	Year	Total
1918 ...	195,023	1944 ...2,372,292		1995 ...	400,051	2006 ...	352,620	2013 ...	333,506	2019 ...	331,332
1920 ...	9,050	1945 ...2,282,259		2000 ...	357,777	2007 ...	340,596	2014 ...	328,791	2020 ...	333,559
1930 ...	13,531	1950 ...	411,277	2001 ...	351,935	2008 ...	328,771	2015 ...	312,195	2021 ...	336,329
1940 ...	51,165	1960 ...	814,213	2002 ...	369,721	2009 ...	333,423	2016 ...	315,786	2022 ...	333,455
1941 ...	152,125	1970 ...	791,078	2003 ...	373,116	2010 ...	337,505	2017 ...	322,559	2023	
1942 ...	764,415	1980 ...	557,969	2004 ...	379,887	2011 ...	333,729	2018 ...	325,222	(May)	328,560
1943 ...2,197,114		1990 ...	535,233	2005 ...	358,705	2012 ...	333,487				

Note: Prior to 1950, data are for U.S. Army Air Corps and Air Service of the Signal Corps. For 2021 and on, data includes Space Force personnel.

U.S. Marine Corps Personnel on Active Duty, 1940-2023
Source: U.S. Dept. of Defense
(as of midyear, except where noted)

Year	Officers	Enlisted	Total	Year	Officers	Enlisted	Total	Year	Officers	Enlisted	Total
1940	1,800	26,545	28,345	2000	17,897	154,744	172,641	2016	20,827	162,543	183,370
1945	37,067	437,613	474,680	2005	19,118	159,113	178,231	2017	21,296	163,234	184,530
1950	7,254	67,025	74,279	2010	21,680	179,446	201,126	2018	21,582	163,637	185,219
1960	16,203	154,418	170,621	2011	22,281	178,546	200,827	2019	21,769	165,045	186,814
1970	24,941	234,796	259,737	2012	22,380	174,748	197,128	2020	21,941	160,788	182,729
1980	18,198	170,271	188,469	2013	22,045	173,048	195,093	2021	22,062	158,074	180,136
1990	19,958	176,694	196,652	2014	21,507	169,327	190,834	2022	21,997	152,487	174,484
1995	18,017	153,929	171,946	2015	21,144	163,144	184,587	2023 (May)..	21,609	147,043	168,652

U.S. Coast Guard Personnel on Active Duty, 1970-2023
Source: U.S. Dept. of Defense
(as of midyear, except where noted)

Year	Officers	Cadets	Enlisted	Total	Year	Officers	Cadets	Enlisted	Total
1970	5,512	653	31,524	37,689	2014	8,572	676	31,233	40,481
1980	6,463	877	32,041	39,381	2015	8,550	623	30,896	40,069
1985	6,775	733	31,087	38,595	2016	8,550	623	30,896	40,069
1990	6,475	820	29,860	37,308	2017	8,483	623	32,015	41,121
1995	7,489	841	28,401	36,731	2018	8,578	807	32,719	42,104
2000	7,154	863	27,695	35,712	2019	8,361	809	32,406	41,576
2005	7,908	1,006	31,900	40,814	2020	9,144	814	31,791	41,749
2010	8,678	744	33,713	43,135	2021	9,031	801	31,705	41,537
2011	8,659	1,053	33,615	43,327	2022	8,941	789	30,823	40,553
2012 (Mar.).....	8,316	988	33,758	43,062	2023 (May)	9,111	811	29,657	39,579
2013 (Jan.).....	8,376	1,010	32,971	42,357					

Women in the U.S. Armed Forces
Source: U.S. Dept. of Defense; U.S. Census Bureau; U.S. Dept. of Commerce; U.S. Coast Guard, U.S. Dept. of Homeland Security; U.S. Dept. of Veterans Affairs

Women in the Army, Navy, Air Force, Marines, and Coast Guard are fully integrated with male personnel. All enlisted jobs were opened to women when the draft ended June 30, 1973. Admission to service academies began in 1976. Under rules instituted in 1993, women began to fly combat aircraft and serve aboard warships. By the mid-1990s, 80% of all jobs and more than 90% of all career fields had been opened to women. A woman first achieved the rank of four-star general in 2008. In 2010, the Navy removed its ban on women serving on submarine crews. The Pentagon in 2013 lifted its ban on women serving in direct ground combat units. In 2015, the first two women graduated from the Army's Ranger School. Adm. Linda Fagan was sworn in as commandant of the Coast Guard in June 2022, making her the first woman to lead a U.S. military branch. Adm. Lisa Franchetti became acting chief of naval operations while awaiting confirmation, Aug. 14, 2023.

Women Active Duty Troops, 2022

Service	% women
Army.................	15.6%
Navy...................	20.8
Marines...............	9.4
Air Force (incl. Space Force)	21.5
Coast Guard (June 2022) ...	15.9

Women on Active Duty, All DOD[1] Services, 1973-2022

Year	% women	Year	% women
1973	2.5%	2015	15.6%
1981	8.9	2017	16.3
1987	10.2	2018	16.6
1993	11.6	2019	17.0
2000	14.4	2020	17.3
2005	14.6	2021	17.4
2010	14.5	2022	17.6

Women Veterans by Period of Service, 2023

Period of service	% of women vets[2]
Gulf War era[3]	67.2%
Vietnam era	12.4
Korean War............	1.3
World War II	0.3
Peacetime only..........	20.4

Note: Numbers on active duty are as of Sept. 30 for all years, except where noted. (1) Does not include Coast Guard. (2) Projected pop. Some women served in multiple periods. (3) Includes women who served both pre- and post-9/11 but not in peacetime only.

African American Service in U.S. Wars
Source: U.S. Dept. of Defense; U.S. Census Bureau, U.S. Dept. of Commerce

American Revolution. About 5,000 served in the Continental Army, mostly in integrated units, some in all-black combat units.

Civil War. Some 180,000 served in 163 units of the Union Army's U.S. Colored Troops, and 200,000 worked in service units—10% of the Union Army in all; about 37,000 died, 31,000 wounded.

World War I. 350,000-400,000 served in the armed forces, 100,000 in France. Some 40,000 fought.

World War II. Some 1 mil served in the armed forces—8% of all troops—mostly in Army service units; all-black fighter and bomber Army Air Force units and infantry divisions gave distinguished service.

Korean War. More than 600,000 served in the military; 3,075 lost their lives in combat. By 1954, armed forces were completely desegregated.

Vietnam War. 274,937 served in the armed forces (1965-74)—9.8% of all troops; 7,243 were killed in combat.

Persian Gulf War. About 104,000 served in the Kuwaiti theater—20% of all U.S. troops; 66 died in combat.

Operation Enduring Freedom/Freedom's Sentinel. 204 military deaths and 1,458 wounded in Afghanistan and elsewhere.

Operation Iraqi Freedom/Operation New Dawn/Operation Inherent Resolve. 465 military deaths and 2,797 wounded.

U.S. Military Personnel by Race and Ethnicity, 2021
Source: *2021 Demographics: Profile of the Military Community*, U.S. Dept. of Defense

| | Active-duty personnel | | | | | Selected reserve personnel | | | | |
| | Hispanic or Latino | | Not Hispanic or Latino | | | Hispanic or Latino | | Not Hispanic or Latino | | |
Race	No.	%	No.	%	Total	No.	%	No.	%	Total
American Indian/AK Native.......	3,696	26.0	10,528	74.0	14,224	1,081	17.7	5,042	82.3	6,123
Asian..............	2,118	3.2	63,818	96.8	65,936	639	1.7	37,278	98.3	37,917
Black or African American	13,486	5.9	216,569	94.1	230,055	5,280	4.1	123,976	95.9	129,256
Native Hawaiian/other Pac. Isl....	1,538	9.9	14,005	90.1	15,543	1,135	15.8	6,058	84.2	7,193
White	183,512	19.9	736,752	80.1	920,264	97,653	16.7	487,175	83.3	584,828
Multi-racial[1]................	6,261	15.6	33,978	84.4	40,239	1,859	12.8	12,630	87.2	14,489
Unknown	25,958	52.3	23,629	47.7	49,587	10,244	50.6	10,014	49.4	20,258
Total	236,569	17.7	1,099,279	82.3	1,335,848	117,891	14.7	682,173	85.3	800,064

Note: As of Sept. Percentages may not add up to 100% due to rounding. (1) The Army and Army Reserve do not report "multi-racial."

U.S. Military Reserve Personnel by Service Branch, 2021
Source: *2021 Demographics: Profile of the Military Community*, U.S. Dept. of Defense

Reserve component	Enlisted	Officers	Total	Pct. of total reserve personnel
Army National Guard	290,736	46,789	337,525	42.2%
Army Reserve.....................	144,710	39,648	184,358	23.0
Navy Reserve.....................	43,535	14,097	57,632	7.2
Marine Corps Reserve	30,819	4,421	35,240	4.4
Air National Guard	92,106	16,377	108,483	13.6
Air Force Reserve..................	55,623	14,947	70,570	8.8
Total Dept. of Defense	657,529	136,279	793,808	99.2
Coast Guard Reserve..............	5,237	1,019	6,256	0.8
Total Selected Reserve.............	662,766	137,298	800,064	NA

Note: As of Sept. Percentages may not add up to 100% due to rounding.

Monthly Military Pay Scale, 2023
Source: U.S. Dept. of Defense
(effective Jan. 1, 2023; salaries rounded to nearest dollar)

| | Cumulative years of service | | | | | | | | | | | | | | |
	<2	2	3	4	6	8	10	12	14	16	18	20	22	24	26
Commissioned officers															
O-10	NA	NA	NA	NA	NA	NA	NA	NA	NA	NA	NA	17,675	17,675	17,675	17,675
O-9	NA	NA	NA	NA	NA	NA	NA	NA	NA	NA	NA	17,201	17,450	17,675	17,675
O-8	12,171	12,570	12,834	12,908	13,238	13,790	13,918	14,442	14,593	15,044	15,697	16,298	16,700	16,700	16,700
O-7	10,113	10,583	10,800	10,973	11,286	11,595	11,953	12,309	12,667	13,790	14,738	14,738	14,738	14,738	14,814
O-6	7,669	8,425	8,978	8,978	9,013	9,399	9,450	9,450	9,987	10,936	11,494	12,050	12,368	12,368	12,368
O-5	6,393	7,202	7,700	7,794	8,106	8,291	8,701	9,002	9,390	9,983	10,265	10,545	10,862	10,862	10,862
O-4	5,516	6,385	6,812	6,906	7,302	7,726	8,255	8,666	8,951	9,116	9,210	9,210	9,210	9,210	9,210
O-3	4,850	5,498	5,933	6,470	6,780	7,121	7,340	7,702	7,891	7,891	7,891	7,891	7,891	7,891	7,891
O-2	4,191	4,773	5,497	5,683	5,799	5,799	5,799	5,799	5,799	5,799	5,799	5,799	5,799	5,799	5,799
O-1	3,637	3,786	4,577	4,577	4,577	4,577	4,577	4,577	4,577	4,577	4,577	4,577	4,577	4,577	4,577
Commissioned officers with over 4 years of active duty service as enlisted member or warrant officer															
O-3E	NA	NA	NA	6,470	6,780	7,121	7,340	7,702	8,007	8,183	8,421	8,421	8,421	8,421	8,421
O-2E	NA	NA	NA	5,683	5,799	5,984	6,296	6,537	6,716	6,716	6,716	6,716	6,716	6,716	6,716
O-1E	NA	NA	NA	4,577	4,887	5,068	5,253	5,434	5,683	5,683	5,683	5,683	5,683	5,683	5,683
Warrant officers															
W-5	NA	NA	NA	NA	NA	NA	NA	NA	NA	NA	NA	8,912	9,364	9,701	10,073
W-4	5,012	5,391	5,546	5,698	5,961	6,220	6,483	6,878	7,224	7,554	7,824	8,088	8,474	8,792	9,154
W-3	4,578	4,768	4,964	5,028	5,232	5,636	6,056	6,254	6,483	6,718	7,142	7,428	7,600	7,781	8,030
W-2	4,050	4,433	4,551	4,632	4,895	5,303	5,506	5,705	5,948	6,139	6,311	6,517	6,653	6,760	6,760
W-1	3,555	3,938	4,041	4,258	4,515	4,894	5,071	5,319	5,562	5,753	5,929	6,143	6,143	6,143	6,143
Enlisted members															
E-9	NA	NA	NA	NA	NA	NA	6,056	6,193	6,366	6,569	6,775	7,103	7,382	7,674	8,122
E-8	NA	NA	NA	NA	NA	4,957	5,177	5,312	5,475	5,651	5,969	6,130	6,404	6,557	6,931
E-7	3,446	3,761	3,905	4,095	4,245	4,501	4,645	4,901	5,114	5,259	5,414	5,473	5,675	5,783	6,194
E-6	2,981	3,280	3,425	3,566	3,712	4,042	4,171	4,420	4,496	4,551	4,616	4,616	4,616	4,616	4,616
E-5	2,730	2,914	3,055	3,199	3,424	3,659	3,852	3,875	3,875	3,875	3,875	3,875	3,875	3,875	3,875
E-4	2,504	2,632	2,774	2,915	3,039	3,039	3,039	3,039	3,039	3,039	3,039	3,039	3,039	3,039	3,039
E-3	2,260	2,402	2,548	2,548	2,548	2,548	2,548	2,548	2,548	2,548	2,548	2,548	2,548	2,548	2,548
E-2	2,149	2,149	2,149	2,149	2,149	2,149	2,149	2,149	2,149	2,149	2,149	2,149	2,149	2,149	2,149
E-1	1,918	1,918	1,918	1,918	1,918	1,918	1,918	1,918	1,918	1,918	1,918	1,918	1,918	1,918	1,918

NA = Not applicable. **Note:** Basic pay rate for Academy cadets/midshipmen and ROTC members/applicants is $1,273. See Dept. of Defense Financial Management Regulations for details on pay-scale limitations and eligibility requirements. (1) Applicable to E-1 with 4 months or more of active duty. Basic pay for an E-1 with less than 4 months of active duty is $1,773.

U.S. Veteran Population, 2023

Source: U.S. Dept. of Veterans Affairs
(projected population, in thousands, as of Sept. 30)

Period of service	Vet. pop.
Total peacetime veterans[1]	**3,979**
Service between Vietnam War era and Gulf War era	2,809
Service between Korean War and Vietnam War era	1,137
Service between WWII and Korean War	33
Total wartime veterans[2]	**14,271**
Total World War II[3]	120
WWII only	104
Total Korean War[3]	783
Korean War with no other wartime service	697
Korean War with service in WWII	11
Total Vietnam War era[3]	5,638
Vietnam War era with no other wartime service	5,191
Vietnam War era with service in Korea	70
Vietnam War era with service in Korea and WWII	5
Total Gulf War era[3]	8,193
Gulf War era pre-9/11 with service in Vietnam era	258
Gulf War era pre-9/11, post-9/11, and with service in Vietnam War era	57
Gulf War era pre-9/11 only	2,601
Gulf War era pre-9/11 and post-9/11	1,536
Gulf War era post-9/11 only	3,684
TOTAL VETERANS IN CIVILIAN LIFE	**18,250**

Note: Figures are for U.S. veterans worldwide. Includes those who served on active duty in Army, Navy, Air Force, Marines, Coast Guard, uniformed Public Health Service and NOAA, and reservists called to federal active duty. According to Dept. of Veterans Affairs projections, as of Sept. 30 there were 338 living veterans who served prior to WWII. Excludes those dishonorably discharged, those whose only active duty was training, and those currently on active duty. (1) Veterans with both wartime and peacetime service are counted only as "wartime veterans." (2) Veterans serving in more than one period are counted only once in total. (3) Total includes veterans who also served in other periods.

Outlays for Individual Payments to Veterans, 1940-2024

Source: White House Office of Management and Budget
(in millions of dollars)

Year	Total	Compensation	Pensions	Hospital, medical	Education	Insurance & burial
1940	$574	$244	$185	$69	—	$76
1950	8,613	1,533	476	764	$2,739	3,101
1960	5,300	2,049	1,263	931	392	665
1970	8,883	2,980	2,255	1,798	1,002	848
1980	21,153	7,446	3,585	6,513	2,421	1,188
1990	28,801	10,735	3,594	12,281	791	1,400
2000	46,835	20,777	2,969	20,090	1,636	1,363
2010	106,454	43,498	4,359	48,506	8,773	1,318
2011	122,524	52,780	4,664	52,681	11,112	1,287
2012	119,544	50,058	4,537	52,972	10,734	1,243
2013	134,083	59,393	5,173	55,067	13,220	1,230
2014	$143,412	$64,360	$5,251	$58,906	$13,729	$1,166
2015	153,506	69,725	5,299	63,652	13,605	1,225
2016	167,046	79,907	5,824	65,810	14,579	926
2017	167,399	79,839	5,505	67,949	13,520	586
2018	170,949	79,986	4,796	72,899	12,703	565
2019	194,241	95,599	4,940	79,661	13,433	608
2020	214,200	105,615	4,751	90,330	13,120	384
2021	230,039	112,134	4,156	101,018	12,245	486
2022	264,668	135,658	4,114	112,412	12,071	413
2023*	285,612	146,178	3,541	123,075	11,999	819
2024*	294,297	152,158	3,109	126,390	11,929	711

— = Not available. * = Estimate. **Note:** Compensation is service-connected; pension is not.

Race and Ethnicity of U.S. Veterans, 2021

Source: American Community Survey, U.S. Census Bureau, U.S. Dept. of Commerce

Age/gender	White, not Hispanic or Latino	Black or African-American	Amer. Ind. or AK Native	Asian	Native Hawaiian or other Pac. Isl.	Some other race	Two or more races	Hispanic or Latino
Male 18 to 34	681,445	130,407	11,312	34,957	4,479	57,995	140,397	182,789
35 to 54	2,148,124	470,803	32,700	80,422	8,509	132,657	354,561	407,204
55 to 64	1,847,538	448,643	20,985	38,726	6,689	71,735	197,601	207,172
65 to 74	3,031,222	408,761	24,244	52,183	5,447	70,743	205,510	213,404
75 and over	3,329,424	247,372	14,922	63,359	3,405	54,836	161,671	177,664
Female 18 to 34	119,098	55,024	3,936	9,598	879	16,102	33,769	46,138
35 to 54	356,135	143,409	6,945	20,809	2,598	22,515	77,319	75,007
55 to 64	262,975	83,637	3,543	6,630	962	10,151	31,553	26,710
65 to 74	175,101	36,836	1,904	4,506	468	5,614	17,547	16,828
75 and over	94,206	9,926	453	1,507	360	945	5,791	6,467

Employment Status of Veterans With Service-Connected Disabilities, 2022

Source: Bureau of Labor Statistics, U.S. Dept. of Labor; as of Aug. 2022

Veteran status, presence of disability, and period of service	Employed (thous.)			Unemployed (thous.)			Unemployment rate (%)			Not in labor force (thous.)		
	Total	Men	Women	Total	Men	Women	Total	Men	Women	Total	Men	Women
Total veterans	8,590	7,370	1,221	252	214	38	2.9%	2.8%	3.0%	9,493	8,723	771
With service-connected disability	2,261	1,879	381	85	72	12	3.6	3.7	3.2	2,575	2,331	243
Without service-connected disability	5,861	5,065	796	163	138	26	2.7	2.6	3.2	6,421	5,921	500
Gulf War era, total	6,145	5,165	980	149	125	24	2.4	2.4	2.4	1,863	1,493	370
With service-connected disability	1,947	1,587	360	74	66	8	3.6	4.0	2.1	942	766	175
Without service-connected disability	3,861	3,270	591	75	59	16	1.9	1.8	2.6	791	606	185
Gulf War era II	3,838	3,201	637	91	75	16	2.3	2.3	2.5	968	757	211
With service-connected disability	1,425	1,129	296	50	49	1	3.4	4.2	0.2	510	392	117
Without service-connected disability	2,177	1,864	313	41	26	16	1.9	1.4	4.8	352	267	85
Gulf War era I	2,308	1,964	343	57	50	7	2.4	2.5	2.1	895	736	159
With service-connected disability	522	458	64	24	16	7	4.3	3.4	NA	432	374	58
Without service-connected disability	1,684	1,406	278	33	33	NA	1.9	2.3	NA	439	339	100
WWII, Korean War, and Vietnam era	773	714	60	47	47	NA	5.7	6.1	NA	5,382	5,195	187
With service-connected disability	126	115	10	6	6	NA	4.7	5.1	NA	1,291	1,259	32
Without service-connected disability	618	575	43	40	40	NA	6.1	6.6	NA	3,822	3,678	144
Other service periods	1,672	1,491	181	57	42	15	3.3	2.8	7.5	2,248	2,035	214
With service-connected disability	187	177	11	5	NA	5	2.4	NA	NA	342	306	36
Without service-connected disability	1,382	1,221	162	48	38	10	3.4	3.0	5.9	1,807	1,637	170

NA = Not available. **Note:** Veterans in survey were on active duty in the U.S. Armed Forces during these periods of service: Gulf War era II (Sept. 2001-present), Gulf War era I (Aug. 1990-Aug. 2001), Vietnam era (Aug. 1964-Apr. 1975), Korean War (July 1950-Jan. 1955), World War II (Dec. 1941-Dec. 1946), and other service periods. Veterans who served in more than one wartime period are classified in the most recent period only. A service-connected disability is a health condition or impairment caused or made worse by military service.

Nations With Largest Armed Forces, 2022

Source: *The Military Balance 2023*, International Institute for Strategic Studies, published by Routledge Journals, Taylor & Francis, UK
(ranked by active-duty troop strength as of 2022)

Rank	Country	Active troops (thous.)	Reserve troops (thous.)	Defense expend. (mil)	Tanks (MBT) (army only)	Cruisers/ frigates/ destroyers	Sub-marines	Combat aircraft (air force only) FGA	Combat aircraft (air force only) FTR
1.	China	2,035	510	$242,409	4,800	7C/41F/42D*	59	1,182+	446
2.	India	1,468	1,155	66,645	3,740	16F/10D*	16	523	61
3.	United States	1,360	817	766,606	2,645	19C/22F/70D*	67	1,063	214
4.	North Korea	1,280	600	—	3,500+	2F	71	30	401+
5.	Russia	1,190	1,500	66,857	1,800	3C/16F/11D*	51	410+	185
6.	Ukraine	688	400	3,547[1]	953	0	0	0	50
7.	Pakistan	652	0	9,768	2,537	8F	8	229	151
8.	Iran	610	350	44,011	1,513+	0	17	80	180+
9.	South Korea	555	3,100	42,991	2,149	3C/17F/6D	19	349	173
10.	Ethiopia	503	0	1,576	220	0	0	6+	11
11.	Vietnam	482	5,000	6,030	1,383	0	8	72	0
12.	Egypt	439	479	5,211	2,480	12F	8	274	32
13.	Indonesia	396	400	9,059	103	7F	4	40	9
14.	Brazil	367	1,340	22,951	296	7F	6	29	47
15.	Thailand	361	200	6,171	394	7F*	0	11	75
16.	Myanmar	356	0	1,876	195+	5F	2	6	63
17.	Turkey	355	379	6,188	2,378	16F	12	279	16
18.	Eritrea	302	—	—	270	0	0	2	8
19.	Saudi Arabia	257	0	45,600	1,010	8F	0	221	81
20.	Colombia	256	35	6,307	0	0	4	22	0
21.	Sri Lanka	255	6	1,154	62	1F	0	1	5
22.	Japan	247	56	48,079	555	4C/8F/34D*	24	122	200
23.	Mexico	216	82	5,743	0	1F	0	0	5
24.	France	203	41	54,417	215	17F/4D*	9	155	34
25.	Morocco	196	150	6,413	656	4F	0	49	22
26.	Iraq	193	0	8,690	391+	0	0	34	0
27.	Germany	183	33	53,371	321	8F/3D	6	0	138
28.	Israel	170	465	19,350	400	0	5	315	0
29.	Taiwan	169	1,657	16,164	650	22F/4D	4	190	215
30.	Syria	169	0	—	—	0	0	79	55

— = Not available. * = Navy with aircraft carrier(s), as follows: China 2, France 1, India 2, Japan 4, Russia 1, Thailand 1, U.S. 11. FGA = Fighter, ground attack. FTR = Fighter. MBT = Main battle tank. (1) Projected to be higher due to Russian invasion that began in Feb. 2022.

U.S. Anti-Terrorism Overseas Contingency Operations (OCO), 2008-21

Source: U.S. Dept. of Defense

(fiscal-year enacted funding, in billions; annual average troop levels, in thousands)

	2008	2009	2010	2011	2012	2013	2014	2015	2016	2017	2018	2019	2020	2021
Total: OCO designated funding	$187	$146	$163	$159	$115	$82	$85	$63	$59	$82	$83	$69	$71[1]	$70
Op. Inherent Resolve[2]	148	94	62	45	10	3	1	5	5	14	13	14	7	7
Op. Freedom's Sentinel[3]	39	52	101	114	105	79	84	54	44	46	47	45	17	13
European Deterrence Initiative/non-war	NA	NA	NA	NA	NA	NA	NA	2	2	4	6	7	6	5
Base requirements	NA	NA	NA	NA	NA	NA	NA	2	8	18	17	2	6	17
Total: OCO troop levels	187	185	180	145	99	63	37	13	14	14	24	26	22*	—
Op. Inherent Resolve[2]	154	141	96	47	9	0	0	3	4	6	6	11	7	—
Op. Freedom's Sentinel[3]	33	44	84	98	90	63	37	10	10	8	18	16	15	—

NA = Not applicable. — = Not available. * = Requested. (1) Total includes $35 bil of in-theater and U.S. stateside costs attributed to individual operations for previous years and excludes funding associated with border security and hurricane reconstruction efforts. (2) Includes Operations Iraqi Freedom, New Dawn, Inherent Resolve, and other activities in Iraq and Syria. (3) Includes Operations Enduring Freedom and Freedom's Sentinel, both in Afghanistan.

Conventional Arms Transfer Agreements With the World by Supplier, 2010-22

Source: Stockholm International Peace Research Institute (SIPRI); as of Mar. 13, 2023

(SIPRI trend-indicator values [TIVs] in millions of current U.S. dollars; ranked by 2010-22 totals)

Supplier	2010	2012	2013	2014	2015	2016	2017	2018	2019	2020	2021	2022	2010-22
United States	$8,336	$8,999	$7,607	$9,588	$9,918	$9,769	$11,732	$9,674	$10,880	$9,426	$10,994	$14,515	$130,387
Russia	6,158	8,171	7,923	5,467	5,927	6,811	6,199	7,173	5,627	3,904	2,857	2,820	77,715
France	864	1,308	1,780	1,755	2,263	2,155	2,355	1,998	3,612	2,378	3,853	3,021	29,575
China	1,472	1,520	2,059	1,308	1,800	2,449	1,617	1,372	1,585	704	1,462	2,017	20,630
Germany	2,373	730	786	1,822	1,820	2,529	1,866	1,106	1,020	1,172	938	1,510	18,888
United Kingdom	1,151	816	1,493	1,658	1,177	1,339	1,117	683	910	625	656	1,504	14,135
Italy	555	784	922	677	687	621	717	539	384	848	1,673	1,825	11,198
Spain	273	266	450	962	977	480	820	705	308	971	594	950	8,753
Israel	644	462	410	386	562	1,226	1,187	1,122	348	381	543	831	8,650
Netherlands	366	869	384	638	469	484	1,067	466	301	462	347	295	6,689
South Korea	177	203	350	220	94	473	738	1,054	682	772	544	209	5,844
Total	25,724	27,809	27,247	27,195	28,484	31,213	31,438	27,807	27,607	24,000	26,792	31,983	367,198

Note: SIPRI data on arms transfers relate to actual deliveries of major conventional weapons, using TIV. TIV is based on the known unit production costs of a core set of weapons and is intended to represent the transfer of military resources rather than the financial value of the transfer. A weapon that has been in service in another armed force is valued at 40% of a new weapon. A significantly refurbished or modified used weapon is valued at 66% of that of a new weapon. Total includes suppliers/countries not shown here.

U.S. Foreign Military Sales, 1950-2022

Source: Defense Security Cooperation Agency (DSCA), Dept. of Defense

Listed are the top 50 foreign government purchasers of military articles, services, and/or training in fiscal years 1950-2022 through the DSCA-administered Foreign Military Sales (FMS) program for the Dept. of Defense. Transfers may in some cases be completed through grants/leases. (in millions)

	1950-2022	2021	2022		1950-2022	2021	2022
Saudi Arabia	$164,229.4	$1,564.8	$1,512.3	Iran	$10,715.4	$0.0	$0.0
Israel	53,483.7	1,478.5	2,428.3	Belgium	10,494.2	109.2	61.6
Japan	52,957.8	3,903.5	2,803.5	Switzerland	10,061.9	36.9	5,698.6
Taiwan	49,683.0	2,678.0	2,057.1	Morocco	9,888.6	53.5	−9.5
Australia	45,795.6	937.5	6,668.6	Lebanon	9,859.2	67.1	144.1
South Korea	44,418.7	1,902.0	947.3	Norway	9,460.5	36.8	162.5
Egypt	43,625.9	2,027.9	1,492.1	Jordan	9,385.0	153.6	1,731.6
Qatar	39,401.3	−68.4	5.4	Thailand	8,878.5	297.8	83.3
United Kingdom	34,899.3	2,861.1	869.0	France	8,877.2	1,516.4	665.1
United Arab Emirates	29,634.7	359.7	203.3	Bahrain	5,910.1	452.0	170.2
Iraq	26,319.2	386.4	449.9	Italy	5,855.9	935.6	114.8
Turkey	21,581.0	256.9	196.6	Denmark	4,632.3	35.2	41.8
Germany	20,764.2	1,097.4	440.0	Ukraine	4,093.8	333.1	2,119.4
Kuwait	20,763.6	1,256.7	240.2	Romania	3,812.1	986.4	103.8
Finland	17,243.4	90.6	11,830.6	Kosovo	3,573.3	22.4	16.2
Poland	16,841.2	126.6	4,825.8	Oman	3,519.4	−41.6	−4.5
Afghanistan	16,428.2	1,263.9	−553.2	Colombia	3,154.2	71.6	24.1
Greece	15,741.8	314.6	728.6	Indonesia	2,890.1	27.6	75.9
Netherlands	15,258.6	522.2	83.3	Armenia	2,747.0	0.0	1.3
Canada	14,711.6	2,555.8	381.4	Brazil	2,739.9	101.7	21.5
Seychelles	14,279.1	0.0	0.3	Philippines	2,487.4	90.3	134.7
India	13,394.9	320.2	−254.0	Benin	2,431.8	0.0	0.0
Spain	12,254.2	186.5	199.1	Slovakia	2,425.0	119.9	43.4
Singapore	11,853.5	24.8	800.6	Chile	2,021.7	585.6	41.5
Pakistan	11,141.4	73.2	35.1	New Zealand	2,002.6	58.6	39.0
				World total	**$1,037,178.3**	**$34,809.7**	**$51,924.8**

Note: World total includes countries not listed. International organizations including NATO and the United Nations are also recipients of the program.

Leading Defense Contract Recipients, 2022

Source: U.S. Dept. of Defense; Federal Procurement Data System, U.S. General Services Administration

Listed are the 50 companies or organizations receiving the largest dollar volume of prime contract awards from the U.S. Dept. of Defense during fiscal year 2022 (Oct. 1, 2021-Sept. 30, 2022), as of Sept. 28, 2023.

Rank	Recipient	Funds awarded	Rank	Recipient	Funds awarded
1.	Lockheed Martin Corp.	$46,213,556,415	26.	The British Petroleum Co. Plc.	$2,089,949,769
2.	Raytheon Technologies Corp.	26,131,041,978	27.	Abbott Laboratories	1,903,042,837
3.	General Dynamics Corp	21,574,860,870	28.	Bell Boeing Joint Project Office	1,887,421,279
4.	Pfizer Inc.	16,669,419,909	29.	Moderna, Inc.	1,859,856,855
5.	The Boeing Co.	14,802,123,520	30.	iHealth Labs Inc.	1,774,999,987
6.	Northrop Grumman Corp.	13,766,613,197	31.	CACI International Inc.	1,755,258,966
7.	Humana Inc.	7,739,712,978	32.	Oshkosh Corp.	1,645,279,966
8.	L3Harris Technologies, Inc.	6,747,701,907	33.	GlaxoSmithKline Holdings (Americas) Inc.	1,633,124,216
9.	Huntington Ingalls Industries, Inc.	5,358,246,653	34.	AmerisourceBergen Corp.	1,615,810,327
10.	BAE Systems PLC	5,088,664,721	35.	Jacobs Engineering Group Inc.	1,504,536,515
11.	Leidos Holdings, Inc.	4,081,300,445	36.	Vectrus Federal Services GmbH	1,480,090,579
12.	Centene Corp.	3,550,059,420	37.	Valero Energy Corp.	1,402,887,022
13.	Analytic Services Inc.	3,282,767,886	38.	Johns Hopkins University	1,217,646,385
14.	Bechtel Corp.	3,207,751,106	39.	United Launch Alliance, L.L.C.	1,213,662,847
15.	Amentum Services, Inc.	3,193,044,698	40.	Hensel Phelps Construction Co.	1,204,195,480
16.	Atlantic Diving Supply, Inc.	3,113,338,552	41.	Massachusetts Institute of Tech.	1,133,916,740
17.	KBR, Inc.	3,087,936,764	42.	Rolls-Royce Holdings plc	1,090,539,490
18.	McKesson Corporation	2,912,482,434	43.	Kokosing Alberici Traylor, LLC	1,070,124,150
19.	Science Applications International Corp.	2,806,561,522	44.	The MITRE Corp.	1,061,316,970
20.	Eli Lilly and Co.	2,752,650,000	45.	Dell Technologies Inc.	1,054,058,467
21.	General Electric Co.	2,628,625,800	46.	Textron Inc.	1,044,104,485
22.	Okinawa Idemitsu K.K.	2,423,675,282	47.	Peraton Inc.	1,040,701,404
23.	Booz Allen Hamilton Holding Corp.	2,421,741,066	48.	The Aerospace Corp.	1,036,405,128
24.	General Atomics	2,183,714,738	49.	Merck & Co. Inc.	997,122,535
25.	Fluor Corp	2,119,220,065	50.	Ministry of Defense (Japan)	994,144,983

Medal of Honor

Source: Congressional Medal of Honor Society; U.S. Army, U.S. Dept. of Defense; as of Aug. 2023

The Medal of Honor is the highest military award for individual bravery in the U.S. On Dec. 21, 1861, Pres. Abraham Lincoln signed a bill to create the Navy Medal of Honor. Lincoln, on July 14, 1862, approved a resolution providing for the presentation of Medals of Honor to enlisted men of the Army and Voluntary Forces. The law was amended on Mar. 3, 1863, so that officers as well as enlisted men were eligible. The first Army Medals of Honor were awarded on Mar. 25, 1863; the first Navy medals went to sailors and Marines on Apr. 3, 1863.

The Medal of Honor is awarded in the name of Congress to a person who, while a member of the armed forces, distinguishes himself or herself conspicuously by gallantry and intrepidity at the risk of life above and beyond the call of duty while engaged in an action against any enemy of the U.S.; while engaged in military operations involving conflict with an opposing foreign force; or while serving with friendly foreign forces engaged in an armed conflict against an opposing armed force in which the U.S. is not a belligerent party.

The deed performed must have been one of personal bravery or self-sacrifice so conspicuous as to clearly distinguish the individual above his or her comrades and must have involved risk of life. Incontestable proof of the performance of service is required, and each recommendation for award of this decoration is considered on the standard of extraordinary merit.

Prior to World War I, the 2,625 Army Medal of Honor awards up to that time were reviewed to determine which met new stringent criteria. The Army removed 911 names from the list, most of them former members of a Civil War volunteer infantry group who had been induced to extend their enlistments when they were promised the medal. However, the medal was restored to Dr. Mary Walker in 1977 and to Buffalo Bill Cody and seven other scouts in 1989. Among recipients, 1,523 received the Medal of Honor for valor in the Civil War; 126 for those during WWI, 472 in WWII, 146 in the Korean War, 268 in the Vietnam War, 20 for actions in Afghanistan, and 8 for Iraq.

Medal of Honor Recipients From Recent Conflicts

Honoree	Rank[1]	Branch of service	Date of action	Date of award
Somalia Campaign				
Gordon, Gary I.*	Master Sgt.	U.S. Army	10/3/1993	5/23/1994
Shughart, Randall D.*	Sgt. First Class	U.S. Army	10/3/1993	5/23/1994
War in Iraq				
Atkins, Travis W.*	Staff Sgt.	U.S. Army	6/1/2007	3/27/2019
Bellavia, David G.	Staff Sgt.	U.S. Army	11/10/2004	6/25/2019
Cashe, Alwyn C.*	Sgt. First Class	U.S. Army	10/17/2005	12/16/2021
Dunham, Jason L.*	Corporal	USMC	4/14/2004	1/11/2007
McGinnis, Ross A.*	Pvt. First Class/Specialist*	U.S. Army	12/4/2006	6/5/2008
Monsoor, Michael A.*	Petty Officer Second Class	U.S. Navy	9/29/2006	4/8/2008
Payne, Thomas P.	Sgt. Major	U.S. Army	10/22/2015	9/11/2020
Smith, Paul R.*	Sgt. First Class	U.S. Army	4/4/2003	4/5/2005
War in Afghanistan				
Byers, Edward C., Jr.	Senior Chief	U.S. Navy	12/8-9/2012	2/29/2016
Carpenter, William Kyle	Lance Cpl.	USMC	11/21/2010	6/19/2014
Carter, Ty M.	Staff Sgt.	U.S. Army	10/3/2009	8/26/2013
Celiz, Christopher A.*	Sgt. First Class	U.S. Army	7/12/2018	12/16/2021
Chapman, John A.*	Technical Sgt.	USAF	3/4/2002	8/22/2018
Giunta, Salvatore A.	Staff Sgt.	U.S. Army	10/25/2007	11/16/2010
Groberg, Florent A.	Capt.	U.S. Army	8/8/2012	11/12/2015
Meyer, Dakota	Sgt.	USMC	9/8/2009	9/15/2011
Miller, Robert J.*	Staff Sgt.	U.S. Army	1/25/2008	10/6/2010
Monti, Jared C.*	Sgt. First Class	U.S. Army	6/21/2006	9/17/2009
Murphy, Michael P.*	Lt.	U.S. Navy	6/28/2005	10/22/2007
Petry, Leroy A.	Sgt. First Class	U.S. Army	5/26/2008	7/12/2011
Pitts, Ryan M.	Staff Sgt.	U.S. Army	7/13/2008	7/21/2014
Plumlee, Earl D.	Master Sgt.	U.S. Army	8/28/2013	12/16/2021
Romesha, Clinton L.	Staff Sgt.	U.S. Army	10/3/2009	2/11/2013
Shurer, Ronald J., II	Staff Sgt.	U.S. Army	4/6/2008	10/1/2018
Slabinski, Britt K.	Master Chief	U.S. Navy	3/4/2002	5/24/2018
Swenson, William D.	Capt.	U.S. Army	9/8/2009	10/15/2013
White, Kyle J.	Sgt.	U.S. Army	11/9/2007	5/13/2014
Williams, Matthew O.	Master Sgt.	U.S. Army	4/6/2008	10/30/2019

* = Awarded posthumously. (1) Rank at date of award.

Other Selected Awards

Source: The Institute of Heraldry, U.S. Army; Navy Department Awards Web Service; Air Force Personnel Center

Distinguished Service Cross

Established by Congress July 9, 1918, on recommendation of Gen. John J. "Black Jack" Pershing, and awarded for extraordinary heroism not justifying the award of a Medal of Honor. The act or acts of heroism must have been so notable and have involved risk of life so extraordinary as to set the individual apart from his or her comrades. The Navy Cross and Air Force Cross are equivalent.

Silver Star

Third-highest military combat honor. An earlier version of this award, the Citation Star, was established by Congress on July 19, 1918, and retroactively awarded to soldiers for "gallantry in action," back to the Spanish-American War. The Silver Star medal replaced the Citation Star in 1932 and is awarded for gallantry in action which, while of a lesser degree than that required for award of the Distinguished Service Cross, must nevertheless have been performed with marked distinction.

Distinguished Flying Cross

Established by Congress July 2, 1926, and awarded for heroism or extraordinary achievement while participating in aerial flight. Awards are made only to recognize single acts of heroism or extraordinary achievement, not sustained operational activities against an armed enemy. Initial awards were given to persons who made record-breaking long-distance and endurance flights or who set altitude records.

Soldier's Medal

Established by Congress July 2, 1926, to recognize acts of heroism not involving actual conflict with an enemy. The same degree of heroism is required as for the award of the Distinguished Flying Cross. The performance must have involved

personal hazard or danger and the voluntary risk of life under conditions not involving conflict with an armed enemy. Awards are not made solely on the basis of having saved a life.

Bronze Star

Established by executive order Feb. 4, 1944, largely to raise the morale of ground troops in WWII, on the recommendation of Gen. George C. Marshall. It is awarded to any person who, while serving in any capacity in or with the U.S. military, distinguishes himself or herself by heroic or meritorious achievement or service not involving participation in aerial flight.

Purple Heart

The original Purple Heart, designated as the Badge of Military Merit, was established by Gen. George Washington on Aug. 7, 1782. Following the American Revolution, the badge fell into disuse until 1932, the 200th anniversary of Washington's birth. During WWII, the Order of the Purple Heart was awarded for both wounds received in action and for meritorious service. Following the introduction of the Legion of Merit, the Purple Heart was awarded only for combat wounds. Today, it is awarded to any armed forces member who, while serving with the U.S. Armed Services, has been wounded or killed, or who has died or may hereafter die after being wounded in action against an enemy of the U.S. or in an armed conflict in which the U.S. or friendly foreign forces are engaged; as the result of an act of any hostile foreign force; as a result of an international terrorist attack against the U.S. or a friendly foreign nation; or as a result of military operations outside the U.S. as part of a peacekeeping force. Wounds must be inflicted directly by enemy action, including while held as a prisoner of war or while being taken captive.

U.S. Army, Navy, Air Force, Marine Corps, and Coast Guard Insignia

Source: Dept. of the Army, Dept. of the Navy, Dept. of the Air Force, U.S. Dept. of Defense; U.S. Coast Guard, U.S. Dept. of Homeland Security

Army

General of the Armies—Gen. John J. Pershing (1860-1948), the only person to have held this rank while living, was authorized to prescribe his own insignia but never wore in excess of four stars. Congress established the rank in 1799 to be bestowed on George Washington; Washington was finally promoted to the rank by joint resolution of Congress, approved by Pres. Gerald Ford, Oct. 19, 1976.

General of the Army—Five silver stars fastened together in a circle and the coat of arms of the U.S. in gold color metal with shield and crest enameled. Reserved for wartime use only.

Rank	Insignia
General of the Army*	Five silver stars
General	Four silver stars
Lieutenant General	Three silver stars
Major General	Two silver stars
Brigadier General	One silver star
Colonel	Silver eagle
Lieutenant Colonel	Silver oak leaf
Major	Gold oak leaf
Captain	Two silver bars
First Lieutenant	One silver bar
Second Lieutenant	One gold bar

Warrant Officers

Grade Five—Silver bar with enamel black line.
Grade Four—Silver bar with 4 enamel black squares.
Grade Three—Silver bar with 3 enamel black squares.
Grade Two—Silver bar with 2 enamel black squares.
Grade One—Silver bar with 1 enamel black square.

Noncommissioned Officers

Sergeant Major of the Army (E-9)—Three chevrons above 3 arcs, with a U.S. coat of arms centered on the chevrons, flanked by 2 stars—1 star on each side of the eagle. Also distinctive red-and-white shield collar insignia.
Command Sergeant Major (E-9)—Three chevrons above 3 arcs with a 5-pointed star with a wreath around the star between the chevrons and arcs.
Sergeant Major (E-9)—Three chevrons above 3 arcs with a 5-pointed star between the chevrons and arcs.
First Sergeant (E-8)—Three chevrons above 3 arcs with a lozenge between the chevrons and arcs.
Master Sergeant (E-8)—Three chevrons above 3 arcs.
Sergeant First Class (E-7)—Three chevrons above 2 arcs.
Staff Sergeant (E-6)—Three chevrons above 1 arc.
Sergeant (E-5)—Three chevrons.
Corporal (E-4)—Two chevrons.

Specialists

Specialist (E-4)—Eagle device only.

Other Enlisted

Private First Class (E-3)—One chevron above 1 arc.
Private (E-2)—One chevron.
Private (E-1)—None.
*Rank reserved for wartime use only.

Air Force

Insignia for Air Force officers are identical to those of the Army. Insignia for enlisted personnel are worn on both sleeves and consist of 1 star and an appropriate number of rockers. Chevrons appear above 5 rockers for the top three noncommissioned officer ranks, as follows (in ascending order): Master Sergeant, 1 chevron; Senior Master Sergeant, 2 chevrons; Chief Master Sergeant, 3 chevrons. The insignia of the Chief Master Sergeant of the Air Force has 3 chevrons and a wreath around the star design, while the Command Chief Master Sergeant insignia features an additional star. General of the Air Force is reserved for wartime use only.

Navy

The following stripes are worn on the lower sleeves of the Service Dress Blue uniform. They are of gold embroidery.

Rank	Insignia
Fleet Admiral*	1 two inch with 4 one-half inch
Admiral	1 two inch with 3 one-half inch
Vice Admiral	1 two inch with 2 one-half inch
Rear Admiral (upper half)	1 two inch with 1 one-half inch
Rear Admiral (lower half)	1 two inch
Captain	4 one-half inch
Commander	3 one-half inch
Lieutenant Commander	2 one-half inch with 1 one-quarter inch between
Lieutenant	2 one-half inch
Lieutenant (jr. grade)	1 one-half inch with 1 one-quarter inch above
Ensign	1 one-half inch
Warrant Officer W-5	½" stripe under ⅛" blue strip with 1 break
Warrant Officer W-4	½" stripe with 1 break
Warrant Officer W-3	½" stripe with 2 breaks, 2" apart
Warrant Officer W-2	½" stripe with 3 breaks, 2" apart

Enlisted personnel (noncommissioned petty officers)—Rating badge worn on the upper left sleeve consisting of a spread eagle, appropriate number of chevrons, and centered specialty mark.
* = Rank reserved for wartime use only.

Marine Corps

Marine Corps' distinctive cap and collar ornament is the Marine Corps emblem—a combination of the American eagle, a globe, and an anchor. Marine Corps and Army officer insignia are similar. Marine Corps enlisted insignia, although basically similar to the Army's, feature crossed rifles beneath the chevrons. Marine Corps enlisted rank insignia are as follows:

Sergeant Major of the Marine Corps (E-9)—Same as Sergeant Major (below) but with Marine Corps emblem in the center with a 5-pointed star on both sides of the emblem.
Sergeant Major (E-9)—Three chevrons above 4 rockers with a 5-pointed star in the center.
Master Gunnery Sergeant (E-9)—Three chevrons above 4 rockers with a bursting bomb insignia in the center.
First Sergeant (E-8)—Three chevrons above 3 rockers with a diamond in the middle.
Master Sergeant (E-8)—Three chevrons above 3 rockers with crossed rifles in the middle.
Gunnery Sergeant (E-7)—Three chevrons above 2 rockers with crossed rifles in the middle.
Staff Sergeant (E-6)—Three chevrons above 1 rocker with crossed rifles in the middle.
Sergeant (E-5)—Three chevrons above crossed rifles.
Corporal (E-4)—Two chevrons above crossed rifles.
Lance Corporal (E-3)—One chevron above crossed rifles.
Private First Class (E-2)—One chevron.
Private (E-1)—None.

Coast Guard

Coast Guard insignia follow Navy custom, with certain minor changes such as the officer cap insignia. The Coast Guard shield is worn on both sleeves of officers and on the right sleeve of all enlisted personnel.

Federal Service Academies

U.S. Military Academy, West Point, NY. Founded 1802. Awards B.S. degree and Army commission for a 5-year service obligation. **Website:** www.usma.edu

U.S. Naval Academy, Annapolis, MD. Founded 1845. Awards B.S. degree and Navy or Marine Corps commission for a 5-year service obligation. **Website:** www.usna.edu

U.S. Air Force Academy, Colorado Springs, CO. Founded 1954. Awards B.S. degree and Air Force commission for a 6-year service obligation. **Website:** www.usafa.af.mil

U.S. Coast Guard Academy, New London, CT. Founded 1876. Awards B.S. degree and Coast Guard commission for a 5-year service obligation. **Website:** www.cga.edu

U.S. Merchant Marine Academy, Kings Point, NY. Founded 1943. Awards B.S. degree; a license as a deck, engineer, or dual officer; and a U.S. Naval Reserve commission. Service obligations vary according to options taken by the graduate. **Website:** www.usmma.edu

Casualties in Principal Wars of the U.S.

Source: U.S. Dept. of Defense; U.S. Coast Guard, U.S. Dept. of Homeland Security

Data prior to World War I are based on incomplete records in many cases. Casualty data are confined to dead and wounded personnel and, therefore, exclude personnel captured or missing in action who were subsequently returned to military control.

	Branch of service	Number serving	Battle deaths	Other deaths	Wounds not mortal[1]	Total[2]
				CASUALTIES		
Revolutionary War .... Total 1775-83	Total	184,000 to 250,000[13]	4,435	—	6,188	10,623
War of 1812 .... Total 1812-15	Total	286,730[14]	2,260	—	4,505	6,765
	Army	—	1,950	—	4,000	5,950
	Navy	—	265	—	439	704
	Marines	—	45	—	66	111
Mexican War .... Total 1846-48	Total	78,718[14]	1,733	11,550	4,152	17,435
	Army	—	1,721	11,550	4,102	17,373
	Navy	—	1	—	3	4
	Marines	—	11	—	47	58
	Coast Guard[8] ..	71 off.	—	—	—	—
Civil War 1861-65 Union forces[3] .... Total	Total	2,213,363	140,414	224,097	281,881	646,392
	Army	2,128,948[14]	138,154	221,374	280,040	639,568
	Navy	84,415	2,112	2,411	1,710	6,233
	Marines	(in Navy total)	148	312	131	591
	Coast Guard[8] ..	219 off.	1	—	—	1
Confederate forces (estimate)[3] ..... Total ...	Total	600,000 to 1.5 mil	74,524	59,297	—	133,821
Spanish-American War .... Total 1898	Total	306,760	385	2,061	1,662	4,108
	Army[9]	280,564	369	2,061	1,594	4,024
	Navy	22,875	10	—	47	57
	Marines	3,321	6	—	21	27
	Coast Guard[8] ..	660	0	—	—	—
World War I .... Total .... Apr. 6, 1917-Nov. 11, 1918	Total	4,734,991	53,402	63,114	204,002	320,518
	Army[10]	4,057,101	50,510	55,868	193,663	300,041
	Navy	599,051	431	6,856	819	8,106
	Marines	78,839	2,461	390	9,520	12,371
	Coast Guard ...	8,835	30	81	—	111
World War II[4] .... Total .... Dec. 7, 1941-Dec. 31, 1946	Total	16,112,566	291,557	113,842	670,846	1,076,245
	Army[11]	11,260,000	234,874	83,400	565,861	884,135
	Navy[12]	4,183,466	36,950	25,664	37,778	100,392
	Marines	669,100	19,733	4,778	67,207	91,718
	Coast Guard ...	241,093	574	1,343	—	1,917
Korean War[5] .... Total .... June 25, 1950-July 27, 1953	Total	5,720,000	33,739	2,835	103,284	139,858
	Army	2,834,000	27,731	2,125	77,596	107,452
	Navy	1,177,000	503	154	1,576	2,233
	Marines	424,000	4,267	242	23,744	28,253
	Air Force	1,285,000	1,238	314	368	1,920
	Coast Guard ...	44,143	—	—	—	—
Vietnam War[6] .... Total .... Aug. 4, 1964-Jan. 27, 1973	Total	8,744,000	47,434	10,786	153,303	211,523
	Army	4,368,000	30,963	7,261	96,802	135,026
	Navy	1,842,000	1,631	935	4,178	6,744
	Marines	794,000	13,095	1,749	51,392	66,236
	Air Force	1,740,000	1,745	841	931	3,517
	Coast Guard ...	8,000	7	2	60	69
Persian Gulf War .... Total 1991	Total	2,225,000	147	235	467	849
	Army	782,000	98	126	354	578
	Navy	669,000	5	50	12	67
	Marines	213,000	24	44	92	160
	Air Force	561,000	20	15	9	44
	Coast Guard ...	400	—	—	—	—
Iraq War[7] .... Total .... Mar. 19, 2003-Dec. 15, 2011	Total	269,363[15]	3,519	973	32,292	36,784
	Army	99,664[15]	2,574	727	22,543	25,844
	Navy	61,018[15]	63	49	672	784
	Marines	66,166[15]	852	171	8,625	9,648
	Air Force	42,515[15]	29	26	452	507
	Coast Guard ...	1,250[15]	1	—	1	2

— = Not available. Off. = Officers. **Note:** As of Aug. 2023, there were 1,845 battle deaths, 504 non-hostile deaths, and 20,149 wounded in Op. Enduring Freedom (Oct. 7, 2001-Dec. 31, 2014), mostly in Afghanistan and the Persian Gulf area; 77 battle deaths, 30 non-hostile deaths, and 620 wounded in Operation Freedom's Sentinel (Jan. 1, 2015-Aug. 30, 2021) in Afghanistan, including 13 killed in attack on Kabul's airport in Aug. 2021 during U.S. withdrawal; 20 battle deaths, 88 non-hostile deaths, and 295 wounded in Operation Inherent Resolve (Aug. 8, 2014-) against ISIS in Iraq and Syria. (1) Marine Corps data for Iraq War, World War II, Spanish-American War, and prior wars represent the number of individuals wounded, whereas all other data in this column represent the total number (incidence) of wounds. (2) Totals for all branches do not include categories for which no data are listed. (3) From the final report of the Provost Marshal General, 1863-66. Authoritative statistics for the Confederate forces are not available. In addition, an estimated 26,000-31,000 Confederate personnel died in Union prisons. New estimates published in Civil War History in 2012 recalculated the death toll for both sides and determined that it was 20% higher than previously thought, at 750,000. (4) Data are for Dec. 1, 1941, through Dec. 31, 1946, when hostilities were officially terminated by presidential proclamation; few battle deaths or wounds not mortal were incurred after Japanese acceptance of Allied peace terms on Aug. 14, 1945. Numbers serving Dec. 1, 1941-Aug. 31, 1945: Total—14,903,213; Army—10,420,000; Navy—3,883,520; Marine Corps—599,693. (5) As a result of an ongoing Dept. of Defense review of available Korean War casualty record information, updates have been made to previously reported figures for battle deaths and other deaths. (6) Number serving Aug. 5, 1964-Jan. 27, 1973 (date of cease-fire). Includes casualties incurred in Mayaguez incident. Wounds not mortal exclude 150,341 persons not requiring hospital care. (7) Military deaths during the invasion phase, which ended Apr. 30, 2003, totaled 115 combat-related and 23 other. (8) Then known as the U.S. Revenue Cutter Services, predecessor to the U.S. Coast Guard. (9) Number serving Apr. 21-Aug. 13, 1898, while dead and wounded data are for May 1-Aug. 31, 1898. Active hostilities ceased on Aug. 13, 1898, but the U.S. and Spain did not exchange ratifications of the treaty of peace until Apr. 11, 1899. (10) Includes Army Air Forces battle deaths and wounds not mortal, as well as casualties suffered by American forces in northern Russia to Aug. 25, 1919, and in Siberia to Apr. 1, 1920. Other deaths cover Apr. 1, 1917-Dec. 31, 1918. (11) Includes Army Air Forces. (12) Battle deaths and wounds not mortal include casualties incurred in Oct. 1941 due to hostile action. (13) Estimated. (14) As reported by Commissioner of Pensions in his Annual Report for Fiscal Year 1903. (15) Number serving as of Mar. 31, 2003, i.e., does not include numbers of troops deployed since then.

Timeline of Major Wars Since 1066

Norman Conquest
1066-71
William I, duke of Normandy, landed on the English coast near Hastings on Sept. 28, 1066, and defeated Harold II, Saxon king of England, at Battle of Hastings Oct. 14. William crowned king Dec. 25 in Westminster Abbey. Most revolts were suppressed by 1071. **Conquest linked England's interests with those of the continent and led to its rise as a powerful monarchy.**

Crusades
1095-1270/1291
Military expeditions undertaken by **Western European Christians**, usually at the behest of the **papacy**, to recover **Jerusalem** and other Biblical places of pilgrimage from **Muslim** control. In the long term, stimulated trade and flow of ideas between East and West. Pope Urban II called Nov. 27, 1095, for the **First Crusade**; Crusaders took Jerusalem on July 15, 1099, massacred inhabitants, and founded four temporary states: Antioch, Edessa, Jerusalem, and Tripoli. The failed **Second Crusade** was prompted by Muslims' capture of Edessa in 1144. Jerusalem was captured by Ayyubid sultan Saladin on Oct. 2, 1187, leading to the **Third Crusade**, which involved the Holy Roman emperor, Frederick I (Barbarossa); the French king, Philip II (Augustus); and the English king, Richard I (Lion-Heart) but did not lead to a Crusader victory. The **Fourth Crusade** sacked Constantinople on Apr. 13, 1204. The **Fifth Crusade** began with capture of Damietta in Egypt (1219) but failed at Cairo. A **Sixth Crusade** led to the Treaty of Jaffa in 1229, giving Jerusalem to the Crusaders until 1244, when its seizure by the Khwarezmians led to the launch of a **Seventh Crusade**. The last crusade abruptly ended when its leader, French King Louis IX, died in 1270. The last major Crusader stronghold, Acre, was lost on May 18, 1291.

Hundred Years War
1337-1453
Series of armed conflicts over rival claims to the French throne, broken by a number of truces and peace treaties. Edward III declared self king of France in 1338 and invaded, with victories at Crécy (1346) and Poitiers (1356). **Treaty of Brétigny** signed May 8, 1360, but French king Charles V renewed fighting in 1369. Truce from 1396 until **Henry V** of England invaded in 1415 and **defeated French army at Agincourt**, capturing land north of Loire River, including Paris. **Treaty of Troyes** in 1420 made Henry VI heir of both thrones. The siege of French stronghold Orléans, lifted in 1429 with help from **Joan of Arc**, turned tide in favor of French, who won last battle (1453). **War ended English claims to France, paved way for French absolute monarchy.**

Wars of the Roses
1455-85
Series of dynastic civil wars for the throne in England fought by the **rival houses of Lancaster and York**. Richard, third duke of York, in conflict with the Lancastrian King **Henry VI**, won victories at St. Albans (1455) and Northampton (1460); Richard died at Battle of Wakefield on Dec. 30, 1460, before coronation, leaving his son to become King Edward IV. Henry VI imprisoned in Tower of London, 1465. Edward died in 1483; his brother became **Richard III** after usurping throne from Edward V, nephew. Henry Tudor defeated Richard III at the Battle of Bosworth Field (1485). As Henry VII, he married Edward IV's daughter Elizabeth, 1486, **uniting the houses.**

Thirty Years' War
1618-48
A series of religious and political conflicts involving **most countries of Western Europe**; majority of fighting in Germany, devastating it. Protestants stormed Habsburg palace in the "Defenestration of Prague" (May 23, 1618). Major conflicts included defeat of King Christian IV of Denmark and Norway by Catholic League (1626); victories by Lutheran King Gustav II Adolph of Sweden at Breitenfeld (1631) and Lützen (1632). France, under cardinal and statesman **Richelieu**, chief minister of King Louis XIII, declared war on the Habsburgs in May 1635; defeated Austro-Bavarian army (Aug. 3, 1645), leading to Truce of Ulm. **Peace of Westphalia** signed at Münster on Oct. 24, 1648, bringing peace by recognizing the rulers' sovereignty within their lands and their right to determine the religious beliefs of their subjects.

English Civil Wars
1638-60
Series of conflicts between followers of King Charles (Cavaliers) and of Parliament (Roundheads), over divine right of king versus Parliament's right to control national finances. Presbyterian Scots, allied with Parliament, rioted and in 1640 occupied the northern counties of England. **Oliver Cromwell**, second in command of Parliament's New Model Army, destroyed the king's army at Battle of Naseby (June 14, 1645); first civil war ended May 1646 when Charles surrendered to the Scots. Charles later allied with Scots but was defeated by Cromwell at Preston Aug. 17-19, 1648, and executed Jan. 30, 1649. Parliament abolished monarchy and House of Lords. Cromwell suppressed Irish and Scottish rebellions, was briefly succeeded by son Richard after death (1658). **Charles II restored to the throne** by the "Long Parliament," May 1660.

War of the Spanish Succession
1701-14
War fought by the Grand Alliance (originally England, Netherlands, Denmark, and Austria; later also Portugal), against coalition of France, Spain, and a number of small Italian and German principalities to preserve balance of power after death of Spanish king Charles II. Opened with invasion of Italy, via Venice, by an Austrian army under Prince Eugène of Savoy in May 1701. France forced to withdraw from Netherlands and Italy in 1706 and were finally defeated in 1709 in bloodiest battle of the war at French village of Malplaquet. Treaties of Rastatt and Baden signed in 1714; **Austria given control of Spanish Netherlands, and peace settled between Austria and France.**

War of the Austrian Succession
1740-48
Conflict over rival claims for the **hereditary dominions of the Habsburg family**, following death (1740) of Charles VI, Holy Roman emperor and archduke of Austria. An alliance of Bavaria, France, Spain, Sardinia, Prussia, and Saxony fought against Austria, allied with Holland and Great Britain. King Frederick the Great of Prussia captured Silesia from Austria in the First (1740-42) and Second (1744-45) Silesian Wars. British king George II defeated French army at Battle of Dettingen am Main (June 27, 1743). French conquered Austrian Netherlands (1745-46). Treaty of Aix-la-Chapelle Oct. 18, 1748, **restored most original borders; Prussia became significant force.**

Seven Years' War
1756-63
Worldwide conflicts fought for **control of Germany** and for **supremacy in colonial N America and India**. French defeated British Gen. Edward Braddock in Battle of Monongahela in 1754, leading to formal declaration of **French-Indian War**, May 1756. Frederick II of Prussia invaded Saxony on Aug. 29, 1756; defeated French at Rossbach (1757), Austrians at Leuthen (1757), Russians at Zorndorf (1758). By 1760, British conquered French Canada. Peter III of Russia signed armistice with Prussia, 1762. Treaty of Paris signed Feb. 10, 1763; Peace of Hubertusburg Feb. 15, 1763, between Prussia and Austria. **England emerged as leading world naval power.**

American Revolution
1775-83
Conflict between Great Britain and 13 British colonies in eastern N America. George Washington took command of the Continental Army, July 3, 1775, and King George III declared colonies traitors on Aug. 23. **Declaration of Independence of colonies adopted July 4, 1776.** France recognized the colonies' independence Feb. 6, 1778, followed by Spain on June 21, 1779; both pledged support. French fleet drove British fleet under Adm. Thomas Graves from Chesapeake Bay on Sept. 5, 1781. French and Americans laid siege to Yorktown, VA, Sept. 28-Oct. 19, forcing British Gen. Cornwallis to surrender. **Treaty of Paris** (Sept. 3, 1783) recognized U.S. independence.

Wars of French Revolution and Napoleonic Wars
1792-1815
Large-scale wars fought between France and two multinational coalitions. France declared war on the Austrian part of the Holy Roman Empire, Apr. 20, 1792. Newly created French Republic declared war on monarchs of Britain and Holland, Feb. 1, 1793, and of Spain, Mar. 7. Napoleon Bonaparte defeated Austria in N Italy (1796-97), captured Egypt from Britain (1798-99; Battle of the Pyramids, July 21, 1798), and became First Consul after coup d'état of Nov. 9-10, 1799. French Grande Armée later swept through Europe using innovative and aggressive tactics. French navy defeated by British under Adm. Horatio Nelson at **Trafalgar** (Oct. 21, 1805), but Napoleon defeated Austro-Russian forces at Austerlitz (Dec. 2) and controlled most of Europe except Russia and Great Britain by 1808. France suffered its first major defeat by Austria at Aspern-Essling, May 21-22, 1809. **Napoleon invaded Russia**, captured Moscow Sept. 14, 1812, but fled the bitter Russian winter and abandoned Germany after defeat at Leipzig, Oct. 16-19, 1813. Paris captured by Allied armies Mar. 30-31, 1814. Napoleon exiled to Elba May 4 but returned for "Hundred Days" reign, Mar. 20-June 28, 1815; **final defeat at Waterloo** by British and Prussian troops (June 18). The **Bourbon monarchy was restored under Louis XVIII**, and Britain, Prussia, Russia, and Austria maintained European peace.

Crimean War
1853-56

Conflict between **Russia** and coalition of **Great Britain, France, Sardinia, and Turkey for influence over Balkans** and the straits between the Black Sea and Mediterranean. Russia destroyed Turkish fleet at Sinope on Nov. 30, 1853. Britain and France declared war in Mar. 1854 and with Turkish troops defeated Russians at Battle of Alma River, Sept. 20. Lord Lucan of Britain prevented Russia from capturing Balaklava on Oct. 25. ("Charge of the Light Brigade" led by Lord Cardigan). Siege of Sevastopol ended when Russia evacuated Sept. 8, 1855. Treaty of Paris signed Mar. 30, 1856; **curbed Russian expansion and loosened European power alignments.**

American Civil War
1861-65

Conflict between the U.S. (the Union) and 11 secessionist Southern states (the Confederate States of America). Union garrison at Fort Sumter in harbor of Charleston, SC, surrendered to Brig. Gen. P.G.T. Beauregard (Apr. 12-13, 1861). Under Beauregard, 22,000 Confederates repelled 30,000 Union troops under Gen. Irvin McDowell along Bull Run stream near Manassas, VA (July 21). The *Merrimack* (renamed *Virginia*) battled the *Monitor* Mar. 9, 1862. In **Battle of Antietam**, MD (Sept. 17), some 12,000 Northerners and 12,700 Southerners were killed or wounded. Pres. Abraham Lincoln announced **Emancipation Proclamation** Sept. 22. Confederate Gen. Robert E. Lee's 75,000 forces battled 88,000 Union troops under Gen. George Meade at **Gettysburg**, PA, July 1-3, 1863; Lee's army forced across the Potomac R. Lee surrendered to Ulysses S. Grant at **Appomattox Court House** in Virginia (Apr. 9, 1865). **The Union was preserved and slavery subsequently abolished.**

Franco-Prussian War
1870-71

German states led by Prussia defeated France, seizing Alsace and part of Lorraine. French defeated in several major battles, culminating at **Sedan** Sept. 1, 1870, when Prussian forces decisively defeated the French army and captured emperor Napoleon III. Prussian king William I was made emperor of unified Germany, Jan 18, 1871. **France surrendered** Jan. 28. Final treaty signed May 10; set the stage for later **German imperialistic expansion.**

Spanish-American War
1898

War waged by the U.S. to **liberate Cuba from Spanish rule.** A mysterious explosion, blamed on Spain by American newspapers, sank the U.S. battleship *Maine* in Havana's harbor (Feb. 15, 1898), killing 260. The U.S. called for Spain's withdrawal from Cuba, and Spain declared war (Apr. 24). William Rufus Shafter led 17,000 U.S. troops from Daiquirí to Santiago de Cuba, taking **San Juan Hill** with help of the Rough Riders under Teddy Roosevelt. Santiago de Cuba surrendered July 17. The Treaty of Paris (Dec. 10, 1898) provided for the **independence of Cuba** and the cession by Spain to the U.S. of **Puerto Rico, Guam, and for a $20 mil payment, the Philippine Islands.**

World War I
1914-18

Local European war that grew into a global war involving 32 nations: the Allies and the Associated Powers—28 nations including Great Britain, France, Russia, Italy, and the U.S.—versus the Central Powers of Germany, Austria-Hungary, Turkey, and Bulgaria. Archduke Francis Ferdinand of Austria assassinated in Sarajevo, Bosnia (June 28, 1914). Germany invaded France through Belgium; advance on Paris halted by the French under Gen. Joseph Jacques Césaire Joffre at the **First Battle of the Marne**, Sept. 5-12. Germany checked the Russian army at the Battle of Tannenberg, Aug. 26-30. The British suffered 57,470 casualties (19,240 dead) in the opening day of the **First Battle of the Somme** (July 1-Nov. 18, 1916), first of 12 battles that forced Germany back to Hindenburg Line. **U.S. declared war on Germany Apr. 6, 1917.** Russian involvement ended when Bolshevik party seized power on Nov. 7; signed armistice Dec. 15. German offensive halted by U.S. and French troops at **Second Battle of the Marne** (July 15-Aug. 5, 1918), turning point of the war. Allied counteroffensive broke the fortified defensive Hindenburg Line, and an armistice was signed Nov. 11.

World War II
1939-45

Global military conflict stemming from European unrest after World War I and Japan's aggressive expansion into Asia and the Pacific. **War in Europe:** Nazi-Soviet nonaggression pact (Aug. 23, 1939) freed Germany and the Soviet Union to attack Poland in Sept. **Britain and France declared war on Germany** Sept. 3. German forces raced through Europe (Apr.-June 1940), captured Paris June 14. **Italy declared war on France and Britain** June 10. German-Italian campaigns won the Balkans and N Africa by June 1941. U.S. entered war Dec. 1941. Three million Axis troops invaded Russia June 22, 1941, but Russian counterthrusts stopped the German advance (**Stalingrad**, Aug. 20, 1942-Feb. 2, 1943), and Allies took N Africa (Nov. 8, 1942-May 13, 1943), Italy (July 10, 1943-May 2, 1945). Normandy invaded on **D-Day**, June 6, 1944; Paris liberated Aug. 25. Leaders at Yalta Conference (Feb. 4-11, 1945) discussed defeat and division of Germany into four. Adolf Hitler committed suicide Apr. 30. **Germany surrendered unconditionally** May 7. **War in the Pacific:** Japan invaded China (July 7, 1937), joined alliance with Germany and Italy (Sept. 27, 1940), and signed nonaggression pact with Russia (Apr. 13, 1941); attacked Hawaii's Pearl Harbor, Dec. 7, 1941; U.S. declared war on Japan Dec. 8. **Battle of Midway** (June 4-7, 1942) repulsed Japanese advance. Marines landed on Guadalcanal Aug. 7. Navy defeated Japanese fleet at **Leyte Gulf**, Oct. 23-26, 1944. B-29 bombing raids on Japan began in Nov. Marines invaded Iwo Jima (Feb. 19-Mar. 16, 1945) with heavy casualties, then Okinawa (Apr. 1-June 21). **U.S. atom bombs dropped** on Hiroshima (Aug. 6) and Nagasaki (Aug. 9) and Soviet invasion of Manchuria (Aug. 8) **forced Japan to agree, on Aug. 14, to surrender;** formal surrender on Sept. 2.

Korean War
1950-53

Military struggle fought on the Korean Peninsula between the Democratic Peoples' Republic of Korea (N Korea) and the Republic of Korea (S Korea) that developed into an international war involving China allied with N Korea against the U.S. and other nations under the UN flag. DPRK army crossed the 38th parallel and invaded S Korea (June 25, 1950), entering Seoul (June 26). Amphibious assault launched at **Inchon** by Gen. Douglas MacArthur (Sept. 15) helped U.S. forces rout DPRK close to Yalu River by Nov. 24. The Chinese, in counterattack, retook Seoul (Jan. 4, 1951) but were forced back to the 38th parallel by Apr. 22. Armistice was signed (July 27, 1953) by the UN, DPRK, and China, but not ROK, **leaving the peninsula partitioned at about the 38th parallel.**

Vietnam War
1959-75

Struggle primarily in S Vietnam that widened into a war between S Vietnam supported mainly by the U.S. and N Vietnam supported by the USSR and China. Viet Minh, led by Communist leader Ho Chi Minh, formed the Democratic Republic of Vietnam (Sept. 2, 1945). Colonial power France withdrew after fortress at Dien Bien Phu fell (May 8, 1954). Pres. John F. Kennedy pledged U.S. commitment to S Vietnamese independence Dec. 14, 1961. USS *Maddox* destroyer damaged in **Gulf of Tonkin** (Aug. 2, 1964), prompting Congress to increase involvement. Regular bombing of N Vietnam began (Feb. 24, 1965), and the first U.S. combat ground forces arrived (Mar. 6). N Vietnamese Army siege of **Khe Sanh** (Jan. 21-Apr. 7, 1968) and the **"Tet" offensive** (Jan. 30) aimed to cause insurrection in the S. **My Lai Massacre** by U.S. soldiers of civilians (Mar. 16, 1968) created scandal, fueled U.S. disaffection with war. U.S. forces peaked at 543,400 in Apr. 1969. NVA **"Easter Offensive"** (Mar. 30, 1972) rebuffed, and U.S. responded with aerial bombings in May and Dec. U.S. withdrew after cease-fire, Jan. 1973. **NVA offensive captured Saigon, Apr. 30, 1975, and unified Vietnam under Communist rule.**

Persian Gulf Wars
1991, 2003-10

Conflicts fought principally between Iraq and the U.S. concerning Iraq's influence in the Middle East and its development of weapons of mass destruction. **First Gulf War:** Iraq under dictator Saddam Hussein invaded Kuwait Aug. 2, 1990, and annexed it; UN Security Council ordered Iraqi forces to withdraw by Jan. 15, 1991. Beginning Jan. 17, a U.S.-led multinational force (**Operation Desert Storm**) bombed military targets in Iraq and Kuwait. A coordinated air-land offensive (**Operation Desert Sabre**, begun Feb. 24) retook Kuwait City Feb. 26, and a permanent cease-fire was signed on Apr. 6. Iraq was ordered to pay reparations to Kuwait, reveal locations of biological and chemical weapons, and eliminate weapons of mass destruction. **Second Gulf War:** The U.S. and UK mistakenly asserted that Iraq was still producing WMDs and posed an imminent threat. The UN passed Resolution 1441, Nov. 8, 2002, warning Iraq of "serious consequences" if it failed to cooperate fully and unconditionally with UN weapons inspectors. Iraq rejected a Mar. 17, 2003, U.S. ultimatum demanding Hussein and his sons leave Iraq. U.S. launched **Operation Iraqi Freedom** Mar. 19, 2003, with support from UK and other allies, but without full UN Security Council support. Baghdad fell Apr. 9, and major combat operations declared over May 1. Hussein was captured Dec. 13, 2003, but guerrilla opposition to U.S. troops and insurgent violence continued. U.S. combat operations in Iraq formally ended Aug. 31, 2010.

FOOD AND AGRICULTURE

Number and Acreage of Farms by State, 2000, 2022

Source: National Agricultural Statistics Service, U.S. Dept. of Agriculture

State	No. of farms (thous.) 2022	2000	Acreage in farms (mil) 2022	2000	Acreage per farm 2022	2000	State	No. of farms (thous.) 2022	2000	Acreage in farms (mil) 2022	2000	Acreage per farm 2022	2000
AL	38.1	47.0	8.2	9.0	215	191	NE	44.3	46.1	44.8	46.1	1,011	887
AK	1.0	0.6	0.9	0.9	850	1,569	NV	3.3	3.1	5.9	6.4	1,788	2,065
AZ	18.8	10.7	26.1	26.9	1,388	2,518	NH	4.1	3.3	0.4	0.4	105	133
AR	41.9	48.0	14.0	14.6	334	304	NJ	9.9	9.7	0.8	0.8	76	86
CA	68.4	83.1	24.0	28.0	351	337	NM	24.1	18.0	40.0	44.9	1,660	2,494
CO	38.8	30.0	31.8	31.6	820	1,060	NY	33.4	37.5	6.9	7.7	207	205
CT	5.5	4.2	0.4	0.4	69	86	NC	45.0	55.5	8.3	9.2	184	166
DE	2.3	2.6	0.5	0.6	230	215	ND	25.9	30.8	39.2	39.4	1,514	1,279
FL	47.3	44.0	9.7	10.4	205	238	OH	76.5	79.0	13.1	14.8	171	187
GA	41.3	49.1	10.2	10.9	247	223	OK	77.2	84.5	34.4	33.8	446	401
HI	7.3	5.5	1.1	1.4	151	251	OR	36.9	40.0	15.7	17.3	425	433
ID	24.4	24.5	11.5	11.9	471	486	PA	52.7	59.0	7.3	7.7	139	130
IL	70.7	77.0	27.0	27.5	382	357	RI	1.1	0.8	0.1	0.1	55	75
IN	54.8	63.4	14.8	15.2	270	240	SC	24.6	24.2	4.8	4.9	195	203
IA	84.9	94.0	30.5	32.5	359	346	SD	29.4	32.4	43.2	44.0	1,469	1,358
KS	57.7	64.5	45.7	47.5	792	736	TN	69.5	88.0	10.7	11.8	154	134
KY	73.5	90.0	12.9	13.7	176	152	TX	246.0	228.3	126.0	130.9	512	573
LA	27.4	29.0	8.0	8.0	292	277	UT	17.9	15.5	10.9	11.6	609	747
ME	7.6	7.1	1.3	1.4	171	190	VT	6.8	6.6	1.2	1.3	176	192
MD	12.4	12.4	2.0	2.1	161	172	VA	41.5	48.5	7.7	8.7	186	180
MA	7.2	6.1	0.5	0.5	69	89	WA	35.2	37.0	14.5	15.6	412	420
MI	44.3	53.0	9.2	10.2	208	192	WV	22.5	20.8	3.5	3.6	156	173
MN	67.1	81.0	25.4	27.9	379	344	WI	64.1	77.5	14.2	16.0	222	206
MS	34.1	42.0	10.3	11.2	302	266	WY	11.9	9.2	28.5	34.5	2,395	3,750
MO	95.0	109.0	27.5	30.2	289	277	U.S.	2,002.7	2,166.8	893.4	945.1	446	436
MT	27.1	27.8	57.9	59.3	2,137	2,133							

Supplemental Nutrition Assistance Program (SNAP), 1969-2022

Source: Food and Nutrition Service (FNS), U.S. Dept. of Agriculture

Fiscal year	Avg. participation (thous.)	Avg. monthly benefit per person	Total benefits (mil)	All other costs (mil)[1]	Total costs (mil)	Fiscal year	Avg. participation (thous.)	Avg. monthly benefit per person	Total benefits (mil)	All other costs (mil)[1]	Total costs (mil)
1969	2,878	$6.63	$228.8	$21.7	$250.5	2009	33,490	$125.31	$50,359.9	$3,260.0	$53,619.9
1970	4,340	10.55	549.7	27.2	576.9	2010	40,302	133.79	64,702.2	3,581.4	68,283.5
1975	17,064	21.40	4,385.5	233.2	4,618.7	2011	44,709	133.85	71,810.9	3,875.6	75,686.5
1980	21,082	34.47	8,720.9	485.6	9,206.5	2012	46,609	133.41	74,619.3	3,791.8	78,411.1
1985	19,899	44.99	10,743.6	959.6	11,703.2	2013	47,636	133.07	76,066.3	3,792.7	79,859.0
1990	20,049	58.78	14,142.8	1,304.5	15,447.3	2014	46,664	125.01	69,998.8	4,061.5	74,060.3
1995	26,619	71.27	22,764.1	1,856.3	24,620.4	2015	45,767	126.81	69,645.1	4,301.6	73,946.8
2000	17,194	72.62	14,983.2	2,070.7	17,054.0	2016	44,220	125.40	66,539.3	4,372.9	70,912.1
2003	21,250	83.94	21,404.3	2,412.0	23,816.3	2017	42,317	125.47	63,711.1	4,464.0	68,175.0
2004	23,811	86.16	24,618.9	2,480.1	27,099.0	2018	40,776	124.50	60,916.9	4,532.0	65,448.8
2005	25,628	92.89	28,567.9	2,504.1	31,072.0	2019	35,702	129.83	55,622.3	4,763.1	60,385.4
2006	26,549	94.75	30,187.4	2,715.7	32,903.1	2020	39,853	155.10	74,174.7	4,999.6	79,174.2
2007	26,316	96.18	30,373.3	2,800.3	33,173.5	2021	41,549	217.65	108,515.9	5,243.7	113,759.7
2008	28,223	102.19	34,608.4	3,031.3	37,639.6	2022	41,189	230.34	113,851.4	5,484.1	119,335.5

(1) Includes the federal share of state administrative expenses, nutrition education, and employment and training programs, in addition to other federal costs (e.g., benefit and retailer redemption and monitoring, payment accuracy, EBT [electronic benefit transfer] systems, program evaluation and modernization, program access, health and nutrition pilot projects).

U.S. Federal Food Assistance Programs, 1990-2022

Source: Food and Nutrition Service (FNS), U.S. Dept. of Agriculture
(in millions of dollars; for fiscal years ending on Sept. 30)

Program	1990	1995	2000	2005	2010	2015	2020	2021	2022
Supplemental Nutrition Assistance Program (SNAP)[1]	$15,491	$24,620	$17,054	$31,073	$68,284	$73,946	$79,173	$113,828	$119,378
Puerto Rico nutrition assistance[2]	937	1,131	1,268	1,495	2,001	1,951	1,938	2,038	2,502
Natl. school lunch[3]	3,834	5,160	6,149	8,031	10,880	13,003	10,317	8,359	21,454
School breakfast[3,4]	596	1,048	1,393	1,927	2,859	3,892	3,548	3,130	6,498
WIC (Women, Infants, and Children)[5]	2,122	3,440	3,982	4,994	6,690	6,241	5,012	5,043	5,740
Summer food service[6]	164	237	267	267	359	488	4,310	10,674	601
Child and adult care[7]	813	1,464	1,683	2,111	2,638	3,307	3,023	3,795	3,931
Special milk[4]	19	17	15	16	12	11	4	3	4
Nutrition for the elderly (NSIP)[8]	142	148	137	4	3	3	2	2	1
Food distrib. on Indian reserv.[9]	66	65	76	76	95	120	167	126	112
Commodity supplemental food[9]	85	99	98	156	165	193	286	296	351
Food distrib. to charitable insts.[10]	104	64	2	4	1	0	0	0	0
Emergency food assistance (TEFAP)[11]	334	135	225	373	631	525	769	1,258	1,046
Total[12]	24,707	37,628	32,349	50,527	94,618	103,680	108,549	148,552	161,618

Note: 2022 data are preliminary. All data subject to revision by the FNS. (1) Formerly known as the Food Stamp Program. Includes benefits and admin. expenses. (2) Provides benefits analogous to SNAP. (3) Nine-month averages (summer months excluded). (4) Cash payments based on federal reimbursement rates to states. (5) Includes food benefits, nutrition services and admin. funds, Farmers' Market Nutrition Program, infrastructure, breastfeeding promotion and peer counseling, program evaluation, and technical assistance. (6) Includes cash payments, entitlement and bonus commodities, and the federal share of state and sponsor admin. costs. (7) Includes cash payments, entitlement and bonus commodities, cash-in-lieu of commodities, sponsor admin. costs, start-up costs, and audits. (8) For 2003 and on, Nutrition Services Incentive Program administered by the Agency on Aging, Dept. of Health and Human Services; FNS costs limited to value of commodities distributed. (9) Includes cost of commodity distrib. (entitlement and bonus) and federal share of state admin. expenses. (10) Includes summer camps. (11) Includes cost of commodities to hunger relief orgs. (e.g., food banks, soup kitchens) and federal share of state admin. expenses. (12) Does not include federal share of state admin. costs for some programs not shown.

U.S. Cost of Food, 2023

Source: Center for Nutrition Policy and Promotion (CNPP), U.S. Dept. of Agriculture (USDA)

(costs for individuals are for those in four-person households)

Age-gender group Individual[3]	Thrifty plan[1] Weekly[2]	Monthly[3]	Low-cost plan[2] Weekly	Monthly	Moderate-cost plan[2] Weekly	Monthly	Liberal plan[2] Weekly	Monthly
Child[3]								
1 year	$25.10	$108.90	$35.80	$155.00	$40.70	$176.30	$49.20	$213.10
2-3 years	37.80	163.70	37.80	163.90	45.40	196.90	55.10	238.70
4-5 years	41.20	178.50	39.10	169.30	48.20	209.10	58.30	252.60
6-8 years	45.90	199.00	55.10	238.70	66.30	287.10	77.40	335.30
9-11 years	53.10	230.00	59.00	255.80	76.10	329.70	88.60	384.10
Male								
12-13 years	56.80	246.20	68.70	297.90	85.30	369.70	100.00	433.30
14-19 years	71.70	310.50	69.80	302.60	87.50	379.10	101.40	439.20
20-50 years	69.80	302.40	68.90	298.30	86.40	374.50	105.10	455.40
51-70 years	61.50	266.50	65.00	281.70	81.40	352.70	97.30	421.50
71+ years	58.60	254.00	64.30	278.70	79.40	343.80	96.90	419.90
Female								
12-13 years	49.10	212.80	58.70	254.10	70.10	303.70	86.70	375.70
14-19 years	56.90	246.70	58.60	254.00	69.90	302.90	86.40	374.40
20-50 years	55.80	241.80	59.70	258.50	73.00	316.20	93.30	404.10
51-70 years	51.70	224.10	58.40	252.90	72.30	313.30	86.70	375.50
71+ years	56.90	246.70	58.00	251.50	71.50	309.70	85.50	370.60
4-person family:[4]	224.60	973.30						

Note: As of June 2023. A basis of all four food plans is that all meals and snacks are prepared at home. All costs are rounded to nearest 10 cents. Monthly costs are calculated by multiplying the weekly costs by 4.333. (1) Represents a nutritious, practical, cost-effective diet. The nutritional bases are the Dietary Reference Intakes and the *Dietary Guidelines for Americans, 2020-2025*. For specific foods and quantities, see *Thrifty Food Plan, 2021*. Plan is based on 2013-16 consumption and 2015-16 price data and updated to current dollars by using the Consumer Price Index for specific food items. (2) Represents a nutritious diet at three different cost levels. The nutritional bases of the food plans are the 1997-2005 Dietary Reference Intakes, 2005 Dietary Guidelines for Americans, and 2005 MyPyramid food intake recommendations. In addition to cost, differences among plans are in specific foods and quantities of foods. For specific foods and quantities of foods in the food plans, see *The Low-Cost, Moderate-Cost, and Liberal Food Plans, 2007*. All three food plans are based on 2001-02 data and updated to current dollars by using the Consumer Price Index for specific food items. (3) Age range varies slightly from standard: 14-19 years and 20-50 years, replacing 14-18 years and 19-50 years, respectively. (4) Defined as a couple (male and female), 20-50 years old, and two children ages 6-8 and 9-11 years.

U.S. Household Food Security by Selected Characteristics, 2021

Source: Economic Research Service, U.S. Dept. of Agriculture

(in thousands of households)

	Total[1]	Food secure No.	%	With low food security No.	%	With very low food security No.	%
All households	132,043	118,533	89.8%	8,428	6.4%	5,082	3.8%
Household composition							
With children under 18 years old	36,765	32,170	87.5	3,277	8.9	1,318	3.6
With children under 6 years old	15,406	13,418	87.1	1,473	9.6	515	3.3
Married-couple families	23,849	22,088	92.6	1,344	5.7	417	1.7
Female head, no spouse	9,197	6,965	75.7	1,497	16.3	735	8.0
Male head, no spouse	3,194	2,678	83.8	374	11.8	142	4.4
Other household with child[2]	524	438	83.6	NA	NA	NA	NA
With no children under 18 years old	95,278	86,364	90.6	5,150	5.4	3,764	4.0
More than one adult	56,113	52,215	93.1	2,458	4.3	1,440	2.6
Women living alone	21,641	18,781	86.8	1,568	7.2	1,292	6.0
Men living alone	17,524	15,367	87.7	1,125	6.4	1,032	5.9
With elderly	42,501	39,473	92.9	1,858	4.3	1,170	2.8
Elderly living alone	16,056	14,530	90.5	798	5.0	728	4.5
Race/ethnicity of households							
White, non-Hispanic	85,866	79,843	93.0	3,754	4.4	2,269	2.6
Black, non-Hispanic	16,951	13,597	80.2	2,019	11.9	1,335	7.9
Other, non-Hispanic	10,144	9,112	89.8	595	5.9	437	4.3
Hispanic[3]	19,082	15,983	83.8	2,059	10.7	1,040	5.5
Area of residence[4]							
Inside metropolitan area	113,842	102,295	89.9	7,219	6.3	4,328	3.8
In principal cities[5]	38,360	33,684	87.8	2,899	7.6	1,777	4.6
Not in principal cities	58,118	53,029	91.2	3,228	5.6	1,861	3.2
Outside metropolitan area	18,201	16,240	89.2	1,208	6.7	753	4.1

NA = Not reported. **Note:** Low food security households report food acquisition problems and reduced diet quality but typically few, if any, indications of reduced food intake. The very low food security category identifies households in which the food intake of one or more members was reduced and eating patterns disrupted because of insufficient money and other resources for food. (1) Totals exclude households of unknown food security status. Exclusions represented 0.2% of all households in 2021. (2) Households with children in complex living arrangements, e.g., children of other relatives or unrelated roommate or boarder. (3) Hispanics may be of any race. (4) Based on 2013 Office of Management and Budget delineations of metropolitan areas. (5) Households within incorporated areas of the largest cities in each metropolitan area. Residence inside or outside of principal cities unknown for about 15% of households in metropolitan statistical areas.

Trends in U.S. Food Insecurity in U.S. Households, 1998-2021
Source: Economic Research Service, U.S. Dept. of Agriculture

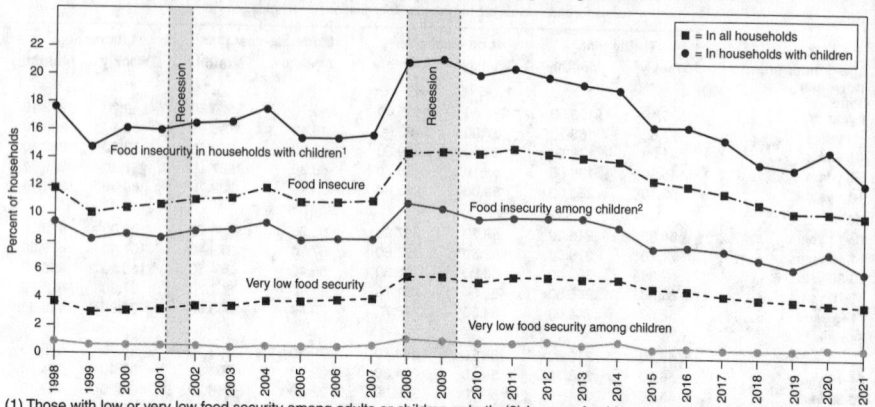

(1) Those with low or very low food security among adults or children or both. (2) In some food-insecure households with children, only adults were food insecure. Households with food-insecure children are those with low or very low food security among children.

U.S. Annual Per Capita Consumption of Selected Foods, 1970-2020
Source: Economic Research Service, U.S. Dept. of Agriculture; Distilled Spirits Council of the U.S.; Beer Institute; Wine Institute
(fruits and vegetables in pounds, beverages in gallons)

	1970	1990	2020	% change, 1970-2020		1970	1990	2020	% change, 1970-2020
Fresh fruit	100.6	117.1	139.4	38.6%	**Fresh vegetables**	154.4	176.4	181.9	17.9%
Apples	17.2	19.8	16.3	-5.6	Broccoli	0.5	3.4	5.9	1,000.5
Avocados	0.5	1.4	9.3	1,952.8	Carrots	6.0	8.3	7.7	29.2
Bananas	17.4	24.3	27.2	56.6	Cucumbers	2.8	4.7	7.5	166.3
Grapes	2.9	7.9	8.2	181.1	Garlic	0.4	1.4	1.7	285.6
Oranges	16.1	12.4	9.4	-41.6	Lettuce head	22.4	27.7	12.3	-44.9
Peaches/nectarines	5.8	5.5	2.4	-59.4	Onions	10.1	15.1	20.4	101.5
Strawberries	1.7	3.2	7.1	311.4	Potatoes	61.8	46.7	31.5	-49.1
Canned vegetables	100.7	110.3	86.6[1]	-14.0[2]	Tomatoes	12.1	15.5	19.3	59.0
Sweet corn	14.3	10.9	4.7[1]	-67.4[2]	**Beverages**				
Tomatoes	62.1	75.3	67.5	8.7	Orange juice	3.6	3.7	2.3	-36.0
Frozen vegetables	43.7	66.7	72.1[1]	64.9[2]	Coffee	33.4	26.8	26.2[3]	-21.5[4]
Broccoli	1.0	2.2	2.6	173.2	Beer	18.5	23.9	19.4	5.0
Carrots	1.4	2.3	1.8[1]	26.2[2]	Wine	1.3	2.0	3.1	136.2
Green peas	1.9	2.2	1.0[1]	-46.3[2]	**Sweeteners**	119.1	132.5	126.7	6.3
Potatoes	28.5	46.4	50.9	78.5	Sugar (refined)	101.8	64.4	68.8	-32.4
Sweet corn	5.7	8.6	6.0[1]	4.0[2]	Honey	1.0	0.8	1.3	34.2
					High fructose corn syrup	0.5	49.6	40.2	7,238.3

Note: All figures are rounded; percent change is calculated based on unrounded original data. Per capita consumption based on total population. Alcoholic beverage consumption would be higher if based on legal drinking age population. (1) As of 2019. (2) Percent change, 1970-2019. (3) As of 2015. (4) Percent change, 1970-2015.

U.S. Meat Production and Consumption, 1940-2023
Source: Economic Research Service, U.S. Dept. of Agriculture
(in millions of pounds)

Year	Beef Prod.	Beef Cons.	Veal Prod.	Veal Cons.	Lamb and mutton Prod.	Lamb and mutton Cons.	Pork Prod.	Pork Cons.	All red meats[1] Prod.	All red meats[1] Cons.	All poultry[2] Prod.	All poultry[2] Cons.
1940	7,175	7,257	981	981	876	873	10,044	9,701	19,076	18,812	NA	NA
1950	9,534	9,825	1,230	1,206	597	602	10,714	10,612	22,075	22,279	3,174	3,097
1960	14,753	15,490	1,109	1,118	768	856	13,905	14,057	30,535	31,521	6,310	6,168
1970	21,684	23,451	588	613	551	669	14,699	14,957	37,522	39,689	10,193	9,981
1980	21,643	23,560	400	420	318	351	16,617	16,838	38,978	41,170	14,173	13,525
1990	22,743	24,030	327	325	363	397	15,354	16,025	38,787	40,778	23,468	22,152
2000	26,888	27,338	225	225	234	354	18,952	18,643	46,299	46,560	36,073	30,508
2010	26,412	26,392	145	150	168	317	22,437	19,072	49,180	45,931	43,058	35,201
2015	23,760	24,771	88	88	155	357	24,517	20,656	48,520	45,872	45,769	38,785
2016	25,221	25,673	81	73	155	381	24,941	20,891	50,388	47,019	47,225	39,577
2017	26,187	26,492	80	78	150	396	25,584	21,035	51,991	48,000	48,178	40,236
2018	26,872	26,762	81	89	158	415	26,315	21,491	53,417	48,757	49,018	40,975
2019	27,155	27,272	79	81	153	422	27,638	22,188	55,015	49,963	50,251	42,081
2020	27,174	27,561	69	66	143	435	28,303	22,121	55,680	50,199	50,876	42,670
2023*	27,161	27,614	NA	NA	NA	NA	27,371	21,541	54,712	49,655	53,114	44,946

NA = Not available. * = July projection. (1) Includes beef, veal, lamb and mutton, and pork. May not add up to totals because of rounding. (2) Includes broilers, turkeys, and mature chicken.

Estimated Calorie Requirements

Source: *Dietary Guidelines for Americans, 2020-2025*, U.S. Dept. of Agriculture and U.S. Dept. of Health and Human Services
Estimated amount of calories, rounded to the nearest 200, needed to maintain energy balance by sex, for various age groups and levels of physical activity. In adults ages 19 and older, calorie needs generally decrease with age.

	Age (years)	Sedentary[1]	Moderately active[2]	Active[3]		Age (years)	Sedentary[1]	Moderately active[2]	Active[3]
Female[4]	2-3	1,000	1,000-1,200	1,000-1,400	Male	2-3	1,000	1,000-1,400	1,000-1,400
	4-8	1,200-1,400	1,400-1,600	1,400-1,800		4-8	1,200-1,400	1,400-1,600	1,600-2,000
	9-13	1,400-1,600	1,600-2,000	1,800-2,200		9-13	1,600-2,000	1,800-2,200	2,000-2,600
	14-18	1,800	2,000	2,400		14-18	2,000-2,400	2,400-2,800	2,800-3,200
	19-30	1,800-2,000	2,000-2,200	2,400		19-30	2,400-2,600	2,600-2,800	3,000
	31-50	1,800	2,000	2,200		31-50	2,200-2,400	2,400-2,600	2,800-3,000
	51+	1,600	1,800	2,000-2,200		51+	2,000-2,200	2,200-2,400	2,400-2,800

Note: Based on Estimated Energy Requirements (EER) equations, using reference heights and weights. The reference man is 5 ft 10 in. tall and weighs 154 lbs. The reference woman is 5 ft 4 in. tall and weighs 126 lbs. (1) Includes only the physical activity of independent living. (2) Includes physical activity equivalent to walking 1.5-3 mi per day at 3-4 mph. (3) Includes physical activity equivalent to walking more than 3 mi per day at 3-4 mph. (4) Calorie needs during the first trimester of pregnancy generally do not increase compared to prepregnancy needs. Additional calories needed for the later trimesters and during lactation include approximately 300-400 additional calories.

Top Sources of Sugars, Saturated Fat, and Sodium in U.S. Diets

Source: *Dietary Guidelines for Americans, 2020-2025*; National Health and Nutrition Examination Survey, 2013-16

Saturated fat		Sodium		Sugars	
Source	**%**	**Source**	**%**	**Source**	**%**
Sandwiches	19	Sandwiches	21	Sugar-sweetened beverages	24
Desserts, sweet snacks	11	Rice, pasta, other grain-based mixed dishes	8	Desserts, sweet snacks	19
Rice, pasta, other grain-based mixed dishes	7	Vegetables, excl. starchy	7	Coffee, tea	11
Higher-fat milk, yogurt	6	Meat, poultry, seafood mixed dishes	5	Candy, sugars	9
Pizza	5	Pizza	5	Breakfast cereals, bars	7
Cheese	4	Poultry, excl. deli and mixed dishes	5	Sandwiches	7
Chips, crackers, savory snacks	4	Chips, crackers, savory snacks	5	Higher-fat milk, yogurt	4
Meat, poultry, seafood mixed dishes	4	Desserts, sweet snacks	4	Other	19
Poultry, excl. deli and mixed dishes	4	Soups	4		
Vegetables, excl. starchy	4	Starchy vegetables	4		
Eggs	3	Breakfast cereals, bars	3		
Meats, excl. deli and mixed dishes	3	Condiments, gravies	3		
Spreads	3	Deli, cured products	3		
Starchy vegetables	3	Eggs	3		
Other	20	Yeast breads, tortillas	3		
		Other	19		

Note: Data are for people ages 1 and older.

Understanding Food Components

Water dissolves and transports other nutrients throughout the body, aiding in the processes of digestion, absorption, circulation, and excretion. It helps regulate body temperature.

Macronutrients

Carbohydrates, of which sugars, fibers, and starches are the major types, are the most important source of energy for the body. The digestive system changes carbohydrates into glucose, which the body uses for energy for cells, tissues, and organs. The body stores extra sugar in the liver and muscles. Best sources: grains, beans, vegetables, fruits.

Fats provide energy by furnishing calories to the body. They also help the body absorb vitamins A, D, E, and K. Best sources of polyunsaturated and monounsaturated fats: olive, canola, and peanut oils; nuts and nut butters; fatty fish; olives; avocado. Sources of saturated fats: meats, cheeses, butter, cream, milk, lard.

Fiber is the portion of plant foods that our bodies cannot digest. There are two basic types: insoluble and soluble. Insoluble fibers help move food materials through the digestive tract; soluble fibers tend to slow them down. Both types absorb water, thus preventing constipation. Soluble fibers are also helpful in reducing blood cholesterol levels. Best sources: beans, bran, fruits, whole grains, vegetables.

Proteins, composed of amino acids, are essential to good nutrition. They build, maintain, and repair the body. Proteins from animal sources (eggs, meat, fish, milk) supply adequate amounts of all indispensable amino acids and are thus called complete. Proteins from plants, legumes, nuts, seeds, and vegetables can be combined to complete protein needs.

Vitamins

Vitamin A promotes good eyesight; plays a role in bone growth, reproduction, the immune system. Best sources: liver, sweet potatoes, carrots, kale, cantaloupe, fortified milk.

Vitamin B$_1$ (thiamin) is essential to energy metabolism and the growth, development, and function of cells. Best sources: whole grains, fortified bread and cereal, pork, fish.

Vitamin B$_2$ (riboflavin) is essential to growth, red blood cell production, and energy metabolism. Best sources: eggs, dairy products, organ meats, lean meats, bread products, fortified cereal, spinach.

Vitamin B$_6$ (pyridoxine and related compounds) is important in making antibodies and hemoglobin, maintaining normal nerve function, and protein metabolism. Best sources: fish, organ meats, beans, poultry, fruits, chickpeas, fortified cereal.

Vitamin B$_{12}$ (cobalamin) is needed to form red blood cells. Best sources: beef liver, clams, meat, fish, poultry, eggs.

Folate (vitamin B$_9$; folic acid is a synthetic form used in supplements and fortified foods) is required for making DNA and other genetic material and for cell division. Best sources: liver, dark green leafy vegetables, fruit, fruit juice, peanuts, beans, enriched breads, fortified cereals.

Niacin (vitamin B$_3$) helps turn food into energy and is important for cell development and function. Best sources: poultry, nuts, fish.

Other B vitamins include pantothenic acid and biotin.

Vitamin C (ascorbic acid) acts as an antioxidant; also needed to make collagen, a protein necessary for wound healing. Best sources: citrus fruits, broccoli, strawberries, cantaloupe, kiwi, Brussels sprouts, potatoes, tomatoes, red and green peppers.

Vitamin D is important for bone development. Best sources: sunlight, fortified dairy products, tuna, salmon.

Vitamin E is an antioxidant and enhances immune function. Best sources: vegetable oils, nuts, seeds, green leafy vegetables.

Vitamin K is necessary for formation of prothrombin, which helps blood to clot. Best dietary sources: green leafy vegetables, plant oils. Also made by intestinal bacteria.

Minerals

Calcium is needed to build and maintain bones and teeth. Best sources: dairy, leafy green vegetables.

Iron is a component of hemoglobin, which transports oxygen within blood, and of myoglobin, which supplies oxygen to the muscles. Best sources: lean meats, beans, green leafy vegetables, seafood, whole grains, fortified cereal.

Phosphorus is present in every cell of the body, and the majority of it can be found in bones and teeth. Best sources: cheese, milk, meats, poultry, fish.

Other minerals include chloride, chromium, copper, fluoride, iodine, magnesium, manganese, molybdenum, potassium, selenium, sodium, zinc.

Understanding Food Label Claims

Source: Center for Food Safety and Applied Nutrition, U.S. Food and Drug Admin. (FDA), U.S. Dept. of Health and Human Services; Food Safety and Inspection Service, Agricultural Marketing Service, U.S. Dept. of Agriculture (USDA)

Nutrition Packaging Terms

Manufacturers can make certain claims on processed food labels only if they meet the definitions specified here.

SUGAR. Sugar free: less than 0.5 g per serving; **No added sugars; Without added sugars:** no sugars or sugar-containing ingredients added during processing; must state if food is not "low calorie" or "reduced calorie"; **Unsweetened; No added sweeteners:** factual statements; **Reduced sugar:** at least 25% less sugar per serving than reference food.

FAT. Fat free: less than 0.5 g of total fat per serving; **Saturated fat free:** less than 0.5 g of saturated fat and less than 0.5 g of trans fatty acids per serving; **Low fat:** 3 g or less of total fat per serving (and per 50 g if the serving size is small, i.e., 30 g or less, 2 tbs or less); **Low saturated fat:** 1 g or less per serving and not more than 15% of calories from saturated fat; **Reduced fat; Less fat:** at least 25% less total fat per serving than reference food.

FIBER. High fiber: 20% or more of the daily value per serving; **Good source of fiber:** 10%-19% of the daily value per serving; **More fiber; Added fiber:** 10% or more of the daily value per serving than reference food.

SODIUM. Sodium free: less than 5 mg per serving; **Low sodium:** 140 mg or less per serving (and per 50 g if the serving size is small, i.e., 30 g or less, 2 tbs or less); **Very low sodium:** 35 mg or less per serving (and per 50 g if the serving size is small); **Reduced sodium; Less sodium:** at least 25% less per serving than reference food.

CALORIES. Calorie free: less than 5 calories per serving; **Low calorie:** 40 calories or less per serving (and per 50 g if the serving size is small, i.e., 30 g or less, 2 tbs or less); **Reduced calories; Fewer calories:** at least 25% fewer calories per serving than reference food.

CHOLESTEROL. Cholesterol claims are only permitted when food contains 2 g or less saturated fat per serving. **Cholesterol free:** less than 2 mg of cholesterol; **Low cholesterol:** 20 mg or less of cholesterol (and per 50 g of food if the serving size is small, i.e., 30 g or less, 2 tbs or less); **Reduced cholesterol; Less cholesterol:** at least 25% less per serving than reference food.

Other Packaging Terms

The FDA allows food producers and marketers to use language on their packaging that advertises the health benefits and production methods of their products. Products marked "certified" have been formally evaluated by a USDA National Organic Program-authorized certifying agent. Below are some common packaging terms and their meanings.

Organic: Organic operations must demonstrate that their practices foster cycling of resources, promote ecological balance, maintain and improve soil and water quality, minimize the use of synthetic materials, and conserve biodiversity. Before a product can be labeled organic, a farm or business must pass a site inspection by a USDA-accredited certifying agent. Organic foods must be produced without genetic engineering, ionizing radiation, or sewage sludge.

Foods that contain all organic ingredients may advertise "100 percent organic" on the "principal display panel" (generally the front of the packaging) along with the USDA organic seal. Foods with at least 95% organic ingredients may be called "organic" and may place the official seal on their packaging. Products with at least 70% organic ingredients may display "made with organic ____" but may not use the organic seal. Products with less than 70% organic ingredients may not make any organic claims on the principal display panel but may list organic ingredients on the information panel.

Natural: Product contains no artificial ingredient or added color and is only minimally processed (i.e., does not fundamentally alter the product).

Free range or **free roaming:** Producers must demonstrate that poultry has been allowed access to the outside.

Fresh poultry: Whole poultry and cuts that have never been below 26°F.

Frozen poultry: Temperature of raw, frozen poultry is 0°F or below.

Gluten free: Products with a gluten limit of 20 parts per million.

Halal and **Zabiah Halal:** Produced in federally inspected meat packing plants and handled in accordance with Islamic law and under Islamic authority.

Kosher: Meat and poultry products prepared under rabbinical supervision.

No hormones: Hormones are not allowed in the raising of hogs or poultry, so those products may not make this claim. If sufficient documentation is provided to the USDA, this term may appear on packages of beef.

No antibiotics: Claim may be made on a package (red meat and poultry) if sufficient documentation is provided to the USDA showing that the animals were raised without antibiotics.

Dietary Guidelines for Americans, 2020-25: Key Recommendations

Source: *Dietary Guidelines for Americans, 2020-2025*, U.S. Dept. of Agriculture and U.S. Dept. of Health and Human Services

The government revises its dietary guidelines every five years. The most recent edition marks the first time the guidelines provide recommendations by life stage, from birth through older adulthood. Each stage of life is distinct and has unique needs that affect health and disease risk. Early food preferences influence food and beverage choices later. And the science has evolved to focus on the importance of a healthy dietary pattern over time. The science also shows it is never too late to start and maintain a healthy dietary pattern, which can yield health benefits in the short term and cumulatively over years.

Core elements of a healthy dietary pattern:

- **Vegetables** of all types—dark green; red and orange; beans, peas, and lentils; starchy; and other vegetables.
- **Fruits,** especially whole fruit.
- **Grains,** at least half of which are whole grain.
- **Dairy,** including fat-free or low-fat milk, yogurt, and cheese, and/or lactose-free versions and fortified soy beverages and yogurt as alternatives.
- **Protein foods,** including lean meats, poultry, and eggs; seafood; beans, peas, and lentils; and nuts, seeds, and soy products.
- **Oils,** including vegetable oils and oils in food, such as seafood and nuts.

Dietary components to limit:

- **Added sugars**—Less than 10% of calories per day starting at age 2. Avoid foods and beverages with added sugars for those younger than age 2.
- **Saturated fat**—Less than 10% of calories per day starting at age 2.
- **Sodium**—Less than 2,300 milligrams per day, and even less for children younger than age 14.
- **Alcoholic beverages**—Adults of legal drinking age can choose not to drink, or to drink in moderation by limiting intake to 2 drinks or less in a day for men and 1 drink or less in a day for women, when alcohol is consumed. Drinking less is better for health than drinking more. There are some adults who should not drink alcohol, such as people who are pregnant.

U.S. Annual Per Capita Consumption of Meat and Dairy, 1910-2021

Source: Economic Research Service, U.S. Dept. of Agriculture
(in pounds per capita per year, unless otherwise noted)

	1910	1930	1950	1970	1990	2000	2010	2015	2018	2021	% change, 1910-2021
Meat											
Beef	48.5	33.7	44.6	79.8	63.9	64.5	56.7	51.4	54.6	56.2	15.8%
Chicken	11.0	11.1	14.3	27.4	42.4	54.2	58.0	62.6	65.2	68.1	520.4
Fish/shellfish	11.2	10.2	11.9	11.7	16.7	16.6	17.4	18.6	18.8	NA	68.0[1]
Pork	38.2	41.1	43.0	48.5	46.4	47.8	44.4	46.3	47.4	47.5	24.2
Total red meat[2]	96.0	83.6	95.8	132.5	112.2	113.7	102.0	98.6	103.0	104.8	9.2
Dairy											
Butter	18.4	17.6	10.9	5.4	4.3	4.5	4.9	5.6	6.0	6.5	−64.9
Cheese, American	2.8	3.2	5.5	7.0	11.1	12.7	13.3	14.0	15.4	16.1	481.9
Cheese, other than American	1.5	1.5	2.2	4.4	13.5	16.9	19.4	21.1	22.6	23.1	1,422.5
Ice cream	1.9	9.3	16.4	16.7	15.4	16.1	14.0	12.9	12.0	12.0	522.0
Milk, skim/lower fat (gallons)	7.1	5.0	2.9	5.8	15.2	14.5	14.8	12.4	10.8	9.3	31.4
Milk, whole (gallons)	25.2	28.2	34.3	25.5	10.5	8.2	5.7	5.5	5.9	5.9	−76.8

NA = Not available. (1) Percent change, 1910-2018. (2) Includes beef, veal, lamb, and pork.

Characteristics of Organic Farms in the U.S., 2017

Source: National Agricultural Statistics Service, U.S. Dept. of Agriculture

	All farms	Organic less than 50% of total sales	Organic 50% or more of total sales	Farms with organic sales, exempt from certification[1]
		Farms with certified organic sales		
Total farms/acreage				
Farms (number)	$2,042,220	$4,301	$11,650	$2,215
Land in farms (acres)	900,217,576	4,082,741	4,912,949	112,809
Average size of farms (acres)	441	949	422	51
Market value of ag. prod. sold/govt. payments				
Total (thous.)	397,466,269	8,473,343	6,744,349	23,698
Average per farm	194,625	1,970,087	578,914	10,699
Total sales (thous.)	388,522,695	8,435,721	6,696,211	22,534
Value of crops[2] (thous.)	193,546,699	7,119,268	3,777,059	16,957
Value of livestock, poultry, and their products (thous.)	194,975,996	1,316,453	2,919,152	5,577
Government payments (thous.)	8,943,574	37,622	48,137	1,164
Land use (acres)				
Total cropland	396,433,817	2,882,881	2,764,555	34,397
Harvested cropland	320,041,858	2,391,939	2,044,553	20,094
Permanent pasture and rangeland	400,771,178	866,997	1,458,601	30,713
Irrigated land	58,013,907	1,272,583	738,351	5,521
Type of farming (no. of farms)				
Oilseed and grain	325,033	695	1,700	18
Vegetable and melon	45,165	531	2,320	573
Fruit and tree nut	95,441	680	2,204	507
Greenhouse, nursery, floriculture	45,477	307	470	300
Tobacco	3,757	69	83	—
Cotton	8,815	26	12	—
Sugarcane, hay, and all other crop farming	443,402	615	1,148	375
Beef cattle ranching and farming	641,496	385	335	98
Cattle feedlots	13,379	49	34	4
Dairy cattle and milk production	37,750	368	2,372	32
Hog and pig	23,048	67	28	105
Poultry and egg production	44,260	260	764	84
Sheep and goat	92,974	105	57	—
Aquaculture[3] and other animal production[4]	222,223	144	123	119

(—) = Not available. (1) Normally less than $5,000 in sales. (2) Including nursery and greenhouse crops. (3) Primarily engaged in the farm raising of finfish, shellfish, or any other kind of animal aquaculture. (4) Primarily engaged in raising animals and insects (except cattle, hogs and pigs, poultry, sheep and goats, and aquaculture) for sale or product production, primarily engaged in one of the following: bees, horses and other equine, rabbits and other fur-bearing animals, etc. and producing products such as honey and other bee products.

Livestock on Farms in the U.S., 1900-2023

Source: National Agricultural Statistics Service, U.S. Dept. of Agriculture
(in thousands as of Jan. 1, unless otherwise noted)

Year	All cattle[1]	Milk cows	Sheep and lambs	Hogs and pigs[2]	Year	All cattle[1]	Milk cows	Sheep and lambs	Hogs and pigs[2]
1900	59,739	16,544	48,105	51,055	2005	95,018	9,004	6,135	60,975
1910	58,993	19,450	50,239	48,072	2010	93,881	9,086	5,620	65,327
1920	70,400	21,455	40,743	60,159	2012	90,769	9,230	5,365	66,361
1930	61,003	23,032	51,565	55,705	2013	89,300	9,218	5,335	66,373
1940	68,309	24,940	52,107	61,165	2014	88,526	9,208	5,245	64,775
1950	77,963	23,853	29,826	58,937	2015	89,143	9,307	5,280	66,145
1960	96,236	19,527	33,170	59,026	2016	91,918	9,310	5,300	68,919
1970	112,369	12,091	20,423	57,046	2017	93,705	9,346	5,250	71,545
1975	132,028	11,220	14,515	54,693	2018	94,298	9,432	5,265	73,145
1980	111,242	10,758	12,699	67,318	2019	94,805	9,353	5,230	74,550
1985	109,582	10,777	10,716	54,073	2020	93,793	9,343	5,200	78,658
1990	95,816	10,015	11,358	53,788	2021	93,790	9,442	5,170	77,312
1995	102,785	9,482	8,886	57,150	2022	92,077	9,377	5,065	74,446
2000	98,199	9,183	7,036	59,335	2023	89,274	9,403	5,020	73,119

(1) For 1970 and on, includes milk cows and heifers that have calved. (2) As of Dec. 1 of preceding year.

Production of Principal U.S. Crops, 1990-2022

Source: National Agricultural Statistics Service, U.S. Dept. of Agriculture

Year	Corn for grain (1,000 bu)	Oats (1,000 bu)	Barley (1,000 bu)	Sorghum for grain (1,000 bu)	All wheat (1,000 bu)	Rye (1,000 bu)	Canola (1,000 lb)	Cotton (upland) (1,000 b)	Cottonseed (1,000 t)
1990	7,934,028	357,654	422,196	573,303	2,729,778	10,176	NA	15,505.4	5,968.5
1995	7,373,876	162,027	359,562	460,373	2,182,591	10,064	548,447	17,532.2	6,848.7
2000	9,915,051	149,545	318,728	470,526	2,232,460	8,386	1,998,310	16,799.2	6,435.6
2005	11,114,082	114,878	211,896	392,933	2,104,690	7,537	1,580,985	23,259.7	8,172.1
2010	12,446,865	81,190	180,268	345,625	2,206,916	7,431	2,447,628	17,600.0	6,098.1
2013	13,828,964	64,642	216,745	392,331	2,134,979	7,626	2,210,505	12,275.0	4,203.0
2014	14,215,532	70,232	181,542	432,575	2,026,310	7,189	2,512,645	15,753.0	5,125.0
2015	13,601,964	89,535	218,187	596,751	2,061,939	11,616	2,878,470	12,455.0	4,043.0
2016	15,148,038	64,770	199,914	480,261	2,308,723	13,451	3,086,340	16,601.0	5,369.0
2017	14,609,407	49,585	143,258	361,871	1,740,910	10,252	3,055,410	20,223.0	6,422.0
2018	14,340,369	56,130	153,527	364,986	1,885,156	8,432	3,615,440	17,566.0	5,631.0
2019	13,619,928	53,258	172,499	341,460	1,932,017	10,622	3,400,865	19,227.0	5,945.0
2020	14,111,449	65,694	170,813	372,960	1,828,043	11,532	3,453,062	14,061.0	4,435.0
2021	15,073,820	39,836	120,090	447,810	1,646,254	9,808	2,720,550	17,191.0	5,323.0
2022	13,729,719	57,655	174,333	187,785	1,649,878	12,301	3,821,810	14,206.0	4,455.0

Year	Tobacco (1,000 lb)	All hay (1,000 t)	Beans, dry edible (1,000 cwt)	Peas, dry edible (1,000 cwt)	Peanuts[1] (1,000 lb)	Soybeans[2] (1,000 bu)	Potatoes (1,000 cwt)	Sweet potatoes (1,000 cwt)
1990	1,626,380	146,212	32,379	2,372	3,602,770	1,925,947	402,110	12,594
1995	1,268,538	154,166	30,812	4,765	4,247,455	2,176,814	443,606	12,906
2000	1,052,999	151,921	26,409	3,474	3,265,505	2,757,810	513,621	13,794
2005	645,015	151,017	26,772	14,003	4,869,860	3,063,237	423,926	15,730
2010	718,190	145,624	31,801	14,221	4,156,840	3,329,181	404,273	23,845
2013	723,579	135,002	24,576	15,620	4,173,170	3,357,984	434,652	24,785
2014	876,415	139,923	28,910	17,155	5,188,665	3,927,090	442,170	29,584
2015	719,171	134,502	30,057	18,283	6,001,357	3,926,339	441,205	31,016
2016	628,720	134,995	28,703	27,762	5,581,570	4,296,086	441,411	31,546
2017	710,161	128,207	35,961	14,195	7,115,410	4,411,633	450,921	35,646
2018	533,241	123,600	37,745	15,929	5,495,935	4,428,150	450,020	27,378
2019	467,956	128,864	20,756	22,210	5,466,487	3,551,908	424,419	31,973
2020	372,877	126,812	32,665	21,629	6,158,350	4,216,302	420,020	30,128
2021	458,126	120,196	22,587	8,636	6,361,331	4,465,382	409,829	29,103
2022	447,367	112,801	25,847	15,092	5,568,150	4,276,123	392,243	25,937

Year	Rice (1,000 cwt)	Sugarcane (1,000 t)	Sugar beets (1,000 t)	Pecans[3] (1,000 lb)	Apples (1,000 t)	Grapes (1,000 t)	Peaches (1,000 t)	Oranges[4] (1,000 bx)	Grapefruit[4] (1,000 bx)
1990	156,088	28,136	27,513	205,000	4,828	5,660	1,121	184,415	49,300
1995	173,871	30,944	27,954	268,000	5,293	5,922	1,150	263,605	71,050
2000	190,872	36,114	32,541	209,850	5,291	7,688	1,276	299,760	66,980
2005	223,235	26,606	27,433	280,250	4,853	7,814	1,185	216,500	25,640
2010	243,104	27,360	32,034	293,740	4,646	7,471	1,150	192,835	30,400
2013	189,953	30,761	32,789	266,330	5,216	8,632	904	189,893	28,950
2014	222,215	30,424	31,285	264,150	5,907	7,884	853	155,977	25,200
2015	193,148	32,122	35,371	254,290	5,023	7,621	847	146,602	21,950
2016	224,145	32,118	36,920	268,770	5,689	7,697	796	141,891	19,400
2017	178,228	33,238	35,317	304,850	5,777	7,384	701	118,520	16,960
2018	223,833	34,542	33,282	240,930	5,120	7,596	652	91,130	12,480
2019	185,104	31,937	28,650	255,600	5,543	6,961	681	126,550	14,810
2020	227,514	36,100	33,610	304,050	5,143	6,040	653	122,840	13,950
2021	191,581	32,838	36,768	256,450	4,966	6,035	691	103,000	10,700
2022	160,368	34,675	32,574	277,700	4,883	5,923	626	81,650	9,130

b = bale; bu = bushel; bx = box; cwt = hundred weight; lb = pound; t = ton. **Note:** Some 2022 figures are preliminary estimates. (1) Harvested for nuts. (2) Harvested for beans. (3) Utilized production only. (4) Crop year ending in year cited.

Animal Products: Average Prices Received by U.S. Farmers, 1940-2022

Source: National Agricultural Statistics Service, U.S. Dept. of Agriculture

Figures represent dollars per 100 lb for veal calves, beef cattle, hogs, lambs, milk (wholesale), and sheep; dollars per head for milk cows; cents per lb for broilers, chickens, turkeys, and wool; and cents per dozen for eggs. Weighted calendar year prices for livestock and livestock products other than wool. For 1943-63, wool prices were weighted on marketing year basis. The marketing year was changed in 1964 from a calendar year to a Dec.-Nov. basis for broilers, chickens, eggs, and hogs.

Year	Broilers	Calves (veal)	Cattle (beef)	Chickens (excl. broilers)	Eggs	Hogs	Lambs[1]	Milk	Milk cows	Sheep[1]	Turkeys	Wool
1940	17.3	8.83	7.56	13.0	18.0	5.39	8.10	1.82	61	3.95	15.2	28.4
1950	27.4	26.30	23.30	22.2	36.3	18.00	25.10	3.89	198	11.60	32.8	62.1
1960	16.9	22.90	20.40	12.2	36.1	15.30	17.90	4.21	223	5.61	25.4	42.0
1970	13.6	34.50	27.10	9.1	39.1	22.70	26.40	5.71	332	7.51	22.6	35.4
1980	27.7	76.80	62.40	11.0	56.3	38.00	63.60	13.05	1,190	21.30	41.3	88.1
1990	32.6	95.60	74.60	9.3	70.9	53.70	55.50	13.74	1,160	23.20	39.4	80.0
2000	33.6	104.00	68.60	5.7	61.8	42.30	79.80	12.40	1,340	34.30	40.7	33.0
2005	43.6	135.00	89.70	6.5	54.0	50.20	110.00	15.19	1,770	45.10	44.9	71.0
2010	48.2	117.00	92.20	8.1	85.7	54.10	125.00	16.35	1,330	49.70	61.5	115.0
2012	50.0	168.00	122.00	8.8	101.1	64.20	NA	18.56	1,430	NA	72.1	153.0
2013	60.6	181.00	125.00	9.5	107.2	67.20	NA	20.12	1,380	NA	66.5	145.0
2014	63.7	261.00	152.00	10.1	122.1	76.50	NA	24.07	1,830	NA	73.5	146.0
2015	53.8	247.00	147.00	10.3	168.0	55.30	NA	17.21	1,990	NA	81.1	145.0
2016	47.8	158.00	119.00	8.1	76.3	49.30	NA	16.34	1,760	NA	82.6	145.0

Year	Broilers	Calves (veal)	Cattle (beef)	Chickens (excl. broilers)	Eggs	Hogs	Lambs[1]	Milk	Milk cows	Sheep[1]	Turkeys	Wool
2017	54.4	168.00	120.00	4.7	85.6	53.10	NA	17.69	1,620	NA	64.6	147.0
2018	55.9	170.00	115.00	4.8	116.1	50.20	NA	16.28	1,360	NA	51.0	175.0
2019	48.6	159.00	116.00	3.7	77.7	51.40	NA	18.63	1,200	NA	57.9	189.0
2020	35.8	161.00	109.00	1.8	93.1	46.90	NA	18.16	1,300	NA	70.9	166.0
2021	53.2	171.00	121.00	1.5	93.9	67.30	NA	18.54	1,360	NA	82.1	170.0
2022	85.0	195.00	142.00	7.6	212.1	72.20	NA	25.39	1,590	NA	106.7	153.0

NA = Not available. (1) Prices not calculated after 2010.

Crops: Average Prices Received by U.S. Farmers, 1940-2022

Source: National Agricultural Statistics Service, U.S. Dept. of Agriculture

Figures represent cents per lb for apples, cotton, and peanuts; dollars per bushel for barley, corn, oats, soybeans, and wheat; dollars per 100 lb for potatoes, rice, and sorghum; and dollars per ton for cottonseed and hay. Weighted crop year prices. The marketing year is described as follows: apples and potatoes, July-June; barley, oats, and wheat, June-May; corn, sorghum, and soybeans, Sept.-Aug.; cottonseed, Aug.-Feb.; cotton, peanuts, and rice, Aug.-July; and hay, May-Apr.

Year	Apples	Barley	Corn	Cotton-seed	Cotton (upland)	Hay	Oats	Peanuts	Pota-toes	Rice	Sor-ghum	Soy-beans	Wheat
1940	NA	0.39	0.62	21.70	9.8	9.78	0.30	3.7	0.85	1.80	0.87	0.89	0.67
1950	NA	1.19	1.52	86.60	39.9	21.10	0.79	10.9	1.50	5.09	1.88	2.47	2.00
1960	2.7	0.84	1.00	42.50	30.1	21.70	0.60	10.0	2.00	4.55	1.49	2.13	1.74
1970	6.5	0.97	1.33	56.40	21.9	26.10	0.62	12.8	2.21	5.17	2.04	2.85	1.33
1980	12.1	2.86	3.11	129.00	74.4	71.00	1.79	25.1	6.55	12.80	5.25	7.57	3.91
1990	20.9	2.14	2.28	121.00	67.1	80.60	1.14	34.7	6.08	6.68	3.79	5.74	2.61
2000	17.8	2.11	1.85	105.00	49.8	84.60	1.10	27.4	5.08	5.61	3.37	4.54	2.62
2005	24.4	2.53	2.00	96.00	47.7	98.20	1.63	17.3	7.06	7.65	3.33	5.66	3.42
2010	25.1	3.86	5.18	161.00	81.5	114.00	2.52	22.5	9.20	12.70	8.96	11.30	5.70
2012	37.1	6.43	6.89	252.00	72.5	191.00	3.89	30.1	8.63	15.10	11.30	14.40	7.77
2013	30.3	6.06	4.46	246.00	77.9	176.00	3.75	24.9	9.71	16.30	7.64	13.00	6.87
2014	25.7	5.30	3.70	194.00	61.3	172.00	3.21	22.0	8.88	13.40	7.20	10.10	5.99
2015	33.6	5.52	3.61	227.00	61.2	145.00	2.12	19.3	8.76	12.20	5.91	8.95	4.89
2016	31.6	4.96	3.36	195.00	68.0	129.00	2.06	19.7	9.08	10.40	4.98	9.47	3.89
2017	32.1	4.47	3.36	142.00	68.6	142.00	2.59	22.9	9.17	12.90	5.75	9.33	4.72
2018	29.9	4.62	3.61	155.00	70.3	166.00	2.66	21.5	8.90	12.60	5.82	8.48	5.16
2019	25.8	4.69	3.56	161.00	59.6	163.00	2.82	20.5	9.94	13.60	5.96	8.57	4.58
2020	29.6	4.75	4.53	194.00	66.3	156.00	2.77	21.0	9.30	14.40	9.90	10.80	5.05
2021	29.6	5.31	6.00	243.00	91.4	193.00	4.55	24.3	10.20	16.10	10.60	13.30	7.63
2022[1]	32.2	7.30	6.70	332.00	83.8	235.00	4.85	26.2	12.90	19.40	12.30	14.30	9.00

NA = Not available. (1) Preliminary.

World Meat Production, 2000, 2021

Source: UN Food and Agriculture Organization; in thousands of metric tons; ranked by top producers in 2021

Rank	Top beef producers Country	2000	2021	Rank	Top pork producers Country	2000	2021	Rank	Top poultry producers Country	2000	2021
1.	U.S.	12,017	12,734	1.	China[1]	39,660	52,959	1.	China[1]	11,890	23,800
2.	Brazil	6,579	9,750	2.	U.S.	8,597	12,560	2.	U.S.	16,575	23,223
3.	China[1]	5,131	7,633	3.	Spain	2,905	5,180	3.	Brazil	6,125	15,216
4.	India	2,781	5,831	4.	Germany	3,982	4,971	4.	Russia	775	4,617
5.	Argentina	2,718	2,982	5.	Brazil	2,600	4,365	5.	Indonesia	818	3,889
6.	Pakistan	886	2,374	6.	Russia	1,578	4,304	6.	India	904	3,714
7.	Mexico	1,409	2,131	7.	Vietnam	1,029	2,590	7.	Mexico	1,849	3,687
8.	Australia	1,988	1,933	8.	Canada	1,640	2,405	8.	Poland	589	2,523
9.	Russia	1,898	1,674	9.	France	2,312	2,204	9.	Japan	1,195	2,436
10.	Türkiye	359	1,472	10.	Poland	1,923	1,986	10.	Argentina	1,000	2,339
11.	France	1,528	1,424	11.	Denmark	1,625	1,724	11.	Egypt	592	2,322
12.	Canada	1,263	1,386	12.	Netherlands	1,623	1,719	12.	Türkiye	668	2,302
13.	Germany	1,304	1,080	13.	Mexico	1,030	1,693	13.	UK	1,513	1,995
14.	South Africa	582	1,051	14.	South Korea	916	1,407	14.	Iran	815	1,994
15.	Uzbekistan	390	1,003	15.	Italy	1,479	1,352	15.	South Africa	821	1,922
16.	UK	705	888	16.	Japan	1,256	1,318	16.	Thailand	1,149	1,845
17.	Zimbabwe	642	806	17.	Philippines	1,213	1,187	17.	Pakistan	332	1,814
18.	Colombia	745	767	18.	Belgium	1,042	1,140	18.	Peru	510	1,752
19.	New Zealand	587	751	19.	UK	899	1,022	19.	Vietnam	365	1,703
20.	Spain	651	718	20.	Thailand	693	928	20.	Colombia	504	1,694
21.	Ireland	577	595	21.	Taiwan	921	825	21.	Malaysia	714	1,625
22.	Uruguay	453	573	22.	Ukraine	676	724	22.	France	2,148	1,616
23.	Poland	349	555	23.	Argentina	214	696	23.	Spain	990	1,561
24.	Kazakhstan	306	540	24.	Chile	261	590	24.	Germany	790	1,546
25.	Paraguay	231	523	25.	Austria	505	502	25.	Canada	1,065	1,502
	Africa	4,704	7,041		Africa	922	2,015		Africa	2,962	7,650
	Asia	13,424	23,570		Asia	47,319	63,071		Asia	22,907	53,152
	Central America	1,766	2,767		Central America	1,132	1,876		Central America	2,351	4,950
	Europe	11,771	10,485		Europe	25,283	30,789		Europe	11,859	21,944
	North America	13,280	14,119		North America	10,237	14,965		Northern America	17,640	24,725
	Oceania	2,591	2,698		Oceania	487	580		Oceania	767	1,593
	South America	11,846	15,900		South America	3,659	6,823		South America	9,696	23,360
	World total	**59,604**	**76,768**		**World total**	**89,249**	**120,372**		**World total**	**68,656**	**137,980**

(1) Not including Hong Kong or Macau.

World Corn, Rice, and Wheat Production, 2000, 2021

Source: UN Food and Agriculture Organization; in millions of metric tons; ranked by top producers in 2021

Top corn producers

Rank Country	2000	2021
1. U.S.	251.9	383.9
2. China	106.0	272.6
3. Brazil	32.3	88.5
4. Argentina	16.8	60.5
5. Ukraine	3.8	42.1
6. India	12.0	31.7
7. Mexico	17.6	27.5
8. Indonesia	9.7	20.0
9. South Africa	11.4	16.9
10. France	16.0	15.4
11. Russia	1.5	15.2
12. Romania	4.9	14.8
13. Canada	7.0	14.0
14. Nigeria	4.1	12.7
15. Ethiopia	2.7	10.7
16. Pakistan	1.6	10.6
17. Philippines	4.5	8.3
18. Egypt	6.5	7.5
19. Poland	0.9	7.3
20. Tanzania	2.0	7.0
21. Türkiye	2.3	6.8
22. Hungary	5.0	6.4
23. Italy	10.1	6.1
24. Serbia	NA	6.0
25. Thailand	4.5	5.3
Africa	43.8	96.6
Asia	149.1	378.9
Central America	20.3	31.6
Europe	63.1	141.8
North America	258.8	397.9
Oceania	0.6	0.5
South America	55.8	162.3
World total	592.0	1,210.2

NA = Not applicable.

Top rice producers

Rank Country	2000	2021
1. China	187.9	212.8
2. India	127.5	195.4
3. Bangladesh	37.6	56.9
4. Indonesia	51.9	54.4
5. Vietnam	32.5	43.9
6. Thailand	25.8	33.6
7. Myanmar	21.0	24.9
8. Philippines	12.4	20.0
9. Pakistan	7.2	14.0
10. Brazil	11.1	11.7
11. Cambodia	4.0	11.4
12. Japan	11.9	10.5
13. U.S.	8.7	8.7
14. Nigeria	3.3	8.3
15. Nepal	4.2	5.6
16. South Korea	7.2	5.2
17. Sri Lanka	2.9	5.1
18. Egypt	6.0	4.8
19. Madagascar	2.5	4.4
20. Laos	2.2	3.9
21. Peru	1.9	3.5
22. Colombia	2.2	3.3
23. Tanzania	0.8	2.7
24. Guinea	1.1	2.5
25. Mali	0.7	2.4
Africa	17.5	37.2
Asia	545.2	708.1
Central America	1.3	1.4
Europe	3.2	3.8
North America	8.7	8.7
Oceania	1.1	0.4
South America	20.5	26.2
World total	598.7	787.3

Top wheat producers

Rank Country	2000	2021
1. China	99.6	136.9
2. India	76.4	109.6
3. Russia	34.5	76.1
4. U.S.	60.6	44.8
5. France	37.4	36.6
6. Ukraine	10.2	32.2
7. Australia	24.8	31.9
8. Pakistan	21.1	27.5
9. Canada	26.5	22.3
10. Germany	21.6	21.5
11. Türkiye	21.0	17.7
12. Argentina	15.5	17.6
13. UK	16.7	14.0
14. Poland	8.5	11.9
15. Kazakhstan	9.1	11.8
16. Romania	4.4	10.4
17. Iran	8.1	10.1
18. Egypt	6.6	9.0
19. Spain	7.3	8.6
20. Brazil	1.7	7.9
21. Morocco	1.4	7.5
22. Bulgaria	2.8	7.3
23. Italy	7.5	7.3
24. Uzbekistan	3.7	6.0
25. Hungary	3.7	5.3
Africa	14.3	29.2
Asia	254.7	340.5
Central America	3.5	3.3
Europe	183.4	269.2
North America	87.2	67.1
Oceania	25.1	32.3
South America	19.6	29.3
World total	587.6	770.9

Value of U.S. Agricultural Trade, 1935-2022

Source: Economic Research Service, U.S. Dept. of Agriculture

(in millions of dollars)

Year	Agric. exports	Agric. imports	Agric. trade balance	Total agric. trade	Year	Agric. exports	Agric. imports	Agric. trade balance	Total agric. trade
1935	$669	$934	−$265	$1,603	2006	$71,231	$68,868	$2,363	$140,099
1940	738	1,239	−501	1,977	2007	85,227	75,171	10,056	160,398
1945	2,191	1,729	462	3,920	2008	117,951	84,227	33,724	202,178
1950	2,986	3,177	−191	6,163	2009	98,644	78,241	20,403	176,886
1955	3,144	3,781	−637	6,925	2010	111,239	82,934	28,304	194,173
1960	4,519	4,010	509	8,529	2011	142,090	97,465	44,625	239,554
1965	6,097	3,986	2,111	10,083	2012	141,200	108,342	32,858	249,542
1970	7,115	5,433	1,682	12,548	2013	145,082	111,002	34,081	256,084
1975	22,220	9,132	13,088	31,352	2014	156,849	115,888	40,961	272,737
1980	41,738	16,526	25,212	58,264	2015	144,068	121,611	22,456	265,679
1985	32,509	19,194	13,315	51,702	2016	133,719	121,083	12,635	254,802
1990	45,348	23,816	21,531	69,164	2017	144,781	127,151	17,630	271,932
1995	60,958	30,480	30,479	91,438	2018	148,620	136,478	12,142	285,098
2000	55,294	41,646	13,648	96,940	2019	140,094	141,437	−1,343	281,530
2002	55,964	44,457	11,507	100,422	2020	139,725	143,404	−3,679	283,129
2003	58,662	49,114	9,548	107,777	2021	171,740	163,341	8,399	335,080
2004	64,896	56,127	8,770	121,023	2022	196,410	193,977	2,433	390,387
2005	64,859	61,567	3,292	126,426					

Note: Data for 1935-65 are for July-June fiscal year; data for 1970-2022 are for Oct.-Sept. fiscal year.

Crop Consumption Per Capita in Selected Nations, 1980-2020

Source: UN Food and Agriculture Organization

(in kilograms per capita per year)

Country	Corn 1980	1990	2010	2020	Rice 1980	1990	2010	2020	Wheat 1980	1990	2010	2020
Afghanistan	33	24	2	3	20	17	21	19	162	140	169	161
Argentina	6	5	11	4	2	6	12	13	115	114	109	120
Australia	2	4	5	4	8	8	17	14	81	70	68	74
Bangladesh	0	0	1	1	144	159	260	257	29	21	15	17
Brazil	22	22	27	28	39	41	47	37	50	44	60	55
Canada	4	3	19	20	3	5	13	16	76	78	86	79
China[1]	5	4	7	7	75	82	124	128	59	78	66	66
Congo Republic	5	3	3	5	2	5	23	16	33	33	37	42
Cuba	0	0	27	27	51	47	64	77	78	74	62	56
Egypt	49	57	64	60	26	31	57	48	129	151	147	148
France	2	13	11	12	4	4	8	9	95	92	108	116
Germany	3	6	9	7	2	2	4	6	69	67	86	64
India	8	8	7	8	64	78	103	102	45	41	59	66
Indonesia	24	29	24	25	125	131	207	185	10	9	22	29
Iran	1	1	3	3	30	30	43	38	154	164	151	157
Iraq	0	3	<1	1	31	37	50	50	144	185	136	144

Country	Corn				Rice				Wheat			
	1980	1990	2010	2020	1980	1990	2010	2020	1980	1990	2010	2020
Israel	12	23	18	17	6	8	16	17	138	124	115	107
Italy	5	3	4	3	5	5	8	8	174	149	143	136
Japan	15	19	13	14	73	65	81	73	44	44	45	44
Kenya	114	88	74	67	2	2	9	22	20	23	40	39
Korea, North	43	56	45	60	71	70	113	100	32	22	21	21
Korea, South	2	13	13	20	138	97	126	85	49	48	51	48
Mexico	118	124	115	121	5	4	8	9	42	42	35	33
New Zealand	1	3	4	7	2	4	9	12	78	69	79	87
Nigeria	6	33	31	34	15	21	45	42	16	3	25	27
Pakistan	7	6	12	23	23	14	22	12	114	128	117	108
Philippines	22	19	22	38	97	94	173	190	17	20	23	40
Russia	NA	NA	1	1	NA	NA	7	8	NA	NA	132	131
Saudi Arabia	11	13	25	29	33	18	55	56	88	104	90	99
South Africa	120	108	96	83	4	8	23	20	56	56	58	57
Thailand	5	5	9	11	137	114	179	168	4	4	10	20
Türkiye	8	21	18	17	3	6	15	17	210	223	184	168
Ukraine	NA	NA	12	22	NA	NA	4	5	NA	NA	112	101
United Arab Emirates	1	1	1	1	43	34	47	28	63	65	80	105
UK	3	3	3	7	2	2	8	9	82	82	97	103
U.S.	8	13	11	12	4	7	11	12	70	81	80	82
Venezuela	55	54	59	51	21	13	49	50	50	51	47	28
Vietnam	7	7	7	17	128	133	231	204	17	3	10	16
Africa	38	41	45	44	15	17	34	35	45	47	49	47
Asia	8	9	9	11	77	82	119	115	53	60	64	67
Central America	107	113	102	107	8	7	15	17	38	38	34	32
Europe	4	5	7	7	5	4	6	7	118	117	109	105
North America	7	12	12	13	4	7	11	12	71	81	81	81
Oceania	2	4	4	3	9	10	19	22	79	69	60	67
South America	22	23	28	28	29	32	42	40	58	53	62	60
World per capita consumption	13	15	17	19	50	54	82	79	64	68	66	67

NA = Not available or not applicable. **Note:** All figures are rounded. Data for 2010 and 2020 are not directly comparable to earlier years because of a change in methodology. (1) Not including Hong Kong or Macau.

Meat Consumption Per Capita in Selected Nations, 1980-2020

Source: UN Food and Agriculture Organization
(in kilograms per capita per year)

Country	Beef				Pork				Poultry			
	1980	1990	2010	2020	1980	1990	2010	2020	1980	1990	2010	2020
Afghanistan	5	7	5	3	NA	NA	NA	0	1	1	2	2
Argentina	85	64	52	47	9	4	8	14	11	11	34	46
Australia	53	47	39	37	15	18	22	24	21	24	46	49
Bangladesh	1	1	1	1	0	0	0	0	1	1	1	2
Brazil	22	28	39	35	8	7	12	14	10	14	38	48
Canada	40	36	28	28	35	28	24	21	22	28	36	40
China[1]	<1	1	5	7	11	19	37	35	1	3	12	15
Congo Republic	4	1	2	2	1	2	1	7	2	5	7	23
Cuba	15	13	6	7	5	10	18	22	9	12	16	38
Egypt	7	8	12	7	<1	<1	<1	<1	4	4	12	14
France	33	33	26	21	37	34	34	31	16	21	23	23
Germany	23	22	13	15	60	60	54	44	10	11	17	18
India	2	2	1	1	<1	<1	<1	<1	<1	<1	2	3
Indonesia	2	3	3	3	1	3	1	1	1	3	7	14
Iran	6	6	7	8	0	0	0	0	6	7	23	26
Iraq	5	7	3	3	0	0	0	0	9	11	12	5
Israel	13	14	25	27	2	2	3	2	35	39	66	69
Italy	26	27	23	16	25	32	42	33	18	20	18	20
Japan	5	8	9	10	13	15	20	21	10	14	17	22
Kenya	12	9	11	5	<1	<1	<1	<1	2	1	1	1
Korea, North	2	1	1	1	10	11	5	4	2	3	2	2
Korea, South	3	6	11	17	8	13	30	38	6	10	32	36
Mexico	11	14	17	15	9	16	19	19	10	17	23	26
New Zealand	57	39	21	21	12	14	22	25	10	17	23	26
Nigeria	5	2	2	2	1	1	1	1	1	1	4	6
Pakistan	5	6	8	10	0	0	0	0	1	1	4	6
Philippines	3	2	5	3	9	12	18	15	5	4	11	16
Russia	NA	NA	16	13	NA	NA	22	28	NA	NA	22	31
Saudi Arabia	6	4	5	4	NA	NA	NA	NA	24	29	45	43
South Africa	20	17	17	17	3	4	4	4	8	15	33	35
Thailand	6	6	3	1	6	9	13	13	7	9	12	11
Türkiye	3	7	10	16	<1	<1	0	0	6	8	19	20
Ukraine	NA	NA	9	7	NA	NA	16	17	NA	NA	24	25
United Arab Emirates	14	13	2	7	NA	NA	NA	NA	43	39	19	31
UK	23	21	19	17	26	25	24	24	14	19	29	33
U.S.	47	43	39	38	33	28	28	31	26	39	51	59
Venezuela	22	18	19	12	6	5	7	4	17	13	45	16
Vietnam	2	2	5	6	5	10	34	38	2	2	12	16
Africa	7	6	6	5	1	1	1	2	2	3	6	6
Asia	2	3	4	5	6	9	15	14	2	3	9	11
Central America	10	12	15	13	14	8	13	15	6	9	28	34
Europe	23	25	16	14	32	35	35	34	12	15	22	25
North America	47	43	38	37	33	28	28	30	26	38	49	57
Oceania	50	43	27	25	14	17	19	20	18	22	33	35
South America	28	23	28	28	7	6	10	12	9	12	34	41
World per capita consumption	11	10	9	9	12	13	16	15	6	8	14	16

NA = Not available or not applicable. **Note:** All figures are rounded. Data for 2010 and 2020 are not directly comparable to earlier years because of a change in methodology. (1) Not including Hong Kong or Macau.

World Capture of Fish, Crustaceans, and Mollusks, 2000-21

Source: UN Food and Agriculture Organization

(in thousands of metric tons; ranked by 2021 captures)

Country	2000	2010	2015	2020	2021	Country	2000	2010	2015	2020	2021
China[1]	13,915	13,643	14,632	12,067	11,607	Chile	4,241	2,444	1,607	1,678	1,911
Indonesia	4,023	5,236	6,260	6,586	6,852	Philippines	1,862	2,435	2,091	1,862	1,788
Peru	10,576	3,923	4,284	5,131	6,007	Myanmar	1,092	1,959	1,969	1,976	1,664
Russia	3,898	3,994	4,390	4,930	5,059	Mexico	1,232	1,456	1,378	1,413	1,525
India	3,570	4,579	4,630	4,469	4,835	Morocco	753	1,082	1,263	1,260	1,288
U.S.	4,580	4,229	4,930	4,194	4,194	Thailand	2,680	1,646	1,339	1,442	1,288
Vietnam	1,435	2,024	2,525	3,146	3,181	Malaysia	1,198	1,353	1,402	1,314	1,251
Japan	4,302	3,742	3,180	3,044	2,981	South Korea	1,392	1,457	1,309	1,238	1,210
Norway	2,699	2,680	2,305	2,472	2,396	Iceland	1,983	1,058	1,318	1,018	1,038
Bangladesh	1,004	1,727	1,624	1,920	1,982	Oman	118	154	252	777	908

(1) Does not include Hong Kong or Macau.

World Aquaculture Production, 2000-21

Source: UN Food and Agriculture Organization; ranked by 2021 production volume

Country	Metric tons (thous.)					Value (mil)				
	2000	2010	2015	2020	2021	2000	2010	2015	2020	2021
China[1]	21,522	35,513	43,748	49,620	51,221	$21,292	$70,830	$126,350	$157,029	$164,186
India	1,943	3,786	5,341	8,636	9,403	2,512	7,073	10,496	15,564	17,262
Indonesia	789	2,305	4,342	5,227	5,515	2,246	4,894	7,900	10,301	11,756
Vietnam	499	2,683	3,462	4,668	4,736	991	5,980	8,885	12,677	13,257
Bangladesh	657	1,309	2,060	2,584	2,639	1,039	2,840	5,140	6,303	6,552
Norway	491	1,020	1,381	1,490	1,665	1,385	5,081	5,811	7,300	9,363
Egypt	340	920	1,175	1,592	1,576	815	1,554	2,230	3,042	3,086
Chile	392	701	1,046	1,486	1,427	1,250	3,753	6,834	8,219	8,821
Thailand	738	1,286	921	1,013	990	2,514	2,813	2,327	3,050	2,994
Myanmar	99	851	997	1,145	929	781	956	1,645	1,889	1,367
Philippines	394	745	782	854	929	681	1,562	1,869	2,090	2,542
Ecuador	61	273	427	775	896	322	1,251	2,305	3,285	3,235
Brazil	172	411	578	629	649	271	1,307	1,228	1,056	1,173
Japan	763	718	705	601	622	3,499	4,042	3,537	3,978	4,078
South Korea	293	476	479	573	582	573	1,480	1,719	2,138	2,493
Iran	41	220	346	481	479	121	638	1,029	1,719	1,739
Turkey (Türkiye)	79	168	240	421	472	220	708	945	1,549	2,088
U.S.	457	497	426	448	448	848	1,023	1,150	1,211	1,211
Cambodia	14	60	143	399	347	28	113	267	1,208	1,050
Russia	74	120	152	270	295	198	397	532	1,295	1,458
World total[2]	32,420	57,759	72,893	87,630	90,862	47,834	131,188	206,912	263,274	280,931

Note: Does not include production of aquatic plants or marine mammals. (1) Does not include Hong Kong. (2) Includes nations not shown.

U.S. Commercial Landings of Fish and Shellfish, 2002-21

Source: Natl. Marine Fisheries Service, Natl. Oceanic and Atmospheric Admin., U.S. Dept. of Commerce

Year	Landings for human food		Landings for industrial purposes[1]		Total	
	Weight (lbs)	Value	Weight (lbs)	Value	Weight (lbs)	Value
2002	7,049,246,187	$2,890,955,208	2,153,425,076	$148,955,631	9,202,671,263	$3,039,910,839
2004	7,723,774,204	3,520,693,350	1,859,072,203	142,879,335	9,582,846,407	3,663,572,685
2005	7,874,565,447	3,763,245,440	1,681,946,018	116,389,034	9,556,511,465	3,879,634,474
2006	7,903,279,001	4,026,097,205	1,699,733,151	115,978,109	9,603,012,152	4,142,075,314
2007	7,508,478,699	4,011,301,024	1,818,824,033	175,860,796	9,327,302,732	4,187,161,820
2008	6,670,498,378	4,264,804,820	1,709,524,710	154,682,040	8,380,023,088	4,419,486,860
2009	6,236,721,255	3,695,837,615	1,841,933,220	158,007,656	8,078,654,475	3,853,845,271
2010	6,562,046,000	4,388,071,094	1,712,917,430	163,869,875	8,274,963,430	4,551,940,969
2011	7,955,723,987	5,320,798,130	1,951,777,865	187,274,468	9,907,501,852	5,508,072,598
2012	7,540,155,560	5,334,152,927	2,176,539,749	193,466,686	9,716,695,309	5,527,619,613
2013	7,974,735,633	5,322,251,178	1,810,216,064	198,756,268	9,784,951,697	5,521,007,446
2014	7,879,863,793	5,370,770,664	1,671,486,259	194,794,791	9,551,350,052	5,565,565,455
2015	7,769,803,945	5,110,257,366	1,979,009,035	235,200,130	9,748,812,980	5,345,457,496
2016	7,507,635,475	5,161,627,244	2,142,281,588	311,996,557	9,649,917,063	5,473,623,801
2017	8,261,065,276	5,543,455,342	1,692,025,418	249,078,976	9,953,090,694	5,792,534,318
2018	7,526,936,397	5,396,753,702	1,893,509,657	254,297,295	9,420,446,054	5,651,050,997
2019	7,596,066,692	5,251,392,288	1,770,230,092	305,636,588	9,366,296,784	5,557,028,876
2020	6,717,484,338	4,516,866,558	1,679,371,084	319,179,007	8,396,855,422	4,836,045,565
2021	7,115,256,901	6,246,743,597	1,457,341,775	335,704,872	8,572,598,676	6,582,448,469

Note: Does not include products of aquaculture, except oysters and clams. Landings reported in round (live) weight for all items except univalve and bivalve mollusks (e.g., clams, oysters, scallops), which are reported in weight of meats (excluding the shell). (1) Processed into meal, oil, solubles, and shell products or used as bait or animal food.

U.S. Domestic Landings by Region, 2021-22

Source: Natl. Marine Fisheries Service, Natl. Oceanic and Atmospheric Admin., U.S. Dept. of Commerce

Region	2021		2022	
	Weight (lbs)	Value	Weight (lbs)	Value
Alaska	5,272,136,213	$2,049,565,003	4,818,006,376	$1,894,105,630
Gulf	1,139,956,130	920,087,400	1,369,522,647	891,242,935
Hawaii	29,637,142	129,108,461	29,183,551	135,188,833
Middle Atlantic	569,089,553	568,361,150	518,799,591	424,756,431
New England	501,143,142	1,968,086,375	415,935,344	1,405,335,181
Pacific Coast	962,983,605	740,528,871	1,038,485,525	668,169,958
South Atlantic	97,650,203	206,698,970	86,852,572	165,492,140
Total[1]	8,572,598,676	6,582,448,469	8,276,790,227	5,584,323,553

Note: Landings reported in round (live) weight for all items except univalve and bivalve mollusks (e.g., clams, oysters, scallops), which are reported in weight of meats (excluding the shell). (1) Includes data for categories not shown.

HEALTH

U.S. Health Expenditures, 1960-2021

Source: Office of the Actuary, Centers for Medicare & Medicaid Services, U.S. Dept. of Health and Human Services

Type of expenditure	1960	1970	1980	1990	2000	2010	2020	2021
				Amount in billions (current dollars)				
NATIONAL HEALTH EXPENDITURES....	$27.1	$74.1	$253.2	$718.8	$1,365.7	$2,589.4	$4,144.1	$4,255.1
				Percent distribution				
Health consumption expenditures	90.5%	89.5%	91.9%	93.2%	93.7%	94.1%	95.3%	95.1%
Personal health care.	85.3	84.2	84.6	85.1	84.7	84.2	81.2	83.5
Hospital care	33.1	36.7	39.7	34.8	30.4	31.2	30.6	31.1
Professional services	29.2	26.7	25.5	28.9	28.3	26.6	26.0	27.2
Physician and clinical services	20.5	19.3	18.8	22.1	21.1	19.8	19.7	20.3
Other professional services	1.4	1.0	1.4	2.4	2.7	2.7	2.8	3.1
Dental services	7.3	6.4	5.3	4.4	4.5	4.1	3.4	3.8
Other health, residential, personal care	1.6	1.8	3.3	3.3	4.7	5.0	5.1	5.3
Home health care[1]	0.2	0.3	0.9	1.7	2.4	2.7	3.0	2.9
Nursing care facilities and continuing care retirement communities[1]	3.0	5.4	6.0	6.2	6.2	5.4	4.8	4.3
Retail outlet sales of medical products . .	18.1	13.3	9.2	10.1	12.7	13.3	11.9	12.7
Prescription drugs	9.9	7.4	4.8	5.6	8.9	9.8	8.5	8.9
Durable medical equipment	2.7	2.4	1.6	1.9	1.9	1.5	1.3	1.6
Other nondurable medical products. .	5.5	3.5	2.8	2.6	1.8	2.0	2.1	2.3
Government administration[2]	0.2	1.0	1.1	1.0	1.3	1.2	1.2	1.2
Net cost of health insurance	3.7	2.5	3.6	4.3	4.6	5.8	7.2	6.0
Government public health activities	1.4	1.8	2.5	2.8	3.2	2.9	5.7	4.4
Investment.	9.5	10.5	8.1	6.8	6.3	5.9	4.7	4.9
Research[3]	2.6	2.6	2.1	1.8	1.9	1.9	1.5	1.4
Structures and equipment.	6.9	7.8	6.0	5.0	4.4	4.0	3.2	3.4
				Average annual percent change from previous year shown				
NATIONAL HEALTH EXPENDITURES....	—	10.6%	13.1%	11.0%	6.6%	6.6%	4.8%	2.7%
Health consumption expenditures	—	10.4	13.4	11.2	6.7	6.7	4.9	2.5
Personal health care	—	10.4	13.1	11.1	6.6	6.5	4.4	5.5
Hospital care	—	11.7	14.0	9.6	5.2	6.9	4.6	4.4
Professional services	—	9.6	12.6	12.4	6.4	5.9	4.6	7.6
Physician and clinical services	—	9.9	12.8	12.8	6.1	5.9	4.8	5.6
Other professional services	—	6.3	17.0	17.4	7.8	6.7	5.3	11.0
Dental services	—	9.0	10.9	9.0	7.0	5.5	2.8	16.1
Other health, residential, personal care	—	11.5	20.5	11.0	10.4	7.2	5.2	6.1
Home health care[1]	—	14.5	26.9	18.1	9.9	8.1	5.9	0.2
Nursing care facilities and continuing care retirement communities[1]	—	17.4	14.2	11.4	6.6	5.2	3.4	−7.9
Retail outlet sales of medical products . .	—	7.3	8.9	12.1	9.1	7.1	3.6	10.5
Prescription drugs	—	7.5	8.2	12.8	11.7	7.6	3.3	7.8
Durable medical equipment	—	9.0	8.8	13.0	6.6	4.4	3.3	21.8
Other nondurable medical products. .	—	5.9	10.5	10.0	3.1	7.5	5.1	14.1
Government administration[2]	—	30.0	14.1	10.0	9.0	5.9	4.7	7.0
Net cost of health insurance	—	6.4	17.2	13.0	7.3	9.1	7.0	−13.9
Government public health activities	—	13.8	16.9	12.0	8.0	5.8	12.2	−21.3
Investment.	—	11.7	10.3	9.0	5.8	5.9	2.5	6.8
Research[3]	—	10.9	10.8	8.9	7.2	6.8	2.0	2.3
Structures and equipment.	—	11.9	10.1	9.0	5.3	5.5	2.7	8.8

— = Not applicable. **Note:** Numbers may not add up to totals due to rounding. (1) Incl. freestanding facilities only. Additional services of this type provided in hospital-based facilities are counted as hospital care. (2) Incl. all administrative costs (e.g., employee salaries) associated with insuring individuals enrolled in federally managed health insurance programs. (3) Research and development expenditures of drug companies and other mfrs. and providers of med. equip. and supplies are included in the expenditure class in which a product falls instead of here.

Health Coverage for Persons Under 65, 1984-2019

Source: National Health Interview Survey, National Center for Health Statistics, CDC, U.S. Dept. of Health and Human Services
(percent of population)

Characteristic	Private insurance				Medicaid[1]				Uninsured[2]			
	1984	2000	2010	2019	1984	2000	2010	2019	1984	2000	2010	2019
Total	76.8%	71.5%	61.7%	64.3%	6.8%	9.5%	16.9%	20.5%	14.5%	17.0%	18.2%	12.0%
Age												
Under 18 years	72.6	66.6	54.1	55.6	11.9	19.6	36.4	37.9	13.9	12.6	7.8	5.1
18-44 years	76.5	70.5	60.0	65.5	5.1	5.6	10.9	15.4	17.1	22.4	27.1	17.0
45-64 years	83.3	78.7	71.3	70.3	3.4	4.5	6.8	12.3	9.6	12.6	15.7	11.1
Race and Hispanic origin												
White only, non-Hispanic	82.4	79.5	72.0	73.8	3.7	6.1	11.0	13.7	11.9	12.5	13.7	8.8
Black only, non-Hispanic.	58.2	56.0	45.1	49.8	20.7	21.0	30.0	34.8	19.7	19.5	20.7	11.2
Hispanic or Latino, any race . . .	55.7	47.8	36.8	44.6	13.3	15.5	28.6	30.9	29.5	35.6	32.0	22.5
Percent of poverty level												
Below 100%	32.2	25.2	16.0	18.4	33.0	38.4	50.8	60.1	33.9	34.2	30.3	19.2
100%-199%	70.3	50.1	34.8	35.8	5.3	16.2	28.5	39.6	21.8	31.0	32.4	20.7
200%-399%[3]	89.3	78.1	70.7	70.4	0.8	4.0	8.4	12.6	7.6	15.4	17.4	13.0
400% or more	95.4	91.9	89.9	90.8	0.2	0.9	2.0	2.7	3.2	5.9	5.6	4.0
Geographic region												
Northeast	80.5	76.3	68.2	67.8	8.6	10.6	17.9	23.2	10.2	12.2	12.4	7.0
Midwest	80.6	78.8	66.7	71.3	7.4	8.0	17.3	17.4	11.3	12.3	14.1	9.3
South	74.3	66.8	57.5	59.4	5.1	9.4	16.0	19.2	17.7	20.5	21.9	16.6
West	71.9	66.5	58.9	63.4	7.0	10.4	17.1	23.3	18.2	20.7	20.6	10.6

Note: Data based on household interviews of a sample of the civilian noninstitutionalized population. Totals incl. groups not shown separately. Because of questionnaire redesigns, data for 1984 are not strictly comparable with data for later years; data for 2019 have not been fully evaluated for comparability with earlier years. (1) Incl. persons who had a state-sponsored health plan or Children's Health Insurance Program (CHIP). (2) Incl. persons who had only Indian Health Service coverage.

Spending on Health in the 50 Most Populous Countries, 2020

Source: Global Health Expenditure Database, World Health Organization (WHO)

Country	As % of GDP	Per capita[1]	Country	As % of GDP	Per capita[1]	Country	As % of GDP	Per capita[1]	Country	As % of GDP	Per capita[1]
Afghanistan	15.5%	$80	France	12.2%	$4,769	Mexico	6.2%	$539	Spain	10.7%	$2,901
Algeria	6.3	215	Germany	12.8	5,930	Morocco	6.0	187	Sudan	3.0	23
Angola	2.9	51	Ghana	4.0	85	Mozambique	7.6	34	Tanzania	3.7	39
Argentina	10.0	864	India	3.0	57	Myanmar	4.6	72	Thailand	4.4	305
Bangladesh	2.6	51	Indonesia	3.4	133	Nepal	5.2	58	Turkey (Türkiye)	4.6	395
Brazil	10.3	701	Iran	5.3	573	Nigeria	3.4	70	Uganda	4.0	34
Canada	12.9	5,619	Iraq	5.1	202	Pakistan	3.0	38	Ukraine	7.6	270
China	5.6	583	Italy	9.6	3,057	Peru	6.3	389	UK	12.0	4,927
Colombia	9.0	477	Japan	10.9	4,388	Philippines	5.1	165	U.S.	18.8	11,702
Congo, Dem. Rep. of	4.1	21	Kenya	4.3	83	Poland	6.5	1,026	Uzbekistan	6.7	121
Egypt	4.4	151	Korea, South	8.4	2,642	Russia	7.6	774	Venezuela	3.8	142
Ethiopia	3.5	29	Madagascar	3.9	18	Saudi Arabia[2]	5.5	1,291	Vietnam	4.7	166
			Malaysia	4.1	419	South Africa	8.6	490	World[3]	10.8	—

(1) At average exchange rate. (2) In 2018. (3) Per capita health spending ranged from $39 in low income countries up to $3,708 in high income countries.

Population Not Covered by Health Insurance by State, 1990-2022

Source: American Community Survey and Current Population Survey, U.S. Census Bureau, U.S. Dept. of Commerce
(numbers in thousands)

	1990		2000		2022			1990		2000		2022	
	No. not covered	% pop. not covered	No. not covered	% pop. not covered	No. not covered	% pop. not covered		No. not covered	% pop. not covered	No. not covered	% pop. not covered	No. not covered	% pop. not covered
AL	710	17.4%	547	12.5%	437	8.8%	MT	115	14.0%	144	16.1%	91	8.3%
AK	77	15.4	108	15.4	77	11.0	NE	138	8.5	134	7.9	130	6.7
AZ	547	15.5	853	16.4	749	10.3	NV	201	16.5	321	15.7	349	11.1
AR	421	17.4	373	14.1	252	8.4	NH	107	9.9	97	7.9	68	4.9
CA	5,683	19.1	5,956	17.5	2,492	6.5	NJ	773	10.0	857	10.2	627	6.8
CO	495	14.7	559	12.9	409	7.1	NM	339	22.2	415	23.0	170	8.2
CT	226	6.9	300	8.9	185	5.2	NY	2,176	12.1	2,730	14.5	945	4.9
DE	96	13.9	66	8.5	57	5.6	NC	883	13.8	964	12.1	973	9.3
DC	109	19.2	71	12.8	19	2.9	ND	40	6.3	61	9.8	49	6.4
FL	2,376	18.0	2,591	16.2	2,448	11.2	OH	1,123	10.3	1,101	9.8	683	5.9
GA	971	15.3	1,126	13.9	1,251	11.7	OK	574	18.6	587	17.4	461	11.7
HI	81	7.3	95	7.9	49	3.5	OR	360	12.4	398	11.6	252	6.0
ID	159	15.2	198	15.4	157	8.2	PA	1,218	10.1	915	7.6	681	5.3
IL	1,272	10.9	1,474	12.0	813	6.6	RI	105	11.1	71	6.9	45	4.2
IN	587	10.7	608	10.1	469	7.0	SC	550	16.2	426	10.7	470	9.1
IA	225	8.1	233	8.1	141	4.5	SD	81	11.6	80	10.8	72	8.1
KS	272	10.8	256	9.6	247	8.6	TN	673	13.7	603	10.7	647	9.3
KY	480	13.2	509	12.7	247	5.6	TX	3,569	21.1	4,555	22.0	4,899	16.6
LA	797	19.7	736	16.8	312	6.9	UT	156	9.0	243	10.8	273	8.1
ME	139	11.2	131	10.4	90	6.6	VT	54	9.5	44	7.4	25	3.9
MD	601	12.7	473	9.0	368	6.1	VA	996	15.7	670	9.6	545	6.5
MA	530	9.1	450	7.1	168	2.4	WA	557	11.4	767	13.1	468	6.1
MI	865	9.4	767	7.8	451	4.5	WV	249	13.8	239	13.4	103	5.9
MN	389	8.9	393	8.0	254	4.5	WI	321	6.7	378	7.1	303	5.2
MS	531	19.9	368	13.2	312	10.8	WY	58	12.5	71	14.7	66	11.5
MO	665	12.7	474	8.6	521	8.6	U.S.	34,719	13.9	36,586	13.1	26,370	8.0

Persons Not Covered by Health Insurance by Selected Characteristics, 2022

Source: Annual Social and Economic Supplement, Current Population Survey, U.S. Census Bureau, U.S. Dept. of Commerce
(numbers without health insurance coverage for entire calendar year, in thousands)

Characteristic	No. not covered	% of tot. pop.	Characteristic	No. not covered	% of tot. pop.
Total uninsured	25,940	7.9%	Household income		
Race and Hispanic origin[1]			Less than $25,000	4,684	13.2%
White	19,540	7.9	$25,000 to less than $50,000	6,147	12.3
White, not Hispanic	9,506	4.9	$50,000 to less than $75,000	5,137	10.1
Black	3,714	8.3	$75,000 to less than $100,000	3,518	8.2
Asian	1,275	5.9	$100,000 to less than $125,000	2,283	6.3
Hispanic (any race)	10,950	17.2	$125,000 to less than $150,000	1,141	4.3
Age[2]			$150,000 or more	3,026	3.4
Under 65 years	25,290	9.3	Work experience[5]		
Under 19 years[3]	4,079	5.4	All workers	15,290	9.7
19 to 64 years	21,210	10.8	Worked full-time, year-round	9,728	8.5
19 to 25 years[4]	4,247	14.0	Less than full-time, year-round	5,563	12.9
26 to 34 years	5,061	12.5	Did not work at least one week	7,084	12.7
35 to 44 years	4,884	11.2	Marital status[6]		
45 to 64 years	7,022	8.6	Married	7,726	7.8
65 years and over	643	1.1	Widowed	444	13.7
Nativity			Divorced	2,021	11.3
Native-born	16,740	6.0	Separated	730	19.2
Foreign-born	9,194	18.8	Never married	10,290	14.5
Naturalized citizen	1,631	6.8			
Not a citizen	7,563	30.4			

(1) Numbers are for one race alone unless otherwise noted. (2) People aged 65 and older as well as certain people under age 65 with long-term disabilities are eligible for Medicare. (3) Eligible for Medicaid/Children's Health Insurance Program (CHIP). (4) May be eligible to be a dependent on a parent's health insurance. (5) Aged 15 to 64 only. (6) Aged 19 to 64 only.

Health Insurance Marketplace Plan Enrollment by Selected Characteristics, 2023

Source: Centers for Medicare & Medicaid Services (CMS), U.S. Dept. of Health and Human Services
(cumulative enrollment-related activity for Nov. 1, 2022-Jan. 15, 2023; exact dates vary for state-based marketplaces)

	Marketplace total		Federal marketplace[1]		State marketplaces[2]	
	Number	Percent	Number	Percent	Number	Percent
Consumers who have selected a plan	16,357,030	100.0%	12,203,622	100.0%	4,153,408	100.0%
Under 18 years of age	1,547,589	9.5	1,225,138	10.0	322,451	7.8
18-25 years of age	1,534,763	9.4	1,200,127	9.8	334,636	8.1
26-34 years of age	2,580,948	15.8	1,871,646	15.3	709,302	17.1
35-44 years of age	2,825,075	17.3	2,142,854	17.6	682,221	16.4
45-54 years of age	3,181,173	19.4	2,407,225	19.7	773,948	18.6
55-64 years of age	4,398,816	26.9	3,142,972	25.8	1,255,844	30.2
65+ years of age.	287,715	1.8	213,660	1.8	74,055	1.8
Consumers receiving financial assistance[3] ...	14,816,459	90.6	11,398,493	93.4	3,417,966	82.3
With advance premium tax credits	14,797,921	90.5	11,382,792	93.3	3,415,129	82.2
With cost-sharing reductions[4]	7,829,201	47.9	6,371,460	52.2	1,457,741	35.1

Note: Figures may not add up to totals due to rounding. (1) For the 33 states using HealthCare.gov, the federally facilitated marketplace. (2) For the 17 states and the Dist. of Columbia with their own marketplaces. (3) Advance premium tax credit (APTC) only, cost-sharing reduction (CSR) only, or both APTC and CSR. (4) Does not include CSR-only data for New York (state-based marketplace) due to reporting limitations.

Health Insurance Marketplace Average Monthly Premiums, 2023

Source: Centers for Medicare & Medicaid Services, U.S. Dept. of Health and Human Services
For the 2023 open enrollment period, 33 states used HealthCare.gov, the eligibility and enrollment platform run by the federal government. Seventeen states and the Dist. of Columbia ran their own exchanges (state-based marketplaces, or SBMs).
(based on enrollment-related activity for Nov. 1, 2022-Jan. 15, 2023; exact dates vary for state-based marketplaces)

State	Avg. premium before tax credits	Avg. premium after tax credits[1]	Avg. tax credits	Avg. % reduction in premium after tax credits	State	Avg. premium before tax credits	Avg. premium after tax credits[1]	Avg. tax credits	Avg. % reduction in premium after tax credits
Alabama	$743	$101	$676	86.4%	Nevada[3]	$531	$156	$439	70.6%
Alaska........	846	224	741	73.5	New Hampshire..	469	228	345	51.4
Arizona	564	162	472	71.3	New Jersey[3]....	658	215	504	67.3
Arkansas[2].....	578	144	481	75.1	New Mexico[3]....	588	162	534	72.4
California[3].....	607	176	486	71.0	New York[3]......	656	451	364	31.3
Colorado[3].....	513	210	404	59.1	North Carolina ..	643	92	583	85.7
Connecticut[3]...	846	243	718	71.3	North Dakota ...	519	126	436	75.7
Delaware	730	197	599	73.0	Ohio	596	196	479	67.1
Dist. of Columbia[3]	657	569	447	13.4	Oklahoma	647	98	577	84.9
Florida	624	78	564	87.5	Oregon[2]	625	224	503	64.2
Georgia	551	96	487	82.6	Pennsylvania[3]...	641	183	523	71.5
Hawaii	655	206	545	68.5	Rhode Island[3]..	519	161	427	69.0
Idaho[3]........	481	132	413	72.6	South Carolina ..	620	84	566	86.5
Illinois	673	196	540	70.9	South Dakota ...	724	111	649	84.7
Indiana	570	187	455	67.2	Tennessee	638	110	572	82.8
Iowa	656	147	568	77.6	Texas	578	65	539	88.8
Kansas	650	139	559	78.6	Utah	431	69	385	84.0
Kentucky[3].....	603	193	495	68.0	Vermont[3]......	786	244	620	69.0
Louisiana	766	126	680	83.6	Virginia[2]	485	127	407	73.8
Maine[3]	614	194	506	68.4	Washington[3]....	576	270	438	53.1
Maryland[3].....	472	183	382	61.2	West Virginia....	1,174	168	1,057	85.7
Massachusetts[3]..	502	219	381	56.4	Wisconsin	668	173	562	74.1
Michigan	521	164	412	68.5	Wyoming.......	965	134	873	86.1
Minnesota[3]....	490	293	346	40.2	**Total HealthCare.**				
Mississippi	624	60	580	90.4	**gov**	607	102	542	83.2
Missouri	669	132	584	80.3	**Total SBMs ....**	598	209	473	65.1
Montana	610	186	491	69.5	**Total marketplace**	605	129	526	78.7
Nebraska	661	132	560	80.0					

(1) Does not reflect any state premium subsidies provided by an SBM. (2) SBM using the HealthCare.gov platform for eligibility determinations, enrollments, and related functions. (3) SBM.

Health Care Visits by Selected Characteristics, 1997-2018

Source: National Health Interview Survey, National Center for Health Statistics, CDC, U.S. Dept. of Health and Human Services

Characteristic	No visits			1-3 visits			4-9 visits			10 visits or more		
	1997	2010	2018	1997	2010	2018	1997	2010	2018	1997	2010	2018
						Percent distribution						
All persons[1]...............	16.5%	15.6%	14.5%	46.2%	45.4%	49.2%	23.6%	25.8%	23.4%	13.7%	13.2%	12.9%
Age												
Under 6 years	5.0	3.7	4.9	44.9	48.9	52.7	37.0	36.8	33.9	13.0	10.6	8.4
6-17 years	15.3	10.4	8.6	58.7	59.1	63.9	19.3	23.6	21.4	6.8	6.9	6.2
18-44 years	21.7	24.2	21.9	46.7	43.9	47.6	19.0	20.6	18.7	12.6	11.3	11.7
45-64 years	16.9	14.8	14.2	42.9	42.8	45.5	24.7	26.1	24.7	15.5	16.4	15.7
65-74 years	9.8	6.3	6.4	36.9	36.1	40.1	31.6	35.7	31.8	21.6	21.9	21.7
75 years and over	7.7	4.1	4.1	31.8	31.0	34.8	33.8	38.0	33.6	26.6	27.0	27.6
Sex												
Male.................	21.3	20.4	18.7	47.1	46.4	49.7	20.6	22.7	21.2	11.0	10.5	10.3
Female...............	11.8	10.9	10.3	45.4	44.4	48.8	26.5	28.8	25.6	16.3	15.9	15.4
Health insurance status[2]												
Insured continuously	14.1	12.1	12.9	49.2	48.6	51.9	23.6	26.2	23.1	13.0	13.0	12.1
Uninsured up to 12 mos. ...	18.9	18.5	21.2	46.0	47.8	48.4	20.8	22.0	20.9	14.4	11.6	9.5
Uninsured 12+ mos.	39.0	43.8	45.3	41.4	39.7	41.6	13.2	12.6	9.9	6.4	3.9	3.1

Note: Totals incl. visits to hospital emergency departments, doctor offices, and clinics as well as home visits by a health care professional during a 12-month period. (1) Incl. persons of unknown health insurance status. (2) Prior to interview, for persons under age 65 only.

Reasons Given by Patients for Physician Office Visits, 2019

Source: National Ambulatory Medical Care Survey, National Center for Health Statistics (NCHS), Centers for Disease Control and Prevention, U.S. Dept. of Health and Human Services

Rank	Principal reason	Number of visits (thous.)	% of all visits	Rank	Principal reason	Number of visits (thous.)	% of all visits
1.	Progress visit, not otherwise specified	221,258	21.3%	12.	Prenatal examination, routine	12,565	1.2%
2.	General medical examination	60,352	5.8	13.	For other and unspecified test results	12,465*	1.2
3.	Postoperative visit	28,479	2.7	14.	Cancer, breast	NA*	NA
4.	Gynecological examination	25,218	2.4	15.	Knee symptoms	10,370	1.0
5.	Counseling, not otherwise specified	22,685	2.2	16.	Skin lesion	10,295*	1.0
6.	Medication, other and unspecified kinds	18,491	1.8	17.	Diagnostic endoscopies	10,264*	NA
7.	Shoulder symptoms	16,436	1.6	18.	Stomach and abdominal pain, cramps, and spasms	10,098	1.0
8.	Hypertension	15,194	1.5	19.	Other special examination	9,939*	1.0
9.	Well-baby examination	15,141	1.5	20.	Preoperative visit for specified and unspecified types of surgery	9,328	0.9
10.	Cough	15,048	1.5		All other reasons	488,995	47.2
11.	Diabetes mellitus	13,393	1.3		All visits	1,036,484	100.0

* = Estimate does not meet NCHS standards of reliability. NA = Not available. **Note:** Based on nationally representative sample survey of visits to nonfederal office-based patient care physicians. Numbers may not add to totals because of rounding.

Visits to Physician Offices and Hospital Outpatient and Emergency Departments, 1995-2018

Source: National Ambulatory Medical Care Survey and National Hospital Ambulatory Medical Care Survey, National Center for Health Statistics, Centers for Disease Control and Prevention, U.S. Dept. of Health and Human Services

(number of visits per 100 persons)

Sex and age	All places[1]			Physician offices				Hospital outpatient depts.			Hospital emergency depts.			
	1995	2000	2011	1995	2000	2011	2018	1995	2000	2011	1995	2000	2011	2018
Total	334	374	400	271	304	314	250	26	31	40	37	40	45	41
Male	290	325	354	232	261	280	214	21	26	32	37	38	42	37
Under 18	273	302	372	209	231	294	179	25	29	37	40	41	41	40
18-44	190	203	208	139	148	145	103	14	17	20	37	38	43	33
45-54	275	316	322	229	260	250	234	20	26	34	26	30	38	35
55-64	351	428	430	300	367	351	277	26	32	45	25	30	34	35
65-74	508	614	655	445	539	566	459	29	38	52	34	36	37	35
75 and over	711	771	869	616	670	758	681	34	42	49	61	59	62	56
Female	377	420	444	309	345	348	286	31	35	48	37	41	48	44
Under 18	277	285	341	217	221	265	172	25	29	38	35	35	39	40
18-44	336	377	393	265	298	286	243	31	33	47	40	46	59	49
45-54	400	451	459	339	384	364	308	32	36	53	29	31	41	39
55-64	446	529	520	382	453	436	383	38	45	54	26	31	31	37
65-74	603	692	707	534	609	611	509	36	46	60	32	37	37	36
75 and over	666	763	790	571	645	657	617	34	49	61	61	69	72	62

(1) Incl. visits to physician offices and hospital outpatient and emergency departments. Prior to 2006, visits to community health centers were not included in survey.

Most Frequently Mentioned Drugs at Office Visits, 2019

Source: National Ambulatory Medical Care Survey, National Center for Health Statistics (NCHS), Centers for Disease Control and Prevention, U.S. Dept. of Health and Human Services

Rank	Therapeutic drug category[1]	No. of mentions (thous.)	% of total[2]	Rank	Therapeutic drug category[1]	No. of mentions (thous.)	% of total[2]
1.	Analgesics[3]	350,354	9.8%	11.	Bronchodilators	112,383	3.1%
2.	Antihyperlipidemic agents	193,096	5.4	12.	Proton pump inhibitors	94,277	2.6
3.	Vitamins	170,853	4.8	13.	Vitamin and mineral combinations	93,902	2.6
4.	Antidepressants	155,241	4.3	14.	Diuretics	92,379	2.6
5.	Antidiabetic agents	145,757	4.1	15.	Immunostimulants	88,972	2.5
6.	Antiplatelet agents	132,183	3.7	16.	Ophthalmic preparations	83,646*	2.3
7.	Anticonvulsants	125,822	3.5	17.	Antihistamines	76,167	2.1
8.	Dermatological agents	124,561	3.5	18.	Minerals and electrolytes	74,588	2.1
9.	Anxiolytics, sedatives, and hypnotics	122,610	3.4	19.	Thyroid drugs	74,477	2.1
10.	Beta-adrenergic blocking agents	119,291	3.3	20.	Calcium channel blocking agents	67,442	1.9

* = Estimate does not meet NCHS standards of reliability. **Note:** A mention is documentation in a patient's record of a drug provided, prescribed, or continued at a visit to a nonfederal office-based patient care physician. (1) Based on the Multum Lexicon second-level therapeutic drug category. (2) Based on an estimated 3,583,272,000 drug mentions. (3) Incl. narcotic and nonnarcotic analgesics and nonsteroidal anti-inflammatory drugs.

U.S. Organ Transplants

Source: Organ Procurement and Transplantation Network (OPTN), United Network for Organ Sharing (UNOS)

Waiting List, Sept. 2023			Transplants Performed, 2022		
Type of transplant	Candidates	% of total	Type of transplant	Number	% of total
All organs	103,389	100.0%	All organs	42,889	100.0%
Kidney	88,620	85.7	Kidney	25,500	59.5
Liver	10,058	9.7	Liver	9,528	22.2
Heart	3,306	3.2	Heart	4,111	9.6
Kidney/pancreas	2,005	1.9	Lung	2,692	6.3
Lung	959	0.9	Kidney/pancreas	810	1.9
Pancreas	836	0.8	Pancreas	108	0.3
Intestine	206	0.2	Intestine	82	0.2
Heart/lung	32	0.03	Heart/lung	51	0.1
VCA—uterus	6	0.006	Genitourinary: uterus	5	0.01
Abdominal wall	3	0.003	Abdominal wall	2	0.005
Upper limb: unilateral	3	0.003			
VCA—head and neck	3	0.003			
VCA—upper limb	3	0.003			

VCA = Vascularized composite allograft. **Note:** Waiting list as of Sept. 27, 2023; numbers may not add up to total because of patients waiting for multiple organs. Total transplants performed include organs not shown separately.

Illicit Drug Use Among Persons Age 12 or Older, 2002-21

Source: National Survey on Drug Use and Health, SAMHSA, U.S. Dept. of Health and Human Services

Of all those age 12 or older who used an illicit drug in the past month in 2021, approximately 1.8 mil were adolescents aged 12-17 (making 7.1% of that age group current drug users). About 8.5 mil current users were young adults aged 18-25 (or 25.3% of that age group).

(numbers in thousands)

Substance	2002 No.	2002 %	2005 No.	2005 %	2010 No.	2010 %	2014 No.	2014 %	2019 No.	2019 %	2021 No.	2021 %
Used in lifetime												
Illicit drugs[1]	—	—	—	—	—	—	—	—	138,027	50.2	138,790	49.6
Marijuana	94,946	40.4	97,545	40.1	106,613	42.0	117,213	44.2	127,139	46.2	128,016	45.7
Cocaine	33,910	14.4	33,673	13.8	37,361	14.7	39,200	14.8	41,445	15.1	40,901	14.6
Crack	8,402	3.6	7,928	3.3	9,208	3.6	9,424	3.6	9,375	3.4	10,640	3.8
Heroin	3,668	1.6	3,534	1.5	4,144	1.6	4,813	1.8	5,696	2.1	6,635	2.4
Hallucinogens	—	—	—	—	—	—	—	—	44,087	16.0	45,826	16.4
LSD	24,516	10.4	22,433	9.2	23,375	9.2	25,035	9.4	27,528	10.0	29,502	10.5
Ecstasy	—	—	—	—	—	—	—	—	20,097	7.3	21,122	7.5
Inhalants	—	—	—	—	—	—	—	—	25,090	9.1	25,596	9.1
Methamphetamine	—	—	—	—	—	—	—	—	16,013	5.8	16,830	6.0
Used in past year												
Illicit drugs[1]	—	—	—	—	—	—	—	—	57,203	20.8	61,203	21.9
Marijuana	25,755	11.0	25,375	10.4	29,301	11.6	35,124	13.2	48,242	17.5	52,454	18.7
Cocaine	5,902	2.5	5,523	2.3	4,533	1.8	4,553	1.7	5,468	2.0	4,765	1.7
Crack	1,554	0.7	1,381	0.6	885	0.3	773	0.3	778	0.3	996	0.4
Heroin	404	0.2	379	0.2	621	0.2	914	0.3	745	0.3	1,099	0.4
Hallucinogens	—	—	—	—	—	—	—	—	6,010	2.2	7,406	2.6
LSD	999	0.4	563	0.2	881	0.3	1,290	0.5	2,470	0.9	2,477	0.9
Ecstasy	—	—	—	—	—	—	—	—	2,539	0.9	2,199	0.8
Inhalants	—	—	—	—	—	—	—	—	2,142	0.8	2,178	0.8
Methamphetamine	—	—	—	—	—	—	—	—	1,999	0.7	2,549	0.9
Misuse of psychotherapeutics[2]	—	—	—	—	—	—	—	—	16,304	5.9	14,284	5.1
Opioids[3]	—	—	—	—	—	—	—	—	10,065	3.7	9,236	3.3
Used in past month												
Illicit drugs[1]	—	—	—	—	—	—	—	—	35,803	13.0	39,995	14.3
Marijuana	14,584	6.2	14,626	6.0	17,409	6.9	22,188	8.4	31,606	11.5	36,363	13.0
Cocaine	2,020	0.9	2,397	1.0	1,472	0.6	1,530	0.6	1,998	0.7	1,833	0.7
Crack	567	0.2	682	0.3	378	0.1	354	0.1	378	0.1	527	0.2
Heroin	166	0.1	136	0.1	239	0.1	435	0.2	431	0.2	589	0.2
Hallucinogens	—	—	—	—	—	—	—	—	1,915	0.7	2,234	0.8
LSD	112	0.0	104	0.1	155	0.1	287	0.1	580	0.2	524	0.2
Ecstasy	—	—	—	—	—	—	—	—	663	0.2	594	0.2
Inhalants	—	—	—	—	—	—	—	—	807	0.3	830	0.3
Methamphetamine	—	—	—	—	—	—	—	—	1,173	0.4	1,617	0.6
Misuse of psychotherapeutics[2]	—	—	—	—	—	—	—	—	5,337	1.9	4,263	1.5
Opioids[3]	—	—	—	—	—	—	—	—	3,101	1.1	2,791	1.0

— = Not comparable due to methodological changes or not reported due to measurement issues. **Note:** Misuse is defined as use in any way not directed by a doctor, including use without a prescription or use in greater amounts, more often, or for a longer period of time. Because of methodological changes, data for 2021 are not comparable with estimates for prior years. (1) Includes marijuana, cocaine (including crack), heroin, hallucinogens, inhalants, methamphetamine, the misuse of psychotherapeutics, and opioids. (2) Includes four categories of prescription drugs (pain relievers, stimulants, tranquilizers, sedatives) but not over-the-counter drugs. (3) Includes the misuse of prescription opioid pain relievers and the use of heroin.

Lifetime Prevalence of Drug Use in 12th Graders, 1975-2022

Source: Monitoring the Future study, Univ. of Michigan Inst. for Social Research; Natl. Inst. on Drug Abuse, Natl. Insts. of Health

(percent who have ever used)

Drug	1975	1980	1985	1990	1995	2000	2005	2010	2015	2019	2020	2021	2022	2021-22 change
Any illicit drug[1]	55.2%	65.4%	60.6%	47.9%	48.4%	54.0%	50.4%	48.2%	48.9%	47.4%	46.6%	41.3%	41.0%	−0.3%
Marijuana/hashish	47.3	60.3	54.2	40.7	41.7	48.8	44.8	43.8	44.7	43.7	43.7	38.6	38.3	−0.3
Inhalants[2]	—	17.3	18.1	18.5	17.4	14.2	11.4	9.0	5.7	5.3	3.8	5.0	5.8	0.9
Nitrites[2]	—	11.1	7.9	2.1	1.5	0.8	1.1	—	—	—	—	—	—	—
Hallucinogens[3]	—	15.6	12.1	9.7	12.7	13.0	8.8	8.6	6.4	6.9	7.5	7.1	7.1	0.0
LSD	11.3	9.3	7.5	8.7	11.7	11.1	3.5	4.0	4.3	5.6	5.9	4.9	4.4	−0.5
PCP	—	9.6	4.9	2.8	2.7	3.4	2.4	1.8	—	—	—	—	—	—
MDMA (Ecstasy, Molly)	—	—	—	—	—	11.0	5.4	7.3	5.9	3.3	3.6	2.8	3.0	0.2
Cocaine	9.0	15.7	17.3	9.4	6.0	8.6	8.0	5.5	4.0	3.8	4.1	2.5	2.4	0.0
Crack	—	—	—	3.5	3.0	3.9	3.5	2.4	1.7	1.7	1.6	1.5	1.3	−0.3
Heroin	2.2	1.1	1.2	1.3	1.6	2.4	1.5	1.6	0.8	0.6	0.4	0.4	0.5	0.0
Narcotics other than heroin[4]	9.0	9.8	10.2	8.3	7.2	10.6	12.8	13.0	8.4	5.3	5.3	2.3	3.2	0.9
Amphetamines[4]	22.3	26.4	26.2	17.5	15.3	15.6	13.1	11.1	10.8	7.7	7.3	4.9	5.3	0.4
Methamphetamine[4]	—	—	—	—	—	7.9	4.5	2.3	1.0	0.8	1.7	0.6	1.1	0.5
Crystal meth (ice)	—	—	—	2.7	3.9	4.0	4.0	1.8	1.2	1.3	0.2	0.7	0.8	0.1
Sedatives (barbiturates)[4]	18.2	14.9	11.8	7.5	7.4	9.2	10.5	7.5	5.9	4.2	4.4	3.5	3.6	0.1
Methaqualone[4]	8.1	9.5	6.7	2.3	1.2	0.8	1.3	0.4	—	—	—	—	—	—
Tranquilizers[4]	17.0	15.2	11.9	7.2	7.1	8.9	9.9	8.5	6.9	6.1	7.0	3.3	3.3	0.0
Alcohol	90.4	93.2	92.2	89.5	80.7	80.3	75.1	71.0	64.0	58.5	61.5	54.1	61.6	7.5
Cigarettes	73.6	71.0	68.8	64.4	64.2	62.5	50.0	42.2	31.1	22.3	24.0	17.8	16.8	−1.0
Smokeless tobacco	—	—	—	—	30.9	23.1	17.5	17.6	13.2	9.8	*	8.6	10.3	1.8
Any vaping[5]	—	—	—	—	—	—	—	—	35.5	45.6	47.2	40.5	40.7	0.2
Steroids[4]	—	—	—	—	2.3	2.5	2.6	2.0	2.3	1.6	2.0	0.8	1.5	0.7

— = Not available. **Note:** Because of changes to question wording, some data may not be directly comparable across years. (1) Incl. marijuana, LSD, other hallucinogens, crack, cocaine other than crack, or heroin; or any use of narcotics other than heroin, amphetamines, sedatives (barbiturates), or tranquilizers not under a doctor's orders. (2) Unadjusted for underreporting of amyl and butyl nitrites. (3) Unadjusted for underreporting of PCP. (4) Incl. only drug use not under a doctor's orders. (5) Incl. vaping nicotine, marijuana, or just flavoring.

Cigarette Use in the U.S., 1985-2021

Source: National Survey on Drug Use and Health, SAMHSA, U.S. Dept. of Health and Human Services
(percentage of persons age 12 or older, unless otherwise noted, reporting use in the month prior to the survey)

	1985	2000	2005	2010	2015	2019	2021
Total	38.7	24.9	24.9	23.0	19.4	16.7	15.6
Sex							
Male	43.4	26.9	27.4	25.4	21.8	18.6	17.2
Female	34.5	23.1	22.5	20.7	17.1	14.9	14.1
Age							
12-17 years	29.4	13.4	10.8	8.4	4.2	2.3	1.5
18-25 years	47.4	38.3	39.0	34.3	26.7	17.5	11.5
26 years or older[1]	45.7	24.2	24.3	22.8	20.0	18.2	17.9

	1985	2000	2005	2010	2015	2019	2021
Race/Hispanic origin							
White, not Hispanic	38.9	25.9	26.0	24.3	20.7	18.0	17.1
Black, not Hispanic	38.0	23.3	24.5	22.6	21.3	18.7	19.3
Hispanic, any race	40.0	20.7	22.1	20.1	15.3	12.2	11.2
Education[2]							
Non-HS graduate	37.3	32.4	34.8	34.3	28.1	26.5	27.3
HS graduate	37.0	31.1	31.8	29.6	27.4	24.9	24.1
Some college	32.6	27.7	28.1	25.8	23.5	20.2	17.7
College graduate	23.0	13.9	13.8	12.8	9.6	8.0	6.3

HS = High school. **Note:** Because of methodological changes in 2002, 2015, and 2021, data may not be comparable across years. (1) Persons age 26 to 34 only in 1985. (2) Persons age 18 or older.

Daily Use of Cigarettes by 8th, 10th, and 12th Graders, 1995-2022

Source: Monitoring the Future study, Univ. of Michigan Inst. for Social Research; Natl. Inst. on Drug Abuse, Natl. Insts. of Health
(percent who smoked daily in last 30 days)

	8th grade					10th grade					12th grade				
	1995	2000	2005	2022	% change, 2005-22	1995	2000	2005	2022	% change, 2005-22	1995	2000	2005	2022	% change, 2005-22
Total	9.3	7.4	4.0	0.3	−92.5%	16.3	14.0	7.5	0.7	−90.7%	21.6	20.6	13.6	1.6	−88.2%
Gender															
Male	9.2	7.0	3.9	0.3	−92.3	16.3	13.7	7.2	0.7	−90.3	21.7	20.9	14.6	2.1	−85.6
Female	9.2	7.5	4.0	0.1	−97.5	16.1	14.1	7.7	0.4	−94.8	20.8	19.7	11.9	0.8	−93.3
College plans															
None/under 4 yrs	22.5	21.7	14.4	1.1	−92.4	32.7	28.8	19.2	1.5	−92.2	33.7	31.7	24.9	3.4	−86.3
Complete 4 yrs	7.5	5.6	2.9	0.1	−96.6	13.3	11.6	5.9	0.5	−91.5	17.4	16.6	10.5	0.8	−92.4
Region															
Northeast	9.2	6.9	3.2	0.3	−90.6	15.8	14.1	7.6	0.3	−96.1	22.5	22.8	13.3	1.1	−91.7
Midwest	11.0	9.0	4.8	0.1	−97.9	17.6	16.3	8.6	0.5	−94.2	25.7	23.6	16.3	1.1	−93.3
South	9.4	7.8	5.0	0.5	−90.0	19.3	15.7	8.8	0.9	−89.8	21.7	19.4	15.4	2.2	−85.7
West	7.0	4.9	2.4	0.3	−87.5	9.4	7.8	4.0	0.8	−80.0	14.5	16.9	7.6	1.4	−81.6
Parental education[1]															
Some HS/less	15.8	13.1	7.8	0.6	−92.3	20.0	18.9	9.9	1.4	−85.9	21.3	22.8	11.7	2.1	−82.1
Some/completed HS	11.3	11.3	6.3	0.7	−88.9	21.6	17.6	11.1	0.4	−96.4	24.6	22.9	18.3	1.2	−93.4
Completed HS/some college	9.4	6.7	4.3	0.2	−95.3	17.0	14.2	7.9	0.6	−92.4	21.6	21.2	14.4	1.9	−86.8
Some/completed college	7.2	3.9	2.2	0.2	−90.9	12.6	11.5	5.2	0.8	−84.6	19.7	18.6	11.7	1.3	−88.9
Completed college/higher	5.7	4.1	1.4	0.2	−85.7	10.3	9.8	4.4	0.4	−90.9	18.5	15.2	8.1	1.2	−85.2
Race/ethnicity[2]															
White	10.5	9.0	4.6	0.4	−91.3	17.6	17.7	9.1	0.7	−92.3	23.9	25.7	17.1	2.1	−87.7
Black	2.8	3.2	2.1	0.4	−81.0	4.7	5.2	3.9	0.4	−89.7	6.1	8.0	5.6	0.8	−85.7
Hispanic	9.2	7.1	3.1	0.1	−96.8	9.9	8.8	5.9	0.4	−93.2	11.6	15.7	7.7	0.9	−88.3

HS = high school. **Note:** Figures may not add up to totals because of rounding. (1) Avg. highest level of education attained by respondent's mother and father. (2) For each of these groups, data for the specified year and previous year have been combined to increase sample size and thus provide more stable estimates.

Tobacco Use by High School and Middle School Students, 2022

Source: National Youth Tobacco Survey, Centers for Disease Control and Prevention, U.S. Dept. of Health and Human Services

In 2022, 11.3% of high school and middle school students in the U.S. reported current use—defined as use on one or more days in the past 30 days—of a tobacco product. While the use of cigarettes, cigars, and smokeless tobacco has declined significantly among students since 2011, electronic cigarette (e-cigarette) use has increased over the same time period. Since 2014, e-cigarettes have been the most commonly used tobacco product among students in grades 6 through 12.

Tobacco product	High school students using tobacco				Middle school students using tobacco			
	Female	Male	All students	Estimated no. of users[1]	Female	Male	All students	Estimated no. of users[1]
E-cigarettes	15.4%	12.8%	14.1%	2,140,000	4.1%	2.5%	3.3%	380,000
Cigars	2.1	3.5	2.8	410,000	0.6	0.6	0.6	70,000
Cigarettes	1.8	2.3	2.0	310,000	1.1	0.8	1.0	110,000
Smokeless tobacco	0.9	2.3	1.6	240,000	0.6	0.7	0.7	80,000
Hookahs	1.3	1.7	1.5	220,000	0.6	0.4	0.5	50,000
Nicotine pouches	0.8	2.1	1.4	210,000	—	0.4	0.5	50,000
Heated tobacco products	1.0	1.3	1.1	160,000	0.7	0.6	0.7	70,000
Pipe tobacco	0.5	0.9	0.7	100,000	—	0.3	0.3	30,000
Any tobacco product[2]	17.6	15.3	16.5	2,510,000	5.3	3.8	4.5	530,000
Any combustible tobacco[3]	4.7	5.8	5.2	790,000	1.9	1.4	1.6	190,000
2+ tobacco products	4.1	5.9	5.0	760,000	1.7	1.3	1.5	170,000

— = Not available. (1) Rounded down to nearest 10,000. (2) Incl. e-cigarettes, cigars, cigarettes, smokeless tobacco (i.e., chewing or dissolvable tobacco, snuff, dip, snus), hookahs, nicotine pouches, heated tobacco products, pipe tobacco, or bidis, not shown separately here. (3) Cigars, cigarettes, hookahs, pipe tobacco, or bidis.

Alcohol Use by 8th and 12th Graders, 1980-2022

Source: Monitoring the Future study, Univ. of Michigan Inst. for Social Research; Natl. Inst. on Drug Abuse, Natl. Insts. of Health

	1980	1990	1995	2000	2005	2010	2013	2015	2021	2022	% change, 2021-22
Alcohol use[1]			Percent using in the 30 days before the survey								
All 8th graders	—	—	24.6%	22.4%	17.1%	13.8%	10.2%	9.7%	7.3%	6.0%	–1.3%
Male	—	—	25.0	22.5	16.2	13.2	9.3	9.1	5.9	5.2	–0.7
Female	—	—	24.0	22.0	17.9	14.3	11.2	9.9	8.5	6.0	–2.4
White	—	—	25.4	24.7	17.9	13.9	9.5	8.9	9.2	7.6	–1.6
Black	—	—	18.7	16.0	14.9	11.8	9.7	8.2	6.9	4.5	–2.4
Hispanic	—	—	32.4	26.7	20.6	18.1	14.3	10.4	6.2	4.8	–1.3
All 12th graders ...	72.0%	57.1%	51.3	50.0	47.0	41.2	39.2	35.3	25.8	28.4	2.5
Male	77.4	61.3	55.7	54.0	50.7	44.2	41.8	36.0	23.1	28.2	5.1
Female	66.8	52.3	47.0	46.1	43.3	37.9	36.3	35.0	28.6	28.3	–0.3
White	75.4	63.8	54.5	55.1	52.3	45.4	43.6	40.9	35.3	33.8	–1.5
Black	47.6	35.8	35.2	30.0	29.0	31.4	28.4	24.0	18.2	13.6	–4.6
Hispanic	63.6	49.1	48.7	51.2	43.3	40.1	39.0	36.3	21.8	19.3	–2.5
Heavy alcohol use[2]			Percent using heavily in the two weeks before the survey								
All 8th graders	—	—	12.3%	11.7%	8.4%	7.2%	5.1%	4.6%	2.8%	2.2%	–0.5%
Male	—	—	12.5	11.7	8.2	6.5	4.5	4.6	2.0	2.1	0.0
Female	—	—	12.1	11.3	8.6	7.8	5.7	4.6	3.2	1.7	–1.5
White	—	—	12.1	13.0	9.0	7.1	4.2	4.0	3.6	2.6	–1.1
Black	—	—	8.3	7.3	6.1	5.3	4.5	4.1	3.4	1.6	–1.8
Hispanic	—	—	18.4	16.0	12.1	10.8	7.8	5.4	2.4	2.1	–0.3
All 12th graders ...	41.2%	32.2%	29.8	30.0	27.1	23.2	22.1	17.2	11.8	12.6	0.8
Male	52.1	39.1	36.9	36.7	32.6	28.0	26.1	19.3	11.1	14.3	3.2
Female	30.5	24.4	23.0	23.5	21.6	18.4	18.1	14.9	12.6	11.2	–1.4
White	44.3	36.6	32.3	34.6	32.5	27.6	25.6	21.2	17.2	16.0	–1.2
Black	17.7	14.4	14.9	11.5	11.3	13.1	12.5	9.8	5.8	4.5	–1.4
Hispanic	33.1	26.5	26.6	31.0	23.9	22.1	22.4	18.5	9.8	8.1	–1.8

— = Not available. **Note:** To derive percentages for each race/ethnicity subgroup, data for the specified year and previous year have been combined to increase sample size and thus provide more stable estimates. (1) In 1993, the alcohol question was changed slightly to indicate that a "drink" is defined as "more than a few sips." (2) Five or more drinks in a row (binge drinking) on one or more occasions.

Acquired Immune Deficiency Syndrome (AIDS)

Source: Centers for Disease Control and Prevention (CDC), U.S. Dept. of Health and Human Services

AIDS (Acquired Immune Deficiency Syndrome) is caused by the human immunodeficiency virus (HIV). HIV disables or kills crucial immune cells known as CD4 cells (also called T cells, or T-lymphocyte or T-helper cells), progressively destroying the body's ability to fight disease.

HIV is commonly spread through unprotected sexual contact with an infected partner's semen or vaginal fluids. It is also spread through contact with infected blood. Modern screening techniques make HIV transmission through transfusions or organ/tissue transplants, rare, but HIV can spread among intravenous drug users who share syringes and similar equipment. HIV can also be spread to a fetus during gestation or delivery or through breastfeeding after a baby's birth. With treatment, the transmission rate can be reduced from about 25% to 1% or less. There is no evidence HIV can spread through saliva or casual contact such as shaking hands or the sharing of food utensils, towels and bedding, or toilet seats.

About two-thirds of people experience flu-like symptoms within 2-4 weeks of being infected with HIV in what is called the acute HIV infection stage. The second stage is chronic infection, also referred to as asymptomatic HIV infection or clinical latency. Even though a person may not have any symptoms, the HIV continues to multiply, infect, and kill CD4 cells.

The term AIDS applies to the final (third) stage of HIV infection. According to the CDC's official case definition, an HIV-infected person 6 years of age or older with fewer than 200 CD4 cells per cubic millimeter of blood can be said to have AIDS. (Healthy adults usually have 500-1,600 CD4 cells per cu mm.) An HIV-infected person who develops an AIDS-defining opportunistic infection (OI) can also be diagnosed with AIDS. In the U.S., the most common OIs include the herpes simplex virus 1, salmonella, candidiasis, and toxoplasmosis.

Months or years prior to the onset of AIDS, people may experience such symptoms as swollen glands, lack of energy, fevers and sweats, and memory loss or other neurologic disorders. Children with AIDS may have delayed development or fail to thrive.

No test can detect HIV immediately after infection. The window period—or time between infection and accurate detection—varies by the type of HIV test used. An antibody test looks for antibodies, disease-fighting proteins of the immune system, to HIV in blood or oral fluid. It can take 23-90 days after exposure for this test to detect HIV antibodies. An antigen/antibody test looks for both HIV antibodies and parts of the virus (antigens); it can detect an infection after 18-90 days. A nucleic acid test (NAT) can detect the presence of HIV in blood 10-33 days following exposure. Most rapid tests and the self-test are antibody tests.

Since 1987, when the U.S. Food and Drug Administration (FDA) approved a drug called zidovudine (or AZT) for the treatment of HIV, more than 40 drugs and drug combinations (fixed doses of two or more medications in a single pill) have received approval. These drugs are grouped into classes: nucleoside reverse transcriptase inhibitors (NRTIs), non-nucleoside reverse transcriptase inhibitors (NNRTIs), protease inhibitors (PIs), fusion inhibitors, CCR5 antagonists, integrase strand transfer inhibitors (INSTIs), attachment inhibitors, post-attachment inhibitors, and capsid inhibitors. Each class of drug attacks the virus at a different point in its life cycle. Patients generally take three different HIV medicines from at least two different classes as part of antiretroviral therapy (ART), which extends the period between HIV infection and the development of serious illness.

Without a vaccine or cure for AIDS, the best way to prevent HIV infection is to avoid activities that carry a risk. The CDC recommends abstinence, mutual monogamy with an uninfected partner, limiting the number of sexual partners, never sharing needles, and using condoms correctly and consistently. People who do not have HIV but are at high risk of exposure can take medication daily to prevent HIV infection, called pre-exposure prophylaxis (PrEP). Daily PrEP reduces the risk of getting HIV from sex by about 99% and from injection drug use by at least 74%. Post-exposure prophylaxis (PEP) is the emergency use of HIV medicines after a single high-risk event. PEP must be started within 72 hours of exposure to HIV, and it is not always effective.

New AIDS Diagnoses in the U.S., by Transmission Category, 1985-2021

Source: National Center for HIV/AIDS, Viral Hepatitis, STD, and TB Prevention; CDC

Transmission category	All years[1]	1985	1990	1995	2000	2005	2010	2015	2018	2021
All persons 13 years of age and older	1,325,509	11,802	47,397	64,418	38,113	34,007	27,354	18,561	17,138	16,054
All males 13 years of age and older	1,048,648	10,942	41,445	51,520	28,118	24,923	20,519	14,060	13,038	12,442
Male-to-male sexual contact (MMSC)	642,202	7,704	26,712	28,881	15,434	15,272	13,925	10,087	9,508	9,304
Injection drug use..................	197,955	1,767	8,790	12,989	5,914	3,465	1,867	947	896	796
MMSC and injection drug use	97,602	1,066	4,010	5,526	2,816	2,442	1,570	914	786	746
Heterosexual contact[2]................	98,768	105	1,052	3,620	1,777	3,609	3,047	2,016	1,764	1,537
Other[3]........................	12,121	299	882	504	177	135	109	95	84	59
All females 13 years of age and older	276,861	860	5,952	12,898	9,995	9,084	6,835	4,501	4,100	3,612
Injection drug use..................	96,728	508	3,408	5,970	3,418	2,417	1,398	827	762	681
Heterosexual contact[2]................	173,579	246	2,232	6,691	6,453	6,543	5,305	3,591	3,253	2,873
Other[3]........................	6,554	107	312	238	124	124	132	83	85	58
All children, under 13 years of age	10,045	—	—	—	—	—	—	—	—	—

— = Not available. Note: Table shows number of persons diagnosed with an HIV infection at stage 3 (AIDS) in the 50 states and DC. The definition of AIDS cases has expanded over time. (1) Includes diagnoses for years not shown, from the beginning of the epidemic (1981) through 2021. Incl. 6 dependent areas. (2) Sexual contact with a person known to have, or with a risk factor for, HIV infection. (3) Incl. hemophilia, blood transfusion, perinatal exposure (13 years of age or older at time of diagnosis), and risk factor not reported or not identified.

New HIV Diagnoses in the U.S., 2017-21

Source: HIV Surveillance Report, 2021, vol. 34; National Center for HIV/AIDS, Viral Hepatitis, STD, and TB Prevention; CDC

Characteristic	Number of diagnoses					Diagnoses per 100,000 pop.				
	2017	2018	2019	2020	2021	2017	2018	2019	2020	2021
All persons	38,433	37,385	36,478	30,335	35,769	11.8	11.4	11.1	9.2	10.8
Gender										
Male	30,444	29,602	28,809	24,174	28,304	—	—	—	—	—
Female	7,288	7,055	6,900	5,421	6,554	—	—	—	—	—
Transgender woman/girl[1]	651	661	692	676	811	—	—	—	—	—
Transgender man/boy[2]	32	48	45	41	56	—	—	—	—	—
Additional gender identity[3]	18	19	32	23	44	—	—	—	—	—
Age at diagnosis										
Under 13 years...............	105	86	57	60	53	0.2	0.2	0.1	0.1	0.1
13-14 years.................	25	20	21	12	15	0.3	0.2	0.3	0.1	0.2
15-19 years.................	1,791	1,722	1,652	1,264	1,452	8.5	8.2	7.8	5.9	6.7
20-24 years.................	6,481	6,123	5,987	4,849	5,460	29.4	28.1	27.7	22.6	25.4
25-29 years.................	7,720	7,682	7,382	6,080	6,713	33.0	32.6	31.4	26.7	30.0
30-34 years.................	5,680	5,664	5,645	5,199	6,368	25.9	25.6	25.1	22.7	27.6
35-39 years.................	4,254	4,186	4,102	3,400	4,403	20.1	19.4	18.9	15.3	19.7
40-44 years.................	2,981	2,964	2,946	2,474	3,140	15.2	15.1	14.8	12.0	14.9
45-49 years.................	2,926	2,759	2,571	2,044	2,326	14.0	13.3	12.6	10.1	11.8
50-54 years.................	2,637	2,435	2,303	1,828	2,116	12.4	11.7	11.3	8.8	10.1
55-59 years.................	1,869	1,824	1,837	1,558	1,786	8.5	8.3	8.4	7.1	8.3
60-64 years.................	1,082	1,042	1,106	879	1,095	5.4	5.1	5.4	4.2	5.2
65 years and over............	882	878	869	688	842	1.7	1.7	1.6	1.3	1.5
Race/ethnicity										
Not Hispanic/Latino										
Amer. Indian/Alaska Native....	193	170	194	190	223	8.0	7.1	8.0	7.8	9.1
Asian......................	919	850	728	612	739	5.0	4.5	3.8	3.1	3.8
Black/African American.......	16,163	15,642	15,327	12,678	14,555	39.8	38.2	37.2	30.4	34.8
Native Hawaiian/other Pac. Isl.	47	51	59	64	76	8.1	9.6	9.8	10.3	12.1
White......................	9,558	9,338	8,992	7,744	9,063	4.8	4.7	4.6	3.9	4.6
Multiracial.................	1,543	1,397	1,320	1,001	1,043	22.0	19.4	17.9	13.1	13.4
Hispanic/Latino (any race)	10,010	9,931	9,858	8,046	10,070	17.1	16.7	16.3	13.0	16.1

— = Not available because of lack of denominator data. Note: Data shown are for the 50 states and DC. They reflect reports to the CDC as of Dec. 31, 2022, of persons who have been diagnosed with an HIV infection, regardless of the stage of disease. 2020 data should be interpreted with caution due to the impact of the COVID-19 pandemic. Numbers less than 12 and rates based on those numbers should be interpreted with caution. (1) Incl. individuals assigned male sex at birth who have ever identified as female gender. (2) Incl. individuals assigned female sex at birth who have ever identified as male gender. (3) Incl., e.g., bigender, gender queer, and two-spirit.

Deaths of Persons in the U.S. With HIV Ever Classified as AIDS, 1981-2021

Source: National Center for HIV/AIDS, Viral Hepatitis, STD, and TB Prevention; CDC

Age at death	Number	% of total	Transmission category[1]	Number	% of total
Under 13 years..................	5,197	0.7%	Male 13 years of age or older........	639,476	80.3%
13-14 years....................	306	0.04	Male-to-male sexual contact (MMSC)	361,065	45.4
15-19 years....................	1,393	0.2	Injection drug use...............	154,887	19.5
20-24 years....................	11,019	1.4	MMSC and injection drug use......	63,498	8.0
25-29 years....................	51,290	6.4	Heterosexual contact[2]...........	50,085	6.3
30-34 years....................	109,420	13.7	Perinatal[3].....................	754	0.1
35-39 years....................	137,683	17.3	Other[4].......................	9,187	1.2
40-44 years....................	132,558	16.7	Female 13 years of age or older......	151,192	19.0
45-49 years....................	108,949	13.7	Injection drug use...............	68,012	8.5
50-54 years....................	84,512	10.6	Heterosexual contact[2]...........	78,408	9.9
55-59 years....................	62,121	7.8	Perinatal[3].....................	868	0.1
60-64 years....................	42,002	5.3	Other[4].......................	3,903	0.5
65 years and over................	49,415	6.2	**Region of residence**		
Race/ethnicity			Northeast......................	229,071	28.8
American Indian/Alaska Native.......	2,185	0.3	Midwest.......................	83,126	10.4
Asian (incl. Asian/Pac. Isl. legacy)....	4,022	0.5	South.........................	310,229	39.0
Black/African American	318,284	40.0	West..........................	145,953	18.3
Native Hawaiian/other Pac. Islander ...	445	0.1	U.S. dependent areas.............	27,486	3.5
White.........................	301,474	37.9	**Total[5]**	**795,865**	**100.0**
Multiracial.....................	21,716	2.7			
Hispanic/Latino (any race)	147,695	18.6			

Note: Deaths of persons with HIV infection, stage 3 (AIDS) may be due to any cause. Numbers are cumulative from the beginning of the epidemic, in 1981, through 2021 in the 50 states, DC, and 6 dependent areas. Numbers may not add up to totals as they are calculated independently. (1) Based on sex assigned at birth. Classified based on risk factor most likely responsible for HIV transmission. (2) Sexual contact with a person known to have, or with a risk factor for, HIV infection. (3) Individual 13 years of age or older at time of death. (4) Incl. hemophilia, blood transfusion, and risk factor not reported or not identified. (5) Incl. persons of unknown race/ethnicity.

Allergies and Asthma

Source: Asthma and Allergy Foundation of America (AAFA), Centers for Disease Control and Prevention (CDC)

An estimated one in six Americans suffers from allergies each year. People with allergies have immune systems that overreact to a normally harmless substance, called an allergen. Common allergens include plant pollens, dust mites, or animal dander; plants such as poison ivy; and certain drugs, such as penicillin. The U.S. Food and Drug Administration recognizes the following as major food allergens, which must be specially manufactured and labeled: milk, eggs, fish, crustacean shellfish, tree nuts, peanuts, wheat, soybeans, and sesame.

The tendency to develop allergies is usually inherited. Though allergies typically manifest in childhood, they can show up at any age. Food allergies and eczema (inflamed or irritated skin) are common allergies among infants. Older children and adults may develop allergic rhinitis, or hay fever, in reaction to an inhaled allergen. Allergic rhinitis symptoms include nasal congestion, runny nose, and sneezing.

People with allergies should avoid contact with an allergen, if feasible. Medications, such as antihistamines and nasal corticosteroids, may be used to decrease an allergic reaction. Other effective allergy treatments include decongestants, eye drops, and ointments. Allergy shots, a form of immunotherapy, aim to desensitize a patient to an allergen through gradual exposure to increasingly higher doses of it. People at risk of anaphylaxis—a severe, whole-body allergic reaction that occurs rapidly—should have access to injectable epinephrine, an emergency medication.

Some allergy sufferers also have asthma. Asthma is a chronic inflammation disease that can develop at any age. It affects the passageways that carry air into and out of the lungs. During an asthma attack, these airways become inflamed and fill with mucus. A person may experience wheezing, tightening of the chest, and coughing. Asthma can become life-threatening if not controlled in its early stages. The following symptoms may be indicative of an emergency: the patient shows no improvement minutes after initial treatment; struggles to breathe while hunched with chest and neck pulled in; has trouble walking or talking; and develops gray or blue lips or fingernails.

Exposure to an allergen can set off an asthma attack. Tobacco smoke, cold air, and expressing strong emotion can also trigger an attack, as can respiratory infections and physical exercise. An accurate diagnosis by a physician is important.
Website: www.aafa.org

Persons With Asthma in the U.S., 2021
Source: National Health Interview Survey, NCHS, CDC

Characteristic	Number (thous.)	Percent
Total	**24,964**	**7.7%**
Children (under age 18)	4,675	6.5
Adults	20,288	8.0
Age		
0-4 years	370	1.9
5-14 years	3,124	7.7
15-19 years	1,862	9.0
20-24 years	1,970	9.5
25-34 years	3,508	7.8
35-64 years	10,080	8.2
65 years and over	4,034	7.2
Sex		
Males	10,274	6.5
Under age 18	2,695	7.3
Age 18 and over	7,579	6.2
Females	14,690	8.9
Under age 18	1,980	5.6
Age 18 and over	12,710	9.7
Race/ethnicity[1]		
White non-Hispanic	14,806	7.6
Black non-Hispanic	4,207	10.9
Asian non-Hispanic	744	4.1
Amer. Ind./Alaska Native non-Hispanic	566	12.3
Hispanic (any race)	3,917	6.4
Mexican	1,968	5.4
Other Hispanic	1,897	8.0

Note: Includes only those with a current asthma diagnosis. Numbers may not add up to totals due to rounding. (1) Data are for 2019-21.

Alzheimer's Disease

Source: Alzheimer's Association

Alzheimer's disease is a degenerative disease in which nerve cells in the brain deteriorate and die. It is the most common cause of dementia. Early symptoms include forgetting newly learned information and apathy or depression. As the disease advances, a person may exhibit disorientation and behavior changes; confusion about events, time, and place; and suspicion towards family, friends, and caregivers.

The rate of the disease's progression varies. Changes to the brain might begin 20 or more years before they are measurable in a stage researchers call preclinical Alzheimer's disease. For example, decreased glucose metabolism, a known biological marker for Alzheimer's disease, can be picked up by a brain scan. In the next stage—mild cognitive impairment (MCI) due to Alzheimer's disease—a person can still perform everyday activities without significant trouble. The disease's third stage, dementia due to Alzheimer's disease, can range from mild to moderate to severe. While a person could remain independent with assistance early on, they ultimately lose the ability to perform basic bodily functions, such as walking or swallowing, making them susceptible to infections of the lungs, urinary tract, and other organs. The average length of time from diagnosis of Alzheimer's dementia until death is 4-8 years for those age 65 and older.

An estimated 6.7 mil persons in the U.S., or 10.8% of the population age 65 and older, were living with Alzheimer's dementia in 2023; 33.3% of those age 85 and older have Alzheimer's dementia. Because women on average live longer than men, and age is the greatest risk factor for Alzheimer's disease, women make up almost two-thirds of Americans with Alzheimer's. Alzheimer's dementia has a higher prevalence in the older Black and Hispanic populations, which may be explained by disparities caused by marginalization of those communities.

Diagnosis involves a comprehensive evaluation that may include a complete health history, physical examination, neurological and mental status assessments, and other tests. Depression, drug interactions, nutritional imbalances, and excessive alcohol consumption can cause symptoms that look similar to dementia. Parkinson's disease, frontotemporal lobar degeneration, and cerebrovascular disease can also cause dementia.

Treatments for cognitive and behavioral symptoms are available, and clinical trials are ongoing for ways to prevent Alzheimer's or to slow its course. The U.S. Food and Drug Administration (FDA) has approved seven drugs, five of which temporarily treat symptoms. The other two drugs target the underlying disease process by removing beta-amyloid from the brain.

Having the e4 form of the APOE (apolipoprotein E) gene and a family history of the disease are also risk factors. Staying physically and mentally active and socially connected may be associated with a lower risk for the disease.

The U.S. cost in 2023 of diagnosing, treating, and providing long-term care for persons age 65 and older with Alzheimer's or other dementias was an estimated $345 bil. That estimate does not include the hours of unpaid care that family members, friends, and others provide, valued at around $339.5 bil in 2022.
Website: www.alz.org

Warning Signs of Alzheimer's Disease

- Memory loss that disrupts daily life
- Challenges in planning or solving problems
- Difficulty completing familiar tasks at home, at work, or at leisure
- Confusion with time or place
- Trouble understanding visual images and spatial relationships
- New problems with words in speaking or writing
- Misplacing things and losing the ability to retrace steps
- Decreased or poor judgment
- Withdrawal from work or social activities
- Changes in mood and personality

Arthritis

Source: Arthritis Foundation; Centers for Disease Control and Prevention (CDC), U.S. Dept. of Health and Human Services

The term arthritis refers to more than 100 different diseases that cause pain, aching, stiffness, and swelling in or around the joints. An estimated 21.6% of the adult population aged 18 and over reported having doctor-diagnosed arthritis in 2022. The cause of most types of arthritis is unknown; scientists are studying the role of genetics, lifestyle, and environment.

Of the three most prevalent forms of arthritis, **osteoarthritis** (OA), also called degenerative arthritis, is the most common, affecting over 32.5 mil Americans. With OA, protective cartilage at a joint breaks down. When the bones of the joint thus rub together, pain and stiffness may result. The most commonly affected joints are in the lower back, hips, knees, hands, and feet.

Fibromyalgia, another common arthritis condition, affects about 2% of American adults, with women twice as likely as men to have it. People suffering from fibromyalgia experience widespread pain, abnormal pain processing, sleep disturbance, and psychological distress. Other symptoms include tingling or numbness in hands and feet and problems with thinking and memory.

Rheumatoid arthritis (RA) is an autoimmune disease that affects an estimated 1.3 mil U.S. adults (or 0.6%–1% of the adult population). It is one of the most serious and disabling forms of arthritis, which women experience at 2-3 times the rate of men. With RA, the body's immune system attacks healthy cells in the joints, causing inflammation that can lead to cartilage and bone damage.

Other forms of arthritis and related conditions include lupus, gout, scleroderma, and Sjögren's syndrome. To diagnose arthritis, a doctor will record a patient's symptoms and look for any swelling or limited movement during a physical. Other signs of arthritis include rashes, mouth sores, and dry eyes. A doctor may test a patient's blood, urine, or joint fluid or take joint X-rays.

Medications that relieve pain and swelling, such as analgesics and anti-inflammatory drugs, can be used to treat arthritis. Regular physical activity, in particular low-impact sports like walking or swimming, can improve mood and ease pain. Maintaining a healthy weight puts less stress on joints. Surgery to replace a joint is an option if OA gets to be too severe.

Website: www.arthritis.org

Attention-Deficit/Hyperactivity Disorder (ADHD)

Source: CDC; Natl. Institute of Mental Health; Children and Adults with Attention-Deficit/Hyperactivity Disorder (CHADD)

Attention-deficit/hyperactivity disorder, or ADHD, is one of the most common neurodevelopmental disorders of childhood, when it is usually first diagnosed. Individuals with ADHD may have trouble paying attention and controlling impulsive behaviors.

Signs and Symptoms of ADHD

Inattention
- Often has trouble paying attention to details, resulting in careless mistakes
- Often loses focus, failing to finish tasks or duties
- Often loses things necessary for tasks (e.g., school materials, eyeglasses, keys)

Hyperactivity and impulsivity
- Often fidgets with hands or feet or squirms while seated
- Often talks too much
- Often has trouble waiting their turn

ADHD may manifest in one of three ways. A person who is **predominantly inattentive** is easily distracted or forgets details of daily routines. Someone who is **predominantly hyperactive-impulsive** may feel restless and impulsive. In the third type, **combined presentation**, an individual displays symptoms of both inattentiveness and hyperactivity-impulsivity. The cause of ADHD is unknown, but current research shows that genetics plays a significant role. Alcohol and tobacco use during pregnancy; low birth weight; and brain injury are being studied as other possible risk factors.

According to the 2019-20 National Survey of Children's Health, 8.9% of children age 3-17 years in the U.S. have a current diagnosis of ADHD. Boys are more likely to be diagnosed because girls with ADHD tend to present more inattentive symptoms. At least one-third of children with ADHD will continue to have it as adults. Studies have found that young adults with ADHD are more likely than those who have never been diagnosed with it to drop out of high school, to be unemployed, or to work an unskilled job.

As no single test exists for diagnosing ADHD, it is usually diagnosed through a checklist of symptoms and patient history. In most cases, ADHD is treated with a combination of medication (stimulants and nonstimulants) and behavior therapy.

Breast Cancer

Source: American Cancer Society, Inc.; National Cancer Institute, National Institutes of Health

In 2023, an estimated 297,790 women and 2,800 men in the U.S. will be newly diagnosed with breast cancer, and about 43,170 women and 530 men will die from it. More than 3.8 mil women live with a history of breast cancer, but mortality rates have been declining, especially among older women, probably because of earlier detection and improved treatment.

The risk for breast cancer is higher for women and increases with age. It is higher for women with a personal or family history of cancer (particularly breast cancer), a longer menstrual history (menstrual periods that started early and ended later in life), recent use of hormonal birth control, use of menopausal hormone therapy, and in those who have no children or had no live birth until after age 30. Other risk factors include alcohol consumption, physical inactivity, and being overweight or obese. About 5%-10% of breast cancers are probably due to inherited mutations, the most common being those in the *BRCA1* and *BRCA2*. Most women who develop breast cancer have no family history of it.

Breast cancer often manifests first as a new lump or mass. Other symptoms include swelling, distortion, tenderness, skin irritation, redness, scaliness, or nipple abnormalities, such as ulceration, retraction, or spontaneous discharge.

Studies show that early detection increases survival and treatment options. Although most detected breast lumps are noncancerous, any suspicious lump should be biopsied.

Treatment for breast cancer may involve breast-conserving surgery (removal of the tumor and surrounding tissue), mastectomy (surgical removal of the breast), radiation, chemotherapy, hormone therapy, and/or targeted therapy. The five-year relative survival rate for female breast cancer patients has improved from 74.8% in 1975-77 to 90.8% in 2013-19; for women diagnosed with localized breast cancer (cancer that has not spread to lymph nodes or other locations outside the breast), survival is 99.3%.

Website: www.cancer.org

Prostate Cancer

Source: Prostate Cancer Foundation (PCF); American Cancer Society, Inc.; National Cancer Institute, National Institutes of Health

The prostate is a male gland located between the bladder and scrotum that secretes seminal fluid. Among men in the U.S., prostate cancer is the most commonly diagnosed non-skin cancer and the second-most common cause, after lung and bronchus cancer, of cancer deaths. In 2023, an estimated 288,300 men will be newly diagnosed with prostate cancer, and about 34,700 will die from the disease. More than 3.1 mil men in the U.S. are living with a history of prostate cancer today.

The most identifiable risk factors for prostate cancer are age, family history, and African ancestry. The median age at diagnosis is 66, and the chances of developing the disease rise dramatically with age. Black men in the U.S. and Caribbean have the world's highest documented incidence rate of prostate cancer. The cause for this disparity remains unclear.

Usually, the disease has no symptoms in its early stages. As the disease advances, a man may experience weak or interrupted urine flow; inability to urinate or difficulty starting or stopping the urine flow; the need to urinate frequently, especially at night; blood in the urine; or pain or burning with urination. Advanced prostate cancer commonly spreads to the bones, causing pain in areas such as the hips, spine, or ribs.

The American Cancer Society recommends that at age 50, men at average risk of prostate cancer should speak with their health care provider about the benefits and limitations of prostate-specific antigen (PSA) testing. An increased PSA level may indicate a higher chance of having prostate cancer, but older age and the use of certain medications, among other factors, can raise or lower PSA levels. Black men or those with a family history of the disease (a close relative who was diagnosed before age 65) should be aware of their screening options beginning at age 45. Men with more than one close relative with prostate cancer should discuss screening at 40. The U.S. Preventive Services Task Force recommends that men ages 55-69 screen for prostate cancer based on individual risk. It advises against routine screening in men age 70 and older. Because prostate cancer is slow-growing, testing is not likely to help men with a life expectancy of less than 10 years. Men under 40 seldom get prostate cancer.

Prostate cancer treatment may include surgery, radiation, hormonal therapy, chemotherapy, or some combination. If caught early on, while tumor cells are localized within the prostate, the five-year relative survival rate approaches 100.0%.

Websites: www.pcf.org; www.cancer.org

Skin Cancer

Source: American Cancer Society, Inc; National Cancer Institute, National Institutes of Health.

Skin cancer—the most common cancer diagnosed in the U.S.—is generally divided into the following types: **basal and squamous cell skin cancers** (or nonmelanomas) and **melanomas**. Invasive melanoma accounts for only about 1% of all skin cancers but the majority of skin cancer deaths. Risk factors include heavy exposure to UV light, multiple moles (more than 50), fair skin, family or personal history of skin cancers, a history of sunburns, and occupational exposure to certain compounds.

Melanomas generally look like abnormal moles on the surface of the skin. Abnormal moles differ from regular skin cells and may be a sign of skin cancer. An irregular mole should be examined by a doctor as soon as possible.

If caught early, melanoma is highly curable. In 2013-19, the five-year relative survival rate for melanoma at the localized stage was 99.6%; at the regional stage, 73.9%; and 35.1% at the distant stage.

Treatment may include simple removal of the melanoma; amputation if the cancer is found on a finger or toe; or chemotherapy, immunotherapy, and/or radiation if the melanoma has spread to other parts of the body.

Warning Signs of Abnormal Moles

- **Asymmetry**: one half does not match the other half
- **Border**: edges are irregular, ragged, notched, or blurred
- **Color**: not uniform; may be shades of brown or black, and patches of pink, red, blue, or white
- **Diameter**: moles wider than ¼ inch are abnormal (however, melanomas can be smaller)
- **Evolving**: mole changes size, shape, or color over time

Website: www.cancer.org

Cancer Risk Factors

Source: American Cancer Society, Inc., www.cancer.org; National Cancer Institute, National Institutes of Health

Alcohol: Alcohol consumption increases the risk of cancers of the mouth, pharynx, larynx, esophagus, liver, colorectum, breast, and possibly pancreas. Alcohol consumption combined with tobacco use increases the risk of cancers of the mouth, pharynx, larynx, and esophagus far more than either drinking or smoking alone.

Diet and physical activity: Overweight and obesity are associated with increased risk for developing many cancers, including cancers of the breast in postmenopausal women, colorectum, kidney, pancreas, and esophagus. Overweight and obesity may also be associated with increased risk of fatal prostate cancer, non-Hodgkin lymphoma, and male breast cancer. It's not yet known for certain how diet, nutrition intake, and the amount and distribution of body fat factor into the development of certain cancers.

Environmental and occupational hazards: Exposure to certain substances, called carcinogens, can increase the risk of various cancers. Carcinogens like arsenic or radon may occur naturally, or they may be manufactured, like vinyl chloride. The risk of lung cancer from asbestos exposure is greatly increased among smokers.

Radon, a form of ionizing radiation, is estimated to be the second-leading cause of U.S. lung cancer deaths. Excessive radon exposure in the home may increase lung cancer risk, especially in cigarette smokers.

Examples of occupational hazards, where workers are in contact with carcinogens at higher levels than the public, include diesel engine exhaust, the foams and flame retardants used by firefighters, and pesticides.

Hormones: Menopausal hormone therapy (MHT, formerly called hormone replacement therapy) without the use of progestin can increase the risk of endometrial and ovarian cancer. Combining progestin with estrogen MHT may help minimize that risk. Studies, however, suggest that use of MHT increases the risk of breast cancer. The benefits and risks of the use of estrogen should be discussed carefully with one's doctor.

Infectious agents: HPV, the Epstein-Barr virus, the hepatitus B and hepatitus C virus, and *Helicobacter pylori* bacteria are known to cause cancer. About 3% of all U.S. cancer cases are due to infections, many of which are treatable and for which vaccines exist.

Tobacco: Smoking is responsible for about 30% of all cancer deaths and 81% of lung cancer deaths in the U.S. Cigarette smoking also increases the risk of the following cancers: larynx, oral cavity and pharynx, esophagus, stomach, pancreas, uterine cervix, kidney, bladder, stomach, colorectum, liver, and acute myeloid leukemia. While electronic cigarettes (e-cigarettes) generally have lower carcinogen levels than combustible tobacco products, the long-term risks of use are not yet clear. Among all lung cancer deaths each year, an estimated 3% are caused by secondhand smoke.

Use of smokeless tobacco products—such as chewing tobacco, snuff, and snus—can increase the risk of oral, esophageal, and pancreatic cancers as well as precancerous mouth lesions.

Ultraviolet radiation: Many of the more than 5 mil skin cancers diagnosed annually in the U.S. could have been prevented by protection from the sun's rays and avoiding indoor tanning. Epidemiological evidence shows that sun exposure is a major factor in the development of melanoma and that incidence rates are increasing.

Screening Guidelines for Early Detection of Cancer

Cancer site	Population	Test or procedure	Frequency
Breast	Women, age 40+	Mammography	The American Cancer Society (ACS) no longer recommends regular breast self-exams or clinical breast exams; research has not found that they reduce the risk of dying from breast cancer. Women should be familiar with how their breasts look and feel and report any changes to a health care professional. For women at average risk (e.g., lack of strong family history of breast cancer), at age 40: begin annual mammography if desired; for ages 45-54: annual mammograms; for ages 55+: mammograms yearly or every two years for those in good health with a life expectancy of 10 or more years. Women at high risk for breast cancer, such as a *BRCA1* or *BRCA2* gene mutation, should get a breast MRI and mammogram yearly.
Cervix	Women, age 21+ or 25+	HPV test, Pap test	The ACS recommends all women begin screening at age 25; the U.S. Preventive Services Task Force (USPSTF) recommends screening start at age 21. For ages 25-65, a primary HPV test every 5 years is preferred. If HPV testing alone is not available, then an HPV/Pap co-test every 5 years or a Pap test every 3 years is acceptable. For ages 65+: women who have had regular screenings with normal results in the previous 10 years should no longer be tested; women with a history of abnormal test results or cervical precancers should continue to be tested for at least 20 years after diagnosis. Women who have had a total hysterectomy for reasons unrelated to cervical cancer should not be screened. Women should not be screened annually by any method at any age.
Colorectal	Men and women, ages 45-75	Guaiac-based fecal occult blood test (gFOBT) **or** fecal immunochemical test (FIT) **or**	The ACS and USPSTF recommend starting at age 45. Annual, for people with average risk. Testing at home with adherence to instructions for collection and number of samples is recommended. A gFOBT or FIT done during a digital rectal examination in a health care setting is not sufficient for screening as only one stool sample is collected.
		Multitargeted stool DNA test (MT-sDNA), **or**	Every 3 years.
		Flexible sigmoidoscopy (FSIG), **or**	Every 5 years, or every 10 years if an FIT is done yearly.
		CT, or virtual, colonography, **or**	Every 5 years.
		Colonoscopy	Every 10 years for people without an increased risk. A colonoscopy should also be done if any of the above tests returns a positive result.
Endometrial	Women, at menopause		Women at average risk should be informed about risks and symptoms of endometrial cancer and encouraged to report any unexpected bleeding or discharge to their physician.
Lung	Current or former smokers, ages 50-80	Low-dose CT scan (LDCT)	People aged 50 to 80 years with a 20 pack-year or more smoking history (number of packs smoked per day multiplied by number of years smoked) who currently smoke or have quit within the past 15 years should be screened annually. People who are older than age 80, or have not smoked for 15 years, or have a limited life expectancy making surgery unlikely should discontinue screening.
Prostate	Men, age 40+ or 55-69	Prostate-specific antigen test (PSA) and digital rectal exam (DRE)	The ACS recommends men with an average risk and an expected life span of 10+ years should talk with their health care provider about the benefits and risks of screening. African Americans—who have a higher rate of prostate cancer—and men with a first-degree relative diagnosed with prostate cancer before age 65 should have this talk at age 45. Men with more than one first-degree relative diagnosed at an early age should have the talk at age 40. The USPSTF recommends PSA-based screening for men ages 55-69 based on individual risk.

New U.S. Cancer Cases and Deaths for Leading Sites, 2023

Source: *Cancer Facts & Figures 2023*, American Cancer Society

The following estimates exclude basal cell and squamous cell skin cancers, also referred to as nonmelanoma skin cancers, and in situ carcinomas (i.e., noninvasive cancers) except of the urinary bladder. In 2023, an estimated 55,720 cases of female breast ductal carcinoma in situ and 89,070 cases of melanoma in situ are expected to be diagnosed. An est. 5.4 mil cases of basal cell and squamous cell skin cancer were diagnosed among 3.3 mil people in 2012 according to the most recent study available.

Estimated New Cases

Both sexes		Male		Female	
Breast	300,590	Prostate	288,300	Breast	297,790
Prostate	288,300	Lung and bronchus	117,550	Lung and bronchus	120,790
Lung and bronchus	238,340	Colon and rectum	81,860	Colon and rectum	71,160
Colon and rectum	153,020	Urinary bladder	62,420	Uterine corpus	66,200
Melanoma of the skin	97,610	Melanoma of the skin	58,120	Melanoma of the skin	39,490
Urinary bladder	82,290	Kidney and renal pelvis	52,360	Non-Hodgkin lymphoma	35,670
Kidney and renal pelvis	81,800	Non-Hodgkin lymphoma	44,880	Thyroid	31,180
Non-Hodgkin lymphoma	80,550	Oral cavity and pharynx	39,290	Pancreas	30,920
Uterine corpus	66,200	Leukemia	35,670	Kidney and renal pelvis	29,440
Pancreas	64,050	Pancreas	33,130	Leukemia	23,940
All sites	**1,958,310**	**All sites**	**1,010,310**	**All sites**	**948,000**

Estimated Deaths

Both sexes		Male		Female	
Lung and bronchus	127,070	Lung and bronchus	67,160	Lung and bronchus	59,910
Colon and rectum	52,550	Prostate	34,700	Breast	43,170
Pancreas	50,550	Colon and rectum	28,470	Colon and rectum	24,080
Breast	43,700	Pancreas	26,620	Pancreas	23,930
Prostate	34,700	Liver and intrahepatic bile duct	19,000	Ovary	13,270
Liver and intrahepatic bile duct	29,380	Leukemia	13,900	Uterine corpus	13,030
Leukemia	23,710	Esophagus	12,920	Liver and intrahepatic bile duct	10,380
Non-Hodgkin lymphoma	20,180	Urinary bladder	12,160	Leukemia	9,810
Brain and other nervous system	18,990	Non-Hodgkin lymphoma	11,780	Non-Hodgkin lymphoma	8,400
Urinary bladder	16,710	Brain and other nervous system	11,020	Brain and other nervous system	7,970
All sites	**609,820**	**All sites**	**322,080**	**All sites**	**287,740**

U.S. Cancer Mortality Rates by Cancer Site, 1975-2020

Source: SEER (Surveillance, Epidemiology, and End Results) Program, National Cancer Institute, National Institutes of Health
(mortality rate per 100,000 pop. by year of death)

Cancer site	1975	1980	1985	1990	1995	2000	2005	2010	2015	2020
All cancer sites combined[1]	199.1	207.0	211.3	214.9	209.9	198.8	185.2	171.8	159.0	143.8
Anus, anal canal, and anorectum	0.04	0.1	0.2	0.2	0.2	0.2	0.2	0.2	0.3	0.4
Bones and joints	0.9	0.6	0.5	0.4	0.5	0.4	0.5	0.4	0.5	0.5
Brain and other nervous system	4.1	4.4	4.6	4.9	4.7	4.5	4.3	4.2	4.4	4.5
Colon and rectum	28.1	28.1	26.9	24.6	22.6	20.7	17.6	15.5	14.0	12.6
Esophagus	3.7	3.8	3.9	4.1	4.3	4.4	4.4	4.3	4.0	3.7
Eye and orbit	0.2	0.1	0.1	0.1	0.1	0.1	0.1	0.1	0.1	0.1
Gallbladder	1.4	1.2	1.1	0.9	0.8	0.7	0.7	0.6	0.6	0.5
Hodgkin lymphoma	1.3	1.0	0.8	0.7	0.5	0.5	0.4	0.4	0.3	0.3
Kidney and renal pelvis	3.6	3.7	4.0	4.2	4.3	4.2	4.1	3.9	3.8	3.4
Larynx	1.7	1.6	1.6	1.6	1.5	1.4	1.2	1.1	1.0	0.9
Leukemia	8.1	8.4	8.1	8.0	7.9	7.7	7.3	6.9	6.3	5.8
Liver and intrahepatic bile duct	2.8	2.8	3.1	3.6	4.4	4.6	5.3	5.9	6.6	6.5
Lung and bronchus	42.6	49.4	54.3	58.9	58.4	55.8	52.9	47.4	40.7	31.8
Melanoma of the skin	2.1	2.3	2.6	2.8	2.7	2.7	2.8	2.7	2.4	2.0
Myeloma	2.9	3.3	3.6	3.8	4.0	3.8	3.6	3.3	3.3	3.0
Non-Hodgkin lymphoma	5.6	6.2	7.1	7.9	8.7	8.2	6.9	6.1	5.5	4.9
Oral cavity and pharynx	4.3	4.2	3.8	3.6	3.2	2.7	2.5	2.5	2.5	2.5
Pancreas	10.7	10.6	10.6	10.7	10.4	10.5	10.8	11.0	11.0	11.0
Small intestine	0.3	0.4	0.4	0.4	0.4	0.4	0.4	0.4	0.4	0.4
Soft tissue including heart	0.9	1.2	1.3	1.4	1.5	1.3	1.3	1.3	1.3	1.3
Stomach	8.5	7.4	6.5	6.1	5.3	4.5	3.8	3.4	3.1	2.8
Thyroid	0.5	0.5	0.4	0.4	0.4	0.5	0.5	0.5	0.5	0.5
Urinary bladder (invasive and in situ)	5.5	5.2	4.7	4.5	4.4	4.3	4.4	4.4	4.4	4.0

(1) Not including cancer sites for which data is not available (breast; cervix uteri; corpus and uterus, not otherwise specified; ovary; prostate; testis; vagina; vulva).

U.S. Cancer Survival Rates by Age at Diagnosis, 2013-19

Source: Surveillance, Epidemiology, and End Results (SEER) Program, National Cancer Institute, National Institutes of Health

Age at diagnosis	All races % total	% male	% female	White % total	% male	% female	Black % total	% male	% female
All ages	68.8%	67.3%	70.3%	69.0%	67.2%	70.8%	64.6%	66.2%	63.0%
Under age 45	84.7	80.9	87.0	85.9	82.5	88.0	75.8	70.2	79.0
Ages 45-54	77.4	71.9	81.4	78.0	72.2	82.2	71.4	69.9	72.7
Ages 55-64	71.5	69.6	73.7	72.0	69.6	74.7	66.0	68.0	63.5
Under age 65	75.8	72.0	79.2	76.4	72.4	80.1	69.3	68.7	69.9
Ages 65-74	68.4	69.0	67.7	68.6	68.8	68.4	64.3	68.1	59.4
Ages 65 and over	61.6	62.9	60.0	61.9	62.8	60.8	57.9	62.7	53.0
Ages 75 and over	52.3	53.6	51.1	53.1	53.9	52.2	46.4	49.5	44.1

Note: Rates are five-year relative (estimated) survival rates for all invasive cancer sites, at all stages of diagnosis; based on follow-up of patients into 2020.

Depression

Source: Substance Abuse and Mental Health Services Admin. and National Institutes of Health, U.S. Dept. of Health and Human Services

Depression is a serious illness that affects thoughts, feelings, and the ability to function in everyday life. It is one of the most common mental disorders in the U.S., affecting all age groups. In 2021, an estimated 21.0 mil adults age 18 and older (or 8.3% of the adult population) in the U.S. had at least one major depressive episode. Over the same 12-month period, 18.6% of persons age 18-25 years experienced at least one major depressive episode versus 4.5% of those 50 or older. More women (13.4 mil) than men (7.7 mil) reported at least one major depressive episode in 2021.

Available treatments can alleviate symptoms. But many depressed people—and those around them—fail to realize that they have an illness or could benefit from medical help.

Symptoms and Types of Depression

- Depressed mood most of the day
- Loss of interest or pleasure in daily activities
- Significant weight loss with appetite and/or weight changes
- Insomnia or hypersomnia (excessive daytime sleepiness or prolonged nighttime sleep)
- Restlessness or moving/talking more slowly
- Fatigue or loss of energy
- Feelings of worthlessness
- Difficulty concentrating, thinking, or making decisions
- Recurrent thoughts of death or suicide, or suicide attempts

A diagnosis of **major depressive disorder** (or **clinical depression**) is made if an individual reports experiencing five or more of these symptoms in the same two-week period.

Bipolar disorder (formerly known as manic-depressive illness), while distinct from depression, is characterized by depressive episodes alternating with manic episodes, when a person may experience an abnormally elevated mood, less need for sleep, increased talkativeness, racing thoughts, agitation, and engagement in risky activities (e.g., spending a lot of money, unprotected sex).

Depression in women who are pregnant or who recently gave birth (**postpartum depression**); **psychotic depression**, where a person also has some type of psychosis, such as delusions or hallucinations; and **seasonal affective disorder** are other forms of depression.

Treatments for Depression

Depression can be treated with medication, psychotherapy, or a combination of the two, which studies have shown to be most effective in treating moderate-to-severe depression. Antidepressants influence the functioning of certain neurotransmitters in the brain. The most popular antidepressants are selective serotonin reuptake inhibitors (SSRIs). Serotonin and norepinephrine reuptake inhibitors (SNRIs) and bupropion are also commonly prescribed as they have fewer side effects than drugs from older classes, such as tricyclics and monoamine oxidase inhibitors (MAOIs). Some people respond better, however, to the older antidepressants.

Research has shown that certain types of psychotherapy, particularly cognitive-behavioral therapy (CBT) and interpersonal therapy (IPT), can help relieve depression. CBT helps patients change the negative thinking and behavior patterns often associated with depression. IPT focuses patients on working through personal relationships that may contribute to depression.

Electroconvulsive therapy (ECT) has been found effective in treating some cases of severe depression, particularly those that have not responded to other treatment. ECT involves using electric currents to produce a seizure in the brain of a patient under general anesthesia. Headaches and memory loss, though common side effects, are typically short-lived. Other types of treatment involving brain stimulation are being studied.

Website: www.nimh.nih.gov

Diabetes

Source: American Diabetes Association; Centers for Disease Control and Prevention (CDC), U.S. Dept. of Health and Human Services

Diabetes is a chronic disease in which the body does not produce or properly use the hormone **insulin**. Insulin is needed to convert sugar, starches, and other foods into energy. Both genetics and environment appear to play roles in the onset of diabetes. This disease, which has no cure, was the eighth leading cause of death in the U.S. in 2021 (25.4 deaths per 100,000 pop.). In 2021, an est. 24.7 mil Americans (6.4% of the population) had diagnosed diabetes. Diagnosed diabetes in the U.S. cost an estimated $327 bil in direct medical costs and in reduced productivity in 2017.

The American Diabetes Association supports studies proving that detection at an earlier stage and modest lifestyle changes, such as eating better and exercising more, will help prevent or delay complications.

There are two major types of diabetes:

Type 1 (formerly known as insulin-dependent or juvenile diabetes). The body does not produce insulin; the disease is usually diagnosed in children and young adults. People with type 1 diabetes must take daily insulin to stay alive.

Type 2 (formerly known as non-insulin dependent or adult-onset diabetes). The body does not produce enough or cannot properly use insulin. It is the most common form of the disease (90%-95% of all diabetes cases) and often begins later in life.

Prediabetes

In 2019, 96.0 mil Americans age 18 and older (or about 1 in 3 adults) had prediabetes, the state that occurs when a person's blood glucose levels are higher than normal but not high enough for a diagnosis of diabetes. People with prediabetes are at increased risk of developing type 2 diabetes unless lifestyle changes are made.

Complications From Diabetes

People often have diabetes for many years before it is diagnosed. During that time, serious complications may develop. Potential complications include the following:

Diabetic eye disease. High blood glucose can damage blood vessels to the eyes. In 2021, about 23.1% of adults age 18 and older with diagnosed diabetes had severe vision difficulty or blindness. Diabetic retinopathy is the most common cause of vision loss among those with diabetes. People with diabetes are also more likely to develop glaucoma or cataracts.

Kidney disease. In 2018, 62,012 people with diagnosed diabetes (181.9 per 100,000 of the total diabetic population) had end-stage renal disease.

Amputations. Diabetes is the most frequent cause for non-traumatic lower-limb amputations. About 1.2 per 1,000 adults age 18 and older with diabetes were hospitalized in 2019 for amputation below the knee; the rate was 0.4 per 1,000 for amputation above the knee and 2.0 for amputation of the foot.

Heart disease and stroke. Among adults age 35 and older with diabetes, 22.0% had major heart disease or a stroke in 2021.

Common Diabetes Symptoms

- Frequent urination
- Thirst
- Hunger
- Fatigue
- Blurry vision
- Cuts and bruises that are slow to heal
- Weight loss, nausea, vomiting (type 1)
- Tingling or numbness in hands or feet (type 2)

Gestational Diabetes

Gestational diabetes mellitus (GDM) is a form of diabetes that develops during or is diagnosed during pregnancy. Hormones released during pregnancy can cause insulin resistance, allowing blood glucose levels to rise. Usually there are no symptoms, or the symptoms are mild. Because GDM usually starts around the 24th week, pregnant women should receive a glucose tolerance test between the 24th and 28th week of pregnancy. Diet and exercise can help keep blood glucose levels within normal limits. Treatment may also include daily blood glucose testing and insulin injections.

Women with GDM tend to have larger babies at birth, which can complicate delivery. Glucose levels usually return to normal after delivery, but the odds of recurrence in future pregnancies and development of type 2 diabetes later in life increase. GDM is a common complication, affecting 2%-10% of U.S. pregnancies annually. In 2020, 7.8 of 100 live births in the U.S. were to women with GDM. In the same year, 10.6 of 1,000 live births were to women diagnosed with diabetes before pregnancy, that is, prepregnancy diabetes mellitus (PDM).

Website: www.diabetes.org

Eating Disorders

Source: National Institute of Mental Health (NIMH), National Institutes of Health, U.S. Dept. of Health and Human Services

Eating disorders are medical illnesses that involve serious disturbances in eating behavior. The main types are anorexia nervosa, bulimia nervosa, and binge-eating disorder. Though they can develop at any age, the median age of onset for anorexia nervosa and bulimia nervosa is 18 years old and 21 years old for binge-eating disorder. They may be caused by a combination of genetics, behavioral, psychological, and social factors. Eating disorders often occur with other illnesses such as depression, substance abuse, and anxiety disorders. If not treated, eating disorders can lead to serious complications, which may result in death.

Anorexia nervosa affects an estimated 0.6% of the U.S. adult population and three times as many women as men. It has the highest mortality rate of any mental disorder in the U.S. People with anorexia see themselves as overweight even when they are dangerously thin. In response, they severely restrict their food intake and take extreme measures to lose weight, such as exercising compulsively or purging by means of vomiting or laxatives. While some fully recover after a single episode, others may relapse frequently or experience chronic deterioration. Symptoms that may develop over time include muscle weakness, lethargy, and infertility.

Bulimia nervosa affects an estimated 1.0% of the U.S. adult population. It is five times more prevalent in women than men. It is characterized by recurrent uncontrolled binge-eating episodes followed by what is believed to be compensatory behavior to prevent weight gain, such as self-induced vomiting, use of laxatives or diuretics, exercising excessively, or fasting. Persons with bulimia can weigh within the normal range for their age and height but still fear gaining weight. Symptoms include a chronically inflamed and sore throat, worn tooth enamel, intestinal distress, and severe dehydration.

Binge-eating disorder affects an estimated 2.8% of the U.S. adult population, with women twice as likely than men to have it. As with bulimia, a binge-eating disorder involves episodes of excessive eating during which a person may feel a complete lack of control. Because these episodes are not followed by purging, exercising, or fasting, persons with binge-eating disorder are often overweight or obese.

Early diagnosis and a comprehensive treatment program are essential to recovery. Some patients may need immediate hospitalization. For anorexia, treatment usually follows three established steps: weight restoration, usually in an inpatient hospital setting; treatment of any accompanying psychological disturbances, including the use of medications; and achieving long-term remission or recovery by reducing or eliminating negative thoughts and behaviors.

Heart and Blood Vessel Disease

Source: American Heart Assn. (AHA); Natl. Center for Chronic Disease Prevention and Health Promotion, Centers for Disease Control and Prevention; Natl. Heart, Blood, and Lung Institute, Natl. Institutes of Health (NIH), U.S. Dept. of Health and Human Services

Warning Signs of Heart Attack

- Discomfort in chest. Most heart attacks involve discomfort, such as pressure, squeezing, or pain, in the center of the chest that lasts more than a few minutes or occurs intermittently. Most common symptom in men and women
- Discomfort in other upper body areas, including one or both arms, the back, neck, jaw, or stomach
- Shortness of breath, with or without chest discomfort
- Breaking out in a cold sweat, nausea, or lightheadedness, among other signs

While chest discomfort is the most common symptom of a heart attack, women are more likely to experience the other symptoms, such as abdominal pain, shortness of breath, dizziness, fainting, and extreme fatigue, without having any chest pain. The AHA advises calling 911 at onset of symptoms so that emergency medical services can begin treatment on the way to the hospital.

Warning Signs of Stroke

- **F**ace drooping or weakness on one side
- **A**rm weakness
- **S**peech difficulty, including slurring
- **T**ime to call 911
  Other stroke symptoms, which may appear separately or in combination with F.A.S.T.:
- Sudden numbness or weakness of the face, arm, or leg, especially on one side of the body
- Sudden confusion or trouble speaking or comprehending
- Sudden vision difficulty in one or both eyes
- Sudden trouble walking, dizziness, or loss of coordination
- Sudden severe headache with no known cause

If someone has one or more stroke symptoms, immediately call 911 or the emergency medical service number so an ambulance, ideally one with advanced life support, can be sent. Prompt treatment of a stroke can prevent death or lessen the long-term effects.

A transient ischemic attack (TIA), also referred to as a mini stroke, is when blood flow to the brain is blocked temporarily, with symptoms typically lasting under five minutes. Immediate medical treatment is still necessary as a TIA could signal a future stroke.

Major Modifiable Risk Factors

Major risk factors for heart and blood vessel (cardiovascular) disease are age, gender, and heredity. People 65 years of age or older are more likely to die of coronary heart disease. Men are at greater risk, as well as African Americans and those with a family history of heart disease. Major risk factors that can be modified include the following:

High blood pressure. High blood pressure, or hypertension, increases the risk of stroke, heart attack, kidney failure, and congestive heart failure. It affects men and women of all races, ethnic origins, and ages. But obesity, physical inactivity, and an unhealthy diet can contribute to this often symptomless disease. Everyone 3 years of age and older should have a blood pressure reading at least once a year.

A blood pressure reading consists of two measurements written one above the other, such as 122/78 mm Hg (millimeters of mercury). The upper number (systolic pressure) represents the amount of pressure in the arteries when the heart contracts (beats) and pushes blood through the circulatory system. The lower number (diastolic pressure) represents the pressure in the arteries between beats, when the heart is resting. According to guidelines revised in 2017, a blood pressure reading below 120/80 is considered normal, while a reading of 130/80 or higher indicates hypertension, of which there are two stages:

Stage 1 is 130-139 (systolic) over 80-89 (diastolic);
Stage 2 is 140+ (systolic) over 90+ (diastolic).

The diagnosis can be based on either the systolic or diastolic reading. Any reading higher than 180/120 is a hypertensive crisis that must be addressed by a doctor immediately.

High blood pressure usually cannot be cured, but it can be controlled in a variety of ways, including through diet, exercise, quitting smoking (where applicable), and medication. Treatment should be at the direction and under the supervision of a physician.

High blood cholesterol. Cholesterol is a waxy fatlike substance produced by the liver and found in all cells of the body. Dietary cholesterol exists in animal foods. Excess levels of cholesterol increase the risk of heart disease. High cholesterol in itself usually does not cause symptoms, so many people are unaware that they have a problem.

There are two major kinds of cholesterol: LDL (low-density lipoprotein), often called "bad" cholesterol, can build up on the inside walls of blood vessels, narrowing them. HDL (high-density lipoprotein), known as "good" cholesterol, helps reduce that risk.

NIH guidelines classify healthy total cholesterol levels (determined by a blood test) as less than 170 mg/dL for those age 19 or younger and 125 to 200 mg/dL for persons age 20 or older. LDL levels of less than 100 mg/dL are considered healthy. Healthy levels of HDL are more than 45 mg/dL for those age 19 or younger, 40 mg/dL or higher for men ages 20+, and 50 mg/dL or higher for women ages 20+. Among U.S. adults age 20 and over, 10.0% had high cholesterol (i.e., total cholesterol level equal to or greater than 240 mg/dL) in 2017-20.

As with high blood pressure, high blood cholesterol can be controlled by lifestyle changes and medication and should be treated by a physician.

Triglycerides, another form of fat in the blood, can also raise the risk of heart disease. Levels that are borderline high (150-199 mg/dL), high (200-499 mg/dL), or very high (500 mg/dL or more) may need treatment.

Diabetes. Adults with diabetes mellitus are two to three times more likely to die of heart disease or stroke.

Tobacco smoke. Cigarette smokers and nonsmokers exposed to secondhand smoke are more likely to develop coronary heart disease (CHD).

Obesity. People with excess body fat, especially around the waist (more than 40 in. for men, more than 35 in. for women), are more likely to develop heart and blood vessel disease even without any other risk factors.

Physical inactivity. A sedentary lifestyle is a risk factor for CHD. The risk increase is comparable to that observed for high blood cholesterol, high blood pressure, or cigarette smoking.

Women and Cardiovascular Disease

Heart disease was the number one cause of death for women in the United States in 2020, accounting for 19.5% of all female deaths; stroke (cerebrovascular disease) was the fifth leading cause, at 5.6%. Many of the major cardiovascular studies were conducted only on men. Researchers are now trying to understand the influence of gender on cardiovascular disease risk and prevention.

One problem in **diagnosis** is that women tend to have heart attacks later in life than men, so symptoms may be masked by other age-related diseases such as arthritis or osteoporosis. Even certain diagnostic tests and procedures such as the exercise stress test may not be as accurate in women, with the result that the disease process leading to heart attack or stroke may not be detected early on, with potentially serious consequences.
Website: www.heart.org

COVID-19

Source: National Center for Immunization and Respiratory Diseases, CDC, U.S. Dept. of Health and Human Services

COVID-19 (coronavirus disease 2019) was discovered in Dec. 2019 in Wuhan, China, and quickly spread around the world. COVID-19 is caused by the SARS-CoV-2 virus. It is part of the coronavirus family, whose viruses cause diseases from the common cold to acute bronchitis to more severe diseases like severe acute respiratory syndrome (SARS) and Middle East respiratory syndrome (MERS). Coronaviruses spread through droplets projected from the mouth or nose when an infected person breathes, coughs, sneezes, or speaks.

The word *corona* means crown and refers to the spike proteins on the surface of coronaviruses. These spike proteins allow the virus to attach to a human cell in order to infect it, replicating inside of the cell and spreading to other cells.

COVID-19 most often causes respiratory symptoms that can feel much like a cold, a flu, or pneumonia. Most experience mild symptoms, but some become severely ill. After infection, some people—even those who experienced minor or no symptoms—may suffer long-term effects, known as post-COVID conditions, or long COVID. Older adults, people with underlying medical conditions, and pregnant people are at increased risk of severe illness from COVID-19. Vaccines against COVID-19 are safe and effective; the first vaccines were made available in the U.S. beginning in Dec. 2020 under emergency authorization.

Symptoms of COVID-19

Symptoms may appear 2-14 days after exposure to the virus. Anyone can have mild to severe symptoms, including the following:

- Fever or chills
- Cough
- Shortness of breath or difficulty breathing
- Fatigue
- Muscle or body aches
- Headache
- New loss of taste or smell
- Sore throat
- Congestion or runny nose
- Nausea or vomiting
- Diarrhea

U.S. COVID-19 Cases, Deaths, and Vaccination Rates

Source: Centers for Disease Control and Prevention, U.S. Dept. of Health and Human Services

The COVID-19 public health emergency in the U.S.—which the Dept. of Health and Human Services first declared on Jan. 31, 2020—expired on May 11, 2023. Authorizations to collect certain public health data also expired on that date. As of May 10, 2023, this data has been archived or will no longer be updated; they may differ from figures elsewhere as the CDC reconciles records. Cumulative totals include confirmed and probable cases and deaths since Jan. 2020. COVID-19 was the third leading cause of death in 2020 and 2021 and the fourth leading cause in 2022.

State/territory	Cumulative total Cases	Cumulative total Deaths	Vaccination rate (% of total pop.) At least one dose	Vaccination rate (% of total pop.) Fully vaccinated[1]
Alabama	1,659,936	21,138	65.1%	53.3%
Alaska	297,588	1,468	73.2	65.3
American Samoa	8,331	34	95.0	85.7
Arizona	2,474,154	33,451	78.4	66.2
Arkansas	995,043	13,115	70.1	57.0
California	12,251,820	101,886	85.1	74.9
Colorado	1,783,663	14,385	84.0	73.8
Connecticut	982,335	12,337	95.0	83.2
Delaware	333,772	3,394	88.5	73.5
Dist. of Columbia	178,904	1,435	95.0	91.3
Florida	7,572,282	88,248	82.9	69.7
Georgia	3,087,729	42,782	68.6	57.5
Guam	61,642	415	94.9	86.0
Hawaii	374,264	1,856	91.7	81.7
Idaho	526,118	5,479	64.1	56.6
Illinois	4,136,659	42,005	79.2	71.5
Indiana	2,076,326	26,446	64.6	57.9
Iowa	908,936	10,797	70.9	64.5
Kansas	945,923	10,214	76.5	65.6
Kentucky	1,743,117	18,623	69.1	59.7
Louisiana	1,600,610	18,971	62.9	55.1
Maine	322,982	3,038	95.0	83.6
Maryland	1,379,385	16,740	92.1	80.0
Massachusetts	2,242,176	24,644	95.0	84.5
Michigan	3,106,362	42,873	69.9	62.6
Minnesota	1,795,771	14,770	79.1	72.4
Mississippi	1,000,415	13,474	61.8	53.8
Missouri	1,790,763	22,931	69.6	59.2
Montana	333,959	3,715	68.4	59.3
Nebraska	575,134	5,089	73.7	66.5
Nevada	898,511	12,008	77.9	63.8
New Hampshire	382,013	3,052	88.5	72.3
New Jersey	3,075,271	36,118	94.9	79.3
New Mexico	681,242	9,236	94.9	75.5
New York[2]	3,572,043	32,341	94.7	81.0
New York City	3,266,726	45,181	NA	NA
North Carolina	3,501,404	29,059	90.2	66.9
North Dakota	291,093	2,513	69.6	58.9
Northern Mariana Islands	13,886	44	90.4	84.9
Ohio	3,441,458	42,207	65.9	60.7
Oklahoma	1,306,350	16,157	74.9	60.6
Oregon	975,856	9,550	82.0	72.7
Pennsylvania	3,559,331	51,047	91.1	73.8
Puerto Rico	1,122,076	5,908	91.0	84.2
Rhode Island	441,466	3,915	95.0	88.0
South Carolina	1,852,019	19,923	71.2	60.1
South Dakota	282,895	3,231	84.3	66.5
Tennessee	2,542,163	29,549	64.6	56.4
Texas	8,508,204	93,780	77.0	63.5
Utah	1,097,475	5,362	75.5	66.9
Vermont	154,243	967	95.0	86.1
Virgin Islands (U.S.)	24,994	131	71.0	55.6
Virginia	2,310,846	23,743	91.3	76.8
Washington	1,957,759	16,186	85.6	76.4
West Virginia	650,556	8,125	67.6	59.8
Wisconsin	2,030,717	16,600	75.3	68.4
Wyoming	187,034	2,031	61.1	53.2
United States[3]	**104,673,730**	**1,133,717**	**81.4**	**69.5**

NA = Not available. (1) Defined as having received two doses on different days of two-dose series or one dose of single-dose vaccine. (2) Excl. New York City, except for vaccination rates, which are for the entire state. (3) U.S. data incl. counts from jurisdictions not shown separately in table, incl. three countries in free association compacts (Marshall Islands, Fed. States of Micronesia, Palau).

Common Infectious Diseases

Source: Centers for Disease Control and Prevention (CDC), U.S. Dept. of Health and Human Services; World Health Organization

State and local officials, in connection with the CDC, monitor certain diseases in the interests of public health. Some diseases must be confirmed in a laboratory while others may be diagnosed based on epidemiologic data (e.g., exposure to a foodborne pathogen linked to confirmed cases of illness in other patients). Statistics may thus appear uneven because of different reporting methods for each disease. This list is meant to be used for reference purposes only and not as a diagnostic tool.

Chickenpox

(Varicella-zoster virus, or VZV) Highly contagious disease commonly associated with children that can be especially serious in babies, adults, pregnant women, and people with weakened immune systems. A person who has had chicken-pox may develop shingles later in life if the virus reactivates. **Transmission:** direct contact with rash or through the air when an infected person coughs or sneezes. **Symptoms:** blister-like rash that can last up to 7 days, fever. **Vaccine:** available since 1995. **Treatment:** for relief of symptoms; antivirals only for those at risk of complications. **Annual U.S. cases:** before 1995, about 4 mil, mostly children; 2,927 in 2020, 3,665 in 2021 (provisional).

Chlamydia

(*Chlamydia trachomatis*) One of the most widely spread sexually transmitted diseases (STDs), and the most common condition reported to the CDC of the diseases that it tracks. **Transmission:** sexually transmitted. A mother can pass an infection to her baby during delivery. **Symptoms:** Most of those infected show no symptoms. In women, abnormal vaginal discharge, infection of the cervix and urinary tract; can cause pelvic inflammatory disease. In men, infection of urinary tract and pain and swelling in one or both testicles; can also infect the throat, rectum, and eyes. **Treatment:** curable with antibiotics. **Annual U.S. cases:** 1,644,416 in 2021 (or 495.5 per 100,000 pop.).

Common cold

(More than 200 different viruses, rhinoviruses being most common) An upper respiratory viral infection. **Transmission:** touching one's nose, eyes, or mouth after touching something contaminated by the virus; inhalation of airborne virus. **Symptoms:** irritated nose or scratchy throat, sneezing and watery green or yellow nasal discharge, coughing, muscle aches, headaches, postnasal drip (mucus dripping down throat). **Treatment:** no cure. Over-the-counter remedies can relieve symptoms. **Annual U.S. cases:** about 1 bil.

Gonorrhea

(*Neisseria gonorrhoeae*) Very common bacterial STD. **Transmission:** sexually transmitted. Can pass from mother to infant during delivery. **Symptoms:** pain or burning during urination. In men, white, yellow, or green discharge from urethra; in women, increased vaginal discharge, vaginal bleeding between periods. Many men and most women do not present symptoms. **Treatment:** curable with antibiotics, although bacteria has become increasingly resistant. **Annual U.S. cases:** 710,151 in 2021 (or 214.0 per 100,000 pop.).

Hepatitis

A viral disease that causes inflammation of the liver. In the U.S., five forms are endemic: A, B, C, D, and E. Forms A, B, and C are the most common. HBV and HCV can cause chronic disease. **Symptoms:** all forms have generally similar symptoms including jaundice, fatigue, abdominal pain, loss of appetite, nausea, mild flu-like symptoms. Many cases cause no symptoms. In extreme cases, infected persons may develop end-stage liver disease.

Hepatitis A (*Hepatovirus picornaviridae*). **Transmission:** consuming food or water contaminated with feces from infected persons. **Vaccine:** effective. (In developing countries, older children and adults may generally be immune after having been infected when young.) **Treatment:** disease usually resolves on its own; alcohol consumption should be avoided. **Annual U.S. cases:** 9,946 acute (i.e., newly acquired) in 2020; 5,726 acute in 2021 (provisional).

Hepatitis B (*Orthohepadnavirus hepadnaviridae*). **Transmission:** unsterilized needle sharing; contaminated blood transfusions; sexual contact; infants during childbirth. **Vaccine:** highly effective. **Treatment:** for chronic cases, drug treatment is necessary. For acute cases, disease usually resolves itself. **Annual U.S. cases:** 2,155 acute, 10 perinatal (pregnant person to child) in 2020; 2,044 acute, 17 perinatal in 2021 (provisional).

Hepatitis C (*Hepacivirus flavinviridae*). **Transmission:** unsterilized needle sharing; contaminated blood transfusions; sexual contact; infants during childbirth. **Vaccine:** none.

Treatment: chronic cases treated with drugs, which can eliminate the virus in more than 90% of patients. For acute cases, the CDC recommends monitoring by a doctor and starting treatment if the infection becomes chronic. **Annual U.S. cases:** 4,798 acute (confirmed), 165 perinatal in 2020; 4,918 acute (confirmed), 200 perinatal in 2021 (provisional).

HPV

(More than 200 related human papillomaviruses) Most common sexually transmitted infection in U.S.; causes nearly all cases of cervical cancer, 91% of anal cancers, and 60%-75% of oropharyngeal, vaginal, vulvar, and penile cancers. The CDC estimates most people in the U.S. will acquire HPV at some point in their lives. **Transmission:** sexually transmitted. **Symptoms:** most of those infected have no symptoms though in some cases, low-risk HPVs result in genital warts and precancerous bumps on anus, cervix or vulva, or penis. High-risk HPVs can persist for years and lead to cell changes that become cancerous, possibly producing symptoms. **Vaccine:** currently only protects against certain HPV types but recommended at age 11 or 12. **Treatment:** while there is no cure, a healthy immune system can usually fight off HPV on its own. Women age 21 and older should be regularly screened for cervical cancer. **Annual U.S. cases:** est. 13 mil new infections, 42.5 mil currently infected in 2020.

Influenza

(Various influenza viruses) Highly contagious viral respiratory infection. **Transmission:** airborne; contact with face after touching infected surface. **Symptoms:** chills, fatigue, fever, headaches, sore throat, sinus congestion, coughing. ("Stomach flu" is not influenza.) **Vaccine:** yearly vaccinations recommended; available as injection or nasal spray. **Treatment:** antiviral drugs; disease normally runs its course in a matter of days. **Annual U.S. cases:** preliminary est. 9.3 mil symptomatic illnesses, 101,262 flu-related hospitalizations, and 4,601 flu-related deaths during the 2021-22 influenza season, with adults 65 years of age and older making up 83.0% of all deaths from influenza.

Lyme disease

(*Borrelia burgdorferi*) Bacterial inflammatory disease, first identified 1975 in Old Lyme, CT. Most common vector-borne disease in the U.S. Concentrated in the Northeast and mid-Atlantic, north-central states (mostly Wisconsin, Minnesota), and the West Coast, particularly Northern California. **Transmission:** bite from infected blacklegged (or deer) tick. Mice and deer are most common tick hosts. **Symptoms:** mimic those of other diseases. Flu-like symptoms: fatigue, stiff neck, joints. A roughly circular rash may appear at site of tick bite and expand to look like a bull's eye. **Treatment:** antibiotics in early stages; anti-inflammatory drugs to relieve symptoms. Some patients continue to experience symptoms after treatment, a condition called Post-Treatment Lyme Disease Syndrome. Without treatment, long-term complications (some fatal) involving joints, heart, and nervous system. **Annual U.S. cases:** from 9,465 reported cases in 1991—the first year the CDC began collecting Lyme disease data—to 18,000 cases (12,123 confirmed; 5,877 probable) in 2020. The CDC estimates about 476,000 people are diagnosed and treated for Lyme disease each year.

Malaria

(*Plasmodium* parasite) Mosquito-borne disease that mostly occurs in tropical and subtropical regions. **Transmission:** bite from infected *Anopheles* mosquito. **Symptoms:** high fever, shaking chills, heavy sweating, headaches, fatigue, enlarged spleen. If left untreated, organ damage and death. **Treatment:** antimalarial drugs, such as doxycycline, for treatment and prevention. **Annual U.S. cases:** 603 in 2020, 1,503 in 2021 (provisional) in the U.S.; est. 247 mil cases and 619,000 deaths worldwide in 2021, with four African countries accounting for just over half of global malaria deaths.

Measles

(*Rubeola* virus) Declared eliminated in the U.S. in 2000; spreads mostly via unvaccinated travelers from abroad.

Transmission: airborne transmission. The virus can survive for up to two hours in the air where an infected person has coughed or sneezed. **Symptoms:** itchy and raised rash, cough, watery eyes, high fever. Complications include ear infections, pneumonia, brain swelling, premature birth, or even death. **Vaccine:** highly effective. **Treatment:** no specific treatment; relief of symptoms. **Annual U.S. cases:** 49 in 2021, 121 in 2022 (both years preliminary).

Mumps

(Mumps virus) Acute and contagious viral infection. **Transmission:** direct contact with mucus or saliva of infected persons. **Symptoms:** headaches, fever, loss of appetite may precede painful, visible swelling of the salivary glands under one or both ears. In severe cases, inflammation of testes, pancreas, ovaries; brain swelling; deafness. **Vaccine:** MMR (measles, mumps, and rubella) vaccine is effective. **Treatment:** no specific treatment; symptoms may be relieved by applying cold or warm compress to swollen glands. **Annual U.S. cases:** 154 in 2021; 322 in 2022 (preliminary).

Peptic ulcer

(Most from *Helicobacter pylori* [*H. pylori*] bacteria; also long-term use of aspirin or other anti-inflammatory drugs) Weakening of the stomach or duodenum's protective mucous coating, allowing stomach acid and bacteria to irritate the lining and cause a sore. **Transmission:** *H. pylori* may be transmitted through food and water; possibly through close contact between infected persons. **Symptoms:** indigestion; bloating; dull, transient abdominal pain or discomfort; nausea; vomiting. **Treatment:** antibiotics, drugs to reduce stomach acid. **Annual U.S. cases:** 4.6 mil people.

Pertussis or Whooping cough

(*Bordetella pertussis*) Upper respiratory bacterial infection. **Transmission:** airborne transmission by infected persons; highly contagious. **Symptoms:** initially, mild cold-like symptoms, fever, difficulty breathing; later, violent coughing with characteristic "whooping" sound when patient tries to breathe between coughs, vomiting. Many babies, instead of coughing, may stop breathing and turn blue. **Vaccine:** available as part of Tdap (tetanus, diphtheria, pertussis) combination vaccine. **Treatment:** antibiotics in early cases; otherwise, disease must run its course. **Annual U.S. cases:** 6,124 in 2020; 2,115 in 2021 (provisional).

Salmonella or Salmonellosis

(Most types of *Salmonella*) Bacterial infection. **Transmission:** eating foods contaminated by feces carrying the bacteria or eating undercooked meats or raw eggs contaminated by bacteria. Contact with infected domestic animals. **Symptoms:** fever, diarrhea, abdominal cramps. **Treatment:** no standard treatment. Runs its course in 4-7 days. Antibiotics in severe cases. **Annual U.S. cases:** (excluding *Salmonella* serotype Typhi and Paratyphi infections, which cause typhoid and paratyphoid fevers, respectively) 45,442 in 2020; 49,249 in 2021 (provisional).

Shigellosis

(Four species of *Shigella* bacteria) Diarrheal disease. **Transmission:** swallowing water or consuming food contaminated by infected feces. **Symptoms:** sometimes bloody diarrhea, fever, stomach pain usually lasting 5-7 days. **Treatment:** replacement of fluids and salts to prevent dehydration. Antibiotics in severe cases. Antidiarrheal medicines may make illness worse. **Annual U.S. cases:** 9,108 in 2020; 9,999 in 2021 (provisional).

Syphilis

(*Treponema pallidum*) Bacterial infection that can cause significant health problems if left untreated. **Transmission:** sexually transmitted; pregnant women can transmit during fetal development or at birth. **Symptoms:** primary stage: painless sore, called a chancre, where bacteria entered the body; usually heals in 3-6 weeks with or without treatment. Without treatment, disease enters secondary stage: skin rash as chancre is healing or weeks after it has healed. Without treatment, enters latent stage (no visible symptoms). Very rarely, can move into tertiary stage 10-30 years after infection and cause death. Syphilis can spread to the brain and nervous system (neurosyphilis) or eyes (ocular syphilis) at any stage; symptoms include fever, fatigue, dementia, vision changes. **Treatment:** antibiotics, though reinfection is possible. **Annual U.S. cases:** 176,713 (all stages and congenital syphilis)/53,767 (primary and secondary) in 2021.

Tetanus or Lockjaw

(*Clostridium tetani*) Bacterial infection. **Transmission:** spores of bacteria commonly found in soil entering body through broken skin. **Symptoms:** muscle stiffness; spasms or "locking" of muscles of the jaw, neck, limbs; seizures, fever. Breathing difficulties may lead to death in 1-2 of every 10 cases. **Vaccine:** four forms of immunization. **Treatment:** tetanus immune globulin to fight infection, drugs to control spasms. **Annual U.S. cases:** 17 in 2020; 28 in 2021 (provisional).

Tuberculosis

(*Mycobacterium tuberculosis*) Bacterial infection that primarily affects the lungs. **Transmission:** airborne transmission by persons with TB disease. **Symptoms:** no symptoms in person with latent TB infection. Person with TB disease may have weight loss, fever, cough with discharge (sometimes with bloody sputum) lasting 3 or more weeks, night sweats. **Vaccine/treatment:** BCG (bacille Calmette-Guérin) vaccine for children where TB is prevalent. Not recommended for use in the U.S. because of low infection risk and variable effectiveness in adults. Antibiotics to treat TB disease or to prevent latent infection from becoming active. **Annual U.S. cases:** 7,874 in 2021; 8,300 in 2022 (provisional).

Yellow fever

(Yellow fever virus, in *flavivirus* genus) Viral infection endemic in tropical areas of Africa and Central and South America. **Transmission:** bite from virus-carrying mosquito. **Symptoms:** head and body aches, nausea and vomiting, fatigue over 3-4 days. Small percentage may then enter more toxic phase, with fever, jaundice (yellowing skin), organ failure, coma, and death in 7-10 days. Most infected people exhibit no symptoms or only mild symptoms. **Vaccine:** safe and effective, conferring lifetime immunity to most who receive it. **Treatment:** symptoms treated until disease runs its course. **Annual cases:** none in the U.S. in 2020 or 2021; est. 200,000 cases and 30,000 deaths worldwide (90% in Africa).

U.S. Vaccine-Preventable Diseases, 1950-2018

Source: Centers for Disease Control and Prevention (CDC), U.S. Dept. of Health and Human Services

Year	Diphtheria Cases	Deaths	Tetanus Cases	Deaths	Pertussis Cases	Deaths	Polio (paralytic) Cases	Deaths	Measles Cases	Deaths	Mumps Cases	Deaths	Rubella Cases	Deaths
1950	5,796	410	486	336	120,718	1,118	33,300[1]	1,904	319,124	468	NR	NA	NR	NA
1960	918	69	368	231	14,809	118	2,525	230	441,703	380	NR	42	NR	12
1970	435	30	148	79	4,249	12	31	7	47,351	89	104,953	16	56,552	31
1980	3	1	95	28	1,730	11	9	2	13,506	11	8,576	2	3,904	1
1990	4	1	64	11	4,570	12	6	0	27,786	64	5,292	1	1,125	8
2000	1	0	35	5	7,867	12	0	0	86	1	338	2	176	0
2005	0	0	27	1	25,616	31	1[2]	0	66	NA	314	0	11	0
2007	0	0	28	5	10,454	9	0	0	43	0	800	0	11	1
2008	0	0	19	3	13,278	6	0	0	140	0	454	2	16	0
2009	0	0	18	6	16,858	1	1[2]	0	71	2	1,991	2	3	2
2010	0	0	26	3	27,550	5	0	0	63	2	2,612	1	5	2
2011	0	0	36	6	18,719	1	0	0	220	0	404	0	4	1
2012	1	0	37	4	48,277	4	0	0	55	2	229	0	3	0
2013	0	0	26	3	28,639	2	1[2]	0	187	0	584	1	9	0
2014	1	0	25	1	32,971	7	0	0	667	0	1,223	0	6	0
2015	0	NA	29	NA	20,762	NA	0	NA	188	NA	1,329	NA	5	NA
2016	0	NA	34	NA	17,972	NA	0	NA	85	NA	6,369	NA	7	NA
2017	0	NA	33	NA	18,975	NA	0	NA	120	NA	6,109	NA	7	NA
2018	1	NA	23	NA	15,609	NA	0	NA	375	NA	2,515	NA	4	NA

NA = Not applicable or available. NR = Not nationally reportable. (1) Incl. non-paralytic reported cases. (2) Vaccine-associated/derived paralytic polio.

Effectiveness of the Seasonal Flu Vaccine, 2004-23

Source: National Center for Immunization and Respiratory Diseases (NCIRD), CDC, U.S. Dept. of Health and Human Services
The CDC conducts studies to determine vaccine effectiveness (VE), or how well each season's flu vaccine worked among a nation-wide sample of patients.

Flu season	VE	Flu season	VE	Flu season	VE
2004-05	10%	2011-12	47%	2017-18	38%
2005-06	21	2012-13	49	2018-19	29
2006-07	52	2013-14	52	2019-20	39
2007-08	37	2014-15	19	2020-21	NA[1]
2008-09	41	2015-16	48	2021-22	36
2009-10	56	2016-17	40	2022-23	NA[2]
2010-11	60				

NA = Not available. (1) VE not estimated due to low influenza virus circulation. (2) VE was 54% for preventing medically attended influenza A infection among persons under 65 years of age, according to one CDC report of interim ests.

Weight Guidelines

Source: National Center for Health Statistics, CDC, U.S. Dept. of Health and Human Services

Federal clinical guidelines on the identification, evaluation, and treatment of overweight and obesity in adults age 20 and over were first released in 1998. The guidelines define overweight and obese in terms of **body mass index (BMI)**. BMI, based on a person's weight and height, can be an indicator of total body fat. A BMI of 18.5-24.9 is within a healthy weight range. A BMI of less than 18.5 is **underweight** while 25-29.9 is considered **overweight**; a BMI of 30 or higher indicates **obesity**. Obesity can be further subdivided into three classes, with class 3 obesity (BMI of 40 or higher) described as severe obesity. BMI can be calculated at www.nhlbi.nih.gov/health/educational/lose_wt/BMI/bmicalc.htm. (BMI in persons ages 2 through 19 is age- and sex-specific. For example, a 10-year-old boy would be at a healthy weight if his BMI were in the 5th to less than 85th percentile of all 10-year-old boys in the reference population.)

Waist circumference should be evaluated along with BMI. Men with a waist circumference of more than 40 inches and non-pregnant women with a waist circumference of more than 35 inches may be at increased risk for disease because of excess abdominal fat. BMI and waist circumference are screening tools, not diagnostics. A health-care provider should also perform other assessments to evaluate risk and diagnose disease, taking into consideration such factors as blood pressure, cholesterol levels, and family medical history.

The National Center for Health Statistics notes that 41.9% of American adults (ages 20 and over) and 19.7% of youth (ages 2-19) in 2017-Mar. 2020 were obese. The prevalence of obesity has increased over time, from 30.5% of adults and 13.9% of youth in 1999-2000 to its current levels. Among all age groups, obesity was more prevalent in the non-Hispanic Black and Hispanic population than among non-Hispanic whites and non-Hispanic Asians.

A high prevalence of overweight and obesity is a public health concern because higher body weights increase a person's risk of developing type 2 diabetes, hypertension, dyslipidemia, cardiovascular disease, stroke, gallbladder disease, sleep and respiratory problems, osteoarthritis, and certain cancers.

Adults Meeting U.S. Fitness Guidelines, 1998-2018

Source: National Health Interview Survey, National Center for Health Statistics, CDC, U.S. Dept. of Health and Human Services

Characteristic	% meeting aerobic activity guidelines					% meeting muscle-strengthening guidelines				
	1998	2000	2005	2010	2018	1998	2000	2005	2010	2018
Sex and age										
Male, 18-44 years	51.5%	53.6%	50.0%	59.0%	63.6%	27.2%	26.3%	28.7%	35.6%	38.3%
Male, 45-54 years	44.3	45.2	42.6	50.7	56.9	18.8	18.0	19.2	24.8	27.3
Male, 55-64 years	38.3	38.9	38.4	46.0	54.8	12.9	13.8	15.7	22.9	22.7
Male, 65-74 years	38.5	41.8	38.3	40.7	50.3	12.0	12.2	14.5	20.6	22.2
Male, 75 years and over	26.1	30.7	28.6	32.3	39.8	9.5	10.1	12.4	14.5	18.5
Female, 18-44 years	40.0	42.0	43.1	48.5	57.2	17.9	17.9	19.8	22.1	28.2
Female, 45-54 years	36.1	39.1	38.1	44.7	48.6	13.7	16.1	19.8	20.4	21.7
Female, 55-64 years	32.5	33.5	34.1	38.6	46.8	10.3	12.4	15.9	17.5	22.2
Female, 65-74 years	26.2	32.6	30.2	31.8	42.4	7.8	10.5	13.3	15.6	19.8
Female, 75 years and over	14.0	16.8	18.8	18.3	26.8	5.7	6.7	6.7	10.8	12.7
Race or Hispanic origin[1]										
White, not Hispanic	43.1	45.7	45.7	51.5	57.6	18.7	19.3	22.5	26.3	29.4
Black, not Hispanic	30.4	31.7	29.1	37.3	45.8	15.6	16.0	15.7	21.6	24.3
Amer. Indian or AK Native	39.7	29.7	41.6	42.0	54.1	18.2	13.9	20.5	16.7	24.2
Asian	37.1	41.7	37.5	44.2	54.7	17.2	17.2	16.9	21.9	26.7
Two or more races	—	43.9	41.1	50.2	56.6	—	22.2	23.6	30.4	30.0
Hispanic or Latino	29.1	30.8	28.5	36.2	47.8	12.7	11.9	12.9	18.1	24.4
Geographic region										
Northeast	39.6	45.3	43.3	46.9	55.5	17.5	20.0	21.6	24.3	28.6
Midwest	42.0	43.5	43.5	46.1	53.4	18.2	19.3	21.9	24.7	28.4
South	35.3	37.3	36.5	45.0	50.5	15.0	15.1	17.6	22.0	25.0
West	46.7	46.9	44.4	52.0	59.9	22.3	19.7	21.3	27.5	30.8
Total, 18 years and over	40.0	42.2	41.1	47.3	54.3	17.7	18.0	20.2	24.4	27.8

— = Not available. **Note:** Measures of physical activity reflect the federal 2008 Physical Activity Guidelines for Americans, which recommend that for substantial health benefits, adults each week perform at least 150 min. of moderate-intensity, 75 min. of vigorous-intensity, or an equivalent combination of moderate- and vigorous-intensity aerobic activity. Aerobic activity should be performed in episodes of at least 10 min., preferably spread throughout the week. The guidelines also recommend that adults perform muscle-strengthening activities that are moderate or high intensity and involve all major muscle groups on two or more days a week. (1) Persons reporting only one race, unless otherwise noted. Persons of Hispanic origin may be of any race.

Obesity Among Adults in the U.S., 2018

Source: National Health Interview Survey, National Center for Health Statistics, CDC, U.S. Dept. of Health and Human Services

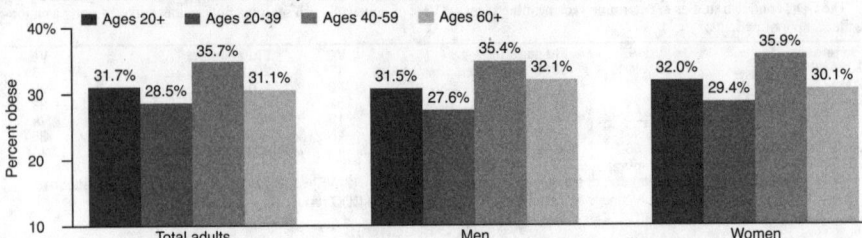

Overweight and Obesity Among U.S. Adults, 1960-2020

Source: National Health and Nutrition Examination Survey, NCHS, CDC, U.S. Dept. of Health and Human Services
(as percent of adults age 20-74 in 1960-80 and age 20 and over for all other years shown here)

Survey period	Total			Men			Women		
	Overweight	Obesity	Severe obesity	Overweight	Obesity	Severe obesity	Overweight	Obesity	Severe obesity
1960-62	31.5%	13.4%	0.9%	38.7%	10.7%	0.3%	24.7%	15.8%	1.4%
1971-74	32.7	14.5	1.3	41.7	12.1	0.6	24.3	16.6	2.0
1976-80	32.1	15.0	1.4	39.9	12.7	0.4	24.9	17.0	2.2
1988-94	33.1	22.9	2.8	40.7	20.2	1.7	25.9	25.4	3.9
1999-2000	34.0	30.5	4.7	39.7	27.5	3.1	28.6	33.4	6.2
2001-02	35.1	30.5	5.1	42.2	27.7	3.6	28.2	33.2	6.5
2003-04	34.1	32.2	4.8	39.7	31.1	2.8	28.6	33.2	6.9
2005-06	32.6	34.3	5.9	39.9	33.3	4.2	25.5	35.3	7.4
2007-08	34.3	33.7	5.7	40.1	32.2	4.2	28.6	35.4	7.3
2009-10	33.0	35.7	6.3	38.4	35.5	4.4	27.9	35.8	8.1
2011-12	33.6	34.9	6.4	37.8	33.5	4.4	29.7	36.1	8.3
2013-14	32.5	37.7	7.7	38.7	35.0	5.5	26.5	40.4	9.9
2015-16	31.6	39.6	7.7	36.5	37.9	5.6	26.9	41.1	9.7
2017-18	30.7	42.4	9.2	34.1	43.0	6.9	27.5	41.9	11.5
2017-20[1]	NA	41.9	9.2	NA	41.8	6.6	NA	41.8	11.7

NA = Not available. **Note:** Overweight is body mass index (BMI) of 25 or greater but less than 30; obesity is BMI greater than or equal to 30; extreme obesity is BMI greater than or equal to 40. Does not include pregnant women. (1) 2017-Mar. 2020 prepandemic data set produced by combining full 2017-18 data with partial 2019-20 data.

Obesity Among Children and Adolescents in the U.S., 1988-2018

Source: National Health and Nutrition Examination Survey, NCHS, CDC, U.S. Dept. of Health and Human Services
(percent of population)

Age/sex/poverty level	1988-94	1999-2002	2003-06	2007-10	2009-12	2011-14	2013-16	2015-18
2-5 years								
Both sexes	7.2%	10.3%	12.5%	11.1%	10.2%	8.9%	11.6%	13.7%
Boys	6.2	10.0	12.8	11.9	12.0	9.2	11.5	14.5
Girls	8.2	10.6	12.2	10.2	8.4	8.6	11.7	12.9
Percent of poverty level[1]								
Below 100%	9.7	10.9	14.3	13.2	12.3	11.6	13.5	15.5
100%-199%	7.3	13.8*	12.7	11.8	11.6	10.2	12.6	16.8
200%-399%	5.6	7.6*	11.9	13.9	11.0	7.7*	10.4	12.7
400% or more	—	—	10.0*	5.8*	5.0*	—	8.2	6.6
6-11 years								
Both sexes	11.3	15.9	17.0	18.8	17.9	17.5	17.9	19.3
Boys	11.6	16.9	18.0	20.7	18.3	17.6	19.6	20.9
Girls.	11.0	14.7	15.8	16.9	17.4	17.5	16.1	17.7
Percent of poverty level[1]								
Below 100%	11.4	19.1	22.0	22.2	24.6	21.5	20.8	24.3
100%-199%	11.1	16.4	19.2	20.7	18.5	20.4	20.8	22.8
200%-399%	11.7	15.3	16.7	18.9	15.8	15.7	17.1	17.1
400% or more	—	12.9*	9.2*	12.5*	12.2*	12.2*	12.2	12.1
12-19 years								
Both sexes	10.5	16.0	17.6	18.2	19.4	20.5	20.6	20.9
Boys	11.3	16.7	18.2	19.4	20.0	20.1	20.0	21.3
Girls	9.7	15.3	16.8	16.9	18.9	21.0	21.2	20.4
Percent of poverty level[1]								
Below 100%	15.8	19.8	19.3	24.3	23.2	22.4	25.7	28.7
100%-199%	11.2	15.1	18.4	20.1	22.5	25.7	24.3	23.1
200%-399%	9.4	15.7	19.3	16.3	17.9	19.7	19.3	21.7
400% or more	—	13.9	12.6	14.0	13.8	13.7*	13.7	11.0

— = Estimate is considered unreliable. * = Estimate has a high relative standard error. **Note:** Obesity is defined as body mass index (BMI) at or above the sex- and age-specific 95th percentile of the 2000 CDC growth charts. (1) Ratio of family's household income to contemporary federal poverty guidelines.

Basic First Aid

Source: Courtesy of the American National Red Cross, www.redcross.org. All rights reserved in all countries.

Note: This information is not intended to be a substitute for formal training. It is recommended that you contact your local American Red Cross chapter to sign up for a First Aid/CPR/AED (automated external defibrillator) course. Similar courses are also offered by organizations like the American Heart Association and National Safety Council.

In an emergency, it is important to get medical assistance as soon as possible, but knowing what to do until a doctor or other trained person gets to the scene can save a life, especially in cases of severe bleeding, choking, poisoning, and shock. The Stop the Bleed initiative provides free training in bleeding control techniques to the general public. **Website:** www.StopTheBleed.org

People with special medical problems, such as diabetes, cardiovascular disease, epilepsy, or allergies, are urged to wear some sort of emblem identifying the problem as a safeguard against receiving medication that might be harmful or even fatal. Emblems can be purchased from MedicAlert Foundation, 101 Lander Ave., Turlock, CA 95380; (800) 432-5378; www.medicalert.org.

Allergic reaction and anaphylaxis: If you know the person has a severe allergy or is having difficulty breathing, call 911 or the local emergency number. Have the person use any emergency medication they might carry, such as epinephrine.

Animal bite: Call 911 or the local emergency number if the wound is bleeding seriously or if the animal was wild or a stray or you suspect it of having rabies. Control any bleeding. Wash minor wounds with soap under running water and apply antibiotic ointment and a dressing. In the U.S., people most commonly get rabies through contact with a bat, which may not leave a noticeable bite mark. When possible, proper authorities should test the animal for rabies.

Bleeding: Use a barrier between your hand and the wound to help prevent infection. Cover wound with a sterile dressing. Apply direct pressure until bleeding stops. Cover compress with a bandage. Call 911 or the local emergency number if bleeding is severe.

Burn: Check for life-threatening conditions. If the burn is mild, with skin unbroken and no blisters, flush with cold running water for at least 10 minutes (at least 15 minutes if the burn was caused by a chemical). Gently wash with soap and water and pat dry. Apply a thin layer of antibiotic ointment and then a loose, sterile dry dressing to prevent infection. If the burn is severe, call 911 or the local emergency number. Care for shock (see separate entry). Keep the person from getting chilled or overheated until advanced medical assistance arrives. Do not try to clean a severe burn or break blisters.

Chemical in eye: Call 911 or the local emergency number. Turn the person's head to the side so that the affected eye is lower than the unaffected eye. Flush the affected eye with large amounts of water for at least 20 minutes.

Choking: See **First Aid for Choking** below.

Convulsions (seizures): Ease the person to the floor and roll them onto one side. Place something soft and flat, like a folded jacket, under the person's head. Do not hold the person down or put anything in their mouth. Stay with the person until they are fully conscious. If convulsions last for longer than 5 minutes or the person has a health condition like diabetes or is pregnant, call 911 or the local emergency number.

Cut (minor): Use a clean barrier between your hand and the wound to prevent infection. Apply direct pressure for a few minutes to control any bleeding. Wash the wound thoroughly with soap and water and apply a thin layer of antibiotic ointment or a microthin film dressing. Cover the wound with a sterile dressing and a bandage.

Diabetic emergency: A person experiencing a diabetic emergency might have a headache or even appear intoxicated, slurring their speech and moving with difficulty. Offer the person some form of sugar only if they are conscious and able to swallow. Call 911 if the person is unresponsive.

Foreign object in eye: If an object is embedded in someone's eye, do not remove it. If the object is not embedded, have the person blink several times. If the object doesn't come out, gently flush the eye with saline solution or water. Do not rub the eye. Seek medical attention if the foreign object remains.

Frostbite: Handle the frostbitten area gently. Do not rub. If there is no danger of the affected area refreezing, soak it in warm water (not warmer than 105°F), without allowing it to touch the side of the water container, until normal color returns and it feels warm. Loosely bandage the area with dry, sterile dressings. Put cotton or gauze between any frostbitten fingers or toes. Do not break any blisters. Call 911 or seek emergency help as soon as possible.

Heart attack and stroke: See **Heart and Blood Vessel Disease** earlier in chapter.

Heat stroke: Remove the person from the heat. Loosen any tight clothing. Immerse person in cold water until they become alert. If a large enough source of water is not available, drench the person with cold water and fan constantly. If the person is conscious, have them slowly drink some cool water. Call 911 if the person's condition does not improve.

Hypothermia: Call 911 or the local emergency number. For mild hypothermia, cover all exposed skin. Replace wet clothes with something dry. If the person is alert, give them simple carbohydrates to eat and warm, nonalcoholic, decaffeinated liquids to drink. Apply heat pads or other heat sources if available but do not place against bare skin.

Loss of limb: Call 911 or the local emergency number and care for any life-threatening conditions. If a limb is severed, properly protect it for possible reattachment. After the victim is cared for, the limb should be wrapped in sterile gauze and placed in a plastic bag. Place bag in a larger bag or container of ice and water slurry, not ice alone. Be sure the limb accompanies the victim to the hospital.

Poisoning: Care for any life-threatening conditions. Contact the National Capital Poison Center (800-222-1222, or access their online tool at www.poison.org), 911, or the local emergency number. Do not give the person any food or drink or induce vomiting unless specified to do so by medical professionals. In cases of **alcohol poisoning**, place the person in a position that keeps their airway clear. In cases of **carbon monoxide poisoning**, remove the person from the area if you can do so safely. Naloxone can be administered as a nasal spray or autoinjectable to reverse an **opioid overdose**. All 50 states and DC have enacted naloxone access laws, which allow for it to be dispensed to persons other than a patient.

Shock (injury-related): Monitor breathing and consciousness. Have the person lie down and keep them as comfortable as possible. Do not give the person anything to eat or drink as it increases the risk of vomiting or aspiration. If the weather is cold or damp, place blankets or extra clothing over and under the person; if the weather is hot, provide shade.

Snakebite: Call 911 or the local emergency number immediately if you're not sure whether the snake was venomous. Do not wait for symptoms to appear. Gently wash the injury with soap and water and keep the area below the level of the heart. Have the person remain still if possible. Do not cut, suck at, or apply a tourniquet or ice to a snakebite. Applying an elastic roller bandage may help slow the spread of venom.

Sprains and strains: Splint any injured bone or joint that the person cannot use.

Sting from bee or wasp: If possible, remove the stinger by scraping it away with your finger or a plastic card (like a credit card) or using tweezers. If you use tweezers, grasp the stinger, not the venom sac. Wash the area with soap and water and cover it with a bandage. Apply cold to the area to reduce swelling and pain. Call 911 or the local emergency number immediately if the wound does not stop swelling, the person collapses, or they are known to be allergic to the sting.

Tick bite: Promptly remove any ticks to lower the chance of infection. Use tweezers to grasp it at its head as close to the skin as possible. Pull it slowly and steadily out. Do not use a match or petroleum jelly to remove an embedded tick. Wash and dress the bite area.

Unconsciousness: Call 911 or the local emergency number immediately. Do not move the person if a spinal injury is suspected.

First Aid for Choking

The recommended first aid for a conscious choking victim who is unable to speak, cough, or breathe is to deliver a series of five blows to the back followed by five thrusts to the abdomen. Have another person call 911 or the local emergency number. Obtain consent from the victim to treat them. Apply the back blows by leaning the victim forward and striking between the shoulder blades with the heel of your hand. If the victim is still choking, stand or kneel behind the victim and wrap your arms around their waist. Make a fist with one hand and place the thumb side against the middle of the person's abdomen, just above the navel and well below the lower tip of the breastbone. Grasp your fist in your other hand and quickly thrust upwards into the abdomen. Continue back blows and abdominal thrusts until the object is dislodged, and the person can breathe or cough forcefully, or the person loses consciousness.

VITAL STATISTICS

Births and Deaths in the U.S., 1960-2022

Source: National Center for Health Statistics (NCHS), CDC, U.S. Dept. of Health and Human Services

Year	BIRTHS Total number	BIRTHS Rate	DEATHS Total number	DEATHS Rate	Year	BIRTHS Total number	BIRTHS Rate	DEATHS Total number	DEATHS Rate
1960	4,257,850	23.7	1,711,982	9.5	2011	3,953,590	12.7	2,515,458	8.1
1970	3,731,386	18.4	1,921,031	9.5	2012	3,952,841	12.6	2,543,279	8.1
1980	3,612,258	15.9	1,989,841	8.8	2013	3,932,181	12.4	2,596,993	8.2
1990	4,092,994	16.7	2,148,463	8.6	2014	3,988,076	12.5	2,626,418	8.2
2000	4,058,814	14.4	2,403,351	8.5	2015	3,978,497	12.4	2,712,630	8.4
2004	4,112,052	14.0	2,397,615	8.2	2016	3,945,875	12.2	2,744,248	8.5
2005	4,138,349	14.0	2,448,017	8.3	2017	3,855,500	11.8	2,813,503	8.6
2006	4,265,555	14.2	2,426,264	8.1	2018	3,791,712	11.6	2,839,205	8.7
2007	4,316,233	14.3	2,423,712	8.0	2019	3,747,540	11.4	2,854,838	8.7
2008	4,247,694	14.0	2,471,984	8.1	2020	3,613,647	11.0	3,383,729	10.3
2009	4,130,665	13.5	2,437,163	7.9	2021	3,664,292	11.0	3,464,231	10.4
2010	3,999,386	13.0	2,468,435	8.0	2022[1]	3,664,000	11.0[2]	3,273,000	9.8[2]

Note: Rates are per 1,000 population; population counts are enumerated as of Apr. 1 for decennial census years and estimated as of July 1 for all other years. Beginning in 1970, statistics exclude births and deaths among nonresidents of the U.S. (1) Provisional. (2) Not directly comparable to previous years due to difference in calculation.

Marriage and Divorce Rates in the U.S., 1920-2021

Source: National Center for Health Statistics (NCHS), CDC, U.S. Dept. of Health and Human Services

(Per 1,000 total population. Rates for 2000-20 may exclude data and populations from nonreporting states. Some data are provisional.)

The U.S. marriage rate dipped during the Depression and peaked sharply just after World War II; the trend after that has been more gradual. The divorce rate generally rose from the 1920s through 1981, when it peaked at 5.3 per 1,000 population, before declining somewhat. The graph below shows marriage and divorce rates since 1920.

U.S. Median Age at First Marriage, 1890-2022

Source: U.S. Census Bureau, U.S. Dept. of Commerce

Year[1]	Men	Women	Year[1]	Men	Women	Year[1]	Men	Women	Year[1]	Men	Women
1890	26.1	22.0	1950	22.8	20.3	1995	26.9	24.5	2017	29.5	27.4
1900	25.9	21.9	1960	22.8	20.3	2000	26.8	25.1	2018	29.8	27.8
1910	25.1	21.6	1970	23.2	20.8	2005	27.1	25.3	2019[2]	29.8	28.0
1920	24.6	21.2	1980	24.7	22.0	2010	28.2	26.1	2020	30.5	28.1
1930	24.3	21.3	1985	25.5	23.3	2015	29.2	27.1	2021	30.3	28.6
1940	24.3	21.5	1990	26.1	23.9	2016	29.5	27.4	2022	30.1	28.2

(1) Figures for 1947 and on are based on Current Population Survey data; earlier figures based on decennial censuses. (2) Starting in 2019, estimates for marriages include same-sex married couples.

Divorce Rates by State, 2021

Source: National Center for Health Statistics (NCHS), CDC, U.S. Dept. of Health and Human Services

(per 1,000 population, estimated as of July 1)

State	Divorce rate	State	Divorce rate	State	Divorce rate
Alabama	3.6	Kentucky	3.3	North Dakota	2.9
Alaska	3.1	Louisiana	2.2	Ohio	2.6
Arizona	2.7	Maine	2.7	Oklahoma	3.8
Arkansas	3.6	Maryland	1.6	Oregon	2.7
California	NA	Massachusetts	1.0	Pennsylvania	2.4
Colorado	3.0	Michigan	2.3	Rhode Island	2.7
Connecticut	2.5	Minnesota	NA	South Carolina	2.4
Delaware	2.6	Mississippi	3.3	South Dakota	2.5
District of Columbia	2.6	Missouri	2.9	Tennessee	3.3
Florida	3.4	Montana	2.5	Texas	1.4
Georgia	2.2	Nebraska	2.6	Utah	3.3
Hawaii	NA	Nevada	4.2	Vermont	2.3
Idaho	3.4	New Hampshire	2.6	Virginia	3.1
Illinois	1.3	New Jersey	2.2	Washington	2.9
Indiana	NA	New Mexico	NA	West Virginia	2.9
Iowa	2.3	New York	2.2	Wisconsin	2.1
Kansas	1.9	North Carolina	3.2	Wyoming	3.7
				United States	**2.5**

NA = Not available. **Note:** Rates based on provisional counts of divorce including annulments and, for certain areas, divorce petitions filed or legal separations.

Birth Rates and Fertility Rates by Age of Mother, 1950-2022

Source: National Center for Health Statistics (NCHS), CDC, U.S. Dept. of Health and Human Services

Year	Birth rate[1]	Fertility rate[2]	10-14 years	15-19 years	15-17 years	18-19 years	20-24 years	25-29 years	30-34 years	35-39 years	40-44 years	45-49 years[3]
			Live births per 1,000 women by age of mother									
1950	24.1	106.2	1.0	81.6	40.7	132.7	196.6	166.1	103.7	52.9	15.1	1.2
1960	23.7	118.0	0.8	89.1	43.9	166.7	258.1	197.4	112.7	56.2	15.5	0.9
1970	18.4	87.9	1.2	68.3	38.8	114.7	167.8	145.1	73.3	31.7	8.1	0.5
1980	15.9	68.4	1.1	53.0	32.5	82.1	115.1	112.9	61.9	19.8	3.9	0.2
1990	16.7	70.9	1.4	59.9	37.5	88.6	116.5	120.2	80.8	31.7	5.5	0.2
2000	14.4	65.9	0.9	47.7	26.9	78.1	109.7	113.5	91.2	39.7	8.0	0.5
2005	14.0	66.7	0.7	40.5	21.4	69.9	102.2	115.5	95.8	46.3	9.1	0.6
2008	14.0	68.6	0.6	41.5	21.7	70.6	103.0	115.1	99.3	46.9	9.8	0.7
2010	13.0	64.1	0.4	34.2	17.3	58.2	90.0	108.3	96.5	45.9	10.2	0.7
2011	12.7	63.2	0.4	31.3	15.4	54.1	85.3	107.2	96.5	47.2	10.3	0.7
2012	12.6	63.0	0.4	29.4	14.1	51.4	83.1	106.5	97.3	48.3	10.4	0.7
2013	12.4	62.5	0.3	26.5	12.3	47.1	80.7	105.5	98.0	49.3	10.4	0.8
2014	12.5	62.9	0.3	24.2	10.9	43.8	79.0	105.8	100.8	51.0	10.6	0.8
2015	12.4	62.5	0.2	22.3	9.9	40.7	76.8	104.3	101.5	51.8	11.0	0.8
2016	12.2	62.0	0.2	20.3	8.8	37.5	73.8	102.1	102.7	52.7	11.4	0.9
2017	11.8	60.3	0.2	18.8	7.9	35.1	71.0	98.0	100.3	52.3	11.6	0.9
2018	11.6	59.1	0.2	17.4	7.2	32.3	68.0	95.3	99.7	52.6	11.8	0.9
2019	11.4	58.3	0.2	16.7	6.7	31.1	66.6	93.7	98.3	52.8	12.0	0.9
2020	10.9	55.7	0.2	15.0	6.1	28.2	63.3	90.9	94.9	51.3	11.8	0.9
2021	11.0	56.3	0.2	13.9	5.6	26.6	61.5	93.0	97.6	53.7	12.0	0.9
2022[4]	11.0[5]	56.1	0.2	13.5	5.5	25.6	60.4	93.4	97.0	54.9	12.5	1.1

(1) Live births per 1,000 population. (2) Live births per 1,000 women 15-44 years of age. (3) Beginning in 1997, rate computed by relating the number of births to women age 45 and over to women 45-49 years of age. (4) Provisional. (5) Not directly comparable to previous years due to difference in calculation.

Cesarean Delivery Rates by State, 2000-22

Source: National Center for Health Statistics (NCHS), CDC, U.S. Dept. of Health and Human Services

State	2000	2010	2020	2022[1]	Percent change, 2000-22	State	2000	2010	2020	2022[1]	Percent change, 2000-22
Alabama	26.3%	35.3%	35.0%	34.5%	31.2%	Montana	19.0%	30.3%	27.6%	27.1%	42.6%
Alaska	17.0	21.5	22.9	22.7	33.5	Nebraska	22.5	31.1	28.8	28.9	28.4
Arizona	18.6	27.0	28.4	28.6	53.8	Nevada	21.7	34.8	32.9	32.9	51.6
Arkansas	26.3	34.8	33.8	33.6	27.8	New Hampshire	21.0	30.4	32.1	32.1	52.9
California	23.4	33.0	30.5	31.0	32.5	New Jersey	27.3	38.4	33.2	32.9	20.5
Colorado	18.3	25.9	27.2	27.9	52.5	New Mexico	17.1	22.8	26.1	27.5	60.8
Connecticut	21.6	35.1	34.1	35.2	63.0	New York	24.6	34.5	33.6	33.9	37.8
Delaware	24.8	33.9	31.7	31.9	28.6	North Carolina	23.0	30.8	29.9	30.2	31.3
District of Columbia	22.6	33.0	32.3	33.3	47.3	North Dakota	20.6	27.7	27.0	26.0	26.2
Florida	24.9	37.8	35.9	35.9	44.2	Ohio	20.0	30.7	31.3	31.4	57.0
Georgia	22.5	33.8	33.9	35.3	56.9	Oklahoma	21.0	34.7	32.1	32.5	54.8
Hawaii	14.6	27.2	26.3	27.7	89.7	Oregon	19.4	29.4	28.8	29.2	50.5
Idaho	18.3	24.8	23.5	24.5	33.9	Pennsylvania	21.7	31.3	30.6	31.1	43.3
Illinois	20.9	31.1	30.8	31.0	48.3	Rhode Island	21.9	33.0	33.4	34.8	58.9
Indiana	21.5	30.3	30.1	30.5	41.9	South Carolina	25.2	35.0	33.5	32.6	29.4
Iowa	20.8	30.3	30.2	29.6	42.3	South Dakota	22.8	26.6	24.7	24.0	5.3
Kansas	22.2	30.5	30.1	30.1	35.6	Tennessee	24.8	34.2	32.1	32.1	29.4
Kentucky	23.6	35.4	34.3	34.5	46.2	Texas	24.7	35.1	34.7	34.7	40.5
Louisiana	26.6	39.6	36.8	35.5	33.5	Utah	16.8	23.1	23.1	24.0	42.9
Maine	22.8	29.8	29.7	31.7	39.0	Vermont	17.3	27.5	26.9	28.1	62.4
Maryland	24.1	34.5	33.7	34.3	42.3	Virginia	23.1	34.3	32.6	32.3	39.8
Massachusetts	23.3	33.0	32.4	33.1	42.1	Washington	20.6	29.5	28.5	29.7	44.2
Michigan	21.9	32.6	32.5	33.2	51.6	West Virginia	25.4	36.0	34.2	34.1	34.3
Minnesota	19.4	27.1	28.5	30.0	54.6	Wisconsin	17.5	26.0	26.7	27.5	57.1
Mississippi	28.2	37.0	38.2	38.5	36.5	Wyoming	19.4	27.9	26.4	27.4	41.2
Missouri	22.3	31.9	29.3	30.4	36.3	**United States**	**22.8**	**32.7**	**31.8**	**32.2**	**41.2**

Note: The cesarean rate is the percentage of all live births by cesarean delivery. (1) Provisional.

Infertility and Use of Infertility Services, by Age and Type of Service, 2015-19

Source: National Survey of Family Growth, National Center for Health Statistics (NCHS), U.S. Dept. of Health and Human Services

A special tabulation in 2015-19 found that for all women 15-49 years of age, 12.2% had ever received any infertility services.

Age	% of all women who have impaired fecundity[1]		% of all women who have ever received any infertility service		Type of infertility service	% of women[2]
	0 births	1 or more births	0 births	1 or more births		
15-29 years	9.2%	12.0%	2.7%	11.5%	Medical help to get pregnant	8.9%
30-39 years	22.2	12.2	13.6	15.5	Advice	6.7
40-49 years	33.4	14.5	21.8	20.0	Tests on woman or man	5.6
Total 15-49 years	**13.8**	**13.1**	**6.4**	**16.6**	Any medical help to prevent miscarriage	5.2
					Ovulation drugs	4.0
					Artificial insemination	1.7
					Surgery to treatment on blocked tubes	0.7
					Assisted Reproductive Technology	0.5

(1) Not surgically sterile, and for whom it is difficult or impossible to get pregnant or carry a pregnancy to term. (2) Age 15-49 years.

Numbers of Multiple Births in the U.S., 1990-2021

Source: National Center for Health Statistics (NCHS), CDC, U.S. Dept. of Health and Human Services

Year	Twins	Triplets	Quad-ruplets	Quin-tuplets[1]	Year	Twins	Triplets	Quad-ruplets	Quin-tuplets[1]
1990	93,865	2,830	185	13	2013	132,324	4,364	270	66
1995	96,736	4,551	365	57	2014	135,336	4,233	246	47
2000	118,916	6,742	506	77	2015	133,155	3,871	228	24
2005	133,122	6,208	418	68	2016	131,723	3,755	217	31
2007	138,961	5,967	369	91	2017	128,310	3,675	193	49
2008	138,660	5,877	345	46	2018	123,536	3,400	115	10
2009	137,217	5,905	355	80	2019	120,291	3,136	114	36
2010	132,562	5,153	313	37	2020	112,437	2,738	108	29
2011	131,269	5,137	239	41	2021	114,161	2,785	133	15
2012	131,024	4,598	276	45					

(1) Quintuplets and other multiple births of five or more.

Origin Countries for U.S. Foreign Adoptions, 2000-22

Source: Annual Report on Intercountry Adoption, Bureau of Consular Affairs, U.S. Dept. of State
(ranked by fiscal year 2022 adoptions)

Country	2022	2021	2020	2019	2018	2017	2016	2015	2013	2010	2005	2000
Colombia	235	297	137	244	229	181	131	153	159	235	291	246
India	223	245	103	241	302	221	194	138	119	243	323	503
South Korea	141	156	188	166	206	276	260	318	138	863	1,630	1,794
Bulgaria	84	108	99	134	134	147	201	185	159	40	30	214
Ukraine	82	235	211	298	248	215	303	303	438	445	821	659
Haiti	79	54	96	130	196	227	178	143	388	1,332	234	131
Taiwan	68	48	42	43	32	44	59	59	94	285	141	28
Philippines	67	68	39	94	105	111	156	150	178	214	271	173
Thailand	49	38	23	38	43	34	45	47	35	53	71	87
Nigeria	44	111	83	116	173	176	121	154	183	189	65	4
Total[1]	**1,517**	**1,785**	**1,622**	**2,971**	**4,059**	**4,714**	**5,372**	**5,648**	**7,094**	**11,059[2]**	**22,710**	**18,120**

(1) Includes countries not shown. (2) Does not reflect approx. 1,090 Haitian children admitted as part of the Special Humanitarian Parole following the 2010 earthquake in Haiti.

Leading Causes of Infant Death in the U.S., 2021

Source: National Vital Statistics System, National Center for Health Statistics (NCHS), CDC, U.S. Dept. of Health and Human Services

Cause of death	Number	Percent of total deaths	Mortality rate[1]
Congenital malformations, deformations, and chromosomal abnormalities	3,963	19 9%	108 2
Disorders related to short gestation and low birth weight, not elsewhere classified	2,946	14 8	80.4
Sudden infant death syndrome	1,459	7.3	39 8
Accidents (unintentional injuries)	1,306	6.6	35 6
Newborn affected by maternal complications of pregnancy	1,113	5.6	30 4
Newborn affected by complications of placenta, cord, and membranes	672	3.4	18 3
Bacterial sepsis[2] of newborn	557	2.8	15 2
Respiratory distress of newborn	414	2.1	11.3
Diseases of the circulatory system	402	2.0	11.0
Intrauterine hypoxia and birth asphyxia	358	1.8	9.8
All other causes	6,730	33.8	—
All causes	**19,920**	**100.0**	**543 6**

— = Not applicable. (1) Deaths of infants under 1 year of age per 100,000 live births. (2) Toxic condition resulting from the spread of bacteria.

Nonmarital Childbearing in the U.S., 1970-2021

Source: National Center for Health Statistics (NCHS), CDC, U.S. Dept. of Health and Human Services

	1970	1975	1980	1985	1990	1995	2000	2005	2010	2015	2020	2021
Live births to unmarried mothers (thous.)	399	448	666	828	1,165	1,254	1,347	1,527	1,633	1,602	1,464	1,464
Race/Hispanic origin of mother	*Percent of live births to unmarried women*											
All races and origins	10.7%	14.3%	18.4%	22.0%	28.0%	32.2%	33.2%	36.9%	40.8%	40.3%	40.5%	40.0%
White	5.5	7.1	11.2	14.7	20.4	25.3	27.1	31.7	35.9	35.8	28.4	27.5
Black	37.5	49.5	56.1	61.2	66.5	69.9	68.5	69.3	72.1	70.1	70.4	70.1
American Indian or Alaska Native	22.4	32.7	39.2	46.8	53.6	57.2	58.4	63.5	65.6	65.8	69.6	68.5
Asian or Pacific Islander[1]	—	—	7.3	9.5	13.2	16.3	14.8	16.2	17.0	16.4	13.9	14.3
Hispanic origin (select states)[2,3]	—	—	23.6	29.5	36.7	40.8	42.7	48.0	53.4	53.0	52.8	53.2
Maternal age	*Percent distribution of live births to unmarried women*											
Under 20 years	50.1%	52.1%	40.8%	33.8%	30.9%	30.9%	28.0%	23.1%	20.1%	12.9%	10.0%	9.3%
20-24 years	31.8	29.9	35.6	36.3	34.7	34.5	37.4	38.3	36.8	35.0	30.8	30.2
25 years and over	18.1	18.0	23.5	29.9	34.4	34.7	34.6	38.7	43.1	52.1	59.2	60.5
Race/Hispanic origin of mother	*Live births per 1,000 unmarried women 15-44 years of age[4]*											
All races and origins	26.4	24.5	29.4	32.8	43.8	44.3	44.0	47.2	47.5	43.4	38.6	37.8
White[5]	13.9	12.4	18.1	22.5	32.9	37.0	38.2	43.2	44.5	40.4	27.6	27.0
Black[5]	95.5	84.2	81.1	77.0	90.5	74.5	70.5	67.2	65.3	59.6	54.9	52.1
Hispanic origin (select states)[2,3]	—	—	—	—	89.6	88.7	87.2	96.2	80.6	67.4	55.8	55.7

— = Not available. (1) For 2020-21, data is for Asian and Native Hawaiian or Other Pacific Islander combined. (2) Hispanic origin data prior to 1995 is not directly comparable with data for more recent years due to differences in reporting area. (3) Hispanics may be of any race. (4) Rates computed by dividing births to unmarried mothers, regardless of mother's age, by the pop. of unmarried women 15-44 years of age. (5) For 1970 and 1975, birth rates are by race of child.

U.S. Teen Birth Rate by State, 2021

Source: National Center for Health Statistics (NCHS), CDC, U.S. Dept. of Health and Human Services

U.S. state	Birth rate[1]	U.S. state	Birth rate[1]	U.S. state	Birth rate[1]	U.S. state	Birth rate[1]
Alabama	22.9	Illinois	11.1	Montana	13.6	Rhode Island	7.8
Alaska	17.5	Indiana	17.0	Nebraska	14.0	South Carolina	18.3
Arizona	15.1	Iowa	12.7	Nevada	15.1	South Dakota	17.0
Arkansas	26.5	Kansas	16.3	New Hampshire	5.4	Tennessee	21.5
California	9.9	Kentucky	22.3	New Jersey	7.9	Texas	20.3
Colorado	11.4	Louisiana	24.5	New Mexico	19.0	Utah	9.7
Connecticut	7.1	Maine	7.8	New York	9.1	Vermont	6.4
Delaware	13.5	Maryland	11.3	North Carolina	16.0	Virginia	11.7
District of Columbia	13.9	Massachusetts	5.7	North Dakota	12.9	Washington	10.1
Florida	13.5	Michigan	12.2	Ohio	15.5	West Virginia	20.9
Georgia	16.6	Minnesota	8.5	Oklahoma	24.1	Wisconsin	10.1
Hawaii	12.3	Mississippi	25.6	Oregon	9.5	Wyoming	16.0
Idaho	12.0	Missouri	17.1	Pennsylvania	11.5	**United States**	**13.9**

(1) Number of births per 1,000 females ages 15-19.

Number, Ratio, and Rate of Legal Abortions in U.S., 1970-2020

Source: *Abortion Surveillance—United States, 2020*, Centers for Disease Control and Prevention, U.S. Dept. of Health and Human Services

Year	Legal abortions	Ratio[1]	Rate[2]	Year	Legal abortions	Ratio[1]	Rate[2]	Year	Legal abortions	Ratio[1]	Rate[2]
1970	193,491	52	5	2001	853,485	249	16	2011	730,322	217	14
1971	485,816	137	11	2002	854,122	250	16	2012	699,202	208	13
1972	586,760	180	13	2003	848,163	245	16	2013	664,435	198	12
1973	615,831	196	14	2004	839,226	241	16	2014	652,639	192	12
1974	763,476	242	17	2005	820,151	235	16	2015	638,169	188	12
1975	854,853	272	18	2006	852,385	233	16	2016	623,471	186	12
1980	1,297,606	359	25	2007	827,609	226	16	2017	612,719	185	11
1990	1,429,247	344	24	2008	825,564	229	16	2018	619,591	189	11
1995	1,210,883	311	20	2009	789,217	224	15	2019	629,898	195	11
2000	857,475	251	16	2010	765,651	225	14	2020	620,327	198	11

Note: After 1998, reporting area varies. (1) Number of abortions per 1,000 live births. (2) Number of abortions per 1,000 women aged 15-44 years.

Reported U.S. Abortions by Weeks of Gestation, Age, and Race, 2020

Source: *Abortion Surveillance—United States, 2020*, Centers for Disease Control and Prevention, U.S. Dept. of Health and Human Services

Characteristic	Weeks of gestation													
	≤6		7-9		10-13		14-15		16-17		18-20		≥21	
	No.	%	No.	%	No.	%	No.	%	No.	%	No.	%	No.	%
Age[1]														
Under 15 years	259	25.6%	358	35.4%	205	20.3%	68	6.7%	40	4.0%	46	4.5%	35	3.5%
15-19 years	14,336	37.9	14,230	37.6	5,837	15.4	1,346	3.6	810	2.1	803	2.1	507	1.3
20-24 years	57,008	43.7	48,095	36.9	16,649	12.8	3,601	2.8	2,087	1.6	1,916	1.5	1,090	0.8
25-29 years	62,751	46.3	48,366	35.7	16,062	11.8	3,497	2.6	2,072	1.5	1,846	1.4	1,064	0.8
30-34 years	43,986	47.5	32,087	34.6	10,599	11.4	2,434	2.6	1,319	1.4	1,350	1.5	921	1.0
35-39 years	23,761	47.5	16,931	33.9	5,696	11.4	1,362	2.7	807	1.6	859	1.7	562	1.1
40 years and over	8,846	50.7	5,505	31.6	1,823	10.5	481	2.8	294	1.7	303	1.7	182	1.0
Total	210,947	45.4	165,572	35.6	56,871	12.2	12,789	2.7	7,429	1.6	7,123	1.5	4,361	0.9
Race/ethnicity[2]														
White[3]	49,617	47.3	36,387	34.7	12,313	11.7	2,692	2.6	1,481	1.4	1,520	1.4	867	0.8
Black[3]	55,749	43.6	46,628	36.5	17,308	13.5	3,608	2.8	1,972	1.5	1,809	1.4	714	0.6
Other[3]	9,564	47.4	6,876	34.1	2,325	11.5	555	2.8	331	1.6	286	1.4	219	1.1
Hispanic	34,236	51.6	21,446	32.3	7,059	10.6	1,514	2.3	878	1.3	816	1.2	425	0.6
Total	149,166	46.7	111,337	34.9	39,005	12.2	8,369	2.6	4,662	1.4	4,431	1.4	2,225	0.7

Note: The CDC requests data annually from the central health agencies of 52 reporting areas (all states, DC, and NYC). Reporting is voluntary. Data exclude areas that did not report, did not report weeks of gestation by age, or did not meet reporting standards. (1) Data from 41 reporting areas; excludes 11 (CA, CT, DC, IL, MD, MA, NH, NY, PA, TN, WI). (2) Data from 28 reporting areas; excludes 24 (CA, CO, CT, DC, HI, IL, IA, LA, ME, MD, MA, NE, NH, NJ, NY, NYC, ND, OH, OK, PA, RI, TN, WA, WI). (3) Non-Hispanic.

Adult LGBT and Transgender Population by State

Source: The Williams Institute, UCLA School of Law

(Adult population self-identifying as LGBT and/or transgender as a percentage of overall population.)

State	LGBT, 2017	Transgender, 2022	State	LGBT, 2017	Transgender, 2022	State	LGBT, 2017	Transgender, 2022
Alabama	3.1%	0.5%	Kentucky	3.4%	0.5%	North Dakota	2.7%	0.4%
Alaska	3.7	0.7	Louisiana	3.9	0.4	Ohio	4.3	0.5
Arizona	4.5	0.7	Maine	4.9	0.5	Oklahoma	3.8	0.6
Arkansas	3.3	0.7	Maryland	4.2	0.5	Oregon	5.6	0.6
California	5.3	0.5	Massachusetts	5.4	0.7	Pennsylvania	4.1	0.6
Colorado	4.6	0.6	Michigan	4.0	0.4	Rhode Island	4.5	0.7
Connecticut	3.9	0.5	Minnesota	4.1	0.4	South Carolina	3.5	0.5
Delaware	4.5	0.8	Mississippi	3.5	0.4	South Dakota	3.0	0.4
District of Columbia	9.8	0.9	Missouri	3.8	0.2	Tennessee	3.5	0.5
Florida	4.6	0.6	Montana	2.9	0.4	Texas	4.1	0.4
Georgia	4.5	0.6	Nebraska	3.8	0.4	Utah	3.7	0.6
Hawaii	4.6	0.7	Nevada	5.5	0.3	Vermont	5.2	0.5
Idaho	2.8	0.5	New Hampshire	4.7	0.6	Virginia	3.9	0.5
Illinois	4.3	0.4	New Jersey	4.1	0.6	Washington	5.2	0.6
Indiana	4.5	0.5	New Mexico	4.5	0.7	West Virginia	4.0	0.4
Iowa	3.6	0.3	New York	5.1	0.5	Wisconsin	3.8	0.3
Kansas	3.3	0.6	North Carolina	4.0	0.9	Wyoming	3.3	0.5
						United States	**4.5**	**0.5**

Sexual Orientation and Gender Identity by Age Group, 2023

Source: *Accelerating Acceptance 2023*, a national survey among U.S. adults using sample sourced by research firm Cint on behalf of GLAAD (percent of survey respondents)

Sexual orientation	Age				Gender identity	Age			
	18-38	39-54	55-73	74+		18-38	39-54	55-73	74+
Strictly straight/heterosexual....	74%	88%	95%	99%	Cisgender..................	88%	92%	97%	99%
Non-heterosexual............	26	14	5	1	Non-cisgender..............	12	8	3	1
Bisexual...................	11	6	1	0	Transgender...............	3	3	0	0
Gay or lesbian..............	5	5	2	1	Nonbinary.................	4	2	—	0
Pansexual..................	4	1	1	0	Unsure or questioning........	5	4	2	0
Queer.....................	2	—	0	0					
Asexual....................	1	1	1	0					
Unsure or questioning........	3	1	—	0					

— = Less than 0.5%. **Note:** Percent distributions may not equal 100 due to rounding. **Asexual:** not experiencing sexual attraction; **bisexual:** experiencing sexual or romantic attraction to more than one gender; **cisgender:** strictly identifying with the sex assigned at birth; **gay/lesbian:** experiencing sexual attraction to the same gender; **nonbinary:** identifying outside of, or beyond, the binary of male and female gender including gender queer, gender fluid, agender, and bigender; **pansexual:** experiencing sexual or romantic attraction to people of any or all gender identities; **queer:** experiencing sexual or romantic attraction in a way that does not fit into the previously mentioned, dominant norms; **transgender:** identifying with a gender that does not correspond to the sex you were assigned at birth.

Sexual Orientation Among U.S. Adults, 2018

Source: *National Health Interview Survey, 2018*, National Center for Health Statistics (NCHS), U.S. Dept. of Health and Human Services

	Gay or lesbian[1]		Straight[2]		Bisexual	
	Number (thous.)	% of group	Number (thous.)	% of group	Number (thous.)	% of group
Total..................	3,955	1.6%	233,360	97.0%	3,143	1.3%
Sex						
Men...................	2,250	1.9	113,250	97.3	895	0.8
Women................	1,705	1.4	120,109	96.8	2,248	1.8
Age						
18-44 years...........	2,113	1.9	105,755	95.8	2,550	2.3
45-64 years...........	1,484	1.8	78,338	97.6	475	0.6
65 years and older........	358	0.7	49,267	99.0	118	0.2

Note: Percent distributions may not equal 100 due to rounding. (1) Response option provided was "gay" for men and "gay or lesbian" for women. (2) Response option provided was "straight, that is, not gay" for men and "straight, that is, not gay or lesbian" for women.

Sexual Behavior of Opposite-Sex and Same-Sex Partners, 2011-19

Source: National Survey of Family Growth, National Center for Health Statistics, U.S. Dept. of Health and Human Services (among population of adults ages 18-49)

	Men			Women		
	Gay	Bisexual	Heterosexual	Lesbian	Bisexual	Heterosexual
Lifetime experience						
Sex with female, ever.......	51.1%	87.3%	94.4%	91.0%	77.7%	12.3%
Sex with male, ever........	94.4	69.5	2.7	74.5	96.6	94.9
Total number of sexual partners in the past 12 months						
None....................	7.9	9.0	6.8	3.6	5.9	6.9
One.....................	37.3	47.0	73.3	71.8	55.8	77.5
Two.....................	17.4	16.5	9.2	12.7	14.5	8.9
Three or more.............	36.5	25.9	10.7	11.3	21.1	6.7

Contraceptive Use in the U.S., 2002-19

Source: National Survey of Family Growth, National Center for Health Statistics (NCHS), U.S. Dept. of Health and Human Services

Method	2002[1]	2006-10[1]	2011-15[1]	2015-17[2]	2017-19[2]	2002[1]	2006-10[1]	2011-15[1]	2015-17[2]	2017-19[2]
			Ever used[3]					Currently using[4]		
Any method of contraception........	98.2%	99.1%	99.3%	99.2%	99.2%	61.9%	62.2%	61.6%	64.9%	65.3%
Male condom..........	89.7	93.4	95.0	94.0	94.8	14.7	10.2	9.2	8.7	8.4
Pill...................	82.3	81.9	79.3	80.5	78.9	19.2	17.1	15.9	12.6	14.0
Withdrawal............	56.1	59.6	64.8	65.9	66.0	5.4	3.2	3.9	3.9	3.7
3-month injectable (Depo-Provera).....	16.8	23.2	25.4	24.2	25.0	3.3	2.3	2.6	2.1	2.0
Female sterilization......	20.7	19.5	17.1	21.5	20.7	16.7	16.5	14.3	18.6	18.1
Calendar rhythm method..	16.2	18.1	15.9	18.3	17.1	NA	NA	NA	1.3	1.4
Male sterilization........	13.0	13.3	11.4	14.7	14.1	6.3	6.2	4.5	5.9	5.6
Emergency contraception	4.2	10.8	20.0	22.0	25.1	NA	NA	NA	NA	NA
Contraceptive patch.....	0.9	10.4	10.6	8.7	7.8	NA	NA	NA	NA	NA
Intrauterine device (IUD)..	5.8	7.7	15.0	18.9	21.5	1.3	3.5	6.8	7.9	8.4
Not currently using contraception[5]........	NA	NA	NA	NA	NA	38.1	37.8	38.4	35.1	34.7

NA = Not available/not applicable. (1) Women ages 15-44. (2) Women ages 15-49. (3) Among women who have ever had intercourse. (4) Percentage of women using specified contraception in month of interview. Women could be using more than one method. Women are classified here according to the one most effective contraceptive method they are using. Additional methods women may be using are not shown. (5) Currently pregnant or postpartum, trying to get pregnant, not having sex, etc.

Sexual Activity of U.S. High School Students, 2021

Source: *Youth Risk Behavior Surveillance—United States, 2021*, CDC, U.S. Dept. of Health and Human Services
(percent of selected population to have engaged in activity)

Race/ethnicity	Ever had sexual intercourse			First sexual intercourse before age 13			Currently sexually active[1]			Condom use during last sexual intercourse[2]		
	Female	Male	Total	Female	Male	Total	Female	Male	Total	Female	Male	Total
Amer. Ind./AK native...	37.2%	29.0%	32.9%	5.5%	2.6%	3.9%	30.7%	11.7%	20.7%	—	—	—
Asian..............	11.1	11.0	11.0	2.0	0.9	1.5	7.0	6.6	6.8	—	—	52.0%
Black or African Amer..	28.7	39.4	33.9	3.2	7.4	5.3	20.7	25.6	23.0	41.4%	55.0%	48.8
Hispanic/Latino.......	31.1	29.8	30.6	3.3	3.5	3.7	22.6	17.9	20.6	42.1	59.6	49.7
Native Hawaiian/other Pac. Isl.............	—	—	28.6	4.2	8.1	6.5	25.9	10.6	16.9	—	—	—
White	32.8	28.0	30.4	2.9	2.2	2.5	24.7	19.3	21.9	52.0	58.1	54.6
Multiple race.........	32.4	34.8	33.5	4.5	4.2	4.3	22.9	20.0	21.6	37.2	51.9	43.2
Grade												
9th................	15.0	16.4	15.9	4.2	3.6	4.0	9.5	8.7	9.2	47.1	58.4	53.4
10th...............	24.4	20.7	22.6	3.6	3.1	3.4	16.7	12.4	14.6	54.8	67.1	59.8
11th...............	34.4	34.8	34.6	2.6	3.0	2.8	25.9	23.9	24.9	50.8	59.8	55.0
12th...............	49.5	47.3	48.4	1.8	3.0	2.4	38.8	31.9	35.4	41.7	52.4	46.4
Sexual identity												
Heterosexual (straight)	28.9	29.4	29.2	1.2	2.8	2.1	22.8	19.1	20.6	51.1	59.1	55.3
Gay, lesbian, or bisexual	40.0	30.7	38.2	6.9	5.2	6.8	27.3	15.3	25.0	38.8	46.4	39.9
Other/questioning.....	24.1	28.5	25.0	4.7	8.9	5.7	15.3	21.4	16.5	47.7	42.6	45.8
Sex of sexual contacts												
Opposite sex only.....	74.0	72.7	73.3	4.3	6.2	5.4	57.2	48.1	52.2	51.7	59.3	55.5
Same sex only or both sexes.............	66.1	69.4	66.8	14.0	24.5	16.2	43.6	38.1	42.4	39.8	38.5	39.5
All students.........	30.6	29.3	30.0	3.1	3.2	3.2	22.6	18.8	20.7	47.3	57.7	51.8

— = Not available. (1) Sexual intercourse with at least 1 person during the 3 months before the survey. (2) Among the students who were currently sexually active.

Sexual Violence Against U.S. High School Students, 2021

Source: *Youth Risk Behavior Surveillance—United States, 2021*, CDC, U.S. Dept. of Health and Human Services
(as percent of selected population)

Race/ethnicity	Ever physically forced to have sexual intercourse[1]			Experienced sexual violence by anyone[2]			Experienced sexual dating violence[3]		
	Female	Male	Total	Female	Male	Total	Female	Male	Total
Amer. Ind./AK native........	31.7%	7.0%	18.3%	25.5%	6.3%	15.8%	14.3%	7.8%	11.0%
Asian....................	7.5	1.5	4.5	7.7	3.7	5.7	9.7	2.2	5.5
Black or African Amer.......	11.3	3.1	7.1	10.6	4.6	7.4	6.2	4.5	5.3
Hispanic/Latino...........	14.9	3.8	9.5	18.4	4.3	11.3	15.7	3.6	10.0
Native Hawaiian/other Pac. Isl................	16.2	5.3	9.8	—	1.2	5.4	—	—	5.5
White	13.7	3.4	8.4	20.5	4.4	11.9	17.6	3.7	10.7
Multiple race..............	15.7	7.1	11.6	19.1	9.5	14.7	15.3	7.6	11.6
Grade									
9	11.5	2.8	7.1	16.9	3.3	9.9	15.9	1.8	8.9
10	13.7	3.1	8.2	19.6	3.7	11.4	17.5	3.7	10.6
11	12.3	4.1	8.2	19.0	6.1	12.3	15.3	6.1	10.8
12	16.4	4.4	10.2	15.9	5.2	10.4	12.8	4.3	8.7
Sexual identity									
Heterosexual (straight)	8.6	2.6	5.0	14.1	3.3	7.6	12.1	2.8	6.6
Gay, lesbian, or bisexual.....	24.9	10.1	21.9	26.4	13.4	23.6	21.1	9.9	19.2
Other/questioning..........	16.7	11.6	15.9	20.0	14.4	18.9	19.3	16.5	20.0
Total	13.5	3.6	8.5	17.9	4.6	11.0	15.3	4.0	9.7

— = Not available. (1) When they did not want to. (2) Including such things as kissing, touching, or being forced to have sexual intercourse that they did not want to do, one or more times during the 12 months before the survey. (3) Being forced to do sexual things (including kissing, touching, or being physically forced to have sexual intercourse) they did not want to do by someone they were dating or going out with, one or more times during the 12 months before the survey, among students who dated or went out with someone during the 12 months before the survey.

Risky Vehicular Behaviors by U.S. High School Students, 2021

Source: *Youth Risk Behavior Surveillance—United States, 2021*, CDC, U.S. Dept. of Health and Human Services
(percent of selected population to have engaged in activity)

Race/ethnicity	Did not always wear a seat belt[1]			Rode with a driver who had been drinking alcohol[2]			Drove when drinking alcohol[2,3]			Texted or emailed while driving[2,3]		
	Female	Male	Total	Female	Male	Total	Female	Male	Total	Female	Male	Total
Amer. Ind./AK native...	41.9%	45.3%	43.6%	20.1%	13.7%	16.6%	—	4.1%	4.1%	—	23.3%	30.8%
Asian...............	28.5	30.6	29.3	9.4	6.5	7.9	3.0%	3.3	3.1	24.9%	26.2	25.5
Black or African Amer..	57.6	61.4	59.2	16.7	12.9	14.9	1.6	3.1	2.4	24.3	28.4	26.4
Hispanic/Latino.......	41.3	45.2	43.6	17.7	16.2	16.9	4.6	5.7	5.3	30.4	30.1	30.5
Native Hawaiian/other Pac. Isl............	—	—	42.2	—	21.4	20.4	—	—	—	—	—	—
White	32.6	37.0	34.9	14.7	12.3	13.4	2.9	6.6	4.8	44.6	40.6	42.3
Multiple race........	39.9	38.1	39.6	11.7	11.4	11.5	6.3	6.4	6.3	35.5	33.6	34.6
Grade												
9................	41.7	47.3	44.5	14.9	12.4	13.7	0.4	3.7	2.2	12.1	12.7	12.4
10...............	42.1	40.6	41.3	17.1	12.1	14.5	2.5	3.1	2.8	20.2	24.6	22.6
11...............	35.6	41.1	38.5	14.3	13.3	13.9	4.0	5.9	5.0	39.2	36.3	37.7
12...............	33.1	36.0	34.6	14.6	14.0	14.3	4.3	8.5	6.3	56.3	52.5	54.3
Total..............	38.1	41.4	39.9	15.2	13.1	14.1	3.4	5.8	4.6	37.1	35.4	36.1

— = Not available. (1) When riding in a car driven by someone else. (2) In a car or other vehicle, one or more times during the 30 days before the survey. (3) Among students who had driven a car or other vehicle during the 30 days before the survey.

U.S. Motor Vehicle Crashes, 2021

Source: National Safety Council (NSC) website: injuryfacts.nsc.org; Natl. Highway Traffic Safety Admin. (NHTSA)

An estimated 46,980 people in the U.S. were killed in motor vehicle crashes in 2021, up 11.0% from the total for 2020. The number of licensed drivers (227.5 mil) decreased, and vehicle miles driven (3.140 tril) increased in 2021; the death rate per 100 mil vehicle miles increased 2.7% to 1.50.

Motor vehicle deaths per 10,000 registered vehicles was 1.66 in 2021. In comparison, the death rate was 1.53 in 2020 and 1.39 in 2011, which represents a 19.4% increase over 10 years. The number of fatalities per 100,000 population increased 26.5% between 2011 and 2021 and increased 10.9% in 2020-21.

In 2021, 6.3 mil male drivers were involved in crashes, whereas 4.5 mil female drivers were involved in crashes. About 72% of fatal crashes (or 44,036) involved male drivers, compared with fatal crashes involving female drivers (15,130).

In 2021, 13,384 motor vehicle traffic fatalities (31%) involved an alcohol-impaired (blood alcohol concentration of 0.08% or greater) driver or motorcycle operator.

Seat belt use was 91.6% in 2022. The least likely seat belt users were those traveling in light traffic (83%) and occupants of pickup trucks (87%). In 2021, the most recent year for which data was available, 50% of passenger vehicle occupants killed in traffic crashes were unrestrained.

Crashes	Deaths	Injuries
All motor vehicle crashes	46,980	5,400,000
Collision between motor vehicles	20,200	4,240,000
Collision with fixed object	12,600	700,000
Collision with pedestrian.............	9,100	160,000
Noncollision accidents (e.g., rollovers)	3,500	140,000
Collision with pedalcycle.............	1,400	130,000
Collision with railroad train	111	0
Collision with animal or animal-drawn vehicle......................	100	33,000

Note: NSC numbers are estimates.

U.S. Passenger Deaths and Death Rates, 1999-2021

Source: National Safety Council website: injuryfacts.nsc.org

Year	Passenger vehicles[1]		Vans, SUVs, pickup trucks[1]		Buses[2]		Railroad passenger trains		Scheduled airlines[3]	
	Deaths	Rate[4]	Deaths	Rate[4]	Deaths	Rate[4]	Deaths	Rate[4]	Deaths	Rate[4]
1999	20,851	0.84	11,295	0.76	40	0.07	14	0.10	23	0.005
2000	20,689	0.81	11,545	0.76	3	0.01	4	0.03	94	0.02
2005	18,509	0.68	13,043	0.76	43	0.07	16	0.10	20	0.003
2010	22,271	0.50	NA	NA	28	0.05	3	0.02	0	0.00
2011	21,315	0.48	NA	NA	36	0.06	6	0.03	0	0.00
2012	21,773	0.49	NA	NA	25	0.04	5	0.02	0	0.00
2013	21,218	0.47	NA	NA	36	0.06	6	0.03	5	0.001
2014	21,039	0.46	NA	NA	28	0.04	4	0.02	0	0.00
2015	22,362	0.49	NA	NA	28	0.01	15	0.07	1	<0.001
2016	23,776	0.50	NA	NA	47	0.01	2	0.01	6	0.001
2017	23,656	0.49	NA	NA	27	0.01	9	0.04	0	0.00
2018	22,840	0.47	NA	NA	30	0.01	6	0.03	1	<0.001
2019	22,367	0.46	NA	NA	27	0.01	1	0.005	2	<0.001
2020	23,907	0.56	NA	NA	12	0.004	2	0.01	5	0.002
2021	26,325	0.57	NA	NA	5	0.001	6	0.05	2	<0.001

NA = Not available. (1) From 2007 on, passenger vehicles include passenger cars, light trucks, vans, and SUVs, which were classified separately in previous years. Drivers of light duty vehicles (except taxis) are considered passengers. Includes taxi passengers. (2) Excludes school buses. (3) Excludes charter, cargo, and on-demand services and deaths due to suicide/sabotage. (4) Deaths per 100 mil passenger miles.

Related Factors in Fatal Crashes, 1995-2021
Source: National Highway Traffic Safety Admin. (NHTSA)

Factor	2021 Number	%	2010 Number	%	2005 Number	%	1995 Number	%
Driving too fast for conditions or in excess of posted limit or racing	11,254	18.5%	9,634	21.6%	11,803	20.0%	11,656	20.8%
Under the influence of alcohol, drugs, or medication	6,835	11.2	6,933	15.5	7,441	12.6	—	—
Operating vehicle in a careless manner[1]	4,601	7.6	—	—	2,712	4.6	2,850	5.1
Failure to yield right of way	4,239	7.0	3,227	7.2	4,306	7.3	4,868	8.7
Failure to keep in proper lane[2]	4,042	6.6	3,482	7.8	16,551	28.0	15,873	28.3
Distracted (phone, talking, eating, object, etc.)[3]	3,346	5.5	3,064	6.9	3,415	5.8	3,323	5.9
Operating vehicle in erratic, reckless, or negligent manner[1]	2,615	4.3	2,574	5.8	—	—	—	—
Failure to obey traffic signs, signals, or officer	2,450	4.0	1,933	4.3	2,354	4.0	3,189	5.7
Overcorrecting/oversteering	1,845	3.0	2,096	4.7	2,319	3.9	1,328	2.4
Vision obscured (rain, snow, glare, lights, building, trees, etc.)	1,584	2.6	1,440	3.2	1,496	2.5	1,309	2.3
Drowsy, asleep, fatigued, ill, or blackout	1,179	1.9	1,234	2.8	1,552	2.6	1,816	3.2
Swerving or avoiding due to wind, slippery surface, etc.	1,310	2.2	1,712	3.8	2,301	3.9	1,926	3.4
Driving wrong way on one-way traffic or wrong side of road	1,278	2.1	1,392	3.1	858	1.5	1,387	2.5
Making improper turn	445	0.7	990	2.2	1,590	2.7	1,253	2.2
Other factors	5,825	9.6	6,362	14.3	9,304	15.7	9,096	16.2
None reported	9,576	15.7	12,793	28.7	21,265	36.0	20,443	36.4
Unknown	19,636	32.2	5,088	11.4	1,187	2.0	990	1.8
Total drivers	**60,904**	**100.0**	**44,599**	**100.0**	**59,104**	**100.0**	**56,155**	**100.0**

— = Not available or not applicable. **Note:** For each year, the sum of the numbers and percentages is greater than total drivers as more than one factor may be present for the same driver. (1) In 1995 and 2005, the two categories were combined; "careless" not mentioned in factor in 2010. (2) "Failure to keep in proper lane or running off road" in 1995, 2005. (3) "Inattentive (talking, eating, etc.)" in 1995, 2005.

U.S. Death Rates for Suicide at Selected Ages, 1960-2019
Source: *Health, United States, 2020-2021*, National Center for Health Statistics (NCHS), CDC, U.S. Dept. of Health and Human Services
(deaths per 100,000 resident population)

Age	2019 Both sexes	Male	Female	2000 Both sexes	Male	Female	1980 Both sexes	Male	Female	1960 Both sexes	Male	Female
15-24 years	13.9	22.0	5.5	10.2	17.1	3.0	12.3	20.2	4.3	5.2	8.2	2.2
25-44 years	17.8	28.0	7.4	13.4	21.3	5.4	15.6	24.0	7.7	12.2	17.9	6.6
45-64 years	19.5	29.9	9.6	13.5	21.3	6.2	15.9	23.7	8.9	22.0	34.4	10.2
65 years and older	17.0	31.7	5.2	15.2	31.1	4.0	17.6	35.0	6.1	24.5	44.0	8.4
All ages[1]	13.9	22.4	6.0	10.4	17.7	4.0	12.2	19.9	5.7	12.5	20.0	5.6

(1) Incl. ages not shown separately here.

Leading Causes of Death in the U.S., 2021
Source: National Vital Statistics System, National Center for Health Statistics, CDC, U.S. Dept. of Health and Human Services

Cause of death	Number	% of total deaths	Death rate[1]	Cause of death	Number	% of total deaths	Death rate[1]
All causes	3,464,231	100.0%	879.7	6. Chronic lower respiratory diseases	142,342	4.1%	34.7
1. Heart disease	695,547	20.1	173.8	7. Alzheimer's disease	119,399	3.4	31.0
2. Cancer	605,213	17.5	146.6	8. Diabetes	103,294	3.0	25.4
3. COVID-19	416,893	12.0	104.1	9. Chronic liver disease and cirrhosis	56,585	1.6	14.5
4. Accidents (unintentional injuries)	224,935	6.5	64.7	10. Kidney disease	54,358	1.6	13.6
5. Stroke	162,890	4.7	41.1	All other causes (residual)	882,775	25.5	—

— = Not applicable. (1) Per 100,000 U.S. population.

Overdose Deaths From Selected Drugs in the U.S., 1999-2021
Source: National Center on Health Statistics (NCHS), CDC WONDER, U.S. Dept. of Health and Human Services

	1999	2000	2005	2010	2015	2018	2019	2020	2021	Percent change 1999-2021	Percent change 2020-21
Total overdose deaths	16,849	17,415	29,813	38,329	52,404	67,367	70,630	91,799	106,699	533.3%	16.2%
Female	5,591	5,852	11,089	15,323	19,447	22,426	22,749	28,071	32,398	479.5	15.4
Male	11,258	11,563	18,724	23,006	32,957	44,941	47,881	63,728	74,301	560.0	16.6
Any opioid	8,050	8,407	14,918	21,089	33,091	46,802	49,860	68,630	80,411	898.9	17.2
Female	2,057	2,264	5,161	7,734	11,420	14,724	15,225	19,970	23,654	1,049.9	18.4
Male	5,993	6,143	9,757	13,355	21,671	32,078	34,635	48,660	56,757	847.1	16.6
Prescription opioids	3,442	3,785	9,612	14,583	12,727	14,975	14,139	16,416	16,706	385.4	1.8
Other synthetic opioids[1]	730	782	1,742	3,007	9,580	31,335	36,359	56,516	70,601	9,571.4	24.9
Heroin	1,960	1,842	2,009	3,036	12,989	14,996	14,019	13,165	9,173	368.0	-30.3
Cocaine	3,822	3,544	6,208	4,183	6,784	14,666	15,883	19,447	24,486	540.7	25.9
Psychostimulants[2]	547	578	1,608	1,854	5,716	12,676	16,167	23,837	32,537	5,848.3	36.5
Benzodiazepines	1,135	1,298	3,084	6,497	8,791	10,724	9,711	12,290	12,499	1,001.2	1.7
Antidepressants	1,749	1,798	2,861	3,889	4,894	5,064	5,175	5,597	5,859	235.0	4.7

Note: Numbers include all deaths with underlying causes of drug poisoning, regardless of intent. (1) Synthetic opioids other than methadone. This category is dominated by fentanyl-related overdoses. (2) This category, "Psychostimulants with abuse potential," is dominated by methamphetamine-related overdoses.

Drug-Overdose Deaths in the U.S., 2021

Source: National Vital Statistics System, National Center for Health Statistics, CDC, U.S. Dept. of Health and Human Services

State	Number	Rate[1]	State	Number	Rate[1]	State	Number	Rate[1]	State	Number	Rate[1]
Alabama	1,408	30.1	Illinois	3,762	29.0	Montana	199	19.5	Rhode Island	455	41.7
Alaska	260	35.6	Indiana	2,811	43.0	Nebraska	214	11.4	South Carolina	2,138	42.8
Arizona	2,730	38.7	Iowa	475	15.3	Nevada	949	29.2	South Dakota	105	12.6
Arkansas	637	22.3	Kansas	680	24.3	New Hampshire	441	32.3	Tennessee	3,813	56.6
California	10,901	26.6	Kentucky	2,381	55.6	New Jersey	3,056	32.4	Texas	4,984	16.8
Colorado	1,887	31.4	Louisiana	2,463	55.9	New Mexico	1,052	51.6	Utah	662	21.1
Connecticut	1,552	42.3	Maine	611	47.1	New York	5,842	28.7	Vermont	252	42.3
Delaware	513	54.0	Maryland	2,737	42.8	North Carolina	3,981	39.2	Virginia	2,626	30.5
Dist. of Columbia	427	61.6	Massachusetts	2,585	36.8	North Dakota	124	17.2	Washington	2,264	28.1
Florida	7,827	37.5	Michigan	3,089	31.5	Ohio	5,397	48.1	West Virginia	1,501	90.9
Georgia	2,500	23.5	Minnesota	1,356	24.5	Oklahoma	960	24.4	Wisconsin	1,775	31.6
Hawaii	269	17.3	Mississippi	787	28.4	Oregon	1,171	26.8	Wyoming	109	18.9
Idaho	354	19.0	Missouri	2,155	36.5	Pennsylvania	5,449	43.2	**U.S.**	**106,699**	**32.4**

(1) Number of deaths due to drug overdose per 100,000 population.

Principal Types of Accidental Deaths in the U.S., 1970-2021

Source: National Safety Council website: injuryfacts.nsc.org; National Center for Health Statistics, U.S. Dept. of Health and Human Services

Year[1]	Total[2]	Motor vehicle	Falls	Poisoning	Choking: Inhalation of food, object	Drowning	Fires, flames, smoke	Mechanical suffocation	Firearms
1970	114,638	54,633	16,926	5,299	2,753	7,860	6,718	NA	2,406
1980	105,718	53,172	13,294	4,331	3,249	7,257	5,822	NA	1,955
1985	93,457	45,901	12,001	5,170	3,551	5,316	4,938	NA	1,649
1990	91,983	46,814	12,313	5,803	3,303	4,685	4,175	NA	1,416
1995	93,320	43,363	13,986	9,072	3,185	4,350	3,761	NA	1,225
2000	97,900	43,354	13,322	12,757	4,313	3,482	3,377	1,335	776
2005	117,809	45,343	19,656	23,617	4,386	3,582	3,197	1,514	789
2010	120,859	35,332	26,009	33,041	4,570	3,782	2,782	1,595	606
2013	130,557	35,369	30,208	38,851	4,864	3,391	2,760	1,737	505
2014	135,928	35,398	31,959	42,032	4,816	3,406	2,701	1,764	461
2015	146,571	37,757	33,381	47,478	5,051	3,602	2,646	1,863	489
2016	161,374	40,327	34,673	58,335	4,829	3,789	2,730	1,781	495
2017	169,936	40,231	36,338	64,795	5,216	3,709	2,812	1,730	486
2018	167,127	39,404	37,455	62,399	5,084	3,710	2,972	1,617	458
2019	173,040	39,107	39,443	65,773	5,228	3,692	2,692	1,848	486
2020	200,955	42,339	42,114	87,404	4,963	4,177	2,951	1,805	535
2021	224,935	46,980	44,686	102,001	5,325	4,337	3,389	1,857	549
				Deaths per 100,000 population					
1970	56.2	26.8	8.3	2.6	1.4	3.9	3.3	NA	1.2
1980	46.5	23.4	5.9	1.9	1.4	3.2	2.6	NA	0.9
1985	39.3	19.3	5.0	2.2	1.5	2.2	2.1	NA	0.7
1990	36.9	18.8	4.9	2.3	1.3	1.9	1.7	NA	0.6
1995	35.5	16.5	5.3	3.4	1.2	1.7	1.4	NA	0.5
2000	35.6	15.7	4.8	4.6	1.6	1.3	1.2	0.5	0.3
2005	39.7	15.3	6.6	8.0	1.5	1.2	1.1	0.5	0.3
2010	39.0	11.4	8.4	10.7	1.5	1.2	0.9	0.5	0.2
2013	41.3	11.2	9.6	12.3	1.5	1.1	0.9	0.5	0.2
2014	42.6	11.1	10.0	13.2	1.5	1.1	0.8	0.6	0.1
2015	45.6	11.7	10.4	14.8	1.6	1.1	0.8	0.6	0.2
2016	49.9	12.5	10.7	18.1	1.5	1.2	0.8	0.6	0.2
2017	52.2	12.4	11.2	19.9	1.6	1.1	0.9	0.5	0.2
2018	51.1	12.0	11.4	19.1	1.6	1.1	0.9	0.5	0.1
2019	52.7	11.9	12.0	20.0	1.6	1.1	0.8	0.6	0.1
2020	60.6	12.8	12.7	26.4	1.5	1.3	0.9	0.5	0.2
2021	67.8	14.2	13.5	30.7	1.6	1.3	1.0	0.6	0.2

NA = Not available. **Note:** All figures include on-the-job deaths. (1) Data after 1999 are not comparable with earlier data because of classification changes. (2) Total incl. other accidental deaths not shown in detail here.

Deaths in the U.S. Involving Firearms by Age and Sex, 2021

Source: National Safety Council website: injuryfacts.nsc.org

Type and sex	All ages	Under 5	5-14 years	15-24 years	25-44 years	45-54 years	55-64 years	65-74 years	75 or older
Total firearms deaths	48,830	153	672	10,132	19,140	5,898	5,189	3,923	3,722
Male	41,866	96	489	8,916	16,403	4,830	4,317	3,388	3,417
Female	6,964	48	183	1,216	2,737	1,068	872	535	305
Preventable/accidental	549	51	53	125	157	46	44	46	20
Male	482	43	50	113	134	40	37	42	18
Female	67	8	3	12	23	6	7	4	2
Suicide	26,328	0	236	3,590	7,865	3,717	3,984	3,430	3,505
Male	22,936	0	181	3,215	6,762	3,072	3,363	3,045	3,297
Female	3,392	0	55	375	1,103	645	621	385	208
Assault	20,958	87	359	6,207	10,610	2,024	1,096	413	162
Male	17,596	44	243	5,413	9,050	1,630	857	277	75
Female	3,362	28	116	794	1,560	394	239	136	87

U.S. Infant Mortality Rates by Race and Sex, 1960-2021

Source: National Center for Health Statistics (NCHS), CDC, U.S. Dept. of Health and Human Services
(deaths of infants under 1 year old per 1,000 live births)

Year	All races[1] Both sexes	Male	Female	White[2] Both sexes	Male	Female	Black[2] Both sexes	Male	Female
1960	26.0	29.3	22.6	22.9	26.0	19.6	44.3	49.1	39.4
1970	20.0	22.4	17.5	17.8	20.0	15.4	32.7	36.2	29.0
1980	12.6	13.9	11.2	10.9	12.1	9.5	22.2	24.2	20.2
1990	9.2	10.3	8.1	7.6	8.5	6.6	18.0	19.6	16.3
2000	6.9	7.6	6.2	5.7	6.3	5.1	14.1	15.5	12.7
2005	6.9	7.6	6.2	5.7	6.7	4.8	14.3	15.8	12.8
2006	6.7	7.3	6.0	5.6	6.2	5.0	13.8	15.0	12.5
2007	6.8	7.4	6.1	5.6	6.2	5.0	13.8	15.0	12.4
2008	6.6	7.2	6.0	5.5	6.0	5.0	13.1	14.4	11.9
2009	6.4	7.0	5.8	5.3	5.8	4.7	13.1	14.6	11.5
2010	6.1	6.7	5.6	5.1	5.5	4.6	12.0	13.1	10.9
2011	6.1	6.6	5.5	5.1	5.5	4.6	12.0	13.1	10.8
2012	6.0	6.5	5.4	5.0	5.4	4.5	11.6	12.8	10.4
2013	6.0	6.5	5.4	5.0	5.5	4.4	11.6	12.5	10.7
2014	5.8	6.3	5.3	4.8	5.3	4.3	11.4	12.3	10.4
2015	5.9	6.4	5.4	4.8	5.3	4.4	11.7	12.8	10.7
2016	5.9	6.4	5.3	4.8	5.2	4.3	11.8	12.7	10.8
2017	5.8	6.3	5.2	4.7	5.1	4.1	11.0	12.6	10.3
2018	5.7	6.3	5.1	4.6	5.1	4.2	10.8	12.0	9.4
2019	5.6	6.1	5.1	4.4	4.9	4.0	11.0	11.9	10.2
2020	5.4	5.9	5.0	4.4	4.8	4.0	10.4	11.2	9.5
2021	5.4	5.8	5.0	4.4	4.7	4.1	10.6	11.6	9.5

Note: Number of live births is tabulated according to mother's race (1980 and on) or parents' race (before 1980) stated on birth certificate. (1) Incl. races not shown. (2) Non-Hispanic.

Years of Life Expected at Birth in U.S., 1900-2020

Source: National Center for Health Statistics (NCHS), CDC, U.S. Dept. of Health and Human Services

Year	All races[1] Both sexes	Male	Female	White[2] Both sexes	Male	Female	Black[2,3] Both sexes	Male	Female
1900[4]	47.3	46.3	48.3	47.6	46.6	48.7	33.0	32.5	33.5
1910[4]	50.0	48.4	51.8	50.3	48.6	52.0	35.6	33.8	37.5
1920[4]	54.1	53.6	54.6	54.9	54.4	55.6	45.3	45.5	45.2
1930	59.7	58.1	61.6	61.4	59.7	63.5	48.1	47.3	49.2
1940	62.9	60.8	65.2	64.2	62.1	66.6	53.1	51.5	54.9
1950	68.2	65.6	71.1	69.1	66.5	72.2	60.8	59.1	62.9
1960	69.7	66.6	73.1	70.6	67.4	74.1	63.6	61.1	66.3
1970	70.8	67.1	74.7	71.7	68.0	75.6	64.1	60.0	68.3
1980	73.7	70.0	77.4	74.4	70.7	78.1	68.1	63.8	72.5
1990	75.4	71.8	78.8	76.1	72.7	79.4	69.1	64.5	73.6
2000	76.8	74.1	79.3	77.3	74.7	79.9	71.8	68.2	75.1
2010	78.7	76.2	81.0	78.8	76.4	81.1	74.7	71.5	77.7
2013	78.8	76.4	81.2	78.8	76.5	81.2	75.1	71.9	78.1
2014	78.9	76.5	81.3	78.8	76.5	81.2	75.3	72.2	78.2
2015	78.7	76.3	81.1	78.7	76.3	81.0	75.1	71.9	78.1
2016	78.7	76.2	81.1	78.6	76.2	81.0	74.9	71.6	78.0
2017	78.6	76.1	81.1	78.5	76.1	81.0	74.9	71.5	78.1
2018	78.7	76.2	81.2	78.6	76.2	81.1	74.7	71.3	78.0
2019	78.8	76.3	81.4	78.8	76.3	81.3	74.8	71.3	78.1
2020	77.0	74.2	79.9	77.4	74.8	80.1	71.5	67.8	75.4

(1) Includes races not shown. (2) Non-Hispanic beginning in 2010. (3) Data for 1900-60 are for the "nonwhite" pop. (4) Data prior to 1930 does not include all states.

U.S. Life Expectancy at Selected Ages, 2021

Source: National Center for Health Statistics (NCHS), CDC, U.S. Dept. of Health and Human Services

In 2021, U.S. life expectancy fell for the second straight year, primarily due to deaths from COVID-19. Life expectancy in 2021 was 76.1 years, declining by 0.9 year from 77.0 in 2020 and by 2.7 years from 78.8 in 2019. The non-Hispanic American Indian or Alaska Native population (not shown separately on the table) saw the largest decline between 2019 and 2021 (6.6 years). Overall, the 2021 life expectancy was the lowest since 1996.

Age (years)	All races and origins Total	Male	Female	Hispanic Total	Male	Female	White[1] Total	Male	Female	Black[1] Total	Male	Female
0	76.1	73.2	79.1	77.7	74.4	81.0	76.4	73.7	79.2	70.8	66.7	74.8
1	75.6	72.6	78.5	77.1	73.8	80.4	75.7	73.0	78.5	70.6	66.5	74.5
5	71.6	68.7	74.6	73.1	69.8	76.4	71.8	69.1	74.6	66.7	62.6	70.7
10	66.7	63.8	69.7	68.2	64.9	71.5	66.8	64.1	69.6	61.8	57.7	65.7
15	61.7	58.8	64.7	63.2	59.9	66.5	61.9	59.2	64.7	56.9	52.8	60.8
20	56.9	54.1	59.8	58.4	55.1	61.6	57.0	54.4	59.8	52.2	48.3	56.0
25	52.2	49.5	55.0	53.7	50.6	56.8	52.3	49.8	54.9	47.8	44.2	51.3
30	47.6	45.1	50.2	49.1	46.1	52.0	47.7	45.3	50.2	43.5	40.0	46.7
35	43.1	40.7	45.5	44.5	41.7	47.2	43.1	40.9	45.5	39.1	35.9	42.1
40	38.6	36.4	40.9	39.9	37.3	42.5	38.7	36.5	40.8	35.0	32.0	37.7
45	34.2	32.1	36.4	35.5	33.0	37.8	34.3	32.3	36.3	30.9	28.1	33.4
50	30.0	28.0	31.9	31.1	28.8	33.3	30.0	28.1	31.9	26.9	24.4	29.2
55	25.9	24.0	27.6	26.9	24.8	28.8	25.9	24.1	27.6	23.2	20.9	25.2
60	22.0	20.4	23.5	23.0	21.1	24.6	21.9	20.4	23.4	19.7	17.6	21.5
65	18.3	16.9	19.6	19.3	17.6	20.6	18.3	16.9	19.5	16.5	14.8	18.0
70	14.8	13.7	15.8	15.7	14.4	16.7	14.7	13.6	15.7	13.6	12.2	14.7
75	11.5	10.6	12.3	12.4	11.3	13.1	11.4	10.5	12.1	10.9	9.7	11.7
80	8.6	7.9	9.1	9.3	8.5	9.7	8.4	7.8	8.9	8.4	7.5	8.9
85	6.1	5.6	6.4	6.7	6.1	6.9	5.9	5.5	6.2	6.2	5.6	6.5

Note: Data are provisional. (1) Non-Hispanic.

NOTED PERSONALITIES

Widely Known Americans of the Present

Political leaders, journalists, other prominent living persons. As of Oct. 2023. Excludes most who fall in categories listed elsewhere in Noted Personalities, such as Writers of the Present and Entertainment Personalities of the Present. Includes some figures who are active in American life but are not U.S. citizens.

Greg Abbott, b 11/13/1957 (Wichita Falls, TX), TX gov. (R).

Stacey Abrams, b 12/9/1973 (Madison, WI), former GA House minority leader (D); 2022 GA gov. contender.

Eric Adams, b 9/1/1960 (New York, NY), NYC mayor (D).

Pete Aguilar, b 6/19/1979 (Fontana, CA), U.S. rep. (D, CA); House Dem. Caucus chair.

Edwin "Buzz" Aldrin, b 1/20/1930 (Montclair, NJ), former astronaut, second person to walk on the Moon.

Samuel A. Alito Jr., b 4/1/1950 (Trenton, NJ), U.S. Supreme Court justice.

Gloria Allred, b 7/3/1941 (Philadelphia, PA), civil rights lawyer.

Marin Alsop, b 10/16/1956 (New York, NY), Baltimore Symphony musical dir. laureate.

Christiane Amanpour, b 1/12/1958 (London, Eng., UK), TV journalist.

Marc Andreessen, b 7/9/1971 (New Lisbon, IA), co-author of web browser Mosaic, cofounder of Netscape.

Lloyd Austin, b 8/8/1953 (Mobile, AL), defense sec.; U.S. Army gen. (ret.).

David Axelrod, b 2/22/1955 (New York, NY), political strategist.

James Baker, b 4/28/1930 (Houston, TX), former sec. of state.

Robert Ballard, b 6/30/1942 (Wichita, KS), oceanographer; found wreck of the *Titanic*.

Steve Ballmer, b 3/24/1956 (Detroit, MI), former Microsoft CEO; L.A. Clippers owner.

Steve Bannon, b 11/27/1953 (Norfolk, VA), former chief strategist to Pres. Trump, Breitbart News exec.

Mike Barnicle, b 10/13/1943 (Worcester, MA), columnist.

William Barr, b 5/23/1950 (New York, NY), U.S. atty. gen. (1991-93, 2019-20).

Mary Barra, b 12/24/1961 (Waterford, MI), General Motors CEO.

Amy Coney Barrett, b 1/28/1972 (New Orleans, LA), U.S. Supreme Court justice.

Dave Barry, b 7/3/1947 (Armonk, NY), humorist.

Glenn Beck, b 2/10/1964 (Mount Vernon, WA), political commentator.

Ben Bernanke, b 12/13/1953 (Augusta, GA), former Federal Reserve chair.

Carl Bernstein, b 2/14/1944 (Washington, DC), journalist; with Bob Woodward cracked Watergate scandal.

Jeff Bezos, b 1/12/1964 (Albuquerque, NM), Amazon founder.

Hunter Biden, b 2/4/1970 (Wilmington, DE), lawyer, son of pres. Joe Biden.

Jill Biden, b 6/5/1951 (Hammonton, NJ), first lady, professor.

Joseph R. Biden Jr., b 11/20/1942 (Scranton, PA), 46th U.S. president.

Deborah Birx, b 4/4/1956 (Baltimore, MD), physician, fmr. White House coronavirus response coordinator.

Antony Blinken, b 4/16/1962 (Yonkers, NY), sec. of state.

Wolf Blitzer, b 3/22/1948 (Augsburg, Germany), TV journalist.

Michael R. Bloomberg, b 2/14/1942 (Brighton, MA), former NYC mayor, financial information/media entrepreneur.

Charles M. Blow, b 8/11/1970 (Gibsland, LA), columnist.

Cory Booker, b 4/27/1969 (Washington, DC), U.S. sen. (D, NJ), former Newark mayor; 2020 pres. contender.

Andy Borowitz, b 1/4/1958 (Cleveland, OH), humorist.

Donna Brazile, b 12/15/1959 (Kenner, LA), political analyst.

Stephen Breyer, b 8/15/1938 (San Francisco, CA), former U.S. Supreme Court justice.

Sergey Brin, b 8/21/1973 (Moscow, Russia), cofounder of Google.

Tom Brokaw, b 2/6/1940 (Webster, SD), TV journalist, retired anchor.

David Brooks, b 8/11/1961 (Toronto, ON, Can.), columnist, political commentator.

Aaron Brown, b 11/10/1948 (Hopkins, MN), broadcast journalist.

Frank Bruni, b 10/31/1964 (White Plains, NY), columnist.

Warren Buffett, b 8/30/1930 (Omaha, NE), investor, leading philanthropist.

Lonnie Bunch III, b 11/18/1952 (Newark, NJ), Smithsonian Institution sec.

Doug Burgum, b 8/1/1956 (Arthur, ND), ND gov. (R); 2024 pres. contender.

Tarana Burke, b 9/12/1973 (New York, NY), activist who started #metoo movement.

Barbara Bush, b 11/25/1981 (Dallas, TX), daughter of former pres. George W. Bush.

George W. Bush, b 7/6/1946 (New Haven, CT), 43rd U.S. president.

Jeb Bush, b 2/11/1953 (Midland, TX), former FL gov. (R).

Laura Bush, b 11/4/1946 (Midland, TX), former first lady.

Pete Buttigieg, b 1/19/1982 (South Bend, IN), transportation sec.; 2020 pres. contender (D).

Gretchen Carlson, b 6/21/1966 (Anoka, MN), TV journalist.

Tucker Carlson, b 5/16/1969 (San Francisco, CA), news commentator.

Jimmy Carter, b 10/1/1924 (Plains, GA), 39th U.S. president; 2002 Nobel Peace Prize winner.

Rosalynn Carter, b 8/18/1927 (Plains, GA), former first lady.

Joaquin Castro, b 9/16/1974 (San Antonio, TX), U.S. rep. (D, TX).

Julián Castro, b 9/16/1974 (San Antonio, TX), fmr. housing and urban dev. sec.; 2020 pres. contender (D).

Dick Cheney, b 1/30/1941 (Lincoln, NE), former U.S. vice president.

Liz Cheney, b 7/28/1966 (Madison, WI), fmr. U.S. rep. (R, WY).

Lynne Cheney, b 8/14/1941 (Casper, WY), political commentator, wife of former U.S. vice pres. Dick Cheney.

Brian Chesky, b 8/29/1981 (Niskayuna, NY), Airbnb founder, CEO.

Judy Chicago, b 7/20/1939 (Chicago, IL), artist.

Dale Chihuly, b 9/20/1941 (Tacoma, WA), glass sculptor.

Noam Chomsky, b 12/7/1928 (Philadelphia, PA), linguist, activist.

Chris Christie, b 9/6/1962 (Newark, NJ), former NJ gov. (R); 2016, 2024 pres. contender.

Connie Chung, b 8/20/1946 (Washington, DC), former TV journalist.

Katherine Clark, b 7/17/1963 (New Haven, CT), House minority whip (D, MA).

Bill Clinton, b 8/19/1946 (Hope, AR), 42nd U.S. president.

Chelsea Clinton, b 2/27/1980 (Little Rock, AR), daughter of former pres. Bill Clinton and Hillary Clinton.

Hillary Rodham Clinton, b 10/26/1947 (Chicago, IL), former sec. of state, U.S. sen. (D, NY), first lady; 2016 presidential nominee.

Kate Clinton, b 11/9/1947 (Buffalo, NY), political humorist.

Jim Clyburn, b 7/21/1940 (Sumter, SC), U.S. rep. (D, SC).

Kenneth Cole, b 3/23/1954 (Brooklyn, NY), fashion designer.

Gail Collins, b 11/25/1945 (Cincinnati, OH), newspaper columnist, writer.

Jason Collins, b 12/2/1978 (Northridge, CA), first openly gay active NBA player.

James Comey, b 12/14/1960 (Yonkers, NY), former FBI director.

Kellyanne Conway, b 1/20/1967 (Camden, NJ), fmr. counselor to Pres. Trump.

Tim Cook, b 11/1/1960 (Robertdale, AZ), CEO of Apple Inc.

Anderson Cooper, b 6/3/1967 (New York, NY), TV news anchor.

Bob Costas, b 3/22/1952 (Astoria, Queens, NY), TV sports journalist.

Ann Coulter, b 12/8/1961 (New Canaan, CT), political commentator, author.

Katie Couric, b 1/7/1957 (Arlington, VA), TV and online journalist.

Harlan Crow, b 10/17/1949 (Dallas, TX), real estate developer.

Candy Crowley, b 12/12/1948 (Kalamazoo, MI), TV journalist.

Ben Crump, b 10/10/1969 (Lumberton, NC), civil rights attorney.

Ted Cruz, b 12/22/1970 (Calgary, AB, Can.), U.S. sen. (R, TX).

Mark Cuban, b 7/31/1958 (Pittsburgh, PA), entrepreneur, Dallas Mavericks owner.

Andrew Cuomo, b 12/6/1957 (New York, NY), former NY gov. (D), state atty. gen.

Chris Cuomo, b 8/9/1970 (Queens, NY), TV journalist.

Ann Curry, b 11/19/1956 (Guam), TV journalist.

Angela Davis, b 1/26/1944 (Birmingham, AL), political activist, professor.

Bill de Blasio, b 5/8/1961 (New York, NY), former NYC mayor (D); 2020 pres. contender.

Michael Dell, b 2/23/1965 (Houston, TX), founder and CEO of tech giant Dell.

Alan Dershowitz, b 9/1/1938 (Brooklyn, NY), attorney, political commentator.

Ron DeSantis, b 9/14/1978 (Jacksonville, FL), FL gov. (R); 2024 pres. contender.

José Díaz-Balart, b 11/7/1960 (Fort Lauderdale, FL), TV journalist.

Barry Diller, b 2/2/1942 (San Francisco, CA), media exec.

Jamie Dimon, b 3/13/1956 (New York, NY), chair, CEO of JPMorgan Chase.

Lou Dobbs, b 9/24/1945 (Childress, TX), TV journalist.

James Dobson, b 4/21/1936 (Shreveport, LA), evangelical Christian leader.

Timothy Dolan, b 2/6/1950 (St. Louis, MO), Rom. Cath. cardinal, archbishop of NY.

Jack Dorsey, b 11/19/1976 (St. Louis, MO), Twitter cofounder.

Maureen Dowd, b 1/14/1952 (Washington, DC), columnist.

Elizabeth Drew, b 11/16/1935 (Cincinnati, OH), journalist.

Matt Drudge, b 10/27/1966 (Takoma Park, MD), Drudge Report founder/editor.

Michael S. Dukakis, b 11/3/1933 (Brookline, MA), former MA gov. (D), 1988 pres. nominee.

David Duke, b 7/1/1950 (Tulsa, OK), white nationalist activist; politician.

Dick Durbin, b 11/21/1944 (East St. Louis, IL), U.S. Senate majority whip (D IL).

Sylvia Earle, b 8/30/1935 (Gibbstown, NJ), marine biologist.

Marian Wright Edelman, b 6/6/1939 (Bennettsville, SC), Children's Defense Fund founder.

Michael Eisner, b 3/7/1942 (Mt. Kisco, NY), former Disney Co. CEO.

Sarah Kate Ellis, b 11/27/1991 (Staten Island, NY), GLAAD CEO.

Lawrence J. Ellison, b 8/17/1944 (New York, NY), Oracle Corp. cofounder.

Rahm Emanuel, b 11/29/1959 (Chicago, IL), amb. to Japan; fmr. Chicago mayor, Obama chief of staff, U.S. rep. (D, IL).

Doug Emhoff, b 10/13/1964 (Brooklyn, NY), husband of vice pres. Kamala Harris.

Tom Emmer, b 3/3/1961 (South Bend, IN), House majority whip (R, MN).

Myrlie Evers-Williams, b 3/17/1933 (Vicksburg, MS), civil rights activist.

Louis Farrakhan, b 5/11/1933 (Roxbury, MA), Nation of Islam leader.

Ronan Farrow, b 12/19/1987 (New York, NY), investigative journalist.

Anthony Fauci, b 12/24/1940 (New York, NY), physician, fmr. National Institute of Allergy and Infectious Diseases dir.

John Fetterman, b 8/15/1969 (West Reading, PA), U.S. sen. (D, PA).

Michael Flynn, b 12/1/1958 (Middletown, RI), U.S. Army gen. (ret.); briefly Pres. Trump's natl. security adviser.

Steve (Malcolm) Forbes Jr., b 7/18/1947 (Morristown, NJ), publisher, former pres. contender.

Christine Blasey Ford, b 11/28/1966 (Potomac, MD), professor; complainant against U.S. Supreme Court justice Brett Kavanaugh.

Tom Ford, b 8/27/1961 (Austin, TX), fashion designer, director.

Thomas Friedman, b 7/20/1953 (Minneapolis, MN), columnist, author.

Tulsi Gabbard, b 4/12/1981 (Leloaloa, Amer. Samoa), former U.S. rep (D, HI); 2020 pres. contender.

Merrick Garland, b 11/13/1952 (Chicago, IL), U.S. atty. gen.; Supreme Court nominee.

Bill Gates, b 10/28/1955 (Seattle, WA), software pioneer; Microsoft exec.

Henry Louis Gates Jr., b 9/16/1950 (Keyser, WV), African American studies scholar; TV host.

Melinda Gates, b 8/15/1964 (Dallas, TX), philanthropist.

David Geffen, b 2/21/1943 (Brooklyn, NY), entertainment exec.

Charles Gibson, b 3/4/1943 (Evanston, IL), TV journalist.

Gabrielle Giffords, b 6/8/1970 (Tucson, AZ), former U.S. rep. (D, AZ); shot in 2011 assassination attempt.

Newt Gingrich, b 6/17/1943 (Harrisburg, PA), former House speaker (R, GA); 2012 pres. contender.

Rudolph Giuliani, b 5/28/1944 (Brooklyn, NY), atty. for fmr. Pres. Trump, fmr. NYC mayor (R).

Ira Glass, b 3/3/1959 (Baltimore, MD), radio host.

Roger Goodell, b 2/19/1959 (Jamestown, NY), NFL commissioner.

Ellen Goodman, b 4/11/1941 (Newton, MA), columnist.

Doris Kearns Goodwin, b 1/4/1943 (Brooklyn, NY), historian, TV commentator.

Berry Gordy, b 11/28/1929 (Detroit, MI), Motown record label founder.

Al Gore Jr., b 3/31/1948 (Washington, DC), former U.S. sen. (D, TN), vice pres., 2000 pres. nominee.

Lindsey Graham, b 7/9/1955 (Central, SC), U.S. sen. (R, SC).

Temple Grandin, b 8/29/1947 (Boston, MA), animal behavioral scientist.

Marjorie Taylor Greene, b 5/27/1974 (Milledgeville, GA), U.S. rep. (R, GA).

Jeff Greenfield, b 6/10/1943 (New York, NY), TV journalist.

Alan Greenspan, b 3/6/1926 (New York, NY), former Federal Reserve chair.

Savannah Guthrie, b 12/27/1971 (Melbourne, Vic., Australia), TV journalist.

Jenna Bush Hager, b 11/25/1981 (Dallas, TX), daughter of former pres. George W. Bush; TV host.

Nikki Haley, b 1/20/1972 (Bamberg, SC), fmr. U.S. ambassador to UN, SC gov. (R); 2024 pres. contender.

Nikole Hannah-Jones, b 4/9/1976 (Waterloo, IA), journalist.

Sean Hannity, b 12/30/1961 (New York, NY), radio and TV host, author, political commentator.

Kamala Harris, b 10/20/1964 (Oakland, CA), U.S. vice pres.; former U.S. sen. (D, CA).

Jaime Harrison, b 2/5/1976 (Orangeburg, SC), Dem. Natl. Committee chair.

Reed Hastings, b 10/8/1960 (Boston, MA), Netflix cofounder, exec. chair.

Carla Hayden, b 8/10/1952 (Tallahassee, FL), librarian of U.S. Congress.

Tommy Hilfiger, b 3/24/1951 (Elmira, NY), fashion designer.

Anita Hill, b 7/30/1956 (Morris, OK), legal scholar; complainant against U.S. Supreme Court justice Clarence Thomas.

Paris Hilton, b 2/17/1981 (New York, NY), heiress.

Perez Hilton, b 3/23/1978 (Miami, FL), gossip columnist.

James P. Hoffa, b 5/19/1941 (Detroit, MI), fmr. Teamsters Union head.

Eric Holder Jr., b 1/21/1951 (Bronx, NY), former U.S. atty. general.

Lester Holt, b 3/8/1959 (San Francisco, CA), TV journalist.

David Horowitz, b 1/10/1939 (New York, NY), consumer advocate, columnist, author.

Steny H. Hoyer, b 6/14/1939 (New York, NY), U.S. rep. (D, MD).

Mike Huckabee, b 8/24/1955 (Hope, AR), former AR gov. (R), TV host; 2008, 2016 pres. contender.

Dolores Huerta, b 4/10/1930 (Dawson, NM), labor activist.

Arianna Huffington, b 7/15/1950 (Athens, Greece), political commentator.

Brit Hume, b 6/22/1943 (Washington, DC), TV journalist.

Asa Hutchinson, b 12/3/1950 (Bentonville, AR), fmr. AR gov. (R); 2024 pres. contender.

Carl Icahn, b 2/16/1936 (Brooklyn, NY), financier.

Bob Iger, b 2/10/1951 (Oceanside, NY), Walt Disney Co. CEO.

Jay Inslee, b 2/9/1951 (Seattle, WA), WA gov. (D); 2020 pres. contender.

Jesse Jackson, b 10/8/1941 (Greenville, SC), civil rights leader, former pres. contender (D).

Ketanji Brown Jackson, b 9/14/1970 (Washington, DC), U.S. Supreme Court justice.

Marc Jacobs, b 4/9/1964 (New York, NY), fashion designer.

Letitia James, b 10/18/1958 (Brooklyn, NY), NY atty. gen.

Andy Jassy, b 1/13/1968 (Scarsdale, NY), Amazon CEO.

Karine Jean-Pierre, b 8/13/1974 (Fort-de-France, Martinique), White House press sec.

Hakeem Jeffries, b 8/4/1970 (Brooklyn, NY), House minority leader (D, NY).

Jasper Johns, b 5/15/1930 (Augusta, GA), painter, printmaker.

Robert L. Johnson, b 4/8/1946 (Hickory, MS), Black Entertainment Television co-founder.

Sheila Johnson, b 1/25/1949 (PA), Black Entertainment Television co-founder.

Alex Jones, b 2/11/1974 (Dallas, TX), InfoWars creator, radio host.

Cleve Jones, b 10/11/1954 (W. Lafayette, IN), AIDS and LGBTQ rights activist.

Colin Kaepernick, b 11/3/1987 (Milwaukee, WI), football player, activist.

Elena Kagan, b 4/28/1960 (New York, NY), U.S. Supreme Court justice.

Tim Kaine, b 2/26/1958 (St. Paul, MN), U.S. sen. (D, VA), 2016 vice-pres. nominee.

Travis Kalanick, b 8/6/1976 (Los Angeles, CA), Uber cofounder and former CEO.

Donna Karan, b 10/2/1948 (Forest Hills, Queens, NY), fashion designer.

Jeffrey Katzenberg, b 12/21/1950 (New York, NY), entertainment exec.

Brett Kavanaugh, b 2/12/1965 (Washington, DC), U.S. Supreme Court justice.

Garrison Keillor, b 8/7/1942 (Anoka, MN), author, broadcaster.

Mark Kelly, b 2/21/1964 (Orange, NJ), U.S. sen. (D, AZ), former NASA shuttle commander.

Megyn Kelly, b 11/18/1970 (Syracuse, NY), TV commentator, host.

Brian Kemp, b 11/2/1963 (Athens, GA), GA gov. (R).

Anthony M. Kennedy, b 7/23/1936 (Sacramento, CA), former U.S. Supreme Court justice.

Caroline Kennedy, b 11/27/1957 (New York, NY), author, diplomat, daughter of Pres. Kennedy.

Robert F. Kennedy Jr., b 1/17/1954 (Washington, DC), environmental lawyer, activist; 2024 pres. contender.

John Kerry, b 12/11/1943 (Aurora, CO), U.S. climate envoy, former sec. of state, U.S. sen. (D, MA); 2004 pres. nominee.

Gayle King, b 12/28/1954 (Chevy Chase, MD), TV and magazine journalist.

Adam Kinzinger, b 2/27/1978 (Kankakee, IL), fmr. U.S. rep. (R, IL).

Henry Kissinger, b 5/27/1923 (Furth, Germany), former sec. of state.

Ron Klain, b 8/8/1961 (Indianapolis, IN), fmr. White House chief of staff.

Calvin Klein, b 11/19/1942 (Bronx, NY), fashion designer.

Amy Klobuchar, b 5/25/1960 (Plymouth, MN), U.S. sen. (D, MN); 2020 pres. contender.

Philip H. Knight, b 2/24/1938 (Portland, OR), founder and chair emeritus of Nike.

Charles G. Koch, b 5/3/1940 (Wichita, KS), Koch Industries exec., philanthropist.

Sarah Koenig, b 7/9/1969 (New York, NY), radio journalist.

Jeff Koons, b 1/21/1955 (York, PA), artist.

Ted Koppel, b 2/8/1940 (Lancashire, Eng., UK), former TV journalist.

Michael Kors, b 8/9/1959 (Merrick, NY), fashion designer.

Hoda Kotb, b 8/9/1964 (Norman, OK), TV host.

Nicholas D. Kristof, b 4/27/1959 (Chicago, IL), columnist, author.

William Kristol, b 12/23/1952 (New York, NY), editor, columnist.

Steve Kroft, b 8/22/1945 (Kokomo, IN), TV journalist.

Paul Krugman, b 2/28/1953 (Albany, NY), economist, columnist.

Jared Kushner, b 1/10/1981 (Livingston, NJ), fmr. Trump senior adviser; real estate developer.

Brian Lamb, b 10/9/1941 (Lafayette, IN), cable TV exec., journalist.

Wayne LaPierre Jr., b 11/8/1949 (Schenectady, NY), National Rifle Assn. exec. VP.

Matt Lauer, b 12/30/1957 (New York, NY), former TV journalist.

Ralph Lauren, b 10/14/1939 (Bronx, NY), fashion designer.

Norman Lear, b 7/27/1922 (New Haven, CT), TV producer, political activist.

Annie Leibovitz, b 10/2/1949 (Waterbury, CT), photographer.

Monica Lewinsky, b 7/23/1973 (San Francisco, CA), former White House intern.

Shannon Lucid, b 1/14/1943 (Shanghai, China), NASA scientist, astronaut.

Loretta Lynch, b 5/21/1959 (Greensboro, NC), former U.S. atty. gen.

Rachel Maddow, b 4/1/1973 (Castro Valley, CA), TV/radio host, political commentator.

Michelle Malkin, b 10/20/1980 (Philadelphia, PA), political commentator.

Joe Manchin, b 8/24/47 (Farmington, WV), U.S. sen. (D, WV).

Rob Manfred, b 9/28/1958 (Rome, NY), MLB commissioner.

Chelsea Manning, b 12/17/1987 (Crescent, OK), Army pvt. convicted on espionage charges.

Ruth Marcus, b 5/15/1958 (Philadelphia, PA), columnist.

Meghan Markle (Duchess of Sussex), b 8/4/1981 (Los Angeles, CA), wife of UK's Prince Harry, actress.

Chris Matthews, b 12/17/1945 (Philadelphia, PA), TV journalist.

Peter Max, b 10/19/1937 (Berlin, Germany), artist.

Kevin McCarthy, b 1/26/1965 (Bakersfield, CA), fmr. U.S. House Speaker (R, CA).

Mitch McConnell, b 2/20/1942 (Tuscumbia, AL), U.S. sen. minority leader (R, KY).

Ronna Romney McDaniel, b 1973 (Austin, TX), Rep. Natl. Committee chair.

Dr. Phil McGraw, b 9/1/1950 (Vinita, OK), TV host, author.

Mark Meadows, b 7/28/1959 (Verdun, France), fmr. White House chief of staff, fmr. U.S. rep. (R, NC).

Lorne Michaels, b 11/17/44 (Toronto, ON, Canada), creator and producer of *Saturday Night Live*.

Kate Michelman, b 8/4/1942 (NJ), activist.

Michael Moore, b 4/23/1954 (Davison, MI), activist, documentary filmmaker, author.

Bill Moyers, b 6/5/1934 (Hugo, OK), TV journalist, author.

Robert S. Mueller III, b 8/7/1944 (New York, NY), special counsel who investigated Russian interference in 2016 U.S. elections; former FBI director.

David Muir, b 11/8/1973 (Syracuse, NY), TV news anchor.

Rupert Murdoch, b 3/11/1931 (Melbourne, Vic., Austral.), media exec.

Bobby Murphy, b 7/19/1988 (Berkeley, CA), Snapchat cofounder.

Patty Murray, b 10/11/1950 (Bothell, WA), Senate pres. pro tempore (D, WA).

Vivek Murthy, b 7/10/1977 (Huddersfield, Eng., UK), U.S. surgeon gen.

Elon Musk, b 6/28/1971 (Pretoria, S. Afr.), Twitter owner; SpaceX and Tesla CEO.

Satya Nadella, b 8/19/1967 (Hyderabad, India), Microsoft CEO.

Ralph Nader, b 2/27/1934 (Winsted, CT), consumer advocate, independent pres. cand. (1996, 2000, '04, '08).

Carl Nassib, b 4/12/1993 (West Chester, PA), first openly gay active NFL player.

Craig Newmark, b 12/6/1952 (Morristown, NJ), founder of Craigslist.com.

Gavin Newsom, b 10/10/1967 (San Francisco, CA), CA gov. (D).

Kristi Noem, b 11/30/1971 (Watertown, SD), SD gov. (R).

Peggy Noonan, b 9/7/1950 (Brooklyn, NY), columnist, speechwriter.

Oliver North, b 10/7/1943 (San Antonio, TX), former NRA pres., Natl. Sec. Council aide, figure in Iran-contra scandal.

Eleanor Holmes Norton, b 6/13/1937 (Washington, DC), DC delegate to U.S. House (D).

Barack Obama, b 8/4/1961 (Honolulu, HI), 44th U.S. president, former U.S. sen. (D, IL).

Michelle Obama, b 1/17/1964 (Chicago, IL), former first lady, lawyer.

Soledad O'Brien, b 9/19/1966 (Smithtown, NY), TV journalist.

Alexandria Ocasio-Cortez, b 10/13/1989 (Bronx, NY), U.S. rep. (D, NY).

Sandra Day O'Connor, b 3/26/1930 (El Paso, TX), former Supreme Court justice.

Ilhan Omar, b 10/4/1981 (Mogadishu, Somalia), U.S. rep. (D, MN).

Bill O'Reilly, b 9/10/1949 (New York, NY), fmr. TV host.

Suze Orman, b 5/5/1951 (Chicago, IL), financial adviser, TV host.

Beto O'Rourke, b 9/26/1972 (El Paso, TX), former U.S. rep. (D, TX); 2020 pres. contender.

Joel Osteen, b 3/5/1963 (Houston, TX), televangelist, author.

Michael Ovitz, b 12/14/1946 (Encino, CA), entertainment exec.

Candace Owens, b 4/29/1989 (Stamford, CT), political activist.

Mehmet Oz, b 6/11/1960 (Cleveland, OH), surgeon, TV host; 2022 U.S. sen. contender (R, PA).

Clarence Page, b 6/2/1947 (Dayton, OH), journalist, TV commentator.

Lawrence Page, b 3/26/1973 (East Lansing, MI), cofounder of Google.

Camille Paglia, b 4/2/1947 (Endicott, NY), scholar, author.

Sarah Palin, b 2/11/1964 (Sandpoint, ID), former AK gov. (R), 2008 vice-pres. nominee.

Leon E. Panetta, b 6/28/1938 (Monterey, CA), former sec. of defense, CIA director, Obama chief of staff, U.S. rep. (D, CA).

Sean Parker, b 12/3/1979 (Herndon, VA), cofounder of Napster, Facebook.

Rand Paul, b 1/7/1963 (Pittsburgh, PA), U.S. sen. (R, KY).

Jane Pauley, b 10/31/1950 (Indianapolis, IN), TV journalist.

Nancy Pelosi, b 3/26/1940 (Baltimore, MD), fmr. U.S. House Speaker (D, CA).

Karen Pence, b 1/1/1957 (Indianapolis, IN), wife of fmr. U.S. vice pres. Mike Pence.

Mike Pence, b 6/7/1959 (Columbus, IN), fmr. U.S. vice pres., IN gov. (R); 2024 pres. contender.

David Petraeus, b 11/7/1952 (Cornwall-on-Hudson, NY), former CIA director, CENTCOM cmdr.

Alexandra Petri, b 3/15/1988 (WI), columnist.

Sundar Pichai, b 6/10/1972 (Madurai, Tamil Nadu, India), Alphabet/Google CEO.

Mike Pompeo, b 12/30/1963 (Orange, CA), former sec. of state, CIA director.

Jerome Powell, b 2/4/1953 (Washington, DC), Federal Reserve chair.

Reince Priebus, b 3/18/1972 (Kenosha, WI), former White House chief of staff, Rep. Natl. Committee chair.

Jen Psaki, b 12/1/1978 (Stamford, CT), former White House press sec; TV commentator.

Dan Quayle, b 2/4/1947 (Indianapolis, IN), former U.S. vice pres., U.S. sen. (R, IN).

Anna Quindlen, b 7/8/1953 (Philadelphia, PA), author, columnist.

Martha Raddatz, b 2/14/1953 (Idaho Falls, ID), TV journalist.

Vivek Ramaswamy, b 8/9/1985 (Cincinnati, OH), biotech entrepreneur, 2024 pres. contender (R).

Jorge Ramos, b 3/15/1958 (Mexico City, Mex.), TV journalist.

Dan Rather, b 10/31/1931 (Wharton, TX), TV journalist, retired anchor.

Robert Redfield, b 7/15/1951, fmr. Centers for Disease Control and Prevention dir.

Ralph Reed Jr., b 6/24/1961 (Portsmouth, VA), political adviser.

Robert B. Reich, b 6/24/1946 (Scranton, PA), economist, author, former labor sec.

Condoleezza Rice, b 11/14/1954 (Birmingham, AL), former sec. of state, natl. security adviser.

Frank Rich, b 6/2/1949 (Washington, DC), essayist, columnist.

John G. Roberts, b 1/27/1955 (Buffalo, NY), U.S. Supreme Court chief justice.

Robin Roberts, b 11/23/1960 (Tuskegee, AL), *Good Morning America* co-host.

Eugene Robinson, b 3/12/1954 (Orangeburg, SC), columnist.

V. Gene Robinson, b 5/29/1947 (Lexington, KY), first openly gay Episcopal bishop (retired).

Al Roker, b 8/20/1954 (Queens, NY), TV weather person.

Mitt Romney, b 3/12/1947 (Detroit, MI), U.S. sen. (R, UT); 2012 pres. nominee, former MA gov.

Charlie Rose, b 1/5/1942 (Henderson, NC), TV journalist.

Rod Rosenstein, b 1/13/65 (Philadelphia, PA), fmr. U.S. deputy atty. gen.

Karl Rove, b 12/25/1950 (Denver, CO), former adviser to Pres. G. W. Bush, political commentator.

Marco Rubio, b 5/28/1971 (Miami, FL), U.S. sen. (R, FL).

Edward Ruscha, b 12/16/1937 (Omaha, NE), artist.

Paul Ryan, b 1/29/1970 (Janesville, WI), 2012 vice-pres. nominee, former U.S. rep. (R, WI) and House Speaker.

Sheryl Sandberg, b 8/28/1969 (Washington, DC), fmr. Facebook exec., author.

Bernie Sanders, b 9/8/1941 (Brooklyn, NY), U.S. sen. (I, VT); 2016 and 2020 Dem. pres. contender.

Sarah Huckabee Sanders, b 8/13/1982 (Hope, AR), AR gov. (R); fmr. White House press sec.

Mark Sanford, b 5/28/1960 (Ft. Lauderdale, FL), fmr. SC gov., U.S. rep. (R); 2020 pres. contender.

George Santos, b 7/22/1988 (Queens, NY), U.S. rep. (R, NY).

Ted Sarandos, b 7/30/1964 (Phoenix, AZ), co-CEO of Netflix.

Diane Sawyer, b 12/22/1945 (Glasgow, KY), TV journalist.

Stephen Scalise, b 10/6/1965 (New Orleans, LA), U.S. rep. (R, LA), House majority leader.

Bob Schieffer, b 2/25/1937 (Austin, TX), TV journalist.

Charles Schumer, b 11/23/1950 (Brooklyn, NY), U.S. Sen. majority leader (D, NY).

Arnold Schwarzenegger, b 7/30/1947 (Thal, Styria, Austria), actor, former CA gov. (R).

Tim Scott, b 9/19/1965 (North Charleston, SC), U.S. sen. (R, SC), 2024 pres. contender.

Richard Serra, b 11/2/1939 (San Francisco, CA), sculptor.

Al Sharpton, b 10/3/1954 (Brooklyn, NY), activist, civil rights leader, TV personality.

Amy Sherald, b 8/30/1973 (Columbus, GA), artist.

Will Shortz, b 8/26/1952 (Crawfordsville, IN), puzzle editor.

Maria Shriver, b 11/6/1955 (Chicago, IL), TV journalist, former CA first lady.

Liz Shuler, b 1970 (OR), AFL-CIO pres.

Adam Silver, b 4/25/1962 (Rye, NY), NBA commissioner.

Nate Silver, b 1/13/1978 (E. Lansing, MI), statistician.

Russell Simmons, b 10/4/1957 (Queens, NY), music producer.

O. J. Simpson, b 7/9/1947 (San Francisco, CA), former NFL star, murder defendant.

Jack Smith, b 6/5/1969, U.S. Dept. of Justice special counsel; fmr. war crimes prosecutor.

Edward Snowden, b 6/21/1983 (Elizabeth City, NC), computer specialist accused of leaking classified information.

George Soros, b 8/12/1930 (Budapest, Hung.), financier, philanthropist.

Sonia Sotomayor, b 6/25/1954 (Bronx, NY), U.S. Supreme Court justice.

Evan Spiegel, b 6/4/1990 (Los Angeles, CA), Snapchat cofounder.

Steven Spielberg, b 12/18/1946 (Cincinnati, OH), movie director, producer.

Lesley Stahl, b 12/16/1941 (Swampscott, MA), TV journalist.

Shelby Steele, b 1/1/1946 (Chicago, IL), scholar, critic.

Elise Stefanik, b 7/2/1984 (Albany, NY), House conference chair (R, NY).

Gloria Steinem, b 3/25/1934 (Toledo, OH), author, feminist.

Frank Stella, b 5/12/1936 (Malden, MA), painter.

George Stephanopoulos, b 2/10/1961 (Fall River, MA), TV journalist, *Good Morning America* co-host; former pres. adviser.

Howard Stern, b 1/12/1954 (Jackson Heights, NY), radio host.

Martha Stewart, b 8/3/1941 (Nutley, NJ), homemaking adviser, entrepreneur, TV personality.

Biz Stone, b 3/10/1974 (Boston, MA), cofounder of Twitter.

Roger Stone, b 8/27/1952 (Norwalk, CT), political consultant.

Chesley Sullenberger III, b 1/23/1951 (Denison, TX), pilot who safely landed a passenger jet in the Hudson River.

Andrew Sullivan, b 8/10/1963 (S. Godstone, Eng., UK), political commentator.

A(rthur) G(regg) Sulzberger, b 8/5/1980 (Washington, DC), *NY Times* publisher and NY Times Co. chair.

Arthur Ochs Sulzberger Jr., b 9/22/1951 (Mt. Kisco, NY), fmr. NY Times Co. chair.

Jake Tapper, b 3/12/1969 (New York, NY), TV journalist.

Marc A. Thiessen, b 1/13/1967, columnist.

Clarence Thomas, b 6/23/1948 (Savannah, GA), U.S. Supreme Court justice.

Linda Thomas-Greenfield, b 1952 (Baker, LA), U.S. amb. to United Nations.

John Thune, b 1/7/1961 (Pierre, SD), U.S. Sen. minority whip (R, SD).

Joseph Tobin, b 5/3/1952 (Detroit, MI), Rom. Cath. cardinal, archbishop of Newark, NJ.

Chuck Todd, b 4/8/1972 (Miami, FL), TV journalist, fmr. *Meet the Press* moderator.

Donald Trump, b 6/14/1946 (Jamaica, Queens, NY), 45th U.S. president; 2024 pres. contender; real estate exec., TV personality.

Donald Trump Jr., b 12/31/1977 (New York, NY), son of Pres. Trump; Trump Org. exec.

Eric Trump, b 1/6/1984 (New York, NY), son of Pres. Trump; Trump Org. exec.

Ivanka Trump, b 10/30/1981 (New York, NY), daughter of and fmr. adviser to Pres. Trump.

Melania Trump, b 4/26/1970 (Novo Mesto, [now] Slovenia), fmr. first lady, model.

Ted Turner, b 11/19/1938 (Cincinnati, OH), TV exec., philanthropist.

Neil deGrasse Tyson, b 10/5/1958 (New York, NY), astrophysicist, author, TV host.

Hamdi Ulukaya, b 10/26/1972 (Erzincan, Turkey), Chobani CEO.

Greta Van Susteren, b 6/11/1954 (Appleton, WI), attorney, TV journalist.

Meredith Vieira, b 12/30/1953 (Providence, RI), TV journalist/host.

Diane von Fürstenberg, b 12/31/1946 (Brussels, Belgium), fashion designer.

Rochelle Walensky, b 4/5/1969 (Peabody, MA), fmr. Centers for Disease Control and Prevention dir.

Jimmy Wales, b 8/8/1966 (Huntsville, AL), cofounder of Wikipedia.

Alexander Wang, b 5/17/1984 (San Francisco, CA), fashion designer.

Vera Wang, b 6/27/1949 (New York, NY), fashion designer.

Elizabeth Warren, b 6/22/1949 (Oklahoma City, OK), U.S. sen. (D, MA); 2020 pres. contender.

James Watson, b 4/6/1928 (Chicago, IL), biochemist, DNA pioneer.

Shannon Watts, b 1971?, founder of Moms Demand Action.

Andrew Weil, b 6/8/1942 (Philadelphia, PA), health adviser.

Harvey Weinstein, b 3/19/1952 (Flushing, Queens, NY), movie exec.; convicted in 2020 on rape and sexual abuse charges.

Bill Weld, b 7/31/1945 (Smithtown, NY), fmr. MA gov. (R); 2020 pres. contender.

Kristen Welker, b 7/1/1976 (Philadelphia, PA), TV journalist, *Meet the Press* moderator.

Jann Wenner, b 1/7/1946 (New York, NY), founder of *Rolling Stone*.

Cornel West, b 6/23/1953 (Tulsa, OK), academic, critic; 2024 pres. contender (People's Party, Green Party).

Ruth Westheimer, b 6/4/1928 (Frankfurt am Main, Germany), human sexuality expert.

Gretchen Whitmer, b 8/23/1971 (Lansing, MI), MI gov. (D).

Kehinde Wiley, b 2/28/1977 (Los Angeles, CA), artist.

George Will, b 5/4/1941 (Champaign, IL), journalist, author.

Brian Williams, b 5/5/1959 (Ridgewood, NJ), TV journalist.

Evan Williams, b 3/31/1972 (Clarks, NE), Twitter cofounder.

Jody Williams, b 10/9/1950 (Brattleboro, VT), peace activist, 1997 Nobel Peace Prize winner.

Marianne Williamson, b 7/8/1952 (Houston, TX), activist and author; 2020, 2024 pres. contender (D).

Oprah Winfrey, b 1/29/1954 (Kosciusko, MS), TV and media personality, entrepreneur, actress.

Anna Wintour, b 11/3/1949 (London, Eng., UK), *Vogue* editor.

Susan Wojcicki, b 7/5/1968 (Santa Clara, CA), former CEO of YouTube.

Judy Woodruff, b 11/20/1946 (Tulsa, OK), TV journalist.

Bob Woodward, b 3/26/1943 (Geneva, IL), journalist; with Carl Bernstein cracked Watergate scandal.

Steve Wozniak, b 8/11/1950 (Sunnyvale, CA), inventor, cofounder of Apple.

Steve Wynn, b 1/27/1942 (New Haven, CT), casino developer.

Andrew Yang, b 1/13/1975 (Schenectady, NY), Venture for America founder; 2020 pres. contender (D).

Janet Yellen, b 8/13/1946 (New York, NY), treasury sec.; former Federal Reserve chair.

David Zaslav, b 1/15/1960 (Brooklyn, NY), CEO of Warner Bros. Discovery.

Jeff Zients, b 11/12/1966 (Washington, DC), White House chief of staff.

Mark Zuckerberg, b 5/14/1984 (Dobbs Ferry, NY), founder of Facebook/Meta.

Mortimer Zuckerman, b 6/4/1937 (Montréal, QC, Can.), publisher, columnist.

Widely Known World Personalities of the Present

Living non-Americans only. Generally excludes current heads of state or government (see Nations of the World) and excludes most others covered elsewhere, such as in Widely Known Americans, Writers, and Entertainment or Sports Personalities.

Mahmoud Abbas (Abu Mazen), b 3/26/1935 (Safed, Palestine [now Israel]), president of the Palestinian National Authority.

Gerry Adams, b 10/6/1948 (Belfast, N. Ireland, UK), fmr. Sinn Fein leader.

Mahmoud Ahmadinejad, b 10/28/1956 (Garmsar, Iran), former Iranian pres.

Ai Weiwei, b 1957 (Beijing, China), visual artist, activist.

Akihito, b 12/23/1933 (Tokyo, Jpn.), Japanese emperor emeritus.

Albert II, b 6/6/1934 (Brussels, Belgium), former king of Belgium (1993-2013).

Prince Andrew (Duke of York), b 2/19/1960 (London, Eng., UK), second son of Queen Elizabeth II.

Princess Anne (Princess Royal), b 8/15/1950 (London, Eng., UK), daughter of Queen Elizabeth II.

Jacinda Ardern, b 7/26/1980 (Hamilton, NZ), former New Zeal. prime min.

Oscar Arias Sánchez, b 9/13/1941 (Heredia, Costa Rica), former Costa Rican pres., 1987 Nobel Peace Prize laureate.

Giorgio Armani, b 7/30/1934 (Piacenza, Italy), fashion designer.

Hanan Ashrawi, b 10/8/1946 (Nablus, Israel), Palestinian activist.

Julian Assange, b 7/3/1971 (Townsville, Qld., Austral.), founder of WikiLeaks media org.

Thomas Bach, b 12/29/1953 (Würzburg, Ger.), president of the Intl. Olympic Cmte.

Ban Ki-moon, b 6/13/1944 (Umsong, [now] South Korea), former UN sec.-gen.

Abdul Ghani Baradar, b 1968? (Yatimak, Afghanistan), Taliban co-founder, leader.

Ehud Barak, b 2/12/1942 (Mishmar Ha-Sharon Kibbutz, Israel), former Israeli min. of defense, prime min.

Beatrix, b 1/31/1938 (Baarn, Netherlands), former Dutch queen (1980-2013).

Jocelyn Bell Burnell, b 7/15/1943 (Belfast, N. Ire.), astrophysicist.

Tim Berners-Lee, b 6/8/1955 (London, Eng., UK), World Wide Web inventor.

Tony Blair, b 5/6/1953 (Edinburgh, Scot., UK), former British prime min.

Hans Blix, b 6/28/1928 (Uppsala, Swed.), former UN weapons inspector.

Bono (Paul David Hewson), b 5/20/1960 (Glasnevin, Dublin, Ire.), musician, social activist, philanthropist.

Fernando Botero, b 4/19/1932 (Medellín, Colombia), artist.

Richard Branson, b 7/18/1950 (S. London, Eng., UK), British Virgin Records and Airways founder.

Gordon Brown, b 2/20/1951 (Glasgow, Scot., UK), former British prime min.

Tina Brown, b 11/21/1953 (Maidenhead, UK), journalist, author.

Gisele Bündchen, b 7/20/1980 (Horizontina, Rio Grande do Sul, Braz.), model.

Mark Burnett, b 7/17/1960 (Myland, Eng., UK), reality TV producer.

Rhonda Byrne, b 3/12/1951 (Australia), author, TV writer and producer.

David Cameron, b 10/9/1966 (London, Eng., UK), former British prime min.

Queen Camilla, b 7/17/1947 (London, Eng., UK), wife of King Charles III.

Kim Campbell, b 3/10/1947 (Port Alberni, BC, Can.), former Canadian prime min.

Magnus Carlsen, b 11/30/1990 (Tonsberg, Norway), fmr. world chess champion.

Princess Caroline, b 1/23/1957 (Monte Carlo, Monaco), Monaco royal (eldest daughter of Prince Rainier and Princess Grace).

Raúl Castro Ruz, b 6/3/1931 (Birán, Cuba), former pres. of Cuba.

Catherine (Kate) Middleton (Princess of Wales), b 1/9/1982 (Reading, Eng., UK), wife of Prince William.

Princess Charlotte Elizabeth Diana (of Wales), b 5/2/2015 (London, Eng., UK), daughter of Prince William and Catherine.

Chen Guangcheng, b 11/12/1971 (Dongshigu, China), civil rights activist.

Yao Chen, b 10/5/1979 (Nanping, Fujian, China), actress, microblogger.

Deepak Chopra, b 1946 (New Delhi, India), writer, alternative medicine advocate.

Jean Chrétien, b 1/11/1934 (Shawinigan, QC, Can.), former Canadian prime min.

Joe (Charles Joseph) Clark, b 6/5/1939 (High River, AB, Can.), former Canadian prime min.

Simon Cowell, b 10/7/1959 (Brighton, East Sussex, Eng., UK), music exec., TV producer, former *American Idol* judge.

Dalai Lama, 14th (Tenzin Gyatso), b 7/6/1935 (Taktser, Amdo, Tibet), Buddhist leader; 1989 Nobel Peace Prize winner.

Richard Dawkins, b 3/26/1941 (Nairobi, Kenya), ethologist, evolutionary biologist, author.

Shirin Ebadi, b 6/21/1947 (Hamadan, Iran), human rights activist, 2003 Nobel Peace Prize winner.

Prince Edward (Duke of Edinburgh), b 3/10/1964 (London, Eng., UK), third son of Queen Elizabeth II.

Daniel Ek, b 2/21/1983 (Stockholm, Sweden), Spotify cofounder/CEO.

Mohamed ElBaradei, b 6/17/1942 (Cairo, Egypt), former director general of the International Atomic Energy Agency (IAEA); 2005 Nobel Peace Prize winner.

Francis (Jorge Mario Bergoglio), b 12/17/1936 (Buenos Aires, Argentina), pope of Roman Catholic Church.

Fumihito, Prince Akishino, b 11/30/1965 (Tokyo, Jpn.), crown prince of Japan.

John Galliano, b 11/28/1960 (Gibraltar, UK), fashion designer.

Prince George Alexander Louis (of Wales), b 7/22/2013 (London, Eng., UK), elder son of Prince William and Catherine.

Wael Ghonim, b 12/23/1980 (Cairo, Egypt), computer engineer and internet activist.

Jane Goodall, b 4/3/1934 (London, Eng., UK), anthropologist, primatologist.

Juan Guaidó, b 7/28/1983 (La Guaira, Venezuela), Venezuelan opposition leader.

António Guterres, b 4/30/1949 (Lisbon, Portugal), UN sec.-gen.

Jürgen Habermas, b 6/18/1929 (Dusseldorf, Ger.), philosopher.

Stephen Harper, b 4/30/1959 (Toronto, ON, Can.), former Canadian prime min.

Prince Henry (Harry) (Duke of Sussex), b 9/15/1984 (London, Eng., UK), younger son of King Charles III and Diana.

Damien Hirst, b 6/7/1965 (Bristol, Eng., UK), artist.

David Hockney, b 7/9/1937 (Bradford, Eng., UK), artist.

Hu Jintao, b 12/21/1942 (Shanghai, China), former pres. of China.

Boris Johnson, b 6/19/1964 (New York, NY), former British prime min.

Juan Carlos I, b 1/5/1938 (Rome, Italy), former king of Spain (1975-2014).

Hamid Karzai, b 12/24/1957 (Kandahar, Afghanistan), former pres. of Afghanistan.

Garry Kasparov, b 4/13/1963 (Baku, Azerbaijan, USSR), former world chess champion; Russian pro-democracy leader.

Ayatollah Ali Khamenei, b 7/17/1939 (Mashhad, Iran), Supreme Leader, cleric; former president of Iran.

Imram Khan, b 10/5/1952 (Lahore, Pakistan), fmr. Pakistani prime min.

Marie Kondo, b 10/9/1984 (Tokyo, Japan), organizing specialist.

Christine Lagarde, b 1/1/1956 (Paris, Fr.), European Central Bank pres.

Carrie Lam, b 5/13/1957 (Wan Chai, Hong Kong), fmr. chief executive of Hong Kong.

Jean-Marie Le Pen, b 6/20/1928 (La Trinité-sur-Mer, Fr.), French right-wing politician.

Marine Le Pen, b 8/5/1968 (Neuilly-sur-Seine, Fr.), head of France's far-right party.

Tzipi Livni, b 7/5/1958 (Tel Aviv, Isr.), attorney, Israeli politician.

Prince Louis Arthur Charles (of Wales), b 4/23/2018 (London, Eng., UK), younger son of Prince William and Catherine.

John Major, b 3/29/1943 (Wimbledon, Eng., UK), former British prime min.

Nouri al-Malaki, b 7/1/1950 (Iraq), former prime min. of Iraq.

Imelda Marcos, b 7/2/1929 (Manila, Philip.), former first lady of the Philippines.

Paul Martin, b 8/28/1938 (Windsor, ON, Can.), former prime min. of Canada.

Empress Masako, b 12/9/1963 (Tokyo, Jpn.), empress of Japan.

Theresa May, b 10/1/1956 (Eastbourne, Eng., UK), former British prime min.

Stella McCartney, b 9/13/1971 (London, Eng., UK), fashion designer.

Dmitry Medvedev, b 9/14/1965 (Leningrad, USSR [now Russia]), fmr. prime min., president of Russia.

Rigoberta Menchú, b 1/9/1959 (Aldea Chimel, Guatemala), human rights activist, 1992 Nobel Peace Prize winner.

Angela Merkel, b 7/17/1954 (Hamburg, Ger.), first woman chancellor of Germany.

Jean-Marie Messier, b 12/13/1956 (Grenoble, Fr.), former CEO of Vivendi Universal.

Michiko, b 10/20/1934 (Tokyo, Japan), empress emerita of Japan.

Kate Moss, b 1/16/1974 (Addiscombe, Surrey, Eng., UK), model.

Archie Harrison Mountbatten-Windsor, b 5/6/2019 (London, Eng., UK), son of Prince Harry and Meghan Markle.

Lilibet Diana Mountbatten-Windsor, b 6/4/2021 (Santa Barbara, CA), daughter of Prince Harry and Meghan Markle.

Brian Mulroney, b 3/20/1939 (Baie-Corneau, QC, Can.), former Canadian prime min.

Renhō Murata, b 11/28/1968 (Tokyo, Japan), first woman leader of Japan's Democratic Party.

Hassan Nasrallah, b 8/31/1960 (Qarantina, Lebanon), sec.-gen. of Hezbollah.

Alexei Navalny, b 6/4/1976 (Butyn', Russia), Russian opposition leader.

Queen Noor (Lisa Halaby), b 8/23/1951 (Washington, DC), American-born widow of Jordan's King Hussein.

Ehud Olmert, b 9/30/1945 (Binyamina, Palestine), former prime min. of Israel.

Daniel Ortega Saavedra, b 11/11/1945 (La Libertad, Nicar.), Nicaraguan pres., Sandinista leader.

Ren Zhengfei, b 10/25/1944 (Guizhou, China), founder and CEO of Huawei Technologies.

Gerhard Richter, b 2/9/1932 (Dresden, Ger.), artist.

Mary Robinson, b 5/21/1944 (Ballina, Co. Mayo, Ire.), former Irish pres., former UN High Commissioner for Human Rights.

Arundhati Roy, b 11/24/1961 (Shillong, Meghalaya, India), author, political activist.

Ségolène Royal, b 9/22/1953 (Dakar, Senegal), French socialist politician.

Muqtada al-Sadr, b 8/4/1974 (Najaf, Iraq), extremist Shiite cleric.

Mohammad bin Salman, b 8/31/1985 (Riyadh, Saudi Arabia), Saudi crown prince.

Nicolas Sarkozy, b 1/28/1955 (Paris, France), former French pres.

Gerhard Schröder, b 4/7/1944 (Mossenburg, Ger.), former German chancellor.

Nawaz Sharif, b 12/25/1949 (Lahore, Pakistan), former Pakistan prime min.

Ayatollah Ali al-Sistani, b 8/4/1930 (Mashhad, Iran), major Iraqi Shiite religious leader.

Carlos Slim Helú, b 1/28/1940 (Mexico City, Mex.), founder of Grupo Carso; former chair of Telmex, América Móvil.

Princess Stephanie, b 2/1/1965 (Monte Carlo, Monaco), youngest child of Prince Rainier and Princess Grace.

Dominique Strauss-Kahn, b 4/25/1949 (Neuilly-sur-Seine, France), former Intl. Monetary Fund managing dir.

Aung San Suu Kyi, b 6/19/1945 (Rangoon, Myanmar), political activist, 1991 Nobel Peace Prize winner; deposed Myanmar govt. leader.

Valentina Tereshkova, b 3/6/1937 (Maslennikovo, Russia, USSR), first woman in space.

Greta Thunberg, b 1/3/2003 (Stockholm, Swed.), environmental activist.

Liz Truss, b 7/26/1975 (Oxford, Eng., UK), former British prime min.

Ursula von der Leyen, b 10/8/1958 (Brussels, Belg.), first woman European Commission pres.

Lech Walesa, b 9/29/1943 (Popowo, Pol.), Solidarity leader, former pres. of Poland; 1983 Nobel Peace Prize winner.

Justin Welby, b 1/6/1956 (London, Eng., UK), archbishop of Canterbury.

Prince William (of Wales), b 6/21/1982 (London, Eng., UK), elder son of King Charles III and Diana; heir apparent to British throne.

Rowan Williams, b 6/14/1950 (Ystradgynlais, Wales, UK), former archbishop of Canterbury.

Malala Yousafzai, b 7/12/1997 (Mingora, Pakistan), activist for girls' education, 2014 Nobel Peace Prize winner.

Muhammad Yunus, b 6/28/1940 (Chittagong, Bangladesh), economist, 2006 Nobel Peace Prize winner.

Mohammad Javad Zarif, b 1/8/1960 (Tehran, Iran), Irani minister of foreign affairs.

Architects

Alvar Aalto, 1898-1976, Säynätsalo Town Hall, Vuoksenniska Church, Finland.

Max Abramovitz, 1908-2004, Avery Fisher Hall, New York, NY; U.S. Steel Tower (Bldg.), Pittsburgh, PA.

Tadao Ando, b 1941, Modern Art Museum, Ft. Worth, TX; Stone Hill Center, MA.

Michael Arad, b 1969, Natl. 9/11 Memorial, New York, NY.

Henry Bacon, 1866-1924, Lincoln Memorial, Washington, DC.

Benjamin Banneker, 1731-1806, African American inventor, astronomer, mathematician; helped design and lay out Washington, DC.

Pietro Belluschi, 1899-1994, Juilliard School, Lincoln Center, Pan Am Bldg.

(now MetLife Bldg.) with Walter Gropius, New York, NY.

Marcel Breuer, 1902-81, Whitney Museum of American Art (now Met Breuer) (with Hamilton Smith), New York, NY.

Filippo Brunelleschi, 1377-1446, Santa Maria del Fiore Cathedral, Florence, Italy.

Charles Bulfinch, 1763-1844, State House, Boston, MA; Capitol (part), Wash., DC.

Gordon Bunshaft, 1909-90, Lever House, New York, NY; Hirshhorn Museum, Washington, DC.

Daniel H. Burnham, 1846-1912, Union Station, Washington, DC; Flatiron Bldg., New York, NY.

Santiago Calatrava, b 1951, World Trade Center transport hub, New York, NY.

Irwin Chanin, 1892-1988, theaters, skyscrapers, New York, NY.

David Childs, b 1941, Washington Mall Master Plan/Constitution Gardens, Washington, DC; One World Trade Center, New York, NY.

Lucio Costa, 1902-98, master plan for city of Brasilia, Brazil (with Oscar Niemeyer).

Ralph Adams Cram, 1863-1942, Cath. of St. John the Divine, New York, NY; U.S. Military Acad. (part), West Point, NY.

Gustave Eiffel, 1832-1923, Eiffel Tower, Paris.

Norman Foster, b 1935, Commerzbank Headquarters, Frankfurt-am-Main, Ger.; London Millennium Bridge, 30 St. Mary Axe ("The Gherkin"), London, Eng., UK.

James Ingo Freed, 1930-2005, Holocaust Memorial Museum, Washington, DC; Jacob K. Javits Center, New York, NY.

R. Buckminster Fuller, 1895-1983, U.S. Pavilion (geodesic domes), Expo 67, Montréal, QC, Can.

Antoni Gaudí, 1852-1926, Basilica and Expiatory Temple of the Sagrada Familia, Barcelona, Spain.

Frank O. Gehry, b 1929, Guggenheim Museum, Bilbao, Spain; Walt Disney Concert Hall, Los Angeles, CA.

Cass Gilbert, 1859-1934, Custom House, Woolworth Bldg., New York, NY; Supreme Court Bldg., Washington, DC.

Bertram G. Goodhue, 1869-1924, Capitol, Lincoln, NE; St. Thomas's Church, St. Bartholomew's Church, New York, NY.

Michael Graves, 1934-2015, Portland Bldg., Portland, OR; Humana Bldg., Louisville, KY.

Walter Gropius, 1883-1969, Pan Am Bldg. (now MetLife Bldg.) (with Pietro Belluschi), New York, NY.

Zaha Hadid, 1950-2016, Rosenthal Center for Contemporary Art, Cincinnati, OH; London Aquatics Centre, Eng., UK.

Lawrence Halprin, 1916-2009, Ghirardelli Sq., San Francisco, CA; Nicollet Mall, Minneapolis, MN; FDR Memorial, Wash., DC.

Peter Harrison, 1716-75, Touro Synagogue, Redwood Library, Newport, RI.

Wallace K. Harrison, 1895-1981, Metropolitan Opera House, Lincoln Center, New York, NY.

Thomas Hastings, 1860-1929, NY Public Library (with John Carrère), Frick Mansion, New York, NY.

James Hoban, 1762-1831, White House, Washington, DC.

Raymond Hood, 1881-1934, Rockefeller Center (part), Daily News Bldg., New York, NY; Tribune Tower, Chicago, IL.

Richard M. Hunt, 1827-95, Metropolitan Museum (part), New York, NY; Biltmore Estate, Asheville, NC.

Arata Isozaki, b 1931, Museum of Contemporary Art, Los Angeles, CA.

Toyo Ito, 1941-22, Sendai Mediatheque, Sendai, Japan; Tower of Winds, Yokohama, Japan.

Helmut Jahn, 1940-2021, United Airlines Terminal, O'Hare Airport, Chicago, IL.

William Le Baron Jenney, 1832-1907, Home Insurance Bldg. (demolished 1931), Chicago, IL.

Philip C. Johnson, 1906-2005, AT&T Bldg. (now 550 Madison Ave.), New York, NY; Transco (now Williams) Tower, Houston, TX.

Albert Kahn, 1869-1942, General Motors Bldg. (now Cadillac Place), Detroit, MI.

Louis Kahn, 1901-74, Salk Laboratory, La Jolla, CA; Yale Art Gallery, New Haven, CT.

Rem Koolhaas, b 1944, Seattle Central Library, Seattle, WA.

Christopher Grant LaFarge, 1862-1938, Roman Catholic Chapel, West Point, NY.

Benjamin H. Latrobe, 1764-1820, Capitol (part), Washington, DC; State Capitol Bldg., Richmond, VA.

Le Corbusier (Charles-Edouard Jeanneret), 1887-1965, Salvation Army Hostel, Swiss Dormitory, Paris, France; master plan for cities of Algiers and Buenos Aires.

William Lescaze, 1896-1969, Philadelphia Savings Fund Society, PA; Borg-Warner Bldg., Chicago, IL.

Daniel Libeskind, b 1946, developed master plan for the rebuilding of World Trade Center site, New York, NY.

Maya Lin, b 1959, Vietnam Veterans Mem., Washington, DC.

Charles Rennie Mackintosh, 1868-1928, Glasgow School of Art; Hill House, Helensburgh, Scot., UK.

Bernard R. Maybeck, 1862-1957, Hearst Hall, Univ. of CA, Berkeley; First Church of Christ Scientist, Berkeley, CA.

Charles F. McKim, 1847-1909, Boston Public Library; Columbia Univ. (part), New York, NY.

Charles M. McKim, 1920-2017, KUHT-TV Transmitter Bldg., Lutheran Church of the Redeemer, Houston, TX.

Richard Meier, b 1934, Getty Center, Los Angeles, CA; High Museum of Art, Atlanta, GA.

Ludwig Mies van der Rohe, 1886-1969, Seagram Bldg. (with Philip C. Johnson), New York, NY; National Gallery, Berlin, Ger.

Robert Mills, 1781-1855, Washington Monument, Washington, DC.

Charles Moore, 1925-93, Sea Ranch, nr. San Francisco, CA; Piazza d'Italia, New Orleans, LA.

Julia Morgan, 1872-1957, Hearst Castle, San Simeon, CA.

John Nash, 1752-1835, Buckingham Palace, London, Eng., UK.

Richard J. Neutra, 1892-1970, Orange Co. Courthouse, Santa Ana, CA.

Oscar Niemeyer, 1907-2012, government buildings, Brasilia Palace Hotel, Brasilia, Braz.

Gyo Obata, 1923-2022, Natl. Air and Space Museum, Smithsonian Inst., Washington, DC; Dallas-Ft. Worth Airport, TX.

Frederick L. Olmsted, 1822-1903, Central Park, New York, NY; Fairmount Park, Philadelphia, PA.

I(eoh) M(ing) Pei, 1917-2019, East Wing, Natl. Gallery of Art, Washington, DC; Pyramid, The Louvre, Paris, Fr.; Rock & Roll Hall of Fame and Museum, Cleveland, OH.

Cesar Pelli, 1926-2019, World Financial Center, Carnegie Hall Tower, New York, NY; Petronas Twin Towers, Malaysia.

William Pereira, 1909-85, Cape Canaveral, FL; Transamerica Pyramid, San Francisco.

Renzo Piano, b 1937, Pompidou Centre, Paris, Fr.; New York Times Bldg., New York, NY; The Shard, London, Eng., UK.

John Russell Pope, 1874-1937, National Gallery, Jefferson Memorial, Wash., DC.

John Portman, 1924-2017, Peachtree Center, Atlanta, GA.

George Browne Post, 1837-1913, NY Stock Exchange, New York, NY; Capitol, Madison, WI.

James Renwick Jr., 1818-95, Grace Church, St. Patrick's Cathedral, New York, NY; Smithsonian Institution (Castle), Washington, DC.

Henry H. Richardson, 1838-86, Trinity Church, Boston, MA.

Kevin Roche, 1922-2019, Oakland Museum, Oakland, CA; Fine Arts Center, Univ. of Massachusetts, Amherst, MA.

James Gamble Rogers, 1867-1947, Columbia-Presbyterian Medical Ctr., New York, NY; Northwestern Univ., Evanston, IL.

John Wellborn Root, 1887-1963, Palmolive Bldg., Chicago, IL; Hotel Statler (now Capital Hilton), Washington, DC.

Paul Rudolph, 1918-97, Jewitt Art Center, Wellesley College, MA; Art & Architecture Bldg., Yale Univ., New Haven, CT.

Eero Saarinen, 1910-61, Gateway to the West Arch, St. Louis, MO; TWA Flight Center, JFK Airport, New York, NY.

Kazuyo Sejima, b 1956, 21st Century Museum of Contemporary Art (with Ryue Nishizawa), Kanazawa, Japan.

Kodja Mimar Sinan, 1489-1588, chief court architect of Ottoman dynasty.

Louis Skidmore, 1897-1962, Atomic Energy Commission town site, Oak Ridge, TN; Terrace Plaza Hotel, Cincinnati, OH.

Norma Merrick Sklarek, 1928-2012, Terminal One, Los Angeles International Airport, CA.

Clarence S. Stein, 1882-1975, Temple Emanu-El, New York, NY.

Edward Durell Stone, 1902-78, interior of Radio City Music Hall, Museum of Modern Art, New York, NY.

Louis H. Sullivan, 1856-1924, Auditorium Bldg., Chicago, IL.

Kenzo Tange, 1913-2005, Hiroshima Peace Park, 1964 Tokyo Olympic stadiums, Japan.

Richard Upjohn, 1802-78, Trinity Church, New York, NY.

Max O. Urbahn, 1912-95, Vehicle Assembly Bldg., Cape Canaveral, FL.

Joern Utzon, 1918-2008, Sydney Opera House, NSW, Australia.

William Van Alen, 1883-1954, Chrysler Building, New York, NY.

Calvert Vaux, 1824-95, Central Park, New York, NY; Prospect Park, Brooklyn, NY.

Robert Venturi, 1925-2018, Gordon Wu Hall, Princeton, NJ; Mielparque Nikko Kirifuri Resort, Japan.

Ralph T. Walker, 1889-1973, NY Telephone (now Verizon) Bldg., Irving Trust Bldg. (now 1 Wall St.), New York, NY.

Wang Shu, b 1963, Ningbo Museum, China.

Roland A. Wank, 1898-1970, Cincinnati Union Terminal, OH; head architect, 1933-44, Tennessee Valley Authority.

Stanford White, 1853-1906, Washington Arch in Washington Square Park, first Madison Square Garden, New York, NY.

Christopher Wren, 1632-1723, St. Paul's Cathedral, London, Eng., UK.

Frank Lloyd Wright, 1867-1959, Imperial Hotel, Tokyo, Japan; Guggenheim Museum, New York, NY; Kaufmann "Fallingwater" house, Mill Run, PA; Taliesin West, Scottsdale, AZ.

Tom Wright, b 1957, Burj Al Arab hotel, Dubai, UAE.

William Wurster, 1895-1973, Ghirardelli Sq., San Francisco, CA.

Minoru Yamasaki, 1912-86, World Trade Center (destroyed 2001), New York, NY.

Artists, Photographers, and Sculptors of the Past

Artists are painters unless otherwise indicated.

Berenice Abbott, 1898-1991, (U.S.) photographer. Documentary of New York City, *Changing New York* (1939).

Ansel Easton Adams, 1902-84, (U.S.) photographer. Landscapes of the American Southwest.

Washington Allston, 1779-1843, (U.S.) landscapist. *Belshazzar's Feast*.

Albrecht Altdorfer, 1480-1538, (Ger.) landscapist.

Fra Angelico, c. 1400-55, (It.) Renaissance muralist. *Madonna of the Linen Drapers' Guild*.

Diane Arbus, 1923-71, (U.S.) photographer. Disturbing images.

Alexsandr Archipenko, 1887-1964, (U.S.) sculptor. *Boxing Match*, *Medranos*.

Jean Arp, 1887-1966, (Fr.) sculptor and painter. Founder of Dada movement.

Richard Artschwager, 1923-2013, (U.S.) painter and sculptor. *Table With Pink Tablecloth*.

Eugène Atget, 1856-1927, (Fr.) photographer. Paris life.

John James Audubon, 1785-1851, (U.S.) *Birds of America*.

Richard Avedon, 1923-2004, (U.S.) fashion and celebrity photographer.

Hans Baldung-Grien, 1484-1545, (Ger.) *Todentanz*.

Ernst Barlach, 1870-1938, (Ger.) Expressionist sculptor. *Man Drawing a Sword*.

Frédéric-Auguste Bartholdi, 1834-1904, (Fr.) sculptor. *Liberty Enlightening the World* (Statue of Liberty).

Fra Bartolommeo, 1472-1517, (It.) *Vision of St. Bernard*.

Romare Bearden, 1911-88, (U.S.) collage and other media. *The Visitation*.

Aubrey Beardsley, 1872-98, (Br.) illustrator. *Salome*, *Lysistrata*, *Morte d'Arthur*, *Volpone*.

Cecil Beaton, 1904-80, (Br.) fashion and celebrity photographer.

Max Beckmann, 1884-1950, (Ger.) Expressionist. *The Descent From the Cross*.

Gentile Bellini, 1426-1507, (It.) Renaissance. *Procession in St. Mark's Square*.

Giovanni Bellini, 1428-1516, (It.) Renaissance. *St. Francis in Ecstasy*.

Jacopo Bellini, 1400-70, (It.) Renaissance. *Crucifixion*.

George Wesley Bellows, 1882-1925, (U.S.) sports artist, portraitist, landscapist. *Stag at Sharkey's*, *Edith Clavell*.

Thomas Hart Benton, 1889-1975, (U.S.) American regionalist. *Threshing Wheat*, *Arts of the West*.

Ruth Bernhard, 1905-2006, (Ger.-U.S.) photographer. Black-and-white studies of female nudes.

Gianlorenzo Bernini, 1598-1680, (It.) Baroque sculptor. *The Assumption*.

Albert Bierstadt, 1830-1902, (U.S.) landscapist. *The Rocky Mountains*, *Mount Corcoran*.

George Caleb Bingham, 1811-79, (U.S.) American frontier. *Fur Traders Descending the Missouri*.

William Blake, 1757-1827, (Br.) engraver. *Book of Job*, *Songs of Innocence*, *Songs of Experience*.

Rosa Bonheur, 1822-99, (Fr.) Realist. *The Horse Fair*.

Pierre Bonnard, 1867-1947, (Fr.) Intimist. *The Breakfast Room*, *Girl in a Straw Hat*.

Gutzon Borglum, 1867-1941, (U.S.) sculptor. Mt. Rushmore Memorial.

Hieronymus Bosch, 1450-1516, (Flem.) religious allegories. *The Crowning With Thorns*.

Fernando Botero, 1932-2023, (Colombia) figurative painter and sculptor.

Sandro Botticelli, 1444-1510, (It.) Renaissance. *Birth of Venus*, *Adoration of the Magi*, *Guliano de' Medici*.

Louise Bourgeois, 1911-2010, (Fr.) sculptor. *Maman*.

Margaret Bourke-White, 1904-71, (U.S.) photographer, photojournalist. WWII, USSR, rural South during the Depression.

Mathew Brady, c. 1823-96, (U.S.) photographer. Civil War.

Constantin Brancusi, 1876-1957, (Romania-Fr.) Nonobjective sculptor. *Flying Turtle*, *The Kiss*.

Georges Braque, 1882-1963, (Fr.) Cubist. *Violin and Palette*.

Pieter Bruegel the Elder, c. 1525-69, (Flem.) Renaissance. *The Peasant Dance*, *Hunters in the Snow*, *Magpie on the Gallows*.

Pieter Bruegel the Younger, 1564-1638, (Flem.) Baroque. *Village Fair*, *The Crucifixion*.

Edward Burne-Jones, 1833-98, (Br.) Pre-Raphaelite artist-craftsman. *The Mirror of Venus*.

Alexander Calder, 1898-1976, (U.S.) sculptor. *Lobster Trap and Fish Tail*.

Julia Margaret Cameron, 1815-79, (Br.) photographer, prominent portraitist.

Robert Capa (Endre Friedmann), 1913-54, (Hung.-U.S.) photographer, war photojournalist. Invasion of Normandy.

Michelangelo Merisi da Caravaggio, 1573-1610, (It.) Baroque. *The Supper at Emmaus*.

Emily Carr, 1871-1945, (Can.) landscapist. *Blunden Harbour*, *Big Raven*, *Rushing Sea of Undergrowth*.

Carlo Carrà, 1881-1966, (It.) Metaphysical school. *Lot's Daughters*, *The Enchanted Room*.

Leonora Carrington, 1917-2011, (Br.) Surrealist. *The Inn of the Dawn Horse (Self-Portrait)*.

Henri Cartier-Bresson, 1908-2004, (Fr.) photographer. *Imagenes à la sauvette*.

Mary Cassatt, 1844-1926, (U.S.) Impressionist. *The Cup of Tea*, *Woman Bathing*, *The Boating Party*.

George Catlin, 1796-1872, (U.S.) American Indian life. *Gallery of Indians*, *Buffalo Dance*.

Benvenuto Cellini, 1500-71, (It.) Mannerist sculptor, goldsmith. *Perseus and Medusa*.

Paul Cézanne, 1839-1906, (Fr.) Post-Impressionist. *Card Players*, *Mont-Sainte-Victoire With Large Pine Trees*.

Marc Chagall, 1887-1985, (Russ.) Jewish life and folklore. *I and the Village*, *The Praying Jew*.

John Chamberlain, 1927-2011, (U.S.) sculptor of automobile metal.

Jean Simeon Chardin, 1699-1779, (Fr.) still lifes. *The Kiss*, *The Grace*.

Giorgio de Chirico, 1888-1978, (It.) founded the Metaphysical school. *Enigma of an Autumn Night*.

Christo (Javacheff), 1935-2020, (Bulg.), large-scale environmental installation artist with wife Jeanne-Claude. *The Gates*, *Surrounded Islands*.

Frederick Church, 1826-1900, (U.S.) Hudson River school. *Niagara*, *Andes of Ecuador*.

Giovanni Cimabue, 1240-1302, (It.) Byzantine mosaicist. *Madonna Enthroned With St. Francis*.

Claude (Lorrain) (Claude Gellée), 1600-82, (Fr.) Ideal-landscapist. *The Enchanted Castle*.

Chuck Close, 1940-2021, (U.S.) photorealistic and conceptual portraitist.

Thomas Cole, 1801-48, (U.S.) Hudson River school. *The Ox-Bow*, *In the Catskills*.

John Constable, 1776-1837, (Br.) landscapist. *Salisbury Cathedral From the Bishop's Garden*.

John Singleton Copley, 1738-1815, (U.S.) portraitist. *Samuel Adams*, *Watson and the Shark*.

Lovis Corinth, 1858-1925, (Ger.) Expressionist. *Apocalypse*.

Jean-Baptiste-Camille Corot, 1796-1875, (Fr.) landscapist. *Souvenir de Mortefontaine*, *Pastorale*.

Correggio, 1494-1534, (It.) Renaissance muralist. *Mystic Marriages of St. Catherine*.

Gustave Courbet, 1819-77, (Fr.) Realist. *The Artist's Studio*.

Lucas Cranach the Elder, 1472-1553, (Ger.) Protestant Reformation portraitist. *Luther*.

Bill Cunningham, 1929-2016, (U.S.) fashion photographer.

Imogen Cunningham, 1883-1976, (U.S.) photographer, portraitist. Plants.

Nathaniel Currier, 1813-88, and **James M. Ives**, 1824-95, (both U.S.) lithographers. *A Midnight Race on the Mississippi*, *American Forest Scene—Maple Sugaring*.

John Steuart Curry, 1897-1946, (U.S.) Americana, murals. *Baptism in Kansas*.

Edward S. Curtis, 1868-1952, (U.S.) photographer. *The North American Indian*.

Louis Daguerre, 1787-1851, (Fr.) photographer. Invented daguerreotype process.

Salvador Dalí, 1904-89, (Sp.) Surrealist. *Persistence of Memory*, *The Crucifixion*.

Honoré Daumier, 1808-79, (Fr.) caricaturist. *The Third-Class Carriage*.

Jacques-Louis David, 1748-1825, (Fr.) Neoclassicist. *The Oath of the Horatii*.

Arthur Davies, 1862-1928, (U.S.) Romantic landscapist. *Unicorns*, *Leda and the Dioscuri*.

Edgar Degas, 1834-1917, (Fr.) Realist/Impressionist. *The Ballet Class*.

Willem de Kooning, 1904-97, (Neth.-U.S.) Abstract Expressionist. *Excavation*, *Woman I*, *Door to the River*.

Eugène Delacroix, 1798-1863, (Fr.) Romantic. *Massacre at Chios*, *Liberty Leading the People*.

Paul Delaroche, 1797-1856, (Fr.) historical themes. *Children of Edward IV*.

Luca Della Robbia, 1400-82, (It.) Renaissance terra-cotta. *Cantoria* (singing gallery), Florence cathedral.

Donatello, 1386-1466, (It.) Renaissance sculptor. *David*, *Gattamelata*.

Aaron Douglas, 1899-79, (U.S.) Harlem Renaissance illustrator and muralist.

Jean Dubuffet, 1902-85, (Fr.) painter, sculptor, printmaker. *Group of Four Trees*.

Marcel Duchamp, 1887-1968, (Fr.) Dadaist. *Nude Descending a Staircase, No. 2*.

Raoul Dufy, 1877-1953, (Fr.) Fauvist. *Chateau and Horses*.

Asher Brown Durand, 1796-1886, (U.S.) Hudson River school. *Kindred Spirits*.

Albrecht Dürer, 1471-1528, (Ger.) Renaissance painter, engraver, woodcuts. *St. Jerome in His Study*, *Melencolia I*.

Anthony van Dyck, 1599-1641, (Flem.) Baroque portraitist. *Portrait of Charles I Hunting*.

Thomas Eakins, 1844-1916, (U.S.) Realist. *The Gross Clinic*.

Alfred Eisenstaedt, 1898-1995, (Ger.-U.S.) photographer, photojournalist. Famous photo, V-J Day, Aug. 14, 1945.

Peter Henry Emerson, 1856-1936, (Br.) photographer. Promoted photography as an independent art form.

Jacob Epstein, 1880-1959, (Br.) religious and allegorical sculptor. *Genesis*, *Ecce Homo*.

Erté (Romain de Tiertoff), 1892-1990, (Fr.) painter, fashion and stage designer.

Walker Evans, 1903-75, (U.S.) photographer. Documented Great Depression.

Jan van Eyck, c. 1390-1441, (Flem.) naturalistic panels. *Adoration of the Lamb*.

Horst Faas, 1933-2012, (Ger.) Vietnam War photographer.

Roger Fenton, 1819-69, (Br.) photographer. Crimean War.

Anselm Feuerbach, 1829-80, (Ger.) Romantic Classicist. *Judgment of Paris*, *Iphigenia*.

John Bernard Flannagan, 1895-1942, (U.S.) animal sculptor. *Triumph of the Egg*.

Jean-Honoré Fragonard, 1732-1806, (Fr.) Rococo. *The Swing*.

Robert Frank, 1924-2019, (Switz.-U.S.) photographer. *The Americans*.

Helen Frankenthaler, 1928-2011, (U.S.) Abstract Expressionist. *Mountains and Sea*.

Daniel Chester French, 1850-1931, (U.S.) sculptor. *The Minute Man of Concord*; seated *Lincoln*, Lincoln Memorial, Washington, DC.

Lucian Freud, 1922-2011, (Ger.-Br.) portraitist. *Girl With Roses.*

Caspar David Friedrich, 1774-1840, (Ger.) Romantic landscapist. *Man and Woman Gazing at the Moon.*

Thomas Gainsborough, 1727-88, (Br.) portraitist. *The Blue Boy, The Watering Place, The Parish Clerk.*

Alexander Gardner, 1821-82, (U.S.) photographer. Civil War, railroad construction, Great Plains Indians.

Paul Gauguin, 1848-1903, (Fr.) Post-Impressionist. *The Tahitians, Spirit of the Dead Watching.*

Lorenzo Ghiberti, 1378-1455, (It.) Renaissance sculptor. "Gates of Paradise" baptistery doors, Florence, It.

Alberto Giacometti, 1901-66, (Switz.) attenuated sculptures of solitary figures. *Man Pointing.*

Giorgione, c. 1477-1510, (It.) Renaissance. *The Tempest.*

Giotto di Bondone, 1267-1337, (It.) Renaissance. *Presentation of Christ in the Temple.*

François Girardon, 1628-1715, (Fr.) Baroque sculptor of classical themes. *Apollo Tended by the Nymphs.*

Milton Glaser, 1929-2020, (U.S.) graphic designer. I ♥ NY logo.

Edward Gorey, 1925-2000, (U.S.) illustrator. *The Doubtful Guest.*

Arshile Gorky, 1905-48, (U.S.) Surrealist. *The Liver Is the Cock's Comb.*

Francisco de Goya y Lucientes, 1746-1828, (Sp.) painter, printmaker. *The Naked Maja, The Disasters of War* (etchings).

El Greco (Domenikos Theotokopoulos), 1541-1614, (Gr.-Sp.) painter, sculptor. *View of Toledo, Assumption of the Virgin.*

Horatio Greenough, 1805-52, (U.S.) Neoclassical sculptor.

Matthias Grünewald, 1480-1528, (Ger.) mystical religious themes. *The Resurrection.*

Frans Hals, c. 1580-1666, (Neth.) portraitist. *Laughing Cavalier, Gypsy Girl.*

Richard Hamilton, 1922-2011, (Br.) Pop Art. *Just What Is It That Makes Today's Homes So Different, So Appealing?*

Austin Hansen, 1910-96, (U.S.) photographer. Harlem, NY, life.

Keith Haring, 1958-90, (U.S.) painter, muralist. *Crack is Wack.*

Childe Hassam, 1859-1935, (U.S.) Impressionist. *Southwest Wind, July 14 Rue Daunon.*

Carmen Herrera, 1915-2022, (Cuba-U.S.) abstract painter.

Edward Hicks, 1780-1849, (U.S.) folk. *The Peaceable Kingdom.*

Lewis Wickes Hine, 1874-1940, (U.S.) photographer. Studies of immigrants, children in industry.

Hans Hofmann, 1880-1966, (U.S.) early Abstract Expressionist. *Spring, The Gate.*

William Hogarth, 1697-1764, (Br.) caricaturist. *The Rake's Progress.*

Katsushika Hokusai, 1760-1849, (Jpn.) printmaker. *Crabs.*

Hans Holbein the Elder, 1460-1524, (Ger.) late Gothic. *Presentation of Christ in the Temple.*

Hans Holbein the Younger, 1497-1543, (Ger.) portraitist. *Henry VIII, The French Ambassadors.*

Winslow Homer, 1836-1910, (U.S.) naturalist, marine themes. *Marine Coast, High Cliff.*

Edward Hopper, 1882-1967, (U.S.) realistic urban scenes. *Nighthawks, House by the Railroad.*

Horst P. Horst, 1906-99, (Ger.) fashion, celebrity photographer.

Jean-Auguste-Dominique Ingres, 1780-1867, (Fr.) Classicist. *Valpincon Bather.*

George Inness, 1825-94, (U.S.) luminous landscapist. *Delaware Water Gap.*

William Henry Jackson, 1843-1942, (U.S.) photographer. American West, building of Union Pacific Railroad.

Jeanne-Claude (Javacheff), 1935-2009, (Moroc.), large-scale environmental installation artist with husband Christo. *The Gates, Surrounded Islands.*

Frances Benjamin Johnston, 1864-1952, (U.S.) photographer. Historic homes.

Donald Judd, 1928-94, (U.S.) sculptor, major Minimalist.

Frida Kahlo, 1907-54, (Mex.) folkloric stylist. *Self-Portrait With Monkey.*

Wassily Kandinsky, 1866-1944, (Russ.) Abstractionist. *Capricious Forms, Improvisation 28 (second version).*

Ellsworth Kelly, 1923-2015, (U.S.) painter, sculptor. *Red Blue Green.*

Paul Klee, 1879-1940, (Switz.) Abstractionist. *Twittering Machine, Pastoral, Death and Fire.*

Gustav Klimt, 1862-1918, (Austria) cofounder of Vienna Secession Movement. *The Kiss.*

Oskar Kokoschka, 1886-1980, (Austria) Expressionist. *View of Prague, Harbor of Marseilles.*

Käthe Kollwitz, 1867-1945, (Ger.) printmaker, social justice themes. *The Peasant War.*

Gaston Lachaise, 1882-1935, (U.S.) figurative sculptor. *Standing Woman.*

John La Farge, 1835-1910, (U.S.) muralist. *Red and White Peonies, The Ascension.*

Edwin (Henry) Landseer, 1802-73, (Br.) painter, sculptor. *Shoeing, Rout of Comus.*

Dorothea Lange, 1895-1965, (U.S.) photographer. Great Depression, migrant farm workers.

Fernand Léger, 1881-1955, (Fr.) Machine art. *The Cyclists.*

Saul Leiter, 1923-2013, (U.S) photographer.

Leonardo da Vinci, 1452-1519, (It.) Renaissance. *Mona Lisa, Last Supper, The Annunciation.*

Emanuel Leutze, 1816-68, (U.S.) historical themes. *Washington Crossing the Delaware.*

Edmonia Lewis, 1844?-1907, (U.S.) sculptor. *The Death of Cleopatra.*

Roy Lichtenstein, 1923-97, (U.S.) Pop Art.

Jacques Lipchitz, 1891-1973, (Fr.) Cubist sculptor. *Harpist.*

Filippino Lippi, 1457-1504, (It.) Renaissance. *Adoration of the Magi.*

Fra Filippo Lippi, 1406-69, (It.) Renaissance. *Coronation of the Virgin, Madonna and Child With Angels.*

Morris Louis, 1912-62, (U.S.) Abstract Expressionist. *Signa, Stripes, Alpha-Phi.*

René Magritte, 1898-1967, (Belg.) Surrealist. *The Descent of Man, The Betrayal of Images.*

Aristide Maillol, 1861-1944, (Fr.) sculptor. *L'Harmonie.*

Édouard Manet, 1832-83, (Fr.) forerunner of Impressionism. *Luncheon on the Grass, Olympia.*

Andrea Mantegna, 1431-1506, (It.) Renaissance frescoes. *Triumph of Caesar.*

Robert Mapplethorpe, 1946-89, (U.S.) photographer.

Franz Marc, 1880-1916, (Ger.) Expressionist. *Blue Horses.*

John Marin, 1870-1953, (U.S.) Expressionist seascapes. *Maine Island.*

Reginald Marsh, 1898-1954, (U.S.) satire. *Tattoo and Haircut.*

Agnes Martin, 1912-2004, (U.S.) abstract artist. *Night Sea.*

Masaccio, 1401-28, (It.) Renaissance. *The Tribute Money.*

Henri Matisse, 1869-1954, (Fr.) Fauvist. *Woman With the Hat.*

John McCracken, 1934-2011, (U.S.) Minimalist sculptor.

Michelangelo Buonarroti, 1475-1564, (It.) Renaissance. *Pietà, David, Moses, The Last Judgment,* Sistine Chapel ceiling.

Jean-Francois Millet, 1814-75, (Fr.) peasants. *The Gleaners, The Man With a Hoe.*

Joan Miró, 1893-1983, (Sp.) exuberant colors, playful images. *Catalan landscape, Dutch Interior.*

Amedeo Modigliani, 1884-1920, (It.) figurative paintings, sculptures. *Reclining Nude.*

Piet Mondrian, 1872-1944, (Neth.) Abstractionist. *Composition With Red, Yellow and Blue.*

Claude Monet, 1840-1926, (Fr.) Impressionist. *The Bridge at Argenteuil, Haystacks, Bridge Over a Pond of Water Lillies.*

Henry Moore, 1898-1986, (Br.) sculptor of large-scale, abstract works. *Reclining Figure* (several).

Gustave Moreau, 1826-98, (Fr.) Symbolist. *The Apparition (Dance of Salome).*

James Wilson Morrice, 1865-1924, (Can.) landscapist. *The Ferry, Quebec, Venice, Looking Over the Lagoon.*

William Morris, 1834-96, (Br.) decorative artist, leader of Arts and Crafts movement.

Grandma Moses (Anna Mary Robertson Moses), 1860-1961, (U.S.) folk. *Out for the Christmas Tree, Catching the Thanksgiving Turkey.*

Samuel Morse, 1791-1872, (U.S.) portraitist. *Gallery of the Louvre.*

Edvard Munch, 1863-1944, (Nor.) Expressionist. *The Cry.*

Bartolome Murillo, 1618-82, (Sp.) Baroque religious artist. *Vision of St. Anthony, The Two Trinities.*

Elizabeth Murray, 1940-2007, (U.S.) abstract colors. *Kitchen Party.*

Eadweard Muybridge, 1830-1904, (Br.-U.S.) photographer. Studies of motion, *Animal Locomotion.*

Nadar (Gaspar-Félix Tournachon), 1820-1910, (Fr.) photographer, caricaturist, portraitist. Invented photo-essay.

LeRoy Neiman, 1921-2012, (U.S.) sports expressionist painter.

Arnold Newman, 1918-2006, (U.S.) portrait photographer.

Barnett Newman, 1905-70, (U.S.) Abstract Expressionist. *Stations of the Cross.*

Isamu Noguchi, 1904-88, (U.S.) abstract sculptor, designer. *Kouros, BirdC(MU),* sculptural gardens.

Kenneth Noland, 1924-2010, (U.S.) Color Field, abstract.

Georgia O'Keeffe, 1887-1986, (U.S.) Southwest motifs. *Cow's Skull: Red, White, and Blue; The Shelton With Sunspots.*

Claes Oldenburg, 1929-2022, (Swed.-U.S.) pop-art sculptor. *Spoonbridge and Cherry.*

José Clemente Orozco, 1883-1949, (Mex.) frescoes. *House of Tears, Pre-Columbian Golden Age.*

Timothy H. O'Sullivan, 1840-82, (U.S.) Civil War photographer.

Gordon Parks, 1912-2006, (U.S.) African American photographer, filmmaker. *Life* photographer, 1948-68.

Charles Willson Peale, 1741-1827, (U.S.) Amer. Revolutionary portraitist. *The Staircase Group,* U.S. presidents.

Rembrandt Peale, 1778-1860, (U.S.) portraitist. *Thomas Jefferson.*

Irving Penn, 1917-2009, (U.S.) portraitist, fashion photographer.

Pietro Perugino, 1446-1523, (It.) Renaissance. *Delivery of the Keys to St. Peter.*

Pablo Picasso, 1881-1973, (Sp.) painter, sculptor. *Guernica, Dove, Head of a Woman, Head of a Bull, Metamorphosis.*

Piero della Francesca, c. 1415-92, (It.) Renaissance. *Duke of Urbino, Flagellation of Christ.*

Camille Pissarro, 1830-1903, (Fr.) Impressionist. *Boulevard des Italiens, Morning, Sunlight; Bather in the Woods.*

Jackson Pollock, 1912-56, (U.S.) Abstract Expressionist. *Autumn Rhythm.*

Nicolas Poussin, 1594-1665, (Fr.) Baroque pictorial classicism. *St. John on Patmos.*

Maurice B. Prendergast, c. 1860-1924, (U.S.) Postimpressionist watercolorist. *Umbrellas in the Rain.*

Pierre-Paul Prud'hon, 1758-1823, (Fr.) Romanticist. *Crime Pursued by Vengeance and Justice.*

Pierre Cecile Puvis de Chavannes, 1824-98, (Fr.) muralist. *The Poor Fisherman.*

Raphael Sanzio, 1483-1520, (It.) Renaissance. *Disputa, School of Athens, Sistine Madonna.*

Robert Rauschenberg, 1925-2008, (U.S.) printmaker. *Combine, Bed, Revolvers, Outpost.*

Man Ray (Emmanuel Radnitsky), 1890-1976, (U.S.) Dadaist and Surrealist. *Observing Time, The Lovers, Marquis de Sade.*

Odilon Redon, 1840-1916, (Fr.) Symbolist painter, lithographer. *In the Dream, Vase of Flowers.*

Rembrandt van Rijn, 1606-69, (Neth.) painter, printmaker. *The Bridal Couple, The Night Watch.*

Frederic Remington, 1861-1909, (U.S.) painter, sculptor. Portrayer of the American West, *Bronco Buster.*

Pierre-Auguste Renoir, 1841-1919, (Fr.) Impressionist. *The Luncheon of the Boating Party, Dance in the Country.*

Joshua Reynolds, 1723-92, (Br.) portraitist. *Mrs. Siddons as the Tragic Muse.*

Herb Ritts, 1952-2002, (U.S.) photographer. Nudes, celebrities.

Diego Rivera, 1886-1957, (Mex.) frescoes. *The Fecund Earth.*

Larry Rivers, 1923-2002, (U.S.) painter, sculptor, often realistic. Dutch Masters series.

Henry Peach Robinson, 1830-1901, (Br.) a leader of "high art" photography.

Norman Rockwell, 1894-1978, (U.S.) painter, illustrator. *Saturday Evening Post* covers.

Auguste Rodin, 1840-1917, (Fr.) sculptor. *The Thinker.*

Milton Rogovin, 1909-2011, (U.S.) documentary photographer.

Willy Ronis, 1910-2009, (Fr.) photographer. *Postwar Paris.*

Joe Rosenthal, 1911-2006, (U.S.) photojournalist. Photographed six Marines raising the U.S. flag over Iwo Jima in WWII.

Mark Rothko, 1903-70, (U.S.) Abstract Expressionist. *Light, Earth and Blue.*

Georges Rouault, 1871-1958, (Fr.) Expressionist. *Three Judges.*

Henri Rousseau, 1844-1910, (Fr.) primitive exotic themes. *The Snake Charmer.*

Theodore Rousseau, 1812-67, (Switz.-Fr.) landscapist. *Under the Birches, Evening.*

Peter Paul Rubens, 1577-1640, (Flem.) Baroque. *Mystic Marriage of St. Catherine.*

Jacob van Ruisdael, c. 1628-82, (Neth.) landscapist. *Jewish Cemetery.*

Charles M. Russell, 1866-1926, (U.S.) Western life.

Salomon van Ruysdael, c. 1600-70, (Neth.) landscapist. *River With Ferry-Boat.*

Albert Pinkham Ryder, 1847-1917, (U.S.) seascapes, allegories. *Toilers of the Sea.*

Augustus Saint-Gaudens, 1848-1907, (U.S.) memorial statues. *Farragut, Mrs. Henry Adams (Grief).*

Niki de Saint Phalle,1930-2002, (Fr.) paintings, sculptures, prints, large public installations.

Andrea Sansovino, 1460-1529, (It.) Renaissance sculptor. *Baptism of Christ.*

Jacopo Sansovino, 1486-1570, (It.) Renaissance sculptor. *St. John the Baptist.*

John Singer Sargent, 1856-1925, (U.S.) Edwardian society portraitist. *The Wyndham Sisters, Madame X.*

Andrea del Sarto, 1486-1530, (It.) frescoes. *Madonna of the Harpies.*

George Segal, 1924-2000, (U.S.) sculptor. Life-sized figures realistically depicting daily life.

Georges Seurat, 1859-91, (Fr.) Pointillist. *Sunday Afternoon on the Island of La Grande Jatte.*

Gino Severini, 1883-1966, (It.) Futurist and Cubist. *Dynamic Hieroglyph of the Bal Tabarin.*

Ben Shahn, 1898-1969, (U.S.) social and political themes. Sacco and Vanzetti series, *Seurat's Lunch, Handball.*

Charles Sheeler, 1883-1965, (U.S.) abstractionist.

David Alfaro Siqueiros, 1896-1974, (Mex.) political muralist. *March of Humanity.*

David Smith, 1906-65, (U.S.) welded metal sculpture. *Hudson River Landscape, Zig, Cubi* series.

Edward Steichen, 1879-1973, (U.S.) photographer. Credited with transforming photography into an art form.

Alfred Stieglitz, 1864-1946, (U.S.) photographer, editor. Helped create acceptance of photography as art.

Paul Strand, 1890-1976, (U.S.) photographer. People, nature, landscapes.

Gilbert Stuart, 1755-1828, (U.S.) portraitist. George Washington, Thomas Jefferson, James Madison.

Thomas Sully, 1783-1872, (U.S.) portraitist. *The Passage of the Delaware.*

William Henry Fox Talbot, 1800-77, (Br.) photographer. *Pencil of Nature*, early photographically illustrated book.

George Tames, 1919-94, (U.S.) photographer. Presidents, political leaders.

Yves Tanguy, 1900-55, (Fr.) Surrealist. *Mama, Papa Is Wounded!*

Giovanni Battista Tiepolo, 1696-1770, (It.) Rococo frescoes. *The Crucifixion.*

Louis Comfort Tiffany, 1848-1933, (U.S.) stained glass, decorative arts.

Jacopo Tintoretto, 1518-94, (It.) Mannerist. *The Last Supper.*

Titian (Tiziano Vecellio), c. 1488-1576, (It.) Renaissance. *Venus and the Lute Player, The Bacchanal.*

Jose Rey Toledo, 1916-94, (U.S.) Native American life. Tribal dances.

George Tooker, 1920-2011, (U.S.) Magic Realist. *Subway.*

Henri de Toulouse-Lautrec, 1864-1901, (Fr.) Postimpressionist. *At the Moulin Rouge.*

John Trumbull, 1756-1843, (U.S.) historical themes. *The Declaration of Independence.*

Deborah Turbeville, 1937-2013, (U.S.) fashion photographer.

J(oseph) M(allord) W(illiam) Turner, 1775-1851, (Br.) Romantic landscapist. *Snow Storm.*

Cy Twombly, 1928-2011, (U.S.) painter and sculptor. *Leda and the Swan.*

Paolo Uccello, 1397-1475, (It.) Gothic-Renaissance. *The Rout of San Romano.*

Maurice Utrillo, 1883-1955, (Fr.) Impressionist. *Sacré-Coeur de Montmartre.*

Vincent van Gogh, 1853-90, (Neth.) *The Starry Night, L'Arlesienne, Bedroom at Arles, Self-Portrait.*

John Vanderlyn, 1775-1852, (U.S.) Neoclassicist. *Ariadne Asleep on the Island of Naxos.*

Diego Velázquez, 1599-1660, (Sp.) Baroque. *Las Meninas, Portrait of Juan de Pareja.*

Jan Vermeer, 1632-75, (Neth.) interior genre subjects. *Young Woman With a Water Jug.*

Paolo Veronese, 1528-88, (It.) Venetian painter. *The Temptation of St. Anthony.*

Andrea del Verrocchio, 1435-88, (It.) sculptor. *Colleoni.*

Maurice de Vlaminck, 1876-1958, (Fr.) Fauvist landscapist. *Red Trees.*

Andy Warhol, 1928-87, (U.S.) Pop Art. *Campbell's Soup Cans, Marilyn Diptych.*

Antoine Watteau, 1684-1721, (Fr.) Rococo "scenes of gallantry." *The Embarkation for Cythera.*

George Frederic Watts, 1817-1904, (Br.) painter and sculptor. Grandiose allegorical themes. *Hope.*

Benjamin West, 1738-1820, (U.S.) realistic historical themes. *Death of General Wolfe.*

Edward Weston, 1886-1958, (U.S.) photographer. Landscapes of American West.

James Abbott McNeill Whistler, 1834-1903, (U.S.) *Arrangement in Grey and Black No. 1 (Portrait of the Artist's Mother).*

Archibald M. Willard, 1836-1918, (U.S.) murals. *The Spirit of '76.*

Grant Wood, 1891-1942, (U.S.) Midwestern regionalist. *American Gothic, Daughters of Revolution.*

Andrew Wyeth, 1917-2009, (U.S.), regionalist. *Christina's World.*

Ossip Zadkine, 1890-1967, (Russ.) School of Paris sculptor. *The Destroyed City, Musicians, Christ.*

Business Leaders and Philanthropists of the Past

Giovanni Agnelli, 1921-2003, (It.) industrialist; principal shareholder of Fiat.

Karl Albrecht, 1920-2014, and **Theo Albrecht**, 1922-2010, (both Ger.) cofounders of Aldi supermarkets.

Paul Allen, 1953-2018, (U.S.) Microsoft cofounder; philanthropist.

Walter Annenberg, 1908-2002, (U.S.) publisher, founder of *TV Guide*, philanthropist.

Elizabeth Arden (F. N. Graham), 1884-1966, (U.S.) Canadian-born founder of cosmetics empire.

Philip D. Armour, 1832-1901, (U.S.) industrialist; streamlined meatpacking.

Brooke Astor, 1902-2007, (U.S.) philanthropist; pres. of Vincent Astor Foundation.

John Jacob Astor, 1763-1848, (U.S.) German-born fur trader, banker, real estate magnate; at death, richest in U.S.

Francis W. Ayer, 1848-1923, (U.S.) ad industry pioneer.

August Belmont, 1816-90, (U.S.) German-born financier.

Liliane Bettencourt, 1922-2017, (Fr.) L'Oreal heiress, philanthropist.

James B. (Diamond Jim) Brady, 1856-1917, (U.S.) financier, philanthropist, legendary bon vivant.

Adolphus Busch, 1839-1913, (U.S.) German-born brewery founder.

Asa Candler, 1851-1929, (U.S.) founded Coca-Cola Co.

Andrew Carnegie, 1835-1919, (U.S.) Scottish-born industrialist, philanthropist; founded Carnegie Steel Co.

Tom Carvel, 1908-89, (Gr.-U.S.) founded ice cream chain.

William Colgate, 1783-1857, (Br.-U.S.) businessman, philanthropist; founded soap-making empire.

Jay Cooke, 1821-1905, (U.S.) financier.

Peter Cooper, 1791-1883, (U.S.) industrialist, inventor, philanthropist; founded Cooper Union college (1859).

Ezra Cornell, 1807-74, (U.S.) businessman, philanthropist; founded Western Union.

Erastus Corning, 1794-1872, (U.S.) financier; headed New York Central Railroad.

Charles Crocker, 1822-88, (U.S.) railroad builder, financier.

Samuel Cunard, 1787-1865, (Can.) pioneered transatlantic steam navigation.

Marcus Daly, 1841-1900, (U.S.) Irish-born copper magnate.

W. Edwards Deming, 1900-93, (U.S.) quality-control expert who revolutionized Japanese manufacturing.

Walt Disney, 1901-66, (U.S.) pioneer in cinema animation; built entertainment empire.

Herbert H. Dow, 1866-1930, (U.S.) founder of chemical co.

Anthony Drexel, 1826-93, (U.S.) banker, philanthropist, university founder.

James Duke, 1856-1925, (U.S.) founded American Tobacco, Duke Univ.

Eleuthere I. du Pont, 1771-1834, (Fr.-U.S.) gunpowder manufacturer.

Thomas C. Durant, 1820-85, (U.S.) railroad official, financier.

William C. Durant, 1861-1947, (U.S.) industrialist; formed General Motors.

George Eastman, 1854-1932, (U.S.) inventor; manufacturer of photographic equipment.

Marshall Field, 1834-1906, (U.S.) founded Chicago's largest department store.

Harvey Firestone, 1868-1938, (U.S.) founded tire company.

Avery Fisher, 1906-94, (U.S.) industrialist, philanthropist; founded Fisher Electronics.

Henry M. Flagler, 1830-1913, (U.S.) financier; helped form Standard Oil, developed FL as resort state.

Malcolm Forbes, 1919-90, (U.S.) magazine publisher.

Henry Ford, 1863-1947, (U.S.) automaker; developed first popular low-priced car.

Henry Ford II, 1917-87, (U.S.) headed auto company founded by grandfather.

Henry C. Frick, 1849-1919, (U.S.) steel and coke magnate; had prominent role in development of U.S. Steel.

Jakob Fugger (Jakob the Rich), 1459-1525, (Ger.) headed leading banking, trading house in 16th-cent. Europe.

Alfred C. Fuller, 1885-1973, (U.S.) Canadian-born businessman; founded brush company.

Elbert H. Gary, 1846-1927, (U.S.) chaired board of U.S. Steel, 1903-27.

Jean Paul Getty, 1892-1976, (U.S.) founded oil empire.

Amadeo Giannini, 1870-1949, (U.S.) founded Bank of America.

Stephen Girard, 1750-1831, (U.S.) French-born financier, philanthropist.

Leonard H. Goldenson, 1905-99, (U.S.) turned ABC into major TV network.

Jay Gould, 1836-92, (U.S.) railroad magnate, financier.

Hetty Green, 1834-1916, (U.S.) financier nicknamed "witch of Wall St."

William Gregg, 1800-67, (U.S.) launched textile industry in the South.

Meyer Guggenheim, 1828-1905, (U.S.) Swiss-born merchant, philanthropist; built merchandising, mining empires.

Armand Hammer, 1898-1990, (U.S.) headed Occidental Petroleum.

Elliot Handler, 1916-2011, (U.S.) cofounder of Mattel; introduced the Barbie doll.

Edward H. Harriman, 1848-1909, (U.S.) railroad financier; headed Union Pacific.

Hugh Hefner, 1926-2017, (U.S.) founded Playboy Enterprises.

Henry J. Heinz, 1844-1919, (U.S.) founded food empire.

Harry, 1909-97, and **Leona Helmsley**, 1920-2007, (both U.S.) real estate magnates, philanthropists.

Milton Snavely Hershey, 1857-1945, (U.S.) chocolate co. founder, philanthropist.

James J. Hill, 1838-1916, (U.S.) Canadian-born railroad magnate, financier; founded Great Northern Railway.

Conrad N. Hilton, 1888-1979, (U.S.) hotel chain founder.

Howard Hughes, 1905-76, (U.S.) industrialist, aviator, filmmaker.

H. L. Hunt, 1889-1974, (U.S.) oil magnate.

Collis P. Huntington, 1821-1900, (U.S.) railroad magnate.

Henry E. Huntington, 1850-1927, (U.S.) railroad builder, philanthropist.

Lee Iacocca, 1924-2019, (U.S.) auto executive (Ford, Chrysler).

Walter L. Jacobs, 1898-1985, (U.S.) founder of the first rental car agency.

Steve Jobs, 1955-2011, (U.S.) Apple cofounder and exec.; Pixar exec.

Howard Johnson, 1896-1972, (U.S.) founded restaurants.

John H. Johnson, 1918-2005, (U.S.) publisher of Ebony and Jet.

Samuel Curtis Johnson, 1928-2004, (U.S.) headed S.C. Johnson & Sons.

Henry J. Kaiser, 1882-1967, (U.S.) industrialist; built empire in steel, aluminum.

Ingvar Kamprad, 1926-2018, (Swed.) Ikea founder.

Minor C. Keith, 1848-1929, (U.S.) railroad magnate; founded United Fruit Co.

Will K. Kellogg, 1860-1951, (U.S.) businessman, philanthropist; founded breakfast food co.

Kirk Kerkorian, 1917-2015, (U.S.) private equity magnate; real estate developer.

Richard King, 1825-85, (U.S.) cattle farmer; founded King Ranch in Texas.

John W. Kluge, 1914-2010, (Ger.-U.S.) Metromedia chair; philanthropist.

William S. Knudsen, 1879-1948, (U.S.) Danish-born auto industry executive.

David Koch, 1940-2019, (U.S.) businessman, chemical engineer, political activist.

Samuel H. Kress, 1863-1955, (U.S.) businessman, art collector, philanthropist; founded "dime store" chain.

Ray A. Kroc, 1902-84, (U.S.) oversaw vast expansion of McDonald's.

Alfred Krupp, 1812-87, (Ger.) armaments magnate.

Estée Lauder, 1908-2004, (U.S.) cofounder of Estée Lauder companies.

Kenneth L. Lay, 1942-2006, (U.S.), former CEO of Enron; indicted on fraud charges.

William Levitt, 1907-94, (U.S.) industrialist; "suburb maker."

Thomas Lipton, 1850-1931, (Scot.) merchant; tea empire.

James McGill, 1744-1813, (Scot.-Can.) funded Montréal's McGill Univ.

Andrew W. Mellon, 1855-1937, (U.S.) financier, industrialist, philanthropist.

Charles E. Merrill, 1885-1956, (U.S.) financier; developed firm of Merrill Lynch.

J(ohn) P(ierpont) Morgan, 1837-1913, (U.S.) most powerful figure in finance and industry at turn of 20th cent.

Akio Morita, 1921-99, (Jpn.) cofounded Sony Corp.

Malcolm Muir, 1885-1979, (U.S.) created Business Week; led Newsweek, 1937-61.

Roy Neuberger, 1903-2010, (U.S.) financier, art patron.

Samuel Newhouse, 1895-1979, (U.S.) publishing and broadcasting magnate.

Jean Nidetch, 1923-2015, (U.S.) Weight Watchers cofounder.

Aristotle Onassis, 1906-75, (Gr.) shipping magnate.

William S. Paley, 1901-90, (U.S.) built CBS communications empire.

Frederick D. Patterson, 1901-88, (U.S.) founder of United Negro College Fund, 1944.

George Peabody, 1795-1869, (U.S.) merchant, financier, philanthropist.

James C. Penney, 1875-1971, (U.S.) businessman; developed department store.

Frank Perdue, 1920-2005, (U.S.) founder of Perdue Farms, chicken-processing co.

Ross Perot, 1930-2019, (U.S.) computer services pioneer, philanthropist; 2-time pres. candidate (Ind.)

William C. Procter, 1862-1934, (U.S.) headed soap co.

Sumner Redstone, 1923-2020, (U.S.) National Amusements owner, incl. subsidiaries Viacom, CBS.

David Rockefeller, 1915-2017, (U.S.) banker, philanthropist.

John D. Rockefeller, 1839-1937, (U.S.) industrialist; established Standard Oil.

John D. Rockefeller Jr., 1874-1960, (U.S.) philanthropist; provided land for UN.

Laurance S. Rockefeller, 1910-2004, (U.S.) philanthropist, conservationist.

Meyer A. Rothschild, 1743-1812, (Ger.) founded international banking house.

Thomas Fortune Ryan, 1851-1928, (U.S.) financier; a founder of American Tobacco.

Edmond J. Safra, 1932-99, (U.S.) banker.

David Sarnoff, 1891-1971, (U.S.) broadcasting pioneer; established first radio network, NBC.

Richard Sears, 1863-1914, (U.S.) founded mail-order co.

Werner von Siemens, 1816-92, (Ger.) industrialist, inventor.

Alfred P. Sloan, 1875-1966, (U.S.) industrialist, philanthropist; headed GM.

A. Leland Stanford, 1824-93, (U.S.) railroad official, philanthropist; founded university.

Frank Stanton, 1908-2006, (U.S.) president of CBS network, 1946-71.

Nathan Straus, 1848-1931, (U.S.) German-born merchant, philanthropist; headed Macy's dept. store.

Levi Strauss, c. 1829-1902, (U.S.) pants manufacturer.

Clement Studebaker, 1831-1901, (U.S.) wagon, carriage maker.

Gustavus Swift, 1839-1903, (U.S.) pioneer meatpacker.

Gerard Swope, 1872-1957, (U.S.) industrialist, economist; headed General Electric.

Dave Thomas, 1932-2002, (U.S.) Wendy's restaurant chain founder.

James Walter Thompson, 1847-1928, (U.S.) ad exec., founder of ad agency.

Alice Tully, 1902-93, (U.S.) arts patron.

Theodore N. Vail, 1845-1920, (U.S.) organized Bell Telephone, led AT&T.

Cornelius Vanderbilt, 1794-1877, (U.S.) financier; established steamship, railroad empires.

Lillian Vernon, 1927-2015, (Ger.-U.S.) catalog merchant, philanthropist.

Henry Villard, 1835-1900, (U.S.) German-born railroad executive, financier.

Charles R. Walgreen, 1873-1939, (U.S.) founded drugstore chain.

Madame C. J. Walker, 1867-1919, (U.S.) African American hair care entrepreneur, philanthropist.

DeWitt, 1889-1981, and **Lila Wallace**, 1889-1984, (both U.S.) cofounders of Reader's Digest magazine.

Sam Walton, 1918-92, (U.S.) Walmart founder.

John Wanamaker, 1838-1922, (U.S.) department-store merchandising pioneer.

Aaron Montgomery Ward, 1843-1913, (U.S.) established first mail-order firm.

Thomas J. Watson, 1874-1956, (U.S.) IBM head, 1914-56.

Jack Welch, 1935-2020, (U.S.) General Electric CEO.

George Westinghouse, 1846-1914, (U.S) inventor, manufacturer; organized Westinghouse Electric Co., 1886.

John Hay Whitney, 1905-82, (U.S.) publisher, sportsman, philanthropist.

Chuck Williams, 1915-2015, (U.S.) Williams-Sonoma founder.

Charles E. Wilson, 1890-1961, (U.S.) auto exec., public official.

Frank W. Woolworth, 1852-1919, (U.S.) created five-and-dime chain.

William Wrigley Jr., 1861-1932, (U.S.) founded Wrigley chewing gum co.

American Cartoonists

Reviewed by Lucy Shelton Caswell, Professor and Curator, Cartoon Research Library, Ohio State University.

Scott Adams, b 1957, Dilbert.

Charles Addams, 1912-88, macabre cartoons.

Brad Anderson, 1924-2015, Marmaduke.

Sergio Aragonés, b 1937, (Span.-Mex.) Mad magazine.

Peter Arno, 1904-68, The New Yorker.

Tex Avery, 1908-80, animator; Bugs Bunny, Porky Pig.

George Baker, 1915-75, The Sad Sack.

Carl Barks, 1901-2000, Donald Duck comic books.

Alison Bechdel, b 1960, graphic novelist.

C. C. Beck, 1910-89, Captain Marvel.

Dave Berg, 1920-2002, Mad magazine.

Jim Berry, 1932-2015, Berry's World.

Herb Block (Herblock), 1909-2001, political cartoonist.

George Booth, 1926-2022, The New Yorker.

Loren Bouchard, b 1969, Bob's Burgers.

Berkeley Breathed, b 1957, Bloom County.

Dik Browne, 1917-89, Hi & Lois, Hagar the Horrible.

Marjorie Buell, 1904-93, Little Lulu.

Ernie Bushmiller, 1905-82, Nancy.

Milton Caniff, 1907-88, Terry & the Pirates, Steve Canyon.

Al Capp, 1909-79, Li'l Abner.

Roz Chast, b 1954, The New Yorker.

Gene Colan, 1926-2011, Daredevil.

Paul Conrad, 1924-2010, political cartoonist.

Roy Crane, 1901-77, Captain Easy, Buz Sawyer.

R(obert) Crumb, b 1943, underground cartoonist.

Shamus Culhane, 1908-96, animator.

Jay N. "Ding" Darling, 1876-1962, political cartoonist.

Jack Davis, 1924-2016, Mad magazine.

Jim Davis, b 1945, Garfield.

Billy DeBeck, 1890-1942, Barney Google.

Rudolph Dirks, 1877-1968, The Katzenjammer Kids.

Walt Disney, 1901-66, produced animated cartoons; Mickey Mouse, Donald Duck.

Steve Ditko, 1927-2018, Spider-Man.

Mort Drucker, 1929-2020, Mad magazine.

Will Eisner, 1917-2005, The Spirit.

Jules Feiffer, b 1929, political cartoonist.

Bud Fisher, 1885-1954, Mutt & Jeff.

Ham Fisher, 1900-55, Joe Palooka.

Max Fleischer, 1883-1972, Betty Boop.

Hal Foster, 1892-1982, Tarzan, Prince Valiant.

Fontaine Fox, 1884-1964, Toonerville Folks.

Isadore "Friz" Freleng, 1905-95, animator; Yosemite Sam, Porky Pig, Sylvester and Tweety Bird.

Rube Goldberg, 1883-1970, Boob McNutt.

Chester Gould, 1900-85, Dick Tracy.

Harold Gray, 1894-1968, Little Orphan Annie.

Matt Groening, b 1954, Life in Hell, The Simpsons.

Cathy Guisewite, b 1950, Cathy.

Bill Hanna, 1910-2001, and Joe Barbera, 1911-2006, animators; Tom & Jerry, Yogi Bear, Flintstones.

Oliver Harrington, 1912-95, Bootsie.

Johnny Hart, 1931-2007, B.C., Wizard of Id.

Alfred Harvey, 1913-94, created Casper the Friendly Ghost.

Jimmy Hatlo, 1898-1963, Little Iodine.

John Held Jr., 1889-1958, Jazz Age.

George Herriman, 1881-1944, Krazy Kat.

Harry Hershfield, 1885-1974, Abie the Agent.

Stephen Hillenburg, 1961-2018, Sponge-Bob SquarePants.

Al Hirschfeld, 1903-2003, NY Times theater caricaturist.

Burne Hogarth, 1911-96, Tarzan.

Helen Hokinson, 1900-49, The New Yorker.

Nicole Hollander, b 1939, Sylvia.

Al Jaffee, 1921-2023, Mad magazine.

Lynn Johnston, b 1947, (Can.) For Better or For Worse.

Oliver Johnston, 1912-2008, Disney animator.

Chuck Jones, 1912-2002, animator; Bugs Bunny, Porky Pig; created Road Runner, Wile E. Coyote.

Mike Judge, b 1962, Beavis and Butt-Head, King of the Hill.

Bob Kane, 1916-98, Batman.

Bil Keane, 1922-2011, The Family Circus.

Walt Kelly, 1913-73, Pogo.

Hank Ketcham, 1920-2001, Dennis the Menace.

Ted Key, 1912-2008, Hazel.

Frank King, 1883-1969, Gasoline Alley.

Jack Kirby, 1917-94, Fantastic Four, The Incredible Hulk.

Rollin Kirby, 1875-1952, political cartoonist.

B(ernard) Kliban, 1935-90, cat books.

Edward Koren, 1935-2023, The New Yorker.

John Kricfalusi, b 1955, Ren & Stimpy.

Joe Kubert, 1926-2012, Sgt. Rock.

Harvey Kurtzman, 1921-93, Mad magazine.

Walter Lantz, 1900-94, Woody Woodpecker.

Gary Larson, b 1950, The Far Side.

Mell Lazarus, 1927-2016, Momma.

Stan Lee, 1922-2018, Marvel Comics.

David Levine, 1926-2009, NY Review of Books caricatures.

Seth MacFarlane, b 1973, Family Guy.

Jeff MacNelly, 1947-2000, political cartoonist; Shoe.

Doug Marlette, 1949-2007, political cartoonist; Kudzu.

Don Martin, 1931-2000, Mad magazine.

Bill Mauldin, 1921-2003, political cartoonist.

Winsor McCay, 1872-1934, Little Nemo.

John T. McCutcheon, 1870-1949, political cartoonist.

Patrick McDonnell, b 1956, Mutts.

Dwayne McDuffie, 1962-2011, Justice League.

Aaron McGruder, b 1974, The Boondocks.

George McManus, 1884-1954, Bringing Up Father.

Dale Messick, 1906-2005, Brenda Starr.

Wiley Miller, b 1951, Non Sequitur.

Norman Mingo, 1896-1980, Alfred E. Neuman.

Bob Montana, 1920-75, Archie.

Dick Moores, 1909-86, Gasoline Alley.

Willard Mullin, 1902-78, sports cartoonist; Dodgers' "Brooklyn Bum," "Mets Kid."

Randall Munroe, b 1984, xkcd.

Russell Myers, b 1938, Broom Hilda.

Thomas Nast, 1840-1902, political cartoonist; Republican elephant, Democratic donkey.

Pat Oliphant, b 1935, political cartoonist.

Frederick Burr Opper, 1857-1937, Happy Hooligan.

Richard Outcault, 1863-1928, Yellow Kid, Buster Brown.

Brant Parker, 1920-2007, Wizard of Id.

Trey Parker, b 1969, South Park co-creator.

Harvey Pekar, 1939-2010, American Splendor.

Mike Peters, b 1943, Mother Goose & Grimm.

George Price, 1901-95, The New Yorker.

Antonio Prohias, 1921-98, Spy vs. Spy.

Alex Raymond, 1909-56, Flash Gordon, Jungle Jim.

Forrest (Bud) Sagendorf, 1915-94, Popeye.

Art Sansom, 1920-91, The Born Loser.

Charles Schulz, 1922-2000, Peanuts.

Elzie C. Segar, 1894-1938, Popeye.

Marie Severin, 1929-2018, Marvel Comics.

Joe Shuster, 1914-92, and Jerry Siegel, 1914-96, Superman.

Sidney Smith, 1887-1935, The Gumps.

Otto Soglow, 1900-75, Little King.

Art Spiegelman, b 1948, Raw, Maus.

William Steig, 1907-2003, The New Yorker.

Matt Stone, b 1971, South Park co-creator.

James Swinnerton, 1875-1974, Little Jimmy, Canyon Kiddies.

Paul Szep, b 1941, political cartoonist.

Paul Terry, 1887-1971, animator of Mighty Mouse.

Bob Thaves, 1924-2006, Frank and Ernest.

James Thurber, 1894-61, The New Yorker.

Garry Trudeau, b 1948, Doonesbury.

Jim Unger, 1937-2012, Herman.

Mort Walker, 1923-2018, Beetle Bailey.

Bill Watterson, b 1958, Calvin and Hobbes.

Russ Westover, 1887-1966, Tillie the Toiler.

Signe Wilkinson, b 1950, political cartoonist.

Frank Willard, 1893-1958, Moon Mullins.

J. R. Williams, 1888-1957, The Willets Family, Out Our Way.

Gahan Wilson, 1930-2019, The New Yorker.

Tom Wilson, 1931-2011, Ziggy.

Art Young, 1866-1943, political cartoonist.

Chic Young, 1901-73, Blondie.

Economists, Educators, Historians, and Social Scientists of the Past

Brooks Adams, 1848-1927, (U.S.) historian, political theoretician; The Law of Civilization and Decay.

Henry Adams, 1838-1918, (U.S.) historian, autobiographer; The Education of Henry Adams.

Stephen Ambrose, 1936-2002, (U.S.) historian; Eisenhower.

Hannah Arendt, 1906-75, (Ger.) political philosopher; The Origins of Totalitarianism.

Francis Bacon, 1561-1626, (Eng.) philosopher, essayist, statesman; championed observation and induction.

George Bancroft, 1800-91, (U.S.) historian; 10-volume History of the United States.

Jack Barbash, 1910-94, (U.S.) labor economist; helped create the AFL-CIO.

Henry Barnard, 1811-1900, (U.S.) public school reformer.

Charles A. Beard, 1874-1948, (U.S.) historian; The Economic Basis of Politics.

(St.) Bede (the Venerable), c. 673-735, (Br.) scholar, historian; Ecclesiastical History of the English People.

Daniel Bell, 1919-2011, (U.S.) sociologist; The End of Ideology.

Ruth Benedict, 1887-1948, (U.S.) anthropologist; studied Indian tribes of the Southwest.

Isaiah Berlin, 1909-97, (Br.) philosopher, historian; The Age of Enlightenment.

Leonard Bloomfield, 1887-1949, (U.S.) linguist; Language.

For psychologists, see Scientists of the Past.

Franz Boas, 1858-1942, (U.S.) German-born anthropologist; studied American Indians.

Van Wyck Brooks, 1886-1963, (U.S.) historian; critic of New England culture, especially literature.

Edmund Burke, 1729-97, (Ire.) British parliamentarian and political philosopher; Reflections on the Revolution in France.

James MacGregor Burns, 1918-2014, (U.S.) historian, political scientist.

Nicholas Murray Butler, 1862-1947, (U.S.) educator; headed Columbia Univ., 1902-45; 1931 Nobel Peace Prize winner.

Joseph Campbell, 1904-87, (U.S.) author, editor, teacher; wrote books on mythology, folklore.

Thomas Carlyle, 1795-1881, (Scot.) historian, critic; Sartor Resartus, Past and Present, The French Revolution.

(Charles) Bruce Catton, 1899-1978, (U.S.) historian; A Stillness at Appomattox.

Edward Channing, 1856-1931, (U.S.) historian; 6-volume History of the United States.

Henry Steele Commager, 1902-98, (U.S.) historian, educator; The Growth of the American Republic.

John R. Commons, 1862-1945, (U.S.) economist, labor historian; Legal Foundations of Capitalism.

James B. Conant, 1893-1978, (U.S.) educator, diplomat; The American High School Today.

Benedetto Croce, 1866-1952, (It.) philosopher, statesman, historian; Philosophy of the Spirit.

Bernard A. De Voto, 1897-1955, (U.S.) historian; wrote trilogy on American West, edited Mark Twain manuscripts.

Melvil Dewey, 1851-1931, (U.S.) devised decimal system of library-book classification.

Donald Herbert Donald, 1920-2009, (U.S.) Pulitzer Prize-winning Civil War and Lincoln historian.

St. Clair Drake, 1911-90, (U.S.) sociologist, Black studies pioneer; Black Metropolis (1945), with Horace R. Cayton.

W(illiam) E(dward) B(urghardt) Du Bois, 1868-1963, (U.S.) historian, sociologist; NAACP founder, 1909.

Will(iam), 1885-1981, (U.S.) and Ariel Durant, 1898-1981, (Ukraine) historians; The Story of Civilization.

Emile Durkheim, 1858-1917, (Fr.) a founder of modern sociology; The Rules of Sociological Method.

Charles Eliot, 1834-1926, (U.S.) educator, Harvard president.

Friedrich Engels, 1820-95, (Ger.) political writer; with Karl Marx wrote the Communist Manifesto.

Irving Fisher, 1867-1947, (U.S.) economist; contributed to the development of modern monetary theory.

John Fiske, 1842-1901, (U.S.) historian and lecturer; popularized Darwinian theory of evolution.

Charles Fourier, 1772-1837, (Fr.) utopian socialist.

John Hope Franklin, 1915-2009, (U.S.) historian; *From Slavery to Freedom: A History of African Americans*.

James George Frazer, 1854-1941, (Br.) anthropologist; studied myth in religion; *The Golden Bough*.

Milton Friedman, 1912-2006, (U.S.) economist; advocate for free markets.

Paul Fussell, 1924-2012, (U.S.) literary historian; *The Great War and Modern Memory*.

John Kenneth Galbraith, 1908-2006, (Can.-U.S.) economist, author, professor, former amb. to India.

Peter Gay, 1923-2015, (Ger.-U.S.) cultural historian; *The Enlightenment: An Interpretation*.

Giovanni Gentile, 1875-1944, (It.) philosopher, educator; reformed Italian educational system.

Henry George, 1839-97, (U.S.) economist, reformer; led single-tax movement.

Edward Gibbon, 1737-94, (Br.) historian; *The History of the Decline and Fall of the Roman Empire*.

Andrew Greeley, 1928-2013, (U.S.) Rom. Cath. priest; sociologist.

Francesco Guicciardini, 1483-1540, (It.) historian; *Storia d'Italia*, principal historical work of the 16th cent.

Thomas Hobbes, 1588-1679, (Eng.) philosopher, political theorist; *Leviathan*.

Richard Hofstadter, 1916-70, (U.S.) historian; *The Age of Reform*.

Charles Hamilton Houston, 1895-1950, (U.S.) African-American lawyer, Howard Univ. instructor; champion of minority rights.

Samuel Huntington, 1927-2008, (U.S.), political scientist, Harvard University professor; *The Clash of Civilizations*.

Alfred Kahn, 1917-2010, (U.S.) economist; deregulated the U.S. airline industry.

John Keegan, 1934-2012, (Br.) war historian; *The Face of Battle*.

George F. Kennan, 1904-2005, (U.S.) diplomat, historian; main architect of U.S. Cold War "containment" strategy.

John Maynard Keynes, 1883-1946, (Br.) economist; principal advocate of deficit spending.

Alfred Kinsey, 1894-1956, (U.S.) zoologist; pioneering human sex researcher.

Russell Kirk, 1918-94, (U.S.) social philosopher; *The Conservative Mind*.

Alfred L. Kroeber, 1876-1960, (U.S.) cultural anthropologist; studied Indians of North and South America.

Elisabeth Kubler-Ross, 1926-2004, (Switz.) psychiatrist, author; *On Death and Dying*.

Christopher Lasch, 1932-94, (U.S.) social critic, historian; *The Culture of Narcissism*.

James L. Laughlin, 1850-1933, (U.S.) economist; helped establish Federal Reserve System.

Margaret Leech, 1893-1974, (U.S.) historian; *Reveille in Washington, 1860-1865*.

Lucien Lévy-Bruhl, 1857-1939, (Fr.) philosopher; studied the psychology of primitive societies; *Primitive Mentality*.

John Locke, 1632-1704, (Eng.) philosopher, political theorist; *Two Treatises of Government*.

Thomas B. Macaulay, 1800-59, (Br.) historian, statesman.

Niccolò Machiavelli, 1469-1527, (It.) writer, statesman; *The Prince*.

Bronislaw Malinowski, 1884-1942, (Pol.) considered the father of social anthropology.

Thomas R. Malthus, 1766-1834, (Br.) economist; *Essay on the Principle of Population*.

Horace Mann, 1796-1859, (U.S.) pioneered modern public school system.

Karl Mannheim, 1893-1947, (Hung.) sociologist, historian; *Ideology and Utopia*.

Harriet Martineau, 1802-76, (Eng.) writer, feminist; *Society in America*.

Karl Marx, 1818-83, (Ger.) political theorist, proponent of Communism; *Communist Manifesto*, *Das Kapital*.

Benjamin Mays, 1895-1984, (U.S.) minister, educator, civil rights leader; headed Morehouse College, 1940-67.

Giuseppe Mazzini, 1805-72, (It.) political philosopher.

David McCullough, 1933-2022, (U.S.) historian; *John Adams*.

William H. McGuffey, 1800-73, (U.S.) his *Reader* was a mainstay of 19th-cent. U.S. public education.

George H. Mead, 1863-1931, (U.S.) philosopher, social psychologist.

Margaret Mead, 1901-78, (U.S.) cultural anthropologist; popularized field; *Coming of Age in Samoa*.

Alexander Meiklejohn, 1872-1964, (U.S.) Br.-born educator; championed academic freedom and experimental curricula.

James Mill, 1773-1836, (Scot.) philosopher, historian, economist; a proponent of utilitarianism.

John Stuart Mill, 1806-73, (Eng.) philosopher, economist; *Utilitarianism*. Eldest son of James Mill.

Perry G. Miller, 1905-63, (U.S.) historian; interpreted 17th-cent. New England.

Theodor Mommsen, 1817-1903, (Ger.) historian; *The History of Rome*.

Ashley Montagu, 1905-99, (Eng.) anthropologist; *The Natural Superiority of Women*.

Charles-Louis Montesquieu, 1689-1755, (Fr.) social philosopher; *The Spirit of Laws*.

Maria Montessori, 1870-1952, (It.) educator, physician; started Montessori method of student self-motivation.

Samuel Eliot Morison, 1887-1976, (U.S.) historian; chronicled voyages of early explorers.

Edmund Morris, 1940-2019, (Br.-U.S.) historian, presidential biographer (T. Roosevelt, Reagan).

Lewis Mumford, 1895-1990, (U.S.) sociologist, critic; *The Culture of Cities*.

Gunnar Myrdal, 1898-1987, (Swed.) economist, social scientist; *Asian Drama: An Inquiry Into the Poverty of Nations*.

Allan Nevins, 1890-1971, (U.S.) historian, biographer; *The Ordeal of the Union*.

José Ortega y Gasset, 1883-1955, (Sp.) philosopher; advocated control by elite; *The Revolt of the Masses*.

Elinor Ostrom, 1933-2012, (U.S.) political economist.

Robert Owen, 1771-1858, (Br.) political philosopher, reformer; pioneer in cooperative movement.

Thomas Paine, 1737-1809, (Br.-U.S.) political theorist, writer; *Common Sense*.

Vilfredo Pareto, 1848-1923, (It.) economist, sociologist.

Francis Parkman, 1823-93, (U.S.) historian; *France and England in North America*.

Elizabeth P. Peabody, 1804-94, (U.S.) education pioneer; founded first kindergarten in U.S., 1860.

William Prescott, 1796-1859, (U.S.) early American historian; *The Conquest of Peru*.

Pierre Joseph Proudhon, 1809-65, (Fr.) social theorist; father of anarchism; *The Philosophy of Property*.

François Quesnay, 1694-1774, (Fr.) economic theorist.

Robert V. Remini, 1921-2013, (U.S.) historian; *The Life of Andrew Jackson*.

David Ricardo, 1772-1823, (Br.) economic theorist; advocated free international trade.

David Riesman, 1909-2002, (U.S.) sociologist; co-author, *The Lonely Crowd*.

Jacqueline de Romilly, 1913-2010, (Fr.) scholar of Greek civilization and language.

Theodore Roszak, 1933-2011, (U.S.) historian; *The Making of a Counter Culture*.

Jean-Jacques Rousseau, 1712-78, (Fr.) social philosopher; the father of romantic sensibility; *Confessions*.

Paul Samuelson, 1915-2009, (U.S.) economist, famed for modern mathematical approach to economics.

Edward Sapir, 1884-1939, (Ger.-U.S.) anthropologist; studied ethnology and linguistics of American Indian groups.

Ferdinand de Saussure, 1857-1913, (Switz.) a founder of modern linguistics.

Arthur Schlesinger Jr., 1917-2007, (U.S.) historian, author; *The Imperial Presidency*.

Joseph Schumpeter, 1883-1950, (Czech.-U.S.) economist, sociologist.

Elizabeth Seton, 1774-1821, (U.S.) nun; established parochial school education in U.S., first native-born American saint.

Georg Simmel, 1858-1918, (Ger.) sociologist, philosopher; helped establish German sociology.

Robert Sklar, 1936-2011, (U.S.) film scholar.

Adam Smith, 1723-90, (Br.) economist; advocated laissez-faire economy, free trade; *The Wealth of Nations*.

Jared Sparks, 1789-1866, (U.S.) historian, educator, editor; *The Library of American Biography*.

Oswald Spengler, 1880-1936, (Ger.) philosopher, historian; *The Decline of the West*.

Leo Steinberg, 1920-2011, (Russ.-U.S.) art historian.

William G. Sumner, 1840-1910, (U.S.) social scientist, economist; laissez-faire economy, Social Darwinism.

Hippolyte Taine, 1828-93, (Fr.) historian, basis of naturalistic school; *The Origins of Contemporary France*.

A(lan) J(ohn) P(ercivale) Taylor, 1906-90, (Br.) historian; *The Origins of the Second World War*.

Nikolaas Tinbergen, 1907-88, (Neth.-Br.) ethologist; pioneer in study of animal behavior.

Alexis de Tocqueville, 1805-59, (Fr.) political scientist, historian; *Democracy in America*.

Francis E. Townsend, 1867-1960, (U.S.) led old-age pension movement, 1933.

Arnold Toynbee, 1889-1975, (Br.) historian; *A Study of History*, sweeping analysis of hist. of civilizations.

George Trevelyan, 1876-1962, (Br.) historian, statesman; favored "literary" over "scientific" history; *History of England*.

Henri Troyat, 1911-2007, (Russ.-Fr.), biographies of major figures in Russian history.

Frederick J. Turner, 1861-1932, (U.S.) historian, educator; *The Frontier in American History*.

Thorstein B. Veblen, 1857-1929, (U.S.) economist, social philosopher; *The Theory of the Leisure Class*.

Giovanni Vico, 1668-1744, (It.) historian, biographer; regarded by many as first modern historian; *New Science*.

Izaak Walton, 1593-1683, (Eng.) biographer; political-philosophical study of fishing, *The Compleat Angler*.

Booker T. Washington, 1856-1915, (U.S.) founder, 1881, and first pres. of Tuskegee Institute; *Up From Slavery*.

Sidney J., 1859-1947, and **Beatrice Webb**, 1858-1943, (both Br.) leading figures in Fabian Society and Labor Party.

Max Weber, 1864-1920, (Ger.) sociologist; *The Protestant Ethic and the Spirit of Capitalism*.

Walter White, 1893-1955, (U.S.) exec. sec., NAACP, 1931-55.

Roy Wilkins, 1901-81, (U.S.) exec. director, NAACP, 1955-77.

Emma Hart Willard, 1787-1870, (U.S.) pioneered higher education for women.

James Q. Wilson, 1931-2012, (U.S.) political scientist; co-authored broken windows theory.

Carter G. Woodson, 1875-1950, (U.S.) historian; founded Assn. for the Study of Negro Life and History.

C. Vann Woodward, 1908-99, (U.S.) historian; *The Strange Career of Jim Crow*.

Howard Zinn, 1922-2010, (U.S.) historian; *A People's History of the United States*.

American Journalists of the Past

Reviewed by Dean Mills, Dean, Missouri School of Journalism.

See also Business Leaders and Philanthropists, American Cartoonists, and Writers of the Past.

Franklin P. Adams (F.P.A.), 1881-1960, humorist; wrote column "The Conning Tower."

Roger Ailes, 1940-2017, Fox News cofounder and CEO.

Joseph W. Alsop, 1910-89, and **Stewart Alsop**, 1914-74, Washington-based political analysts, columnists.

Jack Anderson, 1922-2006, muckraking Washington, DC, syndicated columnist.

Roger Angell, 1920-2022, *New Yorker* fiction editor; sports essayist.

Brooks Atkinson, 1894-1984, theater critic.

Robert L. Bartley, 1937-2003, editorial-page editor for *Wall Street Journal*.

Jessie Tarbox Beals, 1870-1942, photojournalist.

James Gordon Bennett, 1795-1872, editor and publisher; founded *NY Herald*.

James Gordon Bennett Jr., 1841-1918, succeeded father, financed expeditions, founded afternoon paper.

Nellie Bly (Elizabeth Cochrane), 1864?-1922, pioneer woman journalist, investigative reporter; noted for series on trip around the world.

Elias Boudinot, c. 1803-39, founding editor of first Native American newspaper in U.S., *Cherokee Phoenix* (1828-34).

Benjamin Bradlee, 1921-2014, *Washington Post* exec. editor.

Ed Bradley, 1941-2006, TV journalist (*60 Minutes*).

Andrew Breitbart, 1969-2012, conservative commentator and blogger.

Jimmy Breslin, 1928-2017, *NY Daily News* columnist.

David Brinkley, 1920-2003, co-anchor of NBC's *Huntley-Brinkley Report*, host of ABC's *This Week With David Brinkley*.

Arthur Brisbane, 1864-1936, editor; helped introduce "yellow journalism" with sensational, simply written articles.

David Broder, 1929-2011, political journalist for *Washington Post*.

Joyce Brothers, 1927-2013, psychologist, columnist.

Heywood Broun, 1888-1939, author, columnist; founded American Newspaper Guild.

Helen Gurley Brown, 1922-2012, author; editor-in-chief of *Cosmopolitan* magazine (1965-97).

Art Buchwald, 1925-2007, journalist, humorist, syndicated columnist.

William F. Buckley Jr., 1925-2008, columnist and commentator; founder of *National Review*.

Herb Caen, 1916-97, longtime columnist for *San Francisco Chronicle* and *Examiner*.

John Campbell, 1653-1728, published *Boston News-Letter*, first continuing newspaper in the American colonies.

Jimmy Cannon, 1909-73, syndicated sports columnist.

John Chancellor, 1927-96, NBC reporter, anchor.

Harry Chandler, 1864-1944, *L.A. Times* publisher (1917-41).

Otis Chandler, 1928-2006, *Los Angeles Times* publisher (1960-80).

Marquis Childs, 1903-90, reporter and columnist for *St. Louis Post-Dispatch* and United Feature syndicate.

Craig Claiborne, 1920-2000, *NY Times* food editor and critic; key in internationalizing American tastes.

Alexander Cockburn, 1941-2012, left-wing journalist.

Charles Collingwood, 1917-85, CBS news correspondent.

Alistair Cooke, 1908-2004, Brit. journalist, TV narrator; naturalized American citizen, "Letter From America" series.

Howard Cosell, 1920-95, TV and radio sportscaster.

Gardner Cowles, 1861-1946, founded newspaper chain.

Judith Crist, 1922-2012, film critic.

Walter Cronkite, 1916-2009, CBS evening news anchor, TV journalist.

Evelyn Cunningham, 1916-2010, African-American civil rights reporter.

Cyrus Curtis, 1850-1933, publisher of *Saturday Evening Post, Ladies' Home Journal, Country Gentleman*.

John Charles Daly, 1914-91, war correspondent, TV journalist; Voice of America head.

Charles Anderson Dana, 1819-97, editor, publisher; made *NY Sun* famous for its news reporting.

Elmer (Holmes) Davis, 1890-1958, *NY Times* editorial writer, radio commentator.

Richard Harding Davis, 1864-1916, war correspondent, travel writer, fiction writer.

Benjamin Day, 1810-89, published *NY Sun* beginning in 1833, introducing penny press to the U.S.

Dorothy Dix (Elizabeth Meriwether Gilmer), 1861-1951, reporter; pioneer of the advice column genre.

Finley Peter Dunne, 1867-1936, humorist, social critic; wrote "Mr. Dooley" columns.

Roger Ebert, 1942-2013, film critic.

Mary Baker Eddy, 1821-1910, founded Christian Science movement and *Christian Science Monitor*.

Rowland Evans Jr., 1921-2001, Washington columnist.

Fanny Fern (Sara Willis Parton), 1811-72, newspaper columnist, author.

Marshall Field III, 1893-1956, retail magnate; *Chicago Sun* founder.

Doris Fleeson, 1901-70, war correspondent, columnist.

Benjamin Franklin, 1706-90, publisher of *Poor Richard's Almanack*.

James Franklin, 1697-1735, printer, pioneer journalist; publisher of *New England Courant* and *Rhode Island Gazette*.

Fred W. Friendly, 1915-98, radio, TV reporter, producer, executive; collaborator with Edward R. Murrow.

Margaret Fuller, 1810-50, social reformer, transcendentalist, critic and foreign correspondent for *NY Tribune*.

Frank E. Gannett, 1876-1957, founded newspaper chain.

Mary Ellen Garber, 1916-2008, sports journalist.

William Lloyd Garrison, 1805-79, abolitionist; publisher of *The Liberator*.

Jack Germond, 1928-2013, political reporter.

Edwin Lawrence Godkin, 1831-1902, founder of *The Nation*, editor of *NY Evening Post*.

Katharine Graham, 1917-2001, *Washington Post* publisher.

Sheilah Graham, 1904-89, Hollywood gossip columnist.

Horace Greeley, 1811-72, editor, politician; founded *NY Tribune*.

Meg Greenfield, 1930-99, *Newsweek* columnist, *Washington Post* editorial page editor.

Gilbert Hovey Grosvenor, 1875-1966, longtime editor of *National Geographic* magazine.

John Gunther, 1901-70, *Chicago Daily News* foreign correspondent, author.

David Halberstam, 1934-2007, journalist, sports reporter, author; *The Best and the Brightest, Summer of '49*.

Sarah Josepha Buell Hale, 1788-1879, first female magazine editor; *Ladies' Magazine*, later *Godey's Lady's Book*.

Pete Hamill, 1935-2020, NY tabloid journalist.

Paul Harvey, 1918-2009, radio broadcaster and commentator.

William Randolph Hearst, 1863-1951, founder of Hearst newspaper chain, one of the pioneers of yellow journalism.

Gabriel Heatter, 1890-1972, radio commentator.

John Hersey, 1914-98, foreign correspondent for *Time, Life*, and *The New Yorker*; author.

Marguerite Higgins, 1920-66, reporter, war correspondent.

Christopher Hitchens, 1949-2011, columnist and literary critic.

Hedda Hopper, 1885-1966, Hollywood gossip columnist.

Tony Horwitz, 1958-2019, author and journalist.

Roy Howard, 1883-1964, editor, executive; Scripps-Howard papers and United Press (later United Press International).

Chet (Chester Robert) Huntley, 1911-74, co-anchor of NBC's *Huntley-Brinkley Report*.

Ada Louise Huxtable, 1921-2013, architecture critic.

Gwen Ifill, 1955-2016, TV journalist.

Ralph Ingersoll, 1900-85, editor; *Fortune, Time, Life* exec.

Molly Ivins, 1944-2007, author, syndicated political columnist.

Peter Jennings, 1938-2005, ABC correspondent, anchor.

Pauline Kael, 1919-2001, film critic.

H. V. (Hans von) Kaltenborn, 1878-1965, radio commentator, reporter.

Murray Kempton, 1917-97, columnist for magazines and newspapers, including *NY Post*.

Dorothy Kilgallen, 1913-65, crime reporter, columnist.

James J. Kilpatrick, 1920-2010, political columnist, author and television personality.

John S. Knight, 1894-1981, editor, publisher; founded Knight newspaper group, which merged into Knight-Ridder.

Joseph Kraft, 1942-86, foreign policy columnist.

Irving Kristol, 1920-2009, columnist, commentator.

Arthur Krock, 1886-1974, *NY Times* political writer, Washington bureau chief.

Charles Kuralt, 1934-97, TV anchor; host of CBS "On the Road" featuring stories about life in the U.S.

Ann Landers (Eppie Lederer), 1918-2002, advice columnist.

David Lawrence, 1888-1973, reporter, columnist, publisher; founded *U.S. News & World Report*.

Jim Lehrer, 1934-2020, television journalist.

Frank Leslie, 1821-80, engraver, publisher of newspapers and magazines, notably *Leslie's Illustrated Newspaper*.

Anthony Lewis, 1927-2013, legal journalist.

Alexander Liberman, 1912-99, editorial director for Condé Nast magazines.

A(bbott) J(oseph) Liebling, 1904-63, foreign correspondent, critic; principally with *The New Yorker*.

Walter Lippmann, 1889-1974, political analyst, social critic, columnist, author.

Peter Lisagor, 1915-76, Washington bureau chief, *Chicago Daily News*; broadcast commentator.

David Ross Locke, 1833-88, humorist, satirist under pseudonym P.V. Nasby; owned *Toledo (Ohio) Blade*.

Elijah Parish Lovejoy, 1802-37, abolitionist editor in St. Louis and in Alton, IL; killed by proslavery mob.

Clare Booth Luce, 1903-87, war correspondent for *Life*, diplomat, playwright.

Henry R. Luce, 1898-1967, founded *Time, Fortune, Life, Sports Illustrated*.

Dwight Macdonald, 1906-82, reporter, social critic.

Don Marquis, 1878-1937, humor columnist for *NY Sun* and *NY Tribune*; wrote "Archy and Mehitabel" stories.

Nancy Hicks Maynard, 1946-2008, African American publisher, journalist.

Robert Maynard, 1937-93, first African-American editor and then owner of major U.S. paper, the *Oakland Tribune*.

C(harles) K(enny) McClatchy, 1858-1936, founder of McClatchy newspaper chain.

Sarah McClendon, 1910-2003, veteran White House correspondent.

Samuel McClure, 1857-1949, founder (1893) of *McClure's Magazine*, famous for its investigative reporting.

Anne O'Hare McCormick, 1889-1954, foreign correspondent; first woman on *NY Times* editorial board.

Robert R. McCormick, 1880-1955, editor, publisher, executive of *Chicago Tribune* and *NY Daily News*.

Ralph McGill, 1893-1969, crusading editor, publisher of *Atlanta Constitution*.

Mary McGrory, 1918-2004, Washington columnist.

O(scar) O(dd) McIntyre, 1884-1938, feature writer, syndicated columnist on everyday life in New York City.

John McLaughlin, 1927-2016, TV journalist.

Joseph Medill, 1823-99, founder of the *Chicago Tribune*.

H(enry) L(ouis) Mencken, 1880-1956, reporter, editor, columnist with *Baltimore Sun* papers; anti-establishment viewpoint.

Edwin Meredith, 1876-1928, founder of magazine company.

Frank A. Munsey, 1854-1925, owner, editor, and publisher of newspapers and magazines, including *Munsey's Magazine*.

Edward R. Murrow, 1908-65, broadcast reporter, exec.; reported from Britain in WWII; hosted *See It Now, Person to Person*.

Allen Neuharth, 1924-2013, *USA Today* founder.

Edwin Newman, 1919-2010, NBC news correspondent.

P. J. O'Rourke, 1947-2022, political satirist.

Louella Parsons, 1881-1972, Hollywood gossip columnist.

Ethel L. Payne, 1911-91, African American civil rights reporter.

Daniel Pearl, 1963-2002, American journalist; kidnapped and murdered in Pakistan.

Drew (Andrew Russell) Pearson, 1897-1969, investigative reporter, columnist.

(James) Westbrook Pegler, 1894-1969, reporter, columnist.

Shirley Povich, 1905-98, sports columnist.

Joseph Pulitzer, 1847-1911, *NY World* publisher; founded Columbia Journalism School, Pulitzer Prizes.

Joseph Pulitzer II, 1885-1955, longtime *St. Louis Post-Dispatch* editor, publisher; built it into major paper.

Ernie Pyle, 1900-45, reporter, war correspondent; killed in WWII.

William Raspberry, 1935-2012, public affairs columnist.

Henry Raymond, 1820-69, cofounder, editor, *NY Times*.

Harry Reasoner, 1923-91, ABC and CBS news reporter, anchor.

John Reed, 1887-1920, reporter; foreign correspondent famous for coverage of Bolshevik Revolution; buried at the Kremlin.

Whitelaw Reid, 1837-1912, longtime editor, *NY Tribune*.

James Reston, 1909-95, *NY Times* political reporter, columnist.

Frank Reynolds, 1923-83, ABC reporter, anchor.

(Henry) Grantland Rice, 1880-1954, sportswriter.

Jacob Riis, 1849-1914, reporter, photographer; exposed slum conditions in *How the Other Half Lives*.

Cokie Roberts, 1943-2019, broadcast journalist.

Max Robinson, 1939-88, first African American to anchor network news (ABC), 1978.

Andy Rooney, 1919-2011, radio and TV commentator (*60 Minutes*).

A. M. Rosenthal, 1922-2006, reporter, editor for *NY Times*, 1943-99.

Harold Ross, 1892-1951, founder, editor, *The New Yorker*.

Carl T. Rowan, 1925-2000, reporter, columnist, author.

Mike Royko, 1932-97, Chicago newspaper columnist; wrote *Boss*, biography of Mayor Richard J. Daley (1902-76).

Louis Rukeyser, 1933-2006, TV journalist, financial analyst; hosted *Wall Street Week* on public television.

(Alfred) Damon Runyon, 1884-1946, sportswriter, columnist; stories collected in *Guys and Dolls*.

Tim Russert, 1950-2008, TV journalist; moderator of *Meet the Press* (NBC).

John B. Russwurm, 1799-1851, cofounded (1827) nation's first Black newspaper, *Freedom's Journal*, in New York, NY.

Morley Safer, 1931-2016, TV journalist (*60 Minutes*).

William Safire, 1929-2009, Pulitzer Prize-winning columnist, *NY Times*.

Adela Rogers St. Johns, 1894-1988, reporter, sportswriter for Hearst newspapers.

Pierre Salinger, 1925-2004, press sec. under Pres. Kennedy and Johnson, foreign correspondent.

Harrison Salisbury, 1908-93, reporter, foreign correspondent; Soviet specialist.

Andrew Sarris, 1928-2012, film critic, *Village Voice*.

Daniel Schorr, 1916-2010, broadcast and print journalist.

E(dward) W(illis) Scripps, 1854-1926, founded first large U.S. newspaper chain, pioneered syndication.

Eric Sevareid, 1912-92, war correspondent, radio newscaster, CBS commentator.

Anthony Shadid, 1968-2012, foreign correspondent.

Randy Shilts, 1951-94, journalist; author of *And the Band Played On*.

William L. Shirer, 1904-93, broadcaster, foreign correspondent; wrote *The Rise and Fall of the Third Reich*.

Howard K. Smith, 1914-2002, ABC news reporter, anchor.

Liz Smith, 1923-2017, gossip columnist.

Red (Walter) Smith, 1905-82, sportswriter.

Edgar P. Snow, 1905-71, correspondent; expert on Chinese Communist movement.

Tony Snow, 1955-2008, columnist, radio/TV journalist, White House press sec.

Tom Snyder, 1936-2007, television journalist.

Lawrence Spivak, 1900-94, co-creator, moderator, producer of *Meet the Press*.

(Joseph) Lincoln Steffens, 1866-1936, muckraking journalist.

I(sidor) F(einstein) Stone, 1907-89, one-man editor of *I. F. Stone's Weekly*.

Arthur Hays Sulzberger, 1891-1968, longtime publisher of *NY Times*, 1935-61.

Arthur Ochs "Punch" Sulzberger, 1926-2012, longtime publisher of *NY Times*, 1963-92.

C(yrus) L(eo) Sulzberger, 1912-93, *NY Times* foreign correspondent, columnist.

David Susskind, 1920-87, TV producer, public affairs talk-show host (*Open End*).

John Cameron Swayze, 1906-95, early TV newscaster (NBC).

Herbert Bayard Swope, 1882-1958, war correspondent, editor of *NY World*.

André Leon Talley, 1949-2022, creative director of *Vogue*.

Ida Tarbell, 1857-1944, muckraking journalist.

Helen Thomas, 1920-2013, White House correspondent, 1959-2010.

Isaiah Thomas, 1750-1831, printer, publisher; cofounder of revolutionary journal, *Massachusetts Spy*.

Lowell Thomas, 1892-1981, radio newscaster, world traveler.

Dorothy Thompson, 1894-1961, foreign correspondent, columnist, radio commentator.

Hunter S. Thompson, 1937-2005, political journalist, author; *Fear and Loathing on the Campaign Trail* (1972).

Kenneth Thompson, 1923-2006, Canadian media magnate; owned Toronto *Globe and Mail* newspaper.

Abigail Van Buren (Pauline Phillips), 1918-2013, advice columnist.

Mike Wallace, 1918-2012, TV journalist (*60 Minutes*).

Barbara Walters, 1929-2022, first woman co-anchor of network evening news (ABC), 1976; co-creator and co-host of *The View*.

Ida Bell Wells-Barnett, 1862-1931, African-American reporter, editor, anti-lynching crusader.

William Allen White, 1868-1944, newspaper editor, publisher.

Tom Wicker, 1926-2011, *NY Times* political reporter, columnist.

Walter Winchell, 1897-1972, reporter, columnist, broadcaster of celebrity news.

John Peter Zenger, 1697-1746, printer, journalist; acquitted in precedent-setting libel suit (1735).

Military and Naval Leaders of the Past

Reviewed by Alan C. Aimone, U.S. Military Academy Library.

Alexander the Great, 356-323 BCE, (Maced.) conquered Persia and much of the world known to Europeans.

Harold Alexander, 1891-1969, (Br.) led Allied invasion of Italy, 1943, WWII.

Ethan Allen, 1738-89, (U.S.) headed Green Mountain Boys; captured Ft. Ticonderoga, 1775, Amer. Rev.

Edmund Allenby, 1861-1936, (Br.) in Boer War, WWI; led Egyptian expeditionary force, 1917-18.

Benedict Arnold, 1741-1801, (U.S.) victorious at Saratoga; tried to betray West Point to British, Amer. Rev.

Henry "Hap" Arnold, 1886-1950, (U.S.) commanded Army Air Force in WWII.

Ashurnasirpal II, 884-859 BCE, (Assyria) king; began Assyrian conquest of Middle East.

John Barry, 1745-1803, (U.S.) won numerous sea battles during Amer. Rev.

Pierre Beauregard, 1818-93, (U.S.) Confed. general; ordered bombardment of Ft. Sumter that began Civil War.

Belisarius, c. 505-565, (Byzant.) won remarkable victories for Byzantine emperor Justinian I.

Black Hawk, 1767-1838, (Amer. Ind.) Sauk war chief.

Gebhard von Blücher, 1742-1819, (Ger.) helped defeat Napoleon at Waterloo.

Simón Bolívar, 1783-1830, (Venez.) S. Amer. revolutionary who liberated much of the continent from Spanish rule.

Edward Braddock, 1695-1755, (Br.) commanded forces in French and Indian War.

Omar N. Bradley, 1893-1981, (U.S.) headed U.S. ground troops in Normandy invasion, 1944, WWII.

John Burgoyne, 1722-92, (Br.) general; defeated at Saratoga, Amer. Rev.

Julius Caesar, 100-44 BCE, (Rom.) general and politician; conquered northern Gaul, overthrew Roman Republic.

Charlemagne, 742-814, (Fr.) king of the Franks, Holy Roman Emperor; conquered most of Western Europe.

Claire Lee Chennault, 1893-1958, (U.S.) headed Flying Tigers in WWII.

El Cid (Rodrigo Diaz de Vivar), 1040-99, (Sp.) renowned knight; captured Valencia (1094), hero of "Song of Cid" epic.

Mark W. Clark, 1896-1984, (U.S.) helped plan N African invasion in WWII; commander of UN forces, Korean War.

Karl von Clausewitz, 1780-1831, (Prus.) military theorist.

Lucius D. Clay, 1897-1978, (U.S.) led Berlin airlift, 1948-49.

Henry Clinton, 1738-95, (Br.) commander of forces in Amer. Rev., 1778-81.

Cochise, c. 1815-74, (Amer. Ind.) chief of Chiricahua band of Apache Indians in Southwest U.S.

Charles Cornwallis, 1738-1805, (Br.) victorious at Brandywine, 1777; surrendered at Yorktown, Amer. Rev.

Hernán Cortés, 1485-1547, (Sp.) led Spanish conquistadors in the defeat of the Aztec empire, 1519-28.

Crazy Horse, 1849-77, (Amer. Ind.) Sioux war chief victorious at Battle of the Little Bighorn.

George Armstrong Custer, 1839-76, (U.S.) army officer defeated and killed at Battle of the Little Bighorn.

Benjamin O. Davis Jr., 1912-2002, (U.S.) leader of WWII Black aviators; first African American general in U.S. Air Force.

Benjamin O. Davis Sr., 1877-1970, (U.S.) first African American general in U.S. Army, 1940.

Moshe Dayan, 1915-81, (Isr.) directed campaigns in the 1967, 1973 Arab-Israeli wars.

Stephen Decatur, 1779-1820, (U.S.) naval hero of Barbary wars, War of 1812.

Anton Denikin, 1872-1947, (Russ.) led White forces in Russian civil war.

George Dewey, 1837-1917, (U.S.) destroyed Spanish fleet at Manila, 1898, Span.-Amer. War.

Karl Doenitz, 1891-1980, (Ger.) submarine cmdr. in chief and naval cmdr., WWII; last pres. of Third Reich.

Jimmy Doolittle, 1896-1993, (U.S.) led 1942 air raid on Tokyo and other Japanese cities in WWII.

Hugh Dowding, 1882-1970, (Br.) headed RAF Fighter Command, 1936-40, WWII.

Jubal Early, 1816-94, (U.S.) Confed. general; led raid on Washington, DC, 1864, Civil War.

Dwight D. Eisenhower, 1890-1969, (U.S.) commanded Allied forces in Europe, WWII.

Erich von Falkenhayn, 1861-1922, (Ger.) minister of war, general, commander at Verdun in WWI.

David Farragut, 1801-70, (U.S.) Union admiral; captured New Orleans, Mobile Bay, Civil War.

John Arbuthnot Fisher, 1841-1920, (Br.) WWI admiral; naval reformer.

Ferdinand Foch, 1851-1929, (Fr.) headed victorious Allied armies, 1918, WWI.

Nathan Bedford Forrest, 1821-77, (U.S.) Confed. general; led raids against Union supply lines, Civil War.

Frederick the Great, 1712-86, (Prus.) led Prussia in Seven Years' War.

Horatio Gates, 1728-1806, (U.S.) commanded army at Saratoga, Amer. Rev.

Genghis Khan, 1162-1227, (Mongol) unified Mongol tribes, subjugated much of Asia, 1206-21.

Geronimo, 1829-1909, (Amer. Ind.) leader of Chiricahua band of Apache Indians.

Vo Nguyen Giap, 1911?-2013, (Viet.) commanded People's Army of Vietnam against U.S.

Charles G. Gordon, 1833-85, (Br.) led forces in China, Crimean War; killed at Khartoum, Sudan.

Ulysses S. Grant, 1822-85, (U.S.) headed Union army, Civil War, 1864-65; forced Robert E. Lee's surrender, 1865.

Nathanael Greene, 1742-86, (U.S.) defeated British in Southern campaign, 1780-81, Amer. Rev.

Heinz Guderian, 1888-1954, (Ger.) tank theorist; led panzer tank forces in Poland, France, Russia, WWII.

Gustavus Adolphus, 1594-1632, (Swed.) king, military tactician, reformer; led forces in Thirty Years' War.

Douglas Haig, 1861-1928, (Br.) led British armies in France, 1915-18, WWI.

William F. Halsey, 1882-1959, (U.S.) defeated Japanese fleet at Leyte Gulf, 1944, WWII.

Hannibal, 247-183 BCE, (Carthage) invaded Rome, crossing Alps, in Second Punic War, 218-201 BCE.

Arthur Travers Harris, 1895-1984, (Br.) led Britain's WWII bomber command.

Paul von Hindenburg, 1847-1934, (Ger.) chief of general staff, WWI; second pres. of Weimar Republic.

Richard Howe, 1726-99, (Br.) commanded navy in Amer. Rev., 1776-78; June 1 victory against French, 1794.

William Howe, 1729-1814, (Br.) commanded forces in Amer. Rev., 1776-78.

Isaac Hull, 1773-1843, (U.S.) sunk British frigate *Guerriere*, War of 1812.

Thomas "Stonewall" Jackson, 1824-63, (U.S.) Confed. general; led Shenandoah Valley campaign, Civil War.

Daniel James Jr., 1920-78, (U.S.) first Black 4-star general, 1975; commander, N. American Air Defense Command.

Joseph Joffre, 1852-1931, (Fr.) headed Allied armies; won Battle of the Marne, 1914, WWI.

John Paul Jones, 1747-92, (U.S.) commanded *Bonhomme Richard* in victory over *Serapis*, Amer. Rev., 1779.

Chief Joseph, c. 1840-1904, (Amer. Ind.) chief of the Nez Percé; forced by U.S. army to retreat and surrender.

Stephen Kearny, 1794-1848, (U.S.) headed Army of the West in Mexican War.

Albert Kesselring, 1885-1960, (Ger.) field marshal who led the defense of Italy in WWII.

Ernest J. King, 1878-1956, (U.S.) key WWII naval strategist.

Horatio H. Kitchener, 1850-1916, (Br.) led forces in Boer War, victorious at Khartoum, organized army in WWI.

Henry Knox, 1750-1806, (U.S.) general in Amer. Rev.; first sec. of war under U.S. Constitution.

Lavrenti Kornilov, 1870-1918, (Russ.) commander-in-chief, 1917; led counterrevolutionary march on Petrograd.

Thaddeus Kosciuszko, 1746-1817, (Pol.) aided Amer. Rev.

Walter Krueger, 1881-1967, (U.S.) led Sixth Army in WWII in Southwest Pacific.

Mikhail Kutuzov, 1745-1813, (Russ.) fought at Borodino, Napol. Wars, 1812; abandoned Moscow, forced French retreat.

Marquis de Lafayette, 1757-1834, (Fr.) fought in, secured French aid for Amer. Rev.

T(homas) E. Lawrence (of Arabia), 1888-1935, (Br.) organized revolt of Arabs against Turks in WWI.

William Daniel Leahy, 1875-1959, (U.S.) chief of staff to Pres. Roosevelt in WWII, Fleet Admiral.

Henry (Light-Horse Harry) Lee, 1756-1818, (U.S.) cavalry officer in Amer. Rev.

Robert E. Lee, 1807-70, (U.S.) Confed. general; defeated at Gettysburg, Civil War; surrendered to Grant, 1865.

Curtis LeMay, 1906-90, (U.S.) Air Force cmdr. in WWII, Korean War, Vietnam War.

Lyman Lemnitzer, 1899-1988, (U.S.) WWII hero; later general, chairman of Joint Chiefs of Staff.

James Longstreet, 1821-1904, (U.S.) aided Lee at Gettysburg, Civil War.

Erich Ludendorff, 1865-1937, (Ger.) general; victor at Tannenberg, WWI.

Douglas MacArthur, 1880-1964, (U.S.) commanded forces in SW Pacific in WWII; headed occupation forces in Japan, 1945-51; UN commander in Korean War.

Carl Gustaf Mannerheim, 1867-1951, (Fin.) army officer and pres. of Finland, 1944-46.

Erich von Manstein, 1887-1973, (Ger.) served WWI, WWII; planned invasion of France (1940); convicted of war crimes.

Francis Marion, 1733-95, (U.S.) led guerrilla actions in South Carolina during Amer. Rev.

Duke of Marlborough, 1650-1722, (Br.) led forces against Louis XIV in War of the Spanish Succession.

George C. Marshall, 1880-1959, (U.S.) chief of staff in WWII; authored Marshall Plan.

Maurice, Count of Nassau, 1567-1625, (Neth.) military innovator; led forces in Thirty Years' War.

George B. McClellan, 1826-85, (U.S.) Union general; commanded Army of the Potomac, 1861-62, Civil War.

George Meade, 1815-72, (U.S.) commanded Union forces at Gettysburg, Civil War.

Doris "Dorie" Miller, 1919-43, (U.S.) Navy hero of Pearl Harbor attack; first African American awarded Navy Cross.

Billy Mitchell, 1879-1936, (U.S.) WWI airpower advocate; court-martialed for insubordination, later vindicated.

Helmuth von Moltke, 1800-91, (Ger.) victorious in Austro-Prussian, Franco-Prussian wars.

Louis de Montcalm, 1712-59, (Fr.) headed troops in Canada, French and Indian War; defeated at Quebec, 1759.

Bernard Law Montgomery, 1887-1976, (Br.) stopped German offensive at Alamein, 1942, WWII; helped plan Normandy invasion.

Daniel Morgan, 1736-1802, (U.S.) victorious at Cowpens, 1781, Amer. Rev.

Louis Mountbatten, 1900-79, (Br.) Supreme Allied Commander of SE Asia, 1943-46, WWII.

Joachim Murat, 1767-1815, (Fr.) led cavalry at Marengo, Austerlitz, and Jena, Napoleonic Wars.

Napoleon Bonaparte, 1769-1821, (Fr.) defeated Russia and Austria at Austerlitz, 1805; invaded Russia, 1812; defeated at Waterloo, 1815.

Horatio Nelson, 1758-1805, (Br.) naval cmdr.; destroyed French fleet at Trafalgar.

Michel Ney, 1769-1815, (Fr.) commanded forces in Switz., Austria, Russ., Napoleonic Wars; defeated at Waterloo.

Chester Nimitz, 1885-1966, (U.S.) cmdr. of naval forces in Pacific in WWII.

Osceola, 1804-38, (Amer. Ind.) war leader of Seminole people of Florida.

George S. Patton, 1885-1945, (U.S.) led assault on Sicily, 1943, Third Army invasion of Europe, WWII.

Oliver Perry, 1785-1819, (U.S.) won Battle of Lake Erie in War of 1812.

John Pershing, 1860-1948, (U.S.) commanded Mexican border campaign, 1916; Amer. Expeditionary Force, WWI.

Henri Philippe Pétain, 1856-1951, (Fr.) defended Verdun, 1916; headed Vichy government in WWII.

George E. Pickett, 1825-75, (U.S.) Confed. general famed for "charge" at Gettysburg, Civil War.

Pontiac, 1720?-69, (Amer. Ind.) Ottawa war chief.

Charles Portal, 1893-1971, (Br.) chief of staff, Royal Air Force, 1940-45; led in Battle of Britain.

Colin Powell, 1937-2021, (U.S.) army general, chair of the Joint Chiefs of Staff; first Black sec. of state.

Manfred Freiherr von Richthofen (Red Baron), 1892-1918, (Ger.) WWI flying ace, led elite fighter squadron.

Hyman Rickover, 1900-86, (U.S.) father of nuclear navy.

Matthew Bunker Ridgway, 1895-1993, (U.S.) commanded Allied ground forces in Korean War.

Erwin Rommel, 1891-1944, (Ger.) headed Afrika Korps, WWII.

Gerd von Rundstedt, 1875-1953, (Ger.) supreme cmdr. in West, 1942-45, WWII.

Saladin, 1138-93, (Kurdish Muslim) recaptured Jerusalem from Crusaders.

Aleksandr Samsonov, 1859-1914, (Russ.) led invasion of E Prussia, WWI; defeated at Tannenberg, 1914.

Antonio López de Santa Anna, 1794-1876, (Mex.) defeated Texans at the Alamo; defeated in Mexican War.

Maurice, Count of Saxe, 1696-1750, (Fr.) general, noted tactician; War of Austrian Succession, War of Pol. Succession.

H. Norman Schwarzkopf, 1934-2012, (U.S.) army general; led Persian Gulf War, 1991.

Scipio Africanus the Elder, 234?-183 BCE, (Roman) hero of Second Punic War; defeated Hannibal, invaded N Africa.

Winfield Scott, 1786-1866, (U.S.) hero of War of 1812; headed forces in Mexican War, took Mexico City.

Philip Sheridan, 1831-88, (U.S.) Union cavalry officer; headed Army of the Shenandoah, 1864-65, Civil War.

William T. Sherman, 1820-91, (U.S.) Union general; sacked Atlanta during "march to the sea," 1864, Civil War.

Sitting Bull, c. 1831-90, (Amer. Ind.) Hunkpapa Lakota chief victorious at Battle of the Little Bighorn.

Carl Spaatz, 1891-1974, (U.S.) directed strategic bombing against Germany, later Japan, in WWII.

Raymond Spruance, 1886-1969, (U.S.) victorious at Midway Island, 1942, WWII.

Joseph W. Stilwell, 1883-1946, (U.S.) headed forces in the China, Burma, India theater in WWII.

J.E.B. Stuart, 1833-64, (U.S.) Confed. cavalry commander, Civil War.

Sun Tzu, 6th? cent. BCE, (China) general; author of *The Art of War*.

Aleksandr Suvorov, 1729-1800, (Russ.) commanded Allied Russian and Austrian armies, Russo-Turkish War.

Tamerlane, 1336-1405, (Turkoman Mongol) conqueror; established empire from India to Mediterranean Sea.

Tecumseh, 1768-1813, (Amer. Ind.) Shawnee chief; led Indian confederation opposing colonists.

George H. Thomas, 1816-70, (U.S.) saved Union army at Chattanooga, 1863; won at Nashville, 1864, Civil War.

Semyon Timoshenko, 1895-1970, (USSR) defended Moscow, Stalingrad, WWII; led winter offensive, 1942-43.

Alfred von Tirpitz, 1849-1930, (Ger.) responsible for submarine blockade in WWI.

Henri de la Tour d'Auvergne, Viscount of Turenne, 1611-75, (Fr.) marshal; Thirty Years' War, Fronde, War of Devolution.

Sebastien Le Prestre de Vauban, 1633-1707, (Fr.) innovative military engineer, theorist.

Jonathan M. Wainwright, 1883-1953, (U.S.) forced to surrender on Corregidor, Philippines, 1942, WWII.

George Washington, 1732-99, (U.S.) led Continental army, 1775-83, Amer. Rev.

Archibald Wavell, 1883-1950, (Br.) commanded forces in N and E Africa, SE Asia in WWII.

Anthony Wayne, 1745-96, (U.S.) captured Stony Point, NY, 1779, Amer. Rev.

Duke of Wellington, 1769-1852, (Br.) defeated Napoleon at Waterloo, 1815.

William Westmoreland, 1914-2005, (U.S.) commanded forces in Vietnam, 1964-68.

William I (The Conqueror), 1027-87, (Br.) victor, Battle of Hastings, 1066; became first Norman king of England.

James Wolfe, 1727-59, (Br.) captured Quebec from French, 1759, French and Indian War.

Isoroku Yamamoto, 1884-1943, (Jpn.) cmdr. in chief of Japanese fleet; naval planner before and during WWII.

Georgi Zhukov, 1895-1974, (Russ.) defended Moscow, 1941; led assault on Berlin, 1945, WWII.

Philosophers and Religious Figures of the Past

Excludes biblical figures and popes (see Religion chapter). For Greeks and Romans, see also Historical Figures chapter.

Lyman Abbott, 1835-1922, (U.S.) clergyman, reformer; advocate of Christian Socialism.

Pierre Abelard, 1079-1142, (Fr.) philosopher, theologian, teacher; used dialectic method to support Christian beliefs.

Felix Adler, 1851-1933, (U.S.) German-born founder of the Ethical Culture Soc.

Mortimer Adler, 1902-2001, (U.S.) philosopher; helped create "Great Books" program.

(St.) Anselm, c. 1033-1109, (It.) philosopher-theologian, church leader; "ontological argument" for God's existence.

(St.) Thomas Aquinas, 1225-74, (It.) pre-eminent medieval philosopher-theologian; *Summa Theologica*.

Aristotle, 384-322 BCE, (Gr.) pioneering wide-ranging philosopher, logician, ethician, naturalist.

(St.) Augustine, 354-430, (N Africa) philosopher, theologian, bishop; *Confessions, City of God, On the Trinity*.

J. L. Austin, 1911-60, (Br.) ordinary-language philosopher.

Averroes (Ibn Rushd), 1126-98, (Sp.) Islamic philosopher, physician.

Avicenna (Ibn Sina), 980-1037, (Iran) Islamic philosopher, scientist.

A(lfred) J(ules) Ayer, 1910-89, (Br.) philosopher, logical positivist; *Language, Truth, and Logic*.

Roger Bacon, c. 1214-94, (Eng.) philosopher, scientist.

Bahá'u'lláh (Mirza Husayn Ali), 1817-92, (Pers.) founder of Bahá'í faith.

Karl Barth, 1886-1968, (Switz.) theologian; a leading force in 20th-cent. Protestantism.

Thomas à Becket, 1118-70, (Eng.) archbishop of Canterbury; opposed Henry II, murdered by king's men.

(St.) Benedict, c. 480-547, (It.) founded the Benedictine order.

Jeremy Bentham, 1748-1832, (Br.) philosopher, reformer; enunciated utilitarianism.

Henri Bergson, 1859-1941, (Fr.) philosopher of evolution.

George Berkeley, 1685-1753, (Ire.) idealist philosopher, bishop.

John Biddle, 1615-62, (Eng.) founder of English Unitarianism.

Jakob Boehme, 1575-1624, (Ger.) theosophist, mystic.

Dietrich Bonhoeffer, 1906-45, (Ger.) Lutheran theologian, pastor; executed as opponent of Nazis.

William Brewster, 1567-1644, (Eng.) *Mayflower* passenger, Plymouth Colony leader.

Emil Brunner, 1889-1966, (Switz.) Protestant theologian.

Giordano Bruno, 1548-1600, (It.) philosopher, pantheist.

Martin Buber, 1878-1965, (Ger.) Jewish philosopher, theologian; *I and Thou*.

Buddha (Siddhartha Gautama), c. 563-c. 483 BCE, (India) philosopher; founded Buddhism.

John Calvin, 1509-64, (Fr.) theologian; a key figure in the Protestant Reformation.

Rudolph Carnap, 1891-1970, (U.S.) German-born analytic philosopher; a founder of logical positivism.

William Ellery Channing, 1780-1842, (U.S.) clergyman; early spokesman for Unitarianism.

Auguste Comte, 1798-1857, (Fr.) philosopher; originated positivism.

Confucius, 551-479 BCE, (China) founder of Confucianism.

John Cotton, 1584-1652, (Eng.) Puritan theologian.

Thomas Cranmer, 1489-1556, (Eng.) Anglican churchman; wrote much of *Book of Common Prayer*.

Jacques Derrida, 1930-2004, (Fr.) deconstructionist philosopher.

René Descartes, 1596-1650, (Fr.) philosopher, mathematician; "father of modern philosophy"; *Discourse on Method, Meditations on First Philosophy*.

John Dewey, 1859-1952, (U.S.) philosopher, educator; instrumentalist theory of knowledge, progressive education.

Denis Diderot, 1713-84, (Fr.) philosopher, encyclopedist.

John Duns Scotus, c. 1266-1308, (Scot.) Franciscan philosopher, theologian.

Mary Baker Eddy, 1821-1910, (U.S.) founder of Christian Science; *Science and Health*.

Jonathan Edwards, 1703-58, (U.S.) preacher, theologian; "Sinners in the Hands of an Angry God."

(Desiderius) Erasmus, c. 1466-1536, (Neth.) Renaissance humanist; *On the Freedom of the Will*.

Jerry Falwell, 1933-2007, (U.S.) TV evangelist, religious commentator.

Johann Fichte, 1762-1814, (Ger.) idealist philosopher.

Michel Foucault, 1926-84, (Fr.) structuralist philosopher, historian.

George Fox, 1624-91, (Br.) founder of Society of Friends (Quakers).

(St.) Francis of Assisi, 1182-1226, (It.) espoused voluntary poverty, founded Franciscans order.

al-Ghazali, 1058-1111, (Iran) Islamic philosopher.

Billy Graham, 1918-2018, (U.S.) evangelist, adviser to presidents.

Billy James Hargis, 1925-2004, (U.S.) anti-Communist televangelist; founder of the Church of the Christian Crusade.

Georg W. F. Hegel, 1770-1831, (Ger.) idealist philosopher; *Phenomenology of Mind*.

Martin Heidegger, 1889-1976, (Ger.) existentialist philosopher; affected many fields; *Being and Time*.

Johann G. Herder, 1744-1803, (Ger.) philosopher, cultural historian; a founder of German Romanticism.

Thomas Hobbes, 1588-1679, (Eng.) philosopher, political theorist; *Leviathan*.

L. Ron Hubbard, 1911-1986, (U.S.) founder of Scientology.

David Hume, 1711-76, (Scot.) empiricist philosopher; *Enquiry Concerning Human Understanding*.

Jan Hus, 1369-1415, (Czech.) religious reformer.

Edmund Husserl, 1859-1938, (Ger.) philosopher; founded the phenomenological movement.

Thomas Huxley, 1825-95, (Br.) philosopher, educator.

William Ralph Inge, 1860-1954, (Br.) theologian; explored mystic aspects of Christianity.

William James, 1842-1910, (U.S.) philosopher, psychologist, pragmatist; studied religious experience.

Karl Jaspers, 1883-1969, (Ger.) existentialist philosopher.

Joan of Arc, 1412-31, (Fr.) national heroine, a patron saint of France; key figure in the Hundred Years' War.

Immanuel Kant, 1724-1804, (Ger.) philosopher; founder of modern critical philosophy; *Critique of Pure Reason*.

Thomas à Kempis, c. 1380-1471, (Ger.) monk, devotional writer; *Imitation of Christ* attributed to him.

Soren Kierkegaard, 1813-55, (Den.) religious philosopher, pre-existentialist; *Either/Or, The Sickness Unto Death*.

John Knox, 1505-72, (Scot.) leader of Protestant Reformation in Scotland.

Hans Küng, 1928-2021, (Switz.) Catholic priest and theologian.

Lao-Tzu, 604-531 BCE, (China) philosopher; considered the founder of the Taoist religion.

Gottfried von Leibniz, 1646-1716, (Ger.) rationalistic philosopher, logician, mathematician.

John Locke, 1632-1704, (Eng.) political theorist, empiricist philosopher; *Essay Concerning Human Understanding*.

(St.) Ignatius Loyola, 1491-1556, (Sp.) founder of the Jesuits; *Spiritual Exercises*.

Martin Luther, 1483-1546, (Ger.) leader of the Protestant Reformation; founded Lutheran church.

Jean-Francois Lyotard, 1924-98, (Fr.) postmodern philosopher, lecturer; *The Post-Modern Condition*.

Maimonides, 1135-1204, (Sp.) major Jewish philosopher.

Gabriel Marcel, 1889-1973, (Fr.) Rom. Cath. existentialist philosopher, dramatist.

Jacques Maritain, 1882-1973, (Fr.) neo-Thomist philosopher.

Cotton Mather, 1663-1728, (U.S.) defender of orthodox Puritanism; founded Yale, 1701.

Aimee Semple McPherson, 1890-1944, (Can.-U.S.) Pentecostal evangelist.

Philipp Melanchthon, 1497-1560, (Ger.) theologian, humanist; an important voice in the Reformation.

Maurice Merleau-Ponty, 1908-61, (Fr.) existentialist philosopher; *Phenomenology of Perception*.

Thomas Merton, 1915-68, (U.S.) Trappist monk, spiritual writer; *The Seven Story Mountain*.

Dwight Moody, 1837-99, (U.S.) evangelist.

Rev. Sun Myung Moon, 1920-2012, (N. Kor.) Unification Church founder.

G(eorge) E(dward) Moore, 1873-1958, (Br.) philosopher; *Principia Ethica*, "A Defense of Common Sense."

Muhammad, c. 570-632, (Arab.) prophet of Islam.

Elijah Muhammad, 1897-1975, (U.S.) founder of Black Muslim group, Nation of Islam.

Heinrich Muhlenberg, 1711-87, (Ger.) organized the Lutheran Church in America.

John H. Newman, 1801-90, (Br.) Rom. Cath. convert, cardinal; led Oxford Movement; *Apologia pro Vita Sua*.

Thích Nhat Hanh, 1926-2022, (Viet.) Buddhist monk ("father of mindfulness").

Reinhold Niebuhr, 1892-1971, (U.S.) Protestant theologian.

Richard Niebuhr, 1894-1962, (U.S.) Protestant theologian.

Friedrich Nietzsche, 1844-1900, (Ger.) philosopher; *The Birth of Tragedy, Beyond Good and Evil, Thus Spake Zarathustra*.

Robert Nozick, 1938-2002, (U.S.) political philosopher; *Anarchy, State, and Utopia*.

Blaise Pascal, 1623-62, (Fr.) philosopher, mathematician; *Pensées (Thoughts)*.

(St.) Patrick, c. 389-c. 461, (Br.) brought Christianity to Ireland.

Norman Vincent Peale, 1898-1993, (U.S.) minister, author; *The Power of Positive Thinking*.

C(harles) S. Peirce, 1839-1914, (U.S.) philosopher, logician; originated concept of pragmatism, 1878.

Plato, c. 428-347 BCE, (Gr.) philosopher; wrote Socratic dialogues; argued for

immortality of soul, indep. reality of ideas or forms; *Republic, Meno, Phaedo, Apology*.

Plotinus, 205-70, (Rom.) a founder of neo-Platonism; *Enneads*.

W(illard) V(an) O(rman) Quine, 1908-2001, (U.S.) philosopher, logician; "On What There Is."

John Rawls, 1922-2002, (U.S.) political philosopher; *A Theory of Justice*.

Oral Roberts, 1918-2009, (U.S.) televangelist, university founder.

Pat Robertson, 1930-2023, (U.S.) TV evangelist; founder of Christian Broadcasting Network, Christian Coalition.

Moishe Rosen, 1932-2010, (U.S.) Jews for Jesus founder.

Josiah Royce, 1855-1916, (U.S.) idealist philosopher.

Bertrand Russell, 1872-1970, (Br.) philosopher, logician; one of the founders of modern logic; prolific popular writer.

Charles T. Russell, 1852-1916, (U.S.) founder of Jehovah's Witnesses.

Gilbert Ryle, 1900-76, (Br.) analytic philosopher; *The Concept of Mind*.

George Santayana, 1863-1952, (U.S.) philosopher, writer, critic; *The Sense of Beauty, The Realms of Being*.

Jean-Paul Sartre, 1905-80, (Fr.) philosopher, novelist, playwright; *Nausea, No Exit, Being and Nothingness*.

Friedrich von Schelling, 1775-1854, (Ger.) philosopher of romantic movement.

Friedrich Schleiermacher, 1768-1834, (Ger.) theologian; a founder of modern Protestant theology.

Arthur Schopenhauer, 1788-1860, (Ger.) philosopher; *The World as Will and Idea*.

Robert Schuller, 1926-2015, (U.S.) evangelist; Crystal Cathedral founder.

Albert Schweitzer, 1875-1965, (Ger.) theologian, social philosopher, medical missionary.

Joseph Smith, 1805-44, (U.S.) founded Latter-Day Saints (Mormon) movement, 1830.

Socrates, 469-399 BCE, (Gr.) philosopher immortalized by Plato.

Herbert Spencer, 1820-1903, (Br.) philosopher of evolution.

Herbert Spiegel, 1914-2009, (U.S.) psychiatrist who popularized hypnosis.

Baruch de Spinoza, 1632-77, (Neth.) rationalist philosopher; *Ethics*.

John Stott, 1921-2011, (Br.) evangelical Anglican cleric.

Billy Sunday, 1862-1935, (U.S.) evangelist.

Daisetz Teitaro Suzuki, 1870-1966, (Jpn.) Buddhist scholar.

Emanuel Swedenborg, 1688-1772, (Swed.) philosopher, mystic; *Principia*.

Pierre Teilhard de Chardin, 1881-1955, (Fr.) Jesuit priest, paleontologist, philosopher-theologian; *The Divine Milieu*.

(St.) Therese of Lisieux, 1873-97, (Fr.) Carmelite nun ("Little Flower"), revered for everyday sanctity; *The Story of a Soul*.

Paul Tillich, 1886-1965, (U.S.) German-born philosopher, theologian; brought depth psychology to Protestantism.

John Wesley, 1703-91, (Br.) theologian, evangelist; founded Methodism.

Alfred North Whitehead, 1861-1947, (Br.) philosopher, mathematician; *Process and Reality*.

William of Occam, c. 1285-c. 1349, (Eng.) medieval scholastic philosopher, nominalist.

Roger Williams, c. 1603-83, (U.S.) clergyman; championed religious freedom and separation of church and state.

Ludwig Wittgenstein, 1889-1951, (Austria) philosopher; major influence on contemporary language philosophy; *Tractatus Logico-Philosophicus, Philosophical Investigations*.

John Woolman, 1720-72, (U.S.) Quaker social reformer, abolitionist, writer; *The Journal*.

John Wycliffe, 1320-84, (Eng.) theologian, reformer.

(St.) Francis Xavier, 1506-52, (Sp.) Jesuit missionary; "Apostle of the Indies."

Brigham Young, 1801-77, (U.S.) Mormon leader after Joseph Smith's death; colonized Utah.

Huldrych Zwingli, 1484-1531, (Switz.) theologian; led Swiss Protestant Reformation.

Political Leaders of the Past

U.S. presidents, vice presidents, Supreme Court justices, and signers of the Declaration of Independence listed elsewhere. See also Historical Figures.

Shinzo Abe, 1954-2022, (Jpn.) prime minister.

Abu Bakr, 573-634, (Arab.) Muslim leader, first caliph, chosen successor to Muhammad.

Dean Acheson, 1893-1971, (U.S.) sec. of state; architect of Cold War foreign policy.

Samuel Adams, 1722-1803, (U.S.) patriot; Boston Tea Party firebrand.

Konrad Adenauer, 1876-1967, (Ger.) first West German chancellor.

Emilio Aguinaldo, 1869-1964, (Philip.) revolutionary; fought against Spain and the U.S.

Akbar, 1542-1605, Mogul emperor of India.

Madeleine Albright, 1937-2022, (Czech.-U.S.) first woman U.S. sec. of state.

Salvador Allende Gossens, 1908-73, (Chile) Marxist pres., 1970-73; ousted and died in coup.

Idi Amin, 1925-2003, (Uganda) Ugandan ruler, 1971-79; blamed for hundreds of thousands of deaths.

Kofi Annan, 1938-2018, (Ghana) UN sec.- gen.

Corazon Aquino, 1933-2009, (Philip.) pres. of the Philippines, 1986-92.

Yasir Arafat, 1929-2004, (Egypt) leader of the Palestine Liberation Organization (PLO).

Herbert H. Asquith, 1852-1928, (Br.) Liberal prime min.; instituted major social reforms.

Hafez al Assad, 1930-2000, (Syr.) pres. of Syria, 1970-2000.

Atahualpa, 1500?-33, (Inca) last ruling chief of Incan empire (in present-day Peru).

Kemal Atatürk, 1881-1938, (Turk.) founded modern Turkey.

Clement Attlee, 1883-1967, (Br.) Labour leader, prime min.; enacted natl. health service, nationalized many industries.

Stephen F. Austin, 1793-1836, (U.S.) led Texas colonization.

Mikhail Bakunin, 1814-76, (Russ.) revolutionary; leading exponent of anarchism.

Arthur J. Balfour, 1848-1930, (Br.) foreign sec. under Lloyd George; issued Balfour Declaration backing Zionism.

Bernard M. Baruch, 1870-1965, (U.S.) financier, govt. adviser.

Fulgencio Batista y Zaldívar, 1901-73, (Cuba) Cuban pres., 1940-44, 1952-59; overthrown by Castro.

Menachem Begin, 1913-92, (Isr.) Israeli prime min.; shared 1978 Nobel Peace Prize.

Ahmed Ben Bella, 1918-2012, (Alg.) first Algerian pres., 1963-65.

Eduard Benes, 1884-1948, (Czech.) pres. during interwar and post-WWII eras.

David Ben-Gurion, 1886-1973, (Isr.) first prime min. of Israel, 1948-53, 1955-63.

Thomas Hart Benton, 1782-1858, (U.S.) MO senator; championed agrarian interests and westward expansion.

Ernest Bevin, 1881-1951, (Br.) Labour party leader, foreign minister; helped lay foundation for NATO.

King Bhumibol Adulyadej, 1927-2016, (Thai.) monarch, 1946-2016.

Benazir Bhutto, 1953-2007, (Pak.) Pakistan prime min.; first elected woman leader of a majority-Muslim country.

Otto von Bismarck, 1815-98, (Ger.) statesman known as the Iron Chancellor; uniter of Germany, 1870.

Black Kettle, 1803?-68, (Amer. Ind.) Cheyenne peace chief.

James G. Blaine, 1830-93, (U.S.) Republican politician, diplomat; influential in Pan-American movement.

Léon Blum, 1872-1950, (Fr.) socialist leader, writer; headed first Popular Front government.

William E. Borah, 1865-1940, (U.S.) isolationist senator (R, ID); helped block U.S. membership in League of Nations.

Cesare Borgia, 1476-1507, (It.) soldier, politician; Italian Renaissance figure who partly inspired Machiavelli's *The Prince*.

P. W. Botha, 1916-2006, (S. Afr.) S. African president, prime min.

Boutros Boutros-Ghali, 1922-2016, (Egypt), UN sec.-gen.

Willy Brandt, 1913-92, (Ger.) statesman, chancellor of West Germany, 1969-74; promoted East/West peace, *Ostpolitik*.

Joseph Brant, 1742-1807, (Amer. Ind.) Mohawk chief.

Leonid Brezhnev, 1906-82, (USSR) Soviet leader, 1964-82.

Aristide Briand, 1862-1932, (Fr.) foreign min.; chief architect of Locarno Pact and anti-war Kellogg-Briand Pact.

William Jennings Bryan, 1860-1925, (U.S.) Democratic, populist leader, orator; three times lost race for presidency.

Ralph Bunche, 1904-71, (U.S.) first Black person to win the Nobel Peace Prize, 1950; undersecretary of the UN, 1950.

Robert Byrd, 1917-2010, (U.S.) longest serving U.S. senator (D, WV), 1959-2010.

John C. Calhoun, 1782-1850, (U.S.) political leader; champion of states' rights and a symbol of the Old South.

James Callaghan (Baron Callaghan), 1912-2005, (Br.) Labour party politician, prime min., 1976-79.

Robert Castlereagh, 1769-1822, (Br.) foreign sec.; guided Grand Alliance against Napoleon.

Fidel Castro, 1926-2016, (Cuba) prime min./pres., 1959-2008; led Communist revolution.

Camillo Benso Cavour, 1810-61, (It.) statesman; largely responsible for uniting Italy under the House of Savoy.

Nicolae Ceausescu, 1918-89, (Rom.) Communist leader, head of state, 1967-89; executed.

Neville Chamberlain, 1869-1940, (Br.) Conservative prime min. whose appeasement of Hitler led to Munich Pact.

Hugo Chávez, 1954-2013, (Venez.) socialist Venezuelan pres., 1999-2013.

Chiang Kai-shek, 1887-1975, (China) Nationalist Chinese pres. whose govt. was driven from mainland to Taiwan.

Madame Chiang Kai-shek (Mayling Soong), 1898-2003, (China) highly influential wife of Nationalist Chinese leader Chiang Kai-shek.

Jacques Chirac, 1932-2019, (Fr.) pres. of France, 1995-2007.

Shirley Chisholm, 1924-2005, (U.S.) first Black woman elected to U.S. House (1968, D, NY); pres. contender, 1972.

Winston Churchill, 1874-1965, (Br.) prime min., soldier, author; guided Britain through WWII.

Galeazzo Ciano, 1903-44, (It.) Fascist foreign minister; helped create Rome-Berlin Axis; executed by Benito Mussolini.

Henry Clay, 1777-1852, (U.S.) "The Great Compromiser"; one of the most influential pre-Civil War political leaders.

Georges Clemenceau, 1841-1929, (Fr.) twice prem.; Woodrow Wilson's antagonist at Paris Peace Conference after WWI.

DeWitt Clinton, 1769-1828, (U.S.) political leader; promoted Erie Canal.

Robert Clive, 1725-74, (Br.) first administrator of Bengal; laid foundation for British Empire in India.

Jean Baptiste Colbert, 1619-83, (Fr.) statesman; influential under Louis XIV; created the French navy.

David Crockett, 1786-1836, (U.S.) frontiersman, congressman; died defending the Alamo.

Oliver Cromwell, 1599-1658, (Br.) Lord Protector of England; led parliamentary forces during Civil War.

Curzon of Kedleston, 1859-1925, (Br.) viceroy of India, foreign sec.; major force in post-WWI world.

Édouard Daladier, 1884-1970, (Fr.) Radical Socialist politician; arrested by Vichy government, interned by Germans.

Richard J. Daley, 1902-76, (U.S.) Chicago mayor, 1955-76.

Georges Danton, 1759-94, (Fr.) leading French Rev. figure.

Jefferson Davis, 1808-89, (U.S.) pres. of the Confederacy.

Charles G. Dawes, 1865-1951, (U.S.) statesman, banker; advanced plan to stabilize post-WWI German finances.

Alcide De Gasperi, 1881-1954, (It.) prime min.; founder of Christian Democratic party.

Charles De Gaulle, 1890-1970, (Fr.) general, statesman; first pres. of the Fifth Republic.

F. W. (Frederik Willem) de Klerk, 1936-2021, (S. Afr.), former S. Afr. pres.; 1993 Nobel Peace Prize winner.

Deng Xiaoping, 1904-97, (China) "paramount leader" of China; backed economic modernization.

Eamon De Valera, 1882-1975, (Ire.-U.S.) statesman; led fight for Irish independence.

Thomas E. Dewey, 1902-71, (U.S.) NY governor (R); twice lost in try for presidency.

Ngo Dinh Diem, 1901-63, (Viet.) South Vietnamese pres.; assassinated in government takeover.

John Dingell Jr., 1926-2019, (U.S.) longest-serving U.S. rep (D, MI), 1955-2015.

Benjamin Disraeli, 1804-81, (Br.) prime min.; considered founder of modern Conservative party.

Anatoly Dobrynin, 1919-2010, (Russ.) diplomat and Soviet amb. to U.S. (1962-86).

Engelbert Dollfuss, 1892-1934, (Austria) chancellor; assassinated by Nazis.

Andrea Doria, 1466-1560, (It.) Genoese admiral, statesman; called "Father of Peace" and "Liberator of Genoa."

Stephen A. Douglas, 1813-61, (U.S.) Democratic leader, orator; ran against Lincoln for IL sen. seat, presidency.

Alexander Dubcek, 1921-92, (Czech.) statesman whose attempted liberalization was crushed, 1968.

John Foster Dulles, 1888-1959, (U.S.) sec. of state under Eisenhower; Cold War policy maker.

Friedrich Ebert, 1871-1925, (Ger.) Social Democratic movement leader; first pres., Weimar Republic, 1919-25.

Anthony Eden, 1897-1977, (Br.) foreign sec., prime min. during Suez invasion of 1956.

Ludwig Erhard, 1897-1977, (Ger.) economist, West German chancellor; led nation's economic rise after WWII.

King Fahd, 1923-2005, (Saudi Arabia) monarch from 1982 but inactive after 1995 stroke; encouraged U.S. relations.

Geraldine Ferraro, 1935-2011, (U.S.) U.S. rep. (D, NY), first woman vice-pres. nominee (1984).

João Baptista de Figueiredo, 1918-99, (Braz.) pres. of Brazil; restored nation's democracy after military rule.

Hamilton Fish, 1808-93, (U.S.) sec. of state; successfully mediated disputes with Great Britain, Latin America.

James V. Forrestal, 1892-1949, (U.S.) sec. of navy, first sec. of defense.

Francisco Franco, 1892-1975, (Sp.) leader of rebel forces during Spanish Civil War, longtime ruler of Spain.

Benjamin Franklin, 1706-90, (U.S.) printer, publisher, author, inventor, scientist, diplomat.

Louis de Frontenac, 1620-98, (Fr.) governor of New France (Canada).

J. William Fulbright, 1905-95, (U.S.) U.S. senator (D, AR); leading figure in U.S. foreign policy during Cold War years.

Hugh Gaitskell, 1906-63, (Br.) Labour party leader; major force in reversing its stand for unilateral disarmament.

Albert Gallatin, 1761-1849, (U.S.) sec. of treasury; instrumental in negotiating end of War of 1812.

Léon Gambetta, 1838-82, (Fr.) statesman, politician; one of the founders of the Third Republic.

Indira Gandhi, 1917-84, (India) daughter of Jawaharlal Nehru; prime min. of India, 1966-77, 1980-84; assassinated.

Mohandas K. Gandhi, 1869-1948, (India) political leader, ascetic; led movement against British rule; assassinated.

Giuseppe Garibaldi, 1807-82, (It.) patriot, soldier; a leader in the Risorgimento, Italian unification movement.

Valéry Giscard d'Estaing, 1926-2020, (Fr.) pres. of France, 1974-81.

William E. Gladstone, 1809-98, (Br.) prime min.; dominant force of Liberal party, 1868-94.

Paul Joseph Goebbels, 1897-1945, (Ger.) Nazi propagandist; master of mass psychology.

Barry Goldwater, 1909-98, (U.S.) conservative U.S. senator (R, AZ), 1964 pres. nominee.

Mikhail Gorbachev, 1931-2022, (USSR) reformist Soviet leader; 1990 Nobel Peace Prize winner.

Klement Gottwald, 1896-1953, (Czech.) Communist leader.

Haile Selassie (Tafari Makonnen), 1892-1975, (Ethiopia) emperor of Ethiopia.

Alexander Hamilton, 1755-1804, (U.S.) first treasury sec.; champion of strong central government.

Dag Hammarskjöld, 1905-61, (Swed.) statesman; UN sec.-general.

King Hassan II, 1929-99, (Moroc.) ruler of Morocco, 1962-99.

Vaclav Havel, 1936-2011, (Czech.) first president of Czech Republic, 1989-92.

John Hay, 1838-1905, (U.S.) sec. of state; primarily associated with Open Door Policy toward China.

Edward Heath, 1916-2005, (Br.) Conservative prime min., 1970-74; promoted European unity.

Patrick Henry, 1736-99, (U.S.) major Revolutionary War figure, orator.

Édouard Herriot, 1872-1957, (Fr.) Radical Socialist leader; twice prem., pres. of National Assembly.

Theodor Herzl, 1860-1904, (Hung.) founded modern Zionism.

Heinrich Himmler, 1900-45, (Ger.) head of Nazi SS and Gestapo.

Paul von Hindenburg, 1847-1934, (Ger.) field marshal, WWI; second pres. of Weimar Republic, 1925-34.

Adolf Hitler, 1889-1945, (Ger.) dictator; built Nazism, launched WWII, presided over the Holocaust.

Ho Chi Minh, 1890-1969, (Viet.) N. Vietnamese pres., Communist leader.

Harry L. Hopkins, 1890-1946, (U.S.) New Deal administrator; closest adviser to Franklin D. Roosevelt during WWII.

Edward M. House, 1858-1938, (U.S.) diplomat; confidential adviser to Woodrow Wilson.

Samuel Houston, 1793-1863, (U.S.) leader of struggle for Texas independence.

Cordell Hull, 1871-1955, (U.S.) sec. of state, 1933-44; initiated reciprocal trade to lower tariffs, helped organize UN.

John Hume, 1937-2020, (N. Ire.) nationalist party leader; 1998 Nobel Peace Prize winner.

Hubert H. Humphrey, 1911-78, (U.S.) U.S. senator (D, MN), vice pres., pres. nominee (1968).

King Hussein, 1935-99, (Jordan) peacemaker; ruler of Jordan, 1952-99.

Saddam Hussein, 1937-2006, (Iraq) Iraqi ruler; put to death for crimes against humanity.

Muhammad Ali Jinnah, 1876-1948, (Pak.) founder, first gov.-gen. of Pakistan.

Barbara Jordan, 1936-96, (U.S.) U.S. rep. (D, TX), orator, educator; first Black woman to win a seat in the TX state sen., 1966.

Benito Juarez, 1806-72, (Mex.) rallied his country against foreign threats; sought to create democratic, federal republic.

Betty Mae Tiger Jumper, 1923-2011, (Amer. Ind.) first woman Seminole chief.

Constantine Karamanlis, 1907-98, (Gr.) Greek prime min.; restored democracy, later president.

Frank B. Kellogg, 1856-1937, (U.S.) sec. of state; negotiated Kellogg-Briand Pact to outlaw war.

Edward M. Kennedy, 1932-2009, (U.S.) senator (D, MA); championed progressive causes.

Robert F. Kennedy, 1925-68, (U.S.) attorney general, U.S. sen. (D, NY); assassinated while seeking presidency.

Aleksandr Kerensky, 1881-1970, (Russ.) headed provisional government after Feb. 1917 revolution.

Ayatollah Ruhollah Khomeini, 1900-89, (Iran), religious-political leader; spearheaded overthrow of Shah, 1979.

Nikita Khrushchev, 1894-1971, (USSR) prem., first sec. of Communist party; initiated de-Stalinization.

Kim Dae-jung, 1925-2009, (Korea) S. Korean dissident, opposition leader, pres.; 2000 Nobel Peace Prize winner.

Kim Il Sung, 1912-94, (Korea) N. Korean dictator, 1948-94.

Kim Jong Il, 1942-2011, (Korea) N. Korean dictator, 1994-2011.

Edward I. Koch, 1924-2013, (U.S.) New York City mayor, 1978-89.

Helmut Kohl, 1930-2017, (Ger.) chancellor, 1982-98; reunified Germany.

Lajos Kossuth, 1802-94, (Hung.) principal figure in 1848 Hungarian revolution.

Pyotr Kropotkin, 1842-1921, (Russ.) anarchist; championed the peasants but opposed Bolshevism.

Kublai Khan, c. 1215-94, (Mongol) emperor; founder of Yuan dynasty in China.

Béla Kun, 1886-c. 1939, (Hung.) member of Third Communist International; tried to foment worldwide revolution.

Robert M. LaFollette, 1855-1925, (U.S.) Wisconsin public official; leader of progressive movement.

Fiorello La Guardia, 1882-1947, (U.S.) New York City reform mayor, 1933-45.

Pierre Laval, 1883-1945, (Fr.) politician, Vichy foreign min.; executed for treason.

Andrew Bonar Law, 1858-1923, (Can.) Conservative party politician, British prime min.; led opposition to Irish home rule.

Vladimir Ilyich Lenin (Ulyanov), 1870-1924, (Russ.) revolutionary; founded Bolshevism; Soviet leader, 1917-24.

Ferdinand de Lesseps, 1805-94, (Fr.) diplomat, engineer; conceived idea of Suez Canal.

René Lévesque, 1922-87, (Can.) prem. of Quebec, 1976-85; led unsuccessful separatist campaign.

Trygve Lie, 1896-1968, (Nor.) first UN sec.-gen.

Maxim Litvinov, 1876-1951, (Pol.-Russ.) revolutionary, commissar of foreign affairs; favored cooperation with West.

David Lloyd George, 1863-1945, (Br.) Liberal party prime min.; laid foundations for modern welfare state.

Henry Cabot Lodge, 1850-1924, (U.S.) U.S. senator (R, MA); led opposition to participation in League of Nations.

Huey P. Long, 1893-1935, (U.S.) Louisiana political demagogue, governor, U.S. senator (D); assassinated.

Rosa Luxemburg, 1871-1919, (Ger.) revolutionary; leader of the German Social Democratic party and Spartacus party.

J. Ramsay MacDonald, 1866-1937, (Br.) first Labour party prime min. of Great Britain.

Harold Macmillan, 1895-1986, (Br.) prime min. of Great Britain, 1957-63.

Makarios III, 1913-77, (Cyprus) Greek Orthodox archbishop; first pres. of Cyprus.

Nelson Mandela, 1918-2013, (S. Afr.) anti-apartheid leader; first Black pres. of S. Africa, 1994-99.

Wilma Mankiller, 1945-2010, (Amer. Ind.) first female chief of the Cherokee Nation.

Mao Zedong, 1893-1976, (China) chief Chinese Marxist theorist, revolutionary, political leader; led revolution establishing his nation as Communist state.

Jean Paul Marat, 1743-93, (Fr.) revolutionary, politician; identified with radical Jacobins; assassinated.

Thurgood Marshall, 1908-93, (U.S.) first Black U.S. solicitor general, 1965; first Black justice of U.S. Supreme Court, 1967-91.

José Martí, 1853-95, (Cuba) patriot, poet; independence leader.

Jan Masaryk, 1886-1948, (Czech.) foreign min.; died under mysterious circumstances, allegedly by suicide, following Communist coup.

Thomas G. Masaryk, 1850-1937, (Czech.) statesman, philosopher; first pres. of Czechoslovakia.

Jules Mazarin, 1602-61, (Fr.) cardinal, statesman; prime min. under Louis XIII and queen regent Anne of Austria.

Giuseppe Mazzini, 1805-72, (It.) reformer dedicated to Risorgimento movement for renewal of Italy.

Tom Mboya, 1930-69, (Kenya) political leader; instrumental in securing independence for Kenya.

John McCain, 1936-2018, (U.S.) U.S. sen. (R, AZ), 2008 pres. nominee.

Eugene McCarthy, 1916-2005, (U.S.) political leader, author; 1968 Dem. presidential contender.

Joseph R. McCarthy, 1908-57, (U.S.) senator (R, WI); extremist in searching out alleged Communists and pro-Communists.

Cosimo I de' Medici, 1519-74, (It.) Duke of Florence, grand duke of Tuscany.

Lorenzo de' Medici (the Magnificent), 1449-92, (It.) merchant prince; a towering figure in Italian Renaissance.

Catherine de Médicis, 1519-89, (Fr.) queen consort of Henry II, regent of France; influential in Catholic-Huguenot wars.

Golda Meir, 1898-1978, (Ukr.-Isr.) a founder of the state of Israel; prime min., 1969-74.

Klemens W. N. L. Metternich, 1773-1859, (Austria) statesman; arbiter of post-Napoleonic Europe.

Slobodan Milosevic, 1941-2006, (Serb./Yugo.) former Yugoslav pres.; tried for genocide, crimes against humanity.

François Mitterrand, 1916-96, (Fr.) pres. of France, 1981-95.

Mobutu Sese Seko, 1930-97, (Zaire) longtime ruler of Zaire (now Dem. Rep. of Congo), 1965-97; exiled after rebellion.

Guy Mollet, 1905-75, (Fr.) socialist politician, resistance leader.

Walter Mondale, 1928-2021, (U.S.) U.S. senator (D, MN), vice pres., pres. nominee (1984).

Henry Morgenthau Jr., 1891-1967, (U.S.) sec. of treasury; fundraiser for New Deal and U.S. WWII activities.

Gouverneur Morris, 1752-1816, (U.S.) statesman, diplomat, financial expert; helped plan decimal coinage.

Mohammed Morsi, 1951-2019, (Egypt) first democratically elected pres. of Egypt, 2012; deposed 2013.

Daniel Patrick Moynihan, 1927-2003, (U.S.) senator (D, NY), diplomat, social scientist, author.

Hosni Mubarak, 1928-2020, (Egy.) Egyptian president deposed in 2011 uprising.

Robert Mugabe, 1924-2019, (Zimb.) prime min. and pres. of Zimbabwe.

Benito Mussolini, 1883-1945, (It.) leader of the Italian fascist state; assassinated.

Imre Nagy, c. 1896-1958, (Hung.) Communist prem.; assassinated after Soviets crushed 1956 uprising.

Gamal Abdel Nasser, 1918-70, (Egypt) leader of Arab unification; second Egyptian pres.

Jawaharlal Nehru, 1889-1964, (India) prime min.; guided India through its early years of independence.

Kwame Nkrumah, 1909-72, (Ghana) first prime min., 1957-60; pres., 1960-66, of Ghana.

Manuel Noriega, 1934-2017, (Pan.) dictator, 1983-89; military officer, CIA informant.

Frederick North, 1732-92, (Br.) prime min.; his policies led to loss of American colonies.

Julius K. Nyerere, 1922-99, (Tanz.) founding father; first pres., 1962-85, of Tanzania.

Daniel O'Connell, 1775-1847, (Ire.) nationalist political leader; known as The Liberator.

Omar, c. 581-644, (Arab.) Muslim leader; second caliph, led Islam to become an imperial power.

Thomas P. (Tip) O'Neill Jr., 1912-94, (U.S.) U.S. rep. (D, MA), speaker of the House, 1977-86.

Ignace Paderewski, 1860-1941, (Pol.) statesman, pianist, composer, briefly prime min.; ardent patriot.

Ian Paisley, 1926-2014, (Ire.) Unionist Party leader who agreed to power sharing in N. Ireland.

Viscount Palmerston, 1784-1865, (Br.) Whig-Liberal prime min., foreign min.; embodied British nationalism.

Andreas George Papandreou, 1919-96, (Gr.) leftist politician; served as prem., 1981-89, 1993-96.

Georgios Papandreou, 1888-1968, (Gr.) Republican politician; served three times as prime min.

Franz von Papen, 1879-1969, (Ger.) politician; major role in overthrow of Weimar Republic and rise of Hitler.

Charles Stewart Parnell, 1846-91, (Ire.) nationalist leader; "uncrowned king of Ireland."

Lester Pearson, 1897-1972, (Can.) diplomat, Liberal party leader, prime min.

Robert Peel, 1788-1850, (Br.) reformist prime min.; founder of Conservative party.

Shimon Peres, 1922-2016, (Bela.-Isr.) Israel prime min., 1984-86, 1995-96; president, 2007-14.

Javier Pérez de Cuéllar, 1920-2020 (Per.) UN sec.-gen.

Frances Perkins, 1882-1965, (U.S.) first female cabinet member (sec. of labor).

Eva (Evita) Perón, 1919-52, (Arg.) highly influential second wife of Juan Perón.

Juan Perón, 1895-1974, (Arg.) dynamic pres. of Argentina, 1946-55, 1973-74.

H. Ross Perot, 1930-2019, (U.S.) entrepreneur; pres. contender, 1992, 1996.

Joseph Pilsudski, 1867-1935, (Pol.) statesman; instrumental in reestablishing Polish state in the 20th cent.

Charles Pinckney, 1757-1824, (U.S.) founding father; his Pinckney plan largely incorporated into Constitution.

Christian Pineau, 1905-95, (Fr.) leader of French Resistance during WWII; foreign min., 1956-58.

Augusto Pinochet (Ugarte), 1915-2006, (Chile) former Chilean ruler; indicted for human rights abuses while in office.

William Pitt the Elder, 1708-78, (Br.) statesman; the "Great Commoner," transformed Britain into imperial power.

William Pitt the Younger, 1759-1806, (Br.) prime min. during French Revolutionary wars.

Georgi Plekhanov, 1857-1918, (Russ.) revolutionary, social philosopher; called "father of Russian Marxism."

Raymond Poincaré, 1860-1934, (Fr.) French pres.; advocated harsh punishment of Germany after WWI.

Pol Pot, 1925-98, (Camb.) leader of Khmer Rouge; ruled Cambodia, 1975-79; responsible for mass deaths.

Georges Pompidou, 1911-74, (Fr.) Gaullist political leader; pres., 1969-74.

Grigori Potemkin, 1739-91, (Russ.) field marshal; favorite of empress Catherine II.

Adam Clayton Powell Jr., 1908-72, (U.S.) civil rights leader; U.S. rep. (D, NY), 1945-69.

Muammar al-Qaddafi, 1942-2011, (Libya) Libyan ruler, 1969-2011.

Yitzhak Rabin, 1922-95, (Isr.) military, political leader; prime min. of Israel, 1974-77, 1992-95; assassinated.

Joseph H. Rainey, 1832-87, (U.S.) first Black person elected to U.S. House (1869), from SC.

Edmund Randolph, 1753-1813, (U.S.) attorney; prominent in drafting, ratification of Constitution.

John Randolph, 1773-1833, (U.S.) Southern planter; strong advocate of states' rights.

Jeannette Rankin, 1880-1973, (U.S.) pacifist; first woman member of U.S. Congress (R, MT).

Walt(h)er Rathenau, 1867-1922, (Ger.) industrialist, statesman.

Sam Rayburn, 1882-1961, (U.S.) U.S. rep. (D, TX) for 47 years, House speaker for 17.

Red Cloud, 1822?-1909, (Amer. Ind.) leader of the Oglala Lakota.

Janet Reno, 1938-2016, (U.S.) first U.S. woman attorney general.

Hiram R. Revels, 1822-1901, (U.S.) first African American U.S. senator (R); elected in MS, served 1870-71.

Paul Reynaud, 1878-1966, (Fr.) statesman; prem. in 1940 at time of France's defeat by Germany.

Syngman Rhee, 1875-1965, (Korea) first pres. of S. Korea.

Cecil Rhodes, 1853-1902, (Br.) imperialist, industrial magnate; established Rhodes scholarships in his will.

Ann Richards, 1933-2006, (U.S.) former TX gov. (D).

Cardinal de Richelieu, 1585-1642, (Fr.) statesman, known as "red eminence"; chief minister to Louis XIII.

Maximilien Robespierre, 1758-94, (Fr.) leading figure in French Revolution and Reign of Terror.

Eleanor Roosevelt, 1884-1962, (U.S.) influential first lady, humanitarian, UN diplomat.

Elihu Root, 1845-1937, (U.S.) lawyer, statesman, diplomat; leading Republican supporter of the League of Nations.

John Ross, 1790-1866, (Amer. Ind.) longest-serving principal chief of Cherokee Nation (1828-66).

Dean Rusk, 1909-95, (U.S.) statesman; sec. of state, 1961-69.

John Russell, 1792-1878, (Br.) Liberal prime min. during the Irish potato famine.

Anwar al-Sadat, 1918-81, (Egypt) pres., 1970-81; promoted peace with Israel; Nobel laureate; assassinated.

António de Oliveira Salazar, 1889-1970, (Port.) longtime dictator of Portugal.

José de San Martín, 1778-1850, ([now] Arg.) S. Amer. revolutionary; protector of Peru.

Eisaku Sato, 1901-75, (Jpn.) prime min.; presided over Japan's post-WWII emergence as major world power.

Abdul Aziz Ibn Saud, c. 1880-1953, (Saudi Arabia) king of Saudi Arabia, 1932-53.

Helmut Schmidt, 1918-2015, (Ger.) German chancellor, 1974-82.

Robert Schuman, 1886-1963, (Fr.) statesman; founded European Coal and Steel Community.

Carl Schurz, 1829-1906, (Ger.-U.S.) political leader, journalist, orator, reformer.

Kurt Schuschnigg, 1897-1977, (Austria) chancellor; unsuccessful in stopping Austria's annexation by Germany.

William H. Seward, 1801-72, (U.S.) anti-slavery activist; as U.S. sec. of state purchased Alaska.

Carlo Sforza, 1872-1952, (It.) foreign min. of Italy, anti-Fascist.

Yitzhak Shamir, 1915-2012, (Russ.-Isr.) prime min. of Israel, 1983-84, 1986-92.

Ariel Sharon, 1928-2014, (Isr.) prime min. of Israel, 2001-06.

Eduard Shevardnadze, 1928-2014, (Geo.) Georgian pres., 1995-2003.

George Shultz, 1920-2021, (U.S.) sec. of state.

Norodom Sihanouk, 1922-2012, (Camb.) king of Cambodia, 1941-55, 1993-2004.

Sitting Bull, c. 1831-90, (Amer. Ind.) Hunkpapa Lakota leader; defeated Custer at Battle of the Little Bighorn.

Alfred E. Smith, 1873-1944, (U.S.) NY Democratic governor; first Roman Catholic to run for president (1928).

Margaret Chase Smith, 1897-1995, (U.S.) U.S. rep., senator (R, ME); first woman elected to both houses of Congress.

Jan C. Smuts, 1870-1950, (S. Afr.) statesman, philosopher, soldier, prime min.

Paul Henri Spaak, 1899-1972, (Belg.) statesman, socialist leader.

Joseph Stalin, 1879-1953, (USSR) Soviet dictator, 1924-53; instituted forced collectivization, massive purges, and labor camps, causing millions of deaths.

Edwin M. Stanton, 1814-69, (U.S.) sec. of war, 1862-68.

Alexander Stephens, 1812-83, (U.S.) vice pres. of the Confederacy.

Edward R. Stettinius Jr., 1900-49, (U.S.) industrialist; sec. of state who coordinated aid to WWII allies.

Adlai E. Stevenson, 1900-65, (U.S.) Democratic leader, diplomat, governor (IL), presidential nominee (1952, '56).

Henry L. Stimson, 1867-1950, (U.S.) statesman; served in five administrations, foreign policy adviser in 1930s and 1940s.

Carl Stokes, 1927-96, (U.S.) first Black mayor of a major American city (Cleveland, 1967-72).

Suharto, 1921-2008, (Indon.) former longtime Indonesian ruler.

Sukarno, 1901-70, (Indon.) dictatorial first pres. of the Indonesian republic.

Sun Yat-sen, 1866-1925, (China) revolutionary; leader of Kuomintang political party, regarded as father of modern China.

Robert A. Taft, 1889-1953, (U.S.) conservative Senate leader (OH); called "Mr. Republican."

Charles de Talleyrand, 1754-1838, (Fr.) statesman, diplomat; the major force of the Congress of Vienna of 1814-15.

U Thant, 1909-74, (Burma) statesman, UN sec.-general.

Margaret Thatcher, 1925-2013, (Br.) conservative British prime min., 1979-90; first woman UK prime min.

Norman M. Thomas, 1884-1968, (U.S.) social reformer; six times Socialist party presidential candidate.

Josip Broz Tito, 1892-1980, (Yugo.) pres. of Yugoslavia, 1953-80; WWII guerrilla chief, postwar rival of Stalin.

Palmiro Togliatti, 1893-1964, (It.) major Italian Communist leader.

Hideki Tojo, 1885-1948, (Jpn.) statesman; soldier; prime min. during most of WWII.

François Toussaint L'Ouverture, c. 1744-1803, (Haiti) patriot, martyr; thwarted French colonial aims.

Leon Trotsky, 1879-1940, (Russ.) revolutionary; founded Red Army, expelled from party in conflict with Stalin; assassinated.

Pierre Elliott Trudeau, 1919-2000, (Can.) longtime liberal prime min. of Canada, 1968-79, 1980-84; achieved native Canadian constitution.

Rafael L. Trujillo Molina, 1891-1961, (Dom. Rep.) dictator of Dominican Republic, 1930-61; assassinated.

Moise K. Tshombe, 1919-69, (Congo) pres. of secessionist Katanga prov., prem. of Congo (now Dem. Rep. of the Congo).

William M. Tweed, 1823-78, (U.S.) political boss of Tammany Hall, New York City's Democratic political machine.

Walter Ulbricht, 1893-1973, (Ger.) Communist leader of German Democratic Republic.

Arthur H. Vandenberg, 1884-1951, (U.S.) senator (R, MI); proponent of bipartisan anti-Communist foreign policy.

Eleutherios Venizelos, 1864-1936, (Gr.) most prominent Greek statesman of early 20th cent.

Hendrik F. Verwoerd, 1901-66, (S. Afr.) prime min.; rigorously applied apartheid policy despite protest.

Kurt Waldheim, 1918-2007, (Austria) UN sec.-gen., Austrian pres.

George Wallace, 1919-98, (U.S.) former segregationist governor of Alabama, pres. candidate.

Robert Walpole, 1676-1745, (Br.) statesman; generally considered Britain's first prime min.

Nancy Ward (Nan'yehi), 1738?-1824?, (Amer. Ind.) Cherokee peace leader.

Robert C. Weaver, 1907-97, (U.S.) first African American appointed to cabinet; sec. of Housing and Urban Development.

Daniel Webster, 1782-1852, (U.S.) orator, politician; advocate of business interests during Jacksonian agrarianism.

Chaim Weizmann, 1874-1952, (Russ.-Isr.) Zionist leader, scientist; first Israeli pres.

Kevin White, 1929-2012, (U.S.) Boston mayor, 1967-84.

Wendell L. Willkie, 1892-1944, (U.S.) Republican who tried to unseat Franklin D. Roosevelt when he ran for his third term.

Harold Wilson, 1916-95, (Br.) Labour party leader; prime min., 1964-70, 1974-76.

Boris Yeltsin, 1931-2007, (Russ.) first freely elected pres. of post-Soviet Russia.

Emiliano Zapata, c. 1879-1919, (Mex.) revolutionary; major influence on modern Mexico.

Todor Zhivkov, 1911-98, (Bulg.) Communist ruler of Bulgaria from 1954 until ousted in a 1989 coup.

Zhou Enlai, 1898-1976, (China) diplomat, prime min.; a leading figure of the Chinese Communist party.

Scientists of the Past

Revised by Peter Barker, Prof. and Chair, Dept. of the History of Science, Univ. of Oklahoma.

For pre-modern scientists, see also Philosophers and Religious Figures of the Past and the Historical Figures chapter.

Albertus Magnus, c. 1200-80, (Ger.) theologian, philosopher; helped found medieval study of natural science.

Alhazen (Ibn al-Haytham), c. 965-c. 1040, (Arab.) mathematician, astronomer, optical theorist.

Andre-Marie Ampère, 1775-1836, (Fr.) mathematician, chemist; founder of electrodynamics.

Mary Anning, 1799-1847, (Br.) paleontologist.

Neil Armstrong, 1930-2012, (U.S.) astronaut; first man to walk on the Moon.

John V. Atanasoff, 1903-95, (U.S.) physicist; co-invented Atanasoff-Berry electronic digital computer (1939-41).

Amedeo Avogadro, 1776-1856, (It.) chemist, physicist; proposed that equal volumes of gas contain equal numbers of molecules, permitting determination of molecular weights.

John Bardeen, 1908-91, (U.S.) double Nobel laureate in physics (transistor, 1956; superconductivity, 1972).

A. H. Becquerel, 1852-1908, (Fr.) physicist; discovered radioactivity in uranium (1896).

Alexander Graham Bell, 1847-1922, (U.S.) inventor; first to patent and commercially exploit the telephone (1876).

Daniel Bernoulli, 1700-82, (Switz.) mathematician; developed fluid dynamics and kinetic theory of gases.

Clifford Berry, 1918-63, (U.S.) collaborated with John V. Atanasoff on the ABC electronic digital computer (1939-41).

Jöns Jakob Berzelius, 1779-1848, (Swed.) chemist; developed modern chemical symbols and formulas.

Henry Bessemer, 1813-98, (Br.) engineer; invented Bessemer steel-making process.

Hans Bethe, 1906-2005, (Ger.-U.S.) physicist; won Nobel Prize in 1967 for describing how stars generate energy.

Bruno Bettelheim, 1903-90, (Austria-U.S.) psychoanalyst; studied disturbed children; *Uses of Enchantment* (1976).

Louis Blériot, 1872-1936, (Fr.) engineer; monoplane pioneer.

Franz Boas, 1858-1942, (Ger.-U.S.) founded modern anthropology; studied Pacific Coast tribes.

Niels Bohr, 1885-1962, (Den.) atomic and nuclear physicist; founded quantum mechanics.

Norman Borlaug, 1914-2009, (U.S.) plant pathologist and geneticist; father of "green" (agricultural) revolution.

Max Born, 1882-1970, (Ger.) atomic and nuclear physicist; helped develop quantum mechanics.

Satyendranath Bose, 1894-1974, (India) physicist; forerunner of modern quantum theory for integral-spin particles.

Louis de Broglie, 1892-1987, (Fr.) physicist; proposed quantum wave-particle duality.

Robert Bunsen, 1811-99, (Ger.) chemist; pioneered spectroscopic analysis; discovered rubidium, caesium.

Luther Burbank, 1849-1926, (U.S.) naturalist; developed plant breeding into a modern science.

Vannevar Bush, 1890-1974, (U.S.) electrical engineer; developed differential analyzer, an early analogue computer; led WWII Office of Scientific Res. and Dev.

Marvin Camras, 1916-95, (U.S.) inventor, electrical engineer; invented magnetic tape recording.

Alexis Carrel, 1873-1944, (Fr.) surgeon, biologist; developed methods of suturing blood vessels, transplanting organs.

Rachel Carson, 1907-64, (U.S.) marine biologist, environmentalist; *Silent Spring* (1962).

George Washington Carver, 1864-1943, (U.S.) chemist and botanist; promoted alternative crops.

James Chadwick, 1891-1974, (Br.) physicist; discovered the neutron (1932); led Brit. team on Manhattan Project in U.S.

Eugenie Clark, 1922-2015, (U.S.) ichthyologist and oceanographer.

Albert Claude, 1898-1983, (Belg.-U.S.) a founder of modern cell biology; determined role of mitochondria.

Samuel Cohen, 1921-2010, (U.S.) physicist who invented the neutron bomb.

Barry Commoner, 1917-2012, (U.S.) biologist; noted environmentalist.

Nicolaus Copernicus, 1473-1543, (Pol.) first modern astronomer to propose Sun as center of the planets' motions.

Jacques Yves Cousteau, 1910-97, (Fr.) oceanographer; co-inventor, with Emile Gagnan (Fr.), of the Aqualung (1943).

Seymour Cray, 1925-96, (U.S.) computer industry pioneer; developed supercomputers.

Francis Crick, 1916-2004, (Br.) biophysicist; co-discoverer of genetic code; shared 1962 Nobel Prize in Physiology/Medicine.

Marie, 1867-1934, (Pol.-Fr.) and **Pierre Curie**, 1859-1906, (Fr.) physical chemists; pioneer investigators of radioactivity; discovered radium and polonium (1898).

Gottlieb Daimler, 1834-1900, (Ger.) engineer, inventor; pioneer automobile manufacturer.

John Dalton, 1766-1844, (Br.) chemist, physicist; formulated atomic theory, made first table of atomic weights.

Charles Darwin, 1809-82, (Br.) naturalist; established theory of organic evolution; *Origin of Species* (1859).

Lee De Forest, 1873-1961, (U.S.) inventor of triode; pioneer in wireless telegraphy, sound pictures, television.

Pierre-Gilles de Gennes, 1932-2007, (Fr.) physicist whose research aided development of liquid-crystal display (LCD); awarded 1991 Nobel Prize for Physics.

Max Delbrück, 1906-81, (Fr.-Ger.-U.S.) a founder of molecular biology.

Rudolf Diesel, 1858-1913, (Ger.) mechanical engineer; patented Diesel engine (1892).

Theodosius Dobzhansky, 1900-75, (Russ.-U.S.) biologist; reconciled genetics and natural selection.

Christian Doppler, 1803-53, (Austria) physicist; showed change in wave frequency caused by motion of source, now known as Doppler effect.

J. Presper Eckert Jr., 1919-95, (U.S.) co-inventor, with John W. Mauchly, of the ENIAC computer (1943-45).

Thomas A. Edison, 1847-1931, (U.S.) inventor; held more than 1,000 patents, including incandescent electric lamp.

Robert Edwards, 1925-2013, (Br.) physiologist; pioneered in vitro fertilization.

Paul Ehrlich, 1854-1915, (Ger.) medical researcher in immunology and bacteriology; pioneered antitoxin production.

Albert Einstein, 1879-1955, (Ger.-U.S.) theoretical physicist; founded relativity theory.

John F. Enders, 1897-1985, (U.S.) virologist; helped discover vaccines against polio, measles, mumps, and chicken pox.

Erik Erikson, 1902-94, (U.S.) psychoanalyst, author; theory of developmental stages of life; *Childhood and Society* (1950).

Leonhard Euler, 1707-83, (Switz.) mathematician, physicist; pioneer of calculus, revived ideas of Fermat.

Gabriel Fahrenheit, 1686-1736, (Ger.) physicist; improved thermometers and introduced Fahrenheit temperature scale.

Michael Faraday, 1791-1867, (Br.) chemist, physicist; discovered electrical induction and invented dynamo (1831).

Philo T. Farnsworth, 1906-71, (U.S.) inventor; built first television system (San Francisco, 1928).

Pierre de Fermat, 1601-65, (Fr.) mathematician; founded modern theory of numbers.

Enrico Fermi, 1901-54, (It.-U.S.) nuclear physicist; demonstrated first controlled chain reaction (Chicago, 1942).

Richard Feynman, 1918-88, (U.S.) theoretical physicist, author; founder of Quantum Electrodynamics (QED).

Alexander Fleming, 1881-1955, (Br.) bacteriologist; discovered penicillin (1928).

Dian Fossey, 1932-85, (U.S.) primatologist.

Jean B. J. Fourier, 1768-1830, (Fr.) introduced Fourier Series, method of analysis in math and physics.

Sigmund Freud, 1856-1939, (Austria) psychiatrist; founder of psychoanalysis; *Interpretation of Dreams* (1901).

Erich Fromm, 1900-80, (U.S.) psychoanalyst; *Man for Himself* (1947).

Galileo Galilei, 1564-1642, (It.) physicist; used telescope to vindicate Copernicus, founded modern science of motion.

Carl Friedrich Gauss, 1777-1855, (Ger.) mathematician; completed work of Fermat and Euler in number theory.

Josiah W. Gibbs, 1839-1903, (U.S.) theoretical physicist, chemist; founded chemical thermodynamics.

John Glenn, 1921-2016, (U.S.) astronaut, first American to orbit Earth (1962).

Robert H. Goddard, 1882-1945, (U.S.) physicist; invented liquid fuel rocket (1926).

George W. Goethals, 1858-1928, (U.S.) chief engineer who completed Panama Canal (1907-14).

William C. Gorgas, 1854-1920, (U.S.) physician; pioneer in prevention of yellow fever and malaria.

Stephen Jay Gould, 1941-2002, (U.S.) paleontologist, evolutionary biologist, writer.

Ernest Haeckel, 1834-1919, (Ger.) zoologist, evolutionist; early Darwinist, introduced concept of "ecology."

Otto Hahn, 1879-1968, (Ger.) chemist; with Lise Meitner discovered nuclear fission (1938).

Edmund Halley, 1656-1742, (Br.) astronomer; predicted return of 1682 comet (Halley's Comet) in 1759.

William Harvey, 1578-1657, (Br.) physician, anatomist; discovered circulation of the blood (1628).

Stephen Hawking, 1942-2018, (Br.) physicist; explored gravity, black holes; *A Brief History of Time* (1988).

Werner Heisenberg, 1901-76, (Ger.) physicist; developed matrix mechanics and uncertainty principle (1927).

Hermann von Helmholtz, 1821-94, (Ger.) physicist, physiologist; formulated principle of conservation of energy.

Caroline Herschel, 1750-1848, (Ger.-Br.) astronomer.

William Herschel, 1738-1822, (Ger.-Br.) astronomer; discovered Uranus (1781).

Heinrich Hertz, 1857-94, (Ger.) physicist; discovered radio waves and photo-electric effect (1886-87).

David Hilbert, 1862-1943, (Ger.) mathematician; contributed to algebra, calculus, and foundational studies (formalism).

Albert Hofmann, 1906-2008, (Switz.) chemist; inventor of LSD.

Edwin P. Hubble, 1889-1953, (U.S.) astronomer; discovered observational evidence of expanding universe.

Alexander von Humboldt, 1769-1859, (Ger.) naturalist; explored Central, S. America, ideated ecology.

Edward Jenner, 1749-1823, (Br.) physician; pioneered vaccination, introduced term "virus."

Katherine Johnson, 1918-2020, (U.S.) NASA mathematician.

James Joule, 1818-89, (Br.) physicist; found relation between heat and mechanical energy (conservation of energy).

Carl Jung, 1875-1961, (Switz.) psychiatrist; founder of analytical psychology.

Ernest Everett Just, 1883-1941, (U.S.) marine biologist; studied egg development; *Biology of Cell Surfaces* (1941).

Johannes Kepler, 1571-1630, (Ger.) astronomer; discovered laws of planetary motion.

Al-Khwarizmi, early 9th cent., (Arab.) mathematician; regarded as founder of algebra.

Robert Koch, 1843-1910, (Ger.) bacteriologist; isolated bacterial causes of tuberculosis and other diseases.

Georges Köhler, 1946-95, (Ger.) immunologist; with César Milstein developed monoclonal antibody technique.

Willem Kolff, 1911-2009, (Neth.-U.S.) physician, biomedical engineer; developed first practical kidney dialysis machine; considered the "father of artificial organs."

Jacques Lacan, 1901-81, (Fr.) influential psychoanalyst.

Joseph Lagrange, 1736-1813, (Fr.) geometer, astronomer; showed that gravity of Earth and Moon cancel, creating stable points in space around them.

Jean B. Lamarck, 1744-1829, (Fr.) naturalist; forerunner of Darwin in evolutionary theory.

Pierre Simon de Laplace, 1749-1827, (Fr.) astronomer, physicist; proposed nebular origin for solar system.

Lewis H. Latimer, 1848-1928, (U.S.) African American scientist; associate of Edison; supervised installation of first electric street lighting in New York City.

Antoine Lavoisier, 1743-94, (Fr.) a founder of modern chemistry.

Ernest O. Lawrence, 1901-58, (U.S.) physicist; invented the cyclotron.

Louis, 1903-72, and **Mary Leakey**, 1913-96, (both Br.) early hominid paleoanthropologists; discovered remains in Africa.

Richard Leakey, 1944-2022, (Kenya) anthropologist, paleontologist, conservationist.

Anton van Leeuwenhoek, 1632-1723, (Neth.) founder of microscopy.

Jerome Lejeune, 1927-94, (Fr.) geneticist; discovered chromosomal cause of Down syndrome (1959).

Claude Lévi-Strauss, 1908-2009, (Belg.-Fr.) cultural anthropologist, sociologist, philosopher.

Kurt Lewin, 1890-1947, (Ger.-U.S.) social psychologist; studied human motivation and group dynamics.

Justus von Liebig, 1803-73, (Ger.) founded quantitative organic chemistry.

Joseph Lister, 1827-1912, (Br.) physician; pioneered antiseptic surgery.

Hendrik Lorentz, 1853-1928, (Neth.) physicist; developed electron theory of matter, contributed to relativity theory.

Konrad Lorenz, 1903-89, (Austria) ethologist; pioneer in study of animal behavior.

Bernard Lovell, 1913-2012, (Br.) physicist and radio astronomer.

Percival Lowell, 1855-1916, (U.S.) astronomer; predicted the existence of Pluto.

Louis, 1864-1948, and **Auguste Lumière**, 1862-1954, (both Fr.) invented cinematograph, made first motion picture (1895).

Theodore H. Maiman, 1927-2007, (U.S.) physicist; invented the first workable laser, which he displayed in 1960.

Guglielmo Marconi, 1874-1937, (It.) physicist; developed wireless telegraphy.

John W. Mauchly, 1907-80, (U.S.) co-inventor, with J. Presper Eckert Jr., of computer ENIAC (1943-45).

James Clerk Maxwell, 1831-79, (Br.) physicist; unified electricity and magnetism, electromagnetic theory of light.

Maria Goeppert Mayer, 1906-72, (Ger.-U.S.) physicist; developed shell model of atomic nuclei.

Barbara McClintock, 1902-92, (U.S.) geneticist; showed that some genetic elements are mobile.

Lise Meitner, 1878-1968, (Austria) co-discoverer, with Otto Hahn, of nuclear fission (1938).

Gregor J. Mendel, 1822-84, (Austria) botanist, monk; his experiments became the foundation of modern genetics.

Dmitri Mendeleyev, 1834-1907, (Russ.) chemist; established Periodic Table of the Elements.

Bruce H. Merrifield, 1921-2006, (U.S.) chemist; discovered how to synthesize proteins quickly and efficiently.

Franz Mesmer, 1734-1815, (Ger.) physician; introduced hypnotherapy.

Albert A. Michelson, 1852-1931, (U.S.) physicist; invented interferometer.

Robert A. Millikan, 1868-1953, (U.S.) physicist; measured electronic charge.

Thomas Hunt Morgan, 1866-1945, (U.S.) geneticist, embryologist; established role of chromosomes in heredity.

John F. Nash Jr., 1928-2015, (U.S.) mathematician; Nobel Prize winner (1994) in economics for work on game theory.

Isaac Newton, 1642-1727, (Br.) natural philosopher; discovered laws of gravitation, motion; with Gottfried Wilhelm von Leibniz, founded calculus.

Robert N. Noyce, 1927-90, (U.S.) invented microchip.

J. Robert Oppenheimer, 1904-67, (U.S.) physicist; scientific director of Manhattan Project.

Wilhelm Ostwald, 1853-1932, (Ger.) chemist, philosopher; main founder of modern physical chemistry.

Louis Pasteur, 1822-95, (Fr.) chemist; showed that germs cause disease and fermentation; originated pasteurization.

Linus C. Pauling, 1901-94, (U.S.) chemist; studied chemical bonds; campaigned for nuclear disarmament.

Jean Piaget, 1896-1980, (Switz.) psychologist; four-stage theory of intellectual development in children.

Max Planck, 1858-1947, (Ger.) physicist; introduced quantum hypothesis (1900).

Jules Henri Poincaré, 1854-1912, (Fr.) mathematician; founded algebraic topology, many other discoveries.

Walter S. Reed, 1851-1902, (U.S.) Army physician; proved mosquitoes transmit yellow fever.

Theodor Reik, 1888-1969, (Austria-U.S.) psychoanalyst; major Freudian disciple.

Sally Ride, 1951-2012, (U.S.) astronaut; 1st U.S. woman in space.

Bernhard Riemann, 1826-66, (Ger.) mathematician; developed non-Euclidean geometry used by Einstein.

Norbert Rillieux, 1806-94, (U.S.) African American inventor of a vacuum pan evaporator (1846); revolutionized sugar-refining industry.

Wilhelm Roentgen, 1845-1923, (Ger.) physicist; discovered X-rays (1895).

Carl Rogers, 1902-87, (U.S.) psychotherapist, author; originated nondirective therapy.

Ernest Rutherford, 1871-1937, (Br.) physicist; pioneer investigator of radioactivity, identified the atomic nucleus.

Albert B. Sabin, 1906-93, (Russ.-U.S.) developed oral polio live-virus vaccine.

Carl Sagan, 1934-96, (U.S.) astronomer, author.

Jonas Salk, 1914-95, (U.S.) developed first successful polio vaccine, widely used in U.S. after 1955.

Allan Sandage, 1926-2010, (U.S.) astronomer; refined the Hubble Constant, a measure of the universe's expansion.

Frederick Sanger, 1918-2013, (Br.) biochemist; detailed molecular structure of insulin.

Giovanni Schiaparelli, 1835-1910, (It.) astronomer; reported canals on Mars.

Erwin Schrödinger, 1887-1961, (Austria) physicist; developed wave equation for quantum systems.

Glenn T. Seaborg, 1912-99, (U.S.) chemist; Nobel Prize winner (1951); co-discoverer of plutonium.

Harlow Shapley, 1885-1972, (U.S.) astronomer; mapped galactic clusters and position of Sun in Milky Way Galaxy.

Norman E. Shumway, 1923-2006, (U.S.) surgeon; performed world's first successful heart-lung transplant.

B. F. Skinner, 1904-90, (U.S.) psychologist; leading advocate of behaviorism.

Richard E. Smalley, 1943-2005, (U.S.) chemist; with three other scientists, discovered buckminsterfullerenes, a previously unknown class of carbon molecules.

Roger W. Sperry, 1913-94, (U.S.) neurobiologist; established different functions of right and left sides of brain.

Benjamin Spock, 1903-98, (U.S.) pediatrician, child care expert; *Common Sense Book of Baby and Child Care*.

Charles P. Steinmetz, 1865-1923, (Ger.-U.S.) electrical engineer; developed basic ideas on alternating current.

Ernst Stuhlinger, 1913-2008, (Ger.) rocket scientist; elective propulsion for NASA in early space age.

Leo Szilard, 1898-1964, (Hung.-U.S.) physicist; helped on Manhattan Project, later opposed nuclear weapons.

Edward Teller, 1908-2003, (Hung.-U.S.) physicist; aided on Manhattan Project, had key role in development of H-bomb.

Nikola Tesla, 1856-1943, (Serb.-U.S.) invented electrical devices including AC dynamos, transformers, and motors.

William Thomson (Lord Kelvin), 1824-1907, (Br.) physicist; aided in success of transatlantic telegraph cable (1865); proposed Kelvin absolute temperature scale.

Alan Turing, 1912-54, (Br.) mathematician; helped develop basis for computers.

James Van Allen, 1914-2006, (U.S.) physicist; discovered the presence of radiation belts around Earth (Van Allen belts).

Rudolf Virchow, 1821-1902, (Ger.) pathologist; pioneered the modern theory that diseases affect the body through cells.

Alessandro Volta, 1745-1827, (It.) physicist; electricity pioneer.

Wernher von Braun, 1912-77, (Ger.-U.S.) aerospace engineer; developed rockets for warfare and space exploration.

John von Neumann, 1903-57, (Hung.-U.S.) mathematician; originated game theory; basic design for modern computers.

Alfred Russell Wallace, 1823-1913, (Br.) naturalist; proposed concept of evolution independently of Darwin.

John B. Watson, 1878-1958, (U.S.) psychologist; a founder of behaviorism.

James E. Watt, 1736-1819, (Br.) mechanical engineer, inventor; invented modern steam engine (1765).

Alfred L. Wegener, 1880-1930, (Ger.) meteorologist, geophysicist; postulated continental drift.

Norbert Wiener, 1894-1964, (U.S.) mathematician; founder of cybernetics.

Daniel Hale Williams, 1858-1931, (U.S.) African American surgeon; performed one of first two open-heart operations (1893).

Sewall Wright, 1889-1988, (U.S.) evolutionary theorist; helped found population genetics.

Wilhelm Wundt, 1832-1920, (Ger.) founder of experimental psychology.

Qian Xuesen, 1911-2009, (China) rocket scientist; helped found Jet Propulsion Lab, father of China's space program.

Rosalyn Yalow, 1921-2011, (U.S.) physicist; co-developer of radioimmunoassay.

Chuck Yeager, 1923-2020, (U.S.) test pilot, broke the sound barrier.

Ferdinand von Zeppelin, 1838-1917, (Ger.) soldier, aeronaut, airship designer.

Social Reformers, Activists, and Humanitarians of the Past

Ralph David Abernathy, 1926-90, (U.S.) Black civil rights activist; pres., 1968, Southern Christian Leadership Conf.

Jane Addams, 1860-1935, (U.S.) cofounder of Hull House; won Nobel Peace Prize, 1931.

Susan B. Anthony, 1820-1906, (U.S.) a leader in temperance, antislavery, and woman suffrage movements.

Dennis Banks, 1937-2017, (Amer. Ind.) civil rights activist.

Thomas Barnardo, 1845-1905, (Br.) social reformer; pioneer in care of destitute children.

Clara Barton, 1821-1912, (U.S.) organized American Red Cross.

Daisy Bates, 1914-99, (U.S.) Black civil rights leader who fought for integration; advocate for the "Little Rock 9" during Arkansas desegregation crisis in 1957.

Henry Ward Beecher, 1813-87, (U.S.) clergyman, abolitionist.

Peter Benenson, 1921-2005, (Br.) activist; founded Amnesty International, 1961.

Mary McLeod Bethune, 1875-1955, (U.S.) Black educator, civil rights activist; adviser to FDR and Truman; founder, pres., Bethune-Cookman College.

Elizabeth Blackwell, 1821-1910, (Br.) first female physician in the U.S.

Amelia Bloomer, 1818-94, (U.S.) suffragette, social reformer.

Julian Bond, 1940-2015, (U.S.) civil rights leader, NAACP chair, 1998-2015.

Yelena Bonner, 1923-2011, (Russ.) human rights activist in former Soviet Union.

William Booth, 1829-1912, (Br.) founded Salvation Army.

James Brady, 1940-2014, (U.S.) gun control advocate; Reagan press sec.

John Brown, 1800-59, (U.S.) abolitionist who led murder of five pro-slavery men; hanged.

Linda Brown, 1943-2018, (U.S.) civil rights activist; daughter of *Brown v. Board of Education* (1954) plaintiff.

Frances Xavier (Mother) Cabrini, 1850-1917, (It.-U.S.) nun; founded charitable institutions; first American canonized as a saint, 1946.

Stokely Carmichael (Kwame Ture), 1941-98, (Trinidad-U.S.) Black power activist; major proponent of Pan-Africanism; prime min. of Black Panthers.

Carrie Chapman Catt, 1859-1947, (U.S.) suffragette.

Cesar Chavez, 1927-93, (U.S.) labor leader; helped establish United Farm Workers of America.

Eldridge Cleaver, 1935-98, (U.S.) revolutionary social critic; former minister of information for Black Panthers; *Soul on Ice*.

Clarence Darrow, 1857-1938, (U.S.) lawyer; defender of underdog, opponent of capital punishment.

Ossie Davis, 1917-2005, (U.S.) Black civil rights activist, actor, director.

Dorothy Day, 1897-1980, (U.S.) founder of Catholic Worker movement.

Eugene V. Debs, 1855-1926, (U.S.) labor leader; led Pullman Strike, 1894; four-time Socialist presidential candidate.

Vine Deloria Jr., 1933-2005, (U.S.) Native American activist, author; *Custer Died for Your Sins*.

Dorothea Dix, 1802-87, (U.S.) crusader for mentally ill.

Thomas Dooley, 1927-61, (U.S.) "jungle doctor"; noted for efforts to supply medical aid to developing countries.

Marjory Stoneman Douglas, 1890-1998, (U.S.) writer, environmentalist; campaigned to save Florida Everglades.

Frederick Douglass, 1817-95, (U.S.) author, editor, orator, diplomat; edited abolitionist weekly *The North Star*.

Andrea Dworkin, 1946-2005, (U.S.) radical feminist, antipornography crusader.

Medgar Evers, 1925-63, (U.S.) Black civil rights leader; campaigned to register Black voters; assassinated.

James Farmer, 1920-99, (U.S.) Black civil rights leader; founded Congress of Racial Equality (CORE).

Betty Friedan, 1921-2006, (U.S.) author, feminist; *The Feminine Mystique*.

Millard Fuller, 1935-2009, (U.S.) founder of Habitat for Humanity.

William Lloyd Garrison, 1805-79, (U.S.) abolitionist.

Miep Gies, 1909-2010, (Neth.) protector of Anne Frank and her family during WWII.

Emma Goldman, 1869-1940, (Russ.-U.S.) published anarchist *Mother Earth*; birth-control advocate.

Samuel Gompers, 1850-1924, (U.S.) labor leader; first pres. of the American Federation of Labor (AFL).

Juliette Gordon Low, 1860-1927, (U.S.) Girl Scouts founder.

Prince Hall, 1735-1807, (U.S.) activist; founded Black Freemasonry; served in American Revolutionary War.

Michael Harrington, 1928-89, (U.S.) exposed poverty in affluent U.S. in *The Other America*, 1963.

Dorothy Height, 1912-2010, (U.S.) civil rights activist; pres. of the National Council of Negro Women, 1957-97.

Sidney Hillman, 1887-1946, (Lith.-U.S.) labor leader; helped organize CIO.

Benjamin Hooks, 1925-2010, (U.S.) civil rights activist; exec. dir. NAACP, 1977-92.

Samuel G. Howe, 1801-76, (U.S.) social reformer; changed public attitudes toward the blind, deaf, mentally challenged.

Marsha P. Johnson, 1945-92, (U.S.) LGBT rights activist.

Vernon Jordan, 1935-2021, (U.S.) civil rights activist.

Franklin Kameny, 1925-2011, (U.S.) gay rights activist.

Helen Keller, 1880-1968, (U.S.) crusader for better treatment for the disabled; deaf and blind herself.

Jack Kevorkian 1928-2011, (U.S.) pathologist; assisted-suicide activist.

Coretta Scott King, 1927-2006, (U.S.) Black civil rights leader; wife of Rev. Martin Luther King Jr.

Rev. Martin Luther King Jr., 1929-68, (U.S.) civil rights leader; led 1955-56

Montgomery, AL, boycott; founder, pres., Southern Christian Leadership Conference, 1957; Nobel peace laureate, 1964; assassinated.

Larry Kramer, 1935-2020, (U.S.) HIV/AIDS activist.

Maggie Kuhn, 1905-95, (U.S.) founded Gray Panthers, 1970.

William Kunstler, 1919-95, (U.S.) civil liberties attorney.

John Lewis, 1940-2020, (U.S.) U.S. rep. (D, GA), Black civil rights activist.

John L. Lewis, 1880-1969, (U.S.) labor leader; headed United Mine Workers, 1920-60.

Belva Lockwood, 1830-1917, (U.S.) lawyer; first woman to argue before U.S. Supreme Court.

Almena Lomax, 1915-2011, (U.S.) civil rights activist; journalist who founded *The Los Angeles Tribune*.

Rev. Joseph Lowery, 1921-2020, (U.S.) Black civil rights activist.

Clara Luper, 1923-2011, (U.S.) civil rights activist.

Wangari Maathai, 1940-2011, (Kenya) environmental activist; 2004 Nobel Peace Prize winner.

Robert Macauley, 1923-2010, (U.S.) founder of AmeriCares.

Malcolm X (Little), 1925-65, (U.S.) Black Muslim, Black nationalist leader; promoted Black pride; assassinated.

Russell Means, 1939-2012, (Amer. Ind.) civil rights activist.

Karl Menninger, 1893-1990, (U.S.) with brother **William Menninger** (1899-1966), founded Menninger Clinic and Menninger Foundation.

Harvey Milk, 1930-78, (U.S.) LGBT rights activist; assassinated.

Kate Millett, 1934-2017, (U.S.) writer, feminist; *Sexual Politics*.

Lucretia Mott, 1793-1880, (U.S.) reformer, pioneer feminist.

Philip Murray, 1886-1952, (U.S.) Scottish-born labor leader.

Huey P. Newton, 1942-89, (U.S.) co-founded Black Panther Party, 1966.

Florence Nightingale, 1820-1910, (Br.) founder of modern nursing.

Emmeline Pankhurst, 1858-1928, (Br.) suffragette.

Rosa Parks,1913-2005, (U.S.) Black civil rights activist; her actions sparked 1955-56 Montgomery, AL, bus boycott.

A. Philip Randolph, 1889-1979, (U.S.) organized Brotherhood of Sleeping Car Porters, 1925; an organizer of 1941 and 1963 March on Washington movements.

Walter Reuther, 1907-70, (U.S.) labor leader; headed United Auto Workers.

Jacob Riis, 1849-1914, (Den.-U.S.) crusader for urban reforms.

Sylvia Rivera, 1951-2002, (U.S.) LGBT rights activist.

Paul Robeson, 1898-1976, (U.S.) actor, singer, Black civil rights activist.

Bayard Rustin, 1910-87, (U.S.) Black and LGBT civil rights activist; an organizer of the 1963 March on Washington.

Margaret Sanger, 1883-1966, (U.S.) social reformer; pioneered the birth-control movement.

Phyllis Schlafly, 1924-2016, (U.S.) anti-Equal Rights Amendment activist.

Earl of Shaftesbury (A. A. Cooper), 1801-85, (Br.) social reformer.

Eunice Kennedy Shriver, 1921-2009, (U.S.) cofounder of Special Olympics for athletes with intellectual disabilities.

Sargent Shriver, 1915-2011, (U.S.) founding director of Peace Corps; founder of Job Corps, Head Start.

Fred Shuttlesworth, 1922-2011, (U.S.) civil rights activist.

Albertina Sisulu, 1918-2011, (S. Africa) anti-apartheid activist.

Elizabeth Cady Stanton, 1815-1902, (U.S.) woman suffrage pioneer.

Lucy Stone, 1818-93, (U.S.) feminist, abolitionist.

Mother Teresa of Calcutta, 1910-97, (Alban.) nun; founded order to care for sick, dying poor; 1979 Nobel Peace Prize winner; canonized 2016.

Mamie Till-Mobley, 1921-2003, (U.S.) civil rights activist.

Willard Townsend, 1895-1957, (U.S.) organized the United Transport Service Employees (Red Caps), 1935.

Sojourner Truth (Isabella Baumfree), 1797-1883, (U.S.) preacher, abolitionist; worked for Black educ. opportunity.

Harriet Tubman, 1823-1913, (U.S.) prominent figure in the Underground Railroad; nurse, spy for Union Army in the Civil War.

Nat Turner, 1800-31, (U.S.) slave who led the most significant of more than 200 slave revolts in U.S., in Southampton, VA; hanged.

Desmond Tutu, 1931-2021, (S. Afr.) former S. African archbishop; 1984 Nobel Peace Prize winner.

Philip Vera Cruz, 1905-94, (Philip.-U.S.) helped found the United Farm Workers Union.

Rev. C(ordy) T(indell) Vivian, 1924-2020, (U.S.) Black civil rights activist.

Edgar Wayburn, 1906-2010, (U.S.) conservationist; Sierra Club pres.

Elie Wiesel, 1928-2016, (Rom.-U.S.) Holocaust survivor, author, and activist; 1986 Nobel Peace Prize winner.

William Wilberforce, 1759-1833, (Br.) social reformer; prominent in struggle to abolish slave trade.

Frances E. Willard, 1839-98, (U.S.) temperance, women's rights leader.

Betty Williams, 1944-2020, (N. Ire.) peace activist; 1976 Nobel Peace Prize winner.

Edith Windsor, 1929-2007, (U.S.) LGBT civil rights activist.

Mary Wollstonecraft, 1759-97, (Br.) *Vindication of the Rights of Women*.

Victoria Woodhull, 1838-1927, (U.S.) suffragist, first woman to run for president (1872).

Sports Personalities of the Past and Present

Henry (Hank) Aaron, 1934-2021, Milwaukee-Atlanta outfielder; hit then-record 755 home runs, record 2,297 RBI.

Kareem Abdul-Jabbar, b 1947, Milwaukee, L.A. Lakers center; MVP 6 times; second all-time leading NBA scorer, 38,387 pts.

Andre Agassi, b 1970, tennis player; 8 Grand Slam singles titles.

Troy Aikman, b 1966, quarterback; led Dallas Cowboys to Super Bowl wins in 1993-94, '96; Super Bowl MVP, 1993.

Ben Ainslie, b 1977, (Br.) most decorated Olympic sailor; gold, 2000, '04, '08, '12; silver, 1996.

Michelle Akers, b 1966, soccer player; led U.S. to victory in World Cup (1991, '99).

Grover Cleveland "Pete" Alexander, 1887-1950, pitcher; won 373 NL games; pitched 16 shutouts, 1916.

Muhammad Ali, 1942-2016, 3-time heavyweight champion, activist.

Morten Andersen, b 1960, (Den.) NFL kicker, career leader in games played (382).

Sparky Anderson, 1934-2010, first manager to win World Series in the NL (Cincinnati, 1975-76) and AL (Detroit, 1984).

Mario Andretti, b 1940, (It.) race-car driver; won Daytona 500 (1967), Indy 500 (1969); Formula 1 world title (1978).

Giannis Antetokounmpo, b 1994, (Gr.-Nigeria) Milwaukee Bucks forward; NBA MVP 2019, '20.

Earl Anthony, 1938-2001, bowler; 6 PBA Championships (1973-75, '81-'83), 43 career PBA tournaments.

Eddie Arcaro, 1916-97, only jockey to win racing's Triple Crown twice, 1941, '48; rode to 4,779 wins in his career.

Henry Armstrong, 1912-88, first boxer to hold world title in three weight classes simultaneously (1938).

Lance Armstrong, b 1971, cyclist; record 7-time winner of Tour de France (1999-2005); stripped of victories in 2012 for use of performance-enhancing drugs.

Arthur Ashe, 1943-93, tennis player; first Black man to win U.S. Open (1968), Austral. Open (1970), Wimbledon (1975).

YEAR *in* PICTURES

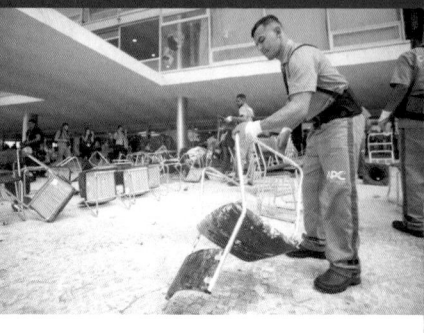

CIVIL DISORDER Supporters of former Brazilian Pres. Jair Bolsonaro stormed government buildings Jan. 8, 2023, in what Pres. Luis Inácio Lula da Silva described as an attempted coup.

SPEAKING OUT A series of unusually public protests in multiple cities in late 2022 called for an end to China's "zero-COVID" policy and ongoing lockdowns.

NIGERIA VOTES Bola Tinubu of Nigeria's ruling centrist All Progressives Congress was elected president of Africa's most populous country in Feb. 25, 2023, voting.

EARTH SHATTERING Powerful earthquakes struck Turkey (Türkiye) and Syria Feb. 6, 2023, causing widespread devastation and destruction and killing tens of thousands.

SITTING IN JUDGMENT Widespread protests in dozens of cities effectively shut down Israel Mar. 26-27, 2023, over a judicial overhaul proposed by the government of Prime Min. Benjamin Netanyahu.

FREE EVAN *Wall Street Journal* reporter Evan Gershkovich, detained in Russia since Mar. 29, 2023, was the first American journalist to be arrested there on spying charges since the Cold War.

PENSION PROTESTS Weeks of sometimes-violent protests greeted the proposal and eventual passing Apr. 14, 2023, of a pension-reform law that raised France's retirement age from 62 to 64.

FIT FOR A KING Charles III was crowned by the Archbishop of Canterbury during his coronation ceremony in Westminster Abbey May 6, 2023, in London, England.

WORLD

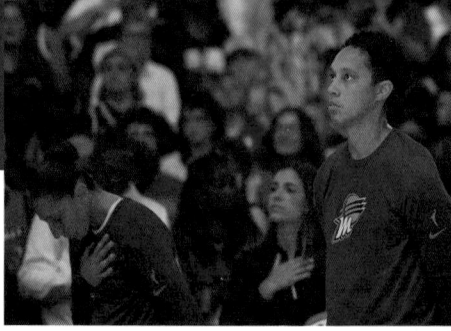

A WAR'S TOLL Nearly 18 months after Russia invaded Ukraine, U.S. officials estimated in Aug. 2023 that nearly half a million Ukrainian and Russian troops had been killed or wounded in the conflict.

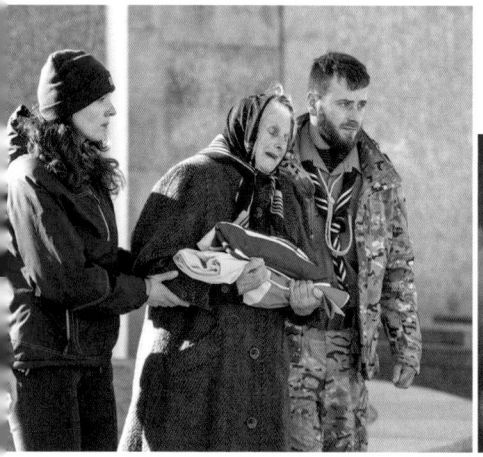

HOMECOMING WNBA star Brittney Griner played her first game back with the Phoenix Mercury May 19, 2023, after ten months in a Russian prison.

FLOODED OUT Ukrainian officials blamed Russian forces for an explosion that breached Ukraine's Kakhovka Dam near Kherson June 6, 2023, causing massive flooding requiring evacuations.

MIGRANT BOAT TRAGEDY An overcrowded fishing trawler that departed Libya days earlier overturned and sank off the coast of Pylos, Greece, June 14, 2023, leaving hundreds dead.

ANOTHER DEADLY QUAKE Morocco's most powerful earthquake in over a century struck Sept. 8, 2023, killing nearly 3,000 and creating massive destruction and need for aid.

WAR GAMES? The Wagner Group launched a short-lived revolt against Kremlin defense leadership June 23-24, 2023, as its mostly Russian mercenary fighters took control of Rostov-on-Don and headed toward Moscow.

SHOCK ATTACK The Palestinian militant group Hamas Oct. 7, 2023, launched a surprise attack on Israel from Gaza by land, sea, and air; within days, hundreds were killed in Israel and in Israeli counterattacks on Gaza.

TO THE SEA Libya's eastern city of Derna was devastated by catastrophic flooding that swept entire neighborhoods out to sea in Sept. 2023, with 4,000-10,000 believed dead and thousands more missing.

NATIONAL

PASS THE GAVEL Elected after a record 15 ballots Jan. 7, 2023, Rep. Kevin McCarthy (R, CA) was removed as Speaker of the House after just nine months.

A TRAIN'S TOLL A Norfolk Southern freight train carrying hazardous chemicals derailed Feb. 3, 2023, in East Palestine, OH, resulting in a massive fire, the mandatory evacuation of hundreds of residents, and lasting concern over the environmental toll.

SPY VS. SPY The U.S. Navy Feb. 5, 2023, began recovery operations to retrieve a large Chinese spy balloon that captured Americans' attention as it tracked across the entire continent before being downed by an Air Force jet off the South Carolina coast.

MEMPHIS TRAGEDY Five police officers were fired and faced various criminal charges in the death of Tyre Nichols, a 29-year-old Black Memphis man, after a violent beating during a traffic stop Jan. 7, 2023.

UP IN THE AIR Canadian wildfire smoke settled heavily over New York City and much of the East Coast for several days in early June 2023.

ONE EXTREME TO ANOTHER Multiple atmospheric river storm events brought damages and flood emergencies to many of California's formerly drought-stricken counties in late 2022 through spring 2023.

ROUGH START Freshman U.S. Rep. George Santos (R, NY), who admitted to lying about his education and work history, was charged with fraud and money laundering in federal court May 10, 2023.

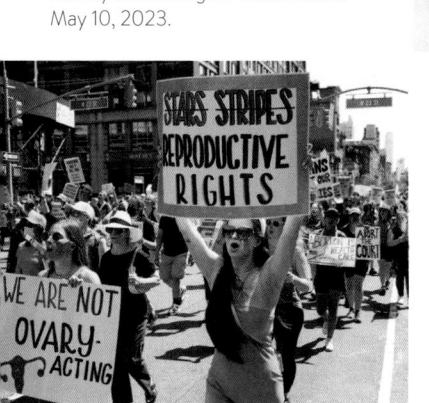

CULTURE WAR FRONT LINES, PART ONE
According to the American Civil Liberties Union, nearly 500 anti-LGBTQ+ bills were introduced in U.S. state legislatures in 2023; many of those targeted access to gender-affirming health care.

CULTURE WAR FRONT LINES, PART TWO
By June 2023, a year after the U.S. Supreme Court overturned the standard set by *Roe v. Wade*, 22 states had banned or added more restrictions on abortion.

199

UNPRECEDENTED PRESIDENT Donald Trump was the first former president to have a mug shot taken when he was booked on 13 charges at the Fulton County Jail in Atlanta, GA, Aug. 24, 2023.

THE SHOW MUST GO ON
Eight Republican presidential contenders met in the first debate of the primary season Aug. 23, 2023; former Pres. Trump declined to attend and other contenders did not meet the threshold for debate inclusion.

MAUI FIRE DISASTER Nearly 100 people were killed and thousands were left homeless after wildfires swept through Lahaina, Kula, and other sites on the island of Maui, HI, Aug. 8, 2023.

BLURRED LINES
U.S. border enforcement policy changed significantly upon the termination May 11, 2023, of the COVID-19 public health emergency and 38-month-old Title 42 asylum rule.

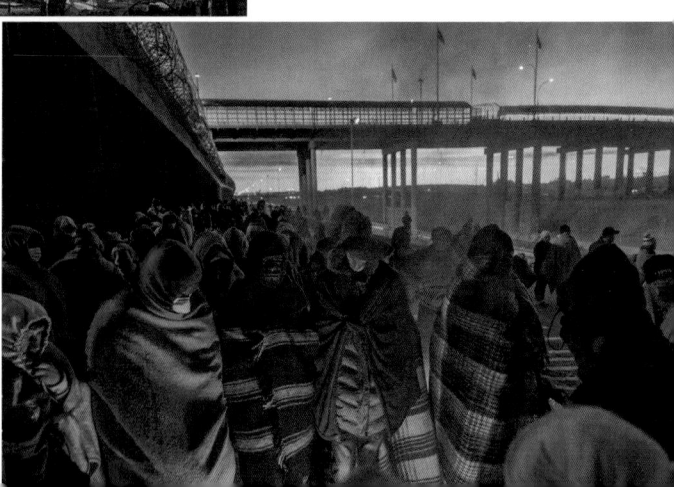

Evelyn Ashford, b 1957, sprinter; won 100m gold (1984) and silver (1988); member of 5 U.S. Olympic teams.

Red Auerbach, 1917-2006, coached Boston to 9 NBA titles.

Geno Auriemma, b 1954, (It.) UConn women's basketball coach; record 11 NCAA women's basketball titles.

Tracy Austin, b 1962, tennis player; youngest to win U.S. Open (age 16 in 1979).

Ernie Banks, 1931-2015, Chicago Cubs slugger; hit 512 NL homers; twice MVP.

Roger Bannister, 1929-2018, (Br.) physician; ran 1st sub-4-min. mile, May 6, 1954 (3 min., 59.4 sec.).

Charles Barkley, b 1963, NBA MVP, 1993; 4th player ever to surpass 20,000 pts., 10,000 rebounds, 4,000 assists.

Rick Barry, b 1944, NBA scoring leader, 1967; ABA scoring leader, 1969.

Sammy Baugh, 1914-2008, Washington Redskins quarterback, punter, defensive back.

Elgin Baylor, 1934-2021, L.A. Lakers forward; 11-time all-star.

Bob Beamon, b 1946, Olympic long jump gold medalist, 1968; world record jump of 29 ft 2½ in. stood until 1991.

Boris Becker, b 1967, (Ger.) tennis player; 6 Grand Slam singles titles.

David Beckham, b 1975, (Br.) soccer midfielder; joined L.A. Galaxy, 2007-12, with record-breaking $250-mil contract.

Bill Belichick, b 1952, NFL coach; led New England to 6 Super Bowl wins.

Jean Béliveau, 1931-2014, (Can.) Montréal Canadiens center; scored 507 career goals; twice MVP.

Johnny Bench, b 1947, Cincinnati Reds catcher; twice MVP; led league in home runs twice, RBIs 3 times.

Patty Berg, 1918-2006, won a record 15 LPGA majors.

Chris Berman, b 1955, sportscaster.

Yogi Berra, 1925-2015, NY Yankees catcher (1946-63); 3-time MVP.

Mookie Betts, b 1992, right fielder; AL MVP (2018).

Abebe Bikila, 1932-73, (Eth.) runner; won consecutive Olympic marathon gold medals in 1960 (barefoot), '64.

Simone Biles, b 1997, gymnast; won 7 Olympic medals, including 4 gold; record 30 world championship medals.

Matt Biondi, b 1965, swimmer; won 5 golds, 1988 Olympics.

Larry Bird, b 1956, Boston Celtics forward (1979-92); NBA MVP, 1984-86; 1998 coach of the year with Indiana Pacers.

Sue Bird, b 1980, point guard; 4-time WNBA champion (2004, '10, '18, '20); Olympic gold (2004, '08, '12, '16, '20).

Bonnie Blair, b 1964, speed skater; won 5 individual gold medals in 3 Olympics (1988, '92, '94).

George Blanda, 1927-2010, quarterback, kicker; 26 years as active player, scored 2,002 career points.

Fanny Blankers-Koen, 1918-2004, (Neth.) track and field athlete; won 4 Olympic medals (1948).

Wade Boggs, b 1958, AL batting champ, 1983, '85-'88; reached 3,000 career hits, 1999 (3,010).

Usain Bolt, b 1986, (Jam.) Olympic sprinter, gold medalist, 2008, '12, '16; world record for men's 100-m, 200-m runs.

Barry Bonds, b 1964, outfielder; hit record 73 homers, 2001; record 7-time NL MVP; 1st all-time in HRs (762); indicted in steroid scandal, 2007.

Björn Borg, b 1956, (Swed.) tennis player; 11 Grand Slam singles titles.

Ray Bourque, b 1960, (Can.) leads NHL defensemen in career goals, assists, points; 5-time Norris Trophy winner.

Bill Bradley, b 1943, led NY Knicks to 2 NBA titles (1970, '73); U.S. senator (NJ), 1979-97.

Donald Bradman, 1908-2001, (Austral.) widely regarded as greatest cricketer ever; set several batting records.

Terry Bradshaw, b 1948, quarterback; led Pittsburgh to 4 Super Bowl wins, 1975-76, '79-'80; NFL MVP, 1978.

Tom Brady, b 1977, quarterback; 7 Super Bowl titles; 5-time Super Bowl MVP; 3-time NFL MVP.

Drew Brees, b 1979, New Orleans Saints quarterback; Super Bowl MVP, 2010.

Christine Brennan, b 1958, sports journalist for *USA Today*, radio and TV commentator specializing in figure skating.

George Brett, b 1953, Kansas City Royals infielder; led AL in batting, 1976, '80, '90; MVP, 1980.

Lou Brock, 1939-2020, St. Louis Cardinals outfielder; stole NL single-season record 118 bases, 1974; led NL 8 times.

Jim Brown, 1936-2023, Cleveland fullback; 12,312 career yds; 3-time NFL MVP.

Paul Brown, 1908-91, football team owner, coach; led eponymous Cleveland Browns to 3 NFL championships.

Bob Bryan, b 1978, tennis player; won 16 Grand Slam doubles titles; Olympic gold, 2012.

Mike Bryan, b 1978, tennis player; won 18 Grand Slam doubles titles; Olympic gold, 2012.

Kobe Bryant, 1978-2020, NBA guard; won 5 titles with Lakers (2000-02, '09, '10); NBA MVP, 2008; NBA Finals MVP, 2009, '10.

Paul "Bear" Bryant, 1913-83, college football coach with 323 wins; led Alabama to 6 national titles (1961, '64-'65, '73, '78-'79).

Sergei Bubka, b 1963, (Ukr.) pole vaulter; first to clear 20 ft; gold medal, 1988 Olympics.

Joe Buck, b 1969, sportscaster.

Don Budge, 1915-2000, won numerous amateur and pro tennis titles; Grand Slam, 1938.

Dick Butkus, 1942-2023, Chicago Bears linebacker; NFL defensive player of the year (1969-70).

Dick Button, b 1929, figure skater; won 1948, '52 Olympic gold medals; world titleholder, 1948-52.

Miguel Cabrera, b 1983, (Venez.) 12-time MLB All-Star; won AL triple crown (2012); AL MVP 2012, '13.

Walter Camp, 1859-1925, Yale football player, coach, athletic director; established many rules for modern football.

Roy Campanella, 1921-93, Brooklyn Dodgers catcher (1948-57); 3-time NL MVP.

Earl Campbell, b 1955, NFL running back; MVP 1978-79.

Jose Canseco, b 1964, outfielder; led Oakland A's to the World Series, 1988; wrote book about steroids in baseball, 2005.

Eric Cantona, b 1966, (Fr.) soccer forward; Manchester United (1992-97).

Rod Carew, b 1945, AL infielder; 7 batting titles, 1977 MVP.

Steve Carlton, b 1944, NL pitcher; 4-time Cy Young winner; 4,136 career strikeouts.

Pete Carroll, b 1951, football coach; NCAA champion (2003, '04); won Super Bowl XLVIII.

Billy Casper, 1931-2015, PGA Player of the Year 2 times; U.S. Open champ twice.

Tamika Catchings, b 1979, basketball forward, WNBA MVP, 2011; 4-time Olympic gold medalist.

Tracy Caulkins, b 1963, swimmer; 3-time Olympic gold medalist.

Wilt Chamberlain, 1936-99, center; 7-time NBA leading scorer, 4-time MVP; scored 100 pts. in a game, 1962.

Nathan Chen, b 1999, figure skater; 2022 Olympic gold medalist; U.S. champion, 2017-22; world champion, 2018-19, '21.

Bobby Clarke, b 1949, (Can.) Philadelphia Flyers center; led team to 2 Stanley Cup championships; 3-time MVP.

Roger Clemens, b 1962, pitcher; 1986 AL MVP; record 7-time Cy Young winner; 354 wins, 4,672 Ks (3rd all-time); accused of lying to Congress about steroids, 2010.

Roberto Clemente, 1934-72, Pittsburgh Pirates outfielder; won 4 batting titles;

MVP, 1966; 3,000 career hits; killed in plane crash on aid mission.

Kim Clijsters, b 1983, (Belg.) tennis player; 4 Grand Slam singles titles.

Ty Cobb, 1886-1961, Detroit Tigers outfielder; record .367 lifetime batting average, 12 batting titles.

Sebastian Coe, b 1956, (Br.) runner; won Olympic 1,500m gold medal and 800m silver medal in both 1980, '84.

Nadia Comaneci, b 1961, (Rom.) gymnast; won 3 gold medals, achieved 7 perfect scores, 1976 Olympics; 9 Olympic medals overall.

Maureen Connolly, 1934-69, tennis player; 9 Grand Slam singles titles.

Jimmy Connors, b 1952, tennis player; 8 Grand Slam singles titles.

Alberto Contador, b 1982, (Sp.) cyclist; won Tour de France 2007, '09; stripped of 2010 title because of doping offense.

Cynthia Cooper-Dyke, b 1963, WNBA player; 4-time finals MVP; 2-time league MVP.

James J. Corbett, 1866-1933, heavyweight champion, 1892-97; credited with being the first "scientific" boxer.

Angel Cordero Jr., b 1942, jockey; leading money winner, 1976, '82-'83; rode 3 Kentucky Derby winners.

Margaret Smith Court, b 1942, (Austral.) tennis player; won 24 Grand Slam singles titles (11 in Open Era).

Bob Cousy, b 1928, Boston guard; 6 NBA titles, 1957 MVP.

Sidney Crosby, b 1987, (Can.) hockey player; Art Ross, Hart Trophies (2007, '14); Olympic gold medal (2010, '14).

Mark Cuban, b 1958, Dallas Mavericks owner; known for outspokenness.

Stephen Curry, b 1988, NBA point guard; 4 NBA titles; NBA MVP, 2015, '16.

Bjoern Daehlie, b 1967, (Nor.) cross-country skier; 8 Olympic gold medals.

Al Davis, 1929-2011, Oakland Raiders owner, former coach.

Oscar De La Hoya, b 1973, boxer; won IBF lightweight (1995), WBC super lightweight (1996) and welterweight (1997-99, 2000) titles.

Donna de Varona, b 1947, swimmer; won 2 Olympic golds, 1964; 1st female sportscaster at a major network, 1965.

Dizzy Dean, 1910-74, pitcher; St. Louis Cardinals' "Gashouse Gang" in the '30s.

Mary Decker Slaney, b 1958, middle-distance runner; numerous U.S./world records.

Frank Deford, 1938-2017, writer for *Sports Illustrated*; author, commentator.

Jack Dempsey, 1895-1983, heavyweight champ, 1919-26.

Gail Devers, b 1966, Olympic 100m gold medalist (1992, '96).

Joe DiMaggio, 1914-99, NY Yankees outfielder; hit safely in record 56 consecutive games, 1941; AL MVP 3 times.

Novak Djokovic, b 1987, (Serb.) tennis player; 24 Grand Slam singles titles.

Landon Donovan, b 1982, soccer forward.

Tony Dorsett, b 1954, Heisman winner who led the Dallas Cowboys to an NFL title in his rookie year, 1977.

Gabrielle Douglas, b 1995, gymnast; Olympic gold in all-around (2012), team (2012, '16).

Caeleb Dressel, b 1996, swimmer; 7-time Olympic gold medalist (2016, '20).

Tim Duncan, b 1976, San Antonio center; NBA MVP, 2002, '03; 3-time Finals MVP.

Margaret Osborne duPont, 1918-2012, tennis player; 6-time Grand Slam singles champion.

Roberto Duran, b 1951, (Pan.) boxer; held titles at 3 weights; lost 1980 "no mas" fight to Sugar Ray Leonard.

Kevin Durant, b 1988, NBA forward; NBA MVP, 2014; Finals MVP, 2017, '18; Olympic gold medalist, 2012, '16, '20.

Leo Durocher, 1905-91, manager; won 3 NL pennants (Brooklyn, 1941; NY Giants, 1951, '54), 1954 World Series.

Dale Earnhardt Jr., b 1974, stock car racer; Daytona 500 winner (2004, '14).

Dale Earnhardt Sr., 1951-2001, 7-time NAS-CAR Winston Cup champ; died in a last-lap crash at 2001 Daytona 500.

Ashton Eaton, b 1988, Olympic decathlon gold medalist, 2012, '16.

Stefan Edberg, b 1966, (Swed.) tennis player; 6 Grand Slam singles titles.

Gertrude Ederle, 1905-2003, first woman to swim English Channel (1926).

Teresa Edwards, b 1964, 5-time basketball Olympian; gold medalist, 1984, '88, '96, 2000; bronze medalist, 1992.

Hicham El Guerrouj, b 1974, (Morocco) runner; holds world records in mile (3:43.13) and 1,500m (3:26); won gold medals in 1,500m and 5,000m, 2004 Olympics.

John Elway, b 1960, quarterback; led Denver Broncos to 2 Super Bowl wins, 1998-99; NFL MVP, 1987; Super Bowl MVP, 1999.

Roy Emerson, b 1936, (Austral.) tennis player; 12 Grand Slam singles titles.

Julius "Dr. J" Erving, b 1950, 3-time ABA MVP, 1981 NBA MVP.

Phil Esposito, b 1942, (Can.) NHL scoring leader 5 times.

Janet Evans, b 1971, 4 Olympic swimming golds, 1988, '92.

Lee Evans, 1947-2021, Olympic 400m gold medalist in 1968 with 43.86-sec. world record not broken until 1988.

Chris Evert, b 1954, tennis player; 18 Grand Slam singles titles.

Ray Ewry, 1873-1937, track and field athlete; won 8 Olympic gold medals (1900, '04, '08).

Nick Faldo, b 1957, (Br.) golfer; won Masters, British Open 3 times each.

Juan Manuel Fangio, 1911-95 (Arg.), 5-time World Grand Prix driving champ (1951, '54-'57).

Marshall Faulk, b 1973, 2000 NFL MVP; scored then-record 26 TDs, 2001; 3-time Off. Player of the Year (1999-2001).

Brett Favre, b 1969, quarterback; led Green Bay to Super Bowl win, 1997; 3-time NFL MVP.

Roger Federer, b 1981, (Switz.) tennis player; 20 Grand Slam singles titles.

Allyson Felix, b 1985, sprinter; 7-time Olympic gold medalist (2008, '12, '16, '20).

Bob Feller, 1918-2010, Cleveland Indians pitcher; won 266 games; pitched 3 no-hitters, 12 one-hitters.

Rollie Fingers, b 1946, pitcher; 341 career saves; AL MVP, Cy Young, 1981; World Series MVP, 1974.

Peggy Fleming, b 1948, world figure skating champion, 1966-68; gold medalist, 1968 Olympics.

Whitey Ford, 1928-2020, NY Yankees pitcher; won 10 World Series games.

George Foreman, b 1949, heavyweight champion, 1973-74, '94-'95; at 45, oldest to win a heavyweight title; gold medalist, 1968 Olympics.

Dick Fosbury, 1947-2023, high jumper; won 1968 Olympic gold medal; developed the "Fosbury Flop."

Jimmie Foxx, 1907-67, Red Sox, Athletics slugger; MVP 3 times; triple crown, 1933.

A. J. Foyt, b 1935, won Indy 500 4 times; U.S. Auto Club champ 7 times.

Dario Franchitti, b 1973, (Scot.) 3-time Indy 500 winner, 2007, '10, '12.

Missy Franklin, b 1995, swimmer; 5-time Olympic gold medalist (2012, '16).

Joe Frazier, 1944-2011, heavyweight champion, 1970-73; gold medalist, 1964 Olympics.

Walt Frazier, b 1945, guard for NY Knicks' NBA championship teams (1970, '73).

Chris Froome, b 1985, (Kenya) 4-time Tour de France winner (2013, '15-'17).

Peter Gammons, b 1945, sportswriter, broadcaster.

Lou Gehrig, 1903-41, NY Yankees 1st baseman; MVP, 1927, '36; triple crown, 1934; played 2,130 straight games (1925-39).

Althea Gibson, 1927-2003, tennis player; first Black woman to compete and win at Wimbledon, U.S. Open; 5 Grand Slam singles titles.

Bob Gibson, 1935-2020, St. Louis Cardinals pitcher; won Cy Young twice; struck out 3,117 batters.

Josh Gibson, 1911-47, Negro Leagues catcher; hit as many as 84 season home runs and 800 in career.

Marc Girardelli, b 1963, (Lux.) skier; won 5 World Cup titles.

Raúl González, b 1977, (Sp.) soccer player; led Real Madrid to 3 Champions League titles (1998, 2000, '02).

Jeff Gordon, b 1971, race-car driver; youngest to win NASCAR title 4 times (1995, '97-'98, 2001).

Steffi Graf, b 1969, (Ger.) tennis player; 22 Grand Slam singles titles (3rd all-time).

Otto Graham, 1921-2003, Cleveland quarterback; 4-time all-pro.

Red Grange, 1903-91, All-American at Univ. of Illinois, 1923-25; played for Chicago Bears, 1925-35.

"Mean" Joe Greene, b 1946, Pittsburgh Steelers lineman; twice NFL outstanding defensive player.

Wayne Gretzky, b 1961, (Can.) top scorer in NHL history with record 894 goals, 1,963 assists, 2,857 pts.; MVP, 1980-87, '89.

Bob Griese, b 1945, All-Pro quarterback; led Miami Dolphins to 17-0 season, 1972, 2 Super Bowl titles, 1973-74.

Ken Griffey Jr., b 1969, outfielder; led AL in homers 1994, '97-'99; 1997 AL MVP; 10 gold gloves.

Archie Griffin, b 1954, Ohio State running back; only 2-time winner of the Heisman Trophy (1974-75).

Florence Griffith Joyner, 1959-98, sprinter; won 3 gold medals at 1988 Olympics; world records for 100m and 200m.

Lefty Grove, 1900-75, pitcher; won 300 AL games.

Janet Guthrie, b 1938, 1st woman driver in Indy 500 (1977).

Tony Gwynn, 1960-2014, 8-time NL batting champ; 3,141 career hits.

Walter Hagen, 1892-1969, golfer; 5 PGA, 4 British Open titles.

Mika Hakkinen, b 1968, (Fin.) Formula One racing driver; Formula One champion, 1998-99.

George Halas, 1895-1983, founder/player/coach of Chicago Bears; won 6 NFL championships as coach.

Roy Halladay, 1977-2017, pitcher; Cy Young, 2003, '10; perfect game, 2010.

Dorothy Hamill, b 1956, figure skater; Olympic gold medalist, 1976.

Lewis Hamilton, b 1985, (Br.) race-car driver; 7-time Formula 1 world champ (2008, '14-'15, '17-'20).

Scott Hamilton, b 1958, U.S. and world figure skating champion, 1981-84; Olympic gold medalist, 1984.

Mia Hamm, b 1972, soccer player; led U.S. teams to World Cup victories (1991, '99) and Olympic gold (1996, 2004).

Yuzuru Hanyu, b 1994, (Jpn.) figure skater; Olympic gold medalist, 2014, '18.

James Harden, b 1989, NBA shooting guard; NBA MVP, 2018.

Franco Harris, 1950-2022, running back; 4 Super Bowls with Steelers (1975-76, '79-'80); 1,000+ season yds. 8 times.

Marvin Harrison, b 1972, Indianapolis Colts wide receiver; 143 single-season receptions, 2002.

Bill Hartack, 1932-2007, jockey; rode 5 Kentucky Derby winners.

Dominik Hasek, b 1965, (Czech.) NHL goaltender; 6 Vezina Trophies; NHL MVP, 1997-98.

John Havlicek, 1940-2019, Boston Celtics forward; scored 26,395 career pts.

Elvin Hayes, b 1945, 12-time NBA All-Star; scored 27,313 career pts.

Eric Heiden, b 1958, speed skater; won 5 Olympic golds, 1980.

Rickey Henderson, b 1958, outfielder; 1990 AL MVP; record 130 stolen bases, 1982; all-time leader in steals, runs.

Sonja Henie, 1912-69, (Nor.) world champion figure skater, 1927-36; Olympic gold medalist, 1928, '32, '36.

Martina Hingis, b 1980, (Switz.) 5 Grand Slam singles titles; youngest number-one player (16 yrs., 6 mos.), 1997.

Ben Hogan, 1912-97, golfer; won 4 U.S. Open titles, 2 PGA Championships, 2 Masters.

Larry Holmes, b 1949, World Heavyweight Champion, 1978-85.

Evander Holyfield, b 1962, 4-time heavyweight champion.

Rogers Hornsby, 1896-1963, NL 2nd baseman; batted record .424, 1924; twice won triple crown.

Paul Hornung, 1935-2020, Green Bay running back, kicker; Heisman Trophy winner, 1956.

Gordie Howe, 1928-2016, (Can.) hockey forward; NHL MVP 6 times; scored 801 goals in 26 NHL seasons.

Carl Hubbell, 1903-88, NY Giants pitcher; 20-game winner 5 consecutive seasons, 1933-37.

Bobby Hull, 1939-2023, (Can.) NHL all-star 10 times; MVP, 1965-66.

Brett Hull, b 1964, (Can.) St. Louis Blues forward; led NHL in goals, 1990-92; MVP, 1991.

Catfish Hunter, 1946-99, pitched perfect game, 1968; 20-game winner 5 times.

Don Hutson, 1913-97, Packers receiver; caught 99 TD passes; 2-time NFL MVP.

Juli Inkster, b 1960, golfer; won 7 career LPGA major titles.

Bo Jackson, b 1962, NFL running back (1987-90) and MLB outfielder (1986-91, '93-'94); 1985 Heisman Trophy winner.

Phil Jackson, b 1945, won 11 NBA titles as coach of Bulls and Lakers; 1970, '73 title as player with NY Knicks.

Reggie Jackson, b 1946, slugger; led AL in home runs 4 times; MVP, 1973; hit 5 World Series home runs, 1977.

"Shoeless" Joe Jackson, 1889-1951, outfielder; .356 career batting average; one of the "Black Sox" banned for allegedly throwing 1919 World Series.

Jaromír Jágr, b 1972, (Czech.) hockey player; NHL MVP, 1999; 5 Art Ross Trophies.

LeBron James, b 1984, NBA forward; 4-time NBA MVP; 4 NBA titles, 4-time Finals MVP; all-time leading NBA scorer.

Ron Jaworski, b 1951, NFL quarterback (1974-89), analyst.

Sally Jenkins, b 1960, sports journalist and writer for Washington Post.

Caitlyn Jenner, b 1949, Olympic men's decathlon gold medalist, 1976; came out as transgender woman, 2015.

Lynn Jennings, b 1960, runner; 3-time World, 9-time U.S. cross country champ; bronze (10,000m), 1992 Olympics.

Derek Jeter, b 1974, shortstop; led NY Yankees to 5 World Series titles; World Series MVP, 2000.

Earvin "Magic" Johnson, b 1959, 3-time NBA MVP; 5 NBA titles; 3-time Finals MVP.

Jack Johnson, 1878-1946, heavyweight champion, 1908-15.

Jimmie Johnson, b 1975, 7-time NASCAR Series champ.

Michael Johnson, b 1967, sprinter; 4-time Olympic gold medalist (1992, '96, 2000).

Rafer Johnson, 1934-2020, Olympic decathlon gold medalist (1960).

Randy Johnson, b 1963, MLB pitcher with 4,875 strikeouts (2nd all-time), perfect game, 2004; 5-time Cy Young winner.

Walter Johnson, 1887-1946, Washington Senators pitcher; won 417 games; record 110 shutouts.

Bobby Jones, 1902-71, won golf's Grand Slam, 1930; U.S. amateur champ 5 times, U.S. Open champ 4 times.

Cobi Jones, b 1970, soccer player; most U.S. national team appearances with 164.

David "Deacon" Jones, 1938-2013, 5-time All-Pro with L.A. Rams (1965-69); "sack" specialist credited with inventing the term.

Marion Jones, b 1975, multi-event Olympic medalist; stripped of medals in 2007 after admitting use of PEDs.

Roy Jones Jr., b 1969, light heavyweight champ, 1999-2004.

Michael Jordan, b 1963, guard; 10-time leading NBA scorer; 5-time MVP; 6-time Finals MVP.

Jackie Joyner-Kersee, b 1962, Olympic gold medalist in heptathlon (1988, '92), long jump (1988).

Dorothy Kamenshek, 1925-2010, 4 All-American Girls Baseball League titles, 1940s.

Mary Keitany, b 1982, (Ken.) distance runner; 4-time NYC marathon winner.

Travis Kelce, b 1989, NFL tight end; 2 Super Bowl wins.

Clayton Kershaw, b 1988, pitcher; NL Cy Young winner (2011, '13, '14).

Harmon Killebrew, 1936-2011, Minnesota Twins slugger; led AL in home runs 6 times; 573 career home runs.

Jean-Claude Killy, b 1943, (Fr.) skier; 3 Olympic golds, 1968.

Ralph Kiner, 1922-2014, Pittsburgh Pirates slugger; led NL in home runs 7 consecutive years, 1946-52.

Billie Jean King, b 1943, 12 Grand Slam singles titles (8 in Open Era); beat Bobby Riggs, 1973.

Peter King, b 1957, sportswriter.

Bob Knight, b 1940, NCAA basketball coach; led Indiana to men's title in 1976, '81, '87.

Brooks Koepka, b 1990, golfer; won U.S. Open, 2017-18; PGA championship, 2018-19, 2023.

Olga Korbut, b 1955, (Belarus) gymnast; 4 Olympic gold medals, 1972, '76.

Sandy Koufax, b 1935, 3-time Cy Young winner; lowest ERA in NL, 1962-66; pitched 4 no-hitters, 1 perfect game.

Jack Kramer, 1921-2009, world's number one tennis player, 1946-53; first at Wimbledon to compete in shorts.

Ingrid Kristiansen, b 1956, (Nor.) only runner to have held simultaneous world records in 5,000m, 10,000m, and marathon.

Julie Krone, b 1963, winningest female jockey; first woman to ride a winner in a Triple Crown race (Belmont, 1993).

Mike Krzyzewski, b 1947, basketball coach; 5 NCAA championships with Duke; led 3 Olympic gold medal teams (2008, '12, '16).

Michelle Kwan, b 1980, figure skater; 9 U.S., 5 World titles; silver medalist at 1998 Olympics, bronze in 2002.

Guy Lafleur, 1951-2022, (Can.) 3-time NHL scoring leader; 1977-78 MVP.

Alexi Lalas, b 1970, soccer player; first modern-era American to play in Italian League Serie A.

Kenesaw Mountain Landis, 1866-1944, 1st commissioner of baseball (1920-44); banned the 8 "Black Sox" involved in fixing 1919 World Series.

Tom Landry, 1924-2000, Dallas Cowboys head coach, 1960-88; won 2 Super Bowls (1972, '78); 270 career wins.

Dick "Night Train" Lane, 1928-2002, defensive back; NFL season record 14 interceptions (1952).

Don Larsen, 1929-2020, as NY Yankee, pitched only World Series perfect game, Oct. 8, 1956—2-0 win over Brooklyn.

Rod Laver, b 1938, (Austral.) tennis player; 11-time Grand Slam singles champion (5 in Open era).

Katie Ledecky, b 1997, swimmer; 10 Olympic medals, incl. 7 gold (2012, '16, '20).

Sunisa Lee, b 2003, gymnast; 3 Olympic medals (2020).

Mario Lemieux, b 1965, (Can.) 6-time NHL leading scorer; 3-time MVP; playoff MVP, 1991-92.

Greg Lemond, b 1961, cyclist; 3-time Tour de France winner (1986, '89-'90); first American to win the event.

Ivan Lendl, b 1960, (Czech.) tennis player; 8 Grand Slam singles titles.

Sugar Ray Leonard, b 1956, boxer; held titles in 5 different weight classes.

Lisa Leslie, b 1972, L.A. Sparks center; 3-time WNBA MVP.

Carl Lewis, b 1961, track and field athlete; won 10 Olympic medals (9 gold) in sprinting and long jump.

Lennox Lewis, b 1965, (Br.) heavyweight champ, 1994, 1997-2004; Olympic gold medalist, 1988.

Ray Lewis, b 1975, linebacker for the Baltimore Ravens; Super Bowl MVP, 2001.

Tara Lipinski, b 1982, youngest figure skater to win world championships, 1997, and Winter Olympic gold, 1998.

Carli Lloyd, b 1982, soccer midfielder; Olympic gold medalist (2008, '12); World Cup champion (2015, '19).

Ryan Lochte, b 1984, swimmer; 12-time Olympic medalist, incl. 6 gold (2004, '08, '12, '16).

Vince Lombardi, 1913-70, Green Bay Packers coach; led team to 5 NFL championships, 2 Super Bowl victories.

Nancy Lopez, b 1957, golfer; 4-time LPGA Player of the Year; 3-time winner of the LPGA Championship.

Greg Louganis, b 1960, won Olympic gold medals in both springboard and platform diving, 1984, '88.

Joe Louis, 1914-81, heavyweight champion, 1937-49.

Sid Luckman, 1916-98, Chicago Bears quarterback; led team to 4 NFL championships; MVP, 1943.

Connie Mack, 1862-1956, Philadelphia Athletics manager, 1901-50; won 9 pennants, 5 championships.

John Madden, 1936-2021, won Super Bowl as coach of Oakland Raiders (1977); NFL TV analyst.

Greg Maddux, b 1966, pitcher; won 4 Cy Young awards, 1992-95; 355 career wins.

Patrick Mahomes, b 1995, youngest QB to win a Super Bowl; NFL MVP (2018, 2022).

Karl Malone, b 1963, Utah Jazz, L.A. Lakers forward; MVP, 1997, '99; 36,928 career pts. (3rd all-time).

Moses Malone, 1955-2015, NBA center; 3-time MVP.

Eli Manning, b 1981, NY Giants quarterback; Super Bowl MVP, 2008, '12.

Peyton Manning, b 1976, quarterback; record 5 NFL MVP awards; Super Bowl MVP, 2007; single-season passing yards record (5,477), 2013.

Mickey Mantle, 1931-95, NY Yankees outfielder; triple crown, 1956; 18 World Series home runs; MVP 3 times.

Diego Maradona, 1960-2020, (Arg.) soccer player; led Argentina to World Cup, 1986.

Pete Maravich, 1947-88, guard; scored NCAA record 44.2 ppg during collegiate career; led NBA in scoring, 1977.

Rocky Marciano, 1923-69, heavyweight champion, 1952-56; retired undefeated.

Dan Marino, b 1961, Miami quarterback; NFL MVP, 1984; 5-time passing yards leader.

Roger Maris, 1934-85, NY Yankees outfielder; hit AL record 61 home runs, 1961, record held 37 years; MVP, 1960-61.

Marta (Marta Vieira da Silva), b 1986, (Braz.) soccer forward; FIFA World Player of the Year a record 6 times.

Eddie Mathews, 1931-2001, Milwaukee-Atlanta Braves 3rd baseman; hit 512 career home runs.

Christy Mathewson, 1880-1925, pitcher; won 373 games.

Bob Mathias, 1930-2006, decathlon gold, 1948, '52 Olympics.

Misty May-Treanor, b 1977, beach volleyball player; 3-time Olympic gold medalist with Kerri Walsh Jennings (2004, '08, '12).

Willie Mays, b 1931, NY-S.F. Giants center fielder; hit 660 home runs, led NL 4 times; had 3,283 hits; twice MVP.

Floyd Mayweather Jr., b 1977, boxer with 50-0 record.

Willie McCovey, 1938-2018, S.F. Giants slugger; hit 521 home runs; led NL 3 times; MVP, 1969.

John McEnroe, b 1959, tennis player; 7 Grand Slam singles titles.

John McGraw, 1873-1934, NY Giants manager; led team to 10 pennants, 3 championships.

Conor McGregor, b 1988, (Ire.) mixed martial artist.

Mark McGwire, b 1963, hit then-record 70 home runs in 1998; 583 career home runs; admitted PED use, 2010.

Rory McIlroy, b 1989, (N. Ire.) golfer; won U.S. Open, 2011; PGA Championship, 2012, '14; British Open, 2014.

Tamara McKinney, b 1962, 1st U.S. skier to win overall Alpine World Cup championship (1983).

Andrea Mead Lawrence, 1932-2009, skier; first woman to win 2 gold medals in alpine skiing at one Olympics (1952).

Lionel Messi, b 1987, (Arg.) soccer forward; 7-time Ballon d'Or winner; led Argentina to World Cup win, 2022.

Mark Messier, b 1961, (Can.) center; NHL MVP, 1990, '92; Conn Smythe Trophy, 1984.

Debbie Meyer, b 1952, 1st swimmer to win 3 individual Olympic golds (1968).

Al Michaels, b 1944, sportscaster.

Phil Mickelson, b 1970, golfer; 6 career major titles.

George Mikan, 1924-2005, Minn. Lakers center; considered the best basketball player of first half of 20th cent.

Stan Mikita, 1940-2018, (Czech.) Chicago Blackhawks center; led NHL in scoring 4 times; MVP twice.

Billy Mills, b 1938, runner; upset winner of the 1964 Olympic 10,000m; only American man ever to win the event.

Joe Montana, b 1956, S.F. 49ers quarterback; 3-time Super Bowl MVP.

Archie Moore, 1913-98, light-heavyweight champ, 1952-62.

Howie Morenz, 1902-37, (Can.) Montréal Canadiens forward; considered best hockey player of first half of 20th cent.

Alex Morgan, b 1989, soccer forward; women's World Cup champion (2015, '19); Olympic gold medalist (2012).

Edwin Moses, b 1955, undefeated in 122 consecutive 400m hurdles races, 1977-87; Olympic gold medalist, 1976, '84.

Shirley Muldowney, b 1940, 1st woman to race Natl. Hot Rod Assn. Top Fuel dragsters; 3-time NHRA points champ.

Andy Murray, b 1987, (Br.) tennis player; 3-time Grand Slam singles champion; Olympic gold medal in men's singles (2012, '16).

Eddie Murray, b 1956, 3rd MLB player with both 3,000+ hits and 500+ home runs.

Stan Musial, 1920-2013, St. Louis Cardinals hitter who won 7 NL batting titles; MVP 3 times.

Rafael Nadal, b 1986, (Sp.) tennis player; 22-time Grand Slam singles champion; Olympic gold medal in men's singles (2008).

Bronko Nagurski, 1908-90, (Can.) Chicago Bears fullback and tackle; gained more than 4,000 yds rushing.

Joe Namath, b 1943, Jets quarterback; 1969 Super Bowl MVP.

Rosie Napravnik, b 1988, jockey.

Steve Nash, b 1974, (Can.) Phoenix Suns point guard; NBA MVP, 2005, '06.

Martina Navratilova, b 1956, (Czech.) tennis player; won 18 Grand Slam singles titles.

Byron Nelson, 1912-2006, won 11 consecutive golf tournaments in 1945; twice Masters and PGA titlist.

Ernie Nevers, 1903-76, Stanford fullback; early pro football star.

Paula Newby-Fraser, b 1962, ([now] Zimbabwe) 8-time Ironman Triathlon world champ.

John Newcombe, b 1944, (Austral.) tennis player; 7 Grand Slam singles and 17 Grand Slam men's doubles titles.

Neymar (Neymar da Silva Santos Júnior), b 1992, (Braz.) soccer forward; led Brazil to Olympic gold, 2016.

Jack Nicklaus, b 1940, PGA Player of the Year, 1967, '72; leading money winner 8 times; won 18 majors (6 Masters).

Chuck Noll, 1932-2014, Pittsburgh Steelers coach; won 4 Super Bowls.

Dirk Nowitzki, b 1978, (Ger.) NBA forward; led Mavericks to NBA title, 2011; NBA MVP, 2007.

Paavo Nurmi, 1897-1973, (Fin.) distance runner; won 9 Olympic gold medals, 1920, '24, '28.

Lorena Ochoa, b 1981, (Mex.) LPGA Player of the Year, 2006-09, money leader 2006-08.

Al Oerter, 1936-2007, discus thrower; won gold medal at 4 consecutive Olympics, 1956, '60, '64, '68.

Apolo Ohno, b 1982, short-track speed skater; most decorated U.S. Winter Olympic athlete with 2 gold, 2 silver, 4 bronze (2002, '06, '10).

Shohei Ohtani, b 1994, (Jpn.) MLB pitcher and designated hitter; AL MVP, 2021.

Hakeem Olajuwon, b 1963, (Nigeria) Houston center; NBA MVP, 1994; playoff MVP, 1994-95; career blocked shots leader (3,830).

Barney Oldfield, 1878-1946, pioneer auto racer; was first to drive a car 60 mph, 1903.

Shaquille O'Neal, b 1972, center; led L.A. Lakers to NBA titles, 2000-02, and Miami Heat to NBA title, 2006; Finals MVP 2000-02; NBA MVP 2000.

Bobby Orr, b 1948, (Can.) Boston Bruins defenseman; 8-time Norris Trophy winner; led NHL in scoring twice, assists 5 times.

Naomi Osaka, b 1997, (Jpn.) tennis player; won U.S. Open (2018, '20), Austral. Open (2019, '21).

Mel Ott, 1909-58, NY Giants right fielder; hit 511 home runs; led NL 6 times.

Alexander Ovechkin, b 1985, (Russ.) hockey player; NHL MVP, 2008, '09, '13.

Jesse Owens, 1913-80, track-and-field athlete; 4 1936 Olympic golds.

Terrell Owens, b 1973, NFL wide receiver.

Satchel Paige, 1906-82, pitcher; starred in Negro Leagues, 1924-48; entered major leagues at age 42.

Arnold Palmer, 1929-2016, golf's first $1 mil winner; won 4 Masters, 2 British Opens.

Jim Palmer, b 1945, Baltimore Orioles pitcher; won Cy Young award 3 times; 20-game winner 8 times.

Inbee Park, b 1988, (S. Kor.) golfer; 2nd woman ever to win first 3 majors of season (2013).

Candace Parker, b 1986, WNBA forward; WNBA MVP (2008, '13); Olympic gold medalist (2008, '12).

Joe Paterno, 1926-2012, Penn St. football coach; national title-winner, 1982, '86; most wins in NCAA Div. I coaching history (409); legacy complicated by child sex abuse scandal at Penn St.

Danica Patrick, b 1982, race car driver; 1st woman to lead Indy 500 and to win NASCAR Sprint Cup series pole.

Floyd Patterson, 1935-2006, 2-time heavyweight champion; first to ever regain the title after losing it.

Walter Payton, 1954-99, Chicago Bears running back; 2nd most rushing yards in NFL history; top NFC rusher, 1976-80.

Pelé (Edson Arantes do Nascimento), 1940-2022, (Braz.) soccer player; led Brazil to 3 World Cups (1958, '62, '70); scored 1,281 goals.

Bob Pettit, b 1932, first NBA player to score 20,000 pts.; twice NBA scoring leader.

Richard Petty, b 1937, NASCAR national champ 7 times; 7-time Daytona 500 winner.

Michael Phelps, b 1985, Olympic swimmer; record-holder, most Olympic medals (28) and gold medals (23) won by a single athlete.

Oscar Pistorius, b 1986, (S. Afr.) sprinter, 1st double-leg amputee to compete in Olympics, 2012; convicted (2015) of murder in girlfriend's death.

Jacques Plante, 1929-86, (Can.) NHL goaltender; 7 Vezina trophies; first goalie to wear mask in a game.

Gary Player, b 1935, (S. Afr.) golfer; won 3 Masters, 3 British Opens, 2 PGA Championships, and U.S. Open.

Mike Powell, b 1963, track-and-field athlete; holds world record for long jump (29 ft 4.5 in.).

Steve Prefontaine, 1951-75, runner; 1st to win 4 NCAA titles in same event (5,000m, 1970-73).

Kirby Puckett, 1960-2006, Minnesota center fielder with .318 career avg.; World Series titles, 1987, '91.

Albert Pujols, b 1980, MLB slugger; NL MVP, 2005, '08-'09.

Paula Radcliffe, b 1973, British runner; fmr. marathon world record holder.

Manny Ramirez, b 1972, (Dom. Rep.) outfielder; 2004 World Series MVP; suspended for violating MLB performance-enhancing drug policy, 2009, '11.

Megan Rapinoe, b 1985, soccer forward; World Cup champion (2015, '19); won Golden Boot, Golden Ball (2019).

Willis Reed, 1942-2023, NY Knicks center; MVP, 1970; playoff MVP, 1970, '73.

Mary Lou Retton, b 1968, gymnast; won all-around gold medal at 1984 Olympics; also won 2 silvers, 2 bronzes.

Jerry Rice, b 1962, receiver; 1989 Super Bowl MVP; NFL record for career touchdowns (208), receptions (1,549).

Maurice Richard, 1921-2000, (Can.) Montréal Canadiens forward; scored 544 regular season goals, 82 playoff goals.

Branch Rickey, 1881-1965, MLB exec.; helped break baseball's color barrier, 1947; initiated farm system, 1919.

Cal Ripken Jr., b 1960, Baltimore shortstop; AL MVP, 1983, '91; most consecutive games played (2,632).

Mariano Rivera, b 1969, (Pan.) relief pitcher; helped NY Yankees to 5 World Series titles; World Series MVP, 1999; all-time MLB leader in regular season and postseason saves.

Oscar Robertson, b 1938, NBA guard; averaged career 25.7 pts. per game; MVP, 1964.

Brooks Robinson, 1937-2023, Baltimore Orioles 3rd baseman; played in 4 World Series; MVP, 1964; 16 gold gloves.

Frank Robinson, 1935-2019, MVP in both NL and AL; triple crown, 1966; 586 career home runs; first Black manager in majors.

Jackie Robinson, 1919-72, broke baseball's color barrier with Brooklyn Dodgers, 1947; NL MVP, 1949.

Sugar Ray Robinson, 1921-89, boxer; middleweight champion 5 times; welterweight champion, 1946-51.

Knute Rockne, 1888-1931, Notre Dame football coach, 1918-31; revolutionized game by stressing forward pass.

Aaron Rodgers, b 1983, NFL quarterback; led Packers to victory in Super Bowl XLV; Super Bowl MVP, 2011; NFL MVP, 2011, '14, '20, '21.

Bill Rodgers, b 1947, runner; won Boston and New York City marathons 4 times each between 1975 and 1980.

Alex Rodriguez, b 1975, MLB infielder; 3-time AL MVP; admitted steroid use 2001-03; suspended 162 games for PED use, 2013-14.

Juan "Chi Chi" Rodriguez, b 1935, champion golfer; 8 PGA tour wins, 22 Champions tour wins.

Ben Roethlisberger, b 1982, Pittsburgh Steelers quarterback; youngest QB to win Super Bowl, 2005.

Ronaldinho (Ronaldo de Assis Moreira), b 1980, (Braz.) soccer midfielder; FIFA World Player of the Year, 2004, '05.

Ronaldo (Ronaldo Luiz Nazario de Lima), b 1976, (Braz.) soccer forward; led Brazil to 2002 World Cup title; 3-time FIFA world player of the year.

Cristiano Ronaldo, b 1985, (Port.) soccer forward; FIFA player of the year, 2008; UEFA career scoring leader (141).

Art Rooney, 1901-88, NFL owner; bought Pittsburgh Pirates in 1933, renamed Steelers, 1940.

Pete Rose, b 1941, won 3 NL batting titles; hit in 44 consecutive games, 1978; most career hits, 4,256; banned for gambling, 1989; admitted betting on his team, 2004.

Ken Rosewall, b 1934, (Austral.) tennis player; 8 Grand Slam singles titles.

Ronda Rousey, b 1987, judoka and mixed martial arts fighter.

Patrick Roy, b 1965, (Can.) Montréal-Colorado goalie; only 3-time NHL playoffs MVP, 1986, '93, 2001.

Wilma Rudolph, 1940-94, sprinter; won 3 1960 Olympic golds.

Adolph Rupp, 1901-77, NCAA basketball coach; led Kentucky to 4 national titles, 1948-49, '51, '58.

Bill Russell, 1934-2022, Boston Celtics center; led team to 11 NBA titles; MVP 5 times; first Black coach of major pro sports team.

Babe Ruth, 1895-1948, NY Yankees outfielder; hit 60 home runs, 1927, 714 lifetime (3rd all-time); led AL 12 times.

Johnny Rutherford, b 1938, auto racer; won 3 Indy 500s.

Nolan Ryan, b 1947, pitcher; holds season (383), career (5,714) strikeout records; won 324 games (7 no-hitters).

Pete Sampras, b 1971, tennis player; 14 Grand Slam singles wins.

Joan Benoit Samuelson, b 1957, won 1st Olympic women's marathon (1984), Boston Marathon (1979, '83).

Barry Sanders, b 1968, running back; won Heisman Trophy, 1988; NFL MVP, 1997.

Deion Sanders, b 1967, NFL cornerback (1989-2000, '04-'05) and MLB outfielder (1989-95, '97, 2005).

Gale Sayers, 1943-2020, Chicago running back; twice led NFL in rushing.

Mike Schmidt, b 1949, Phillies 3rd baseman; led NL in home runs 8 times; 548 lifetime; 3-time NL MVP.

Michael Schumacher, b 1969, (Ger.) race-car driver; 7-time Formula 1 world champ (1994-95, 2000-04).

Vin Scully, 1927-2022, Dodgers broadcaster, 1950-2016.

Tom Seaver, 1944-2020, pitcher; won NL Cy Young award 3 times; won 311 major league games.

Monica Seles, b 1973, (Yugo.) tennis player; won 9 Grand Slam singles titles; stabbed on court by spectator, 1993.

Maria Sharapova, b 1987, (Russ.) tennis player; 5 Grand Slam singles titles.

Patty Sheehan, b 1956, golfer; 3 LPGA Championships (1983-84, '93).

Willie Shoemaker, 1931-2003, jockey; rode 4 Kentucky Derby, 5 Belmont Stakes winners.

Frank Shorter, b 1947, runner; only American to win men's Olympic marathon (1972) since 1908; silver medalist (1976).

Don Shula, 1930-2020, all-time winningest NFL coach (347 games).

Bill Simmons, b 1969, columnist; podcast, TV host; Grantland and theringer.com founder.

O. J. Simpson, b 1947, running back; rushed for 2,003 yds, 1973; AFC leading rusher 4 times; acquitted of murder, 1995; found guilty of robbery and kidnapping, imprisoned 2008-17.

Dean Smith, 1931-2015, basketball coach; 879 Division I wins; led North Carolina to 2 NCAA titles (1982, '93).

Emmitt Smith, b 1969, running back; NFL and Super Bowl MVP, 1993; rushed for career record 18,355 yds.

Conn Smythe, 1895-1980, (Can.) won 7 Stanley Cups as Toronto GM (1929-61); playoff MVP award named in his honor.

Sam Snead, 1912-2002, PGA and Masters champ 3 times each; 82 PGA tournament victories.

Annika Sorenstam, b 1970, (Swed.) golfer; set LPGA 18-hole record of 59 (−13); won 10 LPGA majors, including career Grand Slam.

Sammy Sosa, b 1968, (Dom. Rep.) MLB slugger; NL MVP, 1998; 1st to hit 60+ HR 3 times (1998-99, 2001).

Warren Spahn, 1921-2003, pitcher; won 363 NL games; 20-game winner 13 times; Cy Young winner, 1957.

Tris Speaker, 1888-1958, AL outfielder; batted .345 over 22 seasons; hit record 792 career doubles.

Jordan Spieth, b 1993, golfer; won Masters, 2015; U.S. Open, 2015; British Open, 2017.

Mark Spitz, b 1950, swimmer; won 7 golds at 1972 Olympics.

Amos Alonzo Stagg, 1862-1965, football innovator; Univ. of Chicago football coach for 41 years, 5 undefeated seasons.

Bart Starr, 1934-2019, Green Bay Packers quarterback; led team to 5 NFL titles, 2 Super Bowl victories.

Roger Staubach, b 1942, Dallas Cowboys quarterback; 2-time Super Bowl champ.

George Steinbrenner, 1930-2010, NY Yankees owner.

Casey Stengel, 1890-1975, managed Yankees to 10 pennants, 7 World Series wins between 1949 and 1960.

Breanna Stewart, b 1994, forward; WNBA champion and Finals MVP (2018, '20); WNBA MVP, 2018.

Jackie Stewart, b 1939, (Scot.) auto racer; 27 Grand Prix wins.

John Stockton, b 1962, Utah Jazz guard; NBA career leader in assists, steals; NBA assists leader, 1988-96.

Picabo Street, b 1971, skier; 2-time World Cup downhill champion (1995-96); Olympic super G gold medalist, 1998.

Louise Suggs, 1923-2015, golfer; U.S. Women's Open champ, 1949, '52; 11 major victories.

John L. Sullivan, 1858-1918, last bare-knuckle heavyweight champion, 1882-92.

Pat Summerall, 1930-2013, NFL kicker, radio and TV sportscaster who announced 26 Super Bowls.

Pat Summitt, 1952-2016, women's basketball coach; led Tennessee to 8 NCAA titles; 1,098 career wins.

Ichiro Suzuki, b 1973, (Jpn.) outfielder; AL MVP, 2001; single-season hits record (262), 2004; 3,000th U.S. hit, 2016.

Sheryl Swoopes, b 1971, guard/forward; 1st 3-time WNBA MVP (2000, '02, '05); Olympic gold medalist (1996, 2000, '04).

Fran Tarkenton, b 1940, Minnesota, NY Giants quarterback; 342 career TD passes; 1975 Player of the Year.

Diana Taurasi, b 1982, WNBA guard; leading all-time scorer; 5-time Olympic gold medalist; WNBA MVP, 2009.

Lawrence Taylor, b 1959, linebacker; led NY Giants to 2 Super Bowl titles; played in 10 Pro Bowls.

Daley Thompson, b 1958, (Br.) decathlete; Olympic gold medalist in 1980, '84.

Jenny Thompson, b 1973, swimmer; 12 Olympic medals (8 gold) in 1992, '96, 2000, '04.

Bobby Thomson, 1923-2010, MLB utility player known for pennant-clinching

"Shot Heard 'Round the World" for the NY Giants, 1951.

Jim Thorpe, 1888-1953, football All-American, 1911-12; won pentathlon and decathlon, 1912 Olympics.

Bill Tilden, 1893-1953, tennis player; won 7 U.S. Open titles, 3 Wimbledon.

Y. A. Tittle, 1926-2017, NY Giants quarterback; MVP, 1961, '63.

Alberto Tomba, b 1966, (It.) alpine skier; 5 Olympic medals (3 golds, 2 silver) in 1988, '92, '94.

LaDainian "L.T." Tomlinson, b 1979, running back; NFL single-season record for rushing touchdowns (28).

Joe Torre, b 1940, MLB player, manager; NL MVP, 1971; won 4 World Series in 5 years as NY Yankees manager.

Lee Trevino, b 1939, golfer; 6-time PGA major winner.

Bryan Trottier, b 1956, (Can.) Islanders, Penguins center for 6 Stanley Cup champs.

Mike Trout, b 1991, MLB outfielder; 3-time AL MVP, 2014, '16, '19.

Gene Tunney, 1897-1978, heavyweight champion, 1926-28.

Mike Tyson, b 1966, undisputed heavyweight champ, 1987-90; at 20, youngest to win a heavyweight title (WBC, 1986).

Wyomia Tyus, b 1945, Olympic 100m gold medalist, 1964, '68.

Johnny Unitas, 1933-2002, Baltimore Colts quarterback; passed for more than 40,000 yds; MVP, 1957, '67.

Al Unser, 1939-2021, Indy 500 winner 4 times.

Bobby Unser, 1934-2021, Indy 500 winner 3 times.

Norm Van Brocklin, 1926-83, quarterback; passed for game record 554 yds, 1951; MVP, 1960.

Amy Van Dyken, b 1973, swimmer; first American woman to win 4 gold medals in one Olympics (1996).

Justin Verlander, b 1983, pitcher; won AL MVP, 2011, and Cy Young, 2011, '19, '22.

Sebastian Vettel, b 1987, (Ger.) Formula 1 race car driver.

Michael Vick, b 1980, quarterback; suspended and convicted (2007) of illegal dog fighting, gambling activities.

Lasse Viren, b 1949, (Fin.) runner; Olympic 5,000m and 10,000m gold medalist in 1972, '76.

Lindsey Vonn, b 1984, skier; Olympic gold, 2010; 4 overall World Cup titles 2008-10, '12.

Dwyane Wade, b 1982, guard; led Miami Heat to NBA title, 2006, '12-'13; finals MVP, 2006; NBA scoring title, 2009.

Honus Wagner, 1874-1955, Pittsburgh Pirates shortstop; 8 NL batting titles.

Grete Waitz, 1953-2011, (Nor.) distance runner; 9-time winner of the New York City Marathon (1978-80, '82-'86, '88).

"Jersey" Joe Walcott, 1914-94, boxer; became heavyweight champion at age 37, 1951-52.

Kerri Walsh Jennings, b 1978, beach volleyball player; 3-time Olympic gold medalist with Misty May-Treanor (2004, '08, '12).

Bill Walton, b 1952, center; led Portland Trail Blazers to 1977 NBA title; MVP, 1978; TV commentator.

Abby Wambach, b 1980, soccer player; 2 gold medals in Olympics (2004, '12).

Kurt Warner, b 1971, quarterback; NFL MVP, 1999, 2001; Super Bowl MVP, 2000.

Gerry "Bubba" Watson, b 1978, golfer; won Masters, 2012, '14.

Tom Watson, b 1949, golfer; 6-time PGA Player of the Year; won 5 British Opens, 2 Masters, U.S. Open.

Stan Wawrinka, b 1985, (Switz.) tennis player; won Austral. Open (2014), French Open (2015), U.S. Open (2016).

Karrie Webb, b 1974, (Austral.) golfer; youngest woman (26 yrs., 6 mos.) to win career Grand Slam, 1999-2001.

Johnny Weissmuller, 1903-84, swimmer; won 52 national championships, 5 Olympic gold medals.

Jerry West, b 1938, L.A. Lakers guard; career averaged 27 pts. per game.

Dan Wheldon, 1978-2011, (Br.) race-car driver; 2-time Indy 500 winner (2005, '11).

Byron "Whizzer" White, 1917-2002, running back; led NCAA in scoring and rushing at Colorado, 1937; led NFL in rushing twice, 1938, '40; Supreme Court justice, 1962-93.

Shaun White, b 1986, snowboarder/skateboarder, Olympic gold medalist in half-pipe (2006, '10, '18).

Kathy Whitworth, 1939-2022, 7-time LPGA Player of the Year; 88 tour wins, most on LPGA or PGA tour.

Michelle Wie West, b 1989, golfer; in 2002 became youngest-ever qualifier for LPGA event; turned pro at age 15.

Bradley Wiggins, b 1980, (Br.) cyclist; Tour de France winner, 2012; 8 Olympic medals (5 gold) over 5 Games.

Michael Wilbon, b 1958, commentator/analyst for ESPN.

Lenny Wilkens, b 1937, 3rd winningest coach in NBA history; Hall of Fame player and coach.

Serena Williams, b 1981, tennis player; 23-time Grand Slam singles champion; Olympic gold medals in singles (2012) and doubles (2000, '08, '12) with sister Venus.

Ted Williams, 1918-2002, Boston Red Sox outfielder; won 6 batting titles, 2 triple crowns; hit .406 in 1941.

Venus Williams, b 1980, tennis player; 7-time Grand Slam singles champion; Olympic gold medals in singles (2000) and doubles with sister Serena (2000, '08, '12).

Helen Wills Moody, 1905-98, tennis player; won U.S. Open 7 times, Wimbledon 8 times.

Katarina Witt, b 1965, (Ger.) figure skater; won Olympic gold medal, 1984, '88; world champ, 1984-85, '87-'88.

John Wooden, 1910-2010, UCLA basketball coach; 10 NCAA titles.

Tiger Woods, b 1975, golfer; youngest to win career Grand Slam, at age 24 (1997-2000); 15 career major titles.

Mickey Wright, 1935-2020, golfer; won LPGA and U.S. Open championship 4 times; 82 career wins, including 13 majors.

Eric Wynalda, b 1969, soccer player; scored 1st goal in major league soccer history (1996).

Kristi Yamaguchi, b 1971, figure skater; won national, world, Olympic titles in 1992.

Yao Ming, b 1980, (China) center for Houston Rockets; 8-time NBA All-Star.

Carl Yastrzemski, b 1939, Boston Red Sox slugger; won 3 batting titles; triple crown, 1967.

Cy Young, 1867-1955, pitcher; won record 511 games.

Steve Young, b 1961, 49ers quarterback; NFL MVP, 1992, '94; 3 Super Bowl titles, Super Bowl MVP, 1995.

Babe Didrikson Zaharias, 1911-56, all-around athlete; 3 track-and-field medals (2 golds), 1932 Olympics; won 10 golf majors; also played baseball; 6-time AP Female Athlete of the Year.

Emil Zátopek, 1922-2000, (Czech.) runner; won 3 gold medals at 1952 Olympics (5,000m, 10,000m, marathon).

Zinedine Zidane, b 1972, (Fr.) soccer midfielder; led France to 1998 World Cup title; named top player in 2006; 3-time FIFA world player of the year (1998, 2000, '03).

Writers of the Present

Name	Birthplace	Birthdate
Chimamanda Ngozi Adichie	Enugu, Nigeria	9/15/1977
Mitch Albom	Passaic, NJ.	5/23/1958
Elizabeth Alexander	New York, NY	5/30/1962
Sherman Alexie	Wellpinit, WA.	10/7/1966
Isabel Allende	Lima, Peru	8/2/1942
Dorothy Allison	Greenville, SC.	4/11/1949
Piers Anthony	Oxford, England, UK.	8/6/1934
Jeffrey Archer	Somerset, England, UK	4/15/1940
Margaret Atwood	Ottawa, ON, Canada.	11/18/1939
David Auburn	Chicago, IL	11/30/1969
Jean Auel	Chicago, IL	2/18/1936
Paul Auster	Newark, NJ	2/3/1947
Alan Ayckbourn	Hampstead, England, UK..	4/12/1939
Fredrik Backman	Stockholm, Sweden	6/2/1981
Nicholson Baker	New York, NY	1/7/1957
David Baldacci	Richmond, VA.	8/5/1960
Julian Barnes	Leicester, Eng., UK.	1/19/1946
Sebastian Barry	Dublin, Ireland.	7/5/1955
John Barth	Cambridge, MD	5/27/1930
Ann Beattie	Washington, DC	9/8/1947
Alan Bennett	Leeds, England, UK	5/9/1934
John Berendt	Syracuse, NY	12/5/1939
Elizabeth Berg	St. Paul, MN	12/2/1948
Wendell Berry	Henry County, KY	8/5/1934
Judy Blume	Elizabeth, NJ	2/12/1938
T. Coraghessan Boyle	Peekskill, NY.	12/2/1948
Barbara Taylor Bradford	Leeds, England, UK	5/10/1933
Christopher Bram	Buffalo, NY	2/22/1952
Geraldine Brooks	Sydney, NSW, Australia	9/14/1955
Dan Brown	Exeter, NH	6/22/1964
Rita Mae Brown	Hanover, PA	11/28/1944
Christopher Buckley	New York, NY	9/28/1952
James Lee Burke	Houston, TX	12/5/1936
Augusten Burroughs	Pittsburgh, PA	10/23/1965
Robert Olen Butler	Granite City, IL	1/20/1945
A. S. Byatt	Sheffield, England, UK.	8/24/1936
Ethan Canin	Ann Arbor, MI	7/19/1960
Peter Carey	Bacchus-Marsh, Vic., Australia	5/7/1943
Robert A. Caro	New York, NY	10/30/1935
Caleb Carr	New York, NY	8/2/1955
Michael Chabon	Washington, DC	5/24/1963
Tracy Chevalier	Washington, DC	10/19/1962
Lee Child	Coventry, England, UK.	10/29/1954
Sandra Cisneros	Chicago, IL	12/20/1954
Ta-Nehisi Coates	Baltimore, MD.	9/30/1975
Harlan Coben	Newark, NJ.	1/4/1962
Paulo Coelho	Rio de Janeiro, Brazil	8/24/1947
J(ohn) M(axwell) Coetzee	Capetown, South Africa	2/9/1940
Billy Collins	New York, NY	3/22/1941
Suzanne Collins	Hartford, CT	8/10/1962
Michael Connelly	Philadelphia, PA	7/21/1956
Robin Cook	New York, NY	5/4/1940
Patricia Cornwell	Miami, FL	6/9/1956
Michael Cunningham	Cincinnati, OH	11/6/1952
Don DeLillo	Bronx, NY	11/20/1936
Nelson DeMille	Jamaica, Queens, NY.	8/23/1943
Junot Díaz	Santo Domingo, Dominican Republic	12/31/1968
Annie Dillard	Pittsburgh, PA.	4/30/1945
Anthony Doerr	Cleveland, OH	10/27/1973
Emma Donoghue	Dublin, Ireland.	10/24/1969
Rita Dove	Akron, OH.	8/28/1952
Roddy Doyle	Dublin, Ireland.	5/8/1958
Carol Ann Duffy	Glasgow, Scotland, UK.	12/23/1955
Jennifer Egan	Chicago, IL	9/7/1962
Dave Eggers	Boston, MA.	3/12/1970
Bret Easton Ellis	Los Angeles, CA.	3/7/1964
James Ellroy	Los Angeles, CA.	3/4/1948
Louise Erdrich	Little Falls, MN	6/7/1954
Laura Esquivel	Mexico City, Mexico	9/30/1950
Jeffrey Eugenides	Detroit, MI.	3/8/1960
Janet Evanovich	South River, NJ.	4/22/1943
Helen Fielding	Morley, Yorkshire, Eng., UK..	2/19/1958
Fannie Flagg	Birmingham, AL	9/21/1944
Gillian Flynn	Kansas City, MO.	2/24/1971
Jonathan Safran Foer.	Washington, DC	2/21/1977
Ken Follett	Cardiff, Wales, UK.	6/5/1949
Richard Ford	Jackson, MS.	2/16/1944
Frederick Forsyth	Ashford, England, UK.	8/25/1938
Jonathan Franzen	Western Springs, IL	8/17/1959
Michael Frayn	London, England, UK.	9/8/1933
Charles Frazier	Asheville, NC	11/4/1950
Neil Gaiman	Portchester, England, UK.	11/10/1960
Roxane Gay	Omaha, NE.	10/15/1974
Malcolm Gladwell	Fareham, Hampshire, Eng., UK	9/3/1963
Robert Goddard	Fareham, Hampshire, Eng., UK	11/13/1954
Gail Godwin	Birmingham, AL	6/18/1937
Mary Gordon	Far Rockaway, NY.	12/8/1949
Amanda Gorman	Los Angeles, CA.	3/7/1998
David Grann	New York, NY	3/10/1967
John Green	Indianapolis, IN.	8/24/1977
Andrew Sean Greer	Washington, DC	11/21/1970
John Grisham	Jonesboro, AR	2/8/1955
John Guare	New York, NY	2/5/1938
Matt Haig	Sheffield, England, UK	7/3/1975
Daniel Handler	San Francisco, CA	2/28/1970
David Handler	Los Angeles, CA.	9/14/1952
Kristin Hannah	Garden Grove, CA	9/25/1960
Paul Harding	Wenham, MA	12/19/1967
David Hare	St. Leonards, Sussex, Eng., UK	6/5/1947
Robert Hass	San Francisco, CA	3/1/1941
Paula Hawkins	Harare, Zimbabwe	8/28/1972
Mark Helprin	New York, NY	6/28/1947
Carl Hiaasen	Plantation, FL	3/12/1953
Laura Hillenbrand	Fairfax, VA.	5/15/1967
S. E. Hinton.	Tulsa, OK	7/22/1948
Alice Hoffman	New York, NY	3/16/1952
Alan Hollinghurst	Stroud, Gloucestershire, England, UK	5/26/1954
Colleen Hoover	Sulphur Springs, TX	12/11/1979
Khaled Hosseini	Kabul, Afghanistan	3/4/1965
John Irving	Exeter, NH	3/2/1942
Walter Isaacson	New Orleans, LA	5/20/1952
Kazuo Ishiguro	Nagasaki, Japan.	11/8/1954
E. L. James	London, England, UK.	7/3/1963
Elfriede Jelinek	Müzzuschlag, Austria	10/20/1946
N. K. Jemisin	Iowa City, IA	9/19/1972
Ha Jin	Liaoning, China.	2/21/1956
Adam Johnson	South Dakota	7/12/1967
Edward P. Jones	Washington, DC	10/5/1950
Erica Jong	New York, NY	3/26/1942
Sebastian Junger	Boston, MA.	1/17/1962
Jan Karon	Lenoir, NC.	3/14/1937
Garrison Keillor	Anoka, MN.	8/7/1942
Thomas Keneally	Sydney, NSW, Australia	10/7/1935
William Kennedy	Albany, NY	1/16/1928
Sue Monk Kidd	Sylvester, GA	8/12/1948
Jamaica Kincaid	St. John's, Antigua and Barbuda	5/25/1949
Stephen King	Portland, ME.	9/21/1947
Barbara Kingsolver	Annapolis, MD	4/8/1955
Maxine Hong Kingston	Stockton, CA.	10/27/1940
Jeff Kinney	Andrews Air Force Base, MD	2/19/1971
Dean Koontz.	Everett, PA	7/9/1945
Ted Kooser	Ames, IA.	4/25/1939
Jon Krakauer	Brookline, MA	4/12/1954
Tony Kushner	New York, NY	7/16/1956
Jhumpa Lahiri	London, England, UK.	7/11/1967
Erik Larson	Brooklyn, NY.	1/3/1954
Jean Marie Gustave Le Clézio	Nice, France	4/13/1940
David Leavitt	Pittsburgh, PA.	6/23/1961
Jonathan Lethem	Brooklyn, NY	2/19/1964
Tracy Letts	Tulsa, OK	7/4/1965
David Lodge	South London, England, UK.	1/28/1935
Gregory Maguire	Albany, NY	6/9/1954
David Malouf	Brisbane, Qld., Australia.	3/20/1934
Thomas Mallon	Glen Cove, NY	11/2/1951
David Mamet	Chicago, IL.	11/30/1947
Emily St. John Mandel	Merville, BC, Canada	1979
Yann Martel	Salamanca, Spain	6/25/1963
George R. R. Martin	Bayonne, NJ	9/20/1948
Bobbie Ann Mason	nr. Mayfield, KY.	5/1/1940
Armistead Maupin	Washington, DC	4/13/1944
Colum McCann	Dublin, Ireland.	2/28/1965
Alice McDermott	Brooklyn, NY.	6/27/1953
Ian McEwan	Aldershot, England, UK.	6/21/1948
Thomas McGuane	Wyandotte, MI.	12/11/1939
Jay McInerney	Hartford, CT.	1/13/1955
Terry McMillan	Port Huron, MI	10/18/1951
John McPhee	Princeton, NJ	3/8/1931
Stephenie Meyer	Hartford, CT	12/24/1973
Steven Millhauser	New York, NY	8/3/1943
Walter Mosley	Los Angeles, CA .	1/12/1952
Andrew Motion	London, England, UK.	10/26/1952
Jojo Moyes	Maidstone, England, UK.	8/4/1969
Herta Müller	Nitzkydorf, Banat, Romania	8/17/1953
Alice Munro	Wingham, ON, Canada.	7/10/1931
Haruki Murakami	Kyoto, Japan.	1/12/1949
Celeste Ng	Pittsburgh, PA.	7/30/1980
Viet Thanh Nguyen	Buon Me Thuot, Vietnam	3/13/1971
Lynn Nottage	Brooklyn, NY	11/2/1964
Joyce Carol Oates	Lockport, NY.	6/16/1938
Edna O'Brien	Tuamgraney, Ireland	12/15/1930
Tim O'Brien	Austin, MN	10/1/1946
Kenzaburō Ōe	Uchiko, Japan.	1/31/1935
Michael Ondaatje	Colombo, Sri Lanka	9/12/1943
Delia Owens	GA	4/4/1949?
Cynthia Ozick	New York, NY	4/17/1928
Chuck Palahniuk	Pasco, WA	2/21/1962
Orhan Pamuk	Istanbul, Turkey.	6/7/1952
Suzan-Lori Parks	Fort Knox, KY	5/10/1963
Ann Patchett	Los Angeles, CA.	12/2/1963
James Patterson	Newburgh, NY	3/22/1947
Louise Penny	Toronto, ON, Canada	7/1/1958
Jodi Picoult	New York, NY	5/19/1966

Name	Birthplace	Birthdate	Name	Birthplace	Birthdate
Marge Piercy	Detroit, MI	3/31/1936	Zadie Smith	London, Eng., UK	10/25/1975
Dav Pilkey	Cleveland, OH	3/4/1966	Wole Soyinka	Abeokuta, Nigeria	7/13/1934
Robert Pinsky	Long Branch, NJ	10/20/1940	Nicholas Sparks	Omaha, NE	12/31/1965
Michael Pollan	New York, NY	2/6/1955	Danielle Steel	New York, NY	8/14/1947
Richard Powers	Evanston, IL	6/18/1957	R(obert) L(awrence) Stine	Columbus, OH	10/8/1943
Richard Price	Bronx, NY	10/12/1949	Kathryn Stockett	Jackson, MS	5/17/1969
E. Annie Proulx	Norwich, CT	8/22/1935	Tom Stoppard	Zlin, Czechoslovakia	7/3/1937
Philip Pullman	Norwich, England, UK	10/19/1946	Elizabeth Strout	Portland, ME.	1/6/1956
Thomas Pynchon	Glen Cove, NY	5/8/1937	Amy Tan	Oakland, CA	2/19/1952
David Rabe	Dubuque, IA	3/10/1940	Donna Tartt	Greenwood, MS	12/23/1963
Ishmael Reed	Chattanooga, TN.	2/22/1938	Paul Theroux	Medford, MA.	4/10/1941
Taylor Jenkins Reid	Ocean City, MD	12/20/1983	Olga Tokarczuk	Sulechow, Poland	1/29/1962
Rick Riordan	San Antonio, TX	6/5/1964	Amor Towles	Boston, MA.	10/24/1964
Mary Roach	Etna, NH.	3/20/1959	Calvin Trillin	Kansas City, MO.	12/5/1935
Nora Roberts	Silver Spring, MD	10/10/1950	Scott F. Turow	Chicago, IL	4/12/1949
Marilynne Robinson	Sandpoint, ID	11/26/1943	Anne Tyler	Minneapolis, MN.	10/25/1941
Veronica Roth	New York, NY	8/19/1988	Mario Vargas Llosa	Arequipa, Peru	3/28/1936
J. K. Rowling	Chipping Sodbury, Eng., UK	7/31/1965	Paula Vogel	Washington, DC	11/16/1951
Norman Rush	San Francisco, CA	10/24/1933	Sarah Vowell	Muskogee, OK	12/27/1969
Salman Rushdie	Bombay, India	6/19/1947	Ocean Vuong	Ho Chi Minh City, Vietnam	10/14/1988
Richard Russo	Johnstown, NY	7/15/1949	Alice Walker	Eatonton, GA	2/9/1944
George Saunders	Amarillo, TX	12/2/1958	Joseph Wambaugh	East Pittsburgh, PA.	1/22/1937
Alice Sebold	Madison, WI	9/6/1963	Jesmyn Ward	DeLisle, MS	4/1/1977
David Sedaris	Johnson City, NY	12/26/1956	Andy Weir	Davis, CA	6/16/1972
Vikram Seth	Calcutta, India.	6/20/1952	Edmund White	Cincinnati, OH	1/13/1940
John Patrick Shanley	Bronx, NY	10/13/1950	Colson Whitehead	New York, NY	11/6/1969
Lionel Shriver	Gastonia, NC	5/18/1957	Tobias Wolff	Birmingham, AL	6/19/1945
Jane Smiley	Los Angeles, CA.	9/26/1949	Markus Zusak	Sydney, NSW, Australia	6/23/1975

Writers of the Past

See also Journalists, and Greeks and Romans in Historical Figures chapter.

Chinua Achebe, 1930-2013, (Nigeria) novelist. *Things Fall Apart.*

Alice Adams, 1926-99, (U.S.) novelist, short-story writer. *Superior Woman.*

Richard Adams, 1920-2016, (Br.) novelist. *Watership Down.*

James Agee, 1909-55, (U.S.) novelist. *A Death in the Family.*

S(hmuel) Y(osef) Agnon, 1888-1970, (Isr.) Hebrew novelist. *Only Yesterday.*

Conrad Aiken, 1889-1973, (U.S.) poet, critic. *Ushant.*

Anna Akhmatova, 1889-1966, (Russ.) poet. *Requiem.*

Edward Albee, 1928-2016, (U.S.) playwright. *Who's Afraid of Virginia Woolf?*

Louisa May Alcott, 1832-88, (U.S.) novelist. *Little Women.*

Sholom Aleichem, 1859-1916, (Russ.) Yiddish writer. *Tevye's Daughters, The Old Country.*

Vicente Aleixandre, 1898-1984, (Sp.) poet. *La destrucción o el amor, Dialogalos del conocimiento.*

Horatio Alger, 1832-99, (U.S.) "rags-to-riches" books.

Jorge Amado, 1912-2001, (Brazil) novelist. *Dona Flor and Her Two Husbands, The Violent Land.*

Eric Ambler, 1909-98, (Br.) suspense novelist. *A Coffin for Dimitrios.*

Kingsley Amis, 1922-95, (Br.) novelist, critic. *Lucky Jim.*

Martin Amis, 1949-2023, (Br.) novelist, essayist. *Money, London Fields.*

Hans Christian Andersen, 1805-75, (Den.) author of fairy tales. *The Ugly Duckling.*

Maxwell Anderson, 1888-1959, (U.S.) playwright. *What Price Glory?, High Tor, Winterset, Key Largo.*

Sherwood Anderson, 1876-1941, (U.S.) short-story writer. "Death in the Woods," *Winesburg, Ohio.*

Maya Angelou, 1928-2014, (U.S.) poet, memoirist. *I Know Why the Caged Bird Sings.*

Reinaldo Arenas, 1943-90, (Cuba) short-story writer, novelist. *Before Night Falls.*

Ludovico Ariosto, 1474-1533, (It.) poet. *Orlando Furioso.*

Matthew Arnold, 1822-88, (Br.) poet, critic. "Thyrsis," "Dover Beach," "Culture and Anarchy."

John Ashbery, 1927-2007, (U.S.) poet. *Self-Portrait in a Convex Mirror.*

Isaac Asimov, 1920-92, (U.S.) versatile writer, espec. of science fiction. *I Robot.*

Miguel Angel Asturias, 1899-1974, (Guat.) novelist. *El Señor Presidente.*

Louis Auchincloss, 1917-2010, (U.S.) novelist, memoirist, short-story writer. *The Rector of Justin.*

W(ystan) H(ugh) Auden, 1907-73, (Br.) poet, playwright, literary critic. "The Age of Anxiety."

Jane Austen, 1775-1817, (Br.) novelist. *Pride and Prejudice, Sense and Sensibility, Emma, Mansfield Park.*

Ba Jin (Li Yaotang), 1904-2005, (China) novelist of pre-revolutionary China.

Isaac Babel, 1894-1941, (Russ.) short-story writer, playwright. *Odessa Tales, Red Cavalry.*

Russell Baker, 1925-2019, (U.S.) columnist, essayist. *Growing Up.*

James Baldwin, 1924-87, (U.S.) author, playwright. *The Fire Next Time, Blues for Mister Charlie.*

Honoré de Balzac, 1799-1850, (Fr.) novelist. *Le Père Goriot, Cousine Bette, Eugénie Grandet.*

Russell Banks, 1940-2023, (U.S.) novelist. *Continental Drift.*

James M. Barrie, 1860-1937, (Br.) playwright, novelist. *Peter Pan, Dear Brutus, What Every Woman Knows.*

Charles Baudelaire, 1821-67, (Fr.) poet. *Les Fleurs du Mal.*

L(yman) Frank Baum, 1856-1919, (U.S.) Wizard of Oz series.

Simone de Beauvoir, 1908-86, (Fr.) novelist, essayist. *The Second Sex, Memoirs of a Dutiful Daughter.*

Samuel Beckett, 1906-89, (Ire.) novelist, playwright. *Waiting for Godot, Endgame* (plays); *Murphy, Watt, Molloy* (novels).

Brendan Behan, 1923-64, (Ire.) playwright. *The Quare Fellow, The Hostage, Borstal Boy.*

Saul Bellow, 1915-2005, (U.S.) novelist. *The Adventures of Augie March, Humboldt's Gift.*

Robert Benchley, 1889-1945, (U.S.) humorist.

Stephen Vincent Benét, 1898-1943, (U.S.) poet, novelist. *John Brown's Body.*

Jan Berenstain, 1923-2012, and **Stan Berenstain**, 1923-2005, (both U.S.) co-writers and illustrators of Berenstain Bears series of children's books.

Thomas Berger, 1924-2014, (U.S.) novelist. *Little Big Man.*

John Berryman, 1914-72, (U.S.) poet. *Homage to Mistress Bradstreet.*

Ambrose Bierce, 1842-1914, (U.S.) short-story writer, journalist. *In the Midst of Life, The Devil's Dictionary.*

Maeve Binchy, 1940-2012, (Ire.) novelist, short-story writer. *Circle of Friends, Tara Road.*

Elizabeth Bishop, 1911-79, (U.S.) poet. *North and South—A Cold Spring.*

William Blake, 1757-1827, (Br.) poet, artist. *Songs of Innocence, Songs of Experience.*

Aleksandr Blok, 1880-1921, (Russ.) poet. "The Twelve," "The Scythians."

Harold Bloom, 1930-2019, (U.S.) literary critic. *The Anxiety of Influence.*

Enid Blyton, 1897-1968, (Br.) children's writer. Famous Five series.

Giovanni Boccaccio, 1313-75, (It.) poet. *Decameron.*

Heinrich Böll, 1917-85, (Ger.) novelist, short-story writer. *Group Portrait With Lady.*

Jorge Luis Borges, 1900-86, (Arg.) short-story writer, poet, essayist. *Labyrinths.*

James Boswell, 1740-95, (Scot.) biographer. *The Life of Samuel Johnson.*

Pierre Boulle, 1913-94, (Fr.) novelist. *The Bridge Over the River Kwai, Planet of the Apes.*

Paul Bowles, 1910-99, (U.S.) novelist, short-story writer. *The Sheltering Sky.*

Ray Bradbury, 1920-2012, (U.S.) novelist, short-story writer. *Fahrenheit 451, The Martian Chronicles.*

Anne Bradstreet, c. 1612-72, (U.S.) poet. *The Tenth Muse Lately Sprung Up in America.*

Bertolt Brecht, 1898-1956, (Ger.) dramatist, poet. *The Threepenny Opera, Mother Courage and Her Children.*

Joseph Brodsky, 1940-96, (Russ.-U.S.) poet. *A Part of Speech, Less Than One, To Urania.*

Charlotte Brontë, 1816-55, (Br.) novelist. *Jane Eyre.*

Emily Brontë, 1818-48, (Br.) novelist. *Wuthering Heights.*

Sterling A. Brown, 1901-89, (U.S.) poet, literature professor. *Southern Road.*

William Wells Brown, 1815-84, (U.S.) writer, memoirist; first novel by an African American, *Clotel*, 1853.

Elizabeth Barrett Browning, 1806-61, (Br.) poet. *Sonnets From the Portuguese, Aurora Leigh.*

Robert Browning, 1812-89, (Br.) poet. "My Last Duchess," "Fra Lippo Lippi," *The Ring and the Book.*

Pearl S. Buck, 1892-1973, (U.S.) novelist. *The Good Earth.*

Charles Bukowski, 1920-94, (U.S.) novelist, poet. *Ham on Rye, Women.*

Mikhail Bulgakov, 1891-1940, (Russ.) novelist, playwright. *The Heart of a Dog, The Master and Margarita.*

John Bunyan, 1628-88, (Br.) writer. *Pilgrim's Progress.*

Anthony Burgess, 1917-93, (Br.) author. *A Clockwork Orange.*

Frances Hodgson Burnett, 1849-1924, (Br.-U.S.) novelist. *The Secret Garden.*

Robert Burns, 1759-96, (Scot.) poet. "Flow Gently, Sweet Afton," "My Heart's in the Highlands," "Auld Lang Syne."

Edgar Rice Burroughs, 1875-1950, (U.S.) writer; created Tarzan, John Carter.

William S. Burroughs, 1914-97, (U.S.) novelist. *Naked Lunch.*

Octavia Butler, 1947-2006, (U.S.) science-fiction writer. *Kindred.*

George Gordon, Lord Byron, 1788-1824, (Br.) poet. *Don Juan, Childe Harold, Manfred, Cain.*

Pedro Calderon de la Barca, 1600-81, (Sp.) playwright. *Life Is a Dream.*

Hortense Calisher, 1911-2009, (U.S.) novelist, short-story writer. *False Entry.*

Italo Calvino, 1923-85, (It.) novelist, short-story writer. *If on a Winter's Night a Traveler.*

Luís Vaz de Camões, 1524?-80 (Port.) poet. *The Lusiads.*

Albert Camus, 1913-60, (Fr.) writer. *The Stranger, The Fall.*

Elias Canetti, 1905-94, (Bulg.) novelist, essayist. *Auto-Da-Fe.*

Karel Capek, 1890-1938, (Czech.) playwright, novelist, essayist. *R.U.R. (Rossum's Universal Robots).*

Truman Capote, 1924-84, (U.S.) author. *Other Voices, Other Rooms; Breakfast at Tiffany's; In Cold Blood.*

Eric Carle, 1929-2021, (U.S.) children's author and illustrator. *The Very Hungry Caterpillar.*

Lewis Carroll (Charles Dodgson), 1832-98, (Br.) writer, mathematician. *Alice's Adventures in Wonderland.*

Barbara Cartland 1901-2000, (Br.) romance novelist.

Giacomo Casanova, 1725-98, (It.) adventurer, memoirist.

Willa Cather, 1873-1947, (U.S.) novelist. *O Pioneers!, My Antonia, Death Comes for the Archbishop.*

Constantine Cavafy, 1863-1933, (Gr.) poet. "Ithaka," "Sensual Pleasures."

Camilo Jose Cela, 1916-2001, (Sp.) novelist. *The Family of Pascual Duarte, The Hive.*

Miguel de Cervantes Saavedra, 1547-1616, (Sp.) novelist, dramatist, poet. *Don Quixote.*

Raymond Chandler, 1888-1959, (U.S.) writer of detective fiction. Philip Marlowe series.

Geoffrey Chaucer, c. 1340-1400, (Br.) poet. *The Canterbury Tales, Troilus and Criseyde.*

John Cheever, 1912-82, (U.S.) novelist, short-story writer. *The Wapshot Scandal,* "The Country Husband."

Anton Chekhov, 1860-1904, (Russ.) short-story writer, dramatist. *Uncle Vanya, The Cherry Orchard, The Three Sisters.*

Charles Waddell Chesnutt, 1858-1932, (U.S.) author known for his short stories. *The Conjure Woman.*

G(ilbert) K(eith) Chesterton, 1874-1936, (Br.) critic, novelist, relig. apologist. Father Brown series of mysteries.

Kate Chopin, 1851-1904, (U.S.) writer. *The Awakening.*

Agatha Christie, 1890-1976, (Br.) mystery writer; created Miss Marple, Hercule Poirot. *Murder on the Orient Express, Murder of Roger Ackroyd.*

Tom Clancy, 1947-2013, novelist. *The Hunt for Red October.*

Mary Higgins Clark, 1927-2020, (U.S.) novelist. *Where Are the Children?*

Arthur C. Clarke, 1917-2008, (Br.) science-fiction writer. *2001: A Space Odyssey.*

James Clavell, 1924-94, (Br.-U.S.) novelist. *Shogun, King Rat.*

Beverly Cleary, 1916-2021, (U.S.) children's author. Ramona Quimby books.

Jean Cocteau, 1889-1963, (Fr.) writer, visual artist, filmmaker. *The Beauty and the Beast, Les Enfants Terribles.*

Samuel Taylor Coleridge, 1772-1834, (Br.) poet, critic. "Kubla Khan," "The Rime of the Ancient Mariner."

(Sidonie) Colette, 1873-1954, (Fr.) novelist. *Claudine, Gigi.*

Wilkie Collins, 1824-89, (Br.) novelist. *The Moonstone.*

Evan S. Connell, 1924-2013, (Br.) novelist, short-story writer. *Mrs. Bridge.*

Joseph Conrad, 1857-1924, (Br.) novelist. *Lord Jim, Heart of Darkness, The Secret Agent.*

Pat Conroy, 1945-2016, (U.S.) novelist. *The Prince of Tides, The Great Santini.*

James Fenimore Cooper, 1789-1851, (U.S.) novelist. Leatherstocking Tales, *The Last of the Mohicans.*

Pierre Corneille, 1606-84, (Fr.) dramatist. *Medeé, Le Cid.*

Hart Crane, 1899-1932, (U.S.) poet. "The Bridge."

Stephen Crane, 1871-1900, (U.S.) novelist, short-story writer. *The Red Badge of Courage,* "The Open Boat."

Harry Crews, 1935-2012, (U.S.) novelist. *A Feast of Snakes.*

Michael Crichton, 1942-2008, (U.S.) writer. *The Andromeda Strain, Jurassic Park.*

Countee Cullen, 1903-46, (U.S.) poet, prominent in the Harlem Renaissance of the 1920s. *The Black Christ.*

E. E. Cummings, 1894-1962, (U.S.) poet. *Tulips and Chimneys.*

Roald Dahl, 1916-90, (Br.-U.S.) writer. *Charlie and the Chocolate Factory, James and the Giant Peach.*

Gabriele D'Annunzio, 1863-1938, (It.) poet, novelist, dramatist. *The Child of Pleasure, The Intruder, The Victim.*

Dante Alighieri, 1265-1321, (It.) poet. *The Divine Comedy.*

Robertson Davies, 1913-95, (Can.) novelist, playwright, essayist. Salterton, Deptford, and Cornish trilogies.

Daniel Defoe, 1660-1731, (Br.) writer. *Robinson Crusoe, Moll Flanders, Journal of the Plague Year.*

Philip K. Dick, 1928-82, (U.S.) science-fiction writer. *Do Androids Dream of Electric Sheep?*

Charles Dickens, 1812-70, (Br.) novelist. *David Copperfield, Oliver Twist, Great Expectations, A Tale of Two Cities.*

James Dickey, 1923-97, (U.S.) poet, novelist. *Deliverance.*

Emily Dickinson, 1830-86, (U.S.) poet. "Because I could not stop for Death ...," "Success is counted sweetest ..."

Joan Didion, 1934-2021, (U.S.) essayist, novelist. *The Year of Magical Thinking.*

Isak Dinesen (Karen Blixen), 1885-1962, (Den.) author. *Out of Africa, Seven Gothic Tales, Winter's Tales.*

E(dgar) L(awrence) Doctorow, 1931-2015, (U.S.) novelist. *Ragtime, Billy Bathgate.*

John Donne, 1573-1631, (Br.) poet. *Songs and Sonnets.*

José Donoso, 1924-96, (Chile) novelist and short-story writer. *The Obscene Bird of Night.*

John Dos Passos, 1896-1970, (U.S.) novelist. *U.S.A.*

Fyodor Dostoyevsky, 1821-81, (Russ.) novelist. *Crime and Punishment, The Brothers Karamazov, The Possessed.*

Arthur Conan Doyle, 1859-1930, (Br.) novelist. Sherlock Holmes mystery stories.

Theodore Dreiser, 1871-1945, (U.S.) novelist. *An American Tragedy, Sister Carrie.*

John Dryden, 1631-1700, (Br.) poet, dramatist, critic. *All for Love, Mac Flecknoe, Absalom and Achitophel.*

Alexandre Dumas (père), 1802-70, (Fr.) novelist, dramatist. *The Three Musketeers, The Count of Monte Cristo.*

Alexandre Dumas (fils), 1824-95, (Fr.) dramatist, novelist. *La Dame aux Camélias, Le Demi-Monde.*

Paul Laurence Dunbar, 1872-1906, (U.S.) poet, novelist. *Lyrics of Lowly Life.*

Lawrence Durrell, 1912-90, (Br.) novelist, poet. *Alexandria Quartet.*

Umberto Eco, 1932-2016, (It.) novelist. *The Name of the Rose.*

Ilya G. Ehrenburg, 1891-1967, (Russ.) writer. *The Thaw.*

George Eliot (Mary Ann or Marian Evans), 1819-80, (Br.) novelist. *Silas Marner, Middlemarch.*

T(homas) S(tearns) Eliot, 1888-1965, (Br.) poet, critic. *The Waste Land,* "The Love Song of J. Alfred Prufrock."

Stanley Elkin, 1930-95, (U.S.) novelist, short-story writer. *George Mills.*

Ralph Ellison, 1914-94, (U.S.) writer. *Invisible Man.*

Ralph Waldo Emerson, 1803-82, (U.S.) poet, essayist. "Brahma," "Nature," "The Over-Soul," "Self-Reliance."

James T. Farrell, 1904-79, (U.S.) novelist. *Studs Lonigan.*

Howard Fast, 1914-2003, (U.S.) novelist. *Spartacus, The Immigrants.*

William Faulkner, 1897-1962, (U.S.) novelist. *Sanctuary; Light in August; The Sound and the Fury; Absalom, Absalom!*

Edna Ferber, 1887-1968, (U.S.) novelist, short-story writer, playwright. *So Big, Cimarron, Show Boat.*

Lawrence Ferlinghetti, 1919-2021, (U.S.) poet. *A Coney Island of the Mind.*

Henry Fielding, 1707-54, (Br.) novelist. *Tom Jones.*

F(rancis) Scott Fitzgerald, 1896-1940, (U.S.) short-story writer, novelist. *The Great Gatsby, Tender Is the Night.*

Gustave Flaubert, 1821-80, (Fr.) novelist. *Madame Bovary.*

Ian Fleming, 1908-64, (Br.) novelist. James Bond spy thrillers: *Dr. No, Goldfinger.*

Horton Foote, 1916-2009, (U.S.) playwright, screenwriter. *The Trip to Bountiful.*

Ford Madox Ford, 1873-1939, (Br.) novelist, critic, poet. *The Good Soldier.*

C(ecil) S(cott) Forester, 1899-1966, (Br.) writer. Horatio Hornblower books.

E(dward) M(organ) Forster, 1879-1970, (Br.) novelist. *A Passage to India, Howards End.*

Anatole France, 1844-1924, (Fr.) writer. *Penguin Island, My Friend's Book, The Crime of Sylvestre Bonnard.*

Dick Francis, 1920-2010, (Br.) crime novelist.

Marilyn French, 1929-2009, (U.S.) novelist. *The Women's Room.*

Brian Friel, 1929-2015, (N. Ire.) playwright. *Dancing at Lughnasa.*

Robert Frost, 1874-1963, (U.S.) poet. "Birches," "Fire and Ice," "Stopping by Woods on a Snowy Evening."

Carlos Fuentes, 1928-2012, (Pan.) novelist, essayist. *The Old Gringo.*

William Gaddis, 1922-98, (U.S.) novelist. *The Recognitions.*

Ernest J. Gaines, 1933-2019, (U.S.) novelist. *The Autobiography of Miss Jane Pittman.*

John Galsworthy, 1867-1933, (Br.) novelist, dramatist. *The Forsyte Saga.*

Federico García Lorca, 1898-1936, (Sp.) poet, dramatist. *Blood Wedding.*

Gabriel García Márquez, 1927-2014, (Col.) novelist. *One Hundred Years of Solitude.*

Erle Stanley Gardner, 1889-1970, (U.S.) mystery writer; created Perry Mason.

Jean Genet, 1911-86, (Fr.) playwright, novelist. *The Maids.*

Kahlil Gibran, 1883-1931, (Leban.-U.S.) mystical novelist, essayist, poet. *The Prophet.*

André Gide, 1869-1951, (Fr.) writer. *The Immoralist, The Pastoral Symphony, Strait Is the Gate.*

Allen Ginsberg, 1926-97, (U.S.) Beat poet. "Howl."

Jean Giraudoux, 1882-1944, (Fr.) novelist, dramatist. *Electra, The Madwoman of Chaillot, Ondine, Tiger at the Gate.*

Johann Wolfgang von Goethe, 1749-1832, (Ger.) novelist, dramatist, novelist. *Faust, Sorrows of Young Werther.*

Nikolai Gogol, 1809-52, (Russ.) short-story writer, dramatist, novelist. *Dead Souls, The Inspector General.*

William Golding, 1911-93, (Br.) novelist. *Lord of the Flies.*

William Goldman, 1931-2018, (U.S.) novelist, screenwriter. *The Marathon Man*, *The Princess Bride.*

Oliver Goldsmith, 1728-74, (Br.-Ire.) dramatist, novelist. *The Vicar of Wakefield*, *She Stoops to Conquer.*

Nadine Gordimer, 1923-2014, (S. Afr.) novelist. *Burger's Daughter.*

Maxim Gorky, 1868-1936, (Russ.) dramatist, novelist. *The Lower Depths.*

Sue Grafton, 1940-2017, (U.S.) crime novelist; Kinsey Millhone "alphabet mysteries."

Günter Grass, 1927-2015, (Ger.) novelist, poet. *The Tin Drum.*

Shirley Ann Grau, 1929-2020, (U.S.) novelist. *The Keepers of the House.*

Robert Graves, 1895-1985, (Br.) poet, classical scholar, novelist. *I, Claudius*; *The White Goddess.*

Thomas Gray, 1716-71, (Br.) poet. "Elegy Written in a Country Churchyard," "The Progress of Poesy."

Julien Green, 1900-98, (U.S.-Fr.) expatriate American novelist. *Moira*, *Each Man in His Darkness.*

Graham Greene, 1904-91, (Br.) novelist. *The Power and the Glory*, *The Heart of the Matter*, *The Ministry of Fear.*

Zane Grey, 1872-1939, (U.S.) writer of Western stories.

Jakob Grimm, 1785-1863, philologist, folklorist; with brother **Wilhelm Grimm**, 1786-1859, (both Ger.) collected *Grimm's Fairy Tales.*

Alex Haley, 1921-92, (U.S.) author. *Roots.*

Dashiell Hammett, 1894-1961, (U.S.) detective-story writer; created Sam Spade. *The Maltese Falcon.*

Jupiter Hammon, c. 1720-1800, (U.S.) poet; first African American to have his works published, 1761.

Knut Hamsun, 1859-1952, (Nor.) novelist. *Hunger.*

Lorraine Hansberry, 1930-65, (U.S.) playwright. *A Raisin in the Sun.*

Thomas Hardy, 1840-1928, (Br.) novelist, poet. *The Return of the Native*, *Tess of the D'Urbervilles*, *Jude the Obscure.*

E. Lynn Harris, 1955-2009, (U.S.) novelist. *Invisible Life*, *Basketball Jones.*

Joel Chandler Harris, 1848-1908, (U.S.) writer. Uncle Remus stories.

Jim Harrison, 1937-2016, (U.S.) novelist and essayist. *Legends of the Fall.*

Moss Hart, 1904-61, (U.S.) playwright. *Once in a Lifetime*, *You Can't Take It With You*, *The Man Who Came to Dinner.*

Bret Harte, 1836-1902, (U.S.) short-story writer, poet. *The Luck of Roaring Camp.*

Jaroslav Hasek, 1883-1923, (Czech.) writer, playwright. *The Good Soldier Schweik.*

Vaclav Havel, 1936-2011, (Czech.) essayist, poet, playwright. *The Power of the Powerless.*

John Hawkes, 1925-98, (U.S.) experimental fiction writer. *The Goose on the Grave*, *Blood Oranges.*

Nathaniel Hawthorne, 1804-64, (U.S.) novelist, short-story writer. *The Scarlet Letter*, "Young Goodman Brown."

Seamus Heaney, 1939-2013, (Ire.) poet. *Death of a Naturalist.*

Heinrich Heine, 1797-1856, (Ger.) poet. *Book of Songs.*

Robert Heinlein, 1907-88, (U.S.) science-fiction writer. *Stranger in a Strange Land.*

Joseph Heller, 1923-99, (U.S.) novelist. *Catch-22.*

Lillian Hellman, 1905-84, (U.S.) playwright, memoirist. *The Little Foxes*, *An Unfinished Woman*, *Pentimento.*

Ernest Hemingway, 1899-1961, (U.S.) novelist, short-story writer. *A Farewell to Arms*, *For Whom the Bell Tolls.*

O. Henry (W. S. Porter), 1862-1910, (U.S.) short-story writer. "The Gift of the Magi."

George Herbert, 1593-1633, (Br.) poet. "The Altar," "Easter Wings."

Zbigniew Herbert, 1924-98, (Pol.) poet. "Apollo and Marsyas."

Robert Herrick, 1591-1674, (Br.) poet. "To the Virgins to Make Much of Time."

John Hersey, 1914-93, (U.S.) novelist, journalist. *Hiroshima*, *A Bell for Adano.*

Hermann Hesse, 1877-1962, (Ger.) novelist, poet. *Death and the Lover*, *Steppenwolf*, *Siddhartha.*

Georgette Heyer, 1902-74, (Br.) Regency romance novelist.

Jack Higgins, 1929-2022, (Br.) novelist. *The Eagle Has Landed.*

Oscar Hijuelos, 1951-2013, (U.S.) novelist. *The Mambo Kings Play Songs of Love.*

Tony Hillerman, 1925-2008, (U.S.) novelist. *Dance Hall of the Dead.*

James Hilton, 1900-54, (Br.) novelist. *Lost Horizon.*

Chester Himes, 1909-84, (U.S.) novelist. *Cotton Comes to Harlem.*

Oliver Wendell Holmes, 1809-94, (U.S.) poet, novelist. *The Autocrat of the Breakfast-Table.*

bell hooks, 1952-2021, (U.S.) writer, critic. *All About Love.*

Gerard Manley Hopkins, 1844-89, (Br.) poet. "Pied Beauty," "God's Grandeur."

A(lfred) E. Housman, 1859-1936, (Br.) poet. *A Shropshire Lad.*

William Dean Howells, 1837-1920, (U.S.) novelist, critic. *The Rise of Silas Lapham.*

Langston Hughes, 1902-67, (U.S.) poet, lyric writer, author; a major influence in 1920s Harlem Renaissance.

Ted Hughes, 1930-98, (Br.) British poet laureate, 1984-98. *Crow.*

Victor Hugo, 1802-85, (Fr.) poet, dramatist, novelist. *Notre Dame de Paris*, *Les Misérables.*

Zora Neale Hurston, 1891-1960, (U.S.) novelist, folklorist. *Their Eyes Were Watching God*, *Mules and Men.*

Aldous Huxley, 1894-1963, (Br.) writer. *Brave New World.*

Henrik Ibsen, 1828-1906, (Nor.) dramatist, poet. *A Doll's House*, *Ghosts*, *The Wild Duck*, *Hedda Gabler.*

William Inge, 1913-73, (U.S.) playwright. *Picnic*; *Bus Stop.*

Eugene Ionesco, 1910-94, (Fr.) surrealist dramatist. *The Bald Soprano*, *The Chairs.*

Washington Irving, 1783-1859, (U.S.) writer. "Rip Van Winkle," "The Legend of Sleepy Hollow."

Christopher Isherwood, 1904-86, (Br.) novelist, playwright. *The Berlin Stories.*

Shirley Jackson, 1916-65, (U.S.) short-story writer. "The Lottery."

John Jakes, 1932-2023, (U.S.) novelist. The Kent Family Chronicles.

Henry James, 1843-1916, (U.S.) novelist, short-story writer, critic. *The Portrait of a Lady*, *The Ambassadors*, *Daisy Miller.*

P(hyllis) D(orothy) James, 1920-2014, (Br.) mystery novelist.

Robinson Jeffers, 1887-1962, (U.S.) poet, dramatist. *Tamar and Other Poems*, *Medea.*

James Weldon Johnson, 1871-1938, (U.S.) poet, novelist, diplomat; lyricist for *Lift Every Voice and Sing.*

Samuel Johnson, 1709-84, (Br.) author, scholar, critic. *Dictionary of the English Language*, *Vanity of Human Wishes.*

Ben Jonson, 1572-1637, (Br.) dramatist, poet. *Volpone.*

James Joyce, 1882-1941, (Ire.) writer. *Ulysses*, *Dubliners*, *A Portrait of the Artist as a Young Man*, *Finnegans Wake.*

Ernst Junger, 1895-1998, (Ger.) novelist, essayist. *The Peace*, *On the Marble Cliff.*

Franz Kafka, 1883-1924, (Austria-Hung./Czech.) novelist, short-story writer. *The Trial*, *The Castle*, "The Metamorphosis."

George S. Kaufman, 1889-1961, (U.S.) playwright. *The Man Who Came to Dinner*, *You Can't Take It With You.*

Yasunari Kawabata, 1899-1972, (Jpn.) novelist. *The Sound of the Mountains.*

Nikos Kazantzakis, 1883-1957, (Gr.) novelist. *Zorba the Greek*, *A Greek Passion.*

Alfred Kazin, 1915-98, (U.S.) author, critic. *On Native Grounds.*

John Keats, 1795-1821, (Br.) poet. "Ode on a Grecian Urn," "Ode to a Nightingale," "La Belle Dame Sans Merci."

Jack Kerouac, 1922-69, (U.S.) author, Beat poet. *On the Road*, *The Dharma Bums*, "Mexico City Blues."

Joyce Kilmer, 1886-1918, (U.S.) poet. "Trees."

Galway Kinnell, 1927-2014, (U.S.) poet.

Rudyard Kipling, 1865-1936, (Br.) author, poet. "The White Man's Burden," "Gunga Din," *The Jungle Book.*

Larry Kramer, 1935-2020, (U.S.) playwright. *The Normal Heart.*

Judith Krantz, 1928-2019, (U.S.) novelist. *Scruples.*

Maxine Kumin, 1925-2014, (U.S.) poet, author. *Up Country: Poems of New England.*

Milan Kundera, 1929-2023, (Czech.) novelist. *The Unbearable Lightness of Being.*

Jean de la Fontaine, 1621-95, (Fr.) poet. *Fables choisies* (Selected Fables).

Pär Lagerkvist, 1891-1974, (Swed.) poet, dramatist, novelist. *Barabbas*, *The Sybil.*

Selma Lagerlöf, 1858-1940, (Swed.) novelist. *Jerusalem*, *The Ring of the Lowenskolds.*

Alphonse de Lamartine, 1790-1869, (Fr.) poet, novelist, statesman. *Méditations poétiques.*

Charles Lamb, 1775-1834, (Br.) essayist. *Specimens of English Dramatic Poets*, *Essays of Elia.*

Louis L'Amour, 1908-88, (U.S.) Western author, screenwriter. *Hondo*, *The Cherokee Trail.*

Giuseppe di Lampedusa, 1896-1957, (It.) novelist. *The Leopard.*

William Langland, c. 1332-1400, (Br.) poet. *Piers Plowman.*

Ring Lardner, 1885-1933, (U.S.) short-story writer, humorist.

Steig Larsson, 1954-2004, (Swed.) novelist. *The Girl With the Dragon Tattoo.*

Arthur Laurents, 1917-2011, (U.S.) playwright and director. *West Side Story.*

D(avid) H(erbert) Lawrence, 1885-1930, (Br.) novelist. *Sons and Lovers*, *Women in Love*, *Lady Chatterley's Lover.*

Halldór Laxness, 1902-98, (Iceland) novelist. *Iceland's Bell.*

John le Carré, 1931-2020, (Br.) novelist. *The Spy Who Came in From the Cold*, *Tinker Tailor Soldier Spy.*

Harper Lee, 1926-2016, (U.S.) novelist. *To Kill a Mockingbird.*

Ursula K. Le Guin, 1929-2018, (U.S.) science-fiction writer. *The Left Hand of Darkness.*

Madeleine L'Engle, 1918-2007, (U.S.) young-adult novelist. *A Wrinkle in Time.*

Elmore Leonard, 1925-2013, (U.S.) novelist. *Get Shorty.*

Mikhail Lermontov, 1814-41, (Russ.) novelist, poet. "Demon", *Hero of Our Time.*

Alain-René Lesage, 1668-1747, (Fr.) novelist. *Gil Blas de Santillane.*

Doris Lessing, 1919-2013, (Br.) writer. *The Golden Notebook.*

Gotthold Lessing, 1729-81, (Ger.) dramatist, philosopher, critic. *Miss Sara Sampson*, *Minna von Barnhelm.*

Ira Levin, 1929-2007, (U.S.) novelist, playwright. *Deathtrap*, *Rosemary's Baby.*

C(live) S(taples) Lewis, 1898-1963, (Br.) critic, novelist, religious writer. *Allegory of Love*; *The Lion, the Witch and the Wardrobe*; *Out of the Silent Planet.*

Sinclair Lewis, 1885-1951, (U.S.) novelist. *Babbitt*, *Main Street*, *Dodsworth.*

Li Po, 701-762, (China) poet. "Song Before Drinking," "She Spins Silk."

Vachel Lindsay, 1879-1931, (U.S.) poet. *General William Booth Enters Into Heaven*, *The Congo.*

Hugh Lofting, 1886-1947, (Br.) writer. Dr. Doolittle series.

Jack London, 1876-1916, (U.S.) novelist, journalist. *Call of the Wild*, *The Sea-Wolf*, *White Fang.*

Henry Wadsworth Longfellow, 1807-82, (U.S.) poet. *Evangeline*, *The Song of Hiawatha.*

Lope de Vega, 1562-1635, (Sp.) playwright. *Noche de San Juan*, *Maestro de Danzar.*

H(oward) P(hillips) Lovecraft, 1890- 1937, (U.S.) novelist, short-story writer. "At the Mountains of Madness."

Amy Lowell, 1874-1925, (U.S.) poet, critic. "Lilacs."

James Russell Lowell, 1819-91, (U.S.) poet, editor. *Poems, The Biglow Papers.*

Robert Lowell, 1917-77, (U.S.) poet. "Lord Weary's Castle."

Alison Lurie, 1926-2020, (U.S.) novelist. *Foreign Affairs.*

Joaquim Maria Machado de Assis, 1839-1908, (Brazil) novelist, poet. *The Posthumous Memoirs of Bras Cubas.*

Archibald MacLeish, 1892-1982, (U.S.) poet. *Conquistador.*

Naguib Mahfouz, 1911-2006, (Egypt) novelist; first Arabic-language writer to win the Nobel Prize for Literature. *Cairo Trilogy.*

Norman Mailer, 1923-2007, (U.S.) novelist, essayist, journalist. *The Naked and the Dead.*

Bernard Malamud, 1914-86, (U.S.) short-story writer, novelist. *The Magic Barrel,* *The Assistant, The Fixer.*

Stéphane Mallarmé, 1842-98, (Fr.) poet. *Poésies.*

Thomas Malory, c. 1410-71, (Br.) writer. *Morte d'Arthur.*

Andre Malraux, 1901-76, (Fr.) novelist. *Man's Fate.*

Osip Mandelstam, 1891-1938, (Russ.) poet. *Stone, Tristia.*

Thomas Mann, 1875-1955, (Ger.) novelist, essayist. *Buddenbrooks, The Magic Mountain*, "Death in Venice."

Katherine Mansfield, 1888-1923, (Br.) short-story writer. "Bliss."

Hilary Mantel, 1952-2022, (Br.) novelist. *Wolf Hall, Bring Up the Bodies.*

Christopher Marlowe, 1564-93, (Br.) dramatist, poet. *Tamburlaine the Great, Dr. Faustus, The Jew of Malta.*

Andrew Marvell, 1621-78, (Br.) poet. "To His Coy Mistress."

John Masefield, 1878-1967, (Br.) poet. "Sea Fever," "Cargoes," *Salt Water Ballads.*

Edgar Lee Masters, 1869-1950, (U.S.) poet, biographer. *Spoon River Anthology.*

Peter Matthiessen, 1927-2014, (U.S.) novelist. *The Snow Leopard.*

W(illiam) Somerset Maugham, 1874-1965, (Br.) author. *Of Human Bondage, The Moon and Sixpence.*

Guy de Maupassant, 1850-93, (Fr.) novelist, short-story writer. "A Life," "Bel-Ami," "The Necklace."

François Mauriac, 1885-1970, (Fr.) novelist, dramatist. *Viper's Tangle, The Kiss to the Leper.*

Vladimir Mayakovsky, 1893-1930, (Russ.) poet, dramatist. *The Cloud in Trousers.*

Cormac McCarthy, 1933-2023, (U.S.) novelist. *All the Pretty Horses, The Road.*

Mary McCarthy, 1912-89, (U.S.) critic, novelist, memoirist. *Memories of a Catholic Girlhood.*

Frank McCourt, 1930-2009, (U.S.) memoirist. *Angela's Ashes, 'Tis.*

Carson McCullers, 1917-67, (U.S.) novelist. *The Heart Is a Lonely Hunter, Member of the Wedding.*

Colleen McCullough, 1937-2015, (Austral.) novelist. *The Thorn Birds.*

David McCullough, 1933-2022, (U.S.) historian, biographer. *Truman, John Adams.*

Larry McMurtry, 1936-2021, (U.S.) novelist. *Lonesome Dove.*

Terrence McNally, 1939-2020, (U.S.) playwright. *Love! Valour! Compassion!*

Herman Melville, 1819-91, (U.S.) novelist, poet. *Moby-Dick, Typee, Billy Budd.*

George Meredith, 1828-1909, (Br.) novelist, poet. *The Ordeal of Richard Feverel, The Egoist.*

Prosper Mérimée, 1803-70, (Fr.) author. *Carmen.*

James Merrill, 1926-95, (U.S.) poet. *Divine Comedies.*

W(illiam) S(tanley) Merwin, 1927-2019, (U.S.) poet. *The Lice.*

James Michener, 1907-97, (U.S.) novelist. *Tales of the South Pacific.*

Edna St. Vincent Millay, 1892-1950, (U.S.) poet. *The Harp Weaver and Other Poems.*

Arthur Miller, 1915-2005, (U.S.) playwright. *The Crucible, After the Fall, Death of a Salesman.*

Henry Miller, 1891-1980, (U.S.) novelist. *Tropic of Cancer.*

A(lan) A(lexander) Milne, 1882-1956, (Br.) author. *Winnie-the-Pooh.*

Czeslaw Milosz, 1911-2004, (Pol.) essayist, poet. "Esse," "Encounter."

John Milton, 1608-74, (Br.) poet, writer. *Paradise Lost, Comus, Lycidas, Areopagitica.*

Mishima Yukio (Hiraoka Kimitake) 1925-70, (Jpn.) writer. *Confessions of a Mask.*

Gabriela Mistral, 1889-1957, (Chile) poet. *Sonnets of Death.*

Margaret Mitchell, 1900-49, (U.S.) novelist. *Gone With the Wind.*

Jean Baptiste Molière, 1622-73, (Fr.) dramatist. *Tartuffe, Le Misanthrope, Le Bourgeois Gentilhomme.*

Ferenc Molnár, 1878-1952, (Hung.) dramatist, novelist. *Liliom, The Swan.*

Michel de Montaigne, 1533-92, (Fr.) essayist. *Essais.*

Eugenio Montale, 1896-1981, (It.) poet.

Brian Moore, 1921-99, (Ire.-U.S.) novelist. *The Lonely Passion of Judith Hearne.*

Clement C. Moore, 1779-1863, (U.S.) poet, educator. "A Visit From Saint Nicholas."

Marianne Moore, 1887-1972, (U.S.) poet.

Alberto Moravia, 1907-90, (It.) nov-elist, short-story writer. *The Time of Indifference.*

Thomas More, 1478-1535, (Br.) writer, statesman, saint. *Utopia.*

Wright Morris, 1910-98, (U.S.) novelist. *My Uncle Dudley.*

Toni Morrison, 1931-2019, (U.S.) novelist. *Song of Solomon, Beloved.*

Bharati Mukherjee, 1940-2017, (India-U.S.) novelist, short-story writer. *Jasmine.*

Murasaki Shikibu, c. 978-1026, (Jpn.) novelist. *The Tale of Genji.*

Iris Murdoch, 1919-99, (Br.) novelist, philosopher. *The Sea, the Sea.*

Alfred de Musset, 1810-57, (Fr.) poet, dramatist. *La Confession d'un Enfant du Siècle.*

Vladimir Nabokov, 1899-1977, (Russ.-U.S.) novelist. *Lolita, Pale Fire.*

V. S. Naipaul, 1932-2018, (Trinidad) novelist, travel writer. *A House for Mr. Biswas.*

R. K. Narayan, 1906-2001, (India) novelist. *The Guide.*

Ogden Nash, 1902-71, (U.S.) poet.

Irène Némirovsky, 1903-42, (Ukraine) novelist. *David Golder, Suite Française.*

Pablo Neruda, 1904-73, (Chile) poet. *Twenty Love Poems and One Song of Despair, Toward the Splendid City.*

Patrick O'Brian, 1914-2000, (Br.) historical novelist. *Master and Commander, Blue at the Mizzen.*

Sean O'Casey, 1884-1964, (Ire.) dramatist. *Juno and the Paycock, The Plough and the Stars.*

Flannery O'Connor, 1925-64, (U.S.) novelist, short-story writer. *Wise Blood,* "A Good Man Is Hard to Find."

Frank O'Connor (Michael Donovan), 1903-66, (Ire.) short-story writer. "Guests of a Nation."

Clifford Odets, 1906-63, (U.S.) playwright. *Waiting for Lefty, Awake and Sing, Golden Boy, The Country Girl.*

John O'Hara, 1905-70, (U.S.) novelist, short-story writer. *From the Terrace, Appointment in Samarra, Pal Joey.*

Omar Khayyam, c. 1028-1122, (Per.) poet. *Rubaiyat.*

Eugene O'Neill, 1888-1953, (U.S.) playwright. *Emperor Jones, Anna Christie, Long Day's Journey Into Night.*

George Orwell (Eric Arthur Blair), 1903-50, (Br.) novelist, essayist. *Animal Farm, Nineteen Eighty-Four.*

John Osborne, 1929-95, (Br.) dramatist, novelist. *Look Back in Anger, The Entertainer.*

Wilfred Owen, 1893-1918, (Br.) poet. "Dulce et Décorum Est."

Grace Paley, 1922-2007, (U.S.) short-story writer, poet. *The Little Disturbances of Man.*

Dorothy Parker, 1893-1967, (U.S.) poet, short-story writer. *Enough Rope, Laments for the Living.*

Robert B. Parker, 1932-2010, (U.S.) crime novelist. "Spenser" novels.

Boris Pasternak, 1890-1960, (Russ.) poet, novelist. *Doctor Zhivago.*

Alan Paton, 1903-88, (S. Africa) novelist. *Cry, the Beloved Country.*

Gary Paulsen, 1939-2021, (U.S.) young-adult novelist. *Hatchet, Dogsong.*

Octavio Paz, 1914-98, (Mex.) poet, essayist. *The Labyrinth of Solitude, They Shall Not Pass!, The Sun Stone.*

Samuel Pepys, 1633-1703, (Br.) public official, diarist.

S(idney) J(oseph) Perelman, 1904-79, (U.S.) humorist. *The Road to Miltown, Under the Spreading Atrophy.*

Charles Perrault, 1628-1703, (Fr.) writer. *Tales From Mother Goose (Sleeping Beauty, Cinderella).*

Petrarch (Francesco Petrarca), 1304-74, (It.) poet. *Africa, Trionfi, Canzoniere.*

Harold Pinter, 1930-2008, (Br.) playwright. *The Birthday Party, The Caretaker, The Homecoming.*

Luigi Pirandello, 1867-1936, (It.) novelist, dramatist. *Six Characters in Search of an Author.*

Sylvia Plath, 1932-63, (U.S.) author, poet. *The Bell Jar, The Colossus.*

Edgar Allan Poe, 1809-49, (U.S.) poet, short-story writer, critic. "Annabel Lee," "The Raven," "The Purloined Letter."

Alexander Pope, 1688-1744, (Br.) poet. *The Rape of the Lock, The Dunciad, An Essay on Man.*

Katherine Anne Porter, 1890-1980, (U.S.) novelist, short-story writer. *Ship of Fools.*

Chaim Potok, 1929-2002, (U.S.) novelist. *The Chosen.*

Ezra Pound, 1885-1972, (U.S.) poet. *Cantos.*

Anthony Powell, 1905-2000, (Br.) novelist. *A Dance to the Music of Time* series.

Terry Pratchett, 1948-2015 (Br.) fantasy novelist. *Discworld* series.

Reynolds Price, 1933-2011, (U.S.) novelist, short-story writer, poet. *A Long and Happy Life.*

J(ohn) B(oynton) Priestley, 1894-1984, (Br.) novelist, dramatist. *The Good Companions.*

Marcel Proust, 1871-1922, (Fr.) novelist. *Remembrance of Things Past.*

Aleksandr Pushkin, 1799-1837, (Russ.) poet, novelist. *Boris Godunov, Eugene Onegin.*

Mario Puzo, 1920-99, (U.S.) novelist. *The Godfather.*

François Rabelais, 1495-1553, (Fr.) writer. *Gargantua.*

Jean Racine, 1639-99, (Fr.) dramatist. *Andro-maque, Phèdre, Bérénice, Britannicus.*

David Rakoff, 1964-2012, (Can.-U.S.) essayist. *Fraud, Don't Get Too Comfortable.*

Ayn Rand, 1905-82, (Russ.-U.S.) novelist, moral theorist. *The Fountainhead, Atlas Shrugged.*

Terence Rattigan, 1911-77, (Br.) playwright. *Separate Tables, The Browning Version.*

Erich Maria Remarque, 1898-1970, (Ger.-U.S.) novelist. *All Quiet on the Western Front.*

Mary Renault, 1905-83, (Br.) novelist. *The Last of the Wine.*

Ruth Rendell, 1930-2015, (Br.) novelist. *Chief Inspector Reginald Wexford* mysteries.

Anne Rice, 1941-2021, (U.S.) novelist. *Interview With the Vampire.*

Adrienne Rich, 1929-2012, (U.S.) poet. *Diving Into the Wreck: Poems, 1971-1972.*

Samuel Richardson, 1689-1761, (Br.) novelist. *Pamela; or Virtue Rewarded.*

Rainer Maria Rilke, 1875-1926, (Ger.) poet. *Life and Songs, Duino Elegies, Poems From the Book of Hours.*

Arthur Rimbaud, 1854-91, (Fr.) poet. *A Season in Hell.*

Harold Robbins, 1916-97, (U.S.) novelist. *The Carpetbaggers.*

Edwin Arlington Robinson, 1869-1935, (U.S.) poet. "Richard Cory," "Miniver Cheevy," *Merlin.*

Theodore Roethke, 1908-63, (U.S.) poet. *Open House, The Waking, The Far Field.*

Romain Rolland, 1866-1944, (Fr.) novelist, biographer. *Jean-Christophe.*

Pierre de Ronsard, 1524-85, (Fr.) poet. *Sonnets pour Hélène, La Franciade.*

Christina Rossetti, 1830-94, (Br.) poet. "When I Am Dead, My Dearest."

Dante Gabriel Rossetti, 1828-82, (Br.) poet, painter. "The Blessed Damozel."

Edmond Rostand, 1868-1918, (Fr.) poet, dramatist. *Cyrano de Bergerac.*

Philip Roth, 1933-2018, (U.S.) novelist. *Portnoy's Complaint.*

Damon Runyon, 1880-1946, (U.S.) short-story writer, journalist. *Guys and Dolls, Blue Plate Special.*

John Ruskin, 1819-1900, (Br.) critic, social theorist. *Modern Painters, The Seven Lamps of Architecture.*

Oliver Sacks, 1933-2015, (Br.) neurologist, writer. *The Man Who Mistook His Wife for a Hat.*

François Sagan (Françoise Quoirez), 1935-2004, (Fr.) novelist. *Bonjour Tristesse.*

Antoine de Saint-Exupéry, 1900-44, (Fr.) writer. *Wind, Sand and Stars; The Little Prince.*

Saki (or H[ector] H[ugh] Munro), 1870-1916, (Br.) writer. *The Chronicles of Clovis.*

J. D. Salinger, 1919-2010, (U.S.) novelist. *The Catcher in the Rye.*

George Sand (Amandine Lucie Aurore Dupin), 1804-76, (Fr.) novelist. *Indiana, Consuelo.*

Carl Sandburg, 1878-1967, (U.S.) poet. *The People, Yes; Chicago Poems; Smoke and Steel; Harvest Poems.*

José Saramago, 1922-2010, (Port.) novelist. *Blindness.*

William Saroyan, 1908-81, (U.S.) playwright, novelist. *The Time of Your Life, The Human Comedy.*

Nathalie Sarraute, 1900-99, (Fr.) Nouveau Roman novelist. *Tropismes.*

May Sarton, 1914-95, (Belg.-U.S.) poet, novelist. *Encounter in April, Anger.*

Dorothy L. Sayers, 1893-1957, (Br.) mystery writer; created Lord Peter Wimsey.

Richard Scarry, 1920-94, (U.S.) author and illustrator of children's books. *Richard Scarry's Best Story Book Ever.*

Friedrich von Schiller, 1759-1805, (Ger.) dramatist, poet, historian. *Don Carlos, Maria Stuart, Wilhelm Tell.*

Walter Scott, 1771-1832, (Scot.) novelist, poet. *Ivanhoe.*

Gil Scott-Heron, 1949-2011, (U.S.) poet. "The Revolution Will Not Be Televised."

Jaroslav Seifert, 1902-86, (Czech.) poet.

Maurice Sendak, 1928-2012, (U.S.) children's book author and illustrator. *Where the Wild Things Are.*

Dr. Seuss (Theodor Seuss Geisel), 1904-91, (U.S.) children's book author and illustrator. *The Cat in the Hat.*

William Shakespeare, 1564-1616, (Br.) dramatist, poet. *Romeo and Juliet, Hamlet, King Lear, Julius Caesar,* sonnets.

Karl Shapiro, 1913-2000, (U.S.) poet. "Elegy for a Dead Soldier."

George Bernard Shaw, 1856-1950, (Ire.-Br.) playwright, critic. *St. Joan, Pygmalion, Major Barbara, Man and Superman.*

Sidney Sheldon, 1917-2007, (U.S.) screenwriter, novelist. *Rage of Angels, Memories of Midnight.*

Mary Wollstonecraft Shelley, 1797-1851, (Br.) novelist, feminist. *Frankenstein, The Last Man.*

Percy Bysshe Shelley, 1792-1822, (Br.) poet. *Prometheus Unbound, Adonais,* "Ode to the West Wind," "To a Skylark."

Sam Shepard, 1943-2017, (U.S.) playwright. *Buried Child, True West.*

Richard B. Sheridan, 1751-1816, (Br.) dramatist. *The Rivals, School for Scandal.*

Robert Sherwood, 1896-1955, (U.S.) playwright, biographer. *The Petrified Forest, Abe Lincoln in Illinois.*

Mikhail Sholokhov, 1906-84, (Russ.) writer. *The Silent Don.*

Anne Rivers Siddons, 1936-2019, (U.S.) novelist. *Peachtree Road.*

Shel Silverstein, 1932-99, (U.S.) poet, writer. *The Giving Tree, Where the Sidewalk Ends.*

Georges Simenon (Georges Sims), 1903-89, (Belg.-Fr.) mystery writer; created Inspector Maigret.

Neil Simon, 1927-2018, (U.S.) playwright. *The Odd Couple, Brighton Beach Memoirs.*

Upton Sinclair, 1878-1968, (U.S.) novelist. *The Jungle.*

Isaac Bashevis Singer, 1904-91, (Pol.-U.S.) novelist, short-story writer, in Yiddish. *The Magician of Lublin.*

C(harles) P(ercy) Snow, 1905-80, (Br.) novelist, scientist. *Strangers and Brothers, Corridors of Power.*

Aleksandr Solzhenitsyn, 1918-2008, (Russ.) novelist, dramatist. *One Day in the Life of Ivan Denisovich.*

Susan Sontag, 1933-2004, (U.S.) critic, essayist, novelist. *Notes on Camp, The Volcano Lover, In America.*

Stephen Spender, 1909-95, (Br.) poet, critic, novelist. *Twenty Poems,* "Elegy for Margaret."

Edmund Spenser, 1552-99, (Br.) poet. *The Faerie Queene.*

Mickey Spillane, 1918-2006, (U.S.) novelist; Mike Hammer detective novels. *The Killing Man.*

Johanna Spyri, 1827-1901, (Switz.) children's author. *Heidi.*

Christina Stead, 1903-83, (Austral.) novelist, short-story writer. *The Man Who Loved Children.*

Richard Steele, 1672-1729, (Br.) essayist, playwright; began the *Tatler* and *Spectator. The Conscious Lovers.*

Gertrude Stein, 1874-1946, (U.S.) writer. *Three Lives.*

John Steinbeck, 1902-68, (U.S.) novelist. *The Grapes of Wrath, Of Mice and Men, The Winter of Our Discontent.*

Stendhal (Marie Henri Beyle), 1783-1842, (Fr.) novelist. *The Red and the Black, The Charterhouse of Parma.*

Laurence Sterne, 1713-68, (Br.) novelist. *Tristram Shandy.*

Wallace Stevens, 1879-1955, (U.S.) poet. *Harmonium, The Man With the Blue Guitar, Notes Toward a Supreme Fiction.*

Robert Louis Stevenson, 1850-94, (Br.) novelist, poet, essayist. *Treasure Island, A Child's Garden of Verses.*

Mary Stewart, 1916-2014, (Br.) novelist. Merlin trilogy.

Bram Stoker, 1847-1912, (Br.) writer. *Dracula.*

Rex Stout, 1886-1975, (U.S.) mystery writer; created Nero Wolfe.

Harriet Beecher Stowe, 1811-96, (U.S.) novelist. *Uncle Tom's Cabin.*

Lytton Strachey, 1880-1932, (Br.) biographer, critic. *Eminent Victorians, Queen Victoria, Elizabeth and Essex.*

Mark Strand, 1934-2014, (Can.-U.S.) poet. *Blizzard of One.*

August Strindberg, 1849-1912, (Swed.) dramatist, novelist. *The Father, Miss Julie, The Creditors.*

William Styron, 1925-2006, (U.S.) novelist, essayist. *The Confessions of Nat Turner, Sophie's Choice, Darkness Visible: A Memoir of Madness.*

Jonathan Swift, 1667-1745, (Br.) satirist, poet. *Gulliver's Travels,* "A Modest Proposal."

Algernon C. Swinburne, 1837-1909, (Br.) poet, dramatist. *Atalanta in Calydon.*

John M. Synge, 1871-1909, (Ire.) poet, dramatist. *Riders to the Sea, The Playboy of the Western World.*

Wislawa Szymborska, 1923-2012, (Pol.) poet. "Cat in an Empty Apartment."

Rabindranath Tagore, 1861-1941, (India) author, poet. *Sadhana, The Realization of Life, Gitanjali.*

Booth Tarkington, 1869-1946, (U.S.) novelist. *The Magnificent Ambersons.*

Peter Taylor, 1917-94, (U.S.) novelist. *A Summons to Memphis.*

Sara Teasdale, 1884-1933, (U.S.) poet. *Helen of Troy and Other Poems, Rivers to the Sea.*

Alfred, Lord Tennyson, 1809-92, (Br.) poet. *Idylls of the King, In Memoriam,* "The Charge of the Light Brigade."

William Makepeace Thackeray, 1811-63, (Br.) novelist. *Vanity Fair, Henry Esmond, Pendennis.*

Dylan Thomas, 1914-53, (Wales) poet. *Under Milk Wood, A Child's Christmas in Wales.*

Hunter S. Thompson, 1937-2005, (U.S.) author, journalist. *Hell's Angels, Fear and Loathing in Las Vegas.*

Henry David Thoreau, 1817-62, (U.S.) writer, philosopher, naturalist. *Walden,* "Civil Disobedience."

James Thurber, 1894-1961, (U.S.) humorist. "The Secret Life of Walter Mitty," *My Life and Hard Times.*

J(ohn) R(onald) R(euel) Tolkien, 1892-1973, (Br.) writer. *The Hobbit, Lord of the Rings* trilogy.

Leo Tolstoy, 1828-1910, (Russ.) novelist, short-story writer. *War and Peace, Anna Karenina,* "The Death of Ivan Ilyich."

Lionel Trilling, 1905-75, (U.S.) critic, author. *The Liberal Imagination.*

Anthony Trollope, 1815-82, (Br.) novelist. *The Warden, Barchester Towers,* the Palliser novels.

Ivan Turgenev, 1818-83, (Russ.) novelist, short-story writer. *Fathers and Sons, First Love, A Month in the Country.*

Amos Tutuola, 1920-97, (Nigeria) novelist. *The Palm-Wine Drunkard, My Life in the Bush of Ghosts.*

Mark Twain (Samuel Clemens), 1835-1910, (U.S.) novelist, humorist. *The Adventures of Huckleberry Finn.*

Sigrid Undset, 1881-1949, (Nor.) novelist. *Kristin Lavransdatter.*

John Updike, 1932-2009, (U.S.) novelist, literary critic. *Rabbit Is Rich, The Witches of Eastwick.*

Paul Valéry, 1871-1945, (Fr.) poet, critic. *La Jeune Parque, The Graveyard by the Sea.*

Paul Verlaine, 1844-96, (Fr.) Symbolist poet. *Songs Without Words.*

Jules Verne, 1828-1905, (Fr.) novelist. *Twenty Thousand Leagues Under the Sea.*

Gore Vidal, 1925-2012, (U.S.) novelist. *The City and the Pillar.*

François Villon, 1431-c. 1463, (Fr.) poet. *The Lays, The Grand Testament.*

Voltaire (F. M. Arouet), 1694-1778, (Fr.) writer of "philosophical romances"; philosopher, historian. *Candide.*

Kurt Vonnegut Jr., 1922-2007, (U.S.) novelist, essayist. *Cat's Cradle, Slaughterhouse-Five, Breakfast of Champions.*

Derek Walcott, 1930-2016, (St. Lucia) poet. "Omeros."

David Foster Wallace, 1962-2008, (U.S.) novelist, essayist. *Infinite Jest, A Supposedly Fun Thing I'll Never Do Again.*

Robert Penn Warren, 1905-89, (U.S.) novelist, poet, critic. *All the King's Men.*

Wendy Wasserstein, 1950-2006, (U.S.) playwright. *The Heidi Chronicles.*

Evelyn Waugh, 1903-66, (Br.) novelist. *The Loved One, Brideshead Revisited, A Handful of Dust.*

H(erbert) G(eorge) Wells, 1866-1946, (Br.) novelist. *The Time Machine, The Invisible Man, The War of the Worlds.*

Eudora Welty, 1909-2001, (U.S.) Southern short-story writer, novelist. "Why I Live at the P.O.," "The Ponder Heart."

Rebecca West, 1893-1983, (Br.) novelist, critic, journalist. *Black Lamb and Grey Falcon.*

Edith Wharton, 1862-1937, (U.S.) novelist. *The Age of Innocence, The House of Mirth, Ethan Frome.*

Phillis Wheatley, c. 1753-84, (U.S.) poet; 2nd American woman and first Black woman to be published, 1770.

E(lwyn) B(rooks) White, 1899-1985, (U.S.) essayist, novelist. *Charlotte's Web, Stuart Little.*

Patrick White, 1912-90, (Austral.) novelist. *The Tree of Man.*

T(erence) H(anbury) White, 1906-64, (Br.) author. *The Once and Future King, A Book of Beasts.*

Walt Whitman, 1819-92, (U.S.) poet. *Leaves of Grass.*

John Greenleaf Whittier, 1807-92, (U.S.) poet, journalist. *Snow-Bound.*

Elie Wiesel, 1928-2016, (Rom.) memoirist, novelist. *Night.*

Oscar Wilde, 1854-1900, (Ire.) novelist, playwright. *The Picture of Dorian Gray, The Importance of Being Earnest.*

Laura Ingalls Wilder, 1867-1957, (U.S.) novelist. Little House on the Prairie series of children's books.

Thornton Wilder, 1897-1975, (U.S.) playwright. *Our Town, The Skin of Our Teeth, The Matchmaker.*

Tennessee Williams, 1911-83, (U.S.) playwright. *A Streetcar Named Desire,*

Cat on a Hot Tin Roof, The Glass Menagerie.

William Carlos Williams, 1883-1963, (U.S.) poet, physician. *The Tempers, Al Que Quiere! Paterson, "This Is Just to Say."*

Edmund Wilson, 1895-1972, (U.S.) critic, novelist. *Axel's Castle, To the Finland Station.*

Lanford Wilson, 1937-2011, (U.S.) playwright. *Talley's Folly, Fifth of July.*

P(elham) G(renville) Wodehouse, 1881-1975, (Br.-U.S.) humorist. Jeeves novels, *Anything Goes.*

Thomas Wolfe, 1900-38, (U.S.) novelist, journalist. *Look Homeward, Angel; You Can't Go Home Again.*

Tom Wolfe, 1930-2018, (U.S.) novelist, journalist. *Bonfire of the Vanities, The Right Stuff.*

Virginia Woolf, 1882-1941, (Br.) novelist, essayist. *Mrs. Dalloway, To the Lighthouse, A Room of One's Own.*

William Wordsworth, 1770-1850, (Br.) poet. "Tintern Abbey," "Ode: Intimations of Immortality," *The Prelude.*

Herman Wouk, 1915-2019, (U.S.) novelist. *The Caine Mutiny.*

Richard Wright, 1908-60, (U.S.) novelist, short-story writer. *Native Son, Black Boy, Uncle Tom's Children.*

Elinor Wylie, 1885-1928, (U.S.) poet. *Nets to Catch the Wind.*

William Butler Yeats, 1865-1939, (Ire.) poet, playwright. "The Second Coming," *The Wild Swans at Coole.*

Frank Yerby, 1916-91, (U.S.) first best-selling African American novelist. *The Foxes of Harrow.*

Yevgeny Yevtushenko, 1933-2017, (Russ.) poet. "Babi Yar."

Émile Zola, 1840-1902, (Fr.) novelist. *Nana, Thérèse Raquin.*

Poets Laureate

In England, Henry III (1216-72) reportedly had a Versificator Regis, or King's Poet, paid 100 shillings per year. Other poets said to have filled the role of poet laureate include Geoffrey Chaucer (d 1400), Edmund Spenser (d 1599), Ben Jonson (d 1637), and William d'Avenant (d 1668). The first official English poet laureate was John Dryden, appointed 1668, for life. Then came Thomas Shadwell, in 1689; Nahum Tate, 1692; Nicholas Rowe, 1715; Rev. Laurence Eusden, 1718; Colley Cibber, 1730; William Whitehead, 1757; Rev. Thomas Warton, 1785; Henry James Pye, 1790; Robert Southey, 1813; William Wordsworth, 1843; Alfred, Lord Tennyson, 1850; Alfred Austin, 1896; Robert Bridges, 1913; John Masefield, 1930; C. Day Lewis, 1968; John Betjeman,

1972; Ted Hughes, 1984; Andrew Motion, 1999; Carol Ann Duffy, 2009; and Simon Armitage, 2019.

In the U.S., appointment is by the Librarian of Congress to a term of one year, which may be renewed: Robert Penn Warren, appointed 1986; Richard Wilbur, 1987; Howard Nemerov, 1988; Mark Strand, 1990; Joseph Brodsky, 1991; Mona Van Duyn, 1992; Rita Dove, 1993; Robert Hass, 1995; Robert Pinsky, 1997; Stanley Kunitz, 2000; Billy Collins, 2001; Louise Glück, 2003; Ted Kooser, 2004; Donald Hall, 2006; Charles Simic, 2007; Kay Ryan, 2008; W. S. Merwin, 2010; Philip Levine, 2011; Natasha Trethewey, 2012; Charles Wright, 2014; Juan Felipe Herrera, 2015; Tracy K. Smith, 2017; Joy Harjo, 2019; Ada Limón, 2022.

Composers of Classical and Avant-Garde Music

John Adams, b 1947, (U.S.) *Nixon in China, The Death of Klinghoffer.*

Milton Babbitt, 1916-2011, (U.S.) serial and electronic music.

Carl Philipp Emanuel Bach, 1714-88, (Ger.) cantatas, passions, numerous keyboard and instrumental works.

Johann Christian Bach, 1735-82, (Ger.) concertos, operas, sonatas. Known as the "English" Bach.

Johann Sebastian Bach, 1685-1750, (Ger.) *St. Matthew Passion, The Well-Tempered Clavier.*

Samuel Barber, 1910-81, (U.S.) *Adagio for Strings, Vanessa.*

Béla Bartók, 1881-1945, (Hung.) *Concerto for Orchestra, The Miraculous Mandarin.*

Amy Beach (Mrs. H. H. A. Beach), 1867-1944, (U.S.) *The Year's at the Spring, Fireflies, The Chambered Nautilus.*

Ludwig van Beethoven, 1770-1827, (Ger.) concertos (*Emperor*), sonatas (*Moonlight, Pathétique*), 9 symphonies.

Vincenzo Bellini, 1801-35, (It.) *I Puritani, La Sonnambula, Norma.*

Alban Berg, 1885-1935, (Austria) *Wozzeck, Lulu.*

Hector Berlioz, 1803-69, (Fr.) *Damnation of Faust, Symphonie Fantastique, Requiem.*

Leonard Bernstein, 1918-90, (U.S.) *Chichester Psalms, Jeremiah Symphony, Mass.*

Georges Bizet, 1838-75, (Fr.) *Carmen, Pearl Fishers.*

Ernest Bloch, 1880-1959, (Switz.-U.S.) *Macbeth* (opera), *Schelomo, Voice in the Wilderness.*

Luigi Boccherini, 1743-1805, (It.) chamber music and guitar pieces.

Alexander Borodin, 1833-87, (Russ.) *Prince Igor, In the Steppes of Central Asia, Polovtzian Dances.*

Pierre Boulez, 1925-2016, (Fr.) *Le Visage nuptial, Éclat/Multiples, Domaines.*

Johannes Brahms, 1833-97, (Ger.) Liebeslieder Waltzes, *Academic Festival Overture,* chamber music, 4 symphonies.

Henry Brant, 1913-2008, (Can.) spatial music.

Benjamin Britten, 1913-76, (Br.) *Peter Grimes, Turn of the Screw, A Ceremony of Carols, War Requiem.*

Anton Bruckner, 1824-96, (Austria) 9 symphonies.

Dietrich Buxtehude, 1637-1707, (Den.) organ works, vocal music.

William Byrd, 1543-1623, (Br.) masses, motets.

John Cage, 1912-92, (U.S.) *Winter Music, Fontana Mix.*

Elliott Carter, 1908-2012, (U.S.) *Second String Quartet, Third String Quartet.*

Emmanuel Chabrier, 1841-94, (Fr.) *Le Roi Malgré Lui, España.*

Gustave Charpentier, 1860-1956, (Fr.) *Louise.*

Frédéric Chopin, 1810-49, (Pol.) mazurkas, waltzes, etudes, nocturnes, polonaises, sonatas.

Aaron Copland, 1900-90, (U.S.) *Appalachian Spring, Fanfare for the Common Man, Lincoln Portrait.*

John Corigliano, b 1938, (U.S.) *Symphony No. 2.*

Paul Creston, 1906-85, (U.S.) *Walt Whitman.*

Claude Debussy, 1862-1918, (Fr.) *Pelleas et Melisande, La Mer, Prelude to the Afternoon of a Faun.*

David Del Tredici, b 1937, (U.S.) *Child Alice, In Memory of a Summer Day.*

Gaetano Donizetti, 1797-1848, (It.) *Elixir of Love, Lucia di Lammermoor, Daughter of the Regiment.*

Paul Dukas, 1865-1935, (Fr.) *Sorcerer's Apprentice.*

Antonín Dvořák, 1841-1904, (Czech.) *Songs My Mother Taught Me, Symphony in E Minor (From the New World).*

Edward Elgar, 1857-1934, (Br.) *Enigma Variations, Pomp and Circumstance.*

Manuel de Falla, 1876-1946, (Sp.) *El Amor Brujo, La Vida Breve, The Three-Cornered Hat.*

Louise Farrenc, 1804-75, (Fr.) *Nonet in E flat, Op. 38.*

Gabriel Fauré, 1845-1924, (Fr.) *Requiem, Elègie for Cello and Piano.*

Cesar Franck, 1822-90, (Belg.) *Symphony in D minor, Violin Sonata.*

George Gershwin, 1898-1937, (U.S.) *Rhapsody in Blue, An American in Paris, Porgy and Bess.*

Philip Glass, b 1937, (U.S.) *Einstein on the Beach, The Voyage.*

Mikhail Glinka, 1804-57, (Russ.) *A Life for the Tsar, Ruslan and Ludmilla.*

Christoph W. Gluck, 1714-87, (Ger.) *Alceste, Iphigénie en Tauride.*

Henryk Gorecki, 1933-2010, (Pol.) *Symphony no. 3 (Symphony of Sorrowing Songs).*

Charles Gounod, 1818-93, (Fr.) *Faust, Romeo and Juliet.*

Percy Grainger, 1882-1961, (Austral.) *Country Gardens.*

Edvard Grieg, 1843-1907, (Nor.) *Peer Gynt Suite,* Concerto in A minor for piano.

George Frideric Handel, 1685-1759, (Ger.-Br.) *Messiah, Water Music.*

Howard Hanson, 1896-1981, (U.S.) Symphonies No. 1 (*Nordic*) and No. 2 (*Romantic*).

Roy Harris, 1898-1979, (U.S.) symphonies.

(Franz) Joseph Haydn, 1732-1809, (Austria) symphonies (*Clock, London, Toy*), chamber music, oratorios.

Hildegard von Bingen, 1098-1179, (Ger.) *Ordo virtutum.*

Paul Hindemith, 1895-1963, (U.S.) *Mathis der Maler.*

Gustav Holst, 1874-1934, (Br.) *The Planets.*

Arthur Honegger, 1892-1955, (Fr.) *Judith, Le Roi David, Pacific 231.*

Alan Hovhaness, 1911-2000, (U.S.) symphonies, *Magnificat.*

Engelbert Humperdinck, 1854-1921, (Ger.) *Hansel and Gretel.*

Charles Ives, 1874-1954, (U.S.) *Concord Sonata,* symphonies.

Aram Khachaturian, 1903-78, (Russ.) ballets, piano pieces, *Sabre Dance.*

Zoltán Kodaly, 1882-1967, (Hung.) *Háry János, Psalmus Hungaricus.*

Fritz Kreisler, 1875-1962, (Austria) *Caprice Viennois, Tambourin Chinois.*

Edouard Lalo, 1823-92, (Fr.) *Symphonie Espagnole.*

David Lang, b 1957, (U.S.) *The Little Match Girl Passion.*

Morten Lauridsen, b 1943, (U.S.) *Lux Aeterna.*

Ruggero Leoncavallo, 1857-1919, (It.) *Pagliacci.*

György Ligeti, 1923-2006, (Rom.) *Atmosphères, Requiem.*

Franz Liszt, 1811-86, (Hung.) 20 Hungarian rhapsodies, symphonic poems.

Edward MacDowell, 1861-1908, (U.S.) *To a Wild Rose.*

Gustav Mahler, 1860-1911, (Austria) *Das Lied von der Erde;* 9 complete symphonies.

Pietro Mascagni, 1863-1945, (It.) *Cavalleria Rusticana.*

Jules Massenet, 1842-1912, (Fr.) *Manon, Le Cid, Thaïs.*

Felix Mendelssohn, 1809-47, (Ger.) *A Midsummer Night's Dream, Songs Without Words*, violin concerto.

Gian Carlo Menotti, 1911-2007, (It.-U.S.) *The Medium, The Consul, Amahl and the Night Visitors.*

Olivier Messiaen, 1908-1992, (Fr.) *Apparition de l'Église Éternelle.*

Claudio Monteverdi, 1567-1643, (It.) opera, masses, madrigals.

Wolfgang Amadeus Mozart, 1756-91, (Austria) chamber music, concertos, operas (*Magic Flute, Marriage of Figaro*), 41 symphonies.

Modest Mussorgsky, 1839-81, (Russ.) *Boris Godunov, Pictures at an Exhibition.*

Carl Nielsen, 1865-1931, (Den.) *Saul og David.*

Jacques Offenbach, 1819-80, (Fr.) *Tales of Hoffmann.*

Carl Orff, 1895-1982, (Ger.) *Carmina Burana.*

Johann Pachelbel, 1653-1706, (Ger.) *Canon and Fugue in D major.*

Ignacy Paderewski, 1860-1941, (Pol.) *Minuet in G.*

Niccolò Paganini, 1782-1840, (It.) *Caprices* for violin solo.

Giovanni Palestrina, c. 1525-94, (It.) masses, madrigals.

Arvo Pärt, b 1935, (Eston.) sacred music. *Fratres, Cantus in memoriam Benjamin Britten, Tabula Rasa.*

Krzysztof Penderecki, 1933-2020, (Pol.) *Psalmus, Polymorphia, De natura sonoris.*

Francis Poulenc, 1899-1963, (Fr.) *Dialogues des Carmélites.*

Mel Powell, 1923-98, (U.S.) *Duplicates: A Concerto for Two Pianos and Orchestra, Cantilena Concertante.*

Sergei Prokofiev, 1891-1953, (Russ.) *Classical Symphony, Love for Three Oranges, Peter and the Wolf.*

Giacomo Puccini, 1858-1924, (It.) *La Boheme, Manon Lescaut, Tosca, Madama Butterfly.*

Henry Purcell, 1659-95, (Br.) *Dido and Aeneas.*

Sergei Rachmaninoff, 1873-1943, (Russ.) concertos, preludes (Prelude in C sharp minor), symphonies.

Maurice Ravel, 1875-1937, (Fr.) *Boléro, Daphnis et Chloè*, Piano Concerto in D for Left Hand Alone.

Steve Reich, b 1936, (U.S.) *Double Sextet, Three Tales.*

Nikolai Rimsky-Korsakov, 1844-1908, (Russ.) *Golden Cockerel, Scheherazade, Flight of the Bumblebee.*

Ned Rorem, 1923-2022, (U.S.) "Evidence of Things Not Seen."

Gioachino Rossini, 1792-1868, (It.) *Barber of Seville, Otello, William Tell.*

John Rutter, b 1945, (Br.) *Magnificat, Requiem.*

Camille Saint-Saëns, 1835-1921, (Fr.) *Carnival of Animals* (The Swan), *Samson and Delilah, Danse Macabre.*

Alessandro Scarlatti, 1660-1725, (It.) cantatas, oratorios, operas.

Domenico Scarlatti, 1685-1757, (It.) harpsichord works.

Alfred Schnittke, 1934-98 (Russ.-Ger.) *Life With an Idiot.*

Arnold Schoenberg, 1874-1951, (Austria) *Pelleas and Melisande, Pierrot Lunaire, Verklärte Nacht.*

Franz Schubert, 1797-1828, (Austria) chamber music (*Trout Quintet*), lieder, symphonies ("Unfinished").

Robert Schumann, 1810-56, (Ger.) *Die Frauenliebe und Leben, Träumerei.*

Dmitri Shostakovich, 1906-75, (Russ.) symphonies, *Lady Macbeth of the District Mzensk.*

Jean Sibelius, 1865-1957, (Fin.) *Finlandia.*

Bedrich Smetana, 1824-84, (Czech.) *The Bartered Bride.*

Karlheinz Stockhausen, 1928-2008, (Ger.) *Kontra-Punkte, Kontakte* for Electronic Instruments.

Richard Strauss, 1864-1949, (Ger.) *Salome, Elektra, Der Rosenkavalier, Thus Spake Zarathustra.*

Igor Stravinsky, 1882-1971, (Russ.) *Noah and the Flood, The Rake's Progress, The Rite of Spring.*

Toru Takemitsu, 1930-96, (Jpn.) *Requiem for Strings, Dorian Horizon.*

Thomas Tallis, c. 1505-85, (Br.) anthems, motets.

Peter I. Tchaikovsky, 1840-93, (Russ.) *Nutcracker, Swan Lake, The Sleeping Beauty.*

Georg Philipp Telemann, 1681-1767, (Ger.) church music, orchestral suites, chamber music.

Virgil Thomson, 1896-1989, (U.S.) opera, film music, *Four Saints in Three Acts.*

Dmitri Tiomkin, 1894-1979, (Russ.-U.S.) film scores, including *High Noon.*

Michael Tippett, 1905-98, (Br.) *A Child of Our Time, The Midsummer Marriage, The Knot Garden.*

Michael Torke, b 1961, (U.S.) *Bright Blue Music, Ecstatic Orange.*

Eric Whitacre, b 1970, (U.S.) *Cloudburst.*

Ralph Vaughan Williams, 1872-1958, (Br.) *Fantasia on a Theme by Thomas Tallis*, symphonies, vocal music.

Giuseppe Verdi, 1813-1901, (It.) *Aida, Rigoletto, Don Carlo, Il Trovatore, La Traviata, Falstaff, Macbeth.*

Heitor Villa-Lobos, 1887-1959, (Braz.) *Bachianas Brasileiras.*

Antonio Vivaldi, 1678-1741, (It.) Concerto grossos (*The Four Seasons*).

Richard Wagner, 1813-83, (Ger.) *Rienzi, Tannhäuser, Lohengrin, Tristan und Isolde.*

William Walton, 1902-83, (Br.) *Façade, Belshazzar's Feast.*

Carl Maria von Weber, 1786-1826, (Ger.) *Der Freischutz.*

Judith Weir, b. 1954, (Br.) *King Harald's Saga.*

Composers of Operettas, Musicals, and Popular Music

Richard Adler, 1921-2012, (U.S.) *Pajama Game; Damn Yankees.*

Milton Ager, 1893-1979, (U.S.) "I Wonder What's Become of Sally"; "Hard-Hearted Hannah"; "Ain't She Sweet?"

Leroy Anderson, 1908-75, (U.S.) "Sleigh Ride"; "Blue Tango"; "Syncopated Clock."

Paul Anka, b 1941, (Can.) "My Way"; *Tonight Show Theme.*

Harold Arlen, 1905-86, (U.S.) "Stormy Weather"; "Over the Rainbow"; "Blues in the Night"; "That Old Black Magic."

Burt Bacharach, 1928-2023, (U.S.) "Raindrops Keep Fallin' on My Head"; "Walk on By"; "What the World Needs Now Is Love."

Ernest Ball, 1878-1927, (U.S.) "Mother Machree"; "When Irish Eyes Are Smiling."

John Barry, 1933-2011, (U.S.) *Born Free; Lion in Winter; Out of Africa.*

Irving Berlin, 1888-1989, (U.S.) *Annie Get Your Gun; Call Me Madam*; "God Bless America"; "White Christmas."

Alan Bergman, b 1925, and **Marilyn Bergman**, 1928-2022, (both U.S.) "The Way We Were"; "You Don't Bring Me Flowers."

Leonard Bernstein, 1918-90, (U.S.) *On the Town; Wonderful Town; Candide; West Side Story.*

Eubie Blake, 1883-1983, (U.S.) *Shuffle Along*; "I'm Just Wild About Harry."

Jerry Bock, 1928-2010, (U.S.) *Mr. Wonderful; Fiorello; Fiddler on the Roof; The Rothschilds.*

Carrie Jacobs Bond, 1862-1946, (U.S.) "I Love You Truly."

Nacio Herb Brown, 1896-1964, (U.S.) "Singing in the Rain"; "You Were Meant for Me"; "All I Do Is Dream of You."

Hoagy Carmichael, 1899-1981, (U.S.) "Stardust"; "Georgia on My Mind"; "Old Buttermilk Sky."

James Cleveland, 1931-91, (U.S.) composer, musician, singer; first Black gospel artist to appear at Carnegie Hall.

George M. Cohan, 1878-1942, (U.S.) "Give My Regards to Broadway"; "You're a Grand Old Flag"; "Over There."

Cy Coleman, 1929-2004, (U.S.) *Sweet Charity*; "Witchcraft."

John Frederick Coots, 1895-1985, (U.S.) "Santa Claus Is Coming to Town"; "You Go to My Head"; "For All We Know."

Noël Coward, 1899-1973, (Br.) *Bitter Sweet*; "Mad Dogs and Englishmen"; "Mad About the Boy."

Neil Diamond, b 1941, (U.S.) "I'm a Believer"; "Sweet Caroline."

Walter Donaldson, 1893-1947, (U.S.) "My Buddy"; "Carolina in the Morning"; "Makin' Whoopee."

Vernon Duke, 1903-69, (U.S.) "April in Paris."

Bob Dylan, b 1941, (U.S.) "Blowin' in the Wind"; "Like a Rolling Stone."

Gus Edwards, 1879-1945, (U.S.) "School Days"; "By the Light of the Silvery Moon"; "In My Merry Oldsmobile."

Sherman Edwards, 1919-81, (U.S.) "See You in September"; "Wonderful! Wonderful!"

Duke Ellington, 1899-1974, (U.S.) "Sophisticated Lady"; "Satin Doll"; "It Don't Mean a Thing"; "Solitude."

Sammy Fain, 1902-89, (U.S.) "I'll Be Seeing You"; "Love Is a Many-Splendored Thing."

Fred Fisher, 1875-1942, (U.S.) "Peg O' My Heart"; "Chicago."

Stephen Collins Foster, 1826-64, (U.S.) "My Old Kentucky Home"; "Old Folks at Home"; "Beautiful Dreamer."

Rudolf Friml, 1879-1972, (Czech.-U.S.) *The Firefly; Rose Marie; Vagabond King; Bird of Paradise.*

John Gay, 1685-1732, (Br.) *The Beggar's Opera.*

George Gershwin, 1898-1937, (U.S.) "Someone to Watch Over Me"; "I've Got a Crush on You"; "Embraceable You."

João Gilberto, 1931-2019, (Brazil) bossa nova pioneer.

Morton Gould, 1913-96, (U.S.) "Fall River Suite"; "Holocaust Suite"; "Spirituals for Orchestra"; "Stringmusic."

Ferde Grofe, 1892-1972, (U.S.) "Grand Canyon Suite."

Marvin Hamlisch, 1944-2012, (U.S.) "The Way We Were"; "Nobody Does It Better"; *A Chorus Line.*

Ray Henderson, 1896-1970, (U.S.) *George White's Scandals*; "That Old Gang of Mine"; "Five Foot Two, Eyes of Blue."

Victor Herbert, 1859-1924, (Ire.-U.S.) *Mlle. Modiste; Babes in Toyland; The Red Mill; Naughty Marietta; Sweethearts.*

Jerry Herman, 1931-2019, (U.S.) *Hello, Dolly!; Mame.*

Brian Holland, b 1941, **Lamont Dozier**, 1941-2022, and **Eddie Holland**, b 1939, (all U.S.) "Heat Wave"; "Stop! In the Name of Love"; "Baby, I Need Your Loving."

Rupert Holmes, b 1947, (Br.-U.S.) *The Mystery of Edwin Drood; Curtains.*

James Horner, 1953-2015, (U.S.) *Titanic*; "Somewhere Out There"; "My Heart Will Go On."

Antonio Carlos Jobim, 1927-94, (Brazil) "The Girl From Ipanema"; "Desafinado"; "One Note Samba."

Billy Joel (William Martin), b 1949, (U.S.) "Just the Way You Are"; "Honesty"; "Piano Man."

Elton John, b 1947, (Br.) *The Lion King*; "Candle in the Wind"; "Your Song."

Scott Joplin, 1868-1917, (U.S.) Maple Leaf Rag; *Treemonisha.*

John Kander, b 1927, (U.S.) *Cabaret; Chicago; Funny Lady.*

Jerome Kern, 1885-1945, (U.S.) *Sally; Sunny; Show Boat.*

Carole King, b 1942, (U.S.) "Will You Love Me Tomorrow?"; "Natural Woman"; "One Fine Day"; "Up on the Roof."

Burton Lane, 1912-97, (U.S.) *Finian's Rainbow.*

Jonathan Larson, 1960-96, (U.S.) *tick, tick... BOOM!; Rent.*

Franz Lehar, 1870-1948, (Hung.) *Merry Widow.*

Jerry Leiber, 1933-2011, and **Mike Stoller**, b 1933, (both U.S.) "Hound Dog"; "Searchin'"; "Yakety Yak"; "Love Me Tender."

Mitch Leigh, 1928-2014, (U.S.) *Man of La Mancha.*

John Lennon, 1940-80, and **Paul McCartney**, b 1942, (both Br.) "I Want to Hold Your Hand"; "She Loves You."

Jay Livingston, 1915-2001, (U.S.) "Mona Lisa"; "Que Sera, Sera."

Andrew Lloyd Webber, b 1948, (Br.) *Jesus Christ Superstar; Evita; Cats; The Phantom of the Opera.*

Frank Loesser, 1910-69, (U.S.) *Guys and Dolls; Where's Charley?; The Most Happy Fella; How to Succeed in Business....*

Frederick Loewe, 1901-88, (Austria-U.S.) *Brigadoon; Paint Your Wagon; My Fair Lady; Camelot.*

Robert Lopez, b 1975, (U.S.) *Avenue Q; The Book of Mormon; Frozen.*

Henry Mancini, 1924-94, (U.S.) "Moon River"; "Days of Wine and Roses"; "Pink Panther Theme."

Barry Mann, b 1939, and **Cynthia Weil**, 1940-2023, (both U.S.) "You've Lost That Loving Feeling."

Hugh Martin, 1914-2011, (U.S.) "Have Yourself a Merry Little Christmas"; "The Trolley Song."

Jimmy McHugh, 1894-1969, (U.S.) "Don't Blame Me"; "I'm in the Mood for Love"; "I Feel a Song Coming On."

Christine McVie, 1943-2022, (Br.) "Don't Stop"; "Songbird."

Alan Menken, b 1949, (U.S.) *Little Shop of Horrors; Beauty and the Beast.*

Joseph Meyer, 1894-1987, (U.S.) "If You Knew Susie"; "California, Here I Come"; "Crazy Rhythm."

Lin-Manuel Miranda, b 1980, (U.S.) *In the Heights; Hamilton.*

Joni Mitchell, b 1943, (Can.) "Both Sides Now"; "Big Yellow Taxi."

Ennio Morricone, 1928-2020, (It.) *The Good, the Bad and the Ugly; The Untouchables.*

Willie Nelson, b 1933, (U.S.) "Crazy"; "On the Road Again."

Chauncey Olcott, 1858-1932, (U.S.) "Mother Machree."

Dolly Parton, b 1946, (U.S.) "I Will Always Love You"; "Jolene"; "9 to 5."

Jerome "Doc" Pomus, 1925-91, (U.S.) "Save the Last Dance for Me"; "A Teenager in Love."

Cole Porter, 1891-1964, (U.S.) *Anything Goes; Kiss Me Kate; Can Can; Silk Stockings.*

Smokey Robinson, b 1940, (U.S.) "Shop Around"; "My Guy"; "My Girl"; "Get Ready."

Richard Rodgers, 1902-79, (U.S.) *Oklahoma!; Carousel; South Pacific; The King and I; The Sound of Music.*

Sigmund Romberg, 1887-1951, (Hung.) *Maytime; The Student Prince; Desert Song; Blossom Time.*

Harold Rome, 1908-93, (U.S.) *Pins and Needles; Call Me Mister; Wish You Were Here; Fanny; Destry Rides Again.*

Vincent Rose, 1880-1944, (U.S.) "Avalon"; "Whispering"; "Blueberry Hill."

Harry Ruby, 1895-1974, (U.S.) "Three Little Words"; "Who's Sorry Now?"

Arthur Schwartz, 1900-84, (U.S.) *The Band Wagon;* "Dancing in the Dark"; "By Myself"; "That's Entertainment."

Stephen Schwartz, b 1948, (U.S.) *Godspell; Pippin; Wicked.*

Neil Sedaka, b 1939, (U.S.) "Breaking Up Is Hard to Do."

Marc Shaiman, b 1959, (U.S.) *Hairspray.*

Paul Simon, b 1942, (U.S.) "Sounds of Silence"; "I Am a Rock"; "Mrs. Robinson"; "Bridge Over Troubled Waters."

Stephen Sondheim, 1930-2021, (U.S.) *A Little Night Music; Company; Sweeney Todd; Sunday in the Park With George.*

John Philip Sousa, 1854-1932, (U.S.) *El Capitan;* "Stars and Stripes Forever."

Oskar Straus, 1870-1954, (Austria) *Chocolate Soldier.*

Johann Strauss, 1825-99, (Austria) *Gypsy Baron; Die Fledermaus;* waltzes: Blue Danube; Artist's Life.

Charles Strouse, b 1928, (U.S.) *Bye Bye, Birdie; Annie.*

Jule Styne, 1905-94, (Br.-U.S.) *Gentlemen Prefer Blondes; Bells Are Ringing; Gypsy; Funny Girl.*

Arthur S. Sullivan, 1842-1900, (Br.) *H.M.S. Pinafore; Pirates of Penzance; The Mikado.*

Deems Taylor, 1885-1966, (U.S.) *Peter Ibbetson.*

Jeanine Tesori, b 1971, (U.S.) *Fun Home; Shrek the Musical; Kimberly Akimbo.*

Harry Tobias, 1905-94, (U.S.) *I'll Keep the Lovelight Burning.*

Egbert van Alstyne, 1882-1951, (U.S.) "In the Shade of the Old Apple Tree"; "Memories"; "Pretty Baby."

Jimmy Van Heusen, 1913-90, (U.S.) "Moonlight Becomes You"; "Swinging on a Star"; "All the Way"; "Love and Marriage."

Albert von Tilzer, 1878-1956, (U.S.) "I'll Be With You in Apple Blossom Time"; "Take Me Out to the Ball Game."

Harry von Tilzer, 1872-1946, (U.S.) "Only a Bird in a Gilded Cage"; "Wait 'til the Sun Shines, Nellie."

Fats Waller, 1904-43, (U.S.) "Honeysuckle Rose"; "Ain't Misbehavin'."

Harry Warren, 1893-1981, (U.S.) "You're My Everything"; "We're in the Money"; "I Only Have Eyes for You."

Jimmy Webb, b 1946, (U.S.) "Up, Up and Away"; "By the Time I Get to Phoenix"; "Didn't We?"; "Wichita Lineman."

Kurt Weill, 1900-50, (Ger.-U.S.) *Threepenny Opera; Lady in the Dark; Knickerbocker Holiday; One Touch of Venus.*

Percy Wenrich, 1887-1952, (U.S.) "When You Wore a Tulip"; "Moonlight Bay"; "Put On Your Old Gray Bonnet."

Richard A. Whiting, 1891-1938, (U.S.) "Till We Meet Again"; "Sleepytime Gal"; "Beyond the Blue Horizon"; "My Ideal."

Frank Wildhorn, b 1959, (U.S.) *Jekyll and Hyde; Victor/Victoria; The Civil War.*

John Williams, b 1932, (U.S.) *Jaws; E.T.; Star Wars* series; *Raiders of the Lost Ark* series.

Meredith Willson, 1902-84, (U.S.) *The Music Man.*

Stevie Wonder, b 1950, (U.S.) "You Are the Sunshine of My Life"; "Signed, Sealed, Delivered, I'm Yours."

Vincent Youmans, 1898-1946, (U.S.) *No, No, Nanette;* "Tea for Two"; "I Want to Be Happy."

Lyricists

Dorothy Fields, 1905-74, (U.S.) "On the Sunny Side of the Street"; "Don't Blame Me"; "The Way You Look Tonight."

Ira Gershwin, 1896-1983, (U.S.) "The Man I Love"; "S'Wonderful"; "Embraceable You."

William S. Gilbert, 1836-1911, (Br.) *H.M.S. Pinafore; Pirates of Penzance.*

Gerry Goffin, 1939-2014, (U.S.) "Will You Love Me Tomorrow"; "Take Good Care of My Baby"; "Up on the Roof."

Mack Gordon, 1905-59, (Pol.-U.S.) "You'll Never Know"; "The More I See You"; "Chattanooga Choo-Choo."

Oscar Hammerstein II, 1895-1960, (U.S.) *Show Boat; Oklahoma!; Carousel.*

E.Y. (Yip) Harburg, 1898-1981, (U.S.) "Brother, Can You Spare a Dime"; "April in Paris"; "Over the Rainbow."

Sheldon Harnick, 1924-2023, (U.S.) *Fiddler on the Roof; She Loves Me.*

Lorenz Hart, 1895-1943, (U.S.) "Isn't It Romantic"; "Blue Moon"; "Lover"; "Manhattan"; "My Funny Valentine."

DuBose Heyward, 1885-1940, (U.S.) "Summertime."

Gus Kahn, 1886-1941, (U.S.) "Memories"; "Ain't We Got Fun."

Alan J. Lerner, 1918-86, (U.S.) *Brigadoon; My Fair Lady; Camelot; Gigi; On a Clear Day You Can See Forever.*

Johnny Mercer, 1909-76, (U.S.) "Blues in the Night"; "Come Rain or Come Shine"; "Laura"; "That Old Black Magic."

Bob Merrill, 1921-98, (U.S.) "People"; "(How Much Is That) Doggie in the Window."

Jack Norworth, 1879-1959, (U.S.) "Take Me Out to the Ball Game"; "Shine On Harvest Moon."

Mitchell Parish, 1901-93, (U.S.) "Stardust"; "Stairway to the Stars."

Andy Razaf, 1895-1973, (U.S.) "Honeysuckle Rose"; "Ain't Misbehavin."

Tim Rice, b 1944, (Br.) *Jesus Christ Superstar; Evita; The Lion King.*

Leo Robin, 1900-84, (U.S.) "Thanks for the Memory"; "Diamonds Are a Girl's Best Friend."

Robert Sherman, 1925-2012, (U.S.) *Mary Poppins; The Jungle Book.*

Bernie Taupin, b 1947 (Br.) "Rocket Man"; "Your Song."

Paul Francis Webster, 1907-84, (U.S.) "Secret Love"; "The Shadow of Your Smile"; "Love Is a Many-Splendored Thing."

Jack Yellen, 1892-1991, (U.S.) "Ain't She Sweet"; "Happy Days Are Here Again."

Howard Ashman, 1950-91, (U.S.) *Little Shop of Horrors; The Little Mermaid.*

Johnny Burke, 1908-84, (U.S.) "Misty"; "Imagination."

Irving Caesar, 1895-1996, (U.S.) "Swanee"; "Tea for Two"; "Just a Gigolo."

Sammy Cahn, 1913-93, (U.S.) "High Hopes"; "Love and Marriage"; "The Second Time Around"; "It's Magic."

Leonard Cohen, 1934-2016, (Can.) "Suzanne"; "Hallelujah."

Betty Comden, 1917-2006, and **Adolph Green**, 1915-2002, (both U.S.) "The Party's Over"; "New York, New York."

Hal David, 1921-2012, (U.S.) "What the World Needs Now Is Love."

Buddy De Sylva, 1895-1950, (U.S.) "When Day Is Done"; "Look for the Silver Lining"; "April Showers."

Howard Dietz, 1896-1983, (U.S.) "Dancing in the Dark"; "That's Entertainment."

Al Dubin, 1891-1945, (U.S.) "Tiptoe Through the Tulips"; "Lullaby of Broadway."

Fred Ebb, 1936-2004, (U.S.) *Cabaret; Zorba; Woman of the Year; Chicago.*

Ray Evans, 1915-2007, (U.S.) "Mona Lisa"; "Que Sera, Sera."

Blues and Jazz Artists of the Past

Julian "Cannonball" Adderley, 1928-75, alto sax.

Nat Adderley, 1931-2000, cornet.

Henry "Red" Allen, 1908-67, trumpet.

Mose Allison, 1927-2016, piano.

Louis "Satchmo" Armstrong, 1901-71, trumpet, singer, bandleader.

Albert Ayler, 1936-70, tenor sax, alto sax.

Mildred Bailey, 1907-51, singer.

Chet Baker, 1929-88, trumpet, singer.

Ray Barretto, 1930-2006, conga drummer.

William "Count" Basie, 1904-84, bandleader, piano, composer.

Sidney Bechet, 1897-1959, soprano sax, clarinet.

Bix Beiderbecke, 1903-31, cornet, composer, piano.

Rowland "Bunny" Berigan, 1908-42, trumpet.

Barney Bigard, 1906-80, clarinet.

Eubie Blake, 1883?-1983, composer, piano.

Art Blakey, 1919-90, drums, bandleader.

Jimmy Blanton, 1921-42, bass.

Charles "Buddy" Bolden, 1877-1931, cornet, pioneer bandleader.

Lester Bowie, 1941-99, trumpet, composer, bandleader.

Michael Brecker, 1949-2007, saxophone.

Big Bill Broonzy, 1893-1958, blues singer, guitar.

Clarence "Gatemouth" Brown, 1924-2005, guitar, singer.

Clifford Brown, 1930-56, trumpet.

Ray Brown, 1926-2002, bass.

Dave Brubeck, 1920-2012, piano, bandleader.

Don Byas, 1912-72, tenor sax.

Charlie Byrd, 1925-99, guitar; popularized bossa nova.
Cab Calloway, 1907-94, bandleader, singer.
Harry Carney, 1910-74, baritone sax, clarinet.
Benny Carter, 1907-2003, alto sax.
Betty Carter, 1930-98, jazz singer.
Sidney "Big Sid" Catlett, 1910-51, drums.
Adolphus Anthony "Doc" Cheatham, 1905-97, trumpet.
Don Cherry, 1936-95, trumpet.
Charlie Christian, 1916-42, guitar.
Kenny "Klook" Clarke, 1914-85, drums.
Buck Clayton, 1911-91, trumpet.
Al Cohn, 1925-88, tenor sax.
Nat "King" Cole, 1919-65, piano, singer.
William "Cozy" Cole, 1909-81, drums.
Ornette Coleman, 1930-2015, alto sax, composer.
Alice Coltrane, 1937-2007, piano, composer.
John Coltrane, 1926-67, tenor sax, soprano sax, composer.
Eddie Condon, 1905-73, guitar, bandleader.
Tadd Dameron, 1917-65, piano, composer.
Eddie "Lockjaw" Davis, 1921-86, tenor sax.
Miles Davis, 1926-91, trumpet, composer.
Wild Bill Davison, 1906-89, cornet.
Blossom Dearie, 1924-2009, singer.
Paul Desmond, 1926-77, alto sax.
Vic Dickenson, 1906-84, trombone.
Willie Dixon, 1915-92, composer, bass.
Johnny Dodds, 1892-1940, clarinet.
Warren "Baby" Dodds, 1898-1959, drums.
Eric Dolphy, 1928-64, alto sax, bass clarinet, flute.
Jimmy Dorsey, 1904-57, alto sax, bandleader.
Tommy Dorsey, 1905-56, trombone, bandleader.
Billy Eckstine, 1914-93, singer, bandleader.
Harry "Sweets" Edison, 1915-99, trumpet.
David "Honeyboy" Edwards, 1915-2011, guitar, singer.
Roy Eldridge, 1911-89, trumpet, singer.
Duke Ellington, 1899-1974, piano, bandleader, composer.
Bill Evans, 1929-80, piano.
Gil Evans, 1912-88, composer, arranger, piano.
Art Farmer, 1928-99, trumpet, flugelhorn.
Maynard Ferguson, 1926-2006, trumpet, bandleader.
Ella Fitzgerald, 1917-96, singer.
Tommy Flanagan, 1930-2001, piano.
Pete Fountain, 1930-2016, clarinetist.
Erroll Garner, 1921-77, piano, composer.
Stan Getz, 1927-91, tenor sax.
Dizzy Gillespie, 1917-93, trumpet, composer, bandleader.
Jimmy Giuffre, 1921-2008, clarinetist, composer.
Benny Goodman, 1909-86, clarinet, bandleader.
Dexter Gordon, 1923-90, tenor sax.
Stéphane Grappelli, 1908-97, violin.
Bobby Hackett, 1915-76, trumpet, cornet.
Lionel Hampton, 1908-2002, vibraphone, bandleader.
W. C. Handy, 1873-1958, composer.
Jimmy Harrison, 1900-31, trombone.
Coleman Hawkins, 1904-69, tenor sax.
Percy Heath, 1923-2005, bass.
Fletcher Henderson, 1898-1952, bandleader, arranger.
Woody Herman, 1913-87, clarinet, alto sax, bandleader.
Jay C. Higginbotham, 1906-73, trombone.
Ruiz Hilton, 1952-2006, piano, composer.
Earl "Fatha" Hines, 1903-83, piano.
Milt Hinton, 1910-2000, bass.
Al Hirt, 1922-99, trumpet.
Johnny Hodges, 1906-70, alto sax.
Billie Holiday, 1915-59, singer.
John Lee Hooker, 1917-2001, blues guitar, singer.
Sam "Lightnin'" Hopkins, 1912-82, blues singer, guitar.

Shirley Horn, 1934-2005, piano, singer.
Howlin' Wolf (Chester Burnett), 1910-76, blues singer, harmonica, guitar.
Alberta Hunter, 1895-1984, singer.
Mahalia Jackson, 1911-72, gospel singer.
Milt Jackson, 1923-99, vibraphone.
Elmore James, 1918-63, blues singer, guitar.
Etta James, 1938-2012, blues singer.
Al Jarreau, 1940-2017, jazz singer.
"Blind" Lemon Jefferson, 1897-1929, blues singer, guitar.
J. J. Johnson, 1924-2001, trombone.
James P. Johnson, 1891-1955, piano, composer.
Robert Johnson, 1912-38, blues singer, guitar.
William "Bunk" Johnson, 1879-1949, trumpet.
Elvin Jones, 1927-2004, drums.
Jo Jones, 1911-85, drums.
Philly Joe Jones, 1923-85, drums.
Thad Jones, 1923-86, cornet, bandleader, composer.
Scott Joplin, 1868-1917, ragtime composer.
Louis Jordan, 1908-75, singer, alto sax.
Stan Kenton, 1911-79, bandleader, composer, piano.
Barney Kessel, 1923-2004, guitar.
Albert King, 1923-92, blues guitar.
B. B. King, 1925-2015, blues guitar, singer.
John Kirby, 1908-52, bandleader, bass.
Rahsaan Roland Kirk, 1936-77, saxophone, composer.
Gene Krupa, 1909-73, drums, bandleader.
Scott LaFaro, 1936-61, bass.
Lead Belly (Huddie Ledbetter), 1888-1949, folk and blues singer, guitar.
Peggy Lee, 1920-2002, singer.
John Lewis, 1920-2001, piano, Modern Jazz Quartet founder.
Mel Lewis, 1929-90, drums, bandleader.
Jimmie Lunceford, 1902-47, bandleader.
Machito (Frank Grillo), 1908-84, Latin percussion, singer, bandleader.
Shelly Manne, 1920-84, drums, bandleader.
Ellis Marsalis Jr., 1934-2020, piano.
Jackie McLean, 1931-2006, saxophone, composer.
Jimmy McPartland, 1907-91, trumpet.
Marian McPartland, 1918-2013, pianist.
Carmen McRae, 1920-94, singer.
Glenn Miller, 1904-44, trombone, bandleader.
Charles Mingus, 1922-79, bass, composer, bandleader.
Thelonious Monk, 1917-82, piano, composer.
Wes Montgomery, 1925-68, guitar.
James Moody, 1925-2010, saxophone.
Ferdinand "Jelly Roll" Morton, 1885-1941, composer, piano.
Bennie Moten, 1894-1935, piano, bandleader.
Gerry Mulligan, 1927-96, baritone sax, composer.
Theodore "Fats" Navarro, 1923-50, trumpet.
Red Nichols, 1905-65, cornet, bandleader.
Red Norvo, 1908-99, vibraphone, xylophone, bandleader.
Anita O'Day, 1919-2006, singer.
Arturo "Chico" O'Farrill, 1921-2001, Latin composer, arranger.
King Oliver, 1885-1938, cornet, bandleader.
Sy Oliver, 1910-88, arranger, composer.
Edward "Kid" Ory, 1886-1973, trombone, bandleader.
Johnny Otis, 1921-2012, blues singer.
Oran "Hot Lips" Page, 1908-54, trumpet, singer.
Charlie "Bird" Parker, 1920-55, alto sax, composer.
Joe Pass, 1929-94, guitar.
Jaco Pastorius, 1951-87, bass guitarist.
Art Pepper, 1925-82, alto sax.
Pinetop Perkins, 1913-2011, piano.

Oscar Peterson, 1925-2007, piano.
Oscar Pettiford, 1922-60, bass.
Earl "Bud" Powell, 1924-66, piano.
Chano Pozo, 1915-48, percussionist, singer.
Louis Prima, 1911-78, singer, bandleader.
Tito Puente, 1923-2000, Latin percussion, bandleader.
Gertrude "Ma" Rainey, 1886-1939, blues singer.
Lou Rawls, 1933-2006, singer.
Dewey Redman, 1931-2006, tenor sax.
Don Redman (Robert Rodney Chudnick), 1900-64, composer, arranger.
Django Reinhardt, 1910-53, guitar.
Buddy Rich, 1917-87, drums.
Max Roach, 1924-2007, drums, composer.
Red Rodney (Robert Chudnick), 1927-94, trumpet.
Jimmy Rowles, 1918-96, piano.
Jimmy Rushing, 1903-72, blues and jazz singer.
Charles "Pee Wee" Russell, 1906-69, clarinet.
Artie Shaw, 1910-2004, swing-era bandleader, clarinet.
George Shearing, 1919-2011, piano.
Wayne Shorter, 1933-2023, tenor and soprano sax.
Nina Simone (Eunice Waymon), 1933-2003, singer.
John "Zoot" Sims, 1925-85, tenor sax.
Zutty Singleton, 1898-1975, drums.
Bessie Smith, 1894-1937, blues singer.
Clarence "Pinetop" Smith, 1904-29, piano, singer, boogie woogie pioneer.
Willie "The Lion" Smith, 1897-1973, piano, composer.
Francis "Muggsy" Spanier, 1906-67, cornet.
Edward "Sonny" Stitt, 1924-82, tenor sax, alto sax.
Billy Strayhorn, 1915-67, composer, piano, Duke Ellington collaborator.
Sun Ra (Herman Blount), 1915?-93, bandleader, piano, composer.
Art Tatum, 1910-56, piano.
Art Taylor, 1929-95, drums.
Billy Taylor, 1921-2010, piano.
Jack Teagarden, 1905-64, trombone, singer.
Clark Terry, 1920-2015, trumpet.
Mel Tormé, 1925-99, singer ("The Velvet Fog").
Dave Tough, 1908-48, drums.
Lennie Tristano, 1919-78, piano, composer.
Joe Turner, 1911-85, blues singer.
Sarah Vaughan, 1924-90, singer.
Joe Venuti, 1903-78, violin.
Aaron "T-Bone" Walker, 1910-75, blues guitar.
Thomas "Fats" Waller, 1904-43, piano, singer, composer.
Dinah Washington (Ruth Jones), 1924-63, singer.
Grover Washington Jr., 1943-99, pop-jazz sax, composer.
Ethel Waters, 1896-1977, jazz and blues singer.
Muddy Waters (McKinley Morganfield), 1915-83, blues singer, songwriter.
Julius Watkins, 1921-77, French horn.
William "Chick" Webb, 1902-39, bandleader, drums.
Ben Webster, 1909-73, tenor sax.
Junior Wells (Amos Blackmore), 1934-98, blues singer, harmonica.
Paul Whiteman, 1890-1967, bandleader.
Margaret Whiting, 1924-2011, singer.
Charles "Cootie" Williams, 1910-85, trumpet, bandleader.
Joe Williams, 1918-99, singer.
Mary Lou Williams, 1910-81, piano, composer.
Tony Williams, 1945-97, drums.
John Lee "Sonny Boy" Williamson, 1914-48, blues singer, harmonica.
Sonny Boy Williamson (Aleck "Rice" Miller), 1900?-65, blues singer, harmonica.
Teddy Wilson, 1912-86, piano.
Kai Winding, 1922-83, trombone.
Jimmy Yancey, 1894-1951, piano.
Lester "Pres" Young, 1909-59, tenor sax.

Country Music Artists of the Past and Present

* = Inducted into Country Music Hall of Fame (Nashville, TN) as performer between 1961 and 2023.

*Roy Acuff, 1903-92, fiddler, singer, songwriter; "Wabash Cannon Ball."

*Alabama (Jeff Cook, 1949-2022; Teddy Gentry, b 1952; Mark Herndon, b 1955; Randy Owen, b 1949); "Feels So Right."

Jason Aldean, b 1977, singer; "Don't You Wanna Stay."

*James "Whispering Bill" Anderson, b 1937, singer, songwriter; "Make Mine Night Time."

*Eddy Arnold, 1918-2008, singer, guitarist, known as the Tennessee Plowboy.

*Chet Atkins, 1924-2001, guitarist, composer, producer; helped create the "Nashville sound."

*Gene Autry, 1907-98, singing movie cowboy; "Back in the Saddle Again."

Clint Black, b 1962, singer, songwriter; "Killin' Time."

*Garth Brooks, b 1962, singer, songwriter; "Friends in Low Places."

*Brooks & Dunn (Kix Brooks, b 1955; Ronnie Dunn, b 1953); "Hard Workin' Man."

Kane Brown, b 1993, singer, songwriter; "Lose It."

Luke Bryan, b 1976, singer, songwriter; "Someone Else Calling You Baby."

*Boudleaux, 1920-87, and **Felice Bryant**, 1925-2003, songwriting team; "Hey Joe."

*Glen Campbell, 1936-2017, singer, guitarist; "Gentle on My Mind."

Brandi Carlile, b 1981, singer, songwriter; "The Joke."

Mary Chapin Carpenter, b 1958, singer, songwriter; "I Feel Lucky."

*Carter Family (original members A. P., 1891-1960; "Mother" Maybelle, 1909-78; Sara, 1898-1979); "Wildwood Flower."

*Johnny Cash, 1932-2003, singer, songwriter; "I Walk the Line," "Ring of Fire," "Folsom Prison Blues."

Kenny Chesney, b 1968, singer, songwriter; "You Had Me From Hello."

The Chicks (fmr. Dixie Chicks) (Natalie Maines, b 1974; Emily Strayer, b 1972; Martie Maguire, b 1969); *Wide Open Spaces.*

Eric Church, b 1977, singer, songwriter, guitarist; "Record Year."

*Roy Clark, 1933-2018, guitarist, banjoist, singer, co-host of *Hee Haw*; "Yesterday, When I Was Young."

*Patsy Cline, 1932-63, singer; "Walkin' After Midnight," "Crazy," "Sweet Dreams."

Luke Combs, b 1990, singer, songwriter; "Beautiful Crazy."

Billy Ray Cyrus, b 1961, singer, songwriter; "Achy Breaky Heart."

*Charlie Daniels, 1936-2020, guitarist, fiddler; "The Devil Went Down to Georgia."

*Jimmy Dean, 1928-2010, singer; "Big Bad John."

John Denver, 1943-97, singer, songwriter; "Rocky Mountain High."

Dale Evans, 1912-2001, singer, actress, married Roy Rogers.

Sara Evans, b 1971, singer, songwriter; "Born to Fly."

*Flatt & Scruggs (Lester Flatt, 1914-79; Earl Scruggs, 1924-2012), guitar-banjo duo and soloists; "Foggy Mountain Breakdown."

*Red Foley, 1910-68, singer; "Chattanoogie Shoe Shine Boy."

*Tennessee Ernie Ford, 1919-91, singer, TV host; "Sixteen Tons."

*William "Lefty" Frizzell, 1928-75, singer, guitarist; "Long Black Veil."

*Vince Gill, b 1957, singer, songwriter; "When I Call Your Name."

*Merle Haggard, 1937-2016, singer, songwriter; "Okie From Muskogee."

*Emmylou Harris, b 1947, singer, songwriter, folk-country crossover artist; "If I Could Only Win Your Love."

Hunter Hayes, b 1991, singer; "Wanted."

Faith Hill, b 1967, singer, songwriter; "Breathe."

*Alan Jackson, b 1958, singer, songwriter; "Where Were You (When the World Stopped Turning)."

*Waylon Jennings, 1937-2002, singer, songwriter, outlaw country pioneer; "Luckenbach, Texas."

*George Jones, 1931-2013, singer; "He Stopped Loving Her Today."

*The Judds (Naomi, 1946-2022; Wynonna, b 1964), mother-daughter duo; Wynonna also a solo act.

Toby Keith, b 1961, singer, songwriter, guitarist; "Should've Been a Cowboy."

Alison Krauss, b 1971, bluegrass fiddler, singer, bandleader; "When You Say Nothing at All."

*Kris Kristofferson, b 1936, singer, songwriter, actor; "Me and Bobby McGee."

Lady A (fmr. Lady Antebellum) (Dave Haywood, b 1982; Charles Kelley, b 1981; Hillary Scott, b 1984); *Need You Now.*

Miranda Lambert, b 1983, singer, guitarist; "The House That Built Me."

*Louvin Brothers (Charlie, 1927-2011; Ira, 1924-65), singers; "If I Could Only Win Your Love."

*Patty Loveless, b 1957, singer, songwriter; "How Can I Help You Say Goodbye."

Lyle Lovett, b 1957, singer, songwriter, bandleader, actor; "Cowboy Man."

*Loretta Lynn, 1932-2022, singer; "Coal Miner's Daughter."

*Barbara Mandrell, b 1948, singer; "I Was Country When Country Wasn't Cool."

Kathy Mattea, b 1959, singer, songwriter; "Eighteen Wheels and a Dozen Roses."

Martina McBride, b 1966, singer, songwriter; "Independence Day."

*Reba McEntire, b 1955, singer, songwriter, actress; "Whoever's in New England."

Tim McGraw, b 1967, singer; "It's Your Love," "I Like It, I Love It."

*Roger Miller, 1936-92, singer, songwriter; "King of the Road."

*Ronnie Milsap, b 1943, singer, songwriter; "There's No Gettin' Over Me."

*Bill Monroe, 1911-96, singer, songwriter, mandolin player, "father of bluegrass music"; "Mule Skinner Blues."

Maren Morris, b 1990, singer, songwriter; "My Church."

Anne Murray, b 1945, singer; "You Needed Me."

Kacey Musgraves, b 1988, singer, songwriter; "Space Cowboy."

*Willie Nelson, b 1933, singer, songwriter, actor; "On the Road Again."

Mark O'Connor, b 1961, fiddler, country-classical crossover composer.

*Buck Owens, 1929-2006, singer, guitarist; "Act Naturally."

Brad Paisley, b 1972, singer, songwriter; "Whiskey Lullaby," "When I Get Where I'm Going."

*Dolly Parton, b 1946, singer, songwriter, actress; "Here You Come Again," "9 to 5."

Johnny Paycheck (Don Lytle), 1938-2003, singer, guitarist; "Take This Job and Shove It."

*Minnie Pearl, 1912-96, comedian, Grand Ole Opry star.

Kellie Pickler, b 1986, singer, songwriter.

*Ray Price, 1926-2013, country singer, guitarist, songwriter; "Crazy Arms."

*Charley Pride, 1934-2020, singer, first major Black country star; "Kiss an Angel Good Mornin'."

John Prine, 1946-2020, singer, songwriter; "Angel From Montgomery."

Eddie Rabbitt, 1941-98, singer, songwriter; "I Love a Rainy Night."

Rascal Flatts (Jay DeMarcus, b 1971; Gary LeVox, b 1970; Joe Don Rooney, b 1975); "Life Is a Highway"; "Rewind."

*Jim Reeves, 1923-64, singer, songwriter; "Four Walls."

Thomas Rhett, b 1990, singer, songwriter.

Charlie Rich, 1932-95, singer, songwriter called the "Silver Fox"; "The Most Beautiful Girl."

LeAnn Rimes, b 1982, singer; *Blue.*

*Tex Ritter, 1905-74, singer, songwriter; "Jingle, Jangle, Jingle."

*Marty Robbins, 1925-82, singer, songwriter; "A White Sport Coat and a Pink Carnation."

*Jimmie Rodgers, 1897-1933, singer, songwriter; "T for Texas."

*Kenny Rogers, 1938-2020, singer, songwriter; "The Gambler."

*Roy Rogers (Leonard Slye), 1911-98, singer, actor, "King of the Cowboys," sang with Sons of the Pioneers.

*Fred Rose, 1898-1954, songwriter, singer, producer; "Blue Eyes Cryin' in the Rain."

Blake Shelton, b 1976, singer; "Home."

*Ricky Skaggs, b 1954, singer, songwriter, bandleader; "Don't Cheat in Our Hometown."

Ralph Stanley, 1927-2016, singer, banjo player; "Man of Constant Sorrow."

Chris Stapleton, b 1978, singer, songwriter; *Traveller.*

*George Strait, b 1952, singer, bandleader; "Ace in the Hole."

Sugarland (Kristian Bush, b 1970; Jennifer Nettles, b 1974); "Stay."

Taylor Swift, b 1989, singer, songwriter; "You Belong With Me."

*Lonnie "Mel" Tillis, 1932-2017, singer, songwriter, bandleader; "I Ain't Never."

*Merle Travis, 1917-83, singer, guitarist, songwriter; "Divorce Me C.O.D."

*Randy Travis, b 1959, singer, songwriter; "Forever and Ever, Amen."

*Ernest Tubb, 1914-84, singer, songwriter, guitarist; "Walking the Floor Over You."

*Tanya Tucker, b 1958, singer, songwriter; "Delta Dawn."

Josh Turner, b 1977, singer; "Why Don't We Just Dance."

Shania Twain, b 1965, singer, songwriter; "You're Still the One."

*Conway Twitty, 1933-93, singer, songwriter; "Hello Darlin'."

Carrie Underwood, b 1983, singer, songwriter; *American Idol* winner.

Keith Urban, b 1967, guitarist, singer, songwriter; "Somebody Like You."

*Porter Wagoner, 1927-2007, singer, songwriter, guitarist; "Soul of a Convict."

*Kitty Wells (Ellen Deason), 1919-2012, singer, songwriter; "It Wasn't God Who Made Honky-Tonk Angels."

Dottie West, 1932-91, singer, songwriter; "Here Comes My Baby."

*Hank Williams Jr., b 1949, singer, songwriter; "Bocephus"; "All My Rowdy Friends (Have Settled Down)."

*Hank Williams Sr., 1923-53, singer, songwriter; "Your Cheatin' Heart."

*Bob Wills, 1905-75, Western Swing fiddler, singer, bandleader, songwriter; "New San Antonio Rose."

Lee Ann Womack, b 1966, singer, songwriter; "I Hope You Dance."

*Tammy Wynette, 1942-98, singer; "Stand By Your Man."

Trisha Yearwood, b 1964, singer, songwriter; "How Do I Live."

Dwight Yoakam, b 1957, singer, songwriter, actor; "Ain't That Lonely Yet."

Zac Brown Band (Coy Bowles, b 1979; Zac Brown, b 1978; Clay Cook, b 1978; Jimmy De Martini, b 1976; Chris Fryar, b 1970; John Driskell Hopkins, b 1971); "Chicken Fried."

Dance Figures of the Past

Alvin Ailey, 1931-89, (U.S.) modern dancer, choreographer; melded modern dance and Afro-Caribbean techniques.

Alicia Alonso, 1920-2019, (Cuba) ballerina, founder of National Ballet of Cuba.

Frederick Ashton, 1904-88, (Br.) ballet choreographer; director of Great Britain's Royal Ballet, 1963-70.

Fred Astaire, 1899-1987, dancer, actor; teamed with dancer/actress **Ginger Rogers**, 1911-95, (both U.S.) in movie musicals.

George Balanchine, 1904-83, (Russ.-U.S.) ballet choreographer, teacher; most influential exponent of neoclassical style; founded, with Lincoln Kirstein, School of American Ballet and New York City Ballet.

Pina Bausch, 1940-2009, (Ger.) modern dance choreographer influencing the Tanztheater style of dance.

Carlo Blasis, 1795-1878, (It.) ballet dancer, choreographer, writer; his teaching methods are standards of classical dance.

August Bournonville, 1805-79, (Den.) ballet dancer, choreographer, teacher; exuberant, light style.

Fernando Bujones, 1955-2005, (Cuba-U.S.) ballet dancer.

Gisella Caccianza, 1914-98, (U.S.) ballerina; charter member of Balanchine's American Ballet.

Irene, 1893-1969, (U.S.) and **Vernon Castle**, 1887-1918, (Br.) husband-and-wife ballroom dancers.

Enrico Cecchetti, 1850-1928, (It.) ballet dancer, leading dancer of Russia's Imperial Ballet; his technique was basis for Britain's Imperial Soc. of Teachers of Dancing.

Gower, 1921-80, dancer, choreographer, director; with wife **Marge Champion**, 1919-2020, (both U.S.) choreographed, danced in Broadway musicals and films.

John Cranko, 1927-73, (S. Afr.) choreographer; created narrative ballets based on literary works.

Merce Cunningham, 1919-2009, (U.S.) dancer, choreographer of avant-garde dance.

Jacques d'Amboise, 1934-2021, (U.S.) ballet dancer, choreographer.

Alexandra Danilova, 1903-97, (Russ.) ballerina; noted teacher at the School of American Ballet.

Agnes de Mille, 1905-93, (U.S.) ballerina, choreographer; known for using American themes, she choreographed the ballet *Rodeo* and the musical *Oklahoma!*

Dame Ninette De Valois, 1898-2001, (Br.) choreographer, founding director of London's Royal Ballet; *The Rake's Progress*.

Sergei Diaghilev, 1872-1929, (Russ.) impresario; founded Les Ballet Russes; saw ballet as art unifying dance, drama, music, and decor.

Isadora Duncan, 1877-1927, (U.S.) expressive dancer who united free movement with serious music; one of the founders of modern dance.

Katherine Dunham, 1910-2006, (U.S.) dancer, choreographer; internationally known for African, Caribbean, and African American dance forms.

Fanny Elssler, 1810-84, (Austria) ballerina of the Romantic era; known for dramatic skill, sensual style.

Michel Fokine, 1880-1942, (Russ.) ballet dancer, choreographer, teacher; rejected strict classicism in favor of dramatically expressive style.

Margot Fonteyn, 1919-91, (Br.) prima ballerina, Royal Ballet of Great Britain; famed performance partner of Rudolf Nureyev.

Bob Fosse, 1927-87, (U.S.) jazz dancer, choreographer, director; Broadway musicals and film.

Serge Golovine, 1924-98, (Fr.) ballet dancer with Grand Ballet du Marquis de Cuevas, choreographer.

Martha Graham, 1894-1991, (U.S.) modern dancer, choreographer; created and codified her own dramatic technique.

Melissa Hayden, 1923-2006, (Can.) ballet dancer.

Martha Hill, 1900-95, (U.S.) educator; leading figure in modern dance; founded American Dance Festival.

Gregory Hines, 1946-2003, (U.S.) tap-dance innovator; master of improvisation.

Doris Humphrey, 1895-1958, (U.S.) modern dancer, choreographer, writer, teacher.

Michael Jackson, 1958-2009, (U.S.) singer and dancer who perfected the "moonwalk."

Robert Joffrey, 1930-88, ballet dancer, choreographer; cofounded with **Gerald Arpino**, 1928-2008, (both U.S.) the Joffrey Ballet.

Kurt Jooss, 1901-79, (Ger.) choreographer, teacher; created expressionist works using modern and classical techniques.

Tamara Karsavina, 1885-1978, (Russ.) prima ballerina of Russia's Imperial Ballet and Diaghilev's Ballets Russes; partner of Nijinsky.

Nora Kaye, 1920-87, (U.S.) ballerina with Metropolitan Opera Ballet and Ballet Theater (now American Ballet Theatre).

Gene Kelly, 1912-96, (U.S.) dancer, actor in movie musicals.

Michael Kidd, 1915-2003, (U.S.) dancer, film and theater choreographer.

Lincoln Kirstein, 1907-96, (U.S.) brought ballet as an art form to U.S.; founded, with George Balanchine, School of American Ballet and New York City Ballet.

Serge Lifar, 1905-86, (Russ.-Fr.) prem. danseur; director of dance at Paris Opera, 1930-45, 1947-58.

José Limón, 1908-72, (Mex.-U.S.) modern dancer, choreographer, teacher; developed technique based on Humphrey.

Catherine Littlefield, 1908-51, (U.S.) ballerina, choreographer, teacher; pioneer of American ballet.

Kenneth MacMillan, 1929-92, (Br.) dancer, choreographer; directed Royal Ballet of Great Britain, 1970-77.

Dame Alicia Markova, 1910-2004, (Br.) ballerina known for title role in *Giselle*; helped popularize ballet in U.S. and Britain.

Léonide Massine, 1896-1979, (Russ.-U.S.) ballet dancer, choreographer; known for his "symphonic ballet."

Arthur Mitchell, 1934-2018, (U.S.) dancer, choreographer; cofounded Dance Theatre of Harlem.

Fayard Nicholas, 1914-2006, tap dancer, choreographer, actor; together with brother **Harold Nicholas**, 1921-2000, (both U.S.) formed the Nicholas Brothers.

Vaslav Nijinsky, 1890-50, (Russ.) prem. danseur, choreographer; leading member of Diaghilev's Ballets Russes; his ballets were revolutionary for their time.

Alwin Nikolais, 1910-93, (U.S.) modern choreographer; created dance theater utilizing mixed media effects.

Jean-George Noverre, 1727-1810, (Fr.) ballet choreographer, teacher, writer; "Shakespeare of the Dance."

Rudolf Nureyev, 1938-93, (Russ.) prem. danseur, choreographer; leading male dancer of his generation; director of dance at Paris Opera, 1983-89.

Ruth Page, 1899-1991, (U.S.) ballerina, choreographer; danced, directed ballet at Chicago Lyric Opera.

Anna Pavlova, 1881-1931, (Russ.) prima ballerina; toured with her own company to world acclaim.

Marius Petipa, 1818-1910, (Fr.) ballet dancer, choreographer; ballet master of the Imperial Ballet; established Russian classicism as leading style of late 19th cent.

Roland Petit, 1924-2011, (Fr.) dancer, choreographer; founder of Les Ballets de Paris.

Pearl Primus, 1919-95, (Trinidad-U.S.) modern dancer, choreographer, scholar; combined African, Caribbean, and African American styles.

Jerome Robbins, 1918-98, (U.S.) choreographer, director, dancer; *The King and I*, *West Side Story*, *Fiddler on the Roof.*

Bill "Bojangles" Robinson, 1878-1949, (U.S.) famed tap dancer; called "King of Tapology" on stage and screen.

Ruth St. Denis, 1877-1968, (U.S.) influential interpretive dancer, choreographer, teacher.

Ted Shawn, 1891-1972, (U.S.) modern dancer, choreographer; formed dance company and school with Ruth St. Denis; established Jacob's Pillow Dance Festival.

Marie Taglioni, 1804-84, (It.) ballerina, teacher; in title role of *La Sylphide* established image of the ethereal ballerina.

Maria Tallchief, 1925-2013, (U.S.) prima ballerina, 1st of Amer. Indian descent.

Marjorie Tallchief, 1926-2021, (U.S.) prima ballerina.

Paul Taylor, 1930-2018, (U.S.) dancer, choreographer, teacher.

Glen Tetley, 1926-2007, (U.S.) dancer, choreographer, ballet director; fused elements of modern dance with ballet.

Antony Tudor, 1908-87, (Br.) choreographer, teacher; exponent of the "psychological ballet."

Galina Ulanova, 1910-98, (Russ.) revered ballerina with Bolshoi Ballet.

Agrippina Vaganova, 1879-1951, (Russ.) ballet teacher, director called "queen of variations"; codified Soviet ballet technique.

Mary Wigman, 1886-1973, (Ger.) modern dancer, choreographer, teacher; influenced European expressionist dance.

Opera Singers of the Past

Licia Albanese, 1909-2014, (It.) soprano.

Frances Alda, 1879-1952, (N.Z.) soprano.

Pasquale Amato, 1878-1942, (It.) baritone.

Marian Anderson, 1897-1993, (U.S.) contralto.

Charles Anthony, 1929-2012, (U.S.) tenor.

Jussi Björling, 1911-60, (Swed.) tenor.

Lucrezia Bori, 1887-1960, (It.) soprano.

Grace Bumbry, 1937-2023, (U.S.) mezzo-soprano.

Montserrat Caballé, 1933-2018, (Sp.) soprano.

Maria Callas, 1923-77, (U.S.) soprano.

Emma Calvé, 1858-1942, (Fr.) soprano.

Enrico Caruso, 1873-1921, (It.) tenor.

Feodor Chaliapin, 1873-1938, (Russ.) bass.

Lili Chookasian, 1921-2012, (U.S.) contralto.

Boris Christoff, 1914-93, (Bulg.) bass.

Franco Corelli, 1921-2003, (It.) tenor.

Hughes Cuenod, 1902-2010, (Switz.) tenor.

Victoria De Los Angeles, 1923-2005, (Sp.) soprano.

Giuseppe De Luca, 1876-1950, (It.) baritone.

Fernando De Lucia, 1860-1925, (It.) tenor.

Edouard De Reszke, 1853-1917, (Pol.) bass.

Jean De Reszke, 1850-1925, (Pol.) tenor.

Emmy Destinn, 1878-1930, (Czech.) soprano.

Mattiwilda Dobbs, 1925-2015, (U.S.) coloratura soprano.

Emma Eames, 1865-1952, (U.S.) soprano.

(Carlo Broschi) Farinelli, 1705-82, (It.) castrato.

Geraldine Farrar, 1882-1967, (U.S.) soprano.

Eileen Farrell, 1920-2002, (U.S.) soprano.

Kathleen Ferrier, 1912-53, (Eng.) contralto.

Dietrich Fischer-Dieskau, 1925-2012, (Ger.) baritone.

Kirsten Flagstad, 1895-1962, (Nor.) soprano.

Olive Fremstad, 1871-1951, (Swed.-U.S.) soprano.
Amelita Galli-Curci, 1882-1963, (It.) soprano.
Mary Garden, 1874-1967, (Br.) soprano.
Nicolai Gedda, 1925-2017, (Swed.) tenor.
Nicolai Ghiaurov, 1929-2004, (Bulg.) bass.
Beniamino Gigli, 1890-1957, (It.) tenor.
Tito Gobbi, 1913-84, (It.) baritone.
Giulia Grisi, 1811-69, (It.) soprano.
Frieda Hempel, 1885-1955, (Ger.) soprano.
Jerome Hines, 1921-2003, (U.S.) bass.
Hans Hotter, 1909-2003, (Ger.) bass-baritone.
Maria Jeritza, 1887-1982, (Czech.) soprano.
Sena Jurinac, 1921-2011, (Yugo.) soprano.
Alexander Kipnis, 1891-1978, (Russ.-U.S.) bass.
Dorothy Kirsten, 1910-92, (U.S.) soprano.
Alfredo Kraus, 1927-99, (Sp.) tenor.
Luigi Lablache, 1794-1858, (It.) bass.
Lilli Lehmann, 1848-1929, (Ger.) soprano.
Lotte Lehmann, 1888-1976, (Ger.-U.S.) soprano.
Jenny Lind, 1820-87, (Swed.) soprano.
Christa Ludwig, 1924-2021, (Ger.) mezzo-soprano.
Cornell MacNeil, 1922-2011, (U.S.) baritone.
Maria Malibran, 1808-36, (Sp.) mezzo-soprano.
Giovanni Martinelli, 1885-1969, (It.) tenor.
John McCormack, 1884-1945, (Ire.) tenor.
Nellie Melba, 1861-1931, (Austral.) soprano.
Lauritz Melchior, 1890-1973, (Den.) tenor.
Robert Merrill, 1919-2004, (U.S.) baritone.

Zinka Milanov, 1906-89, (Yugo.) soprano.
Patrice Munsel, 1925-2015, (U.S.) coloratura soprano.
Patricia Neway, 1919-2012, (U.S.) soprano.
Birgit Nilsson, 1918-2005, (Swed.) soprano.
Lillian Nordica, 1857-1914, (U.S.) soprano.
Jessye Norman, 1945-2019, (U.S.) soprano.
Magda Olivero, 1910-2014, (It.) soprano.
Giuditta Pasta, 1797-1865, (It.) soprano.
Adelina Patti, 1843-1919, (It.) soprano.
Luciano Pavarotti, 1935-2007, (It.) tenor.
Peter Pears, 1910-86, (Eng.) tenor.
Jan Peerce, 1904-84, (U.S.) tenor.
Roberta Peters, 1930-2017, (U.S.) soprano.
Ezio Pinza, 1892-1957, (It.) bass.
Lily Pons, 1898-1976, (Fr.) soprano.
Rosa Ponselle, 1897-1981, (U.S.) soprano.
Hermann Prey, 1929-98, (Ger.) baritone.
Margaret Price, 1941-2011, (Br.) soprano.
Regina Resnik, 1922-2013, (U.S.) soprano turned mezzo-soprano.
Elisabeth Rethberg, 1894-1976, (Ger.) soprano.
Giovanni Battista Rubini, 1794-1854, (It.) tenor.
Leonie Rysanek, 1926-98, (Austria) soprano.
Dorothy Sarnoff, 1914-2008, (U.S.) soprano.
Bidú Sayão, 1902-99, (Braz.) soprano.
Friedrich Schorr, 1888-1953, (Hung.) bass-baritone.
Renata Scotto, 1934-2023, (It.) soprano.
Elisabeth Schwarzkopf, 1915-2006, (Ger.) soprano.

Marcella Sembrich, 1858-1935, (Pol.) soprano.
Cesare Siepi, 1923-2010, (It.) bass.
Beverly Sills, 1929-2007, (U.S.) soprano.
Elisabeth Söderström, 1927-2009, (Swed.) soprano.
Eleanor Steber, 1914-90, (U.S.) soprano.
Risë Stevens, 1913-2013, (U.S.) mezzo-soprano.
Joan Sutherland, 1926-2010, (Austral.) soprano.
Ferrucio Tagliavini, 1913-95, (It.) tenor.
Renata Tebaldi, 1922-2004, (It.) soprano.
Luisa Tetrazzini, 1871-1940, (It.) soprano.
Lawrence Tibbett, 1896-1960, (U.S.) baritone.
Giorgio Tozzi, 1923-2011, (U.S.) bass-baritone.
Tatiana Troyanos, 1938-93, (U.S.) mezzo-soprano.
Richard Tucker, 1913-75, (U.S.) tenor.
Shirley Verrett, 1931-2010, (U.S.) mezzo-soprano.
Pauline Viardot, 1821-1910, (Fr.) mezzo-soprano.
Jon Vickers, 1926-2015, (Can.) tenor.
William Warfield, 1920-2002, (U.S.) bass-baritone.
Leonard Warren, 1911-60, (U.S.) baritone.
Ljuba Welitsch, 1913-96, (Bulg.) soprano.
Camilla Williams, 1919-2012, (U.S.) soprano.
Wolfgang Windgassen, 1914-74, (Ger.)

Rock 'n' Roll, Rhythm and Blues, and Rap Artists

Titles in quotation marks are singles; others are albums. * = Inducted into Rock & Roll Hall of Fame as performer between 1986 and 2023; year is in parentheses.

*ABBA (2010): "Dancing Queen"
Paula Abdul: "Straight Up"
*AC/DC (2003): "Back in Black"
Bryan Adams: "Cuts Like a Knife"
Adele: "Rolling in the Deep"
*Aerosmith (2001): "Sweet Emotion"
Christina Aguilera: "What a Girl Wants"
Alice in Chains: "Heaven Beside You"
*The Allman Brothers Band (1995): "Ramblin' Man"
*The Animals (1994): "House of the Rising Sun"
Paul Anka: "Lonely Boy"
Fiona Apple: "Criminal"
Frankie Avalon: "Venus"
Iggy Azalea: "Fancy"
The B-52s: "Love Shack"
Bachman Turner Overdrive: "Takin' Care of Business"
Backstreet Boys: "I Want It That Way"
Bad Company: "Can't Get Enough"
Erykah Badu: "On and On"
*Joan Baez (2017): "The Night They Drove Old Dixie Down"
*La Vern Baker (1991): "I Cried a Tear"
*Hank Ballard[1] and the Midnighters (1990): "Work With Me, Annie"
*The Band (1994): "The Weight"
Barenaked Ladies: "One Week"
*The Beach Boys (1988): "Good Vibrations"
*Beastie Boys (2012): "(You Gotta) Fight for Your Right (to Party)"
*The Beatles (1988): Sgt. Pepper's Lonely Hearts Club Band
Beck: "Loser"
*Jeff Beck (2009): "Escape"
*The Bee Gees (1997): "Stayin' Alive"
*Pat Benatar (2022): "Hit Me With Your Best Shot"
*Chuck Berry (1986): "Johnny B. Goode"
Beyoncé: "Crazy in Love"
The Big Bopper: "Chantilly Lace"
Björk: "Human Behavior"
The Black Crowes: "Hard to Handle"
Black Eyed Peas: Elephunk
*Black Sabbath (2006): "Paranoid"
*Bobby "Blue" Bland (1992): "Turn On Your Love Light"
Mary J. Blige: My Life
Blind Faith: "Can't Find My Way Home"
Blink-182: "All the Small Things"
*Blondie (2006): "Heart of Glass"
Blood, Sweat, and Tears: "Spinning Wheel"
Blues Traveler: "Run-Around"
Gary "U.S." Bonds: "Quarter to Three"
*Bon Jovi (2018): "Livin' on a Prayer"
*Booker T. and the M.G.'s (1992): "Green Onions"

Boston: "More Than a Feeling"
*David Bowie (1996): "Space Oddity"
Boyz II Men: "I'll Make Love to You"
Toni Braxton: "Un-Break My Heart"
Chris Brown: "Kiss Kiss"
*James Brown (1986): "Papa's Got a Brand New Bag"
*Ruth Brown (1993): "Lucky Lips"
*Jackson Browne (2004): "Doctor My Eyes"
*Buffalo Springfield (1997): "For What It's Worth"
Jimmy Buffett: "Margaritaville"
*Solomon Burke (2001): "Over and Over (Huggin' and Lovin')"
*The Paul Butterfield Blues Band (2015): "Born in Chicago"
*The Byrds (1991): "Turn! Turn! Turn!"
Cardi B: "Bodak Yellow"
Mariah Carey: "Always Be My Baby"
The Carpenters: "(They Long to Be) Close to You"
*The Cars (2018): "Shake It Up"
*Johnny Cash (1992): "I Walk the Line"
*Ray Charles (1986): "Georgia on My Mind"
*Cheap Trick (2016): "Surrender"
Chubby Checker: "The Twist"
*Chicago (2016): "Saturday in the Park"
*Eric Clapton (2000): "Layla"
Kelly Clarkson: "Since U Been Gone"
*The Clash (2003): "Rock the Casbah"
*Jimmy Cliff (2010): "I Can See Clearly Now"
*The Coasters (1987): "Yakety Yak"
*Eddie Cochran (1987): "Summertime Blues"
Joe Cocker: "With a Little Help From My Friends"
*Leonard Cohen (2008): "Suzanne"
Coldplay: "Clocks"
Collective Soul: "The World I Know"
Phil Collins: "Against All Odds"
*Sam Cooke (1986): "You Send Me"
Coolio: "Gangsta's Paradise"
*Alice Cooper (2011): "School's Out"
*Elvis Costello and the Attractions (2003): "Alison"
Counting Crows: "Mr. Jones"
*Cream (1993): "Sunshine of Your Love"
Creed: "Arms Wide Open"
*Creedence Clearwater Revival (1993): "Proud Mary"
*Crosby, Stills, and Nash (1997): "Suite: Judy Blue Eyes"
*Sheryl Crow (2023): "All I Want to Do"
The Crystals: "Da Doo Ron Ron"
*The Cure (2019): "Boys Don't Cry"
Daft Punk: "Get Lucky"
Danny and the Juniors: "At the Hop"

*Bobby Darin (1990): "Splish Splash"
Daughtry: "It's Not Over"
*The Dave Clark Five (2008): "Glad All Over"
Dave Matthews Band: "Don't Drink the Water"
*Miles Davis (2006): Bitches Brew
Spencer Davis Group: "Gimme Some Lovin'"
*Deep Purple (2016): "Smoke on the Water"
*Def Leppard (2019): "Photograph"
*The Dells (2004): "Oh, What a Night"
Depeche Mode (2020): "Strange Love"
Destiny's Child: "Survivor"
*Neil Diamond (2011): "Cracklin' Rosie"
*Bo Diddley (1987): "Who Do You Love?
*Dion[1] and the Belmonts (1989): "A Teenager in Love"
Celine Dion: "Because You Loved Me"
*Dire Straits (2018): "Money for Nothing"
DMX: "What's My Name"
Doja Cat: "Kiss Me More"
*Fats Domino (1986): "Blueberry Hill"
*Donovan (2012): "Mellow Yellow"
*The Doobie Brothers (2020): "What a Fool Believes"
*The Doors (1993): "Light My Fire"
Dr. Dre: "Nothin' But a 'G' Thang"
*Dr. John (2011): "Right Place, Wrong Time"
Drake: "Hotline Bling"
*The Drifters (1988): "Save the Last Dance for Me"
*Duran Duran (2022): "Hungry Like the Wolf"
*Bob Dylan (1988): "Like a Rolling Stone"
*The Eagles (1998): "Hotel California"
*Earth, Wind, and Fire (2000): "Shining Star"
*Duane Eddy (1994): "Rebel-Rouser"
Billie Eilish: "Bad Guy"
*Electric Light Orchestra (2017): "Don't Bring Me Down"
*Missy Elliott (2023): "Sock It 2 Me"
*Eminem (2022): "The Real Slim Shady"
En Vogue: "Hold On"
*The Eurythmics (2022): "Sweet Dreams (Are Made of This)"
Everclear: "Father Of Mine"
*The Everly Brothers (1986): "Wake Up, Little Susie"
50 Cent (Curtis Jackson): Get Rich or Die Tryin'
The Five Satins: "In the Still of the Night"
Roberta Flack: "The First Time Ever I Saw Your Face"
*The Flamingos (2001): "I Only Have Eyes for You"
*Fleetwood Mac (1998): Rumours
*The Foo Fighters (2021): "I'll Stick Around"
Foreigner: "Double Vision"
*The Four Seasons (1990): "Sherry"

*The Four Tops (1990): "I Can't Help Myself (Sugar Pie, Honey Bunch)"
*Aretha Franklin (1987): "Respect"
fun.: "We Are Young"
Nelly Furtado: "I'm Like a Bird"
*Peter Gabriel (2014): "Shock the Monkey"
*Gamble (Kenny) and Huff (Leon) (2008): "If You Don't Know Me by Now"
*Marvin Gaye (1987): "I Heard It Through the Grapevine"
*Genesis (2010): "No Reply at All"
*The Go-Go's (2021): "We Got the Beat"
Goo Goo Dolls: "Iris"
Grand Funk Railroad: "We're an American Band"
*Grandmaster Flash and the Furious Five (2007): "The Message"
*The Grateful Dead (1994): "Uncle John's Band"
*Al Green (1995): "Let's Stay Together"
*Green Day (2015): "Boulevard of Broken Dreams"
The Guess Who: "American Woman"
*Guns N' Roses (2012): "Sweet Child o' Mine"
*Buddy Guy (2005): A Man and His Blues
*Bill Haley[1] and His Comets (1987): "Rock Around the Clock"
*Hall (Darryl) and Oates (John) (2014): "Kiss on My List"
*George Harrison (2004): "My Sweet Lord"
*Isaac Hayes (2002): "Theme From 'Shaft'"
*Heart (2013): "Barracuda"
*Jimi Hendrix (1992): "Purple Haze"
Lauryn Hill (2021): "Doo-Wop (That Thing)"
*The Hollies (2010): "Long Cool Woman (In a Black Dress)"
*Buddy Holly (1986): "Peggy Sue"
*John Lee Hooker (1991): "Boogie Chillen"
Hootie and the Blowfish: Cracked Rear View
*Whitney Houston (2020): "I Will Always Love You"
*The Impressions (1991): "For Your Precious Love"
Indigo Girls: "Closer to Fine"
INXS: "Need You Tonight"
*The Isley Brothers (1992): "It's Your Thing"
Ja Rule: Venni, Vetti, Vecci
*The Jackson Five (1997): "ABC"
*Janet Jackson (2019): Rhythm Nation
*Michael Jackson (2001): Thriller
*Etta James (1993): "At Last"
Tommy James and the Shondells: "Crimson and Clover"
Jane's Addiction: "Jane Says"
Jay and the Americans: "This Magic Moment"
*Jay Z (2021): "99 Problems"
*Jefferson Airplane (1996): "White Rabbit"
Jethro Tull: Aqualung
*Joan Jett and the Blackhearts (2015): "I Love Rock 'n' Roll"
Jewel: "You Were Meant for Me"
*Billy Joel (1999): "Piano Man"
*Elton John (1994): "Candle in the Wind"
*Little Willie John (1996): "Sleep"
Norah Jones: Come Away With Me
*Janis Joplin (1995): "Me and Bobby McGee"
*Journey (2017): "Don't Stop Believin'"
K.C. and the Sunshine Band: "Get Down Tonight"
R. Kelly: "I Can't Sleep Baby (If I)"
Alicia Keys: "Fallin'"
Kid Rock: "Cowboy"
*B. B. King (1987): "The Thrill Is Gone"
*Carole King (2021): Tapestry
*The Kinks (1990): "You Really Got Me"
*Kiss (2014): "Rock 'n' Roll All Night"
*Gladys Knight and the Pips (1996): "Midnight Train to Georgia"
Korn: "Blind"
Lenny Kravitz: "Are You Gonna Go My Way?"
Lady Gaga: "Poker Face"
Kendrick Lamar: DAMN.
*Led Zeppelin (1995): "Stairway to Heaven"
*Brenda Lee (2002): "I'm Sorry"
John Legend: "Ordinary People"
*John Lennon (1994): "Imagine"
*Jerry Lee Lewis (1986): "Whole Lotta Shakin' Going On"
Lil' Kim (2021): "No Matter What They Say"
Lil Nas X: "Old Town Road"
Lil Wayne: Tha Block Is Hot
Limp Bizkit: "Break Stuff"
Linkin Park: "One Step Closer"
Dua Lipa: "Levitating"
*Little Anthony and the Imperials (2009): "Tears on My Pillow"

*Little Richard (1986): "Tutti Frutti"
*Little Walter (2008): "Juke"
Lizzo: "Truth Hurts"
LL Cool J: "Mama Said Knock You Out"
Jennifer Lopez: "Love Don't Cost a Thing"
*Darlene Love (2011): "He's a Rebel"
*The Lovin' Spoonful (2000): "Summer in the City"
Ludacris: "Money Maker"
*Frankie Lymon and the Teenagers (1993): "Why Do Fools Fall in Love?"
*Lynyrd Skynyrd (2006): "Free Bird"
*Madonna (2008): "Material Girl"
*The Mamas and the Papas (1998): "Monday, Monday"
Marilyn Manson: "Beautiful People"
*Bob Marley (1994): Exodus
Maroon 5: "Moves Like Jagger"
Bruno Mars: "Just the Way You Are"
*Martha and the Vandellas (1995): "Dancin' in the Streets"
The Marvelettes: "Please, Mr. Postman"
Matchbox 20: "Push"
John Mayer: "Daughters"
*Curtis Mayfield (1999): "Superfly"
*Paul McCartney (1999): "Band on the Run"
Don McLean: "American Pie"
*Clyde McPhatter (1987): "A Lover's Question"
Meat Loaf: "Paradise by the Dashboard Light"
Megan Thee Stallion: "Savage"
*John (Cougar) Mellencamp (2008): "Jack and Diane"
Men at Work: "Who Can It Be Now?"
*Metallica (2009): "Enter Sandman"
*George Michael (2023): "Faith"
*Steve Miller (2016): "Take the Money and Run"
Nicki Minaj: Pink Friday
*Joni Mitchell (1997): Blue
Moby: "Bodyrock"
Janelle Monáe: "Make Me Feel"
The Monkees: "I'm a Believer"
*Moody Blues (2018): "Nights in White Satin"
*The Moonglows (2000): "Blue Velvet"
Alanis Morissette: "Ironic"
*Van Morrison (1993): "Brown-Eyed Girl"
*Mötley Crüe: "Live Wire"
Motörhead: "Ace of Spades"
Jason Mraz: "I'm Yours"
Mumford & Sons: "Little Lion Man"
Nelly: Country Grammar
*Ricky Nelson (1987): "Hello, Mary Lou"
Stevie Nicks (2019): "Edge of Seventeen"
*Nine Inch Nails (2020): "Closer"
*Nirvana (2014): Nevermind
No Doubt: Rock Steady
*The Notorious B.I.G. (2020): "Mo Money Mo Problems"
NSYNC: "Bye, Bye, Bye"
Ted Nugent: "Stranglehold"
*N.W.A. (2016): "Straight Outta Compton"
*The O'Jays (2005): "Back Stabbers"
One Direction: "What Makes You Beautiful"
*Roy Orbison (1987): "Oh, Pretty Woman"
Ozzy Osbourne: "Crazy Train"
OutKast: Speakerboxxx/The Love Below
*Parliament/Funkadelic (1997): "One Nation Under a Groove"
*Pearl Jam (2017): Ten
*Carl Perkins (1987): "Blue Suede Shoes"
Katy Perry: "Firework"
Peter, Paul, and Mary: "Leaving on a Jet Plane"
*Tom Petty and the Heartbreakers (2002): "Refugee"
Liz Phair: Exile in Guyville
Phish: "Sample in a Jar"
*Wilson Pickett (1991): "Land of 1,000 Dances"
Pink: Missundaztood
*Pink Floyd (1996): The Wall
*Gene Pitney (2002): "Only Love Can Break a Heart"
*The Platters (1990): "The Great Pretender"
The Pointer Sisters: "I'm So Excited"
*The Police (2003): "Every Breath You Take"
Iggy Pop: "Lust for Life"
*Elvis Presley (1986): "Love Me Tender"
*The Pretenders (2005): "Back on the Chain Gang"
*Lloyd Price (1998): "Stagger Lee"
*Prince (2004): "Purple Rain"
*Public Enemy (2013): "Fight the Power"
Puff Daddy and the Family: No Way Out
*Queen (2001): "Bohemian Rhapsody"
*Radiohead (2019): OK Computer
*Rage Against the Machine (2023): "Bulls on Parade"

*Bonnie Raitt (2000): "Something to Talk About"
*The Ramones (2002): "I Wanna Be Sedated"
*Red Hot Chili Peppers (2012): "Under the Bridge"
*Otis Redding (1989): "(Sittin' on) The Dock of the Bay"
*Jimmy Reed (1991): "Ain't That Loving You, Baby?"
*Lou Reed (2015): "Walk on the Wild Side"
*R.E.M. (2007): "Losing My Religion"
REO Speedwagon: "Can't Fight This Feeling"
Busta Rhymes: "What's It Gonna Be?"
*The Righteous Brothers (2003): "You've Lost That Lovin' Feelin' "
Rihanna: "Umbrella"
Johnny Rivers: "Poor Side of Town"
*Smokey Robinson[1] and the Miracles (1987): "Shop Around"
*The Rolling Stones (1989): "Satisfaction"
*The Ronettes (2007): "Be My Baby"
*Linda Ronstadt (2014): "You're No Good"
Diana Ross: "I'm Coming Out"
*Roxy Music (2019): "Love Is the Drug"
*Todd Rundgren (2021): "Hello It's Me"
*Run-DMC (2009): "Raisin' Hell"
*Rush (2013): "Tom Sawyer"
Sade: "Smooth Operator"
Salt-N-Pepa: "Shoop"
*Sam and Dave (1992): "Soul Man"
*Santana (1998): "Black Magic Woman"
Seal: "Kiss From a Rose"
Neil Sedaka: "Breaking Up Is Hard to Do"
*Bob Seger (2004): "Old Time Rock & Roll"
*Sex Pistols (2006): "Anarchy in the UK"
Shakira: "Whenever, Wherever"
*Tupac Shakur (2017): "How Do U Want It"
*Del Shannon (1999): "Runaway"
Ed Sheeran: "Thinking Out Loud"
*The Shirelles (1996): "Soldier Boy"
*Carly Simon (2022): "You're So Vain"
Paul Simon (2001): "50 Ways to Leave Your Lover"
*Simon and Garfunkel (1990): "Bridge Over Troubled Water"
*Nina Simone (2018): "Mississippi Goddamn"
*Percy Sledge (2005): "When a Man Loves a Woman"
*Sly and the Family Stone (1993): "Everyday People"
Smashing Pumpkins: "Today"
Patti Smith (2021): "Because the Night"
Sam Smith: "Stay With Me"
Will Smith: "Gettin' Jiggy With It"
The Smiths: "This Charming Man"
Snoop Dogg (a.k.a. Snoop Lion, Snoopzilla): "Gin and Juice"
Sonic Youth: "Bull in the Heather"
Soundgarden: "Black Hole Sun"
Britney Spears: "Hit Me Baby One More Time"
Spice Girls: "Wannabe"
*Dusty Springfield (1999): "I Only Want to Be With You"
*Bruce Springsteen (1999): "Born to Run"
*Staple Singers (1999): "I'll Take You There"
*Steely Dan (2001): "Rikki Don't Lose That Number"
Gwen Stefani: "Hollaback Girl"
Steppenwolf: "Born to Be Wild"
*Cat Stevens (2014): "Wild World"
*Rod Stewart (1994): "Maggie Mae"
Sting: "If You Love Somebody, Set Them Free"
Stone Temple Pilots: "Plush"
*The Stooges (2010): "I Wanna Be Your Dog"
Styx: "Come Sail Away"
The Sugar Hill Gang: "Rapper's Delight"
*Donna Summer (2013): "Bad Girls"
*The Supremes (1988): "Stop! In the Name of Love"
Taylor Swift: "Shake It Off"
Talking Heads (2002): "Once in a Lifetime"
*James Taylor (2001): "You've Got a Friend"
*The Temptations (1989): "My Girl"
Robin Thicke: "Blurred Lines"
Three Dog Night: "Joy to the World"
Justin Timberlake: "SexyBack"
TLC: "Waterfalls"
Traffic (2004): Traffic
*T. Rex (2020): "Bang a Gong (Get It On)"
*Big Joe Turner (1987): "Shake, Rattle & Roll"
*Ike and Tina Turner (1991): "Proud Mary"
*Tina Turner (2021): "What's Love Got to Do With It"
The Turtles: "Happy Together"
*U2 (2005): "With or Without You"
Usher: "You Make Me Wanna"
*Ritchie Valens (2001): "La Bamba"

*Van Halen (2007): "Running With the Devil"
*Stevie Ray Vaughan & Double Trouble (2015): "Change It"
*The Velvet Underground (1996): "Sweet Jane"
*The Ventures (2008): "Walk, Don't Run"
*Gene Vincent (1998): "Be-Bop-A-Lula"
*Tom Waits (2011): "Downtown Train"
The Wallflowers: "One Headlight"
Dionne Warwick: "I Say a Little Prayer"
*Muddy Waters (1987): "I Can't Be Satisfied"

Mary Wells: "My Guy"
Kanye West: "Gold Digger"
The White Stripes: "Seven Nation Army"
Whitesnake: "Here I Go Again"
*The Who (1990): Tommy
Pharrell Williams: "Happy"
*Jackie Wilson (1987): "That's Why"
*Bill Withers (2015): "Lean on Me"
*Bobby Womack (2009): "Lookin' for a Love"
*Stevie Wonder (1989): "You Are the Sunshine of My Life"

Wu-Tang Clan: "Protect Ya Neck"
*The Yardbirds (1992): "For Your Love"
*Yes (2017): "Owner of a Lonely Heart"
*Neil Young (1995): "Down by the River"
*The Young Rascals/The Rascals (1997): "Good Lovin'"
*Frank Zappa[1]/Mothers of Invention (1995): Hot Rats
*The Zombies (2019): "She's Not There"
*ZZ Top (2004): "Legs"

(1) Only individual performer is in Rock and Roll Hall of Fame.

Entertainment Personalities of the Present

Living actors, musicians, dancers, singers, producers, directors, and radio-TV performers.

Name	Birthplace	Birthdate
Abdul, Paula	San Fernando, CA	6/19/1962
Abraham, F. Murray	Pittsburgh, PA	10/24/1939
Abrams, J(effrey) J(acob)	New York, NY	6/27/1966
Adams, Amy	Vicenza, Italy	8/20/1974
Adams, Bryan	Kingston, ON, Canada	11/5/1959
Adams, Yolanda	Houston, TX	8/27/1961
Adele	London, England, UK	5/5/1988
Adjani, Isabelle	Paris, France	6/27/1955
Ad-Rock	South Orange, NJ	10/31/1966
Aduba, Uzo	Boston, MA	2/10/1981
Affleck, Ben	Berkeley, CA	8/15/1972
Affleck, Casey	Falmouth, MA	8/12/1975
Aghdashloo, Shohreh	Tehran, Iran	5/11/1952
Aguilera, Christina	Staten Island, NY	12/18/1980
Ahmed, Riz	Wembley, Eng., UK	12/1/1982
Aiken, Clay	Raleigh, NC	11/30/1978
Aimée, Anouk	Paris, France	4/27/1932
Alba, Jessica	Pomona, CA	4/28/1981
Alberghetti, Anna Maria	Pesaro, Italy	5/15/1936
Albert, Marv	Brooklyn, NY	6/12/1941
Alda, Alan	New York, NY	1/28/1936
Alexander, Jane	Boston, MA	10/28/1939
Alexander, Jason	Newark, NJ	9/23/1959
Ali, Mahershala	Oakland, CA	2/16/1974
Allen, Debbie	Houston, TX	1/16/1950
Allen, Joan	Rochelle, IL	8/20/1956
Allen, Karen	Carrollton, IL	10/5/1951
Allen, Tim	Denver, CO	6/13/1953
Allen, Woody	Bronx, NY	12/1/1935
Alpert, Herb	Los Angeles, CA	3/31/1935
Almodóvar, Pedro	Calzada de Calatrava, Spain	9/24/1949
Ambrose, Lauren	New Haven, CT	2/20/1978
Amos, John	Newark, NJ	12/27/1939
Amos, Tori	Newton, NC	8/22/1963
Anderson, Anthony	Los Angeles, CA	8/15/1970
Anderson, Gillian	Chicago, IL	8/9/1968
Anderson, Ian	Dunfermline, Scotland, UK	8/10/1947
Anderson, Loni	St. Paul, MN	8/5/1945
Anderson, Melissa Sue	Berkeley, CA	9/26/1962
Anderson, Pamela	Ladysmith, BC, Canada	7/1/1967
Anderson, Richard Dean	Minneapolis, MN	1/23/1950
Anderson, Wes	Houston, TX	5/1/1969
André 3000	Atlanta, GA	5/27/1975
Andress, Ursula	Bern, Switzerland	3/19/1936
Andrews, Julie	Walton-on-Thames, Surrey, England, UK	10/1/1935
Andrews, Naveen	London, England, UK	1/17/1969
Aniston, Jennifer	Sherman Oaks, CA	2/11/1969
Anka, Paul	Ottawa, ON, Canada	7/30/1941
Ann-Margret	Stockholm, Sweden	4/28/1941
Ansari, Aziz	Columbia, SC	2/23/1983
Anthony, Marc	New York, NY	9/16/1968
Apatow, Judd	Syosset, NY	12/6/1967
Apple, Fiona	New York, NY	9/13/1977
Applegate, Christina	Los Angeles, CA	11/25/1971
Archer, Anne	Los Angeles, CA	8/24/1947
Arkin, Adam	Brooklyn, NY	8/19/1956
Armisen, Fred	Hattiesburg, MS	12/4/1966
Arnaz, Desi, Jr.	Hollywood, CA	1/19/1953
Arnaz, Lucie	Hollywood, CA	7/17/1951
Arnett, Will	Toronto, ON, Canada	5/4/1970
Arnold, Tom	Ottumwa, IA	3/6/1959
Arquette, David	Winchester, VA	9/8/1971
Arquette, Patricia	Chicago, IL	4/8/1968
Arquette, Rosanna	New York, NY	8/10/1959
Arroyo, Martina	New York, NY	2/2/1937
Ashanti (Douglas)	Glen Cove, NY	10/13/1980
Ashford, Annaleigh	Denvor, CO	6/25/1985
Ashley, Elizabeth	Ocala, FL	8/30/1939
Assante, Armand	New York, NY	10/4/1949
Astin, John	Baltimore, MD	3/30/1930
Astin, Sean	Santa Monica, CA	2/25/1971
Atkins, Eileen	London, England, UK	6/16/1934

Name	Birthplace	Birthdate
Atkinson, Rowan	Newcastle upon Tyne, Eng., UK	1/6/1955
Austin, Patti	New York, NY	8/10/1948
Avalon, Frankie	Philadelphia, PA	9/18/1940
Awkwafina	Stony Brook, NY	6/2/1988
Aykroyd, Dan	Ottawa, ON, Canada	7/1/1952
Azalea, Iggy	Sydney, NSW, Australia	6/7/1990
Azaria, Hank	Forest Hills, Queens, NY	4/25/1964
Babyface	Indianapolis, IN	4/10/1959
Baccarin, Morena	Rio de Janeiro, Brazil	6/2/1979
Bacon, Kevin	Philadelphia, PA	7/8/1958
Bad Bunny	Almirante Sur, PR	3/10/1994
Badalucco, Michael	Brooklyn, NY	12/20/1954
Bader, Diedrich	Alexandria, VA	12/24/1966
Badu, Erykah	Dallas, TX	2/26/1971
Baez, Joan	Staten Island, NY	1/9/1941
Baio, Scott	Brooklyn, NY	9/22/1960
Baker, Anita	Toledo, OH	1/26/1958
Baker, Carroll	Johnstown, PA	5/28/1931
Baker, Diane	Hollywood, CA	2/25/1938
Baker, Joe Don	Groesbeck, TX	2/12/1936
Baker, Kathy	Midland, TX	6/8/1950
Baker, Simon	Launceston, Tas., Australia	7/30/1969
Bakula, Scott	St. Louis, MO	10/9/1954
Baldwin, Alec	Massapequa, NY	4/3/1958
Baldwin, Daniel	Massapequa, NY	10/5/1960
Baldwin, Stephen	Massapequa, NY	5/12/1966
Baldwin, William	Massapequa, NY	2/21/1963
Bale, Christian	Pembrokeshire, Wales, UK	1/30/1974
Balfe, Caitriona	Dublin, Ireland	10/4/1979
Ballas, Mark	Houston, TX	5/24/1986
Bana, Eric	Melbourne, Vic., Australia	8/9/1968
Banderas, Antonio	Málaga, Spain	8/10/1960
Banks, Elizabeth	Pittsfield, MA	2/10/1974
Banks, Jonathan	Washington, DC	1/31/1947
Banks, Tyra	Los Angeles, CA	12/4/1973
Baranski, Christine	Buffalo, NY	5/2/1952
Barbeau, Adrienne	Sacramento, CA	6/11/1945
Bardem, Javier	Las Palmas, Canary Islands, Spain	3/1/1969
Bardot, Brigitte	Paris, France	9/28/1934
Barkin, Ellen	Bronx, NY	4/16/1955
Barrie, Barbara	Chicago, IL	5/23/1931
Barrino, Fantasia	High Point, NC	6/30/1984
Barrymore, Drew	Los Angeles, CA	2/22/1975
Bartlett, Murray	Sydney, NSW, Australia	3/20/1971
Bartoli, Cecilia	Rome, Italy	6/4/1966
Barton, Mischa	London, England, UK	1/24/1986
Baryshnikov, Mikhail	Riga, Latvia	1/28/1948
Basinger, Kim	Athens, GA	12/8/1953
Bass, Lance	Laurel, MS	5/4/1979
Bassett, Angela	New York, NY	8/16/1958
Bassey, Shirley	Cardiff, Wales, UK	1/8/1937
Bateman, Jason	Rye, NY	1/14/1969
Bateman, Justine	Rye, NY	2/19/1966
Bates, Kathy	Memphis, TN	6/28/1948
Batiste, Jon	New Orleans, LA	11/11/1986
Batt, Bryan	New Orleans, LA	3/1/1963
Battle, Kathleen	Portsmouth, OH	8/13/1948
Baxter, Meredith	South Pasadena, CA	6/21/1947
Bean, Sean	Sheffield, England, UK	4/17/1959
Beatty, Warren	Richmond, VA	3/30/1937
Beauvais, Garcelle	St. Marc, Haiti	11/26/1966
Beck	Los Angeles, CA	7/8/1970
Beckham, Victoria	Hertfordshire, England, UK	4/17/1974
Beckinsale, Kate	London, England, UK	7/26/1973
Bedelia, Bonnie	New York, NY	3/25/1948
Bee, Samantha	Toronto, ON, Canada	10/25/1969
Begley, Ed, Jr.	Los Angeles, CA	9/16/1949
Behar, Joy	Brooklyn, NY	10/7/1942
Bell, Kristen	Huntington Woods, MI	7/18/1980
Bello, Maria	Norristown, PA	4/18/1967

Name	Birthplace	Birthdate
Belushi, Jim	Chicago, IL	6/15/1954
Benanti, Laura	Kinnelon, NJ	7/15/1979
Benatar, Pat	Brooklyn, NY	1/10/1953
Benedict, Dirk	Helena, MT	3/1/1945
Benigni, Roberto	Misericordia, Italy.	10/27/1952
Bening, Annette	Topeka, KS	5/29/1958
Benjamin, Richard	New York, NY	5/22/1938
Bennett, Alan	Leeds, England, UK.	5/9/1934
Benson, George	Pittsburgh, PA	3/22/1943
Benson, Robby	Dallas, TX	1/21/1956
Berenger, Tom	Chicago, IL	5/31/1950
Bergen, Candice	Beverly Hills, CA	5/9/1946
Bergeron, Tom	Haverhill, MA.	5/6/1955
Bernard, Crystal	Garland, TX.	9/30/1961
Bernhard, Sandra	Flint, MI.	6/6/1955
Bernsen, Corbin	North Hollywood, CA.	9/7/1954
Berry, Halle	Cleveland, OH.	8/14/1966
Bertinelli, Valerie	Wilmington, DE	4/23/1960
Best, Eve	London, England, UK	7/31/1971
Bettany, Paul.	London, England, UK	5/27/1971
Bialik, Mayim	San Diego, CA.	12/12/1975
Bichir, Demián	Mexico City, Mexico	8/1/1963
Bieber, Justin	Stratford, ON, Canada	3/1/1994
Biel, Jessica	Ely, MN	3/3/1982
Big Boi	Savannah, GA.	2/1/1975
Bigelow, Kathryn	San Carlos, CA	11/27/1951
Biggs, Jason	Pompton Plains, NJ	5/12/1978
Bilson, Rachel	Los Angeles, CA	8/25/1981
Binoche, Juliette	Paris, France	3/9/1964
Birch, Thora	Beverly Hills, CA	3/11/1982
Bisset, Jacqueline.	Weybridge, England, UK..	9/13/1944
Björk (Gudmundsdottir)	Reykjavik, Iceland	11/21/1965
Black, Clint	Long Branch, NJ	2/4/1962
Black, Jack	Santa Monica, CA	8/28/1969
Black, Lewis	Washington, DC	8/30/1948
Blades, Ruben	Panama City, Panama	7/16/1948
Blair, Linda	St. Louis, MO.	1/22/1959
Blanchett, Cate	Melbourne, Vic., Australia	5/14/1969
Bledel, Alexis	Houston, TX	9/16/1981
Bledsoe, Tempestt	Chicago, IL	8/1/1973
Bleeth, Yasmine	New York, NY	6/14/1968
Blethyn, Brenda	Ramsgate, Kent, Eng., UK	2/20/1946
Blige, Mary J.	Bronx, NY	1/11/1971
Bloom, Claire	London, England, UK	2/15/1931
Bloom, Orlando	Canterbury, England, UK	1/13/1977
Bloom, Rachel	Manhattan Beach, CA	4/3/1987
Blunt, Emily.	London, England, UK	2/23/1983
Blyth, Ann	Mt. Kisco, NY.	8/16/1928
Bocelli, Andrea	Lajatico, Italy	9/22/1958
Bogosian, Eric	Woburn, MA	4/24/1953
Bolton, Michael	New Haven, CT	2/26/1953
Bomer, Matt	Spring, TX.	10/11/1977
Bon Jovi, Jon	Sayreville, NJ.	3/2/1962
Bonaduce, Danny	Broomall, PA	8/13/1959
Bonet, Lisa	San Francisco, CA.	11/16/1967
Bonham Carter, Helena.	London, England, UK	5/26/1966
Bonneville, Hugh.	London, England, UK	11/10/1963
Bono	Dublin, Ireland	5/10/1960
Boone, Debby	Hackensack, NJ.	9/22/1956
Boone, Pat	Jacksonville, FL.	6/1/1934
Boreanaz, David	Buffalo, NY	5/16/1969
Borstein, Alex	Chicago, IL	2/15/1971
Bostwick, Barry.	San Mateo, CA	2/24/1945
Bosworth, Kate	Los Angeles, CA	1/2/1983
Bottoms, Timothy	Santa Barbara, CA.	8/30/1951
Bow Wow	Columbus, OH.	3/9/1987
Bowen, Julie	Baltimore, MD	3/3/1970
Boxleitner, Bruce	Elgin, IL.	5/12/1950
Boy George.	Bexleyheath, England, UK	6/14/1961
Boyle, Danny	Manchester, England, UK	10/20/1956
Boyle, Lara Flynn	Davenport, IA	3/24/1970
Boyle, Susan.	Blackburn, Scotland, UK ..	4/1/1961
Bracco, Lorraine	Brooklyn, NY	10/2/1955
Brady, Wayne	Orlando, FL.	6/2/1972
Braff, Zach	South Orange, NJ	4/6/1975
Branagh, Kenneth.	Belfast, N. Ireland, UK	12/10/1960
Brand, Russell	Grays, Essex, UK	6/4/1975
Brandauer, Klaus Maria	Steiermark, Austria	6/22/1944
Brandy (Norwood)	McComb, MS.	2/11/1979
Bratt, Benjamin.	San Francisco, CA	12/16/1963
Braugher, Andre	Chicago, IL	7/1/1962
Braxton, Toni	Severn, MD	10/7/1966
Bremner, Ewen	Edinburgh, Scotland, UK ..	1/23/1972
Brendon, Nicholas	Los Angeles, CA	4/12/1971
Brenneman, Amy	Glastonbury, CT.	6/22/1964
Bridges, Beau	Los Angeles, CA	12/9/1941
Bridges, Jeff	Los Angeles, CA	12/4/1949
Brightman, Sarah	Berkhamsted, England, UK	8/14/1960
Brinkley, Christie.	Monroe, MI	2/2/1954
Britton, Connie	Boston, MA.	3/6/1967
Broadbent, Jim	Lincolnshire, England, UK	5/24/1949
Broderick, Matthew	New York, NY	3/21/1962
Brody, Adam	San Diego, CA.	12/15/1979
Brody, Adrien	New York, NY	4/14/1973
Brolin, James	Los Angeles, CA	7/18/1940
Brolin, Josh	Los Angeles, CA	2/12/1968
Brooks, Albert	Beverly Hills, CA	7/22/1947
Brooks, Garth	Tulsa, OK	2/7/1962
Brooks, James L.	North Bergen, NJ.	5/9/1940
Brooks, Mel.	Brooklyn, NY	6/28/1926
Brosnahan, Rachel	Milwaukee, WI	12/15/1990
Brosnan, Pierce	Navan, Co. Meath, Ireland	5/16/1953
Brown, Blair	Washington, DC	4/23/1946
Brown, Bobby	Roxbury, MA	2/5/1969
Brown, Bryan	Panania, NSW, Australia ..	6/23/1947
Brown, Chris	Tappahannock, VA.	5/5/1989
Brown, Foxy	Brooklyn, NY.	9/6/1979
Brown, Millie Bobby	Marbella, Spain	2/19/2004
Brown, Sterling K.	St. Louis, MO.	4/5/1976
Browne, Jackson	Heidelberg, Germany.	10/9/1948
Bruckheimer, Jerry	Detroit, MI	9/21/1943
Brunson, Quinta	Philadelphia, PA	12/21/1989
Bryan, Luke	Leesburg, GA	7/17/1976
Bryson, Peabo	Greenville, SC.	4/13/1951
Bublé, Michael	Burnaby, BC, Canada ..	9/9/1975
Buckley, Betty	Big Spring, TX.	7/3/1947
Bujold, Geneviève	Montréal, QC, Canada..	7/1/1942
Bullock, Sandra.	Arlington, VA	7/26/1964
Bündchen, Gisele	Horizontina, Brazil	7/20/1980
Burgess, Tituss	Athens, GA	2/21/1979
Burghoff, Gary	Bristol, CT	5/24/1943
Burke, Cheryl	San Francisco, CA.	5/3/1984
Burke, Delta	Orlando, FL.	7/30/1956
Burnett, Carol	San Antonio, TX.	4/26/1933
Burns, Edward	Woodside, Queens, NY ..	1/29/1968
Burns, Ken	New York, NY	7/29/1953
Burrell, Ty	Grants Pass, OR	8/22/1967
Burstyn, Ellen	Detroit, MI	12/7/1932
Burton, LeVar	Landstuhl, Germany	2/16/1957
Burton, Tim	Burbank, CA	8/25/1958
Buscemi, Steve	Brooklyn, NY	12/13/1957
Busey, Gary	Goose Creek, TX.	6/29/1944
Busfield, Timothy	Lansing, MI	6/12/1957
Bush, Kate	Welling, England, UK.	7/30/1958
Butler, Austin	Anaheim, CA.	8/17/1991
Butler, Brett	Montgomery, AL	1/30/1958
Butler, Dan	Fort Wayne, IN.	12/2/1954
Butler, Gerard	Glasgow, Scotland, UK ..	11/13/1969
Butz, Norbert Leo	St. Louis, MO.	1/30/1967
Buzzi, Ruth	Westerly, RI	7/24/1936
Bynes, Amanda	Thousand Oaks, CA	4/3/1986
Byrne, David	Dumbarton, Scotland, UK	5/14/1952
Byrne, Gabriel	Dublin, Ireland	5/12/1950
Byrne, Rose	Sydney, NSW, Australia ..	7/24/1979
Cage, Nicolas	Long Beach, CA	1/7/1964
Cain, Dean	Mt. Clemens, MI	7/31/1966
Caine, Michael	London, England, UK	3/14/1933
Callies, Sarah Wayne	LaGrange, IL	6/1/1977
Callow, Simon	London, England, UK	6/15/1949
Cameron, James	Kapuskasing, ON, Can. ..	8/16/1954
Cameron, Kirk	Panorama City, CA	10/12/1970
Campbell, Bruce	Royal Oak, MI	6/22/1958
Campbell, Naomi	South London, Eng., UK .	5/22/1970
Campbell, Neve	Guelph, ON, Canada	10/3/1973
Campion, Jane	Waikanae, New Zealand ..	4/30/1954
Cannavale, Bobby	Union City, NJ	5/3/1971
Cannon, Dyan	Tacoma, WA	1/4/1937
Cannon, Nick	San Diego, CA.	10/8/1980
Caplan, Lizzy	Los Angeles, CA	6/30/1982
Capshaw, Kate	Ft. Worth, TX.	11/3/1953
Cardellini, Linda	Redwood City, CA	6/25/1975
Cardi B	New York, NY	10/11/1992
Cardinale, Claudia	Tunis, Tunisia.	4/15/1938
Carell, Steve	Concord, MA	8/16/1962
Carey, Drew	Cleveland, OH.	5/23/1958
Carey, Mariah	Huntington, NY.	3/27/1970
Cariou, Len	St. Boniface, MB, Can. ..	9/30/1939
Carlile, Brandi	Ravensdale, WA	6/1/1981
Carlton, Vanessa	Milford, PA.	8/16/1980
Carmen, Eric.	Cleveland, OH.	8/11/1949
Caron, Leslie.	Boulogne, France	7/1/1931
Carpenter, John	Carthage, NY	1/16/1948
Carpenter, Mary Chapin	Princeton, NJ.	2/21/1958
Carr, Vikki	El Paso, TX	7/19/1941
Carreras, Jose	Barcelona, Spain	12/5/1946
Carrere, Tia	Honolulu, HI	1/2/1967
Carrey, Jim	Newmarket, ON, Canada.	1/17/1962
Carter, Jim	Harrogate, Yorkshire, England, UK	8/19/1948
Carter, Lynda	Phoenix, AZ.	7/24/1951
Carter, Nick.	Jamestown, NY	1/28/1980
Carter, Ron	Ferndale, MI	5/4/1937
Cartwright, Nancy	Kettering, OH.	10/25/1957
Caruso, David	Forest Hills, Queens, NY .	1/17/1956
Carvey, Dana	Missoula, MT.	6/2/1955
Cash, Rosanne	Memphis, TN.	5/24/1955
Castellaneta, Dan	Chicago, IL	10/29/1957

Name	Birthplace	Birthdate
Castle-Hughes, Keisha..	Donnybrook, WA, Australia	3/24/1990
Cates, Phoebe	New York, NY	7/16/1963
Cattrall, Kim	Liverpool, England, UK	8/21/1956
Cavanagh, Tom	Ottawa, ON, Canada	10/26/1963
Cavett, Dick	Gibbon, NE	11/19/1936
Caviezel, Jim	Mount Vernon, WA	9/26/1968
Cavill, Henry	Jersey, Channel Isls., UK..	5/5/1983
Cedric the Entertainer..	Jefferson City, MO	4/24/1964
Cera, Michael	Brampton, ON, Canada..	6/7/1988
Chalamet, Timothée	New York, NY	12/27/1995
Chalke, Sarah	Ottawa, ON, Canada	8/27/1976
Chamberlain, Richard..	Beverly Hills, CA	3/31/1934
Chambers, Justin	Springfield, OH	7/11/1970
Chan, Jackie	Hong Kong	4/7/1954
Chance the Rapper	Chicago, IL	4/16/1993
Chandler, Kyle	Buffalo, NY	9/17/1965
Channing, Stockard	New York, NY	2/13/1944
Chaplin, Geraldine	Santa Monica, CA	7/31/1944
Chapman, Tracy	Cleveland, OH	3/30/1964
Chappelle, Dave	Washington, DC	8/24/1973
Charles, Josh	Baltimore, MD	9/15/1971
Charo	Murcia, Spain	1/15/1951?
Chase, Chevy	New York, NY	10/8/1943
Chasez, JC (Joshua)	Washington, DC	8/8/1976
Chastain, Jessica	Sacramento, CA	3/29/1977
Cheadle, Don	Kansas City, MO	11/29/1964
Checker, Chubby	Spring Gulley, SC	10/3/1941
Chen, Julie	New York, NY	1/6/1970
Chenoweth, Kristin	Broken Arrow, OK	7/24/1968
Cher	El Centro, CA.	5/20/1946
Chesney, Kenny	Lutrelle, TN	3/26/1968
Chianese, Dominic	Bronx, NY	2/24/1931
Chiklis, Michael	Lowell, MA.	8/30/1963
Chlumsky, Anna	Chicago, IL	12/3/1980
Chmerkovskiy, Maksim..	Odessa, Ukraine	1/17/1980
Cho, Margaret	San Francisco, CA	12/5/1968
Chong, Thomas	Edmonton, AB, Canada..	5/24/1938
Chopra, Priyanka	Jamshedpur, India	7/18/1982
Chow Yun-Fat	Lamma Island, Hong Kong	5/18/1955
Christensen, Hayden	Vancouver, BC, Canada..	4/19/1981
Christie, Julie	Chukua, Assam, India	4/14/1940
Chuck D	Roosevelt, NY	8/1/1960
Church, Charlotte	Llandaff, Cardiff, Wales, UK	2/21/1986
Church, Thomas Haden	El Paso, TX	6/17/1960
Clapton, Eric	Ripley, Surrey, Eng., UK.	3/30/1945
Clark, Petula	Epson, Surrey, Eng., UK.	11/15/1932
Clarke, Emilia	London, Eng., UK	10/23/1986
Clarkson, Kelly	Burleson, TX	4/24/1982
Clarkson, Patricia	New Orleans, LA	12/29/1959
Clay, Andrew Dice	Brooklyn, NY	9/29/1957
Cleese, John	Weston-super-Mare, Eng., UK	10/27/1939
Clooney, George	Lexington, KY	5/6/1961
Close, Glenn	Greenwich, CT	3/19/1947
Coen, Ethan	St. Louis Park, MN.	9/21/1957
Coen, Joel	St. Louis Park, MN.	11/29/1954
Cohen, Andy	St. Louis, MO.	6/2/1968
Cohen, Sacha Baron	London, England, UK	10/13/1971
Colbert, Stephen	Washington, DC	5/13/1964
Cole, Gary	Park Ridge, IL	9/20/1956
Coleman, Dabney	Austin, TX	1/3/1932
Colfer, Chris	Fresno, CA	5/27/1990
Collette, Toni	Blacktown, NSW, Australia	11/1/1972
Collins, Joan	London, England, UK	5/23/1933
Collins, Judy	Seattle, WA	5/1/1939
Collins, Pauline	Exmouth, England, UK	9/3/1940
Collins, Phil	London, England, UK	1/30/1951
Collins, Stephen	Des Moines, IA	10/1/1947
Colman, Olivia	Norfolk, Eng., UK.	1/30/1974
Columbus, Chris	Spangler, PA	9/10/1958
Colvin, Shawn	Vermillion, SD	1/10/1956
Combs, Sean	New York, NY	11/4/1969
Comer, Jodie	Liverpool, Eng.	3/11/1993
Connelly, Jennifer	Round Top, NY	12/12/1970
Connick, Harry, Jr.	New Orleans, LA	9/11/1967
Connolly, Kevin	Patchogue, NY	3/5/1974
Conroy, Frances	Monroe, GA.	11/13/1953
Consuelos, Mark	Zaragoza, Spain	3/30/1971
Conti, Tom	Paisley, Scotland, UK..	11/22/1941
Coogler, Ryan	Oakland, CA	5/23/1986
Coolidge, Jennifer	Brookline, MA	8/28/1961
Coolidge, Rita	Nashville, TN.	5/1/1945
Coon, Carrie	Copley, OH	1/24/1981
Cooper, Alice	Detroit, MI	2/4/1948
Cooper, Bradley	Philadelphia, PA	1/5/1975
Cooper, Chris	Kansas City, MO	7/9/1951
Copeland, Misty	Kansas City, MO	9/10/1982
Copperfield, David	Metuchen, NJ	9/16/1956
Coppola, Francis Ford	Detroit, MI	4/7/1939
Coppola, Sofia	New York, NY	5/14/1971
Corbett, John	Wheeling, WV	5/9/1961
Corbin, Barry	Lamesa, TX	10/16/1940
Corden, James	Hillingdon, England, UK..	8/22/1978
Corgan, Billy	Elk Grove, IL	3/17/1967
Corwin, Jeff	Norwell, MA.	7/11/1967
Cosby, Bill	Philadelphia, PA	7/12/1937
Cosgrove, Miranda	Los Angeles, CA	5/14/1993
Costas, Bob	Astoria, Queens, NY	3/22/1952
Costello, Elvis	London, England, UK	8/25/1954
Costner, Kevin	Compton, CA.	1/18/1955
Cotillard, Marion	Paris, France	9/30/1975
Cowell, Simon	London, England, UK	10/7/1959
Cox, Brian	Dundee, Scotland, UK..	6/1/1946
Cox, Courteney	Birmingham, AL.	6/15/1964
Cox, Laverne	Mobile, AL	5/29/1972
Cox, Ronny	Cloudcroft, NM.	7/23/1938
Coyote, Peter	New York, NY	10/10/1941
Craig, Daniel	Chester, England, UK	3/2/1968
Cranston, Bryan	San Fernando Valley, CA..	3/7/1956
Crawford, Cindy	DeKalb, IL	2/20/1966
Crawford, Michael	Salisbury, England, UK..	1/19/1942
Criss, Darren	San Francisco, CA.	2/5/1987
Cromwell, James	Los Angeles, CA	1/27/1940
Cross, Marcia	Marlborough, MA.	3/25/1962
Crow, Sheryl	Kennett, MO	2/11/1962
Crowe, Cameron	Palm Springs, CA	7/13/1957
Crowe, Russell	Wellington, New Zealand.	4/7/1964
Crudup, Billy	Manhasset, NY	7/8/1948
Cruise, Tom	Syracuse, NY	7/3/1962
Cruz, Penelope	Madrid, Spain	4/28/1974
Cryer, Jon	New York, NY	4/16/1965
Crystal, Billy	Long Beach, NY	3/14/1948
Cuarón, Alfonso	Mexico City, Mexico..	11/28/1961
Culkin, Kieran	New York, NY	9/30/1982
Culkin, Macaulay	New York, NY	8/26/1980
Cullum, John	Knoxville, TN	3/2/1930
Cumberbatch, Benedict	London, England, UK	7/19/1976
Cumming, Alan	Aberfeldy, Perthshire, Scotland, UK	1/27/1965
Cuoco, Kaley	Camarillo, CA	11/30/1985
Curry, Tim	Grappenhall, Cheshire, England, UK	4/19/1946
Curtin, Jane	Cambridge, MA	9/6/1947
Curtis, Jamie Lee	Los Angeles, CA	11/22/1958
Cusack, Joan	New York, NY	10/11/1962
Cusack, John	Evanston, IL	6/28/1966
Cyrus, Billy Ray	Flatwoods, KY	8/25/1961
Cyrus, Miley	Nashville, TN	11/23/1992
Dafoe, Willem	Appleton, WI	7/22/1955
Dale, Jim	Rothwell, England, UK..	8/15/1935
Dalton, Timothy	Colwyn Bay, Wales, UK..	3/21/1946
Daltrey, Roger	London, England, UK	3/1/1944
Daly, Carson	Santa Monica, CA	6/22/1973
Daly, Timothy	New York, NY	3/1/1956
Daly, Tyne	Madison, WI	2/21/1946
Damon, Matt	Cambridge, MA	10/8/1970
Dane, Eric	San Francisco, CA.	11/9/1972
Danes, Claire	New York, NY	4/12/1979
D'Angelo	Richmond, VA	2/11/1974
D'Angelo, Beverly	Columbus, OH	11/15/1954
Daniels, Anthony	Salisbury, England, UK..	2/21/1946
Daniels, Jeff	Athens, GA	2/19/1955
Daniels, Lee	Philadelphia, PA	12/24/1959
Daniels, William	Brooklyn, NY	3/31/1927
Danner, Blythe	Rosemont, PA	2/3/1943
Danson, Ted	San Diego, CA.	12/29/1947
Danza, Tony	Brooklyn, NY	4/21/1951
Darby, Kim	Hollywood, CA.	7/8/1948
Daughtry, Chris	Roanoke Rapids, NC..	12/26/1979
David, Larry	Brooklyn, NY	7/2/1947
Davidson, John	Pittsburgh, PA	12/13/1941
Davidson, Pete	Staten Island, NY.	11/16/1993
Davis, Clifton	Chicago, IL	10/4/1945
Davis, Geena	Wareham, MA.	1/21/1956
Davis, Hope	Englewood, NJ	3/23/1964
Davis, Judy	Perth, WA, Australia..	4/23/1955
Davis, Kristin	Boulder, CO.	2/24/1965
Davis, Viola	Saint Matthews, SC	8/11/1965
Dawber, Pam	Farmington Hills, MI.	10/18/1951
Dawson, Rosario	New York, NY	5/9/1979
Day, Andra	Edmonds, WA	12/30/1984
Day-Lewis, Daniel	London, England, UK	4/29/1957
de Armas, Ana	Havana, Cuba	4/30/1988
De Mornay, Rebecca	Santa Rosa, CA	8/29/1962
De Niro, Robert	New York, NY	8/17/1943
De Rossi, Portia	Melbourne, Vic., Australia..	1/31/1973
DeBose, Ariana	New Hanover, NC	1/25/1991
DeGeneres, Ellen	Metairie, LA	1/26/1958
DeGraw, Gavin	Middletown, NY	2/4/1977
Del Toro, Benicio	Santurce, Puerto Rico..	2/19/1967
Del Toro, Guillermo	Guadalajara, Jalisco, Mexico	10/9/1964
Delaney, Kim	Philadelphia, PA	11/29/1961
Delany, Dana	New York, NY	3/13/1956
Delon, Alain	Sceaux, France	11/8/1935
Dempsey, Patrick	Lewiston, ME.	1/13/1966
Dench, Judi	York, England, UK	12/9/1934
Deneuve, Catherine	Paris, France	10/22/1943
DePalma, Brian	Newark, NJ	9/11/1940
Depardieu, Gerard	Chateauroux, France..	12/27/1948
Depp, Johnny	Owensboro, KY	6/9/1963

Name	Birthplace	Birthdate
Derek, Bo	Long Beach, CA	11/20/1956
Dern, Bruce	Winnetka, IL	6/4/1936
Dern, Laura	Santa Monica, CA	2/10/1967
Deschanel, Zooey	Los Angeles, CA	1/17/1980
Devine, Loretta	Houston, TX	8/21/1949
DeVito, Danny	Neptune, NJ	11/17/1944
DeWitt, Joyce	Wheeling, WV	4/23/1949
Dey, Susan	Pekin, IL	12/10/1952
Diamond, Neil	Brooklyn, NY	1/24/1941
Diaz, Cameron	San Diego, CA	8/30/1972
Diaz, Guillermo	New Jersey	3/22/1975
Diaz, Justino	San Juan, PR	1/29/1940
DiCaprio, Leonardo	Hollywood, CA	11/11/1974
Dick, Andy	Charleston, SC	12/21/1965
Dickens, Kim	Huntsville, AL	6/18/1965
Dickinson, Angie	Kulm, ND	9/30/1931
Diesel, Vin	New York, NY	7/18/1967
Diggs, Daveed	Oakland, CA	1/24/1982
Diggs, Taye	Newark, NJ	1/2/1972
Dillahunt, Garret	Castro Valley, CA	11/24/1964
Dillon, Kevin	Mamaroneck, NY	8/19/1965
Dillon, Matt	New Rochelle, NY	2/18/1964
Dinklage, Peter	Morristown, NJ	6/11/1969
Dion (DiMucci)	Bronx, NY	7/18/1939
Dion, Celine	Charlemagne, QC, Canada	3/30/1968
Djalili, Omid	London, England, UK	9/30/1965
Dobrev, Nina	Sofia, Bulgaria	1/9/1989
Dockery, Michelle	Barking, Essex, Eng., UK.	12/15/1981
Doherty, Shannen	Memphis, TN	4/12/1971
Dolenz, Micky	Los Angeles, CA	3/8/1945
Domingo, Colman	Philadelphia, PA	11/28/1969
Domingo, Placido	Madrid, Spain	1/21/1941
Donahue, Phil	Cleveland, OH	12/21/1935
D'Onofrio, Vincent	Brooklyn, NY	6/30/1959
Donovan (Leitch)	Glasgow, Scotland, UK	5/10/1946
Donovan, Tate	New York, NY	9/25/1963
Dorn, Michael	Luling, TX	12/9/1952
Douglas, Michael	New Brunswick, NJ	9/25/1944
Dourdan, Gary	Philadelphia, PA	12/11/1966
Dovolani, Tony	Pristina, Kosovo	7/17/1973
Dowd, Ann	Holyoke, MA	1/30/1956
Down, Lesley-Anne	London, England, UK	3/17/1954
Downey, Robert, Jr.	New York, NY	4/4/1965
Downey, Roma	Derry, N. Ireland, UK	5/6/1960
Drake	Toronto, ON, Canada	10/24/1986
Drescher, Fran	Flushing, Queens, NY	9/30/1957
Dreyfuss, Richard	Brooklyn, NY	10/29/1947
Driver, Adam	San Bernardino, CA	11/19/1983
Driver, Minnie	London, England, UK	1/31/1970
Duchovny, David	New York, NY	8/7/1960
Duff, Hilary	Houston, TX	9/28/1987
Duffy (Aimee Anne)	Bangor, Gwynedd, Wales, UK	6/23/1984
Duffy, Julia	Minneapolis, MN	6/27/1951
Duffy, Patrick	Townsend, MT	3/17/1949
Duhamel, Josh	Minot, ND	11/14/1972
Dujardin, Jean	Rueil-Malmaison, France	6/19/1972
Dullea, Keir	Cleveland, OH	5/30/1936
Dunaway, Faye	Bascom, FL	1/14/1941
Duncan, Lindsay	Edinburgh, Scotland, UK	11/7/1950
Duncan, Sandy	Henderson, TX	2/20/1946
Dunham, Lena	New York, NY	5/13/1986
Dunne, Griffin	New York, NY	6/8/1955
Dunst, Kirsten	Point Pleasant, NJ	4/30/1982
Dussault, Nancy	Pensacola, FL	6/30/1936
Dutton, Charles S.	Baltimore, MD	1/30/1951
Duvall, Robert	San Diego, CA	1/5/1931
Duvall, Shelley	Houston, TX	7/7/1949
DuVernay, Ava	Los Angeles, CA	8/24/1972
Dylan, Bob	Duluth, MN	5/24/1941
Dylan, Jakob	New York, NY	12/9/1969
Dzundza, George	Rosenheim, Germany	7/19/1945
Eads, George	Fort Worth, TX	3/1/1967
Easton, Sheena	Bellshill, Scotland, UK	4/27/1959
Eastwood, Clint	San Francisco, CA	5/31/1930
Ebersole, Christine	Chicago, IL	2/21/1953
Eckhart, Aaron	Cupertino, CA	3/12/1968
Eden, Barbara	Tucson, AZ	8/23/1931
Edwards, Anthony	Santa Barbara, CA	7/19/1962
Efron, Zac	San Luis Obispo, CA	10/18/1987
Egerton, Taron	Birkenhead, England, UK.	11/10/1989
Eggold, Ryan	Lakewood, CA	8/10/1984
Ehle, Jennifer	Winston-Salem, NC	12/29/1969
Eichner, Billy	New York, NY	9/18/1978
Eikenberry, Jill	New Haven, CT	1/21/1947
Eilish, Billie	Los Angeles, CA	12/18/2001
Eisenberg, Jesse	Bayside, NY.	10/5/1983
Ejiofor, Chiwetel	London, England, UK	7/10/1974
Ekland, Britt	Stockholm, Sweden	10/6/1942
Elba, Idris	London, England, UK	9/6/1972
Electra, Carmen	Cincinnati, OH	4/20/1972
Elfman, Jenna	Los Angeles, CA	9/30/1971
Elgort, Ansel	New York, NY	3/14/1994
Elizondo, Hector	New York, NY	12/22/1936
Elliott, Chris	New York, NY	5/31/1960
Elliott, Missy	Portsmouth, VA	7/1/1971
Elliott, Sam	Sacramento, CA	8/9/1944
Elvira	Manhattan, KS.	9/17/1951
Emerson, Michael	Cedar Rapids, IA	9/7/1954
Eminem	St. Joseph, MO	10/17/1972
Englund, Robert	Glendale, CA	6/6/1949
Enya	Gweedore, Ireland	5/17/1961
Epps, Omar	Brooklyn, NY	7/23/1973
Erivo, Cynthia	London, England, UK.	1/8/1987
Esposito, Giancarlo	Copenhagen, Den.	4/26/1958
Estefan, Gloria	Havana, Cuba	9/1/1957
Estevez, Emilio	New York, NY	5/12/1962
Estrada, Erik	New York, NY	3/16/1949
Etheridge, Melissa	Leavenworth, KS	5/29/1961
Evans, Chris	Framingham, MA	6/13/1981
Evans, Linda	Hartford, CT	11/18/1942
Evans, Luke	Pontypool, Wales, UK	4/15/1979
Everett, Rupert	Norfolk, England, UK	5/29/1959
Evigan, Greg	South Amboy, NJ	10/14/1953
Fabares, Shelley	Santa Monica, CA	1/19/1944
Fabian	Philadelphia, PA	2/6/1943
Fabio (Lanzoni)	Milan, Italy	3/15/1959
Fabolous	Brooklyn, NY	11/18/1977
Facinelli, Peter	Queens, NY.	11/26/1973
Fairchild, Morgan	Dallas, TX	2/3/1950
Faison, Donald	New York, NY	6/22/1974
Falana, Lola	Philadelphia, PA	9/11/1942
Falco, Edie	Brooklyn, NY	7/5/1963
Fallon, Jimmy	Brooklyn, NY	9/19/1974
Fanning, Dakota	Conyers, GA	2/23/1994
Fanning, Elle	Conyers, GA	4/9/1998
Fargo, Donna	Mt. Airy, NC	11/10/1949
Faris, Anna	Baltimore, MD	11/29/1976
Farmiga, Vera	Clifton, NJ	8/6/1973
Farr, Jamie	Toledo, OH	7/1/1934
Farrell, Colin	Dublin, Ireland	5/31/1976
Farrell, Mike	St. Paul, MN	2/6/1939
Farrell, Perry	Bayside, Queens, NY.	3/29/1959
Farrell, Suzanne	Cincinnati, OH.	8/16/1945
Farrelly, Bobby	Cumberland, RI	6/17/1958
Farrelly, Peter	Phoenixville, PA	12/17/1956
Farrow, Mia	Los Angeles, CA	2/9/1945
Fassbender, Michael	Heidelberg, Germany.	4/2/1977
Fatone, Joey	Brooklyn, NY	1/28/1977
Feinstein, Michael	Columbus, OH.	9/7/1956
Feldman, Corey	Los Angeles, CA	7/16/1971
Feldon, Barbara	Bethel Park, PA	3/12/1933
Feldshuh, Tovah	New York, NY	12/27/1952
Feliciano, Jose	Lares, Puerto Rico.	9/10/1945
Fenn, Sherilyn	Detroit, MI	2/1/1965
Fergie	Hacienda Heights, CA	3/27/1975
Ferguson, Craig	Glasgow, Scotland, UK	5/17/1962
Ferguson, Jesse Tyler	Missoula, MT.	10/22/1975
Ferrara, Jerry	Brooklyn, NY	11/29/1979
Ferrell, Conchata	Charleston, WV	3/28/1943
Ferrell, Will	Irvine, CA	7/16/1967
Ferrera, America	Los Angeles, CA	4/18/1984
Feuerstein, Mark	New York, NY	6/8/1971
Fey, Tina	Upper Darby, PA	5/18/1970
Field, Sally	Pasadena, CA	11/6/1946
Fiennes, Joseph	Salisbury, England, UK	5/27/1970
Fiennes, Ralph	Suffolk, England, UK	12/22/1962
Fierstein, Harvey	Brooklyn, NY	6/6/1954
50 Cent	Jamaica, Queens, NY	7/6/1976
Fillion, Nathan	Edmonton, AB, Canada	3/27/1971
Fincher, David	Denver, CO	8/28/1962
Firth, Colin	Grayshott, England, UK	9/10/1960
Firth, Peter	Bradford, Yorkshire, Eng., UK.	10/27/1953
Fischer, Jenna	Ft. Wayne, IN.	3/7/1974
Fishburne, Laurence	Augusta, GA	7/30/1961
Flack, Roberta	Black Mountain, NC.	2/10/1939
Flanagan, Fionnula	Dublin, Ireland	12/10/1941
Flavor Flav	Roosevelt, NY	3/16/1959
Fleetwood, Mick	Redruth, Cornwall, Eng., UK	6/24/1942
Fleming, Renée	Indiana, PA	2/14/1959
Flockhart, Calista	Freeport, IL	11/11/1964
Florek, Dann	Flat Rock, MI	5/1/1950
Fogerty, John	Berkeley, CA	5/28/1945
Foley, Dave	Etobicoke, ON, Canada	1/4/1963
Foley, Scott	Kansas City, KS.	7/15/1972
Fonda, Bridget	Los Angeles, CA	1/27/1964
Fonda, Jane	New York, NY	12/21/1937
Ford, Faith	Alexandria, LA.	9/14/1964

Name	Birthplace	Birthdate
Ford, Harrison	Chicago, IL	7/13/1942
Forte, Will	Alameda Co., CA	6/17/1970
Foster, Jodie	Los Angeles, CA	11/19/1962
Foster, Sutton	Statesboro, GA	3/18/1975
Fox, Jorja	New York, NY	7/7/1968
Fox, Matthew	Abington, PA	7/14/1966
Fox, Megan	Rockwood, TN	5/16/1986
Fox, Michael J.	Edmonton, AB, Canada	6/9/1961
Fox, Vivica A.	South Bend, IN	7/30/1964
Foxworth, Robert	Houston, TX	11/1/1941
Foxworthy, Jeff	Atlanta, GA	9/6/1958
Foxx, Jamie	Terrell, TX	12/13/1967
Foy, Claire	Stockport, England, UK	4/16/1984
Frampton, Peter	Kent, England, UK	4/22/1950
Francis, Connie	Newark, NJ	12/12/1938
Franco, Dave	Palo Alto, CA	6/12/1985
Franco, James	Palo Alto, CA	4/19/1978
Franken, Al	New York, NY	5/21/1951
Franz, Dennis	Maywood, IL	10/28/1944
Fraser, Brendan	Indianapolis, IN	12/3/1968
Freeman, Martin	Aldershot, Hampshire, Eng., UK	9/8/1971
Freeman, Morgan	Memphis, TN	6/1/1937
French, Dawn	Holyhead, Wales, UK	10/11/1957
Fricker, Brenda	Dublin, Ireland	2/17/1945
Froggatt, Joanne	Littlebeck, North Yorkshire, England, UK	8/21/1980
Fry, Stephen	London, England, UK	8/24/1957
Fuentes, Daisy	Havana, Cuba	11/17/1966
Fuller, Robert	Troy, NY	7/29/1933
Furlong, Edward	Pasadena, CA	8/2/1977
Furtado, Nelly	Victoria, BC, Canada	12/2/1978
Gabriel, Peter	Surrey, England, UK	2/13/1950
Gaines, Boyd	Atlanta, GA	5/11/1953
Galecki, Johnny	Bree, Belgium	4/30/1975
Galifianakis, Zach	Wilkesboro, NC	10/1/1969
Gallagher, Peter	Armonk, NY	8/19/1955
Gallo, Vincent	Buffalo, NY	4/11/1961
Galway, James	Belfast, N. Ireland, UK	12/8/1939
Garber, Victor	London, ON, Canada	3/16/1949
Garcia, Andy	Havana, Cuba	4/12/1956
Garfield, Andrew	Los Angeles, CA	8/20/1983
Garfunkel, Art	Forest Hills, Queens, NY	11/5/1941
Garlin, Jeff	Chicago, IL	6/5/1962
Garner, Jennifer	Houston, TX	4/17/1972
Garner, Julia	Bronx, NY	2/1/1994
Garofalo, Janeane	Newton, NJ	9/28/1964
Garr, Teri	Lakewood, OH	12/11/1944
Garrett, Brad	Woodland Hills, CA	4/14/1960
Garth, Jennie	Urbana, IL	4/3/1972
Gatlin, Larry	Seminole, TX	5/2/1948
Gayle, Crystal	Paintsville, KY	1/9/1951
Gaynor, Mitzi	Chicago, IL	9/4/1931
Geary, Anthony	Coalville, UT	5/29/1947
Gellar, Sarah Michelle	New York, NY	4/14/1977
Gere, Richard	Philadelphia, PA	8/31/1949
Gervais, Ricky	Reading, England, UK	6/25/1961
Gerwig, Greta	Sacramento, CA	8/4/1983
Giamatti, Paul	New Haven, CT	6/6/1967
Giannini, Giancarlo	La Spezia, Italy	8/1/1942
Gibb, Barry	Isle of Man, England, UK	9/1/1946
Gibbons, Leeza	Hartsville, SC	3/26/1957
Gibbs, Marla	Chicago, IL	6/14/1931
Gibson, Debbie	Brooklyn, NY	8/31/1970
Gibson, Mel	Peekskill, NY	1/3/1956
Gibson, Thomas	Charleston, SC	7/3/1962
Gifford, Kathie Lee	Neuilly-sur-Seine, France	8/16/1953
Gilbert, Melissa	Los Angeles, CA	5/8/1964
Gilbert, Sara	Santa Monica, CA	1/29/1975
Gill, Vince	Norman, OK	4/12/1957
Gillette, Anita	Baltimore, MD	8/16/1936
Gilliam, Terry	Minneapolis, MN	11/22/1940
Gilmour, David	Cambridge, England, UK	3/6/1946
Gilpin, Peri	Waco, TX	5/27/1961
Givens, Robin	New York, NY	11/27/1964
Glaser, Paul Michael	Cambridge, MA	3/25/1943
Gleeson, Brendan	Belfast, N. Ireland, UK	3/29/1955?
Glenn, Scott	Pittsburgh, PA	1/26/1941
Gless, Sharon	Los Angeles, CA	5/31/1943
Glover, Crispin	New York, NY	4/20/1964
Glover, Danny	San Francisco, CA	7/22/1947
Glover, Donald	Edwards Air Force Base, CA	9/25/1983
Glover, Julian	London, England, UK	3/27/1935
Glover, Savion	Newark, NJ	11/19/1973
Goldberg, Whoopi	New York, NY	11/13/1955
Goldblum, Jeff	Pittsburgh, PA	10/22/1952
Goldthwait, Bobcat	Syracuse, NY	5/26/1962
Goldwyn, Tony	Los Angeles, CA	5/20/1960
Gomez, Selena	Grand Prairie, TX	7/22/1992
Gooding, Cuba, Jr.	Bronx, NY	1/2/1968
Goodman, John	Affton, MO	6/20/1952
Gordon-Levitt, Joseph	Los Angeles, CA	2/17/1981
Gosling, Ryan	London, ON, Canada	11/12/1980
Gosselaar, Mark-Paul	Panorama City, CA	3/1/1974
Gossett, Louis, Jr.	Brooklyn, NY	5/27/1936
Gould, Elliott	Brooklyn, NY	8/29/1938
Grace, Topher	New York, NY	7/12/1978
Graham, Heather	Milwaukee, WI	1/29/1970
Graham, Lauren	Honolulu, HI	3/16/1967
Grammer, Kelsey	St. Thomas, U.S. Virgin Isls.	2/21/1955
Grande, Ariana	Boca Raton, FL	6/26/1993
Grant, Amy	Augusta, GA	11/25/1960
Grant, Hugh	London, England, UK	9/9/1960
Grant, Lee	Bronx, NY	10/31/1925
Gray, Linda	Santa Monica, CA	9/12/1940
Gray, Macy	Canton, OH	9/6/1969
Green, Al	Forrest City, AR	4/13/1946
Green, Cee Lo	Atlanta, GA	5/30/1974
Green, Seth	Philadelphia, PA	2/8/1974
Green, Tom	Pembroke, ON, Canada	7/30/1971
Greene, Graham	Six Nations Reserve, ON, Canada	6/22/1952
Greene, Shecky	Chicago, IL	4/8/1926
Greenfield, Max	Dobbs Ferry, NY	9/4/1980
Greenwood, Bruce	Noranda, QC, Canada	8/12/1956
Gregory, Cynthia	Los Angeles, CA	7/8/1946
Grenier, Adrian	Santa Fe, NM	7/10/1976
Grey, Jennifer	New York, NY	3/26/1960
Grey, Joel	Cleveland, OH	4/11/1932
Grier, David Alan	Detroit, MI	6/30/1955
Grier, Pam	Winston-Salem, NC	5/26/1949
Griffin, Kathy	Oak Park, IL	11/4/1961
Griffith, Melanie	New York, NY	8/9/1957
Griffiths, Rachel	Melbourne, Vic., Australia	12/18/1968
Grint, Rupert	Walton-at-Stone, Hertfordshire, Eng., UK	8/24/1988
Groban, Josh	Los Angeles, CA	2/27/1981
Groff, Jonathan	Lancaster, PA	3/26/1985
Grohl, Dave	Warren, OH	1/14/1969
Gross, Michael	Chicago, IL	6/21/1947
Guest, Christopher	New York, NY	2/5/1948
Gumbel, Bryant	New Orleans, LA	9/29/1948
Gumbel, Greg	New Orleans, LA	5/3/1946
Gunn, Anna	Santa Fe, NM	8/11/1968
Gunn, Tim	Washington, DC	7/29/1953
Guthrie, Arlo	Brooklyn, NY	7/10/1947
Guttenberg, Steve	Brooklyn, NY	8/24/1958
Guy, Buddy	Lettsworth, LA	7/30/1936
Guy, Jasmine	Boston, MA	3/10/1964
Gyllenhaal, Jake	Los Angeles, CA	12/19/1980
Gyllenhaal, Maggie	New York, NY	11/16/1977
Haas, Shira	Tel Aviv, Israel	5/11/1995
Hackman, Gene	San Bernardino, CA	1/30/1930
Haddish, Tiffany	Los Angeles, CA	12/3/1979
Hader, Bill	Tulsa, OK	6/7/1978
Hagerty, Julie	Cincinnati, OH	6/15/1955
Hahn, Kathryn	Westchester, IL	7/23/1973
Hale, Tony	West Point, NY	9/30/1970
Hall, Anthony Michael	West Roxbury, MA	4/14/1968
Hall, Arsenio	Cleveland, OH	2/12/1955
Hall, Daryl	Pottstown, PA	10/11/1946
Hall, Deidre	Milwaukee, WI	10/31/1947
Hall, Michael C.	Raleigh, NC	2/1/1971
Hall, Tamron	Luling, TX	9/16/1970
Halliwell, Geri	Watford, England, UK	8/6/1972
Hamill, Mark	Oakland, CA	9/25/1951
Hamilton, George	Memphis, TN	8/12/1939
Hamilton, Linda	Salisbury, MD	9/26/1956
Hamlin, Harry	Pasadena, CA	10/30/1951
Hamm, Jon	St. Louis, MO	3/10/1971
Hammer, Armie	Los Angeles, CA	8/28/1986
Hammer (M.C.)	Oakland, CA	3/30/1963
Hammond, Darrell	Melbourne, FL	10/8/1955
Hancock, Herbie	Chicago, IL	4/12/1940
Handler, Chelsea	Livingston, NJ	2/25/1975
Hanks, Colin	Sacramento, CA	11/24/1977
Hanks, Tom	Concord, CA	7/9/1956
Hannah, Daryl	Chicago, IL	12/3/1960
Hannigan, Alyson	Washington, DC	3/24/1974
Hanson, Isaac	Tulsa, OK	11/17/1980
Hanson, Taylor	Tulsa, OK	3/14/1983
Hanson, Zac	Tulsa, OK	10/22/1985
Harden, Marcia Gay	La Jolla, CA	8/14/1959
Hardy, Tom	London, England, UK	9/15/1977
Harewood, Dorian	Dayton, OH	8/6/1950
Hargitay, Mariska	Los Angeles, CA	1/23/1964
Harington, Kit	London, Eng., UK	12/26/1986
Harlow, Jack	Louisville, KY	3/13/1998
Harmon, Angie	Highland Park, TX	8/10/1972
Harmon, Mark	Burbank, CA	9/2/1951
Harper, Ben	Claremont, CA	10/28/1069
Harper, Tess	Mammoth Spring, AR	8/15/1950
Harrelson, Woody	Midland, TX	7/23/1961
Harris, Ed	Tenafly, NJ	11/28/1950
Harris, Emmylou	Birmingham, AL	4/2/1947
Harris, Jared	London, Eng., UK	8/24/1961

Name	Birthplace	Birthdate
Harris, Neil Patrick	Albuquerque, NM	6/15/1973
Harris, Rosemary	Ashby, England, UK	9/19/1927?
Harris, Steve	Chicago, IL	12/3/1965
Harrison, Gregory	Avalon, CA	5/31/1950
Harry, Deborah	Miami, FL	7/1/1945
Hart, Kevin	Philadelphia, PA	7/3/1980
Hart, Mary	Madison, SD	11/8/1950
Hart, Melissa Joan	Smithtown, NY	4/18/1976
Hartley, Mariette	New York, NY	6/21/1940
Hartman, David	Pawtucket, RI	5/19/1935
Hartman Black, Lisa	Houston, TX	6/1/1956
Hartnett, Josh	San Francisco, CA	7/21/1978
Harvey, P. J.	Yeovil, Somerset, Eng., UK	10/9/1969
Harvey, Steve	Welch, WV	1/17/1956
Hasselbeck, Elisabeth	Cranston, RI	5/28/1977
Hasselhoff, David	Baltimore, MD	7/17/1952
Hatcher, Teri	Sunnyvale, CA	12/8/1964
Hatfield, Juliana	Wiscasset, ME	7/27/1967
Hathaway, Anne	Brooklyn, NY	11/12/1982
Hawke, Ethan	Austin, TX	11/6/1970
Hawn, Goldie	Washington, DC	11/21/1945
Hayek, Salma	Coatzacoalcos, Mexico	9/2/1966
Hayes, Hunter	Breaux Bridge, LA	9/9/1991
Hayes, Sean	Glen Ellyn, IL	6/26/1970
Hays, Robert	Bethesda, MD	7/24/1947
Haysbert, Dennis	San Mateo, CA	6/2/1955
Head, Anthony	Camden Town, Eng., UK	2/20/1954
Headey, Lena	Hamilton, Bermuda	10/3/1973
Hearn, George	St. Louis, MO	6/18/1934
Heaton, Patricia	Bay Village, OH	3/4/1958
Heder, Jon	Fort Collins, CO	10/26/1977
Hedges, Lucas	New York, NY	12/12/1996
Hedren, Tippi	New Ulm, MN	1/19/1930
Heigl, Katherine	Washington, DC	11/24/1978
Helberg, Simon	Los Angeles, CA	12/9/1980
Helfgott, David	Melbourne, Vic., Australia	5/19/1947
Helgenberger, Marg	Fremont, NE	11/16/1958
Helms, Ed	Atlanta, GA	1/24/1974
Hemingway, Mariel	Mill Valley, CA	11/22/1961
Hemsworth, Chris	Melbourne, Vic., Australia	8/11/1983
Hemsworth, Liam	Melbourne, Vic., Australia	1/13/1990
Hemsworth, Luke	Melbourne, Vic., Australia	11/5/1980
Hendricks, Christina	Knoxville, TN	5/3/1975
Henley, Don	Gilmer, TX	7/22/1947
Henner, Marilu	Chicago, IL	4/6/1952
Hennessy, Jill	Edmonton, AB, Canada	11/25/1968
Henson, Taraji P.	Washington, DC	9/11/1970
Hershey, Barbara	Hollywood, CA	2/5/1948
Hetfield, James	Downey, CA	8/3/1963
Hewitt, Jennifer Love	Waco, TX	2/21/1979
Hickey, John Benjamin	Plano, TX	6/25/1963
Hicks, Catherine	Scottsdale, AZ	8/6/1951
Hiddleston, Tom	London, England, UK	2/9/1981
Higgins, John Michael	Boston, MA	2/12/1963
Hightower, Chelsie	Las Vegas, NV	7/21/1989
Hill, Dulé	Orange, NJ	5/3/1975
Hill, Faith	Jackson, MS	9/21/1967
Hill, Jonah	Los Angeles, CA	12/20/1983
Hill, Lauryn	South Orange, NJ	5/26/1975
Hines, Cheryl	Miami Beach, FL	9/21/1965
Hirsch, Emile	Palms, CA	3/13/1985
Hirsch, Judd	Bronx, NY	3/15/1935
Hodgman, John	Cambridge, MA	6/3/1971
Hoffman, Dustin	Los Angeles, CA	8/8/1937
Hogan, Hulk	Augusta, GA	8/11/1953
Hogan, Paul	Lightning Ridge, NSW, Australia	10/8/1939
Holliday, Polly	Jasper, AL	7/2/1937
Holloway, Josh	San Jose, CA	7/20/1969
Holly, Lauren	Bristol, PA	10/28/1963
Holmes, Katie	Toledo, OH	12/18/1978
Hopkins, Anthony	Port Talbot, South Wales, UK	12/31/1937
Hopkins, Telma	Louisville, KY	10/28/1948
Horne, Marilyn	Bradford, PA	1/16/1934
Hornsby, Bruce	Williamsburg, VA	11/23/1954
Horsley, Lee	Muleshoe, TX	5/15/1955
Hough, Derek	Salt Lake City, UT	5/17/1985
Hough, Julianne	Salt Lake City, UT	7/20/1988
Hounsou, Djimon	Cotonou, Benin	4/24/1964
Howard, Clint	Burbank, CA	4/20/1959
Howard, Ron	Duncan, OK	3/1/1954
Howard, Terrence	Chicago, IL	3/11/1969
Howell, C. Thomas	Van Nuys, CA	12/7/1966
Hudgens, Vanessa	Salinas, CA	12/14/1988
Hudson, Ernie	Benton Harbor, MI	12/17/1945
Hudson, Jennifer	Chicago, IL	9/12/1981
Hudson, Kate	Los Angeles, CA	4/19/1979
Huffman, Felicity	Bedford, NY	12/9/1962
Hughley, D. L.	Los Angeles, CA	3/6/1963
Hulce, Tom	Detroit, MI	12/6/1953
Humperdinck, Engelbert	Madras, India	5/2/1936
Hunt, Bonnie	Chicago, IL	9/22/1964
Hunt, Helen	Culver City, CA	6/15/1963
Hunt, Linda	Morristown, NJ	4/2/1945
Hunter, Holly	Conyers, GA	3/20/1958
Hurley, Elizabeth	Hampshire, England, UK	6/10/1965
Hurt, Mary Beth	Marshalltown, IA	9/26/1948
Huston, Anjelica	Santa Monica, CA	7/8/1951
Hutcherson, Josh	Union, KY	10/12/1992
Hutton, Lauren	Charleston, SC	11/17/1943
Hutton, Timothy	Malibu, CA	8/16/1960
Ian, Janis	Bronx, NY	4/7/1951
Ice Cube	Los Angeles, CA	6/15/1969
Ice-T	Newark, NJ	2/16/1958
Idle, Eric	S. Shields, England, UK	3/29/1943
Idol, Billy	Middlesex, England, UK	11/30/1955
Iglesias, Enrique	Madrid, Spain	5/8/1975
Iglesias, Julio	Madrid, Spain	9/23/1943
Iler, Robert	New York, NY	3/2/1985
Iman	Mogadishu, Somalia	7/25/1955
Imbruglia, Natalie	Sydney, NSW, Australia	2/4/1975
Imperioli, Michael	Mount Vernon, NY	3/26/1966
Iñárritu, Alejandro G.	Mexico City, Mexico	8/15/1963
Innes, Laura	Pontiac, MI	8/16/1957?
Ireland, Kathy	Glendale, CA	3/20/1963
Irons, Jeremy	Cowes, Isle of Wight, Eng., UK	9/19/1948
Irving, Amy	Palo Alto, CA	9/10/1953
Irwin, Bill	Santa Monica, CA	4/11/1950
Isaac, Oscar	Guatemala	3/9/1979
Ivanek, Željko	Ljubljana, Yugo. (Slovenia)	8/15/1957
Ivey, Judith	El Paso, TX	9/4/1951
Ivory, James	Berkeley, CA	6/7/1928
Izzard, Eddie	Aden, Yemen	2/7/1962
Ja Rule	Hollis, Queens, NY	2/29/1976
Jackée (Harry)	Winston-Salem, NC	8/14/1956
Jackman, Hugh	Sydney, NSW, Australia	10/12/1968
Jackson, Cheyenne	Newport, WA	7/12/1975
Jackson, Janet	Gary, IN	5/16/1966
Jackson, Jermaine	Gary, IN	12/11/1954
Jackson, Jonathan	Orlando, FL	5/11/1982
Jackson, Joshua	Vancouver, BC, Canada	6/11/1978
Jackson, Kate	Birmingham, AL	10/29/1948
Jackson, La Toya	Gary, IN	5/29/1956
Jackson, Peter	Wellington, New Zealand	10/31/1961
Jackson, Samuel L.	Washington, DC	12/21/1948
Jacobi, Derek	London, England, UK	10/22/1938
Jagger, Mick	Dartford, England, UK	7/26/1943
James, Brian d'Arcy	Saginaw, MI	6/29/1968
James, Kevin	Mineola, NY	4/26/1965
James, Lily	Esher, England, UK	4/5/1989
James, Theo	Oxford, England, UK	12/16/1984
Jamison, Judith	Philadelphia, PA	5/10/1943
Janney, Allison	Dayton, OH	11/19/1959
Janssen, Famke	Amsterdam, Netherlands	11/5/1965
Jardine, Al	Lima, OH	9/3/1942
Jarmusch, Jim	Akron, OH	1/22/1953
Jarrett, Keith	Allentown, PA	5/8/1945
Jay-Z	Brooklyn, NY	12/4/1969
Jenkins, Barry	Miami, FL	11/19/1979
Jenkins, Richard	DeKalb, IL	5/4/1947
Jenner, Caitlyn	Mount Kisco, NY	10/28/1949
Jenner, Kendall	Los Angeles, CA	9/3/1995
Jenner, Kris	San Diego, CA	11/5/1955
Jenner, Kylie	Los Angeles, CA	8/10/1997
Jennings, Ken	Edmonds, WA	5/23/1974
Jepsen, Carly Rae	Mission, BC, Canada	11/21/1985
Jett, Joan	Philadelphia, PA	9/22/1958
Jewel (Kilcher)	Payson, UT	5/23/1974
Jewison, Norman	Toronto, ON, Canada	7/21/1926
Jillette, Penn	Greenfield, MA	3/5/1955
Jillian, Ann	Cambridge, MA	1/29/1950
Joel, Billy	Bronx, NY	5/9/1949
Johansson, Scarlett	New York, NY	11/22/1984
John, Elton	Pinner, Middlesex, Eng., UK	3/25/1947
Johns, Glynis	Durban, South Africa	10/5/1923
Johnson, Beverly	Buffalo, NY	10/13/1952
Johnson, Don	Flatt Creek, MO	12/15/1949
Johnson, Dwayne "The Rock"	Hayward, CA	5/2/1972
Johnston, Bruce	Los Angeles, CA	6/24/1942
Johnston, Kristen	Washington, DC	9/20/1967
Jolie, Angelina	Los Angeles, CA	6/4/1975
Jonas, Joe	Casa Grande, AZ	8/15/1989
Jonas, Kevin	Teaneck, NJ	11/5/1987
Jonas, Nick	Dallas, TX	9/16/1992
Jones, Angus T.	Austin, TX	10/8/1993
Jones, Bill T.	Bunnell, FL	2/15/1952
Jones, Cherry	Paris, TN	11/21/1956
Jones, Gemma	London, England, UK	12/4/1942
Jones, Grace	Spanish Town, Jamaica	5/19/1948
Jones, Jack	Hollywood, CA	1/14/1938
Jones, James Earl	Arkabutla, MS	1/17/1931
Jones, John Paul	Sidcup, England, UK	1/3/1946
Jones, January	Sioux Falls, SD	1/5/1978

Name	Birthplace	Birthdate
Jones, Leslie	Memphis, TN	9/7/1967
Jones, Mick	London, England, UK	6/26/1955
Jones, Norah	New York, NY	3/30/1979
Jones, Quincy	Chicago, IL	3/14/1933
Jones, Shirley	Charleroi, PA	3/31/1934
Jones, Star	Badin, NC	3/24/1962
Jones, Tom	Pontypridd, Wales, UK	6/7/1940
Jones, Tommy Lee	San Saba, TX	9/15/1946
Jonze, Spike	Rockville, MD	10/22/1969
Jordan, Michael B.	Santa Ana, CA	2/9/1987
Jovovich, Milla	Kiev, Ukraine	12/17/1975
Judd, Ashley	Granada Hills, CA	4/19/1968
Judd, Wynonna	Ashland, KY	5/30/1964
Kaczmarek, Jane	Milwaukee, WI	12/21/1955
Kaling, Mindy	Cambridge, MA	6/24/1979
Kaluuya, Daniel	London, Eng., UK	2/24/1989
Kanaly, Steve	Burbank, CA	3/14/1946
Kane, Carol	Cleveland, OH	6/18/1952
Kaplan, Gabe	Brooklyn, NY	3/31/1945
Kardashian, Khloe	Los Angeles, CA	6/27/1984
Kardashian, Kim	Los Angeles, CA	10/21/1980
Kardashian, Kourtney	Los Angeles, CA	4/18/1979
Karn, Richard	Seattle, WA	2/17/1956
Katic, Stana	Hamilton, ON, Canada	4/26/1978
Kattan, Chris	Sherman Oaks, CA	10/19/1970
Kaufmann, Jonas	Munich, Germany	1/10/1969
Kavner, Julie	Burbank, CA	9/7/1951
Kaye, Judy	Phoenix, AZ	12/11/1948
Kazan, Lainie	New York, NY	5/15/1940
Keach, Stacy	Savannah, GA	6/2/1941
Keaton, Diane	Santa Ana, CA	1/5/1946
Keaton, Michael	Coraopolis, PA	9/5/1951
Keener, Catherine	Miami, FL	3/23/1959
Keillor, Garrison	Anoka, MN	8/7/1942
Keitel, Harvey	Brooklyn, NY	5/13/1939
Keith, David	Knoxville, TN	5/8/1954
Keith, Penelope	Sutton, Surrey, Eng., UK	4/2/1940
Kelly, Minka	Los Angeles, CA	6/24/1980
Kelly, R(obert)	Chicago, IL	1/8/1967
Kemper, Ellie	Kansas City, MO	5/2/1980
Kendrick, Anna	Portland, ME	8/9/1985
Kennedy, Jamie	Upper Darby, PA	5/25/1970
Kenny G	Seattle, WA	6/5/1956
Kent, Allegra	Santa Monica, CA	8/11/1937
Keoghan, Phil	Christchurch, New Zealand	5/31/1967
Kerns, Joanna	San Francisco, CA	2/12/1953
Kesha	Los Angeles, CA	3/1/1987
Key, Keegan-Michael	Southfield, MI	3/22/1971
Keys, Alicia	New York, NY	1/25/1981
Khaled, DJ	New Orleans, LA	11/26/1975
Khalifa, Wiz	Minot, ND	9/8/1987
Khan, Chaka	Great Lakes, IL	3/23/1953
Kid Rock	Romeo, MI	1/17/1971
Kidman, Nicole	Honolulu, HI	6/20/1967
Kilborn, Craig	Kansas City, KS	8/24/1962
Kilmer, Val	Los Angeles, CA	12/31/1959
Kim, Daniel Dae	Pusan, South Korea	8/4/1968
Kimmel, Jimmy	Brooklyn, NY	11/13/1967
King, Carole	Brooklyn, NY	2/9/1942
King, Gayle	Chevy Chase, MD	12/28/1954?
King, Perry	Alliance, OH	4/30/1948
King, Regina	Los Angeles, CA	1/15/1971
Kingsley, Ben	Scarborough, England, UK	12/31/1943
Kingston, Alex	London, England, UK	3/11/1963
Kinnear, Greg	Logansport, IN	6/17/1963
Kinney, Kathy	Stevens Point, WI	11/3/1954
Kinski, Nastassja	Berlin, W. Germany	1/24/1960
Kirkland, Gelsey	Bethlehem, PA	12/29/1952
Kirkpatrick, Chris	Clarion, PA	10/17/1971
Kirshner, Mia	Toronto, ON, Canada	1/25/1975
Kitsch, Taylor	Kelowna, BC, Canada	4/8/1981
Klein, Robert	Bronx, NY	2/8/1942
Kline, Kevin	St. Louis, MO	10/24/1947
Klum, Heidi	Bergish-Gladbach, Germany	6/1/1973
Knight, Gladys	Atlanta, GA	5/28/1944
Knight, T. R.	Minneapolis, MN	3/26/1973
Knight, Wayne	New York, NY	8/7/1955
Knightley, Keira	Teddington, England, UK	3/26/1985
Knopfler, Mark	Glasgow, Scotland, UK	8/12/1949
Knowles, Beyoncé	Houston, TX	9/4/1981
Knoxville, Johnny	Knoxville, TN	3/11/1971
Kopell, Bernie	Brooklyn, NY	6/21/1933
Krakowski, Jane	Parsippany, NJ	10/11/1968
Krasinski, John	Newton, MA	10/20/1979
Krause, Peter	Aleandria, MN	8/12/1965
Kravitz, Lenny	Brooklyn, NY	5/26/1964
Kravitz, Zoë	Los Angeles, CA	12/1/1988
Kressley, Carson	Allentown, PA	11/11/1969
Kretschmann, Thomas	Dessau, E. Germany	9/8/1962
Kristofferson, Kris	Brownsville, TX	6/22/1936
Kudrow, Lisa	Encino, CA	7/30/1963
Kunis, Mila	Kiev, Ukraine	8/14/1983
Kurtz, Swoosie	Omaha, NE	9/6/1944
Kutcher, Ashton	Cedar Rapids, IA	2/7/1978
Kwan, Daniel	Westborough, MA	2/10/1988
Kwan, Nancy	Hong Kong	5/19/1939
LaBelle, Patti	Philadelphia, PA	5/24/1944
LaBeouf, Shia	Los Angeles, CA	6/11/1986
Lachey, Nick	Harlan, KY	11/9/1973
Ladd, Cheryl	Huron, SD	7/12/1951
Ladd, Diane	Meridian, MS	11/29/1932
Lady Gaga	New York, NY	3/28/1986
Lagasse, Emeril	Fall River, MA	10/15/1959
Lahti, Christine	Birmingham, MI	4/4/1950
Laine, Cleo	Southall, England, UK	10/28/1927
Lake, Ricki	Hastings-on-Hudson, NY	9/21/1968
Lakshmi, Padma	Chennai, India	9/1/1970
Lamar, Kendrick	Compton, CA	6/17/1987
Lamas, Lorenzo	Santa Monica, CA	1/20/1958
Lambert, Adam	Indianapolis, IN	1/29/1982
Lambert, Christopher	Great Neck, NY	3/29/1957
Lambert, Miranda	Longview, TX	11/10/1983
Landis, John	Chicago, IL	8/3/1950
Lane, Diane	New York, NY	1/22/1965
Lane, Nathan	Jersey City, NJ	2/3/1956
lang, k.d.	Consort, AB, Canada	11/2/1961
Lang, Stephen	Jamaica Estates, Queens, NY	7/11/1952
Lange, Jessica	Cloquet, MN	4/20/1949
Langella, Frank	Bayonne, NJ	1/1/1938
LaPaglia, Anthony	Adelaide, SA, Australia	1/31/1959
Larroquette, John	New Orleans, LA	11/25/1947
Larson, Brie	Sacramento, CA	10/1/1989
LaSalle, Eriq	Hartford, CT	6/23/1962
Lauper, Cyndi	Ozone Park, Queens, NY	6/22/1953
Laurie, Hugh	Oxford, England, UK	6/11/1959
Lautner, Taylor	Grand Rapids, MI	2/11/1992
Lavigne, Avril	Belleville, ON, Canada	9/27/1984
Lavin, Linda	Portland, ME	10/15/1937
Law, Jude	London, England, UK	12/29/1972
Lawless, Lucy	Mount Albert, New Zealand	3/29/1968
Lawrence, Carol	Melrose Park, IL	9/5/1934
Lawrence, Jennifer	Louisville, KY	8/15/1990
Lawrence, Joey	Montgomery, PA	4/20/1976
Lawrence, Martin	Frankfurt, Germany	4/16/1965
Lawrence, Steve	Brooklyn, NY	7/8/1935
Lawrence, Vicki	Inglewood, CA	3/26/1949
Lear, Norman	New Haven, CT	7/27/1922
Learned, Michael	Washington, DC	4/9/1939
Leary, Denis	Worcester, MA	8/18/1957
LeBlanc, Matt	Newton, MA	7/25/1967
LeBon, Simon	Bushey, England, UK	10/27/1958
Lee, Ang	Pingtung, Taiwan	10/23/1954
Lee, Brenda	Lithonia, GA	12/11/1944
Lee, Jason	Huntington Beach, CA	4/25/1970
Lee, Michele	Los Angeles, CA	6/24/1942
Lee, Spike	Atlanta, GA	3/20/1957
Leeves, Jane	Ilford, England, UK	4/18/1961
Legend, John	Springfield, OH	12/28/1978
Leguizamo, John	Bogotá, Colombia	7/22/1964
Leigh, Jennifer Jason	Hollywood, CA	2/5/1962
Leighton, Laura	Iowa City, IA	7/24/1968
Lennox, Annie	Aberdeen, Scotland, UK	12/25/1954
Leno, Jay	New Rochelle, NY	4/28/1950
Leo, Melissa	New York, NY	9/14/1960
Leonard, Robert Sean	Westwood, NJ	2/28/1969
Leoni, Tea	New York, NY	2/25/1966
Leto, Jared	Bossier City, LA	12/26/1971
Letterman, David	Indianapolis, IN	4/12/1947
Leung, Tony	Hong Kong	6/27/1962
Levin, Harvey	Los Angeles, CA	9/2/1960
Levine, Adam	Los Angeles, CA	3/18/1979
Levine, Ted	Bellaire, OH	5/29/1957
Levinson, Barry	Baltimore, MD	4/6/1942
Levy, Daniel	Toronto, ON, Canada	8/9/1983
Levy, Eugene	Hamilton, ON, Canada	12/17/1946
Lewis, Damian	London, Eng., UK	2/11/1971
Lewis, Huey	New York, NY	7/5/1950
Lewis, Jason	Newport Beach, CA	6/25/1971
Lewis, Juliette	Los Angeles, CA	6/21/1973
Lewis, Leona	London, England, UK	4/3/1985
Lewis, Richard	Brooklyn, NY	6/29/1947
Li, Jet	Beijing, China	4/26/1963
Light, Judith	Trenton, NJ	2/9/1949
Lil' Kim	Brooklyn, NY	7/11/1975
Lil Nas X	Lithia Springs, GA	4/9/1999
Lil' Romeo	New Orleans, LA	8/19/1989
Lil Wayne	New Orleans, LA	9/27/1982
Lilly, Evangeline	Fort Saskatchewan, AB, Can.	8/3/1979
Lincoln, Andrew	London, England, UK	9/14/1973

Name	Birthplace	Birthdate
Linden, Hal	Bronx, NY	3/20/1931
Ling, Lisa	Sacramento, CA	8/30/1973
Linn-Baker, Mark	St. Louis, MO.	6/17/1954
Linney, Laura	New York, NY	2/5/1964
Lipa, Dua	London, England, UK	8/22/1995
Lithgow, John	Rochester, NY	10/19/1945
Little, Rich	Ottawa, ON, Canada	11/26/1938
Littrell, Brian	Lexington, KY	2/20/1975
Liu, Lucy	Jackson Heights, Queens, NY	12/2/1968
Liu, Simu	Harbin, China	4/19/1989
Lively, Blake	Tarzana, CA.	8/25/1987
LL Cool J	St. Albans, Queens, NY	1/14/1968
Lloyd, Christopher	Stamford, CT.	10/22/1938
Lloyd Webber, Andrew	London, England, UK	3/22/1948
Lockhart, June	New York, NY	6/25/1925
Locklear, Heather	Westwood, CA.	9/25/1961
Loggins, Kenny	Everett, WA	1/7/1948
Lohan, Lindsay	New York, NY	7/2/1986
Lonergan, Kenneth	New York, NY	10/16/1962
Long, Nia	Brooklyn, NY	10/30/1970
Long, Shelley	Ft. Wayne, IN.	8/23/1949
Longoria, Eva	Corpus Christi, TX	3/15/1975
Lopez, George	Mission Hills, CA	4/23/1961
Lopez, Jennifer	Bronx, NY	7/24/1969
Lopez, Mario	San Diego, CA.	10/10/1973
Lorde	Takapuna, New Zealand	11/7/1996
Loren, Sophia	Rome, Italy	9/20/1934
Louis C.K.	Washington, DC	9/12/1967
Louis-Dreyfus, Julia	New York, NY	1/13/1961
Lovato, Demi	Albuquerque, NM.	8/20/1992
Love, Courtney	San Francisco, CA	7/9/1964
Love, Mike	Baldwin Hills, CA.	3/15/1941
Loveless, Patty	Pikeville, KY	1/4/1957
Lovett, Lyle	Klein, TX	11/1/1957
Lovitz, Jon	Tarzana, CA.	7/21/1957
Lowe, Rob.	Charlottesville, VA	3/17/1964
Lucas, George	Modesto, CA	5/14/1944
Lucci, Susan	Scarsdale, NY	12/23/1946
Luckinbill, Laurence	Ft. Smith, AR	11/21/1934
Ludacris	Champaign, IL	9/11/1977
Luhrmann, Baz	Sydney, NSW, Australia	9/17/1962
LuPone, Patti	Northport, NY	4/21/1949
Lynch, David	Missoula, MT.	1/20/1946
Lynch, Jane	Dolton, IL.	7/14/1960
Lynne, Shelby	Quantico, VA	10/22/1968
Lyonne, Natasha	New York, NY	4/4/1979
Ma, Yo-Yo	Paris, France	10/7/1955
Macchio, Ralph	Huntington, NY	11/4/1961
MacDonald, Kelly	Glasgow, Scotland, UK	2/23/1976
MacDowell, Andie	Gaffney, SC	4/21/1958
MacFarlane, Seth	Kent, CT	10/26/1973
MacGowan, Shane	Tunbridge, Kent, Eng., UK	12/25/1957
MacGraw, Ali	Pound Ridge, NY	4/1/1939
Macklemore	Seattle, WA	6/19/1983
MacLachlan, Kyle	Yakima, WA.	2/22/1959
MacLaine, Shirley	Richmond, VA	4/24/1934
MacNicol, Peter	Dallas, TX	4/10/1954
MacPherson, Elle	Sydney, NSW, Australia	3/29/1964
Macy, William H.	Miami, FL	3/13/1950
Madden, Richard	Elderslie, Scot., UK	6/18/1986
Madigan, Amy	Chicago, IL	9/11/1950
Madonna (Ciccone)	Bay City, MI	8/16/1958
Madsen, Michael	Chicago, IL.	9/25/1959
Maguire, Tobey	Santa Monica, CA	6/27/1975
Maher, Bill	New York, NY	1/20/1956
Majors, Lee	Wyandotte, MI	4/23/1939
Makarova, Natalia	Leningrad, Russia	11/21/1940
Malek, Rami	Los Angeles, CA	5/12/1981
Malick, Terrence	Ottawa, IL	11/30/1943
Malick, Wendie	Buffalo, NY	12/13/1950
Malina, Joshua	New York, NY	1/17/1966
Malkovich, John	Christopher, IL.	12/9/1953
Mamet, David	Chicago, IL.	11/30/1947
Manchester, Melissa	Bronx, NY	2/15/1951
Mandel, Howie	Toronto, ON, Canada.	11/29/1955
Mandrell, Barbara	Houston, TX	12/25/1948
Mangione, Chuck	Rochester, NY	11/29/1940
Manheim, Camryn	Caldwell, NJ	3/8/1961
Manilow, Barry	Brooklyn, NY	6/17/1943
Mann, Aimee	Richmond, VA	8/9/1960
Manoff, Dinah	New York, NY	1/25/1958
Manson, Marilyn	Canton, OH	1/5/1969
Mantegna, Joe	Chicago, IL.	11/13/1947
Mantello, Joe	Rockford, IL.	12/27/1962
Mara, Kate	Bedford, NY.	2/27/1983
Mara, Rooney	Bedford, NY.	4/17/1985
Margulies, Julianna	Spring Valley, NY.	6/8/1966
Marie, Constance	Hollywood, CA.	9/9/1965
Marin, Cheech	Los Angeles, CA	7/13/1946
Marinaro, Ed	New York, NY	3/31/1950
Maron, Marc	Jersey City, NJ.	9/27/1963
Mars, Bruno	Honolulu, HI	10/8/1985

Name	Birthplace	Birthdate
Marsalis, Branford	Breaux Bridge, LA	8/26/1960
Marsalis, Wynton	New Orleans, LA	10/18/1961
Marsh, Jean	London, England, UK	7/1/1934
Marshall, Peter	Huntington, WV	3/30/1926
Martin, Chris	Devon, England, UK	3/2/1977
Martin, Jesse L.	Rocky Mount, VA	1/18/1969
Martin, Kellie	Riverside, CA.	10/16/1975
Martin, Ricky	San Juan, Puerto Rico	12/24/1971
Martin, Steve	Waco, TX.	8/14/1945
Martindale, Margo.	Jacksonville, TX.	7/18/1951
Martins, Peter	Copenhagen, Denmark	10/27/1946
Maslany, Tatiana	Regina, SK, Canada	9/22/1985
Mason, Marsha	St. Louis, MO.	4/3/1942
Masterson, Mary Stuart	New York, NY	6/28/1966
Mastrantonio, Mary Elizabeth	Lombard, IL	11/17/1958
Masur, Richard	New York, NY	11/20/1948
Mathers, Jerry	Sioux City, IA.	6/2/1948
Matheson, Tim	Glendale, CA.	12/31/1947
Mathis, Johnny	Gilmer, TX	9/30/1935
Matlin, Marlee	Morton Grove, IL	8/24/1965
Matthews, Dave	Johannesburg, South Africa	1/9/1967
May, Elaine	Philadelphia, PA	4/21/1932
Mayer, John	Bridgeport, CT.	10/16/1977
Mays, Jayma	Bristol, TN	7/16/1979
Mazar, Debi	Jamaica, Queens, NY	8/13/1964
McAdams, Rachel.	London, ON, Canada.	11/17/1978
McArdle, Andrea	Abington, PA	11/5/1963
McAvoy, James	Glasgow, Scotland, UK	4/21/1979
McBride, Patricia	Teaneck, NJ	8/23/1942
McCarthy, Andrew.	Westfield, NJ	11/29/1962
McCarthy, Jenny	Chicago, IL	11/1/1972
McCarthy, Melissa	Plainfield, IL.	8/26/1970
McCartney, Paul	Liverpool, England, UK	6/18/1942
McConaughey, Matthew.	Uvalde, TX.	11/4/1969
McCoo, Marilyn	Jersey City, NJ.	9/30/1943
McCormack, Eric	Toronto, ON, Canada.	4/18/1963
McCormack, Mary	Plainsfield, NJ	2/8/1969
McCrane, Paul	Philadelphia, PA	1/19/1961
McDaniel, James	Washington, DC	3/25/1958
McDermott, Dylan	Waterbury, CT	10/26/1961
McDiarmid, Ian	Carnoustie, Tayside, Scot., UK	4/17/1944?
McDonald, Audra	Berlin, Germany	7/3/1970
McDonnell, Mary	Wilkes-Barre, PA	4/28/1952
McDormand, Frances	Chicago, IL	6/23/1957
McDowell, Malcolm.	Leeds, England, UK.	6/13/1943
McEntire, Reba.	McAlester, OK	3/28/1955
McFerrin, Bobby	New York, NY	3/11/1950
McGillis, Kelly	Newport Beach, CA.	7/9/1957
McGovern, Elizabeth	Evanston, IL	7/18/1961
McGovern, Maureen	Youngstown, OH	7/27/1949
McGraw, Tim.	Delhi, LA	5/1/1967
McGregor, Ewan	Crieff, Scotland, UK.	3/31/1971
McHale, Joel.	Rome, Italy	11/20/1971
McHale, Kevin	Plano, TX.	6/14/1988
McKean, Michael	New York, NY	10/17/1947
McKechnie, Donna	Pontiac, MI	11/16/1942
McKellen, Ian	Burnley, England, UK.	5/25/1939
McKenzie, Ben	Austin, TX	9/12/1978
McKidd, Kevin	Elgin, Scotland, UK	8/9/1973
McKinnon, Kate	Sea Cliff, NY	1/6/1984
McLachlan, Sarah.	Halifax, NS, Canada	1/28/1968
McLean, A. J.	West Palm Beach, FL	1/9/1978
McNichol, Kristy	Los Angeles, CA	9/11/1962
McRaney, Gerald	Collins, MS	8/19/1947
McQueen, Steve	London, England, UK	10/9/1969
McQueen, Steven R.	Los Angeles, CA	7/13/1988
McShane, Ian	Blackburn, England, UK.	9/29/1942
Meester, Leighton	Marco Island, FL	4/9/1986
Megan Thee Stallion.	Bexar County, TX.	2/15/1995
Mehta, Zubin	Bombay, India	4/29/1936
Mellencamp, John.	Seymour, IN	10/7/1951
Meloni, Christopher	Washington, DC	4/2/1961
Mendes, Sam	Redding, England, UK	8/1/1965
Mendes, Sergio	Niteroi, Brazil	2/11/1941
Mendes, Shawn	Toronto, ON, Canada.	8/8/1998
Menzel, Idina	Syosset, NY.	5/30/1971
Menzies, Tobias	London, England, UK	3/7/1974
Merchant, Natalie	Jamestown, NY	10/26/1963
Merkerson, S. Epatha	Saginaw, MI.	11/28/1952
Messing, Debra	Brooklyn, NY	8/15/1968
Metcalf, Laurie	Carbondale, IL.	6/16/1955
Meyers, Seth	Bedford, NH.	12/28/1973
Michaels, Al	Brooklyn, NY	11/12/1944
Michaels, Bret	Butler, PA	3/15/1963
Michaels, Lorne	Toronto, ON, Canada.	11/17/1944
Michele, Lea	Bronx, NY	8/29/1986
Midler, Bette	Honolulu, HI	12/1/1945
Midori (Goto)	Osaka, Japan	10/25/1971
Miguel, Luis	San Juan, PR	4/19/1970

Name	Birthplace	Birthdate
Mike D	Brooklyn, NY	11/20/1965
Milano, Alyssa	Brooklyn, NY	12/19/1972
Miles, Vera	nr. Boise City, OK.	8/23/1930
Miller, Dennis	Pittsburgh, PA	11/3/1953
Miller, Jonny Lee	Kingston Upon Thames, England, UK	11/15/1972
Miller, Penelope Ann	Santa Monica, CA	1/13/1964
Mills, Donna	Chicago, IL	12/11/1943
Mills, Hayley	London, England, UK	4/18/1946
Milnes, Sherrill	Downers Grove, IL	1/10/1935
Milsap, Ronnie	Robinsville, NC	1/16/1943
Minaj, Nicki	St. James, Trinidad and Tobago.	12/8/1982
Ming-Na (Wen)	Coloane Island, Macao	11/20/1963
Minhaj, Hasan.	Davis, CA	9/23/1985
Minnelli, Liza	Los Angeles, CA	3/12/1946
Minogue, Kylie	Melbourne, Vic., Australia.	5/28/1968
Miranda, Lin-Manuel	New York, NY	1/16/1980
Mirren, Helen	London, England, UK	7/26/1945
Mitchell, Brian Stokes	Seattle, WA	10/31/1957
Mitchell, Elizabeth	Los Angeles, CA	3/27/1970
Mitchell, Jerry	Paw Paw, MI	1/15/1960
Mitchell, Joni	Fort McLeod, AB, Canada	11/7/1943
Moby	New York, NY	9/11/1965
Modine, Matthew	Loma Linda, CA	3/22/1959
Molina, Alfred	London, England, UK	5/24/1953
Moll, Richard.	Pasadena, CA	1/13/1943
Moloney, Janel	Woodland Hills, CA	10/3/1969
Monáe, Janelle	Kansas City, KS.	12/1/1985
Monaghan, Dominic	Berlin, Germany	12/8/1976
Monica (Arnold)	College Park, GA.	10/24/1980
Mo'Nique	Woodlawn, MD	12/11/1967
Moore, Demi	Roswell, NM	11/11/1962
Moore, Julianne	Fort Bragg, NC	12/3/1960
Moore, Mandy.	Nashua, NH.	4/10/1984
Moore, Melba	New York, NY	10/29/1945
Moore, Michael	Flint, MI.	4/23/1954
Moore, Terry	Los Angeles, CA	1/7/1929
Morales, Esai	Brooklyn, NY	10/1/1962
Moranis, Rick	Toronto, ON, Canada.	4/18/1953
Moreno, Rita	Humacao, Puerto Rico.	12/11/1931
Morgan, Jeffrey Dean	Seattle, WA	4/22/1966
Morgan, Piers	Guildford, Surrey, UK	3/30/1965
Morgan, Tracy	Bronx, NY	11/10/1968
Moriarty, Michael	Detroit, MI	4/5/1941
Morris, Garrett.	New Orleans, LA	2/1/1937
Morissette, Alanis	Ottawa, ON, Canada	6/1/1974
Morrison, Matthew	Fort Ord, CA	10/30/1978
Morrison, Van	Belfast, N. Ireland, UK	8/31/1945
Morrissey (Steven Patrick)	Manchester, England, UK.	5/22/1959
Morrow, Rob	New Rochelle, NY	9/21/1962
Morse, David.	Beverly, MA	10/11/1953
Mortensen, Viggo	New York, NY	10/20/1958
Mortimer, Emily.	London, England, UK	12/1/1971
Morton, Joe.	New York, NY	10/18/1947
Morton, Samantha	Nottingham, England, UK	5/13/1977
Moses, William	Los Angeles, CA	11/17/1959
Moss, Carrie-Anne	Vancouver, BC, Canada..	8/21/1967
Moss, Elisabeth	Los Angeles, CA	7/24/1982
Moss, Kate	Croydon, Surrey, Eng., UK	1/16/1974
Moyer, Stephen.	Brentwood, UK	10/11/1969
Moynahan, Bridget	Binghamton, NY	4/28/1971
Mueller-Stahl, Armin	Tilsit, E. Prussia	12/17/1930
Mulaney, John.	Chicago, IL	8/26/1982
Muldaur, Diana	Brooklyn, NY	8/19/1938
Mulgrew, Kate	Dubuque, IA	4/29/1955
Mull, Martin.	Chicago, IL	8/18/1943
Mullally, Megan	Los Angeles, CA	11/12/1958
Mullan, Peter.	Peterhead, Scotland, UK .	11/2/1959
Mulligan, Carey.	London, England, UK	5/28/1985
Mulroney, Dermot	Alexandria, VA	10/31/1963
Muniz, Frankie	Wood-Ridge, NJ	12/5/1985
Murphy, Annie.	Ottawa, ON, Canada	12/19/1986
Murphy, Ben	Jonesboro, AR.	3/6/1942
Murphy, Cillian	Cork, Ireland	5/25/1976
Murphy, Donna	Corona, Queens, NY	3/7/1958
Murphy, Eddie.	Brooklyn, NY	4/3/1961
Murphy, Michael	Los Angeles, CA	5/5/1938
Murphy, Ryan	Indianapolis, IN	11/30/1965
Murray, Anne.	Springhill, NS, Canada	6/20/1945
Murray, Bill	Wilmette, IL	9/21/1950
Murray, Don	Hollywood, CA	7/31/1929
Musburger, Brent	Portland, OR	5/26/1939
Muti, Riccardo.	Naples, Italy.	7/28/1941
Myers, Mike	Scarborough, ON, Canada	5/25/1963
Nagra, Parminder	Leicester, England, UK .	10/5/1975
Nanjiani, Kumail	Karachi, Pakistan.	2/21/1978
Nash, Graham	Blackpool, England, UK..	2/2/1942
Nash, Niecy	Palmdale, CA.	2/23/1970
Naughton, James	Middletown, CT	12/6/1945
Navarro, Dave	Santa Monica, CA	6/7/1967

Name	Birthplace	Birthdate
Nealon, Kevin	St. Louis, MO.	11/18/1953
Neeson, Liam	Ballymena, N. Ireland, UK	6/7/1952
Neill, Sam	Ulster, N. Ireland, UK	9/14/1947
Nelligan, Kate	London, ON, Canada.....	3/16/1951
Nelly	Austin, TX	11/2/1974
Nelson, Craig T.	Spokane, WA.	4/4/1944
Nelson, Judd.	Portland, ME.	11/28/1959
Nelson, Tracy	Santa Monica, CA	10/25/1963
Nelson, Willie	Abbott, TX	4/30/1933
Netrebko, Anna	Krasnodar, Russia	9/18/1971
Neuwirth, Bebe	Newark, NJ	12/31/1958
Neville, Aaron	New Orleans, LA	1/24/1941
Newhart, Bob	Oak Park, IL	9/5/1929
Newman, Randy	New Orleans, LA	11/28/1943
Newton, Thandiwe	London, England, UK	11/6/1972
Newton, Wayne.	Norfolk, VA	4/3/1942
Nicholas, Denise	Detroit, MI	7/12/1944
Nicholson, Jack	Neptune, NJ	4/22/1937
Nicks, Stevie	Phoenix, AZ.	5/26/1948
Nighy, Bill	Caterham, Surrey, Eng., UK	12/12/1949
Nixon, Cynthia	New York, NY	4/9/1966
Noah, Trevor	Soweto, South Africa.	2/20/1984
Noble, John	Port Pirie, S. Austral., Australia.	8/20/1948
Nolan, Christopher	London, England, UK	7/30/1970
Nolte, Nick	Omaha, NE.	2/8/1941
Noone, Peter.	Manchester, England, UK..	11/5/1947
Norris, Chuck	Ryan, OK.	3/10/1940
Northam, Jeremy	Cambridge, England, UK..	12/1/1961
Norton, Edward.	Boston, MA	8/18/1969
Noth, Christopher	Madison, WI	11/13/1954
Novak, Kim	Chicago, IL	2/13/1933
Nuyen, France	Marseilles, France	7/31/1939
Nyong'o, Lupita	Mexico City, Mexico....	3/1/1983
Oates, John	New York, NY	4/7/1949
O'Brien, Conan	Brookline, MA	4/18/1963
O'Brien, Margaret	San Diego, CA	1/15/1937
Ocean, Billy	Fyzabad, Trinidad and Tobago.	1/21/1950
Ocean, Frank	Long Beach, CA	10/28/1987
O'Connor, Josh	Cheltenham, England, UK	5/20/1990
Odenkirk, Bob.	Berwyn, IL.	10/22/1962
Odom, Leslie, Jr.	Queens, NY	8/6/1981
O'Donnell, Chris	Winnetka, IL	6/26/1970
O'Donnell, Rosie.	Commack, NY	3/21/1962
Offerman, Nick	Joliet, IL.	6/26/1970
O'Grady, Gail	Detroit, MI	1/23/1963
Oh, Sandra	Nepean, On, Canada	7/20/1971
O'Hara, Catherine.	Toronto, ON, Canada.....	3/4/1954
O'Hare, Denis	Kansas City, MO	1/17/1962
Oka, Masi	Tokyo, Japan.	12/27/1974
Oldman, Gary	South London, Eng., UK .	3/21/1958
Olin, Ken.	Chicago, IL	7/30/1954
Olin, Lena	Stockholm, Sweden	3/22/1955
Oliver, Jamie.	Clavering, England, UK ..	5/27/1975
Oliver, John.	Birmingham, England, UK	4/23/1977
Olmos, Edward James .	E. Los Angeles, CA	2/24/1947
Olsen, Ashley	Sherman Oaks, CA	6/13/1986
Olsen, Elizabeth	Sherman Oaks, CA	2/16/1989
Olsen, Mary-Kate	Sherman Oaks, CA	6/13/1986
Olson, Nancy	Milwaukee, WI	7/14/1928
Olyphant, Timothy	Honolulu, HI	5/20/1968
O'Malley, Mike	Boston, MA.	10/31/1966
O'Neal, Ryan	Los Angeles, CA	4/20/1941
O'Neal, Tatum	Los Angeles, CA	11/5/1963
O'Neill, Ed.	Youngstown, OH	4/12/1946
Ontkean, Michael	Vancouver, BC, Canada..	1/24/1946
O'Quinn, Terry	Newbury, MI	7/15/1952
Orlando, Tony	New York, NY	4/3/1944
Ormond, Julia	Epsom, England, UK	1/4/1965
Osbourne, Jack	London, England, UK	11/8/1985
Osbourne, Kelly	London, England, UK	10/27/1984
Osbourne, Ozzy	Birmingham, England, UK	12/3/1948
Osbourne, Sharon	London, England, UK	10/9/1952
Osment, Haley Joel	Los Angeles, CA	4/10/1988
Osmond, Donny	Ogden, UT	12/9/1957
Osmond, Marie.	Ogden, UT	10/13/1959
Oswalt, Patton.	Portsmouth, VA	1/27/1969
O'Toole, Annette	Houston, TX	4/1/1951
Owen, Clive	Keresley, England, UK..	10/3/1964
Oyelowo, David.	Oxford, England, UK	4/1/1976
Oz, Frank	Herford, England, UK...	5/25/1944
Ozawa, Seiji	Shenyang, China.	9/1/1935
Pacino, Al	New York, NY	4/25/1940
Page, Elliot	Halifax, NS, Canada	2/21/1987
Page, Jimmy	Heston, England, UK...	1/9/1944
Paige, Janis	Tacoma, WA	9/16/1922
Paisley, Brad.	Glen Dale, WV.	10/28/1972
Palin, Michael	Sheffield, England, UK....	5/5/1943
Palmer, Keke	Harvey, IL	8/26/1993
Palminteri, Chazz	Bronx, NY	5/15/1951

Name	Birthplace	Birthdate
Paltrow, Gwyneth	Los Angeles, CA	9/27/1972
Panettiere, Hayden	Palisades, NY	8/21/1989
Panjabi, Archie	Edgware, England, UK	5/31/1972
Pantoliano, Joe	Hoboken, NJ	9/12/1951
Paquin, Anna	Winnipeg, MB, Canada	7/24/1982
Parker, Jameson	Baltimore, MD	11/18/1947
Parker, Mary-Louise	Fort Jackson, SC	8/2/1964
Parker, Sarah Jessica	Nelsonville, OH	3/25/1965
Parsons, Estelle	Marblehead, MA	11/20/1927
Parsons, Jim	Houston, TX	3/24/1973
Parton, Dolly	Sevierville, TN	1/19/1946
Pascal, Pedro	Santiago, Chile	4/2/1975
Pasdar, Adrian	Pittsfield, MA	4/30/1965
Patel, Dev	London, England, UK	4/23/1990
Patinkin, Mandy	Chicago, IL	11/30/1952
Patric, Jason	Flushing, Queens, NY	6/17/1966
Pattinson, Robert	London, England, UK	5/13/1986
Patton, Will	Charleston, SC	6/14/1954
Paul, Aaron	Emmett, ID	8/27/1979
Paul, Adrian	London, England, UK	5/29/1959
Paulson, Sarah	Tampa, FL	12/17/1975
Pearce, Guy	Ely, England, UK	10/5/1967
Peele, Jordan	New York, NY	2/21/1979
Peet, Amanda	New York, NY	1/11/1972
Penn, Kal	Montclair, NJ	4/23/1977
Penn, Sean	Burbank, CA	8/17/1960
Pepper, Barry	Campbell River, BC, Can.	4/4/1970
Perez, Rosie	Brooklyn, NY	9/6/1964
Perkins, Elizabeth	Flushing, Queens, NY	11/18/1960
Perlman, Itzhak	Tel Aviv, Israel	8/31/1945
Perlman, Rhea	Brooklyn, NY	3/31/1948
Perlman, Ron	New York, NY	4/13/1950
Perrine, Valerie	Galveston, TX	9/3/1943
Perry, Katy	Santa Barbara, CA	10/25/1984
Perry, Matthew	Williamstown, MA	8/19/1969
Perry, Tyler	New Orleans, LA	9/13/1969
Pesci, Joe	Newark, NJ	2/9/1943
Peters, Bernadette	Ozone Park, Queens, NY.	2/28/1948
Peters, Evan	St. Louis, MO.	1/20/1987
Petty, Lori	Chattanooga, TN	3/23/1963
Pfeiffer, Michelle	Santa Ana, CA.	4/29/1958
Phair, Liz.	New Haven, CT.	4/17/1967
Phillippe, Ryan	New Castle, DE.	9/10/1974
Phillips, Lou Diamond	Subic Bay, Philippines	2/17/1962
Phillips, Mackenzie	Alexandria, VA.	11/10/1959
Phillips, Michelle	Long Beach, CA	6/4/1944
Phillips, Sian	Bettws, Wales, UK.	5/14/1934
Phoenix, Joaquin	San Juan, Puerto Rico.	10/28/1974
Pierce, David Hyde	Albany, NY.	4/3/1959
Pike, Rosamund	London, England, UK	1/27/1979
Pinchot, Bronson	New York, NY	5/20/1959
Pink.	Doylestown, PA	9/8/1979
Pinkett Smith, Jada	Baltimore, MD	9/18/1971
Pirner, Dave	Green Bay, WI	4/16/1964
Piscopo, Joe	Passaic, NJ	6/17/1951
Pitbull	Miami, FL	1/15/1981
Pitt, Brad	Shawnee, OK	12/18/1963
Piven, Jeremy	New York, NY	7/26/1965
Plant, Robert	W. Bromwich, Eng., UK	8/20/1948
Platt, Ben	Los Angeles, CA	9/24/1993
Plaza, Aubrey	Wilmington, DE	6/26/1984
Plimpton, Martha	New York, NY	11/16/1970
Plowright, Joan	Brigg, England, UK	10/28/1929
Plummer, Amanda	New York, NY	3/23/1957
Poehler, Amy	Newton, MA.	9/16/1971
Polanski, Roman	Paris, France.	8/18/1933
Pompeo, Ellen	Everett, MA	11/10/1969
Pop, Iggy.	Muskegon, MI	4/21/1947
Porter, Billy	Pittsburgh, PA	9/21/1969
Portman, Natalie	Jerusalem, Israel	6/9/1981
Posey, Parker	Baltimore, MD	11/8/1968
Potts, Annie.	Nashville, TN.	10/28/1952
Povich, Maury.	Washington, DC	1/17/1939
Powers, Stefanie	Hollywood, CA.	11/2/1942
Pratt, Chris	Virginia, MN.	6/21/1979
Prentiss, Paula	San Antonio, TX.	3/4/1939
Prepon, Laura	Watchung, NJ	3/7/1980
Presley, Priscilla	Brooklyn, NY	5/24/1945
Pressly, Jaime.	Kinston, NC.	7/30/1977
Price, Leontyne	Laurel, MS.	2/10/1927
Priestley, Jason	Vancouver, BC, Canada.	8/28/1969
Prince, Faith	Augusta, GA	8/5/1957
Principal, Victoria	Fukuoka, Japan.	1/3/1950
Probst, Jeff	Wichita, KS	11/4/1962
Proctor, Emily	Raleigh, NC.	10/8/1968
Pryce, Jonathan	Holywell, N. Wales, UK	6/1/1947
Puck, Wolfgang	St. Veit, Austria	1/8/1949
Pulliam, Keshia Knight	Newark, NJ	4/9/1979
Pullman, Bill	Hornell, NY	12/17/1953
Purcell, Sarah	Richmond, IN	10/8/1948
Purefoy, James	Taunton, England, UK	6/3/1964
Quaid, Dennis	Houston, TX	4/9/1954
Quaid, Randy	Houston, TX	10/1/1950
Quan, Ke Huy	Saigon, Vietnam	8/20/1971
Queen Latifah	Newark, NJ	3/18/1970
Quinn, Aidan	Chicago, IL	3/8/1959
Quinn, Colin	Brooklyn, NY	6/6/1959
Quinn, Martha	Albany, NY.	5/11/1959
Quinto, Zachary	Pittsburgh, PA	6/2/1977
Rachins, Alan	Cambridge, MA	10/3/1942
Radcliffe, Daniel	London, England, UK	7/23/1989
Radnor, Josh	Columbus, OH.	7/29/1974
Rae, Issa	Los Angeles, CA	1/12/1985
Raffi (Cavoukian)	Cairo, Egypt.	7/8/1948
Rainbow, Randy	Plantation, FL	7/6/1981
Raitt, Bonnie	Burbank, CA	11/8/1949
Ralph, Sheryl Lee	Waterbury, CT	12/30/1956
Ramey, Samuel	Colby, KS.	3/28/1942
Ramirez, Sara	Mazatlan, Mexico.	8/31/1975
Ramos, Anthony	Brooklyn, NY	11/1/1991
Rampling, Charlotte	Sturmer, MA	2/5/1946
Ramsay, Gordon	Elderslie, Scotland, UK	11/8/1966
Ramsey, Bella	Nottingham, Eng., UK	9/30/2003
Rancic, Giuliana	Naples, Italy.	8/17/1975
Randolph, Joyce	Detroit, MI	10/21/1924
Raphael, Sally Jessy	Easton, PA.	2/25/1935
Rashad, Phylicia	Houston, TX	6/19/1948
Ratzenberger, John	Bridgeport, CT.	4/6/1947
Raver, Kim	New York, NY	3/15/1969
Ray, Rachael	Glen Falls, NY	8/25/1968
Redford, Robert	Santa Monica, CA	8/18/1936
Redgrave, Vanessa	London, England, UK	1/30/1937
Redmayne, Eddie	London, England, UK	1/6/1982
Reed, Rex.	Ft. Worth, TX.	10/2/1938
Reeves, Keanu	Beirut, Lebanon	9/2/1964
Reeves, Martha	Eufaula, AL	7/18/1941
Regalbuto, Joe	New York, NY	8/24/1949
Reid, Tara	Wyckoff, NJ	11/8/1975
Reid, Tim	Norfolk, VA	12/19/1944
Reid, Vernon	London, England, UK	8/22/1958
Reilly, John C.	Chicago, IL	5/24/1965
Reiner, Rob.	Bronx, NY	3/6/1947
Reinhold, Judge	Wilmington, DE	5/21/1957
Reiser, Paul	New York, NY	3/30/1957
Remini, Leah	Brooklyn, NY	6/15/1970
Renner, Jeremy	Modesto, CA	1/7/1971
Reynolds, Ryan	Vancouver, BC, Canada.	10/23/1976
Reznor, Trent	Mercer, PA.	5/17/1965
Rhames, Ving	New York, NY	5/12/1959
Rhimes, Shonda	Chicago, IL	1/13/1970
Rhymes, Busta	Brooklyn, NY	5/20/1972
Rhys, Matthew	Cardiff, Wales, UK	11/4/1974
Rhys Meyers, Jonathan	Dublin, Ireland.	7/27/1977
Ribisi, Giovanni.	Los Angeles, CA	12/17/1974
Ricci, Christina	Santa Monica, CA	2/12/1980
Richards, Denise	Downers Grove, IL.	2/17/1971
Richards, Keith	Dartford, Kent, Eng., UK	12/18/1943
Richards, Michael	Culver City, CA	7/24/1949
Richardson, Kevin.	Lexington, KY	10/3/1971
Richardson, Miranda	Lancashire, Eng., UK.	3/3/1958
Richardson, Patricia	Bethesda, MD	2/23/1951
Richie, Lionel	Tuskegee, AL.	6/20/1949
Richie, Nicole	Berkeley, CA	9/21/1981
Richter, Andy	Grand Rapids, MI	10/28/1966
Riegert, Peter	New York, NY	4/11/1947
Rihanna	St. Michael, Barbados	2/20/1988
Riley, Amber	Long Beach, CA	2/15/1986
Rimes, LeAnn	Jackson, MS	8/28/1982
Ringwald, Molly	Roseville, CA	2/18/1968
Ripa, Kelly	Stratford, NJ	10/2/1970
Rivera, Chita	Washington, DC	1/23/1933
Rivera, Geraldo	New York, NY	7/4/1943
Robbie, Margot	Dalby, Qld., Australia	7/2/1990
Robbins, Tim.	W. Covina, CA	10/16/1958
Roberts, Eric.	Biloxi, MS	4/18/1956
Roberts, Julia	Smyrna, GA.	10/28/1967
Roberts, Tony	New York, NY	10/22/1939
Robinson, Smokey	Detroit, MI	2/19/1940
Rock, Chris	Andrews, SC	2/7/1965
Rockwell, Sam	Daly City, CA	11/5/1968
Rodrigo, Olivia	Temecula, CA	2/20/2003
Rodriguez, Michelle	Bexar County, TX.	7/12/1978
Rogan, Joe	Newark, NJ	8/11/1967
Rogen, Seth	Vancouver, BC, Canada.	4/15/1982
Rogers, Mimi.	Coral Gables, FL	1/27/1956
Rohm, Elisabeth	Dusseldorf, Germany.	4/28/1973
Rollins, Henry	Washington, DC	2/13/1961
Rollins, Sonny	New York, NY	9/7/1930
Romano, Ray	Forest Hills, Queens, NY.	12/21/1957
Romijn, Rebecca	Berkeley, CA	11/6/1972
Ronan, Saoirse	New York, NY	4/12/1994
Ronson, Mark	London, England, UK	9/4/1975

Name	Birthplace	Birthdate
Ronstadt, Linda	Tucson, AZ	7/15/1946
Root, Stephen	Sarasota, FL	11/17/1951
Rose, Axl	Lafayette, IN	2/6/1962
Roseanne	Salt Lake City, UT	11/3/1952
Sellecca, Connie	Detroit, MI	3/26/1944
Ross, Diana	Hollywood, CA	1/29/1940
Ross, Katharine	Albert Lea, MN	10/25/1928
Ross, Marion	Los Angeles, CA	10/29/1972
Ross, Tracee Ellis	London, England, UK	10/30/1965
Rossdale, Gavin	Rome, Italy	6/18/1952
Rossellini, Isabella	New York, NY	9/12/1986
Rossum, Emmy	Bloomington, IN	10/10/1955
Roth, David Lee	London, England, UK	1/31/1956
Rotten, Johnny	New Rochelle, NY	7/9/1942
Roundtree, Richard	Schenectady, NY	9/16/1952
Rourke, Mickey	Des Moines, IA	10/9/1979
Routh, Brandon	Birkenhead, England, UK	2/17/1929
Routledge, Patricia	Ottawa, ON, Canada	10/26/1965
Rowan, Kelly	Cambria, WI	6/19/1930
Rowlands, Gena	Beverly Hills, CA	12/8/1946
Rubinstein, John	Passaic, NJ	4/6/1969
Rudd, Paul	Miami, FL	9/17/1955?
Rudner, Rita	Gainesville, FL	7/27/1972
Rudolph, Maya	Jackson Heights, Queens,	
Ruehl, Mercedes	NY	2/28/1948
Ruffalo, Mark	Kenosha, WI	11/22/1967
RuPaul	San Diego, CA	11/17/1960
Rupp, Debra Jo	Glendale, CA	2/24/1951
Rush, Barbara	Denver, CO	1/4/1927
Rush, Geoffrey	Toowoomba, Qld.,	
	Australia	7/6/1951
Russell, Keri	Fountain Valley, CA	3/23/1976
Russell, Kurt	Springfield, MA	3/17/1951
Russo, Rene	Burbank, CA	2/17/1954
Ruttan, Susan	Oregon City, OR	9/16/1950
Ryan, Meg	Fairfield, CT	11/19/1961
Ryan, Roz	Detroit, MI	7/7/1951
Ryder, Winona	Winona, MN	10/29/1971
Rylance, Mark	Ashford, England, UK	1/18/1960
Sabato, Antonio, Jr.	Rome, Italy	2/29/1972
Sade (Adu)	Ibadan, Nigeria	1/16/1959
Sagal, Katey	Hollywood, CA	1/19/1954
Saint, Eva Marie	Newark, NJ	7/4/1924
St. James, Susan	Hollywood, CA	8/14/1946
St. John, Jill	Los Angeles, CA	8/19/1940
St. Patrick, Mathew	Philadelphia, PA	3/17/1968
Sajak, Pat	Chicago, IL	10/26/1946
Saldana, Zoë	Passaic, NJ	6/19/1978
Salonga, Lea	Manila, Philippines	2/22/1971
Samberg, Andy	Berkeley, CA	8/18/1978
Samms, Emma	London, England, UK	8/28/1960
San Giacomo, Laura	Hoboken, NJ	11/14/1962
Sandler, Adam	Brooklyn, NY	9/9/1966
Santana, Carlos	Autlan, Mexico	7/20/1947
Sara, Mia	Brooklyn, NY	6/19/1967
Sarandon, Susan	New York, NY	10/4/1946
Savage, Ben	Highland Park, IL	9/13/1980
Savage, Fred	Highland Park, IL	7/9/1976
Sawa, Devon	Vancouver, BC, Canada	9/7/1978
Sayles, John	Schenectady, NY	9/28/1950
Scacchi, Greta	Milan, Italy	2/18/1960
Scaggs, Boz	Canton, OH	6/8/1944
Scales, Prunella	Sutton Abinger, Eng., UK	6/22/1932
Scalia, Jack	Brooklyn, NY	11/10/1951
Scheinert, Daniel	Birmingham, AL	6/7/1987
Schiff, Richard	Bethesda, MD	5/27/1955
Schiffer, Claudia	Rheinbach, Germany	8/25/1970
Schneider, John	Mt. Kisco, NY	4/8/1960
Schneider, Rob	San Francisco, CA	10/31/1963
Schreiber, Liev	San Francisco, CA	10/4/1967
Schroder, Rick	Staten Island, NY	4/13/1970
Schumer, Amy	New York, NY	6/1/1981
Schwarzenegger,		
Arnold	Thal, Austria	7/30/1947
Schwimmer, David	Astoria, Queens, NY	11/2/1966
Sciorra, Annabella	Wethersfield, CT	3/24/1964
Scorsese, Martin	Flushing, Queens, NY	11/17/1942
Scott, Adam	Santa Cruz, CA	4/3/1973
Scott, Ridley	South Shields, Eng.,	
	UK	11/30/1937
Scott, Seann William	Cottage Grove, MN	10/3/1976
Scott Thomas, Kristin	Redruth, England, UK	5/24/1960
Seacrest, Ryan	Atlanta, GA	12/24/1974
Seagal, Steven	Lansing, MI	4/10/1951
Secor, Kyle	Tacoma, WA	5/31/1957
Sedaka, Neil	Brooklyn, NY	3/13/1939
Sedgwick, Kyra	New York, NY	8/19/1965
Seehorn, Rhea	Norfolk, VA	5/12/1972
Segel, Jason	Los Angeles, CA	1/18/1980

Name	Birthplace	Birthdate
Seidelman, Susan	Abington, PA	12/11/1952
Seinfeld, Jerry	Brooklyn, NY	4/29/1954
Sellecca, Connie	Bronx, NY	5/25/1955
Selleck, Tom	Detroit, MI	1/29/1945
Severinsen, Doc	Arlington, OR.	7/7/1927
Sevigny, Chloë	Springfield, MA	11/18/1974
Sewell, Rufus	Twickenham, Middlesex,	
	England, UK	10/29/1967
Seyfried, Amanda	Allentown, PA	12/3/1985
Seymour, Jane	Hillingdon, England, UK	2/15/1951
Shackelford, Ted	Oklahoma City, OK	6/23/1946
Shaffer, Paul	Thunder Bay, ON,	
	Canada	11/28/1949
Shakira (Mebarak Ripoll)	Barranquilla, Colombia	2/2/1977
Shalhoub, Tony	Green Bay, WI	10/9/1953
Shannon, Molly	Shaker Heights, OH.	9/16/1964
Shatner, William	Montréal, QC, Canada	3/22/1931
Shaughnessy, Charles	London, England, UK	2/9/1955
Shaw, Fiona	Cork, Ireland	7/10/1958
Shawkat, Alia	Riverside, CA.	4/18/1989
Shea, John	North Conway, NH.	4/14/1949
Shearer, Harry	Los Angeles, CA	12/23/1943
Sheedy, Ally	New York, NY	6/13/1962
Sheen, Charlie	Los Angeles, CA	9/3/1965
Sheen, Martin	Dayton, OH	8/3/1940
Sheen, Michael	Newport, Wales, UK	2/5/1969
Sheeran, Ed	Hebden Bridge, West	
	Yorkshire, Eng., UK	2/17/1991
Sheindlin, Judy	Brooklyn, NY	10/21/1942
Shelton, Blake	Ada, OK	6/18/1976
Shepherd, Cybill	Memphis, TN.	2/18/1950
Shepherd, Sherri	Chicago, IL	4/22/1967
Sheridan, Nicollette	Worthing, England, UK	11/21/1963
Shields, Brooke	New York, NY	5/31/1965
Shire, Talia	Lake Success, NY	4/25/1946
Short, Martin	Hamilton, ON, Canada.	3/26/1950
Shortz, Will	Crawfordsville, IN.	8/26/1952
Show, Grant	Detroit, MI	2/27/1962
Shue, Andrew	South Orange, NJ	2/20/1967
Shue, Elisabeth	Wilmington, DE	10/6/1963
Shyamalan, M. Night.	Pondicherry, India	8/6/1970
Sidibe, Gabourey	Brooklyn, NY	5/6/1983
Sigler, Jamie-Lynn	Jericho, NY	5/15/1981
Sikking, James B.	Los Angeles, CA	3/5/1934
Silverman, Jonathan	Beverly Hills, CA	8/5/1966
Silverman, Sarah	Bedford, NH.	12/1/1970
Silverstone, Alicia	San Francisco, CA.	10/4/1976
Simmons, Gene	Haifa, Israel	8/25/1949
Simmons, Henry	Stamford, CT.	7/1/1970
Simmons, Richard	New Orleans, LA.	7/12/1948
Simon, Carly	New York, NY	6/25/1945
Simon, Paul	Newark, NJ	10/13/1941
Simpson, Ashlee	Waco, TX.	10/3/1984
Simpson, Jessica	Abilene, TX	7/10/1980
Sinatra, Nancy	Jersey City, NJ.	6/8/1940
Sinbad	Benton Harbor, MI	11/10/1956
Sinise, Gary	Blue Island, IL	3/17/1955
Sisto, Jeremy	Grass Valley, CA	10/6/1974
Skarsgard, Alexander	Stockholm, Sweden.	8/25/1976
Skarsgard, Stellan	Gothenburg, Sweden.	6/13/1951
Skerritt, Tom	Detroit, MI	8/25/1933
Slater, Christian	New York, NY	8/18/1969
Slater, Helen	Massapequa, NY.	12/15/1963
Slattery, John	Boston, MA	8/13/1962
Slezak, Erika	Hollywood, CA.	8/5/1946
Slick, Grace	Evanston, IL	10/30/1939
Smart, Jean	Seattle, WA.	9/13/1951
Smirnoff, Karina	Kharkiv, Ukraine	1/2/1978
Smirnoff, Yakov.	Odessa, Ukraine	1/24/1951
Smith, Allison	New York, NY	12/9/1969
Smith, Jaclyn	Houston, TX	10/26/1945
Smith, Jaden	Malibu, CA.	7/8/1998
Smith, Kevin	Red Bank, NJ	8/2/1970
Smith, Lois	Topeka, KS	11/3/1930
Smith, Maggie	Ilford, England, UK	12/28/1934
Smith, Patti	Chicago, IL	12/30/1946
Smith, Robert	Blackpool, England, UK.	4/21/1959
Smith, Sam	London, England, UK	5/19/1992
Smith, Will	Philadelphia, PA	9/25/1968
Smith, Willow	Los Angeles, CA	10/31/2000
Smits, Jimmy	Brooklyn, NY	7/9/1955
Smothers, Dick	Governor's Island, NY	11/20/1938
Smothers, Tom	Governor's Island, NY	2/2/1937
Smulders, Cobie	Vancouver, BC, Canada.	4/3/1982
Snipes, Wesley	Orlando, FL	7/31/1962
Snooki (Nicole Polizzi)	Santiago, Chile	11/23/1987
Snoop Dogg	Long Beach, CA	10/20/1971
Soderbergh, Steven	Atlanta, GA	1/14/1963
Soloway, Joey	Chicago, IL	9/26/1965

Name	Birthplace	Birthdate
Somerhalder, Ian	Covington, LA	12/8/1978
Sommer, Elke	Berlin, Germany	11/5/1940
Sorbo, Kevin	Mound, MN	9/24/1958
Sorkin, Aaron	New York, NY	6/9/1961
Sorvino, Mira	Tenafly, NJ.	9/28/1967
Soul, David	Chicago, IL	8/28/1943
Spacek, Sissy	Quitman, TX	12/25/1949
Spacey, Kevin	South Orange, NJ	7/26/1959
Spade, David	Birmingham, MI	7/22/1964
Spader, James	Boston, MA	2/7/1960
Spalding, Esperanza	Portland, OR	10/18/1984
Spano, Joe	San Francisco, CA	7/7/1946
Spears, Britney	Kentwood, LA	12/2/1981
Spears, Jamie-Lynn	McComb, MS.	4/4/1991
Spelling, Tori	Los Angeles, CA	5/16/1973
Spencer, Octavia	Montgomery, AL	5/25/1972
Spielberg, Steven	Cincinnati, OH.	12/18/1946
Spiner, Brent	Houston, TX	2/2/1949
Springfield, Rick	Sydney, NSW, Australia.	8/23/1949
Springsteen, Bruce	Long Branch, NJ	9/23/1949
Spurlock, Morgan	Parksburg, WV.	11/7/1970
Stahl, Nick	Harlingen, TX	12/5/1979
Stallone, Sylvester	New York, NY	7/6/1946
Stamos, John	Cypress, CA	8/19/1963
Stamp, Terence	Stepney, England, UK	7/22/1938
Staples, Mavis	Chicago, IL	7/10/1939
Stapleton, Chris	Lexington, KY	4/15/1978
Starr, Ringo	Liverpool, England, UK	7/7/1940
Statham, Jason	Shirebrook, England, UK	7/26/1967
Steenburgen, Mary	Newport, AR	2/8/1953
Stefani, Gwen	Fullterton, CA.	10/3/1969
Stein, Ben	Washington, DC	11/25/1944
Stern, Daniel	Bethesda, MD	8/28/1957
Stern, Howard	Roosevelt, NY	1/12/1954
Sternhagen, Frances	Washington, DC	1/13/1930
Stevens, Andrew	Memphis, TN.	6/10/1955
Stevens, Cat (Yusef Islam)	London, England, UK	7/21/1948
Stevens, Connie	Brooklyn, NY	8/8/1938
Stevenson, Parker	Philadelphia, PA	6/4/1952
Stewart, French	Albuquerque, NM.	2/20/1964
Stewart, Jon	New York, NY	11/28/1962
Stewart, Kristen	Los Angeles, CA	4/9/1990
Stewart, Patrick	Mirfield, England, UK.	7/13/1940
Stewart, Rod	London, England, UK	1/10/1945
Stiles, Julia	New York, NY	3/28/1981
Stiller, Ben	New York, NY	11/30/1965
Stills, Stephen	Dallas, TX	1/3/1945
Sting	Newcastle upon Tyne, England, UK	10/2/1951
Stipe, Michael	Decatur, GA.	1/4/1960
Stoltz, Eric	Whittier, CA	9/30/1961
Stone, Dee Wallace	Kansas City, KS.	12/14/1948
Stone, Emma	Scottsdale, AZ	11/6/1988
Stone, Oliver	New York, NY	9/15/1946
Stone, Sharon	Meadville, PA.	3/10/1958
Stonestreet, Eric	Kansas City, KS.	9/9/1971
Stookey, Paul	Baltimore, MD	12/30/1937
Stowe, Madeleine	Eagle Rock, CA	8/18/1958
Strahan, Michael	Houston, TX	11/21/1971
Strait, George	Pearsall, TX.	5/18/1952
Strasser, Robin	New York, NY	5/7/1945
Strathairn, David	San Francisco, CA.	1/26/1949
Strauss, Peter	Croton-on-Hudson, NY	2/20/1947
Streep, Meryl	Summit, NJ	6/22/1949
Streisand, Barbra	Brooklyn, NY	4/24/1942
Stringfield, Sherry	Colorado Springs, CO	6/24/1967
Stroman, Susan	Wilmington, DE	10/17/1954
Strong, Jeremy	Boston, MA	12/25/1978
Struthers, Sally	Portland, OR	7/28/1948
Styles, Harry	Holmes Chapel, Cheshire, Eng., UK	2/1/1994
Suchet, David	London, England, UK	5/2/1946
Sudeikis, Jason	Fairfax, VA.	9/18/1975
Sullivan, Susan	New York, NY	11/18/1942
Sunjata, Daniel	Evanston, IL	12/30/1971
Sutherland, Donald	St. John, NB, Canada	7/17/1934
Sutherland, Kiefer	London, England, UK	12/21/1966
Suvari, Mena	Newport, RI	2/9/1979
Swank, Hilary	Lincoln, NE	7/30/1974
Swift, Taylor	Wyomissing, PA.	12/13/1989
Swinton, Tilda	London, England, UK	11/5/1960
Swit, Loretta	Passaic, NJ	11/4/1937
Sykes, Wanda	Portsmouth, VA	3/7/1964
Szmanda, Eric	Milwaukee, WI	7/24/1975
T, Mr.	Chicago, IL	5/21/1952
Takei, George	Los Angeles, CA	4/20/1937
Tamblyn, Amber	Santa Monica, CA	5/14/1983
Tamblyn, Russ	Los Angeles, CA	12/30/1934
Tambor, Jeffrey	San Francisco, CA	7/8/1944
Tarantino, Quentin	Knoxville, TN	3/27/1963
Tatum, Channing	Cullman, AL.	4/26/1980
Tautou, Audrey	Beaumont, France	8/9/1976?
Taylor, Buck	Hollywood, CA.	5/13/1938
Taylor, Holland	Philadelphia, PA	1/14/1943
Taylor, James	Boston, MA	3/12/1948
Taylor, Lili	Glencoe, IL.	2/20/1967
Taylor-Joy, Anya	Miami, FL	4/16/1996
Taymor, Julie	Newton, MA.	12/15/1952
Te Kanawa, Kiri	Gisborne, New Zealand	3/6/1944
Teigen, Chrissy	Delta, Utah	11/30/1985
Teller	Philadelphia, PA	2/14/1948
Tennant, David	Bathgate, West Lothian, Scotland, UK	4/18/1971
Tennant, Victoria	London, England, UK	9/30/1950
Tennille, Toni	Montgomery, AL	5/8/1940
Tesh, John	Garden City, NY.	7/9/1952
Tharp, Twyla	Portland, IN	7/1/1941
The Weeknd	Toronto, ON, Canada	2/16/1990
Theron, Charlize	Benoni, South Africa	8/7/1975
Thicke, Robin	Los Angeles, CA	3/10/1977
Thiessen, Tiffani	Long Beach, CA	1/23/1974
Thomas, Jonathan Taylor	Bethlehem, PA.	9/8/1981
Thomas, Marlo	Deerfield, MI	11/21/1937
Thomas, Michael Tilson	Hollywood, CA.	12/21/1944
Thomas, Philip Michael	Columbus, OH.	5/26/1949
Thomas, Richard	New York, NY	6/13/1951
Thomas, Sean Patrick	Wilmington, DE	12/17/1970
Thompson, Emma	London, England, UK	4/15/1959
Thompson, Jack	Sydney, NSW, Australia	8/31/1940
Thompson, Kenan	Atlanta, GA	5/10/1978
Thompson, Lea.	Rochester, MN.	5/31/1961
Thorne-Smith, Courtney	San Francisco, CA.	11/8/1967
Thornton, Billy Bob	Hot Springs, AR.	8/4/1955
Thurman, Uma	Boston, MA	4/29/1970
Tiegs, Cheryl	Breckenridge, MN	9/25/1947
Tierney, Maura	Boston, MA.	2/3/1965
Tilly, Jennifer	Harbor City, CA	9/16/1958
Tilly, Meg.	Long Beach, CA	2/14/1960
Timberlake, Justin.	Memphis, TN.	1/31/1981
Tisdale, Ashley	West Deal, NJ	7/2/1985
Tomei, Marisa	Brooklyn, NY	12/4/1964
Tomlin, Lily	Detroit, MI	9/1/1939
Tonioli, Bruno	Ferrara, Italy	11/25/1955
Tovey, Russell	Billericay, Essex, Eng., UK	11/14/1981
Townsend, Robert	Chicago, IL	2/6/1957
Townshend, Peter.	Chiswick, England, UK	5/19/1945
Travanti, Daniel J.	Kenosha, WI	3/7/1940
Travis, Nancy	Astoria, Queens, NY	9/21/1961
Travis, Randy	Marshville, NC.	5/4/1959
Travolta, John	Englewood, NJ	2/18/1954
Trejo, Danny	Los Angeles, CA	5/16/1944
Tripplehorn, Jean	Tulsa, OK	6/10/1963
Tritt, Travis	Marietta, GA	2/9/1963
Tucci, Stanley	Peekskill, NY	1/11/1960
Tucker, Chris.	Decatur, GA.	8/31/1972
Tucker, Michael	Baltimore, MD	2/6/1944
Tucker, Tanya	Seminole, TX.	10/10/1958
Tune, Tommy	Wichita Falls, TX	2/28/1939
Turlington, Christy	Walnut Creek, CA	1/2/1969
Turner, Janine	Lincoln, NE	12/6/1962
Turner, Kathleen	Springfield, MO	6/19/1954
Turner, Sophie	Northampton, Eng., UK	2/21/1996
Turturro, John	Brooklyn, NY	2/28/1957
Tveit, Aaron	Middletown, NY	10/21/1983
Twain, Shania	Windsor, ON, Canada	8/28/1965
Twiggy (Lawson)	London, England, UK	9/19/1949
Tyler, Liv	New York, NY	7/1/1977
Tyler, Steven	Yonkers, NY	3/26/1948
Uecker, Bob	Milwaukee, WI.	1/26/1934
Uggams, Leslie	New York, NY	5/25/1943
Ullman, Tracey	Slough, England, UK.	12/30/1959
Ullmann, Liv	Tokyo, Japan.	12/16/1938
Ulrich, Skeet	Lynchburg, VA	1/20/1970
Underwood, Blair	Tacoma, WA	8/25/1964
Underwood, Carrie	Muskogee, OK.	3/10/1983
Urban, Keith	Whangarei, North Island, New Zealand	10/26/1967
Urie, Michael	Dallas, TX	8/8/1980
Usher (Raymond IV)	Dallas, TX	10/14/1978
Vaccaro, Brenda	Brooklyn, NY	11/18/1939

Name	Birthplace	Birthdate
Valley, Mark	Ogdensburg, NY	12/24/1964
Valli, Frankie	Newark, NJ	5/3/1934
Van Ark, Joan	New York, NY	6/16/1943
Van Damme, Jean-Claude	Brussels, Belgium	10/18/1960
Van Der Beek, James	Cheshire, CT	3/8/1977
Van Doren, Mamie	Rowena, SD	2/6/1931
Van Dyke, Dick	West Plains, MO	12/13/1925
Van Peebles, Mario	Mexico City, Mexico	1/15/1957
Van Sant, Gus	Louisville, KY	7/24/1952
Van Zandt, Steven	Winthrop, MA	11/22/1950
VanCamp, Emily	Port Perry, ON, Canada	5/12/1986
Vance, Courtney B.	Detroit, MI	3/12/1960
Vardalos, Nia	Winnipeg, MB, Canada	9/24/1962
Vaughn, Vince	Minneapolis, MN	3/28/1970
Vedder, Eddie	Evanston, IL	12/23/1964
Ventimiglia, Milo	Anaheim, CA	7/8/1977
Vereen, Ben	Miami, FL	10/10/1946
Vergara, Sofía	Barranquilla, Colombia	7/10/1972
Vieira, Meredith	Providence, RI	12/30/1953
Vikander, Alicia	Gothenburg, Sweden	10/3/1988
Villella, Edward	Long Island, NY	10/1/1936
Vinton, Bobby	Canonsburg, PA	4/16/1935
Visnjic, Goran	Sibenik, Yugo. (Croatia)	9/9/1972
Vitale, Dick	East Rutherford, NJ	6/9/1939
Voight, Jon	Yonkers, NY	12/29/1938
Von Stade, Frederica	Somerville, NJ	6/1/1945
Von Trier, Lars	Copenhagen, Denmark	4/30/1956
Waddingham, Hannah	London, England, UK	7/28/1974
Wagner, Jack	Washington, MO	10/3/1959
Wagner, Lindsay	Los Angeles, CA	6/22/1949
Wagner, Robert	Detroit, MI	2/10/1930
Wahl, Ken	Chicago, IL	10/31/1954
Wahlberg, Donnie	Dorchester, MA	8/17/1969
Wahlberg, Mark	Dorchester, MA	6/5/1971
Waititi, Taika	Raukokore, New Zealand	8/16/1975
Waits, Tom	Pomona, CA	12/7/1949
Walden, Robert	New York, NY	9/25/1943
Walken, Christopher	Astoria, Queens, NY	3/31/1943
Waller-Bridge, Phoebe	London, England, UK	7/14/1985
Wallis, Quvenzhané	Houma, LA	8/23/2008
Walsh, Kate	San Jose, CA	10/13/1967
Waltz, Christoph	Vienna, Austria	10/4/1956
Warburton, Patrick	Paterson, NJ	11/14/1964
Ward, Fred	San Diego, CA	12/30/1942
Ward, Sela	Meridian, MS	7/11/1956
Warfield, Marsha	Chicago, IL	3/5/1954
Warner, Malcolm-Jamal	Jersey City, NJ	8/18/1970
Warren, Lesley Ann	New York, NY	8/16/1946
Warwick, Dionne	East Orange, NJ	12/12/1940
Washington, Denzel	Mt. Vernon, NY	12/28/1954
Washington, Isaiah	Houston, TX	8/3/1963
Washington, Kerry	Bronx, NY	1/31/1977
Wasikowska, Mia	Canberra, Australia	10/14/1989
Watanabe, Ken	Koide, Niigata, Japan	10/21/1959
Waters, John	Baltimore, MD	4/22/1946
Waters, Roger	Great Bookham, Eng., UK	9/6/1943
Waterston, Sam	Cambridge, MA	11/15/1940
Watson, Emily	London, England, UK	1/14/1967
Watson, Emma	Paris, France	4/15/1990
Watts, Naomi	Shoreham, England, UK	9/28/1968
Wayans, Damon	New York, NY	9/4/1960
Wayans, Keenen Ivory	Brooklyn, NY	6/8/1958
Wayans, Marlon	New York, NY	7/23/1972
Wayans, Shawn	New York, NY	1/19/1971
Weathers, Carl	New Orleans, LA	1/14/1948
Weaver, Sigourney	New York, NY	10/8/1949
Weir, Peter	Sydney, NSW, Australia	8/21/1944
Weisz, Rachel	London, England, UK	3/7/1971
Weld, Tuesday	New York, NY	8/27/1943
Weller, Peter	Stevens Point, WI	6/24/1947
Welling, Tom	Putnam Valley, NY	4/26/1977
Wendt, George	Chicago, IL	10/17/1948
Wentz, Pete	Wilmette, IL	6/5/1979
West, Dominic	Sheffield, Eng., UK	10/15/1969
West, Kanye	Atlanta, GA	6/8/1977
West, Shane	Baton Rouge, LA	6/10/1978
Wettig, Patricia	Cincinnati, OH	12/4/1951
Whalley, Joanne	Manchester, England, UK	8/25/1964
Wheaton, Wil	Burbank, CA	7/29/1972
Whishaw, Ben	Clifton, Eng., UK	10/14/1980
Whitaker, Forest	Longview, TX	7/15/1961
White, Jack	Detroit, MI	7/9/1975
White, Jaleel	Pasadena, CA	11/27/1976
White, Jeremy Allen	Brooklyn, NY	2/17/1991
White, Vanna	N. Myrtle Beach, SC	2/18/1957
Whitford, Bradley	Madison, WI	10/10/1959
Whittaker, Jodie	Skelmanthorpe, West Yorkshire, England, UK	6/17/1982
Wiest, Dianne	Kansas City, MO	3/28/1948
Wiig, Kristen	Canandaigua, NY	8/22/1973
Wilde, Olivia	New York, NY	3/10/1984
Wiley, Samira	Washington, DC	4/15/1987
Wilkinson, Tom	Leeds, England, UK	12/12/1948
Williams, Armstrong	Marion, SC	2/5/1959
Williams, Barry	Santa Monica, CA	9/30/1954
Williams, Billy Dee	New York, NY	4/6/1937
Williams, Hal	Columbus, OH	12/14/1938
Williams, Hank, Jr.	Shreveport, LA	5/26/1949
Williams, Jesse	Chicago, IL	8/5/1981
Williams, JoBeth	Houston, TX	12/6/1948
Williams, Lucinda	Lake Charles, LA	1/26/1953
Williams, Maisie	Bristol, Eng., UK	4/15/1997
Williams, Michelle	Kalispell, MT	9/9/1980
Williams, Montel	Baltimore, MD	7/3/1956
Williams, Paul	Omaha, NE	9/19/1940
Williams, Pharrell	Virginia Beach, VA	4/5/1973
Williams, Vanessa	Millwood, NY	3/18/1963
Williamson, Kevin	New Bern, NC	3/14/1965
Willis, Bruce	Idar-Oberstein, W. Germany	3/19/1955
Wilmore, Larry	Los Angeles, CA	10/30/1961
Wilson, Brian	Inglewood, CA	6/20/1942
Wilson, Cassandra	Jackson, MS	12/4/1955
Wilson, Chandra	Houston, TX	8/27/1969
Wilson, Demond	Valdosta, GA	10/13/1946
Wilson, Luke	Dallas, TX	9/21/1971
Wilson, Owen	Dallas, TX	11/18/1968
Wilson, Rainn	Seattle, WA	1/20/1966
Wilson, Rebel	Sydney, NSW, Australia	2/3/1980
Winfrey, Oprah	Kosciusko, MS	1/29/1954
Winger, Debra	Cleveland, OH	5/16/1955
Winkler, Henry	New York, NY	10/30/1945
Winningham, Mare	Phoenix, AZ	5/16/1959
Winslet, Kate	Reading, England, UK	10/5/1975
Winwood, Steve	Birmingham, Eng., UK	5/12/1948
Witherspoon, Reese	New Orleans, LA	3/22/1976
Witt, Alicia	Worcester, MA	8/21/1975
Wolf, Scott	Boston, MA	6/4/1968
Wonder, Stevie	Saginaw, MI	5/13/1950
Wong, Ali	San Francisco, CA	4/19/1982
Wong, B. D.	San Francisco, CA	10/24/1962
Wong, Faye	Beijing, China	8/8/1969
Woo, John	Guangzhou, China	5/1/1946
Wood, Elijah	Cedar Rapids, IA	1/28/1981
Wood, Evan Rachel	Raleigh, NC	9/7/1987
Woodard, Alfre	Tulsa, OK	11/8/1952
Woodley, Shailene	Simi Valley, CA	11/15/1991
Woods, James	Vernal, UT	4/18/1947
Woodward, Joanne	Thomasville, GA	2/27/1930
Wopat, Tom	Lodi, WI	9/9/1951
Worthington, Sam	Godalming, Surrey, Eng., UK	8/2/1976
Wright, Jeffrey	Washington, DC	12/7/1965
Wright, Robin	Dallas, TX	4/8/1966
Wright, Steven	New York, NY	12/6/1955
Wu, Constance	Richmond, VA	3/22/1982
Wyle, Noah	Hollywood, CA	6/4/1971
Wyman, Bill	London, England, UK	10/24/1936
Yang, Bowen	Brisbane, Qld., Australia	11/6/1990
Yankovic, Weird Al	Lynwood, CA	10/23/1959
Yanni (Chrysomallis)	Kalamata, Greece	11/14/1954
Yarrow, Peter	New York, NY	5/31/1938
Yearwood, Trisha	Monticello, GA	9/19/1964
Yeoh, Michelle	Ipoh, Malaysia	8/6/1962
Yeun, Steven	Seoul, South Korea	12/21/1983
Yoakam, Dwight	Pikesville, KY	10/23/1956
York, Michael	Fulmer, England, UK	3/27/1942
Young, Burt	New York, NY	4/30/1940
Young, Neil	Toronto, ON, Canada	11/12/1945
Young, Sean	Louisville, KY	11/20/1959
Youssef, Ramy	Queens, NY	3/26/1991
Zane, Billy	Chicago, IL	2/24/1966
Zellweger, Renée	Katy, TX	4/25/1969
Zemeckis, Robert	Chicago, IL	5/14/1952
Zendaya	Oakland, CA	9/1/1996
Zerbe, Anthony	Long Beach, CA	5/20/1936
Zeta-Jones, Catherine	Swansea, Wales, UK	9/25/1969
Zhang Ziyi	Beijing, China	2/9/1979
Zhao, Chloé	Beijing, China	3/31/1982
Zimbalist, Stephanie	New York, NY	10/8/1956
Zimmer, Constance	Seattle, WA	10/11/1970
Zimmer, Kim	Grand Rapids, MI	2/2/1955
Zukerman, Pinchas	Tel Aviv, Israel	7/16/1948
Zuniga, Daphne	Berkeley, CA	10/28/1962

Entertainment Personalities of the Past

See also other lists for some deceased entertainers not included here.

Name	Born	Died
Aaliyah (Haughton)	1979	2001
Abbado, Claudio	1933	2014
Abbott, Bud	1895	1974
Abbott, George	1887	1995
Acuff, Roy	1903	1992
Adams, Don	1923	2005
Adams, Edie	1927	2008
Adams, Joey	1911	1999
Adams, Maude	1872	1953
Adler, Jacob P.	1855	1926
Adler, Stella	1902	1992
Adoree, Renee	1898	1933
Agar, John	1921	2002
Aherne, Brian	1902	1986
Aiello, Danny	1933	2019
Ailey, Alvin	1931	1989
Akins, Claude	1918	1994
Albert, Eddie	1906	2005
Albertson, Jack	1907	1981
Alda, Robert	1914	1986
Allen, Fred	1894	1956
Allen, Gracie	1906	1964
Allen, Mel	1913	1996
Allen, Peter	1944	1992
Allen, Steve	1921	2000
Alley, Kirstie	1951	2022
Allgood, Sara	1883	1950
Allman, Gregg	1947	2017
Allyson, June	1917	2006
Altman, Robert	1925	2006
Ameche, Don	1908	1993
Ames, Ed	1927	2023
Ames, Leon	1903	1993
Amsterdam, Morey	1908	1996
Anderson, G. M. "Bronco Billy"	1882	1971
Anderson, Harry	1952	2018
Anderson, Judith	1897	1992
Anderson, Louie	1953	2022
Anderson, Marian	1897	1993
Anderson, Richard	1926	2017
Andersson, Bibi	1935	2019
Andre the Giant	1946	1993
Andrews, Dana	1909	1992
Andrews, Laverne	1913	1967
Andrews, Maxene	1916	1995
Andrews, Patty	1918	2013
Angeli, Pier	1932	1971
Antonioni, Michelangelo	1912	2007
Arbuckle, Fatty (Roscoe)	1887	1933
Archerd, Army	1922	2009
Arden, Eve	1908	1990
Arkin, Alan	1934	2023
Arlen, Richard	1900	1976
Arliss, George	1868	1946
Armstrong, Louis	1901	1971
Arnaz, Desi	1917	1986
Arness, James	1923	2011
Arnold, Eddy	1918	2008
Arnold, Edward	1890	1956
Arquette, Cliff	1905	1974
Arthur, Beatrice	1922	2009
Arthur, Jean	1900	1991
Arzner, Dorothy	1897	1979
Ashcroft, Peggy	1907	1991
Asner, Ed	1929	2021
Astaire, Fred	1899	1987
Astor, Mary	1906	1987
Atkins, Chet	1924	2001
Attenborough, Richard	1923	2014
Atwill, Lionel	1885	1946
Auberjonois, René	1940	2019
Autry, Gene	1907	1998
Avildsen, John	1935	2017
Ayres, Lew	1908	1996
Aznavour, Charles	1924	2018
Bacall, Lauren	1924	2014
Backus, Jim	1913	1989
Bailey, Pearl	1918	1990
Bain, Conrad	1923	2013
Bainter, Fay	1892	1968
Baker, Josephine	1906	1975
Balanchine, George	1904	1983
Ball, Lucille	1911	1989
Ballard, Kaye	1925	2019
Balsam, Martin	1919	1996
Bancroft, Anne	1931	2005
Bankhead, Tallulah	1902	1968
Bara, Theda	1885?	1955
Barker, Bob	1923	2023
Barnum, Phineas T.	1810	1891
Barrett, Syd	1946	2006
Barry, Gene	1919	2009
Barrymore, Ethel	1879	1959
Barrymore, John	1882	1942
Barrymore, Lionel	1878	1954
Barrymore, Maurice	1848	1905
Barthelmess, Richard	1895	1963
Bartholomew, Freddie	1924	1992
Barty, Billy	1924	2000
Basehart, Richard	1914	1984
Basie, Count	1904	1984
Bates, Alan	1934	2003
Bavier, Frances	1902	1989
Baxter, Anne	1923	1985
Baxter, Warner	1889	1951
Beatty, Ned	1937	2021
Beaumont, Hugh	1909	1982
Beavers, Louise	1902	1962
Beck, Jeff	1944	2023
Beery, Noah, Jr.	1913	1994
Beery, Noah, Sr.	1884	1946
Beery, Wallace	1885	1949
Begley, Ed	1901	1970
Bel Geddes, Barbara	1922	2005
Belafonte, Harry	1927	2023
Bell, Art	1945	2018
Bellamy, Ralph	1904	1991
Belmondo, Jean-Paul	1933	2021
Belushi, John	1949	1982
Belzer, Richard	1944	2023
Benaderet, Bea	1906	1968
Bendix, William	1906	1964
Bennett, Constance	1904	1965
Bennett, Joan	1910	1990
Bennett, Michael	1943	1987
Bennett, Tony	1926	2023
Benny, Jack	1894	1974
Berg, Gertrude	1899	1966
Bergen, Edgar	1903	1978
Bergen, Polly	1930	2014
Bergman, Ingmar	1918	2007
Bergman, Ingrid	1915	1982
Berkeley, Busby	1895	1976
Berle, Milton	1908	2002
Berlin, Irving	1888	1989
Berman, Shelley	1925	2017
Bernardi, Herschel	1923	1986
Bernhardt, Sarah	1844	1923
Bernstein, Leonard	1918	1990
Berry, Chuck	1926	2017
Berry, Ken	1933	2018
Bertolucci, Bernardo	1941	2018
Bessell, Ted	1939	1996
Bickford, Charles	1889	1967
Big Bopper, The	1930	1959
Bikel, Theodore	1924	2015
Billingsley, Barbara	1915	2010
Bing, Rudolf	1902	1997
Bishop, Joey	1918	2007
Bitzer, Billy	1872	1944
Bixby, Bill	1934	1993
Black, Karen	1939	2013
Blackstone, Harry, Jr.	1934	1997
Blackstone, Harry, Sr.	1885	1965
Blaine, Vivian	1921	1995
Blake, Amanda	1931	1989
Blake, Eubie	1887	1983
Blake, Robert	1933	2023
Blanc, Mel	1908	1989
Blocker, Dan	1928	1972
Blondell, Joan	1909	1979
Blondin, Charles	1824	1897
Blyden, Larry	1925	1975
Bogarde, Dirk	1921	1999
Bogart, Humphrey	1899	1957
Bogdanovich, Peter	1939	2022
Boland, Mary	1880	1965
Boles, John	1895	1969
Bolger, Ray	1904	1987
Bologna, Joseph	1934	2017
Bond, Ward	1903	1960
Bondi, Beulah	1888	1981
Bono, Sonny	1935	1998
Boone, Richard	1917	1981
Booth, Edwin	1833	1893
Booth, John Wilkes	1838	1865
Booth, Junius Brutus	1796	1852
Booth, Shirley	1898	1992
Borge, Victor	1909	2000
Borgnine, Ernest	1917	2012
Borzage, Frank	1893	1962
Bosco, Philip	1930	2018
Boseman, Chadwick	1976	2020
Bosley, Tom	1927	2010
Bourdain, Anthony	1956	2018
Bow, Clara	1905	1965
Bowes, Maj. Edward	1874	1946
Bowie, David	1947	2016
Bowman, Lee	1914	1979
Boxcar Willie	1931	1999
Boyd, Stephen	1928	1977
Boyd, William	1898	1972
Boyer, Charles	1899	1978
Boyle, Peter	1935	2006
Bracken, Eddie	1915	2002
Brady, Alice	1892	1939
Brando, Marlon	1924	2004
Branigan, Laura	1957	2004
Brazzi, Rossano	1916	1994
Brennan, Eileen	1932	2013
Brennan, Walter	1894	1974
Brenner, David	1936	2014
Brent, George	1904	1979
Brett, Jeremy	1935	1995
Brewer, Teresa	1931	2007
Brice, Fanny	1891	1951
Bridges, Lloyd	1913	1998
Brimley, Wilford	1934	2020
Broderick, Helen	1891	1959
Bronson, Charles	1921	2003
Brooks, Foster	1912	2001
Brooks, Louise	1906	1985
Brown, Clarence	1890	1987
Brown, James	1933	2006
Brown, Joe E.	1892	1973
Brown, Johnny Mack	1904	1974
Brown, Les	1912	2001
Browne, Roscoe Lee	1925	2007
Browning, Tod	1882	1962
Brubeck, Dave	1920	2012
Bruce, Lenny	1925	1966
Bruce, Nigel	1895	1953
Bruce, Virginia	1910	1982
Brynner, Yul	1915	1985
Buchanan, Edgar	1903	1979
Buffett, Jimmy	1946	2023
Bumbry, Grace	1937	2023
Buñuel, Luis	1900	1983
Buono, Victor	1938	1982
Burke, Billie	1885	1970
Burnette, Smiley	1911	1967
Burns, George	1896	1996
Burr, Raymond	1917	1993
Burton, Richard	1925	1984
Busch, Mae	1897	1946
Bushman, Francis X.	1883	1966
Buttons, Red	1919	2006
Byington, Spring	1893	1971
Caan, James	1940	2022
Caballé, Montserrat	1933	2018
Cabot, Bruce	1904	1972
Cabot, Sebastian	1918	1977
Caesar, Sid	1922	2014
Cagney, James	1899	1986
Caldwell, Sarah	1924	2006
Caldwell, Zoe	1933	2020
Calhern, Louis	1895	1956
Calhoun, Rory	1922	1999
Callas, Charlie	1927	2011
Callas, Maria	1923	1977
Calloway, Cab	1907	1994
Cambridge, Godfrey	1933	1976
Campanella, Joseph	1924	2018
Campbell, Glen	1936	2017
Campbell, Mrs. Patrick	1865	1940
Candy, John	1950	1994
Canova, Judy	1916	1983
Cantinflas	1911	1993
Cantor, Eddie	1892	1964
Capra, Frank	1897	1991
Cara, Irene	1959	2022
Carey, Harry	1878	1947
Carey, Harry, Jr.	1921	2012
Carlin, George	1937	2008
Carlisle Hart, Kitty	1910	2007
Carney, Art	1918	2003
Carpenter, Karen	1950	1983
Carradine, David	1936	2009
Carradine, John	1906	1988
Carrillo, Leo	1880	1961
Carroll, Diahann	1935	2019
Carroll, Leo G.	1892	1972
Carroll, Madeleine	1906	1987
Carroll, Pat	1927	2022
Carson, Jack	1910	1963
Carson, Johnny	1925	2005
Carter, Benny	1907	2003
Carter, Dixie	1939	2010
Carter, Jack	1923	2015

Name	Born	Died
Carter, Nell	1948	2003
Caruso, Enrico	1873	1921
Casals, Pablo	1876	1973
Cash, Johnny	1932	2003
Cash, June Carter	1929	2003
Cass, Peggy	1924	1999
Cassavetes, John	1929	1989
Cassidy, David	1950	2017
Cassidy, Jack	1927	1976
Castle, Irene	1893	1969
Castle, Vernon	1887	1918
Champion, Gower	1919	1980
Chandler, Jeff	1918	1961
Chaney, Lon	1883	1930
Chaney, Lon, Jr.	1905	1973
Channing, Carol	1921	2019
Chapin, Harry	1942	1981
Chaplin, Charles	1889	1977
Chapman, Graham	1941	1989
Charisse, Cyd	1922	2008
Charles, Ray	1930	2004
Chase, Ilka	1905	1978
Chatterton, Ruth	1893	1961
Cherrill, Virginia	1908	1996
Chevalier, Maurice	1888	1972
Chiba, Sonny	1939	2021
Child, Julia	1912	2004
Christopher, William	1932	2016
Cimino, Michael	1939	2016
Clair, René	1898	1981
Clark, Dick	1929	2012
Clark, Roy	1933	2018
Clayburgh, Jill	1944	2010
Clayton, Jan	1917	1983
Clemons, Clarence	1942	2011
Cliburn, Van	1934	2013
Clift, Montgomery	1920	1966
Cline, Patsy	1932	1963
Clooney, Rosemary	1928	2002
Cobain, Kurt	1967	1994
Cobb, Lee J.	1911	1976
Coburn, Charles	1877	1961
Coburn, James	1928	2002
Coca, Imogene	1908	2001
Cocker, Joe	1944	2014
Coco, James	1930	1987
Cody, Buffalo Bill	1846	1917
Cody, Iron Eyes	1907	1999
Cohan, George M.	1878	1942
Cohen, Leonard	1934	2016
Cohen, Myron	1902	1986
Colbert, Claudette	1903	1996
Cole, Nat "King"	1919	1965
Cole, Natalie	1950	2015
Coleman, Gary	1968	2010
Coleman, Ornette	1930	2015
Collins, Gary	1938	2012
Collins, Ray	1890	1965
Colman, Ronald	1891	1958
Columbo, Russ	1908	1934
Comden, Betty	1917	2006
Como, Perry	1912	2001
Conklin, Chester	1888	1971
Connery, Sean	1930	2020
Conniff, Ray	1916	2002
Connors, Chuck	1921	1992
Connors, Mike	1925	2017
Conrad, Robert	1935	2020
Conrad, William	1920	1994
Conried, Hans	1917	1982
Constantine, Michael	1927	2021
Conte, Richard	1911	1975
Convy, Bert	1933	1991
Conway, Tim	1933	2019
Coogan, Jackie	1914	1984
Cook, Barbara	1927	2017
Cook, Elisha, Jr.	1904	1995
Cooke, Alistair	1908	2004
Cooke, Sam	1931	1964
Coolio	1963	2022
Cooper, Gary	1901	1961
Cooper, Gladys	1888	1971
Cooper, Jackie	1922	2011
Copland, Aaron	1900	1990
Corby, Ellen	1913	1999
Corea, Chick	1941	2021
Corelli, Franco	1921	2003
Corey, Jeff	1914	2002
Corio, Ann	1914	1999
Corley, Pat	1930	2006
Cornelius, Don	1936	2012
Cornell, Chris	1964	2017
Cornell, Katharine	1893	1974
Correll, Charles	1890	1972
Costello, Dolores	1905	1979
Costello, Lou	1906	1959
Cotten, Joseph	1905	1994
Coward, Noel	1899	1973
Cox, Wally	1924	1973
Crabbe, Buster	1908	1983
Crain, Jeanne	1925	2003
Crane, Bob	1928	1978
Craven, Wes	1939	2015
Crawford, Broderick	1911	1986
Crawford, Joan	1904	1977
Crenna, Richard	1926	2003
Crews, Laura Hope	1880	1942
Crisp, Donald	1880	1974
Crisp, Quentin	1908	1999
Croce, Jim	1942	1973
Cronyn, Hume	1911	2003
Crosby, Bing	1903	1977
Crosby, David	1941	2023
Cross, Ben	1947	2020
Crothers, Scatman	1910	1986
Cruz, Celia	1925	2003
Cugat, Xavier	1900	1990
Cukor, George	1899	1983
Cullen, Bill	1920	1990
Culp, Robert	1930	2010
Cummings, Constance	1910	2005
Cummings, Robert	1908	1990
Curtis, Tony	1925	2010
Curtiz, Michael	1888	1962
Cushing, Peter	1913	1994
Da Silva, Howard	1909	1986
Dahl, Arlene	1925	2021
Dailey, Dan	1915	1978
Damone, Vic	1928	2018
Dandridge, Dorothy	1923	1965
Dangerfield, Rodney	1921	2004
Daniell, Henry	1894	1963
Daniels, Bebe	1901	1971
Daniels, Charlie	1936	2020
Darin, Bobby	1936	1973
Darnell, Linda	1923	1965
Darwell, Jane	1879	1967
Davenport, Harry	1866	1949
Davies, Marion	1897	1961
Davis, Ann B.	1926	2014
Davis, Bette	1908	1989
Davis, Joan	1907	1961
Davis, Mac	1942	2020
Davis, Ossie	1917	2005
Davis, Sammy, Jr.	1925	1990
Dawson, Richard	1932	2012
Day, Dennis	1917	1988
Day, Doris	1922	2019
Day, Laraine	1920	2007
De Carlo, Yvonne	1922	2007
De Havilland, Olivia	1916	2020
De Laurentiis, Dino	1919	2010
de Mille, Agnes	1905	1993
De Mille, Cecil B.	1881	1959
De Wilde, Brandon	1942	1972
De Wolfe, Billy	1907	1974
Dean, James	1931	1955
Dean, Jimmy	1928	2010
Dearie, Blossom	1924	2009
Dee, Frances	1907	2004
Dee, Ruby	1922	2014
Dee, Sandra	1942	2005
Defore, Don	1917	1993
DeFranco, Buddy	1923	2014
DeHaven, Gloria	1925	2016
Dekker, Albert	1905	1968
Del Rio, Dolores	1905	1983
DeLuise, Dom	1933	2009
Demarest, William	1892	1983
Demme, Jonathan	1944	2017
Dennehy, Brian	1938	2020
Dennis, Sandy	1937	1992
Denny, Reginald	1891	1967
Denver, Bob	1935	2005
Denver, John	1943	1997
Derek, John	1926	1998
DeSica, Vittorio	1901	1974
Devine, Andy	1905	1977
Dewhurst, Colleen	1924	1991
Diamond, Selma	1920	1985
Diddley, Bo	1928	2008
Dietrich, Marlene	1901	1992
Diller, Phyllis	1917	2012
Disney, Walt	1901	1966
Dix, Richard	1894	1949
Dmytryk, Edward	1908	1999
Dobson, Kevin	1943	2020
Domino, Fats	1928	2017
Donahue, Troy	1936	2001
Donat, Robert	1905	1958
Donen, Stanley	1924	2019
Donlevy, Brian	1901	1972
Dors, Diana	1931	1984
Dorsey, Jimmy	1904	1957
Dorsey, Tommy	1905	1956
Dotrice, Roy	1923	2017
Douglas, Kirk	1916	2020
Douglas, Melvyn	1901	1981
Dove, Billie	1900	1998
Dow, Tony	1945	2022
Downey, Morton, Jr.	1933	2001
Downs, Hugh	1921	2020
Doyle, David	1929	1997
Drake, Alfred	1914	1992
Draper, Ruth	1884	1956
Dressler, Marie	1869	1934
Drew, Ellen	1915	2003
Drew, Mrs. John	1820	1897
Duchin, Eddy	1909	1951
Duff, Howard	1917	1990
Duggan, Andrew	1923	1988
Dukakis, Olympia	1931	2021
Duke, Patty	1946	2016
Dumbrille, Douglass	1890	1974
Dumont, Margaret	1889	1965
Duncan, Isadora	1878	1927
Duncan, Michael Clarke	1957	2012
Dunham, Katherine	1910	2006
Dunn, James	1905	1967
Dunne, Irene	1898	1990
Dunnock, Mildred	1901	1991
Durante, Jimmy	1893	1980
Durbin, Deanna	1921	2013
Durning, Charles	1923	2012
Duryea, Dan	1907	1968
Duse, Eleanora	1858	1924
Dvorak, Ann	1912	1979
Dysart, Richard	1929	2015
Eagels, Jeanne	1894	1929
Ebert, Roger	1942	2013
Ebsen, Buddy	1908	2003
Eckstine, Billy	1914	1993
Eddy, Nelson	1901	1967
Edelman, Herb	1933	1996
Edwards, Blake	1922	2010
Edwards, Cliff	1895	1971
Edwards, Ralph	1913	2005
Edwards, Vince	1928	1996
Egan, Richard	1923	1987
Eisenstein, Sergei	1898	1948
Ekberg, Anita	1931	2015
Elam, Jack	1916	2003
Ellington, Duke	1899	1974
Elliot, Cass	1941	1974
Elliott, Bob	1923	2016
Elliott, Denholm	1922	1992
Elman, Mischa	1891	1967
Ephron, Nora	1941	2012
Evans, Dale	1912	2001
Evans, Edith	1888	1976
Evans, Maurice	1901	1989
Evans, Robert	1930	2019
Everett, Chad	1937	2012
Everly, Don	1937	2021
Everly, Phil	1939	2014
Ewell, Tom	1909	1994
Fabray, Nanette	1920	2018
Fairbanks, Douglas	1883	1939
Fairbanks, Douglas, Jr.	1909	2000
Falk, Peter	1927	2011
Farentino, James	1938	2012
Farina, Dennis	1944	2013
Farley, Chris	1964	1997
Farmer, Frances	1913	1970
Farnsworth, Richard	1920	2000
Farnum, Dustin	1874	1929
Farnum, William	1876	1953
Farrar, Geraldine	1882	1967
Farrell, Charles	1901	1990
Farrell, Eileen	1920	2002
Fassbinder, Rainer Werner	1946	1982

Name	Born	Died	Name	Born	Died	Name	Born	Died
Fawcett, Farrah	1947	2009	Gershwin, George	1898	1937	Hampton, Lionel	1908	2002
Faye, Alice	1915	1998	Getty, Estelle	1923	2008	Hardwicke, Cedric	1893	1964
Fazenda, Louise	1895	1962	Ghostley, Alice	1926	2007	Hardy, Oliver	1892	1957
Feld, Fritz	1900	1993	Gibb, Andy	1958	1988	Harlow, Jean	1911	1937
Feldman, Marty	1933	1982	Gibb, Maurice	1949	2003	Harper, Valerie	1939	2019
Fell, Norman	1924	1998	Gibb, Robin	1949	2012	Harrington, Pat, Jr.	1929	2016
Fellini, Federico	1920	1993	Gibson, Henry	1935	2009	Harris, Julie	1925	2013
Fenneman, George	1919	1997	Gibson, Hoot	1892	1962	Harris, Phil.	1904	1995
Ferrer, Jose	1912	1992	Gielgud, John	1904	2000	Harris, Richard	1930	2002
Ferrer, Mel.	1917	2008	Gifford, Frank	1930	2015	Harrison, George	1943	2001
Fetchit, Stepin	1898	1985	Gilbert, Billy	1894	1971	Harrison, Rex	1908	1990
Fiedler, Arthur	1894	1979	Gilbert, John	1895	1936	Hart, William S.	1864	1946
Fiedler, John	1925	2005	Gilberto, Astrud	1940	2023	Hartman, Phil	1948	1998
Fields, Gracie	1898	1979	Gilford, Jack	1907	1990	Harvey, Laurence	1928	1973
Fields, Totie	1930	1978	Gillespie, Dizzy	1917	1993	Harvey, Paul	1918	2009
Fields, W. C.	1879	1946	Gillette, William	1853	1937	Harwell, Ernie	1918	2010
Finch, Peter	1916	1977	Gilley, Mickey	1936	2022	Hatfield, Bobby	1940	2003
Fine, Larry	1902	1975	Gingold, Hermione	1897	1987	Hauer, Rutger	1944	2019
Finney, Albert.	1936	2019	Gish, Dorothy	1898	1968	Havens, Richie	1941	2013
Fisher, Carrie	1956	2016	Gish, Lillian	1893	1993	Havoc, June	1912	2010
Fisher, Eddie	1928	2010	Gleason, Jackie	1916	1987	Hawkins, Jack	1910	1973
Fiske, Minnie Maddern	1865	1932	Gleason, James	1886	1959	Hawkins, Screamin' Jay	1929	2000
Fitzgerald, Barry	1888	1961	Gluck, Alma	1884	1938	Hawks, Howard	1896	1977
Fitzgerald, Ella	1917	1996	Gobel, George	1919	1991	Hawthorne, Nigel	1929	2001
Fitzgerald, Geraldine	1913	2005	Godard, Jean-Luc	1930	2022	Hayakawa, Sessue	1890	1973
Fleming, Art	1924	1995	Goddard, Paulette	1905?	1990	Hayden, Sterling	1916	1986
Fleming, Rhonda	1923	2020	Godfrey, Arthur	1903	1983	Hayes, Gabby	1885	1969
Fleming, Victor	1889	1949	Godunov, Alexander	1949	1995	Hayes, Helen	1900	1993
Fletcher, Louise	1934	2022	Goldwyn, Samuel	1882	1974	Hayes, Isaac	1942	2008
Flynn, Errol	1909	1959	Goodman, Benny	1909	1986	Haymes, Dick	1917	1980
Flynn, Joe	1925	1974	Goodman, Len	1944	2023	Hayward, Leland	1902	1971
Foch, Nina	1924	2008	Gorcey, Leo	1917	1969	Hayward, Louis	1909	1985
Fogelberg, Dan	1951	2007	Gordon, Gale	1906	1995	Hayward, Susan	1917	1975
Foley, Red	1910	1968	Gordon, Ruth	1896	1985	Hayworth, Rita	1918	1987
Fonda, Henry	1905	1982	Gorme, Eydie	1932	2013	Head, Edith	1897	1981
Fonda, Peter	1940	2019	Gorshin, Frank	1934	2005	Healy, Ted	1896	1937
Fontaine, Joan	1917	2013	Gosden, Freeman	1899	1982	Heard, John	1945	2017
Fontanne, Lynn	1887	1983	Gottfried, Gilbert	1955	2022	Heche, Anne	1969	2022
Fonteyn, Margot	1919	1991	Gottschalk, Louis	1829	1869	Heckart, Eileen	1919	2001
Ford, Glenn	1916	2006	Gould, Glenn	1932	1982	Heflin, Van	1910	1971
Ford, John	1894	1973	Gould, Harold	1923	2010	Heifetz, Jascha	1901	1987
Ford, Paul	1901	1976	Gould, Morton	1913	1996	Held, Anna	1873	1918
Ford, Tennessee Ernie	1919	1991	Goulet, Robert.	1933	2007	Helm, Levon	1940	2012
Forman, Milos	1932	2018	Grable, Betty	1916	1973	Helmond, Katherine	1929	2019
Forrest, Edwin	1806	1872	Graham, Martha	1894	1991	Hemingway, Margaux	1955	1996
Forrest, Helen	1917	1999	Graham, Virginia	1912	1998	Hemsley, Sherman	1938	2012
Forsythe, John	1918	2010	Grahame, Gloria	1925	1981	Henderson, Florence	1934	2016
Fosse, Bob	1927	1987	Granger, Farley	1925	2011	Henderson, Skitch	1918	2005
Foster, Preston	1901	1970	Granger, Stewart	1913	1993	Hendrix, Jimi	1942	1970
Foxx, Redd	1922	1991	Grant, Cary	1904	1986	Henie, Sonja	1912	1969
Foy, Eddie	1856	1928	Granville, Bonita	1923	1988	Henreid, Paul.	1908	1992
Franchi, Sergio	1926	1990	Grapewin, Charley	1869	1956	Henry, Buck	1930	2020
Franciosa, Anthony	1928	2006	Graves, Peter.	1926	2010	Henson, Jim	1936	1990
Francis, Anne	1930	2011	Gray, Dolores	1924	2002	Hepburn, Audrey	1929	1993
Francis, Arlene	1907	2001	Gray, Spalding	1941	2004	Hepburn, Katharine	1907	2003
Francis, Kay	1905	1968	Grayson, Kathryn	1922	2010	Herrmann, Edward	1943	2014
Franciscus, James	1934	1991	Greco, Jose	1918	2000	Hersholt, Jean	1886	1956
Frankenheimer, John	1930	2002	Green, Adolph	1915	2002	Hesseman, Howard	1940	2022
Franklin, Aretha	1942	2018	Greene, Lorne	1915	1987	Heston, Charlton	1923	2008
Franklin, Bonnie	1944	2013	Greenstreet, Sydney	1879	1954	Hickey, William	1928	1997
Frawley, William	1887	1966	Greenwood, Charlotte	1890	1978	Hickman, Dwayne	1934	2022
Freed, Alan	1921	1965	Gregory, Dick	1932	2017	Hickson, Joan	1906	1998
Freeman, Al, Jr.	1934	2012	Gregory, James	1911	2002	Hildegarde.	1906	2005
Freeman, Mona	1926	2014	Griffin, Merv	1925	2007	Hill, Arthur	1922	2006
French, Victor	1934	1989	Griffith, Andy	1926	2012	Hill, Benny	1925	1992
Frey, Glenn	1948	2016	Griffith, D. W.	1874	1948	Hill, George Roy	1921	2002
Friganza, Trixie	1870	1955	Griffith, Hugh	1912	1980	Hiller, Wendy	1912	2003
Froman, Jane	1907	1980	Griffiths, Richard	1947	2013	Hillerman, John	1932	2017
Frost, David	1939	2013	Grimes, Tammy	1934	2016	Hines, Gregory	1946	2003
Funicello, Annette	1942	2013	Grizzard, George	1928	2007	Hingle, Pat.	1924	2009
Funt, Allen	1914	1999	Grodin, Charles	1935	2021	Hirt, Al	1922	1999
Furness, Betty	1916	1994	Guardino, Harry	1925	1995	Hitchcock, Alfred	1899	1980
Gabin, Jean	1904	1976	Guillaume, Robert	1927	2017	Ho, Don	1930	2007
Gable, Clark	1901	1960	Guinness, Alec	1914	2000	Hodiak, John	1914	1955
Gabor, Eva	1920	1995	Guthrie, Woody	1912	1967	Hoffman, Philip Seymour	1967	2014
Gabor, Zsa Zsa	1917	2016	Guy-Blaché, Alice	1873	1968	Holbrook, Hal.	1925	2021
Gandolfini, James	1961	2013	Gwenn, Edmund	1875	1959	Holden, William	1918	1981
Garagiola, Joe	1926	2016	Gwynne, Fred	1926	1993	Holder, Geoffrey	1930	2014
Garbo, Greta	1905	1990	Hackett, Buddy	1924	2003	Holiday, Billie	1915	1959
Garcia, Jerry	1942	1995	Hackett, Joan	1934	1983	Holliday, Judy	1921	1965
Gardenia, Vincent	1922	1992	Hagen, Jean	1923	1977	Holloway, Sterling	1905	1992
Gardner, Ava	1922	1990	Hagen, Uta	1919	2004	Holly, Buddy	1936	1959
Garfield, John	1913	1952	Haggard, Merle	1937	2016	Holm, Celeste	1919	2012
Garland, Beverly	1926	2008	Hagman, Larry	1931	2012	Holm, Ian.	1931	2020
Garland, Judy	1922	1969	Haines, William	1900	1973	Holt, Jack	1888	1951
Garner, James	1928	2014	Hale, Alan, Jr.	1918	1990	Holt, Tim	1918	1973
Garrett, Betty	1919	2011	Hale, Alan, Sr.	1892	1950	Homolka, Oscar.	1898	1978
Garson, Greer	1904	1996	Hale, Barbara	1922	2017	Hooker, John Lee	1917	2001
Gassman, Vittorio	1922	2000	Haley, Bill	1925	1981	Hope, Bob	1903	2003
Gavin, John	1931	2018	Haley, Jack	1899	1979	Hopkins, Miriam	1902	1972
Gaye, Marvin	1939	1984	Hall, Huntz	1919	1999	Hopper, Dennis	1936	2010
Gaynor, Janet	1906	1984	Hall, Jon	1915	1979	Hopper, DeWolf	1858	1935
Gazzara, Ben	1930	2012	Hall, Monty	1921	2017	Hopper, Hedda	1885	1966
Gebel-Williams, Gunther	1934	2001	Hamilton, Margaret	1902	1985	Horowitz, Vladimir	1904	1989
Geer, Will.	1902	1978	Hammerstein, Oscar	1847	1919	Horne, Lena	1917	2010
			Hammerstein, Oscar, II	1895	1960	Horton, Edward Everett	1886	1970

Name	Born	Died	Name	Born	Died	Name	Born	Died
March, Fredric	1897	1975	Monroe, Vaughn	1911	1973	O'Keefe, Dennis	1908	1968
March, Hal	1920	1970	Montalban, Ricardo	1920	2009	Oland, Warner	1880	1938
Marchand, Nancy	1928	2000	Montand, Yves	1921	1991	Olcott, Chauncey	1860	1932
Markova, Alicia	1910	2004	Monteith, Cory	1982	2013	Oliveira, Manoel de	1908	2015
Marley, Bob	1945	1981	Montgomery, Elizabeth	1933	1995	Oliver, Edna May	1883	1942
Marriner, Neville	1924	2016	Montgomery, George	1916	2000	Olivier, Laurence	1907	1989
Marsh, Mae	1895	1968	Montgomery, Robert	1904	1981	Olsen, Merlin	1940	2010
Marshall, Garry	1934	2016	Moody, Ron	1924	2015	O'Neal, Ron	1937	2004
Marshall, Herbert	1890	1966	Moore, Clayton	1914	1999	O'Neill, James	1849	1920
Marshall, Penny	1943	2018	Moore, Colleen	1900	1988	Ophüls, Max	1902	1957
Martin, Dean	1917	1995	Moore, Dudley	1935	2002	Orbach, Jerry	1935	2004
Martin, Dick	1922	2008	Moore, Garry	1915	1993	Orbison, Roy	1936	1988
Martin, Mary	1913	1990	Moore, Grace	1898	1947	Ormandy, Eugene	1899	1985
Martin, Ross	1920	1981	Moore, Mary Tyler	1936	2017	O'Shea, Milo	1926	2013
Martin, Tony	1913	2012	Moore, Roger	1927	2017	O'Sullivan, Maureen	1911	1998
Marvin, Lee	1924	1987	Moorehead, Agnes	1906	1974	O'Toole, Peter	1932	2013
Marx, Harpo (Arthur)	1888	1964	Moreau, Jeanne	1928	2017	Ouspenskaya, Maria	1876	1949
Marx, Zeppo (Herbert)	1901	1979	Morgan, Dennis	1910	1994	Owen, Reginald	1887	1972
Marx, Groucho (Julius)	1890	1977	Morgan, Frank	1890	1949	Owens, Buck	1929	2006
Marx, Chico (Leonard)	1887	1961	Morgan, Harry	1915	2011	Paar, Jack	1918	2004
Marx, Gummo (Milton)	1893	1977	Morgan, Helen	1900	1941	Paderewski, Ignace	1860	1941
Mason, Jackie	1928	2021	Morgan, Henry	1915	1994	Page, Bettie	1923	2008
Mason, James	1909	1984	Morita, Pat	1932	2005	Page, Geraldine	1924	1987
Massey, Raymond	1896	1983	Morley, Robert	1908	1992	Page, Patti	1927	2013
Mastroianni, Marcello	1924	1996	Morris, Chester	1901	1970	Pakula, Alan	1928	1998
Masur, Kurt	1927	2015	Morris, Greg	1934	1996	Palance, Jack	1919	2006
Matthau, Walter	1920	2000	Morrison, Jim	1943	1971	Pallette, Eugene	1889	1954
Mature, Victor	1913	1999	Morrow, Vic	1929	1982	Palmer, Betsy	1926	2015
Maxwell, Marilyn	1921	1972	Morse, Robert	1931	2022	Palmer, Lilli	1914	1986
Mayer, Louis B.	1885	1957	Morton, Jelly Roll	1885	1941	Palmer, Robert	1949	2003
Mayfield, Curtis	1942	1999	Mostel, Zero	1915	1977	Pangborn, Franklin	1894	1958
Mayo, Virginia	1920	2005	Mowbray, Alan	1897	1969	Papas, Irene	1926	2022
Mazursky, Paul	1930	2014	Mulhare, Edward	1923	1997	Pardo, Don	1918	2014
MCA (Adam Yauch)	1964	2012	Mulligan, Gerry	1927	1996	Parker, Alan	1944	2020
McCallum, David	1933	2023	Mulligan, Richard	1932	2000	Parker, Eleanor	1922	2013
McCambridge, Mercedes	1916	2004	Muni, Paul	1895	1967	Parker, Fess	1925	2010
McCarey, Leo	1898	1969	Murnau, F. W.	1888	1931	Parker, Jean	1915	2005
McCarthy, Kevin	1914	2010	Murphy, Audie	1924	1971	Parks, Bert	1914	1992
McCartney, Linda	1941	1998	Murphy, Brittany	1977	2009	Parks, Larry	1914	1975
McCarver, Tim	1941	2023	Murphy, George	1902	1992	Pasternack, Josef A.	1881	1940
McClanahan, Rue	1934	2010	Murray, Arthur	1895	1991	Pastor, Tony (vaudevillian)	1837	1908
McClure, Doug	1935	1995	Murray, Kathryn	1906	1999	Pastor, Tony (bandleader)	1907	1969
McCormack, John	1884	1945	Murray, Mae	1889	1965	Patrick, Gail	1911	1980
McCrea, Joel	1905	1990	Nabors, Jim	1930	2017	Patti, Adelina	1843	1919
McDaniel, Hattie	1895	1952	Nagel, Conrad	1897	1970	Patti, Carlotta	1840	1889
McDowall, Roddy	1928	1998	Naish, J. Carroll	1900	1973	Paul, Les	1915	2009
McFarland, Spanky (George)	1928	1993	Naldi, Nita	1898	1961	Pavarotti, Luciano	1935	2007
McGoohan, Patrick	1928	2009	Nance, Jack	1943	1996	Pavlova, Anna	1885	1931
McGuire, Al	1931	2001	Natwick, Mildred	1908	1994	Paxton, Bill	1955	2017
McGuire, Dorothy	1916	2001	Nazimova, Alla	1879	1945	Paycheck, Johnny	1938	2003
McHugh, Frank	1898	1981	Neal, Patricia	1926	2010	Payne, John	1912	1989
McIntire, John	1907	1991	Negri, Pola	1897	1987	Pearl, Minnie	1912	1996
McLaglen, Victor	1886	1959	Nelson, David	1936	2011	Peck, Gregory	1916	2003
McMahon, Ed	1923	2009	Nelson, Ed	1928	2014	Peckinpah, Sam	1925	1984
McPartland, Marian	1918	2013	Nelson, Harriet (Hilliard)	1909	1994	Pendergrass, Teddy	1950	2010
McQueen, Butterfly	1911	1995	Nelson, Ozzie	1906	1975	Penn, Arthur	1922	2010
McQueen, Steve	1930	1980	Nelson, Rick	1940	1985	Penner, Joe	1905	1941
Meader, Vaughn	1936	2004	Nero, Peter	1934	2023	Peppard, George	1928	1994
Meadows, Audrey	1924	1996	Nesbit, Evelyn	1884	1967	Perkins, Anthony	1932	1992
Meadows, Jayne	1919	2015	Nesmith, Michael	1942	2021	Perkins, Carl	1932	1998
Meara, Anne	1929	2015	Nettleton, Lois	1927	2008	Perkins, Marlin	1905	1986
Meat Loaf	1947	2022	Newley, Anthony	1931	1999	Perry, Luke	1965	2019
Meek, Donald	1880	1946	Newman, Edwin	1919	2010	Persoff, Nehemiah	1919	2022
Méliès, Georges	1861	1938	Newman, Paul	1925	2008	Peters, Brock	1927	2005
Menjou, Adolphe	1890	1963	Newton-John, Olivia	1948	2022	Peters, Jean	1926	2000
Menuhin, Yehudi	1916	1999	Nicholas, Fayard	1914	2006	Peters, Roberta	1930	2017
Mercer, Marian	1935	2011	Nicholas, Harold	1924	2000	Petersen, Wolfgang	1941	2022
Mercouri, Melina	1925	1994	Nichols, Mike	1931	2014	Peterson, Oscar	1925	2007
Mercury, Freddie	1946	1991	Nielsen, Leslie	1926	2010	Petty, Tom	1950	2017
Meredith, Burgess	1909	1997	Nijinsky, Vaslav	1890	1950	Philbin, Regis	1931	2020
Merman, Ethel	1908	1984	Nilsson, Anna Q.	1888	1974	Phillips, John	1935	2001
Merrick, David	1911	2000	Nimoy, Leonard	1931	2015	Phoenix, River	1970	1993
Merrill, Dina	1925	2017	Niven, David	1910	1983	Piaf, Edith	1915	1963
Merrill, Gary	1915	1990	Nolan, Lloyd	1902	1985	Pickens, Slim	1919	1983
Michael, George	1963	2016	Norman, Jessye	1945	2019	Pickett, Wilson	1941	2006
Mifune, Toshiro	1920	1997	Normand, Mabel	1894	1930	Pickford, Mary	1892	1979
Milland, Ray	1905	1986	North, Sheree	1933	2005	Pidgeon, Walter	1897	1984
Miller, Ann	1923	2004	Notorious B.I.G.	1972	1997	Pinza, Ezio	1892	1957
Miller, Glenn	1904	1944	Novarro, Ramon	1899	1968	Pitney, Gene	1941	2006
Miller, Marilyn	1898	1936	Nureyev, Rudolf	1938	1993	Pitts, Zasu	1898	1963
Miller, Mitch	1911	2010	Oakie, Jack	1903	1978	Plato, Dana	1964	1999
Miller, Roger	1936	1992	Oakley, Annie	1860	1926	Pleasence, Donald	1919	1995
Mills, John	1908	2005	Oates, Warren	1928	1982	Pleshette, Suzanne	1937	2008
Milner, Martin	1931	2015	Oberon, Merle	1911	1979	Plummer, Christopher	1929	2021
Mimieux, Yvette	1942	2022	O'Brien, Edmond	1915	1985	Poitier, Sidney	1927	2022
Mineo, Sal	1939	1976	O'Brien, George	1900	1985	Pollack, Sydney	1934	2008
Minghella, Anthony	1954	2008	O'Brien, Pat	1899	1983	Pons, Lily	1904	1976
Mingus, Charles	1922	1979	O'Connell, Arthur	1908	1981	Ponselle, Rosa	1897	1981
Minnelli, Vincente	1903	1986	O'Connell, Helen	1921	1993	Ponti, Carlo	1912	2007
Miranda, Carmen	1909	1955	O'Connor, Carroll	1924	2001	Porter, Edwin S.	1870	1941
Mitchell, Thomas	1892	1962	O'Connor, Donald	1925	2003	Postlethwaite, Pete	1946	2011
Mitchum, Robert	1917	1997	O'Connor, Sinead	1966	2023	Poston, Tom	1921	2007
Mix, Tom	1880	1940	O'Connor, Una	1880	1959	Powell, Dick	1904	1963
Moffat, Donald	1930	2018	Odetta (Holmes)	1930	2008	Powell, Eleanor	1912	1982
Molinaro, Al	1919	2015	O'Hara, Maureen	1920	2015	Powell, Jane	1929	2021
Monroe, Marilyn	1926	1962	O'Herlihy, Daniel	1919	2005	Powell, William	1892	1984

Name	Born	Died
Power, Tyrone	1914	1958
Preminger, Otto	1905	1986
Presley, Elvis	1935	1977
Preston, Billy	1946	2006
Preston, Robert	1918	1987
Previn, Andre	1929	2019
Price, Ray	1926	2013
Price, Vincent	1911	1993
Pride, Charley	1934	2020
Prima, Louis	1911	1978
Prince	1958	2016
Prince, Hal	1928	2019
Prinze, Freddie	1954	1977
Prosky, Robert	1930	2008
Provine, Dorothy	1937	2010
Prowse, Juliet	1936	1996
Pryor, Richard	1940	2005
Puente, Tito	1923	2000
Pyle, Denver	1920	1997
Quayle, Anthony	1913	1989
Questel, Mae	1908	1998
Quinn, Anthony	1915	2001
Quintero, José	1924	1999
Rabb, Ellis	1930	1998
Rabbitt, Eddie	1941	1998
Radner, Gilda	1946	1989
Rae, Charlotte	1926	2018
Rafferty, Gerry	1947	2011
Raft, George	1895	1980
Rainer, Luise	1910	2014
Rains, Claude	1889	1967
Raitt, John	1917	2005
Ralston, Esther	1902	1994
Ramis, Harold	1944	2014
Ramone, Dee Dee	1952	2002
Ramone, Joey	1951	2001
Ramone, Johnny	1948	2004
Ramone, Tommy	1949	2014
Rampal, Jean-Pierre	1922	2000
Randall, Tony	1920	2004
Randolph, John	1915	2004
Rathbone, Basil	1892	1967
Ratoff, Gregory	1897	1960
Rawls, Lou	1933	2006
Ray, Aldo	1926	1991
Ray, Johnnie	1927	1990
Ray, Nicholas	1911	1979
Rayburn, Gene	1917	1999
Raye, Martha	1916	1994
Raymond, Gene	1908	1998
Reagan, Ronald	1911	2004
Redding, Otis	1941	1967
Reddy, Helen	1941	2020
Redgrave, Corin	1939	2010
Redgrave, Lynn	1943	2010
Redgrave, Michael	1908	1985
Reed, Donna	1921	1986
Reed, Lou	1942	2013
Reed, Oliver	1938	1999
Reed, Robert	1932	1992
Rees, Roger	1944	2015
Reese, Della	1931	2017
Reeve, Christopher	1952	2004
Reeves, George	1914	1959
Reeves, Steve	1926	2000
Reid, Wallace	1891	1923
Reilly, Charles Nelson	1931	2007
Reiner, Carl	1922	2020
Reinhardt, Max	1873	1943
Reinking, Ann	1949	2020
Reitman, Ivan	1946	2022
Remick, Lee	1935	1991
Renaldo, Duncan	1904	1980
Rennie, Michael	1909	1971
Renoir, Jean	1894	1979
Rettig, Tommy	1941	1996
Reubens, Paul	1952	2023
Reynolds, Burt	1936	2018
Reynolds, Debbie	1932	2016
Rich, Charlie	1932	1995
Richardson, Ian	1934	2007
Richardson, Natasha	1963	2009
Richardson, Ralph	1902	1983
Rickles, Don	1926	2017
Rickman, Alan	1946	2016
Riddle, Nelson	1921	1985
Riefenstahl, Leni	1902	2003
Rigg, Diana	1938	2020
Ripperton, Minnie	1947	1979
Ritchard, Cyril	1898	1977
Ritter, John	1948	2003
Ritter, Tex	1905	1974
Ritter, Thelma	1905	1969
Ritz, Al	1901	1965
Ritz, Harry	1906	1986
Ritz, Jimmy	1903	1985
Rivers, Joan	1933	2014
Roach, Hal	1892	1992
Roach, Max	1924	2007
Robards, Jason	1922	2000
Robbins, Jerome	1918	1998
Robbins, Marty	1925	1982
Roberts, Doris	1925	2016
Roberts, Pernell	1928	2010
Roberts, Rachel	1927	1980
Robertson, Cliff	1925	2011
Robertson, Dale	1923	2013
Robeson, Paul	1898	1976
Robinson, Bill	1878	1949
Robinson, Edward G.	1893	1973
Robson, Flora	1902	1984
Roche, Eugene	1928	2004
Rochester (Eddie Anderson)	1905	1977
Roddenberry, Gene	1921	1991
Rodgers, Jimmie	1897	1933
Rodgers, Jimmie F.	1933	2021
Rogers, Buddy	1904	1999
Rogers, Fred	1928	2003
Rogers, Ginger	1911	1995
Rogers, Kenny	1938	2020
Rogers, Roy	1911	1998
Rogers, Wayne	1933	2015
Rogers, Will	1879	1935
Rohmer, Eric	1920	2010
Roland, Gilbert	1905	1994
Rolle, Esther	1920	1998
Rollins, Howard	1950	1996
Roman, Ruth	1924	1999
Romero, Cesar	1907	1994
Rooney, Mickey	1920	2014
Rose Marie	1923	2017
Rose, Billy	1899	1966
Rossellini, Roberto	1906	1977
Rostropovich, Mstislav	1927	2007
Rowan, Dan	1922	1987
Rubinstein, Artur	1887	1982
Rubinstein, Zelda	1933	2010
Ruggles, Charles	1886	1970
Russell, Harold	1914	2002
Russell, Jane	1921	2011
Russell, Ken	1927	2011
Russell, Leon	1942	2016
Russell, Lillian	1861	1922
Russell, Mark	1932	2023
Russell, Nipsey	1923	2005
Russell, Rosalind	1911	1976
Rutherford, Ann	1917	2012
Rutherford, Margaret	1892	1972
Ryan, Irene	1903	1973
Ryan, Robert	1909	1973
Rydell, Bobby	1942	2022
Sabu (Dastagir)	1924	1963
Saget, Bob	1956	2022
Sahl, Mort	1927	2021
St. Cyr, Lili	1917	1999
St. Denis, Ruth	1877	1968
Sakall, S. Z.	1883	1955
Saks, Gene	1921	2015
Sale (Chic), Charles	1885	1936
Sales, Soupy	1926	2009
Sanders, George	1906	1972
Sands, Julian	1958	2023
Sanford, Isabel	1917	2004
Sargent, Dick	1933	1994
Sarrazin, Michael	1940	2011
Savalas, Telly	1922	1994
Saxon, John	1936	2020
Schallert, William	1922	2016
Scheider, Roy	1935	2008
Schell, Maria	1926	2005
Schell, Maximilian	1930	2014
Schenkel, Chris	1923	2005
Schiavelli, Vincent	1948	2005
Schildkraut, Joseph	1896	1964
Schlesinger, John	1926	2003
Schnabel, Artur	1882	1951
Schneider, Maria	1952	2011
Schneider, Romy	1938	1982
Schwartzkopf, Elizabeth	1915	2006
Scofield, Paul	1922	2008
Scolari, Peter	1955	2021
Scott, George C.	1927	1999
Scott, Gordon	1926	2007
Scott, Hazel	1920	1981
Scott, Lizabeth	1922	2015
Scott, Martha	1914	2003
Scott, Randolph	1898	1987
Scott, Stuart	1965	2015
Scott, Zachary	1914	1965
Scott-Heron, Gil	1949	2011
Scott-Siddons, Mrs.	1843	1896
Scully, Vin	1927	2022
Seberg, Jean	1938	1979
Seeger, Pete	1919	2014
Seeley, Blossom	1892	1974
Segal, George	1934	2021
Segovia, Andres	1893	1987
Seldes, Marian	1928	2014
Selena (Quintanilla)	1971	1995
Sellers, Peter	1925	1980
Selznick, David O.	1902	1965
Sennett, Mack	1880	1960
Señor Wences	1896	1999
Serkin, Rudolph	1903	1991
Serling, Rod	1924	1975
Shakur, Tupac	1971	1996
Shandling, Garry	1949	2016
Shankar, Ravi	1920	2012
Sharif, Omar	1932	2015
Shaw, Artie	1910	2004
Shaw, Robert (actor)	1927	1978
Shaw, Robert (conductor)	1916	1999
Shawn, Ted	1891	1972
Shearer, Moira	1926	2006
Shearer, Norma	1902	1983
Shearing, George	1919	2011
Shelley, Carole	1939	2018
Shepard, Sam	1943	2017
Sheppard, Bob	1910	2010
Sheridan, Ann	1915	1967
Shore, Dinah	1917	1994
Short, Bobby	1924	2005
Shorter, Wayne	1933	2023
Shubert, Lee	1875	1953
Shull, Richard B.	1929	1999
Siddons, Sarah	1755	1831
Sidney, Sylvia	1910	1999
Siegel, Don	1912	1991
Signoret, Simone	1921	1985
Sills, Beverly	1929	2007
Silver, Ron	1946	2009
Silverheels, Jay	1912	1980
Silvers, Phil	1912	1985
Sim, Alastair	1900	1976
Simmons, Jean	1929	2010
Simone, Nina	1933	2003
Sinatra, Frank	1915	1998
Sinclair, Madge	1938	1995
Singleton, John	1968	2019
Singleton, Penny	1908	2003
Sirico, Tony	1942	2022
Sirk, Douglas	1900	1987
Siskel, Gene	1946	1999
Sizemore, Tom	1961	2023
Sjostrom, Victor	1879	1960
Skelton, Red	1913	1997
Skinner, Otis	1858	1942
Sledge, Percy	1940	2015
Smith, Alexis	1921	1993
Smith, Bessie	1894?	1937
Smith, Buffalo Bob	1917	1998
Smith, C. Aubrey	1863	1948
Smith, Elliott	1969	2003
Smith, Kate	1907	1986
Smith, Keely	1928	2017
Snodgrass, Carrie	1946	2004
Snow, Hank	1914	1999
Snyder, Tom	1936	2007
Solti, George	1912	1997
Somers, Suzanne	1946	2023
Sondergaard, Gale	1899	1985
Sorvino, Paul	1939	2022
Sothern, Ann	1909	2001
Sousa, John Philip	1854	1932
Spector, Phil	1940	2021
Spector, Ronnie	1943	2022
Spelling, Aaron	1923	2006
Spencer, John	1946	2005
Sperber, Wendie Jo	1958	2005
Springer, Jerry	1944	2023
Springfield, Dusty	1939	1999
Stack, Robert	1919	2003
Stafford, Jo	1917	2008
Stander, Lionel	1908	1994
Stang, Arnold	1918	2009
Stanley, Kim	1925	2001
Stanton, Harry Dean	1926	2017
Stanwyck, Barbara	1907	1990
Stapleton, Jean	1923	2013
Stapleton, Maureen	1925	2006
Steiger, Rod	1925	2002
Sterling, Jan	1921	2004
Stern, Isaac	1920	2001
Stevens, Craig	1918	2000
Stevens, George	1904	1975
Stevens, Inger	1934	1970
Stevens, Mark	1916	1994
Stevens, Risë	1913	2013

Name	Born	Died
Stevens, Stella	1938	2023
Stevenson, McLean	1929	1996
Stewart, James	1908	1997
Stickney, Dorothy	1896	1998
Stiers, David Ogden	1942	2018
Stiller, Jerry	1927	2020
Stockwell, Dean	1936	2021
Stokowski, Leopold	1882	1977
Stone, Lewis	1879	1953
Stone, Milburn	1904	1980
Storch, Larry	1923	2022
Storm, Gale	1922	2009
Straight, Beatrice	1918	2001
Strasberg, Lee	1901	1982
Strasberg, Susan	1938	1999
Stritch, Elaine	1925	2014
Strummer, Joe	1952	2002
Stuart, Gloria	1910	2010
Stuarti, Enzo	1919	2005
Sturges, Preston	1898	1959
Sullavan, Margaret	1911	1960
Sullivan, Barry	1912	1994
Sullivan, Ed	1902	1974
Sumac, Yma	1922	2008
Summer, Donna	1948	2012
Summerville, Slim	1892	1946
Sutherland, Joan	1926	2010
Swanson, Gloria	1899	1983
Swayze, Patrick	1952	2009
Sweet, Blanche	1896	1986
Switzer, Carl "Alfalfa"	1927	1959
Talbot, Lyle	1902	1996
Tallchief, Maria	1925	2013
Talmadge, Constance	1900	1973
Talmadge, Norma	1893	1957
Tamiroff, Akim	1899	1972
Tandy, Jessica	1909	1994
Tanguay, Eva	1878	1947
Tati, Jacques	1908	1982
Taylor, Billy	1921	2010
Taylor, Dub	1907	1994
Taylor, Elizabeth	1932	2011
Taylor, Estelle	1899	1958
Taylor, Laurette	1887	1946
Taylor, Paul	1930	2018
Taylor, Rip	1931	2019
Taylor, Robert	1911	1969
Taylor, Rod	1930	2015
Temple Black, Shirley	1928	2014
Terry, Ellen	1847	1928
Thalberg, Irving	1899	1936
Thaw, John	1942	2002
Thaxter, Phyllis	1919	2012
Thicke, Alan	1947	2016
Thigpen, Lynne	1948	2003
Thomas, Danny	1912	1991
Thomas, Jay	1948	2017
Thompson, Sada	1927	2011
Thorndike, Sybil	1882	1976
Thulin, Ingrid	1926	2004
Tierney, Gene	1920	1991
Tillis, Mel	1932	2017
Tiny Tim	1932	1996
Todd, Michael	1909	1958
Todd, Richard	1919	2009
Tomlinson, David	1917	2000
Tone, Franchot	1905	1968
Tork, Peter	1942	2019
Torme, Mel	1925	1999
Torn, Rip	1931	2019
Toscanini, Arturo	1867	1957
Tracy, Lee	1898	1968
Tracy, Spencer	1900	1967
Travers, Henry	1874	1965
Travers, Mary	1936	2009
Treacher, Arthur	1894	1975
Trebek, Alex	1940	2020
Tree, Herbert Beerbohm	1853	1917
Trevor, Claire	1909	2000
Truffaut, Francois	1932	1984
Tucker, Forrest	1919	1986
Tucker, Richard	1913	1975
Tucker, Sophie	1884	1966
Turner, Big Joe	1911	1985
Turner, Ike	1931	2008
Turner, Lana	1920?	1995
Turner, Tina	1939	2023
Turpin, Ben	1869	1940
Twitty, Conway	1933	1993
Tyson, Cicely	1924	2021
Urich, Robert	1946	2002
Ustinov, Peter	1921	2004
Valens, Ritchie	1941	1959
Valentino, Rudolph	1895	1926
Vallee, Rudy	1901	1986
Van, Bobby	1928	1980
Van Cleef, Lee	1925	1989
Van Fleet, Jo	1922	1996
Van Halen, Eddie	1955	2020
Van Patten, Dick	1928	2015
Vance, Vivian	1912	1979
Vandross, Luther	1951	2005
Varney, Jim	1949	2000
Vaughan, Sarah	1924	1990
Vaughn, Robert	1932	2016
Veidt, Conrad	1893	1943
Velez, Lupe	1908	1944
Vera-Ellen (Rohe)	1926	1981
Verdon, Gwen	1925	2000
Verrett, Shirley	1931	2010
Vicious, Sid	1957	1979
Vickers, Jon	1926	2015
Vidor, King	1894	1982
Vigoda, Abe	1921	2016
Villechaize, Herve	1943	1993
Vincent, Gene	1935	1971
Vincent, Jan-Michael	1944	2019
Von Stroheim, Erich	1885	1957
Von Sydow, Max	1929	2020
Von Zell, Harry	1906	1981
Wain, Bea	1917	2017
Waite, Ralph	1928	2014
Walker, Clint	1927	2018
Walker, Junior	1942	1995
Walker, Nancy	1922	1992
Walker, Paul	1973	2013
Walker, Robert	1918	1951
Wallace, Marcia	1942	2013
Wallach, Eli	1915	2014
Wallenda, Karl	1905	1978
Walsh, J. T.	1943	1998
Walsh, Raoul	1887	1980
Walston, Ray	1914	2001
Walter, Bruno	1876	1962
Walter, Jessica	1941	2021
Walters, Barbara	1929	2022
Ward, Simon	1941	2012
Warden, Jack	1920	2006
Waring, Fred	1900	1984
Warner, H. B.	1876	1958
Warrick, Ruth	1915	2005
Washington, Dinah	1924	1963
Waters, Ethel	1896	1977
Waters, Muddy	1913?	1983
Waxman, Al	1935	2001
Wayne, David	1914	1995
Wayne, John	1907	1979
Weaver, Dennis	1924	2006
Weaver, Fritz	1926	2016
Webb, Clifton	1891	1966
Webb, Jack	1920	1982
Weems, Ted	1901	1963
Weiland, Scott	1967	2015
Weissmuller, Johnny	1904	1984
Welch, Raquel	1940	2023
Welk, Lawrence	1903	1992
Welles, Orson	1915	1985
Wellman, William	1896	1975
Wells, Kitty	1919	2012
Werner, Oskar	1922	1984
Wertmüller, Lina	1928	2021
West, Adam	1928	2017
West, Mae	1893	1980
Weston, Jack	1924	1996
Whale, James	1889	1957
White, Barry	1944	2003
White, Betty	1922	2021
White, Jesse	1919	1997
White, Pearl	1889	1938
Whiteman, Paul	1891	1967
Whiting, Margaret	1924	2011
Whitmore, James	1921	2009
Whitty, May	1865	1948
Wickes, Mary	1910	1995
Widmark, Richard	1914	2008
Wilde, Cornel	1915	1989
Wilder, Billy	1906	2002
Wilder, Gene	1933	2016
Wilding, Michael	1912	1979
Willard, Fred	1939	2020
Williams, Andy	1927	2012
Williams, Bert	1874	1922
Williams, Cindy	1947	2023
Williams, Esther	1921	2013
Williams, Guy	1924	1989
Williams, Hank, Sr.	1923	1953
Williams, Michael K.	1966	2021
Williams, Robin	1951	2014
Williams, Treat	1951	2023
Williamson, Nicol	1936	2011
Wills, Bob	1905	1975
Wills, Chill	1902	1978
Wilson, Carl	1946	1998
Wilson, Dennis	1944	1983
Wilson, Dooley	1894	1953
Wilson, Elizabeth	1921	2015
Wilson, Flip	1933	1998
Wilson, Jackie	1934	1984
Wilson, Marie	1917	1972
Wilson, Nancy	1937	2018
Windom, William	1923	2012
Winehouse, Amy	1983	2011
Winfield, Paul	1941	2004
Winston, George	1949	2023
Winter, Johnny	1944	2014
Winters, Jonathan	1925	2013
Winters, Shelley	1920	2006
Wise, Robert	1914	2005
Wiseman, Joseph	1918	2009
Withers, Bill	1938	2020
Wolfman Jack	1938	1995
Wong, Anna May	1907	1961
Wood, Ed	1924	1978
Wood, Natalie	1938	1981
Wood, Peggy	1892	1978
Wood, Sam	1884	1949
Woodward, Edward	1930	2009
Wooley, Sheb	1921	2003
Woolley, Monty	1888	1963
Worth, Irene	1916	2002
Wray, Fay	1907	2004
Wright, Teresa	1918	2005
Wyatt, Jane	1910	2006
Wyler, William	1902	1981
Wyman, Jane	1917	2007
Wynette, Tammy	1942	1998
Wynn, Ed.	1886	1966
Wynn, Keenan	1916	1986
York, Dick	1928	1992
York, Susannah	1939	2011
Young, Alan	1919	2016
Young, Clara Kimball	1890	1960
Young, Gig	1913	1978
Young, Loretta	1913	2000
Young, Robert	1907	1998
Young, Roland	1887	1953
Youngman, Henny	1906	1998
Zanuck, Darryl F.	1902	1979
Zappa, Frank	1940	1993
Zeffirelli, Franco	1923	2019
Zevon, Warren	1947	2003
Ziegfeld, Florenz	1869	1932
Zimbalist, Efrem, Jr.	1918	2014
Zinneman, Fred	1907	1997
Zukor, Adolph	1873	1976

Original Names of Selected Entertainers

Adele: Adele Laurie Blue Adkins
Ad-Rock: Adam Horovitz
Clay Aiken: Clayton Grissom
Alan Alda: Alphonso D'Abruzzo
Jason Alexander: Jay Greenspan
Woody Allen: Allen Konigsberg
André 3000: Andre Benjamin
Julie Andrews: Julia Wells
Criss Angel: Christopher Sarantakos
Beatrice Arthur: Bernice Frankel
Fred Astaire: Frederick Austerlitz
Awkwafina: Nora Lum

Babyface: Kenneth Edmonds
Lauren Bacall: Betty Joan Perske
Erykah Badu: Erica Wright
Eric Bana: Eric Banadinovich
Anne Bancroft: Anna Maria Italiano
Theda Bara: Theodosia Goodman
Beck: Bek David Campbell
Pat Benatar: Patricia Andrejewski
Tony Bennett: Anthony Benedetto
Jack Benny: Benjamin Kubelsky
Milton Berle: Mendel Berlinger
Irving Berlin: Israel Baline

Sarah Bernhardt: Henriette-Rosine Bernard
Jello Biafra: Eric Reed Boucher
Big Boi: Antwan Patton
The Big Bopper: Jiles Perry "J.P." Richardson
Robert Blake: Michael James Vijencio Gubitosi
Jon Bon Jovi: John Francis Bongiovi
Bono: Paul Hewson
David Bowie: David Robert Jones
Boy George: George Alan O'Dowd
Fanny Brice: Fanny Borach

Charles Bronson: Charles Buchinski
Albert Brooks: Albert Einstein
Mel Brooks: Melvin Kaminsky
Foxy Brown: Inga Marchand
George Burns: Nathan Birnbaum
Ellen Burstyn: Edna Gilhooley
Richard Burton: Richard Jenkins
Red Buttons: Aaron Chwatt
Nicolas Cage: Nicholas Coppola
Michael Caine: Maurice Micklewhite
Maria Callas: Maria Kalogeropoulos
Cardi B: Belcalis Marlenis Almánza
Jackie Chan: Chan Kwong-Sung
Cyd Charisse: Tula Finklea
Ray Charles: Ray Charles Robinson
Charo: María Rosario Pilar Martínez Molina Baeza
Chubby Checker: Ernest Evans
Cher: Cherilyn Sarkisian
Chuck D: Carlton Ridenhour
Patsy Cline: Virginia Patterson Hensley
Claudette Colbert: Lily Chauchoin
Coolio: Artis Leon Ivey Jr.
Alice Cooper: Vincent Furnier
David Copperfield: David Kotkin
Howard Cosell: Howard Cohen
Elvis Costello: Declan McManus
Lou Costello: Louis Cristillo
Peter Coyote: Peter Cohon
Joan Crawford: Lucille LeSueur
Quentin Crisp: Denis Pratt
Tom Cruise: Thomas Cruise Mapother IV
Tony Curtis: Bernard Schwartz
Miley Cyrus: Destiny Hope Cyrus
D'Angelo: Michael D'Angelo Archer
Rodney Dangerfield: Jacob Cohen
Bobby Darin: Walden Robert Cassotto
Andra Day: Cassandra Monique Batie
Doris Day: Doris von Kappelhoff
Yvonne De Carlo: Peggy Middleton
Portia de Rossi: Amanda Lee Rogers
Sandra Dee: Alexandra Zuck
John Denver: Henry John Deutschendorf Jr.
Bo Derek: Mary Cathleen Collins
Danny DeVito: Daniel Michaeli
Angie Dickinson: Angeline Brown
Bo Diddley: Elias Bates
Vin Diesel: Mark Vincent
Phyllis Diller: Phyllis Driver
Divine: Harris Glenn Milstead
DMX: Earl Simmons
Troy Donahue: Merle Johnson Jr.
Kirk Douglas: Issur Danielovitch
Drake: Aubrey Drake Graham
Bob Dylan: Robert Zimmerman
Barbara Eden: Barbara Huffman
Elvira: Cassandra Peterson
Eminem: Marshall Mathers
Enya: Eithne Ni Bhraonain
Dale Evans: Frances Smith
Chad Everett: Raymon Cramton
Fabian: Fabian Anthony Forte
Fabolous: John David Jackson
Douglas Fairbanks: Douglas Ullman
Morgan Fairchild: Patsy McClenny
Jamie Farr: Jameel Farah
Fergie: Stacy Ferguson
Stepin Fetchit: Lincoln Perry
W. C. Fields: William Claude Dukenfield
50 Cent: Curtis Jackson
Flavor Flav: William Drayton
Joan Fontaine: Joan de Havilland
Jodie Foster: Alicia Christian Foster
Jamie Foxx: Eric Bishop
Redd Foxx: John Sanford
Arlene Francis: Arlene Kazanjian
Connie Francis: Concetta Franconero
Greta Garbo: Greta Gustafsson
Judy Garland: Frances Gumm
James Garner: James Bumgarner
Crystal Gayle: Brenda Gail Webb
George Gershwin: Jacob Gershowitz
Kathie Lee Gifford: Kathie Epstein
Whoopi Goldberg: Caryn Johnson
Cary Grant: Archibald Leach
Lee Grant: Lyova Rosenthal
Robert Guillaume: Robert Williams
Buddy Hackett: Leonard Hacker
Hammer: Stanley Kirk Burrell
Jean Harlow: Harlean Carpenter
Helen Hayes: Helen Brown
Susan Hayward: Edythe Marrener
Rita Hayworth: Margarita Cansino
Pee-Wee Herman: Paul Reubenfeld

Charlton Heston: John Charles Carter
Perez Hilton: Mario Lavandeira Jr.
Hulk Hogan: Terry Gene Bollea
Billie Holiday: Eleanora Fagan
Judy Holliday: Judith Tuvim
Bob Hope: Leslie Townes Hope
Harry Houdini: Erik Weisz
Howlin' Wolf: Chester Burnett
Rock Hudson: Roy Scherer Jr. (later Fitzgerald)
Engelbert Humperdinck: Arnold Dorsey
Kim Hunter: Janet Cole
Ice Cube: O'Shea Jackson
Ice-T: Tracy Morrow
Billy Idol: William Broad
Etta James: Jamesetta Hawkins
Ja Rule: Jeffrey Atkins
Jay-Z: Shawn Carter
Elton John: Reginald Dwight
Al Jolson: Asa Yoelson
Jennifer Jones: Phylis Isley
Tom Jones: Thomas Woodward
Spike Jonze: Adam Spiegel
Wynonna Judd: Christina Ciminella
Mindy Kaling: Vera Mindy Chokalingam
Boris Karloff: William Henry Pratt
Diane Keaton: Diane Hall
Michael Keaton: Michael Douglas
Kesha: Kesha Rose Sebert
Alicia Keys: Alicia Augello Cook
Chaka Khan: Yvette Stevens
Kid Rock: Robert Ritchie
Carole King: Carole Klein
Larry King: Larry Zeiger
Ben Kingsley: Krishna Banji
Ted Knight: Tadewurz Wladziu Konopka
Cheryl Ladd: Cheryl Stoppelmoor
Lady Gaga: Stefani Germanotta
Veronica Lake: Constance Ockleman
Kendrick Lamar: Kendrick Lamar Duckworth
Hedy Lamarr: Hedwig Kiesler
Dorothy Lamour: Mary Leta Dorothy Slaton
Michael Landon: Eugene Orowitz
Mario Lanza: Alfredo Cocozza
Queen Latifah: Dana Owens
Stan Laurel: Arthur Jefferson
Brenda Lee: Brenda Mae Tarpley
Gypsy Rose Lee: Rose Louise Hovick
Peggy Lee: Norma Egstrom
Janet Leigh: Jeanette Morrison
Vivien Leigh: Vivian Hartley
Huey Lewis: Hugh Cregg
Jerry Lewis: Joseph Levitch
Lil' Kim: Kimberly Denise Jones
Lil Nas X: Montero Lamar Hill
Little Richard: Richard Penniman
LL Cool J: James Todd Smith
Carole Lombard: Jane Peters
Lorde: Ella Yelich-O'Connor
Sophia Loren: Sophia Scicolone
Peter Lorre: Laszlo Lowenstein
Louis C.K.: Louis Szekely
Myrna Loy: Myrna Williams
Bela Lugosi: Bela Ferenc Blasko
Moms Mabley: Loretta Mary Aiken
Macklemore: Ben Haggerty
Shirley MacLaine: Shirley Beaty
Elle Macpherson: Eleanor Gow
Madonna: Madonna Louise Veronica Ciccone
Lee Majors: Harvey Lee Yeary
Karl Malden: Mladen Sekulovich
Barry Manilow: Barry Alan Pincus
Jayne Mansfield: Vera Jane Palmer
Marilyn Manson: Brian Warner
Bruno Mars: Peter Gene Hernandez
Dean Martin: Dino Crocetti
Ricky Martin: Enrique Jose Martin Morales
MCA: Adam Yauch
Meat Loaf: Marvin Lee Aday
Megan Thee Stallion: Megan Jovon Ruth Pete
Freddie Mercury: Farrokh Bulsara
Ethel Merman: Ethel Zimmermann
George Michael: Georgios Panayiotou
Mike D: Michael Diamond
Nicki Minaj: Onika Tanya Maraj
Helen Mirren: Ilynea Lydia Mironoff
Joni Mitchell: Roberta Joan Anderson
Moby: Richard Melville Hall
Mo'Nique: Monique Imes
Marilyn Monroe: Norma Jean Mortenson (later Baker)

Yves Montand: Ivo Livi
Demi Moore: Demetria Guynes
Rita Moreno: Rosita Alverio
Harry Morgan: Harry Bratsburg
Morrissey: Steven Patrick Morrissey
Mr. T: Lawrence Tureaud
Paul Muni: Mehilem Weisenfreund
Nelly: Cornell Haynes Jr.
Mike Nichols: Michael Igor Peschowsky
Chuck Norris: Carlos Ray Norris
Notorious B.I.G.: Christopher Wallace
Hugh O'Brian: Hugh Krampke
Maureen O'Hara: Maureen FitzSimons
Jack Palance: Vladimir Palanuik
Minnie Pearl: Sarah Ophelia Cannon
Katy Perry: Kathryn Hudson
Bernadette Peters: Bernadette Lazzara
Joaquin Phoenix: Joaquin Bottom
Edith Piaf: Edith Gassion
Slim Pickens: Louis Lindley
Mary Pickford: Gladys Smith
Pink: Alecia Moore
Pitbull: Armando Christian Pérez
Iggy Pop: James Newell Osterberg
Natalie Portman: Natalie Hershlag
Prince: Prince Rogers Nelson
Dee Dee Ramone: Douglas Colvin
Joey Ramone: Jeffrey Hyman
Johnny Ramone: John Cummings
Tommy Ramone: Tom Erdelyi
Tony Randall: Leonard Rosenberg
Della Reese: Delloreese Patricia Early
Busta Rhymes: Trevor Smith Jr.
Joan Rivers: Joan Sandra Molinsky
Edward G. Robinson: Emmanuel Goldenberg
The Rock: Dwayne Johnson
Ginger Rogers: Virginia McMath
Roy Rogers: Leonard Franklin Slye
Mickey Rooney: Joe Yule Jr.
Johnny Rotten: John Lydon
Lillian Russell: Helen Leonard
Meg Ryan: Margaret Hyra
Winona Ryder: Winona Horowitz
Sade: Helen Folsade Abu
Soupy Sales: Milton Supman
Susan Sarandon: Susan Tomaling
Seal: Seal Henry Olusegun Olumide Adeola Samuel
Jane Seymour: Joyce Frankenberg
Omar Sharif: Michael Shalhoub
Charlie Sheen: Carlos Irwin Estevez
Martin Sheen: Ramon Estevez
Talia Shire: Talia Coppola
Beverly Sills: Belle Silverman
Phil Silvers: Philip Silversmith
Gene Simmons: Chaim Witz
Sinbad: David Adkins
Anna Nicole Smith: Vickie Lynn Hogan
Snoop Dogg: Calvin Broadus
Barbara Stanwyck: Ruby Stevens
Jean Stapleton: Jeanne Murray
Ringo Starr: Richard Starkey
Cat Stevens: Stephen Demetre Georgiou
Connie Stevens: Concetta Ingolia
Jon Stewart: Jonathan Stuart Leibowitz
Sting: Gordon Sumner
Joe Strummer: John Graham Mellor
Donna Summer: La Donna Gaines
Rip Taylor: Charles Elmer Taylor Jr.
Robert Taylor: Spangler Brugh
The Weeknd: Abel Makkonen Tesfaye
Danny Thomas: Muzyad Yakhoob (later Amos Jacobs)
Tiny Tim: Herbert Khaury
Rip Torn: Elmore Rual Torn Jr.
Randy Travis: Randy Traywick
Tina Turner: Annie Mae Bullock
Shania Twain: Eilleen Regina Edwards
Twiggy: Lesley Hornby
Conway Twitty: Harold Lloyd Jenkins
Steven Tyler: Stephen Tallarico
Rudolph Valentino: Rudolpho D'Antonguolla
Frankie Valli: Frank Castelluccio
Eddie Vedder: Edward Louis Seversen III
Sid Vicious: John Simon Ritchie
John Wayne: Marion Morrison
Raquel Welch: Raquel Tejada
Gene Wilder: Jerome Silberman
Shelley Winters: Shirley Schrift
Jane Wyman: Sarah Jane Mayfield
Loretta Young: Gretchen Michaels Young
Buckwheat Zydeco: Stanley Dural Jr.

ARTS AND MEDIA

Worldwide Top-Grossing American Movies, 2000-23
Source: Box Office Mojo

Year	Title	Gross (mil)	Year	Title	Gross (mil)
2000	Mission: Impossible II	$546.4	2012	The Avengers	$1,518.8
2001	Harry Potter and the Sorcerer's Stone	974.8	2013	Frozen	1,280.8
2002	The Lord of the Rings: The Two Towers	923.3	2014	Transformers: Age of Extinction	1,104.1
2003	The Lord of the Rings: The Return of the King	1,140.7	2015	Star Wars: Episode VII—The Force Awakens	2,068.2
2004	Shrek 2	928.8	2016	Captain America: Civil War	1,153.3
2005	Harry Potter and the Goblet of Fire	896.0	2017	Star Wars: Episode VIII—The Last Jedi	1,332.5
2006	Pirates of the Caribbean: Dead Man's Chest	1,066.2	2018	Avengers: Infinity War	2,048.4
2007	Pirates of the Caribbean: At World's End	961.0	2019	Avengers: Endgame	2,797.8
2008	The Dark Knight	1,003.0	2020	Bad Boys for Life	426.5
2009	Avatar	2,744.3	2021	Spider-Man: No Way Home	1,905.3
2010	Toy Story 3	1,067.0	2022	Avatar: The Way of Water	2,320.3
2011	Harry Potter and the Deathly Hallows: Part 2	1,341.5	2023	Barbie	1,404.2

Note: Box-office grosses worldwide through Sept. 13, 2023.

All-Time Top-Grossing American Movies
Source: Box Office Mojo

Rank	Title (original release date)	Gross (mil)	Rank	Title (original release date)	Gross (mil)
1.	Star Wars: Episode VII—The Force Awakens (2015)	$936.7	26.	Black Panther: Wakanda Forever (2022)	$453.8
2.	Avengers: Endgame (2019)	858.4	27.	The Dark Knight Rises (2012)	448.1
3.	Spider-Man: No Way Home (2021)	814.1	28.	Shrek 2 (2004)	441.2
4.	Avatar (2009)	785.2	29.	E.T. The Extra-Terrestrial (1982)	437.1
5.	Top Gun: Maverick (2022)	718.7	30.	Toy Story 4 (2019)	434.0
6.	Black Panther (2018)	700.4	31.	Captain Marvel (2019)	426.8
7.	Avatar: The Way of Water (2022)	684.1	32.	The Hunger Games: Catching Fire (2013)	424.7
8.	Avengers: Infinity War (2018)	678.8	33.	Pirates of the Caribbean: Dead Man's Chest (2006)	423.3
9.	Titanic (1997)	674.3	34.	The Lion King (1994)	422.8
10.	Jurassic World (2015)	653.4	35.	Jurassic World: Fallen Kingdom (2018)	417.7
11.	The Avengers (2012)	623.4	36.	Toy Story 3 (2010)	415.0
12.	Barbie (2023)	622.2	37.	Wonder Woman (2017)	412.8
13.	Star Wars: Episode VIII—The Last Jedi (2017)	620.2	38.	Doctor Strange in the Multiverse of Madness (2022)	411.3
14.	Incredibles 2 (2018)	608.6	39.	Iron Man 3 (2013)	409.0
15.	The Super Mario Bros. Movie (2023)	574.9	40.	Captain America: Civil War (2016)	408.1
16.	The Lion King (2019)	543.6	41.	The Hunger Games (2012)	408.0
17.	The Dark Knight (2008)	535.0	42.	Jurassic Park (1993)	407.2
18.	Rogue One: A Star Wars Story (2016)	533.5	43.	Spider-Man (2002)	407.0
19.	Star Wars: Episode IX—The Rise of Skywalker (2019)	515.2	44.	Jumanji: Welcome to the Jungle (2017)	404.5
20.	Beauty and the Beast (2017)	504.5	45.	Transformers: Revenge of the Fallen (2009)	402.1
21.	Finding Dory (2016)	486.3	46.	Frozen (2013)	401.0
22.	Frozen 2 (2019)	477.4	47.	Spider-Man: Far From Home (2019)	390.5
23.	Star Wars: Episode I—The Phantom Menace (1999)	474.5	48.	Guardians of the Galaxy Vol. 2 (2017)	389.8
24.	Star Wars: Episode IV—A New Hope (1977)	461.0	49.	Harry Potter and the Deathly Hallows: Part 2 (2011)	381.4
25.	Avengers: Age of Ultron (2015)	459.0	50.	Spider-Man: Across the Spider-Verse (2023)	381.3

Note: Box-office grosses in the U.S. and Canada through Sept. 15, 2023, in absolute dollars. Rising ticket prices favor newer films. Revenues from re-releases are included.

Top-Grossing American Movies (Adjusted Lifetime Gross)
Source: Box Office Mojo

Rank	Title (original release date)	Adj. gross (mil)	Rank	Title (original release date)	Adj. gross (mil)
1.	Gone With the Wind (1939)	$1,895.4	24.	Fantasia (1940)	$778.1
2.	Star Wars: Episode IV—A New Hope (1977)	1,669.0	25.	The Godfather (1972)	739.5
3.	The Sound of Music (1965)	1,335.1	26.	Forrest Gump (1994)	736.8
4.	E.T. the Extra-Terrestrial (1982)	1,329.2	27.	Mary Poppins (1964)	732.6
5.	Titanic (1997)	1,270.1	28.	Grease (1978)	722.4
6.	The Ten Commandments (1956)	1,227.5	29.	The Avengers (2012)	720.4
7.	Jaws (1975)	1,200.9	30.	Jurassic World (2015)	719.6
8.	Doctor Zhivago (1965)	1,163.1	31.	Black Panther (2018)	715.0
9.	The Exorcist (1973)	1,036.3	32.	Thunderball (1965)	700.9
10.	Snow White and the Seven Dwarfs (1937)	1,021.3	33.	The Dark Knight (2008)	697.7
11.	Star Wars: Episode VII—The Force Awakens (2015)	1,013.0	34.	The Jungle Book (1967)	690.4
12.	101 Dalmatians (1961)	936.2	35.	Sleeping Beauty (1959)	681.0
13.	Star Wars: Episode V—The Empire Strikes Back (1980)	920.8	36.	Avengers: Infinity War (2018)	678.6
			37.	Ghostbusters (1984)	667.9
14.	Ben-Hur (1959)	918.7	38.	Shrek 2 (2004)	665.7
15.	Avatar (2009)	911.8	39.	Spider-Man (2002)	661.8
16.	Avengers: Endgame (2019)	892.7	40.	Butch Cassidy and the Sundance Kid (1969)	661.1
17.	Star Wars: Episode VI—Return of the Jedi (1983)	881.3	41.	Love Story (1970)	656.0
			42.	Independence Day (1996)	649.0
18.	Jurassic Park (1993)	860.2	43.	Home Alone (1990)	634.7
19.	Star Wars: Episode I—The Phantom Menace (1999)	846.2	44.	Star Wars: Episode VIII—The Last Jedi (2017)	633.4
			45.	Pinocchio (1940)	631.6
20.	The Lion King (1994)	835.3	46.	Cleopatra (1963)	629.5
21.	The Sting (1973)	835.3	47.	Beverly Hills Cop (1984)	629.2
22.	Raiders of the Lost Ark (1981)	829.7	48.	Goldfinger (1964)	621.2
23.	The Graduate (1967)	801.9	49.	Incredibles 2 (2018)	621.2
			50.	Airport (1970)	619.5

Note: Adjusted lifetime gross is in 2022 dollars, as of Aug. 15, 2022, and adjusts for ticket price inflation using estimated number of tickets sold.

50 Top-Grossing Movies, 2023

Source: Comscore, Inc.

Rank	Title	Gross (mil)	Rank	Title	Gross (mil)
1.	Barbie	$612.3	26.	Haunted Mansion	$64.7
2.	The Super Mario Bros. Movie	574.9	27.	Cocaine Bear	64.4
3.	Spider-Man: Across the Spider-Verse	381.3	28.	A Man Called Otto	64.2
4.	Guardians of the Galaxy Vol. 3	359.0	29.	Blue Beetle	58.7
5.	Oppenheimer	310.7	30.	Shazam! Fury of the Gods	57.6
6.	The Little Mermaid	298.1	31.	Air	52.5
7.	Avatar: The Way of Water	283.1	32.	Jesus Revolution	52.1
8.	Ant-Man and the Wasp: Quantumania	214.5	33.	No Hard Feelings	50.5
9.	John Wick: Chapter 4	187.1	34.	The Boogeyman	43.2
10.	Sound of Freedom	182.5	35.	The Equalizer 3	42.8
11.	Indiana Jones and the Dial of Destiny	174.4	36.	Talk to Me	40.5
12.	Mission: Impossible–Dead Reckoning Part One	170.6	37.	80 for Brady	39.3
13.	Transformers: Rise of the Beasts	157.1	38.	Knock at the Cabin	35.4
14.	Creed III	156.2	39.	Missing	32.5
15.	Elemental	153.6	40.	Plane	32.1
16.	Fast X	146.0	41.	65	32.1
17.	Puss In Boots: The Last Wish	129.9	42.	Gran Turismo: Based on a True Story	30.9
18.	Scream VI	108.2	43.	Asteroid City	28.1
19.	The Flash	108.1	44.	Magic Mike's Last Dance	26.0
20.	Teenage Mutant Ninja Turtles: Mutant Mayhem	108.0	45.	Strays	21.5
21.	M3GAN	95.0	46.	Are You There God? It's Me, Margaret.	20.4
22.	Dungeons & Dragons: Honor Among Thieves	93.3	47.	The Pope's Exorcist	20.0
23.	Insidious: The Red Door	82.1	48.	The Blackening	17.7
24.	Meg 2: The Trench	79.1	49.	Book Club: The Next Chapter	17.6
25.	Evil Dead Rise	67.2	50.	Pathaan	17.5

Note: Preliminary box-office grosses in the U.S. and Canada, Jan. 1-Aug. 31, 2023; some films had 2022 release dates.

50 Top-Grossing Movies, 2022

Source: Comscore, Inc.

Rank	Title	Gross (mil)	Rank	Title	Gross (mil)
1.	Top Gun: Maverick	$718.7	26.	Puss in Boots: The Last Wish	$73.8
2.	Avatar: The Way of Water	471.8	27.	Everything Everywhere All at Once	70.0
3.	Black Panther: Wakanda Forever	442.0	28.	Ticket to Paradise	68.3
4.	Doctor Strange in the Multiverse of Madness	411.3	29.	The Woman King	67.2
5.	Jurassic World Dominion	376.9	30.	Sing 2	65.7
6.	Minions: The Rise of Gru	369.7	31.	Halloween Ends	64.1
7.	The Batman	369.3	32.	Dog	61.8
8.	Thor: Love and Thunder	343.3	33.	Jackass Forever	57.7
9.	Sonic the Hedgehog 2	190.9	34.	Violent Night	48.7
10.	Spider-Man: No Way Home	178.4	35.	Lyle, Lyle, Crocodile	46.8
11.	Black Adam	168.1	36.	Death on the Nile	45.6
12.	Elvis	151.0	37.	Don't Worry Darling	45.3
13.	Uncharted	148.6	38.	Downton Abbey: A New Era	44.1
14.	Nope	123.3	39.	Barbarian	40.8
15.	Lightyear	118.3	40.	Dragon Ball Super: Super Hero	38.0
16.	Smile (2022)	105.9	41.	Strange World	37.5
17.	The Lost City	105.3	42.	The Menu	36.9
18.	Bullet Train	103.4	43.	Jujutsu Kaisen 0	34.5
19.	The Bad Guys	97.2	44.	The Northman	34.2
20.	Fantastic Beasts: The Secrets of Dumbledore	95.9	45.	The Bob's Burgers Movie	31.9
21.	DC League of Super Pets	93.7	46.	Beast	31.8
22.	Where the Crawdads Sing	90.2	47.	The Invitation	25.1
23.	The Black Phone	90.1	48.	Avatar (2009; rerelease)	24.7
24.	Scream (2022)	81.6	49.	Ambulance	22.8
25.	Morbius	73.9	50.	Marry Me	22.4

Note: Box-office grosses in the U.S. and Canada, Jan. 1, 2022-Jan. 6, 2023; some films had 2021 releases.

National Film Registry, 2022

Source: National Film Registry, Library of Congress

The National Film Registry adds 25 "culturally, historically, or aesthetically significant" American films annually.

Mardi Gras Carnival (1898)
Cab Calloway Home Movies (1948-1951)
Cyrano de Bergerac (1950)
Charade (1963)
Scorpio Rising (1963)
Behind Every Good Man (1967)
Titicut Follies (1967)
Mingus (1968)

Manzanar (1971)
Betty Tells Her Story (1972)
Super Fly (1972)
Attica (1974)
Carrie (1976)
Union Maids (1976)
Word Is Out: Stories of Our Lives (1977)
Bush Mama (1979)

The Ballad of Gregorio Cortez (1982)
Itam Hakim, Hopiit (1984)
Hairspray (1988)
The Little Mermaid (1989)
Tongues Untied (1989)
When Harry Met Sally (1989)
House Party (1990)
Iron Man (2008)
Pariah (2011)

Movie Theaters, 1946-2021

Source: Motion Picture Association of America (MPAA); Comscore, Inc.

Year	Box office (mil)	Admissions (mil)	Admissions per week (mil)	Screens	Avg. ticket price	Films produced	Films released
1946	$1,692.0	4,067.3	78.2	NA	$0.42	NA	400
1950	1,379.0	3,017.5	58.0	NA	0.46	NA	483
1955	1,204.0	2,072.3	39.9	NA	0.58	NA	319
1960	984.4	1,304.5	25.1	NA	0.76	NA	248
1965	1,041.8	1,031.5	19.8	NA	1.01	NA	279
1970	1,429.2	920.6	17.7	NA	1.55	279	306
1975	2,114.8	1,032.8	19.9	15,030	2.03	258	233
1980	2,748.5	1,021.5	19.6	17,590	2.69	214	233
1985	3,749.4	1,056.1	20.3	21,147	3.55	264	470
1990	5,021.8	1,188.6	22.9	23,689	4.22	346	410
1995	5,269.0	1,211.0	23.3	27,805	4.35	631	411
2000	7,468.0	1,383.0	26.6	37,396	5.39	683	475
2005	8,832.0	1,376.0	26.5	38,852	6.41	920	507
2010	10,741.0	1,341.0	25.8	39,547	7.89	795	563
2012	10,774.5	1,358.0	26.0	39,918	7.96	476[1]	690
2013	10,919.7	1,340.0	25.8	42,814	8.13	455[1]	681
2014	10,329.0	1,267.6	24.4	41,518	8.17	482[1]	762
2015	11,081.2	1,321.0	25.4	42,552	8.43	495[1]	753
2016	11,573.4	1,315.0	25.3	42,659	8.65	511[1]	799
2017	11,072.7	1,240.0	23.8	43,216	8.97	549[1]	872
2018	11,852.1	1,304.0	25.1	43,459	9.11	576[1]	862
2019	11,375.3	1,242.0	23.9	43,679	9.16	601[1,2]	987
2020[3]	2,200.0	240.0	4.6	42,623	9.37	341[1,2]	338
2021	4,500.0	470.0	9.0	41,882	9.57	696[1,2]	387

NA = Not available. **Note:** The MPAAs 2022 Theme Report was delayed due to the Writers Guild of America strike. (1) Non-MPAA members with est. budget under $1 mil were not tracked. (2) Incl. Netflix as a member studio. (3) Box office numbers were down 80% in 2020 due to the COVID-19 pandemic.

Best American Movies of All Time

Source: American Film Institute

First unveiled in 1998 based on ballots sent to 1,500 individuals, mostly from the film world, in 1997. Updated in 2007 (the version shown here) to include newly eligible films and reflect shifting cultural perspectives. Criteria for judging included historical significance, cultural impact, critical recognition and awards, and popularity. The year each film was first released is in parentheses.

1. Citizen Kane (1941)
2. The Godfather (1972)
3. Casablanca (1942)
4. Raging Bull (1980)
5. Singin' in the Rain (1952)
6. Gone With the Wind (1939)
7. Lawrence of Arabia (1962)
8. Schindler's List (1993)
9. Vertigo (1958)
10. The Wizard of Oz (1939)
11. City Lights (1931)
12. The Searchers (1956)
13. Star Wars (1977)
14. Psycho (1960)
15. 2001: A Space Odyssey (1968)
16. Sunset Boulevard (1950)
17. The Graduate (1967)
18. The General (1927)
19. On the Waterfront (1954)
20. It's a Wonderful Life (1946)
21. Chinatown (1974)
22. Some Like It Hot (1959)
23. The Grapes of Wrath (1940)
24. E.T. the Extra-Terrestrial (1982)
25. To Kill a Mockingbird (1962)
26. Mr. Smith Goes to Washington (1939)
27. High Noon (1952)
28. All About Eve (1950)
29. Double Indemnity (1944)
30. Apocalypse Now (1979)
31. The Maltese Falcon (1941)
32. The Godfather Part II (1974)
33. One Flew Over the Cuckoo's Nest (1975)
34. Snow White and the Seven Dwarfs (1937)
35. Annie Hall (1977)
36. The Bridge on the River Kwai (1957)
37. The Best Years of Our Lives (1946)
38. The Treasure of the Sierra Madre (1948)
39. Dr. Strangelove (1964)
40. The Sound of Music (1965)
41. King Kong (1933)
42. Bonnie and Clyde (1967)
43. Midnight Cowboy (1969)
44. The Philadelphia Story (1940)
45. Shane (1953)
46. It Happened One Night (1934)
47. A Streetcar Named Desire (1951)
48. Rear Window (1954)
49. Intolerance (1916)
50. The Lord of the Rings: The Fellowship of the Ring (2001)

Film and TV Content Ratings

The Motion Picture Association of America (MPAA) established a ratings system in 1968. It was revised in 1984 and in 1990. The MPAA, Natl. Cable Television Assn., and Natl. Assn. of Broadcasters developed the TV ratings system in 1997, in accordance with the Telecommunications Act of 1996; it was implemented in Oct. 1997.

Film Ratings

G: General Audience. All ages admitted. Does not contain themes, language, nudity, sex, or violence that the MPAA ratings board believes would offend parents whose younger children see the film. Does not necessarily denote a certificate of approval nor children's movie. No nudity, sex scenes, or drug use depicted.

PG: Parental Guidance Suggested. Some material may not be suited for children. The MPAA ratings board recommends that parents determine whether the content of the film is appropriate for their children. The film may contain more mature themes, some profanity, violence, or brief nudity. No drug use depicted.

PG-13: Parents Strongly Cautioned. Some material may be inappropriate for children under 13. Any movie depicting drug use or more than brief nudity is automatically rated at least PG-13. Violence is permitted, though it is generally not both realistic or extreme and persistent violence. The single use of one sexually-derived expletive rates a PG-13; more than one use requires at least an R rating.

R: Restricted. Under 17 requires accompanying parent or adult guardian. Movies given R ratings contain some adult material, defined as adult themes or activity, hard language, intense or persistent violence, sexually-oriented nudity, or drug abuse.

NC-17: No One 17 and Under Admitted. Those films that most parents would consider too adult for children under 17. An NC-17 rating does not mean the film is obscene or pornographic. The rating can be based on violence, sex, aberrational behavior, drug abuse, or any other element.

TV Ratings

TV-Y: All Children. Program designed to be acceptable for children of all ages. Its themes and elements are designed for a very young audience.

TV-Y7: Directed to Older Children. Program designed for children ages 7 and older, and more appropriate for those who have the skills to distinguish between make-believe and reality. May include mild fantasy/comedic violence. Programs with more than mild fantasy violence are denoted TV-Y7-FV.

TV-G: General Audience. Program not necessarily designed for children, but most parents would find it suitable for all ages. Little or no violence, no strong language, and little or no sexual dialogue or situations.

TV-PG: Parental Guidance Suggested. Program might contain material that parents would consider inappropriate for children, such as an adult theme or one or more of the following: suggestive dialogue (D), infrequent coarse language (L), some sexual situations (S), or moderate violence (V).

TV-14: Parents Strongly Cautioned. Program contains material that many parents would consider inappropriate for children under 14, such as one or more of the following: intensely suggestive dialogue (D), strong coarse language (L), intense sexual situations (S), or intense violence (V).

TV-MA: Mature Audience Only. Program specifically designed for adults and may be unsuitable for children under 17. Contains one or more of the following: crude indecent language (L), explicit sexual activity (S), or graphic violence (V).

Most Popular YouTubers, 2023

Source: SocialBlade

Rank	Name	Subscribers (mil)	Rank	Name	Subscribers (mil)	Rank	Name	Subscribers (mil)
1.	T-Series	247.0	20.	Pinkfong Baby Shark - Kids' Songs & Stories	68.8	36.	Infobells - Hindi	54.6
2.	MrBeast	174.0				37.	LooLoo Kids - Nursery Rhymes and Children's Songs	54.5
3.	YouTube Movies	171.0	21.	Canal KondZilla	66.6			
4.	Cocomelon - Nursery Rhymes	163.0	22.	ChuChu TV Nursery Rhymes & Kids Songs	66.4	38.	Ed Sheeran	53.6
5.	SET India	160.0				39.	Taylor Swift	53.4
6.	Kids Diana Show	113.0	23.	Shemaroo Filmi Gaane	65.9	40.	Ariana Grande	52.8
7.	PewDiePie	111.0	24.	Colors TV	65.6	41.	BillionSurpriseToys - Nursery Rhymes & Cartoons	52.6
8.	Like Nastya	106.0	25.	T-Series Bhakti Sagar	61.7			
9.	Vlad and Niki	99.8	26.	Tips Official	60.1	42.	JuegaGerman	48.3
10.	Zee Music Company	97.8	27.	Movieclips	59.6	43.	Billie Eilish	48.2
11.	WWE	96.6	28.	Dude Perfect	59.6	44.	Shemaroo	48.0
12.	BLACKPINK	90.6	29.	El Reino Infantil	59.0	45.	Get Movies	47.8
13.	Goldmines	87.8	30.	Wave Music	58.4	46.	SonyMusicIndiaVEVO	47.0
14.	Sony SAB	84.1	31.	Aaj Tak	58.3	47.	Badabun	46.9
15.	5-Minute Crafts	80.2	32.	Sony Music India	57.5	48.	A4	46.8
16.	BANGTANTV	76.0	33.	EminemMusic	57.1	49.	Bad Bunny	46.3
17.	HYBE LABELS	72.2	34.	Marshmello	56.5	50.	Fernanfloo	46.2
18.	Justin Bieber	71.7	35.	YRF	55.1			
19.	Zee TV	71.3						

Note: Ranked by channel subscribers as of Aug. 14, 2023.

Most Popular Podcasts, 2023

Source: Podtrac

Rank	Podcast	Publisher	Rank	Podcast	Publisher
1.	The Daily	New York Times	12.	The Dan Bongino Show	Dan Bongino
2.	SmartLess	Wondery	13.	My Favorite Murder with Karen Kilgariff and Georgia Hardstark	Exactly Right
3.	Dateline NBC	NBC News			
4.	NPR News Now	NPR	14.	2 Bears 1 Cave with Tom Segura & Bert Kreischer	YMH Studios
5.	Morbid	Wondery			
6.	Up First	NPR	15.	FOX News Hourly Update	FOX News Podcasts
7.	The Ben Shapiro Show	The Daily Wire	16.	CNN 5 Things	WarnerMedia
8.	This Past Weekend	Yardvark	17.	Wait Wait...Don't Tell Me!	NPR
9.	Stuff You Should Know	iHeart Podcasts	18.	Scamanda	Lionsgate Sound
10.	Pardon My Take	Barstool Sports	19.	Hidden Brain	Hidden Brain Media
11.	This American Life	This American Life	20.	48 Hours	Paramount

Note: Rankings based on U.S. unique monthly audience for July 2023.

Top-Selling Video Games, 2022

Source: The NPD Group, Inc.

The U.S. video game industry generated $56.6 bil in revenue in 2022: $9.08 bil on hardware, including peripherals, and $47.5 bil on software, including in-game purchases and subscriptions. Overall spending was down 5% from $59.6 bil in 2021.

Ranked by combined dollar sales of game in physical/digital formats unless noted. Reporting period: Jan. 2, 2022-Dec. 31, 2022.

Rank	Game (console)	Rank	Game (console)
1.	Call of Duty: Modern Warfare 2 (2022) (PC, PS4, PS5, XBO, XBSX)	11.	Mario Kart 8* (Switch, Wii U)
2.	Elden Ring (PC, PS4, PS5, XBO, XBSX)	12.	Call of Duty: Vanguard (PC, PS4, PS5, XBO, XBSX)
3.	Madden NFL 23 (PC, PS4, PS5, XBO, XBSX)	13.	Gran Turismo 7 (PS4, PS5)
4.	God of War: Ragnarok (PS4, PS5)	14.	Kirby and the Forgotten Land* (Switch)
5.	LEGO Star Wars: The Skywalker Saga (PC, PS4, PS5, Switch, XBO, XBSX)	15.	NBA 2K23* (Apple Arcade, PC, PS4, PS5, Switch, XBO, XBSX)
6.	Pokemon: Scarlet/Violet* (Switch)	16.	Sonic Frontiers (PC, PS4, PS5, Switch, XBO, XBSX)
7.	FIFA 23 (PC, PS4, PS5, Switch, XBO, XBSX)	17.	Gotham Knights (PC, PS5, XBSX)
8.	Pokemon Legends: Arceus* (Switch)	18.	Minecraft (Android, iOS, macOS, Nintendo 3DS, PC, PS3, PS4, PS Vita, Switch, XBO, XBO 360, Wii U)
9.	Horizon II: Forbidden West (PS4, PS5)	19.	Nintendo Switch Sports* (Switch)
10.	MLB: The Show 22** (PC, PS4, PS5, Switch, XBO, XBSX)	20.	Super Smash Bros. Ultimate* (Switch)

* = Digital sales not included. ** = Xbox & Switch digital sales not included. **Note:** Includes bundled, collector's, or game-of-the-year editions, except those bundled with hardware. PC = personal computer; PS = PlayStation; XBO = Microsoft Xbox One; XBSX = Microsoft Xbox Series X.

Video Gaming by Age, 2022

Source: Entertainment Software Association

Gamers who said they played—	Age of gamer						Genres gamers played	Age of gamer					
	18-24	25-34	35-44	45-54	55-64	65+		18-24	25-34	35-44	45-54	55-64	65+
On a smartphone	59%	61%	71%	69%	64%	55%	Action games	26%	24%	22%	15%	8%	3%
On a console	64	68	68	43	29	16	Arcade games	30	22	23	21	23	15
On a computer	44	45	44	38	47	59	Fighting games	20	16	15	9	3	0
On a tablet	17	20	24	26	36	34	Puzzle games	22	31	45	54	69	76
On a virtual reality device	10	14	13	8	4	3	Racing games	16	15	18	12	8	5
On only one type of device	40	38	31	46	47	52	Role playing & narrative games	27	28	24	17	9	5
							Shooter games	42	33	24	20	13	6
							Simulation games	20	24	17	14	12	6
							Skill and chance games	10	14	19	37	43	53
							Sports games	21	20	20	17	11	8
							Strategy games	18	18	17	12	8	7

Longest-Running Broadway Shows
Source: The Broadway League

Rank	Title (run)[1]	Performances[2]
1.	The Phantom of the Opera (1988-2023)	13,981
2.	*Chicago (revival) (1996-)	10,377
3.	*The Lion King (1997-)	9,993
4.	*Wicked (2003-)	7,533
5.	Cats (1982-2000)	7,485
6.	Les Misérables (1987-2003)	6,680
7.	A Chorus Line (1975-90)	6,137
8.	Oh! Calcutta! (revival) (1976-89)	5,959
9.	Mamma Mia! (2001-15)	5,758
10.	Beauty and the Beast (1994-2007)	5,462
11.	Rent (1996-2008)	5,123
12.	Jersey Boys (2005-17)	4,642
13.	*The Book of Mormon (2011-)	4,391
14.	Miss Saigon (1991-2001)	4,092
15.	42nd Street (1980-89)	3,486
16.	Grease (1972-80)	3,388
17.	Fiddler on the Roof (1964-72)	3,242
18.	Life With Father (1939-47)	3,224
19.	Tobacco Road (1933-41)	3,182
20.	*Aladdin (2014-)	3,163
21.	Hello, Dolly! (1964-70)	2,844
22.	My Fair Lady (1956-62)	2,717
23.	Hairspray (2002-09)	2,642
24.	Mary Poppins (2006-13)	2,619
25.	*Hamilton (2015-)	2,606
26.	Avenue Q (2003-09)	2,534
27.	Kinky Boots (2013-19)	2,505
28.	The Producers (2001-07)	2,502
29.	Beautiful: The Carole King Musical (2014-19)	2,416
30.	Cabaret (revival) (1998-2004)	2,377
31.	Annie (1977-83)	2,377
32.	Rock of Ages (2009-15)	2,328
32.	Man of La Mancha (1965-71)	2,328
34.	Abie's Irish Rose (1922-27)	2,327
35.	Oklahoma! (1943-48)	2,212
36.	Smokey Joe's Café (1995-2000)	2,036
37.	Pippin (1972-77)	1,944
38.	South Pacific (1949-54)	1,925
39.	The Magic Show (1974-78)	1,920
40.	Aida (2000-04)	1,852
41.	Gemini (1977-81)	1,819
42.	Deathtrap (1978-82)	1,793
43.	Harvey (1944-49)	1,775
44.	Dancin' (1978-82)	1,774
45.	La Cage aux Folles (1983-87)	1,761
46.	Hair (1968-72)	1,750
47.	The Wiz (1975-79)	1,672
	Dear Evan Hansen (2016-22)	1,672
49.	Come From Away (2017-22)	1,669
50.	Born Yesterday (1946-49)	1,642

* = Still running as of Sept. 2023. (1) Unless noted, listings reflect a show's first run on Broadway. (2) Number of performances through May 22, 2023. **Note:** Broadway was shut down as a result of the COVID-19 pandemic beginning Mar. 12, 2020. Shows began officially reopening Sept. 14, 2021.

Broadway Season Statistics, 1959-2023
Source: The Broadway League

Season	Gross (mil $)	Attendance (mil)	Playing weeks	New productions	Avg. ticket price
1959-1960	$46	7.9	1,156	58	$5.82
1964-1965	51	8.2	1,250	67	6.20
1969-1970	53	7.1	1,047	62	7.46
1974-1975	57	6.6	1,101	54	8.64
1979-1980	146	9.6	1,540	61	15.21
1984-1985	209	7.3	1,078	33	28.47
1989-1990	282	8.0	1,070	39	35.07
1994-1995	406	9.0	1,120	33	44.91
1999-2000	603	11.4	1,460	37	52.99
2004-2005	769	11.5	1,494	39	66.70
2005-2006	862	12.0	1,501	39	71.83
2006-2007	939	12.3	1,509	35	76.28
2007-2008	938	12.3	1,560	36	76.45
2008-2009	943	12.2	1,548	43	$77.61
2009-2010	1,020	11.9	1,464	39	85.79
2010-2011	1,081	12.5	1,588	42	86.27
2011-2012	1,139	12.3	1,522	41	92.38
2012-2013	1,139	11.6	1,430	46	98.42
2013-2014	1,269	12.2	1,496	44[1]	103.88
2014-2015	1,365	13.1	1,626	37	104.18
2015-2016	1,373	13.3	1,648	39	103.11
2016-2017	1,449	13.3	1,580	45[2]	109.21
2017-2018	1,697	13.8	1,624	33	123.07
2018-2019	1,829	14.8	1,737	38	123.87
2019-2020[3]	1,358	11.1	1,282	33	121.99
2021-2022[3]	845	6.7	946	39[4]	125.63
2022-2023	1,578	12.3	1,474	40	128.43

(1) Includes one return engagement. (2) Includes two return engagements. (3) Broadway shut down Mar. 12, 2020, due to the COVID-19 pandemic. Broadway shows began reopening on Sept. 14, 2021. (4) Includes five return engagements.

Notable U.S. Museums

This unofficial list of some of the largest museums in the U.S., by budget, was compiled with the assistance of the American Association of Museums (AAM). Zoos, aquariums, arboretums, botanical gardens, and planetariums may be AAM members but are not included here.

Museum	City	State
Academy Museum of Motion Pictures	Los Angeles	CA
American Museum of Natural History	New York	NY
Amon Carter Museum of Western Art	Ft. Worth	TX
The Art Institute of Chicago	Chicago	IL
Boston Children's Museum	Boston	MA
Brooklyn Museum of Art	Brooklyn	NY
Busch-Reisinger Museum	Cambridge	MA
California Academy of Sciences	San Francisco	CA
California Science Center	Los Angeles	CA
Carnegie Museums of Pittsburgh	Pittsburgh	PA
Children's Museum of Indianapolis	Indianapolis	IN
Cincinnati Art Museum	Cincinnati	OH
Cincinnati Museum Center	Cincinnati	OH
Cleveland Museum of Art	Cleveland	OH
Colonial Williamsburg	Williamsburg	VA
Corning Museum of Glass	Corning	NY
Crystal Bridges Museum of American Art	Bentonville	AR
Dallas Museum of Art	Dallas	TX
Denver Art Museum	Denver	CO
Denver Museum of Nature and Science	Denver	CO
Detroit Institute of Arts	Detroit	MI
Exploratorium	San Francisco	CA
The Field Museum	Chicago	IL
Fine Arts Museums of San Francisco	San Francisco	CA
Franklin Institute	Philadelphia	PA
The Frick Collection	New York	NY
J. Paul Getty Museum	Los Angeles	CA
Solomon R. Guggenheim Museum of Art	New York	NY
Harvard University Art Museums	Cambridge	MA
Henry F. DuPont Winterthur Museum	Winterthur	DE
Henry Ford Museum/Greenfield Village	Dearborn	MI
High Museum of Art	Atlanta	GA
Houston Museum of Natural Science	Houston	TX
Jamestown-Yorktown Foundation	Williamsburg	VA
Jewish Museum	New York	NY
L.A. County Museum of Art	Los Angeles	CA
Liberty Science Center, Liberty State Park	Jersey City	NJ
Maryland Science Center	Baltimore	MD
Mashantucket Pequot Museum and Research Center	Mashantucket	CT
Metropolitan Museum of Art	New York	NY
Milwaukee Public Museum	Milwaukee	WI
Minneapolis Institute of Arts	Minneapolis	MN
Museum of African American History	Detroit	MI
Museum of the American Arts and Crafts Movement	St. Petersburg	FL
Museum of the American West	Los Angeles	CA
Museum of Broadway	New York	NY
Museum of Contemporary Art	Los Angeles	CA
Museum of Fine Arts	Boston	MA
Museum of Fine Arts	Houston	TX
Museum of Modern Art	New York	NY

Museum	City	State
Museum of New Mexico	Santa Fe	NM
Museum of Science	Boston	MA
Museum of Science and Industry	Chicago	IL
Musical Instrument Museum	Phoenix	AZ
Mystic Seaport Museum	Mystic	CT
National Air and Space Museum	Washington	DC
National Baseball Hall of Fame and Museum, Inc.	Cooperstown	NY
National Civil Rights Museum	Memphis	TN
National Constitution Center	Philadelphia	PA
National Gallery of Art	Washington	DC
National Museum of African American History and Culture	Washington	DC
National Museum of American History	Washington	DC
National Museum of the American Indian	Washington	DC
National Museum of Natural History	Washington	DC
National 9/11 Memorial & Museum	New York	NY
National World War II Museum	New Orleans	LA
Nelson-Atkins Museum of Art	Kansas City	MO
New-York Historical Society	New York	NY
New York State Museum	Albany	NY
Peabody Essex Museum	Salem	MA
Philadelphia Museum of Art	Philadelphia	PA
Rock and Roll Hall of Fame and Museum, Inc.	Cleveland	OH
St. Louis Science Center	St. Louis	MO
San Diego Museum of Art	San Diego	CA
San Francisco Museum of Modern Art	San Francisco	CA
Science Museum of Minnesota	St. Paul	MN
Toledo Museum of Art	Toledo	OH
U.S. Holocaust Memorial Museum	Washington	DC
Univ. of Pennsylvania Museum of Archaeology and Anthropology	Philadelphia	PA
Virginia Museum of Fine Arts	Richmond	VA
Wadsworth Atheneum	Hartford	CT
Walker Art Center	Minneapolis	MN
Whitney Museum of American Art	New York	NY

Characteristics of Public Libraries by State, 2019

Source: Public Libraries Survey, Institute of Museum and Library Services

State	Libraries[1]	Operating revenue[2] (thous.)	Library visits		Circulation[3]		Internet use[4]	
			Total (thous.)	Per capita	Total (thous.)	Per capita	Total (thous.)	Per capita
AL	220	$112,525	14,450	3.0	20,606	4.3	3,415	0.7
AK	64	39,837	3,062	4.8	5,036	7.8	551	0.9
AZ	89	210,027	23,446	3.3	49,272	6.9	4,246	0.6
AR	60	88,522	9,236	3.4	14,013	5.1	1,449	0.5
CA	185	1,745,727	139,011	3.5	215,768	5.4	24,393	0.6
CO	112	346,011	29,582	5.3	64,123	11.4	5,122	0.9
CT	180	201,517	19,014	5.8	24,927	7.6	3,419	1.0
DE	21	31,574	4,056	4.2	5,593	5.8	509	0.5
DC	1	60,828	3,820	5.4	4,865	6.9	944	1.3
FL	81	673,322	63,289	3.0	103,314	4.9	13,401	0.6
GA	62	214,026	26,003	2.4	35,986	3.3	10,964	1.0
HI	1	40,263	3,436	2.4	5,625	4.0	793	0.6
ID	103	65,518	8,290	5.5	16,379	10.9	1,397	0.9
IL	623	878,783	60,853	5.2	105,752	9.0	9,656	0.8
IN	236	397,598	30,247	5.0	65,173	10.7	4,764	0.8
IA	535	138,270	16,434	5.4	24,515	8.0	2,468	0.8
KS	318	153,380	13,459	5.4	25,225	10.1	2,379	0.9
KY	120	209,295	16,157	3.6	28,888	6.5	3,628	0.8
LA	67	278,802	15,934	3.5	21,990	4.8	4,471	1.0
ME	228	50,760	6,602	5.4	7,993	6.6	693	0.6
MD	24	325,864	24,905	4.1	56,180	9.3	4,979	0.8
MA	367	336,325	39,202	5.8	54,839	8.0	5,195	0.8
MI	396	472,794	43,741	4.4	75,915	7.7	6,976	0.7
MN	136	243,046	21,902	3.9	51,248	9.1	3,875	0.7
MS	53	51,306	6,983	2.3	6,690	2.2	1,712	0.6
MO	149	300,794	24,159	4.4	51,838	9.5	4,237	0.8
MT	82	31,134	4,053	4.1	6,121	6.2	829	0.8
NE	236	64,814	7,158	4.5	13,682	8.6	1,626	1.0
NV	22	104,543	9,391	3.1	17,397	5.7	2,526	0.8
NH	220	66,333	6,836	5.1	10,037	7.5	673	0.5
NJ	296	509,762	42,036	4.8	51,097	5.9	7,398	0.8
NM	88	54,180	6,811	4.6	9,350	6.2	1,529	1.0
NY	756	1,543,388	95,175	4.9	110,536	5.7	15,728	0.8
NC	82	247,597	30,188	2.9	51,051	4.9	4,903	0.5
ND	73	21,436	2,064	3.0	3,542	5.2	393	0.6
OH	251	918,327	67,938	5.9	178,937	15.6	12,598	1.1
OK	119	132,466	13,169	4.1	25,524	7.9	2,793	0.9
OR	132	265,822	19,623	5.6	54,174	15.4	2,652	0.8
PA	452	296,888	40,276	3.2	64,084	5.2	5,218	0.4
RI	48	55,027	5,171	4.9	6,675	6.3	762	0.7
SC	42	158,533	13,592	2.9	24,546	5.3	3,116	0.7
SD	111	28,420	3,693	4.8	5,822	7.5	947	1.2
TN	186	140,358	18,036	2.7	28,621	4.3	4,166	0.6
TX	544	589,149	65,948	2.5	116,451	4.4	11,373	0.4
UT	70	129,792	14,822	4.8	35,488	11.5	1,957	0.6
VT	162	26,035	3,416	5.9	4,201	7.2	427	0.7
VA	93	308,421	33,548	4.0	60,979	7.3	5,759	0.7
WA	60	500,216	36,055	4.8	86,800	11.7	6,109	0.8
WV	97	42,286	4,667	2.5	6,413	3.5	730	0.4
WI	381	266,993	29,071	5.0	54,093	9.3	3,485	0.6
WY	23	32,097	3,124	5.4	4,506	7.8	621	1.1
U.S.	**9,057**	**14,200,729**	**1,243,130**	**3.9**	**2,171,880**	**6.9**	**223,956**	**0.7**

(1) Includes central libraries only. (2) Some operating revenues may be estimated. (3) The total annual circulation of all library materials of all types, including renewals. (4) Total number of sessions accessing the internet using the library's devices.

Opera: Most Performed Works, 2022-23
Source: OPERA America

Title	Composer	Librettist	Productions	Performances
Tosca	Giacomo Puccini	Giuseppe Giacosa, Luigi Illica	22	108
La traviata	Giuseppe Verdi	Francesco Maria Piave	15	69
La bohème	Giacomo Puccini	Giuseppe Giacosa, Luigi Illica	13	67
The Marriage of Figaro	Wolfgang Mozart	Lorenzo Da Ponte	12	40
Carmen	Georges Bizet	Henri Meilhac, Ludovic Halévy	10	43
The Barber of Seville	Gioachino Rossini	Cesare Sterbini	10	21
The Elixir of Love	Gaetano Donizetti	Felice Romani	9	38
Don Giovanni	Wolfgang Mozart	Lorenzo Da Ponte	9	36
Così fan tutte	Wolfgang Mozart	Lorenzo Da Ponte	9	30
Madama Butterfly	Giacomo Puccini	Giuseppe Giacosa, Luigi Illica	8	37

Note: Scheduled productions of a given work during the 2022-23 season (Sept. 1, 2022-Aug. 31, 2023), by members of OPERA America's professional company members. List includes Canadian performances.

Best-Selling U.S. Magazines, 2023
Source: Alliance for Audited Media (AAM)

General magazines, exclusive of comics; also excludes magazines that failed to file reports to AAM. Based on total average paid and verified circulation during the six months ending June 30, 2023; ranked by paid circulation size.

Publication	Paid circ.	Publication	Paid circ.	Publication	Paid circ.
1. AARP The Magazine	22,386,765	17. Smithsonian	1,369,018	34. TV Guide Magazine	1,009,014
2. AARP Bulletin	22,078,961	18. Allrecipes	1,368,050	35. Bon Appétit	969,341
3. COSTCO Connection	15,365,396	19. Food Network Magazine	1,328,790	36. Essence	963,264
4. Better Homes and Gardens	3,109,415	20. Vanity Fair	1,276,661	37. GQ	952,623
5. Southern Living	2,804,808	21. Vogue	1,274,533	38. Food & Wine	936,711
6. Reader's Digest	2,709,208	22. The New Yorker	1,258,436	39. The Atlantic	925,872
7. People	2,545,977	23. Time	1,256,572	40. Outside	889,679
8. Good Housekeeping	2,065,354	24. Sports Illustrated	1,247,283	41. First for Women	887,652
9. Real Simple	2,017,963	25. Golf Magazine	1,232,827	42. The Family Handyman	884,885
10. Us Weekly	1,977,988	26. Woman's Day	1,186,141	43. VFW Magazine	871,379
11. Texas Co-op Power	1,885,022	27. Cosmopolitan	1,153,978	44. Midwest Living	864,256
12. National Geographic	1,708,075	28. HGTV Magazine	1,152,206	45. Architectural Digest	838,197
13. Golf Digest	1,653,821	29. Men's Health	1,136,398	46. Woman's World	831,172
14. American Legion Magazine	1,526,401	30. Women's Health	1,060,247	47. American Hunter	780,545
15. American Rifleman	1,504,881	31. Elle	1,025,424	48. Star Magazine	764,945
16. Taste of Home	1,504,387	32. Magnolia Journal	1,014,759	49. Harper's Bazaar	753,489
		33. Travel + Leisure	1,009,444	50. Carolina Country	747,539

Best-Selling Digital Replica U.S. Magazines, 2023
Source: Alliance for Audited Media (AAM)

General magazines, exclusive of comics; also excludes magazines that failed to file reports to AAM. Based on total average paid and verified circulation during the six months ending June 30, 2023; ranked by paid circulation size.

Publication	Paid circ.	Publication	Paid circ.	Publication	Paid circ.
1. Us Weekly	1,690,237	17. Good Housekeeping	277,907	34. Taste of Home	184,702
2. Golf Digest	847,082	18. Men's Health	274,243	35. Rolling Stone	178,558
3. Star Magazine	633,715	19. Economist (North America)	261,203	36. Allrecipes	173,699
4. Outside	591,130	20. Vanity Fair	251,367	37. House Beautiful	165,625
5. The Atlantic	489,577	21. Real Simple	245,519	38. Prevention	163,781
6. Golf Magazine	479,403	22. New York	239,693	39. Popular Mechanics	154,627
7. Woman's World	463,350	23. Sports Illustrated	230,628	40. Bon Appétit	138,941
8. The New Yorker	460,349	24. Reader's Digest	219,779	41. Food & Wine	138,767
9. First for Women	449,699	25. Women's Health	215,313	42. Elle	138,742
10. National Geographic	413,567	26. Food Network Magazine	214,660	43. Car and Driver	135,351
11. Southern Living	413,100	27. HGTV Magazine	208,377	44. Harvard Business Review	128,970
12. The Knot	408,884	28. Wired	207,056	45. Esquire	123,566
13. People	383,481	29. In Touch Weekly	201,305	46. Dwell	123,115
14. Better Homes and Gardens	362,301	30. Vogue	195,981	47. Architectural Digest	122,372
15. Cosmopolitan	316,294	31. Woman's Day	194,765	48. GQ	121,950
16. Time	311,637	32. Travel + Leisure	188,415	49. Motor Trend	121,776
		33. Fortune (North America)	186,281	50. Harper's Bazaar	115,573

Some Notable New Books, 2023

Source: Reference and User Services Association, American Library Association (ALA)

Fiction

Elsewhere, Alexis Schaitkin
The Haunting of Hajji Hotak: And Other Stories, Jamil Jan Kochai
Horse, Geraldine Brooks
Seeking Fortune Elsewhere, Sindya Bhanoo
Stories From the Tenants Downstairs, Sidik Fofana
The Furrows, Namwali Serpell
The Rabbit Hutch, Tess Gunty
The Swimmers, Julie Otsuka
Trust, Hernan Diaz
Vagabonds! Eloghosa Osunde
What We Fed to the Manticore, Talia Lakshmi Kolluri

Poetry

Alive at the End of the World, Saeed Jones
Bless the Daughter Raised by a Voice in Her Head, Warsan Shire
The Rupture Tense, Jenny Xie
Your Emergency Contact Has Experienced an Emergency, Chen Chen

Nonfiction

Also a Poet: Frank O'Hara, My Father, and Me, Ada Calhoun
An Immense World: How Animal Senses Reveal the Hidden Realms Around Us, Ed Yong
Bitch: On the Female of the Species, Lucy Cooke
Easy Beauty, Chloe Cooper Jones
The Escape Artist: The Man Who Broke Out of Auschwitz to Warn the World, Jonathan Freedland
His Name Is George Floyd: One Man's Life and the Struggle for Racial Justice, Robert Samuels and Toluse Olorunnipa
The Song of the Cell: An Exploration of Medicine and the New Human, Siddhartha Mukherjee
This Body I Wore: A Memoir, Diana Goetsch
Under the Skin: The Hidden Toll of Racism on American Lives and the Health of Our Nation, Linda Villarosa
The Vortex: A True Story of History's Deadliest Storm, an Unspeakable War, and Liberation, Scott Carney and Jason Miklian
We Are the Middle of Forever: Indigenous Voices From Turtle Island on the Changing Earth, edited by Dahr Jamail and Stan Rushworth

Best-Selling Books, 2022

Source: NPD BookScan

Hardcover Fiction

1. Fairy Tale, Stephen King
2. The Boys From Biloxi, John Grisham
3. Lessons in Chemistry, Bonnie Garmus
4. Dreamland, Nicholas Sparks
5. The Last Thing He Told Me, Laura Dave
6. House of Sky and Breath, Sarah J. Maas
7. Mad Honey, Jodi Picoult
8. Verity, Colleen Hoover
9. Demon Copperhead, Barbara Kingsolver
10. No Plan B, Lee Child

Hardcover Nonfiction

1. The Light We Carry: Overcoming in Uncertain Times, Michelle Obama
2. I'm Glad My Mom Died, Jennette McCurdy
3. Atlas of the Heart: Mapping Meaningful Connection and the Language of Human Experience, Brene Brown
4. Go-To Dinners: A Barefoot Contessa Cookbook, Ina Garten
5. Half Baked Harvest Every Day: Recipes for Balanced, Flexible, Feel-Good Meals, Tieghan Gerard
6. Friends, Lovers, and the Big Terrible Thing: A Memoir, Matthew Perry
7. Finding Me, Viola Davis
8. Faith Still Moves Mountains: Miraculous Stories of the Healing Power of Prayer, Harris Faulkner
9. Guinness World Records 2023
10. The Simply Happy Cookbook: 100-Plus Recipes to Take the Stress Out of Cooking, Steve Doocy, Kathy Doocy

Trade Paperback

1. It Ends With Us, Colleen Hoover
2. Verity, Colleen Hoover
3. It Starts With Us, Colleen Hoover
4. Where the Crawdads Sing, Delia Owens
5. Ugly Love, Colleen Hoover
6. The Seven Husbands of Evelyn Hugo, Taylor Jenkins Reid

7. Reminders of Him, Colleen Hoover
8. November 9, Colleen Hoover
9. The Body Keeps the Score: Brain, Mind, and Body in the Healing of Trauma, Bessel Van Der Kolk
10. The Four Agreements: A Practical Guide to Personal Freedom, Don Miguel Ruiz

Mass Market Fiction

1. The Judge's List, John Grisham
2. Invisible, Danielle Steel
3. Wyoming Homecoming, Diana Palmer
4. Blind Tiger, Sandra Brown
5. Steal, James Patterson
6. Cruel Winter of the Mountain Man, William W. Johnstone
7. Bad Days for Bad Men: Smoke Jensen's American Justice, William W. Johnstone
8. A Bend In the Road, Nicholas Sparks
9. The Awakening: The Dragon Heart Legacy, Book 1, Nora Roberts
10. Written in the Stars, Nora Roberts

Children's and Young Adult Hardcover

1. Diper Överlöde (Diary of a Wimpy Kid #17), Jeff Kinney
2. Cat Kid Comic Club: On Purpose: A Graphic Novel (Cat Kid Comic Club #3), Dav Pilkey
3. Harry Potter and the Order of the Phoenix: The Illustrated Edition (Harry Potter, Book 5), J. K. Rowling
4. Cat Kid Comic Club: Collaborations: A Graphic Novel (Cat Kid Comic Club #4), Dav Pilkey
5. Long Live the Pumpkin Queen: Tim Burton's the Nightmare Before Christmas, Shea Ernshaw
6. The Flames of Hope (Wings of Fire #15), Tui T. Sutherland
7. I'm So Glad You Were Born: Celebrating Who You Are, Ainsley Earhardt
8. FGTeeV: The Switcheroo Rescue!, FGTeeV
9. The Final Gambit, Jennifer Lynn Barnes
10. The Pigeon Will Ride the Roller Coaster!, Mo Willems

Note: Hardcover bestsellers include 2021 and 2022 releases. Trade paperback bestsellers are for overall 2022 sales of paperback editions for titles first published in any year. Mass market fiction and children's and young adult bestsellers include frontlist/2022 releases only.

Most Challenged Books, 2022

Source: Office for Intellectual Freedom, American Library Association (ALA)

A challenge is a formal, written complaint filed with a library or school requesting that materials be removed because of content or appropriateness. Book challenges in 2022 were nearly double the number in 2021. The common reasons given for challenges follow each book's title and author.

1. Gender Queer, Maia Kobabe. LGBTQIA+ content, explicit images.
2. All Boys Aren't Blue, George M. Johnson. LGBTQIA+ content, profanity, sexually explicit.
3. The Bluest Eye, Toni Morrison. Sexually explicit.
4. Flamer, Mike Curato. LGBTQIA+ content, sexually explicit.
5. Looking for Alaska, John Green. LGBTQIA+ content, sexually explicit.
   The Perks of Being a Wallflower, Stephen Chbosky. LGBTQIA+ content, drug use, profanity, sexually explicit.

7. Lawn Boy, Jonathan Evison. LGBTQIA+, sexually explicit.
8. The Absolutely True Diary of a Part-Time Indian, Sherman Alexie. Profanity, sexual overtones.
9. Out of Darkness, Ashley Hope Perez. Depictions of abuse, sexually explicit.
10. A Court of Mist and Fury, Sarah J. Maas. Sexually explicit.
    Crank, Ellen Hopkins. Drug use, sexually explicit.
    Me and Earl and the Dying Girl, Jesse Andrews. Profanity, sexually explicit.
    This Book Is Gay, Juno Dawson. LGBTQIA+ content, sexually explicit.

U.S. Daily Newspapers, 2023
Source: *Press Gazette* analysis of Alliance for Audited Media data

Rank	Newspaper	Avg. circulation	% change, 2022-23	Rank	Newspaper	Avg. circulation	% change, 2022-23
1.	Wall Street Journal	609,654	−13%	14.	Arizona Republic	57,660	−18%
2.	New York Times	296,329	−10	15.	Dallas Morning News	57,400	−12
3.	Washington Post	139,232	−12	16.	San Francisco Chronicle[1]	54,340	−14
4.	New York Post	135,983	−7	17.	Houston Chronicle	53,370	−18
5.	USA Today	132,641	−17	18.	Philadelphia Inquirer	51,170	−16
6.	Los Angeles Times	118,758	−17	19.	Chicago Sun-Times	48,690	−15
7.	Star Tribune	91,920	−11	20.	St. Louis Post-Dispatch[2]	48,250	−11
8.	Newsday	86,850	−11	21.	Daily News	45,730	−18
9.	Chicago Tribune	82,190	−23	22.	Denver Post	41,545	−27
10.	Tampa Bay Times[1]	81,890	−25	23.	San Diego Union-Tribune	41,080	−14
11.	Seattle Times	75,910	−12	24.	Atlanta Journal-Constitution	39,070	−32
12.	Honolulu Star-Advertiser	75,457	−5	25.	Las Vegas Review Journal	38,840	−12
13.	Boston Globe	60,500	−12				

Note: Circulation is average Mon.-Fri. figure for six months prior to Mar. 2023. Where this data was not available, Wednesday circulation data was used. (1) Circulation for the six months prior to Sept. 2022. (2) Circulation for the six months prior to Mar. 2022.

Circulation and Revenue for U.S. Local Newspapers, 2015-20
Source: Pew Research Center

	2015	2016	2017	2018	2019	2020
Weekday circulation (Mon.-Fri.)						
Total	13,857,387	12,912,167	11,283,484	10,625,371	8,280,161	8,323,635
Print	11,147,215	10,284,762	8,844,705	7,945,765	5,774,399	5,057,471
Digital	2,710,172	2,627,405	2,438,779	2,679,606	2,505,762	3,266,164
Sunday circulation						
Total	28,106,565	23,653,657	21,044,904	19,395,480	15,746,182	15,384,638
Print	24,985,137	20,578,485	18,195,838	16,185,270	12,692,300	11,430,647
Digital	3,121,428	3,075,172	2,849,066	3,210,210	3,053,882	3,953,991
Average monthly unique visitors	5,691,344	6,400,664	6,821,214	6,474,308	6,935,309	7,574,228
Revenue[1]						
From advertising ($)	3,999,011,000	4,004,563,000	3,776,232,050	3,077,386,330	1,788,180,000	1,068,602,000
From circulation ($)	2,322,594,000	2,569,678,280	2,689,934,680	2,459,659,198	1,527,928,000	1,114,547,000
Digital share of ad revenue (%)	23	28	29	32	31	35

Note: Analysis of local newspapers excludes four publications (*New York Times, Washington Post, Wall Street Journal,* and *USA Today*) that reach large national audiences unless noted. (1) Includes *USA Today.*

U.S. News Consumption by Selected Characteristics, 2022
Source: Pew Research Center
(percent of U.S. adults in each group that get news at least sometimes from each platform)

Characteristic	Television	Radio	Print publications	Total digital	Digital devices News websites or apps	Social media	Search	Podcasts
Total	65%	47%	33%	82%	63%	50%	60%	23%
Men	62	48	33	83	64	47	58	26
Women	67	46	32	81	62	53	62	20
Age								
18-29	44	35	21	91	62	76	70	32
30-49	55	48	27	88	68	58	65	29
50-64	74	55	35	78	64	39	59	18
65+	85	46	49	67	54	27	46	12
Race/ethnicity								
White	64	48	35	82	64	45	58	22
Black	79	48	36	80	64	61	69	26
Asian	47	37	26	89	69	64	68	25
Hispanic	66	42	26	81	57	62	61	22
Education level								
High school or less	72	46	32	71	52	50	53	17
Some college	63	47	31	86	63	53	65	24
College+	58	48	35	90	75	48	65	28
Income level								
Less than $30,000	66	42	29	71	51	55	56	20
$30,000-$79,999	66	47	32	80	60	51	60	22
More than $80,000	62	50	34	90	74	47	64	23
Political affiliation								
Republican/Lean Rep.	64	50	31	80	60	47	58	24
Democratic/Lean Dem.	65	45	35	84	67	54	64	23

Note: White, Black, and Asian adults include those who report being only one race and are not Hispanic; Hispanics are of any race.

National Recording Registry, 2023

Source: Library of Congress

Each year since 2002, the National Recording Registry at the Library of Congress adds 25 recordings showcasing the "range and diversity of American recorded sound heritage."

The Very First Mariachi Recordings, Cuarteto Coculense (1908-09)

"St. Louis Blues," Handy's Memphis Blues Band (1922)

"Sugar Foot Stomp," Fletcher Henderson (1925)

1939 NBC broadcasts, Dorothy Thompson (Aug. 23-Sept. 6, 1939)

"Don't Let Nobody Turn You Around," Fairfield Four (1947)

"Sherry," The Four Seasons (1962)

"Wang Dang Doodle," Koko Taylor (1965)

"What the World Needs Now is Love," Jackie DeShannon (1965)

"Ode to Billie Joe," Bobbie Gentry (1967)

Déjà vu, Crosby, Stills, Nash & Young (1970)

"Imagine," John Lennon (1971)

"Stairway to Heaven," Led Zeppelin (1971)

"Take Me Home, Country Roads," John Denver (1971)

"Margaritaville," Jimmy Buffett (1977)

"Flashdance...What a Feeling," Irena Cara (1983)

"Sweet Dreams (Are Made of This)," Eurythmics (1983)

Synchronicity, The Police (1983)

Like a Virgin, Madonna (1985 reissue)

Black Codes (from the Underground), Wynton Marsalis (1985)

Super Mario theme, Koji Kondo (1985)

All Hail the Queen, Queen Latifah (1989)

"All I Want for Christmas Is You," Mariah Carey (1994)

"Pale Blue Dot," Carl Sagan (1994)

"Gasolina," Daddy Yankee (2004)

"Concerto for Clarinet and Chamber Orchestra," Chamber Music Northwest (2012)

U.S. Commercial Radio Stations by Format, 2013-23

Source: Inside Radio (www.insideradio.com)

(as of July 2023; ranked by 2023 numbers)

Format	2013	2014	2015	2016	2017	2018	2019	2020	2021	2022	2023
1. Country	2,042	2,053	2,112	2,126	2,121	2,143	2,157	2,147	2,150	2,135	2,136
2. News/Talk	1,453	1,409	1,360	1,355	1,330	1,296	1,268	1,241	1,267	1,246	1,225
3. Classic Hits	678	754	805	881	965	1,001	1,046	1,081	1,115	1,143	1,138
4. Spanish	835	844	862	878	858	865	867	886	889	912	899
5. Sports	740	788	788	780	752	726	702	687	653	629	624
6. Classic Rock	486	486	486	492	519	522	548	558	571	606	606
7. Top 40	573	577	579	583	594	595	591	582	579	561	550
8. Adult Contemporary	605	597	609	608	592	581	575	567	551	539	540
9. Hot AC	428	465	462	464	451	452	447	471	452	450	446
10. Religion (Teaching, Variety)	336	324	318	318	332	351	365	392	394	393	402
11. Rock	299	302	304	304	291	285	289	291	290	265	265
12. Oldies	566	476	413	343	293	295	278	262	249	240	231
13. Contemporary Christian	172	157	168	173	193	172	195	201	210	228	216
14. R&B	131	131	143	148	155	158	152	152	160	168	173
15. Urban AC	158	167	166	163	170	170	164	168	171	171	173
16. Inspirational Gospel	212	211	218	213	206	198	198	182	178	171	168
17. Ethnic	142	152	161	168	163	165	159	156	153	151	148
18. Soft Adult Contemporary	141	131	121	108	114	118	122	130	130	121	119
19. Alternative Rock	101	105	103	112	115	117	111	109	110	116	111
20. Southern Gospel	172	169	154	148	130	135	127	125	118	117	111
Total stations	**11,402**	**11,058**	**11,034**	**11,053**	**11,040**	**11,026**	**11,023**	**11,067**	**11,008**	**10,962**	**10,787**

Note: Totals include stations that are changing or did not report format, as well as formats not listed here.

Top-Selling Albums of All Time

Source: Recording Industry Assn. of America (RIAA)

Sales figures represent RIAA multi-platinum certifications; albums ranked by latest sales certification. As of Aug. 15, 2023.

Rank	Title, artist	Unit sales (mil)	Rank	Title, artist	Unit sales (mil)
1.	*Their Greatest Hits (1971-1975)*, Eagles	38.0	24.	*Legend*, Bob Marley and the Wailers	15.0
2.	*Thriller*, Michael Jackson	34.0	25.	*Greatest Hits*, Journey	15.0
3.	*Hotel California*, Eagles	26.0	26.	*Dark Side of the Moon*, Pink Floyd	15.0
4.	*Back in Black*, AC/DC	25.0	27.	*Supernatural*, Santana	15.0
5.	*Led Zeppelin IV*, Led Zeppelin	24.0	28.	*Greatest Hits 1974-1978*, Steve Miller Band	15.0
6.	*The Beatles*, The Beatles	24.0	29.	*The Beatles 1962-1966*, The Beatles	15.0
7.	*Greatest Hits Volume I & Volume II*, Billy Joel	23.0	30.	*21*, Adele	14.0
8.	*The Wall*, Pink Floyd	23.0	31.	*Backstreet Boys*, Backstreet Boys	14.0
9.	*Rumours*, Fleetwood Mac	21.0	32.	*...Baby One More Time*, Britney Spears	14.0
10.	*Double Live*, Garth Brooks	21.0	33.	*Tapestry*, Carole King	14.0
11.	*Cracked Rear View*, Hootie & the Blowfish	21.0	34.	*Ropin' the Wind*, Garth Brooks	14.0
12.	*Come on Over*, Shania Twain	20.0	35.	*Bat Out of Hell*, Meat Loaf	14.0
13.	*No Fences*, Garth Brooks	18.0	36.	*Simon & Garfunkel's Greatest Hits*, Simon & Garfunkel	14.0
14.	*Appetite for Destruction*, Guns N' Roses	18.0	37.	*Whitney Houston*, Whitney Houston	14.0
15.	*The Bodyguard* (soundtrack), Whitney Houston	18.0	38.	*Dirty Dancing* (soundtrack)	14.0
16.	*Boston*, Boston	17.0	39.	*Millennium*, Backstreet Boys	13.0
17.	*Born in the U.S.A.*, Bruce Springsteen	17.0	40.	*Bruce Springsteen & E Street Band Live 1974-'85*, Bruce Springsteen	13.0
18.	*Greatest Hits*, Elton John	17.0	41.	*Ten*, Pearl Jam	13.0
19.	*The Beatles 1967-1970*, The Beatles	17.0	42.	*Purple Rain* (soundtrack), Prince & The Revolution	13.0
20.	*Jagged Little Pill*, Alanis Morissette	16.0	43.	*Wide Open Spaces*, The Chicks	13.0
21.	*Saturday Night Fever* (soundtrack), Bee Gees	16.0			
22.	*Physical Graffiti*, Led Zeppelin	16.0			
23.	*Metallica*, Metallica	16.0			

Top Musical Artists All-Time by Digital Sales

Source: Recording Industry Assn. of America (RIAA)
Units represent digital singles certified as sold, including streaming-equivalent, as of Aug. 15, 2023.

Artist	Units (mil)	Artist	Units (mil)	Artist	Units (mil)	Artist	Units (mil)
Drake	184.0	Ed Sheeran	80.5	Sam Smith	51.0	Sam Hunt	42.5
Rihanna	166.5	Luke Bryan	80.5	A Boogie wit da		Rae Sremmurd	41.5
Eminem	166.0	Morgan Wallen	77.5	Hoodie	50.5	Kendrick Lamar	41.0
Kanye West	150.0	Luke Combs	75.5	Chris Stapleton	50.0	NF	41.0
Taylor Swift	137.5	XXXTentacion	75.0	Pitbull	50.0	Lil Uzi Vert	40.0
Post Malone	134.0	Lil Baby	69.0	DJ Khaled	49.5	Train	40.0
Justin Bieber	119.5	Michael Jackson	65.5	Carrie Underwood	49.0	Thomas Rhett	39.5
Beyoncé	114.5	Ariana Grande	63.5	Kenny Chesney	47.5	Red Hot Chili	
The Weeknd	113.0	J. Cole	61.5	Polo G	46.0	Peppers	39.0
Katy Perry	112.0	Cardi B	57.0	The Chainsmokers	46.0	George Strait	38.5
Imagine Dragons	98.0	SZA	55.5	Billie Eilish	45.5	Jason Aldean	38.5
Chris Brown	94.5	Mariah Carey	55.0	Doja Cat	45.0	Travis Scott	38.5
Lil Wayne	92.0	Florida Georgia Line	54.5	Eric Church	45.0	Linkin Park	38.0
Bruno Mars	91.5	Panic! at the Disco	54.5	Halsey	45.0	Nicki Minaj	38.0
Future	91.5	Khalid	53.0	Big Sean	43.5	Keith Urban	37.5
Maroon 5	87.5	Twenty One Pilots	53.0	Tim McGraw	43.5	Adele	37.0
Juice Wrld	84.0	Flo Rida	52.5	50 Cent	43.0	Alicia Keys	37.0
Lady Gaga	82.5	Blake Shelton	52.0	Original Broadway		Migos	36.5
YoungBoy Never		Miley Cyrus	52.0	Cast of *Hamilton*	43.0	Trippie Redd	36.5
Broke Again	82.0	Harry Styles	51.5	Queen	42.5		

Top Musical Artists All-Time by Album Sales

Source: Recording Industry Assn. of America (RIAA)
Certified album sales in millions, including streaming equivalent where applicable, as of Aug. 15, 2023.

Artist	Certified sales (mil)	Artist	Certified sales (mil)	Artist	Certified sales (mil)
The Beatles	183.0	Metallica	63.0	Guns N' Roses	44.5
Garth Brooks	157.0	Eminem	61.5	Santana	43.5
Elvis Presley	146.5	Whitney Houston	61.0	Queen	43.0
The Eagles	120.0	Van Halen	56.5	Reba McEntire	41.0
Led Zeppelin	112.5	Fleetwood Mac	55.5	Eric Clapton	40.0
Michael Jackson	89.0	Celine Dion	53.0	Tim McGraw	39.5
Billy Joel	86.0	U2	52.0	Chicago	38.5
Elton John	79.0	Taylor Swift	51.0	Simon & Garfunkel	38.5
AC/DC	75.0	Neil Diamond	49.5	Foreigner	38.0
Pink Floyd	75.0	Alabama	49.0	Rod Stewart	38.0
Mariah Carey	74.0	Journey	49.0	Backstreet Boys	37.0
Bruce Springsteen	71.0	Kenny G	48.0	2Pac	36.5
Aerosmith	69.5	Shania Twain	48.0	Bob Dylan	36.0
George Strait	69.0	Kenny Rogers	47.5	Def Leppard	35.5
Barbra Streisand	68.5	Alan Jackson	44.5	Kenny Chesney	35.0
The Rolling Stones	66.5	Bob Seger & the Silver		Bon Jovi	34.5
Madonna	65.5	Bullet Band	44.5	Britney Spears	34.5
				Dave Matthews Band	34.5

Multi-Platinum Awards for Recorded Music, 2022-23

Source: Recording Industry Assn. of America (RIAA)

To be certified platinum, an **album** must sell 1 mil units (LPs, CDs, or digital) with a manufacturer's dollar volume of at least $2 mil based on one-third of the suggested retail list price for each copy sold. To achieve multi-platinum status, an album must reach minimum total sales of at least 2 mil units with a manufacturer's dollar volume of at least $4 mil based on one-third of the list price. RIAA began including streaming in their award formulas in 2018; 1,500 streams count as the equivalent of 10 track sales or 1 album sale. **Digital singles** must sell 2 mil to achieve a multi-platinum award. For digital singles award formulas, 150 streams equal one download sold.

Awards listed here are for albums and digital singles (released Sept. 1, 2021-Aug. 15, 2023) that were certified Sept. 2022-Aug. 15, 2023. Number in parentheses represents millions sold. Alphabetized by artist name.

Albums

Harry's House, Harry Styles (2)
Midnights, Taylor Swift (2)
SOS, SZA (3)

Digital Singles

"Easy on Me" (4), Adele
"Something in the Orange" (4), Zach Bryan
"Fast Car" (2), Luke Combs
"Surface Pressure" (3), Jessica Darrow
"Woman" (3), Doja Cat
"We Don't Talk About Bruno" (4), *Encanto* cast
"Wait for You" (3), Future feat. Drake and Tems
"Tomorrow 2" (2), Glorilla with Cardi B
"I'm Good (Blue)" (2), David Guetta and Bebe Rexha
"First Class" (2), Jack Harlow
"AA" (2), Walker Hayes
"Enemy" (3), Imagine Dragons with JID
"Son of a Sinner" (2), Jelly Roll
"Golden Hour" (2), JVKE
"Big Energy" (3), Latto

"Just Wanna Rock" (2), Lil Uzi Vert
"About Damn Time" (2), Lizzo
"Superhero (Heroes & Villains)" (2), Metro Boomin, Future, and Chris Brown
"Creepin'" (2), Metro Boomin, The Weeknd, and 21 Savage
"Super Freaky Girl" (2), Nicki Minaj
"Calm Down" (3), Rema
"Until I Found You" (2), Stephen Sanchez
"Smokin Out the Window" (2), Silk Sonic
"Sleazy Flow" (2), SleazyWorld Go
"Unholy" (2), Sam Smith feat. Kim Petras
"As It Was" (6), "Late Night Talking" (2), Harry Styles
"I Hate U" (2), "Kill Bill" (5), "Shirt" (2), "Snooze" (2), SZA
"Favorite Song" (2), Toosii
"Thought You Should Know" (2), "You Proof" (4), Morgan Wallen
"Me or Sum" (2), Nardo Wick feat. Future and Lil Baby
"Who Want Smoke??" (3), Nardo Wick feat. G. Herbo, Lil Durk, and 21 Savage
"Sunroof" (2), Nicky Youre and Dazy
"Fall In Love" (2), "Rock and a Hard Place" (2), Bailey Zimmerman

Top-Grossing North American Concert Tours, 1985-2022
Source: Pollstar

Rank	Artist (year)	Total gross[1]	Cities/shows	Rank	Artist (year)	Total gross[1]	Cities/shows
1.	Bad Bunny (2022)	$356.5	43/63	17.	Kenny Chesney (2022)	$135.3	38/41
2.	Taylor Swift (2018)	277.3	27/40	18.	Madonna (2012)	133.7	31/45
3.	Elton John (2022)	201.8	38/50	19.	The Police (2007)	133.2	41/54
4.	Taylor Swift (2015)	199.4	41/62	20.	Guns N' Roses (2016)	130.8	24/31
5.	The Rolling Stones (2019)	177.8	14/16	21.	One Direction (2014)	127.2	21/31
6.	Def Leppard / Mötley Crüe (2022)	177.4	35/36	22.	The Weeknd (2022)	124.5	17/18
7.	U2 (2017)	176.1	26/30	23.	U2 (2009)	123.0	16/20
8.	Beyoncé (2016)	169.4	30/32	24.	Bruce Springsteen & The E Street Band (2016)	122.4	42/48
9.	Jay-Z and Beyoncé (2018)	166.4	24/30	25.	Morgan Wallen (2022)	121.5	51/63
10.	Eagles (2018)	166.0	45/53	26.	The Rolling Stones (1994)	121.2	43/60
11.	The Rolling Stones (2005)	162.0	38/42	27.	Kenny Chesney (2015)	116.4	56/59
12.	Harry Styles (2022)	160.4	12/47	28.	Bruce Springsteen & The E Street Band (2003)	115.9	30/47
13.	Elton John (2019)	157.4	57/81	29.	The Rolling Stones (2021)	115.5	11/12
14.	U2 (2011)	156.0	21/25	30.	Garth Brooks (2015)	114.9	23/120
15.	U2 (2005)	138.9	43/78				
16.	The Rolling Stones (2006)	138.5	35/39				

(1) In millions. Not adjusted for inflation.

Music Sales by Format and Value, 1995-2022
Source: Recording Industry Assn. of America
(in millions, net after returns)

	1995	2000	2005	2010	2015	2020	2021	2022	% change, 2021-22
Physical units shipped	1,112.7	1,079.2	748.8	267.7	135.0	56.8	88.9	75.8	−14.7%
Dollar value	$12,320.3	14,323.7	11,195.0	3,663.7	1,862.2	1,163.3	1,663.8	1,731.0	4.0
Compact discs (CDs)	722.9	942.5	705.4	253.0	117.1	31.6	46.7	33.4	−28.4
Dollar value	$9,377.4	13,214.5	10,520.2	3,389.4	1,445.0	483.3	585.4	482.6	−17.6
LPs/EPs	2.2	2.2	1.0	4.2	13.7	23.7	40.0	41.3	3.2
Dollar value	$25.1	27.7	14.2	88.9	333.4	643.9	1,044.6	1,224.4	17.2
Music videos	12.6	18.2	33.8	9.1	3.1	1.0	1.3	0.7	−49.9
Dollar value	$220.3	281.9	602.2	177.6	70.4	27.4	19.9	11.3	−43.1
Other physical[1]	375.0	116.3	8.6	1.4	1.1	0.5	0.8	0.4	−52.9
Dollar value	$2,697.5	799.6	58.4	7.8	13.4	8.8	14.0	12.7	−9.1
Digital formats: number downloaded	—	—	553.1	1,471.8	1,120.5	314.0	258.3	206.6	−20.0
Digital formats: dollar value	—	—	$925.3	2,699.8	2,314.3	664.7	621.6	494.7	−20.4
Albums downloaded	—	—	13.6	85.8	106.8	33.1	31.1	23.9	−23.0
Dollar value	—	—	$135.7	872.4	1,064.4	319.3	303.3	241.9	−20.2
Singles downloaded	—	—	366.9	1,177.4	986.3	249.3	219.4	177.2	−19.2
Dollar value	—	—	$363.3	1,336.4	1,185.2	303.3	268.9	214.1	−20.4
Ringtones and ringbacks	—	—	170.0	188.5	21.9	8.1	6.3	4.5	−29.0
Dollar value	—	—	$421.6	448.0	54.6	20.2	15.7	11.0	−29.7
Other digital downloads[2]	—	—	2.6	20.1	5.5	1.6	1.5	1.0	−33.7
Dollar value	—	—	$4.7	43.0	10.1	21.9	33.8	27.7	−18.1
Subscription and streaming dollar value	—	—	$169.6	461.6	2,331.3	10,051.3	12,365.4	13,265.7	7.3
Subscription formats[3]	—	—	1.3	1.5	10.8	75.5	84.0	92.0	9.6
Dollar value	—	—	$149.2	212.4	1,156.7	6,972.7	8,562.8	9,179.0	7.2
Limited tier paid subscriptions	—	—	—	—	—	719.9	898.3	1,063.0	18.3
SoundExchange distribution[4]	—	—	$20.4	249.2	802.6	947.4	992.5	959.4	−3.3
On-demand streaming (ad supported)[5]	—	—	—	—	$372.0	1,200.1	1,708.3	1,802.8	5.5
Other ad-supported streaming[6]	—	—	—	—	—	211.2	203.5	261.5	28.5
Synchronization royalties[7]	—	—	—	$188.7	202.9	265.2	306.5	382.5	24.8
Total physical and digital[8]	1,112.7	1,079.2	1,301.9	1,739.5	1,255.5	348.9	347.1	282.4	−18.6
Total value physical and digital	$12,320.3	14,323.7	12,289.9	7,013.8	6,710.8	12,144.7	14,957.3	15,873.9	6.1

— = Not available or not applicable. (1) Includes CD singles, cassettes, vinyl singles, DVD audio, and SACD. (2) Includes kiosk and music video downloads. (3) Streaming, tethered, and other paid subscription services not operating under statutory licenses. Subscription volume is annual average number of subscriptions (excluding limited tier). (4) Estimated payments to performers/copyright holders for digital and customized radio services under statutory licenses. (5) Ad-supported audio and music video services not operating under statutory licenses. (6) Revenues for statutory services that are not distributed by SoundExchange or included in other streaming categories. (7) Includes fees and royalties from sound recordings used in other media. Not included in subscription and streaming dollar value. (8) Units total includes physical and downloaded albums and singles but not streaming, subscriptions, or royalties.

Top Basic Cable TV Networks, 2022
Source: Kagan, a media research group within S&P Global Market Intelligence

Rank	Network (year began)	Subscribers (mil)	Rank	Network (year began)	Subscribers (mil)
1.	C-SPAN (1979)	79.8	11.	Freeform (1977)	75.6
2.	Food Network (1993)	78.5	12.	Disney Channel (1983)	75.5
3.	HGTV (1994)	78.2	13.	AMC (1984)	75.2
4.	TBS (1976)	77.5	14.	CNN (1980)	74.8
5.	TNT (1988)	77.2	15.	E! (1987)	74.8
6.	USA (1980)	77.1	16.	Animal Planet (1996)	74.6
7.	FX (1994)	76.7	17.	Syfy (1992)	74.5
8.	Discovery Channel (1985)	76.5	18.	Bravo (1980)	74.4
9.	TLC (1972)	76.4	19.	ESPN (1979)	73.6
10.	National Geographic Channel (2001)	75.8	20.	ESPN2 (1993)	73.5

Most Watched Original Streaming Shows, 2023

Source: Nielsen Media Research

Shows ranked by estimated total number of minutes the program was viewed using the streaming platform shown by persons aged 2-99 in the U.S., Dec. 26, 2022-Aug. 27, 2023.

Rank	Series, provider	Mins. (mil)
1.	Ted Lasso, Apple	14,299
2.	Ginny & Georgia, Netflix	12,810
3.	The Night Agent, Netflix	12,691
4.	The Mandalorian, Disney	11,314
5.	Outer Banks, Netflix	11,254
6.	Tom Clancy's Jack Ryan, Amazon	11,013
7.	You, Netflix	10,299
8.	Wednesday, Netflix	9,756
9.	The Lincoln Lawyer, Netflix	9,450
10.	Manifest, Netflix	9,298
11.	Gabby's Dollhouse, Netflix	8,888
12.	Love Is Blind, Netflix	8,056
13.	The Witcher, Netflix	7,729
14.	Stranger Things, Netflix	7,027
15.	Queen Charlotte: A Bridgerton Story, Netflix	6,934

Most Watched Acquired Streaming Shows, 2023

Source: Nielsen Media Research

Shows ranked by estimated total number of minutes the program was viewed using the streaming platform shown by persons aged 2-99 in the U.S., Dec. 26, 2022-Aug. 27, 2023.

Rank	Series, provider	Mins. (mil)
1.	Suits, multiple distributors	36,684
2.	Bluey, multiple distributors	28,008
3.	NCIS, multiple distributors	26,525
4.	Cocomelon, Netflix	25,605
5.	Grey's Anatomy, multiple distributors	22,379
6.	The Big Bang Theory, multiple distributors	18,293
7.	Family Guy, multiple distributors	16,469
8.	The Walking Dead, multiple distributors	16,310
9.	South Park, multiple distributors	16,041
10.	Supernatural, multiple distributors	15,919
11.	Heartland, multiple distributors	15,757
12.	Friends, multiple distributors	15,263
13.	Gilmore Girls, multiple distributors	14,956
14.	Criminal Minds, multiple distributors	14,337
15.	Shameless, multiple distributors	13,553

Most Watched Streaming Movies, 2023

Source: Nielsen Media Research

Feature-length films ranked by estimated total number of minutes the movie was viewed using the streaming platform shown by persons aged 2-99 in the U.S., Dec. 26, 2022-Aug. 27, 2023.

Rank	Movie, provider	Mins. (mil)
1.	Moana, multiple distributors	7,838
2.	Encanto, multiple distributors	6,868
3.	Minions: The Rise of Gru, multiple distributors	6,109
4.	Black Panther: Wakanda Forever, multiple distributors	6,051
5.	Glass Onion: A Knives Out Mystery, Netflix	6,023
6.	Avatar: The Way of Water, multiple distributors	5,315
7.	Sing 2, multiple distributors	4,957
8.	You People, Netflix	4,681
9.	Puss in Boots: The Last Wish, multiple distributors	4,463
10.	Trolls, multiple distributors	4,336
11.	A Man Called Otto, multiple distributors	4,325
12.	The Mother, Netflix	3,951
13.	Frozen, multiple distributors	3,801
14.	Cars, multiple distributors	3,594
15.	Zootopia, multiple distributors	3,565

Average U.S. Television Viewing Time, 2022-23

Source: Nielsen Media Research; viewing time given in hours:minutes

Group	Age	Total per week	M-F 7-10 AM	M-F 10 AM-4 PM	M-Sun. 8-11 PM	M-F 11:30 PM-1 AM	Sat. 7 AM-1 PM	Sun. 1-7 PM
Men	18+	21:17	1:22	3:10	4:46	0:52	0:41	1:17
	18-24	4:44	0:12	0:36	1:08	0:13	0:08	0:21
	25-54	12:40	0:42	1:36	3:01	0:35	0:24	0:52
	55+	37:49	2:38	6:01	8:13	1:26	1:13	2:07
Women	18+	23:38	1:37	3:51	5:12	1:00	0:43	1:10
	18-24	4:08	0:12	0:35	0:60	0:12	0:06	0:15
	25-54	13:38	0:53	1:58	3:08	0:38	0:24	0:44
	55+	40:26	2:52	6:54	8:42	1:38	1:14	1:55
Children	2-11	5:02	0:20	0:46	1:03	0:10	0:12	0:20
Teens	12-17	3:18	0:08	0:21	0:51	0:08	0:06	0:16
All viewers[1]		18:48	1:15	2:55	4:10	0:46	0:35	1:02

Note: For viewing period Sept. 19, 2022-May 28, 2023. Includes DVR playback. (1) Ages 2+.

Highest-Rated Prime-Time Television Programs, 2022-23

Source: Nielsen Media Research

Data are for regularly scheduled network programs Sept. 20, 2022-Aug. 31, 2023. Ranked by average audience percentages, or ratings, which are estimates of the percentage of all TV-owning households watching a particular program live or on DVR within seven days of broadcast. Audience share percentages are estimates of the percentage of those watching TV at a certain time that are tuned in to a particular program.

Rank	Program, network	Avg. audience	Audience share	Rank	Program, network	Avg. audience	Audience share
1.	Sunday Night Football, NBC	9.7%	24.9%	26.	Jeopardy! Masters-Wednesday, ABC[1]	4.0%	11.2%
2.	Sunday Night Football Pre-Kick, NBC	7.1	17.8	27.	American Idol, ABC	4.0	11.1
3.	NCIS, CBS	6.0	15.2	28.	The Good Doctor, ABC	4.0	11.6
4.	FBI, CBS	5.8	15.3	29.	The Rookie, ABC	3.9	10.7
5.	Chicago Fire, NBC	5.7	15.2	30.	So Help Me Todd, CBS	3.9	10.4
6.	Blue Bloods, CBS	5.7	17.5	31.	The Neighborhood, CBS	3.9	9.9
7.	Young Sheldon, CBS	5.5	14.8	32.	NCIS: Los Angeles, CBS	3.9	11.8
8.	The OT, FOX	5.5	13.8	33.	Survivor, CBS	3.8	10.3
9.	Ghosts, CBS	5.3	13.8	34.	Will Trent, ABC	3.7	11.4
10.	Chicago Med, NBC	5.3	14.0	35.	Law & Order, CBS	3.7	9.9
11.	60 Minutes, CBS	5.3	13.8	36.	Bob Hearts Abishola, CBS	3.7	9.3
12.	Football Night in America, NBC	5.2	13.1	37.	American Idol-Monday, ABC	3.6	9.3
13.	Chicago P.D., NBC	5.1	15.5	38.	CSI: Vegas, CBS	3.5	10.5
14.	The Equalizer, CBS	5.0	13.1	39.	America's Got Talent-Wednesday, NBC	3.5	10.4
15.	FBI: Most Wanted, CBS	5.0	15.1	40.	911: Lone Star, FOX	3.5	9.2
16.	Fire Country, CBS	5.0	14.3	41.	Law & Order: Organized Crime, CBS	3.5	10.3
17.	FBI International, CBS	4.7	12.6	42.	Grey's Anatomy, ABC	3.4	9.3
18.	NCIS: Hawai'i, CBS	4.6	13.3	43.	Alaska Daily, ABC	3.4	10.0
19.	Law & Order: SVU, CBS	4.4	11.6	44.	Station 19, ABC	3.4	9.0
20.	The Voice-Tuesday, NBC	4.3	11.5	45.	New Amsterdam, NBC	3.3	9.8
21.	The Voice, NBC	4.3	11.0	46.	America's Got Talent All Stars, NBC	3.2	8.3
22.	911, FOX	4.3	10.9	47.	The Conners, ABC	3.1	8.3
23.	East New York, CBS	4.2	11.1	48.	Night Court, NBC	3.1	8.3
24.	America's Got Talent-Tuesday, NBC	4.2	12.5	49.	Big Sky, ABC	3.0	8.9
25.	S.W.A.T., CBS	4.1	11.8	50.	The Price Is Right at Night, CBS	3.0	7.9

(1) Highest-rated night of multiple prime-time broadcasts per week, May 8-24, 2023.

Highest-Rated Basic Cable Programs, 2022-23

Source: Nielsen Media Research

Excl. children's series, miniseries, movies, and news events. Average audience percentages, or ratings, are estimates of the percentage of all TV-owning households watching a program live or within seven days of broadcast, Sept. 20, 2022-Aug. 31, 2023.

Highest-Rated Series

Rank	Program, channel	Avg. audience
1.	Yellowstone, Paramount	6.3%
2.	1923, Paramount	2.6
3.	Tulsa King, Paramount	2.2
4.	Curse of Oak Island, History	2.1
5.	Tucker Carlson Tonight, Fox News Channel	2.1
6.	The Five, Fox News Channel	2.0
7.	When Calls the Heart, Hallmark	1.8
8.	Sister Wives, TLC	1.7
9.	Jesse Watters Primetime, FOX News Channel	1.7
10.	Rachel Maddow Show, MSNBC	1.7
11.	Hannity, Fox News Channel	1.6
12.	The Secret of Skinwalker Ranch, History	1.6
13.	George & Tammy, Paramount	1.6
14.	The Way Home, Hallmark	1.6
15.	90 Day Fiancé - Happily Ever After: Tell All No Limits, TLC	1.6
16.	Chesapeake Shores, Hallmark	1.6
17.	Walking Dead, AMC	1.5
18.	1883, Paramount	1.5
19.	Rock the Block, HGTV	1.5
20.	90 Day: The Single Life, Tell All Part 1, TLC	1.5
21.	Gutfeld!, Fox News Channel	1.4
22.	90 Day Fiancé: Happily Ever After?, TLC	1.4
23.	Special Report, Fox News Channel	1.4
24.	Real Housewives of Beverly Hills, Bravo	1.4
25.	The Ingraham Angle, Fox News Channel	1.3

Highest-Rated Sports Programs

Rank	Program, channel	Avg. audience
1.	College Football Playoff National Semifinal, ESPN	9.6%
2.	College Football Playoff National Championship, ESPN	8.4
3.	NFL Wildcard, ESPN	6.0
4.	NFL Regular season, ESPN	5.5
5.	Rose Bowl, ESPN	5.4
6.	Sugar Bowl, ESPN	4.9
7.	Orange Bowl, ESPN	4.6
8.	NCAA Basketball Championship-Saturday Game 2, (03/25/2023), TBS	4.2
9.	NBA Playoffs Conference Finals, ESPN	4.2
10.	College Football Bowl Game Studio, ESPN	4.1
11.	Exclusive Postgame, NFL Network	4.0
12.	NCAA Basketball Championship Bridge, TBS	3.9
13.	NBA Playoffs Conference Finals, TNT	3.8
14.	Exclusive Game, NFL Netwprk	3.8
15.	NCAA Basketball Championship-Saturday (03/25/2023) Game 1, TBS	3.6
16.	NCAA Basketball Championship-Thursday (03/23/2023) Game 1, TBS	3.2
17.	NBA Playoffs Conference Semifinals, ESPN	3.1
18.	NBA Playoffs Round 2, TNT	2.9
19.	MLB American League Championship Series (10/10/2023), TBS	2.8
20.	Monday Night Kickoff, ESPN	2.7
21.	Home Run Derby, ESPN	2.7
22.	NCAA Basketball Championship, TBS	2.5
23.	NCAA Basketball Championship-Friday (03/24/2023) Game 1, TBS	2.4
24.	Monday Night Football Postgame, ESPN	2.4
25.	Cotton Bowl, ESPN	2.3

Highest-Rated Syndicated Programs, 2022-23

Source: Nielsen Media Research

Average audience percentages, or ratings, are estimates of the percentage of all TV-owning households watching a program live or on DVR within seven days of broadcast, Sept. 20, 2022-Aug. 31, 2023.

Rank	Program	Avg. audience	Rank	Program	Avg. audience
1.	Jeopardy!	5.4%	16.	Access Hollywood (weekend)	1.2%
2.	Wheel of Fortune	4.8	17.	Hot Bench	1.2
3.	Family Feud	4.7	18.	Dateline	1.2
4.	Judge Judy	4.2	19.	Chicago Fire	1.1
5.	Dateline Weekly	3.6	20.	America's Test Kitchen	1.1
6.	Litton's Weekend Adventure	2.4	21.	Chicago P.D.	1.1
7.	Inside Edition	2.2	22.	Last Man Standing	1.0
8.	Entertainment Tonight	2.0	23.	This Old House	1.0
9.	The Big Bang Theory	1.9	24.	Modern Family (weekend)	0.9
10.	Wheel of Fortune (weekend)	1.7	25.	The Big Bang Theory (weekend)	0.9
11.	Family Feud (weekend)	1.7	26.	The Kelly Clarkson Show	0.9
12.	Law & Order: Special Victims Unit	1.7	27.	Cook's Country From America's Test Kitchen	0.8
13.	Live With Kelly and Mark	1.6	28.	People's Court	0.8
14.	Jeopardy! (weekend)	1.3	29.	The Drew Barrymore Show	0.8
15.	Dr. Phil Show	1.2	30.	The Rookie	0.8

Highest-Rated Premium Cable Programs, 2022-23

Source: Nielsen Media Research

Average audience percentages, or ratings, are estimates of the percentage of all TV-owning households watching a program live or on DVR within seven days of broadcast, Sept. 19, 2022-Aug. 31, 2023.

Highest-Rated Original Series

Rank	Program, channel	Avg. audience
1.	House of the Dragon, HBO	1.6%
2.	Real Time With Bill Maher, HBO	0.8
3.	The Last of Us, HBO	0.8
4.	Last Week Tonight With John Oliver, HBO	0.6
5.	Succession, HBO	0.6
6.	The White Lotus, HBO	0.4
7.	Outlander, Starz (Season 7)	0.4
8.	Your Honor, Showtime (Season 2)	0.4
9.	Perry Mason, HBO	0.4
10.	City on a Hill, Showtime	0.4
11.	Power Book II: Ghost, Starz (Season 3)	0.3
12.	The Righteous Gemstones, HBO	0.3
13.	Power Book III: Raising Kanan, Starz (Season 2)	0.3
14.	Billions, Showtime (Season 7)	0.3
15.	Barry, HBO	0.3
16.	George & Tammy, Showtime	0.3
17.	BMF, Starz (Season 2)	0.3
18.	Winning Time, HBO	0.3
19.	Hard Knocks, HBO (Season 23)	0.2
20.	White House Plumbers, HBO	0.2

Highest-Rated Movies

Rank	Program, channel	Avg. audience
1.	The Flash, HBO	0.2%
2.	Avatar: The Way of Water, HBO	0.1
3.	Hot Tub Time Machine, HBO	0.1
4.	Lucy, HBO	0.1
5.	American Gangster, HBO	0.1
6.	Black Adam, HBO	0.1
7.	The Bourne Ultimatum, HBO	0.1
8.	Dr. Seuss' How the Grinch Stole Christmas, HBO	0.1
9.	Big Game, HBO	0.1
10.	Every Secret Thing, HBO	0.1
11.	Gone Girl, HBO	0.1
12.	Live Free or Die Hard, HBO	0.1
13.	Man of Steel, HBO	0.1
14.	A Million Ways to Die in the West, HBO	0.1
15.	Pulp Fiction, HBO	0.1
16.	The Godfather, Showtime	0.1
17.	300: Rise of an Empire, HBO	0.1
18.	Armageddon, HBO	0.1
19.	Casino Royale (2006), HBO	0.1
20.	Edge of Tomorrow, HBO	0.1

All-Time Most Watched Television Programs

Source: Nielsen Media Research, Jan. 1961-Aug. 2023

Estimates exclude unsponsored or joint network telecasts (e.g., presidential addresses) and programs under 30 minutes. Ranked by number of households tuned in to the program (avg. audience). (Rating is percentage of all TV-owning households tuned in.)

Rank	Program	Telecast date	Network	Rating	Avg. audience (thous.)
1.	Super Bowl XLIX	2/1/2015	NBC	48.1%	55,948
2.	Super Bowl 50	2/7/2016	CBS	47.1	54,775
3.	Super Bowl XLVIII	2/2/2014	FOX	47.1	54,585
4.	Super Bowl LI	2/5/2017	FOX	45.8	54,180
5.	Super Bowl XLVI	2/5/2012	NBC	47.0	53,910
6.	Super Bowl XLV	2/6/2011	FOX	46.1	53,435
7.	Super Bowl XLVII	2/3/2013	CBS	46.7	53,363
8.	Super Bowl LII	2/4/2018	NBC	43.5	52,017
9.	Super Bowl XLIV	2/7/2010	CBS	45.2	51,873
10.	Super Bowl XLVII Delay	2/3/2013	CBS	44.5	50,861
11.	Super Bowl LIV	2/2/2020	FOX	42.1	50,726
12.	M*A*S*H (last episode)	2/28/1983	CBS	60.2	50,150
13.	Super Bowl LIII	2/3/2019	CBS	41.4	49,595
14.	Super Bowl XLII	2/3/2008	FOX	43.2	48,721
15.	Super Bowl XLIII	2/1/2009	NBC	42.0	48,139
16.	Super Bowl XLI	2/4/2007	CBS	42.7	47,535
17.	Super Bowl LV	2/7/2021	CBS	38.4	46,446
18.	Super Bowl XL	2/5/2006	ABC	41.6	45,869
19.	XVII Winter Olympics (Women's figure skating)	2/23/1994	CBS	48.5	45,690
20.	Super Bowl LVI	2/13/2022	CBS	37.2	45,533
21.	Super Bowl XXXIX	2/6/2005	FOX	41.1	45,080
22.	Super Bowl XXXVIII	2/1/2004	CBS	41.4	44,910
23.	Super Bowl XXX	1/28/1996	NBC	46.0	44,150
24.	Super Bowl XXXII	1/25/1998	NBC	44.5	43,630
25.	Super Bowl XXXIV	1/30/2000	ABC	43.3	43,620
26.	Super Bowl XXXVII	1/26/2003	ABC	40.7	43,430
27.	Super Bowl XXVIII	1/30/1994	NBC	45.5	42,860
28.	Super Bowl XXXVI	2/3/2002	FOX	40.4	42,660
29.	Cheers (last episode)	5/20/1993	NBC	45.5	42,360

Highest-Rated Television Programs by Season, 1950-2023

Source: Nielsen Media Research; regular series programs (excl. sports), Sept.-May season

Rating is percentage of all TV-owning households tuned in to the program. Data prior to 1988-89 exclude Alaska and Hawaii.

Season	Program	Rating	TV-owning households (thous.)	Season	Program	Rating	TV-owning households (thous.)
1950-51	Texaco Star Theatre	61.6%	10,320	1987-88	The Cosby Show	27.8	88,600
1951-52	Godfrey's Talent Scouts	53.8	15,300	1988-89	Roseanne	25.5	90,400
1952-53	I Love Lucy	67.3	20,400	1989-90	Roseanne	23.4	92,100
1953-54	I Love Lucy	58.8	26,000	1990-91	Cheers	21.6	93,100
1954-55	I Love Lucy	49.3	30,700	1991-92	60 Minutes	21.7	92,100
1955-56	$64,000 Question	47.5	34,900	1992-93	60 Minutes	21.6	93,100
1956-57	I Love Lucy	43.7	38,900	1993-94	Home Improvement	21.9	94,200
1957-58	Gunsmoke	43.1	41,920	1994-95	Seinfeld	20.5	95,400
1958-59	Gunsmoke	39.6	43,950	1995-96	E.R.	22.0	95,900
1959-60	Gunsmoke	40.3	45,750	1996-97	E.R.	21.2	97,000
1960-61	Gunsmoke	37.3	47,200	1997-98	Seinfeld	22.0	98,000
1961-62	Wagon Train	32.1	48,555	1998-99	E.R.	17.8	99,400
1962-63	Beverly Hillbillies	36.0	50,300	1999-2000	Who Wants to Be a Millionaire	18.6	100,800
1963-64	Beverly Hillbillies	39.1	51,600	2000-01	Survivor II	17.4	102,200
1964-65	Bonanza	36.3	52,700	2001-02	Friends	15.3	105,500
1965-66	Bonanza	31.8	53,850	2002-03	CSI	16.3	106,700
1966-67	Bonanza	29.1	55,130	2003-04	CSI	15.9	108,400
1967-68	The Andy Griffith Show	27.6	56,670	2004-05	CSI	16.5	106,900
1968-69	Rowan & Martin's Laugh-In	31.8	58,250	2005-06	American Idol-Tuesday	17.6	110,200
1969-70	Rowan & Martin's Laugh-In	26.3	58,500	2006-07	American Idol-Wednesday	17.3	112,800
1970-71	Marcus Welby, M.D.	29.6	60,100	2007-08	American Idol-Tuesday	15.5	113,050
1971-72	All in the Family	34.0	60,900	2008-09	American Idol-Wednesday	14.4	114,900
1972-73	All in the Family	33.3	64,800	2009-10	American Idol-Tuesday	13.7	114,900
1973-74	All in the Family	31.2	66,200	2010-11	American Idol-Wednesday	14.5	115,900
1974-75	All in the Family	30.2	68,500	2011-12	NCIS	12.3	114,700
1975-76	All in the Family	30.1	69,600	2012-13	NCIS	13.5	114,200
1976-77	Happy Days	31.5	71,200	2013-14	NCIS	12.6	115,800
1977-78	Laverne & Shirley	31.6	72,900	2014-15	The Big Bang Theory	11.6	116,400
1978-79	Laverne & Shirley	30.5	74,500	2015-16	NCIS	12.8	116,400
1979-80	60 Minutes	28.2	76,300	2016-17	The Big Bang Theory	11.5	118,400
1980-81	Dallas	31.2	79,900	2017-18	The Big Bang Theory	11.3	119,600
1981-82	Dallas	28.4	81,500	2018-19	The Big Bang Theory	10.9	119,900
1982-83	60 Minutes	25.5	83,300	2019-20	NCIS	9.5	120,600
1983-84	Dallas	25.7	83,800	2020-21	NCIS	7.7	121,000
1984-85	Dynasty	25.0	84,900	2021-22	NCIS	6.6	122,400
1985-86	The Cosby Show	33.8	85,900	2022-23	NCIS	6.0	123,800
1986-87	The Cosby Show	34.9%	87,400				

All-Time Highest-Rated Television Programs

Source: Nielsen Media Research, Jan. 1961-Aug. 2023

Estimates exclude unsponsored or joint network telecasts (e.g., presidential addresses) and programs under 30 minutes long. Ranked by rating (percentage of all TV-owning households tuned in to the program). Average audience is number of TV-owning households tuned in.

Rank	Program	Telecast date	Network	Rating	Avg. audience (thous.)
1.	M*A*S*H (last episode)	2/28/1983	CBS	60.2%	50,150
2.	Dallas ("Who Shot J.R.?" episode)	11/21/1980	CBS	53.3	41,470
3.	Roots-Pt. 8	1/30/1977	ABC	51.1	36,380
4.	Super Bowl XVI	1/24/1982	CBS	49.1	40,020
5.	Super Bowl XVII	1/30/1983	NBC	48.6	40,480
6.	XVII Winter Olympics (Women's figure skating)	2/23/1994	CBS	48.5	45,690
7.	Super Bowl XX	1/26/1986	NBC	48.3	41,490
8.	Super Bowl XLIX	2/1/2015	NBC	48.1	55,948
9.	Gone With the Wind-Pt. 1	11/7/1976	NBC	47.7	33,960
10.	Gone With the Wind-Pt. 2	11/8/1976	NBC	47.4	33,750
11.	Super Bowl XII	1/15/1978	CBS	47.2	34,410
12.	Super Bowl XLVIII	2/2/2014	FOX	47.1	54,585
12.	Super Bowl XIII	1/21/1979	NBC	47.1	35,090
12.	Super Bowl 50	2/7/2016	CBS	47.1	54,775
15.	Super Bowl XLVI	2/5/2012	NBC	47.0	53,910
16.	Super Bowl XLVII	2/3/2013	CBS	46.7	53,363
17.	Bob Hope Christmas Show	1/15/1970	NBC	46.6	27,260
18.	Super Bowl XVIII	1/22/1984	CBS	46.4	38,880
18.	Super Bowl XIX	1/20/1985	ABC	46.4	39,390
20.	Super Bowl XIV	1/20/1980	CBS	46.3	35,330
21.	Super Bowl XLV	2/6/2011	FOX	46.1	53,435
22.	Super Bowl XXX	1/28/1996	NBC	46.0	44,150
22.	ABC Sunday Night Movie (The Day After)	11/20/1983	ABC	46.0	38,550
24.	Roots-Pt. 6	1/28/1977	ABC	45.9	32,680
24.	The Fugitive (last episode)	8/29/1967	ABC	45.9	25,700
26.	Super Bowl LI	2/5/2017	FOX	45.8	54,180
26.	Super Bowl XXI	1/25/1987	CBS	45.8	40,030
28.	Roots-Pt. 5	1/27/1977	ABC	45.7	32,540
29.	Super Bowl XXVIII	1/30/1994	NBC	45.5	42,860
30.	Cheers (last episode)	5/20/1993	NBC	45.5	42,360
31.	The Ed Sullivan Show (first live U.S. TV appearance of The Beatles)	2/9/1964	CBS	45.3	23,240

AWARDS — MEDALS — PRIZES

Alfred B. Nobel Prizes, 1901-2023

Alfred B. Nobel (1833-96) bequeathed $9 mil, the interest on which was to be distributed yearly to those judged to have most benefited humankind in chemistry, literature, promotion of peace, physics, and physiology or medicine. Prizes were first awarded in 1901. The prize in economics, funded by Sweden's central bank, was first awarded in 1969. Each prize is now worth 11 mil Swedish kronor (about $991,000 in 2023). If year is omitted, no award was given. The Royal Swedish Academy selects prize winners for chemistry, economics, and physics; the Nobel Assembly at Karolinska Institutet, physiology or medicine; the Swedish Academy, literature; and the Norwegian Nobel Committee, the peace prize. Winners sharing a prize are generally listed in alphabetical order, except when the awarding body has given a larger proportion of a shared prize to one or more recipients.

Physics

1901 Wilhelm C. Röntgen, Ger.	**1958** Pavel Cherenkov, Il'ja Frank,	**1993** Russell A. Hulse, Joseph H. Taylor, U.S.
1902 Hendrik A. Lorentz,	Igor Y. Tamm, USSR	**1994** Bertram N. Brockhouse, Can.;
Pieter Zeeman, Neth.	**1959** Owen Chamberlain,	Clifford G. Shull, U.S.
1903 Antoine Henri Becquerel, Pierre	Emilio G. Segre, U.S.	**1995** Martin Perl, Frederick Reines, U.S.
Curie, Fr.; Marie Curie, Pol.-Fr.	**1960** Donald A. Glaser, U.S.	**1996** David M. Lee, Douglas D. Osheroff,
1904 Lord Rayleigh (John W. Strutt), UK	**1961** Robert Hofstadter, U.S.;	Robert C. Richardson, U.S.
1905 Philipp E. A. von Lenard, Ger.	Rudolf L. Mossbauer, Ger.	**1997** Steven Chu, William D. Phillips, U.S.;
1906 Joseph J. Thomson, UK	**1962** Lev D. Landau, USSR	Claude Cohen-Tannoudji, Fr.
1907 Albert A. Michelson, U.S.	**1963** Maria Goeppert-Mayer,	**1998** Robert B. Laughlin, U.S.;
1908 Gabriel Lippmann, Fr.	Eugene P. Wigner, U.S.;	Horst L. Störmer, Ger.-U.S;
1909 Carl F. Braun, Ger.;	J. Hans D. Jensen, Ger.	Daniel C. Tsui, China-U.S.
Guglielmo Marconi, Ital.	**1964** Nicolay G. Basov,	**1999** Gerardus 't Hooft,
1910 Johannes D. van der Waals, Neth.	Aleksandr M. Prokhorov, USSR;	Martinus J. G. Veltman, Neth.
1911 Wilhelm Wien, Ger.	Charles H. Townes, U.S.	**2000** Jack S. Kilby, U.S.;
1912 Nils G. Dalén, Swed.	**1965** Sin-Itiro Tomonaga, Jpn.;	Herbert Kroemer, Ger.-U.S.;
1913 Heike Kamerlingh Onnes, Neth.	Julian S. Schwinger,	Zhores I. Alferov, Russ.
1914 Max von Laue, Ger.	Richard P. Feynman, U.S.	**2001** Eric A. Cornell, Carl E. Wieman,
1915 William H. Bragg,	**1966** Alfred Kastler, Fr.	U.S.; Wolfgang Ketterle, Ger.
William L. Bragg, UK	**1967** Hans A. Bethe, U.S.	**2002** Raymond Davis Jr.,
1917 Charles G. Barkla, UK	**1968** Luis W. Alvarez, U.S.	Riccardo Giacconi, U.S.;
1918 Max K. E. L. Planck, Ger.	**1969** Murray Gell-Mann, U.S.	Masatoshi Koshiba, Jpn.
1919 Johannes Stark, Ger.	**1970** Hannes Alfvén, Swed.; Louis Néel, Fr.	**2003** Alexei A. Abrikosov,
1920 Charles E. Guillaume, Fr.-Switz.	**1971** Dennis Gabor, UK	Vitaly L. Ginzburg, Russ.;
1921 Albert Einstein, Ger.-U.S.	**1972** John Bardeen, Leon N. Cooper,	Anthony J. Leggett, UK
1922 Niels Bohr, Den.	John R. Schrieffer, U.S.	**2004** David J. Gross, H. David Politzer,
1923 Robert A. Millikan, U.S.	**1973** Brian D. Josephson, UK;	Frank Wilczek, U.S.
1924 Karl M. G. Siegbahn, Swed.	Leo Esaki, Jpn.; Ivar Giaever, U.S.	**2005** Roy J. Glauber, John L. Hall, U.S.;
1925 James Franck, Gustav Hertz, Ger.	**1974** Antony Hewish, Martin Ryle, UK	Theodor W. Hänsch, Ger.
1926 Jean B. Perrin, Fr.	**1975** Aage Bohr, Den.;	**2006** John C. Mather, George F. Smoot, U.S.
1927 Arthur H. Compton, U.S.;	Ben Mottelson, U.S.-Den.;	**2007** Albert Fert, Fr.; Peter Grünberg, Ger.
Charles T. R. Wilson, UK	Leo James Rainwater, U.S.	**2008** Yoichiro Nambu, U.S.;
1928 Owen W. Richardson, UK	**1976** Burton Richter,	Makoto Kobayashi,
1929 Prince Louis-Victor de Broglie, Fr.	Samuel C. C. Ting, U.S.	Toshihide Maskawa, Jpn.
1930 Chandrasekhara V. Raman, India	**1977** Philip W. Anderson,	**2009** Charles K. Kao, U.S.-UK;
1932 Werner Heisenberg, Ger.	John H. van Vleck, U.S.;	Willard S. Boyle, U.S.-Can.;
1933 Paul A. M. Dirac, UK;	Nevill F. Mott, UK	George E. Smith, U.S.
Erwin Schrödinger, Austria	**1978** Pyotr Kapitsa, USSR; Arno Penzias,	**2010** Andre Geim, Russ.-Neth.;
1935 James Chadwick, UK	Robert Wilson, U.S.	Konstantin Novoselov, Russ.-UK
1936 Carl D. Anderson, U.S.;	**1979** Sheldon L. Glashow,	**2011** Saul Perlmutter, Adam G. Riess,
Victor F. Hess, Austria	Steven Weinberg, U.S.;	U.S.; Brian P. Schmidt, Austral.-U.S.
1937 Clinton J. Davisson, U.S.;	Abdus Salam, Pakistan	**2012** Serge Haroche, Fr.;
George P. Thomson, UK	**1980** James W. Cronin, Val L. Fitch, U.S.	David J. Wineland, U.S.
1938 Enrico Fermi, Ital.-U.S.	**1981** Nicolaas Bloembergen,	**2013** François Englert, Belg.;
1939 Ernest O. Lawrence, U.S.	Arthur Schawlow, U.S.;	Peter W. Higgs, UK
1943 Otto Stern, U.S.	Kai M. Siegbahn, Swed.	**2014** Isamu Akasaki, Hiroshi Amano, Jpn.;
1944 Isidor Isaac Rabi, U.S.	**1982** Kenneth G. Wilson, U.S.	Shuji Nakamura, Jpn.-U.S.
1945 Wolfgang Pauli, U.S.-Austria	**1983** Subramanyan Chandrasekhar,	**2015** Takaaki Kajita, Jpn.;
1946 Percy W. Bridgman, U.S.	William A. Fowler, U.S.	Arthur B. McDonald, Can.
1947 Edward V. Appleton, UK	**1984** Carlo Rubbia, Ital.;	**2016** David J. Thouless, UK-U.S.;
1948 Patrick M. S. Blackett, UK	Simon van der Meer, Neth.	F. Duncan M. Haldane,
1949 Hideki Yukawa, Jpn.	**1985** Klaus von Klitzing, Ger.	J. Michael Kosterlitz, UK-U.S.
1950 Cecil F. Powell, UK	**1986** Ernest Ruska, Gerd Binnig, Ger.;	**2017** Rainer Weiss, Ger.-U.S.; Barry C.
1951 John D. Cockcroft, UK;	Heinrich Rohrer, Switz.	Barish, Kip S. Thorne, U.S.
Ernest T. S. Walton, Ire.	**1987** J. Georg Bednorz, Ger.;	**2018** Arthur Ashkin, U.S.; Gérard
1952 Felix Bloch, Edward M. Purcell, U.S.	K. Alex Müller, Switz.	Mourou, Fr.; Donna Strickland, Can.
1953 Frits Zernike, Neth.	**1988** Leon M. Lederman, Melvin	**2019** James Peebles, Can.-U.S.;
1954 Max Born, UK; Walter Bothe, Ger.	Schwartz, Jack Steinberger, U.S.	Michel Mayor, Didier Queloz, Switz.
1955 Polykarp Kusch,	**1989** Norman F. Ramsey, U.S.;	**2020** Roger Penrose, UK;
Willis E. Lamb, U.S.	Hans G. Dehmelt, Ger.-U.S.;	Reinhard Genzel, Ger.;
1956 John Bardeen, Walter H. Brattain,	Wolfgang Paul, Ger.	Andrea Ghez, U.S.
William Shockley, U.S.	**1990** Jerome I. Friedman, Henry W.	**2021** Giorgio Parisi, Ital.;
1957 Tsung-Dao Lee, Chen Ning Yang,	Kendall, U.S.; Richard E. Taylor, Can.	Klaus Hasselmann, Ger.;
U.S.-China	**1991** Pierre-Gilles de Gennes, Fr.	Syukuro Manabe, U.S.
	1992 Georges Charpak, Pol.-Fr.	**2022** Alain Aspect, Fr.; John F. Clauser,
		U.S.; Anton Zeilinger, Austria
		2023 Pierre Agostini, Anne L'Huillier, Fr.;
		Ferenc Krausz, Hung.-Austria

Chemistry

1901	Jacobus H. van 't Hoff, Neth.	1958	Frederick Sanger, UK	1997	Paul D. Boyer, U.S.; John E. Walker, UK; Jens C. Skou, Den.
1902	Emil Fischer, Ger.	1959	Jaroslav Heyrovsky, Czech.	1998	Walter Kohn, U.S.; John A. Pople, UK
1903	Svante A. Arrhenius, Swed.	1960	Willard F. Libby, U.S.	1999	Ahmed H. Zewail, U.S.
1904	William Ramsay, UK	1961	Melvin Calvin, U.S.	2000	Alan J. Heeger, U.S.;
1905	Adolf von Baeyer, Ger.	1962	John C. Kendrew, Max F. Perutz, UK		Alan G. MacDiarmid, N.Z.-U.S.;
1906	Henri Moissan, Fr.	1963	Giulio Natta, Ital.; Karl Ziegler, Ger.		Hideki Shirakawa, Jpn.
1907	Eduard Buchner, Ger.	1964	Dorothy C. Hodgkin, UK	2001	K. Barry Sharpless,
1908	Ernest Rutherford, UK	1965	Robert B. Woodward, U.S.		William S. Knowles, U.S.;
1909	Wilhelm Ostwald, Ger.	1966	Robert S. Mulliken, U.S.		Ryoji Noyori, Jpn.
1910	Otto Wallach, Ger.	1967	Manfred Eigen, Ger.; Ronald G. W. Norrish, George Porter, UK	2002	John B. Fenn, U.S.; Koichi Tanaka, Jpn.;
1911	Marie Curie, Pol.-Fr.	1968	Lars Onsager, U.S.		Kurt Wüthrich, Switz.
1912	Victor Grignard, Paul Sabatier, Fr.	1969	Derek H. R. Barton, UK; Odd Hassel, Nor.	2003	Peter Agre, Roderick MacKinnon, U.S.
1913	Alfred Werner, Switz.	1970	Luis F. Leloir, Arg.	2004	Aaron Ciechanover, Avram Hershko, Isr.; Irwin Rose, U.S.
1914	Theodore W. Richards, U.S.	1971	Gerhard Herzberg, Can.	2005	Yves Chauvin, Fr.; Robert H. Grubbs, Richard R. Schrock, U.S.
1915	Richard M. Willstätter, Ger.	1972	Christian B. Anfinsen, Stanford Moore, William H. Stein, U.S.	2006	Roger D. Kornberg, U.S.
1918	Fritz Haber, Ger.	1973	Ernst Otto Fischer, Ger.; Geoffrey Wilkinson, UK	2007	Gerhard Ertl, Ger.
1920	Walther H. Nernst, Ger.	1974	Paul J. Flory, U.S.	2008	Martin Chalfie, Osamu Shimomura, Roger Y. Tsien, U.S.
1921	Frederick Soddy, UK	1975	John Cornforth, Austral.-UK; Vladimir Prelog, Bosnia-Switz.	2009	Venkatraman Ramakrishnan, UK; Thomas A. Steitz, U.S.
1922	Francis W. Aston, UK	1976	William N. Lipscomb, U.S.		Ada E. Yonath, Isr.
1923	Fritz Pregl, Austria	1977	Ilya Prigogine, Belg.	2010	Richard F. Heck, U.S.;
1925	Richard A. Zsigmondy, Ger.	1978	Peter Mitchell, UK		Ei-ichi Negishi, Jpn.-U.S.;
1926	Theodor Svedberg, Swed.	1979	Herbert C. Brown, U.S.; Georg Wittig, Ger.		Akira Suzuki, Jpn.
1927	Heinrich O. Wieland, Ger.	1980	Paul Berg, Walter Gilbert, U.S.; Frederick Sanger, UK	2011	Dan Shechtman, Isr.
1928	Adolf O. R. Windaus, Ger.	1981	Kenichi Fukui, Jpn.; Roald Hoffmann, U.S.	2012	Brian K. Kobilka, Robert J. Lefkowitz, U.S.
1929	Arthur Harden, UK; Hans von Euler-Chelpin, Swed.	1982	Aaron Klug, UK-Lith.	2013	Martin Karplus, Austria-U.S.; Michael Levitt, S. Afr.-U.S.;
1930	Hans Fischer, Ger.	1983	Henry Taube, Can.		Arieh Warshel, Isr.-U.S.
1931	Friedrich Bergius, Carl Bosch, Ger.	1984	Robert Bruce Merrifield, U.S.	2014	Eric Betzig, William E. Moerner, U.S.; Stefan W. Hell, Ger.
1932	Irving Langmuir, U.S.	1985	Herbert A. Hauptman, Jerome Karle, U.S.	2015	Tomas Lindahl, Swed.-UK; Paul Modrich, U.S.;
1934	Harold C. Urey, U.S.	1986	Dudley Herschbach, Yuan T. Lee, U.S.; John C. Polanyi, Can.		Aziz Sancar, Turk.-U.S.
1935	Frédéric Joliot, Irène Joliot-Curie, Fr.	1987	Donald J. Cram, Charles J. Pedersen, U.S.; Jean-Marie Lehn, Fr.	2016	Bernard L. Feringa, Neth.; Jean-Pierre Sauvage, Fr.; J. Fraser Stoddart, UK-U.S.
1936	Peter J. W. Debye, Neth.	1988	Johann Deisenhofer, Robert Huber, Hartmut Michel, Ger.	2017	Jacques Dubochet, Switz.; Joachim Frank, Ger.-U.S.; Richard Henderson, UK
1937	Walter N. Haworth, UK; Paul Karrer, Switz.	1989	Sidney Altman, Thomas R. Cech, U.S.	2018	Frances H. Arnold, George P. Smith, U.S.; Gregory P. Winter, UK
1938	Richard Kuhn, Ger.	1990	Elias James Corey, U.S.	2019	John B. Goodenough, Ger.-U.S.; M. Stanley Whittingham, UK-U.S.; Akira Yoshino, Jpn.
1939	Adolf F. J. Butenandt, Ger.; Leopold Ruzicka, Switz.	1991	Richard R. Ernst, Switz.	2020	Emmanuelle Charpentier, Fr.; Jennifer Doudna, U.S.
1943	George de Hevesy, Hung.	1992	Rudolph A. Marcus, Can.-U.S.	2021	Benjamin List, Ger.; David W.C. MacMillan, UK-U.S.
1944	Otto Hahn, Ger.	1993	Kary B. Mullis, U.S.; Michael Smith, UK-Can.	2022	Carolyn R. Bertozzi, K. Barry Sharpless, U.S.; Morten Meldal, Den.
1945	Artturi I. Virtanen, Fin.	1994	George A. Olah, U.S.	2023	Moungi Bawendi, Fr.-U.S.; Louis Brus, U.S.; Alexei Ekimov, Russ.
1946	James B. Sumner, John H. Northrop, Wendell M. Stanley, U.S.	1995	Paul Crutzen, Neth.; Mario Molina, Mex.-U.S.; Sherwood Rowland, U.S.		
1947	Robert Robinson, UK	1996	Robert F. Curl Jr., Richard E. Smalley, U.S.; Harold W. Kroto, UK		
1948	Arne W. K. Tiselius, Swed.				
1949	William F. Giauque, U.S.				
1950	Kurt Alder, Otto P. H. Diels, Ger.				
1951	Edwin M. McMillan, Glenn T. Seaborg, U.S.				
1952	Archer J. P. Martin, Richard L. M. Synge, UK				
1953	Hermann Staudinger, Ger.				
1954	Linus C. Pauling, U.S.				
1955	Vincent du Vigneaud, U.S.				
1956	Cyril N. Hinshelwood, UK; Nikolay N. Semenov, USSR				
1957	Lord (Alexander R.) Todd, UK				

Physiology or Medicine

1901	Emil A. von Behring, Ger.	1934	George R. Minot, William P. Murphy, G. H. Whipple, U.S.	1958	George W. Beadle, Edward L. Tatum, Joshua Lederberg, U.S.
1902	Ronald Ross, UK	1935	Hans Spemann, Ger.	1959	Arthur Kornberg, Severo Ochoa, U.S.
1903	Niels R. Finsen, Den.	1936	Henry H. Dale, UK; Otto Loewi, U.S.	1960	Frank Macfarlane Burnet, Austral.; Peter B. Medawar, UK
1904	Ivan P. Pavlov, Russ.	1937	Albert Szent-Gyorgyi, Hung.-U.S.	1961	Georg von Békésy, U.S.
1905	Robert Koch, Ger.	1938	Corneille J. F. Heymans, Belg.	1962	Francis H. C. Crick, Maurice H. F. Wilkins, UK; James D. Watson, U.S.
1906	Camillo Golgi, Ital.; Santiago Ramón y Cajal, Spain	1939	Gerhard Domagk, Ger.	1963	John C. Eccles, Austral.; Alan L. Hodgkin, Andrew F. Huxley, UK
1907	Charles L. A. Laveran, Fr.	1943	Henrik C. P. Dam, Den.; Edward A. Doisy, U.S.	1964	Konrad E. Bloch, U.S.; Feodor Lynen, Ger.
1908	Paul Ehrlich, Ger.; Ilya Mechnikov, Fr.	1944	Joseph Erlanger, Herbert S. Gasser, U.S.	1965	François Jacob, André Lwoff, Jacques Monod, Fr.
1909	Emil T. Kocher, Switz.	1945	Ernst B. Chain, Alexander Fleming, Howard W. Florey, UK	1966	Charles B. Huggins, Peyton Rous, U.S.
1910	Albrecht Kossel, Ger.	1946	Hermann J. Muller, U.S.	1967	Ragnar Granit, Swed.; Haldan Keffer Hartline, George Wald, U.S.
1911	Allvar Gullstrand, Swed.	1947	Carl F. Cori, Gerty T. Cori, U.S.; Bernardo A. Houssay, Arg.	1968	Robert W. Holley, H. Gobind Khorana, Marshall W. Nirenberg, U.S.
1912	Alexis Carrel, Fr.	1948	Paul H. Müller, Switz.	1969	Max Delbrück, Alfred D. Hershey, Salvador Luria, U.S.
1913	Charles R. Richet, Fr.	1949	Walter R. Hess, Switz.; Antonio Egas Moniz, Port.	1970	Julius Axelrod, U.S.; Bernard Katz, UK; Ulf von Euler, Swed.
1914	Robert Bárány, Austria	1950	Philip S. Hench, Edward C. Kendall, U.S.; Tadeus Reichstein, Switz.	1971	Earl W. Sutherland Jr., U.S.
1919	Jules Bordet, Belg.	1951	Max Theiler, U.S.	1972	Gerald M. Edelman, U.S.; Rodney R. Porter, UK
1920	Schack A. S. Krogh, Den.	1952	Selman A. Waksman, U.S.	1973	Konrad Lorenz, Austria; Nikolaas Tinbergen, UK; Karl von Frisch, Ger.
1922	Archibald V. Hill, UK; Otto F. Meyerhof, Ger.	1953	Hans A. Krebs, UK; Fritz A. Lipmann, U.S.		
1923	Frederick G. Banting, Can.; John J. R. Macleod, UK	1954	John F. Enders, Frederick C. Robbins, Thomas H. Weller, U.S.		
1924	Willem Einthoven, Neth.	1955	Alex H. T. Theorell, Swed.		
1926	Johannes A. G. Fibiger, Den.	1956	André F. Cournand, Dickinson W. Richards, U.S.; Werner Forssmann, Ger.		
1927	Julius Wagner-Jauregg, Austria	1957	Daniel Bovet, Ital.		
1928	Charles J. H. Nicolle, Fr.				
1929	Christiaan Eijkman, Neth.; Frederick G. Hopkins, UK				
1930	Karl Landsteiner, U.S.				
1931	Otto H. Warburg, Ger.				
1932	Edgar D. Adrian, Charles S. Sherrington, UK				
1933	Thomas H. Morgan, U.S.				

1974 Albert Claude, Lux.-U.S.;
     Christian de Duve, Belg.;
     George Emil Palade, Rom.-U.S.
1975 David Baltimore, Howard Temin,
     U.S.; Renato Dulbecco, Ital.-U.S.
1976 Baruch S. Blumberg,
     Daniel Carleton Gajdusek, U.S.
1977 Rosalyn S. Yalow, Roger Guillemin,
     Andrew V. Schally, U.S.
1978 Werner Arber, Switz.;
     Daniel Nathans, Hamilton O. Smith, U.S.
1979 Allan M. Cormack, U.S.;
     Godfrey N. Hounsfield, UK
1980 Baruj Benacerraf, George Snell,
     U.S.; Jean Dausset, Fr.
1981 Roger W. Sperry, David H. Hubel,
     Torsten N. Wiesel, U.S.
1982 Sune K. Bergström,
     Bengt I. Samuelsson, Swed.;
     John R. Vane, UK
1983 Barbara McClintock, U.S.
1984 Niels K. Jerne, UK-Den.;
     Georges J. F. Köhler, Ger.;
     César Milstein, UK-Árg.
1985 Michael S. Brown,
     Joseph L. Goldstein, U.S.
1986 Stanley Cohen, U.S.;
     Rita Levi-Montalcini, Ital.-U.S.
1987 Susumu Tonegawa, Jpn.
1988 James W. Black, UK;
     Gertrude B. Elion,
     George H. Hitchings, U.S.
1989 J. Michael Bishop,
     Harold E. Varmus, U.S.

1990 Joseph E. Murray,
     E. Donnall Thomas, U.S.
1991 Edwin Neher, Bert Sakmann, Ger.
1992 Edmond H. Fisher, Edwin G. Krebs, U.S.
1993 Richard J. Roberts, UK;
     Phillip A. Sharp, U.S.
1994 Alfred G. Gilman, Martin Rodbell, U.S.
1995 Edward B. Lewis,
     Eric F. Wieschaus, U.S.;
     Christiane Nüsslein-Volhard, Ger.
1996 Peter C. Doherty, Austral.;
     Rolf M. Zinkernagel, Switz.
1997 Stanley B. Prusiner, U.S.
1998 Robert F. Furchgott,
     Louis J. Ignarro, Ferid Murad, U.S.
1999 Günter Blobel, U.S.
2000 Arvid Carlsson, Swed.;
     Paul Greengard, U.S.;
     Eric R. Kandel, Austria-U.S.
2001 Leland H. Hartwell, U.S.;
     R. Timothy (Tim) Hunt,
     Paul M. Nurse, UK
2002 Sydney Brenner, John E. Sulston,
     UK; H. Robert Horvitz, U.S.
2003 Paul C. Lauterbur, U.S.;
     Peter Mansfield, UK
2004 Richard Axel, Linda B. Buck, U.S.
2005 Barry J. Marshall,
     J. Robin Warren, Austral.
2006 Andrew Z. Fire, Craig C. Mello, U.S.
2007 Mario R. Capecchi,
     Oliver Smithies, U.S.;
     Martin J. Evans, UK

2008 Harald zur Hausen, Ger.;
     Françoise Barré-Sinoussi,
     Luc Montagnier, Fr.
2009 Elizabeth H. Blackburn,
     Carol W. Greider,
     Jack W. Szostak, U.S.
2010 Robert G. Edwards, UK
2011 Bruce A. Beutler, U.S.;
     Jules A. Hoffmann, Fr.;
     Ralph M. Steinman, Can.-U.S.
2012 John B. Gurdon, UK
     Shinya Yamanaka, Jpn.-U.S.
2013 James E. Rothman,
     Randy W. Schekman, U.S.;
     Thomas C. Südhof, Ger.-U.S.
2014 John O'Keefe, U.S.-UK; May-Britt
     Moser, Edvard I. Moser, Nor.
2015 William C. Campbell, Ire.-U.S.;
     Satoshi Omura, Jpn.; Youyou Tu, China
2016 Yoshinori Ohsumi, Jpn.
2017 Jeffrey C. Hall, Michael Rosbash,
     Michael W. Young, U.S.
2018 James P. Allison, U.S.;
     Tasuku Honjo, Jpn.
2019 William G. Kaelin Jr.,
     Gregg L. Semenza, U.S.;
     Peter J. Ratcliffe, UK
2020 Harvey J. Alter, Charles M. Rice, U.S.;
     Michael Houghton, UK
2021 David Julius, Ardem Patapoutian, U.S.
2022 Svante Pääbo, Swed.
2023 Katalin Karikó, Hung.-U.S.;
     Drew Weissman, U.S.

Literature

1901 Rene F. A. Sully Prudhomme, Fr.
1902 Theodor Mommsen, Ger.
1903 Bjørnstjerne Bjørnson, Nor.
1904 José Echegaray y Eizaguirre, Spain;
     Fréderic Mistral, Fr.
1905 Henryk Sienkiewicz, Pol.
1906 Giosuè Carducci, Ital.
1907 Rudyard Kipling, UK
1908 Rudolf C. Eucken, Ger.
1909 Selma Lagerlöf, Swed.
1910 Paul J. L. Heyse, Ger.
1911 Maurice Maeterlinck, Belg.
1912 Gerhart Hauptmann, Ger.
1913 Rabindranath Tagore, India
1915 Romain Rolland, Fr.
1916 Verner von Heidenstam, Swed.
1917 Karl A. Gjellerup,
     Henrik Pontoppidan, Den.
1919 Carl F. G. Spitteler, Switz.
1920 Knut Hamsun, Nor.
1921 Anatole France, Fr.
1922 Jacinto Benavente, Spain
1923 William Butler Yeats, Ire.
1924 Wladyslaw S. Reymont, Pol.
1925 George Bernard Shaw, Ire.-UK
1926 Grazia Deledda, Ital.
1927 Henri Bergson, Fr.
1928 Sigrid Undset, Nor.
1929 Thomas Mann, Ger.
1930 Sinclair Lewis, U.S.
1931 Erik A. Karlfeldt, Swed.
1932 John Galsworthy, UK
1933 Ivan A. Bunin, USSR
1934 Luigi Pirandello, Ital.
1936 Eugene O'Neill, U.S.
1937 Roger Martin du Gard, Fr.
1938 Pearl S. Buck, U.S.
1939 Frans E. Sillanpää, Fin.
1944 Johannes V. Jensen, Den.

1945 Gabriela Mistral, Chile
1946 Hermann Hesse, Ger.-Switz.
1947 André Gide, Fr.
1948 T. S. Eliot, UK
1949 William Faulkner, U.S.
1950 Bertrand Russell, UK
1951 Pär F. Lagerkvist, Swed.
1952 François Mauriac, Fr.
1953 Winston Churchill, UK
1954 Ernest Hemingway, U.S.
1955 Halldór K. Laxness, Ice.
1956 Juan Ramón Jiménez, Spain
1957 Albert Camus, Fr.
1958 Boris L. Pasternak, USSR (declined)
1959 Salvatore Quasimodo, Ital.
1960 Saint-John Perse, Fr.
1961 Ivo Andric, Yugo.
1962 John Steinbeck, U.S.
1963 Giorgos Seferis, Greece
1964 Jean-Paul Sartre, Fr. (declined)
1965 Mikhail Sholokhov, USSR
1966 Shmuel Yosef Agnon, Isr.;
     Nelly Sachs, Swed.
1967 Miguel Angel Asturias, Guat.
1968 Yasunari Kawabata, Jpn.
1969 Samuel Beckett, Ire.
1970 Aleksandr I. Solzhenitsyn, USSR
1971 Pablo Neruda, Chile
1972 Heinrich Böll, Ger.
1973 Patrick White, Austral.
1974 Eyvind Johnson,
     Harry Edmund Martinson, Swed.
1975 Eugenio Montale, Ital.
1976 Saul Bellow, U.S.
1977 Vicente Aleixandre, Spain
1978 Isaac Bashevis Singer, U.S.
1979 Odysseus Elytis, Greece
1980 Czeslaw Milosz, Pol.-U.S.
1981 Elias Canetti, Bulg.-UK
1982 Gabriel García Márquez, Colombia

1983 William Golding, UK
1984 Jaroslav Siefert, Czech.
1985 Claude Simon, Fr.
1986 Wole Soyinka, Nigeria
1987 Joseph Brodsky, USSR-U.S.
1988 Naguib Mahfouz, Egypt
1989 Camilo José Cela, Spain
1990 Octavio Paz, Mex.
1991 Nadine Gordimer, S. Afr.
1992 Derek Walcott, St. Lucia
1993 Toni Morrison, U.S.
1994 Kenzaburō Oe, Jpn.
1995 Seamus Heaney, Ire.
1996 Wislawa Szymborska, Pol.
1997 Dario Fo, Ital.
1998 José Saramago, Por.
1999 Günter Grass, Ger.
2000 Gao Xingjian, China-Fr.
2001 V. S. Naipaul, UK
2002 Imre Kertész, Hung.
2003 J. M. Coetzee, S. Afr.
2004 Elfriede Jelinek, Austria
2005 Harold Pinter, UK
2006 Orhan Pamuk, Turk.
2007 Doris Lessing, UK
2008 Jean-Marie Gustave Le Clézio, Fr.
2009 Herta Müller, Ger.
2010 Mario Vargas Llosa, Peru
2011 Tomas Tranströmer, Swed.
2012 Mo Yan, China
2013 Alice Munro, Can.
2014 Patrick Modiano, Fr.
2015 Svetlana Alexievich, Belarus
2016 Bob Dylan, U.S.
2017 Kazuo Ishiguro, Jpn.-UK
2018 Olga Tokarczuk, Pol.
2019 Peter Handke, Austria
2020 Louise Glück, U.S.
2021 Abdulrazak Gurnah, Tanzania
2022 Annie Ernaux, France
2023 Jon Fosse, Nor.

Peace

1901 Jean H. Dunant, Switz.;
     Frédéric Passy, Fr.
1902 Élie Ducommun,
     Charles A. Gobat, Switz.
1903 William R. Cremer, UK
1904 Institute of International Law, Belg.
1905 Baroness Bertha von Suttner, Austria
1906 Theodore Roosevelt, U.S.
1907 Ernesto T. Moneta, Ital.;
     Louis Renault, Fr.
1908 Klas P. Arnoldson, Swed.;
     Fredrik Bajer, Den.
1909 Auguste M. F. Beernaert, Belg.;
     Paul H. B. B. d'Estournelles
     de Constant, Fr.

1910 Permanent Intl. Peace Bureau
1911 Tobias M. C. Asser, Neth.;
     Alfred H. Fried, Austria
1912 Elihu Root, U.S.
1913 Henri La Fontaine, Belg.
1917 Intl. Committee of the Red Cross
1919 Woodrow Wilson, U.S.
1920 Léon V. A. Bourgeois, Fr.
1921 Karl H. Branting, Swed.;
     Christian L. Lange, Nor.
1922 Fridtjof Nansen, Nor.
1925 Austen Chamberlain, UK;
     Charles G. Dawes, U.S.
1926 Aristide Briand, Fr.;
     Gustav Stresemann, Ger.

1927 Ferdinand E. Buisson, Fr.;
     Ludwig Quidde, Ger.
1929 Frank B. Kellogg, U.S.
1930 Nathan Söderblom, Swed.
1931 Jane Addams,
     Nicholas Murray Butler, U.S.
1933 Norman Angell, UK
1934 Arthur Henderson, UK
1935 Carl von Ossietzky, Ger.
1936 Carlos Saavedra Lamas, Arg.
1937 Lord Robert Cecil, UK
1938 Nansen Intl. Office for Refugees
1944 Intl. Committee of the Red Cross
1945 Cordell Hull, U.S.
1946 Emily G. Balch, John R. Mott, U.S.

1947 Friends Service Council, UK; Amer. Friends Service Committee, U.S.	**1979** Mother Teresa of Calcutta, Alb.-India	**2002** Jimmy Carter, U.S.
1949 Lord John Boyd Orr of Brechin, UK	**1980** Adolfo Pérez Esquivel, Arg.	**2003** Shirin Ebadi, Iran
1950 Ralph J. Bunche, U.S.	**1981** Office of UN High Commissioner for Refugees	**2004** Wangari Maathai, Kenya
1951 Léon Jouhaux, Fr.	**1982** Alfonso García Robles, Mex.; Alva Myrdal, Swed.	**2005** Mohamed ElBaradei, Egypt; Intl. Atomic Energy Agency, Austria
1952 Albert Schweitzer, Fr.		
1953 George C. Marshall, U.S.	**1983** Lech Walesa, Pol.	**2006** Muhammad Yunus, Grameen Bank, Bangl.
1954 Office of UN High Commissioner for Refugees	**1984** Bishop Desmond Tutu, S. Afr.	
	1985 Intl. Physicians for the Prevention of Nuclear War, U.S.	**2007** Intergovernmental Panel on Climate Change, Switz.; Al Gore, U.S.
1957 Lester B. Pearson, Can.		
1958 Georges Pire, Belg.	**1986** Elie Wiesel, Rom.-U.S.	**2008** Martti Ahtisaari, Fin.
1959 Philip J. Noel-Baker, UK	**1987** Oscar Arias Sánchez, Costa Rica	**2009** Barack H. Obama, U.S.
1960 Albert J. Lutuli, S. Afr.	**1988** UN Peacekeeping Forces	**2010** Liu Xiaobo, China
1961 Dag Hammarskjöld, Swed.	**1989** Dalai Lama (Tenzin Gyatso), Tibet	**2011** Leymah Gbowee;
1962 Linus C. Pauling, U.S.	**1990** Mikhail S. Gorbachev, USSR	Ellen Johnson Sirleaf, Liberia;
1963 Intl. Committee of the Red Cross, League of Red Cross Societies	**1991** Aung San Suu Kyi, Burma	Tawakkol Karman, Yemen
	1992 Rigoberta Menchú Tum, Guat.	**2012** European Union
1964 Martin Luther King Jr., U.S.	**1993** Frederik W. de Klerk; Nelson Mandela, S. Afr.	**2013** Organization for the Prohibition of Chemical Weapons (OPCW)
1965 UN Children's Fund (UNICEF)		
1968 René Cassin, Fr.	**1994** Yasser Arafat, Pal.; Shimon Peres, Yitzhak Rabin, Isr.	**2014** Kailash Satyarthi, India; Malala Yousafzai, Pakistan
1969 Intl. Labor Organization, Switz.		
1970 Norman E. Borlaug, U.S.	**1995** Joseph Rotblat, Pol.-UK; Pugwash Conferences, Can.	**2015** National Dialogue Quartet, Tunisia
1971 Willy Brandt, Ger.		**2016** Juan Manuel Santos, Colombia
1973 Henry Kissinger, U.S.; Le Duc Tho, N. Viet. (Tho declined)	**1996** Bishop Carlos Ximenes Belo, José Ramos-Horta, Timor-Leste	**2017** Intl. Campaign to Abolish Nuclear Weapons
	1997 Jody Williams, U.S.; Intl. Campaign to Ban Landmines	**2018** Denis Mukwege, Congo; Nadia Murad, Iraq
1974 Seán MacBride, Ire.; Eisaku Sato, Jpn.		
1975 Andrei Sakharov, USSR	**1998** John Hume, David Trimble, N. Ire.	**2019** Abiy Ahmed, Ethiopia
1976 Mairead Corrigan, Betty Williams, N. Ire.	**1999** Médecins Sans Frontières (Doctors Without Borders), Fr.	**2020** World Food Programme
1977 Amnesty International, UK		**2021** Dmitry A. Muratov, Russ.; Maria Ressa, Phil.
1978 Anwar al-Sadat, Egypt; Menachem Begin, Isr.	**2000** Kim Dae Jung, S. Kor.	**2022** Ales Bialiatski, Bela.; Memorial, Russ.; Center for Civil Liberties, Ukr.
	2001 UN; Kofi Annan, Ghana	**2023** Narges Mohammadi, Iran

Nobel Memorial Prize in Economic Sciences

1969 Ragnar Frisch, Nor.; Jan Tinbergen, Neth.	**1992** Gary S. Becker, U.S.	**2010** Peter A. Diamond, Dale T. Mortensen, U.S.; Christopher A. Pissarides, Cyprus-UK
	1993 Robert W. Fogel, U.S. Douglass C. North, U.S.	
1970 Paul A. Samuelson, U.S.		
1971 Simon Kuznets, U.S.	**1994** John C. Harsanyi, John F. Nash, U.S.; Reinhard Selten, Ger.	**2011** Thomas J. Sargent, Christopher A. Sims, U.S.
1972 Kenneth J. Arrow, U.S.; John R. Hicks, UK		
	1995 Robert E. Lucas Jr., U.S.	**2012** Alvin E. Roth, Lloyd S. Shapley, U.S.
1973 Wassily Leontief, U.S.	**1996** James A. Mirrlees, UK; William Vickrey, Can.-U.S.	
1974 Gunnar Myrdal, Swed.; Friedrich A. von Hayek, Austria		**2013** Eugene F. Fama, Lars Peter Hansen, Robert J. Shiller, U.S.
	1997 Robert C. Merton, U.S.; Myron S. Scholes, Can.-U.S.	
1975 Leonid Kantorovich, USSR; Tjalling C. Koopmans, Neth.-U.S.		**2014** Jean Tirole, Fr.
	1998 Amartya Sen, India	**2015** Angus Deaton, UK-U.S.
1976 Milton Friedman, U.S.	**1999** Robert A. Mundell, Can.	**2016** Oliver Hart, U.S.; Bengt Holmström, Fin.-U.S.
1977 James E. Meade, UK; Bertil Ohlin, Swed.	**2000** James J. Heckman, Daniel L. McFadden, U.S.	
		2017 Richard H. Thaler, U.S.
1978 Herbert A. Simon, U.S.	**2001** George A. Akerlof, A. Michael Spence, Joseph E. Stiglitz, U.S.	**2018** William D. Nordhaus, Paul M. Romer, U.S.
1979 Arthur Lewis, UK; Theodore W. Schultz, U.S.		
	2002 Daniel Kahneman, U.S.-Isr.; Vernon L. Smith, U.S.	**2019** Abhijit Banerjee, India-U.S.; Esther Duflo, Fr.-U.S.; Michael Kremer, U.S.
1980 Lawrence R. Klein, U.S.		
1981 James Tobin, U.S.	**2003** Robert F. Engle, U.S.; Clive W. J. Granger, UK	
1982 George J. Stigler, U.S.		**2020** Paul R. Milgrom, Robert B. Wilson, U.S.
1983 Gerard Debreu, Fr.-U.S.	**2004** Finn E. Kydland, Nor.; Edward C. Prescott, U.S.	
1984 Richard Stone, UK		**2021** David Card, Joshua D. Angrist, Guido W. Imbens, U.S.
1985 Franco Modigliani, Ital.-U.S.	**2005** Robert J. Aumann, Isr.-U.S.; Thomas C. Schelling, U.S.	
1986 James M. Buchanan, U.S.		
1987 Robert M. Solow, U.S.	**2006** Edmund S. Phelps, U.S.	**2022** Ben S. Bernanke, Douglas W. Diamond, Philip H. Dybvig, U.S.
1988 Maurice Allais, Fr.	**2007** Leonid Hurwicz, Eric S. Maskin, Roger B. Myerson, U.S.	
1989 Trygve Haavelmo, Nor.		
1990 Harry M. Markowitz, Merton H. Miller, William F. Sharpe, U.S.	**2008** Paul Krugman, U.S.	**2023** Claudia Goldin, U.S.
1991 Ronald H. Coase, UK-U.S.	**2009** Elinor Ostrom, Oliver E. Williamson, U.S.	

Pulitzer Prizes in Journalism, Letters, and Music

Endowed by Joseph Pulitzer (1847-1911), publisher of the *New York World*, in a bequest to Columbia Univ. and awarded annually.

Pulitzer Prizes in Journalism, 2023

Public Service: Associated Press, for the work of Mstyslav Chernov, Evgeniy Maloletka, Vasilisa Stepanenko, and Lori Hinnant, from the besieged city of Mariupol, Ukraine.

Breaking News Reporting: *Los Angeles Times* staff, for coverage of the turmoil and contextual racial issues following their reveal of a secretly recorded racist conversation among city officials.

Investigative Reporting: *Wall Street Journal* staff, for reporting on financial conflicts of interest among officials at 50 federal agencies.

Explanatory Reporting: Caitlin Dickerson, *The Atlantic*, for coverage of the Trump administration policy that separated migrant children from their parents.

Local Reporting: Anna Wolfe, Mississippi Today, Ridgeland, MS, for revealing how a former governor steered state welfare dollars to benefit his family and friends; and John Archibald, Ashley Remkus, Ramsey Archibald, and Challen Stephens of AL.com, Birmingham, AL, for exposing how the Brookside, AL, police force preyed on residents to inflate revenue.

National Reporting: Caroline Kitchener, *Washington Post*, for reporting on consequences after *Roe v. Wade* was overturned.

International Reporting: *NY Times* staff, for unflinching coverage of Russia's invasion of Ukraine.

Feature Writing: Eli Saslow, *Washington Post*, for narratives about people struggling with the pandemic, homelessness, addiction, and inequality.

Commentary: Kyle Whitmire, AL.com, Birmingham, AL, for measured, persuasive columns that document how Alabama's Confederate heritage still colors the present with racism and exclusion.

Criticism: Andrea Long Chu, *New York* magazine, for book reviews that scrutinize authors and their works using multiple lenses.

Editorial Writing: *Miami Herald* editorial board, for series written by Amy Driscoll on the failure of state public officials to deliver taxpayer-funded services and amenities.

Illustrated Reporting and Commentary: Mona Chalabi, *NY Times*, for illustrations to help readers understand the immense wealth and power of Amazon founder Jeff Bezos.

Breaking News Photography: Associated Press photography staff, for images of the first weeks of Russia's invasion of Ukraine.

Feature Photography: Christina House, *L.A. Times*, for an intimate look into the life of a pregnant woman living in a tent.

Audio Reporting: Staff of Gimlet Media, notably Connie Walker, whose investigation of her father's past revealed a larger story of abuse of hundreds of Indigenous children.

Pulitzer Prizes in Letters, 1918-2023

Other Pulitzer Prize Winners, 2023: Biography: Beverly Gage, *G-Man: J. Edgar Hoover and the Making of the American Century.* Memoir/autobiography: Hua Hsu, *Stay True.* History: Jefferson Cowie, *Freedom's Dominion: A Saga of White Resistance to Federal Power.* Poetry: Carl Phillips, *Then the War: And Selected Poems, 2007-2020.*

Fiction

1918 Ernest Poole, *His Family*
1919 Booth Tarkington, *The Magnificent Ambersons*
1921 Edith Wharton, *The Age of Innocence*
1922 Booth Tarkington, *Alice Adams*
1923 Willa Cather, *One of Ours*
1924 Margaret Wilson, *The Able McLaughlins*
1925 Edna Ferber, *So Big*
1926 Sinclair Lewis, *Arrowsmith* (refused)
1927 Louis Bromfield, *Early Autumn*
1928 Thornton Wilder, *The Bridge of San Luis Rey*
1929 Julia Peterkin, *Scarlet Sister Mary*
1930 Oliver La Farge, *Laughing Boy*
1931 Margaret Ayer Barnes, *Years of Grace*
1932 Pearl S. Buck, *The Good Earth*
1933 T. S. Stribling, *The Store*
1934 Caroline Miller, *Lamb in His Bosom*
1935 Josephine W. Johnson, *Now in November*
1936 Harold L. Davis, *Honey in the Horn*
1937 Margaret Mitchell, *Gone With the Wind*
1938 John P. Marquand, *The Late George Apley*
1939 Marjorie Kinnan Rawlings, *The Yearling*
1940 John Steinbeck, *The Grapes of Wrath*
1942 Ellen Glasgow, *In This Our Life*
1943 Upton Sinclair, *Dragon's Teeth*
1944 Martin Flavin, *Journey in the Dark*
1945 John Hersey, *A Bell for Adano*
1947 Robert Penn Warren, *All the King's Men*
1948 James A. Michener, *Tales of the South Pacific*
1949 James Gould Cozzens, *Guard of Honor*
1950 A. B. Guthrie Jr., *The Way West*
1951 Conrad Richter, *The Town*
1952 Herman Wouk, *The Caine Mutiny*
1953 Ernest Hemingway, *The Old Man and the Sea*
1955 William Faulkner, *A Fable*
1956 MacKinlay Kantor, *Andersonville*
1958 James Agee, *A Death in the Family*
1959 Robert Lewis Taylor, *The Travels of Jaimie McPheeters*
1960 Allen Drury, *Advise and Consent*
1961 Harper Lee, *To Kill a Mockingbird*
1962 Edwin O'Connor, *The Edge of Sadness*
1963 William Faulkner, *The Reivers*
1965 Shirley Ann Grau, *The Keepers of the House*
1966 Katherine Anne Porter, *Collected Stories*
1967 Bernard Malamud, *The Fixer*
1968 William Styron, *The Confessions of Nat Turner*
1969 N. Scott Momaday, *House Made of Dawn*
1970 Jean Stafford, *Collected Stories*
1972 Wallace Stegner, *Angle of Repose*
1973 Eudora Welty, *The Optimist's Daughter*
1975 Michael Shaara, *The Killer Angels*
1976 Saul Bellow, *Humboldt's Gift*
1978 James Alan McPherson, *Elbow Room*
1979 John Cheever, *The Stories of John Cheever*
1980 Norman Mailer, *The Executioner's Song*
1981 John Kennedy Toole, *A Confederacy of Dunces*
1982 John Updike, *Rabbit Is Rich*
1983 Alice Walker, *The Color Purple*
1984 William Kennedy, *Ironweed*
1985 Alison Lurie, *Foreign Affairs*
1986 Larry McMurtry, *Lonesome Dove*
1987 Peter Taylor, *A Summons to Memphis*
1988 Toni Morrison, *Beloved*
1989 Anne Tyler, *Breathing Lessons*
1990 Oscar Hijuelos, *The Mambo Kings Play Songs of Love*
1991 John Updike, *Rabbit at Rest*
1992 Jane Smiley, *A Thousand Acres*
1993 Robert Olen Butler, *A Good Scent From a Strange Mountain*
1994 E. Annie Proulx, *The Shipping News*
1995 Carol Shields, *The Stone Diaries*
1996 Richard Ford, *Independence Day*
1997 Steven Millhauser, *Martin Dressler: The Tale of an American Dreamer*
1998 Philip Roth, *American Pastoral*
1999 Michael Cunningham, *The Hours*
2000 Jhumpa Lahiri, *Interpreter of Maladies*
2001 Michael Chabon, *The Amazing Adventures of Kavalier & Clay*
2002 Richard Russo, *Empire Falls*
2003 Jeffrey Eugenides, *Middlesex*
2004 Edward P. Jones, *The Known World*
2005 Marilynne Robinson, *Gilead*
2006 Geraldine Brooks, *March*
2007 Cormac McCarthy, *The Road*
2008 Junot Díaz, *The Brief Wondrous Life of Oscar Wao*
2009 Elizabeth Strout, *Olive Kitteridge*

2010 Paul Harding, *Tinkers*
2011 Jennifer Egan, *A Visit From the Goon Squad*
2013 Adam Johnson, *The Orphan Master's Son*
2014 Donna Tartt, *The Goldfinch*
2015 Anthony Doerr, *All the Light We Cannot See*
2016 Viet Thanh Nguyen, *The Sympathizer*
2017 Colson Whitehead, *The Underground Railroad*
2018 Andrew Sean Greer, *Less*
2019 Richard Powers, *The Overstory*
2020 Colson Whitehead, *The Nickel Boys*
2021 Louise Erdrich, *The Night Watchman*
2022 Joshua Cohen, *The Netanyahus*
2023 Barbara Kingsolver, *Demon Copperhead*; Hernan Diaz, *Trust*

Drama

1918 Jesse Lynch Williams, *Why Marry?*
1920 Eugene O'Neill, *Beyond the Horizon*
1921 Zona Gale, *Miss Lulu Bett*
1922 Eugene O'Neill, *Anna Christie*
1923 Owen Davis, *Icebound*
1924 Hatcher Hughes, *Hell-Bent Fer Heaven*
1925 Sidney Howard, *They Knew What They Wanted*
1926 George Kelly, *Craig's Wife*
1927 Paul Green, *In Abraham's Bosom*
1928 Eugene O'Neill, *Strange Interlude*
1929 Elmer Rice, *Street Scene*
1930 Marc Connelly, *The Green Pastures*
1931 Susan Glaspell, *Alison's House*
1932 George S. Kaufman, Morrie Ryskind, and Ira Gershwin, *Of Thee I Sing*
1933 Maxwell Anderson, *Both Your Houses*
1934 Sidney Kingsley, *Men in White*
1935 Zoe Akins, *The Old Maid*
1936 Robert E. Sherwood, *Idiot's Delight*
1937 George S. Kaufman and Moss Hart, *You Can't Take It With You*
1938 Thornton Wilder, *Our Town*
1939 Robert E. Sherwood, *Abe Lincoln in Illinois*
1940 William Saroyan, *The Time of Your Life*
1941 Robert E. Sherwood, *There Shall Be No Night*
1943 Thornton Wilder, *The Skin of Our Teeth*
1945 Mary Chase, *Harvey*
1946 Russel Crouse and Howard Lindsay, *State of the Union*
1948 Tennessee Williams, *A Streetcar Named Desire*
1949 Arthur Miller, *Death of a Salesman*
1950 Richard Rodgers, Oscar Hammerstein II, and Joshua Logan, *South Pacific*
1952 Joseph Kramm, *The Shrike*
1953 William Inge, *Picnic*
1954 John Patrick, *The Teahouse of the August Moon*
1955 Tennessee Williams, *Cat on a Hot Tin Roof*
1956 Frances Goodrich and Albert Hackett, *The Diary of Anne Frank*
1957 Eugene O'Neill, *Long Day's Journey Into Night*
1958 Ketti Frings, *Look Homeward, Angel*
1959 Archibald MacLeish, *J.B.*
1960 George Abbott, Jerome Weidman, Sheldon Harnick, and Jerry Bock, *Fiorello!*
1961 Tad Mosel, *All the Way Home*
1962 Frank Loesser and Abe Burrows, *How to Succeed in Business Without Really Trying*
1965 Frank D. Gilroy, *The Subject Was Roses*
1967 Edward Albee, *A Delicate Balance*
1969 Howard Sackler, *The Great White Hope*
1970 Charles Gordone, *No Place to Be Somebody*
1971 Paul Zindel, *The Effect of Gamma Rays on Man-in-the-Moon Marigolds*
1973 Jason Miller, *That Championship Season*
1975 Edward Albee, *Seascape*
1976 Michael Bennett, James Kirkwood, Nicholas Dante, Marvin Hamlisch, and Edward Kleban, *A Chorus Line*
1977 Michael Cristofer, *The Shadow Box*
1978 Donald L. Coburn, *The Gin Game*
1979 Sam Shepard, *Buried Child*
1980 Lanford Wilson, *Talley's Folly*
1981 Beth Henley, *Crimes of the Heart*
1982 Charles Fuller, *A Soldier's Play*
1983 Marsha Norman, *'night, Mother*
1984 David Mamet, *Glengarry Glen Ross*
1985 Stephen Sondheim and James Lapine, *Sunday in the Park With George*
1987 August Wilson, *Fences*
1988 Alfred Uhry, *Driving Miss Daisy*
1989 Wendy Wasserstein, *The Heidi Chronicles*
1990 August Wilson, *The Piano Lesson*

1991 Neil Simon, *Lost in Yonkers*
1992 Robert Schenkkan, *The Kentucky Cycle*
1993 Tony Kushner, *Angels in America: Millennium Approaches*
1994 Edward Albee, *Three Tall Women*
1995 Horton Foote, *The Young Man From Atlanta*
1996 Jonathan Larson, *Rent*
1998 Paula Vogel, *How I Learned to Drive*
1999 Margaret Edson, *Wit*
2000 Donald Margulies, *Dinner With Friends*
2001 David Auburn, *Proof*
2002 Suzan-Lori Parks, *Topdog/Underdog*
2003 Nilo Cruz, *Anna in the Tropics*
2004 Doug Wright, *I Am My Own Wife*
2005 John Patrick Shanley, *Doubt, a parable*
2007 David Lindsay-Abaire, *Rabbit Hole*
2008 Tracy Letts, *August: Osage County*
2009 Lynn Nottage, *Ruined*
2010 Tom Kitt and Brian Yorkey, *Next to Normal*
2011 Bruce Norris, *Clybourne Park*
2012 Quiara Alegría Hudes, *Water by the Spoonful*
2013 Ayad Akhtar, *Disgraced*
2014 Annie Baker, *The Flick*
2015 Stephen Adly Guirgis, *Between Riverside and Crazy*
2016 Lin-Manuel Miranda, *Hamilton*
2017 Lynn Nottage, *Sweat*
2018 Martyna Majok, *Cost of Living*
2019 Jackie Sibblies Drury, *Fairview*
2020 Michael R. Jackson, *A Strange Loop*
2021 Katori Hall, *The Hot Wing King*
2022 James Ijames, *Fat Ham*
2023 Sanaz Toossi, *English*

General Nonfiction

1962 Theodore H. White, *The Making of the President 1960*
1963 Barbara W. Tuchman, *The Guns of August*
1964 Richard Hofstadter, *Anti-Intellectualism in American Life*
1965 Howard Mumford Jones, *O Strange New World*
1966 Edwin Way Teale, *Wandering Through Winter*
1967 David Brion Davis, *The Problem of Slavery in Western Culture*
1968 Will and Ariel Durant, *Rousseau and Revolution*
1969 Norman Mailer, *The Armies of the Night*;
 Rene Jules Dubos, *So Human an Animal: How We Are Shaped by Surroundings and Events*
1970 Eric H. Erikson, *Gandhi's Truth*
1971 John Toland, *The Rising Sun*
1972 Barbara W. Tuchman, *Stilwell and the American Experience in China, 1911-1945*
1973 Frances FitzGerald, *Fire in the Lake: The Vietnamese and the Americans in Vietnam*;
 Robert Coles, *Children of Crisis, Vols. II and III*
1974 Ernest Becker, *The Denial of Death*
1975 Annie Dillard, *Pilgrim at Tinker Creek*
1976 Robert N. Butler, *Why Survive? Being Old in America*
1977 William W. Warner, *Beautiful Swimmers*
1978 Carl Sagan, *The Dragons of Eden*
1979 Edward O. Wilson, *On Human Nature*
1980 Douglas R. Hofstadter, *Gödel, Escher, Bach: An Eternal Golden Braid*
1981 Carl E. Schorske, *Fin-de-Siècle Vienna: Politics and Culture*
1982 Tracy Kidder, *The Soul of a New Machine*
1983 Susan Sheehan, *Is There No Place on Earth for Me?*
1984 Paul Starr, *Social Transformation of American Medicine*
1985 Studs Terkel, *The Good War*
1986 Joseph Lelyveld, *Move Your Shadow*;
 J. Anthony Lukas, *Common Ground*
1987 David K. Shipler, *Arab and Jew: Wounded Spirits in a Promised Land*
1988 Richard Rhodes, *The Making of the Atomic Bomb*
1989 Neil Sheehan, *A Bright Shining Lie: John Paul Vann and America in Vietnam*
1990 Dale Maharidge and Michael Williamson, *And Their Children After Them*

1991 Bert Holldobler and Edward O. Wilson, *The Ants*
1992 Daniel Yergin, *The Prize: The Epic Quest for Oil, Money, and Power*
1993 Garry Wills, *Lincoln at Gettysburg*
1994 David Remnick, *Lenin's Tomb: The Last Days of the Soviet Empire*
1995 Jonathan Weiner, *The Beak of the Finch: A Story of Evolution in Our Time*
1996 Tina Rosenberg, *The Haunted Land: Facing Europe's Ghosts After Communism*
1997 Richard Kluger, *Ashes to Ashes: America's Hundred-Year Cigarette War, the Public Health, and the Unabashed Triumph of Philip Morris*
1998 Jared Diamond, *Guns, Germs, and Steel: The Fates of Human Societies*
1999 John McPhee, *Annals of the Former World*
2000 John W. Dower, *Embracing Defeat: Japan in the Wake of World War II*
2001 Herbert P. Bix, *Hirohito and the Making of Modern Japan*
2002 Diane McWhorter, *Carry Me Home: Birmingham, Alabama: The Climactic Battle of the Civil Rights Revolution*
2003 Samantha Power, *A Problem From Hell: America and the Age of Genocide*
2004 Anne Applebaum, *Gulag: A History*
2005 Steve Coll, *Ghost Wars*
2006 Caroline Elkins, *Imperial Reckoning: The Untold Story of Britain's Gulag in Kenya*
2007 Lawrence Wright, *The Looming Tower: Al-Qaeda and the Road to 9/11*
2008 Saul Friedländer, *The Years of Extermination: Nazi Germany and the Jews, 1939-1945*
2009 Douglas A. Blackmon, *Slavery by Another Name: The Re-Enslavement of Black Americans From the Civil War to World War II*
2010 David E. Hoffman, *The Dead Hand: The Untold Story of the Cold War Arms Race and Its Dangerous Legacy*
2011 Siddhartha Mukherjee, *The Emperor of All Maladies: A Biography of Cancer*
2012 Stephen Greenblatt, *The Swerve: How the World Became Modern*
2013 Gilbert King, *Devil in the Grove: Thurgood Marshall, the Groveland Boys, and the Dawn of a New America*
2014 Dan Fagin, *Toms River: A Story of Science and Salvation*
2015 Elizabeth Kolbert, *The Sixth Extinction: An Unnatural History*
2016 Joby Warrick, *Black Flags: The Rise of ISIS*
2017 Matthew Desmond, *Evicted: Poverty and Profit in the American City*
2018 James Forman Jr., *Locking up Our Own: Crime and Punishment in Black America*
2019 Eliza Griswold, *Amity and Prosperity: One Family and the Fracturing of America*
2020 Greg Grandin, *The End of the Myth: From the Frontier to the Border Wall in the Mind of America*; Anne Boyer, *The Undying: Pain, Vulnerability, Mortality, Medicine, Art, Time, Dreams, Data, Exhaustion, Cancer, and Care*
2021 David Zucchino, *Wilmington's Lie: The Murderous Coup of 1898 and the Rise of White Supremacy*
2022 Andrea Elliott, *Invisible Child: Poverty, Survival, & Hope in an American City*
2023 Robert Samuels and Toluse Olorunnipa, *His Name Is George Floyd: One Man's Life and the Struggle for Racial Justice*

Special Citation in Letters

1944 Richard Rodgers and Oscar Hammerstein II, for *Oklahoma!*
1957 Kenneth Roberts, for his historical novels
1960 *The Armada*, by Garrett Mattingly
1961 *American Heritage Picture History of the Civil War*
1973 *George Washington, Vols. I-IV*, by James Thomas Flexner
1977 Alex Haley, for *Roots*
1978 E. B. White
1984 Theodor Seuss Geisel (Dr. Seuss)
1992 Art Spiegelman, for *Maus*
2006 Edmund S. Morgan
2007 Ray Bradbury

Pulitzer Prizes in Music, 1943-2023

1943 William Schuman, *Secular Cantata No. 2, A Free Song*
1944 Howard Hanson, *Symphony No. 4, Op. 34*
1945 Aaron Copland, *Appalachian Spring*
1946 Leo Sowerby, *The Canticle of the Sun*
1947 Charles Ives, *Symphony No. 3*
1948 Walter Piston, *Symphony No. 3*
1949 Virgil Thomson, *Louisiana Story*
1950 Gian-Carlo Menotti, *The Consul*
1951 Douglas Moore, *Giants in the Earth*
1952 Gail Kubik, *Symphony Concertante*
1954 Quincy Porter, *Concerto for Two Pianos and Orchestra*
1955 Gian-Carlo Menotti, *The Saint of Bleecker Street*
1956 Ernest Toch, *Symphony No. 3*
1957 Norman Dello Joio, *Meditations on Ecclesiastes*

1958 Samuel Barber, *Vanessa*
1959 John LaMontaine, *Concerto for Piano and Orchestra*
1960 Elliott Carter, *Second String Quartet*
1961 Walter Piston, *Symphony No. 7*
1962 Robert Ward, *The Crucible*
1963 Samuel Barber, *Piano Concerto No. 1*
1966 Leslie Bassett, *Variations for Orchestra*
1967 Leon Kirchner, *Quartet No. 3*
1968 George Crumb, *Echoes of Time and the River*
1969 Karel Husa, *String Quartet No. 3*
1970 Charles Wuorinen, *Time's Encomium*
1971 Mario Davidovsky, *Synchronisms No. 6*
1972 Jacob Druckman, *Windows*
1973 Elliott Carter, *String Quartet No. 3*

1974 Donald Martino, *Notturno*
1975 Dominick Argento, *From the Diary of Virginia Woolf*
1976 Ned Rorem, *Air Music*
1977 Richard Wernick, *Visions of Terror and Wonder*
1978 Michael Colgrass, *Deja Vu for Percussion and Orchestra*
1979 Joseph Schwantner, *Aftertones of Infinity*
1980 David Del Tredici, *In Memory of a Summer Day*
1982 Roger Sessions, *Concerto for Orchestra*
1983 Ellen Taaffe Zwilich, *Symphony No. 1*
1984 Bernard Rands, *Canti del Sole*
1985 Stephen Albert, *Symphony, RiverRun*
1986 George Perle, *Wind Quintet IV*
1987 John Harbison, *The Flight Into Egypt*
1988 William Bolcom, *12 New Etudes for Piano*
1989 Roger Reynolds, *Whispers Out of Time*
1990 Mel Powell, *Duplicates: A Concerto for Two Pianos
    and Orchestra*
1991 Shulamit Ran, *Symphony*
1992 Wayne Peterson, *The Face of the Night, The Heart[2] of the Dark*
1993 Christopher Rouse, *Trombone Concerto*
1994 Gunther Schuller, *Of Reminiscences and Reflections*
1995 Morton Gould, *Stringmusic*
1996 George Walker, *Lilacs for Voice and Orchestra*
1997 Wynton Marsalis, *Blood on the Fields*
1998 Aaron Jay Kernis, *String Quartet No. 2 (musica instrumentalis)*
1999 Melinda Wagner, *Concerto for Flute, Strings, and Percussion*
2000 Lewis Spratlan, *Life is a Dream, Opera in Three Acts:
    Act II, Concert Version*
2001 John Corigliano, *Symphony No. 2 for String Orchestra*
2002 Henry Brant, *Ice Field*
2003 John Adams, *On the Transmigration of Souls*
2004 Paul Moravec, *Tempest Fantasy*

2005 Steven Stucky, *Second Concerto for Orchestra*
2006 Yehudi Wyner, *Piano Concerto: "Chiavi in Mano"*
2007 Ornette Coleman, *Sound Grammar*
2008 David Lang, *The Little Match Girl Passion*
2009 Steve Reich, *Double Sextet*
2010 Jennifer Higdon, *Violin Concerto*
2011 Zhou Long, *Madame White Snake*
2012 Kevin Puts, *Silent Night: Opera in Two Acts*
2013 Caroline Shaw, *Partita for 8 Voices*
2014 John Luther Adams, *Become Ocean*
2015 Julia Wolfe, *Anthracite Fields*
2016 Henry Threadgill, *In for a Penny, In for a Pound*
2017 Du Yun, *Angel's Bone*
2018 Kendrick Lamar, *DAMN.*
2019 Ellen Reid, *p r i s m*
2020 Anthony Davis, *The Central Park Five*
2021 Tania León, *Stride*
2022 Raven Chacon, *Voiceless Mass*
2023 Rhiannon Giddens and Michael Abels, *Omar*

Special Citation in Music

1974 Roger Sessions
1976 Scott Joplin
1982 Milton Babbitt
1985 William Schuman
1998 George Gershwin
1999 Edward Kennedy "Duke" Ellington
2006 Thelonious Monk
2007 John Coltrane
2008 Bob Dylan
2010 Hank Williams
2019 Aretha Franklin

Booker Prize for Fiction, 1969-2022

The Booker Prize for fiction, named the Man Booker Prize, 2002-18, is £50,000, awarded annually to the author of the best new full-length novel written in English.

Year	Author, book
1969	P. H. Newby, *Something to Answer For*
1970	Bernice Rubens, *The Elected Member*
1971	V. S. Naipaul, *In a Free State*
1972	John Berger, *G*
1973	J. G. Farrell, *The Siege of Krishnapur*
1974	Nadine Gordimer, *The Conservationist*; Stanley Middleton, *Holiday*
1975	Ruth Prawer Jhabvala, *Heat and Dust*
1976	David Storey, *Saville*
1977	Paul Scott, *Staying On*
1978	Iris Murdoch, *The Sea, the Sea*
1979	Penelope Fitzgerald, *Offshore*
1980	William Golding, *Rites of Passage*
1981	Salman Rushdie, *Midnight's Children*[1]
1982	Thomas Keneally, *Schindler's Ark*
1983	J. M. Coetzee, *Life and Times of Michael K*
1984	Anita Brookner, *Hotel du Lac*
1985	Keri Hulme, *The Bone People*
1986	Kingsley Amis, *The Old Devils*
1987	Penelope Lively, *Moon Tiger*
1988	Peter Carey, *Oscar and Lucinda*
1989	Kazuo Ishiguro, *The Remains of the Day*
1990	A. S. Byatt, *Possession*
1991	Ben Okri, *The Famished Road*
1992	Michael Ondaatje, *The English Patient*[2]; Barry Unsworth, *Sacred Hunger*
1993	Roddy Doyle, *Paddy Clarke Ha Ha Ha*
1994	James Kelman, *How Late It Was, How Late*
1995	Pat Barker, *The Ghost Road*
1996	Graham Swift, *Last Orders*
1997	Arundhati Roy, *The God of Small Things*
1998	Ian McEwan, *Amsterdam*
1999	J. M. Coetzee, *Disgrace*
2000	Margaret Atwood, *The Blind Assassin*
2001	Peter Carey, *True History of the Kelly Gang*
2002	Yann Martel, *Life of Pi*
2003	DBC Pierre, *Vernon God Little*
2004	Alan Hollinghurst, *The Line of Beauty*
2005	John Banville, *The Sea*
2006	Kiran Desai, *The Inheritance of Loss*
2007	Anne Enright, *The Gathering*
2008	Aravind Adiga, *The White Tiger*
2009	Hilary Mantel, *Wolf Hall*
2010	Howard Jacobson, *The Finkler Question*
2011	Julian Barnes, *The Sense of an Ending*
2012	Hilary Mantel, *Bring up the Bodies*
2013	Eleanor Catton, *The Luminaries*
2014	Richard Flanagan, *The Narrow Road to the Deep North*
2015	Marlon James, *A Brief History of Seven Killings*
2016	Paul Beatty, *The Sellout*
2017	George Saunders, *Lincoln in the Bardo*
2018	Anna Burns, *Milkman*
2019	Margaret Atwood, *The Testaments*; Bernardine Evaristo, *Girl, Woman, Other*
2020	Douglas Stuart, *Shuggie Bain*
2021	Damon Galgut, *The Promise*
2022	Shehan Karunatilaka, *The Seven Moons of Maali Almeida*

(1) Rushdie's *Midnight's Children* also won the Best of the Bookers prize in 1993 and the Best of the Booker prize in 2008.
(2) Ondaatje's *The English Patient* also won the Golden Man Booker prize in 2018.

Newbery Medal, 1922-2023

The Newbery Medal is awarded annually by the Association for Library Service to Children, a division of the American Library Association, to the most distinguished contribution to American children's literature published in the previous year.

Year	Book, author
1922	*The Story of Mankind*, Hendrik Willem van Loon
1923	*The Voyages of Dr. Dolittle*, Hugh Lofting
1924	*The Dark Frigate*, Charles Boardman Hawes
1925	*Tales From Silver Lands*, Charles J. Finger
1926	*Shen of the Sea*, Arthur Bowie Chrisman
1927	*Smoky, the Cowhorse*, Will James
1928	*Gay-Neck: The Story of a Pigeon*, Dhan Gopal Mukerji
1929	*The Trumpeter of Krakow*, Eric P. Kelly
1930	*Hitty, Her First Hundred Years*, Rachel Field
1931	*The Cat Who Went to Heaven*, Elizabeth Coatsworth
1932	*Waterless Mountain*, Laura Adams Armer
1933	*Young Fu of the Upper Yangtze*, Elizabeth Foreman Lewis
1934	*Invincible Louisa*, Cornelia Meigs
1935	*Dobry*, Monica Shannon
1936	*Caddie Woodlawn*, Carol Ryrie Brink
1937	*Roller Skates*, Ruth Sawyer
1938	*The White Stag*, Kate Seredy
1939	*Thimble Summer*, Elizabeth Enright
1940	*Daniel Boone*, James Daugherty
1941	*Call It Courage*, Armstrong Sperry
1942	*The Matchlock Gun*, Walter D. Edmonds
1943	*Adam of the Road*, Elizabeth Janet Gray
1944	*Johnny Tremain*, Esther Forbes
1945	*Rabbit Hill*, Robert Lawson
1946	*Strawberry Girl*, Lois Lenski
1947	*Miss Hickory*, Carolyn Sherwin Bailey
1948	*The Twenty-One Balloons*, William Pène du Bois
1949	*King of the Wind*, Marguerite Henry

Year	Book, author
1950	*The Door in the Wall*, Marguerite de Angeli
1951	*Amos Fortune, Free Man*, Elizabeth Yates
1952	*Ginger Pye*, Eleanor Estes
1953	*Secret of the Andes*, Ann Nolan Clark
1954	*... And Now Miguel*, Joseph Krumgold
1955	*The Wheel on the School*, Meindert DeJong
1956	*Carry On, Mr. Bowditch*, Jean Lee Latham
1957	*Miracles on Maple Hill*, Virginia Sorensen
1958	*Rifles for Watie*, Harold Keith
1959	*The Witch of Blackbird Pond*, Elizabeth George Speare
1960	*Onion John*, Joseph Krumgold
1961	*Island of the Blue Dolphins*, Scott O'Dell
1962	*The Bronze Bow*, Elizabeth George Speare
1963	*A Wrinkle in Time*, Madeleine L'Engle
1964	*It's Like This, Cat*, Emily Cheney Neville
1965	*Shadow of a Bull*, Maia Wojciechowska
1966	*I, Juan de Pareja*, Elizabeth Borton de Trevino
1967	*Up a Road Slowly*, Irene Hunt
1968	*From the Mixed-Up Files of Mrs. Basil E. Frankweiler*, E. L. Konigsburg
1969	*The High King*, Lloyd Alexander
1970	*Sounder*, William H. Armstrong
1971	*The Summer of the Swans*, Betsy Byars
1972	*Mrs. Frisby and the Rats of NIMH*, Robert C. O'Brien
1973	*Julie of the Wolves*, Jean Craighead George
1974	*The Slave Dancer*, Paula Fox
1975	*M. C. Higgins, the Great*, Virginia Hamilton
1976	*The Grey King*, Susan Cooper
1977	*Roll of Thunder, Hear My Cry*, Mildred D. Taylor
1978	*Bridge to Terabithia*, Katherine Paterson
1979	*The Westing Game*, Ellen Raskin
1980	*A Gathering of Days*, Joan Blos
1981	*Jacob Have I Loved*, Katherine Paterson
1982	*A Visit to William Blake's Inn: Poems for Innocent and Experienced Travelers*, Nancy Willard
1983	*Dicey's Song*, Cynthia Voigt
1984	*Dear Mr. Henshaw*, Beverly Cleary
1985	*The Hero and the Crown*, Robin McKinley

Year	Book, author
1986	*Sarah, Plain and Tall*, Patricia MacLachlan
1987	*The Whipping Boy*, Sid Fleischman
1988	*Lincoln: A Photobiography*, Russell Freedman
1989	*Joyful Noise: Poems for Two Voices*, Paul Fleischman
1990	*Number the Stars*, Lois Lowry
1991	*Maniac Magee*, Jerry Spinelli
1992	*Shiloh*, Phyllis Reynolds Naylor
1993	*Missing May*, Cynthia Rylant
1994	*The Giver*, Lois Lowry
1995	*Walk Two Moons*, Sharon Creech
1996	*The Midwife's Apprentice*, Karen Cushman
1997	*The View From Saturday*, E. L. Konigsburg
1998	*Out of the Dust*, Karen Hesse
1999	*Holes*, Louis Sachar
2000	*Bud, Not Buddy*, Christopher Paul Curtis
2001	*A Year Down Yonder*, Richard Peck
2002	*A Single Shard*, Linda Sue Park
2003	*Crispin: The Cross of Lead*, Avi
2004	*The Tale of Despereaux*, Kate DiCamillo
2005	*Kira-Kira*, Cynthia Kadohata
2006	*Criss Cross*, Lynne Rae Perkins
2007	*The Higher Power of Lucky*, Susan Patron
2008	*Good Masters! Sweet Ladies! Voices From a Medieval Village*, Laura Amy Schlitz
2009	*The Graveyard Book*, Neil Gaiman
2010	*When You Reach Me*, Rebecca Stead
2011	*Moon Over Manifest*, Clare Vanderpool
2012	*Dead End in Norvelt*, Jack Gantos
2013	*The One and Only Ivan*, Katherine Applegate
2014	*Flora & Ulysses: The Illuminated Adventures*, Kate DiCamillo
2015	*The Crossover*, Kwame Alexander
2016	*Last Stop on Market Street*, Matt de la Peña
2017	*The Girl Who Drank the Moon*, Kelly Barnhill
2018	*Hello, Universe*, Erin Entrada Kelly
2019	*Merci Suárez Changes Gears*, Meg Medina
2020	*New Kid*, Jerry Craft
2021	*When You Trap a Tiger*, Tae Keller
2022	*The Last Cuentista*, Donna Barba Higuera
2023	*Freewater*, Amina Luqman-Dawson

Caldecott Medal, 1938-2023

The Caldecott Medal is awarded annually by the Association for Library Service to Children, a division of the American Library Association, to the illustrator of the most distinguished American picture book for children.

Year	Book, illustrator
1938	*Animals of the Bible*, Dorothy P. Lathrop
1939	*Mei Li*, Thomas Handforth
1940	*Abraham Lincoln*, Ingri and Edgar Parin d'Aulaire
1941	*They Were Strong and Good*, Robert Lawson
1942	*Make Way for Ducklings*, Robert McCloskey
1943	*The Little House*, Virginia Lee Burton
1944	*Many Moons*, Louis Slobodkin
1945	*Prayer for a Child*, Elizabeth Orton Jones
1946	*The Rooster Crows*, Maude and Miska Petersham
1947	*The Little Island*, Leonard Weisgard
1948	*White Snow, Bright Snow*, Roger Duvoisin
1949	*The Big Snow*, Berta and Elmer Hader
1950	*Song of the Swallows*, Leo Politi
1951	*The Egg Tree*, Katherine Milhous
1952	*Finders Keepers*, Nicolas, pseud. (Nicholas Mordvinoff)
1953	*The Biggest Bear*, Lynd Ward
1954	*Madeline's Rescue*, Ludwig Bemelmans
1955	*Cinderella, or the Little Glass Slipper*, Marcia Brown
1956	*Frog Went A-Courtin'*, Feodor Rojankovsky
1957	*A Tree Is Nice*, Marc Simont
1958	*Time of Wonder*, Robert McCloskey
1959	*Chanticleer and the Fox*, Barbara Cooney
1960	*Nine Days to Christmas*, Marie Hall Ets
1961	*Baboushka and the Three Kings*, Nicolas Sidjakov
1962	*Once a Mouse*, Marcia Brown
1963	*The Snowy Day*, Ezra Jack Keats
1964	*Where the Wild Things Are*, Maurice Sendak
1965	*May I Bring a Friend?*, Beni Montresor
1966	*Always Room for One More*, Nonny Hogrogian
1967	*Sam, Bangs, and Moonshine*, Evaline Ness
1968	*Drummer Hoff*, Ed Emberley
1969	*The Fool of the World and the Flying Ship*, Uri Shulevitz
1970	*Sylvester and the Magic Pebble*, William Steig
1971	*A Story A Story*, Gail E. Haley
1972	*One Fine Day*, Nonny Hogrogian
1973	*The Funny Little Woman*, Blair Lent
1974	*Duffy and the Devil*, Margot Zemach
1975	*Arrow to the Sun*, Gerald McDermott
1976	*Why Mosquitoes Buzz in People's Ears*, Leo and Diane Dillon
1977	*Ashanti to Zulu: African Traditions*, Leo and Diane Dillon
1978	*Noah's Ark*, Peter Spier
1979	*The Girl Who Loved Wild Horses*, Paul Goble
1980	*Ox-Cart Man*, Barbara Cooney
1981	*Fables*, Arnold Lobel
1982	*Jumanji*, Chris Van Allsburg

Year	Book, illustrator
1983	*Shadow*, Marcia Brown
1984	*The Glorious Flight: Across the Channel With Louis Bleriot*, Alice and Martin Provensen
1985	*Saint George and the Dragon*, Trina Schart Hyman
1986	*The Polar Express*, Chris Van Allsburg
1987	*Hey, Al*, Richard Egielski
1988	*Owl Moon*, John Schoenherr
1989	*Song and Dance Man*, Stephen Gammell
1990	*Lon Po Po: A Red-Riding Hood Story From China*, Ed Young
1991	*Black and White*, David Macaulay
1992	*Tuesday*, David Wiesner
1993	*Mirette on the High Wire*, Emily Arnold McCully
1994	*Grandfather's Journey*, Allen Say
1995	*Smoky Night*, David Diaz
1996	*Officer Buckle and Gloria*, Peggy Rathmann
1997	*Golem*, David Wisniewski
1998	*Rapunzel*, Paul O. Zelinsky
1999	*Snowflake Bentley*, Mary Azarian
2000	*Joseph Had a Little Overcoat*, Simms Taback
2001	*So You Want to be President?*, David Small
2002	*The Three Pigs*, David Wiesner
2003	*My Friend Rabbit*, Eric Rohmann
2004	*The Man Who Walked Between the Towers*, Mordicai Gerstein
2005	*Kitten's First Full Moon*, Kevin Henkes
2006	*The Hello, Goodbye Window*, Chris Raschka
2007	*Flotsam*, David Wiesner
2008	*The Invention of Hugo Cabret*, Brian Selznick
2009	*The House in the Night*, Beth Krommes
2010	*The Lion & the Mouse*, Jerry Pinkney
2011	*A Sick Day for Amos McGee*, Erin E. Stead
2012	*A Ball for Daisy*, Chris Raschka
2013	*This Is Not My Hat*, Jon Klassen
2014	*Locomotive*, Brian Floca
2015	*The Adventures of Beekle: The Unimaginary Friend*, Dan Santat
2016	*Finding Winnie: The True Story of the World's Most Famous Bear*, Sophie Blackall
2017	*Radiant Child: The Story of Young Artist Jean-Michel Basquiat*, Javaka Steptoe
2018	*Wolf in the Snow*, Matthew Cordell
2019	*Hello Lighthouse*, Sophie Blackall
2020	*The Undefeated*, Kadir Nelson
2021	*We Are Water Protectors*, Michaela Goade
2022	*Watercress*, Jason Chin
2023	*Hot Dog*, Doug Salati

National Book Awards, 1950-2022

The National Book Awards (known as American Book Awards 1980-86) are administered by the National Book Foundation and have been given annually since 1950. The $10,000 prizes are awarded for works published in the U.S. In some years, multiple awards were given for nonfiction in various categories; in such cases, the history and biography (if any) or biography winner is listed. Selected additional awards in nonfiction are listed in footnotes.

Other National Book Awards, 2022: Poetry: John Keene, *Punks*. Translated Literature: Samanta Schweblin, Megan McDowell, *Seven Empty Houses*. Young People's Literature: Sabaa Tahir, *All My Rage*. Distinguished Contribution to American Letters: Art Spiegelman. Literarian Award: Tracie D. Hall.

Fiction

Year	Author, book	Year	Author, book
1950	Nelson Algren, *The Man With the Golden Arm*	1986	E. L. Doctorow, *World's Fair*
1951	William Faulkner, *The Collected Stories*	1987	Larry Heinemann, *Paco's Story*
1952	James Jones, *From Here to Eternity*	1988	Pete Dexter, *Paris Trout*
1953	Ralph Ellison, *Invisible Man*	1989	John Casey, *Spartina*
1954	Saul Bellow, *The Adventures of Augie March*	1990	Charles Johnson, *Middle Passage*
1955	William Faulkner, *A Fable*	1991	Norman Rush, *Mating*
1956	John O'Hara, *Ten North Frederick*	1992	Cormac McCarthy, *All the Pretty Horses*
1957	Wright Morris, *The Field of Vision*	1993	E. Annie Proulx, *The Shipping News*
1958	John Cheever, *The Wapshot Chronicle*	1994	William Gaddis, *A Frolic of His Own*
1959	Bernard Malamud, *The Magic Barrel*	1995	Philip Roth, *Sabbath's Theater*
1960	Philip Roth, *Goodbye, Columbus*	1996	Andrea Barrett, *Ship Fever and Other Stories*
1961	Conrad Richter, *The Waters of Kronos*	1997	Charles Frazier, *Cold Mountain*
1962	Walker Percy, *The Moviegoer*	1998	Alice McDermott, *Charming Billy*
1963	J. F. Powers, *Morte d'Urban*	1999	Ha Jin, *Waiting*
1964	John Updike, *The Centaur*	2000	Susan Sontag, *In America*
1965	Saul Bellow, *Herzog*	2001	Jonathan Franzen, *The Corrections*
1966	Katherine Anne Porter, *The Collected Stories*	2002	Julia Glass, *Three Junes*
1967	Bernard Malamud, *The Fixer*	2003	Shirley Hazzard, *The Great Fire*
1968	Thornton Wilder, *The Eighth Day*	2004	Lily Tuck, *The News From Paraguay*
1969	Jerzy Kosinski, *Steps*	2005	William T. Vollmann, *Europe Central*
1970	Joyce Carol Oates, *Them*	2006	Richard Powers, *The Echo Maker*
1971	Saul Bellow, *Mr. Sammler's Planet*	2007	Denis Johnson, *Tree of Smoke*
1972	Flannery O'Connor, *The Complete Stories*	2008	Peter Matthiessen, *Shadow Country*
1973	John Barth, *Chimera*	2009	Colum McCann, *Let the Great World Spin*
1974	Thomas Pynchon, *Gravity's Rainbow*	2010	Jaimy Gordon, *Lord of Misrule*
1974	Isaac Bashevis Singer, *A Crown of Feathers*	2011	Jesmyn Ward, *Salvage the Bones*
1975	Robert Stone, *Dog Soldiers*	2012	Louise Erdrich, *The Round House*
1976	William Gaddis, *JR*	2013	James McBride, *The Good Lord Bird*
1977	Wallace Stegner, *The Spectator Bird*	2014	Phil Klay, *Redeployment*
1978	Mary Lee Settle, *Blood Ties*	2015	Adam Johnson, *Fortune Smiles: Stories*
1979	Tim O'Brien, *Going After Cacciato*	2016	Colson Whitehead, *The Underground Railroad*
1980	William Styron, *Sophie's Choice*	2017	Jesmyn Ward, *Sing, Unburied, Sing*
1981	Wright Morris, *Plains Song*	2018	Sigrid Nunez, *The Friend*
1982	John Updike, *Rabbit Is Rich*	2019	Susan Choi, *Trust Exercise*
1983	Alice Walker, *The Color Purple*	2020	Charles Yu, *Interior Chinatown*
1984	Ellen Gilchrist, *Victory Over Japan*	2021	Jason Mott, *Hell of a Book*
1985	Don DeLillo, *White Noise*	2022	Tess Gunty, *The Rabbit Hutch*

Nonfiction

Year	Author, book	Year	Author, book
1950	Ralph L. Rusk, *Ralph Waldo Emerson*	1975	Richard B. Sewall, *The Life of Emily Dickinson*[6]
1951	Newton Arvin, *Herman Melville*	1976	David Brion Davis, *The Problem of Slavery in the Age of Revolution, 1770-1823*
1952	Rachel Carson, *The Sea Around Us*		
1953	Bernard A. De Voto, *The Course of an Empire*	1977	W. A. Swanberg, *Norman Thomas: The Last Idealist*[7]
1954	Bruce Catton, *A Stillness at Appomattox*	1978	W. Jackson Bate, *Samuel Johnson*
1955	Joseph Wood Krutch, *The Measure of Man*	1979	Arthur M. Schlesinger Jr., *Robert Kennedy and His Times*
1956	Herbert Kubly, *An American in Italy*		
1957	George F. Kennan, *Russia Leaves the War*	1980	Tom Wolfe, *The Right Stuff*
1958	Catherine Drinker Bowen, *The Lion and the Throne*	1981	Maxine Hong Kingston, *China Men*
1959	J. Christopher Herold, *Mistress on an Age: A Life of Madame De Stael*	1982	Tracy Kidder, *The Soul of a New Machine*
		1983	Fox Butterfield, *China: Alive in the Bitter Sea*
1960	Richard Ellman, *James Joyce*	1984	Robert V. Remini, *Andrew Jackson and the Course of American Democracy, 1833-1845*
1961	William L. Shirer, *The Rise and Fall of the Third Reich*		
1962	Lewis Mumford, *The City in History: Its Origins, Its Transformations, and Its Prospects*	1985	J. Anthony Lukas, *Common Ground: A Turbulent Decade in the Lives of Three American Families*
1963	Leon Edel, *Henry James, Vol. II: The Conquest of London* and *Vol. III: The Middle Years*	1986	Barry Lopez, *Arctic Dreams*
		1987	Richard Rhodes, *The Making of the Atom Bomb*
1964	William H. McNeill, *The Rise of the West: A History of the Human Community*	1988	Neil Sheehan, *A Bright Shining Lie: John Paul Vann and America in Vietnam*
1965	Louis Fisher, *The Life of Lenin*	1989	Thomas L. Friedman, *From Beirut to Jerusalem*
1966	Arthur M. Schlesinger Jr., *A Thousand Days: John F. Kennedy in the White House*	1990	Ron Chernow, *The House of Morgan: An American Banking Dynasty and the Rise of Modern Finance*
1967	Peter Gay, *The Enlightenment, An Interpretation, Vol. I: The Rise of Modern Paganism*	1991	Orlando Patterson, *Freedom*
		1992	Paul Monette, *Becoming a Man: Half a Life Story*
1968	George F. Kennan, *Memoirs: 1925-1950*[1]	1993	Gore Vidal, *United States: Essays 1952-1992*
1969	Winthrop D. Jordan, *White Over Black: American Attitudes Toward the Negro, 1550-1812*[2]	1994	Sherwin B. Nuland, *How We Die: Reflections on Life's Final Chapter*
1970	T. Harry Williams, *Huey Long*[3]	1995	Tina Rosenberg, *The Haunted Land: Facing Europe's Ghosts After Communism*
1971	James MacGregor Burns, *Roosevelt: The Soldier of Freedom*	1996	James Carroll, *An American Requiem: God, My Father, and the War That Came Between Us*
1972	Joseph P. Lash, *Eleanor and Franklin: The Story of Their Relationship, Based on Eleanor Roosevelt's Private Papers*	1997	Joseph J. Ellis, *American Sphinx: The Character of Thomas Jefferson*
		1998	Edward Ball, *Slaves in the Family*
1973	James Thomas Flexner, *George Washington, Vol. IV: Anguish and Farewell, 1793-1799*[4]	1999	John W. Dower, *Embracing Defeat: Japan in the Wake of World War II*
1974	John Clive, *Macaulay, The Shaping of the Historian*; Douglas Day, *Malcolm Lowry: A Biography*[5]	2000	Nathaniel Philbrick, *In the Heart of the Sea: The Tragedy of the Whaleship Essex*

Year	Author, book	Year	Author, book
2001	Andrew Solomon, *The Noonday Demon: An Atlas of Depression*	2012	Katherine Boo, *Behind the Beautiful Forevers: Life, Death, and Hope in a Mumbai Undercity*
2002	Robert A. Caro, *Master of the Senate: The Years of Lyndon Johnson*	2013	George Packer, *The Unwinding: An Inner History of the New America*
2003	Carlos Eire, *Waiting for Snow in Havana: Confessions of a Cuban Boy*	2014	Evan Osnos, *Age of Ambition: Chasing Fortune, Truth, and Faith in the New China*
2004	Kevin Boyle, *Arc of Justice: A Saga of Race, Civil Rights, and Murder in the Jazz Age*	2015	Ta-Nehisi Coates, *Between the World and Me*
2005	Joan Didion, *The Year of Magical Thinking*	2016	Ibram X. Kendi, *Stamped From the Beginning: The Definitive History of Racist Ideas in America*
2006	Timothy Egan, *The Worst Hard Time: The Untold Story of Those Who Survived the Great American Dust Bowl*	2017	Masha Gessen, *The Future Is History: How Totalitarianism Reclaimed Russia*
2007	Tim Weiner, *Legacy of Ashes: The History of the CIA*	2018	Jeffrey C. Stewart, *The New Negro: The Life of Alain Locke*
2008	Annette Gordon-Reed, *The Hemingses of Monticello: An American Family*	2019	Sarah M. Broom, *The Yellow House*
2009	T. J. Stiles, *The First Tycoon: The Epic Life of Cornelius Vanderbilt*	2020	Les Payne and Tamara Payne, *The Dead Are Arising: The Life of Malcolm X*
2010	Patti Smith, *Just Kids*	2021	Tiya Miles, *All That She Carried: The Journey of Ashley's Sack, a Black Family Keepsake*
2011	Stephen Greenblatt, *The Swerve: How the World Became Modern*	2022	Imani Perry, *South to America: A Journey Below the Mason-Dixon to Understand the Soul of a Nation*

(1) Science, Philosophy, & Religion: Jonathan Kozol, *Death at an Early Age*. (2) Arts & Letters: Norman Mailer, *The Armies of the Night: History as a Novel, the Novel as History*. (3) Arts & Letters: Lillian Hellman, *An Unfinished Woman: A Memoir*. (4) Contemp. Affairs: Frances FitzGerald, *Fire in the Lake: The Vietnamese and the Americans in Vietnam*. (5) Arts & Letters: Pauline Kael, *Deeper Into the Movies*. (6) Arts & Letters: Roger Shattuck, *Marcel Proust*; Lewis Thomas, *The Lives of a Cell: Notes of a Biology Watcher*. (7) Contemp. Thought: Bruno Bettelheim, *The Uses of Enchantment: The Meaning and Importance of Fairy Tales*.

Journalism Awards, 2023

National Magazine Awards, by American Society of Magazine Editors and Columbia Univ. Graduate School of Journalism. General Excellence—News, Sports, and Entertainment: *The Atlantic*; Service and Lifestyle: *Cook's Illustrated*; Special Interest: *The Marshall Project*; Literature, Science, and Politics: *Grist*. Podcasting: *Stolen: Surviving St. Michael's*, Gimlet Media/Spotify. Video: *Mother Jones*. Design: *GQ*. Photography: *Smithsonian*. Single-Topic Issue: *New York*. Service Journalism: *Romper*. Lifestyle Journalism: *New York*. Reporting: *NY Times Magazine*. Feature Writing: ProPublica and *Milwaukee Journal Sentinel*. Profile Writing: *NY Times Magazine*. Columns and Essays: *The New Yorker*. Reviews and Criticism: *NY Review of Books*. Public Interest: *Glamour*.

George Foster Peabody Awards, by Univ. of Georgia. Career achievement: Lily Tomlin. Institutional award: *Today*, NBC News. Trailblazer award: Issa Rae. Visionary award: Shari Frilot. Arts: *Fire of Love*, Disney+. Documentary: *Aftershock*; *Batata*; "Missing in Brooks County" and "Writing With Fire," *Independent Lens*,

PBS; *Mariupol: The People's Story*, BBC Select; *The Rebellious Life of Mrs. Rosa Parks*, Peacock; *The Territory*, Disney+; *We Need to Talk About Cosby*, Showtime. Entertainment: *Abbott Elementary*, ABC; *Andor*, Disney+; *Atlanta*, FX; *Bad Sisters*, Pachinko*, and *Severance*, Apple TV+; *Better Call Saul*, AMC; *Los Espookys* and *We're Here*, HBO Max; *Mo*, Netflix. Interactive/immersive: "ContraPoints," YouTube; *Life Is Strange: True Colors*; *Lucy and the Wolves in the Walls*, Oculus; "Reeducated," *The New Yorker*; "The Uncensored Library," *Minecraft*. News: "Guns in America," *PBS NewsHour*; "Michael Flynn's Holy War" and "Ukraine: Life Under Russia's Attack," *Frontline*, PBS; "The Gap: Failure to Treat, Failure to Protect," KARE-TV; "No Justice for Women in the Taliban's Afghanistan," VICE News; "One Day in Hebron," AJ+; "Shimon Prokupecz: Unraveling Uvalde," CNN. Podcast/radio: *Stolen: Surviving St. Michael's*, Spotify; *The Divided Dial*, NY Public Radio; "The Pink House at the Center of the World," *This American Life*. Public service: "The Power of Big Oil," *Frontline*, PBS.

Miscellaneous Book Awards, 2023

Coretta Scott King Awards, by American Library Assn., for African American authors and illustrators of outstanding books for children and young adults. Author: *Freewater*, Amina Luqman-Dawson. Illustrator: *Standing in the Need of Prayer: A Modern Retelling of the Classic Spiritual*, illustrated by Frank Morrison. New talent, author: *We Deserve Monuments*, Jas Hammonds. New talent, illustrator: *Choosing Brave: How Mamie Till-Mobley and Emmett Till Sparked the Civil Rights Movement*, illustrated by Janelle Washington.

Edgar Awards, by Mystery Writers of America. Novel: *Notes on an Execution*, Danya Kukafka. First Novel: *Don't Know Tough*, Eli Cranor. Paperback Original: *Or Else*, Joe Hart. Fact Crime: *Tell Me Everything: The Story of a Private Investigation*, Erika Krouse. Critical/Biographical: *The Life of Crime: Detecting the History of Mysteries and Their Creators*, Martin Edwards. Short Story: "Red Flag," Gregory Fallis, *Alfred Hitchcock Mystery Magazine*. Juvenile: *Aggie Morton Mystery Queen: The Seaside Corpse*, Marthe Jocelyn. Young Adult: *The Red Palace*, Jane Hur. TV Episode: "Episode 1," Anthony Horowitz, *Magpie Murders*. Robert L. Fish Memorial Award: "Dogs in the Canyon," Mark Harrison, *Ellery Queen Mystery Magazine*. Mary Higgins Clark Award: *A Dreadful Splendor*, B.R. Myers. Sue Grafton Memorial Award: *Hideout*, Louisa Luna. Lilian Jackson Braun Memorial Award: *Buried in a Good Book*, Tamara Berry. Grand Masters: Michael Connelly, Joanne Fluke. Raven Award: Crime Writers of Color; Eddie Muller for Noir Alley and the Film Noir Foundation. Ellery Queen Award: *The Strand Magazine*.

Golden Kite Awards, by the Society of Children's Book Writers and Illustrators. Picture Book Text: *Fly*, Brittany J. Thurman. Picture Book Illustration: *Kumo the Bashful Cloud*, Nathalie Dion. Middle Grade Fiction: *The Civil War of Amos Abernathy*, Michael Leali. Illustrated Book (older readers): *The Adventures of Team Pom: Squid Happens*, Isabel Roxas. Nonfiction text (younger readers): *Our Planet! There's No Place Like Earth*,

Stacy McAnulty. Nonfiction text (older readers): *Absurd Words: A Kid's Fun and Hilarious Vocabulary Builder for Future Word Nerds*, Tara Lazar. Young Adult Fiction: *Beneath the Wide Silk Sky*, Emily Inouye Huey. Sid Fleischman Award: *The Real Riley Mayes*, Rachel Elliott.

Lambda Literary Awards. Lesbian Fiction: *Gods of Want*, K-Ming Chang. Gay Fiction: *The Foghorn Echoes*, Danny Ramadan. Bisexual Fiction: *Reluctant Immortals*, Gwendolyn Kiste. Transgender Fiction: *The Call-Out*, Cat Fitzpatrick. Bisexual Nonfiction: *Appropriate Behavior*, Maria San Filippo. Transgender Nonfiction: *The Third Person*, Emma Grove. LGBTQ+ Nonfiction: *The Black Period: On Personhood, Race, and Origin*, Hafizah Augustus Geter.

National Book Critics Circle Awards. Fiction: Ling Ma, *Bliss Montage: Stories*. Nonfiction: Isaac Butler, *The Method: How the Twentieth Century Learned to Act*. Biography: Beverly Gage, *G-Man: J. Edgar Hoover and the Making of the American Century*. Autobiography: Hua Hsu, *Stay True*. Criticism: Timothy Bewes, *Free Indirect: The Novel in a Postfictional Age*. Poetry: Cynthia Cruz, *Hotel Oblivion*. John Leonard Prize: Morgan Talty, *Night of the Living Rez*. Gregg Barrios Book in Translation: Andrey Kurkov trans. by Boris Dralyuk, *Grey Bees*. Ivan Sandrof Lifetime Achievement Award: Joy Harjo. Nona Balakian Citation for Excellence in Reviewing: Jennifer Wilson.

Nebula Awards, by the Science Fiction and Fantasy Writers Assn. Novel: *Babel*, R.F. Kuang. Novella: *Even Though I Knew the End*, C.L. Polk. Novelette: "If You Find Yourself Speaking to God, Address God With the Informal You," John Chu. Short Story: "Rabbit Test," Samantha Mills. Ray Bradbury Award: *Everything Everywhere All at Once*, Daniel Kwan, Daniel Scheinert. Andre Norton Award: *Ruby Finley vs. the Interstellar Invasion*, K. Tempest Bradford. Game Writing: *Elden Ring*, Hidetaka Miyazaki, George R.R. Martin.

Printz Award, for young adult literature: *All My Rage*, Sabaa Tahir.

Spingarn Medal, 1915-2023

The Spingarn Medal has been awarded annually in most years since 1915 by the National Assn. for the Advancement of Colored People for outstanding achievement by an African American.

Year	Winner	Year	Winner	Year	Winner	Year	Winner
1915	Ernest E. Just	1943	William H. Hastie	1969	Clarence M. Mitchell Jr.	1996	A. Leon Higginbotham Jr.
1916	Charles Young	1944	Charles Drew	1970	Jacob Lawrence	1997	Carl T. Rowan
1917	Harry T. Burleigh	1945	Paul Robeson	1971	Leon H. Sullivan	1998	Myrlie Evers-Williams
1918	William S. Braithwaite	1946	Thurgood Marshall	1972	Gordon Parks	1999	Earl G. Graves Sr.
1919	Archibald H. Grimké	1947	Dr. Percy L. Julian	1973	Wilson C. Riles	2000	Oprah Winfrey
1920	W. E. B. Du Bois	1948	Channing H. Tobias	1974	Damon Keith	2001	Vernon E. Jordan Jr.
1921	Charles S. Gilpin	1949	Ralph J. Bunche	1976	Henry (Hank) Aaron	2002	John Lewis
1922	Mary B. Talbert	1950	Charles H. Houston	1977	Alvin Ailey	2003	Constance Baker Motley
1923	George W. Carver	1951	Mabel K. Staupers	1977	Alex Haley	2004	Robert L. Carter
1924	Roland Hayes	1952	Harry T. Moore	1979	Andrew Young	2005	Oliver W. Hill
1925	James W. Johnson	1953	Paul R. Williams	1979	Rosa L. Parks	2006	Dr. Benjamin S. Carson
1926	Carter G. Woodson	1954	Theodore K. Lawless	1980	Dr. Rayford W. Logan	2007	John Conyers Jr.
1927	Anthony Overton	1955	Carl Murphy	1981	Coleman Young	2008	Ruby Dee
1928	Charles W. Chesnutt	1956	Jack R. Robinson	1982	Dr. Benjamin E. Mays	2009	Julian Bond
1929	Mordecai W. Johnson	1957	Martin Luther King Jr.	1983	Lena Horne	2010	Cicely Tyson
1930	Henry A. Hunt	1958	Daisy Bates and the	1985	Thomas Bradley	2011	Frankie Muse Freeman
1931	Richard B. Harrison		Little Rock Nine	1985	Bill Cosby	2012	Harry Belafonte
1932	Robert R. Moton	1959	Duke Ellington	1986	Dr. Benjamin L. Hooks	2013	Jessye Norman
1933	Max Yergan	1960	Langston Hughes	1987	Percy E. Sutton	2014	Quincy Jones
1934	William T. B. Williams	1961	Kenneth B. Clark	1988	Frederick D. Patterson	2015	Sidney Poitier
1935	Mary McLeod Bethune	1962	Robert C. Weaver	1989	Jesse Jackson	2016	Nathaniel R. Jones
1936	John Hope	1963	Medgar W. Evers	1990	L. Douglas Wilder	2018	Willie L. Brown Jr.
1937	Walter White	1964	Roy Wilkins	1991	Gen. Colin L. Powell	2019	Patrick Gaspard
1939	Marian Anderson	1965	Leontyne Price	1992	Barbara Jordan	2021	Cato T. Laurencin
1940	Louis T. Wright	1966	John H. Johnson	1993	Dorothy I. Height	2022	Jim Clyburn
1941	Richard Wright	1967	Edward W. Brooke	1994	Maya Angelou	2023	Dr. Hazel N. Dukes
1942	A. Philip Randolph	1968	Sammy Davis Jr.	1995	John Hope Franklin		

Miss America Winners, 1921-2023

Year	Winner, hometown	Year	Winner, hometown
1921	Margaret Gorman, Washington, DC	1976	Tawney Elaine Godin, Saratoga Springs, New York
1922-23	Mary Campbell, Columbus, Ohio	1977	Dorothy Kathleen Benham, Edina, Minnesota
1924	Ruth Malcolmson, Philadelphia, Pennsylvania	1978	Susan Perkins, Columbus, Ohio
1925	Fay Lamphier, Oakland, California	1979	Kylene Barker, Roanoke, Virginia
1926	Norma Smallwood, Tulsa, Oklahoma	1980	Cheryl Prewitt, Ackerman, Mississippi
1927	Lois Delander, Joliet, Illinois	1981	Susan Powell, Elk City, Oklahoma
1933	Marion Bergeron, West Haven, Connecticut	1982	Elizabeth Ward, Russellville, Arkansas
1935	Henrietta Leaver, Pittsburgh, Pennsylvania	1983	Debra Maffett, Anaheim, California
1936	Rose Coyle, Philadelphia, Pennsylvania	1984[1]	Suzette Charles, Mays Landing, New Jersey
1937	Bette Cooper, Bertrand Island, New Jersey	1985	Sharlene Wells, Salt Lake City, Utah
1938	Marilyn Meseke, Marion, Ohio	1986	Susan Akin, Meridian, Mississippi
1939	Patricia Donnelly, Detroit, Michigan	1987	Kellye Cash, Memphis, Tennessee
1940	Frances Marie Burke, Philadelphia, Pennsylvania	1988	Kaye Lani Rae Rafko, Monroe, Michigan
1941	Rosemary LaPlanche, Los Angeles, California	1989	Gretchen Carlson, Anoka, Minnesota
1942	Jo-Caroll Dennison, Tyler, Texas	1990	Debbye Turner, Columbia, Missouri
1943	Jean Bartel, Los Angeles, California	1991	Marjorie Vincent, Oak Park, Illinois
1944	Venus Ramey, Washington, DC	1992	Carolyn Suzanne Sapp, Honolulu, Hawaii
1945	Bess Myerson, New York, New York	1993	Leanza Cornett, Jacksonville, Florida
1946	Marilyn Buferd, Los Angeles, California	1994	Kimberly Aiken, Columbia, South Carolina
1947	Barbara Walker, Memphis, Tennessee	1995	Heather Whitestone, Birmingham, Alabama
1948	BeBe Shopp, Hopkins, Minnesota	1996	Shawntel Smith, Muldrow, Oklahoma
1949	Jacque Mercer, Litchfield, Arizona	1997	Tara Dawn Holland, Overland Park, Kansas
1951	Yolande Betbeze, Mobile, Alabama	1998	Kate Shindle, Evanston, Illinois
1952	Coleen Kay Hutchins, Salt Lake City, Utah	1999	Nicole Johnson, Roanoke, Virginia
1953	Neva Jane Langley, Macon, Georgia	2000	Heather Renee French, Maysville, Kentucky
1954	Evelyn Margaret Ay, Ephrata, Pennsylvania	2001	Angela Perez Baraquio, Honolulu, Hawaii
1955	Lee Meriwether, San Francisco, California	2002	Katie Harman, Gresham, Oregon
1956	Sharon Ritchie, Denver, Colorado	2003	Erika Harold, Urbana, Illinois
1957	Marian McKnight, Manning, South Carolina	2004	Ericka Dunlap, Orlando, Florida
1958	Marilyn Van Derbur, Denver, Colorado	2005	Deidre Downs, Birmingham, Alabama
1959	Mary Ann Mobley, Brandon, Mississippi	2006	Jennifer Berry, Tulsa, Oklahoma
1960	Lynda Lee Mead, Natchez, Mississippi	2007	Lauren Nelson, Lawton, Oklahoma
1961	Nancy Fleming, Montague, Michigan	2008	Kirsten Haglund, Farmington Hills, Michigan
1962	Maria Fletcher, Asheville, North Carolina	2009	Katie Stam, Seymour, Indiana
1963	Jacquelyn Mayer, Sandusky, Ohio	2010	Caressa Cameron, Fredricksburg, Virginia
1964	Donna Axum, El Dorado, Arkansas	2011	Teresa Scanlan, Gering, Nebraska
1965	Vonda Kay Van Dyke, Phoenix, Arizona	2012	Laura Kaeppeler, Kenosha, Wisconsin
1966	Deborah Irene Bryant, Overland Park, Kansas	2013	Mallory Hytes Hagen, Brooklyn, New York
1967	Jane Anne Jayroe, Laverne, Oklahoma	2014	Nina Davuluri, Syracuse, New York
1968	Debra Dene Barnes, Moran, Kansas	2015	Kira Kazantsev, New York, New York
1969	Judith Anne Ford, Belvidere, Illinois	2016	Betty Cantrell, Warner Robins, Georgia
1970	Pamela Anne Eldred, Birmingham, Michigan	2017	Savvy Shields, Fayetteville, Arkansas
1971	Phyllis Ann George, Denton, Texas	2018	Cara Mund, Bismarck, North Dakota
1972	Laurie Lea Schaefer, Bexley, Ohio	2019	Nia Franklin, Brooklyn, New York
1973	Terry Anne Meeuwsen, DePere, Wisconsin	2020	Camille Schrier, Richmond, Virginia
1974	Rebecca Ann King, Denver, Colorado	2022	Emma Broyles, Anchorage, Alaska
1975	Shirley Cothran, Denton, Texas	2023	Grace Stanke, Wausau, Wisconsin

Note: Since the 1950 pageant, winners have been crowned Miss America of the following year (e.g., Miss America 1951 competed in 1950). (1) Miss New York, Vanessa Williams, resigned July 23, 1984.

Tony (Antoinette Perry) Awards, 2023

Play: *Leopoldstadt*, Tom Stoppard
Musical: *Kimberly Akimbo*
Book of a musical: *Kimberly Akimbo*, David Lindsay-Abaire
Original score: *Kimberly Akimbo*, David Lindsay-Abaire, Jeanine Tesori
Play revival: *Topdog/Underdog*
Musical revival: *Parade*
Actor, play: Sean Hayes, *Good Night, Oscar*
Actress, play: Jodie Comer, *Prima Facie*
Actor, musical: J. Harrison Ghee, *Some Like It Hot*
Actress, musical: Victoria Clark, *Kimberly Akimbo*
Featured actor, play: Brandon Uranowitz, *Leopoldstadt*
Featured actress, play: Miriam Silverman, *The Sign in Sidney Brustein's Window*
Featured actor, musical: Alex Newell, *Shucked*
Featured actress, musical: Bonnie Milligan, *Kimberly Akimbo*
Direction, play: Patrick Marber, *Leopoldstadt*
Direction, musical: Michael Arden, *Parade*

Choreography: Casey Nicholaw, *Some Like It Hot*
Orchestrations: Charlie Rosen and Bryan Carter, *Some Like It Hot*
Costume design, play: Brigitte Reiffenstuel, *Leopoldstadt*
Costume design, musical: Gregg Barnes, *Some Like It Hot*
Lighting design, play: Tim Lutkin, *Life of Pi*
Lighting design, musical: Natasha Katz, *Sweeney Todd: The Demon Barber of Fleet Street*
Scenic design, play: Tim Hatley and Andrzej Goulding, *Life of Pi*
Scenic design, musical: Beowulf Boritt, *New York, New York*
Sound design, play: Carolyn Downing, *Life of Pi*
Sound design, musical: Nevin Steinberg, *Sweeney Todd: The Demon Barber of Fleet Street*
Regional theatre: Pasadena Playhouse
Special Tony Award, lifetime achievement: Joel Grey, John Kander
Isabelle Stevenson Award: Jerry Mitchell
Tony Honors for Excellence in the Theatre: Victoria Bailey, Lisa Dawn Cave, Robert Fried

Tony Awards, 1948-2023

Year	Play	Musical	Year	Play	Musical
1948	Mister Roberts	No award	1986	I'm Not Rappaport	The Mystery of Edwin Drood
1949	Death of a Salesman	Kiss Me Kate	1987	Fences	Les Misérables
1950	The Cocktail Party	South Pacific	1988	M. Butterfly	Phantom of the Opera
1951	The Rose Tattoo	Guys and Dolls	1989	The Heidi Chronicles	Jerome Robbins' Broadway
1952	The Fourposter	The King and I	1990	The Grapes of Wrath	City of Angels
1953	The Crucible	Wonderful Town	1991	Lost in Yonkers	The Will Rogers Follies
1954	The Teahouse of the August Moon	Kismet	1992	Dancing at Lughnasa	Crazy for You
1955	The Desperate Hours	The Pajama Game	1993	Angels in America: Millennium Approaches	Kiss of the Spider Woman
1956	The Diary of Anne Frank	Damn Yankees	1994	Angels in America: Perestroika	Passion
1957	Long Day's Journey Into Night	My Fair Lady	1995	Love! Valour! Compassion!	Sunset Boulevard
1958	Sunrise at Campobello	The Music Man	1996	Master Class	Rent
1959	J.B.	Redhead	1997	The Last Night of Ballyhoo	Titanic
1960	The Miracle Worker	Fiorello! and	1998	Art	The Lion King
		The Sound of Music	1999	Side Man	Fosse
1961	Becket	Bye, Bye Birdie	2000	Copenhagen	Contact
1962	A Man for All Seasons	How to Succeed in Business Without Really Trying	2001	Proof	The Producers
			2002	Edward Albee's The Goat or Who Is Sylvia?	Thoroughly Modern Millie
1963	Who's Afraid of Virginia Woolf?	A Funny Thing Happened on the Way to the Forum	2003	Take Me Out	Hairspray
1964	Luther	Hello, Dolly!	2004	I Am My Own Wife	Avenue Q
1965	The Subject Was Roses	Fiddler on the Roof	2005	Doubt	Monty Python's Spamalot
1966	Marat/Sade	Man of La Mancha	2006	The History Boys	Jersey Boys
1967	The Homecoming	Cabaret	2007	The Coast of Utopia	Spring Awakening
1968	Rosencrantz and Guildenstern Are Dead	Hallelujah, Baby!	2008	August: Osage County	In the Heights
1969	The Great White Hope	1776	2009	God of Carnage	Billy Elliot, The Musical
1970	Borstal Boy	Applause	2010	Red	Memphis
1971	Sleuth	Company	2011	War Horse	The Book of Mormon
1972	Sticks and Bones	Two Gentlemen of Verona	2012	Clybourne Park	Once
1973	That Championship Season	A Little Night Music	2013	Vanya and Sonia and Masha and Spike	Kinky Boots
1974	The River Niger	Raisin	2014	All the Way	A Gentleman's Guide to Love & Murder
1975	Equus	The Wiz			
1976	Travesties	A Chorus Line	2015	The Curious Incident of the Dog in the Night-Time	Fun Home
1977	The Shadow Box	Annie			
1978	Da	Ain't Misbehavin'	2016	The Humans	Hamilton
1979	The Elephant Man	Sweeney Todd	2017	Oslo	Dear Evan Hansen
1980	Children of a Lesser God	Evita	2018	Harry Potter and the Cursed Child, Parts One and Two	The Band's Visit
1981	Amadeus	42nd Street			
1982	The Life and Adventures of Nicholas Nickelby	Nine	2019	The Ferryman	Hadestown
			2020	The Inheritance	Moulin Rouge!
1983	Torch Song Trilogy	Cats	2022	The Lehman Trilogy	A Strange Loop
1984	The Real Thing	La Cage aux Folles	2023	Leopoldstadt	Kimberly Akimbo
1985	Biloxi Blues	Big River			

Selected Prime-Time Emmy Awards, 2022

Drama series: *Succession*, HBO
Comedy series: *Ted Lasso*, Apple TV+
Limited series: *The White Lotus*, HBO
Competition program: *Lizzo's Watch Out for the Big Grrrls*, Amazon Prime Video
Variety talk series: *Last Week Tonight With John Oliver*, HBO
Variety sketch series: *Saturday Night Live*, NBC
Lead actor, drama: Lee Jung-jae, *Squid Game*, Netflix
Lead actress, drama: Zendaya, *Euphoria*, HBO
Lead actor, comedy: Jason Sudeikis, *Ted Lasso*, Apple TV+
Lead actress, comedy: Jean Smart, *Hacks*, HBO

Lead actor, limited series: Michael Keaton, *Dopesick*, Hulu
Lead actress, limited series: Amanda Seyfried, *The Dropout*, Hulu
Sup. actor, drama: Matthew Macfadyen, *Succession*, HBO
Sup. actress, drama: Julia Garner, *Ozark*, Netflix
Sup. actor, comedy: Brett Goldstein, *Ted Lasso*, Apple TV+
Sup. actress, comedy: Sheryl Lee Ralph, *Abbott Elementary*, ABC
Sup. actor, limited series: Murray Bartlett, *The White Lotus*, HBO
Sup. actress, limited series: Jennifer Coolidge, *The White Lotus*, HBO

Prime-Time Emmy Awards, 1952-2022

The Academy of Television Arts and Sciences presented the first Emmy Awards in 1949. Through the years, award categories have changed, but since 1952, the Academy has given out an outstanding comedy and drama award annually.

Year	Comedy	Drama	Year	Comedy	Drama
1952	Red Skelton Show, NBC	Studio One, CBS	1984	Cheers, NBC	Hill Street Blues, NBC
1953	I Love Lucy, CBS	Robert Montgomery Presents, NBC	1985	The Cosby Show, NBC	Cagney & Lacey, CBS
			1986	Golden Girls, NBC	Cagney & Lacey, CBS
1954	I Love Lucy, CBS	The U.S. Steel Hour, ABC	1987	Golden Girls, NBC	L.A. Law, NBC
1955	Make Room for Daddy, ABC	The U.S. Steel Hour, ABC	1988	The Wonder Years, ABC	thirtysomething, ABC
1956	Phil Silvers Show, CBS	Producers' Showcase, NBC	1989	Cheers, NBC	L.A. Law, NBC
1957	Phil Silvers Show, CBS	"Requiem for a Heavyweight," CBS[1]	1990	Murphy Brown, CBS	L.A. Law, NBC
			1991	Cheers, NBC	L.A. Law, NBC
1958	Phil Silvers Show, CBS	Gunsmoke, CBS	1992	Murphy Brown, CBS	Northern Exposure, CBS
1959[2]	Jack Benny Show, CBS	2 awards[3]	1993	Seinfeld, NBC	Picket Fences, CBS
1960	Art Carney Special, NBC	Playhouse 90, CBS	1994	Frasier, NBC	Picket Fences, CBS
1961	Jack Benny Show, CBS	Hallmark Hall of Fame: Macbeth, NBC	1995	Frasier, NBC	NYPD Blue, ABC
			1996	Frasier, NBC	ER, NBC
1962	Bob Newhart Show, CBS	The Defenders, CBS	1997	Frasier, NBC	Law & Order, NBC
1963	Dick Van Dyke Show, CBS	The Defenders, CBS	1998	Frasier, NBC	The Practice, ABC
1964	Dick Van Dyke Show, CBS	The Defenders, CBS	1999	Ally McBeal, FOX	The Practice, ABC
1965	Dick Van Dyke Show, CBS	Hallmark Hall of Fame: The Magnificent Yankee, NBC	2000	Will & Grace, NBC	The West Wing, NBC
			2001	Sex and the City, HBO	The West Wing, NBC
1966	Dick Van Dyke Show, CBS	The Fugitive, ABC	2002	Friends, NBC	The West Wing, NBC
1967	The Monkees, NBC	Mission: Impossible, CBS	2003	Everybody Loves Raymond, CBS	The West Wing, NBC
1968	Get Smart, NBC	Mission: Impossible, CBS			
1969	Get Smart, NBC	NET Playhouse, NET	2004	Arrested Development, FOX	The Sopranos, HBO
1970	My World and Welcome to It, NBC	Marcus Welby, M.D., ABC	2005	Everybody Loves Raymond, CBS	Lost, ABC
1971	All in the Family, CBS	The Bold Ones: The Senator, NBC	2006	The Office, NBC	24, FOX
			2007	30 Rock, NBC	The Sopranos, HBO
1972	All in the Family, CBS	Masterpiece Theatre: Elizabeth R, PBS	2008	30 Rock, NBC	Mad Men, AMC
			2009	30 Rock, NBC	Mad Men, AMC
1973	All in the Family, CBS	The Waltons, CBS	2010	Modern Family, ABC	Mad Men, AMC
1974	M*A*S*H, CBS	Masterpiece Theatre: Upstairs, Downstairs, PBS	2011	Modern Family, ABC	Mad Men, AMC
			2012	Modern Family, ABC	Homeland, Showtime
1975	Mary Tyler Moore Show, CBS	Masterpiece Theatre: Upstairs, Downstairs, PBS	2013	Modern Family, ABC	Breaking Bad, AMC
			2014	Modern Family, ABC	Breaking Bad, AMC
1976	Mary Tyler Moore Show, CBS	Police Story, NBC	2015	Veep, HBO	Game of Thrones, HBO
1977	Mary Tyler Moore Show, CBS	Masterpiece Theatre: Upstairs, Downstairs, PBS	2016	Veep, HBO	Game of Thrones, HBO
			2017	Veep, HBO	The Handmaid's Tale, Hulu
1978	All in the Family, CBS	The Rockford Files, NBC	2018	The Marvelous Mrs. Maisel, Amazon	Game of Thrones, HBO
1979	Taxi, ABC	Lou Grant, CBS			
1980	Taxi, ABC	Lou Grant, CBS	2019	Fleabag, Amazon	Game of Thrones, HBO
1981	Taxi, ABC	Hill Street Blues, NBC	2020	Schitt's Creek, Pop	Succession, HBO
1982	Barney Miller, ABC	Hill Street Blues, NBC	2021	Ted Lasso, Apple TV+	The Crown, Netflix
1983	Cheers, NBC	Hill Street Blues, NBC	2022	Ted Lasso, Apple TV+	Succession, HBO

(1) Best single program of the year; shown on Playhouse 90, which was named best new series. (2) Beginning in 1959, Emmys were awarded for work in the season encompassing the previous and current year. (3) Playhouse 90 (CBS) was best dramatic series of one hour or longer, Alcoa-Goodyear Theatre (NBC) of less than one hour.

Selected Daytime Emmy Awards, 2022

Culinary program: Barefoot Contessa: Modern Comfort Food, Food Network
Drama series: General Hospital, ABC
Entertainment news program: Entertainment Tonight, synd.
Game show: Jeopardy!, synd.
Legal/courtroom program: Judy Justice, IMDbTV
Lifestyle program: Sparking Joy With Marie Kondo, Netflix
Talk show, entertainment: The Kelly Clarkson Show, synd.
Talk show, informative: Turning the Tables With Robin Roberts, Disney+
Travel/adventure/nature program: Penguin Town, Netflix
Lead actress, drama: Mishael Morgan, The Young and the Restless, CBS

Lead actor, drama: John McCook, The Bold and the Beautiful, CBS
Supp. actress, drama: Kelly Thiebaud, General Hospital, ABC
Supp. actor, drama: Jeff Kober, General Hospital, ABC
Younger performer, drama: Nicholas Chavez, General Hospital, ABC
Culinary host: Frankie Celenza, Struggle Meals, Tastemade
Game show host: Steve Harvey, Family Feud, synd.
Talk show host, entertainment: Kelly Clarkson, The Kelly Clarkson Show, synd.
Talk show host, informative: Tamron Hall, Tamron Hall, synd.
Directing team: General Hospital, ABC
Writing team: Days of Our Lives, NBC

Golden Globe Awards, 2023

The Hollywood Foreign Press Association (then the Hollywood Foreign Correspondents Association) presented its first awards for achievement in film in 1944; TV in 1955.

Film

Drama: The Fabelmans
Comedy/musical: The Banshees of Inisherin
Actress, drama: Cate Blanchett, Tár
Actor, drama: Austin Butler, Elvis
Actress, comedy/musical: Michelle Yeoh, Everything Everywhere All at Once
Actor, comedy/musical: Colin Farrell, The Banshees of Inisherin
Supporting actress: Angela Bassett, Black Panther: Wakanda Forever
Supporting actor: Ke Huy Quan, Everything Everywhere All at Once
Director: Steven Spielberg, The Fabelmans
Screenplay: Martin McDonagh, The Banshees of Inisherin
Animated film: Guillermo del Toro's Pinocchio
Non-English-language film: Argentina, 1985
Original score: Justin Hurwitz, Babylon
Original song: "Naatu Naatu," RRR, Chandrabose, M.M. Keeravaani

Television

Series, drama: House of the Dragon, HBO
Series, comedy/musical: Abbott Elementary, ABC
Limited series or made-for-TV movie: The White Lotus, HBO
Actress, drama: Zendaya, Euphoria, HBO
Actor, drama: Kevin Costner, Yellowstone, Paramount
Actress, comedy/musical: Quinta Brunson, Abbott Elementary, ABC
Actor, comedy/musical: Jeremy Allen White, The Bear, Hulu
Actress, limited series/TV movie: Amanda Seyfried, The Dropout, Hulu
Actor, limited series/TV movie: Evan Peters, Dahmer – Monster: The Jeffrey Dahmer Story, Netflix
Supporting actress, limited series/TV movie: Jennifer Coolidge, The White Lotus, HBO
Supporting actor, limited series/TV movie: Paul Walter Hauser, Black Bird, Apple TV+
Supporting actress, TV series: Julia Garner, Ozark, Netflix
Supporting actor, TV series: Tyler James Williams, Abbott Elementary, ABC

Academy Awards (Oscars), 1927-2022

Year	Picture	Actor	Actress	Supporting actor[1]	Supporting actress[1]	Director
1927 -28	Wings	Emil Jannings *The Way of All Flesh*	Janet Gaynor *Seventh Heaven*	NA	NA	Frank Borzage *Seventh Heaven;* Lewis Milestone *Two Arabian Knights*
1928 -29	Broadway Melody	Warner Baxter *In Old Arizona*	Mary Pickford *Coquette*	NA	NA	Frank Lloyd *The Divine Lady*
1929 -30	All Quiet on the Western Front	George Arliss *Disraeli*	Norma Shearer *The Divorcee*	NA	NA	Lewis Milestone *All Quiet on the Western Front*
1930 -31	Cimarron	Lionel Barrymore *Free Soul*	Marie Dressler *Min and Bill*	NA	NA	Norman Taurog *Skippy*
1931 -32	Grand Hotel	Fredric March *Dr. Jekyll and Mr. Hyde;* Wallace Beery *The Champ*	Helen Hayes *The Sin of Madelon Claudet*	NA	NA	Frank Borzage *Bad Girl*
1932 -33	Cavalcade	Charles Laughton *The Private Life of Henry VIII*	Katharine Hepburn *Morning Glory*	NA	NA	Frank Lloyd *Cavalcade*
1934	It Happened One Night	Clark Gable *It Happened One Night*	Claudette Colbert *It Happened One Night*	NA	NA	Frank Capra *It Happened One Night*
1935	Mutiny on the Bounty	Victor McLaglen *The Informer*	Bette Davis *Dangerous*	NA	NA	John Ford *The Informer*
1936	The Great Ziegfeld	Paul Muni *The Story of Louis Pasteur*	Luise Rainer *The Great Ziegfeld*	Walter Brennan *Come and Get It*	Gale Sondergaard *Anthony Adverse*	Frank Capra *Mr. Deeds Goes to Town*
1937	The Life of Emile Zola	Spencer Tracy *Captains Courageous*	Luise Rainer *The Good Earth*	Joseph Schildkraut *The Life of Emile Zola*	Alice Brady *In Old Chicago*	Leo McCarey *The Awful Truth*
1938	You Can't Take It With You	Spencer Tracy *Boys Town*	Bette Davis *Jezebel*	Walter Brennan *Kentucky*	Fay Bainter *Jezebel*	Frank Capra *You Can't Take It With You*
1939	Gone With the Wind	Robert Donat *Goodbye, Mr. Chips*	Vivien Leigh *Gone With the Wind*	Thomas Mitchell *Stage Coach*	Hattie McDaniel *Gone With the Wind*	Victor Fleming *Gone With the Wind*
1940	Rebecca	James Stewart *The Philadelphia Story*	Ginger Rogers *Kitty Foyle*	Walter Brennan *The Westerner*	Jane Darwell *The Grapes of Wrath*	John Ford *The Grapes of Wrath*
1941	How Green Was My Valley	Gary Cooper *Sergeant York*	Joan Fontaine *Suspicion*	Donald Crisp *How Green Was My Valley*	Mary Astor *The Great Lie*	John Ford *How Green Was My Valley*
1942	Mrs. Miniver	James Cagney *Yankee Doodle Dandy*	Greer Garson *Mrs. Miniver*	Van Heflin *Johnny Eager*	Teresa Wright *Mrs. Miniver*	William Wyler *Mrs. Miniver*
1943	Casablanca	Paul Lukas *Watch on the Rhine*	Jennifer Jones *The Song of Bernadette*	Charles Coburn *The More the Merrier*	Katina Paxinou *For Whom the Bell Tolls*	Michael Curtiz *Casablanca*
1944	Going My Way	Bing Crosby *Going My Way*	Ingrid Bergman *Gaslight*	Barry Fitzgerald *Going My Way*	Ethel Barrymore *None But the Lonely Heart*	Leo McCarey *Going My Way*
1945	The Lost Weekend	Ray Milland *The Lost Weekend*	Joan Crawford *Mildred Pierce*	James Dunn *A Tree Grows in Brooklyn*	Anne Revere *National Velvet*	Billy Wilder *The Lost Weekend*
1946	The Best Years of Our Lives	Fredric March *The Best Years of Our Lives*	Olivia de Havilland *To Each His Own*	Harold Russell *The Best Years of Our Lives*	Anne Baxter *The Razor's Edge*	William Wyler *The Best Years of Our Lives*
1947	Gentleman's Agreement	Ronald Colman *A Double Life*	Loretta Young *The Farmer's Daughter*	Edmund Gwenn *Miracle on 34th Street*	Celeste Holm *Gentleman's Agreement*	Elia Kazan *Gentleman's Agreement*
1948	Hamlet	Laurence Olivier *Hamlet*	Jane Wyman *Johnny Belinda*	Walter Huston *The Treasure of the Sierra Madre*	Claire Trevor *Key Largo*	John Huston *The Treasure of the Sierra Madre*
1949	All the King's Men	Broderick Crawford *All the King's Men*	Olivia de Havilland *The Heiress*	Dean Jagger *Twelve O'Clock High*	Mercedes McCambridge *All the King's Men*	Joseph L. Mankiewicz *Letter to Three Wives*
1950	All About Eve	José Ferrer *Cyrano de Bergerac*	Judy Holliday *Born Yesterday*	George Sanders *All About Eve*	Josephine Hull *Harvey*	Joseph L. Mankiewicz *All About Eve*
1951	An American in Paris	Humphrey Bogart *The African Queen*	Vivien Leigh *A Streetcar Named Desire*	Karl Malden *A Streetcar Named Desire*	Kim Hunter *A Streetcar Named Desire*	George Stevens *A Place in the Sun*
1952	The Greatest Show on Earth	Gary Cooper *High Noon*	Shirley Booth *Come Back, Little Sheba*	Anthony Quinn *Viva Zapata!*	Gloria Grahame *The Bad and the Beautiful*	John Ford *The Quiet Man*
1953	From Here to Eternity	William Holden *Stalag 17*	Audrey Hepburn *Roman Holiday*	Frank Sinatra *From Here to Eternity*	Donna Reed *From Here to Eternity*	Fred Zinnemann *From Here to Eternity*

Year	Picture	Actor	Actress	Supporting actor[1]	Supporting actress[1]	Director
1954	On the Waterfront	Marlon Brando On the Waterfront	Grace Kelly The Country Girl	Edmond O'Brien, The Barefoot Contessa	Eva Marie Saint On the Waterfront	Elia Kazan On the Waterfront
1955	Marty	Ernest Borgnine Marty	Anna Magnani The Rose Tattoo	Jack Lemmon Mister Roberts	Jo Van Fleet East of Eden	Delbert Mann Marty
1956	Around the World in 80 Days	Yul Brynner The King and I	Ingrid Bergman Anastasia	Anthony Quinn Lust for Life	Dorothy Malone Written on the Wind	George Stevens Giant
1957	The Bridge on the River Kwai	Alec Guinness The Bridge on the River Kwai	Joanne Woodward The Three Faces of Eve	Red Buttons Sayonara	Miyoshi Umeki Sayonara	David Lean The Bridge on the River Kwai
1958	Gigi	David Niven Separate Tables	Susan Hayward I Want to Live	Burl Ives The Big Country	Wendy Hiller Separate Tables	Vincente Minnelli Gigi
1959	Ben-Hur	Charlton Heston Ben-Hur	Simone Signoret Room at the Top	Hugh Griffith Ben-Hur	Shelley Winters Diary of Anne Frank	William Wyler Ben-Hur
1960	The Apartment	Burt Lancaster Elmer Gantry	Elizabeth Taylor Butterfield 8	Peter Ustinov Spartacus	Shirley Jones Elmer Gantry	Billy Wilder The Apartment
1961	West Side Story	Maximilian Schell Judgment at Nuremberg	Sophia Loren Two Women	George Chakiris West Side Story	Rita Moreno West Side Story	Jerome Robbins and Robert Wise West Side Story
1962	Lawrence of Arabia	Gregory Peck To Kill a Mockingbird	Anne Bancroft The Miracle Worker	Ed Begley Sweet Bird of Youth	Patty Duke The Miracle Worker	David Lean Lawrence of Arabia
1963	Tom Jones	Sidney Poitier Lilies of the Field	Patricia Neal Hud	Melvyn Douglas Hud	Margaret Rutherford The V.I.P.s	Tony Richardson Tom Jones
1964	My Fair Lady	Rex Harrison My Fair Lady	Julie Andrews Mary Poppins	Peter Ustinov Topkapi	Lila Kedrova Zorba the Greek	George Cukor My Fair Lady
1965	The Sound of Music	Lee Marvin Cat Ballou	Julie Christie Darling	Martin Balsam A Thousand Clowns	Shelley Winters A Patch of Blue	Robert Wise The Sound of Music
1966	A Man for All Seasons	Paul Scofield A Man for All Seasons	Elizabeth Taylor Who's Afraid of Virginia Woolf?	Walter Matthau The Fortune Cookie	Sandy Dennis Who's Afraid of Virginia Woolf?	Fred Zinnemann A Man for All Seasons
1967	In the Heat of the Night	Rod Steiger In the Heat of the Night	Katharine Hepburn Guess Who's Coming to Dinner	George Kennedy Cool Hand Luke	Estelle Parsons Bonnie and Clyde	Mike Nichols The Graduate
1968	Oliver!	Cliff Robertson Charly	Katharine Hepburn The Lion in Winter; Barbra Streisand Funny Girl	Jack Albertson The Subject Was Roses	Ruth Gordon Rosemary's Baby	Carol Reed Oliver!
1969	Midnight Cowboy	John Wayne True Grit	Maggie Smith The Prime of Miss Jean Brodie	Gig Young They Shoot Horses, Don't They?	Goldie Hawn Cactus Flower	John Schlesinger Midnight Cowboy
1970	Patton	George C. Scott Patton (refused)	Glenda Jackson Women in Love	John Mills Ryan's Daughter	Helen Hayes Airport	Franklin Schaffner Patton
1971	The French Connection	Gene Hackman The French Connection	Jane Fonda Klute	Ben Johnson The Last Picture Show	Cloris Leachman The Last Picture Show	William Friedkin The French Connection
1972	The Godfather	Marlon Brando The Godfather (refused)	Liza Minnelli Cabaret	Joel Grey Cabaret	Eileen Heckart Butterflies Are Free	Bob Fosse Cabaret
1973	The Sting	Jack Lemmon Save the Tiger	Glenda Jackson A Touch of Class	John Houseman The Paper Chase	Tatum O'Neal Paper Moon	George Roy Hill The Sting
1974	The Godfather Part II	Art Carney Harry and Tonto	Ellen Burstyn Alice Doesn't Live Here Anymore	Robert DeNiro The Godfather Part II	Ingrid Bergman Murder on the Orient Express	Francis Ford Coppola The Godfather Part II
1975	One Flew Over the Cuckoo's Nest	Jack Nicholson One Flew Over the Cuckoo's Nest	Louise Fletcher One Flew Over the Cuckoo's Nest	George Burns The Sunshine Boys	Lee Grant Shampoo	Milos Forman One Flew Over the Cuckoo's Nest
1976	Rocky	Peter Finch Network	Faye Dunaway Network	Jason Robards, All the President's Men	Beatrice Straight Network	John G. Avildsen Rocky
1977	Annie Hall	Richard Dreyfuss The Goodbye Girl	Diane Keaton Annie Hall	Jason Robards Julia	Vanessa Redgrave Julia	Woody Allen Annie Hall
1978	The Deer Hunter	Jon Voight Coming Home	Jane Fonda Coming Home	Christopher Walken The Deer Hunter	Maggie Smith California Suite	Michael Cimino The Deer Hunter
1979	Kramer vs. Kramer	Dustin Hoffman Kramer vs. Kramer	Sally Field Norma Rae	Melvyn Douglas Being There	Meryl Streep Kramer vs. Kramer	Robert Benton Kramer vs. Kramer
1980	Ordinary People	Robert DeNiro Raging Bull	Sissy Spacek Coal Miner's Daughter	Timothy Hutton Ordinary People	Mary Steenburgen Melvin and Howard	Robert Redford Ordinary People
1981	Chariots of Fire	Henry Fonda On Golden Pond	Katharine Hepburn On Golden Pond	John Gielgud Arthur	Maureen Stapleton Reds	Warren Beatty Reds
1982	Gandhi	Ben Kingsley Gandhi	Meryl Streep Sophie's Choice	Louis Gossett Jr. An Officer and a Gentleman	Jessica Lange Tootsie	Richard Attenborough Gandhi
1983	Terms of Endearment	Robert Duvall Tender Mercies	Shirley MacLaine Terms of Endearment	Jack Nicholson Terms of Endearment	Linda Hunt The Year of Living Dangerously	James L. Brooks Terms of Endearment
1984	Amadeus	F. Murray Abraham Amadeus	Sally Field Places in the Heart	Haing S. Ngor The Killing Fields	Peggy Ashcroft A Passage to India	Milos Forman Amadeus
1985	Out of Africa	William Hurt Kiss of the Spider Woman	Geraldine Page The Trip to Bountiful	Don Ameche Cocoon	Anjelica Huston Prizzi's Honor	Sydney Pollack Out of Africa
1986	Platoon	Paul Newman The Color of Money	Marlee Matlin Children of a Lesser God	Michael Caine Hannah and Her Sisters	Dianne Wiest Hannah and Her Sisters	Oliver Stone Platoon

Year	Picture	Actor	Actress	Supporting actor[1]	Supporting actress[1]	Director
1987	The Last Emperor	Michael Douglas *Wall Street*	Cher *Moonstruck*	Sean Connery *The Untouchables*	Olympia Dukakis *Moonstruck*	Bernardo Bertolucci *The Last Emperor*
1988	Rain Man	Dustin Hoffman *Rain Man*	Jodie Foster *The Accused*	Kevin Kline *A Fish Called Wanda*	Geena Davis *The Accidental Tourist*	Barry Levinson *Rain Man*
1989	Driving Miss Daisy	Daniel Day-Lewis *My Left Foot*	Jessica Tandy *Driving Miss Daisy*	Denzel Washington *Glory*	Brenda Fricker *My Left Foot*	Oliver Stone, *Born on the Fourth of July*
1990	Dances With Wolves	Jeremy Irons *Reversal of Fortune*	Kathy Bates *Misery*	Joe Pesci *Goodfellas*	Whoopi Goldberg *Ghost*	Kevin Costner *Dances With Wolves*
1991	The Silence of the Lambs	Anthony Hopkins *The Silence of the Lambs*	Jodie Foster *The Silence of the Lambs*	Jack Palance *City Slickers*	Mercedes Ruehl *The Fisher King*	Jonathan Demme *The Silence of the Lambs*
1992	Unforgiven	Al Pacino *Scent of a Woman*	Emma Thompson *Howards End*	Gene Hackman *Unforgiven*	Marisa Tomei *My Cousin Vinny*	Clint Eastwood *Unforgiven*
1993	Schindler's List	Tom Hanks *Philadelphia*	Holly Hunter *The Piano*	Tommy Lee Jones *The Fugitive*	Anna Paquin *The Piano*	Steven Spielberg *Schindler's List*
1994	Forrest Gump	Tom Hanks *Forrest Gump*	Jessica Lange *Blue Sky*	Martin Landau *Ed Wood*	Dianne Wiest, *Bullets Over Broadway*	Robert Zemeckis *Forrest Gump*
1995	Braveheart	Nicolas Cage *Leaving Las Vegas*	Susan Sarandon *Dead Man Walking*	Kevin Spacey *The Usual Suspects*	Mira Sorvino *Mighty Aphrodite*	Mel Gibson *Braveheart*
1996	The English Patient	Geoffrey Rush *Shine*	Frances McDormand *Fargo*	Cuba Gooding Jr. *Jerry Maguire*	Juliette Binoche *The English Patient*	Anthony Minghella *The English Patient*
1997	Titanic	Jack Nicholson *As Good As It Gets*	Helen Hunt *As Good As It Gets*	Robin Williams *Good Will Hunting*	Kim Basinger *L.A. Confidential*	James Cameron *Titanic*
1998	Shakespeare in Love	Roberto Benigni *Life Is Beautiful*	Gwyneth Paltrow *Shakespeare in Love*	James Coburn *Affliction*	Judi Dench *Shakespeare in Love*	Steven Spielberg *Saving Private Ryan*
1999	American Beauty	Kevin Spacey *American Beauty*	Hilary Swank *Boys Don't Cry*	Michael Caine, *The Cider House Rules*	Angelina Jolie *Girl, Interrupted*	Sam Mendes *American Beauty*
2000	Gladiator	Russell Crowe *Gladiator*	Julia Roberts *Erin Brockovich*	Benicio Del Toro *Traffic*	Marcia Gay Harden *Pollock*	Steven Soderbergh *Traffic*
2001	A Beautiful Mind	Denzel Washington *Training Day*	Halle Berry *Monster's Ball*	Jim Broadbent *Iris*	Jennifer Connelly *A Beautiful Mind*	Ron Howard *A Beautiful Mind*
2002	Chicago	Adrien Brody *The Pianist*	Nicole Kidman *The Hours*	Chris Cooper *Adaptation*	Catherine Zeta-Jones, *Chicago*	Roman Polanski *The Pianist*
2003	The Lord of the Rings: The Return of the King	Sean Penn *Mystic River*	Charlize Theron *Monster*	Tim Robbins *Mystic River*	Renée Zellweger *Cold Mountain*	Peter Jackson *The Lord of the Rings: The Return of the King*
2004	Million Dollar Baby	Jamie Foxx *Ray*	Hilary Swank *Million Dollar Baby*	Morgan Freeman *Million Dollar Baby*	Cate Blanchett *The Aviator*	Clint Eastwood *Million Dollar Baby*
2005	Crash	Philip Seymour Hoffman *Capote*	Reese Witherspoon *Walk the Line*	George Clooney *Syriana*	Rachel Weisz *The Constant Gardener*	Ang Lee *Brokeback Mountain*
2006	The Departed	Forest Whitaker, *The Last King of Scotland*	Helen Mirren *The Queen*	Alan Arkin *Little Miss Sunshine*	Jennifer Hudson *Dreamgirls*	Martin Scorsese *The Departed*
2007	No Country for Old Men	Daniel Day-Lewis *There Will Be Blood*	Marion Cotillard *La Vie en Rose*	Javier Bardem *No Country for Old Men*	Tilda Swinton *Michael Clayton*	Joel Coen and Ethan Coen, *No Country for Old Men*
2008	Slumdog Millionaire	Sean Penn *Milk*	Kate Winslet *The Reader*	Heath Ledger *The Dark Knight*	Penelope Cruz, *Vicky Cristina Barcelona*	Danny Boyle *Slumdog Millionaire*
2009	The Hurt Locker	Jeff Bridges *Crazy Heart*	Sandra Bullock *The Blind Side*	Christoph Waltz *Inglourious Basterds*	Mo'Nique *Precious*	Kathryn Bigelow *The Hurt Locker*
2010	The King's Speech	Colin Firth *The King's Speech*	Natalie Portman *Black Swan*	Christian Bale *The Fighter*	Melissa Leo *The Fighter*	Tom Hooper *The King's Speech*
2011	The Artist	Jean Dujardin *The Artist*	Meryl Streep *The Iron Lady*	Christopher Plummer, *Beginners*	Octavia Spencer *The Help*	Michel Hazanavicius *The Artist*
2012	Argo	Daniel Day-Lewis *Lincoln*	Jennifer Lawrence *Silver Linings Playbook*	Christoph Waltz *Django Unchained*	Anne Hathaway *Les Misérables*	Ang Lee *Life of Pi*
2013	12 Years a Slave	Matthew McConaughey *Dallas Buyers Club*	Cate Blanchett *Blue Jasmine*	Jared Leto *Dallas Buyers Club*	Lupita Nyong'o *12 Years a Slave*	Alfonso Cuarón *Gravity*
2014	Birdman	Eddie Redmayne *The Theory of Everything*	Julianne Moore *Still Alice*	J. K. Simmons *Whiplash*	Patricia Arquette *Boyhood*	Alejandro G. Iñárritu *Birdman*
2015	Spotlight	Leonardo DiCaprio *The Revenant*	Brie Larson *Room*	Mark Rylance *Bridge of Spies*	Alicia Vikander *The Danish Girl*	Alejandro G. Iñárritu *The Revenant*
2016	Moonlight	Casey Affleck *Manchester by the Sea*	Emma Stone *La La Land*	Mahershala Ali *Moonlight*	Viola Davis *Fences*	Damien Chazelle *La La Land*
2017	The Shape of Water	Gary Oldman *Darkest Hour*	Frances McDormand *Three Billboards Outside Ebbing, Missouri*	Sam Rockwell *Three Billboards Outside Ebbing, Missouri*	Allison Janney *I, Tonya*	Guillermo del Toro *The Shape of Water*
2018	Green Book	Rami Malek *Bohemian Rhapsody*	Olivia Colman *The Favourite*	Mahershala Ali *Green Book*	Regina King *If Beale Street Could Talk*	Alfonso Cuarón *Roma*
2019	Parasite	Joaquin Phoenix *Joker*	Renée Zellweger *Judy*	Brad Pitt *Once Upon a Time... in Hollywood*	Laura Dern *Marriage Story*	Bong Joon-ho *Parasite*
2020	Nomadland	Anthony Hopkins *The Father*	Frances McDormand *Nomadland*	Daniel Kaluuya *Judas and the Black Messiah*	Yuh-jung Youn *Minari*	Chloé Zhao *Nomadland*
2021	CODA	Will Smith *King Richard*	Jessica Chastain *The Eyes of Tammy Faye*	Troy Kotsur *CODA*	Ariana DeBose *West Side Story*	Jane Campion *The Power of the Dog*

Year	Picture	Actor	Actress	Supporting actor[1]	Supporting actress[1]	Director
2022	*Everything Everywhere All at Once*	Brendan Fraser *The Whale*	Michelle Yeoh *Everything Everywhere All at Once*	Ke Huy Quan *Everything Everywhere All at Once*	Jamie Lee Curtis *Everything Everywhere All at Once*	Daniel Kwan and Daniel Scheinert *Everything Everywhere All at Once*

NA = Not applicable. (1) Award not given until 1936.

Other Academy Award Winners, 2022

Animated film: *Guillermo del Toro's Pinocchio*
Cinematography: *All Quiet on the Western Front*
Costume design: *Black Panther: Wakanda Forever*
Documentary feature: *Navalny*
Film editing: *Everything Everywhere All at Once*
International feature film: *All Quiet on the Western Front*, Germany
Makeup and hairstyling: *The Whale*
Original score: *All Quiet on the Western Front*, Volker Bertelmann
Original song: "Naatu Naatu," *RRR*, M.M. Keeravaani and Chandrabose

Production design: *All Quiet on the Western Front*
Short films: *The Boy, the Mole, the Fox, and the Horse* (animated), *The Elephant Whisperers* (documentary), *An Irish Goodbye* (live action)
Sound: *Top Gun: Maverick*
Visual effects: *Avatar: The Way of Water*
Writing (adapted screenplay): *Women Talking*, Sarah Polley
Writing (original screenplay): *Everything Everywhere All at Once*, Daniel Kwan and Daniel Scheinert

Other Film Awards, 2023

British Academy of Film and Television Awards (BAFTAs)

Awarded in 2023 to films released in the UK in 2022.

Best film: *All Quiet on the Western Front*
Outstanding British film: *The Banshees of Inisherin*
Outstanding debut by a British writer/director/producer: Charlotte Wells, *Aftersun*
Director: Edward Berger, *All Quiet on the Western Front*
Original screenplay: *The Banshees of Inisherin*, Martin McDonagh
Adapted screenplay: *All Quiet on the Western Front*, Edward Berger, Lesley Paterson, Ian Stokell
Animated film: *Guillermo del Toro's Pinocchio*
Documentary: *Navalny*
Film not in the English language: *All Quiet on the Western Front*
Actor: Austin Butler, *Elvis*
Actress: Cate Blanchett, *Tár*
Supporting actor: Barry Keoghan, *The Banshees of Inisherin*
Supporting actress: Kerry Condon, *The Banshees of Inisherin*

Directors Guild of America Awards

Feature film: Daniel Kwan and Daniel Scheinert, *Everything Everywhere All at Once*
First-time feature film: Charlotte Wells, *Aftersun*
Documentary: Sara Dosa, *Fire of Love*

TV movie/limited series: Helen Shaver, *Station Eleven*, "Who's There?"
TV series (drama): Sam Levinson, *Euphoria*, "Stand Still Like the Hummingbird"
TV series (comedy): Bill Hader, *Barry*, "710N"

Screen Actors Guild Awards

Motion picture cast: *Everything Everywhere All at Once*
Female actor in a lead role: Michelle Yeoh, *Everything Everywhere All at Once*
Male actor in a lead role: Brendan Fraser, *The Whale*
Female actor in a supporting role: Jamie Lee Curtis, *Everything Everywhere All at Once*
Male actor in a supporting role: Ke Huy Quan, *Everything Everywhere All at Once*
Drama series ensemble: *The White Lotus*
Female actor in a drama series: Jennifer Coolidge, *The White Lotus*
Male actor in a drama series: Jason Bateman, *Ozark*
Comedy series ensemble: *Abbott Elementary*
Female actor in a comedy series: Jean Smart, *Hacks*
Male actor in a comedy series: Jeremy Allen White, *The Bear*
Female actor in a TV movie/limited series: Jessica Chastain, *George & Tammy*
Male actor in a TV movie/limited series: Sam Elliott, *1883*

Academy of Country Music Awards, 2023

Entertainer: Chris Stapleton
Male artist: Morgan Wallen
Female artist: Lainey Wilson
Duo: Brothers Osborne
Group: Old Dominion
Album: *Bell Bottom Country*, Lainey Wilson

Single: "She Had Me at Heads Carolina," Cole Swindell
Song: "She Had Me at Heads Carolina," Cole Swindell
Visual media: "wait in the truck," HARDY feat. Lainey Wilson
Music event: "wait in the truck," HARDY feat. Lainey Wilson
New female artist: Hailey Whitters
New male artist: Zach Bryan

Selected Grammy Awards, 2022

Source: The Recording Academy
For albums released Oct. 1, 2021–Sept. 30, 2022, awarded in Feb. 2023.

Record of the year (single): "About Damn Time," Lizzo
Album of the year: *Harry's House*, Harry Styles
Song of the year: "Just Like That," Bonnie Raitt
New artist: Samara Joy
Pop performance, solo: "Easy on Me," Adele
Pop performance, duo/group: "Unholy," Sam Smith and Kim Petras
Pop album, traditional vocal: *Higher*, Michael Bublé
Pop album, vocal: *Harry's House*, Harry Styles
Dance/electronic recording: "Break My Soul," Beyoncé
Dance/electronic album: *Renaissance*, Beyoncé
Contemporary instrumental album: *Empire Central*, Snarky Puppy
Rock performance: "Broken Horses," Brandi Carlile
Metal performance: "Degradation Rules," Ozzy Osbourne feat. Tony Iommi
Rock song: "Broken Horses," Brandi Carlile (Brandi Carlile, Phil Hanseroth, Tim Hanseroth, songwriters)
Rock album: *Patient Number 9*, Ozzy Osbourne
Alternative music album: *Wet Leg*, Wet Leg
Alternative music performance: "Chaise Longue," Wet Leg
R&B performance: "Hrs & Hrs," Muni Long
R&B performance, traditional: "Plastic Off the Sofa," Beyoncé
R&B song: "Cuff It," Beyoncé (Denisia "Blu June" Andrews, Beyoncé, Mary Christine Brockert, Brittany "Chi" Coney, Terius "The-Dream" Gesteelde-Diamant, Morten Ristorp, Nile Rodgers, Raphael Saadiq, songwriters)
R&B album: *Black Radio III*, Robert Glasper
Rap performance: "The Heart Part 5," Kendrick Lamar
Rap/sung collaboration: "Wait for U," Future feat. Drake and Tems
Rap song: "The Heart Part 5," Kendrick Lamar (Jake Kosich, Johnny Kosich, Kendrick Lamar, Matt Schaeffer, songwriters)
Rap album: *Mr. Morale & the Big Steppers*, Kendrick Lamar

Country performance, solo: "Live Forever," Willie Nelson
Country performance, duo/group: "Never Wanted to Be That Girl," Carly Pearce and Ashley McBryde
Country song: "'Til You Can't," Cody Johnson (Matt Rogers, Ben Stennis, songwriters)
Country album: *A Beautiful Time*, Willie Nelson
Jazz album, instrumental: *New Standards Vol. 1*, Terri Lyne Carrington, Kris Davis, Linda May Han Oh, Nicholas Payton, and Matthew Stevens
Jazz album, vocal: *Linger Awhile*, Samara Joy
American roots performance: "Stompin' Ground," Aaron Neville with The Dirty Dozen Brass Band and Take Me to the River All-Stars
American roots song: "Just Like That," Bonnie Raitt
Americana album: *In These Silent Days*, Brandi Carlile
Bluegrass album: *Crooked Tree*, Molly Tuttle and Golden Highway
Blues album, traditional: *Get on Board*, Taj Mahal and Ry Cooder
Contemporary Christian album: *Breathe*, Maverick City Music
Folk album: *Revealer*, Madison Cunningham
Gospel album: *Kingdom Book One Deluxe*, Maverick City Music and Kirk Franklin
Latin rock/alternative/urban album: *Motomami*, Rosalía
Música urbana album: *Un Verano Sin Ti*, Bad Bunny
New age album: *Mystic Mirror*, White Sun
Comedy album: *The Closer*, Dave Chappelle
Spoken word album: *Finding Me*, Viola Davis
Soundtrack album, compilation: *Encanto*, Various artists
Soundtrack album, score: *Encanto*, Germaine Franco
Song, visual media: "We Don't Talk About Bruno," *Encanto* (Lin-Manuel Miranda, songwriter)
Music video: "All Too Well: The Short Film," Taylor Swift
Music film: *Jazz Fest: A New Orleans Story*, Frank Marshall and Ryan Suffern

Grammy Awards, 1958-2022

Record of the Year (single)	Year	Album of the Year
Domenico Modugno, "Nel Blu Dipinto Di Blu (Volare)"	1958	Henry Mancini, *The Music From Peter Gunn*
Bobby Darin, "Mack the Knife"	1959	Frank Sinatra, *Come Dance With Me*
Percy Faith, "Theme From a Summer Place"	1960	Bob Newhart, *Button Down Mind*
Henry Mancini, "Moon River"	1961	Judy Garland, *Judy at Carnegie Hall*
Tony Bennett, "I Left My Heart in San Francisco"	1962	Vaughn Meader, *The First Family*
Henry Mancini, "The Days of Wine and Roses"	1963	Barbra Streisand, *The Barbra Streisand Album*
Stan Getz and Astrud Gilberto, "The Girl From Ipanema"	1964	Stan Getz and João Gilberto, *Getz/Gilberto*
Herb Alpert, "A Taste of Honey"	1965	Frank Sinatra, *September of My Years*
Frank Sinatra, "Strangers in the Night"	1966	Frank Sinatra, *A Man and His Music*
5th Dimension, "Up, Up and Away"	1967	The Beatles, *Sgt. Pepper's Lonely Hearts Club Band*
Simon and Garfunkel, "Mrs. Robinson"	1968	Glen Campbell, *By the Time I Get to Phoenix*
5th Dimension, "Aquarius/Let the Sunshine In"	1969	Blood, Sweat & Tears, *Blood, Sweat & Tears*
Simon and Garfunkel, "Bridge Over Troubled Water"	1970	Simon and Garfunkel, *Bridge Over Troubled Water*
Carole King, "It's Too Late"	1971	Carole King, *Tapestry*
Roberta Flack, "The First Time Ever I Saw Your Face"	1972	George Harrison and Friends, *The Concert for Bangla Desh*
Roberta Flack, "Killing Me Softly With His Song"	1973	Stevie Wonder, *Innervisions*
Olivia Newton-John, "I Honestly Love You"	1974	Stevie Wonder, *Fulfillingness' First Finale*
Captain & Tennille, "Love Will Keep Us Together"	1975	Paul Simon, *Still Crazy After All These Years*
George Benson, "This Masquerade"	1976	Stevie Wonder, *Songs in the Key of Life*
Eagles, "Hotel California"	1977	Fleetwood Mac, *Rumours*
Billy Joel, "Just the Way You Are"	1978	Bee Gees, *Saturday Night Fever*
The Doobie Brothers, "What a Fool Believes"	1979	Billy Joel, *52nd Street*
Christopher Cross, "Sailing"	1980	Christopher Cross, *Christopher Cross*
Kim Carnes, "Bette Davis Eyes"	1981	John Lennon and Yoko Ono, *Double Fantasy*
Toto, "Rosanna"	1982	Toto, *Toto IV*
Michael Jackson, "Beat It"	1983	Michael Jackson, *Thriller*
Tina Turner, "What's Love Got to Do With It"	1984	Lionel Richie, *Can't Slow Down*
USA for Africa, "We Are the World"	1985	Phil Collins, *No Jacket Required*
Steve Winwood, "Higher Love"	1986	Paul Simon, *Graceland*
Paul Simon, "Graceland"	1987	U2, *The Joshua Tree*
Bobby McFerrin, "Don't Worry, Be Happy"	1988	George Michael, *Faith*
Bette Midler, "Wind Beneath My Wings"	1989	Bonnie Raitt, *Nick of Time*
Phil Collins, "Another Day in Paradise"	1990	Quincy Jones, *Back on the Block*
Natalie Cole, with Nat "King" Cole, "Unforgettable"	1991	Natalie Cole, with Nat "King" Cole, *Unforgettable*
Eric Clapton, "Tears in Heaven"	1992	Eric Clapton, *Unplugged*
Whitney Houston, "I Will Always Love You"	1993	Whitney Houston, *The Bodyguard*
Sheryl Crow, "All I Wanna Do"	1994	Tony Bennett, *MTV Unplugged*
Seal, "Kiss From a Rose"	1995	Alanis Morissette, *Jagged Little Pill*
Eric Clapton, "Change the World"	1996	Celine Dion, *Falling Into You*
Shawn Colvin, "Sunny Came Home"	1997	Bob Dylan, *Time Out of Mind*
Celine Dion, "My Heart Will Go On"	1998	Lauryn Hill, *The Miseducation of Lauryn Hill*
Santana feat. Rob Thomas, "Smooth"	1999	Santana, *Supernatural*
U2, "Beautiful Day"	2000	Steely Dan, *Two Against Nature*
U2, "Walk On"	2001	Various artists, *O Brother, Where Art Thou?*
Norah Jones, "Don't Know Why"	2002	Norah Jones, *Come Away With Me*
Coldplay, "Clocks"	2003	OutKast, *Speakerboxxx/The Love Below*
Ray Charles and Norah Jones, "Here We Go Again"	2004	Ray Charles and various artists, *Genius Loves Company*
Green Day, "Boulevard of Broken Dreams"	2005	U2, *How to Dismantle an Atomic Bomb*
Dixie Chicks, "Not Ready to Make Nice"	2006	Dixie Chicks, *Taking the Long Way*
Amy Winehouse, "Rehab"	2007	Herbie Hancock, *River: The Joni Letters*
Robert Plant and Alison Krauss, "Please Read the Letter"	2008	Robert Plant and Alison Krauss, *Raising Sand*
Kings of Leon, "Use Somebody"	2009	Taylor Swift, *Fearless*
Lady Antebellum, "Need You Now"	2010	Arcade Fire, *The Suburbs*
Adele, "Rolling in the Deep"	2011	Adele, *21*
Gotye, "Somebody That I Used to Know"	2012	Mumford & Sons, *Babel*
Daft Punk feat. Pharrell Williams and Nile Rodgers, "Get Lucky"	2013	Daft Punk, *Random Access Memories*
Sam Smith, "Stay With Me"	2014	Beck, *Morning Phase*
Mark Ronson feat. Bruno Mars, "Uptown Funk"	2015	Taylor Swift, *1989*
Adele, "Hello"	2016	Adele, *25*
Bruno Mars, "24K Magic"	2017	Bruno Mars, *24K Magic*
Childish Gambino, "This Is America"	2018	Kacey Musgraves, *Golden Hour*
Billie Eilish, "Bad Guy"	2019	Billie Eilish, *When We All Fall Asleep, Where Do We Go?*
Billie Eilish, "Everything I Wanted"	2020	Taylor Swift, *Folklore*
Silk Sonic, "Leave the Door Open"	2021	Jon Batiste, *We Are*
Lizzo, "About Damn Time"	2022	Harry Styles, *Harry's House*

MTV Video Music Awards, 2023

Video of the year: "Anti-Hero," Taylor Swift
Artist of the year: Taylor Swift
Song of the year: "Anti-Hero," Taylor Swift
Best new artist: Ice Spice
Best collaboration: "TQG," Karol G, Shakira
Push performance: "Sugar Rush Ride," Tomorrow X Together
Video for good: "Breakfast," Dove Cameron
Best Afrobeats: "Calm Down," Rema and Selena Gomez
Best alternative: "Candy Necklace," Lana Del Rey feat. Jon Batiste
Best hip-hop: "Super Freaky Girl" Nicki Minaj

Best K-pop: "S-Class," Stray Kids
Best Latin: "Funk Rave," Anitta
Best pop: "Anti-Hero," Taylor Swift
Best rock: "The Loneliest," Måneskin
Best R&B: "Shirt," SZA
Art direction: "Attention," Doja Cat
Choreography: "Pink Venom," BLACKPINK
Cinematography: "Anti-Hero," Taylor Swift
Direction: "Anti-Hero," Taylor Swift
Editing: "vampire," Olivia Rodrigo
Visual effects: "Anti-Hero," Taylor Swift

SCIENCE

Science and Technology News

The following were some of the developments in science and technology in the previous year, as of Sept. 2023.

Energy Efforts

The quest for new sources of relatively clean energy saw advances in two different approaches. One harnessed nuclear fusion—the same process that powers the sun and hydrogen bombs—by which the nuclei of atoms, under high pressure at high temperatures, are fused into heavier nuclei while releasing energy. In Dec. 2022, decades of research on controlled fusion finally yielded a major breakthrough, netting measurably more energy than was put into the fusion reaction. The Lawrence Livermore National Laboratory in California achieved the feat, heating a tiny fuel capsule with 192 laser beams totaling 2.05 megajoules (MJ, or million joules) of energy and releasing 3.15 MJ. Early results from another experiment in July 2023 indicated an even larger energy surplus. Much more development work was needed, however, before fusion can become a practical energy source.

Meanwhile, a team of engineering researchers at the Univ. of Massachusetts Amherst reported in the journal *Advanced Materials* in May 2023 that a broad range of materials could be used in thin films to make a device capable of continuously harvesting electricity from humidity in the air. Much of the same group had discovered in 2020 that tiny wires grown by a certain bacterium could extract electric energy from the air, and subsequently found that what they called the air-gen effect was more general: Nearly any material would do, as long as it contained nanopores having a diameter of less than 100 nanometers, or a thousandth of the width of a human hair. The nanopores "allow air water to pass through and undergo dynamic adsorption–desorption exchange at the porous interface, resulting in surface charging." A single thin film might produce only a small amount of electricity but stacking a large number could conceivably produce a practical device.

Fresh Mayan Finds

Archaeologists continued to make discoveries illuminating the achievements and complexity of the ancient Mayan civilization. A Dec. 2022 paper in *Ancient Mesoamerica* reported that laser scanning, or lidar (light detection and ranging), had enabled the discovery of nearly a thousand Maya settlement sites in a large area of northern Guatemala that had long been hidden by vegetation. The sites, occupied around 1000 BCE to 150 CE, were connected by causeways and canals. The paper's authors argued that "the development of infrastructure demonstrates the presence of complex societies with strong levels of socioeconomic organization and political power."

Mexico's National Institute of Anthropology and History announced in June 2023 that the ruins of a previously unknown Mayan city had been discovered in the Balamkú ecological reserve on the Yucatán Peninsula. The find was initiated by lidar scans, followed by ground exploration by a team led by Slovenian archaeologist Ivan Šprajc (sometimes dubbed a real-life Indiana Jones), who in a translated statement said the site "served as an important center at the regional level, probably during the Classic period (250-1000 AD)." The city's "monumental nucleus" covers more than 50 ha (124 acres) and includes pyramids up to 15 m (50 ft) high and a ball court. The archaeologists named the city Ocomtún (Yucatec Mayan for "stone column"), because of the many stone columns scattered about the area.

Smog and Art

Climate change researchers investigated the possible effects of atmospheric phenomena on creative art in past centuries. A paper published in *Proceedings of the National Academy of Sciences* (*PNAS*) in Jan. 2023 focused on works by painters Claude Monet (1840-1926) and J. M. W. Turner (1775-1851). The researchers analyzed changes in contrast, intensity, and visibility in works by Turner and then Monet over the course of the century and found a marked parallel with data on sulfur dioxide emissions. These artists' depictions of the sky often contained a haziness, a blurring or dulling of colors and edges. The Industrial Revolution of the 19th century in fact fostered a significant increase in atmospheric soot particles (mainly from the burning of coal). The soot absorbed and scattered sunlight—leading, when present in large quantities, to a hazy effect when a person gazed into the distance. The study's results do not mean that the rise of impressionism was "caused" by pollution. Rather, the researchers said their findings showed "that environmental change provided a creative impulse whereby the importance of lines and edges was diminished in favor of demarcating objects using color fields."

In short, "Impressionism—as developed in the works of Turner, Monet, and others—contains elements of polluted realism."

Baseball and Climate Change

When it comes to statistics, baseball leads the sports world, but meteorology also loves numbers. A rigorous statistical analysis of atmospheric and batting data in the May 2023 issue of the *Bulletin of the American Meteorological Society* provided solid evidence for a key factor in the increased number of home runs in Major League Baseball (MLB) in recent years: global warming.

Simple physics mandates that as air temperature rises, the air's density (and consequently air resistance) decreases. But myriad other factors might also play a role in home run output, such as increased use of analytic data by managers and trainers, players' use of steroids and other performance-enhancing drugs, and changes in ball characteristics that could affect air drag. The study's authors analyzed data from more than 100,000 MLB games between 1962 and 2019. They found that in the period from 2010 to 2019, human-caused climate change accounted for, on average, an extra 58 home runs per year. The authors noted that "each degree of global warming is associated with an additional ~95 home runs per baseball season."

Time Reflection

People usually think of the reflection of electromagnetic radiation (such as light) as something that occurs in three-dimensional space. But for more than half a century, scientists have theorized another kind of reflection: one that occurs not at a spatial interface, like a mirror, but a time interface. The phenomenon could presumably occur when the entire medium in which a signal is traveling suddenly changes its properties. Scientists reported in the June 2023 issue of *Nature Physics* that they had found a way to achieve such an abrupt and uniform change in a strip of specially designed "metamaterial" filled with switches linked to capacitors. Triggered simultaneously, the capacitors unloaded their charge, quickly changing the metamaterial's properties. That, in turn, caused signals traveling through the strip to be time reversed.

Further Evidence of Gravitational Waves

In June 2023, astronomers associated with the North American Nanohertz Observatory for Gravitational Waves (NANOGrav), in collaboration with other research groups worldwide, published evidence of extremely low-frequency gravitational waves in the online journal *Astrophysical Journal Letters*.

Gravitational waves, in accordance with Albert Einstein's general theory of relativity, are ripples generated in the fabric of spacetime by the acceleration of enormous masses. Observation of the waves can yield hints about their sources and the history of the universe. But detection is difficult. It involves observing tiny changes that occur in the distance between celestial objects as a wave passes by. The 2023 discovery involved waves of such low frequency—and thus of such an enormous wavelength—that they were likely generated by the motion of truly colossal objects, possibly supermassive black holes up to billions of light-years away. To detect the waves, researchers made use of numerous known pulsars, which are fast-rotating neutron stars that, as seen from Earth, periodically and with extreme punctuality emit electromagnetic signals. The displacement produced by a passing gravitational wave can alter the timing of a pulsar signal's reception by radio telescopes on Earth. NANOGrav's findings were based on analysis of more than 15 years of pulsar observations.

Splitting Phonons

A light beam can be thought of as consisting of waves, but also as tiny indivisible particles, called photons, that obey the laws of quantum mechanics. These laws, which underlie the behavior of quantum computers, allow, for example, a photon under certain conditions to appear to be in two places at once: they let a photon seem to be split in two. A beam of sound can, like that of light, be conceived of as indivisible quantum particles. These phonons, as they are called, arise from the collective motion of a multitude of atoms of the air through which the sound moves. In theory, phonons ought to also behave in a quantum mechanical way, rather like photons. Proof of this, however, has been hard to come by—until now. An article in the June 9, 2023, issue of the journal *Science* reported on the successful creation of a beam splitter for individual phonons. The researchers found that phonons do indeed have key quantum mechanical properties—properties that may permit creating phonon-based devices for computer or communication systems that take advantage of extraordinary capabilities reminiscent of those promised for the photon-based quantum computers currently under development.

Science Glossary

This glossary covers some concepts that come up frequently in the news, in biology, chemistry, geology, and physics.

Biology

Amino acid: any of a group of organic molecules with a certain structure. About 20 are the building blocks of proteins.

Antibiotic: a substance produced by or derived from a bacterium, fungus, or other organism that battles infections and diseases caused by microorganisms, especially bacteria; it works by killing the microorganism or halting its growth.

Archaeon (plural, archaea): one of a group of single-celled microorganisms; archaea are prokaryotes, like bacteria, but they share some similarities with eukaryotes.

Autoimmunity: a condition in which an individual's immune system reacts against his or her own tissues; leads to diseases such as lupus, some forms of diabetes, inflammatory bowel disease, and rheumatoid arthritis.

Bacterium (plural, bacteria): one of a large, varied class of microscopic and simple, single-celled organisms. Bacteria live almost everywhere; some forms cause disease, while others are useful in digestion and other natural processes.

Biodiversity (biological diversity): richness of variety of life-forms—including plants, animals, and other types—in a given environment.

Cell: the smallest unit of life capable of living independently, or with other cells; usually bounded by a membrane. May include a nucleus and other specialized parts.

Cholesterol: a fatty substance in animal tissues. It is produced by the liver in humans; is found in foods such as butter, eggs, and meat; and is an essential body constituent.

Chromosome: one of the rod-like structures in cell nuclei that carry genetic material (DNA).

Cloning: the process of copying a particular piece of DNA to allow it to be sequenced, studied, or used in some other way; can also refer to producing a genetic copy of an organism.

CRISPR (Clustered Regularly Interspaced Short Palindromic Repeats): a segment of DNA in prokaryotes that helps defend against virus attacks; it contains short genetic sequences that, coupled with a special enzyme, permit recognition and cleavage of like sequences in invading viruses. Term is also applied to a technology based on this approach that provides relatively precise targeting of specific bits of genetic code for such purposes as genetic modification or diagnosis.

DNA (deoxyribonucleic acid): a usually double-stranded molecule that carries genetic information, which determines the form and functioning of all known living things.

Ecosystem: an interdependent community of living organisms and their climatic and geographical habitat.

Enzyme: a protein that promotes a particular chemical reaction in the body.

Estrogen: one of a group of hormones that promote development of female secondary sex characteristics and the growth and health of the female reproductive system; males also produce small amounts of estrogen.

Eukaryote: any of the group of single- or multi-celled organisms whose cells have distinct nuclei.

Evolution: the process of gradual change that can occur in a species as it adapts to its environment; natural selection is the process by which evolution occurs.

Gene: a portion of a DNA molecule that provides the blueprint for the assembly of a protein.

Gene pool: the collection and total diversity of genes in an interbreeding population.

Gene therapy: a treatment in which scientists try to implant functioning genes into a person's cells so the genes can produce proteins that the person lacks or that help the person fight disease.

Genetic sequencing: the process of finding the order of subunits in a gene or the order of all an organism's genes.

Genome: the complete set of an organism's genetic material.

Hormone: a substance secreted in one part of an organism that regulates the functioning of other tissues or organs.

Meiosis: the process of cell division that results in gametes (sperm or egg cells), all of which contain half the number of chromosomes as their precursor.

Metabolism: the sum total of the body's chemical processes providing energy for vital functions and enabling new material to be synthesized.

Mitosis: the process by which a cell divides its nucleus and other cell materials into two duplicate daughter cells with the same DNA.

Neuron or **nerve cell:** any of the cells in the nervous system that send electrical and chemical messages to other cells.

Nucleus (plural, nuclei): the center of an atom; or the portion of a eukaryotic cell that contains most of the cell's genetic material. (In most eukaryotic cells, some DNA is also found in the cell's "powerhouses"—tiny components called **mitochondria** that lie outside the nucleus and supply chemical energy.)

Organism: a living entity, capable of growth, metabolism, and usually reproduction.

Phenotype: the observable properties and characteristics of an organism arising at least in part from its genetic makeup.

Pheromone: a chemical secreted by an organism to influence the behavior of other members of its species.

Placebo effect: a phenomenon in which patients show an improvement in their condition after taking a medically inactive substance, called a placebo.

Prokaryote: a single-celled organism that does not have a distinct nucleus, such as a bacterium or archaeon.

Protein: a complex molecule made up of one or more chains of amino acids; essential to the structure and function of all cells.

RNA (ribonucleic acid): a complex molecule similar to the genetic material DNA but usually single-stranded; several forms of RNA translate the genetic code of DNA and use that code to assemble proteins for structural and biological functions in the body. RNA also serves as the genetic material of some viruses.

Species: a population of organisms that breed with each other in nature and produce fertile offspring; other definitions of species exist to accommodate the diversity of life on Earth.

Stem cell: a cell that can develop into other types of cells; for instance, stem cells in bone marrow can differentiate into different types of blood cells.

Steroid: a type of chemical substance with a certain molecular structure. Some steroids are hormones that can suppress immune response or influence stress reaction, blood pressure, or sexual development.

Testosterone: a steroid hormone that stimulates the development and maintenance of male sexual characteristics and the production of sperm; women also produce small amounts of testosterone.

Virus: a microscopic, often disease-causing, agent made of genetic material surrounded by a protein shell; can only reproduce inside a living cell. There also exist "subviral" infectious agents, such as **viroids** (which consist of a short, circular strand of RNA without a protein coat) and **prions** (consisting of protein material).

Chemistry

Acid: a class of compounds that contrasts with bases. Acids taste sour, turn litmus red/pink, and often produce hydrogen gas in contact with some metals. Acids donate protons (hydrogen atoms minus the electron) in chemical reactions.

Base: a substance that yields hydroxyl ions (OH-) when dissolved in water; any of a class of compounds whose aqueous solutions taste bitter, feel slippery, turn litmus blue, and react with acids to form salts; also known as **alkaline**.

Carbon fiber: an extremely strong, thin fiber made by pyrolyzing (decomposing by heat) synthetic fibers, such as rayon, until charred; used to make high-strength composites.

Chlorofluorocarbon (CFC): one of a group of industrial chemicals that contain chlorine, fluorine, and carbon and can damage Earth's ozone layer.

Element: a substance that cannot be chemically decomposed into simpler substances; all the atoms of an element have the same number of protons.

Isotope: an atom of a chemical element with the same number of protons in its nucleus as other atoms of that element, but with a different number of neutrons.

Molecule: the basic unit of a chemical compound, composed of two or more atoms bound together.

Noble gases or **inert gases:** a group of gases including helium, neon, argon, krypton, xenon, and radon that are not reactive except in rare and limited instances.

Osmosis: the transfer of a fluid across a semipermeable membrane, usually from an area of higher concentration to one of lower concentration.

Polymer: a huge molecule containing hundreds or thousands of smaller molecules arranged in repeating units.

Salt: a neutral compound produced by the reaction of an acid and a base.

Geology

Anthropocene: a proposed epoch of geologic time marked by a significant influence of human activity on the environment. Suggested starting points include the mid-20th century (when extensive testing of nuclear and thermonuclear bombs began) and the Industrial Revolution of the 19th century.

Fault, tectonic: a crack or break in Earth's crust, often due to the slippage of tectonic plates past or over one another; usually geologically unstable.

Igneous: a type of rock formed by solidification from a molten state, especially from molten magma.

Magma: hot liquid rock material under Earth's surface, from which igneous rock is formed by cooling.

Metamorphic: in geology, the name given to rocks or minerals that have recrystallized under the influence of heat and pressure since their original formation.

Pangaea: a single supercontinent that scientists believe began to break apart at least 200 mil years ago to form the current continents.

Plate tectonics: theory that Earth's lithosphere—the uppermost layer that includes the crust—is made up of many separate rigid plates of rock that float on top of hot semi-liquid rock.

Sedimentary: a type of rock formed by the buildup of material at the bottoms of bodies of water.

Physics

Absolute zero: the theoretical temperature at which all motion within a molecule stops, corresponding to $-273.15°C$ ($-459.67°F$).

Antimatter: matter that consists of antiparticles, such as antiprotons, that have an opposite charge from normal particles; when matter meets antimatter, both are destroyed, and their combined mass is converted to energy. Antimatter is created in certain radioactive decay processes but appears to be present in only small amounts in the universe.

Atom: the basic unit of a chemical element.

Atomic mass: the total mass of an atom of a given element; atoms of the same element with different atomic masses (different numbers of neutrons but not protons) are called **isotopes**.

Atomic number: the number of protons in an atom of a given element of the periodic table; the characteristic that sets atoms of different elements apart.

Axion: a hypothetical subatomic particle with low mass and energy that has been proposed to exist because of the properties of the strong nuclear force. Axions have been suggested as a candidate for dark matter and also as a possible explanation for the imbalance between matter and antimatter in the universe.

Bose-Einstein condensate (BEC): a "super-atom" comprising thousands of atoms super-cooled to within a few hundred millionths of a degree of absolute zero and thus condensed into the lowest energy state. Atoms bound in the BEC behave synchronously, giving the BEC wavelike properties.

Boson: one of the two primary categories of particles in the Standard Model; bosons include the Higgs boson and force-carrying particles such as photons, gluons, and the W and Z particles.

Dark energy: a mysterious, undefined energy leading to a repulsive force pervading all of space-time; proposed by cosmologists as counteracting gravity and accelerating the expansion of the universe; predicted to make up 68.3% of the universe's composition.

Dark matter: hypothetical, invisible matter that some scientists believe makes up 26.8% of the universe (dark matter and ordinary matter together make up 31.7% of the universe). Its existence was proposed to account for otherwise inexplicable gravitational forces observed in space.

Doppler effect: a change in the frequency of sound, light, or radio waves caused by the motion of the source emitting the waves or the motion of the person or instrument perceiving the waves.

Electron: negatively charged particle that (along with its positively charged counterpart, the **positron**) is the least massive electrically charged fundamental particle; one of six **leptons**.

Energy: capacity to perform work. Energy can take various forms, such as potential energy, kinetic energy, and chemical energy.

Entropy: a measure of disorder in a system.

Fermion: any one of a number of matter particles including electrons, protons, neutrons, neutrinos, leptons, and quarks; one of the two primary categories of particles in the Standard Model, the other being bosons.

Field: the existence of physical effects such as forces (gravitational, electric, etc.) is visualized and described mathematically by physicists in terms of fields, which show the strength and direction of a force at a given position.

Fission: a nuclear reaction that occurs when the nuclei of large, unstable atoms break apart, releasing large amounts of energy.

Fluorescence: luminescence that is caused by the absorption of radiation at one wavelength followed by an almost immediate re-radiation, usually at a different wavelength, that stops almost immediately when the causative radiation stops.

Force: in classical physics, something that causes acceleration in a body; can be thought of as a push or pull.

Fusion: a nuclear reaction occurring when light atomic nuclei collide at high temperatures and combine to form one heavier atomic nucleus, releasing a large amount of energy along with, possibly, a subatomic particle in the process.

Gravity: an attractive force between any two objects or particles, proportional to the mass (or energy) of the objects; strength of the force decreases with greater distance; the only fundamental force still unaccounted for by the Standard Model.

Half-life: the time it takes for half of a given amount of a radioactive element to decay.

Hertz (Hz): a measure of frequency, or how many times a given event occurs per second; applied to sound waves, electrical current, and microchip clock speeds.

Higgs boson: a boson associated with a field accounting for the existence of mass in many particles.

Laser: light consisting of a cascade of photons all having the same wavelength; stands for Light Amplification by Stimulated Emission of Radiation.

Light-emitting diode (LED): a semiconductor that emits light when an electrical current is passed through it. The color of the light depends on the material used in making the diode.

Neutrino: a tiny fundamental particle, classed as a fermion, with no electrical charge and very small mass. Neutrinos move very quickly through the universe; they come in three varieties, or flavors, called electron, muon, and tau.

Neutron: a neutral particle, made up of quarks, found in the nuclei of atoms (except the most common isotope of hydrogen).

Particle accelerator: a machine that accelerates charged particles to extremely high speeds around a circular track or along a straight line. Accelerators are used in scientific research, manufacturing, and medical diagnosis and therapy. Those used to study fundamental physics can be enormous—the Large Hadron Collider in Switzerland has a circumference of 16.8 mi (27 km).

Phosphorescence: luminescence that is caused by the absorption of radiation at one wavelength followed by a delayed re-radiation, usually at a different wavelength, that continues for a time after the causative radiation stops.

Photon: the elementary unit, or quantum, of electromagnetic radiation, such as light. It has no mass or electrical charge and is one of the fundamental force-carrying particles described by the Standard Model.

Plasma: a high-energy state of matter different from solid, liquid, or gas in which atomic nuclei and the electrons orbiting them separate from each other.

Proton: a positively charged subatomic particle, made up of quarks, found in the nuclei of atoms.

Quantum: a natural unit of some physically measurable property, such as energy or electrical charge.

Quark: a fundamental matter particle classed as a fermion; there are six different varieties, or flavors, of quarks grouped in pairs: up and down, charm and strange, top and bottom. Each flavor has a corresponding antiquark. Quarks combine to form such particles as neutrons and protons. Quark-antiquark combinations form the composite particles known as **mesons**.

Radiation: energy emitted as rays or particles. Radiation includes heat, light, ultraviolet rays, gamma rays, X-rays, cosmic rays, alpha particles, and beta particles.

Relativity, general theory of: a theory of space-time proposed by Albert Einstein in 1915; it links gravity to the curvature of space-time.

Relativity, special theory of: Albert Einstein's theory of space and time: all laws of physics are valid in all uniformly moving frames of reference, and the speed of light in a vacuum is always the same, so long as the source and the observer are moving uniformly (not accelerating).

Standard Model: prevailing theory of the interaction of subatomic particles. Particles are either fermions—such as electrons, neutrinos, and quarks—or bosons—such as Higgs bosons, gluons, W or Z bosons, and photons. The theory successfully explains three of the four elementary forces acting on particles (strong, weak, electromagnetic) but thus far has not incorporated gravity.

String theory: a theory that seeks to unify quantum mechanics and general relativity, positing that the basic constituents of matter can best be understood not as pointlike particles but as tiny oscillating "strings."

Subatomic particle: a particle smaller than an atom; three important types—proton, neutron, and electron—are found in most atoms.

Superconductivity: the property of certain materials, usually metals and chemically complex ceramics, to conduct electricity without resistance, generally at very cold temperatures.

Thermodynamics: the branch of physics studying the flow and transformation of heat and other forms of energy, often with a focus on temperature.

Ultraviolet radiation: a form of light, invisible to the human eye, that has a shorter wavelength and greater energy than visible light but a longer wavelength and less energy than X-rays.

Virtual particle: subatomic particles that rapidly pop into and out of existence and can exert real forces; usually occur in particle-antiparticle pairs and are rapidly annihilated.

Mohs Scale of Hardness

Hardness is the ability of a solid substance to resist abrasion or deformation on its surface. Soft minerals scratch more easily than hard ones. For example, a diamond will scratch graphite because graphite is softer. In 1812, German mineralogist Friedrich Mohs (1773-1839) created the arbitrary scale shown below to measure relative hardness using 10 minerals that were readily available at that time. The numbers in the Mohs scale are arranged in order of increasing hardness. An item's hardness is obtained by determining which mineral in the Mohs scale can scratch it.

Mohs scale		**Selected items and their relative hardness**	
1 . . . . . . Talc	6 . . . . . Orthoclase feldspar	2.5 . . . . . .Fingernail	5.5 . . . . .Steel knife blade
2 . . . . . . Gypsum	7 . . . . . Quartz	2.5-3 . . . .Gold, silver	6-7 . . . . .Glass
3 . . . . . . Calcite	8 . . . . . Topaz	3 . . . . . .Copper penny	6.5 . . . . .Iron pyrite
4 . . . . . . Fluorite	9 . . . . . Corundum	4-4.5 . . . . .Platinum	7+. . . . . .Hardened steel file
5 . . . . . . Apatite	10 . . . . . Diamond	4-5 . . . . . .Iron	

Chemical Elements, Atomic Numbers, Year Discovered

Source: International Union of Pure and Applied Chemistry (IUPAC)
See Periodic Table of the Elements on the following page for atomic weights.

Element	Symbol	Atomic number	Year discov.	Element	Symbol	Atomic number	Year discov.	Element	Symbol	Atomic number	Year discov.
Actinium	Ac	89	1899	Gold	Au	79	BCE	Potassium	K	19	1807
Aluminum	Al	13	1825	Hafnium	Hf	72	1923	Praseodymium	Pr	59	1885
Americium	Am	95	1944	Hassium	Hs	108	1984	Promethium	Pm	61	1945
Antimony	Sb	51	1450	Helium	He	2	1868	Protactinium	Pa	91	1917
Argon	Ar	18	1894	Holmium	Ho	67	1878	Radium	Ra	88	1898
Arsenic	As	33	13th cent.	Hydrogen	H	1	1766	Radon	Rn	86	1900
Astatine	At	85	1940	Indium	In	49	1863	Rhenium	Re	75	1925
Barium	Ba	56	1808	Iodine	I	53	1811	Rhodium	Rh	45	1803
Berkelium	Bk	97	1949	Iridium	Ir	77	1804	Roentgenium	Rg	111	1995
Beryllium	Be	4	1798	Iron	Fe	26	BCE	Rubidium	Rb	37	1861
Bismuth	Bi	83	15th cent.	Krypton	Kr	36	1898	Ruthenium	Ru	44	1845
Bohrium	Bh	107	1981	Lanthanum	La	57	1839	Rutherfordium	Rf	104	1969
Boron	B	5	1808	Lawrencium	Lr	103	1961	Samarium	Sm	62	1879
Bromine	Br	35	1826	Lead	Pb	82	BCE	Scandium	Sc	21	1879
Cadmium	Cd	48	1817	Lithium	Li	3	1817	Seaborgium	Sg	106	1974
Calcium	Ca	20	1808	Livermorium	Lv	116	2000	Selenium	Se	34	1817
Californium	Cf	98	1950	Lutetium	Lu	71	1907	Silicon	Si	14	1823
Carbon	C	6	BCE	Magnesium	Mg	12	1829	Silver	Ag	47	BCE
Cerium	Ce	58	1803	Manganese	Mn	25	1774	Sodium	Na	11	1807
Cesium	Cs	55	1860	Meitnerium	Mt	109	1982	Strontium	Sr	38	1790
Chlorine	Cl	17	1774	Mendelevium	Md	101	1955	Sulfur	S	16	BCE
Chromium	Cr	24	1797	Mercury	Hg	80	BCE	Tantalum	Ta	73	1802
Cobalt	Co	27	1735	Molybdenum	Mo	42	1782	Technetium	Tc	43	1937
Copernicium	Cn	112	1996	Moscovium	Mc	115	2004	Tellurium	Te	52	1782
Copper	Cu	29	BCE	Neodymium	Nd	60	1885	Tennessine	Ts	117	2010
Curium	Cm	96	1944	Neon	Ne	10	1898	Terbium	Tb	65	1843
Darmstadtium	Ds	110	1995	Neptunium	Np	93	1940	Thallium	Tl	81	1861
Dubnium (Hahnium)[1]	Db (Ha)	105	1970	Nickel	Ni	28	1751	Thorium	Th	90	1828
Dysprosium	Dy	66	1886	Nihonium	Nh	113	2004	Thulium	Tm	69	1879
Einsteinium	Es	99	1952	Niobium[2]	Nb	41	1801	Tin	Sn	50	BCE
Erbium	Er	68	1843	Nitrogen	N	7	1772	Titanium	Ti	22	1791
Europium	Eu	63	1901	Nobelium	No	102	1958	Tungsten (Wolfram)	W	74	1783
Fermium	Fm	100	1953	Oganesson	Og	118	2006	Uranium	U	92	1789
Flerovium	Fl	114	1999	Osmium	Os	76	1804	Vanadium	V	23	1830
Fluorine	F	9	1771	Oxygen	O	8	1774	Xenon	Xe	54	1898
Francium	Fr	87	1939	Palladium	Pd	46	1803	Ytterbium	Yb	70	1878
Gadolinium	Gd	64	1886	Phosphorus	P	15	1669	Yttrium	Y	39	1794
Gallium	Ga	31	1875	Platinum	Pt	78	1735	Zinc	Zn	30	BCE
Germanium	Ge	32	1886	Plutonium	Pu	94	1941	Zirconium	Zr	40	1789
				Polonium	Po	84	1898				

(1) The name Dubnium (Db) was approved by IUPAC for element 105, but the name Hahnium (Ha) was used in most of the scientific literature before 1998 and is still sometimes used in the U.S. (2) Formerly Columbium.

Periodic Table of the Elements

Source: Los Alamos National Laboratory Division; International Union of Pure and Applied Chemistry (IUPAC)

Shaded elements are commonly regarded as metals.

Legend:
- atomic number
- atomic weight[1]
- symbol
- name

Example:
14 — atomic number
28.08-28.09[— atomic weight[1]
Si — symbol
Silicon — name

1 1.008 **H** Hydrogen																	2 4.003 **He** Helium
3 6.938-6.997[**Li** Lithium	4 9.012 **Be** Beryllium											5 10.81-10.82 **B** Boron	6 12.017 **C** Carbon	7 14.01 **N** Nitrogen	8 16.00 **O** Oxygen	9 19.00 **F** Fluorine	10 20.18 **Ne** Neon
11 22.99 **Na** Sodium	12 24.30-24.31 **Mg** Magnesium											13 26.98 **Al** Aluminum	14 28.08-28.09[**Si** Silicon	15 30.97 **P** Phosphorus	16 32.06-32.08 **S** Sulfur	17 35.45-35.46 **Cl** Chlorine	18 39.79-39.96 **Ar** Argon
19 39.10 **K** Potassium	20 40.08 **Ca** Calcium	21 44.96 **Sc** Scandium	22 47.87 **Ti** Titanium	23 50.94 **V** Vanadium	24 52.00 **Cr** Chromium	25 54.94 **Mn** Manganese	26 55.85 **Fe** Iron	27 58.93 **Co** Cobalt	28 58.69 **Ni** Nickel	29 63.55 **Cu** Copper	30 65.38 **Zn** Zinc	31 69.72 **Ga** Gallium	32 72.63 **Ge** Germanium	33 74.92 **As** Arsenic	34 78.97 **Se** Selenium	35 79.90-79.91 **Br** Bromine	36 83.80 **Kr** Krypton
37 85.47 **Rb** Rubidium	38 87.62 **Sr** Strontium	39 88.91 **Y** Yttrium	40 91.22 **Zr** Zirconium	41 92.91 **Nb** Niobium	42 95.95 **Mo** Molybdenum	43 [98][**Tc** Technetium	44 101.1 **Ru** Ruthenium	45 102.9 **Rh** Rhodium	46 106.4 **Pd** Palladium	47 107.9 **Ag** Silver	48 112.4 **Cd** Cadmium	49 114.8 **In** Indium	50 118.7 **Sn** Tin	51 121.8 **Sb** Antimony	52 127.6 **Te** Tellurium	53 126.9 **I** Iodine	54 131.3 **Xe** Xenon
55 132.9 **Cs** Cesium	56 137.3 **Ba** Barium	57-71 Lanthanoids	72 178.5 **Hf** Hafnium	73 180.95 **Ta** Tantalum	74 183.8 **W** Tungsten	75 186.2 **Re** Rhenium	76 190.2 **Os** Osmium	77 192.2 **Ir** Iridium	78 195.1 **Pt** Platinum	79 197.0 **Au** Gold	80 200.6 **Hg** Mercury	81 204.4 **Tl** Thallium	82 206.14-207.94 **Pb** Lead	83 209.0[**Bi** Bismuth	84 [209][**Po** Polonium	85 [210][**At** Astatine	86 [222][**Rn** Radon
87 [223][**Fr** Francium	88 [226][**Ra** Radium	89-103 Actinoids	104 [265][**Rf** Rutherfordium	105 [270][**Db** Dubnium	106 [269][**Sg** Seaborgium	107 [270][**Bh** Bohrium	108 [270][**Hs** Hassium	109 [278][**Mt** Meitnerium	110 [281][**Ds** Darmstadtium	111 [281][**Rg** Roentgenium	112 [285][**Cn** Copernicium	113 [286][**Nh** Nihonium	114 [289][**Fl** Flerovium	115 [289][**Mc** Moscovium	116 [293][**Lv** Livermorium	117 [293][**Ts** Tennessine	118 [294][**Og** Oganesson

Lanthanoid series

57 138.9 **La** Lanthanum	58 140.1 **Ce** Cerium	59 140.9 **Pr** Praseodymium	60 144.2 **Nd** Neodymium	61 [145][**Pm** Promethium	62 150.4 **Sm** Samarium	63 152.0 **Eu** Europium	64 157.3 **Gd** Gadolinium	65 158.9 **Tb** Terbium	66 162.5 **Dy** Dysprosium	67 164.9 **Ho** Holmium	68 167.3 **Er** Erbium	69 168.9 **Tm** Thulium	70 173.1 **Yb** Ytterbium	71 175.0 **Lu** Lutetium

Actinoid series

89 [227][**Ac** Actinium	90 232.0[**Th** Thorium	91 231.0[**Pa** Protactinium	92 238.0[**U** Uranium	93 [237][**Np** Neptunium	94 [244][**Pu** Plutonium	95 [243][**Am** Americium	96 [247][**Cm** Curium	97 [247][**Bk** Berkelium	98 [251][**Cf** Californium	99 [252][**Es** Einsteinium	100 [257][**Fm** Fermium	101 [258][**Md** Mendelevium	102 [259][**No** Nobelium	103 [262][**Lr** Lawrencium

Note: Atomic weight shown is a weighted average of the atomic masses of normally found isotopes. * = Element has no stable nuclides. A value enclosed in brackets, e.g. [209], indicates the mass number of the longest-lived isotope of the element. However, four such elements (Bi, Th, Pa, and U) do have a characteristic terrestrial isotopic composition, and for these an atomic weight is tabulated. (1) For elements having two or more stable isotopes with a notable variation in atomic-weight values, a range is shown.

Basic Laws of Physics

Newton's Laws of Motion

1. An object in motion moves at a constant velocity in a straight line unless acted upon by a force. Likewise, an object at rest will stay at rest. These two properties are known as inertia.

2. The acceleration of an object is proportional to the force acting on it and inversely proportional to the mass of the object. Force (F) equals mass (m) times acceleration (a):

$$F = ma$$

3. For every action, there is an equal and opposite reaction. For example, if a force of one ton pushes down on an object, the object pushes up with an equal force. As per the second law, the amount of movement (acceleration) produced in the object will depend on the object's mass.

Law of Gravity

In common usage, gravity refers to the gravitational force between planets and objects on or near them. But in scientific parlance, gravitation is one of four basic forces controlling the interactions of matter. (The others are the strong and weak forces, which act on the subatomic level, and the electromagnetic force.) The gravitational force (F) between objects is proportional to the product of their masses (m_1 and m_2) and inversely proportional to the square of the distance (d) between them. G represents the gravitational constant in Newton's law of gravity, a fixed ratio of approximately 6.67408×10^{-11} newton m^2/kg^2.

The basic law of gravity is:

$$F = G\,\frac{m_1 m_2}{d^2}$$

Near Earth's surface, Earth's gravitational force pulls objects downward at a constant acceleration of 9.8 m/s^2 (g). This allows calculation of the vertical velocity (v) of an object with an initial vertical velocity of v_0 in free fall at a given point in time (t) and calculation of the distance (d) of an object from Earth at any given time with a given initial velocity (v_0) and a known initial height (a) via the following equations (here, the effects of air resistance are ignored, and downward velocities and directions are negative):

$$v = v_0 - gt$$

$$d = -\tfrac{1}{2}g(t^2) + v_0 t + a$$

Assuming that height is measured in feet and speeds in feet per second, the maximum height (H) reached by an object with a positive (upward) initial velocity is expressed as:

$$H = a + \frac{v_0^2}{64}$$

For motion not near Earth's surface, more complicated equations are required. Also, if the object's upward velocity is very great, the object may escape Earth's gravity. Even near Earth's surface, there are slight complications. Gravity is lessened by the centrifugal force of the Earth's rotation. At the poles, where centrifugal force is absent, acceleration due to gravity is greater.

Gravity is weaker on a mountaintop than at sea level because the mountaintop is farther from Earth's center.

Conservation Laws

In physics, laws of conservation state that in a closed system, where neither mass nor energy is added or subtracted, certain measurable quantities remain constant.

Conservation of Mass: Mass is neither created nor destroyed within a closed system except when converted from or to energy.

Conservation of Momentum: All moving objects have momentum, and in a closed system, total momentum is always conserved. Linear momentum is the product of the mass of an object and its velocity. In the following equation, M and V represent the initial total mass and velocity of objects within a closed system. After a collision between those objects, the mass and velocity of individual objects may change (for example, one object breaks into smaller pieces, each traveling at a different velocity), but the product of the total mass and velocity in the system after the collision (mv) will remain the same.

$$MV = mv$$

Any object moving in a circle has another kind of momentum—angular momentum. This is because circular motion requires acceleration toward the center of the circle. The amount of acceleration depends on the speed of the object and the square of the radius of the circle. (Angular momentum is the product of this speed, the mass of the object, and the square of the radius.)

Conservation of Energy: The total amount of energy in a closed system will not change except when converted from or to mass.

Conservation of Mass-Energy: Although mass and energy can be converted into one another, the total amount of mass and energy together must be conserved. This is reflected in Einstein's famous equation, where m is mass, E is energy, and c is the speed of light in a vacuum (which is constant):

$$E = mc^2$$

Relativistic mass can describe how mass increases with velocity. The following equation—where m is the mass of a moving object, m_0 is the object's mass when not moving, v is the object's velocity in relation to a stationary observer, and c is the speed of light—shows the relationship:

$$m = \frac{m_0}{\sqrt{1 - \dfrac{v^2}{c^2}}}$$

The theory that no object can travel faster than the speed of light is based in this equation. As an object approaches c, so much energy is converted to mass that it no longer accelerates.

Laws of Thermodynamics

1. Heat is a form of energy. Within a closed system energy must be conserved except in nuclear reactions or other extreme conditions. It is neither created nor destroyed.

2. Within a self-sustaining system, heat can never go from an area of low temperature to an area of high temperature, for that would require added energy. Without added energy, disorder, or entropy, can only increase.

3. Absolute zero cannot be attained by any procedure in a finite number of steps. Although it can be approached asymptotically, it can never be reached.

Laws of Current Electricity

Electric current generally represents the flow of electrons through a conductor. The rate at which electrons flow can be measured in amperes, defined as the number of electrons (measured in a unit called the coulomb, equal to about 6.24 quintillion or 6.24×10^{18} electrons) moving past a particular point every second. One ampere is equal to 1 coulomb of charge passing each second. Like water, electrons tend to move from areas of high pressure to low pressure. The difference between these two pressures, known as potential difference, is measured in volts.

Certain substances, such as copper and carbon, allow electric currents to pass more readily than others—that is, they have greater conductivity. Resistance to conductivity is measured in ohms.

Ohm's Law: Electric current is directly proportional to the potential difference and inversely proportional to the total resistance of the circuit. I is electric current (measured in amperes), V is the potential difference (measured in volts), and R is resistance (measured in ohms):

$$I = \frac{V}{R}$$

Law of Electric Power: Electric power (P), measured in watts, represents the rate at which electricity is converted into some other form of energy (such as light, in the case of a lightbulb). For a direct-current circuit, P is the product of current and potential difference:

$$P = IV$$

Two Basic Laws of Quantum Physics

1. Heisenberg's uncertainty principle: Certain pairs of observable quantities like energy and time or position and momentum cannot be measured with complete accuracy simultaneously. Also known as the indeterminacy principle.

2. Pauli's exclusion principle: Two electrons in an atom cannot simultaneously occupy the same quantum or energy state. This has since been shown to be true also for other types of the subatomic particles known as fermions.

Breaking the Sound Barrier; Speed of Sound

The prefix **Mach** is used to describe supersonic speed. It was named for Ernst Mach (1838-1916), a Czech-born Austrian physicist. Mach may be defined as the ratio of the velocity of an object to the velocity of sound in a particular medium. A plane moving at the speed of sound moves at Mach 1. At twice the speed of sound, it moves at Mach 2.

When a plane passes the sound barrier—that is, flies faster than the speed at which sound travels—people in the area, though not the people on the plane, hear what seem to be thunderclaps. These sounds are sometimes called sonic booms.

Sound is produced by vibrations of an object. It is transmitted by the alternating increase and decrease in pressure that radiates outward from a source through a material medium of molecules, like waves spreading out on a pond after a rock has been tossed in.

The **frequency of sound** is determined by the number of times the vibrating waves undulate per second. It is measured in cycles per second. The slower the cycle of waves, the lower the frequency. As the frequency increases, the sound becomes higher in pitch. The human ear is sensitive to frequencies between 20 and 20,000 vibrations per second, although this range varies among individuals and decreases with age.

Intensity, or loudness, is the strength of the pressure of these radiating waves and is measured in decibels (dB).

The **speed of sound** varies depending on temperature and the medium through which it travels. It moves faster in water than in air, for example. At sea level and a temperature of 59°F (15°C), the speed of sound is approximately 761 mph, or 1,100 ft per sec.

Light and Colors of the Spectrum

Light, a form of electromagnetic radiation similar to radiant heat, radio waves, and X-rays, is emitted from a source in straight lines and spreads in area as it travels. For emission from a point source, light per unit area diminishes in proportion to the square of the distance.

The English mathematician and physicist Isaac Newton (1642-1727) described light as an **emission of particles**; the Dutch astronomer, mathematician, and physicist Christiaan Huygens (1629-95) and others developed the theory that light travels in a **wave motion**. It is now believed that these two theories are essentially complementary. The development of quantum theory has led to results where light acts like a series of particles in some experiments and like a wave in others.

The first relatively accurate measurement of the **speed of light** was made by French physicist Armand Hippolyte Louis Fizeau (1819-96). Today the speed of light is known precisely as 299,792.458 km per sec (or 186,282.397 mi/sec) in a vacuum. In water the speed of light is about 25% less, and in glass, 33% less.

Color sensations are produced through the excitation of the retina of the eye by light vibrating at different frequencies. The different colors of the visible spectrum may be seen by viewing light refracted by passage through a prism, which separates light into its component wavelengths.

Customarily, the basic colors are taken to be the six monochromatic (single) colors that occupy relatively large areas of the spectrum: red, orange, yellow, green, blue, and violet. So-called primary colors can be combined to produce the sensation of other colors. However, scientists disagree about how many and what primary colors to recognize. The color sensation of **black** is due to complete lack of stimulation of the retina, that of **white** to complete stimulation.

Infrared and **ultraviolet rays**, which are below the red (long) end and above the violet (short) end of the visible spectrum, respectively, are invisible to the naked human eye. Heat is the principal effect of infrared rays, and chemical action that of ultraviolet rays. Some animals can see infrared or ultraviolet light.

Life Cycles of Selected Animals

Information reviewed by Ronald M. Nowak, author of *Walker's Mammals of the World* (6th ed., Johns Hopkins University Press, 1999). Average longevity figures supplied by Ronald T. Reuther. These apply to animals in captivity; the potential life span of animals is rarely attained in nature. Figures on gestation and incubation are averages based on estimates.

Animal	Gestation (days)	Average longevity (yrs.)	Maximum longevity (yrs.-mos.)	Animal	Gestation (days)	Average longevity (yrs.)	Maximum longevity (yrs.-mos.)
Ass	365	12	47	Leopard	98	12	23
Baboon	187	20	45	Lion	100	15	30
Bear (black)	219	18	36-10	Monkey (rhesus)	166	15	37
Bear (grizzly)	225	25	50	Moose	240	12	27
Bear (polar)	240	20	45	Mouse (domestic white)	19	3	6
Beaver	105	5	50	Mouse (meadow)	21	3	4
Bison	285	15	40	Opossum (American)	13	1	5
Camel	406	12	50	Pig (domestic)	112	10	27
Cat (domestic)	63	12	38	Puma	90	12	20
Chimpanzee	230	20	60	Rabbit (domestic)	31	5	18-10
Chipmunk	31	6	10	Rhinoceros (black)	450	15	45-10
Cow	284	15	30	Rhinoceros (white)	480	20	50
Deer (white-tailed)	201	8	20	Sea lion (California)	350	12	34
Dog (domestic)	61	12	21	Sheep (domestic)	154	12	23
Elephant (African)	660	35	70	Squirrel (gray)	44	10	23-6
Elephant (Asian)	645	40	77	Tiger	105	16	26-3
Elk	250	15	26-8	Wolf (maned)	63	5	15-8
Fox (red)	52	7	14	Zebra (Grant's)	365	15	50
Giraffe	457	10	36-2				
Goat (domestic)	151	8	18	**Animal**			**Incubation time (days)**
Gorilla	258	20	54	Chicken			21
Guinea pig	68	4	8	Duck			30
Hippopotamus	238	41	61	Goose			30
Horse	330	20	50	Pigeon			18
Kangaroo (gray)	36	7	24	Turkey			26

Geologic Time Scale

Our understanding of Earth's ancient history is largely a result of geoscientists' study of climate, rock strata, ice samples, mineral deposits, and fossils from around the world; clues to the planet's origin have also been found through the study of extraterrestrial bodies. Geologists divide Earth's history into the following units (MYA = million years ago):

PRECAMBRIAN TIME (4,600-541 MYA)

HADEAN EON (4,600-4,000 MYA) Earth initially has no continents, oceans, or life; surface conditions are defined by intense volcanic activity and widespread meteorite impact. Oldest known minerals and rocks, many of meteoric origin, date to this eon, which may also have seen the first appearance of life.

ARCHEAN EON (4,000-2,500 MYA) Earth's surface cools and water vapor in atmosphere condenses to form early oceans, which define small protocontinents; there is substantial evidence for the existence of single-celled organisms, bacteria and archaea, in these oceans.

PROTEROZOIC EON (2,500-541 MYA) Protocontinents merge into larger landmasses as Earth's crust continues to shift. Atmospheric oxygen levels increase, and first known multicellular life appears. Later, soft-bodied marine animals emerge.

PHANEROZOIC EON (541 MYA-present)

Paleozoic Era (541-252 MYA)

Cambrian Period (541-485 MYA). The supercontinent known as Gondwana, or Gondwanaland, dominates the Southern Hemisphere. Seas experience an explosion of invertebrate animal life, including thousands of species of trilobites; the first known vertebrates appear. There is no life on land.

Ordovician Period (485-444 MYA). Gondwanaland extends from South Pole to tropic regions; Northern Hemisphere is mostly ocean. Average global temperatures are warmer than in the current era. First primitive land plants, early ancestors of starfish and mollusks, and first armored, jawless fishes appear. The period ends in mass extinction of a majority of species, possibly a result of a global drop in sea level due to glaciation.

Silurian Period (444-419 MYA). South Pole remains covered by supercontinent, but precursors of present-day N America, Europe, and Asia coalesce around the equator and middle latitudes. Appearance of first known vascular land plants, first freshwater fish, first jawed fish, first coral reefs, and first air-breathing animals (certain eurypterids, also called sea scorpions, largest known arthropods).

Devonian Period (419-359 MYA). Collisions between Gondwanaland and ancestral landmasses of N America and Eurasia produce mountains visible today as northern Appalachians. Newly-formed ozone layer offers protection from sun's rays, allowing first air-breathing spiders and mites to appear on dry land. Fish with fins and scales and first amphibians emerge. Late Devonian mass extinction.

Carboniferous Period (359-299 MYA). Precursors of modern N America and Northern Europe lie in tropical latitudes N of the equator; warm and humid conditions there facilitate spread of lush forests and peat swamps that later form most of the world's coal and limestone. Later period sees emergence of first true conifers, Lepidodendrales ("scale trees") as tall as 100 ft, and first true reptiles.

Permian Period (299-252 MYA). All major landmasses collide to form the supercontinent Pangaea, surrounded by the world ocean Panthalassa. Gradual warming through much of the Permian allows for initial flourishing of species, including dinosaur precursors (up to 10 ft long) and marine species in shallow inland seas. The period ended with the largest of Earth's five mass extinctions. As much as 95% of all marine species and most land species went extinct in the event, which was likely caused by increased greenhouse gases in atmosphere.

Mesozoic Era (252-66 MYA)

Triassic Period (252-201 MYA). Pangaea separates into supercontinents of Laurasia and Gondwana; subtropical conditions extend as far N as present-day Wyoming and New England. Emergence of ichthyosaurs and plesiosaurs (large marine reptiles), pterosaurs (winged reptiles), several species of dinosaurs (up to 15 ft long), first true mammals, and first insects to undergo metamorphosis from larva to pupa to adult. Triassic-Jurassic mass extinction.

Jurassic Period (201-145 MYA). N American continent drifts westward, opening Gulf of Mexico; rift forms between S America and Africa. Warm, moist climate contributes to flourishing of coral reefs and temperate and subtropical forests. Appearance of first angiosperms (flowering plants), the earliest known birds (offshoots of a dinosaur group), and huge dinosaurs such as the carnivorous *Allosaurus* and herbivorous *Apatosaurus*.

Cretaceous Period (145-66 MYA). African continental plate drifts N, creating roots of European Alps; gap between S America and Africa broadens; western movement of N America drives formation of Sierra Nevada and Rocky Mountains, turning the western interior of continent into a vast swamp. Later, sea levels rise and cover about one-third of Earth's present land area. The global climate is warm and mild. The period ends in a mass extinction of plant and animal species (including dinosaurs). Likely causes include an asteroid impact and increased volcanic activity.

Cenozoic Era (66 MYA-present)

Paleogene Period (66-23 MYA)
* Paleocene Epoch (66-56 MYA). Australia begins to separate from Antarctica; N America and Greenland begin to spread apart. Mammalian life predominates, including early marsupials, insectivores, creodonts (carnivorous relatives of cats and dogs), and primitive hoofed mammals.
* Eocene Epoch (56-33.9 MYA). Australia drifts farther from Antarctica; the Indian subcontinent becomes welded to Asia, and tectonic forces drive the upheaval of the Alpine-Himalayan system. Climate in N America and Europe is subtropical and moist, with temperate forests as far N as Greenland and Siberia. Ancestors of modern horses, elephants, rhinoceroses, camels, bats, primates, and squirrel-like rodents emerge; earliest known marine mammals appear in later Eocene.
* Oligocene Epoch (33.9-23 MYA). San Andreas fault develops between N American and Pacific plates. Mammalian species continue to diversify, producing modern horse and multiple rodent, camel, and rhinoceros-like species, as well as first known species of great ape. Long-term cooling trend begins that would later cause Pleistocene ice ages.

Neogene Period (23-2.6 MYA)
* Miocene Epoch (23-5.3 MYA). Crustal plate collisions continue to drive uplift of Alps, Himalayas, and Cordilleran Ranges in Americas; eroded sediment is deposited in shallow marine basins, forming reservoirs for oil fields of California, Romania, and Caspian Sea. Ocean currents prevent Antarctica from receiving warmer waters, fostering growth of Antarctic ice sheet. Northern forests become grassy prairies. Large apes related to the orangutan live in Asia and southern Europe. Oldest hominin fossils from Africa date to this epoch.
* Pliocene Epoch (5.3-2.6 MYA). Alps continue to rise in Europe, and subduction of the Pacific tectonic plate elevates the Sierra Nevada and volcanic Cascade Range. Climate becomes cooler and drier, driving formation of permanent Arctic ice cap. Rapid primate evolution produces *Australopithecus*, an early direct ancestor of modern humans (*Homo sapiens*).

Quarternary Period (2.6 MYA-present)
* Pleistocene Epoch (2.6 MYA-11,700 years ago). Glacier ice covers as much as 25% or more of Earth's land surface, carving numerous present-day features including the Great Lakes; increased rainfall in lower latitudes allows plant and animal life to flourish in northern and eastern Africa. Late Pleistocene brings worldwide extinction of many large mammals, including the mastodon, saber-toothed tiger, and ground sloth. Evidence of Neanderthals, Denisovans, and the small archaic humans *Homo floresiensis* and *Homo luzonensis* dates from the latter part of the Pleistocene.
* Holocene Epoch (11,700 years ago-present). Melting ice caused sea levels to rise 100 ft or more in early Holocene, covering large areas of land and extending continental shelf of N America. Humans proliferate, and civilization begins.

Biological Classification

In biology, classification is the identification, naming, and grouping of organisms into a formal system. The two fields that are most directly concerned with classification are taxonomy and systematics. Although they overlap, taxonomy is more concerned with nomenclature (naming) and with constructing hierarchical systems, and systematics with uncovering evolutionary relationships. Two kingdoms of living forms, Plantae and Animalia, have been recognized since Aristotle established the first taxonomy in the 4th century BCE. Plants and animals are examples of eukaryotes; their cells have nuclei bound by membranes. Two other kingdoms of eukaryotes that have been identified are Protista (mostly one-celled organisms) and Fungi. Single-celled bacteria and archaea lack such nuclei. They are referred to as prokaryotes (or procaryotes) and are commonly placed in separate kingdoms. The seven basic categories of classification (from most general to most specific) are kingdom, phylum (or division), class, order, family, genus, and species. (In addition, many scientists group all eukaryotes in a single "domain," and treat bacteria and archaea as two other domains.) Below are two examples of classification:

ZOOLOGICAL HIERARCHY

Kingdom	Phylum	Class	Order	Family	Genus	Species name	Common name
Animalia	Chordata	Mammalia	Primates	Hominidae	*Homo*	*Homo sapiens*	Human

BOTANICAL HIERARCHY

Kingdom	Division*	Class	Order	Family	Genus	Species name	Common name
Plantae	Magnoliophyta	Magnoliopsida	Magnoliales	Magnoliaceae	*Magnolia*	*M. virginiana*	Sweet bay

*In botany, the division is generally used in place of the phylum.

Selected Endangered or Threatened Animal Species

Source: Fish and Wildlife Service, U.S. Dept. of the Interior

Common name	Scientific name	Range of concern
Albatross, Amsterdam	*Diomedia amsterdamensis*	Amsterdam Island, Indian Ocean
Antelope, giant sable	*Hippotragus niger variani*	Angola
Armadillo, giant	*Priodontes maximus*	Venezuela and Guyana to Argentina
Bandicoot, desert	*Perameles eremiana*	Australia
Bat, gray	*Myotis grisescens*	Central, southeastern U.S.
Bear, grizzly	*Ursus arctos horribilis*	U.S. (mountain-prairie region)
Bobcat, Mexican	*Lynx rufus escuinapae*	Mexico
Bumble bee, rusty patched	*Bombus affinis*	Canada; Eastern, midwestern U.S.
Camel, Bactrian	*Camelus bactrianus*	Mongolia, China
Caribou, woodland	*Rangifer tarandus caribou*	Canada, U.S. (ID, WA)
Cheetah	*Acinonyx jubatus*	Africa to India
Chimpanzee, pygmy	*Pan paniscus*	Dem. Rep. of the Congo
Condor, California	*Gymnogyps californianus*	U.S. (AZ, CA, NV, UT), Mexico (Baja California)
Crane, whooping	*Grus americana*	Canada, central U.S.
Crocodile, American	*Crocodylus acutus*	U.S. (FL); Caribbean; Central, S America
Dolphin, Chinese river	*Lipotes vexillifer*	China
Duck, Hawaiian	*Anas wyvilliana*	U.S. (HI)
Elephant, Asian	*Elephas maximus*	South-central and southeastern Asia
Fox, northern swift	*Vulpes velox hebes*	Canada
Frog, mountain yellow-legged	*Rana muscosa*	U.S. (CA)
Gorilla	*Gorilla gorilla*	Central and western Africa
Hyena, brown	*Parahyaena brunnea*	Southern Africa
Impala, black-faced	*Aepyceros melampus petersi*	Angola, Namibia
Kangaroo, Tasmanian forester	*Macropus giganteus tasmaniensis*	Australia (Tasmania)
Leopard	*Panthera pardus*	Central and Southern Africa, Asia
Monkey, spider	*Ateles geoffroyi frontatus*	Central America
Ocelot	*Leopardus pardalis*	U.S. (AZ, TX), Mexico; Central, S America
Orangutan	*Pongo pygmaeus*	Indonesia
Ostrich, West African	*Struthio camelus spatzi*	Western Sahara
Otter, marine	*Lontra felina*	Peru south to Straits of Magellan
Panda, giant	*Ailuropoda melanoleuca*	China
Panther, Florida	*Puma concolor coryi*	U.S. (FL)
Parrot, imperial	*Amazona imperialis*	Dominica
Penguin, Galapagos	*Spheniscus mendiculus*	Ecuador (Galapagos Islands)
Porpoise, Gulf of California harbor (vaquita)	*Phocoena sinus*	Mexico
Rhinoceros, black	*Diceros bicornis*	Sub-Saharan Africa
Salamander, Chinese giant	*Andrias davidianus*	China
Salmon, sockeye	*Oncorhynchus nerka*	U.S. (OR, WA)
Sea lion, Steller (Western pop.)	*Eumetopias jubatus*	U.S. (AK), Russia
Squirrel, Carolina northern flying	*Glaucomys sabrinus coloratus*	U.S. (NC, TN, VA)
Tiger	*Panthera tigris*	Asia
Tortoise, Galapagos	*Geochelone nigra*	Ecuador (Galapagos Islands)
Whale, gray (Western North Pacific pop.)	*Eschrichtius robustus*	NW Pacific Ocean
Wolf, red	*Canis rufus*	U.S. (FL)
Woodpecker, ivory-billed	*Campephilus principalis*	U.S. (AR)
Yak, wild	*Bos mutus*	China (Tibet), India
Zebra, mountain	*Equus zebra zebra*	South Africa

Status of Endangered and Threatened Species, 2023

Source: Fish and Wildlife Service, U.S. Dept. of the Interior; as of July 2023

Group	Endangered		Threatened		Total species[1]	U.S. species with active recovery plans
	U.S.	Foreign	U.S.	Foreign		
Mammals	67	262	29	23	381	64
Birds	77	217	23	22	339	90
Fishes	96	27	78	9	210	108
Reptiles	17	70	29	25	141	42
Clams	77	2	20	0	99	77
Insects	76	4	17	0	97	69
Snails	38	1	13	1	53	43
Amphibians	23	8	16	1	48	28
Crustaceans	25	0	7	0	32	23
Corals	0	3	7	15	25	0
Arachnids	11	5	0	0	16	11
Annelid worms	0	0	0	0	0	0
Flatworms and roundworms	0	0	0	0	0	0
Hydroids	0	0	0	0	0	0
Millipedes	0	0	0	0	0	0
Sponges	0	0	0	0	0	0
Animal subtotals	**507**	**599**	**239**	**96**	**1,441**	**555**
Plant subtotals	**766**	**1**	**175**	**2**	**944**	**834**
Grand totals	**1,273**	**600**	**414**	**98**	**2,385**	**1,389**

(1) 23 animal species are counted more than once in this table, primarily because these animals have distinct population segments, each with its own individual listing status. The U.S. species tallied more than once as endangered or threatened are Atlantic sturgeon, bearded seal, California tiger salamander, Chinook salmon, chum salmon, coho salmon, gray wolf, lesser prairie-chicken, mountain yellow-legged frog, piping plover, roseate tern, sockeye salmon, and steelhead. The foreign species counted more than once are argali, broad-snouted caiman, humpback whale, leopard, scalloped hammerhead shark, and vicuña. Green sea turtles and loggerhead sea turtles appear on both the U.S. and foreign lists.

Major Venomous Animals

Snakes

Asian pit viper—2 ft to 5 ft long; throughout Asia; reactions and mortality vary, but most bites cause tissue damage; mortality generally low.

Australian brown snake—4 ft to 7 ft long; very slow onset of cardiac or respiratory distress; moderate mortality, but because death can be sudden and unexpected, it is the most dangerous of the Australian snakes; antivenom.

Barba amarilla or fer-de-lance—up to 7 ft long; from tropical Mexico to Brazil; severe tissue damage common; moderate mortality; antivenom.

Black mamba—up to 14 ft long; southern and central Africa; rapid onset of dizziness, difficulty breathing, erratic heartbeat; mortality high, nears 100% without antivenom.

Boomslang—less than 6 ft long; African savannahs; rapid onset of nausea and dizziness, often followed by slight recovery and then sudden death from internal hemorrhaging; bites rare, mortality high; antivenom.

Bushmaster—up to 12 ft long; tropical forests of Central and S America; few bites occur, but mortality high.

Common, or Asian, cobra—4 ft to 8 ft long; throughout S Asia; considerable tissue damage, sometimes paralysis; mortality probably not more than 10%; antivenom.

Copperhead—less than 4 ft long; New England to Texas; pain and swelling; very seldom fatal; antivenom seldom needed.

Coral snake—2 ft to 5 ft long; in Americas S of Canada; bite may be painless; slow onset of paralysis, impaired breathing; mortalities rare but high without antivenom and mechanical respiration.

Cottonmouth water moccasin—up to 5 ft long; wetlands of southern U.S. from Virginia to Texas; rapid onset of severe pain, swelling, tissue destruction can be extensive; mortality low; antivenom.

Death adder—less than 3 ft long; Australia; rapid onset of faintness, cardiac and respiratory distress; at least 50% mortality without antivenom.

Desert horned viper—up to 2 ft long; dry areas of Africa and western Asia; severe tissue damage; mortality low; antivenom.

European viper—1 ft to 3 ft long; throughout Europe; bleeding and tissue damage; mortality low; antivenom.

Gaboon viper—more than 6 ft long; S of the Sahara; massive tissue damage, internal bleeding; few recorded bites.

King cobra—up to 16 ft long; throughout S Asia; rapid swelling, dizziness, loss of consciousness, difficulty breathing, erratic heartbeat; mortality varies with amount of venom involved, but most bites involve nonfatal amounts; antivenom.

Krait—up to 5 ft long; SE Asia; rapid onset of sleepiness, numbness; up to 50% mortality even with use of antivenom.

Puff adder—up to 5 ft long, thick; S of the Sahara, throughout the Middle East; rapid large swelling, great pain, dizziness; moderate mortality, often from internal bleeding; antivenom.

Rattlesnake—2 ft to 6 ft long; throughout Western Hemisphere; rapid onset of severe pain, swelling; mortality low, but amputation of affected digits is sometimes necessary; antivenom. Mojave rattler may produce temporary paralysis.

Ringhals, or spitting, cobra—5 ft to 7 ft long; southern Africa; squirts venom through holes in front of fangs as a defense; venom severely irritating and can cause blindness.

Russell's viper or tic-polonga—more than 5 ft long; throughout Asia; internal bleeding; bite reports common; moderate mortality rate; antivenom.

Saw-scaled, or carpet, viper—up to 2 ft long; dry areas from India to Africa; severe bleeding, fever; high mortality, causes more human fatalities than any other snake; antivenom.

Sea snake—3 ft to 10 ft long; throughout Pacific, Indian Oceans except NE Pacific; almost painless bite; variety of muscle pain, paralysis; mortality low, many bites not envenomed; some antivenoms.

Sharp-nosed pit viper or hundred-pace snake—up to 5 ft long; S Vietnam, Taiwan, and China; the most toxic of Asian pit vipers; very rapid onset of swelling and tissue damage, internal bleeding; moderate mortality; antivenom.

Taipan—up to 11 ft long; Australia and New Guinea; rapid paralysis with severe breathing difficulty; mortality nears 100% without antivenom.

Tiger snake—2 ft to 6 ft long; southern Australia; pain, numbness, mental disturbances with rapid paralysis; may be deadliest of all land snakes; but antivenom is quite effective.

Yellow, or cape, cobra—7 ft long; southern Africa; most toxic venom of any cobra; rapid onset of swelling, breathing and cardiac difficulties; mortality is high without treatment; antivenom.

Note: Not all bites by venomous snakes are actually envenomed. Any animal bite, however, carries the danger of tetanus, and anyone suffering a venomous snake bite should seek medical attention. Antivenoms do not cure; they are only an aid in the treatment of bites. Mortality rates above are for envenomed bites: low mortality, c. 2% or less; moderate, 2%-5%; high, 5%-15%.

Lizards

Gila monster—up to 24 in. long, with heavy body and tail; high desert in SW U.S. and northern Mexico; immediate severe pain, transient low blood pressure; no recent mortality.

Mexican beaded lizard—similar to Gila monster; W coast of Mexico; reaction and mortality similar to Gila monster.

Insects

Ants, bees, hornets, wasps—global distribution; usual reaction is piercing pain in area of sting, though many people suffer allergic reactions (swelling, rashes); not directly fatal, except in cases of massive multiple stings, and a few may die within minutes from severe sensitivity to the venom (anaphylactic shock).

Spiders, scorpions

Black widow—small, round-bodied with red hourglass marking; the widow and its relatives are found in tropical and temperate zones; severe musculoskeletal pain, weakness, breathing difficulty, convulsions, which may be more serious in small children; low mortality; antivenom. The **redback** spider of Australia has the hourglass marking on its back, rather than on its front, but otherwise looks almost identical to the black widow.

Brown recluse, or fiddleback, spider—small, oblong body; throughout U.S.; pain with later ulceration, which may last months, at place of bite; fever, nausea, and stomach cramps in severe cases; very low mortality.

Funnel web spider—several varieties, often large; Australia; slow onset of breathing, circulation difficulties; low mortality; antivenom.

Scorpion—crablike body with stinger in tail, various sizes; many varieties throughout tropical and subtropical areas; severe pain spreading from the wound, numbness, severe agitation, cramps, and even respiratory failure; low mortality, usually in children; antivenoms.

Tarantula—large, hairy spider; worldwide; the American tarantula, and probably all other tarantulas, are harmless to humans, though their bite may cause some pain and swelling.

Sea life

Cone-shell—mollusk in small shell; S Pacific and Indian Oceans; shoots barbs into victims; paralysis; low mortality.

Octopus—global distribution, usually in warm waters; rapid onset of paralysis with breathing difficulty; all varieties produce venom, but only a few can cause death.

Portuguese man-of-war—jellyfish-like siphonophore with tentacles up to 100 ft long; in most warm water areas; immediate severe pain; not directly fatal, though shock may cause death in rare cases.

Sea wasp or box jellyfish—tentacles up to 30 ft long; S Pacific; very rapid onset of circulatory problems; high mortality because of speed of toxic reaction; antivenom.

Stingray—several varieties of differing sizes; tropical and temperate seas and some freshwater; severe pain, rapid onset of nausea, vomiting, breathing difficulties; wound area may ulcerate, gangrene may occur; seldom fatal.

Stonefish—brownish fish that lies motionless on bottom of shallow waters; S Pacific and Indian Oceans; extraordinary pain, rapid paralysis; low mortality; antivenom, warm water relieves pain.

Speeds of Selected Animals

Source: *Natural History* magazine. © American Museum of Natural History

Animal	Speed (mph)	Animal	Speed (mph)	Animal	Speed (mph)
Cheetah	70	Mongolian wild ass	40	Human	27.89
Pronghorn antelope	61	Greyhound	39.35	Elephant	25
Wildebeest	50	Whippet	35.50	Black mamba snake	20
Lion	50	Rabbit (domestic)	35	Six-lined race runner (lizard)	18
Thomson's gazelle	50	Mule deer	35	Wild turkey	15
Quarterhorse	47.5	Jackal	35	Squirrel	12
Elk	45	Reindeer	32	Pig (domestic)	11
Cape hunting dog	45	Giraffe	32	Chicken	9
Coyote	43	White-tailed deer	30	Spider (*Tegenaria atrica*)	1.17
Gray fox	42	Warthog	30	Giant tortoise	0.17
Hyena	40	Grizzly bear	30	Three-toed sloth	0.15
Zebra	40	Cat (domestic)	30	Garden snail	0.03

Note: Most of these measurements are for maximum speeds over approximate quarter-mile distances. Exceptions are the lion and elephant, whose speeds were clocked in the act of charging; the whippet, which was timed over a 200-yd course; the cheetah, timed over a 100-yd distance; a human, timed over a 15-yd segment of a 100-yd run; and the black mamba, six-lined race runner, spider, giant tortoise, three-toed sloth, and garden snail, which were measured over various small distances.

Most Popular Breeds of Cats, 2022

Source: The Cat Fanciers' Association
(ranked by total registrations)

Rank	Breed	Rank	Breed	Rank	Breed	Rank	Breed	Rank	Breed
1.	Ragdoll	10.	Siberian	20.	Burmese	29.	European Burmese	37.	Burmilla
2.	Maine Coon	11.	American Shorthair	21.	Tonkinese	30.	Lykoi	38.	Manx
3.	Devon Rex	12.	Bengal	22.	Ocicat	31.	Turkish Angora	39.	Havana Brown
4.	Exotic	13.	Russian Blue	23.	American Curl	32.	Chartreux	40.	Korat
5.	Persian (including Himalayan)	14.	Norwegian Forest	24.	Somali	33.	Balinese	41.	American Bobtail
		15.	Oriental	25.	RagaMuffin	34.	Singapura	42.	Turkish Van
6.	British Shorthair	16.	Siamese	26.	Egyptian Mau	35.	Colorpoint Shorthair	43.	American Wirehair
7.	Abyssinian	17.	Cornish Rex	27.	Japanese Bobtail			44.	LaPerm
8.	Scottish Fold	18.	Selkirk Rex	28.	Bombay	36.	Toybob	45.	Khao Manee
9.	Sphynx	19.	Birman						

Most Popular American Kennel Club Dog Breed Registrations, 2019-22

Source: American Kennel Club (AKC)
(ranked by 2022 registrations)

Breed	Rank 2022	2021	2020	2019	Breed	Rank 2022	2021	2020	2019
French Bulldogs	1	2	2	4	Doberman Pinschers	15	16	18	19
Labrador Retrievers	2	1	1	1	Boxers	16	14	14	14
Golden Retrievers	3	3	4	3	Miniature Schnauzers	17	18	19	18
German Shepherds	4	4	3	2	Cane Corso	18	21	25	30
Poodles	5	5	6	6	Great Danes	19	17	15	17
Bulldogs	6	6	5	5	Shih Tzu	20	22	20	20
Rottweilers	7	8	8	8	Siberian Huskies	21	19	16	15
Beagles	8	7	7	7	Bernese Mountain Dogs	22	20	22	23
Dachshunds	9	10	10	11	Pomeranians	23	24	23	24
German Shorthaired Pointers	10	9	9	9	Boston Terriers	24	23	21	21
Pembroke Welsh Corgis	11	11	11	10	Havanese	25	25	24	22
Australian Shepherds	12	12	12	13	English Springer Spaniels	26	26	26	27
Yorkshire Terriers	13	13	13	12	Shetland Sheepdogs	27	28	27	25
Cavalier King Charles Spaniels	14	15	17	16	Brittanys	28	27	28	26
					Cocker Spaniels	29	29	30	28
					Border Collies	30	31	32	33

Dog Breeds by Type

Source: American Kennel Club (AKC)

According to the AKC, there are more than 340 dog breeds known throughout the world. As of mid-2023, the AKC recognized about 200 registered breeds and used the following seven groups to classify them, according to functions and other distinctive traits.

Herding Group: Australian Cattle Dog, Australian Shepherd, Bearded Collie, Beauceron, Belgian Laekenois, Belgian Malinois, Belgian Sheepdog, Belgian Tervuren, Bergamasco Sheepdog, Berger Picard, Border Collie, Bouvier des Flandres, Briard, Canaan Dog, Cardigan Welsh Corgi, Collie, Entlebucher Mountain Dog, Finnish Lapphund, German Shepherd Dog, Icelandic Sheepdog, Miniature American Shepherd, Mudi, Norwegian Buhund, Old English Sheepdog, Pembroke Welsh Corgi, Polish Lowland Sheepdog, Puli, Pumi, Pyrenean Shepherd, Shetland Sheepdog, Spanish Water Dog, Swedish Vallhund.

Hound Group: Afghan Hound, American English Coonhound, American Foxhound, Azawakh, Basenji, Basset Hound, Beagle, Black and Tan Coonhound, Bloodhound, Bluetick Coonhound, Borzoi, Cirneco dell'Etna, Dachshund, English Foxhound, Grand Basset Griffon Vendéen, Greyhound, Harrier, Ibizan Hound, Irish Wolfhound, Norwegian Elkhound, Otterhound, Petit Basset Griffon Vendéen, Pharaoh Hound, Plott Hound, Portuguese Podengo Pequeno, Redbone Coonhound, Rhodesian Ridgeback, Saluki, Scottish Deerhound, Sloughi, Treeing Walker Coonhound, Whippet.

Non-Sporting Group: American Eskimo Dog, Bichon Frise, Boston Terrier, Bulldog, Chinese Shar-Pei, Chow Chow, Coton de Tulear, Dalmatian, Finnish Spitz, French Bulldog, Keeshond, Lhasa Apso, Löwchen, Norwegian Lundehund, Poodle (Standard and Miniature), Schipperke, Shiba Inu, Tibetan Spaniel, Tibetan Terrier, Xoloitzcuintli.

Sporting Group: American Water Spaniel, Barbet, Boykin Spaniel, Bracco Italiano, Brittany, Chesapeake Bay Retriever, Clumber Spaniel, Cocker Spaniel, Curly-Coated Retriever, English Cocker Spaniel, English Setter, English Springer Spaniel, Field Spaniel, Flat-Coated Retriever, German Shorthaired Pointer, German Wirehaired Pointer, Golden Retriever, Gordon Setter, Irish Red and White Setter, Irish Setter, Irish Water Spaniel, Labrador Retriever, Lagotto Romagnolo, Nederlandse Kooikerhondje, Nova Scotia Duck Tolling Retriever, Pointer, Spinone Italiano, Sussex Spaniel, Vizsla, Weimaraner, Welsh Springer Spaniel, Wirehaired Pointing Griffon, Wirehaired Vizsla.

Terrier Group: Airedale Terrier, American Hairless Terrier, American Staffordshire Terrier, Australian Terrier, Bedlington Terrier, Border Terrier, Bull Terrier, Cairn Terrier, Cesky Terrier, Dandie Dinmont Terrier, Glen of Imaal Terrier, Irish Terrier, Kerry Blue Terrier, Lakeland Terrier, Manchester Terrier (Standard), Miniature Bull Terrier, Miniature Schnauzer, Norfolk Terrier, Norwich Terrier, Parson Russell Terrier, Rat Terrier, Russell Terrier, Scottish Terrier, Sealyham Terrier, Skye Terrier, Smooth Fox Terrier, Soft Coated Wheaten Terrier, Staffordshire Bull Terrier, Welsh Terrier, West Highland White Terrier, Wire Fox Terrier.

Toy Group: Affenpinscher, Biewer Terrier, Brussels Griffon, Cavalier King Charles Spaniel, Chihuahua, Chinese Crested, English Toy Spaniel, Havanese, Italian Greyhound, Japanese Chin, Maltese, Manchester Terrier (Toy), Miniature Pinscher, Papillon, Pekingese, Pomeranian, Poodle (Toy), Pug, Russian Toy, Shih Tzu, Silky Terrier, Toy Fox Terrier, Yorkshire Terrier.

Working Group: Akita, Alaskan Malamute, Anatolian Shepherd Dog, Bernese Mountain Dog, Black Russian Terrier, Boerboel, Boxer, Bullmastiff, Cane Corso, Chinook, Doberman Pinscher, Dogo Argentino, Dogue de Bordeaux, German Pinscher, Giant Schnauzer, Great Dane, Great Pyrenees, Greater Swiss Mountain Dog, Komondor, Kuvasz, Leonberger, Mastiff, Neapolitan Mastiff, Newfoundland, Portuguese Water Dog, Rottweiler, Saint Bernard, Samoyed, Siberian Husky, Standard Schnauzer, Tibetan Mastiff.

Discoveries and Innovations: Biology, Chemistry, Medicine, Physics

Discovery	Date	Discoverer(s)	Nationality
Acetylene gas	1862	Berthelot	French
ACTH	1927	Evans, Long	U.S.
Adrenaline	1901	Takamine	Japanese
Aluminum, electrolytic process	1886	Hall	U.S.
Aluminum, isolated	1825	Oersted	Danish
Anesthesia, ether	1842	Long	U.S.
Anesthesia, local	1885	Koller	Austrian
Anesthesia, spinal	1898	Bier	German
Aniline dye	1856	Perkin	English
Anti-rabies	1885	Pasteur	French
Antiseptic surgery	1867	Lister	English
Antitoxin, diphtheria	1891	Von Behring	German
Argyrol	1897	Bayer	German
Arsphenamine	1910	Ehrlich	German
Aspirin	1853	Gerhardt	French
Atabrine	1932	Mietzsch, et al.	German
Atomic numbers	1913	Moseley	English
Atomic theory	1803	Dalton	English
Atomic time clock	1948	Lyons	U.S.
Atom-smashing theory	1919	Rutherford	English
Bacitracin	1943	Johnson, Meleneyl	U.S.
Bacteria, description	1676	Leeuwenhoek	Dutch
Bacterial genome, synth.	2010	Venter	U.S.
Bleaching powder	1798	Tennant	English
Blood, circulation	1628	Harvey	English
Bordeaux mixture	1885	Millardet	French
Bromine from the sea	1826	Balard	French
Calcium carbide	1888	Wilson	U.S.
Calculus	1670	Newton	English
Camphor synthetic	1896	Haller	French
Canning (food)	1804	Appert	French
Carbon oxides	1925	Fisher	German
Chemotherapy	1909	Ehrlich	German
Chloamphenicol	1947	Burkholder	U.S.
Chlorine	1774	Scheele	Swedish
Chloroform	1831	Guthrie	U.S.
Chlortetracycline	1948	Duggen	U.S.
Classification of plants and animals	1735	Linnaeus	Swedish
Cloning, DNA	1973	Boyer, Cohen	U.S.
Cloning, mammal	1996	Wilmut, et al.	Scottish
Cocaine	1860	Niermann	German
Combustion explained	1777	Lavoisier	French
Conditioned reflex	1914	Pavlov	Russian
Cortisone	1936	Kendall	U.S.
Cortisone, synthesis	1946	Sarett	U.S.
Cosmic rays	1910	Gockel	Swiss
Cyclotron	1930	Lawrence	U.S.

Discovery	Date	Discoverer(s)	Nationality
DDT (not applied as insecticide until 1939)	1874	Zeidler	German
Denisovan humans (DNA analysis)	2010	Krause, et al.	German
		Pääbo	Swedish
Deuterium	1932	Urey, Brickwedde, Murphy	U.S.
DNA (as carrier of heredity)	1943	Avery, MacLeod, McCarty	U.S.
DNA (structure)	1953	Crick	English
		Watson	U.S.
		Wilkins	N.Z.-Eng.
Electric resistance, law of	1827	Ohm	German
Electric waves	1888	Hertz	German
Electrolysis	1852	Faraday	English
Electromagnetism	1819	Oersted	Danish
Electron	1897	Thomson, J.	English
Electron diffraction	1936	Thomson, G.	English
		Davisson	U.S.
Electroshock treatment	1938	Cerletti, Bini	Italian
Erythromycin	1952	McGuire	U.S.
Evolution, natural selection	1858	Darwin	English
Falling bodies, law of	1590	Galileo	Italian
Gases, law of combining volumes	1808	Gay-Lussac	French
Geometry, analytic	1619	Descartes	French
Gold, cyanidation	1887	MacArthur, R.Forrest, W. Forrest	Scottish
Gravitation, law	1687	Newton	English
Gravitational waves (det.)	2015	LIGO	U.S.-Intl.
Higgs boson	2012	CERN	International
HIV (human immunodeficiency virus)	1984	Montagnier	French
		Gallo	U.S.
Holograph	1948	Gabor	Hung.-Brit.
Homo floresiensis ("hobbit" humans)	2003	Morwood, et al.	New Zea.
Human genome sequence (first draft)	2001	Human Genome Project, Celera Genomics Corp.	U.S.-Intl.
In vitro fertilization	1978	Steptoe, Edwards	English
Indigo, synthesis of	1880	Baeyer	German
Induction, electric	1830	Henry	U.S.
Insulin	1922	Banting, Best	Canadian
		Macleod	Scottish
Intelligence testing	1905	Binet, Simon	French
Isotopes, theory	1912	Soddy	English
Laser	1957	Gould	U.S.
Light, velocity	1675	Roemer	Danish

Discovery	Date	Discoverer(s)	Nationality
Light, wave theory	1690	Huygens	Dutch
Lithography	1796	Senefelder	Bohemian
Logarithms	1614	Napier	Scottish
LSD-25	1943	Hoffman	Swiss
Mendelian laws	1866	Mendel	Austrian
Mercator projection (map)	1568	Mercator (Kremer)	Flemish
Methanol	1661	Boyle	Irish
Milk condensation	1853	Borden	U.S.
Molecular hypothesis	1811	Avogadro	Italian
Motion, laws of	1687	Newton	English
Neomycin	1949	Waksman, Lechevalier	U.S.
Neutrino	1956	Reines, Cowan	U.S.
Neutron	1932	Chadwick	English
Nitric acid	1648	Glauber	German
Nitric oxide	1772	Priestley	English
Nitroglycerin	1846	Sobrero	Italian
Oil cracking process	1891	Dewar	Scottish
Oxygen	1774	Priestley	English
Oxytetracycline	1950	Finlay, et al.	U.S.
Ozone	1840	Schonbein	German
Paper, sulfite process	1867	Tilghman	U.S.
Paper, wood pulp, sulfate process	1884	Dahl	German
Penicillin	1928	Fleming	Scottish
Penicillin, practical use	1941	Florey, Chain	English
Periodic law and table of elements	1869	Mendeleyev	Russian
Physostigmine synthesis	1935	Julian	U.S.
Pill, birth-control	1954	Pincus, Rock	U.S.
Planetary motion, laws	1609	Kepler	German
Plutonium fission	1940	Kennedy, Wahl, Seaborg, Segre	U.S.
Polymyxin	1947	Ainsworth	English
Positron	1932	Anderson	U.S.
Proton	1919	Rutherford	New Zea.
Psychoanalysis	1900	Freud	Austrian
Pulsars	1967	Bell	English
Quantum theory	1900	Planck	German
Quasars	1963	Matthews, Sandage	U.S.
Quinine synthetic	1946	Woodward, Doering	U.S.
Radioactivity	1896	Becquerel	French
Radiocarbon dating	1947	Libby	U.S.
Radium	1898	Curie, Pierre	French
		Curie, Marie	Pol.-Fr.
Relativity theory	1905	Einstein	German
Reserpine	1949	Jal Vakil	Indian
Schick test	1913	Schick	U.S.
Silicon	1823	Berzelius	Swedish
Smallpox eradication	1979	World Health Org.	UN
Streptomycin	1944	Waksman, et al.	U.S.
Sulfanilamide	1935	Bovet, Trefouel	French
Sulfanilamide theory	1908	Gelmo	German
Sulfapyridine	1938	Ewins, Phelps	English
Sulfathiazole	1939	Fosbinder, Walter	U.S.
Sulfuric acid	1831	Phillips	English
Sulfuric acid, lead	1746	Roebuck	English
Superconductivity	1911	Onnes	Dutch
Superconductivity theory	1957	Bardeen, Cooper, Schreiffer	U.S.
Superconductors, high-temp.	1986	Bednorz, Müller	Ger. / Swiss
Syphilis test	1906	Wassermann	German
Transplant, face	2005	Devauchelle, Dubernard	French
Transplant, heart	1967	Barnard	S. African
Tuberculin	1890	Koch	German
Uranium fission, atomic reactor	1942	Fermi, Szilard	U.S.
Uranium fission theory	1939	Hahn, Meitner, Strassmann	German
		Bohr	Danish
		Fermi	Italian
		Einstein, Pegram, Wheeler	U.S.
Vaccine, COVID-19[1]	2020	Pfizer/BioNTech	U.S., Ger.
Vaccine, Ebola	2016	Public Health Agency of Canada	Canadian
Vaccine, malaria (RTS,S)	2021	GlaxoSmithKline	British
Vaccine, measles	1963	Enders	U.S.
Vaccine, MMR	1971	Hilleman	U.S.
Vaccine, meningitis (first conjugate)	1987	Gordon, et al., Connaught Labs	U.S.
Vaccine, polio	1954	Salk	U.S.
Vaccine, polio, oral	1960	Sabin	U.S.
Vaccine, rabies	1885	Pasteur	French
Vaccine, smallpox	1796	Jenner	English
Vaccine, typhus	1909	Nicolle	French
Vaccine, varicella	1974	Takahashi	Japanese
Van Allen belts, radiation	1958	Van Allen	U.S.
Vitamin A	1913	McCollum, Davis	U.S.
Vitamin B	1916	McCollum	U.S.
Vitamin C	1928	Szent-Gyorgyi, King	Hungarian / U.S.
Vitamin D	1922	McCollum	U.S.
Xerography	1938	Carlson	U.S.
X-ray	1895	Roentgen	German

(1) Out of more than 150 COVID-19 vaccine candidates under development at the end of 2020, Pfizer/BioNTech's was the first to receive emergency use validation from the World Health Org.

Inventions

Invention	Date	Inventor(s)	Nationality
Adding machine	1642	Pascal	French
Adding machine	1885	Burroughs	U.S.
Aerosol spray	1926	Rotheim	Norwegian
Air brake	1869	Westinghouse	U.S.
Air conditioning	1902	Carrier	U.S.
Air pump	1654	Guericke	German
Airbag	1952	Hetrick	U.S.
Airplane, automatic pilot	1912	Sperry	U.S.
Airplane, experimental	1896	Langley	U.S.
Airplane, hydro	1911	Curtiss	U.S.
Airplane jet engine	1939	Ohain	German
Airplane with motor	1903	Wright Bros.	U.S.
Airship	1852	Giffard	French
Aqua-Lung	1943	Cousteau, Gagnan	French
Arc welder	1919	Thomson	U.S.
Aspartame	1965	Schlatter	U.S.
ATM (automated cash-dispensing machine)	1967	Shepherd-Barron	Scottish
Autogyro	1920	de la Cierva	Spanish
Automobile, diff. gear	1885	Benz	German
Automobile, electric	1892	Morrison	U.S.
Automobile, exp'mtl	1864	Marcus	Austrian
Automobile, gasoline	1889	Daimler	German
Automobile, gasoline	1892	Duryea	U.S.
Automobile magneto	1897	Bosch	German
Automobile muffler	1904	Pope	U.S.
Automobile self-starter	1911	Kettering	U.S.
Bakelite	1907	Baekeland	Belg.-U.S.
Bar code	1952	Woodland, Silver	U.S.
Barometer	1643	Torricelli	Italian
Bicycle, electric	1895	Bolton	U.S.
Bicycle, modern	1885	Starley	English
Bifocal lens	1780	Franklin	U.S.
Bottle machine	1895	Owens	U.S.
Bluetooth	1994	Haartsen	Dutch
Braille printing	1829	Braille	French
Brassiere, modern	1913	Jacob	U.S.
Bubble gum	1928	Diemer	U.S.
Burner, gas	1855	Bunsen	German
Calculator, electronic pocket	1972	Merryman, Van Tassel	U.S.
Calculator, mechanical	1623	Schickard	German
Camera, digital	1977	Lloyd, Sasson	U.S.
Camera, Kodak	1888	Eastman, Walker	U.S.
Camera, Polaroid Land	1948	Land	U.S.
Can, pop-top	1959	Fraze	U.S.
Car coupler	1873	Janney	U.S.
Carburetor, gasoline	1893	Maybach	German
Carding machine	1797	Whittemore	U.S.
Carpet sweeper	1876	Bissell	U.S.
Cash register	1879	Ritty	U.S.
Cassette, audio	1963	Philips Co.	Dutch
Cassette, videotape	1969	Sony	Japanese
CAT, or CT, scan	1973	Hounsfield	English
Cathode-ray tube	1897	Braun	German
Cellophane	1908	Brandenberger	Swiss
Celluloid	1870	Hyatt	U.S.
Cement, Portland	1824	Aspdin	English
Chronometer	1735	Harrison	English
Circuit breaker	1925	Hilliard	U.S.
Circuit, integrated	1959	Kilby, Noyce, Texas Instr.	U.S.
Clock, pendulum	1657	Huygens	Dutch
Coaxial cable system	1929	Affel, Espensched.	U.S.
Coca-Cola	1885	Pemberton	U.S.
Coffeemaker, auto drip	1963	Bunn Corp.	U.S.
Compressed air rock drill	1871	Ingersoll	U.S.
Comptometer	1887	Felt	U.S.
Computer, electronic	1942	Atanasoff, Berry	U.S.

Invention	Date	Inventor(s)	Nationality
Computer, laptop	1987	Sinclair	English
Computer, large-scale automatic digital	1943	Aiken, et al.	U.S.
Computer, mini	1960	Digital Corp.	U.S.
Condenser microphone (telephone)	1916	Wente	U.S.
Contact lens, corneal	1948	Tuohy	U.S.
Contraceptive, oral	1954	Pincus, Rock.	U.S.
Corn, hybrid	1917	Jones	U.S.
Cotton gin	1793	Whitney	U.S.
Cream separator	1878	DeLaval	Swedish
Cultivator, disc	1878	Mallon	U.S.
Cyclotron	1931	Lawrence	U.S.
Cystoscope	1878	Nitze	German
Diapers, disposable	1950	Donovan	U.S.
Diesel engine	1895	Diesel	German
Disc, compact	1972	RCA	U.S.
Disc player, compact	1979	Sony, Philips Co.	Japanese, Dutch
Dishwasher	1893	Cochrane	U.S.
Disk, floppy	1970	IBM	U.S.
Disk, video	1972	Philips Co.	Dutch
Drone (unmanned aircraft, remotely controlled)	1916	Low	English
Dynamite	1866	Nobel	Swedish
Dynamo, contin. current	1871	Gramme	Belgian
Electric battery	1800	Volta	Italian
Electric fan	1882	Wheeler	U.S.
Electrocardiograph	1903	Einthoven	Dutch
Electroencephalograph	1929	Berger	German
Electromagnet	1824	Sturgeon	English
Electron microscope	1931	Ruska, Knoll	German
Electron spectrometer	1944	Deutsch, Elliott, Evans	U.S.
Electron tube multigrid	1913	Langmuir	U.S.
Electronic cigarette (nicotine-based)	2003	Hon (Han)	Chinese
Electronic paper (e-ink)	1974	Sheridon	U.S.
Electroplating	1805	Brugnatelli	Italian
Electrostatic generator	1929	Van de Graaff	U.S.
Elevator brake	1852	Otis	U.S.
Elevator, push button	1922	Larson	U.S.
Engine, automatic transmission	1910	Fottinger	German
Engine, coal-gas 4-cycle	1876	Otto	German
Engine, compression ignition	1883	Daimler	German
Engine, electric ignition	1883	Benz	German
Engine, gas, compound	1926	Eickemeyer	U.S.
Engine, gasoline	1872	Brayton	U.S.
Engine, gasoline	1889	Daimler	German
Engine, jet	1930	Whittle	English
Engine, steam, piston	1705	Newcomen	English
Engine, steam, piston	1769	Watt	Scottish
Engraving, half-tone	1852	Talbot	U.S.
Ferris wheel	1893	Ferris	U.S.
Fiber optic wire	1970	Keck, Maurer, Schultz	U.S.
Fiber optics	1955	Kapany	English
Fiberglass	1938	Owens-Corning	U.S.
Filament, tungsten	1913	Coolidge	U.S.
Flanged rail	1831	Stevens	U.S.
Flatiron, electric	1882	Seely	U.S.
Food, frozen	1923	Birdseye	U.S.
Freon	1930	Midgley, et al.	U.S.
Furnace (for steel)	1858	Siemens	German
Galvanometer	1820	Sweigger	German
Garbage bag, polyethylene	1950	Wasylyk	Canadian
Gas discharge tube	1922	Hull	U.S.
Gas lighting	1792	Murdoch	Scottish
Gas mantle	1885	Welsbach	Austrian
Gasoline, cracked	1913	Burton	U.S.
Gasoline, high octane	1930	Ipatieff	Russian
Gasoline (lead ethyl)	1922	Midgley	U.S.
Geiger counter	1913	Geiger	German
Geodesic dome	1948	Fuller	U.S.
Glass, laminated safety	1909	Benedictus	French
Glider	1853	Cayley	English
Google search software	1996	Brin, Page	U.S.
Gun, breechloader	1811	Thornton	U.S.
Gun, Browning	1897	Browning	U.S.
Gun, magazine	1875	Hotchkiss	U.S.
Gun, silencer	1908	Maxim, H. P.	U.S.
Guncotton (nitrocellulose)	1847	Schoenbein	German
Gyrocompass	1911	Sperry	U.S.
Gyroscope	1852	Foucault	French
Hard drive, computer	1955	Johnson	U.S.
Harvester-thresher	1818	Lane	U.S.
Heart, artificial	1982	Jarvik	U.S.
Helicopter	1939	Sikorsky	U.S.
Hovercraft	1955	Cockerell	English
Hydrometer	1768	Baume	French
Iron lung	1928	Drinker, Slaw	U.S.
Jet Ski	1973	Jacobsen	U.S.
Kaleidoscope	1817	Brewster	Scottish
Kevlar	1965	Kwolek, Blades	U.S.
Kidney dialysis machine	1941	Kolff	Dutch
Kinetoscope	1889	Edison	U.S.
Lamp, arc	1847	Staite	English
Lamp, fluorescent	1938	General Electric, Westinghouse	U.S.
Lamp, incandescent	1879	Edison	U.S.
Lamp, incand., gas	1913	Langmuir	U.S.
Lamp, klieg	1911	Kliegl, A. and J.	U.S.
Lamp, mercury vapor	1912	Hewitt	U.S.
Lamp, miner's safety	1816	Davy	English
Lamp, neon	1909	Claude	French
Lathe, turret	1845	Fitch	U.S.
Launderette	1934	Cantrell	U.S.
Lens, achromatic	1758	Dollond	English
Lens, fused bifocal	1908	Borsch	U.S.
Leyden jar (condenser)	1745	von Kleist	German
Lightning rod	1752	Franklin	U.S.
Linoleum	1860	Walton	English
Linotype	1884	Mergenthaler	U.S.
Linux	1991	Torvalds	Finnish
Liquid Paper	c.1951	Graham	U.S.
Lock, cylinder	1851	Yale	U.S.
Locomotive, electric	1851	Vail	U.S.
Locomotive, exp'mtl	1802	Trevithick	English
Locomotive, exp'mtl	1812	Fenton, et al.	English
Locomotive, exp'mtl	1814	Stephenson	English
Locomotive, 1st U.S.	1830	Cooper	U.S.
Locomotive, practical	1829	Stephenson	English
Loom, power	1785	Cartwright	English
Loudspeaker, dynamic	1924	Rice, Kellogg	U.S.
Machine gun	1862	Gatling	U.S.
Machine gun, improved	1872	Hotchkiss	U.S.
Machine gun (Maxim)	1883	Maxim, H. S.	U.S.-Eng.
Magnet, electro	1828	Henry	U.S.
Magnetic Resonance Imaging (MRI)	1971	Damadian	U.S.
Maser	1953	Townes	U.S.
Mason jar	1858	Mason	U.S.
Match, friction	1827	Walker	English
Mercerized textiles	1843	Mercer	English
Meter, induction	1888	Shallenberger	U.S.
Metronome	1816	Malezel	German
Microcomputer	1973	Truong, et al.	French
Micrometer	1636	Gascoigne	English
Microphone	1877	Berliner	U.S.
Microprocessor	1971	Intel Corp.	U.S.
Microscope, compound	1590	Janssen	Dutch
Microscope, electronic	1931	Knoll, Ruska	German
Microscope, field ion	1951	Mueller	German
Microwave oven	1947	Spencer	U.S.
Monitor, warship	1861	Ericsson	U.S.
Monotype	1887	Lanston	U.S.
Motor, AC	1892	Tesla	U.S.
Motor, DC	1837	Davenport	U.S.
Motor, induction	1887	Tesla	U.S.
Motorcycle	1885	Daimler	German
Mouse, computer	1967	Engelbart	U.S.
Movie machine	1894	Jenkins	U.S.
Movie, panoramic	1952	Waller	U.S.
Movie, talking	1927	Warner Bros.	U.S.
Mower, lawn	1831	Budding, Ferrabee	English
Mowing machine	1822	Bailey	U.S.
Neoprene	1930	Carothers	U.S.
Nylon	1937	Carothers, DuPont	U.S.
Oil cracking furnace	1891	Gavrilov	Russian
Oil filled power cable	1921	Emanueli	Italian
Oleomargarine	1869	Mege-Mouries	French
Ophthalmoscope	1851	Helmholtz	German
Pacemaker	1952	Zoll	U.S.
Pacemaker, implantable cardiac	1958	Greatbatch	U.S.
Paper	105	Ts'ai	Chinese
Paper clip	1900	Waaler	Norwegian
Paper machine	1809	Dickinson	U.S.
Parachute	1785	Blanchard	French
Pen, ballpoint	1888	Loud	U.S.
Pen, fountain	1884	Waterman	U.S.
Pen, steel	1780	Harrison	English

Invention	Date	Inventor(s)	Nationality
Pendulum	1583	Galileo	Italian
Percussion cap	1807	Forsythe	Scottish
Phonograph	1877	Edison	U.S.
Photo, color	1892	Ives	U.S.
Photo film, celluloid	1893	Reichenbach	U.S.
Photo film, transparent	1884	Eastman, Goodwin	U.S.
Photocopier	1938	Carlson	U.S.
Photoelectric cell	1895	Elster	German
Photographic paper	1835	Talbot	English
Photography	1816	Niepce	French
Photography	1835	Daguerre	French
Photography	1835	Talbot	English
Photophone	1880	Bell	U.S.-Scot.
Phototelegraphy	1925	Bell Labs	U.S.
Piano	1709	Cristofori	Italian
Piano, player	1863	Fourneaux	French
Pin, safety	1849	Hunt	U.S.
Pistol (revolver)	1836	Colt	U.S.
Plow, cast iron	1785	Ransome	English
Plow, disc	1896	Hardy	U.S.
Pneumatic hammer	1890	King	U.S.
Post-it note	1980	Fry, Silver	U.S.
Powder, smokeless	1884	Vieille	French
Printing press, rotary	1845	Hoe	U.S.
Printing press, web	1865	Bullock	U.S.
Propeller, screw	1804	Stevens	U.S.
Propeller, screw	1837	Ericsson	Swedish
Punch card accounting	1889	Hollerith	U.S.
Radar	1940	Watson-Watt	Scottish
Radio amplifier	1906	De Forest	U.S.
Radio beacon	1928	Donovan	U.S.
Radio crystal oscillator	1918	Nicolson	U.S.
Radio FM, 2-path	1933	Armstrong	U.S.
Radio, magnetic detector	1902	Marconi	Italian
Radio receiver, cascade tuning	1913	Alexanderson	U.S.
Radio receiver, heterodyne	1913	Fessenden	Canadian
Radio, signals	1895	Marconi	Italian
Radio transmitter triode modulation	1914	Alexanderson	U.S.
Radio tube diode	1904	Fleming	English
Radio tube oscillator	1915	De Forest	U.S.
Radio tube triode	1906	De Forest	U.S.
Rayon (acetate)	1895	Cross	English
Rayon (cuprammonium)	1890	Despeissis	French
Rayon (nitrocellulose)	1884	Chardonnet	French
Razor, electric	1928	Schick	U.S.
Razor, safety	1895	Gillette	U.S.
Reading machine for the blind	1976	Kurzweil	U.S.
Reaper	1834	McCormick	U.S.
Record, cylinder	1887	Bell, Tainter	U.S.
Record, disc	1887	Berliner	U.S.
Record, long playing	1947	Goldmark	U.S.
Record, wax cylinder	1888	Edison	U.S.
Refrigerator car	1868	David	U.S.
Remote control	1898	Tesla	U.S.
Resin, synthetic	1931	Hill	English
Richter scale	1935	Richter	U.S.
Rifle, repeating	1860	Henry	U.S.
Rocket, liquid fuel	1926	Goddard	U.S.
Rollerblades	1980	Olson	U.S.
Rubber, vulcanized	1839	Goodyear	U.S.
Saccharin	1879	Remsen, Fahlberg	U.S.
Saw, circular	1777	Miller	English
Scotch tape	1930	Drew	U.S.
Seat belt	1959	Volvo	Swedish
Segway human transporter	2001	Kamen	U.S.
Seismograph	1880	Milne, Ewing, Gray	Eng.-Scot.
Sewing machine	1790	Saint	English
Shoe-lasting machine	1883	Matzeliger	U.S.
Shoe-sewing machine	1860	McKay	U.S.
Shrapnel shell	1784	Shrapnel	English
Shuttle, flying	1733	Kay	English
Skates, in-line	1759	Merlin	Belgian
Sleeping-car	1865	Pullman	U.S.
Slide rule	1620	Oughtred	English
Slinky	1943	James	U.S.
Smoke detector	1969	Smith, House	U.S.
Soap, hardwater	1928	Bertsch	German
Spectroscope	1859	Kirchoff, Bunsen	German
Spectroscope (mass)	1918	Dempster	U.S.
Spinning jenny	c.1764	Hargreaves	English
Spinning mule	1779	Crompton	English
Steam car	1770	Cugnot	French
Steam turbine	1884	Parsons	English
Steamboat, exp'mtl	1778	Jouffroy	French
Steamboat, exp'mtl	1785	Fitch	U.S.
Steamboat, exp'mtl	1787	Rumsey	U.S.
Steamboat, exp'mtl	1803	Fulton	U.S.
Steamboat, exp'mtl	1804	Stevens	U.S.
Steamboat, practical	1802	Symington	Scottish
Steamboat, practical	1807	Fulton	U.S.
Steel alloy, high-speed	1901	Taylor, White	U.S.
Steel (converter)	1856	Bessemer	English
Steel, manganese	1884	Hadfield	English
Steel, stainless	1916	Brearley	English
Stereoscope	1838	Wheatstone	English
Stethoscope	1819	Laennec	French
Stethoscope, binaural	1840	Cammann	U.S.
Stock ticker	1870	Edison	U.S.
Storage battery, rechargeable	1859	Plante	French
Stove, electric	1896	Hadaway	U.S.
Submarine	1891	Holland	U.S.
Submarine, even keel	1894	Lake	U.S.
Submarine, torpedo	1776	Bushnell	U.S.
Synthesizer	1964	Moog	U.S.
Tank, military	1914	Swinton	English
Tape recorder, magnetic	1899	Poulsen	Danish
Taser	1974	Cover	U.S.
Teflon	1938	Du Pont	U.S.
Telegraph, magnetic	1837	Morse	U.S.
Telegraph, quadruplex	1864	Edison	U.S.
Telegraph, railroad	1887	Woods	U.S.
Telegraph, wireless high frequency	1895	Marconi	Italian
Telephone[1]	1871	Meucci	U.S.-Italian
Telephone[1]	1876	Bell	U.S.-Scot.
Telephone amplifier	1912	De Forest	U.S.
Telephone answering machine (1st practical)	1954	Hashimoto	Japanese
Telephone, automatic	1891	Strowger	U.S.
Telephone, cellular	1947	Bell Labs	U.S.
Telephone, cordless[2]	1950	Gross	U.S.
Telephone, radio	1900	Poulsen / Fessenden	Danish / Canadian
Telephone, radio	1906	De Forest	U.S.
Telephone, radio, long distance	1915	AT&T	U.S.
Telephone, recording	1898	Poulsen	Danish
Telescope	1608	Lippershey	Dutch
Telescope	1609	Galileo	Italian
Telescope, astronomical	1611	Kepler	German
Telescope, reflecting	1668	Newton	English
Teletype	1928	Morkrum, Kleinschmidt	U.S.
Television, color	1928	Baird	Scottish
Television, electronic	1927	Farnsworth	U.S.
Television, iconoscope	1923	Zworykin	U.S.
Television, mech. scanner	1923	Baird	Scottish
Tesla coil	1891	Tesla	U.S.
Thermometer	1593	Galileo	Italian
Thermometer	1730	Reaumur	French
Thermometer, mercury	1714	Fahrenheit	German
3D printing (stereolithography)	1984	Hull	U.S.
Time recorder	1890	Bundy	U.S.
Tire, double-tube	1845	Thomson	Scottish
Tire, pneumatic	1888	Dunlop	Scottish
Toaster, automatic	1921	Strite	U.S.
Toilet, flush	1589	Harington	English
Torpedo, marine	1804	Fulton	U.S.
Tractor, crawler	1904	Holt	U.S.
Transformer, AC	1885	Stanley	U.S.
Transistor	1947	Shockley, Brattain, Bardeen	U.S.
Trolley car, electric	1884-87	Van DePoele, Sprague	U.S.
Tungsten, ductile	1912	Coolidge	U.S.
Tupperware®	1945	Tupper	U.S.
Turbine, gas	1849	Bourdin	French
Turbine, hydraulic	1849	Francis	U.S.
Turbine, steam	1884	Parsons	English
Type, movable	1447	Gutenberg	German
Typewriter	1867	Sholes, Soule, Glidden	U.S.
Universal Serial Bus (USB)	1994	Bhatt, et al.	U.S.
Vacuum cleaner, electric	1907	Spangler	U.S.
Vacuum evaporating pan	1846	Rillieux	U.S.
Velcro	1948	de Mestral	Swiss

Invention	Date	Inventor(s)	Nationality
Video game ("Pong")	1972	Bushnell	U.S.
Video home system (VHS)	1975	Matsushita, JVC	Japanese
Vinyl	1926	Semon	U.S.
Washer, electric	1901	Fisher	U.S.
Welding, atomic hydrogen	1924	Langmuir, Palmer	U.S.
Welding, electric	1877	Thomson	U.S.
Wheelchair, multiterrain	1986	Twitchell	U.S.
Wheelchair, stair-climbing	1962	Blanco	U.S.
Wiki software	1995	Cunningham	U.S.
Wind tunnel	1912	Eiffel	French
Windshield wiper	1903	Anderson	U.S.
Wire, barbed	1874	Glidden	U.S.
World Wide Web	1989	Berners-Lee	English
Wrench, double-acting	1913	Owen	U.S.
X-ray tube	1913	Coolidge	U.S.
Zamboni	1949	Zamboni	U.S.
Zeppelin	1900	Zeppelin	German
Zipper, early model	1893	Judson	U.S.
Zipper, improved	1913	Sundback	Canadian

(1) While Alexander Graham Bell has traditionally been credited with invention of the telephone, which he patented, Antonio Meucci developed a working model before Bell. (2) Al Gross held a number of important early patents in the field of wireless communication; other people were also involved in the development of practical cordless telephones.

U.S. Patents by Field of Technology, 2000-21

Source: World Intellectual Property Organization Statistics Database

(ranked by number of utility patents, or patents for inventions, for the top 20 fields in 2021, as of June 2023)

Field	2000	2005	2010	2015	2017	2019	2020	2021	% change 2000-21
Computer technology	12,123	14,273	33,428	46,811	46,045	51,600	53,585	52,934	336.64%
Digital communication	3,339	4,982	9,093	23,359	27,616	32,003	32,691	30,745	820.78
Medical technology	8,049	6,121	10,248	16,248	18,217	21,999	21,880	20,746	157.75
Electrical machinery, apparatus, energy	9,533	9,299	14,266	18,692	21,823	23,632	22,125	19,904	108.79
Semiconductors	9,163	9,988	14,288	18,374	19,085	18,746	18,871	17,237	88.12
Audio-visual technology	7,915	8,165	12,139	15,912	16,358	16,853	16,564	15,218	92.27
Measurement	6,874	7,563	10,728	12,273	14,469	16,535	15,876	14,636	112.92
Transport	7,215	6,387	6,805	11,090	12,953	15,144	15,149	14,103	95.47
Optics	7,496	8,303	10,800	11,665	11,622	12,909	12,260	10,932	45.84
Telecommunications	6,173	6,706	11,365	12,839	12,221	12,114	11,203	9,693	57.02
Other special machines	4,957	3,611	4,644	6,142	6,957	8,182	8,384	7,897	59.31
Control	2,722	2,672	4,419	5,646	7,032	8,745	8,654	7,839	187.99
IT methods for management	749	1,170	3,578	3,526	4,829	7,529	7,931	7,791	940.19
Pharmaceuticals	3,997	2,830	5,117	6,902	7,216	7,508	7,820	7,692	92.44
Engines, pumps, turbines	4,141	4,264	4,158	6,302	7,467	8,734	8,621	7,530	81.84
Mechanical elements	4,885	3,796	4,337	6,926	7,514	8,266	7,993	7,199	47.37
Civil engineering	4,419	3,484	4,751	6,434	6,904	8,275	7,980	7,197	62.86
Furniture, games	4,951	3,593	5,040	5,913	6,366	6,924	6,761	6,253	26.30
Biotechnology	3,864	2,811	3,981	5,422	6,025	6,285	6,285	6,043	56.39
Handling	4,400	3,134	4,369	5,161	5,557	6,384	6,295	5,979	35.89

Patent Offices Granting Most Utility Patents, 2000-21

Source: World Intellectual Property Organization Statistics Database

(ranked by 2021 figures; as of June 2023)

National or regional office	2000	2005	2010	2015	2017	2019	2020	2021
China	13,058	53,305	135,110	359,316	420,144	452,804	530,127	695,946
United States	157,496	143,806	219,614	298,407	318,829	354,430	351,993	327,307
Japan	125,880	122,944	222,693	189,358	199,577	179,910	179,383	184,372
South Korea	34,956	73,512	68,843	101,873	120,662	125,661	134,766	145,882
European Patent Office	27,523	53,258	58,108	68,431	105,645	137,782	133,706	108,799
India	1,263	4,320	7,138	6,022	12,387	23,578	26,361	30,721
Brazil	NA	2,439	3,251	3,411	5,450	10,947	20,407	26,872
Russia	17,592	23,390	30,322	34,706	34,254	34,008	28,788	23,662
Canada	12,125	15,516	19,120	22,201	24,099	22,009	21,284	22,687
Germany	14,707	17,063	13,678	14,795	15,653	18,255	17,305	21,113
Australia	13,548	10,979	14,557	23,098	22,742	17,010	17,778	17,155
France	11,274	11,473	9,899	12,699	11,865	13,593	12,874	15,493
Hong Kong	2,737	6,518	5,353	5,963	6,671	6,780	7,658	14,662
United Kingdom	8,253	10,159	5,594	5,464	6,311	5,948	9,772	10,895
Mexico	5,527	8,098	9,399	9,338	8,510	8,702	7,726	10,369
Italy	5,285	5,534	16,106	7,153	4,855	8,617	9,152	7,254
Malaysia	405	2,508	2,160	2,877	5,063	4,106	8,206	6,876
Indonesia	NA	NA	NA	1,911	2,309	10,514	7,981	6,850
Singapore	5,090	7,530	4,442	7,054	6,217	4,188	5,386	6,488
South Africa	3,399	1,831	5,331	4,499	5,535	6,162	3,466	6,107
Israel	2,033	2,269	2,293	4,492	NA	4,197	4,668	5,488
Vietnam	727	668	822	1,388	1,745	2,620	4,319	3,691
World	516,900	632,400	914,200	1,239,600	1,403,000	1,506,900	1,596,500	1,756,500

NA = Not available.

U.S. Utility Patents, 1790-2020

Source: U.S. Patent and Trademark Office, U.S. Dept. of Commerce

Year	Patent applications	Patents granted	Year	Patent applications	Patents granted	Year	Patent applications	Patents granted
1790	NA	3	1990	164,558	90,365	2010	490,226	219,614
1810	NA	223	2000	295,926	157,494	2011	503,582	224,505
1830	NA	544	2001	326,508	166,035	2012	542,815	253,155
1850	2,193	884	2002	334,445	167,331	2013	571,612	277,835
1870	19,171	12,157	2003	342,441	169,023	2014	578,802	300,677
1890	39,884	25,308	2004	356,943	164,290	2015	589,410	298,408
1910	63,293	35,130	2005	390,733	143,806	2016	605,571	303,049
1930	89,554	45,226	2006	425,967	173,772	2017	606,956	318,828
1950	67,264	43,039	2007	456,154	157,282	2018	597,141	307,759
1970	103,175	64,429	2008	456,321	157,772	2019	621,453	354,430
1980	104,329	61,819	2009	456,106	167,349	2020	597,175	352,066

NA = Not available.

TECHNOLOGY

Computer Milestones

1623: German mathematician Wilhelm Schickard developed the first mechanical calculator, capable of adding, subtracting, multiplying, and dividing.

1642: French mathematician Blaise Pascal built the first of more than four dozen copies of an adding and subtracting machine that he invented.

1801: French inventor Joseph Marie Jacquard demonstrated a new control system for looms. He "programmed" the loom, communicating desired weaving operations to the machine via patterns of holes in paper cards.

1833-71: British mathematician and scientist Charles Babbage used the Jacquard punch-card system in his design for a sophisticated, programmable "Analytical Engine" that foreshadowed basic computer features. Babbage's concept was beyond the capabilities of the technology of his time, and the machine remained unfinished at his death in 1871.

1889: American engineer Herman Hollerith patented an electromechanical punch-card tabulating system that facilitated the handling of large amounts of statistical data and quickly found use in censuses in the U.S. and other countries.

1911: Hollerith's Tabulating Machine Company merged with two other enterprises to form the Computing-Tabulating-Recording Company, which was renamed the International Business Machines Corporation (IBM) in 1924.

1941: German engineer Konrad Züse completed the Z3, the first fully functional digital computer to be controlled by a program; the Z3 was not electronic—it was based on electrical switches called relays.

1942: Iowa State Coll. physicist John Vincent Atanasoff and assistant Clifford Berry completed a working model of the first fully electronic computer using vacuum tubes, which could operate much more quickly than relays; the rudimentary machine was not programmable.

1943: IBM and Harvard professor Howard Aiken completed the first large-scale automatic digital computer, the Mark I, a relay-based machine 55-ft long and 8-ft high. British scientists built their first Colossus machine, an electronic computer for breaking German codes during World War II.

1946: ENIAC (Electronic Numerical Integrator and Computer), a 30-ton room-sized electronic computer with more than 18,000 vacuum tubes, was completed by physicist John Mauchly and engineer J. Presper Eckert at the Univ. of Pennsylvania for the U.S. Army. ENIAC could be programmed to do different tasks, but cables had to be plugged in, and switches had to be set by hand.

1951: Eckert and Mauchly's UNIVAC (Universal Automatic Computer) became the first commercially available computer in the U.S. Its first customer was the Census Bureau. CBS-TV used a UNIVAC in 1952 to predict election results.

1955: In the first known use of the term, four U.S. computer scientists proposed a workshop on "artificial intelligence." It took place the next year at Dartmouth Coll.

1959: COBOL, a computer programming language designed for business use, first appeared, based on programming language innovations of American mathematician Grace Hopper.

1967: American computer pioneer Doug Engelbart applied for a patent on the mouse.

1969-71: The powerful Unix operating system was developed at Bell Laboratories; later versions became widely used on large computers and formed the basis for the Macintosh OS X operating system (introduced in 2001).

1971: Intel released the 4004, the first commercial microprocessor (an entire computer processing unit on a chip).

1973: The Alto computer, developed at Xerox's Palo Alto Research Center, became operational, implementing many features of modern commercial personal computers, including a graphical user interface (GUI) featuring windows, icons, and pointers that could be manipulated by a mouse.

1975: The first widely marketed personal computer (PC), the MITS Altair 8800, was introduced in kit form, with no keyboard, video display, or printer, for under $400. Microsoft was founded by Americans Bill Gates and Paul Allen.

1976: The first word-processing program for personal computers, Electric Pencil, was written. Apple Computer Company was founded by Americans Steven Jobs and Stephen Wozniak.

1977: Apple introduced the Apple II; capable of displaying text and graphics in color, the machine enjoyed phenomenal success.

1981: IBM unveiled its Personal Computer (IBM 5150), which used an operating system from Microsoft known as MS-DOS (Disk Operating System).

1984: Apple introduced the first Macintosh. The easy-to-use Macintosh came with a proprietary operating system and was the first popular computer to have a GUI and a mouse.

1990: Microsoft released Windows 3.0, the first workable version of its own GUI. Adobe released the first commercial version of the image-editing software Photoshop.

1991: The Unix-like Linux operating system was invented by Helsinki Univ. student Linus Torvalds and made available for free.

1996: The Palm Pilot, the first widely successful handheld computer and personal information manager, arrived.

1997: The IBM supercomputer Deep Blue beat Russian world chess champion Garry Kasparov in a 6-game match, 2-1, with 3 draws.

2002: The total number of personal computers, including desktop and laptop machines of all types, shipped by manufacturers since 1975 reached 1 bil.

2007: Amazon launched the Kindle, a hardware/software system for displaying books electronically.

2008: Google released the Linux-based Android operating system for mobile devices.

2010: Apple released the iPad tablet computer and sold more than 3 mil devices in the first 80 days.

2012: Microsoft released Windows 8, featuring enhanced support for touchscreens and an interface with a grid of tiles displaying actively updated content and apps.

2015: Microsoft released Windows 10, promising faster startup and improved security, along with features like a personal digital assistant and a new web browser, Microsoft Edge.

2016: Univ. of Maryland scientists developed the first reprogrammable quantum computer; it used lasers to manipulate its five qubits, or bits of quantum information.

2022: Apple became the first company in the world to achieve a stock market value of $3 tril; in 2018, it had become the first company to hit $1 tril. The U.S. supercomputer Frontier became the first "exascale" computer, capable of more than 1 exaflop, or 1 quintillion (billion billion) operations per second.

World's Fastest Supercomputers, 2023

Source: Top500.org, as of midyear 2023

Rank	Name	Location	Manufacturer/ vendor	Processors (cores)	Top speed[1]
1.	Frontier	Oak Ridge National Laboratory, TN, U.S	HPE Cray	8,699,904	1,194.00
2.	Supercomputer Fugaku	RIKEN Center for Computational Science, Japan	Fujitsu	7,630,848	442.01
3.	LUMI	EuroHPC at CSC Data Center, Kajaani, Finland	HPE Cray	2,220,288	309.10
4.	Leonardo	EuroHPC at CINECA, Bologna, Italy	Atos	1,824,768	238.70
5.	Summit	Oak Ridge National Laboratory, TN, U.S.	IBM	2,414,592	148.60
6.	Sierra	Lawrence Livermore National Laboratory, CA, U.S.	IBM	1,572,480	94.64
7.	Sunway TaihuLight	National Supercomputing Center, Wuxi, China	NRCPC[2]	10,649,600	93.01
8.	Perlmutter	National Energy Research Scientific Computing Center, CA, U.S.	HPE Cray	761,856	70.87
9.	Selene	Nvidia, Santa Clara, CA, U.S	Nvidia	555,520	63.46
10.	Tianhe-2A (Milky Way-2A)	National Super Computer Center, Guangzhou, China	NUDT[3]	4,981,760	61.44
11.	Explorer-WUS3	West US3, AZ, U.S.	Microsoft Azure	445,440	53.96
12.	Adastra	GENCI-CINES, Montpellier, France	HPE Cray	319,072	46.10
13.	JUWELS Booster Module	Forschungszentrum Jülich, Jülich, Germany	Atos	449,280	44.12
14.	Pre-Eos 128 Node DGX SuperPOD	Nvidia, U.S.	Nvidia	81,920	40.66
15.	HPC5	Eni S.p.A., Italy	Dell EMC	669,760	35.45

Note: The 500 fastest supercomputers use versions of the Linux operating system. (1) Top speed, in petaflops, achieved as measured according to the Linpack Benchmark. 1 petaflop = 1 quadrillion floating-point operations per sec. (2) NRCPC = National Research Center of Parallel Computer Engineering and Technology. (3) NUDT = National University of Defense Technology.

Top Operating Systems Worldwide, 2009-23

Source: StatCounter Global Stats, gs.statcounter.com

(ranked by 2023 figures)

Operating system	2009	2011	2013	2015	2017	2019	2021	2023
				% of OS market				
Android	0.02	1.39	7.62	25.62	41.24	39.91	41.56	40.12
Windows	93.85	85.45	71.37	50.85	35.24	35.12	30.20	29.34
iOS	0.36	2.18	7.72	11.37	13.20	13.85	16.55	16.78
OS X	4.07	5.79	6.14	4.90	4.66	5.94	6.38	8.62
Unknown	0.37	0.47	0.67	2.28	2.99	3.33	3.36	1.64
Chrome OS	—	—	0.02	0.15	0.19	0.24	0.50	1.36
Linux	0.76	0.71	1.26	1.12	0.77	0.77	0.99	1.33
Xbox	—	—	—	0.03	0.04	0.08	0.03	0.50

— = Not available. **Note:** Percent of users accessing the web with a particular operating system (OS), for July of year shown. Includes desktop, laptop, tablet, console, and mobile devices' operating systems.

U.S. Sales and Household Penetration of Selected Hardware, 2020-22

Source: Consumer Technology Association

(factory sales to dealers in thousands of units and millions of dollars: percent of all households for Jan. of year shown)

Hardware	2020			2021			2022		
	Units	Sales	%	Units	Sales	%	Unit	Sales	%
Smartphones	139,826	$63,307	92%	153,808	$74,512	90%	139,196	$74,177	98%
Televisons	49,478	21,367	93	46,536	21,530	91	40,843	18,689	91
Laptop/notebook/netbook PCs[1]	69,561	40,121	76	76,517	46,259	73	58,685	39,771	72
Tablet computers	50,616	11,409	65	52,704	16,176	61	45,918	14,163	59
Streaming media players	23,898	1,155	53	20,261	928	55	19,507	933	55
Home game consoles	13,496	4,347	48	14,549	6,091	53	14,112	5,613	52
Desktop computers[1,2]	14,577	8,186	55	15,339	11,111	53	16,438	12,756	51
Digital cameras	4,210	1,513	51	3,987	1,480	36	3,829	1,427	34
Smartwatches	25,605	6,521	31	24,438	6,508	35	24,487	6,587	34
E-readers	4,838	299	29	4,450	294	27	4,494	303	26
Action camcorders	2,132	337	9	2,218	367	10	2,251	367	9

Note: Based on sales data tracking and consumer surveys conducted by CTA. (1) Includes commercial and consumer shipments. (2) Includes all-in-one computers.

Device Market Share in the U.S., 2009-23

Source: StatCounter Global Stats, gs.statcounter.com

Device type	2009	2011	2013	2015	2017	2019	2020	2021	2023
					% of market				
Desktops	98.29%	91.64%	78.34%	61.51%	46.32%	47.84%	49.58%	46.44%	65.72%
Mobile devices	1.71	8.36	14.65	29.05	44.10	44.22	45.87	49.86	32.52
Tablets	—	—	7.01	9.44	9.58	7.94	4.55	3.70	1.77

— = Not available. **Note:** Percent of users accessing the web for July of year shown with desktops (including laptops), mobile devices (pocket-sized computing devices typically featuring a display screen with touch input or a miniature keyboard), and tablets (portable computing devices that are larger than a mobile device and have a touchscreen interface).

Device Market Share in the World, 2009-23

Source: StatCounter Global Stats, gs.statcounter.com

Device type	2009	2011	2013	2015	2017	2019	2020	2021	2023
					% of market				
Mobile devices	1.05%	7.02%	16.51%	37.15%	53.99%	51.11%	50.88%	55.89%	55.67%
Desktops	98.95	92.98	78.66	57.00	41.22	45.18	46.39	41.36	42.40
Tablets	—	—	4.83	5.85	4.79	3.71	2.74	2.74	1.93

— = Not available. **Note:** Percent of users accessing the web for July of year shown with desktops (including laptops), mobile devices (pocket-sized computing devices typically featuring a display screen with touch input or a miniature keyboard), and tablets (portable computing devices that are larger than a mobile device and have a touchscreen interface).

Percentage of Households With Access to the Internet by Region and Development Level, 2005-20

Source: ITU World Telecommunication/ICT Indicators Database (estimated data)

	2005	2007	2009	2011	2013	2014	2015	2016	2017	2018	2019	2020
Africa	1.8%	2.3%	4.2%	6.9%	9.6%	11.1%	12.9%	14.2%	15.9%	17.9%	20.0%	22.7%
Americas	34.4	37.5	43.0	48.7	55.8	58.6	60.7	63.3	66.7	69.5	72.2	75.9
Arab States	10.5	15.3	21.6	30.5	37.3	41.2	45.5	47.8	51.8	53.1	57.0	62.4
Asia & Pacific	12.3	17.3	22.5	27.4	34.1	37.3	41.2	44.3	47.9	52.7	58.6	64.1
Commonwealth of Independent States	14.4	21.7	32.9	46.2	62.2	65.7	69.3	72.2	73.4	77.2	78.2	81.7
Europe	39.0	47.9	58.6	67.3	73.3	75.3	76.7	79.0	80.9	82.8	85.4	87.6
Developed Countries	44.9	53.4	62.6	69.7	77.5	78.9	80.1	81.3	83.1	84.4	86.0	87.8
Developing Countries	9.0	12.7	17.7	23.3	29.5	32.9	36.5	39.7	43.0	47.3	52.6	57.8
Least Developed Countries	0.6	1.3	2.5	4.2	6.7	8.6	10.7	13.8	15.9	17.9	19.9	22.0
World	19.6	24.4	30.3	35.8	42.3	45.0	47.9	51.0	53.9	57.3	61.5	65.7

About the Internet

The internet is not owned or funded by any one institution, organization, or government. It has no CEO and is not a commercial service. Its development is guided by the Internet Society (ISOC), a nonprofit formed in 1992. The Internet Society helps fund the Internet Engineering Task Force (IETF), which deals with short-term issues of standards and the internet's architecture. The Internet Architecture Board (IAB), a committee of the IETF, oversees the latter's work and appoints the chair of the Internet Research Task Force (IRTF). The IAB and IRTF focus on long-term issues.

Major Historical Highlights

1969: ARPANET, an experimental four-computer network, was established by the Advanced Research Projects Agency (ARPA) of the U.S. Defense Dept. Two years later, ARPANET linked about 23 computers ("hosts") at 15 sites, including MIT and Harvard.

1971: Engineer Bob Thomas created Creeper, generally considered the first worm, a virus able to self-replicate over a network.

1976: British evolutionary biologist Richard Dawkins coined the term "meme," referring to an idea or a behavior that persists and may spread "virally."

1978: The first spam, or junk email, was sent over ARPANET.

1982: Author William Gibson coined the term "cyberspace" in the story "Burning Chrome."

1983: The set of communications rules (protocol) known as TCP/IP became the main networking protocol of ARPANET. Its adoption was tantamount to the birth of the internet. The military portion of ARPANET was moved onto MILNET.

1986: The U.S. National Science Foundation (NSF) launched NSFNET, the first large-scale network using internet technology.

1988: Internet Relay Chat (IRC) was developed by Finnish student Jarkko Oikarinen, enabling people to communicate via the internet in "real time."

1988: A worm crafted by Cornell Univ. computer science graduate student Robert Morris Jr. infected thousands of computers, shutting many down and causing millions of dollars of damage—the first known case of large-scale damage caused by a computer virus spread via the internet.

1989: Massachusetts-based The World—the first commercial internet service provider supplying dial-up access—debuted.

1989-90: English scientist Tim Berners-Lee invented the World Wide Web. Created as an environment in which scientists at the European Center for Nuclear Research in Switzerland could share information, it gradually evolved into a medium with text, graphics, audio, animation, and video.

1990: ARPANET was disbanded.

1991: NSFNET was opened to commercial traffic. Berners-Lee introduced the first browser, or software for accessing the web.

1993: The National Center for Supercomputing Applications (U.S.) released versions of Mosaic, the first web browser able to present both text and images on a single page.

1993: A coffee pot at England's Cambridge Univ. became the subject of the first live streaming (and the first webcam).

1994: Netscape Communications released the Netscape Navigator browser.

1995: Microsoft released its Internet Explorer browser. It initially failed to make a dent in Netscape's dominance of the browser market, but Internet Explorer surpassed Netscape by 1999.

1995: Amazon and AuctionWeb (now eBay) began operating online.

1997: The initial version of the WiFi network protocol was released.

1998: Under a contract with the U.S. Dept. of Commerce, the nonprofit Internet Corporation for Assigned Names and Numbers (ICANN) took over the management of assigning domain names and internet protocol (IP) addresses.

1999: Release of the free Napster file-sharing service enabled users to easily exchange files containing music or other content without regard to copyright restrictions.

2000: Estonia became the first country to pass a law declaring internet access a fundamental human right of its citizens.

2004: A group of Harvard students founded social network TheFacebook (later just Facebook).

2004: The Mozilla Foundation released the first official version of the open-source browser Mozilla Firefox.

2006: The microblogging and social networking service Twitter was introduced.

2008: Google introduced its Chrome browser. By 2012, Chrome ranked as the most widely used browser in the world, according to StatCounter.com.

2009: The software for Bitcoin, the world's first "cryptocurrency," was released. It relied on cryptography and a complex decentralized public ledger to secure transactions.

2011: ICANN decided to allow the use of almost any characters in any language for the names of generic top-level domains.

2012: The number of Facebook users surpassed 1 bil.

2014: The number of internet hosts (websites) passed 1 bil.

2014: Estonia became the first country in the world to offer noncitizens "e-residency"—a government-issued transnational digital identity.

2016: The leak of more than 11.5 mil documents from Panamanian law firm Mossack Fonseca, which said it was the victim of a hack, exposed large-scale offshore tax evasion.

2016: Global internet traffic surpassed 1 zettabyte (1 tril gigabytes), according to networking giant Cisco.

2017: The number of Facebook users surpassed 2 bil.

2018: Amid growing concern over the misuse of individuals' personal data, the European Union's General Data Protection Regulation (GDPR) went into effect, providing strong safeguards governing personal data held by any organization worldwide that conducts business in Europe.

2018: By year's end the proportion of the world's population using the internet had passed the 50% mark, according to the Intl. Telecommunications Union.

2021: A ransomware cyberattack caused a multi-day shutdown of the Colonial Pipeline, provider of almost half the fuel supply of the U.S. East Coast.

2022: OpenAI released ChatGPT, a chatbot (software capable of human-like conversation) for public use, quickly setting a record for the fastest-growing user base of a consumer internet application. Trained on massive amounts of existing data, and an example of so-called generative artificial intelligence, ChatGPT could upon request produce text, poetry, computer code, and more.

2023: An official advisory from the U.S. surgeon general warned of potential harmful effects of social media use on the mental health and well-being of children and adolescents.

2023: Amid growing public and White House concern over the risks of misuse of artificial intelligence, OpenAI and other leading companies agreed to take steps to ensure the safety, security, and trustworthiness of the technology.

Safety and Security on the Internet

Common sense dictates some basic security rules:

- Avoid using the same password for multiple websites. A password manager can generate passwords and then save them.
- Do not give out your phone number, address, credit card number, or other personal information unless needed for a transaction at a site you trust.
- If you feel someone is being threatening or dangerous, inform your internet service provider.
- Use protective firewall, antivirus, and antispyware software to guard your system against attacks by hackers.
- Be careful about opening email and file attachments from unknown correspondents.
- To avoid falling victim to **phishing**—which uses a forged email message, purportedly from a respectable organization, to elicit personal data—do not click on hyperlinks in emails from companies with which you do business. Phishing emails typically contain a link leading to a fabricated website resembling the site of the ostensible sender. If you want to visit a company's website, open your browser and manually enter the site's address.
- Users of so-called **peer-to-peer** (P2P) file-sharing networks or protocols should open up only part of their computer system, not their entire hard drive, to sharing.
- When manufacturers provide **patches** to solve security flaws or other problems with operating systems, web browsers, or other software, it is usually advisable to install these fixes. If a fix is not available for a serious security problem, consider switching to an alternative program.

Internet Addresses

The fundamental part of an address on the internet is called the domain. The final part of a domain name, known as the **top-level domain (TLD)**, is its most basic part. For example, .com is the top-level domain of many mainstream web addresses. So-called generic top-level domains (gTLDs) consist of three or more letters. Domain names with two letters are generally for countries or regions. Country-code TLDs (ccTLDs) are usually managed by an organization within a certain country.

Worst Data Breaches, 2010-22

Source: Upguard, Inc.

(ranked by approximate number of exposed data records, as of Apr. 2023)

Rank	Company	Year	Records exposed (mil)	Rank	Company	Year	Records exposed (mil)
1.	CAM4	2020	10,880	9.	Yahoo	2014	500
2.	Yahoo	2013	3,000	10.	Marriott/Starwood	2018	500
3.	Aadhaar	2018	1,100	11.	Friend Finder	2016	412
4.	Alibaba	2022	1,100	12.	MySpace	2013	360
5.	First American Financial Corp.	2019	885	13.	Exactis	2018	340
6.	Verifications.io	2019	763	14.	Twitter	2018	330
7.	LinkedIn	2021	700	15.	NetEase	2015	234
8.	Facebook	2019	533	16.	Sociallarks	2021	200

U.S. Internet Crimes by Number of Victims, 2020-22

Source: Internet Crime Complaint Center, Federal Bureau of Investigation (FBI)

(ranked by reported number of victims in 2022)

Rank	Type of crime	2020	2021	2022
1.	Phishing[1]	241,342	323,972	300,497
2.	Personal data breach	45,330	51,829	58,859
3.	Non-payment/non-delivery	108,869	82,478	51,679
4.	Extortion	76,741	39,360	39,416
5.	Tech support	15,421	23,903	32,538
6.	Investment	8,788	20,561	30,529
7.	Identity theft	43,330	51,629	27,922
8.	Credit card/check fraud	17,614	16,750	22,985
9.	Business email compromise/email account compromise	19,369	19,954	21,832
10.	Spoofing[2]	28,218	18,522	20,649
11.	Confidence fraud/romance	23,751	24,299	19,021
12.	Employment	16,879	15,253	14,946
13.	*Harassment/stalking	NA	NA	11,779
14.	Real estate	13,638	11,578	11,727
15.	Government impersonation	12,827	11,335	11,554
16.	Advanced fee	13,020	11,034	11,264
17.	Other	10,372	12,346	9,966
18.	Overpayment[3]	10,988	6,108	6,183
19.	Lottery/sweepstakes/inheritance	8,501	5,991	5,650
20.	Data breach	2,794	1,287	2,795

* = New crime type added in 2022. NA = not available. (1) The use of unsolicited email, text messages, and telephone calls purportedly from a legitimate company requesting personal, financial, and/or login credentials. (2) Contact information (phone number, email, and/or website) is deliberately falsified to mislead and appear to be from a legitimate source. (3) An individual is sent a payment/commission and is instructed to keep a portion of the payment and send the remainder to another individual or business.

U.S. Internet Crimes by Losses, 2020-22

Source: Internet Crime Complaint Center, Federal Bureau of Investigation (FBI)

(ranked by dollar value of reported 2022 losses)

Rank	Type of crime	2020	2021	2022
1.	Investment	$336,469,000	$1,455,943,193	$3,311,742,206
2.	Business email compromise/email account compromise	1,866,642,107	2,395,953,296	2,742,354,049
3.	Tech support	146,477,709	347,657,432	806,551,993
4.	Personal data breach	194,473,055	517,021,289	742,438,136
5.	Confidence fraud/romance	600,249,821	956,039,739	735,882,192
6.	Data breach	128,916,648	151,568,225	459,321,859
7.	Real estate	213,196,082	350,328,166	396,932,821
8.	Non-payment/non-delivery	265,011,249	337,493,071	281,770,073
9.	Credit card/check fraud	129,820,792	172,998,385	264,148,905
10.	Government impersonation	109,938,030	142,643,253	240,553,091
11.	Identity theft	219,484,699	278,267,918	189,205,793
12.	Other	101,523,082	75,837,524	117,686,789
13.	Spoofing	216,513,728	82,169,806	107,926,252
14.	Advanced fee	83,215,405	98,694,137	104,325,444
15.	Lottery/sweepstakes/Inheritance	61,111,319	71,289,089	83,602,376
16.	*SIM swap	NA	NA	72,652,571
17.	Extortion	70,935,939	60,577,741	54,335,128
18.	Employment	62,314,015	47,231,023	52,204,269
19.	Phishing	54,241,075	44,213,707	52,089,159
20.	Overpayment	51,039,922	33,407,671	38,335,772
21.	Ransomware[1]	29,157,405	49,207,908	34,353,237

* = New crime type added in 2022. NA = not available. (1) Does not include estimates of lost business, time, wages, files, or equipment, or any third-party remediation services acquired by a victim. In some cases, victims do not report any loss amount to the FBI. Figure represents only what victims report to the FBI via the Internet Crime Complaint Center and does not account for victim direct reporting to FBI field offices/agents.

Fixed Broadband Penetration in Selected Countries, 2003-22

Source: Organisation for Economic Co-operation and Development (OECD)
(nonmobile broadband subscriptions per 100 inhabitants, for fourth quarter of given year; ranked by 2022 figures)

Nation	2003	2005	2007	2009	2011	2013	2015	2017	2019	2021	2022
France	5.89	15.03	24.38	30.54	34.80	37.80	40.42	42.42	44.12	46.13	46.62
Germany	5.59	12.98	23.74	31.03	33.92	35.49	37.59	40.21	42.26	44.33	44.76
Canada	15.06	20.76	27.25	30.60	32.84	34.46	36.73	38.10	40.85	41.48	42.55
United Kingdom	5.37	16.31	25.59	29.48	32.75	35.50	37.88	39.44	40.14	41.08	41.31
United States	9.59	16.38	23.22	26.04	28.31	30.36	31.85	33.27	34.65	38.45	38.45
Japan	10.90	18.15	22.46	24.72	27.28	28.11	29.66	31.16	32.49	34.77	35.68
Italy	4.17	11.77	17.06	20.28	22.51	23.09	24.89	27.55	28.94	31.61	31.55

Note: Includes internet connections with speeds greater than 256 kilobits per second (256 kbps).

Nations With Highest Percentage of Population Using the Internet, 2000-21

Source: © International Telecommunication Union; ranked by 2021 figures

Rank	Nation	2000	2005	2010	2015	2017	2018	2019	2020	2021
1.	Bahrain	6.15%	21.30%	55.00%	93.48%	95.88%	98.64%	99.70%	99.67%	100.00%
2.	Qatar	4.86	24.73	69.00	92.88	97.39	99.65	99.65	99.65	100.00
3.	Saudi Arabia	2.21	12.71	41.00	69.62	94.18	93.31	95.72	97.86	100.00
4.	United Arab Emirates	23.63	40.00	68.00	90.50	94.82	98.45	99.15	100.00	100.00
5.	Kuwait	6.73	25.93	61.40	82.00	98.00	99.60	99.54	99.11	99.70
6.	Iceland	44.47	87.00	93.39	98.20	98.26	99.01	99.50	99.53	99.69
7.	Norway	52.00	81.99	93.39	96.81	96.36	96.49	98.00	97.00	99.00
8.	Denmark	39.17	82.74	88.72	96.33	97.10	97.32	98.05	96.55	98.87
9.	Luxembourg	22.89	70.00	90.62	96.38	97.36	97.06	97.12	98.82	98.66
10.	Brunei	9.00	36.47	53.00	71.20	94.87	95.00	95.00	96.07	98.08
11.	South Korea	44.70	73.50	83.70	89.90	95.07	96.02	96.16	96.51	97.57
12.	Malaysia	21.38	48.63	56.30	71.06	80.14	81.20	84.19	89.56	96.75
13.	United Kingdom	26.82	70.00	85.00	92.00	90.42	90.69	92.52	94.82	96.68
14.	Oman	3.52	6.68	35.83	73.53	80.19	85.50	90.26	95.23	96.38
15.	Australia	46.76	63.00	76.00	84.56	86.55	90.00	93.61	96.39	96.24
16.	New Zealand	47.38	62.72	80.46	85.20	87.70	89.00	89.86	92.87	95.91
17.	Antigua and Barbuda	6.48	27.00	47.00	70.00	NA	NA	95.71	95.69	95.66
18.	Switzerland	47.10	70.10	83.90	87.48	89.69	91.80	93.15	94.35	95.57
19.	Liechtenstein	36.52	63.37	80.00	96.64	99.55	NA	93.15	94.35	95.57
20.	Ireland	17.85	41.61	69.85	83.49	84.11	87.00	87.00	92.00	95.17
21.	Bahamas	8.00	25.00	43.00	78.00	80.60	83.00	90.69	92.48	94.29
22.	Spain	13.62	47.88	65.80	78.69	84.60	86.11	90.72	93.21	93.90
23.	Andorra	10.54	37.61	81.00	87.90	91.57	NA	90.72	93.21	93.90
24.	Hong Kong	27.83	56.90	72.00	84.95	89.42	90.51	91.74	92.41	93.09
25.	Canada	51.30	71.66	80.30	90.00	92.70	94.64	91.91	92.30	92.83

NA = Not available.

Nations With the Most Internet Users

Source: *The World Factbook*, Central Intelligence Agency (CIA), estimates for nations as of 2021

Rank	Nation	Internet users[1]	% of worldwide users	Rank	Nation	Internet users[1]	% of worldwide users
1.	China	1,022,000,000	21.11%	14.	Turkey (Türkiye)	68,850,000	1.42%
2.	India	644,000,000	13.30	15.	Bangladesh	66,300,000	1.37
3.	United States	312,800,000	6.46	16.	United Kingdom	64,990,000	1.34
4.	Brazil	170,100,000	3.51	17.	Thailand	61,200,000	1.26
5.	Indonesia	167,400,000	3.46	18.	Philippines	58,300,000	1.20
6.	Russia	132,000,000	2.73	19.	France	55,900,000	1.15
7.	Nigeria	115,500,000	2.39	20.	South Korea	50,960,000	1.05
8.	Japan	99,600,000	2.06	21.	Pakistan	48,300,000	1.00
9.	Mexico	98,800,000	2.04	22.	Italy	44,250,000	0.91
10.	Egypt	79,200,000	1.64	23.	Spain	44,180,000	0.91
11.	Germany	75,530,000	1.56	24.	South Africa	42,480,000	0.88
12.	Vietnam	71,780,000	1.48	25.	Argentina	39,150,000	0.81
13.	Iran	69,520,000	1.44		World	4,840,690,000	100.00

(1) Estimated number of individuals who can access the internet at home, via any device type (computer or mobile) and connection.

Top Web Browsers Worldwide, 2009-23

Source: StatCounter Global Stats, gs.statcounter.com
(ranked by 2023 figures)

Browser	% of browser market							
	2009	2011	2013	2015	2017	2019	2021	2023
Chrome	2.98	20.59	36.63	45.09	54.30	63.37	65.12	63.55
Safari	3.35	6.20	11.23	13.20	14.15	15.05	18.65	19.95
Edge	—	—	—	—	—	—	3.40	5.14
Opera	2.88	3.09	3.51	5.48	3.98	2.58	2.13	2.98
Firefox	30.18	25.99	16.84	9.99	5.73	4.49	3.45	2.79
Samsung Internet	—	—	—	—	3.53	3.75	3.13	2.38
UC	—	0.05	1.75	5.61	8.57	3.57	1.18	1.01
QQ	—	—	0.05	0.19	0.11	0.31	0.27	0.28
Yandex	—	—	0.25	0.27	0.29	0.24	0.23	0.27
360 Safe	—	—	0.15	0.09	0.08	0.02	0.29	0.27
Internet Explorer	59.48	39.47	20.49	10.81	3.74	2.26	0.57	0.18
Cốc Cốc	—	—	—	0.07	0.14	0.14	0.05	0.14

— = Not available. **Note:** Percent of desktop, laptop, tablet, console, and mobile device users accessing the web with a particular browser, for July of year shown.

U.S. Internet Use by Selected Characteristics, 2013-21

Source: Pew Research Center

	% who are users			% who are users			% who are users	
	2013	2021		2013	2021		2013	2021
All adults	84%	93%	**Race/ethnicity**			**Annual household income**		
Gender			White, non-Hispanic...	85%	93%	Less than $30,000 ...	72%	86%
Male	84	94	Black, non-Hispanic...	79	91	$30,000-$49,999	86	91
Female	84	93	Hispanic	80	95	$50,000-$74,999	93	98
Age			**Education**			$75,000 or more.....	97	99
18-29	97	99	No high school diploma	54	86[1]	**Geography**		
30-49	92	98	High school graduate..	75	86[1]	Urban	86	95
50-64	81	96	Some college	92	97	Suburban	85	94
65+	56	75	College graduate.....	96	98	Rural	78	90

Note: Percent of U.S. adults, age 18 and over, who use the internet, email, or access the internet via a mobile device. Data for each year based on a pooled analysis of all surveys conducted during that year. (1) The 2021 sample was too small to separate the categories "No high school diploma" and "High school graduate," and so a single figure was reported for "High school or less."

Frequency of Social Media Use by U.S. Teenagers, 2022

Source: Pew Research Center
(percent of teenagers ages 13-17 surveyed)

Site/platform	Almost constantly	Several times a day	About once a day	Several times a week	Less often	Do not use	Daily total
YouTube	19%	41%	17%	12%	6%	5%	77%
TikTok	16	32	9	5	4	33	58
Snapchat	15	29	7	3	5	41	51
Instagram	10	27	12	7	5	38	50
Facebook	2	8	8	6	8	67	19

Frequency of Social Media Use by U.S. Adults, 2021

Source: Pew Research Center

Site/platform	Daily use	Weekly use	Less frequent use
Facebook	70%	17%	12%
Snapchat	59	21	19
Instagram	59	21	20
Twitter	46	27	27
YouTube	54	29	16

Note: Data for users of each platform only; non-users were not included in frequency data.

Most-Visited U.S. Websites, 2023

Source: Comscore, Inc.
Some websites represent an aggregation of domain names; examples added in parentheses.

	All U.S. Sites			Video Sites	
Rank	**Website**	**Visitors[1]**	**Rank**	**Website**	**Visitors[2]**
1.	Google sites (YouTube, Blogger)	276,040	1.	Google sites (YouTube)	255,666
2.	Microsoft sites (Bing, Linkedin, Xbox network)	243,533	2.	The Walt Disney Company	186,951
3.	Facebook (Instagram)	237,066	3.	Comcast NBCUniversal	176,424
4.	Amazon sites	231,357	4.	Paramount Global	174,059
5.	Yahoo (AOL)	229,565	5.	Hulu	171,467
6.	Comcast NBCUniversal	196,707	6.	Universal Music Group	145,551
7.	Warner Bros. Discovery	191,240	7.	WMX - Warner Music Group	134,254
8.	Raptive (formerly CafeMedia)	189,625	8.	BroadbandTV	115,694
9.	Paramount Global	186,730	9.	The Orchard Music	107,498
10.	Apple Inc.	180,623	10.	Fox Corporation	100,952
11.	The Walt Disney Company (ABC, ESPN)	174,221	11.	VEVO	98,122
12.	Universal Music Group	165,185	12.	Studio71 Network	90,392
13.	Dotdash Meredith	160,266	13.	Amazon sites	86,830
14.	WMX - Warner Music Group	158,506	14.	Microsoft sites	78,635
15.	Freestar	156,263	15.	WarnerMedia	77,194
16.	PayPal	156,133	16.	Yahoo	62,282
17.	Hearst	151,170	17.	USA Today Network	50,351
18.	Mediavine	145,037	18.	Enthusiast Gaming	46,095
19.	Fox Corporation	143,689	19.	STN Video	43,648
20.	USA Today Network	139,773	20.	Conde Nast Digital	43,195
21.	Bytedance Inc. (TikTok)	139,241	21.	Nexstar Inc.	39,525
22.	Twitter (a.k.a. X)	130,405	22.	Little Dot Studios	36,749

(1) Number of persons, in thousands, who visited the media property (including website/apps) at least once from any U.S. location in June 2023. Mobile users under age 18 are not measured. (2) Number of persons, in thousands, who visited the media property from a desktop in May 2023. Excludes advertisement videos.

Top Search Engines in the U.S.

Source: StatCounter Global Stats, gs.statcounter.com
(ranked by 2023 figures)

	% of search market								
Search engine	**2009**	**2011**	**2013**	**2015**	**2017**	**2019**	**2020**	**2021**	**2023**
Google	77.54	79.68	78.76	79.64	77.45	80.86	79.05	80.04	77.52
Bing	9.41	8.65	11.58	8.31	12.73	11.86	13.60	11.83	15.62
Yahoo	10.95	9.56	7.59	9.79	8.12	5.49	5.01	4.77	3.94
DuckDuckGo	0.00	0.00	0.05	0.32	0.74	1.21	1.64	2.71	2.39

Note: Percent of desktop (and laptop) computer users utilizing a particular search engine, for July of year shown.

Most Popular U.S. Smartphone Apps, 2023

Source: Comscore, Inc.

Rank	Apps[1]	Reach[2]	Rank	Apps[1]	Reach[2]
1.	YouTube	74%	14.	Google Photos	33%
2.	Gmail	62	15.	PayPal	32
3.	Google Search	59	16.	Temu: Team Up, Price Down	31
4.	Google Maps	58	17.	Walmart	31
5.	Facebook	56	18.	Weather - Native Apple (fmr. Dark Sky Weather)	30
6.	Amazon Mobile	53	19.	Apple News	28
7.	Facebook Messenger	42	20.	Snapchat	28
8.	Google Play	39	21.	Google Drive	25
9.	Instagram	39	22.	Yahoo Stocks	23
10.	TikTok	38	23.	Twitter (a.k.a. X)	22
11.	Spotify	36	24.	Venmo	22
12.	Apple Maps	35	25.	Pinterest	22
13.	Cash App	33			

(1) Includes applications developed for Android and iOS platforms. (2) Percentage of total U.S. smartphone users age 18 and over who used the app in June 2023.

U.S. Internet Use by Race and Ethnicity, 2003-21

Source: U.S. Census Bureau survey for National Telecommunications and Information Administration, U.S. Dept. of Commerce (number in thousands of civilian individuals, age 3 and older)

Survey date	Total U.S.[1] Number	% with internet use	White, non-Hispanic Number	% with internet use	African American, non-Hispanic Number	% with internet use	Asian American, non-Hispanic Number	% with internet use	American Indian or Alaska Native, non-Hispanic Number	% with internet use	Hispanic Number	% with internet use
Oct. 2003	161,636	58.7%	122,243	65.1%	14,898	45.2%	7,043	63.0%	676	48.1%	14,038	37.2%
Oct. 2007	177,987	62.4	130,432	68.9	17,223	50.1	8,686	68.4	793	47.1	17,760	41.6
Oct. 2009	197,941	68.4	141,213	74.3	20,848	59.5	9,243	72.3	1,017	54.9	22,186	49.3
Oct. 2010	209,472	71.7	145,989	76.7	22,389	63.7	9,949	74.2	1,094	62.5	26,246	56.6
July 2011	204,596	69.7	142,827	75.0	21,287	60.2	10,010	73.6	1,142	59.7	25,648	54.4
Oct. 2012	222,038	74.7	149,231	79.1	24,290	68.3	11,643	78.4	1,350	62.5	30,960	62.1
July 2013	213,708	71.4	142,313	75.4	22,996	64.0	11,739	75.3	1,424	61.5	30,771	61.0
July 2015	226,747	74.6	147,408	78.0	25,025	67.8	12,919	77.4	1,423	70.2	34,772	65.8
Nov. 2017	240,270	77.7	151,594	80.2	27,949	73.4	13,993	79.4	1,497	62.7	39,826	72.1
Nov. 2019	248,526	79.4	154,232	81.8	28,814	74.7	14,774	78.3	1,850	73.8	43,129	74.8
Nov. 2021	253,242	80.5	155,071	82.5	29,892	76.9	15,189	80.6	1,885	74.6	45,074	76.7

(1) Includes race categories not shown.

Telecommunications Milestones

1753: Scottish surgeon Charles Morrison proposed using 26 electric lines, one for each letter of the alphabet, to make an electric telegraph. A letter would be indicated by a current in the corresponding line, causing movement of a light object at the receiving end. Swiss scientist Georges-Louis Lesage built such a 26-line "electrostatic" system in 1774.

1837: In England, Charles Wheatstone and William Fothergill Cooke patented an electromagnetic telegraph. To indicate letters, their system used the magnetic field generated by a current to deflect compass needles. In 1839, they built the first commercial electric telegraph along a 13-mi (21-km) route.

1837: American inventor Samuel Morse filed a provisional patent application for a different type of electric telegraph that indicated letters by making marks of various lengths on paper. In 1844, he completed a 30-mi telegraph line from Washington, DC, to Baltimore, MD.

1866: The first successful transatlantic telegraph cable was laid.

1876: Alexander Graham Bell applied for a U.S. patent on the telephone. In his first successful experiment, on Mar. 10, he used the device to call his assistant.

1901: Italian inventor Guglielmo Marconi successfully transmitted the first transatlantic radio signal—from Cornwall, England, to Newfoundland, Canada.

1927: Commercial transatlantic telephone service (via radio) began between New York and London.

1946: The first commercial mobile phone service was launched, in St. Louis, MO.

1947: U.S. scientists invented the transistor, thereby giving birth to a revolution in telecommunications and electronics.

1948: U.S. mathematician/engineer Claude Shannon's epochal paper "A Mathematical Theory of Communication" laid the foundation for modern information theory. Its treatment of such crucial concepts as data compression and error detection and correction opened the way to digital communication.

1951: The mayors of Englewood, NJ, and Alameda, CA, made the first customer-dialed long-distance telephone call, facilitated by the introduction of area codes.

1956: The first transoceanic telephone cable went into service.

1962: NASA launched the world's first active communications satellite, AT&T's *Telstar 1*.

1978: Trials were conducted in Chicago and Newark, NJ, on a cellular approach to mobile telephony. This divided a region into a multitude of small overlapping areas, or cells, and made possible a significant increase in quality of calls and quantity of callers. Callers could be switched from one cell to another as they moved about.

1983: The first commercial cellular system in the U.S. went into operation in Chicago. A similar system was also launched in the Baltimore, MD-Washington, DC, area.

1984: As a result of a 1982 antitrust settlement with the U.S. government, AT&T, which handled most telephone service in the U.S., was broken up into several separate entities.

1994: The first smartphone, IBM's Simon Personal Communicator, went on the market. A bricklike touchscreen device, it combined a cellular phone with such features as an address book, calendar, calculator, email and faxing capability, and games.

2007: Apple released the iPhone, inaugurating an era of multifunctional smartphones.

2012: By late in the year more than 1 bil smartphones of all types were in use worldwide.

2016: Users of Facebook's messaging app Messenger passed the 1 bil mark.

2016: Total sales of Apple's iPhone reached 1 bil units.

2019: Telecommunications carriers began launching commercial "5G" (fifth generation) super-fast cellular networks, with the first large-scale deployments taking place in South Korea and the U.S.

Nations With the Most Cellphone Use, 2000-21

Source: © International Telecommunication Union, estimated; ranked by countries with most cellphone subscriptions in 2021

Country	2000 Subscriptions	Per 100 pop.	2011 Subscriptions	Per 100 pop.	2021 Subscriptions	Per 100 pop.
China	85,260,000	6.74	986,253,000	72.67	1,733,006,000	121.54
India	3,577,095	0.34	893,862,478	71.08	1,154,046,584	81.99
Indonesia	3,669,327	1.71	249,805,619	101.10	365,872,608	133.65
United States	109,478,031	38.77	297,404,000	94.75	361,664,000	107.32
Russia	3,263,200	2.23	203,751,647	141.79	246,569,033	168.98
Brazil	23,188,171	13.18	234,357,507	118.25	219,660,524	102.49
Japan	66,784,374	52.67	132,761,125	103.71	203,334,962	163.17
Nigeria	30,000	0.02	95,167,308	57.52	195,128,265	91.44
Pakistan	306,493	0.20	108,894,518	54.83	188,711,452	81.55
Bangladesh	279,000	0.22	84,368,700	56.17	184,444,949	108.91
Philippines	6,454,359	8.28	94,189,795	97.77	163,345,244	143.44
Iran	962,595	1.47	56,043,006	73.41	135,889,424	154.55
Vietnam	788,559	1.00	127,318,045	144.11	135,349,460	138.87
Mexico	14,077,880	14.38	94,583,253	82.86	125,824,872	99.31
Thailand	3,056,000	4.85	77,449,000	112.71	120,850,000	168.78
Germany	48,202,000	59.11	90,900,000	111.64	106,400,000	127.56
Egypt	1,359,900	1.91	83,425,145	93.53	103,449,734	94.68
South Africa	8,339,000	17.81	64,000,000	122.04	100,328,005	168.92
Turkey (Türkiye)	16,133,405	25.16	65,321,745	88.07	86,288,834	101.79
United Kingdom	43,452,000	73.84	77,162,298	121.93	79,773,000	118.57
Italy	42,246,000	74.16	96,040,913	160.00	78,114,933	131.86
Colombia	2,256,801	5.75	46,200,421	101.97	75,056,111	145.69
South Korea	26,816,398	57.31	52,506,793	106.79	72,855,492	140.57
France	29,052,360	49.52	59,816,000	95.29	72,751,000	112.74
Myanmar (Burma)	13,397	0.03	1,243,619	2.50	67,930,093	126.27

U.S. Wireless Industry, 2010-21

Source: CTIA.org; as of Dec. of year shown

Year	Estimated total subscribers	Cell sites	Mobile wireless data traffic (trillion megabytes)	Annual service revenue (thousand dollars)	Cumulative capital expenditures (thousand dollars)
2010	296,285,629	253,086	0.388	$159,929,649	$310,014,851
2011	315,963,848	283,385	0.867	169,767,314	335,331,967
2012	326,475,248	301,779	1.468	185,013,935	365,426,326
2013	335,652,171	304,360	3.230	189,192,812	398,567,671
2014	355,445,472	298,055	4.061	187,848,447	430,642,374
2015	377,921,241	307,626	9.650	191,949,025	462,605,007
2016	395,881,497	308,334	13.719	188,524,256	488,996,535
2017	400,205,829	323,448	15.687	179,091,135	514,625,256
2018	421,793,010	349,344	28.585	182,779,484	542,033,353
2019	442,456,704	395,562	37.060	187,361,982	571,125,121
2020	468,898,212	417,215	42.205	189,912,441	601,018,145
2021	498,910,316	418,887	53.356	204,214,004	635,759,036

U.S. Smartphone-Only Internet Access by Selected Characteristics, 2013-21

Source: Pew Research Center

(percentage of U.S. adults who do not have home broadband but own smartphones)

	% of adults who say they do not have broadband at home but own smartphones 2013	2021		% of adults who say they do not have broadband at home but own smartphones 2013	2021
All adults	8%	15%	**Education[1]**		
Gender			No high school diploma	14%	23%
Male	9	14	High school graduate	11	23
Female	8	15	Some college	8	15
Age			College graduate	4	4
18-29	12	28	**Annual household income**		
30-49	9	11	Less than $30,000	12	27
50-64	7	13	$30,000-$49,999	9	19
65+	3	12	$50,000-$74,999	5	6
Race/ethnicity			$75,000 or more	5	6
White, non-Hispanic	6	12	**Geography**		
Black, non-Hispanic	10	17	Urban	9	16
Hispanic	16	25	Suburban	7	12
			Rural	9	17

(1) The 2021 sample was too small to separate the categories "No high school diploma" and "High school graduate," so a single figure was reported for "High school or less."

ENVIRONMENT

U.S. Greenhouse Gas Emissions From Human Activities, 1990-2021

Source: U.S. Environmental Protection Agency

Gas and major source(s)	1990	2005	2017	2018	2019	2020	2021	% change, 1990-2021
Carbon dioxide (CO_2)	5,121.0	6,132.2	5,212.2	5,377.8	5,262.1	4,714.6	5,032.2	−1.7%
Fossil fuel combustion	4,728.2	5,747.3	4,852.5	4,989.8	4,855.9	4,344.9	4,639.1	−1.9
Methane (CH_4)	868.7	791.1	762.7	774.0	767.8	742.2	727.4	−16.3
Enteric fermentation[1]	183.1	188.2	195.9	196.8	197.3	196.2	194.9	6.4
Natural gas systems	215.1	203.3	186.2	194.3	193.6	185.3	181.4	−15.7
Landfills	197.8	147.7	123.9	126.7	129.0	124.8	122.6	−38.0
Manure management	39.0	54.9	64.4	66.5	65.7	66.7	66.0	69.2
Nitrous oxide (N_2O)	406.3	415.8	402.8	418.5	399.1	377.7	384.8	−5.3
Agricultural soil management	288.0	291.5	310.6	323.8	309.3	290.5	294.0	2.1
Hydrofluorocarbons (HFCs), etc.[2]	91.3	138.4	172.3	172.8	177.7	180.2	187.2	105.0
Total U.S. emissions	**6,478.3**	**7,477.4**	**6,561.8**	**6,754.8**	**6,617.9**	**6,026.0**	**6,340.2**	**−2.1**
Net U.S. emissions[3]	**5,606.4**	**6,696.3**	**5,787.6**	**5,989.7**	**5,913.9**	**5,249.8**	**5,586.0**	**−0.4**

Note: Emissions given in terms of equivalent emissions of carbon dioxide (CO_2), using units of million metric tons of carbon dioxide equivalent (MMT CO_2 eq.). (1) Digestive process of ruminant animals, such as cattle and sheep, producing methane as a byproduct. (2) Includes HFCs, PFCs (perfluorocarbons), SF_6 (sulfur hexafluoride), and NF_3 (nitrogen trifluoride). (3) Total emissions minus the net sum of all emissions (i.e., sources) of greenhouse gases to the atmosphere plus removals of CO_2 (i.e., sinks or negative emissions) from the atmosphere.

U.S. Greenhouse Gas Emissions, 2021
Source: U.S. Environmental Protection Agency

HFCs, PFCs, SF_6, and NF_3, 3.0%
Methane, 11.5%
Nitrous oxide, 6.2%
Carbon dioxide, 79.4%

World Carbon Dioxide Emissions From the Use of Fossil Fuels, 2021
Source: U.S. Energy Information Administration

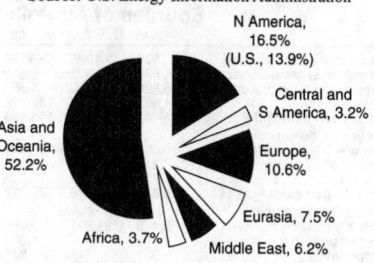

N America, 16.5% (U.S., 13.9%)
Central and S America, 3.2%
Europe, 10.6%
Asia and Oceania, 52.2%
Eurasia, 7.5%
Middle East, 6.2%
Africa, 3.7%

HFC = hydrofluorocarbon; PFC = perfluorocarbon; SF_6 = sulfur hexafluoride; NF_3 = nitrogen trifluoride. **Note:** Emissions sources are independently rounded; percentages may not add up to 100.

Top 20 Nations Producing Carbon Dioxide Emissions, 1980-2021

Source: Energy Information Administration, U.S. Dept. of Energy

(in million metric tons of carbon dioxide emitted from the consumption of energy; ranked by 2021 totals)

Country	1980	1990	2000	2005	2010	2015	2018	2021	% change, 1980-2021	% change, 1990-2021
China	1,597	2,417	3,483	6,120	9,004	10,427	10,606	11,420	615.2%	372.4%
U.S.	4,756	5,038	5,889	6,007	5,594	5,262	5,278	4,904	3.1	−2.6
India	270	541	886	1,119	1,648	2,064	2,310	2,278	743.9	320.9
Russia[1]	3,516	4,024	1,540	1,571	1,661	1,690	1,763	1,867	−46.9	−53.6
Japan	872	1,109	1,233	1,279	1,197	1,215	1,159	1,060	21.6	−4.4
Iran	102	195	303	430	537	613	643	688	576.5	253.3
South Korea	139	264	466	504	612	662	703	679	388.8	157.5
Germany[2]	736	719	872	844	822	788	782	664	−9.7	−7.6
Saudi Arabia	107	199	290	405	497	621	568	603	463.4	203.4
Indonesia	72	149	256	301	409	461	529	580	704.0	290.5
Canada	426	439	515	575	565	592	615	554	30.1	26.2
South Africa	229	329	393	446	479	474	456	446	95.0	35.3
Turkey (Türkiye)	62	128	207	233	268	351	398	405	551.5	217.0
Brazil	188	243	327	342	410	500	453	387	106.0	59.1
Mexico	198	274	383	429	449	465	454	384	94.3	40.2
Australia	216	280	351	381	402	393	412	377	74.6	34.9
UK	613	606	570	585	542	451	409	346	−43.5	−42.8
Italy	337	421	452	473	416	349	340	327	−3.2	−22.3
France	472	385	409	421	388	347	344	317	−33.0	−17.7
Vietnam	10	13	42	84	127	193	244	309	3,144.9	2,220.7
World[3]	**18,705**	**22,151**	**24,262**	**28,691**	**32,514**	**34,747**	**35,556**	**35,341**	**88.9**	**59.5**

(1) Numbers for 1980-90 are for the former Soviet Union. (2) Numbers for 1980-90 are for former West Germany. (3) Includes nations not listed.

Atmospheric Concentration of Carbon Dioxide, 1744-2022

Source: Carbon Dioxide Information Analysis Center, U.S. Dept. of Energy; Earth System Research Laboratory, Natl. Oceanic and Atmospheric Admin., U.S. Dept. of Commerce

Year[1]	CO$_2$ in ppm	Year[1]	CO$_2$ in ppm	Year[1]	CO$_2$ in ppm	Year[1]	CO$_2$ in ppm	Year[1]	CO$_2$ in ppm
1744	277	1878	290	1943	308	1990	354	2015	401
1791	280	1903	295	1960	317	2000	370	2020	414
1816	284	1915	301	1970	326	2005	380	2021	416
1843	287	1927	306	1980	339	2010	390	2022	419
1869	289								

ppm = Parts per million. (1) Measurements for 1744-1943 were derived from a 200-m-deep ice core sample drilled near Siple Station in Antarctica in 1983-84. Measurements for 1960-2021 and most of 2022 were taken directly from the atmosphere at Mauna Loa Observatory in Hawaii; in Dec. 2022, measurements were taken at the Maunakea Observatories, due to the eruption of Mauna Loa Volcano in Nov. 2022.

Emissions of Principal Air Pollutants in the U.S., 1970-2022

Source: U.S. Environmental Protection Agency; in million tons

Pollutant	1970	1980	1990	2000	2005	2010	2015	2020	2021	2022
Carbon monoxide	204.0	185.4	154.2	114.5	86.7	60.2	56.3	62.4	63.4	62.6
Nitrogen oxides[1]	26.9	27.1	25.5	22.6	21.9	15.3	11.1	7.8	7.9	7.6
Particulate matter[2]										
PM10	13.0	7.0	27.8	23.7	17.6	16.2	16.1	16.8	16.8	16.8
PM2.5	NA	NA	7.6	7.3	5.5	4.6	4.7	5.8	5.8	5.8
Sulfur dioxide	31.2	25.9	23.1	16.3	14.6	6.9	3.5	1.8	2.0	1.9
Volatile org. compounds[1]	34.7	31.1	24.1	17.5	16.9	13.6	14.1	16.6	16.6	16.6
Ammonia	NA	NA	4.3	4.9	4.7	4.4	4.5	5.5	5.5	5.5
Black carbon	NA	NA	NA	NA	0.5	0.4	0.3	0.4	0.4	0.4
Organic carbon	NA	NA	NA	NA	1.3	1.2	1.3	2.1	2.1	2.1
Total[3]	309.8	276.5	266.6	206.8	168.4	121.6	110.6	117.1	118.4	117.2

NA = Not available. (1) Ozone, a major air pollutant and the primary constituent of smog, is not emitted directly to the air but is formed by sunlight acting on emissions of nitrogen oxides and volatile organic compounds. (2) PM10 = particulates 10 microns or smaller in diameter. PM2.5 = particulates 2.5 microns or smaller in diameter. (3) Totals are rounded, as are components of totals.

Sources of Air Pollutants in the U.S., 1970-2022

Source: U.S. Environmental Protection Agency; in thousand tons

	1970	1980	1990	2000	2005	2010	2015	2020	2021	2022
Carbon monoxide sources										
Stationary fuel combustion	4,632	7,302	5,511	4,784	4,723	5,007	4,615	4,720	4,720	4,720
Industrial and other processes	16,899	9,250	5,853	4,479	3,469	3,469	3,276	3,075	3,075	3,075
Transportation	174,602	160,512	131,702	92,239	65,632	41,994	34,062	25,955	26,929	26,102
Total carbon monoxide[1]	204,042	185,408	154,188	114,467	86,663	60,247	56,296	62,437	63,412	62,584
Nitrogen oxide sources										
Stationary fuel combustion	10,061	11,320	10,894	8,819	6,316	3,955	3,097	2,333	2,396	2,370
Industrial and other processes	1,215	666	891	943	1,353	1,228	1,168	1,068	1,069	1,067
Transportation	15,276	14,846	13,373	12,560	13,920	9,960	6,596	3,988	3,986	3,755
Total nitrogen oxide[1]	26,882	27,080	25,527	22,598	21,865	15,340	11,114	7,816	7,876	7,618
Sulfur dioxide sources										
Stationary fuel combustion	23,456	21,391	20,290	14,163	12,585	6,073	2,857	1,112	1,281	1,197
Industrial and other processes	7,101	3,807	1,901	1,418	1,063	609	475	484	484	484
Transportation	551	717	874	697	798	165	53	25	30	29
Total sulfur dioxide[1]	31,218	25,926	23,077	16,347	14,563	6,938	3,502	1,845	2,018	1,934

(1) Includes categories not listed.

Average Global Temperature and Atmospheric Carbon Dioxide, 1880-2022

Source: Goddard Institute for Space Studies, National Aeronautics and Space Administration, via Earth Policy Institute; National Centers for Environmental Information, National Oceanic and Atmospheric Admin. (NOAA), U.S. Dept. of Commerce

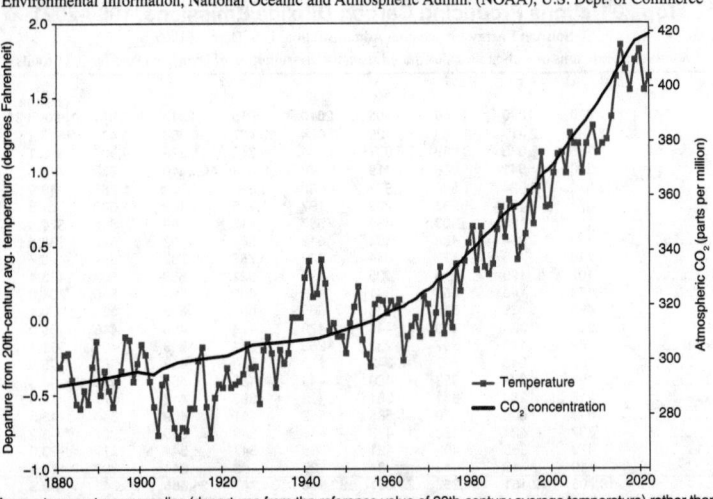

Note: NOAA uses temperature anomalies (departures from the reference value of 20th-century average temperature) rather than absolute temperatures to report average global temperatures.

Climate Change Indicators in the U.S.
Source: U.S. Environmental Protection Agency (EPA)

In May 2021, the EPA's "Climate Change Indicators in the United States" resource (https://www.epa.gov/climate-indicators) relaunched, presenting compelling and clear evidence of changes to climate reflected in rising temperatures, droughts, heat waves, ocean acidity, river flooding, sea level rise, and wildfires, among other indicators. The indicators show:

- Global Temperature: Since 1880, when thermometer-based observations began, 2016 was the warmest year on record, 2020 was the second warmest, and 2012-21 was the warmest decade.
- Arctic Sea Ice: Sept. 2012 had the lowest sea ice extent ever recorded, 44% below the 1981-2010 average for that month. The Sept. 2021 sea ice extent was the 12th smallest on record. It was more than 577,000 square miles less than the historical (1981-2010) average for that month.
- Coastal Flooding: Coastal flooding became more frequent at most locations along the East and Gulf Coasts.
- Heat Waves in U.S. Cities: Frequency of heat waves increased steadily, from an average of two heat waves per year during the 1960s to six per year during the 2010s and 2020s.

- Ice Sheets: Since 1992, Greenland and Antarctica both lost more than 100 bil metric tons of ice per year on average. The loss accounted for about one-third of observed global sea level rise between 2006 and 2015.
- Length of Growing Season: The average length of the growing season in the contiguous 48 states increased by more than two weeks since the beginning of the 20th century.
- Marine Species Distribution: In conjunction with warming ocean waters, many marine species off U.S. coasts shifted northward and moved to deeper waters.
- Sea Level: Sea level (relative to the land) rose along much of the U.S. coastline between 1960 and 2021, particularly the Mid-Atlantic coast and parts of the Gulf Coast, where some stations registered increases of more than 8 in.

Air Pollution in Selected World Cities, 2018-22
Source: IQAir

Particulate matter refers to extremely small particles and liquid droplets in the air that come from vehicle exhaust, burning of fuels, dust, cooking, tobacco smoke, and chemical reactions in the atmosphere. Particulates 2.5 microns or less in diameter (PM2.5) are capable of reaching deep into the respiratory tract and can cause or worsen heart and lung diseases. The World Health Org. (WHO) estimates that exposure to ambient (outdoor) air pollution causes 4.2 mil deaths worldwide every year. Data in this table show the annual average PM2.5 concentration measured in µg/m³. In 2021, the WHO cut the recommended annual PM2.5 concentration from 10.0 to 5.0, with the goal of preventing millions of deaths; around 99% of the world's population lives in places where air quality levels exceed these limits.

City, country	PM2.5 level (µg/m³)			City, country	PM2.5 level (µg/m³)		
	2022	2020	2018		2022	2020	2018
Addis Ababa, Ethiopia	31.3	14.7	27.1	Mexico City, Mexico	22.1	18.8	19.7
Amsterdam, Netherlands	10.1	9.9	11.5	Montréal, QC, Canada	7.9	9.5	7.0
Bangkok, Thailand	18.0	20.6	25.2	Moscow, Russia	10.8	10.5	10.1
Beijing, China	29.8	37.5	50.9	Mumbai, India	46.7	41.3	58.6
Berlin, Germany	12.6	11.8	11.7	New York, NY, U.S.	9.9	NA	NA
Bogotá, Colombia	15.1	14.3	13.9	Oslo, Norway	6.9	6.4	8.2
Chicago, IL, U.S.	11.8	11.1	9.4	Paris, France	12.7	12.2	15.6
Delhi, India	92.6	84.1	113.5	Prague, Czechia	11.9	10.9	17.4
Dhaka, Bangladesh	65.8	77.1	97.1	Rome, Italy	12.6	13.6	NA
Dubai, UAE	43.7	32.6	55.3	Santiago, Chile	25.8	23.6	29.4
Hong Kong, China	14.4	15.4	20.2	São Paulo, Brazil	13.5	14.2	16.2
Johannesburg, South Africa	21.7	22.3	NA	Seoul, South Korea	18.3	20.9	23.3
Kabul, Afghanistan	17.1	46.5	61.8	Shanghai, China	25.4	31.5	36.0
Kolkata, India	50.2	46.6	85.4	Sofia, Bulgaria	19.1	27.5	28.2
Lima, Peru	25.6	18.0	28.0	Sydney, Australia	3.1	7.2	7.6
London, England, UK	9.6	9.6	12.0	Tehran, Iran	36.1	29.0	26.1
Los Angeles, CA, U.S.	10.5	14.6	14.4	Tokyo, Japan	9.2	10.1	13.1
Madrid, Spain	9.5	9.0	10.0	Toronto, ON, Canada	8.5	7.0	7.8

NA = Not available.

Municipal Solid Waste, 2018
Source: U.S. Environmental Protection Agency

In 2018, Americans generated about 292.4 mil tons of refuse collected as municipal solid waste (MSW). Of that MSW, paper represented 23.1%; food 21.6%; plastics 12.2%; yard trimmings 12.1%; rubber, leather, and textiles 8.9%; metals 8.8%; wood 6.2%; glass 4.2%; and other material 2.9%. About 32.1%, or 94 mil tons, was recycled or composted; nearly half of recycled/composted materials consisted of paper and paperboard.

Municipal Solid Waste Generation, 1960-2018

Municipal Solid Waste Recycling and Composting, 1960-2018

Air Quality of Selected U.S. Urban Areas, 1980-2022

Source: Office of Air Quality Planning and Standards, U.S. Environmental Protection Agency

Data indicate the number of days metropolitan statistical areas or corresponding core-based statistical areas failed to meet acceptable air-quality standards based on monitoring of six common pollutants.

Urban area	1980	1990	2000	2005	2010	2015	2018	2020	2021	2022
Atlanta-Sandy Springs-Roswell, GA	28	59	48	17	7	2	0	0	0	1
Bakersfield, CA	72	91	109	79	40	29	27	32	30	2
Baltimore-Columbia-Towson, MD	62	29	17	20	20	1	0	0	0	0
Baton Rouge, LA	27	30	34	20	3	2	1	0	1	0
Boston-Cambridge-Newton, MA-NH	26	6	1	8	1	1	0	0	1	0
Chicago-Naperville-Elgin, IL-IN-WI	40	28	10	25	2	3	6	5	2	2
Cincinnati, OH-KY-IN	43	22	10	19	4	1	2	0	0	1
Cleveland-Elyria, OH	11	9	8	17	4	0	0	1	0	1
Dallas-Fort Worth-Arlington, TX	43	26	35	40	5	5	9	3	4	2
Denver-Aurora-Lakewood, CO	28	3	1	2	2	2	8	4	17	1
Detroit-Warren-Dearborn, MI	28	10	3	17	2	1	2	2	0	0
Fresno, CA	90	55	106	45	22	24	19	40	19	1
Houston-The Woodlands-Sugar Land, TX	79	55	52	44	17	15	9	3	9	3
Indianapolis-Carmel-Anderson, IN	35	9	9	7	0	1	1	0	0	0
Kansas City, MO-KS	34	2	12	16	0	0	1	1	0	0
Las Vegas-Henderson-Paradise, NV	25	10	1	9	0	1	1	3	3	2
Los Angeles-Long Beach-Anaheim, CA	203	145	66	61	15	38	20	63	27	13
Memphis, TN-MS-AR	29	20	23	13	2	0	1	1	0	1
Miami-Fort Lauderdale-West Palm Beach, FL	19	2	1	1	0	0	0	0	0	0
Minneapolis-St. Paul-Bloomington, MN-WI	11	2	1	7	0	0	0	1	3	0
Nashville-Davidson–Murfreesboro–Franklin, TN	11	30	17	6	1	0	1	0	0	0
New Orleans-Metairie, LA	10	4	13	3	2	0	0	0	0	0
New York-Newark-Jersey City, NY-NJ-PA	83	43	18	22	12	3	3	0	3	1
Philadelphia-Camden-Wilmington, PA-NJ-DE-MD	80	36	20	22	12	2	3	0	2	0
Phoenix-Mesa-Scottsdale, AZ	31	15	19	11	2	3	11	143	134	20
Pittsburgh, PA	38	12	10	27	15	1	1	0	1	0
Riverside-San Bernardino-Ontario, CA	170	154	114	93	71	51	66	92	81	31
Sacramento–Roseville–Arden-Arcade, CA	53	42	42	42	9	4	20	27	17	0
Salt Lake City, UT	21	0	13	8	7	2	2	2	9	0
San Francisco-Oakland-Hayward, CA	11	6	4	2	1	0	12	13	1	0
Seattle-Tacoma-Bellevue, WA	5	8	5	1	0	3	7	9	2	0
Tucson, AZ	2	1	0	2	0	0	0	1	0	0
Washington-Arlington-Alexandria, DC-VA-MD-WV	52	22	12	18	13	1	1	1	1	0
Winston-Salem, NC	0	7	18	3	3	0	0	0	0	0

Hazardous Waste Sites in the U.S., 2023

Source: National Priorities List, U.S. Environmental Protection Agency; as of May 2023

State/territory	Proposed Gen.	Proposed Fed.	Final Gen.	Final Fed.	Total	State/territory	Proposed Gen.	Proposed Fed.	Final Gen.	Final Fed.	Total
Alabama	1	0	9	3	13	Nebraska	0	0	17	1	18
Alaska	0	0	1	5	6	Nevada	1	0	1	0	2
Arizona	1	0	7	2	10	New Hampshire	1	0	19	1	21
Arkansas	0	0	9	0	9	New Jersey	1	0	109	6	116
California	1	0	72	24	97	New Mexico	0	0	14	1	15
Colorado	1	0	17	3	21	New York	0	0	82	4	86
Connecticut	0	0	12	1	13	North Carolina	0	0	36	2	38
Delaware	1	0	16	1	18	North Dakota	0	0	0	0	0
District of Columbia	0	0	0	1	1	Ohio	3	1	34	3	41
Florida	1	0	46	6	53	Oklahoma	2	0	7	1	10
Georgia	1	0	15	2	18	Oregon	1	0	11	3	15
Guam	0	0	1	1	2	Pennsylvania	1	0	84	6	91
Hawaii	0	0	1	2	3	Puerto Rico	0	0	18	1	19
Idaho	3	0	4	2	9	Rhode Island	0	0	10	2	12
Illinois	3	0	41	4	48	South Carolina	0	0	26	2	28
Indiana	1	0	39	0	40	South Dakota	0	0	1	1	2
Iowa	1	0	11	1	13	Tennessee	0	0	16	3	19
Kansas	1	0	13	1	15	Texas	1	0	51	4	56
Kentucky	0	0	10	1	11	Utah	3	0	7	5	15
Louisiana	3	0	12	1	16	Vermont	0	0	12	0	12
Maine	0	0	8	3	11	Virgin Islands	0	0	1	0	1
Maryland	1	0	11	10	22	Virginia	0	0	18	11	29
Massachusetts	1	0	26	6	33	Washington	0	0	33	13	46
Michigan	1	1	65	0	67	West Virginia	0	0	9	2	11
Minnesota	0	0	23	2	25	Wisconsin	1	0	36	0	37
Mississippi	0	0	9	0	9	Wyoming	0	0	0	1	1
Missouri	0	0	30	3	33	**Total**	**38**	**2**	**1,178**	**158**	**1,376**
Montana	1	0	18	0	19						

Gen. = Non-federal sites; Fed. = Hazardous waste produced by federal agency. **Note:** Sites that have been proposed for federal Superfund financing are listed under Proposed; sites that have qualified for Superfund financing are under Final.

Renewable Water Resources, 2020

Source: Food and Agriculture Organization (FAO), United Nations

Globally, water supplies are abundant, but they are unevenly distributed among and within countries. In some areas, water withdrawals are so high, relative to supply, that surface water supplies are shrinking, and groundwater reserves are being depleted faster than they can be replenished by precipitation. According to the FAO, the U.S. (including Alaska and Hawaii) has 8,514 cubic meters per capita and 2,818 cubic kilometers of internal renewable water resources total.

The tables below take into account only countries for which data are available, draw upon studies done over a number of years, and use 2020 population data. Numbers represent each country's internal resources. Countries ranked by per capita figures.

Countries With Greatest Internal Water Resources

Country	Cubic m per capita	Total cubic km
Iceland	498,179	170.0
Guyana	306,401	241.0
Suriname	168,760	99.0
Bhutan	101,088	78.0
Papua New Guinea	89,527	801.0
Canada	75,512	2,850.0
Gabon	73,684	164.0
Norway	70,464	382.0
New Zealand	67,811	327.0
Solomon Islands	65,076	44.7

Countries With Lowest Internal Water Resources

Country	Cubic m per capita	Total cubic km
Kuwait	0.0	0.0
Bahrain	2.35	0.004
Egypt	9.77	1.0
United Arab Emirates	15.17	0.15
Qatar	19.44	0.056
Maldives	55.50	0.03
Jordan	66.84	0.682
Saudi Arabia	68.94	2.4
Yemen	70.41	2.1
Mauritania	86.03	0.4

Top Countries by Forest Area, 1990-2020

Source: Food and Agriculture Organization, United Nations
(in square kilometers; ranked by 2020 forest area)

Country	Forest area, 1990	Forest area, 2020	% change, 1990-2020	% of land area covered by forest in 2020	Country	Forest area, 1990	Forest area, 2020	% change, 1990-2020	% of land area covered by forest in 2020
Russia	NA	8,153,116	NA	49.8%	Sweden	280,630	279,800	−0.3%	68.7%
Brazil	5,888,980	4,966,196	−15.7%	59.4	Japan	249,500	249,350	−0.1	68.4
Canada	3,482,729	3,469,281	−0.4	38.7	Gabon	237,616	235,306	−1.0	91.3
United States	3,024,500	3,097,950	2.4	33.9	Finland	218,753	224,090	2.4	73.7
China	1,571,406	2,199,782	40.0	23.4	Central African				
Australia	1,338,822	1,340,051	0.1	17.4	Republic	232,030	223,030	−3.9	35.8
Congo, Dem. Rep. of	1,506,290	1,261,552	−16.2	55.6	Turkey (Türkiye)	197,835	222,204	12.3	28.9
Indonesia	1,185,450	921,332	−22.3	49.1	Congo	223,150	219,460	−1.7	64.3
Peru	764,485	723,304	−5.4	56.5	Nigeria	265,261	216,270	−18.5	23.7
India	639,380	721,600	12.9	24.3	Cameroon	225,000	203,405	−9.6	43.0
Angola	792,628	666,074	−16.0	53.4	Thailand	193,610	198,730	2.6	38.9
Mexico	705,917	656,921	−6.9	33.8	Malaysia	206,185	191,140	−7.3	58.2
Colombia	649,581	591,419	−9.0	53.3	Spain	139,047	185,722	33.6	37.2
Bolivia	578,047	508,338	−12.1	46.9	Guyana	186,022	184,153	−1.0	93.6
Venezuela	520,260	462,309	−11.1	52.4	Sudan	NA	183,596	NA	9.8
Tanzania	573,900	457,450	−20.3	51.6	Chile	152,461	182,107	19.4	24.5
Zambia	474,120	448,140	−5.5	60.3	Zimbabwe	188,267	174,446	−7.3	45.1
Mozambique	433,780	367,438	−15.3	46.7	France	144,360	172,530	19.5	31.5
Papua New Guinea	363,997	358,558	−1.5	79.2	Ethiopia	204,086	170,685	−16.4	15.1
Argentina	352,040	285,730	−18.8	10.4	South Africa	181,421	170,530	−6.0	14.1
Myanmar	392,185	285,439	−27.2	43.7	World	42,315,914	40,589,308	−4.1	31.1

NA = Not available. **Note:** World total includes nations not listed individually.

Largest Trees in the U.S., 2021

Source: American Forests

Nearly 900 native and naturalized species of trees grow in the U.S. The trunk of the world's largest known living tree, the General Sherman giant sequoia in California, weighs almost 1,400 tons—about as much as 15 adult blue whales. To determine the country's largest trees (or "national champions"), American Forests uses a point system whereby trunk circumference, or girth at 4.5 ft above ground level (in inches) + height (in feet) + ¼ average crown spread (in feet) = total points.

Tree type	Location	Girth at 4.5 ft (in.)	Height (ft)	Crown spread (ft)	Total points
Giant sequoia (Gen. Sherman tree)	Tulare, CA	1,231	275	107	1,533
Coast	Del Norte, CA	950	321	75	1,290
Sitka spruce	Grays Harbor, WA	740	191	80	951
Western redcedar	Clallam, WA	746	164	48	922
Coast 1	Grays Harbor, WA	581	294	66	891
Coast	Jefferson, WA	640	221	37	870
Port Orford cedar	Coos, OR	522	242	35	773
Bald cypress	West Feliciana, LA	626	91	87	739
California laurel	Curry, OR	601	101	87	724
Monterey cypress	San Mateo, CA	588	102	111	718

METEOROLOGY

National Weather Service Watches and Warnings

Source: National Weather Service, National Oceanic and Atmospheric Admin. (NOAA), U.S. Dept. of Commerce; *Glossary of Meteorology*, American Meteorological Society

The National Weather Service issues watches, warnings, and advisories for specific geographic areas to alert people to the possibility or imminent arrival of severe weather or of flooding. Often the weather hazard is a convective storm (a storm involving upward and downward movement of heat and moisture). A severe thunderstorm or tornado watch is issued when a severe convective storm, covering a relatively small geographic area or moving in a narrow path, is sufficiently intense to threaten life and property. Excessive localized convective rains are not classified as severe storms but are often the product of severe local storms. Such rainfall may result in phenomena, such as flash floods, that threaten life and property. Lightning occurs with all thunderstorms and, along with flash floods, is a leading cause of storm deaths and injuries.

Cyclone: Atmospheric circulation of winds rotating counterclockwise in the Northern Hemisphere and clockwise in the Southern Hemisphere. Tornadoes, hurricanes/typhoons, and the lows shown on weather maps are all examples of cyclones. Cyclones are usually accompanied by precipitation or stormy weather.

Severe thunderstorm: Thunderstorm (a local storm produced by a cumulonimbus cloud) that produces a tornado, winds of at least 50 knots (58 mph), and/or hail at least 1 in. in diameter. A severe thunderstorm watch indicates conditions are favorable for the development of a severe thunderstorm within 4 to 8 hours. A severe thunderstorm warning indicates a severe thunderstorm has been sighted by radar or reported by a spotter.

Tornado: Violently rotating column of air that extends from the base of a thunderstorm to the ground. On a local scale, it is the most destructive of all atmospheric phenomena. A tornado path can exceed 1 mi wide and 50 mi long and is generally less than 1.25 mi in diameter. The average forward speed is 30 mph, and wind speeds can reach 300 mph. A rotating column of air over water is called a **waterspout**.

Tropical storm: Cyclone that develops over tropical or subtropical waters with 1-min. sustained surface winds between 34 and 63 knots (39-73 mph). A tropical storm watch is issued when tropical storm conditions pose a threat to specified coastal areas within 48 hours. A tropical storm warning is issued when such conditions are expected in a specified coastal area within 36 hours.

Hurricane: Tropical cyclone having 1-min. sustained surface winds of 64 knots (74 mph) or more. (In the western North Pacific Ocean, west of the International Date Line, such storms are known as **typhoons**.) The hurricane-force winds form a circle or oval, sometimes as wide as 300 mi in diameter. In the lower latitudes, hurricanes usually move N or NW at 10-15 mph. When the center approaches 25° to 30° N, the direction of motion often changes to the NE, with increased forward speed. In the Atlantic, hurricane season is June 1-Nov. 30. Hurricane season is May 15-Nov. 30 in the eastern Pacific.

A hurricane warning is issued when a hurricane is forecast for an area within 36 hours.

Winter storm and **blizzard:** A winter storm watch is issued when there is a potential for heavy snow or significant ice accumulations, usually at least 24-36 hours in advance. A winter storm warning is issued when a winter storm is producing or is forecast to produce heavy snow or significant ice accumulations. A blizzard warning is issued for winter storm conditions in which winds are 35 mph or more, there is sufficient falling and/or blowing snow to frequently reduce visibility to less than ¼ mi, and the conditions are expected to prevail for at least 3 hours.

River flooding: Occurs when rains, sometimes coupled with melting snow, quickly fill river basins with an excess of water. Torrential rains from decaying hurricanes or tropical systems are also a major cause. **Coastal flooding:** Tropical storm and hurricane winds or intense offshore low-pressure systems can drive ocean water inland. Coastal floods can also be produced by sea waves called tsunamis, produced by earthquakes or underwater volcanic eruptions or landslides. **Flash flooding:** Usually due to copious amounts of rain falling in a short time. Ice can also cause flash flooding. When ice accumulates at natural or artificial obstructions, it can stop the flow of water. The resulting buildup of water can lead to flooding upstream. If the jam suddenly gives way, a flash flood can happen downstream. Flash flooding typically occurs within 6 hours of the causative event.

Flash floods account for the majority of flood deaths in the U.S. and are the leading cause of deaths associated with thunderstorms. Urbanization significantly increases runoff because less rain is absorbed by the terrain, making flash flooding in urban areas extremely dangerous. Streets can become swift-moving rivers, and basements can fill with water.

A flash flood watch indicates flash flooding is possible within a designated area. A flash flood warning indicates flooding is in progress, imminent, or highly likely.

National Weather Service Marine Warnings and Advisories

Primary sources of dissemination are mobile apps and push notifications, commercial radio, TV, U.S. Coast Guard radio, and National Oceanic and Atmospheric Admin. (NOAA) VHF radio broadcasts. The NOAA Weather Radio All Hazards (NWR) network broadcasts on seven frequencies between 162.400 and 162.550 MHz. These broadcasts can usually be received within about 40 mi of the transmission site using a special radio receiver. The following are examples of the warnings and advisories that may be addressed to mariners.

Small craft advisory: Alerts mariners to sustained weather and/or sea conditions, present or forecast, potentially hazardous to small boats, including winds 20-33 knots (23-38 mph) and/or dangerous wave conditions. The advisory is also issued when sea or lake ice exists that could be hazardous to small boats. Criteria vary depending on region and type of marine environment.

Special marine warning: Indicates potentially hazardous weather conditions not covered by existing marine warnings.

The conditions are usually of short duration (2 hr. or less) and involve wind speeds of 34 knots (39 mph) or more, and/or hail at least ¾ in. in diameter or waterspouts.

Gale warning: Indicates winds of 34-47 knots (39-54 mph) not directly associated with a tropical storm are forecast for the area.

Storm warning: Indicates winds 48-63 knots (55-73 mph) not directly associated with a tropical storm are forecast for the area.

Hurricane and Tornado Classifications

Source: National Weather Service, NOAA, U.S. Dept. of Commerce

The Saffir-Simpson Hurricane Wind Scale, created by Herbert Saffir and expanded upon by Robert Simpson, rates a hurricane's intensity from 1 to 5. The scale, updated in 2012, provides examples of the type of damage and impacts associated with winds of the indicated intensity. The Fujita (or F) Scale was created by T. Theodore Fujita in 1971 to classify tornadoes. The Enhanced Fujita Scale, an update, was implemented in the U.S. in 2007. It uses 3-sec. gusts estimated at the point of damage based on a judgment of eight levels of damage to 28 indicators.

Saffir-Simpson Hurricane Wind Scale			Enhanced Fujita Scale (Tornadoes)	
Category	Wind speed[1]	Summary of damage	Rank	3-sec. gust
1	74-95 mph	Very dangerous winds will produce some damage.	EF-0	65-85 mph
2	96-110 mph	Extremely dangerous winds will cause extensive damage.	EF-1	86-110 mph
3	111-129 mph	Devastating damage will occur.	EF-2	111-135 mph
4	130-156 mph	Catastrophic damage will occur.	EF-3	136-165 mph
5	157 mph or higher	Catastrophic damage will occur.	EF-4	166-200 mph
(1) 1-min. sustained winds.			EF-5	Over 200 mph

Monthly Normal Mean Temperatures, Precipitation in U.S. Cities

Source: National Centers for Environmental Information, NESDIS, NOAA, U.S. Dept. of Commerce

Normals are averages covering a 30-year period. The temperature and precipitation normals given here are based on records for 1991-2020. Temperatures listed below represent means of the normal daily maximum and normal daily minimum temperatures for each month. (*) = City station. Other figures are for airport stations. T = Temperature in Fahrenheit; P = Precipitation in inches.

Station	Jan. T	Jan. P	Feb. T	Feb. P	Mar. T	Mar. P	Apr. T	Apr. P	May T	May P	June T	June P	July T	July P	Aug. T	Aug. P	Sept. T	Sept. P	Oct. T	Oct. P	Nov. T	Nov. P	Dec. T	Dec. P
Albany, NY	24	2.6	27	2.3	36	3.1	48	3.1	60	3.4	68	4.1	73	4.6	71	3.8	64	3.7	51	3.9	41	3.0	30	3.3
Albuquerque, NM	37	0.4	42	0.4	50	0.5	57	0.5	66	0.4	76	0.6	79	1.6	77	1.3	70	1.2	58	0.9	46	0.6	37	0.5
Anchorage, AK	17	0.8	21	0.9	26	0.7	38	0.4	48	0.7	56	1.0	60	1.8	58	2.9	49	3.1	36	1.8	24	1.2	19	1.2
Asheville, NC	39	4.1	42	3.5	48	3.8	57	4.2	65	4.1	72	4.8	75	4.7	74	5.0	68	4.1	58	3.4	48	3.7	41	4.2
Atlanta, GA	45	4.6	49	4.6	56	4.7	63	3.8	71	3.6	78	4.5	81	4.8	80	4.3	75	3.8	65	3.3	54	4.0	47	4.6
Atlantic City, NJ	34	3.4	36	3.2	43	4.5	53	3.3	62	3.3	71	3.6	77	4.5	75	4.6	68	3.6	57	4.1	47	3.4	39	4.5
Baltimore, MD	34	3.1	37	2.9	44	4.0	55	3.4	64	3.9	74	4.0	78	4.5	76	4.1	69	4.4	57	3.9	47	3.1	39	3.7
Birmingham, AL	45	5.0	49	5.0	56	5.7	64	5.1	72	4.9	78	4.8	82	5.4	81	4.4	76	4.0	65	3.3	54	4.2	47	4.9
Bismarck, ND*	13	0.5	17	0.5	29	0.8	42	1.4	55	2.5	65	3.4	71	3.1	70	2.4	60	1.8	45	1.5	30	0.7	18	0.7
Boise, ID	32	1.4	38	1.0	45	1.3	51	1.2	60	1.5	68	0.8	77	0.2	76	0.2	66	0.4	53	0.8	41	1.2	32	1.5
Boston, MA	30	3.4	32	3.2	38	4.2	49	3.6	58	3.3	68	3.9	74	3.3	73	3.2	66	3.6	55	4.0	45	3.7	36	4.3
Buffalo, NY*	26	3.4	26	2.5	34	2.9	46	3.4	58	3.4	67	3.4	72	3.2	70	3.2	63	4.1	52	4.0	41	3.5	31	3.8
Burlington, VT	21	2.1	23	1.8	32	2.2	46	3.1	58	3.8	68	4.3	72	4.1	71	3.5	63	3.7	50	3.8	39	2.7	28	2.5
Caribou, ME	12	3.0	14	2.4	25	2.8	39	3.0	52	3.5	61	3.9	67	4.2	65	3.6	57	3.4	45	4.0	33	3.4	20	3.6
Charleston, SC	50	3.4	53	3.1	59	3.4	66	3.3	73	3.3	79	6.2	83	6.6	81	7.0	77	6.0	68	4.3	58	2.7	52	3.4
Charleston, WV	35	3.3	38	3.4	46	4.1	57	3.6	65	4.9	72	4.7	76	5.4	75	3.8	68	3.5	57	2.9	46	3.2	39	3.6
Chicago, IL	25	2.0	29	2.0	39	2.5	50	3.8	61	4.5	71	4.1	75	3.7	74	4.3	66	3.2	54	3.4	41	2.4	31	2.1
Cleveland, OH	29	1.8	31	1.5	38	2.4	49	3.1	61	3.5	70	2.8	74	3.7	73	3.5	67	2.9	56	3.2	45	2.9	35	2.0
Columbus, OH	30	3.0	33	2.4	42	3.6	53	3.9	63	4.0	72	4.3	75	4.7	74	3.7	67	3.1	55	2.9	44	2.8	35	3.1
Dallas-Ft. Worth, TX	46	2.5	51	2.8	58	3.3	66	3.2	74	4.8	82	3.7	86	2.1	86	2.2	79	2.7	68	4.4	56	2.5	48	2.8
Denver, CO	32	0.4	33	0.4	41	1.0	47	1.9	56	2.0	67	2.0	73	1.8	71	2.3	63	1.3	50	1.0	39	0.5	31	0.4
Des Moines, IA	22	1.1	27	1.3	39	2.2	51	4.0	62	5.2	72	5.3	76	3.8	74	4.2	66	3.2	53	2.8	39	1.9	28	1.6
Detroit, MI	26	2.2	28	2.1	37	2.4	49	3.3	60	3.7	70	3.3	74	3.5	72	3.3	65	3.2	53	2.5	41	2.6	31	2.3
Dodge City, KS*	33	0.6	36	0.6	45	1.4	54	2.0	65	3.0	75	3.3	80	3.1	78	3.0	70	1.3	57	2.0	44	0.8	34	1.0
Duluth, MN*	11	1.0	15	1.0	27	1.5	40	2.5	52	3.4	61	4.4	67	3.9	66	3.7	57	3.5	44	2.9	30	2.0	17	1.5
Fairbanks, AK	-8	0.6	0	0.5	11	0.4	34	0.3	50	0.5	61	1.5	63	2.3	57	2.1	46	1.4	26	0.8	4	0.7	-4	0.6
Fresno, CA	48	2.2	52	1.9	57	1.9	62	1.0	70	0.4	78	0.2	84	0.0	82	0.0	77	0.1	67	0.6	55	0.9	48	1.8
Galveston, TX	56	4.3	59	2.1	65	3.0	72	2.1	78	3.0	84	4.2	86	3.4	86	4.7	82	6.7	75	5.2	66	4.3	59	4.2
Grand Rapids, MI*	25	2.5	27	2.1	36	2.4	48	4.0	59	4.0	69	3.9	73	3.9	71	3.6	64	3.4	52	4.0	40	3.1	30	2.5
Hartford, CT	27	3.3	30	3.1	38	3.8	50	3.9	60	4.0	69	4.3	74	4.2	73	4.2	65	4.4	53	4.5	42	3.5	33	4.1
Helena, MT	23	0.4	27	0.4	36	0.5	45	1.0	54	2.0	62	2.2	71	1.1	69	1.0	59	1.0	46	0.8	33	0.6	23	0.5
Honolulu, HI	74	1.8	74	1.9	75	2.4	77	0.8	79	0.8	80	0.5	82	0.5	82	0.8	82	0.9	80	1.5	78	2.3	76	2.2
Houston, TX	54	3.8	58	3.0	64	3.5	70	4.0	77	5.0	83	6.0	85	3.8	85	4.8	81	4.7	72	5.5	62	3.9	55	4.0
Huron, SD	16	0.6	21	0.8	33	1.2	46	2.5	58	3.2	68	3.9	74	2.8	71	2.6	63	2.4	48	2.0	33	0.8	21	0.7
Indianapolis, IN	29	2.6	33	2.1	43	3.3	54	4.1	64	4.3	73	5.1	76	4.3	74	3.2	68	2.6	56	3.3	43	3.3	34	2.7
Jackson, MS	47	5.4	51	5.1	58	5.7	65	5.8	73	4.4	80	4.4	82	5.0	82	4.7	77	3.5	66	3.8	55	4.4	49	5.1
Jacksonville, FL	55	3.0	58	2.4	63	3.0	68	2.4	74	3.0	80	6.3	82	6.5	82	6.9	79	7.3	72	6.0	63	2.6	58	2.8
Juneau, AK	29	6.0	30	4.3	33	3.7	41	3.5	49	3.5	55	3.8	57	5.1	56	6.4	50	9.2	42	8.4	34	6.5	30	6.5
Kansas City, MO	29	1.2	34	1.5	45	2.4	55	4.1	65	5.3	74	5.3	78	4.6	77	4.2	68	4.0	56	3.3	44	2.0	33	1.6
Knoxville, TN	39	4.7	43	4.8	51	4.9	60	4.7	68	4.1	75	4.2	79	5.3	78	3.6	72	3.5	60	2.8	49	4.2	42	5.0
Lander, WY	21	0.5	25	0.7	36	1.3	43	2.1	53	2.7	63	1.1	72	0.6	70	0.5	60	1.0	49	1.4	32	0.8	22	0.6
Las Vegas, NV	50	0.6	54	0.8	61	0.4	68	0.2	77	0.1	88	0.0	93	0.4	92	0.3	84	0.3	70	0.3	57	0.3	48	0.5
Lexington, KY	34	3.4	38	3.6	46	4.5	56	4.4	65	4.4	73	5.0	77	5.1	76	3.7	69	3.4	58	3.7	46	3.4	38	4.2
Little Rock, AR	41	3.5	45	4.0	53	5.0	61	5.6	70	5.1	78	3.6	81	3.3	81	3.2	74	3.0	63	4.5	51	4.7	43	5.1
Los Angeles, CA	58	2.9	58	3.0	59	1.7	61	0.6	64	0.3	66	0.1	70	0.0	71	0.0	70	0.1	67	0.5	62	0.8	58	2.2
Louisville, KY	36	3.4	40	3.4	48	4.6	59	4.8	68	5.2	76	4.3	80	4.1	79	3.7	72	3.7	60	3.7	49	3.4	40	4.1
Marquette, MI*	19	1.9	20	1.5	28	1.6	38	2.7	50	2.9	59	3.1	66	3.1	66	2.3	59	3.3	47	3.4	35	2.4	24	2.0
Memphis, TN	42	4.1	46	4.6	54	5.7	63	5.9	72	5.3	80	4.0	83	4.8	82	3.4	76	3.0	65	4.0	53	4.7	45	5.5
Miami, FL	69	1.8	71	2.2	73	2.5	77	3.4	80	6.3	83	10.5	84	7.4	84	9.6	83	10.2	80	7.7	75	3.5	71	2.4
Milwaukee, WI	24	1.8	27	1.7	36	2.2	46	3.9	57	3.5	68	4.4	73	3.4	72	3.7	65	3.2	53	2.8	40	2.2	30	1.9
Minneapolis-St. Paul, MN	16	0.9	21	0.9	33	1.7	47	2.9	60	3.9	70	4.6	74	4.1	72	4.3	64	3.0	50	2.6	35	1.6	22	1.2
Mobile, AL	52	5.2	56	3.8	62	5.1	68	4.9	76	4.4	82	5.8	84	6.6	84	7.1	80	4.5	71	3.8	61	4.1	55	5.3
Moline, IL	23	1.7	28	1.8	40	2.6	51	3.8	63	4.7	72	5.0	76	4.2	73	4.0	66	3.3	54	2.8	40	2.3	29	2.0
Nashua, NH*	23	1.7	26	1.8	35	4.1	47	3.9	58	3.6	67	4.2	73	3.6	71	3.7	64	4.2	51	4.7	40	3.7	30	4.5
Nashville, TN	40	4.0	43	4.5	52	4.5	61	4.7	69	5.0	77	4.4	81	4.2	80	3.8	73	3.8	62	3.4	50	3.9	43	4.4
New Orleans, LA	54	5.2	58	4.1	64	4.4	70	5.2	77	5.6	82	7.6	84	6.8	84	6.9	81	5.1	73	3.7	62	3.9	57	4.8
New York, NY	33	3.2	35	2.8	41	3.9	51	3.6	61	3.7	70	3.9	76	3.9	75	4.4	68	3.8	57	3.7	47	3.1	38	4.0
Newark, NJ	33	3.3	36	3.0	43	4.1	53	3.9	63	4.0	73	4.3	78	4.7	76	4.2	69	3.8	58	3.8	47	3.3	39	4.0
Norfolk, VA	42	3.4	44	2.9	51	3.7	60	3.4	68	3.8	77	4.4	81	6.1	79	5.9	74	5.4	64	3.9	53	3.1	46	3.3
Oklahoma City, OK	38	1.3	42	1.4	51	2.6	59	3.6	68	5.3	77	4.5	82	3.6	81	3.6	73	3.7	61	3.3	49	1.7	40	1.8
Omaha, NE	24	0.8	29	1.0	41	1.8	53	3.2	64	4.7	74	4.4	78	3.6	76	4.6	68	3.0	54	2.3	40	1.5	29	1.2
Philadelphia, PA	34	3.1	36	2.8	44	4.0	55	3.5	64	3.7	74	4.0	79	4.4	77	4.3	70	4.4	58	3.5	47	2.9	39	4.0
Phoenix, AZ	57	0.9	60	0.9	66	0.8	73	0.2	82	0.1	91	0.0	96	0.9	94	0.9	89	0.6	77	0.6	65	0.6	56	0.7
Pittsburgh, PA	29	3.0	31	2.6	40	3.2	52	3.3	61	3.8	69	4.1	73	4.3	72	3.5	65	3.3	53	2.8	43	2.9	34	2.8
Portland, ME	24	3.5	26	3.5	34	4.1	45	4.4	55	4.4	65	3.7	72	3.0	69	3.6	62	3.8	50	5.3	40	4.3	30	4.5
Portland, OR	42	5.0	44	3.7	48	4.0	53	2.9	59	2.5	64	1.6	70	0.5	71	0.5	65	1.5	56	3.4	47	5.5	42	5.8
Providence, RI	30	4.0	32	3.4	39	4.9	49	4.3	59	3.6	68	3.8	74	2.9	73	3.6	66	4.2	54	4.2	45	4.3	36	4.7
Raleigh-Durham, NC	42	3.4	45	2.8	52	4.1	61	3.5	69	3.4	77	3.9	81	5.0	79	4.7	73	5.2	62	3.4	52	3.3	45	3.4
Rapid City, SD	24	0.3	26	0.5	35	0.9	44	2.1	54	3.5	65	2.9	72	2.3	71	1.6	61	1.2	47	1.4	35	0.5	26	0.4
Richmond, VA	38	3.2	41	2.6	48	4.0	58	3.2	67	4.0	75	4.6	79	4.4	78	4.9	71	4.6	60	3.4	50	3.1	42	3.5
St. Louis, MO	32	2.6	37	2.2	47	3.5	58	4.7	68	4.8	77	4.5	80	3.9	79	3.4	71	3.0	59	3.2	47	3.4	37	2.5
Salt Lake City, UT	31	1.4	37	1.3	46	1.8	52	2.2	62	1.8	72	1.0	80	0.6	81	1.1	55	1.3	42	1.3	32	1.4		
San Antonio, TX	52	2.0	57	1.7	63	2.3	69	2.4	77	4.4	83	3.3	85	2.4	86	2.2	80	3.9	71	3.8	61	2.1	54	2.0
San Diego, CA	58	2.0	59	2.2	61	1.5	63	0.7	65	0.3	67	0.1	71	0.1	72	0.0	71	0.1	68	0.5	63	0.8	58	1.7
San Francisco, CA	51	3.9	54	4.0	56	2.7	57	1.4	60	0.5	63	0.1	64	0.0	65	0.0	63	0.8	63	0.8	56	2.2	51	4.1
San Juan, PR	78	4.1	78	2.6	79	2.2	80	4.6	82	5.5	83	4.7	84	6.3	83	6.5	83	5.2	83	5.7	81	7.4	79	4.9
Santa Fe, NM	32	0.5	36	0.4	43	0.7	50	0.5	60	0.6	70	0.6	73	1.8	71	2.0	65	1.3	53	1.2	40	0.7	32	0.5
Savannah, GA	51	3.3	54	2.8	60	3.5	67	3.4	74	3.6	80	6.7	83	5.8	82	5.5	78	4.4	69	3.7	59	2.4	53	3.2
Seattle-Tacoma, WA	43	5.8	44	3.8	47	4.2	51	3.2	58	1.9	62	1.5	67	0.6	67	1.0	63	1.6	56	3.4	47	6.3	42	5.7
Spokane, WA	30	2.0	33	1.4	40	1.8	47	1.3	56	1.6	62	1.2	71	0.4	70	0.5	61	0.6	48	1.4	36	2.1	29	2.3
Springfield, MO*	34	2.5	39	2.4	48	3.5	57	4.7	66	5.3	75	4.5	79	3.9	78	3.6	70	4.3	59	3.6	47	3.9	37	2.6
Tampa, FL	62	2.7	65	2.6	69	2.5	74	2.6	80	2.6	83	7.4	84	7.8	84	9.0	83	6.1	77	2.3	70	1.4	65	2.6
Utqiagvik (fmr. Barrow), AK*	-13	0.3	-13	0.3	-12	0.3	3	0.3	21	0.4	34	0.4	40	1.0	39	1.1	34	0.8	21	0.6	5	0.4	-7	0.5
Washington, DC	34	2.9	36	2.6	44	3.5	55	3.5	64	4.7	73	4.3	77	4.2	76	3.5	69	3.9	57	3.7	46	3.1	38	3.3
Wilmington, DE	34	3.2	36	2.8	43	4.2	54	3.5	63	3.6	73	4.7	78	4.4	76	4.0	69	4.4	57	3.7	47	3.1	38	3.9

Normal High and Low Temperatures, Precipitation in U.S. Cities

Source: National Centers for Environmental Information, NESDIS, NOAA, U.S. Dept. of Commerce

The normal temperatures and precipitation data given here are based on records for the period 1991-2020. The extreme temperatures are based on records from the time of each station's installation, through 2022. (*) = City station. Other figures are for airport stations.

State	Station	NORMAL TEMPERATURE (°F) January Max.	Min.	July Max.	Min.	EXTREME TEMPERATURE (°F) Highest	Lowest	AVG. ANNUAL PRECIPITATION (in.)
Alabama	Mobile	62	43	92	75	105	3	60.52
Alaska	Anchorage	23	11	66	53	90	−34	16.42
Alaska	Juneau	33	24	64	50	90	−22	66.99
Alaska	Utqiagvik (fmr. Barrow)*	−6	−19	46	35	79	−56	6.19
Arizona	Phoenix	68	46	107	85	122	17	7.22
Arkansas	Little Rock	51	31	92	71	114	−5	50.42
California	Los Angeles	66	49	75	64	113	28	12.23
California	San Francisco	58	45	73	55	106	20	19.64
Colorado	Denver	45	19	87	59	105	−24	15.02
Connecticut	Hartford	35	19	85	63	103[1]	−26[1]	47.05
Delaware	Wilmington	41	26	87	68	103	−14	45.33
District of Columbia	Washington-Dulles	43	25	88	67	105	−18	43.24
Florida	Jacksonville	65	45	91	73	105	7	51.82
Florida	Miami	76	61	91	78	98	30	67.41
Georgia	Atlanta	54	36	90	72	106	−8	50.43
Georgia	Savannah	61	40	92	74	105	3	48.12
Hawaii	Honolulu	81	67	88	75	95	53	16.41
Idaho	Boise	39	26	93	62	111	−25	11.51
Illinois	Chicago	32	19	85	66	104	−27	37.86
Indiana	Indianapolis	36	21	85	67	105	−27	40.67
Iowa	Des Moines	31	14	86	66	108	−26	36.55
Kansas	Dodge City*	46	20	94	66	111	−21	22.00
Kentucky	Lexington	42	25	87	67	105	−21	49.84
Kentucky	Louisville	44	28	89	71	106	−22	48.34
Louisiana	New Orleans	63	46	91	77	102	11	63.35
Maine	Caribou	21	3	77	56	96	−41	40.70
Maine	Portland	32	16	80	61	103	−39	48.12
Maryland	Baltimore	43	25	89	68	106	−7	45.00
Massachusetts	Boston	37	23	82	66	103	−12	43.59
Michigan	Detroit	32	19	84	64	104	−21	34.32
Michigan	Grand Rapids*	31	19	83	63	104	−22	39.40
Michigan	Sault Ste. Marie	24	8	77	55	98	−36	34.46
Minnesota	Duluth*	20	2	78	56	97	−39	31.18
Minnesota	Minneapolis-St. Paul	24	9	83	65	105	−34	31.62
Mississippi	Jackson	57	37	92	72	107	2	57.35
Missouri	Kansas City	38	20	88	68	109	−23	39.30
Missouri	St. Louis	40	24	90	71	108	−18	41.70
Montana	Helena	32	14	86	55	105	−42	11.40
Nebraska	Omaha	34	15	88	68	114	−23	31.86
Nevada	Las Vegas	59	41	105	82	117	8	4.18
New Hampshire	Concord	32	13	83	59	102	−37	41.95
New Jersey	Atlantic City	43	25	87	67	106	−11	45.96
New Mexico	Albuquerque	48	26	91	67	107	−17	8.84
New York	Albany	33	16	84	62	100	−28	40.68
New York	Buffalo*	32	19	80	63	99	−20	40.68
New York	New York-JFK	40	26	84	69	104	−2	43.29
North Carolina	Raleigh-Durham	52	32	91	70	105	−9	46.07
North Dakota	Bismarck*	23	3	84	58	112	−44	19.21
Ohio	Cleveland	35	24	81	68	104	−20	33.34
Ohio	Columbus	37	22	85	65	104	−22	41.57
Oklahoma	Oklahoma City	49	27	93	70	113	−14	36.39
Oregon	Portland	48	36	82	59	116	−3	36.91
Pennsylvania	Philadelphia	41	26	88	70	104	−7	44.11
Pennsylvania	Pittsburgh	36	21	83	63	103	−22	39.61
Puerto Rico	San Juan	83	72	89	78	98	60	59.87
Rhode Island	Providence	38	22	84	65	104	−13	47.54
South Carolina	Charleston	60	39	91	74	105	6	52.51
South Dakota	Huron	26	6	86	62	112	−41	23.32
South Dakota	Rapid City	36	13	86	59	111	−31	17.44
Tennessee	Memphis	51	33	92	74	108	−13	54.94
Tennessee	Nashville	49	30	91	71	109	−17	50.51
Texas	Dallas-Fort Worth	57	36	96	76	113	−2	37.01
Texas	Houston	64	44	95	76	109	7	51.84
Utah	Salt Lake City	39	24	94	68	107	−30	15.52
Vermont	Burlington	29	13	82	62	101	−30	37.53
Virginia	Norfolk	51	34	89	73	105	−3	49.18
Virginia	Richmond	48	29	90	69	105	−12	45.50
Washington	Seattle-Tacoma	48	38	77	57	108	0	39.34
Washington	Spokane	35	25	84	58	109	−25	16.45
West Virginia	Charleston	44	26	86	66	104	−16	46.24
Wisconsin	Milwaukee	31	17	82	65	103	−26	34.57
Wyoming	Lander	33	10	88	55	101	−37	13.23

Mean annual snowfall (in.), selected cities: Based on climate normals 1991-2020: Albany, NY, 59.2; Anchorage, AK, 77.9; Boston, MA, 49.2; Buffalo, NY, 95.4; Burlington, VT, 87.5; Caribou, ME, 118.2; Duluth, MN, 90.2; Lander, WY, 87.6; Sault Ste. Marie, MI, 120.1.

Wettest spot: Mt. Waialeale in Kauai, HI, may be the rainiest place in the U.S. It has a recorded average annual rainfall of 460 in.

Temperature extremes: The highest temperature ever recorded under standard conditions in the U.S. was 134°F in Death Valley, CA, on July 10, 1913. The record low in the U.S. was −80°F at Prospect Creek, AK, Jan. 23, 1971. (1) Record through 2020.

Annual Climatological Data for U.S. Cities, 2022

Source: National Centers for Environmental Information, NESDIS, NOAA, U.S. Dept. of Commerce

Station	Elev. (ft)	Highest	Date	Lowest	Date	Total (in.)	Greatest in 24 hrs. (in.)	Date	Total snow-fall (in.)	Greatest in 24 hrs. (in.)	Date	MPH	Date	Prec. 0.01 in. or more	Snowfall 1 in. or more
	TEMPERATURE (°F)					PRECIPITATION			Snowfall[1]			FASTEST WIND[2]		NO. OF DAYS	
Albany, NY	281	99	8/4	-6	1/22	37.30	2.24	4/7-8	43.8	6.6	12/11	44	3/7	129	10
Albuquerque, NM	5,308	102	7/19	9	2/5	9.31	1.05	8/21-22	9.4	2.4	3/23	46	4/22	57	4
Anchorage, AK	222	78	7/2	-12	12/20	28.60	1.61	8/7-8	114.3	12.2	3/5	49	12/23	138	33
Asheville, NC	2,174	92	7/23	0	12/24	49.02	2.73	5/22-23	10.9	10.4	1/16	46	1/3	130	1
Atlanta, GA	974	99	6/15	8	12/24	48.15	2.40	6/27	0.6	0.3	1/16	38	3/18	116	0
Atlantic City, NJ	117	99	7/24	8	12/24	52.71	3.62	10/2-3	33.3	14.0	1/29	39	3/8	123	4
Baltimore, MD	196	99	8/4	6	12/24	47.18	2.95	7/6-7	14.4	6.8	1/3	43	12/23	122	4
Barrow, AK	38	69	6/26	-38	2/14	—	—	—	—	—	—	43	2/25	—	—
Birmingham, AL	630	100	7/9	9	12/24+	64.09	6.97	6/8	0.8	0.6	1/16	41	3/30	106	0
Bismarck, ND	1,654	103	8/4	-27	1/1	17.33	1.56	7/4	86.7	17.0	11/10	46	5/13	91	20
Boise, ID	2,861	100	8/31	-3	1/1	11.62	0.80	10/21-22	19.6	3.3	12/12	45	7/3	76	9
Boston, MA	180	100	7/24	4	1/15	31.25	2.22	10/13-14	54.6	23.6	1/29	45	12/23	122	6
Buffalo, NY	717	91	6/25+	1	1/22	45.29	1.98	12/23	188.3	22.3	12/23	48	12/23	164	29
Burlington, VT	348	93	8/6	-14	1/22	39.77	2.59	9/13-14	73.1	8.5	2/4	46	12/23	142	15
Caribou, ME	626	90	5/13	-30	1/27	45.20	1.76	10/14-15	124.6	9.5	2/4	38	12/23	165	34
Charleston, SC	48	98	6/14	18	12/24	50.12	5.64	9/29-30	T	T	1/29+	53	9/30	119	0
Cheyenne, WY	6,128	99	7/18	-25	12/22	9.47	0.49	9/21-22	64.1	7.2	1/5	58	11/5	76	22
Chicago, IL	658	99	6/21	-8	12/23	31.99	1.79	7/23-24	35.2	5.4	2/2	55	6/13	114	12
Cleveland, OH	805	95	6/21+	-4	12/23	40.10	1.86	8/29-30	54.9	8.0	2/3	43	12/23	150	17
Columbus, OH	812	97	6/22	-7	12/24	44.78	4.03	7/5-6	19.5	4.9	12/23	41	7/23	130	8
Dallas-Fort Worth, TX	562	100	7/20+	11	12/23+	36.64	9.19	8/21-22	1.7	1.5	2/3	46	4/6	61	1
Denver, CO	5,382	101	8/5	-24	12/22	11.92	1.14	8/21	68.5	6.4	12/28	46	4/22	72	26
Des Moines, IA	971	99	8/6+	-11	12/22	30.59	2.18	11/4-5	44.4	9.8	1/14	44	12/2	106	12
Detroit, MI	631	96	6/21	-5	12/24	24.31	1.27	2/17	44.2	6.3	2/17	46	11/5	128	15
Duluth, MN	1,429	94	6/20	-23	1/1	34.06	2.21	11/9-10	124.9	11.5	12/14	45	4/13	158	36
Fairbanks, AK	464	86	7/1	-47	1/2	9.30	0.69	9/13-14	59.3	4.4	2/18	33	8/8	113	23
Fresno, CA	375	114	9/6	32	12/17	6.44	1.18	12/27	0.0	0.0	—	35	11/28	27	0
Grand Rapids, MI	788	95	6/21	-2	1/26	37.73	1.91	8/28-29	118.8	10.5	12/24	47	3/6	152	24
Helena, MT	3,867	102	9/7	-35	12/22	11.50	1.09	7/5	34.1	3.5	11/8+	51	7/3	97	13
Honolulu, HI	18	91	9/30+	61	2/14	12.15	3.33	1/1	—	—	—	33	12/19	72	—
Houston, TX	107	105	7/10	15	12/23	41.30	6.30	1/8-9	T	T	3/22	36	4/12	93	0
Huron, SD	1,284	95	6/29	-19	12/22	20.88	3.45	7/5	27.8	6.2	12/15	74	7/5	88	9
Indianapolis, IN	797	99	7/5	-9	12/23	34.88	1.99	8/29	14.9	7.3	2/3	43	3/25	119	3
Jackson, MS	296	99	6/25+	12	12/23	64.55	6.78	8/23-24	T	T	11/21	39	3/30	113	0
Jacksonville, FL	34	100	6/23	20	12/25	55.24	2.90	4/7	0.0	0.0	—	39	11/10	106	0
Kansas City, MO	1,008	101	7/23	-4	12/23	34.57	2.96	5/31	21.4	7.0	2/17	44	4/12	89	7
Knoxville, TN	982	96	6/22+	4	12/24+	53.64	2.99	2/22-23	12.3	6.5	3/12	47	5/6	121	4
Las Vegas, NV	2,091	112	7/22+	28	1/2	2.13	0.59	8/11-12	0.0	0.0	—	48	7/27	17	0
Lexington, KY	984	98	7/6	-5	12/24	45.61	2.79	2/17	26.1	9.9	1/6	43	1/30	126	8
Los Angeles, CA	326	100	9/9	39	2/24	6.40	1.44	11/8	—	—	—	38	3/5	27	—
Louisville, KY	484	101	7/5	-5	12/24	43.04	2.31	2/17	14.2	3.3	1/28	44	4/13	124	6
Marquette, MI	1,415	94	6/20	-17	12/26	42.12	2.04	4/13	280.3	21.6	2/22	—	—	195	65
Memphis, TN	286	103	7/8+	1	12/23	55.84	2.72	4/12-13	4.2	2.0	3/11	35	10/12	110	2
Miami, FL	29	96	9/7	42	1/30	71.55	7.77	6/3-4	—	—	—	32	1/16	162	—
Milwaukee, WI	680	100	6/21	-7	12/23	34.74	5.57	9/11-12	33.3	3.9	1/1	41	3/6	119	11
Minneapolis, MN	874	101	6/20	-17	1/7	22.97	1.94	5/11	60.7	8.4	11/29	39	11/6	116	17
Mobile, AL	212	102	6/23	20	12/24	64.37	2.48	10/29-30	T	T	1/21	44	12/14	135	0
Moline, IL	607	98	6/21	-11	1/3	30.89	2.08	6/25	23.3	4.7	1/1	45	3/5	112	8
Nashville, TN	574	101	6/22	-1	12/23	53.43	2.34	7/9	13.5	6.3	1/6	38	3/30	118	4
New Orleans, LA	7	99	6/24+	25	12/24	57.57	3.61	5/25-26	—	—	—	37	11/14	122	—
New York, NY	161	97	8/9	7	12/24	46.30	2.09	4/18-19	17.7	7.3	1/29	29	12/23	122	4
Newark, NJ	28	102	7/24	6	1/16	40.55	1.84	1/16-17	17.8	6.6	1/29	48	2/18	124	5
Norfolk, VA	69	97	7/24	12	12/24	39.21	3.40	9/30	11.2	3.5	1/22	47	9/30	104	4
North Little Rock, AR	565	103	8/15	1	12/23	45.33	2.32	3/22	9.7	4.3	3/11	—	—	102	3
Oklahoma City, OK	1,284	110	7/19	2	12/22	26.28	2.93	5/23-24	11.7	3.8	2/3	47	10/15	67	4
Philadelphia, PA	62	99	7/24	7	12/24	42.51	2.01	12/15-16	12.9	5.8	1/29	40	3/19	121	4
Phoenix, AZ	1,106	115	7/11	36	12/17	5.78	1.17	12/3-4	—	—	—	55	9/11	33	—
Pittsburgh, PA	1,175	94	6/22	-6	1/27	42.47	2.36	11/11	49.2	8.0	3/12	49	3/7	162	13
Portland, ME	72	96	8/7	-7	1/31	46.66	3.24	10/13-14	36.6	13.2	1/29	41	12/23	118	5
Portland, OR	223	102	7/30+	20	12/23+	40.02	2.74	12/26-27	2.6	1.6	4/11	38	12/22	142	1
Providence, RI	53	98	8/9	2	1/31	45.83	3.69	9/5-6	44.3	18.8	1/29	51	12/23	128	8
Raleigh-Durham, NC	430	102	7/7+	10	12/24	44.74	3.35	9/30	2.7	1.5	1/21	47	5/6	111	1
Rapid City, SD	3,153	105	7/18	-18	12/22+	16.10	2.07	8/25-26	—	—	—	60	4/23	88	—
Reno, NV	4,407	106	9/6	13	2/24	8.34	2.28	12/30-31	23.5	9.0	12/31	54	12/10	34	6
Richmond, VA	167	98	7/24+	7	2/24	39.53	2.27	6/22-23	4.7	2.0	1/16	46	5/27	109	2
St. Louis, MO	710	105	7/23	-6	12/23+	48.94	9.07	7/25-26	15.0	4.9	2/3	43	8/3	109	4
Salt Lake City, UT	4,224	107	9/7	0	1/1	12.57	1.15	3/5-6	43.0	6.9	12/13	45	5/2	86	13
San Antonio, TX	821	105	7/11	16	12/23	11.51	1.69	2/2-3	0.0	0.0	—	44	5/24	63	0
San Diego, CA	81	95	10/19	38	2/25	5.90	0.90	11/8-9	—	—	—	26	11/3	30	—
San Francisco, CA	89	98	6/21	35	1/2	13.42	3.92	12/30-31	—	—	—	43	6/15	42	—
San Juan, PR	10	94	10/2	67	1/24	71.67	4.46	2/5-6	0.0	0.0	—	44	9/18	271	—
Sault Ste. Marie, MI	727	89	7/18	-15	1/15	39.03	1.48	7/27	154.5	17.6	12/24	32	12/3	173	40
Savannah, GA	143	102	6/23	19	12/24	36.87	3.72	7/14	0.0	0.0	—	44	1/3	112	0
Scottsbluff, NE	3,949	108	7/18	-18	1/22	9.83	1.40	5/29-30	46.4	10.0	12/13	52	4/22	72	15
Seattle, WA	434	95	7/31+	18	12/22	40.93	3.31	2/27-28	5.8	2.6	12/3	37	12/27	149	1
Spokane, WA	2,384	102	7/31+	-10	12/22	17.72	1.14	12/26-27	54.5	7.5	11/30	51	4/4	95	16
Springfield, MO	1,280	104	7/26	-8	12/23+	43.26	3.86	5/4-5	20.9	6.8	2/3	37	2/16	100	5
Tampa, FL	40	98	6/18	31	12/25+	61.95	3.64	7/16-17	0.0	0.0	—	40	9/23	113	0
Washington, DC	3	99	6/17	12	12/24	43.51	4.09	7/8-9	13.2	6.9	1/3	48	5/22	115	3
Wilmington, DE	77	97	8/9	7	12/24	43.17	2.86	12/15-16	10.8	3.2	1/7	45	2/18	127	6
Windsor Locks, CT	165	97	7/20	-2	1/31	47.91	3.84	9/5-6	34.4	6.8	1/29	38	2/18	128	8

(+) = Indicates value also occurred on an earlier date(s). (T) = Trace amount. — = Data not available or unreported. (1) Comprises all forms of frozen precipitation, including snow, ice pellets, and hail. (2) Sustained for at least 2 min., not peak gust.

Record Temperatures by State

Source: National Centers for Environmental Information, NOAA, U.S. Dept. of Commerce
(as of Apr. 11, 2023)

State	LOWEST TEMPERATURE				HIGHEST TEMPERATURE			
	°F	Date	Station	Approx. elevation (ft)	°F	Date	Station	Approx. elevation (ft)
Alabama	−27	Jan. 30, 1966	New Market	732	112	Sept. 6, 1925	Centreville	220
Alaska	−80	Jan. 23, 1971	Prospect Creek Camp	955	100	June 27, 1915	Fort Yukon	445
Arizona	−40	Jan. 7, 1971	Hawley Lake	8,180	128	June 29, 1994	Lake Havasu City	449
Arkansas	−29	Feb. 13, 1905	Brook Farm Pond	1,260	120	Aug. 10, 1936	Ozark	390
California	−45	Jan. 20, 1937	Boca	5,575	134	July 10, 1913	Greenland Ranch	−194
Colorado	−61	Feb. 1, 1985	Maybell	5,944	115	July 20, 2019	John Martin Dam	3,814
Connecticut	−32	Jan. 22, 1961[1]	Coventry	480	106	July 15, 1995[1]	Danbury	405
Delaware	−17	Jan. 17, 1893	Millsboro	20	110	July 21, 1930	Millsboro	20
Florida	−2	Feb. 13, 1899	Tallahassee	192	109	June 29, 1931	Monticello	98
Georgia	−17	Jan. 27, 1940	CCC Fire Camp F-16	1,000	112	Aug. 20, 1983[1]	Greenville	960
Hawaii	12	May 17, 1979	Mauna Kea Observ.	13,773	100	Apr. 27, 1931	Pahala	840
Idaho	−60	Jan. 18, 1943	Island Park Dam	6,290	118	July 28, 1934	Orofino	1,320
Illinois	−38	Jan. 31, 2019	Mount Carroll	640	117	July 14, 1954	East St. Louis	410
Indiana	−36	Jan. 19, 1994	New Whiteland	785	116	July 14, 1936	Collegeville	650
Iowa	−47	Feb. 3, 1996[1]	Elkader	788	118	July 20, 1934	Keokuk	651
Kansas	−40	Feb. 13, 1905	Lebanon	1,841	121	July 24, 1936[1]	Alton	1,685
Kentucky	−37	Jan. 19, 1994	Shelbyville	730	114	July 28, 1930	Greensburg	590
Louisiana	−16	Feb. 13, 1899	Minden	185	114	Aug. 10, 1936	Plain Dealing	251
Maine	−50	Jan. 16, 2009	Big Black River	885	105	July 10, 1911[1]	North Bridgton	449
Maryland	−40	Jan. 13, 1912	Oakland	2,420	109	July 10, 1936[2]	Frederick	380
Massachusetts	−35	Jan. 12, 1981[1]	Chester	640	107	Aug. 2, 1975[3]	Chester	640
Michigan	−51	Feb. 9, 1934	Vanderbilt	905	112	July 13, 1936[3]	Stanwood	830
Minnesota	−60	Feb. 2, 1996	Tower	1,430	115	July 29, 1917	Beardsley	1,089
Mississippi	−19	Jan. 30, 1966	Corinth	385	115	July 29, 1930	Holly Springs	502
Missouri	−40	Feb. 13, 1905	Warsaw	705	118	July 14, 1954[3]	Warsaw	705
Montana	−70	Jan. 20, 1954	Rogers Pass	5,545	117	July 5, 1937[1]	Medicine Lake	1,942
Nebraska	−47	Dec. 22, 1989[1]	Oshkosh	3,390	118	July 24, 1936[1]	Minden	2,160
Nevada	−50	Jan. 8, 1937	San Jacinto	5,203	125	June 29, 1994	Laughlin	605
New Hampshire	−50	Jan. 22, 1885	Mt. Washington	6,271	106	July 4, 1911	Nashua	135
New Jersey	−34	Jan. 5, 1904	River Vale	31	110	July 10, 1936	Runyon	20
New Mexico	−50	Feb. 1, 1951	Gavilan	7,425	122	June 27, 1994	Waste Isolat. Pilot Plant	3,411
New York	−52	Feb. 18, 1979	Old Forge	1,748	108	July 22, 1926	Troy	35
North Carolina	−34	Jan. 21, 1985	Mt. Mitchell	6,240	110	Aug. 21, 1983	Fayetteville	186
North Dakota	−60	Feb. 15, 1936	Parshall	1,950	121	July 6, 1936	Steele	1,853
Ohio	−39	Feb. 10, 1899	Milligan	875	113	July 21, 1934	Gallipolis	569
Oklahoma	−31	Feb. 10, 2011	Nowata	NA	120	Aug. 12, 1936[1]	Altus	1,380
Oregon	−54	Feb. 10, 1933[1]	Seneca	4,659	119	June 29, 2021[2]	Pelton Dam	1,410
Pennsylvania	−42	Jan. 5, 1904	Smethport	1,469	111	July 10, 1936[1]	Phoenixville	105
Rhode Island	−28	Jan. 11, 1942	Wood River Junction	49	104	Aug. 2, 1975	Providence	60
South Carolina	−19	Jan. 21, 1985	Caesar's Head	3,200	113	June 29, 2012	Columbia	242
South Dakota	−58	Feb. 17, 1936	McIntosh	2,179	120	July 15, 2006[1]	Fort Pierre	1,590
Tennessee	−32	Dec. 30, 1917	Mountain City	2,503	113	Aug. 9, 1930[1]	Perryville	371
Texas	−23	Feb. 8, 1933[1]	Seminole	3,336	120	June 28, 1994[1]	Monahans	2,547
Utah	−50	Jan. 5, 1913	Strawberry Tunnel (East)	7,615	117	July 10, 2021[1]	Saint George	2,857
Vermont	−50	Dec. 30, 1933	Bloomfield	1,040	107	July 7, 1912	Vernon	226
Virginia	−30	Jan. 21, 1985	Mountain Lake Bio. Station	3,870	110	July 15, 1954[1]	Balcony Falls	732
Washington	−48	Dec. 30, 1968[3]	Winthrop	1,749	120	June 29, 2021	Hanford	NA
West Virginia	−37	Dec. 30, 1917	Lewisburg	2,300	112	July 10, 1936[1]	Martinsburg	534
Wisconsin	−55	Feb. 4, 1996[1]	Couderay	1,300	114	July 13, 1936	Wisconsin Dells	835
Wyoming	−66	Feb. 9, 1933	Riverside Ranger Sta.	6,500	115	July 15, 1988[1]	Diversion Dam	5,590

NA = Not available. (1) Also on earlier dates at the same or other places. (2) Also at other places on the same date and on earlier dates at the same or other places. (3) Also at other places on the same date.

Tropical Cyclone Names in 2024

Source: National Hurricane Center, Central Pacific Hurricane Center, NOAA, U.S. Dept. of Commerce; World Meteorological Org.

NOAA's National Hurricane Center began using name lists in 1953. Presently, six lists, maintained by the World Meteorological Org., are used in rotation. If there are more than 21 named storms in one season, storms take names from supplemental lists, established by the WMO in 2021. Previously, the Greek alphabet had been used if a list was exhausted in a given season (this happened in 2005 and 2020).

Atlantic: Alberto, Beryl, Chris, Debby, Ernesto, Francine, Gordon, Helene, Isaac, Joyce, Kirk, Leslie, Milton, Nadine, Oscar, Patty, Rafael, Sara, Tony, Valerie, William.

Atlantic (supplemental): Adria, Braylen, Caridad, Deshawn, Emery, Foster, Gemma, Heath, Isla, Jacobus, Kenzie, Lucio, Makayla, Nolan, Orlanda, Pax, Ronin, Sophie, Tayshaun, Viviana, Will.

Eastern North Pacific: Aletta, Bud, Carlotta, Daniel, Emilia, Fabio, Gilma, Hector, Ileana, John, Kristy, Lane, Miriam, Norman, Olivia, Paul, Rosa, Sergio, Tara, Vicente, Willa, Xavier, Yolanda, Zeke.

Eastern North Pacific (supplemental): Aidan, Bruna, Carmelo, Daniella, Esteban, Flor, Gerardo, Hedda, Izzy, Jacinta, Kenito, Luna, Marina, Nancy, Ovidio, Pia, Rey, Skylar, Teo, Violeta, Wilfredo, Xinia, Yariel, Zoe.

World Temperature and Precipitation

Source: Natl. Centers of Environmental Information, NOAA, U.S. Dept. of Commerce
Data are for the period 1981-2010 (the most current available as of Apr. 11, 2023) unless otherwise noted. Surface elevations are supplied by the WMO and may differ from figures in other sections of *The World Almanac*.

Station	Surface elevation (ft)	Temperature (°F)						Avg. annual precipitation (in.)
		AVERAGE DAILY				EXTREME		
		January		July				
		Max.	Min.	Max.	Min.	Max.	Min.	
Abu Dhabi, United Arab Emirates[1]	89	75.4	55.0	107.8	83.3	120.6	41.7	2.8
Amsterdam, Netherlands	-13	42.4	33.4	71.6	55.4	NA	NA	33.0
Antwerp, Belgium	39	43.0	33.1	73.4	57.2	NA	NA	32.8
Auckland, New Zealand	23	74.5	60.8	57.7	45.5	NA	NA	43.4
Bangkok, Thailand	10	90.5	72.7	91.8	78.3	103.5	53.6	64.9
Barcelona, Spain	13	56.5	40.5	82.4	67.4	99.3	19.0	22.9
Berlin, Germany	157	37.6	28.6	76.3	58.6	NA	NA	22.6
Bucharest, Romania	295	37.0	23.4	85.6	59.7	108.0	-14.1	23.4
Buenos Aires, Argentina	82	86.2	68.2	59.5	45.3	NA	NA	48.7
Casablanca, Morocco	203	63.1	46.9	78.6	68.2	NA	NA	15.7
Christchurch, New Zealand	121	72.7	53.4	51.6	33.1	NA	NA	23.4
Copenhagen, Denmark	23	38.1	30.7	72.0	57.7	89.8	0.3	25.4
Dubai, United Arab Emirates	26	75.4	57.6	105.6	85.8	117.5	45.3	3.9
Dublin, Ireland	233	46.6	36.5	66.9	52.5	83.7	10.0	29.8
Geneva, Switzerland	1,348	41.2	30.0	80.1	58.3	NA	NA	37.2
Hamburg, Germany	36	39.0	30.0	73.0	55.8	NA	NA	31.3
Helsinki, Finland	10	29.7	20.3	70.7	57.6	87.4	-29.7	25.8
Hong Kong, China	105	65.5	58.1	88.5	80.2	NA	NA	94.4
Islamabad, Pakistan	1,663	64.2	37.8	95.5	75.9	NA	NA	48.4
Jerusalem, Israel	2,657	54.3	43.9	84.7	67.1	NA	NA	20.9
Karachi, Pakistan	69	79.3	52.7	91.9	81.7	NA	NA	7.0
Lhasa, Tibet	11,975	46.6	18.0	73.6	52.0	NA	NA	17.3
Macau, China	361	64.8	54.5	88.9	79.2	NA	NA	81.0
Madrid, Spain	1,998	51.3	32.4	92.3	62.2	108.0	13.1	14.6
Mexico City, Mexico	7,572	71.2	45.7	75.4	54.9	93.0	31.9	33.5
Milan, Italy	354	43.3	31.8	86.2	65.8	NA	NA	26.9
Munich, Germany	1,462	36.1	24.6	75.6	55.6	NA	NA	30.4
Osaka, Japan	75	49.1	37.0	88.9	75.7	NA	NA	50.4
Ottawa, Canada	259	21.6	6.1	79.9	60.3	99.1	-31.0	36.2
Prague, Czech Republic	935	35.4	25.5	76.3	56.7	NA	NA	20.2
Reykjavik, Iceland	171	36.5	27.7	57.6	47.8	78.3	3.7	33.2
Riga, Latvia	20	31.3	23.9	74.3	59.0	NA	NA	29.4
Rio de Janeiro, Brazil	36	88.2	75.4	79.2	65.5	107.6	52.0	65.0
Riyadh, Saudi Arabia	2,034	68.5	48.2	110.3	84.6	NA	NA	3.6
Rome, Italy	423	52.9	37.2	87.6	65.8	NA	NA	30.9
Santiago, Chile	1,581	85.8	53.6	58.5	36.5	NA	NA	10.9
São Paulo, Brazil	2,599	82.8	66.7	72.3	54.1	98.6	33.4	63.6
Sarajevo, Bosnia and Herzegovina	2,067	38.7	26.1	80.6	56.7	101.8	-5.8	36.9
Seoul, South Korea	279	34.7	21.4	83.5	71.4	NA	NA	57.1
Tallinn, Estonia	108	30.2	21.4	71.4	54.9	93.7	-24.5	27.7
Tashkent, Uzbekistan	1,565	44.4	29.3	96.1	67.5	NA	NA	17.5
Tbilisi, Georgia	1,417	44.2	30.9	88.3	67.5	104.0	9.7	19.9
Tehran, Iran	3,907	46.8	33.3	98.2	76.6	108.7	12.6	9.4
Tokyo, Japan	83	49.3	33.6	84.6	71.2	NA	NA	60.2
Ulaanbaatar, Mongolia	4,275	4.1	-15.0	76.3	54.9	100.9	-39.6	10.6
Yerevan, Armenia	3,652	33.4	21.9	90.7	66.4	106.2	-4.0	14.1
Zagreb, Croatia	515	40.1	30.6	81.9	63.9	100.8	1.0	34.3
Zurich, Switzerland	1,824	38.3	29.5	75.7	57.9	NA	NA	43.6

NA = Not available. (1) Data are for 1982-2010.

Speed of Winds in the U.S.

Source: National Centers for Environmental Information, NESDIS, NOAA, U.S. Dept. of Commerce
Based on available records through 2022. Maximum speeds are highest 3-sec. wind speeds.

Station	Avg. mph	Max. mph	Station	Avg. mph	Max. mph	Station	Avg. mph	Max. mph
Albuquerque, NM	8.2	89	Helena, MT	6.9	81	Oklahoma City, OK	11.3	87
Anchorage, AK	6.9	71	Honolulu, HI	10.3	49	Omaha, NE	10.0	96
Atlanta, GA	8.2	76	Houston, TX	7.5	70	Philadelphia, PA	9.2	75
Baltimore, MD	7.2	72	Indianapolis, IN	9.5	85	Phoenix, AZ	6.1	86
Birmingham, AL	6.1	75	Jackson, MS	6.1	75	Pittsburgh, PA	7.8	75
Bismarck, ND	9.4	83	Jacksonville, FL	6.6	86	Portland, ME	7.9	72
Boise, ID	7.6	68	Little Rock, AR	7.0	87	Portland, OR	7.3	67
Boston, MA	11.5	76	Los Angeles, CA	7.4	53	Providence, RI	9.2	66
Buffalo, NY	10.3	75	Louisville, KY	7.8	75	Richmond, VA	7.6	72
Burlington, VT	8.2	70	Miami, FL	8.3	104	St. Louis, MO	9.0	71
Charleston, SC	7.8	69	Milwaukee, WI	10.1	79	Salt Lake City, UT	8.3	75
Chicago, IL	9.9	84	Minneapolis, MN	9.6	71	San Francisco, CA	10.5	71
Cleveland, OH	9.6	72	Mobile, AL	7.4	91	San Juan, PR	8.0	93
Dallas-Ft. Worth, TX	10.5	79	Mount Washington, NH	35.4	231	Seattle, WA	7.9	69
Denver, CO	10.0	80	Nashville, TN	7.0	78	Sioux Falls, SD	10.2	87
Des Moines, IA	9.8	77	New Orleans, LA	7.9	88	Washington, DC	8.9	74
Detroit, MI	9.4	78	New York, NY	6.4	62	Wichita, KS	11.5	101
Fairbanks, AK	4.3	59	Newark, NJ	9.8	78	Wilmington, DE	8.5	78

Wind Chill Temperature

Source: National Weather Service, NOAA, U.S. Dept. of Commerce

Temperature and wind combine to cause heat loss from body surfaces. For example, when the air temperature is 5°F, a 10-mph wind can cause body heat loss equal to that which could occur when the air temperature is –10°F with no wind. In other words, a 10-mph wind can make 5°F feel like –10°F. Wind speeds greater than 45 mph have little additional chilling effect. Direct sunlight can increase the wind chill temperature 10°F to 15°F. When the wind chill temperature falls within the shaded areas, frostbite can occur on exposed skin in the times indicated or less.

	Calm	Air temperature (°F)																	
		40	35	30	25	20	15	10	5	0	–5	–10	–15	–20	–25	–30	–35	–40	–45
		Wind chill temperature (°F)																	
Wind speed (mph)	5	36	31	25	19	13	7	1	–5	–11	–16	–22	–28	–34	–40	–46	–52	–57	–63
	10	34	27	21	15	9	3	–4	–10	–16	–22	–28	–35	–41	–47	–53	–59	–66	–72
	15	32	25	19	13	6	0	–7	–13	–19	–26	–32	–39	–45	–51	–58	–64	–71	–77
	20	30	24	17	11	4	–2	–9	–15	–22	–29	–35	–42	–48	–55	–61	–68	–74	–81
	25	29	23	16	9	3	–4	–11	–17	–24	–31	–37	–44	–51	–58	–64	–71	–78	–84
	30	28	22	15	8	1	–5	–12	–19	–26	–33	–39	–46	–53	–60	–67	–73	–80	–87
	35	28	21	14	7	0	–7	–14	–21	–27	–34	–41	–48	–55	–62	–69	–76	–82	–89
	40	27	20	13	6	–1	–8	–15	–22	–29	–36	–43	–50	–57	–64	–71	–78	–84	–91
	45	26	19	12	5	–2	–9	–16	–23	–30	–37	–44	–51	–58	–65	–72	–79	–86	–93

☐ 30 minutes   ☐ 10 minutes   ☐ 5 minutes

Heat Index

Source: National Weather Service, NOAA, U.S. Dept. of Commerce

The heat index, or apparent temperature, is a measure of how hot it feels when the relative humidity is factored in with the actual air temperature. For example, when air temperature is 100°F, and relative humidity is 50%, it can feel as if it's 118°F with no humidity. Full sunlight can make one feel even hotter. On the chart, the shaded areas indicate the likelihood of heat disorders with prolonged exposure or strenuous activity.

	Air temperature (°F)															
	80	82	84	86	88	90	92	94	96	98	100	102	104	106	108	110
	Apparent temperature (°F)															
Relative humidity (%) 40	80	81	83	85	88	91	94	97	101	105	109	114	119	124	130	136
45	80	82	84	87	89	93	96	100	104	109	114	119	124	130	137	
50	81	83	85	88	91	95	99	103	108	113	118	124	131	137		
55	81	84	86	89	93	97	101	106	112	117	124	130	137			
60	82	84	88	91	95	100	105	110	116	123	129	137				
65	82	85	89	93	98	103	108	114	121	128	136					
70	83	86	90	95	100	105	112	119	126	134						
75	84	88	92	97	103	109	116	124	132							
80	84	89	94	100	106	113	121	129								
85	85	90	96	102	110	117	126	135								
90	86	91	98	105	113	122	131									
95	86	93	100	108	117	127										
100	87	95	103	112	121	132										

☐ Caution   ☐ Extreme caution   ☐ Danger   ☐ Extreme danger

Ultraviolet (UV) Index Forecast

Source: National Weather Service (NWS), NOAA, U.S. Dept. of Commerce; U.S. Environmental Protection Agency (EPA); World Health Organization (WHO)

The NWS and EPA developed and began offering a UV index in 1994 in response to increasing incidences of skin cancer, cataracts, and other effects from exposure to the sun's harmful rays. In 2004, they adapted their index to the Global Solar UV Index sponsored by the WHO. The UV index is now a regular element of NWS atmospheric forecasts. To see the UV index for a given location, visit https://enviro.epa.gov/envirofacts/uv/search or use WHO's app SunSmart Global UV.

The UV index, ranging from 0 to 11+, is an indication of the expected intensity of UV radiation reaching the Earth's surface during the solar noon hour (the time of day, dependent on location and time of year, when the sun appears to have reached its highest point in the sky). The lower the UV index value, the less the expected radiation. The UV index forecast is produced daily for 58 cities by the NWS Climate Prediction Center.

UV levels are influenced by the following:

Ozone. Ozone, a form of oxygen, the molecules of which consist of three atoms rather than two, absorbs UV radiation. The more ozone, the lower the UV radiation at the surface.

Time of day. UV radiation is highest at midday (when the sun peaks in the sky) and is lower in the early morning and late afternoon.

Cloud cover. UV radiation levels are highest under cloudless skies. Even with cloud cover, UV radiation levels can be high due to the scattering of UV radiation by water molecules and fine particles in the atmosphere.

Ground reflection. Reflective surfaces intensify UV exposure. Water reflects about 10% of UV radiation that reaches it; sand, 15%; and snow, as much as 80%.

Altitude. At higher altitudes, a thinner atmosphere filters less UV radiation. For every 1,000 ft (305 m) one travels above sea level, UV levels increase by 2%.

Latitude. The closer a location is to the equator, the higher the UV radiation level.

Seasons. UV radiation is highest in spring and summer, drops in fall, and is lowest in winter.

Land cover. Structures and trees lessen exposure to UV radiation.

Using the UV Forecast

UV index	Exposure	Protective actions
0-2	Low	Sunglasses on bright days, SPF 15+ sunscreen, cover up if you burn easily
3-5	Moderate	Seek shade during midday hours; hat, sunglasses; SPF 30+ sunscreen
6-7	High	Seek shade during midday hours; protective clothing, hat, sunglasses, sunscreen
8-10	Very high	If outside 10 AM-4 PM, seek shade; wear protective clothing, hat, sunglasses, sunscreen; avoid bright surfaces
11+	Extreme	If outside 10 AM-4 PM, seek shade; wear protective clothing, hat, sunglasses, sunscreen; avoid bright surfaces

Lightning

Source: National Weather Service, NOAA, U.S. Dept. of Commerce

Lightning is a powerful electric discharge, or spark, that can occur in the atmosphere when an imbalance of positive and negative charges develops. It can travel within a cloud, between clouds, between a cloud and clear sky, or between a cloud and the ground. Lightning generally accompanies rainstorms, but it can also be seen with snowstorms, volcano eruption clouds, and violent forest fires. In a common form of cloud-to-ground lightning, a negatively charged area in a thunderstorm sends charges down toward positively charged objects. Lightning can travel miles away from the area of a storm.

The transfer of charges in lightning generates a huge amount of heat, sending the temperature in the channel to 50,000°F or more and causing the air within it to expand rapidly. The sound of that expansion is thunder. Sound travels more slowly than light, so lightning is usually observed before thunder is heard.

An estimated 25 mil cloud-to-ground lightning bolts happen in the U.S. each year. They killed an annual average of 36 people in 1993-2022. This is a small number compared to U.S. deaths from fire (3,790 in 2022) and motor vehicle crashes (about 40,000-45,000 annually in recent years), but it is still significant. In comparison, tornadoes caused an average of 71 deaths a year and hurricanes an average of 45 over the same 30-year time period. According to the National Weather Service, 19 people were struck and killed by lightning in 2022; 53 more were injured.

Most lightning deaths and injuries occur in summer when people are outdoors. If outdoors, one should run to a safe building or vehicle when thunder is first heard, lightning is seen, or dark threatening clouds are observed developing overhead. Even while indoors, one is advised to stay away from windows and doors and to avoid contact with anything conducting electricity, including corded phones, computers and other electrical equipment, and tubs, showers, and other plumbing. One should stay inside until 30 min. after the last occurrence of lightning or thunder.

More information about lightning can be found online at https://www.weather.gov/safety/lightning

Global Temperature Extremes and Precipitation Records

Source: World Weather & Climate Extremes Archive, World Meteorological Organization (WMO)

(records in each category ranked from most to least extreme; as of Apr. 12, 2023)

Highest Temperature Extremes

Continent/area	Highest temp. (°F)	Place	Elevation (ft)	Date
North America	134	Death Valley, CA, U.S. (Furnace Creek (fmr. Greenland) Ranch)	−179	July 10, 1913
Africa	131[1]	Kebili, Tunisia	125	July 7, 1931
Europe/Middle East/ Greenland	129	Tirat Tsvi, Israel	−722	June 21, 1942
Asia[2]	129.0	Mitribah, Kuwait	398	July 21, 2016
	128.7	Turbat, Pakistan	495	May 28, 2017
Southwest Pacific	123	Oodnadatta, Australia	367	Jan. 2, 1960
South America	120	Rivadavia, Argentina	673	Dec. 11, 1905
Continental Europe	118.4	Athens, Greece (and Elefsina, Greece)	774	July 10, 1977
Antarctica	67.6	Signy Research Station (UK)	23	Jan. 30, 1982

(1) Previous record of 136.4°F set on Sept. 13, 1922, in El Azizia, Libya, was invalidated in 2012; an error had been made in recording the temperature. (2) Record effectively tied due to margin of error in measurement.

Lowest Temperature Extremes

Continent/area	Lowest temp. (°F)	Place	Elevation (ft)	Date
Antarctica	−128.6	Vostok Station (Soviet Union/Russia)	11,220	July 21, 1983
Europe/Middle East/ Greenland	−93.3	Klinck Auto. Weather Sta., Greenland	10,551	Dec. 22, 1991
Asia	−90	Verkhoyansk, Russia	350	Feb. 5 and 7, 1892
	−90	Oimekon, Russia	2,625	Feb. 6, 1933
North America	−81.4	Snag, Yukon, Canada	2,120	Feb. 3, 1947
Continental Europe	−72.6	Ust'-Shchugor, Russia	279	Dec. 31, 1978
South America	−27	Sarmiento, Argentina	879	June 1, 1907
Southwest Pacific	−14	Eweburn (now Ranfurly), New Zealand	1,388	July 17, 1903
Africa	−11	Ifrane, Morocco	5,364	Feb. 11, 1935
Australia	−9.4	Charlotte Pass, New South Wales	5,758	June 29, 1994

Highest Measured Average Annual Precipitation Extremes

Continent/area	Highest avg. (in.)[1]	Place	Elevation (ft)	Years in averaging period
Asia	467.4	Mawsynram, India	4,695	38
Southwest Pacific	460.0	Mt. Waialeale, Kauai, HI, U.S.	5,148	30
Africa	405.0	Debundscha, Cameroon	30	32
South America	354.0[2]	Quibdo, Colombia	230	29
Australia	316.3	Bellenden Ker, Queensland	5,102	34
North America	276	Henderson Lake, British Columbia, Canada	12	15
Europe	180.8	Crkvice, Montenegro	3,461	30
Antarctica	>31.5[3]	Along coast of E and W and over the Antarctic Peninsula		3[4]

(1) Official greatest average annual precipitation. (2) The frequently cited record of 523.6 in. in Lloro, Colombia (14 mi SE and at a higher elevation than Quibdo) is an estimate. (3) Water equivalent. (4) July 1996-June 1999.

Lowest Measured Average Annual Precipitation Extremes

Continent/area	Lowest avg. (in.)[1]	Place	Elevation (ft)	Years in averaging period
South America	0.03	Arica, Chile	213	59
Antarctica	0.08	Amundsen-Scott South Pole Station (U.S.)	9,301	10
Africa	<0.1	Wadi Halfa, Sudan	590	39
North America	1.2	Batagues, Mexico	69	14
Asia	1.8	Aden, Yemen	63	50
Southwest Pacific	4.05	Troudaninna, Australia	46	42
Continental Europe	6.4	Astrakhan, Russia	66	25

(1) Official lowest average annual precipitation.

OCEANOGRAPHY

Tides and Their Causes

Source: National Ocean Service, NOAA, U.S. Dept. of Commerce

The tides are natural phenomena involving the movement of waves in the Earth's large fluid bodies as a result of the gravitational attraction of the sun and moon. These two variable influences combined produce the complex recurrent cycle of the tides. Tides may occur in both oceans and seas; to a limited extent in large lakes and in the atmosphere; and, to a very minute degree, in the Earth itself. The length of time between succeeding tides can vary.

The tide-generating force represents the difference between (1) the centrifugal force produced by Earth's revolution around the common center of gravity of the Earth-moon system and (2) the gravitational attraction of the moon acting upon the Earth's overlying waters. The moon is about 390 times closer to Earth than is the sun. So despite its smaller mass, the moon's tide-raising force is two times greater.

The tide-generating forces of the moon and sun acting tangentially to the Earth's surface tend to cause a maximum accumulation of waters at two diametrically opposite points on the Earth's surface and to withdraw compensating amounts of water from all points 90° removed from these tidal bulges. As the Earth rotates beneath the maxima and minima of these tide-generating forces, a sequence of two high tides, separated by two low tides, is produced each lunar day (24 hr. and 50 min., the time it takes for a specific site on the Earth to rotate from an exact point under the moon to the same point under the moon) in what is called a **semidiurnal tide**. Each ocean basin reacts differently to tidal forces.

Twice each month, when the sun, moon, and Earth are directly aligned—the moon between the Earth and sun (at new moon) or on the opposite side of Earth from the sun (at full moon)—the sun and moon exert gravitational forces in a mutual or additive fashion. The highest high tides and lowest low tides, called **spring tides**, are produced at these times. At two positions 90° in between, the moon and sun's gravitational forces—imposed at right angles—counteract each other to the greatest extent, and the range between high and low tides is reduced, resulting in **neap tides**.

The inclination of the moon's monthly orbit and of the sun to the equator during Earth's yearly passage through its orbit produce a difference in the height of succeeding high and low tides, known as the diurnal inequality. In most cases, this produces a so-called **mixed tide**. In extreme cases, these phenomena may result in a **diurnal tide**, with only one high tide and one low tide each day. There are other monthly and yearly variations in the tides because of the elliptical shape of the orbits.

The range of tides in the open ocean is generally less than in the coastal regions, where the incoming tide can be augmented by the continental shelves, as well as by bays and estuaries. The largest tidal ranges in the world occur in the Bay of Fundy, Canada, where the range of tide reaches 53 ft. The highest tides in the U.S. occur near Anchorage, AK, with tidal ranges that average around 30 ft.

In every case, actual high or low tide can vary considerably from the average as a result of weather conditions such as strong winds, abrupt barometric pressure changes, or prolonged periods of extreme high or low pressure.

Mean Ranges of Tide

Place	Ft	In.	Place	Ft	In.	Place	Ft	In.
Baltimore, MD.	1	2	Key West, FL	1	3	Provincetown, MA	9	3
Biloxi, MS	1	6	Los Angeles, CA.	3	10	St. Petersburg, FL	1	7
Boston, MA.	9	6	Miami Beach, FL	2	6	San Diego, CA	4	1
Charleston, SC	5	3	New London, CT	2	7	San Francisco, CA	4	1
Eastport, ME.	18	4	New York, NY.	4	6	San Juan, PR.	1	1
Ft. Pulaski, GA	6	11	Newport, RI	3	6	Sandy Hook, NJ	4	8
Galveston, TX.	1	0	Philadelphia, PA.	6	1	Seattle, WA	7	8
Honolulu, HI	1	3	Portland, ME.	9	1	Washington, DC	2	9

Note: Mean range is the difference in height between mean high water and mean low water.

El Niño and La Niña

Source: National Weather Service, NOAA, U.S. Dept. of Commerce

El Niño is a climatically significant disruption of the ocean-atmosphere system characterized by large-scale weakening of trade winds and warming of surface layer waters in the central and eastern equatorial Pacific. The term *El Niño*, Spanish for "the little boy" or "the Christ Child," was originally used by fishing crews to refer to a warm ocean current that appeared around Christmas off the west coast of Ecuador and Peru lasting several months. The term has come to be reserved for exceptionally strong warm currents that bring heavy rains.

El Niño events generally occur at irregular intervals of two to seven years, at an average of once every three to four years. They typically last 12 to 18 months. The intensity of El Niño events varies depending on the area encompassed by the abnormally warm ocean temperatures. Some are strong, such as in 1982-83, 1997-98, and 2015-16. Others are considerably weaker, such as the 2018-19 event. The eastward extent of warmer-than-normal water varies from episode to episode.

El Niño influences weather around the globe, and its impacts are most clearly seen in the winter. During El Niño years, winter temperatures in the continental U.S. tend to be warmer than normal in the northern states and on the West Coast and cooler than normal in the Southeast. Conditions tend to be wetter than normal over central and southern California, the Southwest, and across much of the South, and drier than normal over the northern portions of the Rocky Mountains and in the Ohio Valley. Globally, El Niño brings wetter than normal conditions to Peru and Chile and dry conditions to Australia and Indonesia. It should be noted that El Niño is only one of a number of factors influencing seasonal variations of climate.

La Niña ("the little girl") is characterized by colder than normal sea surface temperatures in the equatorial Pacific. La Niña typically brings wetter, cooler conditions to the Pacific Northwest and drier, warmer conditions to much of the southern U.S. El Niño and La Niña are opposite phases of the El Niño-Southern Oscillation (ENSO) cycle, which involves a shift in tropical sea-level pressure between the Eastern and Western Hemispheres.

NOAA and other agencies monitor these events using satellites, weather balloons, and buoys in the Pacific Ocean. Numerical computer models of the ocean and atmosphere use these data to predict the onset and evolution of El Niño and La Niña. A transition into El Niño conditions began in mid 2023; El Niño conditions were expected to persist through the Northern Hemisphere winter, Dec. 2023-Feb. 2024.

DISASTERS

U.S. Weather and Climate Disasters by Type, 1980-2022

Source: National Centers for Environmental Information, National Oceanic and Atmospheric Admin., U.S. Dept. of Commerce
Does not include disasters causing under $1 billion in 2022 consumer price index-adjusted losses. The worst year for billion-dollar disasters in this period was 2017, with $383.7 billion (CPI-adjusted) in damages from events including Hurricanes Harvey, Irma, and Maria. It easily surpassed the previous U.S. annual record of $260.3 billion, established in 2005. As of Aug. 11, 2023.

Disaster type	Number of events	Losses (bil)	Percent of total losses	Average cost (bil)	Deaths
Drought.................	30	$337.1	13.2%	$11.2	4,275[1]
Flooding[2]...............	40	186.7	7.3	4.7	701
Freeze...................	9	36.2	1.4	4.0	162
Severe storm	167	398.8	15.6	2.4	1,994
Tropical cyclone	60	1,367.6	53.5	22.8	6,890
Wildfire	21	136.6	5.3	6.5	435
Winter storm	21	95.5	3.7	4.5	1,401
All disasters	**348**	**2,558.5**	**100.0**	**7.4**	**15,858**

Note: Tropical cyclones include hurricanes, tropical storms, tropical depressions, and associated storm surges and flooding. (1) Drought-associated deaths are the result of heat waves, which do not always occur with droughts. (2) Does not include inland flood damage caused by tropical cyclone events.

U.S. Weather and Climate Disasters, 2022

Source: National Centers for Environmental Information, National Oceanic and Atmospheric Admin., U.S. Dept. of Commerce
Does not include disasters causing under $1 billion in 2022 consumer price index-adjusted losses.

Date	Event and location	Losses (bil)	Deaths
Jan. 1-Dec. 31	Severe drought, heat wave in western and central states; Lake Mead, largest U.S. reservoir, reached record-low level..........................	$22.9	136
Feb. 21-22	Hail storms, TX (Denton, Collin, Wise Counties)	1.1	0
Mar. 30	83 tornadoes across Gulf Coast states, incl. LA, MS, AL, FL (Washington Co.), AR (Springdale)	1.3	2
Apr. 1-Nov. 30	Severe drought, extreme heat contributed to wildfires, esp. in NM, OR, ID, MT, CA, AK	3.2	17
Apr. 4-6	100 preliminary tornadoes reported across TX, LA, MS, AL, GA (Pembroke), FL, SC..........	1.5	3
Apr. 11-13	High wind, dozens of tornadoes, AR, LA, MS, AL, TX, TN, KY; hail across WI, MN............	2.8	1
May 1-3	Severe weather (high winds, hail), TX, OK, OH, PA	1.2	1
May 9	Hail storms, MN, WI	2.3	0
May 11-12	Severe weather, SD, NE, MN (hail, high winds in St. Cloud, Minneapolis metro area), WI; more than two dozen tornadoes	2.9	1
May 19	Severe hail storms, MN, WI	2.6	0
June 7-8	Severe weather (hail, more than two dozen tornadoes), CO, NE, KS, MO, OK, TX, IA, OH	2.0	0
June 13	Derecho, MI, IL, IN, OH; hail damage, southern WI	3.3	1
July 22-24	Severe weather, 19 tornadoes, ND, MN, WI, MI, IL, IN, OH, PA, VA, MD, NY	1.4	1
July 26-28	Flooding from stalled frontal system, KY, MO................................	1.5	42
Sept. 17-18	Hurricane Fiona, central and western Puerto Rico............................	2.6	25
Sept. 28-30	Hurricane Ian, barrier islands (Captiva, Sanibel, Pine, Fort Myers Beach), central, eastern FL..	115.2	152
Nov. 10-11	Hurricane Nicole, FL..	1.1	5
Dec. 21-26	Winter storm and cold wave, TX to ME; near hurricane-force winds in Buffalo, NY	8.7	87
2022 total	**18 events**	**177.4**	**474**

Note: As of Aug. 11, 2023. Data may be updated as new information becomes available.

Some Notable Aircraft Disasters Since 1937

Source: National Transportation Safety Board; World Almanac research
Particularly notable disasters are in bold. Asterisk (*) indicates number of deaths includes people on ground. As of Sept. 2023.

Date	Aircraft	Incident details, site	Deaths
1937, May 6	**German zeppelin Hindenburg**	**Burned at mooring, Lakehurst, NJ**....................	**36***
1944, Aug. 23	U.S. Air Force B-24 Liberator bomber ...	Hit school, Freckleton, England, UK....................	61*
1945, July 28	U.S. Army B-25............................	Hit Empire State Building after getting lost in fog, New York, NY...	14*
1952, Dec. 20	U.S. Air Force C-124......................	Crashed at Moses Lake, WA........................	87
1953, Mar. 3	**Canadian Pacific DH-106 Comet .....**	**Crashed on takeoff from Karachi, Pakistan; world's first fatal commercial passenger jet crash**	**11**
1953, June 18	U.S. Air Force C-124......................	Crashed, burned near Tokyo, Japan....................	129
1955, Oct. 6	United Airlines DC-4......................	Crashed in Medicine Bow Peak, WY	66
1955, Nov. 1	United Airlines DC-6......................	Bomb on board exploded near Longmont, CO.............	44[1]
1956, June 20	LAV (Venezuela) Super Constellation	Crashed into Atlantic off Asbury Park, NJ	74
1956, June 30	TWA Super Const., United DC-7	Collided over Grand Canyon, AZ	128
1960, Dec. 16	United DC-8, TWA Super Const.	Collided over New York, NY, killing all 128 on planes, 6 on ground	134*
1962, Mar. 16	Flying Tiger (U.S.) Super Constellation ...	Vanished in W Pacific en route to Philippines from Guam........	107
1962, June 3	Air France Boeing 707	Crashed on takeoff from Paris, France...................	130
1962, June 22	Air France Boeing 707	Crashed in storm, Guadeloupe, French W Indies	113
1963, Feb. 1	Lebanese Middle East Airlines Vickers Viscount 754, Turkish Mil. Douglas C-47	Collided over Ankara, Turkey, killing all 17 on planes, 87 on ground..................................	104*
1963, Nov. 29	Trans-Canada Air Lines DC-8	Crashed after takeoff from Montréal, QC, Canada...........	118
1965, May 20	Pakistani Boeing 720	Crashed at airport in Cairo, Egypt	121
1966, Jan. 24	Air India Boeing 707	Crashed on Mont Blanc, France-Italy....................	117
1966, Feb. 4	All-Nippon Boeing 727	Plunged into Tokyo Bay, Japan	133
1966, Mar. 5	BOAC (British Overseas Airways Corp.) Boeing 707........................	Crashed into Mt. Fuji, Japan, after encountering severe turbulence	124
1966, Dec. 24	U.S. military-chartered CL-44	Crashed into village in S Vietnam......................	129*
1967, Apr. 20	Globe Air Bristol Britannia	Crashed on approach to airport, Nicosia, Cyprus............	126
1967, July 19	Piedmont Boeing 727, Cessna 310	Collided over Hendersonville, NC......................	82
1968, Apr. 20	S. African Airways Boeing 707	Crashed on takeoff from Windhoek, Namibia..............	122
1968, May 3	Braniff International Electra	Crashed in storm near Dawson, TX	85
1968, May 12	U.S. Air Force Lockheed C-130B	Hit by mortar while evacuating Kham Duc Camp, S Vietnam.....	155
1969, Mar. 16	VIASA DC-9	Crashed after takeoff from Maracaibo, Venezuela..........	155[2]
1970, July 3	British-chartered DH-106 Comet	Crashed near Barcelona, Spain	112

Date	Aircraft	Incident details, site	Deaths
1970, July 5	Air Canada DC-8	Crashed near Toronto Intl. Airport, ON, Canada	108
1970, Nov. 14	Southern Airways DC-9	Crashed into mountains near Huntington, WV	75[3]
1971, July 30	All-Nippon Boeing 727, Japan Air Force F-86 fighter	Collided over Morioka, Japan	162[4]
1971, Sept. 4	Alaska Airlines Boeing 727	Crashed into mountain near Juneau, AK	111
1972, May 18	Aeroflot Antonov 10A	Wings separated from fuselage on approach to Kharkov, USSR	122
1972, June 18	British European Airways Trident-1C	Crashed near Staines after takeoff from London, Eng., UK	118
1972, Aug. 14	East German Ilyushin 62	Crashed on takeoff from East Berlin, E Germany	156
1972, Aug. 31	Aeroflot Ilyushin 18V	Crashed in field near Magnitogorsk, USSR	101
1972, Oct. 1	Aeroflot Ilyushin 18V	Crashed into Black Sea, USSR	109
1972, Oct. 13	Aeroflot Ilyushin 62	Crashed near Moscow, USSR	174
1972, Dec. 3	Spanish-chartered Convair CV-990	Crashed on takeoff from Canary Islands, Spain	155
1972, Dec. 29	Eastern Airlines Lockheed L-1011 TriStar	Crashed on approach to Miami Intl. Airport, FL	99
1973, Jan. 22	Nigerian-chartered Boeing 707	Burst into flames upon landing at Kano Airport, Nigeria	176
1973, Feb. 21	**Libyan Arab Boeing 727**	**Flew off course, shot down by Israeli fighter planes over Sinai Desert**	**108**
1973, Apr. 10	Invicta Airlines (UK) Vickers Vanguard	Crashed during snowstorm on approach to Basel, Switzerland	108
1973, June 3	Soviet Supersonic Tu-144	Crashed near Goussainville, France	14[5]
1973, July 11	Varig Airlines (Brazil) Boeing 707	Crashed on approach to Orly Airport, Paris, France	123
1973, July 31	Delta Airlines DC-9	Crashed while attempting landing in fog, Logan Airport, Boston, MA	89
1973, Sept. 30	Aeroflot Tupolev 104B	Crashed after takeoff from Sverdlovsk, USSR	108
1973, Oct. 13	Aeroflot Tupolev 104B	Crashed on approach to Moscow, USSR	122
1973, Dec. 22	Royal Air Maroc SE 210 Caravelle VIN	Flew into side of a mountain near Tangier, Morocco	106
1974, Mar. 3	Turkish DC-10	Improperly closed cargo door caused crash, nr. Paris, France	346
1974, Apr. 22	Pan American (U.S.) Boeing 707	Crashed in Bali, Indonesia	107
1974, Apr. 27	Aeroflot Ilyushin 18V	Crashed after takeoff from Leningrad, USSR	109
1974, Dec. 1	TWA Boeing 727	Crashed on approach in storm, Upperville, VA	92
1974, Dec. 4	Dutch-chartered DC-8	Crashed in storm near Colombo, Sri Lanka	191
1975, Apr. 4	U.S. Air Force Galaxy C-5A	Crashed on takeoff nr. Saigon, S Vietnam; carried orphans	155
1975, June 24	Eastern Airlines 727	Crashed in storm, JFK Airport, New York, NY	113
1975, Aug. 3	Alia Royal Jordanian Boeing 707	Hit mountainside in heavy fog near Agadir, Morocco	188
1975, Aug. 20	Czechoslovakian Air Ilyushin 62	Crashed on approach to Damascus, Syria	126
1976, Mar. 6	Aeroflot Ilyushin 18E	Crashed between Moscow, USSR, and Yerevan, Armenia	111
1976, Sept. 10	British Airways Trident, Inex Adria DC-9	Collided near Zagreb, Yugoslavia	176
1976, Sept. 19	Turkish Boeing 727	Hit mountain in southern Turkey	154
1976, Oct. 6	Cubana Airlines DC-8	Bombs set by anti-Castro Cuban exiles detonated mid-flight	73
1976, Oct. 13	Lloyd Aero Boliviano Boeing 707	Crashed into soccer field after takeoff from Santa Cruz, Bolivia	91[6]
1977, Mar. 27	**KLM (Neth.) 747, Pan Am (U.S.) 747**	**Collided on foggy runway, Tenerife, Canary Islands, Spain**	**583**
1977, Nov. 19	TAP Portugal Boeing 727	Crashed in Madeira, Portugal	131
1977, Dec. 4	Malaysian Airlines Boeing 737	Hijacked and forced to fly to Singapore, crashed near Johor Strait	100
1978, Jan. 1	Air India 747	Crashed into sea after takeoff from Bombay, India	213
1978, Sept. 25	Pacific SW Air Boeing 727, Cessna 172	Collided over San Diego, CA	144*
1978, Nov. 15	Indonesian-chartered DC-8	Crashed on approach to airport, Colombo, Sri Lanka	183
1979, May 25	**American Airlines DC-10**	**Crashed after takeoff from O'Hare Airport, Chicago, IL; highest death toll in U.S. aviation history**	**275***
1979, Aug. 11	Aeroflot/Moldova Tu-134, Aeroflot Tu-134	Collided over Ukraine	178
1979, Nov. 26	Pakistani Boeing 707	Crashed near Jidda, Saudi Arabia	156
1979, Nov. 28	Air New Zealand DC-10	Crashed into Mt. Erebus during Antarctica flyover	257
1980, Mar. 14	PLL LOT Ilyushin 62	Crashed making emergency landing, Warsaw, Poland	87[7]
1980, Apr. 25	Dan-Air Services (UK) Boeing 727	Crashed into mountain, Tenerife, Canary Islands, Spain	146
1980, July 8	Aeroflot Tupolev 154B	Crashed after takeoff from Alma-Ata, USSR	166
1980, Aug. 19	Saudi Arabian Lockheed TriStar	Returned to Riyadh airport after fire on board; evacuation delayed	301
1981, Dec. 1	Inex Adria (Yugoslavia) DC-9	Crashed into mountain on island of Corsica, France	180
1982, Jan. 13	Air Florida Boeing 737	Crashed into bridge, Potomac R. after takeoff from Washington, DC	78*
1982, June 8	VASP (Brazil) Boeing 727	Crashed into mountain near Fortaleza, Brazil	137
1982, June 28	Aeroflot Yakovlev 42	Crashed near Mozyr, USSR	132
1982, July 9	Pan Am Boeing 727	Crashed after takeoff from Kenner, LA, near New Orleans	153*
1983, July 11	Ecuadorean Boeing 737	Inexperienced pilot crashed into hill near Cuenca, Ecuador	119
1983, Sept. 1	**S. Korean Boeing 747**	**Shot down after entering restricted Soviet airspace near Sakhalin; plane apparently misidentified**	**269**
1983, Sept. 23	Gulf Air Boeing 737	Bomb exploded in cargo hold over Mina Jebel Ali, UAE	112
1983, Nov. 27	Avianca Boeing 747	Crashed near Barajas Airport, Madrid, Spain	181
1984, Oct. 11	Aeroflot/East Siberia Tu-154	Crashed into vehicles on runway while landing in poor weather, Omsk, Russia	178*
1985, Feb. 19	Spanish Boeing 727	Crashed into Mt. Oiz, Spain	148
1985, June 23	Air India Boeing 747	Crashed into Atlantic off Ireland after bomb allegedly set by Sikh extremists detonated on board	329
1985, July 10	Aeroflot Tupolev 154B	Crashed after takeoff from Uzbekistan, USSR	200
1985, Aug. 2	Delta Air Lines Lockheed L-1011 TriStar	Crashed after encountering microburst near Dallas-Ft. Worth Airport, TX	135*
1985, Aug. 12	**Japan Air Lines Boeing 747**	**Crashed into Mt. Ogura, Japan; world's worst single-plane disaster**	**520**
1985, Dec. 12	Arrow Air (U.S.) DC-8	Crashed after takeoff from Gander, NL, Canada	256[8]
1986, Mar. 31	Mexican Boeing 727	Crashed NW of Mexico City, Mexico	167
1986, Aug. 31	Aeromexico DC-9, Piper PA-28	Collided over Cerritos, CA	82*
1987, May 9	Polish IL-62M	Crashed after takeoff from Warsaw, Poland	183
1987, Aug. 16	Northwest Airlines MD-82	Crashed after takeoff from Romulus, MI	156
1987, Nov. 28	S. African Boeing 747	Crashed into Indian Ocean near Mauritius	159
1987, Nov. 29	Korean Air Boeing 707	Bomb planted by 2 N. Korean agents exploded while plane over Andaman Sea off Burma	115
1988, Mar. 17	Colombian Boeing 707	Crashed into mountainside near Venezuela border	143
1988, July 3	**Iran Air Airbus A300**	**Misidentified as hostile aircraft, shot down by U.S. Navy warship Vincennes over Persian Gulf**	**290**
1988, Oct. 19	Indian Boeing 737	Exploded after striking trees near runway, Ahmedabad, India	131
1988, Dec. 21	**Pan Am (U.S.) Boeing 747**	**Bomb set by Libyan agent; exploded over Lockerbie, Scotland**	**270[9]**
1989, Feb. 8	U.S.-chartered Boeing 707	Crashed into mountain on Azores Isls., off Portugal	144
1989, June 7	Surinam Airways DC-8	Crashed near Paramaribo Airport, Suriname	176
1989, July 19	United Airlines DC-10	Defect in plane forced emergency landing in Sioux City, IA	111
1989, Sept. 3	Cubana Aviacion Ilyushin 62M	Crashed soon after takeoff from Havana, Cuba	171*
1989, Sept. 19	**UTA (France) DC-10**	**Bomb set by Libyan agents exploded on board flight from Congo (Brazzaville) to France while over desert in Niger**	**170**

Date	Aircraft	Incident details, site	Deaths
1989, Oct. 21	TAN-SAHSA (Honduras) Boeing 727	Crashed into mountain near Tegucigalpa, Honduras	131
1989, Nov. 27	Avianca (Colombia) Boeing 727	Bomb exploded on flight from Bogotá, Colombia	107
1990, Jan. 25	Avianca (Colombia) Boeing 707	Crashed on landing at JFK Airport, New York, NY	73
1990, Oct. 2	Xiamen Airlines Boeing 737, China Southern Boeing 757	Hijacked after takeoff fr. Xiamen; collided with China Southern aircraft on runway during emergency landing, Guangzhou, China	128
1991, May 26	Lauda Air (Austria) Boeing 767-300	Broke up following takeoff from Bangkok, Thailand	223
1991, July 11	Nigeria Airways DC-8	Crashed on landing at Jidda, Saudi Arabia	261
1991, Oct. 5	U.S. Air Force Lockheed C-130 Hercules	Crashed after takeoff from Jakarta, Indonesia	135*
1992, July 31	Thai Airbus A300-310	Crashed into mountain N of Kathmandu, Nepal	113
1992, Sept. 26	Nigerian Air Force LC-130 Hercules	Transport full of military officers crashed near Lagos, Nigeria	158
1992, Sept. 28	Pakistan Intl. Air Airbus A300	Crashed into hillside near Kathmandu, Nepal	167
1992, Oct. 4	**El Al (Israel) Boeing 747-200F**	**Crashed into 2 apartment bldgs., Amsterdam, Netherlands**	**120***
1992, Nov. 24	China Southern Airlines Boeing 737	Crashed on approach to Giulin, China	141
1992, Dec. 22	Libyan Arab Air Boeing 727	Collided with Libyan Air Force MiG-23 on approach to Tripoli	159
1993, Feb. 8	Iran Air Tu-154, Iranian Air Force jet	Collided after military jet took off from Tehran, Iran	131
1993, May 19	SAM Colombia Boeing 727	Crashed into mountain near Medellín, Colombia	132
1993, Nov. 20	Macedonian Yakovlev 42D	Crashed into mountain near Skopje, Macedonia	116
1994, Jan. 3	Aeroflot Tu-154	Crashed and exploded after takeoff from Irkutsk, Russia	125*
1994, Apr. 26	China Airlines Airbus A300	Crashed on approach to Nagoya Airport, Japan	264
1994, June 6	China Northwest Airlines Tu-154	Crashed near Xian, China	160
1994, Sept. 8	USAir Boeing 737-300	Crashed near Pittsburgh Intl. Airport, Aliquippa, PA	132
1994, Oct. 31	American Eagle ATR-72-210	Crashed in field near Roselawn, IN	68
1995, Dec. 18	Zairean Lockheed L-188C Electra	Overloaded charter crashed in Lunda Norte, Angola	141
1995, Dec. 20	American Airlines Boeing 757	Crashed into mountain N of Cali, Colombia	159
1996, Jan. 8	African Air Antonov-32 cargo plane	Crashed into a market in Kinshasa, Zaire; all deaths on ground	237*
1996, Feb. 6	Alas Nacionales (Dom. Rep.) Boeing 757	Crashed into Atlantic off Dominican Republic	189
1996, Feb. 29	Faucett (Peru) Boeing 737	Crashed into hillside near Arequipa, Peru	123
1996, Apr. 3	U.S. Air Force Boeing T-43A	Crashed into mountain near Dubrovnik, Croatia	35[10]
1996, May 11	ValuJet DC-9	Crashed into Florida Everglades after improper cargo started fire	110
1996, July 17	Trans World Airlines Boeing 747	Exploded and crashed into Atlantic off Long Island, NY	230
1996, Aug. 29	Vnukovo Airlines (Russia) Tu-154	Crashed into mountain on Arctic island of Spitsbergen	141
1996, Nov. 7	ADC Airlines (Nigeria) Boeing 727	Crashed into lagoon SE of Lagos, Nigeria	144
1996, Nov. 12	**Saudi Arabian Boeing 747, Kazakh Ilyushin 76 cargo plane**	**Collided near New Delhi, India; world's worst midair collision**	**349**
1996, Nov. 23	Ethiopian Airlines Boeing 767	Hijacked; crashed into Indian O. off the Comoros (fuel ran out)	127
1997, Aug. 6	Korean Air Boeing 747-300	Crashed into jungle on Guam on approach to airport	228
1997, Sept. 26	Indonesian Airbus A300	Crashed near airport, Medan, Indonesia	234
1998, Feb. 16	China Airlines Airbus A300	Crashed on approach to airport in Taipei, Taiwan	203*
1998, Sept. 2	Swissair MD-11	Crashed into Atlantic off Nova Scotia, Canada, after onboard fire	229
1999, Oct. 31	EgyptAir Boeing 767	Crashed off Nantucket, MA; result of deliberate actions by copilot, motives unknown	217
2000, Jan. 30	Kenya Airways Airbus A310	Crashed into Atlantic after takeoff from Abidjan, Côte d'Ivoire	169
2000, Jan. 31	Alaska Airlines MD-83	Crashed into Pacific off coast of Southern CA	88
2000, Apr. 19	Air Philippines Boeing 737-200	Crashed on approach to airport, Davao, Philippines	131
2000, July 25	**Air France Concorde**	**Crashed into hotel after takeoff from Paris; world's first Concorde crash**	**113***
2000, Aug. 23	Gulf Air Airbus A320	Crashed into Persian Gulf on approach to airport in Bahrain	143
2001, July 3	Vladivostokavia Tu-154	Crashed on approach to airport, Irkutsk, Russia	145
2001, Sept. 11	**2 Boeing 767s, 2 Boeing 757s**	**September 11 terrorist attacks**	**265[11]**
2001, Oct. 8	Cessna 525A Citation, Scandinavian Airlines System (SAS) MD-87	Collided in heavy fog on takeoff from Milan, Italy	118
2001, Nov. 12	**American Airlines Airbus A300**	**Crashed after takeoff from JFK Airport, New York, NY**	**265***
2002, Feb. 12	Iran Air Tours Tu-154	Crashed into mountain on approach to airport, Khorramabad, Iran	119
2002, Apr. 15	Air China Boeing 767	Crashed into mountain in rain and fog on approach to airport, Pusan, S. Korea	129
2002, May 4	EAS Airlines BAC 1-11	Crashed shortly after takeoff from Kano, Nigeria	149
2002, May 7	China Northern Airlines MD-82	Plunged into sea, apparently after a passenger started fire in cabin, NE China	112
2002, May 25	China Airlines Boeing 747	Broke apart in midair, plunged into Taiwan Strait en route to Hong Kong airport	225
2002, July 27	**Ukraine Air Force Sukhoi Su-27**	**Crashed while performing, Lviv, Ukraine; world's worst air-show crash**	**77[12]**
2002, Aug. 19	Russian Mi-26 transport helicopter	Hit by Chechen missile near Grozny, Chechnya	127
2003, Jan. 8	Turkish Airlines British Aerospace RJ-100	Crashed on approach to airport in Diyarbakir, Turkey	75
2003, Feb. 19	Iranian Revolutionary Guard Ilyushin 76	Crashed into mountain near Kerman, Iran; passengers were Revolutionary Guard members	275
2003, May 26	Ukrain.-Medit. Airlines Yak-42	Crashed into mountain in fog approaching Trabzon, Turkey; passengers incl. Spanish peacekeepers returning from Afghan.	75
2003, July 8	Sudan Airways Boeing 737-200	Mechanical problems reported shortly after takeoff; crashed upon return to Port Sudan Airport	115
2003, Dec. 25	Union Transp. Africains Boeing 727	Overloading caused crash on takeoff from Cotonou, Benin	141
2004, Jan. 3	Flash Airlines Boeing 737-300	Crashed into Red Sea after takeoff from Sharm el Sheikh, Egypt	148
2004, Aug. 24	Volga-Aviaexpress Tu-134, Sibir Airlines Tu-154	2 planes that took off from Moscow crashed within minutes of each other; brought down by Chechen suicide bombers	90
2005, Aug. 14	Helios Airways Boeing 737-300	Crashed after air pressure failure on board, near Athens, Greece	121
2005, Aug. 16	W Caribbean Airways (Colombia) MD-82	Crashed after engine failure, near Machiques, Venezuela	160
2005, Sept. 5	Mandala Airlines Boeing 737-200	Crashed shortly after takeoff from Medan, Sumatra, Indonesia	145*
2005, Oct. 22	Bellview Airlines Boeing 737-200	Crashed during heavy electrical storm near Lagos, Nigeria	117

Date	Aircraft	Incident details, site	Deaths
2005, Dec. 6	Islamic Rep. of Iran Air Force Lockheed C-130	Crashed into apartment building after reportedly attempting emergency landing back at airport, Tehran, Iran	116*
2005, Dec. 10	Sosoliso Airlines DC-9-30	Crashed during storm on approach to Port Harcourt, Nigeria	107
2006, May 3	Armavia Airbus A320	Crashed into Black Sea on approach to airport, Sochi, Russia	113
2006, July 9	S7 Airlines Airbus A310	Skidded off runway, crashed into concrete barrier after landing, Irkutsk, Russia	125
2006, Aug. 22	Pulkovo Aviation Tu-154	Crashed after encountering storm, near Donetsk, Ukraine	170
2006, Sept. 29	Gol Airlines Boeing 737	Crashed into Amazon jungle after midair collision with Embraer Legacy jet (which itself landed safely), Brazil	154
2007, May 5	Kenya Airways Boeing 737-800	Crashed shortly after takeoff from Douala, Cameroon	114
2007, July 17	TAM Airlines Airbus 320	Crashed on runway, caught fire after skidding off runway, São Paulo, Brazil	199*
2008, Aug. 20	Spanair Boeing-MD-82	Swerved off runway, caught fire on takeoff attempt, Madrid, Spain	154
2009, Feb. 12	Colgan Air Bombardier Dash 8 Q400	Crashed into house after pilot error caused stall near Buffalo, NY	50*
2009, June 1	**Air France Airbus A330**	**Plunged into Atlantic Ocean en route from Rio de Janeiro, Brazil, to Paris, France**	**228**
2009, June 30	Yemenia Airbus A310-300	Crashed into Indian Ocean after stalling on approach to Comoros	152
2009, July 15	Caspian Airlines Tupolev 154	Crashed after takeoff from Tehran, Iran	168
2010, Apr. 10	Polish Air Force Tupolev 154M	Crashed on approach to Smolensk Air Base, killing Polish Pres. Lech Kaczynski, his wife, and several members of parliament.	96
2010, May 12	Afriqiyah Airways Airbus A330-200	Crashed short of runway in Tripoli, Libya	103
2010, May 22	Air India Express Boeing 737-800	Overran runway on landing at Mangalore, India	158
2010, July 28	Airblue Airbus 321-231	Crashed into Margalla Hills near Islamabad, Pakistan	152
2012, Apr. 20	Bhoja Airlines Boeing 737-236	Crashed on approach to airport in Islamabad, Pakistan	127
2012, June 3	Dana Air MD-83	Crashed into residential area of Lagos, Nigeria	163*
2014, Mar. 8	Malaysia Airlines Boeing 777	Disappeared over S Indian O. en route fr. Kuala Lumpur to Beijing	239
2014, July 17	Malaysia Airlines Boeing 777	Shot down by Russian missile over disputed eastern Ukraine	298
2014, July 24	Air Algérie Boeing-MD-83	Crashed in desert near Gossi, Mali	116
2014, Dec. 28	Indonesia AirAsia Airbus A320-216	Disappeared over Java Sea between Surabaya and Singapore	162
2015, Mar. 24	Germanwings Airbus A320-211	Copilot deliberately crashed aircraft into French Alps	150
2015, June 30	Indonesian Air Force Lockheed C-130B	Transport plane crashed near Medan Soewondo Air Force Base	139*
2015, Oct. 31	Metrojet Airbus A321-231	Bomb detonated on board after takeoff fr. Sharm el Sheikh, Egypt	224
2016, Nov. 28	LaMia (Bolivia) Avro RJ85	Ran out of fuel and crashed near Medellín, Colombia; passengers incl. Brazilian Chapecoense soccer team	71
2016, Dec. 25	Russian Air Force Tupolev 154B-2	Crashed into Black Sea after takeoff from Sochi, Russia	92
2017, June 7	Myanmar Air Force Shaanxi Y-8-200F	Crashed into Andaman Sea en route to Yangon, Myanmar	122
2018, Apr. 11	Algerian military transport Ilyushin 76	Crashed after takeoff from near Algiers; passengers included Western Sahara separatists, refugees	257
2018, May 18	Cubana de Aviación Boeing 737	Aging aircraft crashed after takeoff from Havana, Cuba	112
2018, Oct. 29	Lion Air Boeing 737 Max 8	Crashed into Java Sea shortly after takeoff from Jakarta, Indonesia	189[13]
2019, Mar. 10	Ethiopian Airlines Boeing 737 Max 8	Crashed minutes after takeoff from Addis Ababa	157[13]
2020, Jan. 8	Ukrainian Airlines Boeing 737-800	Shot down by two Iranian missiles after takeoff from Tehran	176
2020, Jan. 26	Privately-operated Sikorsky S-76B helicopter	Crashed in bad visibility into hillside nr. Calabasas, CA, carrying retired NBA player Kobe Bryant, his daughter, others.	9
2022, Mar. 21	China Eastern Boeing 737-800	Suspected deliberate crash into mountainous area near Wuzhou, Guangxi Prov., China	132
2023, Aug. 23	Embraer ERJ-135BJ Legacy 600	Crashed en route to St. Petersburg, Russia, killing all aboard, including Wagner mercenary group chief, in suspected sabotage	10

(1) Bomb planted by Jack G. Graham in insurance plot to kill his mother, Daisie E. King, a passenger. (2) 84 on plane, 71 on ground killed. (3) Incl. 43 Marshall Univ. (WV) football players and coaches. (4) Fighter pilot parachuted to safety. (5) First supersonic plane crash; killed 8 on ground. (6) Crew of 3, 88 on ground killed. (7) Incl. 22 members of U.S. amateur boxing team. (8) Incl. 8 crew and 248 members of U.S. 101st Airborne Division returning from peacekeeping mission in Sinai, Egypt. (9) Incl. 11 on ground. (10) Incl. U.S. Sec. of Commerce Ron Brown. (11) 4 planes were hijacked and crashed, with all on board killed (265, incl. 19 hijackers). American Airlines Flight 11 (Boeing 767-200) with 81 passengers, 11 crew crashed into Tower 1 of World Trade Center (WTC); United Airlines Flight 175 (Boeing 767-200) with 56 passengers, 9 crew crashed into Tower 2 of WTC; American Airlines Flight 77 (Boeing 757-200) with 58 passengers, 6 crew crashed into Pentagon outside Washington, DC; United Airlines Flight 93 (Boeing 757-200), with 37 passengers, 7 crew crashed near Shanksville, PA. The official death toll of 2,997 includes those who died on the ground at the Pentagon and the WTC, and 3 later victims whose deaths the NYC medical examiner ruled were caused by exposure to toxic dust created by the disaster. Does not include those with cancers and other medical conditions related to WTC site exposure. (12) The two pilots ejected to safety. All spectator deaths. (13) Two fatal crashes, possibly due to faulty sensors and software, led to worldwide grounding of Boeing 737 Max series.

Some Notable Shipwrecks Since 1854

Does not include most wartime disasters.

Date—vessel(s)	Incident	Deaths
1854, Mar. 1—City of Glasgow	British steamer left Liverpool for Philadelphia, never heard from again	480
1854, Sept. 27—Arctic and Vesta	U.S. Collins Line steamer sunk in collision with French steamer nr. Cape Race, Canada	285-351
1856, Jan. 23—Pacific	U.S. Collins Line steamer went missing in N Atlantic	186-286
1857, Sept. 12—Central America	U.S. mail steamship sank off Florida coast with $1.5 mil in gold	427
1858, Sept. 23—Austria	German steamer destroyed by fire in N Atlantic	471
1863, Apr. 27—Anglo-Saxon	British steamer wrecked at Cape Race, Canada	238
1865, Apr. 27—Sultana	Mississippi R. steamer carrying 2,400 released Union prisoners exploded nr. Memphis, TN. Worst maritime disaster in U.S. history	1,800
1869, Feb. 20—Radetzky	Austrian steam frigate exploded in Adriatic Sea	345
1869, Oct. 27—Stonewall	U.S. steamer burned, Mississippi R. below Cairo, IL	200
1872, Nov. 7—Mary Celeste	U.S. half-brig sailing from New York City to Genoa, Italy, with 10 on board found abandoned	Unknown
1873, Jan. 22—Northfleet	British steamer at anchor struck by Spanish steamer Murillo off Dungeness, England, UK	300
1873, Apr. 1—Atlantic	British White Star steamer off Halifax, Nova Scotia, Canada	585
1873, Nov. 23—Ville du Havre and Loch Earn	French steamer sank after collision with British sailing ship	226
1874, Nov. 17—Cospatrick	En route from London to NZ, caught fire off Cape of Good Hope	468
1875, May 7—Schiller	German steamer off Isles of Scilly, UK	312
1875, Nov. 4—Pacific	U.S. steamer sank after collision off Cape Flattery, WA	236
1878, Mar. 24—Eurydice	British frigate sank off Isle of Wight, England, UK	398

Date—vessel(s)	Incident	Deaths
1878, Sept. 3—Princess Alice	British steamer sank after collision with *Bywell Castle* in Thames R.	700
1878, Dec. 18—Byzantin and Rinaldo	French and British steamers collided in Dardanelles, off Turkey.	210
1883, Jan. 19—Cimbria and Sultan	German steamer sank in collision with British steamer in North Sea.	389
1887, Nov. 15—Wah Yeung	Chinese steamer burned in Canton R., Hong Kong	400
1890, Feb. 17—Duburg.	British steamer wrecked, China Sea.	400
1890, Sept. 16—Ertugrul	Ottoman frigate in typhoon off Japan	587
1891, Mar. 17—Utopia and Anson	British steamer sank in collision with British ironclad off Gibraltar	562
1893, June 22—Victoria.	British battleship sank after collision with British warship *Camperdown*, off Syrian coast	358
1895, Jan. 30—Elbe and Craithie.	German steamer sank in collision with British steamer in North Sea.	332
1895, Mar. 11—Reina Regenta	Spanish cruiser foundered nr. Gibraltar	400
1898, Feb. 15—USS Maine	Explosion caused battleship to sink in Havana Harbor, Cuba	260
1898, July 4—La Bourgogne and Cromartyshire	French steamer sank in collision with British sailing ship off Nova Scotia, Canada	549
1904, May 15—Yoshino	Japanese cruiser sank after collision with cruiser *Kasuga* in fog off Liao-Tung Peninsula, China	329
1904, June 15—General Slocum	Excursion steamer burned off N. Brother Isl., New York, NY.	1,021
1904, June 28—Norge	Danish steamer wrecked on Rockall Isl., Scotland, UK	620
1906, Aug. 4—Sirio.	Italian steamer wrecked off Cape Palos, Spain.	350
1907, Feb. 11—Larchmont.	U.S. steamer sank after collision with U.S. schooner *Harry Knowlton* nr. Block Island, RI	131
1908, Mar. 23—Mutsu Maru	Japanese steamer sank in collision with another steamer nr. Hakodate, Japan	300
1909, July 26—Waratah	British steamer vanished en route from Durban to Cape Town, So. Africa	300
1911, Sept. 25—Liberté	French battleship exploded at Toulon	285
1912, Apr. 14-15—Titanic.	British White Star steamer hit iceberg in N Atlantic.	1,503
1912, Sept. 28—Kichemaru	Japanese steamer sank off Japan coast	1,000
1914, May 29—Empress of Ireland	Canadian Pacific steamer collided with Norwegian coal transporter *Storstad* in St. Lawrence R., Canada	1,014
1914, Nov. 26—Bulwark	British battleship exploded in Sheerness Harbor, England, UK	788
1915, May 7—Lusitania	British Cunard Line steamer torpedoed and sunk by German submarine off Ireland	1,198
1915, July 24—Eastland.	Steamer capsized, Chicago R., IL	844
1916, Feb. 26—Provence	French cruiser sank in Mediterranean; then-worst maritime disaster	3,100
1916, Mar. 5—Principe de Asturias	Spanish steamer wrecked nr. Santos, Brazil.	558
1917, Dec. 6—Mont Blanc and Imo	French ammunition ship and Belgian steamer collided in Halifax Harbor, Canada	1,900+
1918, Apr. 25—Kiang-Kwan	Chinese steamer sank after collision with Chinese gunboat *Chutai* off Hankow, China.	500
1918, July 12—Kawachi	Japanese battleship blew up in Tokayama Bay	500
1918, Oct. 25—Princess Sophia.	Canadian-Pacific steamer sank off Vanderbilt Reef, Alaska	398
1919, Jan. 17—Chaonia.	French steamer lost in Straits of Messina, Italy	460
1919, Sept. 9—Valbanera.	Spanish steamer lost off FL coast	500
1920, Jan. 11—Afrique	French liner sank nr. La Rochelle, France.	553
1921, Mar. 18—Hong Kong	Chinese steamer wrecked, S China Sea	1,000
1922, Aug. 26—Niitaka.	Japanese cruiser sank in storm off Kamchatka, USSR	300
1927, Sept. 20—Gentoku Maru	Japanese steamer capsized in Tsingtao Bay, China	278
1927, Oct. 25—Principessa Mafalda	Italian steamer blew up, sank off Porto Seguro, Brazil.	314
1934, Sept. 8—Morro Castle	U.S. steamer en route from Havana to NY, burned off Asbury Park, NJ	134
1940, June 17—Lancastria.	Nazi forces sank Cunard liner evacuating British troops from France	2,500-6,000
1940, July 24—Meknes.	French liner torpedoed by Nazis in English Channel	350
1942, Feb. 18—USS Truxtun and USS Pollux	Destroyer and cargo ship ran aground, sank off Newfoundland, Canada	204
1942, Oct. 2—Curacao and Queen Mary	British cruiser sank off Ireland after collision with liner carrying U.S. troops	338
1943, Nov. 26—HMT Rohna	Transport with U.S. soldiers sunk by German bomber off Algerian coast; largest U.S. troop loss at sea due to enemy action	1,149
1944, Dec. 17-18—Spence, Monaghan, Hull	3 U.S. destroyers sank during typhoon, Philippine Sea	790
1945, Jan. 30—Wilhelm Gustloff	Liner with German refugees, soldiers sunk by Soviet submarine in Baltic	5,000-9,000
1945, Apr. 16—Goya.	Cargo ship carrying German refugees, soldiers sunk by Soviet submarine in Baltic	6,000-7,000
1945, May 3—Cap Arcona and Thielbeck	German ocean liner and freighter carrying concentration camp inmates sunk by British warplanes in Lubeck Bay, Germany	7,000-8,000
1947, Jan. 19—Heimara.	Greek steamer hit rocks off Athens, Greece.	392
1947, Apr. 16—Grandcamp	Ammonium nitrate explosion aboard French freighter caused fires throughout port, Texas City, TX.	576+
1948, Dec. 4—Kiangya.	Ship with Chinese Civil War refugees hit WWII-era landmine on Huangpu R., S of Shanghai	3,920
1949, Jan. 27—Taiping and Chienyuan	Ship with Chinese Civil War refugees collided with cargo ship near Zhoushan Archipelago	1,500
1954, Sept. 26—Toya Maru	Japanese ferry sank, Tsugaru Strait, Japan.	1,172
1956, July 26—Andrea Doria and Stockholm	Italian liner and Swedish liner collided off Nantucket Isl., MA.	51
1957, July 14—Eshghabad.	Soviet fishing boat ran aground in Caspian Sea.	270
1961, Apr. 8—Dara.	British liner exploded in Persian Gulf	236
1961, July 8—Save.	Portuguese ship ran aground off Mozambique.	259
1965, Nov. 13—Yarmouth Castle	Cruise ship burned and sank off Nassau, The Bahamas.	89
1970, Dec. 15—Namyong-Ho.	S. Korean ferry sank in Korea Strait	308
1975, Nov. 10—Edmund Fitzgerald	U.S. cargo ship sank during storm on Lake Superior	29
1976, Oct. 20—George Prince	Mississippi R. ferry collided with Norwegian tanker *Frosta*, Luling, LA.	77
1980, Apr. 22—Don Juan	Sank off Mindoro Isl., Philippines, after colliding with barge	1,000+
1981, Jan. 27—Tamponas II.	Indonesian car ferry caught fire and sank in Java Sea.	580
1983, May 25—10th of Ramadan.	Nile steamer caught fire and sank in Lake Nasser, Egypt	357
1986, May 25—Shamia	Ferry capsized in storm, Meghna R., Bangladesh	500+

Date—vessel(s)	Incident	Deaths
1986, Sept. 1—Admiral Nakhimov and Pyotr Vasev	Soviet cruise ship collided with Soviet freighter in Black Sea	425
1987, Dec. 20—Doña Paz and Vector	Philippine ferry and oil tanker collided in Tablas Strait, Philippines	4,385
1988, Aug. 6	Indian ferry capsized on Ganges R.	400+
1988, Oct. 24—Doña Marilyn	Philippine ferry sank by typhoon near Leyte Isl.	350+
1991, Dec. 14—Salem Express	Ferry rammed coral reef nr. Safaga, Egypt	462
1993, Feb. 17—Neptune	Ferry capsized during heavy rainfall off Port-au-Prince, Haiti	500+
1993, Oct. 10—Seohae	S. Korean ferry capsized in Yellow Sea during storm	292
1994, Sept. 28—Estonia	Ferry en route from Estonia to Sweden sank in Baltic Sea off Finland	852
1996, May 21—Bukoba	Overcrowded Tanzanian ferry sank in Lake Victoria	500+
1997, Sept. 8—Pride of la Gonâve	Haitian ferry sank off Montrouis, Haiti	200+
1999, Feb. 6—Harta Rimba	Cargo ship sank off Indonesia	280+
1999, May 1—Miss Majestic	"Duck" boat on tour sank, Lake Hamilton, AR	13
1999, Nov. 24—Dashun	Passenger ferry sank nr. Yantai, China	280
2000, June 29—Cahaya Bahari	Overloaded ferry carrying refugees from religious strife capsized in storm off Sulawesi Isl., Indonesia	500+
2001, Oct. 19	Fishing boat overloaded with refugees, mainly from Middle East, sank off Indonesia	350+
2002, May 4—Salahuddin-2	Overloaded Bangladesh ferry sank in Meghna R.	300+
2002, Sept. 26—Joola	Overloaded Senegalese ferry capsized in ocean off The Gambia	1,863
2003, July 8—MV-Nasrin 1	Overcrowded ferry sank nr. Chandpur in Bangladesh R.	400
2004, Feb. 27—Superferry 14	Philippine ferry bombed by Islamic militants; deadliest terrorist attack at sea	116
2006, Feb. 3—Al-Salam Boccaccio 98	Ferry caught fire, sank in Red Sea off Egypt	1,000+
2006, Dec. 30—Senopati Nusantara	High waves capsized ferry en route to Java, Indonesia	400+
2007, Nov. 23—Explorer	Canadian cruise ship hit Antarctic iceberg; first commercial passenger ship to sink in region	0
2008, June 23—Princess of the Stars	Philippine ferry capsized during Typhoon Fengshen nr. Manila	800
2011, Sept. 10—MV Spice Islander	Overloaded ferry sank off coast of Tanzania	240+
2012, Jan. 17—Costa Concordia	Cruise ship ran aground off Italian coast; captain abandoned ship before evacuating passengers	32
2013, Oct. 3	Boat carrying migrants fleeing Eritrea sank near Lampedusa Isl., Italy	360
2014, Apr. 16—Sewol	Ferry carrying 476 people, most students, Korea's SW coast	304
2015, June 1—Dongfangzhixing (Eastern Star)	Chinese cruise ship sank in Yangtze R. during torrential rains	442
2015, Oct. 1—El Faro	Cargo ship en route from FL to Puerto Rico sailed into hurricane	33
2018, June 18—Sinar Bangun	Overloaded ferry sank in bad weather, Lake Toba, Sumatra, Indonesia	167
2018, July 19	"Duck" boat sank in a severe storm, Table Rock Lake, nr. Branson, MO	17
2018, Sept. 20—MV Nyerere	Overloaded Tanzanian ferry capsized in Lake Victoria	227+
2019, Sept. 2—Conception	Dive boat caught fire nr. Santa Cruz Isl., CA, while passengers slept	34

Note: Deaths of migrants and refugees trying to cross the Mediterranean Sea began to spike in 2014. The UN's Intl. Organization for Migration reported the following figures for dead and missing in the Mediterranean: 3,538 (2014), 3,771 (2015), 5,096 (2016), 3,139 (2017), 2,277 (2018), 1,510 (2019), 1,881 (2020), 3,231 (2021), 2,439 (2022), and 2,517 (2023, as of Oct. 2, 2023).

Some Notable Railroad Disasters Since 1925

Date	Location	Deaths
1925, June 16	Hackettstown, NJ	50
1933, Dec. 23	Lagny-Pomponne, France	230
1937, July 16	Near Patna, India	107
1938, Dec. 25	Near Kishinev, Romania	150
1939, Dec. 22	Genthin, near Magdeburg, Germany	132
1943, Sept. 6	Frankford Junction, Philadelphia, PA	79
1943, Dec. 16	Between Rennert and Buie, NC	72
1944, Jan. 16	León Province, Spain	500
1944, Mar. 2	Salerno, Italy	521
1944, Dec. 31	Bagley, UT	50
1945, July 16	Munich, Germany	102
1946, Mar. 20	Aracaju, Brazil	185
1949, Oct. 22	Near Nowy Dwór, Poland	200+
1950, Nov. 22	Richmond Hill, Queens, NY	79
1951, Feb. 6	Woodbridge, NJ	84
1952, Mar. 4	Near Rio de Janeiro, Brazil	119
1952, July 9	Rzepin, Poland	160
1952, Oct. 8	Harrow, England, UK	112
1953, Dec. 24	Tangiwai, New Zealand	151
1953, Dec. 24	Sakvice, Czechoslovakia	103
1955, Apr. 3	Guadalajara, Mexico	300
1957, Sept. 1	Kendal, Jamaica	178
1957, Sept. 29	Montgomery, W Pakistan	300
1957, Dec. 4	London, England, UK	90
1958, May 8	Rio de Janeiro, Brazil	128
1960, Nov. 14	Pardubice, Czechoslovakia	117
1962, May 3	Tokyo, Japan	163
1963, Nov. 9	Yokohama, Japan	162
1965, Feb. 27	Near Port Sudan, Sudan	124
1970, Feb. 1	Buenos Aires, Argentina	236
1972, June 16	Near Soissons, France	108
1972, Oct. 6	Near Saltillo, Mexico	204
1974, Aug. 30	Zagreb, Yugoslavia	153
1981, June 6	Bihar, India	268+
1982, Jan. 27	El Asnam, Algeria	120
1982, July 11	Tepic, Mexico	120
1983, Feb. 19	Empalme, Mexico	100
1985, Jan. 13	Awash, Ethiopia	392
1985, Sept. 12	Viseu, Portugal	118
1986, Aug. 6	Bihar, India	202
1987, July 2	Kasumbalesha Shaba, Zaire	125
1987, Aug. 7	Between Moscow and Rostov, USSR	106
1987, Oct. 19	Jakarta, Indonesia	153
1988, June 4	Arzamas, USSR	100
1988, July 8	Kerala, India	108
1989, Jan. 15	Maizdi Khan, Bangladesh	135
1989, June 4	Ufa, USSR	645
1989, Aug. 11	San Rafael R., Sinaloa State, Mexico	112
1990, Jan. 4	Sindh Province, Pakistan	307
1991, Mar. 5	Nacala, Mozambique	109
1991, June 8	Ghotki, Pakistan	100
1991, Sept. 5	Pointe-Noire, Congo Republic	110
1993, Jan. 30	Near Mtito Andei, Kenya	140+
1993, Apr. 25	Near Karachi, Pakistan	150
1994, Sept. 22	Lubango, Angola	300
1994, Dec. 30	Near Namkham, Myanmar	102
1995, Jan. 13	Dinajpur, Bangladesh	150
1995, Aug. 20	Firozabad, Uttar Pradesh, India	350
1995, Nov. 28	Baku, Azerbaijan	337
1997, Mar. 3	Punjab Province, Pakistan	128
1997, May 4	Kisangani, Zaire	100+
1998, Feb. 16	Yaounde, Cameroon	120
1998, June 3	Eschede, Germany	102
1998, Nov. 26	Khanna, India	108
1999, Aug. 2	Gaisal, West Bengal, India	285
2002, Feb. 20	S of Cairo, Egypt	377
2002, May 25	Muamba, Mozambique	195
2002, June 24	Igandu, Tanzania	281
2002, Sept. 10	Bihar, India	112
2004, Feb. 18	Neyshabur, NE Iran	300
2004, Apr. 22	Ryongchon, North Korea	161
2005, Apr. 25	Near Amagasaki, Japan	107
2005, July 13	Ghotki, Pakistan	132
2005, Oct. 29	Veligonda, Andhra Pradesh, India	110
2007, Aug. 2	Nr. Benaleka, Dem. Rep. of Congo	100
2010, May 28	W. Bengal, India	148
2011, July 23	Wenzhou, China	140
2016, Nov. 20	Kanpur, Uttar Pradesh, India	146
2019, Oct. 31	Rahim Yar Khan, Pakistan	75
2021, Apr. 2	Hualien, Taiwan	49
2023, Feb. 28	Tempe, Greece	57
2023, June 2	Odisha, India	293

Notable Droughts

Source: EM-DAT: The International Disaster Database, CRED/Université catholique de Louvain, Brussels, Belgium, www.emdat. be; World Almanac research

Date	Location	Est. deaths	Date	Location	Est. deaths
1900	Bengal, India	1,250,000	1974-76	Somalia	19,000
1900	Cape Verde islands	11,000	1981-85	Mozambique	100,000
1910-14	Zinder Dept., Niger	85,000	1981-85	Chad	3,000
1920	China	500,000	1983	Swaziland	500
1920	Cape Verde islands	24,000	1983-84	Eritrea, Ethiopia	300,000
1921	S Ukraine, Volga, USSR	1,200,000	1983-85	N Sudan	150,000
1928-30	Shaanxi, Henan, Gansu, China	3,000,000	1987	Somalia, Eritrea, Ethiopia	967
1940-44	Cape Verde islands	20,000	1987	NW India	300
1942	Calcutta, Bengal, India	1,500,000	1988	Central China	1,400
1943	Bangladesh	1,900,000	1991	Jiangxi, Hunan Provinces, China	2,000
1946	Cape Verde islands	30,000	1997	Irian Jaya, Indonesia	672
1965	Ethiopia	2,000	1999-2003	Pakistan	143
1965-67	India	1,500,000	2002	Malawi	500
1966	Lombok, Indonesia	8,000	2006	SW China	134
1973-78	Ethiopia	100,000	2014-17	Tharparkar, Pakistan	166

Some Notable Miscellaneous Disasters Since 1950

Date	Event	Location	Details	Est. deaths
1952, Dec.	Pollution	London, England, UK	Heavy smog blanketed city; impeded breathing	4,000
1959-61	Famine	China	Govt. policies compounded by flooding and drought	15-40 mil
1980, summer	Extreme heat	Central, eastern U.S.	Combined direct and indirect deaths est. at 10,000	1,260
1984, Dec. 3	Industrial accident	Bhopal, India	Toxic gas leaked from a Union Carbide factory	16,000
1986, Aug. 21	Gas	Nr. Lake Nyos, Cameroon	Volcanic lake released cloud of carbon dioxide gas	1,700
1990, July 2	Stampede	Mecca, Saudi Arabia	Pilgrims panicked in tunnel leading to the holy city	1,426
1995, June 29	Building collapse	Seoul, South Korea	Improperly built and maintained Sampoong Dept. Store failed with shoppers inside	501
2003, summer	Extreme heat	Europe	France suffered most, with 14,800 dead	35,000
2005, Aug. 31	Stampede	Baghdad, Iraq	Rumors of suicide bomber caused panic among religious pilgrims on al-Aimmah Bridge	965
2010, summer	Extreme heat	Russia	Prolonged heat also triggered wildfires	55,000
2013, Apr. 24	Building collapse	Savar, Bangladesh	Garment factory found to have substandard foundation	1,100+
2015, Sept. 24	Stampede	Mina, Saudi Arabia	Two groups of pilgrims collided during hajj to Mecca	2,411
2017, Aug. 14	Landslide	Freetown, Sierra Leone	Rain, deforestation partially collapsed Sugar Loaf Mt.	1,141
2019, July 21-27	Extreme heat	France	Record temperatures across Europe	868
2021, June 25-July 1	Extreme heat	British Columbia, Canada	Heat dome caused record temperatures	619
2022, summer	Extreme heat	Europe	Europe's hottest summer on record	15,000+

Some Notable U.S. Tornadoes Since 1925

Date	Location	Deaths	Date	Location	Deaths
1925, Mar. 18	MO, IL, IN	747	1979, Apr. 10	TX, OK	60
1927, Apr. 12	Rocksprings, TX	74	1984, Mar. 28	NC, SC	57
1927, May 9	AR; Poplar Bluff, MO	92	1985, May 31	NY; PA; OH; Ontario, Can.	75
1927, Sept. 29	St. Louis, MO	90	1987, May 22	Saragosa, TX	30
1930, May 6	Hill, Navarro, Ellis Cos., TX	41	1989, Nov. 15	Huntsville, AL	18
1932, Mar. 21	Alabama	268	1990, Aug. 28	Northern IL	25
1936, Apr. 5-6	Tupelo, MS; Gainesville, GA	454	1991, Apr. 26	KS, OK	23
1938, Sept. 29	Charleston, SC	32	1992, Nov. 21-23	South, Midwest	26
1942, Mar. 16	Central to NE Mississippi	75	1994, Mar. 27-28	AL, TN, GA, NC, SC	52
1942, Apr. 27	Rogers and Mayes Cos., OK	52	1995, May 6-7	Southern OK, northern TX	23
1944, June 23	OH, PA, WV, MD	150	1997, Mar. 1	Central AR	26
1945, Apr. 12	OK, AR	102	1997, May 27	Jarrell, TX	27
1947, Apr. 9	TX; Woodward, OK; KS	181	1998, Feb. 22-23	Central FL	42
1948, Mar. 19	Bunker Hill and Gillespie, IL	33	1998, Apr. 8	AL, GA, MS	39
1949, Jan. 3	LA, AR	58	1999, May 3	OK, KS	54
1952, Mar. 21-22	AR, MO, TN	208	2000, Feb. 14	SW Georgia	22+
1953, May 11	Waco, TX	114	2002, Nov. 10-11	AL, MS, TN, IN, OH, PA	36
1953, June 8	Flint-Beecher, MI; OH	142	2003, May 4-11	TN, MO, KS, IL, OK, WV, AL	48
1953, June 9	Worcester and vicinity, MA	90	2005, Nov. 6	KY, IN	22
1953, Dec. 5	Vicksburg, MS	38	2007, Mar. 1	AL, GA, MO, Midwest	20
1955, May 25	Udall, KS; MO; Blackwell, OK; TX	115	2008, Feb. 25	TN, AR, KY, AL, MO	57
1957, May 20	KS, MO	48	2008, May 10	MS, OK, GA	23
1958, June 4	NW Wisconsin	30	2011, Apr. 14-16	Southeast, Midwest, OK to VA	38
1959, Feb. 10	St. Louis, MO	21	2011, Apr. 25-28	362 funnels from TX to NY	321
1960, May 5-6	Southeastern OK, AR	30	2011, May 22	Joplin, MO	161
1965, Apr. 11	IA, IN, IL, OH, MI, WI	271	2012, Mar. 2-3	Southeast, Ohio Valley (AL, GA, IN, KY, OH, TN)	42
1966, Mar. 3	Jackson, MS; AL	57			
1967, Apr. 21	IL, MO, IA, MI	33	2013, May 20	Moore, OK	24
1968, May 15	Midwest	71	2013, May 31	El Reno, OK	21
1969, Jan. 23	Mississippi	32	2017, Jan. 20-22	AL, FL, GA, LA, MS, SC, TX	20
1970, May 11	Lubbock, TX	23	2021, Dec. 10-11	AR; Edwardsville, IL; Mayfield, KY; MO; TN	90+
1971, Feb. 21	Mississippi Delta: MS, LA, AR, TN	110			
1973, May 26-27	South, Midwest	47	2023, Mar. 31-Apr. 1	IL, IN, OH, MO, IA, AR, TN, PA	33
1974, Apr. 3-4	AL; GA; KY; Xenia, OH; other states	315			
1977, Apr. 4	AL, MS, GA	22			

Some Notable Hurricanes, Typhoons, Blizzards, Other Storms

C. = cyclone; H. = hurricane; TS. = tropical storm; T. = typhoon[1].

Date	Location	Est. deaths
1881, Aug. 24-29	H., GA, SC	700
1888, Mar. 11-14	Blizzard, Eastern U.S.	400
1893, Aug. 15-Sept. 2	H., GA, SC	1,000+
1893, Oct. 1	H., LA	1,100+
1900, Sept. 8	H., Galveston, TX	8,000+
1906, Sept. 18	T., Hong Kong	10,000+
1906, Sept. 19-24	H., LA, MS	350
1909, Sept. 20	H., LA	350+
1915, Aug. 16	H., Galveston, TX	275
1915, Sept. 29	H., LA	275
1919, Sept. 6-14	H., Carib., FL Keys, Gulf, TX	600+[2]
1922, July 27	T., Swatow, China	100,000
1926, Sept. 11-22	H., FL, AL, MS	370+
1926, Oct. 20	H., Cuba	600
1928, Sept. 6-20	H., southern FL.	2,500+
1930, Sept. 3	H., Dominican Republic	2,000
1935, Aug. 29-Sept. 10	H., Caribbean, SE U.S.	400+
1937, Sept. 2	T., Hong Kong	10,000+
1938, Sept. 21	H., NY, New England	682
1940, Nov. 11-12	NE, Midwest U.S.	154
1942, Oct.	T., W. Sundarbans, Bangladesh	61,000
1942, Oct. 15-16	H., Bengal, India	40,000
1947, Dec. 26	Blizzard, NYC, N Atl. states	55
1952, Oct. 22	T., Philippines	440
1954, Aug. 30	H. Carol, NE U.S.	68
1954, Oct. 5-18	H. Hazel, E Canada, U.S., Haiti	347
1955, Aug. 7-21	H. Diane, Eastern U.S.	400
1955, Sept. 19	H. Hilda, Mexico	200
1956, Feb. 1-29	Blizzard, W Europe	1,000
1957, June 25-30	H. Audrey, TX to AL	390
1958, Feb. 15-16	Blizzard, NE U.S.	171
1959, Sept. 17-19	T. Sarah, Japan, S Korea	2,000
1959, Sept. 26-27	T. Vera, Honshu, Japan	4,466
1960, Sept. 4-12	H. Donna, Caribbean, E U.S.	148
1961, Oct. 31	H. Hattie, Brit. Honduras	400
1962, Sept. 1	T. Wanda, Hong Kong	130-200
1963, May 28-29	Windstorm, Bangladesh	22,000
1963, Oct. 4-8	H. Flora, Caribbean	6,000
1964, June 30	T. Winnie, N Philippines	107
1964, Sept. 5	T. Ruby, Hong Kong, China	735
1965, May 11-12	Windstorm, Bangladesh	17,000
1965, June 1-2	Windstorm, Bangladesh	30,000
1965, Sept. 7-12	H. Betsy, FL, MS, LA	74
1965, Dec. 15	Windstorm, Bangladesh	10,000
1966, June 4-10	H. Alma, Honduras, SE U.S.	51
1966, Sept. 24-30	H. Inez, Carib., FL, Mexico	293
1967, July 9	T. Billie, SW Japan	347
1967, Sept. 5-23	H. Beulah, Carib., Mex., TX	54
1967, Dec. 12-20	Blizzard, SW U.S.	51
1969, Aug. 17-18	H. Camille, MS, LA	256
1970, Sept. 15	T. Pitang (Georgia), Philippines	300
1970, Oct. 14	T. Sening (Joan), Philippines	583
1970, Oct. 15	T. Titang (Kate), Philippines	526
1970, Nov. 13	C. Bhola, Bay of Bengal, Bangladesh	300,000-500,000
1971, Aug. 1	T. Rose, Hong Kong	130
1972, June 19-29	H. Agnes, FL to NY	118
1972, Dec. 3	T. Theresa, Philippines	169
1973, June-Aug.	Monsoon rains, India	1,217
1974, July 11	T. Gilda, Japan, S. Korea	108
1974, Sept. 19-20	H. Fifi, Honduras	2,000
1975, Sept. 13-27	H. Eloise, Caribbean, NE U.S.	71
1976, May 20	T. Olga, floods, Philippines	215
1976, Sept. 25-Oct. 2	H. Liza, western Mexico	630
1978, Oct. 27	T. Rita, Philippines	400
1979, Aug. 30-Sept. 7	H. David, Caribbean, E U.S.	1,100
1980, Aug. 4-11	H. Allen, Caribbean, TX	272
1981, Nov. 25	T. Irma, Luzon Isl., Philippines	176
1983, June	Monsoon, India	900
1984, Sept. 2	T. Ike, southern Philippines	1,363
1985, May 25	C., Bangladesh	15,000
1985, Oct. 26-Nov. 6	T. Juan, SE U.S.	97
1987, Nov. 25	T. Nina, Philippines	650
1988, Sept. 10-17	H. Gilbert, Carib., Gulf of Mex.	260
1989, Sept. 16-22	H. Hugo, Caribbean, SE U.S.	86
1990, May 6-11	C. (mult.), SE India	450
1991, Apr. 30	C. Gorky, Bangladesh	139,000
1991, Nov. 5	TS. Thelma, central Philippines	7,000+
1992, Aug. 24-26	H. Andrew, Southern FL, LA	65
1993, Mar. 12-14	Blizzard, Eastern U.S.	270+
1993, June	Monsoon, Bangladesh	2,000
1994, Nov. 8-18	TS. Gordon, Caribbean, FL	830
1995, Oct. 2-4	H. Opal, S Mexico, FL, AL	59
1995, Nov. 2-3	T. Angela, Philippines	600+
1996, Jan. 7-8	Blizzard, NE U.S.	100
1996, Aug. 22	Blizzard, Himalayas, N India	239
1996, Aug. 29-Sept. 6	H. Fran, Carib., NC, VA, WV	30
1996, Sept. 9	T. Sally, S China	114
1996, Nov. 6	C., Andhra Pradesh, India	1,000+
1996, Dec. 25	TS. Greg, eastern Malaysia	100+
1997, May 19	C., Bangladesh	108
1997, Aug. 18	T. Winnie, Taiwan, E China	140+
1997, Oct. 8-10	H. Pauline, SW Mexico	230
1998, June 9	C., Gujarat, India	1,320
1998, Aug.	Monsoon, Bangladesh	326
1998, Sept. 21-23	H. Georges, Carib., FL, U.S. Gulf	600+
1998, Oct. 27-29	H. Mitch, Central America	11,000+
1999, Sept. 4-17	H. Floyd, The Bahamas, E U.S.	56
1999, Oct. 29	C., E India	9,392
1999, Dec. 26-29	Gales, France, Switz., Germany	120
2000, Dec. 27	Winter storm, TX, OK, AR	40+
2001, July 30	T. Toraji, Taiwan	200
2001, Nov. 6-12	T. Lingling, S Philip., Vietnam	220+
2002, Aug.-Sept.	T. Rusa, N. and S. Korea	115+
2003, Feb. 16-17	Blizzard, E seaboard U.S.	59
2003, Sept. 7-19	H. Isabel, NC, VA, E seaboard	40+
2003, Sept. 12	T. Maemi, S Korea.	130
2004, Mar. 7-19	C. Gafilo, Madagascar	198
2004, May 19	C., Myanmar	220
2004, Aug. 12-15	T. Rananim, eastern China.	164
2004, Aug. 13-14	H. Charley, FL, SC	36
2004, Sept. 5-6	H. Frances, The Bahamas, FL	35
2004, Sept. 7-16	H. Ivan, Barbados, Grenada, U.S. Gulf Coast.	115
2004, Sept. 16-26	H. Jeanne, Dom. Rep., Haiti, FL	2,754
2005, July 7-11	H. Dennis, Jamaica, Haiti, Cuba, FL . . .	50
2005, Aug. 23-30	H. Katrina, LA, MS, FL, GA, AL	1,392+[3]
2005, Aug. 31-Sept. 1	T. Talim, Taiwan, E China	129+
2005, Sept. 21-24	H. Rita, TX, LA	62[4]
2005, Sept. 21-28	T. Damrey, SE Asia; Philippines; Hainan, China	
2005, Oct. 4	H. Stan, Central Amer., Mex.	1,000+[5]
2006, July 14	TS. Bilis, SE China	612
2006, Aug. 10	T. Saomai, SE China	295
2006, Nov. 30	C. Durian, Philippines	450-1,000+
2007, June 6-7	C. Gonu, Oman, Iran	54[6]
2007, Nov. 15	C. Sidr, southern Bangladesh	3,363
2008, May 2-3	C. Nargis, southern Myanmar	138,366
2008, June 20-25	T. Fengshen, Philippines, China	233
2008, Aug. 26-Sept. 1	H. Gustav, Haiti, Dom. Rep., U.S.	138
2008, Sept. 1-4	TS. Hanna, Haiti	529
2008, Sept. 7-13	H. Ike, Haiti; Cuba; TX	164
2009, May 23-26	C. Alia, India, Bangladesh	260
2009, July 9	T. Morakot, mudslides, Taiwan	700+
2009, Sept. 23-30	T. Ketsana, Philippines, Vietnam, Cambodia, Laos	498+
2009, Oct. 3-10	T. Parma, Philippines	375
2009, Oct. 30-Nov. 3	T. Mirinae, Philippines, Vietnam	159+
2010, May 29	TS. Agatha, Guatemala, El Salvador, Honduras	184
2010, July 13-17	T. Conson, Philippines	105+
2011, Oct. 29-30	C., Odisha (Orissa) state, E India	9,893
2011, Dec. 16	TS. Washi, Philippines	1,257
2012, Jan. 24-Feb. 14	Blizzard/cold snap, E Europe	650+
2012, Oct. 22-31	H. Sandy, Cuba, Haiti, Jamaica, Eastern U.S.	245[7]
2012, Dec. 4	T. Bopha, Philippines	1,146
2013, Nov. 8	T. Haiyan, Philippines	7,986
2013, Nov. 10	C., Puntland, Somalia	162
2014, July 15	T. Rammasun, Philippines, China, Vietnam	173
2016, Oct. 4-8	H. Matthew, Haiti, Bahamas, FL, GA, SC, NC	585
2017, Aug. 25-30	H. Harvey, South TX, LA	93+[8]
2017, Aug. 30-Sept. 11	H. Irma, Barbuda, Cuba, FL	134
2017, Sept. 16-30	H. Maria, Dominica, Virgin Isls., Puerto Rico	3,056[9]
2019, Mar. 14-15	C. Idai, Zimbabwe, Mozambique	1,303
2019, May 3	C. Fani, E India, Bangladesh	81
2019, Aug. 28-Sept. 6	H. Dorian, Bahamas, SE U.S.	84
2020, May 16-21	C. Amphan, E India, Bangladesh	98
2020, Oct. 31-Nov. 13	H. Eta, Nicaragua, Honduras, Guatemala, FL, NC	172
2021, Aug. 26-Sept. 1	H. Ida, LA, MS, AL, PA, NJ, NY	91
2021, Aug. 28-30	H. Ian, TX, SC	152

(1) What hurricanes are called W of Intl. Date Line and N of equator. (2) Incl. about 500 lost at sea. (3) A Jan. 2023 assessment accounts for 520 direct deaths—341 in LA, 172 in MS, 6 in FL, and 1 in GA—as well as 565 indirect deaths (most of cardiovascular causes), and 307 deaths of indeterminate cause. (4) Incl. 55 indirect deaths. (5) Incl. deaths from floods and landslides. (6) First documented super cyclone in Arabian Sea. (7) Incl. 87 indirect deaths in the U.S. (8) Downgraded to a tropical storm Aug. 26, Harvey nevertheless caused severe flooding. (9) Puerto Rico's government, Aug. 2018, revised its death toll from 64 to 2,975 in line with a report they commissioned from George Washington Univ. public health experts. A separate Harvard study (May 2018) estimated the death toll to be at least 4,645.

Some Notable Floods, Tidal Waves

Source: EM-DAT: The International Disaster Database, CRED/Université catholique de Louvain, Brussels, Belgium, www.emdat. be; World Almanac research

Date	Location	Est. deaths
1703	Awa, Japan	100,000+
1889, May 31	Johnstown, PA	2,200+
1903, June 15	Heppner, OR.	325
1911	Chang Jiang (Yangtze) R., China.	100,000
1913, Mar. 25-27	OH, IN.	732
1915, Aug. 17	Galveston, TX.	275
1927, Jan.-July	Mississippi Valley	246+
1927, Nov. 1	Mostagenem, Algeria	3,000
1928, Mar. 13	Dam collapse, Saugus, CA.	450
1928, Sept. 16	Lake Okeechobee, FL	1,770+
1931, Aug.	Huang He R., China.	3,700,000
1933	Shandong, China	18,000
1937, Jan. 22	OH, MS valleys	250
1938, June 9	Huang He R., China.	500,000
1946, Apr. 1	HI, AK.	159
1947, Sept. 20	Honshu Isl., Japan	2,000
1949, July	China	57,000
1949, Oct.	Guatemala	40,000
1950	Pakistan	2,900
1951, Aug. 28	Manchuria.	4,800
1953, Jan. 31	Storm surge, Zuiderzee, Netherlands	2,000
1953, June 23	Japan	2,566
1954, Aug.	China	30,000
1954, Aug. 17	Farahzad, Iran	2,000
1955, Oct. 7-12	India, Pakistan	1,700
1959, Nov. 1	Western Mexico	2,000
1959, Dec. 2	Frejus, France.	412
1960, Oct. 10	Bangladesh.	6,000
1960, Oct. 31	Bangladesh.	4,000
1961, July	N India	2,000
1962, Sept. 27	Barcelona, Spain	445
1963, Oct. 9	Dam collapse, Vaiont, Italy	1,800
1967, Jan. 18-24	Eastern Brazil	894
1967, Mar. 19	Rio de Janeiro, Brazil	436
1967, Nov. 26	Lisbon, Portugal	464
1968, July	Rajasthan, Gujarat states, India	4,892
1968, Oct. 7	NE India	780
1969, Jan. 18-26	Southern CA.	100
1969, Aug. 20-22	Western VA.	189
1969, Oct. 1-8	Tunisia	500
1970, July 22	Himalayas, India	500
1972, Feb. 26	Buffalo Creek, WV	118
1972, June 9	Rapid City, SD	238
1972, Aug. 7	Luzon Isl., Philippines	454
1972, Aug. 19-31	Pakistan	1,500
1974, Mar. 29	Tubaro, Brazil	1,000
1974, July	Bangladesh.	28,700
1974, Aug. 12	Monty-Long, Bangladesh	2,500
1975, Aug. 8	Dam collapse, Henan Prov., China.	171,000
1976, July 31	Big Thompson Canyon, CO	140
1978, July	N, NE India	3,800
1979, July 17	Lomblem Isl., Indonesia	539
1979, Aug. 11	Morbi, India.	10,000
1980, June	Sichuan, China	6,200
1981, Apr.	N China.	550
1981, July	Sichuan, Hubei Prov., China	1,300
1982, Jan. 23	Near Lima, Peru	600
1982, May 12	Guangdong, China	430
1982, Sept. 17-21	El Salvador, Guatemala	1,300+
1984, Aug.-Sept.	South Korea	200+
1987, July 22	Bangladesh.	2,055
1987, Aug.-Sept.	Northern Bangladesh	1,000+
1988, June-Sept.	Bangladesh.	2,379
1988, Sept.	N India	1,000+
1989, July 14	China	2,000
1994, May-Oct.	Assam, India.	2,001
1995, July	NE China	1,200
1995, Sept. 1-20	India	1,479
1996, June-July	Guizhou, Hebei, China.	2,775
1997, Oct.-Nov.	Somalia.	2,311
1998, July 17	Papua New Guinea.	3,000
1998, July-Aug.	Hunan, Sichuan, China.	3,656
1998, July-Sept.	Bangladesh.	1,441
1998, Aug.	India	1,811
1999, Oct.-Dec.	Central Vietnam	700+
1999, Dec. 15-20	NW Venezuela	30,000
2000, Feb.-Mar.	Mozambique	700
2000, Sept. 19-30	India, Bangladesh.	1,000+
2001, Aug. 1-6	Taiwan	100+
2001, Nov. 9-10	Northern Algeria	711+
2002, Apr.-Aug.	China	800+
2002, July-Aug.	India, Nepal, Bangladesh	1,100+
2004, May 23-Jun. 1	Dom. Republic, Haiti	2,665
2004, June-Sept.	Bangladesh, India, Myanmar, Nepal	2,000+
2004, June-Sept.	China	500
2004, Nov.-Dec.	Philippines	1,060+
2004, Dec. 26	Indian Ocean nations	227,898
2005, July 26-Aug. 5	W Maharashtra state, India.	1,200
2006, Feb. 17	Leyte Isl., Philippines	1,000
2006, July 17	S of Java, Indonesia	530+
2007, July 21-Aug. 3	Bangladesh.	1,110
2007, July-Sept.	India	1,103
2008, June-July	India	1,063
2009, July-Sept.	India	992
2010, May-Aug.	China	1,691
2010, June 13-24	Cenxi, China.	377+
2010, July-Aug.	Pakistan	1,985
2010, Aug. 1-4	Zhouqu County, China.	1,500+
2011, Jan. 11-12	SE Brazil.	900
2011, Mar. 11	NE Japan.	20,896
2011, Apr.-May	Northern Colombia	425+
2011, July-Dec.	Thailand	708+
2011, July-Dec.	Philippines, Cambodia, Myanmar.	2,000+
2012, July-Oct.	Nigeria	363
2012, Aug.-Oct.	Pakistan	480
2012, Sept.-Oct.	Nigeria	431
2013, June	Uttarakhand, India	6,054
2015, Nov.-Dec.	S India	500
2018, June-Aug.	Kerala, India	504
2018, Dec. 22	Sunda Strait, Indonesia	437
2022, June-Sept.	Pakistan	1,739+
2023, Sept.	Libya	4,000+

Some Major Earthquakes

Source: Global Volcanism Network, Smithsonian Institution; U.S. Geological Survey, U.S. Dept. of the Interior; World Almanac research
Magnitude of earthquakes (mag.) is a relative measurement of an earthquake's energy. Deaths include those in aftershocks or related events.

Date	Location	Deaths	Mag.	Date	Location	Deaths	Mag.
526, May 20	Antioch, Syria	250,000	NA	1755, Nov. 1	Lisbon, Portugal	60,000	8.75[2]
856	Corinth, Greece	45,000	NA	1783, Feb. 4	Calabria, Italy	30,000	NA
856, Dec. 22	Damghan, Iran	200,000	NA	1797, Feb. 4	Quito, Ecuador	41,000	NA
893, Mar. 23	Ardabil, Iran	150,000	NA	1822, Sept. 5	Asia Minor, Aleppo	22,000	NA
1057	Chihli, China	25,000	NA	1828, Dec. 28	Echigo, Japan	30,000	NA
1138, Aug. 9	Aleppo, Syria	230,000	NA	1868, Aug. 13-16	Peru, Ecuador.	40,000	NA
1169, Feb. 11	Nr. Mt. Etna, Sicily	15,000	NA[1]	1875, May 16	Venezuela, Colombia	16,000	NA
1268	Silicia, Asia Minor	60,000	NA	1886, Aug. 31	Charleston, SC	60	6.6
1290, Sept. 27	Chihli, China	100,000	NA	1896, June 15	Sanriku, Japan (tsunami)	27,120	8.5
1293, May 20	Kamakura, Japan	30,000	NA	1902, Apr. 19	Quezaltenango and San		
1531, Jan. 26	Lisbon, Portugal	30,000	NA		Marcos, Guatemala	2,000	7.5
1556, Jan. 24	Shaanxi, China	830,000	NA	1902, Dec. 16	Uzbekistan, Russia.	4,700	6.4
1667, Nov.	Shemakha, Caucasia (now Azerbaijan)	80,000	NA	1903, Apr. 28	Malazgirt, Turkey.	3,500	7.0
				1905, Apr. 4	Kangra, India	19,000	7.5
1693, Jan. 11	Catania, Italy.	60,000	NA	1906, Jan. 31	Off coast of Esmeraldas, Ecuador	1,000	8.8
1737, Oct. 11	India, Calcutta.	300,000	NA				
1755, June 7	N Persia (current-day Iran)	40,000	NA	1906, Mar. 16	Chia-i, Taiwan.	1,250	6.8

Date	Location	Deaths	Mag.
1906, Apr. 18-19	San Francisco, CA	3,000+	7.7[3]
1906, Aug. 17	Valparaiso, Chile	3,882	8.6
1907, Oct. 21	Central Asia	12,000	8.1
1908, Dec. 28	Messina, Italy	72,000	7.2
1909, Jan. 23	Silakhor, Iran	5,000-6,000	7.3
1912, Aug. 9	Murefte, Turkey	2,800	7.4
1914, Oct. 3	Burdur, Turkey	4,000	7.0
1915, Jan. 13	Avezzano, Italy	32,610	7.0
1917, July 30	Yunnan Prov., China	1,800	7.5
1920, Dec. 16	Gansu, China	200,000	7.8[4]
1923, Mar. 24	Sichuan, China	3,500	7.3
1923, Mar. 25	Torbat-e Heydariyeh, Iran.	2,200	5.7
1923, Sept. 1	Yokohama, Japan.	142,800	7.9
1925, Mar. 16	Yunnan Prov., China	5,800	7.0
1927, Mar. 7	Tango, Japan	3,020	7.6
1927, May 22	Gansu, China	40,900	7.6
1929, May 1	Koppeh Dagh, Iran	3,800	7.2
1930, May 6	Salmas, Iran	2,500	7.2
1930, July 23	Irpinia, Italy	1,404	6.5
1931, Mar. 31	Managua, Nicaragua	2,500	6.0
1931, Apr. 27	Armenia-Azerbaijan border.	2,800	5.7
1931, Aug. 10	Xinjiang, China	10,000	8.0
1933, Mar. 2	Sanriku, Japan (tsunami)	2,990	8.4
1933, Mar. 10	Long Beach, CA	115	6.2
1933, Aug. 25	Sichuan, China	9,300	7.5
1934, Jan. 15	Bihar, India-Nepal	10,700	8.1
1935, Apr. 21	Miao-li, Taiwan	3,270	7.1
1935, May 30	Quetta, Pakistan	30,000	7.6
1939, Jan. 25	Chillan, Chile	28,000	7.8
1939, Dec. 26	Erzincan, Turkey	32,700	7.8
1943, Sept. 10	Tottori, Japan	1,190	7.4
1943, Nov. 26	Ladik, Turkey	4,000	7.6
1944, Jan. 15	San Juan, Argentina	8,000	7.4
1944, Feb. 1	Gerede, Turkey.	2,790	7.4
1945, Jan. 12	Mikawa, Japan	1,961	7.1
1945, Nov. 27	Makran Coast, Pakistan	4,000	8.0
1946, May 31	Ustukran, Turkey	1,300	5.9
1946, Nov. 10	Ancash, Peru	1,400	7.3
1946, Dec. 20	Honshu, Japan	1,362	8.1
1948, June 28	Fukui, Japan	3,769	7.3
1948, Oct. 5	Ashgabat, Turkmenistan.	110,000	7.3
1949, July 10	Khait, Tajikistan	12,000	7.5
1949, Aug. 5	Pelileo, Ecuador	5,050	6.8
1950, Aug. 15	Assam, India	1,526	8.6
1954, Sept. 9	Orleansville, Algeria	1,250	6.8
1956, June 10-17	Northern Afghanistan	2,000	7.7
1957, July 2	Northern Iran	1,200	7.1
1960, Feb. 29	Agadir, Morocco	12,000	5.7
1960, May 21-30	Southern Chile	1,655	9.5[5]
1962, Sept. 1	NW Iran	12,255	7.1
1964, Mar. 27	Prince Wm. Sound, AK.	131	9.2[6]
1966, Aug. 19	Eastern Turkey	2,529	6.8
1968, Aug. 31	NE Iran	12,000	7.3
1969, July 25	Guangdong, China	3,000	5.9
1970, Jan. 5	Yunnan Prov., China	10,000	7.5
1970, May 31	Chimbote, Ancash, Peru.	70,000	7.9
1971, Feb. 9	San Fernando Valley, CA.	65	6.6
1972, Apr. 10	Southern Iran	5,054	7.1
1972, Dec. 23	Managua, Nicaragua	5,000	6.2
1974, May 10	Zhaotong, China.	1,540	6.8
1974, Dec. 28	Northern Pakistan	5,300	6.2

Date	Location	Deaths	Mag.
1975, Feb. 4	Haicheng, China.	2,000	7.0
1975, Sept. 6	Eastern Turkey	2,300	6.7
1976, Feb. 4	Guatemala	23,000	7.5
1976, May 6	NE Italy	1,000	6.5
1976, June 25	Irian Jaya, New Guinea	422	7.1
1976, July 28	Tangshan, China	242,769	7.5
1976, Aug. 16	Mindanao, Philippines	8,000	7.9
1976, Nov. 24	NW Iran-Turkey border.	5,000	7.3
1977, Mar. 4	Romania	1,500	7.2
1978, Sept. 16	NE Iran	15,000	7.8
1980, Oct. 10	NW Algeria	5,000	7.7
1980, Nov. 23	Southern Italy	2,735	6.5
1981, June 11	Southern Iran	3,000	6.9
1981, July 28	Southern Iran	1,500	7.3
1982, Dec. 13	W Arabian Peninsula	2,800	6.0
1983, Oct. 30	Eastern Turkey	1,342	6.9
1985, Sept. 19	Michoacan, Mexico.	9,500	8.0
1986, Oct. 10	El Salvador	1,000+	5.5
1987, Mar. 6	Colombia-Ecuador	1,000	7.0
1988, Aug. 20	India-Nepal border	1,000	6.8
1988, Dec. 7	Spitak, Armenia	25,000	6.8
1989, Oct. 17	San Francisco Bay area, CA	63	6.9
1990, June 20	Western Iran	40,000+	7.4
1990, July 16	Luzon, Philippines	1,621	7.7
1991, Feb. 1	Pakistan-Afgh. border.	1,200	6.8
1991, Oct. 19	Northern India	2,000	7.0
1992, Dec. 12	Flores Isl., Indonesia	2,500	7.5
1993, Sept. 30	Maharashtra, S India	9,748	6.2
1994, Jan. 17	Northridge, CA	61	6.7
1994, June 6	Cauca, SW Colombia	1,000	6.8
1995, Jan. 16	Kobe, Japan	5,502	6.9
1995, May 27	Sakhalin Isl., Russia	1,989	7.5
1997, Feb. 28	NW Iran	1,000+	6.1
1997, May 10	Northern Iran	1,567	7.3
1998, Feb. 4	Hindu Kush, Afghanistan	2,323	5.9
1998, May 30	Afgh.-Tajikistan border.	4,000+	6.6
1998, July 17	Papua New Guinea	2,183	7.0
1999, Jan. 25	Armenia, Colombia	1,185+	6.1
1999, Aug. 17	Izmit, western Turkey	17,118+	7.6
1999, Sept. 20	Taichung, Taiwan	2,400	7.6
2001, Jan. 26	Gujarat, India	20,085	7.6
2002, Mar. 25-26	Hindu Kush, Afghanistan	1,000+	6.1
2003, May 21	Northern Algeria	2,266	6.8
2003, Dec. 26	Bam, SE Iran	31,000	6.6
2004, Dec. 26	Sumatra-Andaman Isls., Indonesia	227,898	9.1[7]
2005, Mar. 28	N Sumatra, Indonesia.	1,313	8.6
2005, Oct. 8	Kashmir, Pakistan, India.	86,000	7.6
2006, May 26	Java, Indonesia	5,749	6.3
2008, May 12	E Sichuan Prov., China	87,857	7.9
2009, Sept. 30	Sumatra, Indonesia	1,117	7.5
2010, Jan. 12	Haiti	316,000[8]	7.0
2010, Apr. 13	Southern Qinghai, China	2,698+	6.9
2011, Mar. 11	NE Japan	20,896	9.0[9]
2015, Apr. 25	Nepal	8,669+	7.8
2017, Sept. 19	Mexico City, Mexico	369	7.1
2017, Nov. 12	NW Iran-Iraq border	530	7.3
2018, Sept. 28	Sulawesi, Indonesia	4,340	7.5
2021, Aug. 14	Haiti	2,248+	7.2
2022, June 22	SE Afghanistan	1,036	6.2
2023, Feb. 6	Southern Turkey, NW Syria.	53,227+	7.8
2023, Sept. 8	Morocco	2,946	6.8

NA = Not available. (1) Once thought to have been a volcanic eruption; evidence indicates an earthquake and tsunami occurred on this date. (2) Earthquake caused the most deadly tsunami to date in the Atlantic Ocean. (3) Incl. deaths from resulting fires; revised ests. of magnitude range 7.7-7.9. (4) Commonly referred to as the Gansu quake, actually located within Ningxia autonomous region. (5) Largest recorded earthquake; caused a tsunami that spread across the Pacific Ocean as far as Japan. (6) "Good Friday" earthquake sent a tsunami that hit British Columbia, Canada, and U.S. Pacific coast. (7) Undersea earthquake triggered devastating Indian Ocean tsunamis. (8) Official govt. death toll (Jan. 2011). Ests. from other groups vary widely. (9) The most powerful earthquake in Japan's history set off a tsunami that inundated much of the coast and caused a partial meltdown of the Fukushima nuclear power plant.

Some Notable Fires Since 1940

See also Some Notable Explosions Since 1920.

Date	Location	Deaths
1940, Apr. 23	Nightclub, Natchez, MS	198
1942, Nov. 28	Cocoanut Grove Nightclub, Boston, MA	492
1942, Dec. 12	Hostel, St. John's, NL, Canada	100
1943, Sept. 7	Gulf Hotel, Houston, TX	55
1944, July 6	Ringling Circus, Hartford, CT	168
1946, June 5	LaSalle Hotel, Chicago, IL	61
1946, Dec. 7	Winecoff Hotel, Atlanta, GA	119
1946, Dec. 12	Ice plant, tenement, New York, NY	37
1949, Apr. 5	Hospital, Effingham, IL	77
1950, Jan. 7	Mercy Hospital, Davenport, IA	41
1953, Mar. 29	Nursing home, Largo, FL	35
1953, Apr. 16	Metalworking plant, Chicago, IL	35

Date	Location	Deaths
1957, Feb. 17	Home for aged, Warrenton, MO	72
1958, Mar. 19	Garment factory, New York, NY	24
1958, Dec. 1	Parochial school, Chicago, IL	95
1958, Dec. 16	Store, Bogotá, Colombia	83
1960, Mar. 12	Chemical plant, Pusan, Korea	68
1960, July 14	Psychiatric hospital, Guatemala City	225
1960, Nov. 13	Movie theater, Amude, Syria	152
1960, Dec. 19	USS Constellation, Brooklyn, NY	49
1961, Jan. 6	Thomas Hotel, San Francisco, CA	20
1961, Dec. 17	Circus, Niteroi, Brazil	323
1963, May 4	Theater, Diourbel, Senegal	64
1963, Nov. 18	Surfside Hotel, Atlantic City, NJ	25
1963, Nov. 23	Nursing home, Fitchville, OH	63

Date	Location	Deaths
1963, Dec. 29	Roosevelt Hotel, Jacksonville, FL.....	22
1964, Dec. 18	Nursing home, Fountaintown, IN	20
1965, Aug. 11-16	Watts riot fires, Los Angeles, CA	30+
1966, Dec. 7	Barracks, Erzurum, Turkey.........	68
1967, Feb. 7	Restaurant, Montgomery, AL	25
1967, May 22	Dept. store, Brussels, Belgium	322
1967, July 16	State prison, Jay, FL.............	37
1967, July 29	USS *Forrestal*, off N Vietnam	134
1968, May 11	Wedding hall, Vijayawada, India.....	58
1969, Dec. 2	Nursing home, Notre Dame, QC, Can.	54
1970, Jan. 9	Nursing home, Marietta, OH........	27
1970, Nov. 1	Nightclub, nr. Grenoble, France	146
1970, Dec. 20	Hotel, Tucson, AZ...............	28
1971, Dec. 25	Hotel, Seoul, S. Korea	162
1972, May 13	Nightclub, Osaka, Japan	116
1973, June 24	Bar, New Orleans, LA............	32
1973, Aug. 3	Amusement park, Isle of Man, UK ...	51
1973, Nov. 29	Dept. store, Kumamoto, Japan......	107
1973, Dec. 2	Theater, Seoul, S. Korea	50
1974, Feb. 1	Bank building, São Paulo, Brazil ...	189
1974, Nov. 3	Hotel, disco, Seoul, S. Korea	88
1975, Dec. 12	Pilgrim camp, Mina, Saudi Arabia ...	138
1976, Oct. 24	Social club, Bronx, NY	25
1977, Feb. 25	Rossiya Hotel, Moscow, Russia.....	45
1977, May 28	Nightclub, Southgate, KY..........	164
1977, June 26	Jail, Columbia, TN	42
1977, Nov. 14	Hotel, Manila, Philippines	47
1978, Aug. 19	Movie theater, Abadan, Iran........	425+
1979, July 14	Hotel, Saragossa, Spain.	80
1979, Dec. 31	Social club, Chapais, QC, Can.	42
1980, May 20	Nursing home, Kingston, Jamaica ...	157
1980, Nov. 21	MGM Grand Hotel, Las Vegas, NV ...	84
1980, Dec. 4	Stouffer's Inn, Harrison, NY	26
1981, Jan. 9	Boarding home, Keansburg, NJ	30
1981, Feb. 14	Discotheque, Dublin, Ireland	44
1982, Nov. 8	County jail, Biloxi, MS............	29
1983, Feb. 13	Movie theater, Turin, Italy.........	64
1983, Feb. 16	"Ash Wednesday" bushfires,	
	S Australia and Victoria, Australia...	75
1983, Dec. 17	Discotheque, Madrid, Spain	83
1985, Apr. 21	Movie theaters, Tabaco, Philippines..	44
1985, Apr. 26	Hospital, Buenos Aires, Argentina ...	79
1985, May 11	Soccer stadium, Bradford, Eng., UK..	53
1985, May 13	MOVE headquarters, row houses,	
	Philadelphia, PA...............	11
1986, Dec. 31	Dupont Plaza Hotel, Puerto Rico	96
1987, May 6-		
June 2	Forest fire, Mohe, China..........	191
1987, Nov. 17	Subway, London, England	30
1988, Mar. 20	2,000+ buildings, Lashio, Myanmar ...	134
1990, Mar. 25	Happy Land social club, Bronx, NY ...	87
1991, Mar. 3	Munitions dump, Addis Ababa, Ethiopia	260+
1991, Aug.-Oct.	Wildfires, Sumatra, Borneo, Indonesia	57
1991, Sept. 3	Chicken-processing plant, Hamlet, NC	25
1993, Apr. 19	Cult compound, Waco, TX.........	72
1993, May 10	Toy factory, Bangkok, Thailand	213
1993, Nov. 19	Toy factory, Shenzhen, China	87
1994, Nov. 2	Burning fuel flood, Durunka, Egypt...	500
1994, Nov. 27	Dance hall, Fuxin, China	233
1994, Dec. 8	Theater, Karamay, China	323
1995, Oct. 28	Subway train, Baku, Azerbaijan	300
1995, Dec. 23	School, Mandi Dabwali, India.......	500+
1996, Mar. 19	Nightclub, Quezon City, Philippines ..	150+
1996, Mar. 28	Shopping mall, Bogor, Indonesia	78
1996, Nov. 20	Garley Building, Hong Kong	39
1997, Feb. 23	Worship site, Baripada, India	164
1997, Apr. 15	Encampment, Mina, Saudi Arabia ...	343
1997, June 7	Temple, Thanjavur, India	60+

Date	Location	Deaths
1997, June 13	Movie theater, New Delhi, India	60
1997, July 11	Hotel, Pattaya, Thailand...........	90
1997, Sept.-Nov.	Drought-fueled fire, Sumatra, Indon. ..	240
1998, Apr.-June	Wildfire, Oaxaca, Mexico..........	50
1999, Mar. 24	Mt. Blanc Tunnel, France, Italy......	40
1999, Oct. 30	Karaoke salon, Inchon, S. Korea	55+
2000, Mar. 17	Church, Kanungu, Uganda.........	530
2000, Nov. 11	Cable car, Kaprun, Austria	155
2000, Dec. 25	Shopping center, Luoyang, China ...	309
2001, Mar. 26	School, Machakos, Kenya	64
2001, Aug. 18	Hotel, Quezon City, Philippines	73
2001, Sept. 1	Nightclub, Tokyo, Japan..........	44
2001, Dec. 29	Fireworks accident, Lima, Peru	291
2003, Feb. 18	Subway train, Taegu, S. Korea......	198
2003, Feb. 20	Nightclub pyrotechnics, Warwick, RI ..	100
2003, Sept. 15	Prison, Riyadh, Saudi Arabia	94
2003, Nov. 24	Students' hostel, Moscow, Russia ...	36
2004, May 17	Prison, San Pedro Sula, Honduras....	104
2004, July 16	Pvt. school, Kumbakonam, India	80+
2004, Aug. 1	Market, Asunción, Paraguay	400+
2004, Dec. 30	Club, Buenos Aires, Argentina	194
2005, Feb. 14	Mosque, Tehran, Iran	59
2005, Mar. 7	Prison, Higuey, Dom. Republic......	159
2005, Sept. 5	Theater, Beni Suef, Egypt	32
2006, Dec. 9	Drug treatment center, Moscow, Russ.	45
2007, Mar. 20	Nursing home, Kamyshevatskaya,	
	Russia.......................	62
2007, Mar. 24-		
Sept. 2	Wildfires (arson), Greece	73
2008, Apr. 26	Factory fire, Casablanca, Morocco....	55
2008, Sept.	Wildfires, Mozambique, S. Africa,	
	Swaziland....................	89
2009, Jan. 1	Nightclub fire, Bangkok, Thailand.....	67
2009, Jan.-Feb.	"Black Saturday" wildfires (arson),	
	Victoria, Australia	173
2010, July	Bushfires, Nizhiny Novgorod, Russia..	53
2010, Dec. 2-5	Grassland fire, Israel	44
2012, Feb. 14	Prison fire, Comayagua, Honduras ...	360+
2012, Nov. 24	Garment factory, Bagladesh........	112
2013, Jan. 27	Nightclub, Santa Maria, Brazil	241
2014, May 2	Trade union building, Odessa, Ukraine	40+
2016, Apr. 10	Temple fireworks, Kerala, India.......	110+
2016, Dec. 2	"Ghost Ship" warehouse, Oakland, CA	36
2017, June 14	Grenfell Tower apts., London, Eng., UK	72
2017, June 17-18	Forest fires, central Portugal........	64
2018, July 23	Wildfires, Attica region, Greece	99
2018, Nov. 8-25	Camp Fire wildfire, Butte Co., CA	85
2019, Oct.-		
2020, Feb.	"Black Summer" wildfires, Australia ..	33[1]
2023, Aug. 8	Wildfires, Lahaina, Maui, HI	98
2023, Sept. 28	Wedding venue, Qaraqosh, Iraq	119+

(1) Research published in Mar. 2020 found an additional 417 excess deaths from smoke inhalation.

U.S. Fires, 2022

Source: National Fire Protection Association

- Public fire departments responded to an estimated 1.5 mil fires in 2022, including 522,500 structure fires (360,000 in homes), 222,000 vehicle fires, and 760,000 fires outside or other fires.
- An estimated 3,790 civilians died in fires in 2022.
- There were an estimated 13,250 civilian fire injuries reported, 9,940 of them in home structure fires.
- Direct property damage from fires amounted to an estimated $18.1 bil. Structure fires accounted for $15.0 bil of property damage, and property loss associated with home fires came to $10.5 bil.

Some Notable Explosions Since 1920

See also Principal U.S. Mine Disasters Since 1867. Some bombings related to political conflicts and terrorism are not included.

Date	Location	Deaths
1920, Sept. 16	Wall Street, New York, NY	39
1921, Sept. 21	Chem. storage facility, Oppau, Ger.....	561
1924, Jan. 3	Food plant, Pekin, IL.............	42
1927, May 18	School bombing, Bath, MI	45
1928, Apr. 13	Dance hall, West Plains, MO	40
1937, Mar. 18	School, New London, TX	311
1940, Sept. 12	Hercules Powder factory, Kenvil, NJ ...	55
1942, Apr. 26	Honkeiko (Benxihu) colliery, China.....	1,549

Date	Location	Deaths
1942, June 5	Ordnance plant, Elwood, IL	49
1944, Apr. 14	SS *Fort Stikine*, Bombay docks, India ..	700
1944, July 17	Munitions ships, depot, Port Chicago,	
	CA...........................	322
1944, Oct. 20	Liquid natural gas tanks, Cleveland, OH	130
1947, Apr. 16	Freighter, chemical co. plant,	
	Texas City, TX.................	576
1948, July 28	Farben works, Ludwigshafen, Ger.	184

Date	Location	Deaths
1950, May 19	Munitions barges, S. Amboy, NJ	30
1954, May 26	USS *Bennington*, off RI	103
1956, Aug. 7	Dynamite trucks, Cali, Colombia	1,100
1958, Apr. 18	Sunken munitions ship, Okinawa, Japan	40
1959, Apr. 10	WWII bomb, Philippines	38
1959, June 28	Rail tank cars, Meldrim, GA	25
1959, Aug. 7	Truck with explosives, Roseburg, OR	14
1959, Nov. 2	Explosives, Jamuri Bazar, India	46
1959, Dec. 13	2 apt. bldgs., Dortmund, Germany	26
1960, Mar. 4	Belgian munitions ship, Havana, Cuba	100
1962, Oct. 3	New York Telephone Co. office, New York, NY	23
1963, Jan. 2	Packing plant, Terre Haute, IN	17
1963, Mar. 9	Dynamite plant, S. Africa	45
1963, Aug. 13	Explosives dump, Gauhaiti, India	32
1963, Oct. 31	State Fair Coliseum, Indianapolis, IN	73
1963, Nov. 9	Mitsui Miike coal mine, Japan	458
1964, July 23	Harbor munitions, Bone, Algeria	100
1965, Aug. 9	Missile silo, Searcy, AR	53
1965, Oct. 21	Bridge, Tila Bund, Pakistan	80
1965, Nov. 24	Armory, Keokuk, IA	20
1968, Apr. 6	Sports store, Richmond, IN	43
1969, Mar. 31	Coal mine, nr. Barroteran, Mexico	180
1970, Apr. 8	Subway construction, Osaka, Japan	73
1971, June 24	Tunnel under construction, Sylmar, CA	17
1973, Feb. 10	Liquid gas tank, Staten Island, NY	40
1975, Dec. 27	Coal mine, Chasnala, India	431
1976, Apr. 13	Munitions works, Lapua, Finland	40
1977, Nov. 11	Freight train, Iri, S. Korea	57
1977, Dec. 22	Grain elevator, Westwego, LA	35
1978, July 11	Propylene tank truck, Tarragona, Spain	150
1980, Oct. 23	School, Ortuella, Spain	64
1982, Apr. 25	Antiques exhibition, Todi, Italy	33
1982, Nov. 2	Salang Tunnel, Afghanistan	1,000+
1984, Feb. 25	Oil pipeline, Cubatao, Brazil	508
1984, June 21	Naval supply depot, Severomorsk, USSR	200+
1984, Nov. 19	Gas storage area, NE Mexico City	334
1984, Dec. 3	Chemical plant, Bhopal, India	3,849
1984, Dec. 5	Coal mine, Taipei, Taiwan	94
1985, June 25	Fireworks factory, Hallett, OK	21
1988, Apr. 10	Army ammunitions dump nr. Rawalpindi and Islamabad, Pakistan	100
1988, July 6	Oil rig, North Sea off NE Scotland, UK	167
1989, June 3	Gas pipeline, between Ufa, Asha, USSR	650+
1992, Mar. 3	Coal mine, Kozlu, Turkey	270+
1992, Apr. 22	Gas leak in sewers, Guadalajara, Mexico	200+
1992, May 9	Coal mine, Plymouth, Nova Scotia, Can.	26
1993, Feb. 26	World Trade Center, New York, NY	6
1994, July 18	Jewish community center, Buenos Aires, Argentina	100
1995, Apr. 19	Fed. office building, Oklahoma City, OK	168
1995, Apr. 29	Subway construction, S. Korea	110
1996, Jan. 31	Bank, Colombo, Sri Lanka	53
1996, Mar. 4	Jerusalem and Tel Aviv, Israel	33
1996, June 25	U.S. military housing complex, nr. Dhahran, Saudi Arabia	19
1996, July 24	Train, Colombo, Sri Lanka	86
1996, Nov. 16	Military apt., Dagestan region, Russia	68
1996, Nov. 21	Propane gas leak in bldg., San Juan, PR	33
1996, Nov. 27	Coal mine, Shanxi Prov., China	91+
1996, Dec. 30	Train, Assam, India	59+
1997, Dec. 2	Coal mine, Novokuznetsk, Russia	68
1998, Feb. 14	2 oil tankers, Yaounde, Cameroon	120
1998, Feb. 14	17 bombs, Coimbatore, India	50
1998, Apr. 4	Coal mine, Donetsk, Ukraine	63
1998, Aug. 7	Bomb, U.S. emb., Nairobi, Kenya	213
1998, Aug. 7	Bomb, U.S. emb., Dar-es-Salaam, Tanzania	11
1998, Sept. 8	2 buses, São Paulo, Brazil	59
1998, Oct. 17	Oil pipeline, Jesse, Nigeria	700+
1999, May 16	Fuel truck, Punjab Prov., Pakistan	75
1999, Sept. 9	Apartment building, Moscow, Russia	94
1999, Sept. 13	Apartment building, Moscow, Russia	118
1999, Sept. 16	Apartment building, Moscow, Russia	18
1999, Sept. 26	Fireworks factory, Celaya, Mexico	56
2000, Feb. 25	Bombs on 2 buses, Ozamis, Philippines	41
2000, Mar. 11	Coal mine, Krasnodon, Ukraine	80
2000, Apr. 16	Airport hangar, Dem. Rep. of Congo	100+
2000, Aug. 12	Flaw in torpedo, *Kursk* submarine, off Russia	118
2000, Sept. 9	Truck explosion, Urumqi, China	60
2000, Oct. 12	USS *Cole*, Yemen	17
2001, Mar. 6	School, Jianxi Prov., China	41
2001, Apr. 21	Coal mine, Shaanxi, China	51
2001, June 1	Dance club, Tel Aviv, Israel	21
2001, July 17	Coal mine, Guanxi, China	76+
2001, Aug. 19	Coal mine, Donetsk region, Ukraine	52
2001, Sept. 21	Chem. plant, Toulouse, France	29
2002, Jan. 21	Volcanic lava caused gas station blast, Goma, Dem. Rep. of Congo	50+
2002, Jan. 27	Munitions dump, Lagos, Nigeria	1,000+
2002, May 9	Land mine at parade, Kaspiisk, Russia	34+
2002, June 14	Car bomb outside U.S. consulate, Karachi, Pakistan	12
2002, June 18	Bomb on bus, Jerusalem, Israel	20
2002, July 5	Bomb in market, Larba, Algeria	35+
2002, Aug. 9	Explosion, Jalalabad, Afghanistan	25+
2002, Sept. 5	Car bomb, Kabul, Afghanistan	30
2002, Oct. 12	Nightclub bombings, Bali, Indonesia	202
2003, Aug. 25	Bombs in 2 taxis, Mumbai, India	52
2003, Dec. 5	Bomb on train, Yessentuki, Russia	45
2003, Dec. 23	Gas well explosion, Chongqing, China	233
2004, Feb. 6	Bomb on subway car, Moscow, Russia	39
2004, Mar. 11	Bombs on commuter trains, Madrid, Spain	191
2005, Feb. 14	Coal mine, NE China	214
2005, Mar. 23	Oil refinery, Texas City, TX	15
2005, July 7	Bombs in mass transit, London, Eng., UK	56
2005, Oct. 1	Bombings of restaurants, Bali, Indonesia	26
2005, Nov. 27	Coal mine, NE China	161+
2006, May 12	Oil pipeline, nr. Lagos, Nigeria	200
2006, July 1	Bombings of trains, station, Mumbai, India	207
2007, Mar. 19	Coal mine, Siberia, Russia	108
2007, Mar. 22	Natl. weapons depot, Maputo, Mozambique	117
2007, June 9	Oil pipeline, Pyongan Prov., N. Korea	110
2007, Nov. 18	Methane gas buildup in coal mine, E Ukraine	90
2008, May 15	Pipeline explosion in Lagos, Nigeria	100+
2008, Sept. 20	Truck bomb outside hotel, Islamabad, Pakistan	40+
2009, Feb. 22	Coal mine, N China	74
2010, May 8-9	Coal mine, Siberia, Russia	91
2010, June 17	Coal mine, Amaga, Colombia	73
2011, Mar. 28	Munitions depot, Abyan, Yemen	150+
2011, July 13	Bombs in 3 locations in Mumbai, India	27
2012, Mar. 4	Arms depot, Brazzaville, Congo Rep.	250+
2013, Apr. 17	Fertilizer plant, West, TX	15
2013, June 3	Poultry plant, Mishzai, China	119+
2013, June 30	Fuel tanker, Kampala, Uganda	30+
2013, July 6	Derailed oil train, Lac-Mégantic, QC, Canada	47
2013, Aug. 1	Weapons cache, Homs, Syria	40
2014, May 13	Coal mine, Soma, Turkey	301
2015, Aug. 12	Chemical warehouse, Tianjin, China	173
2017, Oct. 27	Fireworks factory, Tangerang, Indon.	47+
2020, Aug. 4	Chemicals improperly stored at port, Beirut, Lebanon	211
2021, Mar. 7	Explosions at military base, Bata, Equatorial Guinea	107
2022, Apr. 23	Illegal oil refinery, SE Nigeria	100+

Principal U.S. Mine Disasters Since 1867

Source: Bureau of Mines, U.S. Dept. of the Interior; Office of Mine Safety Health Research, Centers for Disease Control
All are bituminous coal mines unless otherwise noted.

Date	Location	Deaths	Date	Location	Deaths	Date	Location	Deaths
1867, Apr. 3	Winterpock, VA....	69	1910, May 5	Palos, AL......	84	1924, Mar. 8	Castle Gate, UT ...	172
1869, Sept. 6	Plymouth, PA....	110	1910, Nov. 8	Delagua, CO	79	1924, Apr. 28	Benwood, WV....	119
1883, Feb. 16	Braidwood, IL.....	69	1911, Apr. 7	Troop, PA......	73	1926, Jan. 13	Wilburton, OK....	91
1884, Mar. 13	Pocahontas, VA....	112	1911, Apr. 8	Littleton, AL.....	128	1927, Apr. 30	Everettville, WV ...	97
1891, Jan. 27	Mt. Pleasant, PA....	109	1911, Dec. 9	Briceville, TN	84	1928, May 19	Mather, PA......	195
1892, Jan. 7	Krebs, OK........	100	1912, Mar. 20	McCurtain, OK....	73	1929, Dec. 17	McAlester, OK....	61
1895, Mar. 20	Red Canyon, WY ..	62	1912, Mar. 26	Jed, WV........	81	1930, Nov. 5	Millfield, OH......	82
1900, May 1	Scofield, UT	200	1913, Apr. 23	Finleyville, PA ...	98	1940, Jan. 10	Bartley, WV......	91
1902, May 19	Coal Creek, TN ...	184	1913, Oct. 22	Dawson, NM.....	263	1940, Mar. 16	St. Clairsville, OH..	72
1902, July 10	Johnstown, PA....	112	1914, Apr. 28	Eccles, WV.....	181	1940, July 15	Portage, PA......	63
1903, June 30	Hanna, WY......	169	1915, Mar. 2	Layland, WV.....	115	1943, Feb. 27	Washoe, MT.....	74
1904, Jan. 25	Cheswick, PA.....	179	1917, Apr. 27	Hastings, CO	121	1944, July 5	Powhatan Pt., OH..	66
1905, Feb. 20	Virginia City, AL ...	112	1917, June 8	Butte, MT[1].......	163	1947, Mar. 25	Centralia, IL	111
1907, Jan. 29	Stuart, WV......	84	1917, Aug. 4	Clay, KY........	62	1951, Dec. 21	West Frankfort, IL..	119
1907, Dec. 6	Monongah, WV ...	362	1919, June 5	Wilkes-Barre, PA ..	92	1968, Nov. 20	Farmington, WV ...	78
1907, Dec. 19	Van Meter, PA....	239	1922, Nov. 6	Spangler, PA	79	1970, Dec. 30	Hyden, KY......	38
1908, Nov. 28	Marianna, PA.....	154	1922, Nov. 22	Dolomite, AL.....	90	1972, Feb. 26	Saunders, WV ...	114
1909, Jan. 12	Switchback, WV ...	67	1923, Feb. 8	Dawson, NM.....	120	1972, May 2	Kellogg, ID[2].....	91
1909, Nov. 13	Cherry, IL.......	259	1923, Aug. 14	Kemmerer, WY....	99	2010, Apr. 5	Montcoal, WV.....	29
1910, Jan. 31	Primero, CO......	75						

Note: The world's worst mine disaster killed 1,549 workers in Manchuria, China, Apr. 26, 1942. (1) Copper mine. (2) Silver mine.

Notable Nuclear Accidents

Sept. 29, 1957: After cooling system failure, nuclear waste at Chelyabinsk-65 in Kyshtym, Russia, exploded. Residents were evacuated but not informed until 1989 about their exposure to radiation.

Oct. 7, 1957: Fire in the Windscale plutonium production reactor N of Liverpool, England, UK, released radioactive material; later blamed for 39 cancer deaths.

Jan. 3, 1961: Reactor explosion at a federal installation near Idaho Falls, ID, killed 3 workers. Radiation contained.

Oct. 5, 1966: Sodium cooling system malfunction caused a partial core meltdown at the Enrico Fermi demonstration breeder reactor, near Detroit, MI. Radiation contained.

Jan. 21, 1969: Coolant malfunction from an experimental underground reactor at Lucens Vad, Switzerland, released radiation into a cavern, which was then sealed.

Mar. 22, 1975: Fire at the Brown's Ferry reactor in Decatur, AL, caused dangerous lowering of cooling water levels.

Mar. 28, 1979: Worst commercial nuclear accident in the U.S. occurred as equipment failures and human mistakes led to a loss of coolant and a partial core meltdown at the Three Mile Island reactor in Middletown, PA.

Feb. 11, 1981: Eight workers were contaminated when 100,000 gallons of radioactive coolant leaked into the containment building of TVA's Sequoyah 1 plant near Chattanooga, TN.

Apr. 25, 1981: Some 100 workers were exposed to radiation during repairs of a nuclear plant at Tsuruga, Japan.

Jan. 6, 1986: Cylinder of nuclear material burst after being improperly heated at a Kerr-McGee plant in Gore, OK. One worker died; 100 were hospitalized.

Apr. 26, 1986: Fires and resulting explosions at the Chernobyl nuclear power plant near Kiev, USSR (now in Ukraine), left at least 31 dead in the immediate aftermath and spread radioactive material over much of Europe. An estimated 135,000 people were evacuated. Tens of thousands of excess cancer deaths (as well as increased birth defects) were expected.

Sept. 1987: Cesium chloride from an improperly discarded hospital irradiation machine contaminated more than 200 people and killed at least 4 in Goiânia, Brazil.

Mar. 11, 2011: A 9.0 magnitude earthquake caused a tsunami that inundated the Fukushima Daiichi nuclear power plant on Japan's NE coast. Three of the plant's reactors suffered partial meltdowns; more than 12,000 tons of radioactive water was released into the sea.

Record Oil Spills

The exact number of barrels in a metric ton varies with the type of oil, but a general approximation is 7 barrels per metric ton. By custom, 42 gallons constitute a barrel of crude oil.

Name, location	Date	Cause	Est. metric tons
BP *Deepwater Horizon* rig, Gulf of Mexico, U.S. ..	Apr. 20-July 15, 2010	Explosion	700,000[1]
Ixtoc I oil well, S Gulf of Mexico	June 3, 1979......	Blowout..........	600,000
Nowruz oil field, Persian Gulf	Feb. 1983........	Blowout..........	600,000
Atlantic Empress, off Trinidad and Tobago	July 19, 1979 ...	Collision with *Aegean*	
		Captain ...	276,000
ABT Summer, off Angola	May 28, 1991	Explosion	260,000
Amoco Cadiz, near Portsall, France	Mar. 16, 1978	Grounding............	223,000
Castillo de Bellver, off Cape Town, South Africa ...	Aug. 6, 1983	Fire	150,000-160,000
Haven, off Genoa, Italy.................	Apr. 11, 1991	Explosion	144,000
Odyssey, off Nova Scotia, Canada	Nov. 10, 1988	Broke apart in storm ...	132,000
Torrey Canyon, off Land's End, England, UK......	Mar. 18, 1967	Grounding.........	119,000
Sea Star, Gulf of Oman	Dec. 19, 1972 ...	Collision	115,000
Sanchi, off Shanghai, China	Jan. 6, 2018	Collision with *CF Crystal*....	113,000
Urquiola, La Coruna, Spain	May 12, 1976	Grounding..........	100,000

(1) The Dept. of Energy estimated the spill at 4.9 mil barrels, or more than 200 mil gallons.

Other Notable Oil Spills

Name, location	Date	Cause	Gallons
Persian Gulf	Jan. 21, 1991	Intentional spillage by Iraq ...	130,000,000[1]
Braer, off Shetland Islands, UK	Jan. 5, 1993	Grounding..........	26,000,000
Taylor Energy platform, Gulf of Mexico, U.S.	Sept. 2004-present	Broke apart during H. *Ivan* ...	Up to 25,000,000
Prestige, off N Spain	Nov. 13-19, 2002	Ship broke in half	22,600,000
Aegean Sea, off N Spain	Dec. 3, 1992	Grounding..........	21,500,000
Sea Empress, off SW Wales, UK............	Feb. 15, 1996	Grounding..........	18,000,000
Newtown Creek, Greenpoint, Brooklyn, NY	Oct. 5, 1950-present	Industrial explosion.........	17,000,000[2]
Hawaiian Patriot, off Hawaii in Pacific	Feb. 23-24, 1977	Hull cracked; ship exploded ..	14,700,000
World Glory, off South Africa	June 13, 1968	Hull failure.............	13,524,000
Exxon Valdez, Prince William Sound, AK.........	Mar. 24, 1989	Grounding..........	10,080,000
Ashland Oil facility, Floreffe, PA; Monongahela R. ..	Jan. 2, 1988	Storage tank collapse.......	3,850,000

(1) Est. by Saudi Arabia. Some estimates as low as 25 mil gal. (2) Legacy of refinery operations since mid-1800s and leaking storage tanks. Spill estimated at up to 30 mil gal.

AEROSPACE

Notable Human Spaceflight Missions

Source: National Aeronautics and Space Administration (NASA); Congressional Research Service; World Almanac research

The spaceflights listed are a selection of notable crewed U.S. missions by NASA, unless otherwise noted, plus crewed non-U.S. missions (shown with an asterisk). The non-U.S. missions were sponsored by the USSR—later, the Commonwealth of Independent States (CIS) and, from 1997, Russia—or by China. Launch dates are Eastern Standard Time. **EVA** = extravehicular activity. **ASTP** = Apollo-Soyuz Test Project. **STS** = Space Transportation System, NASA's name for the overall shuttle program.

For shuttle flights, mission name is in parentheses following name of orbiter. Duration of flight is listed in hours:minutes for 1961-Apr. 1970; days (d.), hours (hr.), and minutes (min.) thereafter. Number of total flights taken by each crew member is given in parentheses when flight listed is not the person's first.

4/12/1961: *Vostok 1*; 1:48; Yuri A. Gagarin. **1st human orbital flight.**

5/5/1961: *Mercury-Redstone 3*; 0:15; Alan B. Shepard Jr. **1st American in space.**

7/21/1961: *Mercury-Redstone 4*; 0:15; Virgil I. Grissom. Flight successful but spacecraft sank shortly after splashdown; Grissom rescued.

8/6/1961: *Vostok 2*; 25:18; Gherman S. Titov. 1st spaceflight of more than 24 hours.

2/20/1962: *Mercury-Atlas 6*; 4:55; John H. Glenn Jr. **1st American in orbit**; three orbits.

5/24/1962: *Mercury-Atlas 7*; 4:56; M. Scott Carpenter. Manual retrofire error caused 250-mi landing overshoot.

8/11/1962: *Vostok 3*; 94:22; Andrian G. Nikolayev. *Vostok 3* and *4* made 1st group flight.

8/12/1962: *Vostok 4*; 70:57; Pavel R. Popovich. On 1st orbit, it came within 3 mi of *Vostok 3*.

10/3/1962: *Mercury-Atlas 8*; 9:13; Walter M. Schirra Jr. Landed 5 mi from target; six orbits.

5/15/1963: *Mercury-Atlas 9*; 34:19; L. Gordon Cooper. 1st U.S. evaluation of effects of one day in space on a person; 22 orbits.

6/14/1963: *Vostok 5*; 119:06; Valery F. Bykovsky. *Vostok 5* and *6* made 2nd group flight.

6/16/1963: *Vostok 6*; 70:50; Valentina V. Tereshkova. **1st woman in space**; passed within 3 mi of *Vostok 5*.

10/12/1964: *Voskhod 1*; 24:17; Vladimir M. Komarov, Konstantin P. Feoktistov, Boris B. Yegorov. 1st three-person orbital flight; 1st without space suits.

3/18/1965: *Voskhod 2*; 26:02; Pavel I. Belyayev, Aleksei A. Leonov. Leonov made **1st spacewalk** (10 min.).

3/23/1965: *Gemini-Titan 3*; 4:53; Virgil I. Grissom (2), John W. Young. 1st piloted spacecraft to change its orbital path.

6/3/1965: *Gemini-Titan 4*; 97:56; James A. McDivitt, Edward H. White II. White was **1st American to "walk in space"** (23 min.).

8/21/1965: *Gemini-Titan 5*; 190:55; L. Gordon Cooper (2), Charles Conrad Jr. Longest-duration human flight to date.

12/4/1965: *Gemini-Titan 7*; 330:35; Frank Borman, James A. Lovell Jr. Longest-duration *Gemini* flight.

12/15/1965: *Gemini-Titan 6A*; 25:51; Walter M. Schirra Jr. (2), Thomas P. Stafford. Completed 1st U.S. space rendezvous, with *Gemini 7*.

3/16/1966: *Gemini-Titan 8*; 10:41; Neil A. Armstrong, David R. Scott. **1st docking of one space vehicle with another**; mission aborted, control malfunction.

6/3/1966: *Gemini-Titan 9A*; 72:21; Thomas P. Stafford (2), Eugene A. Cernan. Performed simulation of lunar module rendezvous.

7/18/1966: *Gemini-Titan 10*; 70:47; John W. Young (2), Michael Collins. 1st use of Agena target vehicle's propulsion systems; 1st orbital docking.

9/12/1966: *Gemini-Titan 11*; 71:17; Charles Conrad Jr. (2), Richard F. Gordon Jr. 1st tethered flight; highest Earth-orbit altitude (850 mi).

11/11/1966: *Gemini-Titan 12*; 94:34; James A. Lovell Jr. (2), Edwin E. "Buzz" Aldrin Jr. Final *Gemini* mission; 5-hr. EVA.

1/27/1967: *Apollo 1*; Virgil I. Grissom, Edward H. White II, and Roger B. Chaffee died in a fire on the ground at Cape Canaveral, FL.

4/23/1967: *Soyuz 1*; 26:40; Vladimir M. Komarov (2). Crashed on reentry, killing Komarov; **1st space fatality.**

10/11/1968: *Apollo-Saturn 7*; 260:09; Walter M. Schirra Jr. (3), Donn F. Eisele, R. Walter Cunningham. **1st piloted flight of Apollo** spacecraft command-service module only; live TV footage of crew.

12/21/1968: *Apollo-Saturn 8*; 147:00; Frank Borman (2), James A. Lovell Jr. (3), William A. Anders. **1st lunar orbit** and piloted lunar return reentry (command-service module only); views of lunar surface televised to Earth.

1/14/1969: *Soyuz 4*; 71:21; Vladimir A. Shatalov. Docked with *Soyuz 5*.

1/15/1969: *Soyuz 5*; 72:54; Boris V. Volyanov, Aleksei S. Yeliseyev, Yevgeny V. Khrunov. Docked with *Soyuz 4*; Yeliseyev and Khrunov transferred to *Soyuz 4* via a spacewalk.

3/3/1969: *Apollo-Saturn 9*; 241:00; James A. McDivitt (2), David R. Scott (2), Russell L. Schweickart. 1st piloted flight of lunar module.

5/18/1969: *Apollo-Saturn 10*; 192:03; Thomas P. Stafford (3), John W. Young (3), Eugene A. Cernan (2). 1st lunar module orbit of moon, 50,000 ft from moon's surface.

7/16/1969: *Apollo-Saturn 11*; 195:18; Neil A. Armstrong (2), Michael Collins (2), Edwin E. "Buzz" Aldrin Jr. (2). **1st moon landing** made by Armstrong and Aldrin (7/20); collected 47.5 lbs of soil, rock samples; lunar stay time 21:36.

10/11/1969: *Soyuz 6*; 118:43; Georgi S. Shonin, Valery N. Kubasov. 1st welding of metals in space.

10/12/1969: *Soyuz 7*; 118:40; Anatoly V. Flipchenko, Vladislav N. Volkov, Viktor V. Gorbatko. Space lab construction test made; *Soyuz 6*, *7*, and *8*: 1st time three spacecraft, seven crew members orbited the Earth at once.

10/13/1969: *Soyuz 8*; 118:51; Vladimir A. Shatalov (2), Aleksei S. Yeliseyev (2). Part of space lab construction team.

11/14/1969: *Apollo-Saturn 12*; 244:36; Charles Conrad Jr. (3), Richard F. Gordon Jr. (2), Alan L. Bean. Conrad and Bean made **2nd moon landing** (11/18); collected 75 lbs of samples; lunar stay time 31:31.

4/11/1970: *Apollo-Saturn 13*; 142:54; James A. Lovell Jr. (4), Fred W. Haise Jr., John L. Swigert Jr. Aborted after service module oxygen tank ruptured; crew returned in lunar module.

6/1/1970: *Soyuz 9*; 17 d., 16 hr., 59 min.; Andrian G. Nikolayev (2), Vitaly I. Sevastyanov. Longest human spaceflight to date.

1/31/1971: *Apollo-Saturn 14*; 9 d., 2 min.; Alan B. Shepard Jr. (2), Stuart A. Roosa, Edgar D. Mitchell. Shepard and Mitchell made **3rd moon landing** (2/5); collected 94 lbs of lunar samples; lunar stay 33:31.

4/19/1971: *Salyut 1*; launched without crew. **1st space station.**

4/22/1971: *Soyuz 10*; 1 d., 23 hr., 46 min.; Vladimir A. Shatalov (3), Aleksei S. Yeliseyev (3), Nikolay N. Rukavishnikov. **1st successful docking with a space station**; failed to enter space station.

6/6/1971: *Soyuz 11*; 23 d., 28 hr., 22 min.; Georgi T. Dobrovolskiy, Vladislav N. Volkov (2), Viktor I. Patsayev. Docked and entered *Salyut 1* space station; **crew died** during reentry from loss of pressurization.

7/26/1971: *Apollo-Saturn 15*; 12 d., 17 hr., 12 min.; David R. Scott (3), James B. Irwin, Alfred M. Worden. Scott and Irwin made **4th moon landing** (7/30). 1st lunar rover use; 1st deep spacewalk; collected 170 lbs of samples; lunar stay 66:55.

4/16/1972: *Apollo-Saturn 16*; 11 d., 1 hr., 51 min.; John W. Young (4), Charles M. Duke Jr., Thomas K. Mattingly II. Young and Duke made **5th moon landing** (4/20); collected 209 lbs of lunar samples; lunar stay 71:02.

12/7/1972: *Apollo-Saturn 17*; 12 d., 13 hr., 52 min.; Eugene A. Cernan (3), Ronald E. Evans, Harrison H. Schmitt. Cernan and Schmitt made 6th and **final crewed landing** (12/11); collected 243 lbs of samples; record lunar stay over 75 hr.

5/14/1973: *Skylab 1*; launched without crew. **1st U.S. space station**; fell out of orbit 7/11/1979.

5/25/1973: *Skylab 2*; 28 d., 49 min.; Charles Conrad Jr. (4), Joseph P. Kerwin, Paul J. Weitz. 1st U.S.-piloted orbiting space station; crew repaired damage caused in boost.

7/28/1973: *Skylab 3*; 59 d., 11 hr., 1 min.; Alan L. Bean (2), Owen K. Garriott, Jack R. Lousma. Crew systems and operational tests; scientific activities; three EVAs, 13:44.

11/16/1973: *Skylab 4*; 84 d., 1 hr., 16 min.; Gerald P. Carr, Edward G. Gibson, William R. Pogue. Final *Skylab* mission.

7/15/1975: *Soyuz 19 (ASTP)*; 6 d., 11 hr., 31 min.; Aleksei A. Leonov (2), Valery N. Kubasov (2). U.S.-USSR joint flight; crews linked up in space (7/17), conducted experiments, shared meals, held a joint news conference.

7/15/1975: *Apollo (ASTP)*; 9 d., 7 hr., 28 min.; Vance D. Brand, Thomas P. Stafford (4), Donald K. Slayton. Joint flight with *Soyuz 19*.

12/10/1977: *Soyuz 26*; 96 d., 10 hr.; Yuri V. Romanenko, Georgiy M. Grechko (2). 1st multiple docking at a space station (*Soyuz 26* and *27* docked at *Salyut 6*).

1/10/1978: *Soyuz 27*; 5 d., 22 hr., 59 min.; Vladimir A. Dzhanibekov. See *Soyuz 26.*

3/2/1978: *Soyuz 28*; 7 d., 22 hr., 16 min.; Aleksei A. Gubarev (2), Vladimir Remek. 1st international crew launch; Remek was 1st Czech in space.

4/12/1981: *Columbia (STS-1)*; 2 d., 6 hr., 21 min.; John W. Young (5), Robert L. Crippen. **1st reusable space shuttle** to fly into Earth's orbit.

11/12/1981: *Columbia (STS-2)*; 3 days; Joe H. Engle, Richard H. Truly. 1st scientific payload; 1st reuse of space shuttle.

11/11/1982: *Columbia (STS-5)*; 6 days; Vance D. Brand (2), Robert F. Overmyer, Joseph P. Allen, William B. Lenoir. 1st four-person crew.

6/18/1983: *Challenger (STS-7)*; 7 days; Robert L. Crippen (2), Frederick H. Hauck, John M. Fabian, Sally K. Ride, Norman E. Thagard. Ride was **1st U.S. woman in space**; 1st 5-person crew.

6/27/1983: *Soyuz T-9*; 150 days; Vladimir A. Lyakhov (2), Aleksandr Pavlovich. Docked at *Salyut 7*. 1st construction in space.

8/30/1983: *Challenger (STS-8)*; 7 days; Richard H. Truly (2), Daniel C. Brandenstein, Dale A. Gardner, Guion S. Bluford Jr., William E. Thornton. Bluford was **1st African-American in space**; 1st night launch.

11/28/1983: *Columbia (STS-9)*; 11 days; John W. Young (6), Brewster H. Shaw Jr., Owen K. Garriott (2), Robert A.R. Parker, Byron K. Lichtenberg, Ulf Merbold. 1st six-person crew; 1st Spacelab mission.

2/3/1984: *Challenger (41-B)*; 8 days; Vance Brand (3), Robert L. Gibson, Ronald E. McNair, Bruce McCandless II, Robert L. Stewart. 1st untethered EVA.

2/8/1984: *Soyuz T-10B*; 63 days; Leonid Kizim, Vladimir Solovyov, Oleg Atkov. Docked with *Salyut 7*; crew set space duration record of 237 days (since eclipsed).

4/3/1984: *Soyuz T-11*; 182 days; Yury Malyshev (2), Gennady Strekalov (3), Rakesh Sharma. Docked with *Salyut 7*; Sharma was 1st Indian in space.

4/6/1984: *Challenger (41-C)*; 7 days; Robert L. Crippen (3), Francis R. Scobee, George D. Nelson, Terry J. Hart, James D. van Hoften. 1st in-orbit satellite repair.

8/30/1984: *Discovery (41-D)*; 7 days; Henry W. Hartsfield Jr. (2), Michael L. Coats, Richard M. Mullane, Steven A. Hawley, Judith A. Resnik, Charles D. Walker. 1st flight of non-astronaut (payload specialist Walker).

10/5/1984: *Challenger (41-G)*; 9 days; Robert L. Crippen (4), Jon A. McBride, Kathryn D. Sullivan, Sally K. Ride (2), David C. Leestma, Marc Garneau, Paul D. Scully-Power. 1st seven-person crew.

11/8/1984: *Discovery (51-A)*; 8 days; Frederick H. Hauck (2), David M. Walker, Anna L. Fisher, Dale A. Gardner (2), Joseph P. Allen (2). 1st satellite retrieval/repair.

4/12/1985: *Discovery (51-D)*; 7 days; Karol J. Bobko, Donald E. Williams, Charles D. Walker (2), M. Rhea Seddon, Jeffrey A. Hoffman, S. David Griggs, E. Jake Garn. Garn (R, UT) was **1st U.S. senator in space**.

6/17/1985: *Discovery (51-G)*; 8 days; Daniel C. Brandenstein (2), John O. Creighton, Shannon W. Lucid, John M. Fabian (2), Steven R. Nagel, Prince Sultan Salman al-Saud, Patrick Baudry. Launched three satellites; Salman al-Saud was 1st Arab in space; Baudry was 1st French person on U.S. mission.

10/3/1985: *Atlantis (51-J)*; 5 days; Karol J. Bobko (3), Ronald J. Grabe, David C. Hilmers, Robert L. Stewart (2), William A. Pailes. 1st *Atlantis* flight.

10/30/1985: *Challenger (61-A)*; 8 days; Henry W. Hartsfield Jr. (3), Steven R. Nagel (2), James F. Buchli (3), Guion S. Bluford Jr. (2), Bonnie J. Dunbar, Wubbo J. Ockels, Reinhard Furrer, Ernst Messerschmid. 1st eight-person crew; 1st German Spacelab mission.

1/12/1986: *Columbia (61-C)*; 7 days; Robert L. Gibson (2), Charles F. Bolden Jr., Franklin R. Chang Díaz, Steven A. Hawley (2), George D. Nelson (2), Robert J. Cenker, Bill Nelson. B. Nelson (D, FL) was **1st U.S. representative in space**.

1/28/1986: *Challenger (51-L)*; 73 seconds; Francis R. Scobee (2), Michael J. Smith, Judith A. Resnik (2), Ellison S. Onizuka (2), Ronald E. McNair, Gregory B. Jarvis, Christa McAuliffe. **Exploded 73 seconds after liftoff; all aboard were killed,** including McAuliffe, a New Hampshire schoolteacher who won competition to become 1st private citizen in space.

2/20/1986: *Mir[1]*; launched without crew. **Space station** with six docking ports launched.

3/13/1986: *Soyuz T-15*; 125 days; Leonid Kizim (3), Vladimir Solovyov (2). Ferry between stations; docked at *Mir.*

9/29/1988: *Discovery (STS-26)*; 4 days; Frederick H. Hauck (3), Richard O. Covey (2), George D. Nelson (3), John M. Lounge (2), David C. Hilmers (2). **1st shuttle flight since *Challenger* explosion** 1/28/1986.

5/4/1989: *Atlantis (STS-30)*; 4 days; David M. Walker (2), Ronald J. Grabe (2), Norman E. Thagard (3), Mary L. Cleave (2), Mark C. Lee. Launched Venus orbiter *Magellan.*

10/18/1989: *Atlantis (STS-34)*; 5 days; Donald E. Williams (2), Michael J. McCulley, Shannon W. Lucid (2), Franklin R. Chang Díaz (2), Ellen S. Baker. Launched Jupiter probe and orbiter *Galileo.*

4/24/1990: *Discovery (STS-31)*; 6 days; Loren J. Shriver (2), Charles F. Bolden Jr. (2), Steven A. Hawley (3), Bruce McCandless (2), Kathryn D. Sullivan (2). **Launched Hubble Space Telescope.**

10/6/1990: *Discovery (STS-41)*; 5 days; Richard N. Richards (2), Robert D. Cabana, Bruce E. Melnick, William M. Shepherd (2), Thomas D. Akers. Launched *Ulysses* spacecraft to investigate interstellar space and the sun.

9/12/1992: *Endeavour (STS-47)*; 8 days; Robert L. Gibson (4), Curtis L. Brown Jr., Mark C. Lee (2), N. Jan Davis, Jay Apt (2), Mae Carol Jemison, Mamoru Mohri. Jemison was **1st black woman in space;** Lee and Davis were **1st married couple to travel together in space**; 1st Japanese Spacelab.

6/21/1993: *Endeavour (STS-57)*; 10 days; Ronald J. Grabe (4), Brian J. Duffy (2), G. David Low (3), Nancy J. Sherlock, Janice E. Voss, Peter J. K. Wisoff. Carried Spacelab commercial payload module.

12/2/1993: *Endeavour (STS-61)*; 11 days; Richard O. Covey (3), Kenneth D. Bowersox (2), F. Story Musgrave (5), Kathryn Thornton (3), Claude Nicollier (2), Jeffrey A. Hoffman (4), Thomas D. Akers (3). Hubble Space Telescope repaired; Akers set new U.S. EVA duration record (29 hr., 40 min.).

3/14/1995: *Soyuz TM-21*; 112 days; Norman E. Thagard (5), Vladimir Dezhurov, Gennady Strekalov (5). Docked with *Mir* 3/16. Thagard was 1st American on board Russian spacecraft; Valery Polyakov returned to Earth, 3/22/1995, after record stay in space (439 days).

6/27/1995: *Atlantis (STS-71)*; 10 days; Robert L. Gibson (5), Charles J. Precourt (2), Ellen S. Baker (3), Bonnie J. Dunbar (4), Gregory J. Harbaugh (3), Anatoly Solovyev (4) (to *Mir*), Nikolai M. Budarin (to *Mir*), Norman E. Thagard (from *Mir*), Gennady Strekalov (from *Mir*), Vladimir Dezhurov (from *Mir*). **1st shuttle-*Mir* docking**; exchanged crew members with *Mir.*

11/12/1995: *Atlantis (STS-74)*; 9 days; Kenneth D. Cameron (3), James D. Halsell Jr. (2), Jerry L. Ross (5), William S. McArthur Jr. (2), Chris A. Hadfield. 2nd shuttle-*Mir* docking (11/15-11/18); erected a 15-ft permanent docking tunnel to *Mir* for future use by U.S. orbiters.

9/16/1996: *Atlantis (STS-79)*; 11 days; William F. Readdy (3), Terry W. Wilcutt (2), Thomas D. Akers (4), John E. Blaha (5) (to *Mir*), Jay Apt (4), Carl E. Walz (3), Shannon W. Lucid (5) (from *Mir*). Docked with *Mir* 9/18; exchanged crew members; Lucid set **U.S. and women's duration in space record** (188 days).

11/19/1996: *Columbia (STS-80)*; 18 days; Kenneth D. Cockrell (3), Kent V. Rominger (2), Tamara E. Jernigan (4), Thomas D. Jones (3), F. Story Musgrave (6). Longest-duration shuttle flight; Musgrave, 61, oldest thus far to fly in space; two science satellites deployed, retrieved.

8/5/1997: *Soyuz TM-26*; 198 days; Anatoly Solovyev (5), Pavel Vinogradov. Docked with *Mir* 8/7; repaired damaged space station.

8/7/1997: *Discovery (STS-85)*; 12 days; Curtis L. Brown Jr. (4), Kent V. Rominger (3), N. Jan Davis (3), Robert L. Curbeam Jr., Stephen K. Robinson, Bjarni V. Tryggvason. Deployed and retrieved satellite designed to study Earth's middle atmosphere; demonstrated robotic arm.

4/17/1998: *Columbia (STS-90)*; 16 days; Richard A. Searfoss (3), Scott D. Altman, Richard M. Linnehan (2), Dave R. Williams, Kathryn P. Hire, Jay C. Buckey, James A. Pawelczyk. Studied effects of microgravity on the nervous systems of the crew and

6/2/1998: *Discovery (STS-91)*; 10 days; Charles J. Precourt (4), Dominic L. Gorie, Wendy B. Lawrence (3), Franklin R. Chang Díaz (6), Janet L. Kavandi, Valery V. Ryumin (4), Andrew S. W. Thomas (2) (from *Mir*). Final docking mission with *Mir*; Thomas from *Mir*, 141 days in space.

10/29/1998: *Discovery (STS-95)*; 10 days; Curtis L. Brown Jr. (5), Steven W. Lindsey (2), Scott E. Parazynski (3), Stephen K. Robinson (2), Pedro Duque, Chiaki Mukai (2), John H. Glenn Jr. (2). The 77-year-old Glenn, one of the original *Mercury* astronauts, and at that point a senator (D, OH), became **oldest person to fly in space**; Duque was 1st Spaniard in space; experiments to study aging performed on Glenn.

12/4/1998: *Endeavour (STS-88)*; 12 days; Robert D. Cabana (4), Frederick W. Sturckow, Nancy J. Currie (3), Jerry L. Ross (6), James H. Newman (3), Sergei K. Krikalev (4). **1st assembly of International Space Station (ISS)**; attached U.S.-built *Unity* connecting module to Russian-built *Zarya* control module; 1st crew to enter ISS.

7/23/1999: *Columbia (STS-93)*; 5 days; Eileen M. Collins (4), Jeffrey S. Ashby, Steven A. Hawley (5), Catherine G. Coleman (2), Michel Tognini (2). Collins was **1st woman space shuttle commander**; deployed Chandra X-ray Observatory telescope.

2/11/2000: *Endeavour (STS-99)*; 12 days; Kevin R. Kregel (4), Dominic L. Gorie (2), Janet L. Kavandi (2), Janice E. Voss (5), Mamoru Mohri (2), Gerhard P.J. Thiele. Used radar to make most complete topographic map of Earth's surface ever produced.

10/31/2000: *Soyuz TM-31*; William M. Shepherd (4), Yuri Gidzenko (2), Sergei Krikalev (5). Established **1st permanent manning of ISS** with three-person crew for a 4-month stay.

7/12/2001: *Atlantis (STS-104)*; 13 days; Steven W. Lindsey (3), Charles O. Hobaugh, Michael L. Gernhardt (4), Janet L. Kavandi (3), James F. Reilly II (2). Installed the Joint Airlock, with nitrogen and oxygen tanks to permit future spacewalks from the ISS; three EVAs.

10/30/2002: *Soyuz TMA-1*[1]; Sergei Zalyotin (2), Frank De Winne (2), Yuri Lonchakov (2). 1st launch of *Soyuz TMA* (crew returned 11/10/2002 on *Soyuz TM-34* already docked at ISS).

1/16/2003: *Columbia (STS 107)*; 16 days; Rick D. Husband (2), William C. McCool, Michael P. Anderson (2), David M. Brown, Kalpana Chawla (2), Laurel B. Clark, Ilan Ramon. **Entire crew lost when Columbia broke apart** upon reentry, 2/1, due to heat shield damage; Ramon was 1st Israeli astronaut.

10/15/2003: *Shenzhou 5*; 21 hr.; Yang Liwei. **1st Chinese manned spacecraft.**

6/21/2004: *SpaceShipOne*[2]; 90 min.; Mike Melvill. **1st privately funded manned spaceflight.**

7/26/2005: *Discovery (STS-114)*; 14 days; Eileen M. Collins (4), James M. Kelly (2), Charles J. Camarda, Wendy B. Lawrence (4), Soichi Noguchi, Stephen K. Robinson (3), Andrew S.W. Thomas (3). **1st space shuttle flight since Columbia disaster**; tested new safety modifications to craft.

6/8/2007: *Atlantis (STS-117)*; 14 days; Frederick W. Sturckow (3), Lee J. Archambault, Patrick G. Forrester (3), John "Danny" Olivas, James F. Reilly (3), Steven R. Swanson, Clayton C. Anderson (to ISS), Sunita L. Williams (from ISS). Delivered truss segments and solar arrays to ISS; Williams set new record for **longest spaceflight by a woman (195 days)**.

8/8/2007: *Endeavour (STS-118)*; 13 days; Scott J. Kelly (2), Charles O. Hobaugh (2), Alvin B. Drew, Barbara R. Morgan, Tracy Caldwell Dyson (to ISS), Rick A. Mastracchio (2), Dave R. Williams (2). Brought **Teacher in Space** project participant Morgan to ISS; attached new truss.

10/10/2007: *Soyuz TMA-11*[1]; Yuri I. Malenchenko (3), Sheikh Muszaphar Shukor (to ISS), Peggy A. Whitson (2) (from ISS), Yi So-yeon (from ISS). Delivered and installed components of ISS; malfunctioned on return to Earth, landing short of its touchdown area but causing no fatalities.

3/11/2008: *Endeavour (STS-123)*; 16 days; Dominic L. Gorie (4), Gregory H. Johnson, Richard M. Linnehan (4), Robert L. Behnken, Michael J. Foreman, Takao Doi (2), Garrett E. Reisman (to ISS), Léopold Eyharts (from ISS). Delivered components of the Japanese Kibo science laboratory.

4/8/2008: *Soyuz TMA-12*[1]; Oleg Kononenko, Sergei Volkov, Yi So-yeon (to ISS), Richard Garriott (from ISS). Yi became **1st S. Korean in space.**

9/25/2008: *Shenzhou 7*; 68 hr.; Jing Haipeng, Liu Boming, Zhai Zhigang. Zhai completed **1st Chinese spacewalk.**

5/11/2009: *Atlantis (STS-125)*; 13 days; Scott D. Altman (4), Gregory C. Johnson, Andrew J. Feustel, Michael T. Good, John M. Grunsfeld (5), Michael J. Massimino (2), K. Megan McArthur. Final Hubble Space Telescope servicing mission.

6/15/2010: *Soyuz TMA-19*[1]; Fyodor Yurchikhin (3), Shannon Walker, Douglas H. Wheelock (2). 100th mission since launching of the International Space Station.

7/8/2011: *Atlantis (STS-135)*; 13 days; Christopher Ferguson (3), Doug Hurley (2), Sandy H. Magnus (3), Rex J. Walheim (3). **Final space shuttle mission.**

5/30/2020: *SpaceX Demo-2*; Robert L. Behnken (3), Douglas G. Hurley (3). **1st commercially operated crewed spaceflight** to carry Americans into orbit.

Note: Four Soviet cosmonauts have died during spaceflight: one person was killed on *Soyuz 1* (1967) when parachute lines tangled during descent; the three-person *Soyuz 11* crew (1971) was asphyxiated. Three Americans died in the *Apollo 1* (1967) fire on the ground at Cape Canaveral, FL; seven Americans died in the *Challenger* (1986) explosion; and six Americans and an Israeli astronaut died aboard *Columbia* (2003). (1) *Soyuz* crew often return from the ISS on spacecraft that launched and were docked at the station before their arrival. (2) Date of first successful flight; later, *SpaceShipOne* flew at least 100 km (62 mi) into space, 9/29/2004, piloted by Mike Melvill, and 10/4/2004, piloted by Brian Binnie, winning the $10-mil Ansari Prize for first private venture to accomplish this feat twice within two weeks.

U.S. Space Shuttles
Source: National Aeronautics and Space Administration (NASA)

After 135 launches, the United States ended its space shuttle program with the safe landing of the *Atlantis* shuttle on July 21, 2011, at Florida's Kennedy Space Center. Two shuttles—*Challenger* in 1986 and *Columbia* in 2003—were destroyed in flight. The surviving shuttles are now on display at museums. *Enterprise* performed atmospheric test flights but never flew in space.

Atlantis: Kennedy Space Center, Titusville, FL; www.kennedyspacecenter.com
Discovery: Udvar-Hazy Center, Smithsonian National Air and Space Museum, Chantilly, VA; discovery.si.edu
Endeavour: California Science Center (CSC), Los Angeles, CA.

(As of mid-2023, began re-installation to vertical position in Samuel Oschin Air and Space Center, under construction at CSC.); www.californiasciencecenter.org
Enterprise: Intrepid Air, Sea, and Space Museum, New York, NY; www.intrepidmuseum.org/Space_Shuttle_Pavilion

International Space Station
Source: National Aeronautics and Space Administration (NASA)

Construction on the International Space Station (ISS) began in 1998 and was completed in 2011. It has been inhabited continuously since 2000 and visited by more than 269 crew members from 21 countries as of May 2023. In July 2022, Russia announced that it would no longer participate in the ISS after 2024.

Cooperating nations: Belgium, Canada, Denmark, France, Germany, Italy, Japan, Netherlands, Norway, Russia, Spain, Sweden, Switzerland, United Kingdom, and U.S. As of May 2023, individuals from all of these countries (except Norway and Switzerland) have flown to the ISS, as have visitors from Brazil, Israel, Kazakhstan, Malaysia, Saudi Arabia, South Africa, South Korea, and the United Arab Emirates.

About the ISS
- It has a mass of 924,739 lbs and is about as long as a football field at 357.5 ft.
- It is entirely powered by an acre of solar panels.
- It requires three people to keep it running but has room for up to 10 people to live aboard.
- Astronauts typically spend 4-6 months aboard.

ISS Research
- Effects of long-term exposure to reduced gravity on humans, plants, crystals, cells, and pathogens
- Recording large-scale long-term changes in Earth's environment by observing the planet from orbit
- Testing recycling technologies for human life support

Summary of Worldwide Successful Launches, 1957-2022

Source: National Aeronautics and Space Administration (NASA); Space Launch Report

Year	1957-59	1960-69	1970-79	1980-89	1990-99	2000-09	2010-19	2020	2021	2022	Total
Russia[1]	6	399	1,028	1,132	542	246	240	17	23	22	3,655
U.S.	18	614	247	191	300	206	209	32	41	73	1,931
China	—	—	8	16	33	52	194	35	52	62	452
ESA[2]	—	2	5	14	55	63	71	4	6	4	224
Ukraine	—	—	—	—	59	57	24	2	2	2	146
Japan	—	—	18	26	23	18	36	4	3	0	128
India	—	—	1	9	11	13	42	2	1	4	83
France[2]	—	4	14	5	16	0	0	0	0	0	39
New Zealand	—	—	—	—	—	—	7	6	5	9	27
UK[2]	—	1	6	4	7	0	0	0	0	0	18
Germany[2]	—	—	3	7	6	0	0	0	0	0	16
Canada	—	—	4	5	4	0	0	0	0	0	13
Israel	—	—	—	—	—	3	3	1	0	0	7
Iran	—	—	—	—	—	1	3	1	0	1	6
South Korea	—	—	—	—	—	1	0	0	0	1	2
North Korea	—	—	—	—	—	—	1	0	0	0	1
Total	**24**	**1,020**	**1,334**	**1,409**	**1,056**	**660**	**830**	**104**	**133**	**178**	**6,748**

— = Not applicable. (1) Data for 1957-91 apply to the Soviet Union, for 1992-96 to the Commonwealth of Independent States, after 1996 to Russia. (2) ESA = European Space Agency, which includes France, Germany, and UK after 2009.

Notable Lunar and Planetary Science Missions

Source: National Aeronautics and Space Administration (NASA)

Spacecraft	Launch date[1]	Mission	Mission notes
Mariner 2	Aug. 27, 1962	Venus	Passed within 22,000 mi of Venus 12/14/1962; confirmed high surface temperature on planet; contact lost 1/3/1963 at 54 mil mi.
Ranger 7	July 28, 1964	Moon	Yielded over 4,000 photos of lunar surface.
Mariner 4	Nov. 28, 1964	Mars	1st probe to fly by Mars; passed behind planet 7/14/1965.
Ranger 8	Feb. 17, 1965	Moon	Yielded over 7,000 photos of lunar surface.
Venera 3	Nov. 16, 1965	Venus	Soviet probe; 1st artificial probe to impact on the surface of another planet, 3/1/1966; probe failed to send back data.
Surveyor 3	Apr. 17, 1967	Moon	Scooped and tested lunar soil.
Mariner 5	June 14, 1967	Venus	In solar orbit; closest Venus flyby 10/19/1967; allowed scientists to obtain accurate readings on the composition of the Venusian atmosphere.
Mariner 6	Feb. 24, 1969	Mars	Came within 2,000 mi of Mars 7/31/1969; collected data, photos.
Mariner 7	Mar. 27, 1969	Mars	Came within 2,000 mi of Mars 8/5/1969.
Venera 7	Aug. 17, 1970	Venus	Soviet probe; 1st probe to land safely on the surface of another planet.
Mariner 9	May 30, 1971	Mars	1st craft to orbit Mars 11/13/1971; sent back over 7,000 photos.
Pioneer 10	Mar. 2, 1972	Jupiter	Passed Jupiter 12/4/1973; took readings on Jupiter's composition. Exited planetary system 6/13/1983; last signal received 1/23/2003 from 7.6 bil mi.
Pioneer 11	Apr. 5, 1973	Jupiter, Saturn	Passed Jupiter 12/3/1974, Saturn 9/1/1979; discovered an additional ring and 2 moons around Saturn. Transmission ended 9/30/1995.
Mariner 10	Nov. 3, 1973	Venus, Mercury	Passed Venus 2/5/1974, arrived at Mercury 3/29/1974. 1st time gravity of a planet (Venus) used to whip spacecraft toward another (Mercury); 1st probe to visit 2 planets.
Viking 1	Aug. 20, 1975	Mars	Landed on Mars 7/20/1976; 1st probe to land safely on Mars; performed chemical analysis of soil; functioned 6 years.
Viking 2	Sept. 9, 1975	Mars	Sister probe of Viking 1; landed on Mars 9/3/1976; functioned 3 years.
Voyager 2	Aug. 20, 1977	Jupiter, Saturn, Uranus, Neptune	Encountered Jupiter 7/9/1979, Saturn 8/25/1981, Uranus 1/24/1986, Neptune 8/25/1989. Confirmed existence of rings around Neptune. As of 9/2023 it was 12.5 bil mi from sun and still returning data to Earth.
Voyager 1	Sept. 5, 1977	Jupiter, Saturn	Encountered Jupiter 3/5/1979; provided evidence of rings around Jupiter; passed Saturn 11/12/1980; became most distant human-made object 2/17/1998. As of 9/2023 it was nearly 15.0 bil mi from sun and still returning data to Earth.
Pioneer Venus 1	May 20, 1978	Venus	Entered Venus orbit 12/4/1978; studied atmosphere, magnetic field, weather, and surface; fuel ran out; probe was destroyed in atmospheric entry, 8/1992.
Pioneer Venus 2 (multiprobe)	Aug. 8, 1978	Venus	Consisted of a "bus" carrying 1 large and 3 small atmospheric probes. All 4 probes entered the Venus atmosphere 12/9/1978.
Magellan	May 4, 1989	Venus	Landed on Venus 8/10/1990; monitored geological activity; mapped more than 99% of planet surface, showed that about 85% is covered by volcanic flows; ceased operating 10/11/1994.
Galileo	Oct. 18, 1989	Jupiter	Used Earth's gravity to propel itself towards Jupiter; encountered Venus 2/10/1990, Jupiter 12/7/1995; encountered moons. Released probe into Jovian atmosphere; intentionally flown into Jupiter 9/21/2003.
Mars Global Surveyor	Nov. 7, 1996	Mars	Began orbiting Mars 9/11/1997; began mapping entire surface 3/9/1999; discovered a weak magnetic field on planet; observed Martian moon Phobos; found evidence of liquid water in past 6/22/2000.
Mars Pathfinder	Dec. 4, 1996	Mars	Landed on Mars 7/4/1997; rover Sojourner measured climate and soil composition, sent surface images; ceased operating 9/27/1997.
Cassini-Huygens	Oct. 15, 1997	Saturn	Began orbiting Saturn 6/30/2004; spotted evidence of a subterranean ocean and hot spots region on moon Titan; detected an atmosphere on moon Enceladus. Intentionally destroyed 9/15/2017. Huygens probe landed on Titan 1/14/2005; found possible water ice, channels carved by liquid methane springs.

Spacecraft	Launch date[1]	Mission	Mission notes
Lunar Prospector	Jan. 6, 1998	Moon	Began orbiting moon 1/11/1998; mapped abundance of 11 elements on moon's surface; discovered evidence of water ice at both lunar poles.
Deep Space 1	Oct. 24, 1998	Comet Borrelly	Flew within 1,500 mi of comet; sent back photos showing 6-mi-long nucleus.
Stardust	Feb. 7, 1999	Comet Wild 2	Reached comet 1/2/2004; gathered dust samples, capsule returned to Earth 1/15/2006. Spacecraft, on new mission Stardust-NExT (follow-up for Deep Impact), reached comet Tempel 1, 2/14/2011.
2001 Mars Odyssey	Apr. 7, 2001	Mars	Reached Mars 10/24/2001; detected evidence of water ice near south pole; primary mission to study climate and geologic history completed 8/2004; began extended mission, aiming to identify minerals on Mars.
Genesis	Aug. 8, 2001	Sun	Orbited sun, collected particles from solar wind; capsule containing specimens crashed to Earth 9/8/2004; some samples survived.
Mars Express/ Beagle 2 lander	June 3, 2003	Mars	1st European Space Agency probe to another planet; arrived at Mars 12/2003; performed remote sensing including photography in search of subsurface water. Beagle 2 lander was deployed 12/19/2003, but contact was lost.
Mars Exploration Rovers	June 7 and July 10, 2003	Mars	Rovers Spirit and Opportunity landed on Mars 1/2004, found further evidence that water existed on surface; Spirit took 1st photo of a Martian meteor; survived severe dust storms in 2007. Opportunity explored massive Victoria Crater 2007-08, set record for most distance driven off-Earth (25 mi) 7/2014.
MESSENGER	Mar. 2, 2004	Mercury	Began returning images of Mercury during initial flyby 1/14/2008; entered orbit 3/17/2011; delivered 100,000th image 5/3/2012; impacted Mercury 4/30/2015.
Deep Impact	Jan. 12, 2005	Comet Tempel 1	Reached Tempel 1; deployed impact probe that slammed into comet 7/4/2005 with force roughly equivalent to 5 tons of TNT. Flyby spacecraft, on supplemental mission EPOXI, reached comet Hartley 2, 11/4/2010.
Mars Reconnaissance Orbiter	Aug. 12, 2005	Mars	Reached Mars 3/10/2006 and began taking detailed images of Martian surface; in 3/2008, found salt deposits suggesting ancient water supplies; in 6/2008, found largest known impact crater in solar system.
New Horizons (Pluto)	Jan. 19, 2006	Pluto, Charon	Flew past Pluto 7/2007 on its way to Pluto and its largest moon, Charon. Returned first-ever photographs of Pluto 7/14/2015. Began examining other objects in the Kuiper Belt in 2019.
Phoenix Mars Lander	Aug. 4, 2007	Mars	Landed on Mars 5/25/2008; examined northern polar region, analyzed weather/minerals; water ice verified 7/31/2008; lost contact 11/2/2008.
Dawn	Sept. 27, 2007	Asteroid Belt (bet. Jupiter and Mars)	Compared evolution of dwarf planet Ceres with Vesta, an asteroid, in an effort to shed light on formation of the solar system. Departed Vesta 8/2012; reached Ceres 3/6/2015.
Kepler/K2	Mar. 9, 2009	Extrasolar planets	Detected potentially habitable Earth-size planets around other Milky Way stars. Kepler confirmed existence of more than 2,600 exoplanets before running out of fuel in Oct. 2018.
Lunar Crater Observation and Sensing Satellite	June 18, 2009	Moon	Impacted the Cabeus crater; detected presence of water ice in moon's surface 10/9/2009. Lunar Reconnaissance Orbiter (LRO), launched with LCROSS, mapped moon's surface.
Juno	Aug. 5, 2011	Jupiter	Entered Jupiter's orbit 7/4/2016; began returning data and color images that improve understanding of the formation of the planet and solar system.
Mars Science Laboratory	Nov. 26, 2011	Mars	Curiosity rover landed on Mars 8/6/2012 and began assessing Mars's past and present ability to support life.
Lunar Atmosphere and Dust Environment Explorer	Sept. 6, 2013	Moon	Studied the fragile lunar atmosphere from orbit for 100 days; impacted with lunar surface 4/17/2014.
Mars Atmosphere and Volatile EvolutioN (MAVEN)	Nov. 18, 2013	Mars	Entered orbit 9/21/2014; exploring Mars's upper atmosphere to determine how planet's loss of atmospheric gas changed its climate from a warmer, wetter environment to a cold desert.
OSIRIS-REx	Sept. 8, 2016	Bennu (asteroid)	First mission to return a sample from an asteroid, aiming to better understand potential asteroid-Earth impacts and the source of Earth's organic materials and water. Entered orbit around Bennu 12/31/2018; returned to Earth 9/24/2023.
Transiting Exoplanet Survey Satellite	Apr. 18, 2018	Extrasolar planets	Survey 200,000 of the brightest nearby stars in search of planets outside our solar system.
InSight	May 5, 2018	Mars	Landed 11/26/2018; began drilling in 2019 beneath surface to investigate how rocky planets form and develop.
Parker Solar Probe	Aug. 12, 2018	Sun	First mission to observe the sun from within its atmosphere. Will fly within 3.8 mil miles of the sun's surface. Passed Venus 10/3/2018.
ICESat-2	Sept. 15, 2018	Earth	Initiated ultra-precise measurements of Earth's ice sheets and glaciers and how changes are affecting rising sea levels.
Mars Perseverance	July 30, 2020	Mars	Landed 2/18/2021; launched drone helicopter on first powered, controlled flight, 4/19/2021.
James Webb Space Telescope	Nov. 2021	Universe	Replaced Hubble Space Telescope as the world's premier astronomical observatory. Returned first high-resolution color images 7/2022.
Double Asteroid Redirection Test (DART)	Nov. 24, 2021	Dimorphos (asteroid)	Crashed into asteroid 9/26/2022 to assess human ability to alter its speed and orbit in order to prevent an asteroid or comet from hitting Earth.
Artemis I	Fall 2022	Moon	Explore lunar surface in preparation for human flight to Mars.
SPHEREx	June 2024	Milky Way galaxy and beyond	Spectro-Photometer for the History of the Universe, Epoch of Reionization and Ices Explorer will collect data on more than 300 million galaxies and 100 million stars to explore the origins of the universe.
Europa Clipper	Oct. 2024	Europa	Assess if Europa, Jupiter's icy, ocean-bearing moon, is suitable for life.
Quesst	2024	Suborbital	First flight of the X-59, aircraft that can travel at supersonic speed without causing thunderous sonic boom
Artemis III	2025	Moon	First human moon landing in more than 50 years. Explore lunar surface in preparation for human flight to Mars and study potential for habitation of the moon.

Note: U.S./NASA missions unless otherwise noted. (1) In Coordinated Universal Time.

General Aviation and Air Taxi Active Aircraft, 2021

Source: Federal Aviation Administration; aircraft not associated with major airlines or the military

Aircraft Type	Total active	Personal	Business	Instructional	Aerial apps.	Aerial observation	Other work	Sightseeing	Air medical	Other	On-demand operations
Fixed Wing......	**164,282**	**107,644**	**22,756**	**15,715**	**2,391**	**1,881**	**1,019**	**409**	**149**	**4,602**	**6,977**
Piston........	138,621	103,016	11,897	15,548	452	1,664	627	391	108	3,407	1,313
Turboprop.....	10,391	2,142	3,089	97	1,900	199	321	—	—	310	1,890
Turbojet......	15,270	2,486	7,770	71	38	—	70	—	27	885	3,762
Rotorcraft....	**10,032**	**1,470**	**482**	**1,056**	**726**	**2,129**	**59**	**187**	**105**	**732**	**2,389**
Piston........	3,012	1,047	114	854	284	236	—	156	0	127	152
Turbine.......	7,020	423	354	202	442	1,893	52	31	105	604	2,237
Other aircraft....	**4,271**	**3,025**	—	**564**	**0**	**0**	**0**	**515**	**0**	**77**	**0**
Gliders........	1,717	1,244	—	409	0	0	0	0	0	49	0
Lighter-than-air..	2,554	1,781	—	155	0	0	0	515	0	28	0
Experimental.....	**27,960**	**26,001**	**257**	**564**	**23**	**41**	**23**	**23**	—	**862**	**73**
Amateur......	21,953	20,759	147	274	—	0	—	—	—	525	73
Exhibition......	1,905	1,555	—	110	—	0	—	0	—	201	0
Experimental light-sport....	3,435	3,218	—	156	0	—	0	—	—	33	0
Other........	667	469	26	25	—	—	0	0	0	103	0
Special Light-sport	**2,650**	**2,167**	**38**	**368**	—	—	—	**0**	—	**56**	**0**
ALL AIRCRAFT...	**209,195**	**140,308**	**23,540**	**18,267**	**3,142**	**4,062**	**1,173**	**1,134**	**262**	**6,329**	**9,455**

— = Insufficient data. **Note:** Columns may not add to totals due to rounding. Totals include some categories not shown. **Personal**—Flying for personal reasons; **Business**—Individual or group use for business transportation with or without a professional crew (includes fractional ownership); **Instructional**—Flying under the supervision of a flight instructor; **Aerial applications**—Includes agriculture, forestry, public health, firefighting, and other applications; **Aerial observation**—Includes aerial mapping/photography, patrol, search and rescue, hunting, traffic advisory, ranching, surveillance, oil and mineral exploration, etc.; **Other work**—Construction work, parachuting, aerial advertising, towing gliders, etc.; **Sightseeing**—Commercial sightseeing; **Air medical services**—Air ambulance services, rescue, human organ transportation, emergency medical services; **Other**—Positioning flights, proficiency flights, training, ferrying, sales demos; **On-demand operations**—On-demand air taxi, air tours, commuter, and air medical services.

Estimated Active Airmen Certificates Held, 2022

Source: Federal Aviation Administration, U.S. Dept. of Transportation

Category	Certificates	Category	Certificates	Category	Certificates
Pilot total.............	756,928	Rotorcraft (helicopters only).............	13,180	Nonpilot total.........	737,582
Student.............	280,582	Glider (only).........	20,804	Mechanic............	320,042
Recreational (only)....	79	**Flight Instructor**		Repairmen..........	37,861
Sport (only)......	6,957	Certificates........	125,075	Parachute Rigger.....	7,495
Airplane[1]		Instrument		Ground Instructor.....	76,109
Private.............	164,090	Ratings........	321,217	Dispatcher...........	24,526
Commercial........	104,498	Remote Pilots[2]........	304,256	Flight Navigator.......	29
Airline Transport.....	166,738			Flight Attendant.......	246,195
				Flight Engineer........	25,325

Note: The term *airmen* includes men and women certified as pilots, mechanics, or other aviation technicians. (1) Includes pilots with an airplane-only certificate as well as those with an airplane and a helicopter and/or glider certificate. (2) Remote pilot certification began in Aug. 2016. These numbers are not included in pilot totals.

World's Most Commonly Flown Aircraft, 2023

Source: Forecast International; World Almanac research

Manufacturer, headquarters, and model	Number in operation	Avg. age (years)	Manufacturer, headquarters, and model	Number in operation	Avg. age (years)
Airbus, Netherlands			**Boeing (continued)**		
A319-100	1,120	17.7	787-8	370	8.3
A320-200	3,975	13.9	787-9 Dreamliner	583	5.5
A320 neo	1,645	3.4	**Bombardier, Canada**		
A321-200	1,549	10.5	RJ200ER	296	21.4
A321 neo	997	2.4	RJ200LR...................	116	21.5
A330-200	459	14.5	RJ700	278	17.9
A330-300	642	12.4	RJ900	418	11.1
A350-900XWB	441	4.3	**British Aerospace, UK**		
A380-800[1]	230	9.3	Jetstream 31 (Turboprop).............	184	34.5
ATR, France			**Cessna, U.S.**		
ATR-42-300 (Turboprop).....	151	33.0	208B (Turboprop)	447	31.0
ATR-72-500 (Turboprop).....	277	16.8	**De Havilland, Canada**		
ATR-72-600 (Turboprop).....	488	6.9	DHC-6-300 (Turboprop)	258	46.3
Boeing, U.S.			DHC-8-400Q[2] (Turboprop).........	448	12.1
717-200	142	21.4	DHC-8-102 (Turboprop)	128	34.6
737 MAX 8	983	3.2	**Embraer, Brazil**		
737 MAX 9	166	2.3	Embraer 175...............	165	9.3
737-300	348	30.6	Embraer 175LR	509	7.3
737-400	261	29.9	Embraer 190AR	208	14.4
737-500	193	29.9	Embraer 190LR	198	12.3
737-700	908	18.1	ERJ 145LR	281	21.8
737-800	4,587	12.1	**Fairchild, US**		
737-900ER	443	9.3	SA-227AC (Turboprop)	173	37.6
747-400[1].................	160	27.6	**Fokker, Netherlands**		
747-400F[1]................	133	23.5	Fokker 50	116	32.6
757-200	453	28.6	Fokker 100	160	31.0
757-200PF	121	29.9	**Raytheon**		
767-300ER	410	24.9	1900D....................	322	26.7
767-300F	227	10.2	**Saab, Sweden**		
777-200ER	300	21.3	SF.340B	192	29.7
777-300ER	774	10.4	**Sukhoi, Russia**		
777F.....................	239	7.2	Superjet 100-95	180	6.7

Note: All aircraft are two-engine planes except where indicated. (1) Four-engine. (2) Manufactured by Bombardier from 1992-2019.

Milestones in Aviation History

Source: National Aeronautics and Space Administration (NASA); Smithsonian National Air and Space Museum; Air Transport Association of America; National Museum of the U.S. Air Force (USAF); National Park Service, U.S. Dept. of the Interior

1903, Dec. 17: Brothers Wilbur and Orville Wright (U.S.) made the first human-carrying, powered flight near Kitty Hawk, NC. Each brother made two flights; the longest, about 852 ft, lasted 59 sec.

1908, May 14: Charles Furnas (U.S.), worker for Wright brothers, became first American airplane passenger.

1911, Feb.: The Burgess Company and Curtiss, Inc. receive authorization to build Wright planes, becoming the first licensed airplane manufacturer in the U.S.

1911, Sept. 23: First transportation of mail by airplane officially approved by the U.S. Postal Service.

1914, Jan. 1: First scheduled passenger airline service began.

1914, June 18: Lawrence Burst Sperry (U.S.) released the controls and stood in his airborne plane, successfully demonstrating his gyrostabilizer, the first autopilot system.

1918, Mar. 6: The Curtiss-Sperry "Flying Bomb" (U.S.) made its first successful flight. The first radio-controlled plane led to the development of cruise missiles.

1918, May 15: First scheduled airmail service began, between New York and Washington, DC, with intermediate stop in Philadelphia. In 1921, scheduled transcontinental airmail service began between New York City and San Francisco.

1919, June 14-15: Capt. John Alcock (UK) and Lt. Arthur W. Brown (U.S.) completed the first nonstop flight across the Atlantic Ocean. They traveled from Newfoundland, Canada, to Ireland in 16 hr., 12 min.

1923, Aug.: Rotating beacons enabled the first U.S. night flights.

1924, Apr. 6-Sept. 28: Two U.S. Army planes landed in Seattle, completing the first circumnavigation of the globe. They completed the 26,000-mi journey in 371 hours of flying time.

1926, May 12-13: Roald Amundsen (Norway), Umberto Nobile (Italy), Lincoln Ellsworth (U.S.), and Oscar Wisting (Norway) made the first flight over the North Pole, in a dirigible that flew between Spitsbergen, Norway, and Teller, AK. Two weeks earlier, Adm. Richard E. Byrd and Floyd Bennett (both U.S.) claimed to have made the first flight over the Pole (May 9, 1926) in a Fokker F-VII. But when Byrd's diary was released to the public in 1996, some historians began to question whether his plane had reached the Pole.

1927, May 20-21: Charles Lindbergh (U.S.) completed the first solo transatlantic flight in the *Spirit of St. Louis.* "Lucky Lindy" traveled 3,610 mi from New York to Paris in 33 hr., 29 min., 30 sec.

1929, Aug. 8-29: Hugo Eckener (Germany) piloted the *Graf Zeppelin* around the world in record time: 20,373 mi in 21 days, 5 hr., 31 min.

1929, Nov. 28: Richard E. Byrd, Harold June, Ashley McKinley (all U.S.) and Bernt Balchen (Norway) became first to fly over the South Pole, in 18 hr., 41 min. round trip from Ross Ice Shelf base.

1930, May 15: Ellen Church (U.S.) became first flight attendant.

1931, June 23-July 1: Wiley Post (U.S.) and Harold Gatty (Austral.-U.S.) broke the speed record for around-the-world flight, traveling 15,474 mi in 8 days, 15 hr., 51 min., in the monoplane *Winnie Mae.*

1931, Oct. 3-5: Clyde Pangborn and Hugh Herndon (both U.S.) completed the first nonstop transpacific flight. They traveled 4,558 mi from Misawa, Japan, to East Wenatchee, WA, in 41 hr., 34 min.

1932, May 20-21: Amelia Earhart (U.S.) completed first solo transoceanic flight by a woman, making the 2,026-mi journey from Newfoundland, Canada, to Ireland in 14 hr., 56 min.

1933, July 15-22: Wiley Post completed the first solo circumnavigation of the globe. His 15,596-mi trip took 7 days, 18 hr., 49 min.

1936, June 25: American Airlines began scheduled passenger service of the first Douglas DC-3 aircraft. The DC-3 was the first aircraft with a kitchen onboard and hence offered the first in-flight hot meal service.

1937, May 6: German *Hindenburg* zeppelin exploded in Lakehurst, NJ, killing 35 of the 97 people aboard (and one on the ground). The airship had made 34 transatlantic flights in 1936.

1938, July 10-13: Howard Hughes (U.S.) and four assistants established a new speed record for circumnavigating the globe: 14,824 mi in 3 days, 9 hr., 17 min.

1939, Aug. 27: The German-made Heinkel He 178 made the first successful flight powered by a jet engine.

1947, Oct. 14: Chuck Yeager (U.S.) broke the sound barrier, reaching Mach 1 in a Bell X-1 rocket-powered aircraft.

1947, Nov. 2: Howard Hughes piloted a Hughes H-4 Hercules on its only flight. The largest plane ever built at the time, the so-called *Spruce Goose* could carry 750 troops or two Sherman tanks.

1949, Mar. 2: James Gallagher (U.S.) piloted the first round-the-world flight refueled in midair. The *Lucky Lady* USAF B-50 covered 23,452 mi in 94 hr., 1 min. and refueled four times.

1950, Sept. 22: Col. David Schilling (USAF) made the first nonstop transatlantic jet flight, covering 3,300 mi in 10 hr., 1 min.

1952, Aug. 26: The UK bomber Canberra made the first round-trip transatlantic crossing on the same day, from Northern Ireland to Newfoundland, Canada, and back in 7 hr., 59 min.

1953, May 18: Jacqueline Cochran (U.S.) became the first woman to fly faster than the speed of sound.

1956, Mar. 10: Britain's Fairey FD-2 aircraft set a world speed record of 1,132 mph.

1956, Nov. 11: Convair B-58 (USAF), the first supersonic bomber, was introduced.

1957, Jan. 15-18: Three USAF B-52 Stratofortresses made the first nonstop global flight by jet planes. They were refueled in flight by KC-97 aerial tankers.

1958, Oct. 24: A Mirage III-A achieved Mach 2 (twice the speed of sound) in level flight, first European plane to do so.

1962, Nov. 29: Britain and France signed an agreement to jointly develop the Concorde, a supersonic plane that could fly twice as fast as most U.S. jets.

1969, June 5: The Soviet Tupolev Tu-144 became the first passenger airliner to break the sound barrier.

1970, May 26: The Tupolev Tu-144 became first passenger airline to exceed Mach 2 with a top speed of about 1,335 mph at 53,475 ft.

1976, Aug. 23: The Concorde began the first scheduled supersonic commercial service.

1977, Aug. 23: The *Gossamer Condor*, built by aeronautical engineer Paul MacCready (U.S.), successfully demonstrated human-powered flight through pedaling.

1979, June 12: MacCready's human-powered *Gossamer Albatross* crossed the English Channel in 2 hr., 49 min.

1981, July 7: MacCready-developed *Solar Challenger* became first solar-powered airplane to cross the English Channel.

1995, Aug. 15-16: The Concorde set a new around-the-world speed record for a passenger plane of 31 hr., 27 min., 49 sec.

1999, Mar. 1-21: Bertrand Piccard (Switz.) and Brian Jones (UK) completed the first around-the-world flight in a hot-air balloon. Their 29,055-mi journey lasted 19 days, 21 hr., 55 min.

2001, Aug. 13: Solar-powered, propeller-driven plane *Helios* (NASA) reached 96,863 ft, breaking altitude record for non-rocket-powered aircraft.

2002, June 19-July 4: Steve Fossett (U.S.) completed the first nonstop solo circumnavigation of globe in a balloon.

2003, Nov. 26: The Concorde flew its final flight.

2005, Mar. 1-3: Steve Fossett achieved the first nonstop solo circumnavigation in an airplane without refueling.

2011, Feb. 4: Northrop Grumman and the U.S. Navy reported the first successful flight for the unmanned X-47B fighter jet.

2012, May 22-31: SpaceX became the first private company to successfully launch (and later recover) a spacecraft to the International Space Station.

2016, July 26: *Solar Impulse 2* became first fuel-free plane to circumnavigate the globe. The 17-leg journey began in Mar. 2015.

2019, Apr. 13: *Stratolaunch* aircraft, with world's longest wingspan, made its maiden voyage (and perhaps its last; the company was put up for sale in June 2019). Its design enabled it to launch satellites into space from 35,000 ft, saving rocket fuel.

2020, May 31: A SpaceX Crew Dragon capsule safely delivered two NASA astronauts to the ISS, marking the first time a private spacecraft carried passengers into orbit without government involvement.

ASTRONOMY

Edited by Laurence A. Marschall, Prof. Emeritus, Dept. of Physics and Astronomy, Gettysburg College

Celestial Events Summary, 2024

There will be four eclipses in 2024: one total solar eclipse, one annular solar eclipse, one penumbral lunar eclipse, and one partial lunar eclipse. The most prominent and accessible solar eclipse, the total solar eclipse of Apr. 8, will be visible in a region stretching from the Eastern Pacific and north central Mexico, across the United States from Texas to Maine, and through New Brunswick and Newfoundland into the North Atlantic, passing through many highly populated urban areas. The other solar eclipse, the annular eclipse of Oct. 2, will be visible primarily in the Pacific Ocean and southernmost South America. The two lunar eclipses, Mar. 25 and Sept. 18, which will be widely visible in the Americas, Europe, and Africa, will produce a barely noticeable dimming of the moon since the full moon, in both cases, passes all or mostly through the outer part of Earth's shadow, the penumbra.

The best meteor showers for viewing may be the Eta Aquarids of May and the Perseids of Aug., which are likely to peak under dark moonless skies after midnight. The Draconids in Oct. also occur in relatively moonless skies and are best seen before midnight (unlike most other showers). Other meteor showers will be hampered by unfavorably bright moon phases in 2024, though some activity will be visible, especially from dark rural sites.

Venus will be visible in the morning sky Jan.-Apr., until it approaches conjunction with the sun in June, and reappears in the evening sky in Aug.-Dec. It will be most visible at the end of the year as it approaches greatest elongation. Mars is in morning sky all year. Jupiter is visible in the evening sky Jan.-May, reaching conjunction with the sun in May, and reappearing in the morning sky in June, where it will be visible until Dec., when it returns to the evening sky at opposition. Saturn is an evening object at the start of the year reaching conjunction in Feb., then visible in the morning sky in Apr. and becoming visible all night around opposition in Sept. and then as an evening object for the remainder of the year. Mercury, frequently too close to the sun for easy viewing, begins the year in the morning sky. It is in the morning sky in Feb., May, Sept., and Dec. and in the evening in Mar., July, and Nov. The best opportunities for seeing Mercury in the morning sky are near western elongation Jan. 12, May 9, Sept. 5 and Dec. 25, while the best opportunities to see it in the evening sky occur at eastern elongation on Mar. 24, July 22, and Nov. 16.

The crescent moon, with its subdued light, regularly pairs with the two brightest planets, Venus and Jupiter. Waxing crescent pairings are visible in the early evening soon after sunset, while waning crescent pairings are visible in the early morning before sunrise. In 2024 the waxing crescent moon pairs with Venus in Aug.-Dec. and with Jupiter in Jan.-Apr. The waning crescent pairs with Venus in Jan.-Mar. and with Jupiter in July-Nov. The moon will occult three bright planets this year: Mars on Apr. 6, May 5, and Dec. 18; Venus on Apr. 7; and Saturn on May 3, May 31, June 27, July 24, Aug. 21, Sept. 17, Oct. 14, Nov. 11, and Dec. 8. The most noticeable planetary conjunctions of the year occur when Venus and Mars pass close to each other on Feb. 22, Mars and Saturn on Apr. 10, and Mars and Jupiter on Aug. 14.

Astronomical Positions and Constants

Two celestial bodies are in **conjunction** when they are due north and south of each other, either in **right ascension** (with respect to the north celestial pole) or in **celestial longitude** (with respect to the north ecliptic pole). Celestial bodies in conjunction will rise and set at nearly the same time. For the inner planets—Mercury and Venus—**inferior conjunction** occurs when either planet passes between Earth and the sun, while **superior conjunction** occurs when either Mercury or Venus is on the far side of the sun. Celestial bodies are in **opposition** when their right ascensions differ by exactly 12 hours, or when their celestial longitudes differ by 180°. In this case one of the two objects in opposition will rise while the other is setting. **Quadrature** refers to the arrangement where the coordinates of two bodies differ by exactly 90°. These terms may refer to the relative positions of any two bodies as seen from Earth, but one of the bodies is so frequently the sun that mention of the sun is omitted in that case.

When objects are in conjunction, the alignment is not perfect, and one usually passes above or below the other. The geocentric angular separation between the sun and an object is termed **elongation**. Elongation is limited only for Mercury and Venus; the greatest elongation for each of these bodies is approximately the time for longest observation. **Perihelion** is the point in an object's orbit when it is nearest to the sun, and **aphelion** is the point when it is farthest from the sun. **Perigee** is the point in an orbit where an object is nearest Earth, **apogee** the point when it is farthest from Earth. An **occultation** of a planet or a star is an eclipse of it by some other body, usually the moon. A **transit** of the sun occurs when Mercury or Venus passes directly between Earth and the sun, appearing to cross the sun's disk.

The following were adopted as part of the International Astronomical Union System of Astronomical Constants (1976/2009): **Speed of light**, 299,792.458 km per sec., or about 186,282 statute mi per sec.; **solar parallax**, 8".794143; **astronomical unit** (AU or au, mean distance between the Earth and sun), 149,597,870,700 m, or 92,955,807 mi; **constant of nutation**, 9".2025; and **constant of aberration**, 20".49552.

Celestial Events Highlights, 2024

(In Coordinated Universal Time, or UTC, the standard time of the prime meridian.)

January

Mercury and **Mars** are low in the E just before sunrise.
Venus is in the E before sunrise.
Jupiter, Saturn, Uranus, and **Neptune** are visible low in the W in early evening.

Jan. 1: Moon at apogee
Jan. 3: Earth at perihelion
Jan. 4: Last quarter moon; Quarantid meteor shower; moon at descending node; Spica 2.0°S of moon
Jan. 8: Antares 0.8°S of moon
Jan. 10: Mars 4.2°N of moon
Jan. 11: New moon
Jan. 12: Mercury at greatest elongation: 23.5°W of sun
Jan. 13: Moon at perigee
Jan. 14: Saturn 2.1°N of moon

Jan. 17: Moon at ascending node
Jan. 18: First quarter moon; Jupiter 2.8°S of moon
Jan. 20: Pleiades 0.9°N of moon
Jan. 24: Pollux 1.7°N of moon
Jan. 25: Full moon
Jan. 27: Mercury 0.2°N of Mars; Regulus 3.6°S of moon
Jan. 29: Moon at apogee
Jan. 31: Moon at descending node

February

Mercury is visible in the SE just before sunrise in the first half of the month.
Venus and **Mars** are visible in the E before sunrise.
Jupiter and **Uranus** are visible in the W in the evening.
Saturn is too close to the sun for easy visibility.
Neptune is visible low in the W just after sunset.

Feb. 1: Spica 1.7°S of moon
Feb. 2: Mercury at aphelion; last quarter moon
Feb. 5: Antares 0.6°S of moon
Feb. 8: Mars 4.2°N of moon
Feb. 9: New moon
Feb. 10: Moon at perigee
Feb. 11: Saturn 1.8°N of moon
Feb. 13: Moon at ascending node
Feb. 15: Jupiter 3.2°S of moon
Feb. 16: First quarter moon; Pleiades 0.6°N of moon
Feb. 21: Pollux 1.6°N of moon
Feb. 22: Venus 0.6°N of Mars
Feb. 23: Regulus 3.6°S of moon
Feb. 24: Full moon
Feb. 25: Moon at apogee
Feb. 27: Moon at descending node
Feb. 28: Mercury at superior conjunction; Spica 1.5°S of moon; Saturn in conjunction with sun

March

Mercury is visible low in the W just after sunset.
Venus is visible low in the E just before sunrise.
Mars is visible in the E before sunrise.
Jupiter and **Uranus** are visible in the W after sunset.
Saturn and **Neptune** are too close to the sun for easy visibility.

Mar. 3: Antares 0.4°S of moon; last quarter moon
Mar. 8: Mars 3.5°N of moon; Venus 3.3°N of moon
Mar. 10: Moon at perigee; new moon
Mar. 12: Moon at ascending node
Mar. 14: Jupiter 3.6°S of moon
Mar. 15: Pleiades 0.4°N of moon
Mar. 17: First quarter moon; Neptune in conjunction with sun; Mercury at perihelion
Mar. 19: Pollux 1.5°N of moon; Venus at aphelion
Mar. 20: Vernal equinox, 03:07 UTC
Mar. 21: Venus 0.3°N of Saturn
Mar. 22: Regulus 3.6°S of moon
Mar. 23: Moon at apogee
Mar. 24: Mercury at greatest elongation: 18.7°E of sun
Mar. 25: Full moon; penumbral lunar eclipse
Mar. 26: Moon at descending node; Spica 1.4°S of moon
Mar. 30: Antares 0.3°S of moon

April

Mercury and **Venus** are too close to the sun for easy visibility.
Mars and **Saturn** are visible in the E before sunrise.
Jupiter and **Uranus** are visible in the W after sunset.
Neptune is visible low in the E just before sunrise.

Apr. 2: Last quarter moon
Apr. 6: Mars 2.0°N of moon; Saturn 1.2°N of moon; occultation of Saturn by moon
Apr. 7: Venus 0.4°S of moon; occultation of Venus by moon; moon at perigee
Apr. 8: Moon at ascending node; total solar eclipse; new moon
Apr. 10: Mars 0.4°N of Saturn; Jupiter 4.0°S of moon
Apr. 11: Pleiades 0.4°N of moon; Mercury at inferior conjunction
Apr. 15: Pollux 1.5°N of moon; first quarter moon
Apr. 18: Regulus 3.6°S of moon
Apr. 20: Moon at apogee
Apr. 22: Lyrid meteor shower; moon at descending node
Apr. 23: Spica 1.5°S of moon; full moon
Apr. 26: Antares 0.3°S of moon

May

Mercury is visible in the E just before sunrise.
Venus, Jupiter, and **Uranus** are too close to the sun for easy visibility.
Mars, Saturn, and **Neptune** are visible in the E before sunrise.

May 1: Last quarter moon
May 3: Saturn 0.8°N of moon; occultation of Saturn by moon
May 4: Eta-Aquarid meteor shower
May 5: Mars 0.2°S of moon; occultation of Mars by moon; moon at ascending node; moon at perigee

May 6: Mercury 3.8°S of moon
May 8: New moon; Mars at perihelion
May 9: Mercury at greatest elongation: 26.4°W of sun
May 12: Pollux 1.6°N of moon
May 13: Uranus in conjunction with sun
May 15: First quarter moon; Regulus 3.5°S of moon
May 17: Moon at apogee
May 18: Jupiter in conjunction with sun
May 19: Moon at descending node
May 20: Spica 1.4°S of moon
May 23: Full moon
May 24: Antares 0.4°S of moon
May 30: Last quarter moon
May 31: Saturn 0.4°N of moon; occultation of Saturn by moon

June

Mercury and **Venus** are too close to the sun for easy visibility.
Mars, Saturn, and **Neptune** are visible in the E before sunrise.
Jupiter and **Uranus** are visible in the E in the just before dawn.

June 2: Moon at ascending node; moon at perigee; Mars 2.4°S of moon
June 4: Venus at superior conjunction
June 5: Pleiades 0.4°N of moon
June 6: New moon
June 9: Pollux 1.7°N of moon
June 12: Regulus 3.3°S of moon
June 13: Mercury at perihelion
June 14: First quarter moon; moon at apogee; Mercury at superior conjunction
June 15: Moon at descending node
June 16: Spica 1.2°S of moon
June 20: Antares 0.3°S of moon; summer solstice, 20:51 UTC
June 22: Full moon
June 27: Moon at perigee; Saturn 0.1°S of moon; occultation of Saturn by moon
June 28: Mercury 4.7°S of Pollux; last quarter moon
June 29: Moon at ascending node

July

Mercury is visible low in the W just after sunset.
Venus is too close to the sun for easy visibility.
Mars, Jupiter, Saturn, Uranus, and **Neptune** are visible in the E before sunrise.

July 1: Mars 4.1°S of moon
July 2: Pleiades 0.3°N of moon
July 5: Earth at aphelion; new moon
July 7: Mercury 3.2°S of moon
July 8: Jupiter 4.7°N of Aldebaran
July 9: Regulus 3.1°S of moon
July 10: Venus at perihelion
July 12: Moon at apogee; moon at descending node
July 13: First quarter moon
July 14: Spica 0.9°S of moon
July 17: Antares 0.2°S of moon
July 20: Mars 4.7°S of Pleiades
July 21: Full moon
July 22: Mercury at greatest elongation: 26.9°E of sun
July 24: Moon at perigee; Saturn 0.4°S of moon; occultation of Saturn by moon
July 25: Mercury 1.7°S of Regulus
July 26: Moon at ascending node
July 27: Mercury at aphelion; Delta-Aquarid meteor shower
July 28: Last quarter moon
July 29: Pleiades 0.1°N of moon

August

Mercury is visible in the W just after sunset at the beginning of the month and low in the E just before sunrise at the end of the month.
Venus is visible low in the W just after sunset.
Mars, Jupiter, Saturn, Uranus, and **Neptune** are visible in the E after midnight.

Aug. 2: Pollux 1.8°N of moon

Aug. 4: Mars 4.9°N of Aldebaran; new moon; Venus 1.0°N of Regulus
Aug. 5: Regulus 2.9°S of moon; Venus 1.7°S of moon
Aug. 9: Moon at descending node; moon at apogee
Aug. 10: Spica 0.7°S of moon
Aug. 12: Perseid meteor shower; first quarter moon
Aug. 14: Antares 0.0°S of moon; Mars 0.3°N of Jupiter
Aug. 19: Mercury at inferior conjunction; full moon
Aug. 21: Saturn 0.4°S of moon; occultation of Saturn by moon; moon at perigee
Aug. 22: Moon at ascending node
Aug. 26: Pleiades 0.1°S of moon; last quarter moon
Aug. 30: Pollux 1.7°N of moon

September

Mercury is visible in the E just before sunrise.
Venus is visible low in the W just after sunset.
Mars and **Jupiter** are visible in the E after midnight.
Saturn and **Neptune** are visible all night, rising a few hours after sunset in the E and near the meridian at midnight.

Sept. 3: New moon
Sept. 5: Mercury at greatest elongation: 18.1°W of sun; moon at descending node; Venus 1.2°N of moon; moon at apogee
Sept. 6: Spica 0.6°S of moon
Sept. 8: Saturn at opposition
Sept. 9: Mercury 0.4°N of Regulus; Mercury at perihelion
Sept. 10: Antares 0.1°N of moon
Sept. 11: First quarter moon
Sept. 17: Saturn 0.3°S of moon; occultation of Saturn by moon
Sept. 18: Full moon; partial lunar eclipse; Venus 2.2°N of Spica; moon at perigee; moon at ascending node
Sept. 20: Neptune at opposition
Sept. 22: Pleiades 0.2°S of moon; autumnal equinox, 12:44 UTC
Sept. 24: Last quarter moon
Sept. 26: Pollux 1.6°N of moon
Sept. 29: Regulus 3.0°S of moon
Sept. 30: Mercury at superior conjunction

October

Mercury is too close to the sun for easy visibility.
Venus, Saturn, and **Neptune** are visible in the W after sunset.
Mars, Jupiter, and **Uranus** are visible in the E after midnight.

Oct. 2: Moon at descending node; annular solar eclipse; new moon; Moon at apogee
Oct. 5: Venus 3.0°N of moon
Oct. 7: Antares 0.2°N of moon
Oct. 10: First quarter moon
Oct. 14: Saturn 0.1°S of moon; occultation of Saturn by moon
Oct. 16: Moon at ascending node
Oct. 17: Moon at perigee; full moon
Oct. 19: Pleiades 0.1°S of moon
Oct. 21: Orionid meteor shower
Oct. 23: Pollux 1.7°N of moon; Mars 3.9°S of moon
Oct. 24: Last quarter moon
Oct. 25: Venus 3.0°N of Antares
Oct. 26: Regulus 2.9°S of moon
Oct. 29: Moon at descending node; Moon at apogee

November

Mercury is visible low in the W just after sunset.
Venus, Saturn, and **Neptune** are visible in the W after sunset.
Mars and **Jupiter** are visible in the E after midnight.
Uranus is visible most of the night, rising in the E after sunset and near the meridian at midnight.

Nov. 1: New moon
Nov. 3: Mercury 2.1°N of moon
Nov. 4: Antares 0.1°N of moon
Nov. 5: Venus 3.1°N of moon; S Taurid meteor shower
Nov. 9: First quarter moon
Nov. 10: Mercury 2.0°N of Antares
Nov. 11: Saturn 0.1°S of moon; occultation of Saturn by moon
Nov. 12: N Taurid meteor shower; moon at ascending node
Nov. 14: Moon at perigee
Nov. 15: Full moon
Nov. 16: Pleiades 0.1°S of moon; Mercury at greatest elongation: 22.5°E of sun
Nov. 17: Uranus at opposition; Leonid meteor shower
Nov. 20: Pollux 1.9°N of moon; Mars 2.4°S of moon
Nov. 22: Regulus 2.7°S of moon
Nov. 23: Last quarter moon
Nov. 25: Moon at descending node
Nov. 26: Moon at apogee
Nov. 27: Spica 0.4°S of moon

December

Mercury is visible in the E just before sunrise.
Venus, Saturn, Uranus, and **Neptune** are visible in the W after sunset.
Mars is visible in the E before sunrise.
Jupiter is visible most of the night, rising in the E after sunset and near the meridian at midnight.

Dec. 1: New moon
Dec. 4: Venus 2.3°N of moon
Dec. 6: Mercury at inferior conjunction; Mercury at perihelion
Dec. 7: Jupiter at opposition
Dec. 8: Saturn 0.3°S of moon; occultation of Saturn by moon; first quarter moon
Dec. 9: Moon at ascending node
Dec. 12: Moon at perigee
Dec. 13: Pleiades 0.1°S of moon
Dec. 14: Geminid meteor shower
Dec. 15: Full moon
Dec. 17: Pollux 2.0°N of moon
Dec. 18: Mars 0.9°S of moon; occultation of Mars by moon
Dec. 20: Regulus 2.5°S of moon
Dec. 21: Winter solstice, 09:20 UTC
Dec. 22: Ursid meteor shower; last quarter moon; moon at descending node
Dec. 24: Moon at apogee; Spica 0.2°S of moon
Dec. 25: Mercury at greatest elongation: 22.0°W of sun
Dec. 28: Antares 0.1°N of moon
Dec. 30: New moon

Moon Phases, 2024

(In Coordinated Universal Time, or UTC, the standard time of the prime meridian.)

New Moon			Waxing Quarter			Full Moon			Waning Quarter		
Date	Hr.	Min.	Date	Hr.	Min.	Date	Hr.	Min.	Date	Hr.	Min.
Jan. 11	11	57	Jan. 18	3	52	Jan. 25	17	54	Jan. 4	3	30
Feb. 9	22	59	Feb. 16	15	01	Feb. 24	12	30	Feb. 2	23	18
Mar. 10	9	00	Mar. 17	4	11	Mar. 25	7	00	Mar. 3	15	23
Apr. 8	18	21	Apr. 15	19	13	Apr. 23	23	49	Apr. 2	3	15
May 8	3	22	May 15	11	48	May 23	13	53	May 1	11	27
June 6	12	38	June 14	5	18	June 22	1	08	May 30	17	13
July 5	22	57	July 13	22	49	July 21	10	17	June 28	21	53
Aug. 4	11	13	Aug. 12	15	19	Aug. 19	18	26	July 28	2	51
Sept. 3	1	55	Sept. 11	6	05	Sept. 18	2	34	Aug. 26	9	26
Oct. 2	18	49	Oct. 10	18	55	Oct. 17	11	26	Sept. 24	18	50
Dec. 1	6	21	Dec. 8	15	26	Dec. 15	9	02	Oct. 24	8	03
Dec. 30	22	27							Dec. 22	22	18

Meteorites and Meteor Showers

When a chunk of material, ice or rock, plunges into Earth's atmosphere and burns up in a fiery display, the event is a **meteor**. While the chunk of material is still in space, it is a **meteoroid**. If a portion of the material survives passage through the atmosphere and reaches the ground, the remnant on the ground is a **meteorite**.

Meteorites found on Earth are classified into types, depending on their composition: **irons**, those composed chiefly of iron, a small percentage of nickel, and traces of other metals such as cobalt; **stones**, stony meteors consisting of silicates; and **stony irons**, containing varying proportions of both iron and stone.

Serious study of meteorites as non-Earth objects began in the 20th century. Scientists use sophisticated chemical analysis, X-rays, and mass spectrography in determining their origin and composition. Although most meteorites are now believed to be fragments of asteroids or comets, geochemical studies have shown that a few Antarctic stones came from the moon or from Mars, presumably ejected by the explosive impact of asteroids.

The largest known meteorite, estimated to weigh about 55 metric tons, is the Hoba meteorite near Grootfontein, Namibia. The Manicouagan impact crater in Quebec, Canada, with an estimated diameter of 60 mi, is one of the largest crater structures still visible on the surface of the Earth. Not obvious to the eye because of erosion, larger impact craters identified include the Vredefort crater in South Africa at 185 mi across

and the Sudbury crater in Ontario, Canada (125 mi). The Bedout impact site off the NW coast of Australia gained attention in 2004 when scientists identified further evidence in support of the idea that it may be linked to the Permian extinction event 250 mil years ago. A 2019 study of the Chicxulub impact crater (93 mi across) in Yucatán Peninsula and the Gulf of Mexico gave evidence of an associated mass extinction event at the end of the Mesozoic Era (66 mil years ago).

Meteor showers vary in strength, but usually the three most visible meteor showers of the year are the **Perseids**, around Aug. 13, the **Orionids**, around Oct. 21, and the **Geminids**, around Dec. 14. These showers feature meteors at the rate of about 60 per hour. Best observing conditions occur in the absence of moonlight, usually when the moon's phase is between waning crescent and waxing quarter.

For most meteor showers the cometary debris is relatively uniformly scattered along the comet's orbit. However, in the case of the **Leonid** meteor shower, which occurs every year around Nov. 17-18, the debris from Comet Temple-Tuttle seems to be bunched up in one stretch. Hence, the meteor shower produced in most years is relatively weak. However, about every 33 years, Earth encounters the bunched-up debris when it crosses the comet's orbit. Sometimes the expected shower is a disappointment, as in 1899 and 1933; at other times, the dense debris provides a spectacular show, as in 1833 and 1866. The Leonids stormed again more recently, producing rates of 1,000-3,000 meteors per hour in 2001.

Morning and Evening "Stars," 2024
(In Coordinated Universal Time, or UTC, the standard time of the prime meridian.)

	Morning	Evening		Morning	Evening
Jan.	Mercury Venus Mars	Jupiter Saturn Uranus Neptune	**July**	Mars Jupiter Saturn Uranus Neptune	Mercury Venus
Feb.	Mercury until Feb. 18 Venus Mars Saturn from Feb. 29	Mercury from Feb. 19 Jupiter Saturn until Feb. 28 Uranus Neptune	**Aug.**	Mercury from Aug. 20 Mars Jupiter Saturn Uranus Neptune	Mercury until Aug. 19 Venus
Mar.	Venus Mars Saturn Neptune from Mar. 18	Mercury Jupiter Uranus Neptune until Mar. 17	**Sept.**	Mercury until Sept. 30 Mars Jupiter Saturn until Sept. 8 Uranus Neptune until Sept. 20	Venus Saturn from Sept. 9 Neptune from Sept. 21
Apr.	Mercury from Apr. 12 Venus Mars Saturn Neptune	Mercury until Apr. 11 Jupiter Uranus	**Oct.**	Mars Jupiter Uranus	Mercury Venus Saturn Neptune
May	Mercury Venus Mars Jupiter from May 19 Saturn Uranus from May 14 Neptune	Jupiter until May 18 Uranus until May 13	**Nov.**	Mars Jupiter Uranus until Nov. 17	Mercury Venus Saturn Uranus from Nov. 18 Neptune
June	Mercury until June 14 Venus until June 4 Mars Jupiter from May 19 Saturn Uranus Neptune	Mercury from June 15 Venus from June 5	**Dec.**	Mercury from Dec. 7 Mars Jupiter to Dec. 7	Mercury until Dec. 6 Venus Jupiter from Dec. 7 Saturn Uranus Neptune

Greenwich Sidereal Time for 0h UTC, 2024
UTC = Coordinated Universal Time. Add 12 hours to obtain right ascension of mean sun.

Date	Hr.	Min.	Date	Hr.	Min.	Date	Hr.	Min.	Date	Hr.	Min.
Jan. 1	6	40.6	Apr. 10	13	14.9	July 9	19	9.7	Oct. 7	1	4.5
Jan. 11	7	20.0	Apr. 20	13	54.3	July 19	19	49.1	Oct.17	1	44.0
Jan. 21	7	59.5	Apr. 30	14	33.7	July 29	20	28.6	Oct. 27	2	23.4
Jan. 31	8	38.9	May 10	15	13.1	Aug. 8	21	8.0	Nov. 6	3	2.8
Feb. 10	9	18.3	May 20	15	52.6	Aug. 18	21	47.4	Nov. 16	3	42.2
Feb. 20	9	57.7	May 30	16	32.0	Aug. 28	22	26.8	Nov. 26	4	21.7
Mar. 1	10	37.1	June 9	17	11.4	Sept. 7	23	6.3	Dec. 6	5	1.1
Mar. 11	11	16.6	June 19	17	50.8	Sept. 17	23	45.7	Dec. 16	5	40.5
Mar. 21	11	56.0	June 29	18	30.3	Sept. 27	0	25.1	Dec. 26	6	19.9
Mar. 31	12	35.4									

Largest Telescopes

Astronomers indicate the size of telescopes not by length or magnification but by the diameter of the primary light-gathering component, such as the lens or mirror. The larger the diameter of the mirror or lens, the fainter the objects that can be detected. In principle, larger telescopes also have better resolving power—the ability to discern small details—than smaller telescopes. However, the Earth's atmosphere limits the details that can be seen using ground-based telescopes. That is why the Hubble Space Telescope, which orbits the Earth outside of its atmosphere, can achieve higher resolutions with its 2.4-m (7.9-ft) mirror than much larger telescopes on Earth. Adaptive optics systems can compensate for the blurring effects of the Earth's atmosphere, allowing ground-based telescopes to achieve higher levels of detail. Telescopes to detect ultraviolet, X-ray, and gamma radiation must be placed in space or high-altitude balloons because the atmosphere absorbs most of these types of radiation; as a result, such telescopes are generally much smaller than optical, infrared, and radio telescopes.

Refracting (lens) telescopes are currently not made with lens diameters of more than 40 in. Because **reflecting telescopes** can be made less expensively and with more precision than refracting telescopes, all modern large optical telescopes are made with mirrors. **Radio telescopes** are larger than optical telescopes because larger diameters are required to obtain equivalent resolution of radio's longer wavelengths. A technique called interferometry, originally developed for radio telescopes, uses arrays of telescopes to achieve better resolution.

Largest refracting (lens) optical telescope: Yerkes Observatory, 1 m (40 in.), at Williams Bay, WI

Largest reflecting (mirror) optical/infrared telescope: Gran Telescopio Canarias, 10.4 m (34 ft), on La Palma, Canary Islands (segmented mirror)

Largest infrared interferometer: Four 8.2-m (27-ft) telescopes of the Very Large Telescope Interferometer (VLTI) with a 200-m (656-ft) baseline on Cerro Paranal in Chile

Largest fully steerable radio dish: Robert Byrd Green Bank Telescope (GBT), 100 m (328 ft), in Green Bank, WV

Largest single radio dish: Five-hundred-meter Aperture Spherical Telescope (FAST), 500 m (1,640 ft), in Guizhou, China

Largest baseline radio interferometer: 10 25-m (82-ft) diameter telescopes of the Very Long Baseline Array (VLBA), dispersed from Hawaii to the Virgin Islands with a resolution equal to a radio dish of 8,600 km (5,000 mi), making it the highest resolution telescope in the solar system

Largest submillimeter interferometer: 54 12-m (39-ft) and 12 7-m (23-ft) antennas of the Atacama Large Millimeter Array (ALMA), located at a site above 5,000 m (16,400 ft) in the Atacama Desert in Chile. The antennas can be spread out over a 16-km (10-mi) distance to increase the resolving power of the array.

Largest airborne telescope: Stratospheric Observatory for Infrared Astronomy (SOFIA), 2.5-m (8.2-ft) infrared telescope aboard a NASA 747

Largest space telescope: The James Webb Space Telescope (JWST), 6.5-m (21-ft) infrared reflecting telescope was successfully launched by NASA on Dec. 25, 2021, and began observations at the sun-earth L_2 point, in 2022.

Constellations

Culturally, constellations are imagined patterns among the stars that, in some cases, have been recognized through millennia. Knowledge of constellations was once necessary in order to function as an astronomer. For today's astronomers, constellations are simply areas of the sky in which objects await observation and interpretation.

Because Western culture has dominated much of modern scientific discourse, constellations and celestial traditions of other cultures are not widely known outside their regions of origin. Even the patterns with which we are most familiar today have undergone considerable change over the centuries.

Today, **88 constellations** are officially recognized. Although many have ancient origins, some are modern, devised out of unclaimed stars by astronomers a few centuries ago. Unclaimed stars were those too faint or inconveniently placed to be included in the more prominent constellations. Stars in a constellation are not necessarily near each other; they are just located in the same direction on the celestial sphere.

Common names of stars often referred to parts of the traditional figures they represented, such as Deneb, the tail of the swan, and Betelgeuse, the giant's shoulder. Astronomers may avoid traditional names by labeling stars with Greek letters, generally to denote order of brightness. The "alpha star" would typically be the brightest in a constellation. The "of" implies possession, so the genitive (possessive) form of the constellation name is used, e.g. Alpha Orionis (the first star of Orion) for Betelgeuse. (While Rigel is brighter than Betelgeuse, its designation is Beta Orionis, possibly because Betelgeuse appeared brighter when they were named.)

Asterisms are widely recognized patterns of stars. The so-called Big Dipper is a small part of the constellation Ursa Major, the big bear; the three stars of the Summer Triangle are each in a different constellation, often with Vega in Lyra the lyre, Deneb in Cygnus the swan, and Altair in Aquila the eagle. The northeast star of the asterism Great Square of Pegasus is Alpha Andromedae.

Name	Abbr.	Meaning	Name	Abbr.	Meaning	Name	Abbr.	Meaning
Andromeda	And	Chained Maiden	Cygnus	Cyg	Swan	Orion	Ori	Hunter
Antlia	Ant	Air Pump	Delphinus	Del	Dolphin	Pavo	Pav	Peacock
Apus	Aps	Bird of Paradise	Dorado	Dor	Dolphinfish	Pegasus	Peg	Flying Horse
Aquarius	Aqr	Water Bearer	Draco	Dra	Dragon	Perseus	Per	Hero
Aquila	Aql	Eagle	Equuleus	Equ	Little Horse	Phoenix	Phe	Phoenix
Ara	Ara	Altar	Eridanus	Eri	River	Pictor	Pic	Painter
Aries	Ari	Ram	Fornax	For	Furnace	Pisces	Psc	Fishes
Auriga	Aur	Charioteer	Gemini	Gem	Twins	Piscis Austrinus	PsA	Southern Fish
Boötes	Boo	Herder	Grus	Gru	Crane (bird)	Puppis	Pup	Stern (deck)
Caelum	Cae	Chisel	Hercules	Her	Hercules	Pyxis	Pyx	Compass (sea)
Camelopardalis	Cam	Giraffe	Horologium	Hor	Clock	Reticulum	Ret	Reticle
Cancer	Cnc	Crab	Hydra	Hya	Water Snake (female)	Sagitta	Sge	Arrow
Canes Venatici	CVn	Hunting Dogs				Sagittarius	Sgr	Archer
Canis Major	CMa	Greater Dog	Hydrus	Hyi	Water Snake (male)	Scorpius	Sco	Scorpion
Canis Minor	CMi	Littler Dog				Sculptor	Scl	Sculptor
Capricornus	Cap	Sea-Goat	Indus	Ind	Indian	Scutum	Sct	Shield
Carina	Car	Keel	Lacerta	Lac	Lizard	Serpens	Ser	Serpent
Cassiopeia	Cas	Queen	Leo	Leo	Lion	Sextans	Sex	Sextant
Centaurus	Cen	Centaur	Leo Minor	LMi	Littler Lion	Taurus	Tau	Bull
Cepheus	Cep	King	Lepus	Lep	Hare	Telescopium	Tel	Telescope
Cetus	Cet	Whale	Libra	Lib	Balance	Triangulum	Tri	Triangle
Chamaeleon	Cha	Chameleon	Lupus	Lup	Wolf	Triangulum Australe	TrA	Southern Triangle
Circinus	Cir	Compass (drawing)	Lynx	Lyn	Lynx	Tucana	Tuc	Toucan
			Lyra	Lyr	Lyre	Ursa Major	UMa	Greater Bear
Columba	Col	Dove	Mensa	Men	Table Mountain	Ursa Minor	UMi	Littler Bear
Coma Berenices	Com	Berenice's Hair	Microscopium	Mic	Microscope	Vela	Vel	Sail
Corona Australis	CrA	Southern Crown	Monoceros	Mon	Unicorn	Virgo	Vir	Maiden
Corona Borealis	CrB	Northern Crown	Musca	Mus	Fly	Volans	Vol	Flying Fish
Corvus	Crv	Crow	Norma	Nor	Square (rule)	Vulpecula	Vul	Fox
Crater	Crt	Cup	Octans	Oct	Octant			
Crux	Cru	Cross (southern)	Ophiuchus	Oph	Serpent Bearer			

Eclipses, 2024

(In Coordinated Universal Time, or UTC, the standard time of the prime meridian.)

There will be four eclipses in 2024: one total solar eclipse, one annular solar eclipse, one penumbral lunar eclipse, and one partial lunar eclipse. The most prominent and accessible solar eclipse, the total solar eclipse of Apr. 8, will be visible stretching from the E Pacific and north central Mexico, across the United States from Texas to Maine, and through New Brunswick and Newfoundland into the N Atlantic. The other solar eclipse, the annular eclipse of Oct. 2, will be visible primarily in the Pacific Ocean and southernmost South America. The penumbral lunar eclipse of Mar. 25 will be visible over much of North and South America, the Atlantic Ocean, easternmost Siberia and Australia, and westernmost Europe and Africa. The partial lunar eclipse of Sept. 18 will be visible over North and South America, the Atlantic Ocean, and most of Europe and Africa.

The tables below give the times in UTC of when the moon or sun will reach certain phases of each event. In the case of the lunar eclipses, the times are relevant for any observer who can see the moon. In the case of solar eclipses, the tabulated times refer to when the given event begins or ends from specific points along the eclipse path; as the moon's shadow sweeps quickly across the Earth, the observed duration and degree of eclipse depends on the observer's precise location. Interactive maps are available on the internet to calculate times for specific locations.

I. Penumbral Eclipse of the Moon: Mar. 25

This eclipse, with the moon passing several lunar radii north of the center of the earth's shadow, promises a relatively dark eclipse of the moon, but since it is penumbral, it will not be as notably dark as an umbral eclipse. It will be visible from sites in easternmost Siberia, Australia, the Pacific Ocean, North America, South America, the Atlantic Ocean, and westernmost Europe and Africa.

Event	Date	Hr.	Min.
Penumbral eclipse begins..	Mar. 25	04	53.1
Greatest eclipse	Mar. 25	07	12.8
Penumbral eclipse ends . . .	Mar. 25	09	33.0

II. Total Eclipse of the Sun: Apr. 8

This eclipse promises to be seen by a wide audience, since the path of totality passes through many heavily populated cities. The moon's shadow will touch down first in the S Pacific, reach land along the west coast of Mexico, cross the United States from central Texas to northern New England, then cross New Brunswick and Newfoundland into the N Atlantic. Times given below are for the midpoint of the eclipse path, just north of the town of Nazas in central Mexico, where the total eclipse lasts for 4 min., 28 sec.

Event	Date	Hr.	Min.
Partial eclipse begins	Apr. 8	16	58.4
Total eclipse begins	Apr. 8	18	15.1
Greatest eclipse	Apr. 8	18	17.3
Total eclipse ends	Apr. 8	18	19.5
Partial eclipse ends	Apr. 8	19	39.7

III. Partial Eclipse of the Moon: Sept. 18

This eclipse, with the moon just grazing the south edge of the umbra of the earth's shadow, will be similar in depth to the penumbral eclipse of Mar. 25, since the moon will be several lunar radii south of the center of the earth's shadow, and the time spent grazing the earth's umbra (the "partial" phase) will be relatively short, lasting about 1 hr., 4 min. It will be visible from North and South America, the Atlantic Ocean, and all of Europe and Africa.

Event	Date	Hr.	Min.
Penumbral eclipse begins. . .	Sept. 18	00	41.0
Partial eclipse begins	Sept. 18	02	12.7
Greatest eclipse	Sept. 18	02	44.2
Partial eclipse ends	Sept. 18	03	16.4
Penumbral eclipse ends . . .	Sept. 18	04	47.9

IV. Annular Eclipse of the Sun: Oct. 2

The partial phases of this eclipse will be visible from the eastern Pacific and central South America, but visibility of the annular eclipse phase is restricted to a narrow path across the central and western Pacific, crossing Easter Island, with the only other landfall a thin strip across southern Chile and Argentina. The times given below are for the midpoint of the eclipse, in the mid-Pacific, NW of Easter Island.

Event	Date	Hr.	Min.
Partial eclipse begins	Oct. 2	17	3.1
Annular eclipse begins	Oct. 2	18	41.3
Greatest eclipse	Oct. 2	18	45.1
Annular eclipse ends	Oct. 2	18	48.7
Partial eclipse ends	Oct. 2	20	32.7

Total Solar Eclipses, 2024-45

Total solar eclipses take place nearly as often as total lunar eclipses. Total lunar eclipses are visible over at least half of the Earth, while total solar eclipses can be seen only along a very narrow path up to a few hundred miles wide and a few thousand miles long. Observing a total solar eclipse is thus a rarity for most people, though the experience is so memorable that many enthusiasts travel long distances just to see totality.

Solar eclipses can be dangerous to observe. This is not because the sun emits more potent rays, but because the sun is always dangerous to observe directly, and people are particularly likely to stare at it during a solar eclipse.

Date	Duration[1] min.	sec.	Width (mi)	Path of totality
2024, Apr. 8	4	28	123	Mexico, U.S., E Canada
2026, Aug. 12	2	18	183	Greenland, Iceland, Spain
2027, Aug. 2	6	24	160	Spain, N Africa, Arabian peninsula
2028, July 22	5	10	140	Indian Ocean, Australia, New Zealand
2030, Nov. 25	3	45	105	Namibia, Botswana, South Africa, Indian Ocean, E Australia
2033, Mar. 30	2	37	485	Alaska, E Russia, Arctic
2034, Mar. 20	4	9	100	Central and NE Africa, Arabian Peninsula, Central and E Asia
2035, Sept. 2	2	54	72	China, Korea, Japan, Pacific Ocean
2037, July 13	3	58	125	Australia, New Zealand
2038, Dec. 26	2	18	96	Australia, New Zealand, South Pacific
2039, Dec. 15	1	51	236	Antarctica
2041, Apr. 30	1	51	45	Angola, Congo, Uganda, Kenya, Somalia
2042, Apr. 20	4	51	130	Malaysia, Indonesia, Philippines, N Pacific
2044, Aug. 23	2	4	281	Greenland, N. Canada, Montana, N. Dakota
2045, Aug. 12	6	6	159	U.S., Caribbean, NE S. America

(1) Length of time at optimal viewing area.

Total Solar Eclipses in the U.S. in the 21st Century

During the 21st century, there are eight total solar eclipses visible somewhere in the continental U.S. The first came after a long gap, in 2017. The last total solar eclipse before that had been on Feb. 26, 1979, in the northwestern U.S.

Date	Path of totality	Date	Path of totality
Aug. 21, 2017	Oregon to South Carolina	Mar. 30, 2052	Florida to Georgia
Apr. 8, 2024	Mexico to Texas and N through Maine	May 11, 2078	Louisiana to North Carolina
Aug. 23, 2044	Montana to North Dakota	May 1, 2079	New Jersey to the lower edge of New England
Aug. 12, 2045	Northern California to Florida	Sept. 14, 2099	North Dakota to Virginia

Beginnings of the Universe

One of the dominating astronomical discoveries of the 20th century was that the galaxies of the universe all seem to be moving away from Earth. Doppler redshifts were observed for spiral nebulae around 1920 even though they were not yet known to be galaxies. By the early 1930s, Edwin Hubble and M. L. Humason had established that the more distant a galaxy, the faster it was receding. It turned out that they were moving away not just from the Earth but from one another—that is, the **universe is expanding**. Scientists conclude that the universe must once, very long ago, have been extremely compact and dense, and a rapid expansion caused the energy and matter to rapidly expand. The beginning of this expansion is referred to as the **Big Bang**.

On the subatomic level, according to this theory, there were vast changes of energy and matter and the way physical laws operated during the first few minutes after the Big Bang. After those early minutes the percentages of the basic matter of the universe—hydrogen, helium, and lithium—were set. Everything was so compact and hot that radiation dominated the early universe and there were no stable, un-ionized atoms. The universe was opaque, in the sense that any energy emitted was quickly absorbed and then re-emitted as the universe expanded, density and temperature continued to drop. A few hundred thousand years after the Big Bang, the temperature dropped far enough that electrons and nuclei could combine to form stable atoms as the universe became transparent. Once that occurred, the radiation that had been trapped was free to escape.

In the 1940s, George Gamow and others predicted that remnants of this escaped radiation should be observable. They had started to search for this background radiation when physicists Arno Penzias and Robert Wilson, using a radio telescope, inadvertently found it, for which they won the 1978 Nobel Prize in Physics.

In 2003, NASA's Wilkinson Microwave Anisotropy Probe made measurements of the temperature of this **cosmic microwave background radiation** to within millionths of a degree. From these measurements, scientists were able to deduce that our universe is 13.7 billion years old and that first-generation stars began to form a mere 200 mil years after the Big Bang.

In 2014, scientists operating a telescope in Antarctica claimed to have found direct evidence for cosmic inflation, the rapid expansion of the universe during the 10-32 sec. after the Big Bang that helps explain why variations of the cosmic background radiation are so small. Follow-up observations cast doubt on this, and higher precision measurements are planned.

A related mystery is evidence suggesting hidden matter and hidden energy that cannot be directly observed. The presence of dark matter is indicated by the rotation curves of galaxies and the dynamics of clusters of galaxies. **Dark matter** may be composed of gas; large numbers of cool, compact objects like dead stars; or even subatomic particles. Evidence for **dark energy** is derived from studies of distant Type Ia supernovae indicating that the expansion of the universe is accelerating rather than slowing. Dark energy seems to work on the very fabric of the universe, acting as a force that increases the rate at which space expands. Visible matter seems to constitute only about 4% of the total mass of the universe while the rest of the universe's mass is in the form of dark matter (27%) and dark energy (68%).

Galaxies

By the 20th century, more than 10,000 **nebulae**—cloud-like luminous objects in the sky—had been discovered. Some were correctly identified as star clusters and others as clouds of gas and dust. Those nebulae which were spiral or elliptical in shape were found in regions of the sky far from the glowing band that is our own Milky Way galaxy. Philosopher Immanuel Kant had written in 1775 that some of these fuzzy objects might be **"island universes"** apart from our own. But the idea remained speculative until 1923-24, when Edwin Hubble discovered variable stars—stars whose varying brightness makes their distance from Earth calculable—in some of these nebulae. This provided conclusive evidence that these systems were far enough away to be outside our own island universe, the Milky Way galaxy.

Galaxies range in size from small dwarf elliptical ones, with perhaps 1 million stars, to spiral galaxies containing 300 billion stars, to giant elliptical galaxies that may be home to more than 10 trillion stars. The diameters of galaxies range from 3,000 light-years in dwarf elliptical galaxies to over 500,000 light-years in giant elliptical galaxies. It is estimated that the Milky Way galaxy is about 100,000 light-years in diameter with about 400 billion stars.

Galaxies also congregate into **clusters**. The smallest are poor clusters of only a few dozen galaxies, while the largest rich clusters may contain thousands. The Milky Way is part of a poor cluster of about three dozen galaxies called the **Local Group**. The largest galaxy of the Local Group is Andromeda, a spiral galaxy visible to the unaided eye in the constellation of Andromeda on a very dark night. The Milky Way is the second largest galaxy in this group; most of the others are small.

The Solar System

The major planets of the solar system, in order of mean distance from the sun, are **Mercury, Venus, Earth, Mars, Jupiter, Saturn, Uranus**, and **Neptune**. The dwarf planets in order of average distance from the sun are **Ceres** (located between Mars and Jupiter), **Pluto, Haumea, Makemake, 2007 OR10**, and **Eris**. All planets orbit counterclockwise around the sun as viewed from above the Earth's North Pole.

Because Mercury and Venus are nearer to the sun than is Earth, their motions about the sun appear from Earth as wide swings first to one side of the sun then to the other, though both planets move around the sun in almost circular orbits. When their passage takes them between Earth and the sun or beyond the sun in relation to Earth, they cannot be seen.

The planets that lie farther from the sun than does Earth may be seen for longer periods. They are invisible only when so located in the sky that they rise and set at about the same time as the sun and are thus overwhelmed by the sun's light.

Mercury and Venus, because they are between Earth and the sun, show phases much as the moon does. The planets farther from the sun are always seen as full, although Mars does occasionally present a slightly gibbous phase, like the moon when it is not quite full.

The planets appear to move rapidly among the stars because they are relatively closer to Earth. The stars are also in motion, some at tremendous speeds, but they are so far away that their motion does not change their apparent positions in the heavens enough to be perceived. The nearest star is about 9,000 times farther away than Neptune. The count for identified **moons** in the solar system orbiting planets and dwarf planets stood at 290 as of mid-2023. Several dwarf planet candidates are also known to have moons.

Planet Superlatives

Largest, most massive planet	Jupiter	Smallest, least massive planet	Mercury
Fastest orbiting planet	Mercury	Slowest orbiting planet	Neptune
Fastest sidereal rotation	Jupiter	Slowest sidereal rotation	Venus
Longest (synodic) day	Mercury	Shortest (synodic) day	Jupiter
Rotational pole closest to ecliptic	Uranus	Hottest planet	Venus
Most moons	Saturn	No moons	Mercury, Venus
Planet with largest moon	Jupiter	Planet with moon with most eccentric orbit	Neptune
Greatest average density	Earth	Lowest average density	Saturn
Tallest mountain	Mars	Deepest oceans	Jupiter
Strongest magnetic fields	Jupiter	Greatest amount of liquid water on surface	Earth
Most circular orbit	Venus		

Selected Characteristics of the Sun and Planets

Object	Radius—at unit distance[1]	Radius—at mean least distance[2]	in mi mean radius	Volume[3]	Mass[3]	Density[3]	Sidereal period d.	hr.	min.	sec.	Gravity at surface[3]	Reflecting power[4]	Daytime surface temp. (°F)
Sun	959.5	976.0	432,500	1,304,000	333,000	0.26	25	9	7		28.00	—	9,941
Mercury	3.36	6.5	1,516	0.0562	0.0553	0.98	58	15	36		0.38	0.11	845
Venus	8.34	33.0	3,760	0.857	0.815	0.95	243		30R		0.91	0.65	867
Earth	8.78	—	3,959	1.000	1.000	1.00		23	56	4.2	1.00	0.37	59
Moon	2.40	986.2	1,079	0.0203	0.0123	0.61	27	7	43	40	0.16	0.12	260
Mars	4.67	12.8	2,106	0.151	0.107	0.71		24	37	22	0.38	0.15	−24
Jupiter	96.40	24.5	43,441	1,321.30	317.83	0.24		9	55	30	2.53	0.52	−162
Saturn	80.29	10.05	36,184	763.6	95.16	0.12		10	39	20	1.06	0.47	−218
Uranus	34.97	2.05	15,759	63.1	14.54	0.23		17	14	20R	0.90	0.51	−323
Neptune	33.95	1.2	15,301	57.7	17.15	0.3		16	6	40	1.14	0.41	−330

R = Retrograde rotation. (1) Angular radius, in seconds of arc, if object were seen at a distance of 1 astronomical unit. (2) Angular radius, in seconds of arc, when object is closest to Earth. (3) Earth = 1. (4) A value of 1 would indicate a perfect reflector.

Planets of the Solar System

The International Astronomical Union (IAU) on Aug. 24, 2006, at their General Assembly in Prague, Czech Republic, agreed on a new definition for planet, and in the process effectively removed Pluto's planet status. The ruling came after years of debate as to whether Pluto, discovered in 1930, should still be considered the ninth planet in our solar system because of its size, orbit, and other characteristics. New discoveries of other Pluto-like objects in the solar system, such as the 2003 discovery of Eris, a **Kuiper Belt object** (KBO) comparable in size to Pluto, also contributed to the debate.

Under the IAU's new definition, Mercury, Venus, Earth, Mars, Jupiter, Saturn, Uranus, and Neptune are regarded as "classical" planets. A **planet** is now defined as a celestial body that (a) is in orbit around the sun, (b) has sufficient mass for its self-gravity to overcome rigid body forces so that it assumes a hydrostatic equilibrium (nearly round) shape, and (c) has cleared the neighborhood around its orbit.

Pluto, Eris, Ceres, Makemake, 2007 OR10, and Haumea are regarded as dwarf planets, with the status of Pluto's largest moon, Charon, still to be determined. A **dwarf planet** is a celestial body that (a) is in orbit around the sun, (b) has sufficient mass for its self-gravity to overcome rigid body forces so that it assumes a hydrostatic equilibrium (nearly round) shape, (c) has not cleared the neighborhood around its orbit, and (d) is not a satellite.

The IAU also created a new category, **small solar system bodies**, for all other objects orbiting the sun, including comets, asteroids, KBOs, and other small objects. It has not yet established a process by which other solar system objects will be classified.

Note: AU = astronomical unit (92.96 mil mi, mean distance of Earth from the sun); **d.** = 1 Earth synodic (solar) day (24 hours); **synodic day** = rotation period of a planet measured with respect to the sun (the "true" day, i.e., the time from midday to midday, or from sunrise to sunrise); **sidereal day** = rotation period of a planet with respect to the stars.

Mercury

Distance from the sun
Perihelion . . . . 28.6 mil mi
Semi-major axis (mean distance). . . . 36 mil mi (0.387 AU)
Aphelion. . . . . 43.4 mil mi
Period of revolution around sun . . . . 87.97 d.
Orbital eccentricity. 0.2056
Orbital inclination. . . . . 7.00°
Synodic day (midday to midday) . . . . .175.94 d.
Sidereal day. . . . . .58.65 d.
Rotational inclination . . . . .0.01°
Mass (Earth = 1) 0.0553
Mean radius . . . . .1,516 mi
Mean density (Earth = 1). 0.984
Natural satellites 0
Average surface temperature . . . . 333°F

Mercury, named for the Roman gods' messenger, is the closest planet to the sun and the smallest planet in the solar system. Mercury orbits so close to the sun that it can never be observed against a dark sky; it is always seen during morning or evening twilights. In 2008, the *Messenger* spacecraft made the first fly-bys of Mercury since the 1970s. *Messenger* went into orbit about Mercury in Mar. 2011 for a reconnaissance mission; the original one-year science program was extended in 2012. The goals of the mission included mapping, imaging, and measuring the surface composition of Mercury, as well as probing the planet's interior structure and interactions with the sun. Among the discoveries were that at least part of Mercury's metallic core is liquid, that there may be water ice in shadowed craters near the poles, and that the planet's magnetic field is offset from the planet's center.

Orbit and rotation. Mercury moves with great speed around the sun, averaging about 30 mi per second to complete its orbit, which takes about 88 Earth days. Mercury takes nearly 59 days to rotate on its axis. Because its orbital period is only about 50% longer than its sidereal rotation, the time from one sunrise to the next on Mercury is about 176 days—twice as long as a Mercurial year. Oddly, Mercury has a magnetic field, albeit a very weak one. It has been held that both a fluid core and rapid rotation—neither of which Mercury was believed to have—are necessary for the generation of a planetary magnetic field. Mercury may demonstrate the contrary.

Atmosphere. Mercury's atmosphere is almost nonexistent. What very little it has is composed of 42% oxygen, 29% sodium, 22% hydrogen, 6% helium, 0.5% potassium, and 0.5% other particles. Because of Mercury's lack of atmosphere, the surface during the day may reach a temperature of about 845°F, while the temperature at night may fall as low as −300°F. Earth-based observation has provided evidence of water ice near the poles.

Surface and composition. Mercury's surface is rocky and cratered similar to that of the Earth's moon. The most imposing feature on Mercury, the Caloris Basin, is a huge impact crater more than 800 mi in diameter. Mercury has a huge iron core that extends out to about 75% of the planet's radius; it has a higher percentage of iron than any other planet in the solar system.

Venus

Distance from the sun
Perihelion . . . . 66.8 mil mi
Semi-major axis (mean distance). . 67.2 mil mi (0.723 AU)
Aphelion. . . . . 67.7 mil mi
Period of revolution around sun . . . . .224.7 d.
Orbital eccentricity. 0.0067
Orbital inclination. . . . . .3.39°
Synodic day (midday to midday) . . . . .116.75 d. (retrograde)
Sidereal day. .243.02 d. (retrograde)
Rotational inclination . . . . .177.4°
Mass (Earth = 1) 0.815
Mean radius . . . . .3,760 mi
Mean density (Earth = 1). 0.951
Natural satellites 0
Average surface temperature . . . . 867°F

Venus, named for the Roman goddess of love, is the second planet out from the sun. Because Venus is almost the same size as Earth, it is believed that the two planets were formed at the same time by the same general process and from the same mixture of chemical elements. Venus can easily be seen from Earth with the naked eye; it is the third-brightest object in the sky, exceeded only by the sun and the moon.

Orbit and rotation. It takes Venus 225 Earth days to complete its orbit around the sun. Its synodic revolution—the amount of time it takes for Venus to return to the same position relative to Earth and the sun, which is a result of the combination of its own motion with that of Earth—is 584 days. Because of this, every 19 months Venus is closer to Earth than to any other planet. The rotation period of Venus appears to be 243 days clockwise. In other words, its rotation is counter to the rotation of the other planets and counter to its own motion around the sun. This rate and sense of rotation make for a solar day (sunrise to sunrise) on Venus of 116.8 Earth days. Night lasts 58 days, and day lasts 58 days. Venus has no detectable magnetic field.

Atmosphere. The Venusian atmosphere is very thick and toxic. It is composed primarily of 96.5% carbon dioxide, 3.5% nitrogen, and trace concentrations of sulfur dioxide, argon, water, carbon monoxide, helium, and neon. In addition, it exerts an atmospheric pressure at the surface more than 90 times Earth's normal sea-level pressure. The planet is covered with a dense, white, cloudy atmosphere that conceals whatever is below. These clouds are believed to contain sulfuric acid, meaning that it rains sulfuric acid on Venus. Due to the thickness of the atmosphere and resulting extreme greenhouse effect, the temperature is essentially the same day and night; the planet has an average surface temperature of about 867°F, making it the hottest planet in the solar system. Winds of about 200 mph in the clouds may account for the consistency in temperature despite the low rotation speed of the planet. However, at the surface, the winds are very slow.

Surface and composition. Radar-produced maps of the planet show large craters, continent-sized highlands, and extensive dry lowlands. No tectonic activity has been found similar to Earth's moving tectonic plates, but a system of global rift zones and numerous broad, low, dome-like structures, called coronae, may have been produced by the upwelling and subsidence of magma from the mantle. Volcanic surface features, such as vast lava plains, fields of small lava domes, and large shield volcanoes, are common. About 1,600 volcanoes and volcanic features appear on the Venusian surface; more than 85% of the surface is covered by volcanic flows. Theia Mons, a huge shield volcano, has a diameter of over 600 mi and a height of over 3.5 mi. (The largest Hawaiian volcano is only about 125 mi in diameter but rises nearly 5.5 mi from the ocean floor.) In recent years, evidence of continuous volcanic activity has been noted by astronomers. Aside from volcanoes, there are highly deformed mountain belts across Venus along with a few meteor-impact craters more than 20 mi wide. Erosion is a very slow process on Venus due to the lack of water. There are indications of some wind movement of dust and sand. The few impact craters on Venus suggest that the surface is generally geologically young—less than 800 mil years old. Despite the fact that probes have landed on Venus, there are very few pictures from the surface because the probes couldn't withstand the high temperature and atmospheric pressure for more than a few hours.

Mars

Distance from the sun	
Perihelion	128.4 mil mi
Semi-major axis (mean distance)	141.6 mil mi (1.524 AU)
Aphelion	154.9 mil mi
Period of revolution around sun	686.98 d. (1.88 yr.)
Orbital eccentricity	0.0935
Orbital inclination	1.85°
Synodic day (midday to midday)	24 hr., 39 min., 35 sec.
Sidereal day	24 hr., 37 min., 22 sec.
Rotational inclination	25.19°
Mass (Earth = 1)	0.107
Mean radius	2,106 mi
Mean density (Earth = 1)	0.713
Natural satellites	2
Average surface temperature	−81°F

Named for the Roman god of war, the Red Planet has some features much like Earth. Mars has climate, seasons, volcanoes, and possibly once had liquid water flowing across its surface. Mars can easily be seen with the naked eye on most clear nights, which is why it was one of the first planets to be studied by ancient astronomers. Later, when telescopes came into use, many observers claimed that canals made by Martians existed on the planet's surface, which led to speculation as to whether there was intelligent life there. Unmanned probes have since put all those theories to rest; the canals turned out to be topographic patterns and dust storms.

Mars is currently being explored by a number of robotic craft, both on the surface and in orbit. The *Curiosity*/Mars Science Laboratory, an SUV-sized robot, landed on the surface in Aug. 2012. Its mission was to understand the history of the Martian geology and climate, search for the presence of organic matter, and assess the planet's past suitability for life. An Indian orbiter is currently using remote sensing to study the Martian surface and atmosphere, while NASA's *MAVEN* spacecraft is studying the upper atmosphere of Mars and its interaction with the solar wind. The European Space Agency *Trace Gas Orbiter* (TGO) began orbiting Mars in Oct. 2016. NASA's *InSight* mission, which landed in 2018, was relaying seismic data that is being used to map the interior of Mars. In 2020, three spacecraft were launched to the red planet, all arriving successfully in 2021: NASA's *Perseverance* lander, equipped with a helicopter named *Ingenuity*, and Mars missions by China and by the United Arab Emirates.

Orbit and rotation. Although Mars's orbital path is nearly circular, it is somewhat more eccentric than that of most other planets. Mars is more than 26 mil mi farther from the sun at its most distant point compared to its closest approach. Its orbit and speed in relation to Earth's bring it fairly close to Earth, at opposition, about every two years. Mars was at opposition on Dec. 8, 2022, and will be close again on Jan. 16, 2025. Every 15-17 years the close approaches are especially favorable for observation. The July 27, 2018, opposition was the last one that was particularly close, and the next such favorable opposition occurs on Sept. 15, 2035.

Mars rotates in 24 hr. and 37 min., almost the same period of time as Earth. Mars's mean distance from the sun is 142 mil mi. Because Mars's axis of rotation is inclined by about 25° from the vertical to the plane of its solar orbit about the sun, the planet has seasons.

Unlike Earth's global magnetic field, the Martian magnetic field is small, weak, and localized and may be the remnant of a stronger field from the planet's past.

Atmosphere. The Martian atmosphere is composed primarily of 95.32% carbon dioxide, 2.7% nitrogen, 1.6% argon, 0.13% oxygen, 0.08% carbon monoxide, and, in very minor quantities, water, hydrogen oxide, and neon. The atmosphere on Mars is very thin. It has an atmospheric pressure between 1% and 2% of Earth's (if Earth's atmosphere were that thin, there would not be enough oxygen to breathe). Because the Martian atmosphere is so thin and because of the planet's weak magnetic field, its surface is bombarded by cosmic radiation about 100 times as intense as on Earth.

Martian weather systems consist mainly of huge dust storms. On the poles, white caps (believed to be both water ice and carbon dioxide ice) grow in winter and shrink in summer. It is mainly the carbon dioxide that comes and goes with the seasons. The water ice is apparently in many layers with dust between them, indicating climatic cycles.

Surface and composition. Mars is an alien world with rust-red sand and pink skies. In the planet's beginning stages when it was much hotter, Mars's surface melted to a sufficient extent to separate into dense and lighter layers. Mars later cooled enough to allow liquid water to possibly flow across its surface. NASA scientists announced in Sept. 2015 the most convincing evidence to date that liquid water flows on the present-day Martian surface. Using imaging and spectroscopy instruments on the Mars Reconnaissance Orbiter, they showed that seasonal flows on Martian slopes contain hydrated minerals that can only form in the presence of liquid water.

Natural satellites. Mars has two small satellites called Phobos and Deimos, each discovered in 1877 by American astronomer Asaph Hall. (Phobos measures about 11 by 17 mi and Deimos about 7 by 9 mi.) Deimos, the outer satellite, revolves around the planet in about 31 hours. Phobos, the inner satellite, whips around Mars in a little more than 7 hours, making three orbits each Martian day. Since it orbits Mars faster than the planet rotates, Phobos rises in the west and sets in the east, opposite to what other bodies appear to do in the Martian sky. Both moons are irregularly shaped and pitted with numerous craters. Their origins are not known; however, some astronomers consider them to be asteroid-like objects that were captured by Mars very early in its history.

Jupiter

Distance from the sun	
Perihelion	460.1 mil mi
Semi-major axis (mean distance)	483.8 mil mi (5.204 AU)
Aphelion	507.4 mil mi
Period of revolution around sun	11.862 yr.
Orbital eccentricity	0.0489
Orbital inclination	1.304°
Synodic day (midday to midday)	9 hr., 55 min., 33 sec.
Sidereal day	9 hr., 55 min., 30 sec.
Rotational inclination	3.13°
Mass (Earth = 1)	317.8
Mean radius	43,441 mi
Mean density (Earth = 1)	0.24
Natural satellites	95
Average temperature*	−162°F

*i.e., temperature where atmospheric pressure equals 1 Earth atmosphere.

Jupiter, named for the Roman ruler of the gods, is the largest planet in the solar system (11 times the diameter of Earth). Its mass is more than twice the mass of all the other planets, moons, and asteroids put together. Visible to the naked eye and known to the ancients, it was a focus of the Italian scientist Galileo Galilei, who viewed the planet and its four largest moons through a homemade telescope.

Orbit and rotation. Jupiter is at an average distance of 484 mil mi from the sun and takes almost 12 Earth years to make a complete revolution. The largest of the planets, Jupiter has an equatorial diameter of 88,846 mi; its polar diameter is more than 5,700 mi shorter. This noticeable oblateness is a result of the liquidity of the planet and its extremely rapid rotation rate—a Jupiter day is less than 10 Earth hours long. A point on Jupiter's equator moves at a speed of 22,000 mph, as compared with 1,000 mph for a point on Earth's equator. Jupiter's magnetic field is by far the strongest of any planet. Electrical activity caused by this field is so strong that it discharges trillions of watts into Jupiter's environment daily. In July 2016, NASA's *Juno* spacecraft entered orbit around the planet to begin a study of Jupiter's composition, magnetic field, and auroras, including close-up views of the poles of the planet. In 2021, it began sending back images of Jupiter's satellites as well as the planet itself. Originally planned for one-year operation, in 2021 the mission was extended until Sept. 2025 or until the spacecraft ceases to function.

Atmosphere. Jupiter's atmosphere is primarily composed of 90% molecular hydrogen and 10% helium. Minor constituents include methane, ammonia, hydrogen deuteride, ethane, and water. Jupiter has a turbulent atmosphere characterized by thick clouds, high winds, and huge lightning storms many times larger than those on Earth. The atmospheric temperature varies, but the temperature at the tops of clouds may be about –280°F. The Great Red Spot seen prominently on Jupiter is a huge hurricane-like storm that is three times the diameter of Earth. In 2006, the Hubble Space Telescope detected the appearance of a second, smaller red spot.

Surface and composition. Gas giant planets like Jupiter, Saturn, and Neptune do not have a surface like Earth or any of the other rocky planets. The gases become denser with depth, until they may turn into a slush or slurry. Jupiter has a liquid hydrogen ocean more than 35,000 mi deep. It likely has a rocky core about the size of Earth, but 13 times more massive. There is no sharp interface between the gaseous atmosphere and the hydrogen ocean that accounts for most of Jupiter's volume. At lower depths, under enormous pressure, the liquid hydrogen takes on the properties of a metal. It is likely that this liquid metallic hydrogen is the source for both Jupiter's persistent radio noise and for its improbably strong magnetic field.

Natural satellites. Jupiter has 95 known satellites, the latest discovered in 2023. Four of the moons (in order of distance from Jupiter), Io, Europa, Ganymede, and Callisto—all discovered by Galileo in 1610—are large and bright and are close in diameter to Earth's moon and Mercury. Because they move so rapidly around Jupiter, their change in position from night to night can be seen from Earth using binoculars.

Io is one of the most volcanically active bodies in the solar system. A gaseous, doughnut-shaped ring, or torus, enveloping Io's orbit around Jupiter may have been formed by material ejected from Io's active volcanoes. (This is not to be confused with Jupiter's rings.) These volcanoes, hotter than Earth's volcanoes, erupt mainly molten sulfur and result in a constantly changing surface appearance.

Europa may have a 30-mi-deep salty, liquid ocean beneath its icy crust, perhaps a small metallic core, and a very tenuous atmosphere. Ganymede is the biggest moon in the solar system. With a diameter of 3,120 mi, it is bigger than both Mercury and Pluto. Ganymede also has its own magnetic field produced by a molten core of perhaps iron sulfide. Callisto has the oldest, most heavily cratered surface in the solar system, a very thin atmosphere of carbon dioxide, and possibly a subsurface liquid ocean.

The other known satellites are much smaller, with four closer to Jupiter than Io, five between Ganymede and Callisto, and the rest farther out. Most of Jupiter's moons orbit the planet at high inclinations from the equator, unlike the innermost satellites. These moons may be captured asteroids.

Rings. Jupiter has a diffuse, dark set of rings that were discovered by the *Voyager 1* spacecraft and cannot be seen from Earth without powerful telescopes. They are composed of small dust grains blasted off the four innermost moons by meteoroid impacts.

Saturn

Saturn, named for the Roman ruler of the Titans, is the sixth planet from the sun and most distant of the planets visible to the unaided eye. Saturn is second in size to Jupiter, but its mass is much smaller. Saturn is the only planet less dense than water, meaning that Saturn would float if there were a pool of water gigantic enough to hold it.

Orbit and rotation. Saturn's diameter is almost 74,900 mi at the equator, while its polar diameter is more than 7,300 mi shorter. Like Jupiter, its noticeable oblateness is a result of the liquidity of the planet and its extremely rapid rate of rotation; a day is little more than 10 Earth hours long.

Distance from the sun	
Perihelion	840.44 mil mi
Semi-major axis (mean distance)	890.8 mil mi (9.582 AU)
Aphelion	941.07 mil mi
Period of revolution around sun	29.458 yr.
Orbital eccentricity	0.0565
Orbital inclination	2.485°
Synodic day (midday to midday)	10 hr., 39 min., 23 sec.
Sidereal day	10 hr., 39 min., 22 sec.
Rotational inclination	26.73°
Mass (Earth = 1)	95.159
Mean radius	36,184 mi
Mean density (Earth = 1)	0.125
Natural satellites	146
Average temperature*	−218°F
*i.e., temperature where atmospheric pressure equals 1 Earth atmosphere.	

Atmosphere. Saturn's atmosphere is composed primarily of 96.3% hydrogen, 3.3% helium, and traces of methane, ammonia, hydrogen deuteride, ethane, and water. Saturn's atmosphere is much like that of Jupiter, except that the temperature at the top of its cloud layer is at least 50°F colder.

Surface and composition. Saturn's atmosphere resembles Jupiter's; it likely has a small dense center surrounded by a deep ocean of hydrogen.

Natural satellites. Saturn has 146 known natural satellites, the discovery of the latest 62 announced in 2023. Saturn's moon Mimas has an impact crater 81 mi across (the moon itself is only 249 mi across). Enceladus has an atmosphere and shows evidence of geysers that spit water ice and vapor. Two tiny moons orbit within the rings, plowing through and making gaps in the rings along their orbits. Pan, the innermost satellite, creates the Encke Gap of Saturn's A-ring. Daphnis creates the Keeler Gap. The most intriguing Saturnian moon is Titan. The second-biggest moon in the solar system, Titan is bigger than Mercury. Its atmosphere is similar to Earth's atmosphere of long ago; it is made up of approximately 95% nitrogen with traces of methane. Titan's atmosphere extends about 360 mi into space whereas most of Earth's atmosphere lies within 37 mi of the surface. Photographs from Titan's surface, taken by the *Huygens* lander in 2005, show a muddy terrain, with possible deposits of water ice, channels carved by liquid methane springs, and an interesting boundary between light and dark material on the surface. In 2006, scientists found sand dunes on Titan's surface. The "sand" is believed to be tiny water ice crystals or organic compounds. Surface phenomena such as sand dunes are signs of erosion and wind. Unlike winds on Earth or Mars, Titan's winds are not the result of uneven solar heating on the moon's surface but rather Saturn's gravitational pull (similar to how the moon acts on the Earth's oceans).

Rings. Saturn's ring system is the planet's most recognizable feature. It begins about 4,000 mi above the visible disk of Saturn lying above its equator and extends about 260,000 mi into space. The diameter of the ring system visible from Earth is about 170,000 mi; the rings are estimated to be about 700 ft thick. The rings are composed of rock and ice and range in size from tiny particles to large chunks of material the size of a bus. There are several divisions in the rings. The 2,920-mi Cassini division, the gap between the A and B rings, is the largest division.

Uranus

Uranus, discovered by Sir William Herschel in 1781, was the first planet discovered using a telescope. It was named for the father of the Titans in Roman mythology.

Orbit and rotation. Uranus has a diameter of over 31,000 mi and spins once in approximately 17.23 hours, according to magnetic data collected by *Voyager 2*. One of the most fascinating features of Uranus is how far over it is tipped. Its north pole is 98° from its orbital plane. Thus, its seasons are extreme. Over its 84-year orbit, when the sun rises at the north pole, it shines there for about 42 Earth years; then it sets, and the north pole is in darkness for 42 Earth years. In addition to its rotational tilt, Uranus's magnetic field axis is tipped 58.6° from its rotational axis and is displaced about 30% of its radius away from the planet's center.

Distance from the sun	
Perihelion	1,703.4 mil mi
Semi-major axis (mean distance)	1,784.8 mil mi
	(19.201 AU)
Aphelion	1,866.4 mil mi
Period of revolution around sun	84.01 yr.
Orbital eccentricity	0.0457
Orbital inclination	0.772°
Synodic day (midday to midday)	17 hr., 14 min., 23 sec. (retrograde)
Sidereal day	17 hr., 14 min., 24 sec. (retrograde)
Rotational inclination	97.77°
Mass (Earth = 1)	14.536
Mean radius	15,759 mi
Mean density (Earth = 1)	0.23
Natural satellites	27
Average temperature*	−323°F
*i.e., temperature where atmospheric pressure equals 1 Earth atmosphere.	

Atmosphere. The atmosphere is composed primarily of 82.5% hydrogen, 15.2% helium, and 2.3% methane, with small amounts of hydrogen deuteride, ammonia ice, water ice, ammonia hydrosulfide, and methane ice.

Surface and composition. Uranus has no solid surface, and likely no rocky core but rather a mixture of rocks and assorted ices with about 15% hydrogen and some helium.

Natural satellites. Uranus has 27 known moons, which have orbits lying in the plane of the planet's equator. Five moons are relatively large, while 22 are very small and were only discovered with the *Voyager 2* mission or in later observations. Miranda has grooved markings, reminiscent of Jupiter's Ganymede, but often arranged in a chevron pattern. Rifts and channels on Ariel provide evidence of liquid flowing over its surface in the past. Umbriel is extremely dark, prompting some observers to regard its surface as among the oldest in the system. Titania has rifts and fractures but not the evidence of flow found on Ariel. Oberon's main feature is its surface saturated with craters, unrelieved by other formations.

Rings. In the equatorial plane there is also a complex of 11 rings, 9 of which were discovered in 1978 by observers watching Uranus pass before a star.

Neptune

Named for the Roman god of the sea, Neptune was the first planet discovered through mathematical predictions before it was directly observed. Its approximate orbit and position were first calculated independently by British astronomer John Couch Adams and French astronomer Urbain Le Verrier in 1845. In 1846, German astronomer Johann Galle first observed Neptune through a telescope.

Orbit and rotation. Neptune orbits the sun in 164.8 Earth years in a nearly circular orbit. Its magnetic field is considerably asymmetric to the planet's structure, similar to, but not so extreme as, Uranus's magnetic field. Neptune's magnetic field axis is tipped 46.9° from its rotational axis and is displaced more than 55% of its radius away from the planet's center.

Ceres

Distance from the sun	
Perihelion	237 mil mi (2.55 AU)
Semi-major axis (mean distance)	257 mil mi (2.77 AU)
Period of revolution around sun	4.6 yr.
Orbital eccentricity	0.0756
Orbital inclination	10.59°
Sidereal day	9.074 hr.
Mass (Earth = 1)	0.00015
Mean radius	292 mi

Ceres was the first asteroid discovered; Italian astronomer Guiseppe Piazzi first observed it on Jan. 1, 1801. In the 1800s, it was considered a planet but lost that designation. Ceres is the largest object in the asteroid belt, comprising nearly one third of

Distance from the sun	
Perihelion	2,761.7 mil mi
Semi-major axis (mean distance)	2,793.1 mil mi
	(30.047 AU)
Aphelion	2,824.5 mil mi
Period of revolution around sun	164.79 yr.
Orbital eccentricity	0.0113
Orbital inclination	1.769°
Synodic day (midday to midday)	16 hr., 6 min., 37 sec.
Sidereal day	16 hr., 6 min., 36 sec.
Rotational inclination	28.32°
Mass (Earth = 1)	17.147
Mean radius	15,301 mi
Mean density (Earth = 1)	0.297
Natural satellites	14
Average temperature*	−330°F
*i.e., temperature where atmospheric pressure equals 1 Earth atmosphere.	

Atmosphere. The Neptunian atmosphere is composed primarily of 80% hydrogen, 19% helium, 1.5% methane, and small amounts of hydrogen deuteride, ethane, ammonia ice, water ice, ammonia hydrosulfide, and methane ice. Neptune's atmosphere is quite blue, with quickly changing white clouds often suspended high above an apparent surface. A Great Dark Spot, reminiscent of Jupiter's Great Red Spot, was discovered in 1989 when *Voyager 2* visited the planet. Observations with the Hubble Space Telescope have shown that the Great Dark Spot originally seen by *Voyager* has apparently dissipated, but a new dark spot has since appeared. Lightning and auroras have been found on other giant planets, but only the aurora phenomenon has been seen on Neptune. As with the other giant planets, Neptune emits more energy than it receives from the sun. The excess has been found to be 2.7 times the solar contribution.

Surface and composition. As with the other giant planets, Neptune may have no solid surface or exact diameter. However, a mean value of 30,600 mi may be assigned to a diameter between atmosphere levels where the pressure is about the same as sea level on Earth.

Natural satellites. The largest of Neptune's 14 satellites is Triton. It is the only large moon in a retrograde orbit, which suggests that it was captured rather than having formed along with the planet. Triton's large size, sufficient to raise significant tides on the planet, may one day, billions of years from now, bring Triton close enough to Neptune for Triton to be torn apart. Triton has a tenuous atmosphere of nitrogen with a trace of hydrocarbons and evidence of active geysers injecting material into it. Triton is the coldest object yet measured in the solar system with a surface temperature of −391°F. Only about half of Triton has been observed, but its terrain shows cratering and a strange regional feature described as resembling the skin of a cantaloupe. Nereid has the highest orbital eccentricity (0.75) of any moon. Its long looping orbit suggests that it was also captured. In 2003, two more moons, which orbit farther from their parent planet than any other moons in the solar system, were discovered. In July 2013, archival Hubble Space Telescope images were used to discover the existence of a 14th natural satellite of Neptune. At less than 20 km diameter, it is the smallest of Neptune's known moons. The *Voyager 2* probe in 1989 confirmed the existence of six rings around Neptune composed of very fine particles. There may be some clumps in the rings' structure. It is not known whether Neptune's satellites influence the formation or maintenance of the rings.

Dwarf Planets

all the mass of asteroids. In Aug. 2006, it was designated a dwarf planet by the Intl. Astronomical Union (IAU).

After a journey of over seven years, the *Dawn* spacecraft entered into orbit around Ceres in Mar. 2015, making *Dawn* the first spacecraft to visit a dwarf planet. Astronomers are particularly interested in asteroids since they are thought to be rocky protoplanets, examples of the building blocks from which planets formed early in the history of the solar system. *Dawn's* scientific instrumentation consists of cameras for surface imaging, a spectrometer for measuring surface mineralogy, and a neutron detector for measuring elemental composition of Ceres. *Dawn* has produced high-resolution maps of the entire surface and the most accurate measurements of Ceres's size and mass. The images show a heavily cratered surface with features such as extremely reflective spots within a crater—thought to be freshly exposed water ice—and at least one mountain several miles high.

Orbit and rotation. Ceres orbits the sun in the asteroid belt region between Mars and Jupiter.

Surface and composition. Ceres's composition is similar to that of the stony meteorites known as carbonaceous chondrites. These are considered to be the oldest materials in the solar system, with a composition reflecting that of the primitive solar nebula. Extremely dark in color, probably because of their hydrocarbon content, they show evidence of having absorbed water. Thus, unlike the Earth and the moon, they have never melted nor been reheated since they first formed. *Dawn* observations suggest that the surface of Ceres consists largely of water ice, though its interior is mostly rock. Up to 25% of Ceres's mass may be water ice. There is evidence for hydrothermal vents at the surface of Ceres, perhaps indicating that liquid water existed below the surface in the recent past. Further study using *Dawn* will try to confirm observations suggesting that water evaporates from the surface and produces a diffuse atmosphere.

Pluto

Distance from the sun	
Perihelion	2,756.9 mil mi
Semi-major axis (mean distance)	3,670.1 mil mi (39.482 AU)
Aphelion	4,583.2 mil mi
Period of revolution around sun	247.74 yr.
Orbital eccentricity	0.2502
Orbital inclination	17.09°
Synodic day (midday to midday)	6 d., 9 hr., 17 min. (retrograde)
Sidereal day	6 d., 9 hr., 18 min. (retrograde)
Rotational inclination	119.59°
Mass (Earth = 1)	0.0022
Mean radius	736.5 mi
Mean density (Earth = 1)	0.339
Natural satellites	5
Average surface temperature	−369°F

Pluto, named for the Roman god of the underworld, is the largest Kuiper Belt object (KBO) by radius, and the second largest by mass. It was first discovered in 1930 by American astronomer Clyde Tombaugh and classified as a planet until 2006, when the IAU changed its designation to dwarf planet. In 2008, Pluto was designated by the IAU as the prototype for a class of objects called **plutoids**, bodies that (a) have an average distance from the sun greater than Neptune's; (b) are large enough that gravity determines their shape; and (c) have not cleared their orbit of other objects. Haumea, Makemake, and Eris are also plutoids. The *New Horizons* spacecraft, launched on a voyage to Pluto and beyond in 2006, made the first flyby of Pluto on July 14, 2015, and traveled on to a flyby of Kuiper belt object 2014 MU69 (Arrokoth), nicknamed Ultima Thule, on Jan. 1, 2019.

Orbit and rotation. Pluto's orbit is highly eccentric; although its average distance from the sun is 3.7 billion mi, it may get as close as 2.76 billion mi and as far as 4.58 billion mi. For about 20 years of its 248-year orbit, it is closer to the sun than Neptune. Currently, it is beyond Neptune's orbit.

Atmosphere and surface. Before the *New Horizons* flyby, all observations of Pluto had been made with telescopes nearly 3 billion mi away, so the mission brought new data to light. The mass and density of Pluto suggests that it is composed of a rocky core with an overlying water-ice mantle. Close-up observations of Pluto from *New Horizons* revealed a mixed surface, with some ancient, heavily cratered terrain and other younger, smoother plains with no craters. The smooth terrain, estimated to be no more than 100 million years old, is much younger than scientists expected and may indicate that geologic processes continue to modify Pluto. Nitrogen ice on the smooth plains appears to be flowing, like glaciers on Earth, onto the more heavily cratered surface. Compositional evidence shows that the smooth areas contain nitrogen, methane, and carbon monoxide ices. Scientists also found several mountain ranges rising more than 2 mi above the smooth plains; they speculated that the mountains are made of water ice thrust up from below Pluto's nitrogen-rich icy surface.

New Horizons also provided the first close-up measurements of Pluto's atmosphere, confirming earlier measurements of methane, nitrogen, and carbon monoxide, the same molecules that form ice on Pluto's surface. Scientists speculate that the atmosphere forms from evaporation of surface ices when the dwarf planet is closer to the sun. The new measurements also revealed hydrocarbon hazes as much as 50 mi above Pluto's surface. The hazes are thought to form when Pluto's tenuous atmosphere is exposed to the sun's ultraviolet rays. Dark regions on Pluto's surface likely result from these hydrocarbons settling. Knowledge of Pluto will continue to improve as more data is analyzed.

Natural satellites. Pluto has five known natural satellites. Charon, the biggest, has a diameter of 750 mi—about half of Pluto's diameter of 1,474 mi. No other planet or dwarf planet has a moon so close to its size. Discovered in 1978, Charon orbits Pluto at a distance of 12,200 mi and takes 6.39 days to move around the dwarf planet. In this same length of time, Pluto and Charon both rotate once on their axes, meaning that the Pluto-Charon system appears to rotate as virtually a rigid body. Both worlds are roughly spherical and have comparable densities. Because of these similarities and their peculiar relationship, there is debate as to whether Charon should one day be designated a dwarf planet. *New Horizons* provided the first detailed look at Charon, revealing a surface with less color and likely dominated by water ice. New evidence suggests Charon may have had a water ocean in the past. Much of Charon's surface is smoother than expected, with few craters, implying that Charon has an active geology capable of resurfacing. The images also reveal fractures extending hundreds of miles and a canyon around 5 mi deep.

Two other moons, discovered in 2005 and 2006, were officially named Nix and Hydra. Two additional moons, discovered in 2011 and 2012, were officially named Kerberos and Styx by the IAU in 2013. In late 2015, NASA released *New Horizons*-sourced images of Nix and Hydra, revealing irregularly shaped objects about 25 and 35 mi across, respectively. Astronomers examining *New Horizons* data have been surprised to find no additional moons, down to the roughly 1-mi-diameter limit of detectability by the spacecraft.

Haumea

Distance from the sun	
Semi-major axis (mean distance)	43.355 AU
Period of revolution around sun	285.48 yr.
Orbital eccentricity	0.189
Orbital inclination	28.20°
Mass (Earth = 1)	0.0007
Mean radius	420 mi
Natural satellites	2

Haumea was discovered in 2004 and was accepted as a dwarf planet by the IAU in 2008.

Orbit and rotation. Haumea has a moderately eccentric orbit and takes about 285 years to go around the sun.

Surface and composition. Spectra of Haumea indicate the presence of almost pure crystalline water ice. The surface reflects about 60% of the sunlight that reaches it. Haumea has a very oblong shape, twice as long as it is wide.

Natural satellites. Haumea has two natural satellites, Hi'iake and Namaka.

Makemake

Distance from the sun	
Semi-major axis (mean distance)	45.715 AU
Period of revolution around sun	309.1 yr.
Orbital eccentricity	0.155
Orbital inclination	28.99°
Mass (Earth = 1)	0.0007
Mean radius	450 mi
Natural satellites	1

Makemake was discovered in 2005 and was accepted as a dwarf planet by the IAU in 2008.

Orbit and rotation. Makemake has a moderately eccentric orbit and takes about 310 years to go around the sun.

Surface and composition. Spectra of Makemake indicate the presence of frozen methane, as well as several organic compounds. The surface is highly reflective and appears similar to that of Pluto.

Natural satellites. Makemake has one natural satellite.

Gonggong (2007 OR10)

Distance from the sun	
Semi-major axis (mean distance)	67.143 AU
Period of revolution around sun	550.19 yr.
Orbital eccentricity	0.505
Orbital inclination	30.87°
Mass (Earth = 1)	0.0006
Mean radius	950 mi
Natural satellites	1

2007 OR10 was discovered in 2007 and was named Gonggong in 2020 pending final approval by the IAU.

Orbit and rotation. 2007 OR10 has a highly elliptical orbit and takes about 550 years to go around the sun.

Surface and composition. Spectra of 2007 OR10 indicate the presence of frozen methane and water ice. The surface is highly reflective and appears similar to that of Pluto.

Natural satellites. One natural satellite of 2007 OR10 was discovered by astronomers using the Hubble Space Telescope in 2017.

Eris

Distance from the sun	
Semi-major axis (mean distance)	67.6497 AU
Period of revolution around sun	556.43 yr.
Orbital eccentricity	0.44171
Orbital inclination	44.204°
Mass (Earth = 1)	0.0027
Mean radius	723 mi
Natural satellites	1

Discovered in 2003 by astronomers at the California Institute of Technology, Eris is the largest dwarf planet by mass, about 27% larger than Pluto, although Pluto has a slightly larger radius.

Orbit and rotation. Eris has a highly elliptical orbit and takes about 560 years to go around the sun—more than twice the time it takes Pluto. Its inclination is steep, tilted at 44° to the planetary plane. It also has an extremely eccentric orbit. It will be at its closest to the sun, actually coming inside part of Pluto's orbit, in about 280 years.

Surface and composition. Eris, with a surface covered in frozen methane, may be similar to Pluto and the Neptunian moon Triton. Observations made by the Hubble Space Telescope show that Eris's surface is almost white and uniform, reflecting 86% of the light that hits it. This makes it the most reflective body in the solar system. The dwarf planet's interior is likely a mixture of rock and ice.

Natural satellites. Eris has one moon, Dysnomia.

Small Solar System Bodies

Asteroids

Besides planets and moons, many smaller objects orbit the sun. In 2006, the International Astronomical Union (IAU) officially designated these objects "small solar system bodies." Asteroids or minor planets are found mainly in a belt between the orbits of Mars and Jupiter. Within this belt there may be millions of asteroids of varying sizes. Most asteroids are very small. Ceres, which can be classified both as an asteroid and a dwarf planet, is 588 mi in diameter, about one-quarter the diameter of our moon.

Some of these asteroids are gravitationally locked with Jupiter and the sun so that they have roughly the same orbit as Jupiter but are either 60° ahead or behind the planet. These are the **Trojan asteroids**. Many of the smaller moons of the solar system, especially those in retrograde orbits, may be captured asteroids. Asteroids whose orbits either cross or come close to the Earth's orbit are labeled **Near Earth asteroids**, or NEAs. A handful of asteroids have actually been imaged by the Arecibo and Goldstone radio telescopes and by the NEAR Shoemaker space probe. The *Galileo* spacecraft imaged the asteroids Gaspra and Ida (including Ida's moon Dactyl) on its way to Jupiter. The Japanese *Hayabusa 2*, after orbiting asteroid Ryugu, returned a sample to Earth in Dec. 2020; and NASA's OSIRIS-REx mission, currently orbiting asteroid Bennu, was scheduled to return a sample to Earth in Sept. 2023. On Sept. 26, 2022, a NASA mission called the Double Asteroid Redirection Test (DART) fired a projectile at Dimorphos, the small moon of the binary asteroid Didymos, successfully altering the orbital by period by over 30 minutes, in a demonstration of how Earth might defend itself against collisions with asteroids. As of 2023, 17 asteroids had been visited by spacecraft.

Comets

Comets are small icy bodies that orbit the sun. When one approaches the sun, the energy from the sun boils off material from the comet's icy nucleus, producing an enlarged head (or coma), and in many cases an extended tail. Because of that, comets are brighter when near the sun. For large comets, the head may be 100,000 mi across and the tail more than a million mi long, though both are mainly empty space.

Comets have been known since ancient times. British astronomer Edmund Halley (1656-1742) ultimately realized that a group of historical reports were just repeated visits of the same object. Comets are the only astronomical objects named after their discoverers. In 1986, the European spacecraft *Giotto* took the first close-up images of a comet's nucleus, specifically of Comet Halley, showing it had a peanut-shaped nucleus with a longest dimension of about 10 mi.

In 1995, U.S. observers Alan Hale (1958-) and Thomas Bopp (1949-2018) independently discovered a comet that was then beyond the orbit of Jupiter. It is one of the brightest comets of all time. It also holds the record for length of time visible to the naked eye—19 months—and is the most photographed comet

in history. In July 2009, an amateur astronomer discovered a large impact scar in the upper atmosphere of Jupiter, likely the result of another cometary impact. In Mar. 2020, astronomers using the *NEOWISE* mission of the Wide-field Infrared Survey Explorer (*WISE*) discovered a comet, which in July 2020 was widely visible to the naked eye. Comet *NEOWISE* was the brightest comet since Hale-Bopp. In 2014, the *Rosetta* spacecraft became the first spacecraft to orbit a comet, 67P/Churyumov-Gerasimenko. *Rosetta* also deployed a lander onto the comet surface. As of summer 2023, eight comets have been studied directly by spacecraft.

Kuiper Belt

The Kuiper Belt is a doughnut-shaped region that extends to about 50 AU (astronomical units) from the sun and is thought to be the source of short-period comets such as Comets Halley or Swift-Tuttle. It is filled with icy bodies that are in solar orbit. The more than 1,000 objects found in this region in recent years are called Kuiper Belt objects (KBOs). It is estimated that there are more than 70,000 objects 60 mi in diameter or larger within the Kuiper Belt. Dwarf planets Pluto and Eris are considered KBOs. There are at least six KBOs larger than 300 mi in diameter.

On Jan. 1, 2019, *New Horizons* made the first close study of a KBO when it flew by the object 2014 MU 69, originally nicknamed Ultima Thule but now provisionally named Arrokoth by the IAU. In the first images sent back to Earth, Arrokoth appears to be a "contact binary," composed of two smaller bodies, 14 mi and 9 mi across, in close contact with each other. No satellite of Arrokoth was observed.

Arrokoth (2014 MU 69)

Distance from the sun	
Semi-major axis (mean distance)	44.539 AU
Period of revolution around sun	298 yr.
Orbital eccentricity	0.04172
Orbital inclination	2.451°
Mass (Earth = 1)	Unknown
Mean radius	14 mi ("Ultima") and 9 mi ("Thule")

Oort Cloud

The Oort Cloud is a vast spherical region hypothesized to exist around the sun and populated by comets. Dutch astronomer Jan Oort (1900-92) proposed its existence as the origin for long-period comets that enter the inner part of the solar system where the planets orbit. Current technology is not sufficient to detect any members of the Oort Cloud other than observed comets whose orbits may reach out as far as 50,000 AU. Recent examples of such long-period comets are Comets Hale-Bopp and Hyakutake.

The Sun

Distance from Earth, mean	92.96 mil mi (1 AU)
Sidereal day (rotation period)	25.38 d.
Mass (Earth = 1)	332,900
Mean radius	432,200 mi
Mean density (Earth = 1)	0.255
Average surface temperature	9,941°F

The sun is the Earth's primary source of light and heat and its closest star. The biggest object in the solar system, the sun is 332,900 times more massive than Earth and contains 99.86% of the mass of the entire solar system. On the whole, the sun is made up of about 92.1% hydrogen and 7.8% helium, with trace amounts of other elements. It has a mass and luminosity greater than that of 90% of the stars in the Milky Way galaxy. Although most of the stars that can be easily seen on a clear night are bigger and brighter than the sun, its proximity to Earth makes it appear tremendously large and bright. The sun is 400,000 times as bright as the full moon, and it gives Earth 6 mil times as much light as do all the other stars put together. Because of the great distance between the sun and Earth, it takes about 499 sec., or slightly more than 8 min., for light from the sun to reach Earth.

Composition. The sun has six regions. The first three from the inside out are the core, the radiative zone, and the convective zone. Together they form the interior. The others, which comprise the visible surface, are the photosphere, the chromosphere, and the outermost region, the corona.

The sun's heat and energy are produced in its core. Through a series of nuclear fusion reactions, hydrogen nuclei are converted to helium nuclei, releasing energy in the process. Temperatures in the core are theorized to be 28 mil °F. In 2017 astronomers discovered that the core rotates nearly four times faster than the surface, a rapidity left over from the time when the sun was formed. From the core, photons transport the energy outward through the radiative zone. It can take photons several million years to pass through this area. In the convective zone, gases move energy outward at a faster rate. Like a boiling pot, bubbles of gas bring energy to the surface.

The photosphere is the visible surface of the sun, that is, the light that we see as sunlight. When sunlight is analyzed with a spectroscope, it is found to consist of a continuous spectrum composed of all the colors of the rainbow, crossed by many dark lines. The dark "absorption lines" are produced by gaseous materials in the outer layers of the sun. More than 60 of the natural terrestrial elements have been identified in the sun, all in gaseous form because of the sun's intense heat.

Just above the photosphere is the chromosphere, which is visible to the naked eye only in total solar eclipses, during which it appears to be a pinkish-violet layer with occasional great prominences projecting above its general level. With proper instruments, the chromosphere can be seen or photographed whenever the sun is visible. Above the chromosphere

is the corona, also visible to the naked eye only at times of total eclipse or with instruments that permit the brighter portions of the corona to be seen. The corona surges millions of miles from the sun; its atoms are all in a state of extreme excitation and high ionization that indicates temperatures nearly 2 mil °F.

Sunspots. These dark, irregularly shaped regions may reach diameters of thousands of miles. There is an intimate connection between sunspots and the corona. At times of low sunspot activity, the fine streamers of the corona are longer above the sun's equator than over the polar regions of the sun; during periods of high sunspot activity, the corona extends fairly evenly outward from all regions of the sun but to a much greater distance in space. The average life of a sunspot group is two months, but some have lasted for more than a year. Sunspots reach a low point, on average, every 11.3 years, with a peak of activity occurring irregularly between two successive periods of minimal activity. The sun experienced an unusually quiet period in 2008 and 2009; its latest period of maximum activity occurred in 2014, though this was among the weakest maximums ever recorded.

Solar wind and magnetic field. Magnetic arches, called prominences, may extend tens of thousands of miles into the corona and may release enormous amounts of energy heating the corona. Coronal mass ejections are enormous releases of solar energy. Coronal holes are regions where the corona appears dark in X-rays, and are associated with open magnetic field lines, where the magnetic field lines project out into space instead of back toward the sun. It is in these regions where the high-speed solar wind originates.

The solar wind carries the sun's magnetic field, which extends beyond the planets. This is called the interplanetary magnetic field (IMF). Far past Pluto and the Kuiper Belt, the solar wind and the IMF lose their influence. The boundary between them and interstellar space is called the heliopause. In 2013, NASA announced that the *Voyager 1* spacecraft, launched in 1977, seemed at last to have reached the heliopause, at a distance 18 billion km (11 billion mi) from the sun.

Searching for Extrasolar Planets

The sun is a typical star in many respects and—with over 400 billion stars in the Milky Way—it is plausible that many other stars might have planets. Since 1995, astronomers have gathered evidence of thousands of planets orbiting stars other than the sun. Astronomers have not directly observed most of these objects but inferred their existence from observations of their parent stars.

Astronomers have used two main techniques to detect planets. The first, called the radial-velocity method, uses the Doppler effect to detect periodic changes in the motion of a star caused by the gravitational tug of an unseen planet. The magnitude of the star's motion and the time it takes to repeat can be used to infer the planet's mass and distance from its host star. This technique is most sensitive to high-mass planets orbiting close to their stars because that situation produces more noticeable changes in a star's motion.

The second technique, the transit method, relies on the dimming of a star's light as an unseen planet repeatedly passes in front of it. Astronomers are able to infer the diameter of the planet and the distance at which the planet orbits the star. When combined with the mass determined from the radial-velocity method, astronomers can determine the density of the unseen planet and begin to infer its similarity to planets in our solar system.

Astronomers have also used optical gravitational lensing to detect extrasolar planets. This technique, which detects the observed brightening of a distant background star as a planet passes in front of it, has allowed Southern Hemisphere astronomers to find the most distant planet yet detected, about halfway to the center of our own Milky Way galaxy.

The first planets to be discovered outside the solar system tended to be massive "hot Jupiters," orbiting close to their parent stars (closer than Mercury's orbit around the sun) and comparable in mass to the gas giant Jupiter. But as detection instruments and techniques have improved, smaller and more distant planets have been discovered. The planets discovered so far seem to fall into several groups: rocky planets as massive as 1.75 times that of Earth; mini-Neptunes, 2-3.5 times as massive as Earth, with gas surrounding a rocky core; "super Earths" more massive than the mini-Neptunes; and gas giants, as massive or more massive than Jupiter.

In 2005, astronomers obtained the first direct image of an extrasolar planet around a normal star called GQ Lupi, which is like Earth's sun but younger. The planet is about 100 AU (astronomical units) away from the star and estimated to be about twice as massive as Jupiter.

In 2006, astronomers discovered what they call a "super Earth" orbiting a red dwarf 9,000 light-years away. The planet appears to have about 13 times Earth's mass and may be composed of rock and ice, but it is believed not to have liquid on its surface. Such super Earths appear to be common in extrasolar planetary systems. In 2007, astronomers detected water in the atmosphere of an extrasolar planet for the first time.

In 2009, NASA launched Kepler, the first telescope sensitive enough to detect Earth-sized planets around other stars. Kepler's first-released data in 2010 indicated that small planets are more common than large planets. Kepler has now detected a large number of planets with diameters similar to that of Earth. Some of the planets are known to orbit within the host star's habitable zone, meaning that the conditions are such that liquid water could exist on the planetary surface. As of July 2023, astronomers had confirmed more than 5,483 planets orbiting more than 4,082 stars; 924 of those stars host more than one planet.

Planets with masses much less than Jupiter's are now regularly discovered. A team of astronomers announced, Aug. 2016, the discovery of a possibly Earth-like planet, Proxima b, in orbit around Proxima Centauri, the star closest to the sun. About 4.2 light-years away, it is the closest known exoplanet. In Feb. 2017, astronomers announced the discovery of at least seven Earth-sized planets orbiting a small star, Trappist-1, located about 40 light-years away. They appear similar in mass and composition to Earth, and three of the planets are in the habitable zone of the star. In June 2017, the Kepler mission announced the discovery of 10 Earth-sized planets, probably rocky in composition, that might support liquid water and could be potentially habitable.

NASA successfully launched the Transiting Exoplanet Survey Satellite (TESS) mission on Apr. 18, 2018, aboard a SpaceX Falcon 9 rocket. This landmark mission was conducting an all-sky survey of extrasolar planets, including those orbiting bright nearby stars, which can be investigated in further detail by large Earth-based and space telescopes. By July 2020, it had finished its primary mission, covering about 75% of space. By 2023, TESS had found 373 confirmed exoplanets as well as over 5,000 candidates needing further detailed observation for confirmation. In Dec. 2019, the European Space Agency launched a complementary mission, Cheops (CHaracterising ExOPlanet Satellite), which is also targeting planets around bright nearby stars.

Earth: Size, Computation of Time, Seasons

Distance from the sun	
Perihelion	91.4 mil mi
Semi-major axis (mean distance)	93 mil mi (1.0000 AU)
Aphelion	94.5 mil mi
Period of revolution	365.256 d.
Orbital eccentricity	0.0167
Orbital inclination	0°
Synodic day (midday to midday)	24 hr., 0 min., 0 sec.
Sidereal day (rotation period)	23 hr., 56 min., 4.2 sec.
Rotational inclination	23.45°
Mass (Earth = 1)	1
Mean radius	3,958.8 mi
Mean density (Earth = 1)	1
Natural satellites	1
Average surface temperature	59°F

Earth is the fifth-largest planet and the third from the sun. Its mass is 5.9736×10^{24} kg. Earth's equatorial diameter is 7,926 mi while its polar diameter is only 7,900 mi.

Size and dimensions. Earth is considered a solid mass, yet it has a large, liquid iron, **magnetic core** with a radius of about 2,160 mi. Surprisingly, it has a solid **inner core** that may be a large iron crystal, with a radius of 760 mi. Around the core is a thick shell, or **mantle**, of dense rock. This mantle is composed of materials rich in iron and magnesium. It is somewhat plastic-like, and under slow steady pressure, it can flow like a liquid. The mantle, in turn, is covered by a thin **crust** forming the solid granite and basalt base of the continents and ocean basins. Over broad areas of Earth's surface, the crust has a thin cover of sedimentary rock such as sandstone, shale, and limestone formed by weathering and by deposits of sands, clays, and plant and animal remains.

The temperature inside the Earth increases about 1°F with every 100 to 200 ft in depth, in the upper 100 km (62 mi) of Earth. It reaches nearly 8,000°F-9,000°F at the center. The heat is believed to come from radioactivity in rocks, pressures within Earth, and the original heat of formation.

Atmosphere. Earth's atmosphere is a blanket composed of 78% nitrogen, 21% oxygen, and 1% argon. Present in minute quantities are carbon dioxide, hydrogen, neon, helium, krypton, and xenon. Water vapor displaces other gases and varies from nearly zero to about 4% by volume. The atmosphere rests on Earth's surface with a weight equivalent to a layer of water 34 ft deep. For about 300,000 ft upward, the gases remain in the proportions stated. Gravity holds the gases to Earth. The weight of the air compresses it at the bottom so that the greatest density is at Earth's surface. Pressure and density decrease as height increases.

The lowest layer of the atmosphere extending up from the Earth's surface about 7.5 mi is the **troposphere**, which contains 90% of the air. This is also where most weather phenomena occur. The temperature drops with increasing height through this layer. The **stratosphere** extends about 23 mi above the troposphere; the temperature generally increases with height within this layer. The stratosphere contains **ozone**, which prevents ultraviolet rays from reaching Earth's surface. Since there is very little convection in the stratosphere, jets regularly cruise in the lower parts to provide a smoother ride for passengers.

Above the stratosphere is the **mesosphere**, where the temperature again decreases with height for another 19 mi. Extending above the mesosphere to the outer fringes of the atmosphere is the **thermosphere**, a region where temperature once more increases with height to a value measured in thousands of degrees Fahrenheit. The lower portion of this region, extending from 50 to about 400 mi in altitude, is characterized by high ion density and is thus called the **ionosphere**. Most meteors are in the lower thermosphere or the mesosphere at the time they are observed.

Longitude and latitude. Position on the globe is measured by meridians and parallels. Meridians, which are imaginary lines drawn around Earth through the poles, determine **longitude**. The meridian running through Greenwich, England, is the **prime meridian** of longitude; all others are either E or W. Parallels, which are imaginary circles parallel with the equator, determine **latitude**. The length of a degree of longitude varies as the cosine of the latitude. At the equator a degree of longitude is 69.171 statute mi; this is gradually reduced toward the poles. Value of a longitude degree at the poles is zero.

Latitude is reckoned by the number of degrees N or S of the **equator**, an imaginary circle on Earth's surface everywhere equidistant between the two poles. According to the International Astronomical Union, the length of a degree of latitude is 68.708 statute mi at the equator and varies slightly N and S because of the oblate form of the globe. At the poles, it is 69.403 statute mi.

Definitions of time. Earth rotates on its axis and follows an elliptical orbit around the sun. The rotation makes the sun appear to move across the sky from E to W. This rotation determines day and night, and the complete rotation, in relation to the sun, is called the **apparent or true solar day**. A sundial thus measures **apparent solar time**. This length of time varies, but an average determines a mean solar day of 24 hours.

The mean solar day and **mean solar time** are in universal use for civil purposes. Mean solar time may be obtained from apparent solar time by correcting observations of the sun for the **equation of time**. Mean solar time may be up to 16 min. different from apparent solar time.

Sidereal time is the measure of time defined by the diurnal motion of the vernal equinox and is determined from observation of the meridian transits of stars. One complete rotation of Earth relative to the equinox is called the **sidereal day**. The **mean sidereal day** is 23 hr., 56 min., 4.2 sec. of mean solar time.

The interval required for Earth to make one absolute revolution around the sun is a **sidereal year**; it consisted of 365 days, 6 hr., 9 min., and 9.5 sec. of mean solar time (approximately 24 hr. per day) in 1900 and has been increasing at the rate of 0.0001 second annually.

The **tropical year**, upon which our calendar is based, is the interval between two consecutive returns of the sun to the vernal equinox. The tropical year consisted of 365 days, 5 hr., 48 min., and 46 sec. in 1900. It has been decreasing at the rate of 0.53 sec. per century. The **calendar year** begins at midnight precisely, local clock time, on the night of Dec. 31-Jan. 1. The day and the calendar month also begin at midnight by the clock.

On Jan. 1, 1972, the Bureau International des Poids et Mesures in Paris introduced **International Atomic Time** (TAI) as the most precisely determined time scale for astronomical usage. The fundamental unit of TAI in the international system of units is the second, defined as the duration of 9,192,631,770 periods of the radiation corresponding to the transition between two hyperfine levels of the ground state of the cesium-133 atom. **Coordinated Universal Time** (UTC), which serves as the basis for civil timekeeping and is the standard time of the prime meridian, is officially defined by a formula which relates UTC to mean sidereal time in Greenwich, England. (UTC replaced Greenwich Mean Time as the basis for standard time for the world.)

Zones and seasons. The five zones of Earth's surface are the Torrid, lying between the Tropics of Cancer and Capricorn; the N Temperate, between Cancer and the Arctic Circle; the S Temperate, between Capricorn and the Antarctic Circle; and the two Frigid Zones, between the Polar Circles and the Poles.

The inclination, or tilt, of Earth's axis, 23°45′ away from a perpendicular to Earth's orbit of the sun, determines the seasons. These are commonly marked in the N Temperate Zone, where spring begins at the vernal equinox, summer at the summer solstice, autumn at the autumnal equinox, and winter at the winter solstice. In the S Temperate Zone, the seasons are reversed. Spring begins at the autumnal equinox, summer at the winter solstice, and so on.

The points at which the sun crosses the equator are the **equinoxes**, when day and night are most nearly equal. The points at which the sun is at a maximum distance from the equator are the **solstices**, when days and nights are most unequal. However, at the equator, day and night are equal throughout the year.

In June, the North Pole is tilted 23°27′ toward the sun, and the days in the Northern Hemisphere are longer than the nights, while the days in the Southern Hemisphere are shorter than the nights. In Dec., the North Pole is tilted 23°27′ away from the sun, and the situation is reversed.

Seasons in 2024. the four seasons begin in the Northern Hemisphere as shown. (Add 1 hour to Eastern Standard Time for Atlantic Time; subtract 1 hour for Central, 2 for Mountain, 3 for Pacific, 4 for Alaska, 5 for Hawaii-Aleutian. Also shown is Coordinated Universal Time.)

Season	Date	UTC	EST/EDT
Vernal Equinox (spring)	Mar. 20	03:07	23:07 EDT Mar. 19
Northern Solstice (summer)	June 20	20:51	16:51 EDT
Autumnal Equinox (fall)	Sept. 22	12:44	0:44 EDT
Southern Solstice (winter)	Dec. 21	09:20	04:20 EST

Poles. The geographic (rotation) poles, or points where Earth's axis of rotation cuts the surface, are not absolutely fixed in the body of Earth. The pole of rotation describes an irregular curve about its mean position.

Two periods have been detected in this motion: (1) an annual period due to seasonal changes in barometric pressure, to load of ice and snow on the surface, and to other seasonal phenomena; (2) a period of about 14 months due to the shape and constitution of Earth. In addition, there are small but as yet unpredictable irregularities. The whole motion is so small that the actual pole at any time remains within a circle of 30 or 40 ft in radius centered at the mean position of the pole.

The pole of rotation for the time being is, of course, the pole having a latitude of 90° and an indeterminate longitude.

Magnetic poles. Although Earth's magnetic field resembles that of an ordinary bar magnet, this magnetic field is probably produced by electric currents in the liquid currents of the Earth's outer core. The **north magnetic pole** of Earth is that region where the magnetic force is downward, and the **south magnetic pole** is that region where the magnetic force is upward. A compass placed at the magnetic poles experiences no directive force in azimuth (i.e., direction).

There are slow changes in the distribution of Earth's magnetic field. This slow temporal change is referred to as the secular change of the main magnetic field, and the magnetic poles shift due to this. The location of the N magnetic pole was first measured in 1831 at Cape Adelaide on the W coast of Boothia Peninsula in Canada's Northwest Territories (about latitude 70° N and longitude 96° W). Since then it has moved over 500 mi. As of 2023 it was estimated to be at latitude 86.15° N, longitude 146.83° E, the Arctic Ocean far north of Siberia. Measurement for several decades by Canadian scientists indicates the motion of the pole has accelerated, now averaging about 34 mi per year.

The direction of the horizontal components of the magnetic field at any point is known as magnetic N at that point, and the

angle by which it deviates E or W of true N is known as the magnetic declination.

A compass without error points in the direction of magnetic north. (In general, this is not the direction of the true rotational North Pole.) If you follow the direction indicated by the N end of the compass, you will go along an irregular curve that eventually reaches the north magnetic pole (though not usually by a great-circle route). However, the action of the compass should not be thought of as due to any influence of the distant pole, but simply as an indication of the distribution of Earth's magnetism at the place of observation.

Rotation. The speed of Earth's rotation about its axis is slightly variable. The variations may be classified as:

(A) **Secular.** Tidal friction acts as a brake on the rotation and causes a slow secular increase in the length of the day, about 1 millisecond per century.

(B) **Irregular.** The speed of rotation may increase for a number of years (about 5 to 10) and then start decreasing. The maximum difference from the mean in the length of the day during a century is about 5 milliseconds. The accumulated difference in time has amounted to approximately 44 seconds since 1900. The cause is probably motion in the interior of Earth.

(C) **Periodic.** Seasonal variations exist with periods of 1 year and 6 months. The cumulative effect is such that each year, Earth is late about 30 milliseconds near June 1 and is ahead about 30 milliseconds near Oct. 1. The maximum seasonal variation in the length of the day is about 0.5 millisecond. It is believed that the principal cause of the annual variation is the seasonal change in the wind patterns of the Northern and Southern Hemispheres. The semiannual variation is due chiefly to tidal action of the sun, which distorts the shape of Earth slightly.

The Moon

Distance from Earth	
Perigee	225,744 mi
Semi-major axis (mean distance)	238,855 mi
Apogee	251,966 mi
Period of revolution	27.322 d.
Orbital eccentricity	0.0549
Orbital inclination	5.145°
Synodic orbital period (period of phases)	29.53 d.
Sidereal day (rotation period)	27.322 d.
Rotational inclination	6.68°
Mass (Earth = 1)	0.0123
Mean radius	1,079 mi
Mean density (Earth = 1)	0.607
Average surface temperature	−100°F

The moon is the second-brightest object in the sky (the sun is the first). Earth's only natural satellite, the moon is the force behind the rising and falling of tides, and it helps to regulate Earth's inclination as they orbit the sun. Many probes have been sent to the moon, and between 1969 and 1972, 12 U.S. astronauts walked on its surface. The moon is the subject of renewed international interest. In 2007, Japan and China orbited satellites around the moon, India orbited a spacecraft in fall 2008, and the U.S. sent an orbiter and impactor in 2009. In Sept. 2009, American scientists announced the discovery of a thin layer of water ice near the lunar poles. Since 2009, NASA has been mapping and measuring the surface composition and other properties of the moon using the Lunar Reconnaissance Orbiter. In Sept. 2013, NASA launched *LADEE*, a mission to study the ephemeral lunar atmosphere and lunar dust from a low orbit. In Dec. 2013, China became the third nation to land a spacecraft on the moon when *Chang'e 3* set down on Mare Imbrium. *Chang'e 3* released the *Yutu* rover to study the lunar surface. On July 22, 2019, India successfully launched the *Chandrayaan-2* mission. Scheduled to land a rover near the south pole of the moon on Sept. 7, 2019, mission control lost contact with the lander 1.3 mi from the surface, though an orbiter remained operational. The *Chandrayaan-3* follow-on mission landed a rover near the south pole of the moon on Aug. 23, 2023.

Orbit and rotation. The moon completes a circuit around Earth in a period that averages 27 days, 7 hr., 43.2 min. This is the moon's sidereal period. Because of the motion of the moon in common with Earth around the sun, the mean duration of the lunar month—the period from one new moon to the next new moon—is 29 days, 12 hr., 44.05 min. This is the moon's synodic period.

The mean distance of the moon from Earth is 238,855 mi, but its orbit about Earth is elliptical, and thus the actual distance varies

considerably. The maximum distance from Earth that the moon may reach is 251,966 mi and the least distance is 225,744 mi.

The moon rotates on its axis in a period of time that is exactly equal to its sidereal revolution about Earth—27.322 days. Thus the backside, or farside, of the moon always faces away from Earth. But this does not mean that the backside is always dark. The farside of the moon gets as much direct sunlight as the nearside; at new moon phase, the farside of the moon is fully lit but not visible from Earth.

The moon's revolution about Earth is irregular because of its elliptical orbit. The moon's rotation, however, is regular, and this, together with the irregular revolution, produces what is called libration in longitude, which permits an observer on Earth to see first farther around the eastern side and then farther around the western side of the moon. The moon's variation north or south of the ecliptic permits one to see farther over first one pole of the moon and then the other; this is called libration in latitude. These two libration effects permit observers on Earth to see a total of about 60% of the moon's surface over a period of time.

Atmosphere and surface. The moon, like the planet Mercury, has no real atmosphere to speak of. What little exists is variable and tenuous. With its long day and night, the daytime temperature can reach 260°F. The coldest nighttime temperature is −280°F. This day-to-night contrast is exceeded only by that on Mercury. The lunar surface has not changed much since humans began observing it. The side visible from Earth has large craters and vast dark areas called maria that were once lava. The farside has almost no maria but is pockmarked with craters; it was first photographed in 1959 by the Soviet space probe *Lunik III*.

Recent findings show that up to 300 mil metric tons of water ice may exist in craters at the lunar poles. In its interior, the moon may have a small core, which supports the idea that most of the moon's mass was ripped away from the early Earth when a Mars-sized object collided with Earth.

Harvest moon and hunter's moon. The harvest moon, the full moon nearest the autumnal equinox, ushers in a period of several days when the moon rises soon after sunset. This phenomenon gives farmers in temperate latitudes extra hours of light in which to harvest their crops. The 2024 harvest moon falls on Sept. 18. Harvest moon in the Southern Hemisphere temperate latitudes in 2024 falls on Mar. 25.

The next full moon after harvest moon is called the hunter's moon; it is accompanied by a similar but less marked phenomenon. In 2024, the hunter's moon occurs on Oct. 17 in the Northern Hemisphere and on Apr. 23 in the Southern Hemisphere.

Western Calendars

The **Julian calendar**, under which all Western nations measured time until 1582 CE, was authorized by Julius Caesar in 46 BCE. It called for a year of 365¼ days, starting in Jan., with every fourth year being a **leap year** of 366 days. St. Bede, an Anglo-Saxon monk also known as the Venerable Bede, announced in 730 CE that the Julian year was 11 min., 14 sec. too long, a cumulative error of about a day every 128 years, but nothing was done about this for centuries.

By 1582 the accumulated error was estimated at 10 days. In that year, Pope Gregory XIII decreed that the day following Oct. 4, 1582, should be called Oct. 15, thus dropping 10 days and initiating the **Gregorian calendar**.

The Gregorian calendar perpetuated a chronological system devised by the monk Dionysius Exiguus (fl. 6th cent.). His chronology started with the first year following the birth of Jesus Christ, which he inaccurately took to be year 753 in the Roman calendar. Leap years were continued, but, to prevent further displacements, centesimal years (years ending in 00) were made common years, not leap years, unless divisible by 400. Under this plan, 1600 and 2000 were leap years; 1700, 1800, and 1900 were not.

The Gregorian calendar was adopted at once by France, Italy, Spain, Portugal, and Luxembourg. Within two years, most German Catholic states, Belgium, and parts of Switzerland and the Netherlands were brought under the new calendar, and Hungary followed in 1587. The rest of the Netherlands, along with Denmark and the German Protestant states, made the change in 1699-1700.

The British government adopted the Gregorian calendar and imposed it on all its possessions, including the American colonies, in 1752, decreeing that the day following Sept. 2, 1752, should be called Sept. 14, a loss of 11 days. All dates preceding were marked OS, for Old Style. In addition, New Year's Day was moved to Jan. 1 from Mar. 25. (Under the old reckoning, for example, Mar. 24, 1700, was followed by Mar. 25, 1701.) Thus George Washington's birth date, which was Feb. 11, 1731, OS, became Feb. 22, 1732, NS (New Style). In 1753, Sweden also went Gregorian.

In 1793, the French revolutionary government adopted a calendar of 12 months of 30 days each with five extra days in Sept. of each common year and six extra days every fourth year. Napoleon reinstated the Gregorian calendar in 1806.

The Gregorian system later spread to non-European regions, replacing traditional calendars at least for official purposes. Japan in 1873, Egypt in 1875, China in 1912, and Turkey in 1925 made the change, usually in conjunction with political upheaval. In China, the republican government began reckoning years from its 1911 founding. After 1949, the People's Republic adopted the Common (or Christian) Era year count, even for the traditional lunar calendar, which it retained. In 1918, the Soviet Union decreed that the day after Jan. 31, 1918, OS, would be Feb. 14, 1918, NS. Greece changed over in 1923. The Russian Orthodox church and some other Christian sects retained the Julian calendar. Saudi Arabia switched to the Gregorian calendar in 2016.

As of 2023, several nations officially used non-Gregorian calendars. Ethiopia used a calendar similar to the Julian system, and Afghanistan and Iran used the traditional Persian, or Solar Hijri, calendar.

To convert from the Julian to the Gregorian calendar, add 10 days to dates Oct. 5, 1582, through Feb. 28, 1700; after that date, add 11 days through Feb. 28, 1800; 12 days through Feb. 28, 1900; and 13 days through Feb. 28, 2100.

A **century** consists of 100 consecutive years. The 1st century CE may be said to have run from the years 1 through 100. The 20th century by this reckoning consisted of the years 1901 through 2000 and ended Dec. 31, 2000, as did the 2nd millennium CE. The 21st century thus technically began on Jan. 1, 2001.

For a **perpetual calendar**, see pages 352-53.

Gregorian Calendar

Choose the desired year from the table below or from the perpetual calendar (for years 1803 to 2080). The number after each year designates which calendar to use for that year, as shown in the perpetual calendar. (The Gregorian calendar was inaugurated Oct. 15, 1582. From that date through Dec. 31, 1582, use calendar 6.)

1583-1802

Year	#	Year	#	Year	#	Year	#	Year	#	Year	#	Year	#	Year	#	Year	#	Year	#	Year	#
1583	7	1603	4	1623	1	1643	5	1663	2	1683	6	1703	2	1723	6	1743	3	1763	7	1783	4
1584	8	1604	12	1624	9	1644	13	1664	10	1684	14	1704	10	1724	14	1744	11	1764	8	1784	12
1585	3	1605	7	1625	4	1645	1	1665	5	1685	2	1705	5	1725	2	1745	6	1765	3	1785	7
1586	4	1606	1	1626	5	1646	2	1666	6	1686	3	1706	6	1726	3	1746	7	1766	4	1786	1
1587	5	1607	2	1627	6	1647	3	1667	7	1687	4	1707	7	1727	4	1747	1	1767	5	1787	2
1588	13	1608	10	1628	14	1648	11	1668	8	1688	12	1708	8	1728	12	1748	9	1768	13	1788	10
1589	1	1609	5	1629	2	1649	6	1669	3	1689	7	1709	3	1729	7	1749	4	1769	1	1789	5
1590	2	1610	6	1630	3	1650	7	1670	4	1690	1	1710	4	1730	1	1750	5	1770	2	1790	6
1591	3	1611	7	1631	4	1651	1	1671	5	1691	2	1711	5	1731	2	1751	6	1771	3	1791	7
1592	11	1612	8	1632	12	1652	9	1672	13	1692	10	1712	13	1732	10	1752	14	1772	11	1792	8
1593	6	1613	3	1633	7	1653	4	1673	1	1693	5	1713	1	1733	5	1753	2	1773	6	1793	3
1594	7	1614	4	1634	1	1654	5	1674	2	1694	6	1714	2	1734	6	1754	3	1774	7	1794	4
1595	1	1615	5	1635	2	1655	6	1675	3	1695	7	1715	3	1735	7	1755	4	1775	1	1795	5
1596	9	1616	13	1636	10	1656	14	1676	11	1696	8	1716	11	1736	8	1756	12	1776	9	1796	13
1597	4	1617	1	1637	5	1657	2	1677	6	1697	3	1717	6	1737	3	1757	7	1777	4	1797	1
1598	5	1618	2	1638	6	1658	3	1678	7	1698	4	1718	7	1738	4	1758	1	1778	5	1798	2
1599	6	1619	3	1639	7	1659	4	1679	1	1699	5	1719	1	1739	5	1759	2	1779	6	1799	3
1600	14	1620	11	1640	8	1660	12	1680	9	1700	6	1720	9	1740	13	1760	10	1780	14	1800	4
1601	2	1621	6	1641	3	1661	7	1681	4	1701	7	1721	4	1741	1	1761	5	1781	2	1801	5
1602	3	1622	7	1642	4	1662	1	1682	5	1702	1	1722	5	1742	2	1762	6	1782	3	1802	6

Julian Period

How many days have you lived? To determine this, multiply your age by 365, add the number of days since your last birthday, and account for all leap years. Chances are your calculations will go wrong somewhere. Astronomers, however, find it convenient to express dates and time intervals in days rather than in years, months, and days. This is done by placing events within the Julian period.

The Julian period was devised in 1583 by the French classical scholar Joseph Scaliger (1540-1609). Some sources postulate Scaliger named it after his father, Julius Caesar Scaliger; others cite Scaliger's references to the Julian calendar.

Scaliger began with a zero hour, or starting time, of noon on Jan. 1, 4713 BCE (on the Julian calendar). This was the most recent time that three major chronological cycles began on the same day: (1) the 28-year solar cycle, after which dates in the Julian calendar return to the same days of the week (e.g., Feb. 11 falls on a Monday); (2) the 19-year lunar cycle, after which the phases of the moon return to the same dates of the year; and (3) the 15-year indiction cycle, used in ancient Rome to regulate taxes.

It will take 7,980 years to complete the period, the product of the numbers 28, 19, and 15, which have no common factors.

Noon (Universal Time) of Jan. 1, 2024, will be Julian date (JD) 2,460,311; that many days will have passed since the start of the current Julian period. The JD at noon of any date in 2024 may be found by adding to that number the day of the year for that date and subtracting one.

Julian Calendar

To find which of the 14 calendars of the perpetual calendar (pages 352-53) applies to any year under the Julian system, find the century for the desired year in the three leftmost columns below. Locate the desired year from among the four top rows. The number at the intersection of that row and column is the calendar designation for that year. For some years and countries, the Julian new year did not start Jan. 1; to find the correct perpetual calendar for Britain and its possessions, you can generally add one year for dates from Jan. 1 to Mar. 24. For example, to look up Feb. 2, 1705, Old Style, use the year 1706.

Year (last 2 digits of desired year)

		01	02	03	04	05	06	07	08	09	10	11	12	13	14	15	16	17	18	19	20	21	22	23	24	25	26	27	28
		29	30	31	32	33	34	35	36	37	38	39	40	41	42	43	44	45	46	47	48	49	50	51	52	53	54	55	56
		57	58	59	60	61	62	63	64	65	66	67	68	69	70	71	72	73	74	75	76	77	78	79	80	81	82	83	84
Century	00	85	86	87	88	89	90	91	92	93	94	95	96	97	98	99													
0	700 1400	12	7	1	2	10	5	6	7	8	3	4	5	13	1	2	3	11	6	7	1	9	4	5	6	14	2	3	4	12
100	800 1500	11	6	7	1	9	4	5	6	14	2	3	4	12	7	1	2	10	5	6	7	8	3	4	5	13	1	2	3	11
200	900 1600	10	5	6	7	8	3	4	5	13	1	2	3	11	6	7	1	9	4	5	6	14	2	3	4	12	7	1	2	10
300	1000 1700	9	4	5	6	14	2	3	4	12	7	1	2	10	5	6	7	8	3	4	5	13	1	2	3	11	6	7	1	9
400	1100 1800	8	3	4	5	13	1	2	3	11	6	7	1	9	4	5	6	14	2	3	4	12	7	1	2	10	5	6	7	8
500	1200 1900	14	2	3	4	12	7	1	2	10	5	6	7	8	3	4	5	13	1	2	3	11	6	7	1	9	4	5	6	14
600	1300 2000	13	1	2	3	11	6	7	1	9	4	5	6	14	2	3	4	12	7	1	2	10	5	6	7	8	3	4	5	13

Signs of the Zodiac

The zodiac is the apparent yearly path of the sun among the stars as viewed from Earth and was divided by the ancients into 12 equal sections or signs, each named for the constellation situated within its limits in ancient times. Astrologers claim that the temperament and destiny of each individual depend on the zodiac sign under which the person was born and the relationships between the planets at that time and throughout the person's life.

Below are the 12 traditional signs and the traditional range of dates pertaining to each:

♈ **Aries** (Ram), March 21-April 19

♉ **Taurus** (Bull), April 20-May 20

♊ **Gemini** (Twins), May 21-June 21

♋ **Cancer** (Crab), June 22-July 22

♌ **Leo** (Lion), July 23-August 22

♍ **Virgo** (Virgin), August 23-September 22

♎ **Libra** (Scales), September 23-October 23

♏ **Scorpio** (Scorpion), October 24-November 21

♐ **Sagittarius** (Archer), November 22-December 21

♑ **Capricorn** (Goat), December 22-January 19

♒ **Aquarius** (Water Bearer), January 20-February 18

♓ **Pisces** (Fishes), February 19-March 20

Chinese Calendar and Asian Festivals

The Chinese calendar, like the Jewish and Islamic calendars (see the Religion chapter), is a lunisolar calendar. It is divided into 12 months of 29 or 30 days (compensating for the lunar month's mean duration of 29 days, 12 hr., 44.05 min.). This calendar is synchronized with the solar year by the addition of extra months at fixed intervals.

The Chinese calendar runs on a 60-year cycle. The last 24 years of the cycle 1864-1923 along with the cycles 1924-83 and 1984-2043, and the first 24 years of the cycle 2044-2103 are shown below grouped by their association with 1 of 12 animals in the Chinese zodiac. Feb. 10, 2024, marks the beginning of the year 4722 in the Chinese calendar and is designated the Year of the Dragon.

Both the Western (Gregorian) and traditional lunar calendars are used publicly in China and in North and South Korea, and two New Year's celebrations are held. In Taiwan and in Vietnam and in overseas Chinese communities, the lunar calendar is used only to set the dates for traditional festivals, with the Gregorian system in general use.

The 4-day Chinese New Year; the 3-day Vietnamese New Year festival, Tet; and the 3-to-4-day Korean festival, Suhl, begin at the second new moon after the winter solstice. The new moon in East Asia, which is west of the international date line, may be a day later than the new moon in the U.S. The festivals may start, therefore, anywhere between Jan. 21 and Feb. 19 of the Gregorian calendar.

Rat	Ox	Tiger	Hare (Rabbit)	Dragon	Snake	Horse	Sheep (Goat)	Monkey	Rooster	Dog	Pig (Boar)
1900	1901	1902	1903	1904	1905	1906	1907	1908	1909	1910	1911
1912	1913	1914	1915	1916	1917	1918	1919	1920	1921	1922	1923
1924	1925	1926	1927	1928	1929	1930	1931	1932	1933	1934	1935
1936	1937	1938	1939	1940	1941	1942	1943	1944	1945	1946	1947
1948	1949	1950	1951	1952	1953	1954	1955	1956	1957	1958	1959
1960	1961	1962	1963	1964	1965	1966	1967	1968	1969	1970	1971
1972	1973	1974	1975	1976	1977	1978	1979	1980	1981	1982	1983
1984	1985	1986	1987	1988	1989	1990	1991	1992	1993	1994	1995
1996	1997	1998	1999	2000	2001	2002	2003	2004	2005	2006	2007
2008	2009	2010	2011	2012	2013	2014	2015	2016	2017	2018	2019
2020	2021	2022	2023	2024	2025	2026	2027	2028	2029	2030	2031
2032	2033	2034	2035	2036	2037	2038	2039	2040	2041	2042	2043
2044	2045	2046	2047	2048	2049	2050	2051	2052	2053	2054	2055
2056	2057	2058	2059	2060	2061	2062	2063	2064	2065	2066	2067

Note: The first 3-7 weeks of each Western year belong to the previous Chinese year.

Calendar for the Year 2024

January
S	M	T	W	T	F	S
	1	2	3	4	5	6
7	8	9	10	11	12	13
14	15	16	17	18	19	20
21	22	23	24	25	26	27
28	29	30	31			

February
S	M	T	W	T	F	S
				1	2	3
4	5	6	7	8	9	10
11	12	13	14	15	16	17
18	19	20	21	22	23	24
25	26	27	28	29		

March
S	M	T	W	T	F	S
					1	2
3	4	5	6	7	8	9
10	11	12	13	14	15	16
17	18	19	20	21	22	23
24	25	26	27	28	29	30
31						

April
S	M	T	W	T	F	S
	1	2	3	4	5	6
7	8	9	10	11	12	13
14	15	16	17	18	19	20
21	22	23	24	25	26	27
28	29	30				

May
S	M	T	W	T	F	S
			1	2	3	4
5	6	7	8	9	10	11
12	13	14	15	16	17	18
19	20	21	22	23	24	25
26	27	28	29	30	31	

June
S	M	T	W	T	F	S
						1
2	3	4	5	6	7	8
9	10	11	12	13	14	15
16	17	18	19	20	21	22
23	24	25	26	27	28	29
30						

July
S	M	T	W	T	F	S
	1	2	3	4	5	6
7	8	9	10	11	12	13
14	15	16	17	18	19	20
21	22	23	24	25	26	27
28	29	30	31			

August
S	M	T	W	T	F	S
				1	2	3
4	5	6	7	8	9	10
11	12	13	14	15	16	17
18	19	20	21	22	23	24
25	26	27	28	29	30	31

September
S	M	T	W	T	F	S
1	2	3	4	5	6	7
8	9	10	11	12	13	14
15	16	17	18	19	20	21
22	23	24	25	26	27	28
29	30					

October
S	M	T	W	T	F	S
		1	2	3	4	5
6	7	8	9	10	11	12
13	14	15	16	17	18	19
20	21	22	23	24	25	26
27	28	29	30	31		

November
S	M	T	W	T	F	S
					1	2
3	4	5	6	7	8	9
10	11	12	13	14	15	16
17	18	19	20	21	22	23
24	25	26	27	28	29	30

December
S	M	T	W	T	F	S
1	2	3	4	5	6	7
8	9	10	11	12	13	14
15	16	17	18	19	20	21
22	23	24	25	26	27	28
29	30	31				

Federal Holidays and Other Notable Dates, 2024

Some dates may be subject to change.

The dates in bold in the calendar above and named below in italics are U.S. federal holidays, designated by the president or Congress and applicable to federal employees and in the District of Columbia. Most U.S. states also observe these holidays, and many states observe others; practices vary by state. In most states the secretary of state's office can provide details.

January
1 *New Year's Day*; Rose Bowl, Sugar Bowl
8 College Football Playoff national championship game (Houston, TX)
15 *Martin Luther King Jr. Day*
15-28 Australian Open tennis tournament
26 Australia Day (observed)

February
2 Groundhog Day
9-14 Carnival, Brazil
10 Chinese New Year
11 Super Bowl LVIII (Las Vegas, NV)
12 Lincoln's Birthday
13 Mardi Gras
14 Ash Wednesday; Valentine's Day
18 NBA All-Star Game (Indianapolis, IN); Daytona 500
19 *Washington's Birthday* (observed), a.k.a. Presidents' Day, or Washington-Lincoln Day (3rd Mon. in Feb.)

March
2 Iditarod Trail Sled Dog Race begins
10 Academy Awards; Daylight saving time begins in U.S.
11 Ramadan (Islamic month of fasting), 1st full day
17 St. Patrick's Day
19 First day of spring (Northern Hemisphere)
21 Benito Juárez's Birthday, Mexico
24 Purim (Feast of Lots) begins previous night
29 Good Friday
31 Easter

April
1 April Fools' Day
5, 7 NCAA Women's Basketball Final Four (Cleveland, OH)
6, 8 NCAA Men's Basketball Final Four (Phoenix, AZ)
8-14 Masters golf tournament
15 Patriots' Day; Boston Marathon (3rd Mon. in Apr.); Tax Day (IRS filing deadline)
22 Earth Day
23 Passover, 1st full day
25 Take Our Daughters and Sons to Work Day
26 Arbor Day

May
1 May Day (International Workers' Day)
4 Kentucky Derby
5 Cinco de Mayo (Battle of Puebla Day), Mexico; Easter (Orthodox)
12 Mother's Day
16-19 PGA Championship (Louisville, KY)
15 Buddha's Birthday, Hong Kong, Korea
18 Armed Forces Day; Preakness Stakes
20 Victoria Day, Canada
26–June 9 French Open tennis tournament
27 *Memorial Day*, or Decoration Day (last Mon. in May)
30–June 2 U.S. Women's Open golf tournament (Lancaster, PA)

June
8 Belmont Stakes
10 Dragon Boat Festival, China
13-16 U.S. Open golf tournament (Pinehurst, NC)
14 Flag Day
16 Father's Day
19 *Juneteenth*
20 First day of summer (Northern Hemisphere)

July
1 Canada Day
1-14 Wimbledon tennis tournament
4 *Independence Day*
7 Islamic New Year (Muharram 1) begins previous night
7-14 Running of the Bulls (Pamplona, Spain)
14 Bastille Day, France
18-21 British Open golf tournament (Troon, Scotland, UK)
26-Aug. 11 Summer Olympic Games (Paris, France)

September
2 *Labor Day*, U.S., Canada (1st Mon. in Sept.)
8 Grandparents' Day, U.S.
16 Independence Day, Mexico (celebration begins previous night)
17 Constitution Day and Citizenship Day, U.S.
22 First day of autumn (Northern Hemisphere)

October
3 Rosh Hashanah (New Year), 1st full day
7 U.S. Supreme Court session begins
12 Yom Kippur (Day of Atonement) begins previous night; Día de la Raza, Spain, Mexico
14 *Columbus Day* (2nd Monday in Oct.); Thanksgiving Day, Canada
31 Halloween

November
1 All Saints' Day
3 Daylight saving time ends in U.S.; New York City Marathon
5 Election Day (1st Tues. after 1st Mon. in Nov.)
10 Remembrance Sunday, UK
11 *Veterans Day*; Remembrance Day, Canada
28 *Thanksgiving Day*

December
10 Nobel Prizes awarded (winners announced in Oct.)
12 Día de la Virgen de Guadalupe, Mexico
21 First day of winter (Northern Hemisphere)
25 *Christmas Day*
26 Boxing Day, Australia, Canada, New Zealand, UK
26-Jan. 1 Kwanzaa
26-Jan. 2 Hanukkah (Festival of Lights) begins previous night

Perpetual Calendar

The number shown for each year indicates which Gregorian calendar to use. For 1583-1802, see "Gregorian Calendar" on page 349. For 1803-20, use numbers for 1983-2000, respectively. The years in the calendar labels are the last and next occurrences of each calendar.

2018/2029 — 2

2017/2023 — 1

2014/2025 — 4

2019/2030 — 3

2021/2027 — 6

2015/2026 — 5

Each calendar block lists the months JANUARY, FEBRUARY, MARCH, APRIL, MAY, JUNE, JULY, AUGUST, SEPTEMBER, OCTOBER, NOVEMBER, DECEMBER with day columns S M T W T F S.

Year	No.	Year	No.	Year	No.	Year	No.
1821	.2	1847	.6	1873	.4	1899	.1
1822	.3	1848	.14	1874	.5	1900	.2
1823	.4	1849	.2	1875	.6	1901	.3
1824	.12	1850	.3	1876	.14	1902	.4
1825	.7	1851	.4	1877	.2	1903	.5
1826	.1	1852	.12	1878	.3	1904	.13
1827	.2	1853	.7	1879	.4	1905	.1
1828	.10	1854	.1	1880	.12	1906	.2
1829	.5	1855	.2	1881	.7	1907	.3
1830	.6	1856	.10	1882	.1	1908	.11
1831	.7	1857	.5	1883	.2	1909	.6
1832	.8	1858	.6	1884	.10	1910	.7
1833	.3	1859	.7	1885	.5	1911	.1
1834	.4	1860	.8	1886	.6	1912	.9
1835	.5	1861	.3	1887	.7	1913	.4
1836	.13	1862	.4	1888	.8	1914	.5
1837	.1	1863	.5	1889	.3	1915	.6
1838	.2	1864	.13	1890	.4	1916	.14
1839	.3	1865	.1	1891	.5	1917	.2
1840	.11	1866	.2	1892	.13	1918	.3
1841	.6	1867	.3	1893	.1	1919	.4
1842	.7	1868	.11	1894	.2	1920	.12
1843	.1	1869	.6	1895	.3	1921	.7
1844	.9	1870	.7	1896	.11	1922	.1
1845	.4	1871	.1	1897	.6	1923	.2
1846	.5	1872	.9	1898	.7	1924	.10

Year	No.	Year	No.	Year	No.	Year	No.
1925	.5	1951	.2	1977	.7	2003	.4
1926	.6	1952	.10	1978	.1	2004	.12
1927	.7	1953	.5	1979	.2	2005	.7
1928	.8	1954	.6	1980	.10	2006	.1
1929	.3	1955	.7	1981	.5	2007	.2
1930	.4	1956	.8	1982	.6	2008	.10
1931	.5	1957	.3	1983	.7	2009	.5
1932	.13	1958	.4	1984	.8	2010	.6
1933	.1	1959	.5	1985	.3	2011	.7
1934	.2	1960	.13	1986	.4	2012	.8
1935	.3	1961	.1	1987	.5	2013	.3
1936	.11	1962	.2	1988	.13	2014	.4
1937	.6	1963	.3	1989	.1	2015	.5
1938	.7	1964	.11	1990	.2	2016	.13
1939	.1	1965	.6	1991	.3	2017	.1
1940	.9	1966	.7	1992	.11	2018	.2
1941	.4	1967	.1	1993	.6	2019	.3
1942	.5	1968	.9	1994	.7	2020	.11
1943	.6	1969	.4	1995	.1	2021	.6
1944	.14	1970	.5	1996	.9	2022	.7
1945	.2	1971	.6	1997	.4	2023	.1
1946	.3	1972	.14	1998	.5	2024	.9
1947	.4	1973	.2	1999	.6	2025	.4
1948	.12	1974	.3	2000	.14	2026	.5
1949	.7	1975	.4	2001	.2	2027	.6
1950	.1	1976	.12	2002	.3	2028	.14

Year	No.	Year	No.
2029	.2	2055	.6
2030	.3	2056	.14
2031	.4	2057	.2
2032	.12	2058	.3
2033	.7	2059	.4
2034	.1	2060	.12
2035	.2	2061	.7
2036	.10	2062	.1
2037	.5	2063	.2
2038	.6	2064	.10
2039	.7	2065	.5
2040	.8	2066	.6
2041	.3	2067	.7
2042	.4	2068	.8
2043	.5	2069	.3
2044	.13	2070	.4
2045	.1	2071	.5
2046	.2	2072	.13
2047	.3	2073	.1
2048	.11	2074	.2
2049	.6	2075	.3
2050	.7	2076	.11
2051	.1	2077	.6
2052	.9	2078	.7
2053	.4	2079	.1
2054	.5	2080	.9

7   2022/2033

JANUARY · FEBRUARY · MARCH · APRIL · MAY · JUNE · JULY · AUGUST · SEPTEMBER · OCTOBER · NOVEMBER · DECEMBER

8   2012/2040

JANUARY · FEBRUARY · MARCH · APRIL · MAY · JUNE · JULY · AUGUST · SEPTEMBER · OCTOBER · NOVEMBER · DECEMBER

9   1996/2024

JANUARY · FEBRUARY · MARCH · APRIL · MAY · JUNE · JULY · AUGUST · SEPTEMBER · OCTOBER · NOVEMBER · DECEMBER

10   2008/2036

JANUARY · FEBRUARY · MARCH · APRIL · MAY · JUNE · JULY · AUGUST · SEPTEMBER · OCTOBER · NOVEMBER · DECEMBER

11   2020/2048

JANUARY · FEBRUARY · MARCH · APRIL · MAY · JUNE · JULY · AUGUST · SEPTEMBER · OCTOBER · NOVEMBER · DECEMBER

12   2004/2032

JANUARY · FEBRUARY · MARCH · APRIL · MAY · JUNE · JULY · AUGUST · SEPTEMBER · OCTOBER · NOVEMBER · DECEMBER

13   2016/2044

JANUARY · FEBRUARY · MARCH · APRIL · MAY · JUNE · JULY · AUGUST · SEPTEMBER · OCTOBER · NOVEMBER · DECEMBER

14   2000/2028

JANUARY · FEBRUARY · MARCH · APRIL · MAY · JUNE · JULY · AUGUST · SEPTEMBER · OCTOBER · NOVEMBER · DECEMBER

Other Calendars: Year and New Year's Day, 2024

Era	Year	Begins in 2024	Era	Year	Begins in 2024
Byzantine	7533	Sept. 14	Islamic/Muslim (Hijra)	1446	July 7[1]
Chinese (Year of the Dragon)	4722	Feb. 10	Japanese[2]	6	May 1
Diocletian	1741	Sept. 11	Jewish	5785	Oct. 3[1]
Grecian (Seleucidae)	2336	Sept. 14 or Oct. 14	Nabonassar (Babylonian)	2773	Apr. 23
Indian (Saka)	1946	Mar. 21	Roman (Ab Urbe Condita)	2777	Jan. 14

(1) Year begins the previous night. (2) Era starts at 0 with new emperor.

Chronological Cycles, 2024

Dominical Letter . . . . GF	Roman Indiction 2	Solar Cycle 17
Golden Number (lunar cycle) XI	Epact 19	Julian Period (year of) 6737

Special Months

There are many thousands of special months, days, and weeks because of anniversaries, official proclamations, and promotional events, both trivial and serious. Here are a few of the special months:

January: Get Organized Month, National Mentoring Month, National Poverty in America Awareness Month

February: Black History Month, American Heart Month, Library Lovers' Month, Youth Leadership Month

March: Irish-American Heritage Month, National Women's History Month, Red Cross Month, National Frozen Food Month, National Colorectal Cancer Awareness Month

April: National Child Abuse Prevention Month, National Humor Month, Stress Awareness Month, Grange Month, Sexual Assault Awareness and Prevention Month

May: Clean Air Month, Get Caught Reading Month, National Barbecue Month, Asian American and Pacific Islander Heritage Month, National Inventors Month, National Mental Health Month

June: Great Outdoors Month; Lesbian, Gay, Bisexual, and Transgender Pride Month; National Safety Month

July: Cell Phone Courtesy Month, National Hot Dog Month, National Make a Difference to Children Month, Women's Motorcycle Month

August: National Black Business Month, Happiness Happens Month, National Immunization Awareness Month

September: Library Card Sign-Up Month, National Hispanic Heritage Month (Sept. 15-Oct. 15), National Biscuit Month

October: Adopt-A-Shelter-Dog Month, National Domestic Violence Awareness Month, National Breast Cancer Awareness Month, Global Diversity Awareness Month, National Popcorn Poppin' Month

November: National American Indian Heritage Month, National Adoption Month, American Diabetes Month, National Peanut Butter Lovers' Month

December: Safe Toys and Gifts Month, National Impaired Driving Prevention Month, National Tie Month

Standard Time Differences: World Cities

The time indicated in the table is fixed by law and is called the legal time or, more generally, standard time. Use of daylight saving time varies widely. An asterisk (*) indicates morning of the following day. At 12:00 noon, Eastern Standard Time, the standard time (in 24-hour time) in selected cities is as shown.

City			City			City			City		
Abu Dhabi	21	00	Denver	10	00	Lisbon	17	00	St. Petersburg	20	00
Addis Ababa	20	00	Dhaka	23	00	London	17	00	Santiago	13	00
Amsterdam	18	00	Dublin	17	00	Los Angeles	9	00	São Paulo	14	00
Ankara	20	00	Edinburgh	17	00	Madrid	18	00	Sarajevo	18	00
Athens	19	00	Geneva	18	00	Manila	1	00*	Seoul	2	00*
Auckland	5	00*	Helsinki	19	00	Mecca	20	00	Shanghai	1	00*
Baghdad	20	00	Ho Chi Minh City	0	00*	Melbourne	3	00*	Singapore	1	00*
Bangkok	0	00*	Hong Kong	1	00*	Montevideo	14	00	Stockholm	18	00
Beijing	1	00*	Honolulu	7	00	Moscow	20	00	Sydney	3	00*
Belfast	17	00	Houston	11	00	Mumbai (Bombay)	22	30	Taipei	1	00*
Belgrade	18	00	Islamabad	22	00	Munich	18	00	Tashkent	22	00
Berlin	18	00	Istanbul	20	00	Nagasaki	2	00*	Tehran	20	30
Bogotá	12	00	Jakarta	0	00*	Nairobi	20	00	Tel Aviv	19	00
Brussels	18	00	Jerusalem	19	00	New Delhi	22	30	Tokyo	2	00*
Bucharest	19	00	Johannesburg	19	00	New York	12	00	Toronto	12	00
Budapest	18	00	Kabul	21	30	Oslo	18	00	Vancouver	9	00
Buenos Aires	14	00	Karachi	22	00	Paris	18	00	Vienna	18	00
Cairo	19	00	Kathmandu	22	45	Prague	18	00	Vladivostok	3	00*
Cape Town	19	00	Kiev	19	00	Pyongyang	2	00*	Warsaw	18	00
Caracas	13	00	Kinshasa	18	00	Quito	12	00	Wellington	5	00*
Casablanca	17	00	Kolkata (Calcutta)	22	30	Rio de Janeiro	14	00	Yangon (Rangoon)	23	30
Chicago	11	00	Lagos	18	00	Riyadh	20	00	Yokohama	2	00*
Copenhagen	18	00	Lima	12	00	Rome	18	00	Zurich	18	00

Wedding Anniversary Gifts

The traditional names for wedding anniversaries go back many years in social usage and have been used to suggest types of appropriate anniversary gifts. Traditional products for gifts are listed here in capital letters, with allowable revisions in parentheses, followed by common modern gifts for each anniversary.

Anniversary	Gift	Anniversary	Gift	Anniversary	Gift
1st	PAPER, clocks	9th	POTTERY (CHINA),	25th	SILVER, sterling silver
2nd	COTTON, china		leather goods	30th	PEARL, diamond
3rd	LEATHER, crystal, glass	10th	TIN, ALUMINUM, diamond	35th	CORAL (JADE), jade
4th	LINEN (SILK), appliances	11th	STEEL, fashion jewelry	40th	RUBY, ruby
5th	WOOD, silverware	12th	SILK, pearls, colored gems	45th	SAPPHIRE, sapphire
6th	IRON, wood objects	13th	LACE, textiles, furs	50th	GOLD, gold
7th	WOOL (COPPER),	14th	IVORY, gold jewelry	55th	EMERALD, emerald
	desk sets	15th	CRYSTAL, watches	60th	DIAMOND, diamond
8th	BRONZE, linens, lace	20th	CHINA, platinum		

Birthstones

Source: American Gem Society

Birth month	Ancient[1] birthstone	Modern birthstone	Birth month	Ancient[1] birthstone	Modern birthstone
January	Garnet	Garnet	July	Onyx	Ruby
February	Amethyst	Amethyst	August	Carnelian	Sardonyx or Peridot
March	Jasper	Bloodstone or Aquamarine	September	Chrysolite	Sapphire
April	Sapphire	Diamond	October	Aquamarine	Opal or Tourmaline
May	Agate, Chalcedony, or Carnelian	Emerald	November	Topaz	Topaz
June	Emerald	Pearl, Moonstone, or Alexandrite	December	Ruby	Turquoise, Tanzanite, or Zircon

(1) Varied by region and culture. Birthstones listed here are those of ancient Hebrew tradition.

Standard Time and Daylight Saving Time

Source: National Institute of Standards and Technology, U.S. Dept. of Commerce

See also Time Zone map, page 492.

Standard Time

Standard time is reckoned from the prime meridian of longitude in Greenwich, England. The world is divided into 24 zones, each 15 deg of arc, or one hour in time apart. The Greenwich meridian (0 deg) extends through the center of the initial zone. Each zone extends 7.5 deg on either side of its central meridian. Zones to the east are numbered from 1 to 12, with the prefix "minus" indicating the number of hours to be subtracted to obtain Greenwich Time.

Westward zones are similarly numbered, but prefixed "plus," showing the number of hours that must be added to get Greenwich Time. The standard time maintained in many countries does not coincide with zone time. For example, China extends across five time zones, but the entire country is on Greenwich Time plus 8 hours.

The U.S. and possessions are divided into nine standard time zones. All places in each zone use, instead of their local time, the time counted from the transit of the mean sun across the standard time meridian that passes near the middle of that zone. These time zones are designated as Atlantic, Eastern, Central, Mountain, Pacific, Alaska, Hawaii-Aleutian, Samoa, and Chamorro (Guam and Northern Mariana Isls.); the time in these zones is reckoned from the 60th, 75th, 90th, 105th, 120th, 135th, 150th, and 165th meridians west of Greenwich and the 150th meridian east of Greenwich. The time zone line wanders to conform to local geography. The time in the various zones in the U.S. and U.S. territories west of Greenwich is earlier than Greenwich Time by 4, 5, 6, 7, 8, 9, 10, and 11 hours, respectively. However, Chamorro crosses the international date line and is 10 hours later than Greenwich Time.

24-Hour Time

With the 24-hour system, the day begins at midnight, and times are designated 00:00 through 23:59. Twenty-four-hour time is widely used in scientific work throughout the world. In the U.S., it is also used in operations of the armed forces. In Europe, it is frequently used by the transportation networks in preference to the 12-hour AM and PM system.

International Date Line

The date line, approximately coinciding with the 180th meridian, separates the calendar dates. The date must be advanced one day when crossing in a westerly direction and set back one day when crossing in an easterly direction. The date line frequently deviates from the 180th meridian because of decisions by affected nations. The line is deflected eastward through the Bering Strait and westward of the Aleutians to prevent separating the islands by date. The line is deflected eastward of the Tonga and New Zealand islands in the South Pacific. In 1995, Kiribati announced that its islands east of the date line would observe the same date as islands to the west, though most maps do not depict this deviation in the date line. In 2011, Samoa moved west of the date line to ease its relationship with Australia and New Zealand. The line is established by international custom; there is no international authority prescribing its exact course.

Daylight Saving Time

Daylight saving time is achieved by advancing the clock one hour. Since 2007, daylight saving time has begun at 2 AM on the second Sunday in Mar. and has ended at 2 AM on the first Sunday in Nov. **In 2024, daylight saving time begins at 2 AM on Mar. 10 and ends at 2 AM on Nov. 3.** Prior to 2007, daylight saving time traditionally ran from the first Sunday in Apr. to the last Sunday in Oct.

Daylight saving time was first observed in the U.S. during World War I and again during World War II. In 1966, Congress passed the Uniform Time Act, which provided that any state or territory choosing to observe daylight saving time must begin and end on the dates established by federal law. Any state could, by law, exempt itself; a 1972 amendment to the act authorized states in more than one time zone to exempt the entire state or one time zone only. Currently, most of Arizona, Hawaii, Puerto Rico, the U.S. Virgin Islands, Guam, American Samoa, and Northern Mariana Isls. do not observe daylight saving time. All of Indiana, which is in two time zones, observed daylight saving time for the first time in 2006.

Congress and the secretary of transportation both have authority to change time zone boundaries, which they have done on a number of occasions since 1966. In 2018, Florida passed legislation that would keep the state on daylight saving time year-round, but either Congress or the Transportation Dept. was required to act before the new law could go into effect. By mid 2023, 17 other U.S. states had also passed laws/regulations maintaining year-round DST. The Senate—but not yet the House—in Mar. 2022 unanimously passed legislation to make DST permanent beginning in 2023; following the bill's expiration, it was reintroduced in the Senate and House in Mar. 2023.

Daylight Saving Time: International Usage

Canada, which extends over six time zones, generally observes daylight saving time during the same period as the U.S. Most provincial governments observe the four-week extension to daylight saving time that went into effect in 2007. Most of Saskatchewan remains on standard time year-round; communities elsewhere in Canada may also exempt themselves from daylight saving time. Beginning in Mar. 2020, the territory Yukon began observing Pacific Daylight Saving Time year-round. Mexico in late Oct. 2022 stopped observing daylight saving time, with the exception of in cities bordering the U.S.

Member nations of the European Union observe a "summertime period," a version of daylight saving time, from the last Sunday of Mar. until the last Sunday in Oct. Although the EU Parliament in Mar. 2019 voted to end mandatory DST starting in 2021 and instead allow member countries to follow permanent standard time if they choose, European Council negotiations to do so had not started as of Aug. 2023.

Turkey stopped observing daylight saving time in 2016, maintaining its "summer hours." Russia, which uses 11 time zones, moved to permanent standard time in 2014 after a three-year experiment to maintain year-round "summer hours" proved unpopular. The country observed "winter hours" year-round beginning in Oct. 2014. Morocco abandoned daylight saving time in Oct. 2018, with a Ramadan exception, and officials in both Jordan and Syria in Oct. 2022 independently announced the countries would remain permanently on daylight saving time, with exceptions within Syria. After an eight-year lapse, Egypt reintroduced daylight saving time in Apr. 2023.

China does not observe daylight saving time. Mongolia discontinued daylight saving time in 2017, two years after it was reintroduced. Japan, which lies within one time zone, also does not modify its legal time during the summer months. Samoa scrapped DST in 2021, after adopting it in 2010, and Fiji suspended its use for both 2022 and 2023.

Many countries in the Southern Hemisphere maintain daylight saving time generally from Oct. to Mar. (Brazil, mostly south of the equator, scrapped daylight saving time in 2019.) However, most countries near the equator do not deviate from standard time.

WEIGHTS AND MEASURES

Source: National Institute of Standards and Technology (NIST), U.S. Dept. of Commerce

International System of Units (SI)

Two systems of weights and measures coexist in the U.S. today: the **U.S. Customary System** and the **International System of Units** (SI, for Système International d'Unités). The SI is a more complete, coherent version of the **metric system**. Throughout U.S. history, the customary system—parts of which were inherited but are now different from the British Imperial System—has been generally used. Federal and state legislation gave it, through implication, standing as the primary weights and measures system. The metric system, however, is the only system that Congress has ever specifically sanctioned, dating back to an 1866 law. The U.S. was one of the original 17 countries to sign the International Metric Convention (or Treaty of the Meter) May 20, 1875, which established several intergovernmental organizations to oversee and refine the SI. The U.S. is represented at these organizations by the Natl. Institute of Standards and Technology (NIST).

Since that time, use of the metric system in the U.S. has slowly increased, particularly in the scientific community, the pharmaceutical industry, and the manufacturing sector—the last motivated by the predominant use of the metric system in international commerce.

On Dec. 23, 1975, Pres. Gerald R. Ford signed the Metric Conversion Act of 1975. It defined the "metric system of measurement" as the SI, as established in 1960 by the General Conference on Weights and Measures and interpreted in the U.S. by the secretary of commerce, who delegated that authority to the director of the NIST. The Trade and Competitiveness Act of 1988 declared the metric system the preferred system of weights and measures for U.S. trade and commerce, but explicitly permitted "the continued use of traditional systems of weights and measures in nonbusiness activities." The Code of Federal Regulations made the use of metric units mandatory for federal agencies in 1991. However, the metric system has not yet become the system of choice for most Americans' daily use.

The following are the seven base SI units: **length**—meter; **mass**—kilogram; **time**—second; **electric current**—ampere; **thermodynamic temperature**—kelvin; **amount of substance**—mole; and **luminous intensity**—candela. All seven were redefined as of May 20, 2019, to emphasize the dependence of base unit definitions on physical constants with fixed numerical values and on the other base units.

Frequently Used Conversions

Boldface indicates exact values. For greater accuracy, use the "multiply by" number in parentheses. For weights, avoirdupois (avdp) weight is the system applied to all goods except medicines, precious metals, and precious stones.

U.S. Customary to Metric

	If you have:	Multiply by:		To get:
Length	inches	**25.4**		millimeters
	inches	**2.54**		centimeters
	inches	**0.0254**		meters
	feet	0.3	**(0.3048)**	meters
	yards	0.9	**(0.9144)**	meters
	miles[1]	1.6	**(1.609344)**	kilometers
Area	sq inches	6.5	**(6.4516)**	sq cm
	sq feet	0.09	**(0.09290304)**	sq meters
	sq yards	0.84	**(0.83612736)**	sq meters
	acres	0.4	(0.4046873)	hectares
	sq miles[1]	2.6	(2.58998811)	sq kilometers
Weight	ounces (avdp)	28	(28.34952)	grams
	pounds (avdp)	454	**(453.59237)**	grams
	pounds (avdp)	0.45	**(0.45359237)**	kilograms
	short tons[2]	0.91	**(0.90718474)**	metric tons
	long tons[3]	1	(1.016047)	metric tons
Liquid	ounces	0.03	(0.02957353)	liters
	cups	0.24	(0.23658824)	liters
	pints	0.47	(0.473176473)	liters
	quarts	0.95	(0.946352946)	liters
	gallons	3.79	(3.785412)	liters

Metric to U.S. Customary

	If you have:	Multiply by:		To get:
Length	millimeters	0.04	(0.03937)	inches
	centimeters	0.4	(0.3937)	inches
	meters	39	(39.37)	inches
	meters	3.3	(3.280840)	feet
	meters	1.1	(1.093613)	yards
	kilometers	0.6	(0.621371)	miles[1]
Area	sq cm	0.16	(0.15500)	sq inches
	sq meters	10.8	(10.76391)	sq feet
	sq meters	1.2	(1.195990)	sq yards
	hectares	2.5	(2.471044)	acres
	sq kilometers	0.39	(0.386102)	sq miles[1]
Weight	grams	0.035	(0.03527396)	ounces (avdp)
	grams	0.002	(0.00220462)	pounds (avdp)
	kilograms	2.2	(2.204623)	pounds (avdp)
	metric tons	1.1	(1.102311)	short tons[2]
	metric tons	0.98	(0.9842065)	long tons[3]
Liquid	liters	33.8	(33.81402)	ounces
	liters	4.2	(4.226752)	cups
	liters	2.1	(2.113376)	pints
	liters	1.1	(1.056688)	quarts
	liters	0.26	(0.264172)	gallons

(1) Survey mile. (2) A short ton is 2,000 pounds. (3) A long ton is 2,240 pounds.

Temperature Conversions

The left-hand column below gives a temperature according to the **Celsius** scale, and the right-hand gives the same temperature according to the **Fahrenheit** scale. The lowest number on each scale is equivalent to absolute zero, the theoretical temperature at which all molecular motion would stop.

For temperatures not shown: To convert Fahrenheit to Celsius, subtract 32 degrees and divide by 1.8; to convert Celsius to Fahrenheit, multiply by 1.8 and add 32 degrees.

Celsius	Fahrenheit	Celsius	Fahrenheit	Celsius	Fahrenheit	Celsius	Fahrenheit	Celsius	Fahrenheit
−273.15	−459.67	−45.6	−50	−1.1	30	30	86	65.6	150
−250	−418	**−40**	**−40**	0	32	32.2	90	70	158
−200	−328	−34.4	−30	4.4	40	35	95	80	176
−184.4	−300	−30	−22	10	50	37	98.6	90	194
−156.7	−250	−28.9	−20	15.6	60	37.8	100	93.3	200
−150	−238	−23.3	−10	20	68	40	104	**100**	**212**
−128.9	−200	−20	−4	21.1	70	43.3	110	121.1	250
−101.1	−150	−17.8	0	23.9	75	48.9	120	148.9	300
−100	−148	−12.2	10	25	77	50	122	150	302
−73.3	−100	−10	14	26.7	80	54.4	130	200	392
−50	−58	−6.7	20	29.4	85	60	140	300	572

Note: Although the term *centigrade* is still frequently used, the International Committee on Weights and Measures and the National Institute of Standards and Technology have recommended since 1948 that this scale be called *Celsius*.

Boiling and Freezing Points

Water boils at 212°F (100°C) at sea level. For every 550 feet above sea level, the boiling point of water is lower by about 1°F. Methyl alcohol (wood alcohol) boils at 148.5°F. Average human oral temperature is 98.6°F. **Water freezes** at 32°F (0°C).

Selected Geometric Formulas

The value of π (the Greek letter pi) is approximately 3.14159265 (equal to the ratio of the circumference of a circle to its diameter). The equivalence is typically rounded further to 3.1416 or 3.14.

Calculating Circumference
Circle: Multiply the diameter by π.

Calculating Area
Circle: Multiply the square of the radius (equal to ½ the diameter) by π.
Rectangle: Multiply the length of the base by the height.
Sphere (surface): Multiply the square of the radius by π and multiply by 4.
Square: Square the length of one side.
Trapezoid: Add the length of the two parallel sides, multiply by the height, and divide by 2.
Triangle: Multiply the base by the height and divide by 2.

Calculating Volume
Cone: Multiply the square of the radius of the base by π, multiply by the height, and divide by 3.
Cube: Cube the length of one edge.
Cylinder: Multiply the square of the radius of the base by π and multiply by the height.
Pyramid: Multiply the area of the base by the height and divide by 3.
Rectangular prism: Multiply the length by the width by the height.
Sphere: Multiply the cube of the radius by π, multiply by 4, and divide by 3.

Playing Cards and Dice Chances

5-Card Poker Hands

Hand	Number possible	Odds against
Royal flush	4	649,739 to 1
Other straight flush	36	72,192 to 1
Four of a kind	624	4,164 to 1
Full house	3,744	693 to 1
Flush	5,108	508 to 1
Straight	10,200	254 to 1
Three of a kind	54,912	46 to 1
Two pairs	123,552	20 to 1
One pair	1,098,240	4 to 3 (1.37 to 1)
Nothing	1,302,540	1 to 1
Total	**2,598,960**	

Bridge

The odds—against suit distribution in a hand of 4-4-3-2 are about 4 to 1; against 5-4-2-2 about 8 to 1; against 6-4-2-1 about 20 to 1; against 7-4-1-1 about 254 to 1; and against 8-4-1-0 about 2,211 to 1; and against 13-0-0-0 about 158,753,389,899 to 1.

Dice
(probabilities on 2 dice)

Total	Odds against (single toss)	Total	Odds against (single toss)
2	35 to 1	8	31 to 5
3	17 to 1	9	8 to 1
4	11 to 1	10	11 to 1
5	8 to 1	11	17 to 1
6	31 to 5	12	35 to 1
7	5 to 1		

Large Numbers

No. of zeros	U.S. term	British[1], French, German	No. of zeros	U.S. term	British[1], French, German
6	million	million	42	tredecillion	septillion
9	billion	milliard	45	quattuordecillion	1,000 septillion
12	trillion	billion	48	quindecillion	octillion
15	quadrillion	1,000 billion	51	sexdecillion	1,000 octillion
18	quintillion	trillion	54	septendecillion	nonillion
21	sextillion	1,000 trillion	57	octodecillion	1,000 nonillion
24	septillion	quadrillion	60	novemdecillion	decillion
27	octillion	1,000 quadrillion	63	vigintillion	1,000 decillion
30	nonillion	quintillion	100	googol	googol
33	decillion	1,000 quintillion	303	centillion	NA
36	undecillion	sextillion	600	NA	centillion
39	duodecillion	1,000 sextillion	googol	googolplex	googolplex

NA = Not available. (1) In recent years, it has become more common in Britain to use U.S. terminology for large numbers.

Prime Numbers to 1,009

A prime number is any positive integer greater than 1 that is divisible only by two positive integers—1 and itself.

	2	3	5	7	11	13	17	19	23
29	31	37	41	43	47	53	59	61	67
71	73	79	83	89	97	101	103	107	109
113	127	131	137	139	149	151	157	163	167
173	179	181	191	193	197	199	211	223	227
229	233	239	241	251	257	263	269	271	277
281	283	293	307	311	313	317	331	337	347
349	353	359	367	373	379	383	389	397	401
409	419	421	431	433	439	443	449	457	461
463	467	479	487	491	499	503	509	521	523
541	547	557	563	569	571	577	587	593	599
601	607	613	617	619	631	641	643	647	653
659	661	673	677	683	691	701	709	719	727
733	739	743	751	757	761	769	773	787	797
809	811	821	823	827	829	839	853	857	859
863	877	881	883	887	907	911	919	929	937
941	947	953	967	971	977	983	991	997	1,009

Common Fractions Converted to Decimals

8ths	16ths	32nds	64ths	= Decimal
			1	= 0.015625
		1	2	= 0.03125
			3	= 0.046875
	1	2	4	= 0.0625
			5	= 0.078125
		3	6	= 0.09375
			7	= 0.109375
1	2	4	8	= 0.125
			9	= 0.140625
		5	10	= 0.15625
			11	= 0.171875
	3	6	12	= 0.1875
			13	= 0.203125
		7	14	= 0.21875
			15	= 0.234375
2	4	8	16	= 0.25

8ths	16ths	32nds	64ths	= Decimal
			17	= 0.265625
	9		18	= 0.28125
			19	= 0.296875
5		10	20	= 0.3125
			21	= 0.328125
	11		22	= 0.34375
			23	= 0.359375
3	6	12	24	= 0.375
			25	= 0.390625
		13	26	= 0.40625
			27	= 0.421875
	7	14	28	= 0.4375
			29	= 0.453125
		15	30	= 0.46875
			31	= 0.484375
4	8	16	32	= 0.5

8ths	16ths	32nds	64ths	= Decimal
			33	= 0.515625
		17	34	= 0.53125
			35	= 0.546875
	9	18	36	= 0.5625
			37	= 0.578125
		19	38	= 0.59375
			39	= 0.609375
5	10	20	40	= 0.625
			41	= 0.640625
		21	42	= 0.65625
			43	= 0.671875
	11	22	44	= 0.6875
			45	= 0.703125
		23	46	= 0.71875
			47	= 0.734375
6	12	24	48	= 0.75

8ths	16ths	32nds	64ths	= Decimal
			49	= 0.765625
		25	50	= 0.78125
			51	= 0.796875
	13	26	52	= 0.8125
			53	= 0.828125
		27	54	= 0.84375
			55	= 0.859375
7	14	28	56	= 0.875
			57	= 0.890625
		29	58	= 0.90625
			59	= 0.921875
	15	30	60	= 0.9375
			61	= 0.953125
		31	62	= 0.96875
			63	= 0.984375
8	16	32	64	= 1.0

Roman Numerals

I — 1	IV — 4	VII — 7	X — 10	XX — 20	L — 50	C — 100	D — 500
II — 2	V — 5	VIII — 8	XI — 11	XXX — 30	LX — 60	CC — 200	CM — 900
III — 3	VI — 6	IX — 9	XIX — 19	XL — 40	XC — 90	CD — 400	M — 1,000

Note: The numerals V, X, L, C, D, or M shown with a horizontal line on top denote 1,000 times the original value.

Ancient Measures

Biblical

Cubit	=	21.8 inches
Omer	=	0.45 peck
	=	3.964 liters
Ephah	=	10 omers
Shekel	=	0.497 ounce
	=	14.1 grams

Greek

Cubit	=	18.3 inches
Stadion	=	607.2 or 622 feet
Obolos	=	715.38 milligrams
Drachma	=	4.2923 grams
Mina	=	0.9463 pound
Talent	=	60 mina

Roman

Cubit	=	17.5 inches
Stadium	=	202 yards
As, libra, pondus	=	325.971 grams
	=	0.71864 pound

Metric System Prefixes

The following prefixes, in combination with the basic unit names, provide the multiples and submultiples in the metric system. For example, the unit name *meter*, with the prefix *kilo* added, produces *kilometer*, meaning "1,000 meters."

Prefix	Symbol	Multiples	Equivalent	Prefix	Symbol	Multiples	Equivalent
yotta	Y	10^{24}	septillionfold	deci	d	10^{-1}	tenth part
zetta	Z	10^{21}	sextillionfold	centi	c	10^{-2}	hundredth part
exa	E	10^{18}	quintillionfold	milli	m	10^{-3}	thousandth part
peta	P	10^{15}	quadrillionfold	micro	µ	10^{-6}	millionth part
tera	T	10^{12}	trillionfold	nano	n	10^{-9}	billionth part
giga	G	10^{9}	billionfold	pico	p	10^{-12}	trillionth part
mega	M	10^{6}	millionfold	femto	f	10^{-15}	quadrillionth part
kilo	k	10^{3}	thousandfold	atto	a	10^{-18}	quintillionth part
hecto	h	10^{2}	hundredfold	zepto	z	10^{-21}	sextillionth part
deka	da	10^{1}	tenfold	yocto	y	10^{-24}	septillionth part

Weight and Measurement Equivalents

The international foot, defined in 1959 as exactly equal to 0.3048 meter, is shorter than the survey foot by exactly 2 parts in 1 million. This means that a mile, also known as an international mile, is about ⅛ inch shorter than the survey mile. The NIST discouraged the use of the survey foot or survey mile for any purposes after Jan. 1, 2023.

When the name of a unit is enclosed in brackets, e.g., [1 hand], either (1) the unit is not in general current use in the U.S. or (2) the unit is believed to be based on custom and usage rather than on formal definition.

Equivalents involving decimals are, in most instances, rounded to the third decimal place; exact equivalents are so designated.

Lengths

1 angstrom (Å)	= 0.1 nanometer (exactly)
	= 0.0001 micrometer (exactly)
	= 0.0000001 millimeter (exactly)
	= 0.000000004 inch
1 cable's length	= 120 fathoms (exactly)
	= 720 feet (exactly)
	= 219 meters
1 centimeter (cm)	= 0.3937 inch
1 chain (ch) (engineer's)	= 30.48 meters (exactly)
	= 100 feet
1 chain (Gunter's or surveyor's)	= 66 feet (exactly)
	= 20.1168 meters
1 decimeter (dm)	= 3.937 inches
1 degree (geographical)	= 364,566.929 feet
	= 69.047 miles (avg.)
	= 111.123 kilometers (avg.)
of latitude	= 68.708 miles at equator
	= 69.403 miles at poles
of longitude	= 69.171 miles at equator
1 dekameter (dam)	= 32.808 feet
1 fathom (fath)	= 6 feet (exactly)
	= 1.8288 meters
1 foot (ft)	= 12 inches (exactly)
	= 0.3048 meters (exactly)
	= 0.015 chains (surveyor's)
1 furlong (fur)	= 660 feet (exactly)
	= ⅛ mile (exactly)
	= 201.168 meters
[1 hand (height measure for horses, from ground to top of their shoulders)]	= 4 inches
1 inch (in.)	= 2.54 centimeters (exactly)
1 kilometer (km)	= 0.621375 mile
	= 3,280.8 feet
1 league (land)	= 3 miles (exactly)
	= 4.828 kilometers
1 link (engineer's)	= 1 foot
	= 0.305 meter
1 link (Gunter's or surveyor's)	= 7.92 inches (exactly)
	= 0.201 meter

1 meter (m)	= 39.37 inches
	= 1.09361 yards
1 micrometer (µm)	= 0.001 millimeter (exactly)
	= 0.00003937 inch
1 mil	= 0.001 inch (exactly)
	= 0.0254 millimeter (exactly)
1 mile (mi) (statute or land)	= 5,280 feet (exactly)
	= 1.609344 kilometers (exactly)
1 mile (nmi) (international nautical)	= 1.852 kilometers (exactly)
	= 1.151 miles
	= 6,076.1 feet
1 millimeter (mm)	= 0.03937 inch
1 nanometer (nm)	= 0.001 micrometer (exactly)
	= 0.00000003937 inch
1 pica (typography)	= 12 points
1 point (pt) (typography)	= 0.013837 inch (exactly)
	= 0.351 millimeter
1 rod (rd), pole, or perch	= 16½ feet (exactly)
	= 5.029 meters
1 yard (yd)	= 3 feet (exactly)
	= 0.9144 meter (exactly)

Areas or Surfaces

1 acre (A)	= 43,560 square feet (exactly)
	= 4,840 square yards
	= 0.405 hectare
1 are (a)	= 119.599 square yards
	= 0.025 acre
1 bolt (cloth measure):	
length	= 100 yards
width	= 45 or 60 inches
1 hectare (ha)	= 2.471 acres
[1 square (building)]	= 100 square feet
1 square centimeter (cm²)	= 0.155 square inch
1 square decimeter (dm²)	= 15.500 square inches
1 square foot (ft²)	= 929.030 square centimeters
1 square inch (in.²)	= 6.4516 square centimeters (exactly)
1 square kilometer (km²)	= 247.104 acres
	= 0.386102 square mile
1 square meter (m²)	= 1.196 square yards
	= 10.764 square feet
1 square mile (mi²)	= 640 acres (exactly)
	= 258.999 hectares
1 square millimeter (mm²)	= 0.002 square inch
1 square rod (rd²), square pole, or square perch	= 25.293 square meters
1 square yard (yd²)	= 0.836127 square meter

Capacities or Volumes

1 barrel (bbl), liquid	= 31 to 42 gallons*

*There are a variety of "barrels" established by law or usage. For example, federal taxes on fermented liquors are based on a barrel of 31 gallons. Many state laws fix the "barrel for liquids" as 31½ gallons; one state fixes a 36-gallon barrel for cistern measurement. Federal law recognizes a 40-gallon barrel for "proof spirits." By custom, 42 gallons constitute a barrel of crude oil or petroleum products for statistical purposes, and this equivalent is recognized "for liquids" by some states.

1 barrel (bbl), standard for fruits, vegetables, and other dry commodities except dry cranberries	= 7,056 cubic inches
	= 105 dry quarts
	= 3.281 bushels, struck measure
1 barrel, standard, cranberry	= 86⁴⁵/₆₄ dry quarts
	= 2.709 bushels, struck measure
	= 5,826 cubic inches
1 board foot (lumber measure)	= a foot-square board 1 inch thick
1 bushel (U.S.) (struck measure)	= 2,150.42 cubic inches (exactly)
	= 35.239 liters
[1 bushel, heaped (U.S.)]	= 2,747.715 cubic inches
	= 1.278 bushels, struck measure**

**Frequently recognized as 1¼ bushels, struck measure.

[1 bushel (bu) (British Imperial) (struck measure)]	= 1.032 U.S. bushels, struck measure
	= 2,219.36 cubic inches
1 cord (cd) (firewood)	= 128 cubic feet (exactly)

1 cubic centimeter (cm³)	= 0.061 cubic inch
1 cubic decimeter (dm³)	= 61.024 cubic inches
1 cubic foot (ft³)	= 7.481 gallons
	= 28.317 cubic decimeters
1 cubic inch (in.³)	= 0.554 fluid ounce
	= 4.433 fluid drams
	= 16.387 cubic centimeters
1 cubic meter (m³)	= 1.308 cubic yards
1 cubic yard (yd³)	= 0.765 cubic meter
1 cup, measuring	= 8 fluid ounces (exactly)
	= ½ liquid pint (exactly)
1 dekaliter (daL)	= 2.642 gallons
	= 1.135 pecks
[1 dram, fluid (fl dr) (British)]	= 0.961 U.S. fluid dram
	= 0.217 cubic inch
	= 3.552 milliliters
1 gallon (gal) (U.S.)	= 4 quarts, liquid (exactly)
	= 231 cubic inches (exactly)
	= 3.785 liters
	= 0.833 British gallon
	= 128 U.S. fluid ounces (exactly)
[1 gallon (British Imperial)]	= 277.42 cubic inches
	= 1.201 U.S. gallons
	= 4.546 liters
	= 160 British fluid ounces (exactly)
1 gill (gi)	= 7.219 cubic inches
	= 4 fluid ounces (exactly)
	= 0.118 liter
1 hectoliter (hL)	= 26.418 gallons
	= 2.838 bushels
1 liter (L) (1 cubic decimeter exactly)	= 1.057 liquid quarts
	= 0.908 dry quart
	= 61.024 cubic inches
1 milliliter (mL) (1 cu cm exactly)	= 0.271 fluid dram
	= 16.231 minims
	= 0.061 cubic inch
1 ounce, liquid (U.S.)	= 1.805 cubic inches
	= 29.573 milliliters
	= 1.041 British fluid ounces
[1 ounce, fluid (fl oz) (British)]	= 0.961 U.S. fluid ounce
	= 1.734 cubic inches
	= 28.412 milliliters
1 peck (pk)	= 8.810 liters
1 pint (pt), dry	= 33.600 cubic inches
	= 0.551 liter
1 pint, liquid	= 28.875 cubic inches (exactly)
	= 0.473 liter
1 quart (qt), dry (U.S.)	= 67.201 cubic inches
	= 1.101 liters
	= 0.969 British quart
1 quart, liquid (U.S.)	= 2 pints, liquid (exactly)
	= 4 cups (exactly)
	= 57.75 cubic inches (exactly)
	= 0.946 liter
	= 0.833 British quart
[1 quart (British)]	= 69.354 cubic inches
	= 1.032 U.S. dry quarts
	= 1.201 U.S. liquid quarts
1 tablespoon (T., Tbs, tbsp.)	= 3 teaspoons (exactly)
	= 4 fluid drams
	= ½ fluid ounce (exactly)
1 teaspoon (t., tsp.)	= ⅓ tablespoon (exactly)
	= 1⅓ fluid drams***

***The equivalent "1 teaspoon = 1⅓ fluid drams" has been found to correspond more closely with the actual capacities of teaspoons in use than the equivalent "1 teaspoon = 1 fluid dram" given by many dictionaries.

Weights or Masses

1 assay ton* (AT)	= 29.167 grams

*Used in assaying. The assay ton bears the same relation to the milligram that a ton of 2,000 pounds avoirdupois bears to the ounce troy; hence, the weight in milligrams of precious metal obtained from one assay ton of ore gives directly the number of troy ounces to the net ton.

1 carat (c)	= 200 milligrams (exactly)
	= 3.086 grains
1 dram avoirdupois (dr avdp)	= 27¹¹/₃₂ (= 27.344) grains
	= 1.772 grams
1 gamma (γ)	= 1 microgram (exactly)
1 grain (gr)	= 64.79891 milligrams (exactly)

1 gram (g) . . . . = 15.432 grains
                                    = 0.035 ounce, avoirdupois

1 hundredweight, gross (or
long)** (gross cwt) . . . . = 112 pounds (exactly)
                                    = 50.802 kilograms

**The gross (or long) ton and hundredweight are used commercially in the U.S. to only a limited extent, usually in restricted industrial fields. These units are the same as the British ton and hundredweight.

1 hundredweight, gross or
short (cwt or net cwt) . . . . . . = 100 pounds (exactly)
                                    = 45.359 kilograms

1 kilogram (kg) . . . . = 2.20462 pounds
1 microgram (µg) . . . . = 0.000001 gram (exactly)
1 milligram (mg) . . . . = 0.015 grain
1 ounce, avoirdupois (oz avdp) = 437.5 grains (exactly)
                                    = 0.911 troy ounce
                                    = 28.3495 grams

1 ounce, troy (oz t) . . . . = 480 grains (exactly)
                                    = 1.097 avoirdupois ounces
                                    = 31.103 grams

1 pennyweight (dwt) . . . . = 1.555 grams
1 pound, avoirdupois (lb avdp) = 7,000 grains (exactly)
                                    = 1.215 troy pounds
                                    = 453.59237 grams (exactly)

1 pound, troy (lb t) . . . . = 5,760 grains (exactly)
                                    = 0.823 avoirdupois pound
                                    = 373.242 grams

1 stone (st) . . . . = 14 pounds avdp (exactly)
                                    = 6.350 kilograms

1 ton, gross or long . . . . = 2,240 pounds (exactly)
                                    = 1.12 net tons (exactly)
                                    = 1.016 metric tons

1 ton, metric (t) . . . . = 2,204.623 pounds
                                    = 0.984 gross ton
                                    = 1.102 net tons

1 ton, net or short (tn) . . . . = 2,000 pounds (exactly)
                                    = 0.893 gross ton
                                    = 0.907 metric ton

Electrical Units

The **watt** (W) is the unit of power (electrical, mechanical, thermal). Electrical power is given by the product of the voltage and the current.

Energy is sold by the **joule** (J), but in common practice the billing of electrical energy is expressed in terms of the **kilowatt-hour** (kWh), which is 3,600,000 joules, or 3.6 megajoules.

The **horsepower** (hp) is a nonmetric unit sometimes used in mechanics. It is equal to 746 watts.

The **ohm** (Ω) is the unit of electrical resistance and represents the physical property of a conductor that offers a resistance to the flow of electricity, permitting just 1 ampere to flow at 1 volt of pressure.

Measures of Force and Pressure

Dyne (dyn) = force necessary to accelerate a 1-gram mass 1 centimeter per second squared = 0.000072 poundal

Poundal (pdl) = force necessary to accelerate a 1-pound mass 1 foot per second squared = 13,825.5 dynes = 0.138255 newton

Newton (N) = force needed to accelerate a 1-kilogram mass 1 meter per second squared = 100,000 dynes (exactly)

Pascal (pressure) (Pa) = 1 newton per square meter = 0.020885 pound per square foot

Atmosphere (air pressure at sea level) (atm) = 2,116.217 pounds per square foot = 14.6959 pounds per square inch = 1.0332 kilograms per square centimeter = 101,325 newtons per square meter

Measures of Alcohol

Pony . . . . = 1.0 fluid ounce
Shot . . . . = varies, usu. 1.0-
                                1.5 fluid ounces
Jigger . . . . = 1.5 fluid ounces
Pint (pt) . . . . = 16 fluid ounces
                                = 0.625 fifth
Fifth . . . . = 25.6 fluid ounces
                                = 1.6 pints
                                = 0.8 quart
                                = 0.757 liter

Quart (qt) . . . . = 32 fluid ounces
                            = 1.25 fifths
Wine bottle
(standard) . . . . . . = 0.75 liter
                        = 25.4 fluid ounces
Magnum . . . . = 1.5 liters

For champagne and brandy:
Jeroboam . . . . = 2 magnums
                            = 3 liters
                            = 101 fluid ounces

For champagne:
Rehoboam . . . . = 3 magnums
Methuselah . . . . = 4 magnums
Salmanazar . . . . = 6 magnums
Balthazar . . . . = 8 magnums
Nebuchadnezzar . . . = 10 magnums

Miscellaneous Measures

Caliber (cal)—the diameter of a gun bore. In the U.S., caliber is traditionally expressed in hundredths of inches, e.g., .22. In Britain, caliber is often expressed in thousandths of inches, e.g., .270. Now it is commonly expressed in millimeters, e.g., the 5.56 mm M16 rifle. The caliber of heavier weapons has long been expressed in millimeters, e.g., the 155 mm howitzer.

Naval guns' caliber refers to the barrel length as a multiple of the bore diameter. For example, a 5-inch, 50-caliber naval gun has a 5-inch bore and a barrel length of 250 inches.

Decibel (dB)—a measure of the relative intensity of sound. The threshold of hearing is given as 0 decibels. A 20-decibel sound is 10 times more intense than a 10-decibel sound; 30 decibels is 100 times more intense. (A 10-decibel increase corresponds generally to the perception of a sound being twice as loud.)

One decibel is the smallest difference between sounds detectable by the human ear. Long or repeated exposure to an 85-decibel-or-higher sound can damage hearing.

10 decibels . . .	breathing
20	rustling leaves
30	whisper
40	refrigerator humming
50	quiet conversation
60	conversation, laughter
70	vacuum cleaner
80	city traffic
90	subway, lawn mower
100	chainsaw

Em—a printer's measure designating the width of any given type size. For example, an em of 10-point type is 10 points. An en is half an em.

Gauge (ga)—the diameter of a shotgun bore. Gauge numbers originally referred to the number of lead balls—of equal diameter as the gun barrel—required to make a pound. Thus, a 16-gauge shotgun's bore was smaller than a 12-gauge shotgun's. Today, an international agreement assigns millimeter measures to each gauge.

Gauge	Bore diameter (mm)	Gauge	Bore diameter (mm)
6	23.34	14	17.60
10	19.67	16	16.81
12	18.52	20	15.90

Horsepower (hp)—the power needed to lift 550 pounds 1 foot in 1 second or to lift 33,000 pounds 1 foot in 1 minute. Equivalent to 746 watts or 2,546 British thermal units per hour.

Karat or carat (k or c)—a measure of fineness for gold equal to 1/24 part of pure gold in an alloy. 24-karat gold is pure; 18-karat gold is 1/4 alloy. The carat is also used as a unit of weight for precious stones; it is equal to 200 milligrams or 3.086 grains.

Knot (kn or kt)—a measure of the speed of ships. A knot equals 1 nautical mile (about 1.151 statute miles) per hour.

Quire (qr)—25 sheets of paper of the same size and quality.

Ream (rm)—500 sheets of paper of the same size and quality.

POSTAL INFORMATION

Administration of the U.S. Postal Service

The Postal Reorganization Act, creating a government-owned postal service under the executive branch and replacing the old executive Post Office Department, was signed into law Aug. 12, 1970. The service officially came into being on July 1, 1971. The U.S. Postal Service is governed by an 11-person board. Nine members are appointed by the president, with Senate approval. These nine choose a postmaster general. The board and the postmaster general choose the 11th member, who serves as deputy postmaster general.

The Postal Service Reform Act of 2022 was signed into law Apr. 6, 2022, altering budget requirements imposed by 2006 legislation and eliminating a provision requiring USPS to pre-fund retiree benefits for 50 years, which had incurred massive annual deficits. (The Postal Service last received a public service subsidy, i.e., taxpayer dollars, in 1982.)

Historical Postage Rates, 1851-2023

Postage cost for a prepaid, 1-oz. letter (the first-class standard after July 1, 1885).

Effective date	Rate	2023 dollars	Effective date	Rate	2023 dollars	Effective date	Rate	2023 dollars
July 1, 1851	$0.06[1]	$2.46	May 29, 1978	$0.15	$0.71	May 11, 2009	$0.44	$0.63
July 1, 1863	0.06	1.50	Mar. 22, 1981	0.18	0.62	Jan. 22, 2012	0.45	0.60
Oct. 1, 1883	0.04	1.25	Nov. 1, 1981	0.20	0.65	Jan. 27, 2013	0.46	0.61
July 1, 1885	0.02	0.64	Feb. 17, 1985	0.22	0.63	Jan. 26, 2014	0.49[3]	0.64
Nov. 2, 1917	0.03[2]	0.68	Apr. 3, 1988	0.25	0.65	Apr. 10, 2016	0.47	0.60
July 1, 1919	0.02[2]	0.35	Feb. 3, 1991	0.29	0.65	Jan. 22, 2017	0.49	0.61
July 6, 1932	0.03	0.67	Jan. 1, 1995	0.32	0.65	Jan. 21, 2018	0.50	0.61
Aug. 1, 1958	0.04	0.42	Jan. 10, 1999	0.33	0.61	Jan. 27, 2019	0.55	0.66
Jan. 7, 1963	0.05	0.50	Jan. 7, 2001	0.34	0.59	Aug. 29, 2021	0.58	0.64
Jan. 7, 1968	0.06	0.54	June 30, 2002	0.37	0.63	July 10, 2022	0.60	0.62
May 16, 1971	0.08	0.60	Jan. 8, 2006	0.39	0.60	Jan. 22, 2023	0.63	—
Mar. 2, 1974	0.10	0.64	May 14, 2007	0.41	0.60	July 9, 2023	0.66	—
Dec. 31, 1975	0.13	0.71	May 12, 2008	0.42	0.59			

— = Not applicable. **Note:** 2023 dollars are as of May. (1) For prepaid domestic letters traveling under 3,000 miles. (2) The price increased one cent during World War I; Congress restored its prewar rate in 1919. (3) The Postal Regulatory Commission approved a 6% total price increase: a 1.7% increase for inflation and an additional 4.3% temporary increase to compensate for USPS losses during the 2008-09 recession.

Status of the U.S. Postal Service, 2001-22

Source: *Postal Facts*, U.S. Postal Service

	2001	2005	2010	2015	2017	2018	2019	2020	2021	2022
Total mail items (bil)	207.5	211.7	170.9	154.3	149.5	146.4	142.6	129.2	128.9	127.3
First-class mail items (bil)	103.7	98.1	77.6	62.6	58.7	56.7	54.9	52.6	50.7	48.9
Stamped mail items (bil)	53.6	45.9	28.9	20.7	18.5	17.5	16.5	15.2	13.9	12.9
Marketing mail items (bil)	89.9	100.9	81.8	80.0	78.3	77.3	75.7	64.0	66.2	67.1
Shipping/package volume (bil)	NA	NA	3.1	4.5	5.7	6.2	6.2	7.3	7.6	7.2
Annual revenue (bil)	$65.8	$69.9	$67.1	$68.8	$69.6	$70.6	$71.1	$73.1	$77.0	$78.8
Total retail revenue (bil)	$14.8	$17.3	$17.5	$19.2	$12.9	$12.7	$12.7	$12.7	$13.0	$12.2
Total customer visits (bil)	1.4	1.3	1.1	0.9	0.9	0.8	0.8	0.8	0.7	0.7
Delivery points (mil)	137.7	144.3	150.9	155.0	157.3	158.6	160.0	161.4	163.1	164.9
Total delivery routes	242,600	243,000	230,600	226,777	228,483	231,843	231,807	231,579	233,171	233,585
Total retail offices	38,123	37,142	36,222	35,520	35,005	34,772	34,613	34,451	34,223	33,641
Career employees	775,903	704,716	583,908	491,863	503,103	497,157	496,934	495,941	516,636	516,750

U.S. Domestic Mail Rates

Source: *Price List* (Notice 123), U.S. Postal Service. Effective July 9, 2023. Rates are for retail customers unless noted. Domestic rates apply to the U.S., its territories and possessions, APOs, FPOs, and Freely Associated States.

First-Class Mail

Includes written matter such as letters, postcards, bills, account statements, and any matter sealed or closed against inspection up to 13 oz. In most cases, delivery is within 2-3 business days.

Letters measuring up to 6⅛ by 11½ in. and not more than ¼ in. thick cost 66¢ for the first oz., 24¢ for each additional oz. or fraction thereof, up to 3.5 oz. Nonmachinable letters (such as those in square, oversized, or unusually shaped envelopes) start at $1.06. Postcard postage is 51¢. Large envelopes up to 12 by 15 in. (or letters over 3.5 oz.) cost $1.35 for the first oz. and 24¢ for each additional oz. or fraction thereof. Presort- and automation-compatible mail can qualify for lower rates if certain piece minimums, mailing permits, and other requirements are met.

Forever Stamps. The USPS introduced the nondenominational "Forever" stamp Apr. 12, 2007, at an initial cost of 41¢. The Forever stamp can be purchased at the current First-Class standard rate and will always be valid as First-Class postage on standard envelopes weighing 1 oz. or less, even after rates increase.

Priority Mail

Priority Mail is delivered within 1-3 business days in most cases, with no additional charge for Saturday deliveries. Can be any mailable article up to 70 lbs and not over 108 in. in length and girth combined.

Priority Mail Flat Rate: $9.65, $9.95, $10.40, regardless of weight, if matter fits into designated USPS flat-rate envelopes. $10.20, $17.10, $22.80 if it fits into flat-rate boxes.

Priority Mail Forever Prepaid Flat Rate packaging can be purchased online at the current priority mail flat rate and remains valid for use after future price increases.

Priority Mail Express

Provides guaranteed expedited service for any mailable article up to 70 lbs and not over 108 in. in combined length and girth. Offers next-day delivery to most destinations; $12.50 additional charge for Sunday or holiday delivery. Includes insurance up to $100, mailing receipt, proof of delivery signature record, and tracking.

Priority Mail Express Flat Rate: $28.75, $28.95, $29.45, regardless of weight, if matter fits into designated USPS flat-rate envelopes.

Domestic Mail Services and Fees

Adult signature required: $9.05 per piece; person 21 years of age or older must sign for shipment.

Adult signature restricted delivery: $9.35 per piece; specific addressee or agent 21 years of age or older must sign for shipment.

Certificate of mailing: $1.95 per piece.

Certified mail: $4.35 per piece; provides proof of mailing and electronic verification of delivery or delivery attempt.

Certified mail restricted delivery: $11.45 per piece.

Collect on delivery (COD): $10.60 for amount to be collected/insurance desired up to $50; $13.15 for $50.01-$100; $2.90 for each additional $100.

Domestic money order: $2.00 for money orders $0.01 to $500; $2.90 for $500.01 to $1,000.

Pickup on demand: $26.50 per pickup; available for Priority Mail, Priority Mail Express, and USPS Retail Ground.

Restricted delivery: $6.90 per item when purchased in combination with COD, Insured Mail, or Registered Mail.

Return receipt: If requested at time of mailing, $3.55 for a receipt by mail, $2.20 for email receipt.

Signature confirmation: $3.40 online, $4.05 at post office.

Sunday/holiday delivery: Available for Priority Mail Express only. Fee: $12.50.

Tracking

Formerly known as Delivery Confirmation, tracking can be used with First-Class Mail parcels, Priority Mail, USPS Retail Ground, and Package Services (Bound Printed Matter, Media Mail, and Library Mail). Available free of charge at time of mailing, except for USPS Marketing Mail parcels ($0.28).

Change of Address

The USPS will forward mail to another address provided a Change of Address (COA) form has been filed in person or mailed to a post office or submitted online at moversguide. usps.com ($1.10 credit card authentication fee). The form can be picked up at any post office or requested by phone at (800) ASK-USPS.

P.O. Box Service

Private P.O. boxes can be rented in five sizes at most post offices. Prices depend on box size and location, ranging from $18.00-$367.00 per 3-month period or $28.00-$639.00 per 6-month period. Keys at most locations require a $5.00 deposit.

Registered Mail

The most secure service provided by the USPS. Full value of item must be declared at time of registration and mailing. Fee: $16.80 for a declared value of $0, up to $31.95 for articles with a declared value of $4,000.01 to $5,000. For each additional $1,000 or fraction thereof above $5,000, add $2.35.

International Mail Rates

Source: *Price List* (Notice 123), U.S. Postal Service. Effective July 9, 2023. Refer to www.usps.com for USPS price groups not shown here and weight limits by country.

First-Class Mail International

Letter-post items weighing up to 1 oz. and single postcards can be sent airmail for $1.50 to all countries.

Priority Mail International

Delivery is in 6-10 business days in many markets. Items must not be more than 108 in. in length and girth combined; max. weight is 70 lbs, though the limit varies by country.

Priority Mail International Flat Rate: $30.35-$44.70, depending on country price group, if matter fits into designated USPS flat-rate envelope (max. weight 4 lbs). Flat-rate boxes are $31.45-$132.05, depending on country price group and box size.

Priority Mail Express International

Priority Mail Express International Flat Rate: $54.75-$75.55, depending on country price group, if matter fits into flat-rate envelope (max. weight 4 lbs).

Global Express Guaranteed

Provides international expedited delivery, in partnership with FedEx, to certain countries. Item to be mailed must not weigh more than 70 lbs nor measure more than 108 in. in combined length and girth. Rate: Starts at $71.10 and $79.20 to Canada and Mexico, respectively, up to $155.50 to countries in price group 4, for items not over 0.5 lb in weight.

International Mail Services and Fees

Business reply: Card: $2.10; envelope (up to 2 oz.): $2.65.

Customs clearance and delivery: $8.30 per inbound letters and flats.

Insurance: Available to many countries for loss of or damage to items. Consult USPS for each country's indemnity limits.

Registered mail: Fee: $20.25 per First-Class mail or package piece.

Return receipt: Shows to whom and when item is delivered. Fee: $5.65 per mail piece.

Postal money order: $49.65 per money order. Only accepted in certain countries.

U.S. Postal Abbreviations

The abbreviations below are approved by the U.S. Postal Service for use in addresses.

Alabama	AL	Illinois	IL	Missouri	MO	Pennsylvania	PA
Alaska	AK	Indiana	IN	Montana	MT	Puerto Rico	PR
American Samoa	AS	Iowa	IA	Nebraska	NE	Rhode Island	RI
Arizona	AZ	Kansas	KS	Nevada	NV	South Carolina	SC
Arkansas	AR	Kentucky	KY	New Hampshire	NH	South Dakota	SD
California	CA	Louisiana	LA	New Jersey	NJ	Tennessee	TN
Colorado	CO	Maine	ME	New Mexico	NM	Texas	TX
Connecticut	CT	Marshall Islands[1]	MH	New York	NY	Utah	UT
Delaware	DE	Maryland	MD	North Carolina	NC	Vermont	VT
District of Columbia	DC	Massachusetts	MA	North Dakota	ND	Virgin Islands	VI
Florida	FL	Michigan	MI	Northern Mariana Isls.	MP	Virginia	VA
Georgia	GA	Micronesia,		Ohio	OH	Washington	WA
Guam	GU	Federated States of[1]	FM	Oklahoma	OK	West Virginia	WV
Hawaii	HI	Minnesota	MN	Oregon	OR	Wisconsin	WI
Idaho	ID	Mississippi	MS	Palau[1]	PW	Wyoming	WY

(1) Although an independent nation, this country is subject to domestic rates and fees.

Canadian Province and Territory Postal Abbreviations

Source: Canada Post

Alberta	AB	Newfoundland and		Nunavut	NU	Quebec	QC
British Columbia	BC	Labrador	NL	Ontario	ON	Saskatchewan	SK
Manitoba	MB	Northwest Territories	NT	Prince Edward Island	PE	Yukon	YT
New Brunswick	NB	Nova Scotia	NS				

SOCIAL SECURITY AND MEDICARE

Social Security Coverage

Source: Social Security Administration; World Almanac research; provisions shown are as under current law, Aug. 2023.

Social Security Benefits

Social Security's **Old-Age, Survivors, and Disability Insurance (OASDI)** program benefits are based on a worker's **primary insurance amount (PIA)**, which is related by law to the average indexed monthly earnings (AIME) on which Social Security contributions have been paid. The full PIA is payable to a worker who retires at full retirement age (FRA), which is 65-67 depending on birth year, and to an entitled disabled worker at any age. Spouses and children of retired or disabled workers and survivors of deceased workers receive set proportions of the PIA subject to a family maximum amount. The PIA is calculated by applying varying percentages to succeeding parts of the AIME. The formula is adjusted annually to reflect changes in average annual wages.

Increases in Social Security benefits are initiated for December of each year, assuming the Consumer Price Index (CPI) for the third calendar quarter of the year increased relative to the base quarter (i.e., the third calendar quarter of the year in which an increase last took effect). The size of the benefit increase is determined by the percentage rise of the CPI between the quarters measured.

The **average monthly benefit** payable to all retired workers amounted to $1,825 in Dec. 2022. The average benefit for disabled workers in that month was $1,483.

Maximum Monthly Retired-Worker Benefits Payable to Individuals Who Retired at Full Retirement Age (FRA)[1]

Retirement year	Maximum benefit— Payable at retirement	Payable effective Dec. 2022
1990	$975	$2,305
1995	1,199	2,388
2000	1,435	2,554
2005	1,939	3,057
2010	2,346	3,179
2015	2,663	3,318
2016	2,639	3,288
2017	2,687	3,338
2018	2,788	3,396
2019	2,861	3,389
2020	3,011	3,511
2021	3,148	3,623
2022	3,345	3,636
2023	3,627	3,627

(1) Benefits in 2000 and earlier are for retirement at age 65 at beginning of a given year. Benefits in 2005 through 2008 are for starting benefits at exact FRA during the year. Benefits in 2009 through 2020 are for retirement at age 66 at beginning of year. Benefits in 2021-23 are for starting benefits at exact FRA during the year. Beneficiaries born in 1938 through 1942 are born in years where the FRA is transitioning from age 65 to age 66, and beneficiaries born in 1955 through 1959 are born in years where the FRA is transitioning from age 66 to age 67.

Amount of Work Required

To qualify for benefits, the worker generally must have worked a certain length of time in covered employment. Just how long depends on when the worker reaches age 62 or, if earlier, when he or she dies or becomes disabled. A person born after 1929 who dies, becomes disabled, or reaches 62 after 1991 must generally have had at least 10 years of work credit to qualify for benefits.

Contribution and Benefit Base

(annual limit on the amount of earnings subject to taxation under OASDI)

Calendar year	OASDI[1]	Calendar year	OASDI[1]	Calendar year	OASDI[1]
1995	$61,200	2008	$102,000	2016	$118,500
2000	76,200	2009	106,800	2017	127,200
2002	84,900	2010	106,800	2018	128,400
2003	87,000	2011	106,800	2019	132,900
2004	87,900	2012	110,100	2020	137,700
2005	90,000	2013	113,700	2021	142,800
2006	94,200	2014	117,000	2022	147,000
2007	97,500	2015	118,500	2023	160,200

(1) Old-Age, Survivors, and Disability Insurance.

A person is **fully insured** when he or she has one quarter of coverage for every year after age 21 is reached (or 1950, if later) up to but not including the year the worker reaches 62, dies, or becomes disabled. In 2023, a person earns one credit, or "quarter of coverage" for each $1,640 of annual earnings in covered employment, up to four credits (or quarters) per year.

To receive **disability benefits**, the worker, in addition to being fully insured, must generally have credit for 20 quarters of coverage out of the 40 calendar quarters before he or she became disabled. A disabled blind worker need meet only the fully insured requirement. Persons disabled before age 31 can qualify with a briefer period of coverage. Certain survivor benefits are payable if the deceased worker had 6 quarters of coverage in the 13 quarters preceding death.

Tax Rate Schedule
(percentage of covered earnings)

Year	Total (for employees and employers, each)	OASDI[1]	HI[2]
1979-80	6.13%	5.08%	1.05%
1981	6.65.	5.35.	1.30
1982-83	6.70.	5.40.	1.30
1984	7.00.	5.70.	1.30
1985	7.05.	5.70.	1.35
1986-87	7.15.	5.70.	1.45
1988-89	7.51.	6.06.	1.45
1990 and after[3]	7.65.	6.20.	1.45

Year	(for self-employed)		
1979-80	8.10%	7.05%	1.05%
1981	9.30.	8.00.	1.30
1982-83	9.35.	8.05.	1.30
1984	14.00.	11.40.	2.60
1985	14.10.	11.40.	2.70
1986-87	14.30.	11.40.	2.90
1988-89	15.02.	12.12.	2.90
1990 and after[3]	15.30.	12.40.	2.90

(1) Old-Age, Survivors, and Disability Insurance. (2) Hospital Insurance (Medicare). (3) Public Law (PL) 111-147 exempted most employers from paying the employer share of OASDI payroll tax on wages paid Mar. 19-Dec. 31, 2010, to certain qualified individuals hired after Feb. 3, 2010. PL 111-312 reduced the OASDI payroll tax rate for 2011 by 2 percentage points for employees and for self-employed workers. PL 112-96 extended the 2011 rate reduction through 2012. The laws required that the general fund of the Treasury reimburse the OASI and DI Trust Funds for these temporary reductions.

What Aged Workers Receive

A person may receive monthly old-age benefits when he or she has enough work in covered employment and has reached retirement age—age 62 for reduced benefits or the age below for full benefits.

Full Retirement Age (FRA) by Birth Year

Year of birth	FRA	Year of birth	FRA
1937 or earlier	65	1955	66 and 2 mos.
1938	65 and 2 mos.	1956	66 and 4 mos.
1939	65 and 4 mos.	1957	66 and 6 mos.
1940	65 and 6 mos.	1958	66 and 8 mos.
1941	65 and 8 mos.	1959	66 and 10 mos.
1942	65 and 10 mos.	1960 or later	67
1943-54	66		

Note: If born on Jan. 1, refer to the previous birth year.

In 2000, the retirement earnings test was eliminated beginning with the month when the beneficiary reaches **full retirement age (FRA)**. A person at or above FRA no longer receives reduced benefits because of earnings. However, a person's benefits are reduced $1 for every $3 of earnings above the limit allowed by law ($56,520 for 2023) if he or she retires in the same calendar year but months prior to FRA. For retirees who have not yet reached the calendar year in which they will attain FRA, the reduction is $1 for every $2 of earnings over the exempt amount ($21,240 for 2023).

For workers who reached age 65 between 1982 and 1989, Social Security benefits are raised by 3% for each year in which the worker did not receive benefits between FRA and 70 (72 before 1984), whether because of earnings from work, because the worker did not apply for benefits, or because the worker declined benefits after entitlement. The **delayed retirement credit** is 1% per year for workers who reached age 65 before 1982. The rate for workers who reached age 65 in 1998-99 is 5.5%; 2000-01, 6.0%; 2002-03, 6.5%; 2004-05, 7.0%; and 2006-07, 7.5%. The delayed retirement credit rose to 8% per year for 2008 and years after.

For workers retiring early, benefits are permanently reduced 5/9 of 1% for each month before the FRA, up to 36 months. If the number of months exceeds 36, then the benefit is further reduced 5/12 of 1% per month.

For example, workers who retire at exactly age 62 have a total of 60 months of reduction if their FRA is 67. The reduction for the first 36 months is 5/9 of 36%, or 20%. The reduction for the remaining 24 months is 5/12 of 24%, or 10%. These workers would see their benefits reduced by 30% by retiring early. The nearer to FRA a person is when he or she begins collecting a benefit, the larger the monthly benefit will be.

Benefits for Worker's Spouse

The spouse of a worker who is getting Social Security retirement or disability payments may become entitled to an insurance benefit of **one-half of the worker's PIA** if claiming benefits at full retirement age. Reduced spouse's benefits are available at age 62 and are permanently reduced 25/36 of 1% for each month before FRA, up to 36 months. If the number of months exceeds 36, then the benefit is further reduced 5/12 of 1% per month. Benefits are also payable to the aged divorced spouse of an insured worker if he or she was married to the worker for at least 10 years. To qualify for divorced spouse benefits, the insured worker does not have to be receiving benefits if the divorce occurred at least two years earlier. Benefits received as a spouse are reduced by the amount of one's PIA.

Benefits for Children of Workers

If a retired or disabled worker has a child under age 18, the **child** will usually get a benefit equal to **one-half of the worker's unreduced benefit**. So will the worker's spouse, regardless of age, if he or she is **caring for an entitled child** of the worker, and the child is under 16 or became disabled before age 22. However, total benefits paid on a worker's earnings record are subject to a family maximum. Total monthly benefits paid to the family of a worker who retired in 2023 at age 66 and 6 months and always had the maximum earnings creditable under Social Security cannot exceed $6,376.

Entitled children generally stop receiving benefits at age 18, though they can continue receiving benefits until age 19 if they attend elementary or secondary school full-time. A child disabled before age 22 may get a benefit as long as the disability meets the definition in the law.

Benefits may also be paid to a grandchild or step-grandchild of a worker or of his or her spouse, in special circumstances.

OASDI Beneficiaries				
Beneficiaries	May 2010	May 2020	May 2022	May 2023
Total (in thous.)[1]	53,349	64,697	65,650	66,665
Age 65 and over, total	36,914	49,199	51,258	52,727
Retired workers. . . .	30,734	43,034	45,248	46,828
Disabled workers. . .	339	550	735	780
Survivors/				
dependents	5,841	5,615	5,275	5,119
Under age 65, total . .	16,435	15,497	14,393	13,938
Retired workers. . . .	3,314	2,699	2,553	2,560
Disabled workers. . .	7,628	7,781	7,076	6,720
Survivors/				
dependents	5,492	5,017	4,763	4,659
Total monthly				
benefits (in mil) . . .	**$56,966**	**$89,936**	**$101,081**	**$113,287**

OASDI = Old-Age, Survivors, and Disability Ins. (1) Numbers may not add up to totals due to rounding or incomplete enumeration.

What Disabled Workers Receive

A worker who becomes unable to work may be eligible for a monthly disability benefit. Benefits continue until it is determined that the individual is no longer disabled. When a disabled-worker beneficiary reaches FRA (see table on previous page), the disability benefit becomes a retired-worker benefit.

Benefits—like those for dependents of retired-worker beneficiaries generally—may be paid to dependents of disabled beneficiaries. However, the maximum family benefit in disability cases is generally lower than in retirement cases.

Survivor Benefits

If an insured worker should die, one or more types of benefits may be payable to survivors, again subject to a maximum family benefit described above.

1. If claiming benefits at FRA, the **surviving spouse** will receive a benefit equal to 100% of the deceased worker's benefit. Benefits claimed before FRA are reduced, with a maximum reduction of 28.5% at age 60. However, if the deceased worker claimed benefits before FRA, the surviving spouse's benefits are limited to the reduced amount the worker would be getting if alive, but not less than 82.5% of the worker's PIA. Remarriage after the worker's death ends the surviving spouse's benefit rights. However, if the widow(er) marries, and the marriage later ends, he or she regains benefit rights. (A marriage after age 60, or age 50 if disabled, is deemed not to have occurred for benefit purposes.) Survivor benefits may also be paid to a divorced spouse if the marriage lasted for at least 10 years.

Disabled widows and widowers may under certain circumstances qualify for benefits after attaining age 50 at the rate of 71.5% of the deceased worker's PIA. The widow or widower must have become totally disabled before or within seven years after the spouse's death or the last month in which he or she received mother's or father's insurance benefits.

2. There is a benefit for each **child under age 18**. The monthly benefit for a child of a deceased worker is 3/4 of the PIA, subject to the family maximum. A child who became disabled before age 22 may also receive benefits. Also, a child can receive benefits until age 19 if he or she is in full-time attendance at an elementary or secondary school.

3. There is a **mother's or father's benefit** for the widow(er) if children of the worker who are under age 16 are in his or her care. The benefit is 75% of the PIA (subject to the family maximum), and it continues until the youngest child reaches age 16, at which time payments stop even if the child's benefit continues. Benefits may continue if the widow(er) has a disabled child beneficiary age 16 or over in his or her care.

4. Dependent parents may be eligible for benefits if they have been receiving at least half their support from the worker before his or her death, have reached age 62, and (except in certain circumstances) have not remarried since the worker's death. Each parent gets 75% of the worker's PIA; if only one parent survives, the benefit is 82% (could be reduced for the family maximum).

5. A **lump sum** cash payment of **$255** is made if the worker was living with a spouse or has a child who is eligible for immediate monthly survivor benefits.

Self-Employed Workers

A self-employed person who has **net earnings of $400 or more** in a year must report such earnings for Social Security tax and credit purposes. Income from real estate, savings, dividends, loans, pensions, or insurance policies are not included unless it is part of a person's business.

A self-employed person receives one credit (also known as a "quarter of coverage") for each $1,640 for 2023, up to a maximum of four credits (or "quarters") per year.

The nonfarm self-employed have the option of reporting their earnings as 2/3 of their gross income from self-employment. This option can be used only if actual net earnings from self-employment income are less than $1,600 and less than 2/3 of their gross income. The option may be used only five times. Also, the self-employed person must have actual net earnings of $400 or more in two of the three taxable years immediately preceding the year in which he or she uses the option.

When a person has both taxable wages and earnings from self-employment, wages are credited for Social Security purposes first; only as much self-employment income as brings total earnings up to the current taxable maximum becomes subject to the self-employment tax.

Farm Owners and Workers

Self-employed farmers whose gross annual earnings from farming are **$8,460** or less may report 2/3 of their gross earnings instead of net earnings for Social Security purposes. Farmers whose gross income is over $8,460 and whose net farm profits were less than $6,107 can report the smaller of 2/3 of gross farm income and $5,640. Cash or crop shares received from a tenant or share farmer count if the owner participated materially in production or management. The self-employed farmer pays contributions at the same rate as other self-employed persons.

Agricultural employees. A worker's earnings from farm work count toward benefits if (1) the employer pays the worker $150 or more in cash during the year or (2) the employer spends $2,500 or more in the year for agricultural labor. Under these rules, a person gets credit for one calendar quarter for each $1,640 in cash pay in 2023.

Foreign farm workers admitted to the U.S. on a temporary basis are not covered.

Household Workers

If an employer pays a household worker (e.g., cleaning person, cook, babysitter, nanny, gardener) who is age 18 or older **$2,600 or more** in wages in 2023, the wages are covered under Social Security. This includes transportation costs paid for in cash. The job need not be regular or full-time. The employee should get a Social Security card at the Social Security office and show it to the employer. The employer deducts the amount of the employee's Social Security tax from the worker's pay, adds an identical amount as the employer's Social Security tax, and sends the total amount to the federal government.

Medicare Coverage

Source: Centers for Medicare & Medicaid Services, U.S. Dept. of Health and Human Services

The Medicare health insurance program provides acute-care coverage for Social Security and Railroad Retirement beneficiaries age 65 and over; workers and spouses age 65 and over with sufficient Medicare-only coverage in federal, state, or local government employment; certain persons entitled to receive Social Security or Railroad Retirement disability benefits; certain disabled persons with Medicare-only coverage through government employment; certain persons with end-stage kidney disease; and certain persons in the vicinity of Libby, MT, with asbestos-related conditions. What follows is a basic description that may not cover all circumstances.

The **basic Medicare plan**, available nationwide, is a fee-for-service arrangement where the beneficiary may use any provider accepting Medicare. Some services are not covered, and there are some out-of-pocket costs.

Hospital insurance (Part A). The basic hospital insurance program pays covered services for hospital and post-hospital care, including:

- All necessary inpatient hospital care for the first 60 days of each benefit period, except for a deductible ($1,600 in 2023). For days 61-90, Medicare pays for services over and above the coinsurance ($400 per day in 2023). After 90 days, the beneficiary has 60 lifetime reserve days for which Medicare helps pay. The coinsurance amount for reserve days was $800 in 2023.
- Up to 100 days of care in a skilled-nursing facility in each benefit period. Hospital insurance pays for all covered services for the first 20 days; for days 21-100, the beneficiary pays coinsurance ($200 per day in 2023).
- Part-time home health care provided by a home health agency (but, as of Jan. 1, 1998, limited to the first 100 visits after a hospital or skilled nursing facility stay of at least 3 days).
- Coverage of hospice care for certain terminally ill beneficiaries.

There is a premium for Part A insurance in certain—but not most—cases.

Medical insurance (Part B). Eligible elderly and disabled persons can receive benefits under this supplementary program only if they sign up and agree to a monthly premium. As of 2007, the monthly premium is tied to annual income. Individuals with an income of $97,000 or less and couples with an income of $194,000 or less pay $164.90 per person if they sign up upon becoming eligible in 2023. Part B covers certain medical services and supplies, including:

- Physicians' and surgeons' services, as well as some services furnished by certain other medical professionals.
- Services in an emergency room, outpatient clinic, or ambulatory surgical center (or, effective Jan. 1, 2023, a rural emergency hospital).
- Home health care not covered under Part A.
- Laboratory tests, X-rays, and other diagnostic radiology services.
- Certain preventative care services and screening tests.
- Most physical and occupational therapy and speech pathology services.
- Comprehensive outpatient rehabilitation facility services and mental health care in a partial hospitalization psychiatric program, if inpatient care would otherwise be required.
- Radiation therapy; renal (kidney) dialysis and transplants; and heart, lung, heart-lung, liver, pancreas, bone marrow, and intestinal transplants.
- Approved durable medical equipment for home use.
- Drugs that are not usually self-administered.
- Certain services for diabetes.
- Ambulance services when other transportation methods are contraindicated.
- Rural health clinic and federally qualified health center services, including some telemedicine.

Part B services are generally subject to a deductible ($226 in 2023), coinsurance (generally 20% of the remaining allowed charges with certain exceptions), a deductible for blood, and amounts above the allowed charge if a doctor or supplier does not accept the Medicare-approved rate as payment in full. For outpatient hospital services, coinsurance varies by service, usually falling between 20% and 50% of allowed charges. There are no deductibles or coinsurance for certain services, such as lab tests paid under the clinical lab fee schedule, home health agency services (except some durable medical equipment, which is subject to 20% coinsurance), and some preventative care services. Payments for certain physical, speech, and occupational therapy services are subject to certain limits. Dental care, hearing aids, and routine eye care are generally not covered under the basic plan.

To get medical insurance (Part B), persons approaching age 65 may enroll during the seven-month initial enrollment period, which includes the month of their 65th birthday as well as the three months before and after. Persons desiring coverage to begin in the month they reach age 65 must enroll in the three months before their birthday. Persons who enroll after their initial enrollment period may be subject to late-enrollment premiums.

The monthly premium is deducted from the cash benefit for persons receiving Social Security, Railroad Retirement, or Civil Service Retirement benefits. Income from the medical premiums and the federal matching payments are put in the Part B Account of the Supplementary Medical Insurance Trust Fund, from which benefits and administrative expenses are paid.

Effective Jan. 2023, there was a new basis for Part B eligibility, for post-kidney-transplant immunosuppressive drug coverage only, upon payment of a monthly premium determined solely for this coverage.

Medicare Advantage (Part C) (formerly Medicare+ Choice). Persons eligible for Medicare may have the option of getting services through a Medicare-certified local coordinated care plan, such as a health maintenance organization (HMO), local preferred provider organization (PPO), provider-sponsored organization (PSO), or other local Medicare-certified **managed care** plan; a regional preferred provider organization (RPPO); a private fee-for-service plan; or, in certain cases, a special-needs plan. Any such plan must provide at least the same benefits as Parts A and B, except for hospice services. They may provide added benefits (such as vision or hearing coverage) or reduce cost sharing or premiums. Enrollees may be required to use the plan's network of participating providers or pay higher out-of-pocket costs to go outside the network.

Prescription Drug Coverage (Part D). Effective Jan. 1, 2006, an optional Medicare prescription drug plan provides insurance coverage for prescription drugs. Medicare recipients pay a monthly premium (averaging about $31.50 in 2023 for basic coverage, depending on the provider) and a portion of drug costs. As of 2011, the monthly premium was tied to annual income; in 2023, individuals with an income greater than $97,000 and couples with an income greater than $194,000 pay more. The open enrollment period is Oct. 15-Dec. 7. Coverage varies depending on the drug plan selected.

Further details are available on the Internet at www.medicare.gov or by calling 1-800-MEDICARE (1-800-633-4227).

Medicare card. Persons qualifying for hospital insurance under Social Security receive a health insurance card. The card indicates whether the individual has taken out medical insurance protection. It is to be shown to the hospital, skilled-nursing facility, home health agency, doctor, or other provider of covered services.

Payments are generally made only in the 50 states, District of Columbia, Puerto Rico, U.S. Virgin Isls., Guam, American Samoa, and Northern Mariana Isls.

Social Security Financing

Social Security is paid for by a tax on certain earnings (for 2023, on earnings up to $160,200) for **Old-Age, Survivors, and Disability Insurance (OASDI)** and on all earnings (no upper limit) for hospital insurance with the **Medicare** program; the taxable earnings base for OASDI is adjusted annually to reflect changes in average wages. The employed worker and his or her employer share Social Security taxes equally.

Employers remit amounts withheld from employee wages for Social Security and income taxes to the Internal Revenue Service; employer Social Security taxes are also payable at the same time. (Self-employed workers pay Social Security taxes when filing their regular income tax forms.) The Social Security taxes (along with revenues arising from partial taxation of the Social Security benefits of certain high-income people) are transferred to the Social Security Trust Funds; they can be used only to pay benefits, the cost of rehabilitation services, and administrative expenses. By law, money not immediately needed for those purposes is invested in obligations of the federal government, which must pay interest on the money borrowed and must repay the principal when the obligations are redeemed or mature.

On Jan. 1, 1974, the **Supplemental Security Income (SSI)** program, established by the Social Security Amendments of 1972, replaced federal grants to the states to aid the needy aged, blind, and disabled. The program provides for federal payments, based on uniform national standards and eligibility requirements, and for state supplementary payments. The Social Security Administration administers the federal payments—financed by general funds of the Treasury—as well as the state supplement for those states that choose to have it federally administered. States may supplement the federal payment of all recipients and must supplement it for persons otherwise adversely affected by the transition from the former public assistance programs. In May 2023, the number of persons receiving federally administered SSI payments was 7,514,206; the payments totaled about $5.3 bil.

The **maximum monthly federal SSI payment** for individuals without an eligible spouse and with no other countable income, living in their own household, was $914 in 2023. For couples where both members were eligible, the maximum payment was $1,371.

For further information, contact the Social Security Administration toll-free at 1-800-772-1213 or visit its website at www.ssa.gov.

Examples of Monthly Social Security Benefits Available, 2023

Benefit or beneficiary	For low earnings ($28,561)[1]	For med. earnings ($63,469)[1]	For max. earnings ($156,123)[1,2]
Primary insurance amount (worker retiring at 66 years, 6 months)	$1,359.70	$2,244.70	$3,627.10
Maximum family benefit (worker retiring at 66 years, 6 months)	2,039.70	4,088.90	6,346.30
Maximum family disability benefit (worker disabled at 55; in 2023)	1,933.70	3,396.90	5,501.50
Disabled worker (worker disabled at 55):			
Worker alone	1,374.00	2,264.00	3,667.00
Worker, spouse, and 1 child	1,932.00	3,396.00	5,499.00
Retired worker claiming benefits at age 62:			
Worker alone[3]	959.00	1,578.00	2,557.00
Worker with spouse claiming benefits at—			
FRA or over	1,644.00	2,705.00	4,383.00
Age 62[3]	1,404.00	2,311.00	3,744.00
Widow or widower claiming benefits at—			
Age 66 or over[4]	1,359.00	2,244.00	3,627.00
Age 60[4]	972.00	1,604.00	2,593.00
Disabled widow or widower claiming benefits at age 50-59[5]	972.00	1,604.00	2,593.00
1 surviving child[4]	1,019.00	1,683.00	2,720.00
Widow or widower at FRA or over and 1 child[4]	2,039.00	3,927.00	6,345.00
Widowed mother or father and 1 child[4]	2,038.00	3,366.00	5,440.00
Widowed mother or father and 2 children[4]	2,037.00	4,086.00	6,345.00

FRA = Full retirement age. **Note:** Effective Jan. 2023. (1) Career average earnings: an average of lifetime earnings indexed to the year prior to entitlement (2022 in this case). (2) Assumes work beginning at age 22. (3) Assumes maximum reduction. (4) Assumes worker lived and worked until FRA without receiving reduced benefits. (5) Effective Jan. 1984, disabled widow(er) claiming a benefit at ages 50-59 receive a benefit equal to 71.5% of the PIA.

Social Security Recipients by Age, Sex, Race, and Hispanic Origin, 2022

Source: Social Security Administration

Characteristic/benefit	Total	White	Black	American Indian, Alaska Native	Asian	Native Hawaiian/ other Pacific Isl.	Hispanic
Social Security beneficiaries (thous.)[1]	55,323	46,358	6,343	916	2,293	128	4,835
Sex							
Male	25,044	21,236	2,632	387	1,034	64	2,176
Female	30,279	25,122	3,711	530	1,259	64	2,660
Age							
15-54 years	4,537	3,428	914	140	153	25	608
55-64 years	5,770	4,604	930	146	178	20	587
65-74 years	25,075	21,120	2,694	421	1,086	52	2,028
75 years or older	19,942	17,206	1,804	209	876	32	1,612
Supplemental Security Income recipients (thous.)[1]	6,035	4,026	1,622	214	297	26	919
Sex							
Male	2,723	1,799	802	90	116	6	386
Female	3,312	2,227	821	123	181	20	533
Age							
15-54 years	2,793	1,860	819	134	64	16	405
55-64 years	1,725	1,226	438	42	32	6	225
65-74 years	927	583	245	35	89	NA	148
75 years or older	591	357	119	3	113	4	141
Average annual benefit in 2021 (dollars)							
Social Security	$17,201	$17,511	$15,321	$15,071	$16,535	$14,687	$14,554
Supplemental Security Income	8,661	8,703	8,748	8,086	7,833	NA	8,060

NA = Not available. **Note:** Race categories include people who reported being of that race, alone or in combination with another race. Persons of Hispanic origin may be of any race. The sum of the individual categories may not add up to totals because of rounding and because the totals include persons who reported being of more than one race. (1) Persons 15 or older receiving Social Security benefits or Supplemental Security Income in Mar. 2022.

Old-Age, Survivors, and Disability Insurance Beneficiaries, 2021

Source: Social Security Administration

State or area	Total benefits (thous.)	Total beneficiaries	Retirement (old-age) Retired workers	Spouses	Children	Survivors Widow(er)s and parents	Children	Disability Disabled workers	Spouses	Children
Alabama	$1,706,991	1,163,871	760,698	27,612	12,587	75,339	44,638	205,681	2,405	34,911
Alaska	162,824	110,006	81,718	2,894	2,042	5,416	4,815	11,023	151	1,947
Arizona	2,298,348	1,449,120	1,105,267	45,184	15,460	78,274	39,981	141,322	1,713	21,919
Arkansas	1,005,891	709,191	468,117	14,405	7,488	43,154	26,302	125,981	1,425	22,319
California	9,340,498	6,166,205	4,636,107	280,801	80,290	357,843	158,316	565,270	8,429	79,149
Colorado	1,467,937	925,084	709,963	32,430	7,956	49,249	24,560	87,507	850	12,569
Connecticut	1,193,327	699,597	532,298	19,471	7,417	35,113	18,600	74,895	616	11,187
Delaware	387,905	229,047	175,408	5,344	1,682	11,562	6,142	25,286	185	3,438
Dist. of Columbia	124,676	83,228	60,292	1,785	815	3,677	3,247	12,097	20	1,295
Florida	7,577,221	4,909,642	3,720,938	147,681	48,222	267,242	120,466	520,045	6,244	78,804
Georgia	2,869,160	1,918,848	1,359,691	45,040	20,960	110,983	71,106	262,794	2,931	45,343
Hawaii	449,099	286,863	230,841	8,470	3,716	14,341	6,235	19,617	305	3,338
Idaho	574,812	377,904	282,455	11,331	4,049	19,823	10,565	41,769	571	7,341
Illinois	3,564,381	2,271,926	1,676,914	72,666	23,438	136,968	70,385	251,128	2,753	37,674
Indiana	2,189,729	1,388,573	987,268	34,766	12,911	83,681	48,724	189,432	2,039	29,752
Iowa	1,039,410	668,984	503,615	16,466	6,474	37,818	18,797	74,363	609	10,842
Kansas	910,440	573,476	422,971	15,444	6,045	32,493	18,359	66,682	616	10,866
Kentucky	1,438,656	1,010,012	647,855	28,545	10,106	71,665	40,000	179,822	3,135	28,884
Louisiana	1,287,133	924,881	583,793	37,246	10,437	79,729	42,803	143,284	2,495	25,094
Maine	521,038	359,152	258,610	9,206	3,412	18,496	9,333	50,945	480	8,670
Maryland	1,710,224	1,038,041	777,516	28,661	10,094	53,947	33,590	116,464	704	17,065
Massachusetts	2,061,173	1,295,088	939,694	38,077	13,901	63,458	35,206	173,945	1,157	29,650
Michigan	3,611,694	2,253,295	1,600,554	64,374	23,142	132,812	70,229	307,554	4,016	50,614
Minnesota	1,756,202	1,082,519	829,789	29,295	10,676	52,033	27,513	114,022	799	18,392
Mississippi	951,295	681,844	446,981	13,849	8,660	44,189	31,842	114,383	1,544	20,396
Missouri	1,990,464	1,329,084	936,580	30,240	12,271	77,123	46,783	194,556	1,981	29,550
Montana	368,099	248,513	189,757	6,689	2,563	13,671	6,994	24,869	319	3,651
Nebraska	559,398	360,240	270,312	9,484	3,621	20,123	10,881	38,910	262	6,647
Nevada	872,772	571,841	438,116	14,748	5,867	29,419	15,079	59,661	597	8,354
New Hampshire	534,012	321,925	236,601	7,646	2,602	14,450	7,714	43,702	274	8,936
New Jersey	2,823,697	1,652,973	1,244,222	53,624	18,529	89,029	44,464	173,632	1,809	27,664
New Mexico	655,876	455,414	326,068	14,726	4,331	26,166	16,061	58,346	678	9,038
New York	5,804,433	3,680,521	2,684,406	130,559	44,722	199,852	96,244	447,428	5,307	72,003
North Carolina	3,388,657	2,202,898	1,611,146	44,814	19,720	114,752	68,099	296,199	2,950	45,218
North Dakota	211,034	140,668	105,753	3,967	1,217	9,092	4,632	13,797	88	2,122
Ohio	3,596,930	2,409,265	1,689,343	77,031	20,420	166,308	84,029	322,274	3,809	46,051
Oklahoma	1,204,224	813,941	561,018	21,085	8,442	53,832	30,413	118,777	1,464	18,910
Oregon	1,420,319	910,086	695,077	27,244	9,101	47,848	20,116	96,685	1,113	12,902
Pennsylvania	4,573,216	2,878,165	2,088,154	82,292	25,308	172,163	82,762	368,244	3,940	55,302
Rhode Island	362,689	230,763	167,529	4,708	2,637	10,659	5,834	33,535	218	5,643
South Carolina	1,886,729	1,215,646	883,812	25,704	11,011	66,880	39,351	161,614	1,694	25,580
South Dakota	283,326	189,232	146,407	4,527	1,616	10,256	5,729	17,723	139	2,835
Tennessee	2,257,993	1,503,361	1,044,660	36,794	14,401	92,126	55,120	222,515	2,662	35,083
Texas	6,664,490	4,475,805	3,149,545	189,980	49,585	314,188	158,275	513,527	7,693	93,012
Utah	693,526	438,581	319,644	19,755	5,433	23,881	17,112	43,781	575	8,400
Vermont	245,387	157,587	116,636	4,048	1,691	7,474	3,871	20,214	135	3,518
Virginia	2,538,995	1,598,078	1,174,814	45,981	15,366	90,389	46,004	192,934	2,181	30,409
Washington	2,303,623	1,413,306	1,068,554	48,634	14,609	73,354	33,218	151,348	1,635	21,954
West Virginia	692,161	475,824	302,162	19,741	5,435	38,978	17,848	77,602	1,942	12,116
Wisconsin	2,046,456	1,289,260	976,275	28,906	11,853	64,405	34,686	147,961	1,198	23,976
Wyoming	192,021	120,816	91,386	3,293	1,043	6,622	3,649	12,878	152	1,793
American Samoa	5,062	6,008	2,678	189	212	583	632	1,226	33	155
Guam	20,019	19,279	12,948	1,039	495	1,573	1,218	1,489	58	459
N. Mariana Isls.	2,735	3,474	2,149	134	166	325	332	281	7	80
Puerto Rico	828,016	821,664	496,598	60,562	9,439	71,879	23,299	136,428	4,582	18,877
U.S. Virgin Isls.	29,211	21,938	17,299	833	395	1,215	646	1,303	20	227
Foreign countries	548,444	695,086	443,546	115,819	11,182	100,183	13,016	8,331	356	2,653
Unknown	861	599	429	26	6	63	16	48	0	11
All areas	99,804,910	65,228,238	47,292,977	2,165,865	687,269	3,888,166	1,975,881	7,877,129	96,063	1,244,888

Outcomes of Applications for Disability Benefits, 2000-20

Source: Social Security Administration

Year of application	Total	Pending final decision	Technical denials[1]	Medical denials Medical	Subsequent nonmedical[2]	Medical allowances Awards	Subsequent denials[2]	Award rate[3]	Allowance rate[4]
2000	1,364,323	0	136,054	456,467	3,817	766,047	1,938	56.1%	62.6%
2005	2,087,733	0	528,760	642,170	6,964	907,877	1,962	43.5	58.4
2010	2,981,615	0	978,627	861,506	19,094	1,120,313	2,075	37.6	56.0
2011	2,952,112	0	981,930	872,759	20,762	1,074,600	2,061	36.4	54.6
2012	2,955,946	0	1,024,477	867,393	23,848	1,037,950	2,278	35.1	53.9
2013	2,790,688	0	971,052	827,416	24,976	964,999	2,245	34.6	53.2
2014	2,687,365	3,820	936,811	800,691	27,033	916,728	2,282	34.2	52.6
2015	2,547,682	4,030	904,263	758,670	27,523	850,895	2,301	33.5	52.0
2016	2,430,101	5,941	875,683	715,441	27,386	803,663	1,987	33.2	52.0
2017	2,306,263	10,626	834,214	672,761	28,181	758,542	1,939	33.0	52.1
2018	2,226,343	35,665	811,115	621,105	29,975	726,398	2,085	33.2	52.8
2019	2,174,707	113,268	774,337	578,744	30,252	676,175	1,941	32.8	52.9
2020	1,882,440	218,510	707,021	468,290	26,321	460,891	1,407	27.7	48.3

Note: Data as of June-July 2021. Applications for more recent years may still be pending; award and allowance rates will change. Does not include Supplemental Security Income-only applications. (1) Application denied for non-medical reason. (2) Denied for non-medical reasons after medical criteria were adjudicated. (3) Percent of all applications, minus pending claims, in which benefits were awarded. (4) Percent of all medical decisions that resulted in an allowance.

OASDI Recipients and Monthly Payments, 1940-2022

Source: Social Security Administration

Year	Total recipients	Monthly benefits Total (thous.)	Avg.[1]	Avg. (2022 dollars)[2]	Year	Total recipients	Monthly benefits Total (thous.)	Avg.[1]	Avg. (2022 dollars)[2]
1940	222,488	$4,070	$18.29	$373.33	2000	45,414,794	$34,848,920	$767.35	$1,307.76
1945	1,288,107	23,801	18.48	294.01	2005	48,434,445	44,351,772	915.71	1,380.13
1950	3,477,243	126,857	36.48	434.05	2010	54,032,097	58,048,364	1,074.33	1,445.98
1955	7,960,616	411,613	51.71	552.30	2015	59,963,425	73,642,029	1,228.12	1,525.74
1960	14,844,589	936,321	63.07	610.19	2016	60,907,307	75,917,962	1,246.45	1,533.51
1965	20,866,767	1,516,802	72.69	659.87	2017	61,903,360	79,732,580	1,288.02	1,551.67
1970	26,228,629	2,628,326	100.21	739.12	2018	62,906,222	84,419,840	1,342.00	1,576.51
1975	32,085,372	5,727,903	178.52	949.21	2019	64,064,496	88,523,452	1,381.79	1,596.71
1980	35,618,840	10,694,022	300.23	1,042.08	2020	64,850,867	92,197,039	1,421.68	1,623.08
1985	37,058,353	15,901,643	429.10	1,155.21	2021	65,228,238	99,804,910	1,530.09	1,659.60
1990	39,832,125	21,686,763	544.45	1,214.40	2022	65,994,457	111,421,667	1,688.35	1,688.35
1995	43,387,259	28,148,078	648.76	1,246.90					

OASDI = Old-Age, Survivors, and Disability Insurance. **Note:** Disability insurance payments began in 1957. (1) Avg. monthly benefit does not necessarily reflect individual payments to OASDI recipients. (2) Adjusted for inflation.

Social Security Trust Funds

Source: Social Security Administration

Old-Age and Survivors Insurance (OASI) Trust Fund, 1940-2022

(in millions)

Fiscal year[1]	Total	INCOME Net payroll tax contribs.	Income from taxing benefits	General fund reimbursements[2]	Net interest[3]	Total	DISBURSEMENTS Benefit pymts.[4]	Admin. expenses	Transfers to Railroad Retirement program	Net increase in fund[5]	Year-end balance
1940	$592	$550	—	—	$42	$28	$16	$12	—	$564	$1,745
1950	2,367	2,106	—	$4	257	784	727	57	—	1,583	12,893
1960	10,360	9,843	—	—	517	11,073	10,270	202	$600	–713	20,829
1970	31,746	29,955	—	442	1,350	27,321	26,268	474	579	4,425	32,616
1980	100,051	97,608	—	557	1,886	103,228	100,626	1,160	1,442	–3,177	24,566
1990	278,607	260,069	$2,924	1,471	14,143	223,481	218,948	1,564	2,969	55,126	203,445
1995	326,067	289,525	5,114	11	31,417	294,456	288,607	1,797	4,052	31,611	447,946
2000	484,228	418,219	12,476	1	53,532	353,396	347,868	1,990	3,538	130,832	893,003
2005	599,992	502,998	15,332	—	81,662	436,919	430,439	2,900	3,579	163,073	1,615,623
2010	682,448	552,037	21,068	737	108,606	579,907	572,515	3,462	3,930	102,541	2,398,377
2015	795,319	672,246	29,627	211	93,235	741,464	733,711	3,496	4,258	53,855	2,766,554
2016	799,892	679,566	31,121	138	89,067	769,827	762,122	3,417	4,287	30,066	2,796,620
2017	822,442	702,123	35,416	15	84,888	798,961	791,094	3,551	4,316	23,481	2,820,101
2018	822,440	706,127	34,718	11	81,583	841,474	833,034	3,672	4,769	–19,034	2,801,066
2019	900,075	785,576	34,896	15	79,589	896,829	888,068	3,881	4,880	3,246	2,804,312
2020	955,571	841,664	37,910	7	75,990	948,702	940,200	3,658	4,844	6,869	2,811,181
2021	935,985	831,124	34,323	2	70,536	991,367	982,673	3,902	4,792	–55,383	2,755,799
2022	1,041,093	929,042	46,970	—	65,081	1,073,262	1,063,896	4,050	5,316	–32,169	2,723,629

— = Not applicable. **Note:** Numbers may not add up to totals due to rounding. (1) Fiscal years 1977 and later consist of the 12 months ending on Sept. 30 of each year. Fiscal years prior to 1977 consisted of the 12 months ending on June 30 of each year. (2) Includes reimbursements from the general fund of the Treasury to the OASI Trust Fund for certain legislated measures since 1957. (3) Includes net profits or losses on marketable investments. Beginning in 1967, the trust fund paid administrative expenses on an estimated basis, with a final adjustment including interest made in the following fiscal year. Net interest includes these interest adjustments. Beginning in Oct. 1973, figures include relatively small gifts to the fund. (4) Beginning in 1967, includes payments for vocational rehabilitation services furnished to disabled persons receiving benefits because of their disabilities; beginning in 1983, includes reimbursements paid from the general fund to the trust fund for unnegotiated benefit checks. (5) Net change in assets during fiscal year, including amounts borrowed or repaid by other funds.

Disability Insurance (DI) Trust Fund, 1960-2022

(in millions)

Fiscal year[1]	Total	INCOME Net payroll tax contribs.	Income from taxing benefits	General fund reimbursements[2]	Net interest[3]	Total	DISBURSEMENTS Benefit pymts.[4]	Admin. expenses	Transfers to Railroad Retirement program	Net increase in fund[5]	Year-end balance
1960	$1,034	$987	—	—	$47	$533	$528	$32	–$27	$501	$2,167
1970	4,380	4,141	—	$16	223	2,954	2,795	149	10	1,426	5,104
1980	17,376	16,805	—	118	453	15,320	14,998	334	–12	2,056	7,680
1990	28,215	27,154	$158	138	766	25,124	24,327	717	80	3,091	11,455
1995	70,209	67,986	335	—	1,888	41,374	40,234	1,072	68	28,835	35,206
2000	77,023	70,001	756	—	6,266	56,008	54,244	1,608	159	21,014	113,752
2005	96,765	85,418	1,164	—	10,183	86,360	83,711	2,301	338	10,405	193,298
2010	105,513	93,739	1,745	125	9,904	126,344	122,935	2,947	462	–20,831	186,946
2015	150,978	146,848	1,209	2	2,918	147,710	144,893	2,751	66	3,267	96,409
2016	147,387	142,898	1,671	1	2,817	146,733	144,084	2,505	144	655	97,063
2017	144,392	141,195	479	—	2,719	143,393	140,742	2,543	107	999	98,063
2018	170,272	167,043	1,000	2	2,227	146,575	143,642	2,759	174	23,698	93,141
2019	150,978	146,848	1,209	2	2,918	147,710	144,893	2,751	66	3,267	96,409
2020	147,387	142,898	1,671	1	2,817	146,733	144,084	2,505	144	655	97,063
2021	144,392	141,195	479	—	2,719	143,393	140,742	2,543	107	999	98,063
2022	162,007	157,816	1,533	—	2,658	145,379	142,459	2,764	156	16,628	114,691

— = Not applicable. **Note:** Numbers may not add up to totals due to rounding. (1) Fiscal years 1977 and later consist of the 12 months ending on Sept. 30 of each year. Fiscal years prior to 1977 consisted of the 12 months ending on June 30 of each year. (2) Includes reimbursements from the general fund of the Treasury to the DI Trust Fund for certain legislated measures since 1957. (3) Includes net profits or losses on marketable investments. Beginning in 1967, the trust fund paid administrative expenses on an estimated basis, with a final adjustment including interest made in the following fiscal year. Net interest includes these interest adjustments. The 1970 report describes the accounting for administrative expenses for years prior to 1967. Beginning in July 1974, figures include relatively small gifts to the fund. (4) Beginning in 1967, includes payments for vocational rehabilitation services furnished to persons receiving benefits because of a disability; beginning in 1983, includes reimbursements paid from the general fund to the trust fund for unnegotiated benefit checks. (5) Net change in assets during fiscal year, including amounts borrowed or repaid by other funds.

Supplementary Medical Insurance Trust Fund (Medicare SMI), 1975-2022

Source: Centers for Medicare & Medicaid Services, U.S. Dept. of Health and Human Services

(in millions)

Fiscal year[1]	INCOME Total	Premium from participants[2]	Govt. contribs.[3]	Transfers from states[4]	Interest and other income[5,6]	DISBURSEMENTS Total	Benefit pymts.[6,7,8]	Admin. expenses	Net change	Year-end balance
1975	$4,322	$1,887	$2,330	—	$106	$4,170	$3,765	$404	$152	$1,424
1980	10,275	2,928	6,932	—	416	10,737	10,144	593	−462	4,532
1990	46,138	11,494	33,210	—	1,434	43,022	41,498	1,524	3,115	14,527
2000	89,239	20,515	65,561	—	3,164	88,992	87,212[9]	1,780	247	45,896
2005	152,505	35,939	115,200	—	1,366	152,735	149,820[10]	2,914	−230	16,885
2010	282,734	61,364[11]	213,709	4,493	3,168	272,224	268,710[11]	3,514	10,510	71,976
2012	290,864	66,067[11]	210,508	8,324	5,965	291,907	287,777[11]	4,130	−1,043	71,783
2013	313,158	71,300[11]	227,208	8,666	5,985	315,123	311,367[11]	3,756	−1,965	69,818
2014	334,943	75,887[11]	244,351	8,727	5,978	333,438	329,141[11]	4,297	1,504	71,323
2015	357,511	79,379[11]	263,484	8,797	5,851	359,393	355,787[11]	3,606	−1,882	69,441
2016	400,623	86,063[11]	299,491	9,755	5,315	403,877	399,456[11]	4,421	−3,254	66,187
2017	422,441	94,794[11]	309,647	11,072	6,928	414,122	409,261[11]	4,861[12]	8,319	74,506
2018	441,569	106,179[11]	316,746	11,670	6,974	414,092	409,408[11]	4,684	27,477	101,983
2019	463,569	113,508[11]	331,830	12,154	6,077	458,359	453,480[11]	4,878	5,210	107,193
2020	497,598	121,973[11]	357,467	11,720	6,439	514,799	509,600[11,13]	5,199	−17,201	89,993
2021	594,895	129,174[11]	448,194[14]	11,859	5,668	511,080	505,736[11,13]	5,345	83,814	173,807
2022	570,759	144,266[11]	406,385[14]	13,330	6,778	573,408	567,749[11,13]	5,659	−2,650	171,158

— = Not applicable. **Note:** Numbers may not add up to totals because of rounding. (1) Fiscal year 1975 ended June 30, 1975; fiscal years 1980 and later ended on Sept. 30 of each year. (2) For Part D, premiums include both amounts withheld from Social Security benefits (and certain other federal benefit payments) and amounts paid directly to Part D plans (estimated). (3) For Part B, includes matching payments from the Treasury's general fund, plus certain interest-adjustment items. For Part D, includes all federal govt. transfers. (4) For full-benefit dually eligible individuals, states pay 90% of estimated costs in 2006, phasing down to 75% in 2015 and after. (5) Other income includes recoveries of amounts reimbursed from the trust fund that are not trust fund obligations and other miscellaneous income. (6) Values after 2005 include additional premiums for Medicare Advantage (MA) plans that are deducted from beneficiaries' Social Security benefits, transferred to HI and SMI trust funds, and then transferred to the plans. (7) Includes costs of Peer Review Organizations in 1983-2001 and costs of Quality Review Organizations beginning in 2002. (8) For Part D, includes payments to plans, subsidies to employer-sponsored retiree drug plans, payments to states for low-income eligibility determinations, and Part D drug premiums (the amount collected from beneficiaries and transferred to plans and an estimated amount for premiums paid directly by enrollees to plans). Includes amounts for transitional assistance benefits in 2004-06. (9) Benefit payments less monies transferred from the HI trust fund for home health agency costs. (10) Certain HI hospice costs were misallocated to, and paid from, the Part B account of the SMI trust fund. (11) Includes an estimated $4.221 bil (2010), $4.843 bil (2011), $5.222 bil (2012), $6.306 bil (2013), $7.450 bil (2014), $8.445 bil (2015), $9.084 bil (2016), $10.175 bil (2017), $10.513 bil (2018), $10.568 bil (2019), $11.467 bil (2020), and $12.173 bil (2022) for premiums paid directly to Part D plans. (12) Reflects a larger-than-usual and upward adjustment for the reallocation of prior-year HI and SMI expenses. (13) Includes $38.4 bil in net Part B payments made through the Medicare Accelerated and Advance Payments (AAP) Program in fiscal year 2020, in light of the COVID-19 public health emergency, and subsequent net repayments of $14.6 bil and $21.7 bil in 2021 and 2022, respectively. (14) Includes (i) a transfer of $37.8 bil in fiscal year 2021 from the general fund of the Treasury to the Part B account, which occurred in Nov. 2020 for the Part B outstanding balance of the Medicare AAP Program, as required by Public Law 116-159, and (ii) subsequent recoveries from Part B providers and suppliers of $8.5 bil in 2021 and $26.5 bil in 2022 transferred to the Treasury's general fund.

Hospital Insurance Trust Fund (Medicare HI), 1975-2022

Source: Centers for Medicare & Medicaid Services, U.S. Dept. of Health and Human Services

(in millions)

Fiscal year[1]	INCOME Total	Payroll taxes	Taxation of benefits	Transfers from Railroad Retirement acct.	Reimb. for uninsured persons	Premiums from voluntary enrollees	Pymts. for military wage credits	Interest and other income[2,3]	DISBURSEMENTS Total	Benefit pymts.[3,4]	Admin. expenses[5]	Net change	Year-end balance
1975	$12,568	$11,291	—	$132	$481	$6	$48	$609	$10,612	$10,353	$259	$1,956	$9,870
1980	25,415	23,244	—	244	697	17	141	1,072	24,288	23,790	497	1,127	14,490
1990	79,563	70,655	—	367	413	113	107	7,908	66,687	65,912	774	12,876	95,631
2000	159,681	137,738	$8,787	465	470	1,392	2	10,827	130,284	127,934[6]	2,350	29,397	168,084
2005	196,921	168,954	8,765	445	286	2,303	0	16,168	184,142	181,292[7]	2,850	12,779	277,723
2010	218,004	183,603	13,760	535	−142	3,314	0	16,933	248,978	245,650	3,328	−30,975	278,939
2012	241,730	204,753	18,643	511	262	3,400	0	14,162	258,155	254,459	3,696	−16,425	229,372
2013	243,560	212,901	14,310	577	0	3,397	0	12,375	266,546	262,411	4,135	−22,986	206,386
2014	262,753	227,579	18,066	612	432	3,259	0	12,805	266,853	262,520	4,332	−4,100	202,286
2015	272,359	237,697	20,208	595	187	3,277	0	10,396	278,736	273,248	5,488	−6,377	195,909
2016	287,106	250,472	23,022	657	158	3,232	0	9,566	290,648	285,574	5,075	−3,542	192,367
2017	298,524	259,744	24,206	637	147	3,492	0	10,302	293,265	290,279	2,986	5,259	197,626
2018	302,839	264,566	24,192	597	132	3,533	0	9,819	297,168	292,078	5,090	5,671	203,297
2019	319,256	281,441	23,781	570	127	3,823	0	9,513	323,726	318,371	5,355	−4,470	198,826
2020	336,116	295,913	26,941	606	109	3,975	0	8,571	400,646	395,823[8]	4,823	−64,530	134,296
2021	333,744	299,147	24,975	568	95	4,141	0	4,819	331,938	326,812[8]	5,126	1,806	136,102
2022	354,619	343,729	32,775	516	82	4,467	0	5,050	344,743	339,554[8]	5,189	41,876	177,979

— = Not applicable. **Note:** Numbers may not add up to totals because of rounding. (1) Fiscal year 1975 ended June 30, 1975; fiscal years 1980 and later ended Sept. 30 of each year. (2) Other income includes recoveries of amounts reimbursed from the trust fund that are not trust fund obligations, receipts from the fraud and abuse control program, and other small amounts of miscellaneous income. In 2008, includes an adjustment of −$853 mil for interest inadvertently earned as a result of HI hospice costs that were misallocated to, and paid from, the Part B account of the Supplementary Medical Insurance (SMI) trust fund from May 2005 to Sept. 2007. (3) Values after 2005 include additional premiums for Medicare Advantage (MA) plans that are deducted from beneficiaries' Social Security benefits, transferred to the HI and SMI trust funds, and then transferred to the plans. (4) Includes costs of Peer Review Organizations in 1983-2001 and costs of Quality Review Organizations beginning in 2002. (5) Includes costs of experiments and demonstration projects. Beginning in 1997, includes fraud and abuse control expenses. (6) Includes monies transferred to the SMI trust fund for home health agency costs. (7) Certain HI hospice costs were misallocated to, and paid from, the Part B account of the SMI trust fund. (8) Includes $65.5 bil in net HI payments made through the Medicare Accelerated and Advance Payments Program in fiscal year 2020, in light of the COVID-19 public health emergency, and subsequent net repayments of $22.2 bil and $39.7 bil in fiscal years 2021 and 2022, respectively.

TAXES

Federal Personal Income Tax Return Facts, 2024
Source: Jessica A. Newport, CPA, Senior Accountant, Andrews Hooper Pavlik PLC

Deadlines. The deadline for filing a 2023 U.S. individual income tax return (Form 1040) is Apr. 15, 2024.

Extensions. Taxpayers who cannot file a 2023 individual income tax return by the deadline can apply for a six-month extension to Oct. 15, 2024. To qualify for an extension, Form 4868 must be filed no later than Apr. 15, 2024.

E-Filing. The electronic filing program began as a pilot program in 1986; by 2011, 1 bil individual tax returns had been e-filed. As of May 12, 2023, 134.9 mil returns for income tax year 2022 had been e-filed, compared to 136.4 mil as of May 13, 2022.

Penalties. The IRS can levy two potential penalties after the filing due date when there is a balance owed. One penalty is for failing to file a timely tax return; the other is for failure to pay the tax when due. In addition, interest is charged on any unpaid tax balance.

Refunds. As of May 12, 2023, the average refund for the 2023 tax filing season was $2,812, compared to $3,033 as of May 13, 2022. The IRS refunded $266.8 bil, of which $253.9 bil was refunded with direct deposit.

Statute of limitations. Taxpayers who have not yet filed their 2020 federal tax return have until three years after the deadline to file and claim their refund. After that date, any refunds for 2020 income tax or withholding tax, including the earned income tax credit, will be lost.

Federal Income Tax Rates for Taxable-Income Brackets, 2023

Tax rate	Unmarried individuals	Married filing jointly or surviving spouses	Married filing separately	Head of household other than surviving spouses
10%	$0 to $11,000	$0 to $22,000	$0 to $11,000	$0 to $15,700
12%	$11,001 to $44,725	$22,001 to $89,450	$11,001 to $44,725	$15,701 to $59,850
22%	$44,726 to $95,375	$89,451 to $190,750	$44,726 to $95,375	$59,851 to $95,350
24%	$95,376 to $182,100	$190,751 to $364,200	$95,376 to $182,100	$95,351 to $182,100
32%	$182,101 to $231,250	$364,201 to $462,500	$182,101 to $231,250	$182,101 to $231,250
35%	$231,251 to $578,125	$462,501 to $693,750	$231,251 to $346,875	$231,251 to $578,100
37%	Over $578,125	Over $693,750	Over $346,875	Over $578,100

Standard Deduction, 2023

The standard deduction is a flat amount subtracted from the adjusted gross income of taxpayers who do not itemize deductions.

Single	$13,850
Married filing jointly or qualifying widow(er)	$27,700
Married filing separately	$13,850
Head of household	$20,800

Additional standard deduction. Elderly and/or blind, single or head of household: $1,850. Elderly and/or blind, married or qualifying widow(er): $1,500.

Personal exemption. The deduction for personal exemptions was suspended until Jan. 1, 2026, under the Tax Cuts and Jobs Act of 2017.

FICA and Medicare tax. For Social Security, wages paid in 2023 are taxable up to $160,200. For Medicare, all wages are taxable.

Common Income Tax Errors

Periodically, the IRS issues a list of the most commonly made income tax errors.

1. Wrong or missing Social Security numbers.
2. Wrong names.
3. Filing status errors, such as Head of Household instead of Single.
4. Math mistakes, for example, when adding or subtracting items on a form or worksheet.
5. Errors in credits or deductions, like the Earned Income Tax Credit, Child and Dependent Care Credit, and standard deductions.
6. Wrong bank and/or account numbers for direct deposit of any tax refund.
7. Forms not signed or dated. An unsigned tax return is not valid. Both spouses must sign a joint return.
8. E-file PIN errors. E-filed returns can be signed electronically with a personal identification number (PIN). Usually, last year's PIN can be used, but if it is unknown, adjusted gross income information from last year's original return needs to be entered for verification.

Retirement Savings Plans and Income Tax

401(k) plan. The maximum amount that an individual can contribute to a 401(k) plan for 2023 is $22,500. Individuals born before 1974 can put away an additional $7,500, for a total of $30,000.

IRAs. Contributions to IRAs and Roth IRAs were limited to $6,500 in 2023. Anyone born before 1974 can contribute an extra $1,000. Funds may be deposited into a traditional IRA for 2023 until Apr. 15, 2024. Contributions after Apr. 15, 2024 will automatically be considered funds deposited for 2024.

Roth IRA. Contributions paid into a Roth IRA are not tax deductible. Distributions of funds including investment earnings held in the account for five years or longer and distributed after age 59½ are free of both income tax and the 10% early-withdrawal penalty. Withdrawals from the account in less than five years can be subject to tax and a 10% withdrawal penalty regardless of age. There are income limitations on contributions.

Distributions. There is a 10% penalty for IRA distributions before age 59½. Distributions paid to a beneficiary due to disability/death of the owner are not subject to this penalty, nor are payments used for certain unreimbursed medical expenses, higher-education expenses, or first-time home buyer acquisition costs (up to $10,000).

The owner of a traditional IRA (or a SIMPLE plan, pension, or profit-sharing plan account) must begin receiving distributions by Apr. 1 of the calendar year following the year in which he or she reaches age 72. Any employee who works beyond 72 and is not a 5% or more owner of the business can continue to defer profit-sharing and pension plan distributions.

Tax Credits

A tax deduction reduces a taxpayer's taxable income whereas tax credits reduce the amount of tax owed.

Adoption credit. The adoption credit in 2023 for qualified expenses is $15,950. The credit limit is per child and is adjusted annually for inflation. The credit is not refundable and phases out for taxpayers at higher income levels.

American Opportunity Tax Credit. This education credit provides up to $2,500 per student per year in the first four years of a student's postsecondary education.

Child and dependent care credit. This credit is for expenses for the care of taxpayers' qualifying children under age 13 or care of a disabled spouse or dependent, while the taxpayer works or looks for work.

Child tax credit. The maximum child tax credit is $2,000 for each qualifying child dependent age 16 and under. The credit is subject to income limitations.

Earned Income Credit. Lower-income workers who maintain a household may be eligible for an Earned Income Credit. This credit is based on total earned income such as wages, commissions, and tips. Military personnel can include tax-free combat pay in income to compute the credit.

Energy credits. There are many energy-related credits—from the purchase of an alternative fuel vehicle and the installation of solar/fuel cell property in a residence, to the production of biodiesel or ethanol.

Alternative Minimum Tax

The Alternative Minimum Tax (AMT) was established in 1969 to prevent individuals with very high incomes from using special tax breaks to pay little or no tax. The AMT 2023 exemption for a single taxpayer is $81,300 and $126,500 for married filing jointly. For married taxpayers filing separate returns, the exemption is $63,250.

Estate and Gift Taxes

Estate tax. The Tax Relief Act of 2010 reinstated the estate tax with a 35% flat rate and increased the exemptions to $5 mil in 2011 and $5.12 mil in 2012. The estate tax rate was increased to 40% for 2013 and subsequent years. The Tax Cuts and Jobs Act of 2017 set the 2023 exemption at $12.92 mil per person, $25.84 mil for married couples.

Gifting. For 2023 U.S. citizens, residents, and non-resident aliens have an annual gift tax exclusion of up to $17,000 per individual to as many individuals as he or she chooses. For married couples the exclusion is $34,000, even if only one spouse does all the gifting.

International property. All property owned worldwide by American citizens is subject to U.S. estate tax rules and regulations.

Resident aliens. Aliens residing in the U.S. are subject to the same rules as American citizens.

Tax Rates for Estates and Trusts

If taxable income is	The tax is
Not over $2,900	10% of the taxable income
Over $2,900 but not over $10,550.	$290 plus 24% of the excess over $2,900
Over $10,550 but not over $14,450.	$2,126 plus 35% of the excess over $10,550
Over $14,450	$3,491 plus 37% of the excess over $14,450

Taxable Social Security Benefits

Earnings limitations. Social Security recipients who have not reached their full retirement age of 67 in 2023 will lose $1 of their benefits for every $2 of earned income over $21,240. Recipients who reached full retirement age in 2023 will not lose any benefits if they earned $56,520 or less. Recipients will have to pay back some benefits if their income exceeded that amount.

Taxable benefits. Up to 50% of Social Security benefits may be taxable if the person's total income is more than $25,000 but less than $34,000 for a single individual, head of household, qualifying widow(er), or a married person who is filing separately if spouses lived apart all year; or more than

$32,000 but less than $44,000 for married individuals filing jointly. For higher incomes, 85% of Social Security benefits may become taxable.

If the only income received during the year was Social Security, these benefits are not taxable, and the recipient probably does not have to file a tax return.

Retention of Income Tax Records

Federal tax returns generally can be audited for up to three years after filing or six years if the IRS suspects underreported income, so it's wise to keep copies of an income tax return and records for at least seven years after filing a return.

Tax Audits

Audit odds. The IRS audit rate for individual income tax returns in tax year 2020 was 0.48%. The odds of an audit generally trend upward with higher taxpayer income, especially on certain types of income. For taxpayers with incomes of $50,000-$75,000, the audit rate was 0.10%. For taxpayers with gross income of $1 mil-$5 mil, the rate was 0.40%. The audit rate was 0.20% for all incomes under $200,000.

The audit selection process is not random. It is based on a set of formulas that are designed to spot questionable returns. If the IRS concludes that a person owes more tax, and he or she disagrees with the findings, the taxpayer can meet with a supervisor.

If the taxpayer still does not agree, he or she can appeal to a separate Appeals Office or take it to the U.S. Tax Court, Federal District Court, or the U.S. Court of Federal Claims.

Tax Court. The U.S. Tax Court is a federal court where taxpayers can dispute tax deficiencies as determined by the Commissioner of Internal Revenue before payment of the disputed amounts. The Tax Court is composed of presidentially appointed members. Many taxpayers choose the Tax Court because they are not required to pay the contested tax up front.

Appeals. For more information about audits, call the IRS at (800) TAX-FORM (829-3676) for its free Publication 556, *Examination of Returns, Appeal Rights, and Claims for Refund* or visit www.irs.gov.

IRS Contact Information

Website: www.irs.gov
Tax questions: (800) 829-1040
Forms/publications: (800) TAX-FORM (829-3676)
Taxpayers can view and download tax forms and publications in Spanish from www.irs.gov/es/spanish/. The IRS site also offers help in Chinese, Korean, Vietnamese, and Russian.

Hearing impaired: (800) 829-4059 (TTY/TDD)
Additional services: The Volunteer Income Tax Assistance (VITA) program offers free tax return preparation help to people who generally make $60,000 or less, persons with disabilities, and taxpayers who speak limited English. Visit www.irs.gov/individuals/free-tax-return-preparation-for-qualifying-taxpayers or (800) 906-9887.

Report wrongdoing: Report misconduct, waste, fraud, or abuse by an IRS employee to the Treasury Inspector General for Tax Administration at (800) 366-4484.

Working With a Tax Preparer

The following are some suggestions when using a tax preparer:

- **Choose** wisely. Regulations require all paid tax return preparers including attorneys, certified public accountants, and IRS-enrolled agents to have a Preparer Tax Identification Number. Check the preparer's qualifications and history. Ask about service fees in advance.
- **Review** last year's tax return. Make note of any changes since then such as marriage, divorce, number of dependents, retirement, job changes, additional income, or new deductions.
- **Organize** your records with income items first, followed by itemized deductions (medical, taxes, interest, and charitable and other miscellaneous deductions), followed by gains, losses, rentals, or other items.
- **Time** spent with your preparer may affect your bill. If you provide disorganized records and deductions, there may be

an additional cost to have your tax preparer organize your information.
- **Prepare** a list of questions in advance. Ask about any invoices or bills that you are not sure apply.
- **Alert** your preparer if you're waiting to receive additional information. He or she can begin preparing your tax return and include the missing data later to finalize your return. Amending a return after it is completed may incur additional fees.
- **Review** your tax return before signing it. Ask questions about any item you don't understand. Even though your preparer is required to sign the return, you are responsible for its contents.

Total U.S. Tax Collections by Type of Tax, 1960-2022

Source: *Internal Revenue Service Data Book, 2022*, Internal Revenue Service, U.S. Dept. of the Treasury
(as percent of total gross collection or total income taxes)

Fiscal year	Total IRS collections (bil)[1]	Income taxes Total	Business[2]	Individual[3]	Estate and trust[3]	Employment taxes[4]	Estate taxes	Gift taxes	Excise taxes[5]
1960	$92	73.1%	33.0%	67.0%	—	12.2%	1.6%	0.20%	12.9%
1965	114	69.7	32.7	67.3	—	14.9	2.1	0.25	12.9
1970	196	70.9	25.3	74.7	—	19.1	1.7	0.22	8.1
1975	294	68.8	22.6	77.4	—	23.9	1.5	0.13	5.7
1980	519	69.3	20.1	79.9	—	24.7	1.2	0.04	4.7
1985	743	63.8	16.3	83.7	—	30.3	0.8	0.04	5.0
1990	1,056	61.6	16.9	83.1	—	34.8	0.9	0.20	2.6
1995	1,376	61.8	20.5	79.5	—	33.8	1.0	0.13	3.3
2000	2,097	65.5	17.2	82.8	—	30.5	1.2	0.20	2.6
2005	2,269	62.3	21.7	78.3	—	34.0	1.0	0.09	2.5
2010	2,345	62.0	19.1	80.0	0.8%	35.1	0.7	0.12	2.0
2015	3,303	66.1	17.9	80.6	1.5	31.0	0.5	0.06	2.3
2018	3,465	64.5	11.8	86.5	1.7	32.7	0.7	0.03	2.1
2019	3,565	63.4	12.3	86.0	1.7	33.9	0.4	0.04	2.3
2020	3,493	61.1	12.3	86.1	1.6	36.3	0.5	0.03	2.1
2021	4,112	67.3	15.1	82.9	2.0	30.6	0.6	0.11	1.4
2022	4,902	69.0	14.1	83.4	2.5	28.9	0.6	0.10	1.4

— = Not available. **Note:** Numbers may not add up to totals because of rounding. (1) Credits to taxpayer accounts excluded beginning with fiscal year 2009. (2) Incl. taxes on corporation income and unrelated business income from tax-exempt organizations. (3) Income tax reported for estates and trusts is included in individual income tax in FY1960-2007. Estate and trust income tax is reported separately from FY2008 on. (4) Incl. taxes for Old-Age, Survivors, Disability, and Hospital Insurance; federal unemployment insurance; and Railroad Retirement. (5) Excl. excise taxes collected by the U.S. Customs and Border Protection and the Alcohol and Tobacco Tax and Trade Bureau. The IRS collected taxes on alcohol and tobacco until FY1988 and taxes on firearms until FY1991.

Taxes Collected by State Governments, 2022

Source: Annual Survey of State Government Tax Collections, U.S. Census Bureau, U.S. Dept. of Commerce
(as percent of total taxes collected or total sales and gross receipts taxes)

State	Total taxes collected in dollars (mil)[1]	Property taxes	Sales and gross receipts taxes Total	General	Selective[2]	License taxes[3]	Individual income taxes	Corporation net income taxes	Other taxes[4]
Alabama	$16,324.9	3.0%	46.2%	57.4%	42.6%	3.7%	37.3%	9.0%	0.9%
Alaska	2,427.8	5.2	11.1	—	100.0	5.7	—	17.0	60.9
Arizona	24,356.8	5.2	55.6	82.5	17.5	2.6	30.9	4.8	0.9
Arkansas	12,768.1	10.3	48.7	73.8	26.2	3.5	29.1	6.5	1.9
California	280,828.4	1.1	25.6	72.5	27.5	3.9	52.1	16.4	0.9
Colorado	21,711.1	—	34.5	57.2	42.8	3.3	53.8	6.9	1.4
Connecticut	22,477.5	—	36.5	63.3	36.7	1.8	43.9	15.5	2.4
Delaware	6,310.9	—	10.2	—	100.0	38.6	38.1	7.9	5.2
DC	10,208.7	28.4	21.3	77.9	22.1	2.2	30.5	9.7	7.8
Florida	59,236.9	0.0	79.4	80.5	19.5	3.8	—	6.4	10.5
Georgia	33,933.8	2.4	33.6	73.0	27.0	2.2	53.9	7.4	0.6
Hawaii	10,279.5	—	54.9	75.5	24.5	3.0	36.6	3.1	2.4
Idaho	7,710.3	—	46.6	80.8	19.2	6.1	33.7	13.5	0.1
Illinois	62,571.2	0.1	41.3	59.1	40.9	5.7	36.3	15.4	1.2
Indiana	29,259.0	0.1	51.5	68.9	31.1	3.0	40.2	5.3	0.0
Iowa	12,909.0	0.0	45.0	72.9	27.1	8.8	38.5	6.7	1.0
Kansas	12,592.6	6.7	44.0	77.1	22.9	3.5	38.4	6.9	0.6
Kentucky	16,546.5	4.4	46.6	66.9	33.1	3.3	37.4	7.1	1.2
Louisiana	14,484.0	0.7	53.4	61.3	38.7	4.4	30.9	7.2	3.4
Maine	6,439.3	0.7	46.2	73.0	27.0	4.9	40.2	6.5	1.5
Maryland	29,361.3	3.2	41.3	54.7	45.3	3.4	41.6	7.3	3.1
Massachusetts	43,492.3	0.0	27.1	74.1	25.9	3.0	56.1	10.6	3.2
Michigan	37,057.0	6.8	45.9	71.7	28.3	6.0	34.8	4.8	1.6
Minnesota	34,911.9	2.2	34.6	60.3	39.7	4.2	43.3	13.5	2.0
Mississippi	10,182.8	0.3	61.3	76.4	23.6	6.0	24.9	7.0	0.5
Missouri	16,887.4	0.2	38.3	70.5	29.5	4.0	53.0	4.5	0.1
Montana	4,622.9	7.8	18.4	—	100.0	10.8	51.6	6.3	5.0
Nebraska	7,476.0	0.0	43.9	80.2	19.8	2.7	43.3	9.6	0.4
Nevada	12,072.2	11.6	73.2	62.3	37.7	5.5	—	—	9.7
New Hampshire	3,497.7	11.6	27.0	—	100.0	15.6	4.4	34.7	6.7
New Jersey	52,771.9	0.0	37.4	71.8	28.2	4.1	39.1	16.4	2.9
New Mexico	8,601.7	1.4	48.7	78.6	21.4	4.3	15.1	3.6	26.9
New York	117,983.7	—	26.5	57.8	42.2	1.6	59.5	6.6	5.8
North Carolina	38,453.6	—	42.5	67.6	32.4	6.9	46.0	4.2	0.4
North Dakota	5,350.8	0.1	29.6	67.7	32.3	3.7	8.8	4.3	53.4
Ohio	37,388.6	—	64.2	65.1	34.9	5.5	30.1	0.0	0.2
Oklahoma	13,188.0	—	40.6	66.3	33.7	8.9	31.5	6.2	12.9
Oregon	18,885.7	0.1	14.1	—	100.0	13.6	62.3	7.9	2.0
Pennsylvania	53,679.8	0.1	48.0	57.3	42.7	5.4	32.4	9.3	4.8
Rhode Island	4,796.0	0.1	49.1	63.7	36.3	3.1	40.4	6.1	1.2
South Carolina	16,051.5	0.5	43.5	69.8	30.2	4.2	42.7	7.5	1.5
South Dakota	2,475.4	—	83.5	73.7	26.3	13.6	—	2.5	0.4
Tennessee	22,650.2	—	73.2	77.7	22.3	11.1	0.0	13.2	2.4
Texas	82,259.7	—	81.3	73.0	27.0	5.3	—	—	13.3
Utah	13,786.2	—	40.3	77.1	22.9	2.8	49.4	6.8	0.7
Vermont	4,415.5	28.0	31.5	39.2	60.8	3.2	28.7	5.4	3.1
Virginia	36,754.6	0.1	35.2	54.9	45.1	3.0	53.7	5.4	2.6
Washington	36,071.8	12.2	74.1	80.3	19.7	5.3	—	—	8.4
West Virginia	7,064.2	0.1	45.3	51.7	48.3	2.7	35.4	5.2	11.2
Wisconsin	23,363.8	0.4	42.3	70.6	29.4	5.7	38.5	12.5	0.6
Wyoming	2,441.0	11.0	48.2	83.0	17.0	8.9	—	—	31.9
United States	**1,461,371.5**	1.7	42.6	69.0	31.0	4.5	38.2	9.1	3.9

— = Tax not collected by state. **Note:** For fiscal year 2022 (July 1, 2021-June 30, 2022) for all states except AL and MI (ends Sept. 30), NY (Mar. 31), and TX (Aug. 31). (1) Incl. taxes not shown separately. (2) Imposed on sales of particular commodities/services, e.g., alcohol and tobacco, motor fuels, public utilities. (3) Related to the exercise of a privilege, such as owning/operating a motor vehicle. (4) Incl. death and gift taxes and severance taxes (on removal of natural resources).

State Government Personal Income Tax Rates, 2023

Source: Reproduced with permission from *CCH State Tax Guide*, published and copyrighted by CCH Inc., a Wolters Kluwer business **Alaska**, **Florida**, **Nevada**, **South Dakota**, **Texas**, **Washington**, and **Wyoming** did not have state income taxes and are thus not listed. Tax rates apply in stages—for example, a single person in Connecticut making $60,000 in taxable income would pay 3% on the first $10,000 of income, 5% on the next $40,000, and 5.5% on the last $10,000. For further details on some states, see notes at end of table.

Alabama

Single, Head of household, or Married filing separately

$0 to $500. . . . . .2%
$501 to $3,000 . . . . .4%
$3,001 and over 5%

Married filing jointly

$0 to $1,000 . . . . .2%
$1,001 to $6,000. . . . . .4%
$6,001 and over 5%

Arizona[1]

2.5% flat tax rate

Arkansas[2]

For net income less than $87,001:

$0 to $5,099 . . . . .0%
$5,100 to $10,299. . . . . .2%
$10,300 to $14,699. . . . . . . .3%
$14,700 to $24,299. . . . . . 3.4%
$24,300 to $87,000. . . . . . 4.7%

For net income greater than $87,000:

$0 to $4,400 . . . . 2.0%
$4,401 to $8,800. . . . . .4%
$8,801 and over 4.7%

For net income over $87,000 but not over $91,300, the amount of tax is reduced by a specified bracket adjustment amount.

California[1,2]

Single or Married/registered domestic partner filing separately

$0 to $10,412 . . . . .1%
$10,413 to $24,684. . . . . .2%
$24,685 to $38,959. . . . . . . .4%
$38,960 to $54,081. . . . . . . .6%
$54,082 to $68,350. . . . . . . .8%
$68,351 to $349,137. . . . . 9.3%
$349,138 to $418,961. . . 10.3%
$418,962 to $698,271. . . 11.3%
$698,272 and over 12.3%

Head of household

$0 to $20,839 . . . . .1%
$20,840 to $49,371. . . . . . . .2%
$49,372 to $63,644. . . . . . . .4%
$63,645 to $78,765. . . . . . . .6%
$78,766 to $93,037. . . . . . . .8%
$93,038 to $474,824. . . . . 9.3%
$474,825 to $569,790. . . 10.3%
$569,791 to $949,649. . . 11.3%
$949,650 and over 12.3%

Married/registered domestic partner filing jointly or Qualifying widow(er)

$0 to $20,824 . . . . .1%
$20,825 to $49,368. . . . . . . .2%
$49,369 to $77,918. . . . . . . .4%
$77,919 to $108,162. . . . . . .6%
$108,163 to $136,700. . . . . .8%
$136,701 to $698,274. . . . 9.3%
$698,275 to $837,922. . . 10.3%
$837,923 to $1,396,542 11.3%
$1,396,543 and over. 12.3%

Colorado

4.4% of federal taxable income

Connecticut

Single or Married filing separately

$0 to $10,000 . . . . .3%
$10,001 to $50,000. . . . . . . .5%
$50,001 to $100,000. . . . . 5.5%
$100,001 to $200,000. . . . . .6%

$200,001 to $250,000. . . . 6.5%
$250,001 to $500,000. . . . 6.9%
$500,001 and over 6.99%

Head of household

$0 to $16,000 . . . . .3%
$16,001 to $80,000. . . . . . . .5%
$80,001 to $160,000. . . . . 5.5%
$160,001 to $320,000. . . . . .6%
$320,001 to $400,000. . . . 6.5%
$400,001 to $800,000. . . . 6.9%
$800,001 and over 6.99%

Married filing jointly or Qualifying widow(er)

$0 to $20,000 . . . . .3%
$20,001 to $100,000. . . . . . .5%
$100,001 to $200,000. . . . 5.5%
$200,001 to $400,000. . . . . .6%
$400,001 to $500,000. . . . 6.5%
$500,001 to $1,000,000. . . 6.9%
$1,000,001 and over. . . . 6.99%

Delaware

$0 to $2,000 . . . . .0%
$2,001 to $5,000. . . . . 2.2%
$5,001 to $10,000. . . . . . . 3.9%
$10,001 to $20,000. . . . . . . 4.8%
$20,001 to $25,000. . . . . . 5.2%
$25,001 to $60,000. . . . . 5.55%
$60,001 and over 6.6%

District of Columbia

$0 to $10,000 . . . . .4%
$10,001 to $40,000. . . . . . . .6%
$40,001 to $60,000. . . . . . 6.5%
$60,001 to $250,000. . . . . 8.5%
$250,001 to $500,000. . . 9.25%
$500,001 to $1,000,000. 9.75%
$1,000,001 and over. . . 10.75%

Georgia

Single

$0 to $750. . . . . .1%
$751 to $2,250. . . . . .2%
$2,251 to $3,750. . . . . .3%
$3,751 to $5,250. . . . . .4%
$5,251 to $7,000. . . . . .5%
$7,001 and over 5.75%

Head of household, Married filing jointly, or Qualifying widow(er)

$0 to $1,000 . . . . .1%
$1,001 to $3,000. . . . . .2%
$3,001 to $5,000. . . . . .3%
$5,001 to $7,000. . . . . .4%
$7,001 to $10,000. . . . . .5%
$10,001 and over 5.75%

Married filing separately

$0 to $500. . . . . .1%
$501 to $1,500. . . . . .2%
$1,501 to $2,500. . . . . .3%
$2,501 to $3,500. . . . . .4%
$3,501 to $5,000. . . . . .5%
$5,001 and over 5.75%

Hawaii

Single or Married filing separately

$0 to $2,400 . . . . 1.4%
$2,401 to $4,800. . . . . 3.2%
$4,801 to $9,600. . . . . 5.5%
$9,601 to $14,400. . . . . . . 6.4%
$14,401 to $19,200. . . . . . . 6.8%
$19,201 to $24,000. . . . . . . 7.2%
$24,001 to $36,000. . . . . . . 7.6%
$36,001 to $48,000. . . . . . . 7.9%
$48,001 to $150,000. . . . 8.25%
$150,001 to $175,000. . . . . .9%
$175,001 to $200,000. . . . . 10%
$200,001 and over 11%

Head of household

$0 to $3,600 . . . . 1.4%
$3,601 to $7,200. . . . . 3.2%
$7,201 to $14,400. . . . . . . 5.5%

$14,401 to $21,600. . . . . . 6.4%
$21,601 to $28,800. . . . . . 6.8%
$28,801 to $36,000. . . . . . 7.2%
$36,001 to $54,000. . . . . . 7.6%
$54,001 to $72,000. . . . . . 7.9%
$72,001 to $225,000. . . . 8.25%
$225,001 to $262,500. . . . . 9%
$262,501 to $300,000. . . . . 10%
$300,001 and over 11%

Married filing jointly or Surviving spouse

$0 to $4,800 . . . . 1.4%
$4,801 to $9,600. . . . . 3.2%
$9,601 to $19,200. . . . . . . 5.5%
$19,201 to $28,800. . . . . . 6.4%
$28,801 to $38,400. . . . . . 6.8%
$38,401 to $48,000. . . . . . 7.2%
$48,001 to $72,000. . . . . . 7.6%
$72,001 to $96,000. . . . . . 7.9%
$96,001 to $300,000. . . . 8.25%
$300,001 to $350,000. . . . . .9%
$350,001 to $400,000. . . . . 10%
$400,001 and over 11%

Idaho[1,2]

Single
5.8% of taxable income over $2,500

Married filing jointly
5.8% of taxable income over $5,000

Illinois

4.95% of federal AGI

Indiana

3.15% of AGI

Iowa[2]

Single, Head of household, or Married filing separately

$0 to $6,000 . . . . 4.4%
$6,001 to $30,000. . . . . . 4.82%
$30,001 to $75,000. . . . . . 5.7%
$75,001 and over 6%

Married filing jointly

$0 to $12,000 . . . . 4.4%
$12,001 to $60,000. . . . . 4.82%
$60,001 to $150,000. . . . . 5.7%
$150,001 and over 6%

Kansas

Single, Head of household, or Married filing separately

$0 to $2,500 . . . . .0%
$2,501 to $15,000. . . . . . . 3.1%
$15,001 to $30,000. . . . . 5.25%
$30,001 and over 5.7%

Married filing jointly

$0 to $5,000 . . . . .0%
$5,001 to $30,000. . . . . . . 3.1%
$30,001 to $60,000. . . . . 5.25%
$60,001 and over 5.7%

Kentucky

4.5% of taxable income

Louisiana[1]

Single, Head of household, or Married filing separately

$0 to $12,500. . . . . 1.85%
$12,501 to $50,000. . . . . . .3.5%
$50,001 and over. 4.25%

Married filing jointly

$0 to $25,000. . . . . 1.85%
$25,001 to $100,000. . . . . .3.5%
$100,001 and over. 4.25%

Maine[2]

Single or Married filing separately

$0 to $24,499 . . . . .5.8%
$24,500 to $58,049. . . . .6.75%
$58,050 and over 7.15%

Head of household

$0 to $36,749 . . . . .5.8%
$36,750 to $87,099. . . . .6.75%
$87,100 and over 7.15%

Married filing jointly or Surviving spouse

$0 to $49,049 . . . . .5.8%
$49,050 to $116,099. . . .6.75%
$116,100 and over 7.15%

Maryland

Single, Married filing separately, or Dependent taxpayers

$0 to $1,000 . . . . 2%
$1,001 to $2,000. . . . . 3%
$2,001 to $3,000. . . . . 4%
$3,001 to $100,000. . . . . 4.75%
$100,001 to $125,000. . . . . 5%
$125,001 to $150,000. . . 5.25%
$150,001 to $250,000. . . . 5.5%
$250,001 and over 5.75%

Head of household, Married filing jointly, or Qualifying widow(er)

$0 to $1,000 . . . . 2%
$1,001 to $2,000. . . . . 3%
$2,001 to $3,000. . . . . 4%
$3,001 to $150,000. . . . . 4.75%
$150,001 to $175,000. . . . . 5%
$175,001 to $225,000. . . 5.25%
$225,001 to $300,000. . . . 5.5%
$300,001 and over 5.75%

Massachusetts

Part A income (short-term capital gains). .12%
Part A income (interest and dividends). . . .5%
Part B income. 5%
Part C income. 5%

Michigan

4.05% of taxable income

Minnesota[2]

Single

$0 to $30,070 . . . . .5.35%
$30,071 to $98,760. . . . . .6.8%
$98,761 to $183,340. . . . 7.85%
$183,341 and over 9.85%

Head of household

$0 to $37,010. . . . . .5.35%
$37,011 to $148,730 . . . .6.8%
$148,731 to $243,720. . . 7.85%
$243,721 and over 9.85%

Married filing jointly

$0 to $43,950 . . . . .5.35%
$43,951 to $174,610. . . . .6.8%
$174,611 to $304,970. . . 7.85%
$304,971 and over 9.85%

Married filing separately

$0 to $21,975 . . . . .5.35%
$21,976 to $87,305 . . . . .6.8%
$87,306 to $152,485 . . . 7.85%
$152,486 and over 9.85%

Mississippi

5% on taxable income over $10,000

Missouri[2]

$0 to $1,207	0%
$1,208 to $2,414	2%
$2,415 to $3,621	2.5%
$3,622 to $4,828	3%
$4,829 to $6,035	3.5%
$6,036 to $7,242	4%
$7,243 to $8,449	4.5%
$8,450 and over	4.95%

Montana[2]

$0 to $3,600	1%
$3,601 to $6,300	2%
$6,301 to $9,700	3%
$9,701 to $13,000	4%
$13,001 to $16,800	5%
$16,801 to $21,600	6%
$21,601 and over	6.75%

Nebraska[2]

Single or Married filing separately

$0 to $3,700	2.46%
$3,701 to $22,170	3.51%
$22,171 to $35,730	5.01%
$35,731 and over	6.64%

Head of household

$0 to $6,900	2.46%
$6,901 to $35,480	3.51%
$35,481 to $52,980	5.01%
$52,981 and over	6.64%

Married filing jointly or Surviving spouse

$0 to $7,390	2.46%
$7,391 to $44,350	3.51%
$44,351 to $71,460	5.01%
$71,461 and over	6.64%

New Hampshire

4% on interest and dividends only

New Jersey

Single or Married/civil-union partner filing separately

$0 to $20,000	1.4%
$20,001 to $35,000	1.75%
$35,001 to $40,000	3.5%
$40,001 to $75,000	5.525%
$75,001 to $500,000	6.37%
$500,001 to $1,000,000	8.97%
$1,000,001 and over	10.750%

Head of household, Married/civil-union couple filing jointly, or Qualifying widow(er)/Surviving civil-union partner

$0 to $20,000	1.4%
$20,001 to $50,000	1.75%
$50,001 to $70,000	2.45%
$70,001 to $80,000	3.5%
$80,001 to $150,000	5.525%
$150,001 to $500,000	6.37%
$500,001 to $1,000,000	8.97%
$1,000,001 and over	10.750%

New Mexico[1]

Single

$0 to $5,500	1.7%
$5,501 to $11,000	3.2%
$11,001 to $16,000	4.7%
$16,001 to $210,000	4.9%
$210,001 and over	5.9%

Head of household, Married filing jointly, or Qualifying widow(er)

$0 to $8,000	1.7%
$8,001 to $16,000	3.2%
$16,001 to $24,000	4.7%
$24,001 to $315,000	4.9%
$315,001 and over	5.9%

Married filing separately

$0 to $4,000	1.7%
$4,001 to $8,000	3.2%
$8,001 to $12,000	4.7%
$12,001 to $157,500	4.9%
$157,501 and over	5.9%

New York

Single or Married filing separately

$0 to $8,500	4%
$8,501 to $11,700	4.5%
$11,701 to $13,900	5.25%
$13,901 to $80,650	5.5%
$80,651 to $215,400	6%
$215,401 to $1,077,550	6.85%
$1,077,551 to $5,000,000	9.65%
$5,000,001 to $25,000,000	10.3%
$25,000,001 and over	10.9%

Head of household

$0 to $12,800	4%
$12,801 to $17,650	4.5%
$17,651 to $20,900	5.25%
$20,901 to $107,650	5.5%
$107,651 to $269,300	6%
$269,301 to $1,616,450	6.85%
$1,616,451 to $5,000,000	9.65%
$5,000,001 to $25,000,000	10.3%
$25,000,001 and over	10.9%

Married filing jointly or Qualifying widow(er)

$0 to $17,150	4%
$17,151 to $23,600	4.5%
$23,601 to $27,900	5.25%
$27,901 to $161,550	5.5%
$161,551 to $323,200	6%
$323,201 to $2,155,350	6.85%
$2,155,351 to $5,000,000	9.65%
$5,000,001 to $25,000,000	10.3%
$25,000,001 and over	10.9%

North Carolina

4.75% on state taxable income

North Dakota[2]

Single

$0 to $44,725	0%
$44,726 to $225,975	1.95%
$225,976 and over	2.5%

Head of household

$0 to $59,950	0%
$59,951 to $250,550	1.95%
$250,551 and over	2.5%

Married filing jointly or Surviving spouse

$0 to $74,750	0%
$74,751 to $275,100	1.95%
$275,101 and over	2.5%

Married filing separately

$0 to $37,375	0%
$37,376 to $137,550	1.95%
$137,551 and over	2.5%

Ohio

$26,051 to $100,000	2.75%
$100,001 to $115,300	3.688%
$115,301 and over	3.75%

Oklahoma

Single or Married filing separately

$0 to $1,000	0.25%
$1,001 to $2,500	0.75%
$2,501 to $3,750	1.75%
$3,751 to $4,900	2.75%
$4,901 to $7,200	3.75%
$7,201 and over	4.75%

Head of household, Married filing jointly, or Qualifying widow(er)

$0 to $2,000	0.25%
$2,001 to $5,000	0.75%
$5,001 to $7,500	1.75%
$7,501 to $9,800	2.75%
$9,801 to $12,200	3.75%
$12,201 and over	4.75%

Oregon[2,3]

Single or Married filing separately

$0 to $3,750	4.75%
$3,751 to $9,450	6.75%
$9,451 to $125,000	8.75%
$125,001 and over	9.9%

Married filing jointly, Head of household, or Qualifying widow(er)

$0 to $7,500	4.75%
$7,501 to $18,900	6.75%
$18,901 to $250,000	8.75%
$250,001 and over	9.9%

Pennsylvania

3.07% of taxable compensation, net profits, net gains from the sale of property, rent, royalties, patents or copyrights, income from estates or trusts, dividends, interest, and winnings

Rhode Island[2]

$0 to $73,450	3.75%
$73,451 to $166,950	4.75%
$166,951 and over	5.99%

South Carolina[2]

$0 to $3,329	0%
$3,330 to $16,679	3%
$16,680 and over	6.4%

Tennessee

0% on interest and dividend income of individuals as of tax year 2021

Utah

4.65% on state taxable income

Vermont[2]

Single

$0 to $45,400	3.35%
$45,401 to $110,050	6.6%
$110,051 to $229,550	7.6%
$229,551 and over	8.75%

Head of household

$0 to $60,850	3.35%
$60,851 to $157,150	6.6%
$157,151 to $254,500	7.6%
$254,501 and over	8.75%

Married or Civil union filing jointly

$0 to $75,850	3.35%
$75,851 to $183,400	6.6%
$183,401 to $279,450	7.6%
$279,451 and over	8.75%

Married or Civil union filing separately

$0 to $37,925	3.35%
$37,926 to $91,700	6.6%
$91,701 to $139,725	7.6%
$139,726 and over	8.75%

Virginia

$0 to $3,000	2%
$3,001 to $5,000	3%
$5,001 to $17,000	5%
$17,001 and over	5.75%

West Virginia

Single, Head of household, Married filing jointly, or Widow(er) with dependent child

$0 to $10,000	2.36%
$10,001 to $25,000	3.15%
$25,001 to $40,000	3.54%
$40,001 to $60,000	4.72%
$60,001 and over	5.12%

Married filing separately

$0 to $5,000	2.36%
$5,001 to $12,500	3.15%
$12,501 to $20,000	3.54%
$20,001 to $30,000	4.72%
$30,001 and over	5.12%

Wisconsin[1,2]

Single or Head of household

$0 to $13,810	3.5%
$13,811 to $27,630	4.4%
$27,631 to $304,170	5.30%
$304,171 and over	7.65%

Married filing jointly

$0 to $18,420	3.5%
$18,421 to $36,840	4.4%
$36,841 to $405,550	5.30%
$405,551 and over	7.65%

Married filing separately

$0 to $9,210	3.5%
$9,211 to $18,420	4.4%
$18,421 to $202,780	5.30%
$202,781 and over	7.65%

AGI = Adjusted gross income; AMT = Alternative minimum tax. (1) Community property state in which, in general, one-half of the community income is taxable to each spouse. (2) Brackets indexed for inflation annually. (3) 2023 adjusted brackets were not available. Bracketed rates listed are for 2022. Other notes, by state: **California:** An additional 1% tax is imposed on taxable income in excess of $1 mil. **Colorado:** Individual taxpayers are subject to an AMT equal to the amount by which 3.47% of their Colorado alternative minimum taxable income exceeds their Colorado normal tax. **Connecticut:** Resident estates and trusts are subject to a 6.99% rate on all income. **Illinois:** Surcharge is imposed on income from the sale or exchange of certain assets. **Indiana:** Counties may impose an AGI tax on residents or on nonresidents, or a county option income tax. **Massachusetts:** An additional 4% tax is imposed on taxable income in excess of $1 mil. Part A income represents either interest and dividends or short-term capital gains, long-term capital gains from collectibles, and long-term capital gains from pre-1996 installment sales. Part B income represents wages, salaries, tips, pensions, business income, rents, etc. Part C income represents gains from the sale of capital assets held for more than one year. 5.85% optional rate may be elected for Part A interest and dividend income, Part B income after exemptions, and Part C income. **Minnesota:** A 6.75% AMT is imposed. **New Mexico:** Qualified nonresident taxpayers may pay an alternative tax of 0.75% of gross receipts from sales in New Mexico. **New York:** A supplemental tax is imposed to recapture the tax table benefit. **Vermont:** The tax amount is increased by 24% for certain items.

EDUCATION STATISTICS

U.S. Public Schools: Students, Staff, Spending, 1899-2021
Source: National Center for Education Statistics, U.S. Dept. of Education

	1899-1900	1919-20	1939-40	1959-60	1979-80	1999-2000	2009-10	2019-20	2020-21[1]
Population (thous.)									
Total U.S. population[2]	75,995	104,514	131,028	177,830	225,055	279,040	306,772	328,330	329,484
Population 5-17 years of age	21,573	27,571	30,151	43,881	48,043	52,811	53,890	53,517	53,521
Percentage 5-17 years of age	28.4%	26.4%	23.0%	24.7%	21.3%	18.9%	17.6%	16.3%	16.2%
Enrollment (thous.)									
Elementary and secondary[3]	15,503	21,578	25,434	35,182	41,651	46,857	49,361	50,796	49,375
Prekindergarten through grade 8	14,984	19,378	18,832	26,911	28,034	33,486	34,409	35,551	34,059
Grades 9-12	519	2,200	6,601	8,271	13,616	13,371	14,952	15,246	15,316
Percent of pop. ages 5-17 enrolled	71.9%	78.3%	84.4%	80.2%	86.7%	88.7%	91.6%	94.9%	92.3%
Grades 9-12 as percent of all enrolled	3.3%	10.2%	26.0%	23.5%	32.7%	28.5%	30.3%	30.0%	31.0%
High school graduates	62	231	1,143	1,627	2,748	2,554	3,128	3,301	3,338
Instructional staff (thous.)									
Total instructional staff	*	678	912	1,449	2,406	3,819	4,279	4,434	NA
Teachers, librarians, and other nonsupervisory instructional staff	423	657	875	1,385	2,300	3,682	4,111	4,240	NA
Revenue and expenditures (mil)									
Total revenue	$220	$970	$2,261	$14,747	$96,881	$372,944	$599,929	$794,568	$837,338
Total expenditures	215	1,036	2,344	15,613	95,962	381,838	608,065	793,719	813,615
Current expenditures[4]	180	861	1,942	12,329	86,984	323,889	518,886	682,217	703,472
Capital outlay	35	154	258	2,662	6,506	43,357	59,843	81,335	79,375
Interest on school debt	*	18	131	490	1,874	9,135	17,720	21,428	21,669
Other programs[5]	*	3	13	133	598	5,457	NA	8,739	9,098
Salaries and pupil cost									
Avg. annual salary of instruct. staff[6]	$325	$871	$1,441	$4,995	$15,970	$41,807	$55,370	$64,172	$65,293
Expenditure per capita total pop.	3	10	18	88	426	1,368	1,982	2,417	2,469
Current expenditure per pupil ADA[4]	17	53	88	375	2,272	7,394	11,427	14,570	15,180

* = Data not collected. NA = Not available. ADA = Average daily attendance. **Note:** Because of rounding, details may not add up to totals. Prior to 1959-60, data do not include Alaska and Hawaii. (1) Revenues and expenditures are provisional data; high school graduates, and expenditure per pupil ADA are projected. (2) Data for 1899-1900 are based on total population from the decennial census. From 1919-20 to 1959-60, total population includes armed forces overseas, as of July 1 preceding the school year. Data for later years are for resident population excluding armed forces overseas. (3) Data for 1899-1940 are school year enrollment; data for later years are fall enrollment. (4) Because of changes in the definition of "current expenditures," data for 1959-60 and later years are not entirely comparable with prior years. (5) Incl. expenditures for community services, adult education, community colleges, private schools, and other progs. not part of public and secondary education. (6) Data prior to 1959-60 include supervisors, principals, teachers, and nonsupervisory instructional staff.

U.S. Public High School Graduation Rates, 2019-20
Source: National Center for Education Statistics, U.S. Dept. of Education

State	Rate[1]	Rank	State	Rate[1]	Rank	State	Rate[1]	Rank	State	Rate[1]	Rank
Alabama	90.6%	6	Illinois	—	—	Montana	85.9%	27	Rhode Island	83.6%	33
Alaska	79.1	46	Indiana	90.9%	5	Nebraska	87.5	22	South Carolina	82.2	42
Arizona	77.3	47	Iowa	91.8	2	Nevada	82.6	38	South Dakota	84.2	30
Arkansas	88.8	14	Kansas	88.2	17	New Hampshire	88.1	19	Tennessee	90.4	7
California	84.3	29	Kentucky	91.1	3	New Jersey	91.0	4	Texas	—	—
Colorado	81.9	44	Louisiana	82.9	37	New Mexico	76.9	48	Utah	88.2	18
Connecticut	88.3	16	Maine	87.4	23	New York	83.5	34	Vermont	83.1	35
Delaware	89.0	11	Maryland	86.8	25	North Carolina	87.6	21	Virginia	88.8	15
Dist. of Columbia	73.0	49	Massachusetts	89.0	12	North Dakota	89.0	13	Washington	83.0	36
Florida	90.2	9	Michigan	82.1	43	Ohio	84.4	28	West Virginia	92.1	1
Georgia	83.8	31	Minnesota	83.8	32	Oklahoma	80.8	45	Wisconsin	90.4	8
Hawaii	86.3	26	Mississippi	87.7	20	Oregon	82.6	39	Wyoming	82.3	40
Idaho	82.2	41	Missouri	89.5	10	Pennsylvania	87.4	24	**Total U.S.**	**86.5**	

— Not available or applicable. (1) The 4-year adjusted cohort graduation rate (ACGR) is the number of students who graduate in 4 years with a regular high school diploma divided by the number of students who form the adjusted cohort for the graduating class. From the beginning of 9th grade (or the earliest high school grade), students who are entering that grade for the first time form a cohort that is "adjusted" by adding any students who subsequently transfer into the cohort and subtracting any students who subsequently transfer out, emigrate to another country, or die.

High School Dropouts by Sex, Race, and Ethnicity, 1960-2021
Source: National Center for Education Statistics, U.S. Dept. of Education
(data for Oct. of year shown unless otherwise noted)

Year[1]	Total dropout rate				Male dropout rate				Female dropout rate			
	All races[2]	White	Black	Hispanic	All races[2]	White	Black	Hispanic	All races[2]	White	Black	Hispanic
1960[3]	27.2%	NA	NA	NA	27.8%	NA	NA	NA	26.7%	NA	NA	NA
1970[4]	15.0	13.2%	27.9%	NA	14.2	12.2%	29.4%	NA	15.7	14.1%	26.6%	NA
1980	14.1	11.4	19.1	35.2%	15.1	12.3	20.8	37.2%	13.1	10.5	17.7	33.2%
1990	12.1	9.0	13.2	32.4	12.3	9.3	11.9	34.3	11.8	8.7	14.4	30.3
2000	10.9	6.9	13.1	27.8	12.0	7.0	15.3	31.8	9.9	6.9	11.1	23.5
2005	9.4	6.0	10.4	22.4	10.8	6.6	12.0	26.4	8.0	5.3	9.0	18.1
2010	7.4	5.1	8.0	15.1	8.5	5.9	9.5	17.3	6.3	4.2	6.7	12.8
2015	5.9	4.6	6.5	9.2	6.3	5.0	6.4	9.9	5.4	4.1	6.5	8.4
2017	5.8	4.6	5.7	9.5	6.6	5.0	7.0	11.5	5.0	4.3	4.4	7.4
2018	5.7	4.5	5.8	9.0	6.3	5.1	6.0	10.4	5.1	3.8	5.6	7.5
2019	5.2	4.5	5.6	7.5	5.9	5.3	6.6	7.8	4.6	3.8	4.6	7.1
2020	5.3	4.8	4.2	7.4	6.2	5.4	5.6	8.9	4.4	4.1	2.9	5.9
2021	5.1	4.4	3.9	8.2	5.7	4.7	4.6	9.2	4.6	4.2	3.3	7.2

NA = Not available. **Note:** Table shows "status" dropouts, defined as 16- to 24-year-olds who are not enrolled in school and who have not completed a high school program, regardless of when they left school. People who have received GED credentials are not shown. Excludes persons in the military and persons living in institutions (e.g., prisons or nursing facilities). Race categories exclude persons of Hispanic ethnicity unless otherwise noted. (1) Because of changes in data collection procedures, data for years prior to 1992 may not be comparable to later years. For 2005 and after, White and Black data exclude persons identifying themselves as being of two or more races. (2) Includes other racial/ethnic groups not separately shown. (3) Based on the Apr. 1960 decennial census. (4) White and Black data include persons of Hispanic ethnicity.

Overview of U.S. Public Schools, 2020-21

Source: National Center for Education Statistics, U.S. Dept. of Education; National Education Association (NEA)

State	Local school districts	Elementary schools[1]	Middle schools[1]	Secondary schools[1]	Classroom teachers	Total enrollment[2]	Pupils per teacher	Teachers' avg. pay	Expend. per pupil[2]
AL	143	698	255	418	46,792	716,084	15.3	$54,271	$10,705
AK	54	172	37	80	7,390	130,394	17.6	73,061	18,708
AZ	691	1,193	231	761	61,180	1,109,774	18.1	52,157	9,920
AR	261	516	211	323	31,079	472,668	15.2	51,668	11,081
CA	1,037	5,978	1,415	2,262	269,850	6,002,523	22.2	85,856	14,801
CO	185	1,043	290	440	57,625	883,199	15.3	58,183	12,996
CT	205	604	182	198	41,822	513,079	12.3	79,742	22,153
DE	45	118	38	42	9,838	138,414	14.1	65,141	16,997
DC	68	140	39	42	7,678	89,883	11.7	80,659	23,181
FL	75	2,216	595	967	142,110	2,791,687	19.6	51,009	10,703
GA	221	1,308	479	483	117,204	1,729,966	14.8	60,553	12,597
HI	1	184	41	42	11,227	176,441	15.7	70,922	17,303
ID	178	379	112	203	17,501	310,605	17.7	51,817	8,376
IL	852	2,390	734	966	132,354	1,893,663	14.3	70,705	17,500
IN	409	1,067	337	418	61,069	1,031,871	16.9	53,072	11,265
IA	327	686	254	345	38,079	506,656	13.3	58,831	12,295
KS	286	727	222	343	35,573	483,303	13.6	53,619	12,828
KY	171	729	221	367	39,977	650,280	16.3	54,139	12,103
LA	165	727	229	286	48,882	699,625	14.3	52,472	12,399
ME	209	350	87	117	14,952	174,446	11.7	57,167	17,293
MD	24	892	228	248	62,767	882,538	14.1	74,006	15,744
MA	400	1,054	320	376	75,147	909,889	12.1	86,755	21,584
MI	830	1,668	516	1,017	81,204	1,398,455	17.2	64,262	11,597
MN	560	982	314	939	56,426	872,083	15.5	66,561	14,122
MS	155	446	187	323	31,856	442,627	13.9	46,862	9,920
MO	555	1,215	390	667	75,928	859,512	11.3	51,557	10,481
MT	401	428	226	172	10,647	145,632	13.7	53,133	12,597
NE	244	540	126	269	25,048	306,910	12.3	56,463	13,133
NV	20	424	114	142	22,435	482,364	21.5	58,167	10,200
NH	166	285	102	100	16,710	167,838	10.0	61,849	19,062
NJ	686	1,513	433	501	116,717	1,343,440	11.5	77,677	22,760
NM	89	455	165	222	21,434	316,489	14.8	54,923	12,963
NY	732	2,570	806	1,217	213,537	2,457,003	11.5	90,222	28,704
NC	115	1,475	490	592	93,461	1,365,199	14.6	53,458	11,052
ND	172	268	40	162	10,360	112,045	10.8	54,837	15,336
OH	1,037	1,789	656	913	101,148	1,739,386	17.2	63,082	13,695
OK	509	937	362	478	42,929	694,113	16.2	54,762	10,553
OR	222	710	204	270	30,813	560,917	18.2	68,565	14,400
PA	787	1,645	528	721	120,717	1,696,022	14.0	71,479	18,847
RI	64	175	58	68	10,669	139,184	13.0	75,966	18,651
SC	84	693	253	292	52,533	766,819	14.6	53,188	12,677
SD	149	327	168	192	9,848	135,984	13.8	49,547	11,102
TN	146	1,013	344	408	64,666	953,917	14.8	52,871	11,128
TX	1,204	4,652	1,746	2,075	369,478	5,359,105	14.5	57,641	10,741
UT	163	622	143	213	30,551	679,431	22.2	57,226	8,968
VT	184	210	25	65	8,176	82,401	10.1	62,483	23,299
VA	132	1,144	351	326	99,783	1,238,176	12.4	58,506	14,003
WA	314	1,208	378	656	62,791	1,060,998	16.9	79,388	17,193
WV	55	423	111	146	18,494	252,357	13.6	50,261	13,671
WI	444	1,138	410	568	56,446	829,935	14.7	59,992	13,833
WY	48	196	61	88	7,408	91,938	12.4	60,234	18,385
Total U.S.	**16,274**	**52,322**	**16,264**	**23,529**	**3,192,309**	**48,847,268**	**15.3**	**65,293**	**14,360**

(1) 2019-20 estimates. (2) Fall enrollment.

Students Falling Behind Their Grade Level, Prepandemic to 2023

Source: School Pulse Panel, Institute of Education Sciences, U.S. Dept. of Education

The School Pulse Panel collected information on the impact of the COVID-19 pandemic from a national sample of approximately 2,400 public elementary, middle, high, and combined-grade schools in June 2022 and Dec. 2022 and released data in Feb. 2023.

(percentage of students behind their grade level at the beginning of the school year)

	Prepandemic	2021-22	2022-23		Prepandemic	2021-22	2022-23
All public schools	36%	50%	49%	**School size**			
Region				Less than 300 students	41%	54%	49%
Northeast	31	45	49	300-499 students	36	51	50
Midwest	34	46	45	500-999 students	34	49	50
South	36	49	48	1,000+ students	23	32	38
West	40	57	54	**School level**			
School location				Elementary	36	52	50
City	47	61	57	Middle/combined	35	49	50
Suburban	32	45	47	High/secondary	36	44	45
Town	33	48	49	**Minority**			
Rural	30	44	41	Up to 25% minority	25	37	36
Poverty				25%-75% minority	32	47	47
IPR[1] up to 200%	48	63	61	Over 75% minority	50	64	61
IPR[1] over 200%	31	45	45				

Note: Schools that responded "don't know" were not included in results. Students' grade level status prepandemic and at the beginning of the 2021-22 school year were collected in June 2022, and grade level status for the 2022-23 school year was collected in Dec. 2022. (1) IPR is the income-to-poverty ratio, which is the percentage of family income that is above or below the federal poverty threshold set for the family's size and structure. A family with income at the poverty threshold has an IPR value of 100.

Revenues for Public Elementary and Secondary Schools by State, 2020-21

Source: National Center for Education Statistics, U.S. Dept. of Education; amounts in thousands

State/territory	Total	Federal Amount	Federal % of tot. rev.	State Amount	State % of tot. rev.	Local and intermediate[1] Amount	Local and intermediate[1] % of tot. rev.
Alabama	$9,634,735	$1,510,373	15.7%	$5,187,636	53.8%	$2,936,726	30.5%
Alaska	2,635,433	436,807	16.6	1,634,812	62.0	563,815	21.4
American Samoa	77,985	54,265	69.6	23,720[2]	30.4	0	0.0
Arizona	12,939,677	2,191,507	16.9	6,193,001	47.9	4,555,169	35.2
Arkansas	6,377,977	1,040,983	16.3	3,044,599	47.7	2,292,396	35.9
California	111,811,428	15,163,382	13.6	60,071,357	53.7	36,576,689	32.7
Colorado	13,390,422	1,599,927	11.9	5,013,783	37.4	6,776,712	50.6
Connecticut	12,433,278	671,481	5.4	4,484,299	36.1	7,277,497	58.5
Delaware	2,773,767	211,068	7.6	1,747,079	63.0	815,619	29.4
District of Columbia	2,886,983	289,214	10.0	NA	NA	2,597,769	90.0
Florida	35,794,107	4,841,583	13.5	14,072,267	39.3	16,880,257	47.2
Georgia	25,099,557	3,068,755	12.2	10,706,159	42.7	11,324,643	45.1
Guam	346,872	116,798	33.7	NA	NA	230,074	66.3
Hawaii	3,241,887	371,018	11.4	2,851,763	88.0	19,106	0.6
Idaho	3,269,320	530,336	16.2	2,023,230	61.9	715,755	21.9
Illinois	40,806,610	3,196,984	7.8	16,117,573	39.5	21,492,053	52.7
Indiana	14,517,671	1,282,480	8.8	8,740,711	60.2	4,494,480	31.0
Iowa	7,909,835	897,141	11.3	4,020,930	50.8	2,991,765	37.8
Kansas	7,448,284	683,749	9.2	4,920,069	66.1	1,844,466	24.8
Kentucky	9,218,839	1,343,277	14.6	4,753,615	51.6	3,121,948	33.9
Louisiana	10,326,354	1,627,228	15.8	4,078,383	39.5	4,620,744	44.7
Maine	3,590,060	497,014	13.8	1,411,382	39.3	1,681,664	46.8
Maryland	17,536,105	1,215,926	6.9	7,620,541	43.5	8,699,638	49.6
Massachusetts	21,032,128	1,290,317	6.1	8,328,725	39.6	11,413,086	54.3
Michigan	23,602,386	2,943,912	12.5	13,498,567	57.2	7,159,908	30.3
Minnesota	15,419,009	1,448,138	9.4	9,833,295	63.8	4,137,576	26.8
Mississippi	5,377,137	1,035,288	19.3	2,493,756	46.4	1,848,093	34.4
Missouri	13,121,987	1,645,054	12.5	3,911,448	29.8	7,565,485	57.7
Montana	2,258,752	429,703	19.0	909,788	40.3	919,260	40.7
Nebraska	5,145,527	497,506	9.7	1,596,679	31.0	3,051,342	59.3
Nevada	5,821,907	680,010	11.7	1,921,522	33.0	3,220,375	55.3
New Hampshire	3,543,958	252,513	7.1	1,093,913	30.9	2,197,532	62.0
New Jersey	35,669,779	1,899,244	5.3	16,224,441	45.5	17,546,094	49.2
New Mexico	4,751,119	596,816	12.6	3,356,381	70.6	797,922	16.8
New York	77,384,806	3,567,146	4.6	29,093,368	37.6	44,724,292	57.8
North Carolina	17,112,494	2,093,422	12.2	10,637,221	62.2	4,381,850	25.6
North Dakota	2,109,305	349,167	16.6	1,078,820	51.1	681,319	32.3
Northern Mariana Islands	97,733	81,124	83.0	16,609[2]	17.0	0	0.0
Ohio	27,616,830	2,681,945	9.7	10,983,197	39.8	13,951,689	50.5
Oklahoma	7,931,412	1,130,566	14.3	3,618,387	45.6	3,182,458	40.1
Oregon	9,863,772	819,250	8.3	5,316,328	53.9	3,728,193	37.8
Pennsylvania	35,182,434	3,265,898	9.3	13,056,288	37.1	18,860,248	53.6
Puerto Rico	2,383,989	751,875	31.5	1,631,653[2]	68.4	461	0.0
Rhode Island	2,911,530	293,372	10.1	1,243,479	42.7	1,374,679	47.2
South Carolina	12,163,885	1,282,235	10.5	6,037,237	49.6	4,844,412	39.8
South Dakota	1,924,967	378,303	19.7	614,051	31.9	932,613	48.4
Tennessee	12,045,679	1,740,443	14.4	5,401,015	44.8	4,904,221	40.7
Texas	72,974,070	9,057,295	12.4	27,559,808	37.8	36,356,966	49.8
Utah	7,355,142	712,100	9.7	4,042,774	55.0	2,600,268	35.4
Vermont	1,986,906	206,938	10.4	1,739,914	87.6	40,054	2.0
Virgin Islands (U.S.)	383,175	218,994	57.2	NA	NA	164,182	42.8
Virginia	19,258,847	1,748,237	9.1	7,836,352	40.7	9,674,259	50.2
Washington	20,577,176	1,691,468	8.2	13,959,388	67.8	4,926,320	23.9
West Virginia	3,981,286	585,850	14.7	2,043,088	51.3	1,352,348	34.0
Wisconsin	13,639,483	1,184,125	8.7	6,708,045	49.2	5,747,313	42.1
Wyoming	1,931,908	234,448	12.1	976,133	50.5	721,327	37.3
United States[3]	837,337,948	88,410,942	10.6	383,806,597	45.8	365,120,409	43.6

NA = Not applicable. **Note:** Percentage totals may not add up to 100 due to rounding. (1) Includes intermediate revenues from education agencies with fundraising capabilities that operate between the state and local government levels. (2) Reported state revenue data are revenues received from the central government of the jurisdiction. (3) U.S. total includes the 50 states and the District of Columbia.

Enrollment in U.S. Public and Private Schools, 1889-2031

Source: National Center for Education Statistics, U.S. Dept. of Education

Of all students enrolled in private schools in fall 2019, 74% attended religious schools and 26% attended nonsectarian schools.

School year[1]	Public school[2]	Private school[2]	% private[3]	School year[1]	Public school[2]	Private school[2]	% private[3]
1889-90	12,723	1,611	11.2%	1969-70	45,550	5,500[4]	10.8%
1899-1900	15,503	1,352	8.0	1979-80	41,651	5,000[4]	10.7
1909-10	17,814	1,558	8.0	1989-90	40,543	5,599	12.1
1919-20	21,578	1,699	7.3	1999-2000	46,857	6,018	11.4
1929-30	25,678	2,651	9.4	2009-10	49,361	5,488	10.0
1939-40	25,434	2,611	9.3	2019-20	50,796	5,486	9.7
1949-50	25,111	3,380	11.9	2029-30[5]	47,357	4,898	9.4
1959-60	35,182	5,675	13.9	2030-31[5]	47,253	4,807	9.2

Note: "Private" includes all nonpublic schools. (1) Fall enrollment. (2) In thousands. Data from fall 1980 onward covers an expanded universe of private schools; comparisons with earlier years should be avoided. (3) Percent of U.S. students enrolled in private schools. (4) Estimated. (5) Projected.

Program for International Student Assessment (PISA) Scores, 2000-18

Source: National Center for Education Statistics, U.S. Dept. of Education

Scores are reported on a scale from 0 to 1,000. The PISA test is administered to 15-year-old students.

Education system	Mathematics 2000	Mathematics 2018	Reading 2000	Reading 2018	Science 2000	Science 2018
Australia*	533	491	528	503	528	503
Austria*	515	499	507	484	519	490
Belgium*	520	508	507	493	496	499
Brazil[1]	334	384	396	413	375	404
Canada*	533	512	534	520	529	518
China[2]	—	591	—	555	—	590
Czechia*	498	499	492	490	511	497
Denmark*	514	509	497	501	481	493
Finland*	536	507	546	520	538	522
France*	517	495	505	493	500	493
Germany*	490	500	484	498	487	503
Greece*	447	451	474	457	461	452
Hungary*	488	481	480	476	496	481
Iceland*	514	495	507	474	496	475
Indonesia	—	379	—	371	—	396
Ireland*	503	500	527	518	513	496
Israel*	—	463	—	470	—	462
Italy*	457	487	487	476	478	468
Japan*	557	527	522	504	550	529
Korea, South*	547	526	525	514	552	519
Latvia*	463	496	458	479	460	487
Luxembourg*	446	483	441	470	443	477
Mexico[1]*	387	409	422	420	422	419
Netherlands*	—	519	—	485	—	503
New Zealand*	537	494	529	506	528	508
Norway*	499	501	505	499	500	490
Philippines[1]	—	353	—	340	—	357
Poland*	470	516	479	512	483	511
Portugal*	454	492	470	492	459	492
Russia	478	488	462	479	460	478
Saudi Arabia	—	373	—	399	—	386
Singapore	—	569	—	549	—	551
Spain*	476	481	493	—	491	483
Sweden*	510	502	516	506	512	499
Switzerland*	529	515	494	484	496	495
Thailand[1]	—	419	—	393	—	426
U.S.*	493	478	504	505	499	502
UK*	529	502	523	504	532	505
UAE	—	435	—	432	—	434
OECD average	500	489	500	487	500	489

— = Not available. * = Organization for Economic Cooperation and Development (OECD) nation as of 2018. (1) 50-75% of the 15-year-old population is covered by the PISA sample. (2) Scores for China only include Beijing, Shanghai, Jiangsu, and Zhejiang provinces.

Mathematics and Reading Scores of U.S. Students, 1971-2023

Source: National Assessment of Educational Progress, National Center for Education Statistics (NCES), U.S. Dept. of Education

Average scores for 9-year-olds in 2022 declined 5 points in reading and 7 points in mathematics compared to 2020. Average scores for 13-year-olds in 2023 declined 4 points in reading and 9 points in math compared to 2020.

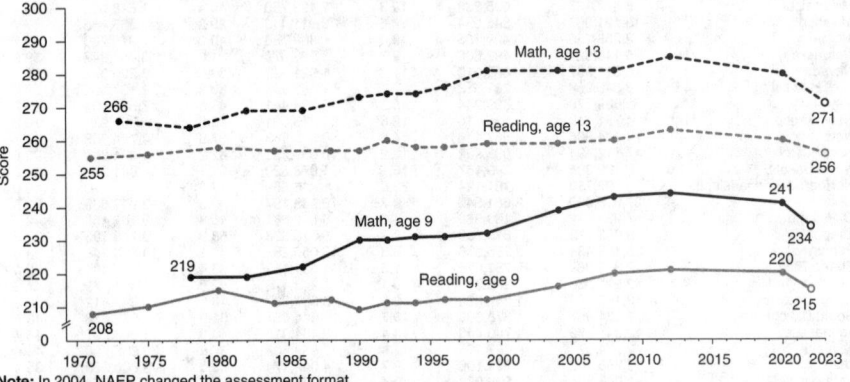

Note: In 2004, NAEP changed the assessment format.

Mathematics, Reading, and Science Achievement of U.S. Students, 1998-2022

Source: National Assessment of Educational Progress, National Center for Education Statistics, U.S. Dept. of Education

(percent of public school students in a grade who scored at or above basic levels in national tests)

State	4th grade Math 2000	4th grade Math 2022	4th grade Reading 1998	4th grade Reading 2022	8th grade Math 2000	8th grade Math 2022	8th grade Reading 1998	8th grade Reading 2022	8th grade Science 2000	8th grade Science 2015
AL	55	71	56	59	53	53	67	61	53	54
AK	—	65	—	51	—	59	—	63	—	—
AZ	57	70	51	61	60	58	72	68	55	61
AR	55	69	54	58	49	55	68	64	53	62
CA	50	67	48	58	50	56	63	67	38	56
CO	—	75	67	68	—	63	77	73	—	—
CT	76	74	76	64	70	63	81	72	64	70
DE	44	53	53	—	51	64	62	—	—	62
DC	24	57	27	50	23	46	44	57	—	—
FL	—	81	53	71	—	58	67	69	—	66
GA	57	73	54	61	54	59	68	69	52	65
HI	55	77	45	64	51	58	59	68	40	58
ID	68	76	—	61	70	71	—	74	71	76
IL	63	76	—	62	67	62	—	71	59	63
IN	77	78	—	63	74	66	—	70	66	70
IA	75	80	67	64	—	67	—	71	—	75
KS	76	75	70	—	76	61	81	67	—	71
KY	59	75	62	62	60	57	74	68	60	73
LA	57	69	44	57	47	53	63	66	44	—
ME	73	75	72	60	73	61	83	66	72	77
MD	60	65	58	56	62	54	70	67	57	67
MA	70	70	70	70	70	70	79	77	70	75
MI	71	71	62	58	68	60	—	68	69	—
MN	76	78	67	61	80	69	78	72	72	76
MS	45	74	47	63	42	54	62	63	41	51
MO	71	72	61	60	64	61	75	67	66	75
MT	72	80	72	65	79	68	83	72	79	78
NE	65	80	—	65	73	68	—	70	71	75
NV	60	69	51	57	55	56	70	68	52	62
NH	—	80	74	67	—	70	—	73	—	81
NJ	—	77	—	67	—	77	—	—	77	—
NM	50	50	51	48	48	45	71	57	48	55
NY	66	66	62	58	63	60	76	70	58	63
NC	73	75	58	61	67	61	74	66	54	64
ND	73	81	—	65	76	69	—	69	72	79
OH	73	76	—	65	73	64	—	71	72	72
OK	67	71	66	55	62	52	80	62	60	66
OR	65	66	58	56	71	57	78	67	68	72
PA	—	76	—	64	—	62	—	68	—	—
RI	65	74	64	62	59	58	76	68	58	64
SC	59	74	53	61	53	56	66	63	48	65
SD	—	80	—	65	—	72	—	73	—	—
TN	59	76	57	59	52	60	71	67	55	71
TX	76	78	59	58	67	61	74	66	52	70
UT	69	78	62	67	66	70	77	75	67	82
VT	73	74	—	62	73	66	—	73	71	79
VA	71	75	62	60	65	65	78	69	61	74
WA	—	74	64	61	—	64	76	71	—	70
WV	65	67	60	52	58	48	75	60	57	63
WI	—	79	69	63	—	70	78	72	—	75
WY	71	84	64	71	69	72	76	71	69	79
U.S.	64	74	58	61	62	60	71	68	57	67

— = Not available.

Fighting, Bullying, and Safety Concerns of High School Students, 2021

Source: *Youth Risk Behavior Surveillance–United States, 2021*, CDC, U.S. Dept. of Health and Human Services

	In a physical fight on school property[1]			Bullied on school property[2]			Electronically bullied[2,3]			Did not go to school because of safety concerns[4]		
	Female	Male	Total	Female	Male	Total	Female	Male	Total	Female	Male	Total
Race/ethnicity												
Amer. Ind./AK native ...	1.8%	4.4%	3.1%	23.5%	12.8%	17.8%	24.2%	18.1%	20.9%	15.9%	11.1%	13.3%
Asian..............	0.4	3.1	1.7	9.6	12.0	10.8	13.5	13.2	13.3	6.4	2.8	4.5
Black or African Amer...	5.7	11.3	8.5	11.6	5.5	8.5	12.1	6.6	9.5	14.6	9.6	12.1
Hispanic/Latino	3.3	7.1	5.4	14.1	10.1	12.4	16.0	9.8	13.2	13.0	8.9	11.3
Native Hawaiian/other Pac. Isl...........	—	—	0.9	4.6	11.8	8.9	15.6	5.5	9.7	7.3	9.0	8.5
White.............	2.4	8.0	5.4	20.5	15.3	17.9	25.8	12.2	18.8	8.7	4.7	6.6
Multiple race	6.0	9.6	7.6	17.6	17.0	17.5	18.0	15.2	16.9	8.6	8.0	8.2
Grade												
9	5.0	11.7	8.5	19.2	14.8	17.1	22.2	11.1	16.6	11.8	7.1	9.3
10	3.3	7.2	5.3	19.1	12.3	15.9	21.9	11.0	16.5	11.9	6.1	9.0
11	2.8	6.3	4.6	15.7	12.8	14.2	19.8	11.5	15.5	9.0	7.0	8.0
12	1.8	6.3	4.1	13.7	10.8	12.2	17.8	11.0	14.4	8.9	5.6	7.3
Sexual identity												
Heterosexual (straight)	2.3	6.9	5.1	13.7	10.8	12.0	16.7	9.8	12.7	8.0	5.6	6.6
Gay, lesbian, or bisexual	5.2	3.4	5.0	23.7	26.7	24.9	28.5	23.3	27.6	14.6	11.7	14.1
Other/questioning	3.3	8.9	4.5	19.9	23.4	21.1	23.8	25.0	24.8	12.7	11.8	12.6
Total..............	3.2	8.1	5.8	17.0	12.8	15.0	20.5	11.2	15.9	10.5	6.6	8.6

(1) One or more times during the 12 months before the survey. (2) During the 12 months before the survey. (3) Including being bullied through texting, Instagram, Facebook, or other social media. (4) On at least one day during the 30 days before the survey.

Characteristics of Public Charter Schools and Students, 2009-22

Source: National Center for Education Statistics, U.S. Dept. of Education

	2009-10	2011-12	2013-14	2015-16	2017-18	2018-19	2019-20	2021-22
Number of charter school students..............	1,610,285	2,057,599	2,519,065	2,845,322	3,143,269	3,290,149	3,431,230	3,674,712
				Percentage of charter school students who were—				
Sex								
Male	49.5%	49.6%	49.6%	49.6%	49.6%	49.7%	49.7%	49.8%
Female	50.5	50.4	50.4	50.4	50.4	50.3	50.3	50.2
Race/ethnicity								
Hispanic	26.0	28.0	30.0	31.7	33.1	33.9	35.3	36.1
White.................	37.3	35.6	34.9	33.1	32.1	31.4	30.4	29.4
Black.................	30.3	28.7	27.1	26.8	25.8	25.4	24.9	24.4
Asian/Pacific Islander ...	3.9	4.0	4.1	4.3	4.4	4.5	4.5	4.7
American Ind./Alaska Native..	1.0	0.9	0.8	0.7	0.7	0.8	0.8	0.7
Two or more races..........	1.4	2.8	3.0	3.4	3.9	3.9	4.2	4.7
Number of charter schools ...	4,952	5,696	6,465	6,855	7,193	7,427	7,547	7,847
				Percentage of charter schools that were—				
School level								
Prekindergarten...........	0.5%	0.5%	0.3%	0.4%	0.3%	0.3%	0.5%	0.3%
Elementary	43.6	44.7	45.9	46.0	46.6	46.5	47.0	47.2
Middle.................	11.6	12.2	11.5	11.2	10.7	10.5	10.5	10.4
Secondary and high	30.9	28.7	28.2	28.3	28.3	27.7	27.7	27.3
Other[1]	13.5	13.9	14.0	14.1	14.0	14.9	14.4	14.8
Locale								
City	54.8	55.4	56.5	56.5	56.1	56.1	56.6	56.3
Suburban	21.1	21.2	26.1	25.9	26.3	26.3	25.7	25.7
Town	8.0	7.4	7.0	6.7	6.1	6.1	6.0	6.0
Rural	16.1	16.0	10.4	10.9	11.5	11.5	11.7	12.0

Note: Race categories exclude persons of Hispanic ethnicity, who may be of any race. (1) Includes other, ungraded, and not applicable/not reported.

Homeschooled Students, 2019

Source: National Center for Education Statistics, U.S. Dept. of Education

A total of 1,456,586 U.S. students in grades K-12 were homeschooled in 2019, down from 1,689,726 in 2016, 1,772,987 in 2012, and 1,520,140 in 2007, and up from 1,095,652 in 2003 and 850,171 in 1999. In a 2019 U.S. Dept. of Education survey of parents who homeschool their children, the reason they gave as most important in their decision to homeschool was concern over the school environment, with such factors as safety, drugs, or negative peer pressure (25%); dissatisfaction with academic instruction in schools (15%); desire to provide religious instruction (13%); emphasis on family life together (8%); desire to provide a nontraditional approach to education (8%); the child has other special needs (7%); desire to provide moral instruction (7%); and the child has a physical or mental health problem (3%). In all, 80% cited concern over school environment as one of their reasons, 75% cited moral instruction, 75% cited emphasis on family life together, 73% cited dissatisfaction with academic instruction, and 59% cited religious instruction.

Characteristic	No. of students (thous.)	% distrib.	Home-schooling rate[1]	Characteristic	No. of students (thous.)	% distrib.	Home-schooling rate[1]
Household locale				**Parents' education**			
City.................	399	27%	2.5%	High school diploma or less	330	23%	2.2%
Suburban	532	37	2.4	Vocational/technical, assoc. degree, or some college........	376	26	2.9
Town................	102	7	2.2				
Rural...............	423	29	4.7				
Race/ethnicity[2]				Bachelor's degree/some graduate school	449	31	3.3
White................	1,014	71	4.0	Graduate/professional degree...............	302	21	3.1
Black................	84	6	1.2				
Other[3].............	83	6	2.7	**Total**...............	1,457	NA	2.8
Hispanic.............	250	17	1.9				

NA = Not applicable. **Note:** Numbers may not add up to totals because of rounding. Homeschooled students are school-age children in a grade equivalent to K-12 who receive instruction at home all or most of the time. Excludes students enrolled in public or private school more than 25 hours per week or homeschooled because of temporary illness only. (1) Percentage of total subgroup (e.g., all "City" students) that is homeschooled. (2) Race categories exclude persons of Hispanic ethnicity, who may be of any race. (3) Includes two or more races and race/ethnicity not reported.

Students With Disabilities Receiving Educational Services, 1976-2022

Source: Office of Special Education Programs, U.S. Dept. of Education

Students served by federally funded educational programs for disabled students include children and young adults 3-21 years old.
(numbers served in thousands)

Type of disability	1976 -77	1980 -81	1990 -91	2000 -01	2010 -11	2015 -16	2016- 17[1,2]	2017- 18[1,3]	2018 -19[1]	2019 -20[1,4]	2020 -20[4,5]	2021 -22[4,6]
Autism.	—	—	—	93	417	617	661	710	762	803	828	882
Deaf-blindness	—	3	1	1	1	1	1	1	2	2	2	2
Developmental delay	—	—	—	213	382	434	446	461	479	502	487	487
Emotional disturbance	283	347	389	480	390	347	348	353	358	365	353	334
Hearing impairment	88	79	58	77	78	75	75	75	74	73	72	71
Intellectual disability	961	830	534	624	448	425	431	436	439	442	429	426
Multiple disabilities	—	68	96	131	130	131	132	132	133	133	128	125
Orthopedic impairment. . . .	87	58	49	82	63	47	42	41	39	37	35	33
Other health impairment[7] . .	141	98	55	303	716	909	955	1,002	1,049	1,094	1,096	1,116
Specific learning disability . .	796	1,462	2,129	2,860	2,361	2,298	2,318	2,342	2,368	2,405	2,346	2,355
Speech/lang. impairment . .	1,302	1,168	985	1,388	1,396	1,337	1,337	1,357	1,378	1,374	1,357	1,378
Traumatic brain injury	—	—	—	16	26	27	27	27	27	27	25	25
Visual impairment.	38	31	23	29	28	27	27	27	27	27	26	25
All disabilities	**3,694**	**4,144**	**4,710[8]**	**6,296**	**6,436**	**6,677**	**6,802**	**6,964**	**7,134**	**7,282**	**7,183**	**7,259**

— = Not available. **Note:** Details may not add up to totals because of rounding and/or incomplete enumeration. (1) Includes Wisconsin's 2015-16 student data (2016-17, 2017-18, 2018-19, and 2019-20 data were not available). (2) Includes Nebraska's 2015-16 data for 3-to-5-year-old students (2016-17 data were not available). (3) Includes 2016-17 data for 3-to-5-year-old students in Minnesota and 6-to-21-year-old students in Maine and Vermont because 2017-18 data were not available. (4) Data by disability type for Iowa are imputed. (5) Includes 2019-20 data for 5-to-21-year-old students in Louisiana (2020-21 data were not available). (6) Includes 2020-21 data for 3-to-5-year-old students in Louisiana (2021-22 data were not available). (7) Includes limited strength, vitality, or alertness due to chronic or acute health problems such as a heart condition, tuberculosis, rheumatic fever, nephritis, asthma, sickle cell anemia, hemophilia, epilepsy, lead poisoning, leukemia, or diabetes. (8) Total includes 390 preschool disabled students. For all other years, preschool children were included in the counts by disability condition.

Population With Upper Secondary Education in Selected Countries, 2021

Source: Organization for Economic Cooperation and Development

Sorted by percentage of the population ages 25-64 that have received at least an upper secondary (senior high school) education.

Country	%	Country	%	Country	%	Country	%	Country	%
Japan	100%	Australia	68%	Poland.	64%	Brazil.	58%	Italy.	46%
South Korea	86	Slovenia	68	Netherlands	63	Latvia	57	Turkey (Türkiye) . .	43
United States	77	France	67	Greece	60	Ireland.	56	Mexico	41
Czechia.	75	Slovakia	67	Belgium.	60	United Kingdom . .	55	Costa Rica	40
Israel.	74	Norway	66	Sweden	59	Iceland	55	Indonesia	38
Canada	72	Switzerland	66	New Zealand	59	Colombia	53	Portugal	36
Finland	71	Denmark	66	Germany	59	Luxembourg	47	China (2020).	35
Chile (2020)	70	Hungary	66	Lithuania	59	South Africa (2020)	47	India (2020)	17
Austria	68	Argentina	65	Estonia	59	Spain	47		

Financial Aid to U.S. Undergraduate Students, 2000-21

Source: National Center for Education Statistics, U.S. Dept. of Education

Type of institution/ year	Number enrolled	Number receiving financial aid	Percent receiving aid	Percent of enrolled students in student aid programs				Average award[1]			
				Federal grants	State/ local grants	Institu- tional grants	Student loans[2]	Federal grants	State/ local grants	Institu- tional grants	Student loans[2]
All institutions											
2000-01	1,976,600	1,390,527	70.3%	31.6%	31.2%	31.1%	40.1%	$4,005	$3,284	$7,634	$6,063
2020-21	2,249,800	1,923,927	85.5	51.2	34.3	52.9	38.4	5,058	4,253	12,568	7,737
Public											
2000-01	1,333,236	872,109	65.4	30.0	33.5	22.7	30.7	3,878	2,749	3,664	4,913
2020-21	1,608,121	1,348,275	83.8	52.0	39.9	46.4	30.7	4,959	4,125	6,057	7,140
4-year											
2000-01	804,793	573,430	71.3	26.6	36.5	29.6	40.7	4,138	3,331	4,214	5,173
2020-21	1,147,973	977,557	85.2	48.6	38.0	56.8	36.8	4,943	4,866	6,609	7,492
2-year											
2000-01	528,443	298,679	56.5	35.2	28.8	12.1	15.3	3,580	1,626	1,617	3,859
2020-21	460,148	370,718	80.6	60.5	44.7	20.6	15.4	4,993	2,550	2,256	5,049
Private nonprofit											
2000-01	439,369	363,044	82.6	28.4	31.8	68.1	57.7	4,637	4,829	11,867	6,474
2020-21	493,415	447,659	90.7	42.4	24.4	82.5	53.6	5,389	4,986	25,243	8,570
4-year											
2000-01	419,499	347,638	82.9	27.4	32.2	70.1	58.1	4,720	4,834	12,013	6,442
2020-21	477,264	432,958	90.7	41.1	25.0	84.4	53.0	5,350	5,001	25,449	8,776
2-year											
2000-01	19,870	15,406	77.5	49.2	23.9	25.7	49.5	3,655	4,658	3,491	7,263
2020-21	16,151	14,701	91.0	79.5	9.0	26.4	73.3	5,971	3,763	5,863	4,171
Private for-profit											
2000-01	203,995	155,374	76.2	49.3	15.2	6.2	63.5	3,724	4,016	2,480	8,887
2020-21	148,264	127,993	86.3	72.2	6.4	24.3	71.5	5,178	3,598	4,318	8,440
4-year											
2000-01	81,075	51,739	63.8	36.1	11.9	8.3	57.7	3,697	4,653	2,603	9,259
2020-21	51,993	44,186	85.0	67.8	9.4	36.7	66.5	5,163	3,907	6,578	8,693
2-year											
2000-01	122,920	103,635	84.3	58.0	17.3	4.8	67.3	3,735	3,727	2,340	8,676
2020-21	96,271	83,807	87.1	74.5	4.8	17.7	74.2	5,159	2,717	1,783	8,317

Note: Data for full-time, first-time, degree/certificate-seeking undergraduate students. (1) Average amounts for students participating in indicated programs, in constant 2021-22 dollars. (2) Includes only loans made directly to students, not parents.

Charges at U.S. Institutions of Higher Education, 1969-2022

Source: National Center for Education Statistics, U.S. Dept. of Education

Data are for the entire academic year and are average charges, in current dollars, for full-time students at degree-granting postsecondary institutions. Room and board based on full-time students. For 1989-90 on, board is based on 20 meals per week.

	Tuition and fees			Board rates			Dormitory charges		
Public (in-state)	**All institutions**	**2-yr**	**4-yr**	**All institutions**	**2-yr**	**4-yr**	**All institutions**	**2-yr**	**4-yr**
1969-70	$323	$178	$358	$508	$465	$510	$366	$308	$369
1979-80	583	355	738	867	893	865	715	574	725
1989-90	1,356	756	1,780	1,635	1,581	1,638	1,513	962	1,557
1999-2000	2,504	1,348	3,349	2,364	1,834	2,406	2,440	1,549	2,519
2008-09	4,512	2,136	6,312	3,507	2,749	3,569	4,190	2,664	4,331
2009-10	4,763	2,283	6,717	3,655	2,571	3,755	4,401	2,854	4,564
2010-11	5,075	2,441	7,132	3,845	2,683	3,956	4,646	2,955	4,832
2011-12	5,563	2,651	7,713	3,946	2,866	4,042	4,849	3,100	5,031
2012-13	5,899	2,792	8,070	4,061	2,888	4,163	5,062	3,247	5,241
2013-14	6,120	2,881	8,312	4,205	2,955	4,308	5,304	3,448	5,479
2014-15	6,370	2,955	8,543	4,313	3,072	4,412	5,504	3,559	5,677
2015-16	6,612	3,038	8,778	4,469	3,118	4,576	5,686	3,759	5,850
2016-17	6,818	3,156	8,804	4,562	3,111	4,666	5,859	3,823	6,018
2017-18	7,051	3,242	9,036	4,682	3,204	4,785	6,060	3,834	6,227
2018-19	7,248	3,312	9,212	4,843	3,582	4,927	6,290	4,057	6,459
2019-20	7,410	3,377	9,349	4,943	3,578	5,031	6,483	4,105	6,655
2020-21	7,635	3,503	9,374	5,107	3,649	5,189	6,630	4,408	6,774
2021-22	7,869	3,564	9,596	5,252	3,626	5,338	6,799	4,430	6,944
Private (nonprofit and for-profit)									
1969-70	$1,533	$1,034	$1,562	$560	$546	$561	$434	$413	$436
1979-80	3,130	2,062	3,225	955	923	957	827	766	831
1989-90	8,147	5,196	8,396	1,948	1,811	1,953	1,923	1,663	1,935
1999-2000	14,100	8,225	14,616	2,877	2,753	2,879	3,236	3,067	3,242
2008-09	21,575	13,567	22,040	4,164	4,603	4,161	5,025	4,553	5,031
2009-10	21,764	14,862	22,269	4,329	4,390	4,329	5,248	5,211	5,248
2010-11	22,042	13,687	22,677	4,430	4,475	4,430	5,403	4,939	5,410
2011-12	22,850	13,961	23,464	4,586	4,475	4,586	5,622	5,169	5,627
2012-13	23,943	14,149	24,523	4,709	3,977	4,712	5,831	5,228	5,837
2013-14	25,110	14,170	25,707	4,864	4,211	4,866	6,021	5,489	6,026
2014-15	26,182	14,261	26,739	5,019	4,560	5,021	6,221	5,506	6,228
2015-16	27,436	14,528	27,942	5,123	4,181	5,128	6,457	5,666	6,464
2016-17	28,945	14,589	29,476	5,268	4,350	5,273	6,710	5,949	6,717
2017-18	30,274	14,894	30,723	5,437	4,645	5,440	6,961	6,057	6,968
2018-19	31,527	15,720	31,883	5,616	6,909	5,608	7,171	5,951	7,179
2019-20	32,411	15,831	32,764	5,756	4,587	5,760	7,397	6,326	7,401
2020-21	32,351	15,473	32,728	5,903	4,619	5,907	7,573	5,571	7,580
2021-22	33,691	16,579	34,041	6,086	4,845	6,090	7,825	5,942	7,831

U.S. Student Loan Balances by Age, 2011-21

Source: *2022 Student Loan Update*, Federal Reserve Bank of New York; Equifax

Note: Total annual balances include loans held by persons of unknown ages. Percentages may not add up to 100 due to rounding.

Student Loan Debt by State, 2004-20

Source: *Student Debt and the Class of 2020*, Project on Student Debt, Institute for College Access & Success

State[1]	Average debt 2004	Average debt 2014	Average debt 2020	% with debt 2004	% with debt 2020	State[1]	Average debt 2004	Average debt 2014	Average debt 2020	% with debt 2004	% with debt 2020
Alabama	$18,042	$29,425	$30,996	57%	51%	Missouri	$15,511	$25,844	$28,713	59%	56%
Alaska	15,648	26,742	26,356	48	47	Montana	18,019	26,946	27,114	68	55
Arizona	18,147	22,609	24,298	48	47	Nebraska	17,384	26,278	26,781	62	60
Arkansas	16,210	25,344	27,319	59	54	Nevada	14,144	20,211	21,357	46	46
California	16,071	21,382	21,125	49	46	New Hampshire	21,441	33,410	39,928	65	70
Colorado	16,352	25,064	26,424	53	49	New Jersey	16,223	28,318	35,117	58	63
Connecticut	18,906	29,750	35,853	57	57	New Mexico	—	18,969	20,868	—	45
Delaware	14,780	33,808	39,705	45	60	New York	18,857	27,822	30,951	62	54
District of						North Carolina	16,863	25,218	29,681	51	55
Columbia	19,357	—	32,966	58	46	North Dakota	22,409	—	31,939	73	66
Florida	18,857	24,947	24,454	51	47	Ohio	19,182	29,353	30,605	62	59
Georgia	15,354	26,518	27,759	53	56	Oklahoma	16,942	23,430	27,876	55	50
Hawaii	13,509	24,554	24,926	29	45	Oregon	17,267	26,106	26,504	63	53
Idaho	22,273	26,091	24,983	68	58	Pennsylvania	19,556	33,264	39,375	69	64
Illinois	15,650	28,984	28,552	56	57	Rhode Island	19,328	31,841	36,791	68	64
Indiana	19,425	29,222	28,521	54	57	South Carolina	16,775	29,163	32,635	55	60
Iowa	24,204	29,732	29,560	76	60	South Dakota	19,023	26,023	32,029	82	73
Kansas	16,266	25,521	26,002	57	60	Tennessee	16,905	25,510	26,852	41	53
Kentucky	14,250	25,939	28,356	52	61	Texas	17,170	26,250	26,273	51	52
Louisiana	18,993	23,025	26,284	61	53	Utah	12,362	18,921	18,344	43	39
Maine	19,410	30,908	32,764	64	63	Vermont	20,706	29,060	34,866	56	57
Maryland	12,597	27,457	30,461	52	55	Virginia	15,831	26,432	29,616	57	55
Massachusetts	17,021	29,391	33,457	60	56	Washington	17,415	24,804	23,993	56	47
Michigan	18,754	29,450	29,863	58	58	West Virginia	18,246	26,854	29,208	69	66
Minnesota	19,580	31,579	32,012	72	64	Wisconsin	16,560	28,810	30,270	60	63
Mississippi	15,503	26,177	29,714	60	58	Wyoming	15,352	23,708	23,510	44	48
						U.S.	**18,550**	**28,950**	**NA**	**65**	**NA**

— = Usable cases covered less than 30% of bachelor's degree recipients, or underlying data showed a state-level change of 30% or more in average debt from previous year. NA = Not available. (1) Location of surveyed colleges (not necessarily location of degree recipient).

College Enrollment by Selected Characteristics, 1947-2021

Source: National Center for Education Statistics, U.S. Dept. of Education

(numbers in thousands)

Year	Total enrollment[1]	Attendance status Full-time	Attendance status Part-time	Attendance status % part-time	Sex of student Male	Sex of student Female	Control of institution Public	Control of institution Total	Control of institution Private Nonprofit	Control of institution For-profit
1947[2]	2,338	NA	NA	NA	1,659	679	1,152	1,186	NA	NA
1950[2]	2,281	NA	NA	NA	1,560	721	1,140	1,142	NA	NA
1955[2]	2,653	NA	NA	NA	1,733	920	1,476	1,177	NA	NA
1965	5,921	4,096	1,825[3]	30.8%	3,630	2,291	3,970	1,951	NA	NA
1970	8,581	5,816	2,765	32.2	5,044	3,537	6,428	2,153	2,134	18
1975	11,185	6,841	4,344	38.8	6,149	5,036	8,835	2,350	2,311	39
1980	12,097	7,098	4,999	41.3	5,874	6,223	9,457	2,640	2,528	112[4]
1985	12,247	7,075	5,172	42.2	5,818	6,429	9,479	2,768	2,572	196
1990	13,819	7,821	5,998	43.4	6,284	7,535	10,845	2,974	2,760	214
1995	14,262	8,129	6,133	43.0	6,343	7,919	11,092	3,169	2,929	240
2000	15,312	9,010	6,303	41.2	6,722	8,591	11,753	3,560	3,109	450
2005	17,487	10,797	6,690	38.3	7,456	10,032	13,022	4,466	3,455	1,011
2006	17,754	10,958	6,797	38.3	7,572	10,182	13,175	4,579	3,513	1,066
2007	18,258	11,271	6,987	38.3	7,820	10,438	13,501	4,757	3,571	1,186
2008	19,082	11,735	7,347	38.5	8,178	10,904	13,971	5,111	3,661	1,450
2009	20,314	12,605	7,708	37.9	8,733	11,581	14,811	5,503	3,768	1,735
2010	21,019	13,087	7,932	37.7	9,046	11,974	15,142	5,877	3,854	2,023
2011	21,011	13,003	8,008	38.1	9,034	11,976	15,116	5,894	3,927	1,967
2012	20,644	12,734	7,910	38.3	8,919	11,725	14,885	5,760	3,951	1,808
2013	20,377	12,597	7,780	38.2	8,861	11,515	14,747	5,630	3,971	1,658
2014	20,209	12,454	7,755	38.4	8,798	11,412	14,655	5,554	3,997	1,557
2015	19,988	12,288	7,701	38.5	8,724	11,264	14,573	5,415	4,066	1,349
2016	19,847	12,125	7,722	38.9	8,638	11,208	14,586	5,261	4,079	1,182
2017	19,778	12,076	7,702	38.9	8,571	11,207	14,572	5,206	4,108	1,098
2018	19,651	11,990	7,662	39.0	8,445	11,207	14,539	5,112	4,132	980
2019	19,630	11,954	7,676	39.1	8,364	11,266	14,504	5,127	4,135	991
2020	19,027	11,609	7,418	39.0	7,885	11,142	13,884	5,143	4,101	1,042
2021	18,660	11,330	7,330	39.3	7,769	10,890	13,544	5,116	4,113	1,003

NA = Not available. **Note:** Data for 1947-95 are for institutions of higher education, while later data are for degree-granting institutions. Degree-granting institutions grant associate's or higher degrees and participate in Title IV federal financial aid programs. The degree-granting classification is very similar to the earlier higher education classification, but it includes more two-year colleges and excludes a few higher education institutions that do not grant degrees. (1) Fall enrollment. (2) Degree-credit enrollment only. (3) Includes part-time resident students and all extension students (students attending courses at sites separate from the primary reporting campus). In later years, part-time student enrollment was collected as a distinct category. (4) Large increases are due to the addition of schools accredited by the Accrediting Commission of Career Schools and Colleges of Technology.

U.S. Bachelor's Degrees Conferred, 1899-2031

Source: National Center for Education Statistics, U.S. Dept. of Education
(*) figures are projected.

Financial Aid for College and Other Postsecondary Education

Reviewed by National Association of Student Financial Aid Administrators; as of June 2023

The cost of postsecondary education in the U.S. continues to increase, but financial aid—in the form of **grants** (no repayment needed), **loans**, and/or **work-study** programs—is widely available to help families meet these expenses. Most federal aid is limited to families that demonstrate financial need as determined by standard formulas and is designed to help students attend the college of their choice regardless of their ability to pay. Financial aid personnel at each school can provide information about all aid programs (federal, state, institutional, and private) available to students, how to apply, and deadlines.

All applicants for federal aid must file a Free Application for Federal Student Aid (**FAFSA**), generally as soon as possible after Oct. 1 for the academic year starting the following Aug. or Sept. This change from Jan. in prior years allows students to apply for aid earlier. Applicants can file a FAFSA form online at fafsa.gov or by completing a printed-out form and mailing it.

Figures provided should match federal income tax forms filed for the previous year. (The use of tax data that has already been filed ensures timely processing.) Thus, the application for the 2023-24 academic year, available Oct. 1, 2022, should be filed with 2021 tax information. This is made easier by the availability of the IRS Data Retrieval Tool, which allows online applicants to access and transfer IRS tax return information directly into their FAFSA. Many other sources of aid—state governments, employers and unions, civic organizations, and the institutions themselves—also use the FAFSA to determine eligibility for aid. Some federal programs pay for postsecondary education in return for service: AmeriCorps, Reserve Officers' Training Corps (Army, Navy, and Air Force), the G.I. Bill, and the National Health Service Corps. A student must reapply for aid annually.

Students, parents, and borrowers are required to use an **FSA ID**, made up of a username and password, to access certain U.S. Dept. of Education websites. An FSA ID is used to confirm identity when accessing financial aid information and electronically signing federal student aid documents.

A **federal formula**, based on information provided on the FAFSA, takes into account such factors as family income in the preceding calendar year, parental and student assets (excluding the parents' home, farm, or certain small businesses), and length of time to parents' retirement. Financial aid personnel have the authority to consider unusual expenses, such as very high medical expenses, which are not reported on the FAFSA. Outside scholarships are also taken into account in determining eligibility for federal, institutional, and state financial aid programs.

The formula determines a family's **expected family contribution** (EFC), which is divided among the number of family members—excluding parents—in college. The EFC is subtracted from the total cost of attending college for each person. The difference determines financial need and the maximum federal aid for which the family may be eligible. (Some institutions use a separate formula for need-based institutional aid.) Some schools guarantee they will meet the full financial need of each admitted student. Schools might try to cover a student's financial need using a combination of tools but be unable to because of a lack of funds.

The **aid package** offered by each school may include one or more of the following: Federal Pell Grants, for those who demonstrate sufficient financial need; Federal Supplemental Educational Opportunity Grants, for those who still have significant need after receiving Federal Pell Grants; grants from the school; Federal Work-Study or other work programs; and federal Direct Subsidized and Unsubsidized Loans (often referred to as Direct Loans). Parents of undergraduates and students in graduate or professional school may apply for a PLUS Loan. Direct Unsubsidized Loans and Direct PLUS Loans are available regardless of financial need, but students and parents must still complete the FAFSA to get these loans. Professional judgment, which allows an institution to take into account current financial circumstances not reflected in the FAFSA, is also available. Students and families that have incurred a loss of income or job elimination can work directly with the financial aid office of their chosen institution to ensure an accurate reflection of their current financial situation.

Loans have varying interest rates and other requirements. Repayment of Direct Subsidized Loans and Direct Unsubsidized Loans generally does not begin until after graduation; deferments, income-based repayment plans, and loan forgiveness are available on federal loans for students who meet certain requirements. For PLUS Loans, parents and graduate-level students must pass a credit check and may need to begin repayment of both principal and interest while the student is still in school.

Terms may vary, but federal student loans must be repaid, even if financial circumstances change, education is incomplete or not as expected, or post-graduation income is less than expected. The loan servicer or lender is required to provide a loan repayment schedule that states the first payment due date, the number and frequency of payments, and the amount due. Some loans have a grace period, a set period of time (in most cases six months) after graduation before repayment begins. Direct loans have a number of repayment plan options—including graduated, extended repayment, income-based repayment—or offer loan consolidation. In most cases, student loan debt cannot be discharged in bankruptcy. Certain federal income **tax credits and refunds** are available to families who meet requirements.

Rules for financial aid are complex and changeable. Comprehensive resources on financial aid from the U.S. Dept. of Education, including fact sheets, videos, worksheets, and other tools, are available online at studentaid.gov/resources.

Further information is available from the Federal Student Aid Information Center: 1-800-4-FED-AID, Mon., 8 ᴀᴍ-9 ᴘᴍ ET; Tues.-Wed., 8 ᴀᴍ-8 ᴘᴍ; Thurs.-Fri., 8 ᴀᴍ-6 ᴘᴍ; studentaid.gov; web chat is also available.

Endowment Assets of Colleges and Universities, 2022

Source: *2022 NACUBO-TIAA Study of Endowments*, National Association of College and University Business Officers (NACUBO)

Rank	College/university	Endowment assets[1]	% change, 2021-22	Rank	College/university	Endowment assets[1]	% change, 2021-22
1.	Harvard University	$49,444,494	−4.73%	21.	Dartmouth College	$8,065,743	−4.93%
2.	University of Texas System	42,668,276	−0.56	22.	Rice University	7,814,267	−3.06
3.	Yale University	41,383,300	−2.13	23.	University of Southern California	7,319,123	−8.62
4.	Stanford University	36,300,000	−3.97	24.	Ohio State University	6,960,782	2.15
5.	Princeton University	35,794,186	−5.05	25.	Brown University	6,141,243	−5.81
6.	Massachusetts Institute of Technology	24,739,862	−10.13	26.	University of Pittsburgh	5,528,910	−2.09
7.	University of Pennsylvania	20,724,351	0.98	27.	University of Minnesota	5,365,669	−1.44
8.	Texas A&M University System	18,243,191	1.19	28.	University of North Carolina at Chapel Hill	5,317,821	2.93
9.	University of Michigan	17,347,188	1.91	29.	New York University	5,148,741	−7.64
10.	University of Notre Dame	16,729,299	−7.44	30.	University of Washington	4,678,009	−0.72
11.	University of California	15,417,663	−5.22	31.	Pennsylvania State University	4,607,961	−0.11
12.	Northwestern University	14,121,488	−5.60	32.	Michigan State University	3,879,500	−1.19
13.	Columbia University	13,279,846	−7.46	33.	Carnegie Mellon University	3,856,808	−2.79
14.	Washington University	12,252,329	−9.48	34.	Purdue University	3,675,960	2.54
15.	Duke University	12,116,260	−4.54	35.	California Institute of Technology	3,635,000	−4.47
16.	Vanderbilt University	10,206,067	−6.61	36.	UCLA	3,560,694	−8.53
17.	Emory University	9,997,742	−9.37	37.	Williams College	3,534,369	−15.26
18.	University of Virginia	9,858,442	−6.40	38.	Indiana University	3,515,282	5.95
19.	Cornell University	9,838,198	−1.90	39.	University of Wisconsin	3,496,791	−13.70
20.	Johns Hopkins University	8,244,472	−11.50	40.	Boston College	3,336,600	−12.82

Note: Market value of endowment assets in the fiscal year. (1) In thousands.

Average ACT Scores and Characteristics of College-Bound Students, 1990-2022

Source: ACT, Inc. (formerly American College Testing)

SCORES[1]	Unit	1990	1995	2000	2005	2010	2015	2017	2018	2019	2020	2021	2022
Composite score	Points	20.6	20.8	21.0	20.9	21.0	21.0	21.0	20.8	20.7	20.6	20.3	19.8
Male	Points	21.0	21.0	21.2	21.1	21.2	21.1	21.0	20.9	20.6	20.5	20.3	19.7
Female	Points	20.3	20.7	20.9	20.9	20.9	21.0	21.1	20.9	20.8	20.8	20.6	20.0
English score	Points	20.5	20.2	20.5	20.4	20.5	20.4	20.3	20.2	20.1	19.9	19.6	19.0
Male	Points	20.1	19.8	20.0	20.0	20.1	20.0	19.9	19.7	19.6	19.3	19.1	18.5
Female	Points	20.9	20.6	20.9	20.8	20.8	20.8	20.8	20.7	20.6	20.5	20.2	19.6
Math score	Points	19.9	20.2	20.7	20.7	21.0	20.8	20.7	20.5	20.4	20.2	19.9	19.3
Male	Points	20.7	20.9	21.4	21.3	21.6	21.3	21.2	20.9	20.8	20.6	20.4	19.7
Female	Points	19.3	19.7	20.2	20.2	20.5	20.4	20.4	20.2	20.0	20.0	19.7	19.1
PARTICIPANTS													
Total number	(Thous.)	817	945	1,065	1,186	1,569	1,924	2,030	1,915	1,783	1,670	1,295	1,350
Male	Percent	46%	44%	43%	44%	45%	47%	46%	47%	46%	46%	46%	47%
White	Percent	79	80	72	66	62	55	52	52	52	52	54	53
Black	Percent	9	9	10	12	14	13	13	13	12	12	12	11
Hispanic[2]	Percent	4	5	5	7	10	16	17	16	16	17	14	16
Composite score													
27 or above	Percent	12	13	14	14	16	18	18	18	18	18	17	15
18 or below	Percent	35	34	32	34	35	37	38	40	41	42	44	48

Note: Minimum score, 1; maximum score, 36. Test scores and characteristics of college-bound students are based on the performance of all ACT-tested students who graduated in the spring of a given school year and took the ACT assessment during junior or senior year of high school. (1) For 2020-22, ACT reported a category of "other responses" for gender that included "another gender" and "prefer not to respond," as well as missing values. (2) Persons of Hispanic origin may be of any race.

Average ACT Composite Scores by State, 2022

Source: ACT, Inc. (formerly American College Testing)

State	Avg. comp. score	% grads taking ACT	State	Avg. comp. score	% grads taking ACT	State	Avg. comp. score	% grads taking ACT
Alabama	18.0	100%	Louisiana	18.1	100%	Ohio	19.4	82%
Alaska	20.4	14	Maine	25.1	2	Oklahoma	17.9	94
Arizona	18.4	64	Maryland	24.4	8	Oregon	23.0	7
Arkansas	18.8	93	Massachusetts	26.5	9	Pennsylvania	24.4	7
California	26.5	4	Michigan	24.6	8	Rhode Island	25.2	5
Colorado	23.2	15	Minnesota	21.0	69	South Carolina	18.9	40
Connecticut	26.3	9	Mississippi	17.8	100	South Dakota	21.5	58
Delaware	24.9	5	Missouri	20.2	66	Tennessee	18.6	100
District of Columbia	26.9	18	Montana	19.3	94	Texas	19.8	22
Florida	19.0	46	Nebraska	19.4	94	Utah	19.9	91
Georgia	21.6	30	Nevada	17.3	100	Vermont	23.7	8
Hawaii	18.8	53	New Hampshire	25.7	5	Virginia	24.6	9
Idaho	22.8	15	New Jersey	24.6	12	Washington	24.6	7
Illinois	24.5	18	New Mexico	19.8	20	West Virginia	20.5	28
Indiana	22.8	13	New York	25.3	10	Wisconsin	19.4	93
Iowa	21.4	49	North Carolina	18.5	88	Wyoming	19.2	100
Kansas	19.9	73	North Dakota	19.2	96	U.S.	19.8	36
Kentucky	18.6	96						

Mean SAT Scores of College-Bound Seniors, 1975-2022

Source: The College Board

(for school year ending in year shown)

	1975	1980	1990	1995	2000	2005	2010	2015	2016[2,3]	2017[3]	2018[3]	2019[3]	2020[3,4]	2021[3,4]	2022[3,4]
Reading and writing[1]	512	502	500	504	505	508	500	495	494	533	536	531	528	533	529
Male	515	506	505	505	507	513	502	497	495	532	534	529	523	530	526
Female	509	498	496	502	504	505	498	493	493	534	539	534	532	535	531
Math score.	498	492	501	506	514	520	515	511	508	527	531	528	523	528	521
Male	518	515	521	525	533	538	533	527	524	538	542	537	531	537	530
Female	479	473	483	490	498	504	499	496	494	516	522	519	516	519	512
Writing score.	NA	NA	NA	NA	NA	NA	491	484	482	NA	NA	NA	NA	NA	NA
Male	NA	NA	NA	NA	NA	NA	485	478	475	NA	NA	NA	NA	NA	NA
Female	NA	NA	NA	NA	NA	NA	497	490	487	NA	NA	NA	NA	NA	NA

NA = Not applicable. **Note:** In 1995, the College Board recentered the scoring scale for the SAT. Earlier scores have been adjusted to account for this recentering. (1) Verbal section, 1975-2005; critical reading, 2006-16. (2) Through Jan. 2016. (3) Beginning in Mar. 2016, students took a redesigned SAT. The College Board advised against comparing 2016-22 SAT results with earlier data. (4) For 2020, 2021, and 2022, 0.1%, 0.2%, and 0.4% of test takers, respectively, responded "another/no response" for gender.

Mean SAT Scores by State, 1990-2022

Source: The College Board; National Center for Education Statistics, U.S. Dept. of Education

(for school year ending in year shown; V = Verbal, M = Math, CR = Critical reading, W = Writing, ERW = Evidence-based reading and writing)

	1990		2000		2010			2020		% grads	2022[1]		% grads
State	V	M	V	M	CR	M	W	ERW	M	taking SAT[1]	ERW	M	taking SAT[2]
Alabama	545	534	559	555	556	550	544	576	551	7%	586	560	4%
Alaska	514	501	519	515	518	515	491	555	543	37	565	545	26
Arizona	521	520	521	523	519	525	500	571	568	29	583	577	14
Arkansas	545	532	563	554	566	566	552	590	567	4	610	581	2
California	494	508	497	518	501	516	500	527	522	67	560	555	21
Colorado	533	534	534	537	568	572	555	511	501	100	518	503	84
Connecticut	506	496	508	509	509	514	513	527	512	100	520	505	89
Delaware	510	496	502	496	493	495	481	497	481	100	491	477	95
District of Columbia	483	467	490	486	474	464	466	498	482	100	502	484	100
Florida	495	493	498	500	496	498	479	512	479	100	510	473	87
Georgia	478	473	488	486	488	490	475	537	516	68	541	520	54
Hawaii	480	505	488	519	483	505	470	549	546	51	566	558	31
Idaho	542	524	540	541	543	541	517	500	484	100	499	488	97
Illinois	542	547	568	586	585	600	577	504	503	98	495	485	97
Indiana	486	486	498	501	494	505	477	540	534	64	540	533	48
Iowa	584	588	589	600	603	613	582	611	609	3	602	594	3
Kansas	566	563	574	580	590	595	567	617	620	4	621	617	2
Kentucky	548	541	548	550	575	575	563	609	598	4	618	600	2
Louisiana	551	537	562	558	555	550	547	597	573	5	597	574	3
Maine	501	490	504	500	468	467	454	504	491	98	549	532	43
Maryland	506	502	507	509	501	506	495	522	507	88	546	529	54
Massachusetts	503	498	511	513	512	526	509	560	559	80	567	561	55
Michigan	529	534	557	569	585	605	576	503	495	100	506	495	84
Minnesota	552	558	581	594	594	607	580	624	633	4	613	612	3
Mississippi	552	538	562	549	566	548	552	610	593	3	623	602	1
Missouri	548	541	572	577	593	595	580	610	603	4	606	594	3
Montana	540	542	543	546	538	538	517	598	587	10	609	597	6
Nebraska	559	562	560	571	585	593	568	615	614	3	613	609	2
Nevada	511	511	510	517	496	501	473	579	567	17	592	580	6
New Hampshire	518	510	520	519	520	524	510	531	524	93	530	521	81
New Jersey	495	498	498	513	495	514	497	541	540	82	543	537	63
New Mexico	554	546	549	543	553	549	534	533	522	19	496	480	42
New York	489	496	494	506	484	499	478	528	530	79	534	533	59
North Carolina	478	470	492	496	497	511	477	553	544	48	573	562	27
North Dakota	579	578	588	609	580	594	559	615	617	2	610	603	1
Ohio	526	522	533	539	538	548	522	536	534	21	528	525	18
Oklahoma	553	542	563	560	569	568	547	490	481	20	485	467	17
Oregon	515	509	527	527	523	524	499	557	547	51	580	563	22
Pennsylvania	497	490	498	497	492	501	480	543	534	67	551	540	48
Rhode Island	498	488	505	500	494	495	488	501	489	100	494	477	93
South Carolina	475	467	484	482	484	495	468	524	503	68	526	504	51
South Dakota	580	570	587	588	592	603	571	609	610	3	608	611	2
Tennessee	558	544	563	553	576	571	565	601	585	7	610	589	5
Texas	490	489	493	500	484	505	473	510	500	73	506	495	64
Utah	566	555	570	569	568	559	547	601	615	3	618	615	2
Vermont	507	493	513	508	519	521	506	559	545	63	538	537	48
Virginia	501	496	509	500	512	512	497	567	549	65	572	552	48
Washington	513	511	526	528	524	532	508	539	534	69	554	542	32
West Virginia	520	514	526	511	515	507	500	480	456	98	481	456	84
Wisconsin	552	559	584	597	595	604	579	615	628	3	622	629	2
Wyoming	534	538	545	545	570	567	546	614	606	3	627	617	2
National average	500	501	505	514	501	516	492	528	523	NA	529	521	NA

NA = Not available. **Note:** In 1995, the College Board recentered the scoring scale for the SAT. In 2005, the Verbal portion became Critical reading, and a writing test was added. In 2016, this portion became Evidence-based reading and writing. (1) Beginning in Mar. 2016, students took a redesigned SAT test. The College Board advised against comparing 2020 and 2022 SAT results with earlier data. (2) Percentage of students from the class of 2022 who took the SAT during high school.

EDUCATION: COLLEGES AND UNIVERSITIES
Four-Year Colleges and Universities

Note: These listings include only accredited degree-granting institutions in the U.S. and U.S. territories with a total enrollment of 1,200 or more. Only four-year colleges and universities that award a bachelor's degree as their highest undergraduate degree are included. Data reported for institutions that provided updated information on Peterson's Annual Survey of Undergraduate Institutions for the 2022-23 academic year, with some exceptions where the previous academic year was the most recent available.

All institutions are coeducational except those where the ZIP code is followed directly by a number in parentheses: (1) = men only; (2) = primarily men; (3) = women only; (4) = primarily women; (5) undergraduate: men only, graduate: coed; (6) undergraduate: women only, graduate: coed.

The **Tuition & fees** column shows the annual tuition and required fees for full-time students or, where indicated, the tuition and standard fees per unit for part-time students. Where tuition varies according to residence, the figure is given for the most local resident and is coded as follows: (A) = area residents; (S) = state residents; all other figures apply to all students regardless of residence. Where annual expenses are expressed as a lump sum (including full-time tuition, mandatory fees, and room and board), the figure is entered under Tuition & fees and coded (C) = comprehensive fee. **Room & board** is the typical cost for one academic year.

Control: (1) independent (nonprofit); (2) independent-religious; (3) proprietary (profit-making); (4) federal; (5) state; (6) commonwealth (Puerto Rico); (7) territory (U.S. territories); (8) county; (9) district; (10) city; (11) state and local; (12) state-related; (13) private—unspecified; (14) public—unspecified. **Degree** means the highest degree offered: B = bachelor's, M = master's, D = doctorate.

Enrollment is the total number of matriculated undergraduate and (if applicable) graduate students.

Faculty is the total number of full-time and part-time faculty members teaching courses.

Grad. rate is the percentage of full-time, first-time bachelor's (or equivalent) degree-seeking undergraduate students entering school in 2016 (or most recent available year prior) who obtained their degrees within six years.

NA indicates category is inapplicable, or data is not available from a consistent source.

Name, address	Year founded	Tuition & fees	Room & board	Control, degree	Enrollment	Faculty	Grad. rate
Abilene Christian Univ., Abilene, TX 79699	1906	$40,500	$11,500	2-D	5,057	464	61.0%
Abraham Baldwin Agr. Coll., Tifton, GA 31793	1933	$3,565 (A)	$7,962	5-B	3,327	162	NA
Acad. of Art Univ., San Francisco, CA 94105-3410	1929	$28,024	$19,431	3-M	6,823	624	36.0
Adams State Univ., Alamosa, CO 81101	1921	$6,072 (A)	NA	5-D	3,090	257	41.7
Adelphi Univ., Garden City, NY 11530-0701	1896	$47,290	$20,028	1-D	7,252	1,067	68.0
Adrian Coll., Adrian, MI 49221-2575	1859	$39,396	$12,870	2-M	1,871	205	52.0
Adventist Univ. of Health Scis., Orlando, FL 32803	1992	$20,880	$22,320	1-D	1,610	278	NA
Alabama Agr. & Mech. Univ., Huntsville, AL 35811	1875	$10,024 (A)	$7,992	5-D	5,969	363	26.8
Alabama State Univ., Montgomery, AL 36101-0271	1867	$11,068 (A)	$6,050	5-D	3,964	327	29.0
Albany State Univ., Albany, GA 31705-2717	1903	$6,500 (A)	$10,904	5-M	6,615	398	33.7
Albertus Magnus Coll., New Haven, CT 06511-1189.	1925	$39,924	$15,338	2-M	1,275	129	50.0
Albion Coll., Albion, MI 49224-1831	1835	$55,746	$12,570	13-B	1,456	154	59.2
Albright Coll., Reading, PA 19612-5234	1856	$28,230	$13,500	2-M	1,539	NA	53.0
Alcorn State Univ., Lorman, MS 39096-7500	1871	NA	NA	5-D	3,321	221	40.0
Allegheny Coll., Meadville, PA 16335	1815	$53,610	$13,796	1-B	1,353	170	67.6
Alliant Intl. Univ.–San Diego, San Diego, CA 92131	1952	$16,631	NA	1-D	3,200	520	NA
Alma Coll., Alma, MI 48801-1599.	1886	$47,430	$13,128	2-M	1,260	138	62.0
Alvernia Univ., Reading, PA 19607-1799	1958	$40,950	$14,030	2-D	2,560	262	61.0
Alverno Coll., Milwaukee, WI 53234-3922 (6)	1887	$32,794	$10,237	2-D	1,596	200	52.0
Amer. InterContinental Univ. Atlanta, Atlanta, GA 30328.	1970	$14,910	$8,057	3-M	1,312	55	NA
Amer. InterContinental Univ. Online, Schaumburg, IL 60173.	1970	$12,860	NA	3-M	12,830	NA	NA
Amer. Intl. Coll., Springfield, MA 01109-3189	1885	$42,970	$16,260	1-D	3,283	NA	NA
Amer. Publ Univ. System, Charles Town, WV 25414.	1991	$7,360	NA	3-D	50,047	NA	NA
Amer. Univ., Washington, DC 20016-8001	1893	$56,543	$16,520	2-D	13,885	1,588	79.0
AmeriTech Coll., Draper, UT 84020-6545	NA	$12,999	NA	3-M	1,309	NA	NA
Amherst Coll., Amherst, MA 01002-5000.	1821	$67,280	$17,560	1-B	1,898	310	92.0
Anderson Univ., Anderson, IN 46012.	1917	$35,640	$12,250	2-D	1,290	186	60.0
Anderson Univ., Anderson, SC 29621	1911	$33,570	$12,030	2-D	4,121	414	69.9
Andrews Univ., Berrien Springs, MI 49104.	1874	$33,710	$10,050	2-D	2,858	323	71.0
Angelo State Univ., San Angelo, TX 76909	1928	$9,443 (A)	$11,800	5-D	10,599	425	41.0
Anna Maria Coll., Paxton, MA 01612	1946	$43,064	$16,240	2-M	1,448	40	42.0
Antelope Valley Coll., Lancaster, CA 93536-5426	1929	$1,150 (A)	NA	9-B	11,105	538	NA
Appalachian State Univ., Boone, NC 28608.	1899	$11,289 (A)	$12,258	5-D	20,436	1,428	75.2
Aquinas Coll., Grand Rapids, MI 49506.	1886	NA	NA	2-M	1,364	180	60.6
Arapahoe Comm. Coll., Littleton, CO 80160-9002.	1965	$5,294 (A)	$12,411	5-B	12,636	507	NA
Arcadia Univ., Glenside, PA 19038-3295.	1853	$48,290	$14,090	2-D	3,026	385	64.0
Arizona State Univ. at the Tempe campus, Tempe, AZ 85287	1885	$13,161 (A)	$14,718	14-D	80,065	4,581	68.6
Arkansas State Univ., State University, AR 72467.	1909	$7,456 (A)	$10,100	5-D	12,142	681	51.8
Arkansas Tech. Univ., Russellville, AR 72801	1909	$8,507 (A)	$9,672	5-D	9,445	517	51.1
Art Ctr. Coll. of Design, Pasadena, CA 91103	1930	$49,942	$14,338	1-M	2,319	NA	76.0
Asbury Univ., Wilmore, KY 40390-1198	1890	$33,640	$9,616	2-M	1,813	186	69.5
Ashford Univ., San Diego, CA 92123	1918	$14,278	NA	3-D	25,425	748	20.0
Ashland Univ., Ashland, OH 44805-3702.	1878	$28,910	$12,510	2-D	7,965	483	62.0
Aspen Univ., Denver, CO 80246-1930.	1987	$5,170	NA	1-D	6,399	NA	NA
Assumption Coll., Worcester, MA 01609-1296.	1904	NA	NA	2-M	2,060	211	71.4
Athens State Univ., Athens, AL 35611	1822	$9,540 (A)	$11,313	5-M	2,894	189	NA
Atlantic Univ. Coll., Guaynabo, PR 00970	1983	$5,440	NA	1-M	1,489	NA	NA
Auburn Univ., Auburn University, AL 36849.	1856	$12,176 (A)	$14,998	5-D	31,764	1,725	80.6
Auburn Univ. at Montgomery, Montgomery, AL 36124-4023.	1967	$11,680 (A)	$10,296	14-D	5,112	332	35.8
Augsburg Coll., Minneapolis, MN 55454-1351.	1869	$43,942	$12,483	2-D	3,088	306	56.0
Augusta Univ., Augusta, GA 30912	1828	$8,122 (A)	$9,672	5-D	7,938	NA	26.4
Augustana Coll., Rock Island, IL 61201-2296	1860	$47,916	$11,782	2-M	2,354	261	77.6
Augustana Univ., Sioux Falls, SD 57197	1860	$39,190	$9,470	2-D	2,086	208	75.5
Aurora Univ., Aurora, IL 60506-4892	1893	$28,220	$13,240	13-D	5,918	548	59.6
Austin Comm. Coll. District, Austin, TX 78752-4390	1973	$2,550 (A)	NA	11-B	39,896	1,814	NA
Austin Peay State Univ., Clarksville, TN 37044	1927	$8,761 (A)	$11,190	5-D	9,326	673	42.0
Averett Univ., Danville, VA 24541-3692.	1859	$38,550	$12,340	2-M	1,317	204	46.0
Azusa Pacific Univ., Azusa, CA 91702-7000	1899	$43,600	$9,724	2-D	8,182	981	68.5
Babson Coll., Babson Park, MA 02457-0310.	1919	$56,032	$20,786	1-M	3,684	NA	94.0
Baker Coll., Flint, MI 48507	1911	$13,300	$6,600	1-D	4,969	832	15.9
Baldwin Wallace Univ., Berea, OH 44017-2088.	1845	$37,938	$13,180	13-M	3,220	417	65.2
Ball State Univ., Muncie, IN 47306.	1918	$10,694 (A)	$14,632	5-D	19,770	1,225	63.5

Name, address	Year founded	Tuition & fees	Room & board	Control, degree	Enroll- ment	Faculty	Grad. rate
Bard Coll., Annandale-on-Hudson, NY 12504	1860	NA	NA	1-D	2,272	274	71.1%
Barnard Coll., New York, NY 10027-6598 (3)	1889	NA	NA	1-B	3,043	NA	92.8
Barry Univ., Miami Shores, FL 33161-6695	1940	$32,500	$11,820	2-D	6,958	880	39.0
Barton Coll., Wilson, NC 27893-7000	1902	$35,600	$13,050	2-M	1,265	144	48.0
Baruch Coll. of the City Univ. of New York, New York, NY 10010-5585	1919	$7,570 (A)	$17,604	11-M	19,969	1,146	74.0
Bates Coll., Lewiston, ME 04240-6028	1855	$63,478	$17,904	1-B	1,790	192	92.6
Bay Path Univ., Longmeadow, MA 01106-2292 (6)	1897	$37,227	$13,316	1-D	1,795	NA	NA
Baylor Univ., Waco, TX 76798	1845	$54,844	$14,378	2-D	20,709	1,526	81.0
Belhaven Univ., Jackson, MS 39202-1789	1883	$29,195	$9,400	2-D	3,627	497	46.0
Bellarmine Univ., Louisville, KY 40205	1950	$46,780	$9,440	2-D	3,293	395	64.0
Bellevue Coll., Bellevue, WA 98007-6484	1966	NA	NA	5-B	10,617	746	NA
Bellevue Univ., Bellevue, NE 68005-3098	1965	$8,310	$10,683	1-D	9,665	NA	37.0
Bellingham Tech. Coll., Bellingham, WA 98225	1957	$4,004 (A)	NA	5-B	1,848	189	NA
Belmont Abbey Coll., Belmont, NC 28012-1802	1876	$19,500	$12,056	2-M	1,501	170	47.0
Belmont Univ., Nashville, TN 37212	1951	$41,250	$13,670	2-D	8,902	931	72.5
Bemidji State Univ., Bemidji, MN 56601-2699	1919	$9,806 (A)	$9,160	5-M	4,577	246	45.0
Benedict Coll., Columbia, SC 29204	1870	$17,938	$7,262	2-D	1,724	NA	NA
Benedictine Coll., Atchison, KS 66002-1499	1859	NA	NA	2-M	2,365	189	67.8
Benedictine Univ., Lisle, IL 60532	1887	NA	NA	2-D	3,123	299	53.0
Bentley Univ., Waltham, MA 02452-4705	1917	$58,150	$19,200	1-D	5,165	512	88.0
Berea Coll., Berea, KY 40404	1855	NA	NA	1-B	1,433	196	61.9
Berkeley Coll.–New York City campus, New York, NY 10017	1936	$28,600	NA	3-M	1,882	142	35.0
Berkeley Coll.–Woodland Park campus, Woodland Park, NJ 07424	1931	$28,600	NA	3-M	2,078	240	43.0
Berklee Coll. of Mus, Boston, MA 02215-3693	1945	$50,270	$19,440	1-M	8,282	1,260	68.0
Berry Coll., Mount Berry, GA 30149	1902	$40,366	$14,230	2-M	2,360	235	65.0
Beth Medrash Govoha, Lakewood, NJ 08701-2797 (1)	1943	$23,656	NA	2-M	5,788	NA	NA
Bethel Coll., Mishawaka, IN 46545-5591	1947	$33,320	$10,560	2-M	1,292	174	57.0
Bethel Univ., McKenzie, TN 38201	1842	$13,981	$9,368	2-M	3,457	469	75.1
Bethel Univ., St. Paul, MN 55112-6999	1871	$42,930	$12,090	2-D	3,945	445	74.7
Bethune-Cookman Univ., Daytona Beach, FL 32114-3099	1904	$14,794	$10,396	2-M	2,727	203	35.0
Big Bend Comm. Coll., Moses Lake, WA 98837-3299	1962	NA	NA	5-B	3,518	96	NA
Binghamton Univ., State Univ. of New York, Binghamton, NY 13902-6000	1946	$10,363 (A)	$18,214	5-D	18,055	1,088	84.0
Biola Univ., La Mirada, CA 90639-0001	1908	$44,382	$10,522	2-D	5,387	482	71.0
Bismarck State Coll., Bismarck, ND 58506-5587	1939	$5,195 (A)	$7,830	5-B	3,771	377	NA
Black Hills State Univ., Spearfish, SD 57799	1883	$9,911 (A)	$7,302	5-M	3,425	NA	42.0
Bloomfield Coll., Bloomfield, NJ 07003-9981	1868	$30,680	$12,900	2-M	1,300	191	37.6
Bloomsburg Univ. of Pennsylvania, Bloomsburg, PA 17815-1301	1839	$11,016 (A)	$10,972	5-D	7,438	372	56.3
Bluefield State Coll., Bluefield, WV 24701-2198	1895	$9,700 (A)	$10,200	5-B	1,243	NA	34.8
Bob Jones Univ., Greenville, SC 29614	1927	$21,890	$9,350	2-D	3,029	NA	63.0
Boise State Univ., Boise, ID 83725-0399	1932	$8,782 (A)	$13,840	5-D	26,162	NA	59.2
Boston Coll., Chestnut Hill, MA 02467-3800	1863	$68,330	$16,120	2-D	14,734	1,475	90.8
Boston Univ., Boston, MA 02215	1839	$65,168	$18,110	1-D	36,714	2,742	89.0
Bowdoin Coll., Brunswick, ME 04011	1794	NA	NA	1-B	1,915	224	94.0
Bowie State Univ., Bowie, MD 20715-9465	1865	$8,999 (A)	$13,239	5-D	6,308	571	41.9
Bowling Green State Univ., Bowling Green, OH 43403	1910	$13,549 (A)	$10,974	5-D	17,645	1,103	60.0
Bowling Green State Univ.–Firelands Coll., Huron, OH 44839-9791	1968	$5,776 (A)	NA	5-B	1,970	102	NA
Bradley Univ., Peoria, IL 61625-0002	1897	$39,680	$12,196	1-D	5,552	577	76.0
Brandeis Univ., Waltham, MA 02454-9110	1948	$62,322	$17,092	1-D	5,585	582	87.0
Brazosport Coll., Lake Jackson, TX 77566-3199	1968	$2,399 (A)	NA	11-B	3,893	NA	NA
Brenau Univ., Gainesville, GA 30501 (4)	1878	$33,275	$12,600	1-D	2,704	258	46.1
Bridgewater Coll., Bridgewater, VA 22812-1599	1880	$41,350	$14,370	1-M	1,421	141	58.0
Bridgewater State Univ., Bridgewater, MA 02325	1840	$10,928 (S)	$14,162	5-M	9,604	736	56.1
Brigham Young Univ., Provo, UT 84602-1001	1875	$6,496	$8,560	2-D	34,454	1,891	79.0
Brigham Young Univ.–Hawaii, Laie, HI 96762-1294	1955	$6,068	$8,034	2-B	3,180	NA	52.0
Brigham Young Univ.–Idaho, Rexburg, ID 83460	1888	$4,536	$4,676	2-B	44,481	NA	44.0
Brookline Coll., Phoenix, AZ 85021	1979	NA	NA	3-M	1,511	43	NA
Brooklyn Coll. of the City Univ. of New York, Brooklyn, NY 11210-2889	1930	$7,570 (A)	$17,604	11-M	15,938	1,298	56.1
Broward Coll., Fort Lauderdale, FL 33301-2298	1960	$2,830 (A)	NA	5-B	33,243	NA	NA
Brown Univ., Providence, RI 02912	1764	$68,230	$16,598	1-D	10,696	1,032	96.0
Bryan Coll., Dayton, TN 37321	1930	$18,900	$8,550	1-M	1,587	64	57.9
Bryant & Stratton Coll.–Orchard Park, Orchard Park, NY 14127	1989	NA	NA	1-B	1,206	75	NA
Bryant & Stratton Coll.–Virginia Beach, Virginia Beach, VA 23462	1952	$17,308	NA	1-B	1,515	60	NA
Bryant & Stratton Coll.–Wauwatosa, Wauwatosa, WI 53226	NA	$19,520	NA	1-B	1,453	NA	NA
Bryant Univ., Smithfield, RI 02917	1863	$51,169	$17,258	1-M	3,483	279	82.5
Bryn Mawr Coll., Bryn Mawr, PA 19010-2899 (6)	1885	$58,940	$18,050	1-D	1,780	195	87.0
Bucknell Univ., Lewisburg, PA 17837	1846	$64,772	$16,118	1-M	3,787	430	86.5
Buena Vista Univ., Storm Lake, IA 50588	1891	$40,190	$10,896	2-M	1,304	91	57.9
Buffalo State Coll., State Univ. of New York, Buffalo, NY 14222-1095	1867	$8,486 (A)	$14,942	5-M	6,445	612	42.2
Butler Univ., Indianapolis, IN 46208-3485	1855	$45,980	$15,350	1-D	5,525	592	80.8
Cabrini Univ., Radnor, PA 19087	1957	$34,645	$13,225	2-D	1,760	213	52.3
Caldwell Univ., Caldwell, NJ 07006-6195	1939	$38,050	$13,399	2-D	2,092	NA	59.0
California Baptist Univ., Riverside, CA 92504-3206	1950	$38,368	$15,150	2-D	11,384	919	63.0
California Coll. of the Arts, San Francisco, CA 94107	1907	$52,312	$19,117	1-M	1,239	485	58.0
California Inst. of Integral Studies, San Francisco, CA 94103	1968	$22,334	NA	1-D	2,145	262	NA
California Inst. of Tech., Pasadena, CA 91125-0001	1891	$63,255	$19,503	1-D	2,401	362	94.0
California Inst. of the Arts, Valencia, CA 91355-2340	1961	$53,466	$12,135	1-D	1,520	400	61.4
California Lutheran Univ., Thousand Oaks, CA 91360-2787	1959	$50,680	$16,210	2-D	3,615	433	74.0
California Polytechnic State Univ., San Luis Obispo, San Luis Obispo, CA 93407	1901	$12,204 (A)	$18,042	5-M	21,778	1,487	87.0
California State Polytechnic Univ., Pomona, Pomona, CA 91768-2557	1938	$7,438 (A)	$16,682	5-D	27,173	1,597	66.0
California State Univ. Channel Islands, Camarillo, CA 93012	2002	$6,802 (A)	$14,200	5-D	6,947	NA	NA
California State Univ., Bakersfield, Bakersfield, CA 93311	1965	$7,708 (A)	$14,430	5-D	9,613	639	49.5

Name, address	Year founded	Tuition & fees	Room & board	Control, degree	Enroll-ment	Faculty	Grad. rate
California State Univ., Chico, Chico, CA 95929-0722	1887	$10,094 (A)	$12,489	5-M	13,840	NA	64.0%
California State Univ., Dominguez Hills, Carson, CA 90747-0001.	1960	$8,376 (A)	$16,200	5-M	15,530	1,013	48.3
California State Univ., East Bay, Hayward, CA 94542-3000	1957	$6,984 (A)	$17,012	5-D	13,141	882	42.2
California State Univ., Fresno, Fresno, CA 93740-8027	1911	$6,973 (A)	$11,634	5-D	24,139	1,377	NA
California State Univ., Fullerton, Fullerton, CA 92831-3599.	1957	$7,074 (A)	$18,464	5-D	40,386	2,052	69.3
California State Univ., Long Beach, Long Beach, CA 90840	1949	$6,988 (A)	$15,612	5-D	39,435	2,454	77.3
California State Univ., Los Angeles, Los Angeles, CA 90032-8530.	1947	$7,884 (A)	$18,658	5-D	26,029	1,633	49.5
California State Univ., Monterey Bay, Seaside, CA 93955-8001 . . .	1994	$5,742 (A)	$16,413	5-M	7,504	517	60.0
California State Univ., Northridge, Northridge, CA 91330	1958	$7,090 (A)	NA	5-D	39,693	1,972	54.2
California State Univ., Sacramento, Sacramento, CA 95819	1947	$7,602 (A)	$13,904	5-D	31,549	1,795	55.6
California State Univ., San Bernardino, San Bernardino, CA 92407	1965	$7,695 (A)	$13,500	5-D	19,467	1,123	54.0
California State Univ., San Marcos, San Marcos, CA 92096-0001.	1990	$7,734 (A)	$14,152	5-M	13,469	854	56.4
California State Univ., Stanislaus, Turlock, CA 95382	1957	$7,818 (A)	$11,234	5-D	10,154	736	55.0
Calvin Coll., Grand Rapids, MI 49546-4388	1876	$38,620	$11,150	2-M	3,257	NA	77.1
Cambridge Coll., Boston, MA 02129	1971	$14,338	$11,000	1-D	2,356	NA	NA
Cameron Univ., Lawton, OK 73505-6377.	1908	NA	NA	5-M	3,418	216	34.0
Campbell Univ., Buies Creek, NC 27506	1887	$39,630	$15,200	2-D	5,272	500	55.7
Campbellsville Univ., Campbellsville, KY 42718-2799.	1906	$26,990	$8,610	2-D	11,521	593	37.3
Canisius Coll., Buffalo, NY 14208-1098.	1870	$32,720	$13,900	2-M	2,492	303	66.0
Capella Univ., Minneapolis, MN 55402	1993	$14,990	$6,870	3-D	11,781	NA	NA
Capital Univ., Columbus, OH 43209-2394	1830	$41,788	$13,446	13-D	2,617	423	61.1
Carleton Coll., Northfield, MN 55057-4001.	1866	$65,457	$16,710	1-B	2,034	300	91.0
Carlow Univ., Pittsburgh, PA 15213-3165 (4).	1929	NA	NA	2-D	1,985	257	52.3
Carnegie Mellon Univ., Pittsburgh, PA 15213-3891	1900	$63,274	$17,468	1-D	16,779	1,237	91.5
Carroll Coll., Helena, MT 59625-0002	1909	$39,028	$10,782	2-B	1,330	145	69.0
Carroll Univ., Waukesha, WI 53186-5593	1846	$37,230	$13,340	2-D	3,299	377	68.0
Carson-Newman Univ., Jefferson City, TN 37760	1851	$34,700	$11,950	13-D	2,586	231	55.5
Carthage Coll., Kenosha, WI 53140.	1847	$36,500	$12,950	2-M	2,667	285	65.0
Cascadia Coll., Bothell, WA 98011.	1994	$3,994 (A)	$16,512	5-B	2,597	129	NA
Case Western Reserve Univ., Cleveland, OH 44106.	1826	$65,351	$18,202	1-D	12,201	991	85.5
Castleton Univ., Castleton, VT 05735	1787	$13,078 (A)	$12,042	5-M	2,210	187	NA
Cecil Coll., North East, MD 21901-1999.	1968	$4,770 (A)	NA	8-B	2,090	160	NA
Cedar Crest Coll., Allentown, PA 18104-6196 (4)	1867	$43,643	$12,722	2-D	1,440	200	73.6
Cedarville Univ., Cedarville, OH 45314	1887	$36,078	$9,094	2-D	4,960	362	75.0
Central Connecticut State Univ., New Britain, CT 06050-4010	1849	$12,460 (A)	$12,710	5-D	9,468	830	53.0
Central Michigan Univ., Mount Pleasant, MI 48859	1892	$14,190 (A)	$11,248	5-D	14,594	940	61.7
Central State Univ., Wilberforce, OH 45384.	1887	$7,596 (A)	$10,900	5-M	5,434	341	25.0
Central Washington Univ., Ellensburg, WA 98926.	1891	$8,339 (A)	$16,314	5-M	9,257	627	53.6
Centre Coll., Danville, KY 40422-1394.	1819	$48,070	$12,300	2-B	1,411	NA	NA
Chadron State Coll., Chadron, NE 69337	1911	$7,178 (A)	$8,534	5-M	2,649	NA	NA
Chamberlain Coll. of Nurs., Addison, IL 60101	1889	$22,172	NA	3-D	23,964	1,055	NA
Chamberlain Coll. of Nurs., Atlanta, GA 30342	NA	$19,952	NA	3-B	1,330	NA	NA
Chamberlain Coll. of Nurs., Houston, TX 77041	NA	$20,156	NA	3-B	1,558	NA	NA
Chaminade Univ. of Honolulu, Honolulu, HI 96816-1578.	1955	$29,970	$16,670	2-D	1,892	126	66.0
Champlain Coll., Burlington, VT 05402-0670	1878	$45,550	$16,900	1-M	2,343	234	65.0
Chapman Univ., Orange, CA 92866.	1861	$62,784	$19,954	13-D	10,014	1,280	83.6
Charleston Southern Univ., Charleston, SC 29423-8087.	1964	$29,615	$14,536	2-D	3,551	303	35.0
Charter Coll., Anchorage, AK 99508	1985	$17,208	NA	3-B	2,120	NA	NA
Charter Oak State Coll., New Britain, CT 06053-2142.	1973	$8,254 (A)	NA	5-M	1,538	182	NA
Chatham Univ., Pittsburgh, PA 15232-2826 (4)	1869	$43,810	$14,327	1-D	2,387	353	68.0
Chestnut Hill Coll., Philadelphia, PA 19118-2693	1924	$39,410	$11,000	2-D	1,548	167	53.0
Chicago State Univ., Chicago, IL 60628.	1867	$9,690 (A)	NA	5-D	2,366	219	21.0
Chipola Coll., Marianna, FL 32446-3065	1947	$3,120 (A)	$4,560	5-B	1,943	NA	NA
Christian Brothers Univ., Memphis, TN 38104-5581	1871	NA	NA	1-M	1,934	247	60.0
Christopher Newport Univ., Newport News, VA 23606-3072.	1960	NA	NA	5-M	4,559	460	76.0
City Coll. of the City Univ. of New York, New York, NY 10031-9198.	1847	$7,340 (A)	$13,536	11-D	14,016	1,356	57.8
Claflin Univ., Orangeburg, SC 29115.	1869	$17,046	$9,480	2-M	1,886	NA	44.0
Claremont McKenna Coll., Claremont, CA 91711	1946	$64,150	$19,650	1-M	1,389	196	91.3
Clark Atlanta Univ., Atlanta, GA 30314	1988	$26,446	$13,446	2-D	4,000	315	46.0
Clark Coll., Vancouver, WA 98663-3598	1933	$5,327 (A)	$17,868	5-B	7,665	NA	NA
Clark Univ., Worcester, MA 01610-1477	1887	$55,187	$10,814	13-D	3,801	341	76.0
Clayton State Univ., Morrow, GA 30260-0285	1969	$5,568 (A)	$10,712	5-M	7,052	348	31.0
Clemson Univ., Clemson, SC 29634	1889	$15,120 (A)	$12,350	5-D	27,341	1,828	85.0
Clover Park Tech. Coll., Lakewood, WA 98499	1942	$5,906 (A)	NA	5-B	3,591	NA	NA
Coastal Carolina Univ., Conway, SC 29528-6054	1954	$11,640 (A)	$11,418	5-D	10,337	790	48.0
Coe Coll., Cedar Rapids, IA 52402-5092.	1851	$52,576	$11,336	2-B	1,264	149	65.0
Colby Coll., Waterville, ME 04901-8840.	1813	$66,600	$17,120	1-B	2,299	240	88.0
Colgate Univ., Hamilton, NY 13346-1386.	1819	$67,024	$16,790	1-M	3,141	380	91.3
Coll. for Creative Stds, Detroit, MI 48202-4034	1906	$51,365	$11,040	1-M	1,517	296	64.0
Coll. of Central Florida, Ocala, FL 34474.	1957	$2,890 (A)	$8,046	11-B	5,492	273	NA
Coll. of Charleston, Charleston, SC 29424-0001	1770	$12,978 (A)	$14,032	5-M	10,885	893	64.7
Coll. of Coastal Georgia, Brunswick, GA 31520.	1961	$4,524 (A)	$13,086	5-B	3,232	143	23.0
Coll. of Mount St. Vincent, Riverdale, NY 10471-1093.	1911	$40,980	$12,000	1-M	2,690	302	63.0
Coll. of St. Benedict, Saint Joseph, MN 56374 (3)	1913	$53,884	$12,160	2-D	1,470	163	78.3
Coll. of Southern Idaho, Twin Falls, ID 83303-1238.	1964	$4,200 (A)	NA	11-B	8,096	354	NA
Coll. of Southern Nevada, Las Vegas, NV 89146	1971	$3,848 (A)	NA	5-B	29,965	NA	NA
Coll. of Staten Island of the City Univ. of New York, Staten Island, NY 10314-6600.	1976	$7,570 (A)	$17,604	11-D	10,258	966	53.5
Coll. of the Holy Cross, Worcester, MA 01610-2395	1843	$60,850	$17,750	2-B	3,233	350	91.0
Coll. of the Ozarks, Point Lookout, MO 65726.	1906	$21,290	$8,500	2-B	1,487	129	63.0
Collin Cty. Comm. Coll. District, McKinney, TX 75069.	1985	$1,860 (A)	$15,210	11-B	35,085	1,737	NA
Colorado Christian Univ., Lakewood, CO 80226	1914	$39,266	$12,362	2-B	1,565	153	62.3
Colorado Mesa Univ., Grand Junction, CO 81501-3122	1925	$10,391 (A)	$16,000	5-D	8,905	579	45.2
Colorado Mountain Coll., Glenwood Springs, CO 81601	1965	$3,100 (A)	$12,120	9-B	5,184	495	NA
Colorado Sch. of Mines, Golden, CO 80401-1887.	1874	$20,040 (A)	$16,110	5-D	7,408	586	81.0
Colorado State Univ., Fort Collins, CO 80523	1870	$12,559 (A)	$13,360	5-D	33,361	1,961	66.9

Name, address	Year founded	Tuition & fees	Room & board	Control, degree	Enrollment	Faculty	Grad. rate
Colorado State Univ.–Global campus, Greenwood Village, CO 80111	NA	$8,400 (A)	NA	5-M	10,844	531	NA
Colorado State Univ.–Pueblo, Pueblo, CO 81001-4901	1933	$7,176 (A)	$11,748	5-D	6,617	341	35.0%
Colorado Tech. Univ. Colorado Springs, Colorado Springs, CO 80907	1965	$12,581	NA	3-D	24,759	NA	NA
Columbia Basin Coll., Pasco, WA 99301-3397	1955	$5,959 (A)	$9,980	5-B	6,745	NA	NA
Columbia Coll. Chicago, Chicago, IL 60605-1996	1890	$32,214	$9,000	1-M	6,646	815	47.2
Columbia Coll., Columbia, SC 29203-5998 (4)	1854	NA	NA	2-M	1,514	179	55.0
Columbia Intl. Univ., Columbia, SC 29203	1923	$27,900	$11,950	2-D	2,481	203	68.3
Columbia Southern Univ., Orange Beach, AL 36561	1993	$5,663	NA	3-D	15,948	586	NA
Columbia Univ., New York, NY 10027	1754	$68,400	$16,156	1-D	6,668	3,206	95.0
Columbia Univ., Sch. of Gen. Studies, New York, NY 10027-6939	1754	$62,466	$15,450	1-B	2,068	NA	NA
Columbus State Univ., Columbus, GA 31907-5645	1958	$6,844 (A)	$11,262	5-D	7,925	512	44.0
Concord Univ., Athens, WV 24712-1000	1872	NA	NA	5-M	1,748	126	40.0
Concordia Univ., Moorhead, MN 56562	1891	$28,916	$9,800	2-D	2,042	210	72.0
Concordia Univ. Chicago, River Forest, IL 60305-1499	1864	$36,258	$11,140	2-D	6,029	463	41.8
Concordia Univ. Irvine, Irvine, CA 92612-3299	1972	$41,390	$13,940	2-D	3,744	471	63.1
Concordia Univ. Texas, Austin, TX 78726	1926	$34,500	$12,270	2-M	1,740	302	35.0
Concordia Univ. Wisconsin, Mequon, WI 53097-2402	1881	$33,262	$12,160	2-D	5,192	313	60.7
Concordia Univ., Nebraska, Seward, NE 68434	1894	$36,310	$9,600	2-M	2,159	253	67.0
Concordia Univ., St. Paul, St. Paul, MN 55104-5494	1893	$25,000	$10,800	2-D	5,502	489	51.0
Connecticut Coll., New London, CT 06320	1911	NA	NA	1-B	1,948	243	83.7
Converse Coll., Spartanburg, SC 29302 (6)	1889	$19,850	$11,948	1-D	1,319	NA	55.0
Coppin State Univ., Baltimore, MD 21216-3698	1900	$6,809 (A)	$11,141	5-M	3,800	312	15.0
Cornell Univ., Ithaca, NY 14853	1865	$66,014	$18,554	1-D	25,898	2,267	95.3
Cornerstone Univ., Grand Rapids, MI 49525-5897	1941	$28,300	$11,360	2-D	1,781	167	60.0
Creighton Univ., Omaha, NE 68178-0001	1878	$47,000	$12,790	2-D	8,397	884	78.0
Cumberland Univ., Lebanon, TN 37087	1842	$26,400	$9,400	1-M	1,481	NA	NA
Curry Coll., Milton, MA 02186-9984	1879	NA	NA	1-M	2,242	289	55.0
Cypress Coll., Cypress, CA 90630-5897	1966	$1,146 (A)	NA	9-B	14,402	NA	NA
Daemen Coll., Amherst, NY 14226-3592	1947	NA	NA	1-D	2,665	274	55.0
Dakota State Univ., Madison, SD 57042-1799	1881	$7,616 (A)	$7,464	5-D	3,241	133	46.0
Dallas Baptist Univ., Dallas, TX 75211-9299	1898	$38,140	$10,215	2-D	4,348	478	58.0
Dalton State Coll., Dalton, GA 30720	1963	$3,924 (A)	$7,104	5-B	4,794	NA	NA
Dartmouth Coll., Hanover, NH 03755	1769	$65,511	$18,759	1-D	6,744	789	95.0
Davenport Univ., Grand Rapids, MI 49512	1866	$23,069	$12,704	1-M	6,429	610	56.0
Davidson Coll., Davidson, NC 28035	1837	$59,510	$16,400	2-B	1,927	219	92.0
Daytona State Coll., Daytona Beach, FL 32114	1957	$3,106 (A)	NA	5-B	12,728	746	NA
Delaware State Univ., Dover, DE 19901-2277	1891	$8,358 (A)	$11,888	5-D	4,353	NA	NA
Delaware Valley Univ., Doylestown, PA 18901-2697	1896	$41,870	$14,750	1-D	2,178	237	54.1
Delta State Univ., Cleveland, MS 38733-0001	1924	NA	NA	5-D	2,558	229	46.0
Denison Univ., Granville, OH 43023	1831	$61,426	$14,400	1-B	2,272	342	81.6
DePaul Univ., Chicago, IL 60604-2287	1898	$42,840	$16,068	2-D	20,917	1,763	69.4
DePauw Univ., Greencastle, IN 46135	1837	$57,070	$14,850	2-B	1,752	228	79.0
DeSales Univ., Center Valley, PA 18034-9568	1964	$44,800	$13,800	2-D	3,016	402	68.0
Dickinson Coll., Carlisle, PA 17013-2896	1773	$63,450	$16,500	1-M	2,137	253	84.0
Dickinson State Univ., Dickinson, ND 58601-4896	1918	$9,118 (A)	$8,250	5-M	1,473	137	44.4
Dillard Univ., New Orleans, LA 70122-3097	1869	$22,594	$11,786	2-B	1,224	134	48.0
Dixie State Univ., St. George, UT 84770-3876	1911	$6,075 (A)	$7,900	5-M	12,266	545	25.0
Dominican Coll., Orangeburg, NY 10962-1210	1952	$33,060	$14,790	1-D	1,407	194	53.0
Dominican Univ. of California, San Rafael, CA 94901-2298	1890	$50,646	$15,986	13-D	1,889	276	78.9
Dominican Univ., River Forest, IL 60305-1099	1901	$37,694	$11,300	2-D	3,196	406	58.4
Dordt Coll., Sioux Center, IA 51250-1697	1955	$34,600	$10,990	2-M	1,737	NA	75.0
Drake Univ., Des Moines, IA 50311-4516	1881	$50,114	$11,858	1-D	4,685	453	78.0
Drew Univ., Madison, NJ 07940-1493	1867	$45,060	$16,404	2-D	2,214	258	74.0
Drexel Univ., Philadelphia, PA 19104-2875	1891	$60,698	$17,550	1-D	23,170	1,999	78.2
Drury Univ., Springfield, MO 65802	1873	$35,335	$10,200	1-M	1,595	112	60.3
Duke Univ., Durham, NC 27708	1838	$65,992	$19,066	2-D	17,620	1,606	96.0
Dunwoody Coll. of Tech., Minneapolis, MN 55403 (2)	1914	$25,878	$14,659	1-B	1,359	146	42.0
Duquesne Univ., Pittsburgh, PA 15282-0001	1878	$47,146	$15,620	2-D	8,107	912	76.0
D'Youville Coll., Buffalo, NY 14201-1084	1908	$33,560	$9,500	1-D	2,523	280	64.0
East Carolina Univ., Greenville, NC 27858-4353	1907	$7,325 (A)	$10,180	5-D	27,151	1,475	65.1
East Central Univ., Ada, OK 74820	1909	$7,052 (A)	$8,858	5-M	4,573	190	31.0
East Georgia State Coll., Swainsboro, GA 30401-2699	1973	$3,136 (A)	$9,811	5-B	3,001	125	NA
East Stroudsburg Univ. of Pennsylvania, East Stroudsburg, PA 18301-2999	1893	$10,108 (A)	$10,490	5-D	5,152	296	48.6
East Tennessee State Univ., Johnson City, TN 37614	1911	$9,950 (A)	$10,270	5-D	13,323	1,121	51.0
East Texas Baptist Univ., Marshall, TX 75670-1498	1912	NA	NA	2-M	1,771	163	42.0
Eastern Connecticut State Univ., Willimantic, CT 06226-2295	1889	$13,292 (A)	$15,608	5-M	4,319	448	57.0
Eastern Florida State Coll., Cocoa, FL 32922-6597	1960	$2,791 (A)	$9,294	5-B	13,937	NA	NA
Eastern Illinois Univ., Charleston, IL 61920	1895	$13,101 (A)	$10,812	5-M	8,857	522	55.0
Eastern Kentucky Univ., Richmond, KY 40475-3102	1906	$9,752 (A)	$9,410	5-D	14,565	1,008	52.0
Eastern Mennonite Univ., Harrisonburg, VA 22802-2462	1917	NA	$12,620	2-D	1,337	154	63.0
Eastern Michigan Univ., Ypsilanti, MI 48197	1849	$16,750 (A)	$12,068	5-D	14,048	1,069	45.0
Eastern New Mexico Univ., Portales, NM 88130	1934	$6,738 (A)	$8,170	5-M	5,106	239	37.0
Eastern Oregon Univ., La Grande, OR 97850-2899	1929	NA	NA	5-M	2,825	107	38.0
Eastern Univ., St. Davids, PA 19087-3696	1925	$37,420	$13,168	2-D	5,769	485	62.7
Eastern Washington Univ., Cheney, WA 99004-2431	1882	$9,381 (A)	$14,880	5-D	10,958	614	49.7
Eckerd Coll., St. Petersburg, FL 33711	1958	$48,900	$13,854	2-B	1,993	191	67.0
ECPI Univ., Virginia Beach, VA 23462	1966	$18,384	NA	3-M	11,740	1,108	55.0
Edgewood Coll., Madison, WI 53711-1997	1927	$33,550	$12,120	2-D	1,377	NA	NA
EDP Univ. of Puerto Rico, Hato Rey, PR 00918	1968	$6,900	$3,000	1-M	1,302	147	53.0
Elizabeth City State Univ., Elizabeth City, NC 27909-7806	1891	NA	NA	5-M	2,002	138	NA
Elizabethtown Coll., Elizabethtown, PA 17022-2298	1899	$36,842	$12,954	1-D	2,021	208	76.5
Elmhurst Coll., Elmhurst, IL 60126-3296	1871	$42,008	$11,858	2-D	3,731	441	68.4
Elms Coll., Chicopee, MA 01013-2839	1928	$42,060	$15,150	2-D	1,275	199	75.0
Elon Univ., Elon, NC 27244-2010	1889	$42,241	$13,886	1-D	7,123	600	83.3
Embry-Riddle Aeron Univ.–Daytona, Daytona Beach, FL 32114-3900	1926	$42,304	$13,670	1-D	7,945	NA	61.6
Embry-Riddle Aeron Univ.–Prescott, Prescott, AZ 86301-3720	1926	NA	NA	1-M	3,004	219	69.6
Emerson Coll., Boston, MA 02116-4624	1880	$55,392	$20,810	1-D	3,708	NA	NA

Name, address	Year founded	Tuition & fees	Room & board	Control, degree	Enrollment	Faculty	Grad. rate
Emmanuel Coll., Boston, MA 02115.	1919	$46,686	$17,500	2-M	2,012	203	66.0%
Emory & Henry Coll., Emory, VA 24327-0947	1836	$35,165	$13,600	2-D	1,230	175	54.0
Emory Univ., Atlanta, GA 30322-1100	1836	$60,774	$18,972	2-D	14,852	1,323	90.0
Emporia State Univ., Emporia, KS 66801-5415	1863	$8,827 (S)	$10,542	5-D	5,615	240	49.9
Endicott Coll., Beverly, MA 01915-2096.	1939	$39,212	$17,372	1-D	4,381	563	78.0
Evangel Univ., Springfield, MO 65802	1955	NA	NA	2-D	2,367	260	94.0
Everglades Univ., Boca Raton, FL 33431	1989	NA	NA	1-M	2,649	56	58.0
Excelsior Coll., Albany, NY 12203-5159.	1970	$16,740	$8,200	1-M	14,633	662	NA
Fairfield Univ., Fairfield, CT 06824	1942	$56,360	$17,500	2-D	6,019	688	84.0
Fairmont State Univ., Fairmont, WV 26554	1865	$7,892 (A)	$10,022	5-M	3,573	NA	36.0
Farmingdale State Coll., Farmingdale, NY 11735	1912	$8,556 (A)	$14,546	5-M	9,314	800	57.0
Fashion Inst. of Tech., New York, NY 10001-5992 (4).	1944	$8,090 (A)	$24,623	11-M	8,125	933	83.0
Faulkner Univ., Montgomery, AL 36109-3398	1942	$23,490	$7,900	2-D	3,350	NA	NA
Fayetteville State Univ., Fayetteville, NC 28301-4298	1867	$3,525 (A)	NA	5-D	6,787	362	44.0
Feather River Coll., Quincy, CA 95971-9124	1968	$1,461 (A)	$10,921	9-B	1,821	108	NA
Felician Univ., Lodi, NJ 07644-2117.	1942	$37,830	$14,190	1-D	2,205	230	52.0
Ferris State Univ., Big Rapids, MI 49307	1884	$13,704 (A)	$10,660	5-D	10,072	651	57.0
FIDM/Fashion Inst. of Design & Merchandising, Los Angeles campus, Los Angeles, CA 90015-1421	1969	$32,795	NA	3-M	1,764	251	74.0
Fisher Coll., Boston, MA 02116-1500.	1903	NA	NA	1-M	1,367	137	38.0
Fitchburg State Univ., Fitchburg, MA 01420-2697	1894	$11,160 (A)	$14,225	5-M	6,554	357	56.0
Flagler Coll., St. Augustine, FL 32085-1027.	1968	$26,710	$14,350	13-M	2,623	292	57.0
Florida Agr. & Mech. Univ., Tallahassee, FL 32307-3200	1887	$4,694 (A)	$11,644	5-D	9,000	715	54.6
Florida Atlantic Univ., Boca Raton, FL 33431-0991	1961	$6,099 (A)	$13,518	5-D	29,592	1,447	62.0
Florida Gateway Coll., Lake City, FL 32025	1962	$3,100 (A)	$5,400	5-B	2,912	188	NA
Florida Gulf Coast Univ., Fort Myers, FL 33965-6565	1991	$7,993 (A)	$10,914	5-D	16,022	873	58.0
Florida Inst. of Tech., Melbourne, FL 32901-6975	1958	$44,320	$12,340	1-D	8,358	476	66.7
Florida Intl. Univ., Miami, FL 33199	1965	$6,566 (A)	$11,600	5-D	55,687	2,430	68.0
Florida Memorial Univ., Miami-Dade, FL 33054	1879	$16,836	$7,486	2-M	1,750	NA	NA
Florida Natl Univ., Hialeah, FL 33012.	1982	$14,888	NA	3-M	2,717	169	43.0
Florida Southern Coll., Lakeland, FL 33801-5698	1883	$41,300	$12,340	2-D	3,386	348	67.7
Florida Southwestern State Coll., Fort Myers, FL 33919	1962	$3,772 (A)	$12,755	11-B	14,337	497	NA
Florida State Coll. at Jacksonville, Jacksonville, FL 32202-4030.	1963	$2,657 (A)	$8,496	5-B	22,344	1,014	NA
Florida State Univ., Tallahassee, FL 32306	1851	$7,493 (A)	$11,565	5-D	44,161	1,980	84.8
Fordham Univ., New York, NY 10458	1841	$61,992	$23,075	2-D	16,556	1,928	83.4
Fort Hays State Univ., Hays, KS 67601-4099	1902	$5,430 (A)	$8,414	5-D	15,033	760	46.0
Fort Lewis Coll., Durango, CO 81301-3999	1911	NA	NA	5-B	3,550	263	44.0
Fort Valley State Univ., Fort Valley, GA 31030	1895	$5,392 (A)	$10,018	5-M	2,776	118	28.0
Framingham State Univ., Framingham, MA 01701-9101	1839	NA	NA	5-M	4,495	307	51.0
Francis Marion Univ., Florence, SC 29502-0547	1970	$11,160 (A)	$8,898	5-D	4,045	332	39.0
Franciscan Univ. of Steubenville, Steubenville, OH 43952-1763 . .	1946	$31,080	$9,390	2-M	3,039	265	76.8
Franklin & Marshall Coll., Lancaster, PA 17604-3003	1787	$63,654	NA	1-B	1,990	246	86.0
Franklin Pierce Univ., Rindge, NH 03461-0060	1962	$43,155	$15,300	1-D	1,436	NA	NA
Franklin Univ., Columbus, OH 43215-5399	1902	$9,577	NA	1-M	4,008	814	13.0
Freed-Hardeman Univ., Henderson, TN 38340-2399	1869	$24,300	$7,950	2-D	2,320	193	64.7
Fresno Pacific Univ., Fresno, CA 93702-4709	1944	$34,188	$8,884	2-D	2,711	479	64.0
Friends Univ., Wichita, KS 67213.	1898	$31,812	$8,938	2-M	1,694	166	40.0
Front Range Comm. Coll., Westminster, CO 80031	1968	$4,293 (A)	$14,679	5-B	18,703	1,112	NA
Frostburg State Univ., Frostburg, MD 21532-1099	1898	$9,998 (A)	$11,352	5-D	4,449	333	47.0
Full Sail Univ., Winter Park, FL 32792-7437 (2).	1979	NA	NA	13-M	26,737	665	NA
Furman Univ., Greenville, SC 29613	1826	$58,312	$15,868	1-M	2,443	323	85.1
Galen Coll. of Nurs., Louisville, KY 40207	1989	$415/cr. hr.	NA	3-B	4,369	197	NA
Galen Coll. of Nurs., San Antonio, TX 78229.	1989	$415/cr. hr.	NA	3-B	3,732	186	NA
Galen Coll. of Nurs., St. Petersburg, FL 33716	1989	$415/cr. hr.	NA	3-B	2,374	132	NA
Gallaudet Univ., Washington, DC 20002-3625.	1864	$18,254	$14,580	1-D	1,451	272	44.0
Galveston Coll., Galveston, TX 77550	1967	$2,546 (A)	$7,880	11-B	2,026	139	NA
Gannon Univ., Erie, PA 16541-0001	1925	$36,676	$15,510	2-D	4,675	423	70.0
Gardner-Webb Univ., Boiling Springs, NC 28017	1905	$32,280	$10,770	2-D	3,884	300	44.0
Geneva Coll., Beaver Falls, PA 15010-3599	1848	$32,350	$10,980	2-M	1,234	220	69.0
George Fox Univ., Newberg, OR 97132-2697	1891	$40,940	$13,600	2-D	4,033	441	71.0
George Mason Univ., Fairfax, VA 22030	1972	$13,404 (A)	$13,120	5-D	39,049	3,032	71.0
Georgetown Coll., Georgetown, KY 40324-1696.	1829	$42,010	$11,386	2-M	1,548	146	46.1
Georgetown Univ., Washington, DC 20057	1789	$65,076	$19,352	2-D	20,984	1,991	96.0
Georgia Coll. & State Univ., Milledgeville, GA 31061	1889	$8,998 (A)	$11,774	5-D	6,315	436	62.0
Georgia Gwinnett Coll., Lawrenceville, GA 30043	2006	$5,262 (A)	$15,320	5-B	11,627	709	21.4
Georgia Highlands Coll., Rome, GA 30161	1970	$2,944 (A)	NA	5-B	6,168	NA	NA
Georgia Inst. of Tech., Atlanta, GA 30332-0001	1885	$11,764 (A)	$15,244	5-D	45,296	1,229	92.6
Georgia Military Coll., Milledgeville, GA 31061-3398	1879	$6,638 (A)	$3,750	14-B	7,014	109	NA
Georgia Southern Univ., Statesboro, GA 30458	1906	$6,998 (A)	$11,106	5-D	25,506	1,167	53.7
Georgia Southwestern State Univ., Americus, GA 31709-4693.	1906	$5,996 (S)	$8,978	5-M	3,076	165	36.0
Georgia State Univ., Atlanta, GA 30302-3083	1913	$10,268 (A)	$13,816	14-D	36,523	1,597	54.0
Georgian Court Univ., Lakewood, NJ 08701-2697.	1908	$37,110	$12,910	2-D	1,962	238	54.0
Gettysburg Coll., Gettysburg, PA 17325-1483.	1832	$64,230	$15,530	2-M	2,241	271	82.0
Glenville State Coll., Glenville, WV 26351-1200	1872	$8,906 (A)	$10,774	5-M	1,577	91	NA
Global Univ., Springfield, MO 65804	1948	NA	NA	2-D	4,551	NA	NA
Golden Gate Univ., San Francisco, CA 94105-2968	1901	NA	NA	1-D	2,685	489	NA
Gonzaga Univ., Spokane, WA 99258.	1887	$53,500	$13,794	2-D	7,295	NA	88.0
Goodwin Univ., East Hartford, CT 06118	1999	$21,188	$6,500	1-B	3,213	312	NA
Gordon Coll., Wenham, MA 01984-1899	1889	$27,000	$12,720	2-M	1,628	219	67.9
Gordon State Coll., Barnesville, GA 30204-1762.	1852	$3,789 (A)	$9,257	5-B	3,986	197	NA
Goucher Coll., Baltimore, MD 21204-2794.	1885	$51,250	$16,650	1-M	1,728	190	59.9
Governors State Univ., University Park, IL 60484	1969	$13,696 (A)	$11,624	5-D	4,427	699	17.2
Grace Coll., Winona Lake, IN 46590-1294.	1948	$25,044	$9,976	2-D	1,587	184	60.0
Graceland Univ., Lamoni, IA 50140	1895	$33,220	$10,540	2-D	1,244	123	45.0
Grambling State Univ., Grambling, LA 71245	1901	$7,683 (A)	$10,990	5-D	5,232	NA	NA
Grand Canyon Univ., Phoenix, AZ 85017-1097.	1949	$17,450	$11,162	2-D	63,752	NA	NA
Grand Valley State Univ., Allendale, MI 49401-9403.	1960	$13,952 (A)	$11,142	5-D	21,648	1,543	67.1
Grand View Univ., Des Moines, IA 50316-1599.	1896	$34,500	$11,032	2-M	1,830	186	52.0
Grantham Univ., Lenexa, KS 66219.	1951	$8,280	NA	3-M	5,445	NA	NA
Grayson Coll., Denison, TX 75020-8299	1964	$2,820 (A)	NA	11-B	5,014	240	NA
Green River Coll., Auburn, WA 98092-3699	1965	$4,332 (A)	NA	5-B	7,494	436	NA
Greenville Tech. Coll., Greenville, SC 29606-5616	1962	$6,710 (A)	NA	5-B	11,380	699	NA
Grinnell Coll., Grinnell, IA 50112-1690.	1846	$64,862	$15,878	1-B	1,759	223	88.0

Name, address	Year founded	Tuition & fees	Room & board	Control, degree	Enrollment	Faculty	Grad. rate
Grove City Coll., Grove City, PA 16127-2104	1876	$20,890	$11,770	2-M	2,316	222	81.0%
Guam Comm. Coll., Mangilao, GU 96913	1977	NA	NA	7-B	1,690	194	NA
Gulf Coast State Coll., Panama City, FL 32401-1058	1957	NA	NA	5-B	4,847	257	NA
Gurnick Acad. of Med. Arts, San Mateo, CA 94403	2004	NA	$15,076	3-B	2,462	NA	NA
Gustavus Adolphus Coll., St. Peter, MN 56082-1498	1862	$54,310	$11,290	2-B	2,088	199	77.8
Gwynedd Mercy Univ., Gwynedd Valley, PA 19437-0901	1948	$38,310	$13,370	2-D	2,521	463	67.1
Hamilton Coll., Clinton, NY 13323-1296	1812	$65,740	$16,690	1-B	2,075	265	92.4
Hamline Univ., St. Paul, MN 55104-1284	1854	$47,336	$11,214	2-D	3,113	251	65.0
Hampton Univ., Hampton, VA 23668	1868	$29,412	$13,636	1-D	3,316	170	57.0
Hardin-Simmons Univ., Abilene, TX 79698-0001	1891	$31,686	$10,393	2-D	2,128	206	55.0
Harding Univ., Searcy, AR 72149-0001	1924	$24,888	$8,580	2-D	4,805	447	69.5
Harris-Stowe State Univ., St. Louis, MO 63103-2136	1857	$5,868 (A)	$9,691	5-B	1,400	161	12.0
Harrisburg Univ. of Sci. & Tech., Harrisburg, PA 17101	2005	NA	NA	1-D	2,727	312	NA
Harvard Univ., Cambridge, MA 02138	1636	$59,076	$20,374	1-D	12,005	1,071	98.0
Haverford Coll., Haverford, PA 19041-1392	1833	$68,020	$18,520	1-B	1,421	185	91.0
Hawai'i Pacific Univ., Honolulu, HI 96813	1965	$33,020	$22,590	13-D	4,876	335	46.0
Henderson State Univ., Arkadelphia, AR 71999-0001	1890	$7,560 (A)	$9,558	5-M	2,626	257	34.0
Herzing Univ., Madison, WI 53718	1948	NA	$11,904	1-M	1,647	NA	NA
High Point Univ., High Point, NC 27268	1924	$41,916	$16,524	2-D	5,860	486	70.0
Hillsdale Coll., Hillsdale, MI 49242-1298	1844	$32,092	$13,180	1-D	1,678	271	86.8
Hiram Coll., Hiram, OH 44234	1850	$25,500	$10,600	1-M	1,354	104	53.0
Hobart & William Smith Colls., Geneva, NY 14456	1822	$61,600	$16,910	1-M	1,684	191	73.1
Hofstra Univ., Hempstead, NY 11549	1935	$55,450	$16,699	1-D	10,243	1,195	69.7
Holy Family Univ., Philadelphia, PA 19114	1954	$32,558	$17,170	2-D	3,081	NA	54.8
Hood Coll., Frederick, MD 21701-8575	1893	$45,870	$14,250	1-D	2,056	231	61.2
Hope Coll., Holland, MI 49422-9000	1866	$37,221	$11,900	2-B	3,251	347	81.4
Houston Baptist Univ., Houston, TX 77074-3298	1960	$37,950	$10,816	13-D	4,257	310	43.9
Howard Univ., Washington, DC 20059-0002	1867	$33,344	$16,474	1-D	12,065	1,188	64.0
Humboldt State Univ., Arcata, CA 95521-8299	1913	$7,864 (A)	$12,540	5-M	5,858	522	45.9
Hunter Coll. of the City Univ. of New York, New York, NY 10065-5085	1870	$7,380 (A)	$17,919	11-D	22,970	1,893	56.4
Huntington Univ., Huntington, IN 46750-1299	1897	$28,930	$9,500	2-D	1,364	185	68.6
Husson Univ., Bangor, ME 04401-2999	1898	NA	NA	1-D	3,088	251	60.0
Idaho State Univ., Pocatello, ID 83209	1901	$10,322 (A)	$6,960	5-D	12,157	761	33.0
Illinois Inst. of Tech., Chicago, IL 60616	1890	$51,763	$16,528	1-D	6,486	674	72.0
Illinois State Univ., Normal, IL 61790	1857	$15,479 (A)	$11,584	5-D	20,683	1,429	67.0
Illinois Wesleyan Univ., Bloomington, IL 61702-2900	1850	$55,704	$12,880	1-B	1,527	192	80.0
Immaculata Univ., Immaculata, PA 19345	1920	$28,550	$12,870	2-D	2,392	297	61.1
Indian River State Coll., Fort Pierce, FL 34981-5596	1959	$2,760 (A)	$4,460	5-B	15,236	NA	NA
Indiana State Univ., Terre Haute, IN 47809	1865	$9,712 (A)	$11,484	5-D	8,658	592	44.0
Indiana Tech., Fort Wayne, IN 46803-1297	1930	$29,560	$13,856	1-D	2,309	212	33.6
Indiana Univ. Bloomington, Bloomington, IN 47405-7000	1820	$11,790 (A)	$12,228	5-D	47,005	2,568	81.1
Indiana Univ. East, Richmond, IN 47374-1289	1971	$8,159 (A)	$10,244	5-M	3,039	257	42.5
Indiana Univ. Kokomo, Kokomo, IN 46902-9003	1945	$8,685 (A)	$10,244	5-M	2,846	235	41.2
Indiana Univ. Northwest, Gary, IN 46408-1197	1959	$8,159 (A)	NA	5-M	3,198	321	38.0
Indiana Univ. of Pennsylvania, Indiana, PA 15705	1875	$11,290 (A)	$10,920	5-D	8,825	453	56.8
Indiana Univ.–Purdue Univ. Fort Wayne, Fort Wayne, IN 46805-1499	1917	$10,155 (A)	$10,111	5-M	9,069	690	34.6
Indiana Univ.–Purdue Univ. Indianapolis, Indianapolis, IN 46202	1969	$10,144 (A)	$13,010	5-D	25,979	4,574	56.4
Indiana Univ. South Bend, South Bend, IN 46615	1922	$8,159 (A)	$7,457	5-M	4,326	384	36.3
Indiana Univ. Southeast, New Albany, IN 47150-6405	1941	$8,159 (A)	$11,654	5-M	3,672	354	34.6
Indiana Wesleyan Univ., Marion, IN 46953-4974	1920	$29,684	$10,050	2-D	3,071	267	65.0
Inter Amer. Univ. of Puerto Rico, Aguadilla, Aguadilla, PR 00605	1957	$5,254	NA	1-M	3,517	199	37.0
Inter Amer. Univ. of Puerto Rico, Arecibo, Arecibo, PR 00614-4050	1957	$5,292	NA	1-M	3,001	NA	NA
Inter Amer. Univ. of Puerto Rico, Bayamón, Bayamón, PR 00957	1912	$5,292	$8,232	1-M	4,500	248	29.0
Inter Amer. Univ. of Puerto Rico, Fajardo, Fajardo, PR 00738-7003	1965	$582/cr. hr.	NA	1-M	1,407	98	61.0
Inter Amer. Univ. of Puerto Rico, Guayama, Guayama, PR 00785	1958	$5,292	NA	1-M	1,927	164	72.0
Inter Amer. Univ. of Puerto Rico, Metropolitan, San Juan, PR 00919-1293	1962	NA	NA	1-D	5,001	394	NA
Inter Amer. Univ. of Puerto Rico, Ponce, Mercedita, PR 00715-1602	1962	$202/cr. hr.	NA	1-D	3,403	284	30.0
Inter Amer. Univ. of Puerto Rico, San Germán, San Germán, PR 00683-5008	1912	$5,580	NA	1-D	3,299	233	46.0
Iona Coll., New Rochelle, NY 10801-1890	1940	$42,828	$17,222	2-M	3,621	325	57.0
Iowa State Univ. of Sci. & Tech., Ames, IA 50011	1858	$10,133 (A)	$9,358	5-D	29,969	1,621	74.0
Ithaca Coll., Ithaca, NY 14850	1892	$49,883	$16,030	13-D	5,054	571	74.3
Jackson State Univ., Jackson, MS 39217	NA	$8,815 (A)	$11,066	5-D	6,906	549	NA
Jacksonville State Univ., Jacksonville, AL 36265-1602	1883	$12,426 (A)	$8,894	5-D	9,540	513	49.7
Jacksonville Univ., Jacksonville, FL 32211	1934	$46,030	$16,550	1-D	3,837	393	53.0
James Madison Univ., Harrisonburg, VA 22807	1908	$19,038 (A)	$11,988	5-D	22,166	1,479	82.3
John Brown Univ., Siloam Springs, AR 72761-2121	1919	$37,496	$9,816	2-M	2,151	157	64.5
John Carroll Univ., University Heights, OH 44118	1886	$49,100	$14,160	2-M	2,922	309	78.0
John Jay Coll. of Criminal Justice of the City Univ. of New York, New York, NY 10019	1964	$7,570 (A)	$17,604	11-M	15,210	1,133	54.2
Johns Hopkins Univ., Baltimore, MD 21218	1876	$62,840	$20,502	1-D	31,275	1,530	94.0
Johnson & Wales Univ., Charlotte, NC 28202	2004	$38,046	$15,112	1-B	1,262	108	NA
Johnson & Wales Univ., Providence, RI 02903-3703	1914	$38,096	$13,734	1-D	5,117	483	NA
Johnson State Coll., Johnson, VT 05656	2018	$12,804 (A)	$12,044	5-M	1,706	179	36.0
Juniata Coll., Huntingdon, PA 16652-2119	1876	$56,402	$13,346	1-M	1,210	151	70.6
Kalamazoo Coll., Kalamazoo, MI 49006-3295	1833	NA	NA	2-B	1,210	127	79.8
Kansas State Univ., Manhattan, KS 66506	1863	$10,942 (A)	$10,100	5-D	19,722	1,032	68.5
Kean Univ., Union, NJ 07083	1855	$13,426 (A)	$15,562	5-D	12,884	1,335	51.0
Keene State Coll., Keene, NH 03435	1909	$14,710 (A)	$14,576	5-M	2,890	305	59.0
Keiser Univ., Fort Lauderdale, FL 33309	1977	$18,176	$4,184	1-D	19,020	4,104	45.0
Kennesaw State Univ., Kennesaw, GA 30144	1963	$6,898 (A)	$13,027	5-D	41,181	NA	46.9
Kent State Univ., Kent, OH 44242-0001	1910	$12,674 (A)	$12,676	5-D	25,854	1,671	65.9
Kent State Univ. at Ashtabula, Ashtabula, OH 44004-2299	1958	NA	NA	14-B	1,723	78	17.2

Name, address	Year founded	Tuition & fees	Room & board	Control, degree	Enroll- ment	Faculty	Grad. rate
Kent State Univ. at Geauga, Burton, OH 44021-9500	1964	NA	NA	5-M	2,095	97	28.4%
Kent State Univ. at Salem, Salem, OH 44460-9412	1966	NA	NA	5-B	1,315	78	28.3
Kent State Univ. at Stark, Canton, OH 44720-7599	1946	$12,845 (A)	$13,040	5-M	3,446	198	32.4
Kent State Univ. at Trumbull, Warren, OH 44483-1998	1954	NA	NA	5-B	1,734	66	25.7
Kent State Univ. at Tuscarawas, New Philadelphia, OH 44663-9403	1962	NA	NA	5-B	1,940	111	31.8
Kentucky State Univ., Frankfort, KY 40601	1886	NA	NA	12-D	2,279	98	35.7
Kenyon Coll., Gambier, OH 43022	1824	$69,330	$14,410	1-B	1,885	213	90.0
Kettering Univ., Flint, MI 48504	1919	NA	NA	1-M	1,769	154	69.3
Keuka Coll., Keuka Park, NY 14478	1890	$38,000	$13,230	2-M	1,344	144	50.0
Keystone Coll., La Plume, PA 18440	1868	$17,450	$12,000	1-M	1,386	151	44.0
King Univ., Bristol, TN 37620-2699	1867	$34,800	$10,262	2-D	1,359	248	46.3
King's Coll., Wilkes-Barre, PA 18711-0801	1946	$42,600	$15,086	2-M	1,994	186	58.0
Kutztown Univ. of Pennsylvania, Kutztown, PA 19530-0730	1866	$11,122 (A)	$11,110	5-D	7,469	398	56.4
La Salle Univ., Philadelphia, PA 19141-1199	1863	$35,570	$15,598	2-D	4,049	360	65.0
La Sierra Univ., Riverside, CA 92505	1922	$34,902	$8,970	2-D	2,278	NA	58.0
Lackawanna Coll., Scranton, PA 18509	1894	$16,130	$10,900	1-B	1,859	195	46.0
Lafayette Coll., Easton, PA 18042	1826	$61,990	$18,290	13-B	2,729	305	89.0
Lake Forest Coll., Lake Forest, IL 60045	1857	$54,202	$12,480	1-M	1,753	184	77.8
Lake Superior State Univ., Sault Sainte Marie, MI 49783	1946	$13,690 (A)	$11,016	5-B	1,812	150	58.0
Lake-Sumter State Coll., Leesburg, FL 34788-8751	1962	$3,292 (A)	NA	11-B	4,760	428	NA
Lakeland Univ., Plymouth, WI 53073	1862	$31,390	$11,258	2-M	3,749	NA	NA
Lamar Univ., Beaumont, TX 77710	1923	$10,894 (A)	$10,154	5-D	17,004	544	66.0
Lancaster Bible Coll., Lancaster, PA 17601	1933	$28,460	$10,220	2-D	1,967	86	60.2
Lander Univ., Greenwood, SC 29649-2099	1872	$11,700 (A)	$10,650	5-M	3,049	249	40.0
Lane Coll., Jackson, TN 38301-4598	1882	$11,790	$7,610	2-B	1,267	66	NA
Langston Univ., Langston, OK 73050	1897	$6,509 (A)	$10,620	5-D	2,222	147	50.0
Laramie Cty. Comm. Coll., Cheyenne, WY 82007-3299	1968	NA	NA	9-B	3,932	257	NA
Lasell Coll., Newton, MA 02466-2709	1851	$26,000	$16,500	1-M	1,639	239	61.0
Lawrence Tech. Univ., Southfield, MI 48075-1058	1932	$41,872	$11,320	1-D	2,966	337	55.3
Lawrence Univ., Appleton, WI 54911	1847	$55,461	$11,838	2-B	1,426	206	78.0
Le Moyne Coll., Syracuse, NY 13214	1946	$38,970	$15,660	2-D	3,301	340	75.8
Lebanon Valley Coll., Annville, PA 17003-1400	1866	$48,620	$13,220	2-D	2,080	302	68.2
Lee Univ., Cleveland, TN 37320-3450	1918	$22,690	$9,340	2-D	3,927	433	63.0
Lehigh Univ., Bethlehem, PA 18015	1865	$62,180	$16,470	2-D	7,394	712	91.2
Lehman Coll. of the City Univ. of New York, Bronx, NY 10468-1589	1931	$7,570 (A)	$17,604	11-D	15,143	961	54.0
Lenoir-Rhyne Univ., Hickory, NC 28601	1891	$43,000	$12,900	2-D	2,686	257	45.0
Lesley Univ., Cambridge, MA 02138-2790 (4)	1909	$31,890	$20,360	1-D	4,510	NA	NA
LeTourneau Univ., Longview, TX 75607-7001	1946	$35,500	$10,570	2-M	3,536	309	66.8
Lewis & Clark Coll., Portland, OR 97219-7899	1867	$62,350	$15,002	1-D	3,601	436	73.3
Lewis Univ., Romeoville, IL 60446	1932	$37,792	$12,140	2-D	6,513	625	62.0
Lewis-Clark State Coll., Lewiston, ID 83501-2698	1893	$8,166 (A)	$7,638	5-B	3,710	212	32.5
Liberty Univ., Lynchburg, VA 24515	1971	$24,600	$12,920	2-D	15,822	NA	71.3
Life Univ., Marietta, GA 30060-2903	1974	$15,036	$14,400	1-D	2,754	210	31.3
LIM Coll., New York, NY 10022-5268 (4)	1939	$31,760	$19,470	3-M	1,314	208	51.0
Limestone Coll., Gaffney, SC 29340-3799	1845	$26,300	$10,777	1-M	1,840	167	29.6
Lincoln Memorial Univ., Harrogate, TN 37752-1901	1897	$26,150	$5,440	1-D	5,418	505	50.4
Lincoln Univ., Jefferson City, MO 65101	1866	NA	NA	5-M	1,833	143	30.0
Lincoln Univ., Lincoln University, PA 19352	1854	$12,272 (A)	$11,314	12-M	1,824	195	44.7
Lindenwood Univ., St. Charles, MO 63301-1695	1832	$21,100	$10,200	1-D	7,000	557	57.0
Lindsey Wilson Coll., Columbia, KY 42728	1903	$27,274	$13,206	2-D	3,159	227	37.0
Lipscomb Univ., Nashville, TN 37204-3951	1891	$37,152	$14,036	2-D	4,778	552	71.3
Lock Haven Univ. of Pennsylvania, Lock Haven, PA 17745-2390	1870	$11,016 (A)	$11,256	5-M	2,859	164	50.3
Logan Univ., Chesterfield, MO 63017	1935	$7,850	$5,400	1-D	1,878	125	NA
Long Island Univ.–LIU Post, Brookville, NY 11548-1300	1954	$41,492	$17,354	1-D	15,740	1,710	47.0
Longwood Univ., Farmville, VA 23909	1839	$14,840 (A)	$14,318	5-M	4,612	338	65.2
Lorain Cty. Comm. Coll., Elyria, OH 44035	1963	$4,135 (A)	$7,982	11-B	10,138	605	NA
Loras Coll., Dubuque, IA 52004-0178	1839	NA	NA	2-M	1,400	139	67.1
Los Angeles Film Sch., Hollywood, CA 90028	1999	NA	NA	3-B	4,900	171	NA
Louisiana State Univ. & Agr. & Mech. Coll., Baton Rouge, LA 70803	1860	$11,956 (A)	$13,154	5-D	37,350	1,573	69.8
Louisiana State Univ. at Alexandria, Alexandria, LA 71302-9121	1960	$6,884 (A)	$9,500	5-B	3,706	172	33.0
Louisiana State Univ. Health Scis. Ctr., New Orleans, LA 70112-2223	1931	$10,376 (A)	NA	5-D	2,804	897	NA
Louisiana State Univ. in Shreveport, Shreveport, LA 71115-2399	1965	$9,515 (A)	NA	5-D	8,721	282	32.5
Louisiana Tech. Univ., Ruston, LA 71272	1894	$10,678 (A)	$9,210	5-D	11,037	594	59.5
Lourdes Univ., Sylvania, OH 43560-2898	1958	$28,830	$12,120	2-D	1,405	185	21.7
Lower Columbia Coll., Longview, WA 98632-0310	1934	NA	NA	5-B	2,435	169	NA
Loyola Marymount Univ., Los Angeles, CA 90045	1911	$58,489	$18,262	2-D	10,165	NA	81.5
Loyola Univ. Chicago, Chicago, IL 60660	1870	$51,706	$13,275	2-D	16,899	1,863	72.5
Loyola Univ. Maryland, Baltimore, MD 21210-2699	1852	$55,480	$18,310	2-D	5,238	447	79.0
Loyola Univ. New Orleans, New Orleans, LA 70118-6195	1912	$47,240	$14,330	2-D	4,397	419	66.9
Lubbock Christian Univ., Lubbock, TX 79407-2099	1957	$27,298	$8,460	2-M	1,596	155	45.0
Luther Coll., Decorah, IA 52101	1861	$50,320	$11,750	2-B	1,610	180	80.0
Lynchburg Coll., Lynchburg, VA 24501-3199	1903	$35,540	$13,250	2-D	2,394	277	60.0
Lynn Univ., Boca Raton, FL 33431-5598	1962	$42,950	$13,750	1-D	3,520	230	52.0
Macalester Coll., St. Paul, MN 55105-1899	1874	$64,908	$14,982	1-B	2,175	249	87.9
Madonna Univ., Livonia, MI 48150-1173	1937	$27,360	$12,840	2-D	2,123	252	49.0
Maharishi Univ. of Mgmt, Fairfield, IA 52557	1971	$16,530	$7,400	1-D	2,015	112	43.0
Manhattan Coll., Riverdale, NY 10471	1853	$48,350	$18,440	2-M	3,569	432	79.0
Mansfield Univ. of Pennsylvania, Mansfield, PA 16933	1857	$11,046 (A)	$10,824	5-M	1,791	104	53.9
Marian Univ., Fond du Lac, WI 54935-4699	1936	$30,000	$8,290	2-D	1,290	NA	NA
Marian Univ., Indianapolis, IN 46222-1997	1851	$39,100	$13,200	2-D	3,928	352	63.5
Marist Coll., Poughkeepsie, NY 12601-1387	1929	$46,010	$19,290	1-D	6,464	599	81.3
Marquette Univ., Milwaukee, WI 53201-1881	1881	$48,700	$15,740	2-D	11,167	1,191	82.5
Marshall Univ., Huntington, WV 25755	1837	$10,018 (A)	$12,852	5-D	10,835	615	50.0
Mary Baldwin Univ., Staunton, VA 24401-3610 (4)	1842	$31,140	$9,730	1-D	1,654	NA	45.0
Maryland Inst. Coll. of Art, Baltimore, MD 21217	1826	$53,815	$17,250	1-M	1,331	NA	69.7
Marymount Manhattan Coll., New York, NY 10021-4597	1936	$38,718	$19,714	1-B	1,608	355	57.0
Marymount Univ., Arlington, VA 22207-4299	1950	$38,150	$14,230	2-D	3,711	310	60.6

Name, address	Year founded	Tuition & fees	Room & board	Control-degree	Enroll-ment	Faculty	Grad. rate
Maryville Univ. of St. Louis, St. Louis, MO 63141-7299	1872	$27,166	$13,300	1-D	10,979	1,136	75.0%
Marywood Univ., Scranton, PA 18509-1598	1915	$39,570	$15,100	2-D	2,606	346	75.5
Massachusetts Coll. of Art & Design, Boston, MA 02115-5882	1873	NA	NA	5-M	1,939	358	66.0
Massachusetts Inst. of Tech., Cambridge, MA 02139-4307	1861	$60,156	$19,390	13-D	11,858	1,705	95.0
Massachusetts Maritime Acad., Buzzards Bay, MA 02532-1803	1891	NA	NA	5-M	1,426	150	79.0
McDaniel Coll., Westminster, MD 21157-4390	1867	$49,647	$13,756	1-M	2,996	581	66.0
McKendree Univ., Lebanon, IL 62254-1299	1828	$33,430	$11,080	2-D	1,958	187	55.6
McNeese State Univ., Lake Charles, LA 70609	1939	$8,380 (A)	$9,344	5-M	7,287	427	NA
MCPHS Univ., Boston, MA 02115-5896	1823	$38,850	$20,400	1-D	3,970	NA	NA
Medaille Coll., Buffalo, NY 14214-2695	1875	$34,000	$16,000	1-D	2,383	411	50.0
Medgar Evers Coll. of the City Univ. of New York, Brooklyn, NY 11225-2298	1969	$7,353 (A)	NA	11-B	4,134	398	25.0
Mercer Univ., Macon, GA 31207	1833	$40,890	$14,528	1-D	8,889	776	73.5
Mercy Coll. of Ohio, Toledo, OH 43604 (4)	1993	$18,825	NA	2-M	1,561	227	33.0
Mercy Coll., Dobbs Ferry, NY 10522-1189	1950	$22,106	$14,700	1-D	8,615	911	45.7
Mercyhurst Univ., Erie, PA 16546	1926	$44,510	$17,070	13-M	2,801	231	68.0
Meredith Coll., Raleigh, NC 27607-5298 (6)	1891	$43,936	$12,920	1-M	1,587	220	68.0
Merrimack Coll., North Andover, MA 01845-5800	1947	$51,786	$21,428	2-M	5,453	489	69.0
Messiah Univ., Mechanicsburg, PA 17055	1909	$40,640	$11,910	2-D	3,231	364	78.0
Methodist Univ., Fayetteville, NC 28311-1498	1956	$38,138	$12,828	2-D	1,916	241	38.0
Metropolitan State Univ., St. Paul, MN 55106-5000	1971	$9,780 (A)	$15,864	5-D	6,649	NA	NA
Metropolitan State Univ. of Denver, Denver, CO 80204	1963	$11,571 (A)	$17,070	5-M	17,678	1,169	29.8
Miami Dade Coll., Miami, FL 33132	1960	$3,054 (A)	NA	11-B	47,245	2,018	NA
Miami Univ. Hamilton, Hamilton, OH 45011-3399	1968	$6,318 (A)	NA	5-M	2,450	184	36.4
Miami Univ. Middletown, Middletown, OH 45042-3497	1966	$6,318 (A)	NA	5-M	1,585	74	27.8
Miami Univ., Oxford, OH 45056	1809	$17,808 (A)	$15,824	12-D	19,107	1,107	80.7
Michigan State Univ., East Lansing, MI 48824	1855	$16,711 (A)	$10,990	5-D	50,023	2,943	81.9
Michigan Tech. Univ., Houghton, MI 49931	1885	$18,392 (A)	$12,058	5-D	7,074	443	67.8
Mid-America Christian Univ., Oklahoma City, OK 73170-4504	1953	$18,838	$8,512	2-M	1,935	NA	NA
MidAmerica Nazarene Univ., Olathe, KS 66062-1899	1966	$36,120	$10,760	2-M	1,508	187	43.4
Middle Georgia State Univ., Macon, GA 31206	2015	$5,332 (A)	$9,476	5-D	7,843	396	26.1
Middle Tennessee State Univ., Murfreesboro, TN 37132	1911	$9,506 (A)	$11,704	5-D	20,857	1,263	53.6
Middlebury Coll., Middlebury, VT 05753-6002	1800	NA	NA	1-D	2,843	328	93.5
Midland Coll., Midland, TX 79705-6329	1969	$2,970 (A)	$3,112	11-B	4,737	NA	NA
Midway Univ., Midway, KY 40347-1120	1847	$26,080	$8,785	2-M	1,901	152	48.0
Midwestern State Univ., Wichita Falls, TX 76308	1922	$9,776 (A)	$10,034	5-D	5,784	362	41.0
Miles Coll., Fairfield, AL 35064	1905	$12,714	$7,348	2-B	1,440	147	NA
Millersville Univ. of Pennsylvania, Millersville, PA 17551-0302	1855	$11,784 (A)	$12,600	5-D	7,192	390	56.7
Millikin Univ., Decatur, IL 62522-2084	1901	$43,570	$12,916	1-D	1,807	244	57.8
Minnesota State Univ. Mankato, Mankato, MN 56001	1868	$9,490 (A)	$11,224	5-D	14,546	662	51.3
Minnesota State Univ. Moorhead, Moorhead, MN 56563	1887	NA	NA	5-D	4,679	282	55.4
Minot State Univ., Minot, ND 58707-0002	1913	$8,634 (A)	$8,058	5-M	2,836	291	46.5
MiraCosta Coll., Oceanside, CA 92056	1934	$1,152 (A)	$30,096	9-B	10,860	668	NA
Misericordia Univ., Dallas, PA 18612-1098	1924	$38,370	$17,140	2-D	2,398	298	74.0
Mississippi Coll., Clinton, MS 39058	1826	NA	NA	2-D	4,250	386	63.0
Mississippi State Univ., Mississippi State, MS 39762	1878	$9,398 (A)	$11,190	5-D	22,649	1,440	63.1
Mississippi Univ. for Women, Columbus, MS 39701-9998	1884	$7,756 (A)	$7,908	5-D	2,673	215	49.0
Mississippi Valley State Univ., Itta Bena, MS 38941-1400	1946	NA	NA	5-M	1,879	142	27.0
Missouri Baptist Univ., St. Louis, MO 63141-8660	1964	$33,122	$10,806	2-D	5,231	244	40.0
Missouri Southern State Univ., Joplin, MO 64801-1595	1937	NA	NA	5-M	4,144	287	34.0
Missouri State Univ., Springfield, MO 65897	1905	$9,024 (A)	$10,308	5-D	22,535	1,017	58.2
Missouri Univ. of Sci. & Tech., Rolla, MO 65409	1870	$11,811 (A)	$11,260	5-D	7,083	438	61.7
Missouri Valley Coll., Marshall, MO 65340-3197	1889	NA	NA	2-M	1,776	133	24.1
Missouri Western State Univ., St. Joseph, MO 64507-2294	1915	$7,200 (A)	$10,200	5-M	4,395	252	38.9
Molloy Coll., Rockville Centre, NY 11571-5002	1955	NA	NA	13-D	4,807	710	70.0
Monmouth Univ., West Long Branch, NJ 07764-1898	1933	$44,850	$16,512	1-D	5,027	626	68.2
Monroe Coll., Bronx, NY 10468	1933	$17,922	$11,500	3-M	7,011	573	69.0
Montana State Univ. Billings, Billings, MT 59101	1927	$6,258 (A)	$7,600	5-M	4,126	223	25.0
Montana State Univ., Bozeman, MT 59717	1893	$7,727 (A)	$11,300	5-D	16,688	968	56.7
Montana Tech. of The Univ. of Montana, Butte, MT 59701-8997	1900	$9,280 (A)	$11,530	5-D	1,625	177	57.0
Montcalm Comm. Coll., Sidney, MI 48885	1965	$3,888 (A)	NA	11-B	1,832	118	NA
Montclair State Univ., Montclair, NJ 07043-1624	1908	$13,762 (A)	$16,170	5-D	21,784	1,952	65.0
Moody Bible Inst, Chicago, IL 60610-3284	1886	$15,022	$12,820	2-M	2,410	187	60.5
Moravian Coll., Bethlehem, PA 18018-6650	1742	$52,000	$15,351	2-D	2,533	366	70.0
Morehead State Univ., Morehead, KY 40351	1887	$9,838 (A)	$8,942	5-D	8,810	388	49.0
Morehouse Coll., Atlanta, GA 30314 (1)	1867	NA	NA	1-B	2,567	145	59.0
Morgan State Univ., Baltimore, MD 21251	1867	$8,110 (A)	$12,755	5-D	8,564	591	44.0
Morningside Coll., Sioux City, IA 51106	1894	$36,610	$10,720	2-M	1,281	240	50.6
Morrisville State Coll., Morrisville, NY 13408	1908	$8,763 (A)	$16,120	5-M	1,803	187	30.0
Mount Aloysius Coll., Cresson, PA 16630-1999	1939	$26,156	$12,694	2-M	2,752	164	NA
Mount Holyoke Coll., South Hadley, MA 01075 (3)	1837	$64,142	$18,838	1-M	2,392	273	82.6
Mount Marty Coll., Yankton, SD 57078-3724	1936	$33,100	$9,300	2-D	1,252	48	57.0
Mount Mary Univ., Milwaukee, WI 53222-4597 (6)	1913	NA	NA	2-D	1,273	201	50.7
Mount Mercy Univ., Cedar Rapids, IA 52402-4797	1928	$39,070	$11,030	2-D	1,526	171	57.0
Mount St. Joseph Univ., Cincinnati, OH 45233-1670	1920	$34,900	$10,650	2-D	2,027	239	50.8
Mount St. Mary Coll., Newburgh, NY 12550-3494	1960	$41,370	$18,820	1-M	1,918	206	61.0
Mount St. Mary's Univ., Emmitsburg, MD 21727-7799	1808	$47,240	$14,750	2-M	2,456	245	64.8
Mount St. Mary's Univ., Los Angeles, CA 90049 (4)	1925	$48,132	$14,154	2-D	2,440	452	70.0
Mount Vernon Nazarene Univ., Mount Vernon, OH 43050-9500	1968	$35,274	NA	2-M	2,068	180	58.2
Muhlenberg Coll., Allentown, PA 18104-5586	1848	NA	NA	2-M	2,095	328	82.3
Murray State Univ., Murray, KY 42071	1922	$9,908 (A)	$12,534	5-D	9,489	461	61.6
Muskingum Univ., New Concord, OH 43762	1837	$31,112	$12,240	2-M	2,169	172	51.0
Natl. Louis Univ., Chicago, IL 60603	1886	$11,520	$13,764	1-D	7,142	650	31.0
Natl. Univ. Coll., Bayamón, PR 00960		$6,919	NA	3-M	24,705	464	5.0
Natl. Univ., La Jolla, CA 92037-1011	1971	$13,320	NA	1-D	18,631	3,265	22.0
Navajo Tech. Univ., Crownpoint, NM 87313	1979	$4,070	$6,270	7-M	1,600	136	14.0
Nazareth Coll. of Rochester, Rochester, NY 14618	1924	$39,070	$15,040	1-D	2,639	506	72.8
Nebraska Wesleyan Univ., Lincoln, NE 68504-2796	1887	$41,762	$12,184	2-M	1,688	180	59.1
Neumann Univ., Aston, PA 19014-1298	1965	$35,350	$15,010	2-D	2,212	234	49.3
Nevada State Coll., Henderson, NV 89002	2002	$6,075 (A)	NA	5-B	3,747	267	15.0
New England Coll., Henniker, NH 03242-3293	1946	$41,454	$16,802	1-D	2,815	273	31.0
New England Inst. of Tech., East Greenwich, RI 02818	1940	$35,625	$15,000	13-D	1,895	231	NA
New Jersey City Univ., Jersey City, NJ 07305-1597	1927	$13,971 (A)	$15,684	5-D	7,550	708	36.0

Name, address	Year founded	Tuition & fees	Room & board	Control, degree	Enroll-ment	Faculty	Grad. rate
New Jersey Inst. of Tech., Newark, NJ 07102	1881	$19,022 (A)	$15,000	5-D	11,901	922	73.7%
New Mexico Highlands Univ., Las Vegas, NM 87701	1893	NA	NA	5-M	2,740	275	31.6
New Mexico Inst. of Mining & Tech., Socorro, NM 87801	1889	NA	NA	5-D	1,690	171	55.0
New Mexico State Univ., Las Cruces, NM 88003-8001	1888	$8,458 (A)	NA	5-D	14,298	980	50.9
New York City Coll. of Tech. of the City Univ. of New York, Brooklyn, NY 11201-2983	1946	$7,331 (A)	NA	11-B	13,087	1,533	30.2
New York Inst. of Tech., Old Westbury, NY 11568-8000	1955	$44,360	$21,836	1-D	7,230	1,016	53.0
New York Univ., New York, NY 10012-1019	1831	$60,438	$24,102	1-D	59,112	6,736	87.1
Newberry Coll., Newberry, SC 29108-2197	1856	$28,250	$11,700	2-M	1,242	135	43.5
Newman Univ., Wichita, KS 67213-2097	1933	$34,400	$9,494	2-M	2,053	233	59.0
Niagara Univ., Niagara University, NY 14109	1856	$37,920	$12,980	2-D	3,858	403	72.0
Nicholls State Univ., Thibodaux, LA 70310	1948	$7,959 (A)	$10,574	5-M	6,134	329	NA
Nichols Coll., Dudley, MA 01571	1815	$40,475	$14,950	1-M	1,553	NA	59.0
Norfolk State Univ., Norfolk, VA 23504	1935	$7,746 (A)	$10,964	5-D	4,992	NA	NA
North Carolina Agr. & Tech. State Univ., Greensboro, NC 27411	1891	$6,747 (A)	$8,832	5-D	12,142	NA	NA
North Carolina Central Univ., Durham, NC 27707-3129	1910	$10,407 (A)	$13,702	5-D	7,553	518	44.0
North Carolina State Univ., Raleigh, NC 27695	1887	$9,128 (A)	$12,748	5-D	36,700	2,156	86.0
North Carolina Wesleyan Coll., Rocky Mount, NC 27804-8677	1956	$34,732	$12,264	2-M	1,603	NA	NA
North Central Coll., Naperville, IL 60566-7063	1861	NA	NA	2-M	2,728	303	64.0
North Dakota State Univ., Fargo, ND 58102	1890	$11,057 (A)	$9,633	5-D	12,461	767	64.9
North Park Univ., Chicago, IL 60625-4895	1891	$33,350	$10,425	2-D	3,138	305	56.0
North Seattle Coll., Seattle, WA 98103-3599	1970	$4,799 (A)	NA	5-B	5,240	262	NA
Northeastern Illinois Univ., Chicago, IL 60625-4699	1961	$14,653 (A)	$9,526	5-M	6,440	553	NA
Northeastern State Univ., Tahlequah, OK 74464-2399	1846	$7,737 (A)	$10,494	5-D	6,631	388	38.0
Northeastern Univ., Boston, MA 02115-5096	1898	$60,192	$18,440	1-D	36,806	2,275	91.2
Northern Arizona Univ., Flagstaff, AZ 86011	1899	$12,274 (A)	$11,728	5-D	28,090	1,585	59.1
Northern Illinois Univ., De Kalb, IL 60115-2854	1895	$12,506 (A)	$11,748	5-D	15,649	1,145	53.0
Northern Kentucky Univ., Highland Heights, KY 41099	1968	$10,684 (A)	$9,860	5-D	15,801	1,133	51.7
Northern Marianas Coll., Saipan, MP 96950	1981	$4,038 (A)	NA	7-B	1,255	99	NA
Northern Michigan Univ., Marquette, MI 49855-5301	1899	$12,648 (A)	$12,150	5-D	6,970	425	56.5
Northern New Mexico Coll., EspaÖola, NM 87532	1909	$4,952 (A)	NA	5-B	1,234	253	NA
Northern State Univ., Aberdeen, SD 57401-7198	1901	NA	NA	5-M	3,344	140	58.7
Northwest Coll., Powell, WY 82435-1898	1946	NA	NA	11-B	1,423	98	NA
Northwest Florida State Coll., Niceville, FL 32578-1295	1963	$3,133 (A)	NA	11-B	5,004	266	NA
Northwest Missouri State Univ., Maryville, MO 64468-6001	1905	$11,878 (A)	$11,002	5-M	7,870	296	53.0
Northwest Nazarene Univ., Nampa, ID 83686-5897	1913	$39,370	$11,550	2-D	1,778	190	58.0
Northwestern Coll., Orange City, IA 51041-1996	1882	$35,300	$10,700	2-M	1,666	205	63.0
Northwestern Michigan Coll., Traverse City, MI 49686-3061	1951	$4,640 (A)	$8,275	11-B	4,609	280	NA
Northwestern Oklahoma State Univ., Alva, OK 73717-2799	1897	$7,883 (A)	$5,250	5-D	1,833	153	25.8
Northwestern State Univ. of Louisiana, Natchitoches, LA 71497	1884	$8,672 (A)	$10,617	5-D	9,389	529	43.0
Northwestern Univ., Evanston, IL 60208	1851	$65,997	$20,334	1-D	22,933	1,742	94.9
Northwood Univ., Michigan campus, Midland, MI 48640-2398	1959	$30,520	$11,440	1-D	1,344	148	58.0
Norwich Univ., Northfield, VT 05663	1819	$45,340	$15,800	1-M	3,672	392	62.5
Notre Dame Coll., South Euclid, OH 44121-4293	1922	$32,595	$12,146	2-M	1,444	160	42.1
Nova Southeastern Univ., Fort Lauderdale, FL 33314-7796	1964	$37,080	$15,950	1-D	20,948	1,665	62.0
Nyack Coll., New York, NY 10004	1882	$27,500	$15,500	2-D	1,944	196	40.3
Oakland Univ., Rochester, MI 48309-4401	1957	$14,694 (A)	$11,309	5-D	17,170	1,207	56.0
Oakwood Univ., Huntsville, AL 35896	1896	$20,090	$10,050	2-M	1,824	NA	46.0
Oberlin Coll., Oberlin, OH 44074	1833	$64,596	$18,942	1-M	2,992	NA	83.4
Occidental Coll., Los Angeles, CA 90041-3314	1887	$63,446	$18,284	1-M	1,942	278	82.7
Oglala Lakota Coll., Kyle, SD 57752-0490	1970	$2,684 (A)	$7,200	11-M	1,300	119	11.0
Oglethorpe Univ., Atlanta, GA 30319-2797	1835	$43,990	$14,400	1-B	1,446	132	58.0
Ohio Christian Univ., Circleville, OH 43113	1948	$23,700	$9,612	2-M	2,007	174	49.0
Ohio Dominican Univ., Columbus, OH 43219-2099	1911	NA	NA	2-M	1,301	128	52.9
Ohio Northern Univ., Ada, OH 45810-1599	1871	$37,600	$13,200	2-D	3,015	266	67.0
Ohio Univ., Athens, OH 45701-2979	1804	$13,352 (A)	$12,336	5-D	23,893	1,136	64.7
Ohio Wesleyan Univ., Delaware, OH 43015	1842	$52,297	$14,832	2-B	1,410	194	66.1
Oklahoma Baptist Univ., Shawnee, OK 74804	1910	$34,050	$8,300	2-M	1,399	125	54.0
Oklahoma Christian Univ., Oklahoma City, OK 73136-1100	1950	$25,148	$8,280	2-M	2,017	NA	57.0
Oklahoma City Univ., Oklahoma City, OK 73106-1402	1904	$33,586	$11,200	2-D	2,551	341	65.0
Oklahoma Panhandle State Univ., Goodwell, OK 73939-0430	1909	$7,490 (A)	$5,872	5-B	1,337	91	91.2
Oklahoma State Univ. Inst. of Tech., Okmulgee, OK 74447-3901	1946	$5,774 (S)	NA	5-B	2,364	141	42.0
Oklahoma State Univ., Stillwater, OK 74078	1890	$9,244 (A)	$11,300	5-D	25,359	1,388	65.0
Oklahoma State Univ.–Oklahoma City, Oklahoma City, OK 73107-6120	1961	$4,439 (A)	$8,092	5-B	4,949	355	NA
Old Dominion Univ., Norfolk, VA 23529	1930	$13,162 (A)	$14,652	5-D	23,107	1,595	48.0
Olivet Nazarene Univ., Bourbonnais, IL 60914	1907	$37,940	$9,790	2-D	3,462	382	63.8
Olympic Coll., Bremerton, WA 98337-1699	1946	$4,198 (A)	$7,944	5-B	11,617	475	NA
Oral Roberts Univ., Tulsa, OK 74171	1963	$34,100	$9,400	2-D	5,186	376	63.0
Oregon Inst. of Tech., Klamath Falls, OR 97601-8801	1947	$12,122 (A)	$9,936	5-M	4,910	293	56.2
Oregon State Univ., Corvallis, OR 97331	1868	$12,330 (A)	$15,075	5-D	32,312	1,735	69.3
Otis Coll. of Art & Design, Los Angeles, CA 90045-9785	1918	$50,040	$16,929	1-M	1,312	338	62.0
Otterbein Univ., Westerville, OH 43081	1847	$34,899	$12,468	2-D	2,458	326	69.5
Ouachita Baptist Univ., Arkadelphia, AR 71998-0001	1886	$32,480	$9,040	13-M	1,784	186	66.0
Our Lady of the Lake Univ., San Antonio, TX 78207-4689	1895	NA	NA	2-D	2,550	NA	35.0
Pace Univ., New York, NY 10038	1906	$50,004	$21,362	1-D	9,157	870	58.4
Pace Univ., Pleasantville campus, Pleasantville, NY 10570	1906	$50,026	$20,480	1-D	4,452	455	68.8
Pacific Lutheran Univ., Tacoma, WA 98447	1890	$50,272	$12,446	2-D	2,633	277	71.8
Pacific Univ., Forest Grove, OR 97116-1797	1849	$54,362	$14,408	1-D	3,751	481	69.9
Palm Beach Atlantic Univ., West Palm Beach, FL 33416-4708	1968	NA	NA	2-D	3,687	351	60.6
Palm Beach State Coll., Lake Worth, FL 33461-4796	1933	$3,050 (A)	$12,825	5-B	30,052	1,170	NA
Park Univ., Parkville, MO 64152-3795	1875	$8,853	$8,084	1-M	10,165	925	27.0
Pasco-Hernando State Coll., New Port Richey, FL 34654-5199	1972	$3,803 (A)	$9,247	5-B	9,886	377	NA
Peninsula Coll., Port Angeles, WA 98362-2779	1961	$4,575 (A)	$17,868	5-B	3,321	156	NA
Penn State Erie, The Behrend Coll., Erie, PA 16563	1948	NA	NA	12-M	3,295	301	67.6
Penn State Harrisburg, Middletown, PA 17057	1966	NA	NA	12-D	4,572	416	70.5
Penn State Univ. Park, University Park, PA 16802	1855	$20,221 (A)	$12,744	12-D	48,765	3,517	84.0
Pennsylvania Coll. of Health Scis., Lancaster, PA 17601	1903	$29,922	NA	1-D	1,793	213	64.0
Pennsylvania Coll. of Tech., Williamsport, PA 17701-5778	1965	NA	NA	12-M	4,241	375	56.2
Pensacola State Coll., Pensacola, FL 32504-8998	1948	$2,367 (A)	$6,750	5-B	10,661	324	74.0

Name, address	Year founded	Tuition & fees	Room & board	Control, degree	Enroll-ment	Faculty	Grad. rate
Pepperdine Univ., Malibu, CA 90263	1937	$66,742	$23,270	2-D	10,030	982	84.0%
Peru State Coll., Peru, NE 68421	1867	$7,800 (A)	$8,680	5-M	1,634	NA	NA
Piedmont Coll., Demorest, GA 30535	1897	$30,440	$12,100	2-D	1,843	200	48.0
Pima Med. Inst, Tucson, AZ 85716	1972	NA	NA	3-B	1,970	NA	NA
Pittsburg State Univ., Pittsburg, KS 66762	1903	$8,156 (A)	$9,710	5-D	6,017	432	NA
Plymouth State Univ., Plymouth, NH 03264-1595	1871	$14,558 (A)	$12,104	5-D	3,872	329	50.6
Point Loma Nazarene Univ., San Diego, CA 92106-2899	1902	$43,550	$12,850	2-D	4,319	500	75.9
Point Park Univ., Pittsburgh, PA 15222-1984	1960	$38,510	NA	1-D	3,591	496	55.0
Point Univ., West Point, GA 31833	1937	$22,300	$8,000	2-M	1,666	184	29.0
Polk State Coll., Winter Haven, FL 33881-4299	1964	$112/cr. hr. (A)	NA	5-B	9,961	368	NA
Polytechnic Univ. of Puerto Rico, Hato Rey, PR 00918	1966	$9,102	$11,928	1-D	4,244	205	20.0
Pomona Coll., Claremont, CA 91711	1887	$59,238	$19,358	1-B	1,764	265	93.0
Pontifical Catholic Univ. of Puerto Rico, Ponce, PR 00717-0777	1948	$5,545	$5,199	2-D	6,614	340	45.5
Pontifical Catholic Univ. of Puerto Rico–Mayaguez campus, Mayaguez, PR 00680	NA	$5,443	NA	2-M	1,273	80	24.0
Portland State Univ., Portland, OR 97207-0751	1946	$9,315 (A)	NA	5-D	21,609	1,469	53.0
Post Univ., Waterbury, CT 06723-2540	1890	$15,458	$11,600	1-D	13,844	996	27.0
Prairie View A&M Univ., Prairie View, TX 77446	1878	$11,078 (A)	$10,317	5-D	9,248	557	37.1
Pratt Inst., Brooklyn, NY 11205-3899	1887	$59,683	$16,710	1-M	5,262	1,284	76.0
Presbyterian Coll., Clinton, SC 29325	1880	NA	NA	2-D	1,231	133	61.0
Princeton Univ., Princeton, NJ 08544-1019	1746	$59,710	$19,380	1-D	8,842	1,195	98.0
Providence Coll., Providence, RI 02918	1917	NA	NA	2-M	4,756	568	85.6
Pueblo Comm. Coll., Pueblo, CO 81004-1499	1933	$4,822 (A)	$14,679	5-B	5,938	321	NA
Purchase Coll., State Univ. of New York, Purchase, NY 10577-1400	1967	$8,953 (A)	$15,400	5-M	3,529	NA	63.5
Purdue Univ. Northwest, Hammond, IN 46323-2094	2016	$8,175 (A)	$8,215	5-D	12,987	456	44.0
Purdue Univ., West Lafayette, IN 47907	1869	$9,992 (A)	$10,030	5-D	50,884	2,945	84.0
Queens Coll. of the City Univ. of New York, Queens, NY 11367-1597	1937	$7,570 (A)	$17,604	11-M	18,772	1,350	55.2
Queens Univ. of Charlotte, Charlotte, NC 28274-0002	1857	$42,790	$19,100	2-M	1,873	285	68.6
Quinnipiac Univ., Hamden, CT 06518-1940	1929	$53,090	$16,910	1-D	8,788	1,091	77.3
Radford Univ., Radford, VA 24142	1910	$12,286 (A)	$11,564	5-D	7,718	737	54.0
Ramapo Coll. of New Jersey, Mahwah, NJ 07430-1680	1969	$15,978 (A)	$14,882	5-M	5,732	500	71.7
Randolph-Macon Coll., Ashland, VA 23005-5505	1830	$48,002	$14,630	2-M	1,490	196	74.0
Ranken Tech. Coll., St. Louis, MO 63113 (2)	1907	$16,164	$7,750	1-B	1,823	NA	NA
Rasmussen Coll. Ocala, Ocala, FL 34474	1984	$12,690	$4,653	3-D	1,422	NA	NA
Reed Coll., Portland, OR 97202-8199	1908	$67,020	$16,820	1-M	1,534	164	80.0
Regent Univ., Virginia Beach, VA 23464-9800	1977	$19,680	$9,952	13-D	10,380	808	55.0
Regis Coll., Weston, MA 02493	1927	$47,770	$17,080	2-D	3,599	400	60.9
Regis Univ., Denver, CO 80221-1099	1877	$43,980	$14,618	2-D	5,858	757	61.1
Reinhardt Univ., Waleska, GA 30183-2981	1883	$27,300	$11,720	2-M	1,524	NA	41.0
Rensselaer Polytechnic Inst., Troy, NY 12180-3590	1824	$61,884	$17,530	1-D	6,991	506	84.0
Renton Tech. Coll., Renton, WA 98056	1942	$5,671 (A)	NA	5-B	3,214	242	NA
Rhode Island Coll., Providence, RI 02908-1991	1854	$10,986 (A)	$13,414	5-D	5,787	597	44.0
Rhode Island Sch. of Design, Providence, RI 02903-2784	1877	$59,760	$15,850	1-M	2,620	523	91.0
Rhodes Coll., Memphis, TN 38112-1690	1848	$54,892	$12,910	1-M	2,008	264	85.0
Rice Univ., Houston, TX 77251-1892	1912	$58,128	$15,000	1-D	8,672	931	93.6
Ringling Coll. of Art & Design, Sarasota, FL 34234-5895	1931	$56,140	$17,350	1-B	1,705	181	76.6
Rivier Univ., Nashua, NH 03060	1933	$35,512	$14,380	2-D	1,296	NA	49.0
Roanoke Coll., Salem, VA 24153-3794	1842	$36,774	$15,366	2-B	1,826	188	71.1
Robert Morris Univ., Moon Township, PA 15108-1189	1921	$34,690	$12,930	1-D	4,608	400	64.7
Roberts Wesleyan Coll., Rochester, NY 14624-1997	1866	NA	NA	2-D	1,658	267	63.6
Rochester Inst. of Tech., Rochester, NY 14623-5603	1829	$54,518	$14,978	1-D	16,615	1,449	73.9
Rockhurst Univ., Kansas City, MO 64110-2561	1910	$42,901	$11,540	2-D	3,405	284	77.0
Rocky Mountain Coll. of Art + Design, Lakewood, CO 80214	1963	$21,615	NA	3-M	1,631	205	48.0
Roger Williams Univ., Bristol, RI 02809	1956	$42,666	$16,690	1-D	4,397	489	67.0
Rogers State Univ., Claremore, OK 74017-3252	1909	$7,920 (A)	$9,432	5-M	3,197	221	35.2
Rollins Coll., Winter Park, FL 32789-4499	1885	$58,300	$16,190	1-D	3,030	217	78.0
Roosevelt Univ., Chicago, IL 60605	1945	$33,398	$12,350	1-D	4,127	578	43.9
Rose-Hulman Inst. of Tech., Terre Haute, IN 47803-3999 (2)	1874	$54,174	$17,718	1-M	2,188	196	81.0
Rowan Univ., Glassboro, NJ 08028-1701	1923	$14,951 (A)	$15,956	5-D	19,568	1,847	68.1
Russell Sage Coll., Troy, NY 12180	1916	$36,756	$13,790	1-D	2,159	234	63.0
Rutgers Univ.–Camden, Camden, NJ 08102-1401	1926	$17,079 (A)	$12,923	5-D	5,966	606	64.8
Rutgers Univ.–New Brunswick, Piscataway, NJ 08854-8097	1766	$17,329 (A)	$14,715	5-D	50,637	3,870	84.4
Rutgers Univ.–Newark, Newark, NJ 07102	1908	$16,586 (A)	$15,060	5-D	11,017	974	66.2
Sacred Heart Univ., Fairfield, CT 06825	1963	$48,160	$12,320	2-D	10,721	1,052	72.9
Saginaw Valley State Univ., University Center, MI 48710	1963	$11,424 (A)	$11,780	5-D	7,613	670	42.5
St. Ambrose Univ., Davenport, IA 52803-2898	1882	$35,598	$12,348	2-D	2,749	328	64.0
St. Anselm Coll., Manchester, NH 03102-1310	1889	$46,800	$16,520	2-M	1,977	210	85.0
St. Bonaventure Univ., St. Bonaventure, NY 14778-2284	1858	$40,150	$15,000	2-M	2,624	277	73.0
St. Catherine Univ., St. Paul, MN 55105 (6)	1905	$49,758	$9,900	2-D	3,589	426	64.0
St. Cloud State Univ., St. Cloud, MN 56301-4498	1869	$10,118 (A)	$9,860	5-D	10,401	621	45.4
St. Edward's Univ., Austin, TX 78704	1885	$50,736	$13,876	2-M	3,014	NA	NA
St. Francis Coll., Brooklyn Heights, NY 11201-4398	1884	$27,298	$17,200	2-M	2,735	339	54.0
St. Francis Univ., Loretto, PA 15940-0600	1847	$41,720	$13,210	2-D	2,856	240	77.0
St. John Fisher Coll., Rochester, NY 14618-3597	1948	$39,666	$14,342	2-D	3,637	452	72.0
St. John's Univ., Collegeville, MN 56321 (5)	1857	$53,942	$12,130	2-M	1,645	146	75.7
St. John's Univ., Queens, NY 11439	1870	$50,110	$19,720	2-D	19,663	1,372	69.0
St. Joseph's Coll. of Maine, Standish, ME 04084	1912	$41,586	$14,935	2-M	1,329	126	50.0
St. Joseph's Coll., Long Island campus, Patchogue, NY 11772-2399	1916	NA	NA	2-M	3,302	395	71.0
St. Joseph's Univ., Philadelphia, PA 19131-1395	1851	$51,340	$15,740	2-D	7,863	787	82.0
St. Lawrence Univ., Canton, NY 13617	1856	$62,020	$15,995	1-M	2,279	206	81.9
St. Leo Univ., Saint Leo, FL 33574-6665	1889	$27,860	$15,724	2-M	2,788	200	47.3
St. Louis Univ., St. Louis, MO 63103	1818	$53,244	$14,570	2-D	12,519	1,194	81.2
St. Martin's Univ., Lacey, WA 98503	1895	NA	NA	2-D	1,614	253	60.2
St. Mary's Coll., Notre Dame, IN 46556 (3)	1844	$51,430	$13,850	2-D	1,519	189	74.7
St. Mary's Coll. of California, Moraga, CA 94575	1863	$53,572	$16,404	2-D	3,169	NA	73.2
St. Mary's Coll. of Maryland, St. Mary's City, MD 20686-3001	1840	$15,236 (A)	$14,672	5-M	1,536	207	71.0
St. Mary's Univ., San Antonio, TX 78228	1852	$35,226	$11,448	2-D	3,432	358	59.0
St. Mary's Univ. of Minnesota, Winona, MN 55987-1399	1912	$43,160	$10,720	2-D	4,133	409	65.4
St. Michael's Coll., Colchester, VT 05439	1904	NA	NA	2-M	1,573	174	78.0
St. Norbert Coll., De Pere, WI 54115-2099	1898	$44,432	$13,523	2-M	1,882	199	72.0
St. Olaf Coll., Northfield, MN 55057-1098	1874	$56,970	$13,000	2-B	3,046	329	84.8

Name, address	Year founded	Tuition & fees	Room & board	Control, degree	Enroll- ment	Faculty	Grad. rate
St. Peter's Univ., Jersey City, NJ 07306-5997	1872	NA	NA	2-D	3,009	270	58.4%
St. Petersburg Coll., St. Petersburg, FL 33733-3489	1927	$3,421 (A)	$17,911	11-B	24,543	1,298	NA
St. Thomas Aquinas Coll., Sparkill, NY 10976	1952	$37,395	$15,500	1-M	2,033	137	53.5
St. Thomas Univ., Miami Gardens, FL 33054-6459	1961	$33,740	$12,460	2-D	4,824	NA	42.8
St. Vincent Coll., Latrobe, PA 15650-2690	1846	$41,526	$14,529	2-D	1,552	227	76.0
St. Xavier Univ., Chicago, IL 60655-3105	1847	$35,770	$11,780	2-M	3,080	360	52.0
Salem State Univ., Salem, MA 01970-5353	1854	$11,979 (A)	$16,003	5-M	5,716	757	57.0
Salisbury Univ., Salisbury, MD 21801-6837	1925	$10,638 (A)	$13,416	5-D	7,123	611	68.6
Salve Regina Univ., Newport, RI 02840-4192	1934	NA	NA	2-D	2,282	304	75.5
Sam Houston State Univ., Huntsville, TX 77341	1879	$15,084 (A)	$11,720	5-D	21,404	1,041	59.0
Samford Univ., Birmingham, AL 35229	1841	$38,144	$12,160	2-D	5,683	525	78.0
San Diego Mesa Coll., San Diego, CA 92111-4998	1964	$1,144 (A)	$30,736	9-B	20,693	723	NA
San Diego State Univ., San Diego, CA 92182	1897	$8,174 (A)	$20,500	5-D	36,637	2,027	78.0
San Francisco State Univ., San Francisco, CA 94132-1722	1899	$8,413 (A)	$19,176	5-D	32,662	1,700	54.0
San Jacinto Coll. District, Pasadena, TX 77504-3323	1961	$2,490 (A)	$14,087	11-B	30,593	1,042	NA
San Jose State Univ., San Jose, CA 95192-0001	NA	$7,992 (A)	$19,866	5-D	35,751	1,937	68.2
Santa Clara Univ., Santa Clara, CA 95053	1851	$59,241	$17,967	2-D	9,178	978	88.6
Santa Fe Coll., Gainesville, FL 32606	1966	$2,568 (A)	$8,604	11-B	12,607	829	NA
Sarah Lawrence Coll., Bronxville, NY 10708-5999	1926	NA	NA	1-M	1,696	260	71.0
Savannah Coll. of Art & Design, Savannah, GA 31402-3146	1978	$40,095	$17,199	1-M	11,679	774	69.0
Savannah State Univ., Savannah, GA 31404	1890	$5,902 (A)	$7,762	5-M	4,827	NA	NA
Sch. of the Art Inst. of Chicago, Chicago, IL 60603-3103	1866	$54,530	$16,100	1-M	3,532	625	74.0
Sch. of Visual Arts, New York, NY 10010-3994	1947	$49,140	$24,200	3-M	4,127	1,053	73.9
Schoolcraft Coll., Livonia, MI 48152-2696	1961	$4,024 (A)	NA	9-B	8,330	404	NA
Seattle Pacific Univ., Seattle, WA 98119-1997	1891	$38,814	$15,498	2-D	3,114	326	63.0
Seattle Univ., Seattle, WA 98122-1090	1891	$54,285	$13,524	2-D	7,268	735	75.0
Seminole State Coll. of Florida, Sanford, FL 32773-6199	1966	$3,131 (A)	NA	11-B	17,706	772	NA
Seton Hall Univ., South Orange, NJ 07079-2697	1856	$54,113	$16,532	2-D	9,623	999	72.0
Seton Hill Univ., Greensburg, PA 15601	1883	$40,224	$13,350	2-D	2,012	219	67.0
Sewanee: The Univ. of the South, Sewanee, TN 37383-1000	1857	$53,704	$15,338	2-D	1,704	236	81.5
Shawnee State Univ., Portsmouth, OH 45662	1986	$9,341 (A)	$11,624	5-D	3,308	378	48.1
Shenandoah Univ., Winchester, VA 22601-5195	1875	$36,028	$11,800	2-D	4,260	449	61.7
Shepherd Univ., Shepherdstown, WV 25443	1871	$7,784 (A)	$10,848	5-D	3,159	281	48.6
Shippensburg Univ. of Pennsylvania, Shippensburg, PA 17257-2299	1871	$13,394 (A)	$11,538	5-D	5,706	319	58.0
Shorter Univ., Rome, GA 30165	1873	$22,810	$9,400	2-M	1,410	NA	43.0
Siena Coll., Loudonville, NY 12211-1462	1937	$42,880	$16,705	2-M	3,651	352	76.5
Siena Heights Univ., Adrian, MI 49221-1796	1919	$29,044	$12,200	2-M	1,966	190	50.0
Simmons Coll., Boston, MA 02115 (6)	1899	$45,538	$17,104	1-D	5,705	1,196	74.0
Skidmore Coll., Saratoga Springs, NY 12866	1922	NA	NA	1-B	2,758	386	84.2
Skyline Coll., San Bruno, CA 94066-1698	1969	$1,464 (A)	$11,164	9-B	14,900	333	NA
Slippery Rock Univ. of Pennsylvania, Slippery Rock, PA 16057-1383	1889	$10,507 (A)	$10,268	5-D	8,243	422	66.5
Smith Coll., Northampton, MA 01063 (6)	1871	NA	NA	1-D	2,873	313	88.5
Sonoma State Univ., Rohnert Park, CA 94928-3609	1960	$8,060 (A)	$16,020	5-M	7,371	NA	59.9
South Carolina State Univ., Orangeburg, SC 29117-0001	1896	$11,060 (A)	$9,000	5-D	2,649	187	34.0
South Coll., Knoxville, TN 37917 (4)	1882	$17,335	NA	3-M	4,175	NA	NA
South Dakota Sch. of Mines & Tech., Rapid City, SD 57701-3995	1885	$12,791 (A)	$7,844	5-D	2,146	NA	NA
South Dakota State Univ., Brookings, SD 57007	1881	$9,300 (A)	$9,564	5-D	11,331	621	59.3
South Florida State Coll., Avon Park, FL 33825-9356	1965	NA	NA	5-B	2,809	160	NA
South Georgia State Coll., Douglas, GA 31533-5098	1906	$3,310 (A)	$8,782	5-B	2,028	115	NA
South Texas Coll., McAllen, TX 78501	1993	$1,968 (A)	NA	9-B	28,233	NA	NA
South Univ., Savannah, GA 31406	1899	$18,000	NA	1-D	9,955	NA	NA
Southeast Missouri State Univ., Cape Girardeau, MO 63701-4799	1873	$10,839 (A)	$11,486	5-M	9,927	496	56.0
Southeastern Baptist Theol Sem, Wake Forest, NC 27587	1950	$10,072	$6,806	2-D	2,764	80	54.0
Southeastern Louisiana Univ., Hammond, LA 70402	1925	$8,373 (A)	$9,430	5-D	13,492	619	37.7
Southeastern Oklahoma State Univ., Durant, OK 74701-0609	1909	$6,990 (A)	$8,210	5-M	4,824	213	34.8
Southeastern Univ., Lakeland, FL 33801-6099	1935	$31,732	$11,020	2-D	10,044	470	44.9
Southern Adventist Univ., Collegedale, TN 37315-0370	1892	$23,210	$8,240	2-D	3,477	172	NA
Southern Arkansas Univ.–Magnolia, Magnolia, AR 71753	1909	NA	NA	5-D	5,094	332	32.9
Southern Connecticut State Univ., New Haven, CT 06515-1355	1893	$11,514 (A)	$14,700	5-D	8,788	990	52.3
Southern Illinois Univ. Carbondale, Carbondale, IL 62901-4701	1869	$13,244 (A)	$14,952	5-D	11,107	991	49.0
Southern Illinois Univ. Edwardsville, Edwardsville, IL 62026	1957	$12,923 (A)	$10,561	5-D	13,010	925	49.1
Southern Methodist Univ., Dallas, TX 75275	1911	$64,460	$18,230	2-D	12,053	1,139	82.0
Southern Nazarene Univ., Bethany, OK 73008	1899	$27,000	$10,300	2-M	1,529	92	60.0
Southern New Hampshire Univ., Manchester, NH 03106-1045	1932	$15,380	$11,800	1-D	3,305	449	68.0
Southern Oregon Univ., Ashland, OR 97520	1926	$11,691 (A)	$15,819	5-M	5,059	263	46.0
Southern Univ. & Agr. & Mech. Coll., Baton Rouge, LA 70813	1880	$9,842 (A)	$9,366	5-D	6,917	441	31.0
Southern Univ. at New Orleans, New Orleans, LA 70126-1009 (4)	1959	$10,486 (A)	$9,020	5-M	1,941	NA	5.2
Southern Utah Univ., Cedar City, UT 84720-2498	1897	$6,770 (A)	$8,824	5-M	13,611	632	47.4
Southwest Baptist Univ., Bolivar, MO 65613-2597	1878	$26,970	$8,290	2-D	3,039	293	48.0
Southwest Minnesota State Univ., Marshall, MN 56258	1963	$10,305 (A)	$11,174	5-M	6,846	NA	NA
Southwest Univ. at El Paso, El Paso, TX 79925	1999	$16,000	NA	3-B	1,558	NA	NA
Southwestern Assemblies of God Univ., Waxahachie, TX 75165-5735	1927	$22,632	$7,600	2-M	1,632	148	NA
Southwestern Univ., Georgetown, TX 78626	1840	$50,558	$14,726	2-B	1,483	151	72.0
Spelman Coll., Atlanta, GA 30314-4399 (3)	1881	$28,885	$15,666	1-B	2,374	288	74.0
Spring Arbor Univ., Spring Arbor, MI 49283-9799	1873	$31,660	$10,650	2-D	1,350	NA	NA
Springfield Coll., Springfield, MA 01109-3797	1885	$43,132	$14,202	1-D	2,965	NA	73.1
Stanbridge Univ., Irvine, CA 92612	NA	NA	NA	3-M	1,508	NA	NA
Stanford Univ., Stanford, CA 94305-2004	1891	$63,936	$19,922	1-D	17,680	2,212	96.0
State Coll. of Florida Manatee-Sarasota, Bradenton, FL 34206-7046	1957	$3,783 (A)	NA	5-B	8,684	430	NA
State Univ. of New York at Fredonia, Fredonia, NY 14063-1136	1826	$8,767 (S)	$14,230	5-M	3,526	389	61.0
State Univ. of New York at New Paltz, New Paltz, NY 12561	1828	$8,524 (A)	$15,616	5-M	6,964	635	73.0
State Univ. of New York at Oswego, Oswego, NY 13126	1861	$8,769 (A)	$15,753	5-M	6,906	540	64.0
State Univ. of New York at Plattsburgh, Plattsburgh, NY 12901-2681	1889	$8,881 (A)	$16,570	5-M	4,474	353	64.8
State Univ. of New York Coll. at Cortland, Cortland, NY 13045	1868	$8,900 (A)	$15,210	5-M	6,691	618	68.7

Name, address	Year founded	Tuition & fees	Room & board	Control, degree	Enroll-ment	Faculty	Grad. rate
State Univ. of New York Coll. at Geneseo, Geneseo, NY 14454-1401	1871	$8,966 (A)	$14,796	5-M	4,210	332	74.4%
State Univ. of New York Coll. at Old Westbury, Old Westbury, NY 11568-0210	1965	$8,489 (A)	$13,760	5-M	4,659	351	43.0
State Univ. of New York Coll. at Oneonta, Oneonta, NY 13820-4015	1889	$8,812 (A)	$15,810	5-M	5,430	461	76.8
State Univ. of New York Coll. at Potsdam, Potsdam, NY 13676	1816	$8,712 (A)	$15,084	5-M	2,427	292	49.8
State Univ. of New York Coll. of Agr. & Tech. at Cobleskill, Cobleskill, NY 12043	1916	$8,634 (A)	$15,310	5-B	1,783	157	50.0
State Univ. of New York Coll. of Environmental Sci. & For., Syracuse, NY 13210-2779	1911	$9,266 (A)	$17,820	5-D	1,976	162	71.0
State Univ. of New York Coll. of Tech. at Alfred, Alfred, NY 14802	1908	$8,862 (A)	$13,620	5-B	3,348	254	42.0
State Univ. of New York Coll. of Tech. at Canton, Canton, NY 13617	1906	$8,689 (A)	$16,700	5-B	2,944	221	45.0
State Univ. of New York Coll. of Tech. at Delhi, Delhi, NY 13753	1913	$8,710 (A)	$14,590	5-B	2,615	204	59.3
State Univ. of New York Empire State Coll., Saratoga Springs, NY 12866-4391	1971	$7,630 (A)	$14,230	5-D	9,462	662	NA
State Univ. of New York Maritime Coll., Throggs Neck, NY 10465-4198	1874	$8,665 (A)	$15,274	5-M	1,427	122	73.0
Stetson Univ., DeLand, FL 32723	1883	$55,220	$16,030	1-D	3,928	433	63.7
Stevens Inst. of Tech., Hoboken, NJ 07030	1870	$60,952	$18,650	1-D	9,314	422	88.0
Stevenson Univ., Stevenson, MD 21153	1947	NA	$13,340	13-D	3,483	392	65.1
Stockton Univ., Galloway, NJ 08205-9441	1969	$15,444 (A)	$13,520	5-D	9,080	770	76.1
Stonehill Coll., Easton, MA 02357	1948	$53,300	$15,300	2-M	2,542	NA	82.0
Stony Brook Univ., State Univ. of New York, Stony Brook, NY 11794	1957	$10,772 (A)	$16,594	5-D	25,710	1,631	78.0
Strayer Univ.–Arlington campus, Arlington, VA 22201	NA	$14,055	$8,613	3-M	3,819	NA	NA
Strayer Univ.–Birmingham campus, Birmingham, AL 35243	NA	$13,725	$8,613	3-M	1,534	NA	NA
Strayer Univ.–Greenville campus, Greenville, SC 29607	NA	$13,515	$8,613	3-M	2,459	NA	NA
Strayer Univ.–Lower Bucks Cty. campus, Trevose, PA 19053	NA	$14,055	$8,613	3-M	1,973	NA	NA
Suffolk Univ., Boston, MA 02108-2770	1906	$45,380	$20,360	13-D	6,790	667	60.2
Sul Ross State Univ., Alpine, TX 79832	1920	$9,334 (A)	$9,744	5-M	1,987	167	26.0
Sullivan Univ., Louisville, KY 40205	1962	NA	NA	3-D	2,265	162	NA
Susquehanna Univ., Selinsgrove, PA 17870	1858	$55,160	$14,960	2-M	2,202	235	70.6
Swarthmore Coll., Swarthmore, PA 19081-1397	1864	$62,412	$18,964	1-B	1,625	235	94.0
Syracuse Univ., Syracuse, NY 13244	1870	$63,061	$18,444	13-D	22,698	1,778	83.4
Tallahassee Comm. Coll., Tallahassee, FL 32304-2895	1966	$3,341 (A)	$11,100	11-B	11,935	740	NA
Tarleton State Univ., Stephenville, TX 76402	1899	$10,294 (A)	$10,846	5-D	14,092	787	62.0
Taylor Univ., Upland, IN 46989-1001	1846	$38,440	$11,552	2-M	2,226	200	78.0
Temple Univ., Philadelphia, PA 19122-6096	1884	$18,060 (A)	$11,968	12-D	33,230	2,675	78.0
Tennessee State Univ., Nashville, TN 37209-1561	1912	$8,336 (A)	$8,716	5-D	9,218	528	33.2
Tennessee Tech. Univ., Cookeville, TN 38505	1915	$10,830 (A)	$5,934	5-D	10,186	NA	NA
Texas A&M Intl. Univ., Laredo, TX 78041	1969	$1,500 (A)	$9,650	5-D	8,525	412	46.7
Texas A&M Univ., College Station, TX 77843	1876	$12,413 (A)	$13,154	5-D	74,014	4,171	83.5
Texas A&M Univ.–Central Texas, Killeen, TX 76549	2009	$5,713 (A)	NA	5-M	2,073	143	NA
Texas A&M Univ.–Commerce, Commerce, TX 75429	1889	$10,026 (A)	$9,584	5-D	10,966	722	44.8
Texas A&M Univ.–Corpus Christi, Corpus Christi, TX 78412	1947	$10,426 (A)	$12,869	5-D	10,778	567	35.0
Texas A&M Univ.–Kingsville, Kingsville, TX 78363	1925	$9,992 (A)	$10,823	5-D	6,932	440	44.7
Texas A&M Univ.–San Antonio, San Antonio, TX 78224	2009	$13,220 (A)	$10,760	5-M	6,078	NA	NA
Texas A&M Univ.–Texarkana, Texarkana, TX 75503	1971	$8,689 (A)	$12,082	5-D	2,138	169	23.7
Texas Christian Univ., Fort Worth, TX 76129-0002	1873	$57,220	$14,800	2-D	12,273	1,212	83.7
Texas Lutheran Univ., Seguin, TX 78155-5999	1891	$34,920	$11,880	2-D	1,441	193	55.3
Texas Southern Univ., Houston, TX 77004-4584	1947	$12,010 (A)	$10,914	5-D	7,524	649	23.0
Texas State Univ., San Marcos, TX 78666	1899	$12,207 (S)	$12,270	5-D	38,111	1,850	56.0
Texas Tech. Univ., Lubbock, TX 79409	1923	$11,852 (A)	$10,460	5-D	40,378	2,170	63.7
Texas Wesleyan Univ., Fort Worth, TX 76105	1890	$36,128	$10,728	2-D	2,619	NA	NA
Texas Woman's Univ., Denton, TX 76204 (4)	1901	$10,540 (A)	$10,950	5-D	15,877	955	48.0
The Catholic Univ. of America, Washington, DC 20064	1887	$55,834	$18,610	2-D	4,968	703	76.0
The Citadel, The Military Coll. of South Carolina, Charleston, SC 29409 (2)	1842	$14,390 (A)	$9,791	5-M	3,721	306	73.0
The Coll. at Brockport, State Univ. of New York, Brockport, NY 14420-2997	1867	$8,698 (A)	$15,752	5-M	6,424	552	62.8
The Coll. of New Jersey, Ewing, NJ 08628	1855	$18,546 (A)	$16,140	5-M	7,629	820	86.0
The Coll. of St. Rose, Albany, NY 12203-1419	1920	$36,398	$13,986	1-M	3,314	264	59.0
The Coll. of St. Scholastica, Duluth, MN 55811-4199	1912	$40,454	$11,380	2-D	3,612	377	65.0
The Coll. of William & Mary, Williamsburg, VA 23187-8795	1693	$25,040 (A)	$14,555	5-D	9,658	958	91.0
The Coll. of Wooster, Wooster, OH 44691-2363	1866	$59,550	$14,000	1-B	1,967	196	74.0
The Colorado Coll., Colorado Springs, CO 80903-3294	1874	$67,932	$15,228	1-M	2,203	253	86.1
The Culinary Inst. of America, Hyde Park, NY 12538-1499	1946	NA	NA	2-M	3,124	207	NA
The Evergreen State Coll., Olympia, WA 98505	1967	$8,250 (A)	$13,806	5-M	2,116	166	43.2
The George Washington Univ., Washington, DC 20052	1821	$64,990	$20,000	1-D	25,939	2,650	84.8
The Master's Univ., Santa Clarita, CA 91321-1200	1927	$28,740	$14,110	2-D	2,435	221	65.0
The Ohio State Univ., Columbus, OH 43210	1870	$12,485 (S)	$13,966	5-D	60,540	6,327	88.0
The Ohio State Univ.–Newark campus, Newark, OH 43055-1797	1957	$8,550 (A)	$10,408	5-M	2,263	148	5.0
The Southern Baptist Theol. Sem., Louisville, KY 40280-0004	1858	$11,896	$7,450	2-D	3,190	NA	NA
The Univ. of Akron Wayne Coll., Orrville, OH 44667-9192	1972	$6,505 (A)	NA	5-B	2,353	119	6.0
The Univ. of Akron, Akron, OH 44325	1870	$10,097 (A)	$11,220	5-D	13,465	1,032	51.7
The Univ. of Alabama at Birmingham, Birmingham, AL 35294	1969	$11,040 (A)	$12,630	5-D	21,639	1,268	64.2
The Univ. of Alabama in Huntsville, Huntsville, AL 35899	1950	$11,878 (A)	$11,540	5-D	9,636	559	60.8
The Univ. of Alabama, Tuscaloosa, AL 35487	1831	$11,900 (A)	$14,426	5-D	38,644	1,969	72.8
The Univ. of Arizona, Tucson, AZ 85721	1885	$13,605 (A)	$14,400	5-D	51,134	2,536	67.9
The Univ. of Findlay, Findlay, OH 45840-3653	1882	$39,646	$11,200	13-D	4,885	365	66.0
The Univ. of Iowa, Iowa City, IA 52242-1316	1847	$12,606 (A)	$12,616	5-D	29,909	1,598	73.7
The Univ. of Kansas, Lawrence, KS 66045	1866	$11,370 (A)	$10,136	5-D	26,708	1,566	67.0
The Univ. of Montana Western, Dillon, MT 59725-3598	1893	$6,431 (S)	$9,464	5-B	1,424	104	47.0
The Univ. of North Carolina at Chapel Hill, Chapel Hill, NC 27599	1789	$8,998 (A)	$13,016	10-D	31,949	2,488	91.0
The Univ. of North Carolina at Charlotte, Charlotte, NC 28223-0001	1946	$7,214 (A)	$12,858	5-D	29,551	1,582	69.9

Name, address	Year founded	Tuition & fees	Room & board	Control, degree	Enroll- ment	Faculty	Grad. rate
The Univ. of North Carolina at Greensboro, Greensboro, NC 27412-5001	1891	$7,498 (A)	$9,924	5-D	17,978	1,113	56.9%
The Univ. of North Carolina at Pembroke, Pembroke, NC 28372-1510	1887	$3,496 (A)	$11,052	5-M	7,666	425	45.1
The Univ. of North Carolina Wilmington, Wilmington, NC 28403-3297	1947	$7,238 (A)	$12,120	5-D	17,843	1,232	74.3
The Univ. of Scranton, Scranton, PA 18510.	1888	NA	NA	2-D	4,692	461	79.0
The Univ. of South Dakota, Vermillion, SD 57069	1862	$9,432 (A)	$8,600	5-D	9,856	667	56.6
The Univ. of Tampa, Tampa, FL 33606-1490	1931	$33,404	$12,686	1-D	10,566	845	65.7
The Univ. of Tennessee, Knoxville, TN 37996	1794	$13,484 (A)	$12,150	5-D	33,805	2,072	72.6
The Univ. of Tennessee at Chattanooga, Chattanooga, TN 37403-2598.	1886	$10,144 (A)	$12,930	5-D	11,283	770	52.0
The Univ. of Tennessee at Martin, Martin, TN 38238.	1900	$5,104 (A)	$6,960	5-M	6,873	479	52.6
The Univ. of Texas at Arlington, Arlington, TX 76019	1895	$11,314 (A)	$10,582	5-D	35,064	NA	42.0
The Univ. of Texas at Austin, Austin, TX 78712-1111	1883	$11,758 (A)	$13,058	5-D	52,484	3,254	87.8
The Univ. of Texas at Dallas, Richardson, TX 75080.	1969	$17,912 (A)	$12,142	5-D	31,570	1,315	73.9
The Univ. of Texas at El Paso, El Paso, TX 79968-0001.	1913	$8,761 (A)	$5,134	5-D	24,879	1,363	44.0
The Univ. of Texas at San Antonio, San Antonio, TX 78249-0617.	1969	$10,581 (A)	$14,248	5-D	34,344	1,339	53.5
The Univ. of Texas at Tyler, Tyler, TX 75799-0001	1971	$9,830 (A)	$10,710	5-D	9,317	616	44.0
The Univ. of Texas of the Permian Basin, Odessa, TX 79762-0001.	1973	$10,904 (A)	$12,780	5-M	5,848	306	39.8
The Univ. of Texas Rio Grande Valley, Edinburg, TX 78539	1927	$9,859 (A)	$9,662	5-D	31,559	1,544	53.0
The Univ. of the Arts, Philadelphia, PA 19102-4944	1876	$54,290	$19,028	1-D	1,313	359	66.0
The Univ. of Toledo, Toledo, OH 43606-3390	1872	$10,679 (A)	$13,506	5-D	15,584	933	56.5
The Univ. of Tulsa, Tulsa, OK 74104-3189	1894	$48,602	$13,622	1-D	3,769	425	72.2
The Univ. of Virginia's Coll. at Wise, Wise, VA 24293	1954	NA	NA	5-B	1,905	182	42.8
The Univ. of West Alabama, Livingston, AL 35470	1835	$10,990 (A)	$9,006	5-D	5,594	273	38.7
Thomas Coll., Waterville, ME 04901-5097.	1894	$29,738	$11,998	1-M	1,601	NA	45.0
Thomas Edison State Univ., Trenton, NJ 08608	1972	$6,638 (A)	NA	5-D	12,504	NA	NA
Thomas Jefferson Univ., Philadelphia, PA 19107	1824	$45,533	$14,715	1-D	8,270	803	71.0
Thomas More Coll., Crestview Hills, KY 41017-3495.	1921	$35,810	$10,014	2-M	1,892	NA	NA
Tiffin Univ., Tiffin, OH 44883-2161	1888	$29,620	$11,700	1-D	2,933	256	41.0
Toccoa Falls Coll., Toccoa Falls, GA 30598	1907	$23,250	$8,600	2-M	2,046	148	46.0
Touro Coll., New York, NY 10010	1971	$18,350	$16,180	1-D	11,222	1,254	70.0
Touro Univ. Worldwide, Los Alamitos, CA 90720.	NA	$14,600	NA	1-D	2,251	135	NA
Towson Univ., Towson, MD 21252-0001	1866	$11,306 (A)	$15,214	5-D	19,793	1,654	70.0
Trevecca Nazarene Univ., Nashville, TN 37210-2877	1901	$30,090	$9,900	2-D	3,327	131	61.0
Trine Univ., Angola, IN 46703-1764	1884	$34,890	$11,920	1-D	3,573	226	NA
Trinity Coll., Hartford, CT 06106-3100	1823	$67,420	$17,990	1-M	2,205	290	83.6
Trinity Univ., San Antonio, TX 78212-7200	1869	$51,352	$14,472	2-M	2,692	344	75.8
Trinity Washington Univ., Washington, DC 20017-1094 (3).	1897	$25,610	$11,750	2-M	1,444	NA	NA
Trocaire Coll., Buffalo, NY 14220-2094 (4)	1958	$18,700	NA	1-B	1,376	172	NA
Troy Univ., Troy, AL 36082.	1887	$12,240 (A)	$7,996	14-D	14,156	927	46.0
Truckee Meadows Comm. Coll., Reno, NV 89512-3901	1971	$3,144 (A)	$16,812	5-B	9,651	658	NA
Truett McConnell Univ., Cleveland, GA 30528.	1946	NA	NA	2-M	2,796	184	44.0
Truman State Univ., Kirksville, MO 63501-4221	1867	$9,456 (A)	$10,701	5-M	4,120	292	71.0
Tufts Univ., Medford, MA 02155	1852	$67,844	$17,660	1-D	13,431	1,196	93.7
Tulane Univ., New Orleans, LA 70118-5669	1834	$58,666	$17,346	1-D	12,592	1,346	87.4
Tusculum Coll., Greeneville, TN 37743-9997.	1794	$29,708	$10,750	2-M	1,386	95	NA
Tuskegee Univ., Tuskegee, AL 36088	1881	$22,614	$10,680	1-D	2,995	207	46.0
Tyler Jr. Coll., Tyler, TX 75711-9020	1926	$4,964 (A)	$9,424	11-B	11,749	563	NA
Union Coll., Schenectady, NY 12308-2311	1795	$66,456	$16,389	13-B	2,107	233	84.6
Union Univ., Jackson, TN 38305-3697	1823	$38,300	$12,166	2-D	2,730	204	67.0
United States Air Force Academy, USAF Academy, CO 80840-5025	1954	NA	NA	4-B	4,085	580	88.1
United States Military Academy, West Point, NY 10996	1802	NA	NA	4-B	4,393	744	87.7
United States Naval Academy, Annapolis, MD 21402-5000	1845	NA	NA	4-B	4,450	588	89.6
Unity Coll., Unity, ME 04988.	1965	$12,640	$10,900	1-M	1,429	165	47.0
Univ. at Albany, State Univ. of New York, Albany, NY 12222-0001.	1844	$10,468 (A)	$16,034	5-D	16,658	1,203	64.4
Univ. at Buffalo, the State Univ. of New York, Buffalo, NY 14260	1846	$10,856 (A)	$16,212	5-D	32,101	2,003	73.5
Univ. of Alaska Anchorage, Anchorage, AK 99508	1954	$8,371 (A)	$15,648	5-D	10,530	804	31.0
Univ. of Alaska Anchorage, Kenai Peninsula Coll., Soldotna, AK 99669-9798.	1964	$6,151 (A)	NA	5-B	2,142	NA	NA
Univ. of Alaska Fairbanks, Fairbanks, AK 99775-7520	1917	$10,334 (A)	$10,650	5-D	6,668	909	41.0
Univ. of Alaska Southeast, Juneau, AK 99801.	1972	$9,920 (A)	$9,800	5-M	1,923	169	27.0
Univ. of Alaska Southeast, Sitka campus, Sitka, AK 99835-9418.	1962	$5,616 (A)	NA	5-M	1,552	59	NA
Univ. of Arkansas, Fayetteville, AR 72701	1871	$9,748 (A)	$12,368	5-D	30,936	1,512	69.2
Univ. of Arkansas at Little Rock, Little Rock, AR 72204-1099	1927	$6,042 (A)	$9,162	5-D	8,266	NA	37.1
Univ. of Arkansas at Monticello, Monticello, AR 71656	1909	$8,421 (A)	$7,360	5-M	2,352	NA	NA
Univ. of Arkansas at Pine Bluff, Pine Bluff, AR 71601-2799	1873	$8,064 (A)	$8,624	5-D	2,658	199	26.0
Univ. of Arkansas for Med. Scis., Little Rock, AR 72205-7199	1879	NA	$7,800	5-D	3,240	989	NA
Univ. of Arkansas–Fort Smith, Fort Smith, AR 72913-3649.	1928	$8,594 (A)	$9,799	11-M	5,887	337	44.0
Univ. of Baltimore, Baltimore, MD 21201-5779	1925	$9,772 (A)	$19,350	5-D	1,899	405	NA
Univ. of Bridgeport, Bridgeport, CT 06604	1927	$35,760	$16,350	1-D	2,350	NA	NA
Univ. of California, Berkeley, Berkeley, CA 94720.	1868	$14,959 (A)	$22,402	14-D	45,745	NA	94.0
Univ. of California, Davis, Davis, CA 95616.	1908	$16,018 (A)	$18,562	5-D	39,075	2,284	NA
Univ. of California, Irvine, Irvine, CA 92697	1965	$15,185 (A)	$18,639	5-D	35,936	1,711	86.7
Univ. of California, Los Angeles, Los Angeles, CA 90095	1919	$14,478 (A)	$17,436	14-D	47,516	2,621	92.0
Univ. of California, Merced, Merced, CA 95343	NA	$13,752 (S)	$20,240	5-D	9,104	471	67.5
Univ. of California, Riverside, Riverside, CA 92521-0102	1954	$15,236 (A)	$17,333	5-D	26,809	1,151	76.0
Univ. of California, San Diego, La Jolla, CA 92093	1959	$18,147 (A)	$17,325	5-D	41,482	1,578	87.7
Univ. of California, Santa Barbara, Santa Barbara, CA 93106-2014.	1909	$15,666 (A)	$18,276	5-D	26,124	1,225	88.7
Univ. of California, Santa Cruz, Santa Cruz, CA 95064.	1965	$13,000 (A)	$18,785	5-D	19,478	917	77.0
Univ. of Central Arkansas, Conway, AR 72035-0001.	1907	$14,667 (A)	$9,194	5-D	9,913	694	50.1
Univ. of Central Florida, Orlando, FL 32816.	1963	$9,584 (A)	$11,498	5-D	68,442	2,236	76.0
Univ. of Central Missouri, Warrensburg, MO 64093.	1871	$9,410 (A)	$9,699	5-M	11,637	537	48.0
Univ. of Central Oklahoma, Edmond, OK 73034-5209.	1890	$8,522 (A)	$9,050	5-M	14,132	876	34.9
Univ. of Charleston, Charleston, WV 25304-1099	1888	$31,900	$10,200	1-D	2,926	239	43.0

Name, address	Year founded	Tuition & fees	Room & board	Control, degree	Enroll-ment	Faculty	Grad. rate
Univ. of Chicago, Chicago, IL 60637-1513.	1890	$65,619	$19,221	1-D	15,946	1,896	96.0%
Univ. of Cincinnati, Cincinnati, OH 45221	1819	$13,570 (A)	$15,350	5-D	40,281	3,459	73.0
Univ. of Cincinnati Blue Ash Coll., Cincinnati, OH 45236-1007	1967	$6,387 (A)	$12,288	5-B	16,098	451	NA
Univ. of Cincinnati Clermont Coll., Batavia, OH 45103-1785	1972	$7,100 (A)	NA	5-B	2,242	284	NA
Univ. of Colorado Boulder, Boulder, CO 80309	1876	$11,976 (A)	$17,590	5-D	37,956	2,347	73.8
Univ. of Colorado Colorado Springs, Colorado Springs, CO 80918	1965	$12,517 (A)	$13,978	5-D	12,031	804	44.1
Univ. of Colorado Denver, Denver, CO 80217-3364	1912	$12,366 (A)	$14,460	5-D	23,744	5,912	44.0
Univ. of Connecticut, Storrs, CT 06269	1881	$20,366 (A)	$13,996	5-D	26,876	1,542	83.0
Univ. of Dallas, Irving, TX 75062-4736.	1956	$50,880	$14,360	2-D	2,328	207	72.0
Univ. of Dayton, Dayton, OH 45469	1850	$47,600	$15,390	2-D	11,674	970	81.0
Univ. of Delaware, Newark, DE 19716.	1743	$14,040 (A)	$14,838	12-D	23,996	1,746	83.6
Univ. of Denver, Denver, CO 80208.	1864	$59,340	$17,049	1-D	13,743	1,641	77.5
Univ. of Detroit Mercy, Detroit, MI 48221	1877	$31,058	$11,222	2-D	5,360	636	73.0
Univ. of Dubuque, Dubuque, IA 52001-5099	1852	$40,065	$11,470	2-D	1,777	318	39.0
Univ. of Evansville, Evansville, IN 47722	1854	$41,336	$13,840	2-D	2,041	262	73.0
Univ. of Florida, Gainesville, FL 32611	1853	$6,380 (A)	$11,500	5-D	55,782	3,382	92.0
Univ. of Georgia, Athens, GA 30602	1785	$11,180 (A)	$10,940	5-D	40,607	2,648	88.1
Univ. of Guam, Mangilao, GU 96923	1952	$6,110 (A)	$7,283	7-M	3,105	263	41.2
Univ. of Hartford, West Hartford, CT 06117-1599	1877	$47,648	$13,945	1-D	5,732	804	60.0
Univ. of Hawaii at Hilo, Hilo, HI 96720-4091	1970	$7,838 (A)	$8,248	5-D	3,924	NA	NA
Univ. of Hawaii at Manoa, Honolulu, HI 96822.	1907	$12,186 (A)	$14,936	5-D	19,074	1,279	62.3
Univ. of Hawaii Maui Coll., Kahului, HI 96732	1967	$3,278 (A)	NA	5-B	4,071	117	NA
Univ. of Hawaii–West Oahu, Kapolei, HI 96707.	1976	$7,584 (A)	NA	5-B	2,913	186	32.7
Univ. of Houston, Houston, TX 77204	1927	$11,882 (A)	$10,830	5-D	46,700	3,139	63.1
Univ. of Houston–Clear Lake, Houston, TX 77058-1002	1971	$17,413 (A)	$9,440	5-D	8,562	530	47.6
Univ. of Houston–Downtown, Houston, TX 77002.	1974	$8,828 (A)	NA	5-M	14,208	761	30.9
Univ. of Houston-Victoria, Victoria, TX 77901-4450	1973	$7,499 (A)	$9,882	5-M	4,407	239	NA
Univ. of Idaho, Moscow, ID 83844-2282	1889	$8,396 (A)	$10,380	5-D	11,507	670	61.1
Univ. of Illinois at Chicago, Chicago, IL 60607-7128	1946	$14,338 (A)	$15,400	5-D	33,747	1,922	62.0
Univ. of Illinois at Springfield, Springfield, IL 62703-5407	1969	$12,262 (A)	$12,088	5-D	3,974	342	52.0
Univ. of Illinois at Urbana–Champaign, Champaign, IL 61820.	1867	$21,802 (A)	$12,354	5-D	56,607	1,936	85.0
Univ. of Indianapolis, Indianapolis, IN 46227-3697	1902	$36,136	$15,878	2-D	5,018	544	60.0
Univ. of Kentucky, Lexington, KY 40506-0032.	1865	$13,212 (A)	$14,676	5-D	31,547	2,261	68.5
Univ. of La Verne, La Verne, CA 91750-4443	1891	$48,300	$15,450	1-D	4,171	515	63.0
Univ. of Louisiana at Lafayette, Lafayette, LA 70504	1898	$10,346 (A)	$13,959	5-D	15,219	831	51.0
Univ. of Louisiana at Monroe, Monroe, LA 71209-0001	1931	$9,207 (A)	$9,770	5-D	8,565	438	54.3
Univ. of Louisville, Louisville, KY 40292-0001	1798	$12,520 (A)	$11,190	5-D	22,017	1,801	62.2
Univ. of Maine, Orono, ME 04469	1865	$12,136 (A)	$12,050	5-D	11,571	836	56.6
Univ. of Maine at Augusta, Augusta, ME 04330-9410	1965	$8,378 (A)	$8,200	5-B	4,683	238	12.1
Univ. of Maine at Farmington, Farmington, ME 04938.	1863	$10,989 (A)	$11,086	5-M	2,051	173	53.0
Univ. of Maine at Fort Kent, Fort Kent, ME 04743-1292	1878	$9,045 (A)	$9,590	5-B	1,517	80	45.3
Univ. of Maine at Presque Isle, Presque Isle, ME 04769-2888	1903	$9,035 (A)	$10,300	5-M	1,590	72	35.0
Univ. of Mary, Bismarck, ND 58504-9652	1959	$20,332	$8,380	2-D	7,263	286	64.0
Univ. of Mary Hardin-Baylor, Belton, TX 76513	1845	$33,150	$10,720	13-D	3,575	326	53.0
Univ. of Mary Washington, Fredericksburg, VA 22401-5358	1908	$14,234 (A)	$12,090	5-M	3,757	316	68.8
Univ. of Maryland Eastern Shore, Princess Anne, MD 21853	1886	$8,724 (A)	$10,085	5-D	2,648	256	40.2
Univ. of Maryland Univ. Coll., Adelphi, MD 20783	1947	$7,704 (A)	NA	5-D	58,526	3,837	NA
Univ. of Maryland, Baltimore Cty, Baltimore, MD 21250	1963	$12,952 (A)	$11,082	5-D	13,991	963	70.0
Univ. of Maryland, Coll. Park, College Park, MD 20742.	1856	$11,233 (A)	$14,896	5-D	40,792	2,609	89.1
Univ. of Massachusetts Amherst, Amherst, MA 01003	1863	$18,123 (A)	$15,437	5-D	32,229	1,761	83.0
Univ. of Massachusetts Boston, Boston, MA 02125-3393	1964	$15,535 (A)	$17,436	5-D	15,586	1,134	51.0
Univ. of Massachusetts Dartmouth, North Dartmouth, MA 02747-2300	1895	$15,208 (A)	$16,000	5-D	7,457	593	54.6
Univ. of Massachusetts Lowell, Lowell, MA 01854.	1894	$16,570 (A)	$13,930	5-D	17,863	NA	69.0
Univ. of Memphis, Memphis, TN 38152	1912	$10,344 (A)	$10,096	5-D	21,917	1,326	48.0
Univ. of Miami, Coral Gables, FL 33124.	1925	$59,926	$21,580	1-D	19,402	1,631	84.0
Univ. of Michigan, Ann Arbor, MI 48109.	1817	$16,736 (A)	$14,460	5-D	51,225	3,706	93.2
Univ. of Michigan–Dearborn, Dearborn, MI 48128.	1959	$14,944 (A)	$2,262	5-M	8,223	494	56.0
Univ. of Michigan–Flint, Flint, MI 48502-1950	1956	$13,524 (A)	$10,628	5-D	5,985	463	46.0
Univ. of Minnesota, Crookston, Crookston, MN 56716-5001	1966	$13,120 (A)	$10,400	5-B	2,303	98	53.0
Univ. of Minnesota, Duluth, Duluth, MN 55812-2496	1947	$14,318 (A)	$10,206	5-D	9,675	561	62.0
Univ. of Minnesota, Twin Cities campus, Minneapolis, MN 55455-0213	1851	$14,496 (A)	$13,028	5-D	54,955	3,512	84.0
Univ. of Mississippi, University, MS 38677.	1844	$9,412 (A)	$12,040	5-D	22,300	1,355	68.0
Univ. of Mississippi Med. Ctr., Jackson, MS 39216-4505	1955	NA	NA	5-D	2,092	NA	NA
Univ. of Missouri, Columbia, MO 65211.	1839	$14,122 (A)	$14,485	5-D	31,318	1,646	75.3
Univ. of Missouri–Kansas City, Kansas City, MO 64110-2499.	1929	$9,840 (A)	$11,269	5-D	15,715	1,158	54.5
Univ. of Missouri–St. Louis, St. Louis, MO 63121	1963	$12,648 (A)	$10,920	5-D	15,189	689	57.6
Univ. of Mobile, Mobile, AL 36613	1961	$25,620	$10,100	2-D	2,016	NA	NA
Univ. of Montana, Missoula, MT 59812	1893	$8,152 (A)	NA	5-D	10,106	610	48.6
Univ. of Montevallo, Montevallo, AL 35115	1896	NA	NA	5-M	2,586	236	55.0
Univ. of Mount Olive, Mount Olive, NC 28365	1951	$24,091	$9,983	2-M	2,350	NA	NA
Univ. of Mount Union, Alliance, OH 44601-3993	1846	$34,400	$11,200	2-D	2,133	263	68.2
Univ. of Nebraska at Kearney, Kearney, NE 68849-0001	1903	$8,270 (A)	$11,566	5-M	6,041	471	54.1
Univ. of Nebraska at Omaha, Omaha, NE 68182	1908	$8,938 (A)	$11,610	5-D	15,328	1,210	58.4
Univ. of Nebraska–Lincoln, Lincoln, NE 68588	1869	$9,579 (A)	$12,430	5-D	23,805	1,607	65.0
Univ. of Nevada, Las Vegas, Las Vegas, NV 89154	1957	$9,143 (A)	$12,072	5-D	30,660	2,226	47.0
Univ. of Nevada, Reno, Reno, NV 89557	1874	$8,994 (A)	$13,700	5-D	20,945	1,349	62.0
Univ. of New England, Biddeford, ME 04005-9526	1831	$40,950	$16,100	1-D	6,434	534	62.1
Univ. of New Hampshire, Durham, NH 03824	1866	$19,112 (A)	$12,992	5-D	13,991	974	78.0
Univ. of New Haven, West Haven, CT 06516	1920	$45,730	$18,400	1-D	8,819	795	61.0
Univ. of New Mexico, Albuquerque, NM 87131-2039.	1889	$10,298 (A)	$11,884	5-D	21,708	1,230	51.4
Univ. of New Orleans, New Orleans, LA 70148	1958	$9,054 (A)	$11,702	5-D	6,895	387	32.0
Univ. of North Alabama, Florence, AL 35632-0001	1830	$12,300 (A)	$10,990	5-D	8,832	566	51.0
Univ. of North Carolina at Asheville, Asheville, NC 28804-3299	1927	$7,380 (A)	$10,556	5-M	2,914	293	58.7
Univ. of North Dakota, Grand Forks, ND 58202	1883	$10,951 (A)	$10,170	5-D	13,876	810	63.0
Univ. of North Florida, Jacksonville, FL 32224	1965	$6,398 (A)	$10,192	5-D	16,406	927	63.0
Univ. of North Georgia, Dahlonega, GA 30597	1873	$7,012 (S)	$11,950	5-D	18,046	939	51.8
Univ. of North Texas, Denton, TX 76203	1890	$11,140 (A)	$10,277	5-D	42,168	NA	NA
Univ. of North Texas at Dallas, Dallas, TX 75241	2001	$9,518 (A)	$9,302	5-D	3,387	285	NA
Univ. of Northern Colorado, Greeley, CO 80639	1890	$14,634 (A)	$12,152	5-D	10,348	724	52.0
Univ. of Northern Iowa, Cedar Falls, IA 50614.	1876	$9,728 (A)	$9,648	5-D	8,949	546	63.6

Name, address	Year founded	Tuition & fees	Room & board	Control, degree	Enroll-ment	Faculty	Grad. rate
Univ. of Northwestern Ohio, Lima, OH 45805-1498	1920	$11,619	$6,900	1-M	3,848	127	57.0%
Univ. of Northwestern–St. Paul, St. Paul, MN 55113-1598	1902	$36,830	$12,282	2-M	3,253	314	70.0
Univ. of Notre Dame, Notre Dame, IN 46556	1842	$62,693	$17,378	2-D	13,105	1,482	96.0
Univ. of Oklahoma, Norman, OK 73019-0390	1890	$10,859 (A)	$15,780	5-D	28,320	1,645	75.8
Univ. of Oregon, Eugene, OR 97403	1876	$14,895 (A)	$15,840	5-D	23,163	1,415	73.4
Univ. of Pennsylvania, Philadelphia, PA 19104	1740	$66,104	$18,496	1-D	23,374	1,875	96.1
Univ. of Phoenix–Phoenix campus, Tempe, AZ 85282-2371	1976	$9,552	$7,770	3-M	69,408	985	NA
Univ. of Pikeville, Pikeville, KY 41501	1889	$24,150	$8,600	2-D	2,425	111	36.0
Univ. of Pittsburgh, Pittsburgh, PA 15260	1787	$21,080 (A)	$12,268	12-D	29,178	NA	83.7
Univ. of Pittsburgh at Greensburg, Greensburg, PA 15601-5860	1963	NA	NA	12-B	1,315	87	34.4
Univ. of Pittsburgh at Johnstown, Johnstown, PA 15904-2990	1927	NA	NA	12-B	2,356	149	57.0
Univ. of Portland, Portland, OR 97203-5798	1901	$51,812	$17,172	2-D	4,029	464	80.8
Univ. of Puerto Rico in Aguadilla, Aguadilla, PR 00604	1972	$5,540 (A)	NA	6-B	3,139	155	46.0
Univ. of Puerto Rico in Arecibo, Arecibo, PR 00614	1967	$4,940 (A)	NA	6-B	3,414	231	46.0
Univ. of Puerto Rico in Bayamón, Bayamón, PR 00959	1971	$6,284 (A)	$11,161	6-B	3,022	183	31.5
Univ. of Puerto Rico in Carolina, Carolina, PR 00984-4800	1974	$7,410 (A)	NA	6-B	3,392	222	48.0
Univ. of Puerto Rico in Cayey, Cayey, PR 00736	1967	$4,940 (A)	NA	6-B	3,830	123	41.6
Univ. of Puerto Rico in Humacao, Humacao, PR 00792	1962	$6,254 (A)	$11,161	6-B	2,634	219	48.0
Univ. of Puerto Rico in Ponce, Ponce, PR 00732-7186	1970	$4,940 (A)	NA	6-B	2,382	152	48.0
Univ. of Puerto Rico in Utuado, Utuado, PR 00641-2500	1979	$4,940 (A)	NA	6-B	1,623	58	NA
Univ. of Puerto Rico, Río Piedras campus, San Juan, PR 00931-3300	1903	NA	NA	6-D	14,932	1,271	47.1
Univ. of Puget Sound, Tacoma, WA 98416	1888	NA	NA	1-D	2,178	271	74.2
Univ. of Redlands, Redlands, CA 92373-0999	1907	$55,678	$15,758	1-D	2,371	NA	NA
Univ. of Rhode Island, Kingston, RI 02881	1892	$16,408 (A)	$14,130	5-D	16,696	NA	69.5
Univ. of Richmond, University of Richmond, VA 23173	1830	$62,600	$15,790	1-D	3,876	627	88.0
Univ. of Rio Grande, Rio Grande, OH 45674	1876	$20,060	$11,166	1-M	2,161	175	43.0
Univ. of Rochester, Rochester, NY 14627	1850	$64,322	$18,784	1-D	12,197	1,030	89.7
Univ. of St. Francis, Fort Wayne, IN 46808-3994	1890	$35,420	$11,240	2-D	1,903	267	54.5
Univ. of St. Francis, Joliet, IL 60435-6169	1920	$36,000	$11,430	2-D	3,426	319	65.0
Univ. of St. Joseph, West Hartford, CT 06117-2700 (4).	1932	$45,908	$13,588	1-D	1,992	346	61.0
Univ. of St. Mary, Leavenworth, KS 66048-5082	1923	$33,890	$10,032	2-D	1,267	152	38.5
Univ. of St. Thomas, Houston, TX 77006-4696	1947	$33,660	$10,248	2-D	3,691	408	66.0
Univ. of St. Thomas, St. Paul, MN 55105-1096	1885	$52,284	$13,764	2-D	9,871	819	76.1
Univ. of San Diego, San Diego, CA 92110-2492	1949	$56,444	$16,380	2-D	8,815	1,046	83.0
Univ. of San Francisco, San Francisco, CA 94117	1855	$58,222	$19,536	2-D	10,034	1,107	76.0
Univ. of Sioux Falls, Sioux Falls, SD 57105-1699	1883	$20,740	$8,960	2-D	1,594	128	58.6
Univ. of South Alabama, Mobile, AL 36688-0002	1963	$10,970 (A)	$8,510	5-D	13,463	1,011	47.0
Univ. of South Carolina Aiken, Aiken, SC 29801	1961	$10,760 (A)	$9,744	5-M	3,840	274	42.0
Univ. of South Carolina Beaufort, Bluffton, SC 29909	1959	$11,080 (A)	$11,710	5-M	2,037	157	30.0
Univ. of South Carolina Lancaster, Lancaster, SC 29721-0889	1959	$12,688 (A)	$13,332	5-B	1,729	105	NA
Univ. of South Carolina Sumter, Sumter, SC 29150-2498	1962	$7,558 (A)	NA	5-B	1,206	66	NA
Univ. of South Carolina Upstate, Spartanburg, SC 29303-4999	1967	$11,758 (A)	$6,726	5-M	4,890	378	43.0
Univ. of South Carolina, Columbia, SC 29208	1801	$12,688 (A)	$13,332	5-D	35,653	2,500	78.0
Univ. of South Florida, Tampa, FL 33620-9951	1956	$6,410 (A)	$13,595	5-D	44,322	2,099	75.0
Univ. of Southern California, Los Angeles, CA 90089	1880	$68,237	$19,200	1-D	49,318	3,603	92.0
Univ. of Southern Indiana, Evansville, IN 47712-3590	1965	NA	NA	5-D	8,446	592	50.0
Univ. of Southern Maine, Portland, ME 04103	1878	$11,700 (A)	$11,370	5-D	7,583	624	40.8
Univ. of Southern Mississippi, Hattiesburg, MS 39406-0001	NA	$9,618 (A)	$11,664	5-D	14,146	843	51.8
Univ. of the Cumberlands, Williamsburg, KY 40769-1372	1889	$9,875	$9,300	2-D	4,511	378	37.0
Univ. of the District of Columbia, Washington, DC 20008-1175	1976	$6,152 (A)	NA	9-D	4,803	576	14.0
Univ. of the Incarnate Word, San Antonio, TX 78209-6397	1881	$35,660	$13,746	2-D	7,405	744	53.0
Univ. of the Pacific, Stockton, CA 95211-0197	1851	$55,340	$16,688	1-D	6,066	837	66.0
Univ. of the Sacred Heart, San Juan, PR 00914-0383	1935	$6,170	$3,650	2-M	4,097	367	NA
Univ. of the Virgin Islands, St. Thomas, VI 00802	1962	$5,559 (S)	$10,650	7-D	1,636	223	26.0
Univ. of Utah, Salt Lake City, UT 84112-1107	1850	$10,287 (A)	$12,398	5-D	34,464	2,161	67.0
Univ. of Vermont, Burlington, VT 05405	1791	$18,890 (A)	$13,354	5-D	13,826	819	77.0
Univ. of Virginia, Charlottesville, VA 22903	1819	$21,381 (A)	$13,600	5-D	28,033	1,619	93.7
Univ. of Washington, Bothell, Bothell, WA 98011	1990	$12,929 (A)	$17,115	5-M	5,757	331	68.8
Univ. of Washington, Seattle, WA 98195	1861	$12,242 (A)	$16,068	5-D	53,083	2,622	84.4
Univ. of Washington, Tacoma, Tacoma, WA 98402-3100	1990	$12,458 (A)	$14,220	5-D	4,801	346	54.2
Univ. of West Florida, Pensacola, FL 32514-5750	1963	$7,129 (A)	$12,432	5-D	13,317	658	52.0
Univ. of West Georgia, Carrollton, GA 30118	1906	$7,034 (A)	$9,920	5-D	11,914	733	42.3
Univ. of Wisconsin–Eau Claire, Eau Claire, WI 54702-4004	1916	$9,276 (A)	$8,795	5-D	9,605	598	65.6
Univ. of Wisconsin–Green Bay, Green Bay, WI 54311-7001	1968	$348/cr. hr. (A)	NA	5-D	6,568	386	54.6
Univ. of Wisconsin–La Crosse, La Crosse, WI 54601-3742	1909	$9,774 (A)	$6,804	5-D	10,279	603	70.0
Univ. of Wisconsin–Madison, Madison, WI 53706-1380	1848	$10,796 (A)	$12,894	5-D	49,886	3,101	89.0
Univ. of Wisconsin–Milwaukee, Milwaukee, WI 53201-0413	1956	$11,585 (A)	$11,139	5-D	23,139	1,576	48.0
Univ. of Wisconsin–Oshkosh, Oshkosh, WI 54901	1871	$9,632 (A)	$8,940	5-D	13,114	533	NA
Univ. of Wisconsin–Parkside, Kenosha, WI 53141-2000	1968	$7,466 (A)	$8,526	5-M	3,966	268	40.0
Univ. of Wisconsin–Platteville, Platteville, WI 53818-3099	1866	$7,663 (A)	$8,530	5-M	6,892	494	NA
Univ. of Wisconsin–River Falls, River Falls, WI 54022	1874	$8,135 (A)	$7,434	5-D	5,184	350	59.0
Univ. of Wisconsin–Stevens Point, Stevens Point, WI 54481-3897	1894	$8,790 (A)	$8,500	5-D	8,019	383	56.0
Univ. of Wisconsin–Stout, Menomonie, WI 54751	1891	$9,869 (A)	$8,718	5-D	7,890	427	60.0
Univ. of Wisconsin–Superior, Superior, WI 54880-4500	1893	$8,232 (A)	$9,870	5-M	2,609	224	43.0
Univ. of Wisconsin–Whitewater, Whitewater, WI 53190-1790	1868	$9,491 (A)	$7,770	5-D	11,460	565	63.5
Univ. of Wyoming, Laramie, WY 82071	1886	$6,801 (A)	$11,610	5-D	11,100	715	60.7
Universidad del Este, Carolina, PR 00984	1949	NA	NA	1-M	5,558	NA	NA
Universidad del Turabo, Gurabo, PR 00778-3030	1972	$5,820	NA	1-D	10,896	NA	19.0
Universidad Metropolitana, San Juan, PR 00928-1150	1980	$5,820	NA	1-D	7,003	NA	26.0
Upper Iowa Univ., Fayette, IA 52142-1857	1857	$33,639	$9,410	1-M	3,031	343	38.0
Ursinus Coll., Collegeville, PA 19426	1869	$59,176	$15,064	1-B	1,527	189	73.0
Utah State Univ., Logan, UT 84322	1888	$8,305 (A)	$8,644	5-D	27,943	1,281	52.5
Utah Valley Univ., Orem, UT 84058-5999	1941	$6,270 (A)	$9,234	5-M	41,262	1,804	33.0
Utica Coll., Utica, NY 13502-4892	1946	NA	NA	1-D	3,861	388	58.0
Valdosta State Univ., Valdosta, GA 31698	1906	$7,100 (A)	$9,120	5-D	10,225	581	40.5
Valencia Coll., Orlando, FL 32802-3028	1967	$3,183 (A)	$13,457	5-B	45,949	NA	NA
Valley City State Univ., Valley City, ND 58072	1890	$8,458 (A)	$6,957	5-M	1,858	143	47.5
Valparaiso Univ., Valparaiso, IN 46383	1859	$46,588	$13,306	2-D	3,085	292	69.8
Vanderbilt Univ., Nashville, TN 37240-1001	1873	$63,946	$21,054	1-D	13,796	1,232	92.8
Vanguard Univ. of Southern California, Costa Mesa, CA 92626	1920	$38,700	$11,950	2-M	2,268	226	61.5

Name, address	Year founded	Tuition & fees	Room & board	Control, degree	Enroll-ment	Faculty	Grad. rate
Vassar Coll., Poughkeepsie, NY 12604	1861	$67,805	$17,415	1-M	2,459	369	92.0%
Vermont Tech. Coll., Randolph Center, VT 05061-0500	1866	$16,539 (A)	$12,404	5-M	1,634	187	37.0
Villanova Univ., Villanova, PA 19085-1699	1842	$64,700	$16,896	2-D	10,383	1,218	90.6
Vincennes Univ., Vincennes, IN 47591	1801	$6,582 (A)	$11,568	5-B	16,389	799	22.0
Virginia Commonwealth Univ., Richmond, VA 23284-9005	1838	$16,233 (A)	$12,689	5-D	28,082	2,138	64.5
Virginia Military Inst, Lexington, VA 24450	1839	NA	NA	5-B	1,512	201	76.9
Virginia Polytechnic Inst. & State Univ., Blacksburg, VA 24061	1872	$15,478 (A)	$14,888	5-D	38,170	2,398	87.0
Virginia State Univ., Petersburg, VA 23806-0001	1882	$6,755 (A)	$11,544	5-D	3,659	NA	44.0
Virginia Union Univ., Richmond, VA 23220-1170	1865	$14,530	$9,798	2-D	1,640	214	42.0
Virginia Wesleyan Univ., Virginia Beach, VA 23455	1961	$36,960	$11,513	2-M	1,538	129	44.0
Viterbo Univ., La Crosse, WI 54601-4797	1890	$31,090	$10,260	2-D	2,520	NA	65.0
Wagner Coll., Staten Island, NY 10301-4495	1883	$6,275/unit	NA	1-D	1,957	295	71.4
Wake Forest Univ., Winston-Salem, NC 27109	1834	$64,758	$17,848	1-D	8,947	919	91.0
Walden Univ., Minneapolis, MN 55401	1970	$10,459	NA	3-D	7,662	NA	NA
Waldorf Univ., Forest City, IA 50436	1903	$23,108	$8,748	2-M	2,523	NA	NA
Walla Walla Univ., College Place, WA 99324	1892	$30,531	$8,358	2-M	1,545	NA	59.3
Walsh Coll. of Accountancy & Bus Admin, Troy, MI 48083	1922	$14,013	NA	1-D	1,811	156	NA
Walsh Univ., North Canton, OH 44720-3396	1958	$33,020	$11,610	2-D	4,987	247	65.2
Wartburg Coll., Waverly, IA 50677-0903	1852	$49,190	$10,280	2-M	1,539	146	69.5
Washburn Univ., Topeka, KS 66621	1865	$9,306 (A)	$10,759	10-D	5,460	419	54.0
Washington & Lee Univ., Lexington, VA 24450	1749	$64,525	$17,685	1-D	2,243	308	94.0
Washington State Univ., Pullman, WA 99164	1890	$12,996 (A)	$16,476	5-D	18,014	1,781	63.1
Washington Univ. in St. Louis, St. Louis, MO 63130-4899	1853	$62,982	$20,778	1-D	17,012	1,568	94.0
Wayland Baptist Univ., Plainview, TX 79072-6998	1908	$23,186	$9,172	2-D	2,978	401	20.0
Wayne State Coll., Wayne, NE 68787	1910	$7,923 (A)	$8,880	5-M	4,773	231	51.0
Wayne State Univ., Detroit, MI 48202	1868	$15,464 (A)	$12,392	5-D	24,931	1,639	55.8
Waynesburg Univ., Waynesburg, PA 15370-1222	1849	$29,460	$12,300	2-D	1,366	137	60.0
Weatherford Coll., Weatherford, TX 76086	1869	$3,660 (A)	$7,695	11-B	5,637	220	NA
Weber State Univ., Ogden, UT 84408-1001	1889	$6,391 (A)	$8,824	5-D	29,774	NA	40.0
Webster Univ., St. Louis, MO 63119-3194	1915	$30,730	$11,980	1-D	3,024	406	59.0
Wellesley Coll., Wellesley, MA 02481 (3)	1870	$64,320	$19,920	1-B	2,447	344	90.0
Wentworth Inst. of Tech., Boston, MA 02115-5998	1904	$41,010	$18,670	1-M	3,920	322	69.0
Wesleyan Univ., Middletown, CT 06459	1831	$67,016	$19,034	1-D	3,253	460	93.2
West Chester Univ. of Pennsylvania, West Chester, PA 19383	1871	$10,575 (A)	$9,644	5-D	17,275	948	72.0
West Coast Univ., Anaheim, CA 92802	NA	$22,516	NA	3-B	2,990	NA	NA
West Coast Univ., North Hollywood, CA 91606	1909	$34,742	NA	3-M	2,413	NA	NA
West Coast Univ., Ontario, CA 91761	NA	$35,178	NA	3-B	2,408	NA	NA
West Liberty Univ., West Liberty, WV 26074	1837	$9,116 (S)	$5,900	5-M	2,315	216	58.0
West Texas A&M Univ., Canyon, TX 79015	1909	$9,204 (A)	$8,512	5-D	9,545	510	45.8
West Virginia State Univ., Institute, WV 25112-1000	1891	$8,833 (A)	$12,886	5-M	2,102	149	26.3
West Virginia Univ., Morgantown, WV 26506	1867	$9,648 (A)	$13,020	5-D	26,839	NA	NA
West Virginia Univ. at Parkersburg, Parkersburg, WV 26104	1961	$5,568 (A)	$7,200	5-B	2,624	NA	NA
West Virginia Univ. Inst. of Tech., Beckley, WV 25801	1895	$7,728 (A)	$11,438	5-B	1,645	124	34.0
West Virginia Wesleyan Coll., Buckhannon, WV 26201	1890	$32,612	$10,054	2-M	1,449	150	49.6
Western Carolina Univ., Cullowhee, NC 28723	1889	$4,631 (A)	$11,179	5-D	11,635	787	60.6
Western Connecticut State Univ., Danbury, CT 06810-6885	1903	$11,781 (A)	$13,876	5-D	5,247	579	51.0
Western Governors Univ., Salt Lake City, UT 84107	1998	$7,454	NA	1-M	150,116	4,059	63.6
Western Illinois Univ., Macomb, IL 61455-1390	1899	$12,848 (A)	$1,630	5-D	7,455	505	51.0
Western Kentucky Univ., Bowling Green, KY 42101	1906	$11,436 (A)	$13,126	5-D	16,493	939	54.0
Western Michigan Univ., Kalamazoo, MI 49008	1903	$14,594 (A)	$11,156	5-D	17,835	1,187	55.1
Western Nevada Coll., Carson City, NV 89703-7316	1971	$3,770 (A)	$14,156	5-B	3,528	226	NA
Western New England Univ., Springfield, MA 01119	1919	$46,430	$14,900	1-D	3,658	327	63.1
Western New Mexico Univ., Silver City, NM 88062-0680	1893	$6,557 (A)	$10,590	5-M	2,822	234	27.2
Western Oregon Univ., Monmouth, OR 97361	1856	$11,025 (A)	$9,895	5-M	3,752	298	47.6
Western State Colorado Univ., Gunnison, CO 81231	1901	$12,997 (A)	$13,131	5-M	3,531	178	47.0
Western Washington Univ., Bellingham, WA 98225-5996	1893	$9,286 (A)	$15,894	5-D	14,747	998	65.0
Western Wyoming Comm. Coll., Rock Springs, WY 82901	1959	NA	NA	11-B	2,473	189	NA
Westfield State Univ., Westfield, MA 01086	1839	$11,882 (A)	$13,510	5-M	5,013	NA	61.0
Westminster Coll., Salt Lake City, UT 84105-3697	1875	$41,416	$13,420	1-D	1,287	244	64.0
Westmont Coll., Santa Barbara, CA 93108-1099	1937	$51,790	$16,360	2-B	1,293	164	73.6
Wheaton Coll., Norton, MA 02766	1834	NA	NA	1-B	1,667	189	79.7
Wheeling Jesuit Univ., Wheeling, WV 26003-6295	1954	$29,290	$11,620	2-D	1,289	109	58.0
Whitman Coll., Walla Walla, WA 99362-2083	1859	$61,492	$14,640	1-B	1,493	185	90.0
Whitworth Univ., Spokane, WA 99251-0001	1890	$50,920	$13,700	2-D	2,417	317	76.0
Wichita State Univ., Wichita, KS 67260	1895	$7,917 (A)	$13,790	5-D	16,921	857	48.0
Widener Univ., Chester, PA 19013-5792	1821	$53,638	$15,550	1-D	5,416	437	68.0
Wilkes Comm. Coll., Wilkesboro, NC 28697	1965	$2,571 (A)	NA	5-B	2,558	NA	NA
Wilkes Univ., Wilkes-Barre, PA 18766-0002	1933	$42,286	$16,006	1-D	5,216	438	59.0
Willamette Univ., Salem, OR 97301-3931	1842	$48,226	$15,380	2-D	1,883	228	76.0
William Carey Univ., Hattiesburg, MS 39401	1906	$14,550	$6,960	2-M	3,233	NA	NA
William Jessup Univ., Rocklin, CA 95765	1939	$37,160	$12,956	2-M	1,685	240	60.0
William Paterson Univ. of New Jersey, Wayne, NJ 07470-8420	1855	$15,150 (A)	$16,920	5-D	9,370	828	53.0
William Penn Univ., Oskaloosa, IA 52577-1799	1873	$28,750	$7,712	2-M	1,473	126	30.0
Williams Coll., Williamstown, MA 01267	1793	$64,860	$16,300	1-M	2,205	350	95.0
Wilmington Univ., New Castle, DE 19720-6491	1967	$11,760	NA	1-D	9,421	2,466	NA
Wingate Univ., Wingate, NC 28174	1896	$41,831	$10,676	2-D	3,396	347	57.9
Winona State Univ., Winona, MN 55987	1858	$10,468 (A)	$9,584	5-D	6,563	455	63.2
Winston-Salem State Univ., Winston-Salem, NC 27110-0003	1892	$6,079 (A)	$10,197	5-M	4,689	NA	NA
Winthrop Univ., Rock Hill, SC 29733	1886	$15,866 (A)	$10,488	5-M	4,712	463	60.9
Wittenberg Univ., Springfield, OH 45501-0720	1845	$43,106	$11,280	2-M	1,299	164	57.3
Wofford Coll., Spartanburg, SC 29303-3663	1854	$54,100	$15,015	2-B	1,823	183	82.5
Worcester Polytechnic Inst, Worcester, MA 01609-2280	1865	$59,070	$18,072	13-D	7,308	598	89.0
Worcester State Univ., Worcester, MA 01602-2597	1874	$11,286 (A)	$13,523	5-M	5,311	462	58.8
Wright State Univ., Dayton, OH 45435	1964	NA	NA	5-D	9,678	NA	43.8
Xavier Univ., Cincinnati, OH 45207	1831	$48,126	$14,220	2-D	6,651	860	75.0
Xavier Univ. of Louisiana, New Orleans, LA 70125	1925	$27,870	$13,058	13-D	3,419	313	47.7
Yale Univ., New Haven, CT 06520	1701	$64,700	$19,180	1-D	14,776	1,929	97.8
Yeshiva Univ., New York, NY 10033-3201	1886	$49,980	$10,750	1-D	5,350	696	84.2
York Coll. of Pennsylvania, York, PA 17403-3651	1787	NA	NA	1-D	3,852	430	65.3
York Coll. of the City Univ. of New York, Jamaica, NY 11451	1967	$7,570 (A)	$17,604	11-M	7,529	NA	NA
Young Harris Coll., Young Harris, GA 30582	1886	$30,900	$11,706	2-B	1,396	NA	NA
Youngstown State Univ., Youngstown, OH 44555-0001	1908	$8,754 (A)	$9,400	5-D	11,296	NA	47.0

DIRECTORY

Associations and Organizations

Source: World Almanac research

Selected list, generally by category and first distinctive key word in each title. Listed by acronym when that is the official name. Year established is in parentheses. Entries for religious organizations include addresses and leadership information for 2023.

Academic and Educational

Academies, Natl. (1863): (202) 334-2000; www.nationalacademies.org
African American Life and History, Assn. for the Study of (1915): (202) 238-5910; www.asalh.org
Alpha Delta Kappa (1947): (816) 363-5525; www.alphadeltakappa.org
AMIDEAST (America-Mideast Educational and Training Services, Inc.) (1951): (202) 776-9600; www.amideast.org
Anthropological Assn., American (1902): (703) 528-1902; www.americananthro.org
Archaeological Institute of America (1879): (857) 305-9350; www.archaeological.org
Arts, Americans for the (1960): (202) 371-2830; www.americansforthearts.org
Arts and Sciences, American Academy of (1780): (617) 576-5000; www.amacad.org
Beta Gamma Sigma Inc. (1913): (314) 432-5650; www.betagammasigma.org
Beta Sigma Phi Intl. (1931): (816) 444-6800; www.bspinternational.org
Biological Sciences, American Institute of (1947): (703) 674-2500; www.aibs.org
Classical Studies, Society for (fmr. American Philological Assn.) (1869): (646) 939-0435; www.classicalstudies.org
College Board (1900): (212) 713-8000; www.collegeboard.org
Colleges and Universities, American Assn. of (1915): (202) 387-3760; www.aacu.org
Community Colleges, American Assn. of (1920): (202) 728-0200; www.aacc.nche.edu
Consumer Interests, American Council on (1953): (727) 940-2658 ext. 2002 www.consumerinterests.org
Delta Kappa Gamma Society Intl. (1929): (512) 478-5748; www.dkg.org
Education, American Council on (1918): (202) 939-9300; www.acenet.edu
Education, Council for Advancement and Support of (1974): (202) 328-2273; www.case.org
Education of Young Children, Natl. Assn. for the (1926): (202) 232-8777; www.naeyc.org
Educators for World Peace, Intl. Assn. of (1973): (256) 534-5501
English-Speaking Union of the U.S. (1920): (212) 818-1200; www.esuus.org
Entomological Society of America (1889): (301) 731-4535; www.entsoc.org
Family Relations, Natl. Council on (1938): (888) 781-9331; www.ncfr.org
Foreign Study, American Institute for (1964): (866) 906-2437; www.aifs.com
Freedom of Information Coalition, Natl. (1989): (757) 276-1413; www.nfoic.org
French Institute/Alliance Française (1898): (212) 355-6100; www.fiaf.org
Genealogical Society, Natl. (1903): (703) 525-0050; www.ngsgenealogy.org
Genetic Assn., American (1914): (541) 264-5612; www.theaga.org
Geological Society of America (1888): (303) 357-1000; www.geosociety.org
Hemispheric Affairs, Council on (1975): (202) 223-4975; www.coha.org
Industrial and Applied Mathematics, Society for (1952): (215) 382-9800; www.siam.org
Intl. Education, Institute of (1919): (212) 883-8200; www.iie.org
Intl. Educational Exchange, Council on (1947): (207) 553-4000; www.ciee.org
Intl. Law, American Society of (1906): (202) 939-6001; www.asil.org
Irish American Cultural Inst. (1962): (973) 605-1991; www.iaci-usa.org
IRTS Foundation (fmr. Intl. Radio and TV Society Foundation) (1939): (212) 867-6650; www.irtsfoundation.org
Law Libraries, American Assn. of (1906): (312) 939-4764; www.aallnet.org
Learned Societies, American Council of (1919): (212) 697-1505; www.acls.org

Libraries Assn., Special (1909): (703) 647-4900; www.sla.org
Linguistic Society of America (1924): (202) 835-1714; www.linguisticsociety.org
Literacy Assn., Intl. (fmr. Intl. Reading Assn.) (1956): (302) 731-1600; www.literacyworldwide.org
Mathematical Society, American (1888): (401) 455-4000; www.ams.org
Mensa, American (1960): (817) 607-0060; www.us.mensa.org
Meteorological Society, American (1919): (617) 227-2425; www.ametsoc.org
Metric Assn., Inc., U.S. (1916): www.usma.org
Microbiology, American Society for (1899): (202) 737-3600; www.asm.org
Modern Language Assn. of America (1883): (646) 576-5000; www.mla.org
Museums, American Alliance of (1906): (202) 289-1818; www.aam-us.org
Music Education, Natl. Assn. for (fmr. Music Educators Natl. Conference) (1907): (703) 860-4000; www.nafme.org
Musicological Society, American (1934): (212) 992-6340; www.amsmusicology.org
Negro College Fund, United (1944): (800) 331-2244; www.uncf.org
Oriental Society, American (1842): (734) 347-1259; https://www.aos-site.org
ORT America (1922): (212) 505-7700; www.ortamerica.org
PEN America (1922): (212) 334-1660; www.pen.org
Phi Beta Kappa Society (1776): (202) 265-3808; www.pbk.org
Phi Theta Kappa Honor Society (1918): (800) 946-9995; www.ptk.org
Philosophical Assn., American (1900): (302) 831-1112; www.apaonline.org
Physics, American Inst. of (1931): (301) 209-3100; www.aip.org
Physiological Society, American (1887): (844) 526-1700; www.physiology.org
Poetry Society of America (1910): (212) 254-9628; www.poetrysociety.org
Poets, Academy of American (1934): (212) 274-0343; www.poets.org
Political Science, Academy of (1880): (212) 870-2500; www.psqonline.org
Religion, American Academy of (1909): (404) 727-3049; www.aarweb.org
Science, American Assn. for the Advancement of (1848): (202) 326-6400; www.aaas.org
Science Fiction Society, World (1939): www.wsfs.org
Sciences, Natl. Academy of (1863): (202) 334-2000; www.nasonline.org
Sigma Beta Delta (1994): (984) 200-8027; www.sigmabetadelta.org
Sociological Assn., American (1905): (202) 383-9005; www.asanet.org
Tau Beta Pi Assn. (1885): (865) 546-4578; www.tbp.org
Teach For America (1990): (212) 279-2080; www.teachforamerica.org
Theological Schools, Assn. of (1918): (412) 788-6505; www.ats.edu
Theosophical Society in America (1875): (630) 668-1571; www.theosophical.org
Universities, Assn. of American (1900): (202) 408-7500; www.aau.edu
World Learning, Inc. (1932): (202) 408-5420; www.worldlearning.org

Animal Welfare and Environment

Animal Welfare Institute (1951): (202) 337-2332; www.awionline.org
Animals, American Society for the Prevention of Cruelty to (ASPCA) (1866): (212) 876-7700; www.aspca.org
Animals, People for the Ethical Treatment of (PETA) (1980): (757) 622-7382; www.peta.org
Appalachian Trail Conservancy (1925): (304) 535-6331; www.appalachiantrail.org
Audubon Society, Natl. (1905): (212) 979-3196; www.audubon.org
Cat Fanciers' Assn., Inc., The (1906): (330) 680-4070; www.cfa.org

Conservation Intl. (1987): (703) 341-2400; www.conservation.org
Defenders of Wildlife (1947): (800) 385-9712; www.defenders.org
Ducks Unlimited (1937): (901) 758-3825; www.ducks.org
Forest History Society (1946): (919) 682-9319; www.foresthistory.org
Foresters, Society of American (1900): (202) 938-3910; www.eforester.org
Friends of the Earth (1969): (202) 783-7400; www.foe.org
Garden Club of America (1913): (212) 753-8287; www.gcamerica.org
Garden Clubs, Inc., Natl. (1929): (314) 776-7574; www.gardenclub.org
Geographic Society, Natl. (1888): (202) 857-7000; www.nationalgeographic.com
Green Mountain Club (1910): (802) 244-7037; www.greenmountainclub.org
Greenpeace (1971): (202) 462-1177; www.greenpeace.org
Hiking Society, American (1976): (301) 565-6704; www.americanhiking.org
Horse Council, American (1969): (202) 296-4031; www.horsecouncil.org
Humane Society of the U.S., The (1954): (202) 452-1100; www.humanesociety.org
Natural Resources Defense Council (1970): (212) 727-2700; www.nrdc.org
Nature Conservancy, The (1951): (703) 841-5300; www.nature.org
Ocean Conservancy (1972): (202) 429-5609; www.oceanconservancy.org
Ornithological Society, American (fmr. Amer. Ornithologists' Union) (1883): (312) 665-7936; www.americanornithology.org
Recreation and Park Assn., Natl. (1965): (703) 858-0784; www.nrpa.org
Recycling Coalition, Inc., Natl. (1978): www.nrcrecycles.org
Rose Society, American (1892): (318) 938-5402; www.rose.org
Save the Redwoods League (1918): (415) 362-2352; www.savetheredwoods.org
Sierra Club (1892): (415) 977-5500; www.sierraclub.org
Water Environment Federation (1928): (800) 666-0206; www.wef.org
Wildflower Center, Lady Bird Johnson (1982): (512) 232-0100; www.wildflower.org
Wildlife Federation, Natl. (1936): (800) 822-9919; www.nwf.org
World Wildlife Fund (1961): (202) 293-4800; www.worldwildlife.org

Children and Social Services

Big Brothers Big Sisters of America (1904): (813) 720-8778; www.bbbs.org
Boy Scouts of America: see Scouts BSA
Boys & Girls Clubs of America (1906): (404) 487-5700; www.bgca.org
Camp Fire (fmr. Camp Fire Boys & Girls) (1910): (816) 285-2010; www.campfire.org
Child Welfare League of America (1920): (202) 688-4200; www.cwla.org
Children's Book Council, The (1944-45): (212) 966-1990; www.cbcbooks.org
Feeding America (fmr. America's Second Harvest) (1979): (800) 771-2303; www.feedingamerica.org
FFA Organization, Natl. (fmr. Future Farmers of America) (1928): (888) 332-2668; www.ffa.org
4-H Council, Natl. (1914): (301) 961-2800; www.4-h.org
Future Business Leaders of America-Phi Beta Lambda, Inc. (1942): (800) 325-2946; www.fbla-pbl.org
Gifted Children, Natl. Assn. for (1954): (202) 785-4268; www.nagc.org
Girl Scouts of the USA (1912): (212) 852-8000; www.girlscouts.org
Honor Society, Natl. (1921): (703) 860-0200; www.nhs.us
Junior Achievement USA® (1919): (719) 540-8000; www.juniorachievement.org
Junior Auxiliaries, Inc., Natl. Assn. of (1941): (662) 332-3000; www.najanet.org

Junior Chamber Intl. USA (1914): (636) 778-3010; www.jciusa.org
Junior Honor Society, Natl. (1929): (703) 860-0200; www.njhs.us
Missing and Exploited Children, Natl. Center for (1984): (703) 224-2150; www.missingkids.com
Pilot Intl. (1921): (478) 477-1208; www.pilotinternational.org
Scouts BSA (fmr. Boy Scouts of America) (1910), (972) 580-2000; www.scouting.org
Student Council, Natl. (1931): (703) 860-0200; www.natstuco.org

Fraternal

Eagles, Fraternal Order of (1898): (614) 883-2200; www.foe.com
Eastern Star, General Grand Chapter, Order of the (1876): (202) 667-4737; www.easternstar.org
Elks of the USA, Benevolent and Protective Order of (1868): (773) 755-4700; www.elks.org
Freemasonry, Scottish Rite of, Supreme Council, 33° Northern Masonic Jurisdiction (1813): (781) 862-4410; www.scottishritenmj.org
Freemasonry, Scottish Rite of, Supreme Council, 33° Southern Jurisdiction (1802): (202) 232-3579; www.scottishrite.org
Kiwanis Intl. (1915): (317) 875-8755; www.kiwanis.org
Knights of Columbus (1882): (203) 752-4000; www.kofc.org
Knights of Pythias, Order of (1864): (781) 341-2422; www.pythias.org
Lions Clubs Intl. (1917): (630) 571-5466; www.lionsclubs.org
Moose Intl., Inc. (1888): (630) 859-2000; www.mooseintl.org
Odd Fellows, Independent Order of (1819): (336) 725-5955; www.odd-fellows.org
Rotary Intl. (1905): (847) 866-3000; www.rotary.org
Shriners Intl. (1872): (813) 281-0300; www.shrinersinternational.org
Sons and Daughters of Italy in America, Order (1905): (202) 547-2900; www.osia.org
Sons of Norway (1895): (612) 827-3611; www.sofn.com
Woodmen of America, Modern (1883): (309) 558-3077; www.modernwoodmen.org

Historical

American Battlefield Trust (1987): (202) 367-1861; www.battlefields.org
Colonial Dames XVII Century, Natl. Soc. (1915): (202) 293-1700; www.colonialdames17c.org
Daughters of the American Revolution (1890): (202) 628-1776; www.dar.org
Daughters of the Confederacy, United (1894): (804) 355-1636; www.hqudc.org
Historic Preservation, Natl. Trust for (1949): (202) 588-6000; www.savingplaces.org
Historical Assn., American (1884): (202) 544-2422; www.historians.org
Lewis and Clark Trail Heritage Foundation (1969): (406) 454-1234; www.lewisandclark.org
Mayflower Descendants, General Soc. of (1897): (508) 746-3188; www.themayflowersociety.org
Pilgrims, Natl. Soc. Sons and Daughters of the (1908): https://www.societyofthepilgrims.org
Railway Historical Society, Inc., Natl. (1935): (215) 557-6606; www.nrhs.com
Sons of the American Revolution, Natl. Soc. of the (1889): (502) 589-1776; www.sar.org
Sons of Confederate Veterans (1896): (931) 380-1844; www.scv.org
State and Local History, American Assn. for (1940): (615) 320-3203; www.aaslh.org
Supreme Court Historical Society (1974): (202) 543-0400; www.supremecourthistory.org
Theodore Roosevelt Assn. (1920): (516) 921-6319; www.theodoreroosevelt.org
Thoreau Society (1941): (978) 369-5310; thoreausociety.org
Titanic Historical Society, Inc. (1963): (413) 543-4770; www.titanichistoricalsociety.org
Victorian Society in America (1966): (856) 216-8124; www.victoriansociety.org

Industrial and Trade

Aerospace Industries Assn. (1919): (703) 358-1000; www.aia-aerospace.org
Better Business Bureaus, Intl. Assn. of (1912): (703) 276-0100; www.bbb.org
Chamber of Commerce, U.S. (1912): (202) 659-6000; www.uschamber.com
Chemistry Council, American (1872): (202) 249-7000; www.americanchemistry.com
Construction Specifications Institute (1948): (800) 689-2900; www.csiresources.org
CropLife America (1933): (202) 296-1585; www.croplifeamerica.org
Electrical Manufacturers Assn., Natl. (1926): (703) 841-3200; www.nema.org
Fire Protection Assn., Natl. (NFPA) (1896): (617) 770-3000; www.nfpa.org
Fisheries Soc., American (1870): (301) 897-8616; www.fisheries.org
Foreign Trade Council, Natl. (1914): (202) 887-0278; www.nftc.org
Funeral Consumers Alliance (1963): (802) 865-8300; www.funerals.org
Hotel & Lodging Assn., American (1910): (202) 289-3100; www.ahla.com
Insurance Assn., American Property Casualty (1866): (847) 297-7800; www.apci.org
Manufacturers, Natl. Assn. of (1895): (202) 637-3000; www.nam.org
News/Media Alliance (fmr. Newspaper Assn. of America; merged with Assn. of Magazine Media, 2022) (1992): (571) 366-1000; www.newsmediaalliance.org
Nuclear Society, American (1954): (708) 352-6611; www.ans.org
Orchestras, League of American (1942): (212) 262-5161; www.americanorchestras.org
Petroleum Institute, American (1919): (202) 682-8000; www.api.org
PRINTING United Alliance (2020, from merger of Printing Industries of America and Specialty Graphic Imaging Assn.): (703) 385-1335; www.printing.org
Publishers, Assn. of American (1970): (202) 347-3375; www.publishers.org
Retail Federation, Natl. (1911): (202) 783-7971; www.nrf.com
Safety Council, Natl. (1913): (630) 285-1121; www.nsc.org
Shipbuilders Council of America (1920): (202) 737-3234; www.shipbuildersusa.org
Small Business Assn., Natl. (1937): (800) 345-6728; www.nsba.biz
Software & Information Industry Assn. (1999): (202) 289-7442; www.siia.net
Tall Buildings and Urban Habitat, Council on (1969): (312) 283-5645; www.ctbuh.org
Toy Assn., Inc. (1916): (212) 675-1141; www.toyassociation.org
Water Works Assn., American (1881): (303) 794-7711; www.awwa.org
Zoos & Aquariums, Assn. of (1924): (301) 562-0777; www.aza.org

Lifestyle and Travel

AAA (American Automobile Assn.) (1902): (407) 444-7000; www.aaa.com
AARP (fmr. American Assn. of Retired Persons) (1958): (888) 687-2277; www.aarp.org
AFS Intercultural Programs USA (1947): (800) 237-4636; www.afsusa.org
Aircraft Owners and Pilots Assn. (1939): (301) 695-2000; www.aopa.org
Appalachian Mountain Club (1876): (617) 523-0636; www.outdoors.org
Boat Owners Assn. of the U.S. (1966): (800) 395-2628; www.boatus.com
Camp Assn., American (1910): (765) 342-8456; www.acacamps.org
Consumer Federation of America (1968): (202) 387-6121; www.consumerfed.org
Consumer Reports, Inc. (fmr. Consumers Union) (1936): (914) 378-2000; www.consumerreports.org
Green America (fmr. Co-op America) (1982): (800) 584-7336; www.greenamerica.org
Hosteling Intl. USA (1934): (240) 650-2100; www.hiusa.org
Jewish Community Centers Assn. of North America (1917): (212) 532-4949; www.jcca.org
Motorcyclist Assn., American (1924): (614) 856-1900; www.americanmotorcyclist.com

Planetary Society (1980): (626) 793-5100; www.planetary.org
Rail Passengers Assn. (1967): (202) 408-8362; www.railpassengers.org
SCRABBLE® Players Assn., N. American (2009): (214) 810-2439; www.scrabbleplayers.org
Sports Car Club of America (1944): (785) 357-7222; www.scca.com
Toastmasters Intl. (1924): (720) 439-5050; www.toastmasters.org
Vertical Flight Society (fmr. American Helicopter Society Intl.) (1943): (703) 684-6777; www.vtol.org
YMCA (Young Men's Christian Assn.) of the USA (1851): (800) 872-9622; www.ymca.org
YWCA (fmr. Young Women's Christian Assn.) USA (1858): (202) 467-0801; www.ywca.org

Military and Veterans

Air & Space Forces Assn. (fmr. Air Force Assn.) (1946): (703) 247-5800; www.afa.org
American Legion (1919): (317) 630-1200; www.legion.org
American Legion Auxiliary (1919): (317) 569-4500; member.legion-aux.org
AMVETS (American Veterans) (1944): (301) 459-9600; www.amvets.org
Army, Assn. of the United States (1950): (703) 841-4300; www.ausa.org
Blinded Veterans Assn. (1945): (800) 669-7079; www.bva.org
Civil Air Patrol (1941): (877) 227-9142; www.gocivilairpatrol.com
Coast Guard Combat Veterans Assn. (1985): (410) 690-8000; www.coastguardcombatvets.org
Disabled American Veterans (1920): (877) 426-2838; www.dav.org
82nd Airborne Division Assn., Inc. (1944): (910) 223-1182; www.82ndairborneassociation.org
Ex-Prisoners of War, American (1942): (817) 649-2979; www.axpow.org
Fleet Reserve Assn. (1924): (703) 683-1400; www.fra.org
Iraq and Afghanistan Veterans of America (2004): (212) 982-9699; www.iava.org
Jewish War Veterans of the U.S.A. (1896): (202) 265-6280; www.jwv.org
Marine Corps League (1937): (703) 207-9588; www.mclnational.org
Military Officers Assn. of America (1929): (703) 549-2311; www.moaa.org
Military Order of the World Wars (1919): (703) 683-4911; www.moww.org
National Guard Assn. of the U.S. (1878): (202) 789-0031; www.ngaus.org
Naval Institute, U.S. (1873): (410) 268-6110; www.usni.org
Navy League of the United States (1902): (703) 528-1775; www.navyleague.org
Ninety-Nines, Inc. (Intl. Org. of Women Pilots) (1929): (405) 685-7969; www.ninety-nines.org
Non Commissioned Officers Assn. (1960): (210) 653-6161; www.ncoausa.org
Paralyzed Veterans of America (1946): (800) 424-8200; www.pva.org
POW/MIA Families, Natl. League of (1970): (703) 465-7432; www.pow-miafamilies.org
Purple Heart, Military Order of the (1932): (703) 642-5360; www.purpleheart.org
Reserve Org. of America (fmr. Reserve Officers Assn. of the U.S.) (1922): (202) 479-2200; www.roa.org
Sons of the American Legion (1932): (317) 630-1200; www.legion.org/sons
Tin Can Sailors (Natl. Assn. of Destroyer Veterans) (1976): (800) 223-5535; www.destroyers.org
Uniformed Services Assn. (2018): www.uniformedservicesassociation.org
USO, Inc. (United Service Orgs.) (1941): (888) 484-3876; www.uso.org
USS Missouri Memorial Assn., Inc. (1994): (808) 455-1600; www.ussmissouri.org
Veterans Memorial Museum (Home of the Legion of Valor) (1991): (559) 498-0510; www.fresnovetsmuseum.com
Veterans of Foreign Wars (1899): (816) 756-3390; www.vfw.org
Veterans of Foreign Wars Auxiliary (1914): (816) 561-8655; vfwauxiliary.org
Vietnam Veterans of America (1978): (301) 585-4000; www.vva.org

Women's Army Corps Veterans' Assn.-Army Women United (1946): (256) 820-6824; www.armywomen.org

Wounded Warrior Project (2003): (877) 832-6997; www.woundedwarriorproject.org

Political

Abortion Federation, Natl. (1977): (202) 667-5881; prochoice.org

Action Network, American (2010): (202) 559-6420; americanactionnetwork.org

Advancement and Support of Education, Council for (1974): (202) 328-2273; www.case.org

American Indians, Natl. Congress of (1944): (202) 466-7767; www.ncai.org

American-Islamic Relations, Council on (1994): (202) 488-8787; www.cair.com

Black Lives Matter (2013): (779) 256-5463; www.blacklivesmatter.com

Brady: United Against Gun Violence (1974): (202) 370-8100; www.bradyunited.org

Cities, Natl. League of (1924): (202) 626-3000; www.nlc.org

Civil Liberties Union, American (ACLU) (1920): (212) 549-2500; www.aclu.org

Coalition to Stop Gun Violence (1974): (202) 408-0061; www.csgv.org

Common Cause (1970): (202) 833-1200; www.commoncause.org

Concerned Women for America (1979): (202) 488-7000; concernedwomen.org

Congress of Racial Equality (CORE) (1942): (702) 637-7968; www.thecongressofracialequality.org

Conservation Voters, League of (1969): (202) 785-8683; www.lcv.org

Constitution Party (1992): (717) 390-1993; www.constitutionparty.com

Counties, Natl. Assn. of (1935): (202) 393-6226; www.naco.org

Crossroads GPS (Grassroots Policy Strategies) (2010): (202) 706-7051; www.crossroadsgps.org

Democratic Natl. Committee (1848): (202) 863-8000; www.democrats.org

Democratic Socialists of America (1982): (212) 727-8610; www.dsausa.org

Everytown for Gun Safety (2013): (646) 324-8250; www.everytown.org

Evident Change (fmr. Natl. Council on Crime and Delinquency) (1907): (800) 306-6223; www.evidentchange.org

Feminists for Life of America (1972): (703) 836-3354; feministsforlife.org

GLAAD (fmr. Gay & Lesbian Alliance Against Defamation) (1985): (212) 629-3322; www.glaad.org

Governors Assn., Natl. (1908): (202) 624-5300; www.nga.org

Grange of the Order of Patrons of Husbandry, Natl. (1867): (202) 628-3507; www.nationalgrange.org

Gray Panthers (1970): (202) 737-6637

Green Party of the U.S. (1984): (202) 319-7191; www.gp.org

Homeless, Natl. Coalition for the (1984): (202) 462-4822; www.nationalhomeless.org

Human Rights Campaign (1980): (202) 628-4160; www.hrc.org

Immigration Equality (1994): (212) 714-2904; immigrationequality.org

Immigration Reform, Federation for American (FAIR) (1979): (202) 328-7004; www.fairus.org

Japanese American Citizens League (1929): (202) 223-1240; jacl.org

Jewish Committee, American (1906): (212) 751-4000; www.ajc.org

John Birch Society (1958): (920) 749-3780; jbs.org

LGBTQ Task Force, Natl. (fmr. Natl. Gay and Lesbian Task Force) (1973): (202) 393-5177; www.thetaskforce.org

Libertarian Natl. Committee, Inc. (1971): (202) 333-0008; www.lp.org

Mayors, U.S. Conference of (1932): (202) 293-7330; www.usmayors.org

Men, Natl. Coalition for (1977): (619) 231-1909; www.ncfm.org

NAACP (Natl. Assn. for the Advancement of Colored People) (1909): (410) 580-5777; www.naacp.org

NRA (National Rifle Assn.) (1871): (800) 672-3888; www.nra.org

OpenSecrets (2021, from merger of Center for Responsive Politics and National Inst. on Money in Politics): (202) 857-0044; www.opensecrets.org

Parliamentarians, Natl. Assn. of (1930): (816) 833-3892; www.parliamentarians.org

Patriot Majority (2005): www.patriot majority.com

National Popular Vote (2006): (650) 472-1587; www.nationalpopularvote.com

Progress, Center for American (2003): (202) 682-1611; www.americanprogress.org

Reform Party Natl. Committee (1995): (972) 275-9297; www.reformparty.org

Republican Natl. Committee (1854): (202) 863-8500; www.gop.com

Southern Christian Leadership Conference (1957): (404) 522-1420; nationalsclc.org

Southern Poverty Law Center (1971): (334) 956-8200; www.splcenter.org

State Governments, Council of (1933): (859) 244-8000; www.csg.org

Tax Foundation (1937): (202) 464-6200; www.taxfoundation.org

Tax Reform, Americans for (1985): (202) 785-0266; www.atr.org

Taxpayers Union, Natl. (1969): (703) 683-5700; www.ntu.org

Tea Party Patriots (2009): (877) 748-3277; www.teapartypatriots.org

Term Limits, U.S. (1991): (202) 261-3532; www.termlimits.com

Urban League, Natl. (1910): (212) 558-5300; www.nul.org

Woman's Christian Temperance Union (1874): (847) 864-1396; www.wctu.org

Women, Natl. Organization for (NOW) (1966): (202) 628-8669; www.now.org

Women and Families, Natl. Partnership for (1971): (202) 986-2600; www.nationalpartnership.org

Women Voters, League of (1920): (202) 429-1965; www.lwv.org

Zionist Organization of America (1897): (212) 481-1500; www.zoa.org

Religious

African Methodist Episcopal Church (1787): 900 13th Ave. S., Ste. 340, Nashville, TN 37212; (615) 254-0911; www.ame-church.com; Gen. Sec., Dr. Jeffery B. Cooper

African Methodist Episcopal Zion Church (1796): 3225 Sugar Creek Rd., Charlotte, NC 28269; (704) 599-4630; www.amez.org; Chief Operating Officer, Rev. Julius Walls Jr.

American Baptist Churches USA (1907): P.O. Box 851, Valley Forge, PA 19482; (610) 768-2000; www.abc-usa.org; Gen. Sec., Rev. Dr. C. Jeff Woods

Antiochian Orthodox Christian Archdiocese of North America (1895): P.O. Box 5238, Englewood, NJ 07631; (201) 871-1355; www.antiochian.org; Primate, Archbishop of New York and Metropolitan Saba Isper

Armenian Apostolic Church of America: *Eastern Prelacy* (1958): 138 E. 39th St., NY, NY 10016; (212) 689-7810; www.armenian-prelacy.org; Prelate, Archbishop Anoushavan Tanielian; *Western Prelacy* (1973): 6252 Honolulu Ave., La Crescenta, CA 91214; (818) 248-7737; www.westernprelacy.org; Prelate, Bishop Torkom Donoyan

Assemblies of God USA (1914): 1445 N. Boonville Ave., Springfield, MO 65802; (417) 862-2781; www.ag.org; Gen. Supt., Doug Clay

Atheists, American (1963): 225 Cristiani St., Cranford, NJ 07016; (908) 276-7300; www.atheists.org; Board Chair, Jen Scott

Bahá'ís of the U.S., Natl. Spiritual Assembly of the (1909): 1233 Central St., Evanston, IL 60201; (847) 733-3400; www.bahai.us; Sec., Kenneth E. Bowers

Baptist Bible Fellowship Intl. (1950): 720 E. Kearney St., Springfield, MO 65803; (417) 862-5001; www.bbfi.org; Pres., Jon Haley

Baptist Convention, Southern (1845): 901 Commerce St., Nashville, TN 37203; (615) 244-2355; www.sbc.net; Pres., Bart Barber

Baptist Convention, USA, Inc., Natl. (1886): 1700 Baptist World Center Dr., Nashville, TN 37207; (615) 228-6292; www.national baptist.com; Pres., Dr. Jerry Young

Baptist Convention of America Intl., Inc., Natl. (1880): 550 W. Kentucky St., Louisville, KY 40203; (844) 610-6222; www.nbcainc.com; Pres., Rev. Samuel C. Tolbert Jr.

Baptist Convention of America, Natl. Missionary (1880): 6925 Wofford Dr., Dallas, TX 75227; (214) 381-3734; www.nmbca.org; Pres., Dr. Anthony E. Sharp

Bible Society, American (1816): 101 N. Independence Mall East FL8, Philadelphia, PA 19106; (215) 309-0900; www.americanbible.org; Interim CEO, Paul Cleckner

Biblical Literature, Society of (1880): 825 Houston Mill Rd., Atlanta, GA 30329; (404) 727-3100; www.sbl-site.org; Exec. Dir., Steed Vernyl Davidson

B'nai B'rith Intl. (1843): 1120 20th St. NW, Ste. 300 N, Washington, DC 20036; (202) 857-6600; www.bnaibrith.org; Pres., Seth J. Riklin

Brethren in Christ Church (c. 1778): 431 Grantham Rd., Mechanicsburg, PA 17055; (717) 697-2634; www.bicus.org; Natl. Dir., Dr. Alan Robinson

Buddhist Churches of America (1899): 1710 Octavia St., San Francisco, CA 94109; (415) 776-5600; www.buddhistchurchesofamerica.org; Pres., Terri Omori

Catholic Bishops, U.S. Conference of (2001): 3211 4th St. NE, Washington, DC 20017; (202) 541-3000; www.usccb.org; Pres., Rev. Timothy P. Broglio

Christian Church (Disciples of Christ) (1832): Disciples Center, P.O. Box 1986, Indianapolis, IN 46206; (317) 635-3100; www.disciples.org; Gen. Min. and Pres., Rev. Teresa Hord Owens

Christian Methodist Episcopal Church (1870): 4466 Elvis Presley Blvd., Memphis, TN 38116; (901) 345-0580; www.thecmechurch.org; Senior Bishop, Lawrence L. Reddick III

Church of the Brethren (1708): General Offices, 1451 Dundee Ave., Elgin, IL 60120; (847) 742-5100; www.brethren.org; Gen. Sec., David A. Steele

Church of Christ (1830): P.O. Box 472, Independence, MO 64051; (816) 206-0147; www.churchofchrist1830.org; Sec., Council of Apostles, Duane L. Ely

Church of God (Anderson, IN) (1881): P.O. Box 2420, Anderson, IN 46018; (765) 642-0256; www.jesusisthesubject.org; Gen. Dir., Jim Lyon

Church of God (Cleveland, TN) (1886): 2490 Keith St., P.O. Box 2430, Cleveland, TN 37320; (423) 472-3361; www.churchofgod.org; Gen. Overseer, Tim Hill

Church of God in Christ (1897): Mason Temple, 930 Mason St., Memphis, TN 38126; (901) 947-9300; www.cogic.org; Presiding Bishop, Bishop John Drew Sheard

Church of Jesus Christ (1862): World Operations Ctr., 110 Walton Tea Room Rd., Greensburg, PA 15601; (724) 837-4425; www.thechurchofjesuschrist.org; Pres., Apostle Joel Gehly

Church of the Nazarene (1908): Global Ministry Center, 17001 Prairie Star Pkwy., Lenexa, KS 66220; (913) 577-0500; www.nazarene.org; Gen. Sec., Gary Hartke

Community of Christ (reorganized Church of Jesus Christ of Latter-day Saints) (1830): Intl. Headquarters, 1001 W. Walnut, Independence, MO 64050; (816) 833-1000; www.cofchrist.org; Pres., Stephen M. Veazey

Community Churches, International Council of (1950): P.O. Box 846, Longmont, CO 80502; (815) 464-5690; www.icccnow.org; Exec. Dir., Rev. Phil Tom

Conservative Judaism, United Synagogue of (1913): 3080 Broadway, Ste. B208, NY, NY 10027; (212) 533-7800; www.uscj.org; CEO, Rabbi Jacob Blumenthal

Converge (fmr. Baptist General Conference) (1852): 11002 Lake Hart Dr., Mail Code 200, Orlando, FL 32832; (800) 323-4215; www.converge.org; Pres., John K. Jenkins Sr.

Cumberland Presbyterian Church (1810): 8207 Traditional Dr., Cordova, TN 38016; (901) 276-4572; www.cumberland.org

Episcopal Church (1789): 815 Second Ave., NY, NY 10017; (212) 716-6000; www.episcopalchurch.org; Presiding Bishop and Primate, Most Rev. Michael B. Curry

Evangelical Lutheran Church in America (1988): 8765 W. Higgins Rd., Chicago, IL 60631; (773) 380-2700; www.elca.org; Presiding Bishop, Rev. Elizabeth A. Eaton

First Church of Christ, Scientist, The (1879): 210 Massachusetts Ave., Boston, MA 02115; (617) 450-2000; www.christianscience.com; Pres., Doris Ulich, C.S.B.

Free Methodist Church USA (1860): 5235 Decatur Blvd., Indianapolis, IN 46241; (317) 244-3660; www.fmcusa.org; COO, Mark Dowley

Freedom From Religion Foundation (1978): P.O. Box 750, Madison, WI 53701; (608) 256-8900; www.ffrf.org; Pres., Annie Laurie Gaylor and Dan Barker

Friends General Conference (1900): 1216 Arch St., #2B, Philadelphia, PA 19107; (215) 561-1700; www.fgcquaker.org; Gen. Sec., Barry Crossno

Gideons Intl., The (1899): P.O. Box 140800, Nashville, TN 37214; (615) 564-5000; www.gideons.org; Exec. Dir., Dan Heighway

Greek Orthodox Archdiocese of America (1922): 8 E. 79th St., NY, NY 10075; (212) 570-3500; www.goarch.org; Primate, Archbishop Elpidophoros

Hadassah, the Women's Zionist Organization of America, Inc. (1912): 40 Wall St., NY, NY 10005; (800) 664-5646; www.hadassah.org; Exec. Dir. and CEO, Naomi Adler

Interfaith Alliance (1994): 110 Maryland Ave., NE, Ste. 509, Washington, DC 20002; (202) 466-0567; www.interfaithalliance.org; Pres., Rev. Paul Brandeis Raushenbush

Islamic Society of North America: 6555 S. County Rd. 750 East, Plainfield, IN 46168; (317) 839-8157; www.isna.net; Pres., Safaa Zarzour

Jehovah's Witnesses (1931): 900 Red Mills Rd., Wallkill, NY 12589; (845) 744-6000; www.jw.org

Jewish Congress, American (1918): 654 Madison Ave., 9th Fl., NY, NY 10065; (212) 879-4500; www.ajcongress.org; Pres., Jack Rosen

Reconstructing Judaism (fmr. Jewish Reconstructionist Communities) (2012): 1299 Church Rd., Wyncote, PA 19095; (215) 576-0800; www.reconstructingjudaism.org; Pres., Rabbi Deborah Waxman

Jewish Women, Natl. Council of (1893): 2055 L St. NW, Ste. 650, Washington, D.C. 20036; (202) 296-2588; www.ncjw.org; Pres., Dana Gershon

Latter-day Saints, The Church of Jesus Christ of (Mormons) (1830): 50 W. North Temple St., Salt Lake City, UT 84150; (801) 240-2640; www.lds.org; Pres., Russell M. Nelson

Lutheran Church—Missouri Synod (1847): 1333 S. Kirkwood Rd., St. Louis, MO 63122; (800) 248-1930; www.lcms.org; Pres., Rev. Dr. Matthew C. Harrison

Mennonite Church USA (2001): 718 N. Main St., Newton, KS 67114; (316) 283-5100; www.mennoniteusa.org; Exec. Dir., Glen Guyton

Moravian Church in North America (1735): www.moravian.org; *Northern Prov.:* 1021 Center St., P.O. Box 1245, Bethlehem, PA 18016; (610) 867-7566; Pres., Rev. Dr. Betsy Miller; *Southern Prov.:* 459 S. Church St., Winston-Salem, NC 27101; (336) 725-5811; Pres., Rev. Dr. Neil Routh

North American Shia Ithna-asheri Muslim Communities, Org. of (1986): P.O. Box 29691, Minneapolis, MN 55429; (905) 763-7512; nasimco.org; Pres., Br. Arif Jacksi

Orthodox Union (1898): 40 Rector St., 4th Fl., NY, NY 10006; (212) 563-4000; www.ou.org; Pres., Mitchel R. Aeder

Pentecostal Assemblies of the World, Inc. (1906): 3939 N. Meadows Dr., Indianapolis, IN 46205; (317) 547-9541; www.pawinc.org; Presiding Bishop, Theodore L. Brooks, Sr.

Presbyterian Church (U.S.A.) (1983): 100 Witherspoon St., Louisville, KY 40202;

(800) 728-7228; www.pcusa.org; Pres., Kathy Lueckert

Progressive Natl. Baptist Convention, Inc. (1961): 601 50th St. NE, Washington, DC 20019; (202) 396-0558; www.pnbc.org; Pres., Rev. David Peoples

Rabbis, Central Conference of American (1889): 355 Lexington Ave., NY, NY 10017; (212) 972-3636; www.ccarnet.org; Pres., Rabbi Erica Ash

Reform Judaism, Union for (1873): 633 3rd Ave., NY, NY 10017; (212) 650-4000; www.urj.org; Pres., Rabbi Rick Jacobs

Secular Humanism, Council for (1980): P.O. Box 664, Amherst, NY 14226; (716) 636-7571; www.secularhumanism.org; Pres., Robyn A. Blumner

Separation of Church and State, Americans United for (1947): 1310 L St. NW, Ste. 200, Washington, DC 20005; (202) 466-3234; www.au.org; Pres. and CEO, Rachel Laser

Seventh-day Adventist Church (1863): 12501 Old Columbia Pike, Silver Spring, MD 20904; (301) 680-6000; www.adventist.org; Pres., Ted N. C. Wilson

Seventh Day Baptist (1802): Box 1678, Janesville, WI 53547; (608) 752-5055; www.seventhdaybaptist.org; Exec. Dir., Rev. Carl F. Greene

Unitarian Universalist Assn. of Congregations (1961): 24 Farnsworth St., Boston, MA 02210; (617) 742-2100; www.uua.org; Pres., Rev. Susan Frederick-Gray

United Church of Christ (1957): 700 Prospect Ave., Cleveland, OH 44115; (216) 736-2100; www.ucc.org; Pres., Rev. John C. Dorhauer

United Methodist Church (1968): 100 Maryland Ave. NE, Washington, DC 20002; (202) 488-5600; www.umc.org; Council of Bishops Pres., Thomas J. Bickerton

United Pentecostal Church Intl. (1945): 36 Research Park Court, Weldon Spring, MO 63304; (636) 229-7900; www.upci.org; Gen. Supt., David K. Bernard

Wesleyan Church, The (1843): 13300 Olio Rd., Fishers, IN 46037; (317) 774-7900; www.wesleyan.org; Gen. Supt., Rev. Dr. Wayne Schmidt

Businesses and Corporations

Source: World Almanac research

Listed below are major corporations offering products and services to U.S. consumers, as of July 2023. Alphabetization is by first key word. Listings generally include examples of products offered.

Company name (NYSE/Nasdaq symbol, if traded on those markets): Address; Telephone number; Website; Top executive; Business, products, or services.

Abbott Laboratories (ABT): 100 Abbott Park Rd., Abbott Park, IL 60064; (224) 667-6100; www.abbott.com; Robert B. Ford; develops, mfr. pharmaceutical, nutritional, diagnostic prods.

AbbVie Inc. (ABBV): 1 N. Waukegan Rd., N. Chicago, IL 60064; (847) 932-7900; www.abbvie.com; Richard A. Gonzalez; pharmaceuticals. Acquired Irish Botox-mfr. Allergan, 5/8/2020.

ABC: see Walt Disney Co.

Accenture Inc. (ACN): 161 N. Clark St., Chicago, IL 60601; (877) 889-9009; www.accenture.com; Julie Sweet; management consulting.

Activision Blizzard Inc. (ATVI): 2701 Olympic Blvd., Bldg. B, Santa Monica, CA 90404; (310) 255-2000; www.activisionblizzard.com; Bobby Kotick; video game publisher (*World of Warcraft, Call of Duty, Candy Crush Saga*). Agreed to acquisition by Microsoft for $68.7 bil, 1/18/2022.

adidas Group: Adi-Dassler-Strasse 1, D-91074 Herzogenaurach, Germany; +49 (0) 9132-84-0; www.adidas-group.com; Bjørn Gulden; apparel and accessories mfr. (Reebok).

Advance Publications, Inc.: One World Trade Ctr., NY, NY, 10007; (718) 981-1234; www.advance.com; Steven Newhouse; communications, newspaper and magazine publisher (Condé Nast subsids.: *New Yorker, Vanity Fair, Vogue*). Acquired The IRONMAN Group sports participation platform, 7/20/2020.

Aetna, Inc.: see CVS Health

Aflac, Inc. (AFL): 1932 Wynnton Rd., Columbus, GA 31999; (706) 596-3264; www.aflac.com; Daniel P. Amos; supplemental health and life insurance.

Airbnb (ABNB): 888 Brannan St., 4th Fl., San Francisco, CA 94117; (415) 800-5959; www.airbnb.com; Brian Chesky; online marketplace for short-term global accommodations. IPO 12/10/2020.

Alaska Air Group, Inc. (ALK): 19300 International Blvd., Seattle, WA 98188; (206) 433-3200; www.alaskaair.com; Ben Minicucci; airline carriers (Alaska Airlines, Horizon Air).

Albertsons Companies, Inc. (ACI): 250 E. Parkcenter Blvd., Boise, ID 83706; (208) 395-6200; www.albertsonscompanies.com; Vivek Sankaran; grocery and drug retail operation (Albertsons, Jewel-Osco, Safeway, Shaw's, Vons). Announced plans to merge with Kroger, 10/14/2022.

Alcoa Corp. (AA): 201 Isabella St., Ste. 500, Pittsburgh, PA 15212; (412) 992-5450; www.alcoa.com; Roy Harvey; prod., mfr. of aluminum, aluminum prods. (aerospace, automotive, industrial materials and components).

Alden Global Capital: 885 3rd Ave., No. 34, NY, NY 10022; (212) 888-5500; aldenglobal.com; Heath Freeman; hedge fund with 2nd largest U.S. portfolio of daily and weekly newspapers. Acquired Tribune Publishing Co. newspapers (*Chicago

Tribune, Baltimore Sun, NY Daily News*), 5/24/2021.

Alibaba Group (BABA): 969 West Wen Yi Rd., Yu Hang District, Hangzhou 311121, China; +86 571-8502-2088; www.alibaba.com; Daniel Zhang; online shopping, logistics, marketing; data mgmt.; financial serv. U.S. IPO, 9/19/2014. Acquired Pakistani online retailer Daraz Group, 5/8/2018. Announced it would split into 6 groups and explore IPOs, 3/28/2023.

Allstate Corp. (ALL): 2775 Sanders Rd., Northbrook, IL 60062; (847) 402-5000; www.allstate.com; Thomas J. Wilson; personal property and casualty insurance; financial services. Acquired personal insurance prov. National General Holdings Corp., 1/4/2021.

Alphabet Inc. (GOOG): 1600 Amphitheatre Pkwy., Mountain View, CA 94043; (650) 253-0000; www.abc.xyz; Sundar Pichai; Google and other internet-related prods. and services (leading search engine, ad sales; YouTube). Reorganized Google as Alphabet, 10/2/2015. Acquired Fitbit, 1/14/2021. Announced plans to buy cybersecurity co. Mandiant, 3/8/2022. Laid off 12,000 employees, 1/20/2023.

Altice USA (ATUS): 1111 Stewart Ave., Bethpage, NY 11714; (516) 803-2300; www.alticeusa.com; Dennis Mathew; telecom, internet, cable provider.

Altria Group, Inc. (MO): 6601 W. Broad St., Richmond, VA 23230; (804) 484-8897; www.altria.com; Billy Gifford; tobacco co. (Marlboro, Merit, Parliament, Virginia Slims). (Altria spun off Philip Morris's intl. operations in 2008 but owns Philip Morris brands in U.S.).

Amazon.com, Inc. (AMZN): 410 Terry Ave. N., Seattle, WA 98109; (206) 266-1000; www.amazon.com; Andy Jassy; online retailer and e-commerce platform; cloud computing (AWS); media streaming/production (Audible, Prime Video, Twitch). Acquired grocer Whole Foods, 8/28/2017. Acquired MGM Studios for $8.5 bil, 3/17/2022. Laid off 27,000 employees, 2023.

American Airlines Group, Inc. (AAL): 1 Skyview Dr., Ft. Worth, TX 76155; (682) 278-9000; www.aa.com; Robert Isom; airlines.

American Electric Power Co., Inc. (AEP): 1 Riverside Plz., Columbus, OH 43215; (614) 716-1000; www.aep.com; Julie Sloat; public utilities.

American Express Co. (AXP): World Financial Ctr., 200 Vesey St., 50th Fl., NY, NY 10285; (212) 640-2000; www.american express.com; Stephen J. Squeri; charge and credit cards, travel-related services.

American Greetings Corp.: 1 American Blvd., Cleveland, OH 44145; (216) 252-7300; www.americangreetings.com; Joe Arcuri; greeting cards, stationery, party goods, gift items.

American Intl. Group, Inc. (AIG): 175 Water St., 15th Fl., NY, NY 10038; (212) 770-7000; www.aigcorporate.com; Peter Zaffino; insurance, financial services. AIG received $182 bil in govt. bailouts, 2008.

AmerisourceBergen (ABC): 1 West First Ave., Conshohocken, PA 19428; (610) 727-7000; www.amerisourcebergen.com; Steven H. Collis; distrib. of generic and brand-name pharmaceuticals.

Amgen, Inc. (AMGN): 1 Amgen Center Dr., Thousand Oaks, CA 91320; (805) 447-1000; www.amgen.com; Robert A. Bradway; biopharmaceuticals.

Anheuser-Busch InBev (BUD): Brouwerijplein 1, 3000 Leuven, Belgium; +32 (16) 276111; www.ab-inbev.com; Michael Doukeris; brewer (Budweiser, Bud Light, Michelob, Corona, Foster's, Stella Artois), soft drinks. Acquired brewing competitor SABMiller for $100 bil+, 10/10/2016.

Anthem, Inc.: see Elevance Health, Inc.

Apple Inc. (AAPL): 1 Apple Park Way, Cupertino, CA 95014; (408) 996-1010; www.apple.com; Tim Cook; mfr. of computers (Mac), digital media devices (iPod, iPhone, iPad) and distrib. (iTunes store, Apple Music). Acquired music ID app Shazam, 9/24/2018; became world's first-ever publicly traded co. worth $1 tril, 8/2018; $2 tril, 8/2020; $3 tril, 1/2022.

ARAMARK Corp. (ARMK): 2400 Market St., Philadelphia, PA 19103; (215) 238-3000; www.aramark.com; John Zillmer; food/support services to institutions and facilities, uniforms and career apparel.

Archer Daniels Midland Co. (ADM): 77 W. Wacker Dr. Ste. 4600, Chicago, IL 60601; (312) 634-8100; www.adm.com; Juan R. Luciano; agricultural commodities and prods.

Armstrong World Industries, Inc. (AWI): 2500 Columbia Ave., P.O. Box 3001, Lancaster, PA 17604; (717) 672-9611; www.armstrong.com; Victor D. Grizzle; mfr. of flooring, ceiling prods., cabinets.

AT&T Inc. (T): 208 S. Akard St., Dallas, TX 75202; (210) 821-4105; www.att.com; John Stankey; telecommunications, global information mgmt., mass media prod., distrib. (WarnerMedia, incl. CNN, HBO; DirecTV). Sold WarnerMedia assets to Discovery for $43 bil, 4/8/2022.

Automatic Data Processing, Inc. (ADP): 1 ADP Blvd., Roseland, NJ 07068; (973) 974-5000; www.adp.com; Maria Black; payroll and tax processing serv.

AutoNation, Inc. (AN): 200 SW 1st Ave., Ste. 1600, Ft. Lauderdale, FL 33301; (954) 769-6000; www.autonation.com; Michael Manley; auto retailer; new and used vehicles; auto parts, maintenance, and repair; auto finance and insurance.

Bank of America Corp. (BAC): 100 N. Tryon St., Charlotte, NC 28255; (704) 386-5681; www.bankofamerica.com; Brian T. Moynihan; banking and financial services.

Barnes & Noble, Inc.: 122 Fifth Ave., NY, NY 10011; (212) 633-3300; www.barnesandnobleinc.com; James Daunt; bookseller, publisher (Sterling Pub. Co.). Acquired by investment firm Elliott Management Corp., 8/7/2019.

Bath & Body Works, Inc. (BBWI) 3 Ltd. Parkway, Columbus, OH 43230; (614) 415-7000; www.bathandbodyworks.com; Gina Boswell; personal care retailer.

Bayer AG: Kaiser-Wilhelm-Allee, D-51368 Leverkusen, Germany; +49 214-30-40126, www.bayer.com; Bill Anderson; pharmaceuticals, health care and biotech prods.; acquired Monsanto for $63 bil, 6/7/2018.

Baxter International Inc. (BAX): 1 Baxter Pkwy., Deerfield, IL 60015; (224) 948-2000; www.baxter.com; José Almeida; mfr. of health care prods.

Bear Stearns Cos. Inc.: see JPMorgan Chase & Co.

Becton, Dickinson & Co. (BDX): 1 Becton Dr., Franklin Lakes, NJ 07417; (201) 847-6800; www.bd.com; Tom Polen; medical, laboratory, diagnostic prods.

Bed Bath & Beyond Inc.: 650 Liberty Ave., Union, NJ 07083; (908) 688-0888; www.bedbathandbeyond.com; Sue Gove; home goods retailer. Filed for Ch. 11 bankruptcy with all stores to close, 4/23/2023. Overstock.com acquired the Bed Bath & Beyond name and trademarks, 6/28/2023.

Berkshire Hathaway Inc. (BRK.A): 3555 Farnam St., Ste. 1440, Omaha, NE 68131; (402) 346-1400; www.berkshirehathaway.com; Warren E. Buffett; diversified holdings incl. insurance (GEICO), building materials (Benjamin Moore & Co., Shaw), apparel (Fruit of the Loom), food (Dairy Queen), Precision Castparts, Duracell.

Bertelsmann AG: Carl-Bertelsmann-Str. 270, 33311 Gütersloh, Germany; +49 (0) 5241-80-62321; www.bertelsmann.de; Thomas Rabe; intl. media corp., trade book publisher (Penguin Random House: Knopf, Doubleday).

Best Buy Co. Inc. (BBY): 7601 Penn Ave. S., Richfield, MN 55423; (612) 291-1000; www.bestbuy.com; Corie Barry; retailer of software, appliances, consumer electronics.

Blackstone Group LP, The (BX): 345 Park Ave., NY, NY 10154; (212) 583-5000; www.blackstone.com; Stephen A. Schwarzman; asset mgmt., financial services. Acquired majority stake in tech co. HealthEdge, 4/9/2020, Australia's Crown Resorts Ltd., 6/24/2022, cloud-based event-software provider Cvent, 6/15/2023.

Boeing Co. (BA): 929 Long Bridge Dr., Arlington, VA 22202; (703) 465-3500; boeing.com; David L. Calhoun; world's leading aerospace co., mfr. of commercial jet and military aircraft; one of the largest U.S. defense contractors. Suspended production of 737 MAX aircraft Jan.-May 2020 following two fatal crashes in 2018 and 2019. Agreed to pay $2.5 bil to settle criminal charges it hid design flaws connected to the crashes, 1/7/2021.

Booking Holdings Inc. (BKNG) (fmr. The Priceline Group): 800 Connecticut Ave., Norwalk, CT 06854; (203) 299-8000; www.bookingholdings.com; Glenn D. Fogel; online travel/hospitality services (Priceline, booking.com, Kayak, Open Table).

Brighthouse Financial, Inc. (BHF): 11225 N. Community House Rd., Charlotte, NC 28277; (800) 638-5000; www.brighthousefinancial.com; Eric Steigerwalt; life insurance, annuities.

Brink's Co., The (BCO): 1801 Bayberry Ct., P.O. Box 18100, Richmond, VA 23226; (804) 289-9600; www.brinks.com; Mark Eubanks; security (armored transport, money processing, trans. of valuables).

Bristol-Myers Squibb Co. (BMY): 430 E. 29th St., 14th Fl., NY, NY 10016; (212) 546-4000; www.bms.com; Giovanni Caforio; development, mfr., and sale of

pharmaceuticals (Plavix, Eliquis, Atripla, Revlimid).

Brown-Forman Corp. (BF.B): 850 Dixie Hwy., Louisville, KY 40210; (502) 585-1100; www.brown-forman.com; Lawson E. Whiting; distilled spirits (Jack Daniel's, Finlandia), wine and champagne (Sonoma-Cutrer, Korbel).

Brunswick Corp. (BC): 26125 N. Riverwoods Blvd., Ste. 500, Mettawa, IL 60045; (847) 735-4700; www.brunswick.com; David M. Foulkes; leisure and recreation prods., incl. marine engines and boats; fitness equip.

Burger King: see Restaurant Brands Intl.

Caesars Entertainment Inc. (CZR): One Caesars Palace Dr., Las Vegas, NV 89109; (702) 407-6000; www.caesars.com; Tom Reeg; casinos; gambling services (Caesars, Harrah's, Horseshoe, World Series of Poker). Acquired by Eldorado Resorts, 7/20/2020.

Campbell Soup Co. (CPB): One Campbell Pl., Camden, NJ 08103; (856) 342-4800; www.campbellsoupcompany.com; Mark A. Clouse; soup mfr.; sauces (Pace, Prego), V8 juice, Pepperidge Farm, Snyder's prods.

Capital One Financial Corporation (COF): 1680 Capital One Dr., McLean, VA 22102; (703) 720-1000; www.capitalone.com; Richard D. Fairbank; financial services.

Cardinal Health, Inc. (CAH): 7000 Cardinal Pl., Dublin, OH 43017; (614) 757-5000; www.cardinalhealth.com; Mike Kaufmann; pharmaceutical and med. equip. dist. co.

Carlyle Group, The (CG): 1001 Pennsylvania Ave. NW, Washington, DC 20004; (202) 729-5626; www.carlyle.com; Harvey M. Schwartz; private equity group.

Caterpillar Inc. (CAT): 510 Lake Cook Rd., Deerfield, IL 60115; (309) 675-2337; www.caterpillar.com; Jim Umpleby; mfr. of construction and mining equip.

CBRE Group, Inc. (CBRE): 2100 McKinney Ave., Ste. 1250, Dallas, TX, 75201; (214) 979-6100; www.cbre.us; Bob Sulentic; commercial real estate.

CBS Corp.: see Paramount Global

CenturyLink, Inc.: see Lumen Technologies

Charter Communications, Inc. (CHTR): 400 Washington Blvd., Stamford, CT 06902; (203) 905-7801; www.charter.com; Tom Rutledge; internet, cable TV, telecom provider (Spectrum).

Chevron Corp. (CVX): 6001 Bollinger Canyon Rd., San Ramon, CA 94583; (925) 842-1000; www.chevron.com; Michael K. Wirth; integrated energy co. Acquired Renewable Energy Group, Inc., 6/13/2022.

Chiquita Brands Intl., Inc.: 1855 Griffin Rd., Ste. C-436, Ft. Lauderdale, FL, 33004; (954) 924-5700; www.chiquita.com; Carlos Lopez Flores; fruits and vegetables. Acquired by Cutrale-Safra, 1/6/2015.

CHS Inc. (CHSCP): 5500 Cenex Dr., Inver Grove Heights, MN 55077; (651) 355-6000; www.chsinc.com; Jay Debertin; grain marketing, oil refining, and pipeline operations.

Chubb Ltd. (CB): 202 Halls Mill Rd., Whitehouse Station, NJ 08889; (908) 572-2000; www.chubb.com; Evan Greenberg; property/casualty insurance. ACE Limited acquired The Chubb Corporation, 1/14/2016.

Church & Dwight Co., Inc. (CHD): Princeton South Corporate Center, 500 Charles Ewing Blvd., Ewing, NJ 08628; (609) 806-1200; www.churchdwight.com; Matthew T. Farrell; ARM & HAMMER baking soda; household and personal care prods. (OxiClean, Arrid, Trojan, First Response).

Cigna Group, The (CI): 900 Cottage Grove Rd., Bloomfield, CT 06002; (860) 226-6000; www.cigna.com; David M. Cordani; insurance provider. Acquired pharmacy benefit manager Express Scripts for $54 bil, 12/20/2018.

Cintas Corp. (CTAS): 6800 Cintas Blvd., Cincinnati, OH 45262; (513) 459-1200; www.cintas.com; Todd M. Schneider; uniform supplier.

Cisco Systems, Inc. (CSCO): 170 W. Tasman Dr., San Jose, CA 95134; (408) 526-4000; www.cisco.com; Chuck Robbins; networking and communication prods.

Citigroup, Inc. (C): 388 Greenwich St., NY, NY 10013; (212) 559-1000; www.citigroup.com; Jane Fraser; diversified financial services.

Clorox Co. (CLX): 1221 Broadway, Oakland, CA 94612; (510) 271-7000; www.clorox.com; Linda Rendle; consumer prods. (Clorox, Formula 409, Pine-Sol, S.O.S., Tilex, Scoop Away, Fresh Step, Kingsford, Hidden Valley, Glad, Brita, Burt's Bees).

Coach, Inc.: see Tapestry, Inc.

Coca-Cola Co. (KO): 1 Coca-Cola Plz. NW, Atlanta, GA 30313; (404) 676-2121; www.coca-cola.com; James Quincey; beverages (Coca-Cola, Sprite, Dasani, Fanta, Minute Maid, Vitaminwater).

Colgate-Palmolive Co. (CL): 300 Park Ave., NY, NY 10022; (212) 310-2000; www.colgate.com; Noel Wallace; soap (Irish Spring, Palmolive), household cleansers (Ajax), toothpaste (Colgate, Tom's of Maine), pet food (Hill's Science Diet).

Comcast Corp. (CMCSA): 1701 JFK Blvd., Philadelphia, PA 19103; (215) 286-1700; www.comcast.com; Brian L. Roberts; cable provider; broadband media services; programming (E!, NBC, Bravo, USA, Telemundo). Acquired DreamWorks Animation, 8/22/2016; majority of UK pay-TV giant SKY, 10/9/2018.

Conagra Brands, Inc. (CAG): 222 W. Merchandise Mart Plaza, Ste. 1300, Chicago, IL 60654; (312) 549-5000; www.conagrafoods.com; Sean Connolly; food processor (Chef Boyardee, Healthy Choice frozen dinners, Egg Beaters, Reddi-wip); food service supplier.

ConocoPhillips Co. (COP): 925 N. Eldridge Pkwy., Houston, TX 77079; (281) 293-1000; www.conocophillips.com; Ryan M. Lance; oil and gas exploration and prod. co.

Consolidated Edison, Inc. (ED): 4 Irving Plc., NY, NY 10003; (212) 460-4600; www.conedison.com; Timothy P. Cawley; electric, natural gas utilities.

Continental Airlines, Inc.: see United Airlines Holdings, Inc.

Corning Inc. (GLW): 1 Riverfront Plz., Corning, NY 14831; (607) 974-9000; www.corning.com; Wendell P. Weeks; mfr. of telecommunications, specialty equip., fiber optics.

Corteva Inc. (CTVA): 9330 Zionsville Rd., Indianapolis, IN 46268; (833) 267-8382; www.corteva.com; Chuck Magro; agricultural chem. dev./mfr. Separated 6/1/2019 from now-dissolved DowDuPont (6/1/2019); see Dow Inc. or Dupont de Nemours, Inc.

Costco Wholesale Corp. (COST): 999 Lake Dr., Issaquah, WA 98027; (425) 313-8100; www.costco.com; W. Craig Jelinek; wholesale warehouse stores.

Countrywide Financial: see Bank of America Corp.

Crown Holdings, Inc. (CCK): 770 Township Line Rd., Yardley, PA 19067; (215) 698-5100; www.crowncork.com; Timothy J. Donahue; producer of packaging prods.

CSX Corp. (CSX): 500 Water St., 15th Fl., Jacksonville, FL 32202; (904) 359-3200; www.csx.com; James M. Foote; rail freight transport.

CVS Health (CVS): 1 CVS Dr., Woonsocket, RI 02895; (401) 765-1500; www.cvs.com; Karen S. Lynch; retail drugstores. Acquired health insurer Aetna for $78 bil, 11/28/2018.

Dairy Farmers of America: 1405 N. 98th St., Kansas City, KS 66111; (816) 801-6455; www.dfamilk.com; Dennis Rodenbaugh; milk marketing cooperative. Acquired Dean Foods Co., 5/1/2020.

Dana Inc. (DAN): 3939 Technology Dr., Maumee, OH 43537; (419) 887-3000; www.dana.com; James Kamsickas; truck and auto parts, supplies.

Darden Restaurants, Inc. (DRI): 1000 Darden Center Dr., Orlando, FL 32837; (407) 245-4000; www.darden.com; Rick Cardenas; casual-dining restaurants (Olive Garden, LongHorn Steakhouse).

Dean Foods Co.: see Dairy Farmers of America

Deere & Co. (DE): One John Deere Pl., Moline, IL 61265; (309) 765-8000; www.deere.com; John C. May; mfr. of farm equip., industrial equip., lawn and garden tractors.

Dell Inc. (DELL): 1 Dell Way, Round Rock, TX 78682; (512) 338-4400; www.dell.com; Michael S. Dell; laptop and desktop computers, network accessories, peripherals, tablets, smartphones. Spun off majority stake in cloud computing co. VMware, 11/1/2021.

Delta Air Lines, Inc. (DAL): 1030 Delta Blvd., Atlanta, GA 30354; (404) 715-2600; www.delta.com; Ed Bastian; air transportation.

Dillard's, Inc. (DDS): 1600 Cantrell Rd., Little Rock, AR 72201; (501) 376-5200; www.dillards.com; William Dillard II; dept. store chain.

Dish Network Corp. (DISH): 9601 S. Meridian Blvd., Englewood, CO 80112; (303) 723-1000; www.dish.com; W. Erik Carlson; satellite media services.

Walt Disney Co., The (DIS): 500 S. Buena Vista St., Burbank, CA 91521; (818) 560-1000; disney.com; Robert Iger; motion pictures (Lucasfilm, Touchstone, Pixar); TV (ABC, ESPN, National Geographic); media streaming (Disney+, Hulu); radio; publishing; theme parks and resorts. Acquired 21st Century Fox's entertainment assets for $71.3 bil, 3/20/2019.

Doctor's Associates Inc.: 325 Sub Way, Milford, CT 06461; (203) 877-4281; www.subway.com; John Chidsey; restaurants (Subway).

Dole plc (DOLE): 29 N. Anne St., Dublin 7, Dublin Ireland DP07; 353-1-887-2600; www.doleplc.com; Rory Byrne; food prods., fresh fruits, vegetables. Formed from merger of Dole Food Co. and Ireland's Total Produce plc, 7/30/2021.

Dollar Tree (DLTR): 500 Volvo Pkwy., Chesapeake, VA 23320; (757) 321-5000; www.dollartree.com; Rick Dreiling; discount retailer. Acquired Family Dollar, 7/6/2015.

Dominion Energy (D): 120 Tredegar St., Richmond, VA, 23219; (804) 771-6115; www.dominionenergy.com; Robert M. Blue; power/energy co.

DoorDash (DASH): 303 2nd St., South Tower, 8th Fl., San Francisco, CA 94107; (650) 487-3970; www.doordash.com; Tony Xu; app-based food delivery.

Dotdash Meredith: 225 Liberty St., 4th Fl., NY, NY, 10281; (202) 204-4000; www.dotdashmeredith.com; Neil Vogel; magazines (*Better Homes & Gardens, Food & Wine, People, Real Simple*), websites (The Balance, Investopedia, Simply Recipes, TreeHugger). Formed from acquisition by IAC-InterActiveCorp. co. Dotdash (fmr. About.com), 12/1/2021.

R. R. Donnelley & Sons Co.: 35 W. Wacker Dr., Chicago, IL 60601; (312) 326-8000; www.rrd.com; Thomas J. Quinlan III; commercial printing; marketing. Acquired by Chatham Asset Management, 2/25/2022.

Dow Inc. (DOW): 2111 H.H. Dow Way, Midland, MI 48674; (989) 636-1000; www.dow.com; Jim Fitterling; commodity chemical prod. Spun off 4/1/2019 from DowDuPont.

Dow Jones & Co., Inc.: see News Corp.

Dr Pepper Snapple Group, Inc.: see Keurig Dr Pepper

Duke Energy Corp. (DUK): 550 S. Tryon St., Charlotte, NC 28202; (704) 594-6200; www.duke-energy.com; Lynn J. Good; utilities, fiber optic networks.

Dun & Bradstreet Corp. (DNB): 5335 Gate Pkwy., Jacksonville, FL 32256; (904) 648-6350; www.dnb.com; Anthony Jabbour; business information, research.

DuPont de Nemours, Inc. (DD): 974 Centre Rd., Chestnut Run Plaza, Bldg. 702, Wilmington, DE 19805; (302) 774-1000; www.dupont.com; Edward Breen; specialty chemical mfr. Separated 6/3/2019 from DowDuPont. Divested majority of mobility and materials business to Celanese Corp. for $11 bil, 11/1/2022.

DXC Technology (DXC): 20408 Bashan Dr., Ste. 231, Ashburn, VA 20147; (470) 690-9512; www.dxc.technology; Mike Salvino; information tech. serv.

Eastman Kodak Co. (KODK): 343 State St., Rochester, NY 14650; (585) 724-4000; www.kodak.com; Jim Continenza; imaging technology and services.

Eaton Corp. (ETN): 1000 Eaton Blvd., Cleveland, OH 44122; (440) 523-5000; www.eaton.com; Craig Arnold; mfr. vehicle components, controls. Acquired rival Tripp Lite, 3/17/2021.

eBay Inc. (EBAY): 2025 Hamilton Ave., San Jose, CA 95125; (408) 376-7400; www.ebay.com; Jamie Iannone; e-commerce (StubHub). Spun off PayPal, 7/17/2015.

Edison Intl. (EIX): 2244 Walnut Grove Ave., Rosemead, CA 91770; (626) 302-2222; www.edison.com; Pedro Pizarro; electric utilities.

Electronic Arts Inc. (EA): 209 Redwood Shores Pkwy., Redwood City, CA 94065; (650) 628-1500; www.ea.com; Andrew Wilson; video game publisher (*Madden NFL, Battlefield, The Sims, UFC*).

Electronic Data Systems: see Hewlett Packard Enterprise

Elevance Health, Inc. (ELV): 220 Virginia Ave., Indianapolis, IN 46204; (317) 488-6000; www.elevancehealth.com; Gail K. Boudreaux; health insurance co. Formerly Anthem, Inc.; renamed 6/28/2022.

Eli Lilly and Co. (LLY): Lilly Corporate Center, Indianapolis, IN 46285; (317) 276-2000; www.lilly.com; David A. Ricks; pharmaceutical research, development, and manufacturing (Prozac, Strattera, Cialis).

EMC Corp.: see Dell Inc.

Emerson Electric Co. (EMR): 8000 W. Florissant Ave., St. Louis, MO 63136; (314) 553-2000; www.emerson.com; Lal Karsanbhai; electrical, electronics prods. and systems.

Energizer Holdings, Inc. (ENR): 533 Maryville Univ. Dr., St. Louis, MO 63141; (314) 985-2000; www.energizer.com; Mark S. LaVigne; batteries, flashlights, personal care prods.

Enterprise Products Partners L.P. (EPD): 1100 Louisiana St., 10th Fl., Houston, TX 77002; (713) 381-6500; www.enterpriseproducts.com; W. Randall Fowler; oil processing/transport and waterborne freight.

Estée Lauder Cos. Inc. (EL): 767 Fifth Ave., NY, NY 10153; (212) 572-4200; www.elcompanies.com; Fabrizio Freda; cosmetics (Clinique, Bobbi Brown), fragrance, skin care prods. (GLAMGLOW).

Exelon Corp. (EXC): 10 S. Dearborn St., 48th Fl., Chicago, IL 60680; (800) 483-3220; www.exeloncorp.com; Calvin Butler; electricity generation/distrib.; natural gas.

Express Scripts Holding Co.: see Cigna Group

ExxonMobil Corp. (XOM): 5959 Las Colinas Blvd., Irving, TX 75039; (972) 444-1000; www.exxonmobil.com; Darren W. Woods; integrated energy, oil co.

Facebook, Inc.: see Meta Platforms, Inc.

Federal Home Loan Mortgage Corp. (Freddie Mac): 8200 Jones Branch Dr., McLean, VA 22102; (703) 903-2000; www.freddiemac.com; Michael DeVito; residential mortgage provider. Under U.S. govt. mgmt. since 9/7/2008.

Federal Natl. Mortgage Assn. (Fannie Mae): Midtown Center, 1100 15th St. NW, Washington, DC 20005; (202) 752-7000; www.fanniemae.com; Priscilla Almodovar; provider of residential mortgage funds. Under U.S. govt. mgmt. since 9/7/2008.

FedEx Corp. (FDX): 942 S. Shady Grove Rd., Memphis, TN 38120; (901) 818-7500; www.fedex.com; Raj Subramaniam; delivery services.

First Data Corp.: see Fiserv, Inc.

FirstEnergy Corp. (FE): 76 S. Main St., Akron, OH 44308; (800) 736-3402; www.firstenergycorp.com; Brian X. Tierney; public electricity supplier.

Fiserv, Inc. (FISV): 255 Fiserv Dr., Brookfield, WI 53045; (800) 872-7882; www.fiserv.com; Frank Bisignano; financial serv. tech. (First Data; Clover).

Fluor Corp. (FLR): 6700 Las Colinas Blvd., Irving, TX 75039; (469) 398-7000; www.fluor.com; David E. Constable; international engineering and construction co.

Foot Locker, Inc. (FL): 330 W. 34th St., NY, NY 10001; (212) 720-3700; www.footlocker-inc.com; Mary N. Dillon; retail athletic stores (Footaction, Foot Locker, Champs Sports).

Ford Motor Co. (F): 1 American Rd., Dearborn, MI 48126; (313) 322-3000; www.ford.com; William C. Ford Jr.; auto mfr.; motor vehicle sales (Ford, Lincoln); auto financing (Ford Motor Credit).

Fox Corp. (FOXA): 1211 Ave. of the Americas, NY, NY 10036; (212) 852-7000; www.foxcorporation.com; Lachlan Murdoch; TV broadcasting (FOX, Fox News). Formed after 3/20/2019 acquisition of most of 21st Century Fox by Walt Disney Co.; see also Disney, News Corp.

Gannett Co., Inc. (GCI): 7950 Jones Branch Dr., McLean, VA 22107; (703) 854-6000; www.gannett.com; Mike Reed; newspaper publisher (*USA Today*).

Gap Inc. (GPS): 2 Folsom St., San Francisco, CA 94105; (650) 952-4400; www.gapinc.com; Bob. L. Martin; casual apparel retailer (Athleta, Banana Republic, Old Navy).

Garrett Motion (GTX): Z.A. La Pièce 16, 1180 Rolle, Switzerland; (862) 812-5013; www.garrettmotion.com; Olivier Rabiller; transport systems and tech.

General Dynamics Corp. (GD): 11011 Sunset Hills Rd., Reston, VA 20190; (703) 876-3000; www.gd.com; Phebe N. Novakovic; defense contractor: aerospace, combat systems, marine systems, computing devices.

General Electric Co. (GE): 5 Necco St., Boston, MA 02210; (617) 443-3000; www.ge.com; H. Lawrence Culp Jr.; electrical, electronic equip., financial services, radio and TV broadcasting, aircraft engines, power generation. Announced plans to split into three cos. specializing in aviation, health care, and energy, 11/9/2021.

General Mills, Inc. (GIS): One General Mills Blvd., Minneapolis, MN 55426; (763) 764-7600; www.generalmills.com; Jeff Harmening; food mfr. (Annie's Homegrown, Betty Crocker, Bisquick, Blue Buffalo, Cheerios, Chex, Häagen-Dazs, Pillsbury, Progresso, Total, Wheaties, Yoplait).

General Motors Co. (GM): 300 Renaissance Ctr., Detroit, MI 48265; (313) 556-5000; www.gm.com; Mary T. Barra; auto mfr. (Chevrolet, Cadillac, Buick, GMC); auto financing (GM Financial); vehicle security (OnStar). General Motors Corp. filed for Ch. 11 reorganization, 6/1/2009; sold profitable components to a new, smaller co. called General Motors Co., 7/10/2009. Sold European brands to France's Peugeot, 7/31/2018.

Genuine Parts (GPC): 2999 Wildwood Pkwy., Atlanta, GA 30339; (678) 934-5000; www.genpt.com; Paul D. Donahue; distrib. auto (NAPA), industrial replacement parts.

Gilead Sciences, Inc. (GILD): 333 Lakeside Dr., Foster City, CA 94404; (650) 574-3000; www.gilead.com; Daniel O'Day; biopharmaceuticals. Acquired Immunomedics for $21 bil, 10/23/2020.

Goldman Sachs Group, Inc. (GS): 200 West St., 29th Fl., NY, NY 10282; (212) 902-1000; www.goldmansachs.com; David Solomon; investment banking, asset mgmt., securities services.

Goodyear Tire & Rubber Co. (GT): 200 Innovation Way, Akron, OH 44316; (330) 796-2121; www.goodyear.com; Richard J. Kramer; tires and other auto prods.

Google, Inc.: see Alphabet Inc.

Graham Holding Co. (GHC): 1300 N. 17th St., 17th Fl., Arlington, VA 22209; (703) 345-6300; www.ghco.com; Timothy O'Shaughnessy; media (newspapers, Slate.com, TV), education (Kaplan), home health care. Fmr. Washington Post Co.; renamed after 2013 sale of newspaper to Nash Holdings LLC.

Halliburton Co. (HAL): 3000 N. Sam Houston Pkwy. E., Houston, TX 77032; (281) 871-4000; www.halliburton.com; Jeff Miller; oil field mgmt., energy services.

Hanesbrands Inc. (HBI): 1000 E. Hanes Mill Rd., Winston-Salem, NC 27105; (336) 519-8080; www.hanesbrands.com; Stephen B. Bratspies; apparel mfr. (Hanes, Barely There, Bali, Champion, Gear for Sports, Just My Size, L'eggs, Maidenform, Playtex, Wonderbra).

Harley-Davidson, Inc. (HOG): 3700 W. Juneau Ave., Milwaukee, WI 53208; (414) 342-4680; www.harley-davidson.com; Jochen Zeitz; mfr. motorcycles, parts, accessories.

Hartford Financial Services Group, Inc. (HIG): One Hartford Plz., Hartford, CT 06155; (860) 547-5000; www.thehartford.com; Christopher J. Swift; insurance, financial services.

Hasbro, Inc. (HAS): 1027 Newport Ave., Pawtucket, RI 02862; (401) 431-8697; www.hasbro.com; Chris Cocks; toy and game mfr. (Playskool, G.I. Joe, Nerf, Play-Doh).

HCA Healthcare, Inc. (HCA): 1 Park Plz., Nashville, TN 37203; (615) 344-9551; www.hcahealthcare.com; Samuel N. Hazen; owns and operates hospitals; other diagnostic, surgical, health treatment centers.

H. J. Heinz Co.: see Kraft Heinz Co.

Henkel Corp.: 200 Elm St., Stamford, CT 06902; (475) 210-0230; www.henkelna.com; Steven Essick; consumer prods. (Dial soap, Purex detergent, Right Guard antiperspirant, Renuzit air fresheners); U.S. subsidiary of Germany's Henkel co.

Hershey Co., The (HSY): 100 Crystal A Dr., Hershey, PA 17033; (717) 534-4200; www.thehersheycompany.com; Michele Buck; chocolate prods. mfr. (Almond Joy, Brookside, Jolly Rancher, Kit Kat, Milk Duds, Reese's, Twizzlers, York).

Hertz Global Holdings, Inc. (HTZ): 8501 Williams Rd., Estero, FL 33928; (201) 307-2000; www.hertz.com; Stephen M. Scherr; car rentals. Filed for Ch. 11 bankruptcy, 5/22/2020; emerged from bankruptcy, 6/30/2021.

Hess Corp. (HES): 1185 Ave. of the Americas, 40th Fl., NY, NY 10036; (212) 997-8500; www.hess.com; John B. Hess; integrated oil and gas co.

Hewlett Packard Enterprise (HPE): 6280 America Center Dr., San Jose, CA 95002; (650) 687-5817; www.hpe.com; Antonio Neri; computer prods. (software, servers, storage), consulting, support. Spun off from Hewlett-Packard Co., now HP Inc., 11/2/2015.

Hillshire Brands Co.: see Tyson Foods, Inc.

Hilton Worldwide (HLT): 7930 Jones Branch Dr., Ste. 1100, McLean, VA 22102; (703) 883-1000; www.hiltonworldwide.com; Christopher J. Nassetta; hotels and resorts (Doubletree, Embassy, Hampton). Sold landmark Waldorf Astoria, 2/2015.

Home Depot, Inc. (HD): 2455 Paces Ferry Rd. NW, Atlanta, GA 30339; (770) 433-8211; www.homedepot.com; Ted Decker; home improvement stores.

Honeywell Intl. (HON): 855 S. Mint St., Charlotte, NC 28202; (877) 841-2840; www.honeywell.com; Vimal Kapur; aerospace systems; performance/building tech.

Hormel Foods Corp. (HRL): 1 Hormel Pl., Austin, MN 55912; (507) 437-5611; www.hormelfoods.com; Jim Snee; food processor, primarily meat (SPAM, Dinty Moore, Jennie-O, Skippy, Applegate Farms).

Hostess Brands (TWNK): 7905 Quivira Rd., Lenexa, KS 66215; (816) 701-4600; www.hostessbrands.com; Andrew P. Callahan; baked goods wholesaler, distrib.

Houghton Mifflin Harcourt Co.: 125 High St., Boston, MA 02110; (617) 351-5000; www.hmhco.com; John J. Lynch Jr.; publisher of textbooks and other educational prods. (Holt McDougal, Clarion), trade and reference books. Acquired by Veritas Capital, 4/7/2022.

HP Inc. (HPQ): 1501 Page Mill Rd., Palo Alto, CA 94305; (650) 857-1501; www8.hp.com; Enrique Lores; computers, electronic prods. and systems.

H&R Block, Inc. (HRB): 1301 Main St., Kansas City, MO 64105; (816) 854-3000; www.hrblock.com; Jeffrey J. Jones II; tax return preparation; business and consulting services.

Humana Inc. (HUM): 500 W. Main St., Louisville, KY 40202; (502) 580-1000; www.humana.com; Bruce D. Broussard; managed health care service provider, related specialty prods. Acquired One Homecare Solutions, 2021.

IAC/InterActiveCorp (IAC): 555 W. 18th St., NY, NY 10011; (212) 314-7300; www.iac.com; Barry Diller; internet conglomerate (Ask.com, Citysearch, The Daily Beast, HomeAdvisor). Spun off Match Group (Match.com, Tinder), 7/1/2020, digital video platform Vimeo, 5/25/2021.

iHeartMedia, Inc. (IHRT) (fmr. Clear Channel Communications): 200 E. Basse Rd., Ste. 100, San Antonio, TX 78209; (210) 822-2828; www.iheartmedia.com; Robert Pittman; radio stations.

Illinois Tool Works Inc. (ITW): 155 Harlem Ave., Glenview, IL 60025; (224) 661-8870; www.itw.com; E. Scott Santi; consumer, industrial tools; food equip. (Hobart), packaging (Zip-Pak).

Ingersoll-Rand Inc. (IR): 800-E, Beaty St., Davidson, NC 28036; (704) 655-4000; ingersollrand.com; Vicente Reynal; mfr. of pumps, compressors, and other tools (ARO, Gardner Denver, CompAir, Nash, Elmo Rietschle, SEEPEX). Formed from merger of Gardner Denver Holdings Inc. and a division of Ingersoll-Rand plc (now Trane Technologies), 3/1/2020.

Intel Corp. (INTC): 2200 Mission College Blvd., Santa Clara, CA 95054; (408) 765-8080; www.intel.com; Pat Gelsinger; mfr. semiconductors, microprocessors (Core, Centrino).

International Business Machines Corp. (IBM): One New Orchard Rd., Armonk, NY 10504; (914) 499-1900; www.ibm.com; Arvind Krishna; advanced information processing technology equip., services.

International Paper Co. (IP): 6400 Poplar Ave., Memphis, TN 38197; (901) 419-9000; www.internationalpaper.com; Mark Sutton; paper/forest prods.

J.C. Penney Co., Inc.: 6501 Legacy Dr., Plano, TX 75024; (972) 431-1000; www.jcpenney.com; Marc Rosen; dept. store retailer, general merchandise catalog sales. Filed for Ch. 11 bankruptcy amid the coronavirus pandemic, 5/15/2020; delisted from NYSE, 5/28/2020; emerged from bankruptcy, 12/7/2020.

J.Crew Group, Inc.: 225 Liberty St., NY, NY 10281; (212) 209-2500; www.jcrew.com; Libby Wadle; retail and mail order apparel and accessories. Filed for Ch. 11 bankruptcy amid the coronavirus pandemic, 5/4/2020; emerged from bankruptcy, 9/10/2020.

JetBlue Airways Corp. (JBLU): 27-01 Queens Plz. N., Long Island City, NY 11101; (718) 286-7900; www.jetblue.com; Robin Hayes; air transportation.

Jo-Ann Stores, LLC (JOAN): 5555 Darrow Rd., Hudson, OH 44236; (330) 656-2600; www.joann.com; Chris DiTullio and Scott Sekella (interim); specialty fabric and craft stores. IPO, 3/12/2021.

Johnson Controls Intl. (JCI): 5757 N. Green Bay Ave., Milwaukee, WI 53209; (414) 524-1200; www.johnsoncontrols.com; George R. Oliver; equip. and controls for heating, ventilating, AC, refrigeration, and building security; auto interiors, batteries.

Johnson & Johnson (JNJ): 1 Johnson & Johnson Plz., New Brunswick, NJ 08933; (732) 524-0400; www.jnj.com; Joaquin Duato; health care prods. (Band-Aid, Neosporin), pharmaceuticals (Tylenol, Motrin, Sudafed), toiletries (Neutrogena, Aveeno, Vogue Intl.). Announced plans to split into two cos. separating consumer products from pharmaceutical/medical devices, 11/12/2021.

S. C. Johnson & Son, Inc.: 1525 Howe St., Racine, WI 53403; (262) 260-2000; www.scjohnson.com; H. Fisk Johnson; cleaning and other household prods. (Windex, Pledge, Fantastik, Raid, OFF!, Shout, Glade, Scrubbing Bubbles, Ziploc).

JPMorgan Chase & Co. (JPM): 383 Madison Ave., NY, NY 10017; (212) 270-6000; www.jpmorganchase.com; James Dimon; financial services.

Kate Spade & Co.: see Tapestry, Inc.

KBR, Inc. (KBR): 601 Jefferson St., Ste. 3400, Houston, TX 77002; (713) 753-2000; www.kbr.com; Stuart Bradie; engineering; construction mgmt. services.

Kellogg Co. (K): One Kellogg Sq., P.O. Box 3599, Battle Creek, MI 49016; (269) 961-2000; www.kelloggcompany.com; Steven A. Cahillane; mfr. of ready-to-eat cereals, other food prods. (Frosted Flakes, Rice Krispies, Pop-Tarts, Nutri-Grain, Keebler, Eggo, Pringles, Gardenburger). Announced plans to split company with global snack business to be named Kellanova and North American cereal business to be named WK Kellogg Co., 3/15/2023.

Kelly Services, Inc. (KELYA): 999 W. Big Beaver Rd., Troy, MI 48084; (248) 362-4444; www.kellyservices.com; Peter Quigley; temporary staffing services.

Keurig Dr Pepper (KDP): 53 South Ave., Burlington, MA 01803; (877) 208-9991; www.keurigdrpepper.com; Robert Gamgort; coffee, tea, and nonalcoholic beverages (Green Mountain Coffee, Caribou Coffee, Straight Up Tea, Dr Pepper, 7UP, Snapple, Mott's).

Kimberly-Clark Corp. (KMB): 351 Phelps Dr., Irving, TX 75038; (972) 281-1200; www.kimberly-clark.com; Michael D. Hsu; personal care prods. (Kleenex, Scott, Cottonelle, Huggies, Kotex).

Kinder Morgan, Inc. (KMI): 1001 Louisiana St., Ste. 1000, Houston, TX 77002; (713) 369-9000; www.kindermorgan.com; Richard D. Kinder; energy trans. and storage.

Kmart Corp.: see Transformco

Koch Industries, Inc.: P.O. Box 2256, Wichita, KS 67201; (316) 828-5500; www.kochind.com; Charles G. Koch; forest prod. mfr.; oil refineries/pipeline; chemicals; pollution-control equip.; ranching.

Kraft Heinz Co. (KHC): 1 PPG Pl., Ste. 3200, Pittsburgh, PA 15222; (412) 456-5700; www.kraftheinzcompany.com; Miguel Patricio; food and beverage mfr. (Ore-Ida, 57 Varieties ketchup, Velveeta, Crystal Light, Maxwell House, Kool-Aid, Lunchables, Jell-O, Oscar Mayer). Formed from merger of Kraft Foods Group with H.J. Heinz Co., 7/2/2015.

Kroger Co. (KR): 1014 Vine St., Cincinnati, OH 45202; (513) 762-4000; www.thekrogerco.com; W. Rodney McMullen; grocery, convenience, and mall jewelry stores. Announced plans to acquire Albertsons for $24.6 bil, 10/14/2022.

L Brands, Inc.: see Bath & Body Works, Inc.; Victoria's Secret & Co.

Las Vegas Sands Corp. (LVS): 3355 Las Vegas Blvd. S., Las Vegas, NV 89109; (702) 414-1000; www.sands.com; Robert Goldstein; casino-resort operator (Venetian, Palazzo, Sands Macao).

La-Z-Boy Inc. (LZB): One La-Z-Boy Dr., Monroe, MI 48162; (855) 802-6636; www.la-z-boy.com; Melinda D. Whittington; reclining chairs, other furniture.

Levi Strauss & Co. (LEVI): 1155 Battery St., San Francisco, CA 94111; (415) 501-6000; www.levistrauss.com; Charles Bergh; blue jeans, casual sportswear (Dockers).

Liberty Mutual Holding Co. Inc.: 175 Berkeley St., Boston, MA 02116; (617) 357-9500; www.libertymutual.com; Timothy Sweeney; insurance prods. and services.

LinkedIn Corp.: see Microsoft Corp.

Liz Claiborne, Inc.: see J.C. Penney Co., Inc.

L.L.Bean, Inc.: 15 Casco St., Freeport, ME 04033; (207) 552-2000; www.llbean.com; Stephen Smith; catalog and retail outdoor apparel, footwear, gear.

Lockheed Martin Corp. (LMT): 6801 Rockledge Dr., Bethesda, MD 20817; (301) 897-6000; www.lockheedmartin.com; Jim Taiclet; leading U.S. defense contractor; aircraft, electronics, missiles, information tech., and communications. Bought Sikorsky Aircraft from United Technologies, 11/6/2015.

Loews Corp. (L): 667 Madison Ave., NY, NY 10065; (212) 521-2000; www.loews.com; James S. Tisch; hotels, insurance (CNA Financial), offshore drilling (Diamond).

Lorillard, Inc.: see Reynolds American Inc.

Lowe's Cos., Inc. (LOW): 1000 Lowe's Blvd., Mooresville, NC 28117; (704) 758-1000; www.lowes.com; Marvin R. Ellison; building material and home improvement superstores.

Lumen Technologies (LUMN) (fmr. CenturyLink): 100 CenturyLink Dr., Monroe, LA 71203; (318) 388-9000; www.lumen.com; Kate Johnson; telecommunications.

Macy's, Inc. (M): 151 W. 34th St., NY, NY 10001; (513) 579-7000; www.macysinc.com; Jeff Gennette; retailer (Macy's, Bloomingdale's, Bluemercury). Announced closure of approx. 125 stores over next 3 years, 2/5/2020.

ManpowerGroup (MAN): 100 Manpower Pl., Milwaukee, WI 53212; (414) 961-1000; www.manpowergroup.com; Jonas Prising; employment services.

Marathon Oil Corp. (MRO): 990 Town and Country Blvd., Houston, TX 77024; (713) 629-6600; www.marathonoil.com; Lee M. Tillman; integrated oil co.

Marriott International, Inc. (MAR): 7750 Wisconsin Ave., Bethesda, MD 20814; (301) 380-3000; www.marriott.com; Anthony Capuano; hotels (Renaissance, Courtyard, Fairfield Inn, Ritz-Carlton).

Mars, Inc.: 6885 Elm St., McLean, VA 22101; (703) 821-4900; www.mars.com; Poul Weihrauch; food mfr., including of chocolate (M&M's, Snickers, Dove), food (Uncle Ben's), pet food (Pedigree, Whiskas, Iams, Eukanuba, Sheba) and services.

Massachusetts Mutual Life Insurance Co. (MassMutual Financial Group): 1295 State St., Springfield, MA 01111; (413) 744-1000; www.massmutual.com; Roger W. Crandall; financial planning and investment, life insurance.

MasterCard Inc. (MA): 2000 Purchase St., Purchase, NY 10577; (914) 249-2000; www.mastercard.com; Michael Miebach; financial services.

Mattel, Inc. (MAT): 333 Continental Blvd., El Segundo, CA 90245; (310) 252-2000; www.mattel.com; Ynon Kreiz; toymaker (Barbie, Fisher-Price, Hot Wheels, Matchbox, American Girls).

McClatchy Co.: 1601 Alhambra Blvd., Ste. 100, Sacramento, CA 95816; (916) 321-1855; www.mcclatchy.com; Tony Hunter; newspaper publisher. Filed for Ch. 11 bankruptcy, 2/13/2020; acquired by hedge fund Chatham Asset Management, 9/4/2020.

McDonald's Corp. (MCD): 110 N. Carpenter St., Ste. 300, Chicago, IL 60607; (844) 534-7211; www.mcdonalds.com; Chris Kempczinski; fast food.

McGraw-Hill Financial: see S&P Global, Inc.

McKesson Corp. (MCK): 6535 N. State Hwy. 161, Irving, TX 75039; (972) 446-4800; www.mckesson.com; Brian Tyler; distrib. of drugs and toiletries; provides mgmt. software and services.

Merck & Co., Inc. (MRK): 126 E. Lincoln Ave., P.O. Box 2000, Rahway, NJ 07065; (908) 740-4000; www.merck.com; Robert M. Davis; pharmaceuticals (Gardasil, Keytruda, Propecia, Singulair, Vytorin, Zocor).

Meredith Corp.: see Dotdash Meredith

Merrill Lynch & Co., Inc.: see Bank of America Corp.

Meta Platforms, Inc. (META): 1 Hacker Way, Menlo Park, CA 94025; (650) 308-7300; www.facebook.com; Mark Zuckerberg; social networking/messaging platforms, services (Facebook, WhatsApp, Instagram, Threads). Rebranded Facebook as Meta, 10/28/2021. Laid off 21,000 employees, 11/2022 to 5/2023.

MetLife, Inc. (MET): 200 Park Ave., NY, NY 10166; (212) 578-2211; www.metlife.com; Michel A. Khalaf; insurance, financial services.

MGM Resorts Intl. (MGM): 3600 S. Las Vegas Blvd., Las Vegas, NV 89109; (702) 693-7120; www.mgmresorts.com; Bill Hornbuckle; hotel-casino operator (Mirage, New York-New York, Luxor, Bellagio, Circus Circus, Monte Carlo).

Microsoft Corp. (MSFT): One Microsoft Way, Redmond, WA 98052; (425) 882-8080; www.microsoft.com; Satya Nadella; software (Windows, Word, Excel); video games (Minecraft, Xbox); networking site LinkedIn; code repository GitHub. Acquired video game co. ZeniMax Media (Doom, Fallout), 3/9/2021. Announced plans to acquire game maker Activision Blizzard for $68.7 bil, 1/18/2022. Laid off 10,000 employees, 1/18/2023.

Molson Coors Beverage Co. (TAP): 250 S. Wacker Dr., Ste. 800, Chicago, IL 60606; (303) 927-2337; www.molsoncoors.com; Gavin Hattersley; brewer. Acquired SABMiller's global Miller brands and majority stake in joint venture, MillerCoors, following Anheuser-Busch InBev's buyout of SABMiller, 10/11/2016.

Mondelēz International, Inc. (MDLZ): 100 Deforest Ave., East Hanover, NJ 07936; (855) 535-5648; www.mondelezinternational.com; Dirk Van de Put; global food mfr., including Nabisco (Oreo), Cadbury, Tang, Trident. Agreed to acquire Clif Bar, 6/20/2022. Agreed to sell its gum business, 12/19/2022.

Monsanto Co.: see Bayer AG

Morgan Stanley (MS): 1585 Broadway, NY, NY 10036; (212) 761-4000; www.morganstanley.com; James P. Gorman; diversified financial services. Acquired online trading firm E-Trade for approx. $13 bil, 10/2/2020; investment firm Eaton Vance, 3/1/2021.

Motorola Solutions, Inc. (MSI): 500 W. Monroe St., Ste. 4400, Chicago, IL 60661; (847) 576-5000; www.motorolasolutions.com; Gregory Q. Brown; electronic equip. and components; communication devices.

Nationwide Mutual Insurance Co.: One Nationwide Plz., Columbus, OH 43215; (614) 249-7111; www.nationwide.com; Kirt Walker; property/casualty, life insurance; financial services.

Navistar Intl. Corp.: 2701 Navistar Dr., Lisle, IL 60532; (331) 332-5000; www.navistar.com; Mathias Carlbaum; mfr. heavy-duty trucks, parts, school buses. Acquired by VW's truck unit, TRATON Group, 7/1/2021.

NBCUniversal: 30 Rockefeller Plz., NY, NY 10112; (212) 664-4444; www.nbcuni.com; Michael Cavanagh (interim); news/entertainment producer; TV and CATV (NBC, Bravo, USA, Telemundo); film production. Owned by Comcast and General Electric.

NCR Corp. (NCR): 864 Spring St. NW, Atlanta, GA 30308; (937) 445-1936; www.ncr.com; Michael Hayford; mfr. ATMs, retail technology, hardware and software; computer services and supplies.

Nestlé USA, Inc.: 800 N. Brand Blvd., Glendale, CA 91203; (818) 549-6000; www.nestleusa.com; Steve Presley; beverages (Nestea, Ovaltine), food (Buitoni, Coffee-Mate), frozen foods (Stouffer's, Häagen-Dazs, Lean Cuisine), pet foods (Purina, Alpo, Friskies). Subsidiary of Nestlé SA in Switzerland.

Netflix, Inc. (NFLX): 100 Winchester Cir., Los Gatos, CA 95032; (408) 540-3700; www.netflix.com; Ted Sarandos and Greg Peters; streaming video.

New York Life Insurance Co.: 51 Madison Ave., NY, NY 10010; (212) 576-7000; www.newyorklife.com; Craig DeSanto; life insurance, annuities, mutual funds.

New York Times Co. (NYT): 620 8th Ave., NY, NY 10018; (212) 556-1234; www.nytco.com; A. G. Sulzberger; newspapers.

Newell Brands (NWL): 6655 Peachtree Dunwoody Rd., Atlanta, GA 30328; (770) 418-7000; www.newellbrands.com; Chris Peterson; housewares (Rubbermaid, Calphalon); writing utensils (Parker, Sharpie, Paper Mate); juvenile prods. (Graco). Sold First Alert to Resideo Technologies, Inc., 4/1/2022.

News Corp. (NWS): 1211 Ave. of the Americas, NY, NY 10036; (212) 416-3400; www.newscorp.com; K. Rupert Murdoch; publisher (HarperCollins; *Wall Street Journal*, *Barron's*); digital media (MarketWatch).

Nexstar Media Group, Inc. (NXST): 545 E. John Carpenter Freeway, Irving, TX 75062; (972) 373-8800; www.nexstar.tv; Perry A. Sook; local TV stations. Acquired Tribune Studios (incl. WGN and 41 other TV stations) in a $7.2 bil deal, 9/19/2019.

NextEra Energy, Inc. (NEE): 700 Universe Blvd., Juno Beach, FL 33408; (561) 694-4000; www.nexteraenergy.com; John W. Ketchum; electricity generation/distrib.

NIKE, Inc. (NKE): 1 Bowerman Dr., Beaverton, OR 97005; (503) 671-6453; www.nike.com; John Donahoe; athletic footwear and apparel mfr.

Nokia (NOK): Karakaari 7, Espoo 02610, Finland; +358 (0) 10 44 88 000; www.nokia.com; Pekka Lundmark; telecom. equip., computer software.

Nordstrom, Inc. (JWN): 1700 7th Ave., Ste. 1500, Seattle, WA 98101; (206) 628-2111; www.nordstrom.com; Erik B. Nordstrom; upscale dept. store chain.

Norfolk Southern Corp. (NSC): 650 W. Peachtree St. NW, Atlanta, GA 30308; (404) 420-4444; www.nscorp.com; Alan H. Shaw; railway operator; freight carrier.

Northrop Grumman Corp. (NOC): 2980 Fairview Park Dr., Falls Church, VA 22042; (703) 280-2900; www.northropgrumman.com; Kathy J. Warden; defense contractor: aircraft, electronics, data systems, information systems, missiles.

Northwest Airlines Corp.: see Delta Air Lines, Inc.

Northwestern Mutual Life Insurance Co.: 720 E. Wisconsin Ave., Milwaukee, WI 53202; (414) 271-1444; www.northwesternmutual.com; John E. Schlifske; life insurance, investment prods. and services, annuities.

Occidental Petroleum Corp. (OXY): Five Greenway Plz., Ste. 110, Houston, TX 77046; (713) 215-7000; www.oxy.com; Vicki A. Hollub; oil, natural gas, chemicals, plastics.

Office Depot, Inc. (ODP): 6600 N. Military Trl., Boca Raton, FL 33496; (561) 438-4800; www.officedepot.com; Gerry P. Smith; office supplier.

Omnicom Group Inc. (OMC): 280 Park Ave., NY, NY, 10017; (212) 415-3672; www.omnicomgroup.com; John D. Wren; advertising, marketing, interactive/digital media.

Oracle Corp. (ORCL): 2300 Oracle Way, Austin, TX 78741; (737) 867-1000; www.oracle.com; Lawrence J. Ellison; database and file mgmt. software. Acquired electronic health record co. Cerner for $28 bil, 6/8/2022.

Paramount Global (PARA): 1515 Broadway, NY, NY 10036; (212) 258-6000; www.paramount.com; Robert M. Bakish; TV networks (CBS), and CATV (BET, Comedy Central, MTV, VH1, Nickelodeon); movies (Paramount); radio stations. Subsidiary of National Amusements. Formerly ViacomCBS Inc.; renamed 2/16/2022.

Payless Inc. (fmr. Payless ShoeSource): 3050 Biscayne Blvd., Miami, FL 33137; (785) 233-5171; www.payless.com; Jared Margolis; shoe mfr./retailer. Emerged from bankruptcy, 1/16/2020.

PepsiCo, Inc. (PEP): 700 Anderson Hill Rd., Purchase, NY 10577; (914) 253-2000; www.pepsico.com; Ramon Laguarta; soft drinks and other beverages (Pepsi-Cola, Mountain Dew, Muscle Milk, Gatorade, Tropicana), snacks and cereals (Fritos, Lay's, Ruffles, Quaker).

Pfizer, Inc. (PFE): 66 Hudson Blvd. E, NY, NY 10001; (212) 733-2323; www.pfizer.com; Albert Bourla; biopharmaceuticals (Celebrex, Hospira, Lipitor, Viagra, Zoloft); human and animal health care prods. With German co. BioNTech, received first emergency use authorization for a COVID-19 vaccine in the U.S., 12/11/2020. Acquired migraine drug maker Biohaven Pharmaceutical Holding for $11.6 bil, 10/3/2022. Agreed to acquire cancer drug maker Seagen for $43 bil, 3/13/2023.

PG&E Corp. (PCG): 300 Lakeside Drive, Oakland, CA 94612; (415) 973-1000; www.pgecorp.com; Patricia K. Poppe; operates Pacific Gas and Electric public utility. Emerged from bankruptcy, 7/1/2020. Pleaded guilty to manslaughter for causing 2018 Camp Fire, 6/16/2020.

Philip Morris Intl. Inc. (PM): 677 Washington Blvd., Ste. 1100, Stamford, CT 06901; (917) 663-2233; www.pmi.com; Jacek Olczak; intl. mfr. and distrib. of tobacco. (Altria spun off intl. Philip Morris operations in 2008 but owns Philip Morris brands in U.S.)

Phillips 66 Co. (PSX): P.O. Box 421959, Houston, TX 77242; (281) 293-6600; www.phillips66.com; Mark Lashier; oil, gas refining and marketing.

Pitney Bowes Inc. (PBI): 3001 Summer St., Stamford, CT 06926; (203) 356-5000; www.pb.com; Marc B. Lautenbach; postage meters and mailing equip.

Post Holdings, Inc. (POST): 2503 S. Hanley Rd., St. Louis, MO 63144; (314) 644-7600; www.postfoods.com; Robert V. Vitale; ready-to-eat cereals.

PPG Industries, Inc. (PPG): 1 PPG Pl., Pittsburgh, PA 15272; (412) 434-3131; www.ppg.com; Tim Knavish; glass prods., silicas, fiberglass, chemicals, sealants.

Priceline Group Inc.: see Booking Holdings Inc.

Procter & Gamble Co. (PG): 1 Procter & Gamble Plz., Cincinnati, OH 45202; (513) 983-1100; www.pg.com; Jon R. Moeller; soaps and detergents (Ivory, Cheer, Tide, Mr. Clean); toiletries (Crest, Scope, Head & Shoulders, Old Spice); pharmaceuticals (Pepto-Bismol, Vicks cough medicines); paper prods. (Charmin toilet tissues, Bounty towels), Tampax tampons; disposable diapers (Pampers, Luvs); Gillette razors.

Prudential Financial, Inc. (PRU): 751 Broad St., Newark, NJ 07102; (973) 802-6000; www.prudential.com; Charles F. Lowrey; insurance, financial services.

Publix Super Markets Inc.: 3300 Publix Corporate Pkwy., Lakeland, FL 33811; (863) 688-1188; www.publix.com; Todd Jones; supermarket chain.

PVH Corp. (PVH): 200 Madison Ave., NY, NY 10016; (212) 381-3500; www.pvh.com; Stefan Larsson; apparel mfr., including licensed brands (Calvin Klein, Tommy Hilfiger). Sold Heritage Brands incl. IZOD, Van Heusen, Arrow, and Geoffrey Beene to Authentic Brands Group, 8/2/2021.

Qualcomm Inc. (QCOM): 5775 Morehouse Dr., San Diego, CA 92121; (858) 587-1121; www.qualcomm.com; Cristiano R. Amon; semiconductor, telecommunications equip. design. Merger with Singapore-based Broadcom blocked by White House over natl. security, 3/12/2018.

Quest Diagnostics (DGX): 500 Plaza Dr., Secaucus, NJ 07094; (973) 520-2700; www.questdiagnostics.com; James E. Davis; leading clinical laboratory.

Ralcorp Holdings, Inc.: see Conagra Brands, Inc.

Ralph Lauren Corp. (RL): 650 Madison Ave., NY, NY 10022; (212) 318-7000; www.ralphlauren.com; Patrice Louvet; men's and women's apparel, home furnishings, fragrances.

Reader's Digest Assn., Inc.: see Trusted Media Brands, Inc.

Republic Services, Inc. (RSG): 18500 N. Allied Way, Phoenix, AZ 85054; (480) 627-2700; www.republicservices.com; Jon Vander Ark; waste mgmt. co.

Resideo Technologies, Inc. (REZI): 16100 N. 71st St., Ste. 550, Scottsdale, AZ 85254; www.resideo.com; Jay Geldmacher; home control systems.

Acquired First Alert from Newell Brands, 4/1/2022.

Restaurant Brands Intl. (QSR): 226 Wyecroft Rd., Oakville, ON L6K 3X7, Canada; (905) 845-6511; www.rbi.com; Joshua Kobza; fast food restaurants (Burger King, Popeyes, Tim Hortons).

Revlon, Inc. (REV): 55 Water St., NY, NY 10041; (212) 527-4000; www.revlon.com; Debra G. Perelman; cosmetics, skin care. Emerged from bankruptcy, 5/2/2023.

Reynolds American Inc.: 401 N. Main St., Winston-Salem, NC 27101; (336) 741-2000; www.reynoldsamerican.com; David Waterfield; cigarettes (Camel, Pall Mall, Doral, Newport), smokeless tobacco (Grizzly, Kodiak), e-cigarettes (VUSE). Subsidiary of British American Tobacco, world's largest tobacco co.

Rite Aid Corp. (RAD): 1200 Intrepid Ave., 2nd Fl., Philadelphia, PA 19112; (717) 761-2633; www.riteaid.com; Elizabeth Burr (interim); retail drugstores.

Rockwell Automation, Inc. (ROK): 1201 S. 2nd St., Milwaukee, WI 53204; (414) 382-2000; www.rockwellautomation.com; Blake Moret; industrial automation co.

RTX Corp. (RTX): 1000 Wilson Blvd., Arlington, VA 22209; (781) 522-3000; www.rtx.com; Gregory J. Hayes; aerospace, defense, communications systems. Formed through merger of Raytheon Corp. with United Technologies Corp.; spun off Carrier and Otis, 4/3/2020.

Ryder System, Inc. (R): 11690 NW 105th St., Miami, FL 33178; (305) 500-3726; www.ryder.com; Robert E. Sanchez; truck-leasing service.

SABMiller plc: see Anheuser-Busch InBev

Safeway Inc.: see Albertsons Companies, Inc.

S&P Global, Inc. (SPGI): 55 Water St., NY, NY 10041; (212) 438-1000; www.spglobal.com; Douglas L. Peterson; financial information, services (Standard & Poor's). Formerly McGraw-Hill Financial; renamed 4/27/2016. Acquired UK-based rival IHS Market for $44 bil, 2/28/2022.

Schering-Plough Corp.: see Merck & Co., Inc.

Schlumberger Limited Co. (SLB): 5599 San Felipe St., 17th Fl., Houston, TX 77056; (713) 375-3400; www.slb.com; Olivier Le Peuch; oil equip. and services.

Sears Holdings Corp.: see Transformco

Shell USA, Inc.: 1000 Main St., Ste. 1700, Houston, TX 77002; (713) 767-5300; www.shell.us; Gretchen Watkins; integrated oil co.; subsidiary of Royal Dutch Shell.

Sherwin-Williams Co. (SHW): 101 W. Prospect Ave., Cleveland, OH 44115; (216) 566-2000; www.sherwin-williams.com; John G. Morikis; paint and varnish producer (Dutch Boy, Krylon, Minwax, Valspar).

Simon Property Group, Inc. (SPG): 225 W. Washington St., Indianapolis, IN 46204; (317) 636-1600; www.simon.com; David E. Simon; global real estate.

Sinclair Broadcast Group, Inc. (SBGI): 10706 Beaver Dam Rd., Hunt Valley, MD 21030; (410) 568-1500; www.sbgi.net; Christopher S. Ripley; TV broadcasting (185 stations); local news producer.

Sirius XM Holdings Inc. (SIRI): 1221 Ave. of the Americas, 35th Fl., NY, NY 10020; (212) 584-5100; www.siriusxm.com; Jennifer Witz; satellite radio.

Smithfield Foods, Inc.: 200 Commerce St., Smithfield, VA 23430; (757) 365-3000; www.smithfieldfoods.com; Shane Smith; pork producer and processor. Subsidiary of China-based WH Group since 9/26/2013.

J. M. Smucker Co. (SJM): One Strawberry Ln., Orrville, OH 44667; (330) 682-3000; www.smuckers.com; Mark T. Smucker; leading producer of fruit spreads, peanut butter (Jif), oils (Crisco), coffee (Folgers), baking prods. (Pillsbury), pet foods (Milk-Bone, Kibbles 'n Bits).

Snap Inc. (SNAP): 2772 Donald Douglas Loop N., Santa Monica, CA 90405; (310) 399-3339; www.snap.com; Evan Spiegel; social media and tech co. (Bitmoji, Snapchat, Spectacles).

Sony Corp. of America: 25 Madison Ave., NY, NY 10016; (212) 833-6800; www.sony.com; Kenichiro Yoshida; U.S. subsidiary of Japan-based Sony Corp.; electronics, movies, music.

Southwest Airlines Co. (LUV): 2702 Love Field Dr., Dallas, TX 75235; (214) 792-4000; www.southwest.com; Robert E. Jordan; air transportation.

Sprint Corp.: see T-Mobile US, Inc.

Stanley Black & Decker, Inc. (SWK): 1000 Stanley Dr., New Britain, CT 06053; (860) 225-5111; www.stanleyblackanddecker.com; Donald Allan Jr.; hand and power tools (DeWalt, Bostitch, Irwin, Lenox), fastening prods. (Gripco, Masterfix).

Staples, Inc.: 500 Staples Dr., Framingham, MA 01702; (508) 253-5000; www.staples.com; John A. Lederer; office-supply retailer.

Starbucks Corp. (SBUX): 2401 Utah Ave. S., Seattle, WA 98134; (206) 447-1575; www.starbucks.com; Laxman Narasimhan; coffee producer; world's leading specialty coffee retailer.

Starwood Hotels & Resorts Worldwide, Inc.: see Marriott International, Inc.

State Farm Mutual Automobile Ins. Co.: 1 State Farm Plz., Bloomington, IL 61710; (309) 766-2311; www.statefarm.com; Michael L. Tipsord; auto/homeowners insurance.

StoneX Group Inc. (SNEX) (fmr. INTL FCStone Inc.): 230 Park Ave., 10th Fl., NY, NY 10169; (212) 485-3500; www.stonex.com; Sean O'Connor; securities and commodities advising. Acquired online foreign exchange provider GAIN Capital Holdings, Inc., 7/31/2020.

Sun Microsystems, Inc.: see Oracle Corp.

SuperValu Inc.: see United Natural Foods, Inc.

Sysco Corp. (SYY): 1390 Enclave Pkwy., Houston, TX 77077; (281) 584-1390; www.sysco.com; Kevin Hourican; food-service distrib.

Tapestry, Inc. (TPR) (fmr. Coach Inc.): 10 Hudson Yards, NY, NY 10001; (212) 946-8400; www.tapestry.com; Joanne Crevoiserat; luxury fashion brands (Coach, Kate Spade, Stuart Weitzman).

Target Corp. (TGT): 1000 Nicollet Mall, Minneapolis, MN 55403; (612) 304-6073; www.target.com; Brian Cornell; discount retailer.

TEGNA, Inc. (TGNA): 8350 Broad St., Ste. 2000, Tysons, VA 22102; (703) 873-6600; www.tegna.com; Dave Lougee; network and cable TV, digital marketing, websites.

Tenneco Inc. (TEN): 500 N. Field Dr., Lake Forest, IL 60045; (847) 482-5000; www.tenneco.com; Jim Voss; automotive parts (Monroe, Walker). Acquired by Apollo Global Management, 11/17/2022.

Tesla Motors, Inc. (TSLA): 1 Tesla Rd., Austin, TX 78725; (650) 681-5000; www.teslamotors.com; Elon Musk; electric vehicles and batteries.

Texas Instruments Inc. (TXN): 12500 TI Blvd., Dallas, TX 75243; (972) 995-2011; www.ti.com; Haviv Ilan; processors, semiconductors, software, handheld calculators.

Textron Inc. (TXT): 40 Westminster St., Providence, RI 02903; (401) 421-2800; www.textron.com; Scott C. Donnelly; aircraft (Cessna, Bell, Beechcraft); pilot training; industrial, auto prods.; financial services.

3M Co. (MMM): 3M Center, St. Paul, MN 55144; (651) 733-1110; www.3m.com; Michael F. Roman; abrasives, adhesives, electrical, health care, printing, consumer prods. (Post-it, Scotch-Brite, Scotch Tape, Scotchgard).

TIAA: 730 Third Ave., NY, NY 10017; (401) 490-9000; www.tiaa.org; Thasunda Brown Duckett; financial services provider.

Time Inc.: see Dotdash Meredith

TJX Cos., Inc. (TJX): 770 Cochituate Rd., Framingham, MA 01701; (508) 390-1000; www.tjx.com; Ernie Herrman; off-price apparel retailer (T.J. Maxx, Marshalls); home furnishing retailer (HomeGoods).

T-Mobile US, Inc. (TMUS): 12920 SE 38th St., Bellevue, WA 98006; (425) 378-4000; www.t-mobile.com; Michael Sievert; wireless telecommunications. Acquired Sprint, 4/1/2020.

Toro Co. (TTC): 8111 Lyndale Ave. S., Bloomington, MN 55420; (952) 888-8801; www.thetorocompany.com; Richard M. Olson; lawn and turf maintenance prods. (Lawn-Boy), snow removal equip.; irrigation systems.

Trane Technologies: 170/175 Lakeview Dr., Airside Business Park, Swords, Dublin, Ireland; tranetechnologies.com; Dave Regnery; HVAC system mfg./services (Ameristar, American Standard, Thermo King, Trane).

Transformco: 3333 Beverly Rd., Hoffman Estates, IL 60179; (847) 286-2500; www.transformco.com; Eddie S. Lampert; retail department stores. Formed in 2019 after Sears Holding Corp. (Kmart, Sears) filed for Ch. 11 bankruptcy in 2018.

The Travelers Companies, Inc. (TRV): 485 Lexington Ave., NY, NY 10017; (917) 778-6000; www.travelers.com; Alan D. Schnitzer; insurance.

Tribune Media Co.: see Nexstar Media Group, Inc.

Tribune Publishing Co.: see Alden Global Capital

Trusted Media Brands, Inc. (fmr. Reader's Digest Assn.): 485 Lexington Ave., NY, NY 10017; (914) 238-1000; www.tmbi.com; Bonnie Kintzer; publisher (Taste of Home, Reader's Digest, Birds & Blooms); marketer of books, music, video prods.

21st Century Fox, Inc.: see Disney, Fox Corp.

Twitter, Inc.: see X Corp.

Tyco Intl. Ltd.: see Johnson Controls Intl.

Tyson Foods, Inc. (TSN): 2200 W. Don Tyson Pkwy., Springdale, AR 72762; (479) 290-4000; www.tysonfoods.com; Donnie King; fresh and processed poultry; beef and pork prods. (Ball Park, Hillshire Farm, Jimmy Dean); Sara Lee prods.

Uber Technologies, Inc. (UBER): 1455 Market St., 4th Fl., San Francisco, CA 94103; (415) 986-2715; www.uber.com; Dara Khosrowshahi; mobile app-based taxi and food delivery services. Acquired Middle Eastern rival Careem, 1/2/2020.

UBS Financial Services Inc.: 1285 Ave. of the Americas, NY, NY 10019; (212) 713-2000; www.ubs.com; Sergio Ermotti; financial services; subsidiary of Switzerland's UBS AG. Acquired Credit Suisse for $3.25 bil, 6/12/2023.

Unilever USA: 800 Sylvan Ave., Englewood Cliffs, NJ 07632; (201) 894-4000; www.unileverusa.com; Hein Schumacher; food (Hellmann's, Knorr, Lipton, Klondike), hygiene prods. (Dove, Q-tips, Vaseline, Dermalogica, Murad). Subsidiary of Unilever NV (Neth.) and Unilever PLC (UK).

Union Pacific Corp. (UNP): 1400 Douglas St., Stop 1560, Omaha, NE 68179; (402) 544-5600; www.up.com; Lance M. Fritz; one of the largest railroad freight cos. in U.S.

Unisys Corp. (UIS): 801 Lakeview Dr., Ste. 100, Blue Bell, PA 19422; (215) 986-4011; www.unisys.com; Peter A. Altabef; designs, manuf. IT systems; IT consulting.

United Airlines Holdings, Inc. (UAL): 233 S. Wacker Dr., Chicago IL 60606; (312) 997-8000; www.united.com; Scott Kirby; air transportation (United Airlines).

United Natural Foods, Inc. (UNFI): 313 Iron Horse Way, Providence, RI 02908; (952) 828-4144; www.unfi.com; Sandy Douglas; wholesale food distrib.

United Parcel Service, Inc. (UPS): 55 Glenlake Pkwy. NE, Atlanta, GA 30328; (404) 828-6000; www.ups.com; Carol Tomé; shipping, logistics.

United States Steel Corp. (X): 600 Grant St., Pittsburgh, PA 15219; (412) 433-1121; www.ussteel.com; David B. Burritt; steel, tin prods.; resource mgmt.

United Technologies Corp.: see RTX.

UnitedHealth Group Inc. (UNH): UHG Center, 9900 Bren Rd. E., Minnetonka, MN 55343; (952) 936-1300;

www.unitedhealthgroup.com; Andrew Witty; health insurance.

U.S. Bancorp (USB): 800 Nicollet Mall, Minneapolis, MN 55402; (651) 466-3000; www.usbank.com; Andrew Cecere; financial services. Acquired MUFG Union Bank from Japan's Mitsubishi UFJ Financial Group, 12/1/2022.

Valero Energy Corp. (VLO): One Valero Way, San Antonio, TX 78249; (210) 345-2000; www.valero.com; Joe Gorder; fuel mfg. and marketing.

Verizon Communications Inc. (VZ): 1 Verizon Way, Basking Ridge, NJ 07920; (908) 559-2001; www.verizon.com; Hans Vestberg; telecom services; digital media. Sold Verizon Media Group (fmr. Oath, Inc., itself fmr. Yahoo) to private equity firm Apollo Global Management, 9/1/2021.

VF Corp. (VFC): 1551 Wewatta St., Denver, CO 80202; (336) 424-6000; www.vfc.com; Bracken Darrell; apparel (North Face, Timberland), backpacks (JanSport), shoes (Vans).

ViacomCBS Inc.: see Paramount Global

Victoria's Secret & Co. (VSCO): 4 Ltd. Parkway, Reynoldsburg, OH 43068; (614) 577-7000; www.victoriassecretandco.com; Martin Waters; lingerie retailer (Victoria's Secret, PINK).

Visa Inc. (V): 900 Metro Center Blvd., Foster City, CA 94404; (650) 432-3200; www.visa.com; Ryan McInerney; financial services.

Visteon Corp. (VC): One Village Center Dr., Van Buren Twp., MI 48111; (734) 710-5000; www.visteon.com; Sachin Lawande; automotive parts mfr.

Walgreens Boots Alliance, Inc. (WBA): 108 Wilmot Rd., Deerfield, IL 60015; (847) 315-3700; www.walgreensbootsalliance.com; Rosalind Brewer; retail drugstores, pharmaceutical wholesale/distrib. (Alliance Healthcare).

Walmart Inc. (WMT): 702 SW 8th St., Bentonville, AR 72716; (479) 273-4000; www.walmartstores.com; Doug McMillon; discount stores, warehouse clubs (Sam's Club).

Warner Bros. Discovery, Inc. (WBD): 230 Park Ave. South, NY, NY 10003; (212) 548-5555; wbd.com; David Zaslav; TV and CATV (Cartoon Network, HBO, CNN, TBS, TNT), motion pictures (Warner Bros.). Formed from Discovery, Inc.'s acquisition of WarnerMedia (fmr. Time Warner) assets from AT&T, 4/8/2022.

Washington Post Co.: see Graham Holdings Co.

Waste Management, Inc. (WM): 800 Capitol St., Ste. 3000, Houston, TX 77002; (713) 512-6200; www.wm.com; James C. Fish Jr.; waste, recycling.

WellPoint, Inc.: see Anthem, Inc.

Wells Fargo & Co. (WFC): 420 Montgomery St., San Francisco, CA 94104; (866) 249-3302; www.wellsfargo.com; Charles W. Scharf; financial services.

Wendy's Co. (WEN): 1 Dave Thomas Blvd., Dublin, OH 43017; (614) 764-3100; www.aboutwendys.com; Todd A. Penegor; fast food restaurants.

Western Union Co. (WU): 7001 E. Belleview, Denver, CO 80237; (720) 332-1000; www.westernunion.com; Devin McGranahan; money transfers, payment services.

WestRock Co. (WRK): 1000 Abernathy Rd. NE, Atlanta, GA 30328; (770) 448-2193; www.westrock.com; David B. Sewell; packaging, shipping containers; chemicals.

Weyerhaeuser Co. (WY): 220 Occidental Ave. S., Seattle, WA 98104; (206) 539-3000; www.weyerhaeuser.com; Devin W. Stockfish; produces, distributes wood prods.; real estate development.

Whirlpool Corp. (WHR): 2000 N. M-63, Benton Harbor, MI 49022; (269) 923-5000; www.whirlpoolcorp.com; Marc Bitzer; mfr. of major home appliances (KitchenAid, Amana, Maytag).

Whole Foods Market, Inc.: see Amazon

Winnebago Industries, Inc. (WGO): 13200 Pioneer Trl., Ste. 150, Eden Prairie, MN 55347; (952) 829-8600; www.winnebagoind.com; Michael J. Happe; mfr. of motor homes, recreational vehicles (RVs).

World Kinect Corp. (WKC): 9800 NW 41st St., Ste. 400, Doral, FL 33178; (305) 392-5621; www.world-kinect.com; Michael J. Kasbar; marketer and financer of fuel to large-scale aviation and marine-related firms.

Wm. Wrigley Jr. Co.: see Mars, Inc.

X Corp.: 1355 Market St., Ste. 900, San Francisco, CA, 94103; (415) 222-9670; twitter.com; Linda Yaccarino; social networking service formerly known as Twitter. Acquired by Elon Musk for $44 bil, 10/27/2022.

Xerox Corp. (XRX): 201 Merritt 7, Norwalk, CT 06851; (203) 968-3000; www.xerox.com; Steve Bandrowczak; printers, multi-function devices, document publishing technology and support.

Yum! Brands, Inc. (YUM): 1900 Colonel Sanders Ln., Louisville, KY 40213; (502) 874-8300; www.yum.com; David Gibbs; fast food restaurants (Pizza Hut, KFC, Taco Bell).

Zoom Video Communications, Inc. (ZM): 55 Almaden Blvd., Ste. 600, San Jose, CA 95113; (888) 799-9666; www.zoom.com; Eric S. Yuan; internet-based video teleconferencing.

Labor Unions and Professional Organizations

Source: Bureau of Labor Statistics, U.S. Dept. of Labor; AFL-CIO; World Almanac research

\# = Member of Strategic Organizing Center (fmr. Change to Win Federation), formed in 2005 by unions disaffiliated from AFL-CIO. * = Independent union or one not otherwise affiliated with Strategic Organizing Center or AFL-CIO. All other unions listed are affiliated with AFL-CIO as of 2023. Year established is in parentheses.

Labor Unions

Air Line Pilots Assn., Intl. (ALPA) (1931): 66,603 members, 42 U.S. and Canadian airlines; (703) 689-2270; www.alpa.org

American Federation of Labor and Congress of Industrial Organizations (AFL-CIO) (1955): federation of 60 unions, 12,471,480 members; (202) 637-5000; www.aflcio.org

Automobile, Aerospace & Agricultural Implement Workers of America, International Union, United (UAW) (1935): 383,003 members, 600+ locals; (313) 926-5000; www.uaw.org

Bakery, Confectionery, Tobacco Workers, and Grain Millers International Union (BCTGM) (1886): 61,475 members, 125 locals; (301) 933-8600; www.bctgm.org

Bricklayers and Allied Craftworkers, International Union of (BAC) (1865): 68,119 members, 40 locals; (202) 783-3788; www.bacweb.org

*Carpenters and Joiners of America, United Brotherhood of (UBC) (1881): 437,216 members, 450+ locals; (202) 546-6206; www.carpenters.org

Communications Workers of America (CWA) (1938): 633,412 members, 1,200 locals; (202) 434-1100; www.cwa-union.org

*Education Assn., Natl. (NEA) (1857): 2,871,908 members, 14,000+ affiliates; (202) 833-4000; www.nea.org

Electrical Workers, International Brotherhood of (IBEW) (1891): 688,937 members, 831 locals; (202) 833-7000; www.ibew.org

Engineers, International Union of Operating (IUOE) (1896): 398,098 members, 123 locals; (202) 429-9100; www.iuoe.org

*Farm Workers of America, United (UFW) (1962): 4,682 members; (661) 823-6151; www.ufw.org

Federal Employees, Natl. Federation of (NFFE; affiliated with IAM) (1917): 110,000 members, around 100 locals; (202) 216-4420; www.nffe.org

Fire Fighters, International Assn. of (IAFF) (1918): 331,151 members, 3,500+ locals; (202) 737-8484; www.iaff.org

Flight Attendants, Assn. of (AFA-CWA) (1945): 39,948 members, 19 airlines; merged with Communications Workers of America in 2004; (202) 434-1300; www.afacwa.org

Food and Commercial Workers International Union, United (UFCW) (1979): 1,165,871 members, 1,000+ locals; (202) 223-3111; www.ufcw.org

Glass, Molders, Pottery, Plastics and Allied Workers Intl. Union (GMP) (1842): 22,290 members, 250+ locals; (610) 565-5051; www.gmpiu.org

Government Employees, American Federation of (AFGE) (1932): 298,102 members, 900 locals; (202) 737-8700; www.afge.org

Iron Workers, Intl. Assn. of Bridge, Structural, Ornamental, and Reinforcing (BSOIW) (1896): 124,937 members, 200+ locals; (202) 383-4800; www.ironworkers.org

Laborers' International Union of North America (LiUNA) (1903): 596,455 members, 400 locals; (202) 737-8320; www.liuna.org

Letter Carriers, Natl. Assn. of (NALC) (1889): 289,753 members, 2,000+ locals; (202) 393-4695; www.nalc.org

\#Locomotive Engineers and Trainmen, Brotherhood of (BLET) (1863): 55,872 members, 500+ locals; (216) 241-2630; www.ble-t.org

Longshoremen's Assn., Intl. (ILA) (1892): 42,881 members, approx. 200 locals; (212) 425-1200; www.ilaunion.org

Machinists and Aerospace Workers, International Assn. of (IAM) (1888): 529,819 members; affiliated with TCU in 2005; (301) 967-4500; www.goiam.org

\#Maintenance of Way Employes, Division of the Intl. Brotherhood of Teamsters; Brotherhood of (BMWED) (1887): 31,656 members, 770 locals; merged with Teamsters in 2004; (248) 662-2660; www.bmwe.org (Note: In honor of tradition, the union maintains the variant spelling of "employes" in its logo.)

Mine Workers of America, United (UMWA) (1890): 50,258 members, 600 locals; (703) 291-2400; www.umwa.org

Musicians of the United States and Canada, American Federation of (AFM) (1896): 65,393 members, 240+ locals; (212) 869-1330; www.afm.org

NewsGuild—Communications Workers of America, The (TNG-CWA) (1933): 24,000 members, 63 locals; (202) 434-7177; www.newsguild.org

*Nurses Assn., American (ANA) (1911): 195,884 members, 50+ constituent state and territorial assns.; (301) 628-5000; www.nursingworld.org

Office and Professional Employees Intl. Union (OPEIU) (1945): 63,290 members, 61 locals; (212) 675-3210; www.opeiu.org

Printing, Packaging, & Production Workers Union of North America (PPPWU) (1983): 54,046 members; merged with Teamsters as Graphic Communications Conference, 2004-23; independent, July 2023; www.pppwu.org

Painters and Allied Trades, International Union of (IUPAT) (1887): 104,842 members, 425 locals; (410) 564-5900; www.iupat.org

Plumbing and Pipe Fitting Industry of the U.S. and Canada, United Assn. of Journeymen and Apprentices of the (UA) (1889): 359,037 members, 274 locals; (410) 269-2000; www.ua.org

*Police, Fraternal Order of (FOP) (1915): 365,409 members, 2,100+ affiliates; (615) 399-0900; www.fop.net

Police Assns., International Union of (IUPA) (1979): 100,000+ members; (941) 487-2560; www.iupa.org

Postal Workers Union, American (APWU) (1971): 222,190 members, 900+ locals; (202) 842-4200; www.apwu.org

Roofers, Waterproofers and Allied Workers, United Union of (RWAW) (1906): 22,231 members; (202) 463-7663; www.unionroofers.com

*Rural Letter Carriers' Assn., Natl. (RLCA) (1903): 107,877 members, 50 state orgs.; (703) 684-5545; www.nrlca.org

*Security, Police, Fire Professionals of America, Intl. Union, (SPFPA) (1948): 16,088 members, 200 locals; (586) 772-7250; www.spfpa.org

\#Service Employees International Union (SEIU) (1921): 1,824,709 members, 150+ locals; (202) 730-7000; www.seiu.org

Sheet Metal, Air, Rail, and Transportation Workers, Int. Assn. of (SMART) (2008, from merger of Sheet Metal Workers' Intl. Assn. and United Transportation Union): 193,055 members, 700 locals; (202) 662-0800; www.smart-union.org

State, County, and Municipal Employees, American Federation of (AFSCME) (1932): 1,238,307 members, 3,400 locals; (202) 429-1000; www.afscme.org

Steel, Paper and Forestry, Rubber, Manufacturing, Energy, Allied Industrial and Service Workers International Union, United (USW) (2005): 532,370 members, 1,800+ locals; formed from merger of United Steelworkers of America (USWA) (1936) and Paper, Allied-Industrial, Chemical and Energy Workers (PACE) (1999); (412) 562-2400; www.usw.org

\#Strategic Organizing Center (SOC) (fmr. Change to Win Federation) (2005): 3 unions, ex-affiliates of AFL-CIO, 2,477,219 members; (202) 721-0660; www.thesoc.org

Teachers, American Federation of (AFT) (1916): 1,686,316 members, 3,000+ locals; (202) 879-4400; www.aft.org

\#Teamsters, International Brotherhood of (IBT) (1903): 1,253,634 members, 380 locals, 1,900 affiliates; (202) 624-6800; www.teamster.org

Theatrical Stage Employees, Moving Picture Technicians, Artists and Allied Crafts of the U.S., Its Territories, and Canada, Intl. Alliance of (IATSE) (1893): 161,792 members, 367 locals; (212) 730-1770; www.iatse.net

Transit Union, Amalgamated (ATU) (1892): 190,378 members, 270 locals; (301) 431-7100; www.atu.org

Transport Workers Union of America (TWU) (1934): 139,993 members, 84 locals; (202) 719-3900; www.twu.org

Transportation Communications Intl. Union (TCU) (1899): affiliated with IAM in 2005; see Machinists and Aerospace Workers.

*Treasury Employees Union, Natl. (NTEU) (1938): 82,860 members, 200+ chapters; (202) 572-5500; www.nteu.org

UNITE HERE (UNITE, 1900; **HERE,** 1891; merged 2004): 262,135 members, 120 locals; (212) 265-7000; www.unitehere.org

\#Workers United (affiliated with SEIU) (WU) (2009): 79,372 members

*Writers Guild of America, East (WGAE) (1954): 6,768; (212) 767-7800; www.wgaeast.org

*Writers Guild of America, West (WGAW) (1933): 26,350 members; (323) 951-4000; www.wga.org

Professional Organizations and Societies

AASA, The School Superintendents Assn. (fmr. American Assn. of School Administrators) (1865): 10,000+ members; (703) 528-0700; www.aasa.org

Accountants, American Institute of Certified Public (1887): 689,000 members; (888) 777-7077; www.aicpa.org

ACMP—Associated Chamber Music Players (1947): 2,500+ members; (212) 645-7424; www.acmp.net

Actuaries, Soc. of (1949): 32,000+ members; (847) 706-3500; www.soa.org

Administrative Professionals, Intl. Assn. of (1942): 40,000+ members; (816) 891-6600; www.iaap-hq.org

Agricultural and Biological Engineers, American Soc. of (1907): 8,000+ members; (269) 429-0300; www.asabe.org

AIGA (fmr. American Institute of Graphic Arts) (1914): 18,000+ members; (212) 807-1990; www.aiga.org

Air & Waste Management Assn. (1907): 5,000+ members; (412) 232-3444; www.awma.org

AMSUS—The Society of Federal Health Professionals (1891): nearly 8,000 members; (301) 897-8800; www.amsus.org

Architects, American Institute of (1857): 96,000+ members; (202) 626-7300; www.aia.org

ASCM—The Assn. for Supply Chain Management (1957): 45,000+ members; (773) 867-1777; www.ascm.org

ASHRAE (Heating, Refrigerating and Air-Conditioning Engineers, Inc., American Soc. of) (1894): 50,000+ members; (404) 636-8400; www.ashrae.org

ASIS Intl. (fmr. Amer. Soc. for Industrial Security) (1955): 34,000 members; (703) 519-6200; www.asisonline.org

Astrologers, Inc., American Federation of (1938): 4,000 members; (480) 838-1751; www.astrologers.com

Astronomical Society, American (1899): 8,260+ members; (202) 328-2010; www.aas.org

Authors Guild, The (1912): 12,000+ members; (212) 563-5904; www.authorsguild.org

Bankers Assn., Independent Community (1930): nearly 5,700 banks; (202) 659-8111; www.icba.org

Bar Assn., American (1878): 194,000+ members; (312) 988-5000; www.americanbar.org

Bar Assn., Federal (1920): 14,000+ members; (571) 481-9100; www.fedbar.org

Biochemistry and Molecular Biology, American Society for (1906): 11,000+ members; (240) 283-6600; www.asbmb.org

Broadcasters, Natl. Assn. of (1923): (202) 429-5300; www.nab.org

Business Women's Assn., American (1949): 40,000 members; (800) 228-0007; www.abwa.org

Cartoonists Society, Natl. (1946): 500+ members; (407) 994-6703; www.nationalcartoonists.com

Ceramic Society, American (1898): 10,000+ members; (614) 890-4700; www.ceramics.org

Chemical Society, American (1876): 173,000+ members; (202) 872-4600; www.acs.org

Chiefs of Police, Intl. Assn. of (1893): 33,000+ members; (703) 836-6767; www.theiacp.org

Chiropractic Assn., American (1963): 15,000+ members; (703) 276-8800; www.acatoday.org

Civil Engineers, American Soc. of (1852): 150,000+ members; (703) 295-6300; www.asce.org

College Admission Counseling, Natl. Assn. for (1937): 26,000+ members; (703) 836-2222; www.nacacnet.org

Communication Assn., Natl. (1914): 8,000+ members; (202) 464-4622; www.natcom.org

Composers, Authors & Publishers, American Soc. of (ASCAP) (1914): 925,000 members; (212) 621-6000; www.ascap.com

Computing Machinery, Assn. for (1947): nearly 100,000 members; (212) 869-7440; www.acm.org

Computing Professionals, Institute for Certification of (1973): 60,000+ members; (847) 299-4227; www.iccp.org

Counseling Assn., American (1952): 56,000+ members; (800) 347-6647; www.counseling.org

Country Music Assn. (1958): 7,300+ members; (615) 244-2840; www.cmaworld.com

Dental Assn., American (1859): 161,000+ members; (312) 440-2500; www.ada.org

Directors Guild of America (1936): 19,000+ members; (310) 289-2000; www.dga.org

Electrical and Electronics Engineers, Institute of (1963): 427,000+ members; (732) 981-0060; www.ieee.org

Electronics Technicians, Intl. Soc. of Certified (1965): 50,000+ members; (817) 921-9061; www.iscet.org

Emergency Medical Technicians, Natl. Assn. of (1975): 75,000+ members; (601) 924-7744; www.naemt.org

Energy Engineers, Assn. of (1977): 18,000+ members; (770) 447-5083; www.aeecenter.org

Engineers, Natl. Society of Professional (1934): 26,000+ members; (888) 285-6773; www.nspe.org

Environmental Assessment Assn. (1972): 3,500 members; (877) 743-6806; www.eaa-assoc.org

Environmental Health Assn., Natl. (1937): 6,000+ members; (303) 756-9090; www.neha.org

Family Physicians, American Academy of (1947): 129,600 members; (800) 274-2237; www.aafp.org

Farm Bureau Federation, American (1919): nearly 6 mil member families; (202) 406-3600; www.fb.org

Farmers Union, Natl. (1902): nearly 220,000+ family farmers, fishers, ranchers; (202) 554-1600; www.nfu.org

Financial Professionals, Assn. for (1979): 16,000+ members; (301) 907-2862; www.afponline.org

Financial Service Professionals, Soc. of (1928): nearly 14,000 members; (610) 526-2500; www.societyoffsp.org

Fire Chiefs, Intl. Assn. of (1873): nearly 12,000 members; (703) 273-0911; www.iafc.org

Fire Protection Engineers, Soc. of (1950): 5,000+ members; (301) 718-2910; www.sfpe.org

Food Technologists, Institute of (1939): 12,000+ members; (312) 782-8424; www.ift.org

Forensic Sciences, American Academy of (1948): 6,500+ members; (719) 636-1100; www.aafs.org

Funeral Directors Assn., Natl. (1882): 20,000 members; (262) 789-1880; www.nfda.org

General Contractors of America, Associated (1918): 27,000+ cos.; (703) 548-3118; www.agc.org

Geographers, American Assn. of (1904): 10,000 members; (202) 234-1450; www.aag.org

Ground Water Assn., Natl. (1948): 10,000+ members; (614) 898-7791; www.ngwa.org

Home Builders, Natl. Assn. of (1942): 140,000 members; (800) 368-5242; www.nahb.org

Human Resource Management, Soc. for (SHRM) (1948): 325,000+ members; (703) 548-3440; www.shrm.org

Illustrators, Society of (1901): 1,000 members; (212) 838-2560; www.societyillustrators.org

Industrial Designers Society of America (1965): 2,500 members; (703) 707-6000; www.idsa.org

Intelligence Officers, Assn. of Former (1975): 24 chap., 4,800 members; (703) 790-0320; www.afio.com

Interior Designers, American Soc. of (1975): 19,000 members; (202) 546-3480; www.asid.org

Jail Assn., American (1981): 3,000 members; (301) 790-3930; www.americanjail.org

Journalists, Society of Professional (1909): 6,000 members; (317) 927-8000; www.spj.org

Landscape Architects, American Society of (1899): 15,000+ members; (202) 898-2444; www.asla.org

Legal Administrators, Assn. of (1971): 8,500+ members; (847) 267-1252; www.alanet.org

Legal Support Professionals, Natl. Assn. for (fmr. Natl. Assn. of Legal Secretaries) (1929): nearly 6,000 members; (918) 582-5188; www.nals.org

Library Assn., American (1876): 50,000+ members; (800) 545-2433; www.ala.org

Lifesaving Assn., U.S. (1964): 100+ chap., 12,600+ members; (866) 367-8752; www.usla.org

Logistics, Intl. Society of (SOLE) (1966): 100+ chap., 3,000+ members; (301) 459-8446; www.sole.org

Magicians, Intl. Brotherhood of (1922): nearly 11,000 members; (636) 724-2400; www.magician.org

Management Accountants, Inst. of (1919): 137,000 members; (201) 573-9000; www.imanet.org

Management Assn., American (1923): 4,100 cos., 38,000 ind.; (877) 566-9441; www.amanet.org

Marketing Assn., American (1937): 30,000+ members; (800) 262-1150; www.ama.org

Master Brewers Assn. of the Americas (1887): 4,000+ members; (651) 454-7250; www.mbaa.com

Material and Process Engineering, Soc. for the Advancement of (1944): 5,000+ members; (626) 521-9460; www.sampe.org

Mechanical Engineers, American Soc. of (1880): 85,000+ members; (646) 616-3100; www.asme.org

Medical Assn., American (1847): 271,660 members; (800) 262-3211; www.ama-assn.org

Medical Library Assn. (1898): 3,600+ members, 1,100+ institutions; (312) 419-9094; www.mlanet.org

Motion Picture Arts & Sciences, Academy of (1927): 10,000+ members; (310) 247-3000; www.oscars.org

Motion Picture and Television Engineers, Soc. of (1916): 7,000+ members; (914) 761-1100; www.smpte.org

Mystery Writers of America (1945): 3,000+ members; (212) 888-8171; www.mysterywriters.org

Notaries, American Society of (1965): 20,000+ members; (850) 671-5164; www.notaries.org

Nursing, Natl. League for (1893): nearly 45,000 members, 1,000+ institutions; (800) 669-1656; www.nln.org

Optometric Assn., American (1898): 45,000+ members; (800) 365-2219; www.aoa.org

Organists, American Guild of (1896): 12,000 members; (212) 870-2310; www.agohq.org

Pharmacists Assn., American (1852): 62,000+ members; (202) 628-4410; www.pharmacist.com

Physical Therapy Assn., American (1921): 100,000+ members; (703) 684-2782; www.apta.org

Plastics Engineers, Society of (1942): 22,500+ members; (203) 740-5400; www.4spe.org

Police Assn.—United States Section, Intl. (1962): 10,000 members; (855) 241-9998; www.ipa-usa.org

Population Assn. of America (1931): nearly 3,000 members; (301) 565-6710; www.populationassociation.org

Postmasters and Managers of America, United (2015): (703) 683-9027; www.unitedpma.org

Press Club, Natl. (1908): 3,000 members; (202) 662-7500; www.press.org

Professional Ball Players of America, Assn. of (1924): 101,500+ members; (602) 730-4528; www.apbpa.org

Professional Beauty Assn. (1904): 100,000+ members; (480) 281-0424; www.probeauty.org

Psychiatric Assn., American (1844): 38,000+ members; (202) 559-3900; www.psychiatry.org

Psychological Assn., American (1892): 146,000+ members; (202) 336-5500; www.apa.org

Public Administration, American Soc. for (1939): 10,000 members; (202) 393-7878; www.aspanet.org

Public Health Assn., American (1872): 25,000+ members; (202) 777-2742; www.apha.org

Public Relations Soc. of America Inc. (1947): nearly 30,000 members; (212) 460-1400; www.prsa.org

Range Management, Society for (1948): 4,000+ members; (303) 986-3309; www.rangelands.org

Real Estate Appraisers, Natl. Assn. of (1966): 10,000+ members; (877) 743-6806; www.narea-assoc.org

Rehabilitation Assn., Natl. (1923): 5,600 members; (703) 836-0850; www.national rehab.org

Road & Transportation Builders Assn., American (1902): 8,000+ members; (202) 289-4434; www.artba.org

Safety Professionals, American Soc. of (1911): 35,000 members; (847) 699-2929; www.assp.org

Science Teaching Assn., Natl. (1944): 40,000 members; (703) 524-3646; www.nsta.org

Screen Actors Guild—American Federation of Television and Radio Artists (2012): 160,000 members; (855) 724-2387; www.sagaftra.org

Songwriters Guild of America, Inc. (1931): 5,000+ members; (615) 742-9945; www.songwritersguild.com

Sportscasters Assn., American (1979): 500+ members; (212) 227-8080; www.americansportscastersonline.com

Supply Chain Management, Assn. for (fmr. Assn. for Operations Management) (1957): 45,000+ members; (773) 867-1777; www.ascm.org

Surgeons, American College of (1913): 84,000 members; (312) 202-5000; www.facs.org

Tax Administrators, Federation of (1937): (202) 624-5890; www.taxadmin.org

Teachers of English, Natl. Council of (1911): 25,000+ members; (217) 328-3870; www.ncte.org

Teachers of French, American Assn. of (1927): 9,000 members; (815) 310-0490; www.frenchteachers.org

Teachers of German, American Assn. of (1926): nearly 3,500 members; (856) 795-5553; www.aatg.org

Teachers of Mathematics, Natl. Council of (1920): 38,000 members; (703) 620-9840; www.nctm.org

Teachers of Spanish and Portuguese, American Assn. of (1917): nearly 10,000 members; (205) 506-0600; www.aatsp.org

Television Arts and Sciences, Natl. Academy of (1955): nearly 20,000 members; (212) 586-8424; www.theemmys.tv

TESOL International Assn. (fmr. Teachers of English to Speakers of Other Languages) (1966): 13,000+ members; (703) 518-2500; www.tesol.org

Theological Library Assn., American (1946): 800+ members; (872) 310-4200; www.atla.org

Transportation Engineers, Inst. of (1930): 17,000+ members; (202) 785-0060; www.ite.org

Travel Advisors, American Soc. of (fmr. Amer. Soc. of Travel Agents) (1931): 12,000 members; (800) 275-2782; www.asta.org

University Women, American Assn. of (1881): 170,000+ members; (202) 785-7700; www.aauw.org

Veterinary Medical Assn., American (1863): 100,000+ members; (847) 925-8070; www.avma.org

Women in Communications, The Assn. for (1909): 1,100+ members; (417) 409-2492; www.womcom.org

Women Engineers, Society of (1950): 40,000+ members; (312) 596-5223; swe.org

Women in Media, Alliance for (1951): nearly 4,000 members; (202) 750-3664; www.allwomeninmedia.org

Professional Sports Organizations

Source: World Almanac research

Major League Baseball

Office of the Commissioner, 1271 Ave. of the Americas, NY, NY 10020; (212) 931-7800; www.mlb.com

American League

Baltimore Orioles (1953): 333 W. Camden St., Baltimore, MD 21201; (410) 685-9800; www.orioles.com

Boston Red Sox (1901): 4 Jersey St., Boston, MA 02215; (617) 267-9440; www.redsox.com

Chicago White Sox (1900, as Chicago White Stockings): 333 W. 35th St., Chicago, IL 60616; (312) 674-1000; www.whitesox.com

Cleveland Guardians (1901, as Cleveland Blues; name changed from Indians after 2021 season): 2401 Ontario St., Cleveland, OH 44115; (216) 420-4200; cleguardians.com

Detroit Tigers (1901): 2100 Woodward Ave., Detroit, MI 48201; (313) 471-2000; www.tigers.com

Houston Astros (1962, as Houston Colt 45s): 501 Crawford St., Houston, TX 77002; (713) 259-8000; www.astros.com (National League, 1962-2012; AL West, 2013-present)

Kansas City Royals (1969): One Royal Way, Kansas City, MO 64129; (816) 921-8000; www.royals.com

Los Angeles Angels (1961): 2000 Gene Autry Way, Anaheim, CA 92806; (714) 940-2000; www.angels.com

Minnesota Twins (1960): 1 Twins Way, Minneapolis, MN 55403; (612) 659-3400; www.twinsbaseball.com

New York Yankees (1903): One E. 161st St., Bronx, NY 10451; (718) 293-4300; www.yankees.com

Oakland Athletics (1901, as Philadelphia Athletics): 7000 Coliseum Way, Oakland, CA 94621; (510) 638-4900; www.athletics.com

Seattle Mariners (1977): 1250 First Ave. S., Seattle, WA 98134; (206) 346-4000; www.mariners.com

Tampa Bay Rays (1995, as Tampa Bay Devil Rays): 1 Tropicana Dr., St. Petersburg, FL 33705; (727) 825-3137; www.raysbaseball.com

Texas Rangers (1960, as Washington Senators): 734 Stadium Dr., Arlington, TX 76011; (817) 533-1972; www.texasrangers.com

Toronto Blue Jays (1976): One Blue Jays Way, Ste. 3200, Toronto, ON M5V 1J1, Canada; (416) 341-1000; www.bluejays.com

National League

Arizona Diamondbacks (1998): 401 E. Jefferson St., Phoenix, AZ 85004; (602) 462-6500; www.dbacks.com

Atlanta Braves (1876, as Boston Red Stockings): 755 Battery Ave., Atlanta, GA 30339; (404) 614-2300; www.braves.com

Chicago Cubs (1876, as Chicago White Stockings): 1060 W. Addison, Chicago, IL 60613; (773) 404-2827; www.cubs.com

Cincinnati Reds (1869, as Cincinnati Red Stockings): 100 Joe Nuxhall Way, Cincinnati, OH 45202; (513) 765-7000; www.reds.com

Colorado Rockies (1991): 2001 Blake St., Denver, CO 80205; (303) 292-0200; www.rockies.com

Los Angeles Dodgers (1890): 1000 Vin Scully Ave., Los Angeles, CA 90012; (323) 224-2611; www.dodgers.com

Miami Marlins (1991, as Florida Marlins): 501 Marlins Way, Miami, FL 33125; (305) 480-1300; www.marlins.com

Milwaukee Brewers (1970): One Brewers Way, Milwaukee, WI 53214; (414) 902-4400; www.brewers.com (American League, 1969-1997; NL Central, 1998-present)

New York Mets (1962): 41 Seaver Way, Queens, NY 11368; (718) 507-6387; www.mets.com

Philadelphia Phillies (1883): One Citizens Bank Way, Philadelphia, PA 19148; (215) 463-6000; www.phillies.com

Pittsburgh Pirates (1887, as Pittsburgh Alleghenies): 115 Federal St., Pittsburgh, PA 15212; (412) 323-5000; www.pirates.com

St. Louis Cardinals (1892, as St. Louis Browns): 700 Clark St., St. Louis, MO 63102; (314) 345-9600; www.cardinals.com

San Diego Padres (1969): 100 Park Blvd., San Diego, CA 92101; (619) 795-5000; www.padres.com

San Francisco Giants (1883, as New York Gothams): 24 Willie Mays Plz., San Francisco, CA 94107; (415) 972-2000; www.sfgiants.com

Washington Nationals (1969, as Montréal Expos): 1500 South Capitol St., SE, Washington, DC 20003; (202) 675-6287; www.nationals.com

National Basketball Association

League Office, 645 Fifth Ave., NY, NY 10022; (212) 407-8000; www.nba.com

Atlanta Hawks (1949, as Tri-Cities Blackhawks): 101 Marietta St. NW, Ste. 1900, Atlanta, GA 30303; (866) 715-1500; www.nba.com/hawks

Boston Celtics (1946): 100 Causeway St., Ste. 1210, Boston, MA 02114; (866) 423-5849; www.nba.com/celtics

Brooklyn Nets (1967, as New Jersey Americans): 168 39th St., 7th Fl., Brooklyn, NY 11232; (718) 933-3000; www.nba.com/nets

Charlotte Hornets (2004, as Charlotte Bobcats): 333 E. Trade St., Charlotte, NC 28202; (704) 688-8600; www.nba.com/hornets

Chicago Bulls (1966): 1901 W. Madison St., Chicago, IL 60612; (312) 455-4000; www.nba.com/bulls

Cleveland Cavaliers (1970): One Center Ct., Cleveland, OH 44115; (216) 420-2000; www.nba.com/cavaliers

Dallas Mavericks (1980): 2500 Victory Ave., Dallas, TX 75219; (214) 747-6287; www.nba.com/mavericks

Denver Nuggets (1967, as Denver Rockets): 1000 Chopper Cir., Denver, CO 80204; (303) 405-1100; www.nba.com/nuggets

Detroit Pistons (1948, as Fort Wayne Pistons): 6201 2nd Ave., Detroit, MI 48202; (313) 747-8667; www.nba.com/pistons

Golden State Warriors (1946, as Philadelphia Warriors): 1 Warriors Way, San Francisco, CA 94158; (888) 479-4667; www.nba.com/warriors

Houston Rockets (1967, as San Diego Rockets): 1510 Polk St., Houston, TX 77002; (713) 758-7200; www.nba.com/rockets

Indiana Pacers (1967): 125 S. Pennsylvania St., Indianapolis, IN 46204; (317) 917-2500; www.nba.com/pacers

Los Angeles Clippers (1970, as Buffalo Braves): 1212 S. Flower St., 5th Fl., Los

Angeles, CA 90015; (213) 204-2800; www.nba.com/clippers

Los Angeles Lakers (1947, as Minneapolis Lakers): 1111 S. Figueroa St., Los Angeles, CA 90015; (310) 426-6000; www.nba.com/lakers

Memphis Grizzlies (1995, as Vancouver Grizzlies): 191 Beale St., Memphis, TN 38103; (901) 888-4667; www.nba.com/grizzlies

Miami Heat (1988): 601 Biscayne Blvd., Miami, FL 33132; (786) 777-1000; www.nba.com/heat

Milwaukee Bucks (1968): 1111 Vel R. Phillips Ave., Milwaukee, WI 53203; (414) 227-0599; www.nba.com/bucks

Minnesota Timberwolves (1989): 600 Hennepin Ave., Ste. 300, Minneapolis, MN 55403; (612) 673-1600; www.nba.com/timberwolves

New Orleans Pelicans (1988, as Charlotte Hornets): 5800 Airline Dr., Metairie, LA 70003; (504) 593-4700; www.nba.com/pelicans

New York Knickerbockers (1946): Two Pennsylvania Plz., NY, NY 10121; (212) 465-6471; www.nba.com/knicks

Oklahoma City Thunder (1967, as Seattle SuperSonics): 208 Thunder Dr., Oklahoma City, OK 73102; (405) 208-4800; www.nba.com/thunder

Orlando Magic (1989): 8701 Maitland Summit Blvd., Orlando, FL 32810; (407) 916-2400; www.nba.com/magic

Philadelphia 76ers (1949, as Syracuse Nationals): 3601 S. Broad St., Philadelphia, PA 19148; (215) 339-7676; www.nba.com/sixers

Phoenix Suns (1968): 201 E. Jefferson St., Phoenix, AZ 85004; (602) 379-2000; www.nba.com/suns

Portland Trail Blazers (1970): One Center Ct., Ste. 200, Portland, OR 97227; (503) 234-9291; www.nba.com/blazers

Sacramento Kings (1945, as Rochester Royals): 500 David J. Stern Walk, Sacramento, CA 95814; (888) 915-4647; www.nba.com/kings

San Antonio Spurs (1967, as Dallas Chaparrals): One AT&T Center, San Antonio, TX 78219; (210) 444-5000; www.nba.com/spurs

Toronto Raptors (1995): 40 Bay St., Toronto, ON M5J 2X2, Canada; (416) 366-3865; www.nba.com/raptors

Utah Jazz (1974, as New Orleans Jazz): 301 W. South Temple, Salt Lake City, UT 84101; (801) 325-2500; www.nba.com/jazz

Washington Wizards (1961, as Chicago Packers): 601 F St. NW, Washington, DC 20004; (202) 661-5000; www.nba.com/wizards

National Hockey League

NHL Headquarters, 1 Manhattan West, 395 Ninth Ave., NY, NY 10001; (212) 789-2000; www.nhl.com

Anaheim Ducks (1993): 2695 E. Katella Ave., Anaheim, CA 92806; (877) 945-3946; ducks.nhl.com

Arizona Coyotes (1979, as Winnipeg Jets): 9400 W. Maryland Ave., Glendale, AZ 85305; (623) 772-3200; coyotes.nhl.com

Boston Bruins (1924): 100 Legends Way, Boston, MA 02114; (617) 624-1900; bruins.nhl.com

Buffalo Sabres (1970): One Seymour H. Knox III Plz., Buffalo, NY 14203; (716) 855-4100; sabres.nhl.com

Calgary Flames (1980): P.O. Box 1540, Station M, Calgary, AB T2P 3B9, Canada; (403) 777-2177; flames.nhl.com

Carolina Hurricanes (1972, as New England Whalers): 1400 Edwards Mill Rd., Raleigh, NC 27607; (919) 467-7825; hurricanes.nhl.com

Chicago Blackhawks (1926): 1901 W. Madison St., Chicago, IL 60612; (312) 455-7000; blackhawks.nhl.com

Colorado Avalanche (1972, as Quebec Nordiques): 1000 Chopper Cir., Denver, CO 80204; (303) 405-1100; avalanche.nhl.com

Columbus Blue Jackets (2000): 200 W. Nationwide Blvd., Suite Level, Columbus, OH 43215; (614) 246-4625; bluejackets.nhl.com

Dallas Stars (1967, as Minnesota North Stars): 2601 Ave. of the Stars, Frisco, TX 75034; (214) 387-5500; stars.nhl.com

Detroit Red Wings (1926, as Detroit Cougars): 2525 Woodward Ave., Detroit, MI 48201; (313) 471-7000; redwings.nhl.com

Edmonton Oilers (1972, as Alberta Oilers): 300, 10214 104 Ave. NW, Edmonton, AB T5J 0H6, Canada; (866) 414-4625; oilers.nhl.com

Florida Panthers (1993): One Panther Pkwy., Sunrise, FL 33323; (954) 835-7000; panthers.nhl.com

Los Angeles Kings (1967): 1111 S. Figueroa St., Los Angeles, CA 90015; (213) 742-7100; kings.nhl.com

Minnesota Wild (2000): 317 Washington St., St. Paul, MN 55102; (651) 602-6000; wild.nhl.com

Montréal Canadiens (1909): 1909 Avenue des Canadiens-de-Montréal, Montréal, QC H3B 5L2, Canada; (514) 932-2582; canadiens.nhl.com

Nashville Predators (1998): 501 Broadway, Nashville, TN 37203; (615) 770-2000; predators.nhl.com

New Jersey Devils (1974, as Kansas City Scouts): Prudential Center, 25 Lafayette St., Newark, NJ 07102; (973) 757-6100; devils.nhl.com

New York Islanders (1972): 200 Merrick Ave., East Meadow, NY 11554; (516) 501-6700; islanders.nhl.com

New York Rangers (1926): Two Pennsylvania Plz., NY, NY 10121; (212) 465-6000; rangers.nhl.com

Ottawa Senators (1992): 1000 Palladium Dr., Ottawa, ON K2V 1A5, Canada; (613) 599-0250; senators.nhl.com

Philadelphia Flyers (1967): 3601 S. Broad St., Philadelphia, PA 19148; (215) 465-4500; flyers.nhl.com

Pittsburgh Penguins (1967): 1001 5th Ave., Pittsburgh, PA 15219; (412) 642-1300; penguins.nhl.com

St. Louis Blues (1967): 1401 Clark Ave. at Brett Hull Way, St. Louis, MO 63103; (314) 622-2500; blues.nhl.com

San Jose Sharks (1991): 525 W. Santa Clara St., San Jose, CA 95113; (408) 287-7070; sharks.nhl.com

Seattle Kraken (2021): 16 W. Harrison St., Ste. 200, Seattle, WA 98119; (206) 460-7825; nhl.com/kraken

Tampa Bay Lightning (1992): 401 Channelside Dr., Tampa, FL 33602; (813) 301-6500; lightning.nhl.com

Toronto Maple Leafs (1919, as Toronto St. Pats): 50 Bay St., Ste. 500, Toronto, ON M5J 2L2, Canada; (416) 815-5700; mapleleafs.nhl.com

Vancouver Canucks (1945, joined NHL in 1970): 89 W. Georgia St., Vancouver, BC V6B 0N8, Canada; (604) 899-7400; canucks.nhl.com

Vegas Golden Knights (2017): 3780 S. Las Vegas Blvd., Las Vegas, NV 89158; (702) 692-1600; goldenknights.nhl.com

Washington Capitals (1974): 627 N. Glebe Rd., Ste. 850, Arlington, VA 22203; (202) 266-2200; capitals.nhl.com

Winnipeg Jets (1999, as Atlanta Thrashers): 600-223 Carlton St., Winnipeg, MB R3C 0V4, Canada; (204) 987-7825; jets.nhl.com

National Football League

League Office, 345 Park Ave., NY, NY 10154; (212) 450-2000; www.nfl.com

Arizona Cardinals (1898, as Morgan Athletic Club): P.O. Box 888, Phoenix, AZ 85001; (602) 379-0101; www.azcardinals.com

Atlanta Falcons (1966): 4400 Falcon Pkwy., Flowery Branch, GA 30542; (770) 965-3115; www.atlantafalcons.com

Baltimore Ravens (1996): 1101 Russell St., Baltimore, MD 21230; (410) 261-7283; www.baltimoreravens.com

Buffalo Bills (1960): One Bills Dr., Orchard Park, NY 14127; (716) 648-1800; www.buffalobills.com

Carolina Panthers (1995): 800 S. Mint St., Charlotte, NC 28202; (704) 358-7000; www.panthers.com

Chicago Bears (1920, as Decatur Staleys): 1920 Football Dr., Lake Forest, IL 60045; (847) 615-2327; www.chicagobears.com

Cincinnati Bengals (1968): One Paycor Stadium, Cincinnati, OH 45202; (513) 621-3550; www.bengals.com

Cleveland Browns (1946): 76 Lou Groza Blvd., Berea, OH 44017; (440) 891-5000; www.clevelandbrowns.com

Dallas Cowboys (1960): 1 Cowboys Way, Ste. 100, Frisco, TX 75034; (972) 497-4900; www.dallascowboys.com

Denver Broncos (1960): 13655 Broncos Pkwy., Englewood, CO 80112; (303) 649-9000; www.denverbroncos.com

Detroit Lions (1930, as Portsmouth Spartans): 222 Republic Dr., Allen Park, MI 48101; (313) 262-2000; www.detroitlions.com

Green Bay Packers (1919): 1265 Lombardi Ave., Green Bay, WI 54304; (920) 569-7500; www.packers.com

Houston Texans (2002): Two NRG Park, Houston, TX 77054; (832) 667-2000; www.houstontexans.com

Indianapolis Colts (1953, as Baltimore Colts): 7001 W. 56th St., Indianapolis, IN 46254; (317) 297-2658; www.colts.com

Jacksonville Jaguars (1995): One TIAA Bank Field Dr., Jacksonville, FL 32202; (904) 633-2000; www.jaguars.com

Kansas City Chiefs (1960, as Dallas Texans): One Arrowhead Dr., Kansas City, MO 64129; (816) 920-9300; www.chiefs.com

Las Vegas Raiders (1960, as Oakland Raiders): 1475 Raiders Way, Henderson, NV 89052; (510) 864-5000; www.raiders.com

Los Angeles Chargers (1960): 3333 Susan St., Costa Mesa, CA 92626; (714) 540-7100; www.chargers.com

Los Angeles Rams (1937, as Cleveland Rams): 29889 Agoura Rd., Agoura Hills, CA 91301; (818) 540-2016; www.therams.com

Miami Dolphins (1966): 347 Don Shula Dr., Miami Gardens, FL 33056; (305) 943-8000; www.miamidolphins.com

Minnesota Vikings (1961): 2600 Vikings Cir., Eagan, MN 55121; (952) 828-6500; www.vikings.com

New England Patriots (1960): One Patriot Pl., Foxborough, MA 02035; (508) 543-8200; www.patriots.com

New Orleans Saints (1967): 5800 Airline Dr., Metairie, LA 70003; (504) 733-0255; www.neworleanssaints.com

New York Giants (1925): 1925 Giants Dr., E. Rutherford, NJ 07073; (201) 935-8111; www.giants.com

New York Jets (1960, as New York Titans): One Jets Dr., Florham Park, NJ 07932; (800) 469-5387; www.newyorkjets.com

Philadelphia Eagles (1933): One NovaCare Way, Philadelphia, PA 19145; (215) 463-2500; www.philadelphiaeagles.com

Pittsburgh Steelers (1933): 3400 S. Water St., Pittsburgh, PA 15203; (412) 432-7800; www.steelers.com

San Francisco 49ers (1946): 4949 Marie P. DeBartolo Way, Santa Clara, CA 95054; (408) 562-4949; www.49ers.com

Seattle Seahawks (1976): 12 Seahawks Way, Renton, WA 98056; (888) 635-4295; www.seahawks.com

Tampa Bay Buccaneers (1976): One Buccaneer Pl., Tampa, FL 33607; (813) 870-2700; www.buccaneers.com

Tennessee Titans (1960, as Houston Oilers): 460 Great Circle Rd., Nashville, TN 37228; (615) 565-4000; www.titansonline.com

Washington Commanders (1932, as Boston Braves): 1600 Fedex Way, Landover, MD 20785; (703) 726-7000; www.commanders.com

Health Organizations

Source: World Almanac research

Entries are roughly alphabetized by the basic condition addressed or organization name. Year established is in parentheses. Always check with a physician before any new health-related undertaking.

Al-Anon Family Groups (1951): (757) 563-1600; al-anon.org

Alcoholics Anonymous (1935): (212) 870-3400; www.aa.org

Aging, Natl. Institute on (1974): (800) 222-2225; www.nia.nih.gov

Aging's Eldercare Locator, Admin. on (1991): (800) 677-1116; www.eldercare.acl.gov

Allergy, Asthma and Immunology, American Academy of (1943): (414) 272-6071; www.aaaai.org

ALS Assn. [Lou Gehrig's disease] (1985): (800) 782-4747; www.als.org

Alzheimer's Assn. (1979): (800) 272-3900; www.alz.org

Anorexia Nervosa and Associated Disorders, Natl. Assn. of (1976): (888) 375-7767; www.anad.org

Arc, The [intellectual/developmental disabilties] (1950): (800) 433-5255; www.thearc.org

Arthritis Foundation (1948): (800) 283-7800; www.arthritis.org

Arthritis and Musculoskeletal and Skin Diseases, Natl. Institute of (1986): (877) 226-4267; www.niams.nih.gov

Asthma and Allergy Foundation of America (1953): (800) 727-8462; www.aafa.org

Autism Society (1965): (800) 328-8476; www.autismsociety.org

Blind, American Council of the (1961): (202) 467-5081; (800) 424-8666; www.acb.org

Blind, Natl. Federation of the (1940): (410) 659-9314; www.nfb.org

Blindness, Foundation Fighting (1971): (800) 683-5555; www.fightingblindness.org

Blindness, Prevent (1908): (800) 331-2020; www.preventblindness.org

Bone Health and Osteoporosis Foundation (1984): (800) 231-4222; www.bonehealthandosteoporosis.org

Brain Tumor Society, Natl. (2008): (617) 924-9997; www.braintumor.org

Breast Cancer Diagnosis, After (ABCD) (1999): (800) 977-4121; www.abcdbreastcancersupport.org

Cancer Institute's Cancer Information Service, Natl. (1975): (800) 422-6237; www.cancer.gov

Cancer Society, American (1913): (800) 227-2345; www.cancer.org

Cerebral Palsy, United (1949): (202) 776-0406; (800) 872-5827; www.ucp.org

Child Abuse and Family Violence, Natl. Council on (1984): (202) 429-6695; www.preventfamilyviolence.org

Childhelp Natl. Child Abuse Hotline (1959): (800) 422-4453; www.childhelp.org

Children, Natl. Center for Missing and Exploited (1984): (703) 224-2150; (800) 843-5678; www.missingkids.org

Children's Tumor Foundation (1978): (212) 344-6633; (800) 323-7938; www.ctf.org

Chronic Pain Assn., American (1980): (913) 991-4740; www.theacpa.org

Continence, Natl. Assn. for (1982): (843) 419-5307; (800) 252-3337; www.nafc.org

Cooley's Anemia Foundation (1954): (212) 279-8090; www.thalassemia.org

Long-COVID Alliance (2020): (704) 364-0016; longcovidalliance.org

Crohn's and Colitis Foundation (1967): (800) 932-2423; www.crohnscolitisfoundation.org

Cystic Fibrosis Foundation (1955): (800) 344-4823; (301) 951-4422; www.cff.org

Deaf, Natl. Assn. of the (1880): (301) 587-1788, TTY (301) 810-3182; www.nad.org

Depression and Bipolar Support Alliance (1985): (800) 826-3632; www.dbsalliance.org

Diabetes Assn., American (1940): (800) 342-2383; www.diabetes.org

Diabetes and Digestive and Kidney Diseases, Natl. Institute of (1950): (800) 860-8747; www.niddk.nih.gov

Disease Control and Prevention, Centers for (CDC) (1946): (800) 232-4636; www.cdc.gov

Domestic Violence Hotline, Natl. (1996): (800) 799-7233, TTY (800) 787-3224; www.thehotline.org

Down Syndrome Congress, Natl. (1973): (800) 232-6372; www.ndsccenter.org

Down Syndrome Society, Natl. (1979): (800) 221-4602; www.ndss.org

Dyslexia Assn., Intl. (1949): (410) 296-0232; dyslexiaida.org

Easterseals [special needs] (1919): (800) 221-6827; www.easterseals.com

Eating Disorders Assn., National (2001): (800) 931-2237; www.nationaleatingdisorders.org

Endometriosis Assn. (1980): (414) 355-2200; www.endometriosisassn.org

Epilepsy Foundation (1968): (800) 332-1000; www.epilepsy.com

Fat Acceptance, Natl. Assn. to Advance (1969): (916) 558-6880; www.naafa.org

First Candle [sudden infant death syndrome] (1987): (800) 221-7437; www.firstcandle.org

FoodSafety.gov: Meat, poultry, eggs: (888) 674-6854; Food (non-meat): (888) 723-3366; Illness or food poisoning: (800) 232-4636 (CDC)

Gamblers Anonymous (1957): (909) 931-9056; www.gamblersanonymous.org

Geriatrics Society, American (1942): (212) 308-1414; www.americangeriatrics.org

Headache Foundation, Natl. (1970): (888) 643-5552; www.headaches.org

HealthyWomen (1988): (877) 986-9472; www.healthywomen.org

Hearing Society, Intl. (1951): (734) 522-7200; www.ihsinfo.org

Heart Assn., American (1924): (800) 242-8721; www.heart.org

Hearts, Inc., Mended (1951): (888) 432-7899; www.mendedhearts.org

HIVinfo: (800) 448-0440; hivinfo.nih.gov

Hospice Foundation of America (1982): (800) 854-3402; www.hospicefoundation.org

Hospice Intl., Children's (1983): (703) 684-0330; www.chionline.org

Hospital Assn., American (1898): (312) 422-3000; (800) 424-4301; www.aha.org

Huntington's Disease Society of America (1967): (800) 345-4372; www.hdsa.org

JDRF (fmr. Juvenile Diabetes Research Foundation) (1970): (800) 533-2873; www.jdrf.org

Kidney Foundation, Natl. (1950): (800) 622-9010; www.kidney.org

Kidney Fund, American (1971): (800) 638-8299; www.kidneyfund.org

La Leche League Intl. [breastfeeding] (1956): (800) 525-3243; www.llli.org

Leukemia and Lymphoma Society (1949): (800) 955-4572; www.lls.org

Lighthouse Guild [visual impairments] (1906): (800) 284-4422; www.lighthouseguild.org

Liver Foundation, American (1976): (800) 465-4837; www.liverfoundation.org

Living Bank [organ donation] (1968): (713) 961-9431; (800) 528-2971; www.livingbank.org

Lung Assn., American (1904): (800) 586-4872; www.lung.org

Lung Line (1983): (800) 222-5864

Lupus Foundation of America (1977): (202) 349-1155; www.lupus.org

March of Dimes [babies' health] (1938): (888) 663-4637; www.marchofdimes.org

Marfan Foundation (1981): (800) 8-MARFAN (862-7326); www.marfan.org

Mayo Clinic (1889): (507) 284-2511; www.mayoclinic.org

ME/CFS Initiative, Solve [myalgic encephalomyelitis/chronic fatigue syndrome] (1987): (704) 364-0016; solvecfs.org

Mental Health, Natl. Institute of (1949): (866) 615-6464; www.nimh.nih.gov

Mental Health America (1909): (703) 684-7722; (800) 969-6642; www.mhanational.org

Mental Illness, Natl. Alliance on (1979): (800) 950-6264; www.nami.org

Multiple Sclerosis Society, Natl. (1946): (800) 344-4867; www.nationalmssociety.org

Muscular Dystrophy Assn. (1950): (800) 572-1717; www.mda.org

Myeloma Foundation, Intl. (1990): (800) 452-2873; www.myeloma.org

Narcotics Anonymous (1953): (818) 773-9999; www.na.org

Natl. Health Council (1920): (202) 785-3910; www.nationalhealthcouncil.org

Natl. Institutes of Health (NIH) (1887): (301) 496-4000; www.nih.gov

Neurological Disorders and Stroke, Natl. Institute of (1950): (800) 352-9424; www.ninds.nih.gov

Organ Sharing, United Network for (1984): (804) 782-4800; (800) 292-9548; www.unos.org

Overeaters Anonymous (1960): (505) 891-2664; www.oa.org

Parkinson's Foundation (1957): (800) 473-4636; www.parkinson.org

Pediatrics, American Academy of (1930): (800) 433-9016; www.aap.org

Phoenix House [substance abuse] (1967): (888) 671-9392; www.phoenixhouse.org

Planned Parenthood Federation of America, Inc. (1916): (800) 230-7526; www.plannedparenthood.org

Plastic Surgeons, American Society of (1931): (847) 228-9900; www.plasticsurgery.org

Poison Control (1980): (800) 222-1222; www.poison.org

Post-Polio Health Intl. (1960): (314) 534-0475; post-polio.org

Psoriasis Foundation, Natl. (1967): (503) 244-7404; (800) 723-9166; www.psoriasis.org

RAINN (Rape, Abuse, & Incest Natl. Network) (1994): (800) 656-4673; www.rainn.org

Rare Disorders, Natl. Org. for (1983): (617) 249-7300; www.rarediseases.org

Rehabilitation Information Center, Natl. (1977): (800) 346-2742, TTY (301) 459-5984; www.naric.com

Reye's Syndrome Foundation, Natl. (1974): (800) 233-7393; www.reyessyndrome.org

Runaway Safeline, Natl. (1971): (800) 786-2929; www.1800runaway.org

Scleroderma Foundation, Natl. (1998): (978) 463-5843; (800) 722-4673; www.scleroderma.org

Sexual Health Assn., American (1914): (919) 361-8400; www.ashasexualhealth.org

Sickle Cell Disease Assn. of America (1971): (410) 528-1555; (800) 421-8453; www.sicklecelldisease.org

Sjögren's Foundation (1983): (301) 530-4420; www.sjogrens.org

Speech-Language-Hearing Assn., American (1925): (800) 638-8255; TTY (301) 296-5650; www.asha.org

Spinal Assn., United (1946): (718) 803-3782; www.unitedspinal.org

Stroke Assn., American (1998): (888) 478-7653; www.stroke.org

Stuttering Assn., Natl. (1977): (800) 937-8888; www.westutter.org

Stuttering Foundation of America (1947): (800) 992-9392; www.stutteringhelp.org

Substance Abuse and Mental Health Services Admin.: (877) 726-4727; www.samhsa.gov

Sudden Infant Death Syndrome Institute, Amer. (1983): (239) 431-5425; www.sids.org

988 Suicide and Crisis Lifeline (fmr. Natl. Suicide Prevention Lifeline) (2004-2005): 988; (800) 273-TALK (8255); 988lifeline.org

Therapy Dogs Intl. (1976): (973) 252-9800; www.tdi-dog.org

Tourette Assn. of America (fmr. Tourette Syndrome Assn.) (1972): (888) 486-8738; www.tourette.org

TSC (Tuberous Sclerosis Complex) Alliance (1974): (301) 562-9890; (800) 225-6872; www.tsalliance.org

Urological Assn., American (1902): (866) 746-4282; www.auanet.org

Women's Health Network, Natl. (1975): (202) 682-2640; www.nwhn.org

UNITED STATES FACTS

Superlative U.S. Statistics

Source: U.S. Geological Survey, U.S. Dept. of the Interior; U.S. Census Bureau, U.S. Dept. of Commerce; World Almanac research

Superlative Statistics for the 50 States

Total area for 50 states and Washington, DC		3,796,742 sq mi
Land area for 50 states and Washington, DC		3,531,905 sq mi
Water area for 50 states and Washington, DC		264,837 sq mi
Largest state	Alaska	665,384 sq mi
Smallest state	Rhode Island	1,545 sq mi
Largest county (excluding Alaska)	San Bernardino County, CA	20,105 sq mi
Smallest county	Arlington County, VA[1]	26 sq mi
Largest incorporated city (by area, pop. 1,000+)	Sitka, AK	4,815 sq mi
Northernmost city	Utqiagvik (formerly Barrow), AK	71°15′ N
Northernmost point	Point Barrow, AK	71°23′ N
Southernmost city	Honolulu, HI	21°19′ N[2]
Southernmost settlement	Discovery Harbour, HI	19°02′ N
Southernmost point	Ka Lae (South Point), island of Hawaii	18°55′ N (155°41′ W)
Easternmost city	Eastport, ME	67°01′ W
Easternmost incorporated place	Lubec, ME	66°59′ W
Easternmost point[3]	Pochnoi Point, Semisopochnoi Island, AK	179°46′ E
Westernmost city	Adak (formerly Adak Station), AK	176°36′ W
Westernmost incorporated place	Adak (formerly Adak Station), AK	176°36′ W
Westernmost point	Amatignak Island, AK	179°07′ W
Highest incorporated city	Leadville, CO	10,158 ft
Lowest settlement	Bombay Beach, CA	−208 ft
Highest point on Atlantic coast	Cadillac Mountain, Mount Desert Island, ME	1,530 ft
Oldest national park	Yellowstone National Park (1872), WY-MT-ID	2,219,791 acres
Largest national park	Wrangell-St. Elias, AK	8,323,146 acres
Longest river system	Mississippi-Missouri-Red Rock	3,710 mi
Highest mountain	Denali (formerly Mt. McKinley), AK	20,310 ft
Lowest point	Death Valley, CA	−282 ft
Deepest lake	Crater Lake, OR	1,949 ft
Rainiest spot	Mount Waialeale, Kauai, HI	annual avg. rainfall 460 in. (30-yr period)
Largest gorge	Grand Canyon, Colorado River, AZ	277 mi long, 600 ft to 18 mi wide, 1 mi deep
Deepest gorge	Hells Canyon, Snake River, OR-ID	7,913 ft
Largest dam	New Cornelia Tailings, Ten Mile Wash, AZ[4]	7.4 bil cu ft material used
Tallest building	One World Trade Center, New York, NY	1,782 ft
Largest building	Boeing Everett Production Facility, Everett, WA	472,000,000 cu ft; covers 98.3 acres
Largest office building	Pentagon, Arlington, VA	77,015,000 cu ft; covers 29 acres
Tallest supported structure	KVLY-TV Tower, Blanchard, ND	2,063 ft
Tallest freestanding tower	Stratosphere Tower, Las Vegas, NV	1,149 ft
Longest bridge span	Verrazzano-Narrows Bridge, New York, NY	4,260 ft
Highest bridge	Royal Gorge Bridge, Cañon City, CO	bridge deck 955 ft above water
Deepest well (onshore)	Bertha Rogers No. 1 (inactive gas well), Washita County, OK	31,441 ft

Superlative Statistics for the 48 Contiguous States

Total area for 48 states and Washington, DC		3,120,426 sq mi
Land area for 48 states and Washington, DC		2,954,841 sq mi
Water area for 48 states and Washington, DC		165,585 sq mi
Largest state	Texas	268,596 sq mi
Northernmost incorporated place	Sumas, WA	49°00′ N
Northernmost settlement	Angle Inlet, MN	49°21′ N
Northernmost point	Northwest Angle, MN	49°21′ N
Southernmost city	Key West, FL	24°34′ N
Southernmost mainland city	Florida City, FL	25°27′ N
Southernmost point	Ballast Key, FL	24°31′ N
Easternmost point[5]	West Quoddy Head, Lubec, ME	66°57′ W
Westernmost city	Port Orford, OR	124°30′ W
Westernmost point	Bodelteh Islands, WA	124°45′ W
Highest mountain	Mount Whitney, CA	14,505 ft

(1) Smallest total area. Smallest county by land area is Kalawao County, Hawaii, at 12 sq mi; its total area (including water) is 53 sq mi. (2) Latitude is for Urban Honolulu census designated place. (3) As measured if the prime meridian and 180° longitude are considered east-west boundaries. (4) Privately owned industrial dam composed of tailings, remnants of a mining process. (5) Some sources give Sail Rock (66°56′50″), off West Quoddy Head (66°57′01″), as the easternmost point.

Highest and Lowest Elevations in U.S. States and Territories

Source: U.S. Geological Survey, U.S. Dept. of the Interior
(negative sign indicates below sea level)

State/territory	Highest point Name	County	Elev. (ft)	Lowest point Name	County	Elev. (ft)
Alabama	Cheaha Mountain	Cleburne	2,413	Gulf of Mexico		Sea level
Alaska	Denali (fmr. Mt. McKinley)	Denali	20,310	Pacific Ocean		Sea level
American Samoa	Lata Mountain	Tau Island	3,160	Pacific Ocean		Sea level
Arizona	Humphreys Peak	Coconino	12,637	Colorado R.	Yuma	70
Arkansas	Magazine Mountain	Logan	2,753	Ouachita R.	Ashley-Union	55
California	Mount Whitney	Inyo-Tulare	14,505	Death Valley	Inyo	−282
Colorado	Mount Elbert	Lake	14,440	Arikaree R.	Yuma	3,315
Connecticut	S. slope of Mt. Frissell (peak in MA)	Litchfield	2,380	Long Island Sound		Sea level
Delaware	Nr. Ebright Azimuth	New Castle	450	Atlantic Ocean		Sea level
Dist. of Columbia	Fort Reno Park	NW quadrant	409	Potomac R.		1
Florida	Britton Hill	Walton	345	Atlantic Ocean		Sea level
Georgia	Brasstown Bald	Towns-Union	4,840	Atlantic Ocean		Sea level
Guam	Mount Lamlam	Agat District	1,332	Pacific Ocean		Sea level
Hawaii	Pu'u Wekiu, Mauna Kea	Hawaii	13,796	Pacific Ocean		Sea level
Idaho	Borah Peak	Custer	12,668	Snake R.	Nez Perce	710
Illinois	Charles Mound	Jo Daviess	1,235	Mississippi R.	Alexander	279
Indiana	Hoosier Hill	Wayne	1,257	Ohio R.	Posey	320
Iowa	Hawkeye Point	Osceola	1,670	Mississippi R.	Lee	480
Kansas	Mount Sunflower	Wallace	4,039	Verdigris R.	Montgomery	679
Kentucky	Black Mountain	Harlan	4,139	Mississippi R.	Fulton	257
Louisiana	Driskill Mountain	Bienville	535	New Orleans	Orleans	−8
Maine	Mount Katahdin	Piscataquis	5,269	Atlantic Ocean		Sea level
Maryland	Hoye Crest	Garrett	3,360	Bloody Point Hole, Chesapeake Bay	Queen Anne	−174
Massachusetts	Mount Greylock	Berkshire	3,491	Atlantic Ocean		Sea level
Michigan	Mount Arvon	Baraga	1,979	Lake Erie		571
Minnesota	Eagle Mountain	Cook	2,301	Lake Superior		601
Mississippi	Woodall Mountain	Tishomingo	806	Gulf of Mexico		Sea level
Missouri	Taum Sauk Mountain	Iron	1,772	St. Francis R.	Dunklin	230
Montana	Granite Peak	Park	12,807	Kootenai R.	Lincoln	1,800
Nebraska	Panorama Point	Kimball	5,424	Missouri R.	Richardson	840
Nevada	Boundary Peak	Esmeralda	13,146	Colorado R.	Clark	479
New Hampshire	Mount Washington	Coos	6,289	Atlantic Ocean		Sea level
New Jersey	High Point	Sussex	1,803	Atlantic Ocean		Sea level
New Mexico	Wheeler Peak	Taos	13,167	Red Bluff Reservoir	Eddy	2,842
New York	Mount Marcy	Essex	5,343	Atlantic Ocean		Sea level
North Carolina	Mount Mitchell	Yancey	6,683	Atlantic Ocean		Sea level
North Dakota	White Butte	Slope	3,506	Red R. of the North	Pembina	750
Northern Mariana Isls.	Mount Agrihan	Agrihan Island	3,166	Pacific Ocean		Sea level
Ohio	Campbell Hill	Logan	1,550	Ohio R.	Hamilton	455
Oklahoma	Black Mesa	Cimarron	4,973	Little R.	McCurtain	289
Oregon	Mount Hood	Clackamas-Hood R.	11,247	Pacific Ocean		Sea level
Pennsylvania	Mount Davis	Somerset	3,213	Delaware R.	Delaware	Sea level
Puerto Rico	Cerro de Punta	Ponce District	4,390	Atlantic Ocean		Sea level
Rhode Island	Jerimoth Hill	Providence	812	Atlantic Ocean		Sea level
South Carolina	Sassafras Mountain	Pickens	3,560	Atlantic Ocean		Sea level
South Dakota	Harney Peak	Pennington	7,244	Big Stone Lake	Roberts	966
Tennessee	Clingmans Dome	Sevier	6,644	Mississippi R.	Shelby	178
Texas	Guadalupe Peak	Culberson	8,751	Gulf of Mexico		Sea level
Utah	Kings Peak	Duchesne	13,518	Beaver Dam Wash	Washington	2,000
Vermont	Mount Mansfield	Chittenden	4,395	Lake Champlain		95
Virgin Islands	Crown Mountain	St. Thomas Island	1,556	Atlantic Ocean		Sea level
Virginia	Mount Rogers	Grayson-Smyth	5,729	Atlantic Ocean		Sea level
Washington	Mount Rainier	Pierce	14,410	Pacific Ocean		Sea level
West Virginia	Spruce Knob	Pendleton	4,863	Potomac R.	Jefferson	240
Wisconsin	Timms Hill	Price	1,951	Lake Michigan		579
Wyoming	Gannett Peak	Fremont	13,810	Belle Fourche R.	Crook	3,099

U.S. Coastline by State

Source: National Oceanic and Atmospheric Administration (NOAA), U.S. Dept. of Commerce
(in statute miles; only states with coastline or shoreline are shown)

	Coastline[1]	Shoreline[2]		Coastline[1]	Shoreline[2]
Atlantic Coast	2,069	28,673	**Gulf Coast**	1,631	17,141
Connecticut	0	618	Alabama	53	607
Delaware	28	381	Florida	770	5,095
Florida	580	3,331	Louisiana	397	7,721
Georgia	100	2,344	Mississippi	44	359
Maine	228	3,478	Texas	367	3,359
Maryland	31	3,190			
Massachusetts	192	1,519	**Pacific Coast**	7,623	40,298
New Hampshire	13	131	Alaska	5,580	31,383
New Jersey	130	1,792	California	840	3,427
New York	127	1,850	Hawaii	750	1,052
North Carolina	301	3,375	Oregon	296	1,410
Pennsylvania	0	89	Washington	157	3,026
Rhode Island	40	384			
South Carolina	187	2,876	**Arctic Coast**	1,060	2,521
Virginia	112	3,315	**United States**	12,383	88,633[3]

(1) Length of general outline of seacoast. Measurements were made in 1948 with a unit measure of 30 minutes of latitude on charts as near the scale of 1:1,200,000 as possible. Includes coastlines of large sounds and bays. (2) Shoreline of outer coast, offshore islands, sounds, bays, rivers, and creeks to the head of tidewater or to a point where tidal waters narrow to a width of 100 ft. Figures obtained in 1939-40 with a recording instrument on the largest-scale charts and maps then available. (3) Total length of U.S. tidal shoreline is 95,471 statute miles, which incl. measurements of outlying U.S. territories and possessions.

States: Capitals, Key Dates, Geographic Data

Source: *Statistical Abstract of the United States*, U.S. Census Bureau, U.S. Dept. of Commerce

The 13 colonies that declared independence from Great Britain and fought the War of Independence (American Revolution) became the 13 original states. They were, in the order in which they ratified the Constitution: Delaware, Pennsylvania, New Jersey, Georgia, Connecticut, Massachusetts, Maryland, South Carolina, New Hampshire, Virginia, New York, North Carolina, and Rhode Island.

State	Settled[1]	Capital	Entered Union Date	Entered Union Order	Length (approx. mean)	Width (approx. mean)	Land	Water	Total	Rank by tot. area
AL	1702	Montgomery	Dec. 14, 1819	22	330	190	50,645	1,775	52,420	30
AK	1784	Juneau	Jan. 3, 1959	49	1,480[2]	810	570,641	94,743	665,384	1
AZ	1776	Phoenix	Feb. 14, 1912	48	400	310	113,594	396	113,990	6
AR	1686	Little Rock	June 15, 1836	25	260	240	52,035	1,143	53,179	29
CA	1769	Sacramento	Sept. 9, 1850	31	770	250	155,779	7,916	163,695	3
CO	1858	Denver	Aug. 1, 1876	38	380	280	103,642	452	104,094	8
CT	1634	Hartford	Jan. 9, 1788	5	110	70	4,842	701	5,543	48
DE	1638	Dover	Dec. 7, 1787	1	96	30	1,949	540	2,489	49
DC	NA	NA	NA	NA	NA	NA	61	7	68	51
FL	1565	Tallahassee	Mar. 3, 1845	27	447	361	53,625	12,133	65,758	22
GA	1733	Atlanta	Jan. 2, 1788	4	300	230	57,513	1,912	59,425	24
HI	1820	Honolulu	Aug. 21, 1959	50	NA	NA	6,423	4,509	10,932	43
ID	1842	Boise	July 3, 1890	43	479	305	82,643	926	83,569	14
IL	1720	Springfield	Dec. 3, 1818	21	390	210	55,519	2,395	57,914	25
IN	1733	Indianapolis	Dec. 11, 1816	19	270	140	35,826	593	36,420	38
IA	1788	Des Moines	Dec. 28, 1846	29	310	200	55,857	416	56,273	26
KS	1727	Topeka	Jan. 29, 1861	34	400	210	81,759	520	82,278	15
KY	1774	Frankfort	June 1, 1792	15	380	140	39,486	921	40,408	37
LA	1699	Baton Rouge	Apr. 30, 1812	18	380	130	43,204	9,174	52,378	31
ME	1624	Augusta	Mar. 15, 1820	23	320	190	30,843	4,537	35,380	39
MD	1634	Annapolis	Apr. 28, 1788	7	250	90	9,707	2,699	12,406	42
MA	1620	Boston	Feb. 6, 1788	6	190	50	7,800	2,754	10,554	44
MI	1668	Lansing	Jan. 26, 1837	26	490	240	56,539	40,175	96,714	11
MN	1805	St. Paul	May 11, 1858	32	400	250	79,627	7,309	86,936	12
MS	1699	Jackson	Dec. 10, 1817	20	340	170	46,923	1,509	48,432	32
MO	1735	Jefferson City	Aug. 10, 1821	24	300	240	68,742	965	69,707	21
MT	1809	Helena	Nov. 8, 1889	41	630	280	145,546	1,494	147,040	4
NE	1823	Lincoln	Mar. 1, 1867	37	430	210	76,824	524	77,348	16
NV	1849	Carson City	Oct. 31, 1864	36	490	320	109,781	791	110,572	7
NH	1623	Concord	June 21, 1788	9	190	70	8,953	397	9,349	46
NJ	1660	Trenton	Dec. 18, 1787	3	150	70	7,354	1,368	8,723	47
NM	1610	Santa Fe	Jan. 6, 1912	47	370	343	121,298	292	121,590	5
NY	1614	Albany	July 26, 1788	11	330	283	47,126	7,429	54,555	27
NC	1660	Raleigh	Nov. 21, 1789	12	500	150	48,618	5,201	53,819	28
ND	1812	Bismarck	Nov. 2, 1889	39	340	211	69,001	1,698	70,698	19
OH	1788	Columbus	Mar. 1, 1803	17	220	220	40,861	3,965	44,826	34
OK	1889	Oklahoma City	Nov. 16, 1907	46	400	220	68,595	1,304	69,899	20
OR	1811	Salem	Feb. 14, 1859	33	360	261	95,988	2,391	98,379	9
PA	1682	Harrisburg	Dec. 12, 1787	2	283	160	44,743	1,312	46,054	33
RI	1636	Providence	May 29, 1790	13	40	30	1,034	511	1,545	50
SC	1670	Columbia	May 23, 1788	8	260	200	30,061	1,960	32,020	40
SD	1859	Pierre	Nov. 2, 1889	40	370	210	75,811	1,305	77,116	17
TN	1769	Nashville	June 1, 1796	16	491	115	41,235	909	42,144	36
TX	1682	Austin	Dec. 29, 1845	28	790	660	261,232	7,365	268,596	2
UT	1847	Salt Lake City	Jan. 4, 1896	45	350	270	82,170	2,727	84,897	13
VT	1724	Montpelier	Mar. 4, 1791	14	160	80	9,217	400	9,616	45
VA	1607	Richmond	June 25, 1788	10	430	200	39,490	3,285	42,775	35
WA	1811	Olympia	Nov. 11, 1889	42	360	240	66,456	4,842	71,298	18
WV	1727	Charleston	June 20, 1863	35	240	130	24,038	192	24,230	41
WI	1766	Madison	May 29, 1848	30	310	260	54,158	11,339	65,496	23
WY	1834	Cheyenne	July 10, 1890	44	360	280	97,093	720	97,813	10

NA = Not applicable. **Note:** Land and water areas, which are as of Jan. 1, 2010, may not add up to totals because of rounding. (1) First permanent settlement by Europeans. (2) Does not include Aleutian Islands or Alexander Archipelago.

Continental Divide of the U.S.

The Continental Divide of the U.S., also known as the Great Divide, is located at the watershed created by the mountain ranges, or tablelands, of the Rocky Mountains. This watershed separates the waters that ultimately drain into the Atlantic Ocean and its marginal seas from those waters that drain into the Pacific Ocean. The majority of water flowing E in the U.S. drains into the Gulf of Mexico and then the Atlantic. The majority of water flowing W drains through the Columbia River or Colorado River, which flows into the Gulf of California before reaching the Pacific.

The location and route of the Continental Divide across the U.S. can be described as follows:

Beginning at the U.S.-Mexico border, near longitude 108°45′ W, the Divide, in a northerly direction, crosses New Mexico along the western edge of the Rio Grande drainage basin, entering Colorado near longitude 106°41′ W. From there by an irregular route N across Colorado along the western summits of the Rio Grande and Arkansas, South Platte, and North Platte river basins, and across Rocky Mountain National Park, entering Wyoming near longitude 106°52′ W.

From there in a northwesterly direction, forming the western rims of the North Platte, Big Horn, and Yellowstone river basins, crossing the SW portion of Yellowstone National Park. From there in a westerly and then northerly direction forming the boundary between Idaho and Montana, to a point on the boundary near longitude 114°00′ W. From there northeasterly and northwesterly through Montana and Glacier National Park, entering Canada near longitude 114°04′ W.

Depending on how a "divide" is defined, the U.S. can also be characterized as having a Northern (or Laurentian) Divide, Eastern Divide, and St. Lawrence Seaway Divide. Some of the waters at the Northern Divide drain into Hudson Bay and the Arctic Ocean. The Appalachian Mountains mark the Eastern Divide, with waters joining the Atlantic or Gulf of Mexico. The waters at the St. Lawrence Seaway Divide, near Chicago, flow into the Gulf of St. Lawrence or Gulf of Mexico.

Chronological List of Territories, With State Admissions to Union

Source: U.S. National Archives and Records Administration

Territory	Date of act creating territory	When act took effect	Date of admission as state	Years as terr.
Northwest Territory[1]	July 13, 1787	No fixed date	Mar. 1, 1803[2]	16
Territory South of Ohio River (Southwest Territory)	May 26, 1790	No fixed date	June 1, 1796[3]	6
Mississippi	Apr. 7, 1798	When president acted	Dec. 10, 1817	19
Indiana	May 7, 1800	July 4, 1800	Dec. 11, 1816	16
Orleans	Mar. 26, 1804	Oct. 1, 1804	Apr. 30, 1812[4]	7
Michigan	Jan. 11, 1805	June 30, 1805	Jan. 26, 1837	31
Louisiana-Missouri[5]	Mar. 3, 1805	July 4, 1805	Aug. 10, 1821	16
Illinois	Feb. 3, 1809	Mar. 1, 1809	Dec. 3, 1818	9
Alabama	Mar. 3, 1817	When MS formed state govt.	Dec. 14, 1819	2
Arkansas	Mar. 2, 1819	July 4, 1819	June 15, 1836	17
Florida	Mar. 30, 1822	No fixed date	Mar. 3, 1845	23
Wisconsin	Apr. 20, 1836	July 3, 1836	May 29, 1848	12
Iowa	June 12, 1838	July 3, 1838	Dec. 28, 1846	8
Oregon	Aug. 14, 1848	Date of act	Feb. 14, 1859	10
Minnesota	Mar. 3, 1849	Date of act	May 11, 1858	9
New Mexico	Sept. 9, 1850	On president's proclamation	Jan. 6, 1912	61
Utah	Sept. 9, 1850	Date of act	Jan. 4, 1896	46
Washington	Mar. 2, 1853	Date of act	Nov. 11, 1889	36
Kansas	May 30, 1854	Date of act	Jan. 29, 1861	6
Nebraska	May 30, 1854	Date of act	Mar. 1, 1867	12
Colorado	Feb. 28, 1861	Date of act	Aug. 1, 1876	15
Dakota	Mar. 2, 1861	Date of act	Nov. 2, 1889	28
Nevada	Mar. 2, 1861	Date of act	Oct. 31, 1864	3
Arizona	Feb. 24, 1863	Date of act	Feb. 14, 1912	49
Idaho	Mar. 3, 1863	Date of act	July 3, 1890	27
Montana	May 26, 1864	Date of act	Nov. 8, 1889	25
Wyoming	July 25, 1868	When officers were qualified	July 10, 1890	22
Alaska	May 17, 1884[6]	No fixed date	Jan. 3, 1959	75
Oklahoma	May 2, 1890	Date of act	Nov. 16, 1907	17
Hawaii	Apr. 30, 1900	June 14, 1900	Aug. 21, 1959	59

Note: California was never organized as a territory. It was administered by the military after its acquisition from Mexico (1848) until its admission as a state (1850). (1) Included what is now Ohio, Indiana, Illinois, Michigan, Wisconsin, and E Minnesota. (2) Date of admission for Ohio, the first state created out of territory, based on the date its General Assembly first met. Congress approved Ohio's entry into the Union on Feb. 19, 1803. (3) Admitted as the state of Tennessee. (4) Admitted as the state of Louisiana. (5) The act renaming Louisiana Territory as Missouri Territory (June 4, 1812) became effective Dec. 7, 1812. (6) Act constituted Alaska as a district, though it was often referred to and administered as a territory. The Territory of Alaska was formally organized by an act of Aug. 24, 1912.

U.S. Geographic Centers

Source: U.S. Geological Survey, U.S. Dept. of the Interior

There is no generally accepted definition of a geographic center and no uniform method for determining it. Geographic center is defined here as the center of gravity of the surface of an area, or that point on which an area would balance if it were a plane of uniform thickness.

No government agency has officially established any points marking the geographic center of the U.S., the conterminous U.S. (48 states), or the North American continent. In 1941, private citizens erected a monument in Lebanon, KS, marking it as the geographic center of the then U.S. (conterminous). Residents of Rugby, ND, installed a cairn after the U.S. Geologic Survey, in 1931, determined it to be the center of the North American continent. In 2017, a Univ. at Buffalo geography professor announced that Center, ND, was the continental center according to a mathematical method he developed. The geographic centers in the following list are approximate. They are indicated by county then city unless otherwise noted.

U.S. (50 states): W of Castle Rock, Butte County, South Dakota; 44°58′ N, 103°46′ W
Conterminous U.S. (48 states): nr. Lebanon, Smith County, Kansas; 39°50′ N, 98°35′ W
North American continent: 6 mi W of Balta, Pierce County, North Dakota; 48°10′ N, 100°10′ W
Alabama: Chilton, 12 mi SW of Clanton
Alaska: 63°50′ N, 152° W, approx. 60 mi NW of Denali
Arizona: Yavapai, 55 mi E-SE of Prescott
Arkansas: Pulaski, 12 mi NW of Little Rock
California: Madera, 38 mi E of Madera
Colorado: Park, 30 mi NW of Pikes Peak
Connecticut: Hartford, at East Berlin
Delaware: Kent, 11 mi S of Dover
District of Columbia: near 4th and L Sts. NW
Florida: Hernando, 12 mi N-NW of Brooksville
Georgia: Twiggs, 18 mi SE of Macon
Hawaii: Hawaii; 20°15′ N, 156°20′ W, off Maui Island
Idaho: Custer, SW of Challis
Illinois: Logan, 28 mi NE of Springfield
Indiana: Boone, 14 mi N-NW of Indianapolis
Iowa: Story, 5 mi NE of Ames
Kansas: Barton, 15 mi NE of Great Bend
Kentucky: Marion, 3 mi N-NW of Lebanon
Louisiana: Avoyelles, 3 mi SE of Marksville
Maine: Piscataquis, 18 mi N of Dover
Maryland: Prince George's, 4.5 mi NW of Davidsonville
Massachusetts: Worcester, N part of city of Worcester
Michigan: Wexford, 5 mi N-NW of Cadillac
Minnesota: Crow Wing, 10 mi SW of Brainerd
Mississippi: Leake, 9 mi W-NW of Carthage
Missouri: Miller, 20 mi SW of Jefferson City
Montana: Fergus, 11 mi W of Lewistown
Nebraska: Custer, 10 mi NW of Broken Bow
Nevada: Lander, 26 mi SE of Austin
New Hampshire: Belknap, 3 mi E of Ashland
New Jersey: Mercer, 5 mi SE of Trenton
New Mexico: Torrance, 12 mi S-SW of Willard
New York: Madison, 12 mi S of Oneida and 26 mi SW of Utica
North Carolina: Chatham, 10 mi NW of Sanford
North Dakota: Sheridan, 5 mi SW of McClusky
Ohio: Delaware, 25 mi N-NE of Columbus
Oklahoma: Oklahoma, 8 mi N of Oklahoma City
Oregon: Crook, 25 mi S-SE of Prineville
Pennsylvania: Centre, 2.5 mi SW of Bellefonte
Rhode Island: Kent, 1 mi S-SW of Crompton
South Carolina: Richland, 13 mi SE of Columbia
South Dakota: Hughes, 8 mi NE of Pierre
Tennessee: Rutherford, 5 mi NE of Murfreesboro
Texas: McCulloch, Brady, 4 mi E of Brady
Utah: Sanpete, 3 mi N of Manti
Vermont: Washington, 3 mi E of Roxbury
Virginia: Buckingham, 5 mi SW of Buckingham
Washington: Chelan, 10 mi W-SW of Wenatchee
West Virginia: Braxton, 4 mi E of Sutton
Wisconsin: Wood, 9 mi SE of Marshfield
Wyoming: Fremont, 58 mi E-NE of Lander

Lengths of U.S. Boundaries

The length of the boundary between the U.S. and Canada is 5,525 mi—3,987 mi between the conterminous U.S. and Canada and 1,538 mi between Alaska and Canada. A 1925 treaty established a permanent International Boundary Commission to maintain the boundary. The U.S.-Mexican border was established by multiple treaties (1848, 1853, 1970) at 1,954-miles long. (The U.S. Census Bureau has put the border at 1,933-miles long.) It largely follows the Rio Grande and Colorado River, from the Gulf of Mexico to the Pacific Ocean. It is overseen by the International Boundary and Water Commission.

Origins of the Names of U.S. States and Territories

Source: State officials; Smithsonian Institution; Topographic Division, U.S. Geological Survey, U.S. Dept. of the Interior

Alabama: Choctaw word for a Chickasaw tribe. First noted in accounts of Hernando de Soto expedition.

Alaska: Russian version of Aleut word *alakshak* for "peninsula," "great lands," or "land that is not an island."

American Samoa: Etymology varies.

Arizona: Spanish version of Pima Indian word for "little spring place" or Aztec *arizuma*, meaning "silver-bearing."

Arkansas: Algonquin name for Quapaw Indians, meaning "south wind."

California: Bestowed by Spanish conquistadors (possibly Hernán Cortés). It was the name of an imaginary island in the 1510 Spanish novel *Las Sergas de Esplandián* (The Exploits of Esplandián), by Garci Rodríguez de Montalvo. The Spanish first visited *Baja* (Lower) *California* in 1533. The present-day U.S. state was called *Alta* (Upper) *California*.

Colorado: From Spanish for "red," first applied to Colorado River.

Connecticut: From Algonquin *quinnehtukqut*, meaning "long river place."

Delaware: Named for Lord De La Warr, early governor of Virginia; first applied to river, then to Indian tribe (Lenni-Lenape).

District of Columbia: For Christopher Columbus, 1791.

Florida: Named by Juan Ponce de León *Pascua Florida*, "Flowery Easter," on Easter Sunday, 1513.

Georgia: Named by colonial administrator James Oglethorpe for King George II of England in 1732.

Guam: From Chamorro name, *Guahan*, meaning "we have."

Hawaii: Possibly derived from *Hawaiki* or *Owhyhee*, Polynesian word for "homeland."

Idaho: George Willing claimed to have coined the name, with the invented meaning "gem of the mountains." He first suggested it for the Pikes Peak mining territory (Colorado) before the name was adopted for the new mining territory of the Pacific Northwest.

Illinois: French for *Illini* or "land of *Illini*," Algonquin word meaning "men" or "warriors."

Indiana: Means "land of the Indians."

Iowa: Indian word variously translated as "here I rest" or "beautiful land." Named for the Iowa River, which was named for the Iowa Indians.

Kansas: Sioux word for "south wind people."

Kentucky: Indian word variously translated as "dark and bloody ground," "meadowland," and "land of tomorrow."

Louisiana: Part of territory called Louisiana by René-Robert Cavelier Sieur de La Salle for French King Louis XIV.

Maine: From Maine, historic French province. Also descriptive, referring to the mainland as distinct from coastal islands.

Maryland: For Queen Henrietta Maria, wife of Charles I of England.

Massachusetts: From Indian tribe whose name meant "at or about the Great Hill" in Blue Hills region south of Boston.

Michigan: From Chippewa *mici gama*, meaning "great water," after lake of the same name.

Minnesota: From Dakota Sioux word meaning "cloudy water" or "sky-tinted water" of the Minnesota River.

Mississippi: Probably Chippewa *mici zibi*, meaning "great river" or "gathering-in of all the waters." Also Algonquin word *messipi*.

Missouri: Algonquin Indian term meaning "river of the big canoes."

Montana: Latin or Spanish for "mountainous."

Nebraska: From Omaha or Otos Indian word meaning "broad water" or "flat river," describing the Platte River.

Nevada: Spanish, meaning "snow-clad."

New Hampshire: Named by Capt. John Mason of Plymouth Council, in 1629, for his home county in England.

New Jersey: The Duke of York, in 1664, gave a patent to Lord John Berkeley and Sir George Carteret for *Nova Caesaria*, or New Jersey, after England's Isle of Jersey.

New Mexico: Spaniards in Mexico applied term to land north and west of Rio Grande in the 16th century.

New York: For James, Duke of York and Albany, who received patent for New Netherland from his brother Charles II and sent an expedition to capture it, 1664.

North Carolina: In 1619, Charles I gave patent to Sir Robert Heath for Province of Carolana, from *Carolus*, Latin name for Charles. Charles II granted a new patent to Earl of Clarendon and others. Divided into North and South Carolina, 1710.

North Dakota: Sioux word *Dakota*, meaning "friend" or "ally."

Northern Mariana Isls.: For Mariana of Austria, queen regent of Spain.

Ohio: Iroquois word for "fine or good river."

Oklahoma: Choctaw word meaning "red man," proposed by Rev. Allen Wright, Choctaw-speaking Indian.

Oregon: Origin unknown. One theory is that the name derives from Mohegan *wauregan*, meaning "beautiful," term used by Indians in Connecticut.

Pennsylvania: William Penn, Quaker who was made full proprietor of area by King Charles II in 1681, suggested "Sylvania," or "woodland," for his tract. The king's government owed 16,000 pounds to Penn's fadm. William Penn, and the land was granted as partial settlement. Charles II added "Penn" to "Sylvania," against the modest proprietor's desires, in honor of the admiral.

Puerto Rico: Spanish for "rich port."

Rhode Island: Origin unknown. One theory notes that Giovanni de Verrazzano recorded observing an island about the size of the Greek island of Rhodes in 1524. Another theory is that Dutch explorer Adriaen Block named the state *Roode Eylandt* for its red clay.

South Carolina: See North Carolina.

South Dakota: See North Dakota.

Tennessee: *Tanasi* was the name of Cherokee villages on the Little Tennessee River. From 1784 to 1788, this was the State of Franklin, or Frankland.

Texas: Variant of word used by Caddo and other Indians meaning "friends" or "allies" and applied to them by the Spanish in eastern Texas. Also written *Texias, Tejas, Teysas*.

Utah: From a Navajo word meaning "upper," or "higher up," as applied to Shoshone tribe called Ute. Proposed name *Deseret*, "land of honeybees," from Book of Mormon, was rejected by Congress.

Vermont: From French words *vert* (green) and *mont* (mountain). The Green Mountains were said to have been named by Samuel de Champlain. When the state was formed in 1777, Dr. Thomas Young suggested combining *vert* and *mont*.

Virgin Islands, U.S.: From Spanish name *Las Once Mil Virgenes* (11,000 Virgins), which Christopher Columbus gave to island group.

Virginia: Named by Sir Walter Raleigh, who outfitted an expedition in 1584, in honor of England's Queen Elizabeth, the Virgin Queen.

Washington: Named after George Washington. When the bill creating the Territory of Columbia was introduced in the 32nd Congress, its name was changed to Washington because of the existence of the District of Columbia.

West Virginia: So named when western counties of Virginia refused to secede from the U.S. in 1863.

Wisconsin: Indian name, spelled *Ouisconsin* or *Mesconsing* by early chroniclers, believed to mean "grassy place" in Chippewa. Congress made it *Wisconsin*.

Wyoming: From Algonquin words for "large prairie place," "at the big plains," or "on the great plain."

Territorial Sea of the U.S.

According to a Dec. 27, 1988, proclamation by Pres. Ronald Reagan, "The territorial sea of the United States henceforth extends to 12 nautical miles from the baselines of the United States determined in accordance with international law. In accordance with international law, as reflected in the applicable provisions of the 1982 United Nations Convention on the Law of the Sea, within the territorial sea of the United States, the ships of all countries enjoy the right of innocent passage and the ships and aircraft of all countries enjoy the right of transit passage through international straits."

Major Accessions of Territory by the U.S.

Source: U.S. Dept. of the Interior; U.S. Census Bureau, U.S. Dept. of Commerce

Not including territories such as the Panama Canal Zone and the Philippines, which are no longer under U.S. jurisdiction.

Accession	Date	Area (sq mi)	Accession	Date	Area (sq mi)	Accession	Date	Area (sq mi)
Territory in 1790[1]	NA	888,685	Mexican Cession	1848	529,017	Guam[3]	1899	212
Louisiana Purchase	1803	827,192	Gadsden Purchase	1853	29,640	American Samoa[4]	1900	76
Treaty of Florida	1819	72,003	Alaska	1867	586,412	U.S. Virgin Islands	1917	133
Texas	1845	390,143	Hawaii	1898	6,450	Northern Marianas[5]	1986	179
Oregon Territory	1846	285,680	Puerto Rico[2]	1899	3,435			

NA = Not applicable. (1) Includes that part of a drainage basin of Red River of the North, south of 49th parallel, sometimes considered part of Louisiana Purchase. (2) Ceded by Spain in 1898, ratified in 1899, and became the Commonwealth of Puerto Rico by Act of Congress on July 25, 1952. (3) Acquired in 1898; ratified 1899. (4) Acquired in 1899; ratified 1900. (5) Part of the UN Trust Territory of the Pacific Islands, which U.S. began administering in 1947; became U.S. commonwealth Nov. 3, 1986.

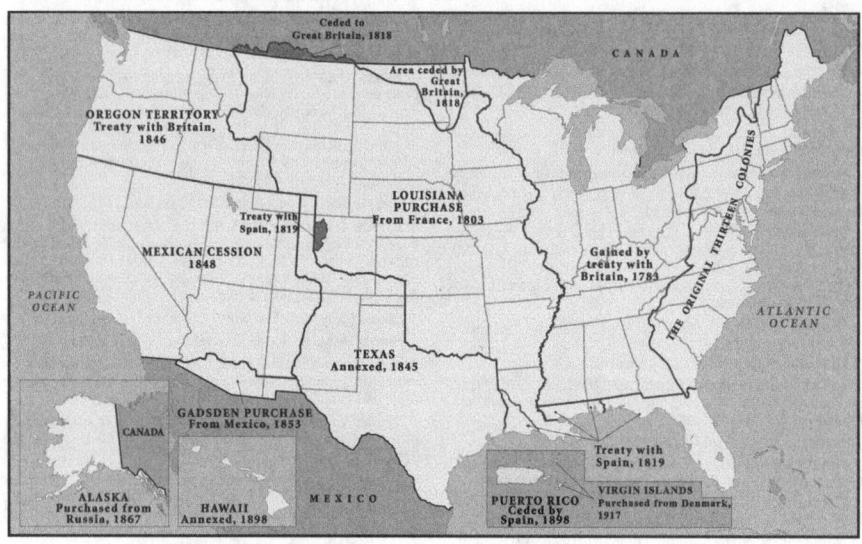

National Park System Recreation Visits, 1904-2022

Source: National Park Service (NPS), U.S. Dept. of the Interior

An NPS-administered site, regardless of its designation (as a park, monument, or preserve, etc.), is generally referred to as a unit. Not all units report public use statistics.

Year	Units reporting visits	Recreation visits	Year	Units reporting visits	Recreation visits	Year	Units reporting visits	Recreation visits
1904	6	120,690	1970	217	168,135,100	2009	360	285,579,941
1905	6	140,954	1975	251	188,085,700	2010	363	281,303,769
1910	9	173,416	1980	275	220,463,211	2011	367	278,939,216
1915	12	314,299	1985	303	263,441,808	2012	367	282,765,682
1920	26	1,022,091	1990	316	255,581,467	2013	370	273,630,895
1925	39	1,900,499	1995	328	269,564,307	2014	370	292,800,082
1930	45	3,038,935	2000	344	285,891,275	2015	372	307,247,252
1935	85	7,435,659	2002	349	277,299,880	2016	376	330,971,689
1940	113	16,410,148	2003	353	266,230,290	2017	379	330,882,751
1945	143	10,855,548	2004	356	276,908,337	2018	379	318,211,833
1950	139	32,706,172	2005	356	273,488,751	2019	379	327,516,619
1955	150	48,891,000	2006	359	272,623,980	2020	383	237,064,332
1960	166	71,586,000	2007	360	275,581,547	2021	388	297,115,406
1965	182	118,662,500	2008	360	274,852,949	2022	389	311,985,998

Most-Visited Sites in the National Park System, 2022

Source: National Park Service (NPS), U.S. Dept. of the Interior

Attendance at 389 of 424 NPS-administered sites totaled 311,985,998 recreation visits in 2022. (Not all units report public use statistics.)

Rank	Site (location)	Rec. visits
1.	Blue Ridge Parkway (NC-VA)	15,711,004
2.	Golden Gate Natl. Recreation Area (CA)	15,638,911
3.	Great Smoky Mountains Natl. Park (NC-TN)	12,937,633
4.	Gateway Natl. Recreation Area (NJ-NY)	8,728,291
5.	Lincoln Memorial (DC)	7,825,397
6.	George Washington Memorial Parkway (DC-MD-VA)	7,397,120
7.	Natchez Trace Parkway (AL-MS-TN)	6,543,533
8.	Gulf Islands Natl. Seashore (FL-MS)	5,685,155
9.	Lake Mead Natl. Recreation Area (AZ-NV)	5,578,226
10.	Vietnam Veterans Memorial (DC)	4,886,254
11.	World War II Memorial (DC)	4,815,309
12.	Grand Canyon Natl. Park (AZ)	4,732,101
13.	Zion Natl. Park (UT)	4,692,417
14.	Delaware Water Gap Natl. Recreation Area (NJ-PA)	4,380,225
15.	Rocky Mountain Natl. Park (CO)	4,300,424
16.	Chesapeake & Ohio Canal Natl. Historical Park (DC-MD-WV)	4,286,185
17.	Korean War Veterans Memorial (DC)	4,010,009
18.	Acadia Natl. Park (ME)	3,970,260
19.	Cape Cod Natl. Seashore (MA)	3,968,672
20.	Yosemite Natl. Park (CA)	3,667,550
21.	Chattahoochee River Natl. Recreation Area (GA)	3,537,848
22.	Castle Clinton Natl. Monument (NY)	3,471,661
23.	Martin Luther King Jr. Memorial (DC)	3,321,897
24.	Franklin Delano Roosevelt Memorial (DC)	3,291,313
25.	Yellowstone Natl. Park (ID-MT-WY)	3,290,242
26.	Statue of Liberty Natl. Monument (NJ-NY)	3,141,213
27.	Joshua Tree Natl. Park (CA)	3,058,294
28.	San Francisco Maritime Natl. Historical Park (CA)	3,034,750
29.	Thomas Jefferson Memorial (DC)	2,975,148
30.	Cuyahoga Valley Natl. Park (OH)	2,913,312
31.	Glacier Natl. Park (MT)	2,908,458
32.	Big Cypress Natl. Preserve (FL)	2,903,159
33.	Cape Hatteras Natl. Seashore (NC)	2,862,844
34.	Glen Canyon Natl. Recreation Area (AZ-UT)	2,842,776
35.	Indiana Dunes Natl. Park (IN)	2,834,180
36.	Grand Teton Natl. Park (WY)	2,806,223
37.	Colonial Natl. Historical Park (VA)	2,762,273
38.	Independence Natl. Historical Park (PA)	2,688,302
39.	Hot Springs Natl. Park (AR)	2,646,133
40.	Mount Rushmore Natl. Memorial (SD)	2,440,449
41.	Olympic Natl. Park (WA)	2,432,972
42.	Bryce Canyon Natl. Park (UT)	2,354,660
43.	Assateague Island Natl. Seashore (MD-VA)	2,340,269
44.	Point Reyes Natl. Seashore (CA)	2,336,202
45.	Boston Natl. Historical Park (MA)	2,123,246
46.	Canaveral Natl. Seashore (FL)	2,122,075
47.	Rock Creek Park (DC)	2,026,156
48.	Valley Forge Natl. Historical Park (PA)	1,645,298
49.	Mount Rainier Natl. Park (WA)	1,622,395
50.	Gateway Arch Natl. Park (MO)	1,618,774

National Parks and Other Areas Administered by National Park Service

As of Dec. 31, 2022, the National Park Service (NPS) administered about 85,135,643 acres of federal and non-federal land across 424 sites. Date when area was authorized or established by Congress or by presidential proclamation is given in parentheses; any date that follows indicates when a site received its current designation or was transferred to the NPS. Figure after the date is gross area acres as of Dec. 31, 2022. Listings do not include parks administered by other agencies, such as the Forest Service or Bureau of Land Management. NA = Not available.

The following units have been authorized but are not yet established: Adams Mem. (DC, authorized 2001), Ronald Reagan Boyhood Home Natl. Historic Site (IL, 2002), Coltsville Natl. Historical Park (CT, 2014), Desert Storm/Desert Shield Mem. (DC, 2014), Global War on Terrorism Mem. (DC, 2017), Amache Natl. Historic Site (CO, 2022), and Blackwell School Natl. Historic Site (TX, 2022).

National Parks

Acadia, ME (1916/1919): 49,071. Incl. Mount Desert Isl., half of Isle au Haut, Schoodic Peninsula on mainland. Highest elevation on Eastern seaboard.

American Samoa, AS (1988): 8,257. Paleotropical rain forest, coral reef.

Arches, UT (1929/1971): 76,679. Contains giant red sandstone arches and other products of erosion.

Badlands, SD (1939/1978): 242,756. Reformations and native prairie; animal fossils 25-37 mil years old.

Big Bend, TX (1935): 801,163. Rio Grande, Chisos Mtns.

Biscayne, FL (1968/1980): 172,971. Aquatic park encompassing chain of islands south of Miami.

Black Canyon of the Gunnison, CO (1933/1999): 30,780. Has canyon 2,900 ft deep and 40 ft wide at narrowest part.

Bryce Canyon, UT (1923/1928): 35,835. Colorful display of erosion effects.

Canyonlands, UT (1964): 337,598. At junction of Colorado and Green Rivers; extensive evidence of prehistoric peoples.

Capitol Reef, UT (1937/1971): 241,905. Nearly 100-mi-long uplift of sandstone cliffs (Waterpocket Fold) dissected by gorges.

Carlsbad Caverns, NM (1923/1930): 46,766. More than 119 limestone caves, incl. Carlsbad Cavern; Chihuahuan Desert.

Channel Islands, CA (1938/1980): 249,561. Sea lion breeding place, nesting seabirds, unique plants.

Congaree, SC (1976/2003): 26,693. Largest intact tract of old-growth bottomland hardwood forest in U.S.

Crater Lake, OR (1902): 183,224. Deepest U.S. lake, in crater of Mt. Mazama, volcano that erupted about 7,700 years ago.

Cuyahoga Valley, OH (1974/2000): 32,572. Along Ohio and Erie Canal system between Akron and Cleveland.

Death Valley, CA-NV (1933/1994): 3,408,396. Large desert. Incl. lowest point in North America and Scotty's Castle (closed until further notice due to flood and fire damage).

Denali, AK (1917/1980): 4,740,911. Highest mountain in U.S.; formerly known as Mt. McKinley.

Dry Tortugas, FL (1935/1992): 64,701. Ft. Jefferson and seven coral reef and sand islands near Key West.

Everglades, FL (1934): 1,508,939. Largest remaining subtropical wilderness in continental U.S; incl. East Everglades Expansion Area acreage added in 1989.

Gates of the Arctic, AK (1978/1980): 7,523,897. Vast wilderness in north central region. Limited federal facilities.

Gateway Arch, St. Louis, MO (1935/2018): 193. Former Jefferson Natl. Expansion Memorial commemorates 19th cent. westward expansion; incl. Gateway Arch (authorized 1954).

Glacier, MT (1910): 1,013,126. Rocky Mt. scenery, numerous glaciers and glacial lakes. Part of Waterton-Glacier Intl. Peace Park established by U.S. and Canada in 1932.

Glacier Bay, AK (1925/1980): 3,223,383. Tidewater glaciers that move down mountainsides and break up into sea.

Grand Canyon, AZ (1919/1919): 1,201,647. Carved by Colorado River.

Grand Teton, WY (1929): 310,044. Incl. highest peaks of Teton Mtns.; summer feeding ground of largest American elk herd.

Great Basin, NV (1922/1986): 77,180. Incl. Wheeler Peak, Lexington Arch, Lehman Caves.

Great Sand Dunes, CO (1932/2004): 107,346. North America's tallest dunes.

Great Smoky Mountains, NC-TN (1926/1934): 522,427. Most biologically diverse NPS unit, with 19,000+ documented species.

Guadalupe Mountains, TX (1966): 86,367. Extensive Permian limestone fossil reef; tremendous earth fault.

Haleakalā, HI (1916/1960): 33,481. Dormant volcano on island of Maui with large craters.

Hawai'i Volcanoes, HI (1916/1961): 344,812. Contains Kilauea and Mauna Loa, active volcanoes.

Hot Springs, AR (1832/1921): 5,554. Waters from park's 47 hot springs used for bathing and drinking.

Indiana Dunes, IN (1966/2019): 15,349. Stretches 15 mi along Lake Michigan.

Isle Royale, MI (1931): 571,790. Largest island in Lake Superior.

Joshua Tree, CA (1936/1994): 795,156. Desert region incl. Joshua trees, other plant and animal life.

Katmai, AK (1918/1980): 3,674,529. "Valley of Ten Thousand Smokes," scene of 1912 volcanic eruption.

Kenai Fjords, AK (1978/1980): 669,650. Marine mammals, birdlife; over 30 glaciers flow from Harding Icefield.

Kings Canyon, CA (1890/1940): 461,901. Mountain wilderness, dominated by Kings River Canyons and High Sierra; giant sequoias.

Kobuk Valley, AK (1978/1980): 1,750,716. Geological and recreational sites. Limited federal facilities.

Lake Clark, AK (1978/1980): 2,619,816. Across Cook Inlet from Anchorage; scenic wilderness, fish and wildlife. Limited federal facilities.

Lassen Volcanic, CA (1907/1916): 106,589. Contains Lassen Peak, recently active volcano; other volcanic phenomena.

Mammoth Cave, KY (1926/1941): 54,016. Longest known cave system in world (more than 426 mi currently surveyed); river 300 ft below surface.

Mesa Verde, CO (1906): 52,485. Most notable and best preserved prehistoric cliff dwellings in U.S.

Mount Rainier, WA (1899): 236,382. Most glaciated peak in contiguous U.S.

New River Gorge (and Preserve), WV (1978/2020): 72,391. Appalachian Mountain forests along 53 mi of the New River.

North Cascades, WA (1968): 504,781. Mountainous region with many glaciers, lakes.

Olympic, WA (1909/1938): 922,649. Wilderness containing glacier-capped mountains, remnant of temperate rain forest, shoreline, endemic animal species.

Petrified Forest, AZ (1906/1962): 221,390. Extensive petrified wood and Indian artifacts. Contains part of Painted Desert.

Pinnacles, CA (1908/2013): 26,686. A release site for captive-bred California condors; talus caves.

Redwood, CA (1968): 138,999. 40 mi of Pacific coastline, groves of ancient redwoods, the world's tallest trees.

Rocky Mountain, CO (1915): 265,848. On Continental Divide; incl. peaks over 14,000 ft.

Saguaro, AZ (1933/1994): 92,877. Part of Sonoran Desert; incl. giant saguaro cacti, unique to region.

Sequoia, CA (1890): 404,063. Giant sequoia groves; world's largest tree (by volume). Mt. Whitney, highest mountain in conterminous U.S.

Shenandoah, VA (1926): 200,446. Portion of Blue Ridge Mtns. Overlooks Shenandoah Valley; Skyline Drive.

Theodore Roosevelt, ND (1947/1978): 70,447. Contains part of Roosevelt's ranch and scenic badlands.

Virgin Islands, VI (1956): 15,052. Covers more than half of St. John Isl. and nearly all of Hassel Isl.; beaches, Carib Indian petroglyphs, evidence of colonial Danes.

Voyageurs, MN (1971): 218,222. Abundant lakes, forests, wildlife.

White Sands, NM (1933/2019): 146,344. World's largest gypsum dunefield.

Wind Cave, SD (1903): 33,971. Limestone caverns in Black Hills; extensive wildlife incl. bison herd.

Wrangell-St. Elias, AK (1978/1980): 8,323,146. Largest area in park system; most peaks over 16,000 ft.

Yellowstone, ID-MT-WY (1872): 2,219,791. World's first national park. More than 10,000 thermal features (geysers, hot springs); Yellowstone River falls and canyons; largest bison herd on U.S. public land.

Yosemite, CA (1890): 761,748. Yosemite Valley, country's highest waterfall, grove of sequoias, mountains.

Zion, UT (1909/1919): 147,243. Unusual shapes, landscapes resulting from erosion, faulting; evidence of past volcanic activity.

National Historical Parks

Abraham Lincoln Birthplace, Hodgenville, KY (1916/2009): 345. Memorial building, sinking spring.

Adams, Quincy, MA (1946/1998): 24. Home of Pres. John Adams, John Quincy Adams, and descendants.

Appomattox Court House, VA (1930/1954): 1,775. Where Confederate Gen. Lee surrendered to Gen. Grant, signaling Civil War's end.

Blackstone River Valley, MA-RI (2014): 1,489. Preserves the valley's industrial heritage.

Boston, MA (1974): 44. Incl. Faneuil Hall, Old North Church, Bunker Hill, Paul Revere House.

Brown v. Board of Education, KS (1992/2022): 1.85. Commemorates landmark 1954 U.S. Supreme Court decision, which ended legal segregation in schools.

Cane River Creole, LA (1994): 206. Preserves Creole culture as it developed along the Cane River.

Cedar Creek and Belle Grove, VA (2002): 3,705. Civil War battle site and an antebellum plantation in Shenandoah Valley.

Chaco Culture, NM (1907/1980): 33,960. Ruins of pueblos built by prehistoric peoples incl. Pueblo, Hopi, and Navajo.

Chesapeake & Ohio Canal, MD-DC-WV (1938/1971): 19,628. 184.5-mi historic canal; DC to Cumberland, MD.

Colonial, VA (1930/1936): 8,675. Incl. most of Jamestown Isl., site of first successful English colony; Yorktown, site of Cornwallis's surrender to George Washington.

Cumberland Gap, KY-TN-VA (1940): 24,547. Mountain pass of Wilderness Road, which carried first great migration of pioneers into America's interior.

Dayton Aviation Heritage, OH (1992): 111. Commemorates area's involvement in aviation.

First State, DE-PA (2013/2014): 1,409. Locations date from colonial past of DE, first state to ratify Constitution.

Fort Sumter and Fort Moultrie, SC (1948/2019): 233. Charleston Harbor sites, where Confederate forces fired the first shots of the Civil War.

George Rogers Clark, Vincennes, IN (1966): 26. Commemorates American defeat of British in West during Revolution.

Golden Spike, UT (1957/2019): 2,735. Commemorates completion of first transcontinental railroad in 1869.

Harpers Ferry, MD-VA-WV (1944/1963): 3,669. At confluence of Shenandoah and Potomac Rivers, the site of John Brown's 1859 raid on the Army arsenal.

Harriet Tubman, NY (2017): 32. Buildings incl. her home, a church, Tubman Home for the Aged.

Harriet Tubman Underground Railroad, MD (2013/2014): 480. Protects landscapes on the Eastern Shore, where Tubman was born and guided other slaves to freedom.

Homestead, NE (1936/2021): 210. Commemorates Homestead Act of 1862, which spurred U.S. westward expansion.

Hopewell Culture, OH (1923/1992): 1,776. Remains of ceremonial mounds built in the Ohio River Valley, 200 BCE-500 CE.

Independence, Philadelphia, PA (1948): 45. Several properties associated with American Revolution and founding of U.S., incl. Independence Hall, Liberty Bell Center.

Jean Lafitte (and Preserve), LA (1907/1978): 25,876. Incl. Chalmette, site of 1815 Battle of New Orleans; French Quarter.

Jimmy Carter, GA (1987/2021): 78. Birthplace and home of 39th president.

Kalaupapa, HI (1980): 10,779. Former colony on Molokai Isl. for those with Hansen's disease (leprosy).

Kaloko-Honokōhau, HI (1978): 1,163. Preserves native culture of Hawaii.

Keweenaw, MI (1992): 1,870. Site of first significant copper mine in U.S.

Klondike Gold Rush, AK-WA (1976): 12,996. Preserves Chilkoot Trail used in 1898 Gold Rush. Museum in Seattle.

Lewis and Clark, OR-WA (1958/2004): 3,410. Lewis and Clark encampment, 1805-06. Incorporates former Fort Clatsop Natl. Mem. Park.

Lowell, MA (1978): 143. Textile mills, canal, 19th-cent. structures; park shows planned city of Industrial Revolution.

Lyndon B. Johnson, TX (1969/1980): 1,572. 36th president's birthplace, boyhood home, ranch.

Manhattan Project, NM-TN-WA (2015): 114. Jointly operated with Dept. of Energy, consists of three sites (Los Alamos, NM; Oak Ridge, TN; Hanford, WA) where U.S. developed world's first atomic weapons.

Marsh-Billings-Rockefeller, VT (1992): 643. Boyhood home of conservationist George Perkins Marsh.

Martin Luther King Jr., Atlanta, GA (1980/2018): 39. Birthplace, grave, church of the civil rights leader.

Minute Man, MA (1959): 1,028. Where Minute Men battled British, Apr. 19, 1775. Also includes The Wayside, home to authors Louisa May Alcott and Nathaniel Hawthorne.

Morristown, NJ (1933): 1,711. Site of important military encampments during the American Revolution; Washington's headquarters, 1779-80.

Natchez, MS (1988): 120. Antebellum estate, other preserved properties related to history of Natchez as a Cotton Belt city.

New Bedford Whaling, MA (1996): 34. Preserves structures and relics associated with the city's 19th-cent. whaling industry.

New Orleans Jazz, LA (1994): 5. Preserves, educates, and interprets jazz as it has evolved in New Orleans.

Nez Perce, ID-MT-OR-WA (1965): 4,565. Illustrates history and culture of Nez Perce, or Nimiipuu, homeland (38 sites).

Ocmulgee Mounds, GA (1934/2019): 3,431. First inhabited by Paleo Indians by c. 15,000 BCE. Ancestral land of the Muscogee (Creek), who were forcibly moved to OK in 1830s.

Palo Alto Battlefield, TX (1978/2009): 3,427. Scene of first battle of the Mexican War.

Paterson Great Falls, NJ (2011): 51. Falls helped make city one of U.S.'s earliest industrial centers.

Pecos, NM (1965/1990): 6,694. Ruins of ancient Pueblo of Pecos, archaeological sites, and two associated Spanish colonial missions from 17th and 18th centuries.

Pullman, IL (2015/2022): 0.4. First planned model industrial community in U.S.; influenced American labor movement.

Pu'uhonua o Hōnaunau, HI (1955/1978): 420. Until 1819, a sanctuary for Hawaiians vanquished in battle and for those guilty of crimes or breaking taboos.

Reconstruction Era, SC (2017/2019): 16. Beaufort Co. sites that tell the story of how formerly enslaved people were integrated into free society.

Rosie the Riveter WWII Home Front, Richmond, CA (2000): 145. Site of shipyard that employed thousands of women during WWII; commemorates women who worked in wartime industries.

Saint-Gaudens, Cornish, NH (1964/2019): 191. Home, studio, and gardens of sculptor Augustus Saint-Gaudens.

Ste. Geneviève, MO (2020): 17. First permanent European settlement in state.

Salt River Bay (and Ecological Preserve), St. Croix, VI (1992): 989. Only known site where, in 1493, members of a Columbus party landed on what is now U.S. territory.

San Antonio Missions, TX (1978): 990. Four Spanish missions, 18th-cent. irrigation system.

San Francisco Maritime, CA (1988): 50. Artifacts, photographs, and historic vessels related to development of the Pacific Coast.

San Juan Island, WA (1966): 2,146. Commemorates peaceful relations between U.S., Canada, and Great Britain since the 1872 boundary disputes.

Saratoga, NY (1938): 3,608. Scene of a major 1777 battle that became a turning point in the American Revolution.

Sitka, AK (1910/1972): 116. Scene of Tlingit Indians' last major resistance to Russian colonizers, 1804.

Thomas Edison, West Orange, NJ (1955/2009): 21. Inventor's home and laboratory.

Tumacacori, AZ (1908/1990): 360. Historic Spanish mission building near site first visited by Father Kino in 1691.

Valley Forge, PA (1976): 3,469. Continental Army campsite in 1777-78 winter.

War in the Pacific, GU (1978): 2,030. Seven units illustrating the Pacific theater of WWII.

Weir Farm, CT (1990/2021): 74. Home and studio of American impressionist painter J. Alden Weir.

Women's Rights, NY (1980): 7. Where Lucretia Mott, Elizabeth Cady Stanton, and others organized movement in 1848.

National Battlefields/Parks/Sites

Antietam, MD (1890/1978): 3,288. Battle here ended first Confederate invasion of North, Sept. 17, 1862.

Big Hole, MT (1910/1963): 976. Site of major battle with Nez Perce Indians, Aug. 9-10, 1877.

Brices Cross Roads, Baldwyn, MS (1929): 1.00. Site of Confederate victory, June 10, 1864.

Cowpens, SC (1929/1972): 842. American Revolution battlefield, Jan. 17, 1781.

Fort Donelson, TN-KY (1928/1985): 1,319. Site of first major Union victory, Feb. 16, 1862.

Fort Necessity, PA (1931/1961): 903. Site of first battle of French and Indian War, July 3, 1754.

Kennesaw Mountain, GA (1917/1935): 2,914. Site of major battle of Atlanta campaign in Civil War.

Manassas, VA (1940): 5,073. Scene of two Civil War battles.

Monocacy, MD (1934/1976): 1,647. Civil War battle in defense of Washington, DC, fought here, July 9, 1864.

Moores Creek, Currie, NC (1926/1980): 88. Commemorates Feb. 27, 1776, battle between Patriots and Loyalists.

Petersburg, VA (1926/1962): 9,350. Scene of Union campaigns, 1864-65.

Richmond, VA (1936): 8,143. Site of battles defending Confederate capital.

River Raisin, Monroe, MI (2010): 42. Site of major battles of War of 1812.

Stones River, TN (1927/1960): 709. Scene of federal offensive to trisect Confederacy, Dec. 31, 1862-Jan. 2, 1863.

Tupelo, MS (1929/1961): 1. Site of crucial battle over Union Gen. Sherman's supply line, July 14-15, 1865.

Wilson's Creek, MO (1960/1970): 2,422. Site of second major Civil War battle, Aug. 10, 1861, for control of Missouri.

National Military Parks

Chickamauga and Chattanooga, GA-TN (1890): 9,523. Where Gen. Sherman and Union armies gained control of TN, 1863.

Fredericksburg and Spotsylvania, VA (1927/1933): 8,405. Sites of several major Civil War battles and campaigns.

Gettysburg, PA (1895/1933): 6,032. Site of decisive Confederate defeat in North, July 1863, and of Gettysburg Address.

Guilford Courthouse, NC (1917/1933): 254. American Revolution battle site.

Horseshoe Bend, AL (1956): 2,040. On Tallapoosa River, where Gen. Andrew Jackson broke power of Upper Creek Indian Confederacy on Mar. 27, 1814.

Kings Mountain, SC (1931/1933): 3,945. Site of American Revolution battle fought on Oct. 7, 1780.

Pea Ridge, AR (1956): 4,300. Civil War battle, Mar. 7-8, 1862.

Shiloh, TN-MS (1894/1933): 9,322. Major Civil War battle site, Apr. 6-7, 1862; incl. Shiloh Indian burial mounds.

Vicksburg, MS-LA (1899/1933): 2,524. Union victory gave North control of Mississippi and split Confederate forces.

National Memorials

Arkansas Post, AR (1960): 758. First permanent French settlement in lower Mississippi River valley.

Arlington House, The Robert E. Lee Memorial, VA (1925/1972): 17. Lee's home overlooking the Potomac River.

Chamizal, El Paso, TX (1966/1974): 55. Commemorates 1963 settlement of 99-year border dispute with Mexico.

Coronado, AZ (1941/1952): 4,830. Commemorates first European exploration of the Southwest.

De Soto, Bradenton, FL (1948): 30. Commemorates 16th-cent. Spanish explorations.

Dwight D. Eisenhower Memorial, Washington, DC (2020): 3.39. Honors his role as Supreme Commander of the Allied Expeditionary Force in WWII and as 34th pres.

Federal Hall, New York, NY (1939/1955): 0.45. First seat of U.S. government under the Constitution.

Flight 93, Shanksville, PA (2002): 2,263. Commemorates passengers and crew of Flight 93, who died thwarting an attack on Sept. 11, 2001.

Fort Caroline, Jacksonville, FL (1950): 138. On St. Johns River, site of first attempt by France, in 16th cent., at permanent North American settlement.

Franklin Delano Roosevelt Memorial, DC (1982): 8. Statues of Pres. Roosevelt and Eleanor Roosevelt; waterfalls and gardens.

General Grant, New York, NY (1958): 0.76. Tomb of Ulysses Grant and wife; largest mausoleum in U.S.

Hamilton Grange, New York, NY (1962): 1.75. Home of Alexander Hamilton.

Johnstown Flood, PA (1964): 178. Commemorates 1889 flood.

Korean War Veterans Memorial, DC (1986/1995): 1.56. Honors those who served in the Korean War.

Lincoln Boyhood, Lincoln City, IN (1962): 200. Site of Abraham Lincoln's boyhood home and grave site of his mother.

Lincoln Memorial, DC (1911/1933): 7. Marble statue of 16th president.

Lyndon Baines Johnson Memorial Grove on the Potomac, DC (1973): 17. Overlooks Potomac River; vista of the Capitol.

Martin Luther King Jr., DC (1996): 2.74. Granite statue of Dr. King close to where he delivered "I Have a Dream" speech.

Mount Rushmore, SD (1925): 1,278. Heads of presidents Washington, Jefferson, Lincoln, T. Roosevelt sculpted into mountain.

Pearl Harbor, HI (2019): 22. Site of Dec. 7, 1941, Japanese attack.

Perry's Victory and International Peace Memorial, Put-in-Bay, OH (1936/1972): 25. World's most massive Doric column promotes pursuit of peace through arbitration and disarmament.

Port Chicago Naval Magazine, Danville, CA (2009): 5. Where 1944 munitions ship explosion killed 320 men.

Roger Williams, Providence, RI (1965): 4.56. Memorial to founder of Rhode Island.

Thaddeus Kosciuszko, Philadelphia, PA (1972): 0.02. Memorial to Polish hero of American Revolution.

Theodore Roosevelt Island, DC (1932/1933): 89. Statue of Roosevelt in wooded island sanctuary.

Thomas Jefferson Memorial, DC (1934/1943): 18. Statue of Jefferson in an inscribed circular, colonnaded structure.

Vietnam Veterans Memorial, DC (1980): 2.18. Black granite wall with names of those missing or killed in action in Vietnam War.

Washington Monument, DC (1876/1933): 106. Obelisk honoring the first U.S. president. Construction began in 1848 with private funding.

World War I Memorial, DC (1981/2014): 1.39. Formerly Pershing Park, dedicated to Gen. John J. Pershing.

World War II Memorial, DC (1993/2004): 8. Oval plaza with central pool commemorating those who fought and died.

Wright Brothers, Kill Devil Hills, NC (1927/1953): 428. Site of first powered flight, by Orville and Wilbur Wright.

National Historic Sites

Allegheny Portage Railroad, PA (1964): 1,284. Linked Pennsylvania Canal system and the West.

Andersonville, GA (1970): 516. Civil War POW camp.

Andrew Johnson, Greeneville, TN (1935/1963): 17. Two homes, his tailor shop, and cemetery where 17th U.S. president is buried.

Bent's Old Fort, CO (1960): 799. Replica of fort on Sante Fe Trail.

Boston African-American, MA (1980): 0.59. Pre-Civil War Black-owned structures.

Carl Sandburg Home, Flat Rock, NC (1968): 268. Home of Pulitzer Prize-winning poet and biographer.

Carter G. Woodson Home, DC (1976/2006): 0.15. Home of "Father of Black History."

Charles Pinckney, Mt. Pleasant, SC (1988): 28. Farm of a principal author and signer of the Constitution.

Christiansted, St. Croix, VI (1952/1961): 27. Preserves historic structures from time of Danish colony.

Clara Barton, Glen Echo, MD (1974): 9. Home of American Red Cross founder.

Edgar Allan Poe, Phila., PA (1978/1980): 0.52. Writer's home.

Eisenhower, Gettysburg, PA (1967): 690. Home of 34th pres.

Eleanor Roosevelt, Hyde Park, NY (1977): 181. Former first lady's personal retreat.

Eugene O'Neill, Danville, CA (1976): 13. Home where playwright wrote his final plays, incl. *The Iceman Cometh*.

First Ladies, Canton, OH (2000): 0.46. Home of first lady Ida Sexton McKinley. Library now devoted to U.S. first ladies.

Ford's Theatre, DC (1866/1970): 0.30. Incl. theater where Lincoln was assassinated, house where he died, and Lincoln Museum.

Fort Bowie, AZ (1964): 999. Focal point of operations against Geronimo and Apaches.

Fort Davis, TX (1961): 523. Frontier outpost in West Texas; established to guard the San Antonio-El Paso Road.

Fort Laramie, WY (1938/1960): 873. Military post on Oregon Trail.

Fort Larned, KS (1964/1966): 718. Military post on Santa Fe Trail.

Fort Point, CA (1970): 29. West Coast fortification; protected San Francisco during and after Civil War.

Fort Raleigh, NC (1941): 516. First attempted English settlement in North America.

Fort Scott, KS (1965/1978): 20. Commemorates U.S. frontier. Focal point of Black troop activity, training during Civil War.

Fort Smith, AR-OK (1961): 75. One of the earliest U.S. posts in Missouri Territory, active 1817-96.

Fort Union Trading Post, MT-ND (1966): 440. Principal fur-trading post on upper Missouri, 1829-67.

Fort Vancouver, WA-OR (1948/1961): 207. Headquarters for Hudson's Bay Company.

Frederick Douglass, DC (1962/1988): 9. Home of Black abolitionist, writer, orator.

Frederick Law Olmsted, Brookline, MA (1979): 7. Home of city planner, famous for designing Central Park in NYC.

Friendship Hill, PA (1978): 675. Home of Albert Gallatin, Jefferson's and Madison's secretary of treasury.

Grant-Kohrs Ranch, MT (1972): 1,618. Ranch house owned by John Grant, 19th-cent. range-cattle industry pioneer.

Hampton, Towson, MD (1948): 62. 18th-cent. Georgian mansion, which in 1790 was largest house in U.S.

Harry S Truman, Independence, MO (1982/1983): 14. House of 33rd pres. from 1919 on and farm where he worked as young man.

Herbert Hoover, West Branch, IA (1965): 187. Birthplace and boyhood home of 31st president.

Home of Franklin D. Roosevelt, Hyde Park, NY (1944): 838. FDR's birthplace, home, and "summer White House."

Honouliuli, HI (2015/2019): 154. Camp where POWs and civilians suspected of disloyalty—mostly Americans of Japanese ancestry—were imprisoned during WWII.

Hopewell Furnace, PA (1938/1985): 848. 19th-cent. iron-making village.

Hubbell Trading Post, AZ (1965): 160. Oldest continuously operating trading post in SW; founded in 1878 on Navajo Nation.

James A. Garfield, Mentor, OH (1980): 8. Home of 20th president; site of his front-porch campaign.

John Fitzgerald Kennedy, Brookline, MA (1967): 0.09. Birthplace and childhood home of 35th president.

John Muir, Martinez, CA (1964): 344. Home of Sierra Club co-founder and "Father of the National Park Service."

Knife River Indian Villages, ND (1974): 1,751. Remnants of villages last occupied by Hidatsa and Mandan Indians.

Lincoln Home, Springfield, IL (1971): 12. Lincoln's residence when he was elected 16th president, 1860.

Little Rock Central High School, AR (1998): 28. Commemorates 1957 desegregation during which federal troops were called in to protect nine Black students.

Longfellow House—Washington's Headquarters, Cambridge, MA (1972/2010): 1.98. Poet's home, 1837-82; Washington's headquarters during Boston siege, 1775-76.

Maggie L. Walker, Richmond, VA (1978): 1.29. Home of Black leader and first female bank president, daughter of former slave.

Manzanar, Lone Pine, CA (1992): 814. Manzanar War Relocation Ctr., a WWII Japanese-American internment camp.

Martin Van Buren, Kinderhook, NY (1974): 285. Lindenwald, home of 8th president.

Mary McLeod Bethune Council House, DC (1982/1991): 0.07. HQ and home of Black women's movement leader.

Minidoka, ID (2001/2008): 396. WWII Japanese internment ctr.

Minuteman Missile, SD (1999): 44. Missile launch facilities dating to Cold War era.

New Philadelphia, IL (2022): 123 (preliminary). First known town planned, legally registered by an African American before the Civil War.

Nicodemus, KS (1996): 4.59. Only remaining Western town established by African Americans during Reconstruction.

Ninety Six, SC (1976): 1,022. Colonial trading village and site of Gen. Nathanael Greene's siege on Loyalist-held fort in 1781.

Pennsylvania Avenue, DC (1965/1996): 18. Incl. area between Capitol and White House, encompassing U.S. Navy Memorial, Freedom Plaza, Old Post Office Pavilion, other sites.

President William Jefferson Clinton Birthplace Home, Hope, AR (2010): 0.68. Birthplace and early home of 42nd pres.

Pu'ukoholā Heiau, Kawaihae, HI (1972): 86. Ruins of temple built by King Kamehameha, first king of united Hawaiian islands.

Sagamore Hill, Oyster Bay, NY (1962): 83. Home of Pres. Theodore Roosevelt from 1885 until his death in 1919.

Saint Paul's Church, Mount Vernon, NY (1943/1978): 6. One of the oldest parishes (1665-1980) in New York State.

Salem Maritime, MA (1938): 9. Major fishing and whaling port famous for 1692 witchcraft trials.

San Juan, PR (1949): 75. 16th-cent. Spanish fortifications.

Sand Creek Massacre, CO (2000): 12,583. Site where around 230 Cheyenne and Arapaho Indians—mostly women, children, and elderly—were killed by U.S. soldiers in 1864.

Saugus Iron Works, MA (1974): 9. Reconstructed 17th-cent. colonial ironworks.

Springfield Armory, MA (1974): 55. Small-arms manufacturing center for nearly 200 years.

Steamtown, Scranton, PA (1986): 62. Rail yard, roadhouse, repair shops of former Delaware, Lackawanna & Western Railroad.

Theodore Roosevelt Birthplace, New York, NY (1962): 0.11. Reconstructed brownstone where 26th president was born.

Theodore Roosevelt Inaugural, Buffalo, NY (1966): 1.18. Wilcox House, where 26th president took oath of office, 1901.

Thomas Stone, Port Tobacco, MD (1978): 328. Haberdeventure, home of signer of Declaration of Independence.

Tuskegee Airmen, AL (1998): 90. Airfield where pilots of all-Black WWII air corps unit received flight training.

Tuskegee Institute, AL (1974): 58. College founded by Booker T. Washington in 1881 for Black students.

Ulysses S. Grant, St. Louis, MO (1989): 10. Home of Grant during pre-Civil War years.

Vanderbilt Mansion, Hyde Park, NY (1940): 212. Mansion of 19th-cent. financier.

Washita Battlefield, OK (1996): 315. Scene of Nov. 27, 1868, battle between Plains tribes and U.S. army.

Whitman Mission, Walla Walla, WA (1936/1963): 139. Site of Protestant missionaries to Cayuse Indians beginning in 1830s.

William Howard Taft, Cincinnati, OH (1969): 3.64. Birthplace and early home of 27th president.

Name	Location	Year[1]	Acreage
National Lakeshores			
Apostle Islands	WI	1970	69,377
Pictured Rocks	MI	1966	73,236
Sleeping Bear Dunes	MI	1970	71,310
National Monuments			
African Burial Ground	NY	2006	0.35
Agate Fossil Beds	NE	1965	3,058
Alibates Flint Quarries	TX	1965	1,371
Aniakchak[2]	AK	1980	137,176
Aztec Ruins	NM	1923	318
Bandelier	NM	1916	33,677
Belmont-Paul Women's Equality	DC	2016	0.34
Birmingham Civil Rights	AL	2017	0.88
Booker T. Washington	VA	1956	239
Buck Island Reef	VI	1961	19,015
Cabrillo	CA	1913	160
Camp Nelson	KY	2018	465
Canyon de Chelly	AZ	1931	83,840
Cape Krusenstern	AK	1978	649,096
Capulin Volcano	NM	1916	793
Casa Grande Ruins	AZ	1918	473
Castillo de San Marcos	FL	1924	19
Castle Clinton	NY	1946	1.00
Castle Mountains	CA	2016	21,026
Cedar Breaks	UT	1933	6,155
César E. Chávez	CA	2012	117
Charles Young Buffalo Soldiers	OH	2013	60
Chiricahua	AZ	1924	12,025
Colorado	CO	1911	20,536
Craters of the Moon	ID	1924	53,438
Devils Postpile	CA	1911	800
Devils Tower	WY	1906	1,347
Dinosaur	CO-UT	1915	210,282
Effigy Mounds	IA	1949	2,526
El Malpais	NM	1987	114,347
El Morro	NM	1906	1,279
Florissant Fossil Beds	CO	1969	6,278
Fort Frederica	GA	1936	305
Fort Matanzas	FL	1924	300
Fort McHenry (and Historic Shrine)	MD	1939	43
Fort Monroe	VA	2011	367
Fort Pulaski	GA	1924	5,623
Fort Stanwix	NY	1935	16
Fort Union	NM	1954	721
Fossil Butte	WY	1972	8,198
Freedom Riders	AL	2017	6
George Washington Birthplace	VA	1930	654
George Washington Carver	MO	1943	240
Gila Cliff Dwellings	NM	1907	533
Governors Island	NY	2001	23
Grand Portage	MN	1958	710
Hagerman Fossil Beds	ID	1988	4,351
Hohokam Pima[3]	AZ	1972	1,690
Hovenweep	CO-UT	1923	785
Jewel Cave	SD	1908	1,274
John Day Fossil Beds	OR	1974	14,062
Katahdin Woods and Waters	ME	2016	87,564
Lava Beds	CA	1925	46,692
Little Bighorn Battlefield	MT	1946	765
Medgar and Myrlie Evers Home	MS	2020	0.74
Mill Springs Battlefield	KY	2020	1,458
Montezuma Castle	AZ	1906	1,016
Muir Woods	CA	1908	554
Natural Bridges	UT	1908	7,636
Navajo	AZ	1909	360
Oregon Caves (and Preserve)	OR	1909	4,554
Organ Pipe Cactus	AZ	1937	330,689
Petroglyph	NM	1990	7,209
Pipe Spring	AZ	1923	40
Pipestone	MN	1937	297
Poverty Point[2]	LA	1988	911
Rainbow Bridge	UT	1910	160

Name	Location	Year[1]	Acreage
Russell Cave..............	AL	1961	310
Salinas Pueblo Missions.......	NM	1909	1,071
Scotts Bluff	NE	1919	3,005
Statue of Liberty	NJ-NY	1924	58
Stonewall	NY	2016	8
Sunset Crater Volcano	AZ	1930	3,040
Timpanogos Cave............	UT	1922	250
Tonto	AZ	1907	1,120
Tule Lake	CA	2019	37
Tule Springs Fossil Beds	NV	2014	22,650
Tuzigoot	AZ	1939	812
Virgin Islands Coral Reef	VI	2001	12,708
Waco Mammoth	TX	2015	107
Walnut Canyon	AZ	1915	3,201
Wupatki...................	AZ	1924	35,402
Yucca House[2]..............	CO	1919	34

National Parkways

Name	Location	Year[1]	Acreage
Blue Ridge	NC-VA	1933	101,102
George Washington Memorial ..	MD-DC-VA	1930	6,774
John D. Rockefeller Jr. Memorial	WY	1972	23,777
Natchez Trace	MS-TN-AL	1938	52,380

National Preserves

Name	Location	Year[1]	Acreage
Aniakchak[2]	AK	1980	464,118
Bering Land Bridge...........	AK	1980	2,697,391
Big Cypress[4]...............	FL	1974	720,564
Big Thicket	TX	1974	113,122
Craters of the Moon	ID	2002	698,940
Denali	AK	1980	1,334,118
Gates of the Arctic	AK	1980	948,608
Glacier Bay................	AK	1980	58,406
Great Sand Dunes	CO	2004	41,686
Katmai...................	AK	1980	418,699
Lake Clark	AK	1980	1,410,294
Little River Canyon	AL	1992	15,292
Mojave	CA	1994	1,549,709
Noatak	AK	1980	6,587,071
Tallgrass Prairie	KS	1996	10,883
Timucuan Ecological and Historic	FL	1988	46,263
Valles Caldera	NM	2014	89,805
Wrangell-St. Elias............	AK	1980	4,852,645
Yukon-Charley Rivers.........	AK	1980	2,526,512

National Recreation Areas

Name	Location	Year[1]	Acreage
Amistad...................	TX	1990	62,945
Bighorn Canyon	MT-WY	1966	120,296
Boston Harbor Islands	MA	1996	2,231
Chattahoochee River	GA	1978	12,417
Chickasaw	OK	1976	9,899
Curecanti	CO	1965	43,591
Delaware Water Gap	NJ-PA	1965	68,709
Gateway	NJ-NY	1972	26,607
Gauley River...............	WV	1988	11,483
Glen Canyon	AZ-UT	1972	1,254,117
Golden Gate	CA	1972	82,116
Lake Chelan	WA	1968	61,939
Lake Mead	AZ-NV	1964	1,495,816
Lake Meredith	TX	1990	44,978
Lake Roosevelt (fmr. Coulee Dam)	WA	1946	100,390
Ross Lake.................	WA	1968	117,575
Santa Monica Mountains.......	CA	1978	153,121
Whiskeytown-Shasta-Trinity[5] ...	CA	1972	42,503

National Reserves

Name	Location	Year[1]	Acreage
City of Rocks...............	ID	1988	14,512
Ebey's Landing Historical	WA	1978	19,334

National Rivers

Name	Location	Year[1]	Acreage
Big South Fork (and Rec. Area)	KY-TN	1991	123,699
Buffalo...................	AR	1972	94,293
Mississippi (and Rec. Area) ...	MN	1988	53,775
Ozark Scenic Riverways.......	MO	1972	80,784

National Seashores

Name	Location	Year[1]	Acreage
Assateague Island[6]..........	MD-VA	1965	41,347
Canaveral	FL	1975	57,662
Cape Cod	MA	1966	43,608
Cape Hatteras..............	NC	1953	30,351
Cape Lookout	NC	1966	28,243
Cumberland Island	GA	1972	36,347
Fire Island	NY	1964	19,581

Name	Location	Year[1]	Acreage
Gulf Islands................	FL-MS	1971	138,306
Padre Island	TX	1968	130,434
Point Reyes	CA	1972	71,053

International Historic Site

Name	Location	Year[1]	Acreage
Saint Croix Island	ME	1984	7

Other Designations

Name	Location	Year[1]	Acreage
Catoctin Mountain Park........	MD	1954	5,891
Constitution Gardens	DC	1974	39
Fort Washington Park.........	MD	1940	345
Greenbelt Park	MD	1950	1,176
National Capital Parks-East ...	DC-MD	1933	8,704
National Mall and Memorial Parks.................	DC	1933	156
Piscataway Park	MD	1961	4,616
Prince William Forest Park	VA	1948	16,059
Rock Creek Park.............	DC	1933	1,755
White House	DC	1933	18
Wolf Trap National Park for the Performing Arts	VA	2002	130

National Wild and Scenic Rivers

Rivers in this system are designated by Congress or the Sec. of the Interior. As of July 2022, the system included 13,396 miles of 226 rivers in 41 states and Puerto Rico. Not all of the rivers that the NPS administers are official units of the park system. Only official NPS units are listed here.

Name	Location	Year[1]	Acreage
Alagnak Wild[2]	AK	1980	30,665
Bluestone Scenic	WV	1988	4,310
Delaware Scenic[7]...........	NJ-PA	1978	1,973
Great Egg Harbor Scenic and Rec.	NJ	1992	43,311
Missouri Recreational	NE-SD	1991	48,457
Niobrara Scenic	NE	1991	29,089
Obed	TN	1976	5,490
Rio Grande	TX	1978	13,123
Saint Croix Scenic Riverway[8] ...	MN-WI	1968	92,743
Upper Delaware Scenic and Rec.	NY-PA	1978	75,000

Affiliated Areas

Affiliated areas are administered in connection with the NPS but are not owned by that agency.

Name	Location	Year[1]	Acreage
Aleutian World War II Natl. Historic Area	AK	1996	135
American Memorial Park......	MP	1978	133
Benjamin Franklin Natl. Memorial (NMEM)	PA	1972	NA
Chicago Portage Natl. Historic Site (NHS)................	IL	1952	91
Chimney Rock NHS	NE	1956	83
Eutaw Springs Battlefield	SC	2021	NA
Fallen Timbers Battlefield and Fort Miamis NHS	OH	1999	185
Father Marquette NMEM	MI	1975	52
Gloria Dei (Old Swedes') Church NHS....................	PA	1942	3.71
Green Springs Natl. Historic Landmark District...........	VA	1974	15,645
Historic Camden Revolutionary War Site.................	SC	1982	107
Ice Age Natl. Scientific Reserve	WI	1964	32,500
International Peace Garden	ND-MB	1949	2,330
Iñupiat Heritage Center........	AK	1999	0
Jamestown NHS	VA	1940	22
Kate Mullany NHS............	NY	2004	0.06
Kettle Creek Battlefield	GA	2021	NA
Lower East Side Tenement NHS	NY	1998	1.2
Natural Bridge State Park......	VA	2016	NA
Oklahoma City NMEM	OK	2004	6
Parkers Crossroads Battlefield ..	TN	2019	NA
Pinelands Natl. Reserve.......	NJ	1978	1,164,025
Red Hill Patrick Henry NMEM ...	VA	1986	NA
Roosevelt Campobello Intl. Park	NB	1964	2,722
Thomas Cole NHS	NY	1999	3.4
Touro Synagogue NHS........	RI	1946	0.23
Wing Luke Museum of the Asian Pacific American Experience ..	WA	2013	NA

NA = Not available. (1) Year established or current designation received. (2) No federal facilities; state services may be available. (3) Located on Gila River Indian Reservation; not open to the public. (4) Incl. acreage added in 1988 expansion. (5) Shasta and Trinity units are administered by the Forest Service. Figure given is NPS acreage only. (6) Figure given includes acreage administered by U.S. Fish and Wildlife Service. (7) Comprises the Lower Delaware Wild and Scenic (2000) and Middle Delaware Scenic, whose year and acreage are given in table. (8) Incl. Lower Saint Croix acreage added in 1972.

National Trails System

Source: National Park Service and Bureau of Land Management, U.S. Dept. of the Interior; U.S. Forest Service, USDA

As of mid-2023, the National Trails System included 11 national scenic trails, 21 national historic trails, almost 1,300 national recreation trails, and 7 connecting and side trails. National scenic trails and national historic trails are established by Congress and administered by the NPS, Forest Service, or BLM. Official NPS units are indicated by an asterisk.

Name	Location	Year[1]	Length (mi)[2]	Name	Location	Year[1]	Length (mi)[2]
National Scenic Trails				Chilkoot	AK	2022	17
*Appalachian	ME to GA	1968	2,180+	El Camino Real de los Tejas	TX-LA	2004	2,580
Arizona	AZ	2009	807	El Camino Real de Tierra Adentro	NM-TX	2000	404
Continental Divide	MT, ID, WY,			Iditarod	AK	1978	2,400
	CO, NM	1978	3,100	Juan Bautista de Anza	AZ-CA	1990	1,200
Florida	FL	1983	1,300	Lewis and Clark	PA to Pacific	1978	4,900
Ice Age	WI	1980	1,200	Mormon Pioneer	IL to UT	1978	1,300
*Natchez Trace	MS-AL-TN	1983	65	Nez Perce (Nee-Me-Poo)	OR to MT	1986	1,170
New England	MA-CT	2009	215	Old Spanish	NM to CA	2002	2,700
North Country	NY to ND	1980	4,600	Oregon	MO to OR	1978	2,170
Pacific Crest	CA-OR-WA	1968	2,650	Overmountain Victory	NC, SC,		
Pacific Northwest	MT-ID-WA	2009	1,200		TN, VA	1980	330
*Potomac Heritage	VA to PA	1983	924	Pony Express	MO to CA	1992	2,000
National Historic Trails[3]				Santa Fe	MO, KS, OK,		
					CO, NM	1987	1,203
Ala Kahakai	HI	2000	175	Selma to Montgomery	AL	1996	54
Butterfield Overland	MO, AR to CA	2023	3,292	Star-Spangled Banner	VA-DC-MD	2008	560
California	MO, NE to			Trail of Tears	GA, NC to OK	1987	5,043
	CA, OR	1978	5,600	Washington-Rochambeau			
Capt. John Smith Chesapeake	NY to VA	2006	3,000	Revolutionary Route	MA to VA	2009	680+

(1) Year designation was received. (2) Authorized or currently completed length. (3) Trails may include both overland and water routes.

U.S. Forest Service Special Designated Areas

Source: U.S. Forest Service, U.S. Dept. of Agriculture; as of Sept. 30, 2022

These areas within the National Forest System have been specially designated by presidential proclamation or act of Congress. Size does not include acreage within National Forest boundaries not federally owned or administered by the Forest Service.

NGR = Natl. Game Refuge; NM = Natl. Monument; NRA = Natl. Recreation Area; NS(A) = Natl. Scenic (Area); NVM = Natl. Volcanic Monument; SMA = Special Management Area.

Area	Location	Estab.	Acreage	Area	Location	Estab.	Acreage
Admiralty Island NM	AK	1980	1,008,069	James Peak Protection Area	CO	2002	17,510
Allegheny NRA	PA	1984	23,789	Jemez NRA	NM	1993	48,872
Ancient Bristlecone Pine Forest	CA	2009	31,799	Jewel Cave NM	SD	1908	2,540
Apache Leap SMA	AZ	2014	714	Kelly Butte SMA	WA	1998	5,673
Arapaho NRA	CO	1978	31,162	Kings River SMA	CA	1987	50,887
Ashley Karst NRA & Geologic Area	UT	2019	173,540	Land Between the Lakes NRA	KY-TN	1998	171,241
Barkshead (Ozark #2) NGR	AR	1926	5,851	Livingston (Ozark #1) NGR	AR	1926	8,755
Bear Creek NSA	VA	2009	5,122	Misty Fiords NM	AK	1980	2,293,162
Bears Ears NM	UT	2016	289,201	Moccasin (Ozark #3) NGR	AR	1926	4,048
Beech Creek NSA & Botanical Area				Mono Basin NSA	CA	1984	51,394
Beech Creek NSA	OK	1988	8,042	Moosalamoo NRA	VT	2006	15,913
Beech Creek Natl. Botanical Area	OK	1988	538	Mount Baker NRA	WA	1984	8,789
Berryessa Snow Mountain NM	CA	2015	197,360	Mount Hood NRA	OR	2009	34,465
Big Levels NGR	VA	1935	12,147	Mount Pleasant NSA	VA	1994	6,864
Black Mountain (Ozark #5) NGR	AR	1926	18,929	Mount Rogers NRA	VA	1966	114,996
Bowen Gulch Protection Area	CO	1993	10,862	Mount St. Helens NVM	WA	1989	112,867
Bridgeport Winter Recreation Area	CA	2009	7,250	Newberry NVM	OR	1990	56,596
Browns Canyon NM	CO	2015	11,822	Noontootly NGR	GA	1938	24,655
Caney Creek (Ouachita #4) NGR	AR	1935	8,038	Norbeck Wildlife Preserve	SD	1920	32,079
Cascade Head NS Research Area	OR	1974	7,156	North Cascades NRA	WA	1984	88,050
Catahoula Wildlife Mgmt. Preserve	LA	1941	37,629	Oak Mountain (Ouachita #2) NGR	AR	1935	8,872
Cherokee Game Refuge #1	TN	1924	9,862	Ocala NGR	FL	1930	68,241
Chimney Rock NM	CO	2012	4,724	Opal Creek Scenic Recreation Area	OR	1996	13,666
Columbia River Gorge NSA	OR-WA	1986	82,795	Oregon Dunes NRA	OR	1972	30,229
Burdoin Mountain SMA	WA	1986	7,294	Ouachita Wildlife Preserve	AR	1933	138,039
Gates of Columbia R. Gorge SMA	OR-WA	1986	53,274	Quinault SMA	WA	1988	5,499
Rowena SMA	OR-WA	1986	3,537	Piedra SMA	CO	1993	60,514
Wind Mountain SMA	WA	1986	14,650	Pigeon Creek (Ouachita #1) NGR	AR	1935	8,107
Coosa NSA	GA	1991	7,044	Pine Ridge NRA	NE	1986	6,651
Cradle of Forestry in America				Pisgah Natl. Game Refuge	NC	1916	71,910
Natl. Historic Area	NC	1968	7,793	Rattlesnake NRA	MT	1980	60,092
Crystal Springs Watershed	OR	2009	2,094	Red Dirt Natl. Wildlife Mgmt. Pres.	LA	1941	40,213
Cultus Creek	OR	2009	280	Robert S. Kerr Botanical Area	OK	1988	7,971
Ed Jenkins NRA	GA	1991	23,540	Robert T. Stafford White Rocks NRA	VT	1984	36,442
Flaming Gorge NRA	UT-WY	1968	188,665	Roubideau SMA	CO	1993	18,837
Fossil Ridge Rec. Mgmt. Area	CO	1993	43,383	Saint Francis Dam NM	CA	2019	353
Frank and Jeanne Moore Wild				San Gabriel Mountains NM	CA	2014	336,926
Steelhead Area	OR	2019	102,762	Sand to Snow NM	CA	2016	70,942
Francis Marion Natl. Forest Wildlife				Santa Rosa/San Jacinto Mtns. NM	CA	2000	70,056
Pres.	SC	1948	53,203	Sawtooth NRA	ID	1972	732,192
F. Church-River of No Return Spec.				Seng Mountain NSA	VA	2009	5,195
Mining Mgmt. Zone-Clear Creek	ID	1980	40,555	Sheep Mountain Game Refuge	WY	1924	21,569
Giant Sequoia NM	CA	2000	328,408	Smith River NRA	CA	1990	323,051
Grand Canyon Natl. Game Preserve	AZ	1906	622,273	Spring Mountains NRA	NV	1993	316,938
Grand Island NRA	MI	1990	13,302	Spruce Knob-Seneca Rocks NRA	WV	1965	57,511
Grey Towers Natl. Historic Site	PA	2004	95	Tabeguache SMA	CO	1993	8,945
Haw Creek (Ozark #4) NGR	AR	1926	3,783	Tahquitz Natl. Game Preserve	CA	1926	18,813
Hells Canyon NRA	OR-ID	1975	635,244	Upper Big Bottom	OR	2009	1,581
Hermosa Creek SMA	CO	2014	70,396	Whiskeytown-Shasta-Trinity NRA	CA	1965	173,075
Indian Nations Scenic Wildlife Area	OK	1988	44,519	Winding Stair Mountain NRA	OK	1988	26,617

National Heritage Areas

Source: National Park Service (NPS), U.S. Dept. of the Interior; Alliance of National Heritage Areas

National Heritage Areas (NHAs) are designated by Congress for their national importance. NHAs are not units of the National Park system, though the NPS advises and provides limited financial assistance. NHC = Natl. Heritage Corridor. As of mid-2023.

Name	Location	Year[1]	Size (sq mi)	Name	Location	Year[1]	Size (sq mi)
Abraham Lincoln	IL	2008	25,975	Mississippi Gulf Coast	MS	2004	4,289
Alabama Black Belt	AL	2023	NA[2]	Mississippi Hills	MS	2009	NA[6]
Appalachian Forest	MD-WV	2019	NA[3]	Mormon Pioneer	UT	2006	16,070
Arabia Mountain	GA	2006	64	MotorCities	MI	1998	10,000+
Atchafalaya	LA	2006	10,400	Mountains to Sound Greenway	WA	2019	2,344
Augusta Canal	GA	1996	3+	Muscle Shoals	AL	2009	3,913
Baltimore	MD	2009	18	National Aviation Heritage Area	OH	2004	NA[7]
Blue Ridge	NC	2003	10,515	National Coal Heritage Area	WV	1996	5,300
Bronzeville-Black Metropolis	IL	2023	NA	Niagara Falls*	NY	2008	13
Cache La Poudre River*	CO	2009	45	Northern Neck	VA	2023	1,070
Cane River	LA	1994	181	Northern Plains	ND	2009	800
Champlain Valley Natl. Heritage Partnership	NY-VT	2006	NA[4]	Northern Rio Grande	NM	2006	10,000
Crossroads of the American Revolution	NJ	2006	2,155	Ohio & Erie Canalway*	OH	1996	110
Delaware & Lehigh NHC*	PA	1988	165	Oil Region	PA	2004	708
Downeast Maine	ME	2023	NA[5]	Rivers of Steel	PA	1996	5,000+
Erie Canalway NHC	NY	2000	4,834	Sacramento-San Joaquin Delta	CA	2019	NA
Essex	MA	1996	550	Saint Croix	VI	2023	84
Freedom's Frontier	KS-MO	2006	31,000	Sangre de Cristo	CO	2009	3,000+
Freedom's Way	MA-NH	2009	994	Santa Cruz Valley	AZ	2019	3,325
Great Basin	NV-UT	2006	15,704	Schuylkill River Greenways	PA	2000	1,700
Gullah Geechee Cultural Heritage Corridor	NC, SC, GA, FL	2006	12,818	Shenandoah Valley Battlefields Natl. Historic District	VA	1996	3,939
Illinois & Michigan Canal NHC	IL	1984	862	Silos & Smokestacks	IA	1996	20,000+
John H. Chafee Blackstone River Valley NHC	MA-RI	1986	720+	South Carolina NHC	SC	1996	NA[8]
Journey Through Hallowed Ground*	PA, MD, WV, VA	2008	180	South Park	CO	2009	1,800
Kenai Mountains-Turnagain Arm	AK	2009	650	Southern Campaign of the Revolution NHC	NC-SC	2023	NA
Lackawanna Heritage Valley	PA	2000	350	Southern Maryland	MD	2023	1,250
The Last Green Valley NHC	CT-MA	1994	1,105	Southwestern Penn. Industrial Heritage Route (Path of Progress)*	PA	1988	500
Maritime Washington*	WA	2019	3,000	Susquehanna	PA	2019	NA[5]
Maurice D. Hinchey Hudson River Valley	NY	1996	6,250	Tennessee Civil War[9]	TN	1996	42,144
Mississippi Delta	MS	2009	10,976	Upper Housatonic Valley	MA-CT	2006	964
				Wheeling	WV	2000	12
				Yuma Crossing	AZ	2000	21

NA = Not available. * = Figure given is length of area. (1) Year designation was received. (2) Covers 19 counties. (3) 18 counties in both states. (4) 11 counties in both states. (5) 2 counties. (6) Parts of 30 counties. (7) 8 counties. (8) 17 counties. (9) Spans state of Tennessee.

Attractions in and Around Washington, DC

Most attractions are free. Hours are subject to change, especially on holidays, when some attractions may be closed. For a free official visitors guide and map, visit washington.org or call Destination DC at 1-800-422-8644. **Note:** Visit the listed websites for updated visitor information on any specific safety guidelines due to COVID-19.

Arlington

Arlington National Cemetery, on the former Custis-Lee estate in Arlington, VA, was first used as a burial site during the Civil War. It is the final resting place of Pres. William Howard Taft and Pres. John F. Kennedy and his wife, Jacqueline Bouvier Kennedy Onassis. More than 400,000 U.S. military personnel from every major war are buried at Arlington. The **Tomb of the Unknown Soldier**, dedicated in 1921, is guarded by soldiers 24 hrs. a day. Unknowns from World War I, World War II, and Korea are interred in the plaza. (Vietnam Unknown was exhumed in 1998 and identified through DNA testing.)

A number of monuments and memorials are located throughout the 639-acre cemetery. They include the **Military Women's Memorial** (dedicated 1997), which honors the more than 3 mil women who have served or currently serve in the U.S. military.

Open daily 8 AM-5 PM (8 AM-7 PM, Apr.-Sept.). Arlington VA; (877) 907-8585. **Website:** www.arlingtoncemetery.mil

The **U.S. Marine Corps War Memorial** stands north of Arlington National Cemetery. A bronze statue depicts the raising of the U.S. flag on Mt. Suribachi, Feb. 23, 1945, during the WWII battle of Iwo Jima. The memorial grounds are open daily 6 AM-midnight; (703) 235-1530. **Website:** www.nps.gov/gwmp/planyourvisit/usmc_memorial.htm

Bureau of Engraving and Printing

The Bureau of Engraving and Printing of the U.S. Treasury Dept. is the headquarters for the making of U.S. paper money. The visitor center remained closed as of mid-2023 while operational improvements were made. 14th and C Sts. SW; (866) 874-2330. **Website:** www.bep.gov

The Capitol

The United States Capitol was originally designed by Dr. William Thornton, an amateur architect, whose submission in 1793 won him $500 and a city lot. Three other architects designed or supervised construction of the Capitol before its completion.

The present cast-iron dome at its greatest exterior height measures 135 ft, 5 in. and is topped by the bronze Statue of Freedom, which stands 19½ ft and weighs 15,000 lbs. On its base are the words *E Pluribus Unum* (out of many, one).

The Capitol Visitor Center is open to the public Mon.-Sat., 8:30 AM-4:30 PM. Free guided tours are available by advance reservations. The Senate and House galleries are not part of the tour. To enter either gallery or to observe Congress in session, those living in the U.S. may obtain tickets from their U.S. representative or senators. Visitors from other countries may inquire at the House and Senate appointment desks. Between Constitution and Independence Aves., bounded by First St.; (202) 226-8000. **Website:** www.visitthecapitol.gov

Federal Bureau of Investigation

The Federal Bureau of Investigation discontinued tours of its headquarters following the Sept. 11, 2001, terrorist attacks. A self-guided tour called the FBI Experience, for U.S. citizens and permanent residents only, is available. Open 9 AM-4:30 PM Mon.-Fri.; visits must be arranged at least four weeks in advance through the office of one's congressional delegate. J. Edgar Hoover Bldg., Pennsylvania Ave., between 9th and 10th Sts. NW; (202) 324-3000. **Website:** www.fbi.gov

Folger Shakespeare Library

The Folger Shakespeare Library, on Capitol Hill, is a research institution with the world's largest collection of Shakespearean materials and other rare books and manuscripts of the Renaissance period. After a three-year renovation, the building expected to reopen to visitors in Nov. 2023. 201 E. Capitol St. SE; (202) 544-4600. **Website:** www.folger.edu

Holocaust Memorial Museum

The U.S. Holocaust Memorial Museum (opened 1993) documents the Holocaust through artifacts and interactive videos and educates the public on other genocides. The permanent exhibition is recommended for visitors age 11 and up.

The museum is open daily, 10 AM-5:30 PM. Entry into the permanent exhibition is timed. Timed passes are available at the door each day on a first-come, first-served basis; advance passes can be ordered online for a fee. 100 Raoul Wallenberg Pl. SW; (202) 488-0400. **Website:** www.ushmm.org

Jefferson Memorial

Dedicated Apr. 13, 1943, the Thomas Jefferson Memorial stands on the south shore of the Tidal Basin in West Potomac Park. The circular stone structure combines architectural elements of the dome of the Pantheon in Rome and the rotunda designed by Jefferson for the Univ. of Virginia.

The memorial is open 24 hrs. a day and staffed 9:30 AM-10 PM. Ohio and E. Basin Drs. SW; (202) 426-6841. **Website:** www.nps.gov/thje/

Kennedy Center

The John F. Kennedy Center for the Performing Arts opened in 1971. Designed by Edward Durell Stone, it includes an opera house, concert hall, theaters, restaurants, and a library. Free tours available Mon.-Fri., 10 AM-4:30 PM, and Sat.-Sun., 10 AM-12:30 PM. 2700 F St. NW; (800) 444-1324. **Website:** www.kennedy-center.org

Martin Luther King Jr. Memorial

The MLK, Jr. Memorial (dedicated 2011) features a 30-ft figure of Dr. King, sculpted by artist Lei Yixin, emerging from a block of granite. The memorial is located on the Tidal Basin, between the Lincoln and Jefferson Memorials.

The memorial is open 24 hrs. a day and staffed 9:30 AM-10 PM. Independence Ave. SW and West Basin Dr. SW; (202) 426-6841. **Website:** www.nps.gov/mlkm/

Korean War Veterans Memorial

The Korean War Veterans Memorial, dedicated 1995 at the Mall's west end, features a multiservice formation of 19 combat-ready soldiers in ponchos. A granite wall, with images of service members, juts into the Pool of Remembrance.

The memorial is open 24 hrs. a day and staffed 9:30 AM-10 PM. Independence Ave. SW and French Dr. SW; (202) 426-6841. **Website:** www.nps.gov/kowa/

Library of Congress

Established by and for Congress in 1800, the Library of Congress extends its services to other government agencies and libraries, scholars, and the public. It contains more than 173 mil items in 470 languages, making it the world's largest library collection.

The Thomas Jefferson Building (Main Reading Room and exhibition galleries) is open to visitors with a free timed-entry pass, reservable online (a limited number of same-day passes are available), Tues.-Sat., 10 AM-5 PM (until 8 on Thursdays). First St. SE between Independence Ave. SE and East Capitol St.; (202) 707-9779. **Website:** www.loc.gov

Lincoln Memorial

Designed by Henry Bacon and dedicated in 1922, the Lincoln Memorial in West Potomac Park is a large marble hall enclosing a statue, designed by Daniel Chester French, of Abraham Lincoln seated in an armchair. The text of the Gettysburg Address is engraved in the south chamber, that of Lincoln's second inaugural speech in the north chamber.

The memorial is open 24 hrs. a day and staffed 9:30 AM-10 PM. Independence Ave. and French Dr. SW; (202) 426-6841. **Website:** www.nps.gov/linc/

Mount Vernon

Mount Vernon, George Washington's estate, is about 15 mi from Washington, DC, in northern Virginia. A one-and-a-half story house was first built on the site by Washington's father, Augustine Washington, in 1734. In 1754, George Washington began running and expanding the estate, named after Adm. Edward Vernon by Washington's half-brother Lawrence. The estate has been restored to its 18th-cent. appearance. Washington and his wife, Martha, are buried on the grounds.

Open all year; hours vary seasonally. Mount Vernon, VA; (703) 780-2000. General admission: adults $28, youth (6-11) $15, ages 5 and under free. **Website:** www.mountvernon.org

National Archives and Records

Original copies of the Declaration of Independence, the Constitution, and the Bill of Rights are on display at the National Archives Museum. The National Archives also holds other U.S. government records, historic maps, photographs, and manuscripts.

The museum is open daily 10 AM-5:30 PM. Constitution Ave. bet. 7th and 9th Sts. NW; (202) 357-5061. **Website:** www.archives.gov

National Gallery of Art

The National Gallery of Art, established by Congress, opened in 1941. The original West Building was designed by John Russell Pope. The East Building, opened in 1978, was designed by I. M. Pei. Galleries are open 10 AM-5 PM. Constitution Ave NW between 3rd and 9th Sts.; (202) 737-4215. **Website:** www.nga.gov

National World War II Memorial

The National WWII Memorial, opened in 2004, is dedicated to the approx. 16 mil veterans who served and the more than 400,000 who died in the war. The 8.25-acre site is at the east end of the Lincoln Memorial Reflecting Pool.

The 43-ft archways at the north and south entrances represent the Atlantic and Pacific theaters. A wall of 4,048 gold stars, each representing 100 American deaths, stands in an oval plaza surrounded by 56 pillars standing for the states, territories, and the Dist. of Columbia.

The memorial is open 24 hrs. a day and staffed 9:30 AM-10 PM. 17th St. and Independence Ave. SW; (202) 426-6841. **Website:** www.nps.gov/wwii/

The Pentagon

The Pentagon, headquarters of the Dept. of Defense, is the largest low-rise office building in the U.S. It houses some 26,000 employees in offices occupying 3,705,793 sq ft. The building was severely damaged when struck by a plane on Sept. 11, 2001.

As of mid-2023, the Pentagon was not providing public tours. Arlington, VA; (703) 697-1776. **Website:** www.defense.gov/Pentagon-Tours/Request-A-Tour/

Franklin Delano Roosevelt Memorial

Opened in 1997, the FDR Memorial features four spaces with bronze statues and panels depicting FDR through his four terms in office. The 8.14-acre memorial is on the Tidal Basin.

Open daily with staff on grounds 9:30 AM-10 PM. Ohio and W. Basin Drs. SW; (202) 426-6841. **Website:** www.nps.gov/frde/

Smithsonian Institution

The Smithsonian Institution, established in 1846, is the world's largest museum and research complex. It holds some 157.2 mil artifacts and specimens in its trust. Seventeen of its 19 museums and the **National Zoo** are in the DC area. The **Smithsonian Institution Building** (or The Castle) houses the Smithsonian Visitor Center. Also on the National Mall are the **National Museum of African American History and Culture**, the **National Museum of African Art**, the **National Air and Space Museum**, **National Museum of American History**, the **National Museum of the American Indian**, the **Arts and Industries Building** (a special-events space), the **Freer Gallery of Art**, the **Hirshhorn Museum and Sculpture Garden**, the **National Museum of Natural History**, and the **Arthur M. Sackler Gallery**. Located nearby are the **National Postal Museum**, the **Smithsonian American Art Museum**, the **National Portrait Gallery**, and the **Renwick Gallery**. The **Anacostia Community Museum** is in SE DC. The Air and Space Museum's **Udvar-Hazy Center** is near Dulles Airport in Virginia.

Most museums are open daily, 10 AM-5:30 PM (later in summer); (202) 633-1000. **Website:** www.si.edu

Vietnam Veterans Memorial

Originally dedicated in 1982, the Vietnam Veterans Memorial recognizes those who served in the Vietnam War. The names of more than 58,000 Americans who lost their lives or remain missing are inscribed on polished black-granite walls arranged to form a V, designed by Maya Ying Lin.

Two additions have been made to Lin's design, the Frederick Hart sculpture Three Servicemen (1984), and the Vietnam Women's Memorial (1993), sculpted by Glenna Goodacre, honoring the approx. 11,000 women who served in Vietnam.

The memorial is open 24 hrs. a day and staffed 9:30 AM-10 PM. Constitution Ave. and Bacon Dr. NW; (202) 426-6841. **Website:** www.nps.gov/vive/

Washington Monument

The Washington Monument (dedicated 1885) is a tapering shaft, or obelisk, of white marble, 555 ft, 5⅛ in. in height and 55 ft, 1½ in. square at the base. Eight small windows, two on each side, are located on the observation deck at the 500-ft level.

The monument is open daily 9 AM-5 PM. 15th St. and Constitution Ave. NW; (202) 426-6841. **Website:** www.nps.gov/wamo/

White House

The White House, the president's residence, stands on 18 acres on the south side of Pennsylvania Ave., between the Treasury and the old Executive Office Building. The sandstone walls, quarried at Aquia Creek, VA, were first made white with lime-based whitewash in 1798, though the name did not become official until 1901.

Free tours of the residence's public areas are available Tues. through Sat., 8 AM-12:30 PM. Tour requests must be made at least 21 but not more than 90 days in advance through one's member of Congress. Foreign visitors may make requests through their embassy. Tours are scheduled on a first-come, first-served basis. 1600 Pennsylvania Ave. NW; (202) 456-7041. **Website:** www.whitehouse.gov

The White House Visitor Center at 1450 Pennsylvania Ave. NW is open daily, 7:30 AM-4 PM; (202) 208-1631. **Website:** www.nps.gov/whho/

U.S. HISTORY: CHRONOLOGY OF EVENTS

1492 Christopher Columbus and crew sighted land Oct. 12 in what is now the Bahamas.

1513 Juan Ponce de León explored Florida coast.

1524 Giovanni da Verrazzano led French expedition along coast from Carolina north to Nova Scotia; entered New York Harbor.

1526 San Miguel de Guadalupe, **first European settlement** in what became U.S. territory, was established in the summer off South Carolina coast; abandoned in Oct.

1539 Hernando de Soto landed in Florida May 28; crossed Mississippi River, 1541.

1540 Francisco Vásquez de Coronado explored Southwest north of Rio Grande. **Hernando de Alarcón** reached Colorado River; **García López de Cárdenas** reached Grand Canyon. Others explored California coast.

1562 First French colony in what became U.S. territory founded on Parris Island off South Carolina coast; abandoned, 1564.

1565 St. Augustine, FL, oldest continuously occupied European settlement in U.S., founded Sept. 8 by Pedro Menéndez de Avilés. Spain ceded settlement to U.S. in 1821.

1579 Sir Francis Drake entered San Francisco Bay and claimed region for Britain.

1585 First English colony in America, sponsored by Sir Walter Raleigh, founded on Roanoke Island, off North Carolina coast; colony failed.

1587 Second colony attempted on Roanoke Island. Virginia Dare of colony became **first English infant born** in the New World. Settlers of second colony seemed to have vanished, 1590.

1607 Capt. John Smith and 105 cavaliers in three ships landed on Virginia coast and started Jamestown, **first permanent English settlement** in New World.

1609 Henry Hudson, English explorer of Northwest Passage, employed by Dutch, sailed into New York Harbor in Sept. and up Hudson to Albany. **Samuel de Champlain** explored Lake Champlain, to the north. Spaniards settled Santa Fe, NM.

1619 House of Burgesses, **first representative assembly** in New World, elected July 30 at Jamestown, VA. **Introduction of slavery:** first Black laborers in English North American colonies, brought to Jamestown in Aug. Chattel slavery laws passed in Massachusetts, 1641, and Virginia, 1661.

1620 Pilgrims, Puritan separatists, left Plymouth, England, Sept. 16 on *Mayflower*; reached Cape Cod Nov. 19; 103 passengers landed at Plymouth, Dec. 26. **Mayflower Compact**, signed Nov. 11, was agreement to form a self-government. Half of colony died during harsh winter.

1624 Dutch settled in Albany and along Hudson River, establishing the colony of **New Netherland** in May.

1626 Peter Minuit bought **Manhattan** for Dutch West India Co. from Manahatta Indians during summer for goods valued at $24; named island **New Amsterdam.**

1630 Settlement of **Boston** established by Massachusetts colonists led by John Winthrop; Winthrop began *The History of New England*. **William Bradford**, a governor of Plymouth Colony, began his chronicle *History of Plymouth Plantation (1620-1647)*, first published in entirety in 1856.

1634 Maryland founded as Catholic colony under charter to Lord Baltimore. Act of Toleration passed 1649 provided for religious tolerance.

1587: The first English baby, Virginia Dare, is born in the Americas in the Roanoke colony.

1635 Boston Latin School, **oldest public school** in continuous existence in U.S., founded Apr. 23.

1636 Roger Williams founded Providence, RI, in June, as a democratically ruled colony with separation of church and state. Charter granted, 1644. **Harvard College** founded; oldest institution of higher learning in U.S.

1640 First book printed in America, the so-called *Bay Psalm Book.*

1647 Liberal constitution drafted in Rhode Island. First law in America providing for **free compulsory basic education** enacted in Massachusetts.

1660 British Parliament passed first **Navigation Act** Dec. 1, regulating colonial commerce to suit English needs.

1661 Missionary John Eliot's translation of the New Testament into Algonquian became the **first Bible printed** in North America.

1664 British troops Sept. 8 seized New Netherland from Dutch. Charles II granted New Netherland and city of New Amsterdam to brother, Duke of York; both renamed **New York.** Dutch recaptured colony 1673 but ceded it to Britain Nov. 10, 1674.

1670 Charles Town, SC, founded by English colonists in Apr.

1673 Regular mail service on horseback instituted Jan. 1 between New York and Boston. **Jacques Marquette** and **Louis Jolliet** reached the upper Mississippi and traveled down it.

1674 Future Salem witch trial judge Samuel Sewall began renowned diary covering events through 1729.

1676 Bloody Indian war in New England ended Aug. 12. King Philip, Wampanoag chief, and Narragansett Indians killed. Nathaniel Bacon led planters against autocratic British Gov. Sir William Berkeley, burned Jamestown, VA, Sept. 19. Rebellion collapsed when Bacon died; 23 followers executed.

1678 A book of poetry by Anne Bradstreet (first published in Britain) revised and expanded for posthumous publication in Massachusetts. Considered first female poet in American colonies.

1679 Fire destroyed 150 houses in Boston. City imported **first fire engines** from England.

1681 John Bunyan's *The Pilgrim's Progress* published in America; became best seller.

1682 René-Robert Cavelier, Sieur de La Salle, claimed lower Mississippi River country for France and called it Louisiana Apr. 9. Had French outposts built in Illinois and Texas, 1684. Killed during mutiny, 1687. Spanish colonists became the **first Europeans to settle Texas**, at site of present-day El Paso.

1683 William Penn signed treaty with Delaware Indians Apr. 23 and made payment for **Pennsylvania** lands. The **first German colonists** in America settled near Philadelphia.

1689 New York's English colonial governor, **Sir Edmund Andros**, resigned after armed uprising in Boston on Apr. 18.

1690 First colonial newspaper, *Publick Occurrences*, published by Benjamin Harris but shut down after one issue for lack of official permission. Harris also published *New England Primer* for use as elementary school textbook. Large-scale whaling operations began in Nantucket, MA.

1692 Hysteria over witchcraft began in Salem Village (now Danvers), MA; 14 women and 6 men were executed by special court.

1697 *The Essays* of Sir Francis Bacon, first published in England in 1597, was published in America; it became a best seller.

1699 Former privateer Capt. **William Kidd** arrested and sent to England; hanged for piracy, 1701. French settlements made in Mississippi, Louisiana.

1702 Legislation enacted making Church of England the established church in Maryland.

1704 Indians and French allies attacked Deerfield, MA, Feb. 29; killed 40, captured and marched off 100. *Boston News Letter*, **first regular newspaper**, started by postmaster John Campbell.

1710 British-colonial troops captured French fort, Port Royal, Nova Scotia, in **Queen Anne's War**, 1702-13. France yielded Nova Scotia by treaty, 1713.

1712 Enslaved Black laborers rebelled against white colonists in New York City Apr. 6 and 9 whites were killed; 40 rebels put on trial and around 20 executed, with 6 committing suicide.

1716 First theater in colonies opened in Williamsburg, VA.

1726 Great Awakening, general revival of evangelical religion, began in colonies.

1776: Thomas Jefferson's final draft of the Declaration of Independence eliminates a phrase in an early draft that called slavery an "execrable commerce."

1731 America's **first subscription library** (paying members could freely borrow books) cofounded in Philadelphia by Benjamin Franklin.

1732 Benjamin Franklin published the **first *Poor Richard's Almanack*;** published annually until 1757. Georgia, last of 13 colonies, chartered.

1733 Influenza epidemic swept through New York City and Philadelphia.

1735 Editor **John Peter Zenger** was acquitted of libel Aug. 5 in New York City after criticizing the British governor's conduct in office.

1739 A series of **slave uprisings** put down in South Carolina.

1741 Famous sermon "Sinners in the Hands of an Angry God," delivered July 8 at Enfield, MA, by Jonathan Edwards, one of the most important preachers in the **Great Awakening** religious revival. Danish navigator **Vitus Bering**, commanding Russian expedition, reached Alaska.

1744 King George's War pitted British and colonials against French. Colonials captured Louisbourg, Cape Breton Isl., Nova Scotia, June 17, 1745. Returned to France 1748 by Treaty of Aix-la-Chapelle.

1752 According to legend, **Benjamin Franklin**, flying kite in thunderstorm, proved lightning is electricity, June 15; invented lightning rod. **Liberty Bell**, cast in England, was delivered to Pennsylvania.

1754 French and Indian War began with Ft. Necessity campaign in Pennsylvania. Skirmish May 28, battle at fort July 3-4. British moved Acadian French from Nova Scotia to Louisiana Oct. 8, 1755. British captured Québec Sept. 18, 1759, in battles in which French Gen. Joseph de Montcalm and British Gen. James Wolfe were killed. Peace pact signed Feb. 10, 1763. French lost Canada and Midwest. Delegates from seven colonies to New York for **Albany Congress**, July 19, approved plan of union by Benjamin Franklin; plan rejected by the colonies.

1757 First streetlights appeared in Philadelphia.

1764 Sugar Act, Apr. 5, placed duties on lumber, foodstuffs in colonies. First law passed by Parliament to specifically raise revenue from colonies, alleviate French and Indian War debts. British enforced this act, unlike with **Molasses Act** of 1733.

1765 Stamp Act, enacted by Parliament Mar. 22, required revenue stamps to help fund royal troops. Nine colonies, at Stamp Act Congress in New York Oct. 7-25, adopted Declaration of Rights. Stamp Act repealed Mar. 17, 1766. **Quartering Act**, requiring colonists to house British troops, went into effect Mar. 24.

1767 Townshend Acts levied taxes on glass, lead, paper, paint, and tea. In 1770 all duties except on tea were repealed.

1770 British troops fired Mar. 5 into Boston mob, killed five including **Crispus Attucks**, a Black man, reportedly leader of group; later called **Boston Massacre**.

1773 East India Co. tea ships turned back at Boston, New York, and Philadelphia in May. Cargo ship burned at Annapolis, Oct. 14; cargo thrown overboard at **Boston Tea Party**, Dec. 16, to protest the tea tax. **First museum** in the colonies was officially established in Charleston, SC; later named the Charleston Museum.

1774 "**Intolerable Acts**" of Parliament curtailed Massachusetts self-rule; barred use of Boston Harbor until dumped tea was paid for. **First Continental Congress** held in Philadelphia

Sept. 5-Oct. 26; called for civil disobedience against British. Rhode Island **abolished slavery**.

1775 Patrick Henry addressed Virginia convention, Mar. 23, said, "Give me liberty, or give me death!" **Paul Revere, William Dawes**, and Dr. **Samuel Prescott**, Apr. 18, rode to alert patriots that British were on their way to Concord, MA, to destroy arms. At **Lexington**, MA, Apr. 19, Minutemen lost eight. On return from **Concord**, British suffered 273 casualties. Col. Ethan Allen (joined by Col. Benedict Arnold) captured **Ft. Ticonderoga** in New York, May 10, also Crown Point. Colonials headed for **Bunker Hill** and fortified nearby Breed's Hill, Charlestown, MA. Repulsed British under Gen. William Howe twice before retreating, June 17. Continental Congress June 15 named **George Washington** commander in chief; established a postal system, July 26. Benjamin Franklin became the **first postmaster general**.

1776 Thomas Paine's *Common Sense*, famous pro-independence pamphlet, published Jan. 10; quickly sold some 100,000 copies. France and Spain agreed May 2 to provide arms to U.S. In Continental Congress June 7, Richard Henry Lee (VA) moved "that these United Colonies are, and of right ought to be, free and independent states." Resolution adopted July 2. **Declaration of Independence** approved July 4, signed Aug. 2. Col. William Moultrie's batteries at **Charleston, SC**, repulsed British sea attack June 28. Washington lost **Battle of Long Island** Aug. 27; evacuated New York. **Nathan Hale** executed as spy by British Sept. 22. Brig. Gen. Arnold's Lake Champlain fleet was defeated in **Battle of Valcour Island** Oct. 11, but British returned to Canada. Howe failed to destroy Washington's army at White Plains, NY, Oct. 28. Hessians captured Ft. Washington, Manhattan, and 3,000 men, Nov. 16; captured Ft. Lee, NJ, Nov. 20. Washington, in Pennsylvania, recrossed **Delaware River** Dec. 25-26, defeated Hessians at **Battle of Trenton**, NJ, Dec. 26.

1777 Washington defeated Lord Charles Cornwallis at **Princeton**, NJ, Jan. 3. Continental Congress, June 14, authorized an **American flag**, the Stars and Stripes. Maj. Gen. John Burgoyne's force of 8,000 from Canada captured **Ft. Ticonderoga**, NY, July 6. Americans beat back Burgoyne at Bemis Heights, Oct. 7, cut off British escape route. Burgoyne surrendered 5,000 men at Saratoga, NY, Oct. 17. **Articles of Confederation** adopted by Continental Congress, Nov. 15; took effect Mar. 1, 1781.

1778 France signed treaty of aid with U.S. Feb. 6; sent fleet. British evacuated Philadelphia, June 18.

1779 George Rogers Clark took Ft. Vincennes in what is now Indiana in Feb. **John Paul Jones** on the *Bonhomme Richard* defeated *Serapis* in British North Sea waters, Sept. 23.

1780 Charleston, SC, fell to the British May 12, but Loyalists were defeated in battle of **Kings Mountain**, NC, Oct. 7 in what Thomas Jefferson called "the turn of the tide of success." **Benedict Arnold** found to be a traitor Sept. 23. Arnold escaped, made brigadier general in British army.

1781 Bank of North America, **first commercial bank**, incorporated May 26. Cornwallis retired to **Yorktown, VA**. French fleet under Adm. François-Joseph-Paul, count de Grasse, gained control of harbor; Washington's troops and French force led by Jean Baptiste de Rochambeau arrived near Yorktown, Sept. 28. After long siege, **Cornwallis surrendered** Oct. 19.

1782 New British cabinet agreed in Mar. to **recognize U.S. independence**. Preliminary agreement signed in Paris, Nov. 30. Use of **scarlet letter A**, sewn on clothing or branded on skin of adulterers, discontinued in New England.

1783 Massachusetts Supreme Court decision in final Quock Walker trial **declared slavery illegal**. Newspapers typically published weekly; **first regular daily newspaper**, *Pennsylvania Evening Post*, went on sale in Philadelphia, May 30. Britain, U.S. signed **Paris peace treaty**, Sept. 3, recognizing American independence; Congress ratified it Jan. 14, 1784. Washington ordered army disbanded Nov. 3, bade farewell to his officers at Fraunces Tavern, New York City, Dec. 4.

1784 Thomas Jefferson's proposal to **ban slavery in new territories** after 1802 was narrowly defeated, Mar. 1.

1785 Regular **stagecoach routes** established between Albany, NY; New York City; and Philadelphia.

1786 Delegates from five states at Annapolis, MD, Sept. 11-14 asked Congress to call a **constitutional convention**.

1787 Shays's Rebellion of debt-ridden farmers in Massachusetts failed, Jan. 25. **Constitutional convention** opened in

Philadelphia, May 25, with Washington presiding. Constitution accepted by delegates, Sept. 17. Delaware was first state to ratify it, Dec. 7; Pennsylvania and New Jersey followed. **Northwest Ordinance** adopted July 13 by Continental Congress for Northwest Territory, north of Ohio River, west of New York; made rules for statehood and guaranteed freedom of religion, support for schools, no slavery. *Federalist Papers* first appeared in *NY Independent Journal.*

1788 A large fire in **New Orleans**, then a Spanish territory, destroyed much of the city, Mar. 21. **Constitution adopted** June 21 after being ratified by the requisite ninth state (New Hampshire); also ratified by Georgia, Connecticut, Massachusetts, Maryland, South Carolina, Virginia, and New York throughout the year. **First U.S. senators elected** Sept. 30, from Pennsylvania.

1789 George Washington chosen president by all electors voting (73 eligible, 69 voting, 4 absent); **John Adams**, vice president, got 34 votes. **First Congress** met at Federal Hall, New York City, and declared Constitution in effect, Mar. 4; Washington inaugurated there Apr. 30; **first inaugural ball** held May 7. U.S. **State Dept.** established by Congress July 27. (Thomas Jefferson installed as first secretary of state Feb. 1790.) **War Dept.** created Aug. 7, with Henry Knox as secretary; **Treasury Dept.** created Sept. 2, with Alexander Hamilton to be secretary. **Supreme Court** created by Federal Judiciary Act, Sept. 24; **John Jay** confirmed by Congress as first Supreme Court chief justice, Sept. 26.

1790 First Supreme Court session held Feb. 2 in New York City. Congress, Mar. 1, authorized decennial **U.S. census**. Collection of data took 18 months. **Naturalization Act** (two-year residency) passed Mar. 26. John Carroll consecrated as **first American Catholic bishop**, Aug. 15. Congress met in **Philadelphia**, new temporary capital, Dec. 6.

1791 Bill of Rights, submitted to states, Sept. 25, 1789, went into effect Dec. 15. First Bank of the United States, **first bank chartered by federal government**, established in Philadelphia.

1792 Coinage Act established **U.S. Mint** in Philadelphia, Apr. 2. Gen. **"Mad" Anthony Wayne** made commander in Ohio-Indiana area, trained American Legion, established string of forts. Routed Indians at Fallen Timbers on Maumee River, Aug. 20, 1794; checked British at Fort Miami, OH, same year. **White House** cornerstone laid Oct. 13.

1793 Washington inaugurated for second term, Mar. 4, having received 132 electoral votes; **John Adams** again became vice president, having received second highest total, 77. Washington declared **U.S. neutrality**, Apr. 22, in war between Britain and France. Eli Whitney invented **cotton gin** (patented 1794), reviving Southern slavery.

1794 Whiskey Rebellion, western Pennsylvania farmers protesting liquor tax of 1791, suppressed by federal militia in Sept. **Jay's Treaty**, controversial treaty with Britain negotiated by John Jay, signed Nov. 19, ratified June 24, 1795. This treaty intended to settle long-standing differences between U.S. and Britain.

1795 U.S. bought peace from **Algerian pirates** by paying $1 mil ransom for 115 seamen Sept. 5, followed by annual tributes. Gen. Wayne signed **Treaty of Greenville** with Indians, opening Northwest Territory to settlers. Univ. of North Carolina became **first operating state university**.

1796 Washington's farewell address as president delivered Sept. 17. Warned against permanent alliances with foreign powers, big public debt, large military establishment, and devices of "small, artful, enterprising minority."

1797 John Adams inaugurated as second president Mar. 4, having received 71 electoral votes; **Thomas Jefferson** became vice president, having received 68. U.S. frigate *United States* launched at Philadelphia, May 10; *Constellation* at Baltimore, Sept. 7; *Constitution* (Old Ironsides) at Boston, Oct. 21.

1798 Alien and Sedition Acts passed by Federalists June-July; intended to silence political opposition. **War with France threatened** over French raids on U.S. shipping and rejection of U.S. diplomats. Navy (45 ships) and 365 privateers captured 84 French ships. USS *Constellation* took French warship *Insurgente*, 1799. Napoleon stopped French raids after becoming first consul.

1800 Federal government moved to **Washington, DC**.

1801 John Marshall named Supreme Court chief justice, Jan. 20. **Thomas Jefferson**, who had received same number of electoral votes as Aaron Burr in 1800 election, won out

1804-06: Meriwether Lewis, William Clark, and the Corps of Discovery—including indispensable guide Sacagawea—explore the Missouri and Columbia Rivers from St. Louis to the Pacific Ocean and back.

over Burr in House vote Feb. 17; Burr named vice president. **Tripoli declared war** June 10 against U.S., which refused added tribute to commerce-raiding Arab corsairs. Land and naval campaigns forced Tripoli to negotiate peace, June 4, 1805. **Oldest U.S. art institution**, Pennsylvania Academy of Fine Arts, founded in Philadelphia.

1802 Congress established U.S. Military Academy at **West Point**, NY.

1803 Supreme Court, in *Marbury v. Madison*, overturned U.S. law for first time, Feb. 24. Napoleon sold all of Louisiana, stretching to Canadian border, to U.S. for $11.25 mil in bonds, plus $3.75 mil indemnities to American citizens with claims against France. U.S. took title Dec. 20. **Louisiana Purchase** doubled U.S. area.

1804 Meriwether Lewis and **William Clark** expedition ordered by Pres. Thomas Jefferson to explore what is now Northwest U.S. Started from St. Louis May 14; ended Sept. 23, 1806, back in St. Louis. Vice Pres. **Aaron Burr** shot Alexander Hamilton in duel July 11 in Weehawken, NJ; Hamilton died next day.

1805 U.S. Marines aided by Arab mercenaries, Apr. 27, captured Tripolitan port of Derna. Major victory in war against **Barbary pirates**; inspiration for "to the shores of Tripoli" in Marines Corps hymn.

1807 Robert Fulton made **first practical steamboat trip**; left New York City Aug. 17 and reached Albany, NY, 150 mi away, in 32 hr. **Embargo Act** banned all trade with foreign countries, forbidding ships to set sail for foreign ports Dec. 22.

1808 Legislation **outlawing slave imports** goes into effect. Some 250,000 people were illegally imported as slaves, 1808-60.

1810 Third U.S. Census found population of 7,239,881. The enslaved population was put at 1,191,364 and the population of all other non-white free persons at 186,446.

1811 Indiana Territory governor William Henry Harrison defeated Indians led by Tenskwatawa, called the Prophet, in **Battle of Tippecanoe**, Nov. 7. Construction began on **Cumberland Road** in Cumberland, MD; road became important route to West. About 400 **slaves revolted** in Louisiana and marched on New Orleans. The insurrection was suppressed; two whites, some 75 slaves killed.

1812 War of 1812 had three main causes: Britain seized U.S. ships trading with France; Britain had seized 4,000 naturalized U.S. sailors by 1810; Britain armed Indians, who raided Western border. U.S. stopped trade with Europe 1807 and 1809. Trade with Britain only was stopped 1810. Unaware that Britain had raised blockade against France two days before, **Congress declared war** June 18. British took **Detroit** Aug. 16.

1813 Oliver H. Perry defeated British fleet at **Battle of Lake Erie**, Sept. 10. U.S. won **Battle of the Thames**, Ontario, Oct. 5, but failed in Canadian invasion attempts. York (Toronto) and Buffalo, NY, were burned.

1814 Troops under Andrew Jackson defeated Creek Indians led by Chief Weatherford at Battle of Horseshoe Bend in Alabama, Mar. 29, ending **Creek Indian War**, begun a year earlier. British landed in Maryland in Aug., defeated U.S.

force Aug. 24, **burned Capitol and White House**. Maryland militia stopped British advance, Sept. 12. British bombardment of Ft. McHenry, Baltimore, for 25 hr., Sept. 13-14, failed, inspiring **Francis Scott Key** to write the words to **"The Star-Spangled Banner."** U.S. won naval **Battle of Lake Champlain** Sept. 11. Peace treaty with Great Britain signed at Ghent, Belgium, Dec. 24.

1815 Some 5,300 British, unaware of peace treaty, attacked U.S. entrenchments near **New Orleans**, Jan. 8. British had more than 2,000 casualties; Americans lost 71. U.S. flotilla finally ended attacks by **pirates** from Ottoman states of Algiers, Tunis, Tripoli.

1816 Second Bank of the U.S. chartered Apr. 10. The **American Colonization Society**, which sought to address slavery issue by encouraging Black people to migrate to Africa, formed in Washington, DC, Dec. 1816-Jan. 1817.

1817 Thomas Hopkins Gallaudet established the **first free public school for the deaf** in Hartford, CT.

1818 Connecticut expanded **suffrage** among white male voters. Massachusetts followed suit in 1820, and New York in 1821, reducing or eliminating property qualifications.

1819 Spain ceded **Florida** to U.S. Feb. 22. American steamship *Savannah* made first part-steam-powered, part-sail-powered **crossing of Atlantic**, traveling from Savannah, GA, to Liverpool, England, in 29 days. **Washington Irving's** *Sketch Book* became best seller.

1820 First organized immigration of Black people from **U.S. to Africa** began with a group of 86 sailing to Sierra Leone in Feb. Henry Clay's **Missouri Compromise** bill passed by Congress, Mar. 3. Slavery was allowed in Missouri but not west of the Mississippi River, north of 36° 30′ (the southern line of Missouri). Compromise repealed 1854.

1821 Emma Willard founded Troy Female Seminary, **first U.S. women's college**. Stephen Austin established **first American community in Texas**, San Felipe de Austin. **James Fenimore Cooper's** *The Spy*, novel set during American Revolution, published and became a best seller.

1822 Tension between sports and academics surfaced when Yale College Pres. Timothy Dwight banned a **primitive form of football**, setting fines for violators.

1823 Monroe Doctrine, opposing European intervention in the Americas, enunciated by Pres. James Monroe Dec. 2. The **Hudson River School**, painters who focused on the beauties of nature, began to receive public attention.

1824 Pawtucket, RI, **weavers strike** is first organized factory strike in U.S. and one of earliest known involving women workers. **Slavery abolished** in state of Illinois Aug. 2.

1825 After a deadlocked election, **John Quincy Adams** was elected president by the House, Feb. 9. **Erie Canal** opened; first boat left Buffalo, NY, Oct. 26, reached New York City Nov. 4. John Stevens, of Hoboken, NJ, built and operated **first experimental steam locomotive** in U.S.

1826 Thomas Jefferson and **John Adams** both died July 4. **James Fenimore Cooper's** *The Last of the Mohicans* published.

1827 Massachusetts became first state to pass a law providing for tax-supported **public high schools**.

1828 Baltimore & Ohio, the **first U.S. passenger railroad**, began operations July 4. South Carolina Dec. 19 declared right of **state nullification of federal laws**, opposing the "Tariff of Abominations." **Noah Webster** published his *American Dictionary of the English Language*.

1829 Andrew Jackson inaugurated as president, Mar. 4.

1830 Famous **debate** culminating Jan. 27 between Sen. **Daniel Webster** (MA) and Robert Hayne (SC), on state right to nullify federal law. **Mormon church** organized by Joseph Smith in Fayette, NY, Apr. 6. Pres. Jackson, May 28, signed **Indian Removal Act**, granting president authority to negotiate treaties whereby Indians living east of Mississippi R. give up lands in exchange for lands in West.

1831 William Lloyd Garrison began **abolitionist newspaper** *The Liberator* Jan. 1. **Nat Turner**, an enslaved man in Virginia, led local rebellion, starting Aug. 21; 57 whites killed. Troops called in, 100 rebellion participants killed. Turner captured, tried, and hanged Nov. 11.

1832 Black Hawk War in Illinois and Wisconsin Apr.-Sept. pushed Sauk and Fox Indians west across Mississippi.

1833 American Anti-Slavery Society founded in Philadelphia, Dec. 4. **Oberlin College** became first to adopt coeducation in U.S.

1835 According to tradition, the **Liberty Bell** cracked July 8 while tolling death of Chief Justice John Marshall. **Seminole Indians** in Florida under Osceola began attacks Nov. 1, protesting forced removal. The unpopular war ended Aug. 14, 1842; most of the Indians sent to Oklahoma. **Texas** proclaimed right to secede from Mexico; **Sam Houston** put in command of Texas army, Nov. 2-4. **Gold** discovered on Cherokee land in Georgia. Indians forced to cede lands, Dec. 20, and to cross Mississippi.

1836 Texans besieged at **Alamo** in San Antonio by Mexicans under Antonio López de Santa Anna, Feb. 23-Mar. 6; entire garrison killed. Texas independence had been declared, Mar. 2. At San Jacinto Apr. 21, Sam Houston and Texans defeated Mexicans. Ralph Waldo Emerson published his first work, *Nature*, espousing his philosophy of **transcendentalism**. Marcus Whitman, H. H. Spaulding, and wives reached Fort Walla Walla on Columbia River, OR, **first white women to cross the Continental Divide**, in the Rocky Mountains.

1838 Cherokee Indians forced to walk **"Trail of Tears"** from southeast U.S. to area in present-day Oklahoma. At least 4,000—nearly one-fifth of Cherokee population—are estimated to have died.

1841 First emigrant wagon train bound for California, 47 people, left Independence, MO, May 1; reached California Nov. 4. Edgar Allan Poe published one of the **first American detective stories**, *The Murders in the Rue Morgue*.

1842 Webster-Ashburton Treaty signed Aug. 9, fixing U.S.-Canada border in Maine and Minnesota. **First use of anesthetic** (sulfuric ether gas) in an operation performed by Georgia doctor Crawford Long.

1843 More than 1,000 settlers left Independence, MO, for Oregon May 22, arriving in Oct. via **Oregon Trail**.

1844 First message over first telegraph line sent May 24 by inventor Samuel F. B. Morse from Washington to Baltimore: "What hath God wrought!"

1845 Congress **overrode a presidential veto for the first time**, Mar. 3, after Pres. John Tyler vetoed a tariff bill. Congress of **Texas** voted for annexation by U.S., July 4; Texas admitted to Union, Dec. 29. **Edgar Allan Poe's** poem "The Raven" published.

1846 Mexican War began after Pres. James K. Polk ordered Gen. Zachary Taylor to seize disputed Texan land settled by Mexicans. After border clash, U.S. declared war May 13; Mexico declared war May 23. About 12,000 U.S. troops took Vera Cruz Mar. 27, 1847, and Mexico City Sept. 14, 1847. Treaty signed Feb. 2, 1848, ended war, and Mexico ceded claims to Texas, California, and other territory. Bear flag of **Republic of California** raised by American settlers at Sonoma, June 14. Treaty with Britain June 15 set **Oregon territory** boundary at 49th parallel (extension of existing line). Expansionists had used slogan "54°40′ or fight." The term **"manifest destiny,"** coined by journalist in 1845, also came into play. **Mormons**, after violent clashes with settlers over polygamy, left Nauvoo, IL, for West under Brigham Young. They settled July 1847 at Salt Lake City, UT. Elias Howe invented **sewing machine**.

1847 First adhesive U.S. postage stamps—Benjamin Franklin 5¢, Washington 10¢—sold July 1. **Henry Wadsworth Longfellow's** *Evangeline* published.

1838: Cherokee population is marched from their home in southeast U.S. to present-day Oklahoma on the "Trail of Tears."

1848 Gold discovered Jan. 24 in California; 80,000 prospectors emigrated in 1849. Lucretia Mott and Elizabeth Cady Stanton led Seneca Falls, NY, **Women's Rights Convention** July 19-20.

1850 Sen. Henry Clay's **Compromise of 1850** admitted California as 31st state Sept. 9, with slavery forbidden; made Utah and New Mexico territories; made **Fugitive Slave Law** harsher; and ended District of Columbia slave trade. **Nathaniel Hawthorne**'s *The Scarlet Letter* published.

1851 Herman Melville's *Moby-Dick* published.

1852 Harriet Beecher Stowe's *Uncle Tom's Cabin* published.

1853 Japan receives Comm. Matthew C. Perry, July 14. He negotiated treaty to **open Japan** to U.S. ships. New York City hosted **first World's Fair** in the U.S., beginning July 14. **Stephen Foster** published "My Old Kentucky Home."

1854 Republican Party formed at Ripon, WI, Feb. 28. Opposed Kansas-Nebraska Act, which left issue of slavery to vote of settlers. Act became law May 30. Treaty ratified with Mexico Apr. 25, providing for **Gadsden Purchase** of a strip of land. **Henry David Thoreau**'s *Walden* published.

1855 First railroad train crossed Mississippi River on river's first bridge, between Rock Island, IL, and Davenport, IA, Apr. 21. **Walt Whitman**'s *Leaves of Grass* published.

1856 Proslavery group sacked **Lawrence, KS**, May 21; abolitionist John Brown led antislavery contingent against Missourians at Osawatomie, KS, Aug. 30. Antislavery Republican Party's **first presidential nominee**, John C. Frémont, defeated by James Buchanan. Abraham Lincoln made 50 speeches for Frémont. **First U.S. kindergarten** opened in Watertown, WI.

1857 In **Dred Scott** case, which involved determination of constitutionality of already-repealed Missouri Compromise, Supreme Court decided Mar. 6 that enslaved individuals did not become free in a free state, and Black persons were not and could not be citizens. **Currier & Ives**, firm of American lithographers, issued their first print.

1858 First Atlantic cable completed by Cyrus W. Field Aug. 5. **Lincoln-Douglas debates** in Illinois, Aug. 21-Oct. 15.

1859 Edwin L. Drake drilled the **first commercially productive oil well** near Titusville, PA, Aug. 27. Abolitionist John Brown, with 21 men, seized U.S. armory at **Harpers Ferry**, WV, Oct. 16. U.S. Marines captured raiders, killing several. Brown was hanged for treason Dec. 2.

1860 Shoeworkers in Lynn, MA, went on strike Feb. 22. Within a week, strike spread to include 20,000 shoeworkers throughout New England in country's **largest strike to date**. **First Pony Express** between Sacramento, CA, and St. Joseph, MO, started Apr. 3. Republican **Abraham Lincoln** elected president Nov. 6 in four-way race.

1861 Seven southern states set up **Confederate States of America** Feb. 8, with **Jefferson Davis** as president. **Civil War** began as Confederates fired on **Ft. Sumter** in Charleston, SC, Apr. 12; they captured it Apr. 14. Pres. Lincoln called for 75,000 volunteers Apr. 15. Lincoln blockaded Southern ports Apr. 19, cutting off vital exports and aid. By May, 11 states had seceded. Confederates repelled Union forces at first **Battle of Bull Run**, July 21. **First transcontinental telegraph line** put in operation.

1862 Union forces were victorious in Western campaigns, took New Orleans May 1. Battles in East were largely inconclusive despite heavy casualties. The **Battle of Antietam**, in western Maryland Sept. 17, was bloodiest one-day battle of war; each side lost more than 2,000 men. **Homestead Act**, which granted free farms to settlers, approved May 20. **Land Grant Act**, which provided for public land sale to benefit agricultural education, approved July 7. It eventually led to establishment of state university systems.

1863 Pres. Lincoln issued **Emancipation Proclamation** Jan. 1, freeing "all slaves in areas still in rebellion." Union forces won major victory at Gettysburg, PA, July 1-3. Confederate forces under siege surrendered **Vicksburg, MS**, to Union forces under Gen. Ulysses S. Grant, July 4; control of Mississippi River in Union hands. About 1,000 were killed or wounded in **draft riots** in New York City; white mobs attacked and hanged Black individuals July 13-16. Pres. Lincoln gave his **Gettysburg Address** Nov. 19. Lincoln declared **Thanksgiving** a national holiday.

1863: President Abraham Lincoln's Emancipation Proclamation frees the enslaved population in seceding states.

1864 Gen. **William Tecumseh Sherman** marched through Georgia, taking Atlanta Sept. 1 and Savannah Dec. 22. **Sand Creek massacre** of Cheyenne and Arapaho Indians Nov. 29. Soldiers drove Indians out of village; about 150 killed.

1865 Gen. **Robert E. Lee surrendered** 27,800 Confederate troops to Gen. Grant at Appomattox Court House in VA, Apr. 9. J. E. Johnston surrendered 31,200 to Sherman at Durham Station, NC, Apr. 18. Last rebel troops surrendered May 26. Pres. Lincoln shot Apr. 14 by **John Wilkes Booth** in Ford's Theater, Washington, DC; died the following morning. Vice Pres. **Andrew Johnson** was sworn in as president. Booth was tracked down and fatally wounded, perhaps by his own hand, Apr. 26. Four co-conspirators were hanged July 7. **13th Amendment**, abolishing slavery except as a punishment for crime, ratified Dec. 6.

1866 Congress took control of Southern **Reconstruction**, backed freedmen's rights in legislation vetoed by Pres. Andrew Johnson; veto overridden by Congress, Apr. 9. **Ku Klux Klan** formed secretly in South to terrorize Black residents who voted. Disbanded 1869-71.

1867 Alaska sold to U.S. by Russia for $7.2 mil Mar. 30, through efforts of Sec. of State William H. Seward. Fraternal society the **Grange** was organized Dec. 4 to protect farmer interests. **Horatio Alger**'s *Ragged Dick* published.

1868 Pres. Andrew Johnson dismissed Sec. of War Edwin M. Stanton without Senate approval. **Johnson impeached** by the House Feb. 24 for violation of Tenure of Office Act, though charges were actually made in response to his opposition to congressional Reconstruction. He was acquitted by the Senate Mar.-May. **14th Amendment**, providing for citizenship of all persons born or naturalized in U.S. and subject to the jurisdiction thereof, ratified July 9. **Louisa May Alcott**'s *Little Women* published. *The World Almanac*, a publication of the *New York World* newspaper, appeared for first time.

1869 First **Transcontinental railroad** completed; golden spike driven at Promontory Summit, UT, May 10, marking junction of Central Pacific and Union Pacific lines. Attempt to "corner" gold led to financial **"Black Friday"** in New York Sept. 24. **Woman suffrage law** passed in Wyoming Territory Dec. 10. **Knights of Labor** labor union formed in Philadelphia. By 1886, it had 700,000 members nationally.

1870 15th Amendment, making race no bar to voting rights, ratified Feb. 8. **First U.S. boardwalk** completed, in Atlantic City, NJ. **U.S. Weather Bureau** founded.

1871 Great Chicago fire destroyed city Oct. 8-11. **National Rifle Association (NRA)** founded.

1872 Amnesty Act May 22 restored civil rights to citizens of the South, except for 500 Confederate leaders. Congress established Yellowstone, **first national park**. James McNeill Whistler painted famous portrait known informally as **"Whistler's Mother."**

1873 First U.S. postal card issued May 1. **Jesse James** and his gang robbed their first passenger train July 21. Banks failed, panic began in Sept. **Depression** lasted five years. **"Boss" William Tweed** of New York City was convicted Nov. 19 of stealing public funds; he died in jail in 1878. New York's Bellevue Hospital started **first nursing school**.

1874 Women's Christian Temperance Union established in Cleveland. **First public zoo** in U.S. established in Philadelphia.

1875 Congress passed **Civil Rights Act** Mar. 1, giving equal rights to Black people in public accommodations and jury duty. Supreme Court invalidated act in 1883. First **Kentucky Derby** held May 17. First **Jim Crow segregation law** enacted, in Tennessee.

1876 Alexander Graham Bell patented the telephone Mar. 7. Col. **George A. Custer** and 264 soldiers of the 7th Cavalry were killed June 25 in "last stand," **Battle of the Little Bighorn**, MT, in Sioux Indian War. Democrat **Samuel J. Tilden** received majority of popular votes for president over Republican **Rutherford B. Hayes**, Nov. 7, but 22 electoral votes were in dispute. Congress agreed to certify Hayes as winner in Feb. 1877 after Republicans agreed to end federal Reconstruction of South.

1877 Molly Maguires—Irish terrorist society in mining areas of Scranton, PA—was broken up by hanging, June 21, of 11 leaders for murders of mine officials and police. Pres. Hayes sent federal troops to control violent national **railroad strike**, which began in July.

1878 First commercial telephone exchange opened, New Haven, CT, Jan. 28. **Thomas A. Edison** founded Edison Electric Light Co. on Oct. 15.

1879 F. W. Woolworth opened his first five-and-ten store, in Utica, NY, Feb. 22. French actress **Sarah Bernhardt** made her U.S. debut Nov. 8 at New York City's Booth Theater. Economist and social philosopher **Henry George** published *Progress & Poverty*, advocating single tax on land.

1881 Clara Barton founded **American Red Cross** May 21. Pres. **James A. Garfield** shot in Washington, DC, July 2, by mentally disturbed office seeker; died Sept. 19. Famous gun battle between the Earp brothers and outlaw rustlers Oct. 26 near the **OK Corral**, Tombstone, AZ. **Booker T. Washington** founded Tuskegee Institute for Black students. **Helen Hunt Jackson**'s *A Century of Dishonor*, about mistreatment of American Indians, published.

1882 Chinese Exclusion Act, barring immigration of Chinese laborers for 10 years, later made permanent, passed by Congress May 6; first significant law to restrict immigration to U.S.

1883 Civil Service Act, or **Pendleton Act**, passed Jan. 16, created foundations of American civil service system. The **Brooklyn Bridge** opened May 24 as world's longest suspension bridge. Transcontinental **Northern Pacific Railroad** was completed Sept. 8. **Buffalo Bill Cody**'s Wild West Show began its 30-year touring run.

1884 Switchback Railway—**first U.S. roller coaster** built as amusement park ride—opened at Coney Island in New York City. **Mark Twain**'s *The Adventures of Huckleberry Finn* published.

1885 Washington Monument dedicated Feb. 21.

1886 Haymarket riot and bombing, May 4, followed labor battles for 8-hr. work day in Chicago; seven police and four workers died. Eight anarchists found guilty Aug. 20; four hanged Nov. 11. **Coca-Cola** first sold, May 8, at Jacob's

Pharmacy in Atlanta. Apache Indian **Geronimo** surrendered Sept. 4, ending last major Indian war. **Statue of Liberty** dedicated Oct. 28. **American Federation of Labor** (AFL) formed Dec. 8 by 25 craft unions.

1887 Interstate Commerce Act enacted Feb. 4, created Interstate Commerce Commission.

1888 Great blizzard struck Eastern U.S. Mar. 11-14, causing about 400 deaths. Ernest Thayer's poem **"Casey at the Bat"** recited for first time in public at New York City theater in May.

1889 U.S. opened 2-mil acre **Oklahoma District** to settlement Apr. 22, initiating land run; "sooner" settlers illegally entered the territory before that date to stake favorable claims. More than 2,200 lives lost in **Johnstown flood** (PA) May 31. **Electric lights** installed at White House.

1890 Sherman Antitrust Act passed July 2, began federal effort to curb monopolies. After decades of broken treaties and diminished reservations, U.S. Army massacre at Wounded Knee, SD, Dec. 29, kills about 250 Lakota Sioux men, women, and children; at least 25 soldiers were killed. **Jacob Riis**'s *How the Other Half Lives*, about city slums, published, instigating reform legislation in New York City. **Emily Dickinson**'s poems published, four years after her death.

1891 Forest Reserve Act, Mar. 3, let president close public forest land to settlement for establishment of national parks. **Carnegie Hall**, in New York City, opened May 5.

1892 Ellis Island, in New York Bay, opened Jan. 1 to receive immigrants; closed 1954. **Homestead strike** (PA) at Carnegie steel mills; 7 guards and 11 strikers and spectators shot to death July 6. James J. Corbett defeated John L. Sullivan Sept. 7 to become **first world heavyweight champion** under Marquess of Queensbury rules.

1893 Columbian Exposition world's fair held May-Oct. in Chicago. Financial panic led to four-year **depression**. **Mormon Temple** dedicated in Salt Lake City, UT.

1894 Thomas A. Edison's **kinetoscope**, for motion pictures (invented 1887), given first public showing Apr. 14. **Jacob S. Coxey** led army of unemployed from the Midwest, reaching Washington, DC, Apr. 30. Coxey arrested May 1 for trespassing on Capitol grounds; his army disbanded. **Pullman strike** began May 11 at railroad car plant in Chicago. Milton Hershey started **Hershey Chocolate Company**.

1895 "America, the Beautiful" appeared for first time, in church publication, July 4. **Stephen Crane**'s *The Red Badge of Courage* published.

1896 Supreme Court, in *Plessy v. Ferguson*, May 18, approved racial segregation under the **"separate but equal"** doctrine. **William Jennings Bryan** delivered "Cross of Gold" speech July 9; won Democratic Party nomination. **John Philip Sousa** composed "Stars and Stripes Forever" on Dec. 25.

1897 Olney-Pauncefote Treaty with Britain, Jan. 11, gave wide scope to arbitration in settling disputes; never ratified by U.S. John J. McDermott won **first Boston Marathon** Apr. 19. First Klondike gold arrived in San Francisco July 14, helping set off **Klondike gold rush**. **First subway service** in country opens to public in Boston, Sept. 1.

1898 U.S. battleship *Maine* exploded Feb. 15 in Havana, Cuba; 260 killed. U.S. blockaded Cuba Apr. 22 in aid of independence forces. U.S. declared **war on Spain** Apr. 24; destroyed Spanish fleet in Philippines May 1; took Guam June 20. U.S. took **Puerto Rico** July 25-Aug. 12. Spain agreed Dec. 10 to cede Philippines, Puerto Rico, and Guam, and approved independence for Cuba. Annexation of **Hawaii** signed by Pres. William McKinley, July 7.

1899 Filipino insurgents, unable to get recognition of independence from U.S., started guerrilla war Feb. 4. Their leader, Emilio Aguinaldo, captured May 23, 1901. **Philippine insurrection** ended 1902. Some 200,000 civilians and 20,000 Filipino troops died, mostly from disease and starvation. Pres. McKinley signed treaty officially ending **Spanish-American War**, Feb. 10. U.S. declared **Open Door Policy** Sept. 6, to make China an open international market. Philosopher **John Dewey**'s *School and Society*, advocating progressive education ("learn by doing"), published. Pianist Scott Joplin's "Maple Leaf Rag" published, popularizing **ragtime music**.

1900 International Ladies' Garment Workers Union founded in New York City June 3. Fought sweatshop working conditions. **Carry Nation**, Kansas temperance leader, began raiding saloons with a hatchet. U.S. helped suppress **Boxer Rebellion** in Beijing, China. Eastman Kodak Co. introduced the **Brownie camera**, popularizing picture-taking.

1882: The Chinese Exclusion Act blocks immigration of new Chinese workers; workers from China played a key role in building the transformational railroads in the West.

1901 Texas had first significant oil strike at **Spindletop** well near Beaumont, Jan. 10. U.S. withdrew troops from **Cuba** May 20, and Cuba became independent. Pres. **McKinley** shot Sept. 6 in Buffalo, NY, by anarchist Leon Czolgosz; died Sept. 14. Vice Pres. **Theodore Roosevelt** sworn in as youngest-ever president, at age 42 years, 11 months. **Booker T. Washington**'s *Up From Slavery* published.

1902 Permanent **Bureau of the Census** established Mar. 6. **Helen Keller** autobiography appeared in serial form.

1903 Treaty between U.S. and Colombia to have U.S. dig **Panama Canal** signed Jan. 22, but rejected by Colombia's Congress. Panama declared independence from Colombia with U.S. support Nov. 3; recognized by Pres. Roosevelt Nov. 6. U.S., Panama signed canal treaty Nov. 18. Wisconsin set first **direct primary voting system**, May 23. **Henry Ford** founded Ford Motor Co., June 16. Boston defeated Pittsburgh, 5 games to 3, Oct. 13 in **first modern World Series**. **First successful flight** in heavier-than-air mechanically propelled airplane by **Orville Wright** Dec. 17 near Kitty Hawk, NC, 120 ft in 12 sec. Later flight same day by **Wilbur Wright**, 852 ft in 59 sec. Improved plane patented, 1906. **Iroquois Theater fire** in Chicago killed about 600 out of 1,900 in audience, Dec. 30. Pioneering film *Great Train Robbery* produced.

1904 St. Louis hosted **first Olympics in U.S.**, July 1-Nov. 23. First section of **New York City subway** system opened, Oct. 27. **Ida Tarbell** published muckraking *The History of the Standard Oil Company*. **Henry James**'s last major novel, *The Golden Bowl*, published.

1905 **Industrial Workers of the World**, which advocated Marxian theory of class struggle between workers and capitalists, founded in Chicago, June 27. **Rotary**, oldest service club organization in U.S., founded in Chicago.

1906 **San Francisco earthquake** and fire, Apr. 18-19, caused more than 3,000 deaths and $400 mil in damages. **Upton Sinclair**'s *The Jungle*, which exposed working conditions in meat-packing industry, published. Helped spur passage of the **Pure Food and Drug Act** and **Meat Inspection Act** June 30.

1907 Financial panic and **depression** started Mar. 13. Pres. Roosevelt sent **"Great White Fleet"** of 16 U.S. battleships around the world in show of power.

1908 Springfield, IL, torn by **anti-Black rioting**, Aug. 14-15. Henry Ford introduced **Model T** car, priced at $850, Oct. 1.

1909 Adm. Robert E. Peary claimed to have reached **North Pole** Apr. 6 on sixth attempt, accompanied by Black explorer Matthew Henson and four Inuit men; may have fallen short. National Conference on the Negro convened May 30, leading to founding of **National Association for the Advancement of Colored People** (NAACP).

1910 **Boy Scouts** of America founded Feb. 8. Former Pres. Roosevelt called for **"new nationalism"** in famous speech in Kansas, Aug. 10.

1911 Building with New York City's **Triangle Shirtwaist Co.** factory caught fire Mar. 25; 146 died. Supreme Court ruled May 15 that **Standard Oil Co.** must be dissolved because it unreasonably restrained trade. **First transcontinental airplane**

flight (with numerous stops) by C. P. Rodgers, from New York, NY, to Pasadena, CA, Sept. 17-Nov. 5; time in air 82 hr., 4 min.

1912 American Girl Guides founded Mar. 12; name changed in 1913 to **Girl Scouts**. U.S. Marines, Aug. 14, sent to **Nicaragua**, which was in default of loans to U.S. and Europe.

1913 **16th Amendment**, authorizing federal income tax, ratified Feb. 3. The **Armory Show** in New York City brought modern art to U.S. for first time, Feb. 17. **17th Amendment**, providing for direct popular election of U.S. senators (originally elected by state legislatures), ratified Apr. 8. **Federal Reserve System** authorized Dec. 23, in major reform of U.S. banking and finance.

1914 **Ford Motor Co.** raised basic wage rates from $2.40 for 9-hr. day to $5 for 8-hr. day, Jan. 5, increasing stability in labor force. When U.S. sailors were arrested in Tampico, Mexico, Apr. 9, Atlantic fleet was sent to **Veracruz**, occupied city. Pres. Woodrow Wilson proclaimed **U.S. neutrality** in the European war, Aug. 4. The **Panama Canal** officially opened Aug. 15. The **Clayton Antitrust Act** passed Oct. 15, strengthening federal antimonopoly powers.

1915 **First transcontinental telephone call**, New York to San Francisco, completed Jan. 25 by Alexander Graham Bell and Thomas A. Watson. British ship *Lusitania* sunk May 7 by German submarine; 1,198 passengers died, including 128 Americans. (In notice in morning newspapers the day *Lusitania* set sail, Germany had warned Americans against taking passage on British vessels.) As result of U.S. campaign, Germany issued apology and promise of payments, Oct. 5. U.S. troops landed in **Haiti**, July 28. Haiti became virtual U.S. protectorate under Sept. 16 treaty. Pres. Wilson asked for a military fund increase, Dec. 7. D. W. Griffith's film *The Birth of a Nation* released. William J. Simmons partly inspired by film to revive **Ku Klux Klan**, which peaks in 1920s.

1916 Gen. **John J. Pershing** entered Mexico in Mar. to pursue **Francisco (Pancho) Villa**, who had raided U.S. border areas. Forces withdrew Feb. 5, 1917. **Rural Credits Acts** passed July 17, followed by **Warehouse Act** Aug. 11; both provided financial aid to farmers. Bomb exploded during **San Francisco Preparedness Day parade** July 22, killed 10. Thomas J. Mooney, labor organizer, and Warren K. Billings, shoeworker, convicted 1917; both later pardoned. U.S. bought **Virgin Islands** from Denmark Aug. 4. U.S. established military government in the **Dominican Republic** Nov. 29. Jeannette Rankin (R, MT) elected to House of Representatives, **first woman to be a member of Congress**.

1917 Germany, suffering from British blockade, declared almost unrestricted **submarine warfare** Jan. 31. U.S. cut diplomatic ties with Germany Feb. 3 and formally **declared war** Apr. 6. Jones Act, passed Mar. 2, made **Puerto Rico** a U.S. territory, its inhabitants U.S. citizens. **Conscription law** passed May 18. First U.S. troops arrived in Europe June 26.

1918 Pres. Wilson set out his **14 Points** as basis for peace, Jan. 8. More than 1 mil American troops were in Europe by July. Allied counteroffensive launched at Château-Thierry July 18. War ended with signing of **armistice** Nov. 11. **Influenza pandemic** killed an estimated 50-100 mil worldwide, 675,000 in U.S.

1919 **18th Amendment**, providing for prohibition of manufacture, sale, or transportation of alcoholic beverages, ratified Jan. 16, to take effect on Jan. 16, 1920. **First transatlantic flight**, by U.S. Navy seaplane, left Rockaway, NY, May 8; stopped at Newfoundland, Azores, Lisbon May 27. **Boston police strike** Sept. 9, earliest strike conducted by government employees. About 250 **foreign-born radicals** deported Dec. 21 to Soviet Union.

1920 In national **Red Scare**, some 2,700 Communists, anarchists, and other radicals were arrested Jan.-May. **League of Women Voters** founded Feb. 14. Senate refused Mar. 19 to ratify **League of Nations Covenant**. Nicola Sacco and Bartolomeo Vanzetti accused of killing two men in Massachusetts payroll holdup Apr. 15; found guilty 1921. A seven-year campaign for their release failed; both executed Aug. 23, 1927. Verdict repudiated 1977 by proclamation of Massachusetts Gov. Michael Dukakis. **19th Amendment** ratified Aug. 18, giving women the vote. **First regular licensed radio broadcasting** began Aug. 20. **Wall St. bombing** in New York

1908: Ford's relatively affordable Model T is introduced, making car ownership more widely accessible.

1920: Women are given the right to vote with the ratification of the 19th Amendment, though voting rights are still difficult or impossible for many Americans to exercise.

City killed 39, injured 200-300, did $2 mil damage, Sept. 16. **Sinclair Lewis**'s *Main Street* published.

1921 Congress sharply curbed immigration, set **national quota system** May 19. **"Black Wall Street"** in Tulsa, OK, looted and burned by white rioters, May 31-June 1. Joint congressional resolution declaring **peace with Germany, Austria, and Hungary** signed July 2 by Pres. Warren G. Harding; treaties were signed in Aug. In so-called **Black Sox scandal**, eight Chicago White Sox players were banned from baseball Aug. 4 for conspiring with gamblers to throw the 1919 World Series. Limitation of Armaments Conference met in Washington, DC, Nov. 12-Feb. 6, 1922. Major powers agreed to curtail naval construction, outlaw poison gas, restrict submarine attacks on merchant vessels, and respect China's integrity.

1922 During nationwide coal strike, union miners killed some 21 strikebreakers at Herrin, IL, June 21-22, in incident referred to as the **Herrin Massacre. T. S. Eliot**'s *The Waste Land* published.

1923 **First sound-on-film motion picture**, *Phonofilm*, shown at Rivoli Theater, New York City, beginning in Apr. Pres. Calvin Coolidge addressed Congress, Dec. 6; **first radio broadcast of president's annual speech.**

1924 Law approved by Congress June 2 made all **Native Americans U.S. citizens. Immigration law** enacted May 24 excluded Asian immigrants and established permanent national quotas favoring N and W Europeans. **Nellie Tayloe Ross** and **Miriam (Ma) Ferguson** elected governor of Wyoming and Texas, respectively. Ross inaugurated as nation's **first woman governor** Jan. 5, 1925. **George Gershwin** wrote and premiered "Rhapsody in Blue."

1925 In so-called Monkey Trial, John T. Scopes found guilty of having taught **evolution** in Dayton, TN, high school and fined, July 24. **F. Scott Fitzgerald**'s *The Great Gatsby* published.

1926 Dr. Robert H. Goddard, Mar. 16, demonstrated **first liquid-fuel rocket.** Congress established **Army Air Corps** July 2. **Air Commerce Act** passed Nov. 2, established government agencies for development of airports, radio navigation, and other services. **Ernest Hemingway**'s *The Sun Also Rises* published.

1927 Capt. **Charles A. Lindbergh** left Roosevelt Field, NY, May 20 alone in *Spirit of St. Louis* on first New York-Paris nonstop flight. Reached Le Bourget airfield May 21, 3,610 mi in 33½ hr. *The Jazz Singer*, **first feature-length film** in which spoken dialogue was part of narrative action, released Oct. 6. The musical *Show Boat* opened in New York City Dec. 27.

1928 **Amelia Earhart** became first woman to fly across the Atlantic, June 17. **Herbert Hoover** elected president Nov. 6, defeating New York Gov. Alfred E. Smith, a Catholic.

1929 Gangsters killed seven rivals in Chicago **St. Valentine's Day massacre** Feb. 14, which won Al Capone control of Chicago's underworld. Stock market crash Oct. 29 marked end of past prosperity as stock prices plummeted. Stock losses for 1929-31 estimated at $50 bil; beginning of **Great Depression**. Albert B. Fall, former interior sec., was convicted of accepting

$10,000 bribe in leasing of the **Elk Hills (Teapot Dome)** naval oil reserve; sentenced Nov. 1 to a year in prison and fined. **William Faulkner**'s *The Sound and the Fury* published.

1930 London **Naval Reduction Treaty** signed by U.S., Britain, Italy, France, and Japan Apr. 22; in effect Jan. 1, 1931; expired Dec. 31, 1936. **Hawley-Smoot Tariff** signed; rate hikes slash world trade. **Sinclair Lewis** became first American to win a Nobel Prize in literature. **Dashiell Hammett**'s *The Maltese Falcon* published.

1931 **Empire State Building** opened in New York City May 1, displacing NYC's Chrysler Building as world's tallest. **Al Capone** convicted of tax evasion Oct. 17. **Charlie Chaplin** film *City Lights* released.

1932 **Reconstruction Finance Corp.** established Jan. 22 to stimulate banking and business. Unemployment at 12 mil. Twenty-month-old **Charles Lindbergh Jr.** kidnapped Mar. 1; found dead May 12. Bruno Hauptmann found guilty Feb. 1935; executed Apr. 3, 1936. Unemployed World War I veterans demanding Congress pay promised bonus early launched **Bonus March** on Washington, DC, May 29. **Franklin D. Roosevelt** elected president for first time in Democratic landslide, Nov. 8. Chicago Bears won **first NFL title game** Dec. 18, defeating the Portsmouth (OH) Spartans, 9-0.

1933 Pres. Roosevelt named **Frances Perkins** U.S. sec. of labor; **first woman in U.S. cabinet**. Pres. Roosevelt ordered **all U.S. banks closed** Mar. 6. In a "100 days" special session, Mar. 9-June 16, Congress passed **New Deal**, including measures to regulate banks, distribute funds to the jobless, create jobs, raise agricultural prices, and set wage and production standards for industry. **Gold standard** dropped by U.S. in favor of "modified gold bullion standard"; announced by Pres. Roosevelt Apr. 19, ratified by Congress June 5. **Tennessee Valley Authority (TVA)** created by act of Congress, May 18. **Prohibition** ended in the U.S. as 36th state ratified **21st Amendment** Dec. 5. Pres. Roosevelt foreswore armed intervention in **Western Hemisphere** nations, Dec. 26.

1934 Pres. Roosevelt signed law creating **Securities and Exchange Commission**, June 6. U.S. troops pulled out of **Haiti**, Aug. 6.

1935 **Works Progress Administration (WPA)** instituted May 6. Rural Electrification Administration created May 11. National Industrial Recovery Act struck down by Supreme Court May 27. **Boulder Dam** (later renamed **Hoover Dam**) completed, May 29. **Social Security Act** passed by Congress Aug. 8-9. Comedian **Will Rogers** and aviator Wiley Post killed Aug. 15 in Alaska plane crash. Sen. **Huey Long**, former Louisiana governor, shot Sept. 8 by a political rival's son-in-law; died Sept. 10. George Gershwin's jazz opera *Porgy and Bess* opened Oct. 10 in New York. **Committee for Industrial Organization** (later Congress of Industrial Organizations) formed to expand industrial unionism Nov. 9.

1936 **Jesse Owens** won four gold medals at the **Berlin Olympics** in Aug. Baseball Hall of Fame founded in Cooperstown, NY. **Margaret Mitchell**'s *Gone With the Wind* published.

1937 Airship *Hindenburg* caught fire May 6 as it was landing in Lakehurst, NJ; 36 killed. **Golden Gate Bridge** in San Francisco opened May 27. **Joe Louis** knocked out James J. Braddock to become world heavyweight champ June 22. Aviator **Amelia Earhart** and copilot Fred Noonan disappeared July 2 near Howland Isl., in the Pacific. Pres. Roosevelt proposed judicial reforms that would allow him to appoint additional Supreme Court justices; his **"court-packing" plan** defeated. Auto, steel labor unions won first big contracts.

1938 National **minimum wage** enacted June 25. Orson Welles's radio dramatization of H. G. Wells's *War of the Worlds*, Oct. 30, caused Martian invasion scare among some who had missed the introduction. **Seabiscuit** beat War Admiral in match race of the century, at Pimlico track, MD, Nov. 1. The work of folk artist Anna Mary Robertson Moses, **"Grandma Moses,"** discovered. **Thornton Wilder**'s *Our Town* produced on Broadway.

1939 Opera singer **Marian Anderson** performed for integrated crowd of 75,000 at Lincoln Memorial Apr. 9 after Daughters of the American Revolution refused to let Anderson sing in DC's Constitution Hall. **New York World's Fair**—theme: "The World of Tomorrow"—opened Apr. 30, closed Oct. 31. Reopened for second season May 11-Oct. 27, 1940. **Lou Gehrig**, seriously ill with disease that would come to bear his name, said farewell to fans at Yankee Stadium, July 4. Albert Einstein alerted Pres. Roosevelt to **A-bomb possibilities** in Aug. 2 letter. **U.S. declared its neutrality** in European war

1942: Pres. Franklin D. Roosevelt orders the relocation of 117,000 Japanese-Americans to detention camps for the duration of the war.

Sept. 5. Pres. Roosevelt proclaimed limited **national emergency** Sept. 8, unlimited emergency May 27, 1941. Both ended by Pres. Harry Truman, Apr. 28, 1952.

Pocket Books, **first paperback publisher** in U.S., established. **John Steinbeck's** *The Grapes of Wrath* published. *The Wizard of Oz* and *Gone With the Wind* released, the latter to become highest-grossing film of all time (inflation-adjusted).

1940 U.S. OK'd sale of **surplus war material** to Britain June 3; announced transfer of 50 overaged destroyers Sept. 3. **First peacetime military draft** in U.S. history approved, Sept. 14. **Forty-hour work week** went into effect, Oct. 24. Pres. **Roosevelt** elected Nov. 5 to third presidential term. **Richard Wright's** *Native Son* published.

1941 **Four Freedoms**—freedom of speech and religion, freedom from want and fear—termed essential by Pres. Roosevelt in speech to Congress Jan. 6. **Lend-Lease Act** signed Mar. 11 provided $7 bil in military credits for Britain. Lend-lease for USSR approved in Nov. Pres. Roosevelt signed executive order June 25 barring federal government and war contractors from **racial discrimination**. Order also established Fair Employment Practice Committee. The **Atlantic Charter**, 8-point declaration of principles, issued by Pres. Roosevelt and British Prime Min. Winston Churchill, Aug. 14. Japan attacked **Pearl Harbor**, Hawaii, 7:55 AM Hawaiian time, Dec. 7; 19 ships sunk or damaged, 2,403 dead. Pres. Roosevelt called it "a date which will live in infamy." U.S. declared war on Japan Dec. 8. Germany and Italy declared war on U.S. Dec. 11. U.S. responded with declaration of war later on same day. Japanese invaded **Philippines**, Dec. 22; Wake Island fell, Dec. 23. *Citizen Kane*, directed by Orson Welles, released.

1942 Pres. Roosevelt issued executive order Feb. 19 authorizing relocation of Japanese-Americans. Federal government began forcibly moving 117,000 Japanese-Americans from West Coast to **detention camps**; exclusion lasted three years. Japanese troops took **Bataan** peninsula Apr. 8 and **Corregidor** May 6. **Battle of Midway** June 4-7 was Japan's first major defeat. Marines landed on **Guadalcanal** Aug. 7; last Japanese not expelled until Feb. 9, 1943. U.S., Britain invaded **North Africa** Nov. 8. **First nuclear chain reaction** (fission of uranium isotope U-235) produced at Univ. of Chicago under physicists Arthur Compton, Enrico Fermi, others, Dec. 2. The movie *Casablanca*, starring Humphrey Bogart and Ingrid Bergman, released.

1943 *Oklahoma!* opened Mar. 31 on Broadway. Pres. Roosevelt signed Jun 10 pay-as-you-go income tax bill. Starting July 1, wage and salary earners were subject to **paycheck withholding tax**. **Detroit race riot** June 21 left 34 dead, 700 injured. Six killed in riot in New York City's **Harlem** section Aug. 2. U.S., Britain invaded **Sicily** July 9, Italian **mainland** Sept. 3. Marines in Nov. recaptured the **Gilbert Islands**, captured by Japan in 1941 and 1942.

1944 U.S., Allied forces invaded Europe at Normandy, France, on **"D-Day,"** June 6, in massive amphibious operation. **GI Bill of Rights**, providing benefits to veterans, signed by Pres. Roosevelt June 22. Representatives of the U.S. and other major powers met at **Dumbarton Oaks**, Washington, DC, Aug. 21-Oct. 7, to work out formation of postwar world organization

that would become the **United Nations**. U.S. forces landed on **Leyte**, Philippines, Oct. 20. Pres. **Roosevelt** elected to fourth term as president Nov. 7. **Battle of the Bulge**, failed Nazi counteroffensive, waged Dec. 16 to Jan. 28, 1945.

1945 **Yalta Conference** met in the Crimea, USSR, Feb. 4-11. Pres. Roosevelt, Prime Min. Churchill, and Soviet leader Joseph Stalin agreed that their countries, plus France, would occupy Germany and that the Soviet Union would enter war against Japan. Marines landed on **Iwo Jima** Feb. 19, declared victory Mar. 26 after heavy casualties. U.S. forces invaded **Okinawa** Apr. 1, captured it June 21. Pres. **Roosevelt** died in Warm Springs, GA, Apr. 12; Vice Pres. **Harry S. Truman** became president. Germany surrendered May 7; May 8 proclaimed **V-E Day**. **First atomic bomb**, produced at Los Alamos, NM, exploded at Alamogordo, NM, July 16. Bomb dropped on **Hiroshima**, Japan, Aug. 6, killing about 75,000; bomb dropped on **Nagasaki**, Japan, Aug. 9, killing about 40,000. Japan agreed to surrender Aug. 14; formally surrendered Sept. 2. At **Potsdam Conference**, July 17-Aug. 2, leaders of U.S., USSR, and Britain agreed on disarmament of Germany, occupation zones, war crimes trials. **Empire State Building** struck accidentally by Army B-25 bomber, July 28, killing 14. U.S. forces entered **Korea** south of 38th parallel to displace Japanese Sept. 8. Gen. **Douglas MacArthur** took over supervision of Japan Sept. 9.

1946 **Steel strike** by 750,000 started Jan. 21, settled in four weeks. Strike by 400,000 **mine workers** began Apr. 1 (settled May 29); other industries (including rail, maritime) followed. Former Prime Min. Winston Churchill employed the phrase **"Iron Curtain"** in Mar. 5 speech at Westminster College in Fulton, MO. Atomic bomb tested off **Bikini Atoll** in Pacific, July 1. In all, U.S. conducted 23 nuclear tests between 1946 and 1958. **Philippines** given independence by U.S. July 4. Mother Frances Xavier Cabrini **first American to be canonized**, July 7. Dr. Benjamin Spock's *Baby and Child Care* published as **baby boom** began.

1947 Pres. Truman asked Congress for financial and military aid for Greece and Turkey to help combat Communist subversion, Mar. 12; **Truman Doctrine** approved May 15. UN Security Council voted Apr. 2 to place under U.S. trusteeship the **Pacific islands** formerly mandated to Japan. **Jackie Robinson** joined Brooklyn Dodgers Apr. 11, breaking color barrier in major league baseball. The **Marshall Plan** for U.S. aid to European countries proposed by Sec. of State George C. Marshall June 5. Congress authorized some $12 bil in next four years. **Taft-Hartley Labor Act** restricting labor union power vetoed by Pres. Truman June 20; Congress overrode veto. Air Force Capt. **Chuck Yeager** broke sound barrier, Oct. 14, in X-1 rocket plane. First families moved to new suburban Levittown, NY, development Oct. 1 (original construction ended 1951).

1948 **Organization of American States** (OAS) founded Apr. 30 by 21 countries. USSR halted all surface traffic into **West Berlin** June 24; in response, U.S. and British troops launched an **airlift**. Soviet blockade halted May 12, 1949; airlift ended Sept. 30. Pres. **Truman** elected Nov. 2, defeating NY Gov. Thomas E. Dewey in historic upset. Former State Dept. official **Alger Hiss** indicted Dec. 15 for perjury, after denying he had passed government documents to Whittaker Chambers to go to a Communist spy ring; convicted Jan. 21, 1950. **Kinsey Report** on sexuality in the human male published.

1949 North Atlantic Treaty Organization **(NATO)** established Aug. 24 by U.S., Canada, and 10 Western European nations, agreeing that an armed attack against one would be considered an attack against all. Eleven leaders of U.S. **Communist Party** convicted Oct. 14 of advocating violent overthrow of U.S. government; sentenced to prison. Supreme Court upheld convictions, 1951. Pres. Truman, Oct. 26, signed legislation raising **federal minimum wage** from 40¢ an hour to 75¢. **Arthur Miller's** *Death of a Salesman* opened on Broadway.

1950 Masked bandits robbed **Brink's, Inc.**, Boston express office, Jan. 17, of $2.8 mil. Case solved 1956; eight sentenced to life. Pres. Truman authorized production of **H-bomb** Jan. 31. Special Senate committee to investigate organized crime established May 3, chaired by Sen. **Estes Kefauver** (D, TN).

North Korean forces **invaded South Korea** June 25. UN asked for troops to restore peace. Pres. Truman ordered Air Force and Navy to Korea June 27. Truman approved ground forces, airstrikes against North Korea June 30. U.S. sent 35 military advisers to **South Vietnam** June 27 and agreed to aid anti-Communist government. U.S. forces landed at **Inchon**, South Korea, Sept. 15. UN forces took Pyongyang Oct. 20, reached China border Nov. 20. China sent troops across border Nov. 26. U.S. banned shipments Dec. 8 to **Communist China** and to Asiatic ports trading with it.

Army **seized all U.S. railroads** Aug. 27 on Truman's order to prevent general strike; returned to owners in 1952. Two members of **Puerto Rican nationalist movement** tried to kill Pres. Truman Nov. 1.

Peanuts comic strip appeared in newspapers. Variety show *Your Show of Shows* debuted on TV. David Riesman's *The Lonely Crowd* published.

1951 **22nd Amendment**, limiting presidential term of office, ratified Feb. 27. **Julius Rosenberg**; his wife, **Ethel Rosenberg**; and **Morton Sobell** found guilty Mar. 29 of conspiracy to commit wartime espionage. Rosenbergs received death penalty. Sobell sentenced to 30 years; released 1969.

Pres. Truman removed Gen. **Douglas MacArthur** from Korea command Apr. 11 for unauthorized policy statements. **Korea cease-fire** talks began in July; lasted two years. Fighting ended July 27, 1953.

Transcontinental TV began Sept. 4 with Pres. Truman's address at Japanese Peace Treaty Conference in San Francisco. **Japanese peace treaty** signed in San Francisco Sept. 8 by U.S., Japan, and 47 other nations. **J. D. Salinger**'s *Catcher in the Rye* published. *I Love Lucy* sitcom premiered on TV.

1952 Pres. Truman ordered seizure of nation's **steel mills** Apr. 8 to avert strike; ruled illegal by Supreme Court June 2. **Peace contract** between West Germany, U.S., Great Britain, and France signed May 26. **Immigration** measure, passed over veto June 26-27, barred those deemed subversive and removed some barriers to Asian immigration, though quotas remained for nationalities and regions. **Puerto Rico** proclaimed commonwealth July 25, after referendum Mar. 3. Richard Nixon, as vice-pres. candidate, gave **"Checkers" speech,** so called because of sentimental reference to his dog Checkers, Sept. 23. **First hydrogen device explosion** Nov. 1 in Pacific. **Ralph Ellison**'s *Invisible Man* published.

1953 Federal jury in New York convicted 13 **Communist** leaders on conspiracy charges, Jan. 20. **Julius and Ethel Rosenberg** executed in electric chair, June 19, for relaying nuclear secrets to Soviet Union. **Korean War armistice** signed July 27. California Gov. **Earl Warren** sworn in Oct. 5 as 14th chief justice of U.S. Supreme Court.

1954 *Nautilus*, **first atomic-powered submarine,** launched at Groton, CT, Jan. 21. Five members of Congress were wounded in the House May 1 by four **Puerto Rican independence supporters** who fired at random from a spectators' gallery.

At televised hearings, Apr. 22-June 17, before a Senate subcommittee, Army officials accused Sen. **Joseph McCarthy** (R, WI) of seeking preferential treatment for a draftee, and McCarthy accused Army of hindering probe of Communist infiltration. McCarthy was cleared in the hearings, but the Senate later voted to condemn him, 67-22, for abuse of the Senate during hearings and debates.

Supreme Court ruled unanimously May 17 that racial segregation in public schools was unconstitutional, in *Brown v. Board of Education* of Topeka. **Ernest Hemingway** won Nobel Prize in literature.

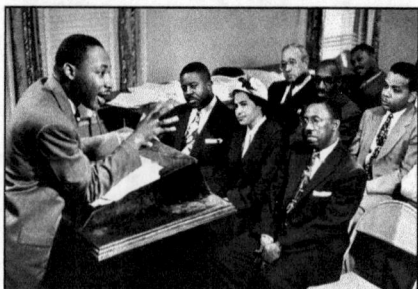

1955: The bus boycott beginning Dec. 5 in Montgomery, AL, led by Martin Luther King Jr., is a foundational event in the burgeoning civil rights movement.

1955 U.S. agreed Feb. 12 to help train **South Vietnamese army.** Supreme Court ordered "all deliberate speed" in **integration** of public schools, May 31. A summit meeting of leaders of **Big 4**—U.S., Britain, France, and USSR—took place July 18-23 in Geneva, Switzerland.

Rosa Parks refused Dec. 1 to give her seat to white man on bus in Montgomery, AL. Her arrest, detention, and conviction provided catalyst for Black community's planned boycott, fronted by Rev. **Martin Luther King Jr.**, of Montgomery's bus system, Dec. 5, 1955-Dec. 20, 1956. Bus segregation ordinance declared unconstitutional by federal court in 1956.

America's two largest labor organizations merged Dec. 5, creating **AFL-CIO**. Russian-born U.S. citizen **Vladimir Nabokov**'s *Lolita* published.

1956 Massive resistance to Supreme Court **desegregation rulings** was called for Mar. 12 by 101 Southern congressmen. U.S. Supreme Court, Apr. 23, unanimously ruled against **racial segregation** on intrastate buses.

Federal-Aid Highway Act signed June 29, creating **interstate highway system. First transatlantic telephone cable** activated Sept. 25. In Game 5, Oct. 8, Yankee right-hander Don Larsen pitched **only perfect World Series game.** Eugene O'Neill's *Long Day's Journey Into Night* opened Nov. 7 on Broadway.

1957 Congress approved **Civil Rights Act of 1957,** Apr. 29, first such bill since Reconstruction to protect voting rights. Pres. Dwight D. Eisenhower signed act into law Sept. 9; provided for creation of Civil Rights Commission. The U.S. surgeon general July 12 said studies showed "direct link" between cigarette **smoking and lung cancer.**

Arkansas Gov. Orval Faubus (D) called National Guard Sept. 4 to bar nine Black students from entering all-white high school in **Little Rock.** Faubus complied Sept. 21 with federal court order to remove Guard, but local authorities ordered Black students to withdraw. Pres. Eisenhower sent troops Sept. 24 to enforce court order.

Jack Kerouac's *On the Road* published.

1958 Army launched **first U.S. Earth-orbiting satellite,** *Explorer I*, Jan. 31 from Cape Canaveral, FL; discovered Van Allen radiation belt. U.S. Marines sent to **Lebanon** to protect elected government from threatened overthrow July-Oct. Nuclear sub *Nautilus* made **first undersea crossing of North Pole** Aug. 5. Presidential aide **Sherman Adams** resigned Sept. 22 over scandal involving alleged improper gifts. **First domestic jet airline passenger service** in U.S. opened by National Airlines Dec. 10 between New York and Miami.

1959 Alaska admitted as 49th state, Jan. 3; **Hawaii** admitted as 50th, Aug. 21. **St. Lawrence Seaway** linking Atlantic Ocean and Great Lakes opened to traffic, Apr. 25.

Vice Pres. Richard Nixon, on tour of USSR, held **"kitchen debate,"** July 24, with Soviet Prem. Nikita Khrushchev at U.S. exhibit in Moscow. Prem. **Khrushchev** paid unprecedented visit to U.S. Sept. 15-27; made transcontinental tour.

Pres. Eisenhower issued injunction Oct. 12, upheld and made effective by Supreme Court Nov. 7, ending record **116-day steel strike.** In quiz show scandal, Columbia Univ. Prof. Charles Van Doren admitted to U.S. House subcommittee Nov. 2 that he had been coached before appearances on NBC-TV's *21* in 1956; he had won $129,000. William Wyler's *Ben-Hur* released; the movie won a record 11 Academy Awards the following year.

1960 Sit-ins began Feb. 1 when four Black college students in Greensboro, NC, refused to move from a Woolworth lunch counter after being denied service. By Sept. 1961, more than 70,000 students had participated in sit-ins. Pres. Eisenhower signed **Civil Rights Act** May 6.

A U.S. **U-2 reconnaissance plane** was shot down in the Soviet Union May 1; pilot Gary Powers captured. The incident led to cancellation of Paris summit conference; Powers traded for Soviet spy, 1962. A **birth control pill** approved as safe for first time by Food and Drug Administration May 9. Vice Pres. **Richard Nixon** and Sen. **John F. Kennedy** faced each other Sept. 26 in first series of televised debates. Kennedy defeated Nixon to win presidency, Nov. 8. U.S. announced Dec. 15 its backing of rightist group in **Laos**, which took power the next day.

Alfred Hitchcock film *Psycho* released.

1961 U.S. severed diplomatic and consular relations with Cuba Jan. 3, after disputes over nationalizations of U.S. firms, U.S. military presence at Guantánamo base. U.S.-directed invasion of Cuba's **Bay of Pigs** Apr. 17 by Cuban exiles unsuccessfully attempted to overthrow the regime of Prem. Fidel Castro.

Peace Corps created by executive order, Mar. 1. **23rd Amendment**, giving DC citizens the right to vote in presidential elections, ratified Mar. 29. Alan B. Shepard Jr. rocketed from Cape Canaveral, FL, in a Mercury capsule May 5, in **first U.S.-crewed suborbital space flight.**

"Freedom Rides" from Washington, DC, across Deep South were launched May 20 to protest segregation in interstate transportation.

Joseph Heller's *Catch-22* published.

1962 Pres. Kennedy said Feb. 14 that U.S. military advisers in **Vietnam** would fire if fired upon. Lt. Col. John H. Glenn Jr. became **first American in orbit** Feb. 20 when he circled the Earth three times in the Mercury capsule *Friendship 7.*

In *Baker v. Carr*, Mar. 26, U.S. Supreme Court ruled that constitutional challenges to unequal distribution of voters among legislative districts could be resolved by federal courts. **James Meredith** became first Black student at Univ. of Mississippi Oct. 1 after 3,000 federal troops put down riots.

A Soviet **offensive missile buildup** in Cuba was revealed Oct. 22 by Pres. Kennedy, who ordered naval and air quarantine on shipment of offensive military equipment to the island. He and Soviet Prem. Khrushchev agreed Oct. 28 on formula to end crisis. Kennedy announced Nov. 2 that missile bases in Cuba were being dismantled. **Rachel Carson's** *Silent Spring* launched environmentalist movement.

1963 In *Gideon v. Wainwright*, Mar. 18, Supreme Court ruled that all criminal defendants have a right to counsel.

March for civil rights began May 2 in Birmingham, AL; led to desegregation accord, which in turn sparked rioting and violence. Univ. of Alabama **desegregated** after Gov. George Wallace stepped aside when confronted by federally deployed National Guard troops June 11. Civil rights leader **Medgar Evers** assassinated June 12. On Aug. 28, 200,000 joined in **March on Washington** in support of Black demands for equal rights led by **Rev. Martin Luther King Jr.**; highlight was King's **"I Have a Dream" speech.**

Supreme Court ruled June 17 that laws requiring **recitation of Lord's Prayer or Bible verses** in public schools were unconstitutional. Pres. Kennedy, on Europe trip, addressed huge crowd in **West Berlin**, June 23. **Limited nuclear test-ban treaty** agreed upon July 25 by the U.S., the Soviet Union, and Britain. Four Black girls killed in bombing of **16th St. Baptist Church** in Birmingham, AL, Sept. 15.

South Vietnam Pres. **Ngo Dinh Diem** assassinated Nov. 2; U.S. had earlier withdrawn support. Pres. **Kennedy** shot and fatally wounded Nov. 22 as he rode in motorcade through downtown Dallas, TX. Vice Pres. **Lyndon B. Johnson** sworn in as president. **Lee Harvey Oswald** arrested and charged with murder but was himself shot and fatally wounded Nov. 24. Nightclub owner **Jack Ruby** convicted of Oswald's murder; Ruby died in 1967 while awaiting retrial following reversal of his conviction. **Betty Friedan's** feminist work *The Feminine Mystique* published.

1964 Panama suspended relations with U.S. Jan. 9 after riots. U.S. offered Dec. 18 to negotiate new canal treaty. **The Beatles** appeared Feb. 9 on *The Ed Sullivan Show.* Supreme Court ruled Feb. 17 that **congressional districts** as near as practicable be equal in population. U.S. reported May 27 it was sending military planes to **Laos.**

Three **civil rights workers** reported missing in Mississippi June 22; bodies found Aug. 4. Eighteen white men tried. On

Oct. 20, 1967, an all-white federal jury convicted seven of conspiracy in the slayings. Omnibus **civil rights bill** signed by Pres. Johnson July 2, banning discrimination in voting, jobs, public accommodations.

Congress Aug. 7 passed **Tonkin Gulf Resolution,** authorizing presidential action in Vietnam, after North Vietnamese boats reportedly attacked U.S. destroyers Aug. 2. (Resolution repealed, 1971.) Congress approved War on Poverty bill Aug. 11, providing for a domestic Peace Corps (**VISTA**), **Job Corps,** and antipoverty funding. The **Warren Commission** released a report Sept. 27 concluding that Lee Harvey Oswald was solely responsible for the Kennedy assassination. Pres. **Johnson** elected to full term, Nov. 3, defeating Sen. **Barry Goldwater** (R, AZ) in landslide. **Verrazzano-Narrows Bridge** opened in New York City, Nov. 21, with world's then-longest suspension span.

1965 In State of the Union address Jan. 4, Pres. Johnson outlined plans for **"Great Society,"** program of civil rights, antipoverty, and health-care legislation. Johnson in Feb. ordered continuous bombing of **North Vietnam** below 20th parallel.

Malcolm X assassinated by Nation of Islam members Feb. 21 at New York City rally. March from **Selma to Montgomery**, AL, Mar. 21-25, by Rev. Martin Luther King Jr. to demand federal protection of voting rights for Black citizens. Some 14,000 U.S. troops sent to **Dominican Republic** during civil war Apr. 28. All troops withdrawn by next year. Bill establishing **Medicare**, government health insurance program for elderly, signed by Pres. Johnson July 30.

New **Voting Rights Act**, which banned literacy tests and other voter qualification tests, signed Aug. 6. Arrest of Black motorist by white police officers precipitated **Watts riot** in predominantly Black Los Angeles neighborhood Aug. 11-16. Riots resulted in 34 deaths and $200 mil in property damage.

Major **immigration law**, signed Oct. 3, replaced national quota system with emphasis on immigrants' skills and family unification. **Electric power failure** blacked out most of northeastern U.S., parts of two Canadian provinces the night of Nov. 9-10.

1966 U.S. forces began firing into **Cambodia** May 1. Bombing of **Hanoi** area of North Vietnam by U.S. planes began June 29. By Dec. 31, 385,300 U.S. troops were stationed in South Vietnam, plus 60,000 offshore and 33,000 in Thailand.

Supreme Court ruled June 13, in *Miranda v. Arizona*, that suspects must be read their rights before police questioning. **Medicare** began July 1. In **Univ. of Texas shooting** rampage, 25-year-old student Charles Whitman killed 15 and wounded 31 from tower observation deck on Austin campus, Aug. 1; shot dead by police.

Dept. of Transportation created, Oct. 15. Edward Brooke (R, MA) elected Nov. 8 as first Black U.S. senator in 85 years. Robert C. Weaver named secretary of newly created Dept. of Housing and Urban Development, becoming **first Black cabinet member**.

1967 Green Bay Packers beat Kansas City Chiefs, 35-10, in **first Super Bowl**, Jan. 15, in Los Angeles. Three astronauts died Jan. 27 in *Apollo 1* fire on ground at Cape Canaveral, FL. **25th Amendment**, providing for presidential succession, ratified Feb. 10. Pres. Johnson and Soviet Prem. **Aleksei Kosygin** met June 23 and 25 at Glassboro State College in New Jersey; agreed not to let any crisis push them into war.

Riots erupted among residents of predominantly Black **Newark**, NJ, July 12-17; 26 killed, 1,500 injured, more than 1,000 arrested. In **Detroit**, MI, July 23-30, 43 died, 2,000 injured; 5,000 left homeless by rioting, looting, and burning in city's Black neighborhoods. **Thurgood Marshall** sworn in Oct. 2 as first Black U.S. Supreme Court justice. **Antiwar march** on Washington, DC, Oct. 21-22, drew at least 70,000 participants. Carl B. Stokes (D, Cleveland) and Richard G. Hatcher (D, Gary, IN) elected **first Black mayors** of major U.S. cities Nov. 7.

1968 In **"Tet offensive,"** Communist troops attacked several provincial capitals and other major cities, including Saigon, Jan. 30, but suffered heavy casualties. Pres. Johnson **curbed bombing** of North Vietnam Mar. 31. Peace talks began in Paris May 10. All bombing of North halted Oct. 31.

Rev. **Martin Luther King Jr.** assassinated Apr. 4 in Memphis, TN. **James Earl Ray**, an escaped convict, pleaded guilty to slaying, was sentenced to 99 years. Students at **Columbia Univ.**, Apr. 23-24, seized school buildings in protest against school's involvement in military research, among other issues. Sen. **Robert F. Kennedy** (D, NY) shot June 5 in Los Angeles

1964: The Beatles' appearance on *The Ed Sullivan Show* **presages a pop cultural shift.**

after celebrating presidential primary victories, died June 6. **Sirhan Sirhan** convicted of murder, 1969; death sentence commuted to life in prison, 1972.

Vice Pres. Hubert Humphrey nominated for president at **Democratic National Convention** in Chicago, marked by clash between police and antiwar protesters, Aug. 26-29. Republican nominee **Richard Nixon** won presidency, defeating Humphrey in close race Nov. 5.

Apollo 8 **orbited moon** in five-day mission, Dec. 21-27. North Korea released 82-man crew of the USS *Pueblo* Dec. 22, 11 months after seizing the ship in Sea of Japan; one crew member had been killed in battle.

1969 Expanded four-party **Vietnam peace talks** began Jan. 18. U.S. force peaked at 543,400 in Apr.; withdrawal started July 8. Pres. Nixon set Vietnamization policy of expanding role of South Vietnamese forces Nov. 3. Earl Warren retired upon swearing in **Warren Burger**, June 23, as Supreme Court chief justice. In incident that marked birth of **gay rights** movement, police clashed with patrons of gay bar, the **Stonewall Inn**, in New York City June 28.

U.S. astronaut **Neil Armstrong**, commander of the *Apollo 11* mission, became the **first person to set foot on the moon**, July 20, followed by astronaut **Edwin "Buzz" Aldrin**. Astronaut **Michael Collins** remained aboard command module.

Woodstock rock music festival near Bethel, NY, drew 400,000 people, Aug. 15-18. **Anti-Vietnam War demonstrations** held in cities across the U.S., marking Vietnam Moratorium day, Oct. 15; on Nov. 12, some 250,000 marched in Washington, DC. Massacre of hundreds of civilians by U.S. troops at **My Lai**, South Vietnam, in 1968 reported Nov. 16. **Kurt Vonnegut**'s *Slaughterhouse Five* published. *Sesame Street* launched on public TV.

1970 A federal jury Feb. 18 found the **"Chicago 7"** antiwar activists not guilty of conspiring to incite riots during 1968 Democratic National Convention. However, five were convicted of crossing state lines with intent to incite riots.

Three astronauts safely returned to Earth Apr. 17 after oxygen tank on *Apollo 13* ruptured. Lunar landing had been canceled. Millions of Americans participated in antipollution demonstrations Apr. 22 to mark **first Earth Day**.

U.S. and South Vietnamese forces crossed **Cambodian** borders Apr. 30 to get at enemy bases. Four students killed May 4 at **Kent State Univ.** in Ohio by National Guardsmen during war protest. In protest at **Jackson State Univ.** in Mississippi, two killed when police fired on protesters.

First female U.S. generals appointed June 11. **Postal reform** measure signed Aug. 12 created an independent U.S. Postal Service. Pres. Nixon, Dec. 31, signed **clean air bill** calling for development of cleaner auto engine and national air quality standards for 10 major pollutants. Garry Trudeau's *Doonesbury* comic strip launched in 30 papers.

1971 Charles Manson and three of his cult followers found guilty Jan. 25 of first-degree murder in 1969 slaying of actress Sharon Tate and six others. A court-martial jury Mar. 29 convicted Lt. **William Calley** in murder of 22 South Vietnamese at **My Lai** on Mar. 16, 1968. He was sentenced to life in prison Mar. 31, later reduced to 20 years.

Pres. Nixon, Apr. 14, relaxed 20-year **trade embargo with China**. *New York Times* began publishing June 13 classified **Pentagon Papers**, secret Pentagon study on U.S. involvement in Vietnam leaked by Daniel Ellsberg, military analyst consulting for government. Supreme Court June 30 upheld, 6-3, right to publish the documents. **26th Amendment**, lowering the minimum voting age to 18, ratified June 30. Pres. Nixon, Aug. 15, instituted 90-day **wage and price freeze**.

U.S. bombers initiated massive five-day strike Dec. 26 in North Vietnam in retaliation for alleged violations of agreements reached prior to 1968 bombing halt.

1972 Pres. Nixon arrived in **Beijing** Feb. 21 for eight-day visit to China, in "journey for peace." Joint communiqué released Feb. 27 called for increased Sino-U.S. contacts. Senate, Mar. 22, approved **Equal Rights Amendment** banning discrimination on basis of sex; sent measure to states for ratification.

North Vietnamese forces launched biggest attacks in four years across the demilitarized zone Mar. 30. The U.S. responded Apr. 15 with **resumption of bombing** of Hanoi and Haiphong. Pres. Nixon announced May 8 the mining of North Vietnam ports.

Gov. **George C. Wallace** (D, AL), campaigning for president at Laurel, MD, shopping center May 15, shot and seriously wounded. **Arthur Bremer** convicted Aug. 4, sentenced

1969: *Apollo 11* lands on the lunar surface; Neil Armstrong and Edwin "Buzz" Aldrin are first humans to walk on the moon.

to 63 years for shooting Wallace and three others. In **first visit of U.S. president to Moscow**, Pres. Nixon arrived May 22 for summit talks with Kremlin leaders that culminated in landmark strategic arms pact (**SALT I**). Five men arrested June 17 for breaking into Democratic National Committee offices in **Watergate** office complex in Washington, DC. U.S. Supreme Court in *Furman v. Georgia* June 29 ruled **capital punishment** as unconstitutional.

Mark Spitz won seven gold medals in world record times at the Munich Olympics in Aug.-Sept.

Pres. **Nixon** reelected Nov. 7 in landslide, carrying 49 states to defeat Sen. George McGovern (D, SD). Three astronauts, part of *Apollo 17*, made 6th and last lunar landing on Dec. 11. Full-scale **bombing of North Vietnam** resumed after Paris peace negotiations reached impasse Dec. 18.

The Godfather, directed by Francis Ford Coppola, is released.

1973 In *Roe v. Wade*, Supreme Court ruled, 7-2, Jan. 22, fetus not a person with constitutional rights and that right to privacy protected woman's decision to have abortion; states may not ban abortions during first three months of pregnancy but may regulate, not ban, abortions during second trimester.

Four-party **Vietnam peace pacts** signed in Paris Jan. 27. **End of military draft** announced on same day. Last U.S. troops left Vietnam Mar. 29. North Vietnam released some 590 U.S. prisoners by Apr. 1. Pres. Nixon announced, Apr. 30, resignation of top Nixon aides H. R. Haldeman and John Ehrlichman and firing of White House Counsel **John Dean** as a consequence of the widening **Watergate** scandal. Dean told Senate hearings June 25 that Nixon, his aides, and Justice Dept. had conspired to cover up Watergate facts. The U.S. officially ceased bombing in **Cambodia** at midnight Aug. 14 in accord with June congressional action.

Vice Pres. **Spiro Agnew**, Oct. 10, resigned and pleaded no contest to charge of tax evasion while Maryland governor. **Gerald R. Ford**, Oct. 12, became **first appointed vice president** under 25th Amendment; sworn in Dec. 6. The **"Saturday Night Massacre"** occurred Oct. 20, when Pres. Nixon ordered Atty. Gen. Elliot Richardson to fire Watergate special prosecutor **Archibald Cox**, who had sought handover of Nixon's subpoenaed **White House tapes**. Richardson refused to comply and resigned; Dep. Atty. Gen. William Ruckelshaus refused and was fired. Solicitor Gen. Robert Bork, as acting atty. gen., then fired Cox. Nixon administration named **Leon Jaworski**, Nov. 1, to succeed Cox.

Skylab, **first U.S. space station**, launched May 14. **Secretariat** became first Triple Crown winner since Citation in 1948 by winning Belmont Stakes June 9 in record time. **Billie Jean King** defeated Bobby Riggs in three straight sets in tennis's nationally televised "Battle of the Sexes," Sept. 20. Total **ban on oil exports** to U.S. imposed by Arab oil-producing nations Oct. 19-21 after outbreak of an Arab-Israeli war; lifted Mar. 1974. Congress overrode Nov. 7 Pres. Nixon's veto of **war powers bill** curbing president's power to commit forces to hostilities abroad without congressional approval.

1974 On Apr. 8, **Hank Aaron** of the Atlanta Braves hit his 715th career home run to break Babe Ruth's record.

House Judiciary Committee opened **impeachment** hearings May 9 against Pres. Nixon. John Ehrlichman and three **White House "plumbers"** found guilty July 12 of conspiring to violate the civil rights of the psychiatrist of **Pentagon Papers** leaker Daniel Ellsberg by breaking into psychiatrist's office. Supreme Court ruled, 8-0, July 24 that Pres. Nixon had to turn over 64 **audio tapes of White House conversations**. House Judiciary Committee, in televised hearings July 24-30, recommended **articles of impeachment** against Pres. Nixon, involving conspiracy to obstruct justice in Watergate cover-up, abuses of power, and defiance of committee subpoenas.

Pres. **Nixon** announced his **resignation**, Aug. 8, and stepped down the next day. His support in Congress had begun to collapse Aug. 5 after release of tapes appearing to implicate him in Watergate cover-up. Vice Pres. **Ford** sworn in Aug. 9 as 38th U.S. president. Pres. Ford, Aug. 20, nominated **Nelson Rockefeller** to be vice president; Rockefeller sworn in Dec. 10. Citing need to move on, Pres. Ford, Sept. 8, issued **pardon to Nixon** for any federal crimes he committed while president.

New York Times published article Dec. 22 on CIA engagement in illegal domestic surveillance. Reports of other apparently illegal CIA activities, recorded in **"family jewels"** file kept by the CIA, leaked out over the years.

1975 Former Atty. Gen. John Mitchell and ex-presidential advisers H. R. Haldeman and John Ehrlichman found guilty Jan. 1 of **Watergate cover-up** charges. Mitchell freed 1979, last of 25 jailed over scandal to leave prison.

Bill Gates and Paul Allen founded Microsoft, Apr. 4. U.S. launched **evacuation from Saigon** of Americans and some South Vietnamese Apr. 29 as Communist forces completed takeover of South Vietnam; **South Vietnam** government officially surrendered Apr. 30. U.S. merchant ship *Mayaguez* and its crew of 39 seized by Cambodian forces in Gulf of Siam May 12. In rescue operation, U.S. Marines attacked Koh Tang Island, recovered ship and crew but inadvertently left three Marines behind. Congress voted $405 mil for **South Vietnam refugees** May 16; 140,000 flown to U.S.

Publishing heiress **Patricia (Patty) Hearst**, kidnapped Feb. 5, 1974, by Symbionese Liberation Army (SLA), captured in San Francisco Sept. 18 with other militants. She was convicted Mar. 20, 1976, of bank robbery.

1976 In **right-to-die** case, New Jersey Supreme Court, Mar. 31, allowed comatose Karen Ann Quinlan to be removed from respirator; she survived until 1985. U.S. Supreme Court reinstated **death penalty**, July 2, subject to conditions.

1974: Pres. Richard Nixon resigns from office and departs the White House.

U.S. celebrated **200th anniversary of independence** July 4 with festivals, parades, and New York City's Operation Sail, gathering of tall ships from around the world. **"Legionnaire's disease"** killed 29 people who attended American Legion convention July 21-24 in Philadelphia.

Viking I made successful landing on Mars, July 20. Two U.S. officers on routine mission near DMZ slain by **North Korean soldiers** Aug. 18; North Korea stated "regret."

1977 Convicted murderer Gary Gilmore executed by Utah firing squad Jan. 17; **first use of capital punishment** in U.S. since 1967. Pres. Jimmy Carter Jan. 21 pardoned most Vietnam War **draft evaders**.

Natural gas shortage caused by severe winter weather led Congress Feb. 2 to approve emergency gas bill temporarily authorizing reallocation from surplus areas. Pres. Carter signed act Aug. 4 creating new cabinet-level **Energy Dept.** FBI Dec. 7 released 40,000 pages of previously secret files relating to **Kennedy assassination**.

George Lucas's first *Star Wars* film released.

1978 Senate voted Apr. 18 to turn over **Panama Canal** to Panama on Dec. 31, 1999; Mar. 16 vote had given approval to treaty guaranteeing area's neutrality after the year 2000. Californians, June 6, approved **Proposition 13**, state constitutional amendment slashing property taxes.

Supreme Court, June 28, ruled that while race could be a factor in admission to institutions of higher education, **numerical quotas** could not be used.

Egyptian Pres. **Anwar al-Sadat** and Israeli Prem. **Menachem Begin** reached accord on "framework for peace," Sept. 17, after Pres. Carter-mediated talks at Camp David. A mass murder-suicide, mostly by poisoning, kills more than 900 American members of the Peoples Temple cult led by Jim Jones in Guyana Nov. 18, 1978.

1979 Partial meltdown released radioactive material Mar. 28 at nuclear reactor on **Three Mile Island** near Middletown, PA. American Airlines DC-10 **jetliner crashed** May 25 after losing an engine following takeoff from Chicago, killing 275 people.

In speech July 15, Pres. Carter spoke of national "crisis of confidence" and outlined proposed 10-year, $140-bil program to reduce **dependence on foreign oil**. Militant followers of **Ayatollah Khomeini** took hostage some 90 people, including 66 Americans, Nov. 4 at **American embassy in Tehran**, Iran. Khomeini demanded return of ailing former Shah Muhammad Reza Pahlavi to stand trial.

1980 Pres. Carter announced, Jan. 4, economic **sanctions against USSR** in retaliation for Soviet invasion of Afghanistan. At his request, U.S. Olympic Committee voted, Apr. 12, against U.S. participation in **Moscow Summer Olympics**. At **Winter Olympics** in Lake Placid, NY, U.S. hockey team defeated Russian team Feb. 22, en route to gold medal in **"miracle on ice."**

Eight Americans were killed, Apr. 24, in **attempt to rescue hostages** held by Iranian militants. **Mt. St. Helens**, in Washington state, erupted May 18; the blast and later ones left 57 dead.

In sweeping victory, Nov. 4, **Ronald Reagan** (R) was elected president, defeating incumbent Pres. Carter. Former Beatle **John Lennon** was shot and killed by Mark David Chapman, Dec. 8, in New York City.

1981 Minutes after Reagan's inauguration Jan. 20, 52 **American hostages in Iran** were freed, after being held 444 days. Pres. **Reagan** was shot and seriously wounded, Mar. 30, in Washington, DC, along with a Secret Service agent, a police officer, and Press Sec. **James Brady**. John W. Hinckley Jr. was arrested, found not guilty by reason of insanity, and committed (released in 2016).

World's **first reusable spacecraft**, space shuttle *Columbia*, sent into space, Apr. 12. U.S. Centers for Disease Control, June 5, reported first cases of what became known as **AIDS**. **Air controllers** went on strike Aug. 3; most were fired by Reagan after defying back-to-work order. Reagan, Aug. 13, signed **tax-cut legislation** expected to save taxpayers $750 bil over five years. The Senate, Sept. 21, confirmed **Sandra Day O'Connor**, 99-0, as **first female Supreme Court justice**.

1982 **Equal Rights Amendment** was defeated when ratification deadline passed June 30 with support from only 35 of the 38 states needed. The economy showed signs of recovery from a **recession** that began in mid-1981, as the Dow Jones industrial average, Oct. 13, hit highest level in 18 months.

NFL strike ended Nov. 16 after 57 days, with $1.6-bil pact. **Michael Jackson**'s album *Thriller* was released Nov. 30.

1987: Under pressure from activists, the FDA approves AZT, the first drug shown to be effective in treating HIV/AIDS.

Dr. Barney Clark became **first permanent artificial heart recipient**, Dec. 2.

1983 Pres. Reagan, Jan. 3, declared **Times Beach**, MO, a federal disaster area because of toxic **dioxin** in soil, prompting town's closure. **Harold Washington** (D) was elected Apr. 12 as **first Black mayor of Chicago**. On Apr. 20, Reagan signed bipartisan bill designed to save **Social Security** from bankruptcy.

Sally Ride became **first American woman to travel in space**, with launch June 18 of space shuttle *Challenger*. On Sept. 1, a **South Korean passenger jet** in Soviet air space was apparently misidentified and shot down; 269 people, including 61 Americans, killed. On Oct. 23, 241 U.S. service members were killed when a **suicide truck bomb** blew up Marine barracks in **Lebanon**. U.S. troops, with small force from six Caribbean nations, invaded **Grenada** Oct. 25; deposed Marxist regime.

1984 Seven regional companies took over local telephone service from **AT&T**, Jan. 1. On May 7, Vietnam War veterans reached $180-mil settlement with chemical companies in suit over the herbicide **Agent Orange**.

Former Vice Pres. **Walter Mondale** won Democratic presidential nomination, June 6. He chose Rep. **Geraldine Ferraro** (D, NY) as vice presidential candidate; first woman nominated to that post by a major party. Pres. Reagan signed bill July 17 cutting federal transportation aid to states that keep their **drinking age** under 21. **Reagan** was reelected Nov. 6 in Republican landslide, carrying 49 states for record 525 electoral votes.

1985 First international **AIDS conference** met in Atlanta, GA, Apr. 15-17. Philadelphia police bombed row house occupied by **MOVE** radical group, May 13; 11 killed, some 60 homes destroyed. On June 14, **terrorists seized TWA jet** after takeoff from Athens, Greece, with 153 aboard; 39 Americans held hostage for 17 days; one U.S. service member killed.

Reversing a highly unpopular decision, **Coca-Cola** said, July 10, it would resume marketing soda made under its original "Classic" formula. **Live Aid** rock concert, broadcast around the world July 13, raised $70 mil for **famine relief** in Ethiopia. On Oct. 7, four **Palestinian hijackers** seized Italian cruise ship *Achille Lauro* in the Mediterranean for two days; one American was killed. U.S. and Soviet leaders met at **summit in Geneva**, Nov. 19-20. **General Electric** agreed Dec. 11 to buy RCA Corp.

1986 U.S. officially observed **Martin Luther King Jr. Day** for first time, Jan. 20. Space shuttle *Challenger* exploded 73 seconds after liftoff, Jan. 28, killing six astronauts and teacher **Christa McAuliffe**. **Robert Penn Warren** named America's **first poet laureate**, Feb. 26.

The **Senate**, Sept. 17, confirmed **William Rehnquist** as Supreme Court chief justice (65-33) and **Antonin Scalia** as associate justice (98-0). Congress completed action Oct. 2 to override a Reagan veto and place economic sanctions on **South Africa**. On Nov. 3, news broke of the **Iran-Contra scandal**, involving secret U.S. sale of arms to Iran and diversion of proceeds to support anti-Communist "Contra" insurgents in Nicaragua.

Pres. Reagan, Nov. 7, signed measure giving legal status to some 2.7 mil **undocumented immigrants** who had applied for amnesty. In plea deal, financier **Ivan Boesky**, Nov. 14, agreed to pay $100 mil and serve time in prison for **insider trading**.

1987 Pres. Reagan produced nation's **first trillion-dollar budget**, Jan. 5. FDA, Mar. 20, approved AZT—first drug shown to be effective in fight against **AIDS**.

Senate and House committees held joint televised hearings, May 5-Aug. 3, investigating **Iran-Contra affair;** Pres. Reagan in speech to nation, Aug. 12, denied knowing of diversion of funds to Contras. An **Iraqi missile** killed 37 sailors on the USS *Stark* in the Persian Gulf, May 17; Iraq called it an accident.

Dow industrial average fell 508 points Oct. 19, ending bull market that began mid-1982. Pres. Reagan and Soviet leader **Mikhail Gorbachev**, Dec. 8, signed pact to dismantle all 1,752 U.S. and 859 Soviet intermediate- and shorter-range missiles.

1988 *Phantom of the Opera* opened Jan. 26; became longest-running Broadway show ever. In report issued May 16, Surgeon Gen. **C. Everett Koop** declared cigarettes addictive. U.S. missile fired from Navy warship *Vincennes* in the Persian Gulf mistakenly struck a commercial **Iranian airliner**, July 3, killing all 290 aboard.

George H. W. Bush (R) was elected president, Nov. 8, decisively defeating Massachusetts Gov. **Michael Dukakis** (D). **Pan Am Flight 103** exploded over **Lockerbie**, Scotland, due to terrorist bomb, Dec. 21; 270 killed, including 11 on the ground. Investment firm **Drexel Burnham Lambert** agreed, Dec. 21, to plead guilty to **insider trading** and other violations, and pay penalties of $650 mil.

U.S. suffered widespread **drought** conditions, the worst in over 50 years.

1989 *Exxon Valdez* struck Bligh Reef in Alaska's Prince William Sound, Mar. 24, spilling 10.8 mil gallons of oil. Former National Security Council staffer **Oliver North** was convicted, May 4, on charges related to **Iran-Contra scandal** (overturned in 1991). TV sitcom *Seinfeld* premiered July 5 on NBC.

Pres. George H. W. Bush signed $125 bil bailout measure, Aug. 9, to rescue **savings and loan industry**. Baseball legend **Pete Rose banned** from game for life, Aug. 24, for involvement with gamblers. **Hurricane Hugo** swept through the Caribbean and SE U.S. in Sept.; caused at least 86 deaths and billions in property damages. Army Gen. **Colin Powell**, Oct. 1, became first Black chairman of **Joint Chiefs of Staff**. An **earthquake** struck **San Francisco Bay** area just before a World Series game, Oct. 17, causing 63 deaths.

U.S. troops invaded **Panama**, Dec. 20, overthrowing government of **Manuel Noriega** Noriega surrendered to U.S. authorities; convicted and imprisoned for drug trafficking. **L. Douglas Wilder** (D) declared governor of Virginia Dec. 22, after recount; first elected Black governor in U.S.

1990 Junk bond financier **Michael Milken** pleaded guilty to fraud-related charges, Apr. 14; agreed to pay $500 mil in restitution and sentenced to 10 years in prison. U.S. fell into **recession** (July 1990-Mar. 1991). Pres. Bush signed **Americans With Disabilities Act** barring discrimination against and requiring accommodations for the disabled, July 26.

Operation Desert Shield forces left for Saudi Arabia Aug. 7, following invasion of **Kuwait** by Iraq. **David Souter** was confirmed Oct. 2 (90-9) to serve on **Supreme Court**, replacing retiring Justice **William Brennan**. Bush Nov. 15 signed new **Clean Air Act**, focused on limiting urban pollution, cancer-causing emissions from industrial sources.

1991 After **Iraq** rebuffed UN resolution to withdraw from **Kuwait**, U.S., with allies, launched massive air attacks against Iraq, Jan. 16, followed by ground war; with Kuwait liberated and Iraqi resistance collapsed, Bush declared cease-fire, Feb. 27.

U.S. Senate, voting 52-48 on Oct. 15, confirmed nomination of **Clarence Thomas** to replace retiring Justice **Thurgood Marshall**, after contentious hearings marked by allegations that Thomas had sexually harassed former aide **Anita Hill**.

1992 Trans World Airlines (**TWA**) filed for bankruptcy, Jan. 31. **Riots** swept South Central **Los Angeles** Apr. 29 after jury acquitted four white police officers on all but one count in the 1991 videotaped beating of Black motorist **Rodney King**. Death toll in L.A. violence was put at 53; two officers convicted Apr. 1993, in federal trial. **27th Amendment**, regarding congressional pay raises, ratified May 7.

Hurricane Andrew ravaged S Florida and Louisiana Aug. 24-26, causing 65 deaths. White supremacist and fugitive **Randall Weaver** surrendered Aug. 31 after 11-day FBI siege at his **Ruby Ridge**, ID, cabin, during which three others were killed.

Arkansas Gov. **Bill Clinton** (D) was elected president, Nov. 3, defeating Pres. **Bush** and independent **Ross Perot**. A UN-sanctioned military force, led by U.S. troops, arrived in **Somalia** Dec. 9. Presidents of U.S., Canada, and Mexico Dec. 17 signed North American Free Trade Agreement (**NAFTA**), which took effect Jan. 1, 1994.

1993 A bomb exploded in garage beneath the **World Trade Center** in New York City, Feb. 26, killing six; seven men found guilty of involvement by 1997. Four federal agents were killed, Feb. 28, during raid on **Branch Davidian** compound near **Waco**, TX; compound burned down Apr. 19, leaving over 70 cult members dead. Eleven members acquitted in deaths of federal agents.

Janet Reno became first female U.S. attorney general, Mar. 12. "Motor-voter" bill was signed by Pres. Clinton, May 20. "**Great Flood of 1993**" inundated parts of nine Midwestern states in summer, leaving about 50 dead and $15 bil in damages.

On July 19 Pres. Clinton announced "**don't ask, don't tell, don't pursue**" policy for homosexuals in the military (rescinded 2010). Senate, voting 96-3 on Aug. 3, confirmed nomination of **Ruth Bader Ginsburg** to Supreme Court, replacing retiring Justice **Byron White**. Clinton, Aug. 10, signed measure to reduce federal budget deficits by $496 bil over five years, through spending cuts and new taxes. **Brady Bill**, mandating background checks for gun buyers, was signed into law Nov. 30.

1994 Predawn **earthquake** in Los Angeles area, Jan. 17, claimed 61 lives. Pres. Clinton Feb. 3 lifted 19-year ban on U.S. trade with **Vietnam**. Byron De La Beckwith was convicted Feb. 5 of 1963 murder of civil rights leader **Medgar Evers**. Longtime CIA officer **Aldrich Ames** pleaded guilty, Apr. 28, to spying for Russians; received life in prison.

U.S. troops, Mar. 25, ended aid and peacekeeping mission in **Somalia**, begun in 1992. **Kenneth Starr** was named Aug. 5 as independent counsel to probe **Whitewater** affair. MLB players went on strike following Aug. 11 games. World Series canceled; strike ended Apr. 25, 1995.

Republicans gained control of Congress in Nov. 8 elections, after many years of Democratic control.

1995 **Newt Gingrich** (R, GA) elected U.S. House speaker. A bill to end Congress's exemption from federal labor laws, first in series of measures in Republicans' "**Contract With America**," cleared Congress Jan. 17; signed into law Jan. 23. Pres. Clinton, Jan. 31, authorized $20-bil loan to **Mexico**. Peacekeeping responsibilities in **Haiti** transferred from U.S. to UN forces Mar. 31, with U.S. providing 2,400 soldiers.

Truck bomb exploded outside **Oklahoma City** federal office building Apr. 19, killing 168 people. Antigovernment extremist Timothy McVeigh was convicted as bomber; executed June 2011; a co-conspirator was sentenced to life. U.S. space shuttle *Atlantis* docked for first time with Russian space station *Mir*, June 29-July 4. The U.S. announced July 11 it was reestablishing **relations with Vietnam**.

Ten **Muslim militants** were convicted, Oct. 1, in failed plot to blow up **UN Headquarters** and assassinate political leaders. Former football star **O.J. Simpson** found not guilty Oct. 3 of June 1994 murders of his former wife and her friend. Hundreds of thousands of Black men participated in **Million Man March** in Washington, DC, Oct. 16, organized by **Louis Farrakhan**. Cumulative number of **AIDS** cases reported in the U.S. passed 500,000 by Oct. 31, with more than 310,000 deaths.

Five Americans were among seven killed, Nov. 13, in bombing of U.S. military post in **Riyadh, Saudi Arabia**. Budget impasse between Congress and Pres. Clinton led to partial **government shutdown** Nov. 14; operations resumed Nov. 20 under continuing resolutions. After U.S.-mediated talks outside Dayton, OH, warring parties in **Bosnia and Herzegovina** reached peace agreement Nov. 21.

A 1973 federal law imposing **55-mph speed limit** was repealed Nov. 28.

1996 U.S. Senate, Jan. 26, approved, 87-4, Second Strategic Arms Reduction Treaty (**START II**) with Russia. Congress, Mar. 28, approved **line-item veto**; struck down by Supreme Court, 1998.

Arkansas Gov. **Jim Guy Tucker** (D) and two other Clinton associates were convicted May 28 of fraud and conspiracy in

Whitewater case. The antitax **Freemen** surrendered to federal authorities June 13 after 81-day standoff near Jordan, MT; four were convicted, July 1998, of conspiring to defraud banks. Bomb exploded at **Khobar Towers** military complex in Saudi Arabia, June 25, killing 19 U.S. service personnel. **Pipe bomb** exploded July 27 in **Atlanta**, GA, park during **Summer Olympics**; one person killed.

Major **welfare reform** bill signed into law, Aug. 22. Defense of Marriage Act (**DOMA**), passed by wide margins and signed Sept. 21, barred federal recognition of same-sex marriages (repealed by Congress, 2022). U.S. signed **Comprehensive Test Ban Treaty**, Sept. 24, which banned all nuclear weapons tests; Senate failed to ratify it.

Pres. **Clinton reelected**, Nov. 5, over Sen. **Bob Dole** (R, KS).

1997 **Madeleine Albright** sworn in as first woman sec. of state, Jan. 23. Former CIA official Harold Nicholson pleaded guilty, Mar. 3, to **spying for Russia**. Thirty-nine members of **Heaven's Gate** religious cult found dead in Rancho Santa Fe, CA, house Mar. 26, in apparent mass suicide.

The film *Titanic* was released Dec. 14; went on to win 11 Oscars, tying record set in 1960 by *Ben-Hur*.

1998 Media outlets Jan. 21 reported evidence of sexual relationship between Pres. Clinton and former White House intern **Monica Lewinsky**. Clinton initially denied affair, but in address to nation, Aug. 17, acknowledged relationship that was "not appropriate." On Sept. 9, independent counsel **Kenneth Starr** sent findings to House, which, Dec. 19, approved two articles of **impeachment**.

"**Unabomber**" Theodore Kaczynski, arrested in Montana in 1993, pleaded guilty Jan. 22 to bombings that killed three people; sentenced to four life terms plus 30 years. **Bombs** at **U.S. embassies** in Kenya and Tanzania killed at least 257, Aug. 7. On Sept. 30, Pres. Clinton announced federal **budget surplus** of $70 bil for fiscal 1998, first since 1969.

Pres. Clinton, Nov. 13, agreed to pay $850,000 to **Paula Jones**, settling suit for an alleged unwanted sexual advance. Biggest U.S. **tobacco companies**, Nov. 23, agreed to pay states and territories $206 bil over 25 years to cover public health costs.

1995: The Murrah Federal Building in Oklahoma City is targeted in the deadliest act of domestic terrorism in U.S. history.

2001: The attacks of Sept. 11, 2001, kill more than 2,750 people in New York City, including 343 firefighters.

1999 *The Sopranos* TV drama debuted, Jan. 10. Pres. Clinton was acquitted, Feb. 12, in **impeachment trial**. Perjury article drew 45 votes; obstruction of justice article drew 50-50 vote, short of the needed two-thirds majority.

Dr. **Jack Kevorkian** convicted of second-degree murder Mar. 26 in death of **terminally ill man**. One man pleaded guilty Apr. 5, another convicted Nov. 4, in 1998 kidnapping and beating death of **Matthew Shepard**, an openly gay student at Univ. of Wyoming.

Two teenagers killed 12 fellow students, a teacher, and themselves, Apr. 20 at **Columbine High School** in Littleton, CO. **John F. Kennedy Jr.** died, with his wife and sister-in-law, in crash of private plane July 16.

2000 Midnight celebrations marked changeover to year 2000; feared **Y2K** computer glitch fizzled. The first state law recognizing **same-sex civil unions** was enacted in **Vermont**, Apr. 26. U.S. and British scientists, June 26, announced they had determined structure of the **human genome**. Six-year-old **Elián González** was returned to his father in **Cuba** June 28, after rescue from a refugee boat wreck in which his mother drowned.

Tiger Woods, at 24, became youngest player to win all four golf majors, July 23. FDA announced, Sept. 28, approval of **RU-486**, a pill that induces **abortion**. Seventeen U.S. sailors died Oct. 12 in terrorist bombing of **USS Cole**, in Aden, Yemen.

With contested Nov. 7 **presidential election** result showing Texas Gov. **George W. Bush** (R) barely ahead of Vice Pres. **Al Gore** (D) in Florida, state's Supreme Court, Dec. 8, ordered partial manual recounts. U.S. Supreme Court reversed order, Dec. 12, leaving Bush as winner.

2001 AOL-Time Warner megamerger completed Jan. 11. **Colin Powell** sworn in Jan. 20 as first Black U.S. sec. of state. **U.S. Navy spy plane** collided with **Chinese fighter plane** over South China Sea Apr. 1, killing fighter pilot; 24 U.S. crew members detained in Hainan until U.S. apology, Apr. 12. Pres. Bush signed, June 7, $1.35-tril **tax-cut** package.

On **Sept. 11**, two hijacked airliners struck **World Trade Center twin towers** in New York City. A third plane destroyed part of the **Pentagon**; a fourth crashed in a field near **Shanksville**, PA. Some 3,000 people were killed, including about 2,750 at the World Trade Center. U.S. and Britain, Oct. 7, launched airstrikes against Afghan-based terrorist organization **al-Qaeda** and Afghanistan's ruling **Taliban** militia. Bush Oct. 26 signed USA **Patriot Act**, with wide-ranging provisions aimed at preventing terrorism.

Taliban surrendered Kabul, Nov. 13, and fled from Kandahar, their stronghold, Dec. 7. U.S. government, Dec. 11, indicted al-Qaeda operative **Zacarias Moussaoui** as **Sept. 11 co-conspirator**; sentenced in 2006 to life. Five people died, Oct. 5-Nov. 21, from exposure to **anthrax** through letters in the U.S. mail; a suspect later died by suicide.

Energy-trading company **Enron** filed for bankruptcy, Dec. 2. Bush announced, Dec. 13, U.S. withdrawal from 1972 **Antiballistic Missile Treaty** with Russians. **"Shoe bomber"** prevented from in-flight attack on airliner, Dec. 22.

2002 Taliban and al-Qaeda fighters captured in Afghanistan sent to U.S. naval base at **Guantánamo Bay** in Cuba, starting Jan. 11. In State of the Union address, Jan. 29, Pres. Bush called Iran, Iraq, and North Korea part of **"axis of evil."** By Mar. 6, 1,200 U.S. troops were involved in **Operation Anaconda** against al-Qaeda and Taliban forces in **Afghanistan**.

Independent prosecutor's report, Mar. 20, found **insufficient evidence** that Pres. Clinton or Hillary Clinton committed a crime in connection with **Whitewater**. Pres. Bush, Mar. 27, signed McCain-Feingold **campaign-finance reform bill** banning unregulated, unrestricted "soft money" donations (part of bill struck down by Supreme Court, 2007). On Oct. 10-11 the House, 296-133, and Senate, 77-23, gave Bush backing to use military force against **Iraq**. Bush administration revealed Oct. 16 that **North Korea** had acknowledged developing **nuclear arms** in violation of a 1994 agreement. Bush signed measure, Nov. 25, creating cabinet **Dept. of Homeland Security**.

U.S. **Catholic bishops**, Nov. 13, tightened policies for dealing with priests who **sexually abuse** minors.

2003 Space shuttle **Columbia** broke apart Feb. 1 during descent; all seven crew were killed. Senate, Mar. 6, approved **Strategic Offensive Reductions Treaty** (SORT) for reducing nuclear stockpiles. U.S.-led offensive aimed at ousting Iraqi dictator **Saddam Hussein** began Mar. 19, as cruise missiles hit Baghdad. Bush, May 1, declared **end of major combat operations**, though insurgent attacks continued.

Bush signed measure May 27 providing $15 bil to fight **AIDS** especially in **Africa**. He signed bill May 28 providing $330 bil in **tax cuts** over several years. A power failure caused **blackouts** affecting some 50 mil people, mostly in NE U.S. and Canada, Aug. 14.

The **archdiocese of Boston** agreed to pay up to $85 mil, in **sex abuse settlement** announced Sept. 9. Californians, Oct. 7, voted to recall Gov. **Gray Davis** (D) and replace him with actor-turned-politician **Arnold Schwarzenegger** (R). Virginia jury, Nov. 17, found **"Beltway sniper"** guilty in 2002 Washington, DC, area attacks that killed 10; he was executed, Nov. 2009; his teen accomplice was convicted and sentenced to life.

Pres. Bush signed bill Dec. 8 adding prescription drug benefit to **Medicare**. **Saddam Hussein captured** by U.S. forces Dec. 13; tried and executed (2006) by Iraqi authorities.

2004 Harvard undergrad **Mark Zuckerberg**, Feb. 4, launched the website that grew into the social media network **Facebook**. *The Lord of the Rings: The Return of the King* became third film to win a record 11 Oscars, Feb. 29.

Photos showing abuse of **Abu Ghraib** prison inmates in Iraq by American soldiers emerged Apr. 3; two soldiers found guilty (2005) and sentenced to prison. U.S.-led coalition transferred power to interim Iraqi government, June 28. **9/11 Commission Report**, released July 22, called for restructuring U.S. intelligence operations.

On May 17, pursuant to a 2003 court decision, Massachusetts became first state to legalize **same-sex marriage**. **Boston Red Sox** won World Series Oct. 27, for first time since 1918.

Pres. **Bush reelected** Nov. 2, defeating Sen. **John Kerry** (D, MA). Bush signed **intelligence reform bill** Dec. 17, creating a director of national intelligence.

2005 **Condoleezza Rice** became first Black woman sec. of state, Jan. 26. **Terri Schiavo**, in vegetative state since 1990, died Mar. 31, after feeding tube was removed following legal battle.

Hurricane Katrina hit Gulf coast, Aug. 29, causing nearly 1,400 deaths and widespread devastation, especially to **New Orleans**. **John G. Roberts Jr.** was confirmed by Senate, Sept. 29, 78-22, to replace Chief Justice **William H. Rehnquist**, who died Sept. 3.

NY Times, Dec. 16, reported that Pres. Bush in 2002 had secretly authorized NSA to **eavesdrop without court warrant** on people in U.S. suspected of terrorist activities. Bush, Dec. 30, signed **anti-torture legislation**.

2006 Former GOP lobbyist **Jack Abramoff** pleaded guilty Jan. 3 to bribery and other charges; sentenced to prison. **Samuel Alito Jr.** confirmed to Supreme Court, Jan. 31, 58-42, to replace retiring Justice **Sandra Day O'Connor**. The Court ruled June 29 that system for trying terrorism detainees at **Guantánamo Bay** was unauthorized.

Pres. Bush, July 19, vetoed bill to end funding constraints on human embryonic **stem cell research**. On Sept. 6 he confirmed existence of **secret overseas prisons**, run by CIA, for terrorism suspects. Democrats won control of House and Senate in **midterm elections** Nov. 7.

2007 Rep. **Nancy Pelosi** (D, CA) chosen Jan. 4 as **first woman Speaker** of the House. On Jan. 10, Pres. Bush announced troop **"surge"** in Iraq. Reports of substandard conditions at **Walter Reed** Army Medical Center led to ousters of officials, Mar. 1-2. A **Virginia Tech** student fatally shot 32 people on campus, Apr. 16, before killing himself.

On Apr. 18, Supreme Court upheld, 5-4, a 2003 federal law banning so-called **partial-birth abortions**. Congress May 24 approved Iraq and Afghanistan war funding, with benchmarks for withdrawal of troops from Iraq; same bill raised federal hourly **minimum wage** from $5.15 to $7.25 over two years. Pres. Bush July 20 banned **"cruel, inhuman, or degrading"** treatment of imprisoned terror suspects.

Harry Potter and the Deathly Hallows, final novel in blockbuster series, released July 21. Congress, Aug. 4, cleared bill allowing **NSA** to monitor communications without warrants if believed related to terrorism. **Barry Bonds** tied Hank Aaron's all-time career **home-run record** at 755 on Aug. 4 and hit No. 756 on Aug. 7. Report by former Sen. **George Mitchell** (D, ME), released Dec. 13, presented evidence of **performance-enhancing drug** use by 86 MLB players. Bush, Dec. 19, signed energy bill increasing automobile **fuel-economy** standards.

2008 To counter economic recession, Pres. Bush, Feb. 13, signed a $168-bil **economic stimulus package** that provided significant tax rebates. With financial system in crisis, federal government Sept. 7 took control of mortgage finance companies **Fannie Mae** and **Freddie Mac**; **Lehman Brothers** declared bankruptcy Sept. 15. U.S., Sept. 16, took over insurance giant **AIG** in $85-bil bailout. A Treasury Dept. plan to purchase up to $700 bil of **"toxic" mortgage-backed securities**. Revised Troubled Asset Relief Program (**TARP**) cleared Congress Oct. 3. On Oct. 21 Fed pledged $540 bil as a backup to protect **money market funds**.

Sen. **Barack Obama** (D, IL) was elected, Nov. 4, as **first Black president** in U.S. history, defeating Sen. **John McCain** (R, AZ). Obama later named nomination campaign rival Sen. **Hillary Clinton** (NY) as sec. of state. California voters approved **Proposition 8**, banning same-sex marriage.

U.S. government Nov. 23 announced massive **bailout** to protect **Citigroup** from mortgage losses. Dow dropped 7.7% Dec. 1 after report that the economy was in **recession** that began Dec. 2007; Dow closed the year down 33.8%, its worst since 1931. Fed, Dec. 16, cut benchmark **interest rate** to near zero. Pres. Bush, Dec. 19, announced that $17 bil in **TARP funds** would be used to help keep **General Motors** and **Chrysler** afloat.

2009 Pres. **Obama** issued executive orders Jan. 22 restricting CIA interrogation practices and calling for U.S. military prison at **Guantánamo Bay**, Cuba, to close (closing blocked by Congress). Illinois Gov. **Rod Blagojevich** (D) was convicted of corruption and removed from office, Jan. 29 (sentence commuted by Pres. Trump, 2020). Treasury Sec. **Timothy Geithner**, Feb. 10, outlined $2-tril program to stabilize banking and ease credit markets with **stress tests** for banks. Obama signed **stimulus** bill Feb. 17, with $212 bil in tax cuts and $575 bil in new spending. **Swine flu outbreak** declared a public health emergency Apr. 26. **Chrysler** filed for bankruptcy, Apr. 30. Obama, May 19, tightened vehicle **fuel efficiency** standards. **General Motors** filed for bankruptcy June 1, under plan providing new federal funds. On June 9, 10 financial firms received go-ahead from U.S. Treasury to return some $68 bil in **TARP funds**.

George Tiller, Kansas doctor and **abortion** provider, was murdered May 31 by anti-abortion extremist. Speaking June 4 in Egypt, Pres. Obama called for **"new beginning"** in relations with Muslim world. Financier **Bernard Madoff** sentenced to prison June 29, after pleading guilty in massive **Ponzi scheme**. **Sonia Sotomayor** confirmed Aug. 6, 68-31, as Supreme Court's **first Hispanic justice**, replacing retiring Justice **David Souter**.

Government reported Oct. 29 that GDP grew at 3.5% annual rate July-Sept., signaling technical **end of recession**. On Nov. 5, 13 were killed in **mass shooting** at **Ft. Hood**, TX; an Army major was convicted and sentenced to death.

Obama, Nov. 6, signed measure to extend unemployment benefits and give $8,000 tax credit to first-time homebuyers. A surge of 30,000 troops to **Afghanistan** was announced Dec. 1. Obama received **Nobel Peace Prize**, Dec. 10, and brokered multination **greenhouse-gas accord**, reached Dec. 18 in Copenhagen.

2010 In *Citizens United v. FEC*, U.S. Supreme Court Jan. 21 held that spending by corporations and unions on advertising to influence election outcomes could not be limited by law. Obama, Mar. 18, signed $18-bil **job-stimulus** measure. On Mar. 21, the House, with no GOP support, gave final approval to **"Obamacare"** health-care reform bill. Pres. Obama and Russian Pres. **Dmitri Medvedev**, Apr. 8, signed New Strategic Arms Reduction Treaty, or **New START**. On Apr. 20, *Deepwater Horizon* drilling platform exploded in Gulf of Mexico, killing 11 and creating huge oil spill; $20-bil settlement against energy giant **BP** approved in 2016. Obama signed **financial reform** bill, July 21. Over 75,000 Afghanistan documents, many of them classified, were published July 25 on **WikiLeaks** website. **Elena Kagan** was confirmed as **Supreme Court** justice, 63-37, Aug. 5, to replace retiring Justice **John Paul Stevens**.

The Fed Nov. 3 announced plan to buy $600 bil in **Treasury securities** to stimulate economy. Bipartisan **Simpson-Bowles** commission, Dec. 1, called for deep spending cuts to stabilize national debt. Obama, Dec. 17, signed $858-bil compromise measure temporarily extending G. W. **Bush-era tax cuts** and unemployment insurance benefits.

2011 Gunman in **Tucson**, AZ, Jan. 8, killed 6 people and injured 13, including Rep. **Gabrielle Giffords** (D, AZ).

On May 2, in Abbottabad, Pakistan, Navy **SEALs** killed al-Qaeda leader **Osama bin Laden**. On May 26 Obama signed measure extending key provisions of **USA Patriot Act**.

Tornado hit Joplin, MO, May 22, claiming about 160 lives. NASA's **space shuttle** program ended with landing of *Atlantis*, July 21. **Budget control act**, Aug. 1-2, raised **debt ceiling** and cut some $900 bil in spending, with another $1.5 tril in cuts to be worked out by **supercommittee**. A left-wing protest movement that began Sept. 17 as **Occupy Wall Street** expanded across the U.S. and abroad.

Anwar al-Awlaki, a Muslim cleric linked to terrorist attacks in U.S., was killed Sept. 30 in U.S. drone attack in **Yemen**. U.S. military mission in **Iraq** formally ended Dec. 15; last troop convoy left Dec. 18.

2012 Pres. Obama Feb. 10 announced compromise **health insurance** mandate that allowed religiously affiliated employers to avoid directly providing **contraceptive coverage**. On June 15 he announced Deferred Action for Childhood Arrivals (**DACA**) program, shielding from deportation certain **undocumented immigrants** who entered as minors.

Former Penn State assistant football coach **Jerry Sandusky** was convicted June 22 in **sexual abuse** of ten boys. Twelve people were killed July 20, in movie-theater shooting in Aurora, CO; shooter sentenced to life. A gunman opened fire Aug. 5 at a **Sikh temple** in Oak Creek, WI, leaving six dead, before killing himself. NASA rover *Curiosity* landed on **Mars** Aug. 6.

2005: Hurricane Katrina and subsequent failure of levees cause unprecedented destruction in New Orleans and along the Gulf Coast.

Islamist terrorists attacked U.S. facility in **Benghazi**, Libya, Sept. 11-12, killing U.S. **ambassador** and three other Americans. **Hurricane Sandy** made landfall in the U.S. Oct. 29, devastating mid-Atlantic coastal areas and leaving over 200 dead.

Pres. **Obama reelected** Nov. 6, defeating former Massachusetts Gov. **Mitt Romney** (R). Colorado and Washington became first states to vote to decriminalize recreational **marijuana**.

A gunman killed 20 young children and 6 adults before killing himself, Dec. 14, at **Sandy Hook** Elementary School in **Newtown**, CT.

2013 Averting **"fiscal cliff,"** Senate passed compromise Jan. 1, making **Bush-era tax** cuts permanent up to certain ceilings, while deferring automatic spending cuts (**sequestration**). Sequestration took effect Mar. 1, triggering $1.2 tril in spending cuts to both defense and domestic programs over ten years.

Bombs at the Boston Marathon, Apr. 15, killed three spectators and injured 264; two Chechen-born brothers were implicated.

The *Guardian*, June 5, disclosed details of classified **NSA electronic surveillance** program; NSA contractor **Edward Snowden** claimed responsibility for leaks, after having fled the country. Army Staff Sgt. **Robert Bales** pleaded guilty, June 5, to killing 16 Afghan civilians; sentenced to life. Supreme Court, June 25, overturned key provision of the 1965 **Voting Rights Act** and, June 26, struck down part of 1996 Defense of Marriage Act.

A jury, July 13, found George Zimmerman not guilty in Feb. 2012 shooting of **Trayvon Martin**, an unarmed Black teenager, in Sanford, FL. **Detroit** filed for **bankruptcy**, July 18. Army Pfc. **Chelsea Manning** was sentenced Aug. 21 to 35 years for releasing military and diplomatic documents to **WikiLeaks** (Obama commuted sentence, 2017). A gunman killed 12 people at the **Navy Yard** in Washington, DC, Sept. 16; he was killed by responding police.

Health insurance exchanges opened Oct. 1 in **Obamacare rollout** plagued by technical glitches. U.S. **government partially shut down** Oct. 1 over budget impasse; resolved by Congress Oct. 16. **JPMorgan Chase** agreed, Nov. 19, to $13-bil settlement on charges of deceptive mortgage-sale practices. Dow up 26.5% in 2013; biggest yearly gain since 1995.

2014 **Janet Yellen** was confirmed Jan. 6 as first woman **Fed** chair. **General Motors**, Feb. 7, began recall of vehicles with defect linked to deaths; fined $900 mil. **Toyota** agreed Mar. 19 to $1.2-bil fine on charges it concealed information about defective parts.

Gunman killed 6 people and injured 13 before killing himself, May 23, near **Univ. of California-Santa Barbara**. U.S. Army Sgt. **Bowe Bergdahl**, captured by Taliban in 2009, was freed May 31 in exchange for U.S. release of five Taliban captives. Veterans Affairs Sec. **Eric Shinseki** resigned May 30 after revelations that **VA hospitals** had hidden long waiting times.

The Sunni extremist Islamic State of Iraq and Syria (**ISIS**) declared a **"caliphate"** June 29. Pres. Obama announced June 19 that the U.S. would send **military advisers** to Iraq; he authorized airstrikes there, Aug. 7. ISIS released videos in Aug.-Nov. showing **beheadings** of three Americans.

A white police officer fatally shot unarmed Black 18-year-old **Michael Brown**, Aug. 9, in **Ferguson**, MO, precipitating sometimes violent **protests**; grand jury declined to indict. **Bank of America** agreed Aug. 21 to $16.65-bil settlement on charges it misled investors.

U.S. jury Oct. 22 convicted four former contract security guards in 2007 shootings that killed 17 **Iraqi civilians**. New York City's new **One World Trade Center** welcomed first tenants Nov. 3.

Tamir Rice, a Black 12-year-old holding a pellet gun, was fatally shot by a white police officer, Nov. 22, in **Cleveland**, OH; grand jury declined to indict. A grand jury decided Dec. 3 not to indict a **New York City** police officer for alleg edly using a nonregulation **chokehold** to detain **Eric Garner**, a Black man who died July 17 in custody. A Black man shot and killed two **New York City police** officers in their patrol car, Dec. 20, then killed himself.

U.S.-led NATO mission in **Afghanistan** ended combat operations Dec. 28, after over 13 years; troops remained in support roles.

2015 **Standard & Poor's** agreed Feb. 3 to pay $1.4 bil, and **Morgan Stanley** agreed Feb. 15 to pay $2.6 bil, to resolve claims of financial deception. Justice Dept. Mar. 4 released report exposing widespread mistreatment of Black individuals by **Ferguson**, MO, police and court system.

A New York court Mar. 5 approved $8.5-bil settlement between **Bank of America** and investors in mortgage securities issued by **Countrywide Financial Corp.** Federal judge, Mar. 20, approved settlement in which **AIG** paid $970.5 mil to shareholders allegedly misled over high-risk mortgage loans. Facing continuing drought, California Gov. **Jerry Brown** (D) issued mandatory **water restrictions** Apr. 1. Pres. Obama met in Panama with Cuban Pres. **Raúl Castro**, Apr. 11; U.S. and Cuba reopened embassies in their countries July 20, reestablishing relations.

The Apr. 19 death of a Black man, **Freddie Gray**, from injury in a **Baltimore** police van, spurred riots and led to indictment of six officers; no convictions resulted. A **white supremacist** fatally shot nine, June 17, at historic Black church in **Charleston**, SC; shooter sentenced to death, 2017.

Obama June 2 signed a bill to end **NSA's bulk collection** of phone data, with telecom companies to hold custody of data instead. **American Pharoah**, June 6, became first in 37 years to take horse racing's **Triple Crown**. On June 26, the Supreme Court ruled that **same-sex couples** had constitutional right to marry.

Iran and six world powers led by the U.S. formally agreed July 14 on deal to limit **Iranian nuclear capability** in return for lifting economic sanctions (Pres. Trump announced U.S. withdrawal, 2018). Pres. Obama Aug. 3 unveiled EPA **Clean Power Plan** limiting carbon dioxide emissions from power plants (Supreme Court ruled it unconstitutional, 2022).

Pope Francis visited the U.S., Sept. 22-27, and addressed joint session of Congress. A student shooter at a community college, Oct. 1, in **Roseburg**, OR, killed nine people before killing himself. U.S. airstrike hit an **Afghanistan hospital** Oct. 3, killing more than 40; military report blamed human error.

U.S. and 11 other nations completed negotiations, Oct. 5, on **Trans-Pacific Partnership** trade agreement. On Oct. 22 U.S.-Iraqi mission freed about 70 hostages held by **ISIS** in Iraq; one U.S. soldier was killed. On Oct. 30, Obama announced he would deploy special operations forces to fight ISIS in **Syria**.

Three people were killed Nov. 27 at **Planned Parenthood** clinic in Colorado Springs, CO; alleged shooter found incompetent to stand trial. A married couple said by the FBI to be **Muslim extremists** fatally shot 14 people at a Dec. 2 office party in **San Bernardino**, CA; both died in shootout with police.

Defense Dept., Dec. 3, announced that all **military combat positions** would be **opened to women**. U.S. and 194 other parties reached agreement in Paris, Dec. 12, on plan to reduce greenhouse gases linked to **climate change**. The **Fed**, Dec. 16, **raised key interest rates** from near-zero levels. Obama signed $1.8-tril **spending and tax relief package** Dec. 18.

2016 Armed protesters, Jan. 2, began 41-day occupation of Oregon's **Malheur National Wildlife Refuge**, in land dispute;

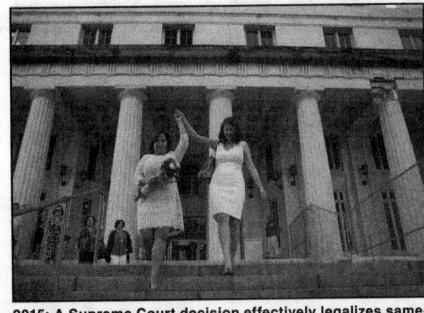

2015: A Supreme Court decision effectively legalizes same-sex marriage nationwide.

2017: A gunman shooting from a high-rise hotel window in Las Vegas kills 58 people and injures hundreds more attending an outdoor country music festival Oct. 1.

one fatally shot, Jan. 26, in confrontation with law enforcement. Obama declared federal state of emergency in **Flint, MI**, Jan. 16, because of **lead-contaminated drinking water**. Following the death in Feb. of conservative Supreme Court Justice **Antonin Scalia**, Obama Mar. 16 nominated appellate court judge **Merrick Garland**, but Senate Republicans declined to schedule confirmation hearings.

North Carolina Gov. **Pat McCrory** (R) Mar. 23 signed **"bathroom bill"** requiring that persons use state facilities corresponding to birth-certificate gender; boycotts followed. (Measure partly repealed, 2017.) Justice Dept. announced Apr. 11 that **Goldman Sachs** would pay $5.1 bil to settle charges of selling faulty mortgage-backed securities.

U.S. **drone strike** killed Afghan Taliban leader **Akhtar Muhammad Mansour** May 21. A gunman who declared allegiance to **ISIS** killed 49 mostly Hispanic people June 12 at **gay nightclub** in **Orlando**, FL; he was killed by responding police. The blockbuster musical *Hamilton* won 11 Tony Awards June 12.

In settlement announced June 28, **Volkswagen** agreed to pay some $15 bil for cheating in emissions tests. Defense Dept. announced, June 30, that **transgender individuals** could serve openly in the military. Protests followed **fatal police shootings** of a Black man in **Baton Rouge**, LA, July 5, and in a **St. Paul**, MN, suburb, July 6. Five police officers were killed by a sniper, July 7 in **Dallas**, TX, and three in an ambush, July 17 in **Baton Rouge**, LA.

After investigating Hillary Clinton's use of a **private email server** as sec. of state, FBI Dir. **James Comey**, July 5, said she was careless but did not show intent to violate the law. Justice Dept. report released Aug. 10 concluded that **Baltimore police** routinely used **excessive force** against Blacks. Riots broke out in **Milwaukee**, WI, Aug. 13-15, following fatal **police shooting** of an armed Black man fleeing a traffic stop. Regulators fined **Wells Fargo** $185 mil Sept. 8 for illicit revenue scheme.

The *Washington Post* Oct. 7 made public 2005 video footage that showed **Trump** bragging about **groping women**. **WikiLeaks** Oct. 7 began releasing apparently hacked emails from Clinton campaign chair **John Podesta**. AT&T agreed Oct. 22 to acquire **Time Warner** for about $85 bil. **Chicago Cubs** won World Series Nov. 2, for first time since 1908.

In Nov. 8 presidential election, **Donald Trump** (R) defeated former Sec. of State **Hillary Clinton** (D), with 304 electoral votes out of 538, though losing popular vote by about 3 mil.

Tech pioneer **Yahoo** Dec. 14 revealed an Aug. 2013 hack, affecting some 3 bil user accounts. Following evidence of **Russian hacking**, Obama Dec. 29 expelled 35 Russian diplomats.

2017 Pres. **Trump inaugurated** Jan. 20. **Women's Marches**, Jan. 21, in Washington, DC, and other cities drew millions of protesters. Trump Jan. 23-27 withdrew U.S. from **Trans-Pacific Partnership** trade agreement, ordered building of a Mexican **border wall**, and issued executive order banning admission of travelers from certain **Muslim-majority nations** (expanded ban later upheld by Supreme Court).

After a suspected **chemical attack** in Syria, Apr. 4, Pres. Trump authorized **cruise-missile strike** against a government airfield. The U.S. military, Apr. 13, bombed a complex

of caves and tunnels in **Afghanistan**; 94 militants reportedly killed.

After Republicans used the so-called **nuclear option** to end a Democratic filibuster, the Senate voted, 54-45, Apr. 7, to confirm nomination of **Neil Gorsuch** to Supreme Court. Pres. Trump fired FBI Dir. **James Comey** May 9; Justice Dept., May 17, appointed former FBI Dir. **Robert Mueller III** as special counsel to head investigation into Russian election meddling.

On June 1 the **Dakota Access oil pipeline**, protested by the **Standing Rock** tribe, became operational. A gunman targeting Republicans June 14 at a practice for the bipartisan **Congressional Baseball Game** critically injured Rep. **Steve Scalise** (R, LA) and wounded four others; perpetrator fatally wounded in shootout.

Iraqi Prime Min. **Haider al-Abadi** declared victory over ISIS, Dec. 9. American student **Otto Warmbier** was returned to U.S., June 13, in a comatose state after imprisonment in **North Korea**; he soon died. Trump Aug. 2 signed bipartisan bill imposing certain economic sanctions against **Russia** as well as Iran and **North Korea**.

A **white nationalist rally** in **Charlottesville**, VA, Aug. 12, erupted in clashes; one counterdemonstrator was killed and 19 others were injured when a white nationalist drove into a crowd. On Aug. 21, millions viewed the first total **solar eclipse** visible coast to coast since 1918. **North Korea** Sept. 3 conducted its sixth nuclear weapons test; UN and U.S. imposed economic sanctions. Credit reporting firm **Equifax** revealed Sept. 7 that hackers had gained access to information on some 143 mil Americans; company later agreed to pay up to $700 mil to resolve claims.

Hurricane Maria hit **Puerto Rico**, Sept. 20, causing widespread devastation and nearly 3,000 deaths. A gunman fatally shot 60 people and injured hundreds at a country music concert, Oct. 1, in **Las Vegas**. *NY Times* Oct. 5 reported multiple accusations of sexual assault or harassment against movie producer **Harvey Weinstein**, beginning a wave of **"Me Too"** allegations.

U.S.-backed militias in Syria reported, Oct. 20, capture of **Raqqa**, de facto capital of ISIS's self-proclaimed caliphate. Former Trump adviser **Michael Flynn** pleaded guilty Nov. 30 to lying to the FBI about conversations with Russia's U.S. ambassador (pardoned by Trump in 2020).

Eight people were rammed and killed by a truck along a **bike path** in New York City, Oct. 31. A gunman killed 26 people, Nov. 5, at a **Baptist church** in Sutherland Springs, TX; shooter died by suicide. U.S. Navy report, Nov. 1, blamed personnel errors for collisions involving the USS *Fitzgerald* (June 17; 7 sailors killed) and USS *John S. McCain* (Aug. 21; 10 sailors killed). Pres. Trump, Dec. 6, recognized **Jerusalem** as Israel's capital. FCC voted 3-2, Dec. 14, to scrap **net neutrality** rules. On Dec. 22, Trump signed measure reducing tax rates, allowing oil drilling in Alaska's **Arctic National Wildlife Refuge**, and repealing Obamacare's individual mandate.

2018 Michigan State Univ. sports physician **Larry Nasser** sentenced to prison, Jan. 24, after pleading guilty to decades of **sexual abuse**. A shooting Feb. 14 at a **Parkland**, FL, high school left 17 dead; an expelled student was indicted for murder and pleaded guilty. Students protesting gun violence led **March for Our Lives** demonstrations, Mar. 24.

Uber suspended its self-driving cars from four North American test cities after pedestrian fatality Mar. 18. Facebook CEO **Mark Zuckerberg** apologized before Congress, Apr. 10-11, after revelations that British consulting firm **Cambridge Analytica** had gained access to data from Facebook users allegedly provided to political campaigns.

After a reported **chemical weapons attack** by Syria's **Assad regime**, U.S., UK, and France launched airstrikes against suspected weapons production sites, Apr. 14. Federal regulators announced $1 bil in fines Apr. 20 against **Wells Fargo** for financial improprieties.

U.S.-led coalition against **ISIS** Apr. 30 closed its land forces command headquarters in Iraq. Pres. Trump declared May 8 he was withdrawing U.S. from the **2015 Iran nuclear deal**. On May 18, eight students and two teachers were killed in shooting at a high school in **Santa Fe**, TX; a student was arrested and charged. **NFL** team owners May 23 announced players must either **stand during national anthem** or remain in locker room.

2018: Pres. Donald Trump continues to call for construction of a new wall on the southern U.S. border.

Following widespread criticism, Trump June 20 signed an executive order to end separation of **undocumented children** at the Mexican border. Cardinal **Theodore McCarrick** was removed from public ministry June 20, amid allegations of **sexual abuse**; later resigned as cardinal and was laicized. A gunman arrested at the scene killed five employees and injured two at *Capital Gazette* offices in Annapolis, MD, June 28 (gunman convicted in 2021).

Justice Dept. charged 12 **Russian intelligence officers** July 13 with hacking the Clinton campaign and Democratic National Committee and leaking emails and data prior to the 2016 presidential election. Pres. Trump and Russian Pres. **Vladimir Putin** held summit in Helsinki, Finland, July 16.

Pennsylvania grand jury Aug. 14 released report detailing decades of **clerical sexual abuse** and cover-up in six Roman Catholic dioceses. Former Trump campaign chair **Paul Manafort** was found guilty Aug. 21 of **financial crimes** (pardoned by Trump, 2020). Former Trump attorney **Michael Cohen** pleaded guilty Aug. 21 to campaign finance violations for **hush money** he said he paid to cover up Trump extramarital affairs.

Saudi dissident journalist **Jamal Khashoggi**, a U.S. resident, was killed after entering the Saudi consulate in Istanbul, Oct. 2; U.S. intelligence implicated Saudi crown prince. A white Chicago police officer was convicted of second-degree murder, Oct. 5, in the 2014 shooting of Black teenager **Laquan McDonald**.

U.S. Senate, 50-48, Oct. 6 confirmed nomination of **Brett Kavanaugh** to Supreme Court, after hearings in which a psychology professor testified he had sexually assaulted her when both were teenagers. **Sears** filed for bankruptcy Oct. 15.

Authorities intercepted **package bombs** addressed to prominent Democrats and CNN and arrested the suspected sender, Oct. 26. A gunman opened fire in **Tree of Life Congregation synagogue** in Pittsburgh, PA, Oct. 27, killing 11. Trump ordered 5,200 troops to the southern border, Oct. 29, to halt **Central American migrants** and, Nov. 9, issued an order to deny asylum to migrants who crossed that border (enforcement suspended under court order).

An ex-Marine fatally shot 12 people at a bar in **Thousand Oaks**, CA, Nov. 7, then killed himself. A **wildfire**, starting on Nov. 8, wiped out the town of **Paradise**, CA; 85 people died. Three U.S. service members were killed Nov. 27 in apparent Taliban bombing in Afghanistan; U.S. airstrike in response reportedly caused civilian deaths. Pres. Trump, Dec. 21, signed bipartisan **criminal justice reform** bill reducing or eliminating mandatory minimum sentences for many drug-related federal crimes. An impasse over border-wall funding led to a partial federal government **shutdown**, Dec. 22, lasting a record 35 days.

2019 Trump administration, Jan. 25, initiated **"Remain in Mexico"** policy for asylum seekers. On Feb. 1 the administration announced it was suspending U.S. obligations under the 1987 Intermediate-Range Nuclear Forces (**INF**) **Treaty**. NASA announced the end of its **Mars** *Opportunity* rover mission Feb. 13, after 15 years.

Justice Dept. Mar. 12, charged some 50 people, including several celebrities, in **college admissions cheating schemes**.

FAA Mar. 13 grounded **Boeing's 737 Max** aircraft after two fatal crashes abroad.

The U.S.-backed **Syrian Democratic Forces** declared victory over ISIS in Syria, Mar. 23. **Disney** Mar. 20 completed $71.3-bil acquisition of most of **21st Century Fox's** film and TV assets. **OxyContin** maker **Purdue Pharma** and its owners, Mar. 26, agreed to pay $270 mil settling suits for allegedly minimizing the drug's addictive potential. **Apple** agreed Apr. 16 to pay wireless chipmaker **Qualcomm** at least $4.5 bil to settle dispute over technology used in iPhones.

Justice Dept. report released Apr. 18 found the **Russian government** had "worked to secure" Trump's election. Pres. Trump May 10 increased **tariffs** on Chinese products. On May 24 Trump declared tensions with **Iran** a national security emergency, allowing U.S. **arms sales** to Saudi Arabia, UAE, and Jordan.

On May 23 Justice Dept. announced charges against Australian **WikiLeaks** founder **Julian Assange**. Gunman killed 12 people in **Virginia Beach**, VA, May 31. The EPA, June 19, repealed Obama's **Clean Power Plan**, replacing it with weaker regulations.

Pres. Trump met June 30 with North Korean leader **Kim Jong Un** at the Demilitarized Zone (DMZ). Trump July 1 signed $4.6-bil package to help U.S. agencies deal with migrant surge at **U.S.-Mexican border**. U.S. won a record fourth FIFA women's **World Cup** title July 7. Financier **Jeffrey Epstein** was indicted, July 8, on federal charges of **sexual abuse** involving dozens of girls; he died Aug. 10, in apparent suicide.

Citing signs of global economic cooling, the Fed July 31 began cutting **interest rates**. As U.S.-China **trade war** heated up, the Dow, Aug. 5, fell 767 points; recession fears contributed to 800-point drop Aug. 14.

On Aug. 3 a shooter reportedly targeting Mexicans fatally shot 23 people at an **El Paso, TX, Walmart**, before surrendering. On Aug. 4 a gunman killed nine people on a **Dayton**, OH, street, before being fatally shot by police.

House Speaker **Nancy Pelosi** (D, CA) announced Sept. 24 that the House would launch a formal **impeachment inquiry** against Pres. Trump, following allegations he had pressured Ukrainian Pres. **Volodymyr Zelenskyy** to investigate dealings of political rival **Joe Biden** and Biden's son Hunter, after temporarily withholding $400 mil in aid to Ukraine.

U.S. unemployment rate for Sept. fell to 3.5%, lowest since 1969. White House, Oct. 6, announced withdrawal of some U.S. troops from **Syria** in the face of an imminent Turkish assault against **Kurdish** forces allied with the U.S. against ISIS. ISIS leader Abu Bakr al-Baghdadi was reported killed during U.S. military raid in Syria, Oct. 26. A **Saudi Arabian** military officer in flight training fatally shot three trainees Dec. 7 at U.S. naval base in **Pensacola**, FL; he was killed in gun battle.

On Nov. 15, Trump political adviser **Roger Stone** was convicted on charges stemming from the election-interference probe; Trump later commuted his sentence. A Justice Dept. **watchdog report**, released Dec. 6, found procedural errors in the probe but no evidence of bias against Trump.

House Judiciary Committee, Dec. 13, approved articles of **impeachment** against Pres. Trump for **abuse of power** and for **obstruction of Congress**. On Dec. 18 the full House, with no Republican support, passed the first article, 230-197, and the second, 229-198.

Dow closed the year up 22.3%. CDC reported 1,282 cases of **measles** for 2019, largest number since 1992.

2020 U.S. **drone strikes** in Iraq, Jan. 3, killed Iranian Islamic Revolutionary Guard Corps Major Gen. **Qassem Soleimani**; another drone attack, in **Yemen** disclosed Feb. 6, killed **Qasim al-Raymi**, leader of al-Qaeda in the Arabian Peninsula. CDC, Jan. 21, announced **first confirmed COVID-19 case** in the U.S., in traveler from China; starting Feb. 2, Trump administration barred U.S. entry for most non-Americans recently in China. Former NBA star **Kobe Bryant** and his daughter Gianna were among nine people killed in helicopter crash in Calabasas, CA, Jan. 26.

After **impeachment trial**, senators on Feb. 5 voted, 52-48, to convict Pres. Trump for abuse of power, and 53-47 for obstruction of Congress, falling short of the needed two-thirds majority.

2020: Spurred by the death of George Floyd and other Black men and women in dealings with police, protests call for an end to systemic racism.

A federal judge Feb. 11 approved **T-Mobile's** $26.5 bil deal to acquire rival **Sprint**. **Morgan Stanley** agreed Feb. 20 to purchase **E-Trade** for $13 bil. **Wells Fargo**, Feb. 21, agreed to pay $3 bil to end probe into unauthorized accounts under customers' names. **Boy Scouts**, facing sex-abuse suits and waning membership, filed for bankruptcy Feb. 18.

The fatal shooting of unarmed Black jogger **Ahmaud Arbery** (by white pursuers, Feb. 23 in Brunswick, GA; later convicted of murder) and Black woman **Breonna Taylor** (by police in botched raid on her apartment, Mar. 13, in Louisville, KY) fueled widespread protests in support of **Black Lives Matter** movement.

First U.S. COVID-19 fatality reported, Feb. 29. The administration declared a national emergency Mar. 13, banned most travel from Europe by non-Americans, and, Mar. 20, began invoking a legal provision (**"Title 42"**) to allow immediate expulsion of **asylum-seeking migrants** as threats to public health during the COVID emergency. The Northeast was especially hard hit initially, with health resources sharply strained.

U.S. and **Taliban** militants approved pact Feb. 29 calling for all U.S. and coalition forces to leave **Afghanistan** within 14 months, with some 5,000 Taliban prisoners to be freed and a Taliban pledge to end attacks and engage in intra-Afghan talks; Taliban subsequently grew in strength.

Dow fell 2,352 points Mar. 12, a day after WHO declared the coronavirus a **global pandemic**, and 2,997 points Mar. 16, despite action by the Fed cutting its benchmark interest rate. Trump, Mar. 27, signed $2-tril economic aid and **stimulus bill**. Dow ended Apr. up 11.1%, but **unemployment** hit 14.7%, highest since the Great Depression. J. Crew, Neiman Marcus, J. C. Penney, and Hertz declared **bankruptcy** in May.

Idaho, Mar. 29, became the first state to bar **transgender** girls and women from participating in female sports. CDC, Apr. 3, urged Americans to wear **face masks** to prevent spread of COVID-19. Trump May 15 announced **Operation Warp Speed**, aimed at facilitating development, manufacture, and distribution of **COVID vaccines**. U.S., May 27-28, became the first country to exceed 100,000 COVID deaths.

On May 25 **Derek Chauvin**, a white **Minneapolis** police officer, kneeled on the neck of a prone Black man in custody, **George Floyd**, who died. Demonstrations followed, with instances of arson, looting, and vandalism; Chauvin later convicted of murder. The incident fueled widespread protests in support of **Black Lives Matter**.

The shooting of **Jacob Blake**, a Black man, in struggle with police in **Kenosha**, WI, Aug. 23, set off demonstrations in which two protesters were fatally shot by a vigilante claiming self-defense; he was acquitted. Amid clashes between Trump supporters and activists in **Portland**, OR, one man was fatally shot Aug. 29. Unrest erupted in **Philadelphia** Oct. 26-27 following fatal shooting of a Black man by police; over 50 police injured.

SpaceX, May 30, became first private company to launch humans into orbit. **Bayer**, which acquired agricultural giant **Monsanto** in 2018, announced June 24 it would pay over $10 bil to resolve lawsuits over cancers allegedly caused by the herbicide **Roundup**.

Supreme Court ruled June 15, 6-3, that employers could not discriminate against workers for being **gay or transgender**. Ruling 7-2, July 8, the Court held that private employers could opt out of Affordable Care Act mandate requiring coverage of **contraceptives**, if on religious or moral grounds. On July 6, the Court ruled, 9-0, that states could compel **presidential electors** to vote for candidates they had pledged to support.

Executions of death row inmates for federal crimes resumed July 14, ending informal moratorium begun in 2003. Trump, in Aug.-Sept., announced agreements between **Israel** and **UAE** and **Bahrain** to normalize relations. Supreme Court Justice **Ruth Bader Ginsburg** died Sept. 18; **Amy Coney Barrett** was confirmed, Oct. 26, to replace her.

More than 3.9 mil acres burnt Aug.-Sept. in California's **wildfire** season; over 30 people died. **GDP** rose an estimated 33.4% in third quarter 2020, having fallen 31.4% in the second quarter. Federal officials Oct. 8 announced indictment of six people over failed right-wing extremist plot to kidnap Michigan Gov. **Gretchen Whitmer** (D). Justice Dept., Oct. 21 announced **OxyContin** maker **Purdue Pharma** would pay $8.3 bil to settle charges of illegal marketing and kickbacks to doctors.

Vote counting continued after **Election Day**, Nov. 3, with news organizations, Nov. 7, projecting **Biden** as winner of the presidential election. Republicans filed over 50 lawsuits challenging results or balloting procedures, to little effect. The Biden-Harris ticket won in Electoral College, 306-232, and came out ahead by 7 mil in popular vote. Trump refused to concede, claiming without evidence to have lost due to fraud.

The U.S., Nov. 4, formally withdrew from the 2015 **Paris climate agreement**. Massive **cyberattack** on U.S. government sites and other targets confirmed by U.S., Dec. 13; attributed to Russia. Congress easily passed a second **economic aid and stimulus** bill, signed Dec. 27 by Trump.

FDA approved **COVID-19 vaccines** from Pfizer, Dec. 11, and Moderna, Dec. 18, on emergency basis; first vaccine in the U.S. administered Dec. 14. By year's end, U.S recorded some **20 mil COVID-19 cases**, with 350,000 deaths, according to Johns Hopkins Univ.'s Coronavirus Resource Center.

2021 On Jan. 6, after Pres. Trump told rally to "fight like hell" against accepting 2020 presidential results, a mob of supporters, some armed, broke into the **Capitol**, temporarily preventing Congress from certifying the election outcome. One woman was fatally shot by police, of whom over 100 were injured. By a 232-197 vote, the House, Jan. 13, voted to **impeach Trump** for a second time, this time for "incitement of insurrection." On Feb. 13, 7 Republican senators joined all 50 joined Democrats in a vote to convict, which fell short of the needed two-thirds majority.

Joe Biden was sworn in as president Jan. 20, at the Capitol. Beginning Jan. 20 he signed a series of **executive orders**, many aimed at revoking or modifying Trump policies. Pres. Biden announced, Feb. 4, that the U.S. would end its support for Saudi-led offensive against Iran-backed Houthi in devastating **Yemen civil war**. On Feb. 11 Biden halted diversion of Pentagon funding for construction of a **border wall**.

NASA's **Perseverance** rover landed on **Mars**, Feb. 18. U.S. officially reentered the **Paris climate accord** Feb. 19. Biden Mar. 11 signed $1.9-tril **COVID relief package**, which included direct payments to nearly all households.

A **gunman** Mar. 16 killed eight people, including six Asian women, at **Atlanta**-area spas. Another shooter killed 10 people Mar. 22 at supermarket in **Boulder**, CO. A police officer, mistakenly firing her handgun instead of her Taser, killed **Daunte Wright**, a Black driver, after a traffic stop struggle in Minneapolis suburb Apr. 11; the officer was convicted of manslaughter. Eight workers at a FedEx facility in **Indianapolis**, IN, were shot and killed Apr. 15 by a former employee, who died by suicide.

Georgia became the first of several states to impose controversial **voting restrictions**, under measure signed Mar. 25 by Gov. **Brian Kemp** (R).

GOP House members May 12 voted to remove Rep. **Liz Cheney** (R, WY), a Trump critic, as chair of the House Republican Conference. Biden administration June 1 suspended oil and gas leases in Alaska's **Arctic National Wildlife Refuge**. Pres. Biden announced plan June 3 to donate **COVID vaccines** to global sharing program and, June 10, to purchase 500

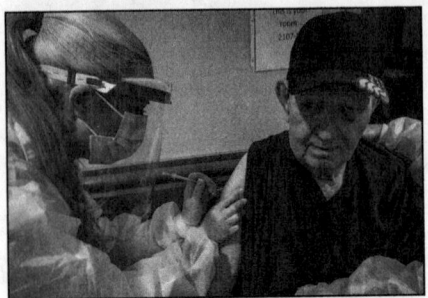

2021: Coronavirus vaccines are widely available by midyear, but virus variants and vaccine reluctance continue to pose challenges.

mil vaccines for lower-income countries. **Boy Scouts** July 1 agreed to pay $850 mil to settle sexual abuse claims.

In Afghanistan, the U.S., July 2, handed over control of its largest military base, **Bagram Airfield**, to Afghan forces; Taliban continued expanding territorial control. A wildfire ignited July 13 in **California** burned nearly 1 mil acres. On July 20, **Jeff Bezos** launched Blue Origin's reusable and pilotless *New Shepard* rocket, with Bezos and three others aboard.

Taliban forces captured 26 provincial capitals and, Aug. 15, retook **Kabul**, while Afghan forces surrendered Bagram Airfield. Under a fixed Aug. 31 deadline, U.S. forces scrambled to evacuate Americans and Afghans who aided them, with many of the latter left behind. An **airport bombing**, Aug. 26, killed 13 U.S. soldiers and at least 169 Afghan civilians.

New York Gov. **Andrew Cuomo** (D) resigned, effective Aug. 23, following probe that reported instances of sexual harassment. **Hurricane Ida** made landfall Aug. 29 in Louisiana, amid heat wave; close to 100 U.S. deaths reported.

A **Texas** law generally prohibiting **abortions** after a detectable fetal heartbeat took effect Sept. 1. Pres. Biden, Sept. 9, announced a COVID **vaccine mandate** for companies with over 100 employees (mandate later struck down by Supreme Court).

Four passengers aboard SpaceX's *Dragon* capsule, launched Sept. 15, became the first all-civilian, nonprofessional crew to orbit Earth. Federal regulators, Nov. 2, recommended the Pfizer vaccine for children aged 5-11 and, Nov. 19, authorized **booster shots** of Pfizer and Moderna vaccines for all adults. Biden, Nov. 15, signed $1.5-tril **infrastructure** package.

Six people were run over and killed at **Waukesha**, WI, Christmas parade, Nov. 21; suspect convicted, sentenced to life. Four students were shot and killed, Nov. 30, at an **Oxford, MI, high school**; the shooter pleaded guilty; his parents were also charged, for allowing him access to the weapon. Five people shot dead, Dec. 27, in and around **Denver** and **Lakewood**, CO; shooter was killed by police.

2022 COVID infection rates in U.S. peaked Jan. 15, driven up by the highly contagious **omicron** variant. U.S. raid in NW Syria, Feb. 3, led to death of **ISIS** leader Abu Ibrahim al-Hashimi al-Qurayshi.

Gun manufacturer **Remington** agreed, Feb. 15, to pay $73 mil to families of nine victims of the 2012 **Newtown**, CT, school shooting. Jury Oct. 12 ordered Infowars host **Alex Jones** to pay $965 mil to families of eight victims, for having portrayed shootings as staged.

In State of the Union address, Mar. 1, Pres. Biden vowed U.S. support for **Ukraine**, in the wake of the Feb. 24 Russian invasion. **Puerto Rico** exited **bankruptcy** Mar. 15, after adopting the largest debt restructuring plan in U.S. history. Florida Gov. **Ron DeSantis** (R) signed a bill, Mar. 28, barring public school "instruction on sexual orientation or gender identity" in primary grades. Pres. Biden signed bipartisan legislation Mar. 29 making **lynching** a federal crime.

Senate voted, 53-47, Apr. 7, to confirm federal appeals court judge **Ketanji Brown Jackson** to the Supreme Court. She replaced Justice **Stephen Breyer** upon his retirement, becoming the Court's **first Black woman** justice.

An 18-year-old armed with an AR-15-style semi-automatic rifle fatally shot 10 Black people at a **Buffalo supermarket**

May 14; shooter sentenced to life. On May 24, an 18-year-old gunman killed 19 students and two teachers at Robb Elementary School in mostly Hispanic **Uvalde**, TX; after long delay, officers entered classrooms, and the shooter was killed. On June 25 Pres. Biden, signed a **gun control bill** which, though limited, was the most extensive passed by Congress in nearly three decades.

COVID-19 deaths in U.S. passed the 1 million mark, according to CDC data released May 16. A House select committee investigating the **Jan. 6, 2021, attack** on the Capitol began televised public hearings June 9; former Trump aides testified that he had been advised his claims of widespread electoral fraud had no basis and had resisted pleas to call off rioters.

Record flooding and landslides forced temporary closure of **Yellowstone National Park**, June 13. Fifty-three **Hispanic migrants** were found dead or dying, June 27, in an abandoned tractor-trailer in San Antonio, TX.

On June 24, in *Dobbs v. Jackson Women's Health Organization*, U.S. Supreme Court voted, 6-3, to uphold Mississippi's 15-week **abortion ban** and, 5-4, to overturn the landmark 1973 *Roe v. Wade* decision that had asserted a constitutional right to abortion. Other 6-3 decisions, June 21-30, also highlighted the impact of Court conservatives.

A rooftop shooter opened fire July 4 into crowd at a parade in the Chicago suburb of **Highland Park**, killing seven and injuring over 30; suspect was indicted. The Fed raised benchmark **interest rates** July 27 by 0.75%, after inflation hit a new high in June, up 9.1% from a year earlier. U.S. House Speaker **Nancy Pelosi** (D, CA) met with Taiwan's president Aug. 3 in Taipei; China, in response, staged military drills around Taiwan and paused or ended cooperation with U.S. in eight policy areas.

On Aug. 8, the FBI executed a **search warrant at Mar-a-Lago**, former Pres. Trump's residence in Palm Beach, FL, seizing boxes of government documents, some marked as classified. Florida Gov. **Ron DeSantis** (R) Sept. 14 sent some 50 asylum **seekers** aboard unannounced chartered flights to **Martha's Vineyard**, MA; the flights followed busing of thousands of migrants from GOP-controlled Texas and Arizona to Democrat-led **big cities**.

Pres. Biden signed an executive order, Aug. 24, canceling up to $20,000 in **student loan debt** for millions of individual borrowers (struck down by Supreme Court decision, 2023). The Fed on Sept. 21 raised benchmark **interest rates** by 0.75% for the third time in three straight meetings. **Hurricane Ian** made landfall in Florida on Sept. 28 and South Carolina on Sept. 30; causing over 150 deaths, nearly all in Florida. In sale finalized Oct. 27, tech magnate **Elon Musk** took over **Twitter**, paying $44 bil; layoffs followed. **Paul Pelosi**, husband of House Speaker **Nancy Pelosi** (D, CA), was assaulted by a home intruder targeting his wife, Oct. 28. The Fed, Nov. 2, hiked **interest rates** by 0.75% to 3.75-4%, their highest levels since 2008, and up from near-zero early in the year, as inflation remained a key concern.

In federal elections Nov. 8, Republicans won control of the **U.S. House** by an unexpectedly modest majority (ultimately 222-213); Democrats kept narrow control of the **Senate**, flipping one seat.

Three students were fatally shot at **Univ. of Virginia**, and four were fatally stabbed in off-campus housing at **Univ. of Idaho**, Nov. 13. Mass shooting, Nov. 22, at Chesapeake, VA, **Walmart** left seven dead, including the killer.

Pres. Biden met with **Chinese Pres. Xi Jinping**, Nov. 14, in Bali. On Nov. 29, **Stewart Rhodes** and another **Oath Keepers** militia leader were convicted of **seditious conspiracy** in Jan. 6 attack on U.S. Capitol. **Trump Org.** Dec. 6 was found guilty of **tax fraud** and other crimes.

WNBA star **Brittney Griner**, imprisoned in Russia (Feb. 2022) on a minor drug offense, was released Dec. 8 in exchange for a notorious Russian arms dealer. On Dec. 13, Pres. Biden signed the Respect for Marriage Act, passed by Congress with some bipartisan support, protecting federal recognition of **same-sex marriages** legal under state laws.

Pres. Volodymyr Zelenskyy met with Pres. Biden and spoke before Congress, Dec. 21, seeking more financial support in fight against Russian invasion. Biden signed $1.7-trillion spending measure, Dec. 29, averting a partial government shutdown.

U.S. HISTORY: DOCUMENTS, SPEECHES, AND SYMBOLS

Patrick Henry's Speech to the Virginia Convention

The following is an excerpt from Patrick Henry's speech to the Virginia Convention, which met at St. John's Church in Richmond, on Mar. 23, 1775, to react to British oppression.

Gentlemen may cry, Peace, Peace—but there is no peace. The war is actually begun! The next gale that sweeps from the north will bring to our ears the clash of resounding arms! Our brethren are already in the field! Why stand we here idle? What is it that gentlemen wish? What would they have? Is life so dear, or peace so sweet, as to be purchased at the price of chains and slavery? Forbid it, Almighty God! I know not what course others may take; but as for me, give me liberty, or give me death!

Adoption of the Declaration of Independence

On June 7, 1776, Richard Henry Lee, who had issued the first call for a congress of the colonies, introduced in the Continental Congress at Philadelphia a resolution declaring "that these United Colonies are, and of right ought to be, free and independent states, that they are absolved from all allegiance to the British Crown, and that all political connection between them and the state of Great Britain is, and ought to be, totally dissolved."

The resolution, seconded by John Adams on behalf of the Massachusetts delegation, came up again June 11 when a committee of five chaired by Thomas Jefferson (VA) was appointed to express the purpose of the resolution in a declaration of independence. The other four were John Adams, Benjamin Franklin (PA), Robert R. Livingston (NY), and Roger Sherman (CT).

Drafting the Declaration was assigned to Jefferson, who worked on a portable desk of his own construction in a room at Market and 7th St. The committee reported the result on June 28, 1776. The members of the Congress suggested a number of changes, which Jefferson called "deplorable." They did not approve Jefferson's arraignment of the British people and King George III for encouraging and fostering the slave trade, which Jefferson called "an execrable commerce." They eliminated 630 words and added 146, leaving 1,322 words in the final draft. In its final form, capitalization was erratic. Jefferson had written that men were endowed with "inalienable" rights; in the final copy it came out as "unalienable."

The Lee-Adams resolution of independence was adopted by 12 yeas on July 2—the actual date of the act of independence. The Declaration, which explains the act, was adopted July 4.

After the Declaration was adopted, July 4, 1776, it was turned over to printer John Dunlap to be printed on broadsides. The original copy was lost and one of his broadsides was attached to a page in the journal of the Congress. It was read aloud July 8 in Philadelphia; Easton, PA; and Trenton, NJ. On July 9, it was read by order of Gen. George Washington to the troops assembled on the Common in New York City (now City Hall Park).

The Continental Congress of July 19, 1776, adopted the following resolution:

"Resolved, That the Declaration passed on the 4th, be fairly engrossed on parchment with the title and stile of 'The Unanimous Declaration of the thirteen United States of America' and that the same, when engrossed, be signed by every member of Congress." (Engrossing meant clearly writing out an official document.)

Not all delegates who signed the engrossed Declaration had been present on July 4. Among them were Robert Morris (PA), William Williams (CT), and Samuel Chase (MD), who signed on Aug. 2. Oliver Wolcott (CT), George Wythe (VA), Richard Henry Lee (VA), and Elbridge Gerry (MA) signed in Aug. and Sept.; Matthew Thornton (NH) joined the Congress Nov. 4 and signed later. Thomas McKean (DE) rejoined Washington's army before signing and said later that he signed in 1781.

Charles Carroll of Carrollton was appointed a delegate by Maryland on July 4, 1776, presented his credentials July 18, and signed the engrossed Declaration on Aug. 2. Born Sept. 19, 1737, he was 95 years old and the last surviving signer when he died Nov. 14, 1832.

Two Pennsylvania delegates who did not support the Declaration July 4, 1776, were replaced. The four New York delegates did not have authority from their state to vote on July 4. On July 9, the New York state convention authorized its delegates to approve the Declaration, and the Congress was so notified on July 15, 1776. The four signed the Declaration on Aug. 2.

Declaration of Independence

The Declaration of Independence was adopted by the Continental Congress in Philadelphia on July 4, 1776. John Hancock was president of the Congress, and Charles Thomson was secretary. A copy of the Declaration, engrossed (i.e., written in a clear hand) on parchment, was signed by members of Congress on and after Aug. 2, 1776. On Jan. 18, 1777, Congress ordered that "an authenticated copy, with the names of the members of Congress subscribing the same, be sent to each of the United States, and that they be desired to have the same put on record." Authenticated copies were printed in broadside form in Baltimore, where the Continental Congress was then in session. The following text is that of the original printed by John Dunlap in Philadelphia for the Continental Congress. The original is on display at the National Archives in Washington, DC.

In CONGRESS, July 4, 1776.
A DECLARATION
By the REPRESENTATIVES of the
UNITED STATES OF AMERICA,
In GENERAL CONGRESS assembled.

When in the Course of human Events, it becomes necessary for one People to dissolve the Political Bands which have connected them with another, and to assume among the Powers of the Earth, the separate and equal Station to which the Laws of Nature and of Nature's God entitle them, a decent Respect to the Opinions of Mankind requires that they should declare the causes which impel them to the Separation.

We hold these Truths to be self-evident, that all Men are created equal, that they are endowed by their Creator with certain unalienable Rights, that among these are Life, Liberty, and the Pursuit of Happiness—That to secure these Rights, Governments are instituted among Men, deriving their just Powers from the Consent of the Governed, that whenever any Form of Government becomes destructive of these Ends, it is the Right of the People to alter or to abolish it, and to institute new Government, laying its Foundation on such Principles, and organizing its Powers in such Form, as to them shall seem most likely to effect their Safety and Happiness. Prudence, indeed, will dictate that Governments long established should not be changed for light and transient Causes; and accordingly all Experience hath shewn, that Mankind are more disposed to suffer, while Evils are sufferable, than to right themselves by abolishing the Forms to which they are accustomed. But when a long Train of Abuses and Usurpations, pursuing invariably the same Object, evinces a Design to reduce them under absolute Despotism, it is their Right, it is their Duty, to throw off such Government, and to provide new Guards for their future Security. Such has been the patient Sufferance of these Colonies; and such is now the Necessity which constrains them to alter their former Systems of Government. The History of the present King of Great-Britain is a History of repeated Injuries and Usurpations, all having in direct Object the Establishment of an absolute Tyranny over these States. To prove this, let Facts be submitted to a candid World.

He has refused his Assent to Laws, the most wholesome and necessary for the public Good.

He has forbidden his Governors to pass Laws of immediate and pressing Importance, unless suspended in their Operation till his Assent should be obtained; and when so suspended, he has utterly neglected to attend to them.

He has refused to pass other Laws for the Accommodation of large Districts of People, unless those People would relinquish the Right of Representation in the Legislature, a Right inestimable to them, and formidable to Tyrants only.

He has called together Legislative Bodies at Places unusual, uncomfortable, and distant from the Depository of their Public Records, for the sole Purpose of fatiguing them into Compliance with his Measures.

He has dissolved Representative Houses repeatedly, for opposing with manly Firmness his Invasions on the Rights of the People.

He has refused for a long Time, after such Dissolutions, to cause others to be elected; whereby the Legislative Powers, incapable of Annihilation, have returned to the People at large for their exercise; the State remaining in the mean time exposed to all the Dangers of Invasion from without, and Convulsions within.

He has endeavoured to prevent the Population of these States; for that Purpose obstructing the Laws for Naturalization of Foreigners; refusing to pass others to encourage their Migrations hither, and raising the Conditions of new Appropriations of Lands.

He has obstructed the Administration of Justice, by refusing his Assent to Laws for establishing Judiciary Powers.

He has made Judges dependent on his Will alone, for the Tenure of their Offices, and the Amount and Payment of their Salaries.

He has erected a Multitude of new Offices, and sent hither Swarms of Officers to harrass our People, and eat out their Substance.

He has kept among us, in Times of Peace, Standing Armies, without the consent of our Legislatures.

He has affected to render the Military independent of and superior to the Civil Power.

He has combined with others to subject us to a Jurisdiction foreign to our Constitution, and unacknowledged by our Laws; giving his Assent to their Acts of pretended Legislation:

For quartering large Bodies of Armed Troops among us:

For protecting them, by a mock Trial, from Punishment for any Murders which they should commit on the Inhabitants of these States:

For cutting off our Trade with all Parts of the World:

For imposing Taxes on us without our Consent:

For depriving us, in many Cases, of the Benefits of Trial by Jury:

For transporting us beyond Seas to be tried for pretended Offences:

For abolishing the free System of English Laws in a neighbouring Province, establishing therein an arbitrary Government, and enlarging its Boundaries, so as to render it at once an Example and fit Instrument for introducing the same absolute Rule into these Colonies:

For taking away our Charters, abolishing our most valuable Laws, and altering fundamentally the Forms of our Governments:

For suspending our own Legislatures, and declaring themselves invested with Power to legislate for us in all Cases whatsoever.

He has abdicated Government here, by declaring us out of his Protection and waging War against us.

He has plundered our Seas, ravaged our Coasts, burnt our Towns, and destroyed the Lives of our People.

He is, at this Time, transporting large Armies of foreign Mercenaries to compleat the Works of Death, Desolation, and Tyranny, already begun with circumstances of Cruelty

and Perfidy, scarcely paralleled in the most barbarous Ages, and totally unworthy the Head of a civilized Nation.

He has constrained our fellow Citizens taken Captive on the high Seas to bear Arms against their Country, to become the Executioners of their Friends and Brethren, or to fall themselves by their Hands.

He has excited domestic Insurrections amongst us, and has endeavoured to bring on the Inhabitants of our Frontiers, the merciless Indian Savages, whose known Rule of Warfare, is an undistinguished Destruction, of all Ages, Sexes and Conditions.

In every stage of these Oppressions we have Petitioned for Redress in the most humble Terms: Our repeated Petitions have been answered only by repeated Injury. A Prince, whose Character is thus marked by every act which may define a Tyrant, is unfit to be the Ruler of a free People.

Nor have we been wanting in Attentions to our British Brethren. We have warned them from Time to Time of Attempts by their Legislature to extend an unwarrantable Jurisdiction over us. We have reminded them of the Circumstances of our Emigration and Settlement here. We have appealed to their native Justice and Magnanimity, and we have conjured them by the Ties of our common Kindred to disavow these Usurpations, which, would inevitably interrupt our Connections and Correspondence. They too have been deaf to the Voice of Justice and of Consanguinity. We must, therefore, acquiesce in the Necessity, which denounces our Separation, and hold them, as we hold the rest of Mankind, Enemies in War, in Peace, Friends.

We, therefore, the Representatives of the UNITED STATES OF AMERICA, in General Congress, Assembled, appealing to the Supreme Judge of the World for the Rectitude of our Intentions, do, in the Name, and by Authority of the good People of these Colonies, solemnly Publish and Declare, That these United Colonies are, and of Right ought to be, Free and Independent States; that they are absolved from all Allegiance to the British Crown, and that all political Connection between them and the State of Great-Britain, is and ought to be totally dissolved; and that as Free and Independent States, they have full Power to levy War, conclude Peace, contract Alliances, establish Commerce, and to do all other Acts and Things which Independent States may of right do. And for the support of this Declaration, with a firm Reliance on the Protection of divine Providence, we mutually pledge to each other our Lives, our Fortunes, and our sacred Honor.

JOHN HANCOCK, President.

Attest.

CHARLES THOMSON, Secretary.

Signers of the Declaration of Independence

Delegate (state)	Occupation	Birthplace	Born	Died
Adams, John (MA)	Lawyer	Braintree (Quincy), MA	Oct. 30, 1735	July 4, 1826
Adams, Samuel (MA)	Merchant, brewer	Boston, MA	Sept. 27, 1722	Oct. 2, 1803
Bartlett, Josiah (NH)	Physician, judge	Amesbury, MA	Nov. 21, 1729	May 19, 1795
Braxton, Carter (VA)	Plantation owner	Newington Plantation, VA	Sept. 10, 1736	Oct. 10, 1797
Carroll, Charles, of Carrollton (MD)	Plantation owner	Annapolis, MD	Sept. 19, 1737	Nov. 14, 1832
Chase, Samuel (MD)	Lawyer, judge	Princess Anne, MD	Apr. 17, 1741	June 19, 1811
Clark, Abraham (NJ)	Surveyor	Elizabethtown, NJ	Feb. 15, 1726	Sept. 15, 1794
Clymer, George (PA)	Merchant	Philadelphia, PA	Mar. 16, 1739	Jan. 23, 1813
Ellery, William (RI)	Lawyer	Newport, RI	Dec. 22, 1727	Feb. 15, 1820
Floyd, William (NY)	Plantation owner, soldier	Brookhaven, NY	Dec. 17, 1734	Aug. 4, 1821
Franklin, Benjamin (PA)	Printer, inventor	Boston, MA	Jan. 17, 1706	Apr. 17, 1790
Gerry, Elbridge (MA)	Merchant	Marblehead, MA	July 17, 1744	Nov. 23, 1814
Gwinnett, Button (GA)	Merchant	Gloucester, England	c. 1735	May 19, 1777
Hall, Lyman (GA)	Physician	Wallingford, CT	Apr. 12, 1724	Oct. 19, 1790
Hancock, John (MA)	Merchant	Braintree (Quincy), MA	Jan. 12, 1737	Oct. 8, 1793
Harrison, Benjamin (VA)	Plantation owner	Charles City County, VA	Apr. 5, 1726	Apr. 24, 1791
Hart, John (NJ)	Plantation owner	Stonington, CT	c. 1713	May 11, 1779
Hewes, Joseph (NC)	Merchant	Kingston, NJ	Jan. 23, 1730	Nov. 10, 1779
Heyward, Thomas, Jr. (SC)	Lawyer, plantation owner	St. Luke's Parish, SC	July 28, 1746	Mar. 6, 1809
Hooper, William (NC)	Lawyer	Boston, MA	June 17, 1742	Oct. 14, 1790
Hopkins, Stephen (RI)	Judge, merchant	Providence, RI	Mar. 7, 1707	July 13, 1785
Hopkinson, Francis (NJ)	Composer, lawyer	Philadelphia, PA	Oct. 2, 1737	May 9, 1791
Huntington, Samuel (CT)	Lawyer, judge	Windham, CT	July 3, 1731	Jan. 5, 1796
Jefferson, Thomas (VA)	Lawyer, plantation owner	Shadwell, VA	Apr. 13, 1743	July 4, 1826
Lee, Francis Lightfoot (VA)	Plantation owner	Westmoreland County, VA	Oct. 14, 1734	Jan. 11, 1797
Lee, Richard Henry (VA)	Plantation owner	Westmoreland County, VA	Jan. 20, 1732	June 19, 1794
Lewis, Francis (NY)	Merchant	Llandaff, Wales	Mar. 21, 1713	Dec. 31, 1802
Livingston, Philip (NY)	Merchant	Albany, NY	Jan. 15, 1716	June 12, 1778
Lynch, Thomas, Jr. (SC)	Plantation owner	Winyah, SC	Aug. 5, 1749	(at sea) 1779
McKean, Thomas (DE)	Lawyer	New London, PA	Mar. 19, 1734	June 24, 1817
Middleton, Arthur (SC)	Plantation owner	Charleston, SC	June 26, 1742	Jan. 1, 1787
Morris, Lewis (NY)	Farmer, judge	Morrisania (Bronx County), NY	Apr. 8, 1726	Jan. 22, 1798
Morris, Robert (PA)	Merchant	Liverpool, England	Jan. 31, 1734	May 8, 1806
Morton, John (PA)	Surveyor	Ridley, PA	c. 1724	Apr. 1777
Nelson, Thomas, Jr. (VA)	Merchant	Yorktown, VA	Dec. 26, 1738	Jan. 4, 1789
Paca, William (MD)	Lawyer, judge	Abingdon, MD	Oct. 31, 1740	Oct. 23, 1799
Paine, Robert Treat (MA)	Lawyer, judge	Boston, MA	Mar. 11, 1731	May 11, 1814
Penn, John (NC)	Lawyer	Caroline County, VA	May 17, 1741	Sept. 14, 1788
Read, George (DE)	Lawyer, judge	Cecil County, MD	Sept. 18, 1733	Sept. 21, 1798
Rodney, Caesar (DE)	Farmer, judge	Dover, DE	Oct. 7, 1728	June 26, 1784
Ross, George (PA)	Lawyer, judge	New Castle, DE	May 10, 1730	July 14, 1779
Rush, Benjamin (PA)	Physician	Byberry Twp. (Philadelphia), PA	Jan. 4, 1746	Apr. 19, 1813
Rutledge, Edward (SC)	Lawyer, plantation owner	Charleston, SC	Nov. 23, 1749	Jan. 23, 1800
Sherman, Roger (CT)	Lawyer, judge	Newton, MA	Apr. 19, 1721	July 23, 1793
Smith, James (PA)	Lawyer	Ireland	c. 1719	July 11, 1806
Stockton, Richard (NJ)	Lawyer	Princeton, NJ	Oct. 1, 1730	Feb. 28, 1781
Stone, Thomas (MD)	Lawyer	Charles County, MD	c. 1743	Oct. 5, 1787
Taylor, George (PA)	Iron mfr., judge	Ireland	c. 1716	Feb. 23, 1781
Thornton, Matthew (NH)	Physician	Ireland	c. 1714	June 24, 1803
Walton, George (GA)	Lawyer, judge	Cumberland County, VA	c. 1749	Feb. 2, 1804
Whipple, William (NH)	Merchant, judge	Kittery, ME	Jan. 14, 1730	Nov. 28, 1785
Williams, William (CT)	Merchant	Lebanon, CT	c. 1731	Aug. 2, 1811
Wilson, James (PA)	Lawyer	Carskerdo, Scotland	Sept. 14, 1742	Aug. 21, 1798
Witherspoon, John (NJ)	Clergyman, educator	Gifford, Scotland	Feb. 5, 1723	Nov. 15, 1794
Wolcott, Oliver (CT)	Lawyer, judge	Windsor, CT	Nov. 20, 1726	Dec. 1, 1797
Wythe, George (VA)	Lawyer	Elizabeth City County, VA	c. 1726	June 8, 1806

Origin of the Constitution

The War of Independence was conducted by delegates from the original 13 states, who composed the Congress of the United States of America, known as the Continental Congress. In 1777 the Congress submitted to the legislatures of the states the Articles of Confederation and Perpetual Union, which were ratified by New Hampshire, Massachusetts, Rhode Island, Connecticut, New York, New Jersey, Pennsylvania, Delaware, Virginia, North Carolina, South Carolina, Georgia, and finally, in 1781, Maryland.

The first article read: "The stile of this confederacy shall be the United States of America." This did not signify a sovereign nation, because the states delegated only those powers they could not handle individually, such as to wage war, make treaties, and contract debts for general expenses (e.g., paying the army). Taxes for payment of such debts were levied by the individual states. The president signed himself "President of the United States in Congress assembled," but here the United States were considered in the plural, a cooperating group.

When the war was over, it became evident that a stronger federal union was needed. The Congress left the initiative to the legislatures. Virginia in Jan. 1786 appointed commissioners to meet with representatives of other states; delegates from Virginia, Delaware, New York, New Jersey, and Pennsylvania met at Annapolis. Alexander Hamilton prepared their call asking delegates from all states to meet in Philadelphia in May 1787 "to render the Constitution of the federal government adequate to the exigencies of the union." Congress endorsed the plan on Feb. 21, 1787. Delegates were appointed by all states except Rhode Island.

The convention was called for May 14, 1787, but a quorum was not present until May 25. George Washington was chosen president (presiding officer). The states certified 65 delegates, but 10 did not attend. The work was done by 55, not all of whom were present at all sessions. Of the 55 attending delegates, 39 signed Sept. 17, 1787, some with reservations, and 16 failed to sign. Some historians have said 74 delegates (nine more than the 65 actually certified) were named, and 19 failed to attend. These additional persons refused the appointment, were never delegates, and were never counted as absentees. Washington sent the Constitution to Congress, and that body, Sept. 28, 1787, ordered it sent to the legislatures, "in order to be submitted to a convention of delegates chosen in each state by the people thereof."

The Constitution was ratified by the votes of each state's convention as follows: Delaware, Dec. 7, 1787, unanimous; Pennsylvania, Dec. 12, 1787, 46 to 23; New Jersey, Dec. 18, 1787, unanimous; Georgia, Jan. 2, 1788, unanimous; Connecticut, Jan. 9, 1788, 128 to 40; Massachusetts, Feb. 6, 1788, 187 to 168; Maryland, Apr. 28, 1788, 63 to 11; South Carolina, May 23, 1788, 149 to 73; New Hampshire, June 21, 1788, 57 to 46; Virginia, June 25, 1788, 89 to 79; New York, July 26, 1788, 30 to 27. Nine states were needed to establish the operation of the Constitution "between the states so ratifying the same," and New Hampshire was the ninth state. The government did not declare the Constitution in effect until the first Wednesday in Mar. 1789, which was Mar. 4. After that, North Carolina ratified it on Nov. 21, 1789, 194 to 77; and Rhode Island, May 29, 1790, 34 to 32. Vermont in convention ratified it on Jan. 10, 1791, and by act of Congress approved on Feb. 18, 1791, was admitted into the Union as the 14th state, Mar. 4, 1791.

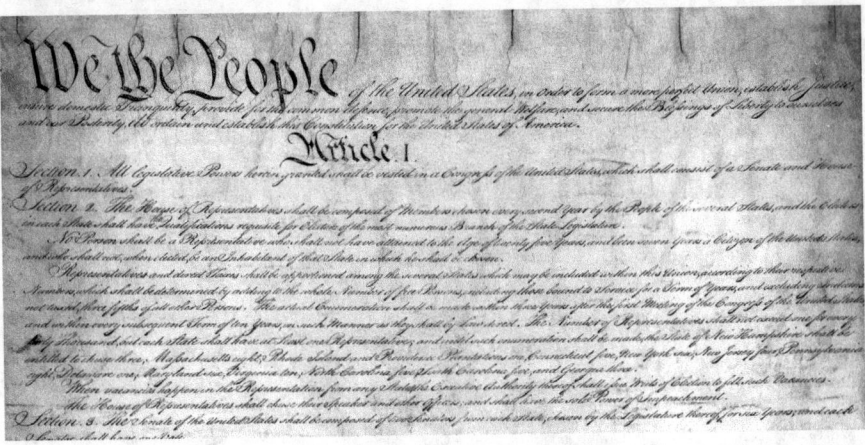

Constitution of the United States

The text of the Constitution given here is from the centennial edition of *The Constitution of the United States of America: Analysis and Interpretation*, prepared by the Library of Congress and issued by the U.S. Government Printing Office. Aug. 26, 2017. Text in brackets indicates that an item has been superseded or amended, or provides background information. **Boldface text** preceding an article, section, or amendment is a brief summary, added by *The World Almanac*.

The Original Seven Articles

PREAMBLE

We the People of the United States, in Order to form a more perfect Union, establish Justice, insure domestic Tranquility, provide for the common defence, promote the general Welfare, and secure the Blessings of Liberty to ourselves and our Posterity, do ordain and establish this Constitution for the United States of America.

ARTICLE I.

Section 1—Legislative powers, in whom vested.

All legislative Powers herein granted shall be vested in a Congress of the United States, which shall consist of a Senate and House of Representatives.

Section 2—House of Representatives, how and by whom chosen. Qualifications of a Representative. Representatives and direct taxes, how apportioned and enumerated. Vacancies to be filled. Choosing of officers and power of impeachment.

The House of Representatives shall be composed of Members chosen every second Year by the People of the several States, and the Electors in each State shall have the Qualifications requisite for Electors of the most numerous Branch of the State Legislature.

No Person shall be a Representative who shall not have attained to the Age of twenty five Years, and been seven Years a Citizen of the United States, and who shall not, when elected, be an Inhabitant of that State in which he shall be chosen.

[Representatives and direct Taxes shall be apportioned among the several States which may be included within this Union, according to their respective Numbers, which shall be determined by adding to the whole Number of free Persons, including those bound to Service for a Term of Years, and excluding Indians not taxed, three fifths of all other Persons.] *[The part of the previous sentence regarding apportionment of representatives among the states was changed by Amendment XIV, section 2, and apportionment of taxes by Amendment XVI.]* The actual Enumeration shall be made within three Years after the first Meeting of the Congress of the United States, and within every subsequent Term of ten Years, in such Manner as they shall by Law direct. The Number of Representatives shall not exceed one for every thirty Thousand, but each State shall have at Least one Representative; and until such enumeration shall be made, the State of New Hampshire shall be entitled to chuse three, Massachusetts eight, Rhode-Island and Providence Plantations one, Connecticut five, New York six, New Jersey four, Pennsylvania eight, Delaware one, Maryland six, Virginia ten, North Carolina five, South Carolina five, and Georgia three.

When vacancies happen in the Representation from any State, the Executive Authority thereof shall issue Writs of Election to fill such Vacancies.

The House of Representatives shall chuse their Speaker and other Officers; and shall have the sole Power of Impeachment.

Section 3—Senators, how and by whom chosen. How assembled. Qualifications of a Senator. President of the Senate. President pro tempore and other officers of the Senate, how chosen. Power to try impeachments. Judgment in cases of impeachment.

The Senate of the United States shall be composed of two Senators from each State, [chosen by the Legislature] *[The preceding words were superseded by Amendment XVII.]* thereof, for six Years; and each Senator shall have one Vote.

Immediately after they shall be assembled in Consequence of the first Election, they shall be divided as equally as may be into three Classes. The Seats of the Senators of the first Class shall be vacated at the Expiration of the second Year, of the second Class at the Expiration of the fourth Year, and of the third Class at the Expiration of the sixth Year, so that one third may be chosen every second Year; [and if Vacancies happen by Resignation, or otherwise, during the Recess of the Legislature of any State, the Executive thereof may make temporary Appointments until the next Meeting of the Legislature, which shall then fill such Vacancies.] *[The words in brackets were superseded by Amendment XVII.]*

No Person shall be a Senator who shall not have attained to the Age of thirty Years, and been nine Years a Citizen of the United States, and who shall not, when elected, be an Inhabitant of that State for which he shall be chosen.

The Vice President of the United States shall be President of the Senate, but shall have no Vote, unless they be equally divided.

The Senate shall chuse their other Officers, and also a President pro tempore, in the Absence of the Vice President, or when he shall exercise the Office of President of the United States.

The Senate shall have the sole Power to try all Impeachments. When sitting for that Purpose, they shall be on Oath or Affirmation. When the President of the United States is tried, the Chief Justice shall preside: And no Person shall be convicted without the Concurrence of two thirds of the Members present.

Judgment in Cases of Impeachment shall not extend further than to removal from Office, and disqualification to hold and enjoy any Office of honor, Trust or Profit under the United States: but the Party convicted shall nevertheless be liable and subject to Indictment, Trial, Judgment and Punishment, according to Law.

Section 4—Times, places, manner of elections. Time of assembly.

The Times, Places and Manner of holding Elections for Senators and Representatives, shall be prescribed in each State by the Legislature thereof; but the Congress may at any time by Law make or alter such Regulations, except as to the Places of chusing Senators.

The Congress shall assemble at least once in every Year, and such Meeting shall be [on the first Monday in December], *[The words in brackets were superseded by Amendment XX, section 2.]* unless they shall by Law appoint a different Day.

Section 5—Membership, quorums, adjournments. Rules of proceedings. Journal of proceedings. Time of adjournments.

Each House shall be the Judge of the Elections, Returns and Qualifications of its own Members, and a Majority of each shall constitute a Quorum to do Business; but a smaller Number may adjourn from day to day, and may be authorized to compel the Attendance of absent Members, in such Manner, and under such Penalties as each House may provide.

Each House may determine the Rules of its Proceedings, punish its Members for disorderly Behaviour, and, with the Concurrence of two thirds, expel a Member.

Each House shall keep a Journal of its Proceedings, and from time to time publish the same, excepting such Parts as may in their Judgment require Secrecy; and the Yeas and Nays of the Members of either House on any question shall, at the Desire of one fifth of those Present, be entered on the Journal.

Neither House, during the Session of Congress, shall, without the Consent of the other, adjourn for more than three days, nor to any other Place than that in which the two Houses shall be sitting.

Section 6—Compensation, privileges. Incompatible offices.

The Senators and Representatives shall receive a Compensation for their Services, to be ascertained by Law, and paid out of the Treasury of the United States. They shall in all Cases, except Treason, Felony and Breach of the Peace, be privileged from Arrest during their Attendance at the Session of their respective Houses, and in going to and returning from the same; and for any Speech or Debate in either House, they shall not be questioned in any other Place.

No Senator or Representative shall, during the Time for which he was elected, be appointed to any civil Office under the Authority of the United States, which shall have been created, or the Emoluments whereof shall have been encreased during such time; and no Person holding any Office under the United States, shall be a Member of either House during his Continuance in Office.

Section 7—House to originate revenue bills. Legislative process; bill presented to the President before becoming law. Passing of bill over objections of President, veto.

All Bills for raising Revenue shall originate in the House of Representatives; but the Senate may propose or concur with Amendments as on other Bills.

Every Bill which shall have passed the House of Representatives and the Senate, shall, before it become a Law, be presented to the President of the United States; If he approve he shall sign it, but if not he shall return it, with his Objections to that House in which it shall have originated, who shall enter the Objections at large on their Journal, and proceed to reconsider it. If after such Reconsideration two thirds of that House shall agree to pass the Bill, it shall be sent, together with the Objections, to the other House, by which it shall likewise be reconsidered, and if approved by two thirds of that House, it shall become a Law. But in all such Cases the Votes of both Houses shall be determined by Yeas and Nays, and the Names of the Persons voting for and against the Bill shall be entered on the Journal of each House respectively. If any Bill shall not be returned by the President within ten Days (Sundays excepted) after it shall have been presented to him, the Same shall be a Law, in like Manner as if he had signed it, unless the Congress by their Adjournment prevent its Return, in which Case it shall not be a Law.

Every Order, Resolution, or Vote to which the Concurrence of the Senate and House of Representatives may be necessary (except on a question of Adjournment) shall be presented to the President of the United States; and before the Same shall take Effect, shall be approved by him, or being disapproved by him, shall be repassed by two thirds of the Senate and House of Representatives, according to the Rules and Limitations prescribed in the Case of a Bill.

Section 8—Powers of Congress.

The Congress shall have Power To lay and collect Taxes, Duties, Imposts and Excises, to pay the Debts and provide for the common Defence and general Welfare of the United States; but all Duties, Imposts and Excises shall be uniform throughout the United States;

To borrow Money on the credit of the United States;

To regulate Commerce with foreign Nations, and among the several States, and with the Indian Tribes;

To establish an uniform Rule of Naturalization, and uniform Laws on the subject of Bankruptcies throughout the United States;

To coin Money, regulate the Value thereof, and of foreign Coin, and fix the Standard of Weights and Measures;

To provide for the Punishment of counterfeiting the Securities and current Coin of the United States;

To establish Post Offices and post Roads;

To promote the Progress of Science and useful Arts, by securing for limited Times to Authors and Inventors the exclusive Right to their respective Writings and Discoveries;

To constitute Tribunals inferior to the supreme Court;

To define and punish Piracies and Felonies committed on the high Seas, and Offences against the Law of Nations;

To declare War, grant Letters of Marque and Reprisal, and make Rules concerning Captures on Land and Water;

To raise and support Armies, but no Appropriation of Money to that Use shall be for a longer Term than two Years;

To provide and maintain a Navy;

To make Rules for the Government and Regulation of the land and naval Forces;

To provide for calling forth the Militia to execute the Laws of the Union, suppress Insurrections and repel Invasions;

To provide for organizing, arming, and disciplining, the Militia, and for governing such Part of them as may be employed in the Service of the United States, reserving to the States respectively, the Appointment of the Officers, and the Authority of training the Militia according to the discipline prescribed by Congress;

To exercise exclusive Legislation in all Cases whatsoever, over such District (not exceeding ten Miles square) as may, by Cession of particular States, and the Acceptance of Congress, become the Seat of the Government of the United States, and to exercise like Authority over all Places purchased by the Consent of the Legislature of the State in which the Same shall be, for the Erection of Forts, Magazines, Arsenals, dock-Yards, and other needful Buildings;—And

To make all Laws which shall be necessary and proper for carrying into Execution the foregoing Powers, and all other Powers vested by this Constitution in the Government of the United States, or in any Department or Officer thereof.

Section 9—Powers denied to Congress: Importation of slaves. Habeas corpus. Bills of attainder. Taxes, how apportioned. Export duty. Preference to ports. Money, how drawn from Treasury. Titles of nobility.

The Migration or Importation of such Persons as any of the States now existing shall think proper to admit, shall not be prohibited by the Congress prior to the Year one thousand eight hundred and eight, but a Tax or duty may be imposed on such Importation, not exceeding ten dollars for each Person.

The Privilege of the Writ of Habeas Corpus shall not be suspended, unless when in Cases of Rebellion or Invasion the public Safety may require it.

No Bill of Attainder or ex post facto Law shall be passed.

No Capitation, or other direct, Tax shall be laid, unless in Proportion to the Census or Enumeration herein before directed to be taken.

No Tax or Duty shall be laid on Articles exported from any State.

No Preference shall be given by any Regulation of Commerce or Revenue to the Ports of one State over those of another: nor shall Vessels bound to, or from, one State, be obliged to enter, clear, or pay Duties in another.

No Money shall be drawn from the Treasury, but in Consequence of Appropriations made by Law; and a regular Statement and Account of the Receipts and Expenditures of all public Money shall be published from time to time.

No Title of Nobility shall be granted by the United States: And no Person holding any Office of Profit or Trust under them, shall, without the Consent of the Congress, accept of any present, Emolument, Office, or Title, of any kind whatever, from any King, Prince, or foreign State.

Section 10—States prohibited from the exercise of certain powers.

No State shall enter into any Treaty, Alliance, or Confederation; grant Letters of Marque and Reprisal; coin Money; emit Bills of Credit; make any Thing but gold and silver Coin a Tender in Payment of Debts; pass any Bill of Attainder, ex post facto Law, or Law impairing the Obligation of Contracts, or grant any Title of Nobility.

No State shall, without the Consent of the Congress, lay any Imposts or Duties on Imports or Exports, except what may be absolutely necessary for executing it's inspection Laws: and the net Produce of all Duties and Imposts, laid by any State on Imports or Exports, shall be for the Use of the Treasury of the United States; and all such Laws shall be subject to the Revision and Controul of the Congress.

No State shall, without the Consent of Congress, lay any Duty of Tonnage, keep Troops, or Ships of War in time of Peace, enter into any Agreement or Compact with another State, or with a foreign Power, or engage in War, unless actually invaded, or in such imminent Danger as will not admit of delay.

ARTICLE II.

Section 1—President, powers and term of office. Electors, number and how appointed. Electors to vote for President. Qualifications of President. On whom duties devolve in case of removal, death, etc., of President. President's compensation. Oath of office.

The executive Power shall be vested in a President of the United States of America. He shall hold his Office during the Term of four Years, and, together with the Vice President, chosen for the same Term, be elected, as follows:

Each State shall appoint, in such Manner as the Legislature thereof may direct, a Number of Electors, equal to the whole Number of Senators and Representatives to which the State may be entitled in the Congress: but no Senator or Representative, or Person holding an Office of Trust or Profit under the United States, shall be appointed an Elector.

[The Electors shall meet in their respective States, and vote by Ballot for two Persons, of whom one at least shall not be an Inhabitant of the same State with themselves. And they shall make a List of all the Persons voted for, and of the Number of Votes for each; which List they shall sign and certify, and transmit sealed to the Seat of the Government of the United States, directed to the President of the Senate. The President of the Senate shall, in the Presence of the Senate and House of Representatives, open all the Certificates, and the Votes shall then be counted. The Person having the greatest Number of Votes shall be the President, if such Number be a Majority of the whole Number of Electors appointed; and if there be more than one who have such Majority, and have an equal Number of Votes, then the House of Representatives shall immediately chuse by Ballot one of them for President; and if no Person have a Majority, then from the five highest on the List the said House shall in like Manner chuse the President. But in chusing the President, the Votes shall be taken by States, the Representation from each State having one Vote; A quorum for this Purpose shall consist of a Member or Members from two thirds of the States, and a Majority of all the States shall be necessary to a Choice. In every Case, after the Choice of the President, the Person having the greatest Number of Votes of the Electors shall be the Vice President. But if there should remain two or more who have equal Votes, the Senate shall chuse from them by Ballot the Vice President.] *[This clause was superseded by Amendment XII.]*

The Congress may determine the Time of chusing the Electors, and the Day on which they shall give their Votes; which Day shall be the same throughout the United States.

No Person except a natural born Citizen, or a Citizen of the United States, at the time of the Adoption of this Constitution, shall be eligible to the Office of President; neither shall any Person be eligible to that Office who shall not have attained to the Age of thirty five Years, and been fourteen Years a Resident within the United States. *[For qualification of the Vice President, see Amendment XII.]*

[In Case of the Removal of the President from Office, or of his Death, Resignation, or Inability to discharge the Powers and Duties of the said Office, the Same shall devolve on the Vice President, and the Congress may by Law provide for the Case of Removal, Death, Resignation or Inability, both of the President and Vice President, declaring what Officer shall then act as President, and such Officer shall act accordingly, until the Disability be removed, or a President shall be elected.] *[This clause was superseded by Amendment XXV.]*

The President shall, at stated Times, receive for his Services, a Compensation, which shall neither be encreased nor diminished during the Period for which he shall have been elected, and he shall not receive within that Period any other Emolument from the United States, or any of them.

Before he enter on the Execution of his Office, he shall take the following Oath or Affirmation:—

"I do solemnly swear (or affirm) that I will faithfully execute the Office of President of the United States, and will to the best of my Ability, preserve, protect and defend the Constitution of the United States."

Section 2—President to be Commander in Chief. Power to make treaties; nominations for, appointments to certain offices. Power to fill vacancies during Senate recess.

The President shall be Commander in Chief of the Army and Navy of the United States, and of the Militia of the several States, when called into the actual Service of the United States; he may require the Opinion, in writing, of the principal Officer in each of the executive Departments, upon any Subject relating to the Duties of their respective Offices, and he shall have Power to Grant Reprieves and Pardons for Offences against the United States, except in Cases of Impeachment.

He shall have Power, by and with the Advice and Consent of the Senate, to make Treaties, provided two thirds of the Senators present concur; and he shall nominate, and by and with the Advice and Consent of the Senate, shall appoint Ambassadors, other public Ministers and Consuls, Judges of the supreme Court, and all other Officers of the United States, whose Appointments are not herein otherwise provided for, and which shall be established by Law: but the Congress may by Law vest the Appointment of such inferior Officers, as they think proper, in the President alone, in the Courts of Law, or in the Heads of Departments.

The President shall have Power to fill up all Vacancies that may happen during the Recess of the Senate, by granting Commissions which shall expire at the End of their next Session.

Section 3—President shall communicate to, may convene and adjourn Congress; shall receive ambassadors, execute laws, and commission officers.

He shall from time to time give to the Congress Information on the State of the Union, and recommend to their Consideration such Measures as he shall judge necessary and expedient; he may, on extraordinary Occasions, convene both Houses, or either of them, and in Case of Disagreement between them, with Respect to the Time of Adjournment, he may adjourn them to such Time as he shall think proper; he shall receive Ambassadors and other public Ministers; he shall take Care that the Laws be faithfully executed, and shall Commission all the Officers of the United States.

Section 4—All civil offices forfeited for certain crimes.

The President, Vice President and all civil Officers of the United States, shall be removed from Office on Impeachment for, and Conviction of, Treason, Bribery, or other high Crimes and Misdemeanors.

ARTICLE III.

Section 1—Judicial powers, tenure, compensation.

The judicial Power of the United States, shall be vested in one supreme Court, and in such inferior Courts as the Congress may from time to time ordain and establish. The Judges, both of the supreme and inferior Courts, shall hold their Offices during good Behaviour, and shall, at stated Times, receive for their Services, a Compensation, which shall not be diminished during their Continuance in Office.

Section 2—Judicial power, cases to which it extends. Jurisdiction of Supreme Court. Trial by jury; where held.

The judicial Power shall extend to all Cases, in Law and Equity, arising under this Constitution, the Laws of the United States, and Treaties made, or which shall be made, under their Authority;—to all Cases affecting Ambassadors, other public Ministers and Consuls;—to all Cases of admiralty and maritime Jurisdiction;—to Controversies to which the United States shall be a Party;—to Controversies between two or more States;—[between a State and Citizens of another State;]—between Citizens of different States;—between Citizens of the same State claiming Lands under Grants of different States, [and between a State, or the Citizens thereof, and foreign States, Citizens or Subjects.] *[This section was modified by Amendment XI.]*

In all Cases affecting Ambassadors, other public Ministers and Consuls, and those in which a State shall be Party, the supreme Court shall have original Jurisdiction. In all the other Cases before mentioned, the supreme Court shall have appellate Jurisdiction, both as to Law and Fact, with such Exceptions, and under such Regulations as the Congress shall make.

The Trial of all Crimes, except in Cases of Impeachment, shall be by Jury; and such Trial shall be held in the State where the said Crimes shall have been committed; but when not committed within any State, the Trial shall be at such Place or Places as the Congress may by Law have directed.

Section 3—Treason defined. Punishment of.

Treason against the United States, shall consist only in levying War against them, or in adhering to their Enemies, giving them Aid and Comfort. No Person shall be convicted of Treason unless on the Testimony of two Witnesses to the same overt Act, or on Confession in open Court.

The Congress shall have Power to declare the Punishment of Treason, but no Attainder of Treason shall work Corruption of Blood, or Forfeiture except during the Life of the Person attainted.

ARTICLE IV.

Section 1—Each State to give credit to the public acts, etc., of every other State.

Full Faith and Credit shall be given in each State to the public Acts, Records, and judicial Proceedings of every other State. And the Congress may by general Laws prescribe the Manner in which such Acts, Records and Proceedings shall be proved, and the Effect thereof.

Section 2—Privileges of citizens of each State. Fugitives from justice to be delivered up. Fugitives from service or labor, to be delivered up.

The Citizens of each State shall be entitled to all Privileges and Immunities of Citizens in the several States.

A Person charged in any State with Treason, Felony, or other Crime, who shall flee from Justice, and be found in another State, shall on Demand of the executive Authority of the State from which he fled, be delivered up, to be removed to the State having Jurisdiction of the Crime.

[No Person held to Service or Labour in one State, under the Laws thereof, escaping into another, shall, in Consequence of any Law or Regulation therein, be discharged from such Service or Labour, but shall be delivered up on Claim of the Party to whom such Service or Labour may be due.] *[This clause was superseded by Amendment XIII.]*

Section 3—Admission of new States. Power of Congress over territory and other property.

New States may be admitted by the Congress into this Union; but no new State shall be formed or erected within the Jurisdiction of any other State; nor any State be formed by the Junction of two or more States, or Parts of States, without the Consent of the Legislatures of the States concerned as well as of the Congress.

The Congress shall have Power to dispose of and make all needful Rules and Regulations respecting the Territory or other Property belonging to the United States; and nothing in this Constitution shall be so construed as to Prejudice any Claims of the United States, or of any particular State.

Section 4—Republican form of government guaranteed; each State to be protected.

The United States shall guarantee to every State in this Union a Republican Form of Government, and shall protect each of them against Invasion; and on Application of the Legislature, or of the Executive (when the Legislature cannot be convened) against domestic Violence.

ARTICLE V.

Constitution, how amended; proviso.

The Congress, whenever two thirds of both Houses shall deem it necessary, shall propose Amendments to this Constitution, or, on the Application of the Legislatures of two thirds of the several States, shall call a Convention for proposing Amendments, which, in either Case, shall be valid to all Intents and Purposes, as Part of this Constitution, when ratified by the Legislatures of three fourths of the several States, or by Conventions in three fourths thereof, as the one or the other Mode of Ratification may be proposed by the Congress; Provided that no Amendment which may be made prior to the Year One thousand eight hundred and eight shall in any Manner affect the first and fourth Clauses in the Ninth Section of the first Article; and that no State, without its Consent, shall be deprived of its equal Suffrage in the Senate.

ARTICLE VI.

Certain debts and engagements shall be valid. Constitution, laws and treaties made, shall be supreme law of the United States. Oath to support Constitution, by whom taken; no religious test shall be required.

All Debts contracted and Engagements entered into, before the Adoption of this Constitution, shall be as valid against the United States under this Constitution, as under the Confederation.

This Constitution, and the Laws of the United States which shall be made in Pursuance thereof; and all Treaties made, or which shall be made, under the Authority of the United States, shall be the supreme Law of the Land; and the Judges in every State shall be bound thereby, any Thing in the Constitution or Laws of any State to the Contrary notwithstanding.

The Senators and Representatives before mentioned, and the Members of the several State Legislatures, and all executive and judicial Officers, both of the United States and of the several States, shall be bound by Oath or Affirmation, to support this Constitution; but no religious Test shall ever be required as a Qualification to any Office or public Trust under the United States.

ARTICLE VII.

Ratification to establish the Constitution.

The Ratification of the Conventions of nine States, shall be sufficient for the Establishment of this Constitution between the States so ratifying the Same.

done in Convention by the Unanimous Consent of the States present the Seventeenth Day of September in the Year of our Lord one thousand seven hundred and Eighty seven and of the Independance of the United States of America the Twelfth. In witness whereof We have hereunto subscribed our Names,

G°. Washington, Presid^t. and deputy from Virginia

New Hampshire—John Langdon, Nicholas Gilman

Massachusetts—Nathaniel Gorham, Rufus King

Connecticut—W^m. Saml. Johnson, Roger Sherman

New York—Alexander Hamilton

New Jersey—Wil: Livingston, David Brearley, W^m. Paterson, Jona: Dayton

Pennsylvania—B Franklin, Thomas Mifflin, Robt. Morris, Geo. Clymer, Thos. FitzSimons, Jared Ingersoll, James Wilson, Gouv Morris

Delaware—Geo: Read, Gunning Bedford jun, John Dickinson, Richard Bassett, Jaco: Broom

Maryland—James McHenry, Dan of St Thos. Jenifer, Danl Carroll

Virginia—John Blair, James Madison Jr.

North Carolina—W^m. Blount, Rich^d. Dobbs Spaight, Hu Williamson

South Carolina—J. Rutledge, Charles Cotesworth Pinckney, Charles Pinckney, Pierce Butler

Georgia—William Few, Abr Baldwin

[George Washington was first to sign the Constitution on Sept. 17, 1787, followed by state delegates in order of geography, from north to south. In total, 38 delegates signed the Constitution, although Delaware delegate George Reed signed for absent delegate John Dickinson, bringing the total signatures to 39. Three delegates abstained from signing in protest of the absent Bill of Rights.]

Origin of the Bill of Rights

Congress, at its first session in New York, NY, submitted to the states 12 amendments Sept. 25, 1789, to clarify certain individual and state rights not named in the Constitution. They are generally called the Bill of Rights.

Influential in framing these amendments was the Declaration of Rights of Virginia, written by George Mason (1725-92) in 1776. Mason, a Virginia delegate to the Constitutional Convention, did not sign the Constitution and opposed its ratification on the ground that it did not sufficiently oppose slavery or safeguard individual rights.

In the preamble to the resolution offering the proposed amendments, Congress said: "The Conventions of a number of the States, having at the time of their adopting the Constitution, expressed a desire, in order to prevent misconstruction or abuse of its powers, that further declaratory and restrictive clauses should be added: And as extending the ground of public confidence in the Government, will best insure the beneficent ends of its institution."

Ten of these amendments, originally three to 12 inclusive, were ratified by the states as follows: New Jersey, Nov. 20, 1789; Maryland, Dec. 19, 1789; North Carolina, Dec. 22, 1789; South Carolina, Jan. 19, 1790; New Hampshire, Jan. 25, 1790; Delaware, Jan. 28, 1790; New York, Feb. 27, 1790; Pennsylvania, Mar. 10, 1790; Rhode Island, June 7, 1790; Vermont, Nov. 3, 1791; Virginia, Dec. 15, 1791; Massachusetts, Mar. 2, 1939; Georgia, Mar. 18, 1939; Connecticut, Apr. 19, 1939. These original 10 ratified amendments follow as Amendments I to X inclusive.

Of the two original proposed amendments that were not ratified promptly by the necessary number of states, the first related to apportionment of Representatives; the second, relating to compensation of members of Congress, was ratified in 1992 and became Amendment XXVII.

The Bill of Rights
In force Dec. 15, 1791

AMENDMENT I.

Religious establishment prohibited. Freedom of speech and of press; right to assemble and to petition.

Congress shall make no law respecting an establishment of religion, or prohibiting the free exercise thereof; or abridging the freedom of speech, or of the press; or the right of the people peaceably to assemble, and to petition the Government for a redress of grievances.

AMENDMENT II.

Right to keep and bear arms.

A well regulated Militia, being necessary to the security of a free State, the right of the people to keep and bear Arms shall not be infringed.

AMENDMENT III.

Conditions for quartering of soldiers.

No Soldier shall, in time of peace be quartered in any house, without the consent of the Owner, nor in time of war, but in a manner to be prescribed by law.

AMENDMENT IV.

Protection from unreasonable search and seizure.

The right of the people to be secure in their persons, houses, papers, and effects, against unreasonable searches and seizures, shall not be violated, and no Warrants shall issue but upon probable cause, supported by Oath or affirmation, and particularly describing the place to be searched, and the persons or things to be seized.

AMENDMENT V.

Provisions concerning prosecution and due process of law. Compensation of private property taken for public use.

No person shall be held to answer for a capital, or otherwise infamous crime, unless on a presentment or indictment of a Grand Jury, except in cases arising in the land and naval forces, or in the Militia, when in actual service in time of War or public danger; nor shall any person be subject for the same offence to be twice put in jeopardy of life or limb; nor shall be compelled in any criminal case to be a witness against himself, nor be deprived of life, liberty, or property, without due process of law; nor shall private property be taken for public use, without just compensation.

AMENDMENT VI.

Rights of accused in criminal prosecutions.

In all criminal prosecutions, the accused shall enjoy the right to a speedy and public trial, by an impartial jury of the State and district wherein the crime shall have been committed, which district shall have been previously ascertained by law, and to be informed of the nature and cause of the accusation; to be confronted with the witnesses against him; to have compulsory process for obtaining witnesses in his favor, and to have the Assistance of Counsel for his defense.

AMENDMENT VII.

Right of trial by jury in civil cases.

In Suits at common law, where the value in controversy shall exceed twenty dollars, the right of trial by jury shall be preserved, and no fact tried by a jury, shall be otherwise reexamined in any Court of the United States, than according to the rules of the common law.

AMENDMENT VIII.

Excessive bail or fines; cruel and unusual punishment.

Excessive bail shall not be required, nor excessive fines imposed, nor cruel and unusual punishments inflicted.

AMENDMENT IX.

Unenumerated rights.

The enumeration in the Constitution, of certain rights, shall not be construed to deny or disparage others retained by the people.

AMENDMENT X.

Rights reserved to States.

The powers not delegated to the United States by the Constitution, nor prohibited by it to the States, are reserved to the States respectively, or to the people.

Amendments Since the Bill of Rights

AMENDMENT XI.

Judicial powers construed.

[Proposed by Congress Mar. 4, 1794. Ratification complete Feb. 7, 1795, though official announcement of ratification not made until Jan. 8, 1798.]

The Judicial power of the United States shall not be construed to extend to any suit in law or equity, commenced or prosecuted against one of the United States by Citizens of another State, or by Citizens or Subjects of any Foreign State.

AMENDMENT XII.

Election of President and Vice-President.

[Proposed by Congress Dec. 9, 1803; ratified June 15, 1804.]
The Electors shall meet in their respective states and vote by ballot for President and Vice-President, one of whom, at least, shall not be an inhabitant of the same state with themselves; they shall name in their ballots the person voted for as President, and in distinct ballots the person voted for as Vice-President, and they shall make distinct lists of all persons voted for as President, and of all persons voted for as Vice-President, and of the number of votes for each, which lists they shall sign and certify, and transmit sealed to the seat of the government of the United States, directed to the President of the Senate;—The President of the Senate shall, in the presence of the Senate and House of Representatives, open all the certificates and the votes shall then be counted;—The person having the greatest number of votes for President, shall be the President, if such number be a majority of the whole number of Electors appointed; and if no person have such majority, then from the persons having the highest numbers not exceeding three on the list of those voted for as President, the House of Representatives shall choose immediately, by ballot, the President. But in choosing the President, the votes shall be taken by states, the representation from each state having one vote; a quorum for this purpose shall consist of a member or members from two-thirds of the states, and a majority of all the states shall be necessary to a choice. [And if the House of Representatives shall not choose a President whenever the right of choice shall devolve upon them, before the fourth day of March next following, then the Vice-President shall act as President, as in the case of the death or other constitutional disability of the President.] *[The words in brackets were superseded by Amendment XX, section 3.]* The person having the greatest number of votes as Vice-President, shall be the Vice-President, if such number be a majority of the whole number of Electors appointed, and if no person have a majority, then from the two highest numbers on the list, the Senate shall choose the Vice-President; a quorum for the purpose shall consist of two-thirds of the whole number of Senators, and a majority of the whole number shall be necessary to a choice. But no person constitutionally ineligible to the office of President shall be eligible to that of Vice-President of the United States.

THE RECONSTRUCTION AMENDMENTS

[Amendments XIII, XIV, and XV are commonly known as the Reconstruction Amendments inasmuch as they followed the Civil War and were drafted by Republicans who wanted to impose their own policy of reconstruction on the South. Southern postbellum legislatures in states including Mississippi, South Carolina, and Georgia had set up laws that effectively perpetuated slavery under other names.]

AMENDMENT XIII.

Slavery abolished.

[Proposed by Congress Jan. 31, 1865; ratified Dec. 6, 1865.]
Section 1. Neither slavery nor involuntary servitude, except as a punishment for crime whereof the party shall have been duly convicted, shall exist within the United States, or any place subject to their jurisdiction.
Section 2. Congress shall have power to enforce this article by appropriate legislation.

AMENDMENT XIV.

Citizenship rights not to be abridged.

[Proposed by Congress June 13, 1866, ratified July 9, 1868, and declared to have been ratified in a proclamation by the Secretary of State, July 28, 1868.]
Section 1. All persons born or naturalized in the United States, and subject to the jurisdiction thereof, are citizens of the United States and of the State wherein they reside. No State shall make or enforce any law which shall abridge the privileges or immunities of citizens of the United States; nor shall any State deprive any person of life, liberty, or property, without due process of law; nor deny to any person within its jurisdiction the equal protection of the laws.
Section 2. Representatives shall be apportioned among the several States according to their respective numbers, counting the whole number of persons in each State, excluding Indians not taxed. But when the right to vote at any election for the choice of electors for President and Vice-President of the United States, Representatives in Congress, the Executive and Judicial officers of a State, or the members of the Legislature thereof, is denied to any of the male inhabitants of such State, being [twenty-one] *[The words in brackets were changed by Amendment XXVI.]* years of age, and citizens of the United States, or in any way abridged, except for participation in rebellion, or other crime, the basis of representation therein shall be reduced in the proportion which the number of such male citizens shall bear to the whole number of male citizens twenty-one years of age in such State.
Section 3. No person shall be a Senator or Representative in Congress, or elector of President and Vice-President, or hold any office, civil or military, under the United States, or under any State, who, having previously taken an oath, as a member of Congress, or as an officer of the United States, or as a member of any State legislature, or as an executive or judicial officer of any State, to support the Constitution of the United States, shall have engaged in insurrection or rebellion against the same, or given aid or comfort to the enemies thereof. But Congress may by a vote of two-thirds of each House, remove such disability.
Section 4. The validity of the public debt of the United States, authorized by law, including debts incurred for payment of pensions and bounties for services in suppressing insurrection or rebellion, shall not be questioned. But neither the United States nor any State shall assume or pay any debt or obligation incurred in aid of insurrection or rebellion against the United States, or any claim for the loss or emancipation of any slave; but all such debts, obligations and claims shall be held illegal and void.
Section 5. The Congress shall have power to enforce, by appropriate legislation, the provisions of this article.

AMENDMENT XV.

Race no bar to voting rights.

[Proposed by Congress Feb. 26, 1869; ratified Feb. 3, 1870.]
Section 1. The right of citizens of the United States to vote shall not be denied or abridged by the United States or by any State on account of race, color, or previous condition of servitude.
Section 2. The Congress shall have power to enforce this article by appropriate legislation.

AMENDMENT XVI.

Taxes on income.

[Proposed by Congress July 12, 1909; ratified Feb. 3, 1913.]
The Congress shall have power to lay and collect taxes on incomes, from whatever source derived, without apportionment among the several States, and without regard to any census or enumeration.

AMENDMENT XVII.

Popular election of Senators.

[Proposed by Congress May 13, 1912; ratified Apr. 8, 1913.]
The Senate of the United States shall be composed of two Senators from each State, elected by the people thereof, for six years; and each Senator shall have one vote. The electors in each State shall have the qualifications requisite for electors of the most numerous branch of the State legislatures.

When vacancies happen in the representation of any State in the Senate, the executive authority of such State shall issue writs of election to fill such vacancies: Provided, That the legislature of any State may empower the executive thereof to make temporary appointments until the people fill the vacancies by election as the legislature may direct.

This amendment shall not be so construed as to affect the election or term of any Senator chosen before it becomes valid as part of the Constitution.

AMENDMENT XVIII.

Liquor prohibition amendment.

[Proposed by Congress Dec. 18, 1917; ratified Jan. 16, 1919. Repealed by Amendment XXI, effective Dec. 5, 1933.]

Section 1. After one year from the ratification of this article the manufacture, sale, or transportation of intoxicating liquors within, the importation thereof into, or the exportation thereof from the United States and all territory subject to the jurisdiction thereof for beverage purposes is hereby prohibited.

Section 2. The Congress and the several States shall have concurrent power to enforce this article by appropriate legislation.

Section 3. This article shall be inoperative unless it shall have been ratified as an amendment to the Constitution by the legislatures of the several States, as provided in the Constitution, within seven years from the date of the submission hereof to the States by the Congress.

AMENDMENT XIX.

Nationwide suffrage to women.

[Proposed by Congress June 4, 1919; ratified Aug. 18, 1920.]

The right of citizens of the United States to vote shall not be denied or abridged by the United States or by any State on account of sex.

Congress shall have power to enforce this article by appropriate legislation.

AMENDMENT XX.

Commencement of terms of office.

[Proposed by Congress Mar. 2, 1932; ratified Jan. 23, 1933.]

Section 1. The terms of the President and Vice President shall end at noon on the 20th day of January, and the terms of Senators and Representatives at noon on the 3d day of January, of the years in which such terms would have ended if this article had not been ratified; and the terms of their successors shall then begin.

Section 2. The Congress shall assemble at least once in every year, and such meeting shall begin at noon on the 3d day of January, unless they shall by law appoint a different day.

Section 3. If, at the time fixed for the beginning of the term of the President, the President elect shall have died, the Vice President elect shall become President. If a President shall not have been chosen before the time fixed for the beginning of his term, or if the President elect shall have failed to qualify, then the Vice President elect shall act as President until a President shall have qualified; and the Congress may by law provide for the case wherein neither a President elect nor a Vice President elect shall have qualified, declaring who shall then act as President, or the manner in which one who is to act shall be selected, and such person shall act accordingly until a President or Vice President shall have qualified.

Section 4. The Congress may by law provide for the case of the death of any of the persons from whom the House of Representatives may choose a President whenever the right of choice shall have devolved upon them, and for the case of the death of any of the persons from whom the Senate may choose a Vice President whenever the right of choice shall have devolved upon them.

Section 5. Sections 1 and 2 shall take effect on the 15th day of October following the ratification of this article.

Section 6. This article shall be inoperative unless it shall have been ratified as an amendment to the Constitution by the legislatures of three-fourths of the several States within seven years from the date of its submission.

AMENDMENT XXI.

Repeal of Amendment XVIII.

[Proposed by Congress Feb. 20, 1933; ratified Dec. 5, 1933.]

Section 1. The eighteenth article of amendment to the Constitution of the United States is hereby repealed.

Section 2. The transportation or importation into any State, Territory, or possession of the United States for delivery or use therein of intoxicating liquors, in violation of the laws thereof, is hereby prohibited.

Section 3. This article shall be inoperative unless it shall have been ratified as an amendment to the Constitution by conventions in the several States, as provided in the Constitution, within seven years from the date of the submission hereof to the States by the Congress.

AMENDMENT XXII.

Limit on presidential terms of office.

[Proposed by Congress Mar. 24, 1947; ratified Feb. 27, 1951.]

Section 1. No person shall be elected to the office of the President more than twice, and no person who has held the office of President, or acted as President, for more than two years of a term to which some other person was elected President shall be elected to the office of the President more than once. But this Article shall not apply to any person holding the office of President when this Article was proposed by Congress, and shall not prevent any person who may be holding the office of President, or acting as President, during the term within which this Article becomes operative from holding the office of President or acting as President during the remainder of such term.

Section 2. This Article shall be inoperative unless it shall have been ratified as an amendment to the Constitution by the legislatures of three-fourths of the several States within seven years from the date of its submission to the States by the Congress.

AMENDMENT XXIII.

Presidential vote for District of Columbia.

[Proposed by Congress June 16, 1960; ratified Mar. 29, 1961.]

Section 1. The District constituting the seat of Government of the United States shall appoint in such manner as the Congress may direct:

A number of electors of President and Vice President equal to the whole number of Senators and Representatives in Congress to which the District would be entitled if it were a State, but in no event more than the least populous State; they shall be in addition to those appointed by the States, but they shall be considered, for the purposes of the election of President and Vice President, to be electors appointed by a State; and they shall meet in the District and perform such duties as provided by the twelfth article of amendment.

Section 2. The Congress shall have power to enforce this article by appropriate legislation.

AMENDMENT XXIV.

Poll tax barred in federal elections.

[Proposed by Congress Sept. 14, 1962; ratified Jan. 23, 1964.]

Section 1. The right of citizens of the United States to vote in any primary or other election for President or Vice President, for electors for President or Vice President, or for Senator or Representative in Congress, shall not be denied or abridged by the United States or any State by reason of failure to pay any poll tax or other tax.

Section 2. The Congress shall have power to enforce this article by appropriate legislation.

AMENDMENT XXV.

Presidential vacancy, inability, and succession.

[Proposed by Congress July 6, 1965; ratified Feb. 10, 1967.]
Section 1. In case of the removal of the President from office or of his death or resignation, the Vice President shall become President.

Section 2. Whenever there is a vacancy in the office of the Vice President, the President shall nominate a Vice President who shall take office upon confirmation by a majority vote of both Houses of Congress.

Section 3. Whenever the President transmits to the President pro tempore of the Senate and the Speaker of the House of Representatives his written declaration that he is unable to discharge the powers and duties of his office, and until he transmits to them a written declaration to the contrary, such powers and duties shall be discharged by the Vice President as Acting President.

Section 4. Whenever the Vice President and a majority of either the principal officers of the executive departments or of such other body as Congress may by law provide, transmit to the President pro tempore of the Senate and the Speaker of the House of Representatives their written declaration that the President is unable to discharge the powers and duties of his office, the Vice President shall immediately assume the powers and duties of the office as Acting President.

Thereafter, when the President transmits to the President pro tempore of the Senate and the Speaker of the House of Representatives his written declaration that no inability exists, he shall resume the powers and duties of his office unless the Vice President and a majority of either the principal officers of the executive department or of such other body as Congress may by law provide, transmit within four days to the President pro tempore of the Senate and the Speaker of the House of Representatives their written declaration that the President is unable to discharge the powers and duties of his office. Thereupon Congress shall decide the issue, assembling within forty-eight hours for that purpose if not in session. If the Congress, within twenty-one days after receipt of the latter written declaration, or, if Congress is not in session, within twenty-one days after Congress is required to assemble, determines by two-thirds vote of both Houses that the President is unable to discharge the powers and duties of his office, the Vice President shall continue to discharge the same as Acting President; otherwise, the President shall resume the powers and duties of his office.

AMENDMENT XXVI.

Voting age lowered to 18 years.

[Proposed by Congress Mar. 23, 1971; ratified July 1, 1971.]
Section 1. The right of citizens of the United States, who are eighteen years of age or older, to vote shall not be denied or abridged by the United States or by any State on account of age.

Section 2. The Congress shall have power to enforce this article by appropriate legislation.

AMENDMENT XXVII.

Congressional pay.

[Proposed by Congress Sept. 25, 1789; ratified May 7, 1992.]
No law, varying the compensation for the services of the Senators and Representatives, shall take effect, until an election of Representatives shall have intervened.

How a Bill Becomes a Law

A senator or representative introduces a bill in Congress by sending it to the clerk of the Senate or the House, who assigns it a number and title. This procedure is termed the first reading. The clerk then refers the bill to the appropriate committee of the Senate or House.

If the committee does not wish to consider the bill, it will table it. Otherwise, the committee holds hearings to gather information, such as by inviting experts and other members of the public to testify. The committee then debates the bill and may offer amendments. A vote is taken, and if favorable, the bill is sent back to the clerk of the Senate or House.

The clerk reads the bill to the house—the second reading. Members may then debate the bill and suggest amendments.

After debate and any amendments, the bill is given a third reading, simply of the title, and put to a voice or roll-call vote.

It should be noted that the Senate has additional rules that can further complicate the process of making laws. Most significantly, the Senate tradition of unlimited debate has allowed for the use of the filibuster, a tactic to prolong debate and thus delay or prevent a vote on measures, even as they may actually have majority support. In an early effort to limit the use of filibusters, the Senate in 1917 provided for "cloture," or a vote to end debate. Originally cloture required a two-thirds supermajority to succeed; in 1975 the Senate reduced the required supermajority to three-fifths of all senators duly chosen and sworn. If the bill passes, it goes to the other house, where it may be defeated or passed, with or without amendments. If defeated, the bill dies. If passed with amendments, a conference committee made up of members of both houses works out the differences between the two bills and arrives at a compromise.

After passage of the final version by both houses, the bill is sent to the president. If the president signs it, the bill becomes a law. The president may instead veto the bill by refusing to sign it and sending it back to the house where it originated, with reasons for the veto.

The president's objections are then read and debated, and a roll-call vote is taken. If the bill receives less than a two-thirds majority, it is defeated. If it receives at least two-thirds, it is sent to the other house. If that house also passes it by at least a two-thirds majority, the president's veto is overridden, and the bill becomes a law.

If the president neither signs nor vetoes the bill within 10 days—not including Sundays—it automatically becomes a law even without the president's signature. However, if Congress adjourns within those 10 days, the bill is automatically killed; this indirect rejection is termed a pocket veto.

Under the Line Item Veto Act, effective Jan. 1, 1997, the president was authorized, under certain circumstances, to veto a bill in part. The legislation was found unconstitutional by the Supreme Court, June 25, 1998.

Presidential Oath of Office

The Constitution (Article II, Section 1) directs that the president-elect shall take the following oath to be inaugurated: "I do solemnly swear [affirm] that I will faithfully execute the office of President of the United States, and will, to the best of my ability, preserve, protect, and defend the Constitution of the United States."

Custom decrees the addition of the words "So help me God" at the end of the oath when taken by the president-elect, with the left hand on the Bible for the duration of the oath, and the right hand slightly raised. However, the use of a Bible, or any other religious book, is not required.

Presidential Succession

If, by reason of death, resignation, removal from office, inability, or failure to qualify, there is neither a president nor vice president to discharge the powers and duties of the office of president, then the speaker of the House of Representatives shall, upon his resignation as speaker and as representative, act as president. The same rule shall apply in the case of the death, resignation, removal from office, or inability of an individual acting as president.

If, at the time when a speaker is to begin the discharge of the powers and duties of the office of president, there is no speaker, or the speaker fails to qualify as acting president, then the president pro tempore of the Senate, upon his resignation as president pro tempore and as senator, shall act as president.

An individual acting as president shall continue to act until the expiration of the then current presidential term, except that (1) if his discharge of the powers and duties of the office is founded in whole or in part in the failure of both the president-elect and the vice president-elect to qualify, then he shall act only until a president or vice president qualifies, and (2) if his discharge of the powers and duties of the office is founded in whole or in part on the inability of the president or vice president, then he shall act only until the removal of the disability of one of such individuals.

If, by reason of death, resignation, removal from office, or failure to qualify, there is no president pro tempore to act as president, then the officer of the United States who is highest on the following list, and who is not under any disability to discharge the powers and duties of president shall act as president: the secretaries of state, treasury, and defense; the attorney general; the secretaries of interior, agriculture, commerce, labor, health and human services, housing and urban development, transportation, energy, education, veterans affairs, and homeland security.

Legislation approved July 18, 1947; amended Sept. 9, 1965, Oct. 15, 1966, Aug. 4, 1977, Sept. 27, 1979, and Mar. 9, 2006. See also Constitutional Amendment XXV.

Confederate States: Secession and Government

The American Civil War (1861-65) grew out of sectional disputes over the continued existence of slavery in the South. Southern legislators contended that the states retained the right to enslave Black people and the right to secede.

The war was not fought by state against state but by one federal regime against another. A Confederate government in Richmond, VA, assumed control over the economic, political, and military life of the seceding states, under protest from Georgia and South Carolina.

South Carolina voted unanimously in convention to secede from the Union, repealing its 1788 ratification of the U.S. Constitution on Dec. 20, 1860, to take effect on Dec. 24. Other states seceded in 1861. Their votes in conventions were Mississippi, Jan. 9, 84-15; Florida, Jan. 10, 62-7; Alabama, Jan. 11, 61-39; Georgia, Jan. 19, 208-89; Louisiana, Jan. 26, 113-17; Texas, Feb. 1, 166-7, ratified by popular vote (34,794 to 11,325) Feb. 23; Virginia, Apr. 17, 88-55, ratified by popular vote (128,884 to 32,134) May 23; Arkansas, May 6, 69-1; Tennessee, May 7, ratified by popular vote (104,019 to 47,238) June 8; and North Carolina, unanimous, May 20.

Missouri Unionists stopped secession in conventions Feb. 28 and Mar. 9, 1861. Under the protection of Confederate troops, secessionist members of the legislature adopted a resolution of secession at Neosho, Oct. 31. The Confederate Congress seated the secessionists' representatives.

Kentucky did not secede, and its government remained Unionist. In a part of the state occupied by Confederate troops, Kentuckians approved secession, and the Confederate Congress admitted their representatives.

The Maryland legislature voted against secession Apr. 27, 1861, 53-13. Delaware did not secede. Pro-Union residents of western Virginia held conventions at Wheeling and, on June 17, 1861, formed the Restored Government of Virginia. It was admitted to the Union as West Virginia on June 20, 1863. Its constitution provided for gradual abolition of slavery.

Forty-two delegates from South Carolina, Georgia, Alabama, Mississippi, Louisiana, and Florida met in convention in Montgomery, AL, on Feb. 4, 1861. They adopted a provisional constitution of the Confederate States of America and elected Jefferson Davis (MS) as provisional president and Alexander H. Stephens (GA) as provisional vice president.

A permanent constitution was adopted Mar. 11. It banned the African slave trade but did not bar interstate commerce in slaves. On July 20 the Congress moved to Richmond. Davis was elected president in Nov. 1861 and was inaugurated Feb. 22, 1862.

The Confederate Congress adopted a flag ("The Stars and Bars") consisting of one white stripe and two red stripes and a blue canton with a circle of white stars. The Confederate battle flag, carried by the Army of Northern Virginia, was more popularly known. It has blue diagonal crossbars with 13 white stars, for the 11 states in the Confederacy plus Kentucky and Missouri, against a red field.

The Gettysburg Address

Delivered by Pres. Abraham Lincoln at the dedication of the Soldiers' National Cemetery in Gettysburg, PA, on Nov. 19, 1863. Five handwritten copies of the Gettysburg Address as made by Lincoln are known to exist. The text differs slightly between copies. The Bliss copy, made for Alexander Bliss, is shown here. The copy is kept on display in the White House.

Four score and seven years ago our fathers brought forth on this continent, a new nation, conceived in Liberty, and dedicated to the proposition that all men are created equal.

Now we are engaged in a great civil war, testing whether that nation, or any nation so conceived and so dedicated, can long endure. We are met on a great battle-field of that war. We have come to dedicate a portion of that field, as a final resting place for those who here gave their lives that that nation might live. It is altogether fitting and proper that we should do this.

But, in a larger sense, we can not dedicate—we can not consecrate—we can not hallow—this ground. The brave men, living and dead, who struggled here, have consecrated it, far above our poor power to add or detract. The world will little note, nor long remember what we say here, but it can never forget what they did here.

It is for us the living, rather, to be dedicated here to the unfinished work which they who fought here have thus far so nobly advanced. It is rather for us to be here dedicated to the great task remaining before us—that from these honored dead we take increased devotion to that cause for which they gave the last full measure of devotion—that we here highly resolve that these dead shall not have died in vain—that this nation, under God, shall have a new birth of freedom—and that government of the people, by the people, for the people, shall not perish from the earth.

Origin of the United States National Motto

In God We Trust, designated as the U.S. National Motto by Congress in 1956, originated during the Civil War as an inscription for U.S. coins. On Nov. 13, 1861, the Rev. M. R. Watkinson, of Ridleyville, PA, wrote to Treasury Sec. Salmon P. Chase requesting "recognition of the Almighty God in some form on our coins." Chase ordered designs prepared with the inscription In God We Trust and backed coinage legislation that authorized use of this slogan. The motto first appeared on some U.S. coins in 1864 and sporadically thereafter until 1938, after which all U.S. coins bear the inscription. A joint resolution passed by the 84th Congress and signed by Pres. Dwight D. Eisenhower July 30, 1956, declared In God We Trust the national motto of the United States.

Great Seal of the U.S.

On July 4, 1776, the Continental Congress appointed a committee consisting of Benjamin Franklin, John Adams, and Thomas Jefferson "to bring in a device for a seal of the United States of America." The designs submitted by this and a subsequent committee were considered unacceptable. After many delays, a third committee, appointed early in 1782, presented a design prepared by lawyer William Barton. Charles Thomson, the secretary of Congress, suggested certain changes, and Congress finally approved the design on June 20, 1782. The obverse of the seal shows a bald eagle. In the eagle's mouth is a ribbon bearing the motto *E Pluribus Unum* (out of many, one). In the eagle's talons are 13 arrows of war and an olive branch of peace. The reverse shows an unfinished pyramid with an eye (Eye of Providence) above it.

The Flag of the U.S.—The Stars and Stripes

The 50-star flag of the United States was raised for the first time officially at 12:01 AM on July 4, 1960, at Ft. McHenry National Monument in Baltimore, MD. The 50th star had been added for Hawaii; just a year earlier, the 49th star was added for Alaska.

There are so many myths and legends surrounding the history of the Stars and Stripes that the facts are difficult, and in some cases impossible, to establish. For example, it is not certain who designed the Stars and Stripes, who made the first such flag, or even whether it ever flew during any battle of the American Revolution.

Historians agree, however, that the Stars and Stripes originated as the result of a resolution offered by the Marine Committee of the Second Continental Congress at Philadelphia and adopted on June 14, 1777. It read:

"Resolved: that the flag of the United States be thirteen stripes, alternate red and white; that the union be thirteen stars, white in a blue field, representing a new constellation."

Congress gave no hint as to the designer of the flag, no instructions as to the arrangement of the stars, and no information on its appropriate uses.

The resolution establishing the flag was not published until Sept. 2, 1777. Despite repeated requests, George Washington did not get the flags until 1783, after the war was over. And there is no certainty that they were the Stars and Stripes.

Early Flags

Many historians consider the first flag of the U.S. to have been the Grand Union (sometimes called Great Union) flag, although the Continental Congress never officially adopted it. This flag was a modification of the British Meteor flag, which had the red cross of St. George and the white cross of St. Andrew combined in the blue canton. For the Grand Union flag, six horizontal stripes were imposed on the red field, dividing it into 13 alternating red and white stripes. On Jan. 1, 1776, when the Continental Army came into formal existence, this flag was unfurled on Prospect Hill, Somerville, MA. Washington wrote that "we hoisted the Union Flag in compliment to the United Colonies."

One of several flags about which controversy has raged is in Easton, PA. Containing the devices of the national flag in reversed order, this flag has been in the public library in Easton for more than 150 years. Some contend that this flag was actually the first Stars and Stripes, first displayed on July 8, 1776. This flag has 13 red and white stripes in the canton and 13 white stars centered in a blue field.

A flag was hastily improvised from garments by the defenders of Ft. Schuyler at Rome, NY, Aug. 3-22, 1777. Historians believe it was the Grand Union Flag.

The Sons of Liberty had a flag of nine red and white stripes, to signify nine colonies, when they met in New York in 1765 to oppose the Stamp Tax. By 1775, the flag had grown to 13 red and white stripes, with a rattlesnake on it.

At Concord, MA, Apr. 19, 1775, the minutemen from Bedford, MA, are said to have carried a flag having a silver arm with sword on a red field. At Cambridge, MA, the Sons of Liberty used a plain red flag with a green pine tree on it.

In June 1775, Washington went from Philadelphia to Boston to take command of the army. He was escorted to New York by the Philadelphia Light Horse Troop, which carried a yellow flag that had an elaborate coat of arms—the shield charged with 13 knots, the motto "For These We Strive"—and a canton of 13 blue and silver stripes.

In Feb. 1776, Col. Christopher Gadsden, a member of the Continental Congress, gave the South Carolina Provincial Congress a flag "such as is to be used by the commander-in-chief of the American Navy." It had a yellow field, with a rattlesnake about to strike and the words "Don't Tread on Me."

At the Battle of Bennington, Aug. 16, 1777, patriots used a flag of seven white and six red stripes with a blue canton extending down nine stripes. Eleven white stars arch over the figure 76 in the canton; a star appears in each of the canton's upper corners. The stars are seven-pointed. This flag is preserved in a museum in Bennington, VT.

At the Battle of Cowpens, Jan. 17, 1781, the 3rd Maryland Regiment is said to have carried a flag of 13 red and white stripes, with a blue canton containing 12 stars in a circle around one star.

Who Designed the Flag? No one knows for certain. Francis Hopkinson, designer of a naval flag, declared he had designed the flag and in 1781 asked Congress to reimburse him for his services. Congress did not do so.

Who Called the Flag "Old Glory"? The flag is said to have been named Old Glory by William Driver, a sea captain of Salem, MA. One legend has it that he did so when he raised the flag on his brig in 1824. But his daughter said he named it at his 21st birthday celebration on Mar. 17, 1824, when his mother presented the homemade flag to him.

The Betsy Ross Legend. The widely publicized legend that Betsy Ross made the first Stars and Stripes in June 1776, at the request of a committee composed of George Washington, Robert Morris, and George Ross, an uncle, was first made public in 1870, by a grandson of Ross. Historians have been unable to find a historical record of such a meeting or committee.

Adding New Stars

On the admission of Vermont and Kentucky to the Union, Congress designated that after May 1, 1795, the flag should have 15 stripes, alternating red and white, and 15 white stars on a blue field.

When more new states were admitted, it became evident that the flag would become burdened with stripes. Congress ordered that after July 4, 1818, the flag should have 13 stripes, symbolizing 13 original states; that the union have 20 stars; and that whenever a new state was admitted a new star should be added on the July 4 following admission.

No law designates the permanent arrangement of the stars. However, since 1912, when a new state has been admitted, the new design has been announced by executive order. No star is specifically identified with any state.

Pledge of Allegiance to the Flag

I pledge allegiance to the flag of the United States of America, and to the republic for which it stands, one nation under God, indivisible, with liberty and justice for all.

This, the current official version of the Pledge of Allegiance, developed from a pledge first published in the Sept. 8, 1892, issue of *Youth's Companion*, a weekly magazine. The original pledge contained the phrase "my flag," which was changed more than 30 years later to "flag of the United States of America." A 1954 act of Congress added the words "under God." (In 2002, the 9th Circuit U.S. Court of Appeals ruled that recitation of the pledge in public schools could not include that phrase. In 2004, however, the U.S. Supreme Court voted to decline to decide the case on a technicality. The lower court's decision was thus overturned.)

The authorship of the pledge was in dispute for many years. *Youth's Companion* stated in 1917 that the original draft was written by James B. Upham, an executive of the magazine who died in 1910. A leaflet circulated by the magazine later named Upham as the originator of the first draft.

Francis Bellamy, a former member of the *Youth's Companion* editorial staff, publicly claimed authorship of the pledge in 1923. In 1939, the United States Flag Association, acting on the advice of a committee named to study the controversy, upheld the claim by Bellamy, who had died eight years earlier. In 1957 the Library of Congress issued a report attributing the authorship to Bellamy.

According to the federal Flag Code, the pledge should be given while standing at attention facing the flag with the right hand over the heart. Those not in military uniform should remove any non-religious head coverings with their right hand and hold it at the left shoulder, the hand being over the heart. Those in uniform should remain silent, face the flag, and render a military salute. Members and veterans of the Armed Forces not in uniform may also render the military salute in the manner provided for persons in uniform.

History of the U.S. National Anthem

"The Star-Spangled Banner" was formally designated the national anthem by Act of Congress, Mar. 3, 1931. The words were written by Francis Scott Key, of Georgetown, in DC, marking the bombardment of Ft. McHenry in Baltimore, MD, Sept. 13-14, 1814. Key was a lawyer, a graduate of St. John's College in Annapolis, MD, and a volunteer in a light artillery company. When a friend, Dr. William Beanes, a Maryland physician, was arrested by the British for interfering with British deserters and straggling ground troops, Key and U.S. Col. John Skinner, with permission from Pres. Madison, went to the fleet under a flag of truce to ask for Beanes's release. The British consented, but as the fleet was about to sail up the Patapsco River to bombard Ft. McHenry, Key was detained for the duration of the battle.

The bombardment of Ft. McHenry began at 7 AM, Sept. 13, and lasted 25 hours. The British fired more than 1,500 shells. They were unable to approach closely because the U.S. had sunk 22 vessels to form a barrier. Only four Americans were killed and 24 wounded. A British bomb ship was disabled.

The morning after the shelling, Sept. 14, inspired by the flag still flying above the garrison, Key began to draft the poem. Released from British custody in Baltimore Sept. 16, Key revised the poem and gave it to his brother-in-law, Joseph Nicholson, who encouraged its printing on handbills. The first versions were titled "The Defence of Fort McHenry" and included a note suggesting use of the tune "Anacreon in Heaven" (attributed to British composer John Stafford Smith). The poem appeared in several newspapers within days and spread quickly.

The garrison flag that Key saw the morning after the bombardment is preserved at the Smithsonian Institution's National Museum of American History in Washington, DC. Major George Armistead, the commander of the militia unit stationed at Fort McHenry, had ordered a flag "so large that the British will have no difficulty seeing it from a distance." A government contract paid Baltimore flagmaker Mary Pickersgill $405.90 in 1813 for the garrison flag and $168.54 for a smaller storm flag (which was flown during the battle itself). The garrison flag originally measured 30 by 42 ft and had 15 alternating red and white stripes and 15 stars, for the original 13 states plus Kentucky and Vermont. The preserved flag measures 30 by 34 ft and is missing one star. Before the flag was placed in a museum, the family holding the flag would give clippings of it away as souvenirs.

The Star-Spangled Banner

I

Oh, say can you see by the dawn's early light
What so proudly we hailed at the twilight's last gleaming?
Whose broad stripes and bright stars through the perilous fight,
O'er the ramparts we watched were so gallantly streaming?
And the rockets' red glare, the bombs bursting in air,
Gave proof through the night that our flag was still there.
Oh, say does that star-spangled banner yet wave
O'er the land of the free and the home of the brave?

II

On the shore, dimly seen through the mists of the deep,
Where the foe's haughty host in dread silence reposes,
What is that which the breeze, o'er the towering steep,
As it fitfully blows, half conceals, half discloses?
Now it catches the gleam of the morning's first beam,
In full glory reflected now shines in the stream:
'Tis the star-spangled banner! Oh long may it wave
O'er the land of the free and the home of the brave!

III

And where is that band who so vauntingly swore
That the havoc of war and the battle's confusion,
A home and a country should leave us no more!
Their blood has washed out their foul footsteps' pollution.
No refuge could save the hireling and slave
From the terror of flight, or the gloom of the grave:
And the star-spangled banner in triumph doth wave
O'er the land of the free and the home of the brave!

IV

Oh! thus be it ever, when freemen shall stand
Between their loved home and the war's desolation!
Blest with victory and peace, may the heav'n rescued land
Praise the Power that hath made and preserved us a nation.
Then conquer we must, when our cause it is just,
And this be our motto: "In God is our trust."
And the star-spangled banner in triumph shall wave
O'er the land of the free and the home of the brave!

Statue of Liberty National Monument

Since 1886, the Statue of Liberty, formally known as "Liberty Enlightening the World," has stood as a symbol of freedom in New York Harbor. A gift from the people of France to the people of the U.S., it initially was conceived by legal philosopher Édouard de Laboulaye and intended to celebrate the U.S. centennial and commemorate the abolition of slavery. It was designed by French sculptor Frédéric Auguste Bartholdi (1834-1904).

On Feb. 22, 1877, Congress approved the use of a site on Bedloe's Island suggested by Bartholdi. This island of 12 acres had been owned in the 17th cent. by a colonist named Isaac Bedloe. (On Aug. 3, 1956, Pres. Dwight Eisenhower approved a measure changing the name to Liberty Island.)

The statue was finished on May 21, 1884, and presented to the U.S. minister to France, Levi Parsons Morton, July 4, 1884, by French diplomat Ferdinand de Lesseps.

On Aug. 5, 1884, the cornerstone for the granite pedestal—designed by architect Richard Morris Hunt—was laid on the foundations of Fort Wood, erected by the government in 1811. The American Committee for the Statue of Liberty had raised an inadequate $125,000, and *New York World* newspaper owner Joseph Pulitzer appealed Mar. 16, 1885, for general donations. By Aug. 11, 1885, he had raised $100,000. The statue itself arrived dismantled, in 214 packing cases, from Rouen, France, in June 1885. The last rivet of the statue was driven on Oct. 28, 1886, when Pres. Grover Cleveland dedicated the monument.

The Statue of Liberty National Monument was designated as such in 1924. It is administered by the National Park Service. A $2.5-mil building housing the American Museum of Immigration was opened by Pres. Richard Nixon on Sept. 26, 1972, at the base of the statue. It houses a permanent exhibition tracing the history of American immigration.

Four years of restoration work funded and led by the Statue of Liberty-Ellis Island Foundation were completed before the statue's 1986 centennial. The $87-mil project included the replacement of the 1,600 wrought iron bands that hold the statue's copper skin to its frame, replacement of the torch, and installation of an elevator. A four-day extravaganza of concerts, tall ships, cultural and heritage festivals, and fireworks, July 3-6, 1986, celebrated the 100th anniversary. U.S. Supreme Court Chief Justice Warren E. Burger swore in 5,000 new citizens on Ellis Island, while 20,000 others across the country were sworn in through a satellite telecast. Other ceremonies followed on Oct. 28, 1986, the statue's exact 100th birthday.

After the Sept. 11, 2001, terrorist attacks, Liberty Island was closed to visitors. The secretary of the interior reopened the island in Dec. 2001 after installing security screening facilities at passenger embarkation areas at Battery Park in Manhattan and Liberty State Park in New Jersey.

The federal government increased security throughout the park before reopening the statue. In addition to federally funded security upgrades, significant building safety improvements were made. Public access to the statue pedestal was restored in Aug. 2004, and the crown reopened July 4, 2009.

Following the 125th anniversary celebration Oct. 28, 2011, the statue was closed. A $30-mil renovation brought it up to contemporary safety standards and allowed for increased visitor access. Although the statue interior reopened Oct. 28, 2012, damages caused by Hurricane Sandy forced all of Liberty Island to close again within days. The island and the statue officially reopened to visitors July 4, 2013. A new, 26,000-sq-ft Statue of Liberty Museum opened in May 2019.

Ferry service to Liberty Island and to Ellis Island, from Battery Park in New York City and from Liberty State Park in New Jersey was suspended Mar. 16, 2020, in response to the COVID-19 outbreak, but resumed in July 2021, available only by specific time of departure.

Liberty Island can be reached by ferry only. As of mid-2023 there was public access to the Statue of Liberty Museum and theater, as well as (with reservations) to the statue pedestal and the crown. (Visitors should note that the crown can only be reached by climbing a long, confining spiral staircase.) Tickets may sell out well beforehand. Reservations are available months in advance and can be made at www.statuecruises.com or by calling 1-877-LADY-TIX. Before visiting, check www.nps.gov/stli for latest information on openings and fees and on guidelines, including age and height restrictions. Park rangers conduct English-language tours throughout the day. Standard self-guided audio tours and a family-friendly audio tour (aimed at children ages 6-10) are available in a number of languages.

Statue Statistics

The statue weighs 450,000 lbs, or 225 tons. The copper sheeting weighs 200,000 lbs. There are 377 steps from the main lobby to the crown platform. There are 146 steps from the top of the pedestal (the statue's feet) to the crown platform.

	Measurement	
Statue feature	Ft	In.
Height from base to torch tip	151	1
Foundation of pedestal to torch tip	305	1
Heel to top of head	111	1
Hand, length	16	5
Index finger, length	8	0
Fingernail size		13x10
Head from chin to cranium	17	3
Head thickness, ear to ear	10	0
Nose, length	4	6
Right arm, length	42	0
Right arm, max. thickness	12	0
Waist, thickness	35	0
Mouth, width	3	0
Tablet, length	23	7
Tablet, width	13	7

Ellis Island

Ellis Island was the gateway to America for over 12 mil immigrants between 1892 and 1924. In the late 18th cent., Samuel Ellis, a New York City merchant, purchased the island. From Ellis, it passed to New York state before the U.S. government bought it in 1808. On Jan. 1, 1892, the government opened the first federal immigration center in the U.S. there. The 27.5-acre site eventually supported over 35 buildings, including the Main Building with its Great Hall, designed to process 5,000 people a day. In Ellis Island's peak year, 1907, it received 1,004,756 immigrants; on its peak day (Apr. 17, 1907), 11,747 immigrants were processed.

Closed as an immigration station in 1954, Ellis Island was proclaimed part of the Statue of Liberty National Monument in 1965 by Pres. Lyndon B. Johnson. After a six-year, $170-mil restoration project funded by the Statue of Liberty-Ellis Island Foundation, Ellis Island was reopened as a museum in 1990, now called the Ellis Island National Museum of Immigration. Artifacts, historic photographs and documents, oral histories, and ethnic music depicting 400 years of American immigration are housed in the museum.

In 1998, the U.S. Supreme Court ruled that nearly 90% of the island (the 24.2 acres that are landfill) lies in New Jersey, while the original 3.3 acres, on which the museum is located, are in New York. (The decision settled the issue of jurisdiction over potential development.)

The American Family Immigration History Center opened in Apr. 2001. Visitors can access arrival records on over 51 mil individuals who entered through the Port of New York and Ellis Island from 1892 to 1957. The searchable digitized archives include ships' images and manifests and passenger information such as age, ethnicity, and port of departure. **Website:** www.libertyellisfoundation.org

Damage caused by storm surges from Hurricane Sandy in late Oct. 2012 forced Ellis Island to close for repairs. It reopened Oct. 28, 2013, and new galleries focusing on post-Ellis Island-era immigration opened May 20, 2015.

Ellis Island was closed Mar. 16, 2020, in response to the COVID-19 outbreak, but reopened in summer 2020, with limited capacity. Access is available by ferry only. For latest information see www.nps.gov/elis

PRESIDENTS OF THE UNITED STATES

U.S. Presidents

	Name	Politics	Born	Birthplace	Inaug.	Age at inaug.	Died	Age at death
1.	George Washington	Fed.	1732, Feb. 22	VA	1789	57	1799, Dec. 14	67
2.	John Adams	Fed.	1735, Oct. 30	MA	1797	61	1826, July 4	90
3.	Thomas Jefferson	Dem.-Rep.	1743, Apr. 13	VA	1801	57	1826, July 4	83
4.	James Madison	Dem.-Rep.	1751, Mar. 16	VA	1809	57	1836, June 28	85
5.	James Monroe	Dem.-Rep.	1758, Apr. 28	VA	1817	58	1831, July 4	73
6.	John Quincy Adams	Dem.-Rep.	1767, July 11	MA	1825	57	1848, Feb. 23	80
7.	Andrew Jackson	Dem.	1767, Mar. 15	SC	1829	61	1845, June 8	78
8.	Martin Van Buren	Dem.	1782, Dec. 5	NY	1837	54	1862, July 24	79
9.	William Henry Harrison	Whig	1773, Feb. 9	VA	1841	68	1841, Apr. 4	68
10.	John Tyler	Whig	1790, Mar. 29	VA	1841	51	1862, Jan. 18	71
11.	James Knox Polk	Dem.	1795, Nov. 2	NC	1845	49	1849, June 15	53
12.	Zachary Taylor	Whig	1784, Nov. 24	VA	1849	64	1850, July 9	65
13.	Millard Fillmore	Whig	1800, Jan. 7	NY	1850	50	1874, Mar. 8	74
14.	Franklin Pierce	Dem.	1804, Nov. 23	NH	1853	48	1869, Oct. 8	64
15.	James Buchanan	Dem.	1791, Apr. 23	PA	1857	65	1868, June 1	77
16.	Abraham Lincoln	Rep.	1809, Feb. 12	KY	1861	52	1865, Apr. 15	56
17.	Andrew Johnson	Dem.[1]	1808, Dec. 29	NC	1865	56	1875, July 31	66
18.	Ulysses S. Grant	Rep.	1822, Apr. 27	OH	1869	46	1885, July 23	63
19.	Rutherford Birchard Hayes	Rep.	1822, Oct. 4	OH	1877	54	1893, Jan. 17	70
20.	James Abram Garfield	Rep.	1831, Nov. 19	OH	1881	49	1881, Sept. 19	49
21.	Chester Alan Arthur	Rep.	1829, Oct. 5	VT	1881	51	1886, Nov. 18	57
22.	(Stephen) Grover Cleveland	Dem.	1837, Mar. 18	NJ	1885	47	1908, June 24	71
23.	Benjamin Harrison	Rep.	1833, Aug. 20	OH	1889	55	1901, Mar. 13	67
24.	(Stephen) Grover Cleveland	Dem.	1837, Mar. 18	NJ	1893	55	1908, June 24	71
25.	William McKinley	Rep.	1843, Jan. 29	OH	1897	54	1901, Sept. 14	58
26.	Theodore Roosevelt	Rep.	1858, Oct. 27	NY	1901	42	1919, Jan. 6	60
27.	William Howard Taft	Rep.	1857, Sept. 15	OH	1909	51	1930, Mar. 8	72
28.	(Thomas) Woodrow Wilson	Dem.	1856, Dec. 28	VA	1913	56	1924, Feb. 3	67
29.	Warren Gamaliel Harding	Rep.	1865, Nov. 2	OH	1921	55	1923, Aug. 2	57
30.	(John) Calvin Coolidge	Rep.	1872, July 4	VT	1923	51	1933, Jan. 5	60
31.	Herbert Clark Hoover	Rep.	1874, Aug. 10	IA	1929	54	1964, Oct. 20	90
32.	Franklin Delano Roosevelt	Dem.	1882, Jan. 30	NY	1933	51	1945, Apr. 12	63
33.	Harry S. Truman	Dem.	1884, May 8	MO	1945	60	1972, Dec. 26	88
34.	Dwight David Eisenhower	Rep.	1890, Oct. 14	TX	1953	62	1969, Mar. 28	78
35.	John Fitzgerald Kennedy	Dem.	1917, May 29	MA	1961	43	1963, Nov. 22	46
36.	Lyndon Baines Johnson	Dem.	1908, Aug. 27	TX	1963	55	1973, Jan. 22	64
37.	Richard Milhous Nixon	Rep.	1913, Jan. 9	CA	1969	56	1994, Apr. 22	81
38.	Gerald Rudolph Ford	Rep.	1913, July 14	NE	1974	61	2006, Dec. 26	93
39.	James Earl (Jimmy) Carter	Dem.	1924, Oct. 1	GA	1977	52		
40.	Ronald Wilson Reagan	Rep.	1911, Feb. 6	IL	1981	69	2004, June 5	93
41.	George Herbert Walker Bush	Rep.	1924, June 12	MA	1989	64	2018, Nov. 30	94
42.	Wm. Jefferson (Bill) Clinton	Dem.	1946, Aug. 19	AR	1993	46		
43.	George Walker Bush	Rep.	1946, July 6	CT	2001	54		
44.	Barack Hussein Obama	Dem.	1961, Aug. 4	HI	2009	47		
45.	Donald John Trump	Rep.	1946, June 14	NY	2017	70		
46.	Joseph Robinette Biden Jr.	Dem.	1942, Nov. 20	PA	2021	78		

(1) Johnson, a Democrat, was nominated vice president by Republicans and elected with Lincoln on National Union ticket.

U.S. Presidents, Vice Presidents, Congresses

President	Service	Vice President	Congresses
1. George Washington	Apr. 30, 1789-Mar. 3, 1797	1. John Adams	1, 2, 3, 4
2. John Adams	Mar. 4, 1797-Mar. 3, 1801	2. Thomas Jefferson	5, 6
3. Thomas Jefferson	Mar. 4, 1801-Mar. 3, 1805	3. Aaron Burr	7, 8
	Mar. 4, 1805-Mar. 3, 1809	4. George Clinton	9, 10
4. James Madison	Mar. 4, 1809-Mar. 3, 1813	George Clinton[1]	11, 12
	Mar. 4, 1813-Mar. 3, 1817	5. Elbridge Gerry[2]	13, 14
5. James Monroe	Mar. 4, 1817-Mar. 3, 1825	6. Daniel D. Tompkins	15, 16, 17, 18
6. John Quincy Adams	Mar. 4, 1825-Mar. 3, 1829	7. John C. Calhoun	19, 20
7. Andrew Jackson	Mar. 4, 1829-Mar. 3, 1833	John C. Calhoun[3]	21, 22
	Mar. 4, 1833-Mar. 3, 1837	8. Martin Van Buren	23, 24
8. Martin Van Buren	Mar. 4, 1837-Mar. 3, 1841	9. Richard M. Johnson	25, 26
9. William Henry Harrison[4]	Mar. 4, 1841-Apr. 4, 1841	10. John Tyler	27
10. John Tyler	Apr. 6, 1841-Mar. 3, 1845	(None)	27, 28
11. James K. Polk	Mar. 4, 1845-Mar. 3, 1849	11. George M. Dallas	29, 30
12. Zachary Taylor[4]	Mar. 5, 1849-July 9, 1850	12. Millard Fillmore	31
13. Millard Fillmore	July 10, 1850-Mar. 3, 1853	(None)	31, 32
14. Franklin Pierce	Mar. 4, 1853-Mar. 3, 1857	13. William R. King[5]	33, 34
15. James Buchanan	Mar. 4, 1857-Mar. 3, 1861	14. John C. Breckinridge	35, 36
16. Abraham Lincoln[4]	Mar. 4, 1861-Mar. 3, 1865	15. Hannibal Hamlin	37, 38
	Mar. 4, 1865-Apr. 15, 1865	16. Andrew Johnson	39
17. Andrew Johnson	Apr. 15, 1865-Mar. 3, 1869	(None)	39, 40
18. Ulysses S. Grant	Mar. 4, 1869-Mar. 3, 1873	17. Schuyler Colfax	41, 42
	Mar. 4, 1873-Mar. 3, 1877	18. Henry Wilson[6]	43, 44
19. Rutherford B. Hayes	Mar. 4, 1877-Mar. 3, 1881	19. William A. Wheeler	45, 46
20. James A. Garfield[4]	Mar. 4, 1881-Sept. 19, 1881	20. Chester A. Arthur	47
21. Chester A. Arthur	Sept. 20, 1881-Mar. 3, 1885	(None)	47, 48
22. Grover Cleveland[7]	Mar. 4, 1885-Mar. 3, 1889	21. Thomas A. Hendricks[8]	49, 50
23. Benjamin Harrison	Mar. 4, 1889-Mar. 3, 1893	22. Levi P. Morton	51, 52
24. Grover Cleveland[7]	Mar. 4, 1893-Mar. 3, 1897	23. Adlai E. Stevenson	53, 54
25. William McKinley[4]	Mar. 4, 1897-Mar. 3, 1901	24. Garret A. Hobart[9]	55, 56
	Mar. 4, 1901-Sept. 14, 1901	25. Theodore Roosevelt	57
26. Theodore Roosevelt	Sept. 14, 1901-Mar. 3, 1905	(None)	57, 58
	Mar. 4, 1905-Mar. 3, 1909	26. Charles W. Fairbanks	59, 60
27. William H. Taft	Mar. 4, 1909-Mar. 3, 1913	27. James S. Sherman[10]	61, 62
28. Woodrow Wilson	Mar. 4, 1913-Mar. 3, 1921	28. Thomas R. Marshall	63, 64, 65, 66

President	Service	Vice President	Congresses
29. Warren G. Harding[4]	Mar. 4, 1921-Aug. 2, 1923	29. Calvin Coolidge	67
30. Calvin Coolidge	Aug. 3, 1923-Mar. 3, 1925	(None)	68
	Mar. 4, 1925-Mar. 3, 1929	30. Charles G. Dawes	69, 70
31. Herbert C. Hoover	Mar. 4, 1929-Mar. 3, 1933	31. Charles Curtis	71, 72
32. Franklin D. Roosevelt[4,11]	Mar. 4, 1933-Jan. 20, 1941	32. John N. Garner	73, 74, 75, 76, 77
	Jan. 20, 1941-Jan. 20, 1945	33. Henry A. Wallace	77, 78, 79
	Jan. 20, 1945-Apr. 12, 1945	34. Harry S. Truman	79
33. Harry S. Truman	Apr. 12, 1945-Jan. 20, 1949	(None)	79, 80, 81
	Jan. 20, 1949-Jan. 20, 1953	35. Alben W. Barkley	81, 82, 83
34. Dwight D. Eisenhower	Jan. 20, 1953-Jan. 20, 1961	36. Richard M. Nixon	83, 84, 85, 86, 87
35. John F. Kennedy[4]	Jan. 20, 1961-Nov. 22, 1963	37. Lyndon B. Johnson	87, 88
36. Lyndon B. Johnson	Nov. 22, 1963-Jan. 20, 1965	(None)	88, 89
	Jan. 20, 1965-Jan. 20, 1969	38. Hubert H. Humphrey	89, 90, 91
37. Richard M. Nixon[13]	Jan. 20, 1969-Jan. 20, 1973	39. Spiro T. Agnew[12]	91, 92, 93
	Jan. 20, 1973-Aug. 9, 1974	40. Gerald R. Ford[14]	93
38. Gerald R. Ford[15]	Aug. 9, 1974-Jan. 20, 1977	41. Nelson A. Rockefeller[16]	93, 94, 95
39. Jimmy Carter	Jan. 20, 1977-Jan. 20, 1981	42. Walter F. Mondale	95, 96, 97
40. Ronald W. Reagan	Jan. 20, 1981-Jan. 20, 1989	43. George H. W. Bush	97, 98, 99, 100, 101
41. George H. W. Bush	Jan. 20, 1989-Jan. 20, 1993	44. Dan Quayle	101, 102, 103
42. Bill Clinton	Jan. 20, 1993-Jan. 20, 2001	45. Al Gore	103, 104, 105, 106, 107
43. George W. Bush	Jan. 20, 2001-Jan. 20, 2009	46. Dick Cheney	107, 108, 109, 110, 111
44. Barack H. Obama	Jan. 20, 2009-Jan. 20, 2017	47. Joe Biden	111, 112, 113, 114, 115
45. Donald J. Trump	Jan. 20, 2017-Jan. 20, 2021	48. Mike Pence	115, 116, 117
46. Joseph R. Biden	Jan. 20, 2021-	49. Kamala Harris	117, 118

(1) Died Apr. 20, 1812. (2) Died Nov. 23, 1814. (3) Resigned Dec. 28, 1832, to become U.S. senator. (4) Died in office. (5) Died Apr. 18, 1853. (6) Died Nov. 22, 1875. (7) Terms not consecutive. (8) Died Nov. 25, 1885. (9) Died Nov. 21, 1899. (10) Died Oct. 30, 1912. (11) First president to be inaugurated under 20th Amendment, Jan. 20, 1937. (12) Resigned Oct. 10, 1973, after pleading no contest to a charge of tax evasion. (13) Resigned Aug. 9, 1974. (14) First nonelected vice president, chosen under 25th Amendment. (15) First president never elected president or vice president. (16) Second nonelected vice president, chosen under 25th Amendment. Confirmed Dec. 19, 1974.

Vice Presidents of the U.S.

The numerals given vice presidents do not coincide with those given presidents because some presidents (Tyler, Fillmore, A. Johnson, Arthur) had none, and some had more than one.

Name	Birthplace	Born	Home	Inaug.	Politics/party	Place of death	Died	Age at death
1. John Adams	Quincy, MA	1735	MA	1789	Fed.	Quincy, MA	1826	90
2. Thomas Jefferson	Shadwell, VA	1743	VA	1797	Dem.-Rep.	Monticello, VA	1826	83
3. Aaron Burr	Newark, NJ	1756	NY	1801	Dem.-Rep.	Staten Island, NY	1836	80
4. George Clinton	Little Britain, NY	1739	NY	1805	Dem.-Rep.	Washington, DC	1812	73
5. Elbridge Gerry	Marblehead, MA	1744	MA	1813	Dem.-Rep.	Washington, DC	1814	70
6. Daniel D. Tompkins	Scarsdale, NY	1774	NY	1817	Dem.-Rep.	Staten Island, NY	1825	51
7. John C. Calhoun[1]	Abbeville, SC	1782	SC	1825	Dem.-Rep.	Washington, DC	1850	68
8. Martin Van Buren	Kinderhook, NY	1782	NY	1833	Dem.	Kinderhook, NY	1862	79
9. Richard M. Johnson[2]	Louisville, KY	1780	KY	1837	Dem.	Frankfort, KY	1850	70
10. John Tyler	Greenway, VA	1790	VA	1841	Whig	Richmond, VA	1862	71
11. George M. Dallas	Philadelphia, PA	1792	PA	1845	Dem.	Philadelphia, PA	1864	72
12. Millard Fillmore	Cayuga Co., NY	1800	NY	1849	Whig	Buffalo, NY	1874	74
13. William R. King	Sampson Co., NC	1786	AL	1853	Dem.	Cahaba, AL	1853	67
14. John C. Breckinridge	Lexington, KY	1821	KY	1857	Dem.	Lexington, KY	1875	54
15. Hannibal Hamlin	Paris, ME	1809	ME	1861	Rep.	Bangor, ME	1891	81
16. Andrew Johnson	Raleigh, NC	1808	TN	1865	Dem.[3]	Carter Co., TN	1875	66
17. Schuyler Colfax	New York, NY	1823	IN	1869	Rep.	Mankato, MN	1885	62
18. Henry Wilson	Farmington, NH	1812	MA	1873	Rep.	Washington, DC	1875	63
19. William A. Wheeler	Malone, NY	1819	NY	1877	Rep.	Malone, NY	1887	68
20. Chester A. Arthur	Fairfield, VT	1829	NY	1881	Rep.	New York, NY	1886	57
21. Thomas A. Hendricks	Zanesville, OH	1819	IN	1885	Dem.	Indianapolis, IN	1885	66
22. Levi P. Morton	Shoreham, VT	1824	NY	1889	Rep.	Rhinebeck, NY	1920	96
23. Adlai E. Stevenson[4]	Christian Co., KY	1835	IL	1893	Dem.	Chicago, IL	1914	78
24. Garret A. Hobart	Long Branch, NJ	1844	NJ	1897	Rep.	Paterson, NJ	1899	55
25. Theodore Roosevelt	New York, NY	1858	NY	1901	Rep.	Oyster Bay, NY	1919	60
26. Charles W. Fairbanks	Unionville Centre, OH	1852	IN	1905	Rep.	Indianapolis, IN	1918	66
27. James S. Sherman	Utica, NY	1855	NY	1909	Rep.	Utica, NY	1912	57
28. Thomas R. Marshall	N. Manchester, IN	1854	IN	1913	Dem.	Washington, DC	1925	71
29. Calvin Coolidge	Plymouth Notch, VT	1872	MA	1921	Rep.	Northampton, MA	1933	60
30. Charles G. Dawes	Marietta, OH	1865	IL	1925	Rep.	Evanston, IL	1951	85
31. Charles Curtis	Topeka, KS	1860	KS	1929	Rep.	Washington, DC	1936	76
32. John Nance Garner	Red River Co., TX	1868	TX	1933	Dem.	Uvalde, TX	1967	98
33. Henry A. Wallace	Adair County, IA	1888	IA	1941	Dem.	Danbury, CT	1965	77
34. Harry S. Truman	Lamar, MO	1884	MO	1945	Dem.	Kansas City, MO	1972	88
35. Alben W. Barkley	Graves Co., KY	1877	KY	1949	Dem.	Lexington, VA	1956	78
36. Richard M. Nixon	Yorba Linda, CA	1913	CA	1953	Rep.	New York, NY	1994	81
37. Lyndon B. Johnson	Stonewall, TX	1908	TX	1961	Dem.	San Antonio, TX	1973	64
38. Hubert H. Humphrey	Wallace, SD	1911	MN	1965	Dem.	Waverly, MN	1978	66
39. Spiro T. Agnew[5]	Baltimore, MD	1918	MD	1969	Rep.	Berlin, MD	1996	77
40. Gerald R. Ford[6]	Omaha, NE	1913	MI	1973	Rep.	Rancho Mirage, CA	2006	93
41. Nelson A. Rockefeller[7]	Bar Harbor, ME	1908	NY	1974	Rep.	New York, NY	1979	70
42. Walter F. Mondale	Ceylon, MN	1928	MN	1977	Dem.	Minneapolis, MN	2021	93
43. George H. W. Bush	Milton, MA	1924	TX	1981	Rep.	Houston, TX	2018	94
44. James Danforth (Dan) Quayle Jr.	Indianapolis, IN	1947	IN	1989	Rep.			
45. Albert A. Gore	Washington, DC	1948	TN	1993	Dem.			
46. Richard B. Cheney	Lincoln, NE	1941	WY	2001	Rep.			
47. Joseph R. Biden Jr.	Scranton, PA	1942	DE	2009	Dem.			
48. Michael R. Pence	Columbus, IN	1959	IN	2017	Rep.			
49. Kamala D. Harris	Oakland, CA	1964	CA	2021	Dem.			

(1) Resigned Dec. 28, 1832, having been elected to the Senate to fill a vacancy. (2) Richard M. Johnson was the only vice president to be chosen by the Senate because of a tied vote in the Electoral College. (3) Democrat Andrew Johnson was nominated vice president by Republicans and elected with Lincoln on the National Union ticket. (4) Grandfather of Democratic candidate for president in 1952 and 1956. (5) Resigned Oct. 10, 1973, after pleading no contest to a charge of tax evasion. (6) First nonelected vice president, chosen under 25th Amendment procedure. (7) Second nonelected vice president, chosen under 25th Amendment.

Biographies of the Presidents

George Washington (1789-97), first president, Federalist, was born on Feb. 22, 1732, in Wakefield on Pope's Creek, Westmoreland Co., VA, the son of Augustine and Mary Ball Washington. He spent his early childhood on a farm near Fredericksburg. His father died when Washington was 11. He studied mathematics and surveying, and at 16, he went to live with his elder half brother, Lawrence, who built and named Mount Vernon in Virginia. Washington surveyed the lands of Thomas Fairfax in the Shenandoah Valley. He accompanied Lawrence to Barbados, West Indies, where he contracted smallpox and was deeply scarred. Lawrence died in 1752, and Washington inherited his property. He valued land, and when he died, he was a slaveholder who owned 70,000 acres in Virginia and 40,000 acres in what is now West Virginia.

Washington's military service began in 1753, when Lt. Gov. Robert Dinwiddie of Virginia sent him on missions deep into Ohio country. He clashed with the French and had to surrender Fort Necessity on July 3, 1754. He was an aide to the British general Edward Braddock and was at his side when the army was ambushed and defeated (July 9, 1755) on a march to Fort Duquesne. He helped take Fort Duquesne from the French in 1758.

After Washington's marriage to Martha Dandridge Custis, a widow, in 1759, he managed his family estate at Mount Vernon. Although not in favor of independence initially, he opposed the repressive measures of the British crown and took charge of the Virginia troops before war broke out. He was made commander of the newly created Continental Army by the Continental Congress on June 15, 1775.

The American victory was due largely to Washington's leadership. He was resourceful, a disciplinarian, and a dependable force for unity. Washington favored a federal government. He became chairman of the Constitutional Convention of 1787 and helped get the Constitution ratified. Unanimously elected president by the Electoral College, he was inaugurated Apr. 30, 1789, on the balcony of New York's Federal Hall. He was reelected in 1792. Washington made an effort to avoid partisan politics as president.

Refusing to consider a third term, Washington retired to Mount Vernon in Mar. 1797. A ride in snow and rain around his estate led to what present-day doctors believe to have been an attack of acute epiglottitis. Doctors were unsuccessful in treating the inflammation in his throat, and Washington died Dec. 14, 1799.

John Adams (1797-1801), second president, Federalist, was born on Oct. 30, 1735, in Braintree (now Quincy), MA, the son of John and Susanna Boylston Adams. He was a great-grandson of Henry Adams, who came from England in 1636. He graduated from Harvard in 1755, then taught school and studied law. He married Abigail Smith in 1764. In 1770, he successfully defended in court the British soldiers who fired on civilians in the Boston Massacre. He was a delegate to the Continental Congress and a signer of the Declaration of Independence. In 1778, Congress sent Adams and John Jay to join Benjamin Franklin as diplomatic representatives in Europe. Because he ran second to Washington in Electoral College balloting in Feb. 1789, Adams became the nation's first vice president, a post he characterized as highly insignificant; he was reelected in 1792.

In 1796 Adams was chosen president by the electors. His administration was marked by growing conflict with fellow Federalist Alexander Hamilton and with those in his cabinet who shared Hamilton's anti-French position. Adams avoided a declared war with France but became unpopular, especially after securing passage of the Alien and Sedition Acts, which restricted speech critical of the government, in 1798. His foreign policy contributed significantly to the election of Thomas Jefferson in 1800.

Adams lived for a quarter century after he left office, during which time he wrote extensively. He died July 4, 1826, on the same day as his rival Thomas Jefferson (the 50th anniversary of the Declaration of Independence).

Thomas Jefferson (1801-09), third president, Democratic-Republican, was born on Apr. 13, 1743, in Shadwell in Goochland (now Albemarle) Co., VA, the son of Peter and Jane Randolph Jefferson. His father died when Jefferson was 14, leaving him 2,750 acres and his slaves. Jefferson attended (1760-62) the College of William and Mary, read Greek and Latin classics, and played the violin. In 1769 he was elected to the Virginia House of Burgesses. In 1770 he began building his home, Monticello, and in 1772 he married Martha Wayles Skelton, a wealthy widow. Jefferson helped establish the Virginia Committee of Correspondence. As a member of the Second Continental Congress he drafted the Declaration of Independence. He also was a member of the Virginia House of Delegates (1776-79) and was elected governor of Virginia in 1779. He resigned in 1781, after British troops invaded Virginia. During his term he wrote the Virginia Statute of Religious Freedom. After his wife's death in 1782, Jefferson again became a delegate to the Congress, and in 1784 he drafted the report that was the basis for the Ordinances of 1784, 1785, and 1787. He was minister to France from 1785 to 1789, when George Washington appointed him secretary of state.

Jefferson's strong faith in the consent of the governed conflicted with the emphasis on executive control, favored by Sec. of the Treasury Alexander Hamilton, and Jefferson resigned as secretary of state on Dec. 31, 1793. In the 1796 election Jefferson was the Democratic-Republican candidate for president; John Adams won the election, and Jefferson became vice president. In 1800, Jefferson and Aaron Burr received equal numbers of Electoral College votes; the House of Representatives elected Jefferson president. Jefferson was a strong advocate of westward expansion; major events of his first term were the Louisiana Purchase (1803) and the Lewis and Clark expedition. His second term saw the passage of the Embargo Act, barring U.S. ships from setting sail to foreign ports and forbidding foreign ships from loading cargo in U.S. ports. Jefferson established the Univ. of Virginia and designed its buildings. He died July 4, 1826, on the same day as John Adams (the 50th anniversary of the Declaration of Independence).

Jefferson called slavery a "moral depravity" and violation of natural rights, but he profited from it as a slaveholder. He advocated gradual emancipation through voting, in conjunction with deportation. Based partly on DNA taken from descendants of Jefferson and of Sally Hemings, an enslaved woman who lived at Monticello from a young age, many historians conclude that Jefferson fathered one or more of her six children.

James Madison (1809-17), fourth president, Democratic-Republican, was born on Mar. 16, 1751, in Port Conway, King George Co., VA, the son of James and Eleanor Rose Conway Madison. Madison graduated from the College of New Jersey in 1771. He served in the Virginia Constitutional Convention (1776), and, in 1780, became a delegate to the Second Continental Congress. He was chief recorder of the Constitutional Convention in 1787 and supported ratification in the *Federalist Papers*, written with Alexander Hamilton and John Jay. In 1789, Madison was elected to the House of Representatives, where he helped frame the Bill of Rights and fought against passage of the Alien and Sedition Acts. In the 1790s, he helped found the Democratic-Republican Party, which ultimately became the Democratic Party. He became Jefferson's secretary of state in 1801.

Madison was elected president in 1808. His first term was marked by tensions with Great Britain, and his conduct of foreign policy was criticized by the Federalists and by his own party. Nevertheless, he was reelected in 1812, the year war was declared on Great Britain. The war that many considered a second American revolution ended with a treaty that did not settle any of the issues. Madison's most important action after the war was demilitarizing the U.S.-Canadian border.

In 1817, Madison retired to his Virginia plantation, Montpelier, which made use of slave labor. He edited his famous papers on the Constitutional Convention and helped found the Univ. of Virginia, of which he became rector in 1826. He died June 28, 1836.

James Monroe (1817-25), fifth president, Democratic-Republican, was born on Apr. 28, 1758, in Westmoreland Co., VA, the son of Spence and Elizabeth Jones Monroe. He entered the College of William and Mary in 1774 but left to serve in the Third Virginia Regiment during the American Revolution. After the war, he studied law with Thomas Jefferson. In 1782 he was elected to the Virginia House of Delegates, and he served (1783-86) as a delegate to the Continental Congress. He opposed ratification of the Constitution because it lacked a bill of rights. Monroe was elected to the U.S. Senate in 1790. In 1794, Pres. Washington appointed Monroe minister to France. He was again minister to France (1803) under Pres. Jefferson as well as minister to Great Britain (1803-07). He served twice as governor of Virginia (1799-1802, 1811).

In 1816 Monroe was elected president; he was reelected in 1820 with all but one Electoral College vote. His administration became known as the Era of Good Feeling. He obtained Florida from Spain, settled boundary disputes with Britain over Canada, and eliminated border forts. Though a slaveholder himself, he supported the anti-slavery position that led to the Missouri Compromise. His most significant contribution was the Monroe Doctrine, which opposed European intervention in the Western Hemisphere and became a cornerstone of U.S. foreign policy.

Although Monroe retired to Oak Hill, VA, financial problems forced him to sell his property and move to New York City. He died there on July 4, 1831.

John Quincy Adams (1825-29), sixth president, independent Federalist, later Democratic-Republican, was born on July 11, 1767, in Braintree (now Quincy), MA, the son of John and Abigail Adams. His father was the second president. He studied abroad and at Harvard College, from which he graduated in 1787. In 1803, he was elected to the U.S. Senate. President Monroe chose him as his secretary of state in 1817. In this capacity he negotiated the cession of Florida from Spain, supported exclusion of slavery in the Missouri Compromise, and helped formulate the Monroe Doctrine.

After no candidate won an Electoral College majority in 1824, the presidential election was decided by the House of Representatives. Adams won with support from rival Henry Clay, whom he named secretary of state, fueling accusations of a "corrupt bargain." His expansion of executive powers was strongly opposed, and in the 1828 election he lost to Andrew Jackson. In 1831 he entered the House of Representatives and served 17 years. He opposed slavery, the annexation of Texas, and the Mexican War. He helped establish the Smithsonian Institution.

Adams suffered a stroke in the House and died in the Speaker's Room on Feb. 23, 1848.

Andrew Jackson (1829-37), seventh president, Democratic-Republican, later a Democrat, was born on Mar. 15, 1767, in the Waxhaw district, on the border of North and South Carolina, the son of Andrew and Elizabeth Hutchinson Jackson. At the age of 13, he joined the militia to fight in the American Revolution and was captured. Orphaned at age 14, Jackson was raised by an uncle. By age 20, he was practicing law, and he later served as prosecuting attorney in Nashville, TN. In 1796 he helped draft the constitution of Tennessee, and for a year he occupied its one seat in the House of Representatives. The next year he served in the U.S. Senate.

In the War of 1812, Jackson crushed the Creek Indians at Horseshoe Bend, AL (1814), and, with a greatly outnumbered army consisting chiefly of militia members, privateers, Choctaw Indians, and other volunteer fighters, defeated Gen. Edward Pakenham's British troops at the Battle of New Orleans (1815). Nicknamed "Old Hickory" for his toughness, he emerged a national hero.

In 1818 Jackson briefly invaded Spanish Florida to quell Seminoles and outlaws who harassed frontier settlements. He ran for president against John Quincy Adams in 1824, but did not achieve a majority despite winning the most popular and electoral votes. The House of Representatives decided the election and chose Adams. In the 1828 election, however, Jackson, a slaveholder, defeated Adams by carrying the West and the South.

As president, Jackson introduced what became known as the spoils system—rewarding party members with government posts. A self-professed champion of the common man, he also viewed the Second Bank of the U.S. as a bastion of privilege and made it a major issue in the election of 1832, the first where candidates were chosen at national conventions rather than in congressional caucuses. Defeating Henry Clay, Jackson increasingly diverted funds from the national bank into so-called pet banks run by members of his own party. When South Carolina refused to collect imports under a federal tariff, which it declared null and void, Jackson won passage of legislation confirming his right to use military force to obtain compliance; eventually the tariff rate was reduced and the nullifiers backed down. After leaving office in 1837, he retired to the Hermitage, his estate outside Nashville, where he died on June 8, 1845.

Martin Van Buren (1837-41), eighth president, Democrat, was born on Dec. 5, 1782, in Kinderhook, NY, the son of Abraham and Maria Hoes Van Buren. After attending local schools, he studied law and became a lawyer at the age of 20. A consummate politician, Van Buren began his career in the New York state senate and then served as state attorney general (1816-19). He was elected to the U.S. Senate in 1821. He helped swing Eastern support to Andrew Jackson in the 1828 election and served as Jackson's secretary of state from 1829 to 1831. In 1832 he was elected vice president. Known as the "Little Magician," Van Buren was extremely influential in Jackson's administration.

In 1836, Van Buren defeated William Henry Harrison for president and took office as the financial panic of 1837 initiated a nationwide depression. Although he instituted the independent treasury system, his refusal to spend land revenues led to his defeat by William Henry Harrison in 1840. In 1844 he lost the Democratic nomination to James K. Polk. In 1848 he again ran for president on the Free Soil ticket but lost. He died in Kinderhook on July 24, 1862.

William Henry Harrison (1841), ninth president, Whig, who served only 31 days, was born on Feb. 9, 1773, in Berkeley, Charles City Co., VA, the son of Benjamin Harrison—a signer of the Declaration of Independence—and of Elizabeth Bassett Harrison. He attended Hampden-Sydney College. Harrison served as secretary of the Northwest Territory in 1798 and was its delegate to the House of Representatives in 1799. He was the first governor of Indiana Territory and served as superintendent of Indian affairs. Leading some 950 troops, he repelled an attack by Shawnee Indians at Tippecanoe, IN, on Nov. 7, 1811. A generation later, in 1840, he waged a rousing presidential campaign using the slogan "Tippecanoe and Tyler Too." The Tyler of the slogan was his running mate, John Tyler.

Although born to one of the wealthiest, most prestigious, and most influential families in Virginia, Harrison also campaigned with the slogan "Log Cabin and Hard Cider." He died Apr. 4, 1841, after only one month in office, of what doctors now believe was typhoid fever.

John Tyler (1841-45), 10th president, independent Whig, was born on Mar. 29, 1790, in Greenway, Charles City Co., VA, the son of John and Mary Armistead Tyler. His father was governor of Virginia (1808-11). Tyler graduated from the College of William and Mary in 1807 and in 1811 was elected to the Virginia legislature. In 1816 he was chosen for the U.S. House of Representatives. He served in the Virginia legislature again from 1823 to 1825, when he was elected governor of Virginia. After a stint in the U.S. Senate (1827-36), he was elected vice president (1840).

When William Henry Harrison died only a month after taking office, Tyler succeeded him. Because he was the first person to occupy the presidency without having been elected to that office, he was referred to as "His Accidency." He gained passage of the Preemption Act of 1841, which gave squatters on government land the right to buy 160 acres at the minimum auction price. His last act as president was to sign a resolution annexing Texas. Tyler accepted renomination in 1844 from some Democrats but withdrew in favor of the official party candidate, James K. Polk. A slaveholder who consistently supported the expansion of slavery, he served briefly in the Confederate House of Representatives before he died in Richmond, VA, on Jan. 18, 1862.

James Knox Polk (1845-49), 11th president, Democrat, was born on Nov. 2, 1795, in Mecklenburg Co., NC, the son of Samuel and Jane Knox Polk. He graduated from the Univ. of North Carolina in 1818 and served in the Tennessee state legislature from 1823 to 1825. He served in the U.S. House of Representatives from 1825 to 1839, the last four years as Speaker. He was governor of Tennessee from 1839 to 1841. In 1844, after the Democratic National Convention became deadlocked, it nominated Polk, who became the first "dark horse" candidate for president. He was nominated primarily because he favored annexation of Texas and tolerated slavery.

As president, Polk reestablished the independent treasury system originated by Van Buren. He was so intent on acquiring California from Mexico that he sent troops to the Mexican border and declared a state of war after Mexicans attacked. The Mexican War ended with the annexation of California and much of the Southwest as part of America's "manifest destiny." Polk compromised on the Oregon boundary ("54-40 or fight!") by accepting the 49th parallel and yielding Vancouver Island to the British. Polk died in Nashville, TN, on June 15, 1849, a few months after leaving office.

Zachary Taylor (1849-50), 12th president, Whig, who served only 16 months, was born on Nov. 24, 1784, in Orange Co., VA, the son of Richard and Sarah Strother Taylor. He grew up on his father's plantation near Louisville, KY, where the work was done by enslaved persons and he was educated by private tutors. In 1808 Taylor joined the regular army and was commissioned first lieutenant. He fought in the War of 1812, the Black Hawk War (1832), and the second Seminole War (beginning in 1837). He was called "Old Rough and Ready" for his military prowess. In 1846 Pres. Polk sent him with an army to the Rio Grande. When the Mexicans attacked him, Polk declared war. Outnumbered four to one, Taylor defeated Antonio López de Santa Anna at Buena Vista (1847).

A national hero, Taylor received the Whig nomination in 1848 and was elected president, even though he had never bothered to vote. He resumed the spoils system and, though a slaveholder, worked to admit California as a free state. He fell ill, likely from a case of acute gastroenteritis, and died in office on July 9, 1850.

Millard Fillmore (1850-53), 13th president, Whig, was born on Jan. 7, 1800, in Cayuga Co., NY, the son of Nathaniel and Phoebe Millard Fillmore. Although he had little schooling, he became a law clerk at the age of 22 and was admitted to the bar a year later. He was elected to the New York state assembly in 1828 and served until 1831. From 1833 until 1835 and again from 1837 to 1843, he represented his district in the U.S. House of Representatives. He opposed the entrance of Texas as a slave state and voted for a protective tariff. In 1844 he was defeated for governor of New York.

In 1848, he was elected vice president; he became president after Taylor's death. Fillmore favored the Compromise of 1850 and signed the Fugitive Slave Law. His policies pleased neither expansionists nor slaveholders, and he was not renominated in 1852. In 1856 he was nominated by the American (Know-Nothing) Party, but despite the support of the Whigs, he was defeated by James Buchanan. He died in Buffalo, NY, on Mar. 8, 1874.

Franklin Pierce (1853-57), 14th president, Democrat, was born on Nov. 23, 1804, in Hillsboro, NH, the son of Benjamin Pierce, Revolutionary War general and governor of New Hampshire, and Anna Kendrick. He graduated from Bowdoin College in 1824 and was admitted to the bar in 1827. He was elected to the New Hampshire state legislature in 1829 and was chosen Speaker in 1831. He went to the U.S. House in 1833 and was elected a U.S. senator in 1837. He enlisted in the Mexican War and became brigadier general under Gen. Winfield Scott.

In 1852 Pierce was nominated as the Democratic presidential candidate on the 49th ballot. He decisively defeated Gen. Scott, his Whig opponent, in the election. Although he was against slavery, Pierce was influenced by proslavery Southerners. He supported the controversial Kansas-Nebraska Act, which left the question of slavery in the new territories of Kansas and Nebraska to popular vote. Pierce signed a reciprocity treaty with Canada and approved the Gadsden Purchase, from Mexico, of a border area on a proposed railroad route. Denied renomination, he spent most of his remaining years in Concord, NH, where he died on Oct. 8, 1869.

James Buchanan (1857-61), 15th president, Federalist, later Democrat, was born on Apr. 23, 1791, near Mercersburg, PA, the son of James and Elizabeth Speer Buchanan. He graduated from Dickinson College in 1809 and was admitted to the bar in 1812. He fought in the War of 1812 as a volunteer. He was twice elected to the Pennsylvania general assembly, and in 1821 he entered the U.S. House of Representatives. After briefly serving (1832-33) as minister to Russia, he was elected U.S. senator from Pennsylvania. As Polk's secretary of state (1845-49), he ended the Oregon dispute with Britain and supported the Mexican War and annexation of Texas. As minister to Great Britain, he signed the Ostend Manifesto (1854), declaring a U.S. right to take Cuba by force should efforts to purchase it fail.

Nominated by Democrats, Buchanan was elected president in 1856. On slavery he favored popular sovereignty and choice by state constitutions but did not consistently uphold this position. He denied the right of states to secede but opposed coercion and attempted to keep peace by not provoking secessionists. Buchanan left office having failed to deal decisively with the situation. He died at Wheatland, his estate, near Lancaster, PA, on June 1, 1868.

Abraham Lincoln (1861-65), 16th president, Whig, then Republican, was born on Feb. 12, 1809, in a log cabin on a farm in Hardin (now Larue) Co., KY, the son of Thomas and Nancy Hanks Lincoln. The Lincolns moved to Spencer Co., IN, near Gentryville, when Lincoln was 7. After Lincoln's mother died, his father married Mrs. Sarah Bush Johnston in 1819. In 1830 the family moved to Macon Co., IL.

Defeated in 1832 in a race for the state legislature, Lincoln was elected on the Whig ticket two years later and served in the lower house from 1834 to 1842. In 1837 Lincoln was admitted to the bar and became partner in a Springfield, IL, law office. In 1846, he was elected to Congress, where he attracted attention during a single term for his opposition to the Mexican War and his position on slavery. In 1856 he campaigned for the newly founded Republican Party, and in 1858 he became its senatorial candidate against Stephen A. Douglas. Although he lost the election, Lincoln gained national recognition from his debates with Douglas.

In 1860, Lincoln was nominated for president by the Republican Party on a platform of restricting slavery. He ran against Douglas, a northern Democrat; John C. Breckinridge, a southern proslavery Democrat; and John Bell, of the Constitutional Union Party. In response to Lincoln's victory, South Carolina seceded from the Union on Dec. 20, 1860, soon followed by six other Southern states.

The Civil War erupted when South Carolina's Fort Sumter, which Lincoln decided to resupply, was attacked by Confederate forces on Apr. 12, 1861. Lincoln called for recruits from the North, and four more Southern states seceded. Hundreds of thousands of Union and Confederate soldiers were killed or wounded in four years of battle that followed. On Sept. 22, 1862, five days after the Battle of Antietam, Lincoln announced that those who were enslaved in territory then in rebellion would be free Jan. 1, 1863, under his Emancipation Proclamation. His speeches, including his Gettysburg and inaugural addresses, are remembered for their eloquence.

Lincoln was reelected, in 1864, over Gen. George B. McClellan, a Democrat. Confederate Gen. Robert E. Lee surrendered on Apr. 9, 1865. On Apr. 14, Lincoln was shot by actor John Wilkes Booth in Ford's Theatre, in Washington, DC. He died the next day.

Andrew Johnson (1865-69), 17th president, Democrat, was born on Dec. 29, 1808, in Raleigh, NC, the son of Jacob and Mary McDonough Johnson. He was apprenticed to a tailor as a youth but ran away after two years and eventually settled in Greeneville, TN, where he was elected councilman and later mayor. In 1835 he was sent to the state general assembly. In 1843 he was elected to the U.S. House of Representatives, where he served for 10 years. Johnson was also governor of Tennessee from 1853 to 1857, when he was elected to the U.S. Senate.

Although Johnson had himself exploited enslaved labor, he opposed secession and tried to prevent Tennessee from seceding. In Mar. 1862, Lincoln appointed him military governor of occupied Tennessee.

In 1864, in order to balance Lincoln's ticket with a Southern Democrat, the Republicans nominated Johnson for vice president. He was elected vice president with Lincoln and succeeded to the presidency upon Lincoln's death. Soon afterward, in conflict with Congress over the president's power over the South, he proclaimed an amnesty to all Confederates, except certain leaders, if they would ratify the 13th Amendment abolishing slavery. States doing so added anti-Negro provisions that enraged Congress, which restored military control over the South. When Johnson removed Sec. of War Edwin M. Stanton without notifying the Senate, the House impeached him in Feb. 1868 on the charge of violating the Tenure of Office Act. In reality, the House was responding to his opposition to harsh congressional Reconstruction, expressed in repeated vetoes. He was acquitted in the Senate by one-vote margins on each of two counts.

Johnson was denied renomination but remained politically active. He was reelected to the Senate in 1874. Johnson died July 31, 1875, at Carter Station, TN.

Ulysses S. Grant (1869-77), 18th president, Republican, was born on Apr. 27, 1822, in Point Pleasant, OH, the son of Jesse R. and Hannah Simpson Grant. The next year the family moved to Georgetown, OH. Grant was named Hiram Ulysses. Upon entering West Point in 1839, he found his name had been put down as Ulysses S. Grant, with his middle name first and his mother's maiden name as his middle name. He eventually adopted it as his true name but maintained the "S" did not stand for anything. Grant graduated in 1843.

During the Mexican War, Grant served under both Gen. Zachary Taylor and Gen. Winfield Scott. In 1854, he resigned his commission because of loneliness and drinking problems, and in the following years he engaged in generally unsuccessful farming and business ventures. With the start of the Civil War, he was named colonel and then brigadier general of the Illinois Volunteers. He took Forts Henry and Donelson and fought at Shiloh. His brilliant campaign against Vicksburg and his victory at Chattanooga made him so prominent that Lincoln placed him in command of all Union armies. Grant accepted Confederate Gen. Robert E. Lee's surrender at Appomattox Court House on Apr. 9, 1865.

Grant was nominated for president by the Republicans in 1868 and elected over Democrat Horatio Seymour. The 15th Amendment, the amnesty bill, and peaceful settlement of disputes with Great Britain were events of his administration. The Liberal Republicans and Democrats opposed him with Horace Greeley in the 1872 election, but Grant was reelected. His second administration was marked by scandals, including the Crédit Mobilier affair, the Whiskey Ring, in which high-ranked officials conspired to defraud the government of taxes, and the impeachment of his secretary of war. An attempt by the Stalwarts (Old Guard Republicans) to nominate him in 1880 failed. Left penniless by the 1884 collapse of an investment firm in which he was a partner, he wrote his well-regarded memoirs while suffering from cancer to provide income for his family. He died at Mt. McGregor, NY, on July 23, 1885.

Rutherford Birchard Hayes (1877-81), 19th president, Republican, was born on Oct. 4, 1822, in Delaware, OH, the son of Rutherford and Sophia Birchard Hayes. He was reared by his uncle, Sardis Birchard. Hayes graduated from Kenyon College in 1842 and from Harvard Law School in 1845. He practiced law in Lower Sandusky (now Fremont), OH, and was city solicitor of Cincinnati from 1858 to 1861. During the Civil War, he was major of the 23rd Ohio Volunteers. He was wounded several times, and by the end of the war he had risen to the rank of brevet major general. While serving (1865-67) in the U.S. House of Representatives, Hayes supported Reconstruction and Johnson's impeachment. He was twice elected governor of Ohio (1867, 1869). After losing a race for the U.S. House in 1872, he was reelected governor of Ohio in 1875.

In 1876, Hayes was nominated for president. He believed he had lost the election to Democrat Samuel J. Tilden. But a few Southern states submitted two sets of electoral votes, and the result was in dispute. An electoral commission, consisting of 8 Republicans and 7 Democrats, awarded all disputed votes to Hayes, allowing him to become president by one electoral vote. Hayes, keeping a promise to Southerners, withdrew troops from areas still occupied in the South, ending the era of Reconstruction. He proposed civil service reforms, alienating those favoring the spoils system, and advocated repeal of the Tenure of Office Act restricting presidential power to dismiss officials. He supported sound money and specie payments.

Hayes died in Fremont, OH, on Jan. 17, 1893.

James Abram Garfield (1881), 20th president, Republican, was born on Nov. 19, 1831, in Orange, Cuyahoga Co., OH, the son of Abram and Eliza Ballou Garfield. His father died in 1833, and he was reared in poverty by his mother. He worked as a canal bargeman, a farmer, and a carpenter. He attended Western Reserve Eclectic Institute and graduated from Williams College in 1856. He returned to Western Reserve to teach and in 1857, at age 25, he became the school's president. In 1859 he was elected to the Ohio legislature. Anti-slavery and anti-secession, he volunteered for military service in the Civil War, becoming colonel of the 42nd Ohio Infantry and brigadier in 1862. He fought at Shiloh, TN, was chief of staff for Gen. William Starke Rosecrans, and was made major general for gallantry at Chickamauga, GA. He entered Congress as a radical Republican in 1863, calling for execution or exile of Confederate leaders, but he moderated his views after the Civil War. On the electoral commission in 1877 he voted for Hayes against Tilden on strict party lines.

Garfield was a senator-elect in 1880 when he became the Republican nominee for president. He was chosen as a compromise over Gen. Grant, James G. Blaine, and John Sherman, and won election despite some bitterness among Grant's supporters. For much of his brief tenure as president, Garfield was concerned with a fight with New York Sen. Roscoe Conkling, who opposed two major appointments made by Garfield. On July 2, 1881, Garfield was shot and seriously wounded by a mentally disturbed office seeker, Charles J. Guiteau, while entering a railroad station in Washington, DC. He died on Sept. 19, 1881, in Elberon, NJ.

Chester Alan Arthur (1881-85), 21st president, Republican, was born on Oct. 5, 1829, in Fairfield, VT, to William and Malvina Stone Arthur. He graduated from Union College in 1848, taught school in Vermont, then studied law and practiced in New York City. In 1853, he argued that fugitives from enslaved labor transported through New York State were thereby freed. In 1871, he was appointed collector of the Port of New York. Pres. Hayes, an opponent of the spoils system, forced him to resign in 1878. This made the New York machine enemies of Hayes. Arthur and the Stalwarts (Old Guard Republicans) tried to nominate Grant for a third term as president in 1880. When Garfield was nominated, Arthur was nominated for vice president in the interests of harmony.

Upon Garfield's assassination, Arthur became president. Despite his past connections, he signed major civil service reform legislation. Arthur tried to dissuade Congress from enacting the high protective tariff of 1883. He was defeated for renomination in 1884 by James G. Blaine. He died in New York City on Nov. 18, 1886.

(Stephen) Grover Cleveland (1885-89; 1893-97) (*According to a State Dept. ruling, Grover Cleveland should be counted as both the 22nd and the 24th president because his two terms were not consecutive*), Democrat, was born Stephen Grover Cleveland on Mar. 18, 1837, in Caldwell, NJ, the son of Richard F. and Ann Neal Cleveland. When he was a small boy, his family moved to New York. Prevented by his father's death from attending college, he studied on his own and was admitted to the bar in Buffalo, NY, in 1859. In succession he became assistant district attorney (1863), sheriff (1871), mayor (1881), and governor of New York (1882). He was an independent, honest administrator who hated corruption. Cleveland was nominated for president with opposition from New York City's Democratic party machine Tammany Hall in 1884 and defeated Republican James G. Blaine.

As president, he enlarged the civil service and vetoed many pension raids on the Treasury. In the 1888 election he was defeated by Benjamin Harrison, although his popular vote was larger. Reelected over Harrison in 1892, he faced a money crisis brought about by a lowered gold reserve, circulation of paper, and exorbitant silver purchases under the Sherman Silver Purchase Act. He obtained a repeal of the Sherman Act but was unable to secure effective tariff reform. A severe economic depression and labor troubles racked his administration, but he refused to interfere in business matters and rejected business owner Jacob Coxey's demand for unemployment relief. In 1894, he broke the Pullman railroad workers' strike. Cleveland was not renominated in 1896. He died in Princeton, NJ, on June 24, 1908.

Benjamin Harrison (1889-93), 23rd president, Republican, was born on Aug. 20, 1833, in North Bend, OH, the son of John Scott and Elizabeth Irwin Harrison. His great-grandfather, Benjamin Harrison, was a signer of the Declaration of Independence; his grandfather, William Henry Harrison, was the ninth president; his father was a member of Congress. He attended school on his father's farm and graduated from Miami Univ. in Oxford, OH, in 1852. He was admitted to the bar in 1854 and practiced in Indianapolis, IN. During the Civil War, he rose to the rank of brevet brigadier general and fought at Kennesaw Mountain, Peachtree Creek, Nashville, and in the Atlanta campaign. He lost the 1876 gubernatorial election in Indiana but succeeded in becoming a U.S. senator in 1881.

In 1888 he defeated Cleveland for president despite receiving fewer popular votes. As president, he expanded the pension list and signed the McKinley high tariff bill, the Sherman Antitrust Act, and the Sherman Silver Purchase Act. During his administration, six states were admitted to the Union. He was defeated for reelection in 1892. He died in Indianapolis, IN, on Mar. 13, 1901.

William McKinley (1897-1901), 25th president, Republican, was born on Jan. 29, 1843, in Niles, OH, the son of William and Nancy Allison McKinley. McKinley briefly attended Allegheny College in Pennsylvania. When the Civil War broke out in 1861, he enlisted and served for the duration. He rose to captain and in 1865 was made brevet major. After studying law in Albany, NY, he opened a law office in Canton, OH (1867). He served twice in the U.S. House (1877-83; 1885-91) and led the fight there for the McKinley Tariff, passed in 1890; he was not reelected to the House as a result. He served two terms (1892-96) as governor of Ohio.

In 1896 he was elected president as a proponent of a protective tariff and sound money (gold standard) over William Jennings Bryan, the Democrat and a proponent of free silver. McKinley was reluctant to intervene in Cuba, but the loss of the battleship *Maine* at Havana, blamed on Spain, crystallized opinion. He demanded Spain's withdrawal from Cuba; Spain made

some concessions, but Congress announced a state of war as of Apr. 21, 1898. He was reelected in the 1900 campaign, defeating Bryan's anti-imperialist arguments with the promise of a "full dinner pail." He was known for a conservative stance on business issues. On Sept. 6, 1901, at the Pan-American Exposition, in Buffalo, NY, he was shot by Leon Czolgosz, an anarchist. He died Sept. 14.

Theodore Roosevelt (1901-09), 26th president, Republican, was born on Oct. 27, 1858, in New York City, the son of Theodore and Martha Bulloch Roosevelt. He was a fifth cousin of Franklin D. Roosevelt and an uncle of Eleanor Roosevelt. Roosevelt graduated from Harvard Univ. in 1880. He attended Columbia Law School briefly but abandoned law to enter politics. He was elected to the New York State Assembly in 1881 and served until 1884. He spent the next two years ranching and hunting in the Dakota Territory. In 1886, he ran unsuccessfully for mayor of New York City. He was civil service commissioner in Washington, DC, from 1889 to 1895. From 1895 to 1897, he served as New York City's police commissioner. He was assistant secretary of the Navy under McKinley. The Spanish-American War made him nationally known. He organized the First U.S. Volunteer Cavalry (Rough Riders) and, as lieutenant colonel, led the charge up Kettle Hill in San Juan, Cuba. Elected New York governor in 1898, he fought the spoils system and achieved taxation of corporation franchises.

Nominated for vice president in 1900, Roosevelt became the nation's youngest president at the age of 42 when McKinley was assassinated. He was reelected in 1904. As president he fought corruption of politics by big business, dissolved the Northern Securities Co. and others for violating antitrust laws, intervened in the 1902 coal strike on behalf of the public, obtained the Elkins Law (1903) forbidding rebates to favored corporations, and helped pass the Hepburn Railway Rate Act of 1906 (extending jurisdiction of the Interstate Commerce Commission). He helped obtain passage of the Pure Food and Drug Act (1906) and of employers' liability laws. Roosevelt vigorously organized conservation efforts. He mediated the peace between Japan and Russia in 1905, for which he won the Nobel Peace Prize. He abetted the 1903 revolution in Panama that led to U.S. acquisition of territory for the Panama Canal.

In 1908 Roosevelt obtained the nomination of William H. Taft, who was elected. Feeling that Taft had abandoned his policies, he unsuccessfully sought the nomination in 1912. He then ran on the Progressive "Bull Moose" ticket against Taft and Woodrow Wilson, splitting the Republicans and ensuring Wilson's election. During the campaign he was shot by a mentally deranged man but was not seriously wounded. In 1916, after unsuccessfully seeking the presidential nomination, he supported the Republican candidate, Charles E. Hughes. He strongly promoted U.S. intervention in World War I.

Roosevelt was a voracious reader and wrote some 40 books, including *The Winning of the West*. He died Jan. 6, 1919, at Sagamore Hill, his home in Oyster Bay, NY.

William Howard Taft (1909-13), 27th president, Republican, and 10th chief justice of the U.S., was born on Sept. 15, 1857, in Cincinnati, OH, the son of Alphonso and Louisa Maria Torrey Taft. His father was secretary of war and attorney general in Grant's cabinet and minister to Austria and Russia under Arthur. Taft graduated from Yale in 1878 and from Cincinnati Law School in 1880. After working as a law reporter for Cincinnati newspapers, he served as assistant prosecuting attorney (1881-82), assistant county solicitor (1885), superior court judge (1887), U.S. solicitor-general (1890), and federal circuit judge (1892). In 1900 he became head of the U.S. Philippines Commission and was the first civil governor of the Philippines (1901-04). In 1904 he was secretary of war, and in 1906 he was sent to Cuba to help avert a threatened revolution.

Taft was groomed for the presidency by Theodore Roosevelt and elected over William Jennings Bryan in 1908. Taft vigorously continued Roosevelt's trust-busting, instituted the Dept. of Labor, and drafted amendments calling for direct election of senators and an income tax. However, his tariff and conservation policies angered progressives. Although renominated in 1912, he was opposed by Roosevelt, who ran on the Progressive Party ticket; the result was Wilson's election.

Taft, with reservations, supported the League of Nations. He became a professor of constitutional law at Yale (1913-21) and was appointed by Pres. Harding to serve as chief justice of the U.S. (1921-30). Taft was the only person to have been both president and chief justice. He died in Washington, DC, on Mar. 8, 1930.

(Thomas) Woodrow Wilson (1913-21), 28th president, Democrat, was born on Dec. 28, 1856, in Staunton, VA, the son of Joseph Ruggles and Janet (Jessie) Woodrow Wilson. He grew up in Georgia and South Carolina. He attended Davidson College in North Carolina before graduating from Princeton Univ. in 1879. He studied law at the Univ. of Virginia and political science at Johns Hopkins Univ., where he received his PhD in 1886. He taught at Bryn Mawr (1885-88) and at Wesleyan (1888-90) before joining the faculty at Princeton. He was president of Princeton from 1902 until 1910, when he was elected governor of New Jersey. In 1912 he was nominated for president with the aid of William Jennings Bryan, who sought to block James "Champ" Clark and New York City's Democratic party machine Tammany Hall. Wilson won because Theodore Roosevelt, running as a "Bull Moose" Progressive, siphoned votes away from Republican candidate Taft.

As president, Wilson protected American interests in revolutionary Mexico and fought for American rights on the high seas. He oversaw the creation of the Federal Reserve system, cut the tariff, and developed a reputation as a reformer. His sharp warnings to Germany led to the resignation of his secretary of state, Bryan, a pacifist. In 1916 he was reelected by a slim margin with the slogan "He kept us out of war," although his attempts to mediate in the war failed. After several American ships were sunk by the Germans, he secured a declaration of war against Germany on Apr. 6, 1917.

Wilson outlined his peace program on Jan. 8, 1918, in the Fourteen Points, a state paper that enunciated a doctrine of self-determination for the settlement of territorial disputes. The Germans accepted his terms and an armistice on Nov. 11, 1918. Wilson went to Paris to help negotiate the peace treaty, the crux of which he considered the League of Nations. The Senate demanded reservations that would not make the U.S. subordinate to the votes of other nations in case of war. Wilson refused and toured the country to get support. After he suffered a severe stroke in Oct. 1919, his wife, Edith Wilson, concealed the extent of his infirmity, controlled access to him, and in effect largely acted in his place.

Wilson was awarded the 1919 Nobel Peace Prize, but the treaty embodying the League of Nations was ultimately rejected by the Senate in 1920. He left the White House in Mar. 1921. He died in Washington, DC, on Feb. 3, 1924.

Warren Gamaliel Harding (1921-23), 29th president, Republican, was born on Nov. 2, 1865, near Corsica (now Blooming Grove), OH, the son of George Tryon and Phoebe Elizabeth Dickerson Harding. He attended Ohio Central College, studied law, and became editor and publisher of a county newspaper. He entered the political arena as state senator (1901-04) and then served as lieutenant governor (1904-06). In 1910 he ran unsuccessfully for governor of Ohio; in 1914 he was elected to the U.S. Senate. In the Senate he voted for anti-strike legislation, women's suffrage, and the Volstead Prohibition Enforcement Act over Pres. Wilson's veto. He opposed the League of Nations.

In 1920 he was nominated for president and defeated James M. Cox in the election. The Republicans capitalized on war weariness and fear that Wilson's League of Nations would curtail U.S. sovereignty. Harding stressed a return to "normalcy" and worked for tariff revision and the repeal of excess profits law and high income taxes. In the so-called Teapot Dome scandal, his secretary of the interior, Albert B. Fall, resigned and was later convicted of accepting bribes in the leasing of government-owned oil reserves to private companies.

As rumors began to circulate about the corruption in his administration, Harding fell ill after a trip to Alaska, and he died suddenly of a likely heart attack in San Francisco on Aug. 2, 1923. Harding's letters to a longtime mistress were made public by the Library of Congress in 2014, and DNA evidence in 2015 confirmed another mistress's claim that he had fathered her daughter.

(John) Calvin Coolidge (1923-29), 30th president, Republican, was born on July 4, 1872, in Plymouth Notch, VT, the son of John Calvin and Victoria J. Moor Coolidge. Coolidge graduated from Amherst College in 1895. He entered Republican state politics and served as mayor of Northampton, MA, as state senator, as lieutenant governor, and, in 1919, as governor. In Sept. 1919, Coolidge attained national prominence by calling out the state guard in the Boston police strike. He declared, "There is no right to strike against the public safety by anybody, anywhere, anytime." This brought his name before the Republican convention of 1920, where he was nominated for vice president.

Coolidge succeeded to the presidency on Harding's death. As president, he opposed the League of Nations and the soldiers' bonus bill, which was passed over his veto. In 1924 he was elected to the presidency by a huge majority. He substantially reduced the national debt. He twice vetoed legislation to aid financially hard-pressed farmers.

With Republicans eager to renominate him, Coolidge simply announced on Aug. 2, 1927, "I do not choose to run for president in 1928." He died in Northampton, MA, on Jan. 5, 1933.

Herbert Clark Hoover (1929-33), 31st president, Republican, was born on Aug. 10, 1874, in West Branch, IA, the son of Jesse Clark and Hulda Randall Minthorn Hoover. Hoover grew up in Indian Territory (now Oklahoma) and Oregon and graduated from Stanford Univ. with a degree in geology in 1895. He worked briefly with the U.S. Geological Survey and then managed mines in Australia, Asia, Europe, and Africa. While chief engineer of imperial mines in China, he directed food relief for victims of the Boxer Rebellion. He gained a reputation not only as an engineer but as a humanitarian as he directed the American Relief Committee, London (1914-15) and the U.S. Commission for Relief in Belgium (1915-19). He was U.S. Food Administrator (1917-19), American Relief Administrator (1918-23), and in charge of Russian Relief (1918-23). He served as secretary of commerce under both Harding and Coolidge.

In 1928 Hoover was elected president over Alfred E. Smith. In 1929 the stock market crashed, and the economy collapsed. During the Great Depression, Hoover inaugurated some government assistance programs, but he was opposed to administration of aid through a federal bureaucracy. As the effects of the Depression continued, he was defeated in the 1932 election by Franklin D. Roosevelt. Hoover remained active after leaving office. Pres. Truman named him coordinator of the European Food Program (1946) and chairman of the Commission on Organization of the Executive Branch (1947-49); he was later appointed by Pres. Eisenhower to serve in the same role (1953-55).

Hoover died in New York City on Oct. 20, 1964.

Franklin Delano Roosevelt (1933-45), 32nd president, Democrat, was born on Jan. 30, 1882, in Hyde Park, NY, the son of James and Sara Delano Roosevelt, and a fifth cousin of former Pres. Theodore Roosevelt. He graduated from Harvard Univ. in 1903. He attended Columbia University Law School without taking a degree and was admitted to the New York State bar in 1907. His political career began when he was elected to the New York State senate in 1910. In 1913 Pres. Wilson appointed him assistant secretary of the navy, a post he held during World War I.

In 1920 Roosevelt ran for vice president with James Cox and was defeated. From 1921 to 1928 he worked in his New York law office and was also vice president of a bank. In Aug. 1921, he was stricken with poliomyelitis, which left his legs paralyzed. As a result of therapy, he was able to stand and walk a few steps with the aid of leg braces.

Roosevelt served two terms as governor of New York (1929-33). In 1932, Democratic convention delegate W. G. McAdoo, pledged to nominee John N. Garner, threw his votes to Roosevelt, who was nominated for president. The Depression and the promise to repeal Prohibition ensured his election. He asked for emergency powers, proclaimed the New Deal, and put into effect a vast number of administrative changes. Foremost was the use of public funds for relief and public works, resulting in deficit financing. He greatly expanded the federal government's regulation of business and by an excess profits tax and progressive income taxes produced a redistribution of earnings on an unprecedented scale. He also promoted legislation establishing the Social Security system. He was the last president inaugurated on Mar. 4 (1933) and the first inaugurated on Jan. 20 (1937).

Roosevelt was the first president to use radio for "fireside chats." When the Supreme Court nullified some New Deal laws, he sought power to "pack" the Court with additional justices, but Congress refused to give him the authority. He was the first president to break the no-third-term tradition (1940) and was elected to a fourth term in 1944 despite failing health.

Roosevelt was openly hostile to fascist governments before World War II and launched a lend-lease program on behalf of the Allies. With British Prime Min. Winston Churchill he wrote a declaration of principles to be followed after Nazi defeat (the Atlantic Charter of Aug. 14, 1941) and urged the Four Freedoms (freedom of speech, of worship, from want, from fear) Jan. 6, 1941. After Japan attacked Pearl Harbor on Dec. 7, 1941, the U.S. entered the war. Roosevelt guided the nation through the war and conferred with allied heads of state but did not live to see the end of the war. He died of a cerebral hemorrhage in Warm Springs, GA, on Apr. 12, 1945.

Harry S. Truman (1945-53), 33rd president, Democrat, was born on May 8, 1884, in Lamar, MO, the son of John Anderson and Martha Ellen Young Truman. Because of a family disagreement over what his middle name should be, he used only the initial S. After graduating from high school (1901) in Independence, MO, he worked in clerical jobs. He ran his family's farm from 1906 to 1917, then fought in France during World War I. Following the war he opened a haberdashery, served as a judge on the Jackson Co. Court (1922-24), and attended Kansas City School of Law (1923-25).

Truman was elected to the U.S. Senate in 1934 and reelected in 1940. Running with Roosevelt, he was elected vice president in 1944 and became president after Roosevelt's death in Apr. 1945. In 1948, in a famous upset, he defeated Republican Gov. Thomas E. Dewey (NY) to win a new term.

Truman authorized the first uses of the atomic bomb (Hiroshima and Nagasaki, Aug. 1945), bringing World War II to a rapid end. Under his leadership the U.S. provided postwar military and economic aid to Greece and Turkey, threatened by Communist takeover (Truman Doctrine), financed economic recovery in Europe (Marshall Plan, 1948), and signed on to the NATO alliance against the Soviet Union in 1949. In 1948-49, he broke a Soviet blockade of West Berlin with a massive airlift. When Communist North Korea invaded South Korea (1950), he won UN approval to send in forces under Gen. Douglas MacArthur. When MacArthur opposed his policy of limited objectives, Truman removed him.

He died in Kansas City, MO, on Dec. 26, 1972.

Dwight David Eisenhower (1953-61), 34th president, Republican, was born on Oct. 14, 1890, in Denison, TX, the son of David Jacob and Ida Elizabeth Stover Eisenhower, as David Dwight Eisenhower. He grew up on a small farm in Abilene, KS, and graduated from West Point in 1915. He was on the staff of Gen. Douglas MacArthur in the Philippines from 1935 to 1939. In 1942, he was made commander of Allied forces landing in North Africa; the next year he became supreme Allied commander in Europe and led the Normandy invasion (June 6, 1944).

On May 7, 1945, Eisenhower received the surrender of Germany at Rheims, France. He returned to the U.S. to serve as chief of staff (1945-48). His memoir, *Crusade in Europe* (1948), was a best-seller. In 1948 he became president of Columbia Univ.; in 1950 he became commander of NATO forces.

Eisenhower won the Republican nomination for president in 1952 and defeated Illinois Gov. Adlai E. Stevenson (D) in the 1952 and 1956 elections. As president he opposed wage and price controls, kept government out of labor disputes, reorganized the defense establishment, and promoted missile development. He helped negotiate a cease-fire truce in the Korean War, endorsed Taiwan and SE Asia defense treaties, advocated

the "open skies" policy of mutual inspection with the USSR, and backed the UN in condemning the Anglo-French raid on Egypt, even as the CIA advanced regime change in Iran and Guatemala. He sent U.S. troops into Little Rock, AR, in Sept. 1957, to enforce school integration.

Eisenhower died on Mar. 28, 1969, in Washington, DC.

John Fitzgerald Kennedy (1961-63), 35th president, Democrat, was born on May 29, 1917, in Brookline, MA, the son of Rose Fitzgerald Kennedy and Joseph P. Kennedy, a wealthy businessman, investor, and onetime U.S. ambassador to Britain. After graduating from Harvard (1940), Kennedy served in the Navy (1941-45), winning a medal for heroism as commander of a PT (patrol torpedo) boat in the Pacific. He served in the U.S. House, 1947-53, and was elected to the Senate in 1952 and 1958. In 1956, after spinal surgery, he published *Profiles in Courage*, which won a Pulitzer Prize.

In 1960, Kennedy narrowly defeated Vice Pres. Richard Nixon (R) for the presidency. He was the first Catholic and, at 43, the youngest person ever elected to that office. Despite his image of youth and vigor, Kennedy suffered from serious medical problems, including Addison's disease and severe back pain that required him to wear a back brace. The extent of these problems was concealed from the public, as were his frequent sexual liaisons.

In Apr. 1961, the new Kennedy administration was stung by the defeat of a CIA-directed invasion force of anti-Communist Cuban exiles, at Cuba's Bay of Pigs. But he successfully demanded, in Oct. 1962, that the Soviet Union dismantle its missile bases in Cuba. He also defied Soviet attempts to force the Allies out of Berlin. Kennedy established the Peace Corps and spurred on a program to land humans on the Moon, but Congress balked at some of his "New Frontier" initiatives, such as medical coverage for the aged. He eventually introduced major civil rights legislation but did not live to see it passed.

On Nov. 22, 1963, Kennedy was assassinated while riding in a motorcade in Dallas, TX. A commission chaired by Supreme Court Chief Justice Earl Warren concluded in Sept. 1964 that the sole assassin had been Lee Harvey Oswald, an ex-Marine and ardent Marxist. Oswald was captured shortly after the assassination but was shot dead by nightclub owner Jack Ruby while being moved to a county jail.

Lyndon Baines Johnson (1963-69), 36th president, Democrat, was born on Aug. 27, 1908, near Stonewall, TX, the son of Rebekah Baines Johnson and Sam Ealy Johnson, a state legislator. He graduated from Southwest Texas State Teachers College in 1930, with formative experience as a student teacher of underprivileged Mexican-American students in a segregated school, and briefly attended Georgetown Univ. Law School. He served as secretary to a congressman and in 1935 became director of the Texas branch of the New Deal National Youth Administration. In 1937 he won an election to fill a vacancy in Congress; he was subsequently elected to five full terms. During 1941-42 he also served in the Navy.

Johnson won a U.S. Senate seat after a close 1948 primary widely regarded as marred by fraud. After reelection in 1954, he served as a skillful Senate majority leader. Elected vice president in 1960 on the ticket headed by Sen. John Kennedy, he succeeded to the presidency when Kennedy was assassinated. He was elected to a full term in 1964, defeating Sen. Barry Goldwater (R, AZ) in a landslide.

As president Johnson won passage of landmark civil rights, anti-poverty, education (Head Start), and health care (Medicare, Medicaid) legislation—the "Great Society" program. However, in the face of objections to his escalation of the Vietnam war, he declined to seek another term. Johnson died on Jan. 22, 1973, at his ranch in Stonewall, TX.

Richard Milhous Nixon (1969-74), 37th president, Republican, was born on Jan. 9, 1913, in Yorba Linda, CA, the son of Francis Anthony and Hannah Milhous Nixon. He graduated from Whittier College in 1934 and from Duke Univ. Law School in 1937. After practicing law and working in the Office of Price Administration he joined the Navy, serving in the Pacific. Elected to the U.S. House in 1946 and 1948, he played a central role in spearheading the prosecution of suspected Communist spy Alger Hiss. Nixon was elected to the Senate in 1950 and served as vice president under Dwight Eisenhower (1953-61). He first ran for president in 1960, narrowly losing to John F. Kennedy, and ran unsuccessfully for governor of California in 1962. In 1968 he was elected president, defeating Vice Pres. Hubert Humphrey (D).

As president, Nixon appointed four Supreme Court justices, including the chief justice, moving the court to the right. He sought to shift greater responsibility to state and local governments, while also supporting broad federal initiatives such as creation of the Office of Management and Budget and the Environmental Protection Agency. The economy suffered periods of high unemployment and inflation, and he imposed wage and price controls in 1971.

In foreign affairs, Nixon dramatically altered relations with China, which he visited in 1972—the first U.S. president to do so. With adviser Henry Kissinger, he pursued détente with the Soviet Union, signing major arms limitation treaties and increasing trade. While beginning a gradual withdrawal from Vietnam, he ordered an incursion into Cambodia (1970) and the bombing of Hanoi and mining of Haiphong Harbor (1972). Reelected by a large majority in Nov. 1972, he secured a Vietnam cease-fire in Jan. 1973.

Nixon's second term was cut short by scandal, after disclosures relating to a June 1972 burglary of Democratic Party headquarters in the Watergate office complex. The courts and Congress sought tapes of Nixon's office conversations; Nixon claimed executive privilege, but the Supreme Court ruled against him. In July 1974, the House Judiciary Committee recommended adoption of impeachment articles charging obstruction of justice, abuse of power, and contempt of Congress. On Aug. 5, he released transcripts of conversations that linked him to cover-up activities. Nixon resigned on Aug. 9, becoming the first president ever to do so.

In later years, Nixon emerged as an elder statesman. He died Apr. 22, 1994, in New York City.

Gerald Rudolph Ford (1974-77), 38th president, Republican, was born on July 14, 1913, in Omaha, NE, the son of Leslie and Dorothy Gardner King, and was named Leslie Lynch King Jr. His parents divorced in Dec. 1913, and in 1917 his mother married Grand Rapids, MI, businessman Gerald R. Ford, whose name the future president ultimately took. He graduated from Univ. of Michigan in 1935 and Yale Law School in 1941. In 1942, he joined the Navy, serving in the Pacific. He won election in 1948 to the U.S. House, where he served for 25 years, eight of them as Republican leader.

On Oct. 12, 1973, after Vice Pres. Spiro Agnew resigned in a corruption scandal, Pres. Nixon nominated Ford to replace him, in the first use of procedures set out in the 25th Amendment (ratified 1967). When Nixon resigned, in Aug. 1974, Ford succeeded him; he was the only president never elected either to the presidency or to the vice presidency.

Ford was widely credited with helping rebuild morale after the Nixon presidency, though his pardoning of Nixon for any federal crimes in office was controversial. He vetoed 48 bills in his first 21 months in office, mostly in the interest of fighting high inflation; he was less successful in curbing high unemployment. Ford was narrowly defeated in the 1976 election. He died Dec. 26, 2006, at home in Rancho Mirage, CA.

James Earl (Jimmy) Carter (1977-81), 39th president, Democrat, was the first president from the Deep South since before the Civil War. He was born on Oct. 1, 1924, in Plains, GA, the son of James and Lillian Gordy Carter. Carter graduated from the U.S. Naval Academy in 1946 and in 1952 entered the Navy's nuclear submarine program as an aide to Capt. (later Adm.) Hyman Rickover. Carter left the Navy to take over the family peanut farming businesses after his father's death in 1953. He served in the Georgia state senate (1963-67) and as governor of Georgia (1971-75). In 1976, he won the Democratic presidential nomination and defeated Pres. Gerald Ford to win the presidency.

On taking office, Carter pardoned Vietnam draft evaders. He played a major role in negotiations leading to the 1979 peace treaty between Israel and Egypt and reached treaties with Panama ending U.S. control of the Panama Canal, effective in 2000. Carter was widely blamed, however, for the poor state of the economy and viewed by some as weak in handling foreign policy. In Nov. 1979, Iranian student militants attacked the U.S. embassy in Tehran and held 52 members of the embassy staff as hostages; efforts to obtain their release became a major preoccupation of the administration. He responded to the Soviet invasion of Afghanistan (Dec. 1979) by imposing a grain embargo and boycotting the 1980 Moscow Olympics.

Carter was defeated by Ronald Reagan in the 1980 election. The hostages in Iran were finally released on inauguration day, 1981, just after Reagan officially became president. After leaving office, Carter played an active role in diplomatic and humanitarian efforts around the world, especially through the Carter Center, which he founded with his wife, Rosalynn, in 1982. He was awarded the Nobel Peace Prize in 2002. In Feb. 2023 he began home hospice care.

Ronald Wilson Reagan (1981-89), 40th president, Republican, was born on Feb. 6, 1911, in Tampico, IL, the son of John Edward and Nellie Wilson Reagan. After graduating from Eureka College, he worked as a sports announcer in Des Moines, IA. In 1937 he began a career as a Hollywood movie actor. He served in the Army Air Force during World War II, making training films, and after the war became president of the Screen Actors Guild. Reagan served two terms as California governor (1967-75). He won a landslide victory in the 1980 presidential election and was reelected in 1984. He was shot and seriously wounded in an assassination attempt in 1981.

As president Reagan forged a bipartisan coalition in Congress, which led to enactment of large-scale tax cuts, cutbacks in government programs, and a major increase in defense spending. In 1982, the U.S. joined in maintaining a peacekeeping force in Beirut, Lebanon; the next year Reagan sent a task force to invade Grenada after two Marxist coups on the island. Reagan ordered airstrikes on Libyan military installations in 1986, after Libyan agents bombed a nightclub in West Berlin, Germany.

Reagan held four summit meetings with Soviet leader Mikhail Gorbachev and signed a major arms-reduction treaty with the Soviet Union in 1987. He also strongly supported anti-Communist governments and forces around the world. In 1986, it was revealed that the U.S. had secretly sold weapons to Iran in exchange for the release of U.S. hostages held in Lebanon and that some of the proceeds had been illegally diverted to anti-Communist contras in Nicaragua. The scandal led to the resignation of leading White House aides, but no proof was found that Reagan himself was involved. As Reagan left office the nation was experiencing its sixth consecutive year of GDP growth, though also piling up large budget deficits.

In 1994, Reagan revealed that he was suffering from Alzheimer's disease. He died on June 5, 2004, in Los Angeles, CA, from complications of the disease.

George Herbert Walker Bush (1989-93), 41st president, Republican, was born June 12, 1924, in Milton, MA, the son of U.S. Sen. Prescott Bush (R, CT, 1952-63) and Dorothy Walker Bush. He was shot down over the Pacific as a Navy pilot in World War II and was awarded the Distinguished Flying Cross. After graduating from Yale Univ. in 1948, he settled in Texas, where he helped found an oil company.

He lost a 1964 U.S. Senate race but was elected to two U.S. House terms, in 1966 and 1968. After losing a second Senate race, he served as U.S. ambassador to the UN, head of the U.S. Liaison Office in Beijing, and director of the CIA. Following an unsuccessful bid for the 1980 GOP presidential nomination, Bush became Ronald Reagan's running mate, and served two terms as vice president (1981-89).

In 1988, Bush defeated Gov. Michael Dukakis (D, MA) to win the presidency. He faced severe budget deficits, struggled with military cutbacks, and vetoed abortion-rights legislation. In 1990 he agreed to a deficit-reduction plan that included tax hikes, despite a campaign promise to the contrary. He success-fully appointed two justices to the U.S. Supreme Court, David Souter and Clarence Thomas; the latter was confirmed after 1991 hearings in which he was accused of sexual harassment.

Abroad, Bush supported Soviet reforms, Eastern Europe democratization, and good relations with Beijing. In Dec. 1989, he sent troops to Panama, where they overthrew the government and captured dictator Manuel Noriega. Reacting to Iraq's Aug. 1990 invasion of Kuwait, Bush assembled a broad U.S.-led, UN-backed Allied force which retook Kuwait (Feb. 1991) after a month-long air war and four-day ground assault. But the coalition did not seek to drive Iraqi leader Saddam Hussein from power. The quick victory, with extremely light U.S. casualties, gave Bush then-record-high approval ratings, but his popularity plummeted as the economy slipped into recession. He was defeated by Bill Clinton in the 1992 election.

Bush saw his son George W. Bush inaugurated as the 43rd president in 2001. He died Nov. 30, 2018, at home in Houston, TX.

William Jefferson (Bill) Clinton (1993-2001), 42nd president, Democrat, was born Aug. 19, 1946, in Hope, AR, son of William Blythe and Virginia Cassidy Blythe, and was named William Jefferson Blythe IV. Blythe died in an auto accident before his son was born; his widow married Roger Clinton, whose last name Bill Clinton took. Clinton earned his undergraduate degree from Georgetown Univ. in 1968. While attending Oxford Univ. as a Rhodes scholar, he legally avoided the draft, according to some critics by misleading his draft board. Clinton worked on George McGovern's 1972 presidential campaign and earned a degree from Yale Law School in 1973. He taught at the Univ. of Arkansas law school until 1976, when he was elected state attorney general. In 1978 he was elected governor, becoming the nation's youngest at the time. Though defeated for reelection in 1980, he was returned to office several times thereafter. He married law school classmate Hillary Rodham in 1975; their daughter Chelsea was born in 1980.

Positioning himself as a centrist "New Democrat" in a crowded field, Clinton won the party's 1992 presidential nomination and was elected president, defeating Pres. George H. W. Bush and independent Ross Perot. In 1993, he won passage of a deficit reduction measure and congressional approval of the North American Free Trade Agreement. In 1994 he won passage of a stringent anti-crime bill, which became controversial over time. A plan for major health care reform legislation died in Congress. The administration did not intervene in 1994 as a massive genocide was committed in Rwanda. In 1995 Clinton sent troops to Bosnia to help implement a peace settlement there.

Buoyed by a strong economy, Clinton easily won reelection in 1996. He achieved federal budget surpluses in several years. Clinton was cleared of involvement in improprieties by associates in the Whitewater land-development venture, but investigation into the matter turned up evidence of a sexual relationship between Clinton and a White House intern. In 1998, he was impeached by the House, charged with perjury and obstruction of justice in an attempted cover-up of the affair. He was acquitted in a Senate trial, but in a separate proceeding agreed to certain penalties. In 1999 the U.S. joined other NATO nations in an aerial bombing campaign that induced Serbia to withdraw troops from Kosovo, where they had been terrorizing ethnic Albanians.

After leaving office, Clinton actively supported his wife's political career. He also founded what became the Bill, Hillary and Chelsea Clinton Foundation.

George Walker Bush (2001-09), 43rd president, Republican, was born on July 6, 1946, in New Haven, CT. He was the oldest of six children born to the 41st president, George Herbert Walker Bush, and the former Barbara Pierce. He became the first son of a former president to take office as president since John Quincy Adams in 1825.

Bush grew up in Midland and Houston, TX. He attended Phillips Academy in Andover, MA, and graduated from Yale Univ. in 1968. After serving with the Texas Air National Guard and earning an MBA from Harvard, he returned to Midland, where he went into the oil business. In 1977 he married Laura Welch, a librarian; they had twin daughters, Barbara and Jenna, in 1981. After aiding his father's winning 1988 presidential campaign, he became managing partner of the Texas Rangers baseball team. He was elected governor of Texas in 1994 and reelected in 1998. In 2000, Bush and running mate Dick Cheney defeated the Democratic ticket led by Vice Pres. Al Gore, in one of the closest-ever U.S. presidential elections. The result was not settled until a mid-Dec. Supreme Court ruling left Florida's crucial electoral votes in Bush's column.

Pres. Bush called his governing philosophy "compassionate conservatism." During his first term he won passage of two major tax cuts, the No Child Left Behind education bill, and a Medicare reform bill addressing prescription drug coverage, and he pioneered a major U.S. initiative to fight the AIDS epidemic, especially targeting Africa.

But Bush's first term was dominated by the Sept. 11, 2001, terrorist attack on the U.S. and the nation's response. In Oct. 2001, he signed the controversial USA Patriot Act, greatly expanding surveillance powers of the federal government, and created what became the U.S. Dept. of Homeland Security. Abroad, the U.S. military, aided by allies, deposed Afghanistan's Taliban regime, which was sheltering al-Qaeda terrorists. A new government that restored liberties but was condemned for corruption sought to hold off Taliban insurgents, with U.S. aid. Meanwhile, an operation to capture al-Qaeda leader Osama bin Laden, architect of the Sept. 11 attack, failed when he escaped to Pakistan. In 2003 the U.S., aided mainly by UK forces, launched an air and ground war against Iraq and deposed its autocratic leader, Saddam Hussein. However, no evidence was found that Hussein's regime had developed weapons of mass destruction, the key rationale for the war. A new Iraqi government was formed in June 2004, but insurgent violence and U.S. troop casualties continued.

Reelected in 2004, Bush pressed unsuccessfully for Social Security and immigration reforms, and his administration drew criticism for its response to Hurricane Katrina in 2005. He won Senate confirmation for John Roberts (2005) as Supreme Court chief justice and Samuel Alito (2006) as associate justice. After Democrats won majorities in 2006 midterm elections, Bush accepted the resignation of Defense Sec. Donald Rumsfeld, a target of widespread criticism over the Iraq war. Two months later, Bush announced a "surge" in U.S. troop strength in Iraq; a sharp drop in casualties ensued, aided by a shift in alliances. In 2008, the administration reached an agreement with Iraq allowing U.S. troops to remain there through 2011. But the Taliban was gaining strength in Afghanistan, and the Bush administration was damaged by revelations of prisoner abuse and extreme interrogation methods.

The U.S. economy fell into recession in Dec. 2007; Bush and congressional leaders responded with a $168-bil stimulus plan. Problems in home finance and credit markets triggered a deep economic crisis by Sept. 2008. The Treasury Dept. bailed out mortgage finance firms Fannie Mae and Freddie Mac, investment bank Lehman Bros. filed for bankruptcy, and the Federal Reserve rescued insurance giant AIG with a line of credit reaching $144 bil. An administration-backed plan to buy up to $700 bil in devalued mortgage-related assets cleared Congress in Oct., after a severe stock market plunge bolstered support.

In retirement Bush published a memoir, a biography of his father, and two books featuring his own paintings of U.S. war veterans and immigrants. He did not vote for GOP nominee Donald Trump in 2016 or 2020.

Barack Hussein Obama (2009-17), 44th president, Democrat, was born Aug. 4, 1961, in Honolulu, HI, son of Barack Obama Sr., a Black Kenyan, and Stanley Ann Dunham, a white American. They divorced, and after his mother remarried, he lived in Indonesia with his mother and stepfather; he also lived for a time with his maternal grandparents in Hawaii, where he attended high school. Obama graduated from Columbia Univ. (1983) and, after working as a community organizer in Chicago, earned a law degree from Harvard Univ. (1991). He practiced civil rights law in Chicago and taught at the Univ. of Chicago Law School. In 1992, he married attorney Michelle Robinson; they have two daughters, Malia (b. 1998) and Sasha (b. 2001).

Obama served eight years (1997-2004) in the Illinois state senate. He wrote a 1995 memoir, *Dreams From My Father*, and gave the keynote address at the 2004 Democratic National Convention. Elected to the U.S. Senate that year, he won the Democratic nomination for president in 2008, stressing opposition to the Iraq war and a message of "hope and change," and was elected the nation's first Black president.

Awarded the 2009 Nobel Peace Prize, Pres. Obama gradually pulled U.S. troops from Iraq, though U.S. forces were reintroduced in noncombat roles as sectarian strife heightened. With Taliban gaining ground in Afghanistan, he authorized a surge in U.S. forces there, aimed at creating conditions for a handover to the Afghan government; he also stepped up drone strikes against Islamist militants abroad. In May 2011, al-Qaeda leader Osama bin Laden was killed in a U.S. raid on his hideout in Pakistan. Soon after, Obama began reducing U.S. forces in Afghanistan. The U.S. joined in NATO airstrikes leading to the overthrow of Libyan dictator Muammar al-Qaddafi, but rival militias refused to disarm and U.S. personnel were killed in a 2012 attack by Islamist radicals on a U.S. consulate in Benghazi.

The administration won passage of a $787-bil economic stimulus package early in 2009, and the U.S. pulled out of recession, though growth was modest. In Mar. 2010, Obama won passage of his signature health care reform bill ("Obamacare"). Democrats lost their House majority in Nov. 2010 elections, limiting Obama's legislative agenda. In 2012, he signed an executive order suspending deportations for most young undocumented immigrants ("dreamers") who came to the U.S. as children. Among other initiatives, his administration finalized regulations tightening fuel emission standards for motor vehicles. After Obama was reelected in Nov. 2012, a compromise in Congress averted a year-end "fiscal cliff" by making expiring G.W. Bush-era tax cuts permanent for most people. Battles over the federal budget, debt ceiling, and Obamacare funding continued.

Abroad, Russian forces annexed Crimea in 2014 and lent support to pro-Russian separatists in eastern Ukraine; Obama joined Europe in imposing economic sanctions. He called for an end to the repressive regime of Syria's Bashar al-Assad, but when Assad's forces apparently launched a chemical weapons attack on civilians, crossing what Obama had called a "red line," he agreed to a Russian-brokered disarmament pact with the regime. After the Sunni militant group Islamic State in Iraq and Syria (ISIS) took over large areas of both countries, proclaiming an Islamic "caliphate" in June 2014 and terrorizing dissenters and religious minorities, Obama sent military advisers. He also authorized U.S. airstrikes against ISIS and eventually provided arms to Syrian rebels.

After 2014 midterm elections, which left Republicans controlling both houses of Congress, Obama issued an executive order expanding protection of undocumented immigrants from deportation, but it was blocked in court. His administration introduced a plan to reduce carbon pollution from power plants and he signed onto the Paris Agreement aimed at global reductions in greenhouse gas emissions. The administration also restored relations with Cuba and entered a multination accord with Iran intended to curb Iranian nuclear weapons development for a time, in return for eased economic sanctions. In Dec. 2014, Obama declared an end to U.S. combat in Afghanistan, limiting U.S. forces to a support role, but he dropped plans for a full withdrawal.

Responding to a 2012 mass shooting at Sandy Hook Elementary School in Newtown, CT, Obama called unsuccessfully for federal gun control legislation. He also confronted racial violence (as in the 2015 massacre at a Black church in Charleston, SC) and racial tensions over the deaths of Black people in encounters with police (as in Ferguson, MO, 2014). After the

death of Supreme Court Justice Antonin Scalia in early 2016, Senate Republicans refused to hold a confirmation hearing for Obama's nominee to replace him, contending it was too near the presidential election.

The first volume of Obama's two-part memoir was published in 2020. The Chicago-based Obama Foundation, founded in 2014, was overseeing creation of the Obama Presidential Center in Chicago.

Donald John Trump (2017-21), 45th president, Republican, was born June 14, 1946, in Queens, NY, the son of Frederick C. Trump, a wealthy real estate developer, and Mary Anne MacLeod Trump, a Scottish immigrant. From age 13 he attended a military boarding school. After earning a bachelor's degree from the Wharton School (1968), he joined the family real estate business. Trump spearheaded an expansion of New York City holdings and developed casinos in Atlantic City, NJ, though those eventually failed. He coauthored business-advice books, hosted two reality TV series (2008-15), and licensed his name to enterprises around the world. Trump's net worth in mid-2023 was estimated by *Forbes* at $2.5 bil, down from $3.2 bil in fall 2022, due mainly to his weak social media business.

After two marriages that ended in divorce, Trump married Melania Knauss in 2005. Their son, Barron, was born in 2006. He also had two sons, Donald Jr. (b. 1977) and Eric (b. 1984), and a daughter, Ivanka (b. 1981), from his first marriage, and a daughter, Tiffany (b. 1993), from his second. As president he surrendered control, but not ownership, of the Trump Organization to his elder sons.

In his 2015-16 campaign for the presidency, Trump portrayed himself as an outsider who would "make America great again." His provocative rhetoric at rallies and in tweets—which he continued in the White House and afterward—energized supporters, and he won nomination over a crowded field. Accusations of sexual misconduct and evidence of his crude remarks about women dogged but did not derail his fall campaign. He defeated former Sec. of State Hillary Clinton (D), though she received more of the popular vote.

Promptly after inauguration, Pres. Trump issued executive orders to ban immigration from seven Muslim-majority nations (upheld by the Supreme Court as later modified) and plan for a wall along the U.S.-Mexican border. His administration instituted a "remain in Mexico" policy for migrants awaiting U.S. asylum (ended under Pres. Biden after legal battle) and sought unsuccessfully to end the Obama-era DACA program, which temporarily protected many undocumented immigrants who had arrived in the U.S. as minors. Reports of inhumane conditions at migrant detention centers, and of children separated from parents, generated much criticism. In 2017, Trump controversially fired FBI director James Comey, who had led a probe into Russian interference in the 2016 presidential election; former FBI director Robert Mueller was appointed as special counsel to oversee the probe. The Mueller report, released Mar. 2019, found there had been Russian interference and possible obstruction of justice by Trump but did not take a position on charging him with a crime.

Abroad, Trump cultivated ties with Russian Pres. Vladimir Putin, met cordially with North Korean leader Kim Jong Un, and intensified U.S. support for Israel. In 2018 he announced U.S. withdrawal from a 2015 multination nuclear deal with Iran; as a counterweight to Iran, the U.S. aided Saudi Arabia in its intervention in the Yemen civil war. In Feb. 2020, the U.S. signed an accord with the Taliban, providing for a phased U.S. withdrawal from Afghanistan, to be completed by May 2021, along with separate intra-Afghan talks, which failed; release of imprisoned Taliban; and a Taliban pledge not to allow threats to security of the U.S. and its allies.

In Dec. 2017 Trump signed a measure lowering income tax rates; in early 2018 he reluctantly signed a federal budget bill, negotiated with Democrats, that set high spending levels and raised the debt ceiling. Support for Trump's impeachment grew after allegations that he had pressured Ukraine to investigate former Vice Pres. Joe Biden and his son, Hunter Biden, by withholding military aid. After congressional hearings at which officials alleged an illicit quid pro quo, the full House, with no Republican support, passed two articles of impeachment, which failed in the Senate.

During Trump's first three years in office the unemployment rate hit historically low levels, but the trend was reversed by the COVID-19 pandemic. The administration limited travel from China, and later from Europe, as health systems became overwhelmed. Trump created a coronavirus task force and promoted successful efforts to develop vaccines, but he often downplayed the role of preventive measures and was accused of spreading misinformation.

The death in May 2020 of a Black man, George Floyd, caused by a white Minneapolis police officer, gave rise to widespread protests against systemic racism and police brutality. Trump disputed or downplayed protesters' grievances, while citing instances of looting and arson.

The Trump administration halted or reversed many environmental regulations and withdrew from the Paris Agreement on climate change. Trump also appointed many conservative-leaning judges to federal courts, including Neil Gorsuch (2017), Brett Kavanaugh (2018), and Amy Coney Barrett (2020) to the Supreme Court.

Former Vice Pres. Biden defeated Trump in Nov. 2020 by an Electoral College vote of 306-232, but Trump claimed victory, despite the dismissal of his suits challenging state vote counts. On Jan. 6, 2021, energized by a Trump rally, a mob invaded the Capitol in an unsuccessful attempt to intimidate Vice Pres. Mike Pence and Congress into rejecting the presidential election certification. The House voted Jan. 13, 2021, to impeach Trump for "incitement to insurrection"; the Senate vote to convict a month later was 57-43, falling short of the needed two-thirds majority. A House select committee later charged that Trump had spurred the attack and pressured officials to put forward fake electors.

In Nov. 2022, Trump announced he would again be a candidate for a second term as president. In 2023, Trump was indicted in four criminal cases; he was the first former president ever indicted. A New York case alleged criminal acts to cover up hush-money payments during the 2016 campaign. A federal indictment in Florida accused Trump of retaining classified documents after leaving office and obstructing government efforts to reclaim them. Two other indictments arose directly from Trump's actions challenging the 2020 election: a federal case charged him with conspiracy to defraud the U.S. and obstruct an official proceeding, and a Georgia state prosecutor brought a racketeering case against Trump and 18 allies for an array of actions aimed at overturning election results. Trials were expected to begin during the 2024 election year.

Joseph Robinette Biden Jr. (2021-), 46th president, Democrat, was born Nov. 20, 1942, in Scranton, PA, the oldest of four children in a middle-class Irish Catholic family. His parents were Joseph Robinette Biden Sr., a businessman, and Catherine Eugenia Finnegan. He graduated from the Univ. of Delaware (1965) and earned a law degree from Syracuse Univ. (1968). Biden worked as a public defender in Wilmington, DE, where he also served on the New Castle County Council, before winning a U.S. Senate seat from Delaware in Nov. 1972. In a car crash the next month, his wife, Neilia Hunter Biden (m. 1966), and infant daughter Naomi were killed, and their sons Beau (b. 1969) and Hunter (b. 1970) were seriously injured. In 1977 he married Jill Tracy Jacobs, an English teacher; they had a daughter, Ashley (b. 1981)

Biden won reelection to the Senate six times. He famously commuted regularly from Delaware to DC. As chair of the Judiciary Committee, he presided over contentious Supreme Court nomination hearings that ended in the defeat of Robert Bork's

nomination (1987) and in Clarence Thomas's confirmation (1991). He was known for often working with Republicans on legislation. In 1987, Biden ran for the 1988 Democratic presidential nomination but withdrew, damaged by charges of plagiarism in a speech. He dropped out of the 2008 nomination battle after the Iowa caucus, but Obama selected him as his running mate. As vice president, Biden worked closely with Obama, serving as his liaison to Congress. He decided against a 2016 run for president, citing bereavement over the recent death of his son Beau, but in 2020 he won the nomination over a wide field of rivals and defeated incumbent Pres. Trump in Nov.

In office, Biden signed executive orders that reversed Trump administration policies on immigration, the environment (recommitted to the 2016 Paris Agreement on climate change goals), and other issues. He gained passage of a $1.9-tril COVID relief bill, opposed by Republicans as inflationary, and a scaled-back bipartisan $1.2-tril infrastructure bill. In Aug. 2022, he signed a major health, tax, and clean energy bill, passed in a party line vote after long negotiations. The administration expanded COVID vaccine supply and access and stressed other preventative measures, but new variants, vaccination resistance, and controversy or confusion over other preventive measures contributed to persistence of the pandemic, which killed more than a million Americans by mid-2022, before starting to show declines.

In June 2022, shortly after mass shootings in a Buffalo, NY, grocery store and an Uvalde, TX, elementary school, Pres. Biden signed a bipartisan federal gun control measure—the first in decades—though it fell short of his objectives. He condemned a series of Supreme Court rulings decided by a conservative majority, including the 2022 decision that ruled abortion was not a constitutional right and reversed *Roe v. Wade* (1973). Biden's successful nomination of Ketanji Brown Jackson as the first Black female Supreme Court justice did not change the Court's ideological composition.

Abroad, Biden sought to revive a 2015 nuclear deal with Iran. He declared an end to U.S. support for a Saudi-led bombing campaign against Iranian-backed rebels in Yemen but sought to repair ties with Saudi Arabia, despite human rights concerns. Biden kept to a U.S. commitment to total U.S. troop withdrawal from the long war in Afghanistan, adopting Aug. 31, 2021, as a deferred but fixed deadline, despite rapid Taliban advances as the Afghan government collapsed. Amid chaos at the Kabul airport, heightened by a terrorist bombing, over 120,000 people were evacuated, but many Afghans who had helped the U.S. were left behind. Later, al-Qaeda leader Ayman al-Zawahiri, apparently sheltered by Taliban, was located by U.S. intelligence and killed by a drone strike. In Dec. 2021 the U.S. officially ended its combat role in Iraq.

After Russia launched a massive invasion of Ukraine in Feb. 2022, Biden had already vowed not to send troops, but he rallied NATO support for economic sanctions on Russia and sent financial aid and weaponry to assist in Ukraine's defense as the war dragged on, with massive effects on the world economy and U.S.-Russian relations. U.S.-China relations grew more tense after a visit to Taiwan by U.S. House Speaker Nancy Pelosi and a decision by the Biden administration to seek congressional authorization for over $1 bil in new arms sales to Taiwan. In Feb. 2023, Biden ordered a Chinese high-altitude spy balloon shot down after it had transited the U.S.

The administration saw strong job growth through mid-2023 and had to contend with historically high inflation along with the threat of recession. In May 2023, Biden negotiated a compromise on the debt ceiling with House Speaker Kevin McCarthy (R); the terms raised concerns on both left and right, but it passed in Congress with comfortable margins, avoiding a default.

In Jan. 2023 Attorney Gen. Merrick Garland appointed a special counsel to investigate Biden's retention and storage of classified documents; Biden indicated the documents had been inadvertently misplaced and pledged to cooperate with the probe. In Apr. 2023 he announced he would be a candidate for reelection. He was the clear front runner for the nomination, though vulnerable because of his age and legal controversies related to the activities of his son Hunter Biden.

Presidential Rankings, 2021

Source: C-SPAN

As assessed by historians and other professional observers of the presidency, 142 of whom participated in the 2021 survey. Participants rated each president on 10 qualities of presidential leadership; rankings here reflect overall score.

2021 rank	President	2017 rank	2009 rank	2000 rank	2021 rank	President	2017 rank	2009 rank	2000 rank
1.	Abraham Lincoln	1	1	1	23.	William Howard Taft	24	24	24
2.	George Washington	2	2	3	24.	Calvin Coolidge	26	26	27
3.	Franklin D. Roosevelt	3	3	2	25.	Grover Cleveland	23	21	17
4.	Theodore Roosevelt	4	4	4	26.	Jimmy Carter	27	25	22
5.	Dwight D. Eisenhower	5	8	9	27.	James A. Garfield	29	28	29
6.	Harry S. Truman	6	5	5	28.	Gerald R. Ford	25	22	23
7.	Thomas Jefferson	7	7	7	29.	George W. Bush	33	36	NA
8.	John F. Kennedy	8	6	8	30.	Chester A. Arthur	35	32	32
9.	Ronald Reagan	9	10	11	31.	Richard M. Nixon	28	27	26
10.	Barack Obama	12	NA	NA	32.	Benjamin Harrison	30	30	31
11.	Lyndon B. Johnson	10	11	10	33.	Rutherford B. Hayes	31	33	25
12.	James Monroe	13	15	14	34.	Martin Van Buren	34	31	30
13.	Woodrow Wilson	11	9	6	35.	Zachary Taylor	32	29	28
14.	William McKinley	16	16	15	36.	Herbert Hoover	36	34	34
15.	John Adams	19	17	16	37.	Warren G. Harding	40	38	38
16.	James Madison	17	20	18	38.	Millard Fillmore	37	37	35
17.	John Quincy Adams	21	19	19	39.	John Tyler	39	35	36
18.	James K. Polk	14	12	12	40.	William Henry Harrison	38	39	37
19.	William J. Clinton	15	14	21	41.	Donald J. Trump	NA	NA	NA
20.	Ulysses S. Grant	22	23	33	42.	Franklin Pierce	41	40	39
21.	George H. W. Bush	20	18	20	43.	Andrew Johnson	42	41	40
22.	Andrew Jackson	18	13	13	44.	James Buchanan	43	42	41

NA = Not applicable.

Presidential Facts

Oldest president: Joe Biden, who was 78 when he took office

Longest-living president: Jimmy Carter, who on Mar. 22, 2019, reached the age of 94 years and 172 days old, surpassing George H. W. Bush, who died at the age of 94 years, 171 days

Youngest president: Theodore Roosevelt, who was 42 when sworn in after McKinley's death

Youngest person elected president: John F. Kennedy, who was 43 when elected in 1960

Tallest president: Abraham Lincoln, who was 6 feet, 4 inches

Shortest president: James Madison, who was 5 feet, 4 inches

Heaviest president: William Howard Taft, who was 332 pounds in 1911

First president to live in the White House: John Adams, who moved there in 1800

First president whose parents were immigrants: Andrew Jackson; his parents emigrated from Ireland in 1765

First president born a U.S. citizen: Martin Van Buren, in Kinderhook, NY, 1782

First president born outside the original colonies: Abraham Lincoln, in Kentucky, 1809

First president born west of the Mississippi: Herbert Hoover, in West Branch, IA, 1874

Most common presidential home state: Virginia, with 8 presidents

First president born in a hospital: Jimmy Carter, in Plains, GA, 1924

First president to have a telephone in the White House: Rutherford B. Hayes, in 1879

First president to travel outside U.S. while in office: Theodore Roosevelt visited Panama Canal site, 1906

First president to address the nation on radio: Warren G. Harding, in 1922

First president to appear on TV: Franklin D. Roosevelt, at opening ceremonies for the 1939 World's Fair

First president to give a live, televised news conference: John F. Kennedy, in 1961

First president to hold an internet chat: Bill Clinton, in 1999

Presidents who lost the popular vote while winning election: John Quincy Adams, in 1824 (elected by the House after general election failed to produce a majority); Rutherford B. Hayes, in 1876; Benjamin Harrison, in 1888; George W. Bush, in 2000; Donald J. Trump, in 2016. (Popular vote totals before 1824 are unknown.)

Only presidents chosen by the House of Representatives: Thomas Jefferson (1st term) and John Quincy Adams

Only president never elected either president or vice president: Gerald Ford; named vice president when Spiro Agnew resigned (1973), became president when Nixon resigned (1974)

Only president who never previously held government or military office: Donald J. Trump

Left-handed presidents: James Garfield, Herbert Hoover, Harry Truman, Gerald Ford, Ronald Reagan, George H. W. Bush, Bill Clinton, and Barack Obama

First Catholic president: John F. Kennedy; the most common religious affiliations have been Episcopalian (11) and Presbyterian (9)

Only bachelor presidents: James Buchanan, who never married, and Grover Cleveland, who married Frances Folsom in the White House in 1886

First divorced president: Ronald Reagan; divorced from Jane Wyman in 1948, married Nancy Davis in 1952

Only president indicted on criminal charges: Donald Trump, in 2023

Presidents who died on July 4: John Adams and Thomas Jefferson (both 1826) and James Monroe (1831)

First Lady Jill Biden

Jill Biden was born June 3, 1951, in Hammonton, NJ. She graduated from Univ. of Delaware (1975) and had a career as an educator, while earning advanced degrees that ultimately included a doctorate in educational leadership (2007). After an early marriage ended in divorce she married then-Sen. Joe Biden, a widower, in 1977, becoming stepmother to his two sons, Beau and Hunter. The Bidens' daughter, Ashley, was born in 1981. After Biden took office in 2021, she balanced her career as a professor of writing with her role as first lady, in which she promoted community college education, support for military families, cancer research, and COVID vaccination. In May 2022 she met with Ukrainian refugees and visited Ukraine itself, where she met with Ukraine's first lady.

Spouses and Children of the Presidents

Name (born-died; married)	Birth-place	Sons/daughters	Name (born-died; married)	Birth-place	Sons/daughters
Martha Dandridge Custis Washington (1731-1802; 1759)	VA	None	Ida Saxton McKinley (1847-1907; 1871)	OH	0/2
Abigail Smith Adams (1744-1818; 1764)	MA	3/2	Alice Hathaway Lee Roosevelt (1861-84; 1880)	MA	0/1
Martha Wayles Skelton Jefferson (1748-82; 1772)	VA	1/5	Edith Kermit Carow Roosevelt (1861-1948; 1886)	CT	4/1
Dolley Payne Todd Madison (1768-1849; 1794)	NC	None	Helen Herron Taft (1861-1943; 1886)	OH	2/1
Elizabeth Kortright Monroe (1768-1830; 1786)	NY	1/2	Ellen Louise Axson Wilson (1860-1914; 1885)	GA	0/3
Louisa Catherine Johnson Adams (1775-1852; 1797)	Eng.[1]	3/1	Edith Bolling Galt Wilson (1872-1961; 1915)	VA	None
Rachel Donelson Robards Jackson (1767-1828; 1791)	VA	1/0[2]	Florence Kling De Wolfe Harding (1860-1924; 1891)	OH	None
Hannah Hoes Van Buren (1783-1819; 1807)	NY	4/0	Grace Anna Goodhue Coolidge (1879-1957; 1905)	VT	2/0
Anna Tuthill Symmes Harrison (1775-1864; 1795)	NJ	6/4	Lou Henry Hoover (1875-1944; 1899)	IA	2/0
Letitia Christian Tyler (1790-1842; 1813)	VA	3/5	Anna Eleanor Roosevelt (1884-1962; 1905)	NY	5/1
Julia Gardiner Tyler (1820-89; 1844)	NY	5/2	Elizabeth Virginia (Bess) Wallace Truman (1885-1982; 1919)	MO	0/1
Sarah Childress Polk (1803-91; 1824)	TN	None	Mamie Geneva Doud Eisenhower (1896-1979; 1916)	IA	2/0
Margaret (Peggy) Mackall Smith Taylor (1788-1852; 1810)	MD	1/5	Jacqueline Lee Bouvier Kennedy (1929-94; 1953)	NY	2/1
Abigail Powers Fillmore (1798-1853; 1826)	NY	1/1	Claudia (Lady Bird) Alta Taylor Johnson (1912-2007; 1934)	TX	0/2
Caroline Carmichael McIntosh Fillmore (1813-81; 1858)	NJ	None	Thelma Catherine Patricia Ryan Nixon (1912-93; 1940)	NV	0/2
Jane Means Appleton Pierce (1806-63; 1834)	NH	3/0	Elizabeth (Betty) Bloomer Warren Ford (1918-2011; 1948)	IL	3/1
Mary Todd Lincoln (1818-82; 1842)	KY	4/0	Eleanor Rosalynn Smith Carter (1927- ; 1946)	GA	3/1
Eliza McCardle Johnson (1810-76; 1827)	TN	3/2	Anne Frances (Nancy) Robbins Davis Reagan (1921-2016; 1952)	NY	1/1[3]
Julia Boggs Dent Grant (1826-1902; 1848)	MO	3/1	Barbara Pierce Bush (1925-2018; 1945)	NY	4/2
Lucy Ware Webb Hayes (1831-89; 1852)	OH	7/1	Hillary Diane Rodham Clinton (1947- ; 1975)	IL	0/1
Lucretia Rudolph Garfield (1832-1918; 1858)	OH	5/2	Laura Lane Welch Bush (1946- ; 1977)	TX	0/2
Ellen Lewis Herndon Arthur (1837-80; 1859)	VA	2/1	Michelle LaVaughn Robinson Obama (1964- ; 1992)	IL	0/2
Frances Folsom Cleveland (1864-1947; 1886)	NY	2/3	Melania Knauss Trump (1970- ; 2005)	Slovenia	1/0[4]
Caroline Lavinia Scott Harrison (1832-92; 1853)	OH	1/1	Jill Tracy Jacobs Biden (1951- ; 1977)	NJ	0/1[5]
Mary Scott Lord Dimmick Harrison (1858-1948; 1896)	PA	0/1			

Note: Pres. Buchanan was unmarried. Children not born to the marriages shown are not listed unless otherwise noted. (1) Born in London, father a MD citizen. (2) Adopted son. (3) Pres. Reagan's first wife, whom he later divorced, was Jane Wyman (m. 1940-48). They had two daughters, one of whom died in infancy, and an adopted son. (4) Pres. Trump had four children from two previous marriages: two sons (Donald Jr., Eric) and one daughter (Ivanka) with Ivana Marie Zelníčková Trump (m. 1977-92) and one daughter (Tiffany) with Marla Maples (m. 1993-99). (5) Pres. Biden also had two sons (Beau and Hunter) and a daughter (Naomi) with his first wife, Neilia Hunter Biden (m. 1966), who died along with Naomi in a car crash in 1972.

Presidential Impeachment in U.S. History

The U.S. Constitution provides for impeachment and removal from office of federal officials on grounds of "Treason, Bribery, or other high Crimes and Misdemeanors" (Article II, Sect. 4). Impeachment is the bringing of charges by the House of Representatives, whose members can adopt impeachment articles on a simple majority vote. It is followed by a Senate trial; a two-thirds majority vote of Senators present is needed for conviction and removal from office.

In 1868, **Andrew Johnson** became the first president impeached by the House, for his removal of Sec. of War Edwin M. Stanton without first notifying the Senate. He was tried but not convicted. In 1974, impeachment articles against Pres. **Richard Nixon**, in connection with the Watergate scandal, were adopted by the House Judiciary Committee. He resigned Aug. 9, and the House accepted the committee report without taking further action. In 1998, Pres. **Bill Clinton** was impeached by the House in connection with his cover-up of a sexual relationship with former White House intern Monica Lewinsky. He was tried in the Senate in 1999 and acquitted. Pres. **Donald Trump** was impeached in 2019 on charges related to allegations that he used his office to pressure the president of Ukraine to investigate a political rival; he was acquitted by the Senate in 2020. Trump was impeached again in Jan. 2021 for "incitement of insurrection" but again was not convicted.

Burial Places of the Presidents

President	Burial place	President	Burial place
Washington	Mt. Vernon, VA	Arthur	Albany, NY
J. Adams	Quincy, MA	Cleveland	Princeton, NJ
Jefferson	Charlottesville, VA	B. Harrison	Indianapolis, IN
Madison	Montpelier Station, VA	McKinley	Canton, OH
Monroe	Richmond, VA	T. Roosevelt	Oyster Bay, NY
J. Q. Adams	Quincy, MA	Taft	Arlington Natl. Cem., VA
Jackson	Nashville, TN	Wilson	Wash. Natl. Cathedral, DC
Van Buren	Kinderhook, NY	Harding	Marion, OH
W. H. Harrison	North Bend, OH	Coolidge	Plymouth Notch, VT
Tyler	Richmond, VA	Hoover	West Branch, IA
Polk	Nashville, TN	F. Roosevelt	Hyde Park, NY
Taylor	Louisville, KY	Truman	Independence, MO
Fillmore	Buffalo, NY	Eisenhower	Abilene, KS
Pierce	Concord, NH	Kennedy	Arlington Natl. Cem., VA
Buchanan	Lancaster, PA	L. B. Johnson	Stonewall, TX
Lincoln	Springfield, IL	Nixon	Yorba Linda, CA
A. Johnson	Greeneville, TN	Ford	Grand Rapids, MI
Grant	New York, NY	Reagan	Simi Valley, CA
Hayes	Fremont, OH	G. H. W. Bush	College Station, TX
Garfield	Cleveland, OH		

Presidential Libraries

Presidential libraries are coordinated by the National Archives and Records Administration (www.archives.gov/presidential-libraries/). Under the Presidential Records Act, material is available through Freedom of Information Act requests starting five years after a president has left office.

NARA's Barack Obama Presidential Library (www.obamalibrary.gov) will be a fully digital library. Ground was broken in Chicago, Sept. 2021, for the Obama Presidential Center (www.obama.org/the-center), a privately operated, non-governmental organization. Records of the Trump administration are housed at National Archives facilities in Washington, DC, and will be available through FOIA requests as of Jan. 2026. Plans to build a privately funded Trump presidential museum and library had not been announced as of mid-2023.

Herbert Hoover Library and Museum
210 Parkside Dr.
West Branch, IA 52358
Phone: (319) 643-5301
Email: hoover.library@nara.gov
Website: hoover.archives.gov

Franklin D. Roosevelt Library and Museum
4079 Albany Post Rd.
Hyde Park, NY 12538-1990
Phone: (800) FDR-VISIT
Email: roosevelt.library@nara.gov
Website: www.fdrlibrary.marist.edu

Harry S. Truman Library and Museum
500 West U.S. Hwy. 24
Independence, MO 64050-2481
Phone: (800) 833-1225
Email: truman.library@nara.gov
Website: www.trumanlibrary.org

Dwight D. Eisenhower Library
200 SE 4th St.
Abilene, KS 67410-2900
Phone: (877) RING-IKE
Email: eisenhower.library@nara.gov
Website: eisenhower.archives.gov

John F. Kennedy Library and Museum
Columbia Pt.
Boston, MA 02125-3312
Phone: (866) JFK-1960
Email: kennedy.library@nara.gov
Website: www.jfklibrary.org

Lyndon Baines Johnson Library and Museum
2313 Red River St.
Austin, TX 78705-5737
Phone: (512) 721-0200
Email: johnson.library@nara.gov
Website: www.lbjlibrary.org

Richard Nixon Library and Museum
18001 Yorba Linda Blvd.
Yorba Linda, CA 92886-3903
Phone: (714) 983-9120
Email: nixon@nara.gov
Website: www.nixonlibrary.gov

Gerald R. Ford Library and Museum
Library: 1000 Beal Ave.
Ann Arbor, MI 48109-2109
Phone: (734) 205-0555
Museum: 303 Pearl St. NW
Grand Rapids, MI 49504-5353
Phone: (616) 254-0400
Email: ford.library@nara.gov
Website: www.fordlibrarymuseum.gov

Jimmy Carter Library and Museum
441 Freedom Pkwy.
Atlanta, GA 30307-1498
Phone: (404) 865-7100

Email: carter.library@nara.gov
Website: www.jimmycarterlibrary.gov

Ronald Reagan Library and Museum
40 Presidential Dr.
Simi Valley, CA 93065-0600
Phone: (800) 410-8354
Email: reagan.library@nara.gov
Website: reaganlibrary.gov

George H. W. Bush Library and Museum
1000 George Bush Dr. West
College Station, TX 77845
Phone: (979) 691-4000
Email: library.bush@nara.gov
Website: www.bush41.org

William J. Clinton Library and Museum
1200 President Clinton Ave.
Little Rock, AR 72201
Phone: (501) 374-4242
Email: clinton.library@nara.gov
Website: www.clintonlibrary.gov

George W. Bush Library and Museum
2943 SMU Blvd.
Dallas, TX 75205
Phone: (214) 346-1650
Email: gwbush.library@nara.gov
Website: www.bushcenter.org

PRESIDENTIAL ELECTIONS

Popular and Electoral Vote for President, 1789-2020

(D) Democrat; (DR) Democratic Republican; (F) Federalist; (LB) Libertarian; (LR) Liberal Republican; (NR) National Republican; (P) People's/Populist; (PR) Progressive; (R) Republican; (W) Whig; * = See notes below table.

Year	President elected	Popular	Elec.	Major losing candidate(s)	Popular	Elec.
1789	George Washington	Unknown	69	No major opposition	—	—
1792	George Washington	Unknown	132	No major opposition	—	—
1796	John Adams (F)	Unknown	71	Thomas Jefferson (DR)	Unknown	68
1800*	Thomas Jefferson (DR)	Unknown	73	Aaron Burr (DR)	Unknown	73
				John Adams (F)	Unknown	65
1804	Thomas Jefferson (DR)	Unknown	162	Charles Pinckney (F)	Unknown	14
1808	James Madison (DR)	Unknown	122	Charles Pinckney (F)	Unknown	47
1812	James Madison (DR)	Unknown	128	DeWitt Clinton (F)	Unknown	89
1816	James Monroe (DR)	Unknown	183	Rufus King (F)	Unknown	34
1820	James Monroe (DR)	Unknown	231	John Quincy Adams (DR)	Unknown	1
1824*	John Quincy Adams (DR)	113,122	84	Andrew Jackson (DR)	151,271	99
				Henry Clay (DR)	46,587	37
				William H. Crawford (DR)	44,282	41
1828	Andrew Jackson (D)	642,553	178	John Quincy Adams (NR)	500,897	83
1832	Andrew Jackson (D)	701,780	219	Henry Clay (NR)	484,205	49
1836	Martin Van Buren (D)	764,176	170	William H. Harrison (W)	550,816	73
1840	William H. Harrison (W)	1,275,390	234	Martin Van Buren (D)	1,128,854	60
1844	James K. Polk (D)	1,339,494	170	Henry Clay (W)	1,300,004	105
1848	Zachary Taylor (W)	1,361,393	163	Lewis Cass (D)	1,223,460	127
				Martin Van Buren (Free Soil)	291,501	—
1852	Franklin Pierce (D)	1,607,510	254	Winfield Scott (W)	1,386,942	42
1856	James Buchanan (D)	1,836,072	174	John C. Frémont (R)	1,342,345	114
				Millard Fillmore (American/Know-Nothing)	873,053	8
1860	Abraham Lincoln (R)	1,865,908	180	Stephen A. Douglas (D)	848,019	12
				John C. Breckinridge (D)	845,763	72
				John Bell (Constitutional Union)	589,581	39
1864	Abraham Lincoln (R)	2,218,388	212	George McClellan (D)	1,812,807	21
1868	Ulysses S. Grant (R)	3,013,650	214	Horatio Seymour (D)	2,708,744	80
1872*	Ulysses S. Grant (R)	3,598,235	286	Horace Greeley (D-LR)	2,834,671	—
1876*	Rutherford B. Hayes (R)	4,034,311	185	Samuel J. Tilden (D)	4,288,546	184
1880	James A. Garfield (R)	4,446,158	214	Winfield S. Hancock (D)	4,444,260	155
1884	Grover Cleveland (D)	4,874,621	219	James G. Blaine (R)	4,848,936	182
1888	Benjamin Harrison (R)	5,443,892	233	Grover Cleveland (D)	5,534,488	168
1892	Grover Cleveland (D)	5,551,883	277	Benjamin Harrison (R)	5,179,244	145
				James Weaver (P)	1,027,329	22
1896	William McKinley (R)	7,108,480	271	William J. Bryan (D-P)	6,511,495	176
1900	William McKinley (R)	7,218,039	292	William J. Bryan (D)	6,358,345	155
1904	Theodore Roosevelt (R)	7,626,593	336	Alton B. Parker (D)	5,082,898	140
1908	William H. Taft (R)	7,676,258	321	William J. Bryan (D)	6,406,801	162
1912	Woodrow Wilson (D)	6,293,152	435	Theodore Roosevelt (PR)	4,119,207	88
				William H. Taft (R)	3,483,922	8
1916	Woodrow Wilson (D)	9,126,300	277	Charles E. Hughes (R)	8,546,789	254
1920	Warren G. Harding (R)	16,153,115	404	James M. Cox (D)	9,133,092	127
1924	Calvin Coolidge (R)	15,719,921	382	John W. Davis (D)	8,386,704	136
				Robert M. La Follette (PR)	4,822,856	13
1928	Herbert Hoover (R)	21,437,277	444	Alfred E. Smith (D)	15,007,698	87
1932	Franklin D. Roosevelt (D)	22,829,501	472	Herbert Hoover (R)	15,760,684	59
1936	Franklin D. Roosevelt (D)	27,757,333	523	Alfred Landon (R)	16,684,231	8
1940	Franklin D. Roosevelt (D)	27,313,041	449	Wendell Willkie (R)	22,348,480	82
1944	Franklin D. Roosevelt (D)	25,612,610	432	Thomas E. Dewey (R)	22,117,617	99
1948	Harry S. Truman (D)	24,179,345	303	Thomas E. Dewey (R)	21,991,291	189
				Strom Thurmond (States' Rights)	1,169,021	39
				Henry A. Wallace (PR)	1,157,172	—
1952	Dwight D. Eisenhower (R)	33,936,234	442	Adlai E. Stevenson (D)	27,314,992	89
1956*	Dwight D. Eisenhower (R)	35,590,472	457	Adlai E. Stevenson (D)	26,022,752	73
1960*	John F. Kennedy (D)	34,226,731	303	Richard M. Nixon (R)	34,108,157	219
1964	Lyndon B. Johnson (D)	43,129,566	486	Barry M. Goldwater (R)	27,178,188	52
1968	Richard M. Nixon (R)	31,785,480	301	Hubert H. Humphrey (D)	31,275,166	191
				George C. Wallace (Amer. Indep.)	9,906,473	46
1972*	Richard M. Nixon (R)	47,169,911	520	George S. McGovern (D)	29,170,383	17
1976*	Jimmy Carter (D)	40,830,763	297	Gerald R. Ford (R)	39,147,793	240
1980	Ronald Reagan (R)	43,904,153	489	Jimmy Carter (D)	35,483,883	49
				John B. Anderson (independent)	5,719,437	—
1984	Ronald Reagan (R)	54,455,075	525	Walter F. Mondale (D)	37,577,185	13
1988*	George H. W. Bush (R)	48,886,097	426	Michael S. Dukakis (D)	41,809,074	111
1992	Bill Clinton (D)	44,909,889	370	George H. W. Bush (R)	39,104,545	168
				H. Ross Perot (independent)	19,742,267	—
1996	Bill Clinton (D)	47,402,357	379	Bob Dole (R)	39,198,755	159
				H. Ross Perot (Reform)	8,085,402	—
2000*	George W. Bush (R)	50,456,002	271	Al Gore (D)	50,999,897	266
				Ralph Nader (Green)	2,882,955	—
2004*	George W. Bush (R)	62,040,610	286	John Kerry (D)	59,028,444	251
2008	Barack H. Obama (D)	69,498,516	365	John McCain (R)	59,948,283	173
2012	Barack H. Obama (D)	65,915,795	332	Mitt Romney (R)	60,933,504	206
2016*	Donald J. Trump (R)	62,984,828	304	Hillary Clinton (D)	65,853,514	227
2020	Joseph R. Biden (D)	81,268,924	306	Donald J. Trump (R)	74,216,154	232

Note: Not all candidates who received electoral votes are shown. ***1800**—Elected by House of Representatives because of tied electoral vote. **1824**—Elected by House of Representatives because no candidate polled a majority. By 1824, the Democratic Republicans had become a loose coalition of competing political groups. By 1828, Andrew Jackson supporters were known as Democrats and John Q. Adams and Henry Clay supporters as National Republicans. **1872**—Greeley died Nov. 29, 1872. His electoral votes were split among four individuals. **1876**—FL, LA, OR, and SC election returns were disputed. Congress in joint session (Mar. 2, 1877) declared Hayes and Wheeler elected president and vice president. **1956**—Democrats elected 74 electors, but one from AL refused to vote for Stevenson. **1960**—Sen. Harry F. Byrd (D, VA) received 15 electoral votes. **1972**—John Hospers of CA received a vote from an elector of VA. **1976**—Ronald Reagan of CA received a vote from an elector of WA. **1988**—Sen. Lloyd Bentsen (D, TX) received a vote from an elector of WV. **2000**—One Gore elector from Washington, DC, abstained. Nader was listed as "independent" on the ballot in some states; he was not on the ballot in all states. **2004**—One MN elector voted for VP candidate John Edwards for both president and vice president. **2016**—Seven electors from three states (HI, TX, WA) did not vote for the candidate to whom they were pledged (two Trump electors defected, as did five pledged to Clinton).

Electoral and Popular Vote, 2016 and 2020

Source: Federal Election Commission

	2016				2020				
	Electoral vote		Popular vote		Electoral vote		Popular vote		
State	Clinton	Trump	Clinton	Trump	Biden	Trump	Biden	Trump	State
AL	0	9	729,547	1,318,255	0	9	849,624	1,441,170	AL
AK	0	3	116,454	163,387	0	3	153,778	189,951	AK
AZ	0	11	1,161,167	1,252,401	11	0	1,672,143	1,661,686	AZ
AR	0	6	380,494	684,872	0	6	423,932	760,647	AR
CA	55	0	8,753,792	4,483,814	55	0	11,110,250	6,006,429	CA
CO	9	0	1,338,870	1,202,484	9	0	1,804,352	1,364,607	CO
CT	7	0	897,572	673,215	7	0	1,080,831	714,717	CT
DE	3	0	235,603	185,127	3	0	296,268	200,603	DE
DC	3	0	282,830	12,723	3	0	317,323	18,586	DC
FL	0	29	4,504,975	4,617,886	0	29	5,297,045	5,668,731	FL
GA	0	16	1,877,963	2,089,104	16	0	2,473,633	2,461,854	GA
HI	3	0	266,891	128,847	4	0	366,130	196,864	HI
ID	0	4	189,765	409,055	0	4	287,021	554,119	ID
IL	20	0	3,090,729	2,146,015	20	0	3,471,915	2,446,891	IL
IN	0	11	1,033,126	1,557,286	0	11	1,242,416	1,729,519	IN
IA	0	6	653,669	800,983	0	6	759,061	897,672	IA
KS	0	6	427,005	671,018	0	6	570,323	771,406	KS
KY	0	8	628,854	1,202,971	0	8	772,474	1,326,646	KY
LA	0	8	780,154	1,178,638	0	8	856,034	1,255,776	LA
ME	3	1	357,735	335,593	3	1	435,072	360,737	ME
MD	10	0	1,677,928	943,169	10	0	1,985,023	976,414	MD
MA	11	0	1,995,196	1,090,893	11	0	2,804,040	2,649,852	MA
MI	0	16	2,268,839	2,279,543	16	0	1,717,077	1,484,065	MI
MN	10	0	1,367,716	1,322,951	10	0	1,717,077	1,484,065	MN
MS	0	6	485,131	700,714	0	6	539,398	756,764	MS
MO	0	10	1,071,068	1,594,511	0	10	1,253,014	1,718,736	MO
MT	0	3	177,709	279,240	0	3	244,786	343,602	MT
NE	0	5	284,494	495,961	1	4	374,583	556,846	NE
NV	6	0	539,260	512,058	6	0	703,486	669,890	NV
NH	4	0	348,526	345,790	4	0	424,937	365,660	NH
NJ	14	0	2,148,278	1,601,933	14	0	2,608,335	1,883,274	NJ
NM	5	0	385,234	319,667	5	0	501,614	401,894	NM
NY	29	0	4,556,118	2,819,533	29	0	5,230,985	3,244,798	NY
NC	0	15	2,189,316	2,362,631	0	15	2,684,292	2,758,775	NC
ND	0	3	93,758	216,794	0	3	114,902	235,595	ND
OH	0	18	2,394,164	2,841,005	0	18	2,679,165	3,154,834	OH
OK	0	7	420,375	949,136	0	7	503,890	1,020,280	OK
OR	7	0	1,002,106	782,403	7	0	1,340,383	958,448	OR
PA	0	20	2,926,441	2,970,733	20	0	3,458,229	3,377,674	PA
RI	4	0	252,525	180,543	4	0	307,486	199,922	RI
SC	0	9	855,373	1,155,389	0	9	1,091,541	1,385,103	SC
SD	0	3	117,458	227,721	0	3	150,471	261,043	SD
TN	0	11	870,695	1,522,925	0	11	1,143,711	1,852,475	TN
TX	0	36	3,877,868	4,685,047	0	38	5,259,126	5,890,347	TX
UT	0	6	310,676	515,231	0	6	560,282	865,140	UT
VT	3	0	178,573	95,369	3	0	242,820	112,704	VT
VA	13	0	1,981,473	1,769,443	13	0	2,413,568	1,962,430	VA
WA	8	0	1,742,718	1,221,747	12	0	2,369,612	1,584,651	WA
WV	0	5	188,794	489,371	0	5	235,984	545,382	WV
WI	0	10	1,382,536	1,405,284	10	0	1,630,866	1,610,184	WI
WY	0	3	55,973	174,419	0	3	73,491	193,559	WY
Total	227	304	65,853,514	62,984,828	306	232	81,268,924	74,216,154	**U.S.**

Note: In 2016, 7 electors (1 from HI, 2 from TX, 4 from WA) voted for candidates to whom they were not pledged; their votes are not included here. Maine and Nebraska are the only two states with laws that allow electoral votes to be split between candidates.

Voter Turnout in Presidential Elections, 1932-2020

Source: U.S. Census Bureau, U.S. Dept. of Commerce; Office of the Clerk, U.S. House of Representatives

		Voter participation				Voter participation	
		% of voting-age citizen pop.	% of voting-age pop.			% of voting-age citizen pop.	% of voting-age pop.
Year	Candidates			Year	Candidates		
1932	F. D. Roosevelt-Hoover ...	NA	52.6%	1980	Reagan-Carter	64.0%	59.3%
1936	F. D. Roosevelt-Landon ...	NA	56.9	1984	Reagan-Mondale	64.9	59.9
1940	F. D. Roosevelt-Willkie ...	NA	58.8	1988	G. H. W. Bush-Dukakis....	62.2	57.4
1944	F. D. Roosevelt-Dewey....	NA	56.1	1992	Clinton-G. H. W. Bush-Perot	67.7	61.3
1948	Truman-Dewey..........	NA	51.1	1996	Clinton-Dole-Perot	58.4	54.2
1952	Eisenhower-Stevenson....	NA	61.6	2000	G. W. Bush-Gore	59.5	54.7
1956	Eisenhower-Stevenson....	NA	59.3	2004	G. W. Bush-Kerry........	63.8	58.3
1960	Kennedy-Nixon..........	NA	62.8	2008	Obama-McCain	63.6	58.2
1964	L. B. Johnson-Goldwater ..	NA	69.3	2012	Obama-Romney.........	61.8	56.5
1968	Nixon-Humphrey.........	NA	67.8	2016	Trump-Clinton..........	61.4	56.0
1972	Nixon-McGovern.........	NA	63.0	2020	Biden-Trump............	66.8	61.3
1976	Carter-Ford............	NA	59.2				

NA = Not available. Note: Data prior to 1964 is from a legacy source and may not be directly comparable to more recent data. The 1972 presidential election was the first for which eligible voters included 18- to 20-year-olds. The voting-age citizen pop. includes those who are ineligible to vote due to imprisonment or prior felony convictions. The voting-age pop. comprises the former group as well as residents who are ineligible to vote because they are not U.S. citizens.

Electoral Votes for President, 2020

Electoral votes based on the 2010 Census were in force beginning with the 2012 elections.

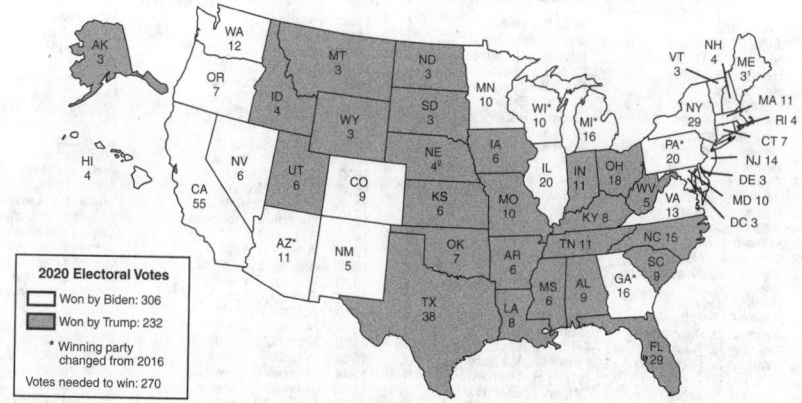

2020 Electoral Votes

☐ Won by Biden: 306
▨ Won by Trump: 232

* Winning party changed from 2016

Votes needed to win: 270

(1) Trump was awarded one of Maine's four electoral votes. (2) Biden was awarded one of Nebraska's five electoral votes.

Presidential Popular Vote, 2020

Source: Federal Election Commission

Candidate (party)	Vote total	Percent of vote
Joseph R. Biden (Democrat)	81,268,924	51.31%
Donald J. Trump (Republican)	74,216,154	46.86
Jo Jorgensen (Libertarian)	1,865,724	1.18
Howie Hawkins (Green)	405,035	0.26
Roque "Rocky" De La Fuente (American Independent)	88,234	0.06
Gloria Estela La Riva (Peace and Freedom/Socialism and Liberation)	85,623	0.05
Kanye West (Independent)	70,296	0.04
Don Blankenship (American Constitution)	60,148	0.04
Brock Pierce (Freedom and Prosperity/Independence)	49,700	0.03
Brian Carroll (American Solidarity)	39,230	0.02
Jade Simmons (Independent)	7,138	<0.01
Alyson Kennedy (Independent/Socialist Workers)	6,791	<0.01
Bill Hammons (Unity Party)	6,647	<0.01
Jerome Segal (Bread and Roses)	5,949	<0.01
Dario Hunter (Progressive)	5,403	<0.01
Phil Collins (Independent/Prohibition)	4,856	<0.01
James G. "Jesse Ventura" Janos (Green)	3,284	<0.01
President Boddie (C.U.P.)	3,185	<0.01

Candidate (party)	Vote total	Percent of vote
Mark Charles (Unaffiliated)	3,098	<0.01%
Joe McHugh (Unaffiliated)	2,843	<0.01
Sheila "Samm" Tittle (Constitution)	1,806	<0.01
C. L. Gammon (Independent)	1,475	<0.01
John Richard Myers (Life and Liberty)	1,372	<0.01
Tom Hoefling (Life, Liberty, Constitution)	1,317	<0.01
H. Brooke Paige (Grumpy Old Patriots)	1,175	<0.01
Christopher LaFontaine (Independent)	856	<0.01
Kyle Kenley Kopitke (Independent American)	815	<0.01
Ricki Sue King (Geneology Know Your Family History)	546	<0.01
Princess Khadijah Maryam Jacob-Fambro (Unaffiliated)	505	<0.01
Blake Huber (Approval Voting)	409	<0.01
Joseph Kishore (Socialist Equality)	350	<0.01
Richard Duncan (Independent)	213	<0.01
Jordan "Cancer" Scott (Unaffiliated)	175	<0.01
Gary Swing (Boiling Frog)	141	<0.01
Keith McCormic (Bull Moose)	126	<0.01
Zachary Scalf (Independent)	29	<0.01
Write-in votes	159,752	0.10
None of these candidates	14,079	<0.01
Total	**158,383,403**	

Note: Party designations vary from one state to another; party label listed may not necessarily represent a political party organization. Vote totals for the candidates listed above include any write-in votes.

The Electoral College

The president and the vice president are the only elective federal officials not chosen by direct vote of the people. They are elected by the members of the Electoral College, an institution provided for in the U.S. Constitution. Under the electoral college system, a candidate who fails to win the popular vote still may win a majority of electoral votes. This happened in the elections of 1876, 1888, 2000, and 2016.

Each state chooses as many electors as it has senators and representatives in Congress. With 100 senators and 435 representatives (plus, since 1964, three electors for Washington, DC), there are 538 members of the Electoral College, with a majority of 270 electoral votes needed to elect the president and vice president.

Each political party chooses its electors, by nomination at a state convention or by vote of the party central committee in each state. An elector cannot be a member of Congress or federal office holder. The electors of the party receiving the

highest vote count are elected under a winner-take-all system. Two states, Maine and Nebraska, allow for proportional allocation.

The electors meet on the first Monday after the second Wednesday in Dec. Certified votes of the electors in each state are sent to the president of the U.S. Senate. He or she then opens them in a joint session of Congress held in early Jan. The electoral votes of all the states are then officially counted.

If no candidate for president has a majority, the House of Representatives chooses a president from the top three candidates, with all representatives from each state combining to cast one vote for that state. The House decided the outcomes of the 1800 and 1824 presidential elections. If no candidate for vice president has a majority, the Senate chooses from the top two, with the senators voting as individuals. The Senate chose the vice president following the 1836 election.

Major-Party Nominees for President and Vice President, 1856-2020

Asterisk (*) denotes winning ticket.

	Democratic			Republican	
Year	President	Vice President	Year	President	Vice President
1856	James Buchanan*	John Breckinridge	1856	John Frémont	William Dayton
1860	Stephen A. Douglas[1]	Herschel V. Johnson	1860	Abraham Lincoln*	Hannibal Hamlin
1864	George McClellan	G. H. Pendleton	1864	Abraham Lincoln*	Andrew Johnson
1868	Horatio Seymour	Francis Blair	1868	Ulysses S. Grant*	Schuyler Colfax
1872	Horace Greeley	B. Gratz Brown	1872	Ulysses S. Grant*	Henry Wilson
1876	Samuel J. Tilden	Thomas Hendricks	1876	Rutherford B. Hayes*	William Wheeler
1880	Winfield Hancock	William English	1880	James A. Garfield*	Chester A. Arthur
1884	Grover Cleveland*	Thomas Hendricks	1884	James G. Blaine	John Logan
1888	Grover Cleveland	A. G. Thurman	1888	Benjamin Harrison*	Levi Morton
1892	Grover Cleveland*	Adlai Stevenson	1892	Benjamin Harrison	Whitelaw Reid
1896	William J. Bryan	Arthur Sewall	1896	William McKinley*	Garret Hobart
1900	William J. Bryan	Adlai Stevenson	1900	William McKinley*	Theodore Roosevelt
1904	Alton Parker	Henry Davis	1904	Theodore Roosevelt*	Charles Fairbanks
1908	William J. Bryan	John Kern	1908	William H. Taft*	James Sherman
1912	Woodrow Wilson*	Thomas Marshall	1912	William H. Taft	James Sherman[2]
1916	Woodrow Wilson*	Thomas Marshall	1916	Charles E. Hughes	Charles Fairbanks
1920	James M. Cox	Franklin D. Roosevelt	1920	Warren G. Harding*	Calvin Coolidge
1924	John W. Davis	Charles W. Bryan	1924	Calvin Coolidge*	Charles G. Dawes
1928	Alfred E. Smith	Joseph T. Robinson	1928	Herbert Hoover*	Charles Curtis
1932	Franklin D. Roosevelt*	John N. Garner	1932	Herbert Hoover	Charles Curtis
1936	Franklin D. Roosevelt*	John N. Garner	1936	Alfred M. Landon	Frank Knox
1940	Franklin D. Roosevelt*	Henry A. Wallace	1940	Wendell L. Willkie	Charles McNary
1944	Franklin D. Roosevelt*	Harry S. Truman	1944	Thomas E. Dewey	John W. Bricker
1948	Harry S. Truman*	Alben W. Barkley	1948	Thomas E. Dewey	Earl Warren
1952	Adlai E. Stevenson	John J. Sparkman	1952	Dwight D. Eisenhower*	Richard M. Nixon
1956	Adlai E. Stevenson	Estes Kefauver	1956	Dwight D. Eisenhower*	Richard M. Nixon
1960	John F. Kennedy*	Lyndon B. Johnson	1960	Richard M. Nixon	Henry Cabot Lodge
1964	Lyndon B. Johnson*	Hubert H. Humphrey	1964	Barry M. Goldwater	William E. Miller
1968	Hubert H. Humphrey	Edmund S. Muskie	1968	Richard M. Nixon*	Spiro T. Agnew
1972	George S. McGovern	R. Sargent Shriver Jr.[3]	1972	Richard M. Nixon*	Spiro T. Agnew
1976	Jimmy Carter*	Walter F. Mondale	1976	Gerald R. Ford	Bob Dole
1980	Jimmy Carter	Walter F. Mondale	1980	Ronald Reagan*	George H. W. Bush
1984	Walter F. Mondale	Geraldine Ferraro	1984	Ronald Reagan*	George H. W. Bush
1988	Michael S. Dukakis	Lloyd Bentsen	1988	George H. W. Bush*	Dan Quayle
1992	Bill Clinton*	Al Gore	1992	George H. W. Bush	Dan Quayle
1996	Bill Clinton*	Al Gore	1996	Bob Dole	Jack Kemp
2000	Al Gore	Joseph Lieberman	2000	George W. Bush*	Richard Cheney
2004	John Kerry	John Edwards	2004	George W. Bush*	Richard Cheney
2008	Barack Obama*	Joe Biden	2008	John McCain	Sarah Palin
2012	Barack Obama*	Joe Biden	2012	Mitt Romney	Paul Ryan
2016	Hillary Clinton	Tim Kaine	2016	Donald J. Trump*	Mike Pence
2020	Joe Biden*	Kamala Harris	2020	Donald J. Trump	Mike Pence

(1) Douglas and Johnson were nominated at the Baltimore convention. An earlier convention in Charleston, SC, failed to reach a consensus and resulted in a split in the party. The Southern faction of the Democrats nominated John Breckinridge for president and Joseph Lane for vice president. (2) Died Oct. 30; replaced on ballot by Nicholas Butler. (3) Chosen by Democratic National Committee after Thomas Eagleton withdrew because of controversy over past treatments for depression.

Third-Party and Independent Presidential Candidates

In most elections since 1860, fewer than one vote in 20 has been cast for a third-party candidate. Still, independent and third-party candidates often bring attention to prominent issues and can affect the outcome between major-party candidates.

Major vote-getters among third-party and independent candidates include James B. Weaver (People's Party), 1892; former Pres. Theodore Roosevelt (Progressive Party), 1912; Robert M. La Follette (Progressive Party), 1924; George C. Wallace (American Independent Party), 1968; and H. Ross Perot, as an independent in 1992 and with the Reform Party in 1996. In these six elections, non-major-party candidates combined polled at least 10% of the vote.

Roosevelt outpolled the Republican candidate, William Howard Taft, in 1912, capturing 28% of the popular vote and 88 electoral votes. In 1948, Strom Thurmond (States' Rights [Dixiecrat]) won 39 electoral votes from five Southern states; however, third-party candidates received only 5.75% of the popular vote. George Wallace's popularity in the same region in 1968 allowed him to get 46 electoral votes and 13.5% of the popular vote.

In 1992, Ross Perot captured 19% of the popular vote but failed to win a single electoral vote. In 1996, Perot won 8% of the popular vote; all third-party candidates combined won just over 10%. In 2000, Ralph Nader (Green, independent) won about 3% of the vote. Gary Johnson (Libertarian) won about 3% in 2016.

Notable Third-Party and Independent Campaigns by Year

Party	Presidential nominee	Year	Issues	Strength in
Free Soil	Martin Van Buren	1848	Anti-slavery	NY, OH
American (Know-Nothing)	Millard Fillmore	1856	Anti-immigrant	Northeast, South
Greenback	Peter Cooper	1876	For "cheap money," labor rights	National
Greenback	James B. Weaver	1880	For "cheap money," labor rights	National
Prohibition	John P. St. John	1884	Anti-liquor	National
People's (Populist)	James B. Weaver	1892	For "cheap money," end of national banks	South, West
Socialist	Eugene V. Debs	1900-12; 1920	For public ownership	National
Progressive (Bull Moose)	Theodore Roosevelt	1912	Against high tariffs	Midwest, West
Progressive	Robert M. La Follette	1924	For farmer and labor rights	Midwest, West
Socialist	Norman Thomas	1928-48	For liberal reforms	National
Union	William Lemke	1936	Anti-New Deal	National
States' Rights (Dixiecrat)	Strom Thurmond	1948	For states' rights	South
Progressive	Henry A. Wallace	1948	Anti-Cold War	NY, CA
American Independent	George C. Wallace	1968	For states' rights	South
American	John G. Schmitz	1972	For "law and order"	West, OH, LA
None (independent)	John B. Anderson	1980	A third choice	National
None (independent)	H. Ross Perot	1992	Federal budget deficit	National
Reform	H. Ross Perot	1996	Deficit, campaign finance	National
Green, independent	Ralph Nader	2000-08	Corporate power, domestic priorities	National
Libertarian	Gary Johnson	2012-16	Public debt, civil liberties	National

489

AFGHANISTAN

ALBANIA

ALGERIA

ANDORRA

ANGOLA

ANTIGUA
AND BARBUDA

ARGENTINA

ARMENIA

AUSTRALIA

AUSTRIA

AZERBAIJAN

THE BAHAMAS

BAHRAIN

BANGLADESH

BARBADOS

BELARUS

BELGIUM

BELIZE

BENIN

BHUTAN

BOLIVIA

BOSNIA AND
HERZEGOVINA

BOTSWANA

BRAZIL

BRUNEI

BULGARIA

BURKINA FASO

BURUNDI

CABO VERDE

CAMBODIA

CAMEROON

CANADA

CENTRAL AFRICAN
REPUBLIC

CHAD

CHILE

CHINA

COLOMBIA

COMOROS

CONGO,
DEM. REP. OF THE

CONGO REPUBLIC

COSTA RICA

CÔTE D'IVOIRE

CROATIA

CUBA

CYPRUS

CZECHIA
(CZECH REPUBLIC)

DENMARK

DJIBOUTI

DOMINICA

DOMINICAN REPUBLIC

ECUADOR

EGYPT

EL SALVADOR

EQUATORIAL GUINEA

ERITREA

Note: Flag proportions have been standardized to fit page.

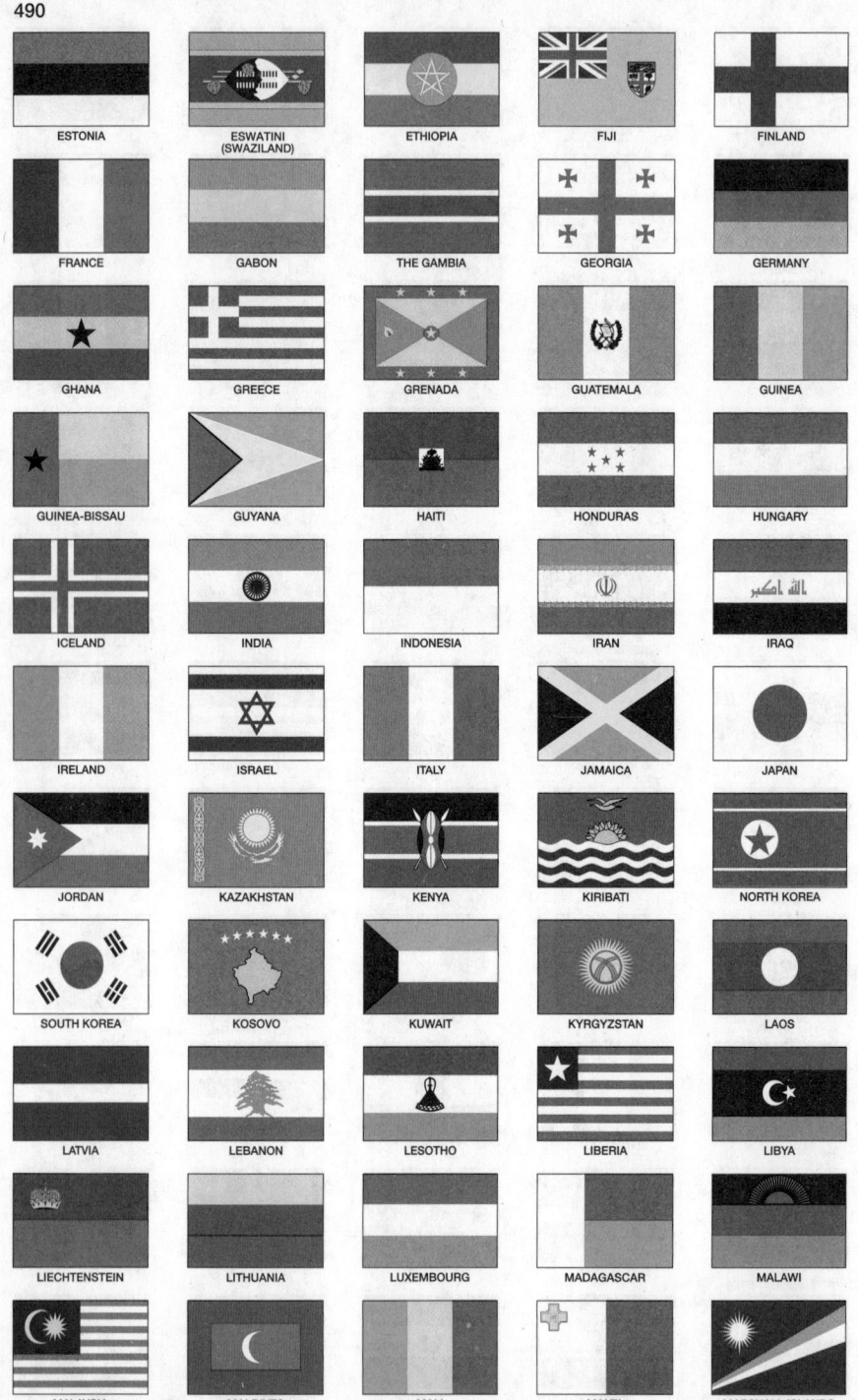

ESTONIA	ESWATINI (SWAZILAND)	ETHIOPIA	FIJI	FINLAND
FRANCE	GABON	THE GAMBIA	GEORGIA	GERMANY
GHANA	GREECE	GRENADA	GUATEMALA	GUINEA
GUINEA-BISSAU	GUYANA	HAITI	HONDURAS	HUNGARY
ICELAND	INDIA	INDONESIA	IRAN	IRAQ
IRELAND	ISRAEL	ITALY	JAMAICA	JAPAN
JORDAN	KAZAKHSTAN	KENYA	KIRIBATI	NORTH KOREA
SOUTH KOREA	KOSOVO	KUWAIT	KYRGYZSTAN	LAOS
LATVIA	LEBANON	LESOTHO	LIBERIA	LIBYA
LIECHTENSTEIN	LITHUANIA	LUXEMBOURG	MADAGASCAR	MALAWI
MALAYSIA	MALDIVES	MALI	MALTA	MARSHALL ISLANDS

Note: Flag proportions have been standardized to fit page.

MAURITANIA MAURITIUS MEXICO MICRONESIA MOLDOVA

MONACO MONGOLIA MONTENEGRO MOROCCO MOZAMBIQUE

MYANMAR (BURMA) NAMIBIA NAURU NEPAL NETHERLANDS

NEW ZEALAND NICARAGUA NIGER NIGERIA NORTH MACEDONIA

NORWAY OMAN PAKISTAN PALAU PANAMA

PAPUA NEW GUINEA PARAGUAY PERU PHILIPPINES POLAND

PORTUGAL QATAR ROMANIA RUSSIA RWANDA

ST. KITTS AND NEVIS ST. LUCIA ST. VINCENT AND THE GRENADINES SAMOA SAN MARINO

SÃO TOMÉ AND PRÍNCIPE SAUDI ARABIA SENEGAL SERBIA SEYCHELLES

SIERRA LEONE SINGAPORE SLOVAKIA SLOVENIA SOLOMON ISLANDS

SOMALIA SOUTH AFRICA SOUTH SUDAN SPAIN SRI LANKA

Note: Flag proportions have been standardized to fit page.

492

SUDAN	SURINAME	SWEDEN	SWITZERLAND	SYRIA
TAIWAN	TAJIKISTAN	TANZANIA	THAILAND	TIMOR-LESTE (EAST TIMOR)
TOGO	TONGA	TRINIDAD AND TOBAGO	TUNISIA	TURKEY
TURKMENISTAN	TUVALU	UGANDA	UKRAINE	UNITED ARAB EMIRATES
UNITED KINGDOM	UNITED STATES	URUGUAY	UZBEKISTAN	VANUATU
VATICAN CITY	VENEZUELA	VIETNAM	YEMEN	ZAMBIA

ZIMBABWE

INTERNATIONAL TIME ZONES

The world is divided into 24 time zones, each 15° longitude wide. The longitudinal meridian passing through Greenwich, England, is the starting point, and is called the *prime meridian*. The 12th zone is divided by the 180th meridian (International Date Line). When the line is crossed going west, the date is advanced one day; when crossed going east, the date becomes a day earlier.

Note: Flag proportions have been standardized to fit page.

UNITED STATES

CANADA

MEXICO

ATLANTIC OCEAN

PACIFIC OCEAN

Gulf of Mexico

THE BAHAMAS

CUBA

Tropic of Cancer

Washington

Lake Superior · Lake Huron · Lake Michigan · Lake Erie · Lake Ontario · Lake of the Woods

Winnipeg · Regina · Quebec · Montreal · Ottawa · Toronto

Vancouver · Victoria · Bellingham · Seattle · Tacoma · Olympia · Spokane · Yakima · Portland · Salem · Eugene · Medford · Klamath Falls

Cape Flattery · Mt. Olympus 2430 m (7,973 ft) · Mt. Rainier 4392 m (14,410 ft) · Mt. Hood 3426 m (11,239 ft) · Mt. Shasta 4317 m (14,163 ft)

Washington · **Oregon** · **Idaho** · **Nevada** · **California** · **Utah** · **Arizona** · **Colorado** · **Wyoming** · **Montana** · **New Mexico**

COAST RANGES · CASCADE RANGE · SIERRA NEVADA · COLUMBIA PLATEAU · GREAT BASIN · COLORADO PLATEAU · ROCKY MOUNTAINS · GREAT PLAINS · EDWARDS PLATEAU · BLACK HILLS · MOJAVE DESERT

San Francisco · Oakland · San Jose · Monterey · Fresno · Bakersfield · Santa Barbara · Los Angeles · Long Beach · Riverside · San Bernardino · San Diego · Tijuana

Sacramento · Redding · Eureka · Coos Bay · Bend · Boise · Twin Falls · Idaho Falls · Pocatello · Salmon · Lewiston · Coeur d'Alene · Sandpoint · Kalispell · Great Falls · Havre · Glasgow · Williston · Minot

Reno · Carson City · Winnemucca · Elko · Ely · Las Vegas · Mt. Whitney 4421 m (14,505 ft) · Death Valley, Lowest point in the U.S. −86 m (−282 ft)

Salt Lake City · Ogden · Provo · Logan · Cedar City · St. George · Richfield · Moab · Grand Junction

Mt. Elbert 4401 m (14,440 ft) · Pikes Peak 4302 m (14,115 ft) · Gannett Pk. 4209 m (13,810 ft/7,244 ft) · Granite Pk. 3904 m (12,807 ft) · Harney Pk. 2208 m · Borah Pk. 3861 m (12,668 ft) · Kings Pk. 4123 m (13,528 ft) · Wheeler Pk. 4013 m (13,165 ft) · Mt. Cleveland 3190 m (10,466 ft)

Phoenix · Tucson · Nogales · Yuma · Casa Grande · Flagstaff · Prescott · Kingman · Winslow · Farmington · Gallup · Albuquerque · Santa Fe · Socorro · Silver City · Las Cruces · El Paso · Roswell · Carlsbad · Tucumcari · Clovis

GRAND CANYON

Denver · Colorado Springs · Pueblo · Boulder · Fort Collins · Alamosa · Durango · Montrose · La Junta · Raton · Trinidad

Cheyenne · Casper · Laramie · Rock Springs · Sheridan · Cody · Jackson · Lander · Vernal · Craig

Helena · Butte · Bozeman · Billings · Miles City · Missoula · Dillon

Rapid City · Hot Springs · Chadron · Scottsbluff · Sterling · Sidney

North Dakota · **South Dakota** · **Nebraska** · **Kansas** · **Oklahoma** · **Texas**

Bismarck · Dickinson · Jamestown · Fargo · Grand Forks · Devils Lake

Pierre · Aberdeen · Watertown · Sioux Falls · Mobridge · Mitchell

North Platte · Broken Bow · Grand Island · Lincoln · Omaha · Kearney · O'Neill

Topeka · Salina · Hays · Goodland · Dodge City · Wichita · Hutchinson · Lawrence · Kansas City

Oklahoma City · Tulsa · Enid · Lawton · Clinton · Durant · Muskogee · McAlester

Amarillo · Lubbock · Midland · Odessa · Abilene · San Angelo · Wichita Falls · Fort Worth · Dallas · Waco · Austin · San Antonio · Laredo · Del Rio · Fort Stockton · Houston · Galveston · Beaumont · Corpus Christi · McAllen · Brownsville · Bryan · Victoria

RIO GRANDE

Monterrey · Chihuahua · Mexicali

Minnesota · **Iowa** · **Missouri** · **Arkansas** · **Louisiana** · **Wisconsin** · **Illinois** · **Mississippi** · **Michigan** · **Indiana** · **Tennessee** · **Alabama** · **Georgia** · **Florida** · **Kentucky** · **Ohio**

International Falls · Bemidji · Duluth · St. Cloud · Minneapolis · St. Paul · Mankato · Rochester · Virginia · Hibbing · Thunder Bay

Sioux City · Council Bluffs · Des Moines · Mason City · Waterloo · Cedar Rapids · Davenport · Dubuque · Ottumwa

St. Joseph · Kansas City · Jefferson City · Columbia · Springfield · Joplin · St. Louis · Hannibal · Rolla · Poplar Bluff · Cape Girardeau

Fayetteville · Fort Smith · Little Rock · Pine Bluff · Jonesboro · Texarkana · El Dorado

Shreveport · Monroe · Alexandria · Lafayette · Baton Rouge · New Orleans · Lake Charles · Morgan City · Natchez · Jackson · Hattiesburg · Biloxi · Meridian · Greenville · Tupelo · Columbus

Eau Claire · La Crosse · Madison · Milwaukee · Green Bay · Appleton · Wausau · Superior · Marquette · Escanaba · Houghton · Sault Ste. Marie

Rockford · Chicago · Peoria · Springfield · Champaign · Rock Island · Carbondale

Mobile · Pensacola · Panama City · Dothan · Montgomery · Birmingham · Huntsville · Tuscaloosa · Gadsden

Traverse City · Alpena · Saginaw · Flint · Grand Rapids · Lansing · Detroit · Kalamazoo · South Bend · Gary · Fort Wayne · Muncie · Indianapolis · Bloomington · Evansville

Louisville · Lexington · Frankfort · Bowling Green · Owensboro · Paducah

Nashville · Memphis · Knoxville · Chattanooga · Jackson

Atlanta · Macon · Columbus · Albany · Valdosta · Savannah · Brunswick · Augusta · Athens

Tallahassee · Gainesville · Jacksonville · St. Augustine · Daytona Beach · Orlando · Melbourne · Cape Canaveral · Tampa · St. Petersburg · Sarasota · Fort Myers · West Palm Beach · Fort Lauderdale · Miami · Key West · Cape Sable

APPALACHIAN MOUNTAINS

Mt. Mitchell 2037 m (6,683 ft) · Mt. Washington 1917 m (6,289 ft) · Mt. Marcy 1629 m (5,344 ft) · Mt. Katahdin 1606 m (5,268 ft) · Spruce Knob 1482 m (4,863 ft)

Maine · **N.H.** · **Vt.** · **Mass.** · **R.I.** · **Conn.** · **New York** · **N.J.** · **Pa.** · **Ohio** · **W. Va.** · **Md.** · **Del.** · **Va.** · **North Carolina** · **South Carolina** · **D.C.**

Saint John · Calais · Houlton · Caribou · Bar Harbor · Bangor · Augusta · Portland · Portsmouth · Manchester · Concord · Rutland · Burlington · Montpelier · Boston · Cape Cod · New Bedford · Providence · New Haven · Hartford · Springfield · Albany · Schenectady · Utica · Syracuse · Rochester · Buffalo · Binghamton · Scranton · New York · Newark · Trenton · Allentown · Philadelphia · Harrisburg · Altoona · Pittsburgh · Youngstown · Akron · Cleveland · Toledo · Mansfield · Columbus · Dayton · Cincinnati · Wheeling · Charleston · Parkersburg · Huntington

Baltimore · Washington · D.C. · Annapolis · Dover · Salisbury · Richmond · Newport News · Norfolk · Roanoke · Lynchburg · Charlottesville · Cape Hatteras · Raleigh · Greensboro · Winston-Salem · Durham · Fayetteville · Wilmington · New Bern · Charlotte · Asheville · Greenville · Columbia · Florence · Charleston

Lake Champlain · Chesapeake Bay · Long Island · Delaware Bay · ADIRONDACK MTS. · GREEN MTS. · WHITE MTS.

ALASKA....See page 494

Hawai'i

Ni'ihau · Kaua'i · Lihu'e · O'ahu · Honolulu · Wailuku · Moloka'i · Lāna'i · Kaho'olawe · Maui · Kahului · Kailua-Kona · Hawai'i · Hilo · Nā'ālehu

Mauna Kea 4205 m (13,796 ft) · Mauna Loa 4169 m (13,680 ft)

PACIFIC OCEAN

0 · 100 Miles · 0 · 150 Kilometers

0 · 250 · 500 · 750 Miles · 0 · 250 · 500 · 750 Kilometers

20° · 30° · 40° · 30° · 70° · 80° · 90° · 100° · 110° · 120° · 155° · 160°

NORTH AMERICA AND THE CARIBBEAN

ATLANTIC OCEAN

PACIFIC OCEAN

UNITED STATES

MEXICO

SOUTH AMERICA

BRAZIL

VENEZUELA

COLOMBIA

Bogotá

Caracas

Port of Spain

Panama City

PANAMA

COSTA RICA

San José

NICARAGUA

Managua

HONDURAS

Tegucigalpa

GUATEMALA

Guatemala City

EL SALVADOR

San Salvador

BELIZE

Belmopan

Lake Nicaragua

Antilles

Lesser Antilles

ANTIGUA and BARBUDA

Anguilla (U.K.)

Guadeloupe (Fr.)

DOMINICA

Martinique (Fr.)

ST. LUCIA

BARBADOS

ST. VINCENT and THE GRENADINES

GRENADA

TRINIDAD and TOBAGO

Virgin Is. (U.K.&U.S.)

NEVIS

ST. KITTS and

Greater Antilles

Puerto Rico (U.S.)

San Juan

Ponce

DOMINICAN REPUBLIC

Santo Domingo

HAITI

Port-au-Prince

JAMAICA

Kingston

Montego Bay

Cayman Is. (U.K.)

CUBA

Havana

Santiago de Cuba

Camagüey

Holguín

Guantánamo

Santa Clara

Santiago

Isla de la Juventud

Turks and Caicos Is. (U.K.)

THE BAHAMAS

Nassau

Freeport

Bermuda (U.K.)

Caribbean Sea

Gulf of Mexico

Straits of Florida

Cape Sable

Florida

Miami

Tampa

St. Petersburg

Sarasota

Jacksonville

Savannah

Charleston

Raleigh

N. Carolina

S. Carolina

Charlotte

Atlanta

Georgia

Birmingham

Alabama

COASTAL PLAIN

Mobile

New Orleans

Jackson

Miss.

Baton Rouge

La.

Shreveport

Memphis

Tennessee

Nashville

Arkansas

Little Rock

Kentucky

Louisville

Cincinnati

Ohio

Columbus

Cleveland

Pittsburgh

Pa.

W. Va.

Richmond

Virginia

Norfolk

Washington, D.C.

Baltimore

Md.

Del.

Philadelphia

New York

Conn.

R.I.

Mass.

Boston

N.H.

Maine

Bangor

Portland

Nova Scotia

Cape Sable

Cape Hatteras

Mt. Mitchell 2037 m (6,684 ft)

APPALACHIAN MTS.

Buffalo

Rochester

N.Y.

Sherbrooke

Montréal

Ottawa

Toronto

Hamilton

L. Ontario

L. Erie

Detroit

Michigan

Chicago

Milwaukee

Madison

Wisconsin

L. Michigan

L. Superior

L. Huron

Sudbury

Duluth

Minneapolis

St. Paul

Minnesota

Sioux Falls

Rapid City

S. Dakota

N. Dakota

Fargo

Bismarck

Williston

Great Falls

Montana

Billings

Missoula

Butte

Spokane

Wash.

Portland

Eugene

Oregon

CASCADE

COAST RANGES

SIERRA NEVADA

Eureka

Sacramento

San Francisco

San José

California

Fresno

Reno

Nevada

Las Vegas

Santa Barbara

Point Conception

Los Angeles

San Diego

Tijuana

Mexicali

BAJA CALIFORNIA

Gulf of California

False Cape

La Paz

Mazatlán

Culiacán

Durango

SIERRA MADRE OCCIDENTAL

Chihuahua

Ciudad Juárez

El Paso

Tucson

Phoenix

Arizona

New Mexico

Albuquerque

COLORADO PLATEAU

Utah

Salt Lake City

Great Salt Lake

GREAT BASIN

Death Valley Lowest point in North America (−282 ft)

Mt. Whitney 4421 m (14,505 ft)

Pocatello

Boise

Idaho

Wyoming

Cheyenne

Casper

Colorado

Denver

Colorado Springs

Pueblo

ROCKY MOUNTAINS

Nebraska

Omaha

Kansas City

Kansas

Wichita

Des Moines

Iowa

St. Louis

Indianapolis

Ind.

Ill.

Oklahoma

Oklahoma City

Amarillo

Lubbock

Fort Worth

Dallas

Texas

Austin

Houston

San Antonio

Laredo

Nuevo Laredo

Brownsville

Matamoros

Monterrey

Saltillo

Ciudad Victoria

Tampico

SIERRA MADRE ORIENTAL

San Luis Potosí

León

Guadalajara

Colima

Mexico City

Puebla

Oaxaca

Acapulco

Veracruz

Villahermosa

Tuxtla Gutiérrez

Mérida

YUCATAN PENINSULA

Campeche

Cancún

Bay of Campeche

Torreón

Hermosillo

Nogales

Ciudad Obregón

Cerro de Orizaba 5675 m (18,619 ft)

Tepic

Tajumulco 4220 m (13,845 ft)

Santa Barbara

4392 m (14,410 ft)

SIERRA MADRE

Tropic of Cancer

0   250   500   750 Miles

0 250 500 750 1,000 Kilometers

SOUTH AMERICA

South Georgia
(claimed by Arg.)

SOUTHERN OCEAN

ANTARCTICA

Curitiba
Joinville
Itajaí
Florianópolis
Foz do Iguaçu
Iguaçu
Passo Fundo
Caxias do Sul
Lajes
Porto Alegre
Santa Maria
Santo Tomé
Rio Grande
Santa Ângelo
Santa Fé
Encarnación
Posadas
Rivera
Pelotas
Salto
Payandú
Melo
Uruguaiana
Minas
URUGUAY
Montevideo
Río de la Plata
La Plata
Mar del Plata
Formosa
Resistencia
Corrientes
Concordia
Paraná
Santiago del Estero
Reconquista
Santa Fe
Rosario
Buenos Aires
Avellaneda
Azul
Tandil
Neocochea
Junín
San Miguel de Tucumán
Córdoba
San Juan
Mendoza
Río Cuarto
Santa Rosa
Bahía Blanca
Punta Alta
Cerro Ojos del Salado
6879 m (22,569 ft)
Copiapó
Catamarca
La Rioja
Cerro Bonete
6872 m (22,546 ft)
Cerro Aconcagua
6959 m (22,831 ft)
Highest point in South America
Cerro Tupungato Cuarto
6800 m (22,310 ft)
San Rafael
Viedma
Valdés Peninsula
Lowest point in South America
San Ambrosio Island
(Chile)
San Miguel
Santiago
Valparaíso
Viña del Mar
San Bernardo
Santiago
ARGENTINA
PAMPAS
CHILE
La Serena
Talca
Chillán
Los Ángeles
San Martín de los Andes
San Antonio Oeste
Viedma
San Félix Island
(Chile)
Talcahuano
Concepción
Temuco
Valdivia
Osorno
Puerto Montt
San Carlos de Bariloche
Esquel
Neuquén
Rawson
Trelew
PATAGONIA
Comodoro Rivadavia
Puerto Deseado
Gulf of San Jorge
Juan Fernández Islands
(Chile)
Los Chonos Archipelago
Chiloé Island
Taitao Peninsula
Coihaique
Río Gallegos
Bahía Grande
Strait of Magellan
Tierra Del Fuego
Ushuaia
Cape Horn
Punta Arenas
Stanley
Falkland Islands
(Islas Malvinas)
(U.K.)
(claimed by Arg.)
San Matías Gulf
Cape Tres Puntas

Tropic of Capricorn

0   250   500   750 Miles
0   250   500   750   1,000 Kilometers

ANTARCTICA

Falkland Is. (U.K.)
ATLANTIC OCEAN
South Georgia
South Orkney Is.
SOUTHERN OCEAN
South Shetland Is.
Elephant I.
Joinville I.
ANTARCTIC PENINSULA
Adelaide I.
Alexander I.
Weddell Sea
Ronne Ice Shelf
Filchner Ice Shelf
Berkner I.
Larsen Ice Shelf
QUEEN MAUD LAND
NEW SCHWABENLAND
COATS LAND
SOUTH AMERICA
Bellingshausen Sea
Thurston I.
Siple I.
ELLSWORTH LAND
ELLSWORTH MTS.
WEST ANTARCTICA
MARIE BYRD LAND
Roosevelt I.
Ross Ice Shelf
Ross Sea
Scott
Cape Adare
Balleny Is.
PACIFIC OCEAN
ANTARCTIC CIRCLE
TRANSANTARCTIC MOUNTAINS
POLAR PLATEAU
South Pole
EAST ANTARCTICA
Optima
Thickest ice
4776 m
(15,669 ft)
AMERICAN HIGHLAND
MAC. ROBERTSON LAND
AMERY Ice Shelf
WILKES LAND
Cape Poinsett
South Magnetic Pole
INDIAN OCEAN
0   800 Miles
0   800 Kilometers

SOUTHERN OCEAN
ANTARCTICA

498

EUROPE

GREENLAND
(KALAALLIT NUNAAT)
(Denmark)

Ísafjörður
Keflavík • Akureyri
• ICELAND
Reykjavík
• Seydhisfjördhur

Norwegian Sea

Arctic Circle

Torshavn • *Faroe Islands* (Den.)

Narvik
Bodø
Namsos

Trondheim
Molde
Ålesund
ÖsterSund
Sundsvall

Shetland Islands (U.K.)

NORWAY   SWEDEN

Bergen
Haugesund
Stavanger
Drammen • Oslo
Skien Karlstad
Kristiansand
Uppsala
Örebro
Stockholm
Norrköping Linköping
Jönköping
Öland

Hebrides
Orkney Islands
Thurso
Inverness
Scotland Aberdeen
Dundee
Glasgow Edinburgh
Ayr
Londonderry
Northern Ireland
Belfast Newcastle
UNITED
KINGDOM
Galway
IRELAND Dublin Leeds
Limerick Liverpool Kingston upon Hull
Cork Waterford Manchester Sheffield

Göteborg
Ålborg
Jutland Århus
Halmstad Växjö
Esbjerg Copenhagen Helsingborg
DENMARK Odense Malmö
Kiel Bornholm (Den.)
Lübeck Rostock Gdansk

ATLANTIC
OCEAN

North
Sea

Birmingham
Wales Swansea Coventry Norwich
Cardiff England
Bristol London
Plymouth
Land's End
Portsmouth Dover
Channel Is. (U.K.)
Brest
Le Havre Caen
Rennes
Nantes

NETHERLANDS
Amsterdam
The Hague
Rotterdam
Antwerp
Lille
BELGIUM
Brussels
Liège Bonn
LUXEMBOURG
Luxembourg
Le Mans
Paris
Orleans
Tours

Groningen
Bremen Hamburg
Hannover Berlin
Bielefeld Magdeburg
Essen GERMANY
Cologne
Kassel Leipzig Dresden
Wiesbaden Erfurt Chemnitz Liberec
Frankfurt
Mannheim Plzen
Saarbrücken Nürnberg Prague
Nancy Regensburg CZECHIA (CZECH REP.)
Strasbourg
Stuttgart
Augsburg Munich Linz

Szczecin
Bydgoszcz
Pozna
POLAND
Wrocław
Walbrzy

Ostrava
Brno
Bratislava
Vienna
Dijon
FRANCE
Limoges
Clermont-Ferrand Lyon
Saint-Étienne SWITZERLAND
Basel Zürich
Bern ALPS
Geneva LIECHTENSTEIN AUSTRIA
Mt. Blanc Matterhorn
4807 m (15,771 ft) 4478 m (14,692 ft)
Grenoble Milan
Turin
Torino Verona
Bergamo
Udine
Salzburg Innsbruck
Klagenfurt
Graz
SLOVENIA
Ljubljana
Trieste
Venice Zagreb
Rijeka CROATIA

Vienna
Györ
HU

Pécs

Bay
of
Biscay

A Coruña
Vigo
Gijón
Santander
Bilbao
Leon Vitoria-Gasteiz
Donostia–
San Sebastián
Pamplona
PYRENEES
Pico de Aneto
3404 m
(11,169 ft)

Porto Braga
Valladolid
IBERIAN
Salamanca
Zaragoza

Bordeaux
Toulouse
Montpellier
Avignon
Marseille Nice
Toulon
MONACO

Genoa
Parma
Bologna
Pisa
Florence
Perugia

SAN
MARINO
Ancona

APENNINES

Banja
Luka BOS. &
HERZ.
Sarajevo

Adriatic
Sea

Split. Dubrovnik

PORTUGAL
Lisbon
Setubal
Badajoz Toledo
Coimbra
Madrid
ANDORRA
Barcelona
Tarragona
Castellon de la Plana

VATICAN CITY
Corsica (Fr.)
Ajaccio
Elba
Rome
ITALY

Foggia
Bari

Cape
St. Vincent
Cádiz
SPAIN
PENINSULA
Valencia
Córdoba
Granada
Alicante
Murcia
Cartagena
Almería
Málaga
GIBRALTAR (U.K.)
Strait of
Gibraltar

Majorca
Palma de
Mallorca
Balearic Is.
(Sp.)
Minorca

Sardinia
(It.)
Cagliari

Sassari

Naples
Vesuvius
1277 m (4,190 ft)
Salerno
Taranto

Palermo
Etna
3369 m (11,053 ft)
Sicily (It.)
Catania
Messina
Reggio di
Calabria

*Tyrrhenian
Sea*

Ionian
Sea

Rabat

AFRICA

MOROCCO

Algiers

Tunis

0   250   500 Miles
0   250   500   750 Kilometers

ALGERIA

TUNISIA MALTA Valletta

Mediterranean Sea

502

AFRICA

AUSTRALIA AND THE PACIFIC

Tropic of Cancer

Equator

Tropic of Capricorn

PACIFIC OCEAN

INDIAN OCEAN

Philippine Sea

Celebes Sea

Banda Sea

Timor Sea

Arafura Sea

Coral Sea

Tasman Sea

Cook Strait

Bass Strait

Gulf of Carpentaria

Great Australian Bight

Great Barrier Reef

PHILIPPINES
Manila

BRUNEI
Bandar Seri Begawan

MALAYSIA

INDONESIA

TIMOR-LESTE
Dili

PALAU
Melekeok
Yap Is.

Northern Mariana Islands (U.S.)
Saipan
Tinian
Guam (U.S.)

Caroline Islands
FEDERATED STATES OF MICRONESIA

MARSHALL ISLANDS
Enewetak Atoll
Bikini Atoll
Ratak Chain
Ralik Chain
Kwajalein Atoll
Majuro
Wake I. (U.S.)

KIRIBATI
Tarawa (Bairiki)
Banaba
Gilbert Islands
Howland I. (U.S.)
Baker I. (U.S.)
Phoenix Islands
Canton I.
Enderbury
Kiritimati (Christmas)
Line Islands
Jarvis I. (U.S.)
Palmyra Atoll (U.S.)
Johnston Atoll (U.S.)

Hawaii (U.S.)
Kaua'i
O'ahu
Honolulu
Maui
Hawai'i

NAURU
Yaren

TUVALU
Funafuti

Tokelau (N.Z.)

SAMOA
Apia
American Samoa (U.S.)
Pago Pago

Wallis and Futuna (Fr.)

TONGA
Nuku'alofa

Niue (N.Z.)

Cook Islands (N.Z.)
Avarua

French Polynesia (Fr.)
Marquesas Islands
Tuamotu Archipelago
Society Islands
Papeete
Tahiti
Austral Islands

PAPUA NEW GUINEA
New Guinea
Mt. Wilhelm 4509 m (14,793 ft)
Admiralty Is.
Bismarck Arch.
New Ireland
New Britain
Rabaul
Madang
Lae
Port Moresby

SOLOMON ISLANDS
Bougainville
Solomon Is.
Guadalcanal
Honiara
Santa Cruz Is.

VANUATU
Espiritu Santo
Malakula
Port-Vila

New Caledonia (Fr.)
Loyalty Is.
Nouméa

FIJI
Vanua Levu
Viti Levu
Suva

Norfolk I. (Aust.)

Kermadec Is. (N.Z.)

NEW ZEALAND
North Island
Auckland
Hamilton
Tauranga
New Plymouth
Gisborne
Napier
Wellington
Nelson
South Island
Christchurch
Aoraki/Mt. Cook 3724 m (12,218 ft)
Dunedin
Stewart I.
Invercargill
Chatham Is. (N.Z.)

AUSTRALIA

Northern Territory
Darwin
Melville I.
Katherine
Alice Springs
Uluru/Ayers Rock 867 m (2,844 ft)

Western Australia
GREAT SANDY DESERT
GIBSON DESERT
GREAT VICTORIA DESERT
Broome
Port Hedland
Dampier
North West Cape
Newman
Carnarvon
Geraldton
Perth
Kalgoorlie-Boulder
Bunbury
Albany
Esperance
NULLARBOR PLAIN
Cape Leveque
Cape Leeuwin

South Australia
SIMPSON DESERT
ARTESIAN BASIN
GREAT BASIN
Lake Eyre
Lowest point in Australia
Coober Pedy
Woomera
Whyalla
Port Lincoln
Port Augusta
Adelaide
Kangaroo I.

Queensland
GREAT DIVIDING RANGE
Cape York
Weipa
Mount Isa
Cairns
Townsville
Mackay
Rockhampton
Bundaberg
Longreach
Charleville
Brisbane
Southport
Toowoomba

New South Wales
MURRAY–DARLING BASIN
Bourke
Broken Hill
Tamworth
Newcastle
Orange
Sydney
Wollongong
Wagga Wagga
Albury
Canberra
Mount Kosciuszko 2228 m (7,310 ft)
Highest point in Australia

Victoria
Bendigo
Ballarat
Geelong
Melbourne

Tasmania
Launceston
Hobart

SCALE
0 400 800 1,200 Miles
0 400 800 1,200 1,600 Kilometers

135° 150° 165° 180° 165° 150° 135° 120°

Presidential Election Results by State and County, 2020

Source: Federal Election Commission (FEC); local secretaries of state and state elections offices. Some candidates who did not appear on ballots are omitted from historical results.

Alabama

County	2020 Biden (D)	Trump (R)	2016 Clinton (D)	Trump (R)
Autauga	7,503	19,838	5,936	18,172
Baldwin	24,578	83,544	18,458	72,883
Barbour	4,816	5,622	4,871	5,454
Bibb	1,986	7,525	1,874	6,738
Blount	2,640	24,711	2,156	22,859
Bullock	3,446	1,146	3,530	1,140
Butler	3,965	5,458	3,726	4,901
Calhoun	15,216	35,101	13,242	32,865
Chambers	6,365	8,753	5,784	7,843
Cherokee	1,624	10,583	1,547	8,953
Chilton	3,073	16,085	2,911	15,081
Choctaw	3,127	4,296	3,109	4,106
Clarke	5,755	7,324	5,749	7,140
Clay	1,267	5,601	1,237	5,245
Cleburne	675	6,484	684	5,764
Coffee	5,076	16,899	4,221	15,875
Colbert	8,343	19,203	7,312	16,746
Conecuh	2,966	3,442	3,080	3,420
Coosa	1,796	3,631	1,782	3,381
Covington	2,721	14,586	2,387	13,267
Crenshaw	1,700	4,864	1,664	4,513
Cullman	4,478	36,880	3,798	32,989
Dale	5,170	14,303	4,413	13,808
Dallas	12,230	5,524	12,836	5,789
DeKalb	4,281	24,767	3,622	21,405
Elmore	10,367	30,164	8,443	27,634
Escambia	4,918	10,869	4,605	9,935
Etowah	11,567	35,528	10,442	32,353
Fayette	1,395	7,300	1,362	6,712
Franklin	2,086	10,376	2,197	9,466
Geneva	1,595	10,848	1,525	9,994
Greene	3,884	875	4,013	838
Hale	4,663	3,192	4,775	3,173
Henry	2,606	6,607	2,292	5,632
Houston	12,917	32,618	10,664	30,728
Jackson	3,717	19,670	3,673	16,672
Jefferson	181,688	138,843	156,873	134,768
Lamar	978	6,174	1,036	5,823
Lauderdale	11,915	31,721	9,952	27,899
Lawrence	3,562	12,322	3,627	10,833
Lee	27,860	42,221	21,230	34,617
Limestone	13,672	34,640	9,468	29,067
Lowndes	4,972	1,836	4,883	1,751
Macon	7,108	1,541	7,566	1,431
Madison	87,286	102,780	62,822	89,520
Marengo	5,488	5,343	5,615	5,233
Marion	1,463	12,205	1,432	11,274
Marshall	5,943	33,191	4,917	29,233
Mobile	79,474	101,243	72,186	95,116
Monroe	4,455	6,147	4,332	5,795
Montgomery	64,529	33,311	58,916	34,003
Morgan	13,234	39,664	11,254	37,486
Perry	3,860	1,339	3,824	1,407
Pickens	4,022	5,594	3,972	5,456
Pike	5,636	8,042	5,056	7,693
Randolph	2,203	8,559	2,291	7,705
Russell	11,228	9,864	9,579	9,210
St. Clair	7,744	36,166	5,589	31,651
Shelby	33,268	79,700	22,977	73,020
Sumter	4,648	1,598	4,746	1,581
Talladega	13,138	22,235	12,121	20,614
Tallapoosa	5,859	14,963	5,519	13,594
Tuscaloosa	37,765	51,117	31,762	47,723
Walker	4,834	26,002	4,497	24,266
Washington	2,258	6,564	2,374	6,042
Wilcox	4,048	1,833	4,339	1,742
Winston	1,066	10,195	872	9,228
Totals	**849,624**	**1,441,170**	**729,547**	**1,318,255**

Alabama Vote Since 1960

2020: Trump, R, 1,441,170; Biden, D, 849,624; Jorgensen, LB, 25,176.
2016: Trump, R, 1,318,255; Clinton, D, 729,547; Johnson, Ind., 44,467; Stein, Ind., 9,391.
2012: Romney, R, 1,255,925; Obama, D, 795,696; Johnson, Ind., 12,328; Stein, Ind., 3,397; Goode, Ind., 2,981.
2008: McCain, R, 1,266,546; Obama, D, 813,479; Nader, Ind., 6,788; Barr, Ind., 4,991; Baldwin, Ind., 4,310.
2004: Bush, R, 1,176,394; Kerry, D, 693,933; Nader, Ind., 6,701; Badnarik, Ind., 3,529; Peroutka, Ind., 1,994.
2000: Bush, R, 941,173; Gore, D, 692,611; Nader, Ind., 18,323; Buchanan, Ind., 6,351; Browne, Ind., 5,893; Phillips, Ind., 775; Hagelin, Ind., 447.

1996: Dole, R, 769,044; Clinton, D, 662,165; Perot, RF, 92,149; Browne, LB, 5,290; Phillips, Ind., 2,365; Hagelin, Natural Law, 1,697; Harris, Ind., 516.
1992: Bush, R, 804,283; Clinton, D, 690,080; Perot, Ind., 183,109; Marrou, LB, 5,737; Fulani, New Alliance, 2,161.
1988: Bush, R, 815,576; Dukakis, D, 549,506; Paul, LB, 8,460; Fulani, Ind., 3,311.
1984: Reagan, R, 872,849; Mondale, D, 551,899; Bergland, LB, 9,504.
1980: Reagan, R, 654,192; Carter, D, 636,730; Anderson, Ind., 16,481; Rarick, Amer. Ind., 15,010; Clark, LB, 13,318; Bubar, Statesman, 1,743; Hall, Comm., 1,629; DeBerry, Soc. Workers, 1,303; McReynolds, Soc., 1,006; Commoner, Citizens, 517.
1976: Carter, D, 659,170; Ford, R, 504,070; Maddox, Amer. Ind., 9,198; Bubar, Prohib., 6,669; Hall, Comm., 1,954; MacBride, LB, 1,481.
1972: Nixon, R, 728,701; McGovern, D, 219,108 plus Natl. Dem. Party of AL, 37,815; Schmitz, Conservative, 11,918; Munn, Prohib., 8,551.
1968: Wallace, 3rd party, 691,425; Humphrey, D, 196,579; Nixon, R, 146,923; Munn, Prohib., 4,022.
1964: Goldwater, R, 479,085; D (electors unpledged), 209,848; scattered, 105.
1960: Kennedy, D, 324,050; Nixon, R, 237,981; Faubus, States' Rights, 4,367; Decker, Prohib., 2,106; King, Afro-Americans, 1,485; scattered, 236.

Alaska

	2020 Biden (D)	Trump (R)	2016 Clinton (D)	Trump (R)
Totals	**153,778**	**189,951**	**116,454**	**163,387**

Alaska Vote Since 1960

2020: Trump, R, 189,951; Biden, D, 153,778; Jorgensen, LB, 8,897; Ventura, Green, 2,673; Blankenship, Const., 1,127; Pierce, petitioning cand., 825; De La Fuente, Alliance, 318.
2016: Trump, R, 163,387; Clinton, D, 116,454; Johnson, LB, 18,725; Stein, Green, 5,735; Castle, Const., 3,866; De La Fuente, unaff., 1,240.
2012: Romney, R, 164,676; Obama, D, 122,640; Johnson, LB, 7,392; Stein, Green, 2,917.
2008: McCain, R, 193,841; Obama, D, 123,594; Nader, Ind., 3,783; Baldwin, AK Ind., 1,660; Barr, LB, 1,589.
2004: Bush, R, 190,889; Kerry, D, 111,025; Nader, Populist, 5,069; Peroutka, AK Ind., 2,092; Badnarik, LB, 1,675; Cobb, Green, 1,058.
2000: Bush, R, 167,398; Gore, D, 79,004; Nader, Green, 28,747; Buchanan, RF, 5,192; Browne, LB, 2,636; Hagelin, Natural Law, 919; Phillips, Const., 596.
1996: Dole, R, 122,746; Clinton, D, 80,380; Perot, RF, 26,333; Nader, Green, 7,597; Browne, LB, 2,276; Phillips, U.S. Taxpayers, 925; Hagelin, Natural Law, 729.
1992: Bush, R, 102,000; Clinton, D, 78,294; Perot, Ind., 73,481; Gritz, Populist/America First, 1,379; Marrou, LB, 1,378.
1988: Bush, R, 119,251; Dukakis, D, 72,584; Paul, LB, 5,484; Fulani, New Alliance, 1,024.
1984: Reagan, R, 138,377; Mondale, D, 62,007; Bergland, LB, 6,378.
1980: Reagan, R, 86,112; Carter, D, 41,842; Clark, LB, 18,479; Anderson, Ind., 11,155; write-in, 857.
1976: Ford, R, 71,555; Carter, D, 44,058; MacBride, LB, 6,785.
1972: Nixon, R, 55,349; McGovern, D, 32,967; Schmitz, Amer., 6,903.
1968: Nixon, R, 37,600; Humphrey, D, 35,411; Wallace, 3rd party, 10,024.
1964: Johnson, D, 44,329; Goldwater, R, 22,930.
1960: Nixon, R, 30,953; Kennedy, D, 29,809.

Arizona

County	2020 Biden (D)	Trump (R)	2016 Clinton (D)	Trump (R)
Apache	23,293	11,442	17,083	8,240
Cochise	23,732	35,557	17,450	28,092
Coconino	44,698	27,052	32,404	21,108
Gila	8,943	18,377	7,003	14,182
Graham	4,034	10,749	3,301	8,025
Greenlee	1,182	2,433	1,092	1,892
La Paz	2,236	5,129	1,575	4,003
Maricopa	1,040,774	995,665	702,907	747,361
Mohave	24,831	78,535	17,455	58,282
Navajo	23,383	27,657	16,459	20,577
Pima	304,981	207,758	224,661	167,428

County	2020		2016	
	Biden (D)	Trump (R)	Clinton (D)	Trump (R)
Pinal	75,106	107,077	47,892	72,819
Santa Cruz	13,138	6,194	11,690	3,897
Yavapai	49,602	91,527	35,590	71,330
Yuma	32,210	36,534	24,605	25,165
Totals	**1,672,143**	**1,661,686**	**1,161,167**	**1,252,401**

Arizona Vote Since 1960

2020: Biden, D, 1,672,143; Trump, R, 1,661,686; Jorgensen, LB, 51,465.

2016: Trump, R, 1,252,401; Clinton, D, 1,161,167; Johnson, LB, 106,327; Stein, Green, 34,345; McMullin, Ind., 17,449; Castle, Const., 1,058.

2012: Romney, R, 1,233,654; Obama, D, 1,025,232; Johnson, LB, 32,100; Stein, Green, 7,816.

2008: McCain, R, 1,230,111; Obama, D, 1,034,707; Barr, LB, 12,555; Nader, New Prog., 11,301; McKinney, Green, 3,406.

2004: Bush, R, 1,104,294; Kerry, D, 893,524; Badnarik, LB, 11,856.

2000: Bush, R, 781,652; Gore, D, 685,341; Nader, Green, 45,645; Buchanan, RF, 12,373; Smith, LB, 5,775; Hagelin, Natural Law, 1,120.

1996: Clinton, D, 653,288; Dole, R, 622,073; Perot, RF, 112,072; Browne, LB, 14,358.

1992: Bush, R, 572,086; Clinton, D, 543,050; Perot, Ind., 353,741; Gritz, Populist/America First, 8,141; Marrou, LB, 6,759; Hagelin, Natural Law, 2,267.

1988: Bush, R, 702,541; Dukakis, D, 454,029; Paul, LB, 13,351; Fulani, New Alliance, 1,662.

1984: Reagan, R, 681,416; Mondale, D, 333,854; Bergland, LB, 10,585.

1980: Reagan, R, 529,688; Carter, D, 246,843; Anderson, Ind., 76,952; Clark, LB, 18,784; DeBerry, Soc. Workers, 1,100; Commoner, Citizens, 551; Hall, Comm., 25; Griswold, Workers World, 2.

1976: Ford, R, 418,642; Carter, D, 295,602; McCarthy, Ind., 19,229; MacBride, LB, 7,647; Camejo, Soc. Workers, 928; Anderson, Amer., 564; Maddox, Amer. Ind., 85.

1972: Nixon, R, 402,812; McGovern, D, 198,540; Jenness, Soc. Workers, 30,945; Schmitz, Amer. Ind., 21,208.

1968: Nixon, R, 266,721; Humphrey, D, 170,514; Wallace, 3rd party, 46,573; McCarthy, New Party, 2,751; Cleaver, Peace/Freedom, 217; Halstead, Soc. Workers, 85; Blomen, Soc. Labor, 75.

1964: Goldwater, R, 242,535; Johnson, D, 237,753; Hass, Soc. Labor, 482.

1960: Nixon, R, 221,241; Kennedy, D, 176,781; Hass, Soc. Labor, 469.

Arkansas

County	2020		2016	
	Biden (D)	Trump (R)	Clinton (D)	Trump (R)
Arkansas	1,818	4,304	1,939	3,826
Ashley	2,125	5,548	2,408	5,338
Baxter	4,635	15,836	4,169	14,682
Benton	42,249	73,965	28,005	60,871
Boone	3,064	13,652	2,926	12,235
Bradley	1,214	2,335	1,317	2,164
Calhoun	479	1,636	639	1,556
Carroll	4,023	7,424	3,342	6,786
Chicot	2,260	1,752	2,350	1,716
Clark	3,438	4,616	3,620	4,404
Clay	962	4,086	1,199	3,781
Cleburne	1,988	10,328	2,101	9,458
Cleveland	651	2,867	723	2,462
Columbia	2,814	5,500	3,140	5,456
Conway	2,615	5,694	2,656	4,849
Craighead	11,921	25,558	10,538	22,892
Crawford	4,959	18,607	4,488	16,686
Crittenden	8,514	7,333	8,410	6,964
Cross	1,772	4,946	1,999	4,584
Dallas	963	1,573	1,165	1,509
Desha	2,016	1,921	2,228	1,919
Drew	2,426	4,349	2,365	3,968
Faulkner	18,347	34,421	14,629	29,346
Franklin	1,300	5,677	1,376	5,039
Fulton	1,035	3,961	1,067	3,471
Garland	14,045	29,069	12,311	26,087
Grant	1,268	6,794	1,373	5,725
Greene	3,058	12,670	3,071	10,720
Hempstead	2,138	4,470	2,377	4,401
Hot Spring	3,082	9,202	3,149	8,172
Howard	1,340	3,367	1,351	3,157
Independence	2,806	11,250	2,881	9,936
Izard	1,021	4,631	1,113	4,042
Jackson	1,365	3,593	1,583	3,267
Jefferson	14,981	9,521	15,772	9,250
Johnson	2,283	6,938	2,427	6,091

County	2020		2016	
	Biden (D)	Trump (R)	Clinton (D)	Trump (R)
Lafayette	839	1,757	1,032	1,758
Lawrence	1,080	4,569	1,263	4,064
Lee	1,423	1,286	1,735	1,229
Lincoln	1,032	2,729	1,252	2,455
Little River	1,226	3,715	1,397	3,605
Logan	1,544	6,441	1,715	5,746
Lonoke	6,686	22,884	5,664	19,958
Madison	1,563	5,658	1,588	4,928
Marion	1,531	5,783	1,434	5,336
Miller	4,245	11,920	4,273	11,294
Mississippi	4,558	7,296	5,670	7,061
Monroe	1,147	1,545	1,312	1,489
Montgomery	731	3,046	748	2,643
Nevada	1,076	2,133	1,157	2,000
Newton	709	3,192	699	2,875
Ouachita	3,995	5,294	4,321	5,351
Perry	1,012	3,479	1,049	3,008
Phillips	3,623	2,417	4,310	2,446
Pike	644	3,519	685	3,150
Poinsett	1,424	5,918	1,880	5,502
Polk	1,246	7,035	1,212	6,618
Pope	5,772	18,081	5,000	16,256
Prairie	654	2,786	814	2,505
Pulaski	101,947	63,687	89,574	61,257
Randolph	1,215	5,355	1,425	4,509
St. Francis	3,604	3,242	4,031	3,195
Saline	16,060	39,556	13,256	35,863
Scott	483	2,962	602	2,731
Searcy	588	3,365	601	2,955
Sebastian	14,487	31,198	12,300	29,127
Sevier	1,116	3,884	1,075	3,282
Sharp	1,398	5,938	1,472	5,407
Stone	1,180	4,616	1,203	4,113
Union	5,584	10,478	5,855	10,456
Van Buren	1,593	6,034	1,549	5,382
Washington	43,824	47,504	33,366	41,476
White	5,978	24,182	5,170	21,077
Woodruff	856	1,543	1,118	1,347
Yell	1,284	5,226	1,480	4,608
Totals	**423,932**	**760,647**	**380,494**	**684,872**

Arkansas Vote Since 1960

2020: Trump, R, 760,647; Biden, D, 423,932; Jorgensen, LB, 13,133; West, Ind., 4,099; Hawkins, Green, 2,980; Collins, Ind., 2,812; Pierce, Ind., 2,141; Blankenship, Const., 2,108; Carroll, Amer. Solidarity, 1,713; Gammon, Ind., 1,475; Myers, other, 1,372; La Riva, Socialism/Liberation, 1,336; De La Fuente, Ind., 1,321.

2016: Trump, R, 684,872; Clinton, D, 380,494; Johnson, LB, 29,949; McMullin, Better For America, 13,176; Stein, Green, 9,473; Hedges, Ind., 4,709; Castle, Const., 4,613; Kahn, Ind., 3,390.

2012: Romney, R, 647,744; Obama, D, 394,409; Johnson, LB, 16,276; Stein, Green, 9,305; Lindsay, Socialism/Liberation, 1,734.

2008: McCain, R, 638,017; Obama, D, 422,310; Nader, Ind., 12,882; Barr, LB, 4,776; Baldwin, Const., 4,023; McKinney, Green, 3,470; La Riva, Socialism/Liberation, 1,139.

2004: Bush, R, 572,898; Kerry, D, 469,953; Nader, Populist, 6,171; Badnarik, LB, 2,352; Peroutka, Const., 2,083; Cobb, Green, 1,488.

2000: Bush, R, 472,940; Gore, D, 422,768; Nader, Green, 13,421; Buchanan, RF, 7,358; Browne, LB, 2,781; Phillips, Const., 1,415; Hagelin, Natural Law, 1,098.

1996: Clinton, D, 475,171; Dole, R, 325,416; Perot, RF, 69,884; Nader, Ind., 3,649; Browne, Ind., 3,076; Phillips, Ind., 2,065; Forbes, Ind., 932; Collins, Ind., 823; Masters, Ind., 749; Moorehead, Ind., 747; Hagelin, Ind., 729; Hollis, Ind., 538; Dodge, Ind., 483.

1992: Clinton, D, 505,823; Bush, R, 337,324; Perot, Ind., 99,132; Phillips, U.S. Taxpayers, 1,437; Marrou, LB, 1,261; Fulani, New Alliance, 1,022.

1988: Bush, R, 466,578; Dukakis, D, 349,237; Duke, Populist, 5,146; Paul, LB, 3,297.

1984: Reagan, R, 534,774; Mondale, D, 338,646; Bergland, LB, 2,220.

1980: Reagan, R, 403,164; Carter, D, 398,041; Anderson, Ind., 22,468; Clark, LB, 8,970; Commoner, Citizens, 2,345; Bubar, Statesman, 1,350; Hall, Comm., 1,244.

1976: Carter, D, 498,604; Ford, R, 267,903; McCarthy, Ind., 639; Anderson, Amer. Ind., 389.

1972: Nixon, R, 445,751; McGovern, D, 198,899; Schmitz, Amer. Ind., 3,016.

1968: Wallace, 3rd party, 235,627; Nixon, R, 189,062; Humphrey, D, 184,901.

1964: Johnson, D, 314,197; Goldwater, R, 243,264; Kasper, Natl. States' Rights, 2,965.

1960: Kennedy, D, 215,049; Nixon, R, 184,508; Faubus, Natl. States' Rights, 28,952.

California

County	2020 Biden (D)	Trump (R)	2016 Clinton (D)	Trump (R)
Alameda	617,659	136,309	514,842	95,922
Alpine	476	244	334	217
Amador	8,153	13,585	6,004	10,485
Butte	50,426	48,730	41,567	45,144
Calaveras	10,046	16,518	7,944	13,511
Colusa	3,239	4,559	2,661	3,551
Contra Costa	416,386	152,877	319,287	115,956
Del Norte	4,677	6,461	3,485	5,134
El Dorado	51,621	61,838	36,404	49,247
Fresno	193,025	164,464	141,341	124,049
Glenn	3,995	7,063	3,065	5,788
Humboldt	44,768	21,770	33,200	18,373
Imperial	34,678	20,847	32,667	12,704
Inyo	4,634	4,620	3,155	4,248
Kern	133,366	164,484	98,689	129,584
Kings	18,699	24,072	13,617	18,093
Lake	14,941	13,123	11,496	10,599
Lassen	2,799	8,970	2,224	7,574
Los Angeles	3,028,885	1,145,530	2,464,364	769,743
Madera	23,168	29,378	17,029	23,357
Marin	128,288	24,612	108,707	21,771
Mariposa	4,088	5,950	3,122	5,185
Mendocino	28,782	13,267	22,079	10,888
Merced	48,991	39,397	37,317	28,725
Modoc	1,150	3,109	877	2,696
Mono	4,013	2,513	2,773	2,111
Monterey	113,953	46,299	89,088	34,895
Napa	49,817	20,676	39,199	17,411
Nevada	36,359	26,779	26,053	23,365
Orange	814,009	676,498	609,961	507,148
Placer	106,869	122,488	73,509	95,138
Plumas	4,561	6,445	3,459	5,420
Riverside	528,340	449,144	373,695	333,243
Sacramento	440,808	259,405	326,023	189,789
San Benito	17,628	10,590	12,521	7,841
San Bernardino	455,859	366,257	340,833	271,240
San Diego	964,650	600,094	735,476	477,766
San Francisco	378,156	56,417	345,084	37,688
San Joaquin	161,137	121,098	121,124	88,936
San Luis Obispo	88,310	67,436	67,107	56,164
San Mateo	291,496	75,584	237,882	57,929
Santa Barbara	129,963	65,736	107,142	56,365
Santa Clara	617,967	214,612	511,684	144,826
Santa Cruz	114,246	26,937	95,249	22,438
Shasta	30,000	60,789	22,301	51,778
Sierra	730	1,142	601	1,048
Siskiyou	9,593	13,290	7,234	11,341
Solano	131,639	69,306	102,360	51,920
Sonoma	199,938	61,825	160,435	51,408
Stanislaus	105,841	104,145	81,647	78,494
Sutter	17,367	24,375	13,076	18,176
Tehama	8,911	19,141	6,809	15,494
Trinity	2,851	3,188	2,214	2,812
Tulare	66,105	77,579	47,585	58,299
Tuolumne	11,978	17,689	9,123	14,551
Ventura	251,388	162,207	194,402	132,323
Yolo	67,598	27,292	54,752	20,739
Yuba	11,230	17,676	7,910	13,170
Totals	**11,110,250**	**6,006,429**	**8,753,792**	**4,483,814**

California Vote Since 1960

2020: Biden, D, 11,110,250; Trump, R, 6,006,429; Jorgensen, LB, 187,895; Hawkins, Green, 81,029; De La Fuente, Amer. Ind., 60,160; La Riva, Peace/Freedom, 51,037.

2016: Clinton, D, 8,753,792; Trump, R, 4,483,814; Johnson, LB, 478,500; Stein, Green, 278,658; Sanders, Ind., 79,341; La Riva, Peace/Freedom, 66,101; McMullin, Ind., 39,596.

2012: Obama, D, 7,854,285; Romney, R, 4,839,958; Johnson, LB, 143,221; Stein, Green, 85,638; Barr, Peace/Freedom, 53,824; Hoefling, Amer. Ind., 38,372.

2008: Obama, D, 8,274,473; McCain, R, 5,011,781; Nader, Peace/Freedom, 108,381; Barr, LB, 67,582; Alan Keyes, Amer. Ind., 40,673; McKinney, Green, 38,774.

2004: Kerry, D, 6,745,485; Bush, R, 5,509,826; Badnarik, LB, 50,165; Cobb, Green, 40,771; Peltier, Peace/Freedom, 27,607; Peroutka, Amer. Ind., 26,645.

2000: Gore, D, 5,861,203; Bush, R, 4,567,429; Nader, Green, 418,707; Browne, LB, 45,520; Buchanan, RF, 44,987; Phillips, Amer. Ind., 17,042; Hagelin, Natural Law, 10,934.

1996: Clinton, D, 5,119,835; Dole, R, 3,828,380; Perot, RF, 697,847; Nader, Green, 237,016; Browne, LB, 73,600; Feinland, Peace/Freedom, 25,332; Phillips, Amer. Ind., 21,202; Hagelin, Natural Law, 15,403.

1992: Clinton, D, 5,121,325; Bush, R, 3,630,575; Perot, Ind., 2,296,006; Marrou, LB, 48,139; Daniels, Ind., 18,597; Phillips, U.S. Taxpayers, 12,711.

1988: Bush, R, 5,054,917; Dukakis, D, 4,702,233; Paul, LB, 70,105; Fulani, Ind., 31,181.

1984: Reagan, R, 5,305,410; Mondale, D, 3,815,947; Bergland, LB, 48,400.

1980: Reagan, R, 4,524,858; Carter, D, 3,083,661; Anderson, Ind., 739,833; Clark, LB, 148,434; Commoner, Ind., 61,063; Smith, Peace/Freedom, 18,116; Rarick, Amer. Ind., 9,856.

1976: Ford, R, 3,882,244; Carter, D, 3,742,284; McCarthy, write-in, 58,412; MacBride, LB, 56,388; Maddox, Amer. Ind., 51,098; Wright, People's, 41,731; Camejo, Soc. Workers, 17,259; Hall, Comm., 12,766; write-in, 4,935.

1972: Nixon, R, 4,602,096; McGovern, D, 3,475,847; Schmitz, Amer. Ind., 232,554; Spock, Peace/Freedom, 55,167; Hospers, LB, 980; Jenness, Soc. Workers, 574; Hall, Comm., 373; Fisher, Soc. Labor, 197; Munn, Prohib., 53; Green, Universal, 21.

1968: Nixon, R, 3,467,664; Humphrey, D, 3,244,318; Wallace, 3rd party, 487,270; Peace/Freedom, 27,707; McCarthy, Alternative, 20,721; Gregory, write-in, 3,230; Blomen, Soc. Labor, 341; Mitchell, Comm., 260; Munn, Prohib., 59; Soeters, Defense, 17.

1964: Johnson, D, 4,171,877; Goldwater, R, 2,879,108; Hass, Soc. Labor, 489; DeBerry, Soc. Workers, 378; Munn, Prohib., 305; Hensley, Universal, 19.

1960: Nixon, R, 3,259,722; Kennedy, D, 3,224,099; Decker, Prohib., 21,706; Hass, Soc. Labor, 1,051.

Colorado

County	2020 Biden (D)	Trump (R)	2016 Clinton (D)	Trump (R)
Adams	134,202	95,657	96,558	80,082
Alamosa	3,759	3,813	3,189	3,046
Arapahoe	213,607	127,323	159,885	117,053
Archuleta	3,738	5,189	2,500	4,264
Baca	317	1,867	283	1,753
Bent	732	1,503	590	1,188
Boulder	159,089	42,501	132,334	41,396
Broomfield	29,077	16,295	19,731	14,367
Chaffee	7,160	6,222	4,888	5,391
Cheyenne	131	993	132	925
Clear Creek	3,604	2,754	2,729	2,575
Conejos	1,959	2,286	1,771	1,914
Costilla	1,311	741	1,125	588
Crowley	437	1,271	339	1,079
Custer	1,112	2,474	797	2,061
Delta	5,887	13,081	4,087	11,655
Denver	313,293	71,618	244,551	62,690
Dolores	341	1,089	242	944
Douglas	104,653	121,270	68,657	102,573
Eagle	18,588	9,892	14,099	8,990
El Paso	161,941	202,828	108,010	179,228
Elbert	4,490	14,027	3,134	11,705
Fremont	7,369	17,517	5,297	15,122
Garfield	15,427	14,717	11,271	13,132
Gilpin	2,223	1,833	1,634	1,566
Grand	4,710	4,883	3,358	4,494
Gunnison	7,132	3,735	5,128	3,289
Hinsdale	255	353	197	339
Huerfano	2,076	2,203	1,633	1,883
Jackson	175	681	171	629
Jefferson	218,396	148,417	160,776	138,177
Kiowa	98	795	91	728
Kit Carson	662	3,144	536	2,967
La Plata	20,548	14,233	15,525	12,587
Lake	2,303	1,497	1,616	1,270
Larimer	126,120	91,489	93,113	83,430

County	2020 Biden (D)	Trump (R)	2016 Clinton (D)	Trump (R)
Las Animas	3,497	4,284	2,650	3,710
Lincoln	470	2,135	409	1,892
Logan	2,218	8,087	1,851	7,282
Mesa	31,536	56,894	21,729	49,779
Mineral	317	427	237	344
Moffat	1,203	5,670	874	5,305
Montezuma	5,836	9,306	3,973	7,853
Montrose	7,687	16,770	5,466	14,382
Morgan	3,876	9,593	3,151	8,145
Otero	3,605	5,756	2,943	4,928
Ouray	2,365	1,577	1,697	1,351
Park	4,903	6,991	3,421	6,135
Phillips	486	1,958	436	1,791
Pitkin	8,989	2,780	7,333	2,550
Prowers	1,458	4,008	1,186	3,531
Pueblo	43,772	42,252	35,875	36,265
Rio Blanco	561	3,061	436	2,791
Rio Grande	2,495	3,660	2,001	3,085
Routt	10,582	5,925	7,600	5,230
Saguache	1,884	1,413	1,417	1,147
San Juan	342	202	265	215
San Miguel	3,924	1,136	2,975	1,033
Sedgwick	301	1,121	267	1,015
Summit	12,631	5,322	9,557	5,100
Teller	5,278	11,241	3,603	9,745
Washington	369	2,595	296	2,249
Weld	66,060	96,145	46,519	76,651
Yuma	785	4,107	726	3,850
Totals	**1,804,352**	**1,364,607**	**1,338,870**	**1,202,484**

Colorado Vote Since 1960

2020: Biden, D, 1,804,352; Trump, R, 1,364,607; Jorgensen, LB, 52,460; Hawkins, Green, 8,986; West, unaff., 8,089; Blankenship, Amer. Const., 5,061; Hammons, Unity, 2,730; Carroll, Amer. Solidarity, 2,515; Charles, unaff., 2,011; La Riva, Socialism/Liberation, 1,035; Kopitke, Ind. Amer., 762; De La Fuente, Alliance, 636; McHugh, unaff., 614; Pierce, unaff., 572; Collins, Prohib., 568; Jacob-Fambro, unaff., 495; Hunter, Progressive, 379; Huber, Approval Voting, 355; Kennedy, Soc. Workers, 354; Kishore, Soc. Equal., 196; Scott, unaff., 175.

2016: Clinton, D, 1,338,870; Trump, R, 1,202,484; Johnson, LB, 144,121; Stein, Green, 38,437; McMullin, unaff., 28,917; Castle, Const., 11,699; Keniston, Veterans, 5,028; Smith, unaff., 1,819; De La Fuente, Amer. Delta, 1,255; Kopitke, Independent Amer., 1,096; Maldonado, Ind., 872; Maturen, Amer. Solidarity, 862; Silva, Nutrition, 751; Scott, unaff., 749; Hoefling, America's Party, 710; La Riva, Socialism/Liberation, 531; Kennedy, Soc. Workers, 452; Kotlikoff, Ind., 392; Lyttle, Nonviolent/Pacifist, 382; Atwood, Approval Voting, 337; Soltysik, Soc. USA, 271; Hedges, Prohib., 185.

2012: Obama, D, 1,323,102; Romney, R, 1,185,243; Johnson, LB, 35,545; Stein, Green, 7,508; Goode, Const., 6,234; Barr, Peace/Freedom, 5,059; Reed, unaff., 2,589; Anderson, Justice, 1,260; Tittle, We the People, 792; Hoefling, Amer. Ind., 679; La Riva, Socialism/Liberation, 317; Alexander, Soc. USA, 308; Miller, A3P, 266; Stevens, Objectivist, 235; Harris, Soc. Workers, 192; White, Soc. Equality, 189.

2008: Obama, D, 1,288,633; McCain, R, 1,073,629; Nader, unaff., 13,352; Barr, LB, 10,898; Baldwin, Const., 6,233; Alan Keyes, Amer., unaff., 3,051; McKinney, Green, 2,822; McEnulty, unaff., 829; Jay, Boston Tea, 598; Allen, HeartQuake '08, 348; Stevens, Objectivist, 336; Moore, Soc. USA, 226; La Riva, Socialism/Liberation, 158; Harris, Soc. Workers, 154; Lyttle, U.S. Pacifist, 110; Amondson, Prohib., 85.

2004: Bush, R, 1,101,255; Kerry, D, 1,001,732; Nader, RF, 12,718; Badnarik, LB, 7,664; Peroutka, Amer. Const., 2,562; Cobb, Green, 1,591; Andress, Ind., 804; Amondson, Concerns of People, 378; Van Auken, Soc. Equal., 329; Harris, Soc. Workers, 241; Brown, Soc., 216; Dodge, Prohib., 140.

2000: Bush, R, 883,748; Gore, D, 738,227; Nader, Green, 91,434; Browne, LB, 12,799; Buchanan, RF, 10,465; Hagelin, RF, 2,240; Phillips, Amer. Const., 1,319; McReynolds, Soc., 712; Harris, Soc. Workers, 216; Dodge, Prohib., 208.

1996: Dole, R, 691,848; Clinton, D, 671,152; Perot, RF, 99,629; Nader, Green, 25,070; Browne, LB, 12,392; Phillips, Amer. Const., 2,813; Collins, Ind., 2,809; Hagelin, Natural Law, 2,547; Hollis, Soc., 669; Moorehead, Workers World, 599; Templin, Amer., 557; Dodge, Prohib., 375; Harris, Soc. Workers, 244.

1992: Clinton, D, 629,681; Bush, R, 562,850; Perot, Ind., 366,010; Marrou, LB, 8,669; Fulani, New Alliance, 1,608.

1988: Bush, R, 728,177; Dukakis, D, 621,453; Paul, LB, 15,482; Dodge, Prohib., 4,604.

1984: Reagan, R, 821,817; Mondale, D, 454,975; Bergland, LB, 11,257.

1980: Reagan, R, 652,264; Carter, D, 367,973; Anderson, Ind., 130,633; Clark, LB, 25,744; Commoner, Citizens, 5,614; Bubar, Statesman, 1,180; Pulley, Soc., 520; Hall, Comm., 487.

1976: Ford, R, 584,367; Carter, D, 460,353; McCarthy, Ind., 26,107; MacBride, LB, 5,330; Bubar, Prohib., 2,882.

1972: Nixon, R, 597,189; McGovern, D, 329,980; Schmitz, Amer., 17,269; Fisher, Soc. Labor, 4,361; Spock, People's, 2,403; Hospers, LB, 1,111; Jenness, Soc. Workers, 555; Munn, Prohib., 467; Hall, Comm., 432.

1968: Nixon, R, 409,345; Humphrey, D, 335,174; Wallace, 3rd party, 60,813; Blomen, Soc. Labor, 3,016; Gregory, New Party, 1,393; Munn, Prohib., 275; Halstead, Soc. Workers, 235.

1964: Johnson, D, 476,024; Goldwater, R, 296,767; DeBerry, Soc. Workers, 2,537; Munn, Prohib., 1,356; Hass, Soc. Labor, 302.

1960: Nixon, R, 402,242; Kennedy, D, 330,629; Hass, Soc. Labor, 2,803; Dobbs, Soc. Workers, 572.

Connecticut

County	2020 Biden (D)	Trump (R)	2016 Clinton (D)	Trump (R)
Fairfield	297,505	169,039	243,852	160,077
Hartford	283,368	159,024	240,403	148,173
Litchfield	50,164	55,601	39,775	53,051
Middlesex	56,848	40,665	45,357	38,867
New Haven	242,630	169,893	205,609	159,048
New London	79,459	57,110	62,278	54,058
Tolland	44,151	34,838	38,506	34,194
Windham	26,706	29,141	21,792	25,747
Totals	**1,080,831**	**714,717**	**897,572**	**673,215**

Connecticut Vote Since 1960

2020: Biden, D, 1,080,831; Trump, R, 714,717; Jorgensen, LB, 20,230; Hawkins, Green, 7,538.

2016: Clinton, D, 897,572; Trump, R, 673,215; Johnson, LB, 48,676; Stein, Green, 22,841; McMullin, Ind., 2,108.

2012: Obama, D, 905,083; Romney, R, 634,892; Johnson, LB, 12,580; Anderson, Ind., 5,487.

2008: Obama, D, 997,772; McCain, R, 629,428; Nader, Ind., 19,162.

2004: Kerry, D, 857,488; Bush, R, 693,826; Nader, petitioning cand., 12,969; Cobb, Green, 9,564; Badnarik, LB, 3,367; Peroutka, Concerned Citizens, 1,543.

2000: Gore, D, 816,015; Bush, R, 561,094; Nader, Green, 64,452; Phillips, Concerned Citizens, 9,695; Buchanan, RF, 4,731; Browne, LB, 3,484.

1996: Clinton, D, 735,740; Dole, R, 483,109; Perot, RF, 139,523; Nader, Green, 24,321; Browne, LB, 5,788; Phillips, Concerned Citizens, 2,425; Hagelin, Natural Law, 1,703.

1992: Clinton, D, 682,318; Bush, R, 578,313; Perot, Ind., 348,771; Marrou, LB, 5,391; Fulani, New Alliance, 1,363.

1988: Bush, R, 750,241; Dukakis, D, 676,584; Paul, LB, 14,071; Fulani, New Alliance, 2,491.

1984: Reagan, R, 890,877; Mondale, D, 569,597.

1980: Reagan, R, 677,210; Carter, D, 541,732; Anderson, Ind., 171,807; Clark, LB, 8,570; Commoner, Citizens, 6,130; scattered, 836.

1976: Ford, R, 719,261; Carter, D, 647,895; Maddox, George Wallace Party, 7,101; LaRouche, U.S. Labor, 1,789.

1972: Nixon, R, 810,763; McGovern, D, 555,498; Schmitz, Amer., 17,239; scattered, 777.

1968: Humphrey, D, 621,561; Nixon, R, 556,721; Wallace, 3rd party, 76,650; scattered, 1,300.

1964: Johnson, D, 826,269; Goldwater, R, 390,996; scattered, 1,313.

1960: Kennedy, D, 657,055; Nixon, R, 565,813.

Delaware

County	2020		2016	
	Biden (D)	Trump (R)	Clinton (D)	Trump (R)
Kent	44,552	41,009	33,351	36,991
New Castle	195,034	88,364	162,919	85,525
Sussex	56,682	71,230	39,333	62,611
Totals	**296,268**	**200,603**	**235,603**	**185,127**

Delaware Vote Since 1960

2020: Biden, D, 296,268; Trump, R, 200,603; Jorgensen, LB, 5,000; Hawkins, Green, 2,139.

2016: Clinton, D, 235,603; Trump, R, 185,127; Johnson, LB, 14,757; Stein, Green, 6,103; McMullin, Ind., 706.

2012: Obama, D, 242,584; Romney, R, 165,484; Johnson, LB, 3,882; Stein, Green, 1,940.

2008: Obama, D, 255,459; McCain, R, 152,374; Nader, Ind. (DE), 2,401; Barr, LB, 1,109; Baldwin, Const., 626; McKinney, Green, 385; Calero, Soc. Workers, 58.

2004: Kerry, D, 200,152; Bush, R, 171,660; Nader, Ind., 2,153; Badnarik, LB, 586; Peroutka, Const., 289; Cobb, Green, 250; Brown, Natural Law, 100.

2000: Gore, D, 180,068; Bush, R, 137,288; Nader, Green, 8,307; Buchanan, RF, 777; Browne, LB, 774; Phillips, Const., 208; Hagelin, Natural Law, 107.

1996: Clinton, D, 140,355; Dole, R, 99,062; Perot, RF, 28,719; Browne, LB, 2,052; Phillips, U.S. Taxpayers, 348; Hagelin, Natural Law, 274.

1992: Clinton, D, 126,054; Bush, R, 102,313; Perot, Ind., 59,213; Fulani, New Alliance, 1,105.

1988: Bush, R, 139,639; Dukakis, D, 108,647; Paul, LB, 1,162; Fulani, New Alliance, 443.

1984: Reagan, R, 152,190; Mondale, D, 101,656; Bergland, LB, 268.

1980: Reagan, R, 111,252; Carter, D, 105,754; Anderson, Ind., 16,288; Clark, LB, 1,974; Greaves, Amer., 400.

1976: Carter, D, 122,596; Ford, R, 109,831; McCarthy, nonpartisan, 2,437; Anderson, Amer., 645; LaRouche, U.S. Labor, 136; Bubar, Prohib., 103; Levin, Soc. Labor, 86.

1972: Nixon, R, 140,357; McGovern, D, 92,283; Schmitz, Amer., 2,638; Munn, Prohib., 238.

1968: Nixon, R, 96,714; Humphrey, D, 89,194; Wallace, 3rd party, 28,459.

1964: Johnson, D, 122,704; Goldwater, R, 78,078; Munn, Prohib., 425; Hass, Soc. Labor, 113.

1960: Kennedy, D, 99,590; Nixon, R, 96,373; Faubus, States' Rights, 354; Decker, Prohib., 284; Hass, Soc. Labor, 82.

District of Columbia

	2020		2016	
	Biden (D)	Trump (R)	Clinton (D)	Trump (R)
Totals	**317,323**	**18,586**	**282,830**	**12,723**

District of Columbia Vote Since 1964

2020: Biden, D, 317,323; Trump, R, 18,586; Jorgensen, LB, 2,036; Hawkins, Green, 1,726; La Riva, Ind., 855; Pierce, Ind., 693.

2016: Clinton, D, 282,830; Trump, R, 12,723; Johnson, LB, 4,906; Stein, Green, 4,258.

2012: Obama, D, 267,070; Romney, R, 21,381; Stein, DC Statehood Green, 2,458; Johnson, LB, 2,083.

2008: Obama, D, 245,800; McCain, R, 17,367; Nader, Ind., 958; McKinney, Green, 590.

2004: Kerry, D, 202,970; Bush, R, 21,256; Nader, Ind., 1,485; Cobb, DC Statehood Green, 737; Badnarik, LB, 502; Harris, Soc. Workers, 130.

2000: Gore, D, 171,923; Bush, R, 18,073; Nader, Green, 10,576; Browne, LB, 669; Harris, Soc. Workers, 114.

1996: Clinton, D, 158,220; Dole, R, 17,339; Nader, Green, 4,780; Perot, RF, 3,611; Browne, LB, 588; Hagelin, Natural Law, 283; Harris, Soc. Workers, 257.

1992: Clinton, D, 192,619; Bush, R, 20,698; Perot, Ind., 9,681; Fulani, New Alliance, 1,459; Daniels, Ind., 1,186.

1988: Dukakis, D, 159,407; Bush, R, 27,590; Fulani, New Alliance, 2,901; Paul, LB, 554.

1984: Mondale, D, 180,408; Reagan, R, 29,009; Bergland, LB, 279.

1980: Carter, D, 130,231; Reagan, R, 23,313; Anderson, Ind., 16,131; Commoner, Citizens, 1,826; Clark, LB, 1,104; Hall, Comm., 369; DeBerry, Soc. Workers, 173; Griswold, Workers World, 52; write-in, 690.

1976: Carter, D, 137,818; Ford, R, 27,873; Camejo, Soc. Workers, 545; McBride, LB, 274; Hall, Comm., 219; LaRouche, U.S. Labor, 157.

1972: McGovern, D, 127,627; Nixon, R, 35,226; Reed, Soc. Workers, 316; Hall, Comm., 252.

1968: Humphrey, D, 139, 566; Nixon, R, 31,012.

1964: Johnson, D, 169,796; Goldwater, R, 28,801.

Florida

County	2020		2016	
	Biden (D)	Trump (R)	Clinton (D)	Trump (R)
Alachua	89,704	50,972	75,820	46,834
Baker	2,037	11,911	2,112	10,294
Bay	25,614	66,097	21,797	62,194
Bradford	3,160	10,334	2,924	8,913
Brevard	148,549	207,883	119,679	181,848
Broward	618,752	333,409	553,320	260,951
Calhoun	1,209	5,274	1,241	4,655
Charlotte	42,273	73,243	33,445	60,218
Citrus	27,092	65,352	22,789	54,456
Clay	38,317	84,480	27,822	74,963
Collier	77,621	128,950	61,085	105,423
Columbia	8,914	23,836	7,601	20,368
DeSoto	4,259	8,313	3,781	6,778
Dixie	1,365	6,759	1,270	5,822
Duval	252,556	233,762	205,704	211,672
Escambia	70,929	96,674	57,461	88,808
Flagler	28,161	43,043	22,026	33,850
Franklin	2,120	4,675	1,744	4,125
Gadsden	16,153	7,465	15,020	6,728
Gilchrist	1,700	7,895	1,458	6,740
Glades	1,385	3,782	1,271	2,996
Gulf	1,985	6,113	1,720	5,329
Hamilton	1,963	3,815	1,904	3,443
Hardee	2,298	6,122	2,149	5,242
Hendry	4,929	7,906	4,615	6,195
Hernando	37,519	70,412	31,795	58,970
Highlands	16,938	34,873	14,937	29,565
Hillsborough	376,367	327,398	307,896	266,870
Holmes	924	8,080	853	7,483
Indian River	37,844	58,872	29,043	48,620
Jackson	6,766	15,488	6,397	14,257
Jefferson	3,897	4,479	3,541	3,930
Lafayette	510	3,128	518	2,809
Lake	83,505	125,859	62,838	102,188
Lee	157,695	233,247	124,908	191,551
Leon	103,517	57,453	92,068	53,821
Levy	6,205	16,749	5,101	13,775
Liberty	694	2,846	651	2,543
Madison	3,747	5,576	3,526	4,851
Manatee	90,166	124,987	71,224	101,944
Marion	74,858	127,826	62,041	107,833
Martin	36,893	61,168	30,185	53,204
Miami-Dade	617,864	532,833	624,146	333,999

County	2020 Biden (D)	Trump (R)	2016 Clinton (D)	Trump (R)
Monroe	21,881	25,693	18,971	21,904
Nassau	15,564	42,566	10,869	34,266
Okaloosa	34,248	79,798	23,780	71,893
Okeechobee	4,390	11,470	3,959	9,356
Orange	395,014	245,398	329,894	195,216
Osceola	97,297	73,480	85,458	50,301
Palm Beach	433,572	334,711	374,673	272,402
Pasco	119,073	179,621	90,142	142,101
Pinellas	277,450	276,209	233,701	239,201
Polk	145,049	194,586	117,433	157,430
Putnam	10,527	25,514	10,094	22,138
St. Johns	63,850	110,946	43,099	88,684
St. Lucie	84,137	86,831	68,881	70,289
Santa Rosa	27,612	77,385	18,464	65,339
Sarasota	120,110	148,370	97,870	124,438
Seminole	132,528	125,241	105,914	109,443
Sumter	29,341	62,761	22,638	52,730
Suwannee	4,485	16,410	3,964	14,287
Taylor	2,299	7,751	2,152	6,930
Union	1,053	5,133	1,014	4,568
Volusia	130,575	173,821	109,091	143,007
Wakulla	5,351	12,874	4,348	10,512
Walton	10,338	32,947	6,876	25,756
Washington	2,347	9,876	2,264	8,637
Totals	**5,297,045**	**5,668,731**	**4,504,975**	**4,617,886**

Florida Vote Since 1960

2020: Trump, R, 5,668,731; Biden, D, 5,297,045; Jorgensen, LB, 70,324; Hawkins, Green, 14,721; De La Fuente, RF, 5,966; La Riva, Socialism/Liberation, 5,712; Blankenship, Const., 3,902.

2016: Trump, R, 4,617,886; Clinton, D, 4,504,975; Johnson, LB, 207,043; Stein, Green, 64,399; Castle, Const., 16,475; De La Fuente, RF, 9,108.

2012: Obama, D, 4,237,756; Romney, R, 4,163,447; Johnson, LB, 44,726; Stein, Green, 8,947; Barr, Peace/Freedom, 8,154; Stevens, Objectivist, 3,856; Goode, Const., 2,607; Anderson, Justice, 1,754; Hoefling, Amer. Ind., 946; Barnett, RF, 820; Alexander, Soc., 799; Lindsay, Socialism/Liberation, 322.

2008: Obama, D, 4,282,074; McCain, R, 4,045,624; Nader, Ecology (FL), 28,124; Barr, LB, 17,218; Baldwin, Const., 7,915; McKinney, Green, 2,887; Keyes, Amer. Ind., 2,550; La Riva, Socialism/Liberation, 1,516; Jay, Boston Tea, 795; Harris, Soc. Workers, 533; Stevens, Objectivist, 419; Moore, Soc. USA, 405; Amondson, Prohib., 293.

2004: Bush, R, 3,964,522; Kerry, D, 3,583,544; Nader, RF, 32,971; Badnarik, LB, 11,996; Peroutka, Const., 6,626; Cobb, Green, 3,917; Brown, Soc., 3,502; Harris, Soc. Workers, 2,732.

2000: Bush, R, 2,912,790; Gore, D, 2,912,253; Nader, Green, 97,488; Buchanan, RF, 17,484; Browne, LB, 16,415; Hagelin, Natural Law, 2,281; Moorehead, Workers World, 1,804; Phillips, Const., 1,371; McReynolds, Soc., 622; Harris, Soc. Workers, 562.

1996: Clinton, D, 2,545,968; Dole, R, 2,243,324; Perot, RF, 483,776; Browne, LB, 23,312.

1992: Bush, R, 2,171,781; Clinton, D, 2,071,651; Perot, Ind., 1,052,481; Marrou, LB, 15,068.

1988: Bush, R, 2,616,597; Dukakis, D, 1,655,851; Paul, LB, 19,796; Fulani, New Alliance, 6,655.

1984: Reagan, R, 2,728,775; Mondale, D, 1,448,344.

1980: Reagan, R, 2,046,951; Carter, D, 1,419,475; Anderson, Ind., 189,692; Clark, LB, 30,524; write-in, 285.

1976: Carter, D, 1,636,000; Ford, R, 1,469,531; McCarthy, Ind., 23,643; Anderson, Amer., 21,325.

1972: Nixon, R, 1,857,759; McGovern, D, 718,117; scattered, 7,407.

1968: Nixon, R, 886,804; Humphrey, D, 676,794; Wallace, 3rd party, 624,207.

1964: Johnson, D, 948,540; Goldwater, R, 905,941.

1960: Nixon, R, 795,476; Kennedy, D, 748,700.

Georgia

County	2020 Biden (D)	Trump (R)	2016 Clinton (D)	Trump (R)
Appling	1,784	6,570	1,434	5,494
Atkinson	825	2,300	697	1,878
Bacon	625	4,017	608	3,364
Baker	652	897	650	775
Baldwin	9,140	8,903	7,970	7,697
Banks	932	7,795	684	6,134
Barrow	10,453	26,804	6,580	21,108
Bartow	12,091	37,672	8,212	29,911
Ben Hill	2,393	4,111	2,101	3,739
Berrien	1,269	6,419	1,047	5,422
Bibb	43,408	26,559	36,787	24,043
Bleckley	1,312	4,329	1,101	3,719
Brantley	700	6,993	619	5,567
Brooks	2,791	4,261	2,528	3,701
Bryan	6,738	14,240	4,014	10,529
Bulloch	11,248	18,387	9,261	15,097
Burke	5,208	5,400	4,731	4,491
Butts	3,274	8,406	2,566	6,717
Calhoun	1,263	923	1,179	830
Camden	7,967	15,249	5,930	12,310
Candler	1,269	3,133	1,026	2,664
Carroll	16,236	37,476	12,464	30,029
Catoosa	6,932	25,167	4,771	20,876
Charlton	1,105	3,419	1,004	2,951
Chatham	78,247	53,232	62,290	45,688
Chattahoochee	667	880	594	751
Chattooga	1,854	8,064	1,613	6,462
Cherokee	42,779	99,585	25,231	80,649
Clarke	36,055	14,450	29,603	12,717
Clay	791	637	697	566
Clayton	95,466	15,811	78,220	12,645
Clinch	744	2,105	686	1,727
Cobb	221,847	165,436	160,121	152,912
Coffee	4,511	10,578	4,094	9,588
Colquitt	4,190	11,777	3,463	9,898
Columbia	29,232	50,013	18,887	43,085
Cook	2,059	4,900	1,753	4,176
Coweta	24,210	51,501	16,583	42,533
Crawford	1,615	4,428	1,421	3,635
Crisp	2,982	4,985	2,837	4,549
Dade	1,261	6,066	965	5,051
Dawson	2,486	13,398	1,448	9,900
Decatur	4,782	6,755	4,124	6,020
DeKalb	308,162	58,377	251,370	51,468
Dodge	2,172	5,843	1,839	5,021
Dooly	1,911	2,159	1,872	1,951
Dougherty	24,568	10,441	23,311	10,232
Douglas	42,814	25,454	31,005	24,817
Early	2,450	2,710	2,168	2,552
Echols	167	1,256	156	1,007
Effingham	7,718	23,361	4,853	17,874
Elbert	2,879	6,226	2,539	5,292
Emanuel	2,886	6,553	2,435	5,335
Evans	1,324	2,888	1,130	2,404
Fannin	2,570	12,169	1,923	9,632
Fayette	33,054	37,956	23,284	35,048
Floyd	11,917	28,906	9,159	24,114
Forsyth	42,208	85,123	23,462	69,851
Franklin	1,593	9,069	1,243	7,054
Fulton	380,212	137,247	297,051	117,783
Gilmer	2,932	13,429	1,965	10,477
Glascock	155	1,402	138	1,235
Glynn	15,882	25,617	11,775	21,512
Gordon	4,384	19,405	3,181	15,191
Grady	3,619	7,034	3,013	6,053
Greene	4,087	7,066	3,199	5,490
Gwinnett	241,994	166,400	166,153	146,989
Habersham	3,562	16,637	2,483	13,190
Hall	25,033	64,183	16,180	51,733
Hancock	2,976	1,154	2,701	843
Haralson	1,791	12,330	1,475	9,585
Harris	5,457	14,319	4,086	11,936
Hart	3,157	9,465	2,585	7,286
Heard	824	4,519	743	3,370
Henry	73,443	48,259	50,057	45,724
Houston	32,239	41,540	22,553	35,430
Irwin	1,008	3,134	891	2,716
Jackson	7,642	29,502	4,491	21,784
Jasper	1,761	5,822	1,544	4,360
Jeff Davis	1,028	4,695	901	4,104
Jefferson	4,058	3,537	3,821	3,063
Jenkins	1,266	2,161	1,123	1,895
Johnson	1,222	2,850	1,136	2,519

County	2020 Biden (D)	Trump (R)	2016 Clinton (D)	Trump (R)
Jones	4,882	9,940	3,961	8,305
Lamar	2,620	6,331	2,270	5,190
Lanier	1,019	2,509	806	1,984
Laurens	8,074	14,493	6,752	12,411
Lee	4,558	12,007	3,170	10,646
Liberty	13,104	7,959	9,556	6,134
Lincoln	1,432	3,173	1,273	2,759
Long	2,035	3,527	1,360	2,626
Lowndes	20,116	25,692	15,064	21,635
Lumpkin	3,126	12,163	2,220	9,619
Macon	2,858	1,783	2,705	1,540
Madison	3,411	11,326	2,425	9,201
Marion	1,312	2,275	1,213	1,921
McDuffie	4,168	6,169	3,699	5,432
McIntosh	2,612	4,016	2,303	3,487
Meriwether	4,287	6,524	3,804	5,222
Miller	748	2,066	623	1,891
Mitchell	3,993	4,935	3,493	4,279
Monroe	4,385	11,057	3,571	8,832
Montgomery	980	2,960	847	2,670
Morgan	3,353	8,231	2,663	6,559
Murray	2,301	12,944	1,800	10,341
Muscogee	49,446	30,107	39,851	26,976
Newton	29,789	23,869	21,943	20,913
Oconee	8,162	16,595	5,581	13,425
Oglethorpe	2,439	5,592	1,831	4,625
Paulding	29,695	54,517	18,025	44,662
Peach	5,922	6,506	5,100	5,413
Pickens	2,824	14,110	1,979	11,651
Pierce	1,100	7,898	903	6,302
Pike	1,505	9,127	1,240	7,278
Polk	3,657	13,587	2,867	11,014
Pulaski	1,230	2,815	1,104	2,437
Putnam	3,448	8,291	2,758	6,544
Quitman	497	604	461	575
Rabun	1,984	7,474	1,444	6,287
Randolph	1,671	1,390	1,598	1,271
Richmond	59,119	26,780	48,814	24,461
Rockdale	31,237	13,014	23,255	13,478
Schley	462	1,800	401	1,472
Screven	2,661	3,915	2,300	3,305
Seminole	1,256	2,613	1,189	2,345
Spalding	11,828	18,104	9,357	15,646
Stephens	2,386	9,367	1,837	7,686
Stewart	1,182	801	1,222	805
Sumter	6,314	5,733	5,520	5,276
Talbot	2,114	1,392	2,002	1,196
Taliaferro	561	360	545	349
Tattnall	2,062	6,054	1,681	5,096
Taylor	1,388	2,420	1,296	2,064
Telfair	1,488	2,825	1,313	2,450
Terrell	2,376	2,004	2,267	1,874
Thomas	8,708	12,969	7,142	11,228
Tift	5,318	10,784	4,347	9,584
Toombs	2,938	7,873	2,338	6,615
Towns	1,550	6,384	1,210	5,383
Treutlen	952	2,101	862	1,809
Troup	11,577	18,142	9,713	15,750
Turner	1,409	2,349	1,246	2,095
Twiggs	2,044	2,370	1,971	2,035
Union	2,800	12,650	1,963	9,852
Upson	4,203	8,606	3,475	7,292
Walker	5,770	23,173	4,215	18,950
Walton	12,683	37,839	8,292	31,125
Ware	4,169	9,903	3,440	8,513
Warren	1,468	1,166	1,314	991
Washington	4,743	4,668	4,200	4,149
Wayne	2,688	9,987	2,041	8,153
Webster	640	748	473	630
Wheeler	689	1,583	646	1,421
White	2,411	12,222	1,674	9,761
Whitfield	10,680	25,644	7,937	21,537
Wilcox	861	2,402	852	2,096
Wilkes	2,160	2,823	1,848	2,572
Wilkinson	2,074	2,665	1,894	2,333
Worth	2,395	6,830	2,020	6,152
Totals	**2,473,633**	**2,461,854**	**1,877,963**	**2,089,104**

Georgia Vote Since 1960

2020: Biden, D, 2,473,633; Trump, R, 2,461,854; Jorgensen, LB, 62,229.

2016: Trump, R, 2,089,104; Clinton, D, 1,877,963 Johnson, LB, 125,306; McMullin, Ind., 13,017; Stein, Ind., 7,674; Castle, Ind., 1,110.

2012: Romney, R, 2,078,688; Obama, D, 1,773,827; Johnson, LB, 45,324.

2008: McCain, R, 2,048,759; Obama, D, 1,844,123; Barr, LB, 28,731.

2004: Bush, R, 1,914,254; Kerry, D, 1,366,149; Badnarik, LB, 18,387.

2000: Bush, R, 1,419,720; Gore, D, 1,116,230; Browne, LB, 36,332; Buchanan, Ind., 10,926.

1996: Dole, R, 1,080,843; Clinton, D, 1,053,849; Perot, RF, 146,337; Browne, LB, 17,870.

1992: Clinton, D, 1,008,966; Bush, R, 995,252; Perot, Ind., 309,657; Marrou, LB, 7,110.

1988: Bush, R, 1,081,331; Dukakis, D, 714,792; Paul, LB, 8,435; Fulani, New Alliance, 5,099.

1984: Reagan, R, 1,068,722; Mondale, D, 706,628.

1980: Carter, D, 890,955; Reagan, R, 654,168; Anderson, Ind., 36,055; Clark, LB, 15,627.

1976: Carter, D, 979,409; Ford, R, 483,743; write-in, 4,306.

1972: Nixon, R, 881,496; McGovern, D, 289,529; Schmitz, Amer., 812; scattered, 2,935.

1968: Wallace, 3rd party, 535,550; Nixon, R, 380,111; Humphrey, D, 334,440; write-in, 162.

1964: Goldwater, R, 616,600; Johnson, D, 522,557.

1960: Kennedy, D, 458,638; Nixon, R, 274,472; write-in, 239.

Hawaii

County	2020 Biden (D)	Trump (R)	2016 Clinton (D)	Trump (R)
Hawaii	58,731	26,897	41,259	17,501
Honolulu	238,869	136,259	175,696	90,326
Kauai	21,225	11,582	16,456	7,574
Maui	47,305	22,126	33,480	13,446
Totals	**366,130**	**196,864**	**266,891**	**128,847**

Hawaii Vote Since 1960

2020: Biden, D, 366,130; Trump, R, 196,864; Jorgensen, LB, 5,539; Hawkins, Green, 3,822; Pierce, Amer. Shop., 1,183; Blankenship, Const., 931.

2016: Clinton, D, 266,891; Trump, R, 128,847; Johnson, LB, 15,594; Stein, Green, 12,737; Castle, Const., 4,508.

2012: Obama, D, 306,658; Romney, R, 121,015; Johnson, LB, 3,840; Stein, Green, 3,184.

2008: Obama, D, 325,871; McCain, R, 120,566; Nader, Ind. (HI), 3,825; Barr, LB, 1,314; Baldwin, Const., 1,013; McKinney, Green, 979.

2004: Kerry, D, 231,708; Bush, R, 194,191; Cobb, Green, 1,737; Badnarik, LB, 1,377.

2000: Gore, D, 205,286; Bush, R, 137,845; Nader, Green, 21,623; Browne, LB, 1,477; Buchanan, RF, 1,071; Phillips, Const., 343; Hagelin, Natural Law, 306.

1996: Clinton, D, 205,012; Dole, R, 113,943; Perot, RF, 27,358; Nader, Green, 10,386; Browne, LB, 2,493; Hagelin, Natural Law, 570; Phillips, Taxpayers, 358.

1992: Clinton, D, 179,310; Bush, R, 136,822; Perot, Ind., 53,003; Gritz, Populist/America First, 1,452; Marrou, LB, 1,119.

1988: Dukakis, D, 192,364; Bush, R, 158,625; Paul, LB, 1,999; Fulani, New Alliance, 1,003.

1984: Reagan, R, 184,934; Mondale, D, 147,098; Bergland, LB, 2,167.

1980: Carter, D, 135,879; Reagan, R, 130,112; Anderson, Ind., 32,021; Clark, LB, 3,269; Commoner, Citizens, 1,548; Hall, Comm., 458.

1976: Carter, D, 147,375; Ford, R, 140,003; MacBride, LB, 3,923.

1972: Nixon, R, 168,865; McGovern, D, 101,409.

1968: Humphrey, D, 141,324; Nixon, R, 91,425; Wallace, 3rd party, 3,469.

1964: Johnson, D, 163,249; Goldwater, R, 44,022.

1960: Kennedy, D, 92,410; Nixon, R, 92,295.

Idaho

County	2020 Biden (D)	Trump (R)	2016 Clinton (D)	Trump (R)
Ada	120,539	130,699	75,677	93,752
Adams	591	1,941	415	1,556
Bannock	14,682	23,331	10,342	17,180
Bear Lake	350	2,914	255	2,203
Benewah	977	3,878	770	3,103

County	2020 Biden (D)	Trump (R)	2016 Clinton (D)	Trump (R)
Bingham	4,124	15,295	2,924	10,907
Blaine	8,919	4,032	6,416	3,340
Boise	1,204	3,485	777	2,673
Bonner	8,310	18,369	5,819	13,343
Bonneville	14,254	37,805	8,930	26,699
Boundary	1,220	4,937	933	3,789
Butte	188	1,202	160	914
Camas	149	507	110	410
Canyon	25,881	61,759	16,883	47,222
Caribou	431	2,906	271	2,275
Cassia	1,464	7,907	1,036	5,949
Clark	41	264	44	203
Clearwater	877	3,453	704	2,852
Custer	603	2,089	427	1,777
Elmore	2,601	7,246	1,814	5,816
Franklin	657	5,845	385	3,901
Fremont	998	5,548	651	4,090
Gem	1,803	7,951	1,229	5,980
Gooding	1,256	4,659	930	3,743
Idaho	1,561	7,826	1,196	6,441
Jefferson	1,661	12,099	976	8,436
Jerome	1,893	5,734	1,329	4,644
Kootenai	24,312	62,837	16,264	44,449
Latah	10,236	9,472	8,093	7,265
Lemhi	1,032	3,592	733	3,011
Lewis	349	1,489	270	1,202
Lincoln	414	1,469	360	1,184
Madison	2,666	13,559	1,201	8,941
Minidoka	1,550	6,265	1,167	4,887
Nez Perce	6,686	13,738	4,828	10,699
Oneida	249	2,148	184	1,531
Owyhee	816	3,819	591	3,052
Payette	2,161	8,862	1,507	6,489
Power	865	2,116	699	1,666
Shoshone	1,693	4,216	1,384	3,297
Teton	3,318	2,858	2,159	2,167
Twin Falls	9,391	25,897	6,233	19,828
Valley	2,976	3,947	1,913	2,906
Washington	1,073	4,154	776	3,283
Totals	287,021	554,119	189,765	409,055

Idaho Vote Since 1960

2020: Trump, R, 554,119; Biden, D, 287,021; Jorgensen, LB, 16,404; West, Ind., 3,632; Pierce, Ind., 2,808; Blankenship, Const., 1,886; De La Fuente, Ind., 1,491.

2016: Trump, R, 409,055; Clinton, D, 189,765; McMullin, Ind., 46,476; Johnson, LB, 28,331; Stein, Ind., 8,496; Castle, Ind., 4,403; Copeland, Const., 2,356; De La Fuente, Ind., 1,373.

2012: Romney, R, 420,911; Obama, D, 212,787; Johnson, LB, 9,453; Stein, Ind., 4,402; Anderson, Ind., 2,499; Goode, Const., 2,222.

2008: McCain, R, 403,012; Obama, D, 236,440; Nader, Ind., 7,175; Baldwin, Const., 4,747; Barr, LB, 3,658.

2004: Bush, R, 409,235; Kerry, D, 181,098; Badnarik, LB, 3,844; Peroutka, Const., 3,084.

2000: Bush, R, 336,937; Gore, D, 138,637; Buchanan, RF, 7,615; Browne, LB, 3,488; Phillips, Const., 1,469; Hagelin, Natural Law, 1,177.

1996: Dole, R, 256,595; Clinton, D, 165,443; Perot, RF, 62,518; Browne, LB, 3,325; Phillips, U.S. Taxpayers, 2,230; Hagelin, Natural Law, 1,600.

1992: Bush, R, 202,645; Clinton, D, 137,013; Perot, Ind., 130,395; Gritz, Populist/America First, 10,281; Marrou, LB, 1,167.

1988: Bush, R, 253,881; Dukakis, D, 147,272; Paul, LB, 5,313; Fulani, Ind., 2,502.

1984: Reagan, R, 297,523; Mondale, D, 108,510; Bergland, LB, 2,823.

1980: Reagan, R, 290,699; Carter, D, 110,192; Anderson, Ind., 27,058; Clark, LB, 8,425; Rarick, Amer., 1,057.

1976: Ford, R, 204,151; Carter, D, 126,549; Maddox, Amer., 5,935; MacBride, LB, 3,558; LaRouche, U.S. Labor, 739.

1972: Nixon, R, 199,384; McGovern, D, 80,826; Schmitz, Amer., 28,869; Spock, People's, 903.

1968: Nixon, R, 165,369; Humphrey, D, 89,273; Wallace, 3rd party, 36,541.

1964: Johnson, D, 148,920; Goldwater, R, 143,557.

1960: Nixon, R, 161,597; Kennedy, D, 138,853.

Illinois

County	2020 Biden (D)	Trump (R)	2016 Clinton (D)	Trump (R)
Adams	8,633	24,220	7,676	22,790
Alexander	1,114	1,486	1,262	1,496
Bond	2,288	5,625	2,068	4,888
Boone	10,542	13,883	8,986	12,282
Brown	486	1,931	476	1,796
Bureau	6,669	10,411	6,029	9,281
Calhoun	677	2,046	739	1,721
Carroll	2,748	5,105	2,447	4434
Cass	1,615	3,625	1,621	3,216
Champaign	57,067	35,285	50,137	33,368
Christian	4,335	11,563	3,992	10,543
Clark	1,993	6,226	1,877	5,622
Clay	1,129	5,629	1,020	5,021
Clinton	4,493	14,304	3,945	12,412
Coles	8,067	14,037	7,309	13,003
Cook	1,725,973	558,269	1,611,946	453,287
Crawford	2,202	7,043	1,992	6,277
Cumberland	1,142	4,601	1,031	4,206
DeKalb	24,643	21,905	20,466	19,091
DeWitt	2,191	5,632	1,910	5,077
Douglas	2,335	6,227	1,949	5,698
DuPage	281,222	193,611	228,622	166,415
Edgar	1,887	6,193	1,793	5,645
Edwards	488	2,833	434	2,778
Effingham	3,716	15,006	3,083	13,635
Fayette	1,826	8,055	1,819	7,372
Ford	1,754	5,048	1,414	4,480
Franklin	4,760	13,622	4,727	13,116
Fulton	6,503	9,867	6,133	8,492
Gallatin	622	2,019	657	1,942
Greene	1,349	4,770	1,205	4,145
Grundy	9,626	16,523	8,065	13,454
Hamilton	824	3,432	802	3,206
Hancock	2,315	6,906	2,139	6,430
Hardin	449	1,691	420	1,653
Henderson	1,187	2,394	1,155	2,155
Henry	9,797	15,300	8,871	13,985
Iroquois	2,908	10,877	2,504	9,750
Jackson	11,181	10,890	11,634	10,843
Jasper	1,007	4,494	924	3,975
Jefferson	4,608	12,476	4,425	11,695
Jersey	2,961	8,712	2,679	7,748
Jo Daviess	5,109	7,166	4,462	6,121
Johnson	1,281	5,059	1,142	4,649
Kane	130,166	96,775	103,665	82,734
Kankakee	20,271	28,532	18,971	25,129
Kendall	33,168	29,492	24,884	24,961
Knox	10,703	12,009	10,083	10,737
Lake	204,032	123,594	171,095	109,767
LaSalle	22,442	30,113	19,543	26,689
Lawrence	1,419	4,886	1,290	4,521
Lee	6,407	9,630	5,528	8,612
Livingston	4,615	12,208	4,023	10,208
Logan	3,840	9,136	3,313	8,181
Macon	19,847	28,589	18,343	26,866
Macoupin	7,365	16,153	6,689	14,322
Madison	57,836	76,031	50,587	70,490
Marion	4,524	12,678	4,369	11,859
Marshall	2,005	4,197	1,789	3,785
Mason	1,985	4,654	2,014	4,058
Massac	1,725	4,997	1,558	4,846
McDonough	4,992	7,027	5,288	6,795
McHenry	78,154	82,260	60,803	71,612
McLean	43,933	40,502	36,196	37,237
Menard	2,022	4,764	1,817	4,231
Mercer	3,280	5,418	3,071	4,807
Monroe	6,569	14,142	5,535	12,629
Montgomery	3,905	9,544	3,504	8,630
Morgan	5,076	9,950	4,696	9,076
Moultrie	1,662	4,964	1,481	4,455
Ogle	9,428	16,248	8,050	14,352
Peoria	43,578	38,252	38,060	35,633
Perry	2,612	7,313	2,462	6,855
Piatt	3,329	6,248	2,645	5,634
Pike	1,484	6,332	1,413	5,754
Pope	433	1,722	375	1,678
Pulaski	891	1,699	962	1,675
Putnam	1,338	1,993	1,147	1,767
Randolph	3,592	11,076	3,439	10,023
Richland	1,830	6,089	1,584	5,739
Rock Island	36,691	28,603	32,298	26,998
St. Clair	68,326	57,150	60,756	53,857
Saline	2,789	8,103	2,572	8,276
Sangamon	48,917	53,485	40,907	49,944
Schuyler	1,068	2,773	1,075	2,524
Scott	572	2,114	535	1,966

County	2020 Biden (D)	Trump (R)	2016 Clinton (D)	Trump (R)
Shelby	2,504	9,426	2,288	8,229
Stark	815	2,004	751	1,778
Stephenson	9,055	12,521	7,768	11,083
Tazewell	24,819	42,513	20,685	38,707
Union	2,579	6,161	2,402	5,790
Vermilion	10,323	20,725	10,039	19,087
Wabash	1,253	4,237	1,151	4,047
Warren	3,090	4,676	2,987	4,275
Washington	1,641	6,115	1,448	5,571
Wayne	1,187	7,176	1,048	6,967
White	1,517	5,791	1,412	5,640
Whiteside	12,253	14,527	11,035	12,615
Will	183,915	155,116	151,927	132,720
Williamson	10,206	22,801	8,581	21,570
Winnebago	64,056	60,861	55,713	55,624
Woodford	6,160	14,799	5,092	13,207
Totals	**3,471,915**	**2,446,891**	**3,090,729**	**2,146,015**

Illinois Vote Since 1960

2020: Biden, D, 3,471,915; Trump, R, 2,446,891; Jorgensen, LB, 66,544; Hawkins, Green, 30,494; Carroll, Amer. Solidarity, 9,548; La Riva, Socialism/Liberation, 8,046.
2016: Clinton, D, 3,090,729; Trump, R, 2,146,015; Johnson, LB, 209,596; Stein, Green, 76,802; McMullin, Ind., 11,655; Castle, Const., 1,138.
2012: Obama, D, 3,019,512; Romney, R, 2,135,216; Johnson, LB, 56,229; Stein, Green, 30,222.
2008: Obama, D, 3,419,348; McCain, R, 2,031,179; Nader, Ind., 30,948; Barr, LB, 19,642; McKinney, Green, 11,838; Baldwin, Const., 8,256; Polachek, New Party, 1,149.
2004: Kerry, D, 2,891,550; Bush, R, 2,345,946; Badnarik, LB, 32,442.
2000: Gore, D, 2,589,026; Bush, R, 2,019,421; Nader, Green, 103,759; Buchanan, Ind., 16,106; Browne, LB, 11,623; Hagelin, RF, 2,127.
1996: Clinton, D, 2,341,744; Dole, R, 1,587,021; Perot, RF, 346,408; Browne, LB, 22,548; Phillips, U.S. Taxpayers, 7,606; Hagelin, Natural Law, 4,606.
1992: Clinton, D, 2,453,350; Bush, R, 1,734,096; Perot, Ind., 840,515; Marrou, LB, 9,218; Fulani, New Alliance, 5,267; Gritz, Populist/America First, 3,577; Hagelin, Natural Law, 2,751; Warren, Soc. Workers, 1,361.
1988: Bush, R, 2,310,939; Dukakis, D, 2,215,940; Paul, LB, 14,944; Fulani, Solidarity, 10,276.
1984: Reagan, R, 2,707,103; Mondale, D, 2,086,499; Bergland, LB, 10,086.
1980: Reagan, R, 2,358,049; Carter, D, 1,981,413; Anderson, Ind., 346,754; Clark, LB, 38,939; Commoner, Citizens, 10,692; Hall, Comm., 9,711; Griswold, Workers World, 2,257; DeBerry, Soc. Workers, 1,302; write-in, 604.
1976: Ford, R, 2,364,269; Carter, D, 2,271,295; McCarthy, Ind., 55,939; Hall, Comm., 9,250; MacBride, LB, 8,057; Camejo, Soc. Workers, 3,615; Levin, Soc. Labor, 2,422; LaRouche, U.S. Labor, 2,018; write-in, 1,968.
1972: Nixon, R, 2,788,179; McGovern, D, 1,913,472; Fisher, Soc. Labor, 12,344; Hall, Comm., 4,541; Schmitz, Amer., 2,471; others, 2,229.
1968: Nixon, R, 2,174,774; Humphrey, D, 2,039,814; Wallace, 3rd party, 390,958; Blomen, Soc. Labor, 13,878; write-in, 325.
1964: Johnson, D, 2,796,833; Goldwater, R, 1,905,946; write-in, 62.
1960: Kennedy, D, 2,377,846; Nixon, R, 2,368,988; Hass, Soc. Labor, 10,560; write-in, 15.

Indiana

County	2020 Biden (D)	Trump (R)	2016 Clinton (D)	Trump (R)
Adams	3,236	10,686	2,805	9,648
Allen	73,189	92,083	55,382	83,930
Bartholomew	12,934	22,410	9,841	20,640
Benton	1,009	3,007	860	2,579
Blackford	1,376	3,841	1,243	3,350
Boone	15,244	22,351	10,181	19,654
Brown	3,036	5,777	2,518	5,016
Carroll	2,224	7,086	1,892	6,273
Cass	4,304	10,552	3,759	9,701
Clark	23,093	33,668	18,808	30,035
Clay	2,552	9,499	2,306	8,531
Clinton	3,361	9,334	2,819	8,531
Crawford	1,355	3,483	1,323	3,015
Daviess	2,169	9,576	1,800	8,545
Dearborn	5,446	19,528	4,883	18,113
Decatur	2,439	9,575	2,121	8,490

County	2020 Biden (D)	Trump (R)	2016 Clinton (D)	Trump (R)
DeKalb	4,966	14,237	3,942	12,054
Delaware	20,474	26,827	18,153	24,263
Dubois	6,292	15,033	5,389	13,365
Elkhart	26,108	46,972	20,740	41,867
Fayette	2,237	7,755	2,252	6,839
Floyd	17,511	23,400	13,945	21,432
Fountain	1,629	6,154	1,476	5,662
Franklin	2,137	9,691	1,969	8,669
Fulton	2,280	6,694	1,960	6,010
Gibson	4,023	11,817	3,721	11,081
Grant	8,015	18,543	7,010	17,008
Greene	3,389	11,103	2,929	10,277
Hamilton	88,390	101,587	57,263	87,404
Hancock	12,895	28,996	8,904	25,074
Harrison	5,343	14,565	4,783	12,943
Hendricks	32,604	53,802	22,600	48,337
Henry	5,544	15,043	5,124	13,895
Howard	13,303	26,449	11,215	23,675
Huntington	4,255	13,147	3,506	11,649
Jackson	4,302	14,555	3,843	12,859
Jasper	3,798	11,383	3,329	9,382
Jay	1,926	6,361	1,889	5,697
Jefferson	4,731	9,663	4,326	8,546
Jennings	2,523	9,490	2,364	8,224
Johnson	24,736	51,219	17,318	45,456
Knox	4,067	11,655	3,772	11,077
Kosciusko	8,364	26,499	6,313	23,935
LaGrange	2,355	8,110	2,080	7,025
Lake	124,870	91,760	116,935	75,625
LaPorte	22,427	25,997	19,798	22,687
Lawrence	4,961	15,601	4,210	14,035
Madison	19,524	31,215	18,595	32,376
Marion	247,772	134,175	212,899	130,360
Marshall	5,712	13,844	4,798	12,288
Martin	1,011	4,029	881	3,697
Miami	3,235	10,925	2,766	9,975
Monroe	39,861	22,071	34,216	20,592
Montgomery	4,213	12,659	3,362	11,059
Morgan	7,781	27,512	6,040	23,674
Newton	1,509	4,942	1,404	4,077
Noble	4,660	14,195	3,904	12,198
Ohio	668	2,054	686	2,118
Orange	2,224	6,432	2,048	5,803
Owen	2,420	7,286	1,946	6,153
Parke	1,503	5,400	1,441	4,863
Perry	3,203	5,345	3,062	4,556
Pike	1,415	4,692	1,297	4,398
Porter	39,746	45,008	33,676	38,832
Posey	3,811	9,206	3,521	8,404
Pulaski	1,463	4,246	1,327	3,854
Putnam	3,946	12,278	3,356	10,637
Randolph	2,513	8,312	2,446	7,517
Ripley	2,774	11,261	2,471	9,806
Rush	1,754	6,035	1,525	5,292
St. Joseph	59,896	53,164	52,252	52,021
Scott	2,701	7,331	2,642	6,074
Shelby	5,023	14,568	4,247	12,718
Spencer	3,213	7,357	2,861	6,572
Starke	2,650	7,466	2,489	6,367
Steuben	4,513	11,327	3,744	10,133
Sullivan	2,153	6,691	2,113	6,138
Switzerland	964	3,133	930	2,558
Tippecanoe	35,017	34,581	27,282	30,768
Tipton	1,834	6,110	1,587	5,589
Union	736	2,688	715	2,445
Vanderburgh	34,415	41,844	28,530	40,496
Vermillion	2,145	5,184	2,081	4,513
Vigo	18,123	24,545	15,931	21,937
Wabash	3,494	10,762	3,018	9,821
Warren	974	3,401	839	2,898
Warrick	11,923	21,326	9,086	19,113
Washington	2,784	9,114	2,636	8,209
Wayne	9,524	17,567	8,322	16,028
Wells	2,928	10,855	2,586	10,005
White	3,032	7,957	2,590	6,893
Whitley	4,234	12,862	3,379	11,358
Totals	**1,242,416**	**1,729,519**	**1,033,126**	**1,557,286**

Indiana Vote Since 1960

2020: Trump, R, 1,729,519; Biden, D, 1,242,416; Jorgensen, LB, 59,232.

2016: Trump, R, 1,557,286; Clinton, D, 1,033,126; Johnson, LB, 133,993; Stein, Green, 7,841; Castle, Const., 1,937.
2012: Romney, R, 1,420,543; Obama, D, 1,152,887; Johnson, LB, 50,111.
2008: Obama, D, 1,374,039; McCain, R, 1,345,648; Barr, LB, 29,257.
2004: Bush, R, 1,479,438; Kerry, D, 969,011; Badnarik, LB, 18,058.
2000: Bush, R, 1,245,836; Gore, D, 901,980; Buchanan, Ind., 16,959; Browne, LB, 15,530.
1996: Dole, R, 1,006,693; Clinton, D, 887,424; Perot, RF, 224,299; Browne, LB, 15,632.
1992: Bush, R, 989,375; Clinton, D, 848,420; Perot, Ind., 455,934; Marrou, LB, 7,936; Fulani, New Alliance, 2,583.
1988: Bush, R, 1,297,763; Dukakis, D, 860,643; Fulani, New Alliance, 10,215.
1984: Reagan, R, 1,377,230; Mondale, D, 841,481; Bergland, LB, 6,741.
1980: Reagan, R, 1,255,656; Carter, D, 844,197; Anderson, Ind., 111,639; Clark, LB, 19,627; Commoner, Citizens, 4,852; Greaves, Amer., 4,750; Hall, Comm., 702; DeBerry, Soc., 610.
1976: Ford, R, 1,185,958; Carter, D, 1,014,714; Anderson, Amer., 14,048; Camejo, Soc. Workers, 5,695; LaRouche, U.S. Labor, 1,947.
1972: Nixon, R, 1,405,154; McGovern, D, 708,568; Reed, Soc. Workers, 5,575; Spock, Peace/Freedom, 4,544; Fisher, Soc. Labor, 1,688.
1968: Nixon, R, 1,067,885; Humphrey, D, 806,659; Wallace, 3rd party, 243,108; Munn, Prohib., 4,616; Halstead, Soc. Workers, 1,293; Gregory, write-in, 36.
1964: Johnson, D, 1,170,848; Goldwater, R, 911,118; Munn, Prohib., 8,266; Hass, Soc. Labor, 1,374.
1960: Nixon, R, 1,175,120; Kennedy, D, 952,358; Decker, Prohib., 6,746; Hass, Soc. Labor, 1,136.

Iowa

County	2020		2016	
	Biden (D)	Trump (R)	Clinton (D)	Trump (R)
Adair	1,198	2,917	1,133	2,461
Adams	590	1,530	565	1,395
Allamakee	2,576	4,735	2,421	4,093
Appanoose	1,891	4,512	1,814	4,033
Audubon	1,071	2,295	1,080	2,136
Benton	5,160	9,188	4,678	8,232
Black Hawk	35,647	29,640	32,233	27,476
Boone	6,303	8,695	5,541	7,484
Bremer	5,958	8,294	5,356	7,208
Buchanan	4,169	6,420	3,970	5,510
Buena Vista	2,961	5,056	2,856	4,903
Butler	2,424	5,542	2,157	4,921
Calhoun	1,470	3,689	1,398	3,468
Carroll	3,454	7,737	3,309	6,638
Cass	2,201	4,969	1,951	4,761
Cedar	4,337	6,161	3,599	5,295
Cerro Gordo	10,941	12,442	9,862	11,621
Cherokee	1,936	4,495	1,679	4,192
Chickasaw	2,233	4,308	2,266	3,742
Clarke	1,466	3,144	1,465	2,713
Clay	2,662	6,137	2,249	5,877
Clayton	3,340	6,106	3,237	5,317
Clinton	10,812	13,361	10,095	11,276
Crawford	2,220	4,854	1,991	4,617
Dallas	26,879	27,987	15,701	19,339
Davis	1,013	3,032	977	2,723
Decatur	1,120	2,615	1,201	2,296
Delaware	3,157	6,666	2,957	5,694
Des Moines	8,893	10,592	8,212	9,529
Dickinson	3,661	7,438	3,056	6,753
Dubuque	25,657	27,214	22,850	23,460
Emmet	1,520	3,265	1,357	3,124
Fayette	3,835	6,145	3,689	5,620
Floyd	3,172	4,732	3,179	4,375
Franklin	1,626	3,422	1,493	3,163
Fremont	1,080	2,711	963	2,407
Greene	1,769	3,223	1,691	2,820
Grundy	2,206	4,929	1,856	4,527
Guthrie	1,985	4,272	1,732	3,628
Hamilton	2,843	4,956	2,726	4,463
Hancock	1,683	4,390	1,587	3,977
Hardin	2,976	5,850	2,787	5,254

County	2020		2016	
	Biden (D)	Trump (R)	Clinton (D)	Trump (R)
Harrison	2,440	5,569	2,131	4,902
Henry	3,275	6,507	2,904	5,779
Howard	1,772	3,127	1,677	2,611
Humboldt	1,442	3,819	1,252	3,568
Ida	917	2,880	792	2,655
Iowa	3,547	6,009	3,084	5,205
Jackson	4,029	6,940	3,837	5,824
Jasper	7,737	12,084	7,109	10,560
Jefferson	4,319	4,443	3,710	3,748
Johnson	59,177	22,925	50,200	21,044
Jones	4,213	6,572	3,787	5,720
Keokuk	1,414	3,797	1,342	3,390
Kossuth	2,696	6,275	2,543	5,653
Lee	6,541	9,773	6,215	8,803
Linn	70,874	53,364	58,935	48,390
Louisa	1,726	3,500	1,648	3,069
Lucas	1,284	3,287	1,239	2,877
Lyon	1,067	5,707	920	5,192
Madison	3,134	6,507	2,678	5,360
Mahaska	2,894	8,297	2,619	7,432
Marion	6,178	12,663	5,482	10,962
Marshall	8,176	9,571	7,652	9,146
Mills	2,508	5,585	2,090	5,067
Mitchell	2,053	3,677	1,888	3,190
Monona	1,407	3,248	1,247	3,120
Monroe	1,078	2,975	1,056	2,638
Montgomery	1,583	3,659	1,314	3,436
Muscatine	9,372	10,823	8,368	9,584
O'Brien	1,569	5,861	1,315	5,752
Osceola	601	2,690	552	2,531
Page	2,086	5,319	1,807	4,893
Palo Alto	1,519	3,370	1,398	3,081
Plymouth	3,494	10,492	2,885	9,680
Pocahontas	933	2,826	963	2,702
Polk	146,250	106,800	119,804	93,492
Pottawattamie	18,575	26,247	15,355	24,447
Poweshiek	4,306	5,657	4,304	4,946
Ringgold	709	1,968	753	1,824
Sac	1,389	4,061	1,270	3,703
Scott	46,926	43,683	40,440	39,149
Shelby	1,959	4,697	1,662	4,362
Sioux	3,019	15,680	2,300	14,785
Story	29,175	20,340	25,709	19,458
Tama	3,577	5,303	3,196	4,971
Taylor	746	2,463	758	2,111
Union	2,061	4,010	1,922	3,525
Van Buren	875	2,859	845	2,527
Wapello	5,821	8,559	5,594	8,715
Warren	12,574	17,782	10,411	14,814
Washington	4,561	6,971	3,943	6,173
Wayne	727	2,338	719	2,069
Webster	6,613	10,938	6,305	10,056
Winnebago	2,135	3,707	1,931	3,447
Winneshiek	5,617	6,235	5,254	5,344
Woodbury	18,704	25,736	16,210	24,727
Worth	1,596	2,738	1,530	2,453
Wright	1,996	4,136	1,896	3,800
Totals	**759,061**	**897,672**	**653,669**	**800,983**

Iowa Vote Since 1960

2020: Trump, R, 897,672; Biden, D, 759,061; Jorgensen, LB, 19,637; West, no party, 3,210; Hawkins, Green, 3,075; Blankenship, Const., 1,707; De La Fuente, Alliance, 1,082; King, other, 546; Pierce, no party, 544.
2016: Trump, R, 800,983; Clinton, D, 653,669; Johnson, LB, 59,186; McMullin, petitioning cand., 12,366; Stein, Green, 11,479; Castle, Const., 5,335; Kahn, New Independent, 2,247; Vacek, Legal Marijuana, 2,246; De La Fuente, petitioning cand., 451; La Riva, Socialism/Liberation, 323.
2012: Obama, D, 822,544; Romney, R, 730,617; Johnson, LB, 12,926; Stein, Green, 3,769; Goode, Const., 3,038; Litzel, Ind., 1,027; Harris, Soc. Workers, 445; La Riva, Socialism/Liberation, 372.
2008: Obama, D, 828,940; McCain, R, 682,379; Nader, Peace/Freedom, 8,014; Barr, LB, 4,590; Baldwin, Const., 4,445; McKinney, Green, 1,423; Harris, Soc. Workers, 292; Moore, Soc. USA, 182; La Riva, Socialism/Liberation, 121.
2004: Bush, R, 751,957; Kerry, D, 741,898; Nader, petitioning cand., 5,973; Badnarik, LB, 2,902; Peroutka, Const., 1,304;

Cobb, Green, 1,141; Harris, Soc. Workers, 373; Van Auken, petitioning cand., 176.

2000: Gore, D, 638,517; Bush, R, 634,373; Nader, Green, 29,374; Buchanan, RF, 5,731; Browne, LB, 3,209; Hagelin, Ind., 2,281; Phillips, Const., 613; Harris, Soc. Workers, 190; McReynolds, Soc., 107.

1996: Clinton, D, 620,258; Dole, R, 492,644; Perot, RF, 105,159; Nader, Green, 6,550; Hagelin, Natural Law, 3,349; Browne, LB, 2,315; Phillips, Taxpayers, 2,229; Harris, Soc. Workers, 331.

1992: Clinton, D, 586,353; Bush, R, 504,891; Perot, Ind., 253,468; Hagelin, Natural Law, 3,079; Gritz, Populist/America First, 1,177; Marrou, LB, 1,076.

1988: Dukakis, D, 670,557; Bush, R, 545,355; LaRouche, Ind., 3,526; Paul, LB, 2,494.

1984: Reagan, R, 703,088; Mondale, D, 605,620; Bergland, LB, 1,844.

1980: Reagan, R, 676,026; Carter, D, 508,672; Anderson, Ind., 115,633; Clark, LB, 13,123; Commoner, Citizens, 2,273; McReynolds, Soc., 534; Hall, Comm., 298; DeBerry, Soc. Workers, 244; Greaves, Amer., 189; Bubar, Statesman, 150; scattered, 519.

1976: Ford, R, 632,863; Carter, D, 619,931; McCarthy, Ind., 20,051; Anderson, Amer., 3,040; MacBride, LB, 1,452.

1972: Nixon, R, 706,207; McGovern, D, 496,206; Schmitz, Amer., 22,056; Jenness, Soc. Workers, 488; Hall, Comm., 272; Green, Universal, 199; Fisher, Soc. Labor, 195; scattered, 321.

1968: Nixon, R, 619,106; Humphrey, D, 476,699; Wallace, 3rd party, 66,422; Halstead, Soc. Workers, 3,377; Cleaver, Peace/Freedom, 1,332; Munn, Prohib., 362; Blomen, Soc. Labor, 241.

1964: Johnson, D, 733,030; Goldwater, R, 449,148; Munn, Prohib., 1,902; Hass, Soc. Labor, 182; DeBerry, Soc. Workers, 159.

1960: Nixon, R, 722,381; Kennedy, D, 550,565; Hass, Soc. Labor, 230; write-in, 634.

Kansas

County	2020 Biden (D)	Trump (R)	2016 Clinton (D)	Trump (R)
Allen	1,570	4,218	1,433	3,651
Anderson	782	2,929	672	2,435
Atchison	2,359	4,906	1,989	4,049
Barber	291	2,014	286	1,850
Barton	2,340	8,608	1,839	7,888
Bourbon	1,541	5,023	1,336	4,424
Brown	1,104	3,262	863	2,906
Butler	9,181	22,634	6,573	19,073
Chase	345	1,123	316	969
Chautauqua	212	1,402	197	1,236
Cherokee	2,194	6,766	2,005	6,182
Cheyenne	224	1,183	181	1,173
Clark	143	904	120	825
Clay	894	3,177	677	2,891
Cloud	920	3,242	761	2,919
Coffey	964	3,489	727	3,050
Comanche	126	762	102	715
Cowley	4,273	9,656	3,551	8,270
Crawford	6,179	10,045	5,199	8,624
Decatur	218	1,260	178	1,210
Dickinson	2,060	7,126	1,609	6,029
Doniphan	686	2,976	587	2,606
Douglas	40,785	17,286	31,195	14,688
Edwards	271	1,141	212	1,037
Elk	195	1,140	160	1,048
Ellis	3,737	9,758	2,742	8,466
Ellsworth	648	2,148	521	1,969
Finney	4,325	7,236	3,195	6,350
Ford	2,947	5,803	2,149	5,114
Franklin	3,690	8,479	2,892	7,185
Geary	3,983	5,323	2,722	4,274
Gove	166	1,291	149	1,140
Graham	228	1,080	188	1,025
Grant	518	1,936	441	1,804
Gray	341	1,911	263	1,698
Greeley	78	549	83	534
Greenwood	569	2,444	485	2,160
Hamilton	141	698	121	705

County	2020 Biden (D)	Trump (R)	2016 Clinton (D)	Trump (R)
Harper	461	2,168	393	1,996
Harvey	6,747	10,182	5,068	8,668
Haskell	268	1,122	245	1,040
Hodgeman	154	875	124	855
Jackson	1,881	4,517	1,512	3,939
Jefferson	3,194	6,334	2,518	5,213
Jewell	212	1,387	180	1,223
Johnson	184,259	155,631	129,852	137,490
Kearny	267	1,164	174	1,075
Kingman	752	3,130	599	2,530
Kiowa	156	980	114	900
Labette	2,655	5,735	2,291	5,335
Lane	115	762	106	718
Leavenworth	13,886	21,610	10,209	17,638
Lincoln	266	1,283	215	1,179
Linn	896	4,048	736	3,484
Logan	186	1,249	149	1,132
Lyon	6,055	7,550	4,649	6,552
Marion	1,516	4,465	1,204	4,003
Marshall	1,259	3,729	1,072	3,307
McPherson	4,134	9,964	3,226	8,549
Meade	263	1,523	210	1,415
Miami	5,247	12,308	3,991	10,003
Mitchell	558	2,504	477	2,308
Montgomery	3,228	9,931	2,637	8,679
Morris	729	2,124	601	1,820
Morton	150	1,034	147	995
Nemaha	927	4,664	725	4,124
Neosho	1,796	4,970	1,501	4,431
Ness	149	1,339	162	1,228
Norton	364	2,007	281	1,840
Osage	2,136	5,705	1,753	4,826
Osborne	281	1,629	233	1,460
Ottawa	506	2,610	424	2,283
Pawnee	643	2,045	579	1,904
Phillips	318	2,418	300	2,233
Pottawatomie	3,313	9,452	2,225	7,612
Pratt	933	3,108	771	2,838
Rawlins	214	1,261	163	1,220
Reno	8,886	18,443	6,837	15,513
Republic	424	2,182	375	2,024
Rice	965	3,262	695	2,837
Riley	12,765	11,610	9,341	10,107
Rooks	339	2,325	275	2,031
Rush	295	1,350	233	1,197
Russell	600	2,790	461	2,574
Saline	8,214	15,722	6,317	13,828
Scott	299	2,014	236	1,865
Sedgwick	95,870	122,416	69,627	104,353
Seward	1,833	3,372	1,628	3,159
Shawnee	43,015	40,443	33,926	35,934
Sheridan	147	1,282	127	1,197
Sherman	396	2,269	347	2,089
Smith	336	1,763	297	1,661
Stafford	357	1,645	304	1,490
Stanton	148	614	115	492
Stevens	237	1,760	220	1,599
Sumner	2,591	8,105	2,076	6,984
Thomas	625	3,130	473	2,908
Trego	242	1,363	198	1,227
Wabaunsee	964	2,845	776	2,372
Wallace	44	770	46	721
Washington	475	2,363	387	2,194
Wichita	149	808	140	769
Wilson	723	3,153	594	2,788
Woodson	294	1,228	273	1,082
Wyandotte	36,788	18,934	30,146	15,806
Totals	**570,323**	**771,406**	**427,005**	**671,018**

Kansas Vote Since 1960

2020: Trump, R, 771,406; Biden, D, 570,323; Jorgensen, LB, 30,574.

2016: Trump, R, 671,018; Clinton, D, 427,005; Johnson, LB, 55,406; Stein, Ind., 23,506; McMullin, Ind., 6,520.

2012: Romney, R, 692,634; Obama, D, 440,726; Johnson, LB, 20,456; Baldwin, RF, 5,017.

2008: McCain, R, 699,655; Obama, D, 514,765; Nader, Ind., 10,527; Barr, LB, 6,706; Baldwin, RF, 4,148.

2004: Bush, R, 736,456; Kerry, D, 434,993; Nader, RF, 9,348; Badnarik, LB, 4,013; Peroutka, Ind., 2,899.

2000: Bush, R, 622,332; Gore, D, 399,276; Nader, Ind., 36,086; Buchanan, RF, 7,370; Browne, LB, 4,525; Hagelin, Ind., 1,373; Phillips, Const., 1,254.

1996: Dole, R, 583,245; Clinton, D, 387,659; Perot, RF, 92,639; Browne, LB, 4,557; Phillips, Ind., 3,519; Hagelin, Ind., 1,655.

1992: Bush, R, 449,951; Clinton, D, 390,434; Perot, Ind., 312,358; Marrou, LB, 4,314.

1988: Bush, R, 554,049; Dukakis, D, 422,636; Paul, Ind., 12,553; Fulani, Ind., 3,806.

1984: Reagan, R, 674,646; Mondale, D, 332,471; Bergland, LB, 3,585.

1980: Reagan, R, 566,812; Carter, D, 326,150; Anderson, Ind., 68,231; Clark, LB, 14,470; Shelton, Amer., 1,555; Hall, Comm., 967; Bubar, Statesman, 821; Rarick, Conservative, 789.

1976: Ford, R, 502,752; Carter, D, 430,421; McCarthy, Ind., 13,185; Anderson, Amer., 4,724; MacBride, LB, 3,242; Maddox, Conservative, 2,118; Bubar, Prohib., 1,403.

1972: Nixon, R, 619,812; McGovern, D, 270,287; Schmitz, Conservative, 21,808; Munn, Prohib., 4,188.

1968: Nixon, R, 478,674; Humphrey, D, 302,996; Wallace, 3rd party, 88,921; Munn, Prohib., 2,192.

1964: Johnson, D, 464,028; Goldwater, R, 386,579; Munn, Prohib., 5,393; Hass, Soc. Labor, 1,901.

1960: Nixon, R, 561,474; Kennedy, D, 363,213; Decker, Prohib., 4,138.

Kentucky

County	2020 Biden (D)	Trump (R)	2016 Clinton (D)	Trump (R)
Adair	1,392	7,276	1,323	6,637
Allen	1,642	7,587	1,349	6,466
Anderson	3,348	9,661	2,634	8,242
Ballard	825	3,356	816	3,161
Barren	5,127	14,654	4,275	13,443
Bath	1,573	3,986	1,361	3,082
Bell	1,789	8,140	1,720	7,764
Boone	20,901	44,814	15,026	39,082
Bourbon	3,296	6,190	2,791	5,569
Boyd	7,083	14,295	6,021	13,591
Boyle	5,298	8,872	4,281	8,040
Bracken	800	3,398	705	2,711
Breathitt	1,301	4,265	1,537	3,991
Breckinridge	2,350	7,701	1,960	6,484
Bullitt	10,552	30,708	8,255	26,210
Butler	1,079	4,960	947	4,428
Caldwell	1,433	4,906	1,260	4,507
Calloway	5,797	11,352	4,749	10,367
Campbell	19,374	28,482	14,658	25,050
Carlisle	463	2,159	432	2,094
Carroll	1,116	2,954	1,106	2,588
Carter	2,642	8,775	2,276	7,587
Casey	918	6,179	767	5,482
Christian	8,296	15,080	7,188	14,108
Clark	6,004	11,811	4,706	10,710
Clay	831	6,677	752	5,861
Clinton	603	4,280	547	3,809
Crittenden	731	3,451	617	3,290
Cumberland	508	2,769	459	2,502
Daviess	17,286	31,025	14,163	28,907
Edmonson	1,227	4,828	979	4,135
Elliott	712	2,246	740	2,000
Estill	1,355	5,100	1,108	4,236
Fayette	90,600	58,860	69,778	56,894
Fleming	1,474	5,347	1,348	4,722
Floyd	3,884	12,250	4,015	11,993
Franklin	12,652	12,900	10,717	11,819
Fulton	794	1,606	774	1,549
Gallatin	822	2,955	749	2,443
Garrard	1,830	6,754	1,453	5,904
Grant	2,205	8,725	1,910	7,268
Graves	3,560	13,206	3,308	12,671
Grayson	2,400	9,453	1,959	8,219
Green	920	4,838	832	4,372
Greenup	4,873	13,064	4,146	11,546
Hancock	1,351	3,145	1,244	2,788
Hardin	18,101	29,832	13,944	26,971
Harlan	1,494	9,367	1,372	9,129
Harrison	2,400	6,334	2,031	5,435
Hart	1,908	6,345	1,730	5,320
Henderson	7,639	12,730	6,707	12,159
Henry	2,142	5,843	1,828	4,944
Hickman	458	1,714	449	1,657
Hopkins	5,439	15,757	4,310	15,277
Jackson	605	5,453	482	4,889
Jefferson	228,358	150,646	190,836	143,768
Jessamine	8,567	17,096	6,144	15,474
Johnson	1,608	8,450	1,250	8,043
Kenton	32,271	48,129	24,214	42,958
Knott	1,412	4,780	1,245	4,357
Knox	2,114	11,012	1,761	9,885
Larue	1,504	5,685	1,278	4,799
Laurel	4,475	23,237	3,440	20,592
Lawrence	1,238	5,633	1,045	4,816
Lee	481	2,273	444	2,151
Leslie	446	4,321	400	4,015
Letcher	1,799	7,226	1,542	7,293
Lewis	823	4,986	785	4,363
Lincoln	2,254	8,489	1,865	7,338
Livingston	939	4,010	887	3,570
Logan	3,094	9,067	2,755	7,778
Lyon	1,092	3,100	1,045	2,789
Madison	15,581	27,356	11,793	23,431
Magoffin	1,214	4,174	1,172	3,824
Marion	2,722	6,113	2,679	5,122
Marshall	4,071	13,297	3,672	12,322
Martin	403	3,496	363	3,503
Mason	2,362	5,477	1,970	4,944
McCracken	11,195	21,820	9,134	20,774
McCreary	725	5,664	664	5,012
McLean	1,074	3,633	988	3,381
Meade	3,632	10,185	3,026	8,660
Menifee	750	2,311	700	2,010
Mercer	3,033	8,506	2,395	7,740
Metcalfe	975	3,959	976	3,491
Monroe	657	4,628	601	4,278
Montgomery	3,630	8,993	3,158	7,856
Morgan	1,175	4,301	1,006	3,628
Muhlenberg	3,545	10,497	3,272	9,393
Nelson	7,188	15,703	6,434	13,431
Nicholas	955	2,408	787	1,957
Ohio	2,404	8,582	2,080	7,942
Oldham	14,505	22,654	10,268	20,469
Owen	1,098	4,292	1,062	3,745
Owsley	216	1,671	256	1,474
Pendleton	1,322	5,515	1,164	4,604
Perry	2,356	8,129	2,136	8,158
Pike	4,866	20,284	4,280	19,747
Powell	1,367	4,041	1,272	3,513
Pulaski	5,666	25,442	4,208	22,902
Robertson	253	884	222	759
Rockcastle	1,134	6,577	915	5,609
Rowan	3,880	5,994	3,295	5,174
Russell	1,331	7,519	1,093	6,863
Scott	10,567	17,767	7,715	15,052
Shelby	8,077	15,055	6,276	13,196
Simpson	2,681	5,888	2,144	5,077
Spencer	2,530	8,737	1,921	7,196
Taylor	2,963	9,376	2,553	8,320
Todd	1,205	4,062	1,042	3,612
Trigg	1,791	5,487	1,587	4,931
Trimble	1,012	3,227	879	2,771
Union	1,529	4,965	1,331	4,701
Warren	22,479	31,791	16,966	28,673
Washington	1,644	4,482	1,420	4,013
Wayne	1,700	7,430	1,431	6,371
Webster	1,412	4,506	1,240	4,397
Whitley	2,552	12,567	2,067	11,312
Wolfe	839	2,097	753	1,804
Woodford	6,530	8,362	4,958	7,697
Totals	**772,474**	**1,326,646**	**628,854**	**1,202,971**

Kentucky Vote Since 1960

2020: Trump, R, 1,326,646; Biden, D, 772,474; Jorgensen, LB, 26,234; West, Ind., 6,483; Pierce, Ind., 3,599.

2016: Trump, R, 1,202,971; Clinton, D, 628,854; Johnson, LB, 53,752; McMullin, Ind., 22,780; Stein, Green, 13,913; De La Fuente, Amer. Delta, 1,128.

2012: Romney, R, 1,087,190; Obama, D, 679,370; Johnson, LB, 17,063; Terry, Ind., 6,872; Stein, Green, 6,337.

2008: McCain, R, 1,048,462; Obama, D, 751,985; Nader, Ind., 15,378; Barr, LB, 5,989; Baldwin, Const., 4,694.

2004: Bush, R, 1,069,439; Kerry, D, 712,733; Nader, Ind., 8,856; Badnarik, LB, 2,619; Peroutka, Const., 2,213.

2000: Bush, R, 872,520; Gore, D, 638,923; Nader, Green, 23,118; Buchanan, RF, 4,152; Browne, LB, 2,885; Hagelin, Natural Law, 1,513; Phillips, Const., 915.

1996: Clinton, D, 636,614; Dole, R, 623,283; Perot, RF, 120,396; Browne, LB, 4,009; Phillips, U.S. Taxpayers, 2,204; Hagelin, Natural Law, 1,493.

1992: Clinton, D, 665,104; Bush, R, 617,178; Perot, Ind., 203,944; Marrou, LB, 4,513.

1988: Bush, R, 734,281; Dukakis, D, 580,368; Duke, Populist, 4,494; Paul, LB, 2,118.

1984: Reagan, R, 815,345; Mondale, D, 536,756.

1980: Reagan, R, 635,274; Carter, D, 616,417; Anderson, Ind., 31,127; Clark, LB, 5,531; McCormack, Respect for Life, 4,233; Commoner, Citizens, 1,304; Pulley, Soc., 393; Hall, Comm., 348.

1976: Carter, D, 615,717; Ford, R, 531,852; Anderson, Amer., 8,308; McCarthy, Ind., 6,837; Maddox, Amer. Ind., 2,328; MacBride, LB, 814.

1972: Nixon, R, 676,446; McGovern, D, 371,159; Schmitz, Amer., 17,627; Spock, People's, 1,118; Jenness, Soc. Workers, 685; Hall, Comm., 464.

1968: Nixon, R, 462,411; Humphrey, D, 397,547; Wallace, 3rd party, 193,098; Halstead, Soc. Workers, 2,843.

1964: Johnson, D, 669,659; Goldwater, R, 372,977; Kasper, Natl. States' Rights, 3,469.

1960: Nixon, R, 602,607; Kennedy, D, 521,855.

Louisiana

Parish	2020 Biden (D)	Trump (R)	2016 Clinton (D)	Trump (R)
Acadia	5,443	22,596	5,638	21,162
Allen	2,108	7,574	2,106	6,867
Ascension	20,399	40,687	16,476	36,143
Assumption	3,833	7,271	3,931	6,714
Avoyelles	4,979	12,028	5,035	11,165
Beauregard	2,542	13,575	2,393	12,238
Bienville	3,067	3,891	3,129	3,756
Bossier	15,662	38,074	12,641	35,474
Caddo	55,110	48,021	53,483	49,006
Calcasieu	25,982	55,066	26,296	54,191
Caldwell	745	3,976	788	3,822
Cameron	324	3,671	323	3,256
Catahoula	1,269	3,541	1,322	3,479
Claiborne	2,731	3,770	2,717	3,585
Concordia	3,177	5,550	3,272	5,477
DeSoto	5,457	9,112	5,165	8,068
East Baton Rouge	115,577	88,420	102,828	84,660
East Carroll	1,900	1,080	1,838	1,059
East Feliciana	4,280	6,064	4,235	5,569
Evangeline	4,158	11,053	4,208	10,360
Franklin	2,658	6,970	2,506	6,514
Grant	1,157	8,117	1,181	7,408
Iberia	11,027	21,251	10,698	20,903
Iberville	8,514	7,893	8,324	7,320
Jackson	2,143	5,394	2,139	5,169
Jefferson	84,477	105,949	73,670	100,398
Jefferson Davis	3,208	11,423	3,080	10,775
Lafayette	39,685	72,519	32,726	68,195
Lafourche	8,672	36,024	8,423	31,959
LaSalle	638	6,378	605	5,836
Lincoln	7,559	11,311	7,107	10,761
Livingston	9,249	54,877	6,950	48,824
Madison	2,654	1,930	2,744	1,927
Morehouse	4,946	6,510	5,155	6,502
Natchitoches	6,896	9,358	7,144	8,968
Orleans	147,854	26,664	133,996	24,292
Ouachita	25,913	42,255	24,428	41,734
Plaquemines	3,414	7,412	3,347	6,900
Pointe Coupee	4,683	7,503	4,764	6,789
Rapides	19,475	38,347	18,322	36,816
Red River	1,644	2,413	1,938	2,391
Richland	3,225	6,607	3,157	6,287
Sabine	1,731	8,776	1,703	7,879
St. Bernard	6,151	11,179	4,960	10,237
St. Charles	9,800	18,233	8,559	16,621
St. Helena	3,346	2,714	3,353	2,497
St. James	6,510	5,954	6,418	5,456
St. John the Baptist	13,582	7,538	12,661	7,569
St. Landry	17,372	23,171	17,209	21,971
St. Martin	8,439	18,203	8,266	16,873
St. Mary	8,055	14,811	8,050	14,359
St. Tammany	37,746	99,666	27,717	90,915
Tangipahoa	18,887	37,806	16,878	33,959
Tensas	1,329	1,197	1,332	1,182
Terrebonne	11,198	34,339	10,665	31,902
Union	2,654	8,407	2,691	7,972
Vermilion	5,009	21,930	4,857	20,063
Vernon	2,898	14,107	2,665	13,471
Washington	5,970	13,307	5,692	12,556
Webster	6,172	11,830	6,260	11,542
West Baton Rouge	6,200	7,684	5,383	6,927
West Carroll	710	4,317	715	3,970
West Feliciana	2,298	3,863	2,248	3,390
Winn	1,543	4,619	1,644	4,608
Totals	**856,034**	**1,255,776**	**780,154**	**1,178,638**

Louisiana Vote Since 1960

2020: Trump, R, 1,255,776; Biden, D, 856,034; Jorgensen, LB, 21,645; West, Birthday Party, 4,897; Carroll, Amer. Solidarity, 2,497; Simmons, Bec. One Nation, 1,626; Boddie, C.U.P., 1,125; La Riva, Socialism/Liberation, 987; Blankenship, Const., 860; Pierce, Freedom/Prosperity, 749; Hoefling, Life/Liberty/Const., 668; Hammons, Unity, 662; Kennedy, Soc. Workers, 536.

2016: Trump, R, 1,178,638; Clinton, D, 780,154; Johnson, LB, 37,978; Stein, Green, 14,031; McMullin, Courage/Char./Serv., 8,547; Castle, Const., 3,129; Keniston, Veterans, 1,881; Hoefling, Life/Fam./Const., 1,581; Kotlikoff, It's Our Children, 1,048; Jacob, Loyal/Trust., 749; Kennedy, Soc. Workers, 480; La Riva, Socialism/Liberation, 446; White, Soc./Eq./Anti-War, 370.

2012: Romney, R, 1,152,262; Obama, D, 809,141; Johnson, LB, 18,157; Stein, Green, 6,978; Goode, Const., 2,508; Tittle, We the People, 1,767; Anderson, Justice, 1,368; Lindsay, Socialism/Liberation, 622; Fellure, Prohib., 518; Harris, Soc. Workers, 389; White, Soc. Equality, 355.

2008: McCain, R, 1,148,275; Obama, D, 782,989; Paul, LA Taxpayers, 9,368; McKinney, Green, 9,187; Nader, Ind., 6,997; Baldwin, Const., 2,581; Harris, Soc. Workers 735; La Riva, Socialism/Liberation, 354; Amondson, Prohib., 275.

2004: Bush, R, 1,102,169; Kerry, D, 820,299; Nader, Better Life, 7,032; Peroutka, Const., 5,203; Badnarik, LB, 2,781; Brown, Protect Working Families, 1,795; Amondson, Prohib., 1,566; Cobb, Green, 1,276; Harris, Soc. Workers, 985.

2000: Bush, R, 927,871; Gore, D, 792,344; Nader, Green, 20,473; Buchanan, RF, 14,356; Phillips, Const., 5,483; Browne, LB, 2,951; Harris, Soc. Workers, 1,103; Hagelin, Natural Law, 1,075.

1996: Clinton, D, 927,837; Dole, R, 712,586; Perot, RF, 123,293; Browne, LB, 7,499; Nader, Liberty, Ecology, Community, 4,719; Phillips, U.S. Taxpayers, 3,366; Hagelin, Natural Law, 2,981; Moorehead, Workers World, 1,678.

1992: Clinton, D, 815,971; Bush, R, 733,386; Perot, Ind., 211,478; Gritz, Populist/America First, 18,545; Marrou, LB, 3,155; Daniels, Ind., 1,663; Phillips, U.S. Taxpayers, 1,552; Fulani, New Alliance, 1,434; LaRouche, Ind., 1,136.

1988: Bush, R, 883,702; Dukakis, D, 717,460; Duke, Populist, 18,612; Paul, LB, 4,115.

1984: Reagan, R, 1,037,299; Mondale, D, 651,586; Bergland, LB, 1,876.

1980: Reagan, R, 792,853; Carter, D, 708,453; Anderson, Ind., 26,345; Rarick, Amer. Ind., 10,333; Clark, LB, 8,240; Commoner, Citizens, 1,584; DeBerry, Soc. Workers, 783.

1976: Carter, D, 661,365; Ford, R, 587,446; Maddox, Amer., 10,058; Hall, Comm., 7,417; McCarthy, Ind., 6,588; MacBride, LB, 3,325.

1972: Nixon, R, 686,852; McGovern, D, 298,142; Schmitz, Amer., 52,099; Jenness, Soc. Workers, 14,398.

1968: Wallace, 3rd party, 530,300; Humphrey, D, 309,615; Nixon, R, 257,535.

1964: Goldwater, R, 509,225; Johnson, D, 387,068.

1960: Kennedy, D, 407,339; Nixon, R, 230,890; States' Rights (unpledged), 169,572.

Maine

County	2020		2016	
	Biden (D)	Trump (R)	Clinton (D)	Trump (R)
Androscoggin	27,617	29,268	23,009	28,227
Aroostook	13,956	21,080	13,386	19,419
Cumberland	128,759	59,584	102,981	57,709
Franklin	8,069	8,754	7,016	7,918
Hancock	19,369	14,982	16,117	13,705
Kennebec	34,902	34,721	29,302	31,675
Knox	15,110	9,982	12,443	9,148
Lincoln	12,684	10,256	10,241	9,727
Oxford	14,755	17,698	12,172	16,210
Penobscot	37,713	44,825	32,838	41,622
Piscataquis	3,517	6,153	3,098	5,406
Sagadahoc	13,528	9,755	10,664	9,304
Somerset	10,199	16,644	9,092	15,001
Waldo	12,345	11,196	10,440	10,378
Washington	6,761	10,194	6,075	9,093
York	71,189	54,817	55,844	50,403
Outside U.S.	4,599	838	3,017	648
Totals	435,072	360,737	357,735	335,593

Maine Vote Since 1960

2020: Biden, D, 435,072; Trump, R, 360,737; Jorgensen, LB, 14,152; Hawkins, Green, 8,230; De La Fuente, Alliance, 1,183.

2016: Clinton, D, 357,735; Trump, R, 335,593; Johnson, LB, 38,105; Stein, Green, 14,251; McMullin, Ind., 1,887; Castle, Const., 333.

2012: Obama, D, 401,306; Romney, R, 292,276; Johnson, LB, 9,352; Stein, Green, 8,119.

2008: Obama, D, 421,923; McCain, R, 295,273; Nader, Ind., 10,636; McKinney, Green, 2,900.

2004: Kerry, D, 396,842; Bush, R, 330,201; Nader, Better Life, 8,069; Cobb, Green, 2,936; Badnarik, LB, 1,965; Peroutka, Const., 735.

2000: Gore, D, 319,951; Bush, R, 286,616; Nader, Green, 37,127; Buchanan, RF, 4,443; Browne, LB, 3,074; Phillips, Const., 579.

1996: Clinton, D, 312,788; Dole, R, 186,378; Perot, RF, 85,970; Nader, Green, 15,279; Browne, LB, 2,996; Phillips, Taxpayers, 1,517; Hagelin, Natural Law, 825.

1992: Clinton, D, 263,420; Perot, Ind., 206,820; Bush, R, 206,504; Marrou, LB, 1,681.

1988: Bush, R, 307,131; Dukakis, D, 243,569; Paul, LB, 2,700; Fulani, New Alliance, 1,405.

1984: Reagan, R, 336,500; Mondale, D, 214,515.

1980: Reagan, R, 238,522; Carter, D, 220,974; Anderson, Ind., 53,327; Clark, LB, 5,119; Commoner, Citizens, 4,394; Hall, Comm., 591; write-in, 84.

1976: Ford, R, 236,320; Carter, D, 232,279; McCarthy, Ind., 10,874; Bubar, Prohib., 3,495.

1972: Nixon, R, 256,458; McGovern, D, 160,584; scattered, 229.

1968: Humphrey, D, 217,312; Nixon, R, 169,254; Wallace, 3rd party, 6,370.

1964: Johnson, D, 262,264; Goldwater, R, 118,701.

1960: Nixon, R, 240,608; Kennedy, D, 181,159.

Maryland

County	2020		2016	
	Biden (D)	Trump (R)	Clinton (D)	Trump (R)
Allegany	9,158	20,886	7,875	21,270
Anne Arundel	172,823	127,821	128,419	122,403
Baltimore	258,540	146,202	218,412	149,477
Calvert	22,587	25,346	18,225	26,176
Caroline	5,095	10,283	4,009	9,368
Carroll	36,456	60,218	26,567	58,215
Cecil	16,809	29,439	13,650	28,868
Charles	62,171	25,579	49,341	25,614
Dorchester	6,857	8,764	6,245	8,413
Frederick	77,675	63,682	56,522	59,522
Garrett	3,281	12,002	2,567	10,776
Harford	63,095	80,930	47,077	77,860
Howard	129,433	48,390	102,597	47,484
Kent	5,329	5,195	4,575	4,876
Montgomery	419,569	101,222	357,837	92,704
Prince George's	379,208	37,090	344,049	32,811
Queen Anne's	10,709	18,741	7,973	16,993
St. Mary's	23,138	30,826	17,534	28,663
Somerset	4,241	5,739	4,196	5,341
Talbot	11,062	10,946	8,653	10,724
Washington	26,044	40,224	21,129	40,998
Wicomico	22,054	22,944	18,050	22,198
Worcester	12,560	18,571	9,753	17,210
City				
Baltimore	207,260	25,374	202,673	25,205
Totals	1,985,023	976,414	1,677,928	943,169

Maryland Vote Since 1960

2020: Biden, D, 1,985,023; Trump, R, 976,414; Jorgensen, LB, 33,488; Hawkins, Green, 15,799; Segal, Bread/Roses, 5,884.

2016: Clinton, D, 1,677,928; Trump, R, 943,169; Johnson, LB, 79,605; Stein, Green, 35,945; McMullin, Ind., 9,630; Castle, Const., 566; Maturen, Ind., 504.

2012: Obama, D, 1,677,844; Romney, R, 971,869; Johnson, LB, 30,195; Stein, Green, 17,110.

2008: Obama, D, 1,629,467; McCain, R, 959,862; Nader, MD Ind., 14,713; Barr, LB, 9,842; McKinney, Green, 4,747; Baldwin, RF, 3,760.

2004: Kerry, D, 1,334,493; Bush, R, 1,024,703; Nader, Populist, 11,854; Badnarik, LB, 6,094; Cobb, Green, 3,632; Peroutka, Const., 3,421.

2000: Gore, D, 1,144,008; Bush, R, 813,827; Nader, Green, 53,768; Browne, LB, 5,310; Buchanan, RF, 4,248; Phillips, Const., 918.

1996: Clinton, D, 966,207; Dole, R, 681,530; Perot, RF, 115,812; Browne, LB, 8,765; Phillips, Taxpayers, 3,402; Hagelin, Natural Law, 2,517.

1992: Clinton, D, 988,571; Bush, R, 707,094; Perot, Ind., 281,414; Marrou, LB, 4,715; Fulani, New Alliance, 2,786.

1988: Bush, R, 876,167; Dukakis, D, 826,304; Paul, LB, 6,748; Fulani, New Alliance, 5,115.

1984: Reagan, R, 879,918; Mondale, D, 787,935; Bergland, LB, 5,721.

1980: Carter, D, 726,161; Reagan, R, 680,606; Anderson, Ind., 119,537; Clark, LB, 14,192.

1976: Carter, D, 759,612; Ford, R, 672,661.

1972: Nixon, R, 829,305; McGovern, D, 505,781; Schmitz, Amer., 18,726.

1968: Humphrey, D, 538,310; Nixon, R, 517,995; Wallace, 3rd party, 178,734.

1964: Johnson, D, 730,912; Goldwater, R, 385,495; write-in, 50.

1960: Kennedy, D, 565,800; Nixon, R, 489,538.

Massachusetts

County	2020		2016	
	Biden (D)	Trump (R)	Clinton (D)	Trump (R)
Barnstable	91,994	55,311	72,430	54,099
Berkshire	51,705	18,064	43,714	16,839
Bristol	153,377	119,872	129,540	105,443
Dukes	9,914	2,631	8,400	2,477
Essex	267,198	144,837	222,310	136,316
Franklin	30,030	11,201	24,478	10,364
Hampden	125,948	87,318	112,590	78,685
Hampshire	63,362	22,281	55,367	21,790
Middlesex	617,196	226,956	520,360	219,793
Nantucket	5,241	1,914	4,146	1,892
Norfolk	273,312	125,294	221,819	119,723
Plymouth	173,630	121,227	135,513	115,369
Suffolk	270,522	58,613	245,751	50,421
Worcester	248,773	171,683	198,778	157,682
Totals	2,382,202	1,167,202	1,995,196	1,090,893

Massachusetts Vote Since 1960

2020: Biden, D, 2,382,202; Trump, R, 1,167,202; Jorgensen, LB, 47,013; Hawkins, Green, 18,658.

2016: Clinton, D, 1,995,196; Trump, R, 1,090,893; Johnson, LB, 138,018; Stein, Green, 47,661; McMullin, Ind., 2,719.

2012: Obama, D, 1,921,290; Romney, R, 1,188,314; Johnson, LB, 30,920; Stein, Green, 20,691.

2008: Obama, D, 1,904,097; McCain, R, 1,108,854; Nader, Ind., 28,841; Barr, LB, 13,189; McKinney, Green, 6,550; Baldwin, RF, 4,971.

2004: Kerry, D, 1,803,800; Bush, R, 1,071,109; Badnarik, LB, 15,022; Cobb, Green, 10,623.

2000: Gore, D, 1,616,487; Bush, R, 878,502; Nader, Green, 173,564; Browne, LB, 16,366; Buchanan, RF, 11,149; Hagelin, Natural Law, 2,884.

1996: Clinton, D, 1,571,509; Dole, R, 718,058; Perot, RF, 227,206; Browne, LB, 20,424; Hagelin, Natural Law, 5,183; Moorehead, Workers World, 3,276.

1992: Clinton, D, 1,318,639; Bush, R, 805,039; Perot, Ind., 630,731; Marrou, LB, 9,021; Fulani, New Alliance, 3,172; Phillips, U.S. Taxpayers, 2,218; Hagelin, Natural Law, 1,812; LaRouche, Ind., 1,027.

1988: Dukakis, D, 1,401,415; Bush, R, 1,194,635; Paul, LB, 24,251; Fulani, New Alliance, 9,561.

1984: Reagan, R, 1,310,936; Mondale, D, 1,239,606.

1980: Reagan, R, 1,057,631; Carter, D, 1,053,802; Anderson, Ind., 382,539; Clark, LB, 22,038; DeBerry, Soc. Workers, 3,735; Commoner, Citizens, 2,056; McReynolds, Soc., 62; Bubar, Statesman, 34; Griswold, Workers World, 19; scattered, 2,382.

1976: Carter, D, 1,429,475; Ford, R, 1,030,276; McCarthy, Ind., 65,637; Camejo, Soc. Workers, 8,138; Anderson, Amer., 7,555; LaRouche, U.S. Labor, 4,922; MacBride, LB, 135.

1972: McGovern, D, 1,332,540; Nixon, R, 1,112,078; Jenness, Soc. Workers, 10,600; Schmitz, Amer., 2,877; Fisher, Soc. Labor, 129; Spock, People's, 101; Hall, Comm., 46; Hospers, LB, 43; scattered, 342.

1968: Humphrey, D, 1,469,218; Nixon, R, 766,844; Wallace, 3rd party, 87,088; Blomen, Soc. Labor, 6,180; Munn, Prohib., 2,369; scattered, 53; blank, 25,394.

1964: Johnson, D, 1,786,422; Goldwater, R, 549,727; Hass, Soc. Labor, 4,755; Munn, Prohib., 3,735; scattered, 159; blank, 48,104.

1960: Kennedy, D, 1,487,174; Nixon, R, 976,750; Hass, Soc. Labor, 3,892; Decker, Prohib., 1,633; others, 31; blank and void, 26,024.

Michigan

County	2020 Biden (D)	Trump (R)	2016 Clinton (D)	Trump (R)
Alcona	2,142	4,848	1,732	4,201
Alger	2,053	3,014	1,663	2,585
Allegan	24,449	41,392	18,050	34,183
Alpena	6,000	10,686	4,877	9,090
Antrim	5,960	9,748	4,448	8,469
Arenac	2,774	5,928	2,384	4,950
Baraga	1,478	2,512	1,156	2,158
Barry	11,797	23,471	9,114	19,202
Bay	26,151	33,125	21,642	28,328
Benzie	5,480	6,601	4,108	5,539
Berrien	37,438	43,519	29,495	38,647
Branch	6,159	14,064	5,061	11,786
Calhoun	28,877	36,221	24,157	31,494
Cass	9,130	16,699	7,270	14,243
Charlevoix	6,939	9,841	5,137	8,674
Cheboygan	5,437	10,186	4,302	8,683
Chippewa	6,648	10,681	5,379	9,122
Clare	5,199	10,861	4,249	8,505
Clinton	21,968	25,098	16,492	21,636
Crawford	2,672	5,087	2,110	4,354
Delta	7,606	13,207	6,436	11,121
Dickinson	4,744	9,617	3,923	8,580
Eaton	31,299	31,798	24,938	27,609
Emmet	9,662	12,135	6,972	10,616
Genesee	119,390	98,714	102,751	84,175

County	2020 Biden (D)	Trump (R)	2016 Clinton (D)	Trump (R)
Gladwin	4,524	9,893	3,794	8,124
Gogebic	3,570	4,600	2,925	4,018
Grand Traverse	28,683	30,502	20,965	27,413
Gratiot	6,693	12,102	5,666	9,880
Hillsdale	5,883	17,037	4,799	14,095
Houghton	7,750	10,378	6,018	8,475
Huron	5,490	12,731	4,579	10,692
Ingham	94,212	47,639	79,110	43,868
Ionia	10,901	20,657	8,352	16,635
Iosco	5,373	9,759	4,345	8,345
Iron	2,493	4,216	2,004	3,675
Isabella	14,072	14,815	11,404	12,338
Jackson	31,995	47,372	25,795	39,793
Kalamazoo	83,686	56,823	67,148	51,034
Kalkaska	3,002	7,436	2,280	6,116
Kent	187,915	165,741	138,683	148,180
Keweenaw	672	862	527	814
Lake	2,288	3,946	1,939	3,159
Lapeer	16,367	35,482	12,734	30,037
Leelanau	8,795	7,916	6,774	7,239
Lenawee	20,918	31,541	16,750	26,430
Livingston	48,220	76,982	34,384	65,680
Luce	842	2,109	681	1,756
Mackinac	2,632	4,304	2,085	3,744
Macomb	223,952	263,863	176,317	224,665
Manistee	6,107	8,321	4,979	6,915
Marquette	20,465	16,286	16,042	14,646
Mason	6,802	10,207	5,281	8,505
Mecosta	7,375	13,267	5,827	10,305
Menominee	4,316	8,117	3,539	6,702
Midland	20,493	27,675	15,635	23,846
Missaukee	1,967	6,648	1,565	5,386
Monroe	32,975	52,710	26,863	43,261
Montcalm	9,703	21,815	7,874	16,907
Montmorency	1,628	4,171	1,287	3,498
Muskegon	45,643	45,133	37,304	36,127
Newaygo	7,873	18,857	6,212	15,173
Oakland	434,148	325,971	343,070	289,203
Oceana	4,944	8,892	3,973	7,228
Ogemaw	3,475	8,253	3,030	6,827
Ontonagon	1,391	2,358	1,176	2,066
Osceola	3,214	8,928	2,705	7,336
Oscoda	1,342	3,466	1,044	2,843
Otsego	4,743	9,779	3,556	8,266
Ottawa	64,705	100,913	44,973	88,467
Presque Isle	2,911	5,342	2,400	4,488
Roscommon	5,166	9,670	4,287	8,141
Saginaw	51,088	50,785	44,396	45,469
St. Clair	31,363	59,185	24,553	49,051
St. Joseph	9,262	18,127	7,526	14,884
Sanilac	5,966	16,194	4,873	13,446
Schoolcraft	1,589	3,090	1,369	2,556
Shiawassee	15,347	23,149	12,546	19,230
Tuscola	8,712	20,297	7,429	17,102
Van Buren	16,803	21,591	13,258	17,890
Washtenaw	157,136	56,241	128,483	50,631
Wayne	597,170	264,553	519,444	228,993
Wexford	5,838	12,102	4,436	10,000
Totals	**2,804,040**	**2,649,852**	**2,268,839**	**2,279,543**

Michigan Vote Since 1960

2020: Biden, D, 2,804,040; Trump, R, 2,649,852; Jorgensen, LB, 60,381; Hawkins, Green, 13,718; Blankenship, U.S. Taxpayers, 7,235; De La Fuente, Natural Law, 2,986.

2016: Trump, R, 2,279,543; Clinton, D, 2,268,839; Johnson, LB, 172,136; Stein, Green, 51,463; Castle, U.S. Taxpayers, 16,139; McMullin, Ind., 8,177; Soltysik, Natural Law, 2,209.

2012: Obama, D, 2,564,569; Romney, R, 2,115,256; Stein, Green, 21,897; Goode, U.S. Taxpayers, 16,119; Johnson, Ind., 7,774, Anderson, Natural Law, 5,147.

2008: Obama, D, 2,872,579; McCain, R, 2,048,639; Nader, Natural Law, 33,085; Barr, LB, 23,716; Baldwin, U.S. Taxpayers, 14,685; McKinney, Green, 8,892.

2004: Kerry, D, 2,479,183; Bush, R, 2,313,746; Nader, Ind., 24,035; Badnarik, LB, 10,552; Cobb, Green, 5,325; Peroutka, U.S. Taxpayers, 4,980; Brown, Natural Law, 1,431.

2000: Gore, D, 2,170,418; Bush, R, 1,953,139; Nader, Green, 84,165; Browne, LB, 16,711; Phillips, U.S. Taxpayers, 3,791; Hagelin, Natural Law, 2,426.

1996: Clinton, D, 1,989,653; Dole, R, 1,481,212; Perot, RF, 336,670; Browne, LB, 27,670; Hagelin, Natural Law, 4,254; Moorehead, Workers World, 3,153; White, Soc. Equality, 1,554.

1992: Clinton, D, 1,871,182; Bush, R, 1,554,940; Perot, Ind., 824,813; Marrou, LB, 10,175; Phillips, U.S. Taxpayers, 8,263; Hagelin, Natural Law, 2,954.

1988: Bush, R, 1,965,486; Dukakis, D, 1,675,783; Paul, LB, 18,336; Fulani, Ind., 2,513.

1984: Reagan, R, 2,251,571; Mondale, D, 1,529,638; Bergland, LB, 10,055.

1980: Reagan, R, 1,915,225; Carter, D, 1,661,532; Anderson, Ind., 275,223; Clark, LB, 41,597; Commoner, Citizens, 11,930; Hall, Comm., 3,262; Griswold, Workers World, 30; Greaves, Amer., 21; Bubar, Statesman, 9.

1976: Ford, R, 1,893,742; Carter, D, 1,696,714; McCarthy, Ind., 47,905; MacBride, LB, 5,406; Wright, People's, 3,504; Camejo, Soc. Workers, 1,804; LaRouche, U.S. Labor, 1,366; Levin, Soc. Labor, 1,148; scattered, 2,160.

1972: Nixon, R, 1,961,721; McGovern, D, 1,459,435; Schmitz, Amer., 63,321; Fisher, Soc. Labor, 2,437; Jenness, Soc. Workers, 1,603; Hall, Comm., 1,210.

1968: Humphrey, D, 1,593,082; Nixon, R, 1,370,665; Wallace, 3rd party, 331,968; Halstead, Soc. Workers, 4,099; Blomen, Soc. Labor, 1,762; Cleaver, New Politics, 4,585; Munn, Prohib., 60; scattered, 29.

1964: Johnson, D, 2,136,615; Goldwater, R, 1,060,152; DeBerry, Soc. Workers, 3,817; Hass, Soc. Labor, 1,704; Prohib. (no candidate listed), 699; scattered, 145.

1960: Kennedy, D, 1,687,269; Nixon, R, 1,620,428; Dobbs, Soc. Workers, 4,347; Decker, Prohib., 2,029; Daly, Tax Cut, 1,767; Hass, Soc. Labor, 1,718; Ind. Amer. (unpledged), 539.

Minnesota

County	2020 Biden (D)	Trump (R)	2016 Clinton (D)	Trump (R)
Aitkin	3,607	6,258	3,134	5,516
Anoka	100,893	104,902	75,500	93,339
Becker	6,589	12,438	5,208	10,880
Beltrami	11,426	12,188	8,688	10,783
Benton	7,280	14,382	5,640	12,872
Big Stone	1,053	1,863	921	1,608
Blue Earth	18,330	16,731	14,428	15,667
Brown	4,753	9,552	3,763	8,708
Carlton	10,098	9,791	8,460	8,160
Carver	30,774	34,009	21,508	29,056
Cass	6,342	11,620	4,949	9,982
Chippewa	2,226	4,250	1,978	3,764
Chisago	11,806	21,916	9,278	18,441
Clay	16,357	15,043	12,971	13,543
Clearwater	1,260	3,372	1,100	2,925
Cook	2,496	1,203	1,912	1,156
Cottonwood	1,834	4,165	1,678	3,679
Crow Wing	13,726	25,676	10,982	22,287
Dakota	146,155	109,638	110,483	99,583
Dodge	4,079	7,783	3,102	6,527
Douglas	7,868	15,799	6,227	13,966
Faribault	2,531	5,191	2,153	4,659
Fillmore	4,551	7,301	3,872	6,271
Freeborn	6,889	9,578	6,041	8,808
Goodhue	11,806	16,052	9,446	14,041
Grant	1,300	2,269	1,105	2,063
Hennepin	532,623	205,973	429,288	191,770
Houston	4,853	6,334	4,145	5,616
Hubbard	4,462	8,202	3,423	7,261
Isanti	7,138	16,491	5,657	13,635
Itasca	10,786	15,239	9,015	12,920
Jackson	1,745	3,948	1,492	3,609
Kanabec	2,774	6,278	2,327	5,230
Kandiyohi	8,440	14,437	7,266	12,785
Kittson	1,006	1,546	823	1,349
Koochiching	2,659	4,131	2,306	3,569
Lac Qui Parle	1,446	2,528	1,305	2,293
Lake	3,647	3,393	3,077	2,932

County	2020 Biden (D)	Trump (R)	2016 Clinton (D)	Trump (R)
Lake of the Woods	671	1,704	553	1,540
Le Sueur	5,672	10,775	4,623	9,182
Lincoln	937	2,121	860	1,931
Lyon	4,634	7,979	3,825	7,256
Mahnomen	1,112	1,142	930	991
Marshall	1,295	3,721	1,225	3,208
Martin	3,305	7,480	2,733	7,062
McLeod	6,413	13,986	4,978	12,155
Meeker	3,867	9,359	3,191	8,104
Mille Lacs	4,404	9,952	3,710	8,340
Morrison	4,367	14,821	3,637	12,925
Mower	8,899	10,025	7,437	8,823
Murray	1,449	3,363	1,295	2,974
Nicollet	9,622	9,018	7,886	8,437
Nobles	2,933	5,600	2,733	5,299
Norman	1,404	1,953	1,264	1,699
Olmsted	49,491	39,692	36,268	35,668
Otter Tail	11,958	23,800	9,340	20,939
Pennington	2,568	4,532	2,147	4,000
Pine	5,419	10,256	4,580	8,191
Pipestone	1,306	3,553	1,127	3,338
Polk	5,439	9,865	4,712	8,979
Pope	2,477	4,417	2,106	3,793
Ramsey	211,620	77,376	177,738	70,894
Red Lake	691	1,454	540	1,141
Redwood	2,355	5,771	1,887	5,137
Renville	2,496	5,467	2,117	4,890
Rice	17,402	17,464	14,437	15,429
Rock	1,556	3,583	1,373	3,091
Roseau	2,188	6,065	1,856	5,451
St. Louis	67,704	49,017	57,771	44,630
Scott	40,040	45,872	28,502	39,948
Sherburne	18,065	36,222	13,293	31,053
Sibley	2,417	5,864	1,954	5,193
Stearns	31,879	50,959	25,576	47,617
Steele	7,917	12,656	6,241	11,198
Stevens	1,922	3,044	2,116	2,799
Swift	1,784	3,316	1,686	2,963
Todd	3,286	9,753	2,783	8,485
Traverse	661	1,172	630	1,049
Wabasha	4,696	8,153	3,866	6,989
Wadena	2,023	5,520	1,684	4,837
Waseca	3,496	6,624	2,838	5,967
Washington	89,165	73,764	67,086	64,428
Watonwan	1,987	3,103	1,814	2,768
Wilkin	1,026	2,328	893	2,129
Winona	13,333	13,227	11,366	12,122
Wright	28,430	51,973	20,334	43,274
Yellow Medicine	1,688	3,734	1,524	3,382
Totals	**1,717,077**	**1,484,065**	**1,367,716**	**1,322,951**

Minnesota Vote Since 1960

2020: Biden, D, 1,717,077; Trump, R, 1,484,065; Jorgensen, LB, 34,976; Hawkins, Green, 10,033; West, Ind., 7,940; Pierce, Ind., 5,651; De La Fuente, Alliance, 5,611; La Riva, Socialism/Liberation, 1,210; Kennedy, Soc. Workers, 643.

2016: Clinton, D, 1,367,716; Trump, R, 1,322,951; Johnson, LB, 112,972; McMullin, Ind., 53,076; Stein, Green, 36,985; Vacek, Legal Marijuana, 11,291; Castle, Const., 9,456; Kennedy, Soc. Workers, 1,672; De La Fuente, Amer. Delta, 1,431.

2012: Obama, D, 1,546,167; Romney, R, 1,320,225; Johnson, LB, 35,098; Stein, Green, 13,023; Goode, Const., 3,722; Carlson, Grassroots, 3,149; Anderson, Justice, 1,996; Morstad, Constitutional, 1,092; Harris, Soc. Workers, 1,051; Lindsay, Socialism/Liberation, 397.

2008: Obama, D, 1,573,354; McCain, R, 1,275,409; Nader, Ind., 30,152; Barr, LB, 9,174; Baldwin, Const., 6,787; McKinney, Green, 5,174; Calero, Soc. Workers, 790.

2004: Kerry, D, 1,445,014; Bush, R, 1,346,695; Nader, Better Life, 18,683; Badnarik, LB, 4,639; Cobb, Green, 4,408; Peroutka, Const., 3,074; Harens, other, 2,387; Van Auken, Soc. Equal., 539; Calero, Soc. Workers, 416.

2000: Gore, D, 1,168,266; Bush, R, 1,109,659; Nader, Green, 126,696; Buchanan, RF MN, 22,166; Browne, LB, 5,282; Phillips, Const., 3,272; Hagelin, RF, 2,294; Harris, Soc. Workers, 1,022.

1996: Clinton, D, 1,120,438; Dole, R, 766,476; Perot, RF, 257,704; Nader, Green, 24,908; Browne, LB, 8,271; Peron,

Grass Roots, 4,898; Phillips, U.S. Taxpayers, 3,416; Hagelin, Natural Law, 1,808; Birrenbach, Ind. Grass Roots, 787; Harris, Soc. Workers, 684; White, Soc. Equality, 347.

1992: Clinton, D, 1,020,997; Bush, R, 747,841; Perot, Ind., 562,506; Marrou, LB, 3,373; Gritz, Populist/America First, 3,363; Hagelin, Natural Law, 1,406.

1988: Dukakis, D, 1,109,471; Bush, R, 962,337; McCarthy, MN Prog., 5,403; Paul, LB, 5,109.

1984: Mondale, D, 1,036,364; Reagan, R, 1,032,603; Bergland, LB, 2,996.

1980: Carter, D, 954,173; Reagan, R, 873,268; Anderson, Ind., 174,997; Clark, LB, 31,593; Commoner, Citizens, 8,406; Hall, Comm., 1,117; DeBerry, Soc. Workers, 711; Griswold, Workers World, 698; McReynolds, Soc., 536; write-in, 281.

1976: Carter, D, 1,070,440; Ford, R, 819,395; McCarthy, Ind., 35,490; Anderson, Amer., 13,592; Camejo, Soc. Workers, 4,149; MacBride, LB, 3,529; Hall, Comm., 1,092.

1972: Nixon, R, 898,269; McGovern, D, 802,346; Schmitz, Amer., 31,407; Fisher, Soc. Labor, 4,261; Spock, People's, 2,805; Jenness, Soc. Workers, 940; Hall, Comm., 662; scattered, 962.

1968: Humphrey, D, 857,738; Nixon, R, 658,643; Wallace, 3rd party, 68,931; Cleaver, Peace/Freedom, 935; Halstead, Soc. Workers, 808; McCarthy, write-in, 585; Mitchell, Comm., 415; Blomen, Industrial Govt., 285; scattered, 2,613.

1964: Johnson, D, 991,117; Goldwater, R, 559,624; Hass, Industrial Govt., 2,544; DeBerry, Soc. Workers, 1,177.

1960: Kennedy, D, 779,933; Nixon, R, 757,915; Dobbs, Soc. Workers, 3,077; Hass, Industrial Govt., 962.

Mississippi

County	2020		2016	
	Biden (D)	Trump (R)	Clinton (D)	Trump (R)
Adams	7,917	5,696	7,757	5,874
Alcorn	2,782	12,818	2,684	11,819
Amite	2,620	4,503	2,697	4,289
Attala	3,542	5,178	3,242	4,897
Benton	1,679	2,570	1,719	2,251
Bolivar	8,904	4,671	9,046	4,590
Calhoun	1,902	4,625	1,910	4,390
Carroll	1,729	3,924	1,680	3,799
Chickasaw	3,810	4,175	3,649	4,127
Choctaw	1,185	3,001	1,218	2,788
Claiborne	3,772	603	3,708	540
Clarke	2,838	5,417	2,585	5,137
Clay	5,844	4,181	5,722	4,150
Coahoma	6,020	2,375	6,378	2,426
Copiah	6,470	6,250	6,741	6,103
Covington	3,416	5,854	3,276	5,435
DeSoto	28,265	46,462	20,591	43,089
Forrest	13,755	17,290	11,716	15,461
Franklin	1,480	2,923	1,502	2,721
George	1,218	9,713	1,027	8,696
Greene	966	4,794	974	4,335
Grenada	4,734	6,081	4,424	5,970
Hancock	4,504	16,132	3,344	13,811
Harrison	27,728	46,822	21,169	40,354
Hinds	73,550	25,141	67,594	25,275
Holmes	6,588	1,369	6,689	1,309
Humphreys	3,016	1,118	3,071	1,151
Issaquena	355	308	395	298
Itawamba	1,249	9,438	1,117	8,470
Jackson	17,375	36,295	14,657	33,629
Jasper	4,341	4,302	4,368	4,038
Jefferson	3,327	531	3,337	490
Jefferson Davis	3,599	2,534	3,720	2,466
Jones	8,517	21,226	7,791	20,133
Kemper	2,887	1,787	2,827	1,778
Lafayette	10,070	12,949	7,969	10,872
Lamar	7,340	20,704	5,190	18,751
Lauderdale	12,960	17,967	11,269	17,741
Lawrence	2,260	4,285	2,195	4,091
Leake	3,897	5,228	3,584	4,782
Lee	12,189	24,207	10,029	22,220

County	2020		2016	
	Biden (D)	Trump (R)	Clinton (D)	Trump (R)
Leflore	7,648	3,129	7,787	3,212
Lincoln	5,040	11,596	4,458	10,550
Lowndes	13,087	13,800	11,819	13,271
Madison	24,440	31,091	20,343	28,265
Marion	3,787	8,273	3,677	7,836
Marshall	8,057	7,566	8,023	6,587
Monroe	5,874	11,177	5,524	10,167
Montgomery	2,121	2,917	2,115	2,818
Neshoba	3,260	8,320	2,715	7,679
Newton	3,075	6,997	2,756	6,548
Noxubee	4,040	1,240	4,347	1,200
Oktibbeha	10,299	9,004	8,859	8,576
Panola	7,403	8,060	7,431	7,449
Pearl River	4,148	19,595	3,604	17,782
Perry	1,362	4,500	1,220	4,135
Pike	8,646	8,479	8,043	8,009
Pontotoc	2,614	11,550	2,386	10,336
Prentiss	2,153	8,370	2,067	7,648
Quitman	2,150	1,026	2,312	1,001
Rankin	18,847	50,895	14,110	47,178
Scott	4,330	6,285	4,268	6,122
Sharkey	1,465	688	1,479	692
Simpson	4,037	7,635	3,874	7,393
Smith	1,791	6,458	1,617	5,928
Stone	1,802	5,964	1,573	5,306
Sunflower	6,781	2,799	6,725	2,794
Tallahatchie	3,105	2,488	3,337	2,462
Tate	4,183	8,707	3,926	7,495
Tippah	1,937	8,054	1,842	7,240
Tishomingo	1,059	7,933	999	7,166
Tunica	2,580	926	2,667	853
Union	2,160	10,373	2,012	9,235
Walthall	2,835	4,220	2,790	4,056
Warren	10,442	10,365	9,284	9,767
Washington	12,503	5,300	11,380	5,244
Wayne	3,624	6,307	3,524	5,990
Webster	1,043	4,291	1,019	3,976
Wilkinson	2,749	1,324	2,857	1,318
Winston	4,040	5,112	3,850	4,910
Yalobusha	2,785	3,671	2,582	3,376
Yazoo	5,496	4,832	5,369	4,598
Totals	**539,398**	**756,764**	**485,131**	**700,714**

Mississippi Vote Since 1960

2020: Trump, R, 756,764; Biden, D, 539,398; Jorgensen, LB, 8,026; West, Ind., 3,657; Hawkins, Green, 1,498; Collins, Ind., 1,317; Blankenship, Amer. Const., 1,279; Carroll, Amer. Solidarity, 1,161; Pierce, Ind., 659.

2016: Trump, R, 700,714; Clinton, D, 485,131; Johnson, LB, 14,435; Castle, Const., 3,987; Stein, Green, 3,731; Hedges, Prohib., 715; De La Fuente, Amer. Delta, 644.

2012: Romney, R, 710,746; Obama, D, 562,949; Johnson, LB, 6,676; Goode, Const., 2,609; Stein, Green, 1,588; Washer, RF, 1,016.

2008: McCain, R, 724,597; Obama, D, 554,662; Nader, Ind., 4,011; Baldwin, Const., 2,551; Barr, LB, 2,529; McKinney, Green, 1,034; Weill, RF, 481.

2004: Bush, R, 684,981; Kerry, D, 458,094; Nader, RF, 3,177; Badnarik, LB, 1,793; Peroutka, Const., 1,759; Harris, Ind., 1,268; Cobb, Green, 1,073.

2000: Bush, R, 572,844; Gore, D, 404,614; Nader, Ind., 8,122; Phillips, Const., 3,267; Buchanan, RF, 2,265; Browne, LB, 2,009; Harris, Ind., 613; Hagelin, Natural Law, 450.

1996: Dole, R, 439,838; Clinton, D, 394,022; Perot, RF, 52,222; Browne, LB, 2,809; Phillips, U.S. Taxpayers, 2,314; Hagelin, Natural Law, 1,447; Collins, Ind., 1,205.

1992: Bush, R, 487,793; Clinton, D, 400,258; Perot, Ind., 85,626; Fulani, New Alliance, 2,625; Marrou, LB, 2,154; Phillips, U.S. Taxpayers, 1,652; Hagelin, Natural Law, 1,140.

1988: Bush, R, 557,890; Dukakis, D, 363,921; Duke, Ind., 4,232; Paul, LB, 3,329.

1984: Reagan, R, 582,377; Mondale, D, 352,192; Bergland, LB, 2,336.

1980: Reagan, R, 441,089; Carter, D, 429,281; Anderson, Ind., 12,036; Clark, LB, 5,465; Griswold, Workers World, 2,402; Pulley, Soc. Workers, 2,347.

1976: Carter, D, 381,309; Ford, R, 366,846; Anderson, Amer., 6,678; McCarthy, Ind., 4,074; Maddox, Ind., 4,049; Camejo, Soc. Workers, 2,805; MacBride, LB, 2,609.

1972: Nixon, R, 505,125; McGovern, D, 126,782; Schmitz, Amer., 11,598; Jenness, Soc. Workers, 2,458.

1968: Wallace, 3rd party, 415,349; Humphrey, D, 150,644; Nixon, R, 88,516.

1964: Goldwater, R, 356,528; Johnson, D, 52,618.

1960: D. (electors unpledged), 116,248; Kennedy, D, 108,362; Nixon, R, 73,561. Mississippi's victorious slate of 8 unpledged Dem. electors cast their votes for Sen. Harry F. Byrd (D, VA).

Missouri

County	2020		2016	
	Biden (D)	Trump (R)	Clinton (D)	Trump (R)
Adair	3,710	6,413	3,500	6,030
Andrew	2,351	7,255	2,045	6,665
Atchison	564	2,199	541	2,060
Audrain	2,704	7,732	2,570	6,981
Barry	2,948	12,425	2,710	11,428
Barton	844	5,168	795	4,959
Bates	1,672	6,597	1,618	6,001
Benton	2,180	8,109	2,025	7,213
Bollinger	750	5,167	705	4,827
Boone	50,064	38,646	41,125	36,200
Buchanan	13,445	22,450	12,013	21,320
Butler	3,301	14,602	3,036	13,650
Caldwell	897	3,725	838	3,232
Callaway	5,870	14,815	4,989	13,057
Camden	5,652	18,850	4,768	16,944
Cape Girardeau	10,760	28,907	8,492	27,017
Carroll	786	3,706	745	3,480
Carter	418	2,451	436	2,324
Cass	19,052	37,197	14,846	33,098
Cedar	1,145	5,788	1,011	5,021
Chariton	916	3,111	888	2,950
Christian	11,131	34,920	8,508	30,946
Clark	678	2,672	724	2,458
Clay	59,400	64,605	45,304	57,476
Clinton	2,896	7,799	2,572	7,067
Cole	12,694	26,086	10,913	24,616
Cooper	2,249	6,272	1,932	5,624
Crawford	2,113	8,725	1,824	7,724
Dade	656	3,414	637	3,184
Dallas	1,380	6,619	1,272	5,895
Daviess	746	3,102	730	2,767
DeKalb	930	3,828	824	3,540
Dent	1,056	5,987	978	5,600
Douglas	1,016	5,898	984	5,486
Dunklin	2,200	8,135	2,360	8,026
Franklin	14,569	38,058	12,341	35,430
Gasconade	1,601	6,222	1,520	5,670
Gentry	613	2,581	605	2,304
Greene	55,068	83,630	42,728	78,035
Grundy	799	3,585	780	3,462
Harrison	597	3,198	574	2,965
Henry	2,619	8,027	2,357	7,075
Hickory	1,056	3,966	1,016	3,542
Holt	338	1,976	347	1,926
Howard	1,413	3,553	1,283	3,277
Howell	3,218	15,181	2,881	13,893
Iron	945	3,596	933	3,173
Jackson	92,182	100,142	71,237	91,557
Jasper	13,549	37,728	10,572	35,070
Jefferson	37,523	77,046	31,568	69,036
Johnson	6,974	15,489	5,930	13,719
Knox	340	1,486	379	1,416
Laclede	2,780	13,762	2,553	12,881
Lafayette	4,472	12,273	4,053	10,988
Lawrence	3,214	14,426	2,901	13,089
Lewis	984	3,553	934	3,344
Lincoln	6,607	21,848	5,575	18,159
Linn	1,275	4,363	1,240	4,088
Livingston	1,410	5,267	1,265	4,879
Macon	1,662	6,076	1,548	5,798
Madison	1,019	4,584	1,005	4,102
Maries	814	3,892	794	3,561
Marion	3,202	9,915	2,994	9,419
McDonald	1,439	7,465	1,329	6,599

County	2020		2016	
	Biden (D)	Trump (R)	Clinton (D)	Trump (R)
Mercer	222	1,541	216	1,486
Miller	2,038	10,176	1,750	9,285
Mississippi	1,178	3,537	1,458	3,600
Moniteau	1,308	5,744	1,237	5,347
Monroe	936	3,477	853	3,159
Montgomery	1,208	4,465	1,119	4,127
Morgan	1,924	7,442	1,768	6,760
New Madrid	1,748	5,447	1,933	5,270
Newton	5,818	22,120	4,990	20,553
Nodaway	2,853	6,865	2,529	6,380
Oregon	823	3,847	865	3,671
Osage	1,037	6,425	998	5,856
Ozark	752	4,064	724	3,639
Pemiscot	1,560	4,120	1,947	3,964
Perry	1,664	7,657	1,520	6,908
Pettis	4,783	13,854	4,324	12,810
Phelps	5,637	13,480	4,766	12,709
Pike	1,717	5,863	1,806	5,274
Platte	27,179	28,917	20,057	25,933
Polk	2,885	11,850	2,631	10,438
Pulaski	3,740	10,329	2,922	9,876
Putnam	361	1,984	353	1,936
Ralls	1,205	4,396	1,138	3,969
Randolph	2,485	8,018	2,283	7,529
Ray	3,109	8,345	3,090	7,104
Reynolds	529	2,733	540	2,406
Ripley	833	4,839	830	4,522
St. Charles	89,530	128,389	68,626	121,650
St. Clair	988	3,932	936	3,501
St. Francois	7,044	20,511	6,250	17,468
St. Louis Co.	328,151	199,493	286,704	202,434
Ste. Genevieve	2,713	6,630	2,542	5,496
Saline	2,904	6,451	2,789	5,977
Schuyler	373	1,606	354	1,505
Scotland	388	1,560	365	1,525
Scott	3,753	13,769	3,575	13,168
Shannon	706	3,165	776	2,966
Shelby	592	2,700	606	2,524
Stoddard	1,819	11,484	1,876	11,079
Stone	3,506	14,800	2,887	13,158
Sullivan	478	1,974	526	1,884
Taney	5,339	20,508	4,373	18,276
Texas	1,716	9,478	1,728	8,875
Vernon	1,903	7,155	1,707	6,533
Warren	4,769	13,222	3,915	11,111
Washington	1,804	8,047	1,926	7,048
Wayne	845	4,987	948	4,658
Webster	3,573	14,880	3,177	12,840
Worth	215	877	195	808
Wright	1,168	7,453	1,170	6,707
City				
Kansas City	107,660	26,393	97,735	24,654
St. Louis	110,089	21,474	104,235	20,832
Totals	**1,253,014**	**1,718,736**	**1,071,068**	**1,594,511**

Missouri Vote Since 1960

2020: Trump, R, 1,718,736; Biden, D, 1,253,014; Jorgensen, LB, 41,205; Hawkins, Green, 8,283; Blankenship, Const., 3,919.

2016: Trump, R, 1,594,511; Clinton, D, 1,071,068; Johnson, LB, 97,359; Stein, Green, 25,419; Castle, Const., 13,092; McMullin, Ind., 7,071.

2012: Romney, R, 1,482,440; Obama, D, 1,223,796; Johnson, LB, 43,151; Goode, Const., 7,936.

2008: McCain, R, 1,445,814; Obama, D, 1,441,911; Nader, Ind., 17,813; Barr, LB, 11,386; Baldwin, Const., 8,201.

2004: Bush, R, 1,455,713; Kerry, D, 1,259,171; Badnarik, LB, 9,831; Peroutka, Const., 5,355.

2000: Bush, R, 1,189,924; Gore, D, 1,111,138; Nader, Green, 38,515; Buchanan, RF, 9,818; Browne, LB, 7,436; Phillips, Const., 1,957; Hagelin, Natural Law, 1,104.

1996: Clinton, D, 1,025,935; Dole, R, 890,016; Perot, RF, 217,188; Phillips, U.S. Taxpayers, 11,521; Browne, LB, 10,522; Hagelin, Natural Law, 2,287.

1992: Clinton, D, 1,053,873; Bush, R, 811,159; Perot, Ind., 518,741; Marrou, LB, 7,497.

1988: Bush, R, 1,084,953; Dukakis, D, 1,001,619; Fulani, New Alliance, 6,656; Paul, write-in, 434.

1984: Reagan, R, 1,274,188; Mondale, D, 848,583.

1980: Reagan, R, 1,074,181; Carter, D, 931,182; Anderson, Ind., 77,920; Clark, LB, 14,422; DeBerry, Soc. Workers, 1,515; Commoner, Citizens, 573; write-in, 31.

1976: Carter, D, 999,163; Ford, R, 928,808; McCarthy, Ind., 24,329.
1972: Nixon, R, 1,154,058; McGovern, D, 698,531.
1968: Nixon, R, 811,932; Humphrey, D, 791,444; Wallace, 3rd party, 206,126.
1964: Johnson, D, 1,164,344; Goldwater, R, 653,535.
1960: Kennedy, D, 972,201; Nixon, R, 962,221.

Montana

County	2020 Biden (D)	Trump (R)	2016 Clinton (D)	Trump (R)
Beaverhead	1,608	3,923	1,143	3,353
Big Horn	2,491	2,207	2,094	1,853
Blaine	1,589	1,469	1,202	1,268
Broadwater	835	3,173	573	2,348
Carbon	2,421	4,468	1,828	3,748
Carter	74	775	70	678
Cascade	15,456	23,315	12,175	19,632
Chouteau	991	1,891	732	1,679
Custer	1,514	4,205	1,176	3,657
Daniels	195	799	168	730
Dawson	962	3,758	787	3,320
Deer Lodge	2,562	2,186	2,058	1,763
Fallon	172	1,375	154	1,279
Fergus	1,496	4,869	1,202	4,269
Flathead	20,274	38,321	13,293	30,240
Gallatin	37,044	31,696	24,246	23,802
Garfield	41	764	34	653
Glacier	3,610	1,884	3,121	1,620
Golden Valley	78	414	71	365
Granite	638	1,419	472	1,192
Hill	2,981	3,957	2,371	3,478
Jefferson	2,625	5,345	1,998	4,177
Judith Basin	275	1,040	235	872
Lake	6,916	9,322	4,776	7,530
Lewis and Clark	19,743	21,409	14,478	16,895
Liberty	249	821	206	698
Lincoln	2,835	8,672	2,041	6,729
Madison	1,771	4,191	1,180	3,297
McCone	155	956	154	862
Meagher	258	833	193	729
Mineral	686	1,828	519	1,330
Missoula	43,357	26,347	31,543	22,250
Musselshell	413	2,423	332	1,967
Park	5,280	6,025	3,595	4,980
Petroleum	39	298	30	278
Phillips	416	1,936	318	1,723
Pondera	903	2,031	738	1,799
Powder River	154	970	127	884
Powell	752	2,355	551	2,029
Prairie	126	603	100	556
Ravalli	8,763	19,114	6,223	14,810
Richland	875	4,800	671	3,908
Roosevelt	1,910	1,996	1,560	1,797
Rosebud	1,199	2,486	987	2,253
Sanders	1,820	5,660	1,218	4,286
Sheridan	574	1,403	477	1,241
Silver Bow	10,392	7,745	8,619	6,376
Stillwater	1,156	4,462	908	3,661
Sweet Grass	549	1,840	402	1,595
Teton	1,007	2,608	808	2,170
Toole	467	1,596	402	1,497
Treasure	78	373	59	351
Valley	1,030	3,135	886	2,698
Wheatland	225	823	179	702
Wibaux	77	516	55	463
Yellowstone	30,679	50,772	22,171	40,920
Totals	**244,786**	**343,602**	**177,709**	**279,240**

Montana Vote Since 1960

2020: Trump, R, 343,602; Biden, D, 244,786; Jorgensen, LB, 15,252.
2016: Trump, R, 279,240; Clinton, D, 177,709; Johnson, LB, 28,037; Stein, Green, 7,970; McMullin, Ind., 2,297; De La Fuente, Amer. Delta, 1,570.
2012: Romney, R, 267,928; Obama, D, 201,839; Johnson, LB, 14,165.
2008: McCain, R, 242,763; Obama, D, 231,667; Paul, Const., 10,638; Nader, Ind., 3,686; Barr, LB, 1,355.
2004: Bush, R, 266,063; Kerry, D, 173,710; Nader, Ind., 6,168; Peroutka, Const., 1,764; Badnarik, LB, 1,733; Cobb, Green, 996.
2000: Bush, R, 240,178; Gore, D, 137,126; Nader, Green, 24,437; Buchanan, RF, 5,697; Browne, LB, 1,718; Phillips, Const., 1,155; Hagelin, Natural Law, 675.
1996: Dole, R, 179,652; Clinton, D, 167,922; Perot, RF, 55,229; Browne, LB, 2,526; Hagelin, Natural Law, 1,754.
1992: Clinton, D, 154,507; Bush, R, 144,207; Perot, Ind., 107,225; Gritz, Populist/America First, 3,658.
1988: Bush, R, 190,412; Dukakis, D, 168,936; Paul, LB, 5,047; Fulani, New Alliance, 1,279.
1984: Reagan, R, 232,450; Mondale, D, 146,742; Bergland, LB, 5,185.
1980: Reagan, R, 206,814; Carter, D, 118,032; Anderson, Ind., 29,281; Clark, LB, 9,825.
1976: Ford, R, 173,703; Carter, D, 149,259; Anderson, Amer., 5,772.
1972: Nixon, R, 183,976; McGovern, D, 120,197; Schmitz, Amer., 13,430.
1968: Nixon, R, 138,835; Humphrey, D, 114,117; Wallace, 3rd party, 20,015; Munn, Prohib., 510; Caton, New RF, 470; Halstead, Soc. Workers, 457.
1964: Johnson, D, 164,246; Goldwater, R, 113,032; Kasper, Natl. States' Rights, 519; Munn, Prohib., 499; DeBerry, Soc. Workers, 332.
1960: Nixon, R, 141,841; Kennedy, D, 134,891; Decker, Prohib., 456; Dobbs, Soc. Workers, 391.

Nebraska

County	2020 Biden (D)	Trump (R)	2016 Clinton (D)	Trump (R)
Adams	4,213	10,085	3,302	9,287
Antelope	452	3,093	383	2,732
Arthur	21	260	17	244
Banner	43	362	19	357
Blaine	35	280	30	276
Boone	499	2,653	414	2,299
Box Butte	1,051	4,002	965	3,617
Boyd	135	1,010	128	983
Brown	191	1,470	153	1,385
Buffalo	6,350	16,640	4,763	14,569
Burt	1,063	2,580	930	2,367
Butler	873	3,542	691	3,079
Cass	4,737	10,121	3,484	8,452
Cedar	725	4,174	571	3,532
Chase	226	1,740	171	1,648
Cherry	373	2,844	317	2,623
Cheyenne	855	3,813	711	3,665
Clay	632	2,848	477	2,422
Colfax	1,025	2,636	859	2,171
Cuming	870	3,507	719	3,122
Custer	786	5,090	641	4,695
Dakota	2,744	3,926	2,314	3,616
Dawes	1,082	2,931	801	2,632
Dawson	2,497	6,524	2,136	5,984
Deuel	141	871	120	809
Dixon	651	2,335	556	2,041
Dodge	5,544	10,984	4,544	9,933
Douglas	150,350	119,159	113,798	108,077
Dundy	105	883	89	823
Fillmore	693	2,359	613	2,130
Franklin	276	1,437	250	1,347
Frontier	189	1,229	161	1,110
Furnas	399	2,163	304	1,921
Gage	3,385	7,445	2,935	6,380
Garden	161	1,016	153	869
Garfield	133	933	121	821
Gosper	215	893	166	794
Grant	20	375	20	367
Greeley	229	1,016	210	912
Hall	7,681	16,189	6,282	14,408
Hamilton	1,118	4,309	878	3,783
Harlan	282	1,615	254	1,496
Hayes	34	494	30	472
Hitchcock	175	1,264	161	1,232
Holt	686	4,769	531	4,354
Hooker	59	376	40	355
Howard	648	2,786	544	2,284
Jefferson	1,016	2,616	837	2,399
Johnson	647	1,518	563	1,355
Kearney	701	2,822	550	2,531

County	2020 Biden (D)	Trump (R)	2016 Clinton (D)	Trump (R)
Keith	763	3,544	571	3,235
Keya Paha	49	476	40	460
Kimball	268	1,563	230	1,330
Knox	905	3,721	720	3,188
Lancaster	82,293	70,092	61,898	61,588
Lincoln	3,692	13,071	2,913	12,164
Logan	38	407	32	400
Loup	75	370	48	323
Madison	3,478	11,940	2,711	10,628
McPherson	17	275	14	257
Merrick	743	3,419	602	2,926
Morrill	386	2,113	284	1,802
Nance	359	1,437	281	1,261
Nemaha	921	2,428	785	2,116
Nuckolls	409	1,857	353	1,726
Otoe	2,490	5,649	2,025	4,860
Pawnee	322	1,071	279	974
Perkins	199	1,321	161	1,217
Phelps	752	4,157	572	3,849
Pierce	480	3,462	382	3,052
Platte	3,260	12,186	2,646	10,965
Polk	530	2,291	413	2,028
Red Willow	811	4,525	645	4,258
Richardson	996	3,073	818	2,769
Rock	84	744	70	687
Saline	1,986	3,631	1,733	3,004
Sarpy	41,206	51,979	28,033	45,143
Saunders	3,331	9,108	2,523	7,555
Scotts Bluff	4,196	10,952	3,207	10,076
Seward	2,438	6,490	1,875	5,454
Sheridan	340	2,292	287	2,211
Sherman	343	1,322	340	1,150
Sioux	72	642	81	616
Stanton	532	2,561	417	2,187
Thayer	624	2,308	499	2,051
Thomas	45	377	30	344
Thurston	1,122	1,180	919	1,043
Valley	412	1,901	339	1,780
Washington	3,554	8,583	2,623	7,424
Wayne	1,022	3,055	835	2,693
Webster	335	1,511	306	1,330
Wheeler	59	438	62	377
York	1,630	5,337	1,186	4,700
Totals	**374,583**	**556,846**	**284,494**	**495,961**

Nebraska Vote Since 1960

2020: Trump, R, 556,846; Biden, D, 374,583; Jorgensen, LB, 20,283.

2016: Trump, R, 495,961; Clinton, D, 284,494; Johnson, LB, 38,946; Stein, petitioning cand., 8,775.

2012: Romney, R, 475,064; Obama, D, 302,081; Johnson, LB, 11,109; Terry, petitioning cand., 2,408.

2008: McCain, R, 452,979; Obama, D, 333,319; Nader, petitioning cand., 5,406; Baldwin, Nebraska, 2,972; Barr, LB, 2,740; McKinney, Green, 1,028.

2004: Bush, R, 512,814; Kerry, D, 254,328; Nader, petitioning cand., 5,698; Badnarik, LB, 2,041; Peroutka, Nebraska, 1,314; Cobb, Green, 978; Calero, petitioning cand., 82.

2000: Bush, R, 433,862; Gore, D, 231,780; Nader, Green, 24,540; Buchanan, Ind., 3,646; Browne, LB, 2,245; Hagelin, Natural Law, 478; Phillips, Ind., 468.

1996: Dole, R, 363,467; Clinton, D, 236,761; Perot, RF, 71,278; Browne, LB, 2,792; Phillips, Ind., 1,928; Hagelin, Natural Law, 1,189.

1992: Bush, R, 343,678; Clinton, D, 216,864; Perot, Ind., 174,104; Marrou, LB, 1,340.

1988: Bush, R, 397,956; Dukakis, D, 259,235; Paul, LB, 2,534; Fulani, New Alliance, 1,740.

1984: Reagan, R, 459,135; Mondale, D, 187,475; Bergland, LB, 2,075.

1980: Reagan, R, 419,214; Carter, D, 166,424; Anderson, Ind., 44,854; Clark, LB, 9,041.

1976: Ford, R, 359,219; Carter, D, 233,287; McCarthy, Ind., 9,383; Maddox, Amer. Ind., 3,378; MacBride, LB, 1,476.

1972: Nixon, R, 406,298; McGovern, D, 169,991; scattered, 817.

1968: Nixon, R, 321,163; Humphrey, D, 170,784; Wallace, 3rd party, 44,904.

1964: Johnson, D, 307,307; Goldwater, R, 276,847.

1960: Nixon, R, 380,553; Kennedy, D, 232,542.

Nevada

County	2020 Biden (D)	Trump (R)	2016 Clinton (D)	Trump (R)
Churchill	3,051	9,372	2,210	7,830
Clark	521,852	430,930	402,227	320,057
Douglas	11,571	21,630	8,454	17,415
Elko	4,557	16,741	3,401	13,551
Esmeralda	74	400	65	329
Eureka	105	895	74	723
Humboldt	1,689	5,877	1,386	4,521
Lander	496	2,198	403	1,828
Lincoln	330	2,067	285	1,671
Lyon	8,473	20,914	6,146	16,005
Mineral	829	1,423	637	1,179
Nye	7,288	17,528	5,094	13,324
Pershing	547	1,731	430	1,403
Storey	902	1,908	752	1,616
Washoe	128,128	116,760	97,379	94,758
White Pine	859	3,403	707	2,723
City				
Carson City	12,735	16,113	9,610	13,125
Totals	**703,486**	**669,890**	**539,260**	**512,058**

Nevada Vote Since 1960

2020: Biden, D, 703,486; Trump, R, 669,890; Jorgensen, LB, 14,783; None of These Candidates, 14,079; Blankenship, Ind. Amer., 3,138.

2016: Clinton, D, 539,260; Trump, R, 512,058; Johnson, LB, 37,384; None of These Candidates, 28,863; Castle, Ind. Amer., 5,268; De La Fuente, unaff., 2,552.

2012: Obama, D, 531,373; Romney, R, 463,567; Johnson, LB, 10,968; None of These Candidates, 5,770; Goode, Ind. Amer., 3,240.

2008: Obama, D, 533,736; McCain, R, 412,827; None of These Candidates, 6,267; Nader, Ind., 6,150; Barr, LB, 4,263; Baldwin, Const., 3,194; McKinney, Green, 1,411.

2004: Bush, R, 418,690; Kerry, D, 397,190; Nader, Ind., 4,838; None of These Candidates, 3,688; Badnarik, LB, 3,176; Peroutka, Ind. Amer., 1,152; Cobb, Green, 853.

2000: Bush, R, 301,575; Gore, D, 279,978; Nader, Green, 15,008; Buchanan, Citizens First, 4,747; None of These Candidates, 3,315; Browne, LB, 3,311; Phillips, Ind. Amer., 621; Hagelin, Natural Law, 415.

1996: Clinton, D, 203,974; Dole, R, 199,244; Perot, RF, 43,986; None of These Candidates, 5,608; Nader, Green, 4,730; Browne, LB, 4,460; Phillips, Ind. Amer., 1,732; Hagelin, Natural Law, 545.

1992: Clinton, D, 189,148; Bush, R, 175,828; Perot, Ind., 132,580; Gritz, Populist/America First, 2,892; Marrou, LB, 1,835.

1988: Bush, R, 206,040; Dukakis, D, 132,738; Paul, LB, 3,520; Fulani, New Alliance, 835.

1984: Reagan, R, 188,770; Mondale, D, 91,655; Bergland, LB, 2,292.

1980: Reagan, R, 155,017; Carter, D, 66,666; Anderson, Ind., 17,651; Clark, LB, 4,358.

1976: Ford, R, 101,273; Carter, D, 92,479; MacBride, LB, 1,519; Maddox, Amer. Ind., 1,497; scattered, 5,108.

1972: Nixon, R, 115,750; McGovern, D, 66,016.

1968: Nixon, R, 73,188; Humphrey, D, 60,598; Wallace, 3rd party, 20,432.

1964: Johnson, D, 79,339; Goldwater, R, 56,094.

1960: Kennedy, D, 54,880; Nixon, R, 52,387.

New Hampshire

County	2020 Biden (D)	Trump (R)	2016 Clinton (D)	Trump (R)
Belknap	16,894	20,899	13,517	19,315
Carroll	16,649	16,150	12,987	14,635
Cheshire	25,522	17,898	22,064	16,876
Coos	7,640	8,617	6,563	7,952
Grafton	33,180	19,905	28,510	19,010
Hillsborough	122,344	104,625	99,589	100,013
Merrimack	48,533	39,711	40,198	37,674
Rockingham	100,064	95,858	79,994	90,447
Strafford	41,721	30,489	34,894	29,072
Sullivan	12,390	11,508	10,210	10,796
Totals	**424,937**	**365,660**	**348,526**	**345,790**

New Hampshire Vote Since 1960

2020: Biden, D, 424,937; Trump, R, 365,660; Jorgensen, LB, 13,236.

2016: Clinton, D, 348,526; Trump, R, 345,790; Johnson, LB, 30,777; Stein, Green, 6,496; De La Fuente, Amer. Delta, 678.

2012: Obama, D, 369,561; Romney, R, 329,918; Johnson, LB, 8,212; Goode, Const., 708.

2008: Obama, D, 384,826; McCain, R, 316,534; Nader, Ind., 3,503; Barr, LB, 2,217; Phillies, LB, 531.

2004: Kerry, D, 340,511; Bush, R, 331,237; Nader, Ind., 4,479.

2000: Bush, R, 273,559; Gore, D, 266,348; Nader, Green, 22,198; Browne, LB, 2,757; Buchanan, Independence, 2,615; Phillips, Const., 328.

1996: Clinton, D, 246,166; Dole, R, 196,486; Perot, RF, 48,387; Browne, LB, 4,214; Phillips, Taxpayers, 1,344.

1992: Clinton, D, 209,040; Bush, R, 202,484; Perot, Ind., 121,337; Marrou, LB, 3,548.

1988: Bush, R, 281,537; Dukakis, D, 163,696; Paul, LB, 4,502; Fulani, New Alliance, 790.

1984: Reagan, R, 267,051; Mondale, D, 120,377; Bergland, LB, 735.

1980: Reagan, R, 221,705; Carter, D, 108,864; Anderson, Ind., 49,693; Clark, LB, 2,067; Commoner, Citizens, 1,325; Hall, Comm., 129; Griswold, Workers World, 76; DeBerry, Soc. Workers, 72; scattered, 68.

1976: Ford, R, 185,935; Carter, D, 147,645; McCarthy, Ind., 4,095; MacBride, LB, 936; Reagan, write-in, 388; LaRouche, U.S. Labor, 186; Camejo, Soc. Workers, 161; Levin, Soc. Labor, 66; scattered, 215.

1972: Nixon, R, 213,724; McGovern, D, 116,435; Schmitz, Amer., 3,386; Jenness, Soc. Workers, 368; scattered, 142.

1968: Nixon, R, 154,903; Humphrey, D, 130,589; Wallace, 3rd party, 11,173; New Party, 421; Halstead, Soc. Workers, 104.

1964: Johnson, D, 182,065; Goldwater, R, 104,029.

1960: Nixon, R, 157,989; Kennedy, D, 137,772.

New Jersey

County	2020		2016	
	Biden (D)	Trump (R)	Clinton (D)	Trump (R)
Atlantic	73,808	64,438	60,924	52,690
Bergen	285,967	204,417	231,211	175,529
Burlington	154,595	103,345	121,725	89,272
Camden	175,065	86,207	146,717	72,631
Cape May	23,941	33,158	18,750	28,446
Cumberland	32,742	28,952	27,771	24,453
Essex	266,820	75,475	240,837	63,176
Gloucester	86,702	83,340	66,870	67,544
Hudson	181,452	65,698	163,917	49,043
Hunterdon	39,457	43,153	28,898	38,712
Mercer	122,532	51,641	104,775	46,193
Middlesex	226,250	143,467	193,044	122,953
Monmouth	181,291	191,808	137,181	166,723
Morris	153,881	141,134	115,249	126,071
Ocean	119,456	217,740	87,150	179,079
Passaic	129,097	92,009	116,759	72,902
Salem	14,479	18,827	11,904	16,381
Somerset	111,173	71,996	85,689	65,505
Sussex	34,481	51,698	24,212	46,658
Union	170,245	80,002	147,414	68,114
Warren	24,901	34,769	17,281	29,858
Totals	**2,608,335**	**1,883,274**	**2,148,278**	**1,601,933**

New Jersey Vote Since 1960

2020: Biden, D, 2,608,335; Trump, R, 1,883,274; Jorgensen, LB, 31,677; Hawkins, Green, 14,202; Hammons, Unity, 3,255; Blankenship, Const., 2,954; La Riva, Socialism/Liberation, 2,928; De La Fuente, Alliance, 2,728.

2016: Clinton, D, 2,148,278; Trump, R, 1,601,933; Johnson, LB, 72,477; Stein, Green, 37,772; Castle, Const., 6,161; Kennedy, Soc. Workers, 2,156; De La Fuente, Amer. Delta, 1,838;

Moorehead, Workers World, 1,749; La Riva, Socialism/Liberation, 1,682.

2012: Obama, D, 2,125,101; Romney, R, 1,477,568; Johnson, LB, 21,045; Stein, Green, 9,888; Goode, Const., 2,064; Anderson, Justice, 1,724; Boss, Ind., 1,007; Harris, Soc. Workers, 710; Miller, A3P, 664; Lindsay, Socialism/Liberation, 521.

2008: Obama, D, 2,215,422; McCain, R, 1,613,207; Nader, Ind., 21,298; Barr, Ind., 8,441; Baldwin, Ind., 3,956; McKinney, Ind., 3,636; Moore, Ind., 699; Boss, Ind., 639; Calero, Ind., 523; La Riva, Ind., 416.

2004: Kerry, D, 1,911,430; Bush, R, 1,670,003; Nader, Ind., 19,418; Badnarik, Ind., 4,514; Peroutka, Ind., 2,750; Cobb, Ind., 1,807; Brown, Ind., 664; Van Auken, Ind., 575; Calero, Ind., 530.

2000: Gore, D, 1,788,850; Bush, R, 1,284,173; Nader, Ind., 94,554; Buchanan, Ind., 6,989; Browne, Ind., 6,312; Hagelin, Ind., 2,215; McReynolds, Ind., 1,880; Phillips, Ind., 1,409; Harris, Ind., 844.

1996: Clinton, D, 1,652,361; Dole, R, 1,103,099; Perot, RF, 262,134; Nader, Green, 32,465; Browne, LB, 14,763; Hagelin, Natural Law, 3,887; Phillips, U.S. Taxpayers, 3,440; Harris, Soc. Workers, 1,837; Moorehead, Workers World, 1,337; White, Soc. Equality, 537.

1992: Clinton, D, 1,436,206; Bush, R, 1,356,865; Perot, Ind., 521,829; Marrou, LB, 6,822; Fulani, New Alliance, 3,513; Phillips, U.S. Taxpayers, 2,670; LaRouche, Ind., 2,095; Warren, Soc. Workers, 2,011; Daniels, Ind., 1,996; Gritz, Populist/America First, 1,867; Hagelin, Natural Law, 1,353.

1988: Bush, R, 1,740,604; Dukakis, D, 1,317,541; Lewin, Peace/Freedom, 9,953; Paul, LB, 8,421.

1984: Reagan, R, 1,933,630; Mondale, D, 1,261,323; Bergland, LB, 6,416.

1980: Reagan, R, 1,546,557; Carter, D, 1,147,364; Anderson, Ind., 234,632; Clark, LB, 20,652; Commoner, Citizens, 8,203; McCormack, Right to Life, 3,927; Lynen, Middle Class, 3,694; Hall, Comm., 2,555; Pulley, Soc. Workers, 2,198; McReynolds, Soc., 1,973; Gahres, Down With Lawyers, 1,718; Griswold, Workers World, 1,288; Wendelken, Ind., 923.

1976: Ford, R, 1,509,688; Carter, D, 1,444,653; McCarthy, Ind., 32,717; MacBride, LB, 9,449; Maddox, Amer., 7,716; Levin, Soc. Labor, 3,686; Hall, Comm., 1,662; LaRouche, U.S. Labor, 1,650; Camejo, Soc. Workers, 1,184; Wright, People's, 1,044; Bubar, Prohib., 554; Zeidler, Soc., 469.

1972: Nixon, R, 1,845,502; McGovern, D, 1,102,211; Schmitz, Amer., 34,378; Spock, People's, 5,355; Fisher, Soc. Labor, 4,544; Jenness, Soc. Workers, 2,233; Mahalchik, America First, 1,743; Hall, Comm., 1,263.

1968: Nixon, R, 1,325,467; Humphrey, D, 1,264,206; Wallace, 3rd party, 262,187; Halstead, Soc. Workers, 8,667; Gregory, Peace/Freedom, 8,084; Blomen, Soc. Labor, 6,784.

1964: Johnson, D, 1,867,671; Goldwater, R, 963,843; DeBerry, Soc. Workers, 8,181; Hass, Soc. Labor, 7,075.

1960: Kennedy, D, 1,385,415; Nixon, R, 1,363,324; Dobbs, Soc. Workers, 11,402; Lee, Conservative, 8,708; Hass, Soc. Labor, 4,262.

New Mexico

County	2020		2016	
	Biden (D)	Trump (R)	Clinton (D)	Trump (R)
Bernalillo	193,757	116,135	143,417	94,698
Catron	595	1,698	427	1,464
Chaves	6,381	15,656	5,534	12,872
Cibola	4,745	3,975	3,741	3,195
Colfax	2,611	3,271	2,129	2,585
Curry	4,307	10,444	3,121	9,035
De Baca	231	656	193	620
Doña Ana	47,957	32,802	37,947	25,374
Eddy	5,424	17,454	5,033	13,147
Grant	7,590	6,553	6,276	5,288
Guadalupe	1,234	917	970	595
Harding	179	319	156	311

County	2020 Biden (D)	2020 Trump (R)	2016 Clinton (D)	2016 Trump (R)
Hidalgo	823	1,120	784	910
Lea	4,061	16,531	3,930	12,495
Lincoln	3,194	6,942	2,331	5,896
Los Alamos	7,554	4,278	5,562	3,359
Luna	3,563	4,408	3,195	3,478
McKinley	18,029	7,801	13,576	5,104
Mora	1,745	903	1,536	665
Otero	8,485	14,521	6,124	11,887
Quay	1,170	2,634	1,017	2,212
Rio Arriba	10,990	5,408	9,592	3,599
Roosevelt	1,802	4,634	1,454	3,884
San Juan	18,083	32,874	12,865	27,946
San Miguel	7,888	3,421	7,285	2,313
Sandoval	40,588	34,174	27,707	25,905
Santa Fe	62,530	18,329	50,793	14,332
Sierra	2,265	3,542	1,612	3,010
Socorro	3,722	3,255	3,313	2,616
Taos	13,121	3,715	10,668	2,727
Torrance	2,344	4,772	1,785	3,714
Union	383	1,388	320	1,216
Valencia	14,263	17,364	10,841	13,215
Totals	501,614	401,894	385,234	319,667

New Mexico Vote Since 1960

2020: Biden, D, 501,614; Trump, R, 401,894; Jorgensen, LB, 12,585; Hawkins, Green, 4,426; Tittle, Const., 1,806; La Riva, Socialism/Liberation, 1,640.

2016: Clinton, D, 385,234; Trump, R, 319,667; Johnson, LB, 74,541; Stein, Green, 9,879; McMullin, Better for Amer., 5,825; Castle, Const., 1,514; La Riva, Socialism/Liberation, 1,184; De La Fuente, Amer. Delta, 475.

2012: Obama, D, 415,335; Romney, R, 335,788; Johnson, LB, 27,788; Stein, Green, 2,691; Anderson, Ind., 1,174; Goode, Const., 982.

2008: Obama, D, 472,422; McCain, R, 346,832; Nader, Ind., 5,327; Barr, LB, 2,428; Baldwin, Const., 1,597; McKinney, Green, 1,552.

2004: Bush, R, 376,930; Kerry, D, 370,942; Nader, Ind., 4,053; Badnarik, LB, 2,382; Cobb, Green, 1,226; Peroutka, Const., 771.

2000: Gore, D, 286,783; Bush, R, 286,417; Nader, Green, 21,251; Browne, LB, 2,058; Buchanan, RF, 1,392; Hagelin, Natural Law, 361; Phillips, Const., 343.

1996: Clinton, D, 273,495; Dole, R, 232,751; Perot, RF, 32,257; Nader, Green, 13,218; Browne, LB, 2,996; Phillips, Taxpayers, 713; Hagelin, Natural Law, 644.

1992: Clinton, D, 261,617; Bush, R, 212,824; Perot, Ind., 91,895; Marrou, LB, 1,615.

1988: Bush, R, 270,341; Dukakis, D, 244,497; Paul, LB, 3,268; Fulani, New Alliance, 2,237.

1984: Reagan, R, 307,101; Mondale, D, 201,769; Bergland, LB, 4,459.

1980: Reagan, R, 250,779; Carter, D, 167,826; Anderson, Ind., 29,459; Clark, LB, 4,365; Commoner, Citizens, 2,202; Bubar, Statesman, 1,281; Pulley, Soc. Workers, 325.

1976: Ford, R, 211,419; Carter, D, 201,148; Camejo, Soc. Workers, 2,462; MacBride, LB, 1,110; Zeidler, Soc., 240; Bubar, Prohib., 211.

1972: Nixon, R, 235,606; McGovern, D, 141,084; Schmitz, Amer., 8,767; Jenness, Soc. Workers, 474.

1968: Nixon, R, 169,692; Humphrey, D, 130,081; Wallace, 3rd party, 25,737; Chavez, 1,519; Halstead, Soc. Workers, 252.

1964: Johnson, D, 194,017; Goldwater, R, 131,838; Hass, Soc. Labor, 1,217; Munn, Prohib., 543.

1960: Kennedy, D, 156,027; Nixon, R, 153,733; Decker, Prohib., 777; Hass, Soc. Labor, 570.

New York

County	2020 Biden (D)	2020 Trump (R)	2016 Clinton (D)	2016 Trump (R)
Albany	99,474	51,081	83,071	47,808
Allegany	6,048	14,135	4,882	12,525
Bronx[1]	355,374	67,740	353,646	37,797
Broome	47,010	43,800	39,212	40,943
Cattaraugus	11,879	22,155	9,497	19,692
Cayuga	16,149	19,512	13,522	17,384
Chautauqua	23,087	34,853	19,091	31,594
Chemung	16,636	21,922	13,757	20,097
Chenango	8,290	13,482	6,775	11,921
Clinton	18,364	16,514	15,059	14,449
Columbia	20,386	14,464	15,284	13,756
Cortland	10,369	10,789	8,771	9,900
Delaware	9,143	13,387	6,627	11,942
Dutchess	81,443	66,872	62,261	61,797
Erie	267,174	197,527	215,456	188,303
Essex	9,947	8,976	7,762	7,958
Franklin	9,253	9,668	7,297	8,221
Fulton	7,931	15,378	6,496	13,462
Genesee	9,625	18,876	7,650	16,915
Greene	10,346	14,271	7,405	13,073
Hamilton	1,178	2,225	949	2,064
Herkimer	9,937	18,870	8,083	16,699
Jefferson	17,307	25,629	13,809	21,763
Kings (Brooklyn)[1]	703,310	202,772	640,553	141,044
Lewis	3,824	8,894	3,146	7,400
Livingston	12,477	18,182	10,697	17,290
Madison	14,807	18,408	11,667	15,936
Monroe	225,746	145,661	188,592	136,582
Montgomery	7,977	12,745	6,695	11,301
Nassau	396,504	326,716	332,154	292,025
New York (Manhattan)[1]	603,040	85,185	579,013	64,930
Niagara	46,029	56,068	35,559	51,961
Oneida	41,567	57,180	33,743	51,437
Onondaga	138,894	90,619	112,337	83,649
Ontario	29,025	29,039	22,233	26,029
Orange	84,684	84,996	68,278	76,645
Orleans	5,587	12,126	4,470	10,936
Oswego	21,143	32,138	17,095	27,688
Otsego	12,975	14,382	10,451	13,308
Putnam	24,953	29,283	19,366	27,024
Queens[1]	569,038	212,665	517,220	149,341
Rensselaer	40,969	36,500	32,717	33,726
Richmond (Staten Island)[1]	90,997	123,320	74,143	101,437
Rockland	75,862	73,186	69,342	60,911
St. Lawrence	19,361	24,608	16,488	19,942
Saratoga	68,471	61,305	50,913	54,575
Schenectady	42,465	30,741	33,747	28,953
Schoharie	5,345	9,903	4,240	8,831
Schuyler	3,903	5,621	3,091	5,050
Seneca	6,914	8,329	5,697	7,236
Steuben	15,790	29,474	12,526	26,831
Suffolk	368,000	375,821	303,951	350,570
Sullivan	15,489	18,665	12,526	15,931
Tioga	9,634	14,791	7,526	13,260
Tompkins	33,619	11,096	28,890	10,371
Ulster	57,970	37,590	44,597	35,239
Warren	17,642	17,699	13,091	15,751
Washington	11,565	15,941	9,098	13,610
Wayne	17,456	26,204	13,473	23,380
Westchester	312,371	144,713	272,926	131,238
Wyoming	5,073	13,898	3,904	12,442
Yates	4,219	6,208	3,659	5,660
Totals	5,230,985	3,244,798	4,556,118	2,819,533

(1) Borough of New York City.

New York Vote Since 1960

2020: Biden, D, 5,230,985; Trump, R, 3,244,798; Jorgensen, LB, 60,234; Hawkins, Green, 32,753; Pierce, Ind., 22,587.

2016: Clinton, D, 4,556,118; Trump, R, 2,819,533; Johnson, LB, 176,598; Stein, Green, 107,935; McMullin, Ind., 10,397.

2012: Obama, D, 4,485,741; Romney, R, 2,490,431; Johnson, LB, 47,256; Stein, Green, 39,982; Goode, Const., 6,274; Lindsay, Socialism/Liberation, 2,050.

2008: Obama, D, 4,804,945; McCain, R, 2,752,771; Nader, Populist, 41,249; Barr, LB, 19,596; McKinney, Green, 12,801; Calero, Soc. Workers, 3,615; La Riva, Socialism/Liberation, 1,639.

2004: Kerry, D, 4,314,280; Bush, R, 2,962,567; Nader, Ind., 99,873; Badnarik, LB, 11,607; Calero, Soc. Workers, 2,405.

2000: Gore, D, 4,112,965; Bush, R, 2,405,570; Nader, Green, 244,360; Buchanan, RF, 24,361; Hagelin, Independence, 24,369; Browne, LB, 7,664; Harris, Soc. Workers, 1,790; Phillips, Const., 1,503.

1996: Clinton, D, 3,756,177; Dole, R, 1,933,492; Perot, RF, 503,458; Nader, Green, 75,956; Phillips, Right to Life, 23,580; Browne, LB, 12,220; Hagelin, Natural Law, 5,011; Moorehead, Workers World, 3,473; Harris, Soc. Workers, 2,762.

1992: Clinton, D, 3,444,450; Bush, R, 2,346,649; Perot, Ind., 1,090,721; Warren, Soc. Workers, 15,472; Marrou, LB, 13,451; Fulani, New Alliance, 11,318; Hagelin, Natural Law, 4,420.

1988: Dukakis, D, 3,347,882; Bush, R, 3,081,871; Marra, Right to Life, 20,497; Fulani, New Alliance, 15,845.

1984: Reagan, R, 3,664,763; Mondale, D, 3,119,609; Bergland, LB, 11,949.

1980: Reagan, R, 2,893,831; Carter, D, 2,728,372; Anderson, Liberal, 467,801; Clark, LB, 52,648; McCormack, Right to Life, 24,159; Commoner, Citizens, 23,186; Hall, Comm., 7,414; DeBerry, Soc. Workers, 2,068; Griswold, Workers World, 1,416; scattered, 1,064.

1976: Carter, D, 3,389,558; Ford, R, 3,100,791; MacBride, LB, 12,197; Hall, Comm., 10,270; Camejo, Soc. Workers, 6,996; LaRouche, U.S. Labor, 5,413; blank, void, and scattered, 143,037.

1972: Nixon, R, 3,824,642; McGovern, D, 2,767,956 and Liberal, 183,128 (total, 2,951,084); Reed, Soc. Workers, 7,797; Fisher, Soc. Labor, 4,530; Hall, Comm., 5,641; blank, void, and scattered, 161,641.

1968: Humphrey, D, 3,378,470; Nixon, R, 3,007,932; Wallace, 3rd party, 358,864; Gregory, Peace/Freedom, 24,517; Halstead, Soc. Workers, 11,851; Blomen, Soc. Labor, 8,432; blank, void, and scattered, 171,624.

1964: Johnson, D, 4,913,156; Goldwater, R, 2,243,559; Hass, Soc. Labor, 6,085; DeBerry, Soc. Workers, 3,215; scattered, 188; blank and void, 151,383.

1960: Kennedy, D, 3,423,909 and Liberal, 406,176 (total, 3,830,085); Nixon, R, 3,446,419; Dobbs, Soc. Workers, 14,319; scattered, 256; blank and void, 88,896.

North Carolina

County	2020		2016	
	Biden (D)	Trump (R)	Clinton (D)	Trump (R)
Alamance	38,825	46,056	29,833	38,815
Alexander	4,145	15,888	3,767	13,893
Alleghany	1,486	4,527	1,306	3,814
Anson	5,789	5,321	5,859	4,506
Ashe	4,164	11,451	3,500	9,412
Avery	2,191	7,172	1,689	6,298
Beaufort	9,633	16,437	8,764	14,543
Bertie	5,939	3,817	5,778	3,456
Bladen	7,326	9,676	7,058	8,550
Brunswick	33,310	55,850	23,282	42,720
Buncombe	96,515	62,412	75,452	55,716
Burke	13,118	31,019	11,251	26,238
Cabarrus	52,162	63,237	35,521	53,819
Caldwell	10,245	32,119	8,425	26,621
Camden	1,537	4,312	1,274	3,546
Carteret	12,093	30,028	9,939	26,569
Caswell	4,860	7,089	4,792	6,026
Catawba	25,689	56,588	21,216	48,324
Chatham	26,787	21,186	21,065	17,105
Cherokee	3,583	12,628	2,860	10,844
Chowan	3,247	4,471	2,992	4,014
Clay	1,699	5,112	1,367	4,437
Cleveland	16,955	33,798	14,964	28,479
Columbus	9,446	16,832	9,063	14,272
Craven	21,148	31,032	17,630	27,731
Cumberland	84,469	60,032	71,605	51,265
Currituck	4,195	11,657	2,913	9,163
Dare	9,936	13,938	7,222	11,460
Davidson	22,636	64,658	18,109	54,317
Davie	6,713	18,228	5,270	15,602
Duplin	8,767	13,793	8,283	12,217
Durham	144,688	32,459	121,250	28,350

County	2020		2016	
	Biden (D)	Trump (R)	Clinton (D)	Trump (R)
Edgecombe	16,089	9,206	16,224	8,261
Forsyth	113,033	85,064	94,464	75,975
Franklin	15,879	20,901	12,874	16,368
Gaston	40,959	73,033	31,177	61,798
Gates	2,546	3,367	2,385	2,874
Graham	905	3,710	768	3,283
Granville	14,565	16,647	12,909	13,591
Greene	3,832	4,874	3,605	4,374
Guilford	173,086	107,294	149,248	98,062
Halifax	15,545	10,080	15,748	9,031
Harnett	22,093	35,177	16,737	27,614
Haywood	13,144	22,834	10,473	18,929
Henderson	27,211	40,032	19,827	35,809
Hertford	7,097	3,479	6,910	3,099
Hoke	11,804	9,453	9,726	7,760
Hyde	1,046	1,418	965	1,288
Iredell	33,888	67,010	24,734	54,754
Jackson	9,591	11,356	7,713	9,870
Johnston	41,257	68,353	28,362	54,372
Jones	2,197	3,280	2,065	2,974
Lee	12,143	16,469	10,469	13,712
Lenoir	13,605	14,590	12,634	13,613
Lincoln	13,274	36,341	9,897	28,806
Macon	6,230	14,211	4,876	12,127
Madison	4,901	7,979	3,926	6,783
Martin	5,911	6,532	5,846	5,897
McDowell	5,832	16,883	4,667	14,568
Mecklenburg	378,107	179,211	294,562	155,518
Mitchell	1,867	7,090	1,596	6,282
Montgomery	4,327	8,411	4,150	7,130
Moore	20,779	36,764	16,329	30,490
Nash	25,947	25,827	23,235	23,319
New Hanover	66,138	63,331	50,979	55,344
Northampton	6,069	3,989	6,144	3,582
Onslow	24,266	46,078	17,514	37,122
Orange	63,594	20,176	59,923	18,557
Pamlico	2,713	4,849	2,448	4,258
Pasquotank	9,832	9,770	8,615	8,180
Pender	11,723	21,956	9,354	17,639
Perquimans	2,492	4,903	2,319	4,177
Person	8,465	13,184	7,833	11,185
Pitt	47,252	38,982	41,824	35,691
Polk	4,518	7,689	3,735	6,768
Randolph	15,618	56,894	13,194	49,430
Richmond	8,754	11,830	8,501	10,383
Robeson	19,020	27,806	19,016	20,762
Rockingham	15,992	31,301	14,228	26,830
Rowan	23,114	49,297	19,400	42,810
Rutherford	9,135	24,891	7,512	21,871
Sampson	10,966	17,411	10,547	14,838
Scotland	7,186	7,473	7,319	6,256
Stanly	8,129	25,458	7,094	21,964
Stokes	5,286	20,142	4,665	17,116
Surry	8,721	27,538	7,488	23,671
Swain	2,780	4,161	2,196	3,565
Transylvania	8,444	11,636	6,558	10,520
Tyrrell	758	1,044	720	975
Union	48,725	80,382	34,337	66,707
Vance	12,431	8,391	12,229	7,332
Wake	393,336	226,197	302,736	196,082
Warren	6,400	3,752	6,413	3,214
Washington	3,396	2,781	3,510	2,564
Watauga	17,122	14,451	14,138	13,697
Wayne	24,215	30,709	21,770	27,540
Wilkes	7,511	27,592	6,638	23,752
Wilson	20,754	19,581	19,663	17,531
Yadkin	3,763	15,933	3,160	13,880
Yancey	3,688	7,516	3,196	6,385
Totals	**2,684,292**	**2,758,773**	**2,189,316**	**2,362,631**

North Carolina Vote Since 1960

2020: Trump, R, 2,758,773; Biden, D, 2,684,292; Jorgensen, LB, 48,678; Hawkins, Green, 12,195; Blankenship, Const., 7,549.

2016: Trump, R, 2,362,631; Clinton, D, 2,189,316; Johnson, LB, 130,126; Stein, Ind., 12,105.

2012: Romney, R, 2,270,395; Obama, D, 2,178,391; Johnson, LB, 44,515.

2008: Obama, D, 2,142,651; McCain, R, 2,128,474; Barr, LB, 25,722.

2004: Bush, R, 1,961,166; Kerry, D, 1,525,849; Badnarik, LB, 11,731.

2000: Bush, R, 1,631,163; Gore, D, 1,257,692; Browne, LB, 13,891; Buchanan, RF, 8,874.

1996: Dole, R, 1,225,938; Clinton, D, 1,107,849; Perot, RF, 168,059; Browne, LB, 8,740; Hagelin, Natural Law, 2,771.

1992: Bush, R, 1,134,661; Clinton, D, 1,114,042; Perot, Ind., 357,864; Marrou, LB, 5,171.

1988: Bush, R, 1,237,258; Dukakis, D, 890,167; Fulani, New Alliance, 5,682; Paul, write-in, 1,263.

1984: Reagan, R, 1,346,481; Mondale, D, 824,287; Bergland, LB, 3,794.

1980: Reagan, R, 915,018; Carter, D, 875,635; Anderson, Ind., 52,800; Clark, LB, 9,677; Commoner, Citizens, 2,287; DeBerry, Soc. Workers, 416.

1976: Carter, D, 927,365; Ford, R, 741,960; Anderson, Amer., 5,607; MacBride, LB, 2,219; LaRouche, U.S. Labor, 755.

1972: Nixon, R, 1,054,889; McGovern, D, 438,705; Schmitz, Amer., 25,018.

1968: Nixon, R, 627,192; Wallace, 3rd party, 496,188; Humphrey, D, 464,113.

1964: Johnson, D, 800,139; Goldwater, R, 624,844.

1960: Kennedy, D, 713,136; Nixon, R, 655,420.

North Dakota

County	2020		2016	
	Biden (D)	Trump (R)	Clinton (D)	Trump (R)
Adams	258	981	216	909
Barnes	1,820	3,568	1,597	3,160
Benson	822	1,094	842	929
Billings	72	541	59	495
Bottineau	821	2,575	736	2,494
Bowman	228	1,395	227	1,446
Burke	137	994	119	895
Burleigh	14,348	34,744	10,881	32,532
Cass	40,311	42,619	31,361	39,816
Cavalier	474	1,499	476	1,357
Dickey	608	1,742	554	1,667
Divide	265	904	245	867
Dunn	342	1,951	358	1,771
Eddy	383	854	355	791
Emmons	237	1,738	215	1,677
Foster	373	1,362	347	1,241
Golden Valley	137	871	99	796
Grand Forks	12,880	16,987	10,851	16,340
Grant	207	1,145	185	1,108
Griggs	308	907	298	847
Hettinger	196	1,091	168	1,050
Kidder	221	1,215	179	1,111
LaMoure	527	1,645	502	1,481
Logan	128	930	114	888
McHenry	564	2,364	490	2,050
McIntosh	261	1,153	235	1,100
McKenzie	814	4,482	698	3,670
McLean	1,230	4,198	1,081	3,860
Mercer	704	3,856	621	3,759
Morton	3,872	12,243	3,080	11,336
Mountrail	1,256	2,824	1,220	2,582
Nelson	586	1,141	536	1,025
Oliver	129	918	119	830
Pembina	786	2,460	681	2,208
Pierce	497	1,585	431	1,437
Ramsey	1,639	3,577	1,505	3,217
Ransom	945	1,418	838	1,210
Renville	220	1,065	201	993
Richland	2,510	5,072	2,064	4,767
Rolette	2,482	1,257	2,099	1,217
Sargent	738	1,266	694	1,088
Sheridan	104	688	95	650
Sioux	804	258	758	260
Slope	44	380	43	362
Stark	2,499	12,110	1,753	9,755
Steele	392	652	361	538
Stutsman	2,676	6,994	2,498	6,718
Towner	317	830	305	733

County	2020		2016	
	Biden (D)	Trump (R)	Clinton (D)	Trump (R)
Traill	1,493	2,522	1,241	2,265
Walsh	1,333	3,324	1,167	2,995
Ward	7,293	19,974	5,806	18,636
Wells	442	1,893	419	1,796
Williams	2,169	11,739	1,735	10,069
Totals	**114,902**	**235,595**	**93,758**	**216,794**

North Dakota Vote Since 1960

2020: Trump, R, 235,595; Biden, D, 114,902; Jorgensen, LB, 9,393.

2016: Trump, R, 216,794; Clinton, D, 93,758; Johnson, LB, 21,434; Stein, Green, 3,780; Castle, Const., 1,833; De La Fuente, Amer. Delta, 364.

2012: Romney, R, 188,163; Obama, D, 124,827; Johnson, LB, 5,231; Stein, Green, 1,361; Goode, Const., 1,185.

2008: McCain, R, 168,601; Obama, D, 141,278; Nader, Ind., 4,189; Barr, LB, 1,354; Baldwin, Const., 1,199.

2004: Bush, R, 196,651; Kerry, D, 111,052; Nader, Ind., 3,756; Badnarik, LB, 851; Peroutka, Const., 514.

2000: Bush, R, 174,852; Gore, D, 95,284; Nader, Ind., 9,486; Buchanan, RF, 7,288; Browne, Ind., 660; Phillips, Const., 373; Hagelin, Ind., 313.

1996: Dole, R, 125,050; Clinton, D, 106,905; Perot, RF, 32,515; Browne, LB, 847; Phillips, Ind., 745; Hagelin, Natural Law, 349.

1992: Bush, R, 136,244; Clinton, D, 99,168; Perot, Ind., 71,084.

1988: Bush, R, 166,559; Dukakis, D, 127,739; Paul, LB, 1,315; LaRouche, Natl. Econ. Recovery, 905.

1984: Reagan, R, 200,336; Mondale, D, 104,429; Bergland, LB, 703.

1980: Reagan, R, 193,695; Carter, D, 79,189; Anderson, Ind., 23,640; Clark, LB, 3,743; Commoner, LB, 429; McLain, Natl. People's League, 296; Greaves, Amer., 235; Hall, Comm., 93; DeBerry, Soc. Workers, 89; McReynolds, Soc., 82; Bubar, Statesman, 54.

1976: Ford, R, 153,470; Carter, D, 136,078; Anderson, Amer., 3,698; McCarthy, Ind., 2,952; Maddox, Amer. Ind., 269; MacBride, LB, 256; scattered, 371.

1972: Nixon, R, 174,109; McGovern, D, 100,384; Schmitz, Amer., 5,646; Jenness, Soc. Workers, 288; Hall, Comm., 87.

1968: Nixon, R, 138,669; Humphrey, D, 94,769; Wallace, 3rd party, 14,244; Halstead, Soc. Workers, 128; Munn, Prohib., 38; Troxell, Ind., 34.

1964: Johnson, D, 149,784; Goldwater, R, 108,207; DeBerry, Soc. Workers, 224; Munn, Prohib., 174.

1960: Nixon, R, 154,310; Kennedy, D, 123,963; Dobbs, Soc. Workers, 158.

Ohio

County	2020		2016	
	Biden (D)	Trump (R)	Clinton (D)	Trump (R)
Adams	2,156	9,870	2,326	8,659
Allen	14,149	33,116	13,294	30,487
Ashland	6,541	19,407	5,740	17,493
Ashtabula	16,497	26,890	15,577	23,318
Athens	14,772	10,862	16,370	11,354
Auglaize	4,651	20,798	3,980	18,658
Belmont	9,138	23,560	8,785	21,108
Brown	4,380	16,480	4,353	14,573
Butler	69,613	114,392	58,642	106,976
Carroll	3,251	10,745	3,154	9,254
Champaign	5,062	14,589	4,594	12,631
Clark	24,076	39,032	23,328	35,205
Clermont	34,092	74,570	26,715	67,518
Clinton	4,697	15,488	4,066	13,838
Columbiana	13,359	35,726	12,432	31,676
Coshocton	4,125	12,325	4,013	10,785
Crawford	4,916	15,436	4,625	13,611
Cuyahoga	416,176	202,699	398,271	184,211
Darke	4,731	22,004	4,470	20,012
Defiance	5,981	13,038	5,368	11,688
Delaware	57,735	66,356	40,872	57,568

County	2020 Biden (D)	Trump (R)	2016 Clinton (D)	Trump (R)
Erie	17,493	22,160	16,057	19,648
Fairfield	31,224	50,797	24,881	44,314
Fayette	2,975	9,473	2,739	7,995
Franklin	409,144	211,237	351,198	199,331
Fulton	6,664	15,731	6,069	13,709
Gallia	2,990	10,645	2,628	9,822
Geauga	21,201	34,143	17,569	30,227
Greene	34,798	52,072	28,943	48,540
Guernsey	4,577	13,407	4,359	11,445
Hamilton	246,266	177,886	215,719	173,665
Hancock	11,757	26,310	9,609	24,183
Hardin	3,062	9,949	2,920	8,717
Harrison	1,768	5,792	1,688	5,098
Henry	4,062	10,479	3,756	9,301
Highland	3,799	15,678	3,773	14,020
Hocking	3,880	9,737	3,775	8,497
Holmes	1,994	10,796	1,788	8,720
Huron	7,759	18,956	7,192	16,226
Jackson	3,311	11,309	3,226	9,949
Jefferson	10,018	22,828	9,675	21,117
Knox	8,589	22,340	8,171	19,131
Lake	55,514	73,278	46,397	64,255
Lawrence	7,489	20,306	6,974	18,689
Licking	33,055	59,514	27,376	51,241
Logan	5,055	17,964	4,647	15,957
Lorain	75,667	79,520	66,949	66,818
Lucas	115,411	81,763	110,833	75,698
Madison	5,698	13,835	4,779	11,631
Mahoning	57,641	59,903	57,381	53,616
Marion	8,269	19,023	7,928	16,961
Medina	39,800	64,598	32,182	54,810
Meigs	2,492	8,316	2,260	7,309
Mercer	4,030	19,452	3,384	17,506
Miami	15,663	41,371	13,120	37,079
Monroe	1,605	5,463	1,662	4,868
Montgomery	135,064	129,034	122,016	123,909
Morgan	1,725	5,041	1,736	4,431
Morrow	4,048	14,077	3,761	11,948
Muskingum	11,971	27,867	11,123	24,056
Noble	1,170	5,135	1,221	4,549
Ottawa	9,008	14,628	8,285	12,653
Paulding	2,213	7,086	2,093	6,500
Perry	4,098	12,357	4,138	10,228
Pickaway	7,304	20,593	6,529	17,076
Pike	3,110	9,157	3,319	7,902
Portage	35,661	45,990	32,397	39,971
Preble	4,493	17,022	4,325	15,446
Putnam	3,195	16,412	2,922	14,961
Richland	17,640	41,472	16,085	36,590
Ross	10,557	22,278	10,356	18,652
Sandusky	10,596	18,896	9,929	16,316
Scioto	9,080	22,609	9,132	20,550
Seneca	8,266	17,086	7,404	14,825
Shelby	4,465	20,422	4,243	18,590
Stark	75,904	111,097	68,146	98,388
Summit	151,668	124,833	134,256	112,026
Trumbull	44,519	55,194	43,014	49,024
Tuscarawas	12,889	30,458	12,188	26,918
Union	11,141	21,669	7,718	18,096
Van Wert	3,067	11,650	2,697	10,469
Vinton	1,331	4,632	1,351	3,883
Warren	46,069	87,988	33,730	77,643
Washington	9,243	22,307	8,026	20,514
Wayne	16,660	36,759	15,031	32,270
Williams	4,842	13,452	4,358	11,939
Wood	30,617	35,757	27,318	32,498
Wyandot	2,733	8,462	2,515	7,468
Totals	**2,679,165**	**3,154,834**	**2,394,164**	**2,841,005**

Ohio Vote Since 1960

2020: Trump, R, 3,154,834; Biden, D, 2,679,165; Jorgensen, LB, 67,569; Hawkins, Ind., 18,812.

2016: Trump, R, 2,841,005; Clinton, D, 2,394,164; Johnson, LB, 174,498; Stein, Green, 46,271; Duncan, Ind., 24,235; McMullin, Ind., 12,574; Castle, Const., 1,887.

2012: Obama, D, 2,827,709; Romney, R, 2,661,437; Johnson, LB, 49,493; Stein, Green, 18,573; Duncan, Ind., 12,502; Goode, Const., 8,152; Alexander, Soc., 2,944.

2008: Obama, D, 2,940,044; McCain, R, 2,677,820; Nader, Ind., 42,337; Barr, LB, 19,917; Baldwin, Const., 12,565; McKinney, Green, 8,518; Duncan, Ind., 3,905; Moore, Soc., 2,735.

2004: Bush, R, 2,859,768; Kerry, D, 2,741,167; Badnarik, nonpartisan, 14,676; Peroutka, nonpartisan, 939.

2000: Bush, R, 2,351,209; Gore, D, 2,186,190; Nader, Ind., 117,857; Buchanan, Ind., 26,724; Browne, LB, 13,475; Hagelin, Natural Law, 6,169; Phillips, Ind., 3,823.

1996: Clinton, D, 2,148,222; Dole, R, 1,859,883; Perot, RF, 483,207; Browne, Ind., 12,851; Moorehead, Ind., 10,813; Hagelin, Natural Law, 9,120; Phillips, Ind., 7,361.

1992: Clinton, D, 1,984,942; Bush, R, 1,894,310; Perot, Ind., 1,036,426; Marrou, LB, 7,252; Fulani, New Alliance, 6,413; Gritz, Populist/America First, 4,699; Hagelin, Natural Law, 3,437; LaRouche, Ind., 2,446.

1988: Bush, R, 2,416,549; Dukakis, D, 1,939,629; Fulani, Ind., 12,017; Paul, Ind., 11,926.

1984: Reagan, R, 2,678,559; Mondale, D, 1,825,440; Bergland, LB, 5,886.

1980: Reagan, R, 2,206,545; Carter, D, 1,752,414; Anderson, Ind., 254,472; Clark, LB, 49,033; Commoner, Citizens, 8,564; Hall, Comm., 4,729; Congress, Ind., 4,029; Griswold, Workers World, 3,790; Bubar, Statesman, 27.

1976: Carter, D, 2,011,621; Ford, R, 2,000,505; McCarthy, Ind., 58,258; Maddox, Amer. Ind., 15,529; MacBride, Ind., 8,961; Hall, Comm., 7,817; Camejo, Soc. Workers, 4,717; LaRouche, U.S. Labor, 4,335; scattered, 130.

1972: Nixon, R, 2,441,827; McGovern, D, 1,558,889; Schmitz, Amer., 80,067; Fisher, Soc. Labor, 7,107; Hall, Comm., 6,437; Wallace, Ind., 460.

1968: Nixon, R, 1,791,014; Humphrey, D, 1,700,586; Wallace, 3rd party, 467,495; Gregory, 372; Blomen, Soc. Labor, 120; Halstead, Soc. Workers, 69; Mitchell, Comm., 23; Munn, Prohib., 19.

1964: Johnson, D, 2,498,331; Goldwater, R, 1,470,865.

1960: Nixon, R, 2,217,611; Kennedy, D, 1,944,248.

Oklahoma

County	2020 Biden (D)	Trump (R)	2016 Clinton (D)	Trump (R)
Adair	1,387	5,585	1,382	4,787
Alfalfa	232	1,978	216	1,933
Atoka	765	4,557	795	4,084
Beaver	190	1,968	176	1,993
Beckham	1,048	6,767	960	6,308
Blaine	688	3,136	711	2,884
Bryan	3,323	12,344	2,804	10,478
Caddo	2,670	7,013	2,420	6,482
Canadian	16,742	43,550	11,674	39,986
Carter	4,470	14,699	4,002	13,752
Cherokee	6,027	11,223	5,456	9,994
Choctaw	1,082	4,698	1,067	4,206
Cimarron	70	970	71	963
Cleveland	49,827	66,677	38,829	62,538
Coal	374	2,091	411	1,898
Comanche	13,747	20,905	11,463	19,183
Cotton	393	2,117	424	2,054
Craig	1,217	4,686	1,252	4,283
Creek	6,577	23,294	5,841	21,575
Custer	2,369	8,060	2,104	7,826
Delaware	3,472	13,557	3,311	11,826
Dewey	214	2,124	222	1,965
Ellis	162	1,688	155	1,611
Garfield	4,919	16,970	4,397	16,009
Garvin	1,865	8,878	1,855	8,253
Grady	4,144	18,538	3,882	17,316
Grant	280	1,916	288	1,827
Greer	328	1,605	323	1,482
Harmon	177	747	225	715
Harper	136	1,327	134	1,318
Haskell	783	4,165	882	3,701
Hughes	919	3,875	961	3,388
Jackson	1,646	6,392	1,473	5,969

County	2020 Biden (D)	Trump (R)	2016 Clinton (D)	Trump (R)
Jefferson	319	2,026	365	1,910
Johnston	738	3,441	786	3,093
Kay	4,040	12,834	3,738	12,172
Kingfisher	854	5,521	786	5,156
Kiowa	699	2,673	767	2,596
Latimer	762	3,437	797	3,100
Le Flore	3,299	15,213	3,250	13,362
Lincoln	2,609	12,013	2,430	10,854
Logan	5,455	15,608	4,248	13,633
Love	711	3,305	735	2,922
Major	320	3,084	310	2,948
Marshall	1,100	4,891	1,096	4,206
Mayes	3,581	12,749	3,423	11,555
McClain	3,582	15,295	2,894	13,169
McCurtain	1,858	9,485	1,802	8,656
McIntosh	2,031	6,172	2,123	5,505
Murray	1,156	4,612	1,087	4,175
Muskogee	8,027	16,526	7,977	15,043
Noble	1,003	3,821	901	3,715
Nowata	712	3,610	742	3,321
Okfuskee	896	3,058	943	2,800
Oklahoma	141,724	145,050	112,813	141,569
Okmulgee	4,357	9,668	4,385	8,944
Osage	6,002	14,121	5,597	12,577
Ottawa	2,686	8,545	2,584	7,631
Pawnee	1,363	5,267	1,344	4,729
Payne	10,904	17,813	8,788	16,651
Pittsburg	3,768	13,851	3,711	12,753
Pontotoc	4,117	10,805	3,637	10,431
Pottawatomie	7,275	20,240	6,015	17,848
Pushmataha	668	4,016	748	3,581
Roger Mills	168	1,629	151	1,547
Rogers	9,589	34,031	7,902	30,913
Seminole	2,150	6,011	2,071	5,613
Sequoyah	3,035	12,113	3,061	10,888
Stephens	3,154	15,560	3,086	14,182
Texas	894	4,505	858	4,621
Tillman	597	2,076	657	1,944
Tulsa	108,996	150,574	87,847	144,258
Wagoner	8,464	26,165	6,723	23,005
Washington	5,790	17,076	5,048	15,825
Washita	598	4,086	588	3,854
Woods	591	2,993	522	2,947
Woodward	1,005	6,611	873	6,347
Totals	**503,890**	**1,020,280**	**420,375**	**949,136**

Oklahoma Vote Since 1960

2020: Trump, R, 1,020,280; Biden, D, 503,890; Jorgensen, LB, 24,731; West, Ind., 5,597; Simmons, Ind., 3,654; Pierce, Ind., 2,547.

2016: Trump, R, 949,136; Clinton, D, 420,375; Johnson, LB, 83,481.

2012: Romney, R, 891,325; Obama, D, 443,547.

2008: McCain, R, 960,165; Obama, D, 502,496.

2004: Bush, R, 959,792; Kerry, D, 503,966.

2000: Bush, R, 744,337; Gore, D, 474,276; Buchanan, RF, 9,014; Browne, LB, 6,602.

1996: Dole, R, 582,315; Clinton, D, 488,105; Perot, RF, 130,788; Browne, LB, 5,505.

1992: Bush, R, 592,929; Clinton, D, 473,066; Perot, Ind., 319,878; Marrou, LB, 4,486.

1988: Bush, R, 678,367; Dukakis, D, 483,423; Paul, LB, 6,261; Fulani, New Alliance, 2,985.

1984: Reagan, R, 861,530; Mondale, D, 385,080; Bergland, LB, 9,066.

1980: Reagan, R, 695,570; Carter, D, 402,026; Anderson, Ind., 38,284; Clark, LB, 13,828.

1976: Ford, R, 545,708; Carter, D, 532,442; McCarthy, Ind., 14,101.

1972: Nixon, R, 759,025; McGovern, D, 247,147; Schmitz, Amer., 23,728.

1968: Nixon, R, 449,697; Humphrey, D, 301,658; Wallace, 3rd party, 191,731.

1964: Johnson, D, 519,834; Goldwater, R, 412,665.

1960: Nixon, R, 533,039; Kennedy, D, 370,111.

Oregon

County	2020 Biden (D)	Trump (R)	2016 Clinton (D)	Trump (R)
Baker	2,346	7,352	1,797	6,218
Benton	35,827	14,878	29,193	13,445
Clackamas	139,043	110,509	102,095	88,392
Clatsop	12,916	10,218	9,252	8,138
Columbia	13,835	17,150	10,167	13,217
Coos	14,243	21,829	10,448	17,865
Crook	3,801	11,287	2,637	8,511
Curry	6,058	8,484	4,300	7,212
Deschutes	65,962	55,646	42,444	45,692
Douglas	19,160	43,298	14,096	34,582
Gilliam	324	834	239	671
Grant	929	3,545	739	3,210
Harney	894	3,475	683	2,912
Hood River	8,764	3,955	6,510	3,272
Jackson	59,478	63,869	44,447	53,870
Jefferson	4,393	7,189	2,980	5,483
Josephine	18,451	31,751	13,453	26,923
Klamath	10,388	25,308	7,210	20,435
Lake	792	3,470	639	3,022
Lane	134,366	80,336	102,753	67,141
Lincoln	17,385	12,460	12,510	10,039
Linn	26,512	43,486	17,995	33,488
Malheur	3,260	8,187	2,246	7,194
Marion	80,872	79,002	57,788	63,377
Morrow	1,371	3,586	1,017	2,721
Multnomah	367,249	82,995	292,561	67,954
Polk	22,917	23,732	16,420	18,940
Sherman	260	921	202	732
Tillamook	8,066	8,354	5,768	6,538
Umatilla	10,707	21,270	7,673	17,059
Union	4,254	10,298	3,249	8,431
Wallowa	1,625	3,404	1,116	2,848
Wasco	6,604	7,035	4,781	5,833
Washington	209,940	99,073	153,251	83,197
Wheeler	217	711	155	591
Yamhill	27,174	29,551	19,301	23,250
Totals	**1,340,383**	**958,448**	**1,002,106**	**782,403**

Oregon Vote Since 1960

2020: Biden, D, 1,340,383; Trump, R, 958,448; Jorgensen, LB, 41,582; Hawkins, Pacific Green, 11,831; Hunter, Progressive, 4,988.

2016: Clinton, D, 1,002,106; Trump, R, 782,403; Johnson, LB, 94,231; Stein, Pacific Green, 50,002.

2012: Obama, D, 970,488; Romney, R, 754,175; Johnson, LB, 24,089; Stein, Pacific Green, 19,427; Christensen, Const., 4,432; Anderson, OR Prog., 3,384.

2008: Obama, D, 1,037,291; McCain, R, 738,475; Nader, Peace Party of OR, 18,614; Baldwin, Const., 7,693; Barr, LB, 7,635; McKinney, Pacific Green, 4,543.

2004: Kerry, D, 943,163; Bush, R, 866,831; Badnarik, LB, 7,260; Cobb, Pacific Green, 5,315; Peroutka, Const., 5,257.

2000: Gore, D, 720,342; Bush, R, 713,577; Nader, Green, 77,357; Browne, LB, 7,447; Buchanan, Ind., 7,063; Hagelin, RF, 2,574; Phillips, Const., 2,189.

1996: Clinton, D, 649,641; Dole, R, 538,152; Perot, RF, 121,221; Nader, Pacific, 49,415; Browne, LB, 8,903; Phillips, Taxpayers, 3,379; Hagelin, Natural Law, 2,798; Hollis, Soc., 1,922.

1992: Clinton, D, 621,314; Bush, R, 475,757; Perot, Ind., 354,091; Marrou, LB, 4,277; Fulani, New Alliance, 3,030.

1988: Dukakis, D, 616,206; Bush, R, 560,126; Paul, LB, 14,811; Fulani, Ind., 6,487.

1984: Reagan, R, 658,700; Mondale, D, 536,479.

1980: Reagan, R, 571,044; Carter, D, 456,890; Anderson, Ind., 112,389; Clark, LB, 25,838; Commoner, Citizens, 13,642; scattered, 1,713.

1976: Ford, R, 492,120; Carter, D, 490,407; McCarthy, Ind., 40,207; write-in, 7,142.

1972: Nixon, R, 486,686; McGovern, D, 392,760; Schmitz, Amer., 46,211; write-in, 2,289.

1968: Nixon, R, 408,433; Humphrey, D, 358,866; Wallace, 3rd party, 49,683; write-ins: McCarthy, 1,496; N. Rockefeller, 69; others, 1,075.

1964: Johnson, D, 501,017; Goldwater, R, 282,779; write-in, 2,509.

1960: Nixon, R, 408,060; Kennedy, D, 367,402.

Pennsylvania

County	2020 Biden (D)	Trump (R)	2016 Clinton (D)	Trump (R)
Adams	18,207	37,523	14,219	31,423
Allegheny	429,065	282,324	367,617	259,480
Armstrong	8,457	27,489	7,178	23,484
Beaver	38,122	54,759	32,531	48,167
Bedford	4,367	23,025	3,645	19,552
Berks	92,895	109,736	78,437	96,626
Blair	17,636	45,306	13,958	39,135
Bradford	8,046	21,600	6,369	18,141
Bucks	204,712	187,367	167,060	164,361
Butler	37,508	74,359	28,584	64,428
Cambria	21,730	48,085	18,867	42,258
Cameron	634	1,771	531	1,589
Carbon	11,212	21,984	8,936	18,743
Centre	40,055	36,372	37,088	35,274
Chester	182,372	128,565	141,682	116,114
Clarion	4,678	14,578	4,273	12,576
Clearfield	9,673	29,203	8,200	24,932
Clinton	5,502	11,902	4,744	10,022
Columbia	10,532	20,098	8,934	18,004
Crawford	12,924	28,559	10,971	24,987
Cumberland	62,245	77,212	47,085	69,076
Dauphin	78,983	66,408	64,706	60,863
Delaware	206,423	118,532	177,402	110,667
Elk	4,522	12,140	3,853	10,025
Erie	68,286	66,869	58,112	60,069
Fayette	20,444	41,227	17,946	34,590
Forest	728	1,882	626	1,683
Franklin	22,422	57,245	17,465	49,768
Fulton	1,085	6,824	912	5,694
Greene	4,911	12,579	4,482	10,849
Huntingdon	5,445	17,061	4,539	14,494
Indiana	12,634	28,089	11,528	24,888
Jefferson	4,527	17,960	3,650	15,192
Juniata	2,253	9,649	1,821	8,273
Lackawanna	61,991	52,324	51,983	48,384
Lancaster	115,847	160,209	91,093	137,914
Lawrence	15,978	29,597	14,009	25,428
Lebanon	23,932	46,731	18,953	40,525
Lehigh	98,288	84,259	81,324	73,690
Luzerne	64,873	86,929	52,451	78,688
Lycoming	16,971	41,462	13,020	35,627
McKean	5,098	14,083	4,025	11,635
Mercer	21,067	36,143	18,733	31,544
Mifflin	4,603	16,670	3,877	14,094
Monroe	44,060	38,726	33,918	33,386
Montgomery	319,511	185,460	256,082	162,731
Montour	3,771	5,844	2,857	5,288
Northampton	85,087	83,854	66,272	71,736
Northumber-land	12,677	28,952	9,788	25,427
Perry	5,950	18,293	4,632	15,616
Philadelphia	603,790	132,740	584,025	108,748
Pike	13,019	19,213	9,256	16,056
Potter	1,726	7,259	1,302	6,251
Schuylkill	20,727	48,871	16,770	44,001
Snyder	4,910	13,983	4,002	11,725
Somerset	8,654	31,466	7,376	27,379
Sullivan	921	2,619	750	2,291
Susquehanna	6,236	15,207	5,123	12,891
Tioga	4,955	15,742	3,901	13,614
Union	7,475	12,356	6,180	10,622
Venango	7,585	18,569	6,309	16,021
Warren	6,066	14,237	5,145	12,477
Washington	45,088	72,080	36,322	61,386
Wayne	9,191	18,843	7,008	16,244
Westmoreland	72,129	130,218	59,669	116,522
Wyoming	4,704	9,936	3,811	8,837
York	88,114	146,733	68,524	128,528
Totals	**3,458,229**	**3,377,674**	**2,926,441**	**2,970,733**

Pennsylvania Vote Since 1960

2020: Biden, D, 3,458,229; Trump, R, 3,377,674; Jorgensen, LB, 79,380.

2016: Trump, R, 2,970,733; Clinton, D, 2,926,441; Johnson, LB, 146,715; Stein, Green, 49,941; Castle, Const., 21,572.

2012: Obama, D, 2,990,274; Romney, R, 2,680,434; Johnson, LB, 49,991; Stein, Green, 21,341.

2008: Obama, D, 3,276,363; McCain, R, 2,655,885; Nader, Ind., 42,977; Barr, LB, 19,912.

2004: Kerry, D, 2,938,095; Bush, R, 2,793,847; Badnarik, LB, 21,185; Cobb, Green, 6,319; Peroutka, Const., 6,318.

2000: Gore, D, 2,485,967; Bush, R, 2,281,127; Nader, Green, 103,392; Buchanan, RF, 16,023; Phillips, Const., 14,428; Browne, LB, 11,248.

1996: Clinton, D, 2,215,819; Dole, R, 1,801,169; Perot, RF, 430,984; Browne, LB, 28,000; Phillips, Const., 19,552; Hagelin, Natural Law, 5,783.

1992: Clinton, D, 2,239,164; Bush, R, 1,791,841; Perot, Ind., 902,667; Marrou, LB, 21,477; Fulani, New Alliance, 4,661.

1988: Bush, R, 2,300,087; Dukakis, D, 2,194,944; McCarthy, Consumer, 19,158; Paul, LB, 12,051.

1984: Reagan, R, 2,584,323; Mondale, D, 2,228,131; Bergland, LB, 6,982.

1980: Reagan, R, 2,261,872; Carter, D, 1,937,540; Anderson, Ind., 292,921; Clark, LB, 33,263; DeBerry, Soc. Workers, 20,291; Commoner, Consumer, 10,430; Hall, Comm., 5,184.

1976: Carter, D, 2,328,677; Ford, R, 2,205,604; McCarthy, Ind., 50,584; Maddox, Const., 25,344; Camejo, Soc. Workers, 3,009; LaRouche, U.S. Labor, 2,744; Hall, Comm., 1,891; others, 2,934.

1972: Nixon, R, 2,714,521; McGovern, D, 1,796,951; Schmitz, Amer., 70,593; Jenness, Soc. Workers, 4,639; Hall, Comm., 2,686; others, 2,715.

1968: Humphrey, D, 2,259,405; Nixon, R, 2,090,017; Wallace, 3rd party, 378,582; Gregory, Peace/Freedom, 7,821; Blomen, Soc. Labor, 4,977; Halstead, Soc. Workers, 4,862; others, 2,264.

1964: Johnson, D, 3,130,954; Goldwater, R, 1,673,657; DeBerry, Soc. Workers, 10,456; Hass, Soc. Labor, 5,092; scattered, 2,531.

1960: Kennedy, D, 2,556,282; Nixon, R, 2,439,956; Hass, Soc. Labor, 7,185; Dobbs, Soc. Workers, 2,678; scattered, 440.

Rhode Island

City	2020 Biden (D)	Trump (R)	2016 Clinton (D)	Trump (R)
Barrington	7,713	2,889	6,153	2,898
Bristol	6,813	4,595	5,771	4,080
Burrillville	3,434	4,906	2,558	4,139
Coventry	9,123	10,461	7,032	9,199
Cranston	23,039	17,313	18,763	15,934
Cumberland	10,869	8,418	8,655	7,444
East Greenwich	5,218	3,227	4,019	3,122
East Providence	14,735	7,930	11,904	7,134
Johnston	6,838	8,222	5,652	7,563
Lincoln	6,633	5,779	5,279	5,410
Middletown	5,529	2,885	4,248	2,745
Narragansett	5,333	3,551	4,214	3,292
Newport	7,866	2,662	6,287	2,644
North Kingstown	10,534	6,633	7,793	6,147
North Providence	9,438	7,129	7,760	6,936
Pawtucket	18,053	7,257	15,574	6,221
Portsmouth	6,649	3,995	4,945	3,922
Providence	45,941	10,186	45,053	7,682
Smithfield	5,566	5,744	4,402	5,254
South Kingstown	11,254	5,003	8,677	4,627
Tiverton	5,123	4,017	4,034	3,797
Warwick	25,845	19,578	20,038	18,338
West Warwick	7,234	6,493	5,540	5,724
Westerly	7,153	5,463	5,291	5,031
Woonsocket	7,289	6,265	6,346	5,442
Other	34,264	29,321	26,537	25,818
Totals	**307,486**	**199,922**	**252,525**	**180,543**

Rhode Island Vote Since 1960

2020: Biden, D, 307,486; Trump, R, 199,922; Jorgensen, LB, 5,053; De La Fuente, Alliance, 923; La Riva, Socialism/Liberation, 847; Carroll, Amer. Solidarity, 767.

2016: Clinton, D, 252,525; Trump, R, 180,543; Johnson, LB, 14,746; Stein, Green, 6,220; De La Fuente, Amer. Delta, 671.

2012: Obama, D, 279,677; Romney, R, 157,204; Johnson, LB, 4,388; Stein, Green, 2,421; Goode, Const., 430; Anderson, Justice, 416; Lindsay, Socialism/Liberation, 132.

2008: Obama, D, 296,571; McCain, R, 165,391; Nader, Ind., 4,829; Barr, LB, 1,382; McKinney, Green, 797; Baldwin, Const., 675; La Riva, Socialism/Liberation, 122.

2004: Kerry, D, 259,765; Bush, R, 169,046; Nader, RF, 4,651; Cobb, Green, 1,333; Badnarik, LB, 907; Peroutka, Const., 339; Parker, Workers World, 253.

2000: Gore, D, 249,508; Bush, R, 130,555; Nader, Ind., 25,052; Buchanan, RF, 2,273; Browne, Ind., 742; Hagelin, Ind., 271; Moorehead, Ind., 199; Phillips, Ind., 97; McReynolds, Ind., 52; Harris, Ind., 34.

1996: Clinton, D, 233,050; Dole, R, 104,683; Perot, RF, 43,723; Nader, Green, 6,040; Browne, LB, 1,109; Phillips, U.S. Taxpayers, 1,021; Hagelin, Natural Law, 435; Moorehead, Workers World, 186.

1992: Clinton, D, 213,299; Bush, R, 131,601; Perot, Ind., 105,045; Fulani, New Alliance, 1,878.

1988: Dukakis, D, 225,123; Bush, R, 177,761; Paul, LB, 825; Fulani, New Alliance, 280.

1984: Reagan, R, 212,080; Mondale, D, 197,106; Bergland, LB, 277.

1980: Carter, D, 198,342; Reagan, R, 154,793; Anderson, Ind., 59,819; Clark, LB, 2,458; Hall, Comm., 218; McReynolds, Soc., 170; DeBerry, Soc. Workers, 90; Griswold, Workers World, 77.

1976: Carter, D, 227,636; Ford, R, 181,249; MacBride, LB, 715; Camejo, Soc. Workers, 462; Hall, Comm., 334; Levin, Soc. Labor, 188.

1972: Nixon, R, 220,383; McGovern, D, 194,645; Jenness, Soc. Workers, 729.

1968: Humphrey, D, 246,518; Nixon, R, 122,359; Wallace, 3rd party, 15,678; Halstead, Soc. Workers, 383.

1964: Johnson, D, 315,463; Goldwater, R, 74,615.

1960: Kennedy, D, 258,032; Nixon, R, 147,502.

South Carolina

County	2020 Biden (D)	Trump (R)	2016 Clinton (D)	Trump (R)
Abbeville	4,101	8,215	3,741	6,763
Aiken	32,275	51,589	25,455	46,025
Allendale	2,718	835	2,735	789
Anderson	27,169	67,565	21,097	56,232
Bamberg	4,010	2,417	3,898	2,204
Barnwell	4,720	5,445	4,490	4,889
Beaufort	43,419	53,194	32,138	42,922
Berkeley	45,223	57,397	30,705	44,587
Calhoun	3,905	4,305	3,573	3,787
Charleston	121,485	93,297	89,299	75,443
Cherokee	6,983	18,043	6,092	15,167
Chester	6,941	8,660	6,579	7,265
Chesterfield	7,431	11,297	6,858	9,312
Clarendon	8,250	8,361	7,732	7,386
Colleton	8,602	10,440	7,627	9,091
Darlington	15,220	16,832	13,888	14,989
Dillon	6,436	6,582	5,834	5,637
Dorchester	33,824	41,913	24,055	34,987
Edgefield	4,953	8,184	4,491	6,842
Fairfield	7,382	4,625	6,945	4,027
Florence	31,153	32,615	26,710	29,573
Georgetown	15,822	20,487	13,310	17,389
Greenville	103,030	150,021	74,483	127,832
Greenwood	12,145	19,431	10,711	16,961
Hampton	5,323	3,906	5,170	3,488
Horry	59,180	118,821	39,410	89,288
Jasper	7,185	7,078	5,956	5,187
Kershaw	12,699	20,471	10,330	17,542

County	2020 Biden (D)	Trump (R)	2016 Clinton (D)	Trump (R)
Lancaster	18,937	30,312	13,812	23,719
Laurens	10,159	20,004	8,889	16,816
Lee	5,329	3,008	5,199	2,803
Lexington	49,301	92,817	35,230	80,026
Marion	8,872	5,711	8,569	5,444
Marlboro	6,290	5,044	5,954	4,267
McCormick	2,687	2,958	2,479	2,652
Newberry	6,958	11,443	6,217	10,017
Oconee	10,414	29,698	7,998	24,178
Orangeburg	27,295	13,603	26,318	11,931
Pickens	13,645	42,907	10,354	36,236
Richland	132,570	58,313	108,000	52,469
Saluda	2,963	6,210	2,813	5,526
Spartanburg	52,926	93,560	39,997	76,277
Sumter	27,379	21,000	24,047	18,745
Union	4,935	8,183	4,729	7,061
Williamsburg	10,289	5,532	9,953	4,864
York	59,008	82,727	41,593	66,754
Totals	**1,091,541**	**1,385,103**	**855,373**	**1,155,389**

South Carolina Vote Since 1960

2020: Trump, R, 1,385,103; Biden, D, 1,091,541; Jorgensen, LB, 27,916; Hawkins, Green, 6,907; De La Fuente, Alliance, 1,862.

2016: Trump, R, 1,155,389; Clinton, D, 855,373; Johnson, LB, 49,204; McMullin, Ind., 21,016; Stein, Green, 13,034; Castle, Const., 5,765; Skewes, American, 3,246.

2012: Romney, R, 1,071,645; Obama, D, 865,941; Johnson, LB, 16,321; Stein, Green, 5,446; Goode, Const., 4,765.

2008: McCain, R, 1,034,896; Obama, D, 862,449; Barr, LB, 7,283; Baldwin, Const., 6,827; Nader, petitioning cand., 5,053; McKinney, Green, 4,461.

2004: Bush, R, 937,974; Kerry, D, 661,699; Nader, Ind., 5,520; Peroutka, Const., 5,317; Badnarik, LB, 3,608; Brown, United Citizens, 2,124; Cobb, Green, 1,488.

2000: Bush, R, 786,892; Gore, D, 566,039; Nader, United Citizens, 20,279; Browne, LB, 4,898; Buchanan, RF, 3,309; Phillips, Const., 1,682; Hagelin, Natural Law, 943.

1996: Dole, R, 573,458; Clinton, D, 506,283; Perot, RF/Patriot, 64,386; Browne, LB, 4,271; Phillips, U.S. Taxpayers, 2,043; Hagelin, Natural Law, 1,248.

1992: Bush, R, 577,507; Clinton, D, 479,514; Perot, Ind., 138,872; Marrou, LB, 2,719; Phillips, U.S. Taxpayers, 2,680; Fulani, New Alliance, 1,235.

1988: Bush, R, 606,443; Dukakis, D, 370,554; Paul, LB, 4,935; Fulani, United Citizens, 4,077.

1984: Reagan, R, 615,539; Mondale, D, 344,459; Bergland, LB, 4,359.

1980: Reagan, R, 439,277; Carter, D, 428,220; Anderson, Ind., 13,868; Clark, LB, 4,807; Rarick, Amer. Ind., 2,086.

1976: Carter, D, 450,807; Ford, R, 346,149; Anderson, Amer., 2,996; Maddox, Amer. Ind., 1,950; write-in, 681.

1972: Nixon, R, 477,044; McGovern, D, 184,559, and United Citizens, 2,265 (total, 186,824); Schmitz, Amer., 10,075; write-in, 17.

1968: Nixon, R, 254,062; Wallace, 3rd party, 215,430; Humphrey, D, 197,486.

1964: Goldwater, R, 309,048; Johnson, D, 215,700; write-ins: Wallace, 5; Nixon, 1; Powell, 1; Thurmond, 1.

1960: Kennedy, D, 198,129; Nixon, R, 188,558; write-in, 1.

South Dakota

County	2020 Biden (D)	Trump (R)	2016 Clinton (D)	Trump (R)
Aurora	317	1,052	340	974
Beadle	2,107	4,808	1,912	4,455
Bennett	466	694	412	666
Bon Homme	721	2,235	704	2,105
Brookings	6,110	8,000	4,879	6,748
Brown	6,538	10,580	5,452	9,613
Brule	673	1,750	571	1,565
Buffalo	352	183	296	171
Butte	939	3,731	696	3,357
Campbell	117	747	105	704

County	2020 Biden (D)	Trump (R)	2016 Clinton (D)	Trump (R)
Charles Mix	1,177	2,552	935	2,382
Clark	437	1,373	398	1,139
Clay	3,083	2,456	2,608	2,109
Codington	3,837	8,958	3,174	7,764
Corson	622	647	535	588
Custer	1,522	3,852	1,121	3,293
Davison	2,648	5,613	2,355	5,157
Day	1,052	1,869	974	1,627
Deuel	609	1,699	570	1,366
Dewey	1,131	790	888	723
Douglas	216	1,468	214	1,338
Edmunds	417	1,538	380	1,433
Fall River	1,053	2,878	821	2,511
Faulk	198	964	204	858
Grant	1,056	2,618	971	2,382
Gregory	455	1,771	391	1,600
Haakon	105	1,026	77	936
Hamlin	647	2,372	555	2,051
Hand	373	1,433	334	1,391
Hanson	557	1,793	424	1,497
Harding	49	748	38	695
Hughes	2,953	5,522	2,450	5,174
Hutchinson	762	2,944	692	2,517
Hyde	136	564	125	543
Jackson	359	738	323	722
Jerauld	270	721	264	648
Jones	90	498	69	450
Kingsbury	819	1,904	703	1,680
Lake	2,068	3,681	2,314	4,038
Lawrence	4,537	8,753	3,356	7,411
Lincoln	11,981	19,617	8,076	15,499
Lyman	525	1,042	369	977
Marshall	858	1,287	754	1,056
McCook	769	2,068	623	1,794
McPherson	222	1,075	192	892
Meade	3,285	9,875	2,223	8,441
Mellette	298	449	238	402
Miner	320	787	281	706
Minnehaha	40,482	49,249	30,610	42,043
Moody	1,179	1,951	1,043	1,731
Oglala Lakota	2,829	297	2,510	241
Pennington	20,606	35,063	14,074	29,804
Perkins	239	1,401	188	1,333
Potter	227	1,139	215	1,071
Roberts	1,828	2,404	1,540	2,144
Sanborn	257	905	241	819
Spink	998	2,104	919	1,854
Stanley	421	1,203	329	1,148
Sully	185	726	137	679
Todd	1,963	532	1,505	487
Tripp	495	2,161	462	2,069
Turner	1,139	3,290	961	2,937
Union	2,725	5,944	2,227	5,290
Walworth	565	1,966	457	1,896
Yankton	4,016	6,581	3,301	5,659
Ziebach	481	404	353	368
Totals	**150,471**	**261,043**	**117,458**	**227,721**

South Dakota Vote Since 1960

2020: Trump, R, 261,043; Biden, D, 150,471; Jorgensen, LB, 11,095.

2016: Trump, R, 227,721; Clinton, D, 117,458; Johnson, LB, 20,850; Castle, Const., 4,064.

2012: Romney, R, 210,610; Obama, D, 145,039; Johnson, LB, 5,795; Goode, Const., 2,371.

2008: McCain, R, 203,054; Obama, D, 170,924; Nader, Ind., 4,267; Baldwin, Const., 1,895; Barr, Ind., 1,835.

2004: Bush, R, 232,584; Kerry, D, 149,244; Nader, Ind., 4,320; Peroutka, Const., 1,103; Badnarik, LB, 964.

2000: Bush, R, 190,700; Gore, D, 118,804; Buchanan, RF, 3,322; Phillips, Ind., 1,781; Browne, LB, 1,662.

1996: Dole, R, 150,543; Clinton, D, 139,333; Perot, RF, 31,250; Browne, LB, 1,472; Phillips, Taxpayers, 912; Hagelin, Natural Law, 316.

1992: Bush, R, 136,718; Clinton, D, 124,888; Perot, Ind., 73,295.

1988: Bush, R, 165,415; Dukakis, D, 145,560; Paul, LB, 1,060; Fulani, New Alliance, 730.

1984: Reagan, R, 200,267; Mondale, D, 116,113.

1980: Reagan, R, 198,343; Carter, D, 103,855; Anderson, Ind., 21,431; Clark, LB, 3,824; Pulley, Soc. Workers, 250.

1976: Ford, R, 151,505; Carter, D, 147,068; MacBride, LB, 1,619; Hall, Comm., 318; Camejo, Soc. Workers, 168.

1972: Nixon, R, 166,476; McGovern, D, 139,945; Jenness, Soc. Workers, 994.

1968: Nixon, R, 149,841; Humphrey, D, 118,023; Wallace, 3rd party, 13,400.

1964: Johnson, D, 163,010; Goldwater, R, 130,108.

1960: Nixon, R, 178,417; Kennedy, D, 128,070.

Tennessee

County	2020 Biden (D)	Trump (R)	2016 Clinton (D)	Trump (R)
Anderson	11,741	23,184	9,013	19,212
Bedford	4,453	14,354	3,395	11,486
Benton	1,529	5,668	1,474	4,716
Bledsoe	971	4,725	897	3,622
Blount	17,932	47,369	12,100	37,443
Bradley	9,851	35,204	7,070	29,768
Campbell	2,441	12,331	2,248	9,870
Cannon	1,261	5,190	1,127	4,007
Carroll	2,559	9,205	2,327	7,756
Carter	4,529	19,584	3,453	16,898
Cheatham	5,514	14,438	3,878	11,297
Chester	1,412	5,952	1,243	5,081
Claiborne	2,202	10,604	1,832	8,602
Clay	735	2,733	707	2,141
Cocke	2,533	12,162	1,981	9,791
Coffee	5,705	17,883	4,743	14,417
Crockett	1,382	4,673	1,303	3,982
Cumberland	6,728	25,168	5,202	20,413
Davidson	199,703	100,218	148,864	84,550
Decatur	904	4,229	894	3,588
DeKalb	1,750	6,672	1,569	5,171
Dickson	6,106	17,643	4,722	13,233
Dyer	3,158	11,768	2,816	10,180
Fayette	7,027	15,690	5,874	13,055
Fentress	1,214	7,441	1,100	6,038
Franklin	4,864	13,987	4,374	11,532
Gibson	5,771	16,259	5,258	13,786
Giles	3,298	9,784	2,917	7,970
Grainger	1,467	8,565	1,154	6,626
Greene	5,199	22,259	4,216	18,562
Grundy	988	4,802	999	3,636
Hamblen	5,500	18,811	4,075	15,857
Hamilton	75,522	92,108	55,316	78,733
Hancock	362	2,372	322	1,843
Hardeman	4,180	5,760	4,185	4,919
Hardin	1,775	9,559	1,622	8,012
Hawkins	4,083	20,405	3,507	16,648
Haywood	4,012	3,343	3,711	3,013
Henderson	2,092	9,797	1,800	8,138
Henry	3,548	11,239	3,063	9,508
Hickman	2,130	7,577	1,824	5,695
Houston	871	2,718	866	2,182
Humphreys	2,017	6,120	1,967	4,930
Jackson	1,135	4,118	1,129	3,236
Jefferson	4,654	18,651	3,494	14,776
Johnson	1,246	6,468	988	5,410
Knox	91,422	124,540	62,878	105,767
Lake	526	1,492	577	1,357
Lauderdale	3,193	5,674	3,056	4,884
Lawrence	3,195	15,334	2,821	12,420
Lewis	1,072	4,474	890	3,585
Lincoln	2,919	12,281	2,554	10,398
Loudon	6,948	21,713	4,919	17,610
Macon	1,307	8,096	1,072	6,263
Madison	18,390	23,943	15,448	21,335
Marion	3,177	9,911	2,832	7,696
Marshall	3,605	11,043	2,852	8,184
Maury	14,418	31,464	10,038	23,799
McMinn	4,361	18,198	3,510	14,691
McNairy	1,943	9,093	1,848	7,841
Meigs	1,008	4,467	856	3,342
Monroe	3,764	16,783	3,186	13,374
Montgomery	32,472	42,187	21,699	32,341
Moore	573	2,888	496	2,325
Morgan	1,167	6,930	1,054	5,441
Obion	2,589	10,790	2,426	9,526
Overton	2,033	7,918	1,945	6,059
Perry	615	2,775	597	2,167

County	2020 Biden (D)	Trump (R)	2016 Clinton (D)	Trump (R)
Pickett	525	2,381	536	2,021
Polk	1,492	6,792	1,252	5,097
Putnam	9,185	23,759	6,851	19,002
Rhea	2,369	11,050	1,942	8,660
Roane	6,043	19,230	4,837	15,880
Robertson	8,692	24,536	6,637	19,410
Rutherford	59,341	81,480	36,706	64,515
Scott	986	8,004	934	6,044
Sequatchie	1,298	5,855	1,053	4,441
Sevier	8,721	33,783	6,297	28,629
Shelby	246,105	129,815	208,992	116,344
Smith	1,802	7,136	1,689	5,494
Stewart	1,232	4,950	1,222	3,864
Sullivan	17,272	55,860	12,578	46,979
Sumner	27,680	63,454	18,161	50,129
Tipton	6,837	20,070	5,785	16,910
Trousdale	1,012	2,936	946	2,103
Unicoi	1,615	6,599	1,262	5,671
Union	1,249	6,803	1,012	5,053
Van Buren	544	2,342	539	1,820
Warren	3,924	11,850	3,535	9,540
Washington	18,638	40,444	13,024	34,252
Wayne	820	5,795	717	5,036
Weakley	3,020	10,396	2,772	9,008
White	2,143	9,606	1,845	7,671
Williamson	50,161	86,469	31,013	68,212
Wilson	22,254	50,296	14,385	39,406
Totals	**1,143,711**	**1,852,475**	**870,695**	**1,522,925**

Tennessee Vote Since 1960

2020: Trump, R, 1,852,475; Biden, D, 1,143,711; Jorgensen, LB, 29,877; West, Ind., 10,279; Blankenship, Ind., 5,365; Hawkins, Ind., 4,545; Kennedy, Ind., 2,576; La Riva, Ind., 2,301; De La Fuente, Ind., 1,860.

2016: Trump, R, 1,522,925; Clinton, D, 870,695; Johnson, Ind., 70,397; Stein, Green, 15,993; McMullin, Ind., 11,991; Smith, Ind., 7,276; De La Fuente, Ind., 4,075; Kennedy, Ind., 2,877; Castle, Ind., 1,584.

2012: Romney, R, 1,462,330; Obama, D, 960,709; Johnson, Ind., 18,623; Stein, Green, 6,515; Goode, Const., 6,022; Anderson, Ind., 2,639, Miller, Ind., 1,739.

2008: McCain, R, 1,479,178; Obama, D, 1,087,437; Nader, Ind., 11,560; Barr, Ind., 8,547; Baldwin, Ind., 8,191; McKinney, Ind., 2,499; Moore, Ind., 1,326; Jay, Ind., 1,011.

2004: Bush, R, 1,384,375; Kerry, D, 1,036,477; Nader, Ind., 8,992; Badnarik, Ind., 4,866; Peroutka, Ind., 2,570.

2000: Bush, R, 1,061,949; Gore, D, 981,720; Nader, Green, 19,781; Browne, LB, 4,284; Buchanan, RF, 4,250; Brown, Ind., 1,606; Phillips, Ind., 1,015; Hagelin, RF, 613; Venson, Ind., 535.

1996: Clinton, D, 909,146; Dole, R, 863,530; Perot, RF, 105,918; Nader, Ind., 6,427; Browne, Ind., 5,020; Phillips, Ind., 1,818; Collins, Ind., 688; Hagelin, Ind., 636; Michael, Ind., 408; Dodge, Ind., 324.

1992: Clinton, D, 933,521; Bush, R, 841,300; Perot, Ind., 199,968; Marrou, LB, 1,847.

1988: Bush, R, 947,233; Dukakis, D, 679,794; Paul, Ind., 2,041; Duke, Ind., 1,807.

1984: Reagan, R, 990,212; Mondale, D, 711,714; Bergland, LB, 3,072.

1980: Reagan, R, 787,761; Carter, D, 783,051; Anderson, Ind., 35,991; Clark, LB, 7,116; Commoner, Citizens, 1,112; Bubar, Statesman, 521; McReynolds, Soc., 519; Hall, Comm., 503; DeBerry, Soc. Workers, 490; Griswold, Workers World, 400; write-in, 152.

1976: Carter, D, 825,879; Ford, R, 633,969; Anderson, Amer., 5,769; McCarthy, Ind., 5,004; Maddox, Amer. Ind., 2,303; MacBride, LB, 1,375; Hall, Comm., 547; LaRouche, U.S. Labor, 512; Bubar, Prohib., 442; Miller, Ind., 316; write-in, 230.

1972: Nixon, R, 813,147; McGovern, D, 357,293; Schmitz, Amer., 30,373; write-in, 369.

1968: Nixon, R, 472,592; Wallace, 3rd party, 424,792; Humphrey, D, 351,233.

1964: Johnson, D, 635,047; Goldwater, R, 508,965; write-in, 34.

1960: Nixon, R, 556,577; Kennedy, D, 481,453; Faubus, States' Rights, 11,304; Decker, Prohib., 2,458.

Texas

County	2020 Biden (D)	Trump (R)	2016 Clinton (D)	Trump (R)
Anderson	3,955	15,110	3,369	13,201
Andrews	850	4,943	836	3,927
Angelina	9,143	25,076	7,538	21,668
Aransas	2,916	9,239	2,465	7,740
Archer	446	4,300	394	3,786
Armstrong	75	1,035	70	924
Atascosa	5,876	12,039	4,651	8,618
Austin	2,951	11,447	2,320	9,637
Bailey	409	1,434	397	1,344
Bandera	2,505	10,057	1,726	8,163
Bastrop	15,474	20,516	10,569	16,328
Baylor	183	1,494	191	1,267
Bee	3,288	6,006	3,444	4,744
Bell	57,014	67,893	37,801	51,998
Bexar	448,452	308,618	319,550	240,333
Blanco	1,911	5,443	1,244	4,212
Borden	16	397	31	330
Bosque	1,561	7,469	1,278	6,339
Bowie	10,747	27,116	8,838	24,924
Brazoria	62,228	90,433	43,200	72,791
Brazos	35,349	47,530	23,121	38,738
Brewster	2,258	2,461	1,873	2,077
Briscoe	78	639	91	625
Brooks	1,470	599	1,937	613
Brown	2,107	13,698	1,621	12,017
Burleson	1,788	6,743	1,491	5,316
Burnet	5,639	18,767	3,797	14,638
Caldwell	6,672	8,031	4,795	6,691
Calhoun	2,148	5,641	2,118	4,638
Callahan	734	6,012	569	4,865
Cameron	64,063	49,032	59,402	29,472
Camp	1,394	3,626	1,260	3,201
Carson	297	2,779	249	2,620
Cass	2,795	11,033	2,391	9,726
Castro	466	1,602	526	1,414
Chambers	3,997	17,353	2,948	13,339
Cherokee	4,210	15,101	3,469	12,919
Childress	310	1,943	253	1,802
Clay	614	5,069	536	4,377
Cochran	177	809	190	679
Coke	178	1,586	140	1,265
Coleman	451	3,641	388	3,177
Collin	230,945	252,318	140,624	201,014
Collingsworth	155	1,048	145	983
Colorado	2,420	7,472	1,987	6,325
Comal	24,826	62,740	14,238	45,136
Comanche	853	5,177	789	4,333
Concho	197	1,058	148	885
Cooke	3,210	15,596	2,352	13,181
Coryell	7,565	15,438	5,064	12,225
Cottle	113	540	92	506
Crane	241	1,247	299	1,049
Crockett	344	1,220	372	980
Crosby	527	1,396	468	1,181
Culberson	438	415	454	280
Dallam	197	1,389	222	1,261
Dallas	598,576	307,076	461,080	262,945
Dawson	808	2,951	835	2,636
Deaf Smith	1,264	3,294	1,185	2,911
Delta	403	2,162	400	1,836
Denton	188,695	222,480	110,890	170,603
DeWitt	1,494	6,567	1,163	5,519
Dickens	130	853	128	755
Dimmit	2,264	1,384	2,173	974
Donley	198	1,438	191	1,225
Duval	2,575	2,443	2,783	1,316
Eastland	983	7,237	776	6,011
Ector	11,367	32,697	10,249	25,020
Edwards	168	893	303	746
El Paso	27,565	56,717	147,843	55,512
Ellis	178,126	84,331	16,253	44,941
Erath	2,916	13,684	2,160	11,210
Falls	1,899	4,177	1,684	3,441
Fannin	2,655	12,171	2,132	9,548
Fayette	2,661	10,171	2,144	8,743
Fisher	352	1,448	403	1,265
Floyd	438	1,584	435	1,474
Foard	99	445	113	383

County	2020 Biden (D)	2020 Trump (R)	2016 Clinton (D)	2016 Trump (R)	County	2020 Biden (D)	2020 Trump (R)	2016 Clinton (D)	2016 Trump (R)
Fort Bend	195,552	157,718	134,686	117,291	McMullen	53	460	40	454
Franklin	804	4,161	665	3,585	Medina	6,773	15,642	4,634	12,085
Freestone	1,635	6,991	1,471	6,026	Menard	197	823	154	682
Frio	2,422	2,823	2,444	1,856	Midland	12,329	45,624	10,025	36,973
Gaines	576	5,355	597	3,907	Milam	2,496	7,984	2,051	6,364
Galveston	58,842	93,911	43,658	73,757	Mills	271	2,217	243	1,951
Garza	231	1,413	230	1,225	Mitchell	397	2,170	354	1,780
Gillespie	3,176	12,514	2,288	10,446	Montague	1,097	8,615	885	7,526
Glasscock	39	611	34	553	Montgomery	74,377	193,382	45,835	150,314
Goliad	877	3,085	973	2,620	Moore	1,062	4,359	1,098	3,977
Gonzales	1,948	5,627	1,571	4,587	Morris	1,669	3,872	1,425	3,446
Gray	829	6,840	701	6,500	Motley	46	604	40	566
Grayson	14,506	44,163	10,301	35,325	Nacogdoches	9,000	17,378	6,846	14,771
Gregg	14,796	32,493	11,677	28,764	Navarro	5,101	13,800	4,002	11,994
Grimes	2,833	9,432	2,194	7,065	Newton	1,173	4,882	1,156	4,288
Guadalupe	28,805	47,553	18,391	36,632	Nolan	1,162	4,131	1,029	3,552
Hale	2,279	7,177	2,101	6,366	Nueces	60,925	64,617	49,198	50,766
Hall	168	995	164	893	Ochiltree	302	2,812	274	2,628
Hamilton	641	3,616	479	3,060	Oldham	81	917	78	850
Hansford	166	1,849	171	1,730	Orange	6,357	29,186	5,735	25,513
Hardeman	241	1,330	249	1,207	Palo Pinto	2,178	10,179	1,708	8,284
Hardin	3,474	23,858	2,780	19,606	Panola	2,057	9,326	1,835	8,445
Harris	918,193	700,630	707,914	545,955	Parker	13,017	62,045	8,344	46,473
Harrison	7,908	21,466	7,151	18,749	Parmer	488	2,135	485	1,915
Hartley	195	1,868	173	1,730	Pecos	1,382	3,215	1,554	2,468
Haskell	353	1,840	314	1,403	Polk	5,387	18,573	4,187	15,176
Hays	59,524	47,680	33,224	33,826	Potter	9,921	22,820	7,657	19,630
Hemphill	206	1,486	181	1,462	Presidio	1,463	721	1,458	652
Henderson	7,060	28,911	5,669	23,650	Rains	842	5,155	628	3,968
Hidalgo	128,199	90,527	118,809	48,642	Randall	12,802	50,796	8,367	43,462
Hill	2,860	11,926	2,547	10,108	Reagan	172	942	167	709
Hockley	1,482	6,536	1,260	5,809	Real	320	1,643	262	1,382
Hood	5,648	26,496	4,008	21,382	Red River	1,246	4,517	1,149	3,926
Hopkins	3,046	12,719	2,510	10,707	Reeves	1,395	2,254	1,659	1,417
Houston	2,314	7,060	1,978	6,205	Refugio	1,108	2,210	1,034	1,830
Howard	2,069	8,054	1,770	6,637	Roberts	17	529	20	524
Hudspeth	371	779	324	503	Robertson	2,374	5,646	2,203	4,668
Hunt	8,906	29,163	6,396	23,910	Rockwall	16,412	36,726	9,655	28,451
Hutchinson	965	7,681	854	7,042	Runnels	552	3,807	453	3,250
Irion	120	759	90	660	Rusk	4,629	16,534	3,935	14,675
Jack	331	3,418	314	2,973	Sabine	669	4,784	614	3,998
Jackson	1,033	5,231	904	4,266	San Augustine	980	3,007	910	2,622
Jasper	2,954	12,542	2,590	10,609	San Jacinto	2,337	10,161	2,038	8,059
Jeff Davis	501	784	422	695	San Patricio	8,988	16,516	7,871	13,030
Jefferson	46,073	47,570	42,443	42,862	San Saba	287	2,308	293	2,025
Jim Hogg	1,197	833	1,635	430	Schleicher	211	940	208	821
Jim Wells	6,119	7,453	6,694	5,420	Scurry	818	4,983	733	4,410
Johnson	16,464	54,628	10,988	44,382	Shackelford	130	1,484	103	1,378
Jones	999	5,660	936	4,819	Shelby	2,068	7,975	1,758	7,179
Karnes	1,234	3,968	1,145	2,965	Sherman	91	886	96	807
Kaufman	18,405	37,624	10,278	29,587	Smith	29,615	69,080	22,300	58,930
Kendall	6,020	20,083	3,643	15,700	Somervell	768	4,105	541	3,206
Kenedy	65	127	99	84	Starr	9,123	8,247	9,289	2,224
Kent	47	411	59	360	Stephens	397	3,385	348	3,034
Kerr	6,524	20,879	4,681	17,727	Sterling	51	584	70	549
Kimble	284	1,987	206	1,697	Stonewall	116	615	135	555
King	8	151	5	149	Sutton	322	1,222	313	1,075
Kinney	446	1,144	458	936	Swisher	478	1,845	462	1,671
Kleberg	5,314	5,504	4,716	4,367	Tarrant	411,567	409,741	288,392	345,921
Knox	265	1,180	247	1,078	Taylor	14,588	39,547	10,085	33,250
La Salle	1,052	1,335	1,129	872	Terrell	119	334	140	288
Lamar	4,458	16,760	3,583	14,561	Terry	757	2,812	753	2,459
Lamb	840	3,521	771	3,111	Throckmorton	82	806	84	715
Lampasas	2,144	8,086	1,483	6,385	Titus	2,856	7,570	2,597	6,511
Lavaca	1,333	8,804	1,170	7,347	Tom Green	12,239	32,313	9,173	27,494
Lee	1,750	6,255	1,372	4,997	Travis	435,860	161,337	308,260	127,209
Leon	1,072	7,523	909	6,391	Trinity	1,323	5,579	1,154	4,737
Liberty	5,785	23,302	4,862	18,892	Tyler	1,403	8,194	1,248	6,624
Limestone	2,213	6,789	1,778	5,796	Upshur	2,877	15,809	2,380	13,209
Lipscomb	131	1,205	135	1,159	Upton	170	1,178	286	1,007
Live Oak	819	4,199	742	3,464	Uvalde	4,073	6,174	3,867	4,835
Llano	2,465	10,079	1,825	8,299	Val Verde	6,771	8,284	6,964	5,890
Loving	4	60	4	58	Van Zandt	3,516	22,270	2,799	18,473
Lubbock	40,017	78,861	28,023	65,651	Victoria	10,380	23,358	8,866	21,275
Lynn	428	1,853	403	1,546	Walker	7,884	15,375	6,091	12,884
Madison	1,088	4,169	881	3,351	Waller	8,191	14,260	5,748	10,531
Marion	1,339	3,470	1,165	2,983	Ward	764	3,241	783	2,547
Martin	288	1,857	266	1,455	Washington	4,261	12,959	3,382	10,945
Mason	457	1,991	354	1,656	Webb	41,820	25,898	42,307	12,947
Matagorda	3,733	9,845	3,500	8,366	Wharton	4,694	11,926	4,238	10,149
Maverick	8,332	6,881	10,397	2,816	Wheeler	168	2,159	194	2,087
McCulloch	490	2,904	482	2,552	Wichita	13,161	32,069	8,770	27,631
McLennan	36,688	59,543	27,063	48,260	Wilbarger	956	3,524	809	3,166

County	2020 Biden (D)	Trump (R)	2016 Clinton (D)	Trump (R)
Willacy	3,108	2,441	3,422	1,547
Williamson	143,795	139,729	84,468	104,175
Wilson	6,350	18,463	4,790	13,998
Winkler	358	1,753	420	1,403
Wise	4,973	27,032	3,412	20,670
Wood	3,509	19,049	2,630	15,700
Yoakum	420	2,174	426	1,797
Young	1,034	7,110	876	6,601
Zapata	1,826	2,033	2,063	1,029
Zavala	2,864	1,490	2,636	694
Totals	5,259,126	5,890,347	3,877,868	4,685,047

Texas Vote Since 1960

2020: Trump, R, 5,890,347; Biden, D, 5,259,126; Jorgensen, LB, 126,243; Hawkins, Green, 33,396.

2016: Trump, R, 4,685,047; Clinton, D, 3,877,868; Johnson, LB, 283,492; Stein, Green, 71,558; McMullin, Ind., 42,366.

2012: Romney, R, 4,569,843; Obama, D, 3,308,124; Johnson, LB, 88,580; Stein, Green, 24,657.

2008: McCain, R, 4,479,328; Obama, D, 3,528,633 Barr, LB, 56,116.

2004: Bush, R, 4,526,917; Kerry, D, 2,832,704; Badnarik, LB, 38,787.

2000: Bush, R, 3,799,639; Gore, D, 2,433,746; Nader, Green, 137,994; Browne, LB, 23,160; Buchanan, Ind., 12,394.

1996: Dole, R, 2,736,167; Clinton, D, 2,459,683; Perot, RF, 378,537; Browne, LB, 20,256; Phillips, U.S. Taxpayers, 7,472; Hagelin, Natural Law, 4,422.

1992: Bush, R, 2,496,071; Clinton, D, 2,281,815; Perot, Ind., 1,354,781; Marrou, LB, 19,699.

1988: Bush, R, 3,036,829; Dukakis, D, 2,352,748; Paul, LB, 30,355; Fulani, New Alliance, 7,208.

1984: Reagan, R, 3,433,428; Mondale, D, 1,949,276.

1980: Reagan, R, 2,510,705; Carter, D, 1,881,147; Anderson, Ind., 111,613; Clark, LB, 37,643; write-in, 528.

1976: Carter, D, 2,082,319; Ford, R, 1,953,300; McCarthy, Ind., 20,118; Anderson, Amer., 11,442; Camejo, Soc. Workers, 1,723; write-in, 2,982.

1972: Nixon, R, 2,298,896; McGovern, D, 1,154,289; Jenness, Soc. Workers, 8,664; Schmitz, Amer., 6,039; others, 3,393.

1968: Humphrey, D, 1,266,804; Nixon, R, 1,227,844; Wallace, 3rd party, 584,269; write-in, 489.

1964: Johnson, D, 1,663,185; Goldwater, R, 958,566; Lightburn, Const., 5,060.

1960: Kennedy, D, 1,167,932; Nixon, R, 1,121,699; Sullivan, Const., 18,169; Decker, Prohib., 3,870; write-in, 15.

Utah

County	2020 Biden (D)	Trump (R)	2016 Clinton (D)	Trump (R)
Beaver	357	2,695	264	1,838
Box Elder	4,473	21,548	2,282	12,230
Cache	16,650	38,032	8,563	21,139
Carbon	2,392	6,693	1,717	5,275
Daggett	111	496	77	331
Davis	57,411	104,135	28,776	62,219
Duchesne	843	7,513	500	5,508
Emery	572	4,207	380	3,425
Garfield	514	2,158	358	1,606
Grand	2,806	2,248	1,960	1,975
Iron	4,892	18,989	2,450	11,561
Juab	645	5,087	442	2,827
Kane	1,083	2,998	741	2,265
Millard	624	5,404	431	3,860
Morgan	1,086	5,181	577	3,188
Piute	86	773	47	626
Rich	180	1,157	104	797
Salt Lake	289,906	230,174	175,863	138,043
San Juan	3,113	3,535	2,042	2,645
Sanpete	1,794	10,459	1,061	6,673
Sevier	1,084	9,052	695	6,740
Summit	15,244	10,252	10,503	7,333
Tooele	8,943	21,014	4,573	11,169
Uintah	1,663	13,261	995	9,810
Utah	76,033	192,812	28,522	102,182
Wasatch	6,187	10,795	3,063	6,115
Washington	20,530	67,294	10,288	42,650

County	2020 Biden (D)	Trump (R)	2016 Clinton (D)	Trump (R)
Wayne	365	1,229	271	966
Weber	40,695	65,949	23,131	40,235
Totals	560,282	865,140	310,676	515,231

Utah Vote Since 1960

2020: Trump, R, 865,140; Biden, D, 560,282; Jorgensen, LB, 38,447; West, unaff., 7,213; Blankenship, Const., 5,551; Hawkins, Green, 5,053; Pierce, unaff., 2,623; McHugh, unaff., 2,229; La Riva, unaff., 1,139.

2016: Trump, R, 515,231; Clinton, D, 310,676; McMullin, unaff., 243,690; Johnson, LB, 39,608; Stein, Green, 9,438; Castle, Const., 8,032; Giordani, Ind. Ameri., 2,752; De La Fuente, unaff., 883; Moorehead, unaff., 544; Kennedy, unaff., 521.

2012: Romney, R, 740,600; Obama, D, 251,813; Johnson, LB, 12,572; Anderson, Justice, 5,335; Stein, Green, 3,817; Goode, Const., 2,871; La Riva, unaff., 393.

2008: McCain, R, 596,030; Obama, D, 327,670; Baldwin, Const., 12,012; Nader, unaff., 8,416; Barr, LB, 6,966; McKinney, unaff., 982; La Riva, unaff., 262.

2004: Bush, R, 663,742; Kerry, D, 241,199; Nader, Ind., 11,305; Peroutka, Const., 6,841; Badnarik, LB, 3,375; Jay, Personal Choice, 946; Harris, Soc. Workers, 393.

2000: Bush, R, 515,096; Gore, D, 203,053; Nader, Green, 35,850; Buchanan, RF, 9,319; Browne, LB, 3,616; Phillips, Ind. American, 2,709; Hagelin, Natural Law, 763; Harris, Soc. Workers, 186; Youngkeit, Ind., 161.

1996: Dole, R, 361,911; Clinton, D, 221,633; Perot, RF, 66,461; Nader, Green, 4,615; Browne, LB, 4,129; Phillips, Taxpayers, 2,601; Templin, Ind. American, 1,290; Crane, Ind., 1,101; Hagelin, Natural Law, 1,085; Moorehead, Workers World, 298; Harris, Soc. Workers, 235; Dodge, Prohib., 111.

1992: Bush, R, 322,632; Perot, Ind., 203,400; Clinton, D, 183,429; Gritz, Populist/America First, 28,602; Marrou, LB, 1,900; Hagelin, Natural Law, 1,319; LaRouche, Ind., 1,089.

1988: Bush, R, 428,442; Dukakis, D, 207,352; Paul, LB, 7,473; Dennis, Amer., 2,158.

1984: Reagan, R, 469,105; Mondale, D, 155,369; Bergland, LB, 2,447.

1980: Reagan, R, 439,687; Carter, D, 124,266; Anderson, Ind., 30,284; Clark, LB, 7,226; Commoner, Citizens, 1,009; Greaves, Amer., 965; Rarick, Amer. Ind., 522; Hall, Comm., 139; DeBerry, Soc. Workers, 124.

1976: Ford, R, 337,908; Carter, D, 182,110; Anderson, Amer., 13,304; McCarthy, Ind., 3,907; MacBride, LB, 2,438; Maddox, Amer. Ind., 1,162; Camejo, Soc. Workers, 268; Hall, Comm., 121.

1972: Nixon, R, 323,643; McGovern, D, 126,284; Schmitz, Amer., 28,549.

1968: Nixon, R, 238,728; Humphrey, D, 156,665; Wallace, 3rd party, 26,906; Peace/Freedom, 180; Halstead, Soc. Workers, 89.

1964: Johnson, D, 219,628; Goldwater, R, 181,785.

1960: Nixon, R, 205,361; Kennedy, D, 169,248; Dobbs, Soc. Workers, 100.

Vermont

County	2020 Biden (D)	Trump (R)	2016 Clinton (D)	Trump (R)
Addison	14,967	6,292	11,219	5,297
Bennington	12,705	7,114	9,539	5,925
Caledonia	9,011	6,551	6,445	5,534
Chittenden	74,961	21,017	54,814	18,601
Essex	1,405	1,773	1,019	1,506
Franklin	13,611	11,274	9,351	8,752
Grand Isle	2,905	1,810	2,094	1,487
Lamoille	10,240	4,163	7,241	3,570
Orange	10,304	6,187	7,541	5,007
Orleans	7,147	6,512	5,185	5,159
Rutland	18,230	14,672	13,635	12,479
Washington	25,191	8,928	18,594	7,993
Windham	18,767	6,440	14,340	5,454
Windsor	23,376	9,971	17,556	8,605
Totals	242,820	112,704	178,573	95,369

Vermont Vote Since 1960

2020: Biden, D, 242,820; Trump, R, 112,704; Jorgensen, LB, 3,608; Hawkins, Green, 1,310; West, Ind., 1,269; Paige, Ind., 1,175; LaFontaine, Ind., 856; Duncan, Ind., 213; Carroll, Amer. Solidarity, 209; Blankenship, Const., 208; Kennedy, Soc. Workers, 195; La Riva, Liberty Union, 166; Swing, other, 141; Collins, Prohib., 137; McCormic, other, 126; Pierce, unaff., 100; Segal, Bread/Roses, 65; Huber, Approval Voting, 54; Kopitke, Ind., 53; De La Fuente, Alliance, 48; Scalf, Ind., 29.

2016: Clinton, D, 178,573; Trump, R, 95,369; Sanders, write-in, 18,218; Johnson, LB, 10,078; Stein, Green, 6,758; De La Fuente, Ind., 1,063; La Riva, Liberty Union, 327.

2012: Obama, D, 199,239; Romney, R, 92,698; Johnson, LB, 3,487; Anderson, Justice, 1,128; Lindsay, Socialism/Liberation, 695.

2008: Obama, D, 219,262; McCain, R, 98,974; Nader, Ind., 3,339; Barr, LB, 1,067; Baldwin, Const., 500; Calero, Soc. Workers, 150; La Riva, Socialism/Liberation, 149; Moore, Liberty Union, 141.

2004: Kerry, D, 184,067; Bush, R, 121,180; Nader, Ind., 4,494; Badnarik, LB, 1,102; Parker, Liberty Union, 265; Calero, Soc. Workers, 244.

2000: Gore, D, 149,022; Bush, R, 119,775; Nader, Green, 20,374; Buchanan, RF, 2,192; Lane, Grass Roots, 1,044; Browne, LB, 784; Hagelin, Natural Law, 219; McReynolds, Liberty Union, 161; Phillips, Const., 153; Harris, Soc. Workers, 70.

1996: Clinton, D, 137,894; Dole, R, 80,352; Perot, RF, 31,024; Nader, Green, 5,585; Browne, LB, 1,183; Hagelin, Natural Law, 498; Peron, Grass Roots, 480; Phillips, Taxpayers, 382; Hollis, Liberty Union, 292; Harris, Soc. Workers, 199.

1992: Clinton, D, 133,590; Bush, R, 88,122; Perot, Ind., 65,985.

1988: Bush, R, 124,331; Dukakis, D, 115,775; Paul, LB, 1,000; LaRouche, Ind., 275.

1984: Reagan, R, 135,865; Mondale, D, 95,730; Bergland, LB, 1,002.

1980: Reagan, R, 94,598; Carter, D, 81,891; Anderson, Ind., 31,760; Commoner, Citizens, 2,316; Clark, LB, 1,900; McReynolds, Liberty Union, 136; Hall, Comm., 118; DeBerry, Soc. Workers, 75; scattered, 413.

1976: Ford, R, 100,387; Carter, D, 77,798 and Ind. Vermonters, 991 (total, 79,789); McCarthy, Ind., 4,001; Camejo, Soc. Workers, 430; LaRouche, U.S. Labor, 196; scattered, 99.

1972: Nixon, R, 117,149; McGovern, D, 68,174; Spock, Liberty Union, 1,010; Jenness, Soc. Workers, 296; scattered, 318.

1968: Nixon, R, 85,142; Humphrey, D, 70,255; Wallace, 3rd party, 5,104; Gregory, New Party, 579; Halstead, Soc. Workers, 295.

1964: Johnson, D, 107,674; Goldwater, R, 54,868.

1960: Nixon, R, 98,131; Kennedy, D, 69,186.

Virginia

County	2020		2016	
	Biden (D)	Trump (R)	Clinton (D)	Trump (R)
Accomack	7,578	9,172	6,740	8,583
Albemarle	42,466	20,804	33,345	19,259
Alleghany	2,243	5,859	2,166	4,874
Amelia	2,411	5,390	2,128	4,708
Amherst	5,672	11,041	5,057	9,719
Appomattox	2,418	6,702	2,023	5,715
Arlington	105,344	22,909	92,016	20,186
Augusta	10,840	30,714	8,177	26,163
Bath	646	1,834	603	1,548
Bedford	12,176	35,600	9,768	30,659
Bland	532	2,903	453	2,573
Botetourt	5,700	15,099	4,494	13,375
Brunswick	4,552	3,357	4,481	3,046
Buchanan	1,587	8,311	1,721	7,296
Buckingham	3,471	4,344	3,128	3,950
Campbell	8,070	21,245	6,664	19,551
Caroline	7,657	8,336	6,432	7,147
Carroll	2,842	12,659	2,559	10,663
Charles City	2,624	1,761	2,496	1,476

County	2020		2016	
	Biden (D)	Trump (R)	Clinton (D)	Trump (R)
Charlotte	2,317	3,815	2,155	3,479
Chesterfield	106,935	93,326	81,074	85,045
Clarke	3,920	5,192	3,051	4,661
Craig	587	2,536	541	2,140
Culpeper	10,617	16,012	7,759	13,349
Cumberland	2,227	3,019	2,036	2,697
Dickenson	1,503	5,748	1,335	4,932
Dinwiddie	6,224	8,695	5,765	7,447
Essex	3,038	3,075	2,542	2,657
Fairfax	419,943	168,401	355,133	157,710
Fauquier	17,565	25,106	12,971	22,127
Floyd	3,004	6,225	2,300	5,293
Fluvanna	7,414	8,155	5,760	7,025
Franklin	8,381	20,895	7,257	18,569
Frederick	17,207	30,558	11,932	26,083
Giles	2,156	6,876	1,950	5,910
Gloucester	6,964	14,875	5,404	13,096
Goochland	6,685	9,966	4,889	8,384
Grayson	1,535	6,529	1,407	5,592
Greene	4,163	6,866	2,924	5,945
Greensville	2,627	1,914	2,558	1,737
Halifax	7,666	10,418	6,897	9,704
Hanover	25,307	44,318	19,382	39,630
Henrico	116,572	63,440	93,935	59,857
Henry	9,127	16,725	8,198	15,208
Highland	417	1,092	371	958
Isle of Wight	9,399	13,707	7,881	12,204
James City	25,553	23,153	19,105	21,306
King and Queen	1,590	2,450	1,468	2,099
King George	5,404	8,446	4,007	7,341
King William	3,260	7,320	2,760	5,975
Lancaster	3,368	3,697	2,869	3,523
Lee	1,489	8,365	1,627	7,543
Loudoun	138,372	82,088	100,795	69,949
Louisa	8,269	13,294	6,212	10,528
Lunenburg	2,418	3,537	2,227	3,204
Madison	2,698	5,300	2,203	4,419
Mathews	1,825	3,901	1,563	3,517
Mecklenburg	6,803	9,266	6,285	8,288
Middlesex	2,491	4,196	2,108	3,670
Montgomery	23,218	20,629	20,021	19,459
Nelson	4,327	4,812	3,689	4,154
New Kent	4,621	9,631	3,546	8,118
Northampton	3,667	2,955	3,255	2,686
Northumberland	3,252	4,485	2,852	4,302
Nottoway	2,971	4,027	2,829	3,712
Orange	7,995	12,426	5,957	10,521
Page	3,007	9,345	2,514	7,831
Patrick	1,954	7,485	1,768	6,454
Pittsylvania	10,115	23,751	9,199	21,554
Powhatan	5,320	14,055	4,060	11,885
Prince Edward	4,973	4,434	4,591	4,101
Prince George	7,103	10,103	6,419	9,157
Prince William	142,863	81,222	113,144	71,721
Pulaski	4,925	12,127	4,172	10,322
Rappahannock	2,096	2,812	1,747	2,539
Richmond	1,513	2,547	1,347	2,213
Roanoke	21,801	34,268	17,200	31,408
Rockbridge	4,086	8,088	3,508	6,680
Rockingham	12,644	30,349	9,366	25,990
Russell	2,373	10,879	2,330	9,521
Scott	1,692	9,063	1,581	8,247
Shenandoah	6,836	16,463	5,273	14,094
Smyth	3,008	10,963	2,665	9,750
Southampton	3,969	5,730	3,595	5,035
Spotsylvania	34,307	39,411	24,207	34,623
Stafford	40,245	37,636	27,908	33,868
Surry	2,397	2,025	2,272	1,819
Sussex	2,827	2,219	2,879	2,055
Tazewell	3,205	16,731	2,895	15,168
Warren	6,603	14,069	5,169	11,773
Washington	6,617	21,679	5,553	19,320
Westmoreland	4,501	5,318	3,836	4,448
Wise	3,110	13,366	2,701	12,086
Wythe	3,143	11,733	2,770	10,046
York	17,683	20,241	12,999	18,837

City	2020 Biden (D)	Trump (R)	2016 Clinton (D)	Trump (R)
Alexandria	66,240	14,544	57,242	13,285
Bristol	2,313	5,347	1,835	4,892
Buena Vista	825	1,863	693	1,430
Charlottesville	20,696	3,094	17,901	2,960
Chesapeake	66,377	58,180	52,627	54,047
Colonial Heights	2,972	6,007	2,367	5,681
Covington	964	1,580	914	1,349
Danville	11,710	7,428	11,059	7,303
Emporia	1,612	754	1,530	789
Fairfax	9,174	4,007	7,367	3,702
Falls Church	7,146	1,490	5,819	1,324
Franklin	2,525	1,487	2,519	1,421
Fredericksburg	8,517	4,037	6,707	3,744
Galax	777	1,838	681	1,603
Hampton	46,220	18,430	41,312	17,902
Harrisonburg	11,022	5,591	10,212	6,262
Hopewell	5,430	4,020	4,724	3,885
Lexington	1,791	906	1,514	766
Lynchburg	18,048	17,097	14,792	17,982
Manassas	10,356	6,256	8,423	5,953
Manassas Park	3,992	1,979	3,204	1,733
Martinsville	3,766	2,165	3,533	2,149
Newport News	53,099	26,377	45,618	25,468
Norfolk	64,440	23,443	57,023	21,552
Norton	464	1,109	383	1,021
Petersburg	12,389	1,584	12,021	1,451
Poquoson	2,054	5,605	1,601	5,092
Portsmouth	30,948	12,755	28,497	12,795
Radford	3,358	2,786	2,925	2,638
Richmond	92,175	16,603	81,259	15,581
Roanoke	26,773	15,607	22,286	14,789
Salem	5,148	7,683	4,202	7,226
Staunton	6,981	5,695	5,333	5,133
Suffolk	28,676	20,082	23,280	18,006
Virginia Beach	117,393	105,087	91,032	98,224
Waynesboro	4,961	5,507	3,764	4,801
Williamsburg	4,790	1,963	5,206	1,925
Winchester	6,610	5,221	5,164	4,790
Totals	2,413,568	1,962,430	1,981,473	1,769,443

Virginia Vote Since 1960

2020: Biden, D, 2,413,568; Trump, R, 1,962,430; Jorgensen, LB, 64,761.

2016: Clinton, D, 1,981,473; Trump, R, 1,769,443; Johnson, LB, 118,274; McMullin, Ind., 54,054; Stein, Green, 27,638.

2012: Obama, D, 1,971,820; Romney, R, 1,822,522; Johnson, LB, 31,216; Goode, Const., 13,058; Stein, Green, 8,627.

2008: Obama, D, 1,959,532; McCain, R, 1,725,005; Nader, Ind., 11,483; Barr, LB, 11,067; Baldwin, Ind. Green, 7,474; McKinney, Green, 2,344.

2004: Bush, R, 1,716,959; Kerry, D, 1,454,742; Badnarik, LB, 11,032; Peroutka, Const., 10,161.

2000: Bush, R, 1,437,490; Gore, D, 1,217,290; Nader, Green, 59,398; Browne, LB, 15,198; Buchanan, RF, 5,455; Phillips, Const., 1,809.

1996: Dole, R, 1,138,350; Clinton, D, 1,091,060; Perot, RF, 159,861; Phillips, Taxpayers, 13,687; Browne, LB, 9,174; Hagelin, Natural Law, 4,510.

1992: Bush, R, 1,150,517; Clinton, D, 1,038,650; Perot, Ind., 348,639; LaRouche, Ind., 11,937; Marrou, LB, 5,730; Fulani, New Alliance, 3,192.

1988: Bush, R, 1,309,162; Dukakis, D, 859,799; Fulani, Ind., 14,312; Paul, LB, 8,336.

1984: Reagan, R, 1,337,078; Mondale, D, 796,250.

1980: Reagan, R, 989,609; Carter, D, 752,174; Anderson, Ind., 95,418; Commoner, Citizens, 14,024; Clark, LB, 12,821; DeBerry, Soc. Workers, 1,986.

1976: Ford, R, 836,554; Carter, D, 813,896; Camejo, Soc. Workers, 17,802; Anderson, Amer., 16,686; LaRouche, U.S. Labor, 7,508; MacBride, LB, 4,648.

1972: Nixon, R, 988,493; McGovern, D, 438,887; Schmitz, Amer., 19,721; Fisher, Soc. Labor, 9,918.

1968: Nixon, R, 590,319; Humphrey, D, 442,387; Wallace, 3rd party, 320,272*; Blomen, Soc. Labor, 4,671; Gregory, Peace/Freedom, 1,680; Munn, Prohib., 601. *10,561 votes for Wallace were omitted in the count.

1964: Johnson, D, 558,038; Goldwater, R, 481,334; Hass, Soc. Labor, 2,895.

1960: Nixon, R, 404,521; Kennedy, D, 362,327; Coiner, Conservative, 4,204; Hass, Soc. Labor, 397.

Washington

County	2020 Biden (D)	Trump (R)	2016 Clinton (D)	Trump (R)
Adams	1,814	3,907	1,299	3,083
Asotin	4,250	7,319	3,134	5,741
Benton	38,706	60,365	26,360	47,194
Chelan	19,349	22,746	13,032	18,114
Clallam	24,721	23,062	17,677	18,794
Clark	140,324	126,303	92,757	92,441
Columbia	668	1,754	526	1,497
Cowlitz	23,938	34,424	17,908	24,185
Douglas	7,811	12,955	4,918	9,603
Ferry	1,486	2,771	1,098	2,202
Franklin	13,340	18,039	8,886	13,206
Garfield	366	1,069	279	851
Grant	11,819	24,764	7,810	18,518
Grays Harbor	17,354	19,877	12,020	14,067
Island	29,213	22,746	20,960	18,465
Jefferson	17,204	6,931	12,656	6,037
King	907,310	269,167	718,322	216,339
Kitsap	90,277	61,563	63,156	49,018
Kittitas	11,421	14,105	7,489	10,100
Klickitat	5,959	7,237	4,194	5,789
Lewis	14,520	29,391	9,654	21,992
Lincoln	1,713	5,150	1,244	4,108
Mason	17,269	18,710	11,993	13,677
Okanogan	8,900	11,840	6,298	9,610
Pacific	6,794	6,953	4,620	5,360
Pend Oreille	2,593	5,728	1,934	4,373
Pierce	249,506	197,730	172,538	146,824
San Juan	9,725	3,057	7,172	2,688
Skagit	38,252	32,762	26,690	24,736
Skamania	3,192	3,885	2,232	2,928
Snohomish	256,728	166,428	185,227	128,255
Spokane	135,765	148,576	93,767	113,435
Stevens	7,839	19,808	5,767	15,161
Thurston	96,608	65,277	68,798	48,624
Wahkiakum	1,165	1,741	832	1,344
Walla Walla	13,690	16,400	9,694	13,651
Whatcom	83,660	50,489	60,340	40,599
Whitman	11,184	9,067	8,146	7,403
Yakima	43,179	50,555	31,291	41,735
Totals	2,369,612	1,584,651	1,742,718	1,221,747

Washington Vote Since 1960

2020: Biden, D, 2,369,612; Trump, R, 1,584,651; Jorgensen, LB, 80,500; Hawkins, Green, 18,289; La Riva, Socialism/Liberation, 4,840; Kennedy, Soc. Workers, 2,487.

2016: Clinton, D, 1,742,718; Trump, R, 1,221,747; Johnson, LB, 160,879; Stein, Green, 58,417; Castle, Const., 17,623; Kennedy, Soc. Workers, 4,307; La Riva, Socialism/Liberation, 3,523.

2012: Obama, D, 1,755,396; Romney, R, 1,290,670; Johnson, LB, 42,202; Stein, Green, 20,928; Goode, Const., 8,851; Anderson, Justice, 4,946; Lindsay, Socialism/Liberation, 1,318; Harris, Soc. Workers, 1,205.

2008: Obama, D, 1,750,848; McCain, R, 1,229,216; Nader, Ind., 29,489; Barr, LB, 12,728; Baldwin, Const., 9,432; McKinney, Green, 3,819; La Riva, Socialism/Liberation, 705; Harris, Soc. Workers, 641.

2004: Kerry, D, 1,510,201; Bush, R, 1,304,894; Nader, Ind., 23,283; Badnarik, LB, 11,955; Peroutka, Const., 3,922; Cobb, Green, 2,974; Parker, Workers World, 1,077; Harris, Soc. Workers, 547; Van Auken, Soc. Equality, 231.

2000: Gore, D, 1,247,652; Bush, R, 1,108,864; Nader, Green, 103,002; Browne, LB, 13,135; Buchanan, Freedom, 7,171; Hagelin, Natural Law, 2,927; Phillips, Const., 1,989; Moorehead, Workers World, 1,729; McReynolds, Soc., 660; Harris, Soc. Workers, 304.

1996: Clinton, D, 1,123,323; Dole, R, 840,712; Perot, RF, 201,003; Nader, Ind., 60,322; Browne, LB, 12,522; Hagelin, Natural Law, 6,076; Phillips, U.S. Taxpayers, 4,578; Collins, Ind., 2,374; Moorehead, Workers World, 2,189; Harris, Soc. Workers, 738.

1992: Clinton, D, 993,037; Bush, R, 731,234; Perot, Ind., 541,780; Marrou, LB, 7,533; Gritz, Populist/America First, 4,854; Hagelin, Natural Law, 2,456; Phillips, U.S. Taxpayers, 2,354; Fulani, New Alliance, 1,776; Daniels, Ind., 1,171.

1988: Dukakis, D, 933,516; Bush, R, 903,835; Paul, LB, 17,240; LaRouche, Ind., 4,412.

1984: Reagan, R, 1,051,670; Mondale, D, 798,352; Bergland, LB, 8,844.

1980: Reagan, R, 865,244; Carter, D, 650,193; Anderson, Ind., 185,073; Clark, LB, 29,213; Commoner, Citizens, 9,403; DeBerry, Soc. Workers, 1,137; McReynolds, Soc., 956; Hall, Comm., 834; Griswold, Workers World, 341.

1976: Ford, R, 777,732; Carter, D, 717,323; McCarthy, Ind., 36,986; Maddox, Amer. Ind., 8,585; Anderson, Amer., 5,046; MacBride, LB, 5,042; Wright, People's, 1,124; Camejo, Soc. Workers, 905; LaRouche, U.S. Labor, 903; Hall, Comm., 817; Levin, Soc. Labor, 713; Zeidler, Soc., 358.

1972: Nixon, R, 837,135; McGovern, D, 568,334; Schmitz, Amer., 58,906; Spock, Ind., 2,644; Hospers, LB, 1,537; Fisher, Soc. Labor, 1,102; Jenness, Soc. Workers, 623; Hall, Comm., 566.

1968: Humphrey, D, 616,037; Nixon, R, 588,510; Wallace, 3rd party, 96,990; Cleaver, Peace/Freedom, 1,609; Blomen, Soc. Labor, 488; Mitchell, Free Ballot, 377; Halstead, Soc. Workers, 270.

1964: Johnson, D, 779,699; Goldwater, R, 470,366; Hass, Soc. Labor, 7,772; DeBerry, Freedom Soc., 537.

1960: Nixon, R, 629,273; Kennedy, D, 599,298; Hass, Soc. Labor, 10,895; Curtis, Const., 1,401; Dobbs, Soc. Workers, 705.

West Virginia

County	2020 Biden (D)	2020 Trump (R)	2016 Clinton (D)	2016 Trump (R)
Barbour	1,457	5,116	1,222	4,527
Berkeley	17,186	33,279	12,321	28,244
Boone	2,041	6,816	1,790	6,504
Braxton	1,457	4,120	1,321	3,537
Brooke	2,947	7,545	2,568	6,625
Cabell	14,994	21,721	11,447	19,850
Calhoun	568	2,364	456	2,035
Clay	641	2,679	568	2,300
Doddridge	435	2,619	362	2,358
Fayette	5,063	11,580	4,290	10,357
Gilmer	599	2,012	545	1,896
Grant	607	4,871	512	4,346
Greenbrier	4,655	10,925	3,765	9,556
Hampshire	1,939	8,033	1,580	6,692
Hancock	3,790	9,806	3,262	8,909
Hardy	1,381	4,859	1,155	4,274
Harrison	9,215	20,683	7,694	18,750
Jackson	3,207	10,093	2,663	9,020
Jefferson	12,127	15,033	9,518	13,204
Kanawha	34,344	46,398	28,263	43,850
Lewis	1,538	5,782	1,347	5,274
Lincoln	1,711	6,012	1,459	5,307
Logan	2,333	10,534	2,092	9,897
Marion	8,901	16,300	6,964	14,668
Marshall	3,455	10,435	2,918	9,666
Mason	2,526	8,491	2,081	7,654
McDowell	1,333	5,148	1,438	4,629
Mercer	5,556	19,237	4,704	17,404
Mineral	2,660	10,040	2,050	9,070
Mingo	1,397	8,544	1,370	7,911
Monongalia	20,282	20,803	14,699	18,432
Monroe	1,345	5,068	1,111	4,443
Morgan	1,998	6,537	1,573	5,732
Nicholas	2,226	8,279	1,840	7,251
Ohio	7,223	12,354	5,493	11,139
Pendleton	820	2,782	729	2,398
Pleasants	699	2,742	621	2,358
Pocahontas	1,047	2,895	928	2,496
Preston	3,163	11,190	2,470	9,538
Putnam	7,878	20,034	5,884	17,788
Raleigh	7,982	24,673	6,443	22,048
Randolph	3,362	8,673	2,735	7,629
Ritchie	586	3,649	496	3,405
Roane	1,455	4,213	1,222	3,781
Summers	1,448	4,074	1,190	3,455
Taylor	1,796	5,477	1,491	4,733
Tucker	938	2,841	751	2,565
Tyler	631	3,226	507	2,996
Upshur	2,256	7,771	1,766	7,005

County	2020 Biden (D)	2020 Trump (R)	2016 Clinton (D)	2016 Trump (R)
Wayne	4,088	12,585	3,357	11,152
Webster	610	2,759	556	2,302
Wetzel	1,539	4,993	1,359	4,519
Wirt	466	2,134	386	1,911
Wood	10,926	27,202	8,400	25,434
Wyoming	1,157	7,353	1,062	6,547
Totals	235,984	545,382	188,794	489,371

West Virginia Vote Since 1960

2020: Trump, R, 545,382; Biden, D, 235,984; Jorgensen, LB, 10,687; Hawkins, Mountain, 2,599.

2016: Trump, R, 489,371; Clinton, D, 188,794; Johnson, LB, 23,004; Stein, Mountain, 8,075; Castle, Const., 3,807.

2012: Romney, R, 417,655; Obama, D, 238,269; Johnson, LB, 6,302; Stein, Mountain, 4,406; Terry, NPA, 3,806.

2008: McCain, R, 397,466; Obama, D, 303,857; Nader, unaff., 7,219; Baldwin, Const., 2,465; McKinney, Mountain, 2,355.

2004: Bush, R, 423,778; Kerry, D, 326,541; Nader, Ind., 4,063; Badnarik, LB, 1,405.

2000: Bush, R, 336,475; Gore, D, 295,497; Nader, Green, 10,680; Buchanan, RF, 3,169; Browne, LB, 1,912; Hagelin, Natural Law, 367.

1996: Clinton, D, 327,812; Dole, R, 233,946; Perot, RF, 71,639; Browne, LB, 3,062.

1992: Clinton, D, 331,001; Bush, R, 241,974; Perot, Ind., 108,829; Marrou, LB, 1,873.

1988: Dukakis, D, 341,016; Bush, R, 310,065; Fulani, New Alliance, 2,230.

1984: Reagan, R, 405,483; Mondale, D, 328,125.

1980: Carter, D, 367,462; Reagan, R, 334,206; Anderson, Ind., 31,691; Clark, LB, 4,356.

1976: Carter, D, 435,864; Ford, R, 314,726.

1972: Nixon, R, 484,964; McGovern, D, 277,435.

1968: Humphrey, D, 374,091; Nixon, R, 307,555; Wallace, 3rd party, 72,560.

1964: Johnson, D, 538,087; Goldwater, R, 253,953.

1960: Kennedy, D, 441,786; Nixon, R, 395,995.

Wisconsin

County	2020 Biden (D)	2020 Trump (R)	2016 Clinton (D)	2016 Trump (R)
Adams	4,329	7,362	3,745	5,966
Ashland	4,801	3,841	4,226	3,303
Barron	9,194	15,803	7,889	13,614
Bayfield	6,147	4,617	4,953	4,124
Brown	65,511	75,871	53,382	67,210
Buffalo	2,860	4,834	2,525	4,048
Burnett	3,569	6,462	2,949	5,410
Calumet	12,116	18,156	9,642	15,367
Chippewa	13,983	21,317	11,887	17,916
Clark	4,524	10,002	4,221	8,652
Columbia	16,410	16,927	13,528	14,163
Crawford	3,953	4,620	3,419	3,836
Dane	260,121	78,794	217,697	71,275
Dodge	16,356	31,355	13,968	26,635
Door	10,044	9,752	8,014	8,580
Douglas	13,218	10,923	11,357	9,661
Dunn	9,897	13,173	9,034	11,486
Eau Claire	31,620	25,341	27,340	23,331
Florence	781	2,133	669	1,898
Fond du Lac	20,588	35,754	17,387	31,022
Forest	1,721	3,285	1,579	2,787
Grant	10,998	14,142	10,051	12,350
Green	10,851	10,169	9,122	8,693
Green Lake	3,344	7,168	2,693	6,216
Iowa	7,828	5,909	6,669	4,809
Iron	1,533	2,438	1,275	2,081
Jackson	4,256	5,791	3,818	4,906
Jefferson	19,904	27,208	16,569	23,417
Juneau	4,746	8,748	4,073	7,130
Kenosha	42,193	44,972	35,799	36,037
Kewaunee	3,976	7,927	3,627	6,618
La Crosse	37,846	28,684	32,406	26,378
Lafayette	3,647	4,821	3,288	3,977
Langlade	3,704	7,330	3,250	6,478
Lincoln	6,261	10,017	5,371	8,401
Manitowoc	16,818	27,218	14,538	23,244

County	2020 Biden (D)	Trump (R)	2016 Clinton (D)	Trump (R)
Marathon	30,808	44,624	26,481	39,014
Marinette	7,366	15,304	6,409	13,122
Marquette	3,239	5,719	2,808	4,709
Menominee	1,303	278	1,002	267
Milwaukee	317,527	134,482	288,822	126,069
Monroe	8,433	13,775	7,052	11,356
Oconto	6,715	16,226	5,940	13,345
Oneida	10,105	13,671	8,109	12,132
Outagamie	47,667	58,385	38,068	49,879
Ozaukee	26,517	33,912	20,170	30,464
Pepin	1,489	2,584	1,344	2,206
Pierce	9,796	12,815	8,399	11,272
Polk	9,370	16,611	7,565	13,810
Portage	20,428	19,299	18,529	17,305
Price	3,032	5,394	2,667	4,559
Racine	50,159	54,479	42,641	46,681
Richland	3,995	4,871	3,569	4,013
Rock	46,658	37,138	39,339	31,493
Rusk	2,517	5,257	2,171	4,564
St. Croix	23,190	32,199	17,482	26,222
Sauk	18,108	17,493	14,690	14,799
Sawyer	4,498	5,909	3,503	5,185
Shawano	7,131	15,173	6,068	12,769
Sheboygan	27,101	37,609	23,000	32,514
Taylor	2,693	7,657	2,393	6,579
Trempealeau	6,285	8,833	5,636	7,366
Vernon	7,457	8,218	6,371	7,004
Vilas	5,903	9,261	4,770	8,166
Walworth	22,789	33,851	18,710	28,863
Washburn	3,867	6,334	3,282	5,436
Washington	26,650	60,237	20,852	51,740
Waukesha	103,906	159,649	79,224	142,543
Waupaca	9,703	18,952	8,451	16,209
Waushara	4,388	9,016	3,791	7,667
Winnebago	44,060	47,796	37,047	43,445
Wood	16,365	24,308	14,225	21,498
Totals	**1,630,866**	**1,610,184**	**1,382,536**	**1,405,284**

Wisconsin Vote Since 1960

2020: Biden, D, 1,630,866; Trump, R, 1,610,184; Jorgensen, LB, 38,491; Carroll, Amer. Solidarity, 5,259; Blankenship, Const., 5,146.

2016: Trump, R, 1,405,284; Clinton, D, 1,382,536; Johnson, LB, 106,674; Stein, WI Green, 31,072; Castle, Const., 12,162; McMullin, Ind., 11,855; Moorehead, Ind., 1,770; De La Fuente, Ind., 1,502.

2012: Obama, D, 1,620,985; Romney, R, 1,407,966; Johnson, LB, 20,439; Stein, Green, 7,665; White, Soc. Equality, 553; La Riva, Socialism/Liberation, 526.

2008: Obama, D, 1,677,211; McCain, R, 1,262,393; Nader, Ind., 17,605; Barr, LB, 8,858; Baldwin, Ind., 5,072; McKinney, Green, 4,216; Wamboldt, Ind., 764; Moore, Ind., 540; La Riva, Ind., 237.

2004: Kerry, D, 1,489,504; Bush, R, 1,478,120; Nader, Ind., 16,390; Badnarik, LB, 6,464; Cobb, Green, 2,661; Brown, Ind., 471; Harris, Ind., 411.

2000: Gore, D, 1,242,987; Bush, R, 1,237,279; Nader, Green, 94,070; Buchanan, RF, 11,446; Browne, LB, 6,640; Phillips, Const., 2,042; Moorehead, Workers World, 1,063; Hagelin, RF, 878; Harris, Soc. Workers, 306.

1996: Clinton, D, 1,071,971; Dole, R, 845,029; Perot, RF, 227,339; Nader, Green, 28,723; Phillips, U.S. Taxpayers, 8,811; Browne, LB, 7,929; Hagelin, Natural Law, 1,379; Moorehead, Workers World, 1,333; Hollis, Soc., 848; Harris, Soc. Workers, 483.

1992: Clinton, D, 1,041,066; Bush, R, 930,855; Perot, Ind., 544,479; Marrou, LB, 2,877; Gritz, Populist/America First, 2,311; Daniels, Ind., 1,883; Phillips, U.S. Taxpayers, 1,772; Hagelin, Natural Law, 1,070.

1988: Dukakis, D, 1,126,794; Bush, R, 1,047,499; Paul, LB, 5,157; Duke, Populist, 3,056.

1984: Reagan, R, 1,198,584; Mondale, D, 995,740; Bergland, LB, 4,883.

1980: Reagan, R, 1,088,845; Carter, D, 981,584; Anderson, Ind., 160,657; Clark, LB, 29,135; Commoner, Citizens, 7,767; Rarick, Const., 1,519; McReynolds, Soc., 808; Hall, Comm., 772; Griswold, Workers World, 414; DeBerry, Soc. Workers, 383; scattered, 1,337.

1976: Carter, D, 1,040,232; Ford, R, 1,004,987; McCarthy, Ind., 34,943; Maddox, Amer. Ind., 8,552; Zeidler, Soc., 4,298;

MacBride, LB, 3,814; Camejo, Soc. Workers, 1,691; Wright, People's, 943; Hall, Comm., 749; LaRouche, U.S. Labor, 738; Levin, Soc. Labor, 389; scattered, 2,839.

1972: Nixon, R, 989,430; McGovern, D, 810,174; Schmitz, Amer., 47,525; Spock, Ind., 2,701; Fisher, Soc. Labor, 998; Hall, Comm., 663; Reed, Ind., 506; scattered, 893.

1968: Nixon, R, 809,997; Humphrey, D, 748,804; Wallace, 3rd party, 127,835; Blomen, Soc. Labor, 1,338; Halstead, Soc. Workers, 1,222; scattered, 2,342.

1964: Johnson, D, 1,050,424; Goldwater, R, 638,495; DeBerry, Soc. Workers, 1,692; Hass, Soc. Labor, 1,204.

1960: Nixon, R, 895,175; Kennedy, D, 830,805; Dobbs, Soc. Workers, 1,792; Hass, Soc. Labor, 1,310.

Wyoming

County	2020 Biden (D)	Trump (R)	2016 Clinton (D)	Trump (R)
Albany	9,092	8,579	6,890	7,602
Big Horn	788	4,806	604	4,067
Campbell	1,935	16,975	1,324	15,778
Carbon	1,427	5,014	1,279	4,409
Converse	861	5,917	668	5,520
Crook	378	3,651	273	3,348
Fremont	5,519	12,007	4,200	11,167
Goshen	1,203	4,878	924	4,418
Hot Springs	482	1,999	400	1,939
Johnson	897	3,881	638	3,477
Laramie	15,217	27,891	11,573	24,847
Lincoln	1,509	8,643	1,105	6,779
Natrona	8,530	25,271	6,577	23,552
Niobrara	155	1,118	115	1,116
Park	3,410	12,813	2,535	11,115
Platte	890	3,898	719	3,437
Sheridan	4,043	11,843	2,927	10,266
Sublette	882	3,957	644	3,409
Sweetwater	3,823	12,229	3,231	12,154
Teton	9,848	4,341	7,314	3,921
Uinta	1,591	7,496	1,202	6,154
Washakie	651	3,245	532	2,911
Weston	360	3,107	299	3,033
Totals	**73,491**	**193,559**	**55,973**	**174,419**

Wyoming Vote Since 1960

2020: Trump, R, 193,559; Biden, D, 73,491; Jorgensen, LB, 5,768; Pierce, Ind., 2,208.

2016: Trump, R, 174,419; Clinton, D, 55,973; Johnson, LB, 13,287; Stein, Ind., 2,515; Castle, Const., 2,042; De La Fuente, Ind., 709.

2012: Romney, R, 170,962; Obama, D, 69,286; Johnson, LB, 5,326; Goode, Const., 1,452.

2008: McCain, R, 164,958; Obama, D, 82,868; Nader, Ind., 2,525; Barr, LB, 1,594; Baldwin, Ind., 1,192.

2004: Bush, R, 167,629; Kerry, D, 70,776; Nader, Ind., 2,741; Badnarik, LB, 1,171; Peroutka, Ind., 631.

2000: Bush, R, 147,947; Gore, D, 60,481; Buchanan, RF, 2,724; Browne, LB, 1,443; Phillips, Ind., 720; Hagelin, Natural Law, 411.

1996: Dole, R, 105,388; Clinton, D, 77,934; Perot, RF, 25,928; Browne, LB, 1,739; Hagelin, Natural Law, 582.

1992: Bush, R, 79,347; Clinton, D, 68,160; Perot, Ind., 51,263.

1988: Bush, R, 106,867; Dukakis, D, 67,113; Paul, LB, 2,026; Fulani, New Alliance, 545.

1984: Reagan, R, 133,241; Mondale, D, 53,370; Bergland, LB, 2,357.

1980: Reagan, R, 110,700; Carter, D, 49,427; Anderson, Ind., 12,072; Clark, LB, 4,514.

1976: Ford, R, 92,717; Carter, D, 62,239; McCarthy, Ind., 624; Reagan, Ind., 307; Anderson, Amer., 290; MacBride, LB, 89; Brown, Ind., 47; Maddox, Amer. Ind., 30.

1972: Nixon, R, 100,464; McGovern, D, 44,358; Schmitz, Amer., 748.

1968: Nixon, R, 70,927; Humphrey, D, 45,173; Wallace, 3rd party, 11,105.

1964: Johnson, D, 80,718; Goldwater, R, 61,998.

1960: Nixon, R, 77,451; Kennedy, D, 63,331.

UNITED STATES GOVERNMENT

EXECUTIVE BRANCH	LEGISLATIVE BRANCH	JUDICIAL BRANCH
President **Vice President** **Executive Office of the President** Council of Economic Advisers Council on Environmental Quality National Security Council Office of Administration Office of Management and Budget Office of National Drug Control Policy Office of Science and Technology Policy Office of the U.S. Trade Representative Office of the Vice President White House Office	**CONGRESS** **Senate/House of Representatives** Architect of the Capitol Congressional Budget Office Government Accountability Office Government Publishing Office Library of Congress U.S. Botanic Garden	**Supreme Court of the United States** Administrative Office of the U.S. Courts Federal Judicial Center Territorial Courts Courts of Appeals Court of Appeals for the Armed Forces Court of Appeals for Veterans Claims District Courts Court of Federal Claims Court of International Trade Sentencing Commission Tax Court

Biden Administration

1600 Pennsylvania Ave. NW, 20500; www.whitehouse.gov
As of Sept. 2023. Mailing addresses are for Washington, DC, except where otherwise noted.
Terms of office of the president and vice president: Jan. 20, 2021, to Jan. 20, 2025.

White House Staff

Assistants to the President:
Chief of Staff: Jeff Zients
Deputy Chiefs of Staff: Jennifer Dillon, Natalie Quillian, Bruce Reed
Senior Advisers: Michael Donilon, Anita Dunn, Mitchell Landrieu, John Podesta
Counselor to the President: Steven J. Ricchetti
White House Counsel: Stuart Delery
National Security Adviser: Jake Sullivan
Principal Deputy National Security Adviser: Jonathan Finer
Deputy National Security Adviser: Elizabeth Sherwood-Randall
Director of Communications: Ben LaBolt
Press Secretary: Karine Jean-Pierre
Cabinet Secretary: Evan M. Ryan
Director of Legislative Affairs: Louisa Terrell
Director of Management and Administration: David Noble
Director of Oval Office Operations: AnnMarie Tomasini
Director of Political Strategy and Outreach: Emma Ruiz
Director of Presidential Personnel: Gautam Raghavan
Director of Scheduling and Advance: Ryan Montoya
Director of Speechwriting: Vinay Reddy
Staff Secretary: Stefanie Feldman
Chief of Staff to the First Lady: Vacant
Senior Adviser to the First Lady: Anthony Bernal

Executive Offices

Climate Policy Office: Ali Zaidi, dir.; https://www.whitehouse.gov/cpo/
Council of Economic Advisers: Jared Bernstein, chair; www.whitehouse.gov/cea/
Council on Environmental Quality: Brenda Mallory, chair; www.whitehouse.gov/ceq/
Domestic Policy Council: Neera Tanden, chair; www.whitehouse.gov/dpc/
Gender Policy Council: Jennifer Klein, chair; www.whitehouse.gov/gpc
National Economic Council: Lael Brainard, dir.; www.whitehouse.gov/nec/
Office of Intergovernmental Affairs: Tom Perez, dir.; www.whitehouse.gov/iga/
Office of Management and Budget: Shalanda Young, dir.; www.whitehouse.gov/omb/
Office of National Drug Control Policy: Rahul Gupta, dir.; www.whitehouse.gov/ondcp/
Office of Public Engagement: Stephen Benjamin, dir.; www.whitehouse.gov/ope/
Office of Science and Technology Policy: Arati Prabhakar, dir.; www.whitehouse.gov/ostp/
Office of the National Cyber Director: Kemba Walden, acting dir.; www.whitehouse.gov/oncd
Office of the U.S. Trade Representative: Katherine Tai, amb.; www.ustr.gov
Office of the Director of National Intelligence (not formally an executive office): Avril Haines, dir.; www.dni.gov

The Cabinet

The heads of major executive departments of the federal government constitute the Cabinet. This institution, not provided for in the U.S. Constitution, developed out of the desire of presidents to consult on policy matters. Aside from its advisory role, the Cabinet as a body has no formal function and wields no executive authority. Individual members exercise authority as heads of their departments, reporting to the president. The Cabinet meets at times set by the president. In addition, the Cabinet commonly includes other officials designated by the president as being of Cabinet rank.

The officials so designated by Pres. Joe Biden include the Vice President, White House Chief of Staff, U.S. Ambassador to the United Nations, Director of National Intelligence, and U.S. Trade Representative, as well as the heads of the Central Intelligence Agency, Environmental Protection Agency, Office of Management and Budget, Council of Economic Advisers, Office of Science and Technology Policy, and Small Business Administration.

Cabinet Department Heads

Secretary of State: Antony Blinken
Secretary of the Treasury: Janet Yellen
Secretary of Defense: Lloyd Austin
Attorney General (Dept. of Justice head): Merrick Garland
Secretary of the Interior: Deb Haaland
Secretary of Agriculture: Tom Vilsack
Secretary of Commerce: Gina Raimondo
Secretary of Labor (acting): Julie Su

Secretary of Health and Human Services: Xavier Becerra
Secretary of Housing and Urban Development: Marcia Fudge
Secretary of Transportation: Pete Buttigieg
Secretary of Energy: Jennifer Granholm
Secretary of Education: Miguel Cardona
Secretary of Veterans Affairs: Denis McDonough
Secretary of Homeland Security: Alejandro Mayorkas

Other Cabinet Rank Officials

Environmental Protection Agency Administrator: Michael Regan
Director of National Intelligence: Avril Haines
U.S. Trade Representative: Katherine Tai
U.S. Ambassador to the United Nations: Linda Thomas-Greenfield
Chair of the Council of Economic Advisers: Jared Bernstein

Small Business Administration Administrator: Isabel Casillas Guzman
Director of the Office of Management and Budget: Shalanda Young
White House Chief of Staff: Jeff Zients
Director of the Central Intelligence Agency: William J. Burns

Cabinet-Level Departments

Department mailing address applies to subordinate bureaus/agencies unless otherwise noted. Mailing addresses are for Washington, DC, except where otherwise noted.

Department of State

2201 C St. NW, 20520; www.state.gov

The Dept. of Foreign Affairs was created by act of Congress on July 27, 1789, and the name changed to Dept. of State on Sept. 15, 1789. Conducts U.S. foreign policy. The Foreign Service protects American citizens and interests through embassies in some 180 countries. Maintains contact with foreign governments, negotiates agreements and treaties, and supports U.S. foreign trade. Promotes democracy, international security, human rights—including issues related to AIDS, human trafficking, war crimes, and migration—and arms and narcotics control. Represents the nation in international organizations. Issues passports to U.S. citizens and visas to foreigners. **Budget:** $32.9 bil (2020); $35.8 bil (2021); $33.2 bil (2022); $34.7 bil (2023 est.); $36.5 bil (2024 est.). Budget for other intl. programs: $21.7 bil (2020); $20.0 bil (2021); $35.8 bil (2022); $44.7 bil (2023 est.); $36.5 bil (2024 est.).

Secretaries of State

President	Secretary	Home	Sworn in
Washington	Thomas Jefferson	VA	1789
	Edmund J. Randolph	VA	1794
	Timothy Pickering	PA	1795
Adams, J.	Timothy Pickering	PA	1797
	John Marshall	VA	1800
Jefferson	James Madison	VA	1801
Madison	Robert Smith	MD	1809
	James Monroe	VA	1811
Monroe	John Quincy Adams	MA	1817
Adams, J. Q.	Henry Clay	KY	1825
Jackson	Martin Van Buren	NY	1829
	Edward Livingston	LA	1831
	Louis McLane	DE	1833
	John Forsyth	GA	1834
Van Buren	John Forsyth	GA	1837
Harrison, W. H.	Daniel Webster	MA	1841
Tyler	Daniel Webster	MA	1841
	Abel P. Upshur	VA	1843
	John C. Calhoun	SC	1844
Polk	John C. Calhoun	SC	1845
	James Buchanan	PA	1845
Taylor	James Buchanan	PA	1849
	John M. Clayton	DE	1849
Fillmore	John M. Clayton	DE	1850
	Daniel Webster	MA	1850
	Edward Everett	MA	1852
Pierce	William L. Marcy	NY	1853
Buchanan	William L. Marcy	NY	1857
	Lewis Cass	MI	1857
	Jeremiah S. Black	PA	1860
Lincoln	Jeremiah S. Black	PA	1861
	William H. Seward	NY	1861
Johnson, A.	William H. Seward	NY	1865
Grant	Elihu B. Washburne	IL	1869
	Hamilton Fish	NY	1869
Hayes	Hamilton Fish	NY	1877
	William M. Evarts	NY	1877
Garfield	William M. Evarts	NY	1881
	James G. Blaine	ME	1881
Arthur	James G. Blaine	ME	1881
	F. T. Frelinghuysen	NJ	1881
Cleveland	F. T. Frelinghuysen	NJ	1885
	Thomas F. Bayard	DE	1885
Harrison, B.	Thomas F. Bayard	DE	1889
	James G. Blaine	ME	1889
	John W. Foster	IN	1892
Cleveland	Walter Q. Gresham	IN	1893
	Richard Olney	MA	1895
McKinley	Richard Olney	MA	1897
	John Sherman	OH	1897
	William R. Day	OH	1898
	John M. Hay	DC	1898
Roosevelt, T.	John M. Hay	DC	1901
	Elihu Root	NY	1905
	Robert Bacon	NY	1909
Taft	Robert Bacon	NY	1909
	Philander C. Knox	PA	1909

President	Secretary	Home	Sworn in
Wilson	Philander C. Knox	PA	1913
	William J. Bryan	NE	1913
	Robert Lansing	NY	1915
	Bainbridge Colby	NY	1920
Harding	Charles E. Hughes	NY	1921
Coolidge	Charles E. Hughes	NY	1923
	Frank B. Kellogg	MN	1925
Hoover	Frank B. Kellogg	MN	1929
	Henry L. Stimson	NY	1929
Roosevelt, F. D.	Cordell Hull	TN	1933
	Edward R. Stettinius Jr.	VA	1944
Truman	Edward R. Stettinius Jr.	VA	1945
	James F. Byrnes	SC	1945
	George C. Marshall	PA	1947
	Dean G. Acheson	CT	1949
Eisenhower	John Foster Dulles	NY	1953
	Christian A. Herter	MA	1959
Kennedy	D. Dean Rusk	GA	1961
Johnson, L. B.	D. Dean Rusk	GA	1963
Nixon	William P. Rogers	NY	1969
	Henry A. Kissinger	DC	1973
Ford	Henry A. Kissinger	DC	1974
Carter	Cyrus R. Vance	NY	1977
	Edmund S. Muskie	ME	1980
Reagan	Alexander M. Haig Jr.	CT	1981
	George P. Shultz	CA	1982
Bush, G. H. W.	James A. Baker III	TX	1989
	Lawrence S. Eagleburger	MI	1992
Clinton	Warren M. Christopher	CA	1993
	Madeleine K. Albright	DC	1997
Bush, G. W.	Colin L. Powell	NY	2001
	Condoleezza Rice	AL	2005
Obama	Hillary Rodham Clinton	NY	2009
	John Kerry	MA	2013
Trump	Rex W. Tillerson	TX	2017
	Mike Pompeo	KS	2018
Biden	Antony Blinken	NY	2021

Department of the Treasury

1500 Pennsylvania Ave. NW, 20220; www.treasury.gov

Organized by act of Congress on Sept. 2, 1789. Responsible for the fiscal affairs of the U.S. Serves as the government's financial agent; collects, borrows, and disburses funds for the federal government. Monitors the nation's financial infrastructure and economic development; recommends domestic and international financial, monetary, economic, trade, and tax policies. Manufactures currency and coins. Carries out monetary and tax law enforcement activities, sanctions, embargoes, and fights illicit finance—counterfeiting, money laundering, narcotics trafficking, terrorist financing. **Budget** (including interest on the public debt): $1.15 tril (2020); $1.63 tril (2021); $1.16 tril (2022); $1.10 tril (2023 est.); $1.43 tril (2024 est.).

- Alcohol and Tobacco Tax and Trade Bureau (1310 G St. NW, Box 12, 20005); www.ttb.gov
- Bureau of Engraving and Printing (14th and C Sts. SW, 20228); www.moneyfactory.gov
- Bureau of the Fiscal Service (401 14th St. SW, 20227); www.fiscal.treasury.gov
- Internal Revenue Service (1111 Constitution Ave. NW, 20224); www.irs.gov
- Office of the Comptroller of the Currency (400 7th St. SW, 20219); www.occ.gov
- U.S. Mint (801 9th St. NW, 20220); www.usmint.gov

Secretaries of the Treasury

President	Secretary	Home	Sworn in
Washington	Alexander Hamilton	NY	1789
	Oliver Wolcott Jr.	CT	1795
Adams, J.	Oliver Wolcott Jr.	CT	1797
	Samuel Dexter	MA	1801
Jefferson	Samuel Dexter	MA	1801
	Albert Gallatin	PA	1801
Madison	Albert Gallatin	PA	1809
	George W. Campbell	TN	1814
	Alexander J. Dallas	PA	1814
	William H. Crawford	GA	1816
Monroe	William H. Crawford	GA	1817
Adams, J. Q.	Richard Rush	PA	1825

President	Secretary	Home	Sworn in
Jackson	Samuel D. Ingham	PA	1829
	Louis McLane	DE	1831
	William J. Duane	PA	1833
	Roger B. Taney	MD	1833
	Levi Woodbury	NH	1834
Van Buren	Levi Woodbury	NH	1837
Harrison, W. H.	Thomas Ewing	OH	1841
Tyler	Thomas Ewing	OH	1841
	Walter Forward	PA	1841
	John C. Spencer	NY	1843
	George M. Bibb	KY	1844
Polk	Robert J. Walker	MS	1845
Taylor	William M. Meredith	PA	1849
Fillmore	Thomas Corwin	OH	1850
Pierce	James Guthrie	KY	1853
Buchanan	Howell Cobb	GA	1857
	Phillip F. Thomas	MD	1860
	John A. Dix	NY	1861
Lincoln	Salmon P. Chase	OH	1861
	William P. Fessenden	ME	1864
	Hugh McCulloch	IN	1865
Johnson, A.	Hugh McCulloch	IN	1865
Grant	George S. Boutwell	MA	1869
	William A. Richardson	MA	1873
	Benjamin H. Bristow	KY	1874
	Lot M. Morrill	ME	1876
Hayes	John Sherman	OH	1877
Garfield	William Windom	MN	1881
Arthur	Charles J. Folger	NY	1881
	Walter Q. Gresham	IN	1884
	Hugh McCulloch	IN	1884
Cleveland	Daniel Manning	NY	1885
	Charles S. Fairchild	NY	1887
Harrison, B.	William Windom	MN	1889
	Charles Foster	OH	1891
Cleveland	John G. Carlisle	KY	1893
McKinley	Lyman J. Gage	IL	1897
Roosevelt, T.	Lyman J. Gage	IL	1901
	Leslie M. Shaw	IA	1902
	George B. Cortelyou	NY	1907
Taft	Franklin MacVeagh	IL	1909
Wilson	William G. McAdoo	NY	1913
	Carter Glass	VA	1918
	David F. Houston	MO	1920
Harding	Andrew W. Mellon	PA	1921
Coolidge	Andrew W. Mellon	PA	1923
Hoover	Andrew W. Mellon	PA	1929
	Ogden L. Mills	NY	1932
Roosevelt, F. D.	William H. Woodin	NY	1933
	Henry Morgenthau Jr.	NY	1934
Truman	Fred M. Vinson	KY	1945
	John W. Snyder	MO	1946
Eisenhower	George M. Humphrey	OH	1953
	Robert B. Anderson	CT	1957
Kennedy	C. Douglas Dillon	NJ	1961
Johnson, L. B.	C. Douglas Dillon	NJ	1963
	Henry H. Fowler	VA	1965
	Joseph W. Barr	IN	1968
Nixon	David M. Kennedy	IL	1969
	John B. Connally	TX	1971
	George P. Shultz	IL	1972
	William E. Simon	NJ	1974
Ford	William E. Simon	NJ	1974
Carter	W. Michael Blumenthal	MI	1977
	G. William Miller	RI	1979
Reagan	Donald T. Regan	NY	1981
	James A. Baker III	TX	1985
	Nicholas F. Brady	NJ	1988
Bush, G. H. W.	Nicholas F. Brady	NJ	1989
Clinton	Lloyd M. Bentsen	TX	1993
	Robert E. Rubin	NY	1995
	Lawrence H. Summers	CT	1999
Bush, G. W.	Paul H. O'Neill	MO	2001
	John W. Snow	OH	2003
	Henry M. Paulson Jr.	FL	2006
Obama	Timothy F. Geithner	NY	2009
	Jack Lew	NY	2013
Trump	Steven T. Mnuchin	NY	2017
Biden	Janet Yellin	NY	2021

Department of Defense

1400 Defense Pentagon, 20301; www.defense.gov

The Dept. of Defense, originally designated the National Military Establishment, was created on Sept. 18, 1947. Directs and controls the armed forces and assists the president in protecting the nation's security. Military departments of the Army, Navy, and Air Force are each separately organized under its own secretary but all function under the command of the secretary of defense. They conduct military operations as unified commands. The chairman of the Joint Chiefs of Staff is the principal military adviser to the president. Undersecretaries supervise acquisition, technology, and logistics; intelligence; personnel and readiness; and policy. **Budget** for military programs: $690.4 bil (2020); $717.6 bil (2021); $726.6 bil (2022); $771.3 bil (2023 est.); $863.0 bil (2024 est.). **Budget** for civil programs: $72.9 bil (2020); $66.0 bil (2021); $65.1 bil (2022); $78.8 bil (2023 est.); $80.7 bil (2024 est.).

- Def. Advanced Research Projects Agency (675 N. Randolph St., Arlington, VA 22203); www.darpa.mil
- Def. Intelligence Agency (200 MacDill Blvd., 20340); www.dia.mil
- Def. Security Cooperation Agency (2800 Defense Pentagon, 20301); www.dsca.mil
- Missile Def. Agency (5700 18th St., Bldg. 245, Fort Belvoir, VA 22060); www.mda.mil
- Natl. Geospatial-Intelligence Agency (7500 GEOINT Dr., MS N73-OCCAE, Springfield, VA 22150); www.nga.mil
- Natl. Security Agency (9800 Savage Rd., Ste. 6272, Ft. Meade, MD 20755); www.nsa.gov

Secretaries of Defense

President	Secretary	Home	Sworn in
Truman	James V. Forrestal	NY	1947
	Louis A. Johnson	WV	1949
	George C. Marshall	PA	1950
	Robert A. Lovett	NY	1951
Eisenhower	Charles E. Wilson	MI	1953
	Neil H. McElroy	OH	1957
	Thomas S. Gates Jr.	PA	1959
Kennedy	Robert S. McNamara	MI	1961
Johnson, L. B.	Robert S. McNamara	MI	1963
	Clark M. Clifford	MD	1968
Nixon	Melvin R. Laird	WI	1969
	Elliot L. Richardson	MA	1973
	James R. Schlesinger	VA	1973
Ford	James R. Schlesinger	VA	1974
	Donald H. Rumsfeld	IL	1975
Carter	Harold Brown	CA	1977
Reagan	Caspar W. Weinberger	CA	1981
	Frank C. Carlucci	PA	1987
Bush, G. H. W.	Richard B. Cheney	WY	1989
Clinton	Les Aspin	WI	1993
	William J. Perry	CA	1994
	William S. Cohen	ME	1997
Bush, G. W.	Donald H. Rumsfeld	IL	2001
	Robert M. Gates	TX	2006
Obama	Robert M. Gates	TX	2009
	Leon E. Panetta	CA	2011
	Chuck Hagel	NE	2013
	Ashton Carter	PA	2015
Trump	James Mattis	WA	2017
	Mark T. Esper	PA	2019
Biden	Lloyd Austin	GA	2021

Secretaries of War

The War Dept. (which included jurisdiction over the Navy until 1798) was created by act of Congress on Aug. 7, 1789.

President	Secretary	Home	Sworn in
Washington	Henry Knox	MA	1789
	Timothy Pickering	PA	1795
	James McHenry	MD	1796
Adams, J.	James McHenry	MD	1797
	Samuel Dexter	MA	1800
Jefferson	Henry Dearborn	MA	1801
Madison	William Eustis	MA	1809
	John Armstrong	NY	1813
	James Monroe	VA	1814
	William H. Crawford	GA	1815
Monroe	John C. Calhoun	SC	1817
Adams, J. Q.	James Barbour	VA	1825
	Peter B. Porter	NY	1828
Jackson	John H. Eaton	TN	1829
	Lewis Cass	MI	1831
	Benjamin F. Butler	NY	1837
Van Buren	Joel R. Poinsett	SC	1837
Harrison, W. H.	John Bell	TN	1841
Tyler	John Bell	TN	1841
	John C. Spencer	NY	1841
	James M. Porter	PA	1843
	William Wilkins	PA	1844
Polk	William L. Marcy	NY	1845
Taylor	George W. Crawford	GA	1849
Fillmore	Charles M. Conrad	LA	1850

President	Secretary	Home	Sworn in
Pierce	Jefferson Davis	MS	1853
Buchanan	John B. Floyd	VA	1857
	Joseph Holt	KY	1861
Lincoln	Simon Cameron	PA	1861
	Edwin M. Stanton	PA	1862
Johnson, A.	Edwin M. Stanton	PA	1865
	John M. Schofield	IL	1868
Grant	John A. Rawlins	IL	1869
	William T. Sherman	OH	1869
	William W. Belknap	IA	1869
	Alphonso Taft	OH	1876
	James D. Cameron	PA	1876
Hayes	George W. McCrary	IA	1877
	Alexander Ramsey	MN	1879
Garfield	Robert T. Lincoln	IL	1881
Arthur	Robert T. Lincoln	IL	1881
Cleveland	William C. Endicott	MA	1885
Harrison, B.	Redfield Proctor	VT	1889
	Stephen B. Elkins	WV	1891
Cleveland	Daniel S. Lamont	NY	1893
McKinley	Russell A. Alger	MI	1897
	Elihu Root	NY	1899
Roosevelt, T.	Elihu Root	NY	1901
	William H. Taft	OH	1904
	Luke E. Wright	TN	1908
Taft	Jacob M. Dickinson	TN	1909
	Henry L. Stimson	NY	1911
Wilson	Lindley M. Garrison	NJ	1913
	Newton D. Baker	OH	1916
Harding	John W. Weeks	MA	1921
Coolidge	John W. Weeks	MA	1923
	Dwight F. Davis	MO	1925
Hoover	James W. Good	IL	1929
	Patrick J. Hurley	OK	1929
Roosevelt, F. D.	George H. Dern	UT	1933
	Harry H. Woodring	KS	1937
	Henry L. Stimson	NY	1940
Truman	Robert P. Patterson	NY	1945
	Kenneth C. Royall[1]	NC	1947

(1) Last member of Cabinet with this title. The War Dept. became the Dept. of the Army with the creation of the Defense Dept. in 1947, though the Army secretary maintained Cabinet-level status until 1949.

Secretaries of the Navy

The Navy Dept. was created by act of Congress on Apr. 30, 1798. The Marine Corps is part of this department.

President	Secretary	Home	Sworn in
Adams, J.	Benjamin Stoddert	MD	1798
Jefferson	Benjamin Stoddert	MD	1801
	Robert Smith	MD	1801
Madison	Paul Hamilton	SC	1809
	William Jones	PA	1813
	Benjamin W. Crowninshield	MA	1814
Monroe	Benjamin W. Crowninshield	MA	1817
	Smith Thompson	NY	1818
	Samuel L. Southard	NJ	1823
Adams, J. Q.	Samuel L. Southard	NJ	1825
Jackson	John Branch	NC	1829
	Levi Woodbury	NH	1831
	Mahlon Dickerson	NJ	1834
Van Buren	Mahlon Dickerson	NJ	1837
	James K. Paulding	NY	1838
Harrison, W. H.	George E. Badger	NC	1841
Tyler	George E. Badger	NC	1841
	Abel P. Upshur	VA	1841
	David Henshaw	MA	1843
	Thomas W. Gilmer	VA	1844
	John Y. Mason	VA	1844
Polk	George Bancroft	MA	1845
	John Y. Mason	VA	1846
Taylor	William B. Preston	VA	1849
Fillmore	William A. Graham	NC	1850
	John P. Kennedy	MD	1852
Pierce	James C. Dobbin	NC	1853
Buchanan	Isaac Toucey	CT	1857
Lincoln	Gideon Welles	CT	1861
Johnson, A.	Gideon Welles	CT	1865
Grant	Adolph E. Borie	PA	1869
	George M. Robeson	NJ	1869
Hayes	Richard W. Thompson	IN	1877
	Nathan Goff Jr.	WV	1881
Garfield	William H. Hunt	LA	1881
Arthur	William E. Chandler	NH	1882

President	Secretary	Home	Sworn in
Cleveland	William C. Whitney	NY	1885
Harrison, B.	Benjamin F. Tracy	NY	1889
Cleveland	Hilary A. Herbert	AL	1893
McKinley	John D. Long	MA	1897
Roosevelt, T.	John D. Long	MA	1901
	William H. Moody	MA	1902
	Paul Morton	IL	1904
	Charles J. Bonaparte	MD	1905
	Victor H. Metcalf	CA	1906
	Truman H. Newberry	MI	1908
Taft	George von L. Meyer	MA	1909
Wilson	Josephus Daniels	NC	1913
Harding	Edwin Denby	MI	1921
Coolidge	Edwin Denby	MI	1923
	Curtis D. Wilbur	CA	1924
Hoover	Charles Francis Adams	MA	1929
Roosevelt, F. D.	Claude A. Swanson	VA	1933
	Charles Edison	NJ	1940
	Frank Knox	IL	1940
	James V. Forrestal	NY	1944
Truman	James V. Forrestal[1]	NY	1945

(1) Last member of Cabinet with this title. The Navy Dept. became a branch of the Dept. of Defense when the latter was created in 1947, though the Navy secretary maintained Cabinet-level status until 1949.

Department of Justice

950 Pennsylvania Ave. NW, 20530; www.justice.gov

The Office of Attorney General was established by act of Congress on Sept. 24, 1789. It officially reached Cabinet rank in Mar. 1792, when the first attorney general, Edmund Randolph, attended his initial Cabinet meeting. The Dept. of Justice, headed by the attorney general, was created June 22, 1870. Provides for the enforcement of federal laws and investigation of violations; furnishes legal counsel in cases involving the federal government and interprets laws relating to the activities of other federal departments; supervises federal penal institutions. The attorney general and Office of Legal Counsel render legal advice, upon request, to the president and department heads. The solicitor general conducts all suits brought before the U.S. Supreme Court in which the federal government is concerned. The Civil Division represents the U.S. government in many civil or criminal matters. The 93 U.S. attorneys (for 94 federal districts) are the principal litigators in the U.S. and its territories.
Budget: $39.6 bil (2020); $39.3 bil (2021); $39.6 bil (2022); $49.6 bil (2023 est.); $48.2 bil (2024 est.).

- Bureau of Alcohol, Tobacco, Firearms and Explosives (99 New York Ave. NE, 20226); www.atf.gov
- Drug Enforcement Admin. (8701 Morrissette Dr., Springfield, VA 22152); www.dea.gov
- Executive Office for Immigration Review (5107 Leesburg Pike, Ste. 1902, Falls Church, VA 22041); www.usdoj.gov/eoir
- Federal Bureau of Investigation (935 Pennsylvania Ave. NW, 20535); www.fbi.gov
- Federal Bureau of Prisons (320 First St. NW, 20534); www.bop.gov
- Foreign Claims Settlement Commission (441 G St. NW, Ste. 6330, 20579); www.justice.gov/fcsc
- INTERPOL Washington (U.S. Natl. Central Bureau) (20530); www.justice.gov/interpol-washington
- Office of Community Oriented Policing Services (145 N St. NE, 20530); www.cops.usdoj.gov
- Office of Justice Programs (810 Seventh St. NW, 20531); www.ojp.gov
- Office on Violence Against Women (145 N St. NE, Ste. 10W-121, 20530); www.justice.gov/ovw
- U.S. Marshals Service (20530); www.usmarshals.gov
- U.S. Parole Commission (90 K St. NE, 20530); www.justice.gov/uspc

Attorneys General

President	Attorney General	Home	Sworn in
Washington	Edmund J. Randolph	VA	1789
	William Bradford	PA	1794
	Charles Lee	VA	1795
Adams, J.	Charles Lee	VA	1797
Jefferson	Levi Lincoln	MA	1801
	John Breckenridge	KY	1805
	Caesar A. Rodney	DE	1807
Madison	Caesar A. Rodney	DE	1807
	William Pinkney	MD	1811
	Richard Rush	PA	1814

President	Attorney General	Home	Sworn in
Monroe	Richard Rush	PA	1817
	William Wirt	VA	1817
Adams, J. Q.	William Wirt	VA	1825
Jackson	John M. Berrien	GA	1829
	Roger B. Taney	MD	1831
	Benjamin F. Butler	NY	1833
Van Buren	Benjamin F. Butler	NY	1837
	Felix Grundy	TN	1838
	Henry D. Gilpin	PA	1840
Harrison, W. H.	John J. Crittenden	KY	1841
Tyler	John J. Crittenden	KY	1841
	Hugh S. Legaré	SC	1841
	John Nelson	MD	1843
Polk	John Y. Mason	VA	1845
	Nathan Clifford	ME	1846
	Isaac Toucey	CT	1848
Taylor	Reverdy Johnson	MD	1849
Fillmore	John J. Crittenden	KY	1850
Pierce	Caleb Cushing	MA	1853
Buchanan	Jeremiah S. Black	PA	1857
	Edwin M. Stanton	PA	1860
Lincoln	Edward Bates	MO	1861
	James Speed	KY	1864
Johnson, A.	James Speed	KY	1865
	Henry Stanbery	OH	1866
	William M. Evarts	NY	1868
Grant	Ebenezer R. Hoar	MA	1869
	Amos T. Akerman	GA	1870
	George H. Williams	OR	1871
	Edwards Pierrepont	NY	1875
	Alphonso Taft	OH	1876
Hayes	Charles Devens	MA	1877
Garfield	I. Wayne MacVeagh	PA	1881
Arthur	Benjamin H. Brewster	PA	1882
Cleveland	Augustus H. Garland	AR	1885
Harrison, B.	William H. H. Miller	IN	1889
Cleveland	Richard Olney	MA	1893
	Judson Harmon	OH	1895
McKinley	Joseph McKenna	CA	1897
	John W. Griggs	NJ	1898
	Philander C. Knox	PA	1901
Roosevelt, T.	Philander C. Knox	PA	1901
	William H. Moody	MA	1904
	Charles J. Bonaparte	MD	1906
Taft	George W. Wickersham	NY	1909
Wilson	James C. McReynolds	TN	1913
	Thomas W. Gregory	TX	1914
	A. Mitchell Palmer	PA	1919
Harding	Harry M. Daugherty	OH	1921
Coolidge	Harry M. Daugherty	OH	1923
	Harlan F. Stone	NY	1924
	John G. Sargent	VT	1925
Hoover	William D. Mitchell	MN	1929
Roosevelt, F. D.	Homer S. Cummings	CT	1933
	Frank Murphy	MI	1939
	Robert H. Jackson	NY	1940
	Francis Biddle	PA	1941
Truman	Thomas C. Clark	TX	1945
	J. Howard McGrath	RI	1949
	James P. McGranery	PA	1952
Eisenhower	Herbert Brownell Jr.	NY	1953
	William P. Rogers	MD	1957
Kennedy	Robert F. Kennedy	MA	1961
Johnson, L. B.	Robert F. Kennedy	MA	1963
	Nicholas Katzenbach	IL	1964
	W. Ramsey Clark	TX	1967
Nixon	John N. Mitchell	NY	1969
	Richard G. Kleindienst	AZ	1972
	Elliot L. Richardson	MA	1973
	William B. Saxbe	OH	1974
Ford	William B. Saxbe	OH	1974
	Edward H. Levi	IL	1975
Carter	Griffin B. Bell	GA	1977
	Benjamin R. Civiletti	MD	1979
Reagan	William French Smith	CA	1981
	Edwin Meese III	CA	1985
	Richard L. Thornburgh	PA	1988
Bush, G. H. W.	Richard L. Thornburgh	PA	1989
	William P. Barr	NY	1991
Clinton	Janet Reno	FL	1993
Bush, G. W.	John Ashcroft	MO	2001
	Alberto R. Gonzales	TX	2005
	Michael B. Mukasey	NY	2007
Obama	Eric H. Holder Jr.	DC	2009
	Loretta E. Lynch	NY	2015
Trump	Jeff Sessions	AL	2017
	William P. Barr	NY	2019
Biden	Merrick Garland	IL	2021

Department of the Interior

1849 C St. NW, 20240; www.doi.gov

Created by act of Congress on Mar. 3, 1849. Custodian of natural resources. Has the responsibility of protecting and conserving the country's land, water, minerals, fish, and wildlife; of promoting the wise use of all these natural resources; of maintaining national parks and recreation areas; and of preserving historic places. It also provides for the welfare of American Indian reservation communities and of inhabitants of island territories under U.S. administration. **Budget:** $16.4 bil (2020); $15.8 bil (2021); $13.9 bil (2022); $23.8 bil (2023 est.); $25.4 bil (2024 est.).

- Bureau of Indian Affairs; www.bia.gov
- Bureau of Indian Education; www.bie.edu
- Bureau of Land Management; www.blm.gov
- Bureau of Ocean Energy Management; www.boem.gov
- Bureau of Reclamation; www.usbr.gov
- Bureau of Safety and Environmental Enforcement; www.bsee.gov
- National Park Service; www.nps.gov
- Office of Surface Mining Reclamation and Enforcement; www.osmre.gov
- U.S. Fish and Wildlife Service; www.fws.gov
- U.S. Geological Survey (12201 Sunrise Valley Dr., Reston, VA 20192); www.usgs.gov

Secretaries of the Interior

President	Secretary	Home	Sworn in
Taylor	Thomas Ewing	OH	1849
Fillmore	Thomas M. T. McKennan	PA	1850
	Alex H. H. Stuart	VA	1850
Pierce	Robert McClelland	MI	1853
Buchanan	Jacob Thompson	MS	1857
Lincoln	Caleb B. Smith	IN	1861
	John P. Usher	IN	1863
Johnson, A.	John P. Usher	IN	1865
	James Harlan	IA	1865
	Orville H. Browning	IL	1866
Grant	Jacob D. Cox	OH	1869
	Columbus Delano	OH	1870
	Zachariah Chandler	MI	1875
Hayes	Carl Schurz	MO	1877
Garfield	Samuel J. Kirkwood	IA	1881
Arthur	Henry M. Teller	CO	1882
Cleveland	Lucius Q. C. Lamar	MS	1885
	William F. Vilas	WI	1888
Harrison, B.	John W. Noble	MO	1889
Cleveland	M. Hoke Smith	GA	1893
	David R. Francis	MO	1896
McKinley	Cornelius N. Bliss	NY	1897
	Ethan A. Hitchcock	MO	1898
Roosevelt, T.	Ethan A. Hitchcock	MO	1901
	James R. Garfield	OH	1907
Taft	Richard A. Ballinger	WA	1909
	Walter L. Fisher	IL	1911
Wilson	Franklin K. Lane	CA	1913
	John B. Payne	IL	1920
Harding	Albert B. Fall	NM	1921
	Hubert Work	CO	1923
Coolidge	Hubert Work	CO	1923
	Roy O. West	IL	1929
Hoover	Ray Lyman Wilbur	CA	1929
Roosevelt, F. D.	Harold L. Ickes	IL	1933
Truman	Harold L. Ickes	IL	1945
	Julius A. Krug	WI	1946
	Oscar L. Chapman	CO	1949
Eisenhower	Douglas McKay	OR	1953
	Fred A. Seaton	NE	1956
Kennedy	Stewart L. Udall	AZ	1961
Johnson, L. B.	Stewart L. Udall	AZ	1963
Nixon	Walter J. Hickel	AK	1969
	Rogers C. B. Morton	MD	1971
Ford	Rogers C. B. Morton	MD	1971
	Stanley K. Hathaway	WY	1975
	Thomas S. Kleppe	ND	1975
Carter	Cecil D. Andrus	ID	1977
Reagan	James G. Watt	CO	1981
	William P. Clark	CA	1983
	Donald P. Hodel	OR	1985
Bush, G. H. W.	Manuel Lujan	NM	1989
Clinton	Bruce Babbitt	AZ	1993
Bush, G. W.	Gale Norton	CO	2001
	Dirk Kempthorne	ID	2006
Obama	Kenneth L. Salazar	CO	2009
	Sally Jewell	WA	2013
Trump	Ryan Zinke	MT	2017
	David Bernhardt	CO	2019
Biden	Deb Haaland	NM	2021

Department of Agriculture

1400 Independence Ave. SW, 20250; www.usda.gov

Created by act of Congress on May 15, 1862. On Feb. 8, 1889, its commissioner was renamed secretary of agriculture and became a member of the Cabinet. Provides leadership on food, agriculture, and natural resources; supports scientific research and education for agriculture, nutrition, and food safety. Develops nutrition assistance programs, promotes healthy eating, supplies food stamps, grades and inspects the commercial supply of food. Responsible for the health of the land through sustainable management and conservation, manages public lands in national forests and grasslands; safeguards against invasive pests and diseases; ensures the health and care of animals and plants. Oversees assistance and conservation programs for farmers and ranchers and programs to improve the rural economy and quality of life. Facilitates domestic and international marketing of U.S. agricultural products. **Budget: $184.2 bil (2020); $235.2 bil (2021); $245.2 bil (2022); $260.6 bil (2023 est.); $229.7 bil (2024 est.).**

- Agricultural Research Service; www.ars.usda.gov
- Economic Research Service; www.ers.usda.gov
- Food and Nutrition Service (1320 Braddock Pl., Alexandria, VA 22314); www.fns.usda.gov
- Food Safety and Inspection Service; www.fsis.usda.gov
- Foreign Agricultural Service; www.fas.usda.gov
- Natl. Agricultural Statistics Service; www.nass.usda.gov
- Natural Resources Conservation Service; www.nrcs.usda.gov
- U.S. Forest Service; www.fs.usda.gov

Secretaries of Agriculture

President	Secretary	Home	Sworn in
Cleveland	Norman J. Colman	MO	1889
Harrison, B.	Jeremiah M. Rusk	WI	1889
Cleveland	J. Sterling Morton	NE	1893
McKinley	James Wilson	IA	1897
Roosevelt, T.	James Wilson	IA	1901
Taft	James Wilson	IA	1909
Wilson	David F. Houston	MO	1913
	Edwin T. Meredith	IA	1920
Harding	Henry C. Wallace	IA	1921
Coolidge	Henry C. Wallace	IA	1923
	Howard M. Gore	WV	1924
	William M. Jardine	KS	1925
Hoover	Arthur M. Hyde	MO	1929
Roosevelt, F. D.	Henry A. Wallace	IA	1933
	Claude R. Wickard	IN	1940
Truman	Clinton P. Anderson	NM	1945
	Charles F. Brannan	CO	1948
Eisenhower	Ezra Taft Benson	UT	1953
Kennedy	Orville L. Freeman	MN	1961
Johnson, L. B.	Orville L. Freeman	MN	1963
Nixon	Clifford M. Hardin	IN	1969
	Earl L. Butz	IN	1971
Ford	Earl L. Butz	IN	1974
	John A. Knebel	VA	1976
Carter	Bob Bergland	MN	1977
Reagan	John R. Block	IL	1981
	Richard E. Lyng	CA	1986
Bush, G. H. W.	Clayton K. Yeutter	NE	1989
	Edward Madigan	IL	1991
Clinton	Mike Espy	MS	1993
	Dan Glickman	KS	1995
Bush, G. W.	Ann M. Veneman	CA	2001
	Mike Johanns	NE	2005
	Ed Schafer	ND	2008
Obama	Tom Vilsack	IA	2009
Trump	Sonny Perdue	GA	2017
Biden	Tom Vilsack	IA	2021

Department of Commerce

1401 Constitution Ave. NW, 20230; www.commerce.gov

The Dept. of Commerce was formed by Congress Mar. 4, 1913, when it divided the Dept. of Commerce and Labor into two departments. Fosters, serves, and promotes the nation's economic development and technological advancement; supports the comprehension and use of the environment and its oceanic life; assists states, communities, and individuals with economic progress; promotes trade abroad and ensures an effective export control and treaty compliance system. Issues trademarks and patents, maintains measurement standards, and manages the federal telecommunications spectrum. Collects, analyzes, and distributes statistics regarding the nation and the economy through the Bureaus of the Census and of Economic Analysis. NOAA explores, monitors, and conserves oceans and coasts, tracks weather and other environmental data. **Budget: $15.9 bil (2020); $13.1 bil (2021); $11.7 bil (2022); $15.8 bil (2023 est.); $20.3 bil (2024 est.).**

- Bureau of Economic Analysis (4600 Silver Hill Rd., Suitland, MD 20746); www.bea.gov
- Minority Business Development Agency; www.mbda.gov
- Natl. Institute of Standards and Technology (100 Bureau Dr., Gaithersburg, MD 20899); www.nist.gov
- Natl. Oceanic and Atmospheric Admin.; www.noaa.gov
- Natl. Technical Information Service (5301 Shawnee Rd., Alexandria, VA 22312); www.ntis.gov
- Natl. Telecommunications and Information Admin.; www.ntia.doc.gov
- U.S. Census Bureau (4600 Silver Hill Rd., 20233); www.census.gov
- U.S. Patent and Trademark Office (600 Dulany St., Alexandria, VA 22314); www.uspto.gov

Secretaries of Commerce

President	Secretary	Home	Sworn in
Wilson	William C. Redfield	NY	1913
	Joshua W. Alexander	MO	1919
Harding	Herbert C. Hoover	CA	1921
Coolidge	Herbert C. Hoover	CA	1923
	William F. Whiting	MA	1928
Hoover	Robert P. Lamont	IL	1929
	Roy D. Chapin	MI	1932
Roosevelt, F. D.	Daniel C. Roper	SC	1933
	Harry L. Hopkins	NY	1939
	Jesse H. Jones	TX	1940
	Henry A. Wallace	IA	1945
Truman	Henry A. Wallace	IA	1945
	W. Averell Harriman	NY	1947
	Charles W. Sawyer	OH	1948
Eisenhower	Sinclair Weeks	MA	1953
	Lewis L. Strauss	NY	1958
	Frederick H. Mueller	MI	1959
Kennedy	Luther H. Hodges	NC	1961
Johnson, L. B.	Luther H. Hodges	NC	1963
	John T. Connor	NJ	1965
	Alex B. Trowbridge	NJ	1967
	Cyrus R. Smith	NY	1968
Nixon	Maurice H. Stans	MN	1969
	Peter G. Peterson	IL	1972
	Frederick B. Dent	SC	1973
Ford	Frederick B. Dent	SC	1974
	Rogers C. B. Morton	MD	1975
	Elliot L. Richardson	MA	1975
Carter	Juanita M. Kreps	NC	1977
	Philip M. Klutznick	IL	1979
Reagan	Malcolm Baldrige	CT	1981
	C. William Verity Jr.	OH	1987
Bush, G. H. W.	Robert A. Mosbacher	TX	1989
	Barbara H. Franklin	PA	1992
Clinton	Ronald H. Brown	DC	1993
	Mickey Kantor	CA	1996
	William M. Daley	IL	1997
	Norman Y. Mineta	CA	2000
Bush, G. W.	Donald L. Evans	TX	2001
	Carlos M. Gutierrez	MI	2005
Obama	Gary F. Locke	WA	2009
	John Bryson	CA	2011
	Penny Pritzker	IL	2013
Trump	Wilbur L. Ross Jr.	NJ	2017
Biden	Gina Raimondo	RI	2021

Secretaries of Commerce and Labor

The Dept. of Commerce and Labor was created by Congress on Feb. 14, 1903.

President	Secretary	Home	Sworn in
Roosevelt, T.	George B. Cortelyou	NY	1903
	Victor H. Metcalf	CA	1904
	Oscar S. Straus	NY	1906
Taft	Charles Nagel	MO	1909

Department of Labor

200 Constitution Ave. NW, 20210; www.dol.gov

The Dept. of Labor was formed by Congress Mar. 4, 1913, when it divided the Dept. of Commerce and Labor into two departments. Administers federal labor laws to foster, promote, and develop the welfare of job seekers, wage earners, and retirees of the U.S.; to improve working conditions; and to advance opportunities for profitable employment. Administers standards for wages and overtime pay, safety and health conditions, workers' compensation. Tracks changes in employment, prices, and other national economic measurements. Regulates pension and welfare benefit plans, the hiring and employment of migrant and seasonal workers, and requirements pertaining to the mining, construction, and transportation industries. Monitors labor unions and their funds. **Budget:** $477.5 bil (2020); $404.8 bil (2021); $51.7 bil (2022); $99.5 bil (2023 est.); $74.8 bil (2024 est.).

- Bureau of Labor Statistics (2 Massachusetts Ave. NE, 20212); www.bls.gov
- Employment and Training Admin.; www.doleta.gov
- Mine Safety and Health Admin. (201 12th St. S, Ste. 401, Arlington, VA 22202); www.msha.gov
- Occupational Safety and Health Admin.; www.osha.gov
- Wage and Hour Div.; www.dol.gov/whd

Secretaries of Labor

President	Secretary	Home	Sworn in
Wilson	William B. Wilson	PA	1913
Harding	James J. Davis	PA	1921
Coolidge	James J. Davis	PA	1923
Hoover	James J. Davis	PA	1929
	William N. Doak	VA	1930
Roosevelt, F. D.	Frances Perkins	NY	1933
Truman	L. B. Schwellenbach	WA	1945
	Maurice J. Tobin	MA	1949
Eisenhower	Martin P. Durkin	IL	1953
	James P. Mitchell	NJ	1953
Kennedy	Arthur J. Goldberg	IL	1961
	W. Willard Wirtz	IL	1962
Johnson, L. B.	W. Willard Wirtz	IL	1963
Nixon	George P. Shultz	IL	1969
	James D. Hodgson	CA	1970
	Peter J. Brennan	NY	1973
Ford	Peter J. Brennan	NY	1974
	John T. Dunlop	CA	1975
	W. J. Usery Jr.	GA	1976
Carter	F. Ray Marshall	TX	1977
Reagan	Raymond J. Donovan	NJ	1981
	William E. Brock	TN	1985
	Ann D. McLaughlin	DC	1987
Bush, G. H. W.	Elizabeth H. Dole	NC	1989
	Lynn Martin	IL	1991
Clinton	Robert B. Reich	MA	1993
	Alexis M. Herman	AL	1997
Bush, G. W.	Elaine L. Chao	KY	2001
Obama	Hilda L. Solis	CA	2009
	Thomas E. Perez	MD	2013
Trump	R. Alexander Acosta	FL	2017
	Eugene Scalia	DC	2019
Biden	Marty Walsh	MA	2021

Department of Housing and Urban Development

451 7th St. SW, 20410; www.hud.gov

Created by act of Congress on Sept. 9, 1965. Responsible for housing needs and the improvement and development of urban areas. Supports affordable housing, provides grants for community development and redevelopment. Enforces fair and safe housing standards. Provides funds to assist homeless individuals and families with emergency and transitional shelters. The Federal Housing Administration provides mortgage insurance on loans made by approved lenders. **Budget:** $33.2 bil (2020); $35.1 bil (2021); $29.3 bil (2022); $61.7 bil (2023 est.); $77.6 bil (2024 est.).

- Fannie Mae (Federal Natl. Mortgage Association) (1100 15th St. NW, 20005); www.fanniemae.com
- Federal Housing Admin.; www.hud.gov/ federal_housing_administration
- Freddie Mac (Federal Home Loan Mortgage Corporation) (8200 Jones Branch Dr., McLean, VA 22102); www.freddiemac.com
- Ginnie Mae (Government Natl. Mortgage Association) (425 3rd St. SW, Ste. 500, 20024); www.ginniemae.gov

Note: Fannie Mae and Freddie Mac are government-sponsored enterprises (GSEs).

Secretaries of Housing and Urban Development

President	Secretary	Home	Sworn in
Johnson, L. B.	Robert C. Weaver	WA	1966
	Robert C. Wood	MA	1969
Nixon	George W. Romney	MI	1969
	James T. Lynn	OH	1973
Ford	James T. Lynn	OH	1974
	Carla Anderson Hills	CA	1975
Carter	Patricia Roberts Harris	DC	1977
	Moon Landrieu	LA	1979
Reagan	Samuel R. Pierce Jr.	NY	1981
Bush, G. H. W.	Jack F. Kemp	NY	1989
Clinton	Henry G. Cisneros	TX	1993
	Andrew M. Cuomo	NY	1997
Bush, G. W.	Mel Martinez	FL	2001
	Alphonso Jackson	TX	2004
	Steve Preston	VA	2008
Obama	Shaun L. S. Donovan	NY	2009
	Julián Castro	TX	2014
Trump	Ben Carson	MD	2017
Biden	Marcia Fudge	OH	2021

Department of Transportation

1200 New Jersey Ave. SE, 20590; www.transportation.gov

Created by act of Congress on Oct. 15, 1966. Promotes and develops rapid, safe, efficient, and convenient transportation in the U.S.; monitors and administers assistance to transportation industries; negotiates and implements international transportation agreements. Manages airspace, commercial space transportation, and the movement of hazardous materials. Resolves railroad rate and service disputes and reviews proposed railroad mergers. Analyzes and shares research and statistics to develop and improve transportation. Develops and enforces regulations on the nation's pipeline transportation system. The Maritime Administration maintains a fleet of cargo ships in reserve for war or national emergencies and commissions officers of the Merchant Marine. Operates the U.S. portion of the St. Lawrence Seaway between Montréal and Lake Erie. **Budget:** $100.3 bil (2020); $104.9 bil (2021); $113.8 bil (2022); $115.0 bil (2023 est.); $125.4 bil (2024 est.).

- Federal Aviation Admin. (800 Independence Ave. SW, 20591); www.faa.gov
- Federal Highway Admin.; www.fhwa.dot.gov
- Federal Motor Carrier Safety Admin.; www.fmcsa.dot.gov
- Federal Railroad Admin.; www.fra.dot.gov
- Federal Transit Admin.; www.transit.dot.gov
- Maritime Admin.; www.maritime.dot.gov
- Natl. Highway Traffic Safety Admin.; www.nhtsa.gov
- Pipeline and Hazardous Materials Safety Admin.; www.phmsa.dot.gov
- St. Lawrence Seaway Development Corp.; www.seaway. dot.gov

Secretaries of Transportation

President	Secretary	Home	Sworn in
Johnson, L. B.	Alan S. Boyd	FL	1966
Nixon	John A. Volpe	MA	1969
	Claude S. Brinegar	CA	1973
Ford	Claude S. Brinegar	CA	1974
	William T. Coleman Jr.	PA	1975
Carter	Brock Adams	WA	1977
	Neil E. Goldschmidt	OR	1979
Reagan	Andrew L. Lewis Jr.	PA	1981
	Elizabeth H. Dole	NC	1983
	James H. Burnley	NC	1987
Bush, G. H. W.	Samuel K. Skinner	IL	1989
	Andrew H. Card Jr.	MA	1992
Clinton	Federico F. Peña	CO	1993
	Rodney E. Slater	AR	1997
Bush, G. W.	Norman Y. Mineta	CA	2001
	Mary E. Peters	AZ	2006
Obama	Raymond L. LaHood	IL	2009
	Anthony Foxx	NC	2013
Trump	Elaine L. Chao	KY	2017
Biden	Pete Buttigieg	IN	2021

Department of Energy

1000 Independence Ave. SW, 20585; www.energy.gov

Created by federal law on Aug. 4, 1977. Secures the nation's energy and promotes scientific and technological innovation. Oversees the national energy supply and electric grid. Investigates and promotes clean and reliable energy. Manages and cleans up nuclear and other radioactive material, including nuclear weapons. The Office of Scientific and Technical Information supports much of America's scientific research through program offices, education initiatives, national laboratories, and technology centers. Four power marketing administrations sell power from federal hydroelectric projects across the West and Southeast. **Budget:** $32.0 bil (2020); $33.7 bil (2021); $22.4 bil (2022); $43.2 bil (2023 est.); $59.5 bil (2024 est.).

- Federal Energy Regulatory Commission (independent regulatory agency) (888 1st St. NE, 20426); www.ferc.gov
- Natl. Nuclear Security Admin.; www.energy.gov/nnsa/national-nuclear-security-administration
- Science Office; www.energy.gov/science/office-science
- U.S. Energy Information Admin.; www.eia.gov

Secretaries of Energy

President	Secretary	Home	Sworn in
Carter	James R. Schlesinger	VA	1977
	Charles W. Duncan Jr.	WY	1979
Reagan	James B. Edwards	SC	1981
	Donald P. Hodel	OR	1982
	John S. Herrington	CA	1985
Bush, G. H. W.	James D. Watkins	CA	1989
Clinton	Hazel R. O'Leary	MN	1993
	Federico F. Peña	CO	1997
	Bill Richardson	NM	1998
Bush, G. W.	Spencer Abraham	MI	2001
	Samuel W. Bodman	MA	2005
Obama	Steven Chu	CA	2009
	Ernest Moniz	MA	2013
Trump	Rick Perry	TX	2017
	Dan Brouillette	TX	2019
Biden	Jennifer Granholm	MI	2021

Department of Health and Human Services

200 Independence Ave. SW, 20201; www.hhs.gov

The Dept. of Health, Education, and Welfare was created by Congress on Apr. 11, 1953. On Sept. 27, 1979, Congress approved creation of a separate Dept. of Education. The existing department was renamed the Dept. of Health and Human Services. Administers a wide range of programs in the fields of health care and social services that affect nearly all Americans. Medicare and Medicaid provide health care insurance for one in four Americans. The HRSA improves health care services for people who are uninsured, isolated, or medically vulnerable; oversees organ, tissue, and blood cell donations. The FDA assures the safety of food, drugs, cosmetics, biological products, and medical devices. The CDC monitors and safeguards against disease outbreaks. The NIH supports research projects nationwide and 27 health institutes and centers. The surgeon general is the nation's chief health educator and leads the U.S. Public Health Service Commissioned Corps. **Budget:** $1.50 tril (2020); $1.47 tril (2021); $1.64 tril (2022); $1.70 tril (2023 est.); $1.69 tril (2024 est.).

- Admin. for Children and Families (330 C St. SW, 20201); www.acf.hhs.gov
- Admin. for Community Living (330 C St. SW, 20201); www.acl.gov
- Agency for Healthcare Research and Quality (5600 Fishers Ln., Rockville, MD 20857); www.ahrq.gov
- Centers for Disease Control and Prevention (1600 Clifton Rd., Atlanta, GA 30333); www.cdc.gov
- Centers for Medicare and Medicaid Services (7500 Security Blvd., Baltimore, MD 21244); www.cms.gov
- Food and Drug Admin. (10903 New Hampshire Ave., Silver Spring, MD 20993); www.fda.gov
- Health Resources and Services Admin. (5600 Fishers Ln., Rockville, MD 20857); www.hrsa.gov
- Indian Health Service (5600 Fishers Ln., Rockville, MD 20857); www.ihs.gov
- Natl. Institutes of Health (9000 Rockville Pike, Bethesda, MD 20892); www.nih.gov
- Substance Abuse and Mental Health Services Admin. (5600 Fishers Ln., Rockville, MD 20857); www.samhsa.gov

Secretaries of Health and Human Services

President	Secretary	Home	Sworn in
Carter	Patricia Roberts Harris	DC	1979
Reagan	Richard S. Schweiker	PA	1981
	Margaret M. Heckler	MA	1983
Reagan	Otis R. Bowen	IN	1985
Bush, G. H. W.	Louis W. Sullivan	GA	1989
Clinton	Donna E. Shalala	WI	1993
Bush, G. W.	Tommy Thompson	WI	2001
	Michael O. Leavitt	UT	2005
Obama	Kathleen Sebelius	KS	2009
	Sylvia Mathews Burwell	WV	2014
Trump	Thomas E. Price	GA	2017
	Alex Azar	IN	2018
Biden	Xavier Becerra	CA	2021

Secretaries of Health, Education, and Welfare

President	Secretary	Home	Sworn in
Eisenhower	Oveta Culp Hobby	TX	1953
	Marion B. Folsom	NY	1955
	Arthur S. Flemming	OH	1958
Kennedy	Abraham A. Ribicoff	CT	1961
	Anthony J. Celebrezze	OH	1962
Johnson, L. B.	Anthony J. Celebrezze	OH	1963
	John W. Gardner	NY	1965
	Wilbur J. Cohen	MI	1968
Nixon	Robert H. Finch	CA	1969
	Elliot L. Richardson	MA	1970
	Caspar W. Weinberger	CA	1973
Ford	Caspar W. Weinberger	CA	1974
	Forrest D. Mathews	AL	1975
Carter	Joseph A. Califano Jr.	DC	1977
	Patricia Roberts Harris	DC	1979

Department of Education

400 Maryland Ave. SW, 20202; www.ed.gov

The Dept. of Health, Education, and Welfare was created by Congress on Apr. 11, 1953. On Sept. 27, 1979, Congress approved creation of a separate Dept. of Education. Works with state agencies and local systems to ensure equal access to all levels of education and seeks to improve the quality of that education through federal support, research programs, and information sharing. Oversees a variety of financial aid distributed through competition, need-based requests, or a set formula. Sets policy goals and initiatives. Conducts research and gathers educational information to disseminate to educators and the general public. **Budget:** $204.4 bil (2020); $260.4 bil (2021); $639.4 bil (2022); $226.2 bil (2023 est.); $171.5 bil (2024 est.).

Secretaries of Education

President	Secretary	Home	Sworn in
Carter	Shirley Hufstedler	CA	1979
Reagan	Terrel H. Bell	UT	1981
	William J. Bennett	NY	1985
	Lauro F. Cavazos	TX	1988
Bush, G. H. W.	Lauro F. Cavazos	TX	1989
	Lamar Alexander	TN	1991
Clinton	Richard W. Riley	SC	1993
Bush, G. W.	Roderick R. Paige	TX	2001
	Margaret Spellings	TX	2005
Obama	Arne Duncan	IL	2009
	John King	NY	2016
Trump	Betsy DeVos	MI	2017
Biden	Miguel Cardona	CT	2021

Department of Veterans Affairs

810 Vermont Ave. NW, 20420; www.va.gov

Pres. Ronald Reagan signed a bill in 1988 granting Cabinet-level status to the Veterans Administration. The agency became the Dept. of Veterans Affairs on Mar. 15, 1989. Supports veterans and their families with nationwide programs for health care, financial assistance, and burial benefits. Compensates for disabilities incurred during wartime. Provides pensions for veterans with low incomes, education assistance, loan guaranty, and life insurance. Manages America's largest medical education and health professions training program, which includes hospitals, clinics, nursing homes, veterans centers, rehabilitation treatment, readjustment counseling, and home-care programs. Also funds medical research pertaining to veterans issues. Manages 143 national cemeteries; provides headstones and markers. **Budget:** $218.4 bil (2020); $233.8 bil (2021); $273.9 bil (2022); $304.5 bil (2023 est.); $320.5 bil (2024 est.).

Secretaries of Veterans Affairs

President	Secretary	Home	Sworn in
Bush, G. H. W.	Edward J. Derwinski	IL	1989
Clinton	Jesse Brown	IL	1993
	Togo D. West Jr.	NC	1998
Bush, G. W.	Anthony J. Principi	CA	2001
	R. James Nicholson	CO	2005
	James B. Peake	MO	2007
Obama	Eric K. Shinseki	VA	2009
	Robert A. McDonald	OH	2014
Trump	David J. Shulkin	PA	2017
	Robert Wilkie	NC	2018
Biden	Denis McDonough	MD	2021

Department of Homeland Security

245 Murray Ln. SW, 20528; www.dhs.gov

Created by act of Congress on Nov. 25, 2002. Provides a unified core for the national network of organizations and institutions involved in efforts to secure the U.S., its borders, infrastructure, and major events. Provides funding, intelligence, and training for law enforcement and disaster relief. Leads and coordinates response teams to natural and manmade emergencies. Identifies threats, administers the Natl. Terrorism Advisory

System. **Budget:** $92.0 bil (2020); $91.1 bil (2021); $80.9 bil (2022); $100.0 bil (2023 est.); $99.5 bil (2024 est.).

- Cybersecurity and Infrastructure Security Agency (245 Murray Ln., 20528); www.cisa.gov
- Fed. Emergency Management Agency (500 C St. SW, 20472); www.fema.gov
- Transportation Security Admin.; www.tsa.gov
- U.S. Citizenship and Immigration Services (111 Massachusetts Ave. NW, MS 2260, 20529); www.uscis.gov
- U.S. Coast Guard (2703 Martin Luther King Jr. Ave. SE, 20593); www.uscg.mil
- U.S. Customs and Border Protection (1300 Pennsylvania Ave. NW, 20229); www.cbp.gov

- U.S. Immigration and Customs Enforcement (500 12th St. SW, 20536); www.ice.gov
- U.S. Secret Service (245 Murray Ln. SW - Bldg. T-5, 20223); www.secretservice.gov

Secretaries of Homeland Security

President	Secretary	Home	Sworn in
Bush, G. W.	Thomas Ridge	PA	2003
	Michael Chertoff	NJ	2005
Obama	Janet A. Napolitano	AZ	2009
	Jeh Johnson	NY	2014
Trump	John F. Kelly	MA	2017
	Kirstjen M. Nielsen	FL	2017
Biden	Alejandro Mayorkas	CA	2021

Other Notable U.S. Government Agencies

Source: *The U.S. Government Manual*; National Archives and Records Administration; World Almanac research
All addresses are for Washington, DC, unless otherwise noted; as of Aug. 2023.

Administrative Conference of the U.S.: Andrew Fois, chair (1120 20th St. NW, Ste. 706S, 20036); www.acus.gov

African Development Foundation: Travis Adkins, pres. and CEO (1400 I St. NW, 20005); www.usadf.gov

AmeriCorps (fmr. Corp. for Natl. and Community Service): Michael D. Smith, CEO (250 E St. SW, 20525); www.americorps.gov

Amtrak: Stephen J. Gardner, CEO (1 Massachusetts Ave. NW, 20001); www.amtrak.com

Central Intelligence Agency: William J. Burns, dir. (Cabinet rank) (20505); www.cia.gov

Commodity Futures Trading Commission: Rostin Behnam, chair (1155 21st St. NW, 20581); www.cftc.gov

Consumer Financial Protection Bureau: Rohit Chopra, dir. (1700 G St. NW, 20552); www.consumerfinance.gov

Consumer Product Safety Commission: Alexander Hoehn-Saric, chair (4330 East-West Hwy., Bethesda, MD 20814); www.cpsc.gov

Defense Nuclear Facilities Safety Board: Joyce L. Connery, chair (625 Indiana Ave. NW, Ste. 700, 20004); www.dnfsb.gov

Election Assistance Commission: Christy McCormick, chair (633 3rd Street NW, Ste. 200, 20001); www.eac.gov

Environmental Protection Agency: Michael S. Regan, admin. (Cabinet rank) (1200 Pennsylvania Ave. NW, 20460); www.epa.gov

Equal Employment Opportunity Commission: Charlotte A. Burrows, chair (131 M St. NE, 20507); www.eeoc.gov

Export-Import Bank of the U.S.: Reta Jo Lewis, chair (811 Vermont Ave. NW, 20571); www.exim.gov

Farm Credit Admin.: Vincent G. Logan, chair and CEO (1501 Farm Credit Dr., McLean, VA 22102); www.fca.gov

Federal Communications Commission: Jessica Rosenworcel, chair (45 L St. NE, 20554); www.fcc.gov

Federal Deposit Insurance Corp.: Martin J. Gruenberg, chair (550 17th St. NW, 20429); www.fdic.gov

Federal Election Commission: Dara Lindenbaum, chair (1050 1st St. NE, 20463); www.fec.gov

Federal Housing Finance Agency: Sandra L. Thompson, dir. (400 7th St. SW, 20219); www.fhfa.gov

Federal Labor Relations Authority: Susan Tsui Grundmann, chair (1400 K St. NW, 20424); www.flra.gov

Federal Maritime Commission: Daniel B. Maffei, chair (800 N. Capitol St. NW, 20573); www.fmc.gov

Federal Mediation and Conciliation Service: Gregory Goldstein, acting dir. (250 E St. SW, 20427); www.fmcs.gov

Federal Mine Safety and Health Review Commission: Mary Lu Jordan, chair (1331 Pennsylvania Ave. NW, Ste. 520N, 20004); www.fmshrc.gov

Federal Reserve System: Jerome H. Powell, chair (20th St. and Constitution Ave. NW, 20551); www.federalreserve.gov

Federal Retirement Thrift Investment Board: Mike Gerber, chair (77 K St. NE, Ste. 1000, 20002); www.frtib.gov

Federal Trade Commission: Lina Khan, chair (600 Pennsylvania Ave. NW, 20580); www.ftc.gov

General Services Admin.: Robin Carnahan, admin. (1800 F St. NW, 20405); www.gsa.gov

Institute of Museum and Library Services: Crosby Kemper III, dir. (955 L'Enfant Plaza North SW, Ste. 4000, 20024); www.imls.gov

Inter-American Foundation: Eddy Arriola, chair (1331 Pennsylvania Ave. NW, Ste. 1200N, 20004); www.iaf.gov

Merit Systems Protection Board: Cathy A. Harris, acting chair (1615 M St. NW, 5th Fl., 20419); www.mspb.gov

Natl. Aeronautics and Space Admin.: Bill Nelson, admin. (300 E St. SW, Ste. 5R30, 20546); www.nasa.gov

Natl. Archives and Records Admin.: Colleen Shogan, archivist (8601 Adelphi Rd., College Park, MD 20740); www.archives.gov

Natl. Capital Planning Commission: Elizabeth A. "Beth" White, chair (401 9th St. NW, Ste. 500N, 20004); www.ncpc.gov

Natl. Council on Disability: Andrés Gallegos, chair (1331 F St. NW, Ste. 850, 20004); www.ncd.gov

Natl. Credit Union Admin.: Todd M. Harper, chair (1775 Duke St., Alexandria, VA 22314); www.ncua.gov

Natl. Endowment for the Arts: Maria Rosario Jackson, chair (400 7th St. SW, 20506); www.arts.gov

Natl. Endowment for the Humanities: Shelly C. Lowe, chair (400 7th St. SW, 20506); www.neh.gov

Natl. Indian Gaming Commission: E. Sequoyah Simermeyer, chair (1849 C St. NW, Mail Stop 1621, 20240); www.nigc.gov

Natl. Labor Relations Board: Lauren McFerran, chair (1015 Half St. SE, 20570); www.nlrb.gov

Natl. Mediation Board: Deirdre Hamilton, chair (1301 K St. NW, Ste. 250E, 20005); www.nmb.gov

Natl. Science Foundation: Sethuraman Panchanathan, dir. (2415 Eisenhower Ave., Arlington, VA 22314); www.nsf.gov

Natl. Transportation Safety Board: Jennifer L. Homendy, chair (490 L'Enfant Plaza SW, 20594); www.ntsb.gov

Nuclear Regulatory Commission: Christopher T. Hanson, chair (20555); www.nrc.gov

Nuclear Waste Technical Review Board: Nathan Siu, chair (2300 Clarendon Blvd., Ste. 1300, Arlington, VA 22201); www.nwtrb.gov

Occupational Safety and Health Review Commission: Cynthia L. Attwood, chair (1120 20th St. NW, 9th Fl., 20036); www.oshrc.gov

Office of the Dir. of Natl. Intelligence: Avril Haines, dir. (Cabinet rank) (20511); www.dni.gov

Office of Government Ethics: Emory A. Rounds III, dir. (1201 New York Ave. NW, Ste. 500, 20005); www.oge.gov

Office of Personnel Management: Kiran Ahuja, dir. (1900 E St. NW, 20415); www.opm.gov

Office of Special Counsel: Henry Kerner, spec. counsel (1730 M St. NW, Ste. 218, 20036); www.osc.gov

Peace Corps: Carol Spahn, dir. (1275 1st St. NE, 20526); www.peacecorps.gov

Pension Benefit Guaranty Corp.: Gordon Hartogensis, dir. (1200 K St. NW, 20005); www.pbgc.gov

Postal Regulatory Commission: Michael M. Kubayanda, chair (901 New York Ave. NW, Ste. 200, 20268); www.prc.gov

Railroad Retirement Board: Erhard R. Chorlé, chair (844 N. Rush St., Chicago, IL 60611); www.rrb.gov

Securities and Exchange Commission: Gary Gensler, chair (100 F St. NE, 20549); www.sec.gov

Selective Service System: Joel C. Spangenberg, acting dir. (Natl. Headquarters, Arlington, VA 22209); www.sss.gov

Small Business Admin.: Isabella Casillas Guzman, admin. (Cabinet rank) (409 3rd St. SW, 20416); www.sba.gov

Social Security Admin.: Kilolo Kijakazi, acting comm. (1100 West High Rise, 6401 Security Blvd., Baltimore, MD 21235); www.ssa.gov

Tennessee Valley Authority: William Kilbride, chair (400 W. Summit Hill Dr., Knoxville, TN 37902); www.tva.gov

U.S. Agency for Global Media (fmr. Broadcasting Board of Governors): Amanda Bennett, CEO (330 Independence Ave. SW, 20037); www.usagm.gov

U.S. Agency for Intl. Development: Samantha Power, admin. (Ronald Reagan Bldg., 20523); www.usaid.gov

U.S. Commission on Civil Rights: chair vacant (1331 Pennsylvania Ave. NW, Ste. 1150, 20425); www.usccr.gov

U.S. Intl. Development Finance Corp. (fmr. Overseas Private Investment Corp.): Scott A. Nathan, CEO (1100 New York Ave. NW, 20527); www.dfc.gov

U.S. Intl. Trade Commission: David S. Johanson, chair (500 E St. SW, 20436); www.usitc.gov

U.S. Postal Service: Louis DeJoy, postmaster general and CEO (475 L'Enfant Plaza SW, 20260); www.usps.com

U.S. Trade and Development Agency: Enoh T. Ebong, dir. (1101 Wilson Blvd., Ste. 1100, Arlington, VA 22209); www.ustda.gov

CONGRESS

Floor Leaders in the U.S. Senate, 1920-2023

MAJORITY LEADERS				MINORITY LEADERS			
Name	Party	State	Tenure	Name	Party	State	Tenure
Charles Curtis[1]	Rep.	KS	1925-1929	Oscar W. Underwood[2]	Dem.	AL	1920-1923
James E. Watson	Rep.	IN	1929-1933	Joseph T. Robinson	Dem.	AR	1923-1933
Joseph T. Robinson	Dem.	AR	1933-1937	Charles L. McNary	Rep.	OR	1933-1944
Alben W. Barkley	Dem.	KY	1937-1947	Wallace H. White	Rep.	ME	1944-1947
Wallace H. White	Rep.	ME	1947-1949	Alben W. Barkley	Dem.	KY	1947-1949
Scott W. Lucas	Dem.	IL	1949-1951	Kenneth S. Wherry	Rep.	NE	1949-1951
Ernest W. McFarland	Dem.	AZ	1951-1953	Henry Styles Bridges	Rep.	NH	1952-1953
Robert A. Taft	Rep.	OH	1953	Lyndon B. Johnson	Dem.	TX	1953-1955
William F. Knowland	Rep.	CA	1953-1955	William F. Knowland	Rep.	CA	1955-1959
Lyndon B. Johnson	Dem.	TX	1955-1961	Everett M. Dirksen	Rep.	IL	1959-1969
Mike Mansfield	Dem.	MT	1961-1977	Hugh D. Scott	Rep.	PA	1969-1977
Robert C. Byrd	Dem.	WV	1977-1981	Howard H. Baker Jr.	Rep.	TN	1977-1981
Howard H. Baker Jr.	Rep.	TN	1981-1985	Robert C. Byrd	Dem.	WV	1981-1987
Robert J. Dole	Rep.	KS	1985-1987	Robert J. Dole	Rep.	KS	1987-1995
Robert C. Byrd	Dem.	WV	1987-1989	Thomas A. Daschle	Dem.	SD	1995-2001[3]
George J. Mitchell	Dem.	ME	1989-1995	Trent Lott	Rep.	MS	2001-2002[3,4]
Robert J. Dole	Rep.	KS	1995-1996	Thomas A. Daschle	Dem.	SD	2003-2005
Trent Lott	Rep.	MS	1996-2001[3]	Harry M. Reid	Dem.	NV	2005-2007
Thomas A. Daschle	Dem.	SD	2001-2003[3]	Mitch McConnell	Rep.	KY	2007-2015
William Frist	Rep.	TN	2003-2007[4]	Harry M. Reid	Dem.	NV	2015-2017
Harry M. Reid	Dem.	NV	2007-2015	Charles E. Schumer	Dem.	NY	2017-2021
Mitch McConnell	Rep.	KY	2015-2021	Mitch McConnell	Rep.	KY	2021-
Charles E. Schumer	Dem.	NY	2021-				

Note: The offices of party (majority and minority) leaders in the Senate did not evolve until the 20th century. (1) First Republican to be formally designated floor leader. Henry Cabot Lodge (MA) served as unofficial party leader prior to Curtis's election. (2) First Democrat to be designated floor leader. (3) Democrats held the majority Jan. 3, 2001, until Dick Cheney (R) was installed as vice pres., Jan. 20. Republicans subsequently lost the majority when Jim Jeffords (VT) switched his affiliation from Republican to Independent, June 6, 2001. (4) Trent Lott resigned from Republican leadership Dec. 20, 2002. William Frist was elected Republican leader Dec. 23, 2002, and began service Jan. 7, 2003, as majority leader.

Speakers of the U.S. House of Representatives, 1789-2023

Name	Party	State	Tenure	Name	Party	State	Tenure
Frederick A. C. Muhlenberg	Federalist	PA	1789-1791	Samuel J. Randall	Dem.	PA	1876-1881
Jonathan Trumbull	Federalist	CT	1791-1793	J. Warren Keifer	Rep.	OH	1881-1883
Frederick A. C. Muhlenberg	Federalist	PA	1793-1795	John G. Carlisle	Dem.	KY	1883-1889
Jonathan Dayton	Federalist	NJ	1795-1799	Thomas B. Reed	Rep.	ME	1889-1891
Theodore Sedgwick	Federalist	MA	1799-1801	Charles F. Crisp	Dem.	GA	1891-1895
Nathaniel Macon	Dem.-Rep.	NC	1801-1807	Thomas B. Reed	Rep.	ME	1895-1899
Joseph B. Varnum	Dem.-Rep.	MA	1807-1811	David B. Henderson	Rep.	IA	1899-1903
Henry Clay	Dem.-Rep.	KY	1811-1814	Joseph G. Cannon	Rep.	IL	1903-1911
Langdon Cheves	Dem.-Rep.	SC	1814-1815	Champ Clark	Dem.	MO	1911-1919
Henry Clay	Dem.-Rep.	KY	1815-1820	Frederick H. Gillett	Rep.	MA	1919-1925
John W. Taylor	Dem.-Rep.	NY	1820-1821	Nicholas Longworth	Rep.	OH	1925-1931
Philip P. Barbour	Dem.-Rep.	VA	1821-1823	John N. Garner	Dem.	TX	1931-1933
Henry Clay	Dem.-Rep.	KY	1823-1825	Henry T. Rainey	Dem.	IL	1933-1934
John W. Taylor	Dem.	NY	1825-1827	Joseph W. Byrns	Dem.	TN	1935-1936
Andrew Stevenson	Dem.	VA	1827-1834	William B. Bankhead	Dem.	AL	1936-1940
John Bell	Dem.	TN	1834-1835	Sam Rayburn	Dem.	TX	1940-1947
James K. Polk	Dem.	TN	1835-1839	Joseph W. Martin Jr.	Rep.	MA	1947-1949
Robert M. T. Hunter	Dem.	VA	1839-1841	Sam Rayburn	Dem.	TX	1949-1953
John White	Whig	KY	1841-1843	Joseph W. Martin Jr.	Rep.	MA	1953-1955
John W. Jones	Dem.	VA	1843-1845	Sam Rayburn	Dem.	TX	1955-1961
John W. Davis	Dem.	IN	1845-1847	John W. McCormack	Dem.	MA	1962-1971
Robert C. Winthrop	Whig	MA	1847-1849	Carl B. Albert	Dem.	OK	1971-1977
Howell Cobb	Dem.	GA	1849-1851	Thomas P. O'Neill Jr.	Dem.	MA	1977-1987
Linn Boyd	Dem.	KY	1851-1855	James C. Wright Jr.	Dem.	TX	1987-1989
Nathaniel P. Banks	American	MA	1856-1857	Thomas S. Foley	Dem.	WA	1989-1995
James L. Orr	Dem.	SC	1857-1859	Newt Gingrich	Rep.	GA	1995-1999
William Pennington	Rep.	NJ	1860-1861	J. Dennis Hastert	Rep.	IL	1999-2007
Galusha A. Grow	Rep.	PA	1861-1863	Nancy Pelosi	Dem.	CA	2007-2011
Schuyler Colfax	Rep.	IN	1863-1869	John Boehner	Rep.	OH	2011-2015
Theodore M. Pomeroy	Rep.	NY	1869	Paul Ryan	Rep.	WI	2015-2019
James G. Blaine	Rep.	ME	1869-1875	Nancy Pelosi	Dem.	CA	2019-2023
Michael C. Kerr	Dem.	IN	1875-1876	Kevin McCarthy	Rep.	CA	2023

Political Divisions of Congress, 1901-2023

Source: Office of the Clerk, U.S. House of Representatives; Congressional Research Service, Library of Congress
All figures reflect post-election party breakdown except where noted; **boldface** denotes party in majority after election.

		SENATE					HOUSE OF REPRESENTATIVES				
Congress	Years	Total members	Dem.	Rep.	Other parties	Vacant	Total members	Dem.	Rep.	Other parties	Vacant
57th	1901-1903	90	29	**56**	3	2	357	153	**198**	5	1
58th	1903-1905	90	32	**58**			386	178	**207**		1
59th	1905-1907	90	32	**58**			386	136	**250**		
60th	1907-1909	92	29	**61**		2	386	164	**222**		
61st	1909-1911	92	32	**59**		1	391	172	**219**		
62nd	1911-1913	92	42	**49**		1	391	**228**	162	1	
63rd	1913-1915	96	**51**	44	1		435	**290**	127	18	
64th	1915-1917	96	**56**	39	1		435	**231**	193	8	3
65th	1917-1919	96	**53**	42	1		435	**210**[1]	216	9	
66th	1919-1921	96	47	**48**	1		435	191	**237**	7	
67th	1921-1923	96	37	**59**			435	132	**300**	1	2
68th	1923-1925	96	43	**51**	2		435	207	**225**	3	

Congress	Years	SENATE Total members	Dem.	Rep.	Other parties	Vacant	HOUSE OF REPRESENTATIVES Total members	Dem.	Rep.	Other parties	Vacant
69th	1925-1927	96	40	54	1	1	435	183	247	5	
70th	1927-1929	96	47	48	1		435	195	237	3	
71st	1929-1931	96	39	56	1		435	163	267	1	4
72nd	1931-1933	96	47	48	1		435	216[2]	218	1	
73rd	1933-1935	96	59	36	1		435	313	117	5	
74th	1935-1937	96	69	25	2		435	322	103	10	
75th	1937-1939	96	75	17	4		435	333	89	13	
76th	1939-1941	96	69	23	-	4	435	262	169	4	
77th	1941-1943	96	66	28	1		435	267	162	6	
78th	1943-1945	96	57	38	1		435	222	209	4	
79th	1945-1947	96	57	38	1		435	243	190	2	
80th	1947-1949	96	45	51			435	188	246	1	
81st	1949-1951	96	54	42			435	263	171	1	
82nd	1951-1953	96	48	47	1		435	234	199	2	
83rd	1953-1955	96	46	48	2		435	213	221	1	
84th	1955-1957	96	48	47	1		435	232	203		
85th	1957-1959	96	49	47			435	234	201		
86th	1959-1961	98	64	34			436[3]	283	153		
87th	1961-1963	100	64	36			437[3]	262	175		
88th	1963-1965	100	67	33			435	258	176	1	
89th	1965-1967	100	68	32			435	295	140		
90th	1967-1969	100	64	36			435	248	187		
91st	1969-1971	100	58	42			435	243	192		
92nd	1971-1973	100	54	44	2		435	255	180		
93rd	1973-1975	100	56	42	2		435	242	192	1	
94th	1975-1977	100	61	37	2		435	291	144		
95th	1977-1979	100	61	38	1		435	292	143		
96th	1979-1981	100	58	41	1		435	277	158		
97th	1981-1983	100	46	53	1		435	242	192	1	
98th	1983-1985	100	46	54			435	269	166		
99th	1985-1987	100	47	53			435	253	182		
100th	1987-1989	100	55	45			435	258	177		
101st	1989-1991	100	55	45			435	260	175		
102nd	1991-1993	100	56	44			435	267	167	1	
103rd	1993-1995	100	57	43			435	258	176	1	
104th	1995-1997	100	48	52			435	204	230	1	
105th	1997-1999	100	45	55			435	207	226	2	
106th	1999-2001	100	45	55			435	211	223	1	
107th	2001-2003	100	50	50[4]			435	212	221	2	
108th	2003-2005	100	48	51	1		435	204	229	1	1
109th	2005-2007	100	44	55	1		435	202	232	1	
110th	2007-2009	100	49	49	2[5]		435	233	202		
111th	2009-2011	100	55	41	2[5]	2	435	256	178		1
112th	2011-2013	100	51	47	2[5]		435	193	242		
113th	2013-2015	100	53	45	2[5]		435	200	234		1
114th	2015-2017	100	44	54	2[5]		435	188	247		
115th	2017-2019	100	46	52	2[5]		435	194	241		
116th	2019-2021	100	45	53	2[5]		435	235	199		1
117th	2021-2023	100	48	50	2[5]		435	222	212		1
118th	2023-	100	48	49	3[5]		435	212	222		1

(1) Democrats organized the House with help of other parties. (2) Democrats organized the House because of Republican deaths. (3) Number of House seats was increased temporarily when proclamations were issued declaring Alaska (Jan. 3, 1959) and Hawaii (Aug. 21, 1959) new states. (4) While the Senate was split 50-50, control was held by whichever party had an incumbent vice president. Republican Sen. Jim Jeffords (VT) changed his party designation to Independent on June 6, 2001, switching control of the Senate to Democrats. (5) Independent senators chose to caucus with the Democrats.

Congressional Bills Vetoed, 1789-2023

Source: Virtual Reference Desk, U.S. Senate; as of Sept. 7, 2023

The president has 10 days (excluding Sundays) to consider a bill or joint resolution passed by Congress. The president can sign it into law or exercise a veto. Only a two-thirds vote in both the Senate and the House can override a regular veto. (A pocket veto cannot be overridden as it takes effect when Congress is adjourned.)

President	Regular vetoes	Pocket vetoes	Total vetoes	Vetoes overridden	President	Regular vetoes	Pocket vetoes	Total vetoes	Vetoes overridden
Washington	2	—	2	—	McKinley	6	36	42	—
J. Adams	—	—	—	—	T. Roosevelt	42	40	82	1
Jefferson	—	—	—	—	Taft	30	9	39	1
Madison	5	2	7	—	Wilson	33	11	44	6
Monroe	1	—	1	—	Harding	5	1	6	—
J. Q. Adams	—	—	—	—	Coolidge	20	30	50	4
Jackson	5	7	12	—	Hoover	21	16	37	3
Van Buren	—	1	1	—	F. D. Roosevelt	372	263	635	9
W. H. Harrison	—	—	—	—	Truman	180	70	250	12
Tyler	6	4	10	1	Eisenhower	73	108	181	2
Polk	2	1	3	—	Kennedy	12	9	21	—
Taylor	—	—	—	—	L. Johnson	16	14	30	—
Fillmore	—	—	—	—	Nixon	26	17	43	7
Pierce	9	—	9	5	Ford	48	18	66	12
Buchanan	4	3	7	—	Carter	13	18	31	2
Lincoln	2	5	7	—	Reagan	39	39	78	9
A. Johnson	21	8	29	15	G. H. W. Bush[3]	29	15	44	1
Grant	45	48	93	4	Clinton[4]	36	1	37	2
Hayes	12	1	13	1	G. W. Bush	12	—	12	4
Garfield	—	—	—	—	Obama	12	—	12	1
Arthur	4	8	12	1	Trump	10	—	10	1
Cleveland[1]	304	110	414	2	Biden	6	—	6	—
B. Harrison	19	25	44	1	**Total[3,4]**	**1,524**	**1,066**	**2,590**	**112**
Cleveland[2]	42	128	170	5					

— = 0. (1) First term only. (2) Second term only. (3) Excluded from the figures are two bills that Pres. George H. W. Bush claimed were pocket vetoed but which Congress considered to be enacted because the president had failed to return them during a Congressional recess. (4) Does not include line-item vetoes, which were ruled unconstitutional by the U.S. Supreme Court on June 25, 1998.

Congressional Firsts and Milestones

House of Representatives

First House meeting: Mar. 4, 1789, at Federal Hall in New York, NY. A quorum of 30 representatives was not reached until Apr. 1, 1789.

First House meeting in its current Capitol Building chamber: Dec. 16, 1857.

First former president to serve as representative: John Quincy Adams (MA, 1831-48); president, 1825-29.

First woman representative: Jeannette Rankin (R, MT, 1917-19, 1941-43).

First woman House speaker: Nancy Pelosi (D, CA), on Jan. 4, 2007.

First Black representative: Joseph Rainey (R, SC, 1870-79).

First Black woman representative: Shirley Chisholm (D, NY, 1969-83).

First American Indian women representatives: Deb Haaland (Laguna Pueblo) (D, NM, 2019-21) and Sharice Davids (Ho-Chunk) (D, KS, 2019-).

First Asian-Pacific American representative: India-born Dalip Saund (D, CA, 1957-63).

First elected Hispanic-American representative: Romualdo Pacheco (R, CA, 1877-83); Pacheco was born in California when it was Mexican territory.

First Jewish representative: Lewis Charles Levin (PA, 1845-51).

First Muslim representative: Keith Ellison (D, MN, 2007-19).

First Muslim women representatives: Ilhan Omar (D, MN, 2019-) and Rashida Tlaib (D, MI, 2019-). Omar was also the first Somali-American member of Congress and the first member to wear a hijab, or headscarf.

First representative to give birth in office: Yvonne Brathwaite Burke (D, CA, 1973-79), on Nov. 23, 1973.

Longest-serving representative: John Dingell Jr. (D, MI, 1955-2015), with more than 59 years of service.

Longest-serving House speaker: Sam Rayburn (D, TX, 1913-61), speaker for 17 years, 2 months, 2 days (non-consecutive).

Oldest representative: Ralph Hall (D-R, TX, 1981-2015); retired at age 91.

Youngest representative: William Charles Cole Claiborne (TN), who was elected at 22 years of age and began service Nov. 23, 1797.

First live-TV broadcast of House proceedings: Mar. 19, 1979, by public television and C-SPAN. Al Gore Jr. (D, TN) was the first representative to give a speech before cameras that day.

First declaration of war made by the House: June 4, 1812, against Great Britain and Ireland.

Senate

First Senate meeting: Mar. 4, 1789, at Federal Hall in New York, NY. A quorum of senators (12) was not reached until Apr. 6, 1789.

First Senate meeting in its current chamber in the Capitol Building: Jan. 4, 1859.

First woman senator: Rebecca Felton (D, GA, 1922). Appointed to a seat left vacant by a death, 87-year-old Felton served only 24 hours after being sworn in Nov. 21. (Felton was also the oldest freshman senator and the last senator to have been a slave owner.)

First elected woman senator: Hattie Caraway (D, AR, 1931-45). Appointed in 1931 to fill the vacancy left by the death of her husband, Thaddeus H. Caraway, she was elected in 1932.

First Black senator: Hiram R. Revels (R, MS, 1870-71).

First Black woman senator: Carol Moseley-Braun (D, IL, 1993-99).

First American Indian senators: Charles Curtis (Kaw) (R, KS, 1907-13, 1915-29) and Robert Owen (Cherokee) (D, OK, 1907-25).

First Hispanic American senator: Mexico-born Octaviano Larrazolo (R, NM, 1928-29).

First Asian American senator: Hiram L. Fong (R, HI, 1959-77).

First Jewish senator: David Levy Yulee (D, FL, 1845-51, 1855-61).

First senator to give birth in office: Tammy Duckworth (D, IL, 2017-), on Apr. 9, 2018.

Longest-serving senator: Robert C. Byrd (D, WV, 1959-2010) died while in office, having served 51 years, 5 months, and 26 days.

Oldest senator: Strom Thurmond (R, SC), who turned 100 years of age on Dec. 5, 2002, one month before he retired from office.

Youngest senator: John H. Eaton (TN), who was 28 years, 5 months old when he was sworn in Nov. 16, 1818.

Longest speech by a senator (since 1900): 24 hours, 18 minutes, by Strom Thurmond (D, SC) in his filibuster against the 1957 Civil Rights Act, Aug. 28-29, 1957.

Number of Senate impeachment trials: 20, resulting in 8 acquittals, 8 convictions, 3 dismissals, and 1 resignation with no further action.

First regular live-TV broadcast from the Senate chamber: June 2, 1986, by the C-SPAN network.

Number of senators who have received the Nobel Peace Prize: 5 (Elihu Root, Frank Kellogg, Cordell Hull, Al Gore, Barack Obama). Root is the only one of the five to receive the award while serving as senator.

Number of senators who have changed party affiliation during their Senate service (since 1890): 22.

Congressional Activity, 1947-2022

Source: *Congressional Record*, U.S. Govt. Publishing Office; Library of Congress

Congress in recent years has been widely perceived as being less productive than in previous sessions. The data below shows the number of public laws and measures passed in every complete session of Congress since 1947.

Congress (years)	Public laws passed	Measures passed	Congress (years)	Public laws passed	Measures passed
80th (1947-48)	906	4,132	99th (1985-86)	664	2,698
81st (1949-50)	921	5,764	100th (1987-88)	713	2,932
82nd (1951-52)	594	4,593	101st (1989-90)	650	2,691
83rd (1953-54)	781	5,201	102nd (1991-92)	590	2,615
84th (1955-56)	1,028	5,713	103rd (1993-94)	465	2,054
85th (1957-58)	936	5,126	104th (1995-96)	333	1,834
86th (1959-60)	800	4,165	105th (1997-98)	394	2,077
87th (1961-62)	885	4,769	106th (1999-2000)	580	2,779
88th (1963-64)	666	3,425	107th (2001-02)	377	2,163
89th (1965-66)	810	4,116	108th (2003-04)	498	2,674
90th (1967-68)	640	3,390	109th (2005-06)	482	2,684
91st (1969-70)	695	3,318	110th (2007-08)	460	3,336
92nd (1971-72)	607	2,840	111th (2009-10)	383	2,939
93rd (1973-74)	649	3,088	112th (2011-12)	283	1,744
94th (1975-76)	588	3,176	113th (2013-14)	297	1,788
95th (1977-78)	633	3,211	114th (2015-16)	328	2,110
96th (1979-80)	613	2,960	115th (2017-18)	338	2,563
97th (1981-82)	473	2,267	116th (2019-20)	284	2,207
98th (1983-84)	623	2,670	117th (2021-22)	242	2,179

Note: Public laws are bills or joint resolutions that have been enacted. Measures passed refers to bills, joint resolutions, concurrent resolutions, or simple resolutions approved by the House or Senate.

Members of the 118th Congress: U.S. Senate

Source: *Statistics of the Congressional Election*, Office of the Clerk, U.S. House of Representatives.

Boldface denotes the 2022 election winner. * = Incumbent. Third-party, independent, or write-in candidates receiving fewer than 70,000 votes are not necessarily listed.

Terms are for six years and end Jan. 3 of the year preceding the senator's name in the following table. Annual salary: $174,000; President Pro Tempore, Majority Leader, and Minority Leader: $193,400. To be eligible to serve in the Senate, a person must be at least 30 years old, a U.S. citizen for at least nine years, and a resident of the state from which elected.

D = Democrat; R = Republican; DFL = Dem.-Farmer-Labor; Ind. = Independent; LB = Libertarian.

Term ends	Senator/candidate (party); service from	2022 election results
Alabama		
2027	Tommy Tuberville (R); 1/3/2021	
2029	**Katie Britt (R).**	942,154
	Will Boyd (D).	436,746
Alaska		
2027	Dan Sullivan (R); 1/6/2015	
2029	**Lisa Murkowski* (R); 12/20/2002**	113,495
	Kelly Tshibaka (R)	111,480
	Patricia Chesbro (D).	27,145
Arizona		
2025	Kyrsten Sinema (Ind.); 1/3/2019	
2029	**Mark Kelly* (D); 12/2/2020**	1,322,027
	Blake Masters (R).	1,196,308
Arkansas		
2027	Tom Cotton (R); 1/6/2015	
2029	**John Boozman* (R); 1/5/2011**	592,437
	Natalie James (D).	280,187
California		
2025	Dianne Feinstein (D); 11/10/1992	
2029	**Alex Padilla* (D); 1/20/2021**	6,621,621
	Mark Meuser (R).	4,222,029
Colorado		
2027	John Hickenlooper (D); 1/3/2021	
2029	**Michael Bennet* (D); 1/22/2009**	1,397,170
	Joe O'Dea (R).	1,031,693
Connecticut		
2025	Christopher S. Murphy (D); 1/3/2013	
2029	**Richard Blumenthal* (D); 1/5/2011**	723,864
	Leora Levy (R)	535,943
Delaware		
2025	Thomas R. Carper (D); 1/3/2001	
2027	Christopher Coons (D); 11/15/2010	
Florida		
2025	Rick Scott (R); 1/8/2019	
2029	**Marco Rubio* (R); 1/5/2011**	4,474,847
	Val Demings (D).	3,201,522
Georgia		
2027	Jon Ossoff (D); 1/20/2021	
2029[1]	**Raphael Warnock* (D); 1/20/2021**	1,820,633
	Herschel Walker (R).	1,721,244
Hawaii		
2025	Mazie K. Hirono (D); 1/3/2013	
2029	**Brian Schatz* (D); 12/26/2012**	290,894
	Bob McDermott (R).	106,358
Idaho		
2027	Jim Risch (R); 1/6/2009	
2029	**Mike Crapo* (R); 1/6/1999.**	358,539
	David Roth (D)	169,808
Illinois		
2027	Richard J. Durbin (D); 1/7/1997	
2029	**Tammy Duckworth* (D); 1/3/2017**	2,329,136
	Kathy Salvi (R)	1,701,055
	Bill Redpath (LB)	68,671
Indiana		
2025	Mike Braun (R); 1/3/2019	
2029	**Todd Young* (R); 1/3/2017**	1,090,165
	Thomas McDermott Jr. (D).	704,411
Iowa		
2027	Joni Ernst (R); 1/6/2015	
2029	**Chuck Grassley* (R); 1/5/1981.**	681,501
	Michael Franken (D).	533,330
Kansas		
2027	Roger Marshall (R); 1/3/2021	
2029	**Jerry Moran* (R); 1/5/2011**	602,976
	Mark R. Holland (D)	372,214
Kentucky		
2027	Mitch McConnell (R); 1/3/1985	
2029	**Rand Paul* (R); 1/5/2011**	913,326
	Charles Booker (D).	564,311

Term ends	Senator/candidate (party); service from	2022 election results
Louisiana		
2027	Bill Cassidy (R); 1/6/2015	
2029	**John Kennedy* (R); 1/3/2017**	851,568
	Gary Chambers Jr. (D)	246,933
	Luke Mixon (D)	182,887
Maine		
2025	Angus King (Ind.); 1/3/2013	
2027	Susan M. Collins (R); 1/7/1997	
Maryland		
2025	Ben Cardin (D); 1/4/2007	
2029	**Chris Van Hollen* (D); 1/3/2017**	1,316,897
	Chris Chaffee (R)	682,293
Massachusetts		
2025	Elizabeth A. Warren (D); 1/3/2013	
2027	Edward Markey (D); 7/16/2013	
Michigan		
2025	Debbie Stabenow (D); 1/3/2001	
2027	Gary Peters (D); 1/6/2015	
Minnesota		
2025	Amy Klobuchar (DFL); 1/4/2007	
2027	Tina Smith (DFL); 1/3/2018	
Mississippi		
2025	Roger F. Wicker (R); 12/31/2007	
2027	Cindy Hyde-Smith (R); 4/9/2018	
Missouri		
2025	Josh Hawley (R); 1/3/2019	
2029	**Eric Schmitt (R).**	1,146,966
	Trudy Busch Valentine (D)	872,694
Montana		
2025	Jon Tester (D); 1/4/2007	
2027	Steve Daines (R); 1/6/2015	
Nebraska		
2025	Deb Fischer (R); 1/3/2013	
2027	Ben Sasse (R); 1/6/2015	
Nevada		
2025	Jacky Rosen (D); 1/3/2019	
2029	**Catherine Cortez Masto* (D); 1/3/2017**	498,316
	Adam Laxalt (R)	490,388
New Hampshire		
2027	Jeanne Shaheen (D); 1/6/2009	
2029	**Maggie Hassan* (D); 1/3/2017**	332,193
	Don Bolduc (R).	275,928
New Jersey		
2025	Robert Menendez (D); 1/18/2006	
2027	Cory Booker (D); 10/31/2013	
New Mexico		
2025	Martin Heinrich (D); 1/3/2013	
2027	Ben Ray Luján (D); 1/3/2021	
New York		
2025	Kirsten E. Gillibrand (D); 1/27/2009	
2029	**Chuck Schumer* (D); 1/6/1999.**	3,320,561
	Joe Pinion (R).	2,501,151
North Carolina		
2027	Thom Tillis (R); 1/6/2015	
2029	**Ted Budd (R).**	1,905,786
	Cheri Beasley (D).	1,784,049
North Dakota		
2025	Kevin Cramer (R); 1/3/2019	
2029	**John Hoeven* (R); 1/5/2011**	135,474
	Katrina Christiansen (D)	59,995
Ohio		
2025	Sherrod Brown (D); 1/4/2007	
2029	**JD Vance (R)**	2,192,114
	Tim Ryan (D)	1,939,489

Term ends	Senator/candidate (party); service from	2022 election results
Oklahoma		
2027[2]	**Markwayne Mullin (R)**	**710,643**
	Kendra Horn (D)	405,389
2029	**James Lankford* (R); 1/6/2015**	**739,960**
	Madison Horn (D)	369,370
Oregon		
2027	Jeff Merkley (D); 1/6/2009	
2029	**Ron Wyden* (D); 2/6/1996**	**1,076,424**
	Jo Rae Perkins (R)	788,991
Pennsylvania		
2025	Bob Casey Jr. (D); 1/4/2007	
2029	**John Fetterman (D)**	**2,751,012**
	Mehmet Oz (R)	2,487,260
Rhode Island		
2025	Sheldon Whitehouse (D); 1/4/2007	
2027	Jack Reed (D); 1/7/1997	
South Carolina		
2027	Lindsey Graham (R); 1/7/2003	
2029	**Tim Scott* (R); 1/3/2013**	**1,066,274**
	Krystle Matthews (D)	627,616
South Dakota		
2027	Mike Rounds (R); 1/6/2015	
2029	**John Thune* (R); 1/4/2005**	**242,316**
	Brian Bengs (D)	91,007
Tennessee		
2025	Marsha Blackburn (R); 1/3/2019	
2027	Bill Hagerty (R); 1/3/2021	

Term ends	Senator/candidate (party); service from	2022 election results
Texas		
2025	Ted Cruz (R); 1/3/2013	
2027	John Cornyn (R); 12/2/2002	
Utah		
2025	Mitt Romney (R); 1/3/2019	
2029	**Mike Lee* (R); 1/5/2011**	**571,974**
	Evan McMullin (Ind.)	459,958
Vermont		
2025	Bernie Sanders (Ind.); 1/4/2007	
2029	**Peter Welch (D)**	**196,575**
	Gerald Malloy (R)	80,468
Virginia		
2025	Timothy M. Kaine (D); 1/3/2013	
2027	Mark Warner (D); 1/6/2009	
Washington		
2025	Maria Cantwell (D); 1/3/2001	
2029	**Patty Murray* (D); 1/3/1993**	**1,741,827**
	Tiffany Smiley (R)	1,299,322
West Virginia		
2025	Joe Manchin III (D); 11/15/2010	
2027	Shelley Moore Capito (R); 1/6/2015	
Wisconsin		
2025	Tammy Baldwin (D); 1/3/2013	
2029	**Ron Johnson* (R); 1/5/2011**	**1,337,185**
	Mandela Barnes (D)	1,310,467
Wyoming		
2025	John Barrasso (R); 6/22/2007	
2027	Cynthia Lummis (R); 1/3/2021	

(1) Result of the runoff between top two candidates Dec. 6, 2022. (2) Special election to replace Sen. James Inhofe (R), who resigned effective Jan. 3, 2023.

Members of the 118th Congress: U.S. House of Representatives

Source: *Statistics of the Congressional Election*, Office of the Clerk, U.S. House of Representatives.

Boldface denotes the 2022 election winner. * = Incumbent. ** = Incumbent running in a different district. Third-party or independent candidates receiving fewer than 10,000 votes are not necessarily listed. Terms are for two years ending on Jan. 3, 2025. Annual salary, $174,000; Majority Leader and Minority Leader, $193,400; Speaker of the House, $223,500. To be eligible to serve in the House, a person must be at least 25 years of age, a U.S. citizen for at least seven years, and a resident of the state from which elected.

D = Democrat; R = Republican; C = Conservative; DFL = Dem.-Farmer-Labor; Ind. = Independent; LB = Libertarian.

Dist.	Representative/candidate (party)	2022 election results
Alabama		
1	**Jerry Carl* (R)**	**140,592**
	Alexander Remrey (LB)	26,369
2	**Barry Moore* (R)**	**137,460**
	Phyllis Harvey-Hall (D)	58,014
3	**Mike Rogers* (R)**	**135,602**
	Lin Veasey (D)	47,859
4	**Robert Aderholt* (R)**	**164,655**
	Rick Neighbors (D)	26,694
5	**Dale Strong (R)**	**142,435**
	Kathy Warner-Stanton (D)	62,740
6	**Gary Palmer* (R)**	**154,233**
	Andria Chieffo (LB)	27,833
7	**Terri Sewell* (D)**	**123,233**
	Beatrice Nichols (R)	67,416
Alaska		
	Mary Sattler Peltola* (D)	**128,553**
	Sarah Palin (R)	67,866
	Nick Begich III (R)	61,513
Arizona		
1	**David Schweikert** (R)**	**182,336**
	Jevin Hodge (D)	179,141
2	**Eli Crane (R)**	**174,169**
	Tom O'Halleran** (D)	149,151
3	**Ruben Gallego** (D)**	**108,599**
	Jeff Zink (R)	32,475
4	**Greg Stanton** (D)**	**148,941**
	Kelly Cooper (R)	116,521
5	**Andy Biggs* (R)**	**182,464**
	Javier Ramos (D)	120,243
	Clint Smith (Ind.)	18,851

Dist.	Representative/candidate (party)	2022 election results
6	**Juan Ciscomani (R)**	**177,201**
	Kirsten Engel (D)	171,969
7	**Raúl M. Grijalva** (D)**	**126,418**
	Luis Pozzolo (R)	69,444
8	**Debbie Lesko* (R)**	**Unopposed**
9	**Paul A. Gosar** (R)**	**Unopposed**
Arkansas		
1	**Rick Crawford* (R)**	**153,774**
	Monte Hodges (D)	54,598
2	**French Hill* (R)**	**147,975**
	Quintessa Hathaway (D)	86,887
	Michael White (LB)	11,584
3	**Steve Womack* (R)**	**142,401**
	Lauren Mallett-Hays (D)	73,541
4	**Bruce Westerman* (R)**	**153,850**
	John White (D)	56,745
California		
1	**Doug LaMalfa* (R)**	**152,839**
	Max Steiner (D)	93,386
2	**Jared Huffman* (D)**	**229,720**
	Douglas Brower (R)	79,029
3	**Kevin Kiley (R)**	**181,438**
	Kermit Jones (D)	156,761
4	**Mike Thompson** (D)**	**176,900**
	Matt Brock (R)	84,007
5	**Tom McClintock** (R)**	**173,524**
	Mike Barkley (D)	109,506
6	**Ami Bera** (D)**	**121,058**
	Tamika Hamilton (R)	95,325
7	**Doris O. Matsui** (D)**	**150,618**
	Max Semenenko (R)	70,033

Dist.	Representative/candidate (party)	2022 election results
8	**John Garamendi** (D)	**145,501**
	Rudy Recile (R)	46,634
9	**Josh Harder** (D)	**95,598**
	Tom Patti (R)	78,802
10	**Mark DeSaulnier** (D)	**198,415**
	Michael Kerr (Green)	52,965
11	**Nancy Pelosi** (D)	**220,848**
	John Dennis (R)	42,217
12	**Barbara Lee** (D)	**217,110**
	Stephen Slauson (R)	22,859
13	**John Duarte** (R)	**67,060**
	Adam Gray (D)	66,496
14	**Eric Swalwell** (D)	**137,612**
	Alison Hayden (R)	60,852
15	**Kevin Mullin** (D)	**108,077**
	David Canepa (D)	86,797
16	**Anna Eshoo** (D)	**139,235**
	Rishi Kumar (D)	101,772
17	**Ro Khanna** (D)	**127,853**
	Ritesh Tandon (R)	52,400
18	**Zoe Lofgren** (D)	**99,776**
	Peter Hernandez (R)	51,737
19	**Jimmy Panetta** (D)	**194,494**
	Jeff Gorman (R)	88,816
20	**Kevin McCarthy** (R)	**153,847**
	Marisa Wood (D)	74,934
21	**Jim Costa** (D)	**68,074**
	Michael Maher (R)	57,573
22	**David Valadao** (R)	**52,994**
	Rudy Salas (D)	49,862
23	**Jay Obernolte** (R)	**103,197**
	Derek Marshall (D)	65,908
24	**Salud Carbajal** (D)	**159,019**
	Brad Allen (R)	103,533
25	**Raul Ruiz** (D)	**87,641**
	Brian Hawkins (R)	65,101
26	**Julia Brownley** (D)	**134,575**
	Matt Jacobs (R)	112,214
27	**Mike Garcia** (R)	**104,624**
	Christy Smith (D)	91,892
28	**Judy Chu** (D)	**150,062**
	Wes Hallman (R)	76,495
29	**Tony Cárdenas** (D)	**69,915**
	Angélica María Dueñas (D)	49,520
30	**Adam Schiff** (D)	**150,100**
	Maebe A. Girl (D)	60,968
31	**Grace Napolitano** (D)	**91,472**
	Daniel Martinez (R)	62,153
32	**Brad Sherman** (D)	**167,411**
	Lucie Volotzky (R)	74,618
33	**Pete Aguilar** (D)	**76,588**
	John Porter (R)	56,119
34	**Jimmy Gomez** (D)	**62,244**
	David Kim (D)	59,223
35	**Norma Torres** (D)	**75,121**
	Mike Cargile (R)	55,832
36	**Ted Lieu** (D)	**194,299**
	Joe Collins III (R)	84,264
37	**Sydney Kamlager** (D)	**84,338**
	Jan Perry (D)	47,542
38	**Linda Sánchez** (D)	**101,260**
	Eric Ching (R)	73,051
39	**Mark Takano** (D)	**75,896**
	Aja Smith (R)	55,701
40	**Young Kim** (R)	**161,589**
	Asif Mahmood (D)	122,722
41	**Ken Calvert** (R)	**123,869**
	Will Rollins (D)	112,769
42	**Robert Garcia** (D)	**99,217**
	John Briscoe (R)	45,903
43	**Maxine Waters** (D)	**95,462**
	Omar Navarro (R)	27,985
44	**Nanette Barragán** (D)	**100,160**
	Paul Jones (R)	38,554

Dist.	Representative/candidate (party)	2022 election results
45	**Michelle Steel** (R)	**113,960**
	Jay Chen (D)	103,466
46	**Lou Correa** (D)	**78,041**
	Christopher Gonzales (R)	48,257
47	**Katie Porter** (D)	**137,374**
	Scott Baugh (R)	128,261
48	**Darrell Issa** (R)	**155,171**
	Stephen Houlahan (D)	101,900
49	**Mike Levin** (D)	**153,541**
	Brian Maryott (R)	138,194
50	**Scott Peters** (D)	**168,816**
	Corey Gustafson (R)	99,819
51	**Sara Jacobs** (D)	**144,186**
	Stan Caplan (R)	88,886
52	**Juan Vargas** (D)	**100,686**
	Tyler Geffeney (R)	50,330
Colorado		
1	**Diana DeGette** (D)	**226,929**
	Jennifer Qualteri (R)	49,530
2	**Joe Neguse** (D)	**244,107**
	Marshall Dawson (R)	97,700
3	**Lauren Boebert** (R)	**163,839**
	Adam Frisch (D)	163,293
4	**Ken Buck** (R)	**216,024**
	Ike McCorkle (D)	129,619
5	**Doug Lamborn** (R)	**155,528**
	David Torres (D)	111,978
6	**Jason Crow** (D)	**170,140**
	Steven Monahan (R)	105,084
7	**Brittany Pettersen** (D)	**204,984**
	Erik Aadland (R)	150,510
8	**Yadira Caraveo** (D)	**114,377**
	Barbara Kirkmeyer (R)	112,745
Connecticut		
1	**John B. Larson** (D)	**149,556**
	Larry Lazor (R)	91,506
2	**Joe Courtney** (D)	**165,946**
	Mike France (R)	114,506
3	**Rosa L. DeLauro** (D)	**137,924**
	Lesley DeNardis (R)	98,704
4	**Jim Himes** (D)	**140,262**
	Jayme Stevenson (R)	95,822
5	**Jahana Hayes** (D)	**127,838**
	George Logan (R)	125,834
Delaware		
	Lisa Blunt Rochester (D)	**178,416**
	Lee Murphy (R)	138,201
Florida		
1	**Matt Gaetz** (R)	**197,349**
	Rebekah Jones (D)	93,467
2	**Neal Dunn** (R)	**180,236**
	Al Lawson (D)	121,153
3	**Kat Cammack** (R)	**178,101**
	Danielle Hawk (D)	103,382
4	**Aaron Bean** (R)	**165,696**
	LaShonda Holloway (D)	108,402
5	**John Rutherford** (R)	**Unopposed**
6	**Michael Waltz** (R)	**226,548**
	Joe Hannoush (LB)	74,207
7	**Cory Mills** (R)	**177,966**
	Karen Green (D)	126,079
8	**Bill Posey** (R)	**222,128**
	Joanne Terry (D)	120,080
9	**Darren Soto** (D)	**108,541**
	Scotty Moore (R)	93,827
10	**Maxwell Alejandro Frost** (D)	**117,955**
	Calvin Wimbish (R)	78,484
11	**Daniel Webster** (R)	**205,995**
	Shante Munns (D)	115,647
12	**Gus Bilirakis** (R)	**226,601**
	Kimberly Walker (D)	95,390
13	**Anna Paulina Luna** (R)	**181,487**
	Eric Lynn (D)	153,876

Dist.	Representative/candidate (party)	2022 election results
14	Kathy Castor* (D)	149,737
	James Judge (R)	113,427
15	Laurel Lee (R)	145,219
	Alan Cohn (D)	102,835
16	Vern Buchanan* (R)	189,762
	Jan Schneider (D)	115,575
17	Greg Steube* (R)	222,483
	Andrea Doria Kale (D)	123,798
18	Scott Franklin** (R)	167,429
	Keith R. Hayden Jr. (Ind.)	56,647
19	Byron Donalds* (R)	213,035
	Cindy Banyai (D)	100,226
20	Sheila Cherfilus-McCormick* (D)	136,215
	Drew Montez Clark (R)	52,151
21	Brian Mast** (R)	208,614
	Corinna Balderramos Robinson (D)	119,891
22	Lois Frankel** (D)	150,010
	Dan Franzese (R)	122,194
23	Jared Moskowitz (D)	143,951
	Joe Budd (R)	130,681
24	Frederica Wilson* (D)	133,442
	Jesus Navarro (R)	52,449
25	Debbie Wasserman Schultz** (D)	129,113
	Carla Spalding (R)	105,239
26	Mario Díaz-Balart** (R)	143,240
	Christine Alexandria Olivo (D)	58,868
27	Maria Elvira Salazar* (R)	136,038
	Annette Taddeo (D)	101,404
28	Carlos Giménez** (R)	134,457
	Robert Asencio (D)	76,665

Georgia

Dist.	Representative/candidate (party)	2022 election results
1	Earl L. "Buddy" Carter* (R)	156,128
	Wade Herring (D)	107,837
2	Sanford D. Bishop Jr.* (D)	132,675
	Chris West (R)	108,665
3	Drew Ferguson* (R)	213,524
	Val Almond (D)	97,057
4	Hank Johnson* (D)	216,332
	Jonathan Chavez (R)	59,302
5	Nikema Williams* (D)	243,687
	Christian Zimm (R)	51,769
6	Rich McCormick (R)	206,886
	Bob Christian (D)	125,612
7	Lucy McBath** (D)	143,063
	Mark Gonsalves (R)	91,962
8	Austin Scott* (R)	178,700
	Darrius Butler (D)	81,886
9	Andrew Clyde* (R)	212,820
	Mike Ford (D)	81,318
10	Mike Collins (R)	198,523
	Tabitha Johnson-Green (D)	109,107
11	Barry Loudermilk* (R)	190,086
	Antonio Daza (D)	113,571
12	Rick Allen* (R)	158,047
	Liz Johnson (D)	107,148
13	David Scott* (D)	216,388
	Caesar Gonzales (R)	48,228
14	Marjorie Taylor Greene* (R)	170,162
	Marcus Flowers (D)	88,189

Hawaii

Dist.	Representative/candidate (party)	2022 election results
1	Ed Case* (D)	143,546
	Conrad Kress (R)	51,217
2	Jill Tokuda (D)	128,407
	Joe Akana (R)	72,874

Idaho

Dist.	Representative/candidate (party)	2022 election results
1	Russ Fulcher* (R)	222,901
	Kaylee Peterson (D)	82,261
2	Mike Simpson* (R)	172,450
	Wendy Norman (D)	98,736

Illinois

Dist.	Representative/candidate (party)	2022 election results
1	Jonathan Jackson (D)	159,142
	Eric Carlson (R)	78,258
2	Robin Kelly* (D)	140,414
	Thomas Lynch (R)	68,761
3	Delia Ramirez (D)	121,764
	Justin Burau (R)	55,995
4	Jesús "Chuy" García* (D)	91,036
	James Falakos (R)	37,352
5	Mike Quigley* (D)	190,999
	Tommy Hanson (R)	79,112
6	Sean Casten* (D)	150,496
	Keith Pekau (R)	126,351
7	Danny K. Davis* (D)	Unopposed
8	Raja Krishnamoorthi* (D)	117,880
	Chris Dargis (R)	89,335
9	Jan Schakowsky* (D)	179,615
	Max Rice (R)	70,915
10	Brad Schneider* (D)	152,566
	Joseph Severino (R)	89,599
11	Bill Foster* (D)	149,172
	Catalina Lauf (R)	115,069
12	Mike Bost* (R)	218,379
	Homer "Chip" Markel (D)	72,791
13	Nikki Budzinski (D)	141,788
	Regan Deering (R)	108,646
14	Lauren Underwood* (D)	128,141
	Scott Gryder (R)	108,451
15	Mary Miller* (R)	213,007
	Paul Lange (D)	86,396
16	Darin LaHood** (R)	197,621
	Elizabeth "Lisa" Haderlein (D)	100,325
17	Eric Sorensen (D)	121,186
	Esther Joy King (R)	111,931

Indiana

Dist.	Representative/candidate (party)	2022 election results
1	Frank Mrvan* (D)	112,656
	Jennifer-Ruth Green (R)	100,542
2	Rudy Yakym (R)	125,313
	Paul Steury (D)	62,891
3	Jim Banks* (R)	131,579
	Gary Snyder (D)	60,577
4	Jim Baird* (R)	134,864
	Roger Day (D)	62,834
5	Victoria Spartz* (R)	146,575
	Jeannine Lee Lake (D)	93,434
6	Greg Pence* (R)	130,686
	Cinde Wirth (D)	62,838
7	André Carson* (D)	117,309
	Angela Grabovsky (R)	53,631
8	Larry Bucshon* (R)	141,995
	Ray McCormick (D)	68,109
9	Erin Houchin (R)	143,166
	Matthew Fyfe (D)	75,700

Iowa

Dist.	Representative/candidate (party)	2022 election results
1	Mariannette Miller-Meeks** (R)	162,947
	Christina Bohannan (D)	142,173
2	Ashley Hinson** (R)	172,181
	Liz Mathis (D)	145,940
3	Zach Nunn (R)	156,262
	Cindy Axne* (D)	154,117
4	Randy Feenstra* (R)	186,467
	Ryan Melton (D)	84,230

Kansas

Dist.	Representative/candidate (party)	2022 election results
1	Tracey Mann* (R)	161,333
	Jimmy Beard (D)	77,092
2	Jake LaTurner* (R)	134,506
	Patrick Schmidt (D)	98,852
3	Sharice Davids* (D)	165,527
	Amanda Adkins (R)	128,839
4	Ron Estes* (R)	144,889
	Bob Hernandez (D)	83,851

Kentucky

Dist.	Representative/candidate (party)	2022 election results
1	James Comer* (R)	184,157
	Jimmy Ausbrooks (D)	61,701
2	Brett Guthrie* (R)	170,487
	Hank Linderman (D)	66,769
3	Morgan McGarvey (D)	160,920
	Stuart Ray (R)	98,637

Dist.	Representative/candidate (party)	2022 election results
4	**Thomas Massie* (R)**	**167,541**
	Matthew Lehman (D)	79,977
5	**Hal Rogers* (R)**	**177,712**
	Conor Halbleib (D)	38,549
6	**Andy Barr* (R)**	**154,762**
	Geoff Young (D)	83,005
Louisiana		
1	**Steve Scalise* (R)**	**177,670**
	Katie Darling (D)	61,467
2	**Troy A. Carter* (D)**	**158,120**
	Dan Lux (R)	46,927
3	**Clay Higgins* (R)**	**144,423**
	Holden Hoggatt (R)	24,474
	Lessie LeBlanc (D)	23,641
	Tia LeBrun (D)	21,172
4	**Mike Johnson* (R)**	**Unopposed**
5	**Julia Letlow* (R)**	**151,080**
	Omar Dantzler (D)	35,149
	Earl Huff (D)	19,383
	Allen Guillory (R)	12,159
6	**Garret Graves* (R)**	**189,684**
	Rufus Holt Craig Jr. (LB)	30,709
	Brian Belzer (R)	15,535
Maine		
1	**Chellie Pingree* (D)**	**219,753**
	Ed Thelander (R)	129,263
2[1]	**Jared Golden* (D)**	**165,136**
	Bruce Poliquin (R)	146,142
	Tiffany Bond (Ind.)	21,655
Maryland		
1	**Andy Harris* (R)**	**159,673**
	Heather Mizeur (D)	126,511
2	**C.A. Dutch Ruppersberger* (D)**	**158,998**
	Nicolee Ambrose (R)	109,075
3	**John Sarbanes* (D)**	**175,514**
	Yuripzy Morgan (R)	115,801
4	**Glenn Ivey (D)**	**144,168**
	Jeff Warner (R)	15,441
5	**Steny Hoyer* (D)**	**182,478**
	Chris Palombi (R)	94,000
6	**David Trone* (D)**	**140,295**
	Neil Parrott (R)	115,771
7	**Kweisi Mfume* (D)**	**151,640**
	Scott Collier (R)	32,737
8	**Jamie Raskin* (D)**	**211,842**
	Gregory Coll (R)	47,965
Massachusetts		
1	**Richard Neal* (D)**	**157,635**
	Dean Martilli (R)	98,386
2	**Jim McGovern* (D)**	**180,639**
	Jeffrey Sossa-Paquette (R)	91,956
3	**Lori Trahan* (D)**	**154,496**
	Dean Tran (R)	88,585
4	**Jake Auchincloss* (D)**	**Unopposed**
5	**Katherine Clark* (D)**	**203,994**
	Caroline Colarusso (R)	71,491
6	**Seth Moulton* (D)**	**198,119**
	Bob May (R)	110,770
7	**Ayanna Pressley* (D)**	**151,825**
	Donnie Palmer (R)	27,129
8	**Stephen F. Lynch* (D)**	**189,987**
	Robert Burke (R)	82,126
9	**Bill Keating* (D)**	**197,823**
	Jesse Brown (R)	136,347
Michigan		
1	**Jack Bergman* (R)**	**233,094**
	Bob Lorinser (D)	145,403
2	**John Moolenaar** (R)**	**216,222**
	Jerry Hilliard (D)	116,452
3	**Hillary Scholten (D)**	**185,989**
	John Gibbs (R)	142,229
4	**Bill Huizenga** (R)**	**183,936**
	Joseph Alfonso (R)	143,690
5	**Tim Walberg** (R)**	**198,020**
	Bart Goldberg (R)	110,946

Dist.	Representative/candidate (party)	2022 election results
6	**Debbie Dingell** (D)**	**241,759**
	Whittney Williams (R)	125,167
7	**Elissa Slotkin** (D)**	**192,809**
	Tom Barrett (R)	172,624
8	**Dan Kildee** (D)**	**178,322**
	Paul Junge (R)	143,850
9	**Lisa McClain** (R)**	**238,300**
	Brian Jaye (D)	123,702
10	**John James (R)**	**159,202**
	Carl Marlinga (D)	157,602
11	**Haley Stevens* (D)**	**224,537**
	Mark Ambrose (R)	141,642
12	**Rashida Tlaib* (D)**	**196,643**
	Steven Elliott (R)	72,888
13	**Shri Thanedar (D)**	**166,650**
	Martell Bivings (R)	56,187
Minnesota		
1	**Brad Finstad* (R)**	**159,621**
	Jeff Ettinger (D)	125,457
2	**Angie Craig* (DFL)**	**165,583**
	Tyler Kistner (R)	148,576
	Paula M. Overby (Legal Marijuana Now)	10,728
3	**Dean Phillips* (DFL)**	**198,883**
	Tom Weiler (R)	134,797
4	**Betty McCollum* (DFL)**	**200,055**
	May Lor Xiong (R)	95,493
5	**Ilhan Omar* (DFL)**	**214,224**
	Cicely Davis (R)	70,702
6	**Tom Emmer* (R)**	**198,145**
	Jeanne Hendricks (DFL)	120,852
7	**Michelle Fischbach* (R)**	**204,766**
	Jill Abahsain (DFL)	84,455
	Travis "Bull" Johnson (Legal Marijuana Now)	16,421
8	**Pete Stauber* (R)**	**188,755**
	Jen Schultz (DFL)	141,009
Mississippi		
1	**Trent Kelly* (R)**	**122,151**
	Dianne Black (D)	45,238
2	**Bennie G. Thompson* (D)**	**108,285**
	Brian Flowers (R)	71,884
3	**Michael Guest* (R)**	**132,481**
	Shuwaski Young (D)	54,803
4	**Mike Ezell (R)**	**127,813**
	Johnny DuPree (D)	42,876
Missouri		
1	**Cori Bush* (D)**	**160,999**
	Andrew Jones (R)	53,767
2	**Ann Wagner* (R)**	**173,277**
	Trish Gunby (D)	135,895
3	**Blaine Luetkemeyer* (R)**	**180,746**
	Bethany Mann (D)	96,851
4	**Mark Alford (R)**	**181,890**
	Jack Truman (D)	67,069
5	**Emanuel Cleaver* (D)**	**140,688**
	Jacob Turk (R)	84,008
6	**Sam Graves* (R)**	**184,865**
	Henry Martin (D)	72,253
7	**Eric Burlison (R)**	**178,592**
	Kristen Radaker-Sheafer (D)	67,485
8	**Jason Smith* (R)**	**186,472**
	Randi McCallian (D)	53,738
Montana		
1	**Ryan Zinke (R)**	**123,102**
	Monica Tranel (D)	115,265
2	**Matt Rosendale** (R)**	**121,979**
	Gary Buchanan (Ind.)	47,195
	Penny Ronning (D)	43,480
Nebraska		
1	**Mike Flood* (R)**	**129,236**
	Patty Pansing Brooks (D)	93,929
2	**Don Bacon* (R)**	**112,663**
	Tony Vargas (D)	106,807
3	**Adrian Smith* (R)**	**172,700**
	David Else (D)	34,836
	Mark Elworth Jr. (Legal Marijuana Now)	13,016

Dist.	Representative/candidate (party)	2022 election results
Nevada		
1	**Dina Titus* (D)**	**115,700**
	Mark Robertson (R)	103,115
2	**Mark Amodei* (R)**	**185,467**
	Elizabeth Mercedes Krause (D)	117,371
3	**Susie Lee* (D)**	**131,086**
	April Becker (R)	121,083
4	**Steven Horsford* (D)**	**116,617**
	Sam Peters (R)	105,870
New Hampshire		
1	**Chris Pappas* (D)**	**167,391**
	Karoline Leavitt (R)	142,229
2	**Ann McLane Kuster* (D)**	**171,636**
	Robert Burns (R)	135,579
New Jersey		
1	**Donald Norcross* (D)**	**139,559**
	Claire Gustafson (R)	78,794
2	**Jeff Van Drew* (R)**	**139,217**
	Tim Alexander (D)	94,522
3	**Andy Kim* (D)**	**150,498**
	Bob Healey (R)	118,415
4	**Chris Smith* (R)**	**173,288**
	Matthew Jenkins (D)	81,233
5	**Josh Gottheimer* (D)**	**145,559**
	Frank Pallotta (R)	117,873
6	**Frank Pallone Jr.* (D)**	**106,238**
	Sue Kiley (R)	75,839
7	**Thomas Kean Jr. (R)**	**159,392**
	Tom Malinowski* (D)	150,701
8	**Rob Menendez Jr. (D)**	**78,382**
	Marcos Arroyo (R)	24,957
9	**Bill Pascrell Jr.* (D)**	**82,457**
	Billy Prempeh (R)	65,365
10	**Donald Payne Jr.* (D)**	**100,710**
	David Pinckney (R)	25,993
11	**Mikie Sherrill* (D)**	**161,436**
	Paul DeGroot (R)	109,952
12	**Bonnie Watson Coleman* (D)**	**125,127**
	Darius Mayfield (R)	71,175
New Mexico		
1	**Melanie Stansbury* (D)**	**156,462**
	Michelle Garcia Holmes (R)	124,151
2	**Gabe Vasquez (D)**	**96,986**
	Yvette Herrell* (R)	95,636
3	**Teresa Leger Fernandez* (D)**	**134,217**
	Alexis Martinez Johnson (R)	96,565
New York		
1	**Nick LaLota (R)**	**177,040**
	Bridget Fleming (D)	141,907
2	**Andrew Garbarino* (R)**	**151,178**
	Jackie Gordon (D)	97,774
3	**George Santos (R)**	**145,824**
	Robert Zimmerman (D)	125,404
4	**Anthony D'Esposito (R)**	**140,622**
	Laura Gillen (D)	130,871
5	**Gregory W. Meeks* (D)**	**104,396**
	Paul King (R)	34,407
6	**Grace Meng* (D)**	**85,049**
	Tom Zmich (R)	47,935
7	**Nydia Velázquez* (D)**	**119,473**
	Juan Pagan (R)	28,597
8	**Hakeem S. Jeffries* (D)**	**99,079**
	Yuri Dashevsky (R)	39,060
9	**Yvette D. Clarke* (D)**	**116,970**
	Menachem Raitport (C)	26,521
10	**Dan Goldman (D)**	**160,582**
	Benine Hamdan (R)	29,058
11	**Nicole Malliotakis* (R)**	**115,992**
	Max Rose (D)	71,801
12	**Jerrold Nadler** (D)**	**200,890**
	Michael Zumbluskas (R)	44,173
13	**Adriano Espaillat* (D)**	**Unopposed**
14	**Alexandria Ocasio-Cortez* (D)**	**82,453**
	Tina Forte (R)	31,935

Dist.	Representative/candidate (party)	2022 election results
15	**Ritchie Torres* (D)**	**76,406**
	Stylo Sapaskis (R)	15,882
16	**Jamaal Bowman* (D)**	**133,567**
	Miriam Levitt Flisser (R)	74,156
17	**Michael Lawler (R)**	**143,550**
	Sean Patrick Maloney** (D)	141,730
18	**Pat Ryan** (D)**	**135,245**
	Colin Schmitt (R)	131,653
19	**Marc Molinaro (R)**	**146,004**
	Josh Riley (D)	141,509
20	**Paul Tonko* (D)**	**160,420**
	Elizabeth Joy (R)	130,869
21	**Elise Stefanik* (R)**	**168,579**
	Matt Castelli (D)	116,421
22	**Brandon Williams (R)**	**135,544**
	Francis Conole (D)	132,913
23	**Nick Langworthy (R)**	**192,694**
	Max Della Pia (D)	104,114
24	**Claudia Tenney** (R)**	**182,054**
	Steven Holden (D)	95,028
25	**Joseph Morelle* (D)**	**152,022**
	La'Ron Singletary (R)	130,190
26	**Brian Higgins* (D)**	**156,883**
	Steven Sams II (R)	88,339
North Carolina		
1	**Don Davis (D)**	**134,996**
	Sandy Smith (R)	122,780
2	**Deborah Ross* (D)**	**190,714**
	Christine Villaverde (R)	104,155
3	**Greg Murphy* (R)**	**166,520**
	Barbara Gaskins (D)	82,378
4	**Valerie Foushee (D)**	**194,983**
	Courtney Geels (R)	96,442
5	**Virginia Foxx* (R)**	**175,279**
	Kyle Parrish (D)	102,269
6	**Kathy Manning* (D)**	**139,553**
	Christian Castelli (R)	116,635
7	**David Rouzer* (R)**	**164,047**
	Charles Graham (D)	120,222
8	**Dan Bishop** (R)**	**183,998**
	Scott Huffman (D)	79,192
9	**Richard Hudson** (R)**	**131,453**
	Ben Clark (D)	101,202
10	**Patrick McHenry* (R)**	**194,681**
	Pam Genant (D)	73,174
11	**Chuck Edwards (R)**	**174,232**
	Jasmine Beach-Ferrara (D)	144,165
12	**Alma Adams* (D)**	**140,494**
	Tyler Lee (R)	83,414
13	**Wiley Nickel (D)**	**143,090**
	Bo Hines (R)	134,256
14	**Jeff Jackson (D)**	**148,738**
	Pat Harrigan (R)	109,014
North Dakota		
	Kelly Armstrong* (R)	**148,399**
	Cara Mund (Ind.)	89,644
Ohio		
1	**Greg Landsman (D)**	**156,416**
	Steve Chabot* (R)	140,058
2	**Brad Wenstrup* (R)**	**192,117**
	Samantha Meadows (D)	65,745
3	**Joyce Beatty* (D)**	**182,324**
	Lee Stahley (R)	76,455
4	**Jim Jordan* (R)**	**200,773**
	Tamie Wilson (D)	89,383
5	**Bob Latta* (R)**	**187,303**
	Craig Swartz (D)	92,634
6	**Bill Johnson* (R)**	**189,883**
	Louis Lyras (D)	90,500
7	**Max Miller (R)**	**168,002**
	Matthew Diemer (D)	135,485
8	**Warren Davidson* (R)**	**180,287**
	Vanessa Enoch (D)	98,629
9	**Marcy Kaptur* (D)**	**150,655**
	J. R. Majewski (R)	115,362

Dist.	Representative/candidate (party)	2022 election results
10	**Mike Turner* (R)**	**168,327**
	David Esrati (D)	104,634
11	**Shontel Brown* (D)**	**167,722**
	Eric Brewer (R)	47,988
12	**Troy Balderson* (R)**	**191,344**
	Amy Rippel-Elton (D)	84,893
13	**Emilia Sykes (D)**	**149,816**
	Madison Gesiotto Gilbert (R)	134,593
14	**David Joyce* (R)**	**183,389**
	Matt Kilboy (D)	113,639
15	**Mike Carey* (R)**	**143,112**
	Gary Josephson (D)	108,139

Oklahoma

Dist.	Representative/candidate (party)	2022 election results
1	**Kevin Hern* (R)**	**142,800**
	Adam Martin (D)	80,974
2	**Josh Brecheen (R)**	**167,843**
	Naomi Andrews (D)	54,194
3	**Frank Lucas* (R)**	**147,418**
	Jeremiah Ross (D)	50,354
4	**Tom Cole* (R)**	**149,879**
	Mary Brannon (D)	74,667
5	**Stephanie Bice* (R)**	**152,699**
	Joshua Harris-Till (D)	96,799

Oregon

Dist.	Representative/candidate (party)	2022 election results
1	**Suzanne Bonamici* (D)**	**210,682**
	Christopher Mann (R)	99,042
2	**Cliff Bentz* (R)**	**208,369**
	Joe Yetter (D)	99,882
3	**Earl Blumenauer* (D)**	**212,119**
	Joanna Harbour (R)	79,766
	David Delk (Progressive)	10,982
4	**Val Hoyle (D)**	**171,372**
	Alek Skarlatos (R)	146,055
5	**Lori Chavez-DeRemer (R)**	**178,813**
	Jamie McLeod-Skinner (D)	171,514
6	**Andrea Salinas (D)**	**147,156**
	Mike Erickson (R)	139,946

Pennsylvania

Dist.	Representative/candidate (party)	2022 election results
1	**Brian Fitzpatrick* (R)**	**201,571**
	Ashley Ehasz (D)	165,809
2	**Brendan Boyle* (D)**	**141,229**
	Aaron Bashir (R)	45,454
3	**Dwight Evans* (D)**	**251,115**
	Christopher Hoeppner (Socialist Workers)	12,820
4	**Madeleine Dean* (D)**	**224,799**
	Christian Nascimento (R)	141,986
5	**Mary Gay Scanlon* (D)**	**205,128**
	David Galluch (R)	110,058
6	**Chrissy Houlahan* (D)**	**190,386**
	Guy Ciarrocchi (R)	136,097
7	**Susan Wild* (D)**	**151,364**
	Lisa Scheller (R)	145,527
8	**Matt Cartwright* (D)**	**146,956**
	Jim Bognet (R)	139,930
9	**Dan Meuser* (R)**	**209,185**
	Amanda Waldman (D)	92,622
10	**Scott Perry* (R)**	**169,331**
	Shamaine Daniels (D)	145,215
11	**Lloyd Smucker* (R)**	**194,991**
	Bob Hollister (D)	121,835
12	**Summer Lee (D)**	**184,674**
	Mike Doyle** (R)	143,946
13	**John Joyce* (R)**	**Unopposed**
14	**Guy Reschenthaler* (R)**	**Unopposed**
15	**Glenn Thompson* (R)**	**213,417**
	Mike Molesevich (D)	91,729
16	**Mike Kelly* (R)**	**190,546**
	Dan Pastore (D)	130,443
17	**Chris Deluzio (D)**	**193,615**
	Jeremy Shaffer (R)	169,013

Rhode Island

Dist.	Representative/candidate (party)	2022 election results
1[2]	**David Cicilline* (D)**	**100,318**
	Allen Waters (R)	56,055
2	**Seth Magaziner (D)**	**101,432**
	Allan Fung (R)	93,969

South Carolina

Dist.	Representative/candidate (party)	2022 election results
1	**Nancy Mace* (R)**	**153,757**
	Annie Andrews (D)	115,796
2	**Joe Wilson* (R)**	**147,699**
	Judd Larkins (D)	98,081
3	**Jeff Duncan* (R)**	**Unopposed**
4	**William Timmons* (R)**	**Unopposed**
5	**Ralph Norman* (R)**	**154,725**
	Evangeline Hundley (D)	83,299
6	**Jim Clyburn* (D)**	**130,923**
	Duke Buckner (R)	79,879
7	**Russell Fry (R)**	**164,440**
	Daryl Scott (D)	89,030

South Dakota

Dist.	Representative/candidate (party)	2022 election results
	Dusty Johnson* (R)	**253,821**
	Collin Duprel (LB)	74,020

Tennessee

Dist.	Representative/candidate (party)	2022 election results
1	**Diana Harshbarger* (R)**	**147,241**
	Cameron Parsons (D)	37,049
2	**Tim Burchett* (R)**	**141,089**
	Mark Harmon (D)	66,673
3	**Chuck Fleischmann* (R)**	**136,639**
	Meg Gorman (D)	60,334
4	**Scott DesJarlais* (R)**	**122,401**
	Wayne Steele (D)	44,648
5	**Andy Ogles (R)**	**123,558**
	Heidi Campbell (D)	93,648
6	**John Rose* (R)**	**129,388**
	Randal Cooper (D)	65,675
7	**Mark Green* (R)**	**108,421**
	Odessa Kelly (D)	68,973
8	**David Kustoff* (R)**	**155,602**
	Lynnette Williams (D)	51,102
9	**Steve Cohen* (D)**	**93,800**
	Charlotte Bergmann (R)	35,123

Texas

Dist.	Representative/candidate (party)	2022 election results
1	**Nathaniel Moran (R)**	**183,224**
	Jrmar Jefferson (D)	51,438
2	**Dan Crenshaw* (R)**	**151,791**
	Robin Fulford (D)	78,496
3	**Keith Self (R)**	**164,240**
	Sandeep Srivastava (D)	100,121
4	**Pat Fallon* (R)**	**170,781**
	Iro Omere (D)	79,179
5	**Lance Gooden* (R)**	**135,595**
	Tartisha Hill (D)	71,930
6	**Jake Ellzey* (R)**	**Unopposed**
7	**Lizzie Fletcher* (D)**	**115,994**
	Johnny Teague (R)	65,835
8	**Morgan Luttrell (R)**	**153,127**
	Laura Jones (D)	68,715
9	**Al Green* (D)**	**125,446**
	Jimmy Leon (R)	38,161
10	**Michael McCaul* (R)**	**159,469**
	Linda Nuno (D)	86,404
11	**August Pfluger* (R)**	**Unopposed**
12	**Kay Granger* (R)**	**152,953**
	Trey Hunt (D)	85,026
13	**Ronny Jackson* (R)**	**161,767**
	Kathleen Brown (D)	52,910
14	**Randy Weber* (R)**	**149,543**
	Mikal Williams (D)	63,606
15	**Monica De La Cruz (R)**	**80,978**
	Michelle Vallejo (D)	68,097
16	**Veronica Escobar* (D)**	**95,510**
	Irene Armendariz-Jackson (R)	54,986
17	**Pete Sessions* (R)**	**144,408**
	Mary Jo Woods (D)	72,801
18	**Sheila Jackson Lee* (D)**	**110,511**
	Carmen Maria Montiel (R)	40,941
19	**Jodey Arrington* (R)**	**152,321**
	Nathan Lewis (Ind.)	37,360

Dist.	Representative/candidate (party)	2022 election results
20	Joaquin Castro* (D)	115,352
	Kyle Sinclair (R)	53,226
21	Chip Roy* (R)	207,426
	Claudia Zapata (D)	122,655
22	Troy Nehls* (R)	150,014
	Jamie Jordan (D)	85,653
23	Tony Gonzales* (R)	116,649
	John Lira (D)	80,947
	Frank Lopez Jr. (Ind.)	11,180
24	Beth Van Duyne* (R)	177,947
	Jan McDowell (D)	119,878
25	Roger Williams* (R)	Unopposed
26	Michael Burgess* (R)	183,639
	Mike Kolls (LB)	81,384
27	Michael Cloud* (R)	133,416
	Maclovio Perez Jr. (D)	73,611
28	Henry Cuellar* (D)	93,803
	Cassy Garcia (R)	71,778
29	Sylvia Garcia* (D)	71,837
	Robert Schafranek (R)	28,765
30	Jasmine Crockett (D)	134,876
	James Rodgers (R)	39,209
31	John Carter* (R)	Unopposed
32	Colin Allred* (D)	116,005
	Antonio Swad (R)	61,494
33	Marc Veasey* (D)	82,081
	Patrick Gillespie (R)	29,203
34	Vicente Gonzalez** (D)	70,896
	Mayra Flores* (R)	59,464
35	Greg Casar (D)	129,599
	Dan McQueen (R)	48,969
36	Brian Babin* (R)	145,599
	Jon Haire (D)	64,016
37	Lloyd Doggett** (D)	219,358
	Jenny Garcia Sharon (R)	59,923
38	Wesley Hunt (R)	163,597
	Duncan Klussmann (D)	92,302

Utah

Dist.	Representative/candidate (party)	2022 election results
1	Blake Moore* (R)	178,434
	Rick Jones (D)	87,986
2	Chris Stewart* (R)	154,883
	Nick Mitchell (D)	88,224
3	John Curtis* (R)	182,497
	Glenn Wright (D)	83,687
4	Burgess Owens* (R)	155,110
	Darlene McDonald (D)	82,181
	January Walker (United Utah)	16,740

Vermont

Dist.	Representative/candidate (party)	2022 election results
	Becca Balint (D)	176,494
	Liam Madden (R)	78,397
	Ericka Redic (LB)	12,590

Virginia

Dist.	Representative/candidate (party)	2022 election results
1	Rob Wittman* (R)	191,828
	Herb Jones Jr. (D)	147,229
2	Jen Kiggans (R)	153,328
	Elaine Luria* (D)	143,219
3	Bobby Scott* (D)	139,659
	Terry Namkung (R)	67,668
4[3]	Jennifer McClellan (D)	82,040
	Leon Benjamin (R)	28,083
5	Bob Good* (R)	177,191
	Joshua Throneburg (D)	129,996

Dist.	Representative/candidate (party)	2022 election results
6	Ben Cline* (R)	173,352
	Jennifer Lewis (D)	95,410
7	Abigail Spanberger* (D)	143,357
	Yesli Vega (R)	130,586
8	Don Beyer* (D)	197,760
	Karina Lipsman (R)	66,589
9	Morgan Griffith* (R)	182,207
	Taysha DeVaughan (D)	66,027
10	Jennifer Wexton* (D)	157,405
	Hung Cao (R)	138,163
11	Gerry Connolly* (D)	193,190
	Jim Myles (R)	95,634

Washington

Dist.	Representative/candidate (party)	2022 election results
1	Suzan DelBene* (D)	181,992
	Vincent Cavaleri (R)	104,329
2	Rick Larsen* (D)	202,980
	Dan Matthews (R)	134,335
3	Marie Gluesenkamp Perez (D)	160,314
	Joe Kent (R)	157,685
4	Dan Newhouse* (R)	150,619
	Doug White (D)	70,710
5	Cathy McMorris Rodgers* (R)	188,648
	Natasha Hill (D)	127,585
6	Derek Kilmer* (D)	208,710
	Elizabeth Kreiselmaier (R)	138,754
7	Pramila Jayapal* (D)	295,998
	Cliff Moon (R)	49,207
8	Kim Schrier* (D)	179,003
	Matt Larkin (R)	155,976
9	Adam Smith* (D)	171,746
	Doug Basler (R)	67,631
10	Marilyn Strickland* (D)	152,544
	Keith Swank (R)	114,777

West Virginia

Dist.	Representative/candidate (party)	2022 election results
1	Carol Miller** (R)	151,511
	Lacy Watson (D)	65,428
	Belinda Fox-Spencer (Ind.)	10,257
2	Alex Mooney** (R)	160,493
	Barry Lee Wendell (D)	84,278

Wisconsin

Dist.	Representative/candidate (party)	2022 election results
1	Bryan Steil* (R)	162,610
	Ann Roe (D)	135,825
2	Mark Pocan* (D)	268,740
	Erik Olsen (R)	101,890
3	Derrick Van Orden (R)	164,743
	Brad Pfaff (D)	152,977
4	Gwen Moore* (D)	191,955
	Tim Rogers (R)	57,660
5	Scott Fitzgerald* (R)	243,741
	Mike Van Someren (D)	134,581
6	Glenn Grothman* (R)	Unopposed
7	Tom Tiffany* (R)	209,224
	Richard Ausman (D)	128,877
8	Mike Gallagher* (R)	223,981
	Paul Boucher (Ind.)	48,896
	Jacob VandenPlas (LB)	32,057

Wyoming

Dist.	Representative/candidate (party)	2022 election results
	Harriet Hageman (R)	132,206
	Lynnette Grey Bull (D)	47,250

(1) Vote results for Golden and Poliquin reflect round two of Maine's ranked-choice general election. (2) Cicilline resigned effective May 31, 2023. (3) Incumbent Donald McEachin (D) died in Nov. 2022 after being reelected. Result of a special election to fill the seat Feb. 21, 2023.

Nonvoting Members of Congress

Delegate/candidate (party)	2022 election results
American Samoa	
Aumua Amata Coleman Radewagen* (R)	Unopposed
District of Columbia	
Eleanor Holmes Norton* (D)	174,238
Nelson Rimensnyder (R)	11,701
Guam	
Jim Moylan (R)	17,260
Judith Won Pat (D)	15,636

Delegate/candidate (party)	2022 election results
Northern Mariana Islands	
Gregorio Kilili Camacho Sablan* (D)	Unopposed
Puerto Rico—Resident Commissioner	
(4-year term; began in Jan. 2021)	
Jenniffer González-Colón* (New Progressive [R])	
Virgin Islands	
Stacey E. Plaskett* (D)	Unopposed

U.S. SUPREME COURT

Justices of the U.S. Supreme Court

The Supreme Court comprises the chief justice of the U.S. and eight associate justices, all appointed for life by the president with advice and consent of the U.S. Senate. Names of chief justices are in **boldface**. Terms of service begin with the year each justice took the judicial oath. Years served is a total of complete years served by a past justice. 2023 salaries: chief justice, $298,500; associate justices, $285,400. The U.S. Supreme Court Building is at 1 First St. NE, Washington, DC 20543.

Website: www.supremecourt.gov

Name, appointed from	Term	Yrs.	Born	Died
John Jay, NY	1789-1795	5	1745	1829
John Rutledge, SC[1]	1790-1791	1	1739	1800
William Cushing, MA	1790-1810*	20	1732	1810
James Wilson, PA	1789-1798	8	1742	1798
John Blair, VA	1789-1795*	5	1732	1800
James Iredell, NC	1790-1799	9	1751	1799
Thomas Johnson, MD	1792-1793	<1	1732	1819
William Paterson, NJ	1793-1806	13	1745	1806
John Rutledge, SC[2,3]	1795	<1	1739	1800
Samuel Chase, MD	1796-1811	15	1741	1811
Oliver Ellsworth, CT	1796-1800	4	1745	1807
Bushrod Washington, VA	1799-1829*	30	1762	1829
Alfred Moore, NC	1800-1804	3	1755	1810
John Marshall, VA	1801-1835	34	1755	1835
William Johnson, SC	1804-1834	30	1771	1834
Henry B. Livingston, NY	1807-1823	16	1757	1823
Thomas Todd, KY	1807-1826	18	1765	1826
Gabriel Duvall, MD	1811-1835	23	1752	1844
Joseph Story, MA	1812-1845*	33	1779	1845
Smith Thompson, NY	1823-1843	20	1768	1843
Robert Trimble, KY	1826-1828	2	1777	1828
John McLean, OH	1830-1861*	31	1785	1861
Henry Baldwin, PA	1830-1844	14	1780	1844
James M. Wayne, GA	1835-1867	32	1790	1867
Roger B. Taney, MD	1836-1864	28	1777	1864
Philip P. Barbour, VA	1836-1841	4	1783	1841
John Catron, TN	1837-1865	28	1786	1865
John McKinley, AL	1838-1852*	14	1780	1852
Peter V. Daniel, VA	1842-1860*	18	1784	1860
Samuel Nelson, NY	1845-1872	27	1792	1873
Levi Woodbury, NH	1845-1851	5	1789	1851
Robert C. Grier, PA	1846-1870	23	1794	1870
Benjamin R. Curtis, MA	1851-1857	5	1809	1874
John A. Campbell, AL	1853-1861*	8	1811	1889
Nathan Clifford, ME	1858-1881	23	1803	1881
Noah H. Swayne, OH	1862-1881	18	1804	1884
Samuel F. Miller, IA	1862-1890	28	1816	1890
David Davis, IL	1862-1877	14	1815	1886
Stephen J. Field, CA	1863-1897	33	1816	1899
Salmon P. Chase, OH	1864-1873	8	1808	1873
William Strong, PA	1870-1880	10	1808	1895
Joseph P. Bradley, NJ	1870-1892	21	1813	1892
Ward Hunt, NY	1873-1882	9	1810	1886
Morrison R. Waite, OH	1874-1888	14	1816	1888
John M. Harlan, KY	1877-1911	33	1833	1911
William B. Woods, GA	1881-1887	6	1824	1887
Stanley Matthews, OH	1881-1889	7	1824	1889
Horace Gray, MA	1882-1902	20	1828	1902
Samuel Blatchford, NY	1882-1893	11	1820	1893
Lucius Q. C. Lamar, MS	1888-1893	5	1825	1893
Melville W. Fuller, IL	1888-1910	21	1833	1910
David J. Brewer, KS	1890-1910	20	1837	1910
Henry B. Brown, MI	1891-1906	15	1836	1913
George Shiras Jr., PA	1892-1903	10	1832	1924
Howell E. Jackson, TN	1893-1895	2	1832	1895
Edward D. White, LA[1]	1894-1910	16	1845	1921
Rufus W. Peckham, NY	1896-1909	13	1838	1909
Joseph McKenna, CA	1898-1925	26	1843	1926
Oliver W. Holmes, MA	1902-1932	29	1841	1935
William R. Day, OH	1903-1922	19	1849	1923
William H. Moody, MA	1906-1910	3	1853	1917
Horace H. Lurton, TN	1910-1914	4	1844	1914
Charles E. Hughes, NY[1]	1910-1916	5	1862	1948
Willis Van Devanter, WY	1911-1937	26	1859	1941
Joseph R. Lamar, GA	1911-1916	5	1857	1916
Edward D. White, LA[2]	1910-1921	10	1845	1921
Mahlon Pitney, NJ	1912-1922	10	1858	1924
James C. McReynolds, TN	1914-1941	26	1862	1946
Louis D. Brandeis, MA	1916-1939	22	1856	1941
John H. Clarke, OH	1916-1922	5	1857	1945
William H. Taft, CT	1921-1930	8	1857	1930
George Sutherland, UT	1922-1938	15	1862	1942
Pierce Butler, MN	1923-1939	16	1866	1939
Edward T. Sanford, TN	1923-1930	7	1865	1930
Harlan F. Stone, NY[1]	1925-1941	16	1872	1946
Charles E. Hughes, NY[2]	1930-1941	11	1862	1948
Owen J. Roberts, PA	1930-1945	15	1875	1955
Benjamin N. Cardozo, NY	1932-1938	6	1870	1938
Hugo L. Black, AL	1937-1971	34	1886	1971
Stanley F. Reed, KY	1938-1957	19	1884	1980
Felix Frankfurter, MA	1939-1962	23	1882	1965
William O. Douglas, CT	1939-1975	36[4]	1898	1980
Frank Murphy, MI	1940-1949	9	1890	1949
Harlan F. Stone, NY[2]	1941-1946	4	1872	1946
James F. Byrnes, SC	1941-1942	1	1879	1972
Robert H. Jackson, NY	1941-1954	13	1892	1954
Wiley B. Rutledge, IA	1943-1949	6	1894	1949
Harold H. Burton, OH	1945-1958	13	1888	1964
Fred M. Vinson, KY	1946-1953	7	1890	1953
Tom C. Clark, TX	1949-1967	17	1899	1977
Sherman Minton, IN	1949-1956	7	1890	1965
Earl Warren, CA	1953-1969	15	1891	1974
John Marshall Harlan, NY	1955-1971	16	1899	1971
William J. Brennan Jr., NJ	1956-1990	33	1906	1997
Charles E. Whittaker, MO	1957-1962	5	1901	1973
Potter Stewart, OH	1958-1981	22	1915	1985
Byron R. White, CO	1962-1993	31	1917	2002
Arthur J. Goldberg, IL	1962-1965	2	1908	1990
Abe Fortas, TN	1965-1969	3	1910	1982
Thurgood Marshall, NY	1967-1991	24	1908	1993
Warren E. Burger, VA	1969-1986	17	1907	1995
Harry A. Blackmun, MN	1970-1994	24	1908	1999
Lewis F. Powell Jr., VA	1972-1987	15	1907	1998
William H. Rehnquist, AZ[1]	1972-1986	14	1924	2005
John Paul Stevens, IL	1975-2010	34	1920	2019
Sandra Day O'Connor, AZ	1981-2006	24	1930	
William H. Rehnquist, VA[2]	1986-2005	18	1924	2005
Antonin Scalia, VA	1986-2016	29	1936	2016
Anthony M. Kennedy, CA	1988-2018	30	1936	
David H. Souter, NH	1990-2009	18	1939	
Clarence Thomas, GA	1991-		1948	
Ruth Bader Ginsburg, NY	1993-2020	27	1933	2020
Stephen G. Breyer, MA	1994-2022	28	1938	
John G. Roberts Jr., MD	2005-		1955	
Samuel A. Alito Jr., NJ	2006-		1950	
Sonia Sotomayor, NY	2009-		1954	
Elena Kagan, MA	2010-		1960	
Neil M. Gorsuch, CO	2017-		1967	
Brett Kavanaugh, MD	2018-		1965	
Amy Coney Barrett, IN	2020-		1972	
Ketanji Brown Jackson, DC	2022-		1970	

* = Because of inadequate government record keeping, date of oath is estimated. (1) Later, chief justice, as listed. (2) Formerly associate justice. (3) Named acting chief justice; confirmation rejected by the Senate. (4) Longest term of service.

Supreme Court History and Notable Firsts

The U.S. Supreme Court first convened Feb. 1, 1790, in New York, NY. Acting on the authority of Congress as outlined in the Judiciary Act of 1789, the court consisted of Chief Justice John Jay and five associate justices who held sessions for a few weeks in Feb. and Aug. The justices also served twice a year in each of the nation's then-13 judicial districts, a requirement known as riding circuit. The number of Justices on the Court changed six times before settling at a total of nine in 1869. Through the 2022-23 term, 116 justices have served on the Court.

The Court's first major legal decision, *Chisholm v. Georgia* (1793), ruled that federal courts held jurisdiction over disputes between individual states and citizens of other states. (The 11th Amendment, which the states ratified in 1795, removed that jurisdiction.) The Court over time has expanded its impact on the nation's affairs. Since 1803 it has declared unconstitutional more than 180 acts of Congress and over 1,000 state, territorial, and municipal laws and statutes. The Court usually hears oral arguments in about 70-80 cases per term. In May 2020 the Court began holding oral arguments by telephone and offering a livestream audio broadcast of the session, both for the first time. Oral arguments in person resumed Oct. 4, 2021.

Of 164 nominations to the Court (including chief justice nominations), the Senate has voted to reject just 12, most recently Robert Bork in 1987. George W. Bush-nominee Harriet Miers withdrew her nomination before the Senate considered it, in 2005. The Senate did not hold hearings on Obama nominee Merrick Garland in 2016, citing the impending presidential election.

Justices may be removed from the Court by impeachment. In 1804, the House of Representatives, in the control of Jeffersonian Republicans, impeached Samuel Chase, a Federalist; he was acquitted by the Senate in 1805.

First fully vested justice: James Wilson, who took the Constitutional Oath of the Court Oct. 5, 1789
First Catholic justice: Roger B.Taney (1836-64)
First Jewish justice: Louis D. Brandeis (1916-39)
Only person to serve as both U.S. president and chief justice: William Howard Taft (pres., 1909-13; chief justice, 1921-30)

First justice to take an oath at the White House: Frank Murphy, Jan. 18, 1940
First Black justice: Thurgood Marshall (1967-91)
First woman justice: Sandra Day O'Connor (1981-2006)
First Hispanic justice: Sonia Sotomayor (2009-)
First Black woman justice: Ketanji Brown Jackson (2022-)

U.S. Supreme Court Decisions by Issue and Leadership Era, 1946-2022

Source: Supreme Court Database, supremecourtdatabase.org

Decisions through the end of the 2021-22 term. Figures are the number of cases decided in each issue category (number of 5-4 decisions in parentheses). The Court begins its term the first Monday in Oct. and typically recesses in late June.

	Number of decisions under Chief Justice—				
Issue	Vinson (1946-53)	Warren (1953-69)	Burger (1969-86)	Rehnquist (1986-2005)	Roberts (2005-)
Attorneys[1]	2 (0)	12 (1)	37 (5)	31 (7)	21 (3)
Civil rights	74 (7)	316 (30)	555 (79)	326 (68)	216 (42)
Criminal procedure	123 (29)	462 (72)	627 (110)	509 (139)	348 (74)
Due process	47 (6)	40 (5)	144 (19)	86 (23)	37 (9)
Economic activity	224 (38)	493 (53)	452 (52)	347 (40)	271 (30)
Federal taxation	49 (2)	118 (6)	75 (7)	56 (3)	17 (3)
Federalism	33 (1)	94 (3)	107 (6)	124 (26)	57 (11)
First amendment	44 (8)	206 (47)	236 (57)	140 (37)	69 (16)
Interstate relations	12 (1)	14 (0)	40 (0)	23 (1)	13 (2)
Judicial power	135 (18)	299 (21)	366 (35)	286 (28)	164 (30)
Miscellaneous[2]	1 (0)	1 (0)	4 (0)	10 (0)	12 (3)
Privacy	4 (0)	2 (0)	48 (10)	42 (7)	24 (3)
Private action[3]	0 (0)	0 (0)	0 (0)	0 (0)	6 (1)
Unions	41 (4)	131 (8)	109 (24)	55 (11)	30 (9)
Total	**789 (115)**	**2,188 (246)**	**2,800 (404)**	**2,035 (390)**	**1,285 (236)**

Note: Decision types include orally argued judgments, per curiams, and opinions; per curiams without oral arguments; equally divided votes; and decrees. (1) Includes cases on commercial fees, attorneys' fees, admission to state or federal bar, attorney discipline, and disbarment. (2) Includes cases that could not be classified. (3) Includes cases on civil procedures, commercial transactions, contracts, evidence, personal and real property, torts, and wills and trusts.

Selected Landmark Decisions of the U.S. Supreme Court

1803: *Marbury v. Madison.* The Court ruled that Congress exceeded its power in the Judiciary Act of 1789. The Court thus established its power to review acts of Congress and to declare invalid those it found to be in conflict with the Constitution.

1819: *Trustees of Dartmouth College v. Woodward.* The Court ruled that a state could not arbitrarily alter the terms of a college's contract. The Court later used a similar principle to limit the states' ability to interfere with business contracts.

1819: *McCulloch v. Maryland.* The Court ruled that Congress had the authority to charter a national bank, under the Constitution's granting of power to enact all laws "necessary and proper" to responsibilities of government.

1824: *Gibbons v. Ogden.* The Court ruled that New York state had overstepped its authority in granting a monopoly to two steamboat operators. According to the ruling, Congress's power to regulate interstate commerce included transportation.

1857: *Dred Scott v. Sandford.* The Court declared unconstitutional the already-repealed Missouri Compromise of 1820 because it deprived a person of "property"—an enslaved person—without due process of law. The Court also ruled that enslaved individuals were not citizens of any state nor of the U.S. The latter part of the decision was overturned by ratification of the 14th Amendment in 1868.

1880: *Strauder v. West Virginia.* The Court struck down a state law mandating that jurors must be white, ruling it a

violation of the right to equal protection under the 14th Amendment.

1896: *Plessy v. Ferguson.* The Court ruled that a state law requiring federal railroad trains to provide "equal but separate" facilities for Black and white passengers neither infringed upon federal authority to regulate interstate commerce nor violated the 13th and 14th Amendments. What became known as the "separate but equal" doctrine remained in effect until the 1954 *Brown v. Board of Education* decision.

1904: *Northern Securities Co. v. U.S.* The Court ruled that a holding company formed solely to eliminate competition between two railroad lines was a combination in restraint of trade, violating the 1890 federal Sherman Antitrust Act.

1908: *Muller v. Oregon.* The Court upheld a state law limiting the working hours of women. (Louis D. Brandeis, counsel for the state, in what is known as the "Brandeis brief," cited evidence from social workers, physicians, and factory inspectors that long work hours were harmful to women.)

1911: *Standard Oil Co. of New Jersey v. U.S.* The Court ruled that the Standard Oil Trust must be dissolved because of its unreasonable restraint of trade.

1919: *Schenck v. U.S.* The Court sustained the Espionage Act of 1917, maintaining that freedom of speech and press could be constrained if "the words used … create a clear and present danger."

1925: *Gitlow v. New York.* The Court ruled that the 1st Amendment free-speech guarantee applied to the states as well as to the federal government. The decision was the first of a number of rulings holding that the 14th Amendment extended the guarantees of the Bill of Rights to state action.

1926: *Myers v. U.S.* The Court held that the president has the power to remove appointed executive-branch officials, without congressional approval. In *Seila Law v. CFPB* (2020) the Court further found that Congress could not make the head of a federal agency, the Consumer Financial Protection Bureau, immune by law from being fired by a president.

1935: *Schechter Poultry Corp. v. U.S.* The Court ruled that Congress exceeded its authority to delegate legislative powers and to regulate interstate commerce when it enacted the National Industrial Recovery Act (1933), which afforded the U.S. president too much discretionary power.

1944: *Korematsu v. U.S.* The Court upheld the constitutionality of an order barring all persons of Japanese ancestry, including U.S. citizens, from much of the West Coast, forcing them into internment camps, ruling that the need to prevent espionage outweighed the petitioner's civil rights. The ruling, never officially overturned, followed *Hirabayashi v. U.S.* (1943), in which the Court upheld the imposition of curfews on minority populations perceived to be a potential wartime threat.

1951: *Dennis v. U.S.* The Court upheld convictions under the Smith Act of 1940 for invoking Communist theory advocating the forcible overthrow of the government. In *Yates v. U.S.* (1957), the Court moderated this ruling by allowing such advocacy in the abstract, if not connected to action to achieve the goal.

1952: *Youngstown Sheet & Tube Co. v. Sawyer.* The Court ruled that the president had exceeded his wartime power in ordering the seizure of private steel mills during a nationwide steelworkers' strike.

1954: *Brown v. Board of Education of Topeka.* The Court ruled that separate public schools for Black and white students were inherently unequal, so state-sanctioned segregation in public schools violated the equal protection guarantee of the 14th Amendment. The Court decided *Bolling v. Sharpe* the same year, ruling that the congressionally mandated segregated public school system in the District of Columbia violated the 5th Amendment's due process guarantee of personal liberty. In *Brown II* (1955), the Court ordered the integration of schools with "all deliberate speed." The Brown rulings also led to abolition of state-sponsored segregation in other public facilities.

1957: *Roth v. U.S.; Alberts v. California.* The Court ruled obscene material—defined as appealing primarily to "prurient interest" in the view of "the average person, applying contemporary community standards"—was not protected by 1st Amendment guarantees of freedom of speech and press, being "utterly without redeeming social importance." This definition was modified in later decisions, including *Miller v. California* (1973).

1958: *Cooper v. Aaron.* The Court held that Arkansas could not nullify *Brown v. Board of Education* (1954) through the passage of legislation or constitutional amendments barring integration. The opinion of the Court affirmed its reading of the Constitution as the "supreme law of the land."

1961: *Mapp v. Ohio.* The Court ruled that evidence obtained in violation of the 4th Amendment guarantee against unreasonable search and seizure must be excluded from use in state as well as federal trials.

1962: *Baker v. Carr.* The Court held that constitutional challenges to the unequal distribution of voters among legislative districts could be resolved by federal courts.

1962: *Engel v. Vitale.* The Court held that government bodies could not encourage the recitation of a state-composed prayer in public schools, even if nondenominational, because that would be an unconstitutional attempt to establish religion.

1963: *Gideon v. Wainwright.* The Court ruled that indigent defendants, even in state cases, have a right to legal counsel as guaranteed by the 6th Amendment.

1964: *New York Times Co. v. Sullivan.* The Court ruled that the 1st Amendment protected the press from libel suits for defamatory reports about public officials unless an injured party could prove "malice," with "reckless disregard" for truth.

1964: *Heart of Atlanta Motel v. U.S.* The Court upheld Title II of the 1964 Civil Rights Act banning racial discrimination in motels/hotels engaged in interstate commerce (by accommodating travelers from other states). The Court in *Katzenbach v. McClung* (1964) held that Title II also applied to many restaurants and businesses.

1965: *Griswold v. Connecticut.* The Court ruled that a state unconstitutionally interfered with privacy in a marriage when it prohibited the use of contraceptives.

1966: *Miranda v. Arizona.* The Court ruled that, under the guarantee of due process, suspects in custody, before being questioned, must be informed that they have the right to remain silent, that anything they say may be used against them, and that they have the right to counsel.

1967: *Loving v. Virginia.* The Court unanimously struck down all state laws banning interracial marriage.

1968: *Terry v. Ohio.* The Court ruled that a "stop and frisk" performed without a warrant or probable cause was not a violation of 4th Amendment rights, provided that the officer had a reasonable suspicion that the subject was armed and dangerous, or had committed or was about to commit a crime.

1969: *Brandenburg v. Ohio.* The Court held that government cannot restrict inflammatory speech unless it is "directed to inciting or producing imminent lawless action AND is likely to incite or produce such action." The so-called Brandenburg test refined the "clear and present danger" test outlined in *Schenck v. U.S.* (1927).

1969: *Tinker v. Des Moines Community School District.* The majority held that students' wearing of armbands in a symbolic political statement did not disrupt school operations and thus was protected under the 1st Amendment.

1973: *Roe v. Wade.* The Court ruled that the fetus was not a "person" with constitutional rights and that a right to privacy inherent in the 14th Amendment's due process guarantee of personal liberty protected a woman's decision to have an abortion. Some regulation of abortion procedures was allowed in the second trimester and some restriction of abortion in the third. In *Planned Parenthood v. Casey* (1992) the Court affirmed the basic right to abortion prior to fetal viability; it allowed states to impose regulations only if they did not impose an "undue burden" on access.

1974: *U.S. v. Nixon.* The Court ruled that neither the separation of powers nor the need to preserve the confidentiality of presidential communications could alone justify an absolute executive privilege of immunity from judicial demands for evidence to be used in a criminal trial.

1976: *Gregg v. Georgia; Proffitt v. Florida; Jurek v. Texas.* The Court held that death, as a punishment for persons convicted of first-degree murder, was not in and of itself cruel and unusual punishment in violation of the 8th Amendment. But the Court ruled that the sentencing judge and jury must consider the character of the offender and the circumstances.

1978: *Regents of the Univ. of Calif. v. Bakke.* The Court ruled that an admissions program for a state medical school that set specific quotas for minorities violated the 1964 Civil Rights Act, which forbids the exclusion of anyone from a federally funded program based on race. But the Court ruled that race could be considered as one of a complex of factors.

1985: *New Jersey v. T.L.O.* The Court ruled that searches on school grounds do not necessarily violate students' 4th Amendment rights because they may be outweighed by schools' need to maintain learning environments.

1986: *Batson v. Kentucky.* The Court ruled that a peremptory challenge cannot be used in a criminal case to exclude a juror solely because of race.

1986: *Bowers v. Hardwick.* The Court refused to extend any right of privacy to homosexual activity, upholding a Georgia antisodomy law that in effect made it a crime. But in *Lawrence v. Texas* (2003), the Court struck down all state antisodomy laws as violating the 14th Amendment's due process clause. In *Romer v. Evans* (1996), the Court struck down a Colorado constitutional provision that barred homosexuals from recognition as a protected class.

1989: *Texas v. Johnson.* The Court held the actions of a political activist who burned an American flag were expressive and thus protected by the 1st Amendment. The ruling invalidated laws in 48 states barring flag desecration.

1990: *Cruzan v. Missouri.* The Court ruled that while a person had the right to refuse life-sustaining medical treatment, a state could require evidence that a comatose patient would not have wanted to live before withholding treatment. In two 1997 rulings, *Washington v. Glucksberg* and *Vacco v. Quill*, the Court ruled that states could ban doctor-assisted suicide.

1995: *U.S. Term Limits, Inc. v. Thornton.* The Court ruled that neither states nor Congress could limit terms of members of Congress because the Constitution reserves to the people the right to choose federal lawmakers.

1995: *Adarand Constructors, Inc. v. Peña.* The Court held that federal programs that classify people by race, unless "narrowly tailored" to further a "compelling governmental interest," are subject to strict scrutiny.

1997: *Clinton v. Jones.* Rejecting an appeal by Pres. Clinton in a sexual harassment suit, the Court ruled that a sitting president did not have temporary immunity from a lawsuit for actions outside the realm of official duties.

1997: *City of Boerne v. Flores.* The Court overturned the portion of a 1993 law banning enforcement of state laws that "substantially burden" religious practice unless there is a "compelling governmental interest" to do so. The Court held that the act was an unwarranted intrusion by Congress on states' prerogatives and an infringement of the judiciary's role.

1997: *Reno v. ACLU.* Citing the right to free expression, the Court overturned a provision making it a crime to display or distribute "obscene or indecent" or "patently offensive" material on the Internet. The Court ruled, however, in *NEA v. Finley*

(1998) that "general standards of decency" may be used as a criterion in federal arts funding.

1998: *Clinton v. City of New York.* The Court struck down the Line-Item Veto Act (1996), holding that it gave presidents "unilateral power to change the text of duly enacted statutes."

1998: *Faragher v. City of Boca Raton; Burlington Industries, Inc. v. Ellerth.* The Court issued new guidelines for workplace sexual harassment suits, holding employers responsible for misconduct by supervisory employees. And in *Oncale v. Sundowner Offshore Services, Inc.* the same year, the Court ruled that the law against discrimination based on sex applies even if the harasser and harassed are the same sex.

1999: *Dept. of Commerce v. U.S. House of Representatives.* Upholding a challenge to plans for the 2000 census, the Court prohibited statistical sampling, favored by Democrats, in apportioning seats in the U.S. House.

1999: *Alden v. Maine; Florida Prepaid v. College Savings Bank; College Savings Bank v. Florida Prepaid.* In a series of rulings, the Court applied the principle of sovereign immunity to shield states in large part from being sued under federal law.

2000: *Boy Scouts of America v. Dale.* The Court ruled that the Boy Scouts could dismiss a troop leader after learning he was gay, holding that the right to freedom of association outweighed a New Jersey antidiscrimination statute.

2000: *Bush v. Gore.* The Court ruled that manual recounts in Florida of ballots cast in the 2000 presidential election could not proceed because inconsistent evaluation standards violated the equal protection clause. In effect, the ruling let the official results stand, making George W. Bush the winner.

2001: *Good News Club v. Milford Central School.* The justices found that a private religious organization could not be denied equal access to a public school facility for after-school meetings because that would violate free speech rights.

2002: *Federal Maritime Commission v. South Carolina State Ports Authority.* The Court ruled that the 11th Amendment gave states immunity from private lawsuits involving federal agencies.

2002: *Atkins v. Virginia.* The Court ruled that executing a person with intellectual disabilities violated the 8th Amendment ban on cruel and unusual punishment.

2002: *Zelman v. Simmons-Harris.* The Court ruled that publicly funded tuition vouchers could be used at religious schools without violating the separation of church and state.

2003: *Grutter v. Bollinger; Gratz v. Bollinger.* The Court upheld the use of race as a factor in the Univ. of Michigan Law School's admissions policies because of the school's interest in a diverse student body. But the Court ruled against a strict point system based on racial and ethnic backgrounds as used in the university's undergraduate admissions process.

2004: *Tennessee v. Lane.* The Court ruled that disabled individuals could sue states under the Americans With Disabilities Act (1990) for failing to provide adequate access to state courthouses, despite states' usual immunity from private lawsuits in federal court under the 11th Amendment.

2004: *Locke v. Davey.* The justices decided that a scholarship program provided by the state of Washington did not violate the right to free exercise of religion in denying aid to students preparing for the clergy.

2004: *Ashcroft v. ACLU.* The Court struck down federal legislation passed in 1998 to restrict online access to pornography by minors, as violating the right of free speech.

2005: *Roper v. Simmons.* The Court barred execution for crimes committed before age 18, as violating the 8th Amendment ban on "cruel and unusual" punishment.

2005: *Kelo v. City of New London.* The Court ruled that local governments could force property owners to sell their land in order to facilitate private development projects deemed to be economically beneficial to the community.

2006: *Garcetti v. Ceballos.* The Court ruled that the 1st Amendment guarantee of free speech did not protect statements made by public employees in the course of their official duties.

2006: *Hamdan v. Rumsfeld.* The Court ruled that Pres. George W. Bush's system for trying terrorism detainees at the U.S. military base in Guantánamo Bay, Cuba, was unauthorized under federal law and the international Geneva Conventions. The Court furthermore ruled in *Boumediene v. Bush* (2008) that detainees had a right to challenge their detention in federal court by applying for a writ of habeas corpus.

2007: *Gonzales v. Carhart; Gonzales v. Planned Parenthood Federation of America.* The Court upheld a 2003 federal law prohibiting the abortion procedure known as intact dilation and extraction, or "partial-birth" abortion.

2007: *Parents Involved in Community Schools v. Seattle School District No. 1; Meredith v. Jefferson County Board of Education.* The Court ruled that two school districts could not, to encourage diversity, use "racial classifications in making school assignments."

2008: *Crawford v. Marion County Election Board.* The Court upheld the constitutionality of an Indiana law requiring in-person voters to present valid government photo identification.

2008: *District of Columbia v. Heller.* The Court overturned DC's handgun ban, ruling that the 2nd Amendment protected an individual's right to own guns for personal use.

2010: *Citizens United v. Federal Election Commission.* The Court ruled that a federal law barring corporations from using general funds to finance campaign advertisements was unconstitutional. The decision cast doubt on many laws restricting political spending by corporations and unions.

2011: *Snyder v. Phelps.* The justices found that an antigay church whose members protested at the funeral of a Marine could not be held liable for intrusion or emotional distress because the protests were protected by the 1st Amendment.

2012: *U.S. v. Jones.* The Court ruled that attaching a GPS tracking device to a suspect's car and monitoring its movements requires a search warrant, as the 4th Amendment prohibition against unreasonable search and seizure applies.

2012: *Miller v. Alabama.* The Court ruled that mandatory life sentences of juveniles without the possibility of parole constitute cruel and unusual punishment, barred by the 8th Amendment. The decision extended *Graham v. Florida* (2010), which barred life sentences for juveniles for nonhomicide crimes. But in *Jones v. Mississippi* (2021) the Court ruled that juvenile offenders need not be deemed permanently incorrigible before they can be so sentenced.

2012: *Natl. Federation of Independent Business v. Sebelius.* The Court ruled Congress acted within its powers of taxation in enacting the individual-mandate provision of the Patient Protection and Affordable Care Act (ACA). But the Court ruled unconstitutional the provision of the act's Medicaid expansion that threatened non-compliant states with loss of funding.

2013: *Shelby County v. Holder.* The justices struck down a key provision of the 1965 Voting Rights Act, meant to prevent discriminatory voting regulations, because it relied on outdated information to identify jurisdictions for additional scrutiny.

2013: *U.S. v. Windsor.* The Court struck down the central provision of the 1996 federal Defense of Marriage Act (DOMA), which prohibited federal recognition of same-sex marriages. A separate decision the same year, in *Hollingsworth v. Perry,* had the effect of legalizing same-sex marriage in California.

2014: *Riley v. California; U.S. v. Wurie.* The Court decided that police generally could not search the mobile telephones of arrested individuals without a search warrant.

2014: *Burwell v. Hobby Lobby Stores; Conestoga Wood Specialties Corp. v. Burwell.* The justices ruled that some closely held corporations could claim an exemption on religious grounds from a 2010 ACA mandate requiring many businesses to provide health insurance that covers contraception.

2015: *Obergefell v. Hodges.* The Court ruled that state bans on same-sex marriage violated couples' rights under the due process and equal protection clauses of the 14th Amendment.

2016: *Whole Woman's Health v. Hellerstedt.* The justices ruled that a Texas law that included stringent regulations on abortion providers did not pass the "undue burden" standard the Court established in 1992's *Planned Parenthood v. Casey.*

2018: *Janus v. American Federation of State, County and Municipal Employees (AFSCME).* The Court struck down rules compelling public employees who opted not to join a union to pay fees in support of its collective-bargaining efforts.

2019: *Rucho v. Common Cause; Lamone v. Benisek.* The Court found that federal courts have no constitutional basis for intervening to block partisan gerrymandering.

2020: *Chiafalo v. Washington.* The Court ruled that a state could require presidential electors to vote for the candidate who won the most popular votes in the state.

2020: *Bostock v. Clayton County.* The Court found that gay and transgender employees were protected from workplace discrimination under 1964 civil rights legislation.

2021: *Edwards v. Vannoy.* The Court ruled that when it issues new rules for criminal procedure that benefit defendants they do not apply retroactively to past final convictions.

2021: *Americans for Prosperity v. Bonta.* The Court found that California violated free speech rights of donors in requiring tax-exempt charities to file federal forms with state regulators that identify major contributors.

2021: *Cedar Point Nursery v. Hassid.* The Court struck down a California regulation giving union organizers a right to visit workers on farms, as a violation of property rights.

2021: *Brnovich v. Democratic National Committee.* The Court ruled that Arizona could enforce measures that restrict collection of mail-in ballots by third parties and disallow votes cast in the wrong precinct, rejecting claims of substantial disproportionate burden on minorities in violation of the 1965 federal Voting Rights Act.

2022: *NY State Rifle & Pistol Assn. v. Bruen.* The Court struck down a New York state law that required "special need" for a license to carry guns outside the home, finding that the 2nd Amendment gives a broad right to carry firearms in public.

2022: *Dobbs v. Jackson Women's Health Organization.* The Court ruled that a Mississippi law banning most abortions after 15 weeks of gestation was constitutional and overturned the decision in *Roe v. Wade* (1973).

See Year in Review: Notable Supreme Court Decisions for major 2022-23 decisions in detail.

Sources: Population: Decennial Censuses and Population Estimates Program, U.S. Census Bureau, U.S. Dept. of Commerce; population as of July 1, 2022, unless otherwise noted. Pop. density is for land area only. **Racial distribution** categories, as of July 1, 2022, are abbreviated; their full forms are white, Black or African American, Asian, American Indian and Alaska Native, Native Hawaiian and other Pacific Islander, two or more races. Categories do not add up to 100% due to rounding. **Hispanic** or Latino persons, as of July 1, 2022, may be of any race. **Area:** Geography Division, U.S. Census Bureau, U.S. Dept. of Commerce. **Acres forested:** U.S. Forest Service, U.S. Dept. of Agriculture; source year may vary. **Chief airports:** Federal Aviation Admin., U.S. Dept. of Transportation preliminary data. Chief airports had 500,000+ boardings in 2022; not all states had airports meeting this threshold. All **Economy** data as of 2022 unless otherwise noted. **Chief manuf. goods:** Manufacturing and Construction Division, U.S. Census Bureau, U.S. Dept. of Commerce. **Chief crops:** Natl. Agricultural Statistics Service, U.S. Dept. of Agriculture. **Farm income:** Economic Research Service, U.S. Dept. of Agriculture; 2021 cash receipts. **Nonfuel minerals:** Office of Mineral Information, U.S. Dept. of Interior; estimated 2022 data. Some states exclude small amounts to avoid disclosing proprietary data. **Commercial fishing:** Natl. Marine Fisheries Service, U.S. Dept. of Commerce; 2021 value. **Gross state product** and **Per cap. pers. income:** Bureau of Economic Analysis, U.S. Dept. of Commerce; as of Dec. 2022. **Sales tax:** Federation of Tax Administrators; as of Jan. 1, 2023. **Gasoline tax:** Energy Information Admin., U.S. Dept. of Energy; as of Jan. 1, 2023; incl. state excise tax, federal excise tax (18.4 cents per gallon), and other state fees. **Employment distrib.** and **Unemployment:** Bureau of Labor Statistics, U.S. Dept. of Labor; distribution is for non-farm jobs as of Apr. 2023; annual unemployment rate for 2022. **Min. wage/hr.:** U.S. Dept. of Labor; as of July 1, 2023. If a state has no minimum wage, or the state minimum wage is lower than the federal minimum wage, the federal rate of $7.25 applies. Small businesses may have lower minimum wages. Some municipalities may have different minimum wages. **New private housing:** Manufacturing and Construction Division, U.S. Census Bureau, U.S. Dept. of Commerce. Figures are building permits issued and est. value of the construction, as of 2022. **Broadband internet:** Industry Analysis and Tech. Division, Fed. Communications Commission; Natl. Telecommunications and Information Administration, U.S. Dept. of Commerce. Broadband connections have minimum speeds of at least 3 megabits per second (Mbps) downstream and 200 kilobits per second (kbps) upstream as of June 2019; figure given is broadband as a percentage of total internet connections. **Commercial banks** and **Savings institutions:** Federal Deposit Insurance Corp., as of June 30, 2022; FDIC-insured institutions only. **Lottery:** North American Assn. of State and Provincial Lotteries, FY 2022. Data may be unaudited and in some cases were gathered by third party; profit is amount of total funds transferred to public beneficiaries, after prizes to players/retailers and administrative costs. **Fed. civ. employees:** Office of Personnel Mgmt., U.S. Dept. of Labor; as of Dec. 2022. **Education:** Natl. Ctr. for Education Statistics; high school graduation rates as of 2019-20 school year; number of colleges/univ. as of 2020-21. Data for 4-yr. private institutions does not include for-profit colleges/universities. **Energy:** Energy Information Admin., U.S. Dept. of Energy; average per capita monthly electricity consumption and cost for residential customers in 2021. **Tourism:** U.S. Travel Assn.; 2022 tourist spending data is preliminary. Other information from sources in individual states. NA = Not available; AFB = Air Force base; JRB = joint reserve base; NAS = naval air station.

Famous persons lists may include non-natives associated with the state as well as persons born there. **Websites** are subject to change and are not endorsed by *The World Almanac*.

Alabama (AL)
Heart of Dixie (unofficial)

People. Population: 5,074,296; rank: 24. **Pop. change** (2010-22): 6.2%. **Pop. density:** 100 per sq mi. **Racial distribution:** 68.9% white; 26.8% Black; 1.6% Asian; 0.7% Amer. Ind.; 0.1% Hawaiian/Pacific Islander; 2 or more races, 2.0%. **Hispanic pop.:** 4.9%.

Geography. Total area: 52,420 sq mi; rank: 30. **Land area:** 50,645 sq mi; rank: 28. **Acres forested:** 23.1 mil. **Location:** East South Central state extending N-S from Tennessee to the Gulf of Mexico; E of the Mississippi River. **Climate:** long, hot summers; mild winters; generally abundant rain. **Topography:** coastal plains, including Prairie Black Belt, give way to hills, broken terrain; highest elevation 2,413 ft. **Capital:** Montgomery. **Chief airports:** Birmingham, Huntsville.

Economy. Chief industries: chemicals, electronics, apparel, primary metals, lumber and wood products, food processing, fabricated metals, automotive tires, oil and gas exploration. **Chief manuf. goods:** poultry processing, paper and paperboard, iron and steel, petroleum, automotive tires, aerospace, aluminum, auto body and parts. **Chief crops:** cotton, greenhouse and nursery, hay, peanuts, corn, soybeans. **Farm income:** Crops: $1.44 bil. Livestock: $4.57 bil. **Nonfuel minerals:** $1.9 bil; cement, lime, sand and gravel (construction), sand and gravel (industrial), stone (crushed). **Commercial fishing:** $81.7 mil. **Chief port:** Mobile. **Gross state product:** $277.8 bil. **Sales tax:** 4.0%. **Gasoline tax:** 47.60 cents/gal. **Employment distrib.:** 18.6% govt.; 19.0% trade/trans./util.; 12.9% mfg.; 11.9% ed./health; 12.5% prof./bus. serv.; 9.5% leisure/hosp.; 4.8% finance; 5.1% constr./mining/log.; 1.1% info.; 4.8% other serv. **Unemployment:** 2.6%. **Min. wage/hr.:** none. **Per cap. pers. income:** $50,637. **New private housing:** 19,506 units/$4.7 bil. **Broadband internet:** 96.6%. **Commercial banks:** 133; deposits $139.7 bil. **Savings institutions:** 3; deposits $422.0 mil.

Federal govt. Fed. civ. employees: 39,054; **avg. salary:** $95,222. **Notable fed. facilities:** Redstone Arsenal; Ft. Novosel (fmr. Rucker); Marshall Space Flight Ctr., Huntsville; Anniston Army Depot; Maxwell AFB and Gunter Annex; Army Corps of Engineers, Mobile District.

Education. High school grad. rate: 90.6%. **4-yr. public coll./univ.:** 14; **2-yr. public:** 25; **4-yr. private:** 19.

Energy. Electricity use/cost: 1,140 kWh, $147.75.

State claims. Motto: Audemus Jura Nostra Defendere (We dare defend our rights). **Flower:** Camellia. **Bird:** Northern flicker (yellowhammer is local nickname). **Tree:** Southern longleaf pine. **Song:** "Alabama". **Entered union:** Dec. 14, 1819; rank: 22nd.

Tourism. Tourist spending: $11.6 bil (2019); change, 2019-20: −27%; change, 2019-22: −5%. **Attractions:** First White House of the Confederacy, Civil Rights Memorial, Alabama Shakespeare Festival, Legacy Museum, National Memorial for Peace and Justice, in Montgomery; Ivy Green (Helen Keller birthplace), Tuscumbia; Barber Vintage Motorsports Museum, Civil Rights Institute, Vulcan Park and Museum (world's largest cast iron statue), in Birmingham; G. W. Carver Interpretive Museum, Tuskegee; W. C. Handy Home, Museum, and Library, Frank Lloyd Wright's Rosenbaum House, in Florence; U.S. Space & Rocket Ctr., Huntsville; Moundville Archaeological Park; USS *Alabama* Memorial Park, Mobile; Gulf State Park, Gulf Shores. **Information:** Alabama Tourism Dept., 401 Adams Ave., P.O. Box 4927, Montgomery, AL 36104; 1-800-ALABAMA, (334) 242-4169; alabama.travel

History. Alabama was inhabited by the Creek, Cherokee, Chickasaw, Alabama, and Choctaw peoples when Spanish explorers arrived in the early 1500s. The French made the first permanent settlement at Ft. Louis, 1702, and founded Mobile, 1711. France later gave up the entire region to England under the Treaty of Paris, 1763. Spanish forces took control of the Mobile Bay area, 1780, and it remained under Spanish control until seized by U.S. troops, 1813. Most of present-day Alabama was held by the Creeks until Gen. Andrew Jackson broke their power, 1814. When Alabama became a state, 1819, enslaved Black people made up about one-third of the population. The Indian Removal Act of 1830 forced most remaining Creeks west. The state seceded, 1861, and the Confederate states were organized Feb. 4, at Montgomery, the first capital. The state was readmitted, 1868. Birmingham, founded 1871, became a center for iron- and steelmaking. The Montgomery bus boycott, 1955, sparked by Rosa Parks, helped launch the civil rights movement. Other confrontations occurred at Birmingham, 1963, and Selma, 1965. The leading political figure from the 1960s through the '80s, four-term Gov. George Wallace, started as a segregationist but later won with Black support. Growth in the auto industry boosted the economy as the 21st cent. began. A string of tornadoes in 2011 killed at least 248. Jefferson County, which includes Birmingham, filed the then-most expensive municipal bankruptcy in 2011. Gov. Robert Bentley pleaded guilty to misdemeanor charges connected with a sex scandal and resigned, 2017. Roy Moore, a former state chief justice, was upset by Doug Jones (D) in a special election for the U.S. Senate in 2017 after several women alleged Moore had a history of sexual misconduct. A tornado in Lee County killed 23 people Mar. 3, 2019. The state in May 2019 passed a law outlawing abortion in nearly all cases, which went into effect after *Roe v. Wade* was overturned in June 2022. In June 2023, the U.S. Supreme Court nullified a congressional map drawn by the GOP-dominated legislature, declaring it violated the voting rights of Black residents.

Famous Alabamians. Hank Aaron, Tallulah Bankhead, Charles Barkley, Hugo L. Black, Paul "Bear" Bryant, George Washington Carver, Nat King Cole, Courteney Cox, William Christopher "W. C." Handy, Polly Holliday, Bo Jackson, Helen Keller, Coretta Scott King, Harper Lee, Joe Louis, Willie Mays, Jim Nabors, Jesse Owens, Terrell Owens, Rosa Parks, Condoleezza Rice, Lionel Richie, Robin Roberts, Octavia Spencer, Channing Tatum, George C. Wallace, Booker T. Washington, Hank Williams.

Website. www.alabama.gov

Alaska (AK)

The Last Frontier (unofficial)

People. Population: 733,583; rank: 48. **Pop. change** (2010-22): 3.3%. **Pop. density:** 1 per sq mi. **Racial distribution:** 64.1% white; 3.7% Black; 6.7% Asian; 15.7% Amer. Ind.; 1.7% Hawaiian/Pacific Islander; 2 or more races, 8.2%. **Hispanic pop.:** 7.7%.

Geography. Total area: 665,384 sq mi; rank: 1. **Land area:** 570,641 sq mi; rank: 1. **Acres forested:** 12.1 mil. **Location:** NW corner of North America, bordered on E by Canada. **Climate:** SE, SW, and central regions, moist and mild; far N extremely dry. Extended summer days, winter nights throughout. **Topography:** includes Pacific and Arctic mountain systems, central plateau, and Arctic slope. Denali, formerly Mt. McKinley, 20,310 ft, is the highest point in N. America. **Capital:** Juneau. **Chief airports:** Anchorage, Fairbanks.

Economy. Chief industries: petroleum, tourism, fishing, mining, forestry, transportation, aerospace. **Chief manuf. goods:** petroleum, seafood. **Chief crops:** greenhouse products, barley, oats, hay, potatoes, carrots. **Farm income:** Crops: $36.64 mil. Livestock: $7.19 mil. **Nonfuel minerals:** $4.5 bil; gold, lead, sand and gravel (construction), silver, zinc. **Commercial fishing:** $1.9 bil. **Chief ports:** Anchorage, Dutch Harbor, Kodiak, Juneau, Sitka, Valdez. **Gross state product:** $63.6 bil. **Sales tax:** none. **Gasoline tax:** 27.35 cents/gal. **Employment distrib.:** 25.0% govt.; 20.0% trade/trans./util.; 3.5% mfg.; 15.9% ed./health; 8.7% prof./bus. serv.; 10.3% leisure/hosp.; 3.5% finance; 8.0% constr./mining/log.; 1.5% info.; 3.6% other serv. **Unemployment:** 4.0%. **Min. wage/hr.:** $10.85. **Per cap. pers. income:** $68,919. **New private housing:** 578 units/$184.6 mil. **Broadband internet:** 94.9%. **Commercial banks:** 6; deposits: $16.4 bil. **Savings institutions:** 1; deposits: $548.0 mil.

Federal govt. Fed. civ. employees: 10,533; **avg. salary:** $92,563. **Notable fed. facilities:** Joint Base Elmendorf-Richardson; Ft. Wainwright; Eielson AFB; Ft. Greely.

Education. High school grad. rate: 79.1%. **4-yr. public coll./univ.:** 4; **2-yr. public:** 0; **4-yr. private:** 2.

Energy. Electricity use/cost: 594 kWh, $133.89.

State data. Motto: North to the future. **Flower:** Forget-me-not. **Bird:** Willow ptarmigan. **Tree:** Sitka spruce. **Song:** "Alaska's Flag." **Entered union:** Jan. 3, 1959; rank: 49th.

Tourism. Tourist spending: $3.2 bil (2019); change, 2019-20: −41%; change, 2019-22: −4%. **Attractions:** Portage Glacier, in Chugach Natl. Forest; Mendenhall Glacier, in Tongass Natl. Forest; Totem Heritage Ctr., Ketchikan; Glacier Bay Natl. Park and Preserve; Denali (formerly Mt. McKinley, N. America's highest peak), in Denali Natl. Park and Preserve; Mt. Roberts Tramway, Juneau; Alaska Maritime Natl. Wildlife Refuge; St. Michael's Cathedral, Alaska Raptor Ctr., in Sitka; White Pass & Yukon Route railroad, Skagway; Katmai Natl. Park and Preserve; Univ. of Alaska Museum of the North, Fairbanks. **Information:** Alaska Travel Industry Association, 610 E. 5th Ave., Ste. 200, Anchorage, AK 99501; 1-800-327-9372; www.travelalaska.com

History. Early inhabitants included the Tlingit-Haida and Athabascan peoples. Ancestors of the Aleut and Inuit (Eskimo) probably arrived from Siberia between 10,000 and 6,000 years ago. Vitus Bering, a Dane sailing for Russia, was the first European to land in Alaska, 1741. Russians, pursuing the fur trade, established a permanent settlement on Kodiak Island, 1784. Sec. of State William H. Seward bought Alaska from Russia for $7.2 mil in 1867, a deal some called "Seward's Folly." Discovery of gold in the Klondike region of Canada's Yukon Territory, 1896, triggered an Alaskan gold rush. Alaska became a territory, 1912, and a state, 1959. A huge oil find at Prudhoe Bay, 1968, led to construction of the Trans-Alaska Pipeline, 1974-77. The *Exxon Valdez* supertanker ran aground, 1989, spilling about 11 mil gallons of crude oil; the cleanup cost more than $2.2 bil. Congress included a measure permitting oil and gas drilling in the Arctic National Wildlife Refuge in the tax bill passed in Dec. 2017, ending a four-decade battle. A magnitude 7.0 earthquake centered near Anchorage struck Nov. 30, 2018, causing at least $75 mil in damage.

Famous Alaskans. Tom Bodett, Susan Butcher, Ernest Gruening, Jewel (Kilcher), Tony Knowles, Sydney Laurence, Sarah Palin, Libby Riddles, Curt Schilling, Jefferson "Soapy" Smith.

Website. www.alaska.gov

Arizona (AZ)

Grand Canyon State

People. Population: 7,359,197; rank: 14. **Pop. change** (2010-22): 15.1%. **Pop. density:** 65 per sq mi. **Racial distribution:** 81.9% white; 5.5% Black; 3.9% Asian; 5.2% Amer. Ind.; 0.3% Hawaiian/Pacific Islander; 2 or more races, 3.2%. **Hispanic pop.:** 32.5%.

Geography. Total area: 113,990 sq mi; rank: 6. **Land area:** 113,594 sq mi; rank: 6. **Acres forested:** 19.1 mil. **Location:** southwestern U.S. **Climate:** clear and dry in southern regions and northern plateau; high central areas have heavy winter snows. **Topography:** Colorado Plateau in the N, containing the Grand Canyon; Mexican Highlands run NW to SE; Sonoran Desert in the SW. **Capital:** Phoenix. **Chief airports:** Phoenix, Tucson, Mesa.

Economy. Chief industries: manufacturing, construction, tourism, mining, agriculture. **Chief manuf. goods:** aerospace, semiconductors, navigational instruments, cement, plastics, structural metals, dairy, printing, furniture. **Chief crops:** cotton, grapes, apples, lettuce, hay, potatoes, sorghum, barley, corn, wheat. **Farm income:** Crops: $2.28 bil. Livestock: $1.72 bil. **Nonfuel minerals:** $10.1 bil; cement, copper, molybdenum mineral concentrates, sand and gravel (construction), stone (crushed). **Gross state product:** $458.9 bil. **Sales tax:** 5.6%. **Gasoline tax:** 37.40 cents/gal. **Employment distrib.:** 13.7% govt.; 19.0% trade/trans./util.; 6.2% mfg.; 15.9% ed./health; 15.1% prof./bus. serv.; 11.0% leisure/hosp.; 7.9% finance; 6.7% constr./mining/log.; 1.6% info.; 3.0% other serv. **Unemployment:** 3.8%. **Min. wage/hr.:** $13.85. **Per cap. pers. income:** $56,667. **New private housing:** 60,994 units/$14.5 bil. **Broadband internet:** 98.2%. **Commercial banks:** 62; deposits: $221.1 bil. **Savings institutions:** 5; deposits: $6.8 bil. **Lottery:** total sales: $1.4 bil; profit: $269.5 mil.

Federal govt. Fed. civ. employees: 32,171; **avg. salary:** $84,778. **Notable fed. facilities:** Luke AFB; Davis-Monthan AFB; Ft. Huachuca; Yuma Proving Ground.

Education. High school grad. rate: 77.3%. **4-yr. public coll./univ.:** 6; **2-yr. public:** 20; **4-yr. private:** 10.

Energy. Electricity use/cost: 1,048 kWh, $131.35.

State data. Motto: Ditat Deus (God enriches). **Flower:** Blossom of the saguaro cactus. **Bird:** Cactus wren. **Tree:** Palo verde. **Song:** "Arizona." **Entered union:** Feb. 14, 1912; rank: 48th.

Tourism. Tourist spending: $23.5 bil (2019); change, 2019-20: −39%; change, 2019-22: −5%. **Attractions:** Grand Canyon; Painted Desert, in Grand Canyon and Petrified Forest Natl. Parks; Glen Canyon Natl. Recreation Area; Canyon de Chelly Natl. Monument; Meteor Crater, near Winslow; London Bridge, Lake Havasu City; Biosphere 2, Oracle; Navajo Natl. Monument; Tombstone historic mining town; Tempe Town Lake. **Information:** Arizona Office of Tourism, 100 N. 7th Ave., Ste. 400, Phoenix, AZ 85007; 1-866-275-5816; www.visitarizona.com

History. Paleo-Indians hunted large game in the area at least 12,000 years ago. Anasazi, Mogollon, and Hohokam civilizations lived there c. 300 BCE-1300 CE; Navajo and Apache came c. 15th cent. Marcos de Niza, a Spanish Franciscan, and Estevanico, a Moroccan-born enslaved Black man, explored, 1539; explorer Francisco Vásquez de Coronado visited, 1540. Eusebio Francisco Kino, a Jesuit missionary, taught Indians, 1692-1711, and left missions. Tubac, a Spanish fort, became the first European settlement, 1752. Spain ceded Arizona to Mexico, 1821. The U.S. took over, 1848, after the Mexican War. The area below the Gila R. came from Mexico in the Gadsden Purchase, 1853. Arizona became a territory, 1863. Apache wars ended with Geronimo's surrender, 1886. Arizona became a state, 1912, and grew rapidly after 1960 with a fourfold rise in population over the next four decades. Barry Goldwater was a leading conservative voice in the U.S. Senate (1953-65, 1969-87). The border with Mexico is a major gateway for illegal immigration to the U.S. In 2012, the U.S. Supreme Court struck down most provisions of a 2010 state immigration law that allowed police to make warrantless arrests of those reasonably suspected of having immigrated illegally. A statewide teacher walkout in Apr. 2018 demanded increased pay and school funding. Gov. Doug Ducey (R) in Apr. 2021 declared a state of emergency in six border counties with increasing migrant numbers. On July 31, 2023, Phoenix ended a record-breaking heat streak of 31 days at or above 110 °F.

Famous Arizonans. Bruce Babbitt, Cochise, Alice Cooper, Geronimo, Gabrielle Giffords, Barry Goldwater, Zane Grey, Carl Hayden, George W. P. Hunt, Helen Hull Jacobs, Bil Keane, Percival Lowell, John McCain, John J. Rhodes, Linda Ronstadt, Emma Stone, Morris K. Udall, Stewart L. Udall, Frank Lloyd Wright.

Website. www.az.gov

Arkansas (AR)

Natural State, Razorback State

People. Population: 3,045,637; rank: 33. **Pop. change** (2010-22): 4.4%. **Pop. density:** 59 per sq mi. **Racial distribution:** 78.5% white; 15.6% Black; 1.8% Asian; 1.1% Amer. Ind.; 0.5% Hawaiian/Pacific Islander; 2 or more races, 2.4%. **Hispanic pop.:** 8.6%.

Geography. Total area: 53,179 sq mi; rank: 29. **Land area:** 52,035 sq mi; rank: 27. **Acres forested:** 18.9 mil. **Location:**

West South Central state. **Climate:** long, hot summers, mild winters; generally abundant rainfall. **Topography:** eastern delta and prairie, southern lowland forests, and the north-western highlands, which include the Ozark Plateaus. **Capital:** Little Rock. **Chief airports:** Little Rock, Bentonville.

Economy. Chief industries: manufacturing, agriculture, tourism, forestry. **Chief manuf. goods:** poultry processing, motor vehicles and parts, iron and steel, paper and paperboard, plastics, preserved fruits and vegetables, aerospace, rubber. **Chief crops:** rice, soybeans, cotton, hay, wheat, corn, sorghum, tomatoes, peaches, watermelons, pecans, blueberries, grapes. **Farm income:** Crops: $4.59 bil. Livestock: $5.81 bil. **Nonfuel minerals:** $1.1 bil; bromine, cement, sand and gravel (construction), sand and gravel (industrial), stone (crushed). **Chief port:** Helena. **Gross state product:** $165.2 bil. **Sales tax:** 6.5%. **Gasoline tax:** 43.30 cents/gal. **Employment distrib.:** 15.7% govt.; 20.1% trade/trans./util.; 12.0% mfg.; 15.0% ed./health; 11.2% prof./bus. serv.; 9.7% leisure/hosp.; 5.2% finance; 4.9% constr./mining/log.; 0.9% info.; 5.4% other serv. **Unemployment:** 3.3%. **Min. wage/hr.:** $11.00. **Per cap. pers. income:** $51,787. **New private housing:** 14,356 units/$3.0 bil. **Broadband internet:** 96.1%. **Commercial banks:** 112; deposits: $95.4 bil. **Savings institutions:** 2; deposits: $234 mil. **Lottery:** total sales: $579.6 mil; profit: $99.4 mil.

Federal govt. Fed. civ. employees: 13,429; **avg. salary:** $81,469. **Notable fed. facilities:** Little Rock AFB; Pine Bluff Arsenal; Natl. Ctr. for Toxicological Research, Jefferson.

Education. High school grad. rate: 88.8%. **4-yr. public coll./univ.:** 11; **2-yr. public:** 22; **4-yr. private:** 12.

Energy. Electricity use/cost: 1,098 kWh, $123.69.

State data. Motto: Regnat Populus (The people rule). **Flower:** Apple blossom. **Bird:** Northern mockingbird. **Tree:** Pine. **Song:** "Arkansas." **Entered union:** June 15, 1836; rank: 25th.

Tourism. Tourist spending: $8.0 bil (2019); change, 2019-20: −25%; change, 2019-22: 9%. **Attractions:** Eureka Springs; Ozark Folk Ctr. State Park, Mountain View; Blanchard Springs Caverns, in Ozark Natl. Forest; Crater of Diamonds State Park, Murfreesboro; Toltec Mounds Archeological State Park, Scott; Buffalo Natl. River; Hot Springs Natl. Park; Pea Ridge Natl. Military Park; William J. Clinton Presidential Library and Museum, Little Rock; Central High School Natl. Historic Site, in Little Rock; Crystal Bridges Museum of American Art, Bentonville. **Information:** Arkansas Dept. of Parks & Tourism, 1 Capitol Mall, Little Rock, AR 72201; 1-800-NATURAL; www.arkansas.com

History. Quapaw, Caddo, Osage, Cherokee, and Choctaw peoples lived in the area at the time of European contact. The first European explorers were Hernando de Soto, 1541; Jacques Marquette and Louis Jolliet, 1673; and René-Robert Cavelier, sieur de La Salle, 1682. French fur trader Henri de Tonty founded the first settlement, 1686, at Arkansas Post. In 1762, the area was ceded by France to Spain, then given back, 1800, and was part of the Louisiana Purchase, 1803. It was made a territory, 1819, and entered the Union as a slave state, 1836. Arkansas seceded in 1861, after the Civil War began; it was readmitted, 1868. Pres. Eisenhower sent federal troops, 1957, to keep Gov. Orval Faubus from blocking racial integration at Central High School in Little Rock. Walmart, now the world's leading retailer, opened its first store in Rogers, 1962. Elected five times as governor, Bill Clinton later served two terms as president (1993-2001). His presidential library opened, 2004, in Little Rock. After 12 years without an execution, the state put to death four inmates in eight days in 2017. The state's legislature in Apr. 2021 overrode Gov. Asa Hutchinson's (R) veto of a bill prohibiting doctors from providing gender-affirming care to transgender youth, making it the first state to ban such medical treatment; a federal judge blocked the ban from going into effect.

Famous Arkansans. Daisy Bates, Dee Brown, Paul "Bear" Bryant, Glen Campbell, Hattie Wyatt Caraway, Johnny Cash, Wesley Clark, Bill Clinton, Jay Hanna "Dizzy" Dean, Orval Faubus, James William Fulbright, Al Green, John Grisham, Levon Helm, John H. Johnson, Douglas MacArthur, John Little McClellan, James S. McDonnell, Scottie Pippen, Dick Powell, Brooks Robinson, Winthrop Rockefeller, Mary Steenburgen, Edward Durell Stone, Billy Bob Thornton, Sam Walton, Archibald Yell.

Website. www.arkansas.gov

California (CA)
Golden State

People. Population: 39,029,342; rank: 1. **Pop. change (2010-22):** 4.8%. **Pop. density:** 251 per sq mi. **Racial distribution:** 70.7% white; 6.5% Black; 16.3% Asian; 1.7% Amer. Ind.; 0.5% Hawaiian/Pacific Islander; 2 or more races, 4.3%. **Hispanic pop.:** 40.3%.

Geography. Total area: 163,695 sq mi; rank: 3. **Land area:** 155,779 sq mi; rank: 3. **Acres forested:** 31.6 mil. **Location:** western coast of U.S. **Climate:** moderate temperatures and rainfall along the coast; extremes in the interior. **Topography:** long mountainous coastline; central valley; Sierra Nevada on the E; desert basins in southern interior; rugged mountains in N. **Capital:** Sacramento. **Chief airports:** Los Angeles, San Francisco, San Diego, Sacramento, San Jose, Santa Ana, Oakland, Burbank, Ontario, Long Beach, Palm Springs, Fresno, Santa Barbara.

Economy. Chief industries: agriculture, tourism, apparel, electronics, telecommunications, entertainment. **Chief manuf. goods:** petroleum, aerospace, precision instruments, semiconductors, telecom and broadcasting equip., pharmaceutical, wineries, plastics, medical equip., preserved fruits and vegetables, printing, dairy, cut and sew apparel, motor vehicles. **Chief crops:** grapes, nursery products, almonds, lettuce, hay, strawberries, floriculture, tomatoes, cotton, oranges, pistachios, walnuts, broccoli, carrots, rice, peaches, lemons. **Farm income:** Crops: $38.47 bil. Livestock: $12.82 bil. **Nonfuel minerals:** $5.6 bil; boron minerals, cement, rare earths, sand and gravel (construction), stone (crushed). **Commercial fishing:** $210.0 mil. **Chief ports:** Long Beach, Los Angeles, San Diego, Port Hueneme, Richmond, Oakland, San Francisco, Stockton. **Gross state product:** $3.6 tril. **Sales tax:** 7.25%. **Gasoline tax:** 83.50 cents/gal. **Employment distrib.:** 14.5% govt.; 17.3% trade/trans./util.; 7.4% mfg.; 17.1% ed./health; 16.1% prof./bus. serv.; 11.3% leisure/hosp.; 4.7% finance; 5.2% constr./mining/log.; 3.3% info.; 3.2% other serv. **Unemployment:** 4.2%. **Min. wage/hr.:** $15.50. **Per cap. pers. income:** $77,339. **New private housing:** 119,667 units/$28.8 bil. **Broadband internet:** 98.5%. **Commercial banks:** 169; deposits: $2.2 tril. **Savings institutions:** 13; deposits: $25.3 bil. **Lottery:** total sales: $8.9 bil; profit: $2.0 bil.

Federal govt. Fed. civ. employees: 141,475; **avg. salary:** $101,012. **Notable fed. facilities:** USMC Camp Pendleton; Naval Base Coronado; Marine Corps Air Ground Combat Ctr., 29 Palms; Marine Corps Air Station Miramar; Travis AFB; Naval Research Lab, Monterey; Lawrence Livermore Natl. Lab; Lawrence Berkeley Natl. Lab; NASA Jet Propulsion Lab, Pasadena; Edwards AFB (NASA Dryden Flight Research Ctr., AF Test Ctr.); San Francisco Mint.

Education. High school grad. rate: 84.3%. **4-yr. public coll./univ.:** 49; **2-yr. public:** 101; **4-yr. private:** 138.

Energy. Electricity use/cost: 542 kWh, $123.67.

State data. Flower: California poppy. **Bird:** California valley quail. **Tree:** California redwood. **Song:** "I Love You, California." **Entered union:** Sept. 9, 1850; rank: 31st.

Tourism. Tourist spending: $159.3 bil (2019); change, 2019-20: −55%; change, 2019-22: −12%. **Attractions:** Queen Mary, Aquarium of the Pacific, in Long Beach; Palomar Observatory, Palomar Mountain; Disneyland Resort, Anaheim; Getty Center, Universal Studios Hollywood, Griffith Observatory, in Los Angeles; Tournament of Roses and Rose Bowl, Pasadena; The California Museum, California State Railroad Museum, in Sacramento; San Diego Zoo, USS Midway Museum, in San Diego; Yosemite Valley; Lassen Volcanic, Sequoia, and Kings Canyon Natl. Parks; Mojave and Sonoran Deserts; Death Valley; Golden Gate Park, Alcatraz Island, in San Francisco; Napa Valley wine region; Monterey Bay Aquarium, Monterey Peninsula; Ancient Bristlecone Pine Forest (oldest known living trees on Earth), in Inyo Natl. Forest; Redwood Natl. and State Parks; Muir Woods Natl. Monument, Mill Valley. **Information:** California Office of Tourism, 555 Capitol Mall, Ste. 465, Sacramento, CA 95814; 1-877-225-4367; www.visitcalifornia.com

History. Early inhabitants included more than 100 different Native American tribes with multiple dialects. The first European explorers were Juan Rodríguez Cabrillo, 1542, and Sir Francis Drake, 1579. The first settlement was the Spanish Alta California mission at San Diego, 1769, first in a string founded by Franciscan Father Junípero Serra. California became a province of independent Mexico, 1821. U.S. traders and settlers arrived in the 19th cent. and staged the Bear Flag revolt, 1846, in protest against Mexican rule; later that year U.S. forces occupied California. At the end of the Mexican War, Mexico ceded the territory to the U.S., 1848; that same year gold was discovered, and the famed gold rush began. California became a state, 1850. An economic downturn in the 1870s spurred riots against Chinese immigrants, who had come as laborers in the boom years. An earthquake and related fires devastated San Francisco, 1906. During World War II, Japanese Americans, many of them U.S. citizens, were held in detention camps, 1942-45. Ronald Reagan, a former movie actor, became state governor (1967-75) and U.S. president (1981-89). A budget crisis, 2003, resulted in the recall of Gov. Gray Davis and the election of another actor, Arnold Schwarzenegger. A 6-year-old drought mostly ended in 2017. Wildfires caused 54 deaths in 2017 and destroyed thousands of homes and other structures. The 2018 fire season was the deadliest—at least 85 killed in Nov. 2018 Camp fire alone—in state history. Gov. Gavin Newsom (D) in 2019 issued a moratorium on the death penalty. More than 4.2 mil acres burned during the 2020 fire season, the most on record and twice the previous high. Beginning June 1, 2022, some 6 mil residents faced unprecedented water restrictions due to continuing drought conditions. Severe "atmospheric river" storms from Dec. 2022 through late Mar. 2023 triggered flooding and landslides causing more than 25 deaths and at least $3.5 bil in damages. Rep. Kevin McCarthy (R, CA) was elected House speaker in Jan. 2023 after 15 floor votes, the most since 1855.

Famous Californians. Tom Brady, Edmund G. (Pat) Brown, Jerry Brown, Luther Burbank, Julia Child, Ted Danson, Cameron Diaz, Leonardo DiCaprio, Joe DiMaggio, Landon Donovan, Clint Eastwood, Billie Eilish, Dianne Feinstein, John C. Fremont, Tom Hanks, Kamala Harris, William Randolph Hearst, Helen Hunt, Steve Jobs, Jimmie Johnson, Angelina Jolie, Jack Kemp, Jason Kidd, Brie Larson, Lisa Leslie, Monica Lewinsky, Jack London, George Lucas, Phil Mickelson, Marilyn Monroe, John Muir, Richard M. Nixon, Gwyneth Paltrow, George S. Patton Jr., Gregory Peck, Nancy Pelosi, Ronald Reagan, Sally K. Ride, William Saroyan, Arnold Schwarzenegger, Junípero Serra, O. J. Simpson, Kevin Spacey, Leland Stanford, Gwen Stefani, John Steinbeck, Shirley Temple, Earl Warren, Serena Williams, Ted Williams, Venus Williams, Tiger Woods.
Website. www.ca.gov

Colorado (CO)
Centennial State

People. Population: 5,839,926; rank: 21. **Pop. change** (2010-22): 16.1%. **Pop. density:** 56 per sq mi. **Racial distribution:** 86.2% white; 4.7% Black; 3.8% Asian; 1.7% Amer. Ind.; 0.2% Hawaiian/Pacific Islander; 2 or more races, 3.4%. **Hispanic pop.:** 22.5%.

Geography. Total area: 104,094 sq mi; rank: 8. **Land area:** 103,642 sq mi; rank: 8. **Acres forested:** 22.8 mil. **Location:** W central U.S. **Climate:** low relative humidity, abundant sun, wide daily/seasonal temperature ranges; alpine conditions in the high mountains. **Topography:** eastern dry high plains; hilly to mountainous central plateau; western Rocky Mts. of high ranges with broad valleys, deep, narrow canyons. **Capital:** Denver. **Chief airports:** Denver, Colorado Springs.

Economy. Chief industries: manufacturing, construction, government, tourism, agriculture, aerospace, electronics equip. **Chief manuf. goods:** animal slaughtering, beer, petroleum, pharmaceuticals, aerospace, medical equip., precision instruments, printing, semiconductors. **Chief crops:** hay, corn, potatoes, wheat, onions, dry edible beans, sunflowers, sugar beets, barley, proso millet, cabbage, peaches, lettuce, apples, cantaloupes. **Farm income:** Crops: $2.63 bil. Livestock: $5.69 bil. **Nonfuel minerals:** $1.9 bil; cement, gold, molybdenum mineral concentrates, sand and gravel (construction), stone (crushed). **Gross state product:** $484.4 bil. **Sales tax:** 2.9%. **Gasoline tax:** 41.65 cents/gal. **Employment distrib.:** 16.2% govt.; 17.0% trade/trans./util.; 5.3% mfg.; 12.3% ed./health; 17.1% prof./bus. serv.; 12.2% leisure/hosp.; 6.0% finance; 7.1% constr./mining/log.; 2.7% info.; 4.2% other serv. **Unemployment:** 3.0%. **Min. wage/hr.:** $13.65. **Per cap. pers. income:** $74,167. **New private housing:** 48,839 units/$12.8 bil. **Broadband internet:** 97.7%. **Commercial banks:** 114; deposits $200.5 bil. **Savings institutions:** 12; deposits $4.8 bil. **Lottery:** total sales: $826.9 mil; profit: $180.3 mil.

Federal govt. Fed. civ. employees: 37,717; **avg. salary:** $99,062. **Notable fed. facilities:** U.S. Air Force Academy; Peterson AFB; Denver Mint; Ft. Carson; Natl. Renewable Energy Lab, Golden; Transportation Tech. Ctr., Pueblo; NORAD and USNORTHCOM Alt. Command Ctr., Cheyenne Mtn. Complex; Denver Fed. Ctr.; Natl. Ctr. for Atmospheric Research, Natl. Inst. of Standards & Technology, NOAA Earth System Research Lab, Boulder; Natl. Wildlife Research Ctr., Fort Collins.

Education. High school grad. rate: 81.9%. **4-yr. public coll./univ.:** 17; **2-yr. public:** 11; **4-yr. private:** 10.

Energy. Electricity use/cost: 704 kWh, $91.96.

State data. Motto: Nil Sine Numine (Nothing without Providence). **Flower:** Rocky Mountain columbine. **Bird:** Lark bunting. **Tree:** Colorado blue spruce. **Songs:** "Where the Columbines Grow"; "Rocky Mountain High." **Entered union:** Aug. 1, 1876; rank: 38th.

Tourism. Tourist spending: $24.3 bil (2019); change, 2019-20: −36%; change, 2019-22: 1%. **Attractions:** Denver Museum of Nature & Science, Denver Botanic Gardens, Denver Zoo; Red Rocks Park and Amphitheatre, Morrison; Natl. Ctr. for Atmospheric Research, Boulder; Rocky Mountain, Black Canyon of the Gunnison, and Mesa Verde (Anasazi cliff dwellings) Natl. Parks; Aspen, Breckenridge, Steamboat, and Vail ski resorts; Garden of the Gods, Colorado Springs; Great Sand Dunes Natl. Park and Preserve; Dinosaur and Colorado Natl. Monuments; Pikes Peak and Mount Evans; Grand Mesa Natl. Forest; historic mining towns of Central City, Silverton, Cripple Creek; Bent's Old Fort Natl. Historic Site, near La Junta; Georgetown Loop Historic Mining and Railroad Park; Durango & Silverton Narrow Gauge Railroad Museum, Durango; Cumbres & Toltec Scenic Railroad, Antonito; gambling in Black Hawk, Central City, Cripple Creek and on tribal land in Ignacio and Towaoc. **Information:** Colorado Tourism Office, 1600 Broadway, Ste. 2500, Denver, CO 80202; 1-800-265-6723; www.colorado.com

History. Paleo-Indians hunted big game in the area at least 11,000 years ago. Anasazi cliff dwellers flourished around Mesa Verde until about 1300 CE; other Native Americans were the Ute, Pueblo, Cheyenne, and Arapaho. The region was claimed by Spain but passed to France, 1800. The U.S. acquired eastern Colorado in the Louisiana Purchase, 1803. Lt. Zebulon M. Pike explored the area, 1806, sighting the peak that bears his name. After the Mexican War, 1846-48, U.S. immigrants settled in the east, former Mexicans in the south. Gold was discovered in 1858, causing a population boom. Congress created Colorado Territory, 1861. Conflict between newcomers and displaced Native Americans led to the Sand Creek Massacre, 1864, in which U.S. soldiers and settlers killed some 150 Cheyenne and Arapaho. U.S. Army troops forced the removal to reservations (mostly in present-day Oklahoma) of most Native Americans in the state, 1867. The 1870s brought statehood, 1876, and rich silver finds that turned Leadville into a boomtown. Federal military and civilian employment in Colorado surged in the 1940s and '50s; since then, tourism and technology have fueled the economy. The state's Hispanic population grew from 5.8% in 1980 to 21.9% in 2020. Colorado became the first state in the U.S. to legalize selling recreational marijuana in 2014. The most destructive wildfire in state history ignited Dec. 30, 2021, about 20 mi. southwest of Denver.

Famous Coloradans. Tim Allen, Chauncey Billups, Frederick Bonfils, Molly Brown, William N. Byers, M. Scott Carpenter, Lon Chaney, Jack Dempsey, Mamie Eisenhower, Douglas Fairbanks, Barney Ford, Neil Gorsuch, Roy Halladay, Ouray, Trey Parker, "Baby Doe" Tabor, Lowell Thomas, Byron R. White, Paul Whiteman.
Website. www.colorado.gov

Connecticut (CT)
Constitution State, Nutmeg State

People. Population: 3,626,205; rank: 29. **Pop. change** (2010-22): 1.5%. **Pop. density:** 749 per sq mi. **Racial distribution:** 78.4% white; 12.9% Black; 5.2% Asian; 0.7% Amer. Ind.; 0.1% Hawaiian/Pacific Islander; 2 or more races, 2.7%. **Hispanic pop.:** 18.2%.

Geography. Total area: 5,543 sq mi; rank: 48. **Land area:** 4,842 sq mi; rank: 48. **Acres forested:** 1.8 mil. **Location:** New England state in NE corner of U.S. **Climate:** moderate; winters avg. slightly below freezing; warm, humid summers. **Topography:** western upland, the Berkshires, in the NW, highest elevations; narrow central lowland N-S; hilly eastern upland drained by rivers. **Capital:** Hartford. **Chief airport:** Windsor Locks.

Economy. Chief industries: manufacturing, retail trade, government, services, finances, insurance, real estate. **Chief manuf. goods:** aerospace, chemicals, fabricated metals, precision instruments, toiletries, medical equip., printing, plastics. **Chief crops:** nursery stock, Christmas trees, mushrooms, sweet corn, apples, tobacco, hay. **Farm income:** Crops: $420.41 mil. Livestock: $169.11 mil. **Nonfuel minerals:** $194 mil; sand and gravel (construction), stone (dimension). **Commercial fishing:** $15.7 mil. **Chief ports:** New Haven, Bridgeport, New London. **Gross state product:** $321.8 bil. **Sales tax:** 6.35%. **Gasoline tax:** 23.40 cents/gal. **Employment distrib.:** 13.9% govt.; 17.5% trade/trans./util.; 9.3% mfg.; 21.1% ed./health; 13.4% prof./bus. serv.; 8.9% leisure/hosp.; 6.8% finance; 3.6% constr./mining/log.; 1.9% info.; 3.7% other serv. **Unemployment:** 4.2%. **Min. wage/hr.:** $15.00. **Per cap. pers. income:** $84,972. **New private housing:** 5,652 units/$1.6 bil. **Broadband internet:** 99.4%. **Commercial banks:** 29; deposits $152.7 bil. **Savings institutions:** 25; deposits $26.4 bil. **Lottery:** total sales $1.5 bil; profit: $405.3 mil.

Federal govt. Fed. civ. employees: 8,388; **avg. salary:** $100,626. **Notable fed. facilities:** U.S. Coast Guard Academy; Naval Sub Base New London.

Education. High school grad. rate: 88.3%. **4-yr. public coll./univ.:** 6; **2-yr. public:** 12; **4-yr. private:** 17.

Energy. Electricity use/cost: 713 kWh, $156.21.

State data. Motto: Qui Transtulit Sustinet (He who transplanted still sustains). **Flower:** Mountain laurel. **Bird:** American robin. **Tree:** White oak. **Song:** "Yankee Doodle." **Fifth** of the 13 original states to ratify the Constitution, Jan. 9, 1788.

Tourism. Tourist spending: $13.3 bil (2019); change, 2019-20: −45%; change, 2019-22: −10%. **Attractions:** Mark Twain House and Museum, Hartford; Yale Univ. Art Gallery, Peabody Museum of Natural History, in New Haven; Mystic Seaport, Mystic Aquarium; Barnum Museum, Bridgeport; Gillette Castle State Park, East Haddam; USS *Nautilus* (1st nuclear-powered submarine) at Submarine Force Library and Museum, Groton; Mashantucket Pequot Museum and Research Ctr.; Foxwoods Resort Casino, Ledyard; Mohegan Sun, Uncasville; Lake Compounce (est. 1846; oldest continuously operating amusement park in U.S.), Bristol; Philip Johnson Glass House, New Canaan. **Information:** Connecticut Office of Tourism, 450 Columbus Blvd., Ste. 5, Hartford, CT 06103; 1-888-CTVISIT, (860) 256-2800; www.ctvisit.com

History. At the time of European contact, inhabitants of the area were Algonquian peoples, including the Mohegan and Pequot. Dutch explorer Adriaen Block was the first European visitor, 1614. By 1634, English settlers from Plymouth had started colonies along the Connecticut R.; in 1637 they defeated the Pequots. The Colony of Connecticut was chartered by England, 1662; New Haven colony was added, 1665. A Patriot stronghold in the American Revolution, the state actively supported the antislavery movement and the Union cause in the Civil War. The state economy prospered in the 20th cent. from insurance- and defense-related industries. *Nautilus*, the first nuclear-powered submarine, was launched at Groton, 1954. Connecticut Sen. Joseph Lieberman was the Democratic nominee for vice president in 2000. American Indian casinos, starting with Foxwoods in 1992, were an economic boon to the state, but tourism revenues declined sharply with the recession that began in late 2007. Twenty children and six staff members were killed in a mass shooting at Sandy Hook Elementary School in Newtown, Dec. 14, 2012. In Oct. 2022, Infowars host Alex Jones was ordered to pay $965 mil to families of some of the victims, over conspiracy theories he spread about the shooting.

Famous "Nutmeggers." Ethan Allen, P. T. Barnum, Michael Bolton, Glenn Close, Samuel Colt, Ann Coulter, Jonathan Edwards, Nathan Hale, Katharine Hepburn, Isaac Hull, Norman Lear, Seth MacFarlane, John Mayer, Robert Mitchum, J. P. Morgan, Ralph Nader, Israel Putnam, Wallace Stevens, Harriet Beecher Stowe, Mark Twain, Noah Webster, Eli Whitney. **Website.** www.ct.gov

Delaware (DE)
First State, Diamond State

People. Population: 1,018,396; rank: 45. **Pop. change** (2010-22): 13.4%. **Pop. density:** 523 per sq mi. **Racial distribution:** 68.0% white; 23.8% Black; 4.4% Asian; 0.7% Amer. Ind.; 0.1% Hawaiian/Pacific Islander; 2 or more races, 3.0%. **Hispanic pop.:** 10.3%.

Geography. Total area: 2,489 sq mi; rank: 49. **Land area:** 1,949 sq mi; rank: 49. **Acres forested:** 0.4 mil. **Location:** Delmarva Peninsula on the Atlantic coastal plain. **Climate:** moderate. **Topography:** Piedmont Plateau to the N, sloping to a near sea-level plain. **Capital:** Dover.

Economy. Chief industries: chemicals, agriculture, finance, poultry, shellfish, tourism, auto assembly, food processing, transportation equip. **Chief manuf. goods:** pharmaceuticals, poultry processing, soap and cleaning compounds, precision instruments, basic chemicals, plastics. **Chief crops:** soybeans, corn, greenhouse and nursery, wheat, potatoes, barley, hay, watermelons, lima beans, green peas, pumpkins, mushrooms, cabbage. **Farm income:** Crops: $373.08 mil. Livestock: $956.55 mil. **Nonfuel minerals:** $25 mil; magnesium compounds, sand and gravel (construction), stone (crushed). **Commercial fishing:** $16.3 mil. **Chief port:** Wilmington. **Gross state product:** $87.5 bil. **Sales tax:** none. **Gasoline tax:** 41.40 cents/gal. **Employment distrib.:** 14.5% govt.; 18.6% trade/trans./util.; 5.7% mfg.; 16.6% ed./health; 14.1% prof./bus. serv.; 10.5% leisure/hosp.; 10.4% finance; 5.0% constr./mining/log.; 0.8% info.; 3.9% other serv. **Unemployment:** 4.5%. **Min. wage/hr.:** $16.50. **Per cap. pers. income:** $61,387. **New private housing:** 6,417 units/$912.9 mil. **Broadband internet:** 99.2%. **Commercial banks:** 36; deposits: $465.2 bil. **Savings institutions:** 4; deposits: $8.5 bil. **Lottery:** total sales: $736.0 mil; profit: $234.5 mil.

Federal govt. Fed. civ. employees: 3,433; avg. salary: $90,134. **Notable fed. facilities:** Dover AFB; Bombay Hook Natl. Wildlife Refuge.

Education. High school grad. rate: 89.0%. **4-yr. public coll./univ.:** 3; **2-yr. public:** 0; **4-yr. private:** 3.

Energy. Electricity use/cost: 950 kWh, $118.85.

State data. Motto: Liberty and independence. **Flower:** Peach blossom. **Bird:** Blue hen chicken. **Tree:** American holly.

Song: "Our Delaware." **First** of original 13 states to ratify the Constitution, Dec. 7, 1787.

Tourism. Tourist spending: $2.5 bil (2019); change, 2019-20: −36%; change, 2019-22: −8%. **Attractions:** Fort Christina (site of founding of colony of New Sweden), Holy Trinity (Old Swedes) Church (erected 1698, oldest church in U.S. still standing as built and in use), Hagley Museum and Library, Nemours Mansion and Gardens, in Wilmington; Winterthur Museum, Garden, and Library, near Wilmington; New Castle Historic District; John Dickinson "Penman of the Revolution" Plantation, First State Heritage Park, Dover Intl. Speedway, in Dover; Rehoboth Beach. **Information:** Delaware Tourism Office, 99 Kings Hwy., Dover, DE 19901; 1-866-2VISITDE; www.visitdelaware.com

History. The Lenni Lenape (Delaware) people lived in the region at the time of European contact. Henry Hudson located the Delaware R., 1609. In 1610, English explorer Samuel Argall entered Delaware Bay and named the area after Virginia's governor, Lord De La Warr. Dutch, Swedish, and Finnish settlers were followed by the British, who took control in 1664. After 1682, Delaware became part of Pennsylvania, and in 1704 it was granted its own assembly. It adopted a constitution as the state of Delaware, 1776, and was the first state to ratify the federal Constitution, 1787. Although it remained in the Union during the Civil War, Delaware retained slavery until the 13th Amendment abolished it in 1865. The DuPont company, founded as a gunpowder mill in 1802, became an industrial giant in the 20th cent. making nylon, Teflon, and other synthetics. Pro-business laws drew many out-of-state firms to incorporate in Delaware. In 2000, Ruth Ann Minner was elected Delaware's first woman governor. Joe Biden, the state's former U.S. senator, served as U.S. vice president, 2009-17, and began serving as president in Jan. 2021.

Famous Delawareans. Thomas F. Bayard, Joe Biden, Henry Seidel Canby, E. I. du Pont, John P. Marquand, Aubrey Plaza, Howard Pyle, Caesar Rodney, Susan Stroman. **Website.** www.delaware.gov

Florida (FL)
Sunshine State

People. Population: 22,244,823; rank: 3. **Pop. change** (2010-22): 18.3%. **Pop. density:** 415 per sq mi. **Racial distribution:** 76.8% white; 17.0% Black; 3.1% Asian; 0.5% Amer. Ind.; 0.1% Hawaiian/Pacific Islander; 2 or more races, 2.4%. **Hispanic pop.:** 27.1%.

Geography. Total area: 65,758 sq mi; rank: 22. **Land area:** 53,625 sq mi; rank: 26. **Acres forested:** 17.0 mil. **Location:** peninsula jutting southward 500 mi between the Atlantic and Gulf of Mexico. **Climate:** subtropical N of Bradenton-Lake Okeechobee-Vero Beach line; tropical S of line. **Topography:** land is flat or rolling; highest point is 345 ft in the NW. **Capital:** Tallahassee. **Chief airports:** Orlando, Miami, Fort Lauderdale, Fort Myers, West Palm Beach, Jacksonville, Sarasota, Sanford, Clearwater, Pensacola, Valparaiso, Punta Gorda, Panama City, Key West.

Economy. Chief industries: tourism, agriculture, manufacturing, construction, services, international trade. **Chief manuf. goods:** navigational instruments, medical equip., cement, broadcasting equip., beverages, phosphatic fertilizer, preserved fruits and vegetables, structural metal, printing. **Chief crops:** greenhouse and nursery, oranges, sugarcane, tomatoes, green peppers, grapefruit, strawberries, snap beans, sweet corn, potatoes, cucumbers, tangerines. **Farm income:** Crops: $6.17 bil. Livestock: $1.57 bil. **Nonfuel minerals:** $2.8 bil; cement, clay (attapulgite and kaolin), phosphate rock, sand and gravel (construction), stone (crushed). **Commercial fishing:** $264.2 mil. **Chief ports:** Pensacola, Tampa, Port Manatee, Miami, Port Everglades, Jacksonville, Canaveral. **Gross state product:** $1.4 tril. **Sales tax:** 6.0%. **Gasoline tax:** 55.70 cents/gal. **Employment distrib.:** 11.6% govt.; 20.2% trade/trans./util.; 4.3% mfg.; 15.1% ed./health; 16.7% prof./bus. serv.; 13.6% leisure/hosp.; 7.0% finance; 6.3% constr./mining/log.; 1.6% info.; 3.6% other serv. **Unemployment:** 2.9%. **Min. wage/hr.:** $11.00. **Per cap. pers. income:** $63,597. **New private housing:** 211,962 units/$51.4 bil. **Broadband internet:** 98.8%. **Commercial banks:** 174; deposits: $839.8 bil. **Savings institutions:** 12; deposits: $38.3 bil. **Lottery:** total sales: $9.3 bil; profit: $2.3 bil.

Federal govt. Fed. civ. employees: 87,878; avg. salary: $90,687. **Notable fed. facilities:** John F. Kennedy Space Ctr.; Eglin AFB; MacDill AFB; Hurlburt Field; Pensacola NAS; Jacksonville NAS; Mayport Naval Sta.

Education. High school grad. rate: 90.2%. **4-yr. public coll./univ.:** 40; **2-yr. public:** 1; **4-yr. private:** 57.

Energy. Electricity use/cost: 1,096 kWh, $130.40.

State data. Motto: In God we trust. **Flower:** Orange blossom. **Bird:** Northern mockingbird. **Tree:** Sabal palmetto palm. **Song:** "Old Folks at Home." **Entered union:** Mar. 3, 1845; rank: 27th.

Tourism. Tourist spending: $112.6 bil (2019); change, 2019-20: −39%; change, 2019-22: 9%. **Attractions:** Miami Beach; Castillo de San Marcos Natl. Monument, St. Augustine Lighthouse & Museum, Lightner Museum, in St. Augustine (oldest permanent European settlement in U.S.); Walt Disney World Resort, SeaWorld Orlando, Universal Studios, Discovery Cove, in Orlando; Kennedy Space Ctr., U.S. Astronaut Hall of Fame; Everglades Natl. Park; Ringling Museum of Art, Ringling Circus Museum, in Sarasota; Cypress Gardens at Legoland Florida, Winter Haven; Busch Gardens, Big Cat Rescue, in Tampa; Florida Caverns State Park, Marianna; Key West. **Information:** Visit Florida, 2540 W. Executive Center Cir., Ste. 200, Tallahassee, FL 32301; 1-888-7FLA-USA; www.visitflorida.com

History. Florida has been inhabited for at least 12,000 years. Timucua, Apalachee, and Calusa peoples were living in the region when the earliest Europeans came; later the Seminole migrated from Georgia to Florida, becoming dominant there in the early 18th cent. The first European to see Florida was Spain's Ponce de León, 1513. France established a colony, Ft. Caroline, on the St. Johns R., 1564. Spain settled St. Augustine, 1565, and Spanish troops massacred most of the French. Britain's Sir Francis Drake burned St. Augustine, 1586. In 1763, Spain ceded Florida to Great Britain, which held the area 20 years before returning it to Spain. Florida was ceded to the U.S. in the Adams-Onís Treaty, 1819. The Seminole War, 1835-42, resulted in the removal of most Native Americans to Indian Territory. Florida joined the Union in 1845, seceded in 1861, and was readmitted in 1868. In the late 19th cent., hotel and railroad builder Henry M. Flagler laid the foundations of the tourism industry. The state experienced phenomenal population growth in the 20th cent., especially after 1950. The first U.S. astronaut was launched into space from Cape Canaveral, 1961. Walt Disney World opened near Orlando, 1971. Hurricane Andrew slammed Florida, 1992, causing at least $25 bil in property damage. A dispute over Florida's presidential vote in 2000 was decided by the U.S. Supreme Court. In June 2016, a gunman carried out the then-deadliest mass shooting in modern U.S. history when he killed 49 people at a gay nightclub in Orlando. The CDC in 2016 issued its first-ever travel warning for part of the continental U.S. amid reports of the Zika virus in a Miami neighborhood. A Feb. 2018 mass shooting at a Parkland high school killed 17 and galvanized a wave of youth-led activism against gun violence. In June 2021, the sudden collapse of a section of a 12-story beachfront condo in the Miami suburb of Surfside killed nearly 100 people. On Mar. 28, 2022, Gov. Ron DeSantis (R) signed a bill that bans classroom instruction related to sexual orientation/gender identity in early grades; in response to Disney's criticism of the law, DeSantis revoked the company's special tax privileges and self-governing status in the state; Disney in 2023 undertook efforts to subvert the governor's attack, resulting in opposing lawsuits. On Sept. 28, 2022, Hurricane Ian made landfall in SW Florida, killing more than 100 people and causing an estimated $109 bil in damages.

Famous Floridians. Edna Buchanan, Jeb Bush, Marjory Stoneman Douglas, Gloria Estefan, Henry Morrison Flagler, Ariana Grande, Carl Hiaasen, Zora Neale Hurston, James Weldon Johnson, Deacon Jones, MacKinlay Kantor, Osceola, Claude Pepper, Tom Petty, Henry B. Plant, A. Philip Randolph, Marjorie Kinnan Rawlings, Janet Reno, Marco Rubio, Deion Sanders, Emmitt Smith, Joseph W. Stilwell, Amar'e Stoudemire, Charles P. Summerall.

Website. www.myflorida.com

Georgia (GA)
Empire State of the South, Peach State

People. Population: 10,912,876; rank: 8. **Pop. change** (2010-22): 12.6%. **Pop. density:** 190 per sq mi. **Racial distribution:** 59.0% white; 33.1% Black; 4.8% Asian; 0.6% Amer. Ind.; 0.1% Hawaiian/Pacific Islander; 2 or more races, 2.4%. **Hispanic pop.:** 10.5%.

Geography. Total area: 59,425 sq mi; rank: 24. **Land area:** 57,513 sq mi; rank: 21. **Acres forested:** 24.3 mil. **Location:** South Atlantic state. **Climate:** maritime tropical air masses dominate in summer; polar air masses in winter; E central area drier. **Topography:** most southerly of the Blue Ridge Mts. cover NE and N central; central Piedmont extends to the fall line of rivers; coastal plain levels to the coast flatlands. **Capital:** Atlanta. **Chief airports:** Atlanta, Savannah.

Economy. Chief industries: services, manufacturing, retail trade. **Chief manuf. goods:** carpet and rugs, animal slaughtering and processing, motor vehicles and parts, plastics, aircrafts, paper, chemicals, food. **Chief crops:** cotton, greenhouse and nursery, peanuts, pecans, corn, tomatoes, cucumbers, onions, watermelons, tobacco, squash, blueberries, hay, cabbage, soybeans, peaches, snap beans, wheat. **Farm income:** Crops: $3.76 bil. Livestock: $5.79 bil. **Nonfuel minerals:** $2.3 bil; cement, clay (kaolin and montmorillonite), sand and gravel (construction),

sand and gravel (industrial), stone (crushed). **Commercial fishing:** $22.9 mil. **Chief ports:** Savannah, Brunswick. **Gross state product:** $755.7 bil. **Sales tax:** 4.0%. **Gasoline tax:** 50.35 cents/gal. **Employment distrib.:** 14.2% govt.; 20.9% trade/trans./util.; 8.5% mfg.; 13.5% ed./health; 15.9% prof./bus. serv.; 10.6% leisure/hosp.; 5.7% finance; 4.7% constr./mining/log.; 2.6% info.; 3.5% other serv. **Unemployment:** 3.0%. **Min. wage/hr.:** $7.25. **Per cap. pers. income:** $57,129. **New private housing:** 77,222 units/$16.0 bil. **Broadband internet:** 97.6%. **Commercial banks:** 187; deposits: $348.6 bil. **Savings institutions:** 10; deposits: $3.0 bil. **Lottery:** total sales: $5.6 bil; profit: $1.5 bil.

Federal govt. civ. employees: 76,788; **avg. salary:** $88,449. **Notable fed. facilities:** Ft. Moore (fmr. Benning); Ft. Stewart; Fed. Law Enforcement Training Ctr. HQ, Brunswick; Robins AFB; Ft. Eisenhower (fmr. Gordon); Naval Sub Base Kings Bay; Moody AFB; Centers for Disease Control, Atlanta; Marine Corps Logistics Base Albany.

Education. High school grad. rate: 83.8%. **4-yr. public coll./univ.:** 27; **2-yr. public:** 23; **4-yr. private:** 32.

Energy. Electricity use/cost: 1,072 kWh, $134.11.

State data. Motto: Wisdom, justice, and moderation. **Flower:** Cherokee rose. **Bird:** Brown thrasher. **Tree:** Southern live oak. **Song:** "Georgia on My Mind." **Fourth** of the 13 original states to ratify the Constitution, Jan. 2, 1788.

Tourism. Tourist spending: $34.9 bil (2019); change, 2019-20: −31%; change, 2019-22: 8%. **Attractions:** Georgia State Capitol, Stone Mountain, Centennial Olympic Park, Six Flags Over Georgia, Martin Luther King Jr. Natl. Historical Park, Jimmy Carter Library and Museum, Atlanta Botanical Garden, Georgia Aquarium (largest in Western Hemisphere); College Football Hall of Fame, in Atlanta; Kennesaw Mountain Natl. Battlefield Park; Chickamauga and Chattanooga Natl. Military Park; Chattahoochee-Oconee Natl. Forest; Dahlonega, site of earliest U.S. gold rush; Brasstown Bald (highest mtn. in state); Franklin D. Roosevelt's Little White House Historic Site, Warm Springs; Callaway Gardens, Pine Mountain; Andersonville Natl. Historic Site; Okefenokee Natl. Wildlife Refuge; Jekyll, St. Simons, and Cumberland barrier islands; Savannah Historic District. **Information:** Dept. of Economic Development, 75 Fifth St., NW, Ste. 1200, Atlanta, GA 30308; 1-800-VISITGA; www.exploregeorgia.org

History. Creek and Cherokee peoples were living in the region when Spaniards founded Santa Catalina mission, 1566, on Saint Catherines Island. Gen. James Oglethorpe established a colony in Savannah, 1733, for the poor and religiously persecuted. Oglethorpe defeated a Spanish army from Florida at Bloody Marsh, 1742. Georgia was a battleground in the American Revolution, with the British finally evacuating Savannah in 1782. When Georgia entered the Union, 1788, its plantation economy relied on enslaving Black workers for rice and cotton growing. The Cherokee were removed to Indian Territory, 1838-39, and thousands died on the long march, known as the Trail of Tears. By 1860 the enslaved population exceeded 462,000 (nearly 44% of the total population). Georgia seceded from the Union, 1861, and was invaded by Union forces, 1864, under Gen. William T. Sherman, who took Atlanta, Sept. 2, and proceeded on his famous "march to the sea," ending in Savannah in Dec. Georgia was readmitted, 1870. Born 1929 in Atlanta, Martin Luther King Jr. made the city his base during the civil rights struggles of the 1960s. Atlanta became the leading city of the "New South," host headquarters of Coca-Cola and CNN, and host of the 1996 Summer Olympic Games. With the state offering significant tax breaks and other economic incentives, film and TV production was a $2.9-bil industry in 2019. Amid groundless claims of voter fraud in the 2020 election, Georgia became the first state to enact new voter restrictions. Three white men were convicted in Nov. 2021 of murdering 25-year-old Black jogger Ahmaud Arbery near Brunswick, in Feb. 2020. The state increasingly found itself in the national political spotlight with Dec. runoff elections to determine its Senate seats extending the biannual federal election cycle.

Famous Georgians. Kim Basinger, Griffin Bell, James Brown, Erskine Caldwell, Jimmy Carter, Ray Charles, Ty Cobb, James Dickey, Walt Frazier, John C. Fremont, Newt Gingrich, Nancy Grace, Joel Chandler Harris, "Doc" Holliday, Larry Holmes, Holly Hunter, Alan Jackson, Martin Luther King Jr., Gladys Knight, Sidney Lanier, Little Richard, Juliette Gordon Low, Margaret Mitchell, Jessye Norman, Sam Nunn, Flannery O'Connor, Otis Redding, Burt Reynolds, Julia Roberts, Jackie Robinson, Ryan Seacrest, Clarence Thomas, Travis Tritt, Ted Turner, Carl Vinson, Alice Walker, Herschel Walker, Joanne Woodward, Trisha Yearwood, Andrew Young.

Website. www.georgia.gov

Hawai'i (HI)
Aloha State

People. Population: 1,440,196; rank: 40. **Pop. change** (2010-22): 5.9%. **Pop. density:** 224 per sq mi. **Racial**

distribution: 25.2% white; 2.2% Black; 37.1% Asian; 0.4% Amer. Ind.; 10.3% Hawaiian/Pacific Islander; 2 or more races, 24.7%. **Hispanic pop.:** 11.1%.

Geography. Total area: 10,932 sq mi; rank: 43. **Land area:** 6,423 sq mi; rank: 47. **Acres forested:** 1.8 mil. **Location:** Pacific archipelago of about 132 islands 2,100 mi SW of U.S. mainland. **Climate:** subtropical, with wide variations in rainfall; Mt. Waialeale, on Kaua'i, wettest spot in U.S. (annual avg. rainfall 422 in., 1912-2015). **Topography:** islands are tops of a chain of submerged volcanic mountains; Mauna Loa, Kilauea are active volcanoes. **Capital:** Honolulu. **Chief airports:** Honolulu, Kahului, Kailua Kona, Lihue, Hilo.

Economy. Chief industries: tourism, defense, sugar, pineapples. **Chief manuf. goods:** concrete, printing, baked goods, sugar, preserved fruits and vegetables, apparel. **Chief crops:** flowers and nursery, pineapples, seed crops, sugarcane, macadamia nuts, coffee, algae, papayas, tomatoes, bananas, basil, ginger. **Farm income:** Crops: $445.91 mil. Livestock: $147.28 mil. **Nonfuel minerals:** $156 mil; sand and gravel (construction), stone (crushed). **Commercial fishing:** $129.3 mil. **Chief ports:** Honolulu, Hilo, Barbers Point, Kahului. **Gross state product:** $98.2 bil. **Sales tax:** 4.0%. **Gasoline tax:** 36.90 cents/gal. **Employment distrib.:** 19.9% govt.; 18.2% trade/trans./util.; 2.0% mfg.; 13.7% ed./health; 11.6% prof./bus. serv.; 18.7% leisure/hosp.; 4.3% finance; 5.9% constr./mining/log.; 1.4% info.; 4.3% other serv. **Unemployment:** 3.5%. **Min. wage/hr.:** $12.00. **Per cap. pers. income:** $61,175. **New private housing:** 4,330 units/$1.8 bil. **Broadband internet:** 99.8%. **Commercial banks:** 10; deposits: $49.8 bil. **Savings institutions:** 3; deposits $10.1 bil.

Federal govt. Fed. civ. employees: 23,675; **avg. salary:** $88,377. **Notable fed. facilities:** Joint Base Pearl Harbor-Hickam; Schofield Barracks; Marine Corps Base Hawaii, Kaneohe Bay; Tripler Army Med. Ctr.; Ft. Shafter; Wheeler Army Airfield; Prince Kuhio Federal Bldg., Honolulu.

Education. High school grad. rate: 86.3%. **4-yr. public coll./univ.:** 4; **2-yr. public:** 6; **4-yr. private:** 4.

Energy. Electricity use/cost: 531 kWh, $177.78.

State data. Motto: Ua mau ke ea o ka aina i ka pono (The life of the land is perpetuated in righteousness). **Flower:** Yellow hibiscus. **Bird:** Nene (Hawaiian goose). **Tree:** Kukui (candlenut). **Song:** "Hawai'i Pono'i" (Hawai'i's Own). **Entered union:** Aug. 21, 1959; rank: 50th.

Tourism. Tourist spending: $29.0 bil (2019); change, 2019-20: −62%; change, 2019-22: −9%. **Attractions:** Oahu Isl.: Natl. Memorial Cemetery of the Pacific, Waikiki Beach, Diamond Head, in Honolulu; USS *Arizona* Memorial, Pearl Harbor; Polynesian Cultural Ctr., Laie; Hanauma Bay; Nu'uanu Pali. Kaua'i Isl.: Waimea Canyon. Maui Isl.: Haleakala Natl. Park. Hawai'i Isl.: Hawaii Volcanoes Natl. Park, Wailoa and Wailuku River State Parks. **Information:** Hawaii Visitors and Conventions Bureau, 2270 Kalakaua Ave., Ste. 801, Honolulu, HI 96815; 1-800-GOHAWAII; www.gohawaii.com

History. Polynesians from islands 2,000 mi to the S settled the Hawaiian Islands, probably 300-600 CE. The first European visitor was British captain James Cook, 1778. King Kamehameha I united the islands by 1810. Christian missionaries arrived, 1819, bringing Western culture. Under the reign, 1825-54, of King Kamehameha III, a constitution, legislature, and public school system were instituted. Sugar production began, 1835, and it became the dominant industry. Queen Liliuokalani was deposed, 1893, and a republic was established, 1894, headed by Sanford B. Dole. Annexation by the U.S. came in 1898. The Japanese attack on Pearl Harbor, Dec. 7, 1941, brought the U.S. into World War II. Hawai'i attained statehood, 1959. Hurricane Iniki pounded Kaua'i, 1992, causing about $1 bil in damage. In 2006, Pres. George W. Bush designated the Northwestern Hawaiian Islands Natl. Monument, a marine area of 140,000 sq mi. The Kilauea volcano on Hawaii's Big Island started to erupt, May 2018, forcing a series of evacuations. Mauna Loa, the world's largest active volcano, erupted in Nov. 2022 for the first time since 1984. Devastating Maui wildfires killed at least 115, Aug. 2023.

Famous Islanders. Bernice Pauahi Bishop, Tia Carrere, Alexander Cartwright, St. Damien de Veuster, Tulsi Gabbard, Don Ho, Daniel K. Inouye, Duke Kahanamoku, King Kamehameha, Nicole Kidman, Brook Mahealani Lee, Jason Scott Lee, Queen Liliuokalani, Bruno Mars, Bette Midler, Barack Obama, Ellison S. Onizuka, Michelle Wie.

Website. portal.ehawaii.gov

Idaho (ID)
Gem State

People. Population: 1,939,033; rank: 38. **Pop. change** (2010-22): 23.7%. **Pop. density:** 24 per sq mi. **Racial distribution:** 92.6% white; 1.0% Black; 1.7% Asian; 1.7% Amer. Ind.; 0.2% Hawaiian/Pacific Islander; 2 or more races, 2.8%. **Hispanic pop.:** 13.5%.

Geography. Total area: 83,569 sq mi; rank: 14. **Land area:** 82,643 sq mi; rank: 11. **Acres forested:** 21.9 mil. **Location:** northwestern Mountain state bordering British Columbia, Canada. **Climate:** tempered by Pacific westerly winds; drier, colder, continental climate in SE; altitude an important factor. **Topography:** Snake R. plains in the S; central region of mountains, canyons, gorges (Hells Canyon, 7,900 ft, deepest in N. America); subalpine northern region. **Capital:** Boise. **Chief airport:** Boise.

Economy. Chief industries: manufacturing, agriculture, tourism, lumber, mining, electronics. **Chief manuf. goods:** computers and electronics, preserved fruits and vegetables, cheese, lumber. **Chief crops:** potatoes, wheat, hay, sugar beets, barley, greenhouse and nursery, onions, dry beans, corn, mint, apples, hops, peaches, lentils, peas, cherries, plums and prunes, oats. **Farm income:** Crops: $3.64 bil. Livestock: $4.94 bil. **Nonfuel minerals:** $371 mil; lead, phosphate rock, sand and gravel (construction), silver, zinc. **Chief port:** Lewiston. **Gross state product:** $109.5 bil. **Sales tax:** 6.0%. **Gasoline tax:** 51.40 cents/gal. **Employment distrib.:** 15.9% govt.; 19.0% trade/trans./util.; 8.5% mfg.; 14.9% ed./health; 13.1% prof./bus. serv.; 10.6% leisure/hosp.; 4.9% finance; 8.7% constr./mining/log.; 1.1% info.; 3.3% other serv. **Unemployment:** 2.7%. **Min. wage/hr.:** $7.25. **Per cap. pers. income:** $54,537. **New private housing:** 18,737 units/$4.7 bil. **Broadband internet:** 97.0%. **Commercial banks:** 28; deposits: $43.9 bil. **Savings institutions:** 1; deposits: $1.2 bil. **Lottery:** total sales $376.3 mil; profit: $73.0 mil.

Federal govt. Fed. civ. employees: 8,762; **avg. salary:** $80,784. **Notable fed. facilities:** Idaho Natl. Lab, Idaho Falls; Mountain Home AFB.

Education. High school grad. rate: 82.2%. **4-yr. public coll./univ.:** 4; **2-yr. public:** 4; **4-yr. private:** 5.

Energy. Electricity use/cost: 961 kWh, $97.62.

State data. Motto: Esto Perpetua (It is perpetual). **Flower:** Syringa. **Bird:** Mountain bluebird. **Tree:** White pine. **Song:** "Here We Have Idaho." **Entered union:** July 3, 1890; rank: 43rd.

Tourism. Tourist spending: $5.7 bil (2019); change, 2019-20: −25%; change, 2019-22: 4%. **Attractions:** Hells Canyon (deepest river gorge in N. America); World Ctr. for Birds of Prey, Boise Art Museum, in Boise; Craters of the Moon Natl. Monument and Preserve; Sun Valley; Shoshone Falls, near Twin Falls; Lava Hot Springs; Lake Coeur d'Alene; Sawtooth Natl. Recreation Area; Frank Church-River of No Return Wilderness Area; Nez Perce Natl. Historical Park. **Information:** Idaho Dept. of Commerce-Tourism Development, 700 W. State St., P.O. Box 83720, Boise, ID 83720; 1-800-VISITID; www.visitidaho.org

History. Paleo-Indian hunters roamed the land over 13,000 years ago; later inhabitants included Shoshone, Northern Paiute, Bannock, and Nez Percé peoples. The Meriwether Lewis and William Clark Expedition took place 1804-06. Next came fur traders, 1809-34, and missionaries, 1830s-50s. Mormons made their first permanent settlement at Franklin, 1860. Idaho's gold rush began the same year and brought thousands of permanent settlers. A series of wars with the territory's Indigenous residents followed, including a campaign by Chief Joseph and the Nez Percé that ended with his surrender in Montana, 1877. Idaho became a territory, 1863, and a state, 1890. In the 20th cent., it emerged as a leader in potato, lumber, and silver output. The Sun Valley ski resort opened in 1936, boosting tourism. Startup of Lewiston's river port, 1975, opened Idaho to oceangoing trade. Fueled by technology job growth, the state's population jumped 21.2%, 2000-10, and 21.3%, 2010-21. In 2020, Idaho became the first state to ban transgender girls and women from sports participation at public schools and colleges/universities, as well as the first, in Apr. 2023, to criminalize helping minors leave the state to receive an abortion without parental consent. Four university students were stabbed to death in Moscow, ID, in Nov. 2022; after a lengthy manhunt, a suspect was arrested in Pennsylvania.

Famous Idahoans. William Borah, Frank Church, Lou Dobbs, Fred Dubois, W. Mark Felt, Chief Joseph, Harmon Killebrew, Aaron Paul, Ezra Pound, Marilynne Robinson, Sacagawea, Picabo Street, Lana Turner.

Website. www.idaho.gov

Illinois (IL)
Prairie State

People. Population: 12,582,032; rank: 6. **Pop. change** (2010-22): −1.9%. **Pop. density:** 227 per sq mi. **Racial distribution:** 76.1% white; 14.7% Black; 6.3% Asian; 0.6% Amer. Ind.; 0.1% Hawaiian/Pacific Islander; 2 or more races, 2.2%. **Hispanic pop.:** 18.3%.

Geography. Total area: 57,914 sq mi; rank: 25. **Land area:** 55,519 sq mi; rank: 24. **Acres forested:** 4.9 mil. **Location:** East North Central state; western, southern, and eastern boundaries formed by Mississippi, Ohio, and Wabash Rivers, respectively. **Climate:** temperate; typically cold, snowy winters, hot summers. **Topography:** prairie and fertile plains throughout; open hills in the southern region. **Capital:** Springfield. **Chief airports:** Chicago (2).

Economy. Chief industries: services, manufacturing, travel, wholesale and retail trade, finance, insurance, real estate, construction, health care, agriculture. **Chief manuf. goods:** food, petroleum, plastics, chemicals, agricultural machinery, pharmaceuticals, motor vehicles, printing. **Chief crops:** corn, soybeans, hay, wheat, greenhouse and nursery, apples, peaches, sorghum. **Farm income:** Crops: $18.60 bil. **Livestock:** $3.10 bil. **Nonfuel minerals:** $1.3 bil; cement, magnesium compounds, sand and gravel (construction); sand and gravel (industrial), stone (crushed). **Chief port:** Chicago. **Gross state product:** $1.0 tril. **Sales tax:** 6.25%. **Gasoline tax:** 85.80 cents/gal. **Employment distrib.:** 13.5% govt.; 19.8% trade/trans./util.; 9.3% mfg.; 15.9% ed./health; 15.8% prof./bus. serv.; 9.6% leisure/hosp.; 6.7% finance; 3.9% constr./mining/log.; 1.5% info.; 4.1% other serv. **Unemployment:** 4.6%. **Min. wage/hr.:** $13.00. **Per cap. pers. income:** $68,822. **New private housing:** 20,550 units/$4.7 bil. **Broadband internet:** 98.5%. **Commercial banks:** 388; deposits: $686.2 bil. **Savings institutions:** 47; deposits: $9.6 bil. **Lottery:** total sales: $3.4 bil; profit: $833.6 mil.

Federal govt. Fed. civ. employees: 42,310; **avg. salary:** $96,973. **Notable fed. facilities:** Great Lakes Naval Station; Fermi Natl. Accelerator Lab, Batavia; Argonne Natl. Lab, Lemont; Scott AFB; Rock Island Arsenal.

Education. High school grad. rate (2018-19): 86.2%. **4-yr. public coll./univ.:** 12; **2-yr. public:** 48; **4-yr. private:** income:

Energy. Electricity use/cost: 728 kWh, $95.86.

State data. Motto: State sovereignty, national union. **Flower:** Native violet. **Bird:** Northern cardinal. **Tree:** White oak. **Song:** "Illinois." **Entered union:** Dec. 3, 1818; rank: 21st.

Tourism. Tourist spending: $45.5 bil (2019); change, 2019-20: −49%; change, 2019-22: 4%. **Attractions:** Art Institute of Chicago, Field Museum of Natural History, Shedd Aquarium, Millennium Park, Navy Pier, in Chicago; Illinois State Museum, Abraham Lincoln Presidential Library and Museum, in Springfield; Cahokia Mounds State Historic Site, Collinsville; Starved Rock State Park; Crab Orchard Natl. Wildlife Refuge; Forts Kaskaskia, de Chartres, Massac; Shawnee Natl. Forest; Dickson Mounds Museum, Lewistown. **Information:** Illinois Office of Tourism, 100 W. Randolph St., Ste. 3-400, Chicago, IL 60601; 1-800-226-6632; www.enjoyillinois.com

History. The region has been inhabited for at least 10,000 years; seminomadic Algonquian peoples, including the Peoria, Illinois, Kaskaskia, and Tamaroa, lived there at the time of European contact. Fur traders were the first Europeans in Illinois, followed shortly by Louis Jolliet and Jacques Marquette, 1673, and René-Robert Cavelier, sieur de La Salle, 1680, who built a fort near present-day Peoria. French priests established the first permanent settlements at Cahokia, near present-day St. Louis, 1699, and Kaskaskia, 1703. France ceded the area to Britain, 1763, and in 1778, American Gen. George Rogers Clark took Kaskaskia from the British without a shot. Illinois became a separate territory, 1809, and a state, 1818. Defeat of Native American tribes in the Black Hawk War, 1832, and canal, rail, and road construction brought rapid change. Mormon settlers at Nauvoo, 1839, met with hostility, and a Carthage mob killed Mormon leader Joseph Smith and his brother, 1844. The Great Chicago Fire, 1871, destroyed the city's downtown. Illinois became a center for the labor movement, leading to bitter conflicts such as the Haymarket riot, 1886, and Pullman strike, 1894. Social reformer Jane Addams founded Hull House, 1889, to aid immigrants and the poor. The expansion of manufacturing, 1900-70, drew African Americans from the South in the Great Migration. Chicago police violently suppressed antiwar protests at the 1968 Democratic National Convention. Barack Obama, elected in 2004 to serve in the U.S. Senate, became the 44th U.S. president in 2009. Political corruption and criminality have plagued the state; since 1960, five former governors have been charged with criminal offenses. A U.S. Justice Dept. investigation of the Chicago Police Dept., launched after a 2014 video of a white officer fatally shooting a Black teen sparked protests, found in 2017 that officers used excessive force too often and without repercussions. The officer was found guilty of 2nd-degree murder and sentenced in Jan. 2019 to 6.75 years in prison. A Chicago public school teachers' strike shut down schools for 11 days in Oct. 2019. On July 4, 2022, a rooftop shooter in the Chicago suburb of Highland Park killed seven people at a parade.

Famous Illinoisans. Jane Addams, Saul Bellow, John Belushi, Jack Benny, Ray Bradbury, Gwendolyn Brooks, St. Frances Xavier Cabrini, Al Capone, Hillary Rodham Clinton, Clarence Darrow, John Deere, Stephen A. Douglas, Katherine Dunham, Wyatt Earp, Roger Ebert, James T. Farrell, Marshall Field, Harrison Ford, Betty Friedan, Benny Goodman, Ulysses S. Grant, Dennis Hastert, Hugh Hefner, Ernest Hemingway, Charlton Heston, Jennifer Hudson, Henry J. Hyde, Abraham Lincoln, Vachel Lindsay, David Mamet, Edgar Lee Masters, Oscar Mayer, Cyrus McCormick, Eliot Ness, Bob Newhart, Michelle Obama, Ronald Reagan, Shonda Rhimes, Donald Rumsfeld, Carl Sandburg, Shel Silverstein, Adlai E. Stevenson, James Watson, Frank Lloyd Wright, Philip K. Wrigley.

Website. www.illinois.gov

Indiana (IN)
Hoosier State

People. Population: 6,833,037; rank: 17. **Pop. change** (2010-22): 5.4%. **Pop. density:** 191 per sq mi. **Racial distribution:** 84.0% white; 10.3% Black; 2.8% Asian; 0.4% Amer. Ind.; 0.1% Hawaiian/Pacific Islander; 2 or more races, 2.4%. **Hispanic pop.:** 7.9%.

Geography. Total area: 36,420 sq mi; rank: 38. **Land area:** 35,826 sq mi; rank: 38. **Acres forested:** 4.8 mil. **Location:** East North Central state; Lake Michigan on N border. **Climate:** four distinct seasons with temperate climate. **Topography:** hilly southern region; fertile rolling plains of central region; flat, heavily glaciated N; dunes along Lake Michigan shore. **Capital:** Indianapolis. **Chief airport:** Indianapolis.

Economy. Chief industries: manufacturing, services, agriculture, government, wholesale and retail trade, transportation, public utilities. **Chief manuf. goods:** motor vehicles and parts, iron and steel mills, pharmaceuticals, petroleum, plastics, medical equip., printing. **Chief crops:** corn, soybeans, greenhouse and nursery, wheat, hay, tomatoes, watermelons, apples. **Farm income:** Crops: $9.71 bil. Livestock: $4.50 bil. **Nonfuel minerals:** $1.4 bil; cement, lime, sand and gravel (construction), stone (crushed), stone (dimension). **Chief ports:** Burns Harbor-Portage, Mt. Vernon, Jeffersonville. **Gross state product:** $455.8 bil. **Sales tax:** 7.0%. **Gasoline tax:** 72.30 cents/gal. **Employment distrib.:** 13.1% govt.; 19.4% trade/trans./util.; 16.6% mfg.; 15.0% ed./health; 11.6% prof./bus. serv.; 9.8% leisure/hosp.; 4.6% finance; 5.2% constr./mining/log.; 0.8% info.; 4.0% other serv. **Unemployment:** 3.0%. **Min. wage/hr.:** $7.25. **Per cap. pers. income:** $57,930. **New private housing:** 28,274 units/$7.2 bil. **Broadband internet:** 98.1%. **Commercial banks:** 109; deposits: $186.4 bil. **Savings institutions:** 23; deposits $8.7 bil. **Lottery:** total sales: $1.7 bil; profit: $346.8 mil.

Federal govt. Fed. civ. employees: 23,622; **avg. salary:** $85,344. **Notable fed. facilities:** Naval Surface Warfare Ctr., Crane Div.; Grissom Air Reserve Base.

Education. High school grad. rate: 90.9%. **4-yr. public coll./univ.:** 15; **2-yr. public:** 1; **4-yr. private:** 39.

Energy. Electricity use/cost: 946 kWh, $126.51.

State data. Motto: Crossroads of America. **Flower:** Peony. **Bird:** Northern cardinal. **Tree:** Tulip poplar. **Song:** "On the Banks of the Wabash, Far Away." **Entered union:** Dec. 11, 1816; rank: 19th.

Tourism. Tourist spending: $13.3 bil (2019); change, 2019-20: −35%; change, 2019-22: −3%. **Attractions:** Lincoln Boyhood Natl. Memorial, Lincoln City; George Rogers Clark Natl. Historical Park, Vincennes; Tippecanoe Battlefield Museum and Park, Battle Ground; Benjamin Harrison Presidential Site, Indianapolis Motor Speedway and Hall of Fame Museum, Indianapolis Museum of Art, in Indianapolis; Indiana Dunes Natl. Park, Chesterton; Studebaker Natl. Museum, in South Bend; Hoosier Natl. Forest. **Information:** Indiana Destination Development Corp., 1 North Capital, Ste. 600, Indianapolis, IN 46204; 1-800-677-9800; www.visitindiana.com

History. When the Europeans arrived, Miami, Potawatomi, Kickapoo, Piankashaw, Wea, and Shawnee peoples inhabited the region. René-Robert Cavelier, sieur de La Salle, visited the present South Bend area, 1679 and 1681. The first French fort was built near present-day Lafayette, 1717. A French trading post was established, 1731-32, at Vincennes. France ceded the area to Britain, 1763. During the American Revolution, American Gen. George Rogers Clark captured Vincennes, 1778, and defeated British forces, 1779. Indiana became a territory, 1800, and a state, 1816. The Miami were beaten, 1794, at Fallen Timbers, and Gen. William H. Harrison defeated Tecumseh's Indian confederation, 1811, at Tippecanoe. Manufacturing grew rapidly after the Civil War. U.S. Steel founded Gary, 1906. An automotive test track was the site of the first Indianapolis 500 race, 1911. The auto industry remains key to the state economy; in 2008, Honda opened a $550-mil plant near Greensburg. Heavy rain in June 2008 flooded southwest and central Indiana. Some rights groups and businesses criticized the state's 2015 Religious Freedom Restoration Act as discriminatory to LGBT individuals. Mike Pence, the state's governor, 2013-17, served as U.S. vice president, 2017-21. A former employee in Apr. 2021 fatally shot eight workers at a FedEx facility in Indianapolis.

Famous "Hoosiers." Larry Bird, Ambrose Burnside, Meg Cabot, Hoagy Carmichael, Jim Davis, James Dean, Eugene V. Debs, John Dillinger, Theodore Dreiser, Paul Dresser, Jeff Gordon, Benjamin Harrison, Gil Hodges, Michael Jackson, David Letterman, Carole Lombard, Marjorie Main, John Mellencamp, Jane Pauley, Cole Porter, Gene Stratton Porter, Ernie Pyle, Dan Quayle, James Whitcomb Riley, Oscar Robertson, Red Skelton, Tony Stewart, Booth Tarkington, Kurt Vonnegut, Lew Wallace, Ryan White, Wendell L. Willkie, Wilbur Wright.
Website. www.in.gov

Iowa (IA)
Hawkeye State

People. Population: 3,200,517; rank: 31. **Pop. change** (2010-22): 5.0%. **Pop. density:** 57 per sq mi. **Racial distribution:** 89.8% white; 4.4% Black; 2.8% Asian; 0.6% Amer. Ind.; 0.2% Hawaiian/Pacific Islander; 2 or more races, 2.2%. **Hispanic pop.:** 6.9%.

Geography. Total area: 56,273 sq mi; rank: 26. **Land area:** 55,857 sq mi; rank: 23. **Acres forested:** 2.9 mil. **Location:** West North Central state bordered by Mississippi R. on the E, Missouri R. on the W. **Climate:** humid, continental. **Topography:** watershed from NW to SE; soil especially rich and sand level in the N central counties. **Capital:** Des Moines. **Chief airports:** Des Moines, Cedar Rapids.

Economy. Chief industries: agriculture, communications, construction, finance, insurance, trade, services, manufacturing. **Chief manuf. goods:** machinery, vegetable oils, animal slaughtering and processing, laundry equip., plastics, motor vehicles and parts. **Chief crops:** corn, soybeans, hay, greenhouse and nursery, oats. **Farm income:** Crops: $18.93 bil. Livestock: $15.99 bil. **Nonfuel minerals:** $846 mil; cement, lime, sand and gravel (construction), sand and gravel (industrial), stone (crushed). **Gross state product:** $231.1 bil. **Sales tax:** 6.0%. **Gasoline tax:** 48.40 cents/gal. **Employment distrib.:** 16.7% govt.; 19.5% trade/trans./util.; 14.3% mfg.; 15.0% ed./health; 9.0% prof./bus. serv.; 8.7% leisure/hosp.; 6.8% finance; 5.4% constr./mining/log.; 1.2% info.; 3.5% other serv. **Unemployment:** 2.7%. **Min. wage/hr.:** $7.25. **Per cap. pers. income:** $58,905. **New private housing:** 12,711 units/$3.2 bil. **Broadband internet:** 96.3%. **Commercial banks:** 277; deposits: $112.3 bil. **Savings institutions:** 7; deposits: $8.5 bil. **Lottery:** total sales: $432.7 mil; profit: $98.0 mil.

Federal govt. Fed. civ. employees: 8,981; **avg. salary:** $84,905. **Notable fed. facilities:** Ames Lab; Natl. Animal Disease Ctr.

Education. High school grad. rate: 91.8%. **4-yr. public coll./univ.:** 3; **2-yr. public:** 16; **4-yr. private:** 34.

Energy. Electricity use/cost: 861 kWh, $109.63.

State data. Motto: Our liberties we prize, and our rights we will maintain. **Flower:** Wild rose. **Bird:** Eastern goldfinch. **Tree:** Oak. **Song:** "The Song of Iowa." **Entered union:** Dec. 28, 1846; rank: 29th.

Tourism. Tourist spending: $9.8 bil (2019); change, 2019-20: −29%; change, 2019-22: 7%. **Attractions:** Des Moines Art Ctr., Iowa State Fairgrounds, Iowa State Capitol, in Des Moines; Natl. Czech & Slovak Museum & Library, Cedar Rapids; Herbert Hoover Natl. Historic Site, Presidential Library and Museum, in West Branch; Effigy Mounds Natl. Monument, Marquette; Amana Colonies (former communal society); Figge Art Museum, Davenport; Living History Farms, Urbandale; Adventureland, Altoona; Boone & Scenic Valley Railroad and Museum; riverboat cruises and casino gambling, Mississippi and Missouri Rivers; Iowa Great Lakes, Okoboji; American Gothic House, Eldon; *Field of Dreams* movie site, Dyersville; Natl. Mississippi River Museum & Aquarium, Dubuque. **Information:** Iowa Tourism Office, Iowa Economic Development Authority, 1963 Bell Ave., Ste. 200, Des Moines, IA 50309; 1-800-345-IOWA; www.traveliowa.com

History. Early inhabitants were Mound Builders who dwelt on Iowa's fertile plains. Later, Iowa and Yankton Sioux lived in the area. The first Europeans, Jacques Marquette and Louis Jolliet, gave France its claim to the area, 1673. In 1762, France ceded the region to Spain, but Napoleon took it back, 1800. It became part of the U.S. through the Louisiana Purchase, 1803. Native American Sauk and Fox tribes moved into the area but relinquished their land in defeat after the 1832 uprising led by Sauk chieftain Black Hawk. Iowa became a territory in 1838 and a free state in 1846, strongly supporting the Union. Fertile land lured farmers from eastern states, 1850-1900, and the population rose rapidly. Growth slowed in the 20th cent., as farming became mechanized. Severe flooding in eastern Iowa in June 2008 caused billions of dollars in damages and forced the evacuation of thousands of residents. The Iowa caucuses have been the first statewide electoral event in the presidential nomination process since 1972. A wind and thunderstorm complex known as a

"derecho" severely affected Iowa in Aug. 2020, with regional damage estimates exceeding $11 bil. An apartment building collapsed in Davenport in May 2023, killing three people.

Famous Iowans. Tom Arnold, Johnny Carson, William F. "Buffalo Bill" Cody, Mamie Dowd Eisenhower, Michael Emerson, Bob Feller, George Gallup, Susan Glaspell, James Norman Hall, Herbert Hoover, Shawn Johnson, Ashton Kutcher, Ann Landers, Cloris Leachman, Glenn Miller, Lillian Russell, Billy Sunday, James A. Van Allen, Abigail Van Buren, Carl Van Vechten, Henry Wallace, Kurt Warner, John Wayne, Meredith Willson, Elijah Wood, Grant Wood.
Website. www.iowa.gov

Kansas (KS)
Sunflower State

People. Population: 2,937,150; rank: 35. **Pop. change** (2010-22): 2.9%. **Pop. density:** 36 per sq mi. **Racial distribution:** 85.9% white; 6.2% Black; 3.2% Asian; 1.2% Amer. Ind.; 0.2% Hawaiian/Pacific Islander; 2 or more races, 3.3%. **Hispanic pop.:** 13.0%.

Geography. Total area: 82,278 sq mi; rank: 15. **Land area:** 81,759 sq mi; rank: 13. **Acres forested:** 2.5 mil. **Location:** West North Central state with Missouri R. on E. **Climate:** temperate but continental, with great extremes between summer and winter. **Topography:** hilly Osage Plains in the E; central region level prairie and hills; high plains in the W. **Capital:** Topeka. **Chief airport:** Wichita.

Economy. Chief industries: manufacturing, finance, insurance, real estate, services. **Chief manuf. goods:** animal slaughtering, aerospace, petroleum, plastics, machinery, navigational instruments, printing. **Chief crops:** wheat, corn, soybeans, hay, sorghum, sunflowers, cotton, potatoes. **Farm income:** Crops: $9.82 bil. Livestock: $11.48 bil. **Nonfuel minerals:** $1.2 bil; cement, helium (Grade-A), salt, sand and gravel (construction), stone (crushed). **Chief port:** Kansas City. **Gross state product:** $210.7 bil. **Sales tax:** 6.5%. **Gasoline tax:** 43.43 cents/gal. **Employment distrib.:** 18.0% govt.; 19.0% trade/trans./util.; 11.9% mfg.; 14.2% ed./health; 12.8% prof./bus. serv.; 9.2% leisure/hosp.; 5.3% finance; 5.1% constr./mining/log.; 1.2% info.; 3.5% other serv. **Unemployment:** 2.7%. **Min. wage/hr.:** $7.25. **Per cap. pers. income:** $60,152. **New private housing:** 9,560 units/$2.5 bil. **Broadband internet:** 97.8%. **Commercial banks:** 247; deposits: $92.6 bil. **Savings institutions:** 11; deposits: $7.4 bil. **Lottery:** total sales: $313.0 mil; profit: $79.1 mil.

Federal govt. Fed. civ. employees: 17,190; **avg. salary:** $82,520. **Notable fed. facilities:** Ft. Riley; Leavenworth Fed. Penitentiary, Dwight D. Eisenhower VA Medical Ctr., Leavenworth; McConnell AFB; Colmery-O'Neil VA Medical Ctr., Topeka.

Education. High school grad. rate: 88.2%. **4-yr. public coll./univ.:** 8; **2-yr. public:** 25; **4-yr. private:** 24.

Energy. Electricity use/cost: 890 kWh, $115.53.

State data. Motto: Ad Astra per Aspera (To the stars through difficulties). **Flower:** Native sunflower. **Bird:** Western meadowlark. **Tree:** Cottonwood. **Song:** "Home on the Range." **Entered union:** Jan. 29, 1861; rank: 34th.

Tourism. Tourist spending: $8.6 bil (2019); change, 2019-20: −26%; change, 2019-21: 6%. **Attractions:** Eisenhower Presidential Library and Museum, Abilene; Natl. Agricultural Ctr. and Hall of Fame, Bonner Springs; Boot Hill Museum, Dodge City; Old Cowtown Museum, Wichita; Ft. Scott and Ft. Larned Natl. Historic Sites; Kansas Cosmosphere and Space Ctr., Hutchinson; U.S. Cavalry Museum, Ft. Riley; Tallgrass Prairie Natl. Preserve, Strong City; Kansas Speedway, Kansas City. **Information:** Kansas Dept. of Commerce, Travel and Tourism Div., 1000 SW Jackson St., Ste. 100, Topeka, KS 66612; (785) 296-2009; www.travelks.com

History. Wichita, Pawnee, Kansa, and Osage peoples lived in the area when Spain's Francisco de Coronado explored it in 1541. These Native Americans—hunters who also farmed— were joined on the Plains by the nomadic Cheyenne, Arapaho, Comanche, and Kiowa about 1800. France claimed the region, 1682, ceded its claim to Spain, 1762, then regained control, 1800, before selling it to the U.S. in the Louisiana Purchase, 1803. After 1830, thousands of Native Americans were removed from more eastern states to Kansas. Organized as a territory, 1854, the area witnessed violent clashes between pro- and antislavery settlers and became known as "Bleeding Kansas." It entered the Union as a free state, 1861. After the Civil War, rail construction and huge cattle drives from Texas turned Abilene and Dodge City into cowboy capitals. Russian Mennonite immigrants brought a new strain of winter wheat, 1874, transforming Kansas agriculture. Carry Nation launched her anti-saloon crusade in the 1890s. Part of the Dust Bowl, the state experienced drought and depression in the 1930s. Topeka was the focus of the famous *Brown v. Board of Education* decision, 1954, that led to desegregation of U.S. public schools. Bob Dole represented Kansas in the U.S. Senate (1969-96) but failed in several efforts to win higher office.

Famous Kansans. Kirstie Alley, Roscoe "Fatty" Arbuckle, Ed Asner, John Brown, Walter P. Chrysler, Glenn Cunningham, John Steuart Curry, Robert Joseph "Bob" Dole, Amelia Earhart, Dwight D. Eisenhower, Melissa Etheridge, Ron Evans, Georgia Neese Clark Gray, Maurice Greene, James Butler "Wild Bill" Hickok, Cyrus K. Holliday, Dennis Hopper, William Inge, Don Johnson, Walter Johnson, Nancy Landon Kassebaum, Buster Keaton, Emmett Kelly, Alfred M. "Alf" Landon, Hattie McDaniel, Oscar Micheaux, Carry Nation, Charlie Parker, Gordon Parks, Jim Ryun, Barry Sanders, Vivian Vance, William Allen White, Jess Willard.

Website. www.kansas.gov

Kentucky (KY)
Bluegrass State

People. Population: 4,512,310; rank: 26. **Pop. change** (2010-22): 4.0%. **Pop. density:** 114 per sq mi. **Racial distribution:** 86.9% white; 8.7% Black; 1.8% Asian; 0.3% Amer. Ind.; 0.1% Hawaiian/Pacific Islander; 2 or more races, 2.3%. **Hispanic pop.:** 4.3%.

Geography. Total area: 40,408 sq mi; rank: 37. **Land area:** 39,486 sq mi; rank: 37. **Acres forested:** 12.4 mil. **Location:** East South Central state bordered on N by Illinois, Indiana, Ohio; on E by West Virginia and Virginia; on S by Tennessee; on W by Missouri. **Climate:** moderate, with plentiful rainfall. **Topography:** mountainous in E; rounded hills of the Knobs region in the N; Bluegrass region in heart of state; wooded rocky hillsides of the Pennyroyal Plateau; Western Coal Field; the fertile Jackson Purchase region in the SW. **Capital:** Frankfort. **Chief airports:** Hebron (Cincinnati metro area), Louisville, Lexington.

Economy. Chief industries: manufacturing, services, finance, insurance and real estate, retail trade, public utilities. **Chief manuf. goods:** motor vehicles and parts, aluminum, basic chemicals, plastics, iron and steel, rubber, printing. **Chief crops:** hay, corn, soybeans, tobacco, wheat. **Farm income:** Crops: $3.38 bil. Livestock: $3.53 bil. **Nonfuel minerals:** $806 mil; cement, clay (common clay), lime, sand and gravel (construction), stone (crushed). **Chief ports:** Louisville, Hickman-Fulton County. **Gross state product:** $260.3 bil. **Sales tax:** 6.0%. **Gasoline tax:** 44.40 cents/gal. **Employment distrib.:** 15.4% govt.; 21.5% trade/trans./util.; 13.0% mfg.; 14.8% ed./health; 11.5% prof./bus. serv.; 10.0% leisure/hosp.; 4.7% finance; 4.6% constr./mining/log.; 1.1% info.; 3.4% other serv. **Unemployment:** 3.9%. **Min. wage/hr.:** $7.25. **Per cap. pers. income:** $52,109. **New private housing:** 15,050 units/$3.3 bil. **Broadband internet:** 96.8%. **Commercial banks:** 148; deposits: $117.5 bil. **Savings institutions:** 10; deposits: $1.2 bil. **Lottery:** total sales: $1.5 bil; profit: $359.3 mil.

Federal govt. Fed. civ. employees: 21,866; avg. salary: $78,957. **Notable fed. facilities:** U.S. Bullion Depository, Ft. Knox; Ft. Campbell; Fed. Medical Ctr., Lexington; Army Corps of Engineers, Louisville District.

Education. High school grad. rate: 91.1%. **4-yr. public coll./univ.:** 8; **2-yr. public:** 16; **4-yr. private:** 25.

Energy. Electricity use/cost: 1,084 kWh, $124.67.

State data. Motto: United we stand, divided we fall. **Flower:** Goldenrod. **Bird:** Northern cardinal. **Tree:** Tulip poplar. **Song:** "My Old Kentucky Home." **Entered union:** June 1, 1792; rank: 15th.

Tourism. Tourist spending: $11.2 bil (2019); change, 2019-20: −27%; change, 2019-22: 12%. **Attractions:** Churchill Downs (Kentucky Derby), Louisville Slugger Museum and Factory, in Louisville; Land Between the Lakes Natl. Recreation Area (Kentucky and Barkley Lakes); Mammoth Cave Natl. Park (world's longest known cave system); Abraham Lincoln Birthplace Natl. Historical Park, Hodgenville; My Old Kentucky Home State Park, Bardstown; Cumberland Gap Natl. Historical Park, Middlesboro; Creation Museum, Petersburg; Kentucky Horse Park, Lexington; Shaker Village of Pleasant Hill, Harrodsburg; Natl. Corvette Museum, Bowling Green. **Information:** Kentucky Dept. of Tourism, 500 Mero St., 5th Fl., Frankfort, KY 40601; 1-800-225-8747; www.kentuckytourism.com

History. Paleo-Indians first arrived about 14,000 years ago. Much later, Shawnee, Wyandot, Delaware, and Cherokee peoples used the area mostly for hunting. Explored by Thomas Walker and Christopher Gist, 1750-51, Kentucky was the first area W of the Alleghenies settled by American pioneers. The first permanent settlement was Harrodsburg, 1774. Daniel Boone blazed the Wilderness Trail through the Cumberland Gap and founded Ft. Boonesborough, 1775. Clashes with Native Americans were frequent, 1774-94. Virginia dropped its claims to the region, and Kentucky became a state, 1792. Tobacco growing, horse breeding, coal mining, and bourbon whiskey making were major industries in the

19th cent. A slave state, Kentucky tried to stay neutral in the Civil War, but then opted for the Union; many Kentuckians sided with the Confederacy. The U.S. gold depository at Ft. Knox opened, 1937. Prior to the 2008 economic downturn, auto manufacturing had grown in recent decades. A statewide teacher walkout in Mar.-Apr. 2018 demanded increased pay and school funding. Tornadoes killed 77 people in western Kentucky Dec. 10-11, 2021, including 17 in Bowling Green and 9 at a candle factory in Mayfield. Record flooding from torrential rains in July 2022 killed nearly 40 people in the state's Appalachian foothills.

Famous Kentuckians. Muhammad Ali, Alben W. Barkley, Ned Beatty, Louis D. Brandeis, John C. Breckinridge, Kit Carson, Albert B. "Happy" Chandler, Henry Clay, George Clooney, Rosemary Clooney, Jefferson Davis, D. W. Griffith, "Casey" Jones, Jennifer Lawrence, Abraham Lincoln, Mary Todd Lincoln, Thomas Hunt Morgan, Carry Nation, Colonel Harland Sanders, Diane Sawyer, Chris Stapleton, Jesse Stuart, Zachary Taylor, Hunter S. Thompson, Robert Penn Warren, Whitney M. Young Jr.

Website. www.kentucky.gov

Louisiana (LA)
Pelican State

People. Population: 4,590,241; rank: 25. **Pop. change** (2010-22): 1.3%. **Pop. density:** 106 per sq mi. **Racial distribution:** 62.5% white; 32.8% Black; 1.9% Asian; 0.8% Amer. Ind.; 0.1% Hawaiian/Pacific Islander; 2 or more races, 1.9%. **Hispanic pop.:** 5.8%.

Geography. Total area: 52,378 sq mi; rank: 31. **Land area:** 43,204 sq mi; rank: 33. **Acres forested:** 14.9 mil. **Location:** West South Central state on the Gulf Coast. **Climate:** subtropical, affected by continental weather patterns. **Topography:** lowlands of marshes and Mississippi R. floodplain; Red R. Valley lowlands; upland hills in the Florida Parishes; avg. elevation, 100 ft. **Capital:** Baton Rouge. **Chief airport:** New Orleans (Kenner).

Economy. Chief industries: wholesale and retail trade, tourism, manufacturing, construction, transportation, communication, public utilities, finance, insurance, real estate, mining. **Chief manuf. goods:** petroleum, chemicals, plastics material and resin, pesticides and fertilizers, cleaning prods., paper and paperboard, ships, structural metals. **Chief crops:** sugarcane, cotton, rice, soybeans, corn, sweet potatoes. **Farm income:** Crops: $2.54 bil. Livestock: $1.11 bil. **Nonfuel minerals:** $1.0 bil; clay (common clay), salt, sand and gravel (construction), sand and gravel (industrial), stone (crushed). **Commercial fishing:** $367.1 mil. **Chief ports:** New Orleans, Baton Rouge, Lake Charles, Port of S. Louisiana (La Place), Shreveport, Plaquemine, St. Bernard, Alexandria. **Gross state product:** $281.4 bil. **Sales tax:** 4.45%. **Gasoline tax:** 39.33 cents/gal. **Employment distrib.:** 16.3% govt.; 18.8% trade/trans./util.; 7.0% mfg.; 17.2% ed./health; 11.4% prof./bus. serv.; 11.2% leisure/hosp.; 4.7% finance; 8.6% constr./mining/log.; 1.2% info.; 3.6% other serv. **Unemployment:** 3.7%. **Min. wage/hr.:** none. **Per cap. pers. income:** $54,622. **New private housing:** 16,270 units/$3.7 bil. **Broadband internet:** 96.9%. **Commercial banks:** 106; deposits: $139.1 bil. **Savings institutions:** 17; deposits: $4.8 bil. **Lottery:** total sales: $582.9 mil; profit: $191.2 mil.

Federal govt. Fed. civ. employees: 18,606; avg. salary: $84,607. **Notable federal facilities:** Ft. Johnson (fmr. Polk) (Joint Readiness Training Ctr.); Barksdale AFB; Strategic Petroleum Reserve, Michoud Assembly Facility, USDA Southern Regional Research Ctr., New Orleans NAS JRB.

Education. High school grad. rate: 82.9%. **4-yr. public coll./univ.:** 17; **2-yr. public:** 14; **4-yr. private:** 11.

Energy. Electricity use/cost: 1,192 kWh, $131.37.

State data. Motto: Union, justice, and confidence. **Flower:** Magnolia blossom. **Bird:** Eastern brown pelican. **Tree:** Bald cypress. **Song:** "Give Me Louisiana." **Entered union:** Apr. 30, 1812; rank: 18th.

Tourism. Tourist spending: $13.9 bil (2019); change, 2019-20: −35%; change, 2019-22: −6%. **Attractions:** Mardi Gras, French Quarter, Bourbon Street, in New Orleans; Jean Lafitte Natl. Historical Park and Preserve; Longfellow-Evangeline State Historic Site, St. Martinville; Kent Plantation House, Alexandria; Oak Alley Plantation, Vacherie; Whitney Plantation, Wallace; Hodges Gardens State Park, Florien; USS *Kidd* Veterans Memorial, Baton Rouge. **Information:** Louisiana Office of Tourism, P.O. Box 94291, Baton Rouge, LA 70804-9291; (225) 342-8100; www.louisianatravel.com

History. Caddo, Tunica, Choctaw, Chitimacha, and Chawash peoples lived in the region at the time of European contact. Spanish explorers in the early 16th cent. reached the mouth of the Mississippi. René-Robert Cavelier, sieur de La Salle, 1682, claimed the region for France. Early French and Spanish settlers were the ancestors of Louisiana Creoles.

Cajuns descended from the Acadians, French settlers expelled by the British from Nova Scotia, Canada, in 1755. France ceded the Louisiana region to Spain, 1762, took it back, 1800, and sold it to the U.S., 1803, in the Louisiana Purchase. Admitted as a state in 1812, Louisiana witnessed the Battle of New Orleans, 1815. Cotton and sugar plantations relied on the enslaved labor of Black workers, who made up close to 47% of the population in 1860, on the eve of the Civil War. Louisiana seceded, 1861, and was readmitted, 1868. Jazz was born in New Orleans in the early 20th cent. As governor (1928-32), Huey Long pushed populist programs. Many tropical storms and floods have battered Louisiana, including Hurricane Katrina and subsequent flooding, 2005, which devastated New Orleans. The offshore oil and gas industry developed after World War II. An oil rig explosion off the state's Gulf coast spilled millions of barrels of oil, damaging coastal wetlands and many of the state's marine-dependent industries in 2010. Rain caused severe flooding in and around Baton Rouge and Lafayette in 2016. In May 2017, New Orleans removed several monuments honoring the Confederacy and a racially motivated Reconstruction-era attack. Category 4 hurricane Laura severely impacted Lake Charles in Aug. 2020, causing the deaths of at least 27. In Aug. 2021, Category 4 hurricane Ida devastated the barrier island town of Grand Isle and was blamed for the deaths of at least 28.

Famous Louisianans. Louis Armstrong, Pierre Beauregard, Judah P. Benjamin, Braxton Bragg, Kate Chopin, Harry Connick Jr., Ellen DeGeneres, Fats Domino, George "Buddy" Guy, Lillian Hellman, Grace King, Jerry Lee Lewis, Bob Livingston, Huey Long, Eli Manning, Peyton Manning, Wynton Marsalis, Tim McGraw, Leonidas K. Polk, Anne Rice, Bill Russell, Henry Miller Shreve, Britney Spears, Madam C. J. Walker (Sarah Breedlove), Edward Douglass White Jr.

Website. www.louisiana.gov

Maine (ME)
Pine Tree State

People. Population: 1,385,340; rank: 42. **Pop. change** (2010-22): 4.3%. **Pop. density:** 45 per sq mi. **Racial distribution:** 93.9% white; 2.0% Black; 1.4% Asian; 0.7% Amer. Ind.; <0.05% Hawaiian/Pacific Islander; 2 or more races, 2.0%. **Hispanic pop.:** 2.1%.

Geography. Total area: 35,380 sq mi; rank: 39. **Land area:** 30,843 sq mi; rank: 39. **Acres forested:** 17.5 mil. **Location:** New England state at northeastern tip of U.S. **Climate:** southern interior and coast influenced by air masses from the S and W; northern clime harsher, avg. over 100 in. snow in winter. **Topography:** Appalachian Mts. extend through state; western borders have rugged terrain; long sand beaches on southern coast; northern coast mainly rocky promontories, peninsulas, fjords. **Capital:** Augusta. **Chief airport:** Portland.

Economy. Chief industries: manufacturing, agriculture, fishing, services, trade, government, finance, insurance, real estate, construction. **Chief manuf. goods:** paper, ships and boats, cardboard, frozen/canned fruits and vegetables, plastics, baked goods. **Chief crops:** potatoes, greenhouse and nursery, wild blueberries, apples, hay, maple syrup. **Farm income:** Crops $493.55 mil. Livestock: $293.45 mil. **Nonfuel minerals:** $100 mil; cement, peat, sand and gravel (construction), stone (crushed), stone (dimension). **Commercial fishing:** $953.8 mil. **Chief ports:** Searsport, Portland, Eastport. **Gross state product:** $84.5 bil. **Sales tax:** 5.5%. **Gasoline tax:** 49.80 cents/gal. **Employment distrib.:** 16.0% govt.; 18.5% trade/trans./util.; 8.6% mfg.; 20.4% ed./health; 12.0% prof./bus. serv.; 9.2% leisure/hosp.; 5.3% finance; 5.3% constr./mining/log.; 1.2% info.; 3.5% other serv. **Unemployment:** 3.0%. **Min. wage/hr.:** $13.80. **Per cap. pers. income:** $59,463. **New private housing:** 7,105 units/$1.7 bil. **Broadband internet:** 96.8%. **Commercial banks:** 11; deposits: $23.6 bil. **Savings institutions:** 18; deposits: $19.2 bil. **Lottery:** total sales: $385.8 mil; profit: $72.1 mil.

Federal govt. Fed. civ. employees: 11,759; **avg. salary:** $81,235. **Notable fed. facilities:** Portsmouth Naval Shipyard.

Education. High school grad. rate: 87.4%. **4-yr. public coll./univ.:** 8; **2-yr. public:** 7; **4-yr. private:** 11.

Energy. Electricity use/cost: 584 kWh, $99.44.

State data. Motto: Dirigo (I direct). **Flower:** White pine cone and tassel. **Bird:** Black-capped chickadee. **Tree:** Eastern white pine. **Song:** "State of Maine Song." **Entered union:** Mar. 15, 1820; rank: 23rd.

Tourism. Tourist spending: $4.9 bil (2019); change, 2019-20: −41%; change, 2019-22: 1%. **Attractions:** Acadia Natl. Park, Bar Harbor, on Mt. Desert Island; Old Orchard Beach; Old Port historic waterfront, Victoria Mansion, Portland; Portland Head Light, Cape Elizabeth; Maine Maritime Museum, Bath; Baxter State Park; L.L. Bean flagship store and outlet shopping, Freeport. **Information:** Maine Office of Tourism,

59 State House Station, Augusta, ME 04330; 1-888-624-6345; www.visitmaine.com

History. Paleo-Indians arrived about 11,500 years ago. Maine was inhabited by Algonquian peoples including the Abnaki, Penobscot, and Passamaquoddy at the time of European contact. French settled, 1604, at the St. Croix R., the English, c. 1607, on the Kennebec; both settlements failed. A royal charter, 1691, made Maine part of Massachusetts. Maine broke off, 1819, and became a separate state, 1820. Drawing on vast forest resources, the pulp and paper industry developed after the Civil War. Bath Iron Works began building U.S. Navy vessels and other ships in the 1890s. Mail-order and retail giant L.L. Bean was founded, 1912. Women have fared well in state politics: Margaret Chase Smith became the first woman to serve in both houses of Congress (House, 1940-49; Senate, 1949-73), and Olympia Snowe and Susan Collins represented Maine in the Senate since the mid-1990s (Snowe retired in Jan. 2013).

Famous "Down Easters." Leon Leonwood (L. L.) Bean, James G. Blaine, Patrick Dempsey, Hannibal Hamlin, Sarah Orne Jewett, Anna Kendrick, Stephen King, Henry Wadsworth Longfellow, Sir Hiram and Hudson Maxim, Edna St. Vincent Millay, George J. Mitchell, Edmund Muskie, Judd Nelson, Edwin Arlington Robinson, Joan Benoit Samuelson, Liv Tyler, Kate Douglas Wiggin, Ben Ames Williams.

Website. www.maine.gov

Maryland (MD)
Old Line State, Free State

People. Population: 6,164,660; rank: 19. **Pop. change** (2010-22): 6.8%. **Pop. density:** 635 per sq mi. **Racial distribution:** 57.3% white; 31.7% Black; 7.1% Asian; 0.7% Amer. Ind.; 0.1% Hawaiian/Pacific Islander; 2 or more races, 3.2%. **Hispanic pop.:** 11.5%.

Geography. Total area: 12,406 sq mi; rank: 42. **Land area:** 9,707 sq mi; rank: 42. **Acres forested:** 2.4 mil. **Location:** South Atlantic state stretching from the ocean to the Allegheny Mts. **Climate:** continental in the W; humid subtropical in the E. **Topography:** coastal plain on Eastern Shore and separated by Chesapeake Bay from coastal plain, Piedmont Plateau, and the Blue Ridge. **Capital:** Annapolis. **Chief airport:** Glen Burnie (Baltimore/Washington).

Economy. Chief industries: manufacturing, biotechnology and information technology, services, tourism. **Chief manuf. goods:** navigational instruments, pharmaceutical and medicine, broadcasting equip., plastics, printing, milk and ice cream. **Chief crops:** greenhouse and nursery, corn, soybeans, wheat, hay, tomatoes, watermelons, barley, potatoes, apples. **Farm income:** Crops: $1.19 bil. Livestock: $1.32 bil. **Nonfuel minerals:** $414 mil; cement, sand and gravel (construction), stone (crushed), stone (dimension). **Commercial fishing:** $68.9 mil. **Chief port:** Baltimore. **Gross state product:** $470.2 bil. **Sales tax:** 6.0%. **Gasoline tax:** 61.29 cents/gal. **Employment distrib.:** 19.5% govt.; 17.2% trade/trans./util.; 4.0% mfg.; 16.8% ed./health; 17.2% prof./bus. serv.; 9.2% leisure/hosp.; 4.9% finance; 5.9% constr./mining/log.; 1.3% info.; 4.0% other serv. **Unemployment:** 3.2%. **Min. wage/hr.:** $13.25. **Per cap. pers. income:** $70,730. **New private housing:** 19,346 units/$4.0 bil. **Broadband internet:** 99.0%. **Commercial banks:** 64; deposits: $205.1 bil. **Savings institutions:** 12; deposits: $3.6 bil. **Lottery:** total sales: $4.7 bil; profit: $1.4 bil.

Federal govt. Fed. civ. employees: 138,892; **avg. salary:** $122,669. **Notable fed. facilities:** U.S. Naval Academy; Beltsville Agriculture Res. Ctr.; Ft. Meade; Aberdeen Proving Ground; Joint Base Andrews; Naval Air Sys. Command; Goddard Space Flight Ctr.; Natl. Inst. of Standards & Technology, Gaithersburg; Food & Drug Admin., Natl. Marine Fisheries Serv., Natl. Oceanic and Atmospheric Admin., Silver Spring; Bureau of the Census, Suitland; Natl. Inst. of Health, Walter Reed Natl. Military Med. Ctr., Bethesda.

Education. High school grad. rate: 86.8%. **4-yr. public coll./univ.:** 13; **2-yr. public:** 16; **4-yr. private:** 18.

Energy. Electricity use/cost: 973 kWh, $127.62.

State data. Motto: Fatti Maschii, Parole Femine (Manly deeds, womanly words). **Flower:** Black-eyed Susan. **Bird:** Baltimore oriole. **Tree:** White oak. **Song:** None. "Maryland, My Maryland" repealed in 2021 over pro-Confederacy lyrics. Seventh of original 13 states to ratify the Constitution, Apr. 28, 1788.

Tourism. Tourist spending: $19.6 bil (2019); change, 2019-20: −37%; change, 2019-22: 1%. **Attractions:** Ocean City; Ft. McHenry (the defense of which inspired Francis Scott Key to write "The Star-Spangled Banner"), Pimlico Race Course (Preakness Stakes), Edgar Allan Poe House and Museum, Oriole Park at Camden Yards, Natl. Aquarium, Inner Harbor, in Baltimore; Antietam Natl. Battlefield, Sharpsburg; South Mountain State Battlefield, Middletown; U.S. Naval Academy,

Maryland State House (oldest in continuous legislative use in U.S.), in Annapolis; Natl. Cryptologic Museum, Ft. Meade. **Information:** Maryland Office of Tourism Development, 401 E. Pratt St., 14th Fl., Baltimore, MD 21202; 1-877-209-5883; www.visitmaryland.org

History. Europeans encountered Algonquian-speaking Nanticoke and Piscataway and Iroquois-speaking Susquehannock when they first visited the area. Italian navigator Giovanni da Verrazzano reached the Chesapeake region in the early 16th cent. English Capt. John Smith explored and mapped the area, 1608. William Claiborne set up a trading post on Kent Island in Chesapeake Bay, 1631. King Charles I granted land to Cecilius Calvert, Lord Baltimore, 1632; Calvert's brother Leonard, with about 200 settlers, founded St. Mary's, 1634. During the Revolutionary War, Baltimore (1776-77) and Annapolis (1783-84) served as temporary capitals of the U.S. When a British fleet tried to take Ft. McHenry in the War of 1812, Marylander Francis Scott Key wrote "The Star-Spangled Banner," 1814. Born into slavery at Tuckahoe in 1818, Frederick Douglass became a leading abolitionist. Although a slaveholding state, Maryland stayed in the Union during the Civil War and was the site of the battle of Antietam, 1862. Gov. Spiro Agnew, elected U.S. vice pres., 1968 and 1972, pleaded no contest to tax evasion and resigned, 1973. Israeli and Egyptian leaders reached a historic peace accord at the Camp David presidential retreat, 1978. A major effort is under way to clean up pollution in the Chesapeake Bay watershed. The death of a young Black man in police custody touched off sometimes violent protests in Baltimore in 2015. Six law enforcement officers were charged in his death; after three were acquitted, charges against the others were dropped. According to a 2016 Justice Dept. report, Baltimore's police dept. regularly violated the constitutional rights of Black residents. A gunman in June 2018 fatally shot five employees at the office of Annapolis's *Capital Gazette*. Baltimore Mayor Catherine Pugh resigned, May 2019, amid a "self-dealing" corruption scandal. In Nov. 2022, the state elected its first Black governor, Wes Moore.

Famous Marylanders. John Astin, Benjamin Banneker, Tom Clancy, Frederick Douglass, Matthew Henson, Francis Scott Key, Thurgood Marshall, H. L. Mencken, Kweisi Mfume, Ogden Nash, Charles Willson Peale, Michael Phelps, William Pinkney, Edgar Allan Poe, Cal Ripken Jr., Babe Ruth, Upton Sinclair, Roger B. Taney, Harriet Tubman, John Waters, Montel Williams.

Website. www.maryland.gov

Massachusetts (MA)
Bay State, Old Colony

People. Population: 6,981,974; rank: 16. **Pop. change** (2010-22): 6.6%. **Pop. density:** 895 per sq. mi. **Racial distribution:** 79.4% white; 9.5% Black; 7.7% Asian; 0.5% Amer. Ind.; 0.1% Hawaiian/Pacific Islander; 2 or more races, 2.7%. **Hispanic pop.:** 13.1%.

Geography. Total area: 10,554 sq mi; rank: 44. **Land area:** 7,800 sq mi; rank: 45. **Acres forested:** 3.0 mil. **Location:** New England state on Atlantic seaboard. **Climate:** temperate, with colder, drier clime in western region. **Topography:** jagged indented coast from Rhode Island around Cape Cod; flat land yields to stony upland pastures near central region and gentle hilly country in W; except in W, land is rocky, sandy, and not fertile. **Capital:** Boston. **Chief airport:** Boston.

Economy. Chief industries: services, trade, manufacturing. **Chief manuf. goods:** electronics and instruments, pharmaceuticals, telecom and broadcasting equip., plastics, medical equip., printing. **Chief crops:** greenhouse and nursery, cranberries, tomatoes, sweet corn, apples, hay, tobacco. **Farm income:** Crops: $385.77 mil. Livestock: $109.20 mil. **Nonfuel minerals:** $206 mil; clay (common clay), lime, sand and gravel (construction), stone (crushed), stone (dimension). **Commercial fishing:** $840.0 mil. **Chief ports:** Boston, Fall River. **Gross state product:** $688.4 bil. **Sales tax:** 6.25%. **Gasoline tax:** 45.60 cents/gal. **Employment distrib.:** 12.4% govt.; 15.1% trade/trans./util.; 6.3% mfg.; 22.4% ed./health; 17.5% prof./bus. serv.; 9.2% leisure/hosp.; 6.2% finance; 4.7% constr./mining/log.; 2.6% info.; 3.6% other serv. **Unemployment:** 3.8%. **Min. wage/hr.:** $15.00. **Per cap. pers. income:** $84,945. **New private housing:** 17,692 units/$5.2 bil. **Broadband internet:** 99.1%. **Commercial banks:** 41; deposits: $492.0 bil. **Savings institutions:** 91; deposits $87.6 bil. **Lottery:** total sales: $5.9 bil; profit: $1.1 bil.

Federal govt. Fed. civ. employees: 24,546; **avg. salary:** $101,212. **Notable fed. facilities:** Thomas P. O'Neill Jr. Fed. Bldg., J.W. McCormack Bldg., JFK Fed. Bldg., Boston; Hanscom AFB; Army Natick Soldier Systems Ctr.

Education. High school grad. rate: 89.0%. **4-yr. public coll./univ.:** 14; **2-yr. public:** 16; **4-yr. private:** 73.

Energy. Electricity use/cost: 596 kWh, $136.37.

State data. Motto: Ense Petit Placidam Sub Libertate Quietem (By the sword we seek peace, but peace only under liberty). **Flower:** Mayflower. **Bird:** Black-capped chickadee. **Tree:** American elm. **Song:** "All Hail to Massachusetts." **Sixth** of original 13 states to ratify the Constitution, Feb. 6, 1788.

Tourism. Tourist spending: $26.5 bil (2019); change, 2019-20: −53%; change, 2019-22: −3%. **Attractions:** Provincetown art colony; Cape Cod; Plymouth Rock, Plimoth Plantation, Mayflower II, in Plymouth; Freedom Trail, Museum of Fine Arts, New England Aquarium, Faneuil Hall, Boston Harbor Isls. Natl. Recreation Area, Boston Public Garden, in Boston; Tanglewood, Hancock Shaker Village, Berkshire Scenic Railway Museum, Norman Rockwell Museum, in the Berkshires region; Peabody Essex Museum, House of the Seven Gables, in Salem; Old Sturbridge Village; Historic Deerfield; Walden Pond, Louisa May Alcott's Orchard House, in Concord; Naismith Memorial Basketball Hall of Fame, Springfield. **Information:** Massachusetts Office of Travel & Tourism, 136 Blackstone St., 5th Fl., Boston, MA 02109; 1-800-227-MASS; www.visitma.com

History. Early inhabitants were Algonquian peoples: Nauset, Wampanoag, Massachuset, Pennacook, Nipmuc, and Pocumtuc. Pilgrims settled in Plymouth, 1620, giving thanks for their survival with a Thanksgiving feast alongside Wampanoag living there, 1621. About 20,000 new settlers arrived, 1630-40. Colonist-Native American relations deteriorated, leading to King Philip's War, 1675-76, which the colonists won. Witch trials at Salem, 1692, led to the execution of 20 people. Demonstrations against British restrictions set off the Boston Massacre, 1770, and the Boston Tea Party, 1773. The first bloodshed of the American Revolution was at Lexington, 1775. After statehood, Massachusetts prospered from shipbuilding, seafaring, and the making of textiles, shoes, and metal goods, while artists, writers, and social reformers flourished. The controversial Sacco-Vanzetti case, 1920-27, ended with the execution of two Italian immigrants on murder and robbery charges. After World War II, old industries declined, knowledge-intensive enterprises thrived, and the Kennedys became a dominant political family. The state's highest court ruled, 2003, that same-sex couples could legally marry. Two bombs exploded Apr. 15, 2013, near the finish line of the Boston Marathon, killing three and injuring more than 250. The surviving of two brothers believed to have planted the bombs was convicted on multiple charges in Apr. 2015 and sentenced to death. U.S. Supreme Court in Mar. 2022 upheld the death sentence.

Famous "Bay Staters." John Adams, John Quincy Adams, Samuel Adams, Louisa May Alcott, Horatio Alger, Susan B. Anthony, Crispus Attucks, Clara Barton, Michael Bloomberg, George H. W. Bush, Steve Carell, John Cheever, E. E. Cummings, Bette Davis, Emily Dickinson, Charles Eliot, Ralph Waldo Emerson, William Lloyd Garrison, Edward Everett Hale, John Hancock, Nathaniel Hawthorne, Oliver Wendell Holmes Jr., Winslow Homer, Elias Howe, John F. Kennedy, Jack Kerouac, John Kerry, Emeril Lagasse, Jack Lemmon, James Russell Lowell, Cotton Mather, Maria Mitchell, Samuel F. B. Morse, Conan O'Brien, Paul Revere, Norman Rockwell, Dr. Seuss (Theodor Seuss Geisel), Henry David Thoreau, Barbara Walters, James Abbott McNeil Whistler, John Greenleaf Whittier.

Website. www.mass.gov

Michigan (MI)
Great Lakes State, Wolverine State

People. Population: 10,034,113; rank: 10. **Pop. change** (2010-22): 1.5%. **Pop. density:** 178 per sq mi. **Racial distribution:** 78.8% white; 14.1% Black; 3.5% Asian; 0.7% Amer. Ind.; <0.05% Hawaiian/Pacific Islander; 2 or more races, 2.8%. **Hispanic pop.:** 5.7%.

Geography. Total area: 96,714 sq mi; rank: 11. **Land area:** 56,539 sq mi; rank: 22. **Acres forested:** 20.1 mil. **Location:** East North Central state bordering four of the Great Lakes, divided into an Upper and Lower Peninsula by the Straits of Mackinac, which link Lakes Michigan and Huron. **Climate:** well-defined seasons tempered by the Great Lakes. **Topography:** low rolling hills give way to northern tableland of hilly belts in Lower Peninsula; Upper Peninsula is level in the E with swampy areas; western region is higher and more rugged. **Capital:** Lansing. **Chief airports:** Detroit, Grand Rapids.

Economy. Chief industries: manufacturing, services, tourism, agriculture, forestry/lumber. **Chief manuf. goods:** motor vehicles and parts, plastics, metalworking machinery, non-wood office furniture, fabricated metals. **Chief crops:** greenhouse and nursery, soybeans, corn, wheat, sugar beets, apples, blueberries, potatoes, dry beans, cherries, hay, cucumbers, tomatoes, grapes. **Farm income:** Crops: $5.86 bil. Livestock: $3.69 bil. **Nonfuel minerals:** $3.4 bil; cement, iron ore, magnesium compounds, nickel sulfide concentrates, salt. **Commercial fishing** (2018): $8.0 mil. **Chief ports:** Detroit, Escanaba, Calcite, Port Inland, Muskegon,

Port Huron. **Gross state product:** $620.7 bil. **Sales tax:** 6.0%. **Gasoline tax:** 68.60 cents/gal. **Employment distrib.:** 14.1% govt.; 18.2% trade/trans./util.; 13.7% mfg.; 15.5% ed./health; 15.1% prof./bus. serv.; 9.0% leisure/hosp.; 5.2% finance; 4.4% constr./mining/log.; 1.3% info.; 3.6% other serv. **Unemployment:** 4.2%. **Min. wage/hr.:** $10.10. **Per cap. pers. income:** $56,813. **New private housing:** 21,983 units/$5.9 bil. **Broadband internet:** 98.2%. **Commercial banks:** 97; deposits: $297.9 bil. **Savings institutions:** 6; deposits: $16.0 bil. **Lottery:** total sales: $4.9 bil; profit: $1.2 bil.

Federal govt. Fed. civ. employees: 27,228; **avg. salary:** $95,634. **Notable fed. facilities:** Army TACOM Life Cycle Mgmt., Detroit Arsenal; DLA Logistics Info. Service; Selfridge Air Natl. Guard Base; Hart-Dole-Inouye Fed. Ctr., Battle Creek.

Education. High school grad. rate: 82.1%. **4-yr. public coll./univ.:** 22; **2-yr. public:** 24; **4-yr. private:** 38.

Energy. Electricity use/cost: 670 kWh, $117.57.

State data. Motto: Si Quaeris Peninsulam Amoenam, Circumspice (If you seek a pleasant peninsula, look about you). **Flower:** Apple blossom. **Bird:** American robin. **Tree:** White pine. **Song:** "Michigan, My Michigan." **Entered union:** Jan. 26, 1837; rank: 26th.

Tourism. Tourist spending: $24.9 bil (2019); change, 2019-20: −28%; change, 2019-22: 2%. **Attractions:** Henry Ford Museum and Greenfield Village, Dearborn; Frederik Meijer Gardens and Sculpture Park, Grand Rapids; Tahquamenon Falls (of Longfellow's poem *Song of Hiawatha*); De Zwaan windmill, Tulip Time Festival, in Holland; Soo Locks (bet. Lakes Superior and Huron), Sault Ste. Marie; Air Zoo, Portage; Mackinac Island; Belle Isle Park, Detroit Institute of Arts, Charles H. Wright Museum of African-American History, Motown Museum, in Detroit. **Information:** Michigan Economic Development Corp., 300 N. Washington Sq., Lansing, MI 48913; 1-888-784-7328; www.michigan.org

History. Hunting and fishing peoples lived in the region as early as 11,000 years ago. Ojibwa, Ottawa, Miami, Potawatomi, and Huron inhabited the area at the time of European contact. French fur traders and missionaries arrived in the 17th cent. and established a settlement at Sault Ste. Marie, 1668. British took over, 1763, and crushed a Native American uprising led by Ottawa chieftain Pontiac. The area was ceded to the U.S. by the Treaty of Paris, 1783, but the British remained until 1796. Michigan was organized as a territory, 1805. The British seized Ft. Mackinac and Detroit, 1812, but the U.S. regained control, 1814. The opening of the Erie Canal, 1825, and new land laws and Native American cessions led the way for a flood of settlers. Strongly antislavery, Michigan became a state, 1837, and supplied 90,000 soldiers to the Union army in the Civil War. Henry Ford launched the Model T car, 1908; the United Auto Workers union was founded, 1935. Motown music flourished in Detroit in the 1960s, but riots in 1967 dealt the city a heavy blow. As the auto industry faltered, Michigan lost more than 20% of its automotive-related jobs in 2002-07. In 2009, the federal government loaned billions of dollars to GM and Chrysler to keep them solvent. Detroit formally emerged from a 17-month bankruptcy process—the largest in U.S. municipal history—in Dec. 2014. In Aug. 2020, the state announced a $600 mil settlement with children/families affected by the lead-contamination crisis that began in 2014 in Flint's municipal water supply system. Michigan State Univ. in May 2018 agreed to pay $500 mil to settle sexual abuse lawsuits related to claims against former MSU doctor Larry Nassar. In Jan. 2022, the Univ. of Michigan agreed to pay $490 mil to settle claims from more than 1,000 people, mostly men, of sexual assault by former Univ. of Michigan sports doctor Robert Anderson. In Dec. 2022, two co-leaders of a foiled right-wing plot to kidnap Gov. Gretchen Whitmer (D) ahead of the 2020 election were sentenced to 16 and 19 years, respectively, in federal prison.

Famous Michiganders. Ralph Bunche, Paul de Kruif, Thomas Edison, Eminem (Marshall Mathers), Edna Ferber, Gerald R. Ford, Henry Ford, Aretha Franklin, Edgar Guest, Lee Iacocca, Magic Johnson, Casey Kasem, Will Kellogg, Ring Lardner, Elmore Leonard, Charles Lindbergh, Joe Louis, Madonna, Malcolm X, Terry McMillan, Michael Moore, Larry Page, Pontiac, Gilda Radner, Smokey Robinson, Mitt Romney, Diana Ross, Tom Selleck, Sinbad (David Adkins), John Smoltz, Lily Tomlin, Serena Williams, Stevie Wonder.

Website. www.michigan.gov

Minnesota (MN)
North Star State, Gopher State

People. Population: 5,717,184; rank: 22. **Pop. change** (2010-22): 7.8%. **Pop. density:** 72 per sq mi. **Racial distribution:** 82.6% white; 7.6% Black; 5.5% Asian; 1.4% Amer. Ind.; 0.1% Hawaiian/Pacific Islander; 2 or more races, 2.8%. **Hispanic pop.:** 6.0%.

Geography. Total area: 86,936 sq mi; rank: 12. **Land area:** 79,627 sq mi; rank: 14. **Acres forested:** 17.7 mil. **Location:** West North Central state bounded on the E by Wisconsin and Lake Superior, on the N by Canada, on the W by the Dakotas, and on the S by Iowa. **Climate:** northern part of state lies in the moist Great Lakes storm belt; the western border lies at the edge of the semiarid Great Plains. **Topography:** central hill and lake region covers approx. half the state; to the NE, rocky ridges and deep lakes; to the NW, flat plain; to the S, rolling plains and deep river valleys. **Capital:** St. Paul. **Chief airport:** Minneapolis.

Economy. Chief industries: agribusiness, forest prods., mining, manufacturing, tourism. **Chief manuf. goods:** petroleum and asphalt, computers and electronics, milk and cheese, printing, animal slaughtering, paper and paper prods., medical equip. **Chief crops:** corn, soybeans, hay, sugar beets, wheat, potatoes, greenhouse and nursery, dry edible beans, green peas, sunflowers. **Farm income:** Crops: $13.46 bil. Livestock: $8.36 bil. **Nonfuel minerals:** $4.8 bil; iron ore, sand and gravel (construction), sand and gravel (industrial), stone (crushed), stone (dimension). **Commercial fishing** (2018): $0.2 mil. **Chief ports:** Two Harbors, Silver Bay, Duluth, St. Paul. **Gross state product:** $446.5 bil. **Sales tax:** 6.875%. **Gasoline tax:** 47.00 cents/gal. **Employment distrib.:** 14.3% govt.; 17.8% trade/trans./util.; 10.9% mfg.; 19.0% ed./health; 13.1% prof./bus. serv.; 8.9% leisure/hosp.; 6.4% finance; 4.5% constr./mining/log.; 1.6% info.; 3.6% other serv. **Unemployment:** 2.7%. **Min. wage/hr.:** $10.59. **Per cap. pers. income:** $68,010. **New private housing:** 31,096 units/$7.5 bil. **Broadband internet:** 97.7%. **Commercial banks:** 302; deposits: $274.8 bil. **Savings institutions:** 14; deposits: $20.8 bil. **Lottery:** total sales: $740.2 mil; profit: $172.6 mil.

Federal govt. Fed. civ. employees: 16,796; **avg. salary:** $92,764. **Notable fed. facilities:** Bishop Henry Whipple Fed. Bldg.; Minneapolis-St. Paul Air Reserve Station.

Education. High school grad. rate: 83.8%. **4-yr. public coll./univ.:** 12; **2-yr. public:** 31; **4-yr. private:** 32.

Energy. Electricity use/cost: 776 kWh, $104.76.

State data. Motto: L'Etoile du Nord (The star of the north). **Flower:** Pink and white lady's-slipper. **Bird:** Common loon. **Tree:** Red pine. **Song:** "Hail! Minnesota." **Entered union:** May 11, 1858; rank: 32nd.

Tourism. Tourist spending: $16.6 bil (2019); change, 2019-20: −47%; change, 2019-22: −9%. **Attractions:** Minneapolis Institute of Arts, Walker Art Center, Minneapolis Sculpture Garden, Minnehaha Falls (in Longfellow's poem *Song of Hiawatha*), Guthrie Theater, in Minneapolis; Mall of America, Bloomington; Ordway Ctr. for the Performing Arts, Science Museum of Minnesota, in St. Paul; Voyageurs Natl. Park; Mayo Clinic, Rochester; North Shore (Lake Superior); Lake Minnetonka; Boundary Waters Canoe Area Wilderness; Superior Natl. Forest; Aerial Lift Bridge, Duluth. **Information:** Explore Minnesota Tourism, Metro Square, 121 7th Pl. E., Ste. 360, St. Paul, MN 55101; 1-888-VISITMN; www.exploreminnesota.com

History. Inhabited for at least 10,000 years, the region was home to Dakota Sioux when Europeans arrived. French fur traders Pierre Esprit Radisson and Médard Chouart, sieur des Groseilliers, explored in the mid-17th cent. In 1679, Daniel Greysolon, sieur Duluth, claimed the entire region for France. Ojibwa arrived in the 18th cent. and warred with the Sioux for over 100 years. Britain took the area east of the Mississippi, 1763. The U.S. took over that portion after the American Revolution and gained the western area, 1803, in the Louisiana Purchase. The U.S. built Ft. St. Anthony (now Ft. Snelling), 1819, and bought Native American lands, 1837, spurring an influx of settlers from the east. Minnesota became a territory, 1849, and a state, 1858. The Sioux staged a bloody uprising, the Battle of Wood Lake, 1862, and were driven from the state. Railroad construction after the Civil War spurred the growth of the grain, timber, and iron mining industries. The opening of the St. Lawrence Seaway, 1959, aided the port of Duluth. Elected as a reformer, former pro wrestler Jesse Ventura served as governor, 1999-2003. Sen. Paul Wellstone (D) died when his campaign plane crashed, 2002. The I-35W Mississippi River Bridge in Minneapolis collapsed in 2007, killing 13. After George Floyd, a Black man, was killed in Minneapolis police custody May 25, 2020, several days of protests/riots damaged about 1,500 businesses in the Twin Cities. The protest movement spread to hundreds of cities, calling for an end to police brutality and other forms of systemic racism. In June 2021, former Minneapolis police officer Derek Chauvin was sentenced to 22.5 years in prison after his conviction on murder and manslaughter charges for his role in Floyd's death; in July 2022, he received a concurrent 21-year federal sentence. Three other officers involved were convicted in Feb. 2022 on lesser federal charges.

Famous Minnesotans. Andrews Sisters, Warren E. Burger, Ethan and Joel Coen, Bob Dylan, F. Scott Fitzgerald, Al Franken, Judy Garland, Cass Gilbert, Hubert H. Humphrey, Garrison Keillor, Sister Elizabeth Kenny, Jessica Lange, Sinclair Lewis, Paul Manship, E. G. Marshall, William J. and Charles H. Mayo,

Eugene McCarthy, Walter F. Mondale, Prince (Prince Rogers Nelson), Charles M. Schulz, Ann Sothern, Harold Stassen, Thorstein Veblen, Jesse Ventura, Lindsey Vonn, Paul Wellstone. **Website.** www.mn.gov

Mississippi (MS)

Magnolia State

People. Population: 2,940,057; rank: 34. **Pop. change** (2010-22): −0.9%. **Pop. density:** 63 per sq mi. **Racial distribution:** 58.8% white; 37.8% Black; 1.2% Asian; 0.6% Amer. Ind.; 0.1% Hawaiian/Pacific Islander; 2 or more races, 1.5%. **Hispanic pop.:** 3.6%.

Geography. Total area: 48,432 sq mi; rank: 32. **Land area:** 46,923 sq mi; rank: 31. **Acres forested:** 19.2 mil. **Location:** East South Central state bordered on the W by the Mississippi R., on the S by the Gulf of Mexico. **Climate:** semitropical, with abundant rainfall and long growing season. **Topography:** low, fertile delta between the Yazoo and Mississippi Rivers; loess bluffs stretch around delta border; sandy gulf coastal terraces followed by piney woods and prairie; rugged, high sandy hills in extreme NE followed by Prairie Black Belt, Pontotoc Ridge, and flatwoods into the N central highlands. **Capital:** Jackson. **Chief airport:** Jackson.

Economy. Chief industries: warehousing and distribution, services, manufacturing, government, wholesale and retail trade. **Chief manuf. goods:** petroleum, upholstered furniture, poultry processing, motor vehicle parts, plastics, ships and boats, chemicals. **Chief crops:** cotton, soybeans, rice, hay, corn, sweet potatoes. **Farm income:** Crops: $2.94 bil. Livestock: $3.21 bil. **Nonfuel minerals:** $225 mil; clay (ball clay, bentonite, common clay, montmorillonite), sand and gravel (construction), sand and gravel (industrial), stone (crushed). **Commercial fishing:** $35.6 mil. **Chief ports:** Pascagoula, Vicksburg, Gulfport, Biloxi, Greenville. **Gross state product:** $138.7 bil. **Sales tax:** 7.0%. **Gasoline tax:** 36.80 cents/gal. **Employment distrib.:** 20.0% govt.; 20.8% trade/trans./util.; 12.5% mfg.; 12.8% ed./health; 9.8% prof./bus. serv.; 11.6% leisure/hosp.; 3.8% finance; 4.6% constr./mining/log.; 0.9% info.; 3.3% other serv. **Unemployment:** 3.9%. **Min. wage/hr.:** none. **Per cap. pers. income:** $46,248. **New private housing:** 7,586 units/$1.4 bil. **Broadband internet:** 95.3%. **Commercial banks:** 84; deposits: $74.7 bil. **Savings institutions:** 4; deposits: $419.0 mil. **Lottery:** total sales: $432.9 mil; profit: $122.9 mil.

Federal govt. Fed. civ. employees: 18,533; **avg. salary:** $80,810. **Notable fed. facilities:** Keesler AFB; Meridian NAS; Columbus AFB; NASA Stennis Space Ctr.; Army Corps of Eng. Waterways Experiment Sta., Vicksburg; Naval Constr. Battalion Ctr., Gulfport.

Education. High school grad. rate: 87.7%. **4-yr. public coll./univ.:** 8; **2-yr. public:** 15; **4-yr. private:** 9.

Energy. Electricity use/cost: 1,171 kWh, $135.31.

State data. Motto: Virtute et Armis (By valor and arms). **Flower:** Magnolia. **Bird:** Northern mockingbird. **Tree:** Magnolia. **Song:** "Go, Mississippi!" **Entered union:** Dec. 10, 1817; rank: 20th.

Tourism. Tourist spending: $7.1 bil (2019); change, 2019-20: −22%; change, 2019-22: −4%. **Attractions:** Vicksburg Natl. Military Park and Cemetery; Natchez Trace Parkway; antebellum home tours in Natchez and other cities; Tupelo Natl. Battlefield, Elvis Presley Birthplace, in Tupelo; Smith Robertson Museum and Cultural Ctr., Mynelle Gardens, Eudora Welty House, in Jackson; Mardi Gras parades on Gulf Coast; Beauvoir (Jefferson Davis Home and Presidential Library), Biloxi; Gulf Islands Natl. Seashore; Delta Blues Museum, Clarksdale. **Information:** Mississippi Division of Tourism, P.O. Box 849, Jackson, MS 39205; 1-866-SEE-MISS; www.visitmississippi.org

History. Choctaw, Chickasaw, and Natchez peoples were living in the region at the time of European contact. The Spaniard Hernando de Soto explored the area, 1540-41. René-Robert Cavelier, sieur de La Salle, claimed the entire Mississippi R. Valley for France, 1682. The first settlement was the French Ft. Maurepas, 1699, on Biloxi Bay. The region was ceded to Britain, 1763, and claimed by Spain, 1779-98, then became a U.S. territory, 1798, and a state, 1817. Slavery spread along with cotton plantations dependent on forced Black labor. By 1860, enslaved Black laborers made up 55% of the population. Mississippi seceded, 1861. In the Civil War, Union forces captured Vicksburg, 1863, and caused extensive damage elsewhere. Mississippi reentered the Union, 1870. For the next 100 years, resistance to desegregation and violence against the Black population made the state a battleground for the civil rights movement. Hurricanes Camille, 1969, and Katrina, 2005, caused substantial damage to the Gulf Coast. Since the early 1990s, casino gambling has boosted the economy, but the state's poverty rate remained the highest in the nation. Legislation retiring the state flag, which featured a Confederate

battle flag emblem, was signed into law June 30, 2020. In its consideration of a Mississippi law banning abortion after 15 weeks, the U.S. Supreme Court on June 24, 2022, more broadly overturned the landmark 1973 decision in *Roe v. Wade* that established a constitutional right to an abortion. Floods shut down water treatment plants in Jackson, Aug. 2022, causing a major crisis. On Mar. 24, Mississippi's Delta region was hit by tornadoes that killed at least 25 people.

Famous Mississippians. Margaret Walker Alexander, Dana Andrews, Jimmy Buffett, Bo Diddley, Medgar Evers, William Faulkner, Brett Favre, Shelby Foote, Morgan Freeman, John Grisham, Fannie Lou Hamer, Jim Henson, Faith Hill, John Lee Hooker, Robert Johnson, James Earl Jones, B. B. King, L. Q. C. Lamar, Trent Lott, Gerald McRaney, Willie Morris, Walter Payton, Elvis Presley, Leontyne Price, Charley Pride, LeAnn Rimes, Robin Roberts, Muddy Waters, Eudora Welty, Tennessee Williams, Oprah Winfrey, Johnny Winter, Richard Wright, Tammy Wynette. **Website.** www.ms.gov

Missouri (MO)

Show Me State

People. Population: 6,177,957; rank: 18. **Pop. change** (2010-22): 3.2%. **Pop. density:** 90 per sq mi. **Racial distribution:** 82.5% white; 11.7% Black; 2.3% Asian; 0.6% Amer. Ind.; 0.2% Hawaiian/Pacific Islander; 2 or more races, 2.7%. **Hispanic pop.:** 4.8%.

Geography. Total area: 69,707 sq mi; rank: 21. **Land area:** 68,742 sq mi; rank: 18. **Acres forested:** 15.4 mil. **Location:** West North Central state near the geographic center of the conterminous U.S.; bordered on the E by Mississippi R., on the NW by Missouri R. **Climate:** continental, susceptible to cold Canadian air; moist, warm Gulf air; and drier SW air. **Topography:** rolling hills, open, fertile plains, and well-watered prairie N of the Missouri R.; S of the river, land is rough and hilly with deep, narrow valleys; alluvial plain in the SE; low elevation in the W. **Capital:** Jefferson City. **Chief airports:** St. Louis, Kansas City, Springfield.

Economy. Chief industries: agriculture, manufacturing, aerospace, tourism. **Chief manuf. goods:** motor vehicles and parts, aerospace, pharmaceuticals, plastics, soap, animal slaughtering and processing, printing. **Chief crops:** soybeans, corn, hay, cotton and cottonseed, wheat, rice, sorghum. **Farm income:** Crops: $7.20 bil. Livestock: $5.05 bil. **Nonfuel minerals:** $3.2 bil; cement, lead, lime, sand and gravel (industrial), stone (crushed). **Gross state product:** $389.9 bil. **Sales tax:** 4.225%. **Gasoline tax:** 40.87 cents/gal. **Employment distrib.:** 14.7% govt.; 18.7% trade/trans./util.; 9.7% mfg.; 16.8% ed./health; 13.2% prof./bus. serv.; 10.4% leisure/hosp.; 6.2% finance; 4.7% constr./mining/log.; 1.6% info.; 3.9% other serv. **Unemployment:** 2.5%. **Min. wage/hr.:** $12.00. **Per cap. pers. income:** $56,551. **New private housing:** 20,963 units/$4.8 bil. **Broadband internet:** 97.0%. **Commercial banks:** 266; deposits $241.2 bil. **Savings institutions:** 9; deposits: $2.4 bil. **Lottery:** total sales: $1.8 bil; profit: $386.4 mil.

Federal govt. Fed. civ. employees: 35,926; **avg. salary:** $79,754. **Notable fed. facilities:** Federal Reserve banks; Ft. Leonard Wood; Jefferson Barracks Natl. Cemetery; Natl. Personnel Records Ctr., St. Louis; Whiteman AFB.

Education. High school grad. rate: 89.5%. **4-yr. public coll./univ.:** 13; **2-yr. public:** 14; **4-yr. private:** 49.

Energy. Electricity use/cost: 1,039 kWh, $118.55.

State data. Motto: Salus Populi Suprema Lex Esto (Let the welfare of the people be the supreme law). **Flower:** Hawthorn. **Bird:** Eastern bluebird. **Tree:** Flowering dogwood. **Song:** "Missouri Waltz." **Entered union:** Aug. 10, 1821; rank: 24th.

Tourism. Tourist spending: $16.5 bil (2019); change, 2019-20: −41%; change, 2019-22: −11%. **Attractions:** Silver Dollar City, Branson; Mark Twain Boyhood Home and Museum, Hannibal; Pony Express Natl. Museum, St. Joseph; Harry S. Truman Library and Museum, Independence; Gateway Arch Natl. Park, Ulysses S. Grant Natl. Historic Site, St. Louis Zoo, in St. Louis; Worlds of Fun amusement park, Kansas City; Lake of the Ozarks; Ozark Natl. Scenic Riverways; Natl. Churchill Museum, Fulton; State Capitol, Jefferson City; Wilson's Creek Natl. Battlefield; George Washington Carver Natl. Monument, Diamond; Bass Pro Shops Outdoor World, Springfield. **Information:** Missouri Division of Tourism, P.O. Box 1055, Jefferson City, MO 65102; 1-800-519-2100; www.visitmo.com

History. In the 17th cent., when French explorers arrived, Algonquian-speaking Sauk, Fox, and Illinois, as well as Siouan-speaking Osage, Missouri, Iowa, and Kansa peoples, were living in the region; few remained by the 1830s. French hunters and lead miners made the first settlement, c. 1735, at Ste. Genevieve. The territory was ceded to Spain by the French, 1762, then returned to France, 1800, and acquired by the U.S. in the Louisiana Purchase, 1803. Powerful earthquakes rocked

New Madrid, 1811-12. Missouri became a territory, 1812, and entered the Union as a slave state, 1821. St. Louis became the gateway for pioneers heading west. Though Missouri stayed with the Union, pro- and antislavery forces battled there during the Civil War. In the late 19th cent., railroad building and the cattle trade made Kansas City a boomtown. The most notable Missourian of the 20th cent., Harry S. Truman, was U.S. president, 1945-53. The state, a political bellwether, voted for the winner in every presidential election from 1960 to 2004. In May 2011, a tornado in Joplin killed about 162. The police-shooting death of Michael Brown in Ferguson in Aug. 2014 touched off major protests that spread nationwide and revived debate over the relationship between law enforcement officers and the communities they serve. With the state legislature considering impeachment, Gov. Eric Greitens resigned his office June 1, 2018, four months after he was indicted on felony charges related to an extramarital affair. More than 200 flood incidents occurred in Mar. 2019; additional flooding affected the NE that June and the NW in July.

Famous Missourians. Maya Angelou, Robert Altman, John Ashcroft, Burt Bacharach, Josephine Baker, Scott Bakula, Thomas Hart Benton, Yogi Berra, Chuck Berry, George Caleb Bingham, Daniel Boone, Omar Bradley, William S. Burroughs, Kate Capshaw, Dale Carnegie, George Washington Carver, Bob Costas, Walter Cronkite, Sheryl Crow, Walt Disney, T. S. Eliot, Richard "Dick" Gephardt, John Goodman, Betty Grable, Jon Hamm, Edwin Hubble, Jesse James, Rush Limbaugh, Marianne Moore, Reinhold Niebuhr, J. C. Penney, John J. Pershing, Brad Pitt, Joseph Pulitzer, Ginger Rogers, Bess Truman, Harry S. Truman, Kathleen Turner, Tina Turner, Mark Twain, Dick Van Dyke, Tennessee Williams, Lanford Wilson, Shelley Winters, Jane Wyman.

Website. www.mo.gov

Montana (MT)
Treasure State

People. Population: 1,122,867; rank: 43. **Pop. change** (2010-22): 13.5%. **Pop. density:** 8 per sq mi. **Racial distribution:** 88.7% white; 0.6% Black; 1.1% Asian; 6.5% Amer. Ind.; 0.1% Hawaiian/Pacific Islander; 2 or more races, 3.0%. **Hispanic pop.:** 4.5%.

Geography. Total area: 147,040 sq mi; rank: 4. **Land area:** 145,546 sq mi; rank: 4. **Acres forested:** 26.3 mil. **Location:** Mountain state bounded on the E by the Dakotas, on the S by Wyoming, on the W and SW by Idaho, on the N by Canada. **Climate:** colder, continental with low humidity. **Topography:** Rocky Mts. in western third of state; eastern two-thirds gently rolling northern Great Plains. **Capital:** Helena. **Chief airport:** Bozeman.

Economy. Chief industries: agriculture, timber, mining, tourism, oil and gas. **Chief manuf. goods:** sawmills, softwood veneer and plywood, petroleum. **Chief crops:** wheat, barley, hay, sugar beets, potatoes, dry beans, flaxseed, cherries, corn, oats. **Farm income:** Crops: $2.33 bil. Livestock: $1.84 bil. **Nonfuel minerals:** $1.6 bil; copper, molybdenum mineral concentrates, palladium, platinum, sand and gravel (construction). **Gross state product:** $65.0 bil. **Sales tax:** none. **Gasoline tax:** 52.15 cents/gal. **Employment distrib.:** 17.8% govt.; 19.4% trade/trans./util.; 4.4% mfg.; 16.2% ed./health; 9.7% prof./bus. serv.; 13.4% leisure/hosp.; 5.6% finance; 8.5% constr./mining/log.; 1.1% info.; 3.8% other serv. **Unemployment:** 2.6%. **Min. wage/hr.:** $9.95. **Per cap. pers. income:** $57,719. **New private housing:** 6,457 units/$1.3 bil. **Broadband internet:** 96.2%. **Commercial banks:** 47; deposits: $37.1 bil. **Savings institutions:** 3; deposits: $110.0 mil. **Lottery:** total sales: $77.8 mil; profit: $16.8 mil.

Federal govt. Fed. civ. employees: 9,282; **avg. salary:** $79,776. **Notable fed. facilities:** Malmstrom AFB and missile silos; Ft. Peck, Hungry Horse, Libby, Yellowtail, and other dams.

Education. High school grad. rate: 85.9%. **4-yr. public coll./univ.:** 9; **2-yr. public:** 9; **4-yr. private:** 3.

Energy. Electricity use/cost: 874 kWh, $97.84.

State data. Motto: Oro y Plata (Gold and silver). **Flower:** Bitterroot. **Bird:** Western meadowlark. **Tree:** Ponderosa pine. **Song:** "Montana." **Entered union:** Nov. 8, 1889; rank: 41st.

Tourism. Tourist spending: $5.3 bil (2019); change, 2019-20: −26%; change, 2019-22: 11%. **Attractions:** Glacier and Yellowstone Natl. Parks; Museum of the Rockies, Bozeman; Museum of the Plains Indian, Blackfeet Reservation, in Browning; Custer Natl. Cemetery at Little Bighorn Battlefield Natl. Monument; Lewis and Clark Caverns State Park, Whitehall; Lewis and Clark Natl. Historic Trail Interpretive Ctr., Great Falls. **Information:** Montana Office of Tourism, Dept. of Commerce, 301 S. Park Ave., P.O. Box 200533, Helena, MT 59620; 1-800-VISITMT; www.visitmt.com

History. Paleo-Indian hunters reached the area over 12,000 years ago. Cheyenne, Blackfoot, Crow, Assiniboin, Salish

(Flatheads), Kootenai, and Kalispel peoples lived in the region before Europeans arrived. French explorers visited the region, 1742. The U.S. acquired the area partly through the Louisiana Purchase, 1803, partly through the Lewis and Clark Expedition, 1804-06. Fur traders and missionaries established posts in the early 19th cent. Gold was discovered on Grasshopper Creek, 1862, and Montana Territory was established, 1864. Indian uprisings reached their peak with the defeat of Gen. George Custer at the Battle of Little Bighorn, 1876. Chief Joseph and the Nez Percé tribe surrendered in Montana, 1877, after being driven from their lands in Oregon. Mining activity and the coming of the Northern Pacific Railway, 1883, brought population growth. Montana became a state, 1889. Copper wealth from the Butte pits resulted in the turn of the century "War of Copper Kings" as feuding factions contended for "the richest hill on earth." During the first half of the 20th cent., the Anaconda Copper firm wielded enormous political influence. Jeannette Rankin, a suffragist and pacifist, was the first woman elected to Congress, 1916. Mike Mansfield served 34 years in Congress and was Senate Democratic leader, 1961-77. An 18-year hunt for notorious "Unabomber" Theodore Kaczynski ended with his arrest, 1996, at his cabin near Lincoln. Ryan Zinke became the first Montanan in the president's cabinet since statehood when he served as interior secretary, 2017-18. Gov. Greg Gianforte (R) signed a bill May 17 banning Chinese-owned app TikTok over privacy concerns, making Montana the first U.S. state to do so.

Famous Montanans. Dana Carvey, Gary Cooper, Marcus Daly, Chet Huntley, Phil Jackson, Will James, Myrna Loy, David Lynch, Mike Mansfield, Brent Musburger, Jeannette Rankin, Charles M. Russell, Lester Thurow.

Website. www.mt.gov

Nebraska (NE)
Cornhusker State

People. Population: 1,967,923; rank: 37. **Pop. change** (2010-22): 7.8%. **Pop. density:** 26 per sq mi. **Racial distribution:** 87.5% white; 5.4% Black; 2.8% Asian; 1.6% Amer. Ind.; 0.1% Hawaiian/Pacific Islander; 2 or more races, 2.5%. **Hispanic pop.:** 12.3%.

Geography. Total area: 77,348 sq mi; rank: 16. **Land area:** 76,824 sq mi; rank: 15. **Acres forested:** 1.4 mil. **Location:** West North Central state with the Missouri R. for a border on NE and E. **Climate:** continental semiarid. **Topography:** till plains of the central lowland in the eastern third rises to the Great Plains and hill country of the N central and NW. **Capital:** Lincoln. **Chief airport:** Omaha.

Economy. Chief industries: agriculture, manufacturing. **Chief manuf. goods:** animal slaughtering, grain and oilseed, farm machinery, medical equip., motor vehicle parts, printing, structural metals. **Chief crops:** corn, sorghum, soybeans, hay, wheat, dry beans, oats, potatoes, sugar beets. **Farm income:** Crops: $13.61 bil. Livestock: $12.92 bil. **Nonfuel minerals:** $256 mil; cement, lime, sand and gravel (construction), sand and gravel (industrial), stone (crushed). **Gross state product:** $161.7 bil. **Sales tax:** 5.5%. **Gasoline tax:** 48.30 cents/gal. **Employment distrib.:** 16.7% govt.; 18.9% trade/trans./util.; 10.1% mfg.; 15.4% ed./health; 11.5% prof./bus. serv.; 9.2% leisure/hosp.; 6.7% finance; 5.8% constr./mining/log.; 1.7% info.; 3.8% other serv. **Unemployment:** 2.3%. **Min. wage/hr.:** $10.50. **Per cap. pers. income:** $63,321. **New private housing:** 11,113 units/$1.9 bil. **Broadband internet:** 97.7%. **Commercial banks:** 163; deposits: $83.1 bil. **Savings institutions:** 7; deposits: $690.0 mil. **Lottery:** total sales: $202.3 mil; profit: $49.4 mil.

Federal govt. Fed. civ. employees: 9,845; **avg. salary:** $86,115. **Notable fed. facilities:** Offutt AFB.

Education. High school grad. rate: 87.5%. **4-yr. public coll./univ.:** 7; **2-yr. public:** 9; **4-yr. private:** 14.

Energy. Electricity use/cost: 1,005 kWh, $108.09.

State data. Motto: Equality before the law. **Flower:** Giant goldenrod. **Bird:** Western meadowlark. **Tree:** Cottonwood. **Song:** "Beautiful Nebraska." **Entered union:** Mar. 1, 1867; rank: 37th.

Tourism. Tourist spending: $5.9 bil (2019); change, 2019-20: −40%; change, 2019-22: −2%. **Attractions:** Univ. of Nebraska State Museum at Morrill Hall, Nebraska State Capitol, in Lincoln; Stuhr Museum of the Prairie Pioneer, Grand Island; Boys Town; Omaha's Henry Doorly Zoo and Aquarium, Joslyn Art Museum, The Durham Museum, in Omaha; Ashfall Fossil Beds State Hist. Park, near Royal; Strategic Air and Space Museum, Ashland; Arbor Lodge State Historical Park, Nebraska City; Buffalo Bill Ranch State Historical Park, North Platte; Pioneer Village, Minden; Oregon Trail landmarks, incl. at Scotts Bluff Natl. Monument and Chimney Rock Natl. Historic Site; Great Platte River Road Archway, Museum of Nebraska Art, in Kearney. **Information:** Nebraska Tourism Commission, 301 Centennial Mall S., P.O. Box 98907, Lincoln,

NE 68509-8907; 1-888-444-1867; www.visitnebraska.com

History. When Europeans arrived, Pawnee, Ponca, Omaha, and Oto peoples lived in the region. Spanish and French explorers and fur traders visited the area prior to its acquisition in the Louisiana Purchase, 1803. Meriwether Lewis and William Clark passed through, 1804-06. The first permanent settlement was Bellevue, near Omaha, 1823. The 1834 Indian Intercourse Act declared Nebraska Indian country and excluded white settlement, but conflicts with settlers eventually forced Native Americans to move to reservations. Nebraska became a territory, 1854, and a state, 1867. Many Civil War veterans settled under free land terms of the 1862 Homestead Act; as agriculture grew, struggles followed between homesteaders and ranchers. Since the mid-1930s, Nebraska has been the only state with a unicameral legislature. A leader in agribusiness, Nebraska has also become a major telemarketing center. Investor Warren Buffett, one of the world's wealthiest men, said in 2006 he would give most of his then-$44-bil fortune to charity. Historic flooding from a so-called "bomb cyclone" Mar. 13-15, 2019, caused nearly $1.4 bil in damage.

Famous Nebraskans. Grover Cleveland Alexander, Fred Astaire, Marlon Brando, Charles W. Bryan, William Jennings Bryan, Warren Buffett, Johnny Carson, Willa Cather, Dick Cavett, Dick Cheney, Loren Eiseley, Father Edward J. Flanagan, Henry Fonda, Bob Gibson, Rollin Kirby, Harold Lloyd, Malcolm X, J. Sterling Morton, John G. Neihardt, Nick Nolte, George W. Norris, Tom Osborne, Roscoe Pound, Red Cloud, Mari Sandoz, Robert Taylor, Darryl F. Zanuck.

Website. www.nebraska.gov

Nevada (NV)
Sagebrush State, Battle Born State, Silver State

People. Population: 3,177,772; rank: 32. **Pop. change** (2010-22): 17.7%. **Pop. density:** 29 per sq mi. **Racial distribution:** 72.1% white; 10.8% Black; 9.4% Asian; 1.7% Amer. Ind.; 0.9% Hawaiian/Pacific Islander; 2 or more races, 5.1%. **Hispanic pop.:** 30.3%.

Geography. Total area: 110,572 sq mi; rank: 7. **Land area:** 109,781 sq mi; rank: 7. **Acres forested:** 10.6 mil. **Location:** Mountain state bordered on N by Oregon and Idaho, on E by Utah, on SE by Arizona, and on SW and W by California. **Climate:** semiarid and arid. **Topography:** rugged N-S mountain ranges; highest elevation, Boundary Peak, 13,146 ft; southern area is within the Mojave Desert; lowest elevation, Colorado R., at southern tip of state, 479 ft. **Capital:** Carson City. **Chief airports:** Las Vegas, Reno.

Economy. Chief industries: gaming, tourism, mining, manufacturing, government, retailing, warehousing, trucking. **Chief manuf. goods:** gaming machines, cement and concrete, plastics, printing, architectural and structural metals, electricity instruments. **Chief crops:** hay, onions, potatoes, alfalfa, wheat, garlic, mint, barley. **Farm income:** Crops: $228.25 mil. Livestock: $546.78 mil. **Nonfuel minerals:** $8.9 bil; copper, diatomite, gold, sand and gravel (construction), stone (crushed). **Gross state product:** $215.9 bil. **Sales tax:** 6.85%. **Gasoline tax:** 42.21 cents/gal. **Employment distrib.:** 11.5% govt.; 18.9% trade/trans./util.; 4.4% mfg.; 10.9% ed./health; 14.3% prof./bus. serv.; 23.0% leisure/hosp.; 4.9% finance; 8.2% constr./mining/log.; 1.2% info.; 2.7% other serv. **Unemployment:** 5.4%. **Min. wage/hr.:** $11.25. **Per cap. pers. income:** $61,282. **New private housing:** 20,031 units/$4.4 bil. **Broadband internet:** 98.9%. **Commercial banks:** 41; deposits: $121.3 bil. **Savings institutions:** 8; deposits $19.1 bil.

Federal govt. Fed. civ. employees: 12,715; **avg. salary:** $88,645. **Notable fed. facilities:** Nevada Natl. Security Site; Hawthorne Army Depot; Creech AFB; Nellis AFB; Fallon NAS; Natl. Wild Horse & Burro Ctr. at Palomino Valley.

Education. High school grad. rate: 82.6%. **4-yr. public coll./univ.:** 6; **2-yr. public:** 1; **4-yr. private:** 4.

Energy. Electricity use/cost: 959 kWh, $110.17.

State data. Motto: All for our country. **Flower:** Sagebrush. **Bird:** Mountain bluebird. **Trees:** Single-leaf piñon and bristlecone pine. **Song:** "Home Means Nevada." **Entered union:** Oct. 31, 1864; rank: 36th.

Tourism. Tourist spending: $45.9 bil (2019); change, 2019-20: −51%; change, 2019-22: 9%. **Attractions:** Legalized gambling, incl. at Lake Tahoe, Reno, Las Vegas, Laughlin, and Elko; Hoover Dam, Lake Mead Natl. Recreation Area, near Boulder City; Great Basin Natl. Park; Valley of Fire State Park; Red Rock Canyon Natl. Conservation Area; Las Vegas Strip, Fremont St., Natl. Atomic Testing Museum, Pinball Hall of Fame, Las Vegas Motor Speedway, in Las Vegas; Natl. Automobile Museum, Reno. **Information:** Travel Nevada, 401 N. Carson St., Carson City, NV 89701; 1-800-NEVADA-8; www.travelnevada.com

History. Shoshone, Paiute, Bannock, and Washoe peoples lived in the area at the time of European contact. Nevada was first explored by Spaniards, 1776. In the 1820s, fur traders Peter Skene Ogden, a Canadian, and Jedediah Smith separately explored the area. It was acquired by the U.S., 1848, at the end of the Mexican War. A trading post at Mormon Station, now Genoa, was established, 1850. Discovery of the Comstock Lode, rich in gold and silver, 1859, spurred a population boom. Nevada became a territory, 1861, and a state, 1864. Hoover Dam was built, 1931-36. With gambling legal since 1931, a surge in resort casino construction after World War II turned Las Vegas into one of the nation's most popular tourist destinations. An influx of both native and foreign-born Hispanics and Asians, attracted by the thriving service and construction industries, helped make Nevada the fastest-growing state in the U.S. in 1990-2005. The 2007-09 recession had an equally powerful effect, with high unemployment and foreclosures. In the deadliest mass shooting in modern U.S. history, a gunman killed 58 when he fired indiscriminately from his 32nd floor Las Vegas hotel suite on an outdoor country music festival in Oct. 2017.

Famous Nevadans. Andre Agassi, Kurt Busch, Kyle Busch, Walter Van Tilburg Clark, George W. G. Ferris, Sarah Winnemucca Hopkins, Paul Laxalt, Dat So La Lee, John William Mackay, Anne Henrietta Martin, Pat McCarran, Key Pittman, William Morris Stewart.

Website. www.nv.gov

New Hampshire (NH)
Granite State

People. Population: 1,395,231; rank: 41. **Pop. change** (2010-22): 6.0%. **Pop. density:** 156 per sq mi. **Racial distribution:** 92.6% white; 2.0% Black; 3.2% Asian; 0.3% Amer. Ind.; 0.1% Hawaiian/Pacific Islander; 2 or more races, 1.9%. **Hispanic pop.:** 4.6%.

Geography. Total area: 9,349 sq mi; rank: 46. **Land area:** 8,953 sq mi; rank: 44. **Acres forested:** 4.7 mil. **Location:** New England state bounded on S by Massachusetts, on W by Vermont, on N by Canada, on E by Maine and the Atlantic Ocean. **Climate:** highly varied, due to its nearness to high mountains and ocean. **Topography:** low, rolling coast followed by countless hills and mountains rising out of a central plateau. **Capital:** Concord. **Chief airport:** Manchester.

Economy. Chief industries: tourism, manufacturing, agriculture, trade, mining. **Chief manuf. goods:** navigational instruments, circuit boards, electrical equip., fabricated metal, machinery, medical equip., plastics. **Chief crops:** greenhouse and nursery, apples, sweet corn, hay, Christmas trees, berries, maple syrup. **Farm income:** Crops: $86.99 mil. Livestock: $102.09 mil. **Nonfuel minerals:** $135 mil; sand and gravel (construction), stone (crushed), stone (dimension). **Commercial fishing:** $48.7 mil. **Chief port:** Portsmouth. **Gross state product:** $105.4 bil. **Sales tax:** none. **Gasoline tax:** 42.23 cents/gal. **Employment distrib.:** 12.9% govt.; 19.8% trade/trans./util.; 10.2% mfg.; 18.0% ed./health; 14.9% prof./bus. serv.; 9.7% leisure/hosp.; 4.9% finance; 4.5% constr./mining/log.; 1.7% info.; 3.5% other serv. **Unemployment:** 2.5%. **Min. wage/hr.:** $7.25. **Per cap. pers. income:** $74,663. **New private housing:** 4,783 units/$1.4 bil. **Broadband internet:** 97.6%. **Commercial banks:** 18; deposits $39.3 bil. **Savings institutions:** 24; deposits $11.7 bil. **Lottery:** total sales: $556.3 mil; profit: $146.6 mil.

Federal govt. Fed. civ. employees: 4,578; **avg. salary:** $101,768. **Notable fed. facilities:** Army Cold Regions Res. and Engineering Lab, Hanover.

Education. High school grad. rate: 88.1%. **4-yr. public coll./univ.:** 6; **2-yr. public:** 7; **4-yr. private:** 10.

Energy. Electricity use/cost: 631 kWh, $125.24.

State data. Motto: Live free or die. **Flower:** Purple lilac. **Bird:** Purple finch. **Tree:** White birch. **Song:** "Old New Hampshire." **Ninth** of original 13 states to ratify the Constitution, June 21, 1788.

Tourism. Tourist spending: $4.6 bil (2019); change, 2019-20: −39%; change, 2019-22: −8%. **Attractions:** Mt. Washington Cog Railway, Mt. Washington (highest peak in Northeast); Lake Winnipesaukee; Crawford, Franconia, Pinkham Notches (mountain passes), Flume Gorge, Cannon Mountain Aerial Tramway, in White Mountains region; Strawbery Banke Museum, Portsmouth; Canterbury Shaker Village; Saint-Gaudens Natl. Historical Park, Cornish; Mt. Monadnock; Santa's Village, Jefferson. **Information:** Dept. of Business and Econ. Affairs, Division of Travel & Tourism Development, 100 N. Main St., Ste. 100, Concord, NH 03301; 1-800-FUN-IN-NH; www.visitnh.gov

History. The area has been inhabited for about 10,000 years. Algonquian-speaking peoples, including the Pennacook, lived in the region when the Europeans arrived. The first explorers to visit the area were England's Martin Pring, 1603, and France's Samuel de Champlain, 1605. The first settlement was Odiorne's Point (now port of Rye), 1623. Before the American Revolution, New Hampshire residents raided a

British fort at Portsmouth, 1774, and drove the royal governor out, 1775. New Hampshire became the first colony to adopt its own constitution, 1776. After statehood, 1788, New Hampshire became a textile manufacturing center. The mill towns declined in the first half of the 20th cent., but tourism and technology industries, lured by low taxes, have revived the economy since the 1960s. A state law requires it to hold the first primary of the presidential campaign season.

Famous New Hampshirites. Dan Brown, Salmon P. Chase, Ralph Adams Cram, Mary Baker Eddy, Daniel Chester French, Robert Frost, Horace Greeley, Sarah Josepha Buell Hale, John Irving, Seth Meyers, Bode Miller, Franklin Pierce, Augustus Saint-Gaudens, Adam Sandler, Alan B. Shepard Jr., Sarah Silverman, David H. Souter, Daniel Webster.

Website. www.nh.gov

New Jersey (NJ)
Garden State

People. Population: 9,261,699; rank: 11. **Pop. change** (2010-22): 5.3%. **Pop. density:** 1,259 per sq mi. **Racial distribution:** 70.7% white; 15.4% Black; 10.5% Asian; 0.7% Amer. Ind.; 0.1% Hawaiian/Pacific Islander; 2 or more races, 2.4%. **Hispanic pop.:** 21.9%.

Geography. Total area: 8,723 sq mi; rank: 47. **Land area:** 7,354 sq mi; rank: 46. **Acres forested:** 2.0 mil. **Location:** Middle Atlantic state bounded on N and E by New York and Atlantic Ocean, on S and W by Delaware and Pennsylvania. **Climate:** moderate, with marked difference between NW and SE extremities. **Topography:** Appalachian Valley in NW also has highest elevation, High Pt., 1,803 ft; Appalachian Highlands, flat-topped NE-SW mountain ranges; Piedmont Plateau, low plains broken by high ridges (Palisades) rising 400-500 ft; Coastal Plain, covering three-fifths of state in SE, rises from sea level to gentle slopes. **Capital:** Trenton. **Chief airport:** Newark.

Economy. Chief industries: pharmaceuticals, telecommunications, biotechnology, printing and publishing. **Chief manuf. goods:** petroleum, pharmaceuticals, toiletries, chemicals, plastics, printing, navigational instruments, medical equip., paper prods. **Chief crops:** greenhouse and nursery, blueberries, peaches, corn, hay, tomatoes, bell peppers, cranberries, soybeans, apples. **Farm income:** Crops: $1.25 bil. Livestock: $116.74 mil. **Nonfuel minerals:** $425 mil; sand and gravel (construction), sand and gravel (industrial), stone (crushed). **Commercial fishing:** $220.5 mil. **Chief ports:** Newark-Elizabeth, Camden. **Gross state product:** $745.4 bil. **Sales tax:** 6.625%. **Gasoline tax:** 59.85 cents/gal. **Employment distrib.:** 13.8% govt.; 21.1% trade/trans./util.; 5.9% mfg.; 18.0% ed./health; 16.8% prof./bus. serv.; 8.9% leisure/hosp.; 6.0% finance; 3.9% constr./mining/log.; 1.8% info.; 3.9% other serv. **Unemployment:** 3.7%. **Min. wage/hr.:** $14.13. **Per cap. pers. income:** $78,700. **New private housing:** 36,974 units/$6.1 bil. **Broadband internet:** 99.1%. **Commercial banks:** 74; deposits: $415.1 bil. **Savings institutions:** 37; deposits: $48.1 bil. **Lottery:** total sales: $3.6 bil; profit: $1.1 bil.

Federal govt. Fed. civ. employees: 21,340; **avg. salary:** $106,917. **Notable fed. facilities:** Joint Base McGuire-Dix-Lakehurst; Picatinny Arsenal; FAA William J. Hughes Technical Ctr.

Education. High school grad. rate: 91.0%. **4-yr. public coll./univ.:** 13; **2-yr. public:** 18; **4-yr. private:** 31.

Energy. Electricity use/cost: 687 kWh, $112.39.

State data. Motto: Liberty and prosperity. **Flower:** Purple violet. **Bird:** Eastern goldfinch. **Tree:** Red oak. Third of the original 13 states to ratify the Constitution, Dec. 18, 1787.

Tourism. Tourist spending: $26.5 bil (2019); change, 2019-20: −37%; change, 2019-22: −2%. **Attractions:** 130 mi of beaches, boardwalks on the Jersey Shore at Atlantic City (with gambling), Seaside Heights, Ocean City, Wildwood; Grover Cleveland Birthplace, Caldwell; Cape May Historic District; Thomas Edison Natl. Historical Park, West Orange; Six Flags Great Adventure, Jackson; Liberty State Park, Liberty Science Ctr., in Jersey City; Pine Barrens wilderness; Princeton Univ., Princeton Battlefield State Park, in Princeton; Morristown Natl. Historical Park; Adventure Aquarium, Battleship *New Jersey*, Walt Whitman House, in Camden. **Information:** Dept. of State, Division of Travel and Tourism, P.O. Box 460, Trenton, NJ 08625; 1-800-VISITNJ; www.visitnj.org

History. The Lenni Lenape (Delaware) peoples lived in the region and had mostly peaceful relations with European colonists, who arrived after the explorers Giovanni da Verrazzano, 1524, and Henry Hudson, 1609. The first permanent European settlement was Dutch, at Bergen (now Jersey City), 1660. When the British took New Netherland, 1664, the area between the Delaware and Hudson Rivers was given to Lord John Berkeley and Sir George Carteret. During the American Revolution, New Jersey was the scene of many major battles, including Trenton, 1776; Princeton, 1777; and Monmouth, 1778. New Jersey was the third state to ratify the Constitution,

1787, and the first to approve the Bill of Rights, 1789. In a duel at Weehawken, 1804, Vice Pres. Aaron Burr fatally shot former Treasury Sec. Alexander Hamilton. Canal and railroad building stimulated the growth of cities and industries in the 19th cent. The 20th-cent. arrival of large numbers of African Americans, Italians, Irish, European Jews, Puerto Ricans, South Asians, and other groups made New Jersey one of the most diverse states in the U.S. Construction of resort casinos in Atlantic City from the late 1970s revitalized tourism. Gov. James McGreevey resigned, 2004, after acknowledging an extramarital affair with a man identified as his former homeland security adviser. An estimated 37 people in New Jersey were killed when Hurricane Sandy (by then downgraded to a tropical storm) made landfall in 2012. Two members of Gov. Chris Christie's administration were convicted in 2016 on federal charges related to allegations that officials had created traffic jams to punish a political opponent. In early Sept. 2021, flash floods from post-tropical storm Ida killed 27 people.

Famous New Jerseyans. Buzz Aldrin, Jason Alexander, Samuel Alito, Count Basie, Judy Blume, Jon Bon Jovi, Bill Bradley, Aaron Burr, Grover Cleveland, Stephen Crane, Danny DeVito, Thomas Edison, Albert Einstein, James Gandolfini, Allen Ginsberg, Alexander Hamilton, Ed Harris, Whitney Houston, Joyce Kilmer, Jack Nicholson, Shaquille O'Neal, Thomas Paine, Bill Parcells, Dorothy Parker, Joe Pesci, Molly Pitcher, Paul Robeson, Philip Roth, Antonin Scalia, Wally Schirra, H. Norman Schwarzkopf, Frank Sinatra, Bruce Springsteen, Martha Stewart, Meryl Streep, Dave Thomas, John Travolta, Walt Whitman, William Carlos Williams, Woodrow Wilson.

Website. www.nj.gov

New Mexico (NM)
Land of Enchantment

People. Population: 2,113,344; rank: 36. **Pop. change** (2010-22): 2.6%. **Pop. density:** 17 per sq mi. **Racial distribution:** 81.1% white; 2.7% Black; 2.0% Asian; 11.2% Amer. Ind.; 0.2% Hawaiian/Pacific Islander; 2 or more races, 2.8%. **Hispanic pop.:** 50.2%.

Geography. Total area: 121,590 sq mi; rank: 5. **Land area:** 121,298 sq mi; rank: 5. **Acres forested:** 24.6 mil. **Location:** southwestern state bounded by Colorado on the N; Oklahoma on NE; Texas on E and S; Mexico on S; Arizona on the W. **Climate:** dry, with temperatures rising or falling 5°F with every 1,000 ft elevation. **Topography:** eastern third, Great Plains; central third, Rocky Mts. (85% of the state is over 4,000-ft elevation); western third, high plateau. **Capital:** Santa Fe. **Chief airport:** Albuquerque.

Economy. Chief industries: government, services, trade. **Chief manuf. goods:** semiconductors, medical equip., navigational/measuring/medical/control instruments, aircraft, chemicals, jewelry. **Chief crops:** hay, pecans, corn, greenhouse and nursery, chiles, onions, cotton, wheat, peanuts. **Farm income:** Crops: $761.56 mil. Livestock: $2.41 bil. **Nonfuel minerals:** $1.5 bil; cement, copper, potash, sand and gravel (construction), stone (crushed). **Gross state product:** $122.1 bil. **Sales tax:** 5.0%. **Gasoline tax:** 37.28 cents/gal. **Employment distrib.:** 21.4% govt.; 16.2% trade/trans./util.; 3.4% mfg.; 16.9% ed./health; 13.9% prof./bus. serv.; 11.1% leisure/hosp.; 4.0% finance; 8.6% constr./mining/log.; 1.2% info.; 3.3% other serv. **Unemployment:** 4.0%. **Min. wage/hr.:** $12.00. **Per cap. pers. income:** $51,500. **New private housing:** 8,838 units/$1.8 bil. **Broadband internet:** 96.3%. **Commercial banks:** 50; deposits: $43.7 bil. **Savings institutions:** 6; deposits: $1.6 bil. **Lottery:** total sales: $136.9 mil; profit: $41.1 mil.

Federal govt. Fed. civ. employees: 21,559; **avg. salary:** $85,194. **Notable fed. facilities:** Kirtland, Cannon, Holloman AF Bases; Los Alamos Natl. Lab; White Sands Missile Range; Natl. Solar Observatory, Sunspot; Natl. Radio Astronomy Observatory (Very Large Array), Socorro; Sandia Natl. Labs, Albuquerque.

Education. High school grad. rate: 76.9%. **4-yr. public coll./univ.:** 9; **2-yr. public:** 19; **4-yr. private:** 3.

Energy. Electricity use/cost: 646 kWh, $87.31.

State data. Motto: Crescit Eundo (It grows as it goes). **Flower:** Yucca. **Bird:** Roadrunner. **Tree:** Piñon. **Songs:** "O, Fair New Mexico"; "Asi Es Nuevo Mexico." **Entered union:** Jan. 6, 1912; rank: 47th.

Tourism. Tourist spending: $8.3 bil (2019); change, 2019-20: −22%; change, 2019-22: 5%. **Attractions:** Carlsbad Caverns Natl. Park (with Lechuguilla Cave, among world's longest caves); Petroglyph Natl. Monument, Sandia Peak Tramway, in Albuquerque; New Mexico History Museum, Museum of Intl. Folk Art, in Santa Fe (oldest U.S. capital); White Sands Natl. Monument (world's largest gypsum dune field); Chaco Culture Natl. Historical Park; Acoma Pueblo, or Sky City, built atop a 367-ft mesa; Taos Art Colony, Taos Ski Valley; Elephant Butte Lake State Park; Shiprock volcanic remnant; Intl. UFO Museum and Research Ctr., Roswell. **Information:** New

Mexico Tourism Dept., 491 Old Santa Fe Trl., Santa Fe, NM 87501; (505) 795-0343; www.newmexico.org

History. Inhabited for more than 10,000 years, the region was home to Sandia, Clovis, Folsom, Mogollon, and Anasazi cultures, followed by the Pueblo people, Anasazi descendants; later, nomadic Navajo and Apache came. Spanish Franciscan Marcos de Niza and Estevanico, a Moroccan-born enslaved Black man, explored the area, 1539, seeking gold; Coronado followed, 1540. First settlements were near San Juan Pueblo, 1598, and at Santa Fe, 1610. Settlers alternately traded and fought with the Apache, Comanche, and Navajo. Trade on the Santa Fe Trail to Missouri started, 1821. After the Mexican War began, 1846, Gen. Stephen Kearny took Santa Fe without firing a shot, and declared New Mexico part of the U.S. All Hispanic New Mexicans and Pueblo became U.S. citizens by terms of the 1848 treaty ending the war. New Mexico became a territory, 1850, but did not attain statehood until 1912. Mexican revolutionary leader Pancho Villa raided Columbus, 1916, and U.S. troops were sent to the area. The world's first atomic bomb was exploded at a test site near Alamogordo, 1945. An underground nuclear waste depository opened near Carlsbad, 1999. Spaceport America, a state-owned commercial spaceport, hosted Virgin Galactic's first space launches with people aboard in 2021. In Oct. 2021, a fatal shooting of a cinematographer by actor Alec Baldwin on a movie set near Santa Fe drew scrutiny to gun safety practices in the film industry. The combined Calf Canyon/Hermits Peak forest fire burned nearly 350,000 acres by July 2022, becoming the state's largest forest fire.

Famous New Mexicans. Ben Abruzzo, Maxie Anderson, Jeff Bezos, William Bonney (Billy the Kid), Kit Carson, Bob Foster, Neil Patrick Harris, Tony Hillerman, Peter Hurd, Jean Baptiste Lamy, Nancy Lopez, Demi Lovato, Bill Mauldin, Georgia O'Keeffe, Bill Richardson, Kim Stanley, Al Unser, Bobby Unser.
Website. www.nm.gov

New York (NY)
Empire State

People. Population: 19,677,151; rank: 4. **Pop. change** (2010-22): 1.5%. **Pop. density:** 418 per sq mi. **Racial distribution:** 68.6% white; 17.7% Black; 9.6% Asian; 1.0% Amer. Ind.; 0.1% Hawaiian/Pacific Islander; 2 or more races, 2.8%. **Hispanic pop.:** 19.7%.

Geography. Total area: 54,555 sq mi; rank: 27. **Land area:** 47,126 sq mi; rank: 30. **Acres forested:** 18.6 mil. **Location:** Middle Atlantic state bordered by the New England states, Atlantic Ocean on E; New Jersey and Pennsylvania on S; Lakes Ontario and Erie on W; Canada on N. **Climate:** variable; the SE region moderated by the ocean. **Topography:** highest and most rugged mountains in the NE Adirondack upland; St. Lawrence-Champlain lowlands extend from Lake Ontario NE along the Canadian border; Hudson-Mohawk lowland follows rivers N and W, 10-30 mi wide; Atlantic coastal plain in the SE; Appalachian Highlands, covering half the state westward from the Hudson Valley, include the Catskill Mts., Finger Lakes; plateau of Erie-Ontario lowlands. **Capital:** Albany. **Chief airports:** New York (2), Buffalo, Albany, Syracuse, Rochester, White Plains, Islip.

Economy. Chief industries: manufacturing, finance, communications, tourism, transportation, services. **Chief manuf. goods:** pharmaceuticals, photographic chemicals, electronics, automotive parts, toiletries, printing, plastics, apparel. **Chief crops:** greenhouse and nursery, apples, corn, hay, cabbage, onions, soybeans, potatoes, snap beans, grapes, squash, pumpkins, tomatoes, wheat, cucumbers, green peas. **Farm income:** Crops: $2.39 bil. Livestock: $3.51 bil. **Nonfuel minerals:** $2.0 bil; cement, salt, sand and gravel (construction), stone (crushed), zinc. **Commercial fishing:** $40.6 mil. **Chief ports:** New York, Buffalo, Albany. **Gross state product:** $2.1 tril. **Sales tax:** 4.0%. **Gasoline tax:** 44.88 cents/gal. **Employment distrib.:** 15.1% govt.; 15.0% trade/trans./util.; 4.4% mfg.; 23.2% ed./health; 14.3% prof./bus. serv.; 9.3% leisure/hosp.; 7.6% finance; 4.1% constr./mining/log.; 3.0% info.; 4.0% other serv. **Unemployment:** 4.3%. **Min. wage/hr.:** $14.20. **Per cap. pers. income:** $78,089. **New private housing:** 41,972 units/$8.4 bil. **Broadband internet:** 99.1%. **Commercial banks:** 144; deposits: $2.5 tril. **Savings institutions:** 40; deposits $84.1 bil. **Lottery:** total sales: $10.4 bil; profit: $3.6 bil.

Federal govt. Fed. civ. employees: 51,038; **avg. salary:** $93,767. **Notable fed. facilities:** Ft. Drum; West Point Military Academy; Merchant Marine Academy, Kings Point; NY Fed. Reserve; U.S. Army Watervliet Arsenal; Brookhaven Natl. Lab; U.S. Mission to the United Nations.

Education. High school grad. rate: 83.5%. **4-yr. public coll./univ.:** 43; **2-yr. public:** 36; **4-yr. private:** 165.

Energy. Electricity use/cost: 599 kWh, $116.70.

State data. Motto: Excelsior (Ever upward). **Flower:** Rose. **Bird:** Eastern bluebird. **Tree:** Sugar maple. **Song:** "I Love

New York." **Eleventh** of original 13 states to ratify the Constitution, July 26, 1788.

Tourism. Tourist spending: $89.6 bil (2019); change, 2019-20: −54%; change, 2019-22: 12%. **Attractions:** New York City; Adirondack and Catskill Mountains; Watkins Glen State Park; Thousand Islands region; Niagara Falls; Saratoga Race Course, Saratoga Springs; Philipsburg Manor, Old Dutch Church of Sleepy Hollow, in Sleepy Hollow; Washington Irving's Sunnyside, Tarrytown; Corning Museum of Glass; Fenimore Art Museum, Natl. Baseball Hall of Fame and Museum, in Cooperstown; Ft. Ticonderoga; New York State Capitol, Albany; LEGOLAND New York Resort, Goshen; Home of Franklin D. Roosevelt Natl. Historic Site, Hyde Park; Long Island beaches; Sagamore Hill (Theodore Roosevelt's "Summer White House"), Oyster Bay. **Information:** Empire State Development, Travel Information Center, 30 South Pearl St., Albany, NY 12245; 1-800-CALLNYS; www.iloveny.com

History. When Europeans arrived, Algonquians including the Mahican, Wappinger, and Lenni Lenape inhabited the region, as did the Iroquoian Mohawk, Oneida, Onondaga, Cayuga, and Seneca tribes, who established the League of the Five Nations. Italian Giovanni da Verrazzano entered New York harbor, 1524. In 1609, England's Henry Hudson sailed the river later named for him, and France's Samuel de Champlain explored the lake that now bears his name. The first permanent settlement was Dutch, near present-day Albany, 1624. New Amsterdam was settled, 1626, at the southern tip of Manhattan island. A British fleet seized New Netherland, 1664. Key battles of the American Revolution included Saratoga, 1777. In the 19th cent., New York City emerged as one of the world's great metropolitan areas, a center for trade, finance, and arts, and a haven for millions of immigrants. Completion of the Erie Canal, 1825, established the state as a gateway to the West. The first women's rights convention was held in Seneca Falls, 1848. Although the state backed the Union in the Civil War, an 1863 military draft triggered three days of riots in New York City. Industry declined in the 20th cent., and California and Texas passed New York in population. Attica was the scene of a bloody prison revolt, 1971. Two jet aircraft hijacked by terrorists on Sept. 11, 2001, destroyed the World Trade Center in lower Manhattan and killed thousands. An estimated 65 people in New York state were killed when Hurricane Sandy (by then downgraded to a tropical storm) made landfall in Oct. 2012. Citing concerns over health risks, Gov. Andrew Cuomo in 2014 announced a statewide ban on hydraulic fracturing (or "fracking"). New York City became an early U.S. epicenter of the coronavirus pandemic beginning in Mar. 2020. Cuomo, accused by multiple women of sexual misconduct, resigned in Aug. 2021. A high-rise apartment fire in the Bronx killed 17 in Jan. 2022. Amazon warehouse workers in Staten Island voted in late Mar. 2022 in favor of unionizing. A white supremacist fatally shot 10 Black people and injured three others at a Buffalo supermarket in May 2022; he was charged with domestic terrorism. In Dec. 2022, a winter storm killed at least 46 in Erie County; snowfall in Buffalo exceeded 56 inches over five days. Freshman U.S. Rep. George Santos (R), who admitted to lying about his education and work history, was charged in May 2023 on 13 federal counts including fraud and money laundering.

Famous New Yorkers. Woody Allen, Susan B. Anthony, James Baldwin, Lucille Ball, Ann Bancroft, L. Frank Baum, Tony Bennett, Milton Berle, Humphrey Bogart, Barbara Boxer, Mel Brooks, Benjamin Cardozo, De Witt Clinton, James Fenimore Cooper, Peter Cooper, Aaron Copland, Francis Ford Coppola, Tom Cruise, Robert De Niro, George Eastman, Jimmy Fallon, Millard Fillmore, Lou Gehrig, George and Ira Gershwin, Ruth Bader Ginsburg, Rudolph Giuliani, Jackie Gleason, Stephen Jay Gould, Julia Ward Howe, Charles Evans Hughes, Washington Irving, Henry and William James, John Jay, Carole King, Edward Koch, Lady Gaga, Fiorello LaGuardia, Herman Melville, Arthur Miller, Lin-Manuel Miranda, J. Pierpont Morgan Jr., Eddie Murphy, Joyce Carol Oates, Carroll O'Connor, Rosie O'Donnell, Eugene O'Neill, Jerry Orbach, George Pataki, Colin Powell, Nancy Reagan, John Roberts, John D. Rockefeller, Nelson Rockefeller, Richard Rodgers, Ray Romano, Eleanor Roosevelt, Franklin D. Roosevelt, Theodore Roosevelt, J. D. Salinger, Caroline Kennedy Schlossberg, Jerry Seinfeld, Al Sharpton, Paul Simon, Alfred E. Smith, Elizabeth Cady Stanton, Barbra Streisand, Donald Trump, William (Boss) Tweed, Martin Van Buren, Luther Vandross, Gore Vidal, Denzel Washington, Edith Wharton, Walt Whitman, Mark Zuckerberg.
Website. www.ny.gov

North Carolina (NC)
Tar Heel State, Old North State

People. Population: 10,698,973; rank: 9. **Pop. change** (2010-22): 12.2%. **Pop. density:** 220 per sq mi. **Racial distribution:** 69.9% white; 22.2% Black; 3.6% Asian; 1.6% Amer.

Ind.; 0.1% Hawaiian/Pacific Islander; 2 or more races, 2.6%. **Hispanic pop.:** 10.5%.

Geography. Total area: 53,819 sq mi; rank: 28. **Land area:** 48,618 sq mi; rank: 29. **Acres forested:** 18.7 mil. **Location:** South Atlantic state bounded on N by Virginia, on S by South Carolina, on SW by Georgia, on W by Tennessee, and on E by Atlantic. **Climate:** subtropical in SE, medium-continental in mountain region; tempered by the Gulf Stream and mountains in W. **Topography:** coastal plain and tidewater in two-fifths of state, extending to the fall line of the rivers; Piedmont Plateau in another two-fifths has gentle to rugged hills; southern Appalachian Mts. contain the Blue Ridge and Great Smoky Mts. **Capital:** Raleigh. **Chief airports:** Charlotte, Raleigh, Asheville, Greensboro, Wilmington.

Economy. Chief industries: manufacturing, agriculture, tourism. **Chief manuf. goods:** transportation, tobacco, pharmaceuticals, toiletries, plastics, animal slaughtering and processing, household furniture, fabric and apparel. **Chief crops:** greenhouse and nursery, tobacco, cotton, soybeans, corn, Christmas trees, sweet potatoes, wheat, peanuts, blueberries, cucumbers, tomatoes, hay, potatoes. **Farm income:** Crops: $4.16 bil. Livestock: $9.23 bil. **Nonfuel minerals:** $1.9 bil; clay (common clay and fire clay), phosphate rock, sand and gravel (construction), sand and gravel (industrial), stone (crushed). **Commercial fishing:** $90.6 mil. **Chief ports:** Morehead City, Wilmington. **Gross state product:** $730.1 bil. **Sales tax:** 4.75%. **Gasoline tax:** 59.15 cents/gal. **Employment distrib.:** 15.2% govt.; 18.8% trade/trans./util.; 9.7% mfg.; 13.8% ed./health; 15.3% prof./bus. serv.; 10.6% leisure/hosp.; 6.0% finance; 5.3% constr./mining/log.; 1.7% info.; 3.6% other serv. **Unemployment:** 3.7%. **Min. wage/hr.:** $7.25. **Per cap. pers. income:** $57,416. **New private housing:** 91,852 units/$21.7 bil. **Broadband internet:** 97.8%. **Commercial banks:** 72; deposits: $542.5 bil. **Savings institutions:** 16; deposits: $2.8 bil. **Lottery:** total sales: $3.9 bil; profit: $930.8 mil.

Federal govt. Fed. civ. employees: 47,502; **avg. salary:** $87,307. **Notable fed. facilities:** Ft. Liberty (fmr. Bragg); Camp Lejeune Marine Base, Marine Corps Air Station Cherry Point; NOAA Natl. Centers for Environmental Information, Asheville; Natl. Inst. of Environmental Health Sciences, EPA Research and Dev. Labs, all in Research Triangle Park.

Education. High school grad. rate: 87.6%. **4-yr. public coll./univ.:** 16; **2-yr. public:** 59; **4-yr. private:** 47.

Energy. Electricity use/cost: 1,063 kWh, $120.38.

State data. Motto: Esse Quam Videri (To be rather than to seem). **Flower:** Dogwood. **Bird:** Cardinal. **Tree:** Pine. **Song:** "The Old North State." **Twelfth** of the original 13 states to ratify the Constitution, Nov. 21, 1789.

Tourism. Tourist spending: $29.2 bil (2019); change, 2019-20: −32%; change, 2019-22: 10%. **Attractions:** Cape Hatteras and Cape Lookout Natl. Seashores; Great Smoky Mountains Natl. Park; Guilford Courthouse Natl. Military Park; Moore's Creek Natl. Battlefield (1776 victory ended British rule in colony); Bennett Place (site of largest troop surrender of Civil War), Durham; Ft. Raleigh Natl. Historic Site, North Carolina Aquarium, on Roanoke Island; Wright Brothers Natl. Mem., Kill Devil Hills; USS *North Carolina*, Wilmington; North Carolina Zoo, Asheboro; North Carolina Symphony, Marbles Kids Museum, North Carolina Museum of Art, North Carolina Museum of Natural Sciences, in Raleigh; Carl Sandburg Home, Flat Rock; Biltmore House and Gardens, North Carolina Arboretum, in Asheville; U.S. Natl. Whitewater Ctr., Discovery Place, in Charlotte; Fort Macon State Park, Atlantic Beach. **Information:** North Carolina Dept. of Commerce, Tourism Div., 301 N. Wilmington St., Raleigh, NC 27601-1058; 1-800-VISIT-NC, (919) 814-4600; www.visitnc.com

History. Algonquian, Siouan, and Iroquoian peoples lived in the region at the time of European contact. Sir Walter Raleigh tried to found a colony, 1584-87; the "Lost Colony" on Roanoke Island, 1587, seemingly disappeared. Permanent settlers came from Virginia in the mid-17th cent. The province's congress was the first to vote for independence, 1776. In the Revolutionary War, Gen. Charles Cornwallis's forces were defeated at Kings Mountain, 1780, and forced out after Guilford Courthouse, 1781. The state ratified the Constitution, 1789, only after Congress passed the Bill of Rights. North Carolina, where one-third of the population was enslaved, seceded from the Union, 1861, and provided more troops to the Confederacy than any other state; it was readmitted, 1868. The Wright brothers made the first powered airplane flight at Kitty Hawk, 1903. Sit-ins at segregated Greensboro lunch counters, 1960, drew national attention to the civil rights movement. Long reliant on tobacco, textiles, and wood products, North Carolina has prospered since the 1960s from advanced technologies in the Raleigh-Durham-Chapel Hill area and banking in Charlotte. The hurricane-prone state was hit hard by Hazel, 1954, Fran, 1996, and Floyd, 1999. The state drew immediate backlash in 2016 after passing a "bathroom bill" requiring people to use public facilities that correspond with the sex assigned on their birth certificate; a revised bill was passed in 2017. The state's election board Feb. 21, 2019, ordered the 9th U.S. Congressional District to redo its 2018 general election, citing ballot fraud allegedly committed by GOP nominee Mark Harris's campaign.

Famous North Carolinians. David Brinkley, Shirley Caesar, John Coltrane, Stephen Curry, Rick Dees, Elizabeth Hanford Dole, Dale Earnhardt Sr., John Edwards, Ava Gardner, Richard Jordan Gatling, Billy Graham, Andy Griffith, O. Henry, Andrew Jackson, Andrew Johnson, Michael Jordan, William Rufus King, Charles Kuralt, Meadowlark Lemon, Dolley Madison, Thelonious Monk, Edward R. Murrow, Richard Petty, James K. Polk, Charlie Rose, Carl Sandburg, Enos Slaughter, Dean Smith, James Taylor, Thomas Wolfe.

Website. www.nc.gov

North Dakota (ND)

Peace Garden State

People. Population: 779,261; rank: 47. **Pop. change** (2010-22): 15.9%. **Pop. density:** 11 per sq mi. **Racial distribution:** 86.6% white; 3.6% Black; 1.7% Asian; 5.3% Amer. Ind.; 0.1% Hawaiian/Pacific Islander; 2 or more races, 2.6%. **Hispanic pop.:** 4.6%.

Geography. Total area: 70,698 sq mi; rank: 19. **Land area:** 69,001 sq mi; rank: 17. **Acres forested:** 0.8 mil. **Location:** West North Central state situated exactly in the middle of North America, bounded on the N by Canada, on the E by Minnesota, on the S by South Dakota, on the W by Montana. **Climate:** continental, with a wide range of temperatures and moderate rainfall. **Topography:** Central Lowland in the E comprises the flat Red R. Valley and the Rolling Drift Prairie; Missouri Plateau of the Great Plains on the W. **Capital:** Bismarck.

Economy. Chief industries: agriculture, mining, tourism, manufacturing, telecommunications, energy, food processing. **Chief manuf. goods:** machinery, wood prods., motor vehicles and parts, furniture, processed foods. **Chief crops:** wheat, soybeans, corn, sugar beets, barley, dry beans, sunflowers, canola, potatoes, flaxseed, hay, dry peas, lentils, oats. **Farm income:** Crops: $7.68 bil. Livestock: $1.39 bil. **Nonfuel minerals:** $105 mil; lime, sand and gravel (construction), sand and gravel (industrial), stone (crushed). **Gross state product:** $73.3 bil. **Sales tax:** 5.0%. **Gasoline tax:** 41.43 cents/gal. **Employment distrib.:** 19.4% govt.; 21.0% trade/trans./util.; 6.3% mfg.; 15.8% ed./health; 8.1% prof./bus. serv.; 9.1% leisure/hosp.; 5.7% finance; 9.8% constr./mining/log.; 1.3% info.; 3.5% other serv. **Unemployment:** 2.1%. **Min. wage/hr.:** $7.25. **Per cap. pers. income:** $66,184. **New private housing:** 3,445 units/$840.8 mil. **Broadband internet:** 98.6%. **Commercial banks:** 74; deposits: $36.6 bil. **Savings institutions:** 2; deposits: $3.0 bil. **Lottery:** total sales: $29.2 mil; profit: $6.7 mil.

Federal govt. Fed. civ. employees: 5,372; **avg. salary:** $79,220. **Notable fed. facilities:** Minot AFB; Grand Forks AFB; Northern Prairie Wildlife Res. Ctr., Jamestown; Garrison Dam Natl. Fish Hatchery; Grand Forks Human Nutrition Res. Ctr.

Education. High school grad. rate: 89.0%. **4-yr. public coll./univ.:** 9; **2-yr. public:** 5; **4-yr. private:** 5.

Energy. Electricity use/cost: 1,041 kWh, $112.93.

State data. Motto: Liberty and union, now and forever, one and inseparable. **Flower:** Wild prairie rose. **Bird:** Western meadowlark. **Tree:** American elm. **Song:** "North Dakota Hymn." **Entered** union: Nov. 2, 1889; rank: 39th.

Tourism. Tourist spending: $3.3 bil (2019); change, 2019-20: −9%; change, 2019-22: 0%. **Attractions:** North Dakota Heritage Ctr., North Dakota State Capitol, in Bismarck; Bonanzaville, West Fargo; Ft. Union Trading Post Natl. Historic Site; Intl. Peace Garden, Dunseith; Elkhorn Ranch site, in Theodore Roosevelt Natl. Park; Ft. Abraham Lincoln State Park and Museum, Mandan; Dakota Dinosaur Museum, Dickinson; Knife River Indian Villages Natl. Historic Site; Scandinavian Heritage Park, Minden. **Information:** North Dakota Tourism Division, Century Center, 1600 E. Century Ave., Ste. 2, P.O. Box 2057, Bismarck, ND 58502-2057; 1-800-435-5663; www.ndtourism.com

History. Paleo-Indian peoples hunted in the area at least 11,000 years ago. At the time of European contact, the Ojibwa, Yanktonai and Teton Sioux, Mandan, Arikara, and Hidatsa peoples lived in the region. Pierre de Varennes, sieur de La Vérendrye, was the first French fur trader in the area, 1738, followed by the English at the end of the 18th cent. Lewis and Clark built Ft. Mandan, near present-day Washburn, 1804-05, and wintered there. The first permanent settlement was at Pembina, 1812. Missouri River steamboats reached the area, 1832. Dakota Territory was organized, 1861. The first railroad arrived, 1872. The "bonanza farm" craze of the 1870s-80s led to statehood, 1889. The Nonpartisan League, a farmers' group favoring state ownership of industries, helped elect Lynn Frazier as governor, 1916, but he and others were ousted in a recall vote, 1921. The predominantly agricultural state has one of the nation's lowest unemployment rates, mostly due to increased oil production since late 2008 in the state's Bakken Formation. Construction of the Dakota Access Pipeline drew international attention and vigorous protests in 2016-17, in particular from the Standing Rock Sioux tribe.

Famous North Dakotans. Maxwell Anderson, Angie Dickinson, Josh Duhamel, John Bernard Flannagan, Phil Jackson, Louis L'Amour, Peggy Lee, Roger Maris, Eric Sevareid, Vilhjalmur Stefansson, Lawrence Welk.

Website. www.nd.gov

Ohio (OH)
Buckeye State

People. Population: 11,756,058; rank: 7. **Pop. change** (2010-22): 1.9%. **Pop. density:** 288 per sq mi. **Racial distribution:** 80.9% white; 13.3% Black; 2.7% Asian; 0.3% Amer. Ind.; 0.1% Hawaiian/Pacific Islander; 2 or more races, 2.7%. **Hispanic pop.:** 4.5%.

Geography. Total area: 44,826 sq mi; rank: 34. **Land area:** 40,861 sq mi; rank: 35. **Acres forested:** 7.8 mil. **Location:** East North Central state bounded on the N by Michigan and Lake Erie; on the E by Pennsylvania; on the E and S by West Virginia; on the S by Kentucky; on the W by Indiana. **Climate:** temperate but variable; weather subject to much precipitation. **Topography:** generally rolling plain; Allegheny Plateau in E; Lake Erie Plains extend southward; central plains in the W. **Capital:** Columbus. **Chief airports:** Cleveland, Columbus, Dayton.

Economy. Chief industries: manufacturing, trade, services. **Chief manuf. goods:** motor vehicles and parts, petroleum, plastics and rubber, iron and steel, aircraft, machinery, fabricated metal, printing. **Chief crops:** corn, soybeans, hay, wheat, grapes, potatoes, tomatoes, apples, strawberries, tobacco. **Farm income:** Crops: $7.13 bil. Livestock: $1.40 bil. **Nonfuel minerals:** $1.5 bil; cement, lime, salt, sand and gravel (construction), stone (crushed). **Commercial fishing** (2018): $3.8 mil. **Chief ports:** Cincinnati, Toledo, Conneaut, Cleveland, Ashtabula. **Gross state product:** $822.7 bil. **Sales tax:** 5.75%. **Gasoline tax:** 56.90 cents/gal. **Employment distrib.:** 14.0% govt.; 18.7% trade/trans./util.; 12.4% mfg.; 16.6% ed./health; 13.2% prof./bus. serv.; 9.9% leisure/hosp.; 5.7% finance; 4.4% constr./mining/log.; 1.2% info.; 3.9% other serv. **Unemployment:** 4.0%. **Min. wage/hr.:** $10.10. **Per cap. pers. income:** $57,880. **New private housing:** 30,913 units/$7.6 bil. **Broadband internet:** 98.1%. **Commercial banks:** 159; deposits: $496.3 bil. **Savings institutions:** 45; deposits: $23.7 bil. **Lottery:** total sales: $5.6 bil; profit: $1.4 bil.

Federal govt. Fed. civ. employees: 52,044; **avg. salary:** $94,421. **Notable fed. facilities:** Wright-Patterson AFB; Defense Supply Ctr., Columbus; NASA Glenn Research Ctr., Cleveland; Joint Systems Manufacturing Ctr., Lima.

Education. High school grad. rate: 84.4%. **4-yr. public coll./univ.:** 35; **2-yr. public:** 25; **4-yr. private:** 65.

Energy. Electricity use/cost: 879 kWh, $112.21.

State data. Motto: With God, all things are possible. **Flower:** Scarlet carnation. **Bird:** Northern cardinal. **Tree:** Ohio buckeye. **Song:** "Beautiful Ohio." **Entered union:** Mar. 1, 1803; rank: 17th.

Tourism. Tourist spending: $23.1 bil (2019); change, 2019-20: −25%; change, 2019-22: 5%. **Attractions:** Hopewell Culture Natl. Historical Park, Chillicothe; Cuyahoga Valley Natl. Park; Armstrong Air and Space Museum, Wapakoneta; Natl. Museum of the U.S. Air Force, near Dayton; Pro Football Hall of Fame, First Ladies Natl. Historic Site, in Canton; Kings Island amusement park, Mason; Lake Erie Islands, Cedar Point amusement park, in Sandusky; birthplaces, homes of, and memorials to presidents W. H. Harrison, Grant, Hayes, Garfield, B. Harrison, McKinley, Taft, and Harding; Amish Country, particularly in Holmes County; German Village historic neighborhood, Franklin Park Conservatory and Botanical Gardens, in Columbus; Rock and Roll Hall of Fame and Museum, West Side Market, Cleveland Metroparks Zoo, in Cleveland; Cincinnati Museum Center at Union Terminal; Toledo Zoo. **Information:** TourismOhio, P.O. Box 1001, Columbus, OH 43216-1001; 1-800-BUCKEYE; www.ohio.org

History. Paleo-Indians hunted in the area about 11,000 years ago; the Adena and Hopewell cultures followed. Wyandot, Delaware, Miami, and Shawnee peoples sparsely occupied the area when the first Europeans arrived. René-Robert Cavelier, sieur de La Salle, visited the region, 1669. France claimed it, 1682, but ceded it to Britain, 1763. After the American Revolution, Ohio became part of the Northwest Territory, 1787. The first permanent settlement was at Marietta, 1788. Cincinnati was also founded, 1788; Cleveland, 1796. Indian warfare abated with the Treaty of Greenville, 1795. Ohio became a state, 1803. In the War of 1812, Oliver Hazard Perry's victory on Lake Erie and William Henry Harrison's invasion of Canada, 1813, ended British incursions. Columbus, founded 1812, became the state capital, 1816. Before the Civil

War, some Ohioans aided the Underground Railroad. Agricultural for much of the 19th cent., the state became an industrial powerhouse in the 20th cent. but struggled to replace well-paying manufacturing jobs that began disappearing even before the 2007-09 recession. Cleveland hosted the Republican Natl. Convention in July 2016; no Republican has ever won the presidency without winning Ohio's electoral votes. A mass shooting in Aug. 2019 killed 10 in a Dayton nightlife district. In Feb. 2023, a Norfolk Southern freight train derailed in East Palestine, spilling highly toxic chemicals that forced the evacuation of thousands and necessitated intensive environmental remediation.

Famous Ohioans. Berenice Abbott, Sherwood Anderson, Neil Armstrong, George Bellows, Halle Berry, Ambrose Bierce, Erma Bombeck, Drew Carey, Hart Crane, George Custer, Clarence Darrow, Paul Laurence Dunbar, Thomas Edison, Clark Gable, John Glenn, Zane Grey, Bob Hope, William Dean Howells, LeBron James, John Legend, Maya Lin, Toni Morrison, Paul Newman, Jack Nicklaus, Annie Oakley, Jesse Owens, Jack Paar, Pontiac, Eddie Rickenbacker, John D. Rockefeller Sr. and Jr., Roy Rogers, Pete Rose, Arthur Schlesinger Jr., Gen. William Sherman, Steven Spielberg, Gloria Steinem, Harriet Beecher Stowe, Robert A. Taft, William H. Taft, Tecumseh, James Thurber, Orville and Wilbur Wright.

Website. www.ohio.gov

Oklahoma (OK)
Sooner State

People. Population: 4,019,800; rank: 28. **Pop. change** (2010-22): 7.1%. **Pop. density:** 59 per sq mi. **Racial distribution:** 73.0% white; 7.9% Black; 2.6% Asian; 9.5% Amer. Ind.; 0.3% Hawaiian/Pacific Islander; 2 or more races, 6.7%. **Hispanic pop.:** 12.1%.

Geography. Total area: 69,899 sq mi; rank: 20. **Land area:** 68,595 sq mi; rank: 19. **Acres forested:** 11.6 mil. **Location:** West South Central state bounded on the N by Colorado and Kansas, on the E by Missouri and Arkansas, on the S and W by Texas, on the W by New Mexico. **Climate:** temperate; southern humid belt merging with colder northern continental; humid eastern and dry western zones. **Topography:** high plains predominate in the W, hills and small mountains in the E; the E central region is dominated by the Arkansas R. Basin, and the S by the Red R. Plains. **Capital:** Oklahoma City. **Chief airports:** Oklahoma City, Tulsa.

Economy. Chief industries: manufacturing, mineral and energy exploration and production, agriculture, services. **Chief manuf. goods:** animal slaughtering and processing, petroleum, plastics and rubber, fabricated metals, machinery, motor vehicles and parts. **Chief crops:** wheat, greenhouse and nursery, hay, cotton, corn, soybeans, pecans, sorghum, peanuts. **Farm income:** Crops: $1.88 bil. Livestock: $5.81 bil. **Nonfuel minerals:** $1.0 bil; cement, iodine, sand and gravel (construction), sand and gravel (industrial), stone (crushed). **Chief port:** Catoosa. **Gross state product:** $240.5 bil. **Sales tax:** 4.5%. **Gasoline tax:** 38.40 cents/gal. **Employment distrib.:** 20.7% govt.; 18.5% trade/trans./util.; 7.8% mfg.; 14.3% ed./health; 11.8% prof./bus. serv.; 10.6% leisure/hosp.; 4.7% finance; 6.6% constr./mining/log.; 1.0% info.; 3.9% other serv. **Unemployment:** 3.0%. **Min. wage/hr.:** $7.25. **Per cap. pers. income:** $54,998. **New private housing:** 13,735 units/$3.4 bil. **Broadband internet:** 97.8%. **Commercial banks:** 202; deposits: $117.6 bil. **Savings institutions:** 2; deposits: $13.6 bil. **Lottery:** total sales: $350.3 mil; profit: $79.3 mil.

Federal govt. Fed. civ. employees: 40,292; **avg. salary:** $79,827. **Notable fed. facilities:** Tinker AFB; FAA Mike Monroney Aeronautical Ctr., Oklahoma City; Ft. Sill; Altus AFB; McAlester Army Ammunition Plant; Vance AFB; Natl. Severe Storms Lab, Norman.

Education. High school grad. rate: 80.8%. **4-yr. public coll./univ.:** 17; **2-yr. public:** 13; **4-yr. private:** 12.

Energy. Electricity use/cost: 1,088 kWh, $119.69.

State data. Motto: Labor Omnia Vincit (Labor conquers all things). **Flower:** Oklahoma rose. **Bird:** Scissor-tailed flycatcher. **Tree:** Redbud. **Song:** "Oklahoma!" **Entered union:** Nov. 16, 1907; rank: 46th.

Tourism. Tourist spending: $9.2 bil (2019); change, 2019-20: −36%; change, 2019-22: −8%. **Attractions:** Cherokee Heritage Ctr., Tahlequah; Oklahoma City Natl. Memorial and Museum, Natl. Cowboy and Western Heritage Museum, White Water Bay and Frontier City amusement parks, Museum of Osteology, Bricktown neighborhood, in Oklahoma City; Will Rogers Memorial Museum and Birthplace Ranch, Claremore and Oologah; Gathering Place, Philbrook Museum of Art, Gilcrease Museum, in Tulsa; Wichita Mountains Wildlife Refuge; Woolaroc Museum and Wildlife Preserve, Price Tower Arts Center, in Bartlesville; Sequoyah's Cabin, Sallisaw; Sam

Noble Museum of Natural History, Norman. **Information:** Oklahoma Tourism Dept., Travel Promotion Division, 123 Robert S. Kerr Ave., Oklahoma City, OK 73102-6406; 1-800-652-6552; www.travelok.com

History. Few Native Americans inhabited the region when Spanish explorer Coronado arrived, 1541; in the 16th and 17th cent., French traders visited. Part of the Louisiana Purchase, 1803, Oklahoma was known as Indian Country and, from 1834, Indian Territory. It became home to the "Five Civilized Tribes"—Cherokee, Choctaw, Chickasaw, Creek, and Seminole—after the forced removal of Indians from the eastern U.S., 1828-46. The land was also used by Comanche, Osage, and other Plains Indians. As white settlers pressed west, land was opened for homesteading by "runs" and lottery. The first run was in 1889; the most famous run, 1893, was to the Cherokee Outlet. Oklahoma became a state, 1907. In the early 20th cent., oil finds brought wealth to the Tulsa area; Tulsa's Greenwood section, then known as the "Negro Wall Street," was looted and destroyed by a white mob, 1921. Depression and drought drove many "Okies" from the Dust Bowl to California in the 1930s. A truck bomb in Oklahoma City, 1995, destroyed a federal office building, killing 168 people; an anti-government extremist was executed for the crime, 2001. A tornado in Moore killed 23 people, May 20, 2013; the widest tornado on record touched down in El Reno, May 31, 2013, killing 10 people. Since 2010, Oklahoma has experienced thousands of earthquakes (more than 1,400 greater than 3 magnitude in 2015-16 alone) believed to be connected with the use of disposal wells for wastewater from oil and gas operations. A teacher walkout in Apr. 2018 demanded increased pay and school funding. Flooding caused major damage in 10 eastern counties, May 2019.

Famous Oklahomans. Troy Aikman, Carl Albert, Gene Autry, Johnny Bench, William Boyd (Hopalong Cassidy), Garth Brooks, Lon Chaney, Gordon Cooper, Ralph Ellison, John Hope Franklin, James Garner, Vince Gill, Woody Guthrie, Paul Harvey, Ron Howard, Patrick J. Hurley, Ben Johnson, Jeane Kirkpatrick, Louis L'Amour, Shannon Lucid, Wilma Mankiller, Mickey Mantle, Reba McEntire, Wiley Post, Tony Randall, Oral Roberts, Will Rogers, Blake Shelton, Barry Switzer, Maria Tallchief, Jim Thorpe, Carrie Underwood, J. C. Watts Jr.

Website. www.oklahoma.gov

Oregon (OR)
Beaver State

People. Population: 4,240,137; rank: 27. **Pop. change** (2010-22): 10.7%. **Pop. density:** 44 per sq mi. **Racial distribution:** 85.9% white; 2.3% Black; 5.1% Asian; 1.9% Amer. Ind.; 0.5% Hawaiian/Pacific Islander; 2 or more races, 4.3%. **Hispanic pop.:** 14.4%.

Geography. Total area: 98,379 sq mi; rank: 9. **Land area:** 95,988 sq mi; rank: 10. **Acres forested:** 29.7 mil. **Location:** Pacific state bounded on N by Washington, on E by Idaho, on S by Nevada and California, on W by the Pacific. **Climate:** mild and humid on coast; continental dryness and extreme temperatures in the interior. **Topography:** Coast Range of rugged mountains; fertile Willamette R. Valley to E and S; Cascade Mt. Range of volcanic peaks E of the valley; plateau E of Cascades, remaining two-thirds of state. **Capital:** Salem. **Chief airports:** Portland, Eugene, Redmond, Medford.

Economy. Chief industries: manufacturing, services, trade, finance, insurance, real estate, government, construction. **Chief manuf. goods:** wood prods., frozen produce, printing, computers and electronics, transportation equip., industrial machinery. **Chief crops:** greenhouse and nursery, grass seed, hay, wheat, potatoes, Christmas trees, onions, pears, hazelnuts, corn, grapes, cherries, blackberries, blueberries, peppermint, snap beans, apples, hops. **Farm income:** Crops: $3.91 mil. Livestock: $1.63 mil. **Nonfuel minerals:** $693 mil; cement, diatomite, pumice and pumicite, sand and gravel (construction), stone (crushed). **Commercial fishing:** $208.1 mil. **Chief ports:** Portland, Coos Bay. **Gross state product:** $299.1 bil. **Sales tax:** none. **Gasoline tax:** 56.40 cents/gal. **Employment distrib.:** 15.6% govt.; 18.2% trade/trans./util.; 9.7% mfg.; 15.8% ed./health; 13.6% prof./bus. serv.; 10.2% leisure/hosp.; 5.3% finance; 6.4% constr./mining/log.; 1.9% info.; 3.3% other serv. **Unemployment:** 4.2%. **Min. wage/hr.:** $14.20. **Per cap. pers. income:** $62,767. **New private housing:** 20,321 units/$4.6 bil. **Broadband internet:** 97.7%. **Commercial banks:** 37; deposits $114.5 bil. **Savings institutions:** 3; deposits $1.1 bil. **Lottery:** total sales $1.7 bil; profit $910.5 mil.

Federal govt. Fed. civ. employees: 18,136; **avg. salary:** $90,904. **Notable fed. facilities:** Bonneville Power Admin.

Education. High school grad. rate: 82.6%. **4-yr. public coll./univ.:** 8; 2-yr. public: 17; 4-yr. private: 22.

Energy. Electricity use/cost: 939 kWh, $106.49.

State data. Motto: She flies with her own wings. **Flower:** Oregon grape. **Bird:** Western meadowlark. **Tree:** Douglas fir. **Song:** "Oregon, My Oregon." **Entered union:** Feb. 14, 1859; rank: 33rd.

Tourism. Tourist spending: $14.1 bil (2019); change, 2019-20: –42%; change, 2019-22: –11%. **Attractions:** John Day Fossil Beds Natl. Monument; Multnomah Falls, Columbia River Gorge; Timberline Lodge, Mount Hood Natl. Forest; Crater Lake Natl. Park; Oregon Dunes Natl. Rec. Area; Ft. Clatsop (Lewis and Clark Natl. Historical Park), Astoria Column, in Astoria; Oregon Caves Natl. Monument and Preserve; Intl. Rose Test Garden, Lan Su Chinese Garden, Pittock Mansion, Oregon Museum of Science and Industry, in Portland; Oregon Shakespeare Festival, Ashland; High Desert Museum, Bend; "Spruce Goose" (largest aircraft ever built), Evergreen Aviation and Space Museum, McMinnville; Yaquina Head Outstanding Natural Area, Oregon Coast Aquarium, in Newport. **Information:** Travel Oregon, 530 Center St. NE, Ste. 200, Salem, OR 97301; 1-800-547-7842; www.traveloregon.com

History. More than 100 Native American tribes inhabited the area at the time of European contact, including the Chinook, Yakima, Cayuse, Modoc, and Nez Percé. Capt. Robert Gray sighted and sailed into the Columbia R., 1792. Lewis and Clark, traveling overland, wintered at its mouth, 1805-06. Fur traders sent by John Jacob Astor established the Astoria trading post in the Columbia River region, 1811. Settlers arrived in the Willamette Valley, 1834. In 1843, the first large wave of settlers arrived via the Oregon Trail. Oregon became a territory, 1848, and a state, 1859. Early in the 20th cent., the "Oregon System"—political reforms that included initiative, referendum, recall, direct primary, and woman suffrage—was adopted. Originally dominated by forest products, the economy diversified after World War II, with technology firms clustering in the "Silicon Forest" area around Portland. Oregonians were the first in the U.S. to pass measures allowing physician-assisted suicide for terminally ill patients, 1994, and establishing an all-mail voting system, 1998. Gov. John Kitzhaber resigned in 2015, amidst an ethics scandal. A 41-day armed occupation of Malheur Natl. Wildlife Refuge ended in Feb. 2016. In July 2020, federal Dept. of Homeland Security agents reportedly detained anti-racism protesters in Portland. Oregon voters in Nov. 2020 voted to legalize possession of small amounts of "hard" drugs such as cocaine and heroin, making it the first state to do so.

Famous Oregonians. Ernest Bloch, Bill Bowerman, Ty Burrell, Beverly Cleary, Matt Groening, Ernest Haycox, Chief Joseph, Ken Kesey, Phil Knight, Ursula K. Le Guin, Edwin Markham, Tom McCall, John McLoughlin, Joaquin Miller, Bob Packwood, Linus Pauling, Steve Prefontaine, John "Jack" Reed, Alberto Salazar, Mary Decker Slaney, William Simon U'Ren.

Website. www.oregon.gov

Pennsylvania (PA)
Keystone State

People. Population: 12,972,008; rank: 5. **Pop. change** (2010-22): 2.1%. **Pop. density:** 290 per sq mi. **Racial distribution:** 80.8% white; 12.2% Black; 4.1% Asian; 0.4% Amer. Ind.; 0.1% Hawaiian/Pacific Islander; 2 or more races, 2.4%. **Hispanic pop.:** 8.6%.

Geography. Total area: 46,054 sq mi; rank: 33. **Land area:** 44,743 sq mi; rank: 32. **Acres forested:** 16.6 mil. **Location:** Middle Atlantic state bordered on the N and NE by New York, E by New Jersey, SE by Delaware, S by Maryland, S and SW by West Virginia, and W by Ohio. **Climate:** continental with wide fluctuations in seasonal temperatures. **Topography:** Allegheny Mts. run SW-NE, with Piedmont and Coast Plain in the SE triangle; Allegheny Front a diagonal spine across the state's center; N and W rugged plateau falls to Lake Erie Lowland. **Capital:** Harrisburg. **Chief airports:** Philadelphia, Pittsburgh, Harrisburg.

Economy. Chief industries: agribusiness, advanced manufacturing, health care, travel and tourism, depository institutions, biotechnology, printing and publishing, research and consulting, trucking and warehousing, transportation by air, engineering and management, legal services. **Chief manuf. goods:** petroleum, pharmaceuticals, plastics, iron and steel, printing, paper and paperboard, confectionery and snacks, animal slaughtering and processing. **Chief crops:** greenhouse and nursery, mushrooms, corn, hay, soybeans, apples, tomatoes, wheat, grapes, peaches, potatoes, strawberries, tobacco. **Farm income:** Crops: $2.95 bil. Livestock: $4.47 bil. **Nonfuel minerals:** $2.1 bil; cement, lime, sand and gravel (construction), sand and gravel (industrial), stone (crushed). **Commercial fishing** (2018): $0.3 mil. **Chief ports:** Philadelphia, Pittsburgh. **Gross state product:** $923.1 bil. **Sales tax:** 6.0%. **Gasoline tax:** 80.60 cents/gal. **Employment distrib.:** 11.4% govt.; 18.8% trade/trans./util.; 9.3%

mfg.; 21.5% ed./health; 14.1% prof./bus. serv.; 9.1% leisure/hosp.; 5.5% finance; 4.7% constr./mining/log.; 1.6% info.; 4.1% other serv. **Unemployment:** 4.4%. **Min. wage/hr.:** $7.25. **Per cap. pers. income:** $65,167. **New private housing:** 28,008 units/$6.6 bil. **Broadband internet:** 97.8%. **Commercial banks:** 120; deposits: $534.0 bil. **Savings institutions:** 51; deposits: $43.7 bil. **Lottery:** total sales: $5.1 bil; profit: $1.2 bil.

Federal govt. Fed. civ. employees: 63,344; **avg. salary:** $88,020. **Notable fed. facilities:** Army War College, Carlisle Barracks; Naval Supply Systems Command (NAVSUP), Mechanicsburg; Philadelphia Mint, Defense Supply Ctr., Naval Surface Warfare Ctr., all in Phila.; DLA Distribution Ctr. Susquehanna, New Cumberland, Mechanicsburg; Tobyhanna Army Depot; Letterkenny Army Depot.

Education. High school grad. rate: 87.4%. **4-yr. public coll./univ.:** 22; **2-yr. public:** 17; **4-yr. private:** 102.

Energy. Electricity use/cost: 851 kWh, $117.11.

State data. Motto: Virtue, liberty, and independence. **Flower:** Mountain laurel. **Bird:** Ruffed grouse. **Tree:** Eastern hemlock. **Song:** "Pennsylvania." **Second** of the original 13 states to ratify the Constitution, Dec. 12, 1787.

Tourism. Tourist spending: $30.3 bil (2019); change, 2019-20: –37%; change, 2019-22: 0%. **Attractions:** Liberty Bell Ctr. at Independence Natl. Historical Park, Franklin Institute, Philadelphia Museum of Art, in Philadelphia; Valley Forge Natl. Historical Park, King of Prussia; Gettysburg Natl. Military Park; Pennsylvania Dutch Country, Lancaster County; Hersheypark, Hershey; Duquesne Incline, Carnegie Museums of Pittsburgh, Heinz Hall for the Performing Arts, in Pittsburgh; Pocono Mountains; Pine Creek Gorge (Pennsylvania Grand Canyon), Allegheny Natl. Forest; Fallingwater (house designed by Frank Lloyd Wright), Mill Run; Johnstown Flood Natl. Memorial; Steamtown Natl. Historic Site, Scranton; U.S. Brig *Niagara*, Erie Maritime Museum, Presque Isle State Park, in Erie; Oil Region Natl. Heritage Area; Longwood Gardens, Kennett Square. **Information:** Pennsylvania Tourism Office, Dept. of Community and Economic Development, Commonwealth Keystone Building, 4th Fl., 400 North St., Harrisburg, PA 17120-0225; 1-800-VISITPA; www.visitpa.com

History. When Europeans came, Algonquian-speaking Lenni Lenape (Delaware) and Shawnee and the Iroquoian Susquehannocks, Erie, and Seneca occupied the region. Swedish explorers made the first permanent settlement, 1643, on Tinicum Island. The Dutch seized the settlement, 1655, but lost it to the British, 1664. The region was given by Charles II to William Penn, 1681. Philadelphia ("brotherly love") was the capital of the colonies during most of the American Revolution and of the U.S., 1790-1800; the Declaration of Independence, 1776, and Constitution, 1787, were signed here. Philadelphia was taken by the British, 1777. George Washington's troops encamped at Valley Forge in the bitter winter of 1777-78. Slavery was abolished, 1780. Union victory at the Battle of Gettysburg, July 1-3, 1863, marked a turning point in the Civil War. A dam collapse at Johnstown, 1889, killed at least 2,200 people. From the late 19th to the mid-20th cent., Pittsburgh prospered from coal and steel; later, heavy industry declined, but the city revived as a hub of finance, health care, and research. The Three Mile Island nuclear plant near Harrisburg had a near-meltdown, 1979. One of four hijacked planes on Sept. 11, 2001, crashed near Shanksville; the Flight 93 national memorial was officially dedicated on the site in 2011. A shooting at Pittsburgh's Tree of Life synagogue, Oct. 2018, killed 11; the shooter was sentenced to death, Aug. 2023. In Oct. 2020, the police shooting of a Black man, Walter Wallace Jr., in Philadelphia, captured on video, triggered multiple days of protests.

Famous Pennsylvanians. Marian Anderson, Maxwell Anderson, George Blanda, Kobe Bryant, James Buchanan, Andrew Carnegie, Rachel Carson, Wilt Chamberlain, Noam Chomsky, Perry Como, Bill Cosby, Cyrus H. K. Curtis, Thomas Eakins, Tina Fey, Stephen Foster, Benjamin Franklin, Robert Fulton, Martha Graham, Milton Hershey, Gene Kelly, Grace Kelly (Princess Grace of Monaco), Dan Marino, George C. Marshall, Chris Matthews, John J. McCloy, Margaret Mead, Andrew W. Mellon, Joe Montana, Stan Musial, Joe Namath, John O'Hara, Arnold Palmer, Robert E. Peary, Mike Piazza, Pink (Alecia Beth Moore), Mary Roberts Rinehart, Fred Rogers, Betsy Ross, Will Smith, Jimmy Stewart, Taylor Swift, Jim Thorpe, Johnny Unitas, John Updike, Honus Wagner, Andy Warhol, Benjamin West.

Website. www.pa.gov

Rhode Island (RI)
Little Rhody, Ocean State

People. Population: 1,093,734; rank: 44. **Pop. change** (2010-22): 3.9%. **Pop. density:** 1,058 per sq mi. **Racial distribution:** 82.8% white; 9.1% Black; 3.7% Asian; 1.2% Amer. Ind.; 0.2% Hawaiian/Pacific Islander; 2 or more races, 3.1%. **Hispanic pop.:** 17.6%.

Geography. Total area: 1,545 sq mi; rank: 50. **Land area:** 1,034 sq mi; rank: 50. **Acres forested:** 0.4 mil. **Location:** New England state. **Climate:** invigorating and changeable. **Topography:** eastern lowlands of Narragansett Basin; western uplands of flat and rolling hills. **Capital:** Providence. **Chief airport:** Warwick.

Economy. Chief industries: services, manufacturing. **Chief manuf. goods:** plastics, fabricated metals, electrical equip., jewelry. **Chief crops:** greenhouse and nursery, sweet corn, berries, potatoes, apples, hay. **Farm income:** Crops: $43.64 mil. Livestock: $21.24 mil. **Nonfuel minerals:** $88 mil; sand and gravel (construction), sand and gravel (industrial), stone (crushed). **Commercial fishing:** $109.9 mil. **Chief ports:** Providence, Davisville, Newport. **Gross state product:** $71.4 bil. **Sales tax:** 7.0%. **Gasoline tax:** 53.52 cents/gal. **Employment distrib.:** 13.3% govt.; 15.2% trade/trans./util.; 8.1% mfg.; 21.5% ed./health; 13.8% prof./bus. serv.; 11.0% leisure/hosp.; 7.1% finance; 4.5% constr./mining/log.; 1.2% info.; 4.4% other serv. **Unemployment:** 3.2%. **Min. wage/hr.:** $13.00. **Per cap. pers. income:** $65,377. **New private housing:** 1,371 units/$387.4 mil. **Broadband internet:** 99.2%. **Commercial banks:** 10; deposits: $39.6 bil. **Savings institutions:** 10; deposits: $4.7 bil. **Lottery:** total sales: $944.5 mil; profit: $388.6 mil.

Federal govt. Fed. civ. employees: 8,080; **avg. salary:** $102,282. **Notable fed. facilities:** Naval War College, Naval Undersea Warfare Ctr., Newport; EPA Atlantic Ecology Div. Lab, Narragansett.

Education. High school grad. rate: 83.6%. **4-yr. public coll./univ.:** 2; **2-yr. public:** 1; **4-yr. private:** 10.

Energy. Electricity use/cost: 585 kWh, $130.40.

State data. Motto: Hope. **Flower:** Common blue violet. **Bird:** Rhode Island red chicken. **Tree:** Red maple. **Song:** "Rhode Island." **Thirteenth** of original 13 states to ratify the Constitution, May 29, 1790.

Tourism. Tourist spending: $2.5 bil (2019); change, 2019-20: –31%; change, 2019-22: –1%. **Attractions:** Block Island; mansions (The Breakers, The Elms, others), Cliff Walk, Intl. Tennis Hall of Fame and Museum, Touro Synagogue (completed 1763, oldest in U.S.), in Newport; First Baptist Church in America, Rhode Island School of Design Museum of Art, WaterFire art installation, in Providence; Slater Mill Historic Site, Pawtucket; Gilbert Stuart Birthplace and Museum, Saunderstown. **Information:** Rhode Island Tourism Division, 315 Iron Horse Way, Ste. 101, Providence, RI 02908; 1-800-556-2484; www.visitrhodeisland.com

History. When Europeans arrived, Narragansett, Niantic, Nipmuc, and Wampanoag peoples lived in the region. Italian Giovanni da Verrazzano visited the area, 1524. The first permanent settlement was founded at Providence, 1636, by Roger Williams, who was exiled from the Massachusetts Bay Colony. Anne Hutchinson, also exiled, settled Portsmouth, 1638. Quaker and Jewish immigrants seeking freedom of worship began arriving, 1650s-60s. The colonists broke the power of the Narragansett in the Great Swamp fight, 1675, the decisive battle in King Philip's War. The colony was the first to formally renounce all allegiance to King George III, May 4, 1776. Initially opposed to joining the Union, Rhode Island was the last of the 13 colonies to ratify the Constitution, 1790. Trade, textiles, and metal goods dominated the economy in the 19th cent., and Newport became a fashionable resort after the Civil War. The U.S. Navy was the state's largest civilian employer, 1945-73, until the destroyer force was relocated from Newport. A nightclub fire in West Warwick killed 100 people in 2003.

Famous Rhode Islanders. Ambrose Burnside, George M. Cohan, Viola Davis, Nelson Eddy, Jabez Gorham, Nathanael Greene, Elisabeth Hasselbeck, Christopher and Oliver La Farge, Cormac McCarthy, John McLaughlin, Matthew C. and Oliver Hazard Perry, Gilbert Stuart, Meredith Vieira.

Website. www.ri.gov

South Carolina (SC)
Palmetto State

People. Population: 5,282,634; rank: 23. **Pop. change** (2010-22): 14.2%. **Pop. density:** 176 per sq mi. **Racial distribution:** 68.9% white; 26.3% Black; 2.0% Asian; 0.6% Amer. Ind.; 0.1% Hawaiian/Pacific Islander; 2 or more races, 2.2%. **Hispanic pop.:** 6.6%.

Geography. Total area: 32,020 sq mi; rank: 40. **Land area:** 30,061 sq mi; rank: 40. **Acres forested:** 12.8 mil. **Location:** South Atlantic state bordered by North Carolina on the N; Georgia on the SW and W; the Atlantic Ocean on the E, SE, and S. **Climate:** humid subtropical. **Topography:** Blue Ridge province in NW has highest peaks; piedmont lies between the mountains and the fall line; coastal plain covers two-thirds of state. **Capital:** Columbia. **Chief airports:** Charleston, Myrtle Beach, Greer (Greenville), Columbia.

Economy. Chief industries: tourism, agriculture, manufacturing. **Chief manuf. goods:** chemicals and synthetics, motor vehicles and parts, plastics, paper and paper prods., turbines, rubber, textiles. **Chief crops:** greenhouse and nursery, tobacco, soybeans, cotton, corn, peaches, wheat, tomatoes, peanuts. **Farm income:** Crops: $1.32 bil. Livestock: $1.40 bil. **Nonfuel minerals:** $1.2 bil; cement, gold, sand and gravel (construction), sand and gravel (industrial), stone (crushed). **Commercial fishing:** $27.4 mil. **Chief ports:** Charleston, Georgetown. **Gross state product:** $295.9 bil. **Sales tax:** 6.0%. **Gasoline tax:** 47.15 cents/gal. **Employment distrib.:** 16.5% govt.; 19.0% trade/trans./util.; 11.4% mfg.; 12.1% ed./health; 13.6% prof./bus. serv.; 12.1% leisure/hosp.; 5.3% finance; 5.0% constr./mining/log.; 1.4% info.; 3.6% other serv. **Unemployment:** 3.2%. **Min. wage/hr.:** none. **Per cap. pers. income:** $53,320. **New private housing:** 45,870 units/$11.9 bil. **Broadband internet:** 98.2%. **Commercial banks:** 63; deposits: $126.5 bil. **Savings institutions:** 13; deposits: $1.7 bil. **Lottery:** total sales: $2.3 bil; profit: $561.8 mil.

Federal govt. Fed. civ. employees: 22,913; **avg. salary:** $86,387. **Notable fed. facilities:** Ft. Jackson; Joint Base Charleston; Marine Corps Recruit Depot Parris Island; Shaw AFB; USMC Air Station Beaufort; Savannah River Site.

Education. High school grad. rate: 82.2%. **4-yr. public coll./univ.:** 13; **2-yr. public:** 20; **4-yr. private:** 22.

Energy. Electricity use/cost: 1,078 kWh, $138.65.

State data. Motto: Dum Spiro Spero (While I breathe, I hope). **Flower:** Yellow jessamine. **Bird:** Carolina wren. **Tree:** Palmetto. **Song:** "Carolina." **Eighth** of the original 13 states to ratify the Constitution, May 23, 1788.

Tourism. Tourist spending: $16.9 bil (2019); change, 2019-20: −34%; change, 2019-22: 2%. **Attractions:** Historic Charleston, Waterfront Park, Charleston Museum (est. 1773, oldest in U.S.), Middleton Place, Magnolia Plantation and Gardens, Drayton Hall, in Charleston; Ft. Sumter Natl. Monument (where first shots of Civil War were fired), in Charleston Harbor; Cypress Gardens, Moncks Corner; Boone Hall Plantation and Gardens, Mt. Pleasant; Brookgreen Gardens, Murrells Inlet; Myrtle Beach; Hilton Head Island; Andrew Jackson State Park, Lancaster; South Carolina State Museum, Riverbanks Zoo, in Columbia. **Information:** SC Dept. of Parks, Recreation, and Tourism, 1205 Pendleton St., Columbia, SC 29201; (803) 734-1700; discoversouthcarolina.com

History. When Europeans arrived, Cherokee, Catawba, and Muskogean peoples lived in the area. Spanish and French came in the 16th cent. The first English colonists settled near the Ashley R., 1670, and moved to the site of present-day Charleston, 1680. The colonists seized the government, 1775, and the royal governor fled. The British took Charleston, 1780, but were defeated at Kings Mountain that same year and at Cowpens, 1781. In the 1830s, South Carolinians, angered by federal protective tariffs, adopted the Nullification Doctrine, holding that a state can void an act of Congress. Plantation agriculture relied on the enslaved labor of Black workers to cultivate rice and cotton. Enslaved Black people made up 57% of the population in 1860, when South Carolina was the first state to secede from the Union. Confederate troops fired on and forced the surrender of U.S. troops at Ft. Sumter, in Charleston Harbor, 1861, launching the Civil War. The state was readmitted to the Union, 1868. Strom Thurmond, who ran for president as a segregationist in 1948, later served 48 years in the U.S. Senate (1955-2003). Formerly dependent on textiles, the state has attracted new industries by courting foreign investment. The state removed the Confederate flag from its capitol grounds in July 2015 after an alleged white supremacist shot and killed nine Black parishioners at a Charleston church the previous month; the shooter was sentenced to death in 2017.

Famous South Carolinians. Aziz Ansari, Charles F. Bolden Jr., Chadwick Boseman, James F. Byrnes, John C. Calhoun, Stephen Colbert, Marian Wright Edelman, Joe Frazier, DuBose Heyward, Ernest F. Hollings, Andrew Jackson, Jesse Jackson, "Shoeless" Joe Jackson, Jasper Johns, Andie MacDowell, Francis Marion, Ronald E. McNair, Charles Pinckney, John Rutledge, Thomas Sumter, Strom Thurmond, John B. Watson.

Website. www.sc.gov

South Dakota (SD)

Coyote State, Mount Rushmore State

People. Population: 909,824; rank: 46. **Pop. change** (2010-22): 11.7%. **Pop. density:** 12 per sq mi. **Racial distribution:** 84.2% white; 2.6% Black; 1.8% Asian; 8.5% Amer. Ind.; 0.1% Hawaiian/Pacific Islander; 2 or more races, 2.8%. **Hispanic pop.:** 4.9%.

Geography. Total area: 77,116 sq mi; rank: 17. **Land area:** 75,811 sq mi; rank: 16. **Acres forested:** 1.9 mil. **Location:**

West North Central state bounded on the N by North Dakota, on the E by Minnesota and Iowa, on the S by Nebraska, on the W by Wyoming and Montana. **Climate:** characterized by extremes of temperature, persistent winds, low precipitation and humidity. **Topography:** Prairie Plains in the E; rolling hills of the Great Plains in the W; the Black Hills, rising 3,500 ft, in the SW corner. **Capital:** Pierre. **Chief airport:** Sioux Falls.

Economy. Chief industries: agriculture, services, manufacturing. **Chief manuf. goods:** animal slaughtering, machinery, semiconductors, surgical appliances. **Chief crops:** corn, soybeans, wheat, hay, sunflowers, sorghum, oats, barley. **Farm income:** Crops: $6.93 bil. Livestock: $4.95 bil. **Nonfuel minerals:** $475 mil; cement, gold, lime, sand and gravel (construction), stone (crushed). **Gross state product:** $67.6 bil. **Sales tax:** 4.5%. **Gasoline tax:** 48.40 cents/gal. **Employment distrib.:** 17.9% govt.; 20.1% trade/trans./util.; 10.1% mfg.; 16.8% ed./health; 8.2% prof./bus. serv.; 10.3% leisure/hosp.; 6.1% finance; 5.4% constr./mining/log.; 1.1% info.; 3.8% other serv. **Unemployment:** 2.1%. **Min. wage/hr.:** $10.80. **Per cap. pers. income:** $65,806. **New private housing:** 9,421 units/$1.8 bil. **Broadband internet:** 98.6%. **Commercial banks:** 76; deposits: $714.9 bil. **Savings institutions:** 3; deposits: $553.0 mil. **Lottery:** total sales: $400.7 mil; profit: $179.3 mil.

Federal govt. Fed. civ. employees: 8,339; **avg. salary:** $76,993. **Notable fed. facilities:** Ellsworth AFB.

Education. High school grad. rate: 84.2%. **4-yr. public coll./univ.:** 8; **2-yr. public:** 5; **4-yr. private:** 6.

Energy. Electricity use/cost: 1,019 kWh, $124.50.

State data. Motto: Under God, the people rule. **Flower:** Pasqueflower. **Bird:** Chinese ring-necked pheasant. **Tree:** Black Hills spruce. **Song:** "Hail, South Dakota." **Entered union:** Nov. 2, 1889; rank: 40th.

Tourism. Tourist spending: $3.1 bil (2019); change, 2019-20: −18%; change, 2019-22: 8%. **Attractions:** Mt. Rushmore Natl. Memorial, Keystone; Harney Peak (tallest E of Rockies); Custer State Park; Crazy Horse Memorial (mtn. carving in progress); Wind Cave Natl. Park, near Hot Springs; Black Hills Natl. Forest; Needles Hwy., part of Peter Norbeck Natl. Scenic Byway; Minuteman Missile Natl. Historic Site; Deadwood (1876 gold rush town); Jewel Cave Natl. Monument, near Custer; Badlands Natl. Park; Great Lakes of South Dakota; Great Plains Zoo and Delbridge Museum of Natural History, Sioux Falls; Corn Palace, Mitchell; Reptile Gardens, Chapel in the Hills, Bear Country USA, in Rapid City. **Information:** Dept. of Tourism, Dolly Reed Plaza, 711 E. Wells Ave., c/o 500 E. Capitol Ave., Pierre, SD 57501-5070; 1-800-SDAKOTA; www.travelsd.com

History. Paleo-Indians hunted in the region at least 11,500 years ago. At the time of first European contact, Mandan, Hidatsa, Arikara, and Sioux lived in the area. The French Vérendrye brothers explored the region, 1742-43. The U.S. acquired the territory in the Louisiana Purchase, 1803, and Meriwether Lewis and William Clark passed through, 1804-06. In 1817, a trading post opened at what would become Ft. Pierre. Dakota Territory was established, 1861. Gold was discovered, 1874, in the Black Hills on Lakota Sioux land; the "Great Dakota Boom" began in 1879. South Dakota became a state, 1889. The massacre of more than 200 Native American men, women, and children at Wounded Knee, 1890, ended Sioux resistance. Armed supporters of the American Indian Movement, a Native American rights group, occupied the area, leading to a 70-day standoff, 1973. Major economic activities include agribusiness and, since the 1980s, credit card services. Republicans scored a key election victory, 2004, with the defeat of three-term U.S. Sen. Tom Daschle, a national Democratic leader. A Smithfield Foods pork processing facility in Sioux Falls in Apr. 2020 became the site of the U.S.'s largest known single-source coronavirus cluster.

Famous South Dakotans. Sparky Anderson, Bob Barker, Black Elk, Tom Brokaw, Crazy Horse, Tom Daschle, Myron Floren, Mary Hart, Cheryl Ladd, Ernest O. Lawrence, George McGovern, Russell Means, Billy Mills, Allen H. Neuharth, Pat O'Brien, Sitting Bull.

Website. www.sd.gov

Tennessee (TN)

Volunteer State

People. Population: 7,051,339; rank: 15. **Pop. change** (2010-22): 11.1%. **Pop. density:** 171 per sq mi. **Racial distribution:** 78.3% white; 16.7% Black; 2.1% Asian; 0.5% Amer. Ind.; 0.1% Hawaiian/Pacific Islander; 2 or more races, 2.2%. **Hispanic pop.:** 6.4%.

Geography. Total area: 42,144 sq mi; rank: 36. **Land area:** 41,235 sq mi; rank: 34. **Acres forested:** 13.8 mil. **Location:** East South Central state bounded on the N by Kentucky and Virginia; on the E by North Carolina; on the S by Georgia, Alabama, and Mississippi; on the W by Arkansas and Missouri.

Climate: humid continental to the N; humid subtropical to the S. **Topography:** rugged country in E; Great Smoky Mts. of the Unaka Range; low ridges of the Appalachian Valley; flat Cumberland Plateau; slightly rolling terrain and knobs of the Interior Low Plateau, the largest region; Eastern Gulf Coastal Plain to the W, laced with streams; Mississippi Alluvial Plain, a narrow strip of swamp and floodplain in extreme W. **Capital:** Nashville. **Chief airports:** Nashville, Memphis, Alcoa (Knoxville).

Economy. Chief industries: manufacturing, trade, services, tourism, finance, insurance, real estate. **Chief manuf. goods:** motor vehicles and parts, computers and electronics, food, chemicals, plastics, printing, appliances, aluminum. **Chief crops:** greenhouse and nursery, soybeans, cotton, corn, tobacco, hay, tomatoes, wheat. **Farm income:** Crops: $2.84 bil. Livestock: $1.56 bil. **Nonfuel minerals:** $1.9 bil; cement, sand and gravel (construction), sand and gravel (industrial), stone (crushed), zinc. **Chief ports:** Memphis, Nashville, Chattanooga. **Gross state product:** $475.8 bil. **Sales tax:** 7.0%. **Gasoline tax:** 45.80 cents/gal. **Employment distrib.:** 13.7% govt.; 20.4% trade/trans./util.; 11.1% mfg.; 14.1% ed./health; 14.2% prof./bus. serv.; 10.8% leisure/hosp.; 5.2% finance; 4.6% constr./mining/log.; 1.7% info.; 3.9% other serv. **Unemployment:** 3.4%. **Min. wage/hr.:** none. **Per cap. pers. income:** $58,279. **New private housing:** 52,512 units/$11.8 bil. **Broadband internet:** 97.9%. **Commercial banks:** 162; deposits: $218.0 bil. **Savings institutions:** 8; deposits: $4.1 bil. **Lottery:** total sales: $2.0 bil; profit: $485.6 mil.

Federal govt. Fed. civ. employees: 29,001; **avg. salary:** $82,304. **Notable fed. facilities:** Tennessee Valley Authority, Knoxville; Oak Ridge Natl. Lab; Arnold Engineering Development Ctr.; Ft. Campbell; NSA Mid-South, Millington.

Education. High school grad. rate: 90.4%. **4-yr. public coll./univ.:** 10; **2-yr. public:** 13; **4-yr. private:** 40.

Energy. Electricity use/cost: 1,183 kWh, $130.98.

State data. Motto: Agriculture and commerce. **Flower:** (cultivated) iris; (wildflower) passion flower, Tennessee coneflower. **Bird:** Northern mockingbird. **Tree:** Tulip poplar. **Songs:** "My Homeland, Tennessee"; "When It's Iris Time in Tennessee"; "My Tennessee"; "Tennessee Waltz"; "Rocky Top"; "Smoky Mountain Rain." **Entered union:** June 1, 1796; rank: 16th.

Tourism. Tourist spending: $24.5 bil (2019); change, 2019–20: –32%; change, 2019–22: 12%. **Attractions:** Lookout Mountain, Tennessee Aquarium, Ruby Falls, in Chattanooga; Great Smoky Mountains Natl. Park; Lost Sea (largest underground lake in U.S.), Sweetwater; Cherokee Natl. Forest; Cumberland Gap Natl. Historical Park; James K. Polk Ancestral Home, Columbia; American Museum of Science and Energy, Oak Ridge; The Hermitage (home of Pres. Andrew Jackson), Country Music Hall of Fame and Museum, Ryman Auditorium, Belle Meade Plantation, Parthenon replica, Grand Ole Opry, in Nashville; Dollywood theme park, Pigeon Forge; Graceland (home of Elvis Presley), Sun Studio, in Memphis; Alex Haley Museum and Interpretive Ctr., Henning; Casey Jones Village, Jackson; Bristol Motor Speedway. **Information:** Dept. of Tourist Development, Wm. Snodgrass/Tennessee Tower, 312 Rosa L. Parks Ave., 13th Fl., Nashville, TN 37243; (615) 741-2159; www.tnvacation.com

History. Inhabited for at least 20,000 years, the region was home to Creek and Yuchi peoples when the first Europeans arrived; the Cherokee moved into the region in the early 18th cent. Spanish explorers visited the area, 1540. English traders crossed the Great Smoky Mtns. from the east, while France's Jacques Marquette and Louis Jolliet sailed down the Mississippi on the west, 1673. The first permanent settlement was of Virginians on the Watauga R., 1769. After the American Revolution, in which Tennesseans fought in eastern campaigns, the region became a territory, 1790, and a state, 1796. Slavery was widespread in western Tennessee, where cotton was the main crop, but much less common in the east. The state seceded, 1861, and saw many Civil War engagements; some 187,000 Tennesseans fought for the Confederacy and 51,000 for the Union. Tennessee was readmitted in 1866, the only former Confederate state not to have a postwar military government. The famous Scopes trial, 1925, questioned the teaching of evolution in public schools. In the 1930s, the Tennessee Valley Authority, a federal program, brought electric power to rural areas. Nashville became the capital of country music while Memphis fostered the blues and, with Elvis Presley in the 1950s, rock 'n' roll. Martin Luther King Jr. was assassinated in Memphis, 1968. Since the 1970s, auto plants have become major employers, as has Federal Express. Al Gore Jr., U.S. vice pres. (1993-2001), lost his 2000 presidential bid partly because he failed to carry his home state of Tennessee. Record amounts of rainfall flooded Nashville in 2010. Wildfires killed 14 in East Tennessee in Nov. 2016. On Mar. 2-3, 2020, tornadoes in central TN killed at least 25 people. In Aug. 2021, flash flooding killed at least 22 people in Humphreys County. Memphis police in Jan. 2023 released

video showing the beating death by officers of 29-year-old Black man Tyre Nichols, sparking protests. Legislation in Mar. 2023 outlawed certain drag shows; a federal judge blocked it, citing First Amendment concerns.

Famous Tennesseans. Roy Acuff, Kenny Chesney, Davy Crockett, Miley Cyrus, David Farragut, Ernie Ford, Aretha Franklin, Bill Frist, Al Gore Jr., Alex Haley, William C. Handy, Sam Houston, Cordell Hull, Andrew Jackson, Andrew Johnson, Casey Jones, Estes Kefauver, Grace Moore, Dolly Parton, Minnie Pearl, James Polk, Elvis Presley, Wilma Rudolph, Dinah Shore, Bessie Smith, Fred Thompson, Justin Timberlake, Tina Turner, Hank Williams Jr., Alvin York. **Website.** www.tn.gov

Texas (TX)
Lone Star State

People. Population: 30,029,572; rank: 2. **Pop. change** (2010-22): 19.4%. **Pop. density:** 115 per sq mi. **Racial distribution:** 77.4% white; 13.4% Black; 5.7% Asian; 1.1% Amer. Ind.; 0.2% Hawaiian/Pacific Islander; 2 or more races, 2.3%. **Hispanic pop.:** 40.2%.

Geography. Total area: 268,596 sq mi; rank: 2. **Land area:** 261,232 sq mi; rank: 2. **Acres forested:** 59.9 mil. **Location:** southwestern state bounded on the SE by the Gulf of Mexico; on the SW by Mexico, separated by the Rio Grande; surrounding states are Louisiana, Arkansas, Oklahoma, New Mexico. **Climate:** extremely varied; driest region is the Trans-Pecos; wettest is the NE. **Topography:** Gulf Coast Plain in the S and SE; North Central Plains slope upward with some hills; the Great Plains extend over the Panhandle, are broken by low mountains; the Trans-Pecos is the southern extension of the Rockies. **Capital:** Austin. **Chief airports:** Fort Worth, Houston (2), Austin, Dallas, San Antonio, El Paso, Midland, Harlingen.

Economy. Chief industries: manufacturing, trade, oil and gas extraction, services. **Chief manuf. goods:** petroleum, chemicals and resins, computers and electronics, animal slaughtering and processing, plastics, aerospace. **Chief crops:** cotton, greenhouse and nursery, corn, wheat, sorghum, hay, peanuts, onions, rice, pecans, grapefruit. **Farm income:** Crops: $8.01 bil. Livestock: $16.78 bil. **Nonfuel minerals:** $8.0 bil; cement, lime, sand and gravel (construction), sand and gravel (industrial), stone (crushed). **Commercial fishing:** $237.5 mil. **Chief ports:** Houston, Galveston, Brownsville, Beaumont, Port Arthur, Corpus Christi, Texas City, Freeport. **Gross state product:** $2.4 tril. **Sales tax:** 6.25%. **Gasoline tax:** 38.40 cents/gal. **Employment distrib.:** 14.9% govt.; 19.9% trade/trans./util.; 6.8% mfg.; 13.5% ed./health; 15.3% prof./bus. serv.; 10.6% leisure/hosp.; 6.5% finance; 7.2% constr./mining/log.; 1.7% info.; 3.4% other serv. **Unemployment:** 3.9%. **Min. wage/hr.:** $7.25. **Per cap. pers. income:** $61,985. **New private housing:** 263,054 units/$52.8 bil. **Broadband internet:** 98.6%. **Commercial banks:** 448; deposits: $1.2 bil. **Savings institutions:** 30; deposits: $549.9 bil. **Lottery:** total sales: $8.3 bil; profit: $2.0 bil.

Federal govt. Fed. civ. employees: 121,511; **avg. salary:** $89,083. **Notable fed. facilities:** Ft. Cavazos (fmr. Hood); Ft. Bliss; Sheppard, Dyess, Goodfellow AF Bases; Joint Base San Antonio; NASA Johnson Space Ctr., Houston; Naval Air Training School, Corpus Christi NAS; Red River Army Depot; Western Currency Facility, Ft. Worth.

Education. High school grad. rate (2018-19): 90.0%. **4-yr. public coll./univ.:** 47; **2-yr. public:** 55; **4-yr. private:** 64.

Energy. Electricity use/cost: 1,094 kWh, $132.40.

State data. Motto: Friendship. **Flower:** Bluebonnet. **Bird:** Northern mockingbird. **Tree:** Pecan. **Song:** "Texas, Our Texas." **Entered union:** Dec. 29, 1845; rank: 28th.

Tourism. Tourist spending: $82.0 bil (2019); change, 2019-20: –39%; change, 2019-22: –2%. **Attractions:** Big Bend and Guadalupe Mountains Natl. Parks; Fort Davis Natl. Historic Site; Six Flags Over Texas, Arlington; SeaWorld San Antonio, Six Flags Fiesta Texas, The Alamo, San Antonio Missions Natl. Historical Park, San Antonio River Walk, in San Antonio; Natl. Cowgirl Museum and Hall of Fame, Kimbell Art Museum, Ft. Worth Zoo, Bureau of Engraving and Printing, in Ft. Worth; Lyndon B. Johnson Natl. Historical Park, Johnson City; LBJ Presidential Library and Museum, Bullock Texas State History Museum, Austin; George H. W. Bush Presidential Library and Museum, College Station; Dallas Arboretum and Botanical Garden, Sixth Floor Museum at Dealey Plaza, George W. Bush Presidential Library and Museum, in Dallas; USS *Lexington*, Texas State Aquarium, Padre Island Natl. Seashore, in Corpus Christi. **Information:** Office of the Governor, Econ. Dev. & Tourism, 1100 San Jacinto Blvd., Austin, TX 78701; 1-800-452-9292, (512) 463-2000; www.traveltexas.com

History. Humans have lived in the region for at least 12,000 years. Coahuiltecan, Karankawa, Caddo, Jumano, and Tonkawa peoples were in the area when the first Europeans came; later, Apache, Comanche, Cherokee, and Wichita arrived. Early Spanish explorers included Alonso Alvarez de Pineda, who sailed along the Texas coast, 1519; Cabeza de Vaca, shipwrecked near Galveston along with Estevanico, a Moroccan-born enslaved black man, 1528; and Coronado, who crossed the Panhandle, 1541. Spaniards made the first settlement at Ysleta, near El Paso, 1682. Americans moved into the land early in the 19th cent. Mexico, of which Texas was a part, won independence from Spain, 1821. Texans rebelled, 1836, losing to Mexican Gen. Santa Anna at the Alamo but winning decisively under Sam Houston at San Jacinto. With Houston as president, 1836-38 and 1841-44, the Republic of Texas functioned as a nation until admitted to the Union. With an enslaved population of 30%, Texas seceded, 1861; mostly unscathed by the Civil War, it was readmitted, 1870. In 1900, a powerful hurricane lashed Galveston, killing at least 8,000. Cotton and cattle were dominant until 1901, when the Spindletop gusher, near Beaumont, launched the petroleum and petrochemical industries. With wealth and population came political power, notably in the presidencies of Lyndon B. Johnson (1963-69), George H. W. Bush (1989-93), and George W. Bush (2001-09). Hurricane Harvey brought historic rainfall and flooding to Houston and surrounding areas in Aug. 2017, displacing thousands. A shooter killed 26 at a Baptist church in Sutherland Springs in Nov. 2017. A shooter at a Santa Fe (TX) high school killed 10 in May 2018. Mass shootings in El Paso, Aug. 2019, and Odessa, Sept. 2019, killed dozens. In Feb. 2021, severe winter weather killed 246 people in the state, mainly through hypothermia brought on by utility outages. In Jan. 2022, a UK national took four people hostage at a synagogue near Fort Worth. Gov. Greg Abbott (R) in Feb. 2022 directed state agencies to investigate gender-affirming medical care for transgender youth as child abuse. On May 24, 2022, a gunman killed 19 students and two teachers at an elementary school in Uvalde. An abandoned tractor trailer with 53 dead migrants was found in San Antonio on June 27, 2022. The Dallas-Fort Worth area received up to 15.3 inches of rain over 24 hours, Aug. 21-22, 2022. Texas's GOP-led state House voted May 27, 2023, to impeach the state's Republican attorney gen., Ken Paxton, over bribery and abuse-of-office allegations.

Famous Texans. Lance Armstrong, Stephen F. Austin, Lloyd Bentsen, James Bowie, Drew Brees, Carol Burnett, George H. W. Bush, George W. Bush, Earl Campbell, Kelly Clarkson, Joan Crawford, Dwight D. Eisenhower, Morgan Fairchild, Farrah Fawcett, George Foreman, Sam Houston, Howard Hughes, Molly Ivins, Lyndon B. Johnson, Tommy Lee Jones, Janis Joplin, Barbara Jordan, Beyoncé Knowles, Mary Martin, Matthew McConaughey, Chester Nimitz, Sandra Day O'Connor, H. Ross Perot, Katherine Anne Porter, Dan Rather, Sam Rayburn, Ann Richards, Michael Strahan, George Strait, Bob Wills, Babe Didrikson Zaharias.

Website. www.texas.gov

Utah (UT)
Beehive State

People. Population: 3,380,800; rank: 30. **Pop. change** (2010-22): 22.3%. **Pop. density:** 41 per sq mi. **Racial distribution:** 90.0% white; 1.6% Black; 2.8% Asian; 1.5% Amer. Ind.; 1.2% Hawaiian/Pacific Islander; 2 or more races, 2.9%. **Hispanic pop.:** 15.1%.

Geography. Total area: 84,897 sq mi; rank: 13. **Land area:** 82,170 sq mi; rank: 12. **Acres forested:** 18.1 mil. **Location:** middle Rocky Mountain state; its SE corner touches Colorado, New Mexico, and Arizona and is the only spot in the U.S. where four states join. **Climate:** arid; ranges from warm desert in SW to alpine in NE. **Topography:** high Colorado Plateau is cut by brilliantly colored canyons of the SE; broad, flat, desertlike Great Basin of the W; the Great Salt Lake and Bonneville Salt Flats to the NW; Middle Rockies in the NE run E-W; valleys and plateaus of the Wasatch Front. **Capital:** Salt Lake City. **Chief airport:** Salt Lake City.

Economy. Chief industries: services, trade, manufacturing, government, transportation, utilities. **Chief manuf. goods:** food, petroleum, nonferrous metal, motor vehicles and parts, aerospace, sporting goods, fabricated metal, computers and electronics. **Chief crops:** hay, greenhouse and nursery, wheat, cherries, onions, apples, barley, peaches, corn. **Farm income:** Crops: $629.19 mil. Livestock: $1.36 bil. **Nonfuel minerals:** $3.6 bil; copper, gold, potash, salt, sand and gravel (construction). **Gross state product:** $248.2 bil. **Sales tax:** 6.1%. **Gasoline tax:** 55.45 cents/gal. **Employment distrib.:** 15.3% govt.; 18.2% trade/trans./util.; 8.9% mfg.; 13.6% ed./health; 14.6% prof./bus. serv.; 10.0% leisure/hosp.; 5.6% finance; 8.4% constr./mining/log.; 2.6% info.; 2.8% other serv. **Unemployment:** 2.3%. **Min. wage/hr.:** $7.25. **Per cap. pers. income:** $57,925. **New private housing:** 31,749 units/$8.0 bil. **Broadband internet:** 98.6%.

Commercial banks: 55; deposits: $782.4 bil. **Savings institutions:** 2; deposits: $67.8 bil.

Federal govt. Fed. civ. employees: 31,374; **avg. salary:** $78,280. **Notable fed. facilities:** Hill AFB; Tooele Army Depot; Army Dugway Proving Ground; NSA Utah Data Ctr.

Education. High school grad. rate: 88.2%. **4-yr. public coll./univ.:** 7; **2-yr. public:** 1; **4-yr. private:** 7.

Energy. Electricity use/cost: 775 kWh, $80.87.

State data. Motto: Industry. **Flower:** Sego lily. **Bird:** (California) sea gull. **Tree:** Blue spruce. **Song:** "Utah, This Is the Place." **Entered union:** Jan. 4, 1896; rank: 45th.

Tourism. Tourist spending: $10.5 bil (2019); change, 2019-20: −29%; change, 2019-22: 11%. **Attractions:** Temple Square (site of Mormon Church headquarters), Salt Lake City; Great Salt Lake; Zion, Canyonlands, Bryce Canyon, Arches, and Capitol Reef Natl. Parks; Dinosaur, Rainbow Bridge, Timpanogos Cave, and Natural Bridges Natl. Monuments; Lake Powell; Flaming Gorge Natl. Recreation Area; Utah Olympic Park, Sundance Film Festival, in Park City. **Information:** Utah Office of Tourism, Council Hall/Capitol Hill, 300 N. State St., Salt Lake City, UT 84114; 1-800-200-1160; visit www.visitutah.com

History. Ute, Gosiute, Southern Paiute, and Navajo peoples lived in the region at the time of European contact. Spanish Franciscans visited the area, 1776; American fur traders followed. Permanent settlement began with the arrival of the Latter-day Saints, or Mormons, 1847, who created a prosperous economy. Organized in 1849, the State of Deseret asked admission to the Union; instead, Congress established Utah Territory, 1850, and appointed Brigham Young governor. The Union Pacific and Central Pacific railroads met near Promontory Point, May 10, 1869, creating the first transcontinental railroad. Statehood was not achieved until 1896, after a long controversy over the Mormon practices of economic isolationism and polygamy (the church renounced the latter in 1890). The 20th cent. brought expansion in mining, defense-related industries, and, more recently, information technologies. More than two-thirds of Utahans are Mormons; the church has its world headquarters in Salt Lake City. Utah experienced 60% population growth, 1990-2010. Environmentalists and tribal groups said they would challenge a Trump administration decision in Dec. 2017 to drastically cut the land area covered by Bears Ears and Grand Staircase-Escalante National Monuments. Pres. Biden ordered a review of the monuments' boundaries, Jan. 2021.

Famous Utahans. Maude Adams, Roseanne Barr, Ezra Taft Benson, John Moses Browning, Butch Cassidy, Marriner S. Eccles, Philo T. Farnsworth, David M. Kennedy, J. Willard Marriott, Merlin Olsen, the Osmonds, Ivy Baker Priest, George W. Romney, Wallace Stegner, Brigham Young, Loretta Young.

Website. www.utah.gov

Vermont (VT)
Green Mountain State

People. Population: 647,064; rank: 50. **Pop. change** (2010-22): 3.4%. **Pop. density:** 70 per sq mi. **Racial distribution:** 93.8% white; 1.5% Black; 2.1% Asian; 0.4% Amer. Ind.; <0.05% Hawaiian/Pacific Islander; 2 or more races, 2.1%. **Hispanic pop.:** 2.3%.

Geography. Total area: 9,616 sq mi; rank: 45. **Land area:** 9,217 sq mi; rank: 43. **Acres forested:** 4.5 mil. **Location:** northern New England state. **Climate:** temperate, with considerable temperature extremes; heavy snowfall in mountains. **Topography:** Green Mts. N-S backbone 20-36 mi wide; avg. altitude 1,000 ft. **Capital:** Montpelier. **Chief airport:** Burlington.

Economy. Chief industries: manufacturing, tourism, agriculture, trade, finance, insurance, real estate, government. **Chief manuf. goods:** dairy, plastics, printing, wood furniture, sporting goods, metalworking machinery. **Chief crops:** greenhouse and nursery, hay, maple syrup, apples, berries, sweet corn. **Farm income:** Crops: $200.85 mil. Livestock: $587.70 mil. **Nonfuel minerals:** $136 mil; sand and gravel (construction), stone (crushed), stone (dimension), talc (crude). **Gross state product:** $40.6 bil. **Sales tax:** 6.0%. **Gasoline tax:** 51.40 cents/gal. **Employment distrib.:** 18.5% govt.; 17.2% trade/trans./util.; 9.2% mfg.; 20.6% ed./health; 10.7% prof./bus. serv.; 10.1% leisure/hosp.; 4.0% finance; 5.1% constr./mining/log.; 1.5% info.; 3.2% other serv. **Unemployment:** 2.6%. **Min. wage/hr.:** $13.18. **Per cap. pers. income:** $63,206. **New private housing:** 2,302 units/$524.4 mil. **Broadband internet:** 94.6%. **Commercial banks:** 16; deposits: $16.0 bil. **Savings institutions:** 8; deposits: $3.5 bil. **Lottery:** total sales: $151.5 mil; profit: $31.1 mil.

Federal govt. Fed. civ. employees: 3,205; **avg. salary:** $92,400. **Notable fed. facilities:** Law Enforcement Support Ctr., Williston.

Education. High school grad. rate: 83.1%. **4-yr. public coll./univ.:** 4; **2-yr. public:** 1; **4-yr. private:** 11.

Energy. Electricity use/cost: 567 kWh, $109.24.

State data. Motto: Freedom and unity. **Flower:** Red clover. **Bird:** Hermit thrush. **Tree:** Sugar maple. **Song:** "These Green Mountains." **Entered union:** Mar. 4, 1791; rank: 14th.

Tourism. Tourist spending: $2.9 bil (2019); change, 2019-20: −44%; change, 2019-22: −3%. **Attractions:** Shelburne Museum; Shelburne Farms; Vermont Marble Museum, Proctor; Bennington Battle Monument; Pres. Calvin Coolidge Homestead, Plymouth; Ben & Jerry's Factory, Waterbury; Stowe, Killington, and Burke ski resorts: Hildene (Robert Todd Lincoln home), Manchester; Marsh-Billings-Rockefeller Natl. Historical Park, Woodstock. **Information:** Vermont Dept. of Tourism and Marketing, Natl. Life Drive, Deane C. Davis Building, 6th Fl., Montpelier, VT 05620; 1-800-VERMONT, (802) 828-3237; www.vermontvacation.com

History. Inhabited for 10,000 years or more, the region attracted Abenaki and Mahican peoples before Europeans arrived. France's Champlain explored the lake that now bears his name, 1609. The first European settlement was on Isle La Motte in Lake Champlain, 1666. During the American Revolution, Ethan Allen and the Green Mountain Boys captured Ft. Ticonderoga (NY), 1775. Under a constitution that provided for public schools and abolished slavery, settlers declared a republic, 1777. Vermont joined the Union, 1791. Agriculture dominated in the 19th cent. Still mainly rural, the state expanded tourism and manufacturing after World War II, and IBM became the largest private employer. Vermont was the first state to recognize same-sex civil unions (2000) and to enact equal same-sex marriage rights via legislation (2009). Legislation to legalize recreational marijuana went into effect in July 2018. Pres. Joe Biden on July 9, 2023, declared a state of emergency in all of the state's 14 counties amid catastrophic flooding.

Famous Vermonters. Ethan Allen, Chester A. Arthur, Calvin Coolidge, Howard Dean, John Deere, George Dewey, John Dewey, Stephen A. Douglas, Dorothy Canfield Fisher, James Fisk, James "Jim" Jeffords, Bernie Sanders, Jody Williams.

Website. www.vermont.gov

Virginia (VA)
Old Dominion

People. Population: 8,683,619; rank: 12. **Pop. change** (2010-22): 8.5%. **Pop. density:** 220 per sq mi. **Racial distribution:** 68.5% white; 20.0% Black; 7.3% Asian; 0.6% Amer. Ind.; 0.1% Hawaiian/Pacific Islander; 2 or more races, 3.4%. **Hispanic pop.:** 10.5%.

Geography. Total area: 42,775 sq mi; rank: 35. **Land area:** 39,490 sq mi; rank: 36. **Acres forested:** 16.0 mil. **Location:** South Atlantic state bounded by the Atlantic Ocean on the E and surrounded by North Carolina, Tennessee, Kentucky, West Virginia, and Maryland. **Climate:** mild and equable. **Topography:** mountain and valley region in the W, including the Blue Ridge Mts.; rolling Piedmont Plateau; tidewater, or coastal plain, including the Eastern Shore. **Capital:** Richmond. **Chief airports:** Arlington, Dulles (Washington), Norfolk, Highland Springs (Richmond).

Economy. Chief industries: services, trade, government, manufacturing, tourism, agriculture. **Chief manuf. goods:** beverages and tobacco, transportation equip., animal slaughtering and processing, plastics, paper and paper prods., printing, pharmaceuticals, furniture, chemicals. **Chief crops:** greenhouse and nursery, soybeans, tomatoes, corn, tobacco, hay, cotton, apples, wheat, peanuts, potatoes. **Farm income:** Crops: $1.43 bil. Livestock: $2.39 bil. **Nonfuel minerals:** $1.5 bil; cement, kyanite, lime, sand and gravel (construction), stone (crushed). **Commercial fishing:** $222.0 mil. **Chief ports:** Norfolk Harbor, Newport News, Richmond, Hopewell. **Gross state product:** $649.4 bil. **Sales tax:** 5.3%. **Gasoline tax:** 55.20 cents/gal. **Employment distrib.:** 17.9% govt.; 15.9% trade/trans./util.; 5.9% mfg.; 13.9% ed./health; 19.6% prof./bus. serv.; 9.9% leisure/hosp.; 5.2% finance; 5.3% constr./mining/log.; 1.7% info.; 4.7% other serv. **Unemployment:** 2.9%. **Min. wage/hr.:** $12.00. **Per cap. pers. income:** $68,211. **New private housing:** 39,701 units/$8.0 bil. **Broadband internet:** 98.0%. **Commercial banks:** 111; deposits: $380.6 bil. **Savings institutions:** 4; deposits: $365.0 mil. **Lottery:** total sales: $3.0 bil; profit: $807.7 mil.

Federal govt. Fed. civ. employees: 140,479; **avg. salary:** $107,959. **Notable fed. facilities:** Pentagon; Norfolk Naval Sta., Shipyard, and other Hampton Roads military bases; Ft. Belvoir; Joint Base Langley-Eustis; NASA Langley Res. Ctr.; CIA George Bush Ctr. for Intelligence, Langley; FBI Academy, Quantico USMC Base; Dahlgren Nav. Surface Warfare Ctr. and Lab; USDA Food and Nutrition Serv., Alexandria; U.S. Geological Survey Natl. Ctr., Reston.

Education. High school grad. rate: 88.8%. **4-yr. public coll./univ.:** 16; **2-yr. public:** 24; **4-yr. private:** 38.

Energy. Electricity use/cost: 1,094 kWh, $130.92.

State data. Motto: Sic Semper Tyrannis (Thus always to tyrants). **Flower:** American dogwood. **Bird:** Northern cardinal.

Tree: American dogwood. **Song emeritus:** "Carry Me Back to Old Virginia." **Tenth** of original 13 states to ratify the Constitution, June 25, 1788.

Tourism. Tourist spending: $29.1 bil (2019); change, 2019-20: −40%; change, 2019-22: 4%. **Attractions:** Colonial Williamsburg, Busch Gardens Williamsburg, Jamestown Settlement, in Williamsburg; Yorktown Victory Ctr.; Wolf Trap Natl. Park for the Performing Arts, near Vienna; Arlington Natl. Cemetery; George Washington's Mount Vernon; Thomas Jefferson's Monticello, Charlottesville; Stratford Hall (Robert E. Lee birthplace); Appomattox Court House Natl. Historical Park; Shenandoah Natl. Park; Blue Ridge Natl. Parkway; Virginia Beach; Kings Dominion amusement park, Doswell. **Information:** Virginia Tourism Corp., 901 E. Cary St., Ste. 900, Richmond, VA 23219; 1-800-VISITVA; www.virginia.org

History. Cherokee and Susquehanna peoples and the Algonquians of the Powhatan Confederacy were in the region when Europeans arrived. English settlers founded Jamestown, 1607. Four of the first five U.S. presidents—Washington, Jefferson, Madison, and Monroe—came from Virginia. The conclusive battle of the American Revolution took place at Yorktown, 1781. The state profited from tobacco, cotton, and the slave trade; in 1860, nearly one-third of the population was enslaved. Virginia seceded from the Union, 1861, and Richmond became the capital of the Confederacy. Western counties, loyal to the Union, split off to become West Virginia, 1863. The war ended with Robert E. Lee's surrender to Ulysses S. Grant at Appomattox, 1865; Virginia was readmitted to the Union, 1870. In the 20th cent., expansion of federal civilian jobs and military facilities transformed the economy. State officials pledged "massive resistance" to racial integration in the mid-1950s. In 1989, L. Douglas Wilder became the first elected Black governor in U.S. history. On Sept. 11, 2001, terrorist hijackers crashed a jet into U.S. defense headquarters at the Pentagon, in Arlington. A driver who steered his car into a crowd of counterprotesters at a 2017 white nationalist rally in Charlottesville was convicted of murder in state court, 2018, and pleaded guilty to federal hate crimes charges in 2019. In 2019, Virginia's top three state officeholders faced calls to resign, over separate blackface and sexual assault scandals.

Famous Virginians. Arthur Ashe, Sandra Bullock, Richard E. Byrd, James B. Cabell, Henry Clay, Katie Couric, Gabby Douglas, Jubal Early, Jerry Falwell, William Henry Harrison, Patrick Henry, A. P. Hill, Thomas Jefferson, Joseph E. Johnston, Robert E. Lee, Meriwether Lewis and William Clark, James Madison, John Marshall, George Mason, James Monroe, Sean Parker, George Pickett, Pocahontas, Edgar Allan Poe, John Randolph, Walter Reed, Rev. Pat Robertson, John Smith, J. E. B. Stuart, William Styron, Zachary Taylor, John Tyler, Maggie Walker, Booker T. Washington, George Washington, L. Douglas Wilder, Woodrow Wilson.

Website. www.virginia.gov

Washington (WA)
Evergreen State

People. Population: 7,785,786; rank: 13. **Pop. change** (2010-22): 15.8%. **Pop. density:** 117 per sq mi. **Racial distribution:** 76.8% white; 4.6% Black; 10.5% Asian; 2.0% Amer. Ind.; 0.8% Hawaiian/Pacific Islander; 2 or more races, 5.3%. **Hispanic pop.:** 14.0%.

Geography. Total area: 71,298 sq mi; rank: 18. **Land area:** 66,456 sq mi; rank: 20. **Acres forested:** 22.1 mil. **Location:** Pacific state bordered by Canada on the N, Idaho on the E, Oregon on the S, the Pacific Ocean on the W. **Climate:** mild, dominated by the Pacific Ocean and protected by the Cascades. **Topography:** Olympic Mts. on NW peninsula; open land along coast to Columbia R.; flat terrain of Puget Sound Lowland; high peaks of Cascade Mts. to the E; Columbia Basin in central portion; highlands to the NE; mountains to the SE. **Capital:** Olympia. **Chief airports:** Seattle, Spokane.

Economy. Chief industries: advanced technology, aerospace, biotechnology, intl. trade, forestry, tourism, recycling, agriculture and food processing. **Chief manuf. goods:** aerospace, petroleum, food, paper, milled lumber, plastics, structural metals, computers and electronics. **Chief crops:** apples, potatoes, wheat, hay, cherries, greenhouse and nursery, forest products, pears, grapes, onions, hops, sweet corn, Christmas trees, mint, raspberries. **Farm income:** Crops: $7.11 bil. Livestock: $3.02 bil. **Nonfuel minerals:** $901 mil; cement, diatomite, sand and gravel (construction), sand and gravel (industrial), stone (crushed). **Commercial fishing:** $295.3 mil. **Chief ports:** Seattle, Tacoma, Vancouver, Kelso-Longview, Anacortes. **Gross state product:** $725.5 bil. **Sales tax:** 6.5%. **Gasoline tax:** 70.78 cents/gal. **Employment distrib.:** 16.2% govt.; 17.0% trade/trans./util.; 7.5% mfg.; 14.9% ed./health; 15.4% prof./bus. serv.; 9.5% leisure/hosp.; 4.6% finance; 6.7% constr./mining/log.; 4.6% info.; 3.5% other serv. **Unemployment:** 4.2%. **Min. wage/hr.:** $15.74. **Per cap. pers. income:**

$75,698. **New private housing:** 49,033 units/$11.2 bil. **Broadband internet:** 97.9%. **Commercial banks:** 67; deposits: $224.7 bil. **Savings institutions:** 8; deposits: $6.7 bil. **Lottery:** total sales: $907.7 mil; profit: $216.8 mil.

Federal govt. Fed. civ. employees: 54,080; **avg. salary:** $91,336. **Notable fed. facilities:** Bonneville Power Admin.; Lewis-McChord Joint Base; Fairchild AFB; Hanford Site (fmr. nuclear weapons production facility); Naval Base Kitsap (Bremerton and Bangor); Whidbey Island NAS; Pacific Northwest Natl. Lab, Richland.

Education. High school grad. rate: 83.0%. **4-yr. public coll./univ.:** 35; **2-yr. public:** 7; **4-yr. private:** 20.

Energy. Electricity use/cost: 984 kWh, $99.45.

State data. Motto: Alki (By and by). **Flower:** Western rhododendron. **Bird:** Willow goldfinch. **Tree:** Western hemlock. **Song:** "Washington, My Home." **Entered union:** Nov. 11, 1889; rank: 42nd.

Tourism. Tourist spending: $22.4 bil (2019), change, 2019-20: −40%; change, 2019-22: 8%. **Attractions:** Seattle Center, Space Needle, EMP Museum, Museum of Flight, Pike Place Market, Underground Tour, in Seattle; Mount Rainier, Olympic, and North Cascades Natl. Parks; Mount St. Helens Natl. Volcanic Monument; Puget Sound; San Juan Islands; Grand Coulee Dam; Columbia R. Gorge Natl. Scenic Area; Riverfront Park, Spokane; Snoqualmie Falls. **Information:** State of Washington Tourism, P.O. Box 16612, Seattle, WA 98116; 1-800-544-1800; www.stateofwatourism.com

History. People of the Clovis culture lived in the region 11,000 years ago. At the time of European contact, Native Americans in the area included Nez Percé, Spokane, Yakima, Cayuse, Okanogan, Walla Walla, and Colville peoples in the interior, and Nooksak, Chinook, Nisqually, Clallam, Makah, Quinault, and Puyallup peoples along the coast. Spain's Bruno de Heceta sailed the coast, 1775. In 1792, British naval officer George Vancouver mapped the Puget Sound area, and American Capt. Robert Gray sailed up the Columbia R. Fur traders and missionaries arrived in the first half of the 19th cent. Final agreement on the border of Washington and Canada was made with Britain, 1846. Completion in 1883 of a transcontinental rail link between Puget Sound and the eastern U.S. aided immigration, and Washington became a state in 1889. In the 20th cent., cheap hydroelectric power spurred growth in the aluminum and aircraft industries. Founded in 1975, Microsoft became a computer software giant. Mount St. Helens erupted, 1980. With Starbucks coffee and Amazon.com, Seattle became a national trendsetter in the 1990s. Violent street protests disrupted a World Trade Organization meeting there in 1999. Gary Locke, in office 1997-2005, was the first U.S. governor of Chinese ancestry. A mudslide in Mar. 2014 killed 43 people in a rural area north of Seattle.

Famous Washingtonians. Paul Allen, Glenn Beck, Raymond Carver, Kurt Cobain, Bing Crosby, William O. Douglas, Bill Gates, Jimi Hendrix, Henry M. Jackson, Gary Larson, Mary McCarthy, Robert Motherwell, Edward R. Murrow, Apolo Ohno, Chris Pratt, Theodore Roethke, Ann Rule, Hope Solo, Hilary Swank, Julia Sweeney, Adam West, Marcus Whitman, Minoru Yamasaki.

Website. access.wa.gov

West Virginia (WV)
Mountain State

People. Population: 1,775,156; rank: 39. **Pop. change** (2010-22): −4.2%. **Pop. density:** 74 per sq mi. **Racial distribution:** 92.8% white; 3.7% Black; 0.9% Asian; 0.3% Amer. Ind.; <0.05% Hawaiian/Pacific Islander; 2 or more races, 2.2%. **Hispanic pop.:** 2.1%.

Geography. Total area: 24,230 sq mi; rank: 41. **Land area:** 24,038 sq mi; rank: 41. **Acres forested:** 12.0 mil. **Location:** South Atlantic state bounded on the N by Pennsylvania, Maryland; on the S, W, and NW by Virginia, Kentucky, Ohio; on the E by Maryland and Virginia. **Climate:** humid continental except for marine modification in the lower panhandle. **Topography:** hilly to mountainous; Allegheny Plateau in the W covers two-thirds of state; mountains here are the highest in the state, over 4,000 ft. **Capital:** Charleston.

Economy. Chief industries: manufacturing, services, mining, tourism. **Chief manuf. goods:** chemicals, aluminum, motor vehicle parts, lumber and plywood, primary and fabricated metals. **Chief crops:** hay, apples, corn, peaches, soybeans, tobacco, wheat. **Farm income:** Crops: $164.68 mil. Livestock: $530.74 mil. **Nonfuel minerals:** $204 mil: cement, lime, salt, sand and gravel (industrial), stone (crushed). **Chief port:** Huntington. **Gross state product:** $95.6 bil. **Sales tax:** 6.0%. **Gasoline tax:** 55.60 cents/gal. **Employment distrib.:** 21.5% govt.; 17.5% trade/trans./util.; 6.5% mfg.; 18.5% ed./health; 10.4% prof./bus. serv.; 9.8% leisure/hosp.; 3.6% finance; 7.5% constr./mining/log.; 1.1% info.; 3.6% other serv. **Unemployment:** 3.9%. **Min. wage/hr.:** $8.75. **Per cap. pers.**

income: $49,169. **New private housing:** 3,406 units/$760.6 mil. **Broadband internet:** 97.3%. **Commercial banks:** 63; deposits: $44.3 bil. **Savings institutions:** 4; deposits: $875.0 mil. **Lottery:** total sales: $1.4 bil; profit: $545.7 mil.

Federal govt. Fed. civ. employees: 16,296; **avg. salary:** $88,421. **Notable fed. facilities:** Natl. Radio Astronomy Observatory, Green Bank; Bureau of the Fiscal Service Bldg.; Alderson Fed. Prison Camp; FBI Criminal Justice Information Services.

Education. High school grad. rate: 92.1%. **4-yr. public coll./univ.:** 13; **2-yr. public:** 9; **4-yr. private:** 10.

Energy. Electricity use/cost: 1,066 kWh, $129.61.

State data. Motto: Montani Semper Liberi (Mountaineers are always free). **Flower:** Big rhododendron. **Bird:** Cardinal. **Tree:** Sugar maple. **Songs:** "The West Virginia Hills"; "This Is My West Virginia"; "West Virginia, My Home, Sweet Home." **Entered union:** June 20, 1863; rank: 35th.

Tourism. Tourist spending: $4.5 bil (2019), change, 2019-20: −34%; change, 2019-22: −8%. **Attractions:** Harpers Ferry Natl. Historical Park, Appalachian Trail Conservancy and Visitor Ctr., in Harpers Ferry; Clay Center for the Arts and Sciences and Avampato Discovery Museum, Charleston; The Greenbrier resort, White Sulphur Springs; Berkeley Springs State Park; Seneca Rocks State Park; New River Gorge Natl. River; Beckley Exhibition Coal Mine; Monongahela Natl. Forest; Fenton Art Glass Company, Williamstown; Mountain State Forest Festival, Elkins; Mountain State Art & Craft Fair, Ripley; Green Bank Telescope (world's largest fully steerable radio telescope); Cass Scenic Railroad State Park. **Information:** West Virginia Tourism Office, Bldg. 3, Ste. 100, State Capitol Complex, 1900 Kanawha Blvd. East, Charleston, WV 25305; 1-800-CALLWVA; wvtourism.com

History. Sparsely inhabited at the time of European contact, the area was primarily Native American hunting grounds. British explorers Thomas Batts and Robert Fallam reached the New R., 1671. Coal, discovered in 1742, was mined extensively by the mid-19th cent. White settlement led to conflicts with Native Americans, including a major battle in which settlers defeated an Indian confederacy at Point Pleasant, 1774. The region joined the Union as part of Virginia, 1788. Longstanding tensions between the E and W parts of the state came to a head in 1861, when Virginia seceded. Delegates of western counties, meeting at Wheeling, repudiated the act and created a new state, Kanawha, later renamed West Virginia, which was admitted to the Union in 1863. Poverty has been a problem for much of the state's subsequent history. It continued to rank low in per capita personal income, despite billions of dollars in federal contracts brought to the state by nine-term U.S. Sen. Robert Byrd, who passed away in 2010. Coal mining, though dangerous and challenged by environmental concerns, continues to be a major industry; nearly 30 miners were killed in a mine explosion in 2010. Flash flooding across the state killed at least 23 people in late June 2016. A statewide teacher walkout in Apr. 2018 demanded increased pay and school funding.

Famous West Virginians. George Brett, Pearl S. Buck, Robert C. Byrd, Henry Louis Gates Jr., Stonewall Jackson, Don Knotts, Michael Joseph Owens, Brad Paisley, Mary Lou Retton, Walter Reuther, Cyrus Vance, Jerry West, Charles "Chuck" Yeager.

Website. www.wv.gov

Wisconsin (WI)
Badger State

People. Population: 5,892,539; rank: 20. **Pop. change** (2010-22): 3.6%. **Pop. density:** 109 per sq mi. **Racial distribution:** 86.6% white; 6.6% Black; 3.2% Asian; 1.2% Amer. Ind.; 0.1% Hawaiian/Pacific Islander; 2 or more races, 2.2%. **Hispanic pop.:** 7.6%.

Geography. Total area: 65,496 sq mi; rank: 23. **Land area:** 54,158 sq mi; rank: 25. **Acres forested:** 16.9 mil. **Location:** East North Central state bounded on the N by Lake Superior and Upper Michigan, on the E by Lake Michigan, on the S by Illinois, on the W by Minnesota and Iowa. **Climate:** long, cold winters and short, warm summers tempered by the Great Lakes. **Topography:** narrow Lake Superior Lowland plain met by Northern Highland, which slopes gently to the sandy crescent Central Plain; Western Upland in the SW; three broad parallel limestone ridges running N-S are separated by wide and shallow lowlands in the SE. **Capital:** Madison. **Chief airports:** Milwaukee, Madison.

Economy. Chief industries: services, manufacturing, trade, government, agriculture, tourism. **Chief manuf. goods:** transportation, dairy, animal slaughtering and processing, paper, printing, plastics, computers and electronics. **Chief crops:** corn, greenhouse and nursery, soybeans, potatoes, cranberries, hay, wheat, snap beans, apples, peas. **Farm income:** Crops: $4.72 bil. Livestock: $8.11 bil. **Nonfuel minerals:** $1.7

mil; lime, sand and gravel (construction), sand and gravel (industrial), stone (crushed), stone (dimension). **Commercial fishing** (2018): $2.9 mil. **Chief ports:** Superior, Milwaukee, Green Bay. **Gross state product:** $401.8 bil. **Sales tax:** 5.0%. **Gasoline tax:** 51.30 cents/gal. **Employment distrib.:** 13.9% govt.; 18.3% trade/trans./util.; 16.1% mfg.; 15.6% ed./health; 10.9% prof./bus. serv.; 8.8% leisure/hosp.; 5.4% finance; 4.5% constr./mining/log.; 1.5% info.; 5.0% other serv. **Unemployment:** 2.9%. **Min. wage/hr.:** $7.25. **Per cap. pers. income:** $61,210. **New private housing:** 21,072 units/$5.8 bil. **Broadband internet:** 97.3%. **Commercial banks:** 180; deposits: $196.3 bil. **Savings institutions:** 25; deposits: $9.6 bil. **Lottery:** total sales: $887.8 mil; profit: $340.6 mil.

Federal govt. civ. employees: 16,605; **avg. salary:** $86,087. **Notable fed. facilities:** Ft. McCoy; USDA Forest Products Lab, Madison.

Education. High school grad. rate: 90.4%. **4-yr. public coll./univ.:** 16; **2-yr. public:** 15; **4-yr. private:** 32.

Energy. Electricity use/cost: 690 kWh, $100.18.

State data. Motto: Forward. **Flower:** Wood violet. **Bird:** American robin. **Tree:** Sugar maple. **Song:** "On, Wisconsin!" **Entered union:** May 29, 1848; rank: 30th.

Tourism. Tourist spending: $13.4 bil (2019); change, 2019-20: −28%; change, 2019-22: 7%. **Attractions:** Wade House, Greenbush; Villa Louis, Prairie du Chien; Circus World Museum, Baraboo; Wisconsin Dells; Old World Wisconsin, Eagle; shoreline and state parks of Door County; Chequamegon-Nicolet Natl. Forest; House on the Rock, Taliesin, in Spring Green; Monona Terrace Community and Convention Ctr., Madison; Milwaukee Art Museum, Pabst Mansion, in Milwaukee. **Information:** Wisconsin Dept. of Tourism, 3319 West Beltline Hwy., P.O. Box 8690, Madison, WI 53708-8690; 1-800-432-TRIP; www.travelwisconsin.com

History. At the time of European contact, Ojibwa, Menominee, Winnebago, Kickapoo, Sauk, Fox, and Potawatomi peoples inhabited the area. French explorer Jean Nicolet reached Green Bay, 1634; French missionaries and fur traders followed. The British took over, 1763. The U.S. won the land after the American Revolution but did not wield control until forts were established at Green Bay and Prairie du Chien, 1816. Native Americans rebelled against the seizure of tribal lands in the Black Hawk War, 1832, but were defeated and relocated to reservations. Wisconsin became a territory, 1836, and a state, 1848. Some 96,000 soldiers served the Union cause during the Civil War. Many immigrants arrived from Germany, Poland, and Scandinavia. Wisconsin agriculture focused on dairy; Milwaukee became a manufacturing center. As governor, 1901-06, Robert La Follette pushed Progressive reforms such as direct primary voting and consumer protection laws. The era of McCarthyism ended when anti-Communist crusader U.S. Sen. Joseph McCarthy of Wisconsin was censured by the Senate, 1954. The state legislature passed controversial measures in 2011 to restrict collective bargaining by some 170,000 public-sector employees, and in 2014 became the 25th state to pass a "right-to-work" law. A Kenosha police officer in Aug. 2020 shot Black man Jacob Blake, sparking multiple nights of unrest quelled by Natl. Guard troops; a pro-police 17-year-old, claiming self-defense, fatally shot two protesters. In Dec. 2021, a driver plowed into a Christmas parade in Waukesha, killing six people.

Famous Wisconsinites. Don Ameche, Carrie Chapman Catt, Willem Dafoe, Edna Ferber, Hamlin Garland, King Camp Gillette, Harry Houdini, Robert La Follette, (Vladzio Valentino) Liberace, Alfred Lunt, Pat O'Brien, Georgia O'Keeffe, Danica Patrick, Les Paul, William H. Rehnquist, John Ringling, Donald K. "Deke" Slayton, Spencer Tracy, Orson Welles, Laura Ingalls Wilder, Thornton Wilder, Frank Lloyd Wright.

Website. www.wisconsin.gov

Wyoming (WY)

Equality State, Cowboy State

People. Population: 581,381; rank: 51. **Pop. change** (2010-22): 3.1%. **Pop. density:** 6 per sq mi. **Racial distribution:** 92.3% white; 1.2% Black; 1.1% Asian; 2.8% Amer. Ind.; 0.1% Hawaiian/Pacific Islander; 2 or more races, 2.4%. **Hispanic pop.:** 10.8%.

Geography. Total area: 97,813 sq mi; rank: 10. **Land area:** 97,093 sq mi; rank: 9. **Acres forested:** 10.8 mil. **Location:** Mountain state in the high western plateaus of the Great Plains. **Climate:** semidesert conditions throughout; true desert in the Bighorn and Great Divide Basins. **Topography:** eastern Great Plains rise to the foothills of the Rocky Mts.; the Continental Divide crosses the state from the NW to the SE. **Capital:** Cheyenne.

Economy. Chief industries: mineral extraction, oil, natural gas, tourism and recreation, agriculture. **Chief manuf. goods:** petroleum, chemicals, fabricated metal, beet sugar, lumber. **Chief crops:** hay, sugar beets, barley, dry beans, wheat,

corn, greenhouse and nursery, oats. **Farm income:** Crops: $456.85 mil. Livestock: $1.29 bil. **Nonfuel minerals:** $2.5 bil; cement, clay (bentonite and common clay), helium (Grade-A), sand and gravel (construction), soda ash. **Gross state product:** $47.4 bil. **Sales tax:** 4.0%. **Gasoline tax:** 42.40 cents/gal. **Employment distrib.:** 24.1% govt.; 18.0% trade/trans./util.; 3.7% mfg.; 10.4% ed./health; 7.0% prof./bus. serv.; 12.4% leisure/hosp.; 4.1% finance; 13.4% constr./mining/log.; 1.1% info.; 5.7% other serv. **Unemployment:** 3.6%. **Min. wage/hr.:** $7.25. **Per cap. pers. income:** $71,342. **New private housing:** 3,004 units/$1.1 bil. **Broadband internet:** 96.4%. **Commercial banks:** 45; deposits: $22.1 bil. **Savings institutions:** 2; deposits: $717.0 mil. **Lottery:** total sales: $27.4 mil; profit: $3.2 mil.

Federal govt. civ. employees: 5,652; **avg. salary:** $77,807. **Notable fed. facilities:** Warren AFB.

Education. High school grad. rate: 82.3%. **4-yr. public coll./univ.:** 1; **2-yr. public:** 7; **4-yr. private:** 0.

Energy. Electricity use/cost: 867 kWh, $96.82.

State data. Motto: Equal rights. **Flower:** Indian paintbrush. **Bird:** Western meadowlark. **Tree:** Plains cottonwood. **Song:** "Wyoming." **Entered union:** July 10, 1890; rank: 44th.

Tourism. Tourist spending: $4.0 bil (2019); change, 2019-20: −27%; change, 2019-22: −5%. **Attractions:** Yellowstone Natl. Park (est. 1872, first U.S. national park); Grand Teton Natl. Park; Natl. Elk Refuge, Jackson; Devils Tower Natl. Monument; Ft. Laramie Natl. Historic Site; Oregon Trail ruts, Guernsey; Buffalo Bill Historical Ctr., Cody; Cheyenne Frontier Days. **Information:** Wyoming Office of Tourism, 5611 High Plains Rd., Cheyenne, WY 82007; 1-800-225-5996; www.travelwyoming.com

History. Inhabited for at least 12,000 years, the region supported Shoshone, Crow, Cheyenne, Oglala Sioux, and Arapaho peoples when Europeans arrived. France's Vérendrye brothers were the first Europeans to see the region, 1742-43. John Colter, an American, traversed the Yellowstone area, 1807-08. Trappers and fur traders followed in the 1820s. Forts Laramie and Bridger became important stops on trails to the West Coast. Population grew after the Union Pacific railroad crossed the state, 1867-68. Wyoming became a territory, 1868, and the first to extend full voting rights to women, 1869. Statehood was attained, 1890. Disputes between large landowners and small ranchers culminated in the Johnson County Cattle War, 1892; federal troops were called in to restore order. Nellie Tayloe Ross was the first woman governor to take office in the U.S., 1925. Wyoming, the least populous state, has relied on the energy, tourism, and ranching industries in recent decades. Dick Cheney, Wyoming's representative in the U.S. House, 1979-89, served as U.S. vice pres., 2001-09. Cheney's daughter, three-term U.S. Rep. Liz Cheney, was stripped of her U.S. House leadership position in May 2021 after refusing to back former Pres. Trump's groundless assertions of election fraud.

Famous Wyomingites. James Bridger, Dick Cheney, William F. "Buffalo Bill" Cody, Curt Gowdy, Esther Hobart Morris, Nellie Tayloe Ross.

Website. www.wyo.gov

District of Columbia (DC)

People. Population: 671,803; rank: 49. **Pop. change** (2010-22): 11.6%. **Pop. density:** 11,013 per sq mi. **Racial distribution:** 46.2% white; 45.0% Black; 4.7% Asian; 0.7% Amer. Ind.; 0.2% Hawaiian/Pacific Islander; 2 or more races, 3.2%. **Hispanic pop.:** 11.7%.

Geography. Total area: 68 sq mi; rank: 51. **Land area:** 61 sq mi; rank: 51. **Acres forested:** NA. **Location:** at the confluence of the Potomac and Anacostia Rivers, flanked by Maryland on the N, E, and SE and by Virginia on the SW. **Climate:** hot humid summers, mild winters. **Topography:** low hills rise toward the N away from the Potomac R. and slope to the S; highest elevation, 409 ft; lowest on Potomac R., 1 ft.

Economy. Chief industries: government, legal, publishing, medical, service, tourism. **Farm income:** NA. **Gross state product:** $162.3 bil. **Sales tax:** 6.0%. **Gasoline tax:** 52.60 cents/gal. **Employment distrib.:** 30.2% govt.; 3.9% trade/trans./util.; 0.1% mfg.; 16.1% ed./health; 22.5% prof./bus. serv.; 9.8% leisure/hosp.; 3.6% finance; 2.0% constr./mining/log.; 2.5% info.; 9.4% other serv. **Unemployment:** 4.7%. **Min. wage/hr.:** $17.00. **Per cap. pers. income:** $96,728. **New private housing:** 7,705 units/$1.0 bil. **Broadband internet:** 98.6%. **Commercial banks:** 31; deposits: $68.6 bil. **Savings institutions:** 1; deposits: $53.0 mil. **Lottery:** total sales: $207.3 mil; profit: $40.7 mil.

Federal govt. Fed. civ. employees: 160,991; **avg. salary:** $131,060.

Education. High school grad. rate: 73.0%. **4-yr. public coll./univ.:** 2; **2-yr. public:** 0; **4-yr. private:** 1.

Energy. Electricity use/cost: 706 kWh, $92.42.

District data. Motto: Justitia omnibus (Justice for all). **Flower:** American beauty rose. **Bird:** Wood thrush. **Tree:** Scarlet oak.

Tourism. Tourist spending: $15.1 bil (2019); change, 2019-20: −61%; change, 2019-22: −14%. **Attractions:** See Attractions in and Around Washington, DC, pp. 429-30. **Information:** Destination DC, 901 7th St. NW, 4th Fl., Washington, DC, 20001-3719; 1-800-422-8644; www.washington.org

History. The District of Columbia, coextensive with the city of Washington, is the seat of the U.S. federal government. It lies on the west central edge of Maryland on the Potomac R., opposite Virginia. The Piscataway, an Algonquian-speaking people, were living in the region when Europeans arrived in the 17th cent. Proposals for a "federal town" for the deliberations of the Continental Congress were made in 1783. Authorized by Congress, 1790, Pres. George Washington chose the Potomac site and persuaded landowners to sell their holdings to the government. Its area was originally 100 sq mi taken from the sovereignty of Maryland and Virginia. Virginia's portion south of the Potomac was given back to that state in 1846.

Pres. Washington chose Pierre Charles L'Enfant, a Frenchman, to plan the capital. Surveyor Andrew Ellicott finished the official map and design of the city, assisted by Benjamin Banneker, a Black architect and astronomer. Washington laid the cornerstone of the north wing of the Capitol building, 1793, and Pres. John Adams moved to the new national capital, 1800. The City of Washington was incorporated, 1802. British troops invaded, 1814, setting fire to the Capitol, the President's House (as the White House was then called), and other buildings. Pres. Abraham Lincoln ended slavery in the district, 1862. Many African Americans arrived after the Civil War, but racial segregation remained legal until the mid-20th

cent. After federal government expansion spurred population growth, 1930-50, an exodus to the suburbs shrank the city's population, 1950-2005.

The 23rd Amendment (1961) granted residents the right to vote for president and vice president. Congress, which has legislative authority over the District under the Constitution, approved legislation in 1970 giving the District one delegate to the House of Representatives, who could vote in committee but not on the floor. Voters approved, 1974, a congressionally drafted charter giving them the right to elect their own mayor and city council. The district won the right to levy taxes, but Congress retained power to veto council actions and approve the city budget. Security measures were dramatically increased after terrorists attacked the U.S. on Sept. 11, 2001. After a 34-year absence, major league baseball returned to the city in 2005. On Jan. 6, 2021, a mob of supporters of outgoing Pres. Donald Trump stormed the Capitol in an apparent attempt to disrupt the joint session of Congress's certification of Pres.-elect Joe Biden's victory. Five deaths resulted, including that of a Capitol police officer and a woman shot by police; as of Aug. 2023, more than 1,000 people had been charged in the insurrection, and more than 560 had been sentenced.

Famous Washingtonians. Edward Albee, Michael Chabon, Frederick Douglass, John Foster Dulles, Kevin Durant, Edward Kennedy, Duke Ellington, Marvin Gaye, Katharine Graham, Goldie Hawn, Taraji P. Henson, J. Edgar Hoover, Bill Nye, Pete Sampras, John Philip Sousa.

Website. www.dc.gov

OUTLYING U.S. AREAS

American Samoa (AS)

People. Population (2023 est.): 44,620. **Pop. change** (2010-23): −19.6%. **Pop. density:** 587 per sq mi. **Racial distribution** (2020 est.): 88.7% Hawaiian/Pacific Islander 88.7% (includes Samoan 83.2%, Tongan 2.2%, other 3.3%), Asian 5.8% (includes Filipino 3.4%, other 2.4%), mixed 4.4%, other 1.1%. **Languages:** Samoan 87.9% (closely related to Hawaiian and other Polynesian languages), English 3.3%, Tongan 2.1%, other Pacific Islander 4.1%, Asian languages 2.1%, other 0.5% (2010 est.).

Geography. Total area: 581 sq mi. **Land area:** 76 sq mi. **Acres forested:** 39,156. **Location:** most southerly of all lands under U.S. sovereignty, about 2,300 mi SW of Honolulu. It is an unincorporated territory consisting of seven islands: Samoan group: **Tutuila** (52.59 sq mi), **Aunu'u** (0.59 sq mi); Manu'a group: **Ta'u** (17.57 sq mi), **Olosega** (2.03 sq mi), **Ofu** (2.83 sq mi); and the atolls **Rose** (0.03 sq mi) and **Swains** (1.38 sq mi). **Climate:** marine tropical, avg. temp 82°F with little seasonal variation; avg. annual rainfall about 36 in. **Topography:** volcanic islands, rugged peaks, and limited coastal plains. About 70% of the land is bush and mountains. **Capital:** Pago Pago, on Tutuila. **Chief airport:** Pago Pago.

Economy. Chief industries: tuna fishing and processing, trade, services, tourism. **Chief crops:** giant taro, taro, yams, coconuts, breadfruits, bananas, papayas. **Livestock** (2008): 35,709 chickens, 16,904 hogs/pigs. **Nonfuel minerals:** crushed stone, trap rock. **Commercial fishing** (2008): $9.7 mil. **Unemployment** (2010): 9.2%. **Min. wage/hr.:** $5.38-$6.79. **Gross domestic product** (2021 est.): $709.0 mil. **Broadband internet** (Dec. 2013): 96.8%. **Commercial banks:** 1; deposits $167.0 mil.

Fed. govt. Fed. civ. employees: 107; **avg. salary:** $72,054. **Education.** 4-yr. public coll./univ.: 1; 2-yr. public: 0; 4-yr. private: 0.

Energy. Total electricity consumption (2019 est.): 151 mil kWh.

Misc. data. Motto: Samoa Muamua le Atua (In Samoa, God is first). **Flower:** Paogo (Ula-fala). **Plant:** Ava. **Song:** "Amerika Samoa."

Tourism. Attractions: Natl. Park of American Samoa; Natl. Marine Sanctuary of American Samoa; Jean P. Haydon Museum. **Information:** American Samoa Visitors Bureau, Ground Fl., Fagatogo Sq., Route 001, Fagatogo, AS 96799; (684) 633-9805; www.americansamoa.travel

History. A tripartite agreement between Great Britain, Germany, and the U.S. in 1899 gave the U.S. sovereignty over the eastern islands of the Samoan group; these islands became American Samoa. Local chiefs ceded Tutuila and Aunu'u to the U.S. in 1900 and the Manu'a group and Rose Island in 1904; Swains Island was annexed in 1925. Samoa (Western), comprising the larger islands of the Samoan group, was a New Zealand mandate and UN Trusteeship until it became independent Jan. 1, 1962 (now called Samoa).

From 1900 to 1951, American Samoa was under the jurisdiction of the U.S. Navy. Since 1951, it has been under the Interior Dept. On Jan. 3, 1978, the first popularly elected

Samoan governor and lieutenant governor were inaugurated. Previously, the governor was appointed by the Sec. of the Interior. American Samoa has a bicameral legislature and elects a delegate to the U.S. House of Representatives who has a voice but no vote, except in committees.

Five of the seven islands are volcanoes. Scientists discovered a rapidly growing volcano, Vailulu'u, between Ta'u and Rose in 1975.

The tuna canning industry has been the backbone of the economy since the 1950s, but one of two canneries closed in 2009, and a third cannery closed in 2016 after opening the year before. An 8.1 magnitude earthquake in Sept. 2009 triggered a tsunami that severely damaged Tutuila.

American Samoans are of Polynesian origin. They are nationals of the U.S. As of 2010, 109,637 lived in the U.S., including 18,287 in Hawaii and 40,100 in California.

Website. www.americansamoa.gov

Guam (GU)

People. Population (2023 est.): 169,330. **Pop change** (2010-23): 6.3%. **Pop. density:** 806 per sq mi. **Racial/ethnic distribution** (2010 est.): 37.3% Chamorro; 26.3% Filipino; 12.0% other Pac. Isl.; 7.1% white. **Languages:** English, Chamorro, Philippine/other Pacific Island languages.

Geography. Total area: 571 sq mi. **Land area:** 210 sq mi. **Land use** (2018 est.): agricultural land, 33.4%; arable land, 1.9%; permanent crops, 16.7%; permanent pasture, 14.8%; forest, 47.9%; other, 18.7%. **Acres forested:** 69,703. **Location:** largest and southernmost of the Mariana Islands in the West Pacific, 3,700 mi W of Hawaii. **Climate:** tropical, with temperatures from 70° to 90°F; rainy July to Nov., avg. annual rainfall about 80-100 in. **Topography:** coralline limestone plateau in the N; southern chain of low volcanic mountains slopes gently to the W, more steeply to coastal cliffs on the E; general elevation, 500 ft; highest point, Mt. Lamlam, 1,332 ft. **Capital:** Hagåtña. **Chief airport:** Tamuning.

Economy. Chief industries: U.S. military, tourism, construction, shipping, concrete prods., printing and publishing. **Chief manuf. goods:** textiles, foods. **Chief crops:** watermelons, cucumbers, eggplant, long beans, bananas, corn. **Livestock** (2007): 533 chickens, 112 cattle, 635 hogs/pigs, 124 goats. **Nonfuel minerals** (2008): $3.8 mil; crushed stone. **Commercial fishing** (2008): $499,095. **Chief port:** Apra Harbor. **Gross domestic product** (2021 est.): $6.1 bil. **Employment distrib.** (Dec. 2022): 24.7% govt.; 25.0% serv.; 21.5% trade; 16.5% constr.; 5.8% pub. util./trans.; 3.5% insur./real estate/finance; 2.4% mfg.; 0.5% agric. **Unemployment** (2022): 6.2%. **Min. wage/hr.:** $9.25. **Per capita income** (2016): $31,961. **Broadband internet** (Dec. 2013): 99.2%. **Commercial banks:** 4; deposits $3.6 bil. **Savings institutions:** 1; deposits $133.0 mil.

Federal govt. Fed. civ. employees: 2,846; **avg. salary:** $74,388. **Notable fed. facilities:** Andersen AFB.

Education. 4-yr. public coll./univ.: 1; 2-yr. public: 1; 4-yr. private: 1.

Energy. Total electricity consumption (2019 est.): 1.7 bil kWh.

Misc. data. Motto: Where America's day begins. **Flower:** Puti Tai Nobio (Bougainvillea). **Bird:** Ko'ko (Guam rail). **Tree:** Ifit (Intsia bijuga). **Song:** "Stand Ye Guamanians."

Tourism. Attractions: Ritidian Point, Guam Natl. Wildlife Refuge; War in the Pacific Natl. Historical Park; Chamorro Village; Two Lovers Point. **Information:** Guam Visitors Bureau, 401 Pale San Vitores Rd., Tumon, Guam 96913; (671) 646-5278; www.visitguam.com

History. Guam was probably settled by voyagers from the Indonesian-Philippine archipelago by 3rd cent. BCE. Pottery, rice cultivation, and megalithic technology show strong East Asian cultural influence. Centralized, village clan-based communities engaged in agriculture and offshore fishing. The estimated population by the early 16th cent. was 50,000-75,000. Portuguese explorer Ferdinand Magellan, sailing for Spain, arrived in the Marianas, Mar. 6, 1521. They were colonized in 1668 by Spanish missionaries, who named them the Mariana Islands in honor of Maria Anna, queen of Spain. When Spain ceded Guam to the U.S., it sold the other Marianas to Germany. Japan obtained a League of Nations mandate over the German islands in 1919; in Dec. 1941, it seized Guam, which was retaken by the U.S. in July-Aug. 1944.

Guam is a self-governing organized unincorporated U.S. territory. The Organic Act of 1950 provided for a governor, elected to a four-year term, and a 21-member unicameral legislature, elected biennially by the residents, who are American citizens. In 1970, the first governor was elected. In 1972, a U.S. law gave Guam one U.S. House delegate, who has a voice but no vote, except in committees.

Guam's quest to change its status to a U.S. commonwealth began in the late 1970s. The Guam Commission on Self-Determination, created in 1984, developed a draft Commonwealth Act. In 1993, legislation proposing a change of status was submitted to the U.S. Congress. In 1994, the U.S. Congress passed legislation transferring 3,200 acres of land on Guam from federal to local control. The Navy approved in 2015 a plan to move 5,000 Marines stationed in Okinawa, Japan, to Guam by 2021. North Korea in Aug. 2017 threatened to target Guam in the wake of new UN sanctions and increasingly heated rhetoric from Pres. Trump.

Website. www.guam.gov

Commonwealth of the Northern Mariana Islands (MP)

People. Population (2023 est.): 51,295. **Pop. change** (2010-23): –4.8%. **Pop. density:** 282 per sq mi. **Racial/ethnic distribution** (2010 est.): 50.0% Asian; 34.9% Hawaiian/Pacific Islander; 2.5% other; 2 or more races/ethnicities, 12.7%. **Languages:** Philippine languages, Chinese, Chamorro (official), English (official), other Pacific Island languages.

Geography. Total area: 1,976 sq mi. **Land area:** 182 sq mi. **Acres forested:** 60,207. **Location:** between Guam and the Tropic of Cancer, the 14 islands of the Northern Marianas form a 300-mi-long archipelago. Indigenous population is concentrated on the three largest of the six inhabited islands: **Saipan,** the seat of government and commerce, **Rota,** and **Tinian. Climate:** tropical, with avg. temperature around 82°F, moderated by NE trade winds; avg. annual rainfall 80-100 in. **Topography:** limestone southern islands with even terraces, coral reefs; volcanic northern isles. **Capital:** Saipan. **Chief airport:** Saipan.

Economy. Chief industries: banking, construction, fishing, mining, tourism, apparel manufacturing, retail. **Chief manuf. goods:** apparel, stone, clay and glass prods. **Chief crops:** bananas, cucumbers, sweet potatoes, taro, watermelons. **Livestock** (2007): 9,700 chickens, 1,395 cattle, 1,483 hogs/pigs. **Commercial fishing** (2010 est.): $608,971. **Chief port:** Saipan. **Gross domestic product** (2020 est.): $858 mil. **Employment distrib.:** 1.9% agriculture; 10.0% industry; 88.1% serv. **Unemployment** (2016): 13.8%. **Min. wage/hr.:** $7.25. **Broadband internet** (Dec. 2013): 80.9%. **Commercial banks:** 3; deposits: $1.0 bil. **Savings institutions:** 1; deposits: $10.0 mil.

Federal govt. Fed. civ. employees: 88; **avg. salary:** $69,218.

Education. 4-yr. public coll./univ.: 1; **2-yr. public:** 0; **4-yr. private:** 0.

Misc. data. Flower: Plumeria. **Bird:** Mariana fruit-dove. **Tree:** Flame tree. **Song:** "Gi Talo Gi Halom Tasi" (In the Middle of the Sea).

Tourism. Attractions: House of Taga; American Memorial Park; Banzai Cliff. **Information:** Marianas Visitors Authority, P.O. Box 500861, Saipan, MP 96950; (670) 664-3200; www.mymarianas.com

History. The people of the Northern Marianas are predominantly of Chamorro cultural extraction, although Carolinians

and immigrants from other areas of E. Asia and Micronesia have also settled in the islands. English is among the several languages commonly spoken.

The German-controlled Northern Marianas were placed under Japanese control by a League of Nations mandate after World War I. The U.S. captured the islands during World War II. From July 18, 1947, the U.S. administered the Northern Marianas under a trusteeship agreement with the UN Security Council. In 1975, the residents voted to become a U.S. commonwealth.

The Northern Mariana Islands has been self-governing since 1978, when a constitution drafted and adopted by the people became effective and a popularly elected bicameral legislature (two-year term), with offices of governor (four-year term) and lieut. governor, was inaugurated. Pres. Ronald Reagan proclaimed the Northern Marianas a commonwealth, 1986, and the UN formally ended its trusteeship, 1990. In 2008, U.S. law gave the islands one delegate to the U.S. House of Representatives who has a voice but no vote, except in committees.

Under the 1976 Commonwealth Covenant with the U.S., the islands are exempt from federal immigration and import laws, and minimum wage was lower than on the mainland. The garment-making industry, which has since boomed, has drawn accusations of sweatshop conditions from some critics. As mandated by legislation passed in 2007, the minimum wage finally reached the federal rate in Sept. 2018.

Website. governor.gov.mp

Commonwealth of Puerto Rico (PR)
Estado Libre Asociado de Puerto Rico

People. Population: 3,221,789 (about 5.8 mil additional Puerto Ricans reside in mainland U.S.). **Pop. change** (2010-22): –13.5%. **Pop. density:** 941 per sq mi. **Racial distribution:** 51.1% white; 10.0% Black; 0.2% Asian; 0.2% Amer. Ind.; <0.05% Hawaiian/Pacific Islander; 2 or more races, 16.9%. **Hispanic pop.:** 98.8%. **Languages:** Spanish and English are joint official languages.

Geography. Total area: 5,325 sq mi. **Land area:** 3,424 sq mi. **Acres forested:** 1.1 mil. **Location:** island between the Atlantic to the N and the Caribbean to the S; it is easternmost of the West Indies group called the Greater Antilles, of which Cuba, Hispaniola, and Jamaica are the larger islands. **Climate:** mild, with a mean temperature of 77°F. **Topography:** mountainous throughout three-fourths of its rectangular area, surrounded by a broken coastal plain; highest peak, Cerro de Punto, 4,390 ft. **Capital:** San Juan. **Chief airport:** San Juan.

Economy. Chief industries: manufacturing, service, tourism. **Chief manuf. goods:** pharmaceuticals, medical equip., electronics, apparel, food products. **Chief crops:** pumpkins, coffee, watermelons, plantains, yams, oranges, pineapples, sugarcane, bananas. **Livestock** (2012): 10.9 mil chickens, 257,285 cattle, 12,539 sheep, 48,262 hogs/pigs. **Nonfuel minerals** (2013): $66.3 mil; crushed stone, lime, salt, cement (portland), clays (common), cement (masonry). **Commercial fishing** (2008): $3.8 mil. **Chief ports:** San Juan, Ponce, Mayagüez. **Gross domestic product** (2020 est.): $105.4 bil. **Employment distrib.:** 26.0% govt.; 18.6% trade/trans./util.; 9.2% mfg.; 14.6% ed./health; 13.2% prof./bus. serv.; 6.3% leisure/hosp.; 5.5% finance; 2.4% constr./mining/log.; 1.9% info.; 2.1% other serv. **Unemployment** (Dec. 2022): 6.0%. **Min. wage/hr.:** $9.50. **Per capita income** (2021): $14,047. **Broadband internet:** 93.4%. **Commercial banks:** 5; deposits: $87.2 bil. **Lottery** (2009): total sales: $421.2 mil; profit: $146.9 mil.

Federal govt. Fed. civ. employees: 13,735; **avg. salary:** $70,355. **Notable fed. facilities:** PR Natl. Guard Training Area at Camp Santiago; Ft. Buchanan; Intl. Inst. of Tropical Forestry, San Juan; Vieques Natl. Wildlife Refuge; USGS Caribbean Water Science Ctr., Guaynabo.

Education. High school grad. rate: 78.1%. **4-yr. public coll./univ.:** 14; **2-yr. public:** 3; **4-yr. private:** 45.

Energy. Total electricity consumption (2019 est.): 15.2 bil kWh.

Misc. data. Motto: Joannes Est Nomen Eius (John is his name). **Flower:** Maga. **Bird:** Reinita. **Tree:** Ceiba. **Anthem:** "La Borinqueña."

Tourism. Tourist spending: $6.1 bil (2019); change, 2019-20: –39%; change, 2019-22: 19%. **Tourism. Attractions:** Museo de Arte de Ponce; San Felipe del Morro and San Cristóbal forts, San Juan Natl. Historic Site, Walled City of Old San Juan, Casa Blanca, in San Juan; Arecibo Observatory; Cordillera Central mtn. range; El Yunque Natl. Forest (only tropical rain forest in Natl. Forest system); Cathedral of San Juan Bautista; Porta Coeli (Doorway to Heaven) Church and Religious Art Museum, San Germán; Rio Camuy Cave Park, Camuy; Mosquito Bay. **Information:** The Puerto Rico Tourism Company, La Princesa Bldg. #2, Paseo La Princesa, Old San Juan, PR 00902; (800) 981-7575; www.prtourism.com

History. Puerto Rico (or Borinquen, after the original Arawak Indian name, Boriquen) was visited by Christopher Columbus on his second voyage, Nov. 19, 1493. In 1508, the Spanish arrived.

Sugarcane was introduced, 1515, and enslaved Black laborers arrived three years later. Gold mining petered out, 1570. Spaniards fought off a series of British and Dutch attacks; slavery was abolished, 1873. Under the Treaty of Paris, Puerto Rico was ceded to the U.S. after the Spanish-American War, 1898. In 1952 the people voted in favor of commonwealth status.

The Commonwealth of Puerto Rico is a self-governing part of the U.S. with a primarily Hispanic culture. The island's citizens have virtually the same control over their internal affairs as do the 50 states of the U.S. However, they do not vote in national general elections, only in national primaries.

Puerto Rico is represented in the U.S. House of Representatives by a Resident Commissioner who has a voice but no vote, except in committees.

No federal income tax is collected from residents on income earned from local sources in Puerto Rico. Nevertheless, as part of the U.S. legal system, Puerto Rico is subject to the provisions of the U.S. Constitution; most federal laws apply as they do in the 50 states.

Puerto Rico's "Operation Bootstrap," begun in the late 1940s, succeeded in changing the island from the "Poorhouse of the Caribbean" to an area with the highest per capita income in Latin America. This program encouraged manufacturing and development of the tourist trade by selective tax exemptions, low-interest loans, and other incentives. Despite the marked success of Puerto Rico's development efforts over an extended period of time, per capita income in Puerto Rico is low in comparison to that of the 50 states.

In plebiscites held in 1967, 1993, and 1998, voters chose to retain commonwealth status. In 2012, a half-million ballots were left blank, with 61.1% of those casting votes favoring statehood over free association (33.3%) or independence (5.6%). In a June 2017 referendum, 97% favored statehood, but only 23% of eligible voters participated, rendering the result indecisive. Protests mounted in the late 1990s over the U.S. Navy's use of Vieques Island for live ammunition training; official military exercises there were terminated, 2003. Puerto Rico went into default for the first time in its history in Aug. 2015 after it missed a bond payment. Pres. Barack Obama signed contentious debt-relief legislation in 2016. Hurricane Maria in Sept. 2017 caused some $90 bil in damages, including widespread devastation of infrastructure. A Harvard study published May 2018 in the *New England Journal of Medicine* estimated at least 4,645 deaths were linked with the hurricane and its aftermath, far greater than the government estimate of 64. A separate analysis, commissioned and accepted by the government, raised the official death toll to 2,975 in Aug. 2018. Gov. Ricardo Rosselló resigned effective Aug. 2, 2019, following weeks of mass protests over corruption allegations and the public leak of offensive private chat messages. In Dec. 2020, the nearly 60-year-old Arecibo Observatory radio telescope, one of the world's largest, collapsed. On Mar. 15, 2022, the territory's govt. formally exited bankruptcy proceedings, capping the largest public debt restructuring in U.S. history, of more than $70 bil it was not able to pay back, initiated in 2017.

Cultural facilities and events. Festival Casals classical music concerts, mid-June; Puerto Rico Symphony Orchestra at Music Conservatory; Botanical Garden and Museum of Anthropology, Art, and History at the Univ. of Puerto Rico; Institute of Puerto Rican Culture, at the Dominican Convent.

Famous Puerto Ricans. Julia de Burgos, Marta Casals Istomin, Pablo Casals, José Celso Barbosa, Orlando Cepeda, Roberto Clemente, José de Diego, José Feliciano, Doña Felisa Rincón de Gautier, Luis A. Ferré, José Ferrer, Commodore Diégo E. Hernández, Miguel Hernández Agosto, Rafael Hernández (El Jibarito), Rafael Hernández Colón, Raúl Juliá, René Marqués, Ricky Martin, Concha Meléndez, Rita Moreno, Luis Muñoz Marín, Luis Palés Matos, Joaquin Phoenix, Adm. Horacio Rivero.

Website. www.pr.gov (in Spanish)

Virgin Islands (VI)

St. John, St. Croix, St. Thomas

People. Population (2023 est.): 104,917. **Pop. change** (2010-23): −1.4%. **Pop. density:** 783 per sq mi. **Racial distribution** (2010): 76.0% Black; 15.6% white; 6.2% other race; 2 or more races, 2.1%. **Languages:** English (official), Spanish, Creole.

Geography. Total area: 733 sq mi. **Land area:** 134 sq mi. **Acres forested:** 46,967. **Location:** 3 larger and 50 smaller islands and cays in the S and W of the V.I. group (British V.I. colony to the N and E), which is situated 70 mi E of Puerto Rico; W of Anegada Passage, a major channel connecting the Atlantic Ocean and Caribbean Sea. **Climate:** subtropical;

sun tempered by gentle trade winds; humidity is low; avg. temperature 78°F. **Topography:** St. Thomas is mainly a ridge of hills running E-W and has little tillable land; St. Croix rises abruptly in the N, slopes to flatlands and lagoons in the S; St. John has steep, lofty hills and valleys with little level tillable land. **Capital:** Charlotte Amalie, on St. Thomas. **Chief airport:** Charlotte Amalie.

Economy. Chief industries: retail, petroleum, tourism, prof. consulting. **Chief manuf. goods:** rum, stone, glass and clay products, electronics, textiles. **Chief crops:** cucumbers, coconuts, mangoes, tomatoes, bananas. **Livestock** (2007): 699 chickens, 776 cattle, 2,981 sheep, 1,125 hogs/pigs, 2,331 goats. **Nonfuel minerals:** crushed stone, limestone, trap rock. **Commercial fishing** (2011): $7.1 mil. **Chief port:** Charlotte Amalie. **Gross domestic product** (2021 est.): $4.4 bil. **Employment distrib.:** 30.7% govt.; 17.4% trade/trans./util.; 2.2% mfg.; 5.8% ed./health; 10.2% prof./bus. serv.; 12.2% leisure/hosp.; 5.0% finance; 10.8% constr./mining/log.; 1.4% info.; 4.4% other serv. **Unemployment** (2022): 12.4%. **Min. wage/hr.:** $10.50. **Per capita income** (2012): $19,982. **Broadband internet:** 99.8%. **Commercial banks:** 4; deposits: $4.0 bil. **Savings institutions:** 1; deposits: $424.0 mil.

Federal govt. Fed. civ. employees: 395; **avg. salary:** $74,572.

Education. 4-yr. public coll./univ.: 1; **2-yr. public:** 0; **4-yr. private:** 0.

Energy. Total electricity consumption (2019 est.): 561.2 mil kWh.

Misc. data. Motto: United in pride and hope. **Flower:** Yellow cedar. **Bird:** Bananaquit (yellow breast). **Song:** "Virgin Islands March."

Tourism. Attractions: St. Croix Isl.: Salt River Bay Natl. Historic Park and Ecological Preserve, Christiansted Natl. Historic Site. St. John and Hassel Isls.: Virgin Islands Natl. Park. St. Thomas Isl.: Blackbeard's Castle, Coral World Ocean Park, Magens Bay, 99 Steps. **Information:** USVI Division of Tourism, P.O. Box 6400, St. Thomas, VI 00804; 1-800-372-USVI; www.visitusvi.com

History. The islands were visited by Columbus in 1493. Spanish forces, 1555, defeated the Caribes and claimed the territory; by 1596 the native population was annihilated. The first permanent settlement in the U.S. territory, 1672, was by the Danes; U.S. purchased the islands, 1917, for defense purposes.

The Virgin Islands has a republican form of government, headed by a governor and lieut. governor elected, since 1970, by popular vote for four-year terms. There is a 15-member unicameral legislature, elected by popular vote for a two-year term. Residents of the V.I. have been U.S. citizens since 1927. Since 1973 they have elected a U.S. House delegate, who has a voice but no vote except in committees. Hurricanes Maria and Irma in Sept. 2017 caused some $5.5 bil in damages, according to Gov. Kenneth Mapp.

Website. www.vi.gov

Other Islands

Navassa lies between Haiti and Jamaica, 100 mi S of Guantánamo Bay, Cuba, in the Caribbean. It covers 1,147 acres and is uninhabited. Claimed 1857, a Coast Guard lighthouse was built 1917, now inoperative. Natl. Wildlife Refuge since 1999. Administered by the Dept. of Interior.

The three coral islands of **Wake Atoll—Wake, Wilkes,** and **Peale**—lie in the Pacific Ocean on a direct route from Hawaii to Hong Kong, about 2,300 mi W of Honolulu and 1,500 mi NE of Guam. The group is 4.5 mi long, 1.5 mi wide. Land area totals 5.2 sq mi. The U.S. annexed Wake Atoll Jan. 17, 1899. Japan occupied Wake 1941-45. Designated a National Historic Landmark in 1985. Wake is owned by the U.S. Air Force, administered by the Dept. of Interior, and used by the Army as a missile launch facility. The population consists of military personnel and contractors. Most infrastructure was damaged by super typhoon Ioke in 2006.

The following mostly uninhabited islands are part of the **Pacific/Remote Islands National Wildlife Refuge Complex,** which along with Wake Atoll are administered by the Dept. of Interior: **Midway Atoll,** acquired in 1867, has three main islands—Sand, Spit, and Eastern—1,250 mi WNW of Honolulu, with an area of about 1,500 acres. Naval activity ended in 1997. Has the world's largest albatross colony (Laysan and black-footed). **Johnston Atoll,** 800 mi WSW of Honolulu, is two natural and two artificial islands across 107 sq mi administered by the Navy. Johnston was a nuclear test site in 1958, 1962; the Army disposed of chemical weapons 1990-2000. Cleanup ended in 2005. **Kingman Reef** is a barren coral atoll 932 mi S of Hawaii, annexed 1922. **Palmyra Atoll** is about 54 islets over 753 sq mi, 1,052 mi S of Hawaii; annexed with Hawaii in 1898. Part privately owned by the Nature Conservancy. **Jarvis Island** covers 1,086 acres, 1,300 mi S of Honolulu near the equator. West of Jarvis are **Howland and Baker Islands,** 36 mi apart and about 1,600 mi SW of Honolulu.

100 MOST POPULOUS U.S. CITIES

Sources: Population: Decennial Census and Population Estimates Program, U.S. Census Bureau, U.S. Dept. of Commerce. Population is as of July 1, 2022; population rank is indicated within parentheses. **Pop. density** specifies the number of persons per square mile (sq mi) of land area. Unless otherwise noted, **all other figures** are estimates for 2017-21 by American Community Survey, U.S. Census Bureau. **Racial distribution** categories are abbreviated; their full forms are white, Black or African American, Asian, American Indian and Alaska Native, Native Hawaiian and Other Pacific Islander, some other race, two or more races. **Hispanic** or Latino persons may be of any race. **Language** is what is spoken at home. **Employment:** Bureau of Labor Statistics, U.S. Dept. of Labor for 2022. **Per capita income:** in 2021 inflation-adjusted dollars. Uninsured is the percentage of people aged 19-64 without health insurance. **Educational attainment** is the percentage of persons age 25 and up who have graduated high school (HS) and who have a bachelor's degree or higher. **Avg. commute** is the time it takes for workers 16 years and over to travel from home to work. "Drive" includes only those who drive to work alone. Forms of transport used by less than 10% are omitted. **Avg. home:** National Association of Realtors®. Figures represent median 2022 sales price of existing single-family homes in the metropolitan area; data not available for all cities. **Avg. rent** is the median gross rent (rent asked plus est. avg. cost of utilities) per month. **Crime rates:** *Crime in the United States, 2021*, Federal Bureau of Investigation, U.S. Dept. of Justice. Rates are per 100,000 in population; data as of 2021 unless otherwise noted. Violent crimes include murder, nonnegligent manslaughter, rape, robbery, aggravated assault; property crimes include burglary, larceny-theft, motor vehicle theft. **Mayor** (or other city leader) and **website:** World Almanac research as of mid-2023; subject to change. A nonpartisan mayor is one whose party affiliation was not indicated on the ballot.

Included here are the 100 most populous U.S. cities, according to U.S. Census Bureau estimates released in May 2023. Most data are for the city proper; some, where noted, apply to the Metropolitan Statistical Area (MSA). Inc. = incorporated; est. = established; NA = Not available.

Albuquerque, New Mexico

Population: 561,008 (32). **Pop. density:** 2,996. **Pop. change (2020-22):** −0.7%. **Area:** 187.3 sq mi. **Racial distribution:** 65.6% white; 3.2% Black; 3.1% Asian; 4.8% Amer. Ind.; 0.1% Pac. Isl.; 9.3% other; 2+ races, 14.1%. **Hispanic pop.** 49.8%. **Foreign born:** 10.2%. **U.S. citizens:** 94.7%. **Language:** 73.3% English only; 20.6% Spanish.

Employment: 273,236 employed; 3.6% unemployment. **Per capita income:** $33,494. **Below poverty:** 14.9%; 11.6% of families. **Uninsured:** 11.1%. **Educational attainment:** 90.9% HS; 37.4% bachelor's. **Avg. commute:** 22.0 min. 76.6% drive. **Housing units:** 252,924; 93.4% occupied. **Home ownership:** 60.1%. **Avg. home:** $336,600; change (2020-22): 35.7%. **Avg. rent:** $932. **Crime rates:** violent: 1,388; property: 4,352.

Mayor: Tim Keller, nonpartisan
History: Founded 1706 by the Spanish; inc. 1891.
Website: www.cabq.gov

Anaheim, California

Population: 344,461 (55). **Pop. density:** 6,850. **Pop. change (2020-22):** −0.8%. **Area:** 50.3 sq mi. **Racial distribution:** 53.1% white; 2.7% Black; 17.3% Asian; 0.7% Amer. Ind.; 0.4% Pac. Isl.; 13.5% other; 2+ races, 12.3%. **Hispanic pop.** 54.0%. **Foreign born:** 35.0%. **U.S. citizens:** 81.9%. **Language:** 40.6% English only; 42.2% Spanish.

Employment: 164,605 employed; 3.4% unemployment. **Per capita income:** $32,053. **Below poverty:** 11.6%; 10.0% of families. **Uninsured:** 15.7%. **Educational attainment:** 77.9% HS; 27.1% bachelor's. **Avg. commute:** 28.7 min. 76.4% drive, 11.3% carpool. **Housing units:** 108,652; 95.3% occupied. **Home ownership:** 46.5%. **Avg. home:** $1,235,000; change (2020-22): 37.2%. **Avg. rent:** $1,823. **Crime rates (2020):** violent: 353; property: 2,519.

Mayor: Ashleigh Aitken, nonpartisan
History: Founded 1857; inc. 1876. Home of Disneyland, the Anaheim Ducks, and the Los Angeles Angels.
Website: www.anaheim.net

Anchorage, Alaska

Population: 287,145 (73). **Pop. density:** 168. **Pop. change (2020-22):** −1.3%. **Area:** 1,706.9 sq mi. **Racial distribution:** 60.3% white; 5.4% Black; 9.7% Asian; 7.2% Amer. Ind.; 2.9% Pac. Isl.; 2.7% other; 2+ races, 11.8%. **Hispanic pop.** 9.5%. **Foreign born:** 11.0%. **U.S. citizens:** 95.9%. **Language:** 82.5% English only; 4.8% Spanish.

Employment: 146,302 employed; 3.3% unemployment. **Per capita income:** $43,125. **Below poverty:** 8.5%; 5.8% of families. **Uninsured:** 13.6%. **Educational attainment:** 94.2% HS; 36.8% bachelor's. **Avg. commute:** 19.0 min. 73.7% drive, 12.1% carpool. **Housing units:** 118,055; 90.4% occupied. **Home ownership:** 62.9%. **Avg. home:** $408,400; change (2020-22): 14.0%. **Avg. rent:** $1,350. **Crime rates (2020):** violent: 1,212; property: 3,447.

Mayor: Dave Bronson, nonpartisan
History: Founded 1914 as a railroad construction port; HQ of Alaska Defense Command, WWII. Severely damaged in earthquake, 1964.
Website: www.muni.org

Arlington, Texas

Population: 394,602 (51). **Pop. density:** 4,117. **Pop. change (2020-22):** 0.1%. **Area:** 95.8 sq mi. **Racial distribution:** 51.9% white; 22.9% Black; 6.7% Asian; 0.4% Amer. Ind.; 0.3% Pac. Isl.; 8.6% other; 2+ races, 9.3%. **Hispanic pop.** 29.9%. **Foreign born:** 20.9%. **U.S. citizens:** 88.0%. **Language:** 65.7% English only; 22.3% Spanish.

Employment: 213,755 employed; 3.6% unemployment. **Per capita income:** $30,659. **Below poverty:** 11.5%; 10.7% of families. **Uninsured:** 25.5%. **Educational attainment:** 85.4% HS; 31.7% bachelor's. **Avg. commute:** 27.0 min. 79.8% drive. **Housing units:** 146,784; 92.8% occupied. **Home ownership:** 55.0%. **Avg. home:** $385,500; change (2020-22): 34.2%. **Avg. rent:** $1,172. **Crime rates:** violent: 564; property: 2,556.

Mayor: Jim Ross, nonpartisan
History: Anglo-Americans began to settle in 1840s; inc. 1884.
Website: www.arlingtontx.gov

Atlanta, Georgia

Population: 499,127 (38). **Pop. density:** 3,690. **Pop. change (2020-22):** −0.1%. **Area:** 135.3 sq mi. **Racial distribution:** 41.0% white; 48.2% Black; 5.0% Asian; 0.3% Amer. Ind.; <0.05% Pac. Isl.; 1.7% other; 2+ races, 3.7%. **Hispanic pop.** 5.0%. **Foreign born:** 8.3%. **U.S. citizens:** 95.5%. **Language:** 89.3% English only; 3.9% Spanish.

Employment: 262,377 employed; 3.4% unemployment. **Per capita income:** $54,466. **Below poverty:** 16.6%; 13.6% of families. **Uninsured:** 13.5%. **Educational attainment:** 92.1% HS; 55.6% bachelor's. **Avg. commute:** 27.8 min. 59.8% drive, 18.6% work from home. **Housing units:** 252,119; 87.7% occupied. **Home ownership:** 45.2%. **Avg. home:** $365,100; change (2020-22): 40.0%. **Avg. rent:** $1,342. **Crime rates:** violent: 884; property: 3,674.

Mayor: Andre Dickens, nonpartisan
History: Founded as Terminus, 1837; renamed Atlanta, 1845; inc. 1847. Played major role in Civil War; became state capital, 1868. Birthplace of civil rights movement; host to 1996 Olympic Games.
Website: www.atlantaga.gov

Aurora, Colorado

Population: 393,537 (52). **Pop. density:** 2,422. **Pop. change (2020-22):** 1.8%. **Area:** 162.5 sq mi. **Racial distribution:** 55.7% white; 16.6% Black; 6.6% Asian; 0.8% Amer. Ind.; 0.3% Pac. Isl.; 9.4% other; 2+ races, 10.6%. **Hispanic pop.** 29.0%. **Foreign born:** 21.2%. **U.S. citizens:** 87.5%. **Language:** 67.3% English only; 20.3% Spanish.

Employment: 203,172 employed; 3.4% unemployment. **Per capita income:** $34,497. **Below poverty:** 8.9%; 7.4% of families. **Uninsured:** 15.6%. **Educational attainment:** 86.9% HS; 31.3% bachelor's. **Avg. commute:** 29.9 min. 72.1% drive, 10.2% carpool, 10.8% work from home. **Housing units:** 145,189; 95.3% occupied. **Home ownership:** 62.3%. **Avg. home:** $670,100; change (2020-22): 36.0%. **Avg. rent:** $1,481. **Crime rates:** violent: 1,006; property: 3,880.

Mayor: Mike Coffman, nonpartisan
History: Founded as Fletcher, 1891; renamed Aurora, 1907; inc. 1928. Early growth stimulated by military bases; fast-growing trade, technology, and med. science center.
Website: www.auroragov.org

Austin, Texas

Population: 974,447 (10). **Pop. density:** 3,040. **Pop. change (2020-22):** 0.9%. **Area:** 320.6 sq mi. **Racial distribution:** 66.4% white; 7.7% Black; 8.2% Asian; 0.8% Amer. Ind.; <0.05% Pac. Isl.; 8.2% other; 2+ races, 8.7%. **Hispanic pop.** 33.1%. **Foreign born:** 18.5%. **U.S. citizens:** 88.1%. **Language:** 69.5% English only; 21.2% Spanish.

Employment: 634,160 employed; 2.7% unemployment. **Per capita income:** $48,550. **Below poverty:** 11.7%; 8.3% of families. **Uninsured:** 15.7%. **Educational attainment:** 90.6% HS; 55.1% bachelor's. **Avg. commute:** 24.5 min. 66.2% drive, 18.4% work from home. **Housing units:** 433,129; 93.3% occupied. **Home ownership:** 44.7%. **Avg. home:** $555,400; change (2020-22): 51.3%. **Avg. rent:** $1,415. **Crime rates:** violent: 491; property: 3,343.

Mayor: Kirk Watson, nonpartisan
History: First permanent Anglo-American settlement, 1830s; capital of Rep. of Texas, 1839; named after Stephen Austin.
Website: www.austintexas.gov

Bakersfield, California

Population: 410,647 (48). **Pop. density:** 2,733. **Pop. change (2020-22):** 1.3%. **Area:** 150.3 sq mi. **Racial distribution:** 57.9% white; 7.0% Black; 7.2% Asian; 0.9% Amer. Ind.; 0.2% Pac. Isl.; 14.4% other; 2+ races, 12.5%. **Hispanic pop.:** 52.0%. **Foreign born:** 19.0%. **U.S. citizens:** 89.9%. **Language:** 58.1% English only; 34.1% Spanish.

Employment: 171,372 employed; 4.8% unemployment. **Per capita income:** $28,837. **Below poverty:** 13.8%; 12.8% of families. **Uninsured:** 11.3%. **Educational attainment:** 81.5% HS; 22.9% bachelor's. **Avg. commute:** 23.9 min. 81.1% drive, 10.2% carpool. **Housing units:** 130,148; 94.8% occupied. **Home ownership:** 59.9%. **Avg. home:** $364,600; change (2020-22): 31.7%. **Avg. rent:** $1,177. **Crime rates (2020):** violent: 517; property: 4,023.

Mayor: Karen Goh, nonpartisan

History: Named after Col. Thomas Baker, an early settler; inc. 1898.

Website: www.bakersfieldcity.us

Baltimore, Maryland

Population: 569,931 (30). **Pop. density:** 7,041. **Pop. change (2020-22):** −2.3%. **Area:** 80.9 sq mi. **Racial distribution:** 29.2% white; 61.6% Black; 2.5% Asian; 0.3% Amer. Ind.; <0.05% Pac. Isl.; 2.4% other; 2+ races, 3.9%. **Hispanic pop.:** 5.6%. **Foreign born:** 8.1%. **U.S. citizens:** 95.5%. **Language:** 89.7% English only; 4.1% Spanish.

Employment: 262,081 employed; 4.3% unemployment. **Per capita income:** $34,378. **Below poverty:** 18.3%; 15.3% of families. **Uninsured:** 7.9%. **Educational attainment:** 86.3% HS; 34.2% bachelor's. **Avg. commute:** 30.7 min. 58.2% drive, 14.4% public trans., 10.8% work from home. **Housing units:** 293,718; 83.4% occupied. **Home ownership:** 47.9%. **Avg. home:** $378,200; change (2020-22): 15.1%. **Avg. rent:** $1,146.

Mayor: Brandon M. Scott, Democrat

History: Founded by Maryland legislature, 1729; inc. 1797. British artillery barrage of Ft. McHenry (1814) inspired "Star-Spangled Banner." Birthplace of America's railroads, 1828; rebuilt after fire, 1904. Site of National Aquarium.

Website: www.baltimorecity.gov

Boise City, Idaho

Population: 236,634 (94). **Pop. density:** 2,806. **Pop. change (2020-22):** 0.3%. **Area:** 84.3 sq mi. **Racial distribution:** 86.4% white; 1.7% Black; 3.4% Asian; 0.7% Amer. Ind.; 0.3% Pac. Isl.; 2.1% other; 2+ races, 5.5%. **Hispanic pop.:** 8.8%. **Foreign born:** 6.5%. **U.S. citizens:** 97.1%. **Language:** 89.9% English only; 4.6% Spanish.

Employment: 133,906 employed; 2.2% unemployment. **Per capita income:** $40,056. **Below poverty:** 11.0%; 6.5% of families. **Uninsured:** 10.8%. **Educational attainment:** 95.2% HS; 43.7% bachelor's. **Avg. commute:** 19.0 min. 73.8% drive, 11.7% work from home. **Housing units:** 101,137; 95.3% occupied. **Home ownership:** 62.4%. **Avg. home:** $491,600; change (2020-22): 38.9%. **Avg. rent:** $1,103. **Crime rates (2020):** violent: 293; property: 1,640.

Mayor: Lauren McLean, nonpartisan

History: Gold discovered in area, 1862; proclaimed capital of Idaho Terr., 1864; inc. 1866; on Oregon Trail.

Website: www.cityofboise.org

Boston, Massachusetts

Population: 650,706 (25). **Pop. density:** 13,461. **Pop. change (2020-22):** −3.1%. **Area:** 48.3 sq mi. **Racial distribution:** 50.1% white; 23.5% Black; 9.7% Asian; 0.3% Amer. Ind.; 0.1% Pac. Isl.; 6.7% other; 2+ races, 9.6%. **Hispanic pop.:** 19.8%. **Foreign born:** 28.1%. **U.S. citizens:** 86.3%. **Language:** 63.4% English only; 16.4% Spanish.

Employment: 379,052 employed; 3.6% unemployment. **Per capita income:** $50,344. **Below poverty:** 16.4%; 12.5% of families. **Uninsured:** 4.2%. **Educational attainment:** 88.2% HS; 52.1% bachelor's. **Avg. commute:** 30.6 min. 36.1% drive, 28.0% public trans., 14.4% walk, 12.3% work from home. **Housing units:** 300,437; 90.5% occupied. **Home ownership:** 34.8%. **Avg. rent:** $1,783. **Crime rates:** violent: 551; property: 1,648.

Mayor: Michelle Wu, nonpartisan

History: Settled 1630 by John Winthrop; capital of Mass. Bay Colony; figured strongly in American Revolution; inc. 1822.

Website: www.boston.gov

Buffalo, New York

Population: 276,486 (79). **Pop. density:** 6,847. **Pop. change (2020-22):** −0.4%. **Area:** 40.4 sq mi. **Racial distribution:** 47.8% white; 33.3% Black; 6.7% Asian; 0.4% Amer. Ind.; <0.05% Pac. Isl.; 5.8% other; 2+ races, 5.9%. **Hispanic pop.:** 12.2%. **Foreign born:** 10.5%. **U.S. citizens:** 94.8%. **Language:** 81.1% English only; 7.9% Spanish.

Employment: 103,350 employed; 4.8% unemployment. **Per capita income:** $27,157. **Below poverty:** 23.4%; 22.0% of families. **Uninsured:** 5.8%. **Educational attainment:** 86.0% HS; 29.4% bachelor's. **Avg. commute:** 19.9 min. 68.1% drive. **Housing units:** 136,664; 86.4% occupied. **Home ownership:** 42.7%. **Avg. home:** $230,000; change (2020-22): 28.9%. **Avg. rent:** $849. **Crime rates:** violent: 943; property: 3,055.

Mayor: Byron W. Brown, Democrat

History: Settled 1780 by Seneca Indians; raided by British in War of 1812; inc. 1832. Served as western terminus for Erie Canal and a center for trade and manufacturing.

Website: www.buffalony.gov

Chandler, Arizona

Population: 280,711 (76). **Pop. density:** 4,285. **Pop. change (2020-22):** 1.2%. **Area:** 65.5 sq mi. **Racial distribution:** 68.1% white; 5.6% Black; 10.9% Asian; 1.7% Amer. Ind.; 0.2% Pac. Isl.; 4.3% other; 2+ races, 9.1%. **Hispanic pop.:** 21.5%. **Foreign born:** 15.1%. **U.S. citizens:** 92.4%. **Language:** 76.4% English only; 12.3% Spanish.

Employment: 152,759 employed; 2.9% unemployment. **Per capita income:** $44,302. **Below poverty:** 6.9%; 5.6% of families. **Uninsured:** 9.3%. **Educational attainment:** 94.1% HS; 45.6% bachelor's. **Avg. commute:** 24.5 min. 71.8% drive, 15.6% work from home. **Housing units:** 108,077; 94.9% occupied. **Home ownership:** 65.0%. **Avg. home:** $477,900; change (2020-22): 43.5%. **Avg. rent:** $1,481. **Crime rates:** violent: 188; property: 1,702.

Mayor: Kevin Hartke, nonpartisan

History: Formed 1912; population doubled in 1990s when marketed as "the high-tech oasis of the Silicon Desert."

Website: www.chandleraz.gov

Charlotte, North Carolina

Population: 897,720 (15). **Pop. density:** 2,896. **Pop. change (2020-22):** 2.6%. **Area:** 310.0 sq mi. **Racial distribution:** 44.7% white; 35.2% Black; 6.5% Asian; 0.4% Amer. Ind.; <0.05% Pac. Isl.; 7.2% other; 2+ races, 5.9%. **Hispanic pop.:** 14.9%. **Foreign born:** 17.3%. **U.S. citizens:** 88.9%. **Language:** 77.8% English only; 12.8% Spanish.

Employment: 500,479 employed; 3.6% unemployment. **Per capita income:** $43,080. **Below poverty:** 9.9%; 8.4% of families. **Uninsured:** 16.5%. **Educational attainment:** 89.7% HS; 45.7% bachelor's. **Avg. commute:** 25.4 min. 68.8% drive, 16.7% work from home. **Housing units:** 374,123; 92.5% occupied. **Home ownership:** 52.7%. **Avg. home:** $397,700; change (2020-22): 34.3%. **Avg. rent:** $1,260. **Crime rates:** violent: 782; property: 3,139.

Mayor: Vi Alexander Lyles, Democrat

History: Scotch-Irish immigrants arrived, c. 1750; inc. 1768 and named after Queen Charlotte, wife of King George III. Site of first major U.S. gold discovery, 1799.

Website: charlottenc.gov

Chesapeake, Virginia

Population: 252,488 (89). **Pop. density:** 746. **Pop. change (2020-22):** 1.1%. **Area:** 338.5 sq mi. **Racial distribution:** 58.3% white; 29.6% Black; 3.5% Asian; 0.2% Amer. Ind.; 0.1% Pac. Isl.; 2.2% other; 2+ races, 6.2%. **Hispanic pop.:** 6.8%. **Foreign born:** 6.3%. **U.S. citizens:** 97.5%. **Language:** 91.3% English only; 3.8% Spanish.

Employment: 120,472 employed; 2.9% unemployment. **Per capita income:** $38,952. **Below poverty:** 6.5%; 6.0% of families. **Uninsured:** 9.6%. **Educational attainment:** 93.5% HS; 35.5% bachelor's. **Avg. commute:** 26.1 min. 80.2% drive. **Housing units:** 94,035; 95.1% occupied. **Home ownership:** 72.7%. **Avg. home:** $323,900; change (2020-22): 17.8%. **Avg. rent:** $1,328. **Crime rates:** violent: 463; property: 1,699.

Mayor: Rick West, Republican

History: First English colonies on banks of Elizabeth River, 1620s; home to Dismal Swamp Canal, first envisioned by George Washington in 1763. Battle of Great Bridge, Dec. 1775; inc. 1963.

Website: www.cityofchesapeake.net

Chicago, Illinois

Population: 2,665,039 (3). **Pop. density:** 11,702. **Pop. change (2020-22):** −2.7%. **Area:** 227.7 sq mi. **Racial distribution:** 45.3% white; 29.2% Black; 6.8% Asian; 0.5% Amer. Ind.; <0.05% Pac. Isl.; 10.7% other; 2+ races, 7.4%. **Hispanic pop.:** 28.7%. **Foreign born:** 20.2%. **U.S. citizens:** 89.4%. **Language:** 64.8% English only; 23.5% Spanish.

Employment: 1,319,764 employed; 5.3% unemployment. **Per capita income:** $41,821. **Below poverty:** 15.2%; 13.3% of families. **Uninsured:** 13.4%. **Educational attainment:** 86.3% HS; 41.7% bachelor's. **Avg. commute:** 34.4 min. 47.4% drive, 23.4% public trans., 12.3% work from home. **Housing units:** 1,252,478; 88.8% occupied. **Home ownership:** 45.6%. **Avg. home:** $345,600; change (2020-22): 20.2%. **Avg. rent:** $1,209.

Mayor: Brandon Johnson, nonpartisan

History: First nonnative residence established by Point Du Sable, 1780s; Fort Dearborn built, 1803; significant white settlement began with completion of Erie Canal, 1825; inc. 1837. Boomed with arrival of railroads and canal to Mississippi R.; one-third of city destroyed by fire, 1871. Major Great Migration destination, 1910-30.

Website: www.chicago.gov

Chula Vista, California

Population: 279,170 (78). **Pop. density:** 5,624. **Pop. change (2020-22):** 1.1%. **Area:** 49.6 sq mi. **Racial distribution:** 48.6% white; 5.3% Black; 15.4% Asian; 0.6% Amer. Ind.; 0.4% Pac. Isl.; 11.6% other; 2+ races, 18.2%. **Hispanic pop.:** 60.2%. **Foreign born:** 30.0%. **U.S. citizens:** 87.8%. **Language:** 42.9% English only; 46.9% Spanish.

Employment: 119,894 employed; 3.9% unemployment. **Per capita income:** $35,019. **Below poverty:** 8.6%; 7.2% of families. **Uninsured:** 10.1%. **Educational attainment:** 84.2% HS; 30.3% bachelor's. **Avg. commute:** 29.2 min. 75.5% drive. **Housing units:** 88,262; 93.3% occupied. **Home ownership:** 59.5%. **Avg. home:** $911,000; change (2020-22): 28.3%. **Avg. rent:** $1,864. **Crime rates:** violent: 316; property: 1,208.

Mayor: John McCann, nonpartisan

History: Visited by Spanish, 1542; became part of Spanish land grant, 1795; claimed by U.S. in Mexican-American War, 1847; inc. 1911. WWII brought aircraft industry and growth.

Website: www.chulavistaca.gov

Cincinnati, Ohio

Population: 309,513 (64). **Pop. density:** 3,972. **Pop. change (2020-22):** 0.0%. **Area:** 77.9 sq mi. **Racial distribution:** 50.6% white; 40.3% Black; 2.4% Asian; 0.1% Amer. Ind.; <0.05% Pac. Isl.; 1.4% other; 2+ races, 5.2%. **Hispanic pop.:** 4.4%. **Foreign born:** 6.6%. **U.S. citizens:** 95.8%. **Language:** 91.3% English only; 3.1% Spanish.

Employment: 142,816 employed; 4.0% unemployment. **Per capita income:** $34,060. **Below poverty:** 21.2%; 18.4% of families. **Uninsured:** 9.4%. **Educational attainment:** 88.6% HS; 39.6% bachelor's. **Avg. commute:** 23.4 min. 69.0% drive. **Housing units:** 159,928; 87.4% occupied. **Home ownership:** 39.1%. **Avg. home:** $263,000; change (2020-22): 25.9%. **Avg. rent:** $814. **Crime rates:** violent: 812; property: 3,285.

Mayor: Aftab Pureval, nonpartisan

History: Founded 1788; named after Society of the Cincinnati, an organization of Revolutionary War officers; chartered as town, 1802; inc. 1819.

Website: www.cincinnati-oh.gov

Cleveland, Ohio

Population: 361,607 (54). **Pop. density:** 4,652. **Pop. change (2020-22):** −2.7%. **Area:** 77.7 sq mi. **Racial distribution:** 38.6% white; 47.4% Black; 2.5% Asian; 0.5% Amer. Ind.; <0.05% Pac. Isl.; 3.9% other; 2+ races, 7.1%. **Hispanic pop.:** 12.2%. **Foreign born:** 6.0%. **U.S. citizens:** 97.0%. **Language:** 85.4% English only; 9.2% Spanish.

Employment: 146,126 employed; 6.0% unemployment. **Per capita income:** $23,415. **Below poverty:** 27.3%; 25.8% of families. **Uninsured:** 10.5%. **Educational attainment:** 82.6% HS; 19.2% bachelor's. **Avg. commute:** 23.5 min. 68.6% drive. **Housing units:** 202,579; 83.0% occupied. **Home ownership:** 41.2%. **Avg. home:** $215,700; change (2020-22): 20.2%. **Avg. rent:** $774. **Crime rates:** violent: 1,665; property: 3,752.

Mayor: Justin M. Bibb, nonpartisan

History: Surveyed in 1796; inc. as village, 1814; inc. as city, 1836; annexed Ohio City 1854. Major Great Lakes port and early hub for steel, oil industries.

Website: www.clevelandohio.gov

Colorado Springs, Colorado

Population: 486,248 (39). **Pop. density:** 2,409. **Pop. change (2020-22):** 1.2%. **Area:** 201.8 sq mi. **Racial distribution:** 75.2% white; 5.9% Black; 3.0% Asian; 1.0% Amer. Ind.; 0.2% Pac. Isl.; 4.8% other; 2+ races, 9.9%. **Hispanic pop.:** 18.4%. **Foreign born:** 7.5%. **U.S. citizens:** 96.6%. **Language:** 87.8% English only; 7.8% Spanish.

Employment: 240,990 employed; 3.2% unemployment. **Per capita income:** $37,979. **Below poverty:** 10.1%; 7.4% of families. **Uninsured:** 11.0%. **Educational attainment:** 93.9% HS; 40.2% bachelor's. **Avg. commute:** 23.2 min. 74.7% drive, 11.4% work from home. **Housing units:** 197,571; 95.5% occupied. **Home ownership:** 61.0%. **Avg. home:** $463,400; change (2020-22): 28.1%. **Avg. rent:** $1,300. **Crime rates:** violent: 574; property: 3,213.

Mayor: Yemi Mobolade, nonpartisan

History: Founded 1871 at the foot of Pikes Peak; inc. 1886.

Website: coloradosprings.gov

Columbus, Ohio

Population: 907,971 (14). **Pop. density:** 4,120. **Pop. change (2020-22):** 0.2%. **Area:** 220.4 sq mi. **Racial distribution:** 56.2% white; 29.2% Black; 5.9% Asian; 0.2% Amer. Ind.; <0.05% Pac. Isl.; 2.5% other; 2+ races, 5.9%. **Hispanic pop.:** 6.5%. **Foreign born:** 13.3%. **U.S. citizens:** 93.0%. **Language:** 83.6% English only; 4.5% Spanish.

Employment: 468,312 employed; 3.6% unemployment. **Per capita income:** $32,481. **Below poverty:** 15.8%; 14.0% of families. **Uninsured:** 11.8%. **Educational attainment:** 90.3% HS; 37.9% bachelor's. **Avg. commute:** 22.0 min. 75.0% drive, 11.0% work from home. **Housing units:** 409,221; 92.3% occupied. **Home ownership:** 44.8%. **Avg. home:** $301,100; change (2020-22): 25.0%. **Avg. rent:** $1,061. **Crime rates:** violent: 588; property: 3,230.

Mayor: Andrew J. Ginther, nonpartisan

History: Laid out as state capital, 1812; inc. 1834.

Website: www.columbus.gov

Corpus Christi, Texas

Population: 316,239 (61). **Pop. density:** 1,949. **Pop. change (2020-22):** −0.6%. **Area:** 162.3 sq mi. **Racial distribution:** 71.9% white; 3.9% Black; 2.3% Asian; 0.3% Amer. Ind.; <0.05% Pac. Isl.; 3.4% other; 2+ races, 18.2%. **Hispanic pop.:** 64.2%. **Foreign born:** 9.3%. **U.S. citizens:** 94.1%. **Language:** 66.7% English only; 31.0% Spanish.

Employment: 142,152 employed; 4.6% unemployment. **Per capita income:** $29,823. **Below poverty:** 14.5%; 13.0% of families. **Uninsured:** 26.9%. **Educational attainment:** 84.6% HS; 22.4% bachelor's. **Avg. commute:** 19.5 min. 82.6% drive. **Housing units:** 133,180; 88.0% occupied. **Home ownership:** 57.0%. **Avg. home:** $273,400; change (2020-22): 21.3%. **Avg. rent:** $1,099. **Crime rates:** violent: 847; property: 3,148.

Mayor: Paulette M. Guajardo, nonpartisan

History: Anglo-Americans settled, 1838-39; inc. 1852. One of the largest U.S. ports.

Website: www.cctexas.com

Dallas, Texas

Population: 1,299,544 (9). **Pop. density:** 3,827. **Pop. change (2020-22):** −0.3%. **Area:** 339.6 sq mi. **Racial distribution:** 53.8% white; 24.0% Black; 3.5% Asian; 0.5% Amer. Ind.; <0.05% Pac. Isl.; 8.8% other; 2+ races, 9.3%. **Hispanic pop.:** 42.0%. **Foreign born:** 23.8%. **U.S. citizens:** 82.5%. **Language:** 57.6% English only; 36.5% Spanish.

Employment: 693,675 employed; 3.7% unemployment. **Per capita income:** $37,719. **Below poverty:** 14.7%; 14.2% of families. **Uninsured:** 30.0%. **Educational attainment:** 79.6% HS; 35.6% bachelor's. **Avg. commute:** 26.9 min. 72.3% drive, 11.2% carpool. **Housing units:** 573,597; 89.8% occupied. **Home ownership:** 41.4%. **Avg. home:** $385,500; change (2020-22): 34.2%. **Avg. rent:** $1,178. **Crime rates:** violent: 825; property: 3,421.

Mayor: Eric Johnson, nonpartisan

History: First nonnatives settled, 1841; inc. 1871. Developed as financial and commercial hub; center of TX oil boom from 1930s.

Website: dallascityhall.com

Denver, Colorado

Population: 713,252 (19). **Pop. density:** 4,660. **Pop. change (2020-22):** −0.6%. **Area:** 153.1 sq mi. **Racial distribution:** 68.8% white; 9.0% Black; 3.6% Asian; 0.8% Amer. Ind.; 0.1% Pac. Isl.; 7.7% other; 2+ races, 9.9%. **Hispanic pop.:** 29.4%. **Foreign born:** 14.2%. **U.S. citizens:** 92.2%. **Language:** 75.5% English only; 17.9% Spanish.

Employment: 423,094 employed; 3.1% unemployment. **Per capita income:** $50,642. **Below poverty:** 10.5%; 8.6% of families. **Uninsured:** 12.2%. **Educational attainment:** 90.0% HS; 52.5% bachelor's. **Avg. commute:** 25.5 min. 62.7% drive, 17.2% work from home. **Housing units:** 335,131; 93.7% occupied. **Home ownership:** 49.6%. **Avg. home:** $670,100; change (2020-22): 36.0%. **Avg. rent:** $1,495. **Crime rates:** violent: 932; property: 5,780.

Mayor: Michael Johnston, nonpartisan

History: Miners arrived, 1858; inc. 1861; became territorial capital, 1867. Growth spurred by gold and silver boom; became financial, industrial, cultural center of Rocky Mtn. region.

Website: www.denvergov.org

Detroit, Michigan

Population: 620,376 (29). **Pop. density:** 4,472. **Pop. change (2020-22):** −2.7%. **Area:** 138.7 sq mi. **Racial distribution:** 12.9% white; 77.9% Black; 1.6% Asian; 0.4% Amer. Ind.; <0.05% Pac. Isl.; 3.8% other; 2+ races, 3.3%. **Hispanic pop.:** 7.8%. **Foreign born:** 5.7%. **U.S. citizens:** 96.5%. **Language:** 89.2% English only; 6.4% Spanish.

Employment: 225,646 employed; 8.0% unemployment. **Per capita income:** $20,780. **Below poverty:** 27.5%; 26.6% of families. **Uninsured:** 11.6%. **Educational attainment:** 82.6% HS; 16.2% bachelor's. **Avg. commute:** 25.7 min. 67.4% drive, 12.2% carpool. **Housing units:** 327,623; 76.3% occupied. **Home ownership:** 48.3%. **Avg. home:** $250,900; change (2020-22): 13.4%. **Avg. rent:** $899. **Crime rates:** violent: 2,154; property: 3,356.

Mayor: Mike Duggan, nonpartisan

History: Founded by French, 1701; controlled by British, 1760; acquired by U.S., 1796; inc. 1815; capital of state 1837-47. First automobile factory opened, 1899. Major Great Migration destination, 1910-30.

Website: detroitmi.gov

Durham, North Carolina

Population: 291,928 (71). **Pop. density:** 2,531. **Pop. change (2020-22):** 2.7%. **Area:** 115.4 sq mi. **Racial distribution:** 47.0% white; 37.2% Black; 5.3% Asian; 0.4% Amer. Ind.; 0.1% Pac. Isl.; 4.0% other; 2+ races, 6.2%. **Hispanic pop.:** 13.2%. **Foreign**

born: 14.6%. **U.S. citizens:** 90.7%. **Language:** 81.7% English only; 11.2% Spanish.

Employment: 152,985 employed; 3.2% unemployment. **Per capita income:** $39,496. **Below poverty:** 11.9%; 8.9% of families. **Uninsured:** 15.4%. **Educational attainment:** 90.6% HS; 52.8% bachelor's. **Avg. commute:** 22.5 min. 70.7% drive, 14.6% work from home. **Housing units:** 126,044; 93.3% occupied. **Home ownership:** 51.9%. **Avg. home:** $453,600; change (2020-22): 39.0%. **Avg. rent:** $1,157. **Crime rates:** violent: 740; property: 3,313.

Mayor: Elaine M. O'Neal, nonpartisan

History: Inc. 1869. Trinity College moved to Durham, 1892, renamed Duke Univ.,1924.

Website: www.durhamnc.gov

El Paso, Texas

Population: 677,456 (22). **Pop. density:** 2,621. **Pop. change (2020-22):** −0.2%. **Area:** 258.5 sq mi. **Racial distribution:** 59.6% white; 3.4% Black; 1.3% Asian; 0.6% Amer. Ind.; 0.2% Pac. Isl.; 14.2% other; 2+ races, 20.7%. **Hispanic pop.** 81.6%. **Foreign born:** 22.8%. **U.S. citizens:** 89.4%. **Language:** 32.8% English only; 65.2% Spanish.

Employment: 296,064 employed; 4.1% unemployment. **Per capita income:** $25,165. **Below poverty:** 15.8%; 15.5% of families. **Uninsured:** 28.8%. **Educational attainment:** 81.4% HS; 26.7% bachelor's. **Avg. commute:** 23.5 min. 79.1% drive, 10.2% carpool. **Housing units:** 258,295; 91.6% occupied. **Home ownership:** 59.8%. **Avg. home:** $237,100; change (2020-22): 33.4%. **Avg. rent:** $910. **Crime rates:** violent: 248; property: 1,247.

Mayor: Oscar Leeser, nonpartisan

History: First nonnatives settled, 1598; inc. 1873; arrival of railroad, 1881, boosted population and industries.

Website: www.elpasotexas.gov

Fort Wayne, Indiana

Population: 267,927 (83). **Pop. density:** 2,421. **Pop. change (2020-22):** 1.3%. **Area:** 110.7 sq mi. **Racial distribution:** 69.7% white; 15.2% Black; 5.5% Asian; 0.2% Amer. Ind.; <0.05% Pac. Isl.; 3.3% other; 2+ races, 6.1%. **Hispanic pop.:** 9.5%. **Foreign born:** 8.6%. **U.S. citizens:** 95.3%. **Language:** 86.5% English only; 6.7% Spanish.

Employment: 127,612 employed; 3.1% unemployment. **Per capita income:** $29,268. **Below poverty:** 12.7%; 11.7% of families. **Uninsured:** 12.5%. **Educational attainment:** 88.9% HS; 28.0% bachelor's. **Avg. commute:** 21.3 min. 80.9% drive. **Housing units:** 115,994; 92.0% occupied. **Home ownership:** 62.5%. **Avg. home:** $214,100; change (2020-22): 26.5%. **Avg. rent:** $823. **Crime rates:** violent: 256; property: 2,242.

Mayor: Tom Henry, Democrat

History: U.S. fort founded, 1794; inc. 1840 prior to Wabash-Erie Canal completion, 1843.

Website: www.cityoffortwayne.org

Fort Worth, Texas

Population: 956,709 (13). **Pop. density:** 2,737. **Pop. change (2020-22):** 3.6%. **Area:** 349.6 sq mi. **Racial distribution:** 55.8% white; 18.8% Black; 4.9% Asian; 0.5% Amer. Ind.; 0.1% Pac. Isl.; 11.3% other; 2+ races, 8.6%. **Hispanic pop.** 35.3%. **Foreign born:** 16.7%. **U.S. citizens:** 89.5%. **Language:** 67.9% English only; 25.4% Spanish.

Employment: 453,953 employed; 3.8% unemployment. **Per capita income:** $32,569. **Below poverty:** 11.2%; 10.1% of families. **Uninsured:** 24.5%. **Educational attainment:** 83.5% HS; 31.0% bachelor's. **Avg. commute:** 27.1 min. 77.3% drive, 11.0% carpool. **Housing units:** 347,206; 91.6% occupied. **Home ownership:** 56.7%. **Avg. home:** $385,500; change (2020-22): 34.2%. **Avg. rent:** $1,187. **Crime rates:** violent: 559; property: 2,621.

Mayor: Mattie Parker, nonpartisan

History: Established as military post, 1849; inc. 1873; oil discovered, 1917.

Website: www.fortworthtexas.gov

Fremont, California

Population: 223,871 (99). **Pop. density:** 2,866. **Pop. change (2020-22):** −2.7%. **Area:** 78.1 sq mi. **Racial distribution:** 21.5% white; 2.8% Black; 61.4% Asian; 0.5% Amer. Ind.; 0.6% Pac. Isl.; 7.1% other; 2+ races, 6.1%. **Hispanic pop.:** 12.5%. **Foreign born:** 48.7%. **U.S. citizens:** 78.2%. **Language:** 36.8% English only; 8.3% Spanish.

Employment: 113,352 employed; 2.8% unemployment. **Per capita income:** $60,881. **Below poverty:** 5.1%; 3.3% of families. **Uninsured:** 2.8%. **Educational attainment:** 92.7% HS; 60.1% bachelor's. **Avg. commute:** 34.5 min. 59.1% drive, 23.0% work from home. **Housing units:** 78,240; 95.4% occupied. **Home ownership:** 61.9%. **Avg. home:** $1,375,000; change (2020-22): 25.0%. **Avg. rent:** $2,591. **Crime rates (2020 MSA):** violent: 440; property: 3,008.

Mayor: Lily Mei, nonpartisan

History: Spanish mission founded, 1797; in 1956 as consolidation of five communities.

Website: www.fremont.gov

Fresno, California

Population: 545,567 (34). **Pop. density:** 4,711. **Pop. change (2020-22):** 0.6%. **Area:** 115.8 sq mi. **Racial distribution:** 49.9% white; 6.8% Black; 14.2% Asian; 1.2% Amer. Ind.; 0.2% Pac. Isl.; 13.1% other; 2+ races, 14.5%. **Hispanic pop.:** 50.0%. **Foreign born:** 19.0%. **U.S. citizens:** 91.0%. **Language:** 56.9% English only; 29.7% Spanish.

Employment: 223,101 employed; 5.0% unemployment. **Per capita income:** $26,368. **Below poverty:** 19.5%; 18.3% of families. **Uninsured:** 10.4%. **Educational attainment:** 79.0% HS; 23.6% bachelor's. **Avg. commute:** 22.4 min. 77.0% drive, 11.3% carpool. **Housing units:** 183,951; 95.0% occupied. **Home ownership:** 47.6%. **Avg. home:** $410,000; change (2020-22): 30.6%. **Avg. rent:** $1,115. **Crime rates (2020):** violent: 665; property: 3,077.

Mayor: Jerry Dyer, nonpartisan

History: Founded by railroad company, 1872; inc. 1885.

Website: www.fresno.gov

Garland, Texas

Population: 240,854 (93). **Pop. density:** 4,217. **Pop. change (2020-22):** −1.9%. **Area:** 57.1 sq mi. **Racial distribution:** 51.4% white; 15.0% Black; 10.9% Asian; 0.8% Amer. Ind.; <0.05% Pac. Isl.; 7.0% other; 2+ races, 14.9%. **Hispanic pop.:** 43.1%. **Foreign born:** 30.1%. **U.S. citizens:** 82.1%. **Language:** 48.9% English only; 36.6% Spanish.

Employment: 125,478 employed; 3.5% unemployment. **Per capita income:** $27,464. **Below poverty:** 9.9%; 9.8% of families. **Uninsured:** 32.1%. **Educational attainment:** 78.2% HS; 23.0% bachelor's. **Avg. commute:** 29.7 min. 76.6% drive, 11.4% carpool. **Housing units:** 82,940; 95.7% occupied. **Home ownership:** 63.0%. **Avg. home:** $385,500; change (2020-22): 34.2%. **Avg. rent:** $1,274. **Crime rates:** violent: 258; property: 2,385.

Mayor: Scott LeMay, nonpartisan

History: Settled 1850s; inc. 1891.

Website: www.garlandtx.gov

Gilbert, Arizona

Population: 275,346 (80). **Pop. density:** 4,013. **Pop. change (2020-22):** 2.3%. **Area:** 68.6 sq mi. **Racial distribution:** 78.2% white; 3.9% Black; 5.7% Asian; 0.8% Amer. Ind.; 0.1% Pac. Isl.; 3.5% other; 2+ races, 7.9%. **Hispanic pop.:** 17.1%. **Foreign born:** 9.3%. **U.S. citizens:** 97.0%. **Language:** 85.6% English only; 7.2% Spanish.

Employment: 143,692 employed; 2.7% unemployment. **Per capita income:** $43,155. **Below poverty:** 5.3%; 3.7% of families. **Uninsured:** 7.4%. **Educational attainment:** 96.4% HS; 46.4% bachelor's. **Avg. commute:** 27.2 min. 71.7% drive, 17.0% work from home. **Housing units:** 92,375; 95.7% occupied. **Home ownership:** 74.2%. **Avg. home:** $477,900; change (2020-22): 43.5%. **Avg. rent:** $1,662. **Crime rates (2020 MSA):** violent: 464 ; property: 2,217.

Mayor: Brigette Peterson, nonpartisan

History: Est. 1902; inc. 1920.

Website: www.gilbertaz.gov

Glendale, Arizona

Population: 252,136 (90). **Pop. density:** 3,820. **Pop. change (2020-22):** 1.3%. **Area:** 66.0 sq mi. **Racial distribution:** 64.0% white; 7.2% Black; 4.2% Asian; 1.8% Amer. Ind.; 0.2% Pac. Isl.; 7.7% other; 2+ races, 15.0%. **Hispanic pop.:** 40.2%. **Foreign born:** 16.9%. **U.S. citizens:** 90.5%. **Language:** 65.9% English only; 26.1% Spanish.

Employment: 125,289 employed; 3.6% unemployment. **Per capita income:** $27,711. **Below poverty:** 14.3%; 13.2% of families. **Uninsured:** 17.0%. **Educational attainment:** 83.5% HS; 22.1% bachelor's. **Avg. commute:** 28.5 min. 73.9% drive, 11.6% carpool. **Housing units:** 89,455; 93.9% occupied. **Home ownership:** 55.9%. **Avg. home:** $477,900; change (2020-22): 43.5%. **Avg. rent:** $1,138. **Crime rates (2020 MSA):** violent: 464 ; property: 2,217.

Mayor: Jerry Weiers, nonpartisan

History: Est. 1892; inc. 1910.

Website: www.glendaleaz.com

Greensboro, North Carolina

Population: 301,115 (69). **Pop. density:** 2,291. **Pop. change (2020-22):** 1.4%. **Area:** 131.4 sq mi. **Racial distribution:** 43.6% white; 43.1% Black; 5.3% Asian; 0.4% Amer. Ind.; 0.1% Pac. Isl.; 3.1% other; 2+ races, 4.4%. **Hispanic pop.:** 8.4%. **Foreign born:** 12.1%. **U.S. citizens:** 93.6%. **Language:** 84.9% English only; 6.1% Spanish.

Employment: 138,397 employed; 4.3% unemployment. **Per capita income:** $31,812. **Below poverty:** 15.4%; 13.2% of families. **Uninsured:** 13.7%. **Educational attainment:** 90.2% HS; 39.5% bachelor's. **Avg. commute:** 21.8 min. 78.2% drive. **Housing units:** 132,010; 89.9% occupied. **Home ownership:** 50.1%. **Avg. home:** $270,300; change (2020-22): 35.7%. **Avg. rent:** $944. **Crime rates:** violent: 874; property: 3,520.

Mayor: Nancy Vaughan, nonpartisan

History: Est. c. 1740; site of Revolutionary War conflict, 1781, between namesake Gen. Nathanael Greene and Gen. Cornwallis; inc. 1807. Origin of civil rights sit-in movement.

Website: www.greensboro-nc.gov

Henderson, Nevada

Population: 331,415 (57). **Pop. density:** 3,114. **Pop. change (2020-22):** 3.9%. **Area:** 106.4 sq mi. **Racial distribution:** 68.9% white; 6.2% Black; 9.1% Asian; 0.7% Amer. Ind.; 0.7% Pac. Isl.; 5.4% other; 2+ races, 8.9%. **Hispanic pop.:** 18.6%. **Foreign born:** 13.8%. **U.S. citizens:** 95.6%. **Language:** 80.5% English only; 10.4% Spanish.

Employment: 159,077 employed; 5.4% unemployment. **Per capita income:** $43,264. **Below poverty:** 7.3%; 5.0% of families. **Uninsured:** 8.8%. **Educational attainment:** 93.9% HS; 34.8% bachelor's. **Avg. commute:** 23.7 min. 77.8% drive, 11.2% work from home. **Housing units:** 131,875; 92.0% occupied. **Home ownership:** 64.6%. **Avg. home:** $466,400; change (2020-22): 40.9%. **Avg. rent:** $1,456. **Crime rates:** violent: 229; property: 1,650.

Mayor: Michelle Romero, nonpartisan
History: Early growth spurred by WWII magnesium mining; inc. 1953.
Website: www.cityofhenderson.com

Honolulu, Hawaii

Population: 343,421 (56). **Pop. density:** 5,665. **Pop. change (2020-22):** –1.4%. **Area:** 60.6 sq mi. **Racial distribution:** 17.3% white; 1.9% Black; 52.6% Asian; 0.2% Amer. Ind.; 8.1% Pac. Isl.; 1.2% other; 2+ races, 18.8%. **Hispanic pop.:** 7.2%. **Foreign born:** 27.5%. **U.S. citizens:** 88.3%. **Language:** 64.6% English only; 1.6% Spanish.

Employment: 442,291 employed; 3.5% unemployment. **Per capita income:** $41,571. **Below poverty:** 10.5%; 7.2% of families. **Uninsured:** 5.8%. **Educational attainment:** 90.4% HS; 38.4% bachelor's. **Avg. commute:** 22.7 min. 57.7% drive, 13.1% carpool. **Housing units:** 155,184; 85.9% occupied. **Home ownership:** 47.6%. **Avg. home:** $1,126,700; change (2020-22): 32.3%. **Avg. rent:** $1,620. **Crime rates:** violent: 227; property: 2,750.

Mayor: Rick Blangiardi, nonpartisan
History: Europeans entered harbor, 1794; declared capital of the Hawaii Kingdom by King Kamehameha III, 1850. Pearl Harbor naval base attacked by Japanese, Dec. 7, 1941.
Website: www.honolulu.gov

Houston, Texas

Population: 2,302,878 (4). **Pop. density:** 3,595. **Pop. change (2020-22):** 0.1%. **Area:** 640.6 sq mi. **Racial distribution:** 46.8% white; 22.6% Black; 6.8% Asian; 0.5% Amer. Ind.; 0.1% Pac. Isl.; 12.5% other; 2+ races, 10.8%. **Hispanic pop.:** 44.5%. **Foreign born:** 28.9%. **U.S. citizens:** 80.6%. **Language:** 51.9% English only; 38.2% Spanish.

Employment: 1,107,526 employed; 4.1% unemployment. **Per capita income:** $35,578. **Below poverty:** 16.1%; 16.0% of families. **Uninsured:** 31.2%. **Educational attainment:** 79.5% HS; 34.7% bachelor's. **Avg. commute:** 27.5 min. 73.7% drive. **Housing units:** 990,632; 88.7% occupied. **Home ownership:** 42.5%. **Avg. home:** $345,000; change (2020-22): 30.8%. **Avg. rent:** $1,136. **Crime rates:** violent: 1,211; property: 4,106.

Mayor: Sylvester Turner, nonpartisan
History: Founded 1836; inc. 1837; capital of Rep. of Texas, 1837-39; developed rapidly after completion of channel to Gulf of Mexico, 1914. World center of oil, natural gas technology.
Website: www.houstontx.gov

Huntsville, Alabama

Population: 221,933 (100). **Pop. density:** 1,006. **Pop. change (2020-22):** 2.6%. **Area:** 220.7 sq mi. **Racial distribution:** 59.9% white; 30.9% Black; 2.2% Asian; 0.4% Amer. Ind.; 0.1% Pac. Isl.; 2.1% other; 2+ races, 4.3%. **Hispanic pop.:** 6.4%. **Foreign born:** 6.4%. **U.S. citizens:** 96.7%. **Language:** 92.0% English only; 4.4% Spanish.

Employment: 103,435 employed; 2.3% unemployment. **Per capita income:** $38,838. **Below poverty:** 12.8%; 10.8% of families. **Uninsured:** 14.4%. **Educational attainment:** 91.1% HS; 44.8% bachelor's. **Avg. commute:** 19.4 min. 81.8% drive. **Housing units:** 98,740; 92.2% occupied. **Home ownership:** 57.0%. **Avg. home:** $324,900; change (2020-22): 31.0%. **Avg. rent:** $912.

Mayor: Tommy Battle, nonpartisan
History: Settled by John Hunt 1805; founded as Twickenham 1809; inc. as Huntsville 1811; temporary state capital 1819-20.
Website: www.huntsvilleal.gov

Indianapolis, Indiana

Population: 880,621 (16). **Pop. density:** 2,435. **Pop. change (2020-22):** –0.7%. **Area:** 361.6 sq mi. **Racial distribution:** 57.7% white; 28.8% Black; 3.9% Asian; 0.2% Amer. Ind.; <0.05% Pac. Isl.; 4.1% other; 2+ races, 5.4%. **Hispanic pop.:** 10.8%. **Foreign born:** 10.0%. **U.S. citizens:** 93.2%. **Language:** 85.6% English only; 8.2% Spanish.

Employment: 447,099 employed; 3.2% unemployment. **Per capita income:** $31,538. **Below poverty:** 14.2%; 11.9% of families. **Uninsured:** 13.1%. **Educational attainment:** 86.7% HS; 32.9% bachelor's. **Avg. commute:** 23.9 min. 77.6% drive. **Housing units:** 395,536; 89.1% occupied. **Home ownership:** 54.5%. **Avg. home:** $294,600; change (2020-22): 29.4%. **Avg. rent:** $962. **Crime rates:** violent: 718; property: 3,442.

Mayor: Joe Hogsett, Democrat
History: Founded 1821; became planned state capital, 1825.
Website: www.indy.gov

Irvine, California

Population: 313,685 (63). **Pop. density:** 4,781. **Pop. change (2020-22):** 1.5%. **Area:** 65.6 sq mi. **Racial distribution:** 43.0% white; 1.9% Black; 42.9% Asian; 0.3% Amer. Ind.; 0.3% Pac. Isl.; 2.8% other; 2+ races, 8.9%. **Hispanic pop.:** 11.9%. **Foreign born:** 39.4%. **U.S. citizens:** 80.7%. **Language:** 50.4% English only; 7.0% Spanish.

Employment: 142,407 employed; 3.1% unemployment. **Per capita income:** $53,857. **Below poverty:** 13.4%; 8.1% of families. **Uninsured:** 5.7%. **Educational attainment:** 96.2% HS; 68.6% bachelor's. **Avg. commute:** 25.1 min. 67.1% drive, 18.5% work from home. **Housing units:** 115,917; 92.5% occupied. **Home ownership:** 44.5%. **Avg. home:** $1,235,000; change (2020-22): 37.2%. **Avg. rent:** $2,533. **Crime rates (2020):** violent: 51; property: 1,499.

Mayor: Farrah N. Khan, nonpartisan
History: Univ. of CA–Irvine campus announced, 1959; planned city developed around campus; inc. 1971.
Website: www.cityofirvine.org

Irving, Texas

Population: 254,715 (88). **Pop. density:** 3,803. **Pop. change (2020-22):** –0.8%. **Area:** 67.0 sq mi. **Racial distribution:** 40.5% white; 13.6% Black; 21.5% Asian; 0.6% Amer. Ind.; <0.05% Pac. Isl.; 14.5% other; 2+ races, 9.2%. **Hispanic pop.:** 43.2%. **Foreign born:** 40.1%. **U.S. citizens:** 71.0%. **Language:** 39.9% English only; 37.8% Spanish.

Employment: 133,700 employed; 3.4% unemployment. **Per capita income:** $34,023. **Below poverty:** 9.3%; 8.3% of families. **Uninsured:** 25.3%. **Educational attainment:** 79.8% HS; 39.4% bachelor's. **Avg. commute:** 24.1 min. 75.0% drive, 10.4% carpool, 11.2% work from home. **Housing units:** 98,176; 93.5% occupied. **Home ownership:** 36.8%. **Avg. home:** $385,500; change (2020-22): 34.2%. **Avg. rent:** $1,277. **Crime rates:** violent: 334; property: 2,440.

Mayor: Rick Stopfer, nonpartisan
History: Founded 1903; inc. 1914; remained small until 1950s.
Website: www.cityofirving.org

Jacksonville, Florida

Population: 971,319 (11). **Pop. density:** 1,300. **Pop. change (2020-22):** 2.1%. **Area:** 747.3 sq mi. **Racial distribution:** 54.5% white; 30.7% Black; 4.9% Asian; 0.2% Amer. Ind.; 0.1% Pac. Isl.; 3.1% other; 2+ races, 6.6%. **Hispanic pop.:** 10.9%. **Foreign born:** 12.0%. **U.S. citizens:** 94.8%. **Language:** 84.3% English only; 7.4% Spanish.

Employment: 469,419 employed; 3.1% unemployment. **Per capita income:** $32,654. **Below poverty:** 13.0%; 11.0% of families. **Uninsured:** 16.6%. **Educational attainment:** 90.3% HS; 30.2% bachelor's. **Avg. commute:** 24.6 min. 77.3% drive. **Housing units:** 406,409; 90.2% occupied. **Home ownership:** 56.6%. **Avg. home:** $386,500; change (2020-22): 38.5%. **Avg. rent:** $1,146. **Crime rates (2020):** violent: 698; property: 2,871.

Mayor: Donna Deegan, Democrat
History: Settled as Cow Ford; renamed after Andrew Jackson, 1822; inc. 1832; scene of Civil War conflict, 1864.
Website: www.coj.net

Jersey City, New Jersey

Population: 286,670 (74). **Pop. density:** 19,438. **Pop. change (2020-22):** –1.8%. **Area:** 14.7 sq mi. **Racial distribution:** 32.1% white; 22.5% Black; 25.4% Asian; 0.6% Amer. Ind.; <0.05% Pac. Isl.; 9.7% other; 2+ races, 9.7%. **Hispanic pop.:** 27.5%. **Foreign born:** 41.6%. **U.S. citizens:** 78.1%. **Language:** 47.9% English only; 21.5% Spanish.

Employment: 140,761 employed; 3.7% unemployment. **Per capita income:** $48,404. **Below poverty:** 14.1%; 12.7% of families. **Uninsured:** 12.7%. **Educational attainment:** 89.5% HS; 51.1% bachelor's. **Avg. commute:** 36.7 min. 29.2% drive, 41.6% public trans., 14.6% work from home. **Housing units:** 127,003; 91.1% occupied. **Home ownership:** 29.6%. **Avg. home:** $589,200; change (2020-22): 33.2%. **Avg. rent:** $1,611.

Mayor: Steven M. Fulop, Democrat
History: Chartered as town by British 1668; scene of Revolutionary War conflict, 1779. Important station on Underground Railroad.
Website: www.jerseycitynj.gov

Kansas City, Missouri

Population: 509,297 (37). **Pop. density:** 1,618. **Pop. change (2020-22):** 0.2%. **Area:** 314.7 sq mi. **Racial distribution:** 59.7% white; 26.5% Black; 2.7% Asian; 0.4% Amer. Ind.; 0.3% Pac. Isl.; 4.1% other; 2+ races, 6.3%. **Hispanic pop.:** 10.7%. **Foreign born:**

8.0%. **U.S. citizens:** 95.6%. **Language:** 88.1% English only; 6.8% Spanish.

Employment: 252,427 employed; 2.8% unemployment. **Per capita income:** $35,352. **Below poverty:** 12.9%; 10.6% of families. **Uninsured:** 16.0%. **Educational attainment:** 91.0% HS; 36.5% bachelor's. **Avg. commute:** 22.1 min. 77.2% drive. **Housing units:** 240,009; 89.0% occupied. **Home ownership:** 53.9%. **Avg. home:** $309,500; change (2020-22): 30.4%. **Avg. rent:** $1,040. **Crime rates:** violent: 1,477; property: 4,284.

Mayor: Quinton Lucas, nonpartisan

History: Est. by 1838 at confluence of Missouri and Kansas Rivers; inc. 1850.

Website: www.kcmo.gov

Laredo, Texas

Population: 256,187 (87). **Pop. density:** 2,398. **Pop. change (2020-22):** 0.3%. **Area:** 106.8 sq mi. **Racial distribution:** 68.0% white; 0.4% Black; 0.5% Asian; 0.2% Amer. Ind.; <0.05% Pac. Isl.; 4.2% other; 2+ races, 26.7%. **Hispanic pop.:** 95.5%. **Foreign born:** 25.2%. **U.S. citizens:** 82.9%. **Language:** 10.3% English only; 88.9% Spanish.

Employment: 107,956 employed; 4.1% unemployment. **Per capita income:** $21,193. **Below poverty:** 18.4%; 19.9% of families. **Uninsured:** 40.5%. **Educational attainment:** 69.7% HS; 20.0% bachelor's. **Avg. commute:** 21.0 min. 79.6% drive, 11.6% carpool. **Housing units:** 79,251; 91.7% occupied. **Home ownership:** 62.2%. **Avg. rent:** $902. **Crime rates:** violent: 301; property: 1,188.

Mayor: Victor D. Treviño, nonpartisan

History: Founded by Spanish colonists, 1755; part of U.S. from 1848. Fast growth fueled by immigration; principal port of entry into Mexico.

Website: www.cityoflaredo.com

Las Vegas, Nevada

Population: 656,274 (24). **Pop. density:** 4,626. **Pop. change (2020-22):** 1.5%. **Area:** 141.9 sq mi. **Racial distribution:** 55.5% white; 11.5% Black; 6.8% Asian; 1.0% Amer. Ind.; 0.8% Pac. Isl.; 13.2% other; 2+ races, 11.1%. **Hispanic pop.:** 34.1%. **Foreign born:** 20.8%. **U.S. citizens:** 89.1%. **Language:** 67.2% English only; 24.9% Spanish.

Employment: 296,106 employed; 6.1% unemployment. **Per capita income:** $33,363. **Below poverty:** 13.2%; 11.0% of families. **Uninsured:** 17.6%. **Educational attainment:** 85.4% HS; 25.9% bachelor's. **Avg. commute:** 25.8 min. 75.5% drive. **Housing units:** 257,779; 91.7% occupied. **Home ownership:** 53.7%. **Avg. home:** $466,400; change (2020-22): 40.9%. **Avg. rent:** $1,219. **Crime rates:** violent: 468; property: 2,543.

Mayor: Carolyn G. Goodman, nonpartisan

History: Occupied by Mormons 1855-57; bought by railroad 1903; city of Las Vegas inc. 1911; gambling legalized 1931.

Website: www.lasvegasnevada.gov

Lexington-Fayette, Kentucky

Population: 320,347 (60). **Pop. density:** 1,129. **Pop. change (2020-22):** –0.7%. **Area:** 283.9 sq mi. **Racial distribution:** 72.8% white; 14.6% Black; 4.0% Asian; 0.2% Amer. Ind.; <0.05% Pac. Isl.; 3.0% other; 2+ races, 5.4%. **Hispanic pop.:** 7.4%. **Foreign born:** 10.1%. **U.S. citizens:** 93.2%. **Language:** 86.6% English only; 6.0% Spanish.

Employment: 170,528 employed; 3.1% unemployment. **Per capita income:** $37,475. **Below poverty:** 14.9%; 9.8% of families. **Uninsured:** 9.4%. **Educational attainment:** 92.4% HS; 45.6% bachelor's. **Avg. commute:** 20.7 min. 77.0% drive. **Housing units:** 145,092; 92.5% occupied. **Home ownership:** 54.1%. **Avg. home:** $242,500; change (2020-22): 20.5%. **Avg. rent:** $967. **Crime rates:** violent: 288; property: 2,718.

Mayor: Linda Gorton, nonpartisan

History: Site founded and named in 1775 after site of the Revolutionary War's opening battle at Lexington, MA; chartered 1782. Merged with Fayette County, 1974.

Website: www.lexingtonky.gov

Lincoln, Nebraska

Population: 292,627 (70). **Pop. density:** 2,953. **Pop. change (2020-22):** 0.4%. **Area:** 99.1 sq mi. **Racial distribution:** 82.8% white; 4.1% Black; 4.6% Asian; 0.7% Amer. Ind.; 0.1% Pac. Isl.; 1.9% other; 2+ races, 5.9%. **Hispanic pop.:** 8.1%. **Foreign born:** 9.1%. **U.S. citizens:** 95.4%. **Language:** 87.3% English only; 4.7% Spanish.

Employment: 159,128 employed; 2.2% unemployment. **Per capita income:** $33,955. **Below poverty:** 12.9%; 7.7% of families. **Uninsured:** 9.9%. **Educational attainment:** 92.9% HS; 40.1% bachelor's. **Avg. commute:** 18.9 min. 78.2% drive. **Housing units:** 122,502; 95.0% occupied. **Home ownership:** 56.6%. **Avg. home:** $273,100; change (2020-22): 24.2%. **Avg. rent:** $920. **Crime rates:** violent: 421; property: 2,724.

Mayor: Leirion Gaylor Baird, nonpartisan

History: Originally called Lancaster; chosen state capital, 1867, renamed after Abraham Lincoln; inc. 1871.

Website: www.lincoln.ne.gov

Long Beach, California

Population: 451,307 (43). **Pop. density:** 8,906. **Pop. change (2020-22):** –3.0%. **Area:** 50.7 sq mi. **Racial distribution:** 47.0% white; 12.1% Black; 13.0% Asian; 1.0% Amer. Ind.; 0.5% Pac. Isl.; 17.7% other; 2+ races, 8.7%. **Hispanic pop.:** 43.9%. **Foreign born:** 25.1%. **U.S. citizens:** 87.6%. **Language:** 54.0% English only; 34.3% Spanish.

Employment: 219,167 employed; 5.0% unemployment. **Per capita income:** $35,856. **Below poverty:** 13.8%; 11.1% of families. **Uninsured:** 12.0%. **Educational attainment:** 80.6% HS; 32.8% bachelor's. **Avg. commute:** 30.7 min. 71.6% drive, 10.6% work from home. **Housing units:** 179,479; 94.7% occupied. **Home ownership:** 40.5%. **Avg. home:** $849,400; change (2020-22): 26.2%. **Avg. rent:** $1,516. **Crime rates (2020):** violent: 506; property: 2,747.

Mayor: Rex Richardson, nonpartisan

History: Settled c. 1784 by Spanish; by 1884, developed as harbor; inc. 1888; oil discovered 1921.

Website: www.longbeach.gov

Los Angeles, California

Population: 3,822,238 (2). **Pop. density:** 8,123. **Pop. change (2020-22):** –1.9%. **Area:** 470.5 sq mi. **Racial distribution:** 44.9% white; 8.6% Black; 11.7% Asian; 0.9% Amer. Ind.; 0.2% Pac. Isl.; 24.0% other; 2+ races, 9.8%. **Hispanic pop.:** 48.4%. **Foreign born:** 36.2%. **U.S. citizens:** 81.6%. **Language:** 41.9% English only; 41.5% Spanish.

Employment: 1,947,280 employed; 5.0% unemployment. **Per capita income:** $39,378. **Below poverty:** 15.0%; 12.2% of families. **Uninsured:** 14.7%. **Educational attainment:** 78.4% HS; 36.2% bachelor's. **Avg. commute:** 31.6 min. 65.2% drive, 12.4% work from home. **Housing units:** 1,503,915; 92.1% occupied. **Home ownership:** 36.9%. **Avg. home:** $849,400; change (2020-22): 26.2%. **Avg. rent:** $1,641. **Crime rates (2020):** violent: 722; property: 2,148.

Mayor: Karen Bass, nonpartisan

History: Est. by Mexicans near Spanish mission, 1781; ceded to U.S., 1848; inc. 1850; grew rapidly after coming of railroads, 1876 and 1885. Film and defense industries drove 20th-century growth.

Website: lacity.gov

Louisville/Jefferson County, Kentucky

Population: 624,444 (27). **Pop. density:** 2,373. **Pop. change (2020-22):** –1.3%. **Area:** 263.2 sq mi. **Racial distribution:** 67.1% white; 23.8% Black; 2.7% Asian; 0.1% Amer. Ind.; 0.1% Pac. Isl.; 1.4% other; 2+ races, 4.8%. **Hispanic pop.:** 6.5%. **Foreign born:** 8.6%. **U.S. citizens:** 95.2%. **Language:** 89.3% English only; 5.2% Spanish.

Employment: 380,623 employed; 3.8% unemployment. **Per capita income:** $34,195. **Below poverty:** 13.1%; 11.2% of families. **Uninsured:** 7.7%. **Educational attainment:** 90.2% HS; 31.6% bachelor's. **Avg. commute:** 22.7 min. 76.6% drive. **Housing units:** 285,274; 90.4% occupied. **Home ownership:** 60.2%. **Avg. home:** $254,200; change (2020-22): 19.8%. **Avg. rent:** $931. **Crime rates:** violent: 981; property: 3,310.

Mayor: Craig Greenberg, Democrat

History: Est. 1778; named for Louis XVI of France; inc. 1828; base for Union forces in Civil War.

Website: louisvilleky.gov

Lubbock, Texas

Population: 263,930 (85). **Pop. density:** 1,912. **Pop. change (2020-22):** 2.3%. **Area:** 138.0 sq mi. **Racial distribution:** 72.2% white; 8.1% Black; 2.7% Asian; 0.7% Amer. Ind.; 0.1% Pac. Isl.; 6.3% other; 2+ races, 9.9%. **Hispanic pop.:** 37.1%. **Foreign born:** 6.7%. **U.S. citizens:** 95.8%. **Language:** 78.8% English only; 17.4% Spanish.

Employment: 133,533 employed; 3.4% unemployment. **Per capita income:** $30,393. **Below poverty:** 19.1%; 12.3% of families. **Uninsured:** 18.0%. **Educational attainment:** 88.2% HS; 33.9% bachelor's. **Avg. commute:** 16.0 min. 78.8% drive, 11.9% carpool. **Housing units:** 110,296; 90.4% occupied. **Home ownership:** 51.1%. **Avg. home:** $229,800; change (2020-22): 25.7%. **Avg. rent:** $1,000. **Crime rates:** violent: 1,062; property: 3,669.

Mayor: Tray Payne, nonpartisan

History: Became county seat, 1891; inc. 1909.

Website: ci.lubbock.tx.us

Madison, Wisconsin

Population: 272,903 (82). **Pop. density:** 3,339. **Pop. change (2020-22):** 1.0%. **Area:** 81.7 sq mi. **Racial distribution:** 76.1% white; 6.8% Black; 8.9% Asian; 0.3% Amer. Ind.; <0.05% Pac. Isl.; 1.6% other; 2+ races, 6.2%. **Hispanic pop.:** 7.8%. **Foreign born:** 12.0%. **U.S. citizens:** 92.6%. **Language:** 86.3% English only; 5.1% Spanish.

Employment: 157,530 employed; 2.1% unemployment. **Per capita income:** $42,693. **Below poverty:** 17.3%; 5.9% of families. **Uninsured:** 5.1%. **Educational attainment:** 95.6% HS; 58.5% bachelor's. **Avg. commute:** 19.6 min. 60.5% drive, 12.1% work from home. **Housing units:** 122,561; 95.7% occupied. **Home**

ownership: 47.6%. Avg. home: $392,700; change (2020-22): 20.3%. Avg. rent: $1,212. Crime rates: violent: 308; property: 2,520.

Mayor: Satya Rhodes-Conway, nonpartisan

History: Selected as site for state capital, named for James Madison, 1836; chartered 1856.

Website: www.cityofmadison.com

Memphis, Tennessee

Population: 621,056 (28). Pop. density: 2,106. Pop. change (2020-22): –1.6%. Area: 294.9 sq mi. Racial distribution: 27.1% white; 64.6% Black; 1.7% Asian; 0.3% Amer. Ind.; <0.05% Pac. Isl.; 3.7% other; 2+ races, 2.7%. Hispanic pop.: 7.7%. Foreign born: 6.1%. U.S. citizens: 96.0%. Language: 90.5% English only; 6.5% Spanish.

Employment: 275,631 employed; 5.1% unemployment. Per capita income: $28,258. Below poverty: 19.6%; 18.9% of families. Uninsured: 20.0%. Educational attainment: 86.6% HS; 27.1% bachelor's. Avg. commute: 21.7 min. 81.0% drive. Housing units: 290,177; 86.0% occupied. Home ownership: 46.8%. Avg. home: $271,600; change (2020-22): 22.8%. Avg. rent: $965. Crime rates: violent: 2,431; property: 5,279.

Mayor: Jim Strickland, nonpartisan

History: French, Spanish, and U.S. forts by 1797; settled by 1819; inc. 1826; surrendered charter to state 1879 after yellow fever epidemics; rechartered as city 1893.

Website: www.memphistn.gov

Mesa, Arizona

Population: 512,498 (36). Pop. density: 3,638. Pop. change (2020-22): 1.3%. Area: 140.9 sq mi. Racial distribution: 75.1% white; 4.4% Black; 2.3% Asian; 2.2% Amer. Ind.; 0.3% Pac. Isl.; 6.6% other; 2+ races, 9.1%. Hispanic pop.: 27.5%. Foreign born: 11.8%. U.S. citizens: 92.4%. Language: 79.2% English only; 17.2% Spanish.

Employment: 260,957 employed; 3.4% unemployment. Per capita income: $33,362. Below poverty: 10.4%; 8.8% of families. Uninsured: 15.8%. Educational attainment: 90.4% HS; 29.5% bachelor's. Avg. commute: 25.3 min. 71.1% drive, 12.2% carpool, 11.6% work from home. Housing units: 217,404; 87.6% occupied. Home ownership: 62.5%. Avg. home: $477,900; change (2020-22): 43.5%. Avg. rent: $1,196. Crime rates (2020): violent: 372; property: 1,846.

Mayor: John Giles, nonpartisan

History: Founded by Mormons from Utah and Idaho, 1878; inc. 1883.

Website: www.mesaaz.gov

Miami, Florida

Population: 449,514 (44). Pop. density: 12,488. Pop. change (2020-22): 1.5%. Area: 36.0 sq mi. Racial distribution: 55.0% white; 15.2% Black; 1.4% Asian; 0.3% Amer. Ind.; <0.05% Pac. Isl.; 5.2% other; 2+ races, 22.9%. Hispanic pop.: 72.3%. Foreign born: 58.1%. U.S. citizens: 71.6%. Language: 22.2% English only; 70.1% Spanish.

Employment: 230,250 employed; 2.6% unemployment. Per capita income: $34,295. Below poverty: 19.4%; 16.9% of families. Uninsured: 26.0%. Educational attainment: 79.2% HS; 33.1% bachelor's. Avg. commute: 28.0 min. 65.9% drive, 10.1% work from home. Housing units: 211,084; 86.0% occupied. Home ownership: 30.0%. Avg. home: $557,500; change (2020-22): 40.1%. Avg. rent: $1,361. Crime rates (2020): violent: 556; property: 2,750.

Mayor: Francis Suarez, nonpartisan

History: Site of fort, 1836; inc. 1896. Modern city developed into financial and tourism center. Land speculation in 1920s added to city's growth.

Website: www.miamigov.com

Milwaukee, Wisconsin

Population: 563,305 (31). Pop. density: 5,857. Pop. change (2020-22): –2.3%. Area: 96.2 sq mi. Racial distribution: 39.9% white; 39.4% Black; 4.5% Asian; 0.6% Amer. Ind.; <0.05% Pac. Isl.; 7.9% other; 2+ races, 7.6%. Hispanic pop.: 19.9%. Foreign born: 10.1%. U.S. citizens: 93.7%. Language: 79.0% English only; 15.2% Spanish.

Employment: 257,768 employed; 4.2% unemployment. Per capita income: $25,564. Below poverty: 20.8%; 19.4% of families. Uninsured: 13.5%. Educational attainment: 84.9% HS; 25.5% bachelor's. Avg. commute: 22.3 min. 71.2% drive. Housing units: 257,267; 89.2% occupied. Home ownership: 40.9%. Avg. home: $345,300; change (2020-22): 18.5%. Avg. rent: $910. Crime rates: violent: 1,586; property: 4,188.

Mayor: Cavalier Johnson, nonpartisan

History: Indian trading post by 1674; inc. 1846. Famous beer industry.

Website: city.milwaukee.gov

Minneapolis, Minnesota

Population: 425,096 (46). Pop. density: 7,872. Pop. change (2020-22): –1.3%. Area: 54.0 sq mi. Racial distribution: 63.1% white; 18.4% Black; 5.7% Asian; 1.3% Amer. Ind.; <0.05% Pac. Isl.; 4.6% other; 2+ races, 6.9%. Hispanic pop.: 9.8%. Foreign born: 14.8%. U.S. citizens: 93.0%. Language: 78.6% English only; 7.4% Spanish.

Employment: 238,268 employed; 2.6% unemployment. Per capita income: $43,925. Below poverty: 16.0%; 10.1% of families. Uninsured: 7.9%. Educational attainment: 90.7% HS; 52.6% bachelor's. Avg. commute: 23.2 min. 56.4% drive, 10.1% public trans., 15.8% work from home. Housing units: 194,532; 93.8% occupied. Home ownership: 48.1%. Avg. home: $375,400; change (2020-22): 19.1%. Avg. rent: $1,159. Crime rates: violent: 1,281; property: 4,189.

Mayor: Jacob Frey, Democrat (DFL)

History: Visited by French missionary Louis Hennepin, 1680; included in area of military reservations, 1819; inc. 1867.

Website: www.minneapolismn.gov

Nashville-Davidson, Tennessee

Population: 683,622 (21). Pop. density: 1,437. Pop. change (2020-22): –0.9%. Area: 475.6 sq mi. Racial distribution: 60.5% white; 27.2% Black; 3.6% Asian; 0.2% Amer. Ind.; <0.05% Pac. Isl.; 3.6% other; 2+ races, 4.9%. Hispanic pop.: 10.6%. Foreign born: 13.7%. U.S. citizens: 91.7%. Language: 82.2% English only; 8.7% Spanish.

Employment: 401,294 employed; 2.8% unemployment. Per capita income: $39,509. Below poverty: 12.4%; 10.7% of families. Uninsured: 15.9%. Educational attainment: 90.0% HS; 43.9% bachelor's. Avg. commute: 25.0 min. 72.8% drive, 12.7% work from home. Housing units: 312,912; 90.4% occupied. Home ownership: 54.1%. Avg. home: $403,700; change (2020-22): 35.1%. Avg. rent: $1,250. Crime rates (2020): violent: 1,156; property: 4,073.

Mayor: John Cooper, nonpartisan

History: Est. 1779; first chartered, 1806; became permanent state capital 1843. Home of Grand Ole Opry.

Website: www.nashville.gov

New Orleans, Louisiana

Population: 369,749 (53). Pop. density: 2,181. Pop. change (2020-22): –3.5%. Area: 169.5 sq mi. Racial distribution: 32.7% white; 58.1% Black; 2.7% Asian; 0.2% Amer. Ind.; <0.05% Pac. Isl.; 2.1% other; 2+ races, 4.1%. Hispanic pop.: 5.6%. Foreign born: 5.4%. U.S. citizens: 97.4%. Language: 91.6% English only; 4.0% Spanish.

Employment: 168,780 employed; 4.5% unemployment. Per capita income: $34,036. Below poverty: 21.3%; 17.1% of families. Uninsured: 12.0%. Educational attainment: 88.2% HS; 39.1% bachelor's. Avg. commute: 23.5 min. 65.6% drive. Housing units: 193,376; 81.0% occupied. Home ownership: 48.0%. Avg. home: $285,600; change (2020-22): 18.8%. Avg. rent: $1,079. Crime rates (2020): violent: 1,324; property: 4,540.

Mayor: LaToya Cantrell, Democrat

History: Founded by French colonists, 1718; became major seaport on Mississippi R.; acquired by U.S. in Louisiana Purchase, 1803; inc. 1805. Hurricane Katrina, 2005, inflicted major damage and killed 1,450+.

Website: www.nola.gov

New York, New York

Population: 8,335,897 (1). Pop. density: 27,744. Pop. change (2020-22): –4.6%. Area: 300.5 sq mi. Racial distribution: 39.8% white; 23.4% Black; 14.2% Asian; 0.5% Amer. Ind.; 0.1% Pac. Isl.; 14.9% other; 2+ races, 7.1%. Hispanic pop.: 28.9%. Foreign born: 36.3%. U.S. citizens: 84.8%. Language: 52.1% English only; 23.5% Spanish.

Employment: 3,867,550 employed; 5.7% unemployment. Per capita income: $43,952. Below poverty: 15.3%; 13.6% of families. Uninsured: 9.8%. Educational attainment: 83.2% HS; 39.6% bachelor's. Avg. commute: 41.4 min. 22.4% drive, 49.7% public trans., 10.7% work from home. Housing units: 3,590,995; 90.5% occupied. Home ownership: 33.2%. Avg. home: $589,200; change (2020-22): 33.2%. Avg. rent: $1,579.

Mayor: Eric Adams, Democrat

History: Trading post est., 1624; British took control from Dutch, 1664, named city New York; U.S. capital, 1785-90. Under new charter, 1898, city expanded to include five boroughs: Bronx, Brooklyn, Queens, and Staten Island, as well as Manhattan. Sept. 11, 2001, terrorist attacks destroyed World Trade Center, killed more than 2,750.

Website: www.nyc.gov

Newark, New Jersey

Population: 305,344 (66). Pop. density: 12,647. Pop. change (2020-22): –1.7%. Area: 24.1 sq mi. Racial distribution: 22.7% white; 48.2% Black; 1.9% Asian; 0.4% Amer. Ind.; 0.1% Pac. Isl.; 18.3% other; 2+ races, 8.5%. Hispanic pop.: 36.8%. Foreign born: 34.0%. U.S. citizens: 80.5%. Language: 49.1% English only; 33.1% Spanish.

Employment: 114,327 employed; 5.8% unemployment. Per capita income: $22,194. Below poverty: 22.4%; 23.2% of families. Uninsured: 24.1%. Educational attainment: 77.0% HS; 16.0%

bachelor's. **Avg. commute:** 33.7 min. 52.9% drive, 21.4% public trans. **Housing units:** 120,733; 90.9% occupied. **Home ownership:** 23.2%. **Avg. home:** $563,300; change (2020-22): 24.6%. **Avg. rent:** $1,167. **Crime rates:** violent: 490; property: 1,457.

Mayor: Ras J. Baraka, nonpartisan

History: Est. by Puritans, 1666; inc. as city, 1836. Major industry and shipping hub from mid-19th century.

Website: www.newarknj.gov

Norfolk, Virginia

Population: 232,995 (95). **Pop. density:** 4,373. **Pop. change (2020-22):** −2.0%. **Area:** 53.3 sq mi. **Racial distribution:** 45.8% white; 40.7% Black; 3.6% Asian; 0.4% Amer. Ind.; 0.1% Pac. Isl.; 3.2% other; 2+ races, 6.2%. **Hispanic pop.:** 8.6%. **Foreign born:** 7.3%. **U.S. citizens:** 96.6%. **Language:** 89.5% English only; 5.1% Spanish.

Employment: 106,458 employed; 3.5% unemployment. **Per capita income:** $32,811. **Below poverty:** 15.0%; 12.7% of families. **Uninsured:** 14.9%. **Educational attainment:** 88.9% HS; 31.8% bachelor's. **Avg. commute:** 21.8 min. 71.3% drive. **Housing units:** 100,967; 92.0% occupied. **Home ownership:** 43.5%. **Avg. home:** $323,900; change (2020-22): 17.8%. **Avg. rent:** $1,114. **Crime rates:** violent: 739; property: 3,199.

Mayor: Kenneth Cooper Alexander, nonpartisan

History: Founded 1682; burned by colonists to prevent capture by British during Revolutionary War. Inc. as city, 1845. Site of world's largest naval base; major commercial port.

Website: www.norfolk.gov

North Las Vegas, Nevada

Population: 280,543 (77). **Pop. density:** 2,742. **Pop. change (2020-22):** 7.4%. **Area:** 102.3 sq mi. **Racial distribution:** 42.9% white; 22.1% Black; 6.7% Asian; 0.8% Amer. Ind.; 0.7% Pac. Isl.; 13.3% other; 2+ races, 13.6%. **Hispanic pop.:** 42.0%. **Foreign born:** 21.6%. **U.S. citizens:** 88.6%. **Language:** 61.2% English only; 32.0% Spanish.

Employment: 111,028 employed; 7.2% unemployment. **Per capita income:** $25,853. **Below poverty:** 11.0%; 10.7% of families. **Uninsured:** 18.0%. **Educational attainment:** 81.5% HS; 17.2% bachelor's. **Avg. commute:** 27.4 min. 79.1% drive, 10.8% carpool. **Housing units:** 85,930; 94.2% occupied. **Home ownership:** 60.3%. **Avg. home:** $466,400; change (2020-22): 40.9%. **Avg. rent:** $1,323. **Crime rates:** violent: 376; property: 1,666.

Mayor: Pamela Goynes-Brown, nonpartisan

History: Inc. 1946.

Website: www.cityofnorthlasvegas.com

Oakland, California

Population: 430,553 (45). **Pop. density:** 7,694. **Pop. change (2020-22):** −2.3%. **Area:** 56.0 sq mi. **Racial distribution:** 33.4% white; 22.0% Black; 15.7% Asian; 1.0% Amer. Ind.; 0.5% Pac. Isl.; 17.9% other; 2+ races, 9.4%. **Hispanic pop.:** 27.2%. **Foreign born:** 26.6%. **U.S. citizens:** 86.3%. **Language:** 60.6% English only; 21.4% Spanish.

Employment: 200,925 employed; 3.9% unemployment. **Per capita income:** $49,970. **Below poverty:** 12.3%; 10.0% of families. **Uninsured:** 8.9%. **Educational attainment:** 84.7% HS; 47.3% bachelor's. **Avg. commute:** 32.3 min. 49.3% drive, 18.8% public trans, 15.6% work from home. **Housing units:** 180,171; 92.9% occupied. **Home ownership:** 41.3%. **Avg. home:** $1,375,000; change (2020-22): 25.0%. **Avg. rent:** $1,676. **Crime rates (2020):** violent: 1,291; property: 5,166.

Mayor: Sheng Thao, nonpartisan

History: Area settled by Spanish, 1820; inc. 1854.

Website: www.oaklandca.gov

Oklahoma City, Oklahoma

Population: 694,800 (20). **Pop. density:** 1,146. **Pop. change (2020-22):** 1.7%. **Area:** 606.5 sq mi. **Racial distribution:** 64.3% white; 13.8% Black; 4.4% Asian; 3.2% Amer. Ind.; 0.1% Pac. Isl.; 4.7% other; 2+ races, 9.4%. **Hispanic pop.:** 19.9%. **Foreign born:** 11.6%. **U.S. citizens:** 92.8%. **Language:** 80.0% English only; 14.8% Spanish.

Employment: 325,314 employed; 2.9% unemployment. **Per capita income:** $33,162. **Below poverty:** 12.7%; 11.3% of families. **Uninsured:** 20.2%. **Educational attainment:** 87.5% HS; 32.3% bachelor's. **Avg. commute:** 21.7 min. 80.0% drive. **Housing units:** 294,960; 90.0% occupied. **Home ownership:** 60.0%. **Avg. home:** $223,400; change (2020-22): 27.7%. **Avg. rent:** $933. **Crime rates:** violent: 643; property: 3,810.

Mayor: David Holt, nonpartisan

History: Settled during land rush, 1889; inc. 1890; became capital, 1910; oil discovered, 1928. Bomb in 1995 destroyed federal office bldg., killed 168 people.

Website: www.okc.gov

Omaha, Nebraska

Population: 485,153 (40). **Pop. density:** 3,401. **Pop. change (2020-22):** −1.5%. **Area:** 142.7 sq mi. **Racial distribution:** 73.6% white; 12.0% Black; 4.0% Asian; 0.6% Amer. Ind.; <0.05% Pac. Isl.; 3.4% other; 2+ races, 6.4%. **Hispanic pop.:** 14.5%. **Foreign born:** 10.8%. **U.S. citizens:** 93.1%. **Language:** 83.4% English only; 10.4% Spanish.

Employment: 245,200 employed; 2.8% unemployment. **Per capita income:** $36,749. **Below poverty:** 10.9%; 7.9% of families. **Uninsured:** 13.8%. **Educational attainment:** 90.3% HS; 38.7% bachelor's. **Avg. commute:** 19.3 min. 77.2% drive. **Housing units:** 208,477; 93.7% occupied. **Home ownership:** 58.3%. **Avg. home:** $272,600; change (2020-22): 23.6%. **Avg. rent:** $999. **Crime rates (2020):** violent: 631; property: 3,174.

Mayor: Jean Stothert, nonpartisan

History: Founded 1854; inc. 1857. Large food-processing, telecommunications, information-processing center.

Website: www.cityofomaha.org

Orlando, Florida

Population: 316,081 (62). **Pop. density:** 2,847. **Pop. change (2020-22):** 2.7%. **Area:** 111.0 sq mi. **Racial distribution:** 53.4% white; 23.5% Black; 4.0% Asian; 0.1% Amer. Ind.; <0.05% Pac. Isl.; 6.5% other; 2+ races, 12.4%. **Hispanic pop.:** 34.2%. **Foreign born:** 22.8%. **U.S. citizens:** 86.9%. **Language:** 59.2% English only; 28.7% Spanish.

Employment: 170,200 employed; 2.9% unemployment. **Per capita income:** $36,596. **Below poverty:** 13.8%; 12.9% of families. **Uninsured:** 19.3%. **Educational attainment:** 91.6% HS; 40.1% bachelor's. **Avg. commute:** 27.1 min. 75.2% drive. **Housing units:** 142,115; 83.6% occupied. **Home ownership:** 38.2%. **Avg. home:** $420,000; change (2020-22): 39.3%. **Avg. rent:** $1,346. **Crime rates (2020):** violent: 860; property: 3,803.

Mayor: Buddy Dyer, nonpartisan

History: Ft. Gatlin built just south of present-day Orlando, 1838; name changed from Jernigan, 1856; inc. 1875. Walt Disney World opened, 1971.

Website: www.orlando.gov

Philadelphia, Pennsylvania

Population: 1,567,258 (6). **Pop. density:** 11,665. **Pop. change (2020-22):** −2.1%. **Area:** 134.4 sq mi. **Racial distribution:** 38.5% white; 40.8% Black; 7.4% Asian; 0.3% Amer. Ind.; <0.05% Pac. Isl.; 7.7% other; 2+ races, 5.3%. **Hispanic pop.:** 15.4%. **Foreign born:** 14.3%. **U.S. citizens:** 93.1%. **Language:** 76.3% English only; 11.0% Spanish.

Employment: 692,255 employed; 5.4% unemployment. **Per capita income:** $32,344. **Below poverty:** 20.3%; 18.3% of families. **Uninsured:** 10.0%. **Educational attainment:** 86.6% HS; 32.5% bachelor's. **Avg. commute:** 33.0 min. 48.3% drive, 21.4% public trans, 10.8% work from home. **Housing units:** 720,688; 89.7% occupied. **Home ownership:** 52.4%. **Avg. home:** $333,100; change (2020-22): 22.1%. **Avg. rent:** $1,149.

Mayor: Jim F. Kenney, Democrat

History: Named Philadelphia, 1682; chartered 1701. Continental Congresses convened 1774, 1775; Declaration of Independence signed, 1776; U.S. capital, 1790-1800.

Website: www.phila.gov

Phoenix, Arizona

Population: 1,644,409 (5). **Pop. density:** 3,173. **Pop. change (2020-22):** 2.0%. **Area:** 518.3 sq mi. **Racial distribution:** 64.4% white; 7.3% Black; 3.9% Asian; 2.1% Amer. Ind.; 0.2% Pac. Isl.; 9.5% other; 2+ races, 12.7%. **Hispanic pop.:** 42.7%. **Foreign born:** 19.2%. **U.S. citizens:** 88.1%. **Language:** 63.1% English only; 30.4% Spanish.

Employment: 856,083 employed; 3.4% unemployment. **Per capita income:** $33,718. **Below poverty:** 12.9%; 11.5% of families. **Uninsured:** 18.7%. **Educational attainment:** 83.5% HS; 30.6% bachelor's. **Avg. commute:** 26.0 min. 70.8% drive, 11.5% carpool, 11.5% work from home. **Housing units:** 624,409; 92.9% occupied. **Home ownership:** 56.1%. **Avg. home:** $477,900; change (2020-22): 43.5%. **Avg. rent:** $1,175. **Crime rates (2020):** violent: 798; property: 2,989.

Mayor: Kate Gallego, nonpartisan

History: Founded 1867; inc. 1881; became territorial capital, 1889.

Website: www.phoenix.gov

Pittsburgh, Pennsylvania

Population: 302,898 (68). **Pop. density:** 5,470. **Pop. change (2020-22):** 0.0%. **Area:** 55.4 sq mi. **Racial distribution:** 65.4% white; 22.9% Black; 5.6% Asian; 0.2% Amer. Ind.; <0.05% Pac. Isl.; 1.1% other; 2+ races, 4.8%. **Hispanic pop.:** 3.5%. **Foreign born:** 9.0%. **U.S. citizens:** 94.3%. **Language:** 88.8% English only; 2.3% Spanish.

Employment: 146,424 employed; 4.1% unemployment. **Per capita income:** $37,655. **Below poverty:** 18.1%; 12.3% of families. **Uninsured:** 7.0%. **Educational attainment:** 93.5% HS; 45.7% bachelor's. **Avg. commute:** 23.9 min. 52.1% drive, 15.1% public trans, 13.9% work from home. **Housing units:** 157,483; 87.5% occupied. **Home ownership:** 47.4%. **Avg. home:** $213,500; change (2020-22): 17.1%. **Avg. rent:** $1,043.

Mayor: Ed Gainey, Democrat

History: Settled around Ft. Pitt, 1758; inc. 1816; became an inland port; a center for iron production by Civil War.

Website: pittsburghpa.gov

Plano, Texas

Population: 289,547 (72). **Pop. density:** 4,039. **Pop. change (2020-22):** 1.1%. **Area:** 71.7 sq mi. **Racial distribution:** 58.7% white; 8.6% Black; 22.3% Asian; 0.3% Amer. Ind.; 0.1% Pac. Isl.; 2.8% other; 2+ races, 7.2%. **Hispanic pop.:** 15.8%. **Foreign born:** 28.6%. **U.S. citizens:** 84.0%. **Language:** 63.1% English only; 12.0% Spanish.
Employment: 167,072 employed; 3.2% unemployment. **Per capita income:** $51,624. **Below poverty:** 6.3%; 4.8% of families. **Uninsured:** 15.0%. **Educational attainment:** 93.3% HS; 58.1% bachelor's. **Avg. commute:** 26.5 min. 71.6% drive, 17.9% work from home. **Housing units:** 112,373; 94.3% occupied. **Home ownership:** 57.6%. **Avg. home:** $385,500; change (2020-22): 34.2%. **Avg. rent:** $1,541. **Crime rates:** violent: 157; property: 1,633.
Mayor: John B. Muns, nonpartisan
History: Settled 1846; inc. 1873.
Website: www.plano.gov

Port St. Lucie, Florida

Population: 231,790 (96). **Pop. density:** 1,944. **Pop. change (2020-22):** 12.1%. **Area:** 119.2 sq mi. **Racial distribution:** 66.7% white; 18.2% Black; 2.0% Asian; 0.2% Amer. Ind.; <0.05% Pac. Isl.; 3.5% other; 2+ races, 9.3%. **Hispanic pop.:** 21.8%. **Foreign born:** 18.8%. **U.S. citizens:** 94.4%. **Language:** 74.3% English only; 16.1% Spanish.
Employment: 100,326 employed; 3.0% unemployment. **Per capita income:** $32,520. **Below poverty:** 7.8%; 5.3% of families. **Uninsured:** 16.7%. **Educational attainment:** 90.4% HS; 25.4% bachelor's. **Avg. commute:** 29.6 min. 82.2% drive. **Housing units:** 78,910; 90.7% occupied. **Home ownership:** 80.4%. **Avg. home:** $400,000; change (2020-22): 47.6%. **Avg. rent:** $1,604. **Crime rates (2020):** violent: 128; property: 807.
Mayor: Shannon Martin, nonpartisan
History: Inc. 1961.
Website: www.cityofpsl.com

Portland, Oregon

Population: 635,067 (26). **Pop. density:** 4,757. **Pop. change (2020-22):** −2.8%. **Area:** 133.5 sq mi. **Racial distribution:** 73.8% white; 5.6% Black; 8.5% Asian; 0.9% Amer. Ind.; 0.5% Pac. Isl.; 2.6% other; 2+ races, 8.0%. **Hispanic pop.:** 10.3%. **Foreign born:** 13.1%. **U.S. citizens:** 94.4%. **Language:** 81.5% English only; 6.5% Spanish.
Employment: 372,811 employed; 3.9% unemployment. **Per capita income:** $47,289. **Below poverty:** 12.3%; 6.9% of families. **Uninsured:** 8.1%. **Educational attainment:** 93.3% HS; 51.9% bachelor's. **Avg. commute:** 25.5 min. 53.8% drive, 18.0% work from home. **Housing units:** 296,479; 94.4% occupied. **Home ownership:** 53.4%. **Avg. home:** $591,000; change (2020-22): 31.0%. **Avg. rent:** $1,406. **Crime rates:** violent: 720; property: 5,577.
Mayor: Ted Wheeler, nonpartisan
History: Est. 1843; developed as trading center, aided by California Gold Rush, 1849; city chartered, 1851.
Website: www.portland.gov

Raleigh, North Carolina

Population: 476,587 (41). **Pop. density:** 3,208. **Pop. change (2020-22):** 2.6%. **Area:** 148.5 sq mi. **Racial distribution:** 56.1% white; 28.6% Black; 4.7% Asian; 0.4% Amer. Ind.; 0.1% Pac. Isl.; 4.7% other; 2+ races, 5.4%. **Hispanic pop.:** 11.3%. **Foreign born:** 13.0%. **U.S. citizens:** 92.3%. **Language:** 82.1% English only; 9.4% Spanish.
Employment: 258,582 employed; 3.3% unemployment. **Per capita income:** $42,632. **Below poverty:** 11.1%; 7.1% of families. **Uninsured:** 13.4%. **Educational attainment:** 92.3% HS; 52.4% bachelor's. **Avg. commute:** 24.0 min. 70.9% drive, 17.2% work from home. **Housing units:** 206,766; 90.6% occupied. **Home ownership:** 51.6%. **Avg. home:** $455,300; change (2020-22): 40.0%. **Avg. rent:** $1,237. **Crime rates:** violent: 464; property: 2,137.
Mayor: Mary-Ann Baldwin, nonpartisan
History: Named after Sir Walter Raleigh; chosen state capital, 1788; inc. 1795; occupied by Union Gen. Sherman, 1865.
Website: raleighnc.gov

Reno, Nevada

Population: 273,448 (81). **Pop. density:** 2,512. **Pop. change (2020-22):** 3.2%. **Area:** 108.9 sq mi. **Racial distribution:** 69.0% white; 3.4% Black; 6.9% Asian; 0.9% Amer. Ind.; 0.9% Pac. Isl.; 10.5% other; 2+ races, 8.5%. **Hispanic pop.:** 23.3%. **Foreign born:** 15.6%. **U.S. citizens:** 92.1%. **Language:** 76.3% English only; 15.2% Spanish.
Employment: 134,455 employed; 3.5% unemployment. **Per capita income:** $39,104. **Below poverty:** 12.3%; 7.1% of families. **Uninsured:** 12.8%. **Educational attainment:** 89.8% HS; 35.5% bachelor's. **Avg. commute:** 20.6 min. 71.1% drive, 12.0% carpool. **Housing units:** 114,268; 93.9% occupied. **Home ownership:** 48.3%. **Avg. home:** $596,600; change (2020-22): 35.3%. **Avg. rent:** $1,213. **Crime rates:** violent: 575; property: 2,858.

Mayor: Hillary Schieve, nonpartisan
History: Originally named Lake's Crossing; name changed to Reno, after a Union Civil War general, 1868, with arrival of transcontinental railroad.
Website: www.reno.gov

Richmond, Virginia

Population: 229,395 (98). **Pop. density:** 3,828. **Pop. change (2020-22):** 1.1%. **Area:** 59.9 sq mi. **Racial distribution:** 44.8% white; 45.2% Black; 2.1% Asian; 0.2% Amer. Ind.; <0.05% Pac. Isl.; 3.0% other; 2+ races, 4.6%. **Hispanic pop.:** 7.3%. **Foreign born:** 7.5%. **U.S. citizens:** 95.1%. **Language:** 89.9% English only; 6.1% Spanish.
Employment: 116,881 employed; 3.4% unemployment. **Per capita income:** $38,132. **Below poverty:** 17.5%; 13.0% of families. **Uninsured:** 13.6%. **Educational attainment:** 87.7% HS; 43.1% bachelor's. **Avg. commute:** 21.7 min. 67.8% drive, 11.5% work from home. **Housing units:** 110,224; 89.7% occupied. **Home ownership:** 43.4%. **Avg. home:** $374,000; change (2020-22): 23.3%. **Avg. rent:** $1,132. **Crime rates:** violent: 374; property: 2,736.
Mayor: Levar M. Stoney, nonpartisan
History: First explored, 1607; became capital of Virginia, 1779; attacked by British, 1781; inc. as city, 1782; capital of Confederate States of America, 1861-65.
Website: www.rva.gov

Riverside, California

Population: 320,764 (59). **Pop. density:** 3,953. **Pop. change (2020-22):** 1.7%. **Area:** 81.1 sq mi. **Racial distribution:** 48.3% white; 5.9% Black; 8.8% Asian; 0.8% Amer. Ind.; 0.4% Pac. Isl.; 25.9% other; 2+ races, 10.0%. **Hispanic pop.:** 54.9%. **Foreign born:** 22.5%. **U.S. citizens:** 89.5%. **Language:** 53.5% English only; 37.4% Spanish.
Employment: 153,810 employed; 3.8% unemployment. **Per capita income:** $28,771. **Below poverty:** 11.9%; 9.2% of families. **Uninsured:** 13.0%. **Educational attainment:** 82.5% HS; 23.9% bachelor's. **Avg. commute:** 31.7 min. 75.5% drive, 11.0% carpool. **Housing units:** 93,117; 94.9% occupied. **Home ownership:** 55.7%. **Avg. home:** $565,000; change (2020-22): 33.7%. **Avg. rent:** $1,568. **Crime rates (2020):** violent: 446; property: 2,985.
Mayor: Patricia Lock Dawson, nonpartisan
History: Founded 1870; inc. 1883. Known for citrus industry; home of the parent navel orange tree.
Website: riversideca.gov

Sacramento, California

Population: 528,001 (35). **Pop. density:** 5,352. **Pop. change (2020-22):** 0.4%. **Area:** 98.6 sq mi. **Racial distribution:** 40.9% white; 13.4% Black; 19.0% Asian; 0.8% Amer. Ind.; 1.8% Pac. Isl.; 12.4% other; 2+ races, 11.7%. **Hispanic pop.:** 28.9%. **Foreign born:** 20.9%. **U.S. citizens:** 91.2%. **Language:** 64.7% English only; 16.5% Spanish.
Employment: 232,029 employed; 4.1% unemployment. **Per capita income:** $35,793. **Below poverty:** 13.8%; 10.3% of families. **Uninsured:** 8.1%. **Educational attainment:** 86.4% HS; 35.1% bachelor's. **Avg. commute:** 26.1 min. 68.9% drive, 12.6% work from home. **Housing units:** 203,906; 95.1% occupied. **Home ownership:** 50.1%. **Avg. home:** $541,000; change (2020-22): 28.5%. **Avg. rent:** $1,434. **Crime rates (2020):** violent: 683; property: 2,745.
Mayor: Darrell Steinberg, nonpartisan
History: Est. 1839; important trading center during Gold Rush; became state capital, 1854.
Website: www.cityofsacramento.org

St. Louis, Missouri

Population: 286,578 (75). **Pop. density:** 4,643. **Pop. change (2020-22):** −4.6%. **Area:** 61.7 sq mi. **Racial distribution:** 46.3% white; 44.8% Black; 3.4% Asian; 0.3% Amer. Ind.; 0.1% Pac. Isl.; 1.2% other; 2+ races, 4.0%. **Hispanic pop.:** 4.2%. **Foreign born:** 6.8%. **U.S. citizens:** 96.3%. **Language:** 90.5% English only; 3.0% Spanish.
Employment: 144,444 employed; 3.1% unemployment. **Per capita income:** $33,326. **Below poverty:** 17.8%; 13.9% of families. **Uninsured:** 14.3%. **Educational attainment:** 89.2% HS; 38.0% bachelor's. **Avg. commute:** 23.3 min. 69.9% drive, 10.5% work from home. **Housing units:** 173,830; 81.2% occupied. **Home ownership:** 44.7%. **Avg. home:** $245,300; change (2020-22): 19.2%. **Avg. rent:** $873. **Crime rates:** violent: 1,484; property: 5,463.
Mayor: Tishaura O. Jones, nonpartisan
History: Founded 1764 as French fur trading post on Mississippi R., near confluence with Missouri R.; acquired by U.S., 1803; chartered as city, 1823.
Website: www.stlouis-mo.gov

St. Paul, Minnesota

Population: 303,176 (67). **Pop. density:** 5,833. **Pop. change (2020-22):** −2.6%. **Area:** 52.0 sq mi. **Racial distribution:** 54.9% white; 16.0% Black; 19.0% Asian; 0.7% Amer. Ind.; <0.05% Pac. Isl.; 2.7% other; 2+ races, 6.6%. **Hispanic pop.:** 8.7%. **Foreign**

born: 19.1%. **U.S. citizens:** 91.9%. **Language:** 71.2% English only; 6.1% Spanish.
Employment: 152,185 employed; 2.8% unemployment. **Per capita income:** $35,547. **Below poverty:** 14.7%; 12.8% of families. **Uninsured:** 8.0%. **Educational attainment:** 87.8% HS; 41.9% bachelor's. **Avg. commute:** 23.7 min. 62.3% drive, 10.6% carpool, 13.0% work from home. **Housing units:** 127,369; 93.8% occupied. **Home ownership:** 51.5%. **Avg. home:** $375,400; change (2020-22): 19.1%. **Avg. rent:** $1,080. **Crime rates:** violent: 780; property: 4,028.
Mayor: Melvin Carter, nonpartisan
History: Est. c. 1840 as Pig's Eye Landing; became capital of Minnesota territory, 1849; chartered as St. Paul, 1854.
Website: www.stpaul.gov

St. Petersburg, Florida

Population: 261,256 (86). **Pop. density:** 4,227. **Pop. change (2020-22):** 0.9%. **Area:** 61.8 sq mi. **Racial distribution:** 67.9% white; 21.0% Black; 3.4% Asian; 0.2% Amer. Ind.; <0.05% Pac. Isl.; 1.6% other; 2+ races, 5.9%. **Hispanic pop.:** 8.2%. **Foreign born:** 10.1%. **U.S. citizens:** 96.5%. **Language:** 87.4% English only; 5.4% Spanish.
Employment: 143,934 employed; 2.7% unemployment. **Per capita income:** $41,493. **Below poverty:** 11.1%; 8.1% of families. **Uninsured:** 14.8%. **Educational attainment:** 93.5% HS; 38.8% bachelor's. **Avg. commute:** 23.6 min. 72.6% drive, 12.9% work from home. **Housing units:** 138,276; 80.9% occupied. **Home ownership:** 62.7%. **Avg. home:** $400,000; change (2020-22): 47.1%. **Avg. rent:** $1,251. **Crime rates (2020):** violent: 662; property: 2,556.
Mayor: Kenneth "Ken" Welch, nonpartisan
History: Founded 1888; inc. 1903. Site of Salvador Dali Museum.
Website: www.stpete.org

San Antonio, Texas

Population: 1,472,909 (7). **Pop. density:** 2,952. **Pop. change (2020-22):** 2.3%. **Area:** 498.9 sq mi. **Racial distribution:** 64.0% white; 6.5% Black; 3.0% Asian; 0.8% Amer. Ind.; 0.1% Pac. Isl.; 8.4% other; 2+ races, 17.2%. **Hispanic pop.:** 65.7%. **Foreign born:** 14.2%. **U.S. citizens:** 91.6%. **Language:** 58.3% English only; 37.9% Spanish.
Employment: 728,473 employed; 3.6% unemployment. **Per capita income:** $28,579. **Below poverty:** 15.0%; 13.7% of families. **Uninsured:** 23.9%. **Educational attainment:** 83.3% HS; 27.3% bachelor's. **Avg. commute:** 24.3 min. 74.6% drive, 11.8% carpool. **Housing units:** 585,402; 91.5% occupied. **Home ownership:** 52.3%. **Avg. home:** $337,700; change (2020-22): 32.8%. **Avg. rent:** $1,090. **Crime rates:** violent: 683; property: 3,814.
Mayor: Ron Nirenberg, nonpartisan
History: First Spanish mission est., 1718; Battle of the Alamo, 1836; city subsequently captured by Texans; inc. 1837.
Website: www.sanantonio.gov

San Diego, California

Population: 1,381,162 (8). **Pop. density:** 4,238. **Pop. change (2020-22):** -0.4%. **Area:** 325.9 sq mi. **Racial distribution:** 58.2% white; 5.8% Black; 17.2% Asian; 0.6% Amer. Ind.; 0.5% Pac. Isl.; 7.3% other; 2+ races, 10.3%. **Hispanic pop.:** 30.1%. **Foreign born:** 25.1%. **U.S. citizens:** 89.2%. **Language:** 61.2% English only; 21.7% Spanish.
Employment: 697,299 employed; 3.3% unemployment. **Per capita income:** $46,460. **Below poverty:** 11.0%; 7.3% of families. **Uninsured:** 9.6%. **Educational attainment:** 89.3% HS; 47.6% bachelor's. **Avg. commute:** 24.3 min. 68.9% drive, 14.0% work from home. **Housing units:** 545,792; 93.3% occupied. **Home ownership:** 47.7%. **Avg. home:** $911,000; change (2020-22): 28.3%. **Avg. rent:** $1,885. **Crime rates:** violent: 377; property: 1,837.
Mayor: Todd Gloria, nonpartisan
History: Claimed by Spanish, 1542; first mission est., 1769; scene of conflict during Mexican-American War, 1846; inc. 1850.
Website: www.sandiego.gov

San Francisco, California

Population: 808,437 (17). **Pop. density:** 17,298. **Pop. change (2020-22):** -7.1%. **Area:** 46.7 sq mi. **Racial distribution:** 43.4% white; 5.2% Black; 34.4% Asian; 0.5% Amer. Ind.; 0.4% Pac. Isl.; 7.8% other; 2+ races, 8.4%. **Hispanic pop.:** 15.4%. **Foreign born:** 34.1%. **U.S. citizens:** 87.2%. **Language:** 57.3% English only; 10.8% Spanish.
Employment: 557,983 employed; 2.5% unemployment. **Per capita income:** $77,267. **Below poverty:** 10.4%; 5.6% of families. **Uninsured:** 4.6%. **Educational attainment:** 88.8% HS; 59.5% bachelor's. **Avg. commute:** 32.8 min. 29.4% drive, 27.8% public trans., 11.0% walk, 18.0% work from home. **Housing units:** 404,720; 89.3% occupied. **Home ownership:** 38.2%. **Avg. home:** $1,375,000; change (2020-22): 25.0%. **Avg. rent:** $2,130. **Crime rates (2020):** violent: 544; property: 4,394.
Mayor: London N. Breed, nonpartisan

History: Est. by 1776; claimed by U.S., 1846; became major city during Gold Rush, 1849; inc. 1850. Devastated by earthquake, 1906.
Website: sf.gov

San Jose, California

Population: 971,233 (12). **Pop. density:** 5,459. **Pop. change (2020-22):** -3.8%. **Area:** 177.9 sq mi. **Racial distribution:** 34.8% white; 3.0% Black; 37.5% Asian; 0.8% Amer. Ind.; 0.5% Pac. Isl.; 13.0% other; 2+ races, 10.4%. **Hispanic pop.:** 31.0%. **Foreign born:** 40.7%. **U.S. citizens:** 82.6%. **Language:** 42.1% English only; 22.2% Spanish.
Employment: 533,297 employed; 2.8% unemployment. **Per capita income:** $53,574. **Below poverty:** 7.5%; 4.9% of families. **Uninsured:** 6.9%. **Educational attainment:** 85.5% HS; 45.4% bachelor's. **Avg. commute:** 29.8 min. 69.2% drive, 10.5% carpool, 13.0% work from home. **Housing units:** 339,550; 95.5% occupied. **Home ownership:** 56.2%. **Avg. home:** $1,797,800; change (2020-22): 29.8%. **Avg. rent:** $2,366. **Crime rates (2020):** violent: 425; property: 2,316.
Mayor: Matt Mahan, nonpartisan
History: Founded by Spanish, 1777, between San Francisco and Monterey; state capital, 1849-51; inc. 1850.
Website: www.sanjoseca.gov

Santa Ana, California

Population: 308,189 (65). **Pop. density:** 11,258. **Pop. change (2020-22):** -0.6%. **Area:** 27.4 sq mi. **Racial distribution:** 29.7% white; 1.0% Black; 11.9% Asian; 0.9% Amer. Ind.; 0.2% Pac. Isl.; 47.5% other; 2+ races, 8.8%. **Hispanic pop.:** 76.7%. **Foreign born:** 41.7%. **U.S. citizens:** 76.4%. **Language:** 21.5% English only; 67.7% Spanish.
Employment: 150,412 employed; 3.3% unemployment. **Per capita income:** $24,766. **Below poverty:** 10.4%; 10.3% of families. **Uninsured:** 20.2%. **Educational attainment:** 63.4% HS; 17.3% bachelor's. **Avg. commute:** 25.3 min. 72.1% drive, 13.5% carpool. **Housing units:** 79,179; 96.8% occupied. **Home ownership:** 45.7%. **Avg. home:** $1,235,000; change (2020-22): 37.2%. **Avg. rent:** $1,726. **Crime rates (2020):** violent: 429; property: 2,079.
Mayor: Valerie Amezcua, nonpartisan
History: Founded by Spanish, 1769; inc. 1886.
Website: www.santa-ana.org

Scottsdale, Arizona

Population: 243,050 (92). **Pop. density:** 1,321. **Pop. change (2020-22):** 0.5%. **Area:** 184.0 sq mi. **Racial distribution:** 85.2% white; 2.2% Black; 4.9% Asian; 0.7% Amer. Ind.; 0.1% Pac. Isl.; 1.6% other; 2+ races, 5.2%. **Hispanic pop.:** 10.4%. **Foreign born:** 11.8%. **U.S. citizens:** 95.2%. **Language:** 87.4% English only; 5.5% Spanish.
Employment: 149,792 employed; 2.8% unemployment. **Per capita income:** $70,040. **Below poverty:** 6.4%; 4.2% of families. **Uninsured:** 7.7%. **Educational attainment:** 97.2% HS; 60.2% bachelor's. **Avg. commute:** 21.6 min. 68.1% drive, 22.4% work from home. **Housing units:** 134,918; 84.1% occupied. **Home ownership:** 66.6%. **Avg. home:** $477,900; change (2020-22): 43.5%. **Avg. rent:** $1,578. **Crime rates:** violent: 214; property: 2,356.
Mayor: David D. Ortega, nonpartisan
History: Founded 1888 by namesake Army Chaplain Winfield Scott; inc. 1951.
Website: www.scottsdaleaz.gov

Seattle, Washington

Population: 749,256 (18). **Pop. density:** 8,920. **Pop. change (2020-22):** 1.2%. **Area:** 84.0 sq mi. **Racial distribution:** 64.9% white; 6.8% Black; 16.3% Asian; 0.5% Amer. Ind.; 0.2% Pac. Isl.; 2.4% other; 2+ races, 8.8%. **Hispanic pop.:** 7.2%. **Foreign born:** 19.3%. **U.S. citizens:** 89.6%. **Language:** 77.9% English only; 4.2% Spanish.
Employment: 481,225 employed; 2.6% unemployment. **Per capita income:** $68,836. **Below poverty:** 10.1%; 5.1% of families. **Uninsured:** 5.6%. **Educational attainment:** 95.5% HS; 65.9% bachelor's. **Avg. commute:** 27.7 min. 40.5% drive, 17.8% public trans., 21.4% work from home. **Housing units:** 362,809; 93.0% occupied. **Home ownership:** 45.2%. **Avg. home:** $756,200; change (2020-22): 26.7%. **Avg. rent:** $1,801. **Crime rates:** violent: 745; property: 5,102.
Mayor: Bruce Harrell, nonpartisan
History: Settled 1851; inc. 1869. Suffered severe fire, 1889; played prominent role in Alaska Gold Rush, 1897; growth followed opening of Panama Canal 1914. Center of aircraft industry during WWII.
Website: www.seattle.gov

Spokane, Washington

Population: 230,160 (97). **Pop. density:** 3,347. **Pop. change (2020-22):** 0.4%. **Area:** 68.8 sq mi. **Racial distribution:** 83.1% white; 2.4% Black; 2.0% Asian; 1.4% Amer. Ind.; 1.0% Pac. Isl.; 1.7% other; 2+ races, 7.5%. **Hispanic pop.:** 6.8%. **Foreign born:** 6.0%. **U.S. citizens:** 97.1%. **Language:** 91.6% English only; 2.6% Spanish.

Employment: 105,372 employed; 5.0% unemployment. **Per capita income:** $32,991. **Below poverty:** 15.1%; 8.9% of families. **Uninsured:** 8.2%. **Educational attainment:** 93.1% HS; 32.4% bachelor's. **Avg. commute:** 20.5 min. 72.0% drive, 10.2% carpool. **Housing units:** 99,933; 94.2% occupied. **Home ownership:** 56.9%. **Avg. home:** $423,900; change (2020-22): 37.9%. **Avg. rent:** $956. **Crime rates:** violent: 651; property: 4,785.
Mayor: Nadine Woodward, nonpartisan
History: Founded 1872; inc. as village of Spokane Falls 1881; destroyed in fire 1889; re-inc. as city of Spokane, 1891.
Website: my.spokanecity.org

Stockton, California

Population: 321,819 (58). **Pop. density:** 5,158. **Pop. change (2020-22):** 0.2%. **Area:** 62.4 sq mi. **Racial distribution:** 35.0% white; 11.3% Black; 20.9% Asian; 0.9% Amer. Ind.; 0.5% Pac. Isl.; 13.8% other; 2+ races, 17.7%. **Hispanic pop.:** 44.9%. **Foreign born:** 25.3%. **U.S. citizens:** 88.3%. **Language:** 53.9% English only; 28.6% Spanish.
Employment: 127,079 employed; 6.0% unemployment. **Per capita income:** $26,403. **Below poverty:** 14.0%; 13.3% of families. **Uninsured:** 10.1%. **Educational attainment:** 78.1% HS; 18.0% bachelor's. **Avg. commute:** 32.3 min. 79.4% drive, 12.5% carpool. **Housing units:** 102,919; 93.5% occupied. **Home ownership:** 51.2%. **Avg. rent:** $1,271. **Crime rates (2020):** violent: 1,277; property: 2,981.
Mayor: Kevin J. Lincoln II, nonpartisan
History: Est. 1849 to serve gold miners; inc. 1850.
Website: www.stocktonca.gov

Tampa, Florida

Population: 398,173 (49). **Pop. density:** 3,504. **Pop. change (2020-22):** 2.6%. **Area:** 113.6 sq mi. **Racial distribution:** 58.8% white; 22.4% Black; 4.6% Asian; 0.2% Amer. Ind.; 0.1% Pac. Isl.; 3.7% other; 2+ races, 10.1%. **Hispanic pop.:** 26.2%. **Foreign born:** 18.1%. **U.S. citizens:** 91.6%. **Language:** 71.8% English only; 20.7% Spanish.
Employment: 211,165 employed; 2.9% unemployment. **Per capita income:** $40,962. **Below poverty:** 15.4%; 12.7% of families. **Uninsured:** 15.3%. **Educational attainment:** 88.4% HS; 41.8% bachelor's. **Avg. commute:** 24.7 min. 71.9% drive, 13.2% work from home. **Housing units:** 169,711; 90.2% occupied. **Home ownership:** 50.0%. **Avg. home:** $400,000; change (2020-22): 47.1%. **Avg. rent:** $1,249. **Crime rates (2020):** violent: 520; property: 1,365.
Mayor: Jane Castor, nonpartisan
History: U.S. army fort on site, 1824; inc. 1855.
Website: www.tampa.gov

Toledo, Ohio

Population: 266,301 (84). **Pop. density:** 3,309. **Pop. change (2020-22):** −1.5%. **Area:** 80.5 sq mi. **Racial distribution:** 60.6% white; 28.1% Black; 1.3% Asian; 0.2% Amer. Ind.; 0.1% Pac. Isl.; 2.9% other; 2+ races, 6.7%. **Hispanic pop.:** 8.8%. **Foreign born:** 3.5%. **U.S. citizens:** 98.3%. **Language:** 93.6% English only; 3.0% Spanish.
Employment: 116,376 employed; 4.9% unemployment. **Per capita income:** $23,795. **Below poverty:** 20.9%; 18.5% of families. **Uninsured:** 10.1%. **Educational attainment:** 87.1% HS; 19.6% bachelor's. **Avg. commute:** 19.9 min. 80.0% drive, 10.2% carpool. **Housing units:** 133,505; 87.1% occupied. **Home ownership:** 51.9%. **Avg. home:** $167,200; change (2020-22): 15.2%. **Avg. rent:** $781. **Crime rates:** violent: 1,077; property: 2,808.
Mayor: Wade Kapszukiewicz, nonpartisan
History: Site of Ft. Industry, 1800; figured in Toledo War between OH and MI over borders, 1835-36; inc. 1837.
Website: toledo.oh.gov

Tucson, Arizona

Population: 546,574 (33). **Pop. density:** 2,260. **Pop. change (2020-22):** 0.7%. **Area:** 241.8 sq mi. **Racial distribution:** 64.8% white; 4.8% Black; 3.1% Asian; 3.4% Amer. Ind.; 0.2% Pac. Isl.; 11.1% other; 2+ races, 12.6%. **Hispanic pop.:** 44.6%. **Foreign born:** 14.2%. **U.S. citizens:** 92.6%. **Language:** 67.5% English only; 27.2% Spanish.
Employment: 250,959 employed; 4.0% unemployment. **Per capita income:** $26,373. **Below poverty:** 18.3%; 14.5% of families. **Uninsured:** 15.3%. **Educational attainment:** 86.3% HS; 28.9% bachelor's. **Avg. commute:** 22.3 min. 71.3% drive, 10.4% carpool. **Housing units:** 242,525; 90.2% occupied. **Home ownership:** 51.3%. **Avg. home:** $371,900; change (2020-22): 40.3%. **Avg. rent:** $907. **Crime rates (2020):** violent: 698; property: 3,621.
Mayor: Regina Romero, Democrat
History: Est. 1775 by Spanish as a presidio; acquired by U.S. in Gadsden Purchase, 1854; inc. 1877.
Website: www.tucsonaz.gov

Tulsa, Oklahoma

Population: 411,867 (47). **Pop. density:** 2,083. **Pop. change (2020-22):** −0.4%. **Area:** 197.8 sq mi. **Racial distribution:** 62.1% white; 14.8% Black; 3.5% Asian; 4.5% Amer. Ind.; 0.2% Pac. Isl.; 4.5% other; 2+ races, 10.5%. **Hispanic pop.:** 17.1%. **Foreign born:** 11.0%. **U.S. citizens:** 92.5%. **Language:** 81.2% English only; 14.1% Spanish.
Employment: 190,758 employed; 3.2% unemployment. **Per capita income:** $33,492. **Below poverty:** 15.1%; 14.0% of families. **Uninsured:** 23.9%. **Educational attainment:** 87.9% HS; 32.4% bachelor's. **Avg. commute:** 18.6 min. 78.4% drive. **Housing units:** 191,753; 87.6% occupied. **Home ownership:** 52.4%. **Avg. home:** $242,300; change (2020-22): 23.7%. **Avg. rent:** $882. **Crime rates:** violent: 1,107; property: 4,977.
Mayor: G.T. Bynum, nonpartisan
History: Settled in 1836 by Creek Indians; modern town founded 1882; inc. 1898; oil discovered early 20th century.
Website: www.cityoftulsa.org

Virginia Beach, Virginia

Population: 455,618 (42). **Pop. density:** 1,862. **Pop. change (2020-22):** −0.9%. **Area:** 244.7 sq mi. **Racial distribution:** 63.9% white; 19.0% Black; 7.0% Asian; 0.2% Amer. Ind.; 0.1% Pac. Isl.; 2.2% other; 2+ races, 7.5%. **Hispanic pop.:** 8.6%. **Foreign born:** 9.3%. **U.S. citizens:** 96.6%. **Language:** 87.8% English only; 4.8% Spanish.
Employment: 225,770 employed; 2.8% unemployment. **Per capita income:** $41,803. **Below poverty:** 7.0%; 6.0% of families. **Uninsured:** 9.9%. **Educational attainment:** 94.5% HS; 38.6% bachelor's. **Avg. commute:** 23.5 min. 79.1% drive. **Housing units:** 189,187; 93.6% occupied. **Home ownership:** 65.0%. **Avg. home:** $323,900; change (2020-22): 17.8%. **Avg. rent:** $1,433. **Crime rates:** violent: 112; property: 1,570.
Mayor: Robert M. "Bobby" Dyer, nonpartisan
History: Settlement by Capt. John Smith, 1607; formed by merger with Princess Anne Co., 1963.
Website: www.vbgov.com

Washington, District of Columbia

Population: 671,803 (23). **Pop. density:** 10,990. **Pop. change (2020-22):** 0.1%. **Area:** 61.1 sq mi. **Racial distribution:** 40.5% white; 44.7% Black; 4.1% Asian; 0.3% Amer. Ind.; 0.1% Pac. Isl.; 4.8% other; 2+ races, 5.7%. **Hispanic pop.:** 11.3%. **Foreign born:** 13.5%. **U.S. citizens:** 92.8%. **Language:** 82.7% English only; 9.0% Spanish.
Employment: 370,229 employed; 4.7% unemployment. **Per capita income:** $63,793. **Below poverty:** 13.7%; 11.6% of families. **Uninsured:** 4.3%. **Educational attainment:** 92.2% HS; 61.4% bachelor's. **Avg. commute:** 30.4 min. 30.7% drive, 27.1% public trans., 11.3% walk, 19.8% work from home. **Housing units:** 344,306; 90.1% occupied. **Home ownership:** 41.5%. **Avg. home:** $585,000; change (2020-22): 23.1%. **Avg. rent:** $1,681.
Mayor: Muriel Bowser, Democrat
History: U.S. capital; planned site on Potomac R. chosen by George Washington, 1790, on land ceded from VA and MD (portion S of Potomac returned to VA, 1846). Congress first met there, 1800; inc. 1802; sacked by British, War of 1812.
Website: dc.gov

Wichita, Kansas

Population: 396,192 (50). **Pop. density:** 2,432. **Pop. change (2020-22):** −0.5%. **Area:** 162.9 sq mi. **Racial distribution:** 70.6% white; 10.3% Black; 4.9% Asian; 1.0% Amer. Ind.; <0.05% Pac. Isl.; 5.2% other; 2+ races, 8.1%. **Hispanic pop.:** 17.6%. **Foreign born:** 9.9%. **U.S. citizens:** 94.6%. **Language:** 82.2% English only; 12.0% Spanish.
Employment: 185,650 employed; 3.3% unemployment. **Per capita income:** $31,558. **Below poverty:** 13.4%; 10.7% of families. **Uninsured:** 17.8%. **Educational attainment:** 88.2% HS; 30.5% bachelor's. **Avg. commute:** 18.7 min. 81.4% drive. **Housing units:** 173,659; 89.4% occupied. **Home ownership:** 57.8%. **Avg. home:** $209,400; change (2020-22): 19.7%. **Avg. rent:** $856.
Mayor: Brandon Whipple, nonpartisan
History: Founded 1864; inc. 1871.
Website: www.wichita.gov

Winston-Salem, North Carolina

Population: 251,350 (91). **Pop. density:** 1,882. **Pop. change (2020-22):** 0.6%. **Area:** 133.5 sq mi. **Racial distribution:** 52.9% white; 33.5% Black; 2.6% Asian; 0.5% Amer. Ind.; 0.1% Pac. Isl.; 4.0% other; 2+ races, 6.5%. **Hispanic pop.:** 16.2%. **Foreign born:** 10.2%. **U.S. citizens:** 93.2%. **Language:** 82.0% English only; 13.7% Spanish.
Employment: 114,265 employed; 4.0% unemployment. **Per capita income:** $30,859. **Below poverty:** 15.5%; 13.8% of families. **Uninsured:** 18.3%. **Educational attainment:** 88.0% HS; 34.6% bachelor's. **Avg. commute:** 21.3 min. 77.7% drive. **Housing units:** 111,293; 87.9% occupied. **Home ownership:** 54.2%. **Avg. home:** $280,500; change (2020-22): 38.6%. **Avg. rent:** $871. **Crime rates:** violent: 1,150; property: 4,041.
Mayor: Allen Joines, Democrat
History: Salem founded, 1766; Winston founded, 1849; became Winston-Salem, 1913. Reynolds Building, completed 1929, used as model for Empire State Building (designed by same architects).
Website: www.cityofws.org

UNITED STATES POPULATION

Census Origins and Methods

A census is conducted in the U.S. every 10 years. The primary purpose is to apportion seats in the House of Representatives. Census data is also used to determine the boundaries of state legislative districts and the distribution of federal funds to local, state, and tribal governments.

The first U.S. census, mandated by the Constitution, was conducted in 1790, a little more than a year after George Washington became president. It counted the numbers of free white males ages 16 and over (as a measure of available workers and military personnel), free white males under 16, free white females, all other free persons, and enslaved persons. The data was collected over 18 months, at a cost of about $44,000, or $1.2 million in current dollars. (The 2020 census cost an est. $14.2 billion, of which $1.1 billion was spent in response to the COVID-19 pandemic.) The 1790 census counted 3.9 million people, resulting in an increase from 65 to 105 U.S. House seats.

As the nation grew, so did the scope of the census. The first inquiries on manufacturing were made in 1810. Questions on "the pursuits, industry, education, and resources of the country" were added to the 1840 census. It took a full 10 years to publish the results of the 1880 and 1890 censuses due to the number of questions asked. Because of those delays, Congress limited the 1900 census to questions on population, mortality, agriculture, and manufacturing.

Today, the secretary of commerce and the Census Bureau are directed by law to collect data on population, housing, employment, trade, and transportation, among other things, at stated intervals. They also conduct smaller-scale surveys on behalf of other federal agencies. After the World Health Organization declared COVID-19 a pandemic in Mar. 2020, the Census Bureau launched the Household Pulse Survey to measure the pandemic's social and economic impact.

U.S. marshals administered the earliest decennial censuses by visiting each household and reporting to the president (1790), to the secretary of state (1800-40), or to the secretary of the interior (1850-70). Trained census-takers were hired for the 1880 census and on. In 1902, Congress authorized a permanent Census Office within the Interior Department. In 1903, the agency was transferred to the new Department of Commerce and Labor and remained with the Commerce Department when a separate labor department was created in 1913.

The 1790 through 1820 decennial censuses were officially enumerated the first Monday in Aug. The 1830-1900 censuses were as of June 1, though the 1890 census was not started until June 2 (June 1 was a Sunday). The 1910 census was as of Apr. 15, the 1920 census as of Jan. 1, and every census since 1930 has been for Apr. 1.

The Census Bureau began using statistical sampling techniques in the 1940s, the first modern computer in the 1950s, and enumeration by mail in the 1960s. Any personally identifiable information gathered is withheld from the public for 72 years, after which records are made available through the National Archives. The 1940 census records, the first to be digitized and released online, can be accessed at 1940census.archives.gov. The 1950 records were made available Apr. 1, 2022, at 1950census.archives.gov.

In 1970 through 2000, about five in six households responded to a short-form census while one in six households answered a long-form questionnaire, which asked about details such as ancestry, marital status, and citizenship status. The annual American Community Survey (ACS) was implemented in 2005 to replace the long-form questionnaire.

The first 2020 Census counts, of the U.S. resident population, were released Apr. 26, 2021. The Census Bureau also delivered the population counts for apportioning Congressional House seats to the president on the same day. States were provided Census results for the redrawing of legislative districts in Sept. 2021. The agency expects to release detailed demographic and housing characteristics data in 2023-24.

U.S. Population by State and Region, 2010-22

Source: Population Estimates Program and Decennial Census, U.S. Census Bureau, U.S. Dept. of Commerce
(ranked by 2022 resident population, estimated as of July 1; 2010 decennial census figures are for Apr. 1)

Rank	State	2022	2010	% change, 2010-22	Rank	State	2022	2010	% change, 2010-22
1.	California	39,029,342	37,253,956	4.8%	29.	Connecticut	3,626,205	3,574,097	1.5%
2.	Texas	30,029,572	25,145,561	19.4	30.	Utah	3,380,800	2,763,885	22.3
3.	Florida	22,244,823	18,801,310	18.3	31.	Iowa	3,200,517	3,046,355	5.1
4.	New York	19,677,151	19,378,102	1.5	32.	Nevada	3,177,772	2,700,551	17.7
5.	Pennsylvania	12,972,008	12,702,379	2.1	33.	Arkansas	3,045,637	2,915,918	4.4
6.	Illinois	12,582,032	12,830,632	−1.9	34.	Mississippi	2,940,057	2,967,297	−0.9
7.	Ohio	11,756,058	11,536,504	1.9	35.	Kansas	2,937,150	2,853,118	2.9
8.	Georgia	10,912,876	9,687,653	12.6	36.	New Mexico	2,113,344	2,059,179	2.6
9.	North Carolina	10,698,973	9,535,483	12.2	37.	Nebraska	1,967,923	1,826,341	7.8
10.	Michigan	10,034,113	9,883,640	1.5	38.	Idaho	1,939,033	1,567,582	23.7
11.	New Jersey	9,261,699	8,791,894	5.3	39.	West Virginia	1,775,156	1,852,994	−4.2
12.	Virginia	8,683,619	8,001,024	8.5	40.	Hawaii	1,440,196	1,360,301	5.9
13.	Washington	7,785,786	6,724,540	15.8	41.	New Hampshire	1,395,231	1,316,470	6.0
14.	Arizona	7,359,197	6,392,017	15.1	42.	Maine	1,385,340	1,328,361	4.3
15.	Tennessee	7,051,339	6,346,105	11.1	43.	Montana	1,122,867	989,415	13.5
16.	Massachusetts	6,981,974	6,547,629	6.6	44.	Rhode Island	1,093,734	1,052,567	3.9
17.	Indiana	6,833,037	6,483,802	5.4	45.	Delaware	1,018,396	897,934	13.4
18.	Missouri	6,177,957	5,988,927	3.2	46.	South Dakota	909,824	814,180	11.7
19.	Maryland	6,164,660	5,773,552	6.8	47.	North Dakota	779,261	672,591	15.9
20.	Wisconsin	5,892,539	5,686,986	3.6	48.	Alaska	733,583	710,231	3.3
21.	Colorado	5,839,926	5,029,196	16.1	49.	Dist. of Columbia	671,803	601,723	11.6
22.	Minnesota	5,717,184	5,303,925	7.8	50.	Vermont	647,064	625,741	3.4
23.	South Carolina	5,282,634	4,625,364	14.2	51.	Wyoming	581,381	563,626	3.2
24.	Alabama	5,074,296	4,779,736	6.2		**United States**	**333,287,557**	**308,745,538**	**7.9**
25.	Louisiana	4,590,241	4,533,372	1.3		Northeast[1]	57,040,406	55,317,240	3.1
26.	Kentucky	4,512,310	4,339,367	4.0		Midwest[2]	68,787,595	66,927,001	2.8
27.	Oregon	4,240,137	3,831,074	10.7		South[3]	128,716,192	114,555,744	12.4
28.	Oklahoma	4,019,800	3,751,351	7.2		West[4]	78,743,364	71,945,553	9.4
						Puerto Rico	3,221,789	3,725,789	−13.5

Note: The U.S. resident population consists of individuals whose usual residence, or where they live and sleep most of the time, is in one of the 50 states or DC. It excludes U.S. military personnel stationed or assigned overseas and civilian U.S. citizens living abroad. 2022 figures are population estimates as of July 1; 2010 figures are decennial census results for Apr. 1 and may reflect revisions/corrections to initial tabulated results. (1) Incl. the states of the New England (Connecticut, Maine, Massachusetts, New Hampshire, Rhode Island, Vermont) and Middle Atlantic (New Jersey, New York, Pennsylvania) divisions. (2) Incl. the states of the East North Central (Illinois, Indiana, Michigan, Ohio, Wisconsin) and West North Central (Iowa, Kansas, Minnesota, Missouri, Nebraska, North Dakota, South Dakota) divisions. (3) Incl. the states of the South Atlantic (Delaware, DC, Florida, Georgia, Maryland, North Carolina, South Carolina, Virginia, West Virginia), East South Central (Alabama, Kentucky, Mississippi, Tennessee), and West South Central (Arkansas, Louisiana, Oklahoma, Texas) divisions. (4) Incl. the states of the Mountain (Arizona, Colorado, Idaho, Montana, Nevada, New Mexico, Utah, Wyoming) and Pacific (Alaska, California, Hawaii, Oregon, Washington) divisions.

U.S. Population by Official

Source: Decennial Censuses, U.S. Census Bureau,
(population figures for 1790-1870

State	1790	1800	1810	1820	1830	1840	1850	1860	1870	1880	1890	1900	1910	1920
AL	—	1	9	128	310	591	772	964	997	1,262,505	1,513,401	1,828,697	2,138,093	2,348,174
AK	—	—	—	—	—	—	—	—	—	33,426	32,052	63,592	64,356	55,036
AZ	—	—	—	—	—	—	—	—	10	40,440	88,243	122,931	204,354	334,162
AR	—	—	1	14	30	98	210	435	484	802,525	1,128,211	1,311,564	1,574,449	1,752,204
CA	—	—	—	—	—	—	93	380	560	864,694	1,213,398	1,485,053	2,377,549	3,426,861
CO	—	—	—	—	—	—	—	34	40	194,327	413,249	539,700	799,024	939,629
CT	238	251	262	275	298	310	371	460	537	622,700	746,258	908,420	1,114,756	1,380,631
DE	59	64	73	73	77	78	92	112	125	146,608	168,493	184,735	202,322	223,003
DC[1]	—	8	15	23	30	34	52	75	132	177,624	230,392	278,718	331,069	437,571
FL	—	—	—	—	35	54	87	140	188	269,493	391,422	528,542	752,619	968,470
GA	83	163	251	341	517	691	906	1,057	1,184	1,542,180	1,837,353	2,216,331	2,609,121	2,895,832
HI	—	—	—	—	—	—	—	—	—	—	—	154,001	191,874	255,881
ID	—	—	—	—	—	—	—	—	15	32,610	88,548	161,772	325,594	431,866
IL	—	—	12	55	157	476	851	1,712	2,540	3,077,871	3,826,352	4,821,550	5,638,591	6,485,280
IN	—	6	25	147	343	686	988	1,350	1,681	1,978,301	2,192,404	2,516,462	2,700,876	2,930,390
IA	—	—	—	—	—	43	192	675	1,194	1,624,615	1,912,297	2,231,853	2,224,771	2,404,021
KS	—	—	—	—	—	—	—	107	364	996,096	1,428,108	1,470,495	1,690,949	1,769,257
KY[1]	74	221	407	564	688	780	982	1,156	1,321	1,648,690	1,858,635	2,147,174	2,289,905	2,416,630
LA	—	—	77	153	216	352	518	708	727	939,946	1,118,588	1,381,625	1,656,388	1,798,509
ME[2]	97	152	229	298	399	502	583	628	627	648,936	661,086	694,466	742,371	768,014
MD	320	342	381	407	447	470	583	687	781	934,943	1,042,390	1,188,044	1,295,346	1,449,661
MA[2]	379	423	472	523	610	738	995	1,231	1,457	1,783,085	2,238,947	2,805,346	3,366,416	3,852,356
MI	—	—	5	7	28	212	398	749	1,184	1,636,937	2,093,890	2,420,982	2,810,173	3,668,412
MN	—	—	—	—	—	—	6	172	440	780,773	1,310,283	1,751,394	2,075,708	2,387,125
MS	—	8	31	75	137	376	607	791	828	1,131,597	1,289,600	1,551,270	1,797,114	1,790,618
MO	—	—	20	67	140	384	682	1,182	1,721	2,168,380	2,679,185	3,106,665	3,293,335	3,404,055
MT	—	—	—	—	—	—	—	—	21	39,159	142,924	243,329	376,053	548,889
NE	—	—	—	—	—	—	—	29	123	452,402	1,062,656	1,066,300	1,192,214	1,296,372
NV	—	—	—	—	—	—	—	7	42	62,266	47,355	42,335	81,875	77,407
NH	142	184	214	244	269	285	318	326	318	346,991	376,530	411,588	430,572	443,083
NJ	184	211	246	278	321	373	490	672	906	1,131,116	1,444,933	1,883,669	2,537,167	3,155,900
NM	—	—	—	—	—	—	62	94	92	119,565	160,282	195,310	327,301	360,350
NY	340	589	959	1,373	1,919	2,429	3,097	3,881	4,383	5,082,871	6,003,174	7,268,894	9,113,614	10,385,227
NC	394	478	557	639	738	753	869	993	1,071	1,399,750	1,617,949	1,893,810	2,206,287	2,559,123
ND[3]	—	—	—	—	—	—	—	—	2	36,909	190,983	319,146	577,056	646,872
OH	—	42	231	581	938	1,519	1,980	2,340	2,665	3,198,062	3,672,329	4,157,545	4,767,121	5,759,394
OK[4]	—	—	—	—	—	—	—	—	—	—	258,657	790,391	1,657,155	2,028,283
OR	—	—	—	—	—	—	12	52	91	174,768	317,704	413,536	672,765	783,389
PA	434	602	810	1,049	1,348	1,724	2,312	2,906	3,522	4,282,891	5,258,113	6,302,115	7,665,111	8,720,017
RI	69	69	77	83	97	109	148	175	217	276,531	345,506	428,556	542,610	604,397
SC	249	346	415	503	581	594	669	704	706	995,577	1,151,149	1,340,316	1,515,400	1,683,724
SD[3]	—	—	—	—	—	—	—	5	12	98,268	348,600	401,570	583,888	636,547
TN	36	106	262	423	682	829	1,003	1,110	1,259	1,542,359	1,767,518	2,020,616	2,184,789	2,337,885
TX	—	—	—	—	—	—	213	604	819	1,591,749	2,235,527	3,048,710	3,896,542	4,663,228
UT	—	—	—	—	—	—	11	40	86	143,963	210,779	276,749	373,351	449,396
VT	85	154	218	236	281	292	314	315	331	332,286	332,422	343,641	355,956	352,428
VA[1]	692	808	878	938	1,044	1,025	1,119	1,220	1,225	1,512,565	1,655,980	1,854,184	2,061,612	2,309,187
WA	—	—	—	—	—	—	1	12	24	75,116	357,232	518,103	1,141,990	1,356,621
WV[1]	56	79	105	137	177	225	302	377	442	618,457	762,794	958,800	1,221,119	1,463,701
WI	—	—	—	—	—	31	305	776	1,055	1,315,497	1,693,330	2,069,042	2,333,860	2,632,067
WY	—	—	—	—	—	—	—	—	9	20,789	62,555	92,531	145,965	194,402
U.S.[5]	3,929	5,308	7,240	9,638	12,861	17,063	23,192	31,443	38,558	50,189,209	62,979,766	76,212,168	92,228,496	106,021,537

Note: With some exceptions, pop. shown is number of residents in a state (or territory of the same name) at the time of each census. Figures may differ from originally reported census data because of corrections through the bureau's Count Question Resolution operation. Excl. U.S. military personnel stationed/assigned overseas and civilian U.S. citizens living abroad. (1) 1790-1860 VA figures are for present-day boundaries: they incl. pop. in areas then part of DC (1800-40) and excl. pop. of areas that went to KY (1790) and WV (1790-1860). (2) 1790-1810 figures for MA do not incl. district taken to form state of ME in 1820. (3) 1860 SD figure is for "unorganized Dakota"; 1870-80 figures are for present-day ND and SD. (4) 1890-1900 figures incl. Indian Terr. pop. 1830-40 totals excl. persons (5,318 in 1830; 6,100 in 1840) on public ships in service of the U.S. not credited to any state. 1890 total incl. Indian Terr. and Indian Reservations pop. (325,464) specially enumerated.

Estimated Population of American Colonies, 1630-1780

Source: U.S. Census Bureau, U.S. Dept. of Commerce
(numbers in thousands)

Colony	1630	1650	1670	1690	1700	1720	1740	1750	1760	1770	1780
Total	4.6	50.4	111.9	210.4	250.9	466.2	905.6	1,170.8	1,593.6	2,148.1	2,780.4
Connecticut	—	4.1	12.6	21.6	26.0	58.8	89.6	111.3	142.5	183.9	206.7
Delaware	—	0.2	0.7	1.5	2.5	5.4	19.9	28.7	33.3	35.5	45.4
Georgia	—	—	—	—	—	—	2.0	5.2	9.6	23.4	56.1
Kentucky[1]	—	—	—	—	—	—	—	—	—	15.7	45.0
Maine (counties)[2]	0.4	1.0	—	—	—	—	—	—	20.0	31.3	49.1
Maryland	—	4.5	13.2	24.0	29.6	66.1	116.1	141.1	162.3	202.6	245.5
Massachusetts and Plymouth[2,3]	0.9	15.6	35.3	56.9	55.9	91.0	151.6	188.0	202.6	235.3	268.6
New Hampshire	0.5	1.3	1.8	4.2	5.0	9.4	23.3	27.5	39.1	62.4	87.8
New Jersey	—	—	1.0	8.0	14.0	29.8	51.4	71.4	93.8	117.4	139.6
New York	0.4	4.1	5.8	13.9	19.1	36.9	63.7	76.7	117.1	162.9	210.5
North Carolina	—	—	3.9	7.6	10.7	21.3	51.8	73.0	110.4	197.2	270.1
Pennsylvania	—	—	—	11.4	18.0	31.0	85.6	119.7	183.7	240.1	327.3
Rhode Island	—	0.8	2.2	4.2	5.9	11.7	25.3	33.2	45.5	58.2	52.9
South Carolina	—	—	0.2	3.9	5.7	17.0	45.0	64.0	94.1	124.2	180.0
Tennessee[4]	—	—	—	—	—	—	—	—	—	1.0	10.0
Vermont[5]	—	—	—	—	—	—	—	—	—	10.0	47.6
Virginia	2.5	18.7	35.3	53.0	58.6	87.8	180.4	231.0	339.7	447.0	538.0

Note: With the exception of KY, ME, Plymouth, TN, and VT, colonies shown are the original 13 states (ratified the Constitution 1787-90). (1) Admitted as state 1792. (2) For 1660-1750, the pop. of ME counties are included with MA. ME was annexed by MA in the 1650s but became a separate state in 1820. (3) Plymouth became part of Prov. of Massachusetts in 1691. (4) Admitted as state 1796. (5) Admitted as state 1791.

Census, 1790-2020

U.S. Dept. of Commerce
only are in thousands)

1930	1940	1950	1960	1970	1980	1990	2000	2010	2020	State
2,646,248	2,832,961	3,061,743	3,266,740	3,444,354	3,894,025	4,040,389	4,447,351	4,779,753	5,024,279	AL
59,278	72,524	128,643	226,167	302,583	401,851	550,043	626,931	710,235	733,391	AK
435,573	499,261	749,587	1,302,161	1,775,399	2,716,546	3,665,339	5,130,632	6,392,017	7,151,502	AZ
1,854,482	1,949,387	1,909,511	1,786,272	1,923,322	2,286,357	2,350,624	2,673,400	2,915,919	3,011,524	AR
5,677,251	6,907,387	10,586,223	15,717,204	19,971,069	23,667,764	29,758,213	33,871,653	37,253,956	39,538,223	CA
1,035,791	1,123,296	1,325,089	1,753,947	2,209,596	2,889,735	3,294,473	4,302,015	5,029,196	5,773,714	CO
1,606,903	1,709,242	2,007,280	2,535,234	3,032,217	3,107,564	3,287,116	3,405,602	3,574,097	3,605,944	CT
238,380	266,505	318,085	446,292	548,104	594,338	666,168	783,600	897,934	989,948	DE
486,869	663,091	802,178	763,956	756,668	638,432	606,900	572,059	601,767	689,545	DC
1,468,211	1,897,414	2,771,305	4,951,560	6,791,418	9,746,961	12,938,071	15,982,824	18,801,332	21,538,187	FL
2,908,506	3,123,723	3,444,578	3,943,116	4,587,930	5,462,982	6,478,149	8,186,816	9,687,650	10,711,908	GA
368,300	422,770	499,794	632,772	769,913	964,691	1,108,229	1,211,537	1,360,301	1,455,271	HI
445,032	524,873	588,637	667,191	713,015	944,127	1,006,734	1,293,956	1,567,652	1,839,106	ID
7,630,654	7,897,241	8,712,176	10,081,158	11,110,285	11,427,409	11,430,602	12,419,647	12,830,632	12,812,508	IL
3,238,503	3,427,796	3,934,224	4,662,498	5,195,392	5,490,210	5,544,156	6,080,517	6,483,802	6,785,528	IN
2,470,939	2,538,268	2,621,073	2,757,537	2,825,368	2,913,808	2,776,831	2,926,382	3,046,355	3,190,369	IA
1,880,999	1,801,028	1,905,299	2,178,611	2,249,071	2,364,236	2,477,588	2,688,824	2,853,118	2,937,880	KS
2,614,589	2,845,627	2,944,806	3,038,156	3,220,711	3,660,324	3,686,892	4,042,285	4,339,367	4,505,836	KY
2,101,593	2,363,880	2,683,516	3,257,022	3,644,637	4,206,116	4,220,164	4,468,958	4,533,372	4,657,757	LA
797,423	847,226	913,774	969,265	993,722	1,125,043	1,227,928	1,274,923	1,328,361	1,362,359	ME
1,631,526	1,821,244	2,343,001	3,100,689	3,923,897	4,216,933	4,780,753	5,296,507	5,773,626	6,177,224	MD
4,249,614	4,316,721	4,690,514	5,148,578	5,689,170	5,737,093	6,016,425	6,349,105	6,547,629	7,029,917	MA
4,842,325	5,256,106	6,371,766	7,823,194	8,881,826	9,262,044	9,295,287	9,938,480	9,883,706	10,077,331	MI
2,563,953	2,792,300	2,982,483	3,413,864	3,806,103	4,075,970	4,375,665	4,919,492	5,303,925	5,706,494	MN
2,009,821	2,183,796	2,178,914	2,178,141	2,216,994	2,520,770	2,575,475	2,844,656	2,967,297	2,961,279	MS
3,629,367	3,784,664	3,954,653	4,319,813	4,677,623	4,916,766	5,116,901	5,596,683	5,988,927	6,154,913	MO
537,606	559,456	591,024	674,767	694,409	786,690	799,065	902,195	989,415	1,084,225	MT
1,377,963	1,315,834	1,325,510	1,411,330	1,485,333	1,569,825	1,578,417	1,711,265	1,826,341	1,961,504	NE
91,058	110,247	160,083	285,278	488,738	800,508	1,201,675	1,998,257	2,700,551	3,104,614	NV
465,293	491,524	533,242	606,921	737,681	920,610	1,109,252	1,235,786	1,316,470	1,377,529	NH
4,041,334	4,160,165	4,835,329	6,066,782	7,171,112	7,365,011	7,730,188	8,414,347	8,791,909	9,288,994	NJ
423,317	531,818	681,187	951,023	1,017,055	1,303,302	1,515,069	1,819,046	2,059,181	2,117,522	NM
12,588,066	13,479,142	14,830,192	16,782,304	18,241,391	17,558,165	17,990,778	18,976,821	19,378,102	20,201,249	NY
3,170,276	3,571,623	4,061,929	4,556,155	5,084,411	5,880,095	6,632,448	8,046,485	9,535,483	10,439,388	NC
680,845	641,935	619,636	632,446	617,792	652,717	638,800	642,200	672,591	779,094	ND
6,646,697	6,907,612	7,946,627	9,706,397	10,657,423	10,797,603	10,847,115	11,353,145	11,536,504	11,799,448	OH
2,396,040	2,336,434	2,233,351	2,328,284	2,559,463	3,025,487	3,145,576	3,450,652	3,751,351	3,959,353	OK
953,786	1,089,684	1,521,341	1,768,687	2,091,533	2,633,156	2,842,337	3,421,436	3,831,074	4,237,256	OR
9,631,350	9,900,180	10,498,012	11,319,366	11,800,766	11,864,720	11,882,842	12,281,054	12,702,379	13,002,700	PA
687,497	713,346	791,896	859,488	949,723	947,154	1,003,464	1,048,319	1,052,567	1,097,379	RI
1,738,765	1,899,804	2,117,027	2,382,594	2,590,713	3,120,729	3,486,310	4,011,816	4,625,364	5,118,425	SC
692,849	642,961	652,740	680,514	666,257	690,768	696,004	754,844	814,191	886,667	SD
2,616,556	2,915,841	3,291,718	3,567,089	3,926,018	4,591,023	4,877,203	5,689,267	6,346,105	6,910,840	TN
5,824,715	6,414,824	7,711,194	9,579,677	11,198,655	14,225,513	16,986,335	20,851,790	25,145,565	29,145,505	TX
507,847	550,310	688,862	890,627	1,059,273	1,461,037	1,722,850	2,233,198	2,763,885	3,271,616	UT
359,611	359,231	377,747	389,881	444,732	511,456	562,758	608,827	625,741	643,077	VT
2,421,851	2,677,773	3,318,680	3,966,949	4,651,448	5,346,797	6,189,197	7,079,030	8,001,024	8,631,393	VA
1,563,396	1,736,191	2,378,963	2,853,214	3,413,244	4,132,353	4,866,669	5,894,141	6,724,540	7,705,281	WA
1,729,205	1,901,974	2,005,552	1,860,421	1,744,237	1,950,186	1,793,477	1,808,350	1,852,994	1,793,716	WV
2,939,006	3,137,587	3,434,575	3,951,777	4,417,821	4,705,642	4,891,769	5,363,715	5,686,986	5,893,718	WI
225,565	250,742	290,529	330,066	332,416	469,557	453,589	493,782	563,626	576,851	WY
123,202,624	132,164,569	151,325,798	179,323,175	203,302,031	226,542,199	248,718,302	281,424,603	308,746,065	331,449,281	U.S.

U.S. Center of Population, 1790-2020

Source: Decennial Censuses, Geography Division, U.S. Census Bureau, U.S. Dept. of Commerce

The country's **(mean) center of population** is the center of population gravity. In other words, it is the point upon which the U.S. would balance if the country were a rigid, weightless plane and its population was distributed thereon, with each individual assuming an equal weight.

Census year	N Latitude			W Longitude			Approximate location
	°	'	"	°	'	"	
1790	39	16	30	76	11	12	Kent Co., MD, 23 miles east of Baltimore
1800	39	16	6	76	56	30	Howard Co., MD, 18 miles west of Baltimore
1810	39	11	30	77	37	12	Loudoun Co., VA, 40 miles northwest by west of Washington, DC
1820	39	5	42	78	33	0	Hardy Co., WV[1], 16 miles east of Moorefield
1830	38	57	54	79	16	54	Grant Co., WV[1], 19 miles west-southwest of Moorefield
1840	39	2	0	80	18	0	Upshur Co., WV[1], 16 miles south of Clarksburg
1850	38	59	0	81	19	0	Wirt Co., WV[1], 23 miles southeast of Parkersburg
1860	39	0	24	82	48	48	Pike Co., OH, 20 miles south by east of Chillicothe
1870	39	12	0	83	35	42	Highland Co., OH, 48 miles east by north of Cincinnati
1880	39	4	8	84	39	40	Boone Co., KY, 8 miles west by south of Cincinnati, OH
1890	39	11	56	85	32	53	Decatur Co., IN, 20 miles east of Columbus
1900	39	9	36	85	48	54	Bartholomew Co., IN, 6 miles southeast of Columbus
1910	39	10	12	86	32	20	Monroe Co., IN, in the city of Bloomington
1920	39	10	21	86	43	15	Owen Co., IN, 8 miles south-southeast of Spencer
1930	39	3	45	87	8	6	Greene Co., IN, 3 miles northeast of Linton
1940	38	56	54	87	22	35	Sullivan Co., IN, 2 miles southeast by east of Carlisle
1950	38	50	21	88	9	33	Richland Co., IL, 8 miles north-northwest of Olney
1950[2]	38	48	15	88	22	8	Clay Co., IL, 3 miles northeast of Louisville
1960[2]	38	35	58	89	12	35	Clinton Co., IL, 6.5 miles northwest of Centralia
1970[2]	38	27	47	89	42	22	St. Clair Co., IL, 5 miles east-southeast of Mascoutah
1980[2]	38	8	13	90	34	26	Jefferson Co., MO, 0.25 mile west of DeSoto
1990[2]	37	52	20	91	12	55	Crawford Co., MO, 9.7 miles southeast of Steelville
2000[2]	37	41	49	91	48	34	Phelps Co., MO, 2.8 miles east of Edgar Springs
2010[2]	37	31	3	92	10	23	Texas Co., MO, 2.7 miles southeast of Plato
2020[2]	37	24	57	92	20	47	Wright Co., MO, 14.6 miles northeast of Hartville

(1) Pres. Lincoln signed a bill Dec. 31, 1862, approving statehood for West Virginia (made up of former Virginia counties). It was admitted to the Union June 20, 1863. (2) Incl. Alaska and Hawaii.

Density of U.S. Population by State, 1930-2020

Source: Decennial Censuses, U.S. Census Bureau, U.S. Dept. of Commerce

(per square mile of land area)

State	1930	1950	1970	1990	2020	State	1930	1950	1970	1990	2020
AL	52.3	60.5	68.0	79.8	99.2	MT	3.7	4.1	4.8	5.5	7.4
AK	0.1	0.2	0.5	1.0	1.3	NE	17.9	17.3	19.3	20.5	25.5
AZ	3.8	6.6	15.6	32.3	62.9	NV	0.8	1.5	4.5	10.9	28.3
AR	35.6	36.7	37.0	45.2	57.9	NH	52.0	59.6	82.4	123.9	153.8
CA	36.4	68.0	128.1	191.0	253.7	NJ	549.5	657.5	974.7	1,051.1	1,263.0
CO	10.0	12.8	21.3	31.8	55.7	NM	3.5	5.6	8.4	12.5	17.5
CT	331.8	414.5	626.1	678.8	744.7	NY	267.1	314.7	387.0	381.7	428.7
DE	122.3	163.2	281.3	341.9	508.0	NC	65.2	83.5	104.5	136.3	214.7
DC	7,975.1	13,140.0	12,392.0	9,941.3	11,280.0	ND	9.9	9.0	9.0	9.3	11.3
FL	27.4	51.7	126.6	241.3	401.4	OH	162.7	194.5	260.7	265.5	288.8
GA	50.6	59.9	79.8	112.6	185.6	OK	34.9	32.6	37.3	45.9	57.7
HI	57.3	77.8	119.7	172.6	226.6	OR	9.9	15.8	21.8	29.6	44.1
ID	5.4	7.1	8.6	12.2	22.3	PA	215.3	234.6	263.6	265.6	290.6
IL	137.4	156.9	200.2	205.9	230.8	RI	665.0	766.0	915.8	970.6	1,061.4
IN	90.4	109.8	145.0	154.8	189.4	SC	57.8	70.4	86.2	116.0	170.2
IA	44.2	46.9	50.6	49.7	57.1	SD	9.1	8.6	8.8	9.2	11.7
KS	23.0	23.3	27.5	30.3	35.9	TN	63.5	79.8	95.2	118.3	167.6
KY	66.2	74.6	81.5	93.3	114.1	TX	22.3	29.5	42.9	65.0	111.6
LA	48.6	62.1	84.3	97.7	107.8	UT	6.2	8.4	12.9	21.0	39.7
ME	25.9	29.6	32.2	39.8	44.2	VT	39.0	41.0	48.2	61.1	69.8
MD	168.1	241.4	404.1	492.6	636.1	VA	61.3	84.0	117.7	156.7	218.6
MA	544.8	601.3	729.4	771.3	901.2	WA	23.5	35.8	51.3	73.2	115.9
MI	85.6	112.7	157.0	164.4	178.0	WV	71.9	83.4	72.6	74.6	74.6
MN	32.2	37.5	47.8	54.9	71.7	WI	54.3	63.4	81.6	90.3	108.8
MS	42.8	46.4	47.2	54.8	63.1	WY	2.3	3.0	3.4	4.7	5.9
MO	52.8	57.5	68.0	74.4	89.5	U.S.	34.7	42.6	57.5	70.4	93.8

Note: For the sake of comparison, the densities of Alaska and Hawaii in 1930 and 1950 are included though they were not yet states.

U.S. Area and Population, 1790-2020

Source: Decennial Censuses, U.S. Census Bureau, U.S. Dept. of Commerce

	AREA (square miles)			RESIDENT POPULATION			
						Increase over preceding census	
Census date	Total area[1]	Land area	Water area[1]	Number	Per sq mi of land	Number	%
1790 (Aug. 2)	891,364	864,746	24,065	3,929,214	4.5	—	—
1800 (Aug. 4)	891,364	864,746	24,065	5,308,483	6.1	1,379,269	35.1%
1810 (Aug. 6)	1,722,685	1,681,828	34,175	7,239,881	4.3	1,931,398	36.4
1820 (Aug. 7)	1,792,552	1,749,462	38,544	9,638,453	5.5	2,398,572	33.1
1830 (June 1)	1,792,552	1,749,462	38,544	12,860,702	7.4	3,222,249	33.4
1840 (June 1)	1,792,552	1,749,462	38,544	17,063,453	9.8	4,203,751	32.7
1850 (June 1)	2,991,655	2,940,042	52,705	23,191,876	7.9	6,128,423	35.9
1860 (June 1)	3,021,295	2,969,640	52,747	31,443,321	10.6	8,251,445	35.6
1870 (June 1)	3,612,299	3,540,705	68,082	38,558,371	10.9	7,115,050	22.6
1880 (June 1)	3,612,299	3,540,705	68,082	50,189,209	14.2	11,630,838	30.2
1890 (June 1)	3,612,299	3,540,705	68,082	62,979,766	17.8	12,790,557	25.5
1900 (June 1)	3,618,770	3,547,314	67,901	76,212,168	21.5	13,232,402	21.0
1910 (Apr. 15)	3,618,770	3,547,045	68,170	92,228,496	26.0	16,016,328	21.0
1920 (Jan. 1)	3,618,770	3,546,931	68,284	106,021,537	29.9	13,793,041	15.0
1930 (Apr. 1)	3,618,770	3,554,608	60,607	123,202,624	34.7	17,181,087	16.2
1940 (Apr. 1)	3,618,770	3,554,608	60,607	132,164,569	37.2	8,961,945	7.3
1950 (Apr. 1)	3,618,770	3,552,206	63,005	151,325,798	42.6	19,161,229	14.5
1960 (Apr. 1)	3,618,770	3,540,911	74,212	179,323,175	50.6	27,997,377	18.5
1970 (Apr. 1)	3,618,770	3,536,855	78,444	203,302,031	57.5	23,978,856	13.4
1980 (Apr. 1)	3,618,770	3,539,289	79,481	226,542,199	64.0	23,240,168	11.4
1990 (Apr. 1)	3,717,796	3,536,278	181,518	248,718,302	70.3	22,176,103	9.8
2000 (Apr. 1)	3,794,083	3,537,438	256,645	281,424,603	79.6	32,706,301	13.1
2010 (Apr. 1)	3,796,742	3,531,905	264,837	308,746,065	87.4	27,321,462	9.7
2020 (Apr. 1)	3,802,820	3,533,038	269,782	331,449,281	93.8	22,703,216	7.4

Note: Area and population density figures represent the area within the boundaries of the U.S. under its jurisdiction on the date in question including, in some cases, considerable areas not organized or settled and not covered by the census. Beginning in 1870, area data include Alaska; from 1900 on, data include Hawaii. Population figures may reflect revisions/corrections to initial tabulated census counts. (1) Figures for 1790-1980 cover inland water only. Figures for 1990 include inland, coastal, and Great Lakes water. Figures for 2000-20 include additional territorial water.

U.S. Congressional Apportionment by Census Year, 1850-2020

Source: Decennial Censuses, U.S. Census Bureau, U.S. Dept. of Commerce

The U.S. Constitution, in Article 1, Section 2, mandates that the population be counted every 10 years so that the number of U.S. representatives can be apportioned among the states. Every state is entitled to at least one House seat, with the size of a state's resident population (citizens and noncitizens) determining any additional representation. Apportionment has been made after every decennial census except for that of 1920. Prior to 1870, an enslaved person was counted as three-fifths of a person in the apportionment population. Since the 1970 census (excluding 1980), U.S. military personnel and federal civilian employees stationed or assigned overseas as well as their dependents have been allocated to a home state for apportionment. Dist. of Columbia, Puerto Rico, and U.S. island area residents are not included in the apportionment population because they lack voting seats in the U.S. House. House seats are allocated using the Huntington-Hill, or equal proportions, method for the least possible variation in the average number of people each House member represents.

The first House of Representatives, in 1789, had 65 members as provided by the Constitution. The number of representatives grew with the nation. A 1911 act fixed the total House membership at 433 (allowing for the addition of one seat each for Arizona and New Mexico upon statehood). Alaska and Hawaii each gained one House seat when they became states, temporarily raising the total to 437 representatives until after the 1960 census.

State	2020	2010	1990	1970	1950	1900	1850	State	2020	2010	1990	1970	1950	1900	1850
AL....	7	7	7	7	9	9	7	NE....	3	3	3	3	4	6	NA
AK....	1	1	1	1	NA	NA	NA	NV....	4	4	2	1	1	1	NA
AZ....	9	9	6	4	2	NA	NA	NH....	2	2	2	2	2	2	3
AR....	4	4	4	4	6	7	2	NJ....	12	12	13	15	14	10	5
CA....	52	53	52	43	30	8	2	NM....	3	3	3	2	2	NA	NA
CO....	8	7	6	5	4	3	NA	NY....	26	27	31	39	43	37	33
CT....	5	5	6	6	6	5	4	NC....	14	13	12	11	12	10	8
DE....	1	1	1	1	1	1	1	ND....	1	1	1	1	2	2	NA
FL....	28	27	23	15	8	3	1	OH....	15	16	19	23	23	21	21
GA....	14	14	11	10	10	11	8	OK....	5	5	6	6	6	5	NA
HI....	2	2	2	2	1	NA	NA	OR....	6	5	5	4	4	2	1
ID....	2	2	2	2	2	1	NA	PA....	17	18	21	25	30	32	25
IL....	17	18	20	24	25	25	9	RI....	2	2	2	2	2	2	2
IN....	9	9	10	11	11	13	11	SC....	7	7	6	6	6	7	6
IA....	4	4	5	6	8	11	2	SD....	1	1	1	2	2	2	NA
KS....	4	4	4	5	6	8	NA	TN....	9	9	9	8	9	10	10
KY....	6	6	6	7	8	11	10	TX....	38	36	30	24	22	16	2
LA....	6	6	7	8	8	7	4	UT....	4	4	3	2	2	1	NA
ME....	2	2	2	2	3	4	6	VT....	1	1	1	1	1	2	3
MD....	8	8	8	8	7	6	6	VA....	11	11	11	10	10	10	13
MA....	9	9	10	12	14	14	11	WA....	10	10	9	7	7	3	NA
MI....	13	14	16	19	18	12	4	WV....	2	3	3	4	6	5	NA
MN....	8	8	8	8	9	9	2	WI....	8	8	9	9	10	11	3
MS....	4	4	5	5	6	8	5	WY....	1	1	1	1	1	1	NA
MO....	8	8	9	10	11	16	7	Total...	435	435	435	435	437	391	237
MT....	2	1	1	2	2	1	NA								

NA = Not applicable.

U.S. Enslaved and "Free Colored" Population, 1790, 1820, 1860

Source: Decennial Censuses, U.S. Census Bureau, U.S. Dept. of Commerce

	1790			1820			1860		
	Enslaved	% enslaved[1]	Free colored	Enslaved	% enslaved[1]	Free colored	Enslaved	% enslaved[1]	Free colored
Northern states[2]	40,354	2.1%	27,070	19,108	0.4%	99,307	18	0.0%	225,224
Connecticut	2,764	1.2	2,808	97	0.0	7,870	0	0.0	8,627
New Jersey...........	11,423	6.2	2,762	7,557	2.7	12,460	18	0.0	25,318
New York............	21,324	6.3	4,654	10,088	0.7	29,279	0	0.0	49,005
Pennsylvania	3,737	0.9	6,537	211	0.0	30,202	0	0.0	56,949
Border/disputed states ..	124,353	27.5	12,056	248,860	22.4	55,794	429,403	13.2	118,652
Delaware	8,887	15.0	3,899	4,509	6.2	12,958	1,798	1.6	19,829
Kansas..............	—	—	—	—	—	—	2	0.0	625
Kentucky.............	12,430	16.9	114	126,732	22.5	2,759	225,483	19.5	10,684
Maryland.............	103,036	32.2	8,043	107,397	26.4	39,730	87,189	12.7	83,942
Missouri.............	—	—	—	10,222	15.4	347	114,931	9.7	3,572
Southern states	532,974	35.3	20,401	1,265,534	37.8	75,775	3,521,110	38.7	132,760
Alabama	—	—	—	41,879	32.7	571	435,080	45.1	2,690
Arkansas	—	—	—	1,617	11.3	59	111,115	25.5	144
Florida	—	—	—	—	—	—	61,745	44.0	932
Georgia..............	29,264	35.5	398	149,656	43.9	1,763	462,198	43.7	3,500
Louisiana	—	—	—	69,064	45.0	10,476	331,726	46.9	18,647
Mississippi	—	—	—	32,814	43.5	458	436,631	55.2	773
North Carolina	100,572	25.5	4,975	204,917	32.1	14,712	331,059	33.4	30,463
South Carolina	107,094	43.0	1,801	258,475	51.4	6,826	402,406	57.2	9,914
Tennessee	3,417	9.6	361	80,107	18.9	2,737	275,719	24.8	7,300
Texas	—	—	—	—	—	—	182,566	30.2	355
Virginia	292,627	39.1	12,866	427,005	39.7	38,173	490,865	30.7	58,042
Total territories[3]	—	—	—	4,520	19.4	2,758	11,434	—	11,434
Total states and territories	697,681	17.8	59,527	1,538,022	16.0	233,634	3,953,760	12.6	488,070

Note: "Free colored" was an official Census Bureau designation in these decades. States are grouped roughly by allegiance in the Civil War. (1) Percentage of total pop., all races. (2) The following states are not listed separately but are included in totals for Northern states (relevant census years in parentheses): CA (1860), IL (1820, 1860), IN (1820, 1860), IA (1860), ME (1790, 1820, 1860), MA (1790, 1820, 1860), MI (1820, 1860), MN (1860), NH (1790, 1820, 1860), OH (1820, 1860), OR (1860), RI (1790, 1820, 1860), VT (1790, 1820, 1860), WI (1820, 1860). (3) Incl. AZ (1860), CO (1860), Dakota (1860), DC (1820, 1860), NE (1860), NV (1860), NM (1860), UT (1860), WA (1860).

U.S. Population by Sex, Race, Residence, and Median Age, 1790-2020

Source: Decennial Censuses, U.S. Census Bureau, U.S. Dept. of Commerce

(numbers in thousands, unless otherwise noted)

Census date	SEX Male	SEX Female	RACE[2,3] White	RACE[2,3] Black Number	RACE[2,3] Black % tot. pop.	RACE[2,3] Other	RESIDENCE Urban[4]	RESIDENCE Rural	MEDIAN AGE (years) All races	MEDIAN AGE (years) White[2,3]	MEDIAN AGE (years) Black[2]
Conterminous U.S.[1]											
1790 (Aug. 2)	NA	NA	3,172	757	19.3%	NA	202	3,728	NA	NA	NA
1800 (Aug. 4)	NA	NA	4,306	1,002	18.9	NA	322	4,986	NA	NA	NA
1810 (Aug. 6)	NA	NA	5,862	1,378	19.0	NA	525	6,714	NA	16.0	NA
1820 (Aug. 7)	4,897	4,742	7,867	1,772	18.4	NA	693	8,945	16.7	16.6	17.2
1830 (June 1)	6,532	6,334	10,537	2,329	18.1	NA	1,127	11,733	17.2	17.3	17.2
1840 (June 1)	8,689	8,381	14,196	2,874	16.8	NA	1,845	15,218	17.8	17.9	17.6
1850 (June 1)	11,838	11,354	19,553	3,639	15.7	NA	3,574	19,617	18.9	19.2	17.4
1860 (June 1)	16,085	15,358	26,923	4,442	14.1	79	6,217	25,227	19.4	19.7	17.5
1870 (June 1)	19,494	19,065	33,589	4,880	12.7	89	9,902	28,656	20.2	20.4	18.5
1880 (June 1)	25,519	24,637	43,403	6,581	13.1	172	14,130	36,059	20.9	21.4	18.0
1890 (June 1)	32,237	30,711	55,101	7,489	11.9	358	22,106	40,874	22.0	22.5	17.8
1900 (June 1)	38,816	37,178	66,809	8,834	11.6	351	30,215	45,997	22.9	23.4	19.4
1910 (Apr. 15).	47,332	44,640	81,732	9,828	10.7	413	42,064	50,164	24.1	24.5	20.8
1920 (Jan. 1)	53,900	51,810	94,821	10,463	9.9	427	54,253	51,768	25.3	25.5	22.3
1930 (Apr. 1).	62,137	60,638	110,287	11,891	9.7	597	69,161	54,042	26.5	26.9	23.5
1940 (Apr. 1).	66,062	65,608	118,215	12,866	9.8	589	74,705	57,459	29.0	29.5	25.3
United States											
1950 (Apr. 1).	74,833	75,864	135,150	15,045	10.0	713	96,847	54,479	30.2	30.8	26.1
1960 (Apr. 1).	88,331	90,992	158,832	18,872	10.5	1,620	125,269	54,054	29.5	30.3	23.5
1970 (Apr. 1).	98,926	104,309	178,098	22,581	11.1	2,557	149,647	53,565	28.1	28.9	22.4
1980 (Apr. 1).	110,053	116,493	194,713	26,683	11.8	5,150	167,051	59,495	30.0	30.9	24.9
1990 (Apr. 1).	121,284	127,507	208,741	30,517	12.3	9,533	187,053	61,656	32.8	33.7	27.9
2000 (Apr. 1).	138,054	143,368	194,553	33,948	12.1	13,013	222,361	59,061	35.3	38.6	30.2
2010 (Apr. 1).	151,781	156,964	196,818	37,686	12.2	17,798	249,253	59,492	37.2	42.0	32.4
2020 (Apr. 1).	162,686	168,763	191,698	39,940	12.1	24,182	265,149	66,300	38.8	44.5	35.1

NA = Not available. **Note:** Population figures may reflect revisions/corrections to initial tabulated census counts. (1) Excludes Alaska and Hawaii. (2) New race categories were introduced in the 2000 census. Race data for 2000 and on are for persons who reported being of one race alone. "Other" comprises Asians, Native Hawaiians and other Pacific Islanders, American Indians and Alaska Natives. Because of these changes, race data from 2000 on are not comparable to figures from previous years. (3) Does not include persons who reported being of Hispanic or Latino origin. (4) The Census Bureau's definition of "urban" has changed over time. Figures for 2000 and 2010 include residents of urbanized areas (50,000 or more inhabitants) and urban clusters (at least 2,500 but fewer than 50,000 inhabitants).

U.S. Population by Race and Hispanic Origin, 2010-20

Source: Decennial Censuses, U.S. Census Bureau, U.S. Dept. of Commerce

	2020 One race alone	2020 One or more races[1]	2010 One race alone	2010 One or more races[1]	% change, 2010-20 One race alone	% change, 2010-20 One or more races[1]
Total population	297,600,338	331,449,281	299,736,465	308,746,065	−0.7%	7.4%
Race						
White.	204,277,273	235,411,507	223,553,265	231,040,398	−8.6	1.9
Black or African American.	41,104,200	46,936,733	38,929,319	42,020,743	5.6	11.7
Asian.	19,886,049	24,000,998	14,674,252	17,320,856	35.5	38.6
American Indian and Alaska Native . . .	3,727,135	9,666,058	2,932,248	5,220,579	27.1	85.2
Native Hawaiian and Other Pac. Isl. . .	689,966	1,586,463	540,013	1,225,195	27.8	29.5
Some other race	27,915,715	49,902,536	19,107,368	21,748,084	46.1	129.5
Hispanic origin and race						
Hispanic or Latino, any race	41,780,084	62,080,044	47,435,002	50,477,594	−11.9	23.0
Not Hispanic or Latino.	255,820,254	269,369,237	252,301,463	258,267,944	1.4	4.3
White.	191,697,641	203,890,286	196,817,552	201,856,108	−2.6	1.0
Black or African American.	39,940,338	44,277,916	37,685,848	40,123,525	6.0	10.4
Asian.	19,618,719	23,142,519	14,465,124	16,722,710	35.6	38.4
American Indian and Alaska Native. .	2,251,699	6,691,567	2,247,098	4,029,675	0.2	66.1
Native Hawaiian and Other Pac. Isl.	622,018	1,336,035	481,576	1,014,888	29.2	31.6
Some other race	1,689,833	4,584,438	604,265	1,033,866	179.7	343.4

Note: Population figures may reflect revisions/corrections to initial tabulated census counts. (1) Alone or in combination with one or more of the other races listed. Numbers do not add up to totals because of individuals reporting more than one race.

U.S. Population Growth by Race and Hispanic Origin, 1970-2030
Source: Decennial Censuses and Population Projections Program, U.S. Census Bureau, U.S. Dept. of Commerce
(numbers in millions)

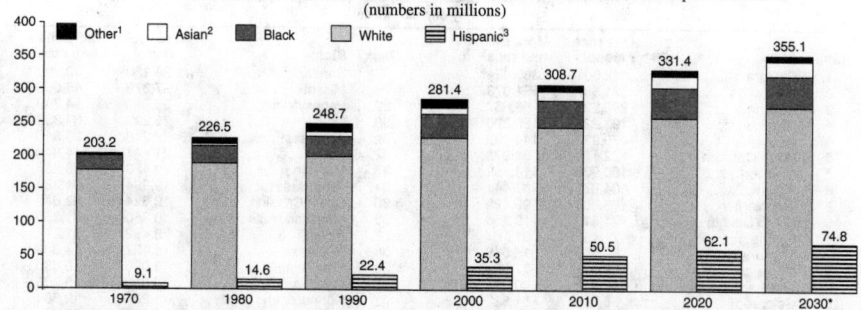

*Projected. **Note:** Because of changes in census questions and methods, data on race and Hispanic origin are not wholly comparable over time. Population figures may reflect revisions/corrections to initial tabulated census counts. (1) Includes American Indians and Alaska Natives as well as other races not shown. For 2000 and on, this category also includes Native Hawaiians and Other Pacific Islanders along with persons reporting two or more races. (2) Figures for 1970-90 include Pacific Islanders. (3) May be of any race. 1970 figure is based on sample of households.

State Population by Race and Hispanic Origin, 2020
Source: Decennial Census, U.S. Census Bureau, U.S. Dept. of Commerce
(percentage of state or country's total population)

State	White	Black or African American	Asian	American Indian and Alaska Native	Native Hawaiian and Other Pacific Islander	Some other race	Two or more races[1]	Hispanic or Latino, any race
Alabama	63.1%	25.6%	1.5%	0.5%	0.05%	0.29%	3.7%	5.3%
Alaska	57.5	2.8	5.9	14.8	1.70	0.62	9.8	6.8
Arizona	53.4	4.4	3.5	3.7	0.20	0.44	3.7	30.7
Arkansas	68.5	14.9	1.7	0.7	0.47	0.27	4.9	8.5
California	34.7	5.4	15.1	0.4	0.35	0.57	4.1	39.4
Colorado	65.1	3.8	3.4	0.6	0.16	0.51	4.5	21.9
Connecticut	63.2	10.0	4.7	0.2	0.03	0.75	3.8	17.3
Delaware	58.6	21.5	4.3	0.3	0.03	0.46	4.3	10.5
Dist. of Columbia	38.0	40.9	4.8	0.2	0.05	0.54	4.3	11.3
Florida	51.5	14.5	2.9	0.2	0.05	0.64	3.7	26.5
Georgia	50.1	30.6	4.4	0.2	0.06	0.52	3.6	10.5
Hawaii	21.6	1.5	36.5	0.2	10.24	0.36	20.1	9.5
Idaho	78.9	0.8	1.4	1.0	0.18	0.45	4.2	13.0
Illinois	58.3	13.9	5.8	0.1	0.02	0.35	3.2	18.2
Indiana	75.5	9.4	2.5	0.2	0.04	0.37	3.9	8.2
Iowa	82.7	4.1	2.4	0.3	0.18	0.27	3.4	6.8
Kansas	72.2	5.6	2.9	0.7	0.11	0.34	5.1	13.0
Kentucky	81.3	7.9	1.6	0.2	0.08	0.33	3.9	4.6
Louisiana	55.8	31.2	1.8	0.6	0.04	0.36	3.4	6.9
Maine	90.2	1.8	1.2	0.5	0.03	0.33	3.9	2.0
Maryland	47.2	29.1	6.8	0.2	0.04	0.57	4.4	11.8
Massachusetts	67.6	6.5	7.2	0.1	0.02	1.31	4.7	12.6
Michigan	72.4	13.5	3.3	0.5	0.03	0.37	4.4	5.6
Minnesota	76.3	6.9	5.2	1.0	0.05	0.37	4.1	6.1
Mississippi	55.4	36.4	1.1	0.5	0.04	0.24	2.8	3.6
Missouri	75.8	11.3	2.1	0.4	0.15	0.36	5.0	4.9
Montana	83.1	0.5	0.7	6.0	0.08	0.40	5.0	4.2
Nebraska	75.7	4.8	2.7	0.8	0.07	0.32	3.7	12.0
Nevada	45.9	9.4	8.6	0.8	0.74	0.55	5.4	28.7
New Hampshire	87.2	1.4	2.6	0.2	0.03	0.43	4.0	4.3
New Jersey	51.9	12.4	10.2	0.1	0.02	0.76	3.1	21.6
New Mexico	36.5	1.8	1.7	8.9	0.07	0.49	2.8	47.7
New York	52.5	13.7	9.5	0.3	0.03	0.98	3.6	19.5
North Carolina	60.5	20.2	3.3	1.0	0.07	0.44	3.9	10.7
North Dakota	81.7	3.4	1.7	4.8	0.11	0.24	3.9	4.3
Ohio	75.9	12.3	2.5	0.2	0.04	0.38	4.3	4.4
Oklahoma	60.8	7.2	2.3	7.9	0.21	0.34	9.4	11.9
Oregon	71.7	1.9	4.5	1.0	0.43	0.54	6.1	13.9
Pennsylvania	73.5	10.5	3.9	0.1	0.02	0.42	3.5	8.1
Rhode Island	68.7	5.0	3.5	0.3	0.03	1.04	4.8	16.6
South Carolina	62.1	24.8	1.7	0.3	0.06	0.38	3.7	6.9
South Dakota	79.6	2.0	1.5	8.4	0.06	0.23	3.9	4.4
Tennessee	70.9	15.7	1.9	0.2	0.05	0.35	3.9	6.9
Texas	39.7	11.8	5.4	0.3	0.10	0.39	3.0	39.3
Utah	75.4	1.1	2.4	0.9	1.10	0.38	3.7	15.1
Vermont	89.1	1.3	1.8	0.3	0.03	0.40	4.6	2.4
Virginia	58.6	18.3	7.1	0.2	0.07	0.53	4.7	10.5
Washington	63.8	3.8	9.4	1.2	0.81	0.56	6.6	13.7
West Virginia	89.1	3.6	0.8	0.2	0.02	0.26	4.0	1.9
Wisconsin	78.6	6.2	3.0	0.8	0.03	0.30	3.5	7.6
Wyoming	81.4	0.8	0.9	2.0	0.08	0.42	4.1	10.2
United States	**57.8**	**12.1**	**5.9**	**0.7**	**0.19**	**0.51**	**4.1**	**18.7**

(1) Not Hispanic or Latino.

American Indian and Alaska Native Population by State, 2010

Source: Decennial Census, U.S. Census Bureau, U.S. Dept. of Commerce
(ranked by one race alone)

Rank	State	One race alone[1]	More than one race[2]	Rank	State	One race alone[1]	More than one race[2]
1.	California	362,801	360,424	27.	Kansas	28,150	30,980
2.	Oklahoma	321,687	161,073	28.	Missouri	27,376	45,000
3.	Arizona	296,529	56,857	29.	Pennsylvania	26,843	54,249
4.	New Mexico	193,222	26,290	30.	Ohio	25,292	64,832
5.	Texas	170,972	144,292	31.	Arkansas	22,248	25,340
6.	North Carolina	122,110	61,972	32.	Idaho	21,441	14,944
7.	New York	106,906	114,152	33.	Maryland	20,420	38,237
8.	Alaska	104,871	33,441	34.	Tennessee	19,994	34,880
9.	Washington	103,869	95,129	35.	South Carolina	19,524	22,647
10.	South Dakota	71,817	10,256	36.	Massachusetts	18,850	31,855
11.	Florida	71,458	91,104	37.	Indiana	18,462	31,276
12.	Montana	62,555	16,046	38.	Nebraska	18,427	11,389
13.	Michigan	62,007	77,088	39.	Mississippi	15,030	10,880
14.	Minnesota	60,916	40,984	40.	Wyoming	13,336	5,260
15.	Colorado	56,010	51,822	41.	Connecticut	11,256	19,884
16.	Wisconsin	54,526	31,702	42.	Iowa	11,084	13,427
17.	Oregon	53,203	56,020	43.	Kentucky	10,120	21,235
18.	Illinois	43,963	57,488	44.	Maine	8,568	9,914
19.	North Dakota	36,591	6,405	45.	Rhode Island	6,058	8,336
20.	Utah	32,927	17,137	46.	Delaware	4,181	5,718
21.	Georgia	32,151	51,873	47.	Hawaii	4,164	29,306
22.	Nevada	32,062	23,883	48.	West Virginia	3,787	9,527
23.	Louisiana	30,579	24,500	49.	New Hampshire	3,150	7,374
24.	Virginia	29,225	51,699	50.	Vermont	2,207	5,172
25.	New Jersey	29,026	41,690	51.	District of Columbia	2,079	4,442
26.	Alabama	28,218	28,900		**United States**	**2,932,248**	**2,288,331**

(1) Respondents who self-identified as American Indian and Alaska Native (AIAN) alone. (2) Respondents who self-identified as AIAN in combination with one or more other races.

American Indian and Alaska Native Population by Selected Tribal Groupings, 2010

Source: Decennial Census, U.S. Census Bureau, U.S. Dept. of Commerce
(ranked by American Indian and Alaska Native [AIAN] alone, one tribal grouping alone)

Tribal grouping	AIAN alone One tribal grouping alone[1]	AIAN alone One or more tribal groupings[2]	AIAN alone or in combination One or more tribal groupings[3]	Tribal grouping	AIAN alone One tribal grouping alone[1]	AIAN alone One or more tribal groupings[2]	AIAN alone or in combination One or more tribal groupings[3]
Total	2,879,638	2,932,248	5,220,579	Crow	10,332	10,860	15,203
AIAN tribes, not specified	693,709	693,709	1,545,963	Kiowa	9,437	10,355	13,787
Amer. Ind. tribes, specified	1,935,363	2,032,133	3,397,251	Paiute	9,340	10,205	13,767
Navajo	286,731	295,016	332,129	Osage	8,938	10,063	18,576
Cherokee	284,247	300,463	819,105	Yakama	8,786	9,096	11,527
Mexican Amer. Ind.	121,221	123,550	175,494	Menominee	8,374	8,627	11,133
Chippewa	112,757	115,402	170,742	Houma	8,169	8,240	10,768
Sioux	112,176	116,477	170,110	Colville	8,114	8,314	10,549
Choctaw	103,910	110,308	195,764	Arapaho	8,014	8,402	10,861
Apache	63,193	69,694	111,810	Shoshone	7,852	8,462	13,002
Lumbee	62,306	62,957	73,691	Delaware	7,843	8,215	18,264
Pueblo	49,695	52,026	62,540	Yuman	7,727	8,278	10,089
Creek	48,352	52,948	88,332	Ute	7,435	8,220	11,491
Iroquois	40,570	42,461	81,002	Ottawa	7,272	8,048	13,033
Chickasaw	27,973	30,206	52,278	Canadian/French Amer. Ind.	6,433	7,051	14,822
Blackfeet	27,279	31,798	105,304	Cree	2,211	2,950	7,983
Pima	22,040	23,205	26,655	All other Amer. Ind. tribes.	270,141	282,747	429,629
Yaqui	21,679	23,195	32,595	Amer. Ind. tribes, not specified	131,943	132,060	234,320
S. Amer. Ind.	20,901	21,380	47,233	AK Native tribes, specified	98,892	103,086	138,850
Potawatomi	20,412	20,874	33,771	Yup'ik	28,927	29,618	33,889
Tohono O'Odham	19,522	20,247	23,478	Inupiat[4]	24,859	25,736	33,360
Central Amer. Ind.	15,882	16,454	27,844	Alaskan Athabascan	15,623	16,427	22,484
Puget Sound Salish	14,320	14,535	20,260	Tlingit-Haida	15,256	16,115	26,080
Seminole	14,080	16,448	31,971	Aleut	11,920	12,643	19,282
Spanish Amer. Ind.	13,460	13,758	19,951	Tsimshian	2,307	2,547	3,755
Hopi	12,580	14,634	18,327	AK Native tribes, not specified	19,731	19,904	29,933
Comanche	12,284	13,471	23,330				
Cheyenne	11,375	12,493	19,051				

Note: This table measures the number of responses, not respondents. Respondents who self-identified with multiple tribal groupings are counted more than once. A tribal grouping refers to combined individual tribes (e.g., Fort Sill Apache and San Carlos Apache as Apache or King Salmon Tribe and Native Village of Kanatak as Aleut). (1) For example, Navajo or Alaskan Athabascan. (2) As in footnote 1 or in combination with other tribal groupings (e.g., Yakama and Aleut). (3) As in footnotes 1 or 2 or in combination with another race (e.g., Apache, Navajo, and white; or Inupiat, white, and Black). (4) Eskimo in previous censuses.

Largest U.S. Cities by Population, 1850-2022

Source: Population Estimates Program and Decennial Censuses, U.S. Census Bureau, U.S. Dept. of Commerce
(ranked by 2022 population)

Rank City	2022	2020	2010	2000	1980	1950	1900	1850
1. New York, NY	8,335,897	8,804,190	8,175,133	8,008,654	7,071,639	7,891,957	3,437,202	515,547
2. Los Angeles, CA	3,822,238	3,898,747	3,792,621	3,694,742	2,968,528	1,970,358	102,479	1,610
3. Chicago, IL	2,665,039	2,746,388	2,695,598	2,896,016	3,005,072	3,620,962	1,698,575	29,963
4. Houston, TX	2,302,878	2,304,580	2,099,451	1,953,631	1,595,138	596,163	44,633	2,396
5. Phoenix, AZ	1,644,409	1,608,139	1,445,632	1,321,045	789,704	106,818	5,544	—
6. Philadelphia, PA	1,567,258	1,603,797	1,526,006	1,517,550	1,688,210	2,071,605	1,293,697	121,376
7. San Antonio, TX	1,472,909	1,434,625	1,327,407	1,144,646	785,940	408,442	53,321	3,488
8. San Diego, CA	1,381,162	1,386,932	1,307,402	1,223,400	875,538	334,387	17,700	—
9. Dallas, TX	1,299,544	1,304,379	1,197,816	1,188,580	904,599	434,462	42,638	—
10. Austin, TX	974,447	961,855	790,390	656,562	345,890	132,459	22,258	629
11. Jacksonville, FL[1]	971,319	949,611	821,784	735,617	540,920	204,517	28,429	1,045
12. San Jose, CA	971,233	1,013,240	945,942	894,943	629,400	95,280	21,500	—
13. Fort Worth, TX	956,709	918,915	741,206	534,694	385,164	278,778	26,688	—
14. Columbus, OH	907,971	905,748	787,033	711,470	565,021	375,901	125,560	17,882
15. Charlotte, NC	897,720	874,579	731,424	540,167	315,474	134,042	18,091	1,065
16. Indianapolis, IN[1]	880,621	887,642	820,445	791,926	710,868	427,173	169,164	8,091
17. San Francisco, CA[2]	808,437	873,965	805,235	776,733	678,974	775,357	342,782	34,776
18. Seattle, WA	749,256	737,015	608,660	563,376	493,846	467,591	80,671	—
19. Denver, CO	713,252	715,522	600,158	553,693	492,686	415,786	133,859	—
20. Oklahoma City, OK	694,800	681,054	579,999	506,132	404,014	243,504	10,037	—
21. Nashville-Davidson, TN[1]	683,622	689,447	601,222	569,892	477,811	174,307	80,865	10,165
22. El Paso, TX	677,456	678,815	649,121	563,662	425,259	130,485	15,906	—
23. Washington, DC	671,803	689,545	601,723	572,059	638,432	802,178	278,718	40,001
24. Las Vegas, NV	656,274	641,903	583,756	479,137	164,674	24,624	—	—
25. Boston, MA	650,706	675,647	617,594	589,141	562,994	801,444	560,892	136,881
26. Portland, OR	635,067	652,503	583,776	529,121	368,148	373,628	90,426	—
27. Louisville/Jefferson Co., KY[1]	624,444	386,884	597,337	256,231	298,694	369,129	204,731	43,194
28. Memphis, TN	621,056	633,104	646,889	650,100	646,174	396,000	102,320	8,841
29. Detroit, MI	620,376	639,111	713,777	951,270	1,203,368	1,849,568	285,704	21,019
30. Baltimore, MD	569,931	585,708	620,961	651,154	786,741	949,708	508,957	169,054
31. Milwaukee, WI	563,305	577,222	594,833	596,974	636,297	637,392	285,315	20,061
32. Albuquerque, NM	561,008	564,559	545,852	448,607	332,619	96,815	6,238	—
33. Tucson, AZ	546,574	542,629	520,116	486,699	330,537	45,454	7,531	—
34. Fresno, CA	545,567	542,107	494,665	427,652	217,491	91,669	12,470	—
35. Sacramento, CA	528,001	524,943	466,488	407,018	275,741	137,572	29,282	6,820
36. Mesa, AZ	512,498	504,258	439,041	396,375	152,404	16,790	722	—
37. Kansas City, MO	509,297	508,090	459,787	441,545	448,028	456,622	163,752	—
38. Atlanta, GA	499,127	498,715	420,003	416,267	425,022	331,314	89,872	2,572
39. Colorado Springs, CO	486,248	478,961	416,427	360,890	215,105	45,472	21,085	—
40. Omaha, NE	485,153	486,051	408,958	390,007	313,939	251,117	102,555	—
41. Raleigh, NC	476,581	467,665	403,892	276,094	150,255	65,679	13,643	4,518
42. Virginia Beach, VA	455,618	459,470	437,994	425,257	262,199	5,390	—	—
43. Long Beach, CA	451,307	466,742	462,257	461,522	361,498	250,767	2,252	—
44. Miami, FL	449,514	442,241	399,457	362,470	346,681	249,276	1,681	—
45. Oakland, CA	430,553	440,646	390,724	399,484	339,337	384,575	66,960	—
46. Minneapolis, MN	425,096	429,954	382,578	382,747	370,951	521,718	202,718	—
47. Tulsa, OK	411,867	413,066	391,906	393,049	360,919	182,740	1,390	—
48. Bakersfield, CA	410,647	403,455	347,483	246,889	105,611	34,784	4,836	—
49. Tampa, FL	398,173	384,959	335,709	303,447	271,577	124,681	15,839	—
50. Wichita, KS	396,192	397,532	382,368	346,753	279,838	168,279	24,671	—
51. Arlington, TX	394,602	394,266	365,438	332,969	160,113	7,692	1,079	—
52. Aurora, CO	393,537	386,261	325,078	275,921	158,588	11,421	202	—
53. New Orleans, LA	369,749	383,997	343,829	484,674	557,927	570,445	287,104	116,375
54. Cleveland, OH	361,607	372,624	396,815	477,459	573,822	914,808	381,768	17,034
55. Anaheim, CA	344,461	346,824	336,265	328,014	219,494	14,556	1,456	—
56. Urban Honolulu, HI[3]	343,421	350,964	337,256	371,657	365,048	248,034	39,306	—
57. Henderson, NV	331,415	317,610	257,729	175,381	24,363	—	—	—
58. Stockton, CA	321,819	320,804	291,707	243,771	148,283	70,853	17,506	—
59. Riverside, CA	320,764	314,998	303,871	255,166	170,591	46,764	7,973	—
60. Lexington-Fayette, KY[1]	320,347	322,570	295,803	260,512	204,165	55,534	26,369	8,159
61. Corpus Christi, TX	316,239	317,863	305,215	277,454	232,134	108,287	4,703	—
62. Orlando, FL	316,081	307,573	238,300	185,951	128,291	52,367	2,481	—
63. Irvine, CA	313,685	307,670	212,375	143,072	62,134	—	—	—
64. Cincinnati, OH	309,513	309,317	296,943	331,285	385,409	503,998	325,902	115,435
65. Santa Ana, CA	308,189	310,227	324,528	337,977	204,023	45,533	4,933	—
66. Newark, NJ	305,344	311,549	277,140	272,537	329,248	438,776	246,070	38,894
67. St. Paul, MN	303,176	311,527	285,068	286,840	270,230	311,349	163,065	1,112
68. Pittsburgh, PA	302,898	302,971	305,704	334,563	423,959	676,806	321,616	46,601
69. Greensboro, NC	301,115	299,035	269,666	223,891	155,642	74,389	10,035	—
70. Lincoln, NE	292,627	291,082	258,379	225,581	171,932	98,884	40,169	—
71. Durham, NC	291,928	283,506	228,330	187,035	101,149	71,311	6,679	—
72. Plano, TX	289,547	285,494	259,841	222,030	72,331	2,126	1,304	—
73. Anchorage, AK	287,145	291,247	291,826	260,283	174,431	11,254	—	—
74. Jersey City, NJ	286,670	292,449	247,597	240,055	223,532	299,017	206,433	6,856
75. St. Louis, MO	286,578	301,578	319,294	348,189	452,801	856,796	575,238	77,860
76. Chandler, AZ	280,711	275,987	236,123	176,581	29,673	3,799	—	—
77. North Las Vegas, NV	280,543	262,527	216,961	115,488	42,739	—	—	—
78. Chula Vista, CA	279,170	275,487	243,916	173,556	83,927	15,927	—	—
79. Buffalo, NY	276,486	278,349	261,310	292,648	357,870	580,132	352,387	42,261
80. Gilbert, AZ	275,346	267,918	208,453	109,697	5,717	1,114	—	—
81. Reno, NV	273,448	264,165	225,221	180,480	100,756	32,497	4,500	—
82. Madison, WI	272,903	269,840	233,209	208,054	170,616	96,056	19,164	1,525
83. Fort Wayne, IN	267,927	263,886	253,691	205,727	172,391	133,607	45,115	4,282
84. Toledo, OH	266,301	270,871	287,208	313,782	354,635	303,616	131,822	3,829
85. Lubbock, TX	263,930	257,141	229,573	199,564	174,361	71,747	—	—
86. St. Petersburg, FL	261,256	258,308	244,769	248,232	238,647	96,738	1,575	—

Rank City	2022	2020	2010	2000	1980	1950	1900	1850
87. Laredo, TX	256,187	255,205	236,091	176,576	91,449	51,910	13,429	—
88. Irving, TX	254,715	256,684	216,290	191,615	109,943	2,621	—	—
89. Chesapeake, VA	252,488	249,422	222,209	199,184	114,486	—	—	—
90. Glendale, AZ	252,136	248,325	226,721	218,812	97,172	8,179	—	—
91. Winston-Salem, NC	251,350	249,545	229,617	185,776	131,885	87,811	13,650	—
92. Scottsdale, AZ	243,050	241,361	217,385	202,705	88,412	2,032	—	—
93. Garland, TX	240,854	246,018	226,876	215,768	138,857	10,571	819	—
94. Boise City, ID	236,634	235,684	205,671	185,787	102,249	34,393	5,957	—
95. Norfolk, VA	232,995	238,005	242,803	234,403	266,979	213,513	46,624	14,326
96. Port St. Lucie, FL	231,790	204,851	164,603	88,769	14,690	—	—	—
97. Spokane, WA	230,160	228,989	208,916	195,629	171,300	161,721	36,848	—
98. Richmond, VA	229,395	226,610	204,214	197,790	219,214	230,310	85,050	27,570
99. Fremont, CA	223,871	230,504	214,089	203,413	131,945	—	—	—
100. Huntsville, AL	221,933	215,006	180,105	158,635	142,513	16,437	8,068	2,863

— = Not available. **Note:** 2022 population estimates are as of July 1. Decennial census figures for 1950-2020 are for Apr. 1; 1850 and 1900 are for June 1. Figures may reflect revisions/corrections to initial tabulated census counts. Cities are incorporated places unless otherwise noted. (1) Consolidated city-county government. For years predating consolidation, city population figures are shown. (2) 1850 figure is for 1852, from state census. 1850 census results were destroyed by fire. (3) Census designated place (CDP). Figures for years prior to 2010 are for Honolulu CDP and are not directly comparable.

Population Change in Largest U.S. Cities, 2010-22

Source: Population Estimates Program and Decennial Census, U.S. Census Bureau, U.S. Dept. of Commerce

(ranked by % change, 2010-22; 2022 estimates are as of July 1; 2010 decennial census figures are for Apr. 1)

Cities With Most Growth

Rank City	Population 2022	2010	% change, 2010-22
1. Irvine, CA	313,685	212,375	47.7%
2. Port St. Lucie, FL	231,790	164,603	40.8
3. Orlando, FL	316,081	238,300	32.6
4. Gilbert, AZ	275,346	208,453	32.1
5. North Las Vegas, NV	280,543	216,961	29.3
6. Fort Worth, TX	956,709	741,206	29.1
7. Henderson, NV	331,415	257,729	28.6
8. Durham, NC	291,928	228,330	27.9
9. Austin, TX	974,447	790,390	23.3
10. Huntsville, AL	221,933	180,105	23.2
11. Seattle, WA	749,256	608,660	23.1
12. Charlotte, NC	897,720	731,424	22.7
13. Reno, NV	273,448	225,221	21.4
14. Aurora, CO	393,537	325,078	21.1
15. Oklahoma City, OK	694,800	579,999	19.8
16. Chandler, AZ	280,711	236,123	18.9
17. Denver, CO	713,252	600,158	18.8
18. Atlanta, GA	499,127	420,003	18.8
19. Omaha, NE	485,153	408,958	18.6
20. Tampa, FL	398,173	335,709	18.6

Cities With Least Growth

Rank City	Population 2022	2010	% change, 2010-22
1. Detroit, MI	620,376	713,777	-13.1%
2. St. Louis, MO	286,578	319,294	-10.2
3. Cleveland, OH	361,607	396,815	-8.9
4. Baltimore, MD	569,931	620,961	-8.2
5. Toledo, OH	266,301	287,208	-7.3
6. Milwaukee, WI	563,305	594,833	-5.3
7. Santa Ana, CA	308,189	324,528	-5.0
8. Norfolk, VA	232,995	242,803	-4.0
9. Memphis, TN	621,056	646,889	-4.0
10. Long Beach, CA	451,307	462,257	-2.4
11. Anchorage, AK	287,145	291,826	-1.6
12. Chicago, IL	2,665,039	2,695,598	-1.1
13. Pittsburgh, PA	302,898	305,704	-0.9
14. San Francisco, CA	808,437	805,235	0.4
15. Los Angeles, CA	3,822,238	3,792,621	0.8
16. Urban Honolulu, HI	343,421	337,256	1.8
17. New York, NY	8,335,897	8,175,133	2.0
18. Anaheim, CA	344,461	336,265	2.4
19. San Jose, CA	971,233	945,942	2.7
20. Philadelphia, PA	1,567,258	1,526,006	2.7

Note: This table shows which of the 100 largest U.S. cities by 2022 population size experienced the most and least population growth since 2010. Figures may reflect revisions/corrections to initial tabulated census counts. Cities are typically incorporated places.

Largest U.S. Counties by Population, 2010-22

Source: Population Estimates Program and Decennial Census, U.S. Census Bureau, U.S. Dept. of Commerce

(ranked by 2022 population, estimated as of July 1; 2010 decennial census figures are for Apr. 1)

Rank County	2022	2010	% change, 2010-22	Rank County	2022	2010	% change, 2010-22
1. Los Angeles Co., CA	9,721,138	9,818,605	-1.0	25. Suffolk Co., NY	1,525,465	1,493,350	2.2
2. Cook Co., IL	5,109,292	5,194,675	-1.6	26. Palm Beach Co., FL	1,518,477	1,320,134	15.0
3. Harris Co., TX	4,780,913	4,092,459	16.8	27. Hillsborough Co., FL	1,513,301	1,229,226	23.1
4. Maricopa Co., AZ	4,551,524	3,817,117	19.2	28. Orange Co., FL	1,452,726	1,145,956	26.8
5. San Diego Co., CA	3,276,208	3,095,313	5.8	29. Nassau Co., NY	1,383,726	1,339,532	3.3
6. Orange Co., CA	3,151,184	3,010,232	4.7	30. Bronx Co., NY	1,379,946	1,385,108	-0.4
7. Miami-Dade Co., FL	2,673,837	2,496,435	7.1	31. Travis Co., TX	1,326,436	1,024,266	29.5
8. Dallas Co., TX	2,600,840	2,368,139	9.8	32. Franklin Co., OH	1,321,820	1,163,414	13.6
9. Kings Co., NY	2,590,516	2,504,700	3.4	33. Oakland Co., MI	1,269,431	1,202,362	5.6
10. Riverside Co., CA	2,473,902	2,189,641	13.0	34. Hennepin Co., MN	1,260,121	1,152,425	9.3
11. Clark Co., NV	2,322,985	1,951,269	19.0	35. Cuyahoga Co., OH	1,236,041	1,280,122	-3.4
12. Queens Co., NY	2,278,029	2,230,722	2.1	36. Allegheny Co., PA	1,233,253	1,223,348	0.8
13. King Co., WA	2,266,789	1,931,249	17.4	37. Salt Lake Co., UT	1,186,257	1,029,655	15.2
14. San Bernardino Co., CA	2,193,656	2,035,210	7.8	38. Wake Co., NC	1,175,021	900,993	30.4
15. Tarrant Co., TX	2,154,595	1,809,034	19.1	39. Collin Co., TX	1,158,696	782,341	48.1
16. Bexar Co., TX	2,059,530	1,714,773	20.1	40. Contra Costa Co., CA	1,156,966	1,049,025	10.3
17. Broward Co., FL	1,947,026	1,748,066	11.4	41. Mecklenburg Co., NC	1,145,392	919,628	24.5
18. Santa Clara Co., CA	1,870,945	1,781,642	5.0	42. Fairfax Co., VA	1,138,331	1,081,726	5.2
19. Wayne Co., MI	1,757,043	1,820,584	-3.5	43. Fulton Co., GA	1,074,634	920,581	16.7
20. Alameda Co., CA	1,628,997	1,510,271	7.9	44. Pima Co., AZ	1,057,597	980,263	7.9
21. Middlesex Co., MA	1,617,105	1,503,085	7.6	45. Montgomery Co., MD	1,052,521	971,777	8.3
22. New York Co., NY	1,596,273	1,585,873	0.7	46. Duval Co., FL	1,016,536	864,263	17.6
23. Sacramento Co., CA	1,584,169	1,418,788	11.7	47. Fresno Co., CA	1,015,190	930,450	9.1
24. Philadelphia Co., PA	1,567,258	1,526,006	2.7	48. Honolulu Co., HI	995,638	953,207	4.5
				49. Westchester Co., NY	990,427	949,113	4.4
				50. St. Louis Co., MO	990,414	998,954	-0.9

Note: Decennial pop. figures may reflect revisions/corrections to initial tabulated census counts. The 10 smallest U.S. counties or county equivalents by estimated 2022 population: (1) Loving Co., TX (pop. 51); (2) Kalawao Co., HI (82); (3) King Co., TX (233); (4) Kenedy Co., TX (358); (5) McPherson Co., NE (372); (6) Arthur Co., NE (433); (7) Blaine Co., NE (453); (8) Petroleum Co., MT (524); and (9) Grant Co., NE, and McMullen Co., TX (576).

Largest U.S. Metropolitan Areas by Population, 2000-22
Source: Population Estimates Program and Decennial Censuses, U.S. Census Bureau, U.S. Dept. of Commerce

Metropolitan Statistical Areas (MSAs) are defined, or delineated geographically, for federal statistical use by the Office of Management and Budget (OMB) with technical assistance from the Census Bureau. An MSA consists of at least one urbanized area of 50,000 or more inhabitants, plus adjacent territory closely integrated socially and economically with the core as measured by commuting ties. The Census Bureau's 2022 population estimates are for delineations issued by the OMB in Mar. 2020, which designated 384 MSAs in the U.S. About 86.4% of the resident population lived in an MSA in 2022.

(ranked by 2022 population, estimated as of July 1; 2000 and 2010 decennial census figures are for Apr. 1)

Rank	Metropolitan Statistical Area	Population 2022	Population 2010	Population 2000	Percent change 2010-22	Percent change 2000-22
1.	New York-Newark-Jersey City, NY-NJ-PA	19,617,869	18,897,109	18,944,519	3.8%	3.6%
2.	Los Angeles-Long Beach-Anaheim, CA	12,872,322	12,828,837	12,365,627	0.3	4.1
3.	Chicago-Naperville-Elgin, IL-IN-WI	9,441,957	9,461,105	9,098,316	−0.2	3.8
4.	Dallas-Fort Worth-Arlington, TX	7,943,685	6,366,542	5,204,126	24.8	52.6
5.	Houston-The Woodlands-Sugar Land, TX	7,340,118	5,920,416	4,693,161	24.0	56.4
6.	Washington-Arlington-Alexandria, DC-VA-MD-WV	6,373,756	5,649,540	4,837,428	12.8	31.8
7.	Philadelphia-Camden-Wilmington, PA-NJ-DE-MD	6,241,164	5,965,343	5,687,147	4.6	9.7
8.	Atlanta-Sandy Springs-Alpharetta, GA	6,222,106	5,286,728	4,263,438	17.7	45.9
9.	Miami-Fort Lauderdale-Pompano Beach, FL	6,139,340	5,564,635	5,007,564	10.3	22.6
10.	Phoenix-Mesa-Chandler, AZ	5,015,678	4,192,887	3,251,876	19.6	54.2
11.	Boston-Cambridge-Newton, MA-NH	4,900,550	4,552,402	4,391,344	7.6	11.6
12.	Riverside-San Bernardino-Ontario, CA	4,667,558	4,224,851	3,254,821	10.5	43.4
13.	San Francisco-Oakland-Berkeley, CA	4,579,599	4,335,391	4,123,740	5.6	11.1
14.	Detroit-Warren-Dearborn, MI	4,345,761	4,296,250	4,452,557	1.2	−2.4
15.	Seattle-Tacoma-Bellevue, WA	4,034,248	3,439,809	3,043,878	17.3	32.5
16.	Minneapolis-St. Paul-Bloomington, MN-WI	3,693,729	3,333,633	3,031,918	10.8	21.8
17.	Tampa-St. Petersburg-Clearwater, FL	3,290,730	2,783,243	2,395,997	18.2	37.3
18.	San Diego-Chula Vista-Carlsbad, CA	3,276,208	3,095,313	2,813,833	5.8	16.4
19.	Denver-Aurora-Lakewood, CO	2,985,871	2,543,482	2,179,240	17.4	37.0
20.	Baltimore-Columbia-Towson, MD	2,835,672	2,710,489	2,552,994	4.6	11.1
21.	St. Louis, MO-IL	2,801,319	2,787,701	2,675,343	0.5	4.7
22.	Orlando-Kissimmee-Sanford, FL	2,764,182	2,134,411	1,644,561	29.5	68.1
23.	Charlotte-Concord-Gastonia, NC-SC	2,756,069	2,243,960	1,717,372	22.8	60.5
24.	San Antonio-New Braunfels, TX	2,655,342	2,142,508	1,711,703	23.9	55.1
25.	Portland-Vancouver-Hillsboro, OR-WA	2,509,489	2,226,009	1,927,881	12.7	30.2
26.	Austin-Round Rock-Georgetown, TX	2,421,115	1,716,289	1,249,763	41.1	93.7
27.	Sacramento-Roseville-Folsom, CA	2,416,702	2,149,127	1,796,857	12.5	34.5
28.	Pittsburgh, PA	2,349,172	2,356,285	2,431,087	−0.3	−3.4
29.	Las Vegas-Henderson-Paradise, NV	2,322,985	1,951,269	1,375,765	19.0	68.9
30.	Cincinnati, OH-KY-IN	2,265,051	2,137,667	1,994,830	6.0	13.5
31.	Kansas City, MO-KS	2,209,494	2,009,342	1,811,254	10.0	22.0
32.	Columbus, OH	2,161,511	1,901,974	1,675,013	13.6	29.0
33.	Indianapolis-Carmel-Anderson, IN	2,141,779	1,887,877	1,658,462	13.4	29.1
34.	Cleveland-Elyria, OH	2,063,132	2,077,240	2,148,143	−0.7	−4.0
35.	Nashville-Davidson—Murfreesboro—Franklin, TN	2,046,828	1,646,200	1,381,287	24.3	48.2
36.	San Jose-Sunnyvale-Santa Clara, CA	1,938,524	1,836,911	1,735,819	5.5	11.7
37.	Virginia Beach-Norfolk-Newport News, VA-NC	1,806,840	1,713,954	1,580,057	5.4	14.4
38.	Jacksonville, FL	1,675,668	1,345,596	1,122,750	24.5	49.2
39.	Providence-Warwick, RI-MA	1,673,802	1,600,852	1,582,997	4.6	5.7
40.	Milwaukee-Waukesha, WI	1,559,792	1,555,908	1,500,741	0.2	3.9
41.	Raleigh-Cary, NC	1,484,338	1,130,490	797,071	31.3	86.2
42.	Oklahoma City, OK	1,459,380	1,252,987	1,095,421	16.5	33.2
43.	Richmond, VA	1,339,182	1,186,501	1,055,683	12.9	26.9
44.	Memphis, TN-MS-AR	1,332,305	1,316,100	1,213,230	1.2	9.8
45.	Louisville/Jefferson County, KY-IN	1,284,553	1,202,718	1,121,109	6.8	14.6
46.	Salt Lake City, UT	1,266,191	1,087,873	939,122	16.4	34.8
47.	New Orleans-Metairie, LA	1,246,176	1,189,866	1,337,726	4.7	−6.8
48.	Hartford-East Hartford-Middletown, CT	1,221,725	1,212,381	1,148,618	0.8	6.4
49.	Buffalo-Cheektowaga, NY	1,161,192	1,135,509	1,170,111	2.3	−0.8
50.	Birmingham-Hoover, AL	1,116,857	1,061,024	1,052,238	5.3	6.1
51.	Grand Rapids-Kentwood, MI	1,094,198	993,670	930,670	10.1	17.6
52.	Rochester, NY	1,081,152	1,079,671	1,062,452	0.1	1.8
53.	Tucson, AZ	1,057,597	980,263	843,746	7.9	25.3
54.	Tulsa, OK	1,034,123	937,478	859,532	10.3	20.3
55.	Fresno, CA	1,015,190	930,450	799,407	9.1	27.0
56.	Urban Honolulu, HI	995,638	953,207	876,156	4.5	13.6

Population by Urban and Rural Residency, 1790-2020
Source: Decennial Censuses, U.S. Census Bureau, U.S. Dept. of Commerce

For the 2020 decennial census, the Census Bureau defined an area as urban if it had 5,000 or more people or at least 2,000 housing units. For the 1990-2010 decennial censuses, an area was considered urban if it had 2,500 or more people, at least 1,500 of whom did not reside in institutional group quarters (e.g., a correctional facility). All other areas were rural. Prior to 1950, the definition of urban was limited to incorporated places and other areas meeting certain criteria.

Year	Total U.S. pop.	No. of places of 2,500 or more	% of total pop. Urban	% of total pop. Rural	Year	Total U.S. pop.	No. of places of 2,500 or more	% of total pop. Urban	% of total pop. Rural
Pre-1950 urban definition					1940	132,164,569	3,485	56.5%	43.5%
					1950	151,325,798	4,077	59.6	40.4
1790	3,929,214	24	5.1%	94.9%	1960	179,323,175	5,023	63.1	36.9
1800	5,308,483	33	6.1	93.9	**1950-90 urban definition**				
1810	7,239,881	46	7.3	92.7	1950	151,325,798	4,307	64.0	36.0
1820	9,638,453	61	7.2	92.8	1960	179,323,175	5,445	69.9	30.1
1830	12,860,702	90	8.8	91.2	1970	203,302,031	6,433	73.6	26.3
1840	17,063,353	131	10.8	89.2	1980	226,542,199	7,749	73.7	26.3
1850	23,191,876	237	15.4	84.6	1990	248,718,302	8,510	75.2	24.8
1860	31,443,321	392	19.8	80.2	**1990-2010 urban definition**				
1870	38,558,371	663	25.7	74.3	1990	248,718,302	8,510	78.0	22.0
1880	50,189,209	939	28.2	71.8	2000	281,424,603	9,063	79.0	21.0
1890	62,979,766	1,348	35.1	64.9	2010	308,746,065	9,644	80.7	19.3
1900	76,212,168	1,740	39.6	60.4	**2020 urban definition**				
1910	92,228,496	2,266	45.6	54.4	2020	331,449,281	2,611[1]	80.0	20.0
1920	106,021,537	2,725	51.2	48.8					
1930	123,202,624	3,183	56.1	43.9					

Note: Figures may not add up to 100 due to rounding. (1) No. of places of 5,000 or more.

Mobility of U.S. Population by Selected Characteristics, 2021-22

Source: Annual Social and Economic Supplement, Current Population Survey (CPS), U.S. Census Bureau, U.S. Dept. of Commerce
(numbers in thousands)

	Total movers	Same county	Previous residence — Diff. county, same state	Diff. state	Abroad		Total movers	Same county	Previous residence — Diff. county, same state	Diff. state	Abroad
Total movers	28,179	15,068	6,857	4,884	1,369	**Educational attainment[2]**					
Age						Not a HS graduate	1,316	727	292	209	88
1 to 14 years	5,281	2,912	1,268	859	241	High school graduate	4,394	2,353	1,079	772	190
1 to 24 years	10,675	5,884	2,568	1,690	532	Some college/associate's degree	4,359	2,391	1,085	717	167
15 years and older	22,899	12,156	5,589	4,025	1,129	Bachelor's degree	4,742	2,411	1,245	851	235
25 years and older	17,506	9,184	4,289	3,196	838	Advanced degree	2,693	1,303	587	646	157
65 years and older	1,848	979	455	374	41	**Income[1]**					
75 years and older	718	386	196	125	11	Without income	2,819	1,403	519	496	400
Marital status[1]						Under $10,000 or loss	2,634	1,261	661	485	227
Married, spouse present	8,346	4,069	2,088	1,742	448	$10,000-$19,999	2,579	1,465	619	400	95
Married, spouse absent, or separated	952	528	216	122	86	$20,000-$29,999	2,687	1,573	672	381	61
Widowed	687	421	161	93	12	$30,000-$39,999	2,453	1,356	650	370	77
Divorced	2,117	1,238	467	351	61	$40,000-$49,999	1,949	1,056	463	385	46
Never married	10,796	5,901	2,656	1,718	521	$50,000-$59,999	1,711	932	468	274	37
Tenure						$60,000-$74,999	1,780	915	455	382	28
In owner-occupied unit	11,601	5,805	3,301	2,128	367	$75,000-$99,999	1,646	905	399	295	47
In renter-occupied unit	16,578	9,263	3,557	2,756	1,002	$100,000 and over	2,641	1,290	683	558	111

Note: Total movers consist of noninstitutionalized persons ages 1 and older whose place of residence one year prior to completing the survey was different. Figures may not add up to totals due to rounding. (1) Ages 15 and older. (2) Ages 25 and older.

Mobility of U.S. Population, 1947-2022

Source: Annual Social and Economic Supplement, Current Population Survey (CPS), U.S. Census Bureau, U.S. Dept. of Commerce
(numbers in thousands unless otherwise noted)

Mobility period	Total movers No.	% of pop.	Same county No.	% distrib.	Diff. county, same state No.	% distrib.	Diff. state No.	% distrib.	Abroad No.	% distrib.
1947-48	28,672	20.2%	19,202	67.0%	4,638	16.2%	4,370	15.2%	462	1.6%
1950-51	31,464	21.2	20,694	65.8	5,276	16.8	5,188	16.5	306	1.0
1955-56	34,040	21.1	22,186	65.2	5,859	17.2	5,053	14.8	942	2.8
1960-61	36,533	20.6	24,289	66.5	5,493	15.0	5,753	15.7	998	2.7
1965-66	37,586	19.8	24,165	64.3	6,275	16.7	6,263	16.7	883	2.3
1970-71	37,705	18.7	23,018	61.0	6,197	16.4	6,946	18.4	1,544	4.1
1975-76	36,793	17.7	22,399	60.9	7,106	19.3	6,140	16.7	1,148	3.1
1980-81	38,200	17.2	23,097	60.5	7,614	19.9	6,175	16.2	1,313	3.4
1985-86	43,237	18.6	26,401	61.1	8,665	20.0	6,971	16.1	1,200	2.8
1990-91	41,539	17.0	25,151	60.5	7,881	19.0	7,122	17.1	1,385	3.3
1995-96	42,537	16.3	26,696	62.8	8,009	18.8	6,471	15.2	1,361	3.2
2000-01	39,007	14.2	21,918	56.2	7,550	19.4	7,783	20.0	1,756	4.5
2005-06	39,837	13.7	24,851	62.4	8,010	20.1	5,679	14.3	1,296	3.3
2010-11	35,038	11.6	23,330	66.6	5,868	16.7	4,756	13.6	1,084	3.1
2015-16	35,138	11.2	21,588	61.4	7,501	21.3	4,768	13.6	1,281	3.6
2021-22	28,179	8.7	15,068	53.5	6,857	24.3	4,884	17.3	1,369	4.9

Note: Total movers consist of noninstitutionalized persons ages 1 and older whose place of residence one year prior to completing the survey was different. Figures may not add up to totals due to rounding. Because of changes in survey processing, numbers may not be comparable over time.

U.S. Households by Size, 1900-2020

Source: Decennial Censuses, U.S. Census Bureau, U.S. Dept. of Commerce

The household population does not include those living in group quarters (either institutionalized like a correctional facility or noninstitutionalized like a college dormitory). Data on households by size not available for 1910, 1920, or 1930; 1960 figures are based on a sample of the population. Average household size is shown above each bar.

Household size (as % of all households): □ 4-or-more-person ▤ 3-person ▥ 2-person ▪ 1-person

Year	Avg	4-or-more	3-person	2-person	1-person
1900	4.60	61.9%	17.8%	15.2%	5.1%
1930	4.01				
1940	3.68	45.2%	22.4%	24.8%	7.7%
1950	3.38	39.8%	22.8%	28.1%	9.3%
1960	3.29	39.8%	18.9%	28.0%	13.3%
1970	3.11	35.6%	17.2%	29.6%	17.6%
1980	2.75	28.6%	17.4%	31.3%	22.7%
1990	2.63	26.0%	17.4%	32.0%	24.6%
2000	2.59	25.1%	16.5%	32.6%	25.8%
2010	2.58	24.4%	16.1%	32.8%	26.7%

Number of persons per household (y-axis: 0 to 5)

Note: Average household size was not yet available from the 2020 Census. Household size as percent of all households for 2020 were as follows: 27.6%, 1-person; 32.9%, 2-person; 15.6%, 3-person; 23.9%, 4-or-more-person.

U.S. Population by Age, Sex, and Household, 2022

Source: American Community Survey (ACS), U.S. Census Bureau, U.S. Dept. of Commerce

	Number	% of tot.			Number	% of tot.
Total population[1]	333,287,562	100.0%		**Sex**		
Age				Male	165,228,214	49.6%
Under 5 years	18,358,199	5.5		Female	168,059,348	50.4
5 to 14 years	40,990,528	12.3		**Total households[2]**	129,870,928	100.0%
15 to 17 years	12,976,875	3.9		Family households	83,304,153	64.1
18 years and over	260,961,960	78.3		2-person household	36,712,153	28.3
Male	128,174,537	38.5		3-person household	18,874,109	14.5
Female	132,787,423	39.8		4-person household	15,581,198	12.0
18 to 24 years	31,254,823	9.4		5-or-more-person household	12,136,693	9.3
25 to 34 years	45,233,264	13.6		Married-couple family household	60,921,873	46.9
35 to 44 years	44,047,644	13.2		Male HH, no spouse present	6,651,201	5.1
45 to 54 years	40,476,446	12.1		Female HH, no spouse present	15,731,079	12.1
55 to 64 years	42,127,468	12.6		Nonfamily households	46,566,775	35.9
65 years and over	57,822,315	17.3		1-person household, or HH living alone	37,161,100	28.6
75 years and over	23,924,243	7.2		HH 65 years and over	14,899,325	11.5
85 years and over	6,159,943	1.8		2-person household	7,821,350	6.0
Median age (years)	39.0	NA		3-or-more-person household	1,584,325	1.2
				Average household size	2.50	NA

NA = Not applicable. HH = Householder, or person in whose name a home is owned or rented. **Note:** Data based on sample and subject to sampling variability. (1) Includes population living in group quarters (institutional and noninstitutional, e.g., correctional facilities, university housing). (2) Number of occupied housing units, not household members. Group quarters are not considered households.

Elderly U.S. Population, 1900-2060

Source: Decennial Censuses and Population Projections Program, U.S. Census Bureau, U.S. Dept. of Commerce
(numbers of resident population in thousands)

	65 and over		85 and over			65 and over		85 and over	
Year	**Number**	**% tot. pop.**	**Number**	**% tot. pop.**	**Year**	**Number**	**% tot. pop.**	**Number**	**% tot. pop.**
1900[1]	3,080	4.1%	122	0.2%	2010	40,268	13.0%	5,493	1.8%
1920[1]	4,933	4.7	210	0.2	2020	55,793	16.8	6,336	1.9
1940[1]	9,019	6.8	365	0.3	2030	73,138	20.6	9,074	2.6
1960	16,560	9.2	929	0.5	2040	80,827	21.6	14,430	3.9
1980	25,549	11.3	2,240	1.0	2050	85,675	22.0	18,561	4.8
2000	34,992	12.4	4,240	1.8	2060	94,676	23.4	19,019	4.7

Note: 1900 figures are for June 1; 1920 figures are for Jan. 1; and 1940-2020 figures are for Apr. 1. 2030-60 projections are as of July 1. (1) Excludes Alaska and Hawaii.

U.S. Population Projections by Age, 2025-60

Source: Population Projections Program, U.S. Census Bureau, U.S. Dept. of Commerce
(numbers of resident population in thousands)

	2025		2030		2040		2050		2060	
Age	**No.**	**% distrib.**	**No.**	**% distrib.**	**No.**	**% distrib.**	**No.**	**% distrib.**	**No.**	**% distrib.**
Total	344,234	100.0%	355,101	100.0%	373,528	100.0%	388,922	100.0%	404,483	100.0%
Under 5 years	20,868	6.1	20,976	5.9	21,106	5.7	21,610	5.6	22,144	5.5
5 to 13 years	37,074	10.8	38,051	10.7	38,568	10.3	39,049	10.0	40,090	9.9
14 to 17 years	16,712	4.9	16,625	4.7	17,447	4.7	17,566	4.5	17,903	4.4
18 to 24 years	30,554	8.9	30,612	8.6	31,369	8.4	32,126	8.3	32,467	8.0
25 to 44 years	92,328	26.8	94,370	26.6	95,067	25.5	97,459	25.1	100,230	24.8
45 to 64 years	81,472	23.7	81,329	22.9	89,135	23.9	95,437	24.5	96,973	24.0
65 years and over	65,226	18.9	73,138	20.6	80,827	21.6	85,675	22.0	94,676	23.4
85 years and over	7,450	2.2	9,074	2.6	14,430	3.9	18,561	4.8	19,019	4.7
100 years and over	120	0.03	140	0.04	196	0.05	386	0.10	589	0.15

Note: Projections are as of July 1 of given year. They are based on assumptions about future births, deaths, and net international migration.

Disability Status of U.S. Population by Age, 2022

Source: American Community Survey (ACS), U.S. Census Bureau, U.S. Dept. of Commerce
(numbers in thousands, by difficulty type)

Characteristic	Number	% of pop.	Characteristic	Number	% of pop.
Total population (all ages)	328,310	100.00%	**Total population (5 years and over)**	309,953	100.00%
With a disability[1]	44,147	13.45	With a cognitive difficulty[2]	17,525	5.65
Under 5 years	139	0.04	5 to 17 years	2,596	0.84
Under 18 years	3,475	1.06	18 to 64 years	10,398	3.35
18 to 64 years	22,007	6.70	65 years and over	4,530	1.46
65 years and over	18,664	5.68	With an ambulatory difficulty[3]	20,905	6.74
With a hearing disability	12,035	3.67	5 to 17 years	322	0.10
Under 5 years	87	0.03	18 to 64 years	8,843	2.85
Under 18 years	380	0.12	65 years and over	11,741	3.79
18 to 64 years	4,009	1.22	With a self-care difficulty[4]	7,999	2.58
65 years and over	7,646	2.33	5 to 17 years	618	0.20
With a vision disability	8,182	2.49	18 to 64 years	3,353	1.08
Under 5 years	80	0.02	65 years and over	4,028	1.30
Under 18 years	608	0.19			
18 to 64 years	4,237	1.29	**Total population (18 years and over)**	256,067	100.00%
65 years and over	3,336	1.02	With an independent living difficulty[5]	15,384	6.01
			18 to 64 years	7,864	3.07
			65 years and over	7,519	2.94

Note: Data based on sample and subject to sampling variability. Does not include military personnel and civilian institutionalized population (i.e., those under formal supervision or custody in a facility). (1) Identified by the ACS as persons "who report difficulty with specific functions and may, in the absence of accommodation, have a disability." (2) Concentrating, remembering, or making decisions. (3) Walking or climbing stairs. (4) Dressing or bathing. (5) Doing errands alone such as visiting a doctor's office or shopping.

Marital Status of the U.S. Population, 1960-2022

Source: Annual Social and Economic Supplements, Current Population Surveys (CPS), U.S. Census Bureau, U.S. Dept. of Commerce
(numbers in millions; data based on sample of occupied households in civilian noninstitutional pop.)

Marital status	Both sexes				Male				Female			
	2022	2000	1980	1960	2022	2000	1980	1960	2022	2000	1980	1960
Total..................	268.6	213.8	171.9	124.9	131.3	103.1	81.9	60.3	137.3	110.7	89.9	64.6
Married[1]............	136.3	120.2	104.8	84.4	67.9	59.7	51.8	41.8	68.4	60.5	53.0	42.6
Never married.........	91.5	60.0	44.5	27.5	48.8	32.3	24.2	15.3	42.7	27.8	20.2	12.3
Divorced	25.6	19.9	9.9	2.8	11.0	8.6	3.9	1.1	14.6	11.3	6.0	1.7
Widowed	15.2	13.7	12.7	10.2	3.7	2.6	2.0	2.1	11.5	11.1	10.8	8.1
% of total or subset pops.												
Married[1]............	50.7%	56.2%	61.0%	67.6%	51.7%	57.9%	63.2%	69.3%	49.9%	54.7%	58.9%	65.9%
Never married	34.1	28.1	25.9	22.0	37.1	31.3	29.6	25.3	31.1	25.1	22.5	19.0
Divorced	9.5	9.3	5.8	2.3	8.4	8.3	4.8	1.8	10.7	10.2	6.6	2.6
Widowed	5.7	6.4	7.4	8.1	2.8	2.5	2.4	3.5	8.4	10.0	12.0	12.5

Note: Total pop. for 1980 and on is persons ages 15 and older and for 1960, persons ages 14 and older. Figures may not add up to totals due to rounding. (1) Comprises subcategories Married, spouse present; Married, spouse absent; and Separated.

Household Characteristics of Couples in the U.S., 2021

Source: American Community Survey (ACS), U.S. Census Bureau, U.S. Dept. of Commerce
(as percent of all households with same relationship type, unless otherwise specified)

Household characteristics	Opposite-sex couples		Same-sex couples					
			Married			Unmarried		
	Married	Unmarried	Total couples	Male-male	Female-female	Total couples	Male-male	Female-female
Total number of households (thous.)	59,650.0	8,697.0	711.1	336.9	374.2	498.3	240.7	257.7
Age of householder								
15 to 24 years..................	1.1%	11.0%	2.2%	1.2%	3.1%	9.7%	6.0%	13.2%
25 to 34 years..................	12.2	35.2	18.3	14.9	21.4	31.7	29.4	33.9
35 to 44 years..................	20.3	21.3	22.3	21.1	23.3	20.1	20.2	20.0
45 to 54 years..................	20.2	14.1	19.7	21.7	18.0	13.6	15.7	11.7
55 to 64 years..................	21.0	10.5	21.6	23.3	20.0	15.3	18.2	12.5
65 years and over..............	25.1	7.9	16.0	17.9	14.2	9.6	10.4	8.8
Average age of householder (years) ...	52.8	39.9	48.9	50.7	47.4	42.0	43.9	40.2
Household income								
Less than $35,000	9.8%	15.7%	8.9%	7.4%	10.2%	12.9%	9.9%	15.7%
$35,000 to $49,999	8.0	11.7	6.7	5.6	7.7	9.0	7.5	10.5
$50,000 to $74,999	15.6	20.5	13.7	12.4	14.8	17.4	15.0	19.6
$75,000 to $99,999	14.9	16.6	14.4	13.2	15.5	15.7	14.6	16.7
$100,000 or more	51.7	35.5	56.3	61.3	51.8	45.0	52.9	37.5
Median household income (dollars)	$102,800	$77,660	$111,700	$125,700	$103,300	$90,010	$105,500	$80,670
Children in household[1]	38.2%	34.9%	18.0%	8.9%	26.2%	10.8%	3.5%	17.6%

Note: Data based on sample and subject to sampling variability. Householder is person in whose name a home is owned or rented. (1) Includes biological, step-, and adopted children and nonrelatives of the householder under 18 years.

Same-Sex Couple Households in the U.S., 2008-21

Source: American Community Survey (ACS), U.S. Census Bureau, U.S. Dept. of Commerce
(in thousands; data based on sample and subject to sampling variability)

Year	Total same-sex couples			Same-sex married couples			Same-sex unmarried partner couples		
	Total	Male-male	Female-female	Total	Male-male	Female-female	Total	Male-male	Female-female
2008..................	539.2	257.9	281.3	142.5	62.2	80.3	396.7	195.8	201.0
2009..................	581.3	280.4	300.9	152.1	66.3	85.8	429.2	214.1	215.0
2010..................	593.3	287.7	305.6	152.3	68.5	83.8	441.0	219.2	221.8
2011..................	605.5	284.3	321.2	168.1	69.5	98.6	437.4	214.8	222.6
2012..................	639.4	305.8	333.6	181.9	80.7	101.2	457.5	225.1	232.5
2013..................	726.6	352.6	374.0	251.7	117.5	134.2	474.9	235.1	239.8
2014..................	783.1	377.9	405.2	334.8	163.2	171.6	448.3	214.7	233.6
2015..................	858.9	412.0	446.9	425.4	201.8	223.6	433.5	210.2	223.3
2016..................	887.5	435.9	451.6	487.0	235.2	251.8	400.5	200.7	199.8
2017..................	935.2	451.5	483.7	555.5	262.3	293.2	379.7	189.2	190.6
2018..................	995.4	485.1	510.4	592.6	285.0	307.6	402.9	200.1	202.8
2019..................	980.3	462.2	518.1	568.1	264.7	303.4	412.2	197.5	214.6
2021..................	1,209.5	577.6	631.9	711.1	336.9	374.2	498.3	240.7	257.7

Note: 2020 estimates were not available because of the COVID-19 pandemic.

Children in the U.S. by Selected Characteristics, 2022

Source: Annual Social and Economic Supplement, Current Population Survey (CPS), U.S. Census Bureau, U.S. Dept. of Commerce
(numbers in thousands; data based on sample of occupied households in civilian noninstitutional pop.)

Characteristic	Number	% of tot.	Characteristic	Number	% of tot.
All children	73,289	100.0%	White alone, non-Hispanic	36,061	49.2%
Age of child			Black alone........................	11,272	15.4
Under 3 year......................	10,864	14.8	Asian alone........................	4,210	5.7
3-5 years.........................	11,666	15.9	Hispanic (any race).................	18,750	25.6
6-8 years.........................	12,093	16.5	**Parents' labor force status**		
9-11 years........................	12,339	16.8	Mother and father in labor force	32,325	44.1
12-14 years.......................	13,019	17.8	Father in labor force, mother not in labor		
15-17 years.......................	13,308	18.2	force	14,839	20.2
Presence of siblings			Mother in labor force, father not present..	12,162	16.6
None.............................	15,196	20.7	Mother not in labor force, father not		
One or more siblings..............	58,092	79.3	present	3,619	4.9
Race and Hispanic origin of child			All other combinations[1]...............	10,343	14.1
White alone.......................	51,907	70.8			

Note: Children are defined as all persons under 18 years of age excluding those who are a family reference person or spouse. Details may not sum to total due to rounding. (1) Incl. Father in labor force, mother not present, and No parent present or parents are same-sex, among others.

Persons Granted Lawful Permanent Resident Status by State, 2022

Source: Office of Immigration Statistics, U.S. Dept. of Homeland Security
(ranked by fiscal year 2022 number)

State/territory	Number	State/territory	Number	State/territory	Number	State/territory	Number
Total	1,018,349	Ohio	18,057	South Carolina	5,854	Idaho	2,050
California	182,921	Arizona	16,984	Louisiana	4,819	Puerto Rico	1,958
Florida	113,653	Michigan	16,881	Iowa	4,737	Mississippi	1,721
New York	111,309	Colorado	11,410	Oklahoma	4,631	Maine	1,363
Texas	109,720	Connecticut	11,219	Kansas	4,449	North Dakota	1,164
New Jersey	54,958	Tennessee	10,821	Nebraska	3,755	West Virginia	814
Illinois	34,551	Minnesota	9,762	Alabama	3,747	South Dakota	683
Massachusetts	32,885	Indiana	8,681	Arkansas	3,391	Alaska	673
Washington	31,835	Nevada	8,587	Rhode Island	3,381	Guam	566
Virginia	28,902	Oregon	8,143	New Mexico	3,327	Vermont	523
Pennsylvania	28,381	Missouri	7,178	Hawaii	2,706	Montana	486
Georgia	26,312	Kentucky	6,476	Dist. of Columbia	2,595	Wyoming	357
Maryland	24,233	Wisconsin	6,109	Delaware	2,385	Other[1]	1,041
North Carolina	21,868	Utah	6,053	New Hampshire	2,086	Unknown	5,198

Note: Applicants for lawful permanent resident (LPR) status, or "green cards," may already live in the U.S. They include refugees and asylees, temp. workers, foreign students, family members of U.S. citizens, and unauthorized immigrants. Applicants from outside the U.S. are granted LPR status upon entry with a visa. (1) Incl. Amer. Samoa, Northern Mariana Isls., U.S. Virgin Isls., and armed forces posts.

Persons Granted Lawful Permanent Resident Status by Top Areas of Residence, 2022

Source: Office of Immigration Statistics, U.S. Dept. of Homeland Security
(ranked by fiscal year 2022 number)

Area of residence[1]	Number	% of total	Area of residence[1]	Number	% of total
Total	1,018,349	100.0%	San Diego-Chula Vista-Carlsbad, CA	13,314	1.3%
New York-Newark-Jersey City, NY-NJ-PA	148,559	14.6	Phoenix-Mesa-Chandler, AZ	12,396	1.2
Los Angeles-Long Beach-Anaheim, CA	63,584	6.2	Tampa-Saint Petersburg-Clearwater, FL	12,271	1.2
Miami-Fort Lauderdale-Pompano Beach, FL	62,475	6.1	Detroit-Warren-Dearborn, MI	11,930	1.2
Washington-Arlington-Alexandria, DC-VA-MD-WV	39,450	3.9	Austin-Round Rock-Georgetown, TX	10,907	1.1
Houston-The Woodlands-Sugar Land, TX	38,186	3.7	Charlotte-Concord-Gastonia, NC-SC	9,500	0.9
San Francisco-Oakland-Berkeley, CA	35,369	3.5	Sacramento-Roseville-Folsom, CA	9,298	0.9
Dallas-Fort Worth-Arlington, TX	35,330	3.5	Minneapolis-Saint Paul-Bloomington, MN-WI	8,203	0.8
Chicago-Naperville-Elgin, IL-IN-WI	31,564	3.1	Baltimore-Columbia-Towson, MD	7,925	0.8
Seattle-Tacoma-Bellevue, WA	26,452	2.6	Denver-Aurora-Lakewood, CO	7,716	0.8
Boston-Cambridge-Newton, MA-NH	26,370	2.6	Las Vegas-Henderson-Paradise, NV	7,101	0.7
San Jose-Sunnyvale-Santa Clara, CA	23,062	2.3	Portland-Vancouver-Hillsboro, OR-WA	6,756	0.7
Atlanta-Sandy Springs-Alpharetta, GA	21,044	2.1	San Antonio-New Braunfels, TX	6,388	0.6
Philadelphia-Camden-Wilmington, PA-NJ-DE-MD	20,234	2.0	Columbus, OH	6,240	0.6
Orlando-Kissimmee-Sanford, FL	17,257	1.7	Nashville-Davidson–Murfreesboro–Franklin, TN	5,874	0.6
Riverside-San Bernardino-Ontario, CA	13,980	1.4	Other CBSAs	76,583	7.5
			Non-CBSA, other, and unknown	203,031	19.9

Note: Applicants for lawful permanent resident (LPR) status, or "green cards," may already live in the U.S. They include refugees and asylees, temporary workers, foreign students, family members of U.S. citizens, and unauthorized immigrants. Applicants from outside the U.S. are granted LPR status upon entry with a visa. (1) Residence by Core Based Statistical Areas, or CBSAs, which refer collectively to metropolitan and micropolitan statistical areas. These areas are defined for federal statistical use by the Office of Management and Budget with Census Bureau assistance.

Unauthorized Immigrant Population in the U.S., 1990-2018

Source: For 2019: Migration Policy Institution (MPI); for 1990-2008: Office of Immigration Statistics, U.S. Dept. of Homeland Security

The unauthorized immigrant population had been increasing steadily since 1990 before it peaked in 2007 with the beginning of the Great Recession. The Migration Policy Institute estimates that in 2019, 23% of the total foreign-born population was unauthorized, while 45% were naturalized citizens, 28% were lawful permanent residents, and 5% were nonimmigrants. About 43% of the unauthorized population had resided in the U.S. for 15 years or more; 21% had been residents for less than five years.
(ranked by 2019 est. population; numbers in thousands)

	Country of Birth					State of Residence			
	Est. population			% change,		Est. population			% change,
Country	2019	2008	1990	2008-19	State	2019	2008	1990	2008-19
Total	11,047	11,600	3,500	−4.8%	Total	11,047	11,600	3,500	−4.8%
Mexico	5,313	7,030	2,040	−24.4	California	2,739	2,850	1,476	−3.9
El Salvador	741	570	298	30.0	Texas	1,739	1,680	438	3.5
Guatemala	724	430	118	68.4	New York	835	640	357	30.5
India	553	160	28	245.6	Florida	772	840	239	−8.1
Honduras	490	300	42	63.3	New Jersey	440	400	95	10.0
China	390	220	70	77.3	Illinois	425	550	194	−22.7
Philippines	370	300	70	23.3	Georgia	339	460	34	−26.3
Venezuela	189	50	10	278.0	North Carolina	296	380	26	−22.1
Brazil	178	180	20	−1.1	Arizona	273	560	88	−51.3
Korea	173	240	24	−27.9	Virginia	251	230	48	9.1
All other countries	1,926	2,120	780	−9.2	All other states	2,938	3,010	504	−2.4

Note: Unauthorized immigrant pop. ests. are made using the residual method. The estimated number of immigrants residing legally in the country is subtracted from the total foreign-born pop. Details may not sum to totals because of rounding. Because of changes in methodology and source, ests. for 1990 may not be directly comparable over time.

Active U.S. DACA Population by Birth Country, 2023

Source: U.S. Citizenship and Immigration Services, U.S. Dept. of Homeland Security

The Deferred Action for Childhood Arrivals (DACA) program grants (1) temporary protection from deportation and (2) permission to legally work to undocumented individuals living in the U.S. who were brought to the country as children.

(number of active DACA recipients as of Mar. 31, 2023, ranked by country of birth)

Country of birth	Number	Country of birth	Number	Country of birth	Number
Total	578,680	Ecuador	4,100	Dominican Republic	1,630
Mexico	468,000	Colombia	3,540	Uruguay	1,450
El Salvador	22,560	Argentina	2,870	Trinidad and Tobago	1,230
Guatemala	15,340	Philippines	2,790	Bolivia	1,220
Honduras	14,120	Jamaica	1,950	Nicaragua	1,130
Peru	5,380	India	1,850	Costa Rica	1,120
South Korea	5,320	Venezuela	1,800	Chile	1,030
Brazil	4,380				

Note: Numbers are approximate and rounded and may not add up to total. Countries with fewer than 1,000 active DACA recipients are not shown here. Does not include individuals who have obtained lawful permanent resident status or U.S. citizenship.

Refugee Arrivals in the U.S. by Region and Nationality, 2001-22

Source: Refugee Processing Center, Bureau of Population, Refugees, and Migration, U.S. Dept. of State

Under the Refugee Act of 1980, the president in consultation with Congress establishes a refugee admissions ceiling and regional allocations before each fiscal year (Oct. 1-Sept. 30). Applicants for refugee status are outside of the U.S. whereas applicants seeking asylum are in the U.S. or at a U.S. port of entry.

(countries ranked by nationality of most refugee arrivals in fiscal year 2022)

Region/country of nationality	2022	2020	2018	2016	2014	2012	2010	2007	2004	2001
Total ceiling	125,000	18,000	45,000	85,000	70,000	76,000	80,000	70,000	70,000	80,000
Total refugee arrivals	25,465	11,814	22,589	84,994	69,987	58,238	73,311	48,282	52,873	69,886
COUNTRY										
Congo, Dem. Rep. of.	7,810	2,868	7,883	16,370	4,540	1,863	3,174	848	569	264
Syria	4,556	481	76	12,587	105	31	25	17	0	8
Myanmar (Burma)	2,156	2,115	3,557	12,347	14,598	14,160	16,693	13,896	1,056	544
Sudan	1,669	254	90	1,458	1,315	1,077	558	705	3,500	5,944
Afghanistan	1,618	604	806	2,737	753	481	515	441	959	2,930
Ukraine	1,610	1,927	2,635	2,543	490	372	449	1,605	3,482	7,313
Guatemala	1,085	247	42	8	0	0	0	0	0	0
El Salvador	519	365	725	364	0	0	0	0	0	0
Moldova	507	364	207	465	142	255	356	565	1,711	1,199
Iraq	498	537	154	9,880	19,769	12,163	18,016	1,608	66	2,465
Somalia	456	149	299	9,020	9,000	4,911	4,884	6,969	13,331	4,946
Honduras	450	91	59	84	0	0	20	0	0	0
Eritrea	325	475	1,269	1,949	1,488	1,346	2,570	963	128	114
South Sudan	293	38	13	189	57	1	—	—	—	—
Colombia	261	215	128	529	252	126	123	54	577	0
Iran	255	137	46	3,750	2,846	1,758	3,543	5,482	1,786	6,461
Ethiopia	252	116	376	1,131	728	620	668	1,028	2,689	1,457
Armenia	200	64	58	55	10	8	1	29	88	26
Burundi	185	46	201	694	68	186	530	4,545	276	109
Central African Republic	181	85	148	401	25	136	45	15	24	1
All other countries	579	636	3,817	8,433	13,801	18,744	21,141	9,512	22,631	36,105
REGION										
Africa	11,358	4,160	10,520	31,624	17,476	10,608	13,305	17,483	29,104	19,020
East Asia	2,215	2,129	3,670	12,518	14,784	14,366	17,716	15,643	8,084	4,163
Europe/Central Asia	2,351	2,578	3,612	3,957	959	1,129	1,526	4,560	9,254	15,794
Former Soviet Union[1]	—	—	—	—	—	—	—	—	—	15,978
Latin America/Caribbean	2,485	948	955	1,340	4,318	2,078	4,982	2,976	3,577	2,975
Near East/South Asia	7,056	1,999	3,832	35,555	32,450	30,057	35,782	7,620	2,854	11,956

— = Not applicable. **Note:** Includes Amerasian immigrants (children born in Cambodia, Korea, Laos, Thailand, or Vietnam in 1950-82 and fathered by a U.S. citizen). (1) Former Soviet Union countries are grouped under Europe from 2004 and on.

Persons Granted Asylum and Refugee Arrivals in the U.S., 1980-2022

Source: U.S. Dept. of Homeland Security; U.S. Dept. of Justice; Refugee Processing Ctr., Bureau of Population, Refugees, and Migration, U.S. Dept. of State

Individuals apply for asylum from within the U.S. or at a U.S. port of entry. Applicants for refugee status are outside of the U.S.

Year	Number granted asylum	Number of refugee arrivals[1]	Year	Number granted asylum	Number of refugee arrivals[1]	Year	Number granted asylum	Number of refugee arrivals[1]
1980	—	207,116	1995	20,703	98,973	2009	22,303	74,602
1981	—	159,252	1996	23,532	75,421	2010	19,777	73,293
1982	—	98,096	1997	22,939	69,653	2011	23,631	56,384
1984	—	70,393	1998	20,507	76,712	2012	27,446	58,179
1985	—	67,704	1999	26,571	85,285	2013	24,657	69,909
1986	—	62,146	2000	32,514	72,165	2014	23,061	69,975
1987	—	64,528	2001	39,148	68,920	2015	25,947	69,920
1988	—	76,483	2002	36,937	26,785	2016	20,313	84,989
1989	—	107,070	2003	28,743	28,286	2017	26,380	53,691
1990	8,472	122,066	2004	27,376	52,840	2018	37,740	22,405
1991	5,035	113,389	2005	25,304	53,738	2019	45,888	29,916
1992	6,307	115,548	2006	26,352	41,094	2020	30,964	11,840
1993	9,543	114,181	2007	25,318	48,218	2021	17,692	11,454
1994	13,828	111,680	2008	23,022	60,107	2022		25,465

— = Not available. Fiscal year (Oct. 1-Sept. 30) data. (1) Excludes Amerasians (children born in Cambodia, Korea, Laos, Thailand, or Vietnam after Dec. 31, 1950, and before Oct. 22, 1982, and fathered by a U.S. citizen) except in FY 1989-91. Figures based on refugee arrival date.

U.S. Foreign-Born Population

Source: Decennial Censuses and Annual Social and Economic Supplements, Current Population Surveys (CPS), U.S. Census Bureau, U.S. Dept. of Commerce

Foreign-Born as a Percentage of U.S. Population, 1900-2021

Foreign-Born Population by Region of Birth, 1995-2021

(numbers in thousands)

Region	2021[1] No.	%	2000	1995
Asia	13,426	30.0%	7,916	6,121
Under 18	768	31.6	696	767
Europe	4,148	9.3	4,382	3,937
Under 18	188	7.7	247	232
Latin America	23,628	52.7	15,323	11,777
Under 18	1,148	47.3	1,786	1,451
Other[2]	3,598	8.0	2,364	2,658
Under 18	326	13.4	249	275
All regions	44,799	100.0	29,985	24,493
Under 18	2,429	100.0	2,977	2,726

(1) Figures are percentage of total foreign-born pop. or of all foreign-born under 18 years of age. (2) Incl. those born at sea.

U.S. Foreign-Born Population: Top Countries of Origin, 1880-2022

Source: Decennial Censuses and American Community Survey (ACS), U.S. Census Bureau, U.S. Dept. of Commerce

(numbers in thousands; percentage is of all foreign-born excluding population born at sea)

1880 Country	No.	%	1920 Country	No.	%	1960 Country	No.	%	2000 Country	No.	%	2022[1] Country	No.	%
Germany	1,967	29.4	Germany	1,686	12.1	Italy	1,257	12.9	Mexico	9,177	29.5	Mexico	10,679	23.1
Ireland	1,855	27.8	Italy	1,610	11.6	Germany	990	10.2	China[3]	1,519	4.9	India	2,840	6.1
UK	918	13.7	USSR	1,400	10.1	Canada	953	9.8	Philippines	1,369	4.4	China[4]	2,455	5.3
Canada	717	10.7	Poland	1,140	8.2	UK	765	7.9	India	1,023	3.3	Philippines	1,982	4.3
Sweden	194	2.9	Canada	1,138	8.2	Poland	748	7.7	Vietnam	988	3.2	El Salvador	1,408	3.0
Norway	182	2.7	UK	1,135	8.2	USSR	691	7.1	Cuba	873	2.8	Vietnam	1,331	2.9
France	107	1.6	Ireland	1,037	7.5	Mexico	576	5.9	Korea[4]	864	2.8	Cuba	1,313	2.8
China[2]	104	1.6	Sweden	626	4.5	Ireland	339	3.5	Canada	821	2.6	Dominican Republic	1,280	2.8
Switzerland	89	1.3	Austria	576	4.1	Austria	305	3.1	El Salvador	817	2.6	Guatemala	1,149	2.5
Czech.	85	1.3	Mexico	486	3.5	Hungary	245	2.5	Germany	707	2.3	Korea[5]	1,045	2.3
Total	6,680	100.0	Total	13,921	100.0	Total	9,738	100.0	Total	31,108	100.0	Total	46,182	100.0

(1) Data based on sample and subject to sampling variability. The Census Bureau collects data from residents regardless of immigration status, so the foreign-born population implicitly includes unauthorized migrants. (2) Incl. Taiwan. (3) Incl. Hong Kong and Taiwan. (4) Incl. Hong Kong. (5) North and South Korea.

Language Spoken at Home by the U.S. Population, 2022

Source: American Community Survey (ACS), U.S. Census Bureau, U.S. Dept. of Commerce

(number of speakers 5 years of age and over by language or language group most often used)

Language	Number (thous.)	% of tot. pop.	% English inability[1]
Total population	314,929	100.00%	8.5%
Speak only English	245,688	78.01	NA
Speak another language	69,242	21.99	38.5
Spanish			
Spanish	42,033	13.35	39.9
Other Indo-European languages			
Armenian	240	0.08	38.3
Bengali	416	0.13	41.1
French (incl. Cajun)	1,223	0.39	21.1
German	876	0.28	15.5
Greek	263	0.08	23.2
Gujarati	457	0.15	31.9
Haitian	910	0.29	37.1
Hindi	881	0.28	16.6
Italian	522	0.17	24.6
Malayalam, Kannada, other Dravidian	294	0.09	20.5
Nepali, Marathi, other Indic	510	0.16	32.2
Persian (incl. Farsi, Dari)	515	0.16	38.0
Polish	483	0.15	37.3
Portuguese	998	0.32	36.8
Punjabi	343	0.11	39.0
Russian	975	0.31	40.2
Serbo-Croatian	247	0.08	31.8
Tamil	341	0.11	15.8
Telugu	506	0.16	18.3
Ukrainian, other Slavic	434	0.14	39.1
Urdu	519	0.16	27.7
Yiddish, Penn. Dutch, other West Germanic	620	0.20	32.8%
Other Indo-European langs.	652	0.21	31.9
Asian and Pacific Island languages			
Chinese (incl. Mandarin, Cantonese)	3,507	1.11	51.1
Hmong	234	0.07	38.7
Ilocano, Samoan, Hawaiian, other Austronesian	485	0.15	35.1
Japanese	432	0.14	39.7
Khmer	198	0.06	54.3
Korean	1,111	0.35	51.0
Tagalog (incl. Filipino)	1,758	0.56	30.3
Thai, Lao, other Tai-Kadai	302	0.10	49.1
Vietnamese	1,538	0.49	57.1
Other langs. of Asia	503	0.16	47.1
All other languages			
Amharic, Somali, other Afro-Asiatic	624	0.20	39.0
Arabic	1,428	0.45	33.5
Hebrew	221	0.07	16.3
Navajo	143	0.05	24.3
Swahili, other langs. of Central/ Eastern/Southern Africa	342	0.11	31.0
Yoruba, Twi, Igbo, other langs. of Western Africa	673	0.21	20.1
Other Native langs. of North America	169	0.05	14.3
Other and unspecified	318	0.10	29.4

NA = Not applicable. Note: Data based on sample and subject to sampling variability. (1) Percent of respondents who speak the language at left who indicated that they spoke English less than "very well." For example, 38.3% of respondents who use Armenian at home do not speak English very well.

U.S. Population by Ancestry Reported, 2022

Source: American Community Survey (ACS), U.S. Census Bureau, U.S. Dept. of Commerce
(numbers in thousands; ranked by number)

Ancestry	Number	% of total	Ancestry	Number	% of total	Ancestry	Number	% of total
Total population	333,288	100.0%	Subsaharan African[1]	4,177	1.3%	Welsh	1,522	0.5%
German	41,137	12.3	Norwegian	3,937	1.2	Portuguese	1,350	0.4
English	31,381	9.4	Swedish	3,317	1.0	Hungarian	1,247	0.4
Irish	30,656	9.2	West Indian (excl. Hispanic groups)[2]	3,155	0.9	Greek	1,201	0.4
American	17,786	5.3	Dutch	3,019	0.9	British	1,196	0.4
Italian	16,010	4.8	Scotch-Irish	2,525	0.8	Czech	1,189	0.4
Polish	8,249	2.5	Arab[3]	2,238	0.7	Other ancestry not shown here	124,919	37.5
French (excl. Basque)	6,311	1.9	Russian	2,099	0.6	Unclassified or not reported	81,555	24.5
Scottish	5,352	1.6	French Canadian	1,626	0.5			
European	4,820	1.4						

Note: Data based on sample and subject to sampling variability. Because respondents could self-identify with more than one ancestry, numbers do not add up to total. (1) Incl. Cabo Verdean, Ethiopian, Ghanian, Kenyan, Liberian, Nigerian, Senegalese, Sierra Leonean, Somali, South African, Sudanese, Ugandan, Zimbabwean, African, and other Subsaharan African. (2) Incl. Bahamian, Barbadian, Belizean, Bermudan, British or Dutch West Indian, Haitian, Jamaican, Trinidadian and Tobagonian, U.S. Virgin Islander, West Indian, and other West Indian. (3) Incl. Egyptian, Iraqi, Jordanian, Lebanese, Moroccan, Palestinian, Syrian, Arab, and other Arab.

U.S. Population by Race, Hispanic Origin, and Age, 2022

Source: American Community Survey (ACS), U.S. Census Bureau, U.S. Dept. of Commerce

Race and origin/age	Number	% of group	Race and origin/age	Number	% of group
White (not Hispanic or Latino)	192,153,076	100.0%	Native Hawaiian and other Pacific Islander	665,807	100.0%
Under 5 years	8,484,914	4.4	Under 5 years	41,369	6.2
Under 18 years	34,292,324	17.8	Under 18 years	171,747	25.8
18 to 64 years	115,090,031	59.9	18 to 64 years	430,678	64.7
65 years and over	42,770,721	22.3	65 years and over	63,382	9.5
85 years and over	4,757,082	2.5	85 years and over	4,445	0.7
Black or African American	40,603,656	100.0	Some other race	24,444,482	100.0
Under 5 years	2,462,102	6.1	Under 5 years	1,634,922	6.7
Under 18 years	9,666,073	23.8	Under 18 years	6,646,584	27.2
18 to 64 years	25,613,809	63.1	18 to 64 years	15,870,140	64.9
65 years and over	5,323,774	13.1	65 years and over	1,927,758	7.9
85 years and over	472,016	1.2	85 years and over	167,381	0.7
American Indian and Alaska Native	3,205,331	100.0	Two or more races	41,782,289	100.0
Under 5 years	185,840	5.8	Under 5 years	3,667,993	8.8
Under 18 years	816,727	25.5	Under 18 years	13,557,948	32.4
18 to 64 years	2,070,729	64.6	18 to 64 years	24,435,537	58.5
65 years and over	317,875	9.9	65 years and over	3,788,804	9.1
85 years and over	21,207	0.7	85 years and over	350,787	0.8
Asian	19,696,980	100.0	Hispanic or Latino (any race)	63,553,639	100.0
Under 5 years	935,429	4.7	Under 5 years	4,851,223	7.6
Under 18 years	3,744,084	19.0	Under 18 years	18,732,013	29.5
18 to 64 years	13,149,196	66.8	18 to 64 years	39,552,462	62.2
65 years and over	2,803,700	14.2	65 years and over	5,269,164	8.3
85 years and over	293,649	1.5	85 years and over	514,332	0.8

Note: Data based on sample and subject to sampling variability. Categories are for one race alone, not in combination with any other race, unless otherwise noted.

Educational Attainment of the U.S. Population, 2022

Source: American Community Survey (ACS), U.S. Census Bureau, U.S. Dept. of Commerce
(numbers in thousands; population 25 years of age and over)

Race and origin/highest ed. completed	Number	% of group	Race and origin/highest ed. completed	Number	% of group
White (not Hispanic or Latino)	141,836	100.0%	Native Hawaiian and other Pacific Islander	422	100.0%
Less than HS diploma	8,184	5.8	Less than HS diploma	52	12.4
HS diploma or equiv. credential	36,711	25.9	HS diploma or equiv. credential	154	36.4
Some college or associate's degree	40,867	28.8	Some college or associate's degree	133	31.5
Bachelor's degree or higher	56,074	39.5	Bachelor's degree or higher	84	19.8
Black or African American	26,714	100.0	Some other race	14,991	100.0
Less than HS diploma	3,115	11.7	Less than HS diploma	4,831	32.2
HS diploma or equiv. credential	8,270	31.0	HS diploma or equiv. credential	4,407	29.4
Some college or associate's degree	8,542	32.0	Some college or associate's degree	3,344	22.3
Bachelor's degree or higher	6,787	25.4	Bachelor's degree or higher	2,409	16.1
American Indian and Alaska Native	2,013	100.0	Two or more races	23,648	100.0
Less than HS diploma	441	21.9	Less than HS diploma	4,421	18.7
HS diploma or equiv. credential	621	30.9	HS diploma or equiv. credential	6,177	26.1
Some college or associate's degree	611	30.4	Some college or associate's degree	6,463	27.3
Bachelor's degree or higher	339	16.8	Bachelor's degree or higher	6,588	27.9
Asian	14,185	100.0	Hispanic or Latino (any race)	37,371	100.0
Less than HS diploma	1,670	11.8	Less than HS diploma	10,036	26.9
HS diploma or equiv. credential	1,982	14.0	HS diploma or equiv. credential	10,517	28.1
Some college or associate's degree	2,390	16.8	Some college or associate's degree	9,212	24.7
Bachelor's degree or higher	8,144	57.4	Bachelor's degree or higher	7,605	20.4

HS = High school. Note: Data based on sample and subject to sampling variability. Categories are for one race alone, not in combination with any other race, unless otherwise noted.

Populations for U.S. Places of 10,000 or More Residents

Source: Decennial Census and Pop. Ests. Program, U.S. Census Bureau, U.S. Dept. of Commerce; NANPA—Somos: www.usps.com

The following is a list of places of 10,000 or more residents according to the Census Bureau's 2022 population estimates, along with each place's 2010 and 2020 census results. Included are **places incorporated** under state law as cities, towns, villages, or boroughs, and **Census designated places (CDPs)**, marked with a (c). The Census Bureau delineates CDPs as statistical counterparts to incorporated places but does not typically include CDPs in its estimates program. This list also includes, in italics, **minor civil divisions (MCDs)** in Connecticut, Maine, Massachusetts, New Hampshire, Rhode Island, and Vermont. MCDs, which are also not incorporated, are often the primary political or administrative divisions of a county. (Balance) indicates the given population is for a consolidated area minus the residents of any separately incorporated places within its boundaries. **Townships are not included.**

An asterisk (*) denotes a **ZIP** code for general delivery; mail routes and/or P.O. boxes within the place may use a different one. More than one area code can serve a geographic area; overlay area codes are separated by slashes. A date within parentheses indicates when a code is expected to be in service. Area codes based on latest information as of mid-2023. — = Not in service.

Alabama
Area codes: 205/659, 251, 256/938, 334

ZIP	Place	2010 population	2020 population	2022 estimate
*35007	Alabaster	30,352	33,284	33,873
*35950	Albertville	21,160	22,386	22,726
*35010	Alexander City	14,875	14,843	14,636
*36201	Anniston	23,106	21,564	21,182
*35611	Athens	21,897	25,406	28,661
*36830	Auburn	53,380	76,143	80,006
*35020	Bessemer	27,456	26,019	25,264
*35203	Birmingham	212,237	200,733	196,910
*35956	Boaz	9,551	10,107	10,292
35040	Calera	11,620	16,494	17,868
*35215	Center Point	16,921	16,406	15,887
35043	Chelsea	10,183	14,982	16,193
*35215	Clay	9,708	10,291	10,290
*35055	Cullman	14,775	18,213	19,251
*36526	Daphne	21,570	27,462	29,670
*35601	Decatur	55,683	57,938	57,922
*36301	Dothan	65,496	71,072	71,235
*36330	Enterprise	26,562	28,711	29,767
*36027	Eufaula	13,137	12,882	12,539
*36532	Fairhope	15,326	22,477	23,859
*35630	Florence	39,319	40,184	41,690
*36535	Foley	14,618	20,335	23,577
35214	Forestdale (c)	10,162	10,409	—
*35967	Fort Payne	14,012	14,877	14,879
*35901	Gadsden	36,856	33,945	33,335
35071	Gardendale	13,893	16,044	16,244
36542	Gulf Shores	9,741	15,014	16,193
35640	Hartselle	14,255	15,455	15,649
*35080	Helena	16,793	20,914	21,862
*35209	Homewood	25,167	26,414	27,864
*35216	Hoover	81,619	92,606	92,435
*35023	Hueytown	16,105	16,776	16,369
*35801	Huntsville	180,105	215,006	221,933
35210	Irondale	12,349	13,497	13,366
*36265	Jacksonville	12,548	14,385	14,432
*35501	Jasper	14,352	14,572	14,338
35094	Leeds	11,773	12,324	12,346
*35758	Madison	42,938	56,933	59,785
35111	McCalla (c)	—	12,965	—
36054	Millbrook	14,640	16,564	17,096
*36602	Mobile	195,111	187,041	183,289
*36104	Montgomery	205,764	200,603	196,986
35004	Moody	11,726	13,170	13,587
*35223	Mountain Brook	20,413	22,461	21,955
*35661	Muscle Shoals	13,146	16,275	17,019
*35476	Northport	23,330	31,125	31,004
*36801	Opelika	26,477	30,995	32,787
36203	Oxford	21,348	22,069	22,002
*36360	Ozark	14,907	14,368	14,299
35124	Pelham	21,352	24,318	24,755
*35125	Pell City	12,695	12,939	13,638
*36867	Phenix City	32,822	38,816	38,267
36064	Pike Road	5,406	9,439	10,701
*36066	Prattville	33,960	37,781	38,776
*36610	Prichard	22,659	19,322	18,870
35906	Rainbow City	9,602	10,191	10,271
*35653	Russellville	9,830	10,855	10,771
36571	Saraland	13,405	16,171	16,358
*35768	Scottsboro	14,770	15,578	15,677
*36701	Selma	20,756	17,971	17,023
36527	Spanish Fort	6,798	10,049	10,656
*35150	Sylacauga	12,749	12,578	12,278
*35160	Talladega	15,676	15,861	14,674
36619	Tillman's Corner (c)	17,398	17,731	—
*36081	Troy	18,033	17,727	17,774
35173	Trussville	19,933	26,123	26,520
*35401	Tuscaloosa	90,468	99,600	110,602
*36854	Valley	9,524	10,529	10,323
*35216	Vestavia Hills	34,033	39,102	38,292

Alaska
Area code: 907 applies to the entire state

ZIP	Place	2010 population	2020 population	2022 estimate
*99501	Anchorage	291,826	291,247	287,145
99711	Badger (c)	19,482	19,031	—
*99708	College (c)	12,964	11,332	—
*99701	Fairbanks	31,535	32,515	32,107
*99801	Juneau	31,275	32,255	31,685
99654	Knik-Fairview (c)	14,923	19,297	—

Arizona
Area codes: 480, 520, 602, 623, 928

ZIP	Place	2010 population	2020 population	2022 estimate
85086	Anthem (c)	21,700	23,190	—
*85119	Apache Junction	35,840	38,499	40,173
*85323	Avondale	76,238	89,334	91,617
*85326	Buckeye	50,876	91,502	105,567
*86442	Bullhead City	39,540	41,348	42,920
86322	Camp Verde	10,873	12,147	12,409
*85122	Casa Grande	48,571	53,658	60,032
85740	Casas Adobes (c)	66,795	70,973	—
85718	Catalina Foothills (c)	50,796	52,401	—
*85225	Chandler	236,123	275,987	280,711
86323	Chino Valley	10,817	13,020	13,669
85128	Coolidge	11,825	13,218	16,711
86326	Cottonwood	11,265	12,029	12,943
*85607	Douglas	17,378	16,534	15,589
*85746	Drexel Heights (c)	27,749	27,523	—
85335	El Mirage	31,797	35,805	35,985
85131	Eloy	16,631	15,635	17,042
*86001	Flagstaff	65,870	76,831	75,907
85132	Florence	25,536	26,785	24,795
85705	Flowing Wells (c)	16,419	15,657	—
*86426	Fort Mohave (c)	14,364	16,190	—
85367	Fortuna Foothills (c)	26,265	27,776	—
*85268	Fountain Hills	22,489	23,820	23,785
*85234	Gilbert	208,453	267,918	275,346
*85301	Glendale	226,721	248,325	252,136
85118	Gold Canyon (c)	10,159	11,404	—
*85338	Goodyear	65,275	95,294	105,406
85622	Green Valley (c)	21,391	22,616	—
*86401	Kingman	28,068	32,689	34,918
*86403	Lake Havasu City	52,527	57,144	58,926
*85653	Marana	34,961	51,908	55,962
*85138	Maricopa	43,482	58,125	66,290
*85201	Mesa	439,041	504,258	512,498
86401	New Kingman-Butler (c)	12,134	12,907	—
85087	New River (c)	14,952	17,290	—
*85621	Nogales	20,837	19,770	19,833
*85737	Oro Valley	41,011	47,070	48,226
85253	Paradise Valley	12,820	12,658	12,606
*85541	Payson	15,301	16,351	16,653
*85345	Peoria	154,065	190,985	197,866
*85003	Phoenix	1,445,632	1,608,139	1,644,409
*86301	Prescott	39,843	45,827	47,603
*86314	Prescott Valley	38,822	46,785	49,075
*85142	Queen Creek	26,361	59,519	70,734
85648	Rio Rico (c)	18,962	20,549	—
85739	Saddlebrooke (c)	9,614	12,574	—
*85546	Safford	9,566	10,129	10,297
85629	Sahuarita	25,259	34,134	35,638
85349	San Luis	25,505	35,257	35,770
*85142	San Tan Valley (c)	81,321	99,894	—
*85251	Scottsdale	217,385	241,361	243,050
*85901	Show Low	10,660	11,732	12,056
*85635	Sierra Vista	43,888	45,308	45,439
*85615	Sierra Vista Southeast (c)	14,797	14,428	—
85350	Somerton	14,287	14,197	14,514
*85351	Sun City (c)	37,499	39,931	—
*85375	Sun City West (c)	24,535	25,806	—
85248	Sun Lakes (c)	13,975	14,868	—
*85374	Surprise	117,517	143,148	154,198
85749	Tanque Verde (c)	16,901	16,250	—
*85281	Tempe	161,719	180,587	185,950
*85701	Tucson	520,116	542,629	546,574
85735	Tucson Estates (c)	12,192	12,069	—
85743	Tucson Mountains (c)	—	10,862	—
85641	Vail (c)	10,208	13,604	—
85757	Valencia West (c)	9,355	14,101	—
86326	Verde Village (c)	11,605	12,019	—
*85364	Yuma	93,064	95,548	98,527

Arkansas
Area codes: 327 (Feb. 20, 2024)/870, 479, 501

ZIP	Place	2010 population	2020 population	2022 estimate
*71923	Arkadelphia.........	10,714	10,380	10,258
*72501	Batesville	10,248	11,191	11,173
*72714	Bella Vista	26,461	30,104	31,733
*72015	Benton	30,681	35,014	36,593
*72712	Bentonville	35,301	54,164	57,868
*72315	Blytheville	15,620	13,406	12,706
72022	Bryant	16,688	20,663	21,501
72023	Cabot	23,776	26,569	26,844
*71701	Camden	12,183	10,612	10,298
72719	Centerton	9,515	17,792	21,525
*72032	Conway	58,908	64,134	67,617
*71730	El Dorado	18,884	17,756	17,063
*72701	Fayetteville	73,580	93,949	99,285
*72335	Forrest City	15,371	13,015	12,676
*72901	Fort Smith	86,209	89,142	89,992
*72601	Harrison	12,943	13,069	13,338
*71901	Hot Springs	35,193	37,930	38,109
*71909	Hot Springs Village (c)	12,807	15,861	—
*72076	Jacksonville	28,364	29,477	29,130
*72401	Jonesboro	67,263	78,576	79,876
*72201	Little Rock	193,524	202,591	202,864
72745	Lowell	7,327	9,839	11,050
*71753	Magnolia	11,577	11,162	10,780
72104	Malvern	10,318	10,867	10,967
72364	Marion	12,345	13,752	13,596
72113	Maumelle	17,163	19,251	19,358
*72653	Mountain Home	12,448	12,825	13,150
*72113	North Little Rock	62,304	64,591	64,627
*72450	Paragould	26,113	29,537	30,178
*71601	Pine Bluff	49,083	41,253	39,495
*72756	Rogers	55,964	69,908	72,999
*72801	Russellville	27,920	28,940	29,113
*72143	Searcy	22,858	22,937	23,009
*72120	Sherwood	29,523	32,731	33,082
*72761	Siloam Springs	15,039	17,287	18,654
*72764	Springdale	69,797	84,161	87,672
*71854	Texarkana	29,919	29,387	29,306
*72956	Van Buren	22,791	23,218	23,755
*72301	West Memphis	26,245	24,520	23,795

California
Area codes: 209/350, 213/323/738 (Nov. 1, 2024), 279/916, 310/424, 341/510, 369/707, 408/669, 415/628, 442/760, 530, 559, 562, 619, 626, 650, 657/714, 661, 747/818, 805/820, 831, 840/909, 858, 949, 951

ZIP	Place	2010 population	2020 population	2022 estimate
92301	Adelanto	31,765	38,046	38,783
*91301	Agoura Hills	20,330	20,299	19,464
*94501	Alameda	73,812	78,280	76,040
94507	Alamo (c)	14,570	15,314	—
*94706	Albany.............	18,539	20,271	19,415
*91801	Alhambra	83,089	82,868	80,259
*92656	Aliso Viejo	47,823	52,176	51,221
*91901	Alpine (c)	14,236	14,696	—
*91001	Altadena (c)	42,777	42,846	—
95127	Alum Rock (c)	15,536	12,042	—
*94503	American Canyon ...	19,454	21,837	21,432
*92805	Anaheim	336,265	346,824	344,461
96007	Anderson	9,932	11,323	11,307
95843	Antelope (c)	45,770	48,733	—
94509	Antioch	102,372	115,291	115,264
*92307	Apple Valley	69,135	75,791	75,867
91006	Arcadia	56,364	56,681	54,857
*95521	Arcata	17,231	18,857	18,555
95825	Arden-Arcade (c)	92,186	94,659	—
*93420	Arroyo Grande	17,252	18,441	18,380
*90701	Artesia	16,522	16,395	15,774
93203	Arvin	19,304	19,495	19,611
94541	Ashland (c)	21,925	23,823	—
*93422	Atascadero	28,310	29,773	29,684
95301	Atwater	28,168	31,970	32,372
*95603	Auburn	13,330	13,776	13,737
93204	Avenal.............	15,505	13,696	13,374
*90601	Avocado Heights (c)	15,411	13,317	—
91702	Azusa	46,361	50,000	48,824
*93301	Bakersfield	347,483	403,455	410,647
91706	Baldwin Park.......	75,390	72,176	69,455
92220	Banning	29,603	29,505	30,683
*92310	Barstow	22,639	25,415	25,231
94565	Bay Point (c).......	21,349	23,896	—
92223	Beaumont..........	36,877	53,036	56,349
*90201	Bell	35,477	33,559	32,466
*90201	Bell Gardens	42,072	39,501	37,927
90706	Bellflower	76,616	79,190	76,405
94002	Belmont	25,835	28,335	26,773
94510	Benicia	26,997	27,131	26,567

ZIP	Place	2010 population	2020 population	2022 estimate
*94704	Berkeley	112,580	124,321	118,950
*90210	Beverly Hills	34,109	32,701	31,326
*92314	Big Bear City (c)	12,304	12,738	—
92316	Bloomington (c)	23,851	24,339	—
*92225	Blythe.............	20,817	18,317	17,358
*91902	Bonita (c)	12,538	12,917	—
92021	Bostonia (c)	15,379	16,882	—
92227	Brawley............	24,953	26,416	26,862
*92821	Brea..............	39,282	47,325	46,993
94513	Brentwood	51,481	64,292	66,127
90620	Buena Park........	80,530	84,034	82,450
*91502	Burbank	103,340	107,337	103,920
94010	Burlingame	28,806	31,386	30,559
*91301	Calabasas..........	23,058	23,241	22,491
92231	Calexico	38,572	38,633	38,249
*93505	California City	14,120	14,973	15,127
92320	Calimesa	7,879	10,026	11,017
*93010	Camarillo	65,201	70,741	70,282
95682	Cameron Park (c) ...	18,228	18,881	—
*92058	Camp Pendleton South (c).........	10,616	12,468	—
*95008	Campbell	39,349	43,959	42,286
*91384	Canyon Lake	10,561	11,082	11,142
*92008	Carlsbad	105,328	114,746	114,160
*95608	Carmichael (c)	61,762	79,793	—
*93013	Carpinteria	13,040	13,264	12,950
*90745	Carson	91,714	95,558	92,388
*91941	Casa de Oro-Mt. Helix (c).........	18,762	19,576	—
*91384	Castaic (c)	19,015	18,937	—
*94546	Castro Valley (c)	61,388	66,441	—
*92234	Cathedral City......	51,200	51,493	52,494
95307	Ceres	45,417	49,302	48,988
90703	Cerritos	49,041	49,578	47,475
*94541	Cherryland (c)......	14,728	15,808	—
95926	Chico	86,187	101,475	101,299
*91708	Chino	77,983	91,403	93,140
91709	Chino Hills	74,799	78,411	77,949
93610	Chowchilla.........	18,720	19,039	18,738
*91910	Chula Vista	243,916	275,487	279,170
91702	Citrus (c)	10,866	10,243	—
*95610	Citrus Heights	83,301	87,583	86,433
91711	Claremont..........	34,926	37,266	36,001
94517	Clayton	10,897	11,070	10,904
95422	Clearlake	15,250	16,685	16,693
*93612	Clovis	95,631	120,124	124,556
92236	Coachella	40,704	41,941	42,835
93210	Coalinga	13,380	17,590	17,024
92324	Colton	52,154	53,909	53,918
*90040	Commerce	12,823	12,378	11,828
90220	Compton	96,455	95,740	91,988
*94520	Concord	122,067	125,410	122,625
93212	Corcoran	24,813	22,339	22,837
*92882	Corona	152,374	157,136	159,567
92118	Coronado	18,912	20,192	18,702
94925	Corte Madera	9,253	10,222	10,006
92626	Costa Mesa	109,960	111,918	109,521
92679	Coto de Caza (c)....	14,866	14,710	—
95204	Country Club (c)	9,379	10,777	—
*91722	Covina	47,796	51,268	49,489
92325	Crestline (c)	10,770	11,650	—
90201	Cudahy	23,805	22,811	21,969
*90230	Culver City	38,883	40,779	39,515
95014	Cupertino	58,302	60,381	57,856
*90630	Cypress............	47,802	50,151	49,243
94015	Daly City	101,123	104,901	100,007
92629	Dana Point	33,351	33,107	32,465
94526	Danville	42,039	43,582	42,732
95616	Davis	65,622	66,850	67,048
90250	Del Aire (c)	10,001	10,338	—
93215	Delano	53,041	51,428	50,843
95315	Delhi (c)	10,755	10,656	—
*92240	Desert Hot Springs..	25,938	32,512	33,091
*91765	Diamond Bar........	55,544	55,072	52,855
95619	Diamond Springs (c)	11,037	11,345	—
93618	Dinuba	21,453	24,563	25,285
*94514	Discovery Bay (c) ...	13,352	15,358	—
95620	Dixon	18,351	18,988	19,143
*90240	Downey	111,772	114,355	109,934
91008	Duarte	21,321	21,727	21,807
94568	Dublin	46,036	72,589	72,060
92544	East Hemet (c)......	17,418	19,432	—
90022	East Los Angeles (c)	126,496	118,786	—
*93306	East Niles (c)	—	28,390	—
94303	East Palo Alto	28,155	30,034	28,383
90221	East Rancho Dominguez (c)....	15,135	15,114	—
91775	East San Gabriel (c)	14,874	22,769	—
90604	East Whittier (c)	—	10,394	—
93117	Eastern Goleta Valley (c).........	—	28,656	—

ZIP	Place	2010 population	2020 population	2022 estimate
*91752	Eastvale	53,668	69,757	71,024
*92020	El Cajon	99,478	106,215	104,414
*92243	El Centro	42,598	44,322	43,811
94530	El Cerrito	23,549	25,962	25,583
95762	El Dorado Hills (c)	42,108	50,547	—
*91731	El Monte	113,475	109,450	105,312
*93446	El Paso de Robles (Paso Robles)	29,793	31,490	31,544
90245	El Segundo	16,654	17,272	16,622
*94803	El Sobrante (c) (Contra Costa Co.)	12,669	15,524	—
92503	El Sobrante (c) (Riverside Co.)	12,723	14,039	—
*95624	Elk Grove	153,015	176,124	177,558
*94608	Emeryville	10,080	12,905	12,913
*92024	Encinitas	59,518	62,007	61,369
*92025	Escondido	143,911	151,038	150,270
*95501	Eureka	27,191	26,512	26,129
93221	Exeter	10,334	10,321	10,267
95628	Fair Oaks (c)	30,912	32,514	—
*94533	Fairfield	105,321	119,881	119,338
*94541	Fairview (c)	10,003	11,341	—
*92028	Fallbrook (c)	30,534	32,267	—
93223	Farmersville	10,588	10,397	10,324
*93015	Fillmore	15,002	16,419	16,657
*90001	Florence-Graham (c)	63,387	61,983	—
95828	Florin (c)	47,513	52,388	—
*95630	Folsom	72,203	80,454	83,269
*92335	Fontana	196,069	208,393	212,475
95841	Foothill Farms (c)	33,121	35,834	—
95540	Fortuna	11,926	12,516	12,516
94404	Foster City	30,567	33,805	32,026
*92704	Fountain Valley	55,313	57,047	55,930
*94538	Fremont	214,089	230,504	223,871
92596	French Valley (c)	23,067	35,280	—
*93721	Fresno	494,665	542,107	545,567
*92831	Fullerton	135,161	143,617	140,541
95632	Galt	23,647	25,383	25,411
95215	Garden Acres (c)	10,648	11,398	—
*92840	Garden Grove	170,883	171,949	169,254
*90247	Gardena	58,829	61,027	58,843
*95020	Gilroy	48,821	59,520	58,005
*91201	Glendale	191,719	196,543	189,221
*91741	Glendora	50,073	52,558	50,824
*93117	Goleta	29,888	32,690	32,432
*92313	Grand Terrace	12,040	13,150	13,109
*95746	Granite Bay (c)	20,402	21,247	—
*95945	Grass Valley	12,860	14,016	13,930
93927	Greenfield	16,330	18,937	19,359
*93433	Grover Beach	13,156	12,701	12,619
91745	Hacienda Heights (c)	54,038	54,191	—
94019	Half Moon Bay	11,324	11,795	11,176
*93230	Hanford	53,967	57,990	58,470
90716	Hawaiian Gardens	14,254	14,149	13,593
*90250	Hawthorne	84,293	88,083	84,563
*94541	Hayward	144,186	162,954	156,754
95448	Healdsburg	11,254	11,340	11,709
*92543	Hemet	78,657	89,833	90,689
94547	Hercules	24,060	26,016	25,920
90254	Hermosa Beach	19,506	19,728	18,985
*92344	Hesperia	90,173	99,818	100,744
*92346	Highland	53,104	56,999	56,705
92103	Hillcrest (c)	—	10,528	—
94010	Hillsborough	10,825	11,387	10,956
*95023	Hollister	34,928	41,678	44,218
*92503	Home Gardens (c)	11,570	11,203	—
*92647	Huntington Beach	189,992	198,711	194,310
90255	Huntington Park	58,114	54,883	52,633
92251	Imperial	14,758	20,263	21,233
*91932	Imperial Beach	26,324	26,137	25,791
*92201	Indio	76,036	89,137	91,980
*90301	Inglewood	109,673	107,762	103,621
*92602	Irvine	212,375	307,670	313,685
93117	Isla Vista (c)	23,096	15,500	—
*91752	Jurupa Valley[1]	—	105,053	107,609
93630	Kerman	13,544	16,016	16,208
93930	King City	12,874	13,332	13,738
93631	Kingsburg	11,382	12,380	12,613
*91011	La Cañada Flintridge	20,246	20,573	19,752
*91024	La Crescenta-Montrose (c)	19,653	19,997	—
*90631	La Habra	60,239	63,097	61,978
*91941	La Mesa	57,065	61,121	60,360
*90638	La Mirada	48,527	48,008	46,323
90623	La Palma	15,568	15,581	15,194
91977	La Presa (c)	34,169	35,033	—
*91744	La Puente	39,816	38,062	36,636
*92253	La Quinta	37,467	37,558	38,392
*95826	La Riviera (c)	10,802	11,252	—
91750	La Verne	31,063	31,334	30,380
92694	Ladera Ranch (c)	22,980	26,170	—
94549	Lafayette	23,893	25,391	25,044
*92651	Laguna Beach	22,723	23,032	22,583
*92653	Laguna Hills	30,344	31,374	30,568
*92677	Laguna Niguel	62,979	64,355	63,742
*92637	Laguna Woods	16,192	17,644	17,192
92352	Lake Arrowhead (c)	12,424	12,401	—
*92530	Lake Elsinore	51,821	70,265	71,898
*92630	Lake Forest	77,264	85,858	85,638
*93535	Lake Los Angeles (c)	12,328	13,187	—
92530	Lakeland Village (c)	11,541	12,364	—
92040	Lakeside (c)	20,648	21,152	—
*90712	Lakewood	80,048	82,496	79,063
93241	Lamont (c)	15,120	14,049	—
*93534	Lancaster	156,633	173,516	169,185
*94939	Larkspur	11,926	13,064	12,754
95330	Lathrop	18,023	28,701	33,670
*90260	Lawndale	32,769	31,807	30,576
*91945	Lemon Grove	25,320	27,627	27,224
95824	Lemon Hill (c)	13,729	14,496	—
*93245	Lemoore	24,531	27,038	27,185
90304	Lennox (c)	22,753	20,323	—
95648	Lincoln	42,819	49,757	52,534
95901	Linda (c)	17,773	21,654	—
93247	Lindsay	11,768	12,659	12,537
95953	Live Oak (c)	17,158	17,038	—
*94550	Livermore	80,968	87,955	84,701
95334	Livingston	13,058	14,172	14,760
*95240	Lodi	62,134	66,348	67,258
*92354	Loma Linda	23,261	24,791	25,129
90717	Lomita	20,256	20,921	20,053
*93436	Lompoc	42,434	44,444	43,736
*90802	Long Beach	462,257	466,742	451,307
90720	Los Alamitos	11,449	11,780	11,550
*94022	Los Altos	28,976	31,625	30,424
*90012	Los Angeles	3,792,621	3,898,747	3,822,238
93635	Los Banos	35,972	45,532	47,044
95030	Los Gatos	29,413	33,529	32,402
*93402	Los Osos (c)	14,276	14,465	—
90262	Lynwood	69,772	67,265	64,086
*93638	Madera	61,416	66,224	68,050
90265	Malibu	12,645	10,654	10,370
*90266	Manhattan Beach	35,135	35,506	34,137
*95336	Manteca	67,096	83,498	86,928
93933	Marina	19,718	22,359	22,503
*90292	Marina del Rey (c)	8,866	11,373	—
94553	Martinez	35,824	37,287	36,447
95901	Marysville	12,072	12,844	12,704
90270	Maywood	27,395	25,138	24,122
93250	McFarland	12,707	14,161	14,019
*95521	McKinleyville (c)	15,177	16,262	—
92570	Mead Valley (c)	18,510	19,819	—
93640	Mendota	11,014	12,595	12,618
*92586	Menifee	77,519	102,527	109,399
*94025	Menlo Park	32,026	33,780	32,295
*95340	Merced	78,958	86,333	91,563
94941	Mill Valley	13,903	14,231	14,006
94030	Millbrae	21,532	23,216	22,071
95035	Milpitas	66,790	80,273	77,738
*92691	Mission Viejo	93,305	93,653	91,776
*95350	Modesto	201,165	218,464	218,069
*91016	Monrovia	36,590	37,931	36,893
*91763	Montclair	36,664	37,865	37,714
90640	Montebello	62,500	62,640	60,569
*93940	Monterey	27,810	30,218	29,571
*91754	Monterey Park	60,269	61,096	58,554
*93021	Moorpark	34,421	36,284	35,514
94556	Moraga	16,016	16,870	16,707
*92551	Moreno Valley	193,365	208,634	211,924
95037	Morgan Hill	37,882	45,483	44,973
*93442	Morro Bay	10,234	10,757	10,696
95391	Mountain House (c)	9,675	24,499	—
*94041	Mountain View	74,066	82,376	81,059
*92562	Murrieta	103,466	110,949	113,783
92407	Muscoy (c)	10,644	10,719	—
*94558	Napa	76,915	79,246	78,315
*91950	National City	58,582	56,173	55,550
94560	Newark	42,573	47,529	47,312
95360	Newman	10,224	12,351	12,272
*92651	Newport Beach	85,186	85,239	83,993
93444	Nipomo (c)	16,714	18,176	—
92860	Norco	27,063	26,316	25,042
*95602	North Auburn (c)	13,022	13,452	—
*94025	North Fair Oaks (c)	14,687	14,027	—
95660	North Highlands (c)	42,694	49,327	—
92705	North Tustin (c)	24,917	25,718	—
*90650	Norwalk	105,549	102,773	98,537
*94947	Novato	51,904	53,225	52,184
*91377	Oak Park (c)	13,811	13,898	—
95361	Oakdale	20,675	23,181	23,176
*94601	Oakland	390,724	440,646	430,553
94561	Oakley	35,432	43,357	44,688

ZIP	Place	2010 population	2020 population	2022 estimate
*92054	Oceanside	167,086	174,068	172,199
93308	Oildale (c)	32,684	36,135	—
95961	Olivehurst (c)	13,656	16,595	—
*91761	Ontario	163,924	175,265	179,061
*92866	Orange	136,416	139,911	136,178
95662	Orangevale (c)	33,960	35,569	—
*93455	Orcutt (c)	28,905	32,034	—
94563	Orinda	17,643	19,514	19,355
*95965	Oroville	15,546	20,042	20,041
*93030	Oxnard	197,899	202,063	200,415
93950	Pacific Grove	15,041	15,090	14,791
94044	Pacifica	37,234	38,640	36,517
*92260	Palm Desert	48,445	51,163	51,583
92262	Palm Springs	44,552	44,575	45,223
*93550	Palmdale	152,750	169,450	163,463
*94303	Palo Alto	64,403	68,572	66,010
*90274	Palos Verdes Estates	13,438	13,347	12,792
90723	Paramount	54,098	53,733	51,653
95823	Parkway (c)	14,670	15,962	—
93648	Parlier	14,494	14,576	14,554
*91101	Pasadena	137,122	138,699	134,211
	Paso Robles. See El Paso de Robles			
95363	Patterson	20,413	23,781	23,833
*92570	Perris	68,386	78,700	80,263
*94952	Petaluma	57,941	59,776	58,652
*92371	Phelan (c)	14,304	13,859	—
90660	Pico Rivera	62,942	62,088	59,781
*94611	Piedmont	10,667	11,270	10,811
94564	Pinole	18,390	19,022	18,582
94565	Pittsburg	63,264	76,416	77,572
*92870	Placentia	50,533	51,824	51,951
95667	Placerville	10,389	10,747	10,664
94523	Pleasant Hill	33,152	34,613	33,913
*94566	Pleasanton	70,285	79,871	76,689
*91765	Pomona	149,058	151,713	146,017
*93041	Port Hueneme	21,723	21,954	21,407
*93257	Porterville	54,165	62,623	62,998
*92064	Poway	47,811	48,841	48,078
93907	Prunedale (c)	17,560	18,885	—
*93536	Quartz Hill (c)	10,912	11,447	—
92065	Ramona	20,292	21,468	—
*95670	Rancho Cordova	64,776	79,332	80,598
*91730	Rancho Cucamonga	165,269	174,453	176,336
92270	Rancho Mirage	17,218	16,999	17,633
92694	Rancho Mission Viejo	—	10,378	—
90275	Rancho Palos Verdes	41,643	42,287	40,527
*92019	Rancho San Diego (c)	21,208	21,858	—
92688	Rancho Santa Margarita	47,853	47,949	46,722
96080	Red Bluff	14,076	14,710	14,416
*96001	Redding	89,861	93,611	92,906
*92373	Redlands	68,747	73,168	73,849
90277	Redondo Beach	66,748	71,576	68,918
*94063	Redwood City	76,815	84,292	80,512
93654	Reedley	24,194	25,227	25,441
*92376	Rialto	99,171	104,026	103,545
94801	Richmond	103,701	116,448	114,301
*93555	Ridgecrest	27,616	27,959	28,346
95673	Rio Linda (c)	15,106	15,944	—
94571	Rio Vista	7,360	10,005	10,375
95366	Ripon	14,297	16,013	16,272
95387	Riverbank	22,678	24,865	24,826
*92501	Riverside	303,871	314,998	320,764
*95677	Rocklin	56,974	71,601	73,857
*94928	Rohnert Park	40,971	44,390	44,326
93560	Rosamond (c)	18,150	20,961	—
93314	Rosedale (c)	14,058	18,639	—
*91770	Rosemead	53,764	51,185	49,791
95826	Rosemont (c)	22,681	23,510	—
*95678	Roseville	118,788	147,773	154,817
90720	Rossmoor (c)	10,244	10,625	—
91748	Rowland Heights (c)	48,993	48,231	—
*95814	Sacramento	466,488	524,943	528,001
95368	Salida (c)	13,722	13,886	—
*93901	Salinas	150,441	163,542	161,020
*94960	San Anselmo	12,336	12,830	12,569
*92401	San Bernardino	209,924	222,101	220,328
94066	San Bruno	41,114	43,908	41,533
*93001	San Buenaventura (Ventura)	106,433	110,763	109,527
94070	San Carlos	28,406	30,722	29,586
*92672	San Clemente	63,522	64,293	63,457
*92101	San Diego	1,307,402	1,386,932	1,381,162
92065	San Diego Country Estates (c)	10,109	10,395	—
91773	San Dimas	33,371	34,924	33,535
*91340	San Fernando	23,645	23,946	23,685
*94102	San Francisco	805,235	873,965	808,437
91775	San Gabriel	39,718	39,568	38,140
*92582	San Jacinto	44,199	53,898	55,470
*95113	San Jose	945,942	1,013,240	971,233
*92675	San Juan Capistrano	34,593	35,196	34,548
*94577	San Leandro	84,950	91,008	86,762
94580	San Lorenzo (c)	23,452	29,581	—
*93401	San Luis Obispo	45,119	47,063	48,341
92069	San Marcos	83,781	94,833	94,854
*91108	San Marino	13,147	12,513	12,039
*94403	San Mateo	97,207	105,661	100,984
*94806	San Pablo	29,139	32,127	31,389
*94901	San Rafael	57,713	61,271	59,971
*94583	San Ramon	72,148	84,605	85,953
93657	Sanger	24,270	26,617	26,600
*92701	Santa Ana	324,528	310,227	308,189
*93101	Santa Barbara	88,410	88,665	87,533
*95050	Santa Clara	116,468	127,647	126,930
*91355	Santa Clarita	176,320	228,673	221,345
*95060	Santa Cruz	59,946	62,956	61,800
95670	Santa Fe Springs	16,223	19,219	18,439
*93454	Santa Maria	99,553	109,707	110,125
*90401	Santa Monica	89,736	93,076	89,947
93060	Santa Paula	29,321	30,657	31,018
*95401	Santa Rosa	167,815	178,127	177,181
*92071	Santee	53,413	60,037	59,051
*95070	Saratoga	29,926	31,051	29,903
*95066	Scotts Valley	11,580	12,224	12,073
90740	Seal Beach	24,168	25,242	24,627
93955	Seaside	33,025	32,366	31,478
*93662	Selma	23,219	24,674	24,430
93263	Shafter	16,988	19,953	21,282
*96019	Shasta Lake	10,164	10,371	10,335
91024	Sierra Madre	10,917	11,268	10,809
*90755	Signal Hill	11,016	11,848	11,381
93065	Simi Valley	124,237	126,356	124,398
92075	Solana Beach	12,867	12,941	12,802
93960	Soledad	25,738	24,925	24,190
95476	Sonoma	10,648	10,739	10,466
91733	South El Monte	20,116	19,567	19,602
90280	South Gate	94,396	92,726	90,926
96150	South Lake Tahoe	21,403	21,330	21,175
*91030	South Pasadena	25,619	26,943	25,850
94080	South San Francisco	63,632	66,105	63,484
91744	South San Jose Hills (c)	20,551	19,855	—
90605	South Whittier (c)	57,156	56,415	—
*91977	Spring Valley (c) (San Diego Co.)	28,205	30,998	—
*94305	Stanford (c)	13,809	21,150	—
90680	Stanton	38,186	37,962	38,952
91381	Stevenson Ranch (c)	17,557	20,178	—
*95202	Stockton	291,707	320,804	321,819
*94585	Suisun City	28,111	29,518	28,949
93543	Sun Village (c)	11,565	12,345	—
*94086	Sunnyvale	140,081	155,805	153,091
96130	Susanville	17,947	16,728	13,707
94941	Tamalpais-Homestead Valley (c)	10,735	11,492	—
*93561	Tehachapi	14,414	12,939	12,389
*92590	Temecula	100,097	110,003	111,752
92883	Temescal Valley (c)	22,535	26,232	—
91780	Temple City	35,558	36,494	35,296
*91360	Thousand Oaks	126,683	126,966	124,265
*90503	Torrance	145,438	147,067	141,126
*95376	Tracy	82,922	93,000	97,328
*96161	Truckee	16,180	16,729	16,850
*93274	Tulare	59,278	68,875	70,693
*95380	Turlock	68,549	72,740	72,309
*92780	Tustin	75,540	80,276	78,418
92277	Twentynine Palms	25,048	28,065	28,158
*95482	Ukiah	16,075	16,607	16,144
*94587	Union City	69,516	70,143	67,039
*91784	Upland	73,732	79,040	78,841
95687	Vacaville	92,428	102,386	101,918
91744	Valinda (c)	22,822	22,437	—
92544	Valle Vista (c)	14,578	16,194	—
*94590	Vallejo	115,942	126,090	123,564
92082	Valley Center (c)	9,277	10,087	—
	Ventura. See San Buenaventura			
*92392	Victorville	115,903	134,810	137,221
*90043	View Park-Windsor Hills (c)	11,075	11,419	—
*91702	Vincent (c)	15,922	15,714	—
95829	Vineyard (c)	24,836	43,935	—
*93277	Visalia	124,442	141,384	143,966
*92084	Vista	93,834	98,381	97,766
*91789	Walnut	29,172	28,430	27,356
*94596	Walnut Creek	64,173	70,127	68,969
90255	Walnut Park (c)	15,966	15,214	—
*93280	Wasco	25,545	27,047	27,731
*95076	Watsonville	51,199	52,590	51,525
90502	West Carson (c)	21,699	22,870	—
*91790	West Covina	106,098	109,501	105,013
*90069	West Hollywood	34,399	35,757	34,514
91746	West Puente Valley (c)	22,636	22,959	—
*90220	West Rancho Dominguez (c)	5,669	24,347	—

ZIP	Place	2010 population	2020 population	2022 estimate
*95691	West Sacramento . . .	48,744	53,915	55,064
*90606	West Whittier-Los Nietos (c)	25,540	25,325	—
*92683	Westminster	89,701	90,911	89,397
*90047	Westmont (c)	31,853	33,913	—
*90602	Whittier	85,331	87,306	84,496
92595	Wildomar	32,176	36,875	37,214
*90222	Willowbrook (c)	35,983	24,295	—
95492	Windsor	26,801	26,344	25,789
92040	Winter Gardens (c) . . .	20,631	22,380	—
95388	Winton (c)	10,613	11,709	—
92504	Woodcrest (c)	14,347	15,378	—
*95695	Woodland	55,468	61,032	61,462
*92886	Yorba Linda	64,234	68,336	67,089
*95991	Yuba City	64,925	70,117	69,014
92399	Yucaipa	51,367	54,542	54,420
*92284	Yucca Valley	20,700	21,738	21,662

(1) Incorporated after 2010 Census.

Colorado

Area codes: 303/720/983, 719, 970

ZIP	Place	2010 population	2020 population	2022 estimate
*80004	Arvada	106,433	124,402	121,581
*80010	Aurora	325,078	386,261	393,537
*80211	Berkley (c)	11,207	12,536	—
80513	Berthoud	5,105	10,332	12,710
*80908	Black Forest (c)	13,116	15,097	—
*80302	Boulder	97,385	108,250	105,485
*80601	Brighton	33,352	40,083	41,881
*80020	Broomfield	55,889	74,112	76,121
*81212	Cañon City	16,400	17,141	17,258
80108	Castle Pines	3,614	11,036	13,486
*80104	Castle Rock	48,231	73,158	80,191
*80015	Centennial	100,377	108,418	105,865
80206	Cherry Creek (c)	11,120	11,488	—
80915	Cimarron Hills (c)	16,161	19,311	—
81520	Clifton (c)	19,889	20,413	—
*80903	Colorado Springs	416,427	478,961	486,248
*80128	Columbine (c)	24,280	25,229	—
*80022	Commerce City	45,913	62,418	66,115
*80127	Dakota Ridge (c).	32,005	33,892	—
*80202	Denver	600,158	715,522	713,252
*81301	Durango	16,887	19,071	19,531
81632	Edwards (c)	10,266	11,246	—
*80110	Englewood	30,255	33,659	33,642
*80516	Erie	18,135	30,038	33,104
*80620	Evans	18,537	22,165	22,619
*80260	Federal Heights	11,467	14,382	14,001
*80504	Firestone	10,147	16,381	18,314
*80913	Fort Carson (c)	13,813	17,693	—
*80521	Fort Collins	143,986	169,810	169,249
*80701	Fort Morgan	11,315	11,597	11,453
80817	Fountain	25,846	29,802	28,907
*80231	Four Square Mile (c). .	—	22,872	—
*80530	Frederick	8,679	14,513	17,158
81521	Fruita	12,646	13,395	13,760
*81601	Glenwood Springs . . .	9,614	9,963	10,264
*80401	Golden	18,867	20,399	20,460
*81501	Grand Junction	58,566	65,560	68,034
*80631	Greeley	92,889	108,795	109,209
*80111	Greenwood Village . . .	13,925	15,691	15,365
*80126	Highlands Ranch (c). .	96,713	103,444	—
80534	Johnstown.	9,887	17,303	18,636
*80127	Ken Caryl (c).	32,438	33,811	—
80026	Lafayette	24,453	30,411	30,699
*80226	Lakewood	142,980	155,984	156,120
*80120	Littleton	41,737	45,652	44,755
*80124	Lone Tree	10,218	14,253	14,177
*80501	Longmont	86,270	98,885	98,687
80027	Louisville	18,376	21,226	20,560
*80537	Loveland	66,859	76,378	77,884
*81401	Montrose.	19,132	20,291	21,003
80132	Monument.	5,530	10,399	11,793
*80233	Northglenn	35,789	38,131	38,106
*80134	Parker	45,297	58,512	61,222
*81003	Pueblo	106,595	111,876	111,456
81007	Pueblo West (c)	29,637	33,086	—
81650	Rifle	9,172	10,437	10,551
80911	Security-Widefield (c)	32,882	38,639	—
80524	Severance	3,165	7,683	10,581
80221	Sherrelwood (c)	18,287	19,228	—
*80487	Steamboat Springs . . .	12,088	13,224	13,302
80751	Sterling	14,777	13,735	13,102
80027	Superior	12,483	13,094	13,292
80134	The Pinery (c)	10,517	11,311	—
*80229	Thornton	118,772	141,867	143,282
80229	Welby (c).	14,846	15,553	—
80549	Wellington	6,289	11,047	11,978
*80031	Westminster	106,114	116,317	114,533
*80033	Wheat Ridge	30,166	32,398	31,879
*80550	Windsor	18,644	32,716	38,510

Connecticut

Area codes: 203/475, 860/959. See introductory note.

ZIP	Place	2010 population	2020 population	2022 estimate
06401	Ansonia.	19,249	18,918	18,923
06001	Avon	18,098	18,932	18,871
06037	Berlin	19,866	20,175	20,197
06801	Bethel	18,584	20,358	20,684
06801	Bethel (c)	9,549	11,582	—
06002	Bloomfield	20,486	21,535	21,560
06405	Branford	28,026	28,273	28,148
*06604	Bridgeport.	144,229	148,654	148,377
*06010	Bristol	60,477	60,833	61,330
06804	Brookfield	16,452	17,528	17,543
06019	Canton	10,292	10,124	10,091
*06410	Cheshire	29,261	28,733	28,994
06413	Clinton	13,260	13,185	13,399
*06415	Colchester	16,068	15,555	15,572
06238	Coventry	12,435	12,235	12,285
06416	Cromwell	14,005	14,225	14,317
*06810	Danbury	80,893	86,518	86,967
06820	Darien	20,732	21,499	21,926
06418	Derby	12,902	12,325	12,358
*06424	East Hampton	12,959	12,717	12,960
*06108	East Hartford	51,252	51,045	50,718
*06512	East Haven	29,257	27,923	27,682
06333	East Lyme	19,159	18,693	18,788
06088	East Windsor	11,162	11,190	11,176
06029	Ellington	15,602	16,426	16,977
*06082	Enfield.	44,654	42,141	41,245
*06824	Fairfield	59,404	61,512	62,871
*06032	Farmington	25,340	26,712	26,728
06033	Glastonbury	34,427	35,159	35,199
06035	Granby	11,282	10,903	11,041
*06830	Greenwich	61,171	63,518	63,638
*06830	Greenwich (c)	12,942	13,836	—
06351	Griswold	11,951	11,402	11,509
*06340	Groton	40,115	38,411	37,743
06437	Guilford	22,375	22,073	22,019
*06514	Hamden	60,960	61,169	60,809
*06103	Hartford	124,775	121,054	120,686
*06239	Killingly	17,370	17,752	17,837
*06339	Ledyard	15,051	15,413	15,456
*06443	Madison	18,269	17,691	17,565
*06040	Manchester	58,241	59,713	59,461
*06040	Manchester (c)	30,577	36,379	—
*06250	Mansfield	26,543	25,892	31,949
*06450	Meriden	60,868	60,850	60,242
*06457	Middletown	47,648	47,717	48,729
*06460	Milford (balance).	51,271	50,558	50,471
*06460	Milford	52,759	52,044	52,679
06468	Monroe	19,479	18,825	18,796
06353	Montville	19,571	18,387	17,891
06770	Naugatuck	31,862	31,519	31,705
*06051	New Britain	73,206	74,135	74,396
06840	New Canaan	19,738	20,622	20,775
06812	New Fairfield	13,881	13,579	13,536
*06511	New Haven	129,779	134,023	138,915
06320	New London	27,620	27,367	27,980
06776	New Milford	28,142	28,115	28,275
*06111	Newington	30,562	30,536	30,356
06470	Newtown	27,560	27,173	27,577
06473	North Branford	14,407	13,544	13,464
06471	North Haven	24,093	24,253	24,114
*06850	Norwalk.	85,603	91,184	91,401
*06360	Norwich	40,493	40,125	40,009
06475	Old Saybrook	10,242	10,481	10,535
06477	Orange	13,956	14,280	14,258
06478	Oxford	12,683	12,706	12,941
06374	Plainfield	15,405	14,973	15,143
06062	Plainville	17,716	17,525	17,479
06782	Plymouth	12,243	11,671	11,711
*06877	Ridgefield	24,638	25,033	25,007
06067	Rocky Hill	19,709	20,845	20,712
*06483	Seymour	16,540	16,748	16,809
06484	Shelton	39,559	40,869	41,897
06070	Simsbury	23,511	24,517	24,935
06074	South Windsor	25,709	26,918	26,783
06488	Southbury	19,904	19,879	19,979
06489	Southington	43,069	43,501	43,753
*06075	Stafford	12,087	11,472	11,449
*06901	Stamford	122,643	135,470	136,188
06378	Stonington	18,545	18,335	18,480
*06268	Storrs (c).	15,344	15,979	—
*06614	Stratford	51,384	52,355	52,477
*06078	Suffield	15,735	15,752	15,731
06084	Tolland	15,052	14,563	14,577
*06790	Torrington	36,383	35,515	35,563
*06611	Trumbull	36,018	36,827	37,135
06066	Vernon	29,179	30,215	30,625
*06492	Wallingford	45,135	44,396	44,017

ZIP	Place	2010 population	2020 population	2022 estimate
*06492	Wallingford Center (c)	18,209	18,278	—
*06702	Waterbury	110,366	114,403	115,016
06385	Waterford	19,517	19,571	19,603
*06795	Watertown	22,514	22,105	22,183
*06105	West Hartford	63,268	64,083	64,271
06516	West Haven	55,564	55,584	55,004
06883	Weston	10,179	10,354	10,354
*06880	Westport	26,391	27,141	27,427
*06109	Wethersfield	26,668	27,298	27,129
06226	Willimantic (c)	17,737	18,149	—
06897	Wilton	18,062	18,503	18,457
*06098	Winchester	11,242	10,224	10,240
06280	Windham	25,268	24,425	24,399
*06095	Windsor	29,044	29,492	29,453
06096	Windsor Locks	12,498	12,613	12,537
*06716	Wolcott	16,680	16,142	16,190

Delaware
Area code: 302 applies to the entire state

ZIP	Place	2010 population	2020 population	2022 estimate
19701	Bear (c)	19,371	23,060	—
19713	Brookside (c)	14,353	14,974	—
*19901	Dover	36,047	39,403	38,594
19702	Glasgow (c)	14,303	15,288	—
19707	Hockessin (c)	13,527	13,478	—
19709	Middletown	18,871	23,192	24,698
19963	Milford	9,559	11,190	12,981
*19711	Newark	31,454	30,601	30,453
19808	Pike Creek Valley (c)	11,217	11,692	—
19977	Smyrna	10,023	12,883	13,294
*19801	Wilmington	70,851	70,898	71,569

District of Columbia
Area codes: 202/771 apply to the entire district

ZIP	Place	2010 population	2020 population	2022 estimate
*20001	Washington	601,723	689,545	671,803

Florida
Area codes: 239, 305/645/786, 321 (part)/407, 324 (Feb. 26, 2024)/904, 352, 386, 407/689, 448/850, 561/728, 656/813, 727, 754/954, 772, 863, 941

ZIP	Place	2010 population	2020 population	2022 estimate
*32624	Alachua	9,059	10,574	10,773
*32828	Alafaya (c)	78,113	92,452	—
*32701	Altamonte Springs	41,496	46,231	45,538
33572	Apollo Beach (c)	14,055	26,002	—
*32712	Apopka	41,542	54,873	57,017
32043	Asbury Lake (c)	8,700	11,036	—
32233	Atlantic Beach	12,655	13,513	13,283
33823	Auburndale	13,507	15,616	18,579
*33180	Aventura	35,762	40,242	38,930
32807	Azalea Park (c)	12,556	14,141	—
*33830	Bartow	17,298	19,309	19,888
34667	Bayonet Point (c)	23,467	26,713	—
34207	Bayshore Gardens (c)	16,323	19,904	—
32073	Bellair-Meadowbrook Terrace (c)	13,343	14,482	—
33430	Belle Glade	17,467	16,698	16,777
32526	Bellview (c)	23,355	25,541	—
*33596	Bloomingdale (c)	22,711	22,947	—
*33431	Boca Raton	84,392	97,422	99,009
*34135	Bonita Springs	43,914	53,644	56,370
*33436	Boynton Beach	68,217	80,380	80,859
*34201	Bradenton	49,546	55,698	56,961
32312	Bradfordville (c)	—	19,183	—
*33510	Brandon (c)	103,483	114,626	—
32503	Brent (c)	21,804	23,447	—
33142	Brownsville (c)	15,313	16,583	—
34743	Buenaventura Lakes (c)	26,079	30,251	—
32404	Callaway	14,405	13,045	13,391
*33990	Cape Coral	154,305	194,016	216,992
*33618	Carrollwood (c)	33,365	34,352	—
*32707	Casselberry	26,241	28,794	29,901
34747	Celebration (c)	7,427	11,178	—
33558	Cheval (c)	10,702	12,522	—
33625	Citrus Park (c)	24,252	28,178	—
34433	Citrus Springs (c)	8,622	10,246	—
*33755	Clearwater	107,685	117,292	117,027
*34711	Clermont	28,742	43,021	46,506
*32922	Cocoa	17,140	19,041	19,559
*32931	Cocoa Beach	11,231	11,354	11,341
*33063	Coconut Creek	52,909	57,833	57,348
32806	Conway (c)	13,467	13,596	—
*33328	Cooper City	28,547	34,401	34,106
*33134	Coral Gables	46,780	49,248	49,193
*33065	Coral Springs	121,096	134,394	133,369
33155	Coral Terrace (c)	24,376	23,142	—
33015	Country Club (c)	47,105	49,967	—
*33186	Country Walk (c)	15,997	16,951	—
*32536	Crestview	20,978	27,134	28,234
*33189	Cutler Bay	40,286	45,425	43,958
33884	Cypress Gardens (c)	8,917	10,169	—
33919	Cypress Lake (c)	11,846	13,727	—
33004	Dania Beach	29,639	31,723	31,658
*33837	Davenport	2,888	9,043	13,485
*33314	Davie	91,992	105,691	106,513
*32114	Daytona Beach	61,005	72,647	77,958
32713	DeBary	19,320	22,260	22,956
*33441	Deerfield Beach	75,018	86,859	86,772
32720	DeLand	27,031	37,351	41,324
*33444	Delray Beach	60,522	66,846	67,030
32738	Deltona	85,182	93,692	97,267
*32541	Destin	12,305	13,931	14,119
*32819	Doctor Phillips (c)	10,981	12,328	—
*33166	Doral	45,704	75,874	76,983
*34698	Dunedin	35,321	36,068	36,059
*34685	East Lake (c)	30,962	32,344	—
*33610	East Lake-Orient Park (c)	22,753	28,050	—
32583	East Milton (c)	11,074	14,309	—
*32132	Edgewater	20,750	23,097	23,506
33614	Egypt Lake-Leto (c)	35,282	36,644	—
*34680	Elfers (c)	13,986	14,573	—
*34223	Englewood (c)	14,863	20,800	—
*32514	Ensley (c)	20,602	23,817	—
*33928	Estero	22,612	36,939	37,730
*32726	Eustis	18,558	23,189	23,961
*32789	Fairview Shores (c)	10,239	10,722	—
*32034	Fernandina Beach	11,487	13,052	13,401
32514	Ferry Pass (c)	28,921	29,921	—
33547	Fish Hawk (c)	14,087	24,625	—
*32003	Fleming Island (c)	27,126	29,142	—
33034	Florida City	11,245	13,085	12,644
*32962	Florida Ridge (c)	18,164	21,302	—
32703	Forest City (c)	13,854	14,623	—
*33301	Fort Lauderdale	165,521	182,760	183,146
*33901	Fort Myers	62,298	86,395	95,949
*34950	Fort Pierce	41,590	47,297	48,305
*32548	Fort Walton Beach	19,507	20,922	20,998
*33144	Fountainebleau (c)	59,764	59,870	—
*33896	Four Corners (c)	26,116	56,381	—
32259	Fruit Cove (c)	29,362	32,143	—
*34432	Fruitville (c)	13,224	15,484	—
*33860	Fuller Heights (c)	8,758	10,467	—
*32601	Gainesville	124,354	141,085	145,214
33913	Gateway (c)	8,401	10,376	—
33534	Gibsonton (c)	14,234	18,566	—
*33147	Gladeview (c)	11,535	14,927	—
*33143	Glenvar Heights (c)	16,898	20,786	—
34116	Golden Gate (c)	23,961	25,321	—
*33161	Golden Glades (c)	33,145	32,499	—
32733	Goldenrod (c)	12,039	13,431	—
*32533	Gonzalez (c)	13,273	14,586	—
33170	Goulds (c)	10,103	11,446	—
32043	Green Cove Springs	6,908	9,786	10,042
*33463	Greenacres	37,573	43,990	43,795
*34736	Groveland	8,729	18,505	22,374
*33707	Gulfport	12,029	11,783	11,726
*33844	Haines City	20,535	26,669	33,629
*33009	Hallandale Beach	37,113	41,217	41,202
*33010	Hialeah	224,669	223,109	220,292
*33016	Hialeah Gardens	21,744	23,068	22,364
*33813	Highland City (c)	10,834	12,355	—
*33455	Hobe Sound (c)	11,521	13,163	—
*34690	Holiday (c)	22,403	24,939	—
32117	Holly Hill	11,659	12,958	13,076
*33019	Hollywood	140,768	153,067	152,650
33030	Homestead	60,512	80,737	81,562
*34446	Homosassa Springs (c)	13,791	14,283	—
*34786	Horizon West (c)	14,000	58,101	—
*34667	Hudson (c)	12,158	12,944	—
32837	Hunters Creek (c)	14,321	24,433	—
*34142	Immokalee (c)	24,154	24,557	—
33908	Iona (c)	15,369	16,908	—
33179	Ives Estates (c)	19,525	25,005	—
*32202	Jacksonville	821,784	949,611	971,319
*32250	Jacksonville Beach	21,362	23,830	23,521
*34668	Jasmine Estates (c)	18,989	21,525	—
34957	Jensen Beach (c)	11,707	12,652	—
*33458	Jupiter	55,156	61,047	61,126
*33478	Jupiter Farms (c)	11,994	12,572	—
*33183	Kendale Lakes (c)	56,148	55,646	—
*33156	Kendall (c)	75,371	80,241	—
*33185	Kendall West (c)	36,154	36,536	—
33149	Key Biscayne	12,344	14,809	14,435
33037	Key Largo (c)	10,433	12,447	—
*33040	Key West	24,649	26,444	25,597

ZIP	Place	2010 population	2020 population	2022 estimate
*33556	Keystone (c)	24,039	25,211	—
*34741	Kissimmee	59,682	79,226	80,003
*32159	Lady Lake	13,926	15,970	16,661
32054	Lake Butler (c)	15,400	18,851	—
32055	Lake City	12,046	12,329	12,449
*33612	Lake Magdalene (c)	28,509	30,742	—
*32746	Lake Mary	13,822	16,798	16,765
*33853	Lake Wales	14,225	16,361	16,774
*33460	Lake Worth Beach	34,910	42,219	43,201
*33801	Lakeland	97,422	112,641	120,071
33813	Lakeland Highlands (c)	11,056	12,187	—
*32065	Lakeside (c)	30,943	31,275	—
*34951	Lakewood Park (c)	11,323	12,510	—
*34202	Lakewood Ranch (c)	—	34,877	—
*34639	Land O' Lakes (c)	31,996	35,929	—
*33462	Lantana	10,423	11,504	12,084
*33770	Largo	77,648	82,485	82,487
*33319	Lauderdale Lakes	32,593	35,954	35,799
*33313	Lauderhill	66,887	74,482	73,633
34272	Laurel (c)	8,171	12,186	—
*33702	Lealman (c)	19,879	21,189	—
*34748	Leesburg	20,117	27,000	29,178
*33936	Lehigh Acres (c)	86,784	114,287	—
33030	Leisure City (c)	22,655	26,324	—
34476	Liberty Triangle (c)	—	23,759	—
*33064	Lighthouse Point	10,344	10,486	10,420
32810	Lockhart (c)	13,060	14,058	—
*32750	Longwood	13,657	15,087	16,842
*33548	Lutz (c)	19,344	23,707	—
32444	Lynn Haven	18,493	18,695	20,044
*32751	Maitland	15,751	19,543	19,356
*33548	Mango (c)	11,313	12,699	—
*34145	Marco Island	16,413	15,760	16,172
*33063	Margate	53,284	58,712	58,209
34473	Marion Oaks (c)	—	19,034	—
32824	Meadow Woods (c)	25,558	43,790	—
*33811	Medulla (c)	8,892	10,871	—
*32901	Melbourne	76,068	84,678	86,441
*32953	Merritt Island (c)	34,743	34,518	—
*33125	Miami	399,457	442,241	449,514
*33140	Miami Beach	87,779	82,890	80,017
*33014	Miami Gardens	107,167	111,640	110,497
*33014	Miami Lakes	29,361	30,467	30,830
*33138	Miami Shores	10,493	11,567	11,569
*33166	Miami Springs	13,809	13,859	13,416
*32068	Middleburg (c)	13,008	12,881	—
32563	Midway (c) (Santa Rosa Co.)	16,115	19,567	—
*32570	Milton	8,826	10,197	10,687
34715	Minneola	9,403	13,843	16,149
*33023	Miramar	122,041	134,721	137,228
*32757	Mount Dora	12,370	16,341	17,160
32526	Myrtle Grove (c)	15,870	17,224	—
*34102	Naples	19,537	19,115	19,618
*33032	Naranja (c)	8,303	13,509	—
32566	Navarre (c)	31,378	40,817	—
*34652	New Port Richey	14,911	16,728	17,332
34653	New Port Richey East (c)	10,036	11,015	—
*32168	New Smyrna Beach	22,464	30,142	32,119
32578	Niceville	12,749	15,772	16,218
34268	Nocatee (c)	4,524	22,503	—
*33917	North Fort Myers (c)	39,407	42,719	—
*33068	North Lauderdale	41,023	44,794	44,541
*33161	North Miami	58,786	60,191	58,906
*33160	North Miami Beach	41,523	43,676	43,023
*33408	North Palm Beach	12,015	13,162	13,083
*34286	North Port	57,357	74,793	85,099
*33624	Northdale (c)	22,079	23,033	—
*32809	Oak Ridge (c)	22,685	25,062	—
*33334	Oakland Park	41,363	44,229	43,824
32065	Oakleaf Plantation (c)	20,315	31,034	—
*34470	Ocala	56,315	63,591	65,478
34761	Ocoee	35,579	47,295	48,198
33163	Ojus (c)	18,036	19,673	—
34677	Oldsmar	13,591	14,898	14,886
*33165	Olympia Heights (c)	13,488	12,873	—
34481	On Top of the World (c)	—	12,668	—
*33054	Opa-locka	15,219	16,463	15,888
*32763	Orange City	10,599	12,632	14,897
*32801	Orlando	238,300	307,573	316,081
*32174	Ormond Beach	38,137	43,080	44,052
*32765	Oviedo	33,342	40,059	39,580
32571	Pace (c)	20,039	24,684	—
*32177	Palatka	10,558	10,446	10,574
*32905	Palm Bay	103,190	119,760	129,234
*33410	Palm Beach Gardens	48,452	59,182	60,175
*34990	Palm City (c)	23,120	25,883	—
*32137	Palm Coast	75,180	89,258	98,411
*34683	Palm Harbor (c)	57,439	61,366	—
*33619	Palm River-Clair Mel (c)	21,024	26,142	—
33406	Palm Springs	18,928	26,890	26,844
32082	Palm Valley (c)	20,019	21,827	—
34238	Palmer Ranch (c)	—	14,966	—

ZIP	Place	2010 population	2020 population	2022 estimate
*34221	Palmetto	12,606	13,323	13,614
*33157	Palmetto Bay	23,410	24,439	24,237
33157	Palmetto Estates (c)	13,535	13,498	—
*32401	Panama City	36,484	32,939	34,690
*32413	Panama City Beach	12,018	18,054	19,056
*33067	Parkland	23,962	34,670	36,895
35541	Pasadena Hills (c)	7,570	11,120	—
*33026	Pembroke Pines	154,750	171,178	169,876
*32502	Pensacola	51,923	54,312	53,876
*32809	Pine Castle (c)	10,805	11,122	—
*32808	Pine Hills (c)	60,076	66,111	—
34465	Pine Ridge (c) (Citrus Co.)	9,598	11,042	—
*33156	Pinecrest	18,223	18,388	17,973
*33781	Pinellas Park	49,079	53,093	53,653
*33147	Pinewood (c)	16,520	17,246	—
*33566	Plant City	34,721	39,764	40,367
*33311	Plantation	84,955	91,750	96,042
*34758	Poinciana (c)	53,193	69,309	—
*33060	Pompano Beach	99,845	112,046	112,302
*33952	Port Charlotte (c)	54,392	60,625	—
32129	Port Orange	56,048	62,596	64,870
32927	Port St. John (c)	12,267	23,474	—
*34953	Port St. Lucie	164,603	204,851	231,790
*34997	Port Salerno (c)	10,091	10,401	—
*33032	Princeton (c)	22,038	39,308	—
*33578	Progress Village (c)	5,392	11,188	—
*33950	Punta Gorda	16,641	19,471	20,608
*33177	Richmond West (c)	31,973	35,884	—
*33569	Riverview (c)	71,050	107,396	—
*33404	Riviera Beach	32,488	37,604	38,344
*32955	Rockledge	24,926	27,678	28,490
33947	Rotonda (c)	8,759	10,114	—
*33411	Royal Palm Beach	34,140	38,932	39,259
*33570	Ruskin (c)	17,208	28,620	—
34695	Safety Harbor	16,884	17,072	17,021
*32084	Saint Augustine	12,975	14,329	15,180
*34769	Saint Cloud	35,183	58,964	64,489
*33701	Saint Petersburg	244,769	258,308	261,256
*33912	San Carlos Park (c)	16,824	18,563	—
*32771	Sanford	53,570	61,051	63,154
*34231	Sarasota	51,917	54,842	57,376
*34232	Sarasota Springs (c)	14,395	12,521	—
32937	Satellite Beach	10,109	11,226	11,273
*32958	Sebastian	21,929	25,054	26,364
*33870	Sebring	10,491	10,729	11,379
*33772	Seminole	17,233	19,364	19,331
34610	Shady Hills (c)	11,523	11,690	—
34472	Silver Springs Shores (c)	6,539	24,846	—
*34207	South Bradenton (c)	22,178	26,858	—
*32119	South Daytona	12,252	12,865	13,654
*33143	South Miami	11,657	12,026	11,744
33157	South Miami Heights (c)	35,696	36,770	—
34293	South Venice (c)	13,949	15,619	—
32824	Southchase (c)	15,921	16,276	—
*34604	Spring Hill (c)	98,621	113,568	—
*34994	Stuart	15,593	17,425	18,253
34446	Sugarmill Woods (c)	8,287	11,204	—
*33573	Sun City Center (c)	19,258	30,952	—
33160	Sunny Isles Beach (c)	20,832	22,342	21,996
*33325	Sunrise	84,439	97,335	96,306
*33165	Sunset (c)	16,389	15,912	—
*33144	Sweetwater	13,499	19,363	19,588
*32301	Tallahassee	181,376	196,169	201,731
*33321	Tamarac	60,427	71,897	71,912
*33184	Tamiami (c)	55,271	54,212	—
*33602	Tampa	335,709	384,959	398,173
*34689	Tarpon Springs	23,484	25,117	25,890
32778	Tavares	13,951	19,003	20,372
*33617	Temple Terrace	24,541	26,690	27,207
*33412	The Acreage (c)	38,704	41,654	—
33186	The Crossings (c)	22,758	23,276	—
33196	The Hammocks (c)	51,003	59,480	—
*32162	The Villages (c)	51,442	79,077	—
33592	Thonotosassa (c)	13,014	15,238	—
33186	Three Lakes (c)	15,047	16,540	—
*32780	Titusville	43,761	48,789	49,319
33615	Town 'n' Country (c)	78,442	85,951	—
34655	Trinity (c)	10,907	11,924	—
32817	Union Park (c)	9,765	10,452	—
*33612	University (c) (Hillsborough Co.)	41,163	50,893	—
32826	University (c) (Orange Co.)	31,084	45,284	—
*32407	Upper Grand Lagoon (c)	13,963	15,778	—
*33594	Valrico (c)	35,545	37,895	—
*34285	Venice	20,748	25,463	27,272
*32960	Vero Beach	15,220	16,354	17,096
*32960	Vero Beach South (c)	23,092	28,020	—
32955	Viera East (c)	10,757	11,687	—
32940	Viera West (c)	6,641	16,688	—

ZIP	Place	2010 population	2020 population	2022 estimate
*33907	Villas (c)	11,569	12,687	—
32507	Warrington (c)	14,531	15,218	—
32779	Wekiwa Springs (c)	21,998	23,428	—
*33414	Wellington	56,508	61,637	61,438
*33544	Wesley Chapel (c)	44,092	64,866	—
*33709	West Lealman (c)	15,651	16,438	—
33147	West Little River (c)..	34,699	34,128	—
*32904	West Melbourne	18,355	25,924	28,837
*33401	West Palm Beach	99,919	117,415	120,932
33023	West Park	14,156	15,130	15,014
*32505	West Pensacola (c)	21,339	21,019	—
33157	West Perrine (c)	9,460	10,602	—
32966	West Vero Corridor (c)	7,138	10,039	—
33626	Westchase (c)	21,747	25,952	—
33165	Westchester (c)	29,862	56,384	—
*33326	Weston	65,333	68,107	67,677
33165	Westwood Lakes (c)..	11,838	11,373	—
34785	Wildwood	6,709	15,730	17,731
*33305	Wilton Manors	11,632	11,426	11,342
*34787	Winter Garden	34,568	46,964	47,049
*33880	Winter Haven	33,874	49,219	55,024
*32789	Winter Park	27,852	29,795	29,816
*32708	Winter Springs	33,282	38,342	38,705
32092	World Golf Village (c)	12,310	22,117	—
32547	Wright (c)	23,127	26,277	—
*32097	Yulee (c)	11,491	14,195	—
*33540	Zephyrhills	13,288	17,194	19,285

Georgia

Area codes: 229, 404/470/678/770/943, 478, 706/762, 912

ZIP	Place	2010 population	2020 population	2022 estimate
*30101	Acworth	20,425	22,440	22,276
*31701	Albany	77,434	69,647	67,192
*30004	Alpharetta	57,551	65,818	67,267
*31709	Americus	17,041	16,230	15,642
*30601	Athens-Clarke Co. (balance)	115,452	127,315	128,561
*30303	Atlanta	420,003	498,715	499,127
*30901	Augusta-Richmond Co. (balance)	195,844	202,081	202,096
*39817	Bainbridge	12,697	14,468	14,242
30032	Belvedere Park (c)	15,152	15,113	—
30517	Braselton	7,511	13,403	14,855
*30319	Brookhaven[1]	—	55,161	57,934
*31520	Brunswick	15,383	15,210	15,159
*30518	Buford	12,225	17,144	18,130
39827	Cairo	9,607	10,179	10,027
*30701	Calhoun	15,650	16,949	17,976
30032	Candler-McAfee (c)	23,025	22,468	—
*30114	Canton	22,958	32,973	35,809
*30116	Carrollton	24,388	26,738	27,262
*30120	Cartersville	19,731	23,187	23,904
30125	Cedartown	9,750	10,190	10,278
*30341	Chamblee	9,892	30,164	29,869
30021	Clarkston	7,554	14,756	14,537
*30337	College Park	13,942	13,930	13,914
*31901	Columbus	189,885	206,922	202,616
*30013	Conyers	15,195	17,305	17,926
*30014	Covington	13,118	14,192	14,381
*30132	Dallas	11,544	14,042	14,763
*30720	Dalton	33,128	34,417	34,366
*30030	Decatur	19,335	24,928	24,338
*30340	Doraville	8,330	10,623	10,888
*31533	Douglas	11,589	11,722	11,685
*30134	Douglasville	30,961	34,650	37,948
*31021	Dublin	16,201	16,074	15,946
*30096	Duluth	26,600	31,873	32,034
*30338	Dunwoody	46,267	51,683	52,201
*30344	East Point	33,712	38,358	38,380
30809	Evans (c)	29,011	34,536	—
30213	Fairburn	12,950	16,483	16,956
30214	Fayetteville	15,945	18,957	19,687
30542	Flowery Branch	5,679	9,391	10,938
*30297	Forest Park	18,468	19,932	19,400
30742	Fort Oglethorpe	9,263	10,423	10,537
*30501	Gainesville	33,804	42,296	45,282
*31405	Garden City	8,778	10,289	10,426
39854	Georgetown (c)	11,823	11,916	—
*30223	Griffin	23,643	23,478	23,693
30813	Grovetown	11,216	15,577	17,148
*31313	Hinesville	33,437	34,891	35,441
30549	Jefferson	9,432	13,233	15,286
*30097	Johns Creek	76,728	82,453	82,453
*30144	Kennesaw	29,783	33,036	33,552
31548	Kingsland	15,946	18,337	19,896
*30240	LaGrange	29,588	30,858	31,773
*30045	Lawrenceville	28,546	30,629	30,588
*30047	Lilburn	11,596	14,502	15,673
30122	Lithia Springs (c)	15,491	16,644	—
30248	Locust Grove	5,402	8,947	10,734
30052	Loganville	10,458	14,127	15,239

ZIP	Place	2010 population	2020 population	2022 estimate
30250	Lovejoy	6,422	10,122	11,638
30126	Mableton (c)	37,115	40,834	—
*31201	Macon-Bibb Co.	91,351	157,346	156,197
*30060	Marietta	56,579	60,972	62,602
30907	Martinez (c)	35,795	34,535	—
*30253	McDonough	22,084	29,051	30,340
*31061	Milledgeville	17,715	17,070	16,837
*30004	Milton	32,661	41,296	41,836
30655	Monroe	13,234	14,928	15,673
*31768	Moultrie	14,268	14,638	14,494
30075	Mountain Park (c)	11,554	13,089	—
*30263	Newnan	33,039	42,549	44,485
*30071	Norcross	9,116	17,209	17,706
30033	North Decatur (c)	16,698	18,511	—
*30329	North Druid Hills (c)..	18,947	20,385	—
30034	Panthersville (c)	9,749	11,237	—
*30269	Peachtree City	34,364	38,244	39,562
*30092	Peachtree Corners[1]..	—	42,243	42,133
31069	Perry	13,839	20,624	23,538
31322	Pooler	19,140	25,711	28,766
31407	Port Wentworth	5,359	10,878	12,347
30127	Powder Springs	13,940	16,887	17,337
30074	Redan (c)	33,015	31,749	—
31324	Richmond Hill	9,281	16,633	18,091
31326	Rincon	8,836	10,934	11,248
*30274	Riverdale	15,134	15,129	14,715
*30161	Rome	36,303	37,713	37,913
*30075	Roswell	88,346	92,833	92,950
31558	Saint Marys	17,121	18,256	18,980
31522	Saint Simons (c)	12,743	14,982	—
*30350	Sandy Springs	93,853	108,080	107,763
*31401	Savannah	136,286	147,780	148,004
30079	Scottdale (c)	10,631	10,698	—
*30080	Smyrna	51,271	55,663	56,160
*30078	Snellville	18,242	20,573	22,024
*30336	South Fulton[1]	—	107,436	111,158
*30458	Statesboro	28,422	33,438	34,353
30281	Stockbridge	25,636	28,973	29,064
*30038	Stonecrest[1]	—	59,194	61,087
30518	Sugar Hill	18,522	25,076	25,407
30024	Suwanee	15,355	20,786	22,477
*31792	Thomasville	18,413	18,881	18,460
*31794	Tifton	16,350	17,045	17,253
*30084	Tucker	27,581	37,005	36,969
30291	Union City	19,456	26,830	27,895
*31601	Valdosta	54,518	55,378	55,074
*30474	Vidalia	10,473	10,785	10,668
30180	Villa Rica	13,956	16,970	18,452
30339	Vinings (c)	9,734	12,581	—
*31088	Warner Robins	66,588	80,308	82,175
*31501	Waycross	14,649	13,942	13,741
31410	Wilmington Island (c)	15,138	15,129	—
30680	Winder	14,099	18,338	19,400
*30188	Woodstock	23,896	35,065	37,350

(1) Incorporated after 2010 Census.

Hawaii

Area code: 808 applies to the entire state

ZIP	Place	2010 population	2020 population	2022 estimate
96701	Aiea (c)	9,338	10,408	—
*96821	East Honolulu (c)	49,914	50,922	—
96706	Ewa Beach (c)	14,955	16,415	—
96706	Ewa Gentry (c)	22,690	25,707	—
96701	Halawa (c)	14,014	15,016	—
96749	Hawaiian Paradise Park (c)	11,404	14,957	—
*96720	Hilo (c)	43,263	44,186	—
*96813	Honolulu, urban (c)..	337,256	350,964	343,421
*96732	Kahului (c)	26,337	28,219	—
*96740	Kailua (c) (Hawaii Co.)	11,975	19,713	—
96734	Kailua (c) (Honolulu Co.)	38,635	40,514	—
*96725	Kaimini (c)	—	12,590	—
*96744	Kaneohe (c)	34,597	37,430	—
96746	Kapaa (c)	10,699	11,652	—
*96707	Kapolei (c)	15,186	21,411	—
96753	Kihei (c)	20,881	21,423	—
*96761	Lahaina (c)	11,704	12,702	—
96792	Maili (c)	9,488	11,535	—
96707	Makakilo (c)	18,248	19,877	—
96789	Mililani (c)	27,629	28,121	—
96789	Mililani Mauka (c)	21,039	21,075	—
96792	Nanakuli (c)	12,666	12,195	—
96706	Ocean Pointe (c)	8,361	14,965	—
96782	Pearl City (c)	47,698	45,295	—
96797	Royal Kunia (c)	14,525	14,896	—
96857	Schofield Barracks (c)	16,370	14,904	—
96786	Wahiawa (c)	17,821	18,658	—
96792	Waianae (c)	13,177	13,614	—
96793	Wailuku (c)	15,313	17,697	—
96701	Waimalu (c)	13,730	13,817	—
96797	Waipahu (c)	38,216	43,485	—
*96797	Waipio (c)	11,674	12,082	—

Idaho

Area codes: 208/986 apply to the entire state

ZIP	Place	2010 population	2020 population	2022 estimate
*83401	Ammon	13,816	17,694	19,000
83221	Blackfoot	11,899	12,346	12,702
*83702	Boise	205,671	235,684	236,634
83318	Burley	10,345	11,704	12,142
*83605	Caldwell	46,237	59,996	65,920
83202	Chubbuck	13,922	15,570	16,165
*83814	Coeur d'Alene	44,137	54,628	56,733
*83616	Eagle	19,908	30,346	32,399
*83714	Garden City	10,972	12,316	12,927
83835	Hayden	13,294	15,570	16,531
*83402	Idaho Falls	56,813	64,818	67,723
83338	Jerome	10,890	12,349	13,037
83634	Kuna	15,210	24,011	27,229
83501	Lewiston	31,894	34,203	34,896
*83642	Meridian	75,092	117,635	129,736
83644	Middleton	5,524	9,425	10,651
*83843	Moscow	23,800	25,435	26,249
83647	Mountain Home	14,206	15,979	16,469
*83651	Nampa	81,557	100,200	110,951
*83201	Pocatello	54,255	56,320	57,730
*83854	Post Falls	27,574	38,485	44,194
83858	Rathdrum	6,826	9,211	10,651
*83440	Rexburg	25,484	39,409	40,462
83669	Star	5,793	11,117	14,646
*83301	Twin Falls	44,125	51,807	54,300

Illinois

Area codes: 217/447, 224/847, 309/861, 312/773/872, 331/630, 464/708, 618/730, 779/815

ZIP	Place	2010 population	2020 population	2022 estimate
60101	Addison	36,942	35,702	35,127
*60102	Algonquin	30,046	29,700	29,951
60803	Alsip	19,277	19,063	18,357
62002	Alton	27,865	25,676	25,217
60002	Antioch	14,430	14,622	14,773
*60005	Arlington Heights	75,101	77,676	75,195
*60505	Aurora	197,899	180,542	177,866
*60010	Barrington	10,327	10,722	10,545
*60103	Bartlett	41,208	41,105	40,154
*60510	Batavia	26,045	26,098	26,122
*60099	Beach Park	13,638	14,249	14,092
*62220	Belleville	44,478	42,404	41,295
60104	Bellwood	19,071	18,789	18,081
61008	Belvidere	25,585	25,339	25,169
*60106	Bensenville	18,352	18,813	18,402
60402	Berwyn	56,657	57,250	55,021
*60108	Bloomingdale	22,018	22,382	22,324
*61701	Bloomington	76,610	78,680	78,864
60406	Blue Island	23,706	22,558	21,714
*60440	Bolingbrook	73,366	73,922	74,031
60914	Bourbonnais	18,631	18,164	18,008
60915	Bradley	15,895	15,419	15,232
60455	Bridgeview	16,446	17,027	16,467
60513	Brookfield	18,978	19,476	18,776
60089	Buffalo Grove	41,496	43,212	42,569
60459	Burbank	28,925	29,439	28,433
60527	Burr Ridge	10,559	11,192	11,037
*62203	Cahokia Heights[1]	—	—	17,366
60409	Calumet City	37,042	36,033	34,709
*60175	Campton Hills	11,131	10,885	10,779
61520	Canton	14,704	13,242	13,054
*62901	Carbondale	25,902	21,857	21,717
*60188	Carol Stream	39,711	39,854	39,044
60110	Carpentersville	37,691	37,983	37,288
60013	Cary	18,271	17,826	17,830
62801	Centralia	13,032	12,182	11,931
*61820	Champaign	81,055	88,302	89,241
60410	Channahon	12,560	13,383	13,926
61920	Charleston	21,838	17,286	17,119
62629	Chatham	11,500	14,377	14,466
*60602	Chicago	2,695,598	2,746,388	2,665,039
*60411	Chicago Heights	30,276	27,480	26,465
60415	Chicago Ridge	14,305	14,433	13,971
60804	Cicero	83,891	85,268	81,919
62234	Collinsville	25,579	24,366	23,972
62236	Columbia	9,707	10,999	10,970
60478	Country Club Hills	16,541	16,775	16,170
*60403	Crest Hill	20,837	20,459	20,158
*60418	Crestwood	10,950	10,826	10,483
*60014	Crystal Lake	40,743	40,269	40,661
*61832	Danville	33,027	29,204	28,472
60561	Darien	22,086	22,011	21,544
*62521	Decatur	76,122	70,522	69,097
60015	Deerfield	18,225	19,196	18,950
60115	DeKalb	43,862	40,290	40,220
*60018	Des Plaines	58,364	60,675	58,594

ZIP	Place	2010 population	2020 population	2022 estimate
61021	Dixon	15,733	15,274	15,177
60419	Dolton	23,153	21,426	20,621
*60515	Downers Grove	47,833	50,247	49,354
61244	East Moline	21,302	21,374	20,874
*61611	East Peoria	23,402	22,484	22,136
*62201	East St. Louis	27,006	18,469	17,919
*62025	Edwardsville	24,293	26,808	26,654
62401	Effingham	12,328	12,252	12,209
*60120	Elgin	108,188	114,797	113,177
*60007	Elk Grove Village	33,127	32,812	31,659
60126	Elmhurst	44,121	45,786	45,272
60707	Elmwood Park	24,883	24,521	23,604
*60201	Evanston	74,486	78,110	75,544
60805	Evergreen Park	19,852	19,943	19,211
62208	Fairview Heights	17,078	16,706	16,324
60130	Forest Park	14,167	14,339	13,802
60020	Fox Lake	10,579	10,978	10,849
60423	Frankfort	17,782	20,296	20,677
60131	Franklin Park	18,333	18,467	18,059
61032	Freeport	25,638	23,973	23,413
60030	Gages Lake (c)	10,198	10,637	—
*61401	Galesburg	32,195	30,052	29,255
60134	Geneva	21,495	21,393	21,228
62034	Glen Carbon	12,934	13,842	13,847
*60137	Glen Ellyn	27,450	28,846	28,364
*60139	Glendale Heights	34,208	33,176	32,484
*60025	Glenview	44,692	48,705	47,258
62035	Godfrey	17,982	17,825	17,688
62040	Granite City	29,849	27,549	27,121
60030	Grayslake	20,957	21,248	20,968
60031	Gurnee	31,295	30,706	30,303
60133	Hanover Park	37,973	37,470	36,376
*60426	Harvey	25,282	20,324	19,590
60429	Hazel Crest	14,100	13,382	12,897
62948	Herrin	12,501	12,352	12,202
60457	Hickory Hills	14,049	14,505	14,007
62249	Highland	9,919	9,991	10,009
*60035	Highland Park	29,763	30,176	30,163
*60521	Hinsdale	16,816	17,395	17,235
*60195	Hoffman Estates	51,895	52,530	50,682
*60491	Homer Glen	24,220	24,543	24,446
*60430	Homewood	19,323	19,463	18,735
60142	Huntley	24,291	27,740	28,138
*62650	Jacksonville	19,446	17,616	17,279
*60436	Joliet	147,433	150,362	150,033
60458	Justice	12,926	12,600	12,199
60901	Kankakee	27,537	24,052	23,602
61443	Kewanee	12,916	12,509	12,229
*60525	La Grange	15,550	16,321	15,821
60526	La Grange Park	13,579	13,475	13,009
60045	Lake Forest	19,375	19,367	19,252
*60102	Lake in the Hills	28,965	28,982	28,700
60047	Lake Zurich	19,631	19,759	19,624
60438	Lansing	28,331	29,076	28,000
60439	Lemont	16,000	17,629	17,531
60048	Libertyville	20,315	20,579	20,402
62656	Lincoln	14,504	13,288	13,084
*60712	Lincolnwood	12,590	13,463	12,989
60046	Lindenhurst	14,462	14,406	14,318
60532	Lisle	22,390	24,223	23,258
*60441	Lockport	24,839	26,094	26,105
60148	Lombard	43,165	44,476	43,856
*61111	Loves Park	23,996	23,397	23,365
60534	Lyons	10,729	10,817	10,411
*61115	Machesney Park	23,499	22,950	22,752
61455	Macomb	19,288	15,051	14,857
61853	Mahomet	7,258	9,434	10,070
60442	Manhattan	7,051	9,385	10,340
62959	Marion	17,193	16,855	16,729
*60428	Markham	12,508	11,661	11,241
60443	Matteson	19,009	19,073	18,439
61938	Mattoon	18,555	16,870	16,666
*60153	Maywood	24,090	23,512	22,932
*60050	McHenry	26,992	27,135	28,117
*60160	Melrose Park	25,411	24,796	23,897
60445	Midlothian	14,819	14,325	13,815
60447	Minooka	10,924	12,758	12,805
60448	Mokena	18,740	19,887	19,766
*61265	Moline	43,483	42,985	42,028
60538	Montgomery	18,438	20,262	21,799
60450	Morris	13,636	14,163	14,360
61550	Morton	16,267	17,117	17,334
60053	Morton Grove	23,270	25,297	24,371
60056	Mount Prospect	54,167	56,852	54,843
62864	Mount Vernon	15,277	14,600	14,284
60060	Mundelein	31,064	31,560	31,612
*60540	Naperville	141,853	149,540	149,936
60451	New Lenox	24,394	27,214	27,594
60714	Niles	29,803	30,912	29,805
*61761	Normal	52,497	52,736	52,838
60706	Norridge	14,572	15,251	14,769
60542	North Aurora	16,760	18,261	18,403
*60064	North Chicago	32,574	30,759	30,490

ZIP	Place	2010 population	2020 population	2022 estimate
*60062	Northbrook	33,170	35,222	34,182
60164	Northlake	12,323	12,840	12,401
60452	Oak Forest	27,962	27,478	26,460
*60453	Oak Lawn	56,690	58,362	56,286
*60301	Oak Park	51,878	54,583	52,553
62269	O'Fallon	28,281	32,289	32,140
*60462	Orland Park	56,767	58,703	57,511
60543	Oswego	30,355	34,585	35,850
61350	Ottawa	18,768	18,840	18,668
*60067	Palatine	68,557	67,908	65,485
60463	Palos Heights	12,515	12,068	11,632
60465	Palos Hills	17,484	18,530	17,883
*60466	Park Forest	21,975	21,687	20,954
60068	Park Ridge	37,480	39,656	38,278
*61554	Pekin	34,094	31,731	31,260
*61602	Peoria	115,007	113,150	111,021
60140	Pingree Grove	4,532	10,365	11,034
*60544	Plainfield	39,581	44,762	46,243
60545	Plano	10,856	11,847	12,472
61764	Pontiac	11,931	11,150	11,085
60070	Prospect Heights	16,256	16,058	15,486
*62301	Quincy	40,633	39,463	38,942
61866	Rantoul	12,941	12,371	12,122
60471	Richton Park	13,646	12,775	12,441
60305	River Forest	11,172	11,717	11,327
60171	River Grove	10,227	10,612	10,391
60827	Riverdale	13,549	10,663	10,266
*61201	Rock Island	39,018	37,108	36,256
*61101	Rockford	152,871	148,655	146,713
60008	Rolling Meadows	24,099	24,200	23,564
60446	Romeoville	39,680	39,863	40,117
61073	Roscoe	10,785	10,983	10,874
60172	Roselle	22,763	22,897	22,505
60073	Round Lake	18,289	18,721	18,491
60073	Round Lake Beach	28,175	27,252	26,879
*60174	Saint Charles	32,974	33,081	32,750
60193	Schaumburg	74,227	78,723	76,225
*60176	Schiller Park	11,793	11,709	11,283
*62269	Shiloh	12,651	14,098	14,496
*60404	Shorewood	15,615	18,186	18,271
60077	Skokie	64,784	67,824	65,497
60177	South Elgin	21,985	23,865	24,007
60473	South Holland	22,030	21,465	20,685
*62701	Springfield	116,250	114,394	113,273
61081	Sterling	15,370	14,764	14,566
60107	Streamwood	39,858	39,577	38,151
*61364	Streator	13,710	12,500	12,263
60501	Summit	11,054	11,161	10,732
*62226	Swansea	13,430	14,386	14,112
60178	Sycamore	17,519	18,577	18,652
62568	Taylorville	11,246	10,506	10,312
*60477	Tinley Park	56,703	55,971	54,287
62294	Troy	9,888	10,960	11,131
*61801	Urbana	41,250	38,336	38,468
60061	Vernon Hills	25,113	26,850	26,759
60181	Villa Park	21,904	22,263	21,791
60555	Warrenville	13,140	13,553	14,841
61571	Washington	15,134	16,071	15,890
62298	Waterloo	9,811	11,013	11,130
60084	Wauconda	13,603	14,084	13,932
*60085	Waukegan	89,078	89,321	87,976
*60185	West Chicago	27,086	25,614	25,166
60154	Westchester	16,718	16,892	16,262
60558	Western Springs	12,975	13,629	13,313
60559	Westmont	24,685	24,429	23,976
*60187	Wheaton	52,894	53,970	52,984
60090	Wheeling	37,648	39,137	37,936
60091	Wilmette	27,087	28,170	27,264
60190	Winfield	9,080	9,835	10,046
60093	Winnetka	12,187	12,744	12,370
*60191	Wood Dale	13,770	14,012	13,714
62095	Wood River	10,657	10,464	10,351
60517	Woodridge	32,971	34,158	33,587
60098	Woodstock	24,770	25,630	25,665
60842	Worth	10,789	10,970	10,590
60560	Yorkville	16,921	21,533	23,835
60099	Zion	24,413	24,655	24,315

(1) Incorporated after 2020 Census.

Indiana
Area codes: 219, 260, 317/463, 574, 765, 812/930

ZIP	Place	2010 population	2020 population	2022 estimate
*46011	Anderson	56,129	54,788	55,099
46706	Auburn	12,731	13,412	13,724
46123	Avon	12,446	21,474	23,611
46106	Bargersville	4,013	9,560	10,717
47421	Bedford	13,413	13,792	13,897
46107	Beech Grove	14,192	14,717	14,492
*47408	Bloomington	80,405	79,168	79,107
46714	Bluffton	9,897	10,308	10,379
46112	Brownsburg	21,285	28,973	31,193
*46032	Carmel	79,191	99,757	101,964
46303	Cedar Lake	11,560	14,106	15,592

ZIP	Place	2010 population	2020 population	2022 estimate
46304	Chesterton	13,068	14,241	14,554
*47129	Clarksville	21,724	22,333	21,782
46725	Columbia City	8,750	9,892	10,086
*47201	Columbus	44,061	50,474	51,268
47331	Connersville	13,481	13,324	13,292
47933	Crawfordsville	15,915	16,306	16,479
*46307	Crown Point	27,317	33,899	34,526
46122	Danville	9,001	10,559	10,927
*46311	Dyer	16,390	16,517	16,361
46312	East Chicago	29,698	26,370	25,968
46514	Elkhart	50,949	53,923	53,801
*47708	Evansville	117,429	117,298	115,749
*46038	Fishers	76,794	98,977	101,966
*46802	Fort Wayne	253,691	263,886	267,927
*46041	Frankfort	16,422	16,715	16,474
46131	Franklin	23,712	25,313	25,728
*46402	Gary	80,294	69,093	67,972
46526	Goshen	31,719	34,517	34,375
46530	Granger (c)	30,465	30,337	
46140	Greenfield	20,602	23,488	24,785
47240	Greensburg	11,492	12,312	12,377
*46142	Greenwood	49,791	63,830	65,406
46319	Griffith	16,893	16,528	16,287
*46320	Hammond	80,830	77,879	76,575
46322	Highland	23,727	23,984	23,622
46342	Hobart	29,059	29,752	29,458
46750	Huntington	17,391	17,022	17,023
*46201	Indianapolis (balance)	820,445	887,642	880,621
*47546	Jasper	15,038	16,703	16,757
*47130	Jeffersonville	44,953	49,447	51,030
46755	Kendallville	9,862	10,271	10,222
*46902	Kokomo	45,468	59,604	59,671
46350	La Porte	22,053	22,471	22,198
*47901	Lafayette	67,140	70,783	71,402
46405	Lake Station	12,572	13,235	13,096
46226	Lawrence	46,001	49,370	49,276
46052	Lebanon	15,792	16,662	16,982
46947	Logansport	18,396	18,366	18,194
46356	Lowell	9,276	10,680	11,128
47250	Madison	11,967	12,357	12,211
*46952	Marion	29,948	28,310	28,030
46151	Martinsville	11,828	11,932	11,858
46055	McCordsville	4,797	8,503	10,369
*46410	Merrillville	35,246	36,444	36,233
*46360	Michigan City	31,479	32,075	31,792
*46544	Mishawaka	48,252	51,063	50,913
*47302	Muncie	70,085	65,194	65,076
46321	Munster	23,603	23,894	23,664
*47150	New Albany	36,372	37,841	37,506
47362	New Castle	18,114	17,396	17,345
46774	New Haven	14,794	15,583	15,843
*46060	Noblesville	51,969	69,604	72,748
46970	Peru	11,417	11,073	10,828
*46168	Plainfield	27,631	34,625	36,074
46563	Plymouth	10,033	10,214	10,705
46368	Portage	36,828	37,926	38,327
*47374	Richmond	36,812	35,720	35,513
46373	Saint John	14,850	20,303	22,847
46375	Schererville	29,243	29,646	29,668
47172	Sellersburg	6,128	9,310	10,057
47274	Seymour	17,503	21,569	21,618
46176	Shelbyville	19,191	20,067	20,159
*46601	South Bend	101,168	103,453	103,110
46224	Speedway	11,812	13,952	13,695
*47802	Terre Haute	60,785	58,389	58,335
*46383	Valparaiso	31,730	34,151	34,565
47591	Vincennes	18,423	16,759	16,484
46992	Wabash	10,666	10,440	10,347
*46580	Warsaw	13,559	15,804	16,111
47501	Washington	11,509	12,017	12,171
*47906	West Lafayette	29,596	44,595	45,060
46074	Westfield	30,068	46,410	54,605
46075	Whitestown	2,867	10,178	11,958
47396	Yorktown	9,405	11,548	11,689
46077	Zionsville	14,160	30,603	31,982

Iowa
Area codes: 319, 515, 563, 641, 712

ZIP	Place	2010 population	2020 population	2022 estimate
50009	Altoona	14,541	19,565	21,503
*50010	Ames	58,965	66,427	66,950
50021	Ankeny	45,582	67,887	72,222
52722	Bettendorf	33,217	39,102	39,548
*50036	Boone	12,661	12,460	12,406
52601	Burlington	25,663	23,982	23,611
51401	Carroll	10,103	10,321	10,184
50613	Cedar Falls	39,260	40,713	40,746
*52401	Cedar Rapids	126,326	137,710	136,429
52732	Clinton	26,885	24,469	24,391
50325	Clive	15,447	18,601	18,908
52241	Coralville	18,907	22,318	23,125
*51501	Council Bluffs	62,230	62,799	62,405

ZIP	Place	2010 population	2020 population	2022 estimate
*52801	Davenport	99,685	101,724	100,486
*50309	Des Moines	203,433	214,133	211,034
*52001	Dubuque	57,637	59,667	58,873
50501	Fort Dodge	25,206	24,871	24,657
52627	Fort Madison	11,051	10,270	10,134
50111	Grimes	8,246	15,392	16,295
50125	Indianola	14,782	15,833	16,069
*52240	Iowa City	67,862	74,828	75,233
50131	Johnston	17,278	24,064	24,390
51031	Le Mars	9,826	10,571	10,605
52302	Marion	34,768	41,535	41,864
50158	Marshalltown	27,552	27,591	27,433
*50401	Mason City	28,079	27,338	26,924
52761	Muscatine	22,886	23,797	23,413
50208	Newton	15,254	15,760	15,688
52317	North Liberty	13,374	20,479	21,399
50211	Norwalk	8,945	12,799	14,177
52577	Oskaloosa	11,463	11,558	11,482
52501	Ottumwa	25,023	25,529	25,175
50219	Pella	10,352	10,464	10,744
*50327	Pleasant Hill	8,785	10,147	11,186
*51101	Sioux City	82,684	85,797	85,497
51301	Spencer	11,233	11,325	11,413
50588	Storm Lake	10,600	11,269	11,307
*50322	Urbandale	39,463	45,580	46,648
*50701	Waterloo	68,406	67,314	66,562
50263	Waukee	13,790	23,940	29,167
50677	Waverly	9,874	10,394	10,522
*50265	West Des Moines	56,609	68,723	70,741

Kansas
Area codes: 316, 620, 785, 913

ZIP	Place	2010 population	2020 population	2022 estimate
67002	Andover	11,791	14,892	15,628
67005	Arkansas City	12,415	11,974	11,923
66002	Atchison	11,021	10,885	10,730
67037	Derby	22,158	25,625	25,939
*67801	Dodge City	27,340	27,788	27,422
67042	El Dorado	13,021	12,870	12,865
66801	Emporia	24,916	24,139	23,941
*67846	Garden City	26,658	28,151	27,519
66030	Gardner	19,123	23,287	24,206
67530	Great Bend	15,995	14,733	14,489
*67601	Hays	20,510	21,116	21,136
67060	Haysville	10,826	11,262	11,287
*67501	Hutchinson	42,080	40,006	39,699
*66441	Junction City	23,353	22,932	22,264
*66101	Kansas City	145,786	156,607	153,345
66043	Lansing	11,265	11,239	11,187
*66044	Lawrence	87,643	94,934	95,794
*66048	Leavenworth	35,251	37,351	37,081
*66211	Leawood	31,867	33,902	33,713
*66215	Lenexa	48,190	57,434	58,617
*67901	Liberal	20,525	19,825	19,274
*66502	Manhattan	52,281	54,100	53,829
67460	McPherson	13,155	14,082	13,865
*66202	Merriam	11,003	11,098	10,966
*67114	Newton	19,132	18,602	18,392
*66061	Olathe	125,872	141,290	145,616
66067	Ottawa	12,649	12,625	12,613
*66212	Overland Park	173,372	197,238	197,726
*66762	Pittsburg	20,233	20,646	20,658
*66208	Prairie Village	21,447	22,957	22,947
*67401	Salina	47,707	46,889	46,231
*66203	Shawnee	62,209	67,311	69,198
*66603	Topeka	127,473	126,587	125,449
*67202	Wichita	382,368	397,532	396,192
67156	Winfield	12,301	11,777	11,701

Kentucky
Area codes: 270/364, 502, 606, 859

ZIP	Place	2010 population	2020 population	2022 estimate
41001	Alexandria	8,477	10,341	10,570
*41101	Ashland	21,684	21,625	21,342
40004	Bardstown	11,700	13,567	13,739
*40403	Berea	13,561	15,539	15,494
*42101	Bowling Green	58,067	72,294	74,926
41005	Burlington (c)	15,926	17,318	—
*42718	Campbellsville	9,108	11,426	11,599
*41011	Covington	40,640	40,961	40,956
*40422	Danville	16,218	17,234	17,303
*42701	Elizabethtown	28,531	31,394	31,892
*41018	Erlanger	18,082	19,611	19,756
*41042	Florence	29,951	31,946	32,618
42223	Fort Campbell North (c)	13,685	12,825	—
41075	Fort Thomas	16,325	17,438	17,133
*40601	Frankfort	25,527	28,602	28,391
*42134	Franklin	8,408	10,176	10,344
40324	Georgetown	29,098	37,086	38,780

ZIP	Place	2010 population	2020 population	2022 estimate
*42141	Glasgow	14,028	15,014	15,282
*42420	Henderson	28,757	27,981	27,697
*42240	Hopkinsville	31,577	31,180	30,927
41051	Independence	24,757	28,676	29,326
*40299	Jeffersontown	26,595	28,474	28,621
*40031	La Grange	8,082	10,067	10,295
40342	Lawrenceburg	10,505	11,728	11,919
*40507	Lexington-Fayette	295,803	322,570	320,347
*40202	Louisville-Jefferson Co. (balance)	597,337	386,884	624,444
*40222	Lyndon	11,002	11,008	10,917
42431	Madisonville	19,591	19,542	19,214
40047	Mount Washington	9,117	18,090	18,424
42071	Murray	17,741	17,307	17,522
*41071	Newport	15,273	14,150	13,901
*40356	Nicholasville	28,015	31,093	31,955
*42301	Owensboro	57,265	60,183	60,037
*42003	Paducah	25,024	27,137	26,834
*40361	Paris	8,553	10,171	10,075
*40160	Radcliff	21,688	23,042	22,953
*40475	Richmond	31,364	34,585	36,129
*40207	Saint Matthews	17,472	17,534	17,362
*40066	Shelbyville	14,045	17,282	17,565
40165	Shepherdsville	11,222	14,201	14,486
*40216	Shively	15,264	15,636	15,482
*42501	Somerset	11,196	11,924	12,218
*40383	Versailles	8,568	10,347	10,416
*40391	Winchester	18,368	19,134	19,142

Louisiana
Area codes: 225, 318, 337, 504, 985

ZIP	Place	2010 population	2020 population	2022 estimate
*70510	Abbeville	12,257	11,186	10,962
*71301	Alexandria	47,723	45,275	44,004
70714	Baker	13,895	12,455	12,172
*70801	Baton Rouge	229,493	227,470	221,453
*70360	Bayou Blue (c)	12,352	13,352	—
*70360	Bayou Cane (c)	19,355	19,770	—
*70037	Belle Chasse (c)	12,679	10,579	—
*70427	Bogalusa	12,232	10,659	10,419
*71111	Bossier City	61,315	62,701	62,635
70518	Broussard	8,197	13,417	14,186
70520	Carencro	7,526	9,272	12,365
70837	Central	26,864	29,565	29,735
*70043	Chalmette (c)	16,751	21,562	—
70433	Claiborne (c)	11,507	12,631	—
70433	Covington	8,765	11,564	11,636
*70526	Crowley	13,265	11,710	11,373
70047	Destrehan (c)	11,535	11,340	—
*70810	Gardere (c)	10,580	13,203	—
70072	Estelle (c)	16,377	17,952	—
70737	Gonzales	9,781	12,231	13,059
*70053	Gretna	17,736	17,814	17,195
*70401	Hammond	20,019	19,584	21,588
*70058	Harvey (c)	20,348	22,236	—
*70360	Houma	33,727	33,406	31,775
70121	Jefferson (c)	11,193	10,633	—
*70062	Kenner	66,702	66,448	64,007
*70501	Lafayette	120,623	121,374	121,389
*70601	Lake Charles	71,993	84,872	79,113
*70068	LaPlace (c)	29,872	28,841	—
70070	Luling (c)	12,119	13,716	—
*70448	Mandeville	11,560	13,192	13,343
*70072	Marrero (c)	33,141	32,382	—
*70001	Metairie (c)	138,481	143,507	—
*71055	Minden	13,082	11,928	11,397
*71201	Monroe	48,815	47,702	46,820
*70380	Morgan City	12,404	11,472	11,078
*71457	Natchitoches	18,323	18,039	17,440
*70560	New Iberia	30,617	28,555	27,473
*70112	New Orleans	343,829	383,997	369,749
*70570	Opelousas	16,634	15,786	15,494
*71360	Pineville	14,555	14,384	14,109
70769	Prairieville (c)	26,895	33,197	—
70123	River Ridge (c)	13,494	13,591	—
*71270	Ruston	21,859	22,166	22,295
70817	Shenandoah (c)	18,399	19,292	—
*71101	Shreveport	199,311	187,593	180,153
*70458	Slidell	27,068	28,781	28,649
*70663	Sulphur	20,410	21,809	20,342
70056	Terrytown (c)	23,319	25,278	—
*70301	Thibodaux	14,566	15,948	15,543
70056	Timberlane (c)	10,243	10,364	—
*71291	West Monroe	13,065	13,103	12,635
70058	Woodmere (c)	12,080	11,238	—
70592	Youngsville	8,105	15,929	17,361
70791	Zachary	14,960	19,316	19,916

Maine

Area code: 207 applies to the entire state. See introductory note.

ZIP	Place	2010 population	2020 population	2022 estimate
*04210	Auburn	23,055	24,061	24,193
*04330	Augusta	19,136	18,899	19,066
*04401	Bangor	33,039	31,753	31,588
*04005	Biddeford	21,277	22,552	22,450
04011	Brunswick	20,278	21,756	21,831
04011	Brunswick (c)	15,175	17,033	—
04105	Falmouth	11,185	12,444	12,857
04038	Gorham	16,381	18,336	17,785
04043	Kennebunk	10,798	11,536	11,757
03904	Kittery	9,490	10,070	10,235
*04240	Lewiston	36,592	37,121	38,493
04473	Orono	10,362	11,183	11,251
04473	Orono (c)	9,474	10,185	—
*04101	Portland	66,194	68,408	68,424
04072	Saco	18,482	20,381	20,872
04073	Sanford	9,761	21,982	22,266
*04074	Scarborough	18,919	22,135	23,218
*04106	South Portland	25,002	26,498	27,026
04084	Standish	9,874	10,244	10,836
*04901	Waterville	15,722	15,828	15,828
04090	Wells	9,589	11,314	11,731
*04092	Westbrook	17,494	20,400	20,645
*04062	Windham	17,001	18,434	19,128
03909	York	12,529	13,723	13,998

Maryland

Area codes: 227/240/301, 410/443/667

ZIP	Place	2010 population	2020 population	2022 estimate
21001	Aberdeen	14,959	16,254	16,859
20607	Accokeek (c)	10,573	13,927	—
20783	Adelphi (c)	15,086	16,823	—
*21401	Annapolis	38,394	40,812	40,648
21403	Annapolis Neck (c)	10,950	10,973	—
21227	Arbutus (c)	20,483	21,655	—
21012	Arnold (c)	23,106	24,064	—
*20906	Aspen Hill (c)	48,759	51,063	—
21220	Ballenger Creek (c)	18,274	24,999	—
*21202	Baltimore	620,961	585,708	569,931
*21014	Bel Air	10,120	10,661	10,596
21050	Bel Air North (c)	30,568	31,841	—
*21015	Bel Air South (c)	47,709	57,648	—
*20705	Beltsville (c)	16,772	20,133	—
20603	Bensville (c)	11,923	15,288	—
20814	Bethesda (c)	60,858	68,056	—
*20715	Bowie	54,727	58,329	57,192
20613	Brandywine (c)	6,719	10,550	—
20772	Brock Hall (c)	9,552	13,181	—
21225	Brooklyn Park (c)	14,373	16,112	—
20619	California (c)	11,857	12,947	—
20705	Calverton (c)	17,724	17,316	—
21613	Cambridge	12,326	13,096	13,129
*20748	Camp Springs (c)	19,096	22,734	—
21234	Carney (c)	29,941	29,363	—
21228	Catonsville (c)	41,567	44,701	—
20657	Chesapeake Ranch Estates (c)	10,519	10,308	—
*20815	Chevy Chase (c)	9,545	10,176	—
20782	Chillum (c)	33,513	36,039	—
20871	Clarksburg (c)	13,766	29,051	—
20735	Clinton (c)	35,970	38,760	—
20904	Cloverly (c)	15,126	15,285	—
21030	Cockeysville (c)	20,776	24,184	—
*20904	Colesville (c)	14,647	15,421	—
*20740	College Park	30,413	34,740	34,190
*21044	Columbia (c)	99,615	104,681	—
21114	Crofton (c)	27,348	29,641	—
*21502	Cumberland	20,859	19,076	18,769
20872	Damascus (c)	15,257	17,224	—
21222	Dundalk (c)	63,597	67,796	—
20737	East Riverdale (c)	15,509	18,459	—
21601	Easton	15,945	17,101	17,342
21040	Edgewood (c)	25,562	25,713	—
21784	Eldersburg (c)	30,531	32,582	—
21075	Elkridge (c)	15,593	25,171	—
*21921	Elkton	15,443	15,807	15,913
*21042	Ellicott City (c)	65,834	75,947	—
21221	Essex (c)	39,262	40,505	—
20904	Fairland (c)	23,681	25,396	—
21061	Ferndale (c)	16,746	17,091	—
20879	Flower Hill (c)	—	14,108	—
20747	Forestville (c)	12,353	12,831	—
*20744	Fort Washington (c)	23,717	24,261	—
*21701	Frederick	65,239	78,171	82,175
*20877	Gaithersburg	59,933	69,657	68,952
*20874	Germantown (c)	86,395	91,249	—
20745	Glassmanor (c)	17,295	18,430	—
*21061	Glen Burnie (c)	67,639	72,891	—

ZIP	Place	2010 population	2020 population	2022 estimate
20906	Glenmont (c)	13,529	16,710	—
20769	Glenn Dale (c)	13,466	14,698	—
21770	Green Valley (c)	—	12,643	—
*20770	Greenbelt	23,068	24,921	24,360
*21740	Hagerstown	39,662	43,527	43,701
21740	Halfway (c)	10,701	11,896	—
21078	Havre de Grace	12,952	14,807	14,996
20748	Hillcrest Heights (c)	16,469	15,793	—
21128	Honeygo (c)	—	12,927	—
*20781	Hyattsville	17,557	21,187	20,675
21043	Ilchester (c)	23,476	26,824	—
20794	Jessup (c)	7,137	10,535	—
21085	Joppatowne (c)	12,616	13,425	—
20902	Kemp Mill (c)	12,564	13,378	—
*20774	Kettering (c)	12,790	14,424	—
20646	La Plata	8,753	10,159	10,676
*20774	Lake Arbor (c)	9,776	14,541	—
*21122	Lake Shore (c)	19,477	19,551	—
20785	Landover (c)	23,078	25,998	—
20787	Langley Park (c)	18,755	20,126	—
*20706	Lanham (c)	10,157	11,282	—
*20774	Largo (c)	10,709	11,605	—
20707	Laurel	25,115	30,060	29,352
20653	Lexington Park (c)	11,626	13,317	—
21771	Linganore (c)	8,543	12,351	—
21090	Linthicum (c)	10,324	11,190	—
21207	Lochearn (c)	25,333	25,511	—
20724	Maryland City (c)	16,093	19,153	—
21093	Mays Chapel (c)	11,420	12,224	—
21220	Middle River (c)	25,191	33,203	—
*21244	Milford Mill (c)	29,042	30,622	—
20716	Mitchellville (c)	10,967	11,136	—
*20886	Montgomery Village (c)	32,032	34,893	—
20784	New Carrollton	12,135	13,715	13,403
*20852	North Bethesda (c)	43,828	50,094	—
20723	North Laurel (c)	4,474	25,379	—
20878	North Potomac (c)	24,410	23,790	—
21811	Ocean Pines (c)	11,710	12,145	—
21113	Odenton (c)	37,132	42,947	—
20832	Olney (c)	33,844	35,820	—
21236	Overlea (c)	12,275	12,832	—
21117	Owings Mills (c)	30,622	35,674	—
*20745	Oxon Hill (c)	17,722	18,791	—
21234	Parkville (c)	30,734	31,812	—
21401	Parole (c)	15,922	17,877	—
*21122	Pasadena (c)	24,287	32,979	—
21128	Perry Hall (c)	28,474	29,409	—
21207	Pikesville (c)	30,764	34,168	—
*20850	Potomac (c)	44,965	47,018	—
21133	Randallstown (c)	32,430	33,655	—
20855	Redland (c)	17,242	18,592	—
*21136	Reisterstown (c)	25,968	26,822	—
*21122	Riviera Beach (c)	12,677	12,384	—
*20850	Rockville	61,209	67,117	66,924
20772	Rosaryville (c)	10,697	11,548	—
21237	Rosedale (c)	19,257	19,961	—
21221	Rossville (c)	15,147	16,029	—
*21801	Salisbury	30,343	33,050	33,209
21146	Severna Park (c)	37,634	39,933	—
*20901	Silver Spring (c)	71,452	81,015	—
20707	South Laurel (c)	26,112	29,602	—
20746	Suitland (c)	25,825	25,839	—
21842	Summerfield (c)	10,898	14,758	—
*20912	Takoma Park	16,715	17,629	17,390
21093	Timonium (c)	9,925	10,458	—
*21204	Towson (c)	55,197	59,553	—
20854	Travilah (c)	12,159	11,985	—
21704	Urbana (c)	9,175	13,304	—
*20602	Waldorf (c)	67,752	81,410	—
20743	Walker Mill (c)	11,302	12,187	—
*21157	Westminster	18,590	20,126	20,393
20774	Westphalia (c)	7,266	11,770	—
*20902	Wheaton (c)	48,284	52,150	—
21162	White Marsh (c)	9,513	10,287	—
20904	White Oak (c)	17,403	16,347	—
21207	Woodlawn (c) (Balt. Co.)	37,879	39,986	—

Massachusetts

Area codes: 339/781, 351/978, 413, 508/774, 617/857. See introductory note.

ZIP	Place	2010 population	2020 population	2022 estimate
02351	Abington	15,985	17,062	16,965
*01720	Acton	21,924	24,021	23,829
*02743	Acushnet	10,303	10,559	10,585
01001	Agawam	28,438	28,692	28,393
01913	Amesbury	16,283	17,366	17,179
*01002	Amherst	37,819	39,263	40,059
*01810	Andover	33,201	36,569	36,363

ZIP	Place	2010 population	2020 population	2022 estimate
*02476	Arlington	42,844	46,308	45,522
01721	Ashland	16,593	18,832	18,466
01331	Athol	11,584	11,945	11,897
02703	Attleboro	43,593	46,461	46,601
01501	Auburn	16,188	16,889	16,762
02630	Barnstable	45,193	48,916	49,532
*01730	Bedford	13,320	14,383	14,161
01007	Belchertown	14,649	15,350	15,316
02019	Bellingham	16,332	16,945	17,407
02478	Belmont	24,729	27,295	26,710
01915	Beverly	39,502	42,670	42,235
*01821	Billerica	40,243	42,119	41,319
02108	Boston	617,594	675,647	650,706
02532	Bourne	19,754	20,452	20,667
*02184	Braintree	35,744	39,143	38,567
02631	Brewster	9,820	10,318	10,444
*02324	Bridgewater	26,563	28,633	28,780
02301	Brockton	93,810	105,643	104,826
02446	Brookline	58,732	63,191	62,535
*01803	Burlington	24,498	26,377	25,966
*02139	Cambridge	105,162	118,403	118,488
02021	Canton	21,561	24,370	24,609
02330	Carver	11,509	11,645	11,626
01507	Charlton	12,981	13,315	13,360
01824	Chelmsford	33,802	36,392	35,906
02150	Chelsea	35,177	40,787	38,637
*01020	Chicopee	55,298	55,560	54,980
01510	Clinton	13,606	15,428	15,484
01742	Concord	17,668	18,491	17,954
01923	Danvers	26,493	28,087	27,781
*02747	Dartmouth	34,032	33,783	33,406
*02026	Dedham	24,729	25,364	24,997
02638	Dennis	14,207	14,674	14,432
01826	Dracut	29,457	32,617	32,060
01571	Dudley	11,390	11,921	11,850
*02332	Duxbury	15,059	16,090	16,107
02333	East Bridgewater	13,794	14,440	14,338
*01028	East Longmeadow	15,720	16,430	16,343
01027	Easthampton	16,053	16,211	16,045
*02356	Easton	23,112	25,058	25,240
02149	Everett	41,667	49,075	49,350
02719	Fairhaven	15,873	15,924	15,837
*02720	Fall River	88,857	94,000	93,682
*02540	Falmouth	31,531	32,517	33,104
01420	Fitchburg	40,318	41,946	41,502
02035	Foxborough	16,865	18,618	18,488
*01701	Framingham	68,318	72,362	70,963
02038	Franklin	31,635	33,261	33,656
01440	Gardner	20,228	21,287	20,902
*01930	Gloucester	28,789	29,729	29,836
01519	Grafton	17,765	19,664	19,815
*01301	Greenfield	17,456	17,768	17,656
01450	Groton	10,646	11,315	11,162
02339	Hanover	13,879	14,833	14,758
02341	Hanson	10,209	10,639	10,587
02645	Harwich	12,243	13,440	13,647
*01830	Haverhill	60,879	67,787	67,153
*02043	Hingham	22,157	24,284	24,130
02343	Holbrook	10,791	11,405	11,285
01520	Holden	17,346	19,905	19,880
01746	Holliston	13,547	14,996	14,856
*01040	Holyoke	39,880	38,238	37,720
01748	Hopkinton	14,925	18,758	19,249
01749	Hudson	19,063	20,092	19,744
01749	Hudson (c)	14,907	15,749	—
02045	Hull	10,293	10,072	10,142
01938	Ipswich	13,175	13,785	13,848
02364	Kingston	12,629	13,708	13,829
*02347	Lakeville	10,602	11,523	11,895
*01840	Lawrence	76,377	89,143	87,954
01524	Leicester	10,970	11,087	11,033
01453	Leominster	40,759	43,782	43,646
*02420	Lexington	31,394	34,454	34,074
01460	Littleton	8,924	10,141	10,139
*01106	Longmeadow	15,784	15,853	15,632
01850	Lowell	106,519	115,554	113,608
01056	Ludlow	21,103	21,002	20,871
01462	Lunenburg	10,086	11,782	11,835
*01901	Lynn	90,329	101,253	100,891
01940	Lynnfield	11,596	13,000	12,951
02148	Malden	59,450	66,263	64,712
02048	Mansfield	23,184	23,860	23,816
01945	Marblehead	19,808	20,441	20,233
01752	Marlborough	38,499	41,793	40,971
*02050	Marshfield	25,132	25,825	25,713
02649	Mashpee	14,006	15,060	15,468
01754	Maynard	10,106	10,746	10,546
02052	Medfield	12,024	12,799	13,072
*02155	Medford	56,173	59,659	65,399
02053	Medway	12,752	13,115	13,393
02176	Melrose	26,983	29,817	29,155
01844	Methuen	47,255	53,059	53,241
*02346	Middleborough	23,116	24,245	24,376
01757	Milford	27,999	30,379	30,196
01757	Milford (c)	25,055	26,971	—
*01527	Millbury	13,261	13,831	13,936
02186	Milton	27,003	28,630	28,364
*02554	Nantucket	10,172	14,255	14,421
*02554	Nantucket (c)	7,446	10,166	—
01760	Natick	33,006	37,006	36,272
02494	Needham	28,886	32,091	32,114
02740	New Bedford	95,072	101,079	100,682
01950	Newburyport	17,416	18,289	18,662
02456	Newton	85,146	88,923	87,381
02056	Norfolk	11,227	11,662	11,552
01247	North Adams	13,708	12,961	12,777
01845	North Andover	28,352	30,915	31,295
*02760	North Attleborough	28,712	30,834	30,930
*01864	North Reading	14,892	15,554	15,549
*01060	Northampton	28,549	29,571	29,327
01532	Northborough	14,155	15,741	15,663
01534	Northbridge	15,707	16,335	16,337
02766	Norton	19,031	19,202	19,108
02061	Norwell	10,506	11,351	11,280
02062	Norwood	28,602	31,599	31,317
01540	Oxford	13,709	13,347	13,287
01069	Palmer	12,140	12,448	12,337
*01960	Peabody	51,251	54,481	53,896
02359	Pembroke	17,837	18,361	18,297
01463	Pepperell	11,497	11,604	11,620
*01201	Pittsfield	44,737	43,927	43,310
*02360	Plymouth	56,468	61,217	64,269
*02169	Quincy	92,271	101,636	101,727
02368	Randolph	32,112	34,984	34,530
02767	Raynham	13,383	15,142	15,474
01867	Reading	24,747	25,518	25,205
02769	Rehoboth	11,608	12,502	13,023
02151	Revere	51,755	62,186	58,528
02370	Rockland	17,489	17,803	17,609
*01970	Salem	41,340	44,480	44,722
02563	Sandwich	20,675	20,259	20,611
01906	Saugus	26,628	28,619	28,547
02066	Scituate	18,133	19,063	19,190
02771	Seekonk	13,722	15,531	15,649
02067	Sharon	17,612	18,575	18,408
*01545	Shrewsbury	35,608	38,325	39,805
02725	Somerset	18,165	18,303	18,192
*02143	Somerville	75,754	81,045	79,762
01075	South Hadley	17,514	18,150	18,046
02664	South Yarmouth (c)	11,092	11,703	—
*01745	Southborough	9,767	10,450	10,409
01550	Southbridge	16,719	17,740	17,619
01562	Spencer	11,688	11,992	11,911
*01103	Springfield	153,060	155,929	154,064
02180	Stoneham	21,437	23,244	22,705
02072	Stoughton	26,962	29,281	28,969
01776	Sudbury	17,659	18,934	18,965
01907	Swampscott	13,787	15,111	15,280
02777	Swansea	15,865	17,144	17,307
*02780	Taunton	55,874	59,408	59,922
01876	Tewksbury	28,961	31,342	30,833
01879	Tyngsborough	11,292	12,380	12,368
01569	Uxbridge	13,457	14,162	14,386
01880	Wakefield	24,932	27,090	27,069
02081	Walpole	24,070	26,383	26,277
*02451	Waltham	60,632	65,218	64,065
01082	Ware	9,872	10,066	10,385
02571	Wareham	21,822	23,303	23,151
*02472	Watertown	31,915	35,329	35,022
01778	Wayland	12,994	13,943	13,664
01570	Webster	16,767	17,776	17,601
01570	Webster (c)	11,412	12,194	—
*02457	Wellesley	27,982	29,550	30,524
*01089	West Springfield	28,391	28,835	28,501
01581	Westborough	18,272	21,567	21,506
*01085	Westfield	41,094	40,834	40,535
01886	Westford	21,951	24,643	24,353
02493	Weston	11,261	11,851	11,661
02790	Westport	15,532	16,339	16,413
02090	Westwood	14,618	16,266	16,231
*02188	Weymouth	53,743	57,437	57,410
02382	Whitman	14,489	15,121	15,259
01095	Wilbraham	14,219	14,613	14,526
01887	Wilmington	22,325	23,349	22,904
01475	Winchendon	10,300	10,364	10,385
01890	Winchester	21,374	22,970	22,640
02152	Winthrop	17,497	19,316	18,510
*01801	Woburn	38,120	40,876	41,248
*01602	Worcester	181,045	206,518	205,319
*02093	Wrentham	10,955	12,178	12,457
*02664	Yarmouth	23,793	25,023	25,244

Michigan

Area codes: 231, 248/947, 269, 313, 517, 586, 616, 734, 810, 906, 989

ZIP	Place	2010 population	2020 population	2022 estimate
49221	Adrian	21,133	20,645	20,442
48101	Allen Park	28,210	28,638	28,040
49401	Allendale (c)	17,579	27,073	
49707	Alpena	10,483	10,197	10,142
*48103	Ann Arbor	113,934	123,851	119,875
*48326	Auburn Hills	21,412	24,360	25,485
*49014	Battle Creek	52,347	52,721	52,123
48708	Bay City	34,932	32,661	32,268
48072	Berkley	14,970	15,194	14,961
48025	Beverly Hills	10,267	10,584	10,435
*48009	Birmingham	20,103	21,813	21,715
*48509	Burton	29,999	29,715	29,449
49601	Cadillac	10,355	10,371	10,499
48017	Clawson	11,825	11,389	11,204
49036	Coldwater	10,945	13,822	13,296
49321	Comstock Park (c)	10,088	10,500	
*49508	Cutlerville (c)	14,370	17,849	
*48120	Dearborn	98,153	109,976	107,710
48127	Dearborn Heights	57,774	63,292	61,980
*48201	Detroit	713,777	639,111	620,376
*49506	East Grand Rapids	10,694	11,371	11,402
*48823	East Lansing	48,579	47,741	47,340
48021	Eastpointe	32,442	34,318	33,806
49829	Escanaba	12,616	12,450	12,347
*48335	Farmington	10,372	11,597	11,406
*48331	Farmington Hills	79,740	83,986	82,737
48430	Fenton	11,756	12,050	11,906
48220	Ferndale	19,900	19,190	18,969
48134	Flat Rock	9,878	10,541	10,424
*48502	Flint	102,434	81,252	79,854
49506	Forest Hills (c)	25,867	28,573	—
48026	Fraser	14,480	14,726	14,488
*48135	Garden City	27,692	27,380	26,815
49417	Grand Haven	10,412	11,011	10,982
*49503	Grand Rapids	188,040	198,917	196,908
*49418	Grandville	15,378	16,083	15,866
*48230	Grosse Pointe Park	11,555	11,595	11,358
*48236	Grosse Pointe Woods	16,135	16,487	16,137
*48212	Hamtramck	22,423	28,433	27,834
48225	Harper Woods	14,236	15,492	15,167
48840	Haslett (c)	19,220	19,670	
48030	Hazel Park	16,422	14,983	14,838
*49423	Holland	33,051	34,378	34,006
48842	Holt (c)	23,973	25,625	—
*48843	Howell	9,489	10,068	10,081
48141	Inkster	25,369	26,088	25,527
48846	Ionia	11,394	13,378	12,935
*49201	Jackson	33,534	31,309	31,031
*49428	Jenison (c)	16,538	16,640	—
*49001	Kalamazoo	74,262	73,598	72,873
*49508	Kentwood	48,707	54,304	54,077
48144	Lambertville (c)	9,953	10,433	—
*48915	Lansing	114,297	112,644	112,537
48146	Lincoln Park	38,144	40,245	39,371
*48150	Livonia	96,942	95,535	93,779
48071	Madison Heights	29,694	28,468	28,281
49855	Marquette	21,355	20,629	20,786
48122	Melvindale	10,715	12,851	12,632
*48640	Midland	41,863	42,547	42,512
*48161	Monroe	20,733	20,462	20,295
48043	Mount Clemens	16,314	15,697	15,409
*48858	Mount Pleasant	26,016	21,688	21,094
*49440	Muskegon	38,401	38,318	38,220
*48047	New Baltimore	12,084	12,117	12,005
49120	Niles	11,600	11,988	11,761
49525	Northview (c)	14,541	15,301	
*49441	Norton Shores	23,994	25,030	25,003
*48374	Novi	55,224	66,243	66,372
48237	Oak Park	29,319	29,560	29,108
*48864	Okemos (c)	21,369	25,121	—
*48867	Owosso	15,194	14,714	14,629
*48340	Pontiac	59,515	61,606	61,854
*48060	Port Huron	30,184	28,983	28,626
49024	Portage	46,292	48,891	48,978
*48193	Riverview	12,486	12,490	12,236
*48307	Rochester	12,711	13,035	12,832
*48306	Rochester Hills	70,995	76,300	75,936
48174	Romulus	23,989	25,178	25,082
48066	Roseville	47,299	47,710	46,812
*48067	Royal Oak	57,236	58,211	57,495
*48601	Saginaw	51,508	44,202	43,477
*48080	Saint Clair Shores	59,715	58,874	57,742
*49783	Sault Ste. Marie	14,144	13,337	13,333
48178	South Lyon	11,327	11,746	11,827
*48033	Southfield	71,739	76,618	75,431
48195	Southgate	30,047	30,014	29,699
*48310	Sterling Heights	129,699	134,346	132,567
49091	Sturgis	10,994	11,082	11,010
48180	Taylor	63,131	63,409	62,258
*49684	Traverse City	14,674	15,678	15,702
48183	Trenton	18,853	18,544	18,202
*48083	Troy	80,980	87,294	87,201
*49534	Walker	23,537	25,132	25,086
*48088	Warren	134,056	139,387	137,107
48917	Waverly (c)	23,925	23,812	—
48184	Wayne	17,593	17,713	17,354
*48185	Westland	84,094	85,420	84,037
48393	Wixom	13,498	17,193	17,152
48183	Woodhaven	12,875	12,941	12,763
*48192	Wyandotte	25,883	25,058	24,503
*49509	Wyoming	72,125	76,501	76,726
*48197	Ypsilanti	19,435	20,648	19,732

Minnesota

Area codes: 218, 320, 507/924 (Aug. 30, 2024), 612, 651, 763, 952

ZIP	Place	2010 population	2020 population	2022 estimate
56007	Albert Lea	18,016	18,492	18,396
56308	Alexandria	11,070	14,335	14,861
*55304	Andover	30,598	32,601	32,928
*55303	Anoka	17,142	17,921	17,990
55124	Apple Valley	49,084	56,374	55,416
55912	Austin	24,718	26,174	26,208
*56601	Bemidji	13,431	14,574	15,946
55309	Big Lake	10,060	11,686	12,413
*55014	Blaine	57,186	70,222	71,739
*55420	Bloomington	82,893	89,987	87,797
*56401	Brainerd	13,590	14,395	14,580
*55430	Brooklyn Center	30,104	33,782	32,217
*55443	Brooklyn Park	75,781	86,478	83,324
55313	Buffalo	15,453	16,168	16,502
*55337	Burnsville	60,306	64,317	63,936
55008	Cambridge	8,111	9,611	10,482
*55316	Champlin	23,089	23,919	23,112
55317	Chanhassen	22,952	25,947	26,224
55318	Chaska	23,770	27,810	28,262
55720	Cloquet	12,124	12,568	12,603
55421	Columbia Heights	19,496	21,973	22,243
*55433	Coon Rapids	61,476	63,599	62,785
55016	Cottage Grove	34,589	38,839	41,033
*55422	Crystal	22,151	23,330	22,265
*56501	Detroit Lakes	8,569	9,869	10,011
*55802	Duluth	86,265	86,697	86,619
*55121	Eagan	64,206	68,855	67,534
*55011	East Bethel	11,626	11,786	12,184
*55344	Eden Prairie	60,797	64,198	62,476
*55424	Edina	47,941	53,494	52,437
55330	Elk River	22,974	25,835	26,750
*56031	Fairmont	10,666	10,487	10,260
55021	Faribault	23,352	24,453	24,518
55024	Farmington	21,086	23,632	23,566
*56537	Fergus Falls	13,138	14,119	14,187
55025	Forest Lake	18,375	20,611	20,857
*55432	Fridley	27,208	29,590	30,289
*55427	Golden Valley	20,371	22,552	21,545
*55744	Grand Rapids	10,869	11,126	11,268
55304	Ham Lake	15,296	16,464	16,613
55033	Hastings	22,172	22,154	21,712
*55810	Hermantown	9,414	10,221	10,126
55746	Hibbing	16,361	16,214	16,052
*55343	Hopkins	17,591	19,079	18,269
55038	Hugo	13,332	15,766	16,408
55350	Hutchinson	14,178	14,599	14,678
*55076	Inver Grove Heights	33,880	35,801	35,701
55042	Lake Elmo	8,069	11,335	13,449
55044	Lakeville	55,954	69,490	74,553
*55014	Lino Lakes	20,216	21,399	21,973
*55117	Little Canada	9,773	10,819	10,261
*56001	Mankato	39,309	44,488	45,140
*55311	Maple Grove	61,567	70,253	70,582
55109	Maplewood	38,018	42,088	40,000
56258	Marshall	13,680	13,628	13,680
*55118	Mendota Heights	11,071	11,744	11,492
*55401	Minneapolis	382,578	429,954	425,096
*55345	Minnetonka	49,734	53,781	52,544
55362	Monticello	12,759	14,455	14,804
*56560	Moorhead	38,065	44,505	44,861
55112	Mounds View	12,155	13,249	12,636
55112	New Brighton	21,456	23,454	22,413
*54427	New Hope	20,339	21,986	21,035
56073	New Ulm	13,522	14,120	14,035
55056	North Branch	10,125	10,787	11,492
*56002	North Mankato	13,394	14,275	14,251
55109	North St. Paul	11,460	12,364	12,659
55057	Northfield	20,007	20,790	20,924
*55128	Oakdale	27,378	28,303	27,799
*55330	Otsego	13,571	19,966	22,424

ZIP	Place	2010 population	2020 population	2022 estimate
55060	Owatonna	25,599	26,420	26,470
*55446	Plymouth	70,576	81,026	78,683
*55372	Prior Lake	22,796	27,617	28,133
*55303	Ramsey	23,668	27,646	28,333
55066	Red Wing	16,459	16,547	16,672
55423	Richfield	35,228	36,994	36,710
55422	Robbinsdale	13,953	14,646	14,210
*55901	Rochester	106,769	121,395	121,878
55374	Rogers	8,597	13,295	13,500
55068	Rosemount	21,874	25,650	27,081
*55113	Roseville	33,660	36,254	35,627
*55418	Saint Anthony	8,226	9,257	10,124
*56301	Saint Cloud	65,842	68,881	69,568
*55416	Saint Louis Park	45,250	50,010	48,827
55376	Saint Michael	16,399	18,235	19,995
*55101	Saint Paul	285,068	311,527	303,176
56082	Saint Peter	11,196	12,066	12,156
*56377	Sartell	15,876	19,351	19,696
56379	Sauk Rapids	12,773	13,862	13,801
55378	Savage	26,911	32,465	32,893
*55379	Shakopee	37,076	43,698	45,735
55126	Shoreview	25,043	26,921	26,632
*55075	South St. Paul	20,160	20,759	20,506
55082	Stillwater	18,225	19,394	19,276
*55127	Vadnais Heights	12,302	12,912	12,713
55318	Victoria	7,345	10,546	11,297
55387	Waconia	10,697	13,033	13,384
*55118	West St. Paul	19,540	20,615	21,794
*55110	White Bear Lake	23,797	24,883	23,588
56201	Willmar	19,610	21,015	21,282
55987	Winona	27,592	25,948	25,842
*55125	Woodbury	61,961	75,102	78,561
56187	Worthington	12,764	13,947	13,743

Mississippi
Area codes: 228, 601/769, 662

ZIP	Place	2010 population	2020 population	2022 estimate
*39520	Bay St. Louis	9,260	9,284	10,596
*39530	Biloxi	44,054	49,449	49,118
*39042	Brandon	21,705	25,138	25,502
*39601	Brookhaven	12,513	11,674	11,608
*39272	Byram	11,489	12,666	12,721
39046	Canton	13,189	10,948	10,744
*38614	Clarksdale	17,962	14,903	13,969
*38732	Cleveland	12,334	11,199	10,545
*39056	Clinton	25,216	28,100	26,996
*39701	Columbus	23,640	24,084	23,273
*38834	Corinth	14,573	14,622	14,312
39540	D'Iberville	9,486	12,721	13,309
*39232	Flowood	7,823	10,202	10,530
39553	Gautier	18,572	19,024	18,977
*38701	Greenville	34,400	29,670	28,017
*38930	Greenwood	15,205	14,490	13,541
*38901	Grenada	13,092	12,700	12,302
*39501	Gulfport	67,793	72,926	72,236
*39401	Hattiesburg	45,989	48,730	48,455
38632	Hernando	14,090	17,138	18,053
38637	Horn Lake	26,066	26,736	26,550
*39201	Jackson	173,514	153,701	145,995
*39440	Laurel	18,540	17,161	17,066
39560	Long Beach	14,792	16,780	17,101
*39110	Madison	24,149	27,747	27,775
*39648	McComb	12,790	12,413	12,041
*39301	Meridian	41,148	35,052	33,816
*39563	Moss Point	13,704	12,147	11,931
*39120	Natchez	15,792	14,520	13,812
*39564	Ocean Springs	17,442	18,429	18,662
38654	Olive Branch	33,484	39,711	47,086
*38655	Oxford	18,916	25,416	26,437
*39567	Pascagoula	22,392	22,010	21,650
*39208	Pearl	25,092	27,115	27,682
39465	Petal	10,454	11,010	11,230
39466	Picayune	10,878	11,885	11,826
39157	Ridgeland	24,047	24,340	24,404
*38671	Southaven	48,982	54,648	56,360
39759	Starkville	23,888	24,360	24,168
*38801	Tupelo	34,546	37,923	37,748
*39180	Vicksburg	23,856	21,573	20,391

Missouri
Area codes: 235 (Mar. 24, 2024)/573, 314/557, 417, 636, 660, 816/975

ZIP	Place	2010 population	2020 population	2022 estimate
63123	Affton (c)	20,307	20,417	—
63010	Arnold	20,808	20,858	20,845
*63011	Ballwin	30,404	31,103	30,622
63137	Bellefontaine Neighbors	10,860	10,740	10,447
64012	Belton	23,116	23,953	25,420
*64015	Blue Springs	52,575	58,603	59,518
*65613	Bolivar	10,325	10,679	11,110

ZIP	Place	2010 population	2020 population	2022 estimate
*65616	Branson	10,520	12,638	12,947
63044	Bridgeton	11,550	11,445	11,338
*63701	Cape Girardeau	37,941	39,540	40,377
64836	Carthage	14,378	15,522	15,491
*63017	Chesterfield	47,484	49,999	49,327
*63105	Clayton	15,939	17,355	17,130
*65201	Columbia	108,500	126,254	128,555
*63128	Concord (c)	16,421	17,668	
63126	Crestwood	11,912	12,404	12,221
63141	Creve Coeur	17,833	18,834	18,565
*63366	Dardenne Prairie	11,494	12,743	13,564
63025	Eureka	10,189	11,646	12,729
64024	Excelsior Springs	11,084	10,553	10,580
63640	Farmington	16,240	18,217	18,143
63135	Ferguson	21,203	18,527	18,143
63028	Festus	11,602	12,706	13,193
*63031	Florissant	52,158	52,533	51,506
65473	Fort Leonard Wood (c)	15,061	15,959	
65251	Fulton	12,790	12,600	12,710
*64118	Gladstone	25,410	27,063	26,907
64029	Grain Valley	12,854	15,627	16,178
64030	Grandview	24,475	26,209	25,610
63401	Hannibal	17,916	17,108	16,938
*63042	Hazelwood	25,703	25,458	25,047
*64050	Independence	116,830	123,011	121,202
63755	Jackson	13,758	15,481	15,702
*65101	Jefferson City	43,079	43,228	42,528
63136	Jennings	14,712	12,895	12,824
*64801	Joplin	50,150	51,762	52,518
*64106	Kansas City	459,787	508,090	509,297
64060	Kearney	8,381	10,404	10,913
63857	Kennett	10,932	10,515	10,229
63501	Kirksville	17,505	17,530	17,474
63122	Kirkwood	27,540	29,461	29,279
63367	Lake St. Louis	14,545	16,707	18,337
65536	Lebanon	14,474	15,013	15,232
*64063	Lee's Summit	91,364	101,108	103,465
63125	Lemay (c)	16,645	17,117	
*64068	Liberty	29,149	30,167	30,775
*63011	Manchester	18,094	18,333	18,076
65340	Marshall	13,065	13,806	13,622
63043	Maryland Heights	27,472	28,284	27,769
64468	Maryville	11,972	10,633	10,461
63129	Mehlville (c)	28,380	28,955	
65265	Mexico	11,543	11,469	11,496
65270	Moberly	13,974	13,783	13,774
*64850	Neosho	11,835	12,590	13,061
65714	Nixa	19,022	23,257	24,749
63129	Oakville (c)	36,143	36,301	
*63366	O'Fallon	79,329	91,316	93,663
63034	Old Jamestown (c)	19,184	19,790	
63114	Overland	16,062	15,955	15,616
65721	Ozark	17,820	21,284	22,512
*63901	Poplar Bluff	17,023	16,225	16,232
*64083	Raymore	19,206	22,941	24,203
*64133	Raytown	29,526	30,012	29,312
65738	Republic	14,751	18,750	19,728
*65401	Rolla	19,559	19,943	20,322
63074	Saint Ann	13,020	13,019	12,755
*63301	Saint Charles	65,794	70,493	71,184
*64501	Saint Joseph	76,780	72,473	70,656
*63101	Saint Louis	319,294	301,578	286,578
*63376	Saint Peters	52,575	57,732	58,523
*65301	Sedalia	21,387	21,725	21,947
63801	Sikeston	16,318	16,291	16,073
64089	Smithville	8,425	10,406	10,653
63138	Spanish Lake (c)	19,650	18,413	
*65802	Springfield	159,498	169,176	170,067
63017	Town and Country	10,815	11,640	11,584
63379	Troy	10,540	12,686	13,951
63084	Union	10,204	12,348	12,756
*63130	University City	35,371	35,065	34,355
64093	Warrensburg	18,838	19,337	19,458
63090	Washington	13,982	14,500	15,075
64870	Webb City	10,996	13,031	13,165
63119	Webster Groves	22,995	24,010	23,610
63385	Wentzville	29,070	44,372	47,197
65775	West Plains	11,986	12,184	12,528
*63040	Wildwood	35,517	35,417	34,954

Montana
Area code: 406 applies to the entire state

ZIP	Place	2010 population	2020 population	2022 estimate
59714	Belgrade	7,389	10,460	11,966
*59101	Billings	104,170	117,116	119,960
*59715	Bozeman	37,280	53,293	56,123
*59701	Butte-Silver Bow (balance)	33,525	34,494	35,416
*59401	Great Falls	58,505	60,442	60,382
*59601	Helena	28,190	32,091	33,885
*59901	Kalispell	19,927	24,558	28,450
*59801	Missoula	66,788	73,489	76,955

Nebraska
Area codes: 308, 402/531

ZIP	Place	2010 population	2020 population	2022 estimate
68310	Beatrice	12,459	12,261	12,223
*68005	Bellevue	50,137	64,176	63,015
68138	Chalco (c)	10,994	11,064	—
*68601	Columbus	22,111	24,028	24,195
*68025	Fremont	26,397	27,141	27,318
*68801	Grand Island	48,520	53,131	52,513
68901	Hastings	24,907	25,152	24,927
*68847	Kearney	30,787	33,790	34,277
*68128	La Vista	15,758	16,746	16,379
68850	Lexington	10,230	10,348	10,725
*68502	Lincoln	258,379	291,082	292,627
*68701	Norfolk	24,210	24,955	25,928
*69101	North Platte	24,733	23,390	22,722
*68102	Omaha	408,958	486,051	485,153
68046	Papillion	18,894	24,159	23,794
*69361	Scottsbluff	15,039	14,436	14,283
68776	South Sioux City	13,353	14,043	13,706

Nevada
Area codes: 702/725, 775

ZIP	Place	2010 population	2020 population	2022 estimate
*89005	Boulder City	15,023	14,885	14,890
*89701	Carson City	55,274	58,639	58,130
89508	Cold Springs (c)	8,544	10,153	—
89403	Dayton (c)	8,964	15,153	—
*89801	Elko	18,297	20,564	20,756
89124	Enterprise (c)	108,481	221,831	—
89408	Fernley	19,368	22,895	24,261
*89410	Gardnerville Ranchos (c)	11,312	11,318	—
*89015	Henderson	257,729	317,610	331,415
*89101	Las Vegas	583,756	641,903	656,274
89027	Mesquite	15,276	20,471	21,992
*89030	North Las Vegas	216,961	262,527	280,543
*89048	Pahrump (c)	36,441	44,738	—
89121	Paradise (c)	223,167	191,238	—
*89501	Reno	225,221	264,165	273,448
*89436	Spanish Springs (c)	15,064	17,314	—
*89431	Sparks	90,264	108,445	109,226
89815	Spring Creek (c)	12,361	14,967	—
*89117	Spring Valley (c)	178,395	215,597	—
89135	Summerlin South (c)	24,085	30,744	—
89433	Sun Valley (c)	19,299	21,178	—
*89110	Sunrise Manor (c)	189,372	205,618	—
89122	Whitney (c)	38,585	49,061	—
*89109	Winchester (c)	27,978	36,403	—

New Hampshire
Area code: 603 applies to the entire state. See introductory note.

ZIP	Place	2010 population	2020 population	2022 estimate
03031	Amherst	11,201	11,753	11,898
03110	Bedford	21,203	23,322	23,704
03743	Claremont	13,355	12,949	13,149
*03301	Concord	42,695	43,976	44,503
03818	Conway	10,115	9,822	10,244
03038	Derry	33,109	34,317	34,411
03038	Derry (c)	22,015	22,879	—
*03820	Dover	29,987	32,741	33,416
03824	Durham	14,638	15,490	14,473
03824	Durham (c)	10,345	11,147	—
03833	Exeter	14,306	16,049	16,178
03833	Exeter (c)	9,242	10,109	—
03045	Goffstown	17,651	18,577	18,550
*03842	Hampton	15,430	16,214	16,484
03755	Hanover	11,260	11,870	10,348
03106	Hooksett	13,451	14,871	14,740
03051	Hudson	24,467	25,394	25,570
*03431	Keene	23,409	23,047	22,774
*03246	Laconia	15,951	16,871	17,086
*03766	Lebanon	13,151	14,282	15,044
*03053	Londonderry	24,129	25,826	26,543
*03053	Londonderry (c)	11,037	11,645	—
*03101	Manchester	109,565	115,644	115,141
03054	Merrimack	25,494	26,632	28,589
03055	Milford	15,115	16,131	16,376
*03060	Nashua	86,494	91,322	91,161
03076	Pelham	12,897	14,222	14,473
*03801	Portsmouth	20,779	21,956	22,713
03077	Raymond	10,138	10,684	10,989
*03867	Rochester	29,752	32,492	33,169
03079	Salem	28,776	30,089	30,647
03878	Somersworth	11,766	11,855	12,159
03087	Windham	13,592	15,817	16,034

New Jersey
Area codes: 201/551, 609/640, 732/848, 856, 862/973, 908

ZIP	Place	2010 population	2020 population	2022 estimate
07712	Asbury Park	16,116	15,188	15,146
*08401	Atlantic City	39,558	38,497	38,561

ZIP	Place	2010 population	2020 population	2022 estimate
07001	Avenel (c)	17,011	16,920	—
07002	Bayonne	63,024	71,686	69,527
08722	Beachwood	11,045	10,859	11,128
*08031	Bellmawr	11,583	11,707	11,683
07621	Bergenfield	26,764	28,321	28,163
08805	Bound Brook	10,402	11,988	11,971
08807	Bradley Gardens (c)	14,206	14,077	—
08302	Bridgeton	25,349	27,263	26,410
08015	Browns Mills (c)	11,223	10,734	—
08016	Burlington	9,920	9,743	10,016
*08102	Camden	77,344	71,791	70,996
07008	Carteret	22,844	25,326	25,176
08002	Cherry Hill Mall (c)	14,171	14,805	—
07010	Cliffside Park	23,594	25,693	25,560
*07013	Clifton	84,136	90,296	88,709
*08108	Collingswood	13,926	14,186	14,150
07067	Colonia (c)	17,795	18,609	—
*07801	Dover	18,157	18,460	18,422
07628	Dumont	17,479	17,863	18,182
*07018	East Orange	64,270	69,612	68,446
07073	East Rutherford	8,913	10,022	10,397
*07724	Eatontown	12,709	13,597	13,545
08043	Echelon (c)	10,743	11,896	—
07020	Edgewater	11,513	14,336	14,604
*07201	Elizabeth	124,969	137,298	134,283
07407	Elmwood Park	19,403	21,422	21,233
*07631	Englewood	27,147	29,308	29,034
07410	Fair Lawn	32,457	34,927	35,279
07022	Fairview	13,835	15,025	14,893
07932	Florham Park	11,696	12,585	13,325
08863	Fords (c)	15,187	12,941	—
07024	Fort Lee	35,345	40,191	39,688
07417	Franklin Lakes	10,590	11,079	10,936
08823	Franklin Park (c)	13,295	13,430	—
07728	Freehold	12,052	12,538	12,497
07026	Garfield	30,487	32,655	32,412
08028	Glassboro	18,579	23,149	23,600
07452	Glen Rock	11,601	12,133	12,039
08030	Gloucester City	11,456	11,484	11,464
*08053	Greentree (c)	11,367	12,012	—
07093	Guttenberg	11,176	12,017	11,446
*07601	Hackensack	43,010	46,030	45,633
07840	Hackettstown	9,724	10,248	10,130
08033	Haddonfield	11,593	12,550	12,514
08690	Hamilton Square (c)	12,784	12,679	—
08037	Hammonton	14,791	14,711	14,833
07029	Harrison	13,620	19,450	19,801
07604	Hasbrouck Heights	11,842	12,125	12,018
*07506	Hawthorne	18,791	19,637	19,231
08904	Highland Park	13,982	15,072	14,988
08844	Hillsborough (c)	—	22,214	—
07642	Hillsdale	10,219	10,143	10,044
07030	Hoboken	50,005	60,419	57,703
*08753	Holiday City-Berkeley (c)	12,831	12,943	—
07843	Hopatcong	15,147	14,362	14,531
08830	Iselin (c)	18,695	20,088	—
*07302	Jersey City	247,597	292,449	286,670
*07032	Kearny	40,684	41,999	39,862
07034	Lake Hiawatha (c)	—	10,194	—
07849	Lake Hopatcong (c)	—	10,232	—
08701	Lakewood (c)	53,805	69,398	—
07035	Lincoln Park	10,521	10,915	10,923
07036	Linden	40,499	43,738	43,352
08021	Lindenwold	17,613	21,641	21,595
07643	Little Ferry	10,626	10,987	10,892
07644	Lodi	24,136	26,206	25,786
07740	Long Branch	30,719	31,667	32,434
07940	Madison	15,845	16,937	16,261
08835	Manville	10,344	10,953	10,875
08053	Marlton (c)	10,133	10,594	—
08836	Martinsville (c)	11,980	12,147	—
07607	Maywood	9,555	10,080	10,000
08619	Mercerville (c)	13,230	13,447	—
08840	Metuchen	13,574	15,049	14,985
08846	Middlesex	13,635	14,636	14,512
08332	Millville	28,400	27,491	27,308
08057	Moorestown-Lenola (c)	14,217	14,240	—
*07960	Morristown	18,411	20,180	20,339
*08901	New Brunswick	55,181	55,266	55,998
07646	New Milford	16,341	16,923	16,875
07974	New Providence	12,171	13,650	13,519
07102	Newark	277,140	311,549	305,344
07031	North Arlington	15,392	16,457	16,309
07060	North Plainfield	21,936	22,808	22,637
07438	Oak Ridge (c)	—	10,996	—
07436	Oakland	12,754	12,748	12,653
08050	Ocean Acres (c)	16,142	18,185	—
08226	Ocean City	11,701	11,229	11,303
08857	Old Bridge (c)	23,753	27,210	—
07650	Palisades Park	19,622	20,292	20,106
07652	Paramus	26,342	26,698	26,359
07054	Parsippany (c)	—	22,778	—
07055	Passaic	69,781	70,537	69,128
*07505	Paterson	146,199	159,732	156,661
08070	Pennsville (c)	11,888	12,043	—

ZIP	Place	2010 population	2020 population	2022 estimate
*08861	Perth Amboy	50,814	55,436	55,357
08865	Phillipsburg	14,950	15,249	15,320
08021	Pine Hill	10,233	10,743	10,738
*07060	Plainfield	49,808	54,586	54,513
08232	Pleasantville	20,249	20,629	20,662
08742	Point Pleasant	18,392	18,941	19,382
07442	Pompton Lakes	11,097	11,127	10,907
07444	Pompton Plains (c)	—	11,144	
07470	Preakness (c)	—	18,487	
*08540	Princeton	12,307	30,681	30,377
08536	Princeton Meadows (c)	13,834	14,776	
07065	Rahway	27,346	29,556	29,693
07446	Ramsey	14,473	14,798	14,671
*07701	Red Bank	12,206	12,936	12,856
07657	Ridgefield	11,032	11,501	11,392
07660	Ridgefield Park	12,729	13,224	13,110
*07450	Ridgewood	24,958	25,979	26,168
07456	Ringwood	12,228	11,735	11,489
07661	River Edge	11,340	12,049	11,986
07751	Robertsville (c)	11,297	11,399	
07203	Roselle	21,085	22,695	22,327
07204	Roselle Park	13,297	13,967	13,819
07070	Rutherford	18,061	18,834	18,662
*08872	Sayreville	42,704	45,345	45,123
*07094	Secaucus	16,264	22,181	21,108
07078	Short Hills (c)	13,165	14,422	—
08081	Sicklerville (c)	—	45,084	—
08244	Somers Point	10,795	10,469	10,495
*08873	Somerset (c)	22,083	22,968	
08876	Somerville	12,098	12,346	12,712
07080	South Plainfield	23,385	24,338	24,228
08882	South River	16,008	16,118	15,990
08003	Springdale (c)	14,518	14,811	
07876	Succasunna (c)	9,152	10,338	
*07901	Summit	21,457	22,719	22,342
07670	Tenafly	14,488	15,409	15,219
07920	The Hills (c)	—	11,410	
*07724	Tinton Falls	17,892	19,181	19,462
08753	Toms River (c)	88,791	92,830	
*07512	Totowa	10,804	11,065	10,822
*08608	Trenton	84,913	90,871	89,661
07087	Union City	66,455	68,589	65,366
07043	Upper Montclair (c)	11,565	13,146	
*08360	Vineland	60,724	60,780	60,491
07463	Waldwick	9,625	10,058	10,048
07057	Wallington	11,335	11,868	11,786
07465	Wanaque	11,116	11,317	11,041
07728	West Freehold (c)	13,613	13,596	
07093	West New York	49,708	52,912	51,981
*07090	Westfield	30,316	31,032	30,539
08108	Westmont (c)	—	13,726	
*07675	Westwood	10,908	11,282	11,186
08094	Williamstown (c)	15,567	15,082	
07075	Wood-Ridge	7,626	10,137	10,074
07095	Woodbridge (c)	19,265	19,839	—
*08096	Woodbury	10,174	9,963	10,048
07424	Woodland Park	11,819	13,484	13,191

New Mexico
Area codes: 505, 575

ZIP	Place	2010 population	2020 population	2022 estimate
*88310	Alamogordo	30,403	30,898	31,309
*87102	Albuquerque	545,852	564,559	561,008
*88210	Artesia	11,301	12,875	12,381
*88220	Carlsbad	26,138	32,238	31,612
*88021	Chaparral (c)	14,631	16,551	
*88101	Clovis	37,775	38,567	37,902
*88030	Deming	14,855	14,758	14,930
*87532	Española	10,224	10,526	10,446
*87401	Farmington	45,877	46,624	46,127
*87301	Gallup	21,678	21,899	20,932
*88240	Hobbs	34,122	40,508	39,648
*88001	Las Cruces	97,618	111,385	113,888
*87701	Las Vegas	13,753	13,166	13,053
*87544	Los Alamos (c)	12,019	13,179	
87031	Los Lunas	14,835	17,242	18,533
88260	Lovington	11,009	11,668	11,268
87107	North Valley (c)	11,333	11,149	
*88130	Portales	12,280	12,137	11,973
*87124	Rio Rancho	87,521	104,046	108,082
*88201	Roswell	48,366	48,422	47,390
*87501	Santa Fe	67,947	87,505	89,008
87105	South Valley (c)	40,976	38,338	—
*88063	Sunland Park	14,106	16,702	17,414

New York
Area codes: 212/332/646/917, 315/680, 329/845, 347/718/917/929, 363/516, 518/838, 585, 607, 624/716, 631/934, 914

ZIP	Place	2010 population	2020 population	2022 estimate
*10901	Airmont	8,628	10,166	10,104
*12202	Albany	97,856	99,224	100,826

ZIP	Place	2010 population	2020 population	2022 estimate
12010	Amsterdam	18,620	18,219	18,244
*13021	Auburn	27,687	26,866	26,081
*11702	Babylon	12,166	12,188	12,146
11510	Baldwin (c)	24,033	33,919	
*14020	Batavia	15,465	15,600	15,459
11706	Bay Shore (c)	26,337	29,244	
12508	Beacon	15,541	13,769	14,290
11710	Bellmore (c)	16,218	16,297	
11714	Bethpage (c)	16,429	16,658	
*13901	Binghamton	47,376	47,969	47,115
11717	Brentwood (c)	60,664	62,387	—
*14610	Brighton (c)	36,609	37,137	—
*14201	Buffalo	261,310	278,349	276,486
*14424	Canandaigua	10,545	10,576	10,539
11720	Centereach (c)	31,578	30,980	—
*11722	Central Islip (c)	34,450	36,714	—
*14227	Cheektowaga (c)	75,178	76,829	—
*10952	Chestnut Ridge	7,916	10,505	10,450
12047	Cohoes	16,168	18,147	17,876
11725	Commack (c)	36,124	36,536	—
11726	Copiague (c)	22,993	23,429	—
11727	Coram (c)	39,113	40,220	—
*14830	Corning	11,183	10,551	10,683
13045	Cortland	19,204	17,556	17,314
13214	De Witt (c)	—	11,247	—
11729	Deer Park (c)	27,745	28,837	—
14043	Depew	15,303	15,178	14,991
*11746	Dix Hills (c)	26,892	26,180	—
10522	Dobbs Ferry	10,875	11,541	11,337
*14048	Dunkirk	12,563	12,743	12,563
12302	East Glenville (c)	6,616	11,896	—
11730	East Islip (c)	14,475	13,931	—
11758	East Massapequa (c)	19,069	19,854	—
11554	East Meadow (c)	38,132	37,796	—
11731	East Northport (c)	20,217	20,048	—
11772	East Patchogue (c)	22,469	21,580	—
11518	East Rockaway (c)	9,818	10,159	10,028
11733	East Setauket (c)	—	10,998	—
*10709	Eastchester (c)	19,554	20,901	—
14226	Eggertsville (c)	15,019	15,561	—
*14901	Elmira	29,200	26,523	25,852
11003	Elmont (c)	33,198	35,265	—
11731	Elwood (c)	11,177	11,426	—
*13760	Endicott	13,392	13,667	13,338
*13760	Endwell (c)	11,446	11,762	—
*13219	Fairmount (c)	10,224	10,248	—
11738	Farmingville (c)	15,481	14,983	—
*11001	Floral Park	15,863	16,172	15,925
*13602	Fort Drum (c)	12,955	15,896	—
11010	Franklin Square (c)	29,320	30,903	—
11520	Freeport	42,860	44,472	43,886
13069	Fulton	11,896	11,389	11,318
*11530	Garden City	22,371	23,272	22,891
14456	Geneva	13,261	12,812	12,503
11542	Glen Cove	26,964	28,365	27,997
*12801	Glens Falls	14,700	14,830	14,603
12078	Gloversville	15,665	15,131	14,932
*11023	Great Neck	9,989	11,145	11,034
*14612	Greece (c)	14,519	14,429	—
11740	Greenlawn (c)	13,742	13,661	—
11946	Hampton Bays (c)	13,603	15,228	—
10528	Harrison	27,472	28,218	29,369
*11788	Hauppauge (c)	20,882	20,083	—
10927	Haverstraw	11,910	12,323	12,213
*11550	Hempstead	53,891	59,169	58,331
*11801	Hicksville (c)	41,547	43,869	—
11741	Holbrook (c)	27,195	26,487	—
*11742	Holtsville (c)	19,714	18,937	—
11743	Huntington (c)	18,046	19,943	—
*11746	Huntington Station (c)	33,029	34,878	—
11096	Inwood (c)	9,792	11,340	—
*14617	Irondequoit (c)	51,692	51,043	—
11751	Islip (c)	18,689	18,418	—
*14850	Ithaca	30,014	32,108	32,870
*14701	Jamestown	31,146	28,712	28,243
10535	Jefferson Valley-Yorktown (c)	14,142	14,444	—
*11753	Jericho (c)	13,567	14,808	—
13790	Johnson City	15,174	15,343	15,080
14217	Kenmore (c)	15,423	15,205	15,012
11754	Kings Park (c)	17,282	17,085	—
*12401	Kingston	23,893	24,069	23,916
10950	Kiryas Joel	20,175	32,954	38,998
14218	Lackawanna	18,141	19,949	19,716
11755	Lake Grove	11,163	11,072	11,041
11779	Lake Ronkonkoma (c)	20,155	18,619	—
14086	Lancaster	10,352	10,027	10,111
*12110	Latham (c)	—	13,680	—
11756	Levittown (c)	51,881	51,758	—
11757	Lindenhurst	27,253	27,148	27,064
*14094	Lockport	21,165	20,876	20,602
11561	Long Beach	33,275	35,029	34,604
12211	Loudonville (c)	—	10,296	—
11563	Lynbrook	19,427	20,438	20,128

642   U.S. POPULATION — POPULATIONS FOR U.S. PLACES OF 10,000+

ZIP	Place	2010 population	2020 population	2022 estimate
10543	Mamaroneck........	18,929	20,151	19,669
11949	Manorville (c).....	14,314	14,317	—
11758	Massapequa (c).....	21,685	21,355	—
11762	Massapequa Park....	17,008	17,109	16,873
13662	Massena..........	10,936	10,151	10,158
11950	Mastic (c)........	15,481	15,404	—
11951	Mastic Beach (c).....	12,930	14,199	—
11763	Medford (c).......	24,142	24,247	—
*11747	Melville (c).......	18,985	19,284	—
11566	Merrick (c).......	22,097	22,040	—
11953	Middle Island (c).....	10,483	10,546	—
*10940	Middletown........	28,086	30,345	30,207
11764	Miller Place (c).....	12,339	11,723	—
11501	Mineola..........	18,799	20,800	21,225
10952	Monsey (c).......	18,412	26,954	—
10549	Mount Kisco.......	10,877	10,959	10,646
11766	Mount Sinai (c).....	12,118	11,623	—
*10550	Mount Vernon......	67,292	73,893	71,714
	Myers Corner (c)....	6,790	10,598	—
10954	Nanuet (c)........	17,882	18,886	—
11767	Nesconset (c).....	13,387	13,207	—
11590	New Cassel (c).....	14,059	14,199	—
10956	New City (c).......	33,559	34,135	—
*11040	New Hyde Park.....	9,712	10,257	10,161
10801	New Rochelle......	77,062	79,726	82,288
*10001	New York.........	8,175,133	8,804,190	8,335,897
12550	Newburgh........	28,866	28,856	28,501
*14301	Niagara Falls......	50,193	48,671	47,993
12309	Niskayuna (c).....	—	20,787	—
11701	North Amityville (c)..	17,862	18,643	—
11703	North Babylon (c)....	17,509	17,927	—
11706	North Bay Shore (c)..	18,944	19,619	—
11710	North Bellmore (c)...	19,941	20,583	—
11713	North Bellport (c)...	11,545	11,900	—
11757	North Lindenhurst (c)	11,652	12,000	—
11758	North Massapequa (c)	17,886	17,829	—
11566	North Merrick (c)...	12,272	12,238	—
*11040	North New Hyde Park (c)	14,899	15,657	—
14120	North Tonawanda....	31,568	30,496	30,235
11580	North Valley Stream (c)	16,628	18,197	—
11793	North Wantagh (c)...	11,960	11,931	—
11572	Oceanside (c).....	32,109	32,637	—
14760	Olean...........	14,452	13,937	13,764
13421	Oneida..........	11,393	10,329	10,140
13820	Oneonta.........	13,901	13,079	15,518
10562	Ossining.........	25,060	27,551	26,633
13126	Oswego..........	18,142	16,921	17,150
11772	Patchogue........	11,798	12,408	12,344
10965	Pearl River (c).....	15,876	16,567	—
10566	Peekskill.........	23,583	25,431	25,514
11803	Plainview (c)......	26,217	27,100	—
*12901	Plattsburgh.......	19,989	19,841	19,904
*10573	Port Chester......	28,967	31,693	30,823
11050	Port Washington (c)..	15,846	16,753	—
12601	Poughkeepsie......	32,736	31,577	32,010
11961	Ridge (c).........	13,336	13,271	—
11901	Riverhead (c).....	13,299	14,993	—
*14604	Rochester........	210,565	211,328	209,352
*11570	Rockville Centre....	24,023	26,016	25,662
11778	Rocky Point (c)....	14,014	13,633	—
12205	Roessleville (c)....	—	11,518	—
*13440	Rome...........	33,725	32,127	31,735
*11779	Ronkonkoma (c)....	19,082	18,955	—
11575	Roosevelt (c).....	16,258	18,066	—
12306	Rotterdam (c).....	20,652	22,968	—
10580	Rye............	15,720	16,592	16,248
11780	Saint James (c)....	13,338	13,487	—
11590	Salisbury (c)......	12,093	12,618	—
12866	Saratoga Springs ...	26,586	28,491	28,593
11782	Sayville (c).......	16,853	16,569	—
*10583	Scarsdale........	17,166	18,253	17,822
*12305	Schenectady......	66,135	67,047	68,809
*10940	Scotchtown (c).....	9,212	10,578	—
11783	Seaford (c).......	15,294	15,251	—
11784	Selden (c)........	19,851	21,262	—
11967	Shirley (c)........	27,854	26,360	—
10591	Sleepy Hollow......	9,870	9,986	11,001
*11787	Smithtown (c).....	26,470	25,629	—
11735	South Farmingdale (c)	14,486	14,345	—
10977	Spring Valley......	31,347	33,066	32,884
*11790	Stony Brook (c)....	13,740	13,467	—
11794	Stony Brook University (c)..	9,216	10,409	—
10980	Stony Point (c)....	12,147	12,126	—
10901	Suffern..........	10,723	11,441	11,338
*11791	Syosset (c).......	18,829	19,259	—
*13202	Syracuse.........	145,170	148,620	144,451
10591	Tarrytown........	11,277	11,860	11,769
11776	Terryville (c)......	11,849	11,472	—
*14150	Tonawanda.......	15,130	15,129	14,991
*14150	Tonawanda (c).....	58,144	57,431	—
*12180	Troy...........	50,129	51,401	50,895
11553	Uniondale (c).....	24,759	32,473	—
*13501	Utica...........	62,235	65,283	64,081

ZIP	Place	2010 population	2020 population	2022 estimate
*11580	Valley Stream......	37,511	40,634	40,115
11793	Wantagh (c).......	18,871	18,613	—
*13601	Watertown........	27,023	24,685	24,451
12189	Watervliet........	10,254	10,375	10,219
*11704	West Babylon (c)...	43,213	43,213	—
10993	West Haverstraw....	10,165	10,678	10,612
11552	West Hempstead (c)..	18,862	19,835	—
11795	West Islip (c)......	28,335	27,048	—
*14224	West Seneca (c)....	44,711	45,500	—
*11590	Westbury.........	15,146	15,864	15,734
*10601	White Plains.......	56,853	59,559	59,316
11797	Woodbury........	10,686	11,526	11,531
11598	Woodmere (c).....	17,121	18,669	—
11798	Wyandanch (c).....	11,647	12,990	—
*10701	Yonkers..........	195,976	211,569	208,121

North Carolina
Area codes: 252, 336/743, 472/910, 704/980, 828, 919/984

ZIP	Place	2010 population	2020 population	2022 estimate
*28001	Albemarle........	15,903	16,432	16,766
28390	Anderson Creek (c)...	—	13,636	—
*27502	Apex...........	37,476	58,780	71,065
27263	Archdale.........	11,415	11,907	12,003
*27203	Asheboro........	25,012	27,156	27,482
*28801	Asheville........	83,393	94,589	93,776
28012	Belmont.........	10,076	15,010	15,353
*28607	Boone..........	17,122	19,092	19,756
*27215	Burlington........	49,963	57,303	59,287
27510	Carrboro.........	19,582	21,295	21,298
*27511	Cary...........	135,234	174,721	180,388
27514	Chapel Hill.......	57,233	61,960	62,098
*28202	Charlotte........	731,424	874,579	897,720
*27520	Clayton.........	16,116	26,307	29,445
27012	Clemmons........	18,627	21,163	21,823
*28025	Concord.........	79,066	105,240	109,896
28031	Cornelius........	24,866	31,412	32,294
28036	Davidson........	10,944	15,106	15,771
*27701	Durham.........	228,330	283,506	291,928
*27288	Eden...........	15,527	15,421	15,325
*27909	Elizabeth City.....	18,683	18,631	18,756
27244	Elon...........	9,419	11,336	11,250
*28301	Fayetteville......	200,564	208,501	208,873
27540	Fuquay-Varina.....	17,937	34,152	40,810
27529	Garner..........	25,745	31,159	33,669
*28052	Gastonia........	71,741	80,411	82,653
27530	Goldsboro........	36,437	33,657	33,215
27253	Graham.........	14,153	17,157	17,856
*27401	Greensboro.......	269,666	299,035	301,115
*27834	Greenville.......	84,554	87,521	89,233
28075	Harrisburg.......	11,526	18,967	19,822
*28532	Havelock........	20,735	16,621	16,188
*27536	Henderson.......	15,368	15,060	14,822
*28792	Hendersonville.....	13,137	15,137	15,321
*28601	Hickory.........	40,010	43,490	44,084
*27260	High Point.......	104,371	114,059	115,067
27540	Holly Springs.....	24,661	41,239	45,945
28348	Hope Mills.......	15,176	17,808	17,824
28078	Huntersville......	46,773	61,376	63,035
28079	Indian Trail......	33,518	39,997	41,724
*28540	Jacksonville......	70,145	72,723	70,420
*28081	Kannapolis.......	42,625	53,114	55,448
*27284	Kernersville......	23,123	26,449	27,763
28086	Kings Mountain....	10,296	11,142	11,638
*28501	Kinston.........	21,677	19,900	19,365
27545	Knightdale.......	11,401	19,435	19,703
28117	Lake Norman of Iredell (c)......	7,411	11,395	—
*28352	Laurinburg.......	15,962	14,978	14,908
*28451	Leland..........	13,527	22,908	28,591
*28645	Lenoir..........	18,228	18,352	18,255
27023	Lewisville........	12,639	13,381	13,811
*27292	Lexington........	18,931	19,632	19,679
28092	Lincolnton.......	10,486	11,091	11,818
*28358	Lumberton........	21,542	19,025	18,841
28105	Matthews........	27,198	29,435	30,124
27302	Mebane.........	11,393	17,797	19,376
28227	Mint Hill........	22,722	26,450	27,143
*28110	Monroe.........	32,797	34,562	36,018
28115	Mooresville......	32,711	50,193	52,656
*28655	Morganton.......	16,918	17,474	17,602
27560	Morrisville.......	18,576	29,630	31,493
27030	Mount Airy.......	10,388	10,676	10,617
28120	Mount Holly......	13,656	17,703	18,170
28411	Murraysville (c)....	14,215	16,582	—
28409	Myrtle Grove (c)....	8,875	11,476	—
*28560	New Bern........	29,524	31,291	31,539
28658	Newton.........	12,968	13,148	13,337
28374	Pinehurst........	13,124	17,581	18,416
28134	Pineville........	7,479	10,602	10,886
28544	Piney Green (c)...	13,293	14,386	—
*27601	Raleigh.........	403,892	467,665	476,587

ZIP	Place	2010 population	2020 population	2022 estimate
*27320	Reidsville	14,520	14,583	14,566
*27870	Roanoke Rapids	15,754	15,229	14,856
*27801	Rocky Mount	57,477	54,341	54,013
27511	Rolesville	3,786	9,475	10,661
*28144	Salisbury	33,662	35,540	35,808
*27330	Sanford	28,094	30,261	31,224
*28150	Shelby	20,323	21,918	21,855
27577	Smithfield	10,966	11,292	12,129
*28387	Southern Pines	12,334	15,545	16,596
28326	Spout Springs (c)		11,040	
28390	Spring Lake	11,964	11,660	11,762
28104	Stallings	13,831	16,112	16,768
*28677	Statesville	24,532	28,419	29,681
27358	Summerfield	10,232	10,951	11,111
27886	Tarboro	11,415	10,721	10,668
*27360	Thomasville	26,757	27,183	27,399
*27587	Wake Forest	30,117	47,601	51,113
28173	Waxhaw	9,859	20,534	22,533
*28785	Waynesville	9,869	10,140	10,620
28104	Weddington	9,459	13,181	13,717
27591	Wendell	5,845	9,793	12,440
*28401	Wilmington	106,476	115,451	120,324
*27893	Wilson	49,167	47,851	47,606
*27101	Winston-Salem	229,621	249,545	251,350
28590	Winterville	9,269	10,462	10,724

North Dakota

Area code: 701 applies to the entire state

ZIP	Place	2010 population	2020 population	2022 estimate
*58501	Bismarck	61,272	73,622	74,445
*58601	Dickinson	17,787	25,679	24,979
*58102	Fargo	105,549	125,990	131,444
*58201	Grand Forks	52,838	59,166	58,692
*58401	Jamestown	15,427	15,849	15,754
58554	Mandan	18,331	24,206	24,486
*58701	Minot	40,888	48,377	47,759
58078	West Fargo	25,830	38,626	39,985
*58801	Williston	14,716	29,160	27,029

Ohio

Area codes: 216, 220/740, 234/330, 283/513, 326/937, 380/614, 419/567, 436 (Mar. 1, 2024)/440

ZIP	Place	2010 population	2020 population	2022 estimate
*44301	Akron	199,110	190,469	188,509
44601	Alliance	22,322	21,672	21,414
45102	Amelia (c)	4,801	12,575	—
44001	Amherst	12,021	12,681	12,892
44805	Ashland	20,362	19,225	19,015
*44004	Ashtabula	19,124	17,975	17,806
45701	Athens	23,832	23,849	20,820
44202	Aurora	15,548	17,239	17,528
44011	Avon	21,193	24,847	25,375
44012	Avon Lake	22,581	25,206	25,617
44203	Barberton	26,550	25,191	24,826
44140	Bay Village	15,651	16,163	15,880
44122	Beachwood	11,953	14,040	13,788
*45432	Beavercreek	45,193	46,549	46,942
44146	Bedford	13,074	13,149	12,838
*44146	Bedford Heights	10,751	11,020	10,776
43311	Bellefontaine	13,370	14,115	14,077
44017	Berea	19,093	18,545	18,395
43209	Bexley	13,057	13,928	12,887
*45242	Blue Ash	12,114	13,394	13,355
*43402	Bowling Green	30,028	30,808	29,647
44141	Brecksville	13,656	13,635	13,506
45211	Bridgetown (c)	14,407	14,731	
44147	Broadview Heights	19,400	19,936	19,635
44142	Brook Park	19,212	18,595	18,171
44144	Brooklyn	11,169	11,359	11,088
44212	Brunswick	34,255	35,426	35,196
44820	Bucyrus	12,362	11,684	11,538
*44702	Canton	73,007	70,872	69,671
*45822	Celina	10,400	10,935	10,881
*45458	Centerville	23,999	24,240	25,156
45601	Chillicothe	21,901	22,059	21,921
*45202	Cincinnati	296,943	309,317	309,513
43113	Circleville	13,314	13,927	14,284
45315	Clayton	13,209	13,310	13,235
*44102	Cleveland	396,815	372,624	361,607
*44118	Cleveland Heights	46,121	45,312	44,201
*43201	Columbus	787,033	905,748	907,971
44030	Conneaut	12,841	12,318	12,400
43812	Coshocton	11,216	11,050	11,016
*44221	Cuyahoga Falls	49,652	51,114	50,655
*45402	Dayton	141,527	137,644	135,944
43512	Defiance	16,494	17,066	16,990

ZIP	Place	2010 population	2020 population	2022 estimate
43015	Delaware	34,753	41,302	43,895
*45247	Dent (c)	10,497	12,301	—
44622	Dover	12,826	13,112	12,997
*43016	Dublin	41,751	49,328	48,998
*44112	East Cleveland	17,843	13,792	13,446
*44095	Eastlake	18,577	17,670	17,383
*44035	Elyria	54,533	52,656	52,908
45322	Englewood	13,465	13,463	13,301
*44117	Euclid	48,920	49,692	48,496
45324	Fairborn	32,352	34,510	34,977
*45011	Fairfield	42,510	44,907	44,456
44126	Fairview Park	16,826	17,291	16,885
*45840	Findlay	41,202	40,313	40,249
*45224	Finneytown (c)	12,741	12,399	—
45240	Forest Park	18,720	20,189	19,878
45255	Forestville (c)	10,532	10,615	—
44830	Fostoria	13,441	13,046	13,035
45005	Franklin	11,771	11,690	11,644
43420	Fremont	16,734	15,930	15,825
43230	Gahanna	33,248	35,726	35,127
44833	Galion	10,512	10,453	10,308
*44125	Garfield Heights	28,849	29,781	29,072
44232	Green	25,699	27,475	27,269
45331	Greenville	13,227	12,786	12,720
43123	Grove City	35,575	41,252	42,233
*45011	Hamilton	62,477	63,399	62,937
45030	Harrison	9,897	12,563	13,079
43056	Heath	10,310	10,412	10,621
43026	Hilliard	28,435	37,114	37,377
45424	Huber Heights	38,101	43,439	43,321
*44236	Hudson	22,262	23,110	22,917
45638	Ironton	11,129	10,571	10,290
44240	Kent	28,904	28,215	27,147
*45429	Kettering	56,163	57,862	57,027
44107	Lakewood	52,131	50,942	49,658
43130	Lancaster	38,780	40,552	41,174
45036	Lebanon	20,033	20,841	21,483
*45801	Lima	38,771	35,579	34,977
43140	London	9,904	10,279	10,442
*44052	Lorain	64,097	65,211	65,365
*45140	Loveland	12,081	13,307	13,131
44124	Lyndhurst	14,001	14,050	13,721
44056	Macedonia	11,188	12,168	12,148
*45211	Mack (c)	11,585	11,088	—
*44902	Mansfield	47,821	47,534	47,865
44137	Maple Heights	23,138	23,701	23,136
45750	Marietta	14,085	13,385	13,178
*43302	Marion	36,837	35,999	35,327
*43040	Marysville	22,094	25,571	27,157
*45036	Mason	30,712	34,792	35,520
*44646	Massillon	32,149	32,146	32,292
43537	Maumee	14,286	13,896	13,689
44124	Mayfield Heights	19,155	20,351	19,907
*44256	Medina	26,678	26,094	26,033
*44060	Mentor	47,159	47,450	47,044
*45343	Miamisburg	20,181	19,923	19,780
44130	Middleburg Heights	15,946	16,004	15,682
*45042	Middletown	48,694	50,987	51,229
*45247	Monfort Heights (c)	11,948	12,070	—
*45050	Monroe	12,442	15,412	15,489
45242	Montgomery	10,251	10,853	10,773
43050	Mount Vernon	16,990	16,956	16,679
43054	New Albany	7,724	10,825	11,043
*44216	New Franklin	14,227	13,877	13,762
44663	New Philadelphia	17,288	17,677	17,437
*43055	Newark	47,573	49,934	50,763
44446	Niles	19,266	18,443	18,286
*44720	North Canton	17,488	17,842	17,687
44070	North Olmsted	32,718	32,442	31,724
*44039	North Ridgeville	29,465	35,280	36,824
44133	North Royalton	30,444	31,322	30,793
*45251	Northbrook (c)	10,668	10,912	—
44203	Norton	12,085	11,673	11,516
44857	Norwalk	17,012	17,068	17,069
45212	Norwood	19,207	19,043	19,108
*43616	Oregon	20,291	19,950	19,760
45056	Oxford	21,371	23,035	19,645
44077	Painesville	19,563	20,312	20,642
*44129	Parma	81,601	81,146	79,358
44130	Parma Heights	20,718	20,863	20,389
*43062	Pataskala	14,962	17,886	18,229
*43551	Perrysburg	20,623	25,041	25,161
43147	Pickerington	18,291	23,094	24,524
45356	Piqua	20,522	20,354	20,607
*45662	Portsmouth	20,226	18,252	17,587
43065	Powell	11,500	14,163	14,390
*45502	Ravenna	11,724	11,323	11,251
*45215	Reading	10,385	10,600	10,397

ZIP	Place	2010 population	2020 population	2022 estimate
*43068	Reynoldsburg	35,893	41,076	41,117
44143	Richmond Heights . . .	10,546	10,801	10,564
45431	Riverside	25,201	24,474	24,355
44116	Rocky River	20,213	21,755	21,346
44460	Salem	12,303	11,915	11,729
*44870	Sandusky	25,793	25,095	24,526
44131	Seven Hills	11,804	11,720	11,557
*44120	Shaker Heights	28,448	29,439	28,723
45241	Sharonville	13,560	14,117	13,899
44878	Shiloh (c)	—	10,952	—
*45365	Sidney	21,229	20,589	20,290
44139	Solon	23,348	24,262	23,792
*44121	South Euclid	22,295	21,883	21,395
45066	Springboro	17,409	19,062	19,427
45246	Springdale	11,223	11,007	10,869
*45502	Springfield	60,608	58,662	58,106
*43952	Steubenville	18,659	18,161	18,030
44224	Stow	34,837	34,483	34,216
44241	Streetsboro	16,028	17,260	17,720
*44136	Strongsville	44,750	46,491	45,725
43560	Sylvania	18,965	19,011	19,051
44278	Tallmadge	17,537	18,394	18,275
44883	Tiffin	17,963	17,953	17,765
45371	Tipp City	9,689	10,274	10,424
*43604	Toledo	287,208	270,871	266,301
45067	Trenton	11,869	13,021	13,486
*45426	Trotwood	24,431	23,070	22,959
*45373	Troy	25,058	26,305	26,679
44087	Twinsburg	18,795	19,248	19,416
*44122	University Heights	13,539	13,914	13,319
*43221	Upper Arlington	33,771	36,800	36,010
43078	Urbana	11,793	11,115	11,124
45891	Van Wert	10,846	11,092	11,063
45377	Vandalia	15,246	15,209	14,999
*44089	Vermilion	10,594	10,659	10,694
*44281	Wadsworth	21,567	24,007	24,521
*44481	Warren	41,557	39,201	38,906
*44122	Warrensville Heights . .	13,542	13,789	13,457
43160	Washington Court House	14,192	14,401	14,399
*45449	West Carrollton	13,143	13,129	12,929
*43081	Westerville	36,120	39,190	38,466
44145	Westlake	32,729	34,228	33,907
*45239	White Oak (c)	19,167	19,541	—
43213	Whitehall	18,062	20,127	19,911
44092	Wickliffe	12,750	12,652	12,610
*44094	Willoughby	22,268	23,959	24,130
44095	Willowick	14,171	14,204	14,139
45177	Wilmington	12,520	12,664	12,656
44691	Wooster	26,119	27,232	27,031
43085	Worthington	13,575	14,786	14,629
45385	Xenia	25,719	25,441	25,612
*44503	Youngstown	66,982	60,068	59,144
*43701	Zanesville	25,487	24,765	24,600

Oklahoma
Area codes: 405/572, 539/918, 580

ZIP	Place	2010 population	2020 population	2022 estimate
*74820	Ada	16,810	16,481	16,542
*73521	Altus	19,813	18,729	18,556
*73401	Ardmore	24,283	24,725	24,869
*74003	Bartlesville	35,750	37,290	37,795
73008	Bethany	19,051	20,831	20,447
74008	Bixby	20,884	28,609	29,800
*74012	Broken Arrow	98,850	113,540	117,911
*73018	Chickasha	16,036	16,051	16,549
73020	Choctaw	11,146	12,182	12,218
*74017	Claremore	18,581	19,580	20,174
74429	Coweta	9,943	9,654	10,456
*73115	Del City	21,332	21,822	21,388
73533	Duncan	23,431	22,692	23,045
*74701	Durant	15,856	18,589	19,628
*73034	Edmond	81,405	94,428	96,286
73036	El Reno	16,749	16,989	18,560
*73644	Elk City	11,693	11,561	11,290
*73701	Enid	49,379	51,308	50,499
74033	Glenpool	10,808	13,691	14,211
73044	Guthrie	10,191	10,749	11,191
73942	Guymon	11,442	12,965	12,378
74037	Jenks	16,924	25,949	27,141
*73501	Lawton	96,867	90,381	91,542
*74501	McAlester	18,383	18,171	18,108
*74354	Miami	13,570	12,969	12,913
*73110	Midwest City	54,371	58,409	57,950
*73160	Moore	55,081	62,793	63,223
*74401	Muskogee	39,223	36,878	36,738
73064	Mustang	17,395	19,879	22,232

ZIP	Place	2010 population	2020 population	2022 estimate
73065	Newcastle	7,685	10,984	13,055
*73069	Norman	110,925	128,026	129,627
*73102	Oklahoma City	579,999	681,054	694,800
74447	Okmulgee	12,321	11,322	11,402
74055	Owasso	28,915	38,240	39,328
*74601	Ponca City	25,387	24,424	24,340
74063	Sand Springs	18,906	19,874	20,031
74066	Sapulpa	20,544	21,929	22,580
*74801	Shawnee	29,857	31,377	31,720
*74074	Stillwater	45,688	48,394	49,160
*74464	Tahlequah	15,753	16,209	16,828
*74103	Tulsa	391,906	413,066	411,867
*73122	Warr Acres	10,043	10,452	10,371
73096	Weatherford	10,833	12,076	11,859
*73801	Woodward	12,051	12,133	11,789
*73099	Yukon	22,709	23,630	25,556

Oregon
Area codes: 458/541, 503/971

ZIP	Place	2010 population	2020 population	2022 estimate
*97321	Albany	50,158	56,472	56,891
*97003	Aloha (c)	49,425	53,828	—
*97603	Altamont (c)	19,257	20,233	—
97520	Ashland	20,078	21,360	21,285
97103	Astoria	9,477	10,181	10,182
97814	Baker City	9,828	10,099	10,247
*97005	Beaverton	89,803	97,494	97,053
*97701	Bend	76,639	99,178	103,254
97229	Bethany (c)	20,646	31,350	—
97013	Canby	15,829	18,171	18,074
*97229	Cedar Mill (c)	14,546	17,259	—
97502	Central Point	17,169	18,997	19,222
97420	Coos Bay	15,967	15,985	15,840
*97113	Cornelius	11,869	12,694	14,431
*97330	Corvallis	54,462	59,922	60,956
97424	Cottage Grove	9,686	10,574	10,713
97338	Dallas	14,583	16,854	17,488
*97009	Damascus (c)	10,539	11,050	—
*97401	Eugene	156,185	176,654	177,923
97024	Fairview	8,920	10,424	10,768
97116	Forest Grove	21,083	26,225	26,784
*97301	Four Corners (c)	15,947	16,740	—
97027	Gladstone	11,497	12,017	11,951
*97526	Grants Pass	34,533	39,189	39,079
*97030	Gresham	105,594	114,247	111,621
*97015	Happy Valley	13,903	23,733	26,456
97305	Hayesville (c)	19,936	21,891	—
97838	Hermiston	16,745	19,354	19,423
*97123	Hillsboro	91,611	106,447	107,299
97351	Independence	8,590	9,828	10,255
*97303	Keizer	36,478	39,376	38,704
*97601	Klamath Falls	20,840	21,813	21,977
97850	La Grande	13,082	13,026	13,106
*97034	Lake Oswego	36,619	40,731	40,108
97355	Lebanon	15,518	18,447	19,415
97128	McMinnville	32,187	34,319	34,530
*97501	Medford	74,907	85,824	85,556
*97222	Milwaukie	20,291	21,119	21,375
97038	Molalla	8,108	10,228	10,171
97361	Monmouth	9,534	11,110	11,274
97132	Newberg	22,068	25,138	25,777
*97365	Newport	9,989	10,256	10,412
97459	North Bend	9,695	10,317	10,218
*97222	Oak Grove (c)	16,629	17,290	—
97006	Oak Hills (c)	11,333	11,903	—
97267	Oatfield (c)	13,415	13,977	—
97914	Ontario	11,366	11,645	11,732
97045	Oregon City	31,859	37,572	37,327
97801	Pendleton	16,612	17,107	17,070
*97201	Portland	583,776	652,503	635,067
97754	Prineville	9,253	10,736	11,497
97756	Redmond	26,215	33,274	36,409
*97470	Roseburg	21,181	23,683	23,853
97051	Saint Helens	12,883	13,817	14,369
*97301	Salem	154,637	175,535	177,487
97055	Sandy	9,570	12,612	12,953
97404	Santa Clara (c)	—	11,239	—
97140	Sherwood	18,194	20,450	20,030
97381	Silverton	9,222	10,484	10,443
*97477	Springfield	59,403	61,851	61,400
97386	Sweet Home	8,925	9,828	10,090
97058	The Dalles	13,620	16,010	15,932
*97223	Tigard	48,035	54,539	55,762
97060	Troutdale	15,962	16,300	15,686
97062	Tualatin	26,054	27,942	27,797
97068	West Linn	25,109	27,373	26,931

ZIP	Place	2010 population	2020 population	2022 estimate
97070	Wilsonville.........	19,509	26,664	26,597
97071	Woodburn..........	24,080	26,013	27,290

Pennsylvania

Area codes: 215/267/445, 223/717, 272/570, 412/724/878, 484/610/835, 582/814

ZIP	Place	2010 population	2020 population	2022 estimate
*18101	Allentown	118,032	125,845	125,094
15101	Allison Park (c)	21,552	21,864	—
*16601	Altoona............	46,320	43,963	43,071
19003	Ardmore (c)........	12,455	13,566	—
15234	Baldwin...........	19,767	21,510	20,956
18603	Berwick...........	10,477	10,327	10,270
15102	Bethel Park........	32,313	33,577	32,782
*18016	Bethlehem	74,982	75,781	77,617
17815	Bloomsburg	14,855	12,711	12,730
19008	Broomall (c).......	10,789	11,718	—
*16001	Butler............	13,757	13,502	13,176
*17013	Carlisle	18,682	20,118	22,203
15108	Carnot-Moon (c)....	11,372	13,151	—
*17201	Chambersburg	20,268	21,903	22,172
*19013	Chester...........	33,972	32,605	33,449
19320	Coatesville	13,100	13,350	13,320
*17109	Colonial Park (c)...	13,229	16,243	—
17512	Columbia	10,400	10,207	10,126
19021	Croydon (c)........	9,950	10,014	—
19023	Darby............	10,687	10,715	10,608
19026	Drexel Hill (c).....	28,043	29,191	—
*18512	Dunmore..........	14,057	14,042	14,118
*18042	Easton	26,800	28,127	30,341
17022	Elizabethtown	11,545	11,639	11,943
*18049	Emmaus	11,211	11,652	11,672
17522	Ephrata	13,394	13,794	13,693
*16501	Erie..............	101,786	94,831	93,511
15237	Franklin Park......	13,470	15,479	15,165
18052	Fullerton (c)	14,925	16,588	—
*15601	Greensburg........	14,892	14,976	14,715
*17331	Hanover	15,289	16,429	16,548
*17101	Harrisburg........	49,528	50,099	50,183
*18201	Hazleton..........	25,340	29,963	29,993
16148	Hermitage	16,220	16,230	16,077
17033	Hershey (c)	14,257	13,858	—
19044	Horsham (c)	14,842	15,193	—
*15701	Indiana	13,975	14,044	14,205
15025	Jefferson Hills	10,619	12,424	12,301
*15901	Johnstown........	20,978	18,411	18,091
*19406	King of Prussia (c) ...	19,936	24,695	—
18704	Kingston	13,182	13,349	13,323
*17601	Lancaster	59,322	58,039	57,453
19446	Lansdale	16,269	18,773	18,935
19050	Lansdowne	10,620	11,107	11,070
*17042	Lebanon	25,477	26,814	26,473
*19055	Levittown (c)......	52,983	52,699	—
15068	Lower Burrell......	11,761	11,758	11,585
*15132	McKeesport.......	19,731	17,727	17,334
*16335	Meadville	13,388	13,050	12,680
*15146	Monroeville	28,386	28,640	28,259
18936	Montgomeryville (c) .	12,624	12,998	—
18707	Mountain Top (c)...	10,982	11,489	—
15120	Munhall	11,406	10,774	10,500
*15668	Murrysville	20,079	21,006	20,724
18634	Nanticoke	10,465	10,628	10,607
*16101	New Castle	23,273	21,926	21,532
15068	New Kensington	13,116	12,170	11,971
*19401	Norristown	34,324	35,748	35,795
18067	Northampton	9,926	10,395	10,323
*19107	Philadelphia	1,526,006	1,603,797	1,567,258
*19460	Phoenixville	16,440	18,602	19,354
*15201	Pittsburgh	305,704	302,971	302,898
15239	Plum.............	27,126	27,144	26,662
*19464	Pottstown	22,377	23,433	23,377
17901	Pottsville	14,324	13,346	13,338
17109	Progress (c)	9,765	11,168	—
*19601	Reading	88,082	95,112	94,858
15857	Saint Marys.......	13,070	12,738	12,908
*18503	Scranton	76,089	76,328	75,848
*16146	Sharon	14,038	13,147	12,952
17404	Shiloh (c)	11,218	11,524	—
*16801	State College	42,034	40,501	40,745
15301	Washington	13,663	13,176	13,483
17268	Waynesboro	10,568	10,951	11,027
17315	Weigelstown (c)....	12,875	15,136	—
*19380	West Chester	18,461	18,671	19,531
*15122	West Mifflin	20,313	19,589	19,140
18052	Whitehall	13,944	15,064	14,785
*18701	Wilkes-Barre	41,498	44,328	44,261
15221	Wilkinsburg	15,930	14,349	13,981

ZIP	Place	2010 population	2020 population	2022 estimate
*17701	Williamsport	29,381	27,754	27,403
19090	Willow Grove (c)	15,726	13,730	—
19610	Wyomissing	10,461	11,114	11,127
19050	Yeadon	11,443	12,054	12,140
*17401	York..............	43,718	44,800	44,845

Rhode Island

Area code: 401 applies to the entire state. See introductory note.

ZIP	Place	2010 population	2020 population	2022 estimate
02806	Barrington........	16,310	17,153	17,113
02809	Bristol	22,954	22,493	22,128
*02830	Burrillville	15,955	16,158	16,300
02863	Central Falls	19,376	22,583	22,490
*02816	Coventry	35,014	35,688	35,898
*02910	Cranston	80,387	82,934	82,421
02864	Cumberland	33,506	36,405	36,382
02818	East Greenwich ...	13,146	14,312	14,573
02914	East Providence ...	47,037	47,139	46,691
*02814	Glocester	9,746	9,974	10,110
02919	Johnston	28,769	29,568	29,506
*02865	Lincoln	21,105	22,529	22,605
02842	Middletown.......	16,150	17,075	16,815
*02882	Narragansett......	15,868	14,532	14,504
*02840	Newport	24,672	25,163	24,684
02842	Newport East (c)...	11,769	12,337	—
02852	North Kingstown...	26,486	27,732	27,802
*02904	North Providence	32,078	34,114	33,871
02896	North Smithfield ...	11,967	12,588	12,477
*02860	Pawtucket	71,148	75,604	75,066
02871	Portsmouth	17,389	17,871	17,659
*02903	Providence	178,042	190,934	189,563
*02857	Scituate	10,329	10,384	10,409
*02917	Smithfield	21,430	22,118	21,987
*02879	South Kingstown ...	30,639	31,931	32,056
02878	Tiverton..........	15,780	16,359	16,196
02864	Valley Falls (c)	11,547	12,094	—
02885	Warren	10,611	11,147	11,119
*02886	Warwick	82,672	82,823	83,016
02893	West Warwick	29,191	31,012	31,115
*02891	Westerly	22,787	23,359	23,298
02891	Westerly (c)	17,936	18,423	—
02895	Woonsocket	41,186	43,240	42,942

South Carolina

Area codes: 605, 803/839, 821 (Aug. 19, 2024)/864, 843/854

ZIP	Place	2010 population	2020 population	2022 estimate
*29801	Aiken.............	29,524	32,025	32,463
*29621	Anderson	26,686	28,106	29,771
*29902	Beaufort	12,361	13,607	13,722
29611	Berea (c).........	14,295	15,578	—
*29910	Bluffton	12,530	27,716	34,493
29316	Boiling Springs (c) ..	8,219	10,405	—
29579	Carolina Forest (c) ...	—	23,342	—
*29033	Cayce	12,528	13,781	13,649
*29401	Charleston	120,083	150,227	153,672
*29631	Clemson	13,905	17,681	17,843
*29201	Columbia	129,272	136,632	139,698
29526	Conway	17,103	24,489	27,346
29223	Dentsville (c)......	14,062	14,431	—
*29640	Easley...........	19,993	22,921	24,463
29681	Five Forks (c)	14,140	17,737	—
*29501	Florence	37,056	39,899	40,072
29206	Forest Acres	10,361	10,617	10,403
*29715	Fort Mill.........	10,811	24,521	30,940
29644	Fountain Inn	7,799	10,416	11,758
*29341	Gaffney	12,414	12,764	12,454
29605	Gantt (c)	14,229	15,006	—
29576	Garden City (c)....	9,209	10,235	—
29445	Goose Creek	35,938	45,946	47,618
*29601	Greenville	58,409	70,720	72,310
*29646	Greenwood	23,222	22,545	22,454
*29650	Greer	25,515	35,308	42,090
29410	Hanahan	17,997	20,325	21,462
29927	Hardeeville	2,952	7,473	10,283
*29928	Hilton Head Island ...	37,099	37,661	38,069
29063	Irmo	11,097	11,569	11,942
29412	James Island[1]	—	11,621	11,762
*29456	Ladson (c)........	13,790	15,550	—
29710	Lake Wylie (c).....	8,841	13,655	—
*29072	Lexington	17,870	23,568	24,626
29566	Little River (c)	8,960	11,711	—
29662	Mauldin	22,889	24,724	26,918
*29461	Moncks Corner	7,885	13,297	15,262
*29464	Mount Pleasant......	67,843	90,801	94,545
*29572	Myrtle Beach	27,109	35,682	38,417

ZIP	Place	2010 population	2020 population	2022 estimate
29108	Newberry	10,277	10,691	10,726
*29841	North Augusta.	21,348	24,379	25,258
*29410	North Charleston	97,471	114,852	118,608
*29582	North Myrtle Beach . .	13,752	18,790	19,836
29073	Oak Grove (c)	10,291	12,899	—
*29115	Orangeburg.	13,964	13,240	13,349
29611	Parker (c)	11,431	13,407	—
29935	Port Royal	10,678	14,220	15,632
*29611	Powdersville (c).	7,618	10,025	—
29072	Red Bank (c).	9,617	10,924	—
*29020	Red Hill (c)	13,223	15,906	—
*29730	Rock Hill	66,154	74,372	75,349
29407	Saint Andrews (c) . . .	20,493	20,675	—
29210	Seven Oaks (c).	15,144	14,652	—
*29681	Simpsonville	18,238	23,354	26,748
29588	Socastee (c)	19,952	22,213	—
*29306	Spartanburg	37,013	38,732	38,584
*29483	Summerville	43,392	50,915	51,617
*29150	Sumter	40,524	43,463	42,757
*29687	Taylors (c).	21,617	23,222	—
29708	Tega Cay.	7,620	12,832	13,689
*29607	Wade Hampton (c) . . .	20,622	21,482	—
*29169	West Columbia	14,988	17,416	17,618

(1) Incorporated after 2010 Census.

South Dakota
Area code: 605 applies to the entire state

ZIP	Place	2010 population	2020 population	2022 estimate
*57401	Aberdeen	26,091	28,495	28,210
57719	Box Elder	7,800	11,746	12,581
57005	Brandon	8,785	11,048	11,110
*57006	Brookings	22,056	23,377	23,993
*57350	Huron	12,592	14,263	14,462
57301	Mitchell	15,254	15,660	15,659
57501	Pierre	13,646	14,091	13,969
*57701	Rapid City.	67,956	74,703	78,824
*57103	Sioux Falls	153,888	192,517	202,078
*57783	Spearfish	10,494	12,193	12,914
57069	Vermillion	10,571	11,695	11,915
57201	Watertown.	21,482	22,655	23,019
57078	Yankton	14,454	15,411	15,534

Tennessee
Area codes: 423, 615/629, 731, 865, 901, 931

ZIP	Place	2010 population	2020 population	2022 estimate
37701	Alcoa.	8,449	10,978	11,803
38002	Arlington	11,517	14,549	14,396
*37303	Athens	13,458	14,084	14,371
38004	Atoka	8,387	10,008	10,464
*38133	Bartlett	54,613	57,786	56,798
*37027	Brentwood	37,060	45,373	45,136
*37620	Bristol	26,702	27,147	27,705
*37402	Chattanooga	167,674	181,099	184,086
*37040	Clarksville	132,929	166,722	176,974
*37311	Cleveland	41,285	47,356	48,557
*37716	Clinton	9,841	10,056	10,245
37315	Collegedale	8,282	11,109	11,255
*38017	Collierville	43,965	51,324	51,594
*38401	Columbia	34,681	41,690	45,792
*38501	Cookeville	30,435	34,842	35,988
38555	Crossville	10,795	12,071	12,470
*37055	Dickson.	14,538	16,058	16,343
*38024	Dyersburg	17,145	16,164	15,957
37412	East Ridge	20,979	22,167	21,936
*37643	Elizabethton	14,176	14,546	14,244
*37922	Farragut	20,676	23,506	24,817
*37064	Franklin	62,487	83,454	86,895
37066	Gallatin	30,278	44,431	48,194
*38138	Germantown	38,844	41,333	40,816
*37072	Goodlettsville	15,921	17,789	17,183
*37743	Greeneville	15,062	15,479	15,614
38040	Halls (c)	—	10,341	—
37074	Hartsville/Trousdale Co.	7,870	11,615	12,111
*37075	Hendersonville	51,372	61,753	62,896
*38301	Jackson	65,211	68,205	68,380
*37601	Johnson City.	63,152	71,046	72,514
*37660	Kingsport	48,205	55,442	56,150
*37902	Knoxville	178,874	190,740	195,889
*37086	La Vergne	32,588	38,719	39,281
38002	Lakeland	12,430	13,904	13,772
38464	Lawrenceburg	10,428	11,633	11,825
*37087	Lebanon	26,190	38,431	44,166
*37771	Lenoir City	8,642	10,117	11,292
37091	Lewisburg	11,100	12,288	12,786
*37355	Manchester.	10,102	12,212	13,020
*38237	Martin	11,473	10,825	10,894

ZIP	Place	2010 population	2020 population	2022 estimate
*37801	Maryville	27,465	31,907	32,716
*37110	McMinnville	13,605	13,788	13,787
*38103	Memphis	646,889	633,104	621,056
37343	Middle Valley (c)	12,684	11,695	—
*38053	Millington	10,176	10,582	10,442
*37813	Morristown	29,137	30,431	31,425
*37122	Mount Juliet	23,671	39,289	42,548
*37130	Murfreesboro	108,755	152,769	162,398
*37201	Nashville-Davidson (bal.)	601,222	689,447	683,622
37135	Nolensville	5,861	13,829	16,872
*37830	Oak Ridge.	29,330	31,402	32,614
*38060	Oakland	6,623	8,936	10,028
38242	Paris	10,156	10,316	10,339
37148	Portland	11,480	13,156	13,482
37849	Powell (c)	—	13,802	—
37415	Red Bank	11,651	11,899	11,959
*37862	Sevierville	14,807	17,889	17,987
37865	Seymour (c)	10,919	14,705	—
*37160	Shelbyville	20,335	23,557	24,452
37167	Smyrna	39,974	53,070	56,516
*37379	Soddy-Daisy	12,714	13,070	13,159
37714	Spring Hill	29,036	50,005	55,800
37172	Springfield.	16,440	18,782	19,221
*37388	Tullahoma	18,655	20,339	20,830
*38261	Union City.	10,895	11,170	10,985
37188	White House	10,255	12,982	14,516

Texas
Area codes: 210/726, 214/469/945/972, 254, 281/346/713/832, 325, 361, 409, 430/903, 432, 512/737, 682/817, 806, 830, 915, 936, 940, 956, 979

ZIP	Place	2010 population	2020 population	2022 estimate
*79601	Abilene	117,063	125,182	127,385
75001	Addison.	13,056	16,661	17,310
78516	Alamo	18,353	19,493	20,305
77039	Aldine (c)	15,869	15,999	—
*78332	Alice	19,104	17,891	17,697
*75002	Allen	84,246	104,627	111,551
78573	Alton	12,341	18,198	19,673
*77511	Alvin	24,236	27,098	28,205
*79101	Amarillo	190,695	200,393	201,291
79714	Andrews	11,088	13,487	13,276
*77515	Angleton	18,862	19,429	19,610
75409	Anna	8,249	16,896	23,558
*76001	Arlington	365,438	394,266	394,602
77346	Atascocita (c)	65,844	88,174	—
*75751	Athens	12,710	12,857	13,007
*78701	Austin	790,390	961,855	974,447
*76020	Azle	10,947	13,369	13,956
*75180	Balch Springs	23,728	27,685	26,947
78602	Bastrop	7,218	9,688	11,189
*77414	Bay City	17,614	18,061	17,505
*77520	Baytown	71,802	83,701	84,324
*77701	Beaumont	118,296	115,282	112,089
*76021	Bedford	46,979	49,928	48,724
*78102	Beeville	12,863	13,669	13,332
77401	Bellaire	16,855	17,202	16,991
*76704	Bellmead	9,901	10,494	10,580
76513	Belton	18,216	23,054	24,327
*76126	Benbrook	21,234	24,520	24,437
*79720	Big Spring	27,282	26,144	25,318
*78006	Boerne	10,471	17,850	20,707
75418	Bonham	10,127	10,408	10,746
*79007	Borger.	13,251	12,551	12,249
*77833	Brenham	15,716	17,369	18,469
*78520	Brownsville	175,023	186,738	189,382
*76801	Brownwood	19,288	18,862	18,709
78717	Brushy Creek (c).	21,764	22,519	—
*77801	Bryan	76,201	83,980	87,792
78610	Buda	7,295	15,108	16,086
76354	Burkburnett	10,811	10,939	11,102
*76028	Burleson.	36,690	47,641	53,381
*79015	Canyon	13,303	14,836	15,771
78130	Canyon Lake (c)	21,262	31,124	—
*75006	Carrollton	119,097	133,434	133,820
*75104	Cedar Hill	45,028	49,148	48,341
*78613	Cedar Park	48,937	77,595	77,642
75009	Celina	6,028	16,739	34,229
77530	Channelview (c)	38,289	45,688	—
78108	Cibolo	15,349	32,276	34,814
*77494	Cinco Ranch (c)	18,274	16,899	—
*76031	Cleburne	29,337	31,352	33,826
77015	Cloverleaf (c)	22,942	24,100	—
77531	Clute.	11,211	10,604	10,634
*77840	College Station	93,857	120,511	124,319
76034	Colleyville	22,807	26,057	25,850
*77301	Conroe	56,207	89,956	101,405
78109	Converse	18,198	27,466	29,603
*75019	Coppell	38,659	42,983	41,926

ZIP	Place	2010 population	2020 population	2022 estimate
76522	Copperas Cove	32,032	36,670	37,964
*76208	Corinth	19,935	22,634	22,875
*78401	Corpus Christi	305,215	317,863	316,239
*75110	Corsicana	23,770	25,109	25,566
76036	Crowley	12,838	18,070	19,478
*75201	Dallas	1,197,816	1,304,379	1,299,544
77536	Deer Park	32,010	34,495	33,468
*78840	Del Rio	35,591	34,673	34,543
75020	Denison	22,682	24,479	26,328
*76201	Denton	113,383	139,869	150,353
75115	DeSoto	49,047	56,145	55,968
77539	Dickinson	18,680	20,847	21,738
78537	Donna	15,798	16,797	16,774
79029	Dumas	14,691	14,501	14,166
*75116	Duncanville	38,524	40,706	39,413
*78852	Eagle Pass	26,248	28,130	28,255
*78539	Edinburg	77,100	100,243	104,294
77437	El Campo	11,602	12,350	12,179
*79901	El Paso	649,121	678,815	677,456
78621	Elgin	8,135	9,784	11,359
*75119	Ennis	18,513	20,159	22,890
76039	Euless	51,277	61,032	60,169
*78015	Fair Oaks Ranch	5,986	9,833	11,104
75069	Fairview	7,248	10,372	10,851
*75234	Farmers Branch	28,616	35,991	36,286
*75087	Fate	6,357	17,958	22,811
*75022	Flower Mound	64,669	75,956	78,486
*76119	Forest Hill	12,355	13,955	13,701
75126	Forney	14,661	23,455	32,108
*79906	Fort Bliss (c)	8,591	11,260	—
76544	Fort Hood (c)	29,589	28,295	—
*76102	Fort Worth	741,206	918,915	956,709
*77498	Four Corners (c)	12,382	12,103	—
78624	Fredericksburg	10,530	10,875	11,257
*77541	Freeport	12,049	10,696	10,546
77545	Fresno (c)	19,069	24,486	—
*77546	Friendswood	35,805	41,213	40,833
*75034	Frisco	116,989	200,509	219,587
*77441	Fulshear	1,134	16,856	34,264
*76240	Gainesville	16,002	17,394	17,912
77547	Galena Park	10,887	10,740	10,370
*77550	Galveston	47,743	53,695	53,089
*75040	Garland	226,876	246,018	240,854
*76528	Gatesville	15,751	16,135	16,198
*78626	Georgetown	47,400	67,176	86,507
75154	Glenn Heights	11,278	15,819	18,299
*76048	Granbury	7,978	10,958	12,391
*75051	Grand Prairie	175,396	196,100	201,843
*76051	Grapevine	46,334	50,631	51,226
*75401	Greenville	25,557	28,164	31,060
77619	Groves	16,144	17,335	16,798
*76117	Haltom City	42,409	46,073	45,525
76548	Harker Heights	26,700	33,097	34,102
*78550	Harlingen	64,849	71,829	71,678
*75032	Heath	6,921	9,769	10,733
*75652	Henderson	13,712	13,271	13,385
79045	Hereford	15,370	14,972	14,765
76643	Hewitt	13,549	16,026	16,431
78557	Hidalgo	11,198	13,964	14,437
75077	Highland Village	15,056	15,899	16,105
*79927	Horizon City	16,735	22,489	23,314
78725	Hornsby Bend (c)	6,791	12,168	—
*77002	Houston	2,099,451	2,304,580	2,302,878
*77338	Humble	15,133	16,795	16,336
*77340	Huntsville	38,548	45,941	47,351
*76053	Hurst	37,337	40,413	39,634
78634	Hutto	14,698	27,577	36,655
78362	Ingleside	9,387	9,519	10,106
77583	Iowa Colony	1,170	8,154	13,031
*75060	Irving	216,290	256,684	254,715
75766	Jacksonville	14,544	13,997	14,215
*77449	Katy	14,102	21,894	25,253
*76248	Keller	39,627	45,776	45,252
*78028	Kerrville	22,347	24,278	24,752
*75662	Kilgore	12,975	13,376	13,476
*76541	Killeen	127,921	153,095	159,172
*78363	Kingsville	26,213	25,402	24,833
*78640	Kyle	28,016	45,697	57,470
*78572	La Homa (c)	11,985	11,267	—
77568	La Marque	14,509	18,030	19,147
*77571	La Porte	33,800	35,124	36,569
77566	Lake Jackson	26,849	28,177	27,668
*78734	Lakeway	11,391	19,189	19,429
*75146	Lancaster	36,361	41,275	40,449
76226	Lantana (c)	6,874	10,785	—
*78040	Laredo	236,091	255,205	256,187
*77573	League City	83,560	114,392	115,418
*78641	Leander	26,521	59,202	74,375
*78238	Leon Valley	10,151	11,542	11,429
*79336	Levelland	13,542	12,652	12,337

ZIP	Place	2010 population	2020 population	2022 estimate
*75057	Lewisville	95,290	111,822	131,215
75068	Little Elm	25,898	46,453	55,357
*78233	Live Oak	13,131	15,781	15,953
78644	Lockhart	12,698	14,379	14,985
*75601	Longview	80,455	81,638	82,531
*79401	Lubbock	229,573	257,141	263,930
*75901	Lufkin	35,067	34,143	34,152
77657	Lumberton	11,943	13,554	14,045
78653	Manor	5,037	13,652	19,009
76063	Mansfield	56,368	72,602	76,724
77578	Manvel	5,179	9,992	14,803
*75670	Marshall	23,523	23,392	23,641
*78501	McAllen	129,877	142,210	144,579
*75070	McKinney	131,117	195,308	207,507
75454	Melissa	4,695	13,901	19,357
78570	Mercedes	15,570	16,258	16,717
*75149	Mesquite	139,824	150,108	147,899
*79701	Midland	111,147	132,524	134,444
76065	Midlothian	18,037	35,125	38,635
76067	Mineral Wells	16,788	14,820	15,173
*78572	Mission	77,058	85,778	86,635
77083	Mission Bend (c)	36,501	36,914	—
*77489	Missouri City	67,358	74,259	76,500
75455	Mount Pleasant	15,564	16,047	16,015
*75094	Murphy	17,708	21,013	21,175
75961	Nacogdoches	32,996	32,147	31,990
77627	Nederland	17,547	18,856	18,189
*78130	New Braunfels	57,740	90,403	104,707
*76117	North Richland Hills	63,343	69,917	70,663
*79761	Odessa	99,940	114,428	112,906
*77630	Orange	18,595	19,324	19,081
*75801	Palestine	18,712	18,544	18,981
*78572	Palmview	5,460	15,830	15,863
*79065	Pampa	17,994	16,867	16,612
*75460	Paris	25,171	24,476	24,695
*77502	Pasadena	149,043	151,950	147,662
*77581	Pearland	91,252	125,828	126,949
*77406	Pecan Grove (c)	15,963	22,782	—
79772	Pecos	8,780	12,916	11,122
*78660	Pflugerville	46,936	65,191	65,556
78577	Pharr	70,400	79,715	80,179
*79072	Plainview	22,194	20,187	19,599
*75074	Plano	259,841	285,494	289,547
78064	Pleasanton	8,934	10,648	11,004
*77640	Port Arthur	53,818	56,039	55,579
77979	Port Lavaca	12,248	11,557	11,262
77651	Port Neches	13,040	13,692	13,614
78374	Portland	15,099	20,383	20,350
75407	Princeton	6,807	17,027	22,900
75078	Prosper	9,423	30,174	37,746
*78580	Raymondville	11,284	10,236	10,167
75154	Red Oak	10,769	14,222	17,396
*76028	Rendon (c)	12,552	13,533	—
*75080	Richardson	99,223	119,469	118,802
*77469	Richmond	11,679	11,627	12,520
78582	Rio Grande City	13,834	15,317	15,269
76706	Robinson	10,509	12,443	12,923
78380	Robstown	11,487	10,143	10,177
*78382	Rockport	8,766	10,070	10,713
75087	Rockwall	37,490	47,251	51,461
78584	Roma	9,765	11,561	11,520
*77471	Rosenberg	30,618	38,282	40,739
*78681	Round Rock	99,887	119,468	126,697
*75088	Rowlett	56,199	62,535	65,113
75189	Royse City	9,349	13,508	19,782
75048	Sachse	20,329	27,103	30,610
*76179	Saginaw	19,806	23,890	25,319
*76901	San Angelo	93,200	99,893	99,112
*78201	San Antonio	1,327,407	1,434,625	1,472,909
78586	San Benito	24,250	24,881	24,665
79849	San Elizario	13,603	10,116	10,138
78589	San Juan	33,856	35,294	35,782
*78666	San Marcos	44,894	67,553	70,301
*77510	Santa Fe	12,222	12,735	12,843
78006	Scenic Oaks (c)	4,957	10,458	—
*78154	Schertz	31,465	42,002	43,010
77586	Seabrook	11,952	13,618	13,708
75159	Seagoville	14,835	18,446	19,491
*78155	Seguin	25,175	29,433	33,408
78154	Selma	5,540	10,952	11,721
*75090	Sherman	38,521	43,645	45,264
77459	Sienna (c)		20,204	
*79549	Snyder	11,202	11,438	11,230
*79927	Socorro	32,013	34,306	37,772
77587	South Houston	16,983	16,153	15,860
76092	Southlake	26,575	31,265	31,102
*77373	Spring (c)	54,298	62,559	—
*77477	Stafford	17,693	17,666	17,427
78732	Steiner Ranch (c)		16,713	
*76401	Stephenville	17,123	20,897	21,641

ZIP	Place	2010 population	2020 population	2022 estimate
*75478	Sugar Land........	78,817	111,026	109,414
*75482	Sulphur Springs	15,449	15,941	16,408
79556	Sweetwater.........	10,906	10,622	10,408
76574	Taylor.............	15,191	16,267	16,975
*76501	Temple	66,102	82,073	89,458
75160	Terrell	15,816	17,465	20,050
*75501	Texarkana	36,411	36,193	35,778
*77510	Texas City	45,099	51,898	55,667
75056	The Colony	36,328	44,534	45,367
*77381	The Woodlands (c) ...	93,847	114,436	—
78260	Timberwood Park (c)	13,447	35,217	—
*77575	Tomball	10,753	12,341	13,585
76262	Trophy Club.........	8,024	13,688	13,758
*75702	Tyler	96,900	105,995	109,286
*78148	Universal City	18,530	19,720	19,990
75205	University Park	23,068	25,278	25,032
*78801	Uvalde	15,751	15,217	15,430
*77901	Victoria	62,592	65,534	65,372
*76701	Waco	124,805	138,486	143,984
*76148	Watauga	23,497	23,650	23,050
*75165	Waxahachie	29,621	41,140	45,476
*76086	Weatherford	25,250	30,854	36,251
77598	Webster	10,400	12,499	12,177
78728	Wells Branch (c)	12,120	14,000	—
*78596	Weslaco	35,670	40,160	42,231
79764	West Odessa (c).....	22,707	33,340	—
77005	West University Place	14,787	14,955	14,792
76108	White Settlement	16,116	18,269	18,046
*76301	Wichita Falls	104,553	102,316	102,664
75098	Wylie	41,427	57,526	60,943

Utah
Area codes: 385/801 apply to the entire state

ZIP	Place	2010 population	2020 population	2022 estimate
84004	Alpine	9,555	10,251	10,304
84003	American Fork	26,263	33,337	37,268
84065	Bluffdale	7,598	17,014	19,080
*84010	Bountiful	42,552	45,762	44,481
84302	Brigham City........	17,899	19,650	19,963
*84720	Cedar City.........	28,857	35,235	38,692
84014	Centerville.........	15,335	16,884	16,502
*84015	Clearfield..........	30,112	31,909	34,062
84015	Clinton	20,426	23,386	23,538
*84047	Cottonwood Heights ..	33,433	33,617	32,420
84020	Draper.............	42,274	51,017	50,731
*84005	Eagle Mountain......	21,415	43,623	54,149
84025	Farmington	18,275	24,531	25,660
*84029	Grantsville.........	8,893	12,617	14,417
84032	Heber	11,362	16,856	17,865
*84096	Herriman	21,785	55,144	59,179
84003	Highland	15,523	19,348	19,902
*84117	Holladay	26,472	31,965	30,816
84737	Hurricane	13,748	20,036	23,077
84319	Hyrum	7,609	9,362	10,594
84738	Ivins	6,753	8,978	10,012
84037	Kaysville	27,300	32,945	32,761
84118	Kearns	35,731	36,723	37,249
*84041	Layton	67,311	81,773	82,601
*84043	Lehi...............	47,407	75,907	84,373
84042	Lindon	10,070	11,397	11,704
*84321	Logan	48,174	52,778	54,680
84044	Magna.............	26,505	29,251	29,668
84664	Mapleton...........	7,979	11,365	12,999
84047	Midvale...........	27,964	36,028	35,637
*84106	Millcreek	62,139	63,380	63,034
84107	Murray	46,746	50,637	49,463
84341	North Logan	8,269	10,986	11,616
*84404	North Ogden	17,357	20,916	21,855
84054	North Salt Lake.....	16,322	21,907	22,537
*84401	Ogden.............	82,825	87,321	86,825
*84057	Orem	88,328	98,129	95,910
84651	Payson	18,294	21,101	22,516
84062	Pleasant Grove	33,509	37,726	37,630
*84414	Pleasant View	7,979	11,083	11,258
*84601	Provo.............	112,488	115,162	113,523
*84065	Riverton	38,753	45,285	44,599
*84067	Roy	36,884	39,306	38,785
*84770	Saint George	72,897	95,342	102,519
84653	Salem	6,423	9,298	10,393
*84101	Salt Lake City	186,440	199,723	204,657
*84070	Sandy	87,461	96,904	93,022
84655	Santaquin	9,128	13,725	16,898
*84043	Saratoga Springs ...	17,781	37,696	49,354
84335	Smithfield	9,495	13,571	14,425
*84095	South Jordan	50,418	77,487	83,513
*84403	South Ogden	16,532	17,488	17,716
*84115	South Salt Lake	23,617	26,777	26,003
84660	Spanish Fork	34,691	42,602	44,102

ZIP	Place	2010 population	2020 population	2022 estimate
*84663	Springville	29,466	35,268	35,832
*84075	Syracuse..........	24,331	32,141	35,561
*84118	Taylorsville........	58,652	60,448	57,879
84074	Tooele.............	31,605	35,742	38,588
84337	Tremonton.........	7,647	9,894	11,840
*84078	Vernal	9,089	10,079	10,432
*84058	Vineyard	139	12,543	14,535
84780	Washington.........	18,761	27,993	32,709
84401	West Haven	10,272	16,739	22,395
*84084	West Jordan	103,712	116,961	116,664
84015	West Point	9,511	10,963	11,892
*84119	West Valley City ...	129,480	140,230	136,650
*84087	Woods Cross	9,761	11,410	11,487

Vermont
Area code: 802 applies to the entire state. See introductory note.

ZIP	Place	2010 population	2020 population	2022 estimate
05201	Bennington	15,764	15,333	15,312
*05301	Brattleboro	12,046	12,184	12,106
*05401	Burlington	42,417	44,743	44,595
*05446	Colchester	17,067	17,524	17,604
*05452	Essex	19,587	22,094	22,408
05452	Essex Junction	9,271	10,590	10,917
05047	Hartford	9,952	10,686	10,764
05468	Milton	10,352	10,723	10,689
*05701	Rutland	16,495	15,807	15,695
*05403	South Burlington ...	17,904	20,292	20,624
05495	Williston	8,698	10,103	10,104

Virginia
Area codes: 276, 434, 540/826, 571/703, 686 (Feb. 1, 2024)/804, 757/948

ZIP	Place	2010 population	2020 population	2022 estimate
*22314	Alexandria.........	139,966	159,467	155,525
22003	Annandale (c)	41,008	43,363	—
*22201	Arlington (c)	207,627	238,643	—
*20147	Ashburn (c)........	43,511	46,349	—
22041	Bailey's Crossroads (c)	23,643	24,749	—
20147	Belmont (c)........	5,966	10,268	—
*24060	Blacksburg	42,620	44,826	45,610
23235	Bon Air (c)........	16,366	18,022	—
20148	Brambleton (c)	9,845	23,486	—
23112	Brandermill (c)	13,173	13,730	—
*24201	Bristol............	17,835	17,219	16,975
20148	Broadlands (c)	12,313	14,021	—
20111	Buckhall (c)........	16,293	20,420	—
20109	Bull Run (c) (Prince William Co.)..	14,983	16,794	—
*22015	Burke (c)..........	41,055	42,312	—
22015	Burke Centre (c)	17,326	17,518	—
24069	Cascades (c)	11,912	12,366	—
24018	Cave Spring (c)....	24,922	26,755	—
*20120	Centreville (c)......	71,135	73,518	—
*20151	Chantilly (c)........	23,039	24,301	—
*22901	Charlottesville	43,475	46,553	45,373
22026	Cherry Hill (c)	16,000	23,683	—
23320	Chesapeake	222,209	249,422	252,488
*23831	Chester (c)	20,987	23,414	—
24073	Christiansburg	21,041	23,348	22,562
23834	Colonial Heights	17,411	18,170	18,294
20165	Countryside (c).....	10,072	10,418	—
22701	Culpeper..........	16,379	20,062	20,764
22193	Dale City (c)	65,969	72,088	—
24541	Danville...........	43,055	42,590	42,229
20191	Difficult Run (c).....	—	10,600	—
20170	Dranesville (c)	11,921	11,785	—
*23222	East Highland Park (c)	14,796	15,131	—
22033	Fair Oaks (c).......	30,223	34,052	—
*22030	Fairfax............	22,565	24,146	24,835
22039	Fairfax Station (c) ...	12,030	12,420	—
*22046	Falls Church	12,332	14,658	14,586
24551	Forest (c)	9,106	11,709	—
22308	Fort Hunt (c)	16,045	17,231	—
22310	Franconia (c).......	18,245	18,943	—
20171	Franklin Farm (c) ...	19,288	19,189	—
*22401	Fredericksburg	24,286	27,982	28,757
22630	Front Royal	14,440	15,011	15,263
*20155	Gainesville (c)	11,481	18,112	—
22030	George Mason (c)...	9,496	11,162	—
23059	Glen Allen (c)	14,774	16,187	—
23062	Gloucester Point (c) ..	9,402	10,587	—
22066	Great Falls (c)	15,427	15,953	—
22306	Groveton (c)........	14,598	15,725	—
*23669	Hampton	137,436	137,148	138,037
*22801	Harrisonburg	48,914	51,814	51,158
*20170	Herndon	23,292	24,655	24,167
23075	Highland Springs (c)..	15,711	16,604	—
24019	Hollins (c)	14,673	15,574	—
23860	Hopewell..........	22,591	23,033	22,962

ZIP	Place	2010 population	2020 population	2022 estimate
22303	Huntington (c)	11,267	13,749	—
22306	Hybla Valley (c)	15,801	16,319	—
22043	Idylwood (c)	17,288	17,954	—
20112	Independent Hill (c) . . .	7,419	10,165	—
22032	Kings Park West (c) . . .	13,390	13,465	—
22315	Kingstowne (c)	15,556	16,825	—
22963	Lake Monticello (c) . . .	9,920	10,126	—
22192	Lake Ridge (c)	41,058	46,162	—
23228	Lakeside (c)	11,849	12,203	—
20176	Lansdowne (c)	11,253	12,427	—
23228	Laurel (c)	16,713	17,769	—
*20175	Leesburg (c)	42,616	48,250	48,974
22191	Leesylvania (c)	—	21,193	—
22312	Lincolnia (c)	22,855	22,922	—
20136	Linton Hall (c)	35,725	41,754	—
*22079	Lorton (c)	18,610	20,072	—
20148	Loudoun Valley Estates (c)	3,656	11,436	—
20165	Lowes Island (c)	10,756	11,023	—
*24501	Lynchburg	75,568	79,009	79,287
24572	Madison Heights (c) . .	11,285	10,893	—
*20110	Manassas	37,821	42,772	42,642
*20111	Manassas Park	14,273	17,219	16,703
23224	Manchester (c)	10,804	12,129	—
*24112	Martinsville	13,821	13,485	13,725
*22101	McLean (c)	48,115	50,773	—
20171	McNair (c)	17,513	21,598	—
23234	Meadowbrook (c)	18,312	20,898	—
*23111	Mechanicsville (c)	36,348	39,482	—
22081	Merrifield (c)	15,212	20,488	—
*23112	Midlothian (c)	—	18,320	—
22025	Montclair (c)	19,570	22,279	—
22121	Mount Vernon (c)	12,416	12,914	—
20187	New Baltimore (c)	8,119	11,251	—
22122	Newington (c)	12,943	13,223	—
22153	Newington Forest (c)	12,442	12,957	—
*23607	Newport News	180,719	186,247	184,306
*23502	Norfolk	242,803	238,005	232,995
*22124	Oakton (c)	34,166	36,732	—
*23704	Petersburg	32,420	33,458	33,394
23662	Poquoson	12,150	12,460	12,582
*23704	Portsmouth	95,535	97,915	97,029
*24141	Radford	16,408	16,070	16,738
*20190	Reston (c)	58,404	63,226	—
23219	Richmond	204,214	226,610	229,395
*24011	Roanoke	97,032	100,011	97,847
24281	Rose Hill (c) (Fairfax Co.)	20,226	21,045	—
24153	Salem	24,802	25,346	25,523
23233	Short Pump (c)	24,729	30,626	—
20152	South Riding (c)	24,256	33,877	—
*22150	Springfield (c)	30,484	31,339	—
*24401	Staunton	23,746	25,750	25,904
*20164	Sterling (c)	27,822	30,337	—
20105	Stone Ridge (c)	7,214	15,039	—
24477	Stuarts Draft (c)	9,235	12,142	—
20109	Sudley (c)	16,203	19,008	—
*23434	Suffolk	84,585	94,324	98,537
20164	Sugarland Run (c)	11,799	12,345	—
24502	Timberlake (c)	12,183	13,267	—
23229	Tuckahoe (c)	44,990	48,051	—
*22102	Tysons (c)	19,627	26,374	—
*22180	Vienna (c)	15,687	16,473	16,276
*23451	Virginia Beach	437,994	459,470	455,618
23888	Wakefield (c)	11,275	11,805	—
*20186	Warrenton	9,611	10,057	10,197
22980	Waynesboro	21,006	22,196	22,808
22042	West Falls Church (c)	29,207	30,243	—
22152	West Springfield (c) . .	22,460	23,369	—
*23185	Williamsburg	14,068	15,425	15,909
*22601	Winchester	26,203	28,120	27,936
*22182	Wolf Trap (c)	16,131	16,496	—
*22191	Woodbridge (c)	4,055	44,668	—
24381	Woodlawn (c) (Fairfax Co.)	20,804	20,859	—
23059	Wyndham (c)	9,785	11,087	—
20111	Yorkshire (c)	7,541	10,992	—

Washington
Area codes: 206, 253, 360/564, 425, 509

ZIP	Place	2010 population	2020 population	2022 estimate
98520	Aberdeen	16,896	17,013	17,113
99001	Airway Heights	6,114	10,757	10,842
*98001	Alderwood Manor (c)	8,442	10,198	—
*98221	Anacortes	15,778	17,637	18,003
98223	Arlington	17,926	19,868	21,059
98335	Artondale (c)	12,653	13,641	—
*98001	Auburn	70,180	87,256	84,858
98110	Bainbridge Island	23,025	24,825	24,494
98604	Battle Ground	17,571	20,743	21,628
*98004	Bellevue	122,363	151,854	152,767

ZIP	Place	2010 population	2020 population	2022 estimate
*98225	Bellingham	80,885	91,482	93,896
*98230	Birch Bay (c)	8,413	10,115	—
98391	Bonney Lake	17,374	22,487	22,885
*98011	Bothell	33,505	48,161	49,017
*98021	Bothell East (c)	8,018	13,970	—
*98021	Bothell West (c)	16,607	22,015	—
*98337	Bremerton	37,729	43,505	45,415
98178	Bryn Mawr-Skyway (c)	15,645	17,397	—
*98166	Burien	33,313	52,066	50,806
98282	Camano (c)	—	17,356	—
98607	Camas	19,355	26,065	27,371
98531	Centralia	16,336	18,183	18,773
99004	Cheney	10,590	13,255	12,747
98072	Cottage Lake (c)	22,494	22,855	—
98042	Covington	17,575	20,777	21,374
*98198	Des Moines	29,673	32,888	32,408
98609	East Renton Highlands (c)	11,140	11,937	—
98802	East Wenatchee	13,190	14,158	14,043
98024	Eastmont (c)	20,101	24,059	—
*98372	Edgewood	9,387	12,327	12,896
*98020	Edmonds	39,709	42,853	42,593
98387	Elk Plain (c)	14,205	14,534	—
*98926	Ellensburg	18,174	18,666	18,703
98022	Enumclaw	10,669	12,543	12,721
*98201	Everett	103,019	110,629	111,337
98058	Fairwood (c) (King Co.)	19,102	19,396	—
99218	Fairwood (c) (Spokane Co.)	7,905	10,541	—
*98001	Federal Way	89,306	101,030	97,863
98248	Ferndale	11,415	15,048	15,840
98424	Fife	9,173	10,999	10,809
98662	Five Corners (c)	18,159	20,973	—
98433	Fort Lewis (c)	11,046	14,052	—
98875	Frederickson (c)	18,719	24,906	—
*98329	Gig Harbor	7,126	12,029	12,484
98338	Graham (c)	23,491	32,658	—
98930	Grandview	10,862	10,907	11,043
98665	Hazel Dell (c)	19,435	23,569	—
*98027	Issaquah	30,434	40,051	39,344
98626	Kelso	11,925	12,720	12,691
98028	Kenmore	20,460	23,914	23,478
99336	Kennewick	73,917	83,921	84,750
*98031	Kent	92,411	136,588	134,392
*98033	Kirkland	48,787	92,175	92,151
*98503	Lacey	42,393	53,526	58,552
98155	Lake Forest Park	12,598	13,630	13,186
98042	Lake Morton-Berrydale (c)	10,160	10,474	—
98258	Lake Stevens	28,069	35,630	39,848
*98087	Lake Stickney (c)	7,777	15,413	—
98391	Lake Tapps (c)	11,859	12,962	—
98001	Lakeland North (c) . . .	12,942	13,663	—
98001	Lakeland South (c) . . .	11,574	13,169	—
*98498	Lakewood	58,163	63,612	62,572
*99016	Liberty Lake	7,591	12,003	12,651
98632	Longview	36,648	37,818	37,782
98264	Lynden	11,951	15,749	16,175
*98036	Lynnwood	35,836	38,568	43,212
98296	Maltby (c)	10,830	11,277	—
98038	Maple Valley	22,684	28,013	28,220
*98807	Martha Lake (c)	15,473	21,660	—
*98270	Marysville	60,020	70,714	72,275
98040	Mercer Island	22,699	25,748	25,172
*98012	Mill Creek	18,244	20,926	20,828
98012	Mill Creek East (c) . . .	15,709	24,912	—
98661	Minnehaha (c)	9,771	11,871	—
98272	Monroe	17,304	19,699	19,243
98837	Moses Lake	20,366	25,146	25,888
*98273	Mount Vernon	31,743	35,219	35,527
*98686	Mount Vista (c)	7,850	10,051	—
98043	Mountlake Terrace . . .	19,909	21,286	21,543
98275	Mukilteo	20,254	21,538	21,096
*98506	Newcastle	10,380	13,017	12,902
98807	North Lynnwood (c) . . .	16,574	22,802	—
*98277	Oak Harbor	22,075	24,622	24,403
*98501	Olympia	46,478	55,605	55,669
98662	Orchards (c)	19,556	27,729	—
*98444	Parkland (c)	35,803	38,623	—
99301	Pasco	59,781	77,108	79,315
*98362	Port Angeles	19,038	19,960	20,060
98366	Port Orchard	11,144	15,587	17,089
98368	Port Townsend	9,113	10,148	10,388
98370	Poulsbo	9,200	11,975	12,039
98391	Prairie Ridge (c)	11,464	12,288	—
*99163	Pullman	29,799	32,901	32,508
*98371	Puyallup	37,022	42,973	42,452
*98052	Redmond	54,144	73,256	76,732

ZIP	Place	2010 population	2020 population	2022 estimate
*98057	Renton	90,927	106,785	104,047
*99352	Richland	48,058	60,560	62,821
98642	Ridgefield	4,763	10,319	14,251
*98685	Salmon Creek (c)	19,686	21,293	—
*98074	Sammamish	45,780	67,455	65,845
*98148	SeaTac	26,909	31,454	30,525
*98101	Seattle	608,660	737,015	749,256
98284	Sedro-Woolley	10,540	12,421	12,912
98584	Shelton	9,834	10,371	10,814
*98133	Shoreline	53,007	58,608	59,690
98208	Silver Firs (c)	20,891	22,174	—
*98315	Silverdale (c)	19,204	20,733	—
*98290	Snohomish	9,098	10,126	10,150
98065	Snoqualmie	10,670	14,121	13,621
*98373	South Hill (c)	52,431	64,708	—
*98387	Spanaway (c)	27,227	35,476	—
*99201	Spokane	208,916	228,989	230,160
*99206	Spokane Valley	89,755	102,976	107,325
*98390	Sumner	9,451	10,621	10,595
98944	Sunnyside	15,858	16,375	16,296
*98402	Tacoma	198,397	219,346	221,776
*98188	Tukwila	19,107	21,798	21,377
*98501	Tumwater	17,371	25,350	26,369
98053	Union Hill-Novelty Hill (c)	18,805	22,683	—
*98466	University Place	31,144	34,866	34,634
*98660	Vancouver	161,791	190,915	194,512
*98070	Vashon (c)	10,624	11,055	—
99362	Walla Walla	31,731	34,060	33,492
98671	Washougal	14,095	17,039	16,926
*98801	Wenatchee	31,925	35,508	35,433
*99353	West Richland	11,811	16,295	17,795
*98106	White Center (c)	13,495	16,631	—
*98072	Woodinville	10,938	13,069	13,261
*98901	Yakima	91,067	96,968	97,012
98597	Yelm	6,848	10,617	10,668

West Virginia
Area codes: 304/681 apply to the entire state

ZIP	Place	2010 population	2020 population	2022 estimate
*25801	Beckley	17,614	17,286	16,749
*25301	Charleston	51,400	48,864	47,129
*26301	Clarksburg	16,578	16,061	15,647
*26554	Fairmont	18,704	18,416	18,242
*25701	Huntington	49,138	46,842	45,746
*25401	Martinsburg	17,227	18,777	18,953
*26505	Morgantown	29,660	30,347	30,277
*26101	Parkersburg	31,492	29,738	29,193
25177	Saint Albans	11,044	10,861	10,456
*25303	South Charleston	13,450	13,647	13,175
*25526	Teays Valley (c)	13,175	14,350	—
26105	Vienna	10,749	10,652	10,506
26062	Weirton	19,746	19,163	18,481
26003	Wheeling	28,486	27,052	26,391

Wisconsin
Area codes: 274/920, 353/608, 414, 534/715

ZIP	Place	2010 population	2020 population	2022 estimate
54301	Allouez	13,975	14,156	13,892
*54911	Appleton	72,623	75,644	74,511
*54304	Ashwaubenon	16,963	16,991	16,817
53913	Baraboo	12,048	12,556	12,633
53916	Beaver Dam	16,214	16,708	16,582
54311	Bellevue	14,570	15,935	16,588
*53511	Beloit	36,966	36,657	36,449
*53045	Brookfield	37,920	41,464	41,958
*53223	Brown Deer	11,999	12,507	12,609
53105	Burlington	10,464	11,047	11,005
53108	Caledonia	24,705	25,361	25,208
53012	Cedarburg	11,412	12,121	12,421
*54729	Chippewa Falls	13,661	14,731	14,645
53110	Cudahy	18,267	18,204	17,796
54115	De Pere	23,800	25,410	25,361
53532	DeForest	8,936	10,811	10,893
*54701	Eau Claire	65,883	69,421	69,737
53121	Elkhorn	10,084	10,247	10,240
*53711	Fitchburg	25,260	29,609	30,834
*54935	Fond du Lac	43,021	44,678	44,339
53538	Fort Atkinson	12,368	12,579	12,412
*54956	Fox Crossing[1]	—	18,974	18,827
53132	Franklin	35,451	36,816	36,066
53022	Germantown	19,749	20,917	21,015
*53209	Glendale	12,872	13,357	12,983
53024	Grafton	11,459	12,094	12,433

ZIP	Place	2010 population	2020 population	2022 estimate
*54301	Green Bay	104,057	107,395	106,095
53129	Greendale	14,046	14,854	14,540
*53220	Greenfield	36,720	37,803	37,071
54942	Greenville[2]	—	—	10,259
54952	Harrison[1]	—	12,418	14,359
53027	Hartford	14,223	15,626	15,829
*54155	Hobart	6,182	10,211	10,535
54636	Holmen	9,005	10,661	11,416
54303	Howard	17,399	19,950	20,460
54016	Hudson	12,719	14,755	15,186
53545	Janesville	63,575	65,615	65,911
*54130	Kaukauna	15,462	17,089	17,372
53140	Kenosha	99,218	99,986	98,484
*54601	La Crosse	51,320	52,680	51,380
*54140	Little Chute	10,449	11,619	12,154
*53703	Madison	233,209	269,840	272,903
*54220	Manitowoc	33,736	34,626	34,570
54143	Marinette	10,968	11,119	11,053
*54449	Marshfield	19,118	18,929	18,789
54952	Menasha	17,353	18,268	17,889
*53051	Menomonee Falls	35,626	38,527	39,246
54751	Menomonie	16,264	16,843	16,650
*53092	Mequon	23,132	25,142	25,337
53562	Middleton	17,442	21,827	22,328
*53202	Milwaukee	594,833	577,222	563,305
53566	Monroe	10,827	10,661	10,457
*53406	Mount Pleasant	26,197	27,732	27,597
53150	Muskego	24,135	25,032	25,150
*54956	Neenah	25,501	27,319	27,361
*53151	New Berlin	39,584	40,451	40,315
54017	New Richmond	8,375	10,079	10,592
53154	Oak Creek	34,451	36,497	36,087
53066	Oconomowoc	15,759	18,203	18,505
54650	Onalaska	17,736	18,803	18,975
53575	Oregon	9,231	11,179	11,610
*54901	Oshkosh	66,083	66,816	65,948
53072	Pewaukee	13,195	15,914	16,169
53818	Platteville	11,224	11,836	11,139
53158	Pleasant Prairie	19,719	21,250	21,840
54467	Plover	12,123	13,519	13,806
53074	Port Washington	11,250	12,353	12,753
53901	Portage	10,324	10,581	10,200
*53402	Racine	78,860	77,816	76,462
*53959	Reedsburg	9,200	9,984	10,057
*53076	Richfield	11,300	11,739	11,855
54022	River Falls	15,000	16,182	16,609
53168	Salem Lakes[1]	—	14,601	14,397
*53081	Sheboygan	49,288	49,929	49,773
53211	Shorewood	13,162	13,859	13,526
53172	South Milwaukee	21,156	20,795	20,309
*54481	Stevens Point	26,717	25,666	25,716
53589	Stoughton	12,611	13,173	12,846
54313	Suamico	11,346	12,820	13,184
*53590	Sun Prairie	29,364	35,967	36,653
54880	Superior	27,244	26,751	26,459
53089	Sussex	10,518	11,487	11,819
54241	Two Rivers	11,712	11,271	11,166
53593	Verona	10,619	14,030	14,521
*53094	Watertown	23,861	22,926	22,784
*53186	Waukesha	70,718	71,158	70,454
53597	Waunakee	12,097	14,879	14,998
53963	Waupun	11,340	11,344	10,785
*54403	Wausau	39,106	39,994	39,833
*53213	Wauwatosa	46,396	48,387	47,289
*53214	West Allis	60,411	60,325	58,950
*53095	West Bend	31,078	31,752	31,604
*54476	Weston	14,868	15,723	15,829
*53217	Whitefish Bay	14,110	14,954	14,631
*53190	Whitewater	14,390	14,889	15,638
*54494	Wisconsin Rapids	18,367	18,877	18,716

(1) Incorporated after 2010 Census. (2) Incorporated after 2020 Census.

Wyoming
Area code: 307 applies to the entire state

ZIP	Place	2010 population	2020 population	2022 estimate
*82601	Casper	55,316	59,038	58,543
*82001	Cheyenne	59,466	65,132	64,610
82414	Cody	9,520	10,028	10,224
*82930	Evanston	12,359	11,747	11,845
*82716	Gillette	29,087	33,403	33,264
*82935	Green River	12,515	11,825	11,535
*83001	Jackson	9,577	10,760	10,698
*82070	Laramie	30,816	31,407	32,035
82501	Riverton	10,615	10,682	10,776
*82901	Rock Springs	23,036	23,526	23,021
82801	Sheridan	17,444	18,737	19,235

Note: In this section, the notation BCE (before the common era) is applied to years dating to the traditional BC (before Christ) era, and CE (common era) is applied to AD (anno domini) dates. This notation is now preferred in many scientific and academic publications. The traditional Gregorian calendar system and its dates and years are unaltered except by these labels.

Other abbreviations used in this chapter include the following: KYA = thousand years ago, MYA = million years ago, c. = circa, fl. = flourished, r. = ruled, b. = born, d. = died.

Prehistory: Our Ancestors Emerge

Reviewed by Marc Kissel, Ph.D., Univ. of Notre Dame, 2016; other updates per World Almanac research.

Evidence of the origins of *Homo sapiens*, the genus and species to which all living humans belong, comes from an ever increasing number of fossils and DNA studies, and from the archaeological record. Put together, the latest evidence suggests that humans evolved from an ape-like ancestor that lived in eastern and central Africa 8 to 5 million years ago.

Current theories trace the first hominin[1] (primates more closely related to humans than to any other living primate) to Africa, where several distinct genera appear in the fossil record 6-4 MYA. Skeletally, hominins are defined by signs of bipedalism (walking on two legs). They lived in a variety of environments, including swampy forest margins, woodlands, and open savannas (usually near lakes or springs).

Claims of the earliest hominin are inherently controversial. The earliest currently proposed species are *Sahelanthropus tchadensis* (c. 7 MYA, Chad) and *Orrorin tugenensis* (c. 6 MYA, Kenya). The recently described species *Ardipithecus ramidus* (4.4 MYA, Ethiopia) had a chimp-sized brain and a fairly primitive body plan but was bipedal.

Although all humans living today are members of a single species, the fossil record confirms that our ancestors coexisted with a number of similar species throughout our evolutionary history. Starting around 4 MYA one of these earliest hominins gave rise to the australopithecines, a genus of early hominins referred to as "bipedal apes." Scientists divided these into two groups, "gracile" and "robust," each containing a number of species.

The robust australopithecines were characterized by larger molar and premolar teeth; they probably went extinct around 1 MYA. Members of this species adapted a new dietary niche of eating hard foods such as nuts and tubers and have been found in both E and S Africa.

The gracile lineage most likely led to modern humans. *Australopithecus sediba* (2 MYA, South Africa) shows a mosaic of both Australopithecus and early *Homo* traits, leading some to suggest that this is the predecessor to our genus; the morphology of its hand is very suggestive of tool-use. However, while originally believed to arise solely within the genus *Homo*, recent work at the sites of Dikika (3.3 MYA, Ethiopia) and Lomekwi (3.3 MYA, Kenya) suggest that earlier hominins were making stone tools.

Our genus, *Homo*, arose 3-2 MYA, with fossils showing early members of our genus being fully bipedal, having larger brains, and hands well-adapted to tool use. The Oldowan tools first appear 2.6 MYA and were used to cut and scrape meat. It is not known whether these early hominins had the ability to speak, but they were social primates, had campsites, and subsisted by gathering plants and small animals and by scavenging other kills, as well as perhaps hunting.

Homo ergaster appeared in E Africa around 1.9 MYA and was the first to leave the continent, spreading throughout Eurasia by c. 1.8 MYA. *H. ergaster* is sometimes grouped with *H. erectus*, a species first identified on the Indonesian island of Java. It was capable of hunting large and medium-sized animals, such as antelopes and horses, learned to make and control fire, and produced bifacially-flaked tools (sharpened on both sides).

The ability to control fire enormously expanded the human food niche as well as creating new opportunities in the social

Cave paintings in Lascaux, France, discovered in 1940, have been carbon-dated to 11,000 to 30,000 years before the present.

world. Fire-making possibly began as early as 1 MYA in Africa and is clearly documented throughout Eurasia after c. 500 KYA. Hearths were found in northern Israel by c. 750 KYA, and by 465 KYA in southwestern France.

After about 800 KYA, Europe provides a particularly rich set of fossil evidence usually assigned to *H. erectus, H. antecessor*, or *H. heidelbergensis*. This population gave rise to the Neanderthals, who appeared c. 350 KYA. While originally portrayed as savage and unhuman-like, recent research suggests they could probably speak, were proficient hunters of large game, had sophisticated tools and weapons, had ornamentation and other forms of symbolic expression, and a well-developed social organization. On the island of Flores, Indonesia, remains of a species known as *Homo floresiensis*, a 1.1-m (3.5-ft) tall hominin, date from c. 100-60 KYA. Its small stature may be due to limited food and few predators on the small island.

The remains of *Homo naledi*, dating to c. 335-236 KYA, raised questions about a possible overlap in existence and behaviors with early humans. It has a human-like foot and lower limbs, but other aspects of the skeleton, such as the pelvis and shoulder, are more primitive looking. They seem to have been deliberately deposited into a cave system, suggesting an early form of burial.

Improved dating techniques call into question the age of modern humans. The oldest modern human fossils (*Homo sapiens*) were dated to c. 300 KYA and were found at the Jebel Irhoud site in Morocco. Until that 2017 analysis, the oldest, found in Omo Kibish, Ethiopia, were believed to date to c. 195 KYA. Fossils considered some of the oldest modern humans were also found at the Herto site in Ethiopia's Middle Awash Valley. The species spread out of Africa, reaching Israel by c. 100 KYA, and parts of Europe perhaps as early as 54 KYA. Migration from Asia to Australia took place as early as 60 KYA. What happened when they met other hominins is a subject of intense research. Genetic evidence in the form of ancient DNA suggests that Neanderthals interbred with modern humans. Genetic data also provide information about the Denisovans, a population of early humans dated to perhaps c. 200 KYA, fossils of which were found in caves in Siberia and Tibet. Some contemporary human populations retain Denisovan DNA, suggesting a complex web of interactions between these populations. Researchers studying (2021) fossilized skull found in NE China contended it represents another separate species (dated to c. 150 KYA or earlier), which they named *Homo longi*.

Most evidence for the crossing from Asia to the Americas by the Bering land bridge dates to the end of the last Ice Age, at c. 14 KYA, but recent evidence suggests some arrived sooner, especially the 2021 reported discovery of fossilized human footprints in New Mexico dated at earlier than 20 KYA. The arrival of humans was followed by the extinction of the indigenous Pleistocene megafauna (e.g., mammoths, mastodons) due either to overexploitation by humans, climate change, or a combination of both.

Wooden throwing spears about 3 m (10 ft) long were fashioned by big-game hunters 300 KYA at Schöningen, Germany. Scraping tools, dated after 750 KYA in Europe, N Africa, the Middle East, and Central Asia, suggest the preparation of hides for clothing. Some of the oldest evidence of personal adornment date to around 300 KYA in the form of ochre, while various sites around 100 KYA from South Africa, Morocco, and Israel show the use of perforated shell beads, suggestive of symbolic expression. Although they were probably invented much earlier, impressions in burnt clay from the Czech Republic document the ability to weave cloth baskets and nets by 28 KYA.

Some of the earliest well-dated cave paintings come from the island of Sulawesi, Indonesia, where they date to around the same time as the earliest cave paintings in Europe. The painted caves of Cosquer and Chauvet in southern France have (contested) radiocarbon dates of c. 32 KYA. Painting, engraving, and bodily decoration flourished in Europe 15 KYA, along with stone and ivory sculpture. More than 200 western European caves show remarkable examples of naturalistic wall painting. A few musical instruments—bone flutes with precisely bored holes—have been found in sites dated after 40 KYA.

Skeletal data suggests that after 60-30 KYA the number of people who survived to become grandparents increased. With more adults available to provide child care, humans began to develop more complex, multigenerational social systems. In general, as human cognitive capacities slowly expanded over the Pleistocene, a variety of behavioral modes—in toolmaking, diet, shelter, social arrangements, and spiritual expression—arose as humans adapted to different geographic and climatic zones. By about 13,000 years ago, sites from all over the world show seasonal migration patterns and efficient exploitation of a wide range of plant and animal foods, some of which were eventually domesticated.

Shortly after 12 KYA, among widely separated foraging communities in both hemispheres, a series of dramatic technological and social changes occurred, marking the Neolithic, or New Stone Age. As the world climate became drier and warmer, population/resource imbalances ensued, creating the conditions that allowed for increased human interference in the life cycles of certain plants and animals. This interference ultimately resulted in the appearance of domestication, initially in the northern Middle East.

Domesticated plants and animals encouraged population growth and the appearance of permanent settlements. Agricultural economies increasingly replaced or assimilated hunting and gathering. Reliance upon domesticated plants and animals, coupled with technological advances like pottery-making, precipitated a dramatic increase in world population and social complexity. Genetic research suggests that mutations related to traits currently found in some human populations, such as Europeans' ability to process lactose, arose after this time.

Sites in the Americas, SE Europe, and the Middle East show roughly contemporaneous (12-6 KYA) evidence of Neolithic domestication economies; similar evidence of E and S Asian, W European, and sub-Saharan African Neolithic adaptations dates to 10-7 KYA. From W Asian sources, farming and the herding of sheep and goats spread rapidly throughout the Mediterranean Basin, perhaps in as short a time interval as 100-200 years. The variety of crops—wheat, barley, rice, maize, squash, beans, and tubers—and a mix of other characteristics suggest that this adaptation occurred independently in as many as 12 or 13 places in both hemispheres.

Evidence for fermented beverages likewise coincides with the early Neolithic settled farming lifestyle. Northern Chinese farmers concocted a wine-like drink from rice, honey, and fruit between 9 and 8 KYA. In highland W Asia, in what is today Iran, vintners were fermenting grapes and making wine by c. 7.4 KYA. The plants and animals associated with the Neolithic Revolution provided the basis for all subsequent social and cultural evolution worldwide.

---

(1) Although "hominid" was standard usage several decades ago, "hominin" is now more commonly used in reference to human ancestors because of developments in the interpretation of primate evolution.

Earliest Civilizations: 4000-1000 BCE

Mesopotamia. Recorded history began with writing in Mesopotamia in the Tigris-Euphrates river valley. The Sumerians used clay tablets with pictographs to keep records after 4000 BCE. A **cuneiform** (wedge-shaped) script, evolved by 3000 BCE as a full syllabic alphabet. Neighboring peoples adapted the script for their own use.

Sumerian life centered, from 4000 BCE, on large cities (Eridu, Ur, Uruk, Nippur, Kish, and Lagash) organized around temples and priestly bureaucracies, with surrounding plains watered by vast irrigation works and worked with traction plows. Sailboats, wheeled vehicles, potter's wheels, and kilns were used. Copper was smelted and tempered from c. 4000 BCE; bronze was produced not long after. Ores, as well as precious stones and metals, were obtained through long-distance ship and caravan trade. Iron was used from c. 2000 BCE. Improved ironworking, developed partly by the Hittites, became widespread by 1200 BCE.

Sumerian political primacy passed among cities and their kingly dynasties. Semitic-speaking peoples, with cultures derived from the Sumerian, founded a succession of dynasties that ruled in Mesopotamia and neighboring areas for most of 1,800 years. Among them were the **Akkadians** (first under Sargon I, c. 2350 BCE), the Amorites (whose laws, codified by **Hammurabi**, c. 1792-1750 BCE, have biblical parallels), and the Assyrians, with interludes of rule by the Hittites, Kassites, and Mitanni.

Mesopotamian learning, preserved in vast libraries, was practically oriented. Scribes maintained lists of astronomical phenomena, plants, animals, and stones. Medical texts listed ailments and herbal cures. The Sumerians worshiped anthropomorphic gods representing natural forces. Sacrifices were made at **ziggurats**, or huge stepped temples.

The Syria-Palestine area, site of some of the earliest urban remains (Jericho, 7000 BCE) and of the **Ebla** civilization (fl. 2500 BCE), experienced Egyptian cultural and political influence along with Mesopotamian. The **Phoenician** coast was an active commercial center. A phonetic alphabet was invented here before 1600 BCE. It became the ancestor of many other alphabets.

Egypt. Agricultural villages along the Nile R. were united by around 3300 BCE into two kingdoms, Upper and Lower Egypt. They were unified (c. 3100 BCE) under the pharaoh Menes, as detailed on the Narmer Palate. A bureaucracy supervised construction of canals and monuments (**pyramids** starting 2700 BCE). Control over Nubia to the S was asserted from 2600 BCE.

Brilliant **Old Kingdom** period achievements in architecture, sculpture, and painting reached their height during the 3rd and 4th dynasties. **Hieroglyphic writing** appeared by 3200 BCE, recording a sophisticated literature that included religious writings, philosophy, history, and science. An ordered hierarchy of gods, including totemistic animal elements, was served by a powerful priesthood in Memphis. The pharaoh was identified with the falcon god Horus. Other trends included belief in an afterlife and short-lived quasi-monotheistic reforms introduced by the pharaoh **Akhenaton** (c. 1379-1362 BCE), who was married to Nefertiti.

After a period of dominance by Semitic Hyksos from Asia (c. 1700-1550 BCE), the **New Kingdom** established an empire in Syria. Egypt became increasingly embroiled in Asiatic wars and diplomacy. Conquered by Persia in 525 BCE, it eventually faded away as an independent culture.

South Asia. The Bronze Age Indus Civilization spanned more than a million square kilometers in Pakistan and Northwestern India with many sites that expanded beyond the fertile core area of the Indus river system. The civilization independently grew out of local traditions developing complex trade networks and technologies during the Regionalization Era (5500-2600 BCE). The fully urban Harappan 2600-1900 BCE phase featured a standardized system of weights, uniform bricks, stamp seals featuring animals and unicorns, well laid out streets, and water management systems. Long distance trade with Mesopotamia and complex technologies were important. The writing system is one of the last to not be fully deciphered.

The major urban centers such as Dholavira, Harappa, and **Mohenjo-daro** were independent states. The civilization gradually changed due to environmental and cultural changes during the Localization Era (1900-1300 BCE). Post-Indus cultural complexes include the Gandara Grave culture (Swat, c. 1500-500 BCE) and the Painted Grey Ware (1200-800 BCE) culture, which some have associated with Vedic chiefdoms of the **Rig Veda**.

Europe. On Crete, the Bronze Age **Minoan civilization** emerged c. 2500 BCE. A prosperous economy and richly decorative art was supported by seaborne commerce. Mycenae and other cities in mainland Greece and Asia Minor (e.g., **Troy**) preserved elements of the culture until c. 1200 BCE. Cretan Linear A script (c. 2000-1700 BCE) remains undeciphered; Linear B script (c. 1300-1200 BCE) records an early Greek dialect. The possible connection between Mycenaean monumental stonework and the megalithic monuments of Western Europe, Iberia, and Malta (c. 4000-1500 BCE) is unclear.

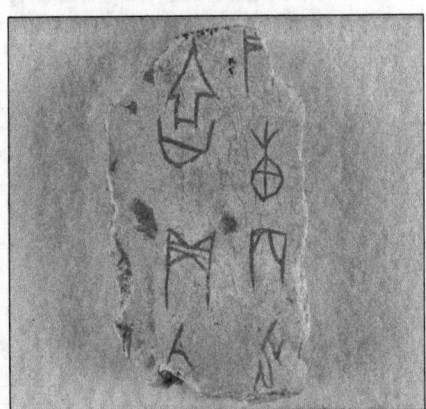

Under the Shang dynasty (c. 1523 BCE), an early writing system was developed.

China. Proto-Chinese Neolithic cultures had long covered N and SE China when the first large political state was organized in the N by the **Shang dynasty** (c. 1523 BCE). Shang kings called themselves Sons of Heaven, and they presided over a cult of human and animal sacrifice to ancestors and nature gods. The Zhou dynasty, starting c. 1027 BCE, expanded the area of the Sons of Heaven's dominion, but feudal states exercised most temporal power.

A writing system with 2,000 characters was already in use under the Shang, with **pictographs** later supplemented by phonetic characters. Many of its principles and symbols, despite changes in spoken Chinese, were preserved in later writing systems. Technical advances allowed urban specialists to create fine ceramic and jade products, and bronze casting after 1500 BCE was the most advanced in the world. Bronze artifacts discovered in northern Thailand date from 3600 BCE, hundreds of years before similar Middle Eastern finds.

Americas. Olmecs settled (1500 BCE) on the Gulf coast of Mexico and developed the first known civilization in the Western Hemisphere. Temple cities and huge stone sculptures date from 1200 BCE. A rudimentary calendar and writing system existed. Olmec religion—centered on a jaguar god—and art forms influenced later Mesoamerican cultures.

Formation of Classical Societies: 1000-400 BCE

Greece. After a period of decline during the Dorian Greek invasions (1200-1000 BCE), the Aegean area developed a unique civilization. Drawing on Mycenaean traditions, Mesopotamian learning (weights and measures, lunisolar calendar, astronomy, musical scales), the Phoenician alphabet (modified for Greek), and Egyptian art, **Greek city-states** saw a rich elaboration of intellectual life. The two great epic poems attributed to **Homer**, the *Iliad* and the *Odyssey*, were probably composed around the 8th cent. BCE. Long-range commerce was aided by metal coinage (introduced by the Lydians in Asia Minor before 700 BCE). Colonies were founded around the Mediterranean (Cumae in Italy in 760 BCE; Massalia in France c. 600 BCE) and Black Sea shores.

Philosophy, starting with Ionian speculation on the nature of matter (Thales, c. 634-546 BCE), continued by other "Pre-Socratics" (e.g., Heraclitus, c. 540-480 BCE; Parmenides, b. c. 515 BCE), reached a high point in Athens in the rationalist idealism of **Plato** (c. 428-347 BCE), a disciple of **Socrates** (c. 469-399 BCE; executed for alleged impiety), and in **Aristotle** (384-322 BCE), a pioneer in many fields, from natural sciences to logic, ethics, and metaphysics. The arts were highly valued. Architecture culminated in the **Parthenon** (438 BCE) by Phidias (fl. 490-430 BCE). Poetry (Sappho, c. 610-580 BCE; Pindar, c. 518-438 BCE) and drama (Aeschylus, 525-456 BCE; Sophocles, c. 496-406 BCE; Euripides, c. 484-406 BCE) thrived. Male beauty and strength, a chief artistic theme, were celebrated at the national games at Olympia.

Ruled by local tyrants or **oligarchies**, the Greeks were not politically united but managed to resist inclusion in the Persian Empire. Persian king Darius was defeated at Marathon (490 BCE), his son Xerxes at Salamis (480 BCE), and the Persian army at Plataea (479 BCE). Democracy sprouted in Athens as statesman Pericles (495-429 BCE) sought participation in government from all citizens. Local warfare was common; the **Peloponnesian Wars** (431-404 BCE) ended in Sparta's victory over Athens. Greek political power subsequently waned, but Greek cultural forms spread far and wide.

Hebrews. Nomadic Hebrew tribes entered Canaan before 1200 BCE, settling among other Semitic peoples speaking the same language. They brought from the desert a **monotheistic** faith said to have been revealed to Abraham in Canaan c. 1800 BCE and Moses at Mt. Sinai c. 1250 BCE, after the Hebrews' escape from bondage in Egypt. David (r. 1000-961 BCE) and Solomon (r. 961-922 BCE) united them in a kingdom that briefly dominated the area. **Phoenicians** to the N founded Mediterranean colonies (Carthage, c. 814 BCE) and sailed into the Atlantic.

A temple in Jerusalem became the national religious center, with sacrifices performed by a hereditary priesthood. Polytheistic influences, especially of the fertility cult of Baal, were opposed by **prophets** (Elijah, Amos, Isaiah).

Divided into **two kingdoms** after Solomon, the Hebrews were unable to resist the revived Assyrian empire, which conquered **Israel**, the northern kingdom, in 722 BCE. **Judah**, the southern kingdom, was conquered in 586 BCE by the Babylonians under Nebuchadnezzar II. With the fixing of most of the biblical canon by the mid-4th cent. BCE and the emergence of rabbis, Judaism successfully survived the loss of Hebrew autonomy. A Jewish kingdom was revived under the Hasmoneans (168-42 BCE).

China. During the **Eastern Zhou** dynasty (770-256 BCE), Chinese culture spread E to the sea and S to the Yangtze R. Large feudal states on the periphery of the empire contended for preeminence but continued to recognize the Son of Heaven (king), who retained a purely ritual role enriched with courtly music and dance. In the Age of Warring States (403-221 BCE), when the first sections of the **Great Wall** were built, the Qin state in the W gained supremacy and finally united all of China.

Iron tools entered China c. 500 BCE. Casting techniques were advanced, aiding agriculture. Peasants owned their land and owed civil and military service to nobles. China's cities grew in number and size; barter remained the chief trade medium.

Intellectual ferment among noble scribes and officials produced a classical age of Chinese literature and philosophy. **Confucius** (551-479 BCE) urged a restoration of a supposedly harmonious social order of the past through proper conduct in accordance with one's station and through filial and ceremonial piety. The *Analects* attributed to him are revered throughout E Asia.

Among other thinkers, **Mencius** (d. 289 BCE) added the view that the Mandate of Heaven can be removed from an unjust dynasty. The Legalists sought to curb the supposed natural wickedness of people through new institutions and harsh laws. The Naturalists emphasized the balance of opposites—yin, yang—in the world. **Daoists** sought mystical knowledge through meditation and disengagement.

India. The political and cultural center of India shifted from the Indus to the Ganges River Valley. Buddhism, Jainism, and mystical revisions of orthodox Vedism all developed c. 500-300 BCE. The *Upanishads*, last part of the *Veda*, urged escape from the cycle of rebirth into the physical world. Vedism remained the preserve of the Brahman caste.

In contrast, **Buddhism**, founded by Siddhartha Gautama (c. 563-c. 483 BCE)—Buddha ("Enlightened One")—appealed to merchants in the urban centers and took hold at first (and most lastingly) on the geographic fringes of Indian civilization. The classic Indian epics were composed in this era: the *Ramayana* perhaps c. 300 BCE, the *Mahabharata* over a period starting around 400 BCE.

Northern India was divided into a large number of monarchies and aristocratic republics, probably derived from tribal groupings, when the Magadha kingdom was formed in Bihar c. 542 BCE. It soon became the dominant power. The **Maurya** dynasty, founded by Chandragupta c. 321 BCE, expanded the kingdom, uniting most of Northern India in a centralized bureaucratic empire. The third Mauryan king, **Asoka** (r. c. 274-236 BCE), conquered most of the subcontinent. He converted to Buddhism, inscribed its tenets on pillars throughout India, and downplayed the caste system.

Before its final decline in India, Buddhism developed into a popular worship of heavenly Bodhisattvas ("enlightened beings"), and it produced a refined architecture (the Great Stupa [shrine] at Sanchi, 100 CE) and sculpture (Gandhara reliefs, 1-400 CE).

The Parthenon, a Doric temple, is part of the Acropolis in Athens, which took shape in Greece in the 5th century BCE.

Persia. Aryan peoples (Persians, Medes) dominated the area of present Iran by the beginning of the 1st millennium BCE.

The prophet **Zoroaster** (b. c. 628 BCE) introduced a dualistic religion in which the forces of good (Ahura Mazda, "Lord of Wisdom") and evil (Ahriman) battle for dominance; individuals are judged by their actions and earn damnation or salvation. Zoroaster's hymns (*Gathas*) are included in the *Avesta*, the Zoroastrian scriptures. A version of this faith became the established religion of the Persian Empire.

Africa. Nubia, periodically occupied by Egypt since about 2600 BCE, ruled Egypt c. 750-661 BCE and survived as

an independent Egyptianized kingdom (**Kush**; capital Meroe) for 1,000 years. The Iron Age Nok culture flourished c. 500 BCE-200 CE on the Benue Plateau of **Nigeria**.

Americas. The Chavin culture controlled Northern Peru c. 900 BCE to 200 BCE. Its ceremonial centers, featuring the jaguar god, survived long after. Its architecture, ceramics, and textiles had influenced other Peruvian cultures. **Mayan civilization** began to develop in Central America as early as 1500 BCE.

Great Empires Unite the Classical World: 400 BCE-400 CE

Persia and the Mediterranean. **Cyrus**, ruler of a small kingdom in Persia from 559 BCE, united the Persians and Medes within 10 years and conquered Asia Minor and Babylonia in another 10. His son Cambyses, followed by **Darius** (r. 522-486 BCE), added vast lands to the E and N as far as the Indus Valley and Central Asia, as well as Egypt and Thrace. The whole empire was ruled by an international bureaucracy and army, with Persians holding the chief positions. The resources and styles of all the subject civilizations were exploited to create a rich syncretic art.

The kingdom of Macedon, which under Philip II dominated the Greek world and Egypt, was passed on to Philip's son **Alexander** in 336 BCE. Within 13 years, Alexander had conquered all the Persian dominions. Imbued by his tutor Aristotle with Greek ideals, Alexander encouraged colonization, and Greek-style cities were founded. After his death in 323 BCE, wars of succession divided the empire into three significant dynasties—the **Antigonids** in Asia Minor and Macedon, the **Ptolemies** in Egypt, and the **Seleucids** in Mesopotamia. In the ensuing 300 years (the **Hellenistic Era**), a cosmopolitan Greek-oriented culture permeated the ancient world from Western Europe to the borders of India, absorbing native elites everywhere.

Hellenistic philosophy stressed the private individual's search for happiness. The Cynics followed Diogenes (c. 400-c. 325 BCE), who stressed self-sufficiency and restriction of desires and expressed contempt for luxury and social convention. Zeno (c. 335-c. 263 BCE) and the **Stoics** exalted reason, identified it with virtue, and counseled an ascetic disregard for misfortune. The **Epicureans** tried to build lives of moderate pleasure without emotional or emotional involvement. Hellenistic arts imitated life realistically, especially in sculpture and literature (comedies of Menander, 342-292 BCE).

The sciences thrived, especially at Alexandria, where the Ptolemies financed a great library and museum. Fields of study included mathematics (**Euclid**'s geometry, c. 300 BCE); astronomy (heliocentric theory of Aristarchus, 310-230 BCE; Julian calendar, 45 BCE; **Ptolemy**'s *Almagest*, c. 150 CE); geography (world map of Eratosthenes, 276-194 BCE); hydraulics (**Archimedes**, 287-212 BCE); medicine (Galen, 130-200 CE); and chemistry. Inventors refined uses for siphons, valves, gears, springs, screws, levers, cams, and pulleys.

A restored Persian empire under the **Parthians** (northern Iranian tribespeople) controlled the eastern Hellenistic world from 250 BCE to 229 CE. The Parthians and the succeeding **Sassanian dynasty** (c. 224-651 CE) fought with Rome periodically. The Sassanians revived Zoroastrianism as a state religion and patronized a nationalistic artistic and scholarly renaissance.

Rome. The city of Rome was founded, according to legend, by Romulus in 753 BCE. Through military expansion and colonization, and by granting citizenship to leading members of conquered tribes, the city annexed all of Italy S of the Po R. in the 100-year period before 268 BCE. The Latin and other Italic tribes were annexed first, followed by the **Etruscans** (founders of a great civilization N of Rome) and Greek colonies in the S. With a large standing army and reserve forces of several hundred thousand, Rome was able to defeat **Carthage** in the three **Punic Wars** (264-241 BCE, 218-201 BCE, 149-146 BCE), despite the invasion of Italy by **Hannibal** (218 BCE), thus gaining Sicily and territory in Spain and N Africa.

Rome exploited local disputes to conquer Greece and Asia Minor in the 2nd cent. BCE and Egypt in the 1st (after the defeat and suicide of **Antony and Cleopatra**, 30 BCE). The Mediterranean civilized world, up to the disputed Parthian border, was now Roman and remained so for 500 years. Less civilized regions were added to the Empire: Gaul (conquered by **Julius Caesar**, 58-51 BCE), Britain (43 CE), and Dacia NE of the Danube (107 CE).

The original aristocratic republican government, with democratic features added in the 5th and 4th cent. BCE, deteriorated under the pressures of empire and class conflict (**Gracchus** brothers, social reformers, murdered in 133 BCE and 121 BCE; slave revolts in 135 BCE and 73 BCE). After a series of civil wars (Marius vs. Sulla, 88-82 BCE; Caesar vs. **Pompey**, 49-45 BCE; triumvirate vs. Caesar's assassins, 44-43 BCE; Antony vs. Octavian, 32-30 BCE), the empire came under the rule of a deified monarch (first emperor, **Augustus**, 27 BCE-14 CE).

Provincials (nearly all granted citizenship by Caracalla, 212 CE) came to dominate the army and civil service. Traditional **Roman law**, systematized and interpreted by independent jurists, and local self-rule in provincial cities were supplanted by a vast tax-collecting bureaucracy in the 3rd and 4th cent. The legal rights of women, children, and slaves were strengthened.

Roman innovations in **civil engineering** included water mills, windmills, and rotary mills and the use of cement that hardened under water. Monumental architecture (baths, theaters, temples) relied on the arch and the dome. A network of roads (some still standing) stretched 53,000 mi, passing through mountain tunnels as long as 3.5 mi. Aqueducts brought water to cities; underground sewers removed waste.

Roman art and literature were derivative of Greek models. Innovations were made in sculpture (naturalistic busts, equestrian statues), decorative wall painting (as at Pompeii), satire (**Juvenal**, 60-127 CE), history (**Tacitus**, 56-120 CE), and prose romance (**Petronius**, d. 66 CE). Gladiatorial contests dominated public amusements, which were supported by the state.

India. The **Gupta** monarchs reunited Northern India c. 320 CE. Their peaceful and prosperous reign saw a revival of Hindu religious thought and Brahman power. The old Vedic traditions were combined with devotion to many indigenous deities (who were seen as manifestations of Vedic gods). Caste lines were reinforced, and Buddhist practices gradually disappeared or were integrated with **Hindu** traditions. The art (often erotic), architecture, and literature of the period, patronized by the Gupta court, are considered among India's finest achievements (Kalidasa, poet and dramatist, fl. c. 400 CE). Mathematical innovations included the use of zero and decimal numbers. Invasions by White Huns from the NW led to the empire's destruction c. 550 CE. Rich cultures also developed in Southern India during this period. Emotional Tamil religious poetry contributed to the Hindu revival. The Pallava kingdom controlled much of Southern India c. 350-880 CE and helped to spread Indian civilization to SE Asia.

China. The Qin ruler Shi Huang (r. 221-210 BCE), known as the First Emperor, centralized political authority; standardized the written language, laws, weights, measures, and coinage; and conducted a census. But he tried to destroy most philosophical texts. The **Han** dynasty (202 BCE-220 CE) instituted the Mandarin bureaucracy, which lasted 2,000 years. Local officials were selected by examination in Confucian classics and trained at the imperial university and provincial schools.

The invention of **paper** facilitated this bureaucratic system. Agriculture was promoted, but peasants bore most of the tax burden. Irrigation was improved, water clocks and sundials were used, astronomy and mathematics thrived, and landscape painting was perfected.

With the expansion S and W (to nearly the present borders of today's China), trade was opened with India, SE Asia, and the Middle East over sea and caravan routes. Indian missionaries brought Mahayana Buddhism to China by the 1st cent. CE and spawned a variety of sects. Daoism was revived and merged with popular superstitions. **Daoist and Buddhist monasteries** and convents multiplied in the turbulent centuries after the collapse of the Han dynasty in 220 CE.

Monotheism Spreads: 1-750 CE

Roman Empire. Polytheism was practiced in the Roman Empire, and religions indigenous to particular Middle Eastern nations became international. Roman citizens worshiped **Isis** of Egypt, **Mithras** of Persia, **Demeter** of Greece, and the great mother **Cybele** of Phrygia. Their cults centered on mysteries (secret ceremonies) and the promise of an afterlife, symbolized by the death and rebirth of the god. The Jews of the empire preserved their monotheistic religion, Judaism, the world's oldest (c. 1300 BCE) continuous religion. Its teachings are contained in the Bible (the Old Testament). 1st-cent. CE Judaism embraced several sects, including the **Sadducees**, mostly drawn from the Temple priesthood, who were culturally Hellenized; the **Pharisees**, who upheld the full range of traditional customs and practices as of equal weight to literal scriptural law and elaborated synagogue worship; and the **Essenes**, an ascetic, millenarian sect. Messianic fervor led to repeated, unsuccessful rebellions against Rome (66-70, 135 CE). As a result, the Temple in Jerusalem was destroyed and the population decimated; this event marked the beginning of the Diaspora (living in exile). To preserve the faith, codification of law was begun at the academy of Yavneh. The work continued for some 500 years in Palestine and in Babylonia, ending in the final redaction (c. 600) of the **Talmud**, a huge collection of legal and moral debates, rulings, liturgy, biblical exegesis, and legendary materials.

Christianity. Emerging as a distinct sect by the second half of the 1st cent. CE, Christianity is based on the teachings of **Jesus**, whom believers considered the Savior (Messiah or Christ) and son of God. Missionary activities of the Apostles and such early leaders as **Paul of Tarsus** spread the faith. Intermittent persecution, as in Rome under Nero in 64 CE, on grounds of suspected disloyalty, failed to disrupt Christian communities. Each congregation, generally urban and of plebeian character, was tightly organized under a leader (bishop), elders (presbyters or priests), and assistants (deacons). The four Gospels (accounts of the life and teachings of Jesus) and the Acts of the Apostles were written down in the late 1st and early 2nd cent. and circulated along with letters of Paul and other Christian leaders. An authoritative canon of these writings was not fixed until the 4th cent.

A school for priests was established at Alexandria in the 2nd cent. Its teachers (**Origen**, c. 182-251) helped define doctrine and promote the faith in Greek-style philosophical works. Neoplatonism underwent Christian coloration in the writings of Church Fathers such as **Augustine** (354-430). Christian hermits began to associate in monasteries, first in Egypt (St. Pachomius, c. 290-345), then in other eastern lands, then in the W (**St. Benedict's rule**, 529). Devotion to saints, especially Mary, mother of Jesus, spread. Under **Constantine** (r. 306-37), Christianity became in effect the established religion of the Empire. Pagan temples were expropriated, state funds were used to build churches and support the hierarchy, and laws were adjusted in accordance with Christian ideas. Pagan worship was banned by the end of the 4th cent., and severe restrictions were placed on Judaism.

The newly established church was rocked by doctrinal disputes, often exacerbated by regional rivalries. Chief heresies (as defined by church councils, backed by imperial authority) were **Arianism**, which denied the divinity of Jesus; **Monophysitism**, denying the human nature of Christ; **Donatism**, which regarded as invalid any sacraments administered by sinful clergy; and **Pelagianism**, which denied the necessity of unmerited divine aid (grace) for salvation.

Islam. The earliest Arab civilization emerged by the end of the 2nd millennium BCE in the watered highlands of Yemen. Seaborne and caravan trade in frankincense and myrrh connected the area with the Nile and Fertile Crescent. The Minaean, Sabean (Sheba), and Himyarite states successively held sway. By Muhammad's time (7th cent. CE), the region was a province of Sassanian Persia. In the N, the Nabataean kingdom at Petra and the kingdom of Palmyra were Aramaicized, Romanized, and finally absorbed, as neighboring Judea had been, into the Roman Empire. Nomads shared the central region with a few trading towns and oases. Wars between tribes and raids on communities were common and were celebrated in a poetic tradition that by the 6th cent. helped establish a classic literary Arabic.

About 610, **Muhammad**, a 40-year-old Arab man of Mecca, emerged as a prophet. He proclaimed a revelation from the one true God, calling on contemporaries to abandon idolatry and restore the faith of Abraham. He introduced his religion as **Islam**, meaning "submission" to the one God, Allah, as a continuation of the biblical faith of Abraham, Moses, and Jesus, all respected as prophets in this system. His teachings, recorded in the Quran, in many ways were inclusive of Abrahamic monotheistic ideas known to the Jews and Christians in Arabia. A key aspect of the Abrahamic connection was insistence on justice in society, which led to severe opposition among the aristocrats in Mecca. As conditions worsened for Muhammad and his followers, he decided in 622 to make a *hegira* (flight) to Medina, 200 mi to the N. This event marks the beginning of the Muslim lunar calendar. Hostilities between Mecca and Medina increased, and in 629 Muhammad conquered Mecca. By the time he died in 632, nearly all the Arabian peninsula accepted his political and religious leadership.

After his death the majority of Muslims (later known as **Sunni** Muslims) recognized the leadership of the **caliph** (successor) Abu Bakr (632-34), followed by Umar (634-44), Uthman (644-56), and Ali (656-60). A minority, the **Shiites**, insisted instead on the leadership of Ali, Muhammad's cousin and son-in-law. By 644, **Muslim rule** over Arabia was confirmed. Muslim armies had threatened the Byzantine and Persian empires, which were weakened by wars and disaffection among subject peoples (including Coptic and Syriac Christians opposed to the Byzantine Orthodox establishment). Syria, Palestine, Egypt, Iraq, and Persia fell to Muslim armies. The new administration assimilated existing systems in the region; hence the conquered peoples participated in running the empire. The Quran recognized the so-called Peoples of the Book, i.e., Christians, Jews, and Zoroastrians, as tolerated monotheists, and Muslim policy was relatively tolerant to minorities living as "protected" peoples. An expanded tax system, based on conquests of the Persian and Byzantine empires, provided revenue to organize campaigns against neighboring non-Muslim regions.

Under the **Umayyads** (661-750) and **Abbasids** (750-1256), territorial expansion led Muslim armies across N Africa and into Spain (711). Muslim armies in the W were stopped at Tours, France, in 732 by the Frankish ruler **Charles Martel**. Asia Minor, the Indus Valley, and Transoxiana were conquered in the E. The conversion of conquered peoples to Islam was gradual. In many places the official Arabic language supplanted the local tongues. But in the eastern regions the Arab rulers and their armies adopted Persian cultures and language as part of their Muslim identity.

Disputes over succession and pious opposition to injustices in society led to a number of oppositional movements, which led to the factionalization of Muslim community. The **Shiites** supported leadership candidates descended from Muhammad, believing them to be carriers of some kind of divine authority. The **Kharijites** supported an egalitarian system derived from the Quran, opposing and even engaging in battle against those who did not agree with them.

Islam's primary religious text, the Quran, contains 114 chapters known as *sura*.

New Peoples Enter World History: 400-900 CE

Barbarian invasions and fall of Rome. Germanic tribes infiltrated S and E from their Baltic homeland during the 1st millennium BCE, reaching southern Germany by 100 BCE and the Black Sea by 214 CE. Organized into large federated tribes under elected kings, most resisted Roman domination and raided the empire in times of civil war (Goths took Dacia in 214, raided Thrace in 251-69). Germanic troops and commanders dominated the Roman armies by the end of the 4th cent. **Huns,** invaders from Asia, entered Europe in 372, driving more Germans into the empire. Emperor Valens allowed Visigoths to cross the Danube in 376. Huns under Attila (d. 453) raided Gaul, Italy, and the Balkans.

The western empire, weakened by overtaxation and social stagnation, was overrun in the 5th cent. Gaul was effectively lost in 406-07, Spain in 409, Britain in 410, and Africa in 429-39. Rome was sacked in 410 by Visigoths under Alaric and in 455 by Vandals. The **last western emperor,** Romulus Augustulus, was deposed in 476 by the Germanic chief Odoacer.

Celts. Celtic cultures, which in pre-Roman times covered most of W Europe, were confined almost entirely to the British Isles after the Germanic invasions. **St. Patrick** completed (c. 457-92) the conversion of Ireland and a strong monastic tradition took hold. Irish monastic missionaries in Scotland, England, and on the continent (Columba, c. 521-97; Columbanus, c. 543-615) helped restore Christianity after the Germanic invasions. **Monasteries** became centers of classic and Christian learning and presided over the recording of a Christianized Celtic mythology, elaborated by secular writers and bards. An intricate decorative art style developed, especially in book illumination (Lindisfarne Gospels, c. 700; Book of Kells, 8th cent.).

Successor states. The Visigothic kingdom in Spain (from 419) and much of France (to 507) saw continuation of Roman administration, language, and law (Breviary of Alaric, 506) until its destruction by Muslim forces from North Africa (711). The Vandal kingdom in Africa (from 429) was conquered by the Byzantines in 533. Italy was ruled successively by an Ostrogothic kingdom under Byzantine suzerainty (489-554), direct Byzantine government, and German Lombards (568-774). The Lombards divided the peninsula with the Byzantines and papacy under the dynamic reformer **Pope Gregory the Great** (590-604) and successors.

King Clovis (r. 481-511) united the Franks on both sides of the Rhine and, after his conversion to Christianity, defeated the Arian heretics, Burgundians (after 500), and Visigoths (507) with the support of native clergy and the papacy. Under the **Merovingian** kings, a feudal system emerged: power was fragmented among hierarchies of military landowners. Social stratification, which in late Roman times had acquired legal, hereditary sanction, was reinforced.

The **Carolingians** (747-987) expanded the kingdom and restored central power. **Charlemagne** (r. 768-814) conquered nearly all the Germanic lands, including Lombard Italy. He was crowned emperor by Pope Leo III in Rome in 800. A centuries-long decline in commerce and arts was reversed under Charlemagne's patronage. He welcomed Jews to his kingdom, which became a center of Jewish learning (Rashi, 1040-1105). He sponsored the Carolingian Renaissance of learning under the Anglo-Latin scholar Alcuin (c. 732-804), who reformed church liturgy.

The pyramid of Kukulkan (El Castillo) at Chichen Itza is one of the existing examples of Mayan architecture in present-day Mexico.

Byzantine Empire. Under **Diocletian** (r. 284-305) the Roman empire had been divided into two parts to facilitate administration and defense. **Constantine** founded (330) **Constantinople** (at old Byzantium) as a fully Christian city. Commerce and taxation financed a sumptuous, orientalized court, a class of hereditary bureaucratic families, and magnificent urban construction (Hagia Sophia, 532-37). The city's fortifications and naval innovations repelled assaults by Goths, Huns, Slavs, Bulgars, Avars, Arabs, and Scandinavians. Greek replaced Latin as the official language by c. 700. **Byzantine art,** a solemn, sacral, and stylized variation of late classical styles (mosaics at the Church of San Vitale, Ravenna, Italy, 526-48), was a starting point for medieval art in Eastern and Western Europe.

Justinian (r. 527-65) finally reconquered parts of Spain, N Africa, and Italy, codified **Roman law** (Codex Justinianus [529] was medieval Europe's chief legal text), closed the Platonic Academy at Athens, and ordered all pagans to convert. Lombards in Italy and Arabs in Africa retook most of his conquests. The Isaurian dynasty from Anatolia (from 717) and the Macedonian dynasty (867-1054) restored military and commercial power. The Iconoclast controversy (726-843) over the permissibility of images helped alienate the Eastern Church from the papacy.

Abbasid Empire. Baghdad (established 762) became seat of the **Abbasid dynasty** (established 750), while Umayyads continued to rule in Spain. A brilliant cosmopolitan civilization emerged, inaugurating a Muslim-Arab golden age. Arabic was the lingua franca of the empire; intellectual sources from Persian, Sanskrit, Greek, and Syriac were rendered into Arabic. Christians and Jews equally participated in this translation movement, which also involved interaction between Jewish legal thought and Islamic law, as much as between Christian theology and Muslim scholasticism. Persian-style court life, with art and music, flourished at the court of **Harun al-Rashid** (786-809), celebrated in the masterpiece known to English readers as *The Arabian Nights.* The sciences, medicine, and mathematics were pursued at Baghdad, Cordova, and Cairo (c. 969). The culmination of this intellectual synthesis in Islamic civilization came with the scientific and philosophical works of **Avicenna** (Ibn Sina, 980-1037), **Averroes** (Ibn Rushd, 1126-98), and **Maimonides** (1135-1204), a Jew who wrote in Arabic. This intellectual tradition was translated into Latin and opened a new period in Christian thought.

The decentralization of the Abbasid empire, from 874, led to the establishment of various Muslim dynasties under different ethnic groups. Persians, Berbers, and Turks ruled different regions, retaining connection with the Abbasid caliph at the religious level. The Abbasid period also saw various religious movements against the orthodox position held by governing authorities. This situation in Islam led to the establishment of different legal, theological, and mystical schools of thought. The most influential mass movement was **Sufism,** which aimed at the reaching out of the average individual in quest of a spiritual path. Al-Ghazali (1058-1111) is credited with reconciling personal Sufism with orthodox Sunni tradition.

Africa. Immigrants from Saba in S Arabia helped set up the **Axum** kingdom in Ethiopia in the 1st cent. (their language, Ge'ez, is preserved by the Ethiopian Church). In the 3rd cent., when the kingdom became Christianized, it defeated Kushite Meroe and expanded its influence into Yemen. Axum was the center of a vast ivory trade and controlled the Red Sea coast until c. 1100. Arab conquest in Egypt cut Axum's political and economic ties with Byzantium.

The Iron Age entered W Africa by the end of the 1st millennium BCE. **Ghana,** the first known sub-Saharan state, ruled in the upper Senegal-Niger region c. 400-1240, controlling the trade of gold from mines in the S to trans-Sahara caravan routes to the N. The **Bantu** peoples, probably of W African origin, began to spread E and S perhaps 2,000 years ago, displacing the Pygmies and Bushmen of central and southern Africa during a 1,500-year period.

Japan. The advanced Neolithic Yayoi period, when irrigation, rice farming, and iron and bronze casting techniques were introduced from China or Korea, persisted to c. 400 CE. The myriad Japanese states were then united by the **Yamato** clan, under an emperor who acted as chief priest of the animistic Shinto cult. Japanese political and military intervention in Korea, then under strong Chinese influence, quickened a Chinese cultural invasion of Japan, bringing Buddhism, the Chinese language (which long remained a literary and governmental medium), Chinese ideographs, and Buddhist styles in painting, sculpture, literature, and architecture (7th cent., Horyuji temple at Nara). The Taika Reforms (646) tried unsuccessfully to centralize Japan according to Chinese bureaucratic and Buddhist philosophical values.

A nativist reaction against the Buddhist **Nara** period (710-94) ushered in the **Heian** period (794-1185) centered at the new capital, Kyoto. Japanese elegance and simplicity modified Chinese styles in architecture, scroll painting, and literature; the writing system was also simplified. The courtly novel *Tale of Genji* (1010-20) testifies to the enhanced role of women in medieval Japanese literature and culture.

Southeast Asia. The historic peoples of SE Asia began arriving some 2,500 years ago from China and Tibet, displacing scattered aborigines. Their agriculture relied on rice and yams. Indian cultural influences were strongest; literacy and Hindu and Buddhist ideas followed the S India-China trade route. From the southern tip of Indochina, the kingdom of **Funan** (1st-7th cent.) traded as far W as Persia. It was absorbed by Chenla, itself conquered by the **Khmer** empire (800-1300). The Khmers, under Hindu god-kings (Suryavarman II, 1113-c. 1150), built the monumental Angkor Wat temple center for the royal phallic cult. The **Nam-Viet** kingdom in Annam, dominated by China and Chinese culture for 1,000 years, emerged in the 10th cent., growing at the expense of the Khmers, who also lost ground in the NW to the new, highly organized **Thai** kingdom. On Sumatra, the **Srivijaya** empire controlled vital sea lanes (7th-10th cent.). A Buddhist dynasty, the Sailendras, ruled central **Java**

(8th-9th cent.), building at Borobudur one of the largest stupas (dome-shaped Buddhist shrines) in the world.

China. The Sui dynasty (581-618) ushered in a period of commercial, artistic, and scientific achievement in China, which continued under the **Tang** dynasty (618-906). Inventions like the magnetic compass, gunpowder, the abacus, and printing were introduced or perfected. Medical innovations included cataract surgery. The state, from its cosmopolitan capital, Chang-an, supervised foreign trade, which exchanged Chinese silks, porcelains, and art for spices and ivory over Central Asian caravan routes and sea routes reaching Africa. A golden age of poetry bequeathed valuable works to later generations (Tu Fu, 712-70; Li Po, 701-62). Landscape painting flourished.

Commercial and industrial expansion continued under the **Northern Song** (960-1126), facilitated by paper money and credit notes. But commerce never achieved full respectability; government monopolies expropriated successful merchants. The population, long stable at 50 million, doubled in 200 years with the introduction of early-ripening rice and the double harvest. In art, native Chinese styles were revived.

Americas. From 300 to 600, a Native American empire stretched from the Valley of Mexico to Guatemala, centering on the huge city **Teotihuacán** (founded 100 BCE). To the S, in Guatemala, a high **Mayan** civilization developed (150-900) around hundreds of rural ceremonial centers. The Mayans improved on Olmec writing and the calendar and pursued astronomy and mathematics. In South America, a widespread pre-Inca culture grew from **Tiahuanacu**, Bolivia, near Lake Titicaca (Gateway of the Sun doorway, c. 700).

Christian Europe Regroups and Expands: 900-1300

Scandinavia. Pagan Danish and Norse (Viking) adventurers, traders, and pirates raided the coasts of the British Isles (Dublin, c. 831), France, and even the Mediterranean for over 200 years beginning in the late 8th cent. Inland settlement in the W was limited to Great Britain (King Canute, 994-1035) and Normandy, settled (911) under Rollo, as a fief of France. Vikings also reached Iceland (874), Greenland (c. 986), and North America (**Leif Ericson** and others, c. 1000). Norse traders (**Varangians**) developed Russian river commerce from the 8th to the 11th cent. and helped set up a state at Kiev in the late 9th cent. Conversion to Christianity occurred in the 10th century, reaching Sweden 100 years later. In the 11th cent., Norman bands conquered Southern Italy and Sicily, and Duke **William of Normandy** conquered (1066) England, bringing feudal government and the French language, essential elements in later English civilization.

Central and East Europe. Slavs began to expand from about 150 CE in all directions in Europe. By the 7th cent. they reached as far S as the Adriatic and Aegean seas. In the Balkan Peninsula they dislocated Romanized local populations or assimilated newcomers (Bulgarians, a Turkic people). The first **Slavic states** were Moravia (628) in Central Europe and the Bulgarian state (680) in the Balkans. Byzantine missions of St. Methodius and Cyril (whose Greek-based cyrillic alphabet is still used by some Southern and Eastern Slavs) converted (863) Moravia. The Eastern Slavs, part-civilized under the overlordship of the Turkish-Jewish **Khazar** trading empire (7th-10th cent.), gravitated toward Constantinople by the 9th cent. The **Kievan** state adopted (989) Eastern Christianity under Prince Vladimir. King Boleslav I (992-1025) began **Poland**'s long history of conquest. The Magyars (**Hungarians**), in present-day Hungary since 896, accepted (1001) Latin Christianity.

Germany. The German kingdom that emerged after the breakup of Charlemagne's Western Empire remained a confederation of largely autonomous states. Otto I, a Saxon who was king from 936, established the **Holy Roman Empire**—a union of Germany and Northern Italy—in alliance with Pope John XII, who crowned (962) him emperor; he defeated (955) the Magyars. Imperial power was greatest under the **Hohenstaufens** (1138-1254), despite the growing opposition of the papacy, which ruled central Italy, and the Lombard League cities. Frederick II (1194-1250) improved administration and patronized the arts. After his death, German influence was removed from Italy.

Christian Spain. From its northern mountain redoubts, Christian rule slowly migrated S through the 11th cent., when Muslim unity collapsed. After the capture (1085) of **Toledo**, the kingdoms of Portugal, Castile, and Aragon undertook repeated crusades of reconquest, finally completed in 1492. Elements of Islamic civilization persisted in recaptured areas, influencing all Western Europe.

Crusades. Pope Urban II called for a crusade (1095) to restore Asia Minor to Byzantium and the Holy Land to Christendom. This first crusade captured Jerusalem and led to the foundation of four Frankish states in the Levant. The defeat inflicted upon crusaders at the Battle of Hattin (1187) by **Saladin** (c. 1137-93), the Kurdish ruler of Egypt and Syria, effectively negated territorial gains. Many crusades followed until 1291. The 4th crusade sacked Constantinople (1204). Other crusades were launched against Christian heretics (Albigensian Crusade, 1229), pagans, and enemies of the papacy.

Economy. The agricultural base of European life benefited from improvements in **plow design** (c. 1000) and by the draining of lowlands and clearing of forests, leading to a rural population increase. Towns grew in Northern Italy, Flanders, and Northern Germany (Hanseatic League). Improvements in **loom design** permitted factory textile production. **Guilds** dominated urban trades from the 12th cent. Banking (centered in Italy, 12th-15th cent.) facilitated long-distance trade.

Christianity. The split between the Eastern and Western churches was formalized in 1054. Western and Central Europe was divided into 500 bishoprics under one united hierarchy, but conflicts between secular and church authorities were frequent (German **Investiture Controversy**, 1075-1122). Clerical power was first strengthened through the international monastic reform begun at Cluny in 910. Popular religious enthusiasm often expressed itself in heretical movements (Waldensians from 1173), but was channeled by the **Dominican** (1215) and **Franciscan** (1223) friars into the religious mainstream.

Arts. Romanesque architecture (9th to mid-12th cent.) expanded on late Roman models, using the rounded arch and massed stone to support enlarged basilicas. Painting and sculpture followed Byzantine models. The literature of **chivalry** was exemplified by the epic (*Chanson de Roland*, c. 1100) and by courtly love poems of the troubadours of Provence and minnesingers of Germany. **Gothic** architecture emerged in France (choir of St. Denis, c. 1140) and spread along with French cultural influence. Rib vaulting and pointed arches were used to combine soaring heights with delicacy, and they freed walls for display of stained glass. Exteriors were covered with painted relief sculpture and embellished with elaborate architectural detail.

Learning. Law, medicine, and philosophy were advanced at independent **universities** (Bologna, Paris, 12th cent.), originally corporations of students and masters. Twelfth-cent. translations of Greek classics, especially by Aristotle, encouraged an analytic approach. Scholastic philosophy, from Anselm (1033-1109) to **Aquinas** (1225-74), attempted to understand revelation through reason.

Apogee of Central Asian Power and the Spread of Islam: 1250-1500

Turks. Turkic peoples, of Central Asian ancestry, were a military threat to the Byzantine and Persian Empires from the 6th cent. After several waves of invasions, during which most of the Turks adopted Islam, the **Seljuk Turks** took (1055) Baghdad. They ruled Persia, Iraq, and, after 1071, Asia Minor, where massive numbers of Turks settled. The empire was divided in the 12th cent. into smaller states ruled by Seljuks, Kurds, and Mamluks (a military caste of former Turk, Kurd, and Circassian slaves), which governed Egypt and the Middle East until the Ottoman era (c. 1290-1922).

Osman I (r. c. 1290-1326) and succeeding sultans united Anatolian Turkish warriors in a militaristic state that waged holy war against Byzantium and Balkan Christians. Most of the Balkans had been subdued and Anatolia united when Constantinople fell (1453). By the mid-16th cent., Hungary, the Middle East, and N Africa had been conquered. The Turkish advance was stopped at Vienna (1529) and at the naval battle of Lepanto (1571) by Spain, Venice, and the papacy.

The **Ottoman state** was governed in accordance with orthodox Muslim law. Greek, Armenian, and Jewish communities were segregated and were ruled by religious leaders responsible for taxation; they dominated trade. Many state offices and most army ranks were filled by slaves, in part through a system of child conscription among Christians.

India. Mahmud of Ghazni (971-1030) led repeated Turkish raids into N India. Turkish power was consolidated in 1206 with the start of the **Sultanate at Delhi**. Centralization of state power under the early Delhi sultans went far beyond traditional Indian practice. Muslim rule of much of the subcontinent lasted until the British conquest 600 years later, though Hinduism remained the majority religion.

Mongols. Genghis Khan (c. 1167-1227) first united the feuding Mongol tribes and built their armies into an effective offensive force around a core of highly mobile cavalry. He and his immediate successors created the largest land empire in history; by 1279 it stretched from the E coast of Asia to the Danube and from the Siberian steppes to the Arabian Sea. East-West trade and contacts were facilitated (Marco Polo, c. 1254-1324). The western Mongols were Islamized by 1295; successor states soon lost their Mongol character by assimilation. They were briefly reunited under the Turk Tamerlane (1336-1405).

Kublai Khan ruled China from his new capital Beijing (established c. 1264). Naval campaigns against Japan (1274, 1281) and Java (1293) were defeated, the latter by the Hindu-Buddhist maritime kingdom of Majapahit. The **Yuan** dynasty used Mongols and other foreigners (including Europeans) in official posts and tolerated the return of Nestorian Christianity

(suppressed 841-45) and the spread of Islam in the S and W. A native reaction expelled the Mongols in 1367-68.

Russia. The Kievan state in Russia, weakened by the decline of Byzantium and the rise of the Catholic Polish-Lithuanian state, was overrun (1238-40) by the Mongols. Only the northern trading republic of Novgorod remained independent. The grand dukes of Moscow emerged as leaders of a coalition of princes that eventually (by 1481) defeated the Mongols. After the fall of Constantinople in 1453, the **Tsars** (Caesars) at Moscow (from Ivan III, r. 1462-1505) set up an independent Russian Orthodox Church. Commerce failed to revive. The isolated Russian state remained agrarian with the peasant class falling into serfdom.

Persia. A revival of Persian literature, making use of the Arab alphabet and literary forms, began in the 10th cent. (epic of Firdausi, 935-1020). An art revival, influenced by Chinese styles introduced after the Mongols came to power in Iran, began in the 13th cent. Persian cultural and political forms, and often the Persian language, were used for centuries by Turkish and Mongol elites from the Balkans to India. Persian mystics from Rumi (1207-73) to Jami (1414-92) promoted **Sufism** in their poetry.

Africa. Two militant Islamic Berber dynasties emerged from the Sahara to carve out empires from the Sahel to central Spain—the **Almoravids** (c. 1050-1140) and the fanatical **Almohads** (c. 1125-1269). The Ghanaian empire was replaced in the upper Niger by Mali (c. 1230-1340), whose Muslim rulers imported Egyptians to help make **Timbuktu** a center of commerce (in gold, leather, and slaves) and learning. The Songhay empire (to 1590) replaced Mali. To the S, forest kingdoms produced refined artworks (Ife terra cotta, **Benin** bronzes).

Other **Muslim states** in Nigeria (Hausas) and Chad originated in the 11th cent. and continued in some form until the 19th-cent. European conquest. Less-developed Bantu kingdoms existed across central Africa.

Some 40 Muslim Arab-Persian trading colonies and city-states were established all along the E African coast from the 10th cent. (Kilwa, Mogadishu). The interchange with Bantu peoples produced the **Swahili** language and culture. Gold, palm oil, and people to enslave were brought from the interior, stimulating the growth of the Monamatapa kingdom of the Zambezi (15th cent.). The Christian Ethiopian empire (from 13th cent.) continued the traditions of Axum.

Southeast Asia. Islam was introduced into Malaya and the Indonesian islands by Arab, Persian, and Indian traders. Coastal Muslim cities and states (starting before 1300) soon dominated the interior. Chief among these was the **Malacca** state (c. 1400-1511), on the Malay peninsula.

Arts and Statecraft Thrive in Europe; New Asian Empires Rise: 1350-1600

Italy. Distinctive Italian achievements in literature and fine arts during the late Middle Ages (Dante, 1265-1321; Giotto, 1276-1337) led to the vigorous new styles of the Renaissance (14th-16th cent.). Patronized by the rulers of the quarreling petty states of Italy (Medicis in Florence and the papacy, c. 1400-1737), the plastic arts perfected realistic techniques, including perspective (Masaccio, 1401-28; Leonardo **da Vinci**, 1452-1519). Classical motifs were used in architecture, and increased talent and expense were put into secular buildings. The Florentine dialect was refined as a national literary language (Petrarch, 1304-74). Greek refugees from the E strengthened the respect of humanist scholars for the classic sources. Soon an international movement aided by the spread of printing (Gutenberg, c. 1397-1468), humanism was optimistic about the power of human reason (Erasmus of Rotterdam, 1466-1536, More's Utopia, 1516) and valued individual effort in the arts and in politics (Machiavelli, 1469-1527).

France. The French monarchy, strengthened in its repeated struggles with powerful nobles (Burgundy, Flanders, Aquitaine) by alliances with the growing commercial towns, consolidated bureaucratic control under Philip IV (r. 1285-1314) and extended French influence into Germany and Italy (popes at Avignon, France, 1309-1417). The **Hundred Years War** (1337-1453) ended English dynastic claims in France (battles of Crécy, 1346, and Poitiers, 1356; Joan of Arc executed, 1431). A French Renaissance, dating from royal invasions (1494, 1499)

of Italy, was encouraged at the court of Francis I (r. 1515-47), who centralized taxation and law. French vernacular literature consciously asserted its independence (La Pléiade, 1549).

England. The evolution of England's political institutions began with the **Magna Carta** (1215), by which King John guaranteed the privileges of nobles and church against the monarchy and assured jury trial. After the **Wars of the Roses** (1455-85), the **Tudor** dynasty reasserted royal prerogatives (Henry VIII, r. 1509-47), but the trend toward independent departments and ministerial government also continued. English trade (wool exports from c. 1340) was protected by the nation's growing maritime power (Spanish Armada destroyed, 1588).

English replaced French and Latin in the late 14th cent. in law and literature (Chaucer, c. 1340-1400), and English translation of the Bible began (Wycliffe, 1380s). Elizabeth I (r. 1558-1603) presided over the development of poetry (Spenser, 1552-99), drama (Shakespeare, 1564-1616), and music.

German Empire. From among a welter of minor feudal states, church lands, and independent cities, the Habsburgs assembled a far-flung territorial domain, based in Austria from 1276. Family members held the title of Holy Roman Emperor from 1438 to the Empire's dissolution in 1806 but failed to centralize its domains, leaving Germany disunited for centuries. Resistance to Turkish expansion brought Hungary and Austrian control over the 16th cent. The Netherlands, Luxembourg, and Burgundy were added in 1477, curbing French expansion.

The Flemish painting tradition of naturalism, technical proficiency, and bourgeois subject matter began in the 15th cent. (Jan van Eyck, c. 1390-1441), the earliest northern manifestation of the Renaissance. Albrecht **Dürer** (1471-1528) typified the merging of late Gothic and Italian trends in 16th-cent. German art. Imposing civic architecture flourished in the prosperous commercial cities.

Black Death. The bubonic plague reached Europe from the E in 1348, killing up to half the population by 1350 (and recurring periodically in most areas until the early 18th cent.). Labor scarcity forced wages to rise and brought greater freedom to the peasantry, making possible **peasant uprisings** (Jacquerie in France, 1358; Wat Tyler's rebellion in England, 1381).

Spain. Despite the unification of Castile and Aragon in 1479, the two countries retained separate governments, and the nobility, especially in Aragon and Catalonia, retained many privileges. Spanish lands in Italy (Naples, Sicily) and the Netherlands entangled the country in European wars through the mid-17th cent., while explorers, traders, and conquerors built up a Spanish empire in the Americas and the Philippines.

From the late 15th cent., a **golden age** of literature and art produced works of social satire (plays of Lope de Vega, 1562-1635; **Cervantes**, 1547-1616), as well as spiritual intensity (**El Greco**, 1541-1614; **Velázquez**, 1599-1660).

Explorations. Organized European maritime exploration began, seeking to evade the Venice-Ottoman monopoly of eastern trade and to promote Christianity. A key goal was to satisfy a growing taste for Asian goods. Beginning in 1418, expeditions from Portugal explored the W coast of Africa, until Vasco da Gama rounded the Cape of Good Hope in 1497 and reached India. A Portuguese trading empire was consolidated by the seizure of Goa (1510) and Malacca (1551). Japan was reached in 1542. The voyages of Christopher **Columbus** (1492-1504) uncovered a world new to Europeans, which Spain hastened to subdue. Navigation schools in Spain and Portugal, the development of large sailing ships (carracks) mounted with cannons, and the invention (c. 1475) of the rifle aided European penetration.

Mughals and Safavids. E of the Ottoman Empire, two Muslim dynasties ruled unchallenged in the 16th and 17th cent. The Mughal dynasty of India, founded by Persianized Turkish invaders from the NW under Babur, dates from their 1526 conquest of the Delhi Sultanate. The dynasty ruled most of India for more than 200 years, surviving nominally until 1857. **Akbar** (r. 1556-1605) consolidated administration at his glorious court, where the Urdu language (Persian-influenced Hindi) developed. Trade relations with Europe increased. Under Shah Jahan (1629-58), a secularized art fusing Hindu and Muslim elements flourished in miniature painting and in architecture (**Taj Mahal**). **Sikhism** (founded late 15th cent.) combined elements of both faiths. Suppression of Hindus and Shiite Muslims in S India in the late 17th cent. weakened the empire.

Intense devotion to the Shiite sect characterized the Safavids (1502-1736) of Persia and led to hostilities with the Sunni Ottomans for more than a century. The prosperity and the strength of the empire are evidenced by the mosques at its

The population of Western Europe was so reduced by the bubonic plague, or "Black Death," that it would not reach pre-plague levels again until the early 16th century.

capital city, **Isfahan.** The Safavids enhanced Iranian national consciousness.

China. The **Ming** emperors (1368-1644), the last native dynasty in China, wielded strong personal power. European trade (Portuguese monopoly through **Macau** from 1557) was strictly controlled. Jesuit scholars and scientists (Matteo Ricci, 1552-1610) introduced some Western sciences; their writings familiarized the West with China. The arts thrived, especially in the areas of painting and ceramics. Chinese manufacturing boomed, bringing in new profits from world trade.

Japan. After the decline of the first hereditary *shogunate* (chief generalship) at **Kamakura** (1185-1333), fragmentation of power accelerated, as did the consequent social mobility. Under Kamakura and the Ashikaga shogunate (1338-1573), the *daimyos* (lords) and *samurai* (warriors) grew more powerful and promoted a martial ideology. Japanese pirates and traders plied the China coast. Popular Buddhist movements included the nationalist Nichiren sect (from c. 1250) and **Zen** (brought from China, 1191), which stressed meditation and a disciplined aesthetic (tea ceremony, gardening, martial arts, *No* drama).

Change and Development in Europe: 1500-1700

Reformation. Theological debate and protests against real and perceived clerical corruption existed in the medieval Christian world, expressed by such dissenters as John **Wycliffe** (c. 1320-84) and his followers (the Lollards) in England, and Huss (burned as a heretic, 1415) in Bohemia.

Martin **Luther** (1483-1546) preached that faith alone, without the mediation of clergy or good works, leads to salvation. He attacked the authority of the pope, rejected priestly celibacy, and recommended individual study of the Bible (which he translated into German c. 1525). His 95 Theses (1517) led to his excommunication (1521). John **Calvin** (1509-64) said that God's elect were predestined for salvation and all others for damnation; good conduct and success were signs of election. Calvin in Geneva and John **Knox** (1505-72) in Scotland established theocratic states.

Henry VIII asserted English national authority and secular power by breaking away (1534) from the Catholic Church, creating what would become the Anglican Church. Monastic property was confiscated, and some Protestant doctrines given official sanction.

Religious wars. A century and a half of religious wars began with a southern German peasant uprising (1524),

repressed with Luther's support. Radical sects—democratic, pacifist, millenarian—arose (Anabaptists ruled Münster, 1534-35) and were suppressed violently. Civil war in France from 1562 between **Huguenots** (Protestant nobles and merchants) and Catholics ended with the 1598 **Edict of Nantes**, tolerating Protestants (revoked 1685). Habsburg attempts to restore Catholicism in Germany were resisted in 25 years of fighting. The 1555 Peace of Augsburg guarantee of religious independence to local princes and cities was confirmed only after the **Thirty Years' War** (1618-48), when much of Germany was devastated by local and foreign armies (Sweden, France).

A Catholic Reformation, or **Counter-Reformation**, met the Protestant challenge, defining an official theology at the Council of Trent (1545-63). The **Jesuit** order (Society of Jesus), founded in 1534 by Ignatius Loyola (1491-1556), helped reconvert large areas of Poland, Hungary, and S Germany and sent missionaries to the New World, India, and China. The **Inquisition** suppressed heresy in Catholic countries. A revival of religious fervor appeared in devotional literature (Teresa of Avila, 1515-82) and in grandiose **Baroque** art (Bernini, 1598-1680).

Scientific Revolution. The late nominalist thinkers (Ockham, c. 1300-49) of Paris and Oxford challenged Aristotelian orthodoxy, allowing for a freer scientific approach. At the same time, metaphysical values, such as the Neoplatonic faith in an orderly, mathematical cosmos, still motivated and directed inquiry. Nicolaus **Copernicus** (1473-1543) promoted the heliocentric theory, which was confirmed when Johannes **Kepler** (1571-1630) discovered the mathematical laws describing the elliptical orbits of the planets. The traditional Christian-Aristotelian belief that the heavens and the Earth were fundamentally different collapsed when **Galileo Galilei** (1564-1642) discovered moving sunspots, irregular moon topography, and moons around Jupiter, but he faced religious opposition (Galileo's retraction, 1633). He and Sir Isaac **Newton** (1642-1727) developed a mechanics that unified cosmic and earthly phenomena. Newton and Gottfried von **Leibniz** (1646-1716) invented calculus. René **Descartes** (1596-1650), best known for his influential philosophy, also invented analytic geometry.

An explosion of **observational science** included the discovery of blood circulation (Harvey, 1578-1657) and microscopic life (Leeuwenhoek, 1632-1723) and advances in anatomy (Vesalius, 1514-64, dissected corpses) and chemistry (Boyle, 1627-91). Scientific research institutes were founded in Florence (1657), London (**Royal Society**, 1660), and Paris (1666). Inventions proliferated (Savery's steam engine, 1698).

Arts. Mannerist trends of the High Renaissance (**Michelangelo**, 1475-1564) exploited virtuosity, grace, novelty, and exotic subjects and poses. The notion of artistic genius was promoted. Private connoisseurs entered the art market. These trends were elaborated in the 17th cent. **Baroque** era on a grander scale. Dynamic movement in painting and sculpture was emphasized by sharp lighting effects, rich materials (colored marble, gilt), and realistic details. Curved facades, broken lines, rich detail, and ceiling decoration characterized Baroque architecture. Monarchs, princes, and prelates, usually Catholic, used Baroque art to enhance and embellish their authority, as in royal portraits (Velázquez, 1599-1660; Van Dyck, 1599-1641).

National styles emerged. In France, a taste for rectilinear order and serenity (Poussin, 1594-1665), linked to the new rational philosophy, was expressed in classical forms. The influence of **classical values** in French literature (tragedies of **Racine**, 1639-99) gave rise to the "battle of the Ancients and Moderns." New forms included the essay (**Montaigne**, 1533-92) and novel (*Princesse de Clèves*, La Fayette, 1678).

Dutch painting of the 17th cent. was unique in its wide social distribution. The Flemish tradition of undemonstrative realism reached its peak in **Rembrandt** (1606-69) and Jan Vermeer (1632-75).

Economy. European economic expansion, known as the **commercial revolution**, was stimulated by new trade with the East, by New World gold and silver, and by a doubling of population (50 million in 1450, 100 million in 1600). **New business and financial techniques** were developed and refined, such as joint-stock companies, insurance, and letters of credit and exchange. The Bank of Amsterdam (1609) and the Bank of England (1694) broke the old monopoly of private banking families. The rise of a business mentality was typified by the spread of clock towers in cities in the 14th cent. By the mid-15th cent., portable clocks were available; the first watch was invented in 1502.

By 1650, most governments had adopted the **mercantile system**, in which they sought to amass metallic wealth by protecting merchants' foreign and colonial trade monopolies. The rise in prices and the new coin-based economy undermined craft guild and feudal manorial systems. Expanding industries (clothweaving, mining) benefited from technical advances. Coal began to replace wood as the chief fuel; it was used to fuel new 16th-cent. blast furnaces making cast iron.

New World. The Aztecs united much of the Mesoamerican area in a militarist empire by 1519 from their capital, Tenochtitlán (pop. 300,000), which was the center of a cult requiring ritual human sacrifice. Most of the civilized areas of South America were ruled by the centralized Inca Empire (1476-1534), stretching 2,000 mi from Ecuador to NW Argentina. Lavish and sophisticated traditions in pottery, weaving, sculpture, and architecture were maintained in both regions.

These empires, beset by revolts, fell in two short campaigns to gold-seeking Spanish forces based in the Antilles and Panama. Hernán **Cortés** took Mexico (1519-21); Francisco **Pizarro**,

The exact purpose of the Incan city of Machu Picchu, built in the 15th century and abandoned less than 150 years later, is unknown; one theory is that it served as a royal retreat.

Peru (1532-35). From these centers, land and sea expeditions claimed most of North and South America for Spain. The indigenous high cultures did not survive the impact of **Christian missionaries** and the new upper class of whites. Although the Spanish administration intermittently concerned itself with their welfare, the population was devastated by European diseases and remained impoverished at most levels. New World silver and such native products as potatoes, tobacco, corn, peanuts, chocolate, and rubber exercised a major economic influence on Europe.

Brazil, which the Portuguese reached in 1500 and settled after 1530, and the Caribbean colonies of several European nations developed a plantation economy where sugarcane, tobacco, cotton, coffee, rice, indigo, and lumber were grown by enslaved people. From the early 16th to late 19th cent., 10 million Africans were transported to **slavery** in the Americas and Caribbean islands.

Netherlands. The urban, Calvinist northern provinces of the Netherlands rebelled (1568) against Habsburg Spain and founded an oligarchic mercantile republic. Their control of the Baltic grain market enabled them to exploit Mediterranean food shortages. Religious refugees—French and Belgian Protestants, Iberian Jews—added to the commercial talent pool. After Spain absorbed Portugal (1580), the Dutch seized Portuguese possessions and created a vast commercial empire ultimately centered in parts of the Caribbean and in Indonesia. The Dutch also challenged or supplanted Portuguese traders in China and Japan. Revolution in 1640 restored Portuguese independence.

England. Anglicanism became firmly established under **Elizabeth I** after a brief Catholic interlude under "Bloody" Mary I (1553-58). But religious and political conflicts led to a rebellion (1642) by Parliament. Forces of the Roundheads (Puritans) defeated the Cavaliers (Royalists); Charles I was beheaded (1649). The new Commonwealth was ruled as a military dictatorship by Oliver **Cromwell**, who also brutally crushed (1649-51) an Irish rebellion. Conflicts within the Puritan camp (democratic Levelers defeated, 1649) aided the Stuart restoration (1660), but Parliament was strengthened and the peaceful **"Glorious Revolution"** (1688) advanced political and religious liberties (writings of **Locke**, 1632-1704). British privateers (Drake, 1540-96) challenged Spanish control of the New World and penetrated Asian trade routes (Madras taken, 1639). North American colonies (Jamestown, 1607; Plymouth, 1620) provided an outlet for private enterprise and religious dissenters from Europe. The British East India Co. gained growing sway in 18th-cent. India, as Mughal power declined.

France. Emerging from the religious civil wars in 1628, France regained military and commercial great power status (under the ministries of **Richelieu**, Mazarin, and Colbert). Under **Louis XIV** (r. 1643-1715), royal absolutism triumphed over nobles and local *parlements* (defeat of Fronde, 1648-53). Durable colonies were founded in Canada (1608), the Caribbean (1626), and India (1674).

Sweden. Sweden seceded from the Scandinavian Union in 1523. The thinly populated agrarian state (with copper, iron, and timber exports) was united by the Vasa kings, whose conquests by the mid-17th cent. made Sweden the dominant Baltic power. The empire collapsed in the Great Northern War (1700-21).

Poland. After the union with Lithuania in 1447, Poland ruled vast territories from the Baltic to the Black Sea, resisting German and Turkish incursions. Catholic nobles failed to gain the loyalty of their Orthodox Christian subjects in the E; commerce and trades were practiced by German and Jewish immigrants. The bloody 1648-49 Cossack uprising began the kingdom's dismemberment.

Russia. Growing authority of the tsars continued with advancing serfdom. Around 1700, **Peter the Great** imported new Western styles and technologies. Steady territorial expansion created a vast territory touching China, the Ottoman Empire, and east-central Europe.

China. A new dynasty, the **Manchus**, invaded from the NE, seized power in 1644, and expanded Chinese control to its greatest extent in Central and SE Asia. Trade and diplomatic contact with Europe grew, carefully controlled by China. New crops (sweet potato, maize, peanut) allowed economic and population growth (pop. 300 million, in 1800). Traditional arts and literature were pursued with increased sophistication (*Dream of the Red Chamber*, novel, mid-18th cent.).

Japan. Tokugawa Ieyasu, shogun from 1603, finally unified and pacified feudal Japan. Hereditary nobles (daimyos and samurai) monopolized government office and the professions. An urban merchant class grew, literacy spread, and a cultural renaissance occurred (**haiku**, a verse innovation of the poet Basho, 1644-94). Fear of European domination led to persecution of Christian converts from 1597 and to substantial isolation from outside contact from 1640.

Philosophy, Industry, and Revolution: 1700-1800

Science and reason. Greater faith in reason and empirical observation, instead of tradition and religious beliefs, espoused since the Renaissance (Francis Bacon, 1561-1626), was bolstered by scientific discoveries. René Descartes (1596-1650) used a rationalistic approach modeled on geometry and introspection to discover "self-evident" truths as a foundation of knowledge. Sir Isaac **Newton** emphasized induction from experimental observation. Baruch de **Spinoza** (1632-77), who called for political and intellectual freedom, developed a systematic rationalistic philosophy in his classic work *Ethics*.

French philosophers assumed leadership of the **Enlightenment** in the 18th cent. Montesquieu (1689-1755) used British history to support his notions of limited government. **Voltaire**'s (1694-1778) diaries and novels of exotic travel illustrated the intellectual trends toward secular ethics and relativism. Jean-Jacques **Rousseau**'s (1712-78) radical concepts of the **social contract** and of the inherent goodness of the common man gave impetus to antimonarchical republicanism. The *Encyclopedia* (1751-72), edited by Diderot and d'Alembert, designed as a monument to reason, was largely devoted to practical technology.

In England, ideals of liberty were connected with empiricist philosophy and science in the followers of John **Locke**. But British empiricism, especially as developed by the skeptical David **Hume** (1711-76), radically reduced the role of reason in philosophy, as did the evolutionary approach to law and politics of Edmund Burke (1729-97) and the utilitarian ethics of Jeremy Bentham (1748-1832). Adam Smith (1723-90) and other economists called for a rationalization of economic activity by removing artificial barriers to a supposedly natural free exchange of goods known as *laissez-faire*.

German writers participated in the new philosophical trends popularized by Christian von Wolff (1679-1754). Immanuel **Kant**'s (1724-1804) transcendental idealism, unifying an empirical epistemology with a priori moral and logical concepts, directed German thought away from skepticism. Italian contributions included work on electricity (Galvani, 1737-98; Volta, 1745-1827), the pioneer historiography of Vico (1668-1744), and writings on penal reform (Beccaria, 1738-94).

Benjamin Franklin (1706-90) was celebrated in Europe for his varied achievements.

The growth of the **press** (*Spectator*, 1711-12) and the wide distribution of sentimental **novels** attested to the increase of a large bourgeois public.

Arts. Rococo art, characterized by extravagant decorative effects, asymmetries copied from organic models, and artificial pastoral subjects, was favored by the continental aristocracy for most of the century (Watteau, 1684-1721) and had musical analogies in the ornamentalized polyphony of late Baroque. The Neoclassical art after 1750, associated with the new scientific archaeology, was more streamlined and was infused with the supposed moral and geometric rectitude of the Roman Republic (David, 1748-1825). In England, **town planning** on a grand scale began.

Industrial Revolution in England. Agricultural improvements, such as the sowing drill (1701) and livestock breeding, were implemented on the large fields provided by enclosure of common lands by private owners. Profits from agriculture and from colonial and foreign trade (1800 volume, £54 million) were channeled through hundreds of banks and the **Stock Exchange** (est. 1773) into new industrial processes.

The Newcomen steam pump (1712) aided coal mining. Coal fueled the new efficient steam engines patented by James Watt in 1769, and coke-smelting produced cheap, sturdy iron for machinery by the 1730s. The **flying shuttle** (1733) and **spinning jenny** (c. 1764) were used in the large new cotton textile factories, where women and children were much of the workforce. Goods were transported cheaply over **canals** (2,000 mi; built 1760-1800). By the early 19th cent., industrialization spread in Western Europe and North America.

American Revolution. The British colonies in North America attracted a mass immigration of religious dissenters and poor people throughout the 17th and 18th cent., coming from the British Isles, Germany, the Netherlands, and other countries, along with Africans to serve as enslaved labor. The population reached 3 million non-natives by the 1770s. The Indigenous population was greatly reduced by European diseases and by wars with the various colonies. British attempts to control colonial trade and to tax the colonists to pay for the costs of colonial administration and defense clashed with local self-government and eventually provoked the colonies to a successful rebellion.

Central and East Europe. The monarchs of the three states that dominated E Europe—Austria, Prussia, and Russia—expanded royal power and centralized institutions in their kingdoms, which were enlarged by the division (1772-95) of Poland.

Under **Frederick II** (the Great) (r. 1740-86), Prussia, with its efficient modern army, doubled in size. State monopolies and tariff protection fostered industry, and some legal reforms were introduced. Austria's heterogeneous realms were unified under **Maria Theresa** (r. 1740-80) and **Joseph II** (r. 1765-90). Reforms in education, law, and religion were enacted, and the Austrian serfs were freed (1781). With its defeat in the Seven Years' War in 1763, Austria failed to regain Silesia, which had been seized by Prussia, but it was compensated by expansion to the E and S (Hungary, Slavonia, 1699; Galicia, 1772).

Russia, whose borders continued to expand, adopted some Western bureaucratic and economic policies under **Peter I** (r. 1682-1725) and **Catherine II** (r. 1762-96). Trade and

Between the 16th and 19th centuries, an estimated 10-12 million people were transported from Africa in deplorable conditions to serve as enslaved labor in the Americas.

cultural contacts with the West multiplied from the new Baltic Sea capital, **St. Petersburg** (est. 1703).

French Revolution. The growing French middle class lacked political power and resented aristocratic tax privileges, especially in light of the successful American Revolution. Peasants lacked adequate land and were burdened with feudal obligations to nobles. War with Britain led to the loss of French Canada and drained the treasury, finally forcing the king to call the **Estates-General** in 1789 for the first time since 1614, in an atmosphere of food riots (poor crop in 1788).

Aristocratic resistance to absolutism was soon overshadowed by the reformist Third Estate (middle class), which proclaimed itself the **National Constituent Assembly** June 17 and took the "Tennis Court Oath" on June 20 to secure a constitution. The storming of the **Bastille** fortress/prison on July 14, 1789, by Parisian artisans was followed by looting and the seizure of aristocratic property throughout France. Assembly reforms included abolition of class and regional privileges, a Declaration of Rights, suffrage by taxpayers (75% of male population), and the **Civil Constitution of the Clergy** providing for election and loyalty oaths for priests. A republic was declared Sept. 22, 1792, in spite of royalist pressure from Austria and Prussia, which had declared war in Apr. (joined by Britain the next year). Louis XVI was beheaded Jan. 21, 1793, and Queen Marie Antoinette was beheaded Oct. 16, 1793.

Royalist uprisings in La Vendée and military reverses led to institution of a **reign of terror** in which tens of thousands of opponents of the Revolution and criminals were executed. Radical reforms in the **Convention** period (Sept. 1793-Oct. 1795) included the abolition of colonial slavery, economic measures to aid the poor, support of public education, and a short-lived de-Christianization.

Division among radicals (execution of Hebert, Danton, and Robespierre, 1794) aided the ascendancy of a moderate **Directory**, which consolidated military victories. **Napoleon Bonaparte** (1769-1821), a popular young general, exploited political divisions and participated in a coup Nov. 9, 1799, making himself first consul (dictator).

India. Sikh and Hindu rebels (Rajputs, Marathas) and Afghans destroyed the power of the Mughals during the 18th cent. After France's defeat (1763) in the Seven Years' War, Britain was the primary European trade power in India. Its control of inland **Bengal** and **Bihar** was recognized (1765) by the Mughal shah, who granted the **British East India Co.** (under Clive, 1725-74) the right to collect land revenue there. Despite objections from Parliament (1784 India Act), the company's involvement in local wars and politics led to repeated acquisitions of new territory. The company exported Indian textiles, sugar, and indigo, but industry was discouraged to promote British imports.

Nationalism Gathers Momentum: 1800-40

French ideals and empire spread. Inspired by the ideals of the French Revolution, and supported by the expanding French armies, new republican regimes arose near France: the **Batavian** Republic in the Netherlands (1795-1806), the **Helvetic** Republic in Switzerland (1798-1803), the **Cisalpine** Republic in Northern Italy (1797-1805), the **Ligurian** Republic in Genoa (1797-1805), and the **Parthenopean** Republic in Southern Italy (1799). A Roman Republic existed briefly in 1798 after Pope Pius VI was arrested by French troops. In Italy and Germany, new nationalist sentiments were stimulated both in imitation of and in reaction to developments in France (anti-French and anti-Jacobin peasant uprisings in Italy, 1796-99).

From 1804, when Napoleon declared himself emperor, to 1812, a succession of military victories (Austerlitz, 1805; Jena, 1806) extended his control over most of Europe through puppet states (**Confederation of the Rhine** united W German states for the first time and **Grand Duchy of Warsaw** revived Polish national hopes), expansion of the empire, and alliances.

Among the lasting reforms initiated under Napoleon's absolutist reign were establishment of the Bank of France, centralization of tax collection, codification of law along Roman models (Code Napoléon), and reform and extension of secondary and university education. In an 1801 concordat, the papacy recognized the effective autonomy of the French Catholic Church.

Napoleon's continental successes were offset by a British victory under Adm. Horatio Nelson in the **Battle of Trafalgar** (1805). Some 400,000 French soldiers were killed in the Napoleonic Wars, along with about 600,000 foreign troops.

Louis Daguerre's 10-minute exposure of Boulevard du Temple in Paris (1838) omits moving traffic but includes the earliest candid image of a person: a man having his shoes polished.

Last gasp of old regimes. The disastrous 1812 invasion of Russia exposed Napoleon's overextension. After Napoleon's 1814 exile to Elba, his armies were defeated (1815) at **Waterloo** by British and Prussian troops.

At the **Congress of Vienna**, the monarchs and princes of Europe redrew their boundaries, to the advantage of Prussia (in Saxony and the Ruhr), Austria (in Illyria and Venetia), and Russia (in Poland and Finland). British conquest of Dutch and French colonies (S Africa, Ceylon, Mauritius) was recognized. France, under the restored Bourbons, retained its expanded 1792 borders. The settlement brought 50 years of international peace to Europe.

But the Congress was unable to check the advance of liberal ideals and of nationalism among the smaller European nations. The 1825 **Decembrist uprising** by liberal officers in Russia was easily suppressed. But an independence movement in **Greece**, stirred by commercial prosperity and a cultural revival, succeeded in expelling Ottoman rule by 1831, with the aid of Britain, France, and Russia.

A constitutional monarchy was secured in France by the **1830 Revolution**; Louis Philippe became king. The revolutionary contagion spread to **Belgium**, which gained its independence (1830) from the Dutch monarchy, to **Poland**, whose rebellion was defeated (1830-31) by Russia, and to Germany.

Romanticism. A new style in intellectual and artistic life replaced Neoclassicism and Rococo after the mid-18th cent. By the early 19th cent., Romanticism prevailed in Europe.

Rousseau had begun the reaction against rationalism; in education (*Émile*, 1762) he stressed subjective spontaneity over regularized instruction. German writers (Lessing, 1729-81; Herder, 1744-1803) favorably compared the German folk song to classical forms and began a cult of Shakespeare, whose passion and "natural" wisdom was a model for the romantic *Sturm und Drang* (Storm and Stress) movement. **Goethe**'s *Sorrows of Young Werther* (1774) set the model for the tragic, passionate genius.

A new interest in **Gothic architecture** in England after 1760 (Walpole, 1717-97) spread through Europe, associated with an aesthetic Christian and mystic revival (**Blake**, 1757-1827). Celtic, Norse, and German mythology and folk tales were revived or imitated (Grimm's Fairy Tales, 1812-22). The medieval revival (Scott's *Ivanhoe*, 1819) led to a new interest in history, stressing national differences and organic growth (**Carlyle**, 1795-1881; Michelet, 1798-1874), corresponding to theories of natural evolution (Lamarck's *Philosophie Zoologique*, 1809; Lyell's *Geology*, 1830-33). A reaction against classicism characterized the English **romantic poets** (beginning with **Wordsworth**, 1770-1850). Revolution and war fed an emphasis on freedom and conflict, expressed by both poets (**Byron**, 1788-1824; **Hugo**, 1802-85) and philosophers (**Hegel**, 1770-1831).

Wild gardens replaced the formal French variety, and painters favored rural, stormy, and mountainous landscapes (**Turner**, 1775-1851; **Constable**, 1776-1837). Clothing became freer, with wigs, hoops, and ruffles discarded. Originality and genius were expected in the life and work of inspired artists (Murger's *Scenes From Bohemian Life*, 1847-49). Exotic locales and themes (as in Gothic horror stories) were used in art and literature (Delacroix, 1798-1863; **Poe**, 1809-49). Music exhibited the new dramatic style and a breakdown of classical forms (**Beethoven**, 1770-1827). The use of folk melodies and modes aided the growth of distinct national traditions (Glinka in Russia, 1804-57).

Latin America.
François **Toussaint L'Ouverture** led a successful slave revolt in Haiti, which subsequently became the first Caribbean state to achieve independence (1804). The mainland Spanish colonies won their independence (1810-24) under such leaders as Simón **Bolívar** (1783-1830). Brazil became an independent empire (1822) under the Portuguese prince regent.

A new class of military officers divided power with large landholders and the church.

United States.
Territory under U.S. control nearly doubled in size with the **Louisiana Purchase** (1803). Heavy immigration and exploitation of ample natural resources fueled rapid economic growth. The spread of the franchise, public education, and antislavery sentiment were signs of a widespread democratic ethic.

China.
Failure to keep pace with Western arms technology exposed China to greater European influence and hampered efforts to bar imports of opium, which had damaged Chinese society and drained wealth overseas. In the **Opium War** (1839-42), Britain forced China to expand trade opportunities and to cede Hong Kong.

New Complexities: Reforms and Imperialism: 1840-80

Idea of progress.
As a result of the cumulative scientific, economic, and political changes of the preceding eras, the idea took hold among literate people in the West that continuing growth and improvement constituted the usual state of human and natural life.

Charles **Darwin**'s statement of the **theory of evolution** and survival of the fittest (*On the Origin of Species*, 1859), defended by intellectuals and scientists against theological objections, was taken as confirmation that progress was the natural direction of life. The controversy helped define popular ideas of the dedicated scientist and of science's increasing control over the world (Foucault's demonstration of Earth's rotation, 1851; **Pasteur**'s germ theory, 1861).

Liberals following Ricardo (1772-1823) in their faith that unrestrained competition would bring continuous economic expansion sought to adjust political life to new social realities and believed that unregulated competition of ideas would yield truth (**Mill**, 1806-73). In England, successive reform bills (1832, 1867, 1884) gave representation to the new industrial towns and extended the franchise to the middle and lower classes and to Catholics, Dissenters, and Jews. On both sides of the Atlantic, reformists strove to improve conditions for the mentally ill (**Dix**, 1802-87), women (Anthony, 1820-1906), and prisoners. Slavery was barred in the British Empire (1833), the U.S. (1865), and Brazil (1888).

Socialist theories based on ideas of human perfectibility or progress were widely disseminated. Utopian socialists such as Saint-Simon (1760-1825) envisaged an orderly, just society directed by a technocratic elite. A model factory town, New Lanark, Scotland, was set up by utopian Robert Owen (1771-1858), and communal experiments were tried in the U.S. (Brook Farm, MA, 1841-47). Bakunin's (1814-76) anarchism represented the opposite extreme of total freedom. Karl **Marx** (1818-83) posited the inevitable triumph of socialism in industrial countries through a dialectical process of class conflict. Effective development of oceanic steamship lines (Cunard Lines, 1840s) and the opening of the **Suez Canal** accelerated shipping and commerce. Telegraph lines (Australia-Europe, 1871) sped communication. International organizations included the General (later Universal) Postal Union (1874) and conferences to limit epidemics like cholera. The initial **Geneva Convention** (1864) regulated treatment of prisoners of war.

Spread of industry.
The technical processes and managerial innovations of the English industrial revolution spread to Europe (especially Germany) and the U.S., causing an explosion of industrial production, demand for raw materials, and competition for markets. Inventors, both trained and self-taught, provided means for larger-scale production (Bessemer steel, 1856; sewing machine, 1846). Many inventions were shown at the universal prosperity-themed 1851 London Great Exhibition at the **Crystal Palace**.

Local specialization and long-distance trade were aided by a revolution in transportation and communication. Railroads were first introduced in the 1820s in England and the U.S. Over 150,000 mi of track had been laid worldwide by 1880, with another 100,000 mi laid in the next decade. Steamships were improved (*Savannah* crossed Atlantic, 1819). The **telegraph**, perfected by 1844 (Morse), connected the Old and New Worlds by cable in 1866 and quickened the pace of international commerce and politics. The first commercial **telephone** exchange went into operation in the U.S. in 1878.

The new class of industrial workers, uprooted from their rural homes, lacked job security and suffered from dangerous overcrowding at work and at home. Many responded by organizing **trade unions** (legalized in England, 1824; France, 1884).

The U.S. Knights of Labor had 700,000 members by 1886. The First International (1864-76) tried to unite workers worldwide around a Marxist program. The quasi-Socialist Paris Commune uprising (1871) was violently suppressed. Acts to reduce child labor and regulate conditions were passed (1833-50 in England). Social security measures were introduced by the Bismarck regime (1883-89) in Germany.

Revolutions of 1848.
Among the causes of the continent-wide revolutions were an international collapse of credit and resulting unemployment, bad harvests in 1845-47, and a cholera epidemic. The new urban proletariat and expanding bourgeoisie demanded greater political roles. Republics were proclaimed in France, Rome, and Venice. Nationalist feelings reached fever pitch in the Habsburg empire, as Hungary declared independence under Kossuth, a Slav Congress demanded equality, and Piedmont tried to drive Austria from Lombardy. A national liberal assembly at Frankfurt called for German unification.

But riots fueled bourgeois fear of socialism (**Marx** and **Engels**, *Communist Manifesto*, 1848), and peasants remained conservative. The old establishment—the Papacy, the Habsburgs with the help of the Tsarist Russian army—was able to rout the revolutionaries by 1849. The French Republic succumbed to a renewed monarchy by 1852 (Emperor Napoleon III).

Great nations unified.
Using the "blood and iron" tactics of Bismarck from 1862, Prussia controlled N Germany by 1867 (war with Denmark, 1864; Austria, 1866). After defeating France in 1870 (annexation of Alsace-Lorraine), it won the allegiance of S German states. A new **German Empire** was proclaimed (1871). **Italy**, inspired by Giuseppe Mazzini (1805-72) and Giuseppe Garibaldi (1807-82), was unified by the reformed Piedmont kingdom through uprisings, plebiscites, and war.

The **United States** expanded its area after the 1846-48 Mexican War and defeated (1861-65) a secession attempt by Southern states in the **Civil War**. Canadian provinces were united in an autonomous **Dominion of Canada** (1867). Control in **India** was removed from the East India Co. and centralized under British administration after the 1857-58 Sepoy rebellion, laying the groundwork for the modern Indian state. Queen Victoria was named Empress of India (1876).

Europe dominates Asia.
The Ottoman Empire began to weaken in the face of Balkan nationalisms and European imperial incursions in N Africa (Suez Canal, 1869). The Ottomans had lost control of most of both regions by 1882. Russia completed its expansion S by 1884 (despite the temporary setback of the **Crimean War** with Turkey, Britain, and France, 1853-56), taking Turkestan, all the Caucasus, and Chinese areas in the E and sponsoring Balkan Slavs against the Turks. A succession of reformist and reactionary regimes presided over a slow modernization (serfs freed, 1861). Persian independence suffered as Russia and British India competed for influence.

China was forced to sign a series of unequal treaties with European powers and Japan. Overpopulation and an inefficient dynasty brought misery and caused rebellions (Taiping, Muslims) leaving tens of millions dead. **Japan** was forced by the U.S. (Commodore Perry's visits, 1853-54) and Europe to end its isolation. The Meiji restoration (1868) gave power to a Westernizing oligarchy, abolishing feudalism and expanding education. Intensified empire-building gave Burma to Britain (1824-85) and Indochina to France (1862-95). Christian missionary activity followed imperial and trade expansion in Asia.

Arts.
The official **Beaux Arts** school in Paris set an international style of imposing public buildings (Paris Opera, 1861-74; Vienna Opera, 1861-69) and uplifting statues (Bartholdi's Statue of Liberty, 1884). Realist painting, influenced by photography

(Daguerre, 1837), appealed to a new mass audience with social or historical narrative (Wilkie, 1785-1841; Poynter, 1836-1919) or with serious religious, moral, or social messages (pre-Raphaelites, Millet's *Angelus*, 1858), often drawn from ordinary life. The **Impressionists** (Monet, 1840-1926; Pissarro, 1830-1903; Renoir, 1841-1919) rejected the formalism, sentimentality, and precise techniques of academic art in favor of a spontaneous,

undetailed rendering of the world through careful representation of the effect of natural light on objects. They were strongly influenced by Asian and African styles.

Realistic **novelists** presented the full panorama of social classes and personalities but retained sentimentality and moral judgment (**Dickens**, 1812-70; **Eliot**, 1819-80; **Tolstoy**, 1828-1910; **Balzac**, 1799-1850).

Veneer of Stability: 1880-1900

Imperialism triumphant. The vast **African** interior, visited by European explorers (Barth, 1821-65; Livingstone, 1813-73), was conquered by the European powers in rapid, competitive thrusts from their coastal bases after 1880, mostly for domestic political and international strategic reasons. W African Muslim kingdoms (Fulani), Arab slave traders (Zanzibar), and Bantu military confederations (Zulu) were alike subdued. Only Christian Ethiopia (defeat of Italy, 1896) and Liberia resisted successfully. France (W Africa) and Britain ("Cape to Cairo," **Boer War**, 1899-1902) were the major beneficiaries. The ideology of "the white man's burden" (Kipling, *Barrack Room Ballads*, 1892) justified the conquests, which in fact reflected Europe's weapons superiority.

W European foreign capital investment soared to nearly $40 billion by 1914, but most was in E Europe (France, Germany), the Americas (Britain), and Europe's colonies. The foundation of the modern interdependent world economy was laid, with cartels dominating raw material trade. Global developments included a new agreement on international patents (1883), the modern Olympics (1896), and the worldwide spread of department stores.

An industrious world. Industrial and technological proficiency characterized the two new great powers—Germany and the U.S. Coal and iron deposits enabled Germany to reach second- or third-place status in iron, steel, and shipbuilding by the 1900s. German electrical and chemical industries were world leaders. The U.S. post-Civil War boom (interrupted by financial panics—1873, 1884, and 1893) was shaped by massive immigration from S and E Europe from 1880, government subsidy of railroads, and huge private monopolies (Standard Oil, 1870; U.S. Steel, 1901). The **Spanish-American War**, 1898 (Philippine Insurrection, 1899-1902), and the **Open Door policy** in China (1899) made the U.S. a world power.

England led in **urbanization**, with London the world capital of finance, insurance, and shipping. Sewer systems (Paris, 1850s), electric subways (London, 1890), parks, and bargain department stores helped improve living standards for most of the urban population of the industrial world. Birthrates declined in the West while infant mortality rates plunged (demographic transition, 1880-1920).

Upheavals in Asia. Asian reaction to European economic, military, and religious incursions took the form of imitation of Western techniques and adoption of Western ideas of progress and freedom. The Chinese "self-strengthening" movement of the 1860s and 1870s included rail, port, and arsenal improvements and metal and textile mills. Reformers such as K'ang Yu-wei (1858-1927) won liberalizing reforms

in 1898, right after the European and Japanese "scramble for concessions."

A universal education system in Japan and importation of foreign industrial, scientific, and military experts aided Japan's rapid modernization after 1868 under the authoritarian Meiji regime. Japan's victory in the **Sino-Japanese War** (1894-95) put Formosa and Korea in its power. Industrialization began in earnest by 1890.

In India, the British alliance with the remaining princely states masked reform sentiment among the Westernized urban elite; higher education had been conducted largely in English for 50 years. The **Indian National Congress**, founded in 1885, demanded a larger government role for Indians.

Fin-de-siècle sophistication. Naturalist writers pushed realism to its extreme limits, adopting a quasi-scientific attitude and writing about formerly taboo subjects such as sex, crime, extreme poverty, and corruption (Flaubert, 1821-80; Zola, 1840-1902; Hardy, 1840-1928). Unseen or repressed psychological motivations were explored in the clinical and theoretical works of Sigmund **Freud** (1856-1939) and in works of fiction (**Dostoyevsky**, 1821-81; Henry James, 1843-1916; Schnitzler, 1862-1931).

A contempt for bourgeois life or a desire to shock a complacent audience was shared by the French **symbolist** poets (Verlaine, 1844-96; Rimbaud, 1854-91), by neopagan English writers (Swinburne, 1837-1909), by continental dramatists (**Ibsen**, 1828-1906), and by satirists (**Wilde**, 1854-1900). The German philosopher Friedrich **Nietzsche** (1844-1900) was influential in his elitism and pessimism.

Postimpressionist art neglected long-cherished conventions of representation (**Cézanne**, 1839-1906) and showed a willingness to learn from primitive and non-European art (**Gauguin**, 1848-1903; Japanese prints).

Racism. Gobineau (1816-82) gave a pseudobiological foundation to modern racist theories, which spread in Europe in the latter 19th cent., along with **Social Darwinism**, the belief that societies are and should be organized as a struggle for survival of the fittest. The medieval period was interpreted as an era of natural Germanic rule (Chamberlain, 1855-1927), and notions of racial superiority were associated with German national aspirations (Treitschke, 1834-96). **Anti-Semitism**, with a new racist rationale, became a significant political force in Germany (Anti-Semitic Petition, 1880), Austria (Lueger, 1844-1910), and France (**Dreyfus affair**, 1894-1906).

Imperialism's High Point: 1900-09

Alliances. While the peace of Europe (and its dependencies) continued to hold (1907 **Hague Conference** extended the rules of war and international arbitration procedures), imperial rivalries, protectionist trade practices (in Germany and France), and the escalating arms race (British *Dreadnought* battleship launched; Germany widens Kiel canal, 1906) exacerbated minor disputes (German-French Moroccan "crises," 1905, 1911).

Security was sought through balance-of-power alliances: **Triple Alliance** (Germany, Austria-Hungary, Italy; renewed in 1902 and 1907); Anglo-Japanese Alliance (1902), Franco-Russian Alliance (1899), **Entente Cordiale** (Britain, France, 1904), Anglo-Russian Treaty (1907), German-Ottoman friendship. Global developments included the establishment of an international court in The Hague, the first transatlantic radio transmission (1901), and the creation of the first international association for European football (1904).

Ottomans decline. The Ottoman government was unable to resist further loss of territory, and earlier reform efforts gave way to greater authoritarianism. Nearly all European lands were lost in 1912 to Serbia, Greece, Montenegro, and Bulgaria. Italy took Libya and the Dodecanese islands the same year. Britain took Kuwait (1899) and the Sinai (1906). The **Young Turk** revolution in 1908 forced the sultan to restore a constitution, and it introduced some social reform and secularization.

British Empire. British trade and cultural influence remained dominant in the empire, but constitutional reforms presaged its eventual dissolution. The colonies of **Australia** were united in 1901 under a self-governing commonwealth. **New Zealand** acquired dominion status in 1907. The old Boer republics joined Cape Colony and Natal in the self-governing Union of **South Africa** in 1910.

The 1909 Indian Councils Act enhanced the role of elected province legislatures in **India**. The Muslim League (founded 1906) sought separate communal representation.

East Asia. Japan exploited its growing industrial power to expand its empire. Victory in the 1904-05 war against Russia (naval battle of Tsushima, 1905) assured Japan's domination of **Korea** (annexed 1910) and Manchuria (Port Arthur taken, 1905).

In China, central authority began to crumble (empress died, 1908). Reforms (Confucian exam system ended 1905, modernization of the army, building of railroads) were inadequate, and secret societies of reformers and nationalists, inspired by the Westernized **Sun** Yat-sen (1866-1925), fomented periodic uprisings in the S.

Siam, whose independence had been guaranteed by Britain and France in 1896, was split into spheres of influence by those countries in 1907.

Russia. The population of the Russian Empire approached 150 million in 1900. Reforms in education, in law, and in local institutions (*zemstvos*) and an industrial boom starting in the 1880s (oil, railroads) created the beginnings of a modern society, despite the autocratic tsarist regime. Liberals (1903 Union of Liberation), Socialists (Social Democrats founded 1898, Bolsheviks split off 1903), and populists (Social Revolutionaries founded 1901) were periodically repressed, and national minorities were persecuted (anti-Jewish pogroms, 1903, 1905-06).

An industrial crisis after 1900 and harvest failures aggravated poverty among urban workers, and the 1904-05 defeat by Japan (which checked Russia's Asian expansion) sparked the **Revolution of 1905-06**. A **Duma** (parliament) was created under Tsar Nicholas II. Agricultural reform (under Stolypin, prime minister, 1906-11) created a large class of land-owning peasants (*kulaks*).

The world shrinks. Developments in transportation and communication and mass population movements helped create an awareness of an interdependent world. Early **automobiles** (Daimler, Benz, 1885) were experimental or were designed as luxuries. Assembly-line mass production (Ford Motor Co., 1903) made the invention practical, and by 1910 nearly 500,000 motor vehicles were registered in the U.S. alone. **Heavier-than-air flights** began in 1903 in the U.S. (Wright brothers' *Flyer*), preceded by glider, balloon, and model plane advances in several countries. Trade was advanced by improvements in **ship design** (gyrocompass, 1910), speed (*Lusitania* crossed Atlantic in five days, 1907), and reach (Panama Canal begun, 1904).

The first transatlantic **radio** telegraphic transmission occurred in 1901, six years after Marconi discovered radio. Radio transmission of human speech had been made in 1900. Telegraphic transmission of photos was achieved in 1904, lending immediacy to news reports. **Phonographs**, popularized by Caruso's recordings (starting 1902), made for quick international spread of musical styles (Dickson, Lumière brothers), became a popular and artistic medium after 1900; newsreels appeared in 1909.

Emigration from crowded European centers soared in the decade: 9 million migrated to the U.S., and millions more went to Siberia, Canada, Argentina, Australia, South Africa, and Algeria. Some 70 million Europeans emigrated in the century before 1914. Several million Chinese, Indians, and Japanese migrated to SE Asia, where their urban skills often enabled them to take a predominant economic role.

Social reform. The social and economic problems of the poor were kept in the public eye by realist fiction writers (Dreiser's *Sister Carrie*, 1900; Gorky's *Lower Depths*, 1902; Sinclair's *The Jungle*, 1906), journalists (U.S. **muckrakers**—Steffens, Tarbell), and artists (Ashcan school). Frequent labor strikes and occasional assassinations by anarchists or radicals (Empress Elizabeth of Austria, 1898; King Umberto I of Italy, 1900; U.S. Pres. McKinley, 1901; Russian Interior Min. Plehve, 1904; Portugal's King Carlos, 1908) added to social

Emigration from densely populated European countries to the Americas soared in the early 20th century; many landed on Ellis Island, in New York Harbor, en route to U.S. cities.

tension and fear of revolution. Feminist agitators for the vote surfaced in several countries.

But democratic reformism responded in part. In Germany, Bernstein's (1850-1932) **revisionist Marxism**, downgrading revolution, was accepted by the powerful Social Democrats and trade unions. The British Fabian Society (the Webbs, Shaw) and the Labour Party (founded 1906) worked for reforms such as social security and union rights (1906), while woman suffragists grew more militant. U.S. **progressives** fought big business (Pure Food and Drug Act, 1906). In France, the 10-hour workday (1904) and separation of church and state (1905) were reform victories, as was universal suffrage in Austria (1907).

Arts. An unprecedented period of experimentation, centered in France, produced several new **painting styles**: Fauvism exploited bold color areas (Matisse, *Woman With Hat*, 1905); expressionism reflected powerful inner emotions (Brücke group, 1905); Cubism combined several views of an object on one flat surface (Picasso, *Demoiselles*, 1906-07); futurism tried to depict speed and motion (Italian Futurist Manifesto, 1910). **Architects** explored new uses of steel structures, with facades either neoclassical (Adler and Sullivan in U.S.), curvilinear Art Nouveau (Gaudí's Casa Mila, 1905-10), or functionally streamlined (Wright's Robie House, 1909).

Music and dance shared the experimental spirit. Ruth St. Denis (1877-1968) and Isadora Duncan (1878-1927) pioneered modern dance, while Sergei Diaghilev in Paris revitalized classic ballet from 1909. Composers explored atonal music (Debussy, 1862-1918) and dissonance (Schoenberg, 1874-1951) or revolutionized classical forms (Stravinsky, 1882-1971), often showing jazz or folk music influences.

War and Revolution: 1910-19

War threatens. Germany under Wilhelm II sought a political and imperial role consonant with its industrial strength, challenging Britain's world supremacy and threatening France, which was still resenting the loss (1871) of Alsace-Lorraine. Austria wanted to curb an expanded Serbia (after 1912) and the threat it posed to its own Slav lands. Russia feared Austrian and German political and economic aims in the Balkans and Turkey.

An accelerated arms race resulted from these circumstances. The German standing army rose to more than 2 million men by 1914. Russia and France had more than a million each, and Austria and the British Empire nearly a million each. Dozens of enormous battleships were built by the powers after 1906.

The **assassination of Austrian Archduke Franz Ferdinand** by a Serbian nationalist, June 28, 1914, was the trigger for war. The system of alliances made the conflict Europe-wide; Germany's invasion of Belgium to outflank France forced Britain to enter the war. Patriotic fervor was nearly unanimous among all classes in most countries.

War unfolds. German forces were stopped in France in one month. The rival armies dug **trench networks**. Artillery and improved machine guns prevented either side from any lasting advance despite repeated assaults (600,000 dead at **Verdun**, Feb.-July 1916). German deployment of poisonous chlorine gas (Ypres, 1915) was first major use of lethal **chemical weapons**. The entrance of more than 1 million U.S. troops tipped the

balance after mid-1917, forcing Germany to sue for peace the next year. The formal armistice was signed on Nov. 11, 1918, and the German emperor abdicated.

In the E, the Russian armies were thrown back (battle of **Tannenberg**, Aug. 20, 1914), and the war grew unpopular in Russia. An allied attempt to relieve Russia through Turkey failed (**Gallipoli**, 1915). The **Russian Revolution** (1917) abolished the monarchy. The new Bolshevik regime signed the capitulatory Brest-Litovsk peace in Mar. 1918. Italy entered the war on the allied side in May 1915 but was pushed back by Oct. 1917. A renewed offensive with Allied aid in Oct.-Nov. 1918 forced Austria to surrender.

The British Navy successfully blockaded Germany, which responded with submarine U-boat attacks; **unrestricted submarine warfare** against neutrals after Jan. 1917 helped bring the U.S. into the war. Other battlefields included Palestine and Mesopotamia, both of which Britain wrested from the Turks in 1917, and the African and Pacific colonies of Germany, most of which fell to Britain, France, Australia, Japan, and South Africa.

Settlement. At the **Paris Peace Conference** (Jan.-June 1919), concluded by the **Treaty of Versailles**, and in subsequent negotiations and local wars (Russian-Polish War, 1920), the **map of Europe** was redrawn with a nod to U.S. Pres. Woodrow Wilson's principle of self-determination. Austria and Hungary were separated, and much of their land was given to Yugoslavia

Both sides in World War I developed elaborate networks of dug-in trenches from which to fight.

(formerly Serbia), Romania, Italy, and the newly independent Poland and Czechoslovakia. Germany lost territory in the W, N, and E, while Finland and the Baltic states were detached from Russia. The Ottoman Empire ended (1922) and most of its Arab lands went to British-sponsored Arab states or to direct French and British rule. Belgium's sovereignty was recognized.

From 1916, the civilian populations and economies of both sides were mobilized to an unprecedented degree. Hardships intensified among fighting nations in 1917 (French mutiny crushed in May). More than 10 million soldiers died in the war.

A huge **reparations** burden and partial demilitarization were imposed on Germany. Pres. Wilson proposed a League of Nations, but the U.S. Senate voted against U.S. involvement.

Pandemic. The presence and movement of World War I troops facilitated the spread of a deadly form of **influenza** caused by an H1N1 virus, its place of origin not clearly known. With no vaccine or drug treatment available, an estimated 500 million people, about one-third of the world population, were infected, 1918-19, and some 50 million believed to have died, in the worst pandemic of recent history.

Russian revolution. Military defeats and high casualties caused a contagious lack of confidence in Tsar Nicholas, who was forced to abdicate Mar. 1917. A liberal provisional government failed to end the war, and massive desertions, riots, and fighting between factions followed. A moderate socialist government under Aleksandr Kerensky was overthrown (Nov. 1917) in a violent coup by the **Bolsheviks** in Petrograd under **Lenin**, who later disbanded the elected Constituent Assembly.

The Bolsheviks brutally suppressed all opposition and ended the war with Germany in Mar. 1918. **Civil war** broke out in the summer between the Red Army (the Bolsheviks and their supporters), and monarchists, anarchists, minority nationalities (Ukrainians, Georgians, Poles), and others. Small U.S., British, French, and Japanese units also opposed the Bolsheviks (1918-19; Japan in Vladivostok to 1922). The civil war, anarchy, and pogroms devastated the country until the 1920 Red Army victory. The **Communist Party** leadership retained absolute power.

Other European revolutions. An unpopular monarchy in **Portugal** was overthrown in 1910. The new republic took severe anticlerical measures in 1911.

After a century of Home Rule agitation, during which **Ireland** was devastated by famine (1 million dead, 1846-47) and emigration, republican militants staged an unsuccessful uprising in Dublin during **Easter 1916**. The execution of the leaders and mass arrests by the British won popular support for the rebels. The **Irish Free State**, comprising all but the six northern counties, achieved dominion status in 1922.

In the aftermath of the world war, radical revolutions were attempted in Germany (**Spartacist** uprising, Jan. 1919), **Hungary** (Kun regime, 1919), and elsewhere. All were suppressed or failed for lack of support.

Chinese revolution. The Qinq, or Manchu, Dynasty was overthrown and a republic proclaimed, 1911-12. Revolutionary leader Sun Yat-sen, who organized the nationalist **Kuomintang** party and led a provisional republican government in Nanjing, resigned in a unification compromise with former imperial viceroy Yuan Shikai. Yuan became president upon the abdication of the emperor in Feb. 1912.

Students launched protests on May 4, 1919, against League of Nations concessions in China to Japan. Nationalist, liberal, and socialist ideas and political groups spread. The **Chinese Communist Party** was founded in 1921. A Communist regime took power in Mongolia with Soviet support in 1921.

India restive. Indian objections to British rule erupted in nationalist riots as well as in the nonviolent tactics of Mahatma **Gandhi** (1869-1948). Nearly 400 unarmed demonstrators were shot at **Amritsar** in Apr. 1919. Britain approved limited self-rule that year.

Mexican revolution. Under the long **Díaz** dictatorship (1877-1911) the economy advanced, but Indian and mestizo lands were confiscated, and concessions to foreigners (mostly U.S.) damaged the middle class. A revolution in 1910 led to civil wars and U.S. intervention (1914, 1916-17). Land reform and a more democratic constitution (1917) were achieved.

Sciences. Scientific specialization continued to advance, with key discoveries especially in **physics**. Physicists challenged common-sense views of causality, observation, and a mechanistic universe, putting science further beyond popular grasp (**Einstein**'s general theory of relativity, 1915-16; Bohr's quantum mechanics, 1913; Heisenberg's uncertainty principle, 1927).

Aftermath of War: 1920-29

U.S. Easy credit, technological ingenuity, and war-related industrial decline in Europe caused a long economic boom, in which ownership of new products—**autos**, **phones**, **radios**—became more democratized. **Prosperity**, an increase in women workers, women's suffrage (19th Amendment ratified, 1920), and drastic change in fashion (**flappers**, mannish bob for women, clean-shaven men) created a wide perception of social change despite prohibition of alcoholic beverages (1919-33). Union membership and strikes increased. Fear of radicals led to Palmer raids (1919-20) and the Sacco-Vanzetti case (1921-27).

Europe sorts itself out. Germany's liberal **Weimar constitution** (1919) could not guarantee a stable government in the face of rightist violence (Foreign Min. Rathenau assassinated, 1922) and Communist refusal to cooperate with Socialists. Reparations and Allied occupation of the Rhineland caused staggering inflation that destroyed middle-class savings, but economic expansion resumed after mid-decade, aided by U.S. loans. A sophisticated, **innovative culture** developed in architecture and design (Bauhaus, 1919-28), film (Lang, *M*, 1931), painting (Grosz), music (Weill, *Threepenny Opera*, 1928), theater (Brecht, *A Man's a Man*, 1926), criticism (Benjamin), philosophy (Jung), and fashion. This culture was considered decadent and socially disruptive by rightists.

England elected its first Labour governments (Jan. 1924, June 1929). A 10-day general strike in support of coal miners failed in May 1926. In **Italy**, strikes, political chaos, and violence by small Fascist bands culminated in the Oct. 1922 Fascist March on Rome, which established **Mussolini**'s dictatorship. Strikes were outlawed (1926), and Italian influence was pressed in the Balkans (Albania made a protectorate, 1926). A conservative dictatorship was also established in **Portugal** in a 1926 military coup.

Czechoslovakia, the only stable democracy to emerge from the war in Central or E Europe, faced opposition from Germans (in the Sudetenland), Ruthenians, and some Slovaks. As the industrial heartland of the old Habsburg empire, it remained fairly prosperous. With French backing, it formed the Little Entente with Yugoslavia (1920) and **Romania** (1921) to block Austrian or Hungarian irredentism. Croats and Slovenes in **Yugoslavia** demanded a federal state until King Alexander I proclaimed (1929) a royal dictatorship. Poland faced internal nationality problems as well (Germans, Ukrainians, Jews; Pilsudski ruled as dictator from 1926. The Baltic states were threatened by traditionally dominant ethnic Germans and by Soviet-supported Communists.

An economic collapse and famine in **Russia** (1921-22) claimed 5 million lives. The New Economic Policy (1921) allowed land ownership by peasants and some private commerce and industry. **Stalin** was absolute ruler within four years of Lenin's death (1924). He inaugurated a brutal collectivization program (1929-32) and used foreign Communist parties for Soviet state advantage. Industrialization advanced rapidly.

Internationalism. Revulsion against World War I led to pacifist agitation, to the Kellogg-Briand Pact renouncing aggressive war (1928), and to **naval disarmament** pacts (Washington, 1922; London, 1930). But the League of Nations was able to arbitrate only minor disputes (Greece-Bulgaria, 1925). A number of countries pulled back from global contacts, as with American isolationism and Russia's separation from international capitalism.

Middle East. Mustafa Kemal (**Ataturk**) led **Turkish** nationalists in resisting Italian, French, and Greek military advances (1919-23). The sultanate was abolished (1922), and elaborate reforms were passed, including secularization of law and adoption of the Latin alphabet. Ethnic conflict led to persecution of **Armenians** (more than 1 million dead in 1915, 1 million expelled), Greeks (forced Greek-Turk population exchange, 1923), and Kurds (1925 uprising).

With evacuation of the Turks from **Arab** lands, the puritanical Wahabi dynasty of E Arabia conquered (1919-25) what is now Saudi Arabia. British, French, and Arab dynastic and nationalist maneuvering resulted in the creation of two more Arab monarchies in 1921—Iraq and Transjordan (both under British control)—and two French mandates—Syria and Lebanon. Jewish immigration into British-mandated **Palestine**, inspired by the Zionist movement, was resisted by Arabs, at times violently (1921, 1929 riots).

Reza Khan ruled **Persia** after his 1921 coup (shah from 1925), centralized control, and created the trappings of a modern secular state.

In 1922, English archaeologist Howard Carter discovered the tomb of the boy pharaoh **Tutankhamun** in the Valley of the Kings in Egypt.

China. The Kuomintang under **Chiang Kai-shek** (1887-1975) subdued the warlords by 1928. The Communists were brutally suppressed after their alliance with the Kuomintang was broken in 1927. Relative peace thereafter allowed for industrial and financial improvements, with some Russian, British, and U.S. cooperation.

Arts. Nearly all bounds of subject matter, style, and attitude were broken in the arts of the period. **Abstract** art first took inspiration from natural forms or narrative themes (Kandinsky from 1911) and then worked free of any representational aims (Malevich's suprematism, 1915-19; Mondrian's geometric style from 1917). The **Dada** movement (from 1916) mocked artistic pretension with absurd collages and constructions. Paradox, illusion, and psychological taboos were exploited by **surrealists** by the late 1920s (Dali, Magritte). Architectural schools celebrated industrial values, whether vigorous abstract constructivism (Tatlin, *Monument to the Third International*, 1919) or the machined, streamlined **Bauhaus** style, which was extended to many design fields (Helvetica typeface).

Prose writers explored revolutionary narrative modes related to dreams (Kafka's *Trial*, 1925), internal monologue (Joyce's *Ulysses*, 1922), and word play (Stein's *Making of Americans*, 1925). Poets and novelists wrote of modern alienation (Eliot's *Waste Land*, 1922) and aimlessness ("The Lost Generation").

Rise of Totalitarians: 1930-39

Depression. A worldwide financial panic and economic depression began with the Oct. 1929 U.S. stock market crash and the May 1931 failure of the Austrian Credit-Anstalt. A credit crunch caused international bankruptcies and **unemployment**: 12 million jobless by 1932 in the U.S., 5.6 million in Germany, 2.7 million in England. Governments responded with **tariff restrictions** (Smoot-Hawley Act, 1930; Ottawa Imperial Conference, 1932), which dried up world trade. Government public works programs were vitiated by deflationary budget balancing.

Germany. As **Nazi Party** leader, **Adolf Hitler** built up a mass movement (feeding on economic hardship, ideas of racial superiority, fear of leftist influence). With a plurality in the Reichstag, he persuaded Pres. **Hindenburg** to name him chancellor (Jan. 1933); Hindenburg further granted him emergency powers after the Reichstag fire in Feb. Other parties and most forms of opposition, including strikes, were banned, and the media and most aspects of life fell under Nazi control. Severe persecution of Jews began (**Nuremberg Laws**, Sept. 1935). Many Jews, political opponents, and others were sent to concentration camps (Dachau, 1933), where thousands died or were killed. Public works, renewed conscription (1935), arms production, and a four-year plan (1936) all but ended unemployment.

Hitler's expansionism started with reincorporation of the Saar (1935), occupation of the **Rhineland** (Mar. 1936), and annexation of Austria (Mar. 1938). At **Munich** (Sept. 1938) Britain and France attempted to appease Hitler and avoid war by successfully encouraging Czechoslovakia's surrender of the Sudetenland territory.

Russia. Rapid industrialization was achieved through successive **five-year plans** starting in 1928, using severe labor discipline and mass forced labor. Industry was financed by exploitation of agriculture, which was almost totally collectivized by the early 1930s. Millions perished in a series of manufactured disasters: extermination (1929-34) of kulaks (peasant landowners), severe famine (1932-33), party purges and show trials (Great Purge, 1936-38), suppression of nationalities, and poor conditions in labor camps. Purges also increased Stalin's power in the Communist party.

Spain. An industrial revolution during World War I created an urban proletariat, which was attracted to socialism and anarchism; Catalan nationalists challenged central authority. The five years after King Alfonso left Spain in Apr. 1931

were dominated by tension between intermittent leftist and anticlerical governments and clericals, monarchists, and other rightists. Anarchist and Communist rebellions were crushed, but a July 1936 extreme right rebellion led by Gen. Francisco **Franco** and aided by Nazi Germany and Fascist Italy succeeded after a three-year **civil war** (more than 1 million dead in battles and atrocities). The war polarized international public opinion.

Italy. Despite propaganda for the ideal of the Corporate State, few domestic reforms were attempted. An entente with Hungary and Austria (Mar. 1934), a pact with Germany and Japan (Nov. 1937), and intervention by 50,000-75,000 troops in Spain (1936-39) sealed Italy's identification with the fascist bloc (anti-Semitic laws after Mar. 1938). Ethiopia was conquered (1935-36) and Albania annexed (Jan. 1939) in conscious imitation of ancient Rome.

Eastern Europe. Repressive regimes fought for power against an active opposition (liberals, socialists, Communists, peasants, Nazis). Minority groups and Jews were restricted

Mahatma Gandhi (right) led efforts for Indian autonomy and independence for more than 25 years.

within national boundaries that did not coincide with ethnic population patterns. In the destruction of **Czechoslovakia**, Hungary occupied S Slovakia (Nov. 1938) and Ruthenia (Mar. 1939), and a pro-Nazi regime took power in the rest of Slovakia. Other boundary disputes (e.g., Poland-Lithuania, Yugoslavia-Bulgaria, and Romania-Hungary) doomed attempts to build joint fronts against Germany or Russia. Economic depression was severe.

East Asia. After a period of liberalism in **Japan**, nativist militarists dominated the government with peasant support. Manchuria was seized (Sept. 1931-Feb. 1932), and a puppet state was set up (Manchukuo). Adjacent Jehol (Inner Mongolia) was occupied in 1933. **China** proper was invaded in July 1937; large areas were conquered by Oct. 1938. Hundreds of thousands of rapes, murders, and other atrocities were attributed to the Japanese.

Communist forces left Kuomintang-besieged strongholds in the S of China in a Long March (1934-35) to the N. The Kuomintang-Communist civil war was suspended in Jan. 1937 in the face of threatening Japan.

Democracies. The Franklin Roosevelt administration, in office Mar. 1933, embarked on an extensive program of **New Deal** social reform and economic stimulation, including protection for labor unions (heavy industries organized), Social Security, public works, wage-and-hour laws, and assistance to farmers. Isolationist sentiment (1937 Neutrality Act) prevented U.S. intervention in Europe, but military expenditures were increased in 1939.

French political instability and polarization prevented resolution of economic and international security questions. The Popular Front government under Léon Blum (June 1936-Apr. 1938) passed social reforms (40-hour work week) and raised arms spending. National coalition governments, which ruled Britain from Aug. 1931, brought economic recovery but failed to define a consistent international policy until Chamberlain's government (from May 1937), which practiced **appeasement** of Germany and Italy.

India. Twenty years of agitation for autonomy and then for independence (Gandhi's **salt march**, 1930) achieved some constitutional reform (extended provincial powers, 1935) despite Muslim-Hindu strife. Social issues assumed prominence with peasant uprisings (1921), strikes (1928), Gandhi's efforts for untouchables (1932 "fast unto death"), and social and agrarian reform by the provinces after 1937.

Arts. The streamlined, geometric design motifs of Art Deco (from 1925) prevailed through the 1930s. **Abstract art** flourished (Moore sculptures from 1931) alongside a new **realism** related to social and political concerns (Socialist Realism, the official Soviet style from 1934; Mexican muralist Rivera, 1886-1957; Orozco, 1883-1949), which were also expressed in fiction and poetry (Steinbeck's *Grapes of Wrath*, 1939; Sandburg's *The People, Yes*, 1936). Modern architecture (International Style, 1932) was unchallenged in its use of artificial materials (concrete, glass), lack of decoration, and monumentality (Rockefeller Center, 1929-40). Larger-than-life U.S.-made films captured a worldwide audience *(Gone With the Wind, The Wizard of Oz,* both 1939).

War, Hot and Cold: 1940-49

War in Asia-Pacific. Japan occupied Indochina in Sept. 1940, dominated Thailand in Dec. 1941, and attacked Hawaii (**Pearl Harbor**), the Philippines, Hong Kong, and Malaya on Dec. 7, 1941 (precipitating U.S. entrance into the war). Indonesia was attacked in Jan. 1942, and Burma was conquered in Mar. 1942. The Battle of **Midway** (June 1942) turned back the Japanese advance. "Island-hopping" battles (**Guadalcanal**, Aug. 1942-Jan. 1943; **Leyte Gulf**, Oct. 1944; **Iwo Jima**, Feb.-Mar. 1945; **Okinawa**, Apr. 1945) and massive bombing raids on Japan from June 1944 wore out Japanese defenses. U.S. atom bombs, dropped Aug. 6 and 9 on **Hiroshima** and **Nagasaki**, forced Japan to agree, on Aug. 14, to surrender; formal surrender was on Sept. 2, 1945.

The U.S. bombing of Hiroshima and Nagasaki, Japan, in 1945 demonstrated the deadly, destructive power of atomic weapons.

War in Europe. The **Nazi-Soviet nonaggression** pact (Aug. 1939) freed Germany to attack Poland (Sept. 1939). Britain and France, which had guaranteed Polish independence, declared war on Germany. Russia seized E Poland (Sept. 1939), attacked Finland (Nov. 1939), and took the Baltic states (July 1940). Mobile German forces staged *blitzkrieg* attacks during Apr.-June 1940, conquering neutral Belgium, Denmark, Luxembourg, Netherlands, and Norway and defeating France; 350,000 British and French troops were evacuated at **Dunkirk**, France (May). The **Battle of Britain** (June-Dec. 1940) denied Germany air superiority. German-Italian campaigns won the Balkans by Apr. 1941. Three million Axis troops **invaded Russia** in June 1941, marching through Ukraine to the Caucasus, and through White Russia and the Baltic republics to Moscow and Leningrad.

Russian winter counterthrusts (1941-42 and 1942-43) stopped the German advance (**Stalingrad**, Sept. 1942-Feb. 1943). Sustaining great casualties, the Russians drove the Axis from all E Europe and the Balkans in the next two years. Invasions of N Africa (Nov. 1942), Italy (Sept. 1943), and **Normandy** (launched on D-Day, June 6, 1944) brought U.S., British, Free French, and allied troops to Germany by spring 1945. In Feb. 1945, the three Allied leaders, Winston **Churchill** (Britain), Joseph **Stalin** (USSR), and Franklin D. **Roosevelt** (U.S.), met in **Yalta** to discuss strategy and resolve political issues, including the postwar Allied occupation of Germany. Germany surrendered May 7, 1945.

Atrocities. The war brought 20th-cent. cruelty to its peak. The Nazi regime systematically killed an estimated 5-6 million Jews, including some 3 million who died in death camps (e.g., **Auschwitz**). The Nazis also killed Roma (also known as Gypsies), political opponents, people with mental or physical disabilities, homosexuals, others deemed undesirable, and vast numbers of Slavs.

German bombs killed 70,000 British civilians. More than 100,000 Chinese civilians were killed by Japanese forces in the capture and occupation of Nanking. Severe retaliation by the Soviet army, E European partisans, Free French, and others took a heavy toll. U.S. and British bombing of Germany killed hundreds of thousands, as did U.S. bombing of Japan (80,000-200,000 at Hiroshima alone). Some 45 million people died in the war.

Settlement. The United Nations charter was signed in San Francisco on June 26, 1945, by 50 nations. The International Tribunal at **Nuremberg** convicted 22 German leaders for war crimes in Sept. 1946; 23 Japanese leaders were convicted in Nov. 1948. Postwar border changes included large gains in territory for the USSR, losses for Germany, a shift to the W in Polish borders, and minor losses for Italy. Communist regimes, supported by Soviet troops, took power in most of Eastern Europe, including Soviet-occupied Germany (GDR, a.k.a. East Germany, proclaimed Oct. 1949). Japan lost all overseas lands. Global developments involved establishing new economic coordinating bodies like the International Monetary Fund (1944) and the Universal Declaration of Human Rights (1948).

Recovery. Basic political and social changes were imposed on Japan and W Germany by the Western allies (Japan constitution adopted, Nov. 1946; W German basic law, May 1949). U.S. **Marshall Plan** aid ($12 billion, 1947-51) spurred W European economic recovery after a period of severe inflation and strikes in Europe and the U.S. The British Labour Party introduced a national health service and nationalized basic industries in 1946.

Cold War. Western fears of further Soviet advances (Cominform formed in Oct. 1947; Czechoslovakia coup, Feb. 1948; Berlin blockade, Apr. 1948-Sept. 1949) led to the formation of **NATO**. Civil war in Greece and Soviet pressure on Turkey led to U.S. aid under the **Truman Doctrine** (Mar. 1947). Other anti-Communist security pacts were the Organization of American States (Apr. 1948) and the SE Asia Treaty Organization (Sept. 1954). A new wave of **Soviet purges** and repression intensified in the last years of Stalin's rule, extending to E Europe (Slansky trial in Czechoslovakia, 1951). Only Yugoslavia resisted Soviet control (expelled by Cominform, June 1948; U.S. aid, June 1949).

China, Korea. Communist forces emerged from World War II strengthened by the Soviet takeover of industrial Manchuria. In four years of fighting, the Kuomintang was driven from the mainland; the People's Republic of China was proclaimed Oct. 1, 1949. Korea was divided by USSR and U.S. occupation forces. Separate republics were proclaimed in the two zones in Aug.-Sept. 1948.

India. India and Pakistan became independent dominions on Aug. 15, 1947. Millions of Hindu and Muslim refugees were created by the partition. Riots (1946-47) took hundreds of thousands of lives. Mahatma **Gandhi** was assassinated in Jan. 1948. Burma became completely independent in Jan. 1948; Ceylon (later Sri Lanka) took dominion status in Feb.

Middle East. The UN approved partition of Palestine into Jewish and Arab states. **Israel** was proclaimed a state, May 14, 1948. Arabs rejected partition, but failed to defeat Israel in war (May 1948-July 1949). Immigration from Europe and the Middle East swelled Israel's Jewish population. British and French forces left Lebanon and Syria in 1946. Transjordan occupied most of Arab Palestine.

Southeast Asia. Communists and others fought against restoration of French rule in **Indochina** from 1946; a non-Communist government was recognized by France in Mar. 1949, but fighting continued. Both Indonesia and the Philippines became independent; the former in 1949 after four years of war with the Netherlands, the latter in 1946. Philippine economic and military ties with the U.S. remained strong; a Communist-led peasant rising was checked in 1948.

Arts. New York City became the center of the world art market; **abstract expressionism** was the chief mode (Pollock from 1943; de Kooning from 1947). Literature and philosophy explored **existentialism** (Camus's *The Stranger*, 1942; Sartre's *Being and Nothingness*, 1943). Non-Western attempts to revive or create regional styles (Senghor's Négritude, Mishima's novels) were responses to global cultural influences. Radio and phonograph records spread American popular music (swing, bebop) around the world.

The Cold War Decade: 1950-59

Decolonization. The relatively peaceful decline of European political and military power in Asia and Africa accelerated in the 1950s. Nearly all of **N** Africa was freed by 1956, but France fought bitterly to retain Algeria, with its large European minority, until 1962. **Ghana**, independent in 1957, led a parade of new self-led African nations (more than two dozen by 1962), which altered the political character of the UN. Ethnic, political, and other factional disputes often exploded in the new nations after decolonization (UN troops in Cyprus, 1964; **Nigerian civil war**, 1967-70). Leaders of the new states, mostly sharing socialist ideologies, tried to create an Afro-Asian bloc (Bandung Conference, 1955), but Western economic influence and U.S. political ties remained strong (Baghdad Pact, 1955).

Trade. World trade volume soared, in an atmosphere of monetary stability assured by international accords (**Bretton Woods**, 1944). In Europe, economic integration advanced (**European Economic Community**, 1957; European Free Trade Association, 1960). Comecon (1949) coordinated the economies of Soviet-bloc countries. Global developments included transcontinental jet travel (first South Africa to Britain flight, 1952; introduction of term "jet lag," 1965) and the increasing spread of English in global business, sports, and transportation.

U.S. Economic growth produced an abundance of consumer goods (9.3 million motor vehicles sold, 1955). Suburban housing changed life patterns for middle and working classes (Levittown, NY, 1947-51). Pres. Dwight **Eisenhower**'s landslide election victories (1952, 1956) reflected consensus politics. A system of alliances and military bases bolstered U.S. influence on all continents. Trade and payments surpluses were balanced by overseas investments and foreign aid ($50 billion, 1950-59).

USSR. In the "thaw" after Stalin's death in 1953, relations with the West improved (evacuation of Vienna, Geneva summit conference, both 1955). Repression of scientific and cultural life eased, and many prisoners were freed culminating in **de-Stalinization** (1956). Nikita **Khrushchev**'s leadership aimed at consumer sector growth, but farm production lagged, despite the virgin lands program (from 1954). Soviet crushing of the 1956 Hungarian revolution, the 1960 U-2 spy plane episode, and other incidents renewed E-W tension and domestic curbs.

Eastern Europe. Resentment of Russian domination and Stalinist repression combined with nationalist, economic, and religious factors to produce periodic violence. E Berlin workers rioted (1953), Polish workers rioted in Poznan (June 1956), and a broad-based **revolution** broke out in **Hungary** (Oct. 1956). All were suppressed by Soviet force or threats (at least 7,000 dead in Hungary), but Poland was allowed to restore private ownership of farms, and a degree of personal and economic freedom returned to Hungary. Yugoslavia experimented with worker self-management and a market economy.

Korea. The 1945 division of Korea along the 38th parallel left industry in the N, which was organized into a militant regime and armed by the USSR. The S was politically disunited. More than 60,000 N Korean troops invaded the S on June 25, 1950. The U.S., backed by the UN Security Council, sent troops. **UN troops** reached the Chinese border in Nov. Some 200,000 Chinese troops crossed the Yalu R. and drove back UN forces. By spring 1951, battle lines had become stabilized near the original 38th parallel border, but heavy fighting continued. Finally, an armistice was signed on July 27, 1953. U.S. troops remained in the S, and U.S. economic and military aid continued. The war stimulated rapid economic recovery in Japan.

China. Starting in 1952, industry, agriculture, and social institutions were forcibly collectivized. In a massive purge, as many as several million people were executed as Kuomintang supporters or as class and political enemies. The **Great Leap Forward** (1958-60) unsuccessfully tried to force the pace of development by substituting labor for investment.

Southeast Asia. Ho Chi Minh's forces, aided by the USSR and the new Chinese Communist government, fought French and pro-French Vietnamese forces to a standstill and captured the strategic **Dien Bien Phu** camp in May 1954. The Geneva Agreements divided Vietnam in half pending elections (never held) and recognized Laos and Cambodia as independent. The U.S. aided the anti-Communist Republic of Vietnam in the S.

Middle East. Arab revolutions placed leftist, militantly nationalist regimes in power in Egypt (1952) and Iraq (1958). But Arab unity attempts failed (United Arab Republic joined Egypt, Syria, Yemen, 1958-61). Arab refusal to recognize Israel (Arab League economic blockade began Sept. 1951) led to a permanent **state of war**, with repeated incidents (Gaza, 1955). Israel occupied Sinai, and Britain and France took (Oct. 1956) the Suez Canal, but were replaced by the UN Emergency Force. The Mossadegh government in Iran nationalized (May 1951) the British-owned oil industry in May, but was overthrown (Aug. 1953) in a U.S.-aided coup.

Latin America. Argentinian dictator Juan Perón, in office 1946, crushed opposition and enforced land reform, some nationalization, welfare state measures, and curbs on the Roman Catholic Church. A Sept. 1955 coup deposed Perón. The 1952 revolution in Bolivia brought land reform, nationalization of tin mines, and improvement in the status of the Indigenous population, who nevertheless remained poor. The Batista regime in Cuba was overthrown (Jan. 1959) by Fidel **Castro**, who imposed a Communist dictatorship, aligned Cuba with the

USSR, and improved education and health care. A U.S.-backed anti-Castro invasion (**Bay of Pigs**, Apr. 1961) was crushed. Self-government advanced in the British Caribbean.

Technology. Large outlays on research and development in the U.S. and the USSR focused on military applications (H-bomb in U.S., 1952; USSR, 1953; Britain, 1957; intercontinental missiles, late 1950s). Soviet launching of the **Sputnik** satellite (Oct. 4, 1957) spurred increases in U.S. science education funds (National Defense Education Act).

Literature and film. Alienation from social and literary conventions reached an extreme in the theater of the absurd (Beckett's *Waiting for Godot*, 1952), the "new novel" (Robbe-Grillet's *Voyeur*, 1955), and avant-garde film (Antonioni's *L'Avventura*, 1960). U.S. beatniks (Kerouac's *On the Road*, 1957) and others rejected the supposed conformism of Americans (Riesman's *The Lonely Crowd*, 1950).

Rising Expectations and New Protests: 1960-69

Global economy. The longest sustained economic boom on record spanned almost the entire decade in the capitalist world; the closely watched GNP figure doubled (1960-70) in the U.S., fueled by **Vietnam War**-related budget deficits. The **General Agreement on Tariffs and Trade** (1967) stimulated Western European prosperity, which spread to peripheral areas (Spain, Italy, E Germany). Japan became a top economic power. Foreign investment aided the industrialization of Brazil. There were limited Soviet economic reform attempts. Outside the Soviet zone the global economy was marked by the growing role of multinational corporations (3,000 in 1914; 6,000 by 1970). International nongovernmental organizations (NGOs) also multiplied rapidly (Amnesty International, 1961).

Reform and radicalization. Pres. John F. **Kennedy**, inaugurated 1961, emphasized youthful idealism and vigor; his assassination Nov. 22, 1963, was a national trauma. Political and social reform movements took root in U.S. and other countries. Blacks demonstrated nonviolently and with partial success against segregation and poverty (1963 March on Washington; 1964 **Civil Rights Act**), but some urban areas erupted in riots (Watts, 1965; Detroit, 1967; more than 100 cities following **Martin Luther King Jr.** assassination, Apr. 4, 1968). New concern for the poor (Harrington's *Other America*, 1963) helped lead to Pres. Lyndon Johnson's **"Great Society"** programs (Medicare, Water Quality Act, Higher Education Act, all 1965). Concern for the **environment** surged (Carson's *Silent Spring*, 1962).

Feminism revived as a cultural and political movement (Friedan's *Feminine Mystique*, 1963; National Organization for Women founded, 1966), and a movement for homosexual rights emerged (Stonewall riot in NYC, 1969). Pope John XXIII called the **Second Vatican Council** (1962-65), which liberalized Roman Catholic liturgy and some other aspects of Catholicism.

Opposition to U.S. involvement in Vietnam, especially among university students (**Moratorium** protest, Nov. 1969), turned violent (Weatherman Chicago riots, Oct. 1969). **New Left** and Marxist theories became popular, and membership in radical

groups (Students for a Democratic Society, Black Panthers) increased. Maoist groups, especially in Europe, called for total transformation of society. In France, students sparked a nationwide strike affecting 10 million workers in May-June 1968.

China. China's revolutionary militancy under Mao Zedong led to border disputes and other conflict with the USSR under "revisionist" Khrushchev, starting in 1960. The **"Great Proletarian Cultural Revolution"** tried to impose a utopian egalitarian program in China and spread revolution abroad; political struggle, often violent, convulsed China in 1965-68.

Southeast Asia. Communist-led guerrillas aided by N Vietnam fought from 1960 against the S Vietnam government of Ngo Dinh Diem (killed 1963). The U.S. military role increased after the 1964 **Tonkin Gulf** incident. Laotian and Cambodian neutrality were threatened by Communist insurgencies, with N Vietnamese aid, and U.S. intrigues.

Developing world. A bloc of authoritarian leftist regimes among the newly independent nations came to dominate the conference of nonaligned nations (Belgrade, 1961; Cairo, 1964; Lusaka, 1970). Soviet political ties and military bases were established in Cuba, Egypt, Algeria, Guinea, and other countries. Some leaders were ousted in coups by pro-Western groups— Dem. Rep. of the Congo's Patrice Lumumba (killed 1961), Ghana's Kwame Nkrumah (exiled 1966), and Indonesia's Sukarno (effectively ousted in 1965 after a Communist coup failed).

Middle East. Arab-Israeli tension erupted into a brief war June 1967. Israel emerged from the war as a major regional power. Military shipments before and after the war increased Soviet influence in much of the Arab world. Most Arab states broke U.S. diplomatic ties, while Communist countries cut their ties to Israel. Intra-Arab disputes continued: Egypt and Saudi Arabia supported rival factions in a bloody Yemen civil war 1962-70; Lebanese troops fought Palestinian commandos 1969.

Eastern Europe. To stop the large-scale exodus of citizens, E German authorities built (Aug. 1961) a fortified **wall across Berlin** that enclosed West Berlin. Soviet sway in the Balkans was weakened by Albania's realignment with China (USSR broke ties with Albania in Dec. 1961) and Romania's assertion (1964) of limited autonomy. Liberalization (spring 1968) in **Czechoslovakia** was crushed with massive force by troops of five Warsaw Pact countries. W German treaties (1970) with the USSR and Poland facilitated transfer of German technology and confirmed postwar boundaries.

Arts and styles. The boundary between fine and popular arts was blurred to some extent by Pop Art (Warhol) and rock musicals (*Hair*, 1968). Informality and exaggeration prevailed in fashion (beards, miniskirts). A nonpolitical "counterculture" developed, rejecting traditional bourgeois life goals and personal habits, and use of marijuana and hallucinogens spread (**Woodstock** festival, Aug. 1969). **The Beatles** brought unprecedented sophistication to rock music.

East Germany in 1961 began construction on a barrier to slow the exodus of its population to West Berlin.

Science. The decade saw great scientific and technological progress, epitomized by landing of **U.S. astronauts on the Moon** (July 1969). There were major advances in **electronics** (lasers, integrated circuits), **agriculture** ("green revolution"), **medicine** (heart transplants, 1967), and other areas, as well as attempts to control spread of **nuclear weapons** (1963 Limited Test Ban Treaty, 1968 Nuclear Nonproliferation Treaty).

New Global Balances and Religious Revivals: 1970-79

U.S. trends. The decade was marked by a sluggish economy, energy shortages, and environmental problems. Communist forces' takeover of **South Vietnam** (evacuation of U.S. civilians, Apr. 1975), revelations of **CIA** misdeeds (Rockefeller Commission report, June 1975), and **Watergate** scandal (Nixon resignation, Aug. 1974) reduced faith in U.S. influence and leadership. Social issues spurred controversy—school busing and racial quotas were challenged (**Bakke** case decided by Supreme Court, June 1978), and proposed **Equal Rights Amendment**, sent to states for approval in Mar. 1972, fell short of ratification. **Three Mile Island** nuclear reactor accident (Mar. 1979) reinforced fears of nuclear energy.

Economic woes. The 1960s boom faltered in the 1970s; a severe **recession** in U.S. and Europe (1974-75) followed a huge oil price hike (Dec. 1973), precipitated by the Oct. 1973 Arab **oil embargo**. Monetary instability (U.S. cut ties to gold, 1971), decline of the dollar, and protectionist moves by industrial countries (1977-78) threatened trade. Business investment declined. Severe **inflation** plagued many countries (25% in Britain, 1975; 18% in U.S., 1979).

China readjusts. After the 1976 deaths of **Mao** Zedong and **Zhou** Enlai, relative pragmatists won the struggle for leadership. Orthodox Maoists were purged; Mao's widow and other members of the so-called **Gang of Four** were arrested. New leaders freed many political prisoners. Political and trade ties to Japan, Europe, and the U.S. (Nixon visit, 1972) expanded, as relations with the USSR, Cuba, and Vietnam eventually worsened (four-week invasion by China, 1979). Some ideological restrictions were reversed (bonuses to workers, exams for college entrance allowed, 1977); some restrictions on cultural expression were eased.

Europe. European unity (EEC-EFTA trade accord, 1972) faltered as economic problems developed (Britain floated pound, 1972; France floated franc, 1974). Germany and Switzerland curbed guest workers from S Europe, while Greece and Turkey quarreled over Cyprus and Aegean oil rights. The authoritarian regime in **Portugal** was overthrown (Apr. 1974), **Greece**'s seven-year military dictatorship yielded power (July 1974), and **Spain** held free elections (June 1977) after Francisco Franco's death.

A surge of terrorist attacks in **Germany** and elsewhere (1972 **Munich Olympics** killings) raised security concerns. France's Socialist-Communist coalition lost 1978 election bid. Disruptive strikes in **Britain** (1978-79 "winter of discontent") contributed to Labour government defeat in May 1979 elections, bringing Conservative Margaret **Thatcher** to power as UK's first woman prime minister.

Religion and politics. Along with the growth of Arab oil wealth, there was a resurgence of activism, often religiously motivated. Libyan dictator Muammar al-**Qaddafi** mixed Islamic laws with socialism. The illegal **Muslim Brotherhood** in Egypt was accused of violence, while extreme groups bombed (1977) theaters to protest Western and secular values. In **Turkey**, the National Salvation Party became the first Islamic group to win a share in power (1974) since secularization in the 1920s. In **Iran**, Ayatollah Ruhollah **Khomeini** led a revolution that deposed the secular shah (Jan. 1979) and created an Islamic republic. Religiously motivated insurrectionists in **Saudi Arabia** briefly seized (1979) the Grand Mosque in Mecca. Muslim puritan opposition to **Pakistan** Pres. Zulfikar Ali-**Bhutto** contributed to his overthrow in July 1977. Bengali nationalism was a driving force behind a successful fight for the independence of Pakistan's eastern province (**Bangladesh**) in Dec. 1971, after a bloody civil war.

Muslim and Hindu opposition to coerced sterilization in **India** helped defeat the Indira **Gandhi** government, to be replaced (Mar. 1977) by a coalition including Hindu religious parties. Muslims in the S **Philippines**, aided by Libya, rebelled against

central rule from 1973. The **Buddhist** Soka Gakkai movement launched (1964) the Komeito party in **Japan**, a major opposition party in 1972 and 1976 elections. Israel's secularist **Israeli** Labor party was ousted in 1977 by conservatives led by Menachem **Begin**; religious militants founded settlements on the disputed **West Bank**, part of biblically promised Israel.

Religious wars raged in **Northern Ireland** (Catholic vs. Protestant, 1969-97) and **Lebanon** (Christian vs. Muslim, 1975-90), while religious militancy complicated the Israel-Arab dispute (1973 Israel-Arab war). The **Camp David Accords**, negotiated in 1978 by Egyptian Pres. Anwar al-**Sadat**, Israeli Prime Min. Menachem **Begin**, and U.S. Pres. Jimmy **Carter**, facilitated landmark 1979 **Egypt-Israel** peace treaty, but increased militancy on the West Bank impeded further progress. **Evangelical Protestant** groups grew in influence in the U.S. Reform **Judaism** in U.S. expanded and ordained first woman rabbi (1972).

Latin America. Right-wing forces strengthened their hold, with a violent coup against the elected (Sept. 1973) leftist **Allende** government in **Chile**, a military coup in **Argentina** (1976), and coups against left-wing regimes in **Bolivia** (1971, 1979) and **Peru** (1976). In Central America, increasing liberal and leftist militancy led to ouster (1979) of the **Somoza** regime of **Nicaragua** and to civil conflict in **El Salvador**.

Southeast Asia. Communist victories in Vietnam, Cambodia, and Laos by May 1975 led to new turmoil. **Pol Pot**'s **Khmer Rouge** regime in **Cambodia** ordered millions to resettle in rural areas, in a program of forced labor and terrorism that cost more than 1 million lives (1975-79) and caused hundreds of thousands to flee. The Vietnamese invasion of Cambodia (1979) swelled the refugee population and contributed to widespread starvation.

Russian expansion. Soviet influence, checked in some countries (troops ousted by **Egypt**, 1972), was projected farther afield (**Angola**, 1975-89; **Ethiopia**, 1977-88). **Détente** with the West—1972 Berlin pact, 1972 strategic arms pact (**SALT**)—was marred in the late 1970s by revelations of Soviet atrocities (Solzhenitsyn's *Gulag Archipelago*, 1974) and the 1979 Soviet invasion of **Afghanistan**.

Africa. The last European colonies won independence (**Spanish Sahara**, 1976; **Djibouti**, 1977), and, after 10 years of civil war, a Black government took over (1979) in **Zimbabwe** (Rhodesia); white domination remained in **South Africa**. Ethnic or tribal conflicts were widespread, with European intervention in local wars (France in **Chad**, **Mauritania**) and heavy involvement of Cuban troops. Dominant figures included Ugandan dictator Idi **Amin**, toppled in Apr. 1979 after eight years of chaotic rule.

The Vietnam War, in which an estimated 2 million Vietnamese and 58,000 Americans died, also engulfed Laos and Cambodia in deadly violence.

End of the Cold War and Demand for Democracy: 1980-89

Global developments. International contacts accelerated thanks to **new openness** in China (from 1978) and USSR (from 1985). **Global consumerism** was symbolized by rapid spread of McDonald's restaurants (Japan, 1971; Russia, 1990). New forms of home media proliferated (VCRs, personal computers, video gaming systems). HIV/AIDS was identified; WHO estimated 400,000 cases worldwide by 1989.

USSR, Eastern Europe. The late 1980s saw the remaking of the Soviet state and the beginning of the disintegration of the Soviet empire. After the deaths of Gen. Sec. Leonid **Brezhnev** (1982) and two successors, emigration restrictions and repression of dissent were eased. Gen. Sec. Mikhail **Gorbachev** (in office 1985-91) promoted *glasnost* and *perestroika*—economic, political, and social reform. Four Reagan-Gorbachev **summits** (1985-88) yielded the **INF disarmament treaty** (1987; expired 2019). Military withdrawal from **Afghanistan** was completed in Feb. 1989, and the Soviet people chose (Mar. 1989) part of the new Congress of People's Deputies from competing candidates.

In **Poland**, Solidarity, the labor union founded (1980) by Lech **Walesa**, was outlawed in 1982 but legalized in 1988, after years of unrest. Free elections (June 1989) brought in a Walesa adviser as prime minister in a government with the Communists. In fall 1989 failing Marxist economies in **Hungary**, **East Germany**, **Czechoslovakia**, **Bulgaria**, and **Romania** brought the collapse of the Communist monopoly and a demand for democracy. In a historic step, the **Berlin Wall** was opened in Nov. 1989.

U.S. Under Pres. Ronald **Reagan** (1981-88) conservative economic policies yielded budget and tax cuts, deregulation, "junk bond" financing, leveraged buyouts, and mergers. Federal budget deficits rose, and a stock market crash in Oct. 1987 (Black Monday) had global repercussions. Foreign policy took a **strong anti-Communist** turn, with increased defense spending, invasion of Cuba-threatened **Grenada** (Oct. 1983), a **"Star Wars"** missile defense program, and the **Iran-contra scandal**.

Middle East. The Middle East remained militarily unstable, with sharp divisions along economic, political, racial, and religious lines. The 1979 Islamic revolution in **Iran**, bringing Ayatollah Ruhollah **Khomeini** to power, fueled antagonism toward U.S. and the West (**hostage crisis**, Nov. 1979-Jan. 1981; first U.S. sanctions imposed). In Sept. 1980, **Iraq** repudiated its border agreement with Iran, and hostilities between the two countries led to an eight-year war in which hundreds of thousands died. After the death of Khomeini (June 1989), his chosen successor, former Pres. Ali Hosseini **Khamenei**, became Iran's supreme leader, retaining office over the next three decades and beyond. **Libya's** support for **terrorism** poisoned relations with the West; U.S. closed (1981) its diplomatic mission there and embargoed Libyan oil (1982). Following an attack on a West Berlin disco frequented by U.S. military (Apr. 1986, 3 killed), U.S. bombed targets in Libya.

Israel affirmed (July 1980) all **Jerusalem** as its capital, destroyed (June 1981) an **Iraqi atomic reactor**, and invaded **Lebanon**, citing terrorism from the Palestine Liberation Organization; PLO withdrew from Lebanon after cease-fire.

Palestinian uprising began (Dec. 1987) in Israeli-occupied Gaza and spread to the West Bank; troops responded with force, leaving hundreds dead and thousands in detention camps. Israel began (Feb. 1985) withdrawal from **war-torn Lebanon**; artillery duels (Mar.-Apr. 1989) between Christian East Beirut and Muslim West Beirut left 200 dead.

Latin America. In **Nicaragua**, the leftist **Sandinista** National Liberation Front, in power after the 1979 civil war, gave military aid to guerrillas in El Salvador, while U.S. aided anti-Sandinista **contras**, utilizing profits from secret arms sales to Iran (**Iran-contra scandal**) and the **CIA** directed the mining of Nicaraguan ports. In **El Salvador**, a military coup (Oct. 1979) failed to halt a leftist insurgency armed by Cuba and Nicaragua. Salvadoran Archbishop Oscar **Romero**, advocate for poor, was assassinated Mar. 1980; right-wing death squads killed thousands in ensuing decade of civil war. In **Chile**, Gen. Augusto **Pinochet**—in power since 1973, and known for harsh measures against leftists and dissidents—yielded the presidency after elections (Dec. 1989) but remained head of the army. In **Panama**, U.S. troops overthrew dictator Manuel **Noriega** (Dec. 1989); later convicted on drug and human rights charges, he served time in the U.S., France, and Panama.

Africa. African countries suffered severe hardship, fueled by accelerating desertification, heavy foreign debt, worldwide recession, rapid population growth, and wars and political instability. Some 60 million Africans faced prolonged hunger in 1981, and severe **drought** in 1983 left one-third of the population, or about 150 million, near **famine**. Western nations sent aid, and **Live Aid**, a marathon rock concert (July 1985), raised relief funds. Wars in **Ethiopia** and **Sudan** and military strife in several other nations continued.

Anti-apartheid sentiment gathered force in **South Africa**, with demonstrations meeting violent police response. White voters approved (Nov. 1983) the first constitution to give Asians and people of mixed-race backgrounds a voice, while still excluding the Black majority. Twelve nations imposed economic **sanctions** in Aug.-Sept. 1985, and Pres. P. W. **Botha** was succeeded (Sept. 1989) by F.W. **de Klerk**, who promised negotiation with the Black population.

Asia and Pacific. Benazir **Bhutto** became the first woman to lead a majority-Muslim nation as prime minister of **Pakistan** (Dec. 1988). "People power" revolt in the **Philippines** ousted Ferdinand **Marcos** (Feb. 1986) after two decades as president; he was replaced by Corazon **Aquino**. Trade imbalances favoring **Japan** dominated that nation's foreign relations.

During the 1980s **China's** Communist government and paramount leader **Deng** Xiaoping expanded ties to the West and the role of market forces. But in Apr. 1989 pro-democracy demonstrators camped out in **Tiananmen Square**, Beijing, and peaceful protest marches spread to at least 20 other cities. Troops and tanks crushed the demonstration in and around Tiananmen Square (June 3-4), leaving an estimated 500-7,000 dead; up to 10,000 were arrested, 31 tried and executed. The conciliatory Communist Party chief was ousted; the Politburo adopted (1989) reforms against official corruption.

Europe. With the addition of Greece, Portugal, and Spain, the **European Community** became a common market of more than 300 million people. In the UK, Conservative Margaret **Thatcher** won three elections (1979, 1983, 1987) to serve as prime minister; she pursued a policy of deregulation and privatization, and presided over British victory in the 1982 **Falklands war**. **France** elected (1981) its first socialist president, François **Mitterrand** (reelected, 1988). Elections in 1983 brought **Italy** its first socialist premier, Bettino **Craxi**.

International terrorism. With the 1979 overthrow of the shah of **Iran** and instability in the **Middle East** and elsewhere, terrorism became a prominent tactic. In 1979-81, Iranian militants held 52 **U.S. hostages** in Iran for 444 days. In Oct. 1983, in **Lebanon**, truck bombs exploded at U.S. Marine headquarters, killing 241 Americans, and at a French paratrooper barracks, killing 58. The *Achille Lauro* cruise ship was hijacked in Oct. 1985. **Assassinated leaders** included Egypt's Pres. Anwar al-Sadat (1981), India's Prime Min. Indira **Gandhi** (1984), and Lebanese Prem. Rashid **Karami** (1987).

The Chinese government responded to pro-democracy demonstrations in Tiananmen Square with force (1989).

New Regional Tensions in a Post-Cold War World: 1990-99

Soviet Empire collapse. Breakup of the Soviet Union into 15 independent states began with declarations of independence by **Lithuania**, **Latvia**, and **Estonia** during abortive coup against Mikhail **Gorbachev** (Aug. 1991). Other republics followed. In Dec. 1991, **Russia**, **Ukraine**, and **Belarus** declared the Soviet Union dead; Gorbachev resigned. The **Warsaw Pact** and Council for Mutual Economic Assistance (**Comecon**) disbanded. Most former Soviet republics joined in loose confederation (**Commonwealth of Independent States**). Hardship ensued as Russia, under Pres. Boris **Yeltsin**, moved to reboot the economy under a free-market system. When the Muslim-majority Russian republic of **Chechnya** declared independence, Russian forces invaded (Dec. 1994), causing massive destruction and civilian casualties before withdrawing after a 1996 cease-fire. In 1999, Russia forcibly suppressed Muslim insurgents in Russian republic of **Dagestan** and again invaded Chechnya, with heavy civilian casualties. **Yeltsin** resigned Russia's presidency, Dec. 1999, with Prime Min. Vladimir **Putin** becoming acting president.

Europe. **Yugoslavia** broke apart, and hostilities ensued along ethnic and religious lines. **Croatia**, **Slovenia**, and **Macedonia** declared independence (1991), followed by **Bosnia-Herzegovina** (1992). **Serbia** and **Montenegro** remained as the republic of Yugoslavia. Bitter fighting followed, especially in Bosnia; Serbian forces laid siege to the town of **Srebrenica**, slaughtering more than 7,000 Bosnian Muslim men and boys (July 1995), and expelling some 20,000 people in an **ethnic cleansing** of the Muslim population; peace plan (**Dayton accord**) reached Nov. 1995 was brokered by the U.S., with **NATO** policing its implementation. In spring 1999, NATO conducted a bombing campaign aimed at stopping Yugoslavia from driving ethnic Albanians from the **Kosovo** region; a June accord brought in NATO peacekeepers.

The **two Germanys were reunited** after 45 years, in Oct. 1990. Czechoslovakia broke apart (Jan. 1993) into the **Czech Republic** and **Slovakia**. Labor leader Lech **Walesa** was elected president of **Poland** (Dec. 1991). In Jan. 1994, NATO approved the **Partnership for Peace**, coordinating defense of E and Central European countries; Russia later joined. NATO signed pact with **Russia** (May 1997) allowing for NATO expansion into former Soviet-bloc countries; Czech Republic, **Hungary**, and **Poland** joined NATO in Jan. 1999. Efforts toward European unity continued with adoption of a single market (Jan. 1993) and conversion of the European Community to the **European Union** as the **Maastricht Treaty** took effect (Nov. 1993). The **euro** was launched as common currency, Jan. 1999, initially only for non-cash uses, in 12 EU countries.

An intraparty revolt forced Margaret **Thatcher** out as UK prime minister, to be succeeded by John **Major** (Nov. 1990); Labour took power under Tony **Blair** (May 1997). Prince **Charles** and **Diana** divorced (Aug. 1996); Diana died in car crash a year later. Talks on **Northern Ireland** led to **peace plan**, approved in all-Ireland vote (May 1998). In Dec. 1999, Northern Ireland was granted home rule. Voters in **Scotland** (overwhelmingly) and **Wales** (narrowly) approved creation of regional legislatures (1997). In **France**, socialist Pres. François **Mitterrand** declined to run for a third term and conservative Jacques **Chirac** was elected (May 1995) to the office.

Middle East. In Aug. 1990, **Iraq's Saddam Hussein** ordered troops to invade **Kuwait**. A UN-approved international force, led by U.S., bombed Iraq (Jan. 1991) and launched a land attack, crushing the invasion. After a cease-fire, agreed to, Apr. 1991, the UN extended sanctions on Iraq for failure to abide by its terms. Iraq's reported failure to cooperate with UN inspectors seeking to eliminate **weapons of mass destruction** led to airstrikes by U.S. and Britain (1998).

Israel and the **PLO** signed peace accord (Sept. 1993) providing for Palestinian self-government in **West Bank** and **Gaza** Strip; Prime Min. Yitzhak **Rabin** and Foreign Min. Shimon **Peres** of Israel and Yasir **Arafat** of the PLO shared 1994 Nobel Peace Prize. Six Arab nations relaxed boycott against Israel (1994), and Israel and **Jordan** signed peace treaty (Oct. 1994). Rabin was assassinated (Nov. 1995) by an Israeli extremist; Benjamin **Netanyahu** became prime minister (May 1996).

Asia and Pacific. Longtime **North Korean** dictator **Kim Il Sung** died (July 1994) and was succeeded by son **Kim Jong Il**.

In Oct. 1994 North Korea signed agreement with U.S. setting timetable for ending **nuclear weapons** program (deal collapsed in 2002). Well over 200,000 (perhaps more than 2 million) North Koreans died in the 1990s from **famine**. **Palau** achieved independence, Oct. 1994. **Hong Kong** was returned to **China** (July 1997), after 156 years as a British colony, and **Macau** reverted to China (Dec. 1999) after over 400 years of Portuguese rule. **Jiang** Zemin, general secretary of the Chinese Communist Party, also became China's president (Mar. 1993). China released several well-known dissidents but continued to jail and execute many. U.S. and China signed trade pact (Nov. 1999). In **Japan** members of a religious cult released the nerve gas sarin on **Tokyo subway**, killing 12 and injuring over 5,500 (Mar. 1995).

After years of growing prosperity, **Thailand**, **Indonesia**, and **South Korea** in 1997 began to suffer economic reverses, with worldwide ripple effect, and received IMF **bailout** packages. In Indonesia, protests over mismanagement led to the resignation of Pres. **Suharto** (May 1998) after 32 years of rule. In a referendum (Aug. 1999), **East Timorese** voted for independence; pro-Indonesian militias rampaged, but a multinational peacekeeping force helped restore order (Sept. 1999).

In **Afghanistan** the radical Islamist **Taliban** gained control of Kabul (Sept. 1996) and, eventually, most of the country. **Indian** forces repeatedly clashed with pro-independence demonstrators in the disputed majority-Muslim region of **Kashmir**, exacerbating relations with **Pakistan**. India and Pakistan both conducted **nuclear tests** in 1998. Conflict between government and the military led to a **bloodless coup** in Pakistan (Oct. 1999).

Africa. **South Africa's** Pres. F. W. **de Klerk** released dissident Black leader Nelson **Mandela** from prison (Feb. 1990) after 27 years, and the white minority government repealed **apartheid** laws (1990, 1991); also dismantled its **nuclear weapons** program. The African National Congress won in multiracial elections (Apr. 1994), making Mandela president, and a new constitution became law (Dec. 1996). **Namibia** became independent in Mar. 1990, after long UN trusteeship. **Eritrea** won independence from **Ethiopia**, July 1993, after over 30 years of war. **Mobutu** Sese Seko, longtime ruler of **Zaire**, was deposed (May 1997) by rebel forces under Laurent **Kabila**, who changed country's name back to **Democratic Republic of the Congo**. In **Nigeria**, former Gen. Olusegun **Obasanjo** was elected (Feb. 1999) as the nation's first civilian leader in 15 years.

Civil war broke out in **Liberia** (Dec. 1989) and lasted, with interruptions, through the 1990s and beyond, leaving hundreds of thousands dead. Factional fighting erupted in **Somalia** (Jan. 1991); a U.S.-led UN peacekeeping force failed to restore order and left (Mar. 1995). In **Algeria**, the army canceled parliamentary elections (Jan. 1992) when the Islamic party won a first round; after ensuing civil war, a peace and amnesty plan was approved in a Sept. 1999 referendum. Assassination of **Burundi's** president (June 1993) renewed ethnic violence between **Hutus** and **Tutsis** there. A suspicious plane crash that killed the

South Africa abandoned apartheid and transitioned to a non-racial democratic government, with Nelson Mandela (pictured, with U.S. Pres. Bill Clinton) elected president in 1994.

presidents of Burundi and Rwanda (Apr. 1994) led to **genocide** in **Rwanda**; some 800,000 died, mostly Tutsis massacred by Hutu militias.

North America. U.S. Pres. Bill Clinton (D) (elected 1992, 1996) presided over growing economy, promoted free trade, intervened in Bosnia. Impeached by House (Dec. 1998) on charges stemming from affair with intern, he was acquitted by the Senate. In **Canada**, Liberal Jean **Chrétien** became prime minister (Nov. 1993; reelected 1997). The Canadian territory of **Nunavut** was created, Apr. 1999. In **Mexico**, Ernesto **Zedillo** of the ruling PRI party was elected president (July 1994) after PRI's first candidate was assassinated. The country weathered a **monetary crisis** with the help of a 1995 U.S. bailout. The North American Free Trade Agreement (**NAFTA**), liberalizing trade between U.S., Canada, and Mexico, took effect Jan. 1994. Globalization trends drew protests from radical activists (**World Trade Org.** meeting, Nov.-Dec. 1999).

Central America and Caribbean. In **Haiti**, Jean-Bertrand **Aristide** was elected president, Dec. 1990; ousted in Sept. 1991 military coup, he was restored to office (Oct. 1994) through U.S.-led negotiations. In Feb. 1990 elections in **Nicaragua** the opposition won a surprise victory over **Sandinista** Pres. Daniel **Ortega**. A 12-year civil war in **El Salvador** ended with peace treaty, Jan. 1992, between government and leftist rebels. In Dec. 1999, Panama assumed full control of the **Panama Canal**, in accord with 1977 treaty with U.S.

South America. Alberto **Fujimori** was elected president of **Peru** in June 1990; condemned for human rights abuses but popular for reducing terrorism; reelected in 1995. Leftist guerrillas took hostages in Lima (Dec. 1996); one hostage killed during rescue operation (Apr. 1997). Peronist Pres. Carlos Saúl **Menem** was **Argentina**'s president for much of the decade,

imposing economic austerity. Former **Chilean** Pres. Augusto **Pinochet** was arrested in London (Oct. 1998) and charged with human-rights violations but judged unfit for trial. In **Brazil**, Fernando Henrique **Cardoso** was elected president (Oct. 1994) and reelected in 1998 despite economic slump; the IMF announced a $42-billion aid package (Nov. 1998). In **Venezuela** two coups were thwarted (1992), but leftist coup leader Hugo **Chávez** was elected president, Dec. 1998.

Terrorism. A bomb exploded in garage beneath New York City's **World Trade Center**, killing six (Feb. 1993); six Islamic fundamentalists were convicted. Bombs outside U.S. embassies in **Kenya** and **Tanzania** killed over 220 (Aug. 1998); U.S. retaliated with airstrikes in Afghanistan and Sudan. Anti-government U.S. radicals bombed a federal building in **Oklahoma City**, OK (Apr. 1995), killing 168.

Science, technology, environment. Hubble Space Telescope was launched, Apr. 1990. U.S. space shuttle *Atlantis* docked with the orbiting Russian space station *Mir* (June 1995) in first of several joint missions. In Nov. 1998 the first component for a new **International Space Station** was launched into space from Kazakhstan. Scottish scientists announced (Feb. 1997) **cloning** of a sheep. Tim **Berners-Lee** launched first **World Wide Web** server (1990); user-friendly graphical browsers (Mosaic, 1993; Netscape, 1994) and consumer internet service providers followed, beginning a global transformation of communications and information access. Efforts to limit **global climate change** intensified with tentative agreements adopted in **Kyoto**, Japan (Dec. 1997). In 1999, World Health Org. announced 33 million people were living with **HIV**, and **AIDS** was fourth leading cause of death worldwide (No. 1 cause in Africa), with an estimated 14 million deaths since the epidemic began.

Globalization and Global Realignments: 2000-09

Terrorism. In Oct. 2000, 17 U.S. Navy sailors were killed aboard the USS *Cole* in Aden, **Yemen**, in suicide bombing tied to **al-Qaeda** terrorist network, based in Afghanistan. Hijackers

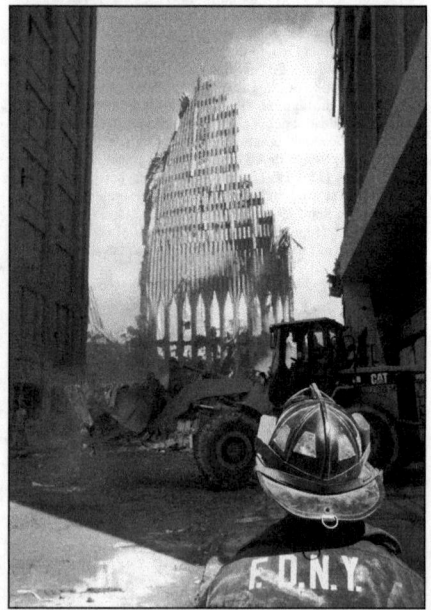

The attacks of Sept. 11, 2001, killed more than 2,750 people in New York.

on Sept. 11, 2001, crashed two jetliners into the twin towers of the **World Trade Center** in New York City and another into the **Pentagon** outside Washington, DC, with a fourth crashing in a Pennsylvania field. The attacks, linked to al-Qaeda and its leader, **Osama bin Laden**, killed nearly 3,000.

Islamic radicals also planted a car bomb on the Indonesian island of **Bali** (Oct. 2002; over 200 killed) and bombed mass transit systems in **Madrid** (Mar. 2004; some 200 killed), **London** (July 2005; 56 killed), and **Mumbai** (July 2006; over 180 killed). Jihadists in Mumbai attacked sites frequented by foreigners in Nov. 2008 (over 160 died). **Chechen** separatist guerrillas were implicated in an attack on a **Moscow** movie theater (Oct. 2002; at least 120 hostages died) and takeover of a school in Beslan (Sept. 2004; over 330 killed). Bombing attacks on **Yazidi** towns in **Iraq** (Aug. 2007) killed at least 500.

Economic crisis. Rapid economic growth in **China** and other developing countries contrasted with sluggish rates in traditional economic powers. A global **recession**, beginning in late 2007, combined with **financial meltdown** (Sept. 2008). **Iceland**'s banking system collapsed (Oct. 2008); rescued by loans and austerity. **Dubai**'s state-controlled investment company was bailed out (Dec. 2009) by Abu Dhabi. Soaring food and fuel prices sparked unrest in **Egypt** and **Haiti** (Apr. 2008). **Austerity** measures spurred protests in Europe.

War in Iraq and Afghanistan. The U.S., with the UK, invaded **Iraq** (Mar. 2003) to oust the regime of Saddam **Hussein**. U.S. Pres. George W. **Bush** declared major combat ended by May, but insurgents caused continuing casualties. Though cited as grounds for the invasion, **weapons of mass destruction** were not found. Hussein was captured by U.S. troops (Dec. 2003) and executed by Iraq (2006) for crimes against humanity. Iraqi **elections** led to a **Shiite coalition government** under Prime Min. Nouri al-**Maliki** (May 2006). With **insurgent** violence intensifying, Bush announced (Jan. 2007) a **"surge"** of additional U.S. troops; casualties fell sharply, aided by changing sectarian aims. In **Afghanistan**, a U.S.-led military coalition ousted the **Taliban** regime. A transitional government was installed (Dec. 2001), and NATO assumed control of multinational forces (Aug. 2003).

Afghans elected Hamid **Karzai** president (Nov. 2004; reelected 2009); Taliban and other Islamist militants stepped up attacks.

Middle East. Palestinian suicide bombings continued, and **Israel** mounted a major offensive (Mar. 2002), reoccupying much of the **West Bank**. The U.S., Russia, UN, and EU introduced (Apr. 2003) **"road map"** for peace negotiations, but made little progress. After Palestinian leader Yasir **Arafat** died (Nov. 2004), Mahmoud **Abbas** was elected in his place; in Jan. 2006 the militant Palestinian party **Hamas** won a parliamentary majority. Israel launched attacks on **Lebanon** (July 2006) after a raid by Lebanon-based **Hezbollah** guerrillas, and in reaction to **Hamas** launched an offensive in the **Gaza Strip** (Dec. 2008), with heavy Palestinian casualties. Feb. 2009 elections in Israel led to a coalition government headed by conservative former Prime Min. Benjamin **Netanyahu**. In **Yemen**, U.S. used drones to kill suspected **al-Qaeda** terrorists (Nov. 2002), and the government, from 2004 onward, battled a growing insurgency from **Shiite Houthi** rebels, believed aided by Iran.

Asia and Pacific. Gen. Pervez **Musharraf**, brought to power in Oct. 1999 coup, assumed **Pakistan**'s presidency, June 2001; former Prime Min. Benazir **Bhutto** was assassinated, Dec. 2007. Riots in the mostly Hindu state of Gujarat, **India** (Feb.-Apr. 2002), left more than 1,200 dead, mostly Muslims. Pakistan and **India** restored ties (May 2003) and declared ceasefire in disputed **Kashmir** (Nov. 2003); relations remained tense.

Leaders of **North** and **South Korea** met (June 2000) in first-ever summit. But North Korea withdrew from nuclear nonproliferation treaty Jan. 2003. The country agreed, Feb. 2007, to end **nuclear weapons** development in exchange for aid, but reneged in 2009. East Timor (**Timor-Leste**) achieved independence, May 2002. In **China**, **Hu** Jintao succeeded **Jiang** Zemin as party chief (Nov. 2002) and president (Mar. 2003).

The UN Intl. Atomic Energy Agency (IAEA) censured **Iran** (Dec. 2003) for covering up aspects of its nuclear program; UN sanctions imposed, Dec. 2006, after Iran continued enriching uranium. Hardline Pres. Mahmoud **Ahmadinejad** was declared landslide winner in June 2009 Iranian elections widely perceived as rigged; massive protests were crushed, with dozens killed, hundreds jailed, some tortured. In **Kyrgyzstan**, protests (Mar. 2005) against election fraud brought down Pres. Askar **Akayev** in **"tulip revolution."** **Myanmar**'s military junta cracked down on hundreds of thousands of protesters (Sept. 2007). In **Australia** the center-left Labor Party won landslide victory in Nov. 2007 elections. **Tamil** guerrillas in **Sri Lanka**, soundly defeated in bloody battles against government forces, ended their rebellion (May 2009), which in 26 years had claimed at least 80,000 lives.

In Dec. 2004 a **tsunami** devastated Indian Ocean nations, leaving some 228,000 dead. **Earthquakes** struck the Indian subcontinent (Oct. 2005; nearly 80,000 died) and China's Sichuan province (May 2008; nearly 70,000 died). Over 80,000 died in a May 2008 **cyclone** in Myanmar.

Europe. The **European Union** admitted 12 E European nations by Jan. 2007. Voters in France and Netherlands rejected treaty to establish a new EU constitution (May-June 2005); modified plan (**Treaty of Lisbon**) came into force Dec. 2009. Yugoslav strongman Slobodan Milosevic yielded power in Oct. 2000 and died, Mar. 2006, while on trial for **war crimes**. **Serbia** and **Montenegro** separated into two independent nations, May-June 2006. **Kosovo** declared independence, Feb. 2008.

Vladimir **Putin**, elected Mar. 2000, began long tenure as Russian president, interrupted (2008-12) when his protégé, Dmitri **Medvedev**, held that office. Russians captured capital of **Chechnya** (Feb. 2000) and established direct rule, but the insurgency continued. In **Ukraine**, a tainted presidential runoff election (Nov. 2004) led to the country's **"orange revolution"**; recount gave victory to nationalist Viktor **Yushchenko**.

British Labour Prime Min. Tony **Blair** won reelection twice (2001, 2005). Angela **Merkel**, of the center-right Christian Democratic Union, began (Nov. 2005) her long tenure as German

A 2004 tsunami killed more than 200,000 people in African and Asian countries.

chancellor. Riots broke out in **France**'s immigrant community, Nov. 2005. French voters elected conservative Nicolas **Sarkozy** president (May 2007), and France rejoined **NATO** military command (Apr. 2009) after more than 40 years.

Netherlands became first country to legalize **same-sex marriage**, effective Apr. 2001.

Africa. Ethiopia and **Eritrea** signed peace treaty (Dec. 2000), ending two-year border war, but clashes continued. Laurent **Kabila**, president of Dem. Rep. of the Congo (**DRC**), was assassinated, Jan. 2001. A peace agreement in DRC (Apr. 2003) did not end violence there. Pres. Charles **Taylor** went into exile (Aug. 2003) in deal to end 14-year civil war in **Liberia**; other accords aimed at ending civil wars in **Angola** (Apr. 2002) and Côte d'Ivoire (Jan. 2003). In **Sudan** the Muslim-led government and rebels from the Christian south signed power-sharing agreement, Jan. 2005. Rebellion in the **Darfur** area of W Sudan led to large-scale violence, especially by Arab militias (**janjaweed**) reportedly backed by the government; over 2 million people were displaced and 300,000 killed. The Intl. Criminal Court issued an arrest warrant for Sudanese Pres. Omar al-**Bashir** for war crimes (Mar. 2009), to no avail. Disputed elections sparked violence in **Kenya** (Jan. 2008) and **Zimbabwe** (Apr. 2008). Under longtime Pres. Robert **Mugabe**, Zimbabwe sustained soaring unemployment and hyperinflation. **Guinea-Bissau**'s defense chief and president were assassinated, Mar. 2009.

Americas and the Caribbean. George W. Bush (R) served as U.S. president, 2001-09, after close election. He pursued wars in Afghanistan and Iraq following Sept. 2001 terror attack. Barack **Obama** (D), first-ever Black U.S. president, elected in 2008, pledged to end Afghanistan and Iraq conflicts. The long-supreme Institutional Revolutionary Party (**PRI**) lost power in **Mexico** with election of center-right presidents Vicente **Fox** (2000) and Felipe **Calderón** (2006); drug violence claimed over 30,000 lives. After 12 years in power, **Canada**'s Liberal Party was defeated in Jan. 2006 elections.

Leftists held power in **Chile** under Ricardo **Lagos** Escobar (from 2000) and Michelle **Bachelet** (from 2006), in **Brazil** under Luiz Inácio **Lula** da Silva (elected 2002; reelected 2006), and in **Bolivia** under Evo **Morales** (elected 2005). In **Venezuela**, leftist populist Pres. Hugo **Chávez** regained power after a failed coup (2002). Peronist Néstor **Kirchner** was elected president of **Argentina** (Apr. 2003); his wife **Cristina** was elected (2007) to succeed him. In **Honduras**, leftist leader Manuel **Zelaya** was elected president (Nov. 2005) but was ousted by the military (June 2009). In **Nicaragua** Sandinista leader Daniel **Ortega** won back the presidency, Nov. 2006, and strengthened ties with Cuba and Iran.

In **Peru**, right-wing Pres. Alberto **Fujimori** was reelected (May 2000) but fled the country; he was extradited (2007) and convicted on human rights and corruption charges. **Haiti** was wracked by antigovernment protests, leading to resignation of Jean-Bertrand **Aristide** in Feb. 2004; a UN peacekeeping mission was brought in. Ailing Pres. Fidel **Castro**, **Cuba**'s strongman leader since 1959, ceded powers (July 2006) to his brother, **Raúl**.

Religion. John Paul II died, Apr. 2005, after 26 years as pope; German Cardinal Joseph Ratzinger succeeded him, under the name **Benedict XVI**. The Catholic Church was shaken by **sexual abuse scandal**.

Science and technology. The U.S. **space shuttle** *Columbia* broke up on reentering Earth's atmosphere (Feb. 2003), killing seven crewmembers. NASA landed two rovers, *Spirit* and *Opportunity*, on **Mars** (Jan. 2004); **China** launched its first manned space flight, Oct. 2003. **Internet** penetration and access to technology expanded exponentially; online commerce, use of **social media** (Facebook, 2004; Twitter, 2006), mobile computing (iPhone, 2007), and file-sharing services became common.

Environment and health. Under the **Kyoto Protocol** (effective Feb. 2005), most industrialized nations agreed to specific reductions in emissions of **greenhouse gases** linked to global warming. Worldwide **AIDS** estimates showed (Nov. 2007) new infections had peaked in the late 1990s. A pandemic of **swine flu**, or influenza A (H1N1), broke out in **Mexico** (Apr. 2009) and spread, killing more than 150,000.

Searching for Resolutions: 2010-19

Middle East. UN General Assembly granted observer-state status to **Palestine** (Nov. 2012). Arab-Israeli **peace talks** foundered as **Fatah** and militant **Hamas** factions agreed (Apr. 2014) to aim for unification. **Israel** launched airstrikes on **Gaza** (July-Aug. 2014) after sustaining rocket attacks; heavy Palestinian casualties were recorded.

Poverty, religious and ethnic conflict, and government corruption and repression fueled revolts against entrenched Arab regimes (**Arab Spring**), yielding mixed results. In **Tunisia**, protests forced out Pres. Zine al-Abidine **Ben Ali** (Jan. 2011); elections and a new constitution followed. In **Egypt**, mass demonstrations led to overthrow of longtime Pres. Hosni **Mubarak** (Feb. 2011), but the elected **Muslim Brotherhood**-dominated government fell in a military coup, July 2013; mass arrests followed, and coup leader Abdel Fattah al-**Sisi** was elected president (May 2014). In **Libya**, insurgents backed by NATO overthrew Muammar al-**Qaddafi**, who was killed (Oct. 2011), but Libya became a battleground for rival Islamist factions and a hub for extralegal migration to Europe. In **Yemen**, Pres. Ali Abdullah **Saleh** yielded power, Feb. 2012, after protests; **Houthi** rebels, backed by Iran, took over the capital, Sept. 2014. A **Saudi**-led coalition of Arab states (Mar. 2015) launched bombings against Houthi, with massive casualties. In Oct. 2018 Saudi dissident journalist Jamal **Khashoggi** was killed inside Saudi consulate in Istanbul; a 2021 CIA report implicated the Saudi crown prince.

In **Iraq**, U.S. military left, Dec. 2011. Death toll, 2003-11: about 4,500 U.S. service members, 300 from allied countries, over 100,000 civilians. Government forces and Shia militia continued to fight insurgents, including the Sunni extremist Islamic State in Iraq and Syria (**ISIS**). U.S. and allies conducted airstrikes against ISIS and sent in advisers; separatist **Kurds** fought ISIS on the ground. ISIS imposed strict Islamic law, murdered minorities and resisters, and sponsored terrorism, but by Dec. 2017 was routed from virtually all its territory in Iraq.

Ashraf **Ghani** was sworn in, Sept. 2014, as president of **Afghanistan**, in power-sharing government (reelected 2020). U.S. and NATO ended combat operations against Taliban insurgents, Dec. 2014, but troops remained in support roles. In **Syria**, Pres. Bashar al-**Assad**, Mar. 2011, launched offensive against protesters, giving rise to **civil war**. After about 1,400 people died in **chemical attacks**, the government, Sept. 2013, agreed to a Russian-backed plan for surrender of chemical weapons; fighting and sporadic chemical attacks continued. In Dec. 2016, Syrian government forces, supported by Russia and Iran, gained control of **Aleppo**. U.S.-backed rebels conquered last remnant of **ISIS** territory in Syria, Mar. 2019.

Iran, July 2015, accepted multinational agreement to cut back **nuclear weapons** capability in return for lifting of sanctions and release of over $100 bil in frozen assets; U.S. withdrew from agreement, 2018, and Iran reduced compliance. Iran was shaken by antigovernment strikes and protests (thousands arrested, many allegedly tortured); in demonstrations, Nov. 2019, 300-1,500 protesters were killed by security forces.

Terrorism. Despite killing of leader Osama **bin Laden**, in U.S. raid in **Pakistan** (May 2011), **al-Qaeda** remained entrenched along Afghan-Pakistan border, while **ISIS** and al-Qaeda affiliates were active on a wide scale. Al-**Shabab** militants were behind Oct. 2017 bombings in Mogadishu, **Somalia** (over 350 killed) and repeated attacks in **Kenya**. In **Yemen**, al-Qaeda in the Arabian Peninsula (**AQAP**) attacked military parade rehearsal (May 2012; over 100 killed). **Boko Haram** jihadists abducted over 200 schoolgirls in **Nigeria** (Apr. 2014).

Taliban gunmen in **Pakistan** killed some 150 at a Peshawar school (Dec. 2014).

Attackers possibly linked to AQAP killed 17 in and around **Paris**, Jan. 2015, most at offices of a magazine. Jihadists linked to ISIS murdered 130 in or near Paris, Nov. 2015. Islamists also launched attacks in **Belgium, Tunisia,** and **Turkey**. An ISIS-inspired shooter killed 49 (June 2016) at gay nightclub in **Orlando**, FL; ISIS claimed responsibility for truck attack killing 86 (July 2016) in **Nice**, France. In **Egypt**, ISIS-affiliated terrorists attacked Coptic Christian churches (Apr.-May 2017; about 75 killed) and a non-Sunni mosque (Nov. 2017; over 300 died). Jihadist targets also included churches and hotels in **Sri Lanka** (Easter Sunday, 2019; over 250 killed).

An anti-Muslim extremist killed 77 people in **Norway**, July 2011, and over 50 died in mass shooting at two mosques in Christchurch, **New Zealand**, Mar. 2019. In Oct. 2017 a shooter killed 58 at a **Las Vegas** music festival before dying by suicide.

Europe. The EU, with IMF help, provided loans to bail out **Greece** (beginning May 2010). Also receiving **bailouts** were **Ireland** (2010), **Portugal** (2011), **Spain** (2013), and **Cyprus** (2013). **Croatia** became 28th EU member, July 2013; **Lithuania** became 19th nation to adopt the **euro**, Jan. 2015. Millions of **migrants**, mostly from Middle East and Africa, sought asylum in Europe, 2014-19; thousands drowned attempting to cross the Mediterranean. EU, Sept. 2015, approved plan aimed at redistributing migrants from heavily impacted **Greece** and **Italy**. Migrant influx fueled anti-EU sentiment and support for right-wing populist parties in some countries.

Apr. 2018 elections in **Hungary** brought right-wing former Prime Min. Viktor **Orbán** back into office (reelected 2014, 2018). Conservatives returned to power in **UK**, under David **Cameron**, May 2010, but he resigned after British voters, in a June 2016 referendum, opted to leave the EU ("**Brexit**"). His successor, Conservative Prime Min. Theresa **May**, left office in June 2019, after failing to win support for her negotiated Brexit terms. Conservatives, led by Boris **Johnson**, won a big majority in a snap general election (Dec. 2019), and Parliament approved Johnson's Brexit agreement.

Centrist Emmanuel **Macron** was elected president of **France**, May 2017; "**yellow-vest**" mass protests followed, initially targeting fuel-tax hike. In **Turkey**, Recep Tayyip **Erdogan**, prime minister since 2003, was elected president (2014, 2018); he cracked down on opposition following July 2016 coup attempt

In one of the deadliest natural disasters in history, 300,000 people were killed in a massive earthquake in Haiti (2010).

Fleeing violence, overcrowded camps, or poverty in Northern Africa, the Middle East, and Afghanistan, millions of refugees and migrants sought refuge in Europe in a wave that peaked 2014-16.

(160,000 jailed) and launched offensives against Kurds in N Syria. **Spain**, in Oct. 2017, imposed direct rule over **Catalonia**. In May 2018, ETA, the Basque separatist group responsible for over 800 deaths in Spain over some 40 years, announced its dissolution.

After interregnum as prime minister, Vladimir **Putin** was reelected as **Russia**'s president (Mar. 2012, 2018). He sent troops to annex Ukrainian territory of **Crimea**, Mar. 2014, resulting in international sanctions. Russia also intervened in **Syrian** civil war and interfered in 2016 **U.S. elections**. Hundreds were arrested in anti-corruption protests, June 2017. Pro-Russian Viktor **Yanukovych**, elected president of **Ukraine** in Feb. 2010, fled in Feb. 2014 after mass protests. War soon broke out in E Ukraine between Ukrainian forces and pro-Russian separatists, aided by Russia. During the fighting a Malaysia Airlines passenger jet crashed over E Ukraine, allegedly shot down by Russian missile (July 2014; 298 killed). Ukraine's central government pursued **westernization** under two successive presidents.

Ireland became first country to legalize **same-sex marriage** by popular vote, May 2015. Over 20 years after the **Srebrenica massacre** in **Bosnia**, former Bosnian Serb leader Radovan **Karadzic** (Mar. 2016) and commander Ratko **Mladic** (Nov. 2017) were convicted of war crimes. So-called **Panama Papers**, leaked Apr. 2016, showed how politicians concealed assets abroad; implicated were leaders in **Russia, Ukraine, UK**, and **Iceland**.

Asia and Pacific. A UN-backed tribunal convicted a prison guard (July 2010) and, later, two high officials, of war crimes in **Cambodia** during the Khmer Rouge regime. An **earthquake** and **tsunami** (Mar. 2011) struck **Japan**, killing more than 16,000 and leading to meltdowns at nuclear reactors. Over 8,500 were killed in two earthquakes in **Nepal** (Apr.-May 2015); over 2,000 in **Indonesia** quake and tsunami (Sept. 2018).

Kyrgyzstan's president was ousted, Apr. 2010, after clashes with protesters; up to 2,000 killed in ethnic violence; voters (Dec. 2016) approved constitutional changes strengthening executive power. In **Kazakhstan**, autocratic Pres. Nursultan **Nazarbayev**, in office since 1990, resigned, Mar. 2019, but retained some powers.

North Korean dictator **Kim Jong Il** died, Dec. 2011; his son and successor **Kim Jong Un** resumed missile tests, leading to international sanctions. In **South Korea**, Pres. **Park** Geunhye was removed, Mar. 2017 (later convicted of corruption); replaced by center-left **Moon** Jae-in. Moon and Kim met in historic summits Apr.-Sept. 2018. **Myanmar**'s military-backed party lost Nov. 2015 election to party of dissident leader Aung San Suu Kyi, but sectarian and government violence against Myanmar's **Rohingya** Muslim minority surged; thousands were killed and hundreds of thousands fled.

In **China**, **Xi** Jinping succeeded **Hu** Jintao as Communist party chief, Nov. 2012, and president, Mar. 2013; term limit on presidency removed, Mar. 2018. Mass demonstrations in **Hong Kong** opposed new anti-democratic policies ("umbrella" protests, 2014; extradition law protests, from Apr. 2019). UN human rights panel (Aug. 2018) denounced China's mass confinement of **Uyghur** minorities. First reported cases of new coronavirus known as **COVID-19** emerged in **Wuhan**, China, Dec. 2019.

Hindu nationalists won majority in May 2014 elections in **India**; Narendra **Modi** became prime minister (reelected 2019). In Muslim-majority **Kashmir** hundreds died in clashes with security forces (beginning July 2016). Anti-crime hardliner Rodrigo **Duterte** was elected **Philippines** president, May 2016; thousands of alleged drug dealers and users were killed in Duterte **anti-drug campaign.**

Thailand's King **Bhumibol** Adulyadej died Oct. 2016, ending 70-year reign; new king **Vajiralongkorn** signed army-drafted constitution. In **Malaysian** elections, May 2018, the ruling coalition since independence fell to the opposition. In **Indonesia** protests followed the May 2019 reelection of Pres. Joko **Widodo**. In **Japan**, Prince **Naruhito** acceded to the throne, May 2019, following abdication of Emperor **Akihito**.

Trans-Pacific Partnership (TPP), trade pact covering 12 Pacific nations, was signed Feb. 2016; after new U.S. administration repudiated it, remaining nations signed replacement, Mar. 2018.

Africa. Coups ousted **Niger**'s president (Feb. 2010) and ended elections in **Guinea-Bissau** (Apr. 2012); in both cases, civilian rule returned. Drought conditions triggered famine in **Somalia** (2010-12); more than 250,000 died. After southern Sudanese (mostly Christian or indigenous religion) voted overwhelmingly for separation from the north (mostly Arab Muslim), **South Sudan** was granted independence, as of July 2011; civil war there (2013-18) left thousands dead, millions displaced. Following a Mar. 2012 coup, **Mali's** junta ceded power to civilians, but Islamic rebels seized control in the north. French and West African forces intervened; a peace deal (June 2013) proved fragile. Armed attackers killed over 130 mostly Islamic villagers in central Mali, Mar. 2019; ISIS attacks on military posts in Mali and **Niger**, Sept.-Dec. 2019, killed close to 200 soldiers. Former Liberian Pres. Charles **Taylor** was convicted of war crimes, Apr. 2012. The Muslim Seleka coalition seized power in **Central African Republic** (Mar. 2013), precipitating civil war; UN peacekeepers were brought in; new president elected, Feb. 2016.

In **Burkina Faso**, longtime Pres. Blaise **Campaoré** fled amid protests (Oct. 2014); elections in Dec. 2015 brought in new government. In **Nigeria**, former dictator Muhammadu **Buhari** was elected president, Mar. 2015; reelected 2019. During the decade, thousands of Nigerians were killed in attacks by **Boko Haram** jihadists and in conflicts between mostly Christian farmers and mostly Muslim herders. In **Burundi** hundreds died and thousands were displaced in violent antigovernment clashes (starting Apr. 2015) and their repression.

An African Union court, June 2016, convicted Hissène **Habré** of crimes against humanity while ruler of **Chad** in the 1980s. In **Gambia** longtime Pres. Yahya **Jammeh** reluctantly yielded power, Jan. 2017, after election defeat. In **Zimbabwe** Pres. Robert **Mugabe**, in power since 1980, resigned, Nov. 2017, after house arrest by military and impeachment threat. In **South Africa**, Jacob **Zuma**, president since 2009, resigned Feb. 2018, amid corruption charges. **Ethiopia** and **Eritrea** opened their common border, closed for 20 years (Sept. 2018). Ailing **Algerian** Pres. Abdelaziz **Bouteflika** stepped down, Apr. 2019, following protests over his plans to seek fifth term. Omar al-**Bashir**, president of **Sudan** since a 1989 coup, was deposed in Apr. 2019 and imprisoned; protests demanding civilian rule were repressed (over 100 protesters killed); a power-sharing agreement, July 2019, led to transitional government. Bashir was convicted of money laundering and corruption, Dec. 2019.

An **Ebola** epidemic in W Africa (2014-15) caused over 11,000 deaths, mostly in Guinea, Liberia, and Sierra Leone.

Americas and the Caribbean. In **Haiti** an earthquake (Jan. 2010) killed over 300,000; lingering **cholera** epidemic introduced by aid workers left thousands more dead, with violence and political instability continuing. Entrepreneur Jovenel **Moïse** became president, Feb. 2017, after disputed election. Poverty and violence fueled by drug cartels spurred **migration** to the U.S. from **Mexico, El Salvador, Honduras**, and **Guatemala**.

Cuba and U.S. restored relations, July 2015; Miguel **Díaz-Canel** succeeded Raúl Castro as Cuba's president, Apr. 2018. Real estate magnate Donald **Trump** won election, Nov. 2016, as

U.S. president; he campaigned on illegal immigration, deregulation, and "America First" stance.

In **Canada**, Conservatives, under Prime Min. Stephen **Harper**, won a majority in May 2011 elections. Liberals came back in Oct. 2015 under party leader Justin **Trudeau**, who led the party to minority governments in two later elections (2019, 2021).

Left and right factions battled in Latin America: Chilean Pres. Michelle **Bachelet** was replaced by billionaire conservative Sebastián **Piñera** following Jan. 2010 election; after she returned for second term, Piñera regained office, Dec. 2017. In **Nicaragua** leftist Pres. Daniel **Ortega** twice won reelections challenged as flawed (2011, 2016); protests, beginning Apr. 2018, were violently suppressed (over 300 killed). In **Venezuela**, Pres. Hugo **Chávez** died Mar. 2013. Under his ally and successor Nicolás **Maduro** Moros, the economy collapsed into chaos; millions fled; results of a legislative election (Dec. 2015) won by the opposition were cast aside; mass protests saw heavy casualties. Maduro was installed for new term, Jan. 2019, after reelection denounced as fraudulent. In **Mexico**, leftist anti-establishment candidate Andrés Manuel **López Obrador** was elected president, July 2018, following a campaign season during which over 100 politicians were murdered. In **Brazil**, after leftist presidents **Lula** da Silva and Dilma **Rousseff** were damaged by corruption scandals, far-right populist Jair **Bolsonaro** was elected president, Oct. 2018. In Bolivia longtime leftist Pres. Evo **Morales** resigned, Nov. 2019, amid protests over his disputed reelection; leftist Luis **Arce** was subsequently elected president (Oct. 2020).

Argentine voters ended 12 years of Peronist rule, choosing center-right candidate Mauricio **Macri** as president (Nov. 2015). After decades of fighting, the **Colombian** government signed peace accord (Nov. 2016) with Revolutionary Army of Colombia (**FARC**) guerrillas; conflicts continued, along with mass protests over government cuts.

Uruguay (Dec. 2013) and **Canada** (June 2018) became first countries to fully legalize **marijuana**. Extradited Mexican drug kingpin known as **"El Chapo"** was convicted on drug trafficking and other charges by U.S. jury, Feb. 2019.

Miscellaneous. After 30 years, NASA's **space shuttle** program ended with return of *Atlantis* to Earth (July 2011). NASA's rover *Curiosity* landed on **Mars**, Aug. 2012; **China** landed unmanned *Yulu* rover on moon, Dec. 2013, and space probe on moon's far side, Dec. 2018. NASA's Kepler/K2 missions ended, Oct. 2018, having found over 2,600 **exoplanets**. **Ransomware** emerged as increasing global threat with launch of CryptoLocker (Sept. 2013) and other cyberattacks. Scientists, Feb. 2016, reported direct observation of **gravitational waves**, confirming Einstein prediction. Two new **Boeing 737 Max 8 jets** with automated anti-stall system crashed after takeoff (Oct. 2018, Mar. 2019; 346 died); model was temporarily grounded.

Pope **Benedict XVI** resigned, Feb. 2013; Argentinean Cardinal Jorge Mario Bergoglio was elected to succeed him, taking the name **Francis**. He stressed poverty, environment, and migrant rights as concerns, along with addressing **clerical sex abuse**.

Representatives of 195 nations, meeting in Paris (Dec. 2015), committed to individual plans for reducing greenhouse gas emissions linked to **climate change**. Global Climate Strike protests (Sept. 2019) drew millions of participants around the world. Europe experienced **heat waves**, breaking temperature records (2019). **Flooding** in **Venice** (Nov. 2019) reached highest level since 1966.

New Conflicts and Challenges, 2020–mid 2023

COVID-19 Pandemic. In Mar. 2020, WHO declared **COVID-19** to be a global pandemic, with some 120,000 cases worldwide. China, Iran, Italy, and South Korea accounted for over 90% of very early cases; by Mar. 2020 the U.S. had recorded the most. Global health resources, personnel, and infrastructure were strained and economies badly damaged. **Vaccines** were developed rapidly and distributed to the public beginning Dec. 2020. More contagious **Omicron variant** was identified, Nov. 2021. By mid-2022 the world had recorded over 6 mil COVID deaths, more than 1 mil in the U.S. alone. **China's** actual toll was uncertain, but severe restrictions were eased there starting Dec. 2022. In May 2023, with new cases and deaths generally declining globally, WHO declared an end to the **"public emergency"** phase.

Ukraine War. In Feb. 2022, **Russia invaded Ukraine**, in what Pres. Vladimir Putin called a "special military operation" to "denazify" the country. Millions were displaced or fled as artillery shelled cities and towns, and invading troops killed and terrorized civilians. The UN General Assembly condemned the invasion; Western nations imposed escalating economic sanctions. Stirred by Ukrainian Pres. Volodymyr **Zelenskyy**, and bolstered by Western military aid and intelligence, Ukrainian forces turned massing Russian troops away from **Kyiv**, but had to surrender the port city of **Mariupol**, May 2022. Russians sought to consolidate gains in the east (Sievierodonetsk surrendered, June 2022) and took full control of the devastated city of **Bakhmut** (May 2023). In June 2023 part of a vital Ukrainian dam and hydroelectric plant, under Russian control, was blown up, and various Russian territorial losses triggered a temporary rebellion by Russia's paramilitary Wagner Group, posing a challenge to Putin's authority. Ukrainian troops began a long-planned counteroffensive in mid-2023, met with strong Russian resistance.

World Economy. As a result of COVID-19, war, drought, and other factors, nations around the world suffered from high inflation, and, often, food scarcity. World economic growth in the early 2020s was generally slow, impacted also by tight monetary policies in many countries.

Americas and Caribbean. Former Vice Pres. Joe **Biden** defeated incumbent Pres. Donald **Trump** to win the Nov. 2020 U.S. presidential election. Trump disputed the election result and a mob of his supporters, Jan. 2021, broke into the **Capitol** by force, seeking to prevent certification of the vote. The Biden administration encountered challenges such as a divided legislature, high inflation, the spread of COVID, racial tensions and gun violence, and responding to Russia's invasion of Ukraine. An influx of **Latin American migrants** at the southern U.S. border created a humanitarian crisis.

A gunman dressed as a police officer killed 22 people in **Nova Scotia, Canada**, Apr. 2020. **Mass graves** found in Canada, beginning May 2021, brought attention to abuses at former residential schools for Indigenous children. Canadian truckers' **"freedom convoy"** blocked Ottawa streets (Jan.-Feb. 2022) protesting COVID-19 **vaccine mandates** for crossing U.S.-Canadian border. Beginning in spring 2023, massive **wildfires** spread through Canada's provinces and territories, generating toxic smoke that spread far into the U.S.

Leftist **Venezuelan** Pres. Nicolás **Maduro** survived coup attempt, May 2020. **Haitian** Pres. Jovenel **Moïse** was **assassinated**, July 2021, in a raid on his residence; the following month an **earthquake** killed over 2,200 Haitians. Protests in **Cuba**, July 2021, met with beatings and arrests.

Pedro **Castillo**, a leftist and political novice, won the presidency in sharply divided **Peru** (June 2021). Ousted by Congress and arrested after attempting to rule by decree (Dec. 2022), he was replaced by Vice-Pres. Dina **Boluarte**, of the same party; anti-government protests continued. Former rebel Gustavo **Petro** narrowly won election in **Colombia**, June 2022, as the country's first left-wing president. In **Brazil**, right-wing populist Jair **Bolsonaro** narrowly lost his bid for reelection (Oct. 2022), as leftist Luiz Inácio **Lula** da Silva returned to power.

Europe. UK formalized **Brexit** terms and left the EU Jan. 2020; replacement trade agreement reached, Dec. 2020. UK Prime Min. Boris **Johnson** resigned amid scandal, July 2022, to be succeeded briefly by Liz **Truss**, and then in Oct. 2022 by Rishi **Sunak**. Britain's **Queen Elizabeth II** died in Sept. 2022, three months after her platinum jubilee; her eldest son was formally crowned **King Charles III** in May 2023.

After Sept. 2021 elections, Olaf **Scholz**, of the SPD, was sworn in as German chancellor, heading a three-party coalition; he replaced Angela **Merkel**, of the CDU, who retired after 16 years. In Dec. 2022, dozens were arrested in Germany for planning a far-right coup. French Pres. Emmanuel **Macron** was reelected Apr. 2022, overcoming challenge from far-right populist Marine **Le Pen**; he encountered mass protests in 2023 over unpopular **pension reform**. **Italy's** first center-right coalition government since World War II came to power following Sept. 2022 elections.

Russian anticorruption activist Alexei **Navalny** was poisoned nearly fatally by a nerve agent, Aug. 2020; Russian agents implicated. He was imprisoned, Jan. 2021. **Russia** was also implicated, Dec. 2020, in massive **cyberattack** on U.S. government and other targets in the West. American WNBA star Brittney **Griner**, arrested in Russia (Feb. 2022) for possession of small amount of a cannabis product, was freed Dec. 2022 in exchange for U.S. release of notorious Russian arms dealer Viktor **Bout**. Intl. Criminal Court issued arrest warrant for **Putin**, Mar. 2023, in connection with forced deportation of Ukrainian children to Russia.

In **Belarus**, longtime authoritarian Pres. Aleksandr **Lukashenko** retained power after Aug. 2020 election widely considered rigged; in May 2021 a passenger plane was forced to land in Belarus so a dissident on board could be arrested. In June 2021 a UN war crimes tribunal convicted two top **Serbian** officials in 1990s **ethnic cleansing** in the Balkans.

Finland joined NATO, Apr. 2023; **Sweden** applied, May 2022.

Middle East. U.S. drone strike, Jan. 2020, killed **Iranian** Islamic Revolutionary Guard Corps Major Gen. **Qassem Soleimani**. Russia and Turkey agreed, Mar. 2020, on cease-fire deal for a contested area of **Syria**. Massive explosion in a **Beirut** chemical warehouse, Aug. 2020, killed some 200. **Suez Canal** was blocked for six days (Mar. 2021) by grounded container ship. "**Abraham Accords**," signed Sept. 2020, normalized relations between Israel and two Arab nations, **UAE** and **Bahrain**. Over 250 Palestinians died, along with 12 Israeli civilians, in violence May 2021 between **Hamas** and Israel. Longtime Israeli Prime Min. Benjamin **Netanyahu** was ousted June 2021 amid corruption charges; he was returned to office after Nov. 2022 elections while still facing trial.

Ebrahim **Raisi**, protégé of Supreme Leader Ayatollah Ali **Khamenei**, won the presidency of **Iran**, June 2021, in widely boycotted election. Death of a woman arrested for dress code violations triggered protests in Iran, Sept. 2022. U.S. raid in NW **Syria**, Feb. 2022, took down **ISIS** leader Abu Ibrahim al-Hashimi al-Qurayshi.

Earthquake, Feb. 2023, killed over 50,000 people in **Turkey** and over 8,000 in **Syria**. Longtime Turkish Pres. **Erdogan**, May 2023, survived a tough challenge to win reelection.

Asia and Pacific. In 2023 India surpassed China as world's most populous nation.

A U.S.-Taliban peace agreement in **Afghanistan**, Feb. 2020, called for phased U.S. withdrawal, with Taliban prisoner releases and intra-Afghan talks, which failed. Attacks often targeted civilians (at least 90 killed in bombing outside school, May 2021). With little resistance, **Taliban** forces captured most provincial capitals and (Aug. 2021) retook Kabul, as Pres. Ashraf **Ghani** fled. At a fixed Aug. 31 deadline, the last foreign forces left, amid chaotic evacuation (at least 169 Afghans killed in airport bombing). Taliban imposed **sharia law** and suppressed protests; terrorist bombings continued (120 killed in bombing of Shiite mosques, Oct. 2021).

China's parliament, June 2020, approved sweeping security law for **Hong Kong**. Chinese Pres. **Xi** Jinping secured third

The bumpy, deadly withdrawal of U.S. forces (2021) marked an end to 20 years of war in Afghanistan.

five-year term as party leader, Oct. 2022; elected president for third term, Mar. 2023.

Azerbaijan and **Armenia** accepted Russian-brokered cease-fire agreement, Nov. 2020, following flare-up over disputed **Nagorno-Karabakh** region. Protests in **Kazakhstan** against the authoritarian regime, Jan. 2022, left over 200 dead.

In **India** some 250 million workers joined in one-day nationwide general strike (Nov. 2020). After **Myanmar**'s ruling party, led by Aung San Suu Kyi, won landslide victory in Nov. 2020 elections, the military staged a coup (Feb. 2021); protests were crushed, leaders arrested, hundreds killed. Repression of **Rohingya** Muslims continued, with over 700,000 in refugee camps in **Bangladesh**.

India and Pakistan reached cease-fire, Feb. 2021, after border clashes. Record monsoon **flooding**, June-Oct. 2022, devastated Pakistan, leaving over 1,700 dead. Pakistani Prime Min. Imran **Khan** lost no-confidence vote, Apr. 2022; arrested May 2023, sparking demonstrations. Over 80 killed in Pakistan mosque attack, Jan. 2023. Close to 300 killed in **train crash** in E **India**, June 2023.

Ferdinand Marcos Jr., son of the late dictator, won May 2022 presidential election in the **Philippines**. In **Australian** elections, May 2022, Labor, led by Anthony **Albanese**, ended nine years of Conservative government. Former **Japanese** Prime Min. Shinzo **Abe** was assassinated July 2022.

Africa. Transitional unity government formed in **South Sudan**, Feb. 2020, as unrest continued. In **Sudan**, peace agreement was reached, Oct. 2020, with most rebel groups, but the transitional government was deposed in a military coup (Oct. 2021); a power-sharing arrangement followed. **New violence** broke out, Apr. 2023, between two rival military factions.

Libya's UN-backed government reached cease-fire with rival factions, Oct. 2020, ending six-year civil war. Hostilities broke out in **Ethiopia**, Nov. 2020, between Tigray separatists and Ethiopian and Eritrean troops; millions were displaced, as famine spread and atrocities were reported; a truce was agreed to, Nov. 2022.

W Africa saw repeated attacks by Islamic terrorists—such as a June 2021 raid on a village in **Burkina Faso** (at least 160 killed) and raids in June 2022 on three villages in **Mali** (132 killed). The region also saw political instability. **Mali**'s Pres. Ibrahim Boubacar **Keita** was removed in an Aug. 2020 military coup; a transitional government went down in a second coup, May 2021. Longtime **Chad** Pres. Idriss **Déby** was killed Apr. 2021, while visiting troops fighting rebels. Military coups took down governments in **Guinea** (Sept. 2021) and **Burkina Faso** (Jan. 2022). However, despite a coup attempt days before, **Niger** enjoyed its first democratic transfer of power, with the inauguration of Pres. Mohamed **Bazoum**, Apr. 2021.

Longtime **Ugandan** Pres. Yoweri **Museveni** was returned, Jan. 2021, for sixth term, after disputed elections. Imprisonment of former **South African** Pres. Jacob **Zuma**, for refusing to testify before corruption commission, triggered riots, July 2021, with over 300 deaths. After long delay, lawmakers in **Somalia** elected a new president, May 2022, amid continuing violence by **al-Shabab** rebels (car bombings in Mogadishu, Oct. 2022, killed at least 120 people). In Jan. 2023, Nigeria's governing party retained power with the election of Bola **Tinubu** as president, Feb. 2023. **Uganda** enacted a new **anti-gay law**, May 2023.

WHO, Oct. 2021, endorsed a partially effective vaccine for **malaria**, a disease fatal to hundreds of thousands of African children every year.

Miscellaneous. The year 2020 tied with 2016 as **warmest on record**; average global temperatures for 2021 and 2022 were, respectively, the sixth and fifth highest on record.

SpaceX became the first private company to launch humans into orbit, May 2020. **China** landed a robotic *Change'e-5* spacecraft on the **moon**, Dec. 2020, and its *Tianwen-1* spacecraft on **Mars**, May 2021. NASA's *Perseverance* rover landed on Mars, Feb. 2021. **ChatGPT**, an artificial intelligence chatbot, was launched, Nov. 2022.

"**Pandora Papers**," leaked and made public Oct. 2021, exposed complex tax avoidance schemes by billionaires and political leaders.

Retired **Pope Benedict XVI** died, Dec. 2022.

HISTORICAL FIGURES

Note: Information accurate as of Sept. 2023.

Ancient Greeks and Romans

Greeks

Aeschines, orator, 389-314 BCE
Aeschylus, dramatist, 525-456 BCE
Aesop, fableist, c. 620-c. 560 BCE
Alcibiades, politician, 450-404 BCE
Anacreon, poet, c. 582-c. 485 BCE
Anaxagoras, philosopher, c. 500-428 BCE
Anaximander, philosopher, 611-546 BCE
Anaximenes, philosopher, c. 570-500 BCE
Antiphon, speechwriter, c. 480-411 BCE
Apollonius, mathematician, c. 265-170 BCE
Archimedes, mathematician, 287-212 BCE
Aristophanes, dramatist, c. 448-380 BCE
Aristotle, philosopher, 384-322 BCE
Athenaeus, scholar, fl. c. 200
Callicrates, architect, fl. 5th cent. BCE
Callimachus, poet, c. 305-240 BCE
Cratinus, comic dramatist, 520-421 BCE
Democritus, philosopher, c. 460-370 BCE
Demosthenes, orator, 384-322 BCE
Diodorus, historian, fl. 20 BCE
Diogenes, philosopher, c. 400-c. 325 BCE
Dionysius, historian, d. c. 7 BCE
Empedocles, philosopher, c. 490-430 BCE
Epicharmus, dramatist, c. 530-440 BCE
Epictetus, philosopher, c. 55-c. 135
Epicurus, philosopher, 341-270 BCE
Eratosthenes, scientist, 276-194 BCE
Euclid, mathematician, fl. c. 300 BCE
Euripides, dramatist, c. 484-406 BCE
Galen, physician, 129-200
Heraclitus, philosopher, c. 540-c. 480 BCE
Herodotus, historian, c. 484-420 BCE
Hesiod, poet, 8th cent. BCE
Hippocrates, physician, c. 460-377 BCE
Homer, poet, fl. c. 8th cent. BCE
Isocrates, orator, 436-338 BCE
Menander, dramatist, 342-292 BCE
Parmenides, philosopher, c. 515-440 BCE
Pericles, statesman, c. 495-429 BCE
Phidias, sculptor, fl. 490-430 BCE
Pindar, poet, c. 518-c. 438 BCE
Plato, philosopher, c. 428-347 BCE
Plutarch, biographer, c. 46-120
Polybius, historian, c. 200-c. 118 BCE
Praxiteles, sculptor, 400-330 BCE
Pythagoras, phil., math., c. 580-c. 500 BCE
Sappho, poet, c. 610-c. 580 BCE
Simonides, poet, 556-c. 468 BCE
Socrates, philosopher, 469-399 BCE
Solon, statesman, 640-560 BCE
Sophocles, dramatist, c. 496-406 BCE
Strabo, geographer, c. 63 BCE-24 CE
Thales, philosopher, c. 634-546 BCE
Themistocles, politician, c. 524-c. 460 BCE
Theocritus, poet, c. 310-250 BCE
Theophrastus, phil., c. 372-c. 287 BCE
Thucydides, historian, fl. 5th cent. BCE
Timon, philosopher, c. 320-c. 230 BCE
Xenophon, historian, c. 434-c. 355 BCE
Zeno, philosopher, c. 335-c. 263 BCE

Romans

Ammianus, historian, c. 330-395
Apuleius, satirist, c. 124-c. 170
Boethius, scholar, c. 480-524
Caesar, Julius, leader, 100-44 BCE
Catiline, politician, c. 108-62 BCE
Cato (Elder), statesman, 234-149 BCE
Catullus, poet, c. 84-54 BCE
Cicero, orator, 106-43 BCE
Claudian, poet, c. 370-c. 404
Ennius, poet, 239-170 BCE
Gellius, author, c. 130-c. 165
Horace, poet, 65-8 BCE
Juvenal, satirist, 60-127
Livy, historian, 59 BCE-17 CE
Lucan, poet, 39-65
Lucilius, poet, c. 180-c.102 BCE
Lucretius, poet, c. 99-c. 55 BCE
Martial, epigrammatist, c. 38-c. 103
Nepos, historian, c. 100-c. 25 BCE
Ovid, poet, 43 BCE-17 CE
Persius, satirist, 34-62
Plautus, dramatist, c. 254-c. 184 BCE
Pliny the Elder, scholar, 23-79
Pliny the Younger, author, 62-113
Quintilian, rhetorician, c. 35-c. 97
Sallust, historian, 86-34 BCE
Seneca, philosopher, 4 BCE-65 CE
Silius, poet, c. 25-101
Statius, poet, c. 45-c. 96
Suetonius, biographer, c. 69-c. 122
Tacitus, historian, 56-120
Terence, dramatist, 195/185-c. 159 BCE
Tibullus, poet, c. 55-c. 19 BCE
Virgil (or Vergil), poet, 70-19 BCE
Vitruvius, architect, fl. late 1st cent. BCE

Roman Rulers

From Romulus to the end of the Empire in the West (Rome). Rulers in the East sat in Constantinople and, for a brief period, in Nicaea, until the capture of Constantinople by the Turks in 1453, when Byzantium was succeeded by the Ottoman Empire.

The Kingdom

BCE
753 Romulus (Quirinus)
715 Numa Pompilius
673 Tullus Hostilius
641 Ancus Marcius
616 L. Tarquinius Priscus
579 Servius Tullius
534 L. Tarquinius Superbus

The Republic

509 Consulate established;
    Quaestorship instituted
498 Dictatorship introduced
494 Plebeian Tribunate created;
    Plebeian Aedileship created
444 Consular Tribunate organized
435 Censorship instituted
366 Praetorship established;
    Curule Aedileship created
362 Military Tribunate elected
326 Proconsulate introduced
311 Naval Duumvirate elected
217 Dictatorship of Fabius Maximus
133 Tribunate of Tiberius Gracchus
123 Tribunate of Gaius Gracchus
82 Dictatorship of Sulla
60 First Triumvirate formed
    (Caesar, Pompeius, Crassus)
47 Dictatorship of Caesar
43 Second Triumvirate formed
    (Octavianus, Antonius, Lepidus)

The Empire

27 Augustus (or Octavian)
CE
14 Tiberius
37 Caligula
41 Claudius
54 Nero
68 Galba
69 Otho; Vitellius; Vespasian,
    established Flavian Dynasty
79 Titus
81 Domitian, end of Flavian Dynasty

96 Nerva
98 Trajan
117 Hadrian
138 Antoninus Pius
161 Marcus Aurelius and Lucius Verus
169 Marcus Aurelius (alone)
177 Marcus Aurelius and Commodus
180 Commodus
193 Pertinax
193 Didius Julianus
193 Septimius Severus, founded
    Severan Dynasty
211 Caracalla and Geta
212 Caracalla (alone)
217 Macrinus
218 Elagabalus (or Heliogabalus)
222 Alexander Severus, end of dynasty
235 Maximinus (the Thracian)
238 Gordian I and Gordian II
238 Pupienus and Balbinus
238 Gordian III
244 Philip (the Arabian)
249 Decius
251 Gallus and Volusianus
253 Aemilian
253 Valerian and Gallienus
258 Gallienus (alone)
268 Claudius II (or Claudius Gothicus)
270 Quintillus
270 Aurelian
275 Tacitus
276 Florian
276 Probus
282 Carus
283 Carinus and Numerian
284 Diocletian
286 Diocletian and Maximian
305 Galerius and Constantius I
306 Galerius, Maximinus (or
    Maximinus Daia), Severus
307 Galerius, Maximinus (Daia),
    Constantine I, Licinius, Maxentius
311 Maximinus (Daia), Constantine I,
    Licinius, Maxentius

314 Constantine I, Licinius
324 Constantine I (the Great), first
    Christian emperor
337 Constantine II, Constans I,
    Constantius II
340 Constantius II and Constans I
353 Constantius II (alone)
361 Julian (the Apostate)
363 Jovian

West (Rome) and East (Constantinople)

364 Valentinian I (West),
    Valens (East)
367 Valentinian I with Gratian (W),
    Valens (E)
375 Gratian with Valentinian II (W),
    Valens (E)
379 Gratian with Valentinian II (W),
    Theodosius I (E)
383 Magnus Maximus and
    Valentinian II (W),
    Theodosius I (E)
388 Valentinian II (W), Theodosius I (E)
392 Eugenius (W), Theodosius I (E)
394 Theodosius I (the Great)
395 Honorius (W), Arcadius (E)
408 Honorius (W), Theodosius II (E)
423 Valentinian III (W),
    Theodosius II (E)
450 Valentinian III (W), Marcian (E)
455 Petronius Maximus (W),
    Marcian (E)
455 Avitus (W), Marcian (E)
457 Majorian (W), Leo I (E)
461 Libius Severus (W), Leo I (E)
467 Anthemius (W), Leo I (E)
472 Olybrius (W), Leo I (E)
473 Glycerius (W), Leo I (E)
474 Julius Nepos (W), Leo II (E)
475 Romulus Augustulus (W), Zeno (E)
476 End of Empire in W when Romulus
    Augustulus deposed by Germanic
    chief Odoacer, who was later
    murdered by King Theodoric of
    Ostrogoths, 493

Rulers of England and the United Kingdom

Reign began	England: Saxons and Danes	Age at death[1]
829	Egbert, king of Wessex, won allegiance of all English	NA
839	Ethelwulf, son, king of Wessex, Sussex, Kent, Essex	NA
858	Ethelbald, eldest son, displaced father in Wessex	NA
860	Ethelbert, 2nd son of Ethelwulf, united Kent and Wessex	NA
866	Ethelred I, 3rd son of Ethelwulf, king of Wessex, fought Danes	NA
871	Alfred (the Great), 4th son of Ethelwulf, defeated Danes, fortified London	52
899	Edward (the Elder), son, united English, claimed Scotland	55
924	Athelstan (the Glorious), eldest son, king of Mercia, Wessex	45
940	Edmund, 3rd son of Edward, king of Wessex, Mercia	25
946	Edred, 4th son of Edward	32
955	Edwy (the Fair), eldest son of Edmund, king of Wessex	18
959	Edgar (the Peaceful), 2nd son of Edmund, ruled all English	32
975	Edward (the Martyr), eldest son, murdered by stepmother	17
978; 1014[2]	Ethelred II (the Unready), 2nd son of Edgar, married Emma of Normandy	48
1016	Edmund II (Ironside), son, king of London	27
1016	Canute (the Dane), son of Sweyn, who conquered English territory; gave Wessex to Edmund II; married Emma, Ethelred II's widow	40
1035	Harold I (Harefoot), illegitimate son	NA
1040	Hardecanute, son of Canute by Emma, also king of Denmark	24
1042	Edward (the Confessor), son of Ethelred II, canonized 1161	62
1066	Harold II, brother-in-law, last Saxon king	44

Reign began	England: House of Normandy	Age at death[1]
1066	William I (the Conqueror), son of Duke Robert I of Normandy, defeated Harold II at Hastings	60
1087	William II (Rufus), 3rd son, killed by arrow while hunting in possible assassination	43
1100	Henry I (Beauclerc), youngest son of William I	67

Reign began	England: House of Blois	Age at death[1]
1135	Stephen, son of Adela, daughter of William I, and Count of Blois	50

Reign began	England: House of Plantagenet	Age at death[1]
1154	Henry II, son of Geoffrey Plantagenet (Angevin), son of Matilda, daughter of Henry I	56
1189	Richard I (Coeur de Lion), son, crusader	42
1199	John (Lackland), son of Henry II, approved Magna Carta, 1215	50
1216	Henry III, son, acceded at 9, under regency until 1227	65
1272	Edward I (Longshanks), son	68
1307	Edward II, son, deposed by Parliament	43
1327	Edward III (of Windsor), son	65
1377	Richard II, grandson of Edward III, deposed	33

Reign began	England: House of Lancaster	Age at death[1]
1399	Henry IV (of Bolingbroke), son of John of Gaunt, duke of Lancaster, son of Edward III	47
1413	Henry V, son, victor over French at Agincourt	34
1422; 1470	Henry VI, son, overthrown by Edward IV in 1461 but was returned to throne in 1470. Deposed, died in Tower of London, 1471	49

Reign began	England: House of York	Age at death[1]
1461; 1471	Edward IV, great-great-grandson of Edward III, son of duke of York. Acclaimed king by Parliament, 1461. Driven into exile in 1470 but regained throne, 1471	40
1483	Edward V, son, murdered in Tower of London	13
1483	Richard III, brother of Edward IV, fell in battle at Bosworth Field against Henry Tudor	32

Reign began	England: House of Tudor	Age at death[1]
1485	Henry VII, son of Edmund Tudor, earl of Richmond, whose father had married Henry V's widow. Descended from Edward III through mother, Margaret Beaufort, via John of Gaunt. Married Elizabeth of York, eldest daughter of Edward IV, to unite Lancaster and York	53
1509	Henry VIII, 2nd son, by Elizabeth	56
1547	Edward VI, son, by Jane Seymour, his 3rd queen. Was persuaded by John Dudley to name Lady Jane Grey, his cousin and Dudley's daughter-in-law, his successor. Council of State proclaimed her queen, July 10, 1553, but she ruled only nine days before Mary Tudor overthrew her	16
1553	Mary I, daughter of Henry VIII, by his 1st wife, Catherine of Aragon	43
1558	Elizabeth I, daughter of Henry VIII, by his 2nd wife, Anne Boleyn	69

Reign began	Great Britain: House of Stuart	Age at death[1]
1603	James I (James VI of Scotland), son of Mary, Queen of Scots. First to call self king of Great Britain; this became official with Acts of Union, 1707	59
1625	Charles I, only surviving son of James I	48

Reign began	Great Britain: Commonwealth	Age at death[1]
1649	Declared upon execution of Charles I	NA

Reign began	Great Britain: Protectorate	Age at death[1]
1653	Oliver Cromwell, served on Council of State, executive body of Commonwealth, following overthrow of monarchy. Named Lord Protector upon creation of Protectorate by 1653 Instrument of Government	59
1658	Richard Cromwell, 3rd son, resigned as Lord Protector amid civil war, 1659	86

Reign began	Great Britain: House of Stuart (restored)	Age at death[1]
1660	Charles II, eldest son of Charles I, acceded to throne by Restoration, died without issue	55
1685	James II, 2nd son of Charles I, deposed 1688	68
1689	William III, son of William, Prince of Orange, by Mary, daughter of Charles I. Offered joint rule of throne with wife by Parliament	51
1689	Mary II, eldest daughter of James II and wife of William III, died 1694	33
1702	Anne, 2nd daughter of James II, sister-in-law of William III, assumed throne on William's death	49

Reign began	United Kingdom of Great Britain[3]: House of Hanover	Age at death[1]
1714	George I, son of Elector of Hanover by Sophia, granddaughter of James I	67
1727	George II, only son, married Caroline of Brandenburg	77
1760	George III, grandson, married Charlotte of Mecklenburg	81
1820	George IV, eldest son, prince regent from Feb. 1811	67
1830	William IV, 3rd son of George III, married Adelaide of Saxe-Meiningen	71
1837	Victoria, daughter of Edward, 4th son of George III; married Prince Albert of Saxe-Coburg and Gotha, 1840	81

Reign began	United Kingdom of Great Britain[3]: House of Saxe-Coburg-Gotha	Age at death[1]
1901	Edward VII, eldest son, married Alexandra, Princess of Denmark	68

Reign began	United Kingdom of Great Britain[3]: House of Windsor[4]	Age at death[1]
1910	George V, 2nd son, married Princess Mary of Teck	70
1936	Edward VIII, eldest son, acceded Jan. 20, abdicated Dec. 11	77
1936	George VI, 2nd son of George V, married Lady Elizabeth Bowes-Lyon	56
1952	Elizabeth II, elder daughter, acceded Feb. 6	96
2022	Charles III, eldest son, acceded Sept. 8	NA

NA = Age/birthdate not certain or not applicable. (1) Except where noted, year of death is the same year the next ruler's reign began. (2) King Sweyn I of Denmark invaded England in 1013 and declared himself king. Ethelred II fled England but reclaimed the throne upon Sweyn's death in 1014. (3) Officially the United Kingdom of Great Britain and Ireland after Act of Union 1801 and the United Kingdom of Great Britain and Northern Ireland after Anglo-Irish Treaty of 1921 (name formalized 1927). (4) Name adopted by proclamation of George V, July 17, 1917, because of anti-German feeling during World War I.

Rulers of Scotland

Reign began	Name	Reign began	Name
846	Kenneth I, first Scot to rule both Scots and Picts	1306	Robert I (the Bruce), victor at Bannockburn, 1314. Treaty with England and secured throne, 1328
1005	Malcolm II, son of Kenneth II		
1034	Duncan I, grandson, first general ruler	1329	David II, only surviving son
1040	Macbeth, seized kingdom, slain by Malcolm Canmore	1371	Robert II (the Steward), son of Robert I's daughter Marjorie and Walter, steward of Scotland. First of Stewart line
1057	Malcolm III (Canmore), eldest son of Duncan I	1390	Robert III, son
1093	Donald III (the Fair), younger brother	1406	James I, son, assassinated
1094	Duncan II, eldest son of Malcolm III by first wife	1437	James II, son
1095	Donald III (restored)	1460	James III, eldest son, possibly assassinated
1097	Edgar, 4th son of Malcolm III and Queen Margaret	1488	James IV, eldest son
1107	Alexander I, brother	1513	James V, eldest son, died at Battle of Flodden
1124	David I, brother	1542	Mary (Queen of Scots), daughter, became queen before she was 1 week old. Married Francis II (d. 1560), son of King Henry II of France, 1558. Married her cousin, Henry Stewart, Lord Darnley (d. 1567), 1565. Married James Hepburn, Earl of Bothwell, 1567. Imprisoned by her cousin Elizabeth I of England, 1568; beheaded, 1587
1153	Malcolm IV (the Maiden), grandson		
1165	William (the Lion), brother		
1214	Alexander II, son		
1249	Alexander III, son		
1286	Margaret (Maid of Norway), granddaughter; died 1290 at age 8. (Interregnum, 1290-92)		
1292	John Balliol, proclaimed king of Scotland by Edward I of England. (Interregnum, 1296-1306[1])	1567	James VI, son of Mary and Lord Darnley, became James I, king of England, on Elizabeth's death, 1603. (Legislative union of Scotland and England as United Kingdom of Great Britain not official until Acts of Union, 1707)

Note: Not all rulers before 1005 are shown. (1) Edward I decreed annexation of Scotland to England, 1296, after defeating Balliol in battle. William Wallace led resistance, 1297-1305.

Prime Ministers of the United Kingdom

Titles are given on first mention only. C = Conservative; La. = Labour; Li. = Liberal; P = Peelite; T = Tory; W = Whig.

Entered office	Name (party)	Entered office	Name (party)	Entered office	Name (party)
1721	Sir Robert Walpole (W)[1]	1827	Frederick John Robinson, Viscount Goderich (T)	1895	Robert Gascoyne-Cecil (C)
1742	Spencer Compton, 1st Earl of Wilmington (W)	1828	Arthur Wellesley, 1st Duke of Wellington (T)	1902	Arthur James Balfour (C)
				1905	Sir Henry Campbell-Bannerman (Li.)
1743	Henry Pelham (W)	1830	Charles Grey, 2nd Earl Grey (W)	1908	Herbert Henry Asquith (Li.[2])
1754	Thomas Pelham-Holles, 1st Duke of Newcastle (W)	1834	William Lamb, 2nd Viscount Melbourne (W)	1916	David Lloyd George (Li.[2])
1756	William Cavendish, 4th Duke of Devonshire (W)	1834	Arthur Wellesley (T)	1922	Andrew Bonar Law (C)
1757	Thomas Pelham-Holles (W)	1834	Sir Robert Peel, 2nd Baronet (C)	1923	Stanley Baldwin (C)
1762	John Stuart, 3rd Earl of Bute (T)	1835	William Lamb (W)	1924	Ramsay MacDonald (La.)
1763	George Grenville (W)	1841	Sir Robert Peel (C)	1924	Stanley Baldwin (C)
1765	Charles Watson-Wentworth, 2nd Marquess of Rockingham (W)	1846	John Russell, 1st Earl Russell (W)	1929	Ramsay MacDonald (La.[2])
1766	William Pitt the Elder, 1st Earl of Chatham (W)	1852	Edward Stanley, 14th Earl of Derby (C)	1935	Stanley Baldwin (C[2])
1768	Augustus Henry Fitzroy, 3rd Duke of Grafton (W)	1852	George Hamilton Gordon, 4th Earl of Aberdeen (P[2])	1937	Neville Chamberlain (C[2])
1770	Lord Frederick North (T)	1855	Henry John Temple, 3rd Viscount Palmerston (W-Li.)	1940	Winston Churchill (C[2])
1782	Charles Watson-Wentworth (W)			1945	Clement Attlee (La.)
1782	William Petty, 2nd Earl of Shelburne (W)	1858	Edward Stanley (C)	1951	Winston Churchill (C)
		1859	Henry John Temple (W-Li.)	1955	Anthony Eden (C)
1783	William Cavendish-Bentinck, 3rd Duke of Portland (W[2])	1865	John Russell (Li.)	1957	Harold Macmillan (C)
		1866	Edward Stanley (C)	1963	Alec Douglas-Home (C)
1783	William Pitt the Younger (W)	1868	Benjamin Disraeli (C)	1964	Harold Wilson (La.)
1801	Henry Addington (T)	1868	William E. Gladstone (Li.)	1970	Edward Heath (C)
1804	William Pitt the Younger (T)	1874	Benjamin Disraeli (C)	1974	Harold Wilson (La.)
1806	William Wyndham Grenville, 1st Baron Grenville (W)	1880	William E. Gladstone (Li.)	1976	James Callaghan (La.)
		1885	Robert Gascoyne-Cecil, 3rd Marquess of Salisbury (C)	1979	Margaret Thatcher (C)
1807	William Cavendish-Bentinck (T)			1990	John Major (C)
1809	Spencer Perceval (T)	1886	William E. Gladstone (Li.)	1997	Tony Blair (La.)
1812	Robert Banks Jenkinson, 2nd Earl of Liverpool (T)	1886	Robert Gascoyne-Cecil (C)	2007	Gordon Brown (La.)
		1892	William E. Gladstone (Li.)	2010	David Cameron (C[2])
1827	George Canning (T)	1894	Archibald Primrose, 5th Earl of Rosebery (Li.)	2016	Theresa May (C)
				2019	Boris Johnson (C)
				2022	Liz Truss (C)
				2022	Rishi Sunak (C)

Note: Prime ministers prior to 1801 are for Great Britain. The Conservative Party was formed in 1834, an outgrowth of the Tory party. (1) Walpole is traditionally regarded as the first prime minister of Britain though the title was not commonly used then and did not become official until 1905. (2) Led a coalition government for all or part of time in office.

Prime Ministers of Canada

C = Conservative; Lib. = Liberal; PC = Progressive Conservative; U = Unionist

Entered office	Name (party)	Entered office	Name (party)	Entered office	Name (party)
1867	John A. Macdonald (C)	1921	W. L. Mackenzie King (Lib.)	1979	Joe Clark (PC)
1873	Alexander Mackenzie (Lib.)	1926[3]	Arthur Meighen (C)	1980	Pierre Trudeau (Lib.)
1878	John A. Macdonald (C)	1926	W. L. Mackenzie King (Lib.)	1984[3]	John Turner (Lib.)
1891	John Abbott (C)	1930	Richard Bedford Bennett (C)	1984	Brian Mulroney (PC)
1892	John Thompson (C)	1935	W. L. Mackenzie King (Lib.)	1993[4]	Kim Campbell (PC)
1894	Mackenzie Bowell (C)	1948	Louis St. Laurent (Lib.)	1993	Jean Chrétien (Lib.)
1896[1]	Charles Tupper (C)	1957	John G. Diefenbaker (PC)	2003	Paul Martin (Lib.)
1896	Wilfrid Laurier (Lib.)	1963	Lester B. Pearson (Lib.)	2006	Stephen Harper (C)
1911	Robert Borden (C/U)[2]	1968	Pierre Trudeau (Lib.)	2015	Justin Trudeau (Lib.)
1920	Arthur Meighen (U)				

(1) May-July. (2) Conservative 1911-17, Unionist 1917-20. (3) June-Sept. (4) June-Nov.

Rulers of France

Caesar to Charlemagne

Julius Caesar subdued the Gauls, native tribes of Gaul (France), 58 to 51 BCE. The Romans ruled 500 years. The Franks, a Teutonic tribe, reached the Somme from the east c. 250 CE. By the 5th cent., the Merovingian Franks ousted the Romans. In 451, with the help of Visigoths, Burgundians, and others, they defeated Attila and the Huns at Châlons-sur-Marne.

Childeric I became leader of the Merovingians, 458. After son Clovis I (crowned 481) defeated the Alemanni (Germans), 496, he was baptized a Christian and made Paris his capital. Line ended when Childeric III was deposed, 751.

The West Merovingians were called Neustrians, the eastern Austrasians. Pepin of Herstal (687-714), major domus (head of the palace) of Austrasia, took over Neustria as dux (leader) of the Franks. Pepin's son, Charles, called Martel (the Hammer), defeated the Saracens at Tours-Poitiers, 732; was succeeded in 741 by his sons, Pepin the Short and Carloman (abdicated 747). Pepin deposed Childeric III and ruled as king until 768.

His son, Charlemagne, or Charles the Great (742-814), became king of the Franks, 768, with his brother Carloman (751-71). Charlemagne ruled France, Germany, parts of Italy, Spain, and Austria, and enforced Christianity. Crowned Emperor of the Romans by Pope Leo III in Rome, 800. Succeeded by son, Louis I (the Pious), 814. At death, 840, Louis left empire to sons Lothair (Roman emperor), Pepin I (king of Aquitaine), Louis II (the German), and Charles II (the Bald, of France). They quarreled and, by the Treaty of Verdun, 843, divided the empire.

The date preceding each entry is year of accession.

Carolingian Dynasty

843 Charles II (the Bald), Roman emperor, 875
877 Louis II (the Stammerer), son
879 Louis III (d. 882), son, and brother Carloman
885 Charles III (the Fat), son of Louis the German, Roman emperor, 881
888 Eudes (Odo), son of Robert the Strong, elected by nobles
898 Charles III (the Simple), son of Louis II the Stammerer, deposed
922 Robert I, brother of Eudes, defeated forces of Charles III but died in battle
923 Rudolph (Raoul), Robert I's son-in-law, duke of Burgundy
936 Louis IV, son of Charles III (the Simple); struggled with Hugh the Great, son of Robert I
954 Lothair, son, dominated by Hugh the Great
986 Louis V (the Sluggard), left no heirs

House of Capet

987 Hugh Capet, son of Hugh the Great
996 Robert II (the Pious), son
1031 Henry I, son
1060 Philip I (the Fair), son
1108 Louis VI (the Fat), son
1137 Louis VII (the Younger), son
1180 Philip II Augustus, son, crowned at Reims
1223 Louis VIII (the Lion), son
1226 Louis IX, son, arbitrated disputes with English King Henry III; led crusades, 1248 (captured in Egypt, 1250) and 1270, when he died of plague in Tunis. Canonized as St. Louis, 1297
1270 Philip III (the Bold), son
1285 Philip IV (the Fair), son, king at 17
1314 Louis X (the Headstrong), son. His posthumous son, John I, lived and reigned only five days.
1316 Philip V (the Tall), brother of Louis X
1322 Charles IV (the Fair), brother of Louis X

House of Valois

1328 Philip VI (of Valois), grandson of Philip III
1350 John II (the Good), son, retired to England
1364 Charles V (the Wise), son
1380 Charles VI (the Beloved), son
1422 Charles VII (the Victorious), son. In 1429, Joan of Arc defeated English at Orleans and Patay and had Charles crowned at Reims. Joan was captured, 1430, and executed, 1431, at Rouen for heresy.
1461 Louis XI (the Cruel), son, civil reformer
1483 Charles VIII (the Affable), son
1498 Louis XII, great-grandson of Charles V
1515 Francis I, of Angouleme, nephew, son-in-law. Fought four major wars, was patron of the arts
1547 Henry II, son, killed at joust. Husband of Catherine (daughter of Lorenzo) de Médicis and lover of Diane de Poitiers. By marriage to Henry II, Catherine became the mother of Francis II, Charles IX, Henry III, and Queen Margaret (Reine Margot), wife of Henry IV (of Navarre).
1559 Francis II, son. Betrothed in 1548 at age 4 to Mary, Queen of Scots, aged 6; they were married 1558. Francis died 1560, aged 16. Mary returned to rule Scotland, 1561.

1560 Charles IX, brother
1574 Henry III, brother, assassinated

House of Bourbon

1589 Henry IV (of Navarre), grandson of Queen Margaret of Navarre. Made enemies when he gave tolerance to Protestants by Edict of Nantes, 1598. Married Margaret of Valois, daughter of Henry II and Catherine de Médicis; was divorced. Married Marie de Médicis, 1600. She became regent upon Henry's assassination, 1610-17, for her son, Louis XIII; she was exiled by Richelieu, 1631.
1610 Louis XIII (the Just), son, married Anne of Austria. His chief minister (1622-42), Cardinal Richelieu, determined his policies.
1643 Louis XIV (the Sun King), son; was king 72 years. Until 1661, Anne of Austria was regent with Cardinal Mazarin as chief minister; Louis then ruled absolutely. Known for lavish court and arts patronage, he exhausted the economy with wars for territory.
1715 Louis XV (the Beloved), great-grandson. Married a Polish princess, lost Canada to England. Favorite mistresses Mme. de Pompadour and Mme. Du Barry influenced policies. Pompadour's saying "Après moi, le déluge" (After me, the deluge) is often incorrectly attributed to Louis XV.
1774 Louis XVI, grandson, married Marie Antoinette, daughter of Empress Maria Therese of Austria. Couple executed by guillotine in French Revolution, 1793. Louis XVII, son, never ruled and died in prison.

First Republic

1792 National Convention of the French Revolution
1795 Directory, under Viscount of Barras and others
1799 Consulate, Napoleon Bonaparte, first consul. Elected consul for life, 1802

First Empire

1804 Napoleon I (Napoleon Bonaparte), emperor. Josephine (de Beauharnais), empress, 1804-09; Marie Louise, empress, 1810-14. Son, Napoleon II (1811-32), titular king of Rome, later duke of Reichstadt, never ruled. Napoleon I abdicated 1814; died in exile, 1821.

House of Bourbon (restored)

1814 Louis XVIII, brother of Louis XVI, king
1824 Charles X, brother, reactionary, deposed by the July Revolution, 1830

House of Orleans

1830 Louis-Philippe (the Citizen King)

Second Republic

1848 Louis Napoleon Bonaparte, nephew of Napoleon I, president

Second Empire

1852 Napoleon III (Louis Napoleon Bonaparte), emperor; Eugenie (de Montijo) (d. 1920), empress. Lost Franco-Prussian war, deposed 1870. Son, Prince Imperial (1856-79), died in Zulu War.

Third Republic

1871 Adolphe Thiers (1797-1877), president
1873 Patrice de Mac-Mahon (1808-93)
1879 Jules Grévy (1807-91)
1887 Sadi Carnot (1837-94), assassinated
1894 Jean Casimir-Périer (1847-1907)
1895 Félix Faure (1841-99)
1899 Émile Loubet (1838-1929)
1906 Armand Fallières (1841-1931)
1913 Raymond Poincaré (1860-1934)
1920 Paul Deschanel (1855-1922)
1920 Alexandre Millerand (1859-1943)
1924 Gaston Doumergue (1863-1937)
1931 Paul Doumer (1857-1932), assassinated
1932 Albert Lebrun (1871-1950), resigned 1940

Vichy Regime

1940 Philippe Pétain (1856-1951), chief of state, 1940-44, under German armistice

Provisional Government

1944 Charles de Gaulle (1890-1970)
1946 Félix Gouin (1884-1977)
1946 Georges Bidault (1899-1983)

Fourth Republic

1947 Vincent Auriol (1884-1966), president
1954 René Coty (1882-1962)

Fifth Republic

1959 Charles de Gaulle (1890-1970), president; resigned 1969. Alain Poher (1909-96), interim pres., Apr.-June 1969
1969 Georges Pompidou (1911-74); Poher, interim pres., Apr.-May 1974
1974 Valéry Giscard d'Estaing (1926-2020)
1981 François Mitterrand (1916-96)
1995 Jacques Chirac (1932-2019)
2007 Nicolas Sarkozy (1955-)
2012 François Hollande (1954-)
2017 Emmanuel Macron (1977-)

Rulers of Middle Europe and Germany

Carolingian Dynasty

Charles I (the Great), or Charlemagne, made Roman emperor by pope in Rome, 800. Ruled France, Italy, and Middle Europe; established Ostmark (later Austria). Died 814.

Louis I (Ludwig) (the Pious), son, crowned co-emperor by Charlemagne, 813. Divided empire among sons. Died 840; sons fought for control.

Louis II (the German), son, succeeded to East Francia (Germany), 843-76, with Treaty of Verdun.

Charles III (the Fat), son, inherited Swabia, 876. With brothers' deaths, acquired East Francia and West Francia (France), reuniting empire. Crowned emperor by pope, 881; deposed 887.

Arnulf, nephew, 887-99, took over East Francia; partition of empire.

Louis IV (the Child), son, 900-11, last direct descendant of Charlemagne.

Conrad I, duke of Franconia, first elected German king, 911-18.

Saxon Dynasty; First Reich

Henry I (the Fowler), duke of Saxony, elected king 919-36.

Otto I (the Great), son, 936-73, crowned Holy Roman Emperor by pope, 962.

Otto II, son, 961-83, ruled with Otto I as king, then emperor, 967.

Otto III, son, 983-1002, crowned Holy Roman Emperor, 996.

Henry II (the Saint), great-grandson of Otto the Great, duke of Bavaria, 1002-24. Crowned emperor, 1014.

Salian Dynasty

Conrad II, 1024-39, elected king of Germany.

Henry III (the Black), son, 1039-56, deposed three popes; annexed Burgundy.

Henry IV, son, 1056-1106, with mother, Agnes of Poitou, as regent in early years. He and Pope Gregory VII tried to depose each other. Civil war lasted about 20 years.

Henry V, son, 1106-25, last of Salian Dynasty.

Lothair, duke of Saxony, elected king 1125-37. Crowned emperor in Rome, 1133.

Hohenstaufen Dynasty

Conrad III, duke of Franconia, 1138-52, in Second Crusade.

Frederick I (Barbarossa, Italian for "Redbeard"), nephew, 1152-90.

Henry VI, son, 1190-97, gained kingdom of Sicily through marriage.

Philip of Swabia, brother, 1197-1208. Otto IV, nephew of King Richard I of England, 1198-1215, was elected rival king. Philip's murder, in 1208, led to Otto's win in new election same year. Civil war followed before Otto was deposed, 1215.

Frederick II, son of Henry VI, elected 1212-50. Had earlier succeeded father as king of Sicily; crowned himself king of Jerusalem, 1229, in Sixth Crusade.

Conrad IV, son, 1250-54. Conquered Naples.

(Interregnum, 1254-73. Conradin, son of Conrad IV and last legitimate Hohenstaufen, defeated by Charles of Anjou—brother of King Louis IX of France—and executed, 1268. Rise of electors of German monarch.)

Transition

Rudolf I, of Habsburg, 1273-91, defeated King Ottocar II of Bohemia, 1278. Bequeathed duchies of Austria and Styria to sons.

Adolf of Nassau, 1292-98, killed in war with Albert I.

Albert I, elder son of Rudolf I, 1298-1308, assassinated.

Henry VII, of Luxembourg, 1308-13. Gained Bohemia, 1310; crowned Holy Roman Emperor, 1312.

Louis IV, of Wittelsbach, 1314-46. Also elected was a son of Albert I, Frederick of Austria, whom Louis defeated in 1322. Rejected need for papal confirmation of elected German king.

Charles IV, of Luxemburg, grandson of Henry VII, 1346-78. Took Brandenburg.

Wenceslaus, son, 1378-1400; deposed.

Rupert, of Wittelsbach, elector palatine, 1400-10.

Sigismund, brother of Wenceslaus, 1410-37.

Habsburg Dynasty

Albert II, duke of Austria, son-in-law of Sigismund, elected German king, 1438-39; king of Hungary and Holy Roman Emperor.

Frederick III, cousin, 1440-93, fought Turks.

Maximilian I, son, 1493-1519, archduke of Austria.

Charles V, grandson, 1519-58. King of Spain; assumed title of Holy Roman Emperor. Martin Luther, who had been excommunicated by pope, appeared at Diet of Worms, 1521. Charles attempted church reform and conciliation between Catholicism and Protestantism; abdicated.

Ferdinand I, brother, 1558-64; king of Hungary and Bohemia, 1526 (successive leaders through Maria Theresa will rule these lands as well).

Maximilian II, son, 1564-76.

Rudolf II, son, 1576-1612.

Matthias, brother, 1612-19.

Ferdinand II, grandson of Ferdinand I, 1619-37. Bohemian Protestants, unhappy with Ferdinand's support of Catholic Counter-Reformation, crowned Frederick V, elector palatine. Frederick became known as "Winter King" with defeat in battle, 1620; start of Thirty Years' War.

Ferdinand III, son, 1637-57. Treaties signed, 1648, in Peace of Westphalia ended war.

Leopold I, son, 1658-1705.

Joseph I, son, 1705-11.

Charles VI, brother, 1711-40; died without male heir.

Maria Theresa, daughter, 1740-80. Appointed husband, Francis Stephen of Lorraine, co-regent. Dispute over her inheritance led to War of the Austrian Succession. Charles VII, also known as Charles Albert, elected in opposition to Francis, 1742-45. After Charles's death, Maria Theresa obtained election of her husband as Holy Roman Emperor Francis I, 1745-65. Fought Seven Years' War with Frederick II of Prussia.

Habsburg-Lorraine Dynasty

Joseph II, son, 1765-90, reformer. Ruled jointly with Maria Theresa until her death. Participated in first partition of Poland, with Prussia and Russia.

Leopold II, brother, 1790-92; king of Hungary and Bohemia.

Francis II, son, 1792-1806; king of Hungary and Bohemia. Proclaimed first emperor of Austria, 1804-35. Unsuccessfully fought against Napoleon; forced to abdicate, 1806, as Holy Roman Emperor, last use of title.

Ferdinand, son, 1835-48, emperor of Austria; king of Hungary and Bohemia. Abdicated in favor of nephew after revolution broke out in Vienna.

Austro-Hungarian Monarchy

Francis Joseph I, nephew, 1848-1916, emperor of Austria and king of Hungary. Defeated in Austro-Prussian War, 1866. Formed dual monarchy of Austria-Hungary, 1867. After Serbian nationalist assassinated Francis Joseph's nephew and heir, Archduke Francis Ferdinand, June 28, 1914, Austrian diplomacy precipitated World War I.

Charles I, grandnephew, 1916-18, last emperor of Austria and king of Hungary. Abdicated Nov. 1918; died in exile, 1922.

Second and Third Reichs

William I, brother of Frederick William IV, 1861-88, king of Prussia. Appointed Otto von Bismarck chancellor, 1862. Franco-Prussian War, also known as Franco-German War, 1870-71, unified German states. William proclaimed German emperor, 1871; beginning of Second Reich.

Frederick III, son, 1888.

William II, son, 1888-1918, led Germany into World War I. Abdicated Nov. 1918; died in exile in the Netherlands, 1941.

Germany adopted constitution at Weimar, July 1, 1919, setting up Weimar Republic. Presidents included Friedrich Ebert, 1919-25, and Paul von Hindenburg, 1925-34, field marshal in World War I. Hindenburg appointed Adolf Hitler chancellor, 1933, at beginning of Third Reich. Following Hindenburg's death, Hitler succeeded as Führer and chancellor, 1934-45, with dictatorial powers. Annexed Austria, 1938. Precipitated World War II, 1939-45. Hitler committed suicide, 1945.

Germany After 1945

After World War II, Germany was split between democratic West and Soviet-dominated East. West German chancellors: Konrad Adenauer, 1949-63; Ludwig Erhard, 1963-66; Kurt Georg Kiesinger, 1966-69; Willy Brandt, 1969-74; Helmut Schmidt, 1974-82; Helmut Kohl, 1982-90. East German Communist party leaders: Walter Ulbricht, 1950-71; Erich Honecker, 1971-89; Egon Krenz, 1989. (Berlin Wall fell, Nov. 1989.)

Germany reunited Oct. 3, 1990. Post-reunification chancellors: Helmut Kohl, 1990-98; Gerhard Schröder, 1998-2005; Angela Merkel, 2005-21; Olaf Scholz, 2021- .

Rulers of Hungary

The first king of Hungary was Stephen I, of the Arpad Dynasty, 1000-38. Feuds followed his death.

Charles I, also known as Charles Robert, became king, 1308-42.

Louis I (the Great), son, 1342-82. Succeeded uncle Casimir III as ruler of Poland, 1370.

Mary, elder daughter, 1382-95, ruled with husband, Sigismund of Luxemburg, 1387-1437, who also became king of Bohemia, Germany and Holy Roman Emperor. Hedwig (Jadwiga), younger daughter of Louis I, became queen of Poland. (See **Rulers of Poland**.)

Albert II, duke of Austria, son-in-law of Sigismund, 1438-39. Also king of Germany and Holy Roman Emperor.

Vladislaus I, 1440-44, king of Poland.

Ladislaus V, posthumous son of Albert II, 1444-57, not crowned until 1453. Janos Hunyadi acted as governor under young king, 1446-52; fought Turks.

Matthias I (Corvinus), son of Janos Hunyadi, 1458-90. Shared title of king of Bohemia. Captured Vienna, 1485; annexed Styria, Carinthia.

Vladislaus II, 1490-1516, king of Bohemia.

Louis II, son, 1516-26. Died in Battle of Mohács against Suleiman (the Magnificent), head of Ottoman Empire.

Ferdinand I, of Austria, brother-in-law, and John I, also known as John Zapolya of Transylvania, elected rival kings. Suleiman claimed part of Hungary for Ottoman Empire. Hungary partitioned. (Refer to **Habsburg Dynasty** for continuation.)

Rulers of Prussia

Nucleus of Prussia was the margravate of Brandenburg, an electorate of the Holy Roman Empire. Frederick VI, burgrave of Nuremberg, was made elector of Brandenburg, 1415. Rise of Hohenzollern Dynasty in territory that included Brandenburg and duchy of Prussia.

Frederick William (the Great Elector), 1640-88, elector of Brandenburg.

Frederick III, son, 1688-1713, elector of Brandenburg. Crowned Frederick I, king in Prussia, 1701.

Frederick William I, son, 1713-40.

Frederick II (the Great), son, 1740-86; military strategist who expanded Prussia's holdings.

Frederick William II, nephew, 1786-97.

Frederick William III, son, 1797-1840; Napoleonic Wars.

Frederick William IV, son, 1840-61. Revolution of 1848; constitution adopted, 1850. (Refer to **Second and Third Reichs** for continuation.)

Rulers of Poland

House of Piast

Mieszko I, c. 963-92, duke of Poland; Poland Christianized, 966. Expansion under three with name Boleslaus (reigns not consecutive): Boleslaus I (the Brave), son, 992-1025, crowned first king of Poland, 1025; Boleslaus II (the Bold), great-grandson, 1058-79, exiled after killing bishop of Krakow, Stanislaus (who became a patron saint of Poland); Boleslaus III (the Wry-Mouthed), nephew, 1102-38, divided Poland among four sons with oldest also in control of crown. Period of feudal division followed.

A Polish duke, Conrad of Masovia, asked the Teutonic Knights—a German military religious order—to crusade against Prussia, 1226. Teutonic Knights conquered lands; thereafter warred with Poland. Mongols/Tatars invaded Poland, 1241.

Vladislaus I, 1306-33, reunited most Polish territories; crowned king, 1320. Casimir III (the Great), son, 1333-70, developed economy, cultural life, foreign policy. No male heir. Succeeded by Louis I, nephew, 1370-82, who was also Louis I (the Great) of Hungary.

Jadwiga, daughter, 1384-99.

House of Jagiello

Vladislaus Jagiello, grand duke of Lithuania, married Jadwiga, 1386, and ruled jointly as Vladislaus II, 1386-1434. Poland and Lithuania united; Lithuania converted to Christianity. Defeated Teutonic Knights at Grunwald (Tannenberg), 1410.

Vladislaus III, son, 1434-44, also king of Hungary. Fought Turks; killed in Battle of Varna, 1444.

Casimir IV, brother, 1447-92, put son Vladislaus on throne of Bohemia and Hungary. Victorious over Teutonic Knights; signed treaty, 1466, after 13-year war.

John I, son, 1492-1501.

Alexander I, brother, 1501-05.

Sigismund I, brother, 1506-48, patronized sciences and arts; his and son's reign were golden age. Grand Master of Teutonic Order, Albert Hohenzollern, converted to Protestantism; secularized his state and made first duke of Prussia by Sigismund, 1525.

Sigismund II, son, 1548-72; Union of Lublin, 1569, established dual state of Poland and Lithuania. No male heir.

Elective Kings

Henry of Valois, 1573-74, first king elected by nobility. Left Poland to assume crown of France after brother's death. Interregnum.

Stephen Bathory, 1576-86, prince of Transylvania, married Anna, sister of Sigismund II. Fought Russians.

Sigismund III Vasa, nephew of Sigismund II and son of king of Sweden, 1587-1632. Fought to reclaim Swedish crown, which he'd lost because of his Catholicism; battled Russians and Turks.

Vladislaus IV Vasa, son, 1632-48.

John II Casimir Vasa, brother, 1648-68. Fought Cossacks, Swedish, Russians, Turks, Tatars; period of invasions known as "the Deluge."

Michael Korybut Wisniowiecki, 1669-73.

John III Sobieski, 1674-96, freed Vienna from besieging Turks, 1683.

Augustus II (the Strong), 1697-1733, elector of Saxony.

Augustus III, son, 1733-63, elector of Saxony.

Stanislaus II, 1764-95, last king. Encouraged reforms; first modern constitution in Europe, 1791. Poland lost territory to Russia, Austria, and Prussia in three partitions (1772, 1793, 1795). Thaddeus Kosciusko, American-Polish general, attempted unsuccessful insurrection, 1794.

Poland Under Foreign Rule

Grand duchy of Warsaw created by Napoleon I out of Prussian (formerly Polish) territory. Frederick Augustus I, king of Saxony, ruled grand duchy, 1807-15. Defeat of Napoleon led to Congress of Vienna, 1814-15; part of Poland claimed as kingdom by Russia. Polish uprisings against Russia (1830, 1863) and Austria (1846) repressed. Poland regained independence following World War I.

Second Republic

Jozef Pilsudski, 1918-22, head of state. Presidents: Gabriel Narutowicz, 1922, assassinated by extremist; Stanislaus Wojciechowski, 1922-26, resigned after coup d'état by Pilsudski; Ignacy Moscicki, 1926-39, ruled with Pilsudski (d. 1935) and Pilsudski's military colleagues as virtual dictator during what came to be known as Sanacja (meaning "cleansing" or "healing") regime.

Poland Under Foreign Occupation, Influence

After Hitler and Stalin signed nonaggression pact, Germany invaded Poland Sept. 1, 1939; Russia invaded Sept. 17. Polish government-in-exile was in France, then England. Vladislaus Raczkiewicz, 1939-47, president; Gen. Vladislaus Sikorski, 1939-43, and Stanislaus Mikolajczyk, 1943-44, prime ministers. Polish residents were sent to German concentration camps and Soviet labor camps; about 3 million Jewish Poles were killed in the Holocaust. Thousands of Polish prisoners of war, mostly military officers, massacred in Katyn Forest by Soviet secret police, 1940. Soviet-sponsored Polish Committee of National Liberation took formative role in new government, 1945, renamed Polish People's Republic in 1952. Communist Polish United Workers' Party ruled the country. Brief period of liberalization followed Stalin's death in 1953. Vladislaus Gomulka, 1956-70, and Edward Gierek, 1970-80, led country as first secretary of Polish United Workers' Party.

Election of Cardinal Karol Wojtyla, archbishop of Krakow, as pope (John Paul II) inspired Poles, 1978. Strikes in 1980 prompted creation of Solidarity, an independent trade union headed by Lech Walesa. Solidarity gained control of government in partly free elections, 1985.

Third Republic

Presidents: Lech Walesa, 1990-95; Aleksander Kwasniewski, 1995-2005; Lech Kaczynski, 2005-10, died in plane crash; Bronislaus Komorowski and Grzegorz Schetyna, acting, 2010; Komorowski, 2010-15; Andrzej Duda, 2015- .

Rulers of Denmark, Sweden, Norway

Denmark

Canute (the Great) ruled area that included England, Denmark, and Norway, 1016-35. Valdemar IV Atterdag reunited Denmark, 1361. Margrethe I, daughter, married to Haakon VI, king of Norway, 1363. After Valdemar's death, Olaf, Margrethe's infant son, made king of Denmark, 1375. He was also crowned king of Norway after death of Haakon, 1380. Following Olaf's death, 1387, Margrethe served as regent of Denmark, Norway, and Sweden. She effected the Union of Kalmar of the three kingdoms, 1397. She had her grandnephew, Eric of Pomerania, crowned (she held actual power until her death, 1412).

Succeeding rulers were unable to enforce their claims on Sweden until Christian II, 1512-23, conquered the country, 1520. He was soon deposed; accession of Gustav I as king of Sweden, 1523, ended Kalmar Union. Denmark continued to dominate Norway until the Napoleonic Wars when Frederik VI, 1808-39, allied with Napoleon I after Danish fleet was attacked by Britain, 1807. By 1814 treaty, Denmark was forced to cede Norway to Sweden.

Succession: House of Oldenborg (began with Christian I, 1448): Christian VIII, 1839-48; Frederik VII, son, 1848-63. House of Glücksborg: Christian IX, 1863-1906; Frederik VIII, son, 1906-12; Christian X, son, 1912-47; Frederik IX, son, 1947-72; Margrethe II, daughter, 1972- .

Sweden

Under King Magnus Ladulas, hereditary nobility established around 1280. Swedish nobles opposed to Albrekt of Mecklenburg accepted Margareta (Margrethe), regent of Denmark, as ruler, 1389. Sweden joined Kalmar Union, 1397. After internal unrest, Sweden was conquered anew by Denmark's Kristian II, 1520. Execution of Kristian's opponents in "Stockholm Bloodbath" led to uprising under Gustav I Eriksson (Vasa), who was elected Swedish king, 1523-60. Gustav established an independent kingdom with centralized power, state church, and hereditary throne. Gustav II Adolf (Lion of the North), 1611-32, fought Russia, Poland, Germany; died in battle.

Later rulers: Kristina, daughter, 1632-54, abdicated; Karl X Gustav, cousin, 1654-60; Karl XI, son, 1660-97; Karl XII, son, 1697-1718; Ulrika Eleonora, sister, 1718-20, abdicated; Fredrik I, of Hesse, husband, 1720-51; Adolf Fredrik, 1751-71; Gustaf III, son, 1771-92; Gustaf IV Adolf, son, 1792-1809, deposed; Karl XIII, uncle, 1809-18. Karl XIV Johan (born Jean Baptiste Bernadotte, a general under Napoleon I), 1818-44, founded House of Bernadotte.

Succession: Oskar I, son, 1844-59; Karl XV, son, 1859-72; Oskar II, brother, 1872-1907; Gustaf V, son, 1907-50; Gustaf VI Adolf, son, 1950-73; Carl XVI Gustaf, grandson, 1973- .

Norway

Harald I (Fairhair) overcame rivals to become first king of Norway, c. 885-c. 933. Olaf II Haraldsson, 1015-28, Christianized country; became patron saint of Norway. Haakon V Magnusson, 1299-1319, died without male heir. His daughter Ingeborg was married to Erik, a son of the Norwegian king; their son Magnus VII Eriksson became ruler of Norway, 1319-55, and Sweden, 1319-63. Haakon VI Magnusson, son, 1355-80, married Margaret of Denmark. Olaf IV, son, became king of Norway, 1380-87, and Denmark, 1375-87, with mother as regent. Margaret took over rule upon his death, 1387. Union of Kalmar, 1397, united Norway, Denmark, and Sweden.

After Napoleonic Wars, Denmark ceded Norway to Sweden, 1814. A strong nationalist movement forced Sweden to recognize Norway as an independent kingdom under the Swedish kings. Norwegian constitution, adopted 1814, allowed for creation of the Storting (Norwegian parliament), which governed country domestically. In 1905, the union was dissolved. Prince Charles of Denmark elected king of Norway as Haakon VII, 1905-57; founded House of Glücksburg. Succession: Olav V, son, 1957-91; Harald V, son, 1991- .

Rulers of the Netherlands and Belgium

The Netherlands

Willem I, son of Prince Willem V of Orange, came to power after French rule ended in the Netherlands, 1813; crowned king with approval of Congress of Vienna, 1815. Started House of Orange-Nassau. Northern Netherlands was known as Holland. Belgians, in southern Netherlands, rebelled against the Dutch and seceded, Oct. 4, 1830. Dutch formally recognized Belgian independence, Apr. 19, 1839. Willem I abdicated, 1840.

Succession: Willem II, son, 1840-49; Willem III, son, 1849-90; Wilhelmina, daughter, 1890-1948; Juliana, daughter, 1948-80; Beatrix, daughter, 1980-2013; Willem-Alexander, son, 2013- .

Belgium

A national congress elected Prince Leopold of Saxe-Coburg as king. He took the throne July 21, 1831, as Leopold I.

Succession: Leopold II, son, 1865-1909; Albert I, nephew, 1909-34; Leopold III, son, 1934-51, in exile after Germany invaded Belgium, later abdicated; Prince Charles, brother, acted as regent 1944-50; Baudouin I, son of Leopold III, 1951-93; Albert II, brother, 1993-2013; Philippe, son, 2013- .

Rulers of Modern Italy

After the fall of Napoleon, the Congress of Vienna, 1814-15, restored Italy as a political patchwork, comprising the Kingdom of the Two Sicilies (Naples and Sicily), the Papal States, and smaller units. King Victor Emmanuel I of Savoy ruled Sardinia, Piedmont, and Genoa.

Victor Emmanuel I abdicated 1821. Charles Felix, brother, 1821-31, died without issue. Succeeded by Charles Albert, 1831-49; he abdicated upon defeat by the Austrians. Succeeded by Victor Emmanuel II, son, 1849-61. United Italy emerged under Camillo Benso di Cavour, prime minister of the Kingdom of Sardinia, 1852-61. Giuseppe Mazzini and Giuseppe Garibaldi were also figures in Risorgimento ("resurgence") period before Italy's unification.

In 1859, France forced Austria to cede Lombardy to Sardinia. In 1860, Garibaldi led more than 1,000 volunteers in a campaign against King Francis II of the Two Sicilies, taking Sicily and Naples. The House of Savoy subsequently annexed the Two Sicilies, Tuscany, Parma, Modena, Romagna, the Marches, and Umbria. Victor Emmanuel II assumed leadership of a united Kingdom of Italy, Mar. 17, 1861.

In 1866, Victor Emmanuel II allied with Prussia in the Austro-Prussian War and, with Prussia's victory, received Venetia. On Sept. 20, 1870, Italian troops entered Rome, ending the temporal power of the Roman Catholic Church. (The 1929 Lateran Treaty established papal sovereignty in Vatican City.)

Succession: Umberto I, son, 1878-1900, assassinated; Victor Emmanuel III, son, 1900-46; Umberto II, son, 1946, ruled only one month before voters in a referendum chose to establish a republic. In 1919, Benito Mussolini helped found the nationalist Fasci di Combattimento (Fighting Leagues), or Fascists. After Mussolini organized March on Rome, 1922, Victor Emmanuel III agreed to a coalition government. Mussolini eventually became dictator (Il Duce). He entered World War II as an ally of Hitler, 1940. He was dismissed by the king, 1943; captured and executed by partisans, 1945.

At a plebiscite, 1946, voters approved a republic. Prime minister Alcide de Gasperi was chief of state, 1945-53; Enrico de Nicola was provisional president. Successive presidents: Luigi Einaudi, 1948-55; Giovanni Gronchi, 1955-62; Antonio Segni, 1962-64; Giuseppe Saragat, 1964-71; Giovanni Leone, 1971-78; Alessandro Pertini, 1978-85; Francesco Cossiga, 1985-92; Oscar Luigi Scalfaro, 1992-99; Carlo Azeglio Ciampi, 1999-2006; Giorgio Napolitano, 2006-15; Sergio Mattarella, 2015- .

Rulers of Spain

From 8th to 11th centuries, Spain was dominated by the Moors (Muslims from North Africa of Arab and Berber origin). A number of small kingdoms—Aragon, Asturias, Castile, Catalonia, Leon, Navarre, and Valencia—undertook a Christian reconquest. In 1474, Isabella I became Queen of Castile and Leon. By the Catholic Monarchs' request, Pope Sixtus IV authorized the Inquisition, 1478. Isabella's husband, Ferdinand V, acceded to the throne of Aragon, 1479. Last Moorish kingdom, Granada, seized 1492. Spain sponsored Christopher Columbus, who led European exploration of New World, 1492. Isabella was succeeded by daughter, Joanna (the Mad), but Ferdinand acted as regent until his death, 1516.

Charles I, son of Joanna and grandson of Habsburg Emperor Maximilian I, became Holy Roman Emperor as Charles V, 1520;

abdicated 1556. Philip II, son, 1556-98, inherited only part of empire. He conquered Portugal, fought against Ottoman Empire, sent Armada in unsuccessful invasion of England. Succession: Philip III, son, 1598-1621; Philip IV, son, 1621-65; Charles II, son, 1665-1700, no issue, left Spain to Philip of Anjou, grandson of Louis XIV of France. As Philip V, he was first of Bourbon dynasty in Spain, 1700-46 (his son Louis ruled briefly in 1724); Ferdinand VI, son, 1746-59; Charles III, brother, 1759-88; Charles IV, son, 1788-1808, abdicated.

Joseph Bonaparte made king of Spain, 1808-13, by his brother Napoleon. Ferdinand VII, son of Charles IV, 1808, 1814-33, lost American colonies except Cuba, Puerto Rico. Maria Christina of the Two Sicilies, wife, was regent until 1843 for Isabella II, daughter, who was driven into exile by revolution, 1868. Amadeo of Savoy elected king by the Cortes (parliament), 1870-73. First Republic, 1873-74. Alfonso XII, son of Isabella II, 1875-85; Alfonso XIII, posthumous son, 1901-31, with mother Maria Christina as regent before he assumed throne. Spain ceded territory after loss in Spanish-American War, 1898. Primo de Rivera ruled as dictator, 1923-30, after military coup but was forced to resign after losing support. Alfonso agreed to exile without formal abdication. Monarchy abolished; Second Republic established with socialist backing. Presidents: Niceto Alcala Zamora, 1931-36; Manuel Azaña, 1936-39.

Revolt by military started Spanish Civil War, 1936-39. Gen. Francisco Franco ruled as head of Nationalist regime, 1939-73. Monarchy restored after 1947 referendum. Juan Carlos, grandson of Alfonso XIII, acceded to throne after Franco's death in 1975; abdicated, 2014. Felipe VI, son, 2014- .

Leaders in the South American Wars of Liberation

Francisco de Miranda, José de San Martín, and Simón Bolívar led early 19th-cent. struggles of South American nations to free themselves from Spain.

Miranda (1750-1816), a Venezuelan, served as an officer in the Spanish army. After a dispute with the army, he fled to the U.S., 1783, where he met leaders of the American Revolution. He traveled seeking support for South American independence from other world leaders. Miranda unsuccessfully attempted a revolt in Venezuela, 1806. Napoleon's invasion of Spain, 1808, prompted the start of a revolution in Venezuela. Miranda returned, 1810, and headed the revolution with dictatorial powers. Venezuela declared independence, 1811. Overcome by royalist forces, 1812, Miranda surrendered and was arrested; he died in a Spanish prison.

San Martín (1778-1850) was born in present-day Argentina. He served in Spanish campaigns in Europe until 1811. He returned to Argentina and joined the independence movement, 1812. In 1817, he invaded Chile through the Andean mountain passes. He and Bernardo O'Higgins defeated the Spanish at Chacabuco, 1817. Chile gained independence, 1819; O'Higgins became first director of Chile, 1817-23. In 1821, San Martín entered Lima and took the port of Callao; he became protector of an independent Peru.

Bolívar (1783-1830) was born into an aristocratic family in Venezuela. He served under Miranda until Miranda's surrender in 1812. Bolívar continued to fight; he captured Caracas and was named Liberator, 1813. But he was forced to flee by royalist forces, 1814. In 1817, Bolívar again fought for control of Venezuela. With Francisco de Paula Santander and José Antonio Páez, he defeated the Spanish at the Battle of Boyacá, 1819, freeing New Granada (present-day Colombia). New Granada, Venezuela, and the area that is now Panama and Ecuador were joined as the Republic of Colombia, or Gran Colombia, with Bolívar as president later that same year, though parts of the republic remained under Spanish control. He decisively defeated the Spanish in the Battle of Carabobo in Venezuela, 1821.

Antonio José de Sucre, Bolívar's chief lieutenant, overcame Spanish forces at the Battle of Pichincha in Ecuador, 1822. Bolívar convinced San Martín to resign as protector of Peru. Peru was declared independent after Bolívar and Sucre won the Battle of Junin, Aug. 1824, and Sucre triumphed at the Battle of Ayacucho, Dec. 1824.

Sucre organized Upper Peru as Republica Bolívar (now Bolivia), 1825, and acted as president in place of Bolívar, who wrote its constitution.

Civil strife caused the Colombian federation to break apart. Bolívar gave up the presidency, 1830.

Rulers of Russia; Leaders of the USSR and Russian Federation

The Varangian (Viking) prince Rurik is considered to be the first leader of the Russians; he established himself at Novgorod, c. 862 CE. His successor, Oleg, and those who followed Oleg ruled as princes of Kiev. Vladimir I, or Saint Vladimir, married sister of Byzantine emperor and converted to Christianity, 988. Yaroslav I (the Wise), brother, 1019-54, was important organizer and lawgiver; his daughters married kings of Norway, Hungary, and France. In 1169, Andrew Bogolyubsky conquered Kiev and began the line of Vladimir.

Daniel, a son of grand prince of Vladimir, Alexander Nevsky, was first to be called prince of Muscovy (Moscow), 1263-1303. Dmitri Ivanovich (Donskoi), prince of Moscow, defeated the Tatars at the Battle of Kulikovo, 1380. His successors were grand princes of Moscow. Ivan III (the Great), 1462-1505, achieved considerable territorial expansion.

Ivan III married Sofia Palaeologus, niece of the last Byzantine emperor. Succession: Vasily III, son. Ivan IV (the Terrible), son, crowned 1547 as Tsar of Russia. Fyodor I, son, reigned 1584-98, but his brother-in-law Boris Godunov had real control before becoming tsar himself, 1598-1605. After years of internal strife ("Time of Troubles"), the Russians united under 16-year-old Michael Romanov, distantly related to Ivan IV's first wife. He ruled 1613-45, establishing the Romanov line.

Tsars, or emperors, of Russia (Romanovs): Peter I (the Great), 1682-1725, with Ivan V, brother, as co-ruler, 1682-96. Catherine I, his widow, 1725-27. Peter II, grandson of Peter I, 1727-30. Anna, daughter of Ivan V and niece of Peter I, 1730-40. Ivan VI, nephew, 1740-41; deposed by Elizabeth, daughter of Peter I, 1741-62. Peter III, nephew, 1762; deposed by his wife, Catherine II (the Great), former princess of Anhalt Zerbst (Germany), 1762-96. Paul I, son, 1796-1801, assassinated. Alexander I, son, 1801-25, defeated Napoleon. Nicholas I, brother, 1825-55. Alexander II, son, 1855-81, assassinated. Alexander III, son, 1881-94. Nicholas II, son, 1894-1917, last tsar of Russia, was forced to abdicate by revolutionaries following losses to Germany in WWI. The tsar, empress, tsarevich (crown prince), and tsar's four daughters were murdered by the Bolsheviks, July 1918.

Premiers of provisional government: Prince Georgi Lvov, followed by Alexander Kerensky, 1917.

Union of Soviet Socialist Republics

Bolshevik Revolution, Nov. 7, 1917, (also known as the October Revolution, based on Russia's then use of the Julian calendar) removed Kerensky from power. Council of People's Commissars formed with Lenin (Vladimir Ilyich Ulyanov), as chair (or premier), 1917-24. Aleksei Rykov (executed 1938) and Vyacheslav M. Molotov held the office, but effective ruler was Joseph Stalin (Joseph Vissarionovich Dzhugashvili), general secretary of the Communist Party. Stalin was chair of the Council of People's Commissars from 1941 until his death in 1953. Succeeded by Georgi M. Malenkov, who also briefly served as general secretary of the Communist Party before being ousted from the position by Nikita S. Khrushchev. Malenkov was forced to resign as premier, 1955, and was expelled from the Communist Party, 1961. Nikolai A. Bulganin was premier, 1955-58, until his replacement by Khrushchev, 1958-64.

Leonid I. Brezhnev ousted Khrushchev as general secretary of the party, a post he held until his death in 1982. Aleksei N. Kosygin was premier, 1964-80. The Central Committee elected former KGB (state security) head Yuri V. Andropov general secretary, 1982-84. After Andropov's death, Konstantin U. Chernenko was chosen for the position, 1984-85. Upon Chernenko's death, he was succeeded by Mikhail Gorbachev. Gorbachev assumed the newly created position of president of the Soviet Union, 1990. Boris Yeltsin was sworn in July 1991 as the Russian Republic's first elected president. Under Yeltsin, Russia became a founding member of the Commonwealth of Independent States. Gorbachev resigned the presidency, Dec. 25, 1991, and the Soviet Union officially disbanded Dec. 31. Each of the 15 former Soviet constituent republics became independent.

Post-Soviet Russia

Presidents of the Russian Federation: Boris Yeltsin, 1991-99; Vladimir Putin, 2000-08; Dmitry Medvedev, 2008-12; Putin, 2012- .

Rulers of China

Where dynastic dates overlap, the rulers or events referred to appeared in different areas of China.

Years in power	Dynasty/ruler(s)
c. 1994-c. 1766 BCE	Xia dynasty, first hereditary Chinese dynasty
c. 1766-c. 1045 BCE	Shang dynasty, first Chinese dynasty with historical records
c. 1045-771 BCE	Western Zhou dynasty, capital near present-day Xi'an
770-256 BCE	Eastern Zhou dynasty, new capital established at Luoyang. During Chunqiu (Spring and Autumn) period (722-481 BCE), Zhou began to lose authority. Period of the Warring States (403-221 BCE) involved major powers of Qi, Chu, Yan, Han, Zhao, Wei, and Qin
221-207 BCE	Qin dynasty, quasi-feudal states unified for first time under self-proclaimed Shi Huang Di, or First Emperor. Prefectures/counties organized under central govt., uniform laws; written language, weights standardized
206 BCE-9 CE	Earlier, or Western Han dynasty, founded by rebel leader Liu Bang. Expansion under Emperor Wudi (born Liu Che), 140-87 BCE; civil service system established
9-23	Xin dynasty, established by Wang Mang, who deposed infant emperor for whom he was regent
25-220	Later, or Eastern Han dynasty
220-265[1]	Wei dynasty, established by son of Han general Cao Cao
221-263[1]	Shu Han dynasty in SW China
222-280[1]	Wu dynasty in SE China
265-317	Western Jin dynasty, established by Sima Yan, Wei dynasty general
317-420	Eastern Jin dynasty, established by prince of Sima family
420-589	Southern dynasties, four short-lived dynasties with capital at Jiankang (present-day Nanjing)
581-618	Sui dynasty, reunified China; established by Emperor Wendi (born Yang Jian), military appointee who usurped throne of non-Chinese Northern Zhou, 581
618-906	Tang dynasty, founded by Li Yuan (known as Emperor Gaozu of Tang), who led rebellion against the Sui. Notable rulers include former imperial concubine Empress Wu, 683-705; Xuanzong, 712-56
907-960	Five Dynasties. Period of disunion with short-lived dynasties in N; Ten Kingdoms (states) in S and W
907-1125	Liao dynasty, of Khitan Mongols, capital at Yanjing (present-day Beijing)
960-1126	Northern Song dynasty, established by military leader Zhao Kuangyin (Emperor Taizu), capital at Kaifeng
1122-1234	Jin dynasty, of Juchen people of Manchuria; drove Song out of N China
1127-1279	Southern Song dynasty, capital at Lin'an (present-day Hangzhou)
1279-1368	Yuan, or Mongol dynasty; Kublai Khan, grandson of Genghis Khan, high point of Mongol power
1368-1644	Ming dynasty, founded by Buddhist monk turned rebel general Zhu Yuanzhang. Country again under Chinese rule; capital in present-day Nanjing, then Beijing after Mongolian tribes' defeat
1644-1912	Qing, or Manchu dynasty, under rule of Manchu people. Last imperial dynasty; Emperor Xuantong, or Puyi, last emperor. Sun Yat-sen organized Kuomintang (Nationalist party) and led provisional republican government in Nanjing, 1911-12. Sun resigned in unification compromise with former imperial viceroy Yuan Shikai, who became president upon emperor's abdication in Feb. 1912
1912-1949	Rep. of China, power passed to provincial warlords upon Yuan's death, 1916. Gen. Chiang Kai-shek sought to reunify China under Kuomintang with new government at Nanjing, 1928. War with Japan, then civil war, led to Nationalist authority collapse, Communist declaration of People's Rep. of China, 1949

(1) Also known as the period of the Three Kingdoms because of warfare between the Wei, Shu Han, and Wu dynasties.

Leaders of People's Republic of China

Name	Title/position, years in power
Mao Zedong	People's Rep. of China (PRC) Chairman, 1949-59; Chinese Communist Party (CCP) Chairman, 1949-76
Zhou Enlai	Premier, 1949-76
Liu Shaoqi	PRC Chairman, 1959-68; one-time Mao successor removed from power during Cultural Revolution (1966-76)
Lin Biao	Red Army cmdr. designated Mao's successor, 1966; govt. reported his death in plane crash, 1971, after coup attempt
Hua Guofeng	Premier, 1976-80; CCP Chairman, 1976-81
Deng Xiaoping	"Paramount leader," 1977-97
Hu Yaobang	CCP General Secretary, 1980-87; CCP Chairman, 1981-82
Zhao Ziyang	Premier, 1980-87; CCP General Secretary, 1987-89
Li Xiannian	President, 1983-88
Yang Shangkun	President, 1988-93
Li Peng	Premier, 1988-98
Jiang Zemin	CCP General Secretary, 1989-2002; President, 1993-2003
Zhu Rongji	Premier, 1998-2003
Hu Jintao	CCP General Secretary, 2002-12; President, 2003-13
Wen Jiabao	Premier, 2003-13
Xi Jinping	CCP General Secretary, 2012- ; President, 2013-
Li Keqiang	Premier, 2013-23
Li Qiang	Premier, 2023-

Historical Periods of Japan

Years in power	Period	Founding event
c. 300-592	Yamato	The Yamato clan united various Japanese states. Also called Tumulus, or Tomb, period for its large burial mounds
593-710	Asuka	Accession of Empress Suiko, with her nephew Prince Shotoku as regent. The Taika reforms (from 645) established a centralized government under the emperor; capital moved to Asuka
710-794	Nara	Capital moved to Nara
794-1185	Heian	Capital moved to Heian (present-day Kyoto) by Emperor Kammu
858-1160	Fujiwara	Fujiwara no Yoshifusa became regent for his grandson
1160-1185	Taira	Taira no Kiyomoro assumed control; Minamoto no Yoritomo defeated Taira, 1185
1192-1333	Kamakura	Yoritomo became shogun, head of military government, with the emperor as titular leader
1334-1392	Namboku	Emperor Go-Daigo returned to power in Kemmu Restoration; 1336 revolt drove him from Kyoto to establish Southern Court at Yoshino
1392-1573	Muromachi	Unification of Southern and Northern Courts; Ashikaga family dominates
1467-1600	Sengoku	Onin War began; also known as Warring States period
1573-1603	Momoyama	Oda Nobunaga entered Kyoto, 1568, deposed last Ashikaga shogun, 1573. Tokugawa Ieyasu victor at Battle of Sekigahara, 1600
1603-1867	Edo	Ieyasu established Tokugawa shogunate, became shogun
1868-1912	Meiji	Meiji Restoration of imperial power, with Meiji (reign name of Mutsuhito) ascending throne; Charter Oath, 1868, led to Westernization
1912-1926	Taisho	Accession of Emperor Taisho (reign name of Yoshihito)
1926-1989	Showa	Accession of Emperor Hirohito (posthumous name Showa)
1989-2019	Heisei	Accession of Emperor Akihito[1]
2019-	Reiwa	Accession of Emperor Naruhito[1]

(1) A 2017 law allowed Akihito to abdicate, the first Japanese emperor to do so in about 200 years, on Apr. 30, 2019, and assume the title of emperor emeritus. His eldest son acceded to the throne the next day.

WORLD EXPLORATION AND GEOGRAPHY

Early Explorers of the Western Hemisphere

Genetic evidence suggests that humans reached the Americas by sailing along the Pacific coast or by crossing the Bering Land Bridge between Siberia and Alaska. Scientists dated fossilized footprints in New Mexico's White Sands National Park to 21,000-23,000 years before the present (BP), in a study published in 2021. Previously discovered remains of early arrivals include Anzick-1 (c. 12,600 BP), a male infant of the Clovis people found buried in present-day Montana; Xach'itee'aanenh T'eede Gaay (Sunrise Girl-Child) (c. 11,500 BP) of the Ancient Beringians, in Alaska; Luzia Woman (11,500 BP) in Brazil; and Kennewick Man (8,500 BP), in Washington. Modern Native Americans appear to be descended from peoples indigenous to N and Central Asia who split into two Native American populations—Northern and Southern—as they dispersed across the continents.

The Americas were populated mostly by hunter-gatherers and small-scale horticulturalists, but complex chiefdoms and state-level societies appeared in a few areas (SE U.S., Mesoamerica, coastal Chile). The earliest known state in the Americas, established by the Caral, or Caral-Supe, civilization, spanned 700 sq mi across river valleys in coastal Peru about 5,000 BP.

The Norse, led by Leif Ericson, are usually credited as being the first Europeans to reach America, with at least five voyages occurring about 1000 CE to areas they called Helluland, Markland, and Vinland—possibly present-day Baffin Island, Labrador, and either Newfoundland or New England. L'Anse aux Meadows, Newfoundland, is the only documented settlement, with evidence of a village dating to c. 1000 CE.

Sustained contact between the hemispheres began with Christopher Columbus (born Cristoforo Colombo, c. 1451, near Genoa, Italy), who made four voyages to the Americas with funding from the Spanish monarchs and private investors. He left Spain, Aug. 3, 1492, with 88 men and a fleet of three vessels—the Niña, Pinta, and Santa María—and landed on the island of San Salvador in present-day Bahamas on Oct. 12, 1492. He also visited Cuba, Hispaniola, and many smaller Caribbean islands, then populated by the Taíno. A second expedition, in 1493, reached the island of Dominica in the Lesser Antilles; a third, in 1498, took Columbus to Trinidad and the adjacent S American coast. A fourth voyage reached Mexico, Honduras, Panama, and what he christened Santiago (the present-day island of Jamaica) in 1502.

In 1497 and 1499, Amerigo Vespucci (for whom the Americas are named), an Italian sailing for Spain, passed along the N and E coasts of S America. He was the first to claim these lands were previously unknown and not part of Asia. Some early explorations are listed below.

Year	Explorer	Nationality (sponsor, if different)	Area reached or explored
1497	John Cabot	Italian (English)	Newfoundland, possibly Nova Scotia
1497-98	Vasco da Gama	Portuguese	Cape of Good Hope (Africa), India
1499	Alonso de Ojeda	Spanish	Northern S Amer. coast, Venezuela
1500	Vicente Yañez Pinzón	Spanish	S American coast, Amazon R.
1500	Pedro Álvarez Cabral	Portuguese	Brazil
1501	Rodrigo de Bastidas	Spanish	Central America
1513	Vasco Núñez de Balboa	Spanish	Panama, Pacific Ocean
1513	Juan Ponce de León	Spanish	Florida, Yucatán Peninsula
1515	Juan de Solis	Spanish	Río de la Plata
1519	Alonso de Pineda	Spanish	Mouth of Mississippi R.
1519	Hernán Cortés	Spanish	Mexico
1519-20	Ferdinand Magellan	Portuguese (Spanish)	Straits of Magellan, Tierra del Fuego
1524	Giovanni da Verrazano	Italian (French)	Atlantic coast, incl. New York Harbor
1528	Álvar Núñez Cabeza de Vaca	Spanish	Texas coast and interior
1532	Francisco Pizarro	Spanish	Peru
1534	Jacques Cartier	French	Canada, Gulf of St. Lawrence
1536	Pedro de Mendoza	Spanish	Up Río de la Plata, Buenos Aires
1539	Francisco de Ulloa	Spanish	California coast
1539	Marcos de Niza	Italian (Spanish)	SW United States
1539-41	Hernando de Soto	Spanish	Mississippi R., near Memphis, TN
1540	Francisco de Coronado	Spanish	SW United States
1540	Hernando de Alarcón	Spanish	Colorado R.
1540	Garcia Lopez de Cárdenas	Spanish	Colorado, Grand Canyon
1541	Francisco de Orellana	Spanish	Amazon R.
1542	Juan Rodriguez Cabrillo	Portuguese (Spanish)	Western Mexico, San Diego Harbor
1565	Pedro Menéndez de Avilés	Spanish	St. Augustine, FL
1576	Sir Martin Frobisher	English	Frobisher Bay, Canada
1577-80	Sir Francis Drake	English	CA coast, on voyage around world
1582	Antonio de Espejo	Spanish	SW U.S. (New Mexico)
1584	Philip Amadas and Arthur Barlowe (for Raleigh)	English	Virginia, Roanoke Isl.
1585-87	Sir Walter Raleigh's men	English	Roanoke Isl., NC
1595	Sir Walter Raleigh	English	Orinoco R., Venezuela
1603-09	Samuel de Champlain	French	Canadian interior, Lake Champlain
1607	John Smith	English	Atlantic coast
1609-10	Henry Hudson	English (Dutch)	Hudson R., Hudson Bay
1634	Jean Nicolet	French	Lake Michigan, Wisconsin
1673	Jacques Marquette and Louis Jolliet	French	Mississippi R., south to Arkansas
1682	René-Robert Cavelier, sieur de La Salle	French	Mississippi R., south to Gulf of Mexico
1727-29	Vitus Bering	Danish (Russian)	Bering Strait, Alaska
1789	Sir Alexander Mackenzie	Canadian	NW Canada
1804-06	Meriwether Lewis and William Clark	American	Missouri R., Rocky Mts., Columbia R.

Arctic Exploration

1596-97: Willem Barents (Dutch) touched Spitsbergen, 79°49′N, and rounded Novaya Zemlya, where he and crew were forced to winter ashore, first W Europeans to successfully do so in the Arctic.

1610: Henry Hudson (Eng.) explored Hudson Strait, Hudson Bay on search for Northwest Passage. After winter ashore, crew mutinied, 1611, and set him, his son, and some others adrift on small boat.

1733-43: Great Northern Expedition (Russ.), led by Vitus Bering (Dan./Russ.), surveyed Siberian Arctic coast. Bering had sailed through what would become known as Bering Strait,

1728, but this second expedition proved that Asia and North America were separate.

1827: William Edward Parry (Eng.), attempting to reach North Pole, made it to 82°45′N via sledge, setting record for farthest north.

1831: James Clark Ross (Eng.) was first to north magnetic pole.

1878-79: Baron Adolf Erik Nordenskiöld (Swed.) was first to navigate Northeast Passage—ocean route connecting Europe's North Sea to Pacific O.

1881-84: Adolphus Greely led 25-person U.S. expedition to Ellesmere Isl. as part of first Intl. Polar Year (1882-83). Only he and five others survived scurvy and starvation after relief ships failed to reach them.

1893-96: Fridtjof Nansen (Nor.) deliberately allowed *Fram* to become icebound and drift from New Siberian Isls. Leaving others in charge of ship, he tried polar dash in 1895 but only reached 86°14′N.

1903-06: Roald Amundsen (Nor.) was first to sail length of Northwest Passage—route linking Atlantic and Pacific via Canada's marine waterways.

1909: Robert E. Peary (U.S.) began dash for North Pole, Mar. 1, from Ellesmere Isl. Reportedly reached the pole, 90°N, Apr. 6, with Matthew Henson and four Inuit. Research suggests he may have fallen short of goal by c. 30-60 mi. (Dr. Frederick Cook [U.S.] claimed to have reached the North Pole in 1908.)

1926: Richard E. Byrd and Floyd Bennett (both U.S.) reputedly flew over North Pole, May 9. Amundsen, Lincoln Ellsworth

(U.S.), and Umberto Nobile (Ital.) flew over North Pole May 12 in dirigible *Norge*.

1958: Nuclear-powered submarine USS *Nautilus* crossed the North Pole beneath the ice.

1968: Ralph Plaisted (U.S.) and three amateur explorers on snowmobiles became first independently confirmed surface expedition to reach North Pole.

1978: Naomi Uemura (Jpn.) became first person to reach the North Pole alone, traveling by dog sled in 54-day, 600-mi trek.

1982: Ranulph Fiennes (Eng.) and Charles Burton (S. Afr.-UK) reached the North Pole and became first to circle the Earth from pole to pole. They had reached the South Pole 16 months earlier. The 52,000-mi trek took three years at an est. cost of $18 mil.

1995: Richard Weber (Can.) and Mikhail Malakhov (Russ.) became first to North Pole and back without any mechanical assistance. The 940-mi trip on skis took 121 days.

Antarctic Exploration

Research published in 2021 suggests Polynesian (Māori) explorer Hui Te Rangiora and his crew may have sighted Antarctica in the early 600s. Western explorers have approached Antarctica since 1773-75, when Capt. James Cook (Eng.) reached 71°10′S. Fabian von Bellingshausen (Russ.) mapped the region on an expedition for Tsar Alexander I, 1819-21. In 1823, James Weddell (Brit.) reached 74°15′S and found the Weddell Sea.

First to announce existence of the continent of Antarctica was Charles Wilkes (U.S.), who followed the coast for 1,500 mi, 1840. Ross Ice Shelf was found by James Clark Ross (Brit.), 1841-42.

1895: Leonard Kristensen (Nor.) landed a party on Victoria Land, first ashore on main continental mass. C. E. Borchgrevink, a member of that party, returned in 1899 with a Brit. expedition, first to winter on Antarctica.

1901-04: Robert Falcon Scott (Eng.), commander of Brit. Natl. Antarctic Expedition, crossed Ross Ice Shelf to 82°17′S, farthest south then reached.

1911: Roald Amundsen (Nor.) with four men and dog teams were first to South Pole, Dec. 14. Scott and four companions reached South Pole on Jan. 17, 1912; they died on return trip.

1929: Richard E. Byrd (U.S.) crossed South Pole, Nov. 29, with three others in 1,600-mi airplane flight.

1934-35: Byrd led second expedition to Little America base camp, explored 450,000 sq mi, wintered alone at 80°08′S.

1935: Lincoln Ellsworth (U.S.) made first transcontinental crossing by air, flying south along E coast of Palmer Peninsula then across to Little America.

1946-48: Ronne Antarctic Research Expedition Cmdr. Finn Ronne determined Antarctic to be one continent with no strait between Weddell and Ross Seas.

1955-57: Supporting U.S. scientific efforts for Intl. Geophysical Year (IGY), the U.S. Navy's Operation Deep Freeze, led by Byrd, established five coastal stations and three interior stations; explored more than 1 mil sq mi in Wilkes Land.

1957-58: During the IGY, scientists from 12 countries conducted research within network of some 60 stations on Antarctica. Vivian E. Fuchs (Eng.) led 12-person Trans-Antarctic Expedition on first land crossing of Antarctica; completed in Mar. 1958 after traveling 2,158 mi in 99 days.

1959: Argentina, Australia, Belgium, Chile, France, Japan, New Zealand, Norway, South Africa, USSR, UK, and U.S. signed a treaty (in force 1961) affirming the use of Antarctica (specifically the area south of 60°S) "for peaceful purposes only." Territorial claims suspended.

1961-62: Scientists discovered Bentley Trench, running from Ross Ice Shelf into Marie Byrd Land, near the end of the Ellsworth Mts., toward Weddell Sea.

1985: Ocean Drilling Project finds that E Antarctic Ice Sheet is 37 mil years old, W Antarctic Ice Sheet 8 mil years old.

1991: Protocol to the Antarctic Treaty on Environmental Protection, or Madrid Protocol, adopted (in force 1998); it banned activities, except research, related to mineral resources.

1995: After 1994 solo expedition to North Pole, Borge Ousland (Nor.) reached South Pole on skis, becoming first to reach both poles alone. He later became the first to traverse both Antarctica (1996-97) and the Arctic (2001) solo.

2018: Colin O'Brady (U.S.) makes first solo Antarctic crossing without assistance or wind aid (54 days). Louis Rudd (Brit.) completed the same feat a little over two days later (56 days).

Volcanoes

Source: *Volcanoes of the World*, Geoscience Press; Global Volcanism Program, Smithsonian Institution, volcano.si.edu

Eruptions have been confirmed in some 859 volcanoes. More than half to three-quarters of historically active volcanoes can be found on the so-called **Ring of Fire**, which runs along the W coast of the Americas from the southern tip of Chile to Alaska, down the E coast of Asia from Kamchatka to Indonesia, and continues from New Guinea to New Zealand. The Ring of Fire marks boundaries between tectonic plates underlying the Pacific Ocean and the surrounding continents. Volcanic activity also occurs along rift zones like Iceland, where plates pull apart, or over hot spots such as Hawaii, where molten material rises from the mantle to Earth's crust. The majority of Earth's volcanism takes place at submarine rift zones, on the seafloor.

Notable Volcanic Eruptions

In approximately 5,700 BC, Mount Mazama, in southern Oregon, erupted violently, ejecting large amounts of ash and pumice and sending out pyroclastic flows (mixture of volcanic debris and gases). The top of the mountain collapsed, leaving a caldera about 6 mi across and 1 mi deep. This depression filled with water from rain and snow to form Crater Lake.

Date	Volcano	Est. deaths	Date	Volcano	Est. deaths
Aug. 24, 79 CE	Vesuvius, Italy	16,000[1]	Jan. 30, 1911	Taal, Philippines	1,400
1586	Kelut, Java, Indon.	10,000	June 6-8, 1912	Novarupta, AK, U.S.[5]	1
Dec. 15, 1631	Vesuvius, Italy	4,000	May 19, 1919	Kelut, Java, Indon.	5,000
Aug. 12, 1772	Papandayan, Java, Indon.	3,000	Jan. 17-21, 1951	Lamington, Papua New Guinea	3,000
June 8, 1783	Laki, Iceland	9,350	May 18, 1980	St. Helens, WA, U.S.	57
May 21, 1792	Unzen, Japan	14,500	Mar. 28, 1982	El Chichón, Mexico	1,880
Apr. 10-12, 1815	Tambora, Sumbawa, Indon.	92,000[2]	Nov. 13, 1985	Nevado del Ruiz, Colombia	23,000
Aug. 26-27, 1883	Krakatau, Indon.	36,000[3]	Aug. 21, 1986	Lake Nyos, Cameroon	1,700[6]
Apr. 24, 1902	Santa María, Guatemala	1,000[4]	June 15, 1991	Pinatubo, Luzon, Philippines	800[7]
May 8, 1902	Pelée, Martinique	28,000			

(1) Heated mud and ash engulfed Pompeii, Herculaneum, and Stabiae with debris more than 60 ft deep. About 10% of the three towns' pop. were killed. (2) Of these, about 10,000 were directly related to the eruption. Released gases and particles altered the global climate, leading to additional deaths from starvation and disease when crops failed. (3) At least 2,000 died in pyroclastic flows, Aug. 26. Collapse of volcano, Aug. 27, sank most of island, killing over 3,000. Resulting tsunamis were responsible for the majority of deaths, in Java and Sumatra. (4) An additional 3,000 deaths due to a malaria outbreak are sometimes attributed to the eruption. (5) Biggest eruption of 20th cent. by volume. (6) Caused by release of massive amount of carbon dioxide from crater lake. (7) Of these, about 500 were associated with post-eruption lahars (volcanic mudflows).

Notable Active Volcanoes

Source: Global Volcanism Program, Smithsonian Inst.; Volcano Hazards Program, U.S. Geological Survey, U.S. Dept. of the Interior

Active volcanoes display a wide range of activity, including the production of ash plumes and seismic swarms. An eruption may involve the explosive ejection of fragmental material and escape of liquid lava. Year of a volcano's last known or confirmed eruption, as of June 2023, is given. Volcanoes are listed by elevation, which does not reflect eruptive magnitude. Submarine volcanoes are not included.

Volcano (last eruption)	Location	Elev. (ft)
Africa		
Cameroon (2000)	Cameroon	13,435
Nyiragongo (2023)	Dem. Rep. of the Congo	11,385
Nyamuragira (2023)	Dem. Rep. of the Congo	10,033
Ol Doinyo Lengai (2023)	Tanzania	9,718
Fogo (2015)	Cape Verde Isls.	9,281
Piton de la Fournaise (2022)	Réunion Isl. (Fr.), Indian O.	8,635
Karthala (2007)	Comoros	7,746
Nabro (2012)	Eritrea	7,277
Antarctica		
Erebus (2023)	Ross Isl.	12,448
Melbourne (1892)	Victoria Land	8,963
Asia and Oceania		
Ararat (1840)	Turkey	16,946
Klyuchevskoy (2022)	Kamchatka, Russia	15,597
Kerinci (2020)	Sumatra, Indon.	12,467
Fuji (1708)	Honshu, Japan	12,388
Rinjani (2016)	Lombok, Indon.	12,224
Semeru (2023)	Java, Indon.	11,998
Tolbachik (2013)	Kamchatka, Russia	11,847
Koryaksky (2009)	Kamchatka, Russia	11,253
Slamet (2014)	Java, Indon.	11,247
Shiveluch (Sheveluch) (2023)	Kamchatka, Russia	10,771
Raung (2021)	Java, Indon.	10,696
Dempo (2022)	Sumatra, Indon.	10,308
Ontake (2014)	Honshu, Japan	10,062
Agung (2019)	Bali, Indon.	9,833
Merapi (2023)	Java, Indon.	9,547
Zhupanovsky (2016)	Kamchatka, Russia	9,511
Marapi (2018)	Sumatra, Indon.	9,465
Bezymianny (2023)	Kamchatka, Russia	9,455
Ruapehu (2007)	North Isl., New Zealand	9,177
Heard (2023)	Heard Isl., Australia	9,006
Changbaishan (1903)	China-North Korea	9,003
Avachinsky (2001)	Kamchatka, Russia	8,914
Papandayan (2002)	Java, Indon.	8,743
Talang (2007)	Sumatra, Indon.	8,448
Asama (1973)	Honshu, Japan	8,425
Dieng Volcanic Complex (2021)	Java, Indon.	8,415
Mayon (2023)	Luzon, Philippines	8,077
Sinabung (2021)	Sumatra, Indon.	8,071
Kanlaon (2017)	Negros, Philippines	7,989
Niigata-Yakeyama (1998)	Honshu, Japan	7,874
Kizimen (2013)	Kamchatka, Russia	7,657
Ulawun (2022)	Papua New Guinea	7,657
Tengger Caldera (2020)	Java, Indon.	7,641
Alaid (2022)	Kuril Isls., Russia	7,497
Chokai (1974)	Honshu, Japan	7,336
Galunggung (1984)	Java, Indon.	7,113
Kusatsu-Shirane (2018)	Honshu, Japan	7,103
Sorikmarapi (1986)	Sumatra Isl., Indon.	7,037
Kambalny (2017)	Kamchatka, Russia	6,942
Tangkubanparahu (2019)	Java, Indon.	6,837
Tongariro (2012)	North Isl., New Zealand	6,490
Azuma (1977)	Honshu, Japan	6,394
Kaba (2000)	Sumatra Isl., Indon.	6,365
Nasu (1963)	Honshu, Japan	6,283
Sangeang Api (2022)	Lesser Sunda Isls., Indon.	6,273
Bagana (2023)	Papua New Guinea	6,086
Karkar (2014)	Papua New Guinea	6,033
Chachadake (Tiatia) (1981)	Kunashir Isl., Japan-admin. by Russia	5,978
Bandai (1888)	Honshu, Japan	5,958
Manam (2023)	Papua New Guinea	5,928
Gorely (2010)	Kamchatka, Russia	5,902
Karangetang (Api Siau) (2023)	Siau Isl., Indon.	5,896
Kuju (1996)	Kyushu, Japan	5,876
Soputan (2020)	Sulawesi, Indon.	5,856
Chikurachki (2022)	Kuril Isls., Russia	5,843
Kelut (2014)	Java, Indon.	5,679
Adatara (1996)	Honshu, Japan	5,669
Batur (2000)	Bali, Indon.	5,633
Gamalama (2018)	Ternate, Indon.	5,627
Lewotobi (2003)	Flores Isl., Indon.	5,587
Kirishima (2018)	Kyushu, Japan	5,577
Egon (2008)	Flores, Indon.	5,449
Gamkonora (2007)	Halmahera, Indon.	5,364
Aso (2020)	Kyushu, Japan	5,223
Lokon-Empung (2015)	Sulawesi, Indon.	5,184
Bulusan (2022)	Luzon, Philippines	5,036
Karymsky (2022)	Kamchatka, Russia	4,964
Akan (2008)	Hokkaido, Japan	4,918
Pinatubo (2021)	Luzon, Philippines	4,875
Central America and West Indies		
Tacaná (1986)	Mexico-Guatemala	13,333
Acatenango (1972)	Guatemala	13,045
Fuego (2023)	Guatemala	12,346
Santa María (2023)	Guatemala	12,287
Irazú (1994)	Costa Rica	11,260
Turrialba (2022)	Costa Rica	10,958
Poás (2022)	Costa Rica	8,848
Pacaya (2020)	Guatemala	8,428
Santa Ana (2005)	El Salvador	7,812
San Miguel (2023)	El Salvador	6,988
Rincón de la Vieja (2023)	Costa Rica	6,286
San Cristóbal (2022)	Nicaragua	5,725
Concepción (2011)	Nicaragua	5,577
Arenal (2010)	Costa Rica	5,479
Soufrière Guadeloupe (1977)	Guadeloupe (France)	4,813
Pelée (1932)	Martinique (France)	4,573
Momotombo (2016)	Nicaragua	4,167
North America		
Pico de Orizaba (1846)	Mexico	18,255
Popocatépetl (2023)	Mexico	17,694
Rainier (1450)	Washington	14,409
Shasta (1250)	California	14,163
Wrangell (1912)	Alaska	14,035
Colima (2019)	Mexico	12,631
Hood (1866)	Oregon	11,240
Spurr (1992)	Alaska	11,070
Lassen Peak (1917)	California	10,456
Redoubt (2009)	Alaska	10,197
Iliamna (1876)	Alaska	10,016
Shishaldin (2020)	Unimak Isl., Aleutians, AK	9,373
St. Helens (2008)	Washington	8,363
Veniaminof (2021)	Alaska	8,225
Pavlof (2022)	Alaska	8,179
Fourpeaked (2006)	Alaska	6,906
Katmai (1912)	Alaska	6,716
Makushin (1995)	Unalaska Isl., Aleutians, AK	5,906
Great Sitkin (2023)	Great Sitkin Isl., Aleutians, AK	5,709
Cleveland (2020)	Chuginadak Isl., Aleutians, AK	5,676
South America		
Llullaillaco (1877)	Chile-Argentina	22,110
San Pedro-San Pablo (1960)	Chile	20,151
Guallatiri (1960)	Chile	19,918
San José (1960)	Chile-Argentina	19,915
Sabancaya (2023)	Peru	19,554
Cotopaxi (2023)	Ecuador	19,393
El Misti (1985)	Peru	19,101
Ubinas (2019)	Peru	18,609
Tupungatito (1987)	Chile-Argentina	18,570
Láscar (2023)	Chile	18,346
Nevado del Huila (2012)	Colombia	17,598
Sangay (2023)	Ecuador	17,343
Nevado del Ruiz (2023)	Colombia	17,320
Irruputuncu (1995)	Chile-Bolivia	16,939
Tungurahua (2016)	Ecuador	16,480
Guagua Pichincha (2002)	Ecuador	15,696
Puracé (2022)	Colombia	15,256
Galeras (2014)	Colombia	14,029
Planchón-Peteroa (2019)	Chile	13,048
Lautaro (1979)	Chile	11,834
Reventador (2023)	Ecuador	11,686
Nevados de Chillán (2022)	Chile	10,433
Llaima (2009)	Chile	10,253
Europe		
Etna (2023)	Italy	11,014
Vesuvius (1944)	Italy	4,203
Stromboli (2023)	Italy	3,031
Mid-Atlantic		
La Palma (2021)	Canary Isls. (Spain)	7,959
Beerenberg (1985)	Jan Mayen (Norway)	7,208
Bardarbunga (2015)	Iceland	6,562
Grímsvötn (2011)	Iceland	5,640
Eyjafjallajökull (2010)	Iceland	5,417
Hekla (2000)	Iceland	4,888
Mid-Pacific		
Mauna Loa (2022)	Hawaii, HI	13,681
Haleakala (1750)	Maui, HI	10,023
Kilauea (2023)	Hawaii, HI	4,009

Mountains
North America

Source: U.S. Geological Survey, U.S. Dept. of the Interior; National Geodetic Survey, NOAA, U.S. Dept. of Commerce; Natural Resources Canada. Survey dates and elevation sources may differ.

Peak, state/prov., country	Height (ft)	Peak, state/prov., country	Height (ft)	Peak, state/prov., country	Height (ft)
Denali (fmr. McKinley), AK	20,308	La Malinche (Matlalcuéyetl),		Wilson, CO	14,246
Logan, Yukon, Canada	19,551	Mexico	14,636	Cameron, CO	14,238
Pico de Orizaba, Mexico	18,619	Hunter, AK	14,573	Shavano, CO	14,231
St. Elias, AK-YT, U.S.-Can.	18,009	Browne Tower, AK	14,530	Princeton, CO	14,204
Popocatépetl, Mexico	17,802	Whitney, CA	14,505	Belford, CO	14,203
Foraker, AK	17,400	Alverstone, AK-YT, U.S.-Can.	14,500	Yale, CO	14,200
Iztaccíhuatl, Mexico	17,159	University Peak, AK	14,470	Crestone Needle, CO	14,197
Lucania, YT, Canada	17,146	Elbert, CO	14,440	Bross, CO	14,172
King Peak, YT, Canada	16,972	Massive, CO	14,421	Kit Carson, CO	14,165
Steele, YT, Canada	16,624	Harvard, CO	14,421	Point Success, WA	14,164
Bona, AK	16,500	Rainier, WA	14,410	Shasta, CA	14,163
Blackburn, AK	16,390	Williamson, CA	14,376	Wrangell, AK	14,163
Sanford, AK	16,237	Blanca Peak, CO	14,345	Maroon Peak, CO	14,163
South Buttress, AK	15,885	La Plata Peak, CO	14,336	Tabeguache, CO	14,162
Wood, YT, Canada	15,873	Uncompahgre Peak, CO	14,321	Oxford, CO	14,160
Vancouver, AK-YT, U.S.-Can.	15,699	Crestone Peak, CO	14,294	El Diente Peak, CO	14,159
Churchill, AK	15,638	Lincoln, CO	14,293	Sill, CA	14,159
Nevado de Toluca (Xinantécatl),		Castle Peak, CO	14,279	Democrat, CO	14,155
Mexico	15,354	Grays Peak, CO	14,278	Sneffels, CO	14,150
Fairweather, AK-BC, U.S.-Can.	15,299	Antero, CO	14,276	Capitol Peak, CO	14,130
Macaulay, YT, Canada	15,299	Torreys Peak, CO	14,275	Liberty Cap, WA	14,118
Slaggard, YT, Canada	15,299	Quandary Peak, CO	14,271	Pikes Peak, CO	14,115
Hubbard, AK-YT, U.S.-Can.	15,016	Evans, CO	14,265	Snowmass, CO	14,099
Bear, AK	14,831	Longs Peak, CO	14,259	Russell, CA	14,094
Walsh, YT, Canada	14,780	McArthur, YT, Canada	14,253	Eolus, CO	14,083
East Buttress, AK	14,730	White Mountain Peak, CA	14,252	Windom, CO	14,082
		North Palisade, CA	14,248	Challenger Point, CO	14,081

Note: The highest point in the West Indies is Pico Duarte (10,417 ft), in the Dominican Republic.

Other Notable U.S. Mountains

Peak, state	Height (ft)	Peak, state	Height (ft)	Peak, state	Height (ft)
Gannett, WY	13,810	Adams, WA	12,281	Mitchell, NC	6,683
Grand Teton, WY	13,775	San Gorgonio, CA	11,503	Clingmans Dome, NC-TN	6,644
Kings, UT	13,518	Hood, OR	11,247	Washington, NH	6,289
Cloud, WY	13,171	Cleveland, MT	10,466	Rogers, VA	5,729
Wheeler, NM	13,167	Lassen, CA	10,461	Marcy, NY	5,343
Boundary, NV	13,146	Granite, CA	10,325	Katahdin, ME	5,269
Granite, MT	12,807	Guadalupe, TX	8,751	Spruce Knob, WV	4,863
Borah, ID	12,668	Olympus, WA	7,973	Mansfield, VT	4,395
Humphreys, AZ	12,637	Harney, SD	7,244	Black Mountain, KY	4,139

South America

Peak, country	Height (ft)	Peak, country	Height (ft)	Peak, country	Height (ft)
Aconcagua, Argentina	22,835	Coropuna, Peru	21,083	Solo, Argentina	20,492
Ojos del Salado, Arg.-Chile	22,569	Laudo, Argentina	20,997	Polleras, Argentina	20,456
Bonete, Argentina	22,546	Ancohuma, Bolivia	20,958	Pular, Chile	20,423
Tupungato, Argentina-Chile	22,310	Ausangate, Peru	20,945	Chani, Argentina	20,341
Pissis, Argentina	22,241	Toro, Argentina-Chile	20,932	Aucanquilcha, Chile	20,295
Mercedario, Argentina	22,211	Illampu, Bolivia	20,873	Juncal, Argentina-Chile	20,276
Huascarán, Peru	22,205	Tres Cruces, Argentina-Chile	20,853	Negro, Argentina	20,184
Llullaillaco, Argentina-Chile	22,110	Huandoy, Peru	20,852	Quela, Argentina	20,128
El Libertador, Argentina	22,047	Parinacota, Bolivia-Chile	20,768	Condoriri, Bolivia	20,095
Cachi, Argentina	22,047	Tortolas, Argentina-Chile	20,745	Palermo, Argentina	20,079
Yerupajá, Peru	21,765	Ampato, Peru	20,702	Solimana, Peru	20,068
Incahuasi, Argentina-Chile	21,720	El Condor, Argentina	20,669	San Juan, Argentina-Chile	20,049
Galan, Argentina	21,654	Salcantay, Peru	20,574	Sierra Nevada, Argentina-Chile	20,023
Nevado Sajama, Bolivia	21,463	Chimborazo, Ecuador	20,564	Antofalla, Argentina	20,013
El Muerto, Argentina-Chile	21,457	Huancarhuas, Peru	20,531	Marmolejo, Argentina-Chile	20,013
Nacimiento, Argentina	21,302	Famatina, Argentina	20,505	Chachani, Peru	19,931
Illimani, Bolivia	21,201	Pumasillo, Peru	20,492		

Africa

Peak, country	Height (ft)	Peak, country	Height (ft)	Peak, country	Height (ft)
Kilimanjaro, Tanzania	19,341	Karisimbi, Congo-Rwanda	14,787	Guna, Ethiopia	13,881
Kenya, Kenya	17,057	Tullu Dimtu, Ethiopia	14,360	Gughe, Ethiopia	13,780
Margherita Pk., Uganda-Congo	16,765	Elgon, Kenya-Uganda	14,178	Jebel Toubkal, Morocco	13,665
Meru, Tanzania	14,977	Batu, Ethiopia	14,131	Cameroon, Cameroon	13,435
Ras Dashen, Ethiopia	14,872				

Australia, New Zealand, SE Asian Islands

Peak, country	Height (ft)	Peak, country	Height (ft)	Peak, country	Height (ft)
Jaya, New Guinea, Indon.	16,024	Wilhelm, Papua New Guinea	14,793	Aoraki/Cook, New Zealand	12,218
Trikora, New Guinea, Indon.	15,585	Kinabalu, Malaysia	13,436	Semeru, Java, Indon.	12,060
Mandala, New Guinea, Indon.	15,420	Kerinci, Sumatra, Indon.	12,467	Kosciusko, Australia	7,313

Height of Mount Everest

Mt. Everest, the world's highest mountain, was considered 29,002 ft when Edmund Hillary and Tenzing Norgay became the first to scale it, in 1953. In 1954, the Surveyor General of the Republic of India set the height at 29,028 ft, plus or minus 10 ft because of snow. In 1999, a team of climbers sponsored by Boston's Museum of Science and the National Geographic Society measured the height at the summit using satellite-based technology. The new measurement, of 29,035 ft, was accepted by other authorities, including the U.S. National Imagery and Mapping Agency, but not by Nepal. Government surveyors from Nepal and China, in 2019 and 2020, respectively, ascended Everest in order to determine a new official height. They jointly announced Everest's height as 29,031.693 ft (8,848.86 m) in Dec 2020.

Climbers typically ascend Everest on its north (Tibet) or south face (Nepal). By the end of the 2022 climbing season, which runs from April through May, a total of about 6,338 different climbers had made successful ascents; around 316 climbers had died, among them 16 Sherpas killed in 2014 when falling ice set off an avalanche. A 7.8 magnitude earthquake hit Nepal Apr. 25, 2015, triggering avalanches that swept through Everest Base Camp on the south side, killing 19. The 2015 season was subsequently canceled, making it the first year since 1974 that no one reached the top. The 2019 climbing season included 11 deaths, raising concerns about overcrowding and the number of permits issued to inexperienced climbers. The COVID-19 pandemic forced the closure of the 2020 climbing season. Lax procedures and poor communication led to a COVID-19 outbreak in spring 2021 at Everest Base Camp in Nepal. Nepal issued a record 478 permits for climbing parties in 2023.

Europe

Peak, country	Height (ft)
Alps	
Mont Blanc, France-Italy	15,774
Dufourspitze (highest of Monte Rosa group), Switzerland	15,203
Dom, Switzerland	14,911
Liskamm, It.-Switzerland	14,852
Weisshorn, Switzerland	14,780
Taschhorn, Switzerland	14,733
Matterhorn, It.-Switzerland	14,692
Dent Blanche, Switzerland	14,293
Nadelhorn, Switzerland	14,196
Grand Combin, Switzerland	14,154
Lenzspitze, Switzerland	14,088
Finsteraarhorn, Switzerland	14,022
Castor, Switzerland	13,865
Zinalrothorn, Switzerland	13,849
Hohberghorn, Switzerland	13,842
Alphubel, Switzerland	13,799
Rimpfischhorn, Switzerland	13,776
Aletschorn, Switzerland	13,763
Strahlhorn, Switzerland	13,747
Dent D'Herens, Switzerland	13,686
Breithorn, It.-Switzerland	13,665
Bishorn, Switzerland	13,645
Jungfrau, Switzerland	13,642
Ecrins, France	13,461
Monch, Switzerland	13,448
Pollux, Switzerland	13,422
Schreckhorn, Switzerland	13,379
Ober Gabelhorn, Switzerland	13,330
Gran Paradiso, Italy	13,323
Bernina, It.-Switzerland	13,284
Fiescherhorn, Switzerland	13,283
Grunhorn, Switzerland	13,266
Lauteraarhorn, Switzerland	13,261
Durrenhorn, Switzerland	13,238
Allalinhorn, Switzerland	13,213
Weissmies, Switzerland	13,199
Lagginhorn, Switzerland	13,156
Zupo, Switzerland	13,120
Fletschhorn, Switzerland	13,110
Adlerhorn, Switzerland	13,081
Gletscherhorn, Switzerland	13,068
Schalihorn, Switzerland	13,040
Scerscen, Switzerland	13,028
Eiger, Switzerland	13,025
Jagerhorn, Switzerland	13,024
Rottalhorn, Switzerland	13,022
Pyrenees	
Aneto, Spain	11,168
Posets, Spain	11,073
Perdido, Spain	11,007
Vignemale, France-Spain	10,820
Long, Spain	10,479
Estats, Spain	10,304
Montcalm, Spain	10,105
Caucasus (Europe-Asia)	
Elbrus, Russia	18,481
Shkhara, Georgia	17,064
Dykh Tau, Russia	17,054
Kashtan Tau, Russia	16,877
Janqi, Georgia	16,565
Kazbek, Georgia	16,558

Asia (Mainland)

Peak, country/region	Height (ft)
Everest, Nepal-Tibet	29,032
K2 (Godwin Austen), Kashmir	28,251
Kanchenjunga, India-Nepal	28,169
Lhotse I (Everest), Nepal-Tibet	27,923
Makalu I, Nepal-Tibet	27,824
Lhotse II (Everest), Nepal-Tibet	27,560
Dhaulagiri, Nepal	26,795
Manaslu I, Nepal	26,781
Cho Oyu, Nepal-Tibet	26,750
Nanga Parbat, Kashmir	26,660
Annapurna I, Nepal	26,545
Annapurna II, Nepal	26,545
Gasherbrum, Kashmir	26,470
Broad, Kashmir	26,400
Gosainthan, Nepal-Tibet	26,287
Gyachung Kang, Nepal-Tibet	25,910
Disteghil Sar, Kashmir	25,868
Himalchuli, Nepal	25,801
Nuptse (Everest), Nepal-Tibet	25,726
Masherbrum, Kashmir	25,660
Nanda Devi, India	25,645
Rakaposhi, Kashmir	25,550
Kamet, India-Tibet	25,447
Namcha Barwa, Tibet	25,445
Gurla Mandhata, Tibet	25,355
Kungur, Xinjiang, China	25,325
Tirich Mir, Pakistan	25,230
Makalu II, Nepal-Tibet	25,120
Minya Konka, China	24,900
Annapurna III, Nepal	24,786
Kula Gangri, Bhutan-Tibet	24,784
Changtse (Everest), Nepal-Tibet	24,780
Muztagh Ata, Xinjiang, China	24,757
Skyang Kangri, Kashmir	24,750
Annapurna IV, Nepal	24,688
Ismail Samani Peak, Tajikistan	24,590
Noshaq, Afghanistan	24,580
Jongsong Peak, India-Nepal-Tibet	24,472
Jengish Chokusu, Xinjiang, China-Kyrgyzstan	24,406
Sia Kangri, Kashmir	24,350
Haramosh Peak, Pakistan	24,270
Istoro Nal, Pakistan	24,240
Kirat Chuli, India-Nepal	24,165
Chomo Lhari, Bhutan-Tibet	24,040
Chamlang, Nepal	24,012
Kabru, India-Nepal	24,002
Alung Gangri, Tibet	24,000
Baltoro Kangri, Kashmir	23,990
Mana, India	23,860
Baruntse, Nepal	23,688
Nepal Peak, India-Nepal	23,500
Amne Machin, China	23,490
Gauri Sankar, Nepal-Tibet	23,440
Badrinath, India	23,420
Nunkun, Kashmir	23,410
Lenin Peak, Tajikistan	23,406
Pyramid, India-Nepal	23,400
Api, Nepal	23,399
Pauhunri, India-Tibet	23,385
Trisul, India	23,360
Kangto, India-Tibet	23,260
Nyenchen Thanglha, Tibet	23,255
Trisuli, India	23,210
Pumori, Nepal-Tibet	23,190
Dunagiri, India	23,184
Lombo Kangra, Tibet	23,165
Saipal, Nepal	23,100
Macha Pucchare, Nepal	22,958
Khan Tengri, Kazakhstan-Kyrgyzstan-Xinjiang, China	22,949
Ulugh Muztagh, Xinjiang, China-Tibet	22,877
Numbar, Nepal	22,817
Kanjiroba, Nepal	22,580
Ama Dablam, Nepal	22,350
Cho Polu, Nepal	22,093
Lingtren, Nepal-Tibet	21,972
Khumbutse, Nepal-Tibet	21,785
Hlako Gangri, Tibet	21,266

Antarctica

Peak	Height (ft)
Vinson Massif	16,066
Tyree	15,919
Shinn	15,750
Gardner	15,375
Epperly	15,100
Kirkpatrick	14,855
Elizabeth	14,698
Markham	14,290
Bell	14,117
Mackellar	14,098
Anderson	13,957
Bentley	13,934
Kaplan	13,878
Andrew Jackson	13,750
Sidley	13,720
Ostenso	13,710
Minto	13,668
Miller	13,650
Long Gables	13,620
Dickerson	13,517
Giovinetto	13,412
Wade	13,400
Fisher	13,386
Fridtjof Nansen	13,350
Wexler	13,202
Lister	13,200
Shear	13,100
Odishaw	13,008
Donaldson	12,894
Ray	12,808
Sellery	12,779
Waterman	12,730
Anne	12,703
Press	12,566
Falla	12,549
Rucker	12,520
Goldthwait	12,510
Morris	12,500
Erebus	12,448

Notable Islands and Their Areas

Figures are for total area in square miles. Boldface figures in parentheses show rank among the world's 10 largest individual islands. Only the largest islands in an island group are shown. Table does not include islands smaller than 10 sq mi in area. Canada's Manitoulin Island (1,068 sq mi), in Lake Huron, is the world's largest island in a freshwater lake.

Antarctica

Adelaide	1,400
Alexander	16,700
Berkner	18,500
Roosevelt	2,900

Arctic Ocean

Amund Ringnes, NU, Can.	2,029
Axel Heiberg, NU, Can.	16,671
Baffin, NU, Can. (5).	195,928
Banks, NT, Can.	27,038
Bathurst, NU, Can.	6,194
Bolshoy Lyakhovsky, Russia	1,776
Borden, NT-NU, Can.	1,079
Bylot, NU, Can.	4,273
Coats, NU, Can.	2,123
Cornwallis, NU, Can.	2,701
Devon, NU, Can.	21,331
Disko, Greenland, Denmark	3,312
Ellef Ringnes, NU, Can.	4,361
Ellesmere, NU, Can. (10)	75,767
Faddayevskiy, Russia.	1,930
Franz Josef Land, Russia	8,000
Iturup (Etorofu), Russia	2,596
King William, NU, Can.	5,062
Kotelny, Russia.	4,504
Mackenzie King, NT, Can.	1,949
Melville, NT-NU, Can.	16,274
Milne Land, Greenland, Den.	1,400
New Siberian Isls., Russia	14,500
Novaya Zemlya, Russia (2 isls.)	31,730
Prince Charles, NT, Can.	3,676
Prince Patrick, NT, Can.	6,119
Prince of Wales, NU, Can.	12,872
Severnaya Zemlya, Russia (tot. group)	14,175
Bol'shevik	4,368
Komsomolets	3,477
Oktyabr'skoy Revolyutsii.	5,471
Somerset, NU, Can.	9,570
Southampton, NU, Can.	15,913
Svalbard, Norway (tot. group).	23,561
Nordaustlandet	5,576
Spitsbergen	14,546
Traill, Greenland, Denmark	1,300
Victoria, NT-NU, Can. (8)	83,897
Wrangel, Russia	2,937

Atlantic Ocean

Anticosti, QC, Can.	3,066
Ascension, UK	35
Azores, Portugal (tot. group)	868
Faial	67
San Miguel	291
Bahama Isls. (tot. group)	5,382
Andros	2,300
Bermuda Isls., UK (tot. group)	21
Bioko Isl., Equatorial Guinea	785
Block Island, RI, U.S.	21
Cabo Verde	1,557
Canary Isls., Spain (tot. group).	2,807
Fuerteventura	688
Gran Canaria	592
Tenerife	795
Cape Breton, NS, Can.	3,981
Caviana, Pará, Brazil	1,918
Channel Isls., UK (tot. group)	75
Guernsey	24
Jersey	45
Falkland Isls., UK (tot. group)	4,700
East Falkland	2,550
West Falkland	1,750
Faroe Isls., Denmark	538
Great Britain, UK (9)	80,823
Greenland, Denmark (1)	836,330
Gurupá, Pará, Brazil	1,878
Hebrides, Scotland, UK	2,744
Iceland	39,958
Ireland, Ireland-UK	32,589
Isle of Man, UK	221
Isle of Wight, England, UK	147
Long Island, NY, U.S.	1,320
Madeira Isls., Portugal	306
Marajó, Brazil	15,444
Martha's Vineyard, MA, U.S.	89

Atlantic Ocean

Mount Desert, ME, U.S.	104
Nantucket, MA, U.S.	45
Newfoundland, Canada	42,031
Orkney Isls., Scotland, UK	383
Prince Edward Isl. (main), Can.	2,170
St. Helena, UK	47
Shetland Isls., Scotland, UK	555
Skye, Scotland, UK.	647
South Georgia, UK	1,450
Tierra del Fuego, Chile-Arg.	18,800
Tristan da Cunha, UK.	38

Baltic Sea

Aland Isls., Finland	610
Bornholm, Denmark	227
Funen, Denmark	1,154
Gotland, Sweden	1,159
Zealand, Denmark	2,722

Caribbean Sea

Antigua	108
Aruba, Netherlands.	69
Barbados	166
Cayman Isls., UK (tot. group)	102
Cuba	40,285
Isle of Youth	934
Curaçao, Netherlands.	171
Dominica	290
Guadeloupe, France.	687
Hispaniola (Haiti and Dominican Rep.)	29,389
Jamaica	4,244
Martinique, France	436
Montserrat, UK	39
Nevis	36
Puerto Rico, U.S.	3,425
St. Kitts	65
St. Lucia	238
St. Vincent	133
Tobago	116
Trinidad	1,864
Virgin Isls., UK	59
Virgin Isls., U.S.	134

East Indies

Bali, Indonesia	2,171
Bangka, Indonesia	4,375
Borneo, Indonesia-Malaysia-Brunei (3)	290,321
Bougainville, Papua New Guinea	3,880
Buru, Indonesia	3,670
Flores, Indonesia	5,500
Halmahera, Indonesia	6,865
Java (Jawa), Indonesia.	48,900
Madura, Indonesia	2,113
Moluccas, Indonesia.	32,307
New Britain, PNG	14,093
New Guinea, Indon.-PNG (2)	303,381
New Ireland, PNG.	3,707
Seram, Indonesia	6,621
Sulawesi (Celebes), Indonesia.	69,000
Sumatra, Indonesia (6).	182,543
Sumba, Indonesia.	4,306
Sumbawa, Indonesia	5,965
Timor, Indon.–Timor-Leste	13,094
Yos Sudarsa, Indonesia	4,500

Indian Ocean

Andaman Isls., India	2,500
Kerguelen, France	2,247
Madagascar (4)	226,917
Mauritius	720
Pemba, Tanzania	380
Réunion, France	970
Seychelles	176
Sri Lanka	25,332
Zanzibar, Tanzania.	640

Mediterranean Sea

Balearic Isls., Spain	1,927
Corfu, Greece	229
Corsica, France	3,369
Crete, Greece	3,189
Cyprus	3,572
Elba, Italy	86
Euboea, Greece	1,411

Mediterranean Sea

Malta.	95
Rhodes, Greece	540
Sardinia, Italy	9,301
Sicily, Italy.	9,926

Pacific Ocean

Admiralty, AK, U.S.	1,709
Aleutian Isls., AK, U.S. (tot. group)	6,912
Adak	275
Attu	350
Tanaga	195
Umnak	686
Unalaska.	1,051
Unimak	1,571
Baranof, AK, U.S.	1,636
Chichagof, AK, U.S.	2,062
Chiloe, Chile	3,241
Easter Isl. (Rapa Nui), Chile	63
Fiji (tot. group)	7,056
Vanua Levu	2,242
Viti Levu	4,109
Galapagos Isls., Ecuador	3,043
Graham Isl., BC, Can.	2,456
Guadalcanal, Solomon Isls.	2,180
Guam, U.S.	210
Hainan, China.	13,000
Hawaiian Isls., HI, U.S. (tot. group)	6,428
Hawaii.	4,028
Oahu.	597
Hong Kong, China	31
Hoste, Chile	1,590
Japan (tot. group)	145,937
Hokkaido.	32,210
Honshu (7)	89,280
Kyushu	16,305
Okinawa	881
Shikoku.	7,260
Kangaroo, South Australia	1,705
Kiritimati (Christmas), Kiribati	150
Kodiak, AK, U.S.	3,485
Kupreanof, AK, U.S.	1,084
Marquesas Isls., France	492
Marshall Islands	70
Melville, Northern Terr., Australia	2,234
Micronesia	271
New Caledonia, France	6,530
New Zealand (tot. group)	103,362
Chatham Isls.	372
North.	44,075
South	58,076
Stewart	649
Northern Mariana Isls., U.S.	179
Nunivak, AK, U.S.	1,600
Palau	188
Philippines (tot. group)	115,831
Leyte.	2,787
Luzon	40,680
Mindanao	36,775
Mindoro.	3,690
Negros	4,907
Palawan	4,554
Panay	4,446
Samar.	5,050
Prince of Wales, AK, U.S.	2,770
Revillagigedo, AK, U.S.	1,134
Riesco, Chile	1,973
St. Lawrence, AK, U.S.	1,780
Sakhalin, Russia.	29,500
Samoa Isls. (tot. group)	1,177
American Samoa, U.S.	77
Savaii, Samoa	659
Tutuila, U.S.	55
Upolu, Samoa	432
Santa Catalina, CA, U.S.	75
Santa Ines, Chile	1,407
Tahiti, France	402
Taiwan (tot. group)	13,892
Jinmen Dao (Quemoy)	56
Tasmania, Australia	26,178
Tonga	288
Vancouver Isl., BC, Can.	12,079
Vanuatu	4,707
Wellington, Chile	2,549

Persian Gulf

Bahrain	295

Notable Deserts of the World

Deserts are defined as regions of the Earth receiving less than 10 in. of precipitation annually, usually in combination with an evaporation rate exceeding precipitation.

In addition to areas listed below, the continent of Antarctica, with an area of about 5.48 mil sq mi (of which 110,039 sq mi is ice free), is generally considered a desert. Average annual precipitation for the continent as a whole is 2-6 in., with most precipitation falling along the coast; there is little evaporation.

Arabian, 899,618 sq mi, spanning almost all of Arabian Peninsula

Atacama, 600-mi-long area rich in nitrate and copper deposits in northern Chile

Chihuahuan, 139,769 sq mi in TX, NM, AZ, and Mexico

Dasht-e Kavir, approx. 500 mi long by 200 mi wide in north-central Iran

Dasht-e Lut, approx. 300 mi long by 200 mi wide in south-central Iran

Death Valley, 3,300 sq mi in CA and NV

Eastern (Arabian), 86,000 sq mi in Egypt between the Nile R. and Red Sea, extending south into Sudan

Gibson, 60,232 sq mi in the interior of western Australia

Gobi, 500,002 sq mi in Mongolia and China

Great Sandy, 103,186 sq mi in western Australia

Great Victoria, 134,653 sq mi in southwestern Australia

Kalahari, 347,492 sq mi in southern Africa

Karakum, 135,136 sq mi in Turkmenistan

Kyzyl Kum, 115,000 sq mi in Kazakhstan and Uzbekistan

Libyan, 425,000 sq mi in the Sahara, extending from Libya through southwestern Egypt into Sudan

Mojave, 15,000 sq mi in southern CA

Namib, long narrow area (varies 30-100 mi wide) extending 800 mi along SW coast of Africa

Nubian, 157,000 sq mi in the Sahara in northeastern Sudan

Painted Desert, section of high plateau in northern AZ extending 200 mi southeast from Grand Canyon

Patagonia, 259,847 sq mi in southern Argentina

Rub al-Khali (Empty Quarter), 250,000 sq mi in the S Arabian Peninsula

Sahara, 3,552,140 sq mi in N Africa, extending west to the Atlantic. Largest desert in the world

Sonoran, 120,000 sq mi in southwestern AZ and southeastern CA extending into NW Mexico

Syrian, 193,051 sq mi over much of northern Saudi Arabia, eastern Jordan, southern Syria, and western Iraq

Taklamakan, 130,000 sq mi in Xinjiang Prov., China

Tanami, 71,236 sq mi in northern Australia

Thar (Great Indian), 100,000-sq-mi area extending 400 mi along India-Pakistan border

Areas and Average Depths of Oceans, Seas, and Gulfs

Four major bodies of water were historically recognized: the Pacific, Atlantic, Indian, and Arctic Oceans. The Atlantic and Pacific Oceans are considered divided at the equator into N and S. The Arctic Ocean is the name for waters north of the continental landmasses in the region of the Arctic Circle. The International Hydrographic Organization (IHO) delimited a fifth world ocean—the Southern (Antarctic)—in 2000. The Southern Ocean extends from the coast of Antarctica north to 60°S latitude, encompassing portions of the Atlantic, Indian, and Pacific Oceans, although its boundaries have yet to be agreed on by all IHO member countries. A Woods Hole Oceanographic Institution study published in 2010 calculated a mean depth of 12,081 ft for the world's oceans.

Body of water	Area (sq mi)	Avg. depth (ft)	Body of water	Area (sq mi)	Avg. depth (ft)
Pacific Ocean	60,060,893	14,040	Sea of Japan	391,100	5,468
Atlantic Ocean	29,637,974	11,810	Hudson Bay	281,900	305
Indian Ocean	26,469,620	12,800	East China Sea	256,600	620
Southern Ocean	7,848,299	14,450	Andaman Sea	218,100	3,667
Arctic Ocean	5,427,052	4,300	Black Sea	196,100	3,906
South China Sea	1,388,385	4,802	Red Sea	174,900	1,764
Caribbean Sea	1,094,214	8,448	North Sea	164,900	308
Bering Sea	972,977	4,893	Baltic Sea	147,500	180
Mediterranean Sea	953,286	4,926	Yellow Sea	113,500	121
Gulf of Mexico	582,100	5,297	Persian Gulf	88,800	328
Sea of Okhotsk	537,500	3,192	Gulf of California	59,100	2,375

Principal Ocean Depths

Source: Intl. Hydrographic Org. (IHO); Intergovernmental Oceanographic Commission (IOC) of UNESCO; National Geospatial-Intelligence Agency, U.S. Dept. of Defense

Body of water	Location (lat.)	(long.)	Depth (meters)	(fathoms)	(feet)
Pacific Ocean					
Mariana Trench	11°22′ N	142°36′ E	10,994	6,012	36,069
Tonga Trench	23°16′ S	174°44′ W	10,800	5,906	35,433
Philippine Trench	10°38′ N	126°36′ E	10,057	5,499	32,995
Kermadec Trench	31°53′ S	177°21′ W	10,047	5,494	32,963
Bonin Trench	24°30′ N	143°24′ E	9,994	5,464	32,788
Kuril Trench	44°15′ N	150°34′ E	9,750	5,331	31,988
Izu Trench	31°05′ N	142°10′ E	9,695	5,301	31,808
New Britain Trench	06°19′ S	153°45′ E	8,940	4,888	29,331
Yap Trench	08°33′ N	138°02′ E	8,527	4,663	27,976
Japan Trench	36°08′ N	142°43′ E	8,412	4,600	27,599
Peru-Chile Trench	23°18′ S	71°14′ W	8,064	4,409	26,457
Palau Trench	07°52′ N	134°56′ E	8,054	4,404	26,424
Aleutian Trench	50°51′ N	177°11′ E	7,679	4,199	25,194
New Hebrides Trench	20°36′ S	168°37′ E	7,570	4,139	24,836
North Ryukyu Trench	24°00′ N	126°48′ E	7,181	3,927	23,560
Middle America Trench	14°02′ N	93°39′ W	6,662	3,643	21,857
Atlantic Ocean					
Puerto Rico Trench	19°55′ N	65°27′ W	8,605	4,705	28,232
South Sandwich Trench	55°42′ S	25°56′ W	8,325	4,552	27,313
Romanche Gap	0°13′ S	18°26′ W	7,728	4,226	25,354
Cayman Trench	19°12′ N	80°00′ W	7,535	4,120	24,721
Brazil Basin	09°10′ S	23°02′ W	6,119	3,346	20,076
Indian Ocean					
Java Trench	10°19′ N	109°58′ E	7,125	3,896	23,376
Ob′ Trench	09°45′ S	67°18′ E	6,874	3,759	22,553
Diamantina Trench	35°50′ S	105°14′ E	6,602	3,610	21,660
Vema Trench	09°08′ S	67°15′ E	6,402	3,501	21,004
Agulhas Basin	45°20′ S	26°50′ E	6,195	3,387	20,325
Arctic Ocean					
Eurasia Basin	82°23′ N	19°31′ E	5,450	2,980	17,881
Mediterranean Sea					
Ionian Basin	36°32′ N	21°06′ E	5,150	2,816	16,896

Note: Greater depths have been reported in some areas but have not been officially confirmed by research vessels.

Major World Rivers

North American rivers are listed in a separate table.

River	Source or upper limit of length	Outflow	Length (mi)
Africa			
Chari	Bamingui-Bangoran region, Central African Republic	Lake Chad	650
Congo	Junction of Lualaba and Luvua Rivers, Dem. Rep. of Congo	Atlantic Ocean	2,720
Cubango (fmr. Okavango)	Central Angola	Okavango Delta	1,000
Gambia	Fouta Djallon Highlands, Guinea	Atlantic Ocean	700
Kasai	Central Angola	Congo River	1,100
Limpopo	Junction of Marico and Ngotwane Rivers, South Africa	Indian Ocean	1,100
Lualaba	Southeastern Dem. Rep. of Congo	Congo River	1,100
Niger	Fouta Djallon Highlands, Guinea	Gulf of Guinea	2,600
Nile	Luvironza River, Burundi	Mediterranean Sea	4,132
Orange	Maluti Mountains, northern Lesotho	Atlantic Ocean	1,300
Sénégal	Junction of Bafing and Bakoy Rivers, Mali	Atlantic Ocean	1,000
Ubangi	Junction of Uele and Bomu Rivers, Dem. Rep. of Congo	Congo River	700
Zambezi	Northwestern Zambia	Indian Ocean	1,700
Asia			
Amu Darya	Junction of Vakhsh and Panj Rivers, Afghanistan-Tajikistan	Aral Sea	1,660
Amur	Junction of Shilka and Argun Rivers, China-Russia	Tartar Strait	1,780
Angara	Lake Baikal, Russia	Yenisei River	1,150
Ayeyarwady (fmr. Irrawaddy)	Junction of Mali and Nmai Rivers, Myanmar	Andaman Sea	1,000
Brahmaputra	Kailas Range, Himalayas, southwestern Tibet	Bay of Bengal	1,800
Chang-Jiang	Tibetan Plateau, southwestern Qinghai, China	East China Sea	3,450
Euphrates	Junction of Kara (Sarasu) and Murat Rivers, Turkey	Shatt al-Arab	1,700
Ganges	Gangotri glacier, Himalayas, India	Bay of Bengal	1,560
Godavari	Western Ghats, Maharashtra, India	Bay of Bengal	900
Hsi (see Xi He)			
Huang-He	Kunlun Mountains, Qinghai, China	Yellow Sea	3,000
Indus	Kailas Range, Himalayas, Tibet	Arabian Sea	1,900
Irtysh	Kazakhstan-Russia	Ob River	2,650
Jordan	Junction of Dan, Banias, and Hazbani streams, Israel	Dead Sea	200
Kolyma	Kolyma and Cherskogo Ranges, Russia	Arctic Ocean	1,500
Krishna	Western Ghats, Maharashtra, India	Bay of Bengal	800
Kura	Northeastern Turkey	Caspian Sea	950
Lena	Western Baikal Range, Russia	Laptev Sea	2,734
Mekong	Eastern Tibetan Plateau, China	South China Sea	2,700
Narmada	Madhya Pradesh, India	Arabian Sea	775
Ob	Junction of Biya and Katun Rivers, Russia	Gulf of Ob	2,300
Salween	Eastern Tibet, China	Gulf of Martaban	1,750
Songhua Jiang	Changbai Mountains, Jilin, China	Amur River	1,150
Sungari (see Songhua Jiang)			
Sutlej	Kailas Range, Himalayas, Tibet	Indus River	900
Syr	Junction of Naryn and Kara Darya Rivers, Uzbekistan	Aral Sea	1,380
Tarim	Junction of Kashi and Yarkant Rivers, China	Lop Nor	1,300
Tigris	Taurus Mountains, Turkey	Shatt al-Arab	1,150
Xi He	Eastern Yunnan, China	South China Sea	1,250
Yamuna	Yamnotri glacier, Uttarakhand, India	Ganges River	850
Yangtze (see Chang-Jiang)			
Yellow (see Huang-He)			
Yenisei	Kyzyl, Tuva Republic, Russia	Kara Sea	2,500
Australia			
Darling	Eastern Highlands, NE New South Wales/SE Queensland	Murray River	1,703
Murray	Australian Alps, SE New South Wales	Southern Ocean	1,558
Murrumbidgee	Australian Alps, SE New South Wales	Murray River	923
Europe			
Buh, Southern	Podolian Upland, Ukraine	Black Sea	532
Buh, Western	Western Ukraine	Vistula River	500
Danube	Brege and Brigach Rivers, Black Forest, southwestern Germany	Black Sea	1,770
Dnieper	Valdai Hills, western Russia	Black Sea	1,420
Dniester	Carpathian Mountains, Ukraine	Black Sea	850
Don	SE of Tula, Russia	Sea of Azov	1,200
Drava	Carnic Alps, northern Italy	Danube River	450
Dvina, North	Near Veliki Ustyug, Vologda, Russia	White Sea	465
Dvina, West	Valdai Hills, Russia	Gulf of Riga	635
Ebro	Cantabrian Mountains, northern Spain	Mediterranean Sea	575
Elbe	Giant Mountains, northwestern Czech Republic	North Sea	725
Garonne	Central Pyrenees, Spain	Bay of Biscay	402
Kama	Ural Mountains, N of Kuliga, Russia	Volga River	1,260
Loire	Mt. Gerbier-de-Jonc, Vivrais Mountains, France	Atlantic Ocean	630
Marne	Langres Plateau, northeastern France	Seine River	325
Meuse	Langres Plateau, northeastern France	North Sea	560
Oder	Sudetes Mountains, northeastern Czech Republic	Baltic Sea	562
Oka	S of Orël, Russia	Volga River	925
Pechora	Northern Ural Mountains, Russia	Barents Sea	1,120
Po	Cottian Alps, Piedmont, northwestern Italy	Adriatic Sea	405
Rhine	Swiss Alps	North Sea	766

River	Source or upper limit of length	Outflow	Length (mi)
Rhône	Rhône glacier, northeastern Valais, Switzerland	Mediterranean Sea	505
Seine	Langres Plateau, northern Burgundy, France	English Channel	480
Shannon	Near Cuilcagh Mountain, northwestern Cavan County, Ireland	Atlantic Ocean	240
Tagus	E of Madrid, Spain	Atlantic Ocean	585
Thames	4 headstreams in the Cotswold Hills, Gloucestershire, England, UK	North Sea	215
Tiber	Etruscan Apennines, Italy	Tyrrhenian Sea	251
Tisza	N of Rakhiv, western Ukraine	Danube River	700
Ural	Southern Ural Mountains, northeastern Bashkortostan, Russia	Caspian Sea	1,580
Vistula (Wisla)	W Beskid range, Carpathian Mountains, southwestern Poland	Gulf of Gdansk	665
Volga	Valdai Hills, Smolensk, Russia	Caspian Sea	2,290
Weser	Junction of Fulda and Werra Rivers, Germany	North Sea	273
South America			
Amazon	Junction of Ucayali and Marañón Rivers, Andes Mountains, Peru	Atlantic Ocean	4,000
Araguaía	Serra das Araras, Goiás-Mato Grosso, Brazil	Tocantins River	1,100
Beni	Cordillera Real, La Paz, Bolivia	Madeira River	1,000
Caquetá-Japura	Andes Mountains, southwestern Colombia	Amazon River	1,750
Juruá	Cerros de Canchyuaya, eastern Peru	Amazon River	1,500
Madeira	Junction of Beni and Mamoré Rivers, Bolivia	Amazon River	2,100
Magdalena	Cordillera Central, southwestern Colombia	Caribbean Sea	1,000
Negro	Southeastern Colombia	Amazon River	1,400
Orinoco	Near Mt. Delgado Chalbaud, Guiana Highlands, S Venezuela	Atlantic Ocean	1,600
Paraguay	Central Mato Grosso highlands, Brazil	Paraná River	1,584
Paraná	Junction of Paranaíba and Rio Grande Rivers, SE Brazil	Río de la Plata	2,485
Pilcomayo	E of Lake Poopó, Bolivia	Paraguay River	1,000
Purus	Andes Mountains, eastern Peru	Amazon River	2,100
Putumayo	Andes Mountains, southern Colombia	Amazon River	1,000
Río de la Plata	Estuary of Paraná and Uruguay Rivers, Argentina-Uruguay	Atlantic Ocean	170
São Francisco	Serra de Canastra, southwestern Minas Gerais, Brazil	Atlantic Ocean	1,800
Tocantins	South-central Goiás, Brazil	Para River	1,640
Ucayali	Junction of Apurímac and Urubamba Rivers, eastern Peru	Marañón River	1,000
Uruguay	Southern Brazil	Río de la Plata	1,000
Xingu	Central Mato Grosso, Brazil	Amazon River	1,230

Major Rivers in North America

River	Source or upper limit of length	Outflow	Length (mi)
Alabama	Gilmer County, GA	Mobile River	729
Albany	Lake St. Joseph, ON, Can.	James Bay	610
Allegheny	Potter County, PA.	Ohio River, Pittsburgh, PA.	325
Altamaha-Ocmulgee	Junction of Yellow and South Rivers, Newton Co., GA	Atlantic Ocean	392
Apalachicola-Chattahoochee	Towns County, GA	Gulf of Mexico	524
Arkansas	Lake County, CO	Mississippi River	1,459
Assiniboine	Eastern Saskatchewan, Can.	Red River	450
Athabasca	Columbia Icefield, AB, Can.	Lake Athabasca	765
Attawapiskat	Attawapiskat, ON, Can.	James Bay	465
Back (NT)	Contwoyto Lake, NT, Can.	Chantrey Inlet, Arctic Ocean	605
Big Black	Webster County, MS	Mississippi River	330
Brazos	Junction of Salt and Double Mountain Forks, Stonewall Co., TX	Gulf of Mexico	1,280
Canadian	Las Animas County, CO.	Arkansas River	906
Cedar (IA)	Dodge County, MN.	Iowa River	329
Cheyenne	Junction of Antelope Creek and Dry Fork, Converse Co., WY	Missouri River	290
Churchill, Labrador	Lake Ashuanipi, NL, Can.	Atlantic Ocean	532
Churchill, Manitoba	Methy Lake, SK, Can.	Hudson Bay	1,000
Cimarron	Colfax County, NM	Arkansas River	600
Colorado (AZ)	Rocky Mountain Natl. Park, CO	Gulf of California	1,450
Colorado (TX)	Dawson County, TX	Matagorda Bay	862
Columbia	Columbia Lake, BC, Can.	Pacific Ocean, Astoria, OR	1,243
Columbia, Upper	Columbia Lake, BC, Can.	Mouth of Snake River	890
Connecticut	Third Connecticut Lake, NH	Long Island Sound, CT	407
Coppermine	Lac de Gras, NT, Can.	Coronation Gulf, Arctic Ocean	525
Cumberland	Letcher County, KY	Ohio River	720
Delaware	Schoharie County, NY	Liston Point, Delaware Bay	390
Fraser	Near Mount Robson (on Continental Divide)	Strait of Georgia	851
Gila	Catron County, NM.	Colorado River	649
Green (UT-WY)	Junction of Wells and Trail Creeks, Sublette County, WY	Colorado River	730
Hudson	Henderson Lake, Essex County, NY	Upper New York Bay	306
Illinois	St. Joseph County, IN.	Mississippi River	420
James (ND-SD)	Wells County, ND	Missouri River	710
James (VA)	Junction of Jackson and Cowpasture Rivers, Botetourt Co., VA	Hampton Roads	340
Kanawha-New	Junction of North and South Forks of New River, NC	Ohio River	352
Kentucky	Junction of North and Middle Forks, Lee County, KY	Ohio River	259
Klamath	Lake Ewauna, Klamath Falls, OR.	Pacific O., Klamath, CA	250

River	Source or upper limit of length	Outflow	Length (mi)
Kootenay (Kootenai)	Rocky Mountains, BC, Can.	Columbia River	485
Koyukuk	Endicott Mountains, AK	Yukon River	470
Kuskokwim	Alaska Range	Kuskokwim Bay	724
Liard	Southern Yukon, AK	Mackenzie River	693
Little Missouri	Crook County, WY	Missouri River	560
Mackenzie	Great Slave Lake, NT, Can.	Arctic Ocean	2,635
Milk	Junction of North and South Forks, AB, Can.	Missouri River	624
Minnesota	Big Stone Lake, MN	Mississippi River	332
Mississippi	Lake Itasca, Clearwater County, MN	Gulf of Mexico	2,340
Mississippi-Missouri-Red Rock	Source of Red Rock, Beaverhead County, MT	Gulf of Mexico	3,710
Missouri	Junction of Jefferson, Madison, and Gallatin Rivers, Gallatin County, MT	Mississippi River	2,315
Missouri-Red Rock	Source of Red Rock, Beaverhead County, MT	Mississippi River	2,540
Mobile-Alabama-Coosa	Gilmer County, GA	Mobile Bay	774
Nelson	Lake Winnipeg, MB, Can.	Hudson Bay	400
Neosho	Morris County, KS	Arkansas River, OK	460
Niobrara	Niobrara County, WY	Missouri River, NE	431
North Canadian	Union County, NM	Canadian River, OK	800
North Platte	Junction of Grizzly and Little Grizzly Creeks, Jackson Co., CO	Platte River, NE	618
Ohio	Junction of Allegheny and Monongahela Rivers, Pittsburgh, PA	Mississippi River, Cairo, IL	981
Osage	East-central Kansas	Missouri River	500
Ottawa	Lake Capimitchigama, QC, Can.	St. Lawrence River	790
Ouachita	Polk County, AR	Black River	605
Peace	Junction of Finlay and Parsnip Rivers, BC, Can.	Slave River	1,195
Pearl	Neshoba County, MS	Gulf of Mexico	411
Pecos	Mora County, NM	Rio Grande	926
Pee Dee-Yadkin	Watauga County, NC	Winyah Bay	435
Pend Oreille-Clark Fork	Near Butte, MT	Columbia River	531
Platte	Junction of North Platte and South Platte Rivers, NE.	Missouri River	990
Porcupine	West-central Yukon, Can.	Yukon River, AK	569
Potomac	Garrett County, MD	Chesapeake Bay	383
Powder	Junction of South and Middle Forks, WY	Yellowstone River	375
Red (River of the South)	Curry County, NM	Atchafalaya River, LA	1,290
Red River of the North	Junction of Otter Tail and Bois de Sioux Rivers, Wilkin Co., MN	Lake Winnipeg	545
Republican	Junction of North Fork and Arikaree Rivers, NE	Kansas River	445
Rio Grande (Rio Bravo)	San Juan County, CO	Gulf of Mexico	1,900
Roanoke	Junction of North and South Forks, Montgomery Co., VA	Albemarle Sound	380
Rock (IL-WI)	Dodge County, WI	Mississippi River	300
Sabine	Junction of Cowleech and Caddo Forks, Hunt Co., TX	Sabine Lake	380
Sacramento	Siskiyou County, CA	Suisun Bay	377
Saguenay	Lake St. John, QC, Can.	St. Lawrence River	434
St. Francis	Iron County, MO	Mississippi River	425
St. John	Northwestern Maine	Bay of Fundy	418
St. Lawrence	Lake Ontario, NY-ON, Can.	Gulf of St. Lawrence, Atlantic Ocean	800
Salmon (ID)	Custer County, ID	Snake River	420
San Joaquin	Junction of South and Middle Forks, Madera Co., CA	Suisun Bay	350
San Juan	Silver Lake, Archuleta County, CO	Colorado River	360
Santee-Wateree-Catawba	McDowell County, NC	Atlantic Ocean	538
Saskatchewan, North	Rocky Mountains, AB, Can.	Saskatchewan R.	800
Saskatchewan, South	Rocky Mountains, AB, Can.	Saskatchewan R.	865
Savannah	Junction of Seneca and Tugaloo Rivers, Anderson Co., SC	Atlantic Ocean, GA-SC.	314
Severn (ON)	Sandy Lake, ON, Can.	Hudson Bay	610
Smoky Hill	Cheyenne County, CO	Kansas River, KS	540
Snake	Teton County, WY	Columbia River, WA	1,038
South Platte	Junction of South and Middle Forks, Park County, CO	Platte River	424
Susitna	Alaska Range	Cook Inlet	313
Susquehanna	Otsego Lake, Otsego County, NY	Chesapeake Bay	447
Tallahatchie	Tippah County, MS	Yazoo River	301
Tanana	Wrangell Mountains, AK	Yukon River	659
Tennessee	Junction of French Broad and Holston Rivers, TN	Ohio River	652
Tennessee-French Broad	Courthouse Creek, Transylvania County, NC	Ohio River	886
Tombigbee	Prentiss County, MS	Mobile River	525
Trinity	N of Dallas, TX	Galveston Bay	360
Usumacinta	Junction of Pasión and Chixoy Rivers, Guatemala	Bay of Campeche, Mex.	600
Wabash	Darke County, OH	Ohio River	512
Washita	Hemphill County, TX	Red River, OK	500
White (AR-MO)	Madison County, AR	Mississippi River	722
Willamette	Douglas County, OR	Columbia River	309
Wind-Bighorn	Junction of Wind and Little Wind Rivers, Fremont Co., WY (source of Wind R. is Togwotee Pass, Teton Co., WY)	Yellowstone River	338
Wisconsin	Lac Vieux Desert, Vilas County, WI	Mississippi River	430
Yellowstone	Park County, WY	Missouri River	682
Yukon	McNeil River, YT, Can.	Bering Sea	1,979

Major Natural Lakes of the World
Source: U.S. Geological Survey, U.S. Dept. of the Interior; Natural Resources Canada

A lake is generally defined as a body of water surrounded by land. By this definition some bodies of water that are called seas, such as the Caspian Sea and the Aral Sea, are really lakes. In the following table, the word "lake" is omitted when it is part of the name.

Name	Continent	Area (sq mi)	Length (mi)	Maximum depth (ft)	Elevation (ft)
Caspian Sea[1]	Asia-Europe	144,001	760	3,363	-92
Superior	North America	31,700	350	1,333	601
Victoria	Africa	26,828	209	270	3,720
Huron	North America	23,000	206	750	578
Michigan	North America	22,300	307	923	578
Tanganyika	Africa	12,700	420	4,823	2,534
Baikal	Asia	12,162	395	5,315	1,493
Great Bear	North America	12,096	192	1,463	512
Nyasa (Malawi)	Africa	11,150	360	2,280	1,550
Great Slave	North America	11,030	298	2,014	512
Erie	North America	9,910	241	210	569
Winnipeg	North America	9,416	266	200	712
Ontario	North America	7,340	193	802	243
Balkhash[1]	Asia	7,115	376	85	1,115
Ladoga	Europe	6,835	124	738	13
Maracaibo	South America	5,217	133	115	sea level
Aral Sea[1,2]	Asia	4,040	260	180	175
Onega	Europe	3,710	145	328	108
Eyre[1]	Australia	3,600[3]	90	4	-49
Titicaca	South America	3,200	122	922	12,500
Nicaragua	North America	3,100	102	230	102
Athabasca	North America	3,064	208	407	699
Reindeer	North America	2,568	143	720	1,106
Tonle Sap	Asia	2,500[3]	70	45	NA
Turkana (Rudolf)	Africa	2,473	154	240	1,230
Issyk Kul[1]	Asia	2,355	115	2,303	5,279
Torrens[1]	Australia	2,230[3]	130	NA[3]	92
Vänern	Europe	2,181	91	328	144
Nettilling	North America	2,140	67	NA[3]	98
Winnipegosis	North America	2,075	141	38	833
Albert	Africa	2,075	100	168	2,030
Nipigon	North America	1,872	72	540	853
Gairdner[1]	Australia	1,840[3]	90	NA[3]	112
Manitoba	North America	1,799	140	21	813
Urmia[1]	Asia	888	90	49	4,177
Chad	Africa	521[4]	175	24	787

NA = Not available. (1) Salt lake. (2) The diversion of its two feeder rivers since the 1960s has devastated the Aral—once the world's fourth-largest lake (26,000 sq mi) with length, max. depth, and elevation shown. By 2000, the Aral had effectively become three lakes, with the total area shown. (3) Subject to great seasonal variation. (4) Once fourth-largest lake in Africa (about 10,000 sq mi in the 1960s), Chad had shrunk to around 5% of its original size by 2006 as a result of irrigation and long-term drought.

The Great Lakes
Source: National Ocean Service, National Oceanic and Atmospheric Administration, U.S. Dept. of Commerce

The Great Lakes form the world's **largest freshwater body** (in surface area) and with their connecting waterways are the largest inland water transportation unit. Draining the north-central basin of the U.S., they enable shipping to get to the Atlantic via their outlet, the St. Lawrence R.; the Gulf of Mexico can be reached via the Illinois Waterway, between Lake Michigan and the Mississippi R. A third outlet connects with the Hudson R. and then the Atlantic via the New York State Barge Canal System. Illinois Waterway and NYS Barge Canal System traffic is limited to recreational boating and small shipping vessels.

Only Lake Michigan is wholly in the U.S.; the other lakes are shared with Canada. Ships move from the shores of Lake Superior to Whitefish Bay in the east, then through the Soo Locks in Sault Ste. Marie, MI, onto St. Mary's R. and into Lake Huron. To reach the Port of Indiana-Burns Harbor and South Chicago, IL, ships travel west from Lake Huron to Lake Michigan through the Straits of Mackinac. Low water datum is based on the International Great Lakes Datum (1985), with Rimouski, Quebec, as the reference zero point. The distance between Duluth, MN, and Lake Ontario's east end is 1,156 mi.

	Superior	Michigan	Huron	Erie	Ontario
Length (mi)	350	307	206	241	193
Breadth (mi)	160	118	183	57	53
Deepest soundings (ft)	1,333	923	750	210	802
Volume of water (cu mi)	2,935	1,180	850	116	393
Area (sq mi) water surface—U.S.	20,600	22,300	9,100	4,980	3,460
Canada	11,100	NA	13,900	4,930	3,880
Area (sq mi) entire drainage basin—U.S.	16,900	45,600	16,200	18,000	15,200
Canada	32,400	NA	35,500	4,720	12,100
Total area (sq mi), U.S. and Canada	**81,000**	**67,900**	**74,700**	**32,630**	**34,850**
Low water datum above mean water level at Rimouski, QC, avg. level (ft)	601.10	577.50	577.50	569.20	243.30
Latitude, N	46°25′	41°37′	43°00′	41°23′	43°11′
	49°00′	46°06′	46°17′	42°52′	44°15′
Longitude, W	84°22′	84°45′	79°43′	78°51′	76°03′
	92°06′	88°02′	84°45′	83°29′	79°53′
National boundary line (mi)	282.8	NA	260.8	251.5	174.6
U.S. shoreline (mainland only) (mi)	863	1,400	580	431	300

NA = Not applicable.

Notable Waterfalls

The magnitude of a waterfall is determined not only by height but also by volume and steadiness of flow, crest width, the angle of a drop, and the number of leaps it may make. A series of low falls over a considerable distance is known as a cascade. Waterfalls are highly variable and few authoritative figures exist. For more information and some alternative measurements, see the World Waterfall Database at www.worldwaterfalldatabase.com.

Estimated mean annual flow (ft³/sec): Niagara, 205,000; Paulo Afonso, 100,000; Iguazú, 61,000; Victoria, 35,400.

Height is total drop in feet in one or more leaps. If river name is not shown, it is the same as the waterfall. # = more than one leap; * = diminishes greatly seasonally; ** = reduces to a trickle or is dry for part of each year; R. = river; (C) = cascade.

Name, location	Height (ft)
Africa	
Angola-Namibia	
Ruacana, Cunene R.	352
Lesotho	
Maletsunyane*	630
South Africa	
Augrabies, Orange R.*	480
Tugela#	2,800
Tanzania-Zambia	
Kalambo*	704
Zimbabwe-Zambia	
Victoria, Zambezi R.*	344
Asia and Oceania	
Australia	
New South Wales	
Wentworth	614
Wollomombi	722
Queensland	
Tully**	984
Wallaman, Stony Creek	879
India	
Jog, Sharavati R.*	829
Sivasamudram	320
Japan	
Kegon, Lake Chuzenji*	350
New Zealand	
Helena	722
Sutherland, Arthur R.#	1,904
Europe	
Austria	
Gastein#	487
Krimml#	1,246
France	
Gavarnie*	1,385
Italy	
Toce (C)	470
Norway	
Mardalsfossen#**	2,154
Skykje**	984
Vetti, Morka-Koldedola R.	900
Sweden	
Handol#	345

Name, location	Height (ft)
Switzerland	
Giessbach (C).	984
Reichenbach#	394
Staubbach	974
Trümmelbach#	950
United Kingdom	
Glomach, Scotland	370
Pistyll Rhaeadr, Wales	240
North America	
Canada	
Alberta	
Panther, Nigel Creek	600
British Columbia	
Della#	1,444
Takakkaw, Daly Glacier#	992
Ontario	
Niagara (Horseshoe)	167
Québec	
Montmorency	276
United States	
Alabama	
Noccalula Falls	90
California	
Feather*	640
Yosemite National Park	
Bridalveil*	620
Nevada, Merced R.*	594
Ribbon**	1,612
Silver Strand,	
Meadow Brook**	574
Vernal, Merced R.*	317
Wapama*	1,310
Yosemite#**	2,425
Colorado	
Seven Falls,	
S. Cheyenne Creek#	300
Hawaii	
Akaka, Kolekole Stream	420
Idaho	
Shoshone, Snake R.**	212
Kentucky	
Cumberland	68

Name, location	Height (ft)
Maryland	
Great, Potomac R. (C)*	76
Minnesota	
Minnehaha**	53
New Jersey	
Great, Passaic R.	70
New York	
Kaaterskill, Lake Creek*	231
Niagara (American)	120
Taughannock*	215
Oregon	
Multnomah#	620
Tennessee	
Fall Creek	256
Washington	
Colonial Creek	2,568
Sluiskin, Paradise R.	300
Snoqualmie**	268
Wisconsin	
Big Manitou, Black R. (C)*	165
Wyoming	
Tower	132
Yellowstone (lower)*	308
Yellowstone (upper)*	109
South America	
Argentina-Brazil	
Iguazú	269
Brazil	
Cachoeira da Fumaça*	1,312
Paulo Afonso, São Francisco R.	275
Colombia	
Tequendama, Bogotá R.*	482
Ecuador	
Agoyan, Pastaza R.*	200
Guyana	
Kaieteur, Potaro R.	741
King George VI, Kamarang R.	1,600
Marina, Ipobe R.#	500
Venezuela	
Angel (Kerepakupai Merú), Churún#*	3,212
Cuquenan	2,000

Latitude and Longitude of World Cities

Source: National Geospatial-Intelligence Agency, U.S. Dept. of Defense

City, country	Lat. °	′	Long. °	′
Athens, Greece	37	59 N	23	44 E
Bangkok, Thailand	13	45 N	100	31 E
Beijing, China	39	55 N	116	23 E
Berlin, Germany	52	31 N	13	24 E
Bogotá, Colombia	4	38 N	74	3 W
Buenos Aires, Argentina	34	35 S	58	40 W
Cairo, Egypt	30	4 N	31	17 E
Jakarta, Indonesia	6	10 S	106	49 E
Jerusalem, Israel	31	45 N	35	0 E
Johannesburg, South Africa	26	12 S	28	2 E
Kiev, Ukraine	50	26 N	30	31 E
Lagos, Nigeria	6	35 N	3	45 E
London, UK (Greenwich)	51	28 N	0	0
Manila, Philippines	14	35 N	121	0 E
Mexico City, Mexico	19	26 N	99	8 W
Moscow, Russia	55	45 N	37	36 E
Mumbai (Bombay), India	18	59 N	72	50 E
New Delhi, India	28	36 N	77	12 E
Paris, France	48	52 N	2	20 E
Rio de Janeiro, Brazil	22	52 S	43	16 W
Rome, Italy	41	54 N	12	29 E
Santiago, Chile	33	27 S	70	40 W
Seoul, South Korea	37	35 N	127	0 E
Sydney, Australia	33	51 S	151	12 E
Tehran, Iran	35	40 N	51	25 E
Tokyo, Japan	35	41 N	139	45 E

Highest and Lowest Continental Elevations

Continent	Highest point	Elev. (ft)
Asia	Everest, Nepal-Tibet	29,032
South America	Aconcagua, Argentina	22,835
North America	Denali (fmr. McKinley), Alaska, U.S.	20,308
Africa	Kilimanjaro, Tanzania	19,341
Europe	Elbrus, Russia	18,481
Antarctica	Vinson Massif	16,066
Australia	Kosciusko, New South Wales	7,313

Continent	Lowest point	Ft below sea level
Antarctica	Denman Glacier	11,483
Asia	Dead Sea, Israel-Jordan	1,414
Africa	Lake Assal, Djibouti	509
South America	Laguna del Carbón, Argentina	344
North America	Death Valley, California, U.S.	282
Europe	Caspian Sea, Azer.-Kazakh.-Russ.	92
Australia	Lake Eyre, South Australia	49

Latitude, Longitude, and Elevation of U.S. and Canadian Cities

Source: U.S. geographic positions and altitudes provided by U.S. Geological Survey, U.S. Dept. of the Interior. Canadian geographic positions and altitudes provided by Natural Resources Canada.

City, state/province	Lat. N °	′	″	Long. W °	′	″	Elev. (ft)
Albany, NY	42	39	9	73	45	22	149
Albuquerque, NM	35	5	4	106	39	4	4,956
Anchorage, AK	61	13	5	149	54	1	104
Annapolis, MD	38	58	42	76	29	32	43
Atlanta, GA	33	44	56	84	23	17	1,050
Augusta, GA	33	28	15	81	58	29	141
Augusta, ME	44	18	38	69	46	46	123
Austin, TX	30	16	2	97	44	35	489
Baltimore, MD	39	17	25	76	36	44	36
Baton Rouge, LA	30	27	3	91	9	16	46
Billings, MT	45	47	0	108	30	2	3,124
Birmingham, AL	33	31	14	86	48	9	610
Bismarck, ND	46	48	30	100	47	1	1,695
Boise, ID	43	36	49	116	12	12	2,699
Boston, MA	42	21	30	71	3	35	45
Buffalo, NY	42	53	11	78	52	42	600
Burlington, VT	44	28	33	73	12	43	196
Calgary, AB	51	2	45	114	3	27	3,557
Carson City, NV	39	9	50	119	46	3	4,681
Casper, WY	42	52	0	106	18	47	5,105
Cedar Rapids, IA	42	0	30	91	38	39	808
Charleston, SC	32	46	36	79	55	51	11
Charleston, WV	38	20	59	81	37	57	596
Charlotte, NC	35	13	38	80	50	35	762
Charlottetown, PE	46	14	25	63	8	5	160
Cheyenne, WY	41	8	24	104	49	13	6,087
Chicago, IL	41	51	0	87	39	0	586
Churchill, MB	58	46	51	94	11	13	94
Cleveland, OH	41	29	58	81	41	43	653
Colorado Springs, CO	38	50	2	104	49	17	6,010
Columbia, SC	34	0	3	81	2	5	300
Columbus, OH	39	57	40	82	59	56	780
Concord, NH	43	12	29	71	32	15	273
Corpus Christi, TX	27	48	2	97	23	47	7
Dallas, TX	32	46	59	96	48	24	421
Denver, CO	39	44	21	104	59	5	5,277
Des Moines, IA	41	36	2	93	36	33	873
Detroit, MI	42	19	53	83	2	45	598
Dover, DE	39	9	29	75	31	27	28
Durham, NC	35	59	39	78	53	55	400
Edmonton, AB	53	32	4	113	29	25	2,200
El Paso, TX	31	45	31	106	29	13	3,717
Eugene, OR	44	3	7	123	5	12	430
Evansville, IN	37	58	29	87	33	21	388
Fairbanks, AK	64	50	16	147	42	59	445
Fargo, ND	46	52	38	96	47	23	902
Ft. Smith, AR	35	23	9	94	23	55	440
Ft. Wayne, IN	41	7	50	85	7	44	810
Ft. Worth, TX	32	43	31	97	19	15	653
Frankfort, KY	38	12	3	84	52	24	507
Fredericton, NB	45	56	43	66	40	0	67
Greensboro, NC	36	4	21	79	47	31	827
Greenville, SC	34	51	9	82	23	38	984
Gulfport, MS	30	22	3	89	5	34	21
Halifax, NS	44	52	0	63	42	58	477
Hamilton, ON	43	14	34	79	59	22	780
Harrisburg, PA	40	16	25	76	53	4	332
Hartford, CT	41	45	49	72	41	6	29
Helena, MT	46	35	34	112	2	10	4,047
Hilo, HI	19	43	47	155	5	24	59
Honolulu, HI	21	18	25	157	51	30	17
Houston, TX	29	45	48	95	21	48	37
Idaho Falls, ID	43	28	0	112	2	3	4,705
Indianapolis, IN	39	46	6	86	9	29	720
Iqaluit, NU	63	45	0	68	31	0	112
Jackson, MS	32	17	56	90	11	5	280
Jacksonville, FL	30	19	56	81	39	20	15
Jefferson City, MO	38	34	36	92	10	25	630
Jersey City, NJ	40	43	41	74	4	40	34
Juneau, AK	58	18	7	134	25	11	33
Kansas City, MO	39	5	59	94	34	43	898
Knoxville, TN	35	57	38	83	55	15	904
Lansing, MI	42	43	57	84	33	20	853
Laredo, TX	27	30	23	99	30	27	415
Las Vegas, NV	36	10	30	115	8	14	2,001
Lexington, KY	37	59	19	84	28	40	968
Lincoln, NE	40	48	0	96	40	0	1,200
Little Rock, AR	34	44	47	92	17	23	333
Los Angeles, CA	34	3	8	118	14	37	291
Louisville, KY	38	15	15	85	45	34	466
Madison, WI	43	4	23	89	24	4	873
Manchester, NH	42	59	44	71	27	17	258
Memphis, TN	35	8	58	90	2	56	260
Miami, FL	25	46	27	80	11	37	8
Milwaukee, WI	43	2	20	87	54	23	615
Minneapolis, MN	44	58	48	93	15	50	830
Mobile, AL	30	41	40	88	2	35	10
Montgomery, AL	32	22	0	86	18	0	238
Montpelier, VT	44	15	36	72	34	31	526
Montréal, QC	45	31	0	73	39	0	221
Nashville, TN	36	9	57	86	47	4	567
New Orleans, LA	29	57	17	90	4	30	1
New York, NY	40	42	51	74	0	22	35
Newark, NJ	40	44	8	74	10	21	32
Nome, AK	64	30	4	165	24	23	37
Oklahoma City, OK	35	28	3	97	30	59	1,198
Olympia, WA	47	2	16	122	54	3	93
Omaha, NE	41	15	31	95	56	16	1,059
Ottawa, ON	45	20	0	75	35	3	382
Overland Park, KS	38	58	56	94	40	15	1,084
Philadelphia, PA	39	57	8	75	9	50	45
Phoenix, AZ	33	26	54	112	4	27	1,085
Pierre, SD	44	22	6	100	21	3	1,479
Pittsburgh, PA	40	26	26	79	59	45	766
Portland, OR	45	31	24	122	40	34	33
Providence, RI	41	49	26	71	24	46	9
Provo, UT	40	14	2	111	39	31	4,551
Québec, QC	46	49	0	71	13	0	244
Raleigh, NC	35	46	20	78	38	19	315
Rapid City, SD	44	4	50	103	13	52	3,243
Regina, SK	50	27	17	104	36	24	1,894
Reno, NV	39	31	47	119	48	50	4,505
Richmond, VA	37	33	14	77	27	37	213
Rochester, NY	43	9	17	77	36	56	504
Sacramento, CA	38	34	54	121	29	40	27
St. John's, NL	47	28	56	52	47	49	461
St. Louis, MO	38	37	38	90	11	52	464
St. Paul, MN	44	56	34	93	5	36	789
Salem, OR	44	56	35	123	2	6	157
Salt Lake City, UT	40	45	39	111	53	28	4,265
San Antonio, TX	29	25	27	98	29	37	649
San Diego, CA	32	42	55	117	9	26	63
San Francisco, CA	37	46	30	122	25	10	54
San Jose, CA	37	20	22	121	53	42	82
San Juan, PR	18	27	59	66	6	21	26
Santa Fe, NM	35	41	13	105	56	16	6,995
Saskatoon, SK	52	8	23	106	41	10	1,653
Savannah, GA	32	5	1	81	5	59	20
Seattle, WA	47	36	22	122	19	55	177
Shreveport, LA	32	31	31	93	45	1	151
Sioux City, IA	42	30	0	96	24	1	1,201
Sioux Falls, SD	43	33	0	96	42	1	1,473
Spokane, WA	47	39	35	117	25	45	1,732
Springfield, IL	39	48	6	89	38	37	600
Tacoma, WA	47	15	10	122	26	39	250
Tampa, FL	27	56	51	82	27	30	15
Topeka, KS	39	2	54	95	40	41	948
Toronto, ON	43	44	30	79	22	24	251
Trenton, NJ	40	13	1	74	44	35	61
Tucson, AZ	32	13	18	110	55	35	2,490
Tulsa, OK	36	9	14	95	59	34	721
Vancouver, BC	49	15	40	123	6	50	14
Victoria, BC	48	25	42	123	21	53	63
Virginia Beach, VA	36	51	11	75	58	41	11
Washington, DC	38	53	42	77	2	11	24
Whitehorse, YT	60	41	46	135	4	51	2,305
Wichita, KS	37	41	32	97	20	15	1,302
Wilmington, DE	39	44	45	75	32	48	91
Wilmington, NC	34	13	33	77	56	41	36
Winnipeg, MB	49	53	4	97	8	47	783
Yakima, WA	46	36	7	120	30	21	1,068
Yellowknife, NT	62	27	13	114	22	12	675

RELIGION

Religious Affiliation in the U.S., 2024

Source: Gina A. Zurlo, ed., *World Religion Database* (Leiden/Boston: Brill, July 2023)

Affiliation	2024 pop.	Percent	Affiliation	2024 pop.	Percent	Affiliation	2024 pop.	Percent
Agnostics	59,884,000	17.7%	Christians	244,990,000	72.4%	Muslims	5,301,000	1.6%
Atheists	11,868,000	3.5	Daoists	13,800	—	New religionists...	1,820,000	0.5
Baha'is	607,000	0.2	Ethnic religionists..	1,152,000	0.3	Shintoists	69,400	—
Buddhists	4,619,000	1.4	Hindus	1,759,000	0.5	Sikhs	420,000	0.1
Chinese			Jains	114,000	—	Spiritists	268,000	0.1
folk-religionists ..	119,000	—	Jews	5,518,000	1.6	Zoroastrians	18,200	—
— = Less than 0.05%.								

Religious Group Membership in the U.S., 2015

Source: Todd M. Johnson and Gina A. Zurlo, eds., *World Christian Database* (Leiden/Boston: Brill, July 2023)

Figures generally are based on collected reports made by each denomination as of 2015 and include only persons affiliated with a congregation of the denomination. Reporting practices vary from one denomination to another but generally include all members, not only full communicants. Denominations with fewer than 28,000 members not generally shown. Broad religious groups are indicated in **boldface**.

Group (congregations)	Members	Group (congregations)	Members
African Methodist Episcopal Church (9,000)	2,800,000	Cumberland Presbyterian Church (920)	70,800
African Methodist Episcopal Zion Church (3,400)	1,750,000	Czechoslovak Hussite Church (20)	50,000
Agnosticism	**51,565,000**	**Daoism**	**13,000**
Albanian Orthodox Archdiocese in America (15)	35,000	Defenders of the Christian Faith (90)	30,000
American Baptist Assn. (1,500)	100,000	Elim Assemblies Fellowship (260)	40,000
American Baptist Churches in the USA (5,100)	1,469,000	Episcopal Church in the USA (4,800)	1,917,000
Antiochian Orthodox Christian (270)	480,000	Ethiopian Orthodox Church in the USA (80)	85,000
Apostolic Assemblies of Christ Intl. (260)	50,000	**Ethnic religions[2]**	**1,137,000**
Apostolic Assembly of the Faith in Christ		Evangelical Covenant Church of America (900)	160,000
Jesus (760)	89,700	Evangelical Fellowship Intl. (300)	90,000
Armenian Apostolic Church of America (37)	360,000	Evangelical Free Church of America (1,500)	375,000
Armenian Church of North America (100)	370,000	Evangelical Lutheran Church in America (10,500)	4,300,000
Armenian Evangelical Union of Churches (60)	40,000	Evangelical Presbyterian Church (600)	145,000
Assemblies of God USA (13,700)	3,522,000	Evangelistic Messengers Assn. (650)	65,000
Assemblies of the Lord Jesus Christ (440)	62,000	Faith Christian Fellowship Intl. (150)	75,000
Assembly of Christian Churches (140)	28,000	Fellowship of Christian Believers (70)	30,000
Assn. of Free Lutheran Congregations (280)	48,000	Free Methodist Church of North America (1,100)	76,000
Assn. of Intl. Gospel Assemblies (260)	270,000	Friends General Conference (600)	28,000
Associate Reformed Presbyterian Church (290)	50,000	Friends United Meeting (600)	40,000
Assyrian Church of the East (23)	115,000	Full Gospel Baptist Church Fellowship (600)	180,000
Atheism	**8,820,000**	Full Gospel Fellowship of Churches and	
Baha'i Faith	**544,000**	Ministers (800)	450,000
Baptist Bible Fellowship Intl. (4,500)	1,730,000	General Assn. of General Baptists (820)	59,200
Baptist General Conference (1,300)	399,000	General Assn. of Regular Baptist Churches (1,200)	200,000
Baptist Missionary Assn. of America (1,300)	230,000	Global Christian Ministry Forum (75)	37,500
Bible Way Churches of Our Lord Jesus Christ		Global Network of Christian Ministries (280)	45,000
World-Wide (750)	150,000	Grace Communion International (130)	30,000
Buddhism	**4,209,000**	Grace Intl. (110)	130,000
Calvary Chapels Intl. (1,200)	525,000	Greater Emmanuel Intl. Fellowship (50)	50,000
Catholic Church in the USA[1] (18,000)	72,798,000	Greek Orthodox Archdiocese of America (540)	1,500,000
Charis Fellowship (260)	36,500	Gulf States Pastors & Churches Fellowship (360)	28,000
Chinese folk-religions[2]	**114,000**	**Hinduism**	**1,553,000**
Christian and Missionary Alliance (2,100)	653,000	Independent Assemblies Fellowship (500)	80,000
Christian Brethren (Open) (1,300)	112,000	Independent Assemblies of God Intl. (310)	122,000
Christian Church (Disciples of Christ) (3,600)	786,000	Independent Fundamental Churches of	
Christian Churches and Churches of Christ (4,800)	1,150,000	America (620)	58,000
Christian Congregation (1,600)	130,000	Intl. Church of the Foursquare Gospel (1,900)	327,000
Christian International Ministries (150)	36,000	Intl. Churches of Christ (170)	52,100
Christian Methodist Episcopal Church (3,900)	1,000,000	Intl. Convention of Faith Ministries (420)	105,000
Christian Reformed Church in N. America (1,100)	236,000	Intl. Council of Community Churches (130)	66,000
Christianity	**240,445,000**	Intl. Pentecostal Holiness Church (1,700)	265,000
Church of Christ, Scientist (1,200)	140,000	**Islam[3]**	**4,433,000**
Church of God (Anderson, IN) (2,000)	277,000	**Jainism**	**92,000**
Church of God (Cleveland, OH) (6,500)	1,454,000	Jehovah's Witnesses (13,600)	2,834,000
Church of God (Huntsville, AL) (1,600)	83,000	**Judaism[4]**	**5,554,000**
Church of God in Christ (24,000)	8,046,000	Korean American Presbyterian Church (670)	72,000
Church of God of Prophecy (1,700)	108,000	Korean Full Gospel Churches of America (850)	260,000
Church of Jesus Christ (400)	100,000	Korean Presbyterian Church in America (310)	60,000
Church of Jesus Christ of Latter-day Saints (14,200)	6,642,000	Korean Presbyterian Church of America (1,900)	600,000
Church of Our Lord Jesus Christ of Apostolic		Latin American Council of Christian Churches (200)	36,000
Faith (550)	670,000	Lutheran Church-Missouri Synod (6,100)	2,061,000
Church of the Brethren (970)	138,000	Malankara Orthodox Syrian Church of the	
Church of the Living God (170)	42,000	East (100)	50,000
Church of the Nazarene (4,500)	773,000	Mennonite Church USA (850)	130,000
Churches of Christ (Non-Instrumental) (12,200)	1,510,000	Ministers Fellowship Intl. (210)	55,000
Churches of God General Conference (330)	39,000	Missionary Church (400)	50,000
Churches of God (Holiness) (30)	30,000	Moravian Church in America (170)	40,000
Churches on the Rock Intl. (100)	100,000	Native American Church of North America (400)	200,000
Community of Christ (900)	170,000	Natl. Assn. of Free Will Baptists (2,100)	178,000
Conservative Baptist Assn. of America (1,100)	186,000	Natl. Baptist Convention of America (12,500)	4,250,000
Conservative Congregational Christian		Natl. Baptist Convention, USA (40,000)	9,200,000
Conference (320)	40,000	Natl. Missionary Baptist Conv. of America (270)	440,000
Coptic Orthodox Church (250)	500,000	Natl. Primitive Baptist Convention (1,600)	600,000
Covenant Ministries Intl. (35)	95,000	New Apostolic Church USA (220)	38,400
Crenshaw Christian Center (2)	28,000	**New Religions[2]**	**1,680,000**

Group (congregations)	Members	Group (congregations)	Members
North American Baptist Conference (380)	61,900	Southern Baptist Convention (47,300)	18,836,000
North American Old Roman Catholic Church (140)	66,000	**Spiritism**	**235,000**
Old Order Amish Mennonite Church (1,000)	126,000	Syriac Orthodox Church of Antioch (33)	31,000
Old Order & Wisler Mennonite Church (64)	28,000	Unitarian Universalist Assn. (1,000)	216,000
Open Bible Churches (320)	42,000	United Baptist churches (400)	55,000
Orthodox Church in America (530)	2,900,000	United Brethren in Christ (200)	37,000
Orthodox Presbyterian Church (270)	32,000	United Church of Christ (5,000)	880,000
Pentecostal Assemblies of the World (1,600)	1,300,000	United Church of Jesus Christ (Apostolic) (120)	36,000
Pentecostal Church of God (1,100)	100,000	United Free Will Baptist Church (700)	100,000
Pentecostal Churches of the Apostolic Faith (350)	75,000	United House of Prayer for All People (140)	1,700,000
Potter's House (10)	35,000	United Methodist Church (33,000)	7,067,000
Presbyterian Church in America (1,900)	372,000	United Pentecostal Church Intl. (4,500)	875,000
Presbyterian Church (USA) (9,600)	1,705,000	Unity School of Christianity (680)	140,000
Primitive Baptists (3,000)	135,000	Universal Fellowship of MCCs (220)	40,000
Progressive Natl. Baptist Convention (1,200)	1,857,000	U.S. Conference of Mennonite Brethren	
Redeemed Christian Church of God (700)	35,000	Churches (200)	45,000
Reformed Church in America (890)	214,000	Vineyard Churches (USA) (590)	180,000
Rhema Bible Churches (600)	180,000	Way of the Cross Church of Christ (75)	80,000
Romanian Orthodox Episcopate of America (100)	110,000	Wesleyan Church (1,600)	135,000
Salvation Army (1,100)	400,000	Willow Creek Assn. of Churches (2,200)	440,000
Serbian Orthodox Church in N. and S. Amer. (120)	68,000	Wisconsin Evangelical Lutheran Synod (1,300)	367,000
Seventh-day Adventist Church (5,000)	1,309,000	World Council of Independent Christian Chs. (240)	40,000
Shintoism	**65,800**	World Harvest Ministerial Alliance (140)	40,000
Sikhism	**399,000**	**Zoroastrianism**	**18,500**

(1) According to the U.S. Center for Applied Research in the Apostolate, there were 75.4 mil self-identified Catholics in the U.S. in 2015 and 73.5 mil in 2022. (2) **Chinese folk-religionists** include followers of traditional Chinese religion; it may involve worship of local deities, ancestor veneration, Confucian ethics, divination, and Buddhist or Taoist elements, among other beliefs and practices. **Ethnic religionists** include followers of local, tribal, animistic, or shamanistic religions, generally belonging to a single ethnic group. **New religionists** include followers of Asian new religions, neoreligious movements, radical new crisis religions, and syncretistic mass religions. (3) Other sources vary. In 2017, the Council on American-Islamic Relations estimated a total of 2,000 mosques and 6-7 mil Muslims in the U.S., and a 2021 Pew Research Center report estimated the U.S. Muslim pop. at 3.85 mil in 2020. (4) Includes Jewish Reconstructionist Communities (about 90), Union of Orthodox Jewish Congregations of America (500), Other Orthodox congregations (1,200), Chabad (over 2,000), Union for Reform Judaism (850), and United Synagogue of Conservative Judaism (580). Among Jewish adherents in the U.S., about 35% classify themselves as Reform, 18% as Conservative, 10% as Orthodox, 2% as Reconstructionist, the rest as "just Jewish." Source: Ira M. Sheskin and Arnold Dashefsky, "United States Jewish Population, 2019," in *The American Jewish Year Book* (Dordrecht: Springer, 2019). (This source estimates the total American Jewish population at 6.7 mil.)

World Adherents of Religions by Continental Area, 2024

Source: Gina A. Zurlo, ed., *World Religion Database* (Leiden/Boston: Brill, July 2023). All adherents figures are midyear estimates, in thous.

Religion (no. of countries/territories)	Africa	Asia	Europe	Latin America	Northern America	Oceania	World	% of world pop.
Baha'is (224)	3,089	4,162	175	1,114	669	150	9,358	0.1%
Buddhists (152)	403	548,869	2,073	990	5,327	1,046	558,708	6.9
Chinese folk-religionists (120)	268	483,666	701	228	936	207	486,005	6.0
Christians (234)	729,873	399,514	563,349	621,304	268,709	28,934	2,611,683	32.2
Catholics (234)	261,439	157,898	246,322	508,674	88,074	10,127	1,272,535	15.7
Protestants (231)	279,718	112,655	85,487	67,380	57,489	13,492	616,220	7.6
Independents (231)	139,556	132,121	12,531	63,082	66,029	2,237	415,559	5.1
Orthodox (142)	63,953	18,827	204,499	1,523	8,688	1,198	298,687	3.7
Confucianists (17)	39	8,740	18	1	—	87	8,884	0.1
Ethnoreligionists (148)	110,617	156,029	1,186	3,966	1,304	447	273,547	3.4
Hindus (144)	3,789	1,078,993	1,412	821	2,311	861	1,088,187	13.4
Jains (20)	134	6,347	25	2	133	9	6,649	0.1
Jews (148)	89	7,303	1,276	393	5,883	114	15,058	0.2
Muslims (217)	615,701	1,354,018	56,591	1,956	6,938	991	2,036,194	25.1
Sunnis (214)	609,648	1,145,099	53,816	1,423	4,836	750	1,815,571	22.4
Shiites (149)	1,033	196,932	2,733	519	1,346	237	202,801	2.5
New religionists (121)	165	60,659	404	1,974	1,922	151	65,276	0.8
Shintoists (9)	—	2,730	—	10	69	—	2,810	—
Sikhs (64)	101	27,011	763	9	964	206	29,054	0.4
Spiritists (59)	4	2	161	14,628	288	10	15,092	0.2
Taoists (7)	—	9,849	—	—	14	15	9,879	0.1
Zoroastrians (29)	1	146	6	—	26	3	183	—
All religious adherents (234)	**1,464,274**	**4,148,038**	**628,139**	**647,395**	**295,491**	**33,230**	**7,216,567**	**89.0**
Nonreligious (233)	10,136	640,042	118,343	29,158	82,193	11,581	892,038	11.0
Agnostics (233)	9,370	530,595	102,861	25,722	69,151	9,534	747,233	9.2
Atheists (223)	767	110,033	15,482	3,436	13,042	2,047	144,806	1.8

— = Less than 500 adherents or 0.05% of world pop. **Note:** Figures may not add up to totals due to rounding. Continental areas are as per UN demographic terminology; "Asia" is defined to include the former Soviet Central Asian states, while "Europe" includes all of Russia, extending to the Pacific coast. Figures in parentheses indicate the number of countries/territories where the religion or type of belief has a significant following. **Buddhists** include Mahayana (72%), Theravada or Hinayana (25%), and Tantrayana (incl. Lamaists, Tibetans) (3%). **Chinese folk-religionists** are followers of traditional Chinese religion; it may involve worship of local deities, ancestor veneration, Confucian ethics, divination, and Buddhist or Daoist elements, among other beliefs and practices. **Christians** are usually baptized members of a church belonging to one of the major Christian traditions shown here. Those characterized as Independents belong to groups that consider themselves independent of historical mainstream institutionalized Christianity; these include groups such as Unitarians, Church of Jesus Christ of Latter-day Saints, and Jehovah's Witnesses. **Confucianists** are followers of Confucius, mostly living in China or elsewhere in East/Southeast Asia. **Ethnic religionists** are followers of local, tribal, animistic, or shamanistic religions, generally belonging to a single ethnic group. **Hindus** include Vaishnavites (38%); Shaivites (36%); and Shaktas, neo-Hindi, and reformed Hindi (26%). **New religionists** include followers of Asian new religions, neoreligious movements, radical new crisis religions, and syncretistic mass religions.

Episcopal Church Liturgical Colors and Calendar, 2023-27

The most common liturgical colors in the Episcopal Church are as follows: **White**—Christmas Day through first Sunday after Epiphany; Maundy Thursday (as an alternative to crimson at the Eucharist); from the Vigil of Easter to the Day of Pentecost (Whitsunday); Trinity Sunday; Feasts of the Lord (except Holy Cross Day); the Confession of St. Peter; the Conversion of St. Paul; St. Joseph; St. Mary Magdalene; St. Mary the Virgin; St. Michael and All Angels; All Saints' Day; St. John the Evangelist; memorials of other saints who were not martyred; Independence Day and Thanksgiving Day; weddings and funerals. **Red**—the Day of Pentecost; Holy Cross Day; feasts of apostles and evangelists (except those previously mentioned); feasts and memorials of martyrs (including Holy Innocents' Day). **Violet**—Advent and Lent. **Crimson** or oxblood (dark red)—Holy Week. **Green**—the seasons after Epiphany and after Pentecost. **Black**—optional alternative for funerals and Good Friday.

The days of fasting are Ash Wednesday and Good Friday. Other days of special devotion (penitence) include the 40 days of Lent. Ember days are days of prayer for the church's ministry. They fall on the Wednesday, Friday, and Saturday after the first Sunday in Lent, the Day of Pentecost, Holy Cross Day, and Dec. 13. Rogation Days, the three days before Ascension Day, are days of prayer for God's blessing on the crops, on commerce and industry, and for conservation of the Earth's resources.

Holy days and other variables	2023	2024	2025	2026	2027
Golden Number	10	11	12	13	14
Sunday Letter	A	G/F	E	D	C
Sundays after Epiphany	7	6	8	6	5
Ash Wednesday	Feb. 22	Feb. 14	Mar. 5	Feb. 18	Feb. 10
First Sunday in Lent	Feb. 26	Feb. 18	Mar. 9	Feb. 22	Feb. 14
Passion/Palm Sunday	Apr. 2	Mar. 24	Apr. 13	Mar. 29	Mar. 21
Good Friday	Apr. 7	Mar. 29	Apr. 18	Apr. 3	Mar. 26
Easter Day	Apr. 9	Mar. 31	Apr. 20	Apr. 5	Mar. 28
Ascension Day	May 18	May 9	May 29	May 14	May 6
Day of Pentecost	May 28	May 19	June 8	May 24	May 16
Trinity Sunday	June 4	May 26	June 15	May 31	May 23
Numbered Proper of 2 Pentecost	#5	#4	#7	#5	#4
First Sunday of Advent	Dec. 3	Dec. 1	Nov. 30	Nov. 29	Nov. 28

Greek Orthodox Movable Ecclesiastical Dates, 2023-27

Feast days and fasting days are determined annually on the basis of the date of Holy Pascha (Easter). Western Easter dates are also included for reference. This ecclesiastical cycle begins with the first day of the Triodion and ends with the Sunday of All Saints, a total of 18 weeks. In years where Pascha falls on or after May 3, Fast of Holy Apostles lasts zero days.

Holy days and observances	2023	2024	2025	2026	2027
Triodion begins	Feb. 5	Feb. 25	Feb. 9	Feb. 1	Feb. 21
1st Saturday of Souls	Feb. 18	Mar. 9	Feb. 22	Feb. 14	Mar. 6
Meat-Fare Sunday	Feb. 19	Mar. 10	Feb. 23	Feb. 15	Mar. 7
2nd Saturday of Souls	Feb. 25	Mar. 16	Mar. 1	Feb. 21	Mar. 13
Lent begins	Feb. 27	Mar. 18	Mar. 3	Feb. 23	Mar. 15
St. Theodore—3rd Saturday of Souls	Mar. 4	Mar. 23	Mar. 8	Feb. 28	Mar. 20
Sunday of Orthodoxy	Mar. 5	Mar. 24	Mar. 9	Mar. 1	Mar. 21
Saturday of Lazarus	Apr. 8	Apr. 27	Apr. 12	Apr. 4	Apr. 24
Palm Sunday	Apr. 9	Apr. 28	Apr. 13	Apr. 5	Apr. 25
Holy (Good) Friday	Apr. 14	May 3	Apr. 18	Apr. 10	Apr. 30
Western Easter	Apr. 9	Mar. 31	Apr. 20	Apr. 5	Mar. 28
Orthodox Pascha (Easter)	Apr. 16	May 5	Apr. 20	Apr. 12	May 2
Ascension	May 25	June 13	May 29	May 21	June 10
Saturday of Souls	June 3	June 22	June 7	May 30	June 19
Pentecost	June 4	June 23	June 8	May 31	June 20
All Saints	June 11	June 30	June 15	June 7	June 27
Fast of Holy Apostles (first day)	June 12	NA	June 16	June 8	June 28
Fast of Holy Apostles lasts—	17 days	0 days	13 days	21 days	1 day

Jewish Holy Days, 5783-5787 (2022-27)

The Jewish calendar consists of 12 lunar months, alternating between 29 and 30 days. It is lunisolar and adjusts for the solar cycle by adding an extra month (Adar II) in the 3rd, 6th, 8th, 11th, 14th, 17th, and 19th years of a 19-year cycle. The calendar starts on the day of Creation, reckoned in the 2nd-3rd cent. BCE as Tishrei 1, 3,761 years before the common era.

The religious calendar begins with the month Nisan, from which all other months are counted, and the civil calendar with Tishrei. The months are 1) Nisan, 2) Iyar, 3) Sivan, 4) Tammuz, 5) Av (also Abh), 6) Elul, 7) Tishrei, 8) Cheshvan (also Marcheshvan), 9) Kislev, 10) Tevet (also Tebeth), 11) Shevat (also Shebhat), 12) Adar, and 12a) Adar Sheni (II), added in leap years.

All holidays listed below begin at sunset of the previous day and end at nightfall on the last day shown.

Holiday	Date on Jewish cal.	5783 (2022-23)		5784 (2023-24)		5785 (2024-25)		5786 (2025-26)		5787 (2026-27)	
Rosh Hashanah (New Year)	Tishrei 1	Sept. 26	Mon.	Sept. 16	Sat.	Oct. 3	Thu.	Sept. 23	Tue.	Sept. 12	Sat.
	Tishrei 2	Sept. 27	Tue.	Sept. 17	Sun.	Oct. 4	Fri.	Sept. 24	Wed.	Sept. 13	Sun.
Yom Kippur (Day of Atonement)	Tishrei 10	Oct. 5	Wed.	Sept. 25	Mon.	Oct. 12	Sat.	Oct. 2	Thu.	Sept. 21	Mon.
Sukkot	Tishrei 15	Oct. 10	Mon.	Sept. 30	Sat.	Oct. 17	Thu.	Oct. 7	Tue.	Sept. 26	Sat.
	Tishrei 21	Oct. 16	Sun.	Oct. 6	Fri.	Oct. 23	Wed	Oct. 13	Mon.	Oct. 2	Fri.
Shemini Atzeret	Tishrei 22	Oct. 17	Mon.	Oct. 7	Sat.	Oct. 24	Thu.	Oct. 14	Tue.	Oct. 3	Sat.
Simchat Torah	Tishrei 23	Oct. 18	Tue.	Oct. 8	Sun.	Oct. 25	Fri.	Oct. 15	Wed.	Oct. 4	Sun.
Hanukkah	Kislev 25	Dec. 19	Mon.	Dec. 8	Fri.	Dec. 26	Thu.	Dec. 15	Mon.	Dec. 5	Sat.
	Tevet 2 or 3	Dec. 26	Mon.	Dec. 15	Fri.	Jan. 2	Thu.	Dec. 22	Mon.	Dec. 12	Sat.
Purim	Adar 14	Mar. 7	Tue.	Mar. 24	Sun.	Mar. 14	Fri.	Mar. 3	Tue.	Mar. 23	Tue.
Pesach (Passover)	Nisan 15	Apr. 6	Thu.	Apr. 23	Tue.	Apr. 13	Sun.	Apr. 2	Thu.	Apr. 22	Thu.
	Nisan 21	Apr. 13	Thu.	Apr. 30	Tue.	Apr. 20	Sun.	Apr. 9	Thu.	Apr. 29	Thu.
Shavuot	Sivan 6	May 26	Fri.	June 12	Wed.	June 2	Mon.	May 22	Fri.	June 11	Fri.
	Sivan 7	May 27	Sat.	June 13	Thu.	June 3	Tue.	May 23	Sat.	June 12	Sat.
Fast of the 9th of Av	Av 9	July 27	Thu.	Aug. 13	Tue.	Aug. 3	Sun.	July 23	Thu.	Aug. 12	Thu.

Hindu Festivals, 2023-27

There are various traditional lunisolar Hindu calendars. Most have similar names for the 12 lunar months, with days beginning at dawn or sunrise, but they differ in various ways, including the numbering of years and the starting point of months. The Indian civil (Saka) calendar, adopted in 1957, is solar-based, and begins Mar. 22 (Mar. 21 in leap years). There are many Hindu holidays and festivals; some are observed only in certain regions. Below are three of the most widely observed.

Festival	2023	2024	2025	2026	2027
Maha Shivaratri (Night of Shiva)[1]	Feb. 18	Mar. 8	Feb. 26	Feb. 15	Mar. 6
Holi (Festival of Color)	Mar. 7	Mar. 25	Mar. 14	Mar. 3	Mar. 22
Diwali (Festival of Lights)	Nov. 12	Oct. 31	Oct. 20	Nov. 8	Oct. 29

(1) Begins the night of the previous day.

Islamic Holy Days, 1444-1448 AH (2022-27)

The Islamic calendar is a strict lunar calendar reckoned from the year of the Hijra (anno Hegirae, or AH)—Muhammad's flight from Mecca to Medina, in 622 CE. Each year consists of 12 lunar months of 29 or 30 days beginning and ending with each new moon's visible crescent. Common years have 354 days; leap years have 355 days. Some Muslim countries employ a conventionalized calendar with the leap day added to the last month, Dhu'l-Hijja, but for religious purposes the leap date is taken into account by tracking each new moon sighting.

Holy days begin at sunset of the day previous to the day cited. The actual dates may vary slightly from what is shown below, depending on the locality and the times of actual moon sightings as determined by different authorities.

Holy day (date)	1444 (2022-23)	1445 (2023-24)	1446 (2024-25)	1447 (2025-26)	1448 (2026-27)
New Year's Day (Muharram 1)	July 30, 2022	July 19, 2023	July 7, 2024	June 26, 2025	June 16, 2026
Ashura (Muharram 10)	July 8, 2022	July 28, 2023	July 16, 2024	July 5, 2025	June 25, 2026
Mawlid (Rabi' I 12)	Oct. 8, 2022	Sept. 27, 2023	Sept. 15, 2024	Sept. 4, 2025	Aug. 25, 2026
Ramadan begins (Ramadan 1)	Mar. 23, 2023	Mar. 11, 2024	Mar. 1, 2025	Feb. 18, 2026	Feb. 8, 2027
Eid al-Fitr (Shawwal 1)	Apr. 22, 2023	Apr. 10, 2024	Mar. 30, 2025	Mar. 20, 2026	Mar. 9, 2027
Eid al-Adha (Dhu'l-Hijja 10)	June 29, 2023	June 17, 2024	June 6, 2025	May 27, 2026	May 16, 2027

Ash Wednesday and Easter Sunday (Western Churches), 2001-2100

Year	Ash Wed.	Easter Sunday	Year	Ash Wed.	Easter Sunday	Year	Ash Wed.	Easter Sunday	Year	Ash Wed.	Easter Sunday	Year	Ash Wed.	Easter Sunday
2001	Feb. 28	Apr. 15	2021	Feb. 17	Apr. 4	2041	Mar. 6	Apr. 21	2061	Feb. 23	Apr. 10	2081	Feb. 12	Mar. 30
2002	Feb. 13	Mar. 31	2022	Mar. 2	Apr. 17	2042	Feb. 19	Apr. 6	2062	Feb. 8	Mar. 26	2082	Mar. 4	Apr. 19
2003	Mar. 5	Apr. 20	2023	Feb. 22	Apr. 9	2043	Feb. 11	Mar. 29	2063	Feb. 28	Apr. 15	2083	Feb. 17	Apr. 4
2004	Feb. 25	Apr. 11	2024	Feb. 14	Mar. 31	2044	Mar. 2	Apr. 17	2064	Feb. 20	Apr. 6	2084	Feb. 9	Mar. 26
2005	Feb. 9	Mar. 27	2025	Mar. 5	Apr. 20	2045	Feb. 22	Apr. 9	2065	Feb. 11	Mar. 29	2085	Feb. 28	Apr. 15
2006	Mar. 1	Apr. 16	2026	Feb. 18	Apr. 5	2046	Feb. 7	Mar. 25	2066	Feb. 24	Apr. 11	2086	Feb. 13	Mar. 31
2007	Feb. 21	Apr. 8	2027	Feb. 10	Mar. 28	2047	Feb. 27	Apr. 14	2067	Feb. 16	Apr. 3	2087	Mar. 5	Apr. 20
2008	Feb. 6	Mar. 23	2028	Mar. 1	Apr. 16	2048	Feb. 19	Apr. 5	2068	Mar. 7	Apr. 22	2088	Feb. 25	Apr. 11
2009	Feb. 25	Apr. 12	2029	Feb. 14	Apr. 1	2049	Mar. 3	Apr. 18	2069	Feb. 27	Apr. 14	2089	Feb. 16	Apr. 3
2010	Feb. 17	Apr. 4	2030	Mar. 6	Apr. 21	2050	Feb. 23	Apr. 10	2070	Feb. 12	Mar. 30	2090	Mar. 1	Apr. 16
2011	Mar. 9	Apr. 24	2031	Feb. 26	Apr. 13	2051	Feb. 15	Apr. 2	2071	Mar. 4	Apr. 19	2091	Feb. 21	Apr. 8
2012	Feb. 22	Apr. 8	2032	Feb. 11	Mar. 28	2052	Mar. 6	Apr. 21	2072	Feb. 24	Apr. 10	2092	Feb. 13	Mar. 30
2013	Feb. 13	Mar. 31	2033	Mar. 2	Apr. 17	2053	Feb. 19	Apr. 6	2073	Feb. 8	Mar. 26	2093	Feb. 25	Apr. 12
2014	Mar. 5	Apr. 20	2034	Feb. 22	Apr. 9	2054	Feb. 11	Mar. 29	2074	Feb. 28	Apr. 15	2094	Feb. 17	Apr. 4
2015	Feb. 18	Apr. 5	2035	Feb. 7	Mar. 25	2055	Mar. 3	Apr. 18	2075	Feb. 20	Apr. 7	2095	Mar. 9	Apr. 24
2016	Feb. 10	Mar. 27	2036	Feb. 27	Apr. 13	2056	Feb. 16	Apr. 2	2076	Mar. 4	Apr. 19	2096	Feb. 29	Apr. 15
2017	Mar. 1	Apr. 16	2037	Feb. 18	Apr. 5	2057	Mar. 7	Apr. 22	2077	Feb. 24	Apr. 11	2097	Feb. 13	Mar. 31
2018	Feb. 14	Apr. 1	2038	Mar. 10	Apr. 25	2058	Feb. 27	Apr. 14	2078	Feb. 16	Apr. 3	2098	Mar. 5	Apr. 20
2019	Mar. 6	Apr. 21	2039	Feb. 23	Apr. 10	2059	Feb. 12	Mar. 30	2079	Mar. 8	Apr. 23	2099	Feb. 25	Apr. 12
2020	Feb. 26	Apr. 12	2040	Feb. 15	Apr. 1	2060	Mar. 3	Apr. 18	2080	Feb. 21	Apr. 7	2100	Feb. 10	Mar. 28

Roman Catholic Church Hierarchy

The Roman Catholic Church is headed by the pope, or bishop of Rome. He is assisted and advised by members of the College of Cardinals. The church is governed through a central administrative body, the Roman Curia. Dioceses around the world are headed by bishops appointed by the pope; collectively they also play a part in leadership of the church as a whole.

The Papacy

Roman Catholics consider Peter the Apostle to have been the first bishop of Rome and first in a line of popes extending to the present. He is said to have arrived in Rome c. 42 CE and to have been martyred there c. 67; he was later canonized as a saint. Popes through history have had both religious and secular roles. The pope today is the head of state of Vatican City as well as leader of the church.

German-born Pope **Benedict XVI**, formerly Cardinal Joseph Ratzinger, who was elected in Apr. 2005, resigned effective Feb. 28, 2013, citing his age (85) and declining health. Assuming the title of supreme pontiff emeritus, he took up residence in a restored convent near the Vatican. He died Dec. 31, 2022.

At a papal conclave in Mar. 2013, 115 cardinals from 48 countries chose Argentinean Cardinal Jorge Mario Bergoglio as pope. He took the name **Francis**, after St. Francis of Assisi (1182-1226), known for his life of poverty and devotion to the poor. Pope Francis was the first member of the Society of Jesus (Jesuits), a Roman Catholic order, to become pope, and the first born outside Europe since Syrian-born Gregory III, who died in 741.

Chronological List of Popes

Source: *Annuario Pontificio*

Table lists year of accession of each pope. * = antipope, an illegitimate claimant to the papal throne.

Year	Pope	Year	Pope	Year	Pope	Year	Pope	Year	Pope
NA	St. Peter	530	Boniface II	884	St. Adrian III	1102	Albert*	1431	Eugene IV
67	St. Linus	530	Dioscorus*	885	Stephen V (VI)	1105	Sylvester IV*	1439	Felix V*
76	St. Anacletus,	533	John II	891	Formosus	1118	Gelasius II	1447	Nicholas V
	or Cletus	535	St. Agapitus I	896	Boniface VI	1118	Gregory VIII*	1455	Callistus III
88	St. Clement I	536	St. Silverius, Martyr	896	Stephen VI (VII)	1119	Callistus II	1458	Pius II
97	St. Evaristus	537	Vigilius	897	Romanus	1124	Honorius II	1464	Paul II
105	St. Alexander I	556	Pelagius I	897	Theodore II	1124	Celestine II*	1471	Sixtus IV
115	St. Sixtus I	561	John III	898	John IX	1130	Innocent II	1484	Innocent VIII
125	St. Telesphorus	575	Benedict I	900	Benedict IV	1130	Anacletus II*	1492	Alexander VI
136	St. Hyginus	579	Pelagius II	903	Leo V	1138	Victor IV*	1503	Pius III
140	St. Pius I	590	St. Gregory I	903	Christopher*	1143	Celestine II	1503	Julius II
155	St. Anicetus	604	Sabinian	904	Sergius III	1144	Lucius II	1513	Leo X
166	St. Soter	607	Boniface III	911	Anastasius III	1145	Bl. Eugene III	1522	Adrian VI
175	St. Eleutherius	608	St. Boniface IV	913	Landus	1153	Anastasius IV	1523	Clement VII
189	St. Victor I	615	St. Deusdedit,	914	John X	1154	Adrian IV	1534	Paul III
199	St. Zephyrinus		or Adeodatus	928	Leo VI	1159	Alexander III	1550	Julius III
217	St. Callistus I	619	Boniface V	928	Stephen VII (VIII)	1159	Victor IV*	1555	Marcellus II
217	St. Hippolytus*	625	Honorius I	931	John XI	1164	Paschal III*	1555	Paul IV
222	St. Urban I	640	Severinus	936	Leo VII	1168	Callistus III*	1559	Pius IV
230	St. Pontian	640	John IV	939	Stephen VIII (IX)	1179	Innocent III*	1566	St. Pius V
235	St. Anterus	642	Theodore I	942	Marinus II	1181	Lucius III	1572	Gregory XIII
236	St. Fabian	649	St. Martin I, Martyr	946	Agapitus II	1185	Urban III	1585	Sixtus V
251	St. Cornelius	654	St. Eugene I	955	John XII	1187	Clement III	1590	Urban VII
251	Novatian*	657	St. Vitalian	963	Leo VIII	1187	Gregory VIII	1590	Gregory XIV
253	St. Lucius I	672	Adeodatus II	964	Benedict V	1191	Celestine III	1591	Innocent IX
254	St. Stephen I	676	Donus	965	John XIII	1198	Innocent III	1592	Clement VIII
257	St. Sixtus II	678	St. Agatho	973	Benedict VI	1216	Honorius III	1605	Leo XI
259	St. Dionysius	682	St. Leo II	974	Boniface VII*	1227	Gregory IX	1605	Paul V
269	St. Felix I	684	St. Benedict II	974	Benedict VII	1241	Celestine IV	1621	Gregory XV
275	St. Eutychian	685	John V	983	John XIV	1243	Innocent IV	1623	Urban VIII
283	St. Caius	686	Conon	984	Boniface VII*	1254	Alexander IV	1644	Innocent X
296	St. Marcellinus	687	Theodore*	985	John XV	1261	Urban IV	1655	Alexander VII
308	St. Marcellus I	687	Paschal*	996	Gregory V	1265	Clement IV	1667	Clement IX
309	St. Eusebius	687	St. Sergius I	997	John XVI*	1271	Bl. Gregory X	1670	Clement X
311	St. Melchiades	701	John VI	999	Sylvester II	1276	Bl. Innocent V	1676	Bl. Innocent XI
314	St. Sylvester I	705	John VII	1003	John XVII	1276	Adrian V	1689	Alexander VIII
336	St. Marcus	708	Sisinnius	1004	John XVIII	1276	John XXI	1691	Innocent XII
337	St. Julius I	708	Constantine	1009	Sergius IV	1277	Nicholas III	1700	Clement XI
352	Liberius	715	St. Gregory II	1012	Benedict VIII	1281	Martin IV	1721	Innocent XIII
355	Felix II*	731	St. Gregory III	1012	Gregory*	1285	Honorius IV	1724	Benedict XIII
366	St. Damasus I	741	St. Zachary	1024	John XIX	1288	Nicholas IV	1730	Clement XII
366	Ursinus*	752	Stephen II (III)[1]	1032	Benedict IX	1294	St. Celestine V	1740	Benedict XIV
384	St. Siricius	757	St. Paul I	1045	Sylvester III	1294	Boniface VIII	1758	Clement XIII
399	St. Anastasius I	767	Constantine*	1045	Benedict IX	1303	Bl. Benedict XI	1769	Clement XIV
401	St. Innocent I	768	Philip*	1045	Gregory VI	1305	Clement V	1775	Pius VI
417	St. Zosimus	768	Stephen III (IV)	1046	Clement II	1316	John XXII	1800	Pius VII
418	St. Boniface I	772	Adrian I	1047	Benedict IX	1328	Nicholas V*	1823	Leo XII
418	Eulalius*	795	St. Leo III	1048	Damasus II	1334	Benedict XII	1829	Pius VIII
422	St. Celestine I	816	Stephen IV (V)	1049	St. Leo IX	1342	Clement VI	1831	Gregory XVI
432	St. Sixtus III	817	St. Paschal I	1055	Victor II	1352	Innocent VI	1846	Pius IX
440	St. Leo I	824	Eugene II	1057	Stephen IX (X)	1362	Bl. Urban V	1878	Leo XIII
461	St. Hilary	827	Valentine	1058	Benedict X*	1370	Gregory XI	1903	St. Pius X
468	St. Simplicius	827	Gregory IV	1059	Nicholas II	1378	Urban VI	1914	Benedict XV
483	St. Felix III (II)	844	John*	1061	Alexander II	1378	Clement VII*	1922	Pius XI
492	St. Gelasius I	844	Sergius II	1061	Honorius II*	1389	Boniface IX	1939	Pius XII
496	Anastasius II	847	St. Leo IV	1073	St. Gregory VII	1394	Benedict XIII*	1958	St. John XXIII
498	St. Symmachus	855	Benedict III	1080	Clement III*	1404	Innocent VII	1963	Paul VI
498	Lawrence* (also in	855	Anastasius*	1086	Bl. Victor III	1406	Gregory XII	1978	John Paul I
	501-505)	858	St. Nicholas I	1088	Bl. Urban II	1409	Alexander V*	1978	St. John Paul II
514	St. Hormisdas	867	Adrian II	1099	Paschal II	1410	John XXIII*	2005	Benedict XVI
523	St. John I, Martyr	872	John VIII	1100	Theodoric*	1417	Martin V	2013	Francis
526	St. Felix IV (III)	882	Marinus I						

NA = Not available. Bl. = Blessed. (1) A Roman priest named Stephen was elected but died before assuming the papacy. Another Stephen was then elected to succeed St. Zachary, as Stephen II. He is sometimes listed as Stephen III.

Pope Francis

Pope Francis was born Jorge Mario Bergoglio in Buenos Aires, Argentina, Dec. 17, 1936; his parents were Italian immigrants. He joined the Jesuits in 1958 and was ordained a priest in 1969. Bergoglio served as a parish priest, theology professor, and college administrator. Ordained a bishop in 1992, he was named archbishop of Buenos Aires in 1998 and made a cardinal in 2001.

Soon after his election in 2013, Francis approved measures for reform of the scandal-ridden Vatican Bank and established a commission on clerical sex abuse. In 2015, Francis released an encyclical focusing on consumerism and the environment, and the next year addressed family life, divorce, and inclusion. A 2018 publication offered guidance on holy behavior, including the need to care for poor, sick, and migrant populations. Francis convened a summit on clergy sex abuse in Rome in Feb. 2019 and in May 2019 issued guidance mandating that church officials worldwide report clergy sexual abuse and cover-ups to their church superiors.

College of Cardinals

Members of the Sacred College of Cardinals are chosen by the pope to be his chief assistants and advisers in the administration of the church. Among their duties is the election of the pope.

In its present form, the College of Cardinals dates from the 12th century. The first cardinals, from about the 6th century, were deacons and priests of the leading churches of Rome and were bishops of neighboring dioceses. The title of cardinal was limited to members of the college in 1567. The number of cardinals was set at 70 in 1586. Pope John XXIII began to increase the number in 1959; however, the number eligible to participate in papal elections was limited to 120. Previous limitations were set aside by Pope John Paul II when he created new cardinals. In 1918, the Code of Canon Law specified that all cardinals must be priests. Pope John XXIII in 1962 ruled that cardinals must ordinarily be bishops. In 1971, Pope Paul VI decreed that at age 80, cardinals must retire from curial departments and offices and cannot be summoned to participate in papal elections. As of Sept. 2023, there were 221 cardinals from 88 countries, of whom 120 from 65 countries remained eligible to vote.

North American Cardinals

Name	Office	Born	Named cardinal
Carlos Aguiar Retes	Archbishop of Mexico City	1950	2016
Felipe Arizmendi Esquivel[2]	Bishop emeritus of San Cristóbal de las Casas, Mexico	1940	2020
Raymond L. Burke	Archbishop emeritus of St. Louis	1948	2010
Thomas C. Collins	Archbishop of Toronto, Canada	1947	2012
Blase J. Cupich	Archbishop of Chicago	1949	2016
Michael Czerny	Undersecretary of Migrant and Refugee Section, Dicastery for Promoting Integral Human Development	1946	2019
Daniel N. DiNardo	Archbishop of Galveston-Houston	1949	2007
Timothy M. Dolan	Archbishop of New York	1950	2012
Kevin J. Farrell	Prefect, Dicastery for Laity, Family, and Life; bishop emer. of Dallas	1947	2016
Wilton Daniel Gregory	Archbishop of Washington, DC	1947	2020
James M. Harvey	Archpriest of St. Paul Outside-the-Walls	1949	2012
Gérald Cyprien Lacroix[1]	Archbishop of Québec, Canada	1957	2014
Roger Mahony[2]	Archbishop emeritus of Los Angeles	1936	1991
Adam Joseph Maida[2]	Archbishop emeritus of Detroit	1930	1994
Robert Walter McElroy	Bishop of San Diego	1954	2022
Edwin F. O'Brien[2]	Archbishop emeritus of Baltimore	1939	2012
Sean O'Malley[3]	Archbishop of Boston	1944	2006
Marc Ouellet	Prefect emeritus, Dicastery for Bishops; pres. emeritus, Pontifical Commission for Latin America	1944	2003
Robert Francis Prevost	Prefect, Dicastery for Bishops, pres., Pontifical Commission for Latin America	1955	2023
Justin F. Rigali[2]	Archbishop emeritus of Philadelphia	1935	2003
Norberto Rivera Carrera[2]	Archbishop emeritus of Mexico City, Mexico	1942	1998
José Francisco Robles Ortega	Archbishop of Guadalajara, Mexico	1949	2007
Juan Sandoval Iñiguez[2]	Archbishop emeritus of Guadalajara, Mexico	1933	1994
James F. Stafford[2]	Archbishop emeritus of Denver	1932	1998
Alberto Suárez Inda[2]	Archbishop emeritus of Morelia, Mexico	1939	2015
Joseph W. Tobin	Archbishop of Newark	1952	2016
Donald W. Wuerl[2,4]	Archbishop emeritus of Washington, DC	1940	2010

Note: (1) Member, Council for the Economy. (2) Ineligible to vote in a papal conclave because of age. (3) Member, Council of Cardinals and Pres., Pontifical Commission for the Protection of Minors. (4) Resigned as archbishop in Oct. 2018 after allegations he concealed clergy sexual abuse.

The Ten Commandments

In the Hebrew Bible (Old Testament) the Ten Commandments (also called the Decalogue, from the Greek meaning "ten words") were revealed by God to Moses on Mt. Sinai. They form the covenant between God and the Israelites and the moral code that is the basis for the Jewish and Christian religions. The Ten Commandments appear in two places in the Old Testament—Exodus 20:1-17 and Deuteronomy 5:6-21.

Most Protestant, Anglican, and Orthodox Christians follow Jewish tradition, as shown here, which considers the introduction ("I am the Lord ...") the first commandment and makes the prohibition against idolatry the second. Roman Catholic and Lutheran traditions combine I and II and split the last commandment into two that separately prohibit coveting of a neighbor's wife and of a neighbor's goods. This arrangement alters the numbering of the other commandments by one.

Following is the text as it appears in Exodus 20:1-17 in the King James version of the Bible [Roman numerals added]:

And God spake all these words, saying,

I. I *am* the LORD thy God, which have brought thee out of the land of Egypt, out of the house of bondage. Thou shalt have no other gods before me.

II. Thou shalt not make unto thee any graven image, or any likeness of *any thing* that *is* in heaven above, or that *is* in the earth beneath, or that *is* in the water under the earth. Thou shalt not bow down thyself to them, nor serve them: for I the LORD thy God *am* a jealous God, visiting the iniquity of the fathers upon the children unto the third and fourth *generation* of them that hate me; and shewing mercy unto thousands of them that love me, and keep my commandments.

III. Thou shalt not take the name of the LORD thy God in vain: for the LORD will not hold him guiltless that taketh his name in vain.

IV. Remember the sabbath day, to keep it holy. Six days shalt thou labour, and do all thy work: but the seventh day *is* the sabbath of the LORD thy God: *in it* thou shalt not do any work, thou, nor thy son, nor thy daughter, thy manservant, nor thy maidservant, nor thy cattle, nor thy stranger that *is* within thy gates: for *in* six days the LORD made heaven and earth, the sea, and all that in them *is*, and rested the seventh day: wherefore the LORD blessed the sabbath day, and hallowed it.

V. Honour thy father and thy mother: that thy days may be long upon the land which the LORD thy God giveth thee.

VI. Thou shalt not kill.

VII. Thou shalt not commit adultery.

VIII. Thou shalt not steal.

IX. Thou shalt not bear false witness against thy neighbour.

X. Thou shalt not covet thy neighbour's house, thou shalt not covet thy neighbour's wife, nor his manservant, nor his maidservant, nor his ox, nor his ass, nor any thing that *is* thy neighbour's.

Major Christian Denominations:

Brackets indicate some features that tend to

Denomination	Origins	Organization	Authority	Special rites
Baptists	In radical Reformation, objections to infant baptism, demands for church and state separation; John Smyth, English Separatist, in 1609; Roger Williams, 1638, Providence, RI.	Congregational; each local church is autonomous.	Scripture; some Baptists, particularly in the South, interpret the Bible literally.	[Baptism, usually early teen years and after, by total immersion]; Lord's Supper.
Church of Christ (Disciples)	Among evangelical Presbyterians in KY (1804) and PA (1809), in distress over Protestant factionalism and decline of fervor; organized in 1832.	Congregational.	["Where the Scriptures speak, we speak; where the Scriptures are silent, we are silent."]	Adult baptism; Lord's Supper (weekly).
Episcopalians	Henry VIII separated English Catholic Church from Rome, 1534, for political reasons; Protestant Episcopal Church in U.S. founded in 1789.	[Diocesan bishops, in apostolic succession, are elected by parish representatives; the national Church is headed by General Convention and Presiding Bishop; part of the Anglican Communion.]	Scripture as interpreted by tradition, especially 39 Articles (1563); tri-annual convention of bishops, priests, and lay people.	Infant baptism, Eucharist, and other sacraments; sacrament taken to be symbolic, but as having real spiritual effect.
Jehovah's Witnesses	Founded in 1870 in PA by Charles Taze Russell; incorporated as Watch Tower Bible and Tract Society of PA, 1884; name Jehovah's Witnesses adopted in 1931.	A governing body located in NY coordinates worldwide activities; each congregation cared for by a body of elders; each Witness considered a minister.	The Bible.	Baptism by immersion; annual Lord's Meal ceremony.
Latter-day Saints (Mormons)	In a vision of the Father and the Son reported by Joseph Smith (1820s) in NY; Smith also reported receiving new scripture on golden tablets: the Book of Mormon.	Theocratic; 1st Presidency (church president, two counselors), 12 Apostles preside over international church; local congregations headed by lay priesthood leaders.	Revelation to living prophet (church president). The Bible, Book of Mormon, and other revelations to Smith and his successors.	Baptism at age 8; laying on of hands (which confers the gift of the Holy Ghost); Lord's Supper; temple rites: baptism for the dead, marriage for eternity, others.
Lutherans	Begun by Martin Luther in Wittenberg, Germany, in 1517; objection to Catholic doctrine of salvation and sale of indulgences; break complete, 1519.	Varies from congregational to episcopal; in U.S., a combination of regional synods and congregational polities is most common.	Scripture alone; the Book of Concord (1580), which includes the three Ecumenical Creeds, is subscribed to as a correct exposition of Scripture.	Infant baptism; Lord's Supper; Christ's true body and blood present "in, with, and under the bread and wine."
Methodists	Rev. John Wesley began movement in 1738, within Church of England; first U.S. denomination in Baltimore (1784).	Conference and superintendent system; [in United Methodist Church, general superintendents are bishops— not a priestly order, only an office—who are elected for life].	Scripture as interpreted by tradition, reason, and experience.	Baptism of infants or adults; Lord's Supper commanded; other rites: marriage, ordination, solemnization of personal commitments.
Orthodox	Developed in original Christian proselytizing; broke with Rome in 1054 after centuries of doctrinal disputes and diverging theology.	Synods of bishops in autonomous, usually national, churches elect a patriarch, archbishop, or metropolitan; these men, as a group, are the heads of the church.	Scripture, tradition, and the first seven church councils up to Nicaea II in 787; bishops in council have authority in doctrine and policy.	Seven sacraments: infant baptism and anointing, Eucharist, ordination, penance, marriage, and anointing of the sick.
Pentecostal	In Topeka, KS (1901) and Los Angeles (1906), in reaction to perceived loss of evangelical fervor among Methodists and others.	Originally a movement, not a formal organization, Pentecostalism now has a variety of organized forms and continues also as a movement.	Scripture; individual charismatic leaders, the teachings of the Holy Spirit.	[Spirit baptism, especially as shown in "speaking in tongues"; faith healing; sometimes exorcism]; adult baptism; Lord's Supper.
Presbyterians	In 16th-cent. Calvinist reformation; differed with Lutherans over sacraments, church government; John Knox founded Scotch Presbyterian church about 1560.	[Highly structured representational system of ministers and lay persons (presbyters) in local, regional, and national bodies (synods).]	Scripture.	Infant baptism; Lord's Supper; bread and wine symbolize Christ's spiritual presence.
Roman Catholics	Traditionally, founded by Jesus who named St. Peter the first vicar; developed in early Christian proselytizing, especially after the conversion of imperial Rome in the 4th cent.	[Hierarchy with supreme power vested in pope elected by cardinals]; councils of bishops advise on matters of doctrine and policy.	[The pope, when speaking for the whole church in matters of faith and morals, and tradition (which is expressed in church councils and in part contained in Scripture).]	Mass; seven sacraments: baptism, reconciliation, Eucharist, confirmation, marriage, ordination, and anointing of the sick (unction).
United Church of Christ	By ecumenical union, in 1957, of Congregationalists and Evangelical and Reformed, representing both Calvinist and Lutheran traditions.	Congregational; a General Synod, representative of all congregations, sets general policy.	Scripture.	Infant baptism; Lord's Supper.

How Do They Differ?

distinguish a denomination sharply from others.

Practice	Ethics	Doctrine	Other	Denomination
Worship style varies from staid to evangelistic; extensive missionary activity.	Usually opposed to alcohol and tobacco; some tendency toward a perfectionist ethical standard.	[No creed; true church is of believers only, who are all equal.]	Believing no authority can stand between the believer and God, the Baptists are strong supporters of church and state separation.	**Baptists**
Tries to avoid any rite not considered part of the 1st-cent. church; some congregations may reject instrumental music.	Some tendency toward perfectionism; increasing interest in social action programs.	Simple New Testament faith; avoids any elaboration not firmly based on Scripture.	Highly tolerant in doctrinal and religious matters; strongly supportive of scholarly education.	**Church of Christ (Disciples)**
Formal, based on *Book of Common Prayer*, updated 1979; services range from austerely simple to highly liturgical.	Tolerant, sometimes permissive; some social action programs.	Scripture; the "historic creeds," which include the Apostles, Nicene, and Athanasian, and the *Book of Common Prayer*; ranges from Anglo-Catholic to low church, with Calvinist influences.	Strongly ecumenical, holding talks with many branches of Christendom.	**Episco-palians**
Meetings are held in Kingdom Halls and members' homes for study and worship; [extensive door-to-door visitations].	High moral code; stress on marital fidelity and family values; avoidance of tobacco and blood transfusions.	[God, by his first creation, Christ, will soon destroy all wickedness; 144,000 faithful ones will rule in heaven with Christ over others on a paradise earth.]	Total allegiance proclaimed only to God's kingdom or heavenly government by Christ.	**Jehovah's Witnesses**
Simple service with prayers, hymns, sermon; private temple ceremonies may be more elaborate.	Temperance; strict moral code; [tithing]; a strong work ethic with communal self-reliance; [strong missionary activity]; family emphasis.	Jesus Christ is the Son of God, the Eternal Father. Jesus's atonement saves all humans; those who are obedient to God's laws may become joint-heirs with Christ in God's kingdom.	Mormons believe theirs is the true church of Jesus Christ, restored by God through Joseph Smith. Official name: The Church of Jesus Christ of Latter-day Saints.	**Latter-day Saints (Mormons)**
Relatively simple, formal liturgy with emphasis on the sermon.	Generally conservative in personal and social ethics; doctrine of "two kingdoms" (worldly and holy) supports conservatism in secular affairs.	Salvation by grace alone through faith; Lutheranism has made major contributions to Protestant theology.	Though still somewhat divided along ethnic lines (German, Swedish, etc.), main divisions are between fundamentalists and liberals.	**Lutherans**
Worship style varies widely by denomination, local church, geography.	Originally pietist and perfectionist; always strong social activist elements.	No distinctive theological development; 25 articles abridged from Church of England's 39, not binding.	In 1968, The United Methodist Church was formed by the union of The Methodist Church and The Evangelical United Brethren Church.	**Methodists**
Elaborate liturgy, usually in the vernacular, though extremely traditional; the liturgy is the essence of Orthodoxy; veneration of icons.	Tolerant; little stress on social action; divorce, remarriage permitted in some cases; bishops are celibate; priests need not be.	Emphasis on Christ's resurrection, rather than crucifixion; the Holy Spirit proceeds from God the Father only.	Orthodox Church in America originally under Patriarch of Moscow, was granted autonomy in 1970; Greek Orthodox do not recognize this autonomy.	**Orthodox**
Loosely structured service with rousing hymns and sermons, culminating in spirit baptism.	Usually, emphasis on perfectionism, with varying degrees of tolerance.	Simple traditional beliefs, usually Protestant with emphasis on the immediate presence of God in the Holy Spirit.	Once appealed mostly to lower classes; formation of charismatic fellowships in mainline churches expanded reach.	**Pentecostal**
A simple, sober service in which the sermon is central.	Traditionally, a tendency toward strictness, with firm church- and self-discipline; otherwise tolerant.	Emphasizes the sovereignty and justice of God; no longer dogmatic.	Although traces of belief in predestination (that God has foreordained salvation for the "elect") remain, this idea is no longer a central element in Presbyterianism.	**Presby-terians**
Relatively elaborate ritual centered on the Mass; also rosary recitation, novenas.	Traditionally strict but increasingly tolerant in practice; divorce and remarriage not accepted, but annulments sometimes granted; celibate clergy, except in Eastern rite.	Highly elaborated; salvation by merit gained through grace; dogmatic; special veneration of Mary, the mother of Jesus.	Relatively rapid changes followed Vatican Council II (1962-65). Mass held in vernacular instead of Latin; more stress on social action, tolerance, ecumenism.	**Roman Catholics**
Usually simple service with emphasis on the sermon.	Tolerant; some social action emphasis.	Standard Protestant; Statement of Faith (1959) is not binding.	Two main churches in the 1957 union represented earlier unions with small groups of almost every Protestant denomination.	**United Church of Christ**

Books of the Bible

Old Testament—Standard Protestant List

Genesis	I Kings	Ecclesiastes	Obadiah
Exodus	II Kings	Song of Solomon	Jonah
Leviticus	I Chronicles	Isaiah	Micah
Numbers	II Chronicles	Jeremiah	Nahum
Deuteronomy	Ezra	Lamentations	Habakkuk
Joshua	Nehemiah	Ezekiel	Zephaniah
Judges	Esther	Daniel	Haggai
Ruth	Job	Hosea	Zechariah
I Samuel	Psalms	Joel	Malachi
II Samuel	Proverbs	Amos	

New Testament List

Matthew	Ephesians	Hebrews
Mark	Philippians	James
Luke	Colossians	I Peter
John	I Thessalonians	II Peter
Acts	II Thessalonians	I John
Romans	I Timothy	II John
I Corinthians	II Timothy	III John
II Corinthians	Titus	Jude
Galatians	Philemon	Revelation

The standard Protestant Old Testament consists of the same 39 books as in the Bible of Judaism, but the latter is organized differently. The Old Testament used by Roman Catholics has 7 additional deuterocanonical books, plus some additional parts of books. The 7 are **Tobit, Judith, Wisdom, Sirach (Ecclesiasticus), Baruch, I Maccabees,** and **II Maccabees.** Both Catholic and Protestant versions of the New Testament have 27 books with the same names.

Figures in the Hebrew Bible (Old Testament)

Aaron: First of Hebrew high priests; brother of Moses and Miriam.

Abel: Second son of Adam and Eve; slain by Cain.

Abraham: Founder of monotheism; patriarch; also called Abram.

Adam: First human according to Genesis.

Amos: Herdsman; prophesized against social injustice and oppression of the poor.

Bathsheba: Seduced by King David; mother of King Solomon.

Cain: First son of Adam and Eve; killed his brother Abel.

Cyrus: Persian ruler; sent Jews home to Jerusalem from exile.

Daniel: Cast into lion's den for violating decree of King Darius; saved.

David: Israel's greatest king; shepherd, warrior, musician, psalmist.

Deborah: Prophet and judge; ruled over Israel.

Elijah: Great prophet; was victorious over the priests of the Phoenician god Baal.

Elisha: Prophet; successor to Elijah.

Esther: Jewish wife of the king of Persia; saved Jews from annihilation.

Eve: First woman according to Genesis.

Ezekiel: Visionary; prophesized hope to exiled Jews in Babylon.

Ezra: Great Jewish leader; rededicated worship and Torah law after exile.

Goliath: Giant Philistine warrior; slain by David.

Hannah: Childless; promised child to God; mother to the prophet Samuel.

Hosea: Enacted prophecy; asked God's forgiveness for Israel's unfaithfulness.

Isaac: Son of Abraham and Sarah; saved from sacrificial altar.

Isaiah: Highly educated prophet; avoided war with Assyria; Israel destroyed; Jerusalem survived.

Jacob: Son of Isaac; father of the Twelve Tribes; renamed "Israel" by angel.

Jeremiah: Confronted leaders and urged surrender to Babylon.

Jezebel: Phoenician queen of King Ahab of Israel; had Israelite prophets killed.

Job: "Blameless" man; allowed by God to lose family, health, and possessions in a test of his faith.

Jonah: Swallowed by a great fish; prophesied destruction of the city of Nineveh, averted when the people repented.

Jonathan: Son of King Saul; friend of David.

Joseph: Favorite of Jacob; interpreted Pharaoh's dreams; brought Hebrews to Egypt.

Joshua: Successor of Moses; led Hebrews into Canaan.

Josiah: Reformist king; repaired Solomon's Temple; restored worship; reintroduced Passover.

Leah: Matriarch; older sister of Rachel; Jacob's wife.

Micah: Prophet; predicted the end of war and beginning of peace.

Miriam: Prophet and great leader of the Hebrews; sister to Moses and Aaron.

Moses: Most important Hebrew prophet; leader of the Israelites; received the Torah.

Nathan: Prophet; confronted King David over his seduction of the married Bathsheba.

Nebuchadnezzar: Babylonian king; destroyed Jerusalem.

Nehemiah: Led Jews back to Jerusalem from Babylonian exile.

Noah: Man of great faith who, according to Genesis, saved his family and two of every living thing on Earth from a great flood.

Rachel: Matriarch; younger sister of Leah; Jacob's wife; Joseph's mother.

Rebecca: Matriarch; wife of Isaac; mother of Jacob.

Ruth: Moabite convert; ancestor of David.

Samson: Judge and military leader of Israel; possessed super-human strength.

Samuel: Prophet; anointed Saul king of Israel and later anointed David to succeed him.

Sarah: First matriarch of Israel; wife of Abraham; mother of Isaac.

Saul: First king of Israel; father of Jonathan.

Solomon: King of Israel at its zenith; known for great wisdom.

Zechariah: Prophet; encouraged rebuilding of Solomon's Temple, which had been destroyed by Babylonians.

Figures in the New Testament

Andrew: One of the Twelve Apostles; brother of Peter and former fisherman; one of the earlier disciples.

Barabbas: Imprisoned with Jesus; set free by Pilate on Passover.

Barnabas: Disciple of Jesus; closely connected with Paul.

Bartholomew: A lesser-known member of the Twelve Apostles; cheerful and prayed often.

Cornelius: Roman convert; defended by Peter, allowing Gentiles to become Christians.

Elizabeth: Mother of John the Baptist; relation of the Virgin Mary.

Gabriel: Archangel; appeared to the Virgin Mary to announce that she was to give birth to the Messiah.

Herod: May refer to Herod the Great, who ordered the death of children after Jesus's birth, or to his son, Herod, who had John the Baptist beheaded.

James: May refer to either of two apostles: James, son of Zebedee, brother of John the Apostle, or the lesser-known James, son of Alphaeus.

Jesus: Central figure of the Gospels; believed to be the Messiah and son of God; crucified by the Romans.

John (Apostle): Beloved disciple of Jesus; one of the Twelve Apostles; possible author of fourth Gospel; brother of James.

John (Baptist): Known as John the Baptist; important prophet and forerunner to Jesus; relation of the Virgin Mary.

Joseph: Husband of the Virgin Mary; descendant of King David.

Judas Iscariot: Betrayer of Jesus; prominent member of the Apostles; committed suicide.

Judas Thaddeus: One of the Twelve Apostles; also called Jude to distinguish him from Judas Iscariot.

Lazarus: Brother of the disciples Martha and Mary of Bethany; raised from the dead by Jesus at their request; possibly the same Lazarus who appears in Jesus's parable of the rich man.

Luke: Traditional author of the Gospel of Luke; possibly a follower of Paul.

Mark: Traditional author of the Gospel of Mark; possibly a disciple of Peter.

Mary, the mother of Jesus: Traditionally believed to be a virgin who conceived without sin; wife of Joseph.

Mary Magdalene: Important female disciple of Jesus; witness to his death and resurrection.

Matthew: One of the Twelve Apostles; possible author of the Gospel of Matthew; former tax collector.

Matthias: Often included on lists of the Twelve Apostles as the apostle who replaced Judas Iscariot after his betrayal.

Paul (Saul): Writer of nearly a quarter of the New Testament; a former persecutor of Christians, converted after a vision; played a significant role in spreading Christianity.

Peter: Considered the foremost of the Twelve Apostles; traditionally the first pope and "rock" of the Christian church; author of epistles; also called Simon and Simon Peter.

Philip: One of the Twelve; considered pragmatic and sensible.

Pilate, Pontius: A Roman prefect; played large role in the trial and crucifixion of Jesus.

Simon: One of the Twelve Apostles; known as "the Zealot" to distinguish from Simon Peter.

Stephen: Fervently preached that Jesus was the Messiah; stoned to death by angry mob, including Saul (Paul); important figure in Saul's conversion.

Thomas: One of the Twelve Apostles; known as "Doubting Thomas" because he did not believe Jesus was risen until he could touch him.

Timothy: A disciple closely connected with Paul; recipient of epistles.

Zacharias: Father of John the Baptist; husband of Elizabeth; struck dumb when he doubted his barren wife could become pregnant.

Major Religions

Islam

Founded: Muhammad received his first revelation in 610 CE.

Founder: Muhammad (c. 570-632 CE), the Prophet.

Sacred texts: Two texts constitute the Muslim sacred canon, the *Quran* (Koran) and the *Hadith*. The Quran provides the foundation for Islamic religion and culture. It is regarded as the final, perfect, and complete word of God as revealed to Muhammad over the course of his life. Received by Muhammad in the Arabic language, it is memorized in Arabic by adherents regardless of their native language. It is divided into 114 chapters of unequal length, the shortest containing only 3 verses, and the longest containing 286 verses. The Quran is the ultimate source of everything Islamic, from metaphysics to theology to sacred history, to ethics and law, to art. The Hadith, which describes Muhammad's actions, attitudes, and teachings, complements the Quran. Due to its long history of oral transmission, the Hadith's lessons are seen as somewhat vulnerable to human error. It is not said to contain God's unadulterated voice as is the Quran but functions as a powerful spiritual and behavioral code nonetheless.

Organization: Muhammad was both the last prophet and a statesman. Muslim leaders have often assumed both civil and moral functions within Islamic states. Within the larger community, there are cultural and national groups, held together by a common religious law, the *Sharia*. Muslims believe that God is the ultimate lawgiver and that human beings cannot devise laws that oppose divine laws. Still, the Sharia is approached differently in different parts of the Islamic world. Over the centuries, Sunnis have developed four major schools of law: the Hanafi, the Shafi'i, the Hanbali, and the Maliki. The Ja'fari is the most important and well-known Shiite school. Before the 20th century, religious scholars known as the *ulama* held much legal power. Judges (*qadis*) and law-interpreters (*muftis*) are people learned in religious law who lead congregational prayers in mosques and perform other religious duties.

Practice: Five duties (of both men and women), known as the Pillars of Islam, are regarded as cardinal in Islam and as central to the life of the Islamic community. In accordance with Islam's absolute commitment to monotheism, the first duty is the profession of faith (the *Shahadah*): "There is no God but Allah and Muhammad is His Prophet." A Muslim must profess this belief publicly at least once in his or her lifetime; it defines the membership of an individual in the Islamic community. The second duty is that of five daily prayers organized in intervals throughout the day: sunrise, early afternoon, late afternoon, immediately after sunset, and before midnight. During prayer, Muslims face the Kaaba, a small, cube-shaped structure in the courtyard of al-Haram (the "inviolate place"), at the Grand Mosque of Mecca in Saudi Arabia. All five prayers in Islam are congregational and are to be offered in a mosque, but they may be offered individually if one cannot be present with a congregation. Congregational prayer is required only at the early afternoon prayer on Friday for men. The third cardinal duty of a Muslim is to pay alms, or *zakat*, which should be 2.5% of one's total wealth. This was originally the tax levied by Muhammad on the wealthy members of the community, primarily to help the poor. Only when zakat has been paid is the rest of a Muslim's property considered purified and legitimate. The fourth duty is the fast of the lunar month of Ramadan. During the fasting month, one must abstain from eating, drinking, smoking, impure thoughts, and sexual intercourse from dawn until sunset, and feed at least one poor person, if able. The fifth duty is the pilgrimage to the Kaaba, known as the hajj, which a Muslim must undertake, with exceptions for poverty and ill health, at least once during his or her lifetime.

Divisions: There are two major groups: the majority Sunni (85%-90% of the worldwide Muslim population) and the minority Shiites. Sects first appeared in Islam at the time of Muhammad's death. The group that came to be known as Sunni accepted Abu Bakr, an early convert, as his successor (caliph), while a smaller number, which became the Shia, believed that Ali ibn Abi Talib, the son-in-law and first cousin of the prophet, should have become his successor (Imam). Imams are believed to interpret the Quran infallibly. **Shiites** fall into three major branches: Fivers, Seveners, and Twelvers, reflecting the number of Imams they recognize. Twelvers believe that the 12th Imam has lived an invisible existence since 874, and will return as the Mahdi (a messiah figure) who will usher in a 1,000-year reign of peace and justice. **Sufism** (mystical dimension of Islam) emphasizes personal relation to God and obedience informed by love of God; it is prevalent among both Sunni and Shiites.

Location: W Africa to Philippines, across a band including E Africa, Central Asia and western China, India, Malaysia, Indonesia. Islam has several million adherents in North America and about 30 mil in Europe.

Beliefs: Strictly monotheistic. God is creator of the universe, omnipotent, omniscient, just, forgiving, and merciful. God revealed the Quran to Muhammad to guide humanity to truth and justice. Those who sincerely "submit" (literal meaning of "Islam") to God attain salvation.

World's Largest Muslim Populations, 2024

Source: Gina A. Zurlo, ed., *World Religion Database* (Leiden/Boston: Brill, July 2023).

Rank	Country	Muslim population	% of country's pop.
1.	Pakistan	230,135,000	96.7%
2.	Indonesia	226,505,000	79.6
3.	India	215,654,000	15.1
4.	Bangladesh	151,843,000	88.8
5.	Nigeria	106,673,000	46.8
6.	Egypt	99,291,000	90.4
7.	Iran	86,575,000	98.5
8.	Turkey	84,833,000	98.3
9.	Algeria	45,878,000	98.2
10.	Sudan	44,552,000	92.4
11.	Ethiopia	43,345,000	34.2
12.	Iraq	43,176,000	97.7
13.	Afghanistan	42,555,000	99.9
14.	Morocco	38,485,000	99.7
15.	Uzbekistan	33,912,000	96.3
16.	Saudi Arabia	33,227,000	90.3
17.	Yemen	32,224,000	99.2
18.	Niger	27,146,000	96.7
19.	China	26,345,000	1.8
20.	Tanzania	21,824,000	32.6
21.	Syria	20,960,000	95.6
22.	Mali	20,316,000	89.3
23.	Malaysia	18,969,000	55.8
24.	Russia	18,566,000	12.8
25.	Somalia	17,827,000	99.9

Baha'i

Founded: Mid-19th century.

Founder: Mirza Husayn-Ali Nuri (1817-92), later known as Baha'u'llah (Arabic for "Glory of God").

Sacred texts: The writings of Baha'u'llah and of his herald the Bab (Siyyid Ali-Muhammad, 1819-50). The primary text is *Kitab-i-Aqdas* (Most Holy Book).

Organization: The Baha'i administrative system consists of elected nine-member councils at the local, national, and international levels. There are also more than 180 National Spiritual Assemblies and an elected, international governing body known as the Universal House of Justice.

Practice: Prayer, meditation, and fasting are key components of the Baha'i Faith. Work performed in a spirit of service to humanity is considered an important form of worship. The Baha'i Faith has no clergy and minimal ritual and congregational worship.

Divisions: In a religion in which unity is perhaps the central spiritual value, the Baha'i Faith has avoided separating into sects with differentiated theologies and practices.

Location: Worldwide.

Beliefs: God has progressively revealed His will and purpose through a series of Divine manifestations including Jesus, Buddha, Muhammad, Zoroaster, and Baha'u'llah. Baha'u'llah's teachings include the oneness of humanity, the equality of men and women, the harmony of science and religion, and the need to abandon all forms of prejudice and eliminate extremes of poverty and wealth.

Buddhism

Founded: About 525 BCE, reportedly near Benares, India.

Founder: Gautama Siddhartha (c. 563-483 BCE), the Buddha, who achieved enlightenment through intense meditation.

Sacred texts: The *Tripitaka*, a collection of the Buddha's teachings, rules of monastic life, and philosophical commentaries on the teachings; also a vast body of Buddhist teachings and commentaries, many of which are called *sutras*.

Organization: The basic institution is the *sangha*, or monastic order, through which traditions are passed down. Monastic life tends to be democratic and antiauthoritarian.

Practice: Varies widely according to the sect and ranges from austere meditation to magical chanting and elaborate temple rites. Many practices, such as exorcism of devils, reflect pre-Buddhist beliefs.

Divisions: A variety of sects grouped into three primary branches: Theravada, which emphasizes the importance of pure thought and deed; Mahayana (includes Zen and Soka-gakkai), which ranges from philosophical schools to belief in the saving grace of higher beings or ritual practices and to practical meditative disciplines; and Vajrayana, or Tantrism, a combination of belief in ritual magic and sophisticated philosophy.

Location: Mainly in Asia, from Sri Lanka to Japan.

Beliefs: Life is suffering, and there is no ultimate reality behind it. The cycle of birth and rebirth continues because of desire and attachment to the unreal "self." Meditation and deeds will end the cycle and achieve Nirvana (nothingness, enlightenment).

Hinduism

Founded: About 1500 BCE to 300 CE as a religion and *dharma* (way of life); a diverse synthesis of primarily Indian traditions, practices, and beliefs.

Sacred texts: The *Vedas* (Rig, Sama, Yajur, Atharva); the *Upanishads*, a collection of rituals and commentaries; a vast number of epic stories about gods, heroes, and saints, including the *Puranas*, *Ramayana*, and *Mahabharata*; the *Bhagavad Gita*; and the *Agamas*.

Organization: None, strictly speaking. No single founder, establishment date, authoritative scripture, or central religious organization exist.

Practice: *Sanskara*, or rites of passage (e.g., initiation, marriage, death), and devotionals (*bhakti*). Bhakti may be practiced privately, as at a household shrine, or in a group.

Divisions: There is no concept of orthodoxy in Hinduism, which presents a variety of sects. Three major traditions are those devoted to the gods Vishnu and Shiva and to the goddess Shakti, but others believe in *brahman* (the All) as a more impersonal but infinite spiritual core. Numerous beliefs and practices, often in amalgamation, exist side by side with various philosophical schools.

Location: Mainly India, Nepal, Malaysia, Mauritius, Guyana, Suriname, and Sri Lanka.

Beliefs: Two basic tenets of Hinduism include a belief in the unity of existence as well as in the process of transmigration and rebirth (*samsara*) with no clear beginning or end. Life in all its forms is an aspect or manifestation of the divine or of divine qualities.

Judaism

Founded: About 2000 BCE.

Founder: Abraham is regarded as the founding patriarch.

Sacred texts: The five books of Moses (the Torah), the basic source of teachings.

Organization: Originally theocratic, Judaism has evolved into a congregational polity. The basic institution is the local synagogue or temple, operated by the congregation and led by a rabbi of their choice. Chief rabbis in France and Great Britain have authority only over those who accept it; in Israel, the two chief rabbis (one each from the Sephardic Jewish and Ashkenazi Jewish communities) have civil authority in family law.

Practice: Among traditional practitioners, almost all areas of life are governed by strict discipline. Sabbath and holidays are marked by observances, and attendance at public worship is considered especially important. Chief annual observances are Passover, celebrating liberation of the Israelites from Egypt and marked by the Seder meal in homes, and the 10 days from Rosh Hashanah (New Year) to Yom Kippur (Day of Atonement), a period of penitence.

Divisions: Judaism is an unbroken spectrum from ultraconservative to ultraliberal, largely reflecting different points of view regarding the binding character of the prohibitions and duties—particularly the dietary and Sabbath observations—traditionally prescribed for the daily life of the Jew.

Location: Mainly in Israel and the U.S.

Beliefs: Strictly monotheistic. God is the creator and ruler of the universe. God established a particular relationship with the Hebrew people: by obeying a divine law God gave them, they would be a special witness to God's mercy and justice. Judaism stresses ethical behavior (and, among the traditional, careful ritual obedience) as true worship of God.

Sikhism

Founded: Late 15th century in South Asia.

Founder: Guru Nanak Dev ji, Sikhism's first Guru.

Sacred texts: The *Guru Granth Sahib* was compiled by the Sikh Gurus and contains their experiences of the Divine. It also contains writings by other saintly figures of different faiths.

Organization: Each Sikh must make her or his own spiritual journey and not depend on clergy. Congregational prayer led by both men and women takes place in local *Gurdwaras* ("doorway to the Guru"). Harmandir Sahib in Amritsar, Punjab (northern India), is the central place of worship.

Practice: Prayers are required in the morning, evening, and before sleeping. The most important mode of congregational prayer is the singing of hymns from the Guru Granth Sahib. The "Five Ks" are five articles of faith required of all Sikhs: *Kes* (uncut hair), *Kangha* (comb), *Kara* (steel bracelet), *Kirpan* (sword), and *Kaccha* (short pants).

Divisions: The last living Guru, Guru Gobind Singh (1666-1708), crystallized the practices and beliefs of the faith and determined that no future living Guru was needed. Today the religion is guided by joint sovereignty of Guru Granth and Guru Panth. Guru Granth is the Sikh scripture, as the spiritual manifestation of the Guru, while the Guru Panth is the collectivity of all initiated Sikhs worldwide, as the physical manifestation of the Guru.

Location: Many Sikhs have Punjabi backgrounds. The Punjab region was divided between India and Pakistan with the end of British rule.

Beliefs: Sikhism preaches a message of devotion, remembrance of God at all times, truthful living, equality between all human beings, and social justice, while denouncing what is considered superstition and blind ritualism. Sikhism is a monotheistic religion based on revelation.

LANGUAGE

New Words in English

The following new words and definitions were provided by Merriam-Webster, Inc., publishers of *Merriam-Webster's Collegiate Dictionary, Eleventh Edition*, and other language references. The words are among those added in 2023 by Merriam-Webster's editors to the digital version of the dictionary, available as the *Merriam-Webster Dictionary* app and online at www.merriam-webster.com.

alt text: a short piece of usually hidden text that is associated with a digital image on the internet

bad actor: a person, group, country, etc. who purposely and usually repeatedly engages in very bad behavior

bingo card *slang:* a list of possible, expected, or likely scenarios—usually used in the phrase *on one's bingo card*

cheffy: characteristic of or befitting a professional chef (as in showiness, complexity, or exoticness)

chonky *informal:* plump or chubby especially in an endearing way

cold open: a scene of a film or television episode that precedes the title sequence or opening credits

drip *African American English:* a fashionable style or look

dunk on *slang:* to publicly make fun of (someone or something) especially on social media

emotional intelligence: the ability to recognize, understand, and deal skillfully with one's own emotions and the emotions of others

e-scooter: a scooter propelled by an electric motor

friend zone: a state of friendship in which one's romantic or sexual interest in someone is not reciprocated

gameplay: the characteristic way in which the action of a game (such as a video game) occurs or is experienced

'grammable: suitable to be posted on the Instagram photo-sharing service

jollof rice: a West African dish of rice cooked in a sauce of tomatoes and onions seasoned usually with garlic, thyme, hot pepper, and other spices and often accompanied by meat, fish, or vegetables

JOMO *informal:* joy of missing out: joy experienced when not attending events to which one has been invited

jump scare: a scripted moment (as in a film or video game) intended to startle the audience

kayfabe: the tacit agreement between professional wrestlers and their fans to pretend that overtly staged wrestling events, stories, characters, etc., are genuine

love language: a person's characteristic means of showing love or care for another

mooncake: a small pastry filled with sweet or savory ingredients and traditionally associated with the Mid-Autumn Festival in Chinese culture and various other East and Southeast Asian cultures

nanoplastic: an extremely small piece of plastic especially when occurring as an environmental pollutant

non-player character: a character in a video game that does not represent and cannot be manipulated by a player

nurdle: a plastic pellet that is usually less than 0.2 inch (0.5 centimeter) in diameter or length, that is the raw material from which plastic products are manufactured, and that is a common pollutant of global waters and beaches

performativity *often disapproving:* the state of being made or done for show (as to bolster one's own image or make a positive impression on others)

quiet quitting: the practice of doing the minimum amount of work required for one's job

review bomb: to post a usually negative online review of (a product, business, etc.) especially as part of a coordinated campaign

rewild: to return (an animal) to the wild

slacktivism: the practice of conspicuously showing support for a cause without taking any real steps to effect change

smishing: the practice of sending text messages to someone in order to trick the person into revealing personal or confidential information which can then be used for criminal purposes

solar farm: a large installation of typically ground-mounted solar panels that generates electricity for distribution by a public utility

spoolie: a very small brush used especially to groom the eyebrows or to apply mascara

the tea *slang:* private or inside information especially of a personal nature—usually used in the phrase *spill the tea*

world-building: the creation of a fictional world that is believable and consistent within the context of the story

National Spelling Bee

The Scripps National Spelling Bee, conducted each year since 1925, allows students under age 16 in 8th grade or lower to compete for a chance to advance to national championship finals in Washington, DC. After announcing it was running out of challenging words, the competition named eight spellers co-champions in 2019; the 2020 Bee was canceled due to the COVID-19 pandemic. The contest format was changed repeatedly 2021-23 to help avert ties that had become increasingly common in recent years. In 2023, Dev Shah, a 14-year-old from Largo, FL, was named the winner. The runner-up, Charlotte Walsh of Merrifield, VA, was eliminated in round 14 after misspelling *daviely*.

Here are the last words given and spelled correctly at the National Spelling Bee in recent years:

1982	psoriasis	1992	lyceum	2002	prospicience	2012	guetapens	2018	koinonia
1983	purim	1993	kamikaze	2003	pococurante	2013	knaidel	2019	auslaut, erysipelas,
1984	luge	1994	antediluvian	2004	autochthonous	2014	feuilleton		palama, aiguillette,
1985	milieu	1995	xanthosis	2005	appoggiatura		stichomythia		odylic, cernuous,
1986	odontalgia	1996	vivisepulture	2006	Ursprache	2015	scherenschnitte		pendeloque,
1987	staphylococci	1997	euonym	2007	serrefine		nunatak		bougainvillea
1988	elegiacal	1998	chiaroscurist	2008	guerdon	2016	Feldenkrais	2021	murraya
1989	spoliator	1999	logorrhea	2009	Laodicean		gesellschaft	2022	moorhen
1990	fibranne	2000	demarche	2010	stromuhr	2017	marocain	2023	psammophile
1991	antipyretic	2001	succedaneum	2011	cymotrichous				

Non-English Words and Phrases Commonly Used by English Speakers

A = Arabic; F = French; Ger = German; Gr = Greek; I = Italian; J = Japanese; L = Latin; R = Russian; S = Spanish; Y = Yiddish

ad hoc (L; ad-HOK): for the end or purpose at hand; impromptu

ad hominem (L; ad-HOH-mee-nem): argument that criticizes an opponent, often unfairly, rather than addressing an issue directly

al fresco (F; ahl-FRAYS-koh): outdoors

anime (J: A-nuh-may): Japanese-style animation

apparatchik (R: ap-per-AT-chik): functionary; blindly devoted official or working member of a party/other organization

au courant (F; oh-koo-RAHN): up-to-date, fashionable

belles lettres (F; bel-LET-truh): writing aspiring to artistic merit

bête noire (F; bet-NWAHR): literally, black beast; a thing or person viewed with particular dislike or fear

bildungsroman (Ger; BIL-doongs-roh-mahn): novel embodying coming-of-age story

bodega (S; boh-DAY-gah): grocery store

bon vivant (F; bon-vee-VAHN): a person with refined tastes, esp. for food and drink

bonhomie (F; boh-noh-MEE): friendliness

bourgeois (F; boo-ZHWAH): middle-class; materialistic

carte blanche (F; kahrt-BLANSH): full discretionary power

cause célèbre (F; kawz-suh-LEB): a notorious incident

chutzpah (Y, HUHTS-pah): audacity, nerve

coup de grâce (F; kooh-duh-GRAHS): the decisive final blow

cum laude/magna cum laude/summa cum laude (L; kuhm-LOU-day; MAG-na ... ; SOO-ma ...): with praise or honor/with great praise or honor/with the highest praise or honor

de facto (L; day-FAK-toh): in fact, if not by law

de jure (L; dee-JOOR-ee, day-YOOR-ay): by right or by law

de rigueur (F; duh-ree-GUR): required by convention or etiquette

détente (F; day-TAHNT): an easing of strained relations

deus ex machina (L; DAY-uhs-eks-MAH-keh-nah): person/event that provides a solution unexpectedly or suddenly, esp. (in literature) a contrived solution to a plot

doppelgänger (Ger; DAH-pul-gang-ur): a double or ghostly counterpart of a person

double entendre (F; DOO-blahn-TAHN-druh): expression with a double meaning, one meaning of which is often risqué

e pluribus unum (L; eh-PLOO-ree-boos-OO-noom): out of many, one (U.S. motto)

éminence grise (F; ay-meh-nahns-GREEZ): one who wields power behind the scenes

ennui (F; ah-NOOEE): boredom; world-weariness; annoyance

ersatz (Ger; EHR-zats): artificial; being a (usually inferior) substitute

ex post facto (L; eks-pohst-FAK-toh): retroactive(ly)

fait accompli (F; fayt-uh-kom-PLEE): an accomplished fact

fatwa (A; FAHT-wah): in Islam, a legal or religious decree

faux pas (F; foh-PAH): false step; breach of etiquette

habeas corpus (L; HAY-bee-ahs-KOR-pus): an order for a prisoner to be brought to court to challenge his or her detention

hoi polloi (Gr; hoy-puh-LOY): the masses

impresario (I; im-prah-SAH-ri-oh): manager, promoter, or sponsor of a musical or theatrical program or company

imprimatur (L; im-prah-MAH-toor): approval or official permission to print, esp. by the Roman Catholic church

in loco parentis (L; in-LOH-koh-puh-REN-tis): in place of a parent

in medias res (L; in-MAY-dee-oos-rays): into the middle of things

intelligentsia (R; in-te-luh-JEN-see-uh): elite social class made up of intellectuals and educated people

ipso facto (L; ip-soh-FAK-toh): by that fact itself

je ne sais quoi (F; zhuh-nuh-say-KWAH): literally, "I don't know what"; the little something that eludes description

jihad (A; jih-HAHD): Islamic holy war; struggle in devotion to Islam

joie de vivre (F; zhwah-duh-VEEV-ruh): zest for life

kvetch (Y; Kuh-VETCH): complain, gripe

leitmotif (Ger; lyt-moh-TEEF): the central theme or idea, particularly in art and literature

mano a mano (S; MAH-noh-ah-MAH-noh): hand to hand; in direct combat

mea culpa (L; MAY-uh-CUL-puh): through my fault

mensch (Y; MENTSCH): an upright, noble, admirable person

modus operandi (L; MOH-duhs-op-uh-RAN-dee): method of operation

mujahedeen (A; moo-jah-ha-DEEN): Islamic holy warrior

noblesse oblige (F; nuh-BLES-oh-BLEEZH): the obligation of nobility to help the less fortunate

nolo contendere (L; NOH-loh-kohn-TEN-duh-ree): a plea of no contest to charges, without admitting guilt

non compos mentis (L; non-KOM-puhs-MEN-tis): not of sound mind

non sequitur (L; non-SEH-kwi-tour): a conclusion that does not logically follow from what preceded it

nouveau riche (F; noo-voh-REESH): a newly rich person, esp. one who spends money conspicuously

ombudsman (Swedish; AHM-budz-muhn): person who receives, investigates, and settles complaints

pariah (Tamil; par-EYE-ah): an outcast; member of low caste in India

persona non grata (L; per-SOH-nah-non-GRAH-tah): unwelcome person

pièce de résistance (F; pee-es-duh-ray-ZEES-tonz): the outstanding item in a series or group

prima facie (L; pry-muh-FAY-shee-ee; pry-muh-FAY-shuh): true at first glance; presumptively valid

pro bono (L; proh-BOH-noh): (work) donated for the public good

quid pro quo (L; kwid-proh-KWOH): something given or received for something else

raison d'être (F; RAY-zohnn-DET-ruh): reason for being

savoir faire (F; sav-wahr-FAIR): dexterity in social affairs

schadenfreude (Ger; SHAH-duhn-froy-deh): joy at another's misfortune

semper fidelis (L; SEM-puhr-fee-DAY-lis): always faithful

sobriquet (F; SOH-bri-kay): nickname or informal descriptive name for someone

sotto voce (I; sah-toh-VOH-chee); in a low voice

sui generis (L; soo-ee-JEN-er-is); unique; one of a kind

terra firma (L; TER-uh-FUR-muh): solid ground

verboten (Ger; ver-BOH-ten): forbidden

vis-à-vis (F; vee-zuh-VEE): compared with; with regard to

voir dire (F; vwar-DEER): examination by lawyers or judge to determine the suitability of a witness or a prospective juror

zeitgeist (Ger; ZITE-gyste): the general intellectual, moral, and cultural climate of an era

Names for Animal Young

calf: cattle, elephant, hippo, camel, others
cheeper: grouse, partridge, quail
chick: chicken, penguin, other birds
cockerel: rooster
codling, sprag: codfish
colt: horse, zebra (male)
cria: llama, alpaca
cub: lion, bear, shark, fox, others
cygnet: swan
duckling: duck
elver: eel
ephyra: jellyfish
eyas: hawk, other birds

fawn: deer, antelope
filly: horse, zebra (female)
fingerling, fry: fish generally
fledgling, nestling: birds generally
foal: horse, zebra, others
gosling: goose
heifer: cow
hoglet: hedgehog
joey: kangaroo, opossum, wombat
kid: goat
kit: beaver, rabbit, ferret, others
kitten: cat, other small mammals
lamb: sheep

larva: frog, sea urchin, insects generally
parr, smolt, grilse: salmon
piglet, shoat, farrow, suckling: pig
polliwog, tadpole: frog
poult: turkey
pullet: hen
pup: dog, fox, seal, rat, others
spat: oyster, other bivalves
spiderling: spider
spike, blinker, tinker: mackerel
squab: pigeon
whelp: dog, tiger, other carnivores
yearling: cattle, sheep, horse, others

Names for Animal Collectives

alligators: congregation
ants: army, colony, swarm
apes: shrewdness, troop
bears: sleuth, sloth
bees: colony, swarm, hive
birds: flight, volery
buffalo: gang, obstinacy
butterflies: flutter
buzzards: wake
camels: caravan, flock, train
cats: clowder, cluster, pounce
cattle: drove
cheetahs: coalition
cockroaches: intrusion
cranes: sedge, siege
crocodiles: bask, nest, float
crows: murder, horde
dolphins: pod
doves: dule, pitying

ducks: brace, team
eagles: convocation, aerie
ferrets: business
finches: charm
fish: school, shoal
flamingos: stand, flamboyance
foxes: skulk
geese: flock, gaggle, skein
giraffes: corps, herd, tower
goats: tribe, trip
gorillas: band, troop, whoop
grasshoppers: cloud
hawks: cast, kettle
hedgehogs: array, prickle
hippopotamuses: bloat
horses: pair, team
hounds: cry, mute, pack
hyenas: cackle

iguanas: mess
jellyfish: smack
kangaroos: mob, troop
larks: exaltation
leopards: leap
lions: pride
locusts: plague, swarm
mice, rats: mischief
moles: labor
monkeys: troop
mules: barren, span
nightingales: watch
otters: romp
owls: parliament
oxen: yoke
peacocks: muster
pheasants: nest, nide, bouquet
ponies: string

raccoons: gaze
ravens: unkindness
rhinoceroses: crash
seals: pod
sheep: flock, drove, hurtle
snakes: nest
squirrels: dray, scurry
starlings: flock, murmuration
swans: bevy
tigers: streak
toads: knot
trout: hover
turkeys: rafter
turtles: bale
vultures: committee
whales: gam, herd, pod
woodchucks: fall
woodpeckers: descent
zebras: herd, zeal

Some Common Abbreviations

(See also Abbreviations in the General Index.) Abbreviations include acronyms, pronounceable words formed from first letters, or syllables, of other words, e.g., AIDS. Some acronyms are words coined as abbreviations and written in lowercase (e.g., sonar). Italicized words below are Latin unless otherwise noted.

A: ampere
AA: Alcoholics Anonymous
ABA: American Bar Association
AC: alternating current; air-conditioning
ACA: Affordable Care Act
ACLU: American Civil Liberties Union
AD: *anno Domini* (in the year of the Lord)
AD(H)D: attention deficit (hyperactivity) disorder
AFL-CIO: American Federation of Labor-Congress of Industrial Organizations
AFSCME: American Federation of State, County, and Municipal Employees
AFT: American Federation of Teachers
AI: artificial intelligence
AIDS: acquired immune deficiency syndrome

ALA: American Library Association
a.m. or **AM:** *ante meridiem* (before noon)
AP: Associated Press
APO: army post office
APR: annual percentage rate
AQAP: al-Qaeda in the Arabian Peninsula
ARM: adjustable rate mortgage
ASAP: as soon as possible
ASCAP: American Society of Composers, Authors, and Publishers
ASCII: American Standard Code for Information Interchange
ATM: automated teller machine
Ave.: Avenue
AWOL: absent without leave
BA: Bachelor of Arts
bbl: barrel(s)

BC: before Christ
BCE: before Common, or Christian, Era
Benelux: Belgium, Netherlands, Luxembourg
bpd or **b/d:** barrels per day
BRB: be right back
Brexit: BRitish EXIT (from the EU)
BS: Bachelor of Science
Btu: British thermal unit(s)
BTW: by the way
B2B: business-to-business (company)
bu: bushel(s)
BYOB: bring your own bottle
C: Celsius, centigrade
c.: *circa* (about); copyright
C(A)T: computerized (axial) tomography
CD: compact disc

CDC: Centers for Disease Control and Prevention; Community Development Corporation

CE: Common Era; Christian Era

CEO: chief executive officer

cf.: *confer* (compare)

CFO: chief financial officer

CIA: Central Intelligence Agency

COBRA: Consolidated Omnibus Budget Reconciliation Act (health insurance continuation)

COD: cash (or collect) on delivery

COL or **Col.:** Colonel

COLA: cost of living adjustment

COO: chief operating officer

CPA: certified public accountant

CPI: consumer price index

CPL or **Cpl.:** Corporal

CPR: cardiopulmonary resuscitation

CPU: central processing unit

CRT: critical race theory

CST: central standard time

CV: curriculum vitae

DA: district attorney

DACA: Deferred Action for Childhood Arrivals

DC: direct current

DD: Doctor of Divinity

DDS: Doctor of Dental Surgery

DEA: Drug Enforcement Administration

DHS: Department of Homeland Security

DJ or **deejay:** disc jockey

DM: direct message

DMD: Doctor of Dental Medicine

DMZ: demilitarized zone

DNA: deoxyribonucleic acid

DNC: Democratic National Committee

DNR: do not resuscitate

DOA: dead on arrival

DOB: date of birth

DoD: Department of Defense

dpi: dots per inch

DPT: diphtheria, pertussis, tetanus

DUI: driving under the influence

DVD: digital video disc

DVM: Doctor of Veterinary Medicine

DWI: driving while intoxicated

ECB: European Central Bank

ed.: edited; editor; editor

EEG: electroencephalogram

e.g.: *exempli gratia* (for example)

EKG or **ECG:** electrocardiogram

EMT: emergency medical technician

EOE: equal opportunity employer

EP: extended play

EPA: Environmental Protection Agency

ERA: Equal Rights Amendment; earned run average

ESL: English as a second language

ESP: extrasensory perception

Esq.: Esquire

EST: eastern standard time

et al.: *et alii* (and others)

etc.: *et cetera* (and so forth)

EU: European Union

F: Fahrenheit

Fannie Mae: Federal National Mortgage Association

FAQ: frequently asked questions

FBI: Federal Bureau of Investigation

FDA: Food and Drug Administration

FDIC: Federal Deposit Insurance Corporation

FEC: Federal Election Commission

FEMA: Federal Emergency Management Agency

ff.: and those following

FICA: Federal Insurance Contributions Act (Social Security)

FIFA: Fédération Internationale de Football Association

fl.: *floruit* (flourished), used for historical figures when life dates uncertain

FLOTUS: First Lady of the United States

FOMO: Fear of missing out

Freddie Mac: Federal Home Loan Mortgage Corporation

FTP: file transfer protocol

FWIW: for what it's worth

FY: fiscal year

FYI: for your information

GB: gigabyte(s)

GDP: gross domestic product

GED: general equivalency diploma

GMO: genetically modified organism

GMT: Greenwich mean time

GOP: Grand Old Party (Republican Party)

GPS: Global Positioning System

GTG: got to go

GUI: graphical user interface

ha: hectare

hazmat: HAZardous MATerial

HDTV: high-definition television

HIV: human immunodeficiency virus

HMO: health maintenance organization

HMS: His/Her Majesty's Ship (UK)

Hon.: the Honorable

HOV: high-occupancy vehicle

HRH: Her (His) Royal Highness (UK)

HTML: hypertext markup language

HTTP: hypertext transfer protocol

HUD: Department of Housing and Urban Development

HVAC: heating, ventilating, and air-conditioning

Hz: hertz

ibid.: *ibidem* (in the same place)

ICE: Immigration and Customs Enforcement (agency)

ICU: intensive care unit

ICYMI: in case you missed it

i.e.: *id est* (that is)

IM: instant messaging

IMF: International Monetary Fund

IM(H)O: in my (humble) opinion

INS: Immigration and Naturalization Service

IPO: initial public offering

IQ: intelligence quotient

IRA: individual retirement account; Irish Republican Army

IRS: Internal Revenue Service

ISBN: International Standard Book Number

ISIL or **ISIS:** Islamic State of Iraq in the Levant, or of Iraq and Syria

ISP: Internet service provider

IVF: in vitro fertilization

JD: *Juris Doctor* (Doctor of Law)

k: karat; **K:** Kelvin

kWh: kilowatt-hour(s)

laser: Light Amplification by Stimulated Emission of Radiation

lb: pound

LGBT(QIA): lesbian, gay, bisexual, transgender (queer/questioning, intersex, asexual)

LLP: limited liability partnership

loc. cit.: *loco citato* (in the place cited)

LOL: laughing out loud

LSAT: Law School Admission Test

LT or **Lt.:** Lieutenant

MA: Master of Arts

MB: megabyte(s)

MBA: Master of Business Administration

MCAT: Medical College Admission Test

MD: *Medicinae Doctor* (Doctor of Medicine)

MIA: missing in action

modem: MOdulator-DEModulator

MP: member of Parliament (UK)

mph: miles per hour

MRI: magnetic resonance imaging

ms, mss: manuscript(s)

MS: Master of Science; multiple sclerosis

MSG: monosodium glutamate

MST: mountain standard time

MVP: most valuable player

MYOB: mind your own business

NA: not applicable; not available

NAACP: National Association for the Advancement of Colored People

NAFTA: North American Free Trade Agreement

NASA: National Aeronautics and Space Administration

NATO: North Atlantic Treaty Organization

NB or **n.b.:** *nota bene* (note carefully)

NCAA: National Collegiate Athletic Association

NEA: National Education Association; National Endowment for the Arts

NFT: non-fungible token

NIH: National Institutes of Health

NIMBY: not in my backyard

NOW: National Organization for Women

NPR: National Public Radio

NRA: National Rifle Association

NSA: National Security Agency

NSC: National Security Council

obs.: obsolete

OECD: Organization for Economic Cooperation and Development

OED: Oxford English Dictionary

OMB: Office of Management and Budget

OMG: Oh my goodness/gosh/God!

op., opp.: *opus* (work[s])

OPEC: Organization of Petroleum Exporting Countries

OTC: over-the-counter

oz: ounce

p., pp.: page(s)

PA: public address

PAC: political action committee

PC: personal computer; politically correct

PDA: personal digital assistant

PET: positron emission tomography

PETA: People for the Ethical Treatment of Animals

PhD: *Philosophiae Doctor* (Doctor of Philosophy)

PIN: personal identification number

p.m. or **PM:** *post meridiem* (after noon)

PM: private message; prime minister

POTUS: President of the United States

PPE: personal protective equipment

PPO: preferred provider organization, a type of health-care provider network

PS: *post scriptum* (postscript)

PST: Pacific standard time

pt: part(s); pint(s); point(s)

PT: physical therapy/training

PTSD: post-traumatic stress disorder

PVT or **Pvt.:** Private

QC: Queen's Council (UK)

QED: *quod erat demonstrandum* (which was to be demonstrated)

radar: RAdio Detecting And Ranging

RAM: random access memory

RC: Roman Catholic

RCMP: Royal Canadian Mounted Police

REM: rapid eye movement

Rev.: Reverend

rev.: revised; reviewed

RIP: *requiescat in pace* (may he/she rest in peace)

RN: registered nurse

RNA: ribonucleic acid

RNC: Republican National Committee

ROFL: rolling on the floor laughing

ROM: read only memory

ROTC: Reserve Officers' Training Corps

rpm: revolutions per minute
RSVP: *répondez s'il vous plaît* (Fr.) (please reply)
SARS: severe acute respiratory syndrome
SCOTUS: Supreme Court of the United States
scuba: self-contained underwater breathing apparatus
SEC: Securities and Exchange Commission
SEO: search engine optimization
SETI: Search for Extraterrestrial Intelligence
SGT or Sgt.: Sergeant
SIDS: sudden infant death syndrome
SJ: Society of Jesus (Jesuits)
SMH: shaking my head
sonar: SOund NAvigation and Ranging
SOTU: State of the Union
SPCA: Society for the Prevention of Cruelty to Animals
SSI: Supplementary Security Income
St.: Saint; Street

STEM: science, technology, engineering, math
TB: tuberculosis; terabyte(s)
TBA/TBD: to be announced/determined
tbsp: tablespoon
TBT: Throwback Thursday
TEFL: teaching English as a foreign language
TIA: transient ischemic attack
TMI: too much information
TPP: Trans-Pacific Partnership (trade agreement)
TSA: Transportation Security Administration
tsp: teaspoon
UFO: unidentified flying object
UPC: Universal Product Code
URL: Universal Resource Locator
USDA: United States Department of Agriculture
USS: United States ship

UTC: coordinated universal time
VA: Department of Veterans Affairs
VAT: value-added tax
VCR: videocassette recorder
VISTA: Volunteers in Service to America
viz: *videlicet* (namely)
VP: vice president
W: watt(s)
WHO: World Health Organization
WMD: weapon of mass destruction
WPM: words per minute
WTF: what the f--- [expletive]
WTO: World Trade Organization
WWW: World Wide Web
YMCA/YWCA: Young Men's/Women's Christian Association
YOLO: you only live once
YTD: year to date
yuppie: young urban professional
ZIP: zone improvement plan (U.S. Postal Service)

Most Popular U.S. First Names by Decade or Year of Birth

Source: U.S. Social Security Administration

All names are from Social Security card applications for births that occurred in the United States after 1879. Rankings are based on one spelling of the name; variant spellings and similar sounding names are considered separate names.

BOYS

1880-1889	John, William, James, George, Charles, Frank, Joseph, Henry, Robert, Thomas
1890-1899	John, William, James, George, Charles, Joseph, Frank, Robert, Edward, Henry
1900-1909	John, William, James, George, Charles, Robert, Joseph, Frank, Edward, Thomas
1910-1919	John, William, James, Robert, Joseph, George, Charles, Edward, Frank, Thomas
1920-1929	Robert, John, James, William, Charles, George, Joseph, Richard, Edward, Donald
1930-1939	Robert, James, John, William, Richard, Charles, Donald, George, Thomas, Joseph
1940-1949	James, Robert, John, William, Richard, David, Charles, Thomas, Michael, Ronald
1950-1959	Michael, David, James, John, Robert, Mark, William, Richard, Thomas, Jeffrey
1960-1969	Michael, David, John, James, Robert, Mark, William, Richard, Thomas, Jeffrey
1970-1979	Michael, Christopher, Jason, David, James, John, Robert, Brian, William, Matthew
1980-1989	Michael, Christopher, Matthew, Joshua, David, James, Daniel, Robert, John, Joseph
1990-1999	Michael, Christopher, Matthew, Joshua, Jacob, Nicholas, Andrew, Daniel, Tyler, Joseph
2000-2009	Jacob, Michael, Joshua, Matthew, Daniel, Christopher, Andrew, Ethan, Joseph, William
2010-2019	Noah, Liam, Jacob, William, Mason, Ethan, Michael, Alexander, James, Elijah
2022	Liam, Noah, Oliver, James, Elijah, William, Henry, Lucas, Benjamin, Theodore

GIRLS

1880-1889	Mary, Anna, Emma, Elizabeth, Margaret, Minnie, Ida, Bertha, Clara, Alice
1890-1899	Mary, Anna, Margaret, Helen, Elizabeth, Ruth, Florence, Ethel, Emma, Marie
1900-1909	Mary, Helen, Margaret, Anna, Ruth, Elizabeth, Dorothy, Marie, Florence, Mildred
1910-1919	Mary, Helen, Dorothy, Margaret, Ruth, Mildred, Anna, Elizabeth, Frances, Virginia
1920-1929	Mary, Dorothy, Helen, Betty, Margaret, Ruth, Virginia, Doris, Mildred, Frances
1930-1939	Mary, Betty, Barbara, Shirley, Patricia, Dorothy, Joan, Margaret, Nancy, Helen
1940-1949	Mary, Linda, Barbara, Patricia, Carol, Sandra, Nancy, Sharon, Judith, Susan
1950-1959	Mary, Linda, Patricia, Susan, Deborah, Barbara, Debra, Karen, Nancy, Donna
1960-1969	Lisa, Mary, Susan, Karen, Kimberly, Patricia, Linda, Donna, Michelle, Cynthia
1970-1979	Jennifer, Amy, Melissa, Michelle, Kimberly, Lisa, Angela, Heather, Stephanie, Nicole
1980-1989	Jessica, Jennifer, Amanda, Ashley, Sarah, Stephanie, Melissa, Nicole, Elizabeth, Heather
1990-1999	Jessica, Ashley, Emily, Sarah, Samantha, Amanda, Brittany, Elizabeth, Taylor, Megan
2000-2009	Emily, Madison, Emma, Olivia, Hannah, Abigail, Isabella, Samantha, Elizabeth, Ashley
2010-2019	Emma, Olivia, Sophia, Isabella, Ava, Mia, Abigail, Emily, Charlotte, Madison
2022	Olivia, Emma, Charlotte, Amelia, Sophia, Isabella, Ava, Mia, Evelyn, Luna

Words and Expressions in Common Languages

English	Arabic	Chinese[1]	French	German	Hebrew	Russian	Spanish
Hello/hi	Salam	Ni hao	Bonjour	Hallo	Shalom	Privet (informal)	Hola
Good morning	Sabah el kheer	Zao shang hao	Bonjour	Guten Morgen	Boker tov	Dobraye utra	Buenos días
Good night	Tosbeho 'ala khair	Wan an	Bonne nuit	Gute Nacht	Layla tov	Spakoynay noci	Buenas noches
Goodbye	Ma'a salama	Zai jian	Au revoir	Auf wiedersehen	Lehitraot	Da svidan'ya	Adiós
Please	Men fadlek	Qing	S'il vous plaît	Bitte	Bevakasha	Pazhalusta	Por favor
Thank you very much	Shokran jazeelan	Xie xie	Merci beaucoup	Danke schön	Toda raba	Spasiba	Muchas gracias
You're welcome	Al' afw	Huan ying	De rien/pas de quoi	Bitte schön	Bevakasha	Pazhalusta	De nada
How are you?	Kaifa haloka?	Ni hao?	Comment allez-vous?	Wie geht's dir/Ihnen?	Ma shelomkha?	Kak dela?	¿Cómo estás?
I'm fine	Ana bekhair	Hen hao	Je vais bien	Mir geht's gut	Tov	Harasho	Estoy bien
I'm sorry	Aasef	Bao qian	Je suis désolé	Entschuldigung	Ani mamash mitstaer	Prastite	Lo siento
Excuse me	Alma'derah	Bao qian	Pardon	Darf ich mal vorbei?	Selikha	Izvinite	Perdone
yes	na'am	shi [it is so]	oui	ja	ken	da	sí
no	laa	bu [not]	non	nein	lo	nyet	no
one	wahed	yi	un	eins	ekhad	adin	uno
two	ithnaan	er	deux	zwei	shenayim	dva	dos
three	thalatha	san	trois	drei	shelosha	tri	tres
four	arba'a	si	quatre	vier	arbaa	chityri	cuatro
five	khamsa	wu	cinq	fünf	khamisha	p'at	cinco

Note: Actual form or usage of some words and expressions may vary depending on dialect, grammar, or circumstances. Transliterations for languages not in Latin alphabet vary. (1) Mandarin.

Principal Languages of the World

Source: Used by permission. © 2023 SIL International, from *Ethnologue: Languages of the World, 26th Edition*

Languages shown in italics are macrolanguages, or language groups that are equivalent in some ways to individual languages. Each language group consists of a number of variants, which may be mutually unintelligible; these variants, when they have 2.5 mil speakers or more, appear in the larger table below, and occasionally have the same name as the macrolanguage. Numbers are estimates and count only speakers for whom the language is a first language, or mother tongue.

Languages Spoken by the Most People

Language	Speakers (mil)	Language	Speakers (mil)	Language	Speakers (mil)
Chinese	1,346.2	Turkish	84.0	Italian	64.6
Spanish	485.1	Marathi	83.2	Gujarati	57.1
English	379.7	Telugu	83.0	*Pushto*	53.8
Arabic	372.6	*Malay*	82.2	Bhojpuri	52.3
Hindi	344.7	Korean	81.7	Hausa	51.7
Portuguese	236.3	French	80.8	Yoruba	43.8
Bengali	233.8	Tamil	78.6	Kannada	43.7
Russian	147.0	German	75.3	Polish	39.9
Japanese	123.3	Urdu	70.6	*Oromo*	37.4
Lahnda	103.0	Javanese	68.3	*Oriya*	37.1
Vietnamese	85.0	*Persian*	67.5	*Fulah*	36.9

Languages With at Least 2.5 Million Speakers

Primary country is country of origin, not necessarily the country where the most speakers reside (e.g., Portugal is the primary country for Portuguese, but more Portuguese speakers live in Brazil). Number of speakers is worldwide total for each language.

Primary country	Language	Countries	Speakers (mil)
Afghanistan	Pashto, Southern	4	16.4
	Dari	3	10.3
	Hazaragi	3	3.7
	Uzbek, Southern	2	3.4
Albania	*Albanian*	26	6.3
	Albanian, Gheg	6	4.2
Algeria	Arabic, Algerian Spoken	2	35.7
	Amazigh	2	7.5
	Tachawit	2	2.6
Angola	Umbundu	1	7.8
	Chokwe	3	2.7
Armenia	Armenian	4	3.7
Austria	Bavarian	4	14.6
Azerbaijan	Azerbaijani, North	4	9.1
Bangladesh	Bengali	4	233.8
	Chittagonian	1	13.0
	Rangpuri	2	10.5
	Sylheti	2	10.0
Bosnia and Herzegovina	Bosnian	6	2.6
Botswana	Setswana	4	5.9
Brazil	Hunsrik	1	3.0
Bulgaria	Bulgarian	8	6.5
Burkina Faso	Mòoré	5	11.9
Burundi	Rundi	1	12.9
Côte d'Ivoire	Baoulé	1	5.3
	Jula	3	2.6
Cambodia	Khmer	2	17.0
Cameroon	Fulfulde, Adamawa	5	3.0
China	*Chinese*	94	1,346.2
	Chinese, Mandarin	18	939.2
	Chinese, Yue	15	86.1
	Chinese, Wu	1	83.4
	Chinese, Min Nan	10	49.9
	Chinese, Jinyu	1	48.0
	Chinese, Hakka	14	44.0
	Chinese, Xiang	1	38.1
	Chinese, Gan	1	22.6
	Zhuang	2	14.9
	Chinese, Min Bei	2	11.7
	Chinese, Min Dong	6	10.9
	Uyghur	6	10.5
	Hmong	9	8.1
	Chinese, Huizhou	1	5.4
	Chinese Sign Language	1	4.2
	Chinese, Min Zhong	1	3.7
	Mongolian, Peripheral	2	3.4
	Chinese, Pu-Xian	3	3.2
	Bouyei	3	3.0
Congo, Dem. Rep of the	Lingala	2	20.3
	Kituba	1	11.6
	Kongo	3	7.0
	Luba-Kasai	2	6.4
	Koongo	3	6.3
Croatia	Croatian	8	5.5
Czechia	Czech	8	9.6
Denmark	Danish	5	5.6

Primary country	Language	Countries	Speakers (mil)
Egypt	Arabic, Egyptian Spoken	2	77.4
	Arabic, Sa'idi Spoken	1	25.1
	Arabic, Eastern Egyptian Bedawi Spoken	4	2.8
Eritrea	Tigrigna	3	8.7
Ethiopia	*Oromo*	6	37.4
	Amharic	2	32.4
	Oromo, West Central	1	19.2
	Oromo, Eastern	1	9.7
	Oromo, Borana-Arsi-Guji	3	8.4
	Sidamo	1	4.3
Finland	Finnish	5	5.0
France	French	102	80.8
Georgia	Georgian	4	3.7
Germany	German, Standard	46	75.3
Ghana	Akan	1	8.9
	Ewé	2	5.0
Greece	Greek	10	13.0
Guinea	*Mandingo*	7	9.0
	Pular	5	4.8
	Maninkakan, Eastern	3	3.7
Haiti	Haitian Creole	5	13.0
Hungary	Hungarian	9	12.6
India	Hindi	5	344.7
	Marathi	1	83.2
	Telugu	4	83.0
	Tamil	10	78.6
	Gujarati	8	57.1
	Bhojpuri	3	52.3
	Punjabi, Eastern	6	48.3
	Kannada	1	43.7
	Oriya	7	37.1
	Malayalam	2	36.6
	Odia	1	34.5
	Maithili	2	21.6
	Magahi	2	20.7
	Marwari	3	20.6
	Chhattisgarhi	1	16.3
	Rajasthani	3	16.2
	Assamese	1	15.3
	Deccan	1	12.8
	Bajjika	2	12.3
	Haryanvi	1	9.8
	Marwari	2	7.9
	Santhali	3	7.6
	Kashmiri	2	7.1
	Varhadi-Nagpuri	1	7.0
	Indian Sign Language	4	6.8
	Kanauji	1	6.0
	Konkani	1	5.9
	Bundeli	1	5.6
	Malvi	1	5.4
	Sadri	2	5.1
	Lambadi	1	5.1
	Awadhi	2	4.4
	Mewari	1	4.2
	Merwari	1	3.9
	Konkani, Goan	2	3.7
	Dogri	1	3.7

Primary country	Language	Countries	Speakers (mil)
India (cont.)	Wagdi	1	3.4
	Bhili	1	3.3
	Shekhawati	1	3.0
	Godwari	1	3.0
	Haroti	1	2.9
	Bagheli	1	2.7
	Sambalpuri	1	2.6
	Dogri	1	2.6
Indonesia	Javanese	3	68.3
	Indonesian	2	43.7
	Sunda	1	32.4
	Madura	2	7.8
	Betawi	1	5.0
	Minangkabau	1	4.9
	Bugis	2	3.9
	Banjar	2	3.7
	Bali	1	3.3
	Musi	1	3.1
	Aceh	1	2.8
Iran	*Persian*	34	67.5
	Persian, Iranian	7	57.2
	Azerbaijani	21	24.0
	Azerbaijani, South	5	14.9
	Kurdish, Southern	2	3.8
	Gilaki	1	2.6
Iraq	*Kurdish*	31	24.9
	Arabic, Mesopotamian Spoken	4	18.2
	Arabic, North Mesopotamian Spoken	4	10.3
	Kurdish, Central	2	5.3
Israel	Hebrew	2	6.0
Italy	Italian	17	64.6
	Napoletano-Calabrese	1	5.7
	Sicilian	1	4.7
	Lombard	2	3.9
	Venetian	5	3.9
Jamaica	Jamaican English Creole	3	3.1
Japan	Japanese	4	123.3
Kazakhstan	Kazakh	6	16.4
Kenya	Gikuyu	1	8.2
	Dholuo	2	5.3
	Kamba	2	4.7
	Kalenjin	3	4.6
	Oluluyia	3	3.3
	Ekegusii	2	2.7
Korea	Korean	7	81.7
Kuwait	Arabic, Gulf Spoken	10	11.1
Kyrgyzstan	Kyrgyz	5	5.2
Laos	Lao	3	3.7
Lesotho	Sotho, Southern	2	5.6
Libya	Arabic, Libyan Spoken	3	5.4
Lithuania	Lithuanian	2	2.8
Madagascar	*Malagasy*	6	18.1
	Malagasy, Merina	2	7.5
Malawi	Chichewa	4	14.4
	Lomwe, Malawi	1	4.0
	Yao	4	3.7
Malaysia	*Malay*	29	82.2
	Malay	3	16.2
	Malay, Kedah	2	2.6
Mali	Bamanankan	3	4.2
	Tamashek	7	2.8
Mauritania	Hassaniyya	7	5.2
Mongolia	*Mongolian*	12	6.2
	Mongolian, Halh	2	2.8
Morocco	Arabic, Moroccan Spoken	4	29.5
	Tachelhit	4	5.8
	Tamazight, Central Atlas	3	3.1
Mozambique	Makhuwa	2	4.0
	Lomwe	1	2.5
Myanmar	Burmese	1	33.0
	Shan	3	4.7
	Rohingya	2	2.5
Nepal	*Nepali*	24	17.7
	Nepali	3	16.9
Netherlands	Dutch	8	22.9
Niger	Zarma	4	6.0
	Fulfulde, Western Niger	3	3.1
Nigeria	Hausa	9	51.7
	Yoruba	4	43.8
	Igbo	1	30.9
	Fulfulde, Nigerian	3	16.6
	Kanuri	6	9.5
	Kanuri, Yerwa	5	8.5
	Ibibio	1	6.3
	Pidgin, Nigerian	1	4.7

Primary country	Language	Countries	Speakers (mil)
Nigeria (cont.)	Tiv	2	4.6
	Anaang	1	2.9
Norway	Norwegian	1	5.3
Oman	Arabic, Omani Spoken	5	2.9
Pakistan	*Lahnda*	14	103.0
	Urdu	8	70.6
	Punjabi, Western	2	66.7
	Pushto	19	53.8
	Sindhi	4	33.2
	Pashto, Northern	4	28.9
	Saraiki	2	26.2
	Baluchi	10	8.8
	Pashto, Central	1	8.5
	Hindko, Northern	1	5.3
	Balochi, Southern	4	3.6
	Pahari-Potwari	2	3.5
	Balochi, Eastern	2	2.9
	Brahui	3	2.9
Paraguay	*Guaraní*	5	6.7
	Guaraní, Paraguayan	1	6.5
Peru	*Quechua*	6	6.9
Philippines	Tagalog	5	28.7
	Cebuano	1	16.0
	Ilocano	1	6.5
	Hiligaynon	1	6.3
	Waray-Waray	1	2.6
Poland	Polish	10	39.9
Portugal	Portuguese	16	236.3
Romania	Romanian	6	24.5
Russia	Russian	22	147.0
	Tatar	4	4.3
Rwanda	Kinyarwanda	3	14.5
Saudi Arabia	*Arabic*	97	372.6
	Arabic, Najdi Spoken	4	18.1
	Arabic, Hijazi Spoken	3	10.8
Senegal	*Fulah*	20	36.9
	Wolof	2	6.1
	Pulaar	6	5.9
Serbia	*Serbo-Croatian*	31	18.5
	Serbian	11	10.2
Sierra Leone	Mende	2	2.5
Slovakia	Slovak	8	5.3
Somalia	Somali	4	21.9
	Maay	1	2.6
South Africa	Zulu	5	12.1
	Xhosa	3	8.2
	Afrikaans	6	7.4
	Tsonga	4	6.6
	Sotho, Northern	1	4.6
South Sudan	*Dinka*	3	4.2
Spain	*Spanish*	43	485.1
	Catalan	4	4.2
	Galician	3	3.1
Sri Lanka	Sinhala	2	15.5
Sudan	Arabic, Sudanese Spoken	5	33.4
Sweden	Swedish	4	9.9
Switzerland	German, Swiss	6	6.5
Syria	Arabic, Levantine	7	47.2
Tajikistan	Tajik	5	8.3
Tanzania	*Swahili*	23	18.2
	Swahili	9	16.2
	Sukuma	1	8.1
Thailand	Thai	2	20.8
	Thai, Northeastern	1	15.0
	Thai, Northern	2	6.0
	Thai, Southern	1	4.5
Tunisia	Arabic, Tunisian Spoken	2	11.7
Turkey	Turkish	13	84.0
	Kurdish, Northern	9	15.8
Turkmenistan	Turkmen	6	6.6
Uganda	Ganda	1	5.6
	Nyankore	2	3.4
	Soga	1	3.0
	Ateso	2	2.8
Ukraine	Ukrainian	7	26.9
United Kingdom	English	170	379.7
Uzbekistan	*Uzbek*	17	31.4
	Uzbek, Northern	6	27.9
Vietnam	Vietnamese	5	85.0
Yemen	Arabic, Sanaani Spoken	1	12.6
	Arabic, Ta'izzi-Adeni Spoken	3	11.9
	Arabic, Hadrami Spoken	1	5.1
Zambia	Bemba	2	4.1
Zimbabwe	Shona	3	7.4

BUILDINGS, BRIDGES, AND TUNNELS

100 Tallest Buildings in the World

Source: SKYDB, www.skydb.net; Council on Tall Buildings and Urban Habitat (CTBUH), www.ctbuh.org

Only buildings that are completed or under construction and topped out as of Oct. 2023, are shown here. Structures under construction and topped out architecturally are denoted by an asterisk (*). Year in parentheses is date of completion or projected completion. Height is generally measured from the lowest significant open-air pedestrian entrance to the architectural top, including spires and other decorative features that are an integral part of the design, but not including flagpoles and antennae. Stories generally counted from street level. NA = Not available.

Building	Ht. (ft)	Stories	Building	Ht. (ft)	Stories
Burj Khalifa, Dubai, United Arab Emirates (2010)	2,717	163	PIF Tower, Riyadh, Saudi Arabia (2021)	1,260	76
Merdeka 118, Kuala Lumpur, Malaysia (2023)	2,227	118	Shun Hing Square, Shenzhen, China (1996)	1,260	69
Shanghai Tower, Shanghai, China (2015)	2,074	128	Eton Place Dalian Tower 1, Dalian, China (2016)	1,257	80
Makkah Royal Clock Tower Hotel, Mecca, Saudi Arabia (2013)	1,972	120	Autograph Tower, Jakarta, Indonesia (2022)	1,256	75
Ping An Finance Center, Shenzhen, China (2016)	1,965	115	Burj Mohammed Bin Rashid Tower, Abu Dhabi, UAE (2014)	1,251	88
*Goldin Finance 117, Tianjin, China (On hold)	1,957	128	Logan Century Center 1, Nanning, China (2019)	1,251	82
Lotte World Tower, Seoul, South Korea (2017)	1,819	123	Empire State Building, New York, NY, U.S. (1931)	1,250	102
One World Trade Center, New York, NY, U.S. (2014)	1,782	94	Elite Residence, Dubai, UAE (2012)	1,248	87
CTF Finance Center, Guangzhou, China (2016)	1,739	111	1 Corporate Avenue, Wuhan, China (2021)	1,234	73
Tianjin CTF Finance Center, Tianjin, China (2019)	1,739	97	Shenzhen Center, Shenzhen, China (2021)	1,232	71
Citic Tower, Beijing, China (2018)	1,732	108	*Guangdong Business Center, Guangzhou, China (2024)	1,232	60
Taipei 101, Taipei, Taiwan (2004)	1,667	101	Central Plaza, Hong Kong, China (1992)	1,227	78
Shanghai World Financial Center, Shanghai, China (2008)	1,614	101	Vostok, Moscow, Russia (2017)	1,226	93
International Commerce Centre, Hong Kong, China (2010)	1,588	108	*Hengfeng Guiyang Ctr. Twr. 1, Guiyang, China (2023)	1,225	77
Wuhan Greenland Center, Wuhan, China (2023)	1,560	97	Dalian Intl. Trade Center, Dalian, China (2019)	1,214	86
Central Park Tower, New York, NY, U.S. (2021)	1,550	95	*Shanghai Intl. Trade Center Tower 1, Shanghai, China (2024)	1,214	67
Lakhta Center, St. Petersburg, Russia (2019)	1,516	87	Hai Tian Center Tower 2, Qingdao, China (2021)	1,211	72
Vincom Landmark 81, Ho Chi Minh City, Vietnam (2018)	1,513	81	Golden Eagle Tiandi Tower A, Nanjing, China (2019)	1,207	76
*International Land-Sea Center, Chongqing, China (2024)	1,503	98	Address Boulevard, Dubai, UAE (2017)	1,207	72
The Exchange 106, Kuala Lumpur, Malaysia (2019)	1,488	97	Bank of China Tower, Hong Kong, China (1989)	1,205	72
Changsha IFS Tower T1, Changsha, China (2018)	1,483	94	Bank of America Twr., New York, NY, U.S. (2009)	1,200	55
Petronas Tower I, Kuala Lumpur, Malaysia (1998)	1,483	88	*Ciel Tower, Dubai, UAE (2024)	1,199	81
Petronas Tower II, Kuala Lumpur, Malaysia (1998)	1,483	88	St. Regis Chicago, Chicago, IL, U.S. (2020)	1,191	101
Suzhou IFS, Suzhou, China (2019)	1,476	95	Almas Tower, Dubai, UAE (2008)	1,181	68
Zifeng Tower, Nanjing, China (2010)	1,476	66	*Ping'an Finance Ctr. Twr. 1, Jinan, China (2023)	1,181	63
Wuhan Center, Wuhan, China (2019)	1,454	88	Huiyin Center, Shenzhen, China (2023)	1,178	80
Willis (fmr. Sears) Twr., Chicago, IL, U.S. (1974)	1,451	108	Hanking Center, Shenzhen, China (2018)	1,177	65
KK100, Shenzhen, China (2011)	1,449	100	*Greenland Group Suzhou Center, Suzhou, China (2023)	1,175	77
Guangzhou International Finance Center, Guangzhou, China (2010)	1,439	103	Gevora Hotel, Dubai, UAE (2017)	1,169	76
111 West 57th St., New York, NY, U.S. (2021)	1,428	82	Il Primo Tower 1, Dubai, UAE (2023)	1,168	79
*Shandong IFC, Jinan, China (2024)	1,404	88	Galaxy World Tower 1, Shenzhen, China (2023)	1,168	71
Minying International Trade Center T2, Dongguan, China (2021)	1,401	88	Galaxy World Tower 2, Shenzhen, China (2023)	1,168	71
One Vanderbilt, New York, NY, U.S. (2020)	1,401	62	JW Marriott Marquis Hotel Dubai Tower 2, Dubai, UAE (2013)	1,166	82
432 Park Avenue, New York, NY, U.S. (2015)	1,397	85	JW Marriott Marquis Hotel Dubai Tower 1, Dubai, UAE (2012)	1,166	82
Marina 101, Dubai, UAE (2017)	1,394	101	Chongqing Raffles City T3N, Chongqing, China (2019)	1,163	81
Trump Intl. Hotel & Tower, Chicago, IL, U.S. (2009)	1,389	98	Chongqing Raffles City T4N, Chongqing, China (2019)	1,163	81
Jin Mao Tower, Shanghai, China (1999)	1,380	88	Emirates Office Tower, Dubai, UAE (2000)	1,163	54
Princess Tower, Dubai, UAE (2012)	1,356	101	OKO South Tower, Moscow, Russia (2015)	1,162	90
Al Hamra Tower, Kuwait City, Kuwait (2011)	1,354	80	The Torch, Dubai, UAE (2011)	1,155	86
Two International Finance Centre, Hong Kong, China (2003)	1,352	88	*Central Bank of the Republic of Turkey, Istanbul, Turkey (2024)	1,155	59
LCT Landmark Tower, Busan, South Korea (2019)	1,350	101	Forum 66 Tower 1, Shenyang, China (2015)	1,150	67
*Ningbo Central Plaza Tower 1, Ningbo, China (2024)	1,342	80	The Pinnacle, Guangzhou, China (2012)	1,149	60
Guangxi China Resources Tower, Nanning, China (2020)	1,321	85	Glory-Xi'an Intl. Finance Ctr., Xi'an, China (2022)	1,148	75
Guiyang Financial Ctr. Twr. 1, Guiyang, China (2021)	1,316	79	Spring City 66, Kunming, China (2019)	1,145	61
*Iconic Tower, Cairo, Egypt (2023)	1,292	80	Tuntex Sky Tower, Kaohsiung, Taiwan (1998)	1,140	85
China Resources HQ, Shenzhen, China (2018)	1,288	66	Shimao Hunan Center, Changsha, China (2019)	1,138	76
23 Marina, Dubai, UAE (2012)	1,287	88	Aon Center, Chicago, IL, U.S. (1973)	1,136	83
CITIC Plaza, Guangzhou, China (1997)	1,280	80	The Center, Hong Kong, China (1998)	1,135	73
Citimark Center, Shenzhen, China (2023)	1,274	70	Neva Towers 2, Moscow, Russia (2020)	1,132	79
Sum Yip Upperhills Twr. 1, Shenzhen, China (2020)	1,273	80			
30 Hudson Yards, New York, NY (2019)	1,268	73			

Tallest Free-Standing Towers in the World

Source: SKYDB, www.skydb.net; Council on Tall Buildings and Urban Habitat (CTBUH), www.ctbuh.org
Year is date of completion or projected completion. As of Oct. 2023.

Tower	Ht. (ft)	Year	Tower	Ht. (ft)	Year
Tokyo Sky Tree, Tokyo, Japan	2,080	2012	Tashkent Tower, Tashkent, Uzbekistan	1,230	1985
Canton Tower, Guangzhou, China	1,969	2010	Liberation Tower, Kuwait City, Kuwait	1,220	1996
CN Tower, Toronto, ON, Canada	1,815	1976	Alma-Ata Tower, Almaty, Kazakhstan	1,217	1982
Ostankino Tower, Moscow, Russia	1,772	1967	Camlica TV Tower, Istanbul, Turkey	1,211	2019
Oriental Pearl Television Tower, Shanghai, China	1,535	1995	TV Tower, Riga, Latvia	1,208	1987
Milad Tower, Tehran, Iran	1,427	2008	Berliner Fernsehturm, Berlin, Germany	1,207	1969
Manara Kuala Lumpur, Kuala Lumpur, Malaysia	1,379	1996	Stratosphere Tower, Las Vegas, NV, U.S.	1,149	1996
Tianjin Radio & TV Tower, Tianjin, China	1,362	1991	Lotus Tower, Colombo, Sri Lanka	1,148	2019
Central Radio & TV Tower, Beijing, China	1,347	1992	West Pearl Tower, Chengdu, China	1,112	2004
Henan Province Radio & Television Emission Tower, Zhengzhou, China	1,273	2010	Macau Tower, Macau, China	1,109	2001
			Europaturm, Frankfurt, Germany	1,106	1979
Kiev TV Tower, Kiev, Ukraine	1,263	1974	Dragon Tower, Harbin, China	1,102	2000

Tall Buildings in Selected North American Cities

Source: SKYDB, www.skydb.net; Council on Tall Buildings and Urban Habitat (CTBUH), www.ctbuh.org

List includes freestanding towers and other structures that do not have stories and are not technically considered buildings. Structures under construction and topped out architecturally as of Oct. 2023 are denoted by an asterisk (*). Year in parentheses is date of completion or projected completion. Height is generally measured from the lowest significant open-air pedestrian entrance to the architectural top, including penthouses, spires, and other decorative features that are an integral part of the design, but not including flagpoles and antennae. Stories generally counted from street level. NA = Not applicable/available.

Atlanta, GA

Building/structure	Ht. (ft)	Stories
Bank of America Plaza (incl. spire), 600 Peachtree St. NE (1992)	1,023	55
Truist Plaza, 303 Peachtree St. NE[1] (1993)	867	60
One Atlantic Center, 1201 W. Peachtree St. (1987)	820	50
191 Peachtree Tower (1991)	770	50
Westin Peachtree Plaza, 210 Peachtree St. NW[2] (1976)	723	73
Georgia Pacific Tower, 133 Peachtree St. NE (1981)	697	51
Promenade II (incl. spire), 1230 Peachtree St. NE (1989)	691	40
AT&T Bldg., 675 W. Peachtree St. (1980)	677	47
Sovereign, 3344 Peachtree (2008)	665	48
1180 Peachtree (2006)	657	41
GLG Grand/Four Seasons Hotel, 75 14th St. NE (1992)	609	53
The Mansion on Peachtree, 3376 Peachtree Rd. NE (2008)	580	42
Atlantic, 270 17th St. NW (2009)	577	46
State of Georgia Bldg., 2 Peachtree St. NW[3] (1967)	556	44
Marriott Marquis, 265 Peachtree Center Ave. NE (1985)	554	52

(1) 902 ft incl. antenna. (2) 883 ft incl. antenna. (3) 599 ft incl. antenna.

Austin, TX

Building/structure	Ht. (ft)	Stories
*Waterline, 98 Red River St. (2026)	1,021	74
*6 X Guadalupe, 400 W. 6th St. (2023)	847	66
*The Republic, 308 Guadalupe St. (2025)	708	46
The Independent, 301 West Ave. (2019)	694	58
Austonian, 200 Congress Ave. (2010)	683	56
*ATX Tower, 325 W. 6th St. (2025)	675	58
*Modern Austin, 90 Rainey St. (2025)	655	55
*415 Colorado (2025)	633	47
*The Travis Phase I, 80 Red River St. (NA)	594	52
601 W. 2nd St. (2022)	594	35
Fairmont Austin (incl. spire), 101 Red River St. (2018)	591	36
360 Condominiums (incl. spire), 360 Nueces St. (2008)	581	44
*44 East Avenue (2023)	573	48
*Paseo, 80 Rainey St. (2025)	567	44
Indeed Tower, 200 W. 6th St. (2021)	542	36

Boston, MA

Building/structure	Ht. (ft)	Stories
200 Clarendon (1976)	790	62
Prudential Tower, 800 Boylston St.[1] (1964)	750	52
Four Seasons Hotel and Private Residences One Dalton Street (2020)	743	61
115 Winthrop Square (2023)	691	48
Millennium Tower, 426 Washington St. (2016)	681	54
*South Station Tower (2024)	678	51
Federal Reserve Bldg., 600 Atlantic Ave. (1978)	604	32
BNY Mellon Center at One Boston Place, 201 Washington St. (1970)	602	41
One International Place, 100 Oliver St. (1987)	600	46
*One Congress Street Tower 2 (2023)	600	43
100 Federal St. (1971)	591	37
One Financial Center, 10 Dewey Square (1984)	590	46
111 Huntington Ave. (2002)	564	36
Two International Place (1993)	538	35
One Post Office Square (1981)	525	40

(1) 920 ft incl. antenna.

Burnaby, BC, Canada

Building/structure	Ht. (ft)	Stories
*Grand Tower at Sky Park (2025)	755	65
*Two Gilmore Place (2024)	708	64
Solo District-Altus (2017)	616	49
Brentwood One (2019)	611	53
Brentwood Two (2019)	611	53
Brentwood Three (2021)	597	55
*Hillside East C (2023)	597	55
*Highline, 6511 Sussex Ave. (2023)	581	53
Station Square V, 6000 McKay Ave. (2022)	564	54
*Central Tower at Sky Park (2025)	542	45
4670 Assembly Way (2018)	535	48

Calgary, AB, Canada

Building/structure	Ht. (ft)	Stories
Brookfield Place Tower One, 225 6th Ave. (2017)	810	56
The Bow, 510 Centre St. (2012)	779	57
Telus Sky (2019)	737	59
Petro Canada Centre West Tower, 150 6th Ave. SW (1984)	705	53
Eighth Avenue Place East Tower, 8th Ave. & 5th St. SW (2011)	696	49
Bankers Hall West Tower, 888 3rd St. SW (2000)	645	50
Bankers Hall East Tower, 855 2nd St. SW (1989)	645	50
Calgary Tower, 101 9th Ave. SW (1967)	626	NA
Centennial Place 1 (incl. spire), 520 3rd Ave. SW (2010)	599	40

Building/structure	Ht. (ft)	Stories
TransCanada Tower, 450 1st St. SW (2001)	581	38
Canterra Tower, 400 3rd Ave. SW (1988)	580	46
Eighth Avenue Place West Tower, 8th Ave. & 5th St. SW (2014)	580	40
Jamieson Place (incl. spires), 302 4th Ave. SW (2009)	568	38
First Canadian Centre, 350 7th Ave. SW (1982)	547	41
Western Canadian Place-North Tower, 707 6th St. SW (1983)	538	41
Canada Trust, Calgary Eatons Centre, 421 7th Ave. SW (1991)	530	40

Charlotte, NC

Building/structure	Ht. (ft)	Stories
Bank of America Corp. Center, 100 N. Tryon St. (1992)	871	60
Duke Energy Center, 534 S. Tryon St. (2010)	786	48
Hearst Tower, 214 N. Tryon St. (2002)	659	47
Bank of America Tower, 620 Tryon St. (2019)	632	33
Charlotte Metro, S. Tryon St. (2023)	629	40
One Wells Fargo Center, 301 S. College St. (1988)	588	42
The Vue, 400 W. 5th St. (2010)	574	50

Chicago, IL

Building/structure	Ht. (ft)	Stories
Willis (fmr. Sears) Tower, 233 S. Wacker Dr.[1] (1974)	1,451	108
Trump International Hotel & Tower (incl. spire), 401 N. Wabash Ave. (2009)	1,389	98
St. Regis Chicago, 381 E. Wacker Dr. (2020)	1,191	101
Aon Center, 200 E. Randolph St. (1973)	1,136	83
875 N. Michigan Ave. (fmr. John Hancock Ctr.)[2] (1969)	1,128	100
Franklin Center-North Tower (incl. spires), 227 W. Monroe St. (1989)	1,007	60
Two Prudential Plaza (incl. spire), 180 N. Stetson Ave. (1990)	978	64
One Chicago Square East Tower, 732 N. State St. (2022)	971	78
311 S. Wacker Drive (1990)	961	65
NEMA Chicago, 1200 S. Indiana Ave. (2019)	896	81
900 N. Michigan Ave. (1989)	871	66
Chase Tower, 21 S. Clark St. (1969)	868	61
Aqua at Lakeshore East, 225 N. Columbus Dr. (2009)	859	86
Water Tower Place, 845 N. Michigan Ave. (1976)	859	74
Park Tower, 800 N. Michigan Ave. (2000)	844	68
One Bennett Park, 451 E. Grand Ave. (2018)	837	67
Salesforce Tower, 333 Wolf Point Plaza (2023)	835	60
The Legacy at Millennium Park, 21-39 S. Wabash (2010)	818	73
110 N. Wacker Dr. (2020)	817	55
*1000M, 1000 S. Michigan Ave. (2024)	805	73
300 N. LaSalle (2009)	785	60
3 First National Plaza, 70 W. Madison St. (1981)	767	57
Grant Thornton Tower, 161 N. Clark St. (1992)	756	50
Blue Cross Headquarters, 300 E. Randolph St. (2010)	744	54
River Point, 444 W. Lake St. (2017)	732	52
Olympia Centre, 737 N. Michigan Ave. (1986)	731	63
BMO Tower, 310 S. Canal St. (2021)	727	50
One Museum Park, 1215 S. Prairie Ave. (2009)	726	62
150 North Riverside (2017)	725	53
AMA Plaza, 330 N. Wabash Ave. (1973)	695	52
Waldorf Astoria Chicago, 940 N. Rush St. (2009)	686	60
111 S. Wacker Dr. (2005)	681	51
181 W. Madison St. (1990)	680	50
71 S. Wacker (2005)	679	48
One Magnificent Mile, 980 N. Michigan Ave. (1983)	673	57
340 on the Park, 340 E. Randolph St. (2007)	672	64
Wolf Point East Tower, 350 N. Orleans St. (2020)	668	60
United Bldg., 77 W. Wacker Dr. (1992)	668	49
UBS Tower, 1 N. Wacker Dr. (2001)	652	50
Daley Center, 55 W. Washington St. (1965)	648	31
55 E. Erie St. (2004)	647	56
Lake Point Tower, 505 N. Lake Shore Dr. (1968)	645	70
River East Center, 350 E. Illinois St. (2001)	644	58
Grand Plaza I (incl. spire), 540 N. State St. (2003)	641	57
155 N. Wacker Dr. (2009)	638	45
Leo Burnett Bldg., 35 W. Wacker Dr. (1989)	635	46
The Heritage at Millennium Park, 125 N. Wabash Ave. (2005)	631	57
NBC Tower (incl. spire), 455 N. Cityfront Plaza Dr. (1989)	627	37
353 N. Clark (2009)	623	44
OneEleven, 111 West Wacker (2014)	616	58
Millennium Centre, 33 W. Ontario St. (2003)	610	58
Board of Trade (incl. statue), 141 W. Jackson Blvd. (1930)	609	44
Chicago Place, 700 N. Michigan Ave. (1991)	608	49
Essex on the Park, 812 S. Michigan Ave. (2019)	607	56
CNA Plaza, 325 S. Wabash St. (1972)	601	44
One Prudential Plaza, 130 E. Randolph St.[3] (1955)	601	41

Building/structure	Ht. (ft)	Stories
500 W. Monroe St. (1992)	600	45
One Madison Plaza, 200 W. Madison St. (1982)	599	44
The Grant, 201 E. Roosevelt Rd. (2010)	595	54
1000 Lake Shore Plaza (1964)	590	55
The Clare at Water Tower, 55 East Pearson St. (2008)	589	52
Marina City I, 300 N. State St. (1964)	588	61
Marina City II, 301 N. Dearborn St. (1964)	588	61
Accenture Tower, 500 W. Madison St. (1987)	588	42
Optima Signature, 220 E. Illinois St. (2017)	587	57
The Park Monroe, 65 E. Monroe St. (1972)	583	49
Crain Communications Bldg., 150 N. Michigan Ave. (1983)	582	41
North Pier Apts., 474 N. Lake Shore Dr. (1990)	581	61
Citadel Center, 131 S. Dearborn St. (2003)	580	39
The Fordham, 25 E. Superior St. (2003)	574	52
23 W. Chicago Ave. (2022)	574	49
190 S. LaSalle St. (1987)	573	40
One S. Dearborn (2005)	571	39
Onterie Center, 446 E. Ontario St. (1986)	570	58
Loews Chicago Hotel, 455 North Park Dr. (2015)	569	52
Chicago Temple, 77 W. Washington St. (1924)	568	23
Palmolive Bldg. (incl. beacon), 919 N. Michigan Ave. (1929)	565	37
Kluczynski Federal Bldg., 230 S. Dearborn St. (1974)	562	42
Huron Plaza Apts., 30 E. Huron St. (1983)	560	56
Boeing International Headquarters, 100 N. Riverside Plaza (1990)	560	36
Cirrus, 211 N. Harbor Dr. (2021)	559	47
The Parkshore, 195 N. Harbor Dr. (1991)	556	56
North Harbor Tower, 175 N. Harbor Dr. (1988)	556	55
Civic Opera Bldg., 20 N. Wacker Dr. (1929)	555	45
Streeter Place, 351 E. Ohio St. (2009)	554	55
Harbor Point, 155 N. Harbor Dr. (1975)	554	54
Newberry Plaza, 1000 N. State St. (1974)	553	53
Michigan Plaza South, 205 N. Michigan Ave. (1985)	553	46
30 N. LaSalle St. (1975)	553	44
Pittsfield Bldg., 55 E. Washington St. (1927)	551	38
One S. Wacker Dr. (1982)	550	40
(1) 1,729 ft incl. antenna. (2) 1,499 ft incl. antenna. (3) 912 ft incl. antenna.		

Cleveland, OH

Key Tower (incl. spire), 127 Public Sq. (1991)	947	57
Terminal Tower, 50 Public Sq.[1] (1928)	708	52
200 Public Square (1985)	658	46
*Sherwin-Williams HQ, 145 W. 3rd St. (2024)	616	36
Tower at Erieview, 1301 E. 9th St. (1964)	529	40
(1) 771 ft incl. flagpole.		

Columbus, OH

James A. Rhodes State Office Tower, 30 E. Broad St. (1973)	624	41
Leveque-Lincoln Tower, 50 W. Broad St. (1927)	555	47
William Green Bldg., 30 W. Spring St. (1990)	530	33

Dallas, TX

Bank of America Plaza, 901 Main St. (1985)	921	72
Renaissance Tower (incl. spire), 1201 Elm St. (1974)	886	56
Comerica Bank Tower, 1717 Main St. (1987)	787	60
Dallas Arts Tower, 2200 Ross Ave. (1987)	738	55
Fountain Place, 1445 Ross Ave. (1986)	720	58
2001 Ross Ave. (1984)	686	50
1700 Pacific Ave. (1983)	655	50
Santander Tower, 1600 Pacific Ave. (1982)	645	50
Energy Plaza, 1601 Bryan St. (1983)	629	49
The Drever, 1401 Elm St. (1965)	628	52
Gables Republic Tower (incl. spire), 300 N. Ervay (1954)	602	36
Republic Center Tower II, 325 N. St. Paul (1964)	598	50
One AT&T Plaza, 208 S. Akard St. (1984)	580	37
Ross Tower, 500 N. Akard St. (1984)	579	45
AMLI Fountain Place, 1800 N. Field St. (2020)	562	46
Museum Tower, 2112 Flora St. (2013)	560	42
Tower at Cityplace, 2711 N. Haskell Ave. (1989)	560	42
Reunion Tower, 300 Reunion Blvd. (1976)	560	NA
Sheraton Dallas Hotel Center Tower, 400 Olive St. (1959)	550	42

Denver, CO

Republic Plaza, 330 17th St. (1984)	714	50
1801 California Street (1982)	709	52
Wells Fargo Center, 1700 Lincoln Ave. (1983)	698	50
Four Seasons Hotel & Private Residences, 1111 14th St. (2010)	639	45
1144 Fifteenth (2018)	602	42
1999 Broadway (1985)	544	43

Detroit, MI

Marriott Hotel, Renaissance Center I[1] (1977)	727	70
*Hudsons Tower, 1246 Woodward Ave. (2024)	680	51
One Detroit Center, 500 Woodward Ave. (1991)	619	43
Penobscot Bldg., 633 Griswold Ave.[2] (1928)	565	47
(1) 755 ft incl. antenna. (2) 665 ft incl. antenna.		

Fort Worth, TX

Burnett Plaza, 801 Cherry St. (1983)	567	40
D.R. Horton Tower, 301 Commerce St. (1984)	547	38
Carter Burgess Plaza, 777 Main St. (1982)	525	40

Houston, TX

600 Travis St. (1982)	1,002	75
Wells Fargo Plaza, 1000 Louisiana St. (1983)	992	71
Williams Tower, 2800 Post Oak Blvd. (1982)	901	64
TC Energy Center, 700 Louisiana St. (1983)	780	56
Texaco Heritage Plaza, 1111 Bagby St. (1987)	762	53
Enterprise Plaza, 1100 Louisiana St.[1] (1980)	756	55
609 Main at Texas (2017)	755	48
Centerpoint Energy Plaza, 1111 Louisiana St. (1996)	741	53
Texas Tower, 801 Texas Ave. (2021)	735	47
1600 Smith St. (1984)	732	55
Fulbright Tower, 1301 McKinney St. (1982)	725	52
One Shell Plaza, 900 Louisiana St.[2] (1970)	714	50
1400 Smith St. (1983)	691	50
3 Allen Center, 333 Clay St. (1980)	685	50
LyondellBassell Tower, 1221 McKinney St. (1978)	678	47
First City Tower, 1001 Fannin St. (1984)	662	47
BG Group Place, 811 Main St. (2011)	632	46
San Felipe Plaza, 5847 San Felipe Blvd. (1984)	625	45
ExxonMobil Bldg., 800 Bell Ave. (1962)	606	44
1500 Louisiana St. (2002)	600	40
America General Center, 2929 Allen Pkwy. (1983)	590	42
Two Houston Center, 909 Fannin St. (1974)	579	40
San Jacinto Monument, La Porte (1939)	570	NA
Marathon Oil Tower, 5555 San Felipe Blvd. (1983)	562	41
1415 Louisiana (1983)	550	44
KBR Tower, 601 Jefferson St. (1973)	550	40
Brava, 414 Milam St. (2022)	549	46
Memorial Hermann Tower (incl. spires), 929 Gessner Rd. (2009)	542	30
2929 Weslayan (2015)	533	40
Bank of America Tower, 800 Capitol St. (2019)	532	35
(1) 782 ft incl. antenna. (2) 999 ft incl. antenna.		

Huixquilucan, Mexico

*Nua Interlomas Torre 1 (2025)	591	47
*Nua Interlomas Torre 2 (2025)	591	47
Bosque Real Residence Torre 3-4 (2021)	558	52
Bosque Real Residence Torre 1-2 (2019)	558	52

Jersey City, NJ

99 Hudson St. (2020)	889	76
30 Hudson St. (2004)	781	42
Journal Squared 2, 537 Summit Ave. (2021)	759	72
*One Journal Square Tower I (2026)	710	64
*One Journal Square Tower II (2026)	710	64
URL Harborside Tower 1 (2016)	700	70
*Journal Squared 3 (2024)	633	60
Haus25, 25 Columbus Dr. (2022)	626	57
Journal Squared 1, 615 Pavonia Ave. (2016)	574	53
101 Hudson St. (1992)	548	42
235 Grand St. (2019)	537	45
Trump Plaza I, 88 Morgan St. (2008)	532	55
Newport Tower, 525 Washington Blvd. (1990)	531	37
90 Columbus (2018)	529	50
70 Columbus (2015)	529	50

Las Vegas, NV

Stratosphere Twr., 2000 Las Vegas Blvd. S. (1996)	1,149	NA
*The Drew Las Vegas, 2755 Las Vegas Blvd. S. (2023)	735	63
Resorts World Las Vegas Tower I, 3000 Las Vegas Blvd. S. (2021)	674	57
The Palazzo, 3339 Las Vegas Blvd. S. (2007)	642	53
Encore at Wynn Las Vegas, 3145 Las Vegas Blvd. S. (2008)	631	52
Trump International Hotel and Tower 1, 3128 Las Vegas Blvd. S. (2008)	622	64
Wynn Las Vegas, 3145 Las Vegas Blvd. S. (2005)	613	45
Cosmopolitan Casino Spa Tower, Las Vegas Blvd. S. and Harmon Ave. (2010)	603	52
Cosmopolitan Beach Resort Twr., Las Vegas Blvd. S. and Harmon Ave. (2010)	603	50
Aria Resort & Casino (2009)	600	60
Elara-Hilton Grand Vacations Hotel, 3667 Las Vegas Blvd. S. (2009)	597	50
VDARA, 2551 W. Harmon Ave. (2009)	556	55
Eiffel Tower, Paris Hotel and Casino, 3645 Las Vegas Blvd. S. (1998)	540	NA
Mandarin Oriental Las Vegas, 3750 Las Vegas Blvd. S. (2009)	539	47
New York, New York Hotel & Casino, 3790 Las Vegas Blvd. S. (1997)	529	48

Los Angeles, CA

Wilshire Grand Center (2017)	1,100	62
US Bank Tower, 633 W. 5th St. (1990)	1,018	72
Aon Center, 707 Wilshire Blvd. (1974)	858	62
Two California Plaza, 350 S. Grand Ave. (1992)	750	52
Gas Company Tower, 555 W. 5th St. (1991)	749	52
Wells Fargo North Tower, 333 S. Grand Ave. (1983)	740	54
Bank of America Plaza, 333 S. Hope St. (1975)	735	55
777 Tower, 777 S. Figueroa St. (1991)	725	53
Figueroa at Wilshire, 601 S. Figueroa St. (1989)	717	53
City National Tower, 555 S. Flower St. (1971)	699	52
Paul Hastings Tower, 515 S. Flower St. (1971)	699	52

Building/structure	Ht. (ft)	Stories
Beaudry, 945 W. 8th St. (2023)	695	64
*Oceanwide Plaza Tower I (on hold)	677	53
Ritz Carlton/Marriott Marquis Los Angeles, 900 W. Olympic Blvd. (2010)	667	54
Thea at Metropolis Tower 3, 1000 W. 8th St. (2019)	627	56
FourFortyFour South Flower (1982)	625	48
611 W. 6th St. (1969)	620	42
Wells Fargo South Tower, 355 S. Grand Ave. (1984)	606	45
*Olympic & Hill, 1000 S. Hill St. (2022)	594	54
One California Plaza, 300 S. Grand Ave. (1985)	578	42
Century Plaza Tower 1, 2029 Century Park East (1973)	571	44
Century Plaza Tower 2, 2049 Century Park East (1973)	571	44
*Century City Center, 1950 Ave. of the Stars (2026)	564	37
825 S. Hill (2019)	563	53
Century Plaza N. Twr., 2025 Ave. of the Stars (2022)	537	46
Century Plaza S. Twr., 2025 Ave. of the Stars (2022)	537	46
Ernst & Young, LLP Plaza, 725 S. Figueroa St. (1986)	534	41
SunAmerica Center, 1999 Ave. of the Stars (1989)	533	39
*Oceanwide Plaza Tower II (on hold)	530	40
*Oceanwide Plaza Tower III (on hold)	530	40
Mexico City, Mexico		
Torre Mitikah, Rio Churubusco 601 (2022)	877	67
Torre Reforma, Paseo de la Reforma 483 (2016)	807	57
Chapultepec Uno, Paseo de la Reforma 509 (2019)	789	59
Torre BBVA, Paseo de la Reforma 506 (2015)	771	50
Torre Mayor, Paseo de la Reforma 505 (2003)	738	55
Torre Ejecutiva Pemex, Marina Nacional 329 Col. Huasteca (1984)	693	51
*The University Tower, Paseo de la Reforma 150 (2024)	666	58
*Torre Aeromexico, Paseo de la Reforma 445 (on hold)	660	47
*Expansion Antara (2025)	660	42
*Rosewood Mexico City (2025)	659	48
*Downtown & Be Grand Reforma, La Fragura 7 (2023)	657	50
Torre Paradox, Av. Santa Fe 562 (2018)	644	60
Torre Reforma Latino, Paseo de la Reforma 296 (2016)	599	47
Torre Cuarzo, Paseo de la Reforma 26 (2017)	591	40
Torre M, Rio Churubusco 601 (2019)	577	35
Torre 300, Santa Fe 578 (2019)	574	51
Torre Altus, Paseo de los Laureles 416 (1998)	571	47
World Trade Center, Montecito 38 Col. Napoles (1972)	565	50
Miyana Torre Chapulin, Av. Ejecito Nacional (2020)	563	49
Siroco Elite Residences, Av. Santa Fe 482 (2015)	561	43
Sofitel Hotel Mexico City, Paseo de la Reforma 297 (2019)	558	41
Torre Latino Americana, Eje Central Lazaro Cardenas 2[1] (1956)	545	44
Peninsula Tower, Av. Santa Fe 1240 (2014)	539	50
Torre Punta Reforma, Paseo de la Reforma 180 (2015)	537	37
Arcos Torre II East, Paseo de los Tamarindos 400 (2008)	529	35
Arcos Torre II West, Paseo de los Tamarindos 400 (2008)	529	35
Arcos Torre I, Paseo de los Tamarindos 400 (1997)	529	35
(1) 595 ft incl. antenna.		
Miami, FL		
*Waldorf Astoria Hotel and Residences, 300 Biscayne Blvd. (2026)	1,041	98
*Okan Tower, 501 N. Miami Ave. (2026)	890	70
Panorama Tower, 1101 Brickell Ave. (2018)	828	81
Aston Martin Residences, 300 Biscayne Blvd. Way (2023)	817	66
Four Seasons Hotel & Tower, 1441 Brickell Ave. (2003)	789	64
*1 Southside Park, 191 SW 12th St. (2024)	773	64
Wachovia Financial Center, 200 S. Biscayne Blvd. (1983)	764	55
*830 Brickell, 830 SE 1st Ave. (2023)	724	55
Paramount Miami Worldcenter, 129 NE 8th St. (2019)	706	57
Marquis, 1100 Biscayne Blvd. (2009)	702	63
One Thousand Museum, 1000 Biscayne Blvd. (2019)	699	60
Brickell Flatiron, 1001 S. Miami Ave. (2019)	698	64
*Legacy Hotel & Residences, 942 NE 1st Ave. (2025)	690	51
Wells Fargo Tower, 200 SE 3rd St. (2010)	655	47
900 Biscayne Bay, 900 Biscayne Blvd. (2008)	650	63
*Missoni Baia, 700 NE 26th Ter. (2023)	646	57
Elysee, 700 NE 23rd St. (2021)	644	57
*Miami River Phase 1, 265 SW 6th St. (2025)	640	54
Echo Brickell, 1451 Brickell Ave. (2017)	637	57
Mint at Riverfront, 90 SW 3rd St. (2009)	631	55
Infinity at Brickell, 60 W. 13th St. (2008)	630	52
Miami Tower, 100 SE Second St. (1987)	625	47
Marinablue, 888 Biscayne Blvd. (2007)	615	57
*Una Residences, 175 SE 25th Rd. (2023)	613	47
Plaza on Brickell Tower I, 901 Brickell Ave. (2007)	610	56
Epic Residences & Hotel, 300 Biscayne Blvd. Way (2009)	601	54
One Paraiso, 620 NE 31st St. (2018)	601	53
SLS Brickell, 1300 S. Miami Ave. (2016)	599	52
SLS Lux Brickell, 801 S. Miami Ave. (2018)	595	57
*Nativo, 159 NE 6th St. (2023)	588	51
Icon Brickell North Tower, 495 Brickell Ave. (2008)	586	58
Icon Brickell South Tower, 495 Brickell Ave. (2008)	586	58

Building/structure	Ht. (ft)	Stories
*Miami World Tower (NA)	579	52
400 Biscayne (2022)	573	49
*Downtown 1st, 34 SW 1st St. (2023)	560	57
Paramount at Edgewater Square, 2066 N. Bayshore Dr. (2009)	555	47
50 Biscayne Blvd. (2007)	554	55
Quantum on the Bay South Tower, 1900 N. Bayshore Dr. (2008)	554	51
Biscayne Beach, 701 NE 29th St. (2017)	550	51
Solitair Brickell, 80 SW 8th St. (2018)	550	49
Brickell Heights North Tower, 850 S. Miami Ave. (2017)	549	52
GranParaiso, 600 NE 31st St. (2018)	548	55
ParaisoBay, 600 NE 31st St. (2017)	548	55
1010 Brickell (2017)	548	50
Opera Tower, 1750 N. Bayshore Dr. (2007)	543	56
Viceroy, 495 Brickell Ave. (2009)	542	50
Vizcayne North Tower, 244 Biscayne Blvd. (2008)	538	49
Vizcayne South Tower, 244 Biscayne Blvd. (2008)	538	49
Avant at Met Square, 340 SE 3rd St. (2018)	538	46
Quantum on the Bay North Tower, 1900 N. Bayshore Dr. (2008)	536	44
Aria on the Bay, 1770 N. Bayshore Dr. (2018)	535	53
Ten Museum Park, 1040 Biscayne Blvd. (2007)	530	50
Brickell Heights South Tower, 850 S. Miami Ave. (2017)	529	52
Jade at Brickell Bay, 1331 Brickell Bay Dr. (2004)	528	49
Plaza on Brickell Tower II, 901 Brickell Ave. (2007)	525	48
Minneapolis, MN		
IDS Center, 80 8th St. South[1] (1973)	792	55
Capella Tower, 225 South Sixth (1992)	776	56
Wells Fargo Center, 90 7th St. South (1988)	775	56
33 South Sixth St. (1983)	668	52
Two22 Tower, 222 9th St. South (1985)	582	42
US Bank Plaza I, 200 6th St. South (1981)	561	40
Eleven, 1111 West River Parkway (2022)	547	44
RBC Plaza, 60 6th St. South (1992)	539	40
(1) 910 ft incl. antenna.		
Mississauga, ON, Canada		
*M City Tower 3 (2024)	854	77
*Exchange District Condos, EX3 (2026)	761	72
*M City Tower 4 (2026)	707	67
*Exchange District Condos, EX1 (2024)	659	60
*M City Tower 2, 3883 Quartz Rd. (2023)	650	61
*M City Tower 1, 3980 Burnhamthorpe Rd. (2022)	650	61
Absolute World 56, 50 Absolute Ave. (2012)	576	56
*Oro at Edge Towers (2025)	525	51
Monterrey, Mexico		
*Torre Rise (2026)	1,558	94
T.Op Corporativo (2020)	1,002	64
Torre Koi, San Pedro Garza Garcia (2017)	916	65
*Sohl, Constitucion 999 (2026)	879	62
Hotel Safi Metropolitan, San Pedro Garza Garcia (2020)	764	56
Pabellon M (2015)	681	47
Santa Maria Torre 6 (2020)	620	43
*Torre ¡LoLa! (2023)	604	44
Metropolitan Center Torre II, San Pedro Garza Garcia (2017)	594	52
Centro de Gobierno Plaza Civica (2010)	591	36
*Ikon Tower, Av. Lazaro Cardenas 2305, San Pedro Garza Garcia (2024)	574	38
LIU East, San Pedro Garza Garcia (2013)	564	39
Torre Avalanz, San Pedro Garza Garcia (2000)	548	41
*Torre LaLo (2024)	525	42
Montréal, QC, Canada		
*1 Square Phillips, 539 Rue St. Catherine O. (2024)	763	61
1250 Boulevard Rene-Levesque O. (incl. spire) (1992)	743	47
1000 Rue de la Gauchetiere (1992)	673	51
*Le 900 Saint James (2025)	656	62
*Victoria Sur le Parc, 700 Rue Saint James (2023)	656	58
*National Bank HQ, 800 Rue Saint James (2023)	656	40
*Maestra Tour B (2023)	651	58
Tour de la Bourse, 800 Place Victoria (1964)	624	47
1 Place Villa Marie (1962)	616	43
*Maestra Tour A (2023)	606	55
L'Avenue, 1175 Avenue des Canadiens (2017)	605	51
La Tour CIBC, 1155 Boul. Rene-Levesque O.[1] (1962)	604	45
Montreal Tower (1987)	574	NA
Tour des Canadiens 3, 1250 Rue St. Antoine O. (2021)	551	53
Tour des Canadiens 2, 1150 Rue St. Antoine O. (2021)	551	53
Tour des Canadiens, 1288 Ave. des Canadiens (2016)	548	50
(1) 740 ft incl. antenna.		
New Orleans, LA		
Hancock Whitney Center, 701 Poydras St. (1972)	697	51
CapitalOne Center, 201 St. Charles Ave. (1985)	645	53
Plaza Tower, 1001 Howard Ave. (1969)	531	45
Energy Centre, 1100 Poydras St. (1984)	530	39
New York, NY		
One World Trade Center (incl. spire) (2014)	1,782	94
Central Park Tower, 217 W. 57th St. (2021)	1,550	98

Building/structure	Ht. (ft)	Stories
111 W. 57th St. (2021)	1,428	82
One Vanderbilt Place, 51 E. 42nd St. (2020)	1,401	62
432 Park Avenue (2015)	1,397	85
*JPMorgan Chase World HQ, 270 Park Ave. (2025)	1,388	63
30 Hudson Yards (2019)	1,268	73
Empire State Building, 350 5th Ave.[1] (1931)	1,250	102
Bank of America Tower (incl. spire), One Bryant Park (2009)	1,200	55
Three World Trade Center, 175 Greenwich St. (2018)	1,079	69
The Brooklyn Tower, 340 Flatbush Ext., Brooklyn (2023)	1,073	74
*740 8th Ave. (2027)	1,067	52
53 West 53rd (2019)	1,050	77
Chrysler Bldg. (incl. spire), 405 Lexington Ave. (1930)	1,046	77
New York Times Twr. (incl. spire), 620 8th Ave. (2007)	1,046	52
The Spiral, 435 10th Ave. (2023)	1,031	66
One57, 157 W. 57th St. (2014)	1,005	75
*520 5th Ave. (2026)	1,000	76
35 Hudson Yards (2019)	1,000	72
One Manhattan West, 401 9th Ave. (2019)	996	67
50 Hudson Yards, 504 W. 34th St. (2022)	981	58
4 World Trade Center, 150 Greenwich St. (2014)	977	65
220 Central Park South (2019)	952	70
70 Pine (incl. spire) (1932)	952	67
Two Manhattan West, 401 W. 31st St. (2023)	935	58
The Trump Bldg., 40 Wall St. (1930)	927	71
30 Park Place, 99 Church St. (2016)	926	67
Citigroup Center, 153 E. 53rd St. (1977)	915	63
15 Hudson Yards (2019)	914	70
*125 Greenwich St. (2024)	912	72
10 Hudson Yards (2016)	878	50
New York by Gehry at Eight Spruce Street (2011)	870	76
Trump World Tower, 845 UN Plaza (2001)	861	72
*262 5th Ave. (2024)	860	54
425 Park Avenue (2021)	860	44
Comcast Bldg., 30 Rockefeller Center (1933)	850	70
One Manhattan Square, 250 South St. (2019)	847	72
Sutton 58, 428-432 E. 58th St. (2022)	847	65
Cityspire Center, 150 W. 56th St. (1987)	814	75
28 Liberty (1961)	813	60
56 Leonard St. (2016)	813	57
4 Times Square[2] (1999)	809	48
MetLife Bldg., 200 Park Ave. (1963)	808	59
Bloomberg Tower, 731 Lexington Ave.[3] (2005)	806	54
Madison House, 126 Madison Ave. (2022)	805	56
The Centrale, 138 E. 50th St. (2019)	803	64
*42-02 Orchard St., Queens (2026)	794	69
Woolworth Building, 233 Broadway (1913)	792	58
111 Murray St. (2019)	788	60
520 Park Avenue (2018)	781	52
50 West, 50 West St. (2018)	779	64
Madison Square Park Tower, 41 E. 22nd St. (2017)	778	61
55 Hudson Yards (2019)	778	51
1 Worldwide Plaza, 935 8th Ave. (1989)	778	47
*50 W. 66th St. (2025)	775	52
Skyline Tower, 23-15 44th Dr., Queens (2021)	762	67
19 Dutch St. (2018)	758	63
Carnegie Hall Tower, 152 W. 57th St. (1991)	757	60
Sven, 29-55 Northern Blvd., Queens (2021)	755	67
The Wall Street Tower, 130 William St. (2021)	755	61
383 Madison Ave. (2001)	755	47
1717 Broadway (2013)	753	67
AXA Center, 787 7th Ave. (1985)	752	51
One Penn Plaza, 250 W. 34th St. (1972)	750	57
1251 Ave. of the Americas (1971)	750	54
Time Warner Center North Tower, 10 Columbus Cir. (2004)	749	55
Time Warner Center South Tower, 10 Columbus Cir. (2004)	749	55
Goldman Sachs HQ, 200 Murray St. (2010)	749	44
60 Wall Street (1989)	745	55
One Astor Plaza, 1515 Broadway (1972)	745	54
One Liberty Plaza, 165 Broadway (1972)	743	54
7 World Trade Center, 250 Greenwich St. (2006)	743	49
Twenty Exchange, 20 Exchange Pl. (1931)	741	57
Three World Financial Center, 200 Vesey St. (1986)	739	51
ARO, 242 W. 53rd St. (2018)	738	62
*43-03 24th St., Queens (2026)	732	66
1540 Broadway (incl. spire) (1990)	732	42
Times Square Tower, 1459 Broadway (2004)	726	47
Brooklyn Point, 138 Willoughby St., Brooklyn (2020)	723	57
Metropolitan Tower, 142 W. 57th St. (1985)	716	68
252 E. 57th St. (2016)	715	59
100 E. 53rd St. (2018)	711	61
General Motors Bldg., 767 5th Ave. (1968)	705	50
The Eugene, 401 W. 31st St. (2017)	702	64
25 Park Row (2020)	702	54
Metropolitan Life Tower, 1 Madison Ave. (1909)	700	50
500 5th Ave. (1931)	697	59
Americas Tower, 1177 Ave. of the Americas (1992)	692	48
Solow Bldg., 9 W. 57th St. (1974)	689	49
Marine Midland Bldg., 140 Broadway (1967)	688	52
55 Water St. (1972)	687	53
277 Park Ave. (1963)	687	50
The Beekman Hotel & Residences, 5 Beekman St. (2017)	687	47
1585 Broadway (1989)	685	42
Random House/Park Imperial, 1739 Broadway (2003)	684	52
Four Seasons Hotel, 57 E. 57th St. (1993)	682	52
Sky, 605 W. 42nd St (2015)	676	61
McGraw-Hill Bldg., 1221 Ave. of the Americas (1972)	674	51
Barclay Tower, 10 Barclay St. (2007)	673	56
One Grand Central Place, 60 E. 42nd St. (1930)	673	53
277 5th Ave. (2019)	673	52
One Court Square, Queens (1990)	673	50
*One Seaport, 161 Maiden Ln. (on hold)	670	60
Paramount Plaza, 1633 Broadway (1970)	670	48
200 Amsterdam Ave. (2021)	668	55
*45 Park Place (on hold)	667	43
Trump Tower, 725 5th Ave. (1982)	664	58
Bank of New York Bldg., 1 Wall St. (1932)	654	50
Silver Towers East, 600 W. 42nd St. (2009)	653	58
Silver Towers West, 600 W. 42nd St. (2009)	653	58
599 Lexington Ave. (1986)	653	51
712 5th Ave. (1990)	650	53
Chanin Bldg., 122 E. 42nd St. (1929)	649	56
245 Park Avenue (1967)	648	47
550 Madison Avenue (1983)	647	37
Two World Financial Center, 225 Liberty St. (1986)	645	44
1095 Ave. of the Americas (1974)	645	43
*450 11th Ave. (2024)	642	51
570 Lexington Ave. (1931)	642	50
1 New York Plaza, 1 Water St. (1969)	640	50
Rose Hill, 30 E. 29th St. (2021)	639	45
1 MiMA Tower, 440 W. 42nd St. (2011)	638	63
Tower 28, 42-12 28th St., Queens (2017)	638	58
3Eleven, 311 11th Ave. (2022)	637	59
1 Dag Hammarskjold Plaza, 885 2nd Ave. (1972)	637	48
345 Park Ave. (1968)	634	44
Langham Place, 400 5th Ave. (2010)	632	58
Mercantile Bldg., 10 E. 40th St. (1929)	632	48
W New York Downtown Hotel & Residences, 123 Washington St. (2010)	631	57
Grace Plaza, 1114 Ave. of the Americas (1972)	630	50
Home Insurance Plaza, 59 Maiden Ln. (1966)	630	44
101 Park Ave. (1982)	629	49
Central Park Place, 301 W. 57th St. (1988)	628	56
888 7th Ave. (1971)	628	45
11 Hoyt St., Brooklyn (2020)	626	51
Burlington House, 1345 Ave. of the Americas (1969)	625	50
Waldorf Astoria New York, 301 Park Ave. (1931)	625	47
Avalon Willoughby West, 100 Willoughby St., Brooklyn (2015)	624	57
Trump Palace, 200 E. 69th St. (1991)	623	54
One Madison Park, 20 E. 23rd St. (2010)	621	51
Olympic Tower, 645 5th Ave. (1976)	620	51
425 Fifth Ave. (2003)	618	55
The Epic, 125 W. 31st St. (2007)	615	61
919 3rd Ave. (1970)	615	47
Tower 49, 12 E. 49th St. (1985)	615	44
750 7th Ave. (incl. spire) (1989)	615	35
New York Life, 51 Madison Ave. (1928)	615	33
835 6th Ave. (2010)	614	53
Gotham Point, 1-15 57th Ave., Queens (2023)	612	57
551 10th Ave. (2016)	612	52
Baccarat Hotel & Residences, 20 W. 53rd St. (2014)	610	46
Credit Lyonnais Bldg., 1301 Ave. of the Amer. (1964)	609	46
The Orion, 350 W. 42nd St. (2006)	604	58
590 Madison Ave. (1983)	603	41
The Hub, 333 Schermerhorn St., Brooklyn (2017)	602	54
250 W. 55th St. (2013)	602	40
Eleven Times Square, 644 8th Ave. (2011)	601	40
1166 Avenue of the Americas (1974)	600	40
Eagle Lofts, 43-22 Queens St., Queens (2018)	598	55
Hawthorn Park, 160 W. 62nd St. (2014)	598	54
Hearst Magazine Tower, 959 8th Ave. (2006)	597	46
3 Lincoln Center, 160 W. 66th St. (1993)	595	60
Celanese Bldg., 1211 Ave. of the Amer. (1973)	592	45
The London NYC, 151 W. 54th St. (1990)	590	54
388 Bridge St., Brooklyn (2014)	590	51
Thurgood Marshall U.S. Courthouse, 505 Pearl St. (1936)	590	37
Museum Tower Apts., 21 W. 53rd St. (1985)	589	52
The Millennium Hilton Hotel, 55 Church St. (1992)	588	58
Sky House, 11 E. 29th St. (2008)	588	55
Hunter's Point South Phase 2 Tower A, 52-03 Center Blvd., Queens (2022)	587	56
1271 Ave. of the Americas (1959)	587	48
451 10th Ave. Residential Tower (2022)	587	45
Jacob K. Javits Federal Bldg., 26 Federal Plz. (1967)	587	41
W Times Square, 1567 Broadway (2000)	584	53
Trump Intl. Hotel & Twr., 15 Columbus Cir. (1970)	583	44
3 Jackson Park, 28-30 Jackson Ave., Queens (2018)	581	54
Stevens Tower, 1185 Ave. of the Amer. (1971)	580	42
Ritz-Carlton NoMad, 1185 Broadway (2022)	580	40
Municipal Bldg., 1 Centre St. (1914)	580	34
520 Madison Ave. (1981)	577	43

Building/structure	Ht. (ft)	Stories
One World Financial Center, 200 Liberty St. (1985)	577	37
Merchandise Mart, 41 Madison Ave. (1973)	576	42
*346 Kent Ave., Brooklyn (2024)	575	52
Park Ave. Plaza, 55 E. 52nd St. (1981)	575	44
300 Madison Ave. (2003)	575	38
Lehman Bldg., 745 7th Ave. (2001)	575	38
32 Old Slip (1987)	575	37
Marriott Marquis Times Sq., 1531 Broadway (1985)	574	50
299 Park Ave. (1967)	574	42
5 Times Square, 590 7th Ave. (2002)	574	40
Socony Mobil Bldg., 150 E. 42nd St. (1956)	572	42
Lyra, 555 W. 38th St. (2022)	571	52
1290 Ave. of the Americas (1963)	571	43
780 3rd Ave. (1983)	570	49
600 3rd Ave. (1971)	570	42
The Ashland, 590 Fulton St., Brooklyn (2016)	568	51
450 Lexington Ave. (1991)	568	38
Paramount Tower, 240 E. 39th St. (1998)	567	51
230 Park Ave. (1928)	565	35
New York Palace Hotel, 455 Madison Ave. (1980)	563	51
Continental Bank Bldg., 30 Broad St. (1932)	562	48
Turkevi Center, 821 UN Plaza (2021)	561	36
Park Ave. Tower, 65 E. 55th St. (1986)	561	36
Nelson Tower, 450 7th Ave. (1931)	560	46
Sherry-Netherland, 781 5th Ave. (1927)	560	40
623 5th Ave. (1990)	560	36
South Park Tower, 124 W. 60th St. (1986)	558	51
100 UN Plaza, 327 E. 48th St. (1986)	557	52
Continental Can, 633 3rd Ave. (1962)	557	39
Summit New York, 222 E. 44th St. (2018)	556	42
3 Park Ave. (1975)	556	42
Continental Center, 180 Maiden Ln. (1983)	555	41
330 Madison Ave. (1964)	555	41
Equitable Bldg., 120 Broadway (1915)	555	38
3 Times Square[4] (2001)	555	30
Tower 111, 885 6th Ave. (2011)	554	48
Instrada Nomad, 10 E. 29th St. (1999)	554	48
Inmont Bldg., 1133 Ave. of the Americas (1970)	553	44
One Willoughby Square, 420 Albee Sq., Brooklyn (2021)	552	35
Downtown by Philippe Starck, 15 Broad St. (1927)	551	42
*3 W. 29th St. (on hold)	551	34
Hyatt Times Square, 135 W. 45th St. (2013)	550	53
Biltmore Tower, 267 W. 47th St. (2003)	550	51
Unisys Bldg., 605 3rd Ave. (1963)	550	44
The Tower at 15 Central Park West (2008)	550	35
AT&T Long Lines Bldg., 33 Thomas St. (1974)	550	29

(1) 1,455 ft incl. antenna. (2) 1,118 ft incl. antenna. (3) 941 ft incl. antenna. (4) 659 ft incl. antenna.

Philadelphia, PA

Building/structure	Ht. (ft)	Stories
Comcast Technology Center, 1800 Arch St. (2018)	1,121	59
Comcast Center, 1701 JFK Blvd. (2008)	974	57
One Liberty Place (incl. spire), 1650 Market St. (1987)	945	61
Two Liberty Place (incl. spire), 1601 Chestnut St. (1989)	848	58
BNY Mellon Bank Center, 1735 Market St. (1990)	792	54
Three Logan, 1717 Arch St. (1991)	739	55
FMC Tower at Cira Centre South (2017)	730	49
G. Fred DiBona Jr. Bldg., 1901 Market St. (1990)	625	45
The W Philadelphia and Element, 1441 Chestnut St. (2019)	617	51
The Laurel, 1911 Walnut St. (2022)	599	50
Commerce Square #1, 2005 Market St. (1990)	572	40
Commerce Square #2, 2001 Market St. (1992)	572	40
City Hall (incl. statue) (1901)	548	7
Arthaus, 309 S. Broad St. (2022)	528	47

Pittsburgh, PA

Building/structure	Ht. (ft)	Stories
US Steel Tower, 600 Grant St. (1970)	841	64
BNY Mellon Center, 500 Grant St. (1983)	725	54
One PPG Place (1984)	635	40
Fifth Ave. Place, 120 5th Ave. (1987)	616	32
One Oxford Centre, 301 Grant St. (1982)	615	46
Gulf Tower, 707 Grant St. (1932)	582	44
The Tower at PNC Plaza (2015)	545	33
University of Pittsburgh Cathedral of Learning, 4200 5th Ave. (1936)	535	42

Portland, OR

Building/structure	Ht. (ft)	Stories
Wells Fargo Center, 1300 SW 5th Ave. (1973)	546	40
Park Avenue West (incl. spire), 728 SW 9th Ave. (2016)	537	30
U.S. Bancorp Tower, 111 SW 5th Ave. (1983)	536	42

Puebla, Mexico

Building/structure	Ht. (ft)	Stories
*Oak 58 Torre Orso, San Andres Cholula (on hold)	761	58
Inxignia (2023)	738	45

Building/structure	Ht. (ft)	Stories
*Torre NVBOLA (on hold)	650	40
*Oak 58 Torre Lupo, San Andres Cholula (on hold)	630	48

St. Louis, MO

Building/structure	Ht. (ft)	Stories
Gateway Arch, 11 N. 4th St. (1965)	630	NA
Metropolitan Square Tower, 211 N. Broadway (1988)	593	42
900 Pine St. (1986)	588	44
Thomas F. Eagleton Federal Courthouse, 111 S. 10th St. (2000)	557	29

San Francisco, CA

Building/structure	Ht. (ft)	Stories
Salesforce Tower, 415 Mission St. (2018)	1,070	61
Sutro Tower (1972)	977	NA
Transamerica Pyramid, 600 Montgomery St. (1972)	853	48
181 Fremont (2018)	810	56
555 California St. (1969)	779	52
345 California Center (1986)	695	48
Millennium Tower, 301 Mission St. (2009)	645	58
The Avery, 400 Folsom St. (2019)	618	56
One Rincon Hill South Tower, 425 First St. (2008)	605	54
Park Tower at Transbay (2018)	605	43
101 California St. (1982)	600	48
50 Fremont Center (1985)	600	43
575 Market St. (1975)	573	40
Four Embarcadero Center, 55 Clay St. (1984)	570	45
One Embarcadero Center, 355 Clay St. (1970)	569	45
44 Montgomery St. (1967)	565	43
Spear Tower, 1 Market St. (1976)	565	42
One Sansome Street (1984)	550	43
One Rincon Hill North Tower, 425 First St. (2014)	541	45
*Hayes Point, 30 Van Ness Ave. (2025)	540	47
Shaklee Terrace Bldg., 444 Market St. (1982)	537	38
First Market Tower, 525 Market St. (1972)	529	38
McKesson Plaza, 1 Post St. (1969)	529	38

Seattle, WA

Building/structure	Ht. (ft)	Stories
Columbia Center, 701 5th Ave. (1985)	933	76
Rainier Square Tower, 1301 5th Ave. (2020)	852	58
1201 Third Avenue Tower, 1201 3rd Ave. (1988)	772	55
Two Union Square, 601 Union St. (1989)	740	56
Seattle Municipal Tower, 700 5th Ave. (1990)	722	57
F5 Tower, 811 5th Ave. (2017)	660	44
Safeco Plaza, 1001 4th Ave. (1969)	630	50
City Centre, 1420 5th Ave. (1989)	606	44
Space Needle, 203 6th Ave. (1962)	605	NA
Russell Investments Center, 1301 2nd Ave. (2006)	598	42
Wells Fargo Center, 999 3rd Ave. (1983)	574	47
Madison Centre, 505 Madison St. (2017)	560	36
Bank of America Fifth Avenue Plaza, 800 Fifth Ave. (1981)	543	42
901 5th Ave. (1973)	536	41
2+U, 1201 2nd Ave. (2019)	527	38

Sunny Isles Beach, FL

Building/structure	Ht. (ft)	Stories
Estates at Acqualina Boutique North Tower, 17901 Collins Ave. (2023)	672	52
Estates at Acqualina South Tower, 17901 Collins Ave. (2022)	672	52
Turnberry Ocean Club, 18501 Collins Ave. (2020)	649	52
Muse, 17141 Collins Ave. (2018)	649	47
Porsche Design Tower, 18555 Collins Ave. (2016)	644	58
Mansions at Acqualina, 17749 Collins Ave. (2015)	643	46
The Ritz-Carlton Residences, 15701 Collins Ave. (2020)	642	52
Residences by Armani Casa, 18975 Collins Ave. (2019)	639	55
Jade Signature, 16901 Collins Ave. (2017)	636	57
Jade on the Beach Condominiums, 17001 Collins Ave. (2008)	574	51
Trump Royale, 18201 Collins Ave. (2008)	551	43
Trump Palace, 18101 Collins Ave. (2005)	551	43
Acqualina Resort & Spa, 17875 Collins Ave. (2004)	550	51
Jade Ocean, 17121 Collins Ave. (2009)	543	51

Tampa, FL

Building/structure	Ht. (ft)	Stories
Regions Bldg., 100 N. Tampa St. (1992)	579	42
Bank of America Plaza, 101 E. Kennedy Blvd. (1986)	577	42
One Tampa City Center, 201 N. Franklin St. (1981)	537	39
Truist Place, 401 E. Jackson St. (1992)	525	36

Toronto, ON, Canada

Building/structure	Ht. (ft)	Stories
CN Tower, 310 Front St. West (1976)	1,815	NA
*The One, 1 Bloor St. West (2024)	1,077	91
*Sky Tower, 1 Yonge St. (2025)	1,025	95
*Concord Sky, 385 Yonge St. (2027)	981	85
First Canadian Place, 100 King St. West[1] (1975)	978	72
The St. Regis Toronto (incl. spire), 325 Bay St. (2012)	963	63
Scotia Tower, 40 King St. West (1989)	902	68
Aura at College Park, 388 Yonge St. (2014)	892	78

Building/structure	Ht. (ft)	Stories
*Forma East, 260 King St. West (2026)	874	73
Brookfield Place (incl. spire), 161 Bay St. (1990) . . .	856	53
Number One Bloor, 1 Bloor St. East (2017)	844	75
*CIBC Square II, 141 Bay St. (2024)	792	53
*160 Front (2023)	787	46
Commerce Court West, 199 Bay St.[2] (1973)	784	57
CIBC Square I, 81 Bay St. (2021)	780	49
Ice Condos at York Centre 2, 16 York St. (2015)	768	67
Harbour Plaza Residences E., 90 Harbour St. (2017)	764	71
*Canada House 1, 23 Spadina Ave. (2024)	759	69
*Sugar Wharf Tower D, 95 Lakeshore East (2023) . .	755	70
Eau de Soleil Sky Tower, 2183 Lake Shore Blvd. W., Etobicoke (2019)	747	67
Harbour Plaza Residences W., 90 Harbour St. (2017)	735	67
Ten York (2018)	735	65
TD Centre-Toronto Dominion Bank Tower, 66 Wellington St. West (1967)	730	56
*Sugar Wharf Tower E, 95 Lakeshore East (2023) . .	717	65
*8 Elm St. (2026)	716	69
The Prestige at Pinnacle One Yonge (2022)	712	65
*The Pemberton, 33 Yorkville Ave. (2024)	708	68
Bay-Adelaide Center West Twr., 335 Bay St. (2010)	704	52
Living Shangri-La Toronto, 180 University Ave. (2012)	702	65
*Cru Condos, 11 Yorkville Ave. (2024)	699	62
Ritz-Carlton Hotel and Residences, 185 Wellington St. West (2011)	687	54
The Residences of 488 University Avenue (2019) . .	679	58
BCE Place, Bay-Wellington Tower, 181 Bay St. (1991)	679	49
L Tower, 1 Front St. (2014)	673	58
Massey Tower, 199 Yonge St. (2019)	670	62
88 Scott St. (2017)	669	58
Four Seasons Private Residences West, 48 Yorkville Ave. (2012)	669	55
YC Condos, 460 Yonge St. (2018)	664	60
*Canada House 2, 23 Spadina Ave. (2024)	663	59
Ice Condos at York Centre 1, 16 York St. (2014)	663	57
Bay-Adelaide Center East Twr., 40 Adelaide St. (2016)	643	44
E Condos South, 8 Eglinton Ave. (2019).	642	58
Wellesley on the Park, 11 Wellesley St. W. (2021) . .	637	60
22I21 Yonge, 2221 Yonge St. (2021)	632	58
EY Tower, 100 Adelaide St. West (2017)	617	40
*19 Duncan St. (2023)	612	58
Rosedale on Bloor, 403 Bloor St. East (2023)	610	55
*Water's Edge at the Cove, 38 The Marginal Blvd., Etobicoke (2024)	607	56
RBC Centre, 155 Wellington St. West (2009)	607	42
CASA II, 42 Charles St. East (2016).	605	57
U Condominiums East Tower, 50 St. Joseph St. (2016)	604	55
One Yorkville (2020)	601	58
TD North Tower, 77 King St. West (1969)	600	46
*8 Wellesley West (2024)	595	55
Maple Leaf Square North Tower, 65 Bremner Blvd. (2010)	595	54
Eau de Soleil Water Tower, 2183 Lake Shore Blvd. West, Etobicoke (2019)	593	49
CASA III, 50 Charles St. East (2018)	589	56
*United Bldg., 481 University Ave. (2024)	589	52
Vita on the Lake, 2165 Lake Shore Blvd. West, Etobicoke (2022)	587	58
INDX Condominiums, 70 Temperance St. (2016). . . .	585	54
1 King West (2005)	578	51
The Well Office Tower, 410 Front St. West (2022). . .	571	38
Success Tower 2, 33 Bay St. (2010)	569	55
Royal Bank Plaza-South Tower, 200 Bay St. (1976)	567	41
Maple Leaf Square South Tower, 55 Bremner Blvd. (2010)	562	50
Teahouse Condominiums South, 501 Yonge St. (2022)	561	52
The Selby Condominiums, 592 Shelbourne St. (2019)	560	51
*Eight Cumberland, 826 Yonge St. (2023)	557	51
Hullmark Centre I, 4789 Yonge St. (2015)	557	45
*4800 Yonge (2025)	552	49
Lago at the Waterfront, 2151 Lake Shore Blvd. Ave., Etobicoke (2016)	550	49

(1) 1,116 ft incl. antenna. (2) 942 ft incl. antenna.

Vancouver, BC, Canada

Building/structure	Ht. (ft)	Stories
Shangri-La Vancouver, 1120 W. Georgia St. (2009)	659	59
Paradox Hotel and Residences, 1133 W. Georgia (2016).	616	58
*The Butterfly, 969 Burrard St. (2023)	586	57
One Burrard Place (2021)	551	54
The Stack, 1133 Melville St. (2023)	550	37

Vaughan, ON, Canada

Building/structure	Ht. (ft)	Stories
*Festival Tower A (2024)	615	59
*CG Tower, 2900 Hwy. 7 (2025)	608	60
Transit City Condos 3 (2021)	587	55
*Festival Tower C (2024).	583	55
Transit City Condos 1 (2021)	575	55
Transit City Condos 2 (2021)	575	55
*TC4 (2023)	546	50

Other Tall Buildings in North America

Building/structure	City	Ht. (ft)	Stories
Devon Energy Center (2012)	Oklahoma City, OK	844	52
Stantec Tower (2019)	Edmonton, AB, Can.	816	66
RSA Battle House Tower (incl. spire) (2007)	Mobile, AL.	745	35
Ocean Resort Casino (2012). .	Atlantic City, NJ	718	53
Salesforce Tower[1] (1990)	Indianapolis, IN	701	49
*Mutual of Omaha HQ (2026)	Omaha, NE.	677	44
Hotel Riu Plaza Guadalajara (incl. spire) (2011)	Guadalajara, Mexico	669	42
BOK Tower (1975)	Tulsa, OK	667	52
Great American Twr. at Queen City Square (2011).	Cincinnati, OH	665	40
Cityplex Central Tower (1979)	Tulsa, OK	648	60
The Tower at First National Center (2002)	Omaha, NE.	634	45
801 Grand (1991)	Des Moines, IA	630	44
JW Marriott-Legends Private Residences (2024)	Edmonton, AB, Can.	627	56
One Kansas City Place (incl. spire) (1988)	Kansas City, MO . . .	623	42
Tower of the Americas (1968)	San Antonio, TX . . .	622	NA
Bank of America Tower (1990)	Jacksonville, FL . . .	617	42
AT&T Building (1994)	Nashville TN	617	33
U.S. Bank Center (1973).	Milwaukee, WI.	601	42
*Bellevue 600 (2024)	Bellevue, WA.	600	43
*555 108th Ave. NE (2023) . . .	Bellevue, WA	600	42
Town Pavilion (1986)	Kansas City, MO . . .	591	38
Erastus Corning II Twr. (1973).	Albany, NY	589	44
*Pier West 1 (2023)	New Westminster, BC, Can.	584	53
Niagara Falls Hilton Phase 2 (2009)	Niagara Falls, ON, Can.	581	58
Carew Tower[2] (1931)	Cincinnati, OH	574	49
Concourse Corporate Ctr. V (incl. spire) (1988)	Sandy Springs, GA	570	34
Hyatt Regency Andares (2017)	Zapopan, Mexico . .	568	41
Torre Aura Altitude (2008). . . .	Zapopan, Mexico . .	563	44
Blue Diamond Tower (2000) . .	Miami Beach, FL. . .	559	44
Green Diamond Tower (2000)	Miami Beach, FL. . .	559	44
*Parkway II (2025)	Surrey, BC, Can. . . .	555	50
Washington Monument (1884)	Washington, DC . . .	555	NA
Concourse Corporate Ctr. VI (incl. spire) (1991)	Sandy Springs, GA	553	34
Northwestern Mutual Tower (2017)	Milwaukee, WI.	550	33
400 West Market (1992)	Louisville, KY	549	35
Simmons Tower (1986).	Little Rock, AR	546	40
Marriott Rivercenter (incl. spires) (1988)	San Antonio, TX . . .	546	38
Four Seasons Hotel & Residences (2022)	Nashville, TN	539	40
PNC Plaza (incl. spire) (2008)	Raleigh, NC	538	32
City Place I (1980)	Hartford, CT	535	38
Modis Tower (1975)	Jacksonville, FL . . .	535	37
One America Tower (1982) . . .	Indianapolis, IN	533	38
567 Clarke + Como (2021). . . .	Coquitlam, BC, Can.	532	49
Corporativo Bansi (2019)	Guadalajara, Mexico	532	32
Torre 40 Residencial Gran Jardin (2020).	León, Mexico	531	44
Transamerica Tower (1973) . .	Baltimore, MD	529	40
Seneca One (1970)	Buffalo, NY	529	38
*Highpoint (2023)	Coquitlam, BC, Can.	528	50
Travelers Tower (1919)	Hartford, CT	527	24
Vehicle Assembly Bldg. (1965)	Cape Canaveral, FL	526	40
Harrah's Waterfront Twr. (2008)	Atlantic City, NJ . . .	525	44
*The Sky (2024)	Mérida, Mexico	525	37

(1) 811 ft incl. antenna. (2) 623 ft incl. antenna.

Selected Bridge Styles

Bridges support weight through tension (pulling), compression (pushing), or a combination of both. **Suspension** and **cable-stayed** bridges are characterized by cables under tension. While the deck of a suspension bridge hangs from suspenders, that of a cable-stayed bridge ties directly to a bridge tower. The elements of a **truss** form triangles, which distribute the forces of tension and compression. Truss bridges can thus carry more weight than beam bridges. Steel plates can be welded or bolted together to make a **plate girder**, a kind of beam. A common form is the **box girder**.

A bridge can have a **simple** configuration, whereby its load is supported at both ends. If a bridge is **continuous**, its load extends across multiple supports. In a **cantilever** configuration, structural elements (e.g., trusses or girders) supported at one end project out, or cantilever, to carry a span.

Notable North American Bridges

Source: World Almanac research; Office of Bridge Technology, Federal Highway Administration, U.S. Dept. of Transportation Asterisk (*) designates a bridge that carries railroads only. All other bridges carry roads or roads and rail unless otherwise noted. Year is date of completion or projected completion. Span of bridge is the distance between its main supports. As of mid-2023.

Suspension

Year	Bridge	Location	Main span (ft)
1964	Verrazzano-Narrows	New York, NY	4,260
1937	Golden Gate	San Francisco Bay, CA	4,200
1957	Mackinac	Straits of Mackinac, MI	3,800
1931	George Washington	New York, NY-Fort Lee, NJ	3,500
1950/2007	Tacoma Narrows (twin)	Tacoma, WA	2,800
2003	Al Zampa Mem. (New Carquinez) (westbound)	Carquinez Strait, CA	2,388
1936	San Francisco-Oakland Bay (West Span)[1]	San Francisco-Yerba Buena Isl., CA	2,310
1939	Bronx-Whitestone	East R., New York, NY	2,300
1970	Pierre Laporte	Quebec City, QC, Can.	2,190
1951/68	Delaware Mem. (twin)	Pennsville, NJ-New Castle, DE	2,150
1957	Walt Whitman	Philadelphia, PA-NJ	2,000
1929	Ambassador	Detroit, MI-Windsor, ON, Can.	1,850
1961	Throgs Neck	New York, NY	1,801
1926	Benjamin Franklin	Phila., PA-Camden, NJ	1,750
1924	Bear Mountain	Hudson R., Peekskill, NY	1,632
1969	Claiborne Pell/Newport	Narragansett Bay, RI	1,600
1952/73	William Preston Lane Jr. Memorial (twin)	Sandy Point, MD	1,600
1903	Williamsburg	East R., New York, NY	1,600
1883	Brooklyn	East R., New York, NY	1,596
1938	Lions Gate	Vancouver, BC, Can.	1,549
1963	Vincent Thomas	L.A. Harbor, CA	1,500
1930	Mid-Hudson	Poughkeepsie, NY	1,495
1909	Manhattan	East R., New York, NY	1,470
1955	Angus L. Macdonald	Halifax, NS, Can.	1,447
1970	A. Murray MacKay	Halifax, NS, Can.	1,400
1936	Triborough (Harlem R. Lift/Bronx Crossing/East R. Suspension)	East R., New York, NY	1,380
2013	San Francisco-Oakland Bay (SAS)[2]	San Francisco Bay, CA	1,263

Cantilever

Year	Bridge	Location	Main span (ft)
1917	Quebec	Quebec City, QC, Can.	1,800
1974	Commodore Barry	Chester, PA-Bridgeport, NJ	1,644
1958/88	Crescent City Connection (twin)	Mississippi R., New Orleans, LA	1,575
1995	Veterans Memorial	Gramercy, LA	1,460
1968	Baton Rouge	Mississippi R., LA	1,235
1930	Lewis and Clark	Longview, WA-Rainier, OR	1,200
1909	Queensboro	East R., New York, NY	1,182
1958	Carquinez (eastbound)	San Francisco Bay, CA	1,100
1930	Jacques Cartier	Montreal, QC, Can.	1,097
1968	Isaiah D. Hart	Jacksonville, FL	1,088
1956	Richmond-San Rafael (twin)	San Francisco Bay, CA	1,070
1963/80	Newburgh-Beacon (twin)	Hudson R., NY	1,000

Truss

Year	Bridge	Location	Main span (ft)
1966	Astoria-Megler (U.S. 101)	Columbia R., OR-WA	1,232
1976	Francis Scott Key	Baltimore, MD	1,200
1981	Ravenswood	Ohio R., Ravenswood, WV	902
1995	Taylor-Southgate	Ohio R., Cincinnati, OH-Newport, KY	850
1943	Julien Dubuque (U.S. 20)	Mississippi R., IA-IL	845
1966	Charles Braga	Fall River, MA	840
1963	Brent Spence (I-71/I-75)	Ohio R., OH-KY	831
1956	Shawneetown (KY 56) (twin)	Ohio R., IL-KY.	825
1953	John E. Mathews	Jacksonville, FL	810
1992	Cooper R.	Charleston, SC	800
1957	Kingston-Rhinecliff	Hudson R., NY	800
1950	Maurice J. Tobin	Boston, MA	800
1988	Phil G. McDonald (Glade Creek)	Beckley, WV	784
1986	Rochester-Monaca	Rochester-Monaca, PA	780
1973/88	Atchafalaya R. (U.S. 190) (twin)	Krotz Springs, LA	780
1917	*Sciotoville RR (twin)	Sciotoville, OH-KY	775
1981	Sewickley	Sewickley, PA	750
1977	Jennings Randolph	Chester, PA-E. Liverpool, OH	750
1974	Carroll C. Cropper (I-275)	Ohio R., IN-KY	750
1940	Glover Cary	Ohio R., Owensboro, KY-IN	750
1984	13th Street	Ohio R., Ashland, KY-OH	740
1959	Monaca-E. Rochester	Monaca-E. Rochester, PA	730
1976	Betsy Ross	Phila., PA-Pennsauken, NJ	729
2013	Milton-Madison (U.S. 421)	Ohio R., KY-IN	727
1967	Matthew E. Welsh	Ohio R., Mauckport, IN-KY	725
1994	Robert C. Byrd	Huntington, WV.	720
1971	Atchafalaya R. (LA 1)	Simmesport, LA	720
1962	U.S. 41 Twin	Ohio R., Evansville, IN-Henderson, KY	720
1929	Irvin S. Cobb (U.S. 45)	Ohio R., Brookport, IL-Paducah, KY	716
1970	Vanport	Vanport, PA	715
1973	Girard Point	Philadelphia, PA	700
1963	John F. Kennedy (I-65)	Ohio R., Louisville, KY-Jeffersonville, IN	700
1923	*Mears Mem., Tanana R.	Nenana, AK	700

Plate and Box Girder

Year	Bridge	Location	Main span (ft)
1997	Confederation[3]	Prince Edward Isl.-NB, Can.	820
2010	Kanawha R. (I-64)	S. Charleston-Dunbar, WV	760
1982	Jesse H. Jones Memorial	Houston, TX	750
1977	LA 27, Intracoastal Canal.	Gibbstown, LA	750
1976	LA 82, Intracoastal Canal.	Forked Isl., LA	750
1967	San Mateo-Hayward	San Francisco Bay, CA	750
1992	Jamestown-Verrazano	Narragansett Bay, RI.	674
2002	Vietnam Veterans Mem.	James R., Richmond, VA.	672
1986	Umatilla	Columbia R., OR-WA	660
1969	San Diego-Coronado (twin)	San Diego Bay, CA	660
2007	Benicia-Martinez (new)	Carquinez Strait, CA	659

Cable-Stayed

Year	Bridge	Location	Main span (ft)
2025	Gordie Howe Intl.	Detroit, MI-Windsor, ON, Can.	2,798
2012	Baluarte Bicentennial	Sinaloa-Durango, Mex.	1,706
2025	New Harbor (U.S. 181)	Corpus Christi Ship Channel, TX	1,661
2011	John James Audubon	St. Francisville, LA	1,583
2005	Arthur Ravenel Jr.	Charleston, SC	1,546
2012	Port Mann	Vancouver, BC, Can.	1,542
1986	Alex Fraser	Vancouver, BC, Can.	1,526
2014	Stan Musial Veterans Memorial (I-70)	Miss. R., St. Louis, MO-IL	1,500
2010	Greenville (U.S. 82)	MS-Lake Village, AR	1,378
1994	Clark	Alton, IL-MO	1,360
1989	Dames Point	Jacksonville, FL	1,300
2003	Sidney Lanier	Brunswick, GA	1,250
1995	Fred Hartman	Houston Ship Channel, Baytown, TX	1,250
2007	Veterans' Glass City Skyway	Maumee R., Toledo, OH	1,225
1983	Hale Boggs Memorial	Luling, LA	1,222
2017	Mario Cuomo (I-287) (twin)	Hudson R., Tarrytown-Nyack, NY	1,200
2002	William Natcher, Ohio R.	Owensboro, KY-IN	1,200
1987	Sunshine Skyway (I-275)	Tampa Bay, FL	1,200
2012	Margaret Hunt Hill	Trinity R., Dallas, TX	1,197
1988	Tampico	Panuco R., Mex.	1,181
2006	Penobscot Narrows	Bucksport, ME	1,161
2003	Bill Emerson Memorial	Cape Girardeau, MO-IL	1,150
1988	Skybridge[4]	Vancouver, BC, Can.	1,115
1991	Talmadge Memorial	Savannah, GA	1,100
2000	Maysville (Wm. H. Harsha)	Ohio R., KY-Aberdeen, OH	1,050

Steel Arch

Year	Bridge	Location	Main span (ft)
1977	New River Gorge	Fayetteville, WV	1,700
1931	Bayonne (Kill Van Kull)	Bayonne, NJ-New York, NY	1,675
1973	Fremont	Portland, OR	1,255
1964	Port Mann	Vancouver, BC, Can.	1,200
1967	Laviolette	Trois-Rivières, QC, Can.	1,100
1990	Roosevelt Lake	Roosevelt Lake, AZ	1,080
1959	Glen Canyon	Page, AZ	1,028
1962	Lewiston-Queenston	NY-ON, Can.	1,001
1976	Perrine	Twin Falls, ID	993
1916	*Hell Gate	East R., New York, NY	978
1941	Rainbow	Niagara Falls, NY-ON, Can.	950
1997	Second Blue Water	Port Huron, MI-ON, Can.	922
1977	Moundsville	Ohio R., WV	912

Land Vehicular Tunnels in the U.S.

Source: World Almanac research; Federal Highway Administration, U.S. Dept. of Transportation

Name	Location	Length (ft)	Name	Location	Length (ft)
Anton Anderson Memorial[1]	Whittier, AK	13,300	Kittatinny Mountain (twin)	Franklin Co., PA	4,727
SR 99 (Alaskan Way)	Seattle, WA	12,244	Lehigh (twin)	Lehigh Co.-Carbon	
Edwin C. Johnson Memorial	I-70, Clear Creek Co.-			Co., PA	4,383
	Summit Co., CO	8,877	Tom Lantos/Devil's		4,342/
Eisenhower Memorial	I-70, Clear Creek Co.-		Slide (twin)	San Mateo Co., CA	4,265
	Summit Co., CO	8,856	Blue Mountain (twin)	Newburg, PA	4,340
Ted Williams[2]	MA Turnpike, Boston, MA	8,448	Wawona	Yosemite Natl. Pk., CA	4,237
Thomas P. O'Neill Jr.	I-93, Boston, MA	7,920	Big Walker Mountain (twin)	Bland Co., VA	4,228
Tetsuo Harano (twin)	Oahu, HI	6,336	Squirrel Hill (twin)	Pittsburgh, PA	4,225
Allegheny (twin)	Somerset Co., PA	6,069	Hanging Lake (twin)	Glenwood Canyon, CO	4,035/
Liberty (twin)	PA Turnpike, Pittsburgh,				3,941
	PA	5,898	Cave Rock (eastbound)	Douglas Co., NV	3,915
East River Mountain (twin)	I-77, Rocky Gap,		Wabash HOV	Pittsburgh, PA	3,661
	VA-Bluefield, WV	5,661	Caldecott (4 tubes)	Oakland, CA	3,616/3,610/
Zion-Mount Carmel	Zion Natl. Park, UT	5,613			3,371/3,399
Tuscarora Mountain (twin)	Franklin Co.-Huntingdon		Fort Pitt (twin)	Pittsburgh, PA	3,614
	Co., PA	5,324	Mount Washington Transit	Pittsburgh, PA	3,549
Cumberland Gap (twin)	U.S. 25E, KY-TN	4,860	I-395 Mall (Third St.)	Washington, DC	3,400

(1) Vehicles and trains take turns using the tunnel's one lane. (2) Total length of tunnel is 8,448 ft, of which 3,960 ft is underwater.

Major U.S. Dams and Reservoirs

Source: National Inventory of Dams, U.S. Army Corps of Engineers

Highest U.S. Dams

Rank	Dam (year completed)	River	Location	Type	Height (ft)
1.	Oroville (1968)	Feather	California	Embankment earthfill	770
2.	Hoover (1935)	Colorado	Nevada-Arizona	Arch-Gravity	730
3.	Dworshak (1973)	N. Fork Clearwater	Idaho	Gravity	717
4.	Glen Canyon (1963)	Colorado	Arizona	Arch	710
5.	New Bullards Bar (1970)	North Yuba	California	Arch	645
6.	New Melones (1979)	Stanislaus	California	Embankment rockfill	625
7.	Mossyrock (1968)	Cowlitz	Washington	Arch	606
8.	Shasta (1945)	Sacramento	California	Gravity	602
9.	Don Pedro (1971)	Tuolumne	California	Embankment earthfill	585
10.	Hungry Horse (1952)	S. Fork Flathead	Montana	Arch	564

Note: The height of a dam is the vertical distance between the original streambed or excavated foundation and the dam's crest, parapet wall, or maximum design water level. Tailings and other mining dams (i.e., dams built from the waste generated by mining operations) are not included in this list.

Largest U.S. Embankment Dams

Rank	Dam (year completed)	River	Location	Volume in cubic yards (thous.)
1.	Fort Peck (1957)	Missouri	Montana	125,628
2.	Oahe (1966)	Missouri	South Dakota	92,000
3.	Oroville (1968)	Feather	California	80,000
4.	B. F. Sisk (San Luis) (1967)	San Luis Creek	California	77,664
5.	Garrison (1953)	Missouri	North Dakota	66,500
6.	Scotts Flat (1948)	Deer Creek	California	66,300
7.	Cochiti (1975)	Rio Grande	New Mexico	65,000
8.	Herbert Hoover (1965)	Kissimmee River Basin	Florida	54,700
9.	Fort Randall (1954)	Missouri	South Dakota	50,200
10.	Castaic (1973)	Castaic Creek	California	44,000

Note: An embankment dam is any dam constructed with excavated material, including earth, rocks, and mining or other industrial waste. (In contrast, gravity, arch, and buttress dams are generally made out of concrete or masonry.) The majority of the world's dams are embankment dams. All dams in this list are earthfill, or formed primarily out of layers of compacted earth.

Largest-Capacity U.S. Reservoirs

Rank	Dam (year completed)	Reservoir	Location	Maximum capacity (thous. acre-feet)
1.	Hoover (1935)	Lake Mead	Nevada-Arizona	30,237
2.	Glen Canyon (1963)	Lake Powell	Arizona	29,875
3.	Garrison (1953)	Lake Sakakawea	North Dakota	26,000
4.	Oahe (1966)	Lake Oahe	South Dakota	23,600
5.	Fort Peck (1957)	Fort Peck Lake	Montana	19,100
6.	Grand Coulee (1941)	Lake Roosevelt	Washington	9,562
7.	Herbert Hoover (1965)	Lake Okeechobee	Florida	8,519
8.	Kentucky (1944)	Kentucky Lake	Kentucky	7,535
9.	Sam Rayburn (1965)	Sam Rayburn Lake	Texas	6,520
10.	Wright Patman (1954)	Wright Patman Lake	Texas	6,505

Note: A reservoir is a body of water created by a dam for storage. This water may serve a single or multiple purposes, such as irrigation, flood reduction, and electricity generation.

Major Dams and Reservoirs of the World

Source: World Register of Dams, Intl. Commission on Large Dams (ICOLD)
Asterisk (*) designates structure is planned or under construction as of mid-2023. NA = Not available.

World's Highest Dams

Rank	Dam	Country	Meters	Feet
1.	*Rogun	Tajikistan	335	1,099
2.	*Shuangjiangkou	China	312	1,023
3.	Jinping 1	China	305	1,001
4.	Nurek	Tajikistan	300	984
5.	*Lianghekou	China	295	968
6.	Xiaowan	China	294	965
7.	Xiluodu	China	286	938
8.	Grande Dixence	Switzerland	285	935
9.	*Baihetan	China	277	909
10.	*Bakhtiyari	Iran	275	902
11.	*Diamer-Bhasha	Pakistan	272	892
12.	Enguri	Georgia	272	892
13.	*Yusufeli	Turkey	270	886
14.	Manuel Moreno Torres (Chicoasén)	Mexico	262	860
15.	Nuozhadu	China	262	860

World's Largest-Capacity Reservoirs

Rank	Dam	Country	Max. capacity (thous. cubic meters)
1.	Kariba	Zambia/Zimbabwe	180,600,000
2.	Bratsk	Russia	169,000,000
3.	Akosombo	Ghana	150,000,000
4.	Daniel Johnson	Canada	141,851,350
5.	Guri	Venezuela	135,000,000
6.	High Aswan	Egypt	132,000,000
7.	W.A.C. Bennett	Canada	74,300,000
8.	*Grand Ethiopian Renaissance	Ethiopia	74,000,000
9.	Krasnoyarsk	Russia	73,300,000
10.	Zeya	Russia	68,400,000
11.	Robert-Bourassa	Canada	61,400,000
12.	La Grande-3	Canada	59,994,000
13.	Ust-Ilimsk	Russia	59,300,000
14.	Cutarm Creek	Canada	58,595,982
15.	Boguchany	Russia	58,200,000

World's Largest-Capacity Hydroelectric Plants

Rank	Dam	Country	Installed capacity (MW)	Energy generated (GWh/year)
1.	Sanxia (Three Gorges)	China	22,500	98,100
2.	*Baihetan	China	16,000	51,500
3.	Itaipu	Brazil/Paraguay	14,000	98,300
4.	Xiluodu	China	13,860	57,120
5.	Belo Monte	Brazil	11,234	NA
6.	Guri	Venezuela	10,235	53,400
7.	Tucurui	Brazil	8,370	41,400
8.	*Ta Sang	Myanmar	7,100	35,446
9.	Grand Coulee	U.S.	6,809	NA
10.	*Grand Ethiopian Renaissance	Ethiopia	6,420	NA
11.	Sayano-Shushenskaya	Russia	6,400	22,800
12.	Xiangjiaba	China	6,400	30,747
13.	Longtan	China	6,300	18,710
14.	Krasnoyarsk	Russia	6,000	20,400
15.	Nuozhadu	China	5,850	23,912

Dams by Purpose, Worldwide

Purpose	Single-purpose dams		Multi-purpose dams	
	Number	Percent distrib.	Number	Percent distrib.
Irrigation	13,580	47.2%	6,278	23.8%
Hydropower	6,115	21.2	4,135	15.7
Water supply	3,376	11.7	4,587	17.4
Flood control	2,539	8.8	4,911	18.6
Recreation	1,361	4.7	3,035	11.5
Fish farming, navigation, tailing, and others	1,820	6.3	3,463	13.1

Note: Based on a survey of 28,791 single-purpose dams and 10,319 multi-purpose dams registered with ICOLD. Percentages may not sum to 100 due to rounding.

Timeline of Selected Architectural Styles and Structures

Asterisk (*) denotes part of a UNESCO World Heritage site as of mid-2023.

Style and period	Location; characteristics; significant examples
Mesopotamian c. 3500-539 BCE	City-states of Sumer, Akkad, Babylon, Assyria (modern-day Iraq). Mud-brick rectangular temples on oval platforms with simple corbel vaults, later ziggurats. Painted terra-cotta mosaics and murals; carved reliefs on columns and walls. **Ziggurat of Nanna**, Ur (Muqayyar, Iraq), ordered by Ur-Nammu, c. 2100 BCE **Anu Ziggurat and White Temple**, Uruk (Warka, Iraq), c. 3000 BCE
Egyptian c. 3000-30 BCE	Along Nile R. Mud-brick and limestone tombs and massive, geometric pyramids, post-and-lintel construction. Highly decorative with colorful hieroglyphics, carvings, columns, obelisks, paintings, and sculpture. ***Stepped Pyramid of Pharaoh Djoser** (Saqqara, Egypt), by Imhotep, c. 2737-2717 BCE ***Great Pyramid of Khufu** (Giza, Egypt), c. 2250 BCE ***Great Temple of Amon-Ra** (Karnak, Egypt), c. 1530-300 BCE ***Mortuary Temple of Queen Hatshepsut**, Deir el-Bahari (Thebes, Egypt), by Senenmut, c. 1479-1458 BCE
Three Dynasties c. 2100-221 BCE	China. Single-level mud-brick or mud-smeared timber structures on earthen platforms with thatched roofs. Later, bracketed wooden-framed structures with brick-tiled floors, roofs with overhanging eaves. **City of Erlitou** (Yanshi, China), c. 1900-1500 BCE

Style and period	Location; characteristics; significant examples
Minoan c. 1800-1450 BCE	Crete. Palaces, tombs in monumental style adapted from Mesopotamia and Egypt. Multilevel stone palaces with large central court, no fortifications. Walls made of doors (*polythyron*); stone porticoes and lintels; wooden ceilings and columns; beehive-shaped tombs (*tholi*). **Palace at Knossos** (Heraklion, Crete, Greece), c. 1700 BCE
Mycenaean c. 1600-1100 BCE	Greece. Adapted Minoan style, with large stone masonry, huge walls, and fortified citadels with complex palaces (*megaron*). ***Treasury of Atreus** (Mycenae, Greece), c. 1250 BCE
Olmec c. 1200-400 BCE	Mexico Gulf Coast. Many religious structures, including stone temple-pyramids centered in cities; also large stone sculptures and mosaic pavement with natural and animistic themes. **Great Pyramid** (La Venta, Mexico), c. 800-400 BCE
Mayan c. 900 BCE-900 CE	Central America. Religious structures with plaster-surfaced stone temple-pyramids with stairs containing tombs. Decorative animistic and geometric relief sculptures, lintels, and stone monuments with hieroglyphics. ***Pyramid of the Magician** (Uxmal, Mexico), c. 700-910 CE ***North Acropolis** (Tikal, Guatemala), c. 200 BCE
Greek c. 750-323 BCE	Greek peninsula, Asia Minor, North Africa, western Mediterranean. Religious, civic buildings in monumental style, inspired by Egypt, based on strict rules of form and human proportion; many ornamental details. Marble and limestone structures (including rectangular temples) with pediment, colonnaded porticoes in diverse regional styles, defined by orders of architecture like Ionic, Doric, Corinthian. Most early buildings with timber supports; solid stone in later temples. ***Parthenon, Acropolis** (Athens, Greece), by Ictinus and Callicrates, 447-436 BCE ***Temple of Zeus** (Olympia, Greece), by Libon of Elis, mid-5th cent. BCE **Mausoleum of Halicarnassus** (Bodrum, Turkey), by Pythis, c. 353 BCE (destroyed) ***Temple of Apollo Epicurius** (Bassae, Greece), by Ictinus, c. 420 BCE
Achaemenid c. 550-334 BCE	Persian Empire (Eastern Mediterranean to Indus R.). Palatial complexes influenced by cultures absorbed by the empire; limestone and mud-brick complexes on raised stone terraces with ornamental stairways, rectangular pillared audience halls with porticoes and corner towers; pleasure gardens (*bâgh*) as focal point of architecture. ***Pasargadae** (Iran), founded by Cyrus II, after 547 BCE ***Persepolis** (Iran), founded by Darius I, around 518 BCE
Roman c. 500 BCE-400 CE	Roman Empire. Civic and religious structures with grandiose limestone brick and concrete construction in systematic, practical layout. Adapted Greek orders in many structures, including circular temples and large covered halls (basilica), but emphasized movement with rounded arches and domes, geometric vaults. ***Pantheon** (Rome, Italy), ordered by Emperor Hadrian, 118-128 CE ***Colosseum** (Rome, Italy), ordered by Emperor Vespasian, 70-82 CE ***Roman Forum** (Rome, Italy), 500s BCE-608 CE
Qin and Han c. 221 BCE-220 CE	China. Massive public works, palaces, tombs, and planned cities; systematic layout and design determined by divination techniques (geomancy). Multistoried timber palace complexes with gardens, courtyards laid along a long hall with a south-north axis for weather; decorative roof with overhanging eaves. ***The Great Wall** (China), ordered by Qin Shi Huang, 220 BCE-c. 1600 CE ***Mausoleum of the First Qin Emperor** (Xianyang [Xi'an], China), c. 210 BCE
Sassanian 226-651	Iran. Mud-brick, mortared rubble, and stone palaces on platforms. Tall, vaulted entry chambers with one open side (*iwans*). Three-aisled hall chambers covered with rudimentary barrel vaults. Parabolic domes abandoned for square courtyards in later Sassanian period. ***Palace of Ardashir I** (Firuzabad, Iran), c. 224 **Taq-i Kisra** [Arch of Khosrau] (Ctesiphon, Iraq), c. 260 or c. 550
Byzantine 330-1453	Byzantine Empire, Italy, Russia. Religious structures with masonry construction based on Roman architecture, many salvaged pieces. Centralized cross-in-square layout, with large central dome supported by vaults. Highly decorative, with iconographic frescoes, glass mosaics. ***Hagia Sophia** (Istanbul, Turkey), by Anthemius and Isidorus, 532-37 ***St. Mark's Basilica** (Venice, Italy), ordered by Domenico Contarini, 1063-94
Sui and Tang 581-906	China. Includes influences from other cultures; geomancy used to enhance harmony and social status. Rectangular, multistory modular timber structures with interlinking corridors; single-eaved roofs with exposed beams. **Daming Palace** (Xi'an, China), 634 (destroyed) ***Hall of the Great Buddha**, Foguang Temple (Mount Wutai, China), ordered rebuilt by Xuan Zhong, 857
Early Islamic (Umayyad) 692-c. 1000	Syria, Middle East, North Africa, southern Spain. Mosques in adapted Sassanian style. Austere exteriors; simple columned halls with minarets and mihrabs (prayer niches), walled courtyards and gardens, onion domes. Highly decorative interiors with patterned marble, mosaics. ***Dome of the Rock** [Qubbat al-Sakhra] (Jerusalem), ordered by Abd al-Malik, 692 ***Great Mosque of Córdoba** (Spain), ordered by Abd al-Rahman I, 784-86
Khmer c. 880-1200s	Indochina. Hindu or Buddhist temple complexes, including brick, later sandstone beehive-shaped shrines with arches atop terraced temple "mountains" symbolizing Mount Meru, Hindu and Buddhist center of the universe, where the gods dwell. Concentric layout of structures mimics the cosmos, relating religious narrative in carved reliefs. ***Angkor Wat** (Cambodia), ordered by Suryavarman II, 12th cent.
Romanesque (Norman) c. 900s-1100s	Western Europe. Churches and monasteries in localized Roman style; many reused material from Roman structures. Austere, heavy, simple masonry construction with thick walls, concealed buttresses, small windows, barrel arches, and vaults. Churches like Roman basilica with arched central nave, lower side aisles, apse, transept formed Latin cross. Monumental art and ornaments with Christian narrative throughout, especially on façade and portals. ***Durham Cathedral** (England, UK), ordered by Bishop William de Saint-Calais, 1093-1133 ***Cathedral, Baptistery, and "Leaning" Tower** (Pisa, Italy), by various architects, begun in 1063, tower not completed until 1372
Gothic c. 1100s-1500s	France, Europe. Cathedrals meant to inspire spirituality with design like Roman basilica: pointed arches and spires that reach toward heavens, skeletal masonry, revealed structure like flying buttresses, ribbed vaults to allow larger lighting, large stained-glass windows. **Abbey Church of Saint-Denis** (France), ordered by Abbot Suger, 1135-44 ***Cathedral of Notre-Dame** (Paris, France), ordered by Bishop Maurice de Sully, 1163-1351 ***Cologne Cathedral** (Cologne, Germany), ordered by Archbishop Konrad von Hochstaden, 1248-1880 ***St. Vitus Cathedral** (Prague, Czech Republic), by Matthias of Arras, later Peter Parler, 1344-1929
Yuan and Ming 1279-1644	China. Mongol-influenced timber and some brick structures influenced by geomancy. Emphasized monumental mass in low-lying, sprawling structures with simple rectangular pavilions, great halls, elaborate wooden latticework, carved and painted details. ***Forbidden City** (Beijing, China), ordered by Emperor Yongle, 1406-20

Style and period	Location; characteristics; significant examples
Renaissance 1420s-1520s	Italy. The rebirth or rediscovery of ancient Roman design, grounded in a scholarly approach to architecture. Followed rules of proportion in perspective and symmetry, classical orders, and simple but perfected geometric forms; emphasis on human scale. *Pazzi Chapel (Florence, Italy), by Filippo Brunelleschi, 1429-61 *Palazzo Medici-Riccardi (Florence, Italy), by Michelozzo di Bartolomeo, 1444-60 *Tempietto San Pietro (Rome, Italy), by Donato Bramante, 1502-10 *Villa Almerico Capra, or La Rotonda (near Vicenza, Italy), by Andrea Palladio, later Vincenzo Scamozzi, 1566-1610
Mughal 1526-1858	India. Monumental palaces and mosques blending Hindu and Islamic architecture. Sandstone with marble inlay; highly decorative, with semiprecious stones, vegetal and Koranic motifs. Formulaic four-part pleasure gardens (*charbâgh*), exemplified by grounds of Taj Mahal. *Humayun's Tomb (Delhi, India), by Sayyid Muhammad, 1562-72 *Taj Mahal (Agra, India), ordered by Emperor Shah Jahan, 1631-48
Baroque 1630s-1700s	Italy, later Western Europe. Elaborate and theatrical religious and civic structures, focused on dramatic overall effect. Complex geometric shapes and elaborate sculptures meant to be viewed from many angles. St. Carlo alle Quattro Fontane (Rome, Italy), by Francesco Borromini, 1638-41 *Palace of Versailles (Versailles, France), royal hunting lodge (built 1631-34) expanded under Louis XIV, 1661-1710 Church of San Lorenzo (Turin, Italy), by Guarino Guarini, 1666-79 Church of St. John of Nepomuk, or Asamkirche (Munich, Germany), by Cosmas Damian and Egid Quirin Asam, 1733-46
Rococo 1690s-1700s	Europe. Mostly interior, simplified but still fanciful Baroque designs; ornate with natural motifs, gold trim, light and creamy colors, asymmetrical designs, and unusual materials. *Sanssouci Palace (Potsdam, Germany), by Georg Wenzeslaus von Knobelsdorff, 1745-47
Neoclassicism 1750-1830	Europe, Americas. Civic, commercial, and religious structures; chaste, non-decorative designs in reaction to Baroque excess. Grounded in Enlightenment-era principles and simple, strict adherence to classic (Greek, Roman, Renaissance) forms and details. Palladian style in England, Federal style in U.S. Chiswick House (Chiswick, England, UK), by Richard Boyle, 1725-29 *Monticello (Charlottesville, VA), by Thomas Jefferson, 1768-1809
Neo-Gothic 1837-1900s	Britain, U.S. Civic, commercial, and religious structures utilizing Gothic forms in new commercial enterprises like railway stations and hotels. Traditional masonry façade disguised modern structural material like iron and glass. *Westminster Palace (London, England, UK), by Charles Barry and A.W.N. Pugin, 1840-47 Hotel fronting St. Pancras Railway Station (London, England, UK), by George Gilbert Scott, 1865-71
Arts and Crafts 1850s-1930s	England, U.S. Residential structures made of brick and other indigenous materials, with pastoral and traditional elements like gabled roofs. Conceived as a reaction against homogenization of style following the Industrial Revolution. Red House (Bexley Heath, England, UK), by Philip Webb, 1859 Tigbourne Court (Surrey, England, UK), by Edwin Lutyens, 1898
Beaux-Arts 1870s-1930s	France, U.S. Grandiose, highly decorative style, using a mix of classical forms taught at the École des Beaux-Arts (School of Fine Arts) in Paris: columns, wall projections, elaborate rooftops, high-relief decoration. Boston Public Library (Boston, MA), by McKim, Mead, and White, 1888-95 Grand Central Terminal (New York, NY), Reed & Stem and Warren & Wetmore, 1903-13
Art Nouveau 1884-1905	Europe (esp. Brussels, Belgium; France). Civic and residential structures using industrial products like metal and glass to mimic natural forms; airy, fluid, and ornate. *Hôtel Tassel (Brussels, Belgium), by Victor Horta, 1892-93 Entrances to Métro (subway) (Paris, France), by Hector Guimard, 1900
Prairie 1893-1917	U.S. Mostly residences, some civic buildings in adapted Arts and Crafts style. Inspired by American Midwest and small-town values. Frank Lloyd Wright most notable architect of the style. Buildings centered on chimney, with overhanging eaves and horizontal emphasis, long bands of windows. *Robie House (Chicago, IL), by Frank Lloyd Wright, 1908-10 National Farmer's Bank (Owatonna, MN), by Louis Sullivan, 1906-08
Futurism 1913-14	Italy. Purely theoretical style that produced no actual structures. Emphasized concrete, glass, and steel construction; pure geometric forms and straight lines; and exposed structure and utilities. La Città Nuova (The New City) (sketches), by Antonio Sant'Elia, 1913
Constructivism 1914-20s	Russia, Europe. Public buildings based on socialist philosophies. Purely utilitarian industrial design, modern materials. Rusakov Club (Moscow, Russia), by Konstantin Melnikov, 1927-28
De Stijl 1917-31	Netherlands. Building and fixtures designed as a complete, sculpture-like piece of art; emphasis on primary colors, simple but asymmetrical geometry. Name is Dutch for "The Style." *Schröder House (Utrecht, Netherlands), by Gerrit Thomas Rietveld, 1924
Bauhaus 1919-33	Weimar Republic Germany. Art and design school founded by Walter Gropius with philosophy that the machine is the modern medium. Concrete, glass, and steel construction that united industrial crafts and fine arts with simple geometric forms and colors. *Bauhaus (Dessau, Germany), by Walter Gropius, 1925-26
International Style 1920s-70s	Asia, Europe, North America. Reinforced concrete and steel structures, mostly commercial buildings with some residences and civic structures. Post-and-slab construction meant walls no longer supported weight so façades could be continuous strip (ribbon) glass "curtain-walls" with modular interiors. Emphasis on simple forms; glass, marble, and stainless steel; minimal decoration. Philadelphia Savings Fund Society Building (Philadelphia, PA), by George Howe and William Lescaze, 1926-32 *Villa Savoye (Poissy, France), by Le Corbusier, 1928-31 Seagram Building (New York, NY), by Ludwig Mies Van Der Rohe with Philip Johnson, 1954-58
Art Deco 1925-30s	Europe, U.S. Traditional, symmetric, elegant construction like Beaux-Arts whimsically mixed with modern styles like geometric forms and steel or chrome features. Chrysler Building (New York, NY), by William van Alen, 1928-30 Empire State Building (New York, NY), by Shreve, Lamb & Harmon, 1930-31
Postmodernism 1970s-present	Asia, Europe, North America. Playful reaction against generic, mainstream "orthodox modern architecture," according to Robert Venturi. Token references to traditional architectural elements like pediments or gables on houses; aim to present, Venturi wrote, "old clichés in new settings." Vanna Venturi House (Philadelphia, PA), by Robert Venturi, 1962 Public Service Building (Portland, OR), by Michael Graves, 1980-82

World Population Growth

There were perhaps 50 mil people in the world in 1000 BCE. The United Nations (UN) Population Division estimates a figure of 300 mil for 1 CE. This diagram shows estimated population growth since then.

Although different sources may provide varying numbers, they agree that the world's population began growing more rapidly in the 18th and 19th centuries and increased at an even greater rate in the 20th century. According to the UN, the total population reached 1 bil in 1804; rose to 2 bil 123 years later, in 1927; to 3 bil 33 years after that, in 1960; to 4 bil in 1975; to 5 bil in 1987; to 6 bil in 1999; and to 7 bil in 2011.

The UN put the world population in mid-2023 at 8.05 bil. It projected that the population would reach 9 bil by 2037 and 10 bil by 2058. Between 2023 and 2050, eight countries are expected to account for more than half the increase in the world population: Dem. Rep. of the Congo, Egypt, Ethiopia, India, Nigeria, Pakistan, the Philippines, and Tanzania. Almost all increases in the population under age 65 will occur in low-income and lower-middle-income countries. In high-income and upper-middle-income countries, growth will be in the proportion of the population age 65 and older (10.0% in 2023).

Year	Population
2022	8 bil
2011	7 bil
1999	6 bil
1987	5 bil
1975	4 bil
1960	3 bil
1927	2 bil
1804	1 bil
1500	500 mil
1250	400 mil
1 CE	300 mil

Area and Population of the World by Continent, 1950-2035

Source: International Data Base, International Programs Center, U.S. Census Bureau, U.S. Dept. of Commerce; *The World Factbook*, Central Intelligence Agency (CIA)

Continent/region	Land area (sq mi)	Land area (sq km)	% of Earth's land	Population (midyear) 1950	1975	2000	2023	% of world total, 2023	2035[1]
Asia	11,922,585	30,879,354	21.1	1,437,565,483	2,412,768,719	3,727,477,124	4,699,843,209	58.9	5,030,470,543
Africa	11,533,768	29,872,321	20.5	229,049,683	417,040,599	807,568,544	1,446,531,252	18.1	1,890,100,532
Europe[2]	8,559,255	22,168,368	15.2	547,140,324	678,635,710	731,570,664	748,613,648	9.4	742,751,210
N. America	7,880,511	20,410,430	14.0	165,945,185	238,783,486	313,388,419	378,317,402	4.7	406,417,366
Latin America[3]	7,723,205	20,003,010	13.7	165,442,794	320,977,684	521,642,616	661,046,777	8.3	713,337,086
Oceania	3,277,072	8,487,578	5.8	12,476,128	21,181,359	30,808,618	44,909,722	0.6	51,791,810
Antarctica[4]	5,482,651	14,200,000	9.7	NA	NA	NA	NA	NA	NA
World[5]	56,379,047	146,021,061	100.0	2,557,619,597	4,089,387,557	6,132,455,985	7,979,262,010	100.0	8,834,868,547

NA = Not applicable. **Note:** Composition of geographical (continental) regions are as defined by the United Nations. Figures may not add up to totals due to rounding. (1) Projected. (2) Includes all of Russia. (3) Includes the Caribbean. (4) Antarctica has no indigenous inhabitants, though people are present at permanent and seasonal research stations. Only an est. 110,039 sq mi are ice free. (5) Total pops. do not include countries for which ests. or projections are not available.

Population of the World's Largest Urban Areas, 1975-2035

Source: *World Urbanization Prospects: The 2018 Revision*, Dept. of Economic and Social Affairs, UN Population Division

Population figures are midyear estimates or projections for urban agglomerations, i.e., whole metropolitan areas comprising an urban center and surrounding settlements of lower density. In 2023, 57.5% of the world's population lived in an urban area. That proportion is expected to increase to an est. 62.5% in 2035.

Data may differ from figures elsewhere in *The World Almanac*. MMA = Major Metropolitan Area.

(ranked by mid-2023 population)

Rank	Urban area, country	Population (thous.) 1975	2000	2023	2035	Rate of change (%) 1975-2000	2000-23	2023-35	Pop. of urban area as % of country's 2023 pop.
1.	Tokyo, Japan	26,615	34,450	37,194	36,014	29.4%	8.0%	-3.2%	29.7%
2.	Delhi, India	4,436	15,692	32,941	43,345	253.7	109.9	31.6	2.3
3.	Shanghai, China	5,658	14,247	29,211	34,341	151.8	105.0	17.6	2.0
4.	Dhaka, Bangladesh	2,221	10,285	23,210	31,234	363.1	125.7	34.6	13.3
5.	São Paulo, Brazil	9,614	17,014	22,620	24,490	77.0	32.9	8.3	10.4
6.	Mexico City, Mexico	10,734	18,457	22,281	25,415	72.0	20.7	14.1	16.1
7.	Cairo, Egypt	6,450	13,626	22,183	28,504	111.3	62.8	28.5	20.5
8.	Beijing, China	4,828	10,285	21,766	25,366	113.0	111.6	16.5	1.5
9.	Mumbai (Bombay), India	7,685	16,147	21,297	27,343	110.1	31.9	28.4	1.5
10.	Kinki MMA (Osaka), Japan	16,298	18,660	19,013	18,346	14.5	1.9	-3.5	15.2
11.	New York, NY-Newark, NJ, U.S.	15,880	17,813	18,937	20,817	12.2	6.3	9.9	5.6
12.	Chongqing, China	2,545	7,863	17,341	20,531	209.0	120.5	18.4	1.2
13.	Karachi, Pakistan	3,989	9,825	17,236	23,128	146.3	75.4	34.2	7.9
14.	Kinshasa, Dem. Rep. of the Congo	1,482	6,140	16,316	26,682	314.4	165.7	63.5	16.6
15.	Lagos, Nigeria	1,890	7,281	15,946	24,419	285.3	119.0	53.1	7.2
16.	Istanbul, Turkey	3,600	8,744	15,848	17,986	142.9	81.2	13.5	18.6
17.	Buenos Aires, Argentina	9,143	12,504	15,490	17,128	36.8	23.9	10.6	33.2
18.	Kolkata (Calcutta), India	8,166	13,097	15,333	19,564	60.4	17.1	27.6	1.1
19.	Manila, Philippines	4,999	9,958	14,667	18,649	99.2	47.3	27.2	12.8
20.	Guangzhou, Guangdong, China	1,698	7,812	14,284	16,741	360.0	82.9	17.2	1.0
21.	Tianjin, China	3,527	6,989	14,239	16,446	98.1	103.7	15.5	1.0
22.	Lahore, Pakistan	2,399	5,576	13,979	19,117	132.5	150.7	36.7	6.4
23.	Rio de Janeiro, Brazil	7,733	11,307	13,728	14,810	46.2	21.4	7.9	6.3
24.	Bangalore, India	2,111	5,581	13,608	18,066	164.4	143.8	32.8	1.0
25.	Shenzhen, China	36	6,550	13,073	15,185	18,327.5	99.6	16.2	0.9
26.	Moscow, Russia	7,623	10,005	12,680	12,823	31.2	26.7	1.1	8.9
27.	Los Angeles-Long Beach-Santa Ana, CA, U.S.	8,926	11,798	12,534	13,778	32.2	6.2	9.9	3.7
28.	Chennai (Madras), India	3,594	6,593	11,776	15,376	83.5	78.6	30.6	1.0
29.	Bogotá, Colombia	3,040	6,329	11,508	12,753	108.2	81.8	10.8	22.5
30.	Jakarta, Indonesia	4,813	8,390	11,249	13,688	74.3	34.1	21.7	4.0

National Rankings by Population, Area, Population Density, 2023

Source: International Data Base (IDB), International Programs Center, U.S. Census Bureau, U.S. Dept. of Commerce; *The World Factbook*, Central Intelligence Agency (CIA)

Pop. figures are for midyear. In mid-2023, the world had an estimated pop. of 8.0 bil, of which China and India each represented one-sixth. (The IDB projected that India's pop. will overtake China's in 2024-25; the UN Population Division estimated that date occurred in mid-2023.) Pop. density is calculated using land area, which does not include inland water.

Largest Populations

Rank	Country	Population
1.	China[1]	1,413,142,846
2.	India	1,399,179,585
3.	United States	339,665,118
4.	Indonesia	279,476,346
5.	Pakistan	247,653,551
6.	Nigeria	230,842,743
7.	Brazil	218,689,757
8.	Bangladesh	167,184,465
9.	Russia	141,698,923
10.	Mexico	129,875,529

Smallest Populations

Rank	Country	Population
1.	Vatican City[2]	1,000
2.	Nauru	9,852
3.	Tuvalu	11,639
4.	Palau	21,779
5.	Monaco	31,597
6.	San Marino	34,892
7.	Liechtenstein	39,993
8.	Saint Kitts and Nevis	54,817
9.	Dominica	74,656
10.	Marshall Islands	80,966

Largest Land Areas

Rank	Country	Area (sq mi)	Area (sq km)
1.	Russia	6,323,482	16,377,742
2.	China[1]	3,600,947	9,326,410
3.	United States	3,533,044	9,150,541
4.	Canada	3,511,023	9,093,507
5.	Brazil	3,227,096	8,358,140
6.	Australia	2,966,153	7,682,300
7.	India	1,147,956	2,973,193
8.	Argentina	1,056,642	2,736,690
9.	Kazakhstan	1,042,360	2,699,700
10.	Algeria	919,595	2,381,740

Smallest Land Areas

Rank	Country	Area (sq mi)	Area (sq km)
1.	Vatican City	0.17	0.44
2.	Monaco	0.77	2
3.	Nauru	8	21
4.	Tuvalu	10	26
5.	San Marino	24	61
6.	Liechtenstein	62	160
7.	Marshall Islands	70	181
8.	Saint Kitts and Nevis	101	261
9.	Maldives	115	298
10.	Malta	122	316

Most Densely Populated

Rank	Country	Persons per sq mi	Persons per sq km
1.	Monaco	41,035.1	15,798.5
2.	Singapore	21,808.0	8,427.9
3.	Vatican City[2]	5,882.4	2,272.7
4.	Bahrain	5,303.4	2,044.6
5.	Malta	3,829.0	1,478.3
6.	Maldives	3,387.5	1,307.3
7.	Bangladesh	3,326.5	1,284.4
8.	Taiwan	1,893.8	731.2
9.	Barbados	1,827.9	705.7
10.	Mauritius	1,670.2	645.0

Least Densely Populated

Rank	Country	Persons per sq mi	Persons per sq km
1.	Mongolia	5.43	2.10
2.	Namibia	8.74	3.37
3.	Australia	8.92	3.44
4.	Iceland	9.32	3.60
5.	Guyana	10.42	4.02
6.	Suriname	10.62	4.10
7.	Mauritania	10.67	4.12
8.	Libya	10.68	4.12
9.	Canada	10.97	4.24
10.	Botswana	11.05	4.27

(1) Does not include Hong Kong (mid-2023 pop., 7,288,167; area, 414 sq mi) and Macau (639,971; 11 sq mi). (2) 2022 pop. est.

Current Population and Projections for Countries and Other Areas

Source: International Data Base, International Programs Center, U.S. Census Bureau, U.S. Dept. of Commerce; *The World Factbook*, Central Intelligence Agency (CIA)

(midyear figures)

Country/area	2023	2035	2050	Country/area	2023	2035	2050
Afghanistan	39,232,003	49,971,066	63,197,340	Burundi	13,162,952	18,294,904	25,611,635
Albania	3,101,621	3,088,040	2,894,358	Cabo Verde	603,901	680,565	745,776
Algeria	44,758,398	50,313,187	56,117,140	Cambodia	16,891,245	18,651,681	20,202,507
American Samoa	44,620	37,849	31,305	Cameroon	30,135,732	41,067,264	57,310,971
Andorra	85,468	83,961	78,031	Canada	38,516,736	41,420,185	44,002,894
Angola	35,981,281	53,282,768	82,021,832	Cayman Islands	65,483	78,906	93,381
Anguilla	19,079	23,061	27,546	Central African			
Antigua and				Republic	5,552,228	6,771,878	8,322,886
Barbuda	101,489	114,077	124,705	Chad	18,523,165	26,161,691	37,418,108
Argentina	46,621,847	50,803,301	54,950,409	Chile	18,549,457	19,631,668	20,126,545
Armenia	2,989,091	2,813,532	2,521,147	China	1,413,142,846	1,419,797,578	1,361,613,688
Aruba	123,702	138,571	153,739	Colombia	49,336,454	51,529,656	51,491,975
Australia	26,461,166	29,791,638	33,374,282	Comoros	888,378	1,026,481	1,172,195
Austria	8,940,860	9,202,329	9,383,858	Congo, Dem.			
Azerbaijan	10,420,515	11,031,759	11,361,504	Rep of the	111,859,928	160,911,174	240,710,111
Bahamas, The	358,508	387,949	408,923	Congo Republic	5,677,493	7,472,548	10,192,844
Bahrain	1,553,886	1,700,439	1,847,256	Cook Islands	7,939	6,328	5,392
Bangladesh	167,184,465	183,161,334	194,343,726	Costa Rica	5,256,612	5,785,418	6,188,395
Barbados	303,431	307,710	298,257	Côte d'Ivoire	29,344,847	37,217,421	46,939,672
Belarus	9,383,853	8,987,651	8,461,760	Croatia	4,169,239	3,939,174	3,623,602
Belgium	11,913,633	12,539,867	13,095,652	Cuba	10,985,974	10,703,968	10,100,436
Belize	419,137	499,528	592,243	Curaçao	152,849	155,690	153,245
Benin	14,219,908	20,785,031	32,070,919	Cyprus	1,308,120	1,413,331	1,428,212
Bermuda	72,576	74,001	71,717	Czechia	10,706,242	10,602,485	10,470,774
Bhutan	876,181	968,448	1,047,471	Denmark	5,946,984	6,215,716	6,416,507
Bolivia	12,186,079	13,504,069	14,596,934	Djibouti	976,143	1,189,701	1,391,020
Bosnia and				Dominica	74,656	73,032	66,443
Herzegovina	3,807,764	3,649,137	3,303,663	Dominican Republic	10,790,744	11,799,664	12,608,829
Botswana	2,417,596	2,795,948	3,199,855	Ecuador	17,483,326	19,561,162	21,348,217
Brazil	218,689,757	232,129,523	238,435,974	Egypt	109,546,720	127,733,072	150,738,197
Brunei	484,991	563,881	646,799	El Salvador	6,602,370	6,693,932	6,492,154
Bulgaria	6,827,736	6,315,986	5,740,967	Equatorial Guinea	1,737,695	2,399,813	3,052,647
Burkina Faso	22,489,126	29,082,087	36,938,704	Eritrea	6,274,796	7,353,464	8,921,842

Country/area	2023	2035	2050
Estonia	1,202,762	1,093,594	970,580
Eswatini (Swaziland)	1,130,043	1,216,135	1,309,186
Ethiopia	116,462,712	151,372,229	195,982,344
Faroe Islands	52,600	55,974	58,360
Fiji	947,760	986,402	1,018,845
Finland	5,614,571	5,671,447	5,620,077
France	68,521,974	70,717,443	71,416,579
French Polynesia	301,488	320,833	330,218
Gabon	2,397,368	3,132,314	4,081,893
Gambia, The	2,468,569	3,101,196	3,826,233
Gaza Strip	2,037,744	2,520,726	3,060,115
Georgia	4,936,390	4,904,446	4,815,328
Germany	84,220,184	82,632,717	79,776,607
Ghana	33,846,114	43,079,646	55,437,373
Gibraltar	29,629	29,806	28,946
Greece	10,497,595	10,066,836	9,504,172
Greenland	57,777	56,560	53,424
Grenada	114,299	116,330	116,072
Guam	169,330	168,948	159,508
Guatemala	17,980,803	21,096,354	24,442,800
Guernsey	67,642	68,819	68,777
Guinea	13,607,249	18,812,686	27,517,931
Guinea-Bissau	2,078,820	2,817,191	4,036,411
Guyana	791,739	830,909	843,728
Haiti	11,470,261	12,999,321	14,521,985
Honduras	9,571,352	10,819,671	11,934,762
Hong Kong	7,288,167	7,271,766	6,890,901
Hungary	9,670,009	9,254,346	8,664,334
Iceland	360,872	391,869	417,620
India	1,399,179,585	1,522,819,483	1,622,372,511
Indonesia	279,476,346	301,603,148	318,393,046
Iran	87,590,873	95,163,155	100,972,304
Iraq	41,266,109	51,251,890	63,087,363
Ireland	5,323,991	5,875,210	6,478,153
Isle of Man	91,840	95,321	95,693
Israel	9,043,387	10,637,373	12,563,059
Italy	61,021,855	60,887,498	61,036,680
Jamaica	2,820,982	2,869,074	2,972,457
Japan	123,719,238	116,494,761	106,156,887
Jersey	102,785	107,852	110,111
Jordan	11,086,716	13,207,868	15,735,443
Kazakhstan	19,543,464	20,944,420	22,380,770
Kenya	57,052,004	71,838,265	89,573,347
Kiribati	115,372	128,289	139,289
Korea, North	26,072,217	26,986,455	27,200,057
Korea, South	51,966,948	52,598,115	50,217,135
Kosovo	1,964,327	2,121,219	2,243,316
Kuwait	3,103,580	3,492,016	3,896,539
Kyrgyzstan	6,122,781	6,635,711	7,097,955
Laos	7,852,377	8,934,325	9,920,518
Latvia	1,821,750	1,586,003	1,341,195
Lebanon	5,331,203	5,652,938	5,744,987
Lesotho	2,210,646	2,423,048	2,638,694
Liberia	5,506,280	7,520,214	10,557,787
Libya	7,252,573	8,369,582	9,734,776
Liechtenstein	39,993	42,897	44,924
Lithuania	2,655,755	2,346,636	2,050,440
Luxembourg	660,924	769,014	884,664
Macau	639,971	679,863	697,801
Madagascar	28,812,195	36,418,409	45,355,015
Malawi	21,279,597	27,022,619	33,877,000
Malaysia	34,219,975	37,957,793	41,286,972
Maldives	389,568	416,544	449,604
Mali	21,359,722	29,679,103	41,603,635
Malta	467,138	484,290	490,187
Marshall Islands	80,966	92,725	103,319
Mauritania	4,244,878	5,249,163	6,467,891
Mauritius	1,309,448	1,305,007	1,232,670
Mexico	129,875,529	142,051,813	152,646,592
Micronesia, Federated States of	100,319	90,317	74,899
Moldova	3,250,532	2,802,592	2,287,079
Monaco	31,597	33,636	32,661
Mongolia	3,255,468	3,497,963	3,699,569
Montenegro	602,445	563,539	494,545
Montserrat	5,440	5,707	5,546
Morocco	37,067,420	40,402,356	43,116,499
Mozambique	32,513,805	44,206,049	63,366,021
Myanmar (Burma)	57,970,293	62,244,488	64,837,457
Namibia	2,777,232	3,398,921	4,151,610
Nauru	9,852	10,351	11,329
Nepal	30,899,443	33,250,249	35,274,683
Netherlands	17,463,930	18,096,999	18,405,073
New Caledonia	300,682	339,444	376,851
New Zealand	5,109,702	5,591,053	5,990,813
Nicaragua	6,359,689	6,953,360	7,287,372
Niger	25,396,840	38,971,565	62,099,731
Nigeria	230,842,743	310,623,910	428,438,012
North Macedonia	2,133,410	2,135,941	2,074,629
Northern Mariana Islands	51,295	49,497	45,315
Norway	5,597,924	6,069,685	6,518,282
Oman	3,833,465	4,594,402	5,421,335
Pakistan	247,653,551	303,043,639	366,569,839
Palau	21,779	22,628	22,478
Panama	4,404,108	5,123,749	5,796,506
Papua New Guinea	9,819,350	12,576,047	15,933,221
Paraguay	7,439,863	8,305,805	8,954,539
Peru	32,440,172	35,145,177	37,977,511
Philippines	116,434,200	137,176,759	158,108,572
Poland	37,991,766	36,269,582	33,491,484
Portugal	10,223,150	10,083,359	9,728,863
Puerto Rico	3,057,311	2,646,152	2,163,684
Qatar	2,532,104	2,587,812	2,586,967
Romania	18,326,327	16,854,271	15,560,475
Russia	141,698,923	137,323,001	131,733,062
Rwanda	13,400,541	16,065,002	19,133,170
Saint Barthélemy	7,093	6,997	6,721
Saint Helena, Ascension, and Tristan da Cunha	7,935	7,935	7,569
Saint Kitts and Nevis	54,817	57,569	57,519
Saint Lucia	167,591	171,168	167,817
Saint Martin	32,897	34,033	35,182
Saint Pierre and Miquelon	5,195	4,475	3,685
Saint Vincent and the Grenadines	100,804	98,989	95,383
Samoa	207,501	224,906	246,912
San Marino	34,892	36,771	36,514
São Tomé and Príncipe	220,372	258,415	306,603
Saudi Arabia	35,939,806	42,536,636	47,966,097
Senegal	18,384,660	23,938,019	30,635,314
Serbia	6,693,375	6,238,163	5,692,788
Seychelles	97,617	102,137	101,082
Sierra Leone	8,908,040	11,399,388	14,356,255
Singapore	5,975,383	6,536,522	6,959,346
Sint Maarten	45,677	50,943	54,257
Slovakia	5,425,319	5,275,705	4,972,634
Slovenia	2,099,790	2,059,546	1,983,776
Solomon Islands	714,766	855,336	1,006,932
Somalia	12,693,796	16,987,551	22,655,319
South Africa	58,048,332	63,582,370	68,434,347
South Sudan	12,118,379	17,304,109	23,592,886
Spain	47,222,613	47,798,695	47,250,516
Sri Lanka	23,326,272	24,706,443	25,595,389
Sudan	49,197,555	66,369,914	88,749,624
Suriname	639,759	716,199	784,492
Sweden	10,536,338	11,108,774	11,771,380
Switzerland	8,563,760	9,172,236	9,822,717
Syria	22,933,531	28,091,447	33,355,509
Taiwan	23,588,613	23,481,565	22,132,472
Tajikistan	9,245,937	10,643,899	12,088,991
Tanzania	65,642,682	89,502,233	124,222,573
Thailand	69,794,997	70,086,586	66,768,316
Timor-Leste	1,476,042	1,824,351	2,184,155
Togo	8,703,961	11,447,738	15,344,759
Tonga	105,221	100,169	90,196
Trinidad and Tobago	1,407,460	1,409,512	1,359,882
Tunisia	11,976,182	12,553,077	12,895,172
Turkey (Türkiye)	83,593,483	88,693,414	90,656,580
Turkmenistan	5,690,818	6,216,739	6,627,470
Turks and Caicos Islands	59,367	71,821	86,092
Tuvalu	11,639	12,551	13,341
Uganda	47,729,952	67,953,747	96,972,729
Ukraine	43,306,477	40,597,628	37,422,979
United Arab Emirates	9,973,449	10,965,355	12,429,115
United Kingdom	68,138,484	71,307,950	74,268,354
United States	339,665,118	364,862,145	388,922,201
Uruguay	3,416,264	3,504,442	3,560,420
Uzbekistan	31,360,836	33,775,322	35,560,973
Vanuatu	313,046	370,413	432,719
Vatican City[1]	1,000	NA	NA
Venezuela	30,518,260	34,187,388	36,513,281
Vietnam	104,799,174	114,434,819	121,027,926
Virgin Islands, British	39,369	47,666	56,060
Virgin Islands, U.S.	104,917	96,072	82,348
Wallis and Futuna	15,929	16,126	15,971
West Bank	3,050,760	3,628,844	4,240,579
Yemen	31,565,602	38,207,444	45,693,399
Zambia	20,216,029	27,807,418	38,476,482
Zimbabwe	15,418,674	19,323,074	24,837,643
World[2]	7,979,261,010	8,834,868,547	9,740,512,435

NA = Not available. **Note:** Figures for countries do not include the population of any dependencies listed separately in this table. For example, China's population estimate and projections do not include Hong Kong or Macau. (1) 2022 pop. est. (2) Total projected populations do not include countries for which projections were not available.

Countries Ranked by Gross Domestic Product and Per Capita GDP, 2022

Source: The World Bank

Estimates of gross domestic product (GDP)—the value of all final goods and services that a country produced in a year—were made based on purchasing power parity exchange rates. Per capita GDP is calculated using the estimated population size as of July 1 in a given year. GDP figures are 2022 ests. unless otherwise noted.

GDP (in mil)		Per capita GDP	
Highest	**Lowest**	**Highest**	**Lowest**
1. China[1] ... $30,327,320	1. Tuvalu $61	1. Luxembourg .. $142,214	1. Burundi $836
2. U.S. 25,462,700	2. Nauru 166	2. Singapore 127,565	2. Central African Republic 967
3. India ... 11,874,583	3. Palau[2] 274	3. Ireland 126,905	3. Congo, Dem. Rep. of 1,337
4. Japan 5,702,287	4. Marshall Islands ... 300	4. Norway 114,899	4. Somalia........ 1,364
5. Russia...... 5,326,855	5. Kiribati.......... 310	5. Qatar........ 114,648	5. Mozambique.... 1,468
6. Germany.... 5,309,606	6. Micronesia, Fed. States 440	6. United Arab Emirates ... 87,729	6. Niger........... 1,505
7. Indonesia ... 4,036,901	7. Tonga[2] 719	7. Switzerland ... 83,598	7. Chad 1,668
8. Brazil ... 3,837,261	8. Dominica 987	8. U.S. 76,399	8. Afghanistan[2] ... 1,674
9. France...... 3,769,924	9. Vanuatu 1,075	9. Denmark..... 74,005	9. Liberia.......... 1,725
10. UK......... 3,656,809	10. São Tomé and Príncipe 1,077	10. Netherlands ... 69,577	10. Malawi 1,732
11. Turkey (Türkiye) .. 3,180,984	11. Samoa 1,343	11. Brunei 69,275	11. Madagascar 1,774
12. Italy 3,052,609	12. St. Kitts and Nevis.. 1,623	12. Iceland 69,081	12. Sierra Leone...... 1,931
13. Mexico...... 2,742,903	13. St. Vincent and the Grenadines..... 1,789	13. San Marino[2] .. 67,983	13. Guinea-Bissau.... 2,190
14. South Korea.. 2,585,011	14. Solomon Islands... 1,922	14. Austria 67,936	14. Kiribati........ 2,365
15. Canada..... 2,273,489	15. Grenada 2,131	15. Belgium...... 65,027	15. Gambia, The.... 2,510
16. Spain 2,181,968	16. San Marino[2] 2,294	16. Sweden...... 64,578	16. Mali........... 2,517
17. Saudi Arabia ... 2,150,487	17. Antigua and Barbuda 2,376	17. Germany..... 63,150	17. Zimbabwe...... 2,531
18. Egypt 1,674,951	18. St. Lucia 3,194	18. Australia 62,625	18. Burkina Faso ... 2,546
19. Australia ... 1,626,940	19. Comoros 3,207	19. Bahrain...... 61,228	19. Togo 2,608
20. Poland..... 1,625,236	20. Seychelles 3,525	20. Saudi Arabia .. 59,065	20. Solomon Islands.. 2,654

(1) Does not include Hong Kong ($507.2 bil GDP) or Macau ($38.5 bil GDP). (2) 2021 est.

Budget Deficits as Percent of GDP in Selected Countries, 1995-2023

Source: *OECD Economic Outlook*, Organisation for Economic Co-operation and Development (OECD); as of June 1, 2023

Country	1995	2000	2005	2010	2014	2018	2020	2021	2022	2023
Australia	−1.7%	0.9%	2.2%	−4.2%	−1.8%	−0.6%	−12.2%	−4.8%	−1.8%	−0.8%
Austria	−6.1	−2.4	−2.5	−4.4	−2.7	0.2	−8.0	−5.8	−3.2	−3.2
Belgium	−4.5	−0.1	−2.7	−4.1	−3.1	−0.9	−9.0	−5.5	−3.9	−5.2
Brazil*	NA	−3.3	−3.5	−2.4	−6.0	−7.0	−13.3	−4.6	−4.7	−6.7
Canada	−5.5	2.6	1.6	−4.7	0.2	0.4	−10.9	−4.4	−0.8	−0.4
China*	−1.0	−2.6	−0.6	−0.4	−0.3	−3.1	−7.0	−6.6	−6.7	−6.7
Colombia	NA	−4.7	−2.5	−0.8	−3.1	−5.2	−8.8	−7.8	−5.3	−3.8
Czechia	−12.4	−3.6	−3.0	−4.2	−2.1	0.9	−5.8	−5.1	−3.6	−3.8
Denmark	−3.6	1.9	5.0	−2.7	1.1	0.8	0.2	3.6	3.3	2.4
Estonia	1.0	−0.1	1.1	0.2	0.7	−0.6	−5.5	−2.4	−0.9	−3.2
Finland	−5.9	6.9	2.7	−2.5	−3.0	−0.9	−5.6	−2.8	−0.9	−1.6
France	−5.1	−1.3	−3.4	−6.9	−3.9	−2.3	−9.0	−6.5	−4.7	−4.8
Germany	−9.4	−1.6	−3.3	−4.4	0.6	1.9	−4.3	−3.7	−2.6	−1.8
Greece	−8.7	−4.0	−6.2	−11.4	−3.7	0.9	−9.7	−7.1	−2.3	−1.5
Hungary	−8.6	−3.0	−7.8	−4.4	−2.8	−2.1	−7.5	−7.1	−6.2	−4.2
Iceland	−2.9	1.4	5.0	−6.7	0.4	1.0	−8.9	−8.4	−4.3	−2.5
India*	−6.5	−9.4	−6.6	−7.0	−6.7	−5.8	−13.1	−10.4	−8.9	−7.9
Ireland	−2.1	4.9	1.6	−32.6	−3.6	0.1	−5.0	−1.6	1.6	1.7
Israel	NA	−0.8	−2.7	−3.7	−2.3	−3.6	−10.8	−3.7	0.3	−1.1
Italy	−7.2	−2.4	−4.1	−4.2	−3.0	−2.2	−9.7	−9.0	−8.0	−4.1
Japan	−4.3	−7.3	−4.4	−9.1	−5.6	−2.5	−9.0	−6.2	−5.9	−5.3
Korea, South	2.8	4.2	1.4	0.9	1.2	3.0	−2.7	−0.8	−0.6	−0.1
Latvia	−1.4	−2.7	−0.5	−8.6	−1.6	−0.8	−4.4	−7.1	−4.4	−3.6
Lithuania	−1.5	−3.2	−0.3	−6.9	−0.6	0.5	−6.5	−1.2	−0.6	−1.4
Luxembourg	2.7	5.5	−0.2	−0.3	1.3	3.0	−3.4	0.7	0.2	−2.3
Netherlands	−8.7	1.2	−0.5	−5.3	−2.3	1.5	−3.7	−2.4	0.0	−1.0
New Zealand	2.4	1.7	4.8	−6.8	0.5	0.9	−8.0	−6.6	−4.4	−4.3
Norway	3.1	15.0	14.7	10.9	8.6	7.8	−2.6	10.6	26.0	17.1
Poland	−4.3	−4.0	−3.9	−7.5	−3.7	−0.2	−6.9	−1.8	−3.7	−4.7
Portugal	−5.2	−3.2	−6.1	−11.4	−7.4	−0.3	−5.8	−2.9	−0.4	−0.1
Slovakia	−3.5	−12.6	−2.9	−7.5	−3.1	−1.0	−5.4	−5.4	−2.0	−5.8
Slovenia	−8.1	−3.6	−1.3	−5.6	−5.5	0.7	−7.7	−4.6	−3.0	−4.1
South Africa*	−3.1	−2.1	−1.3	−3.1	−4.0	−3.7	−11.3	−6.6	−5.4	−6.4
Spain	−6.8	−1.2	1.2	−9.5	−6.1	−2.6	−10.1	−6.9	−4.8	−3.5
Sweden	−7.0	3.1	1.8	−0.1	−1.5	0.8	−2.8	0.0	0.7	−0.4
Switzerland	−1.9	0.3	−0.6	0.4	−0.2	1.3	−3.1	−0.5	1.0	0.1
United Kingdom	−5.0	3.4	−2.9	−9.2	−5.5	−2.2	−13.1	−8.0	−5.2	−4.8
United States	−4.7	0.3	−4.5	−12.5	−5.4	−6.2	−14.9	−12.1	−4.2	−5.1
OECD countries	**−5.2**	**−0.9**	**−2.9**	**−8.1**	**−3.7**	**−2.8**	**−10.2**	**−7.5**	**−3.6**	**−3.6**

* = Not an OECD member nation; excluded from OECD country total. NA = Not available.

Gold Reserves of Selected Central Banks and Governments, 1975-2022

Source: *International Financial Statistics*, International Monetary Fund (IMF)
(in mil fine troy ounces)

Year-end	World[1]	China[2]	France	Germany[3]	India	IMF	Italy	Japan	Russia	Saudi Arabia	Switzerland	Turkey (Türkiye)	U.S.
1975	1,179.8	NA	100.9	117.6	7.0	153.4	82.5	21.1	NA	3.1	83.2	3.6	274.7
1980	1,152.9	12.8	81.9	95.2	8.6	103.4	66.7	24.2	NA	4.6	83.3	3.8	264.3
1985	1,146.7	12.7	81.9	95.2	9.4	103.4	66.7	24.2	NA	4.6	83.3	3.9	262.7
1990	1,144.2	12.7	81.9	95.2	10.7	103.4	66.7	24.2	NA	4.6	83.3	4.1	261.9
1995	1,114.7	12.7	81.9	95.2	12.8	103.4	66.7	24.2	9.4	4.6	83.3	3.7	261.7
2000	1,067.8	12.7	97.2	111.5	11.5	103.4	78.8	24.5	12.4	4.6	77.8	3.7	261.6
2005	992.9	19.3	90.9	110.2	11.5	103.4	78.8	24.6	12.4	4.6	41.5	3.7	261.6
2008	964.6	19.3	80.1	109.7	11.5	103.4	78.8	24.6	16.7	10.4	33.4	3.7	261.5
2010	991.8	33.9	78.3	109.3	17.9	90.5	78.8	24.6	25.4	10.4	33.4	3.7	261.5
2012	1,018.6	33.9	78.3	109.0	17.9	90.5	78.8	24.6	30.8	10.4	33.4	11.6	261.5
2014	1,037.5	33.9	78.3	108.8	17.9	90.5	78.8	24.6	38.8	10.4	33.4	17.0	261.5
2016	1,080.1	59.2	78.3	108.6	17.9	90.5	78.8	24.6	51.9	10.4	33.4	12.1	261.5
2017	1,093.1	59.2	78.3	108.5	17.9	90.5	78.8	24.6	59.1	10.4	33.4	18.2	261.5
2018	1,100.6	59.6	78.3	108.3	19.3	90.5	78.8	24.6	67.9	10.4	33.4	15.7	261.5
2019	1,118.3	62.6	78.3	108.2	20.4	90.5	78.8	24.6	73.0	10.4	33.4	17.8	261.5
2020	1,134.5	62.6	78.3	108.1	21.8	90.5	78.8	24.6	73.9	10.4	33.4	23.0	261.5
2021	1,141.8	62.6	78.3	108.0	24.2	90.5	78.8	27.2	74.0	10.4	33.4	21.1	261.5
2022	1,140.8	64.6	78.3	107.9	25.3	90.5	78.8	27.2	75.0	10.4	33.4	25.3	261.5

IMF = International Monetary Fund. NA = Not available. (1) Includes countries and international organizations not shown here. (2) Figures are for mainland China only and do not include Hong Kong (0.07 mil oz t in 2022) or Macau. (3) West Germany prior to 1991.

Unemployment Rates in Selected Countries, 1960-2023

Source: *OECD Economic Outlook*, Organisation for Economic Co-operation and Development (OECD); as of June 1, 2023

Year	Canada	Chile	France	Germany	Greece	Italy	Japan	South Korea	Turkey (Türkiye)	UK	U.S.	OECD countries[1]
1960	6.9%	NA	1.3%	NA	NA	4.0%	1.6%	NA	8.8%	2.8%	5.6%	3.4%
1965	3.9	NA	1.4	NA	NA	3.8	1.2	7.3%	9.1	2.7	4.5	3.1
1970	5.7	NA	2.2	NA	NA	3.8	1.2	4.4	5.7	3.5	5.0	3.2
1975	6.9	NA	3.6	NA	NA	4.1	1.9	4.1	6.9	4.5	8.5	5.0
1980	7.5	NA	5.6	NA	NA	5.4	2.0	5.2	7.5	6.8	7.2	5.4
1985	10.5	NA	9.1	NA	NA	8.3	2.6	4.0	6.6	11.4	7.2	7.3
1990	8.2	7.9%	8.0	NA	NA	8.8	2.1	2.4	7.5	7.1	5.6	5.7
1995	9.5	7.5	10.0	8.2%	9.7%	11.3	3.1	2.1	7.1	8.6	5.6	7.4
2000	6.8	9.9	8.6	7.9	11.6	10.0	4.7	4.4	6.0	5.5	4.0	6.2
2005	6.7	9.4	8.9	11.0	10.0	7.7	4.4	3.7	9.5	4.8	5.1	6.8
2010	8.1	8.3	9.3	6.6	12.7	8.5	5.0	3.7	11.1	7.9	9.6	8.5
2013	7.2	6.1	10.4	4.9	27.5	12.3	4.0	3.1	9.0	7.6	7.4	8.0
2015	6.9	6.3	10.4	4.4	24.9	12.0	3.4	3.6	10.3	5.4	5.3	6.9
2016	7.0	6.7	10.1	3.9	23.5	11.7	3.1	3.7	10.9	4.9	4.9	6.5
2017	6.4	7.0	9.5	3.6	21.5	11.3	2.8	3.7	10.9	4.4	4.4	5.9
2018	5.8	7.4	9.1	3.2	19.3	10.6	2.4	3.9	10.9	4.1	3.9	5.5
2019	5.7	7.2	8.5	3.0	17.3	9.9	2.4	3.8	13.7	3.8	3.7	5.4
2020	9.7	10.7	8.1	3.7	16.3	9.3	2.8	4.0	13.1	4.6	8.1	7.2
2021	7.5	8.8	7.9	3.6	14.7	9.5	2.8	3.6	12.0	4.5	5.4	6.2
2022	5.3	7.9	7.3	3.1	12.4	8.1	2.6	2.9	10.5	3.7	3.6	5.0
2023	5.2	8.5	7.2	2.9	11.2	8.1	2.5	3.0	10.0	4.2	3.7	5.0

NA = Not available. **Note:** Labor market data are subject to differences in definitions across countries. Because of changes in methodology, some data may not be fully comparable over time. (1) Includes countries not shown here.

Personal Tax Rates in Selected Countries, 2022

Source: *Taxing Wages*, Organisation for Economic Co-operation and Development (OECD)
Rates are averages for a single person without children at the income level of the average full-time worker.
(as % of gross wage earnings before taxes in U.S. dollars with equal purchasing power; ranked by total payment rate)

Country	Total payment rate[1]	Income tax	Employee soc. sec. contribs.	Gross wage earnings	Country	Total payment rate[1]	Income tax	Employee soc. sec. contribs.	Gross wage earnings
Belgium	40.3%	26.4%	14.0%	$74,273	Sweden	24.3	17.3	7.0	$57,432
Germany	38.0	17.7	20.3	75,137	Slovakia	24.3	10.9	13.4	28,711
Lithuania	37.1	17.6	19.5	41,708	United Kingdom	23.6	14.3	9.3	64,134
Denmark	35.5	35.5	0.0	69,941	Australia	23.0	23.0	0.0	65,455
Slovenia	33.6	11.5	22.1	41,498	Greece	23.0	9.0	14.0	35,772
Hungary	33.5	15.0	18.5	39,542	Poland	22.8	4.9	17.8	38,493
Austria	33.2	15.2	18.0	69,202	Japan	22.3	7.9	14.5	53,769
Luxembourg	32.1	19.8	12.3	82,660	Spain	21.4	15.0	6.4	47,019
Finland	31.1	20.8	10.3	61,778	New Zealand	20.1	20.1	0.0	47,539
Italy	28.8	20.1	8.7	53,498	Czechia	19.5	8.5	11.0	36,411
Iceland	28.2	28.1	0.1	73,897	Israel	19.1	10.9	8.3	46,020
Portugal	28.1	17.1	11.0	38,546	Switzerland	18.5	12.1	6.4	94,601
Netherlands	27.7	16.1	11.7	76,635	Estonia	18.4	16.8	1.6	34,099
France	27.7	16.2	11.4	59,445	South Korea	15.8	6.6	9.3	60,090
Ireland	27.5	23.5	4.0	69,624	Mexico	11.3	9.9	1.4	15,204
Norway	27.3	19.3	8.0	70,726	Costa Rica	10.5	0.0	10.5	28,169
Latvia	26.5	16.0	10.5	31,864	Chile	7.0	0.0	7.0	26,719
Turkey (Türkiye)	26.2	11.2	15.0	29,336	Colombia	0.0	0.0	0.0	14,644
Canada	25.6	19.2	6.4	64,941	OECD[2]	24.7	15.0	9.7	52,195
United States	24.8	17.2	7.7	64,889					

(1) Income tax and soc. sec. contribs. may not add up to total due to rounding. (2) The 38 countries shown here.

Inflation Rates in Selected Countries, 1975-2022

Source: *International Financial Statistics*, International Monetary Fund (IMF)
(annual average consumer price % change)

Country	1975-80	1980-85	1985-90	1990-95	1995-2000	2000-05	2005-10	2010-15	2015-18	2018-19	2019-20	2020-21	2021-22
Canada	8.8%	7.5%	4.5%	2.3%	1.7%	2.3%	1.7%	1.7%	1.8%	1.9%	0.7%	3.4%	6.8%
Chile	82.5	21.5	19.4	13.9	5.2	2.6	3.7	3.4	2.8	2.6	3.0	4.5	11.6
China[1]	NA	NA	11.8[2]	13.1	1.9	1.3	3.0	2.8	1.9	2.9	2.4	1.0	2.0
France	10.5	9.7	3.0	2.2	1.2	1.9	1.5	1.1	1.0	1.1	0.5	1.6	5.2
Germany	4.0	3.9	1.4	3.6	1.3	1.5	1.6	1.4	1.2	1.4	0.1	3.1	6.9
Greece	16.3	20.7	17.4	13.9	4.9	3.4	3.2	0.2	0.3	0.3	−1.2	1.2	9.6
India	4.2	9.3	8.6	10.5	7.6	4.0	8.7	8.0	4.1	3.7	6.6	5.1	6.7
Japan	6.6	2.8	1.4	1.4	0.3	−0.4	−0.1	0.7	0.4	0.5	−0.02	−0.2	2.5
Spain	18.6	12.2	6.5	5.2	2.6	3.2	2.4	1.3	1.1	0.7	−0.3	3.1	8.4
Turkey (Türkiye)	52.6	38.3	53.2	79.3	74.1	27.5	8.7	7.9	11.8	15.2	12.3	19.6	72.3
United Kingdom	14.4	7.2	5.1	3.9	2.0	1.6	2.6	2.1	2.0	1.7	1.0	2.5	7.9
United States	8.9	5.5	4.0	3.1	2.5	2.6	2.2	1.7	1.9	1.8	1.2	4.7	8.0

NA = Not available. (1) Figures for mainland China only and do not include Hong Kong (1.9% in 2021-22) or Macau (1.0% in 2021-22). (2) For 1986-90.

Number of Days Off Work Per Year in Selected Countries

Source: Organisation for Economic Co-operation and Development (OECD); Center for Economic and Policy Research

Entitlements are generally for full-time, full-year private-sector employees working a five-day week who have been with their current employer for at least one year. The U.S. is the only OECD country without a national statute that entitles workers to a minimum number of days off per year.

Country	Paid days off[1]	Public holidays[2]	Total minimum days off	Country	Paid days off[1]	Public holidays[2]	Total minimum days off	Country	Paid days off[1]	Public holidays[2]	Total minimum days off
Australia	20	7	27	Germany	20	10-14	30-34	Netherlands	20	9	29
Austria	25	13	38	Greece	20	11	31	New Zealand	20	11	31
Belgium	20	10	30	Hungary	20	11	31	Norway	21	10	31
Bulgaria	20	12	32	Iceland	24	12	36	Poland	20	13	33
Canada	10	9	19	Ireland	20	9	29	Portugal	22	13	35
Chile	15	5	20	Israel	16	9	25	Romania	20	13	33
Colombia	15	18	33	Italy	20	12	32	Slovakia	20	15	35
Costa Rica	10	11	21	Japan	10	16	26	Slovenia	20	13	33
Croatia	20	13	33	Korea, South	15	15	30	Spain	22	14	36
Cyprus	20	14-17	34-37	Latvia	20	15	35	Sweden	25	11	36
Czechia	20	13	33	Lithuania	20	15	35	Switzerland	20	9-13	29
Denmark	25	11	36	Luxembourg	26	10	36	Turkey (Türkiye)	14	15	29
Estonia	20	11	31	Malta	24	14	38	UK	28	8	28
Finland	24	11	35	Mexico	6	8	14	U.S.	0	NA[3]	0
France	25	11	36								

NA = Not applicable. (1) Statutory minimum. (2) Generally set at the national or federal level. May vary at the state level. In some countries, including the U.S., public holidays do not have to be given as paid leave. (3) The government designates 11 federal holidays per year (Inauguration Day is also a holiday for federal employees in the Washington, DC, metro area). Private sector employers decide how much paid leave to offer.

International Migrants by Destination and Origin, 2000, 2020

Source: *International Migrant Stock 2020*, Dept. of Economic and Social Affairs, UN Population Division
(numbers in thousands)

	Places hosting the most international migrants				Places of origin with the largest diaspora populations			
	2020		**2000**			**2020**		**2000**	
	Country/terr.	Migrants	Country/terr.	Migrants		Country/terr.	Migrants	Country/terr.	Migrants
1.	U.S.	50,632.8	U.S.	34,814.1	1.	India	17,869.5	Russia	10,664.8
2.	Germany	15,762.5	Russia	11,900.3	2.	Mexico	11,185.7	Mexico	9,562.9
3.	Saudi Arabia	13,454.8	Germany	8,992.6	3.	Russia	10,756.7	India	7,928.1
4.	Russia	11,636.9	India	6,411.3	4.	China[1]	10,461.2	China[1]	5,884.9
5.	UK	9,359.6	France	6,278.7	5.	Syria	8,457.2	Ukraine	5,596.5
6.	UAE	8,716.3	Ukraine	5,527.1	6.	Bangladesh	7,401.8	Bangladesh	5,441.1
7.	France	8,524.9	Canada	5,511.9	7.	Pakistan	6,328.4	Afghanistan	4,750.7
8.	Canada	8,049.3	Saudi Arabia	5,263.4	8.	Ukraine	6,139.1	UK	3,860.0
9.	Australia	7,685.9	UK	4,730.2	9.	Philippines	6,094.3	Kazakhstan	3,554.5
10.	Spain	6,842.2	Australia	4,386.3	10.	Afghanistan	5,853.8	Pakistan	3,406.4
11.	Italy	6,387.0	Pakistan	4,181.9	11.	Venezuela	5,415.3	Germany	3,235.2
12.	Turkey (Türkiye)	6,052.7	Kazakhstan	2,874.2	12.	Poland	4,825.1	Italy	3,067.5
13.	Ukraine	4,997.4	Hong Kong	2,669.1	13.	UK	4,732.5	Philippines	3,062.7
14.	India	4,878.7	Iran	2,476.5	14.	Indonesia	4,601.4	Turkey (Türkiye)	2,847.3
15.	Kazakhstan	3,732.1	UAE	2,447.0	15.	Kazakhstan	4,203.9	Palestine	2,767.3
16.	Thailand	3,632.5	Côte d'Ivoire	2,163.6	16.	Palestine	4,022.8	Indonesia	2,415.1
17.	Malaysia	3,476.6	Italy	2,121.7	17.	Romania	3,987.1	Vietnam	2,158.5
18.	Jordan	3,457.7	Jordan	1,927.8	18.	Germany	3,855.3	Morocco	2,077.0
19.	Pakistan	3,276.6	Israel	1,851.3	19.	Myanmar	3,711.8	Poland	2,047.6
20.	Kuwait	3,110.2	Japan	1,686.4	20.	Egypt	3,610.5	Portugal	1,993.8
21.	Hong Kong	2,962.5	Spain	1,657.3	21.	Turkey (Türkiye)	3,411.4	U.S.	1,979.3
22.	South Africa	2,860.5	Switzerland	1,570.8	22.	Vietnam	3,392.0	South Korea	1,875.4
23.	Iran	2,797.2	Netherlands	1,556.3	23.	Morocco	3,262.2	Egypt	1,708.3
24.	Japan	2,771.0	Argentina	1,540.2	24.	Italy	3,258.8	Belarus	1,685.6
25.	Côte d'Ivoire	2,564.9	Malaysia	1,463.6	25.	Colombia	3,024.3	Azerbaijan	1,630.6
26.	Singapore	2,523.6	Uzbekistan	1,406.5	26.	U.S.	2,996.2	Puerto Rico	1,600.1
27.	Switzerland	2,491.2	Singapore	1,351.7	27.	Nepal	2,599.7	Uzbekistan	1,576.0
28.	Oman	2,372.8	Turkey (Türkiye)	1,281.0	28.	South Sudan	2,575.9	France	1,555.4
29.	Netherlands	2,358.3	Belgium	1,268.4	29.	France	2,341.9	Bosnia and Herzegovina	1,496.7
30.	Argentina	2,281.7	Thailand	1,257.8	30.	South Korea	2,204.6	Colombia	1,433.9
	World	280,598.1	World	173,230.6		World	280,598.1	World	173,230.6

(1) Not incl. Hong Kong or Macau.

Refugees and Other Populations of Concern, 2013-22

Source: *UNHCR Global Trends*, United Nations High Commissioner for Refugees (UNHCR)

Refugees are persons recognized under the 1951 UN Refugee Convention/1967 Protocol, the 1969 OAU (Org. of African Unity) Refugee Convention, the refugee definition in the 1984 Cartagena Declaration as incorporated into national laws, those recognized in accordance with the UNHCR Statute, and persons granted or receiving protection. The UNHCR also extends assistance to internally displaced persons (IDPs), although they legally remain under their home country's protection. Stateless persons are not considered nationals under any state under the operation of its laws. Others of concern comprises persons who do not necessarily belong in any one category. All data are provisional; population as of year-end.

Category	2013	2015	2017	2018	2020	2021	2022	% change, 2021-22
Refugees	11,699,300	16,111,300	19,941,300	20,360,600	20,650,300	21,326,917	29,413,033	37.9%
Asylum-seekers (pending cases)	1,164,400	3,225,000	3,090,900	3,503,300	4,139,300	4,623,754	5,438,929	17.6
Others in need of intl. protection[1]	NA	NA	NA	2,592,900	3,856,300	4,406,409	5,217,456	18.4
Returned refugees[2]	414,600	201,400	667,400	593,800	251,000	429,234	339,260	−21.0
IDPs[3]	23,925,500	37,494,200	39,118,500	41,425,100	48,557,400	51,322,623	57,321,197	11.7
Returned IDPs[2]	1,356,200	2,317,300	4,229,000	2,312,900	3,184,100	5,265,622	5,708,166	8.4
Stateless persons	3,469,200	3,687,800	2,796,200	2,820,300	4,176,900	4,337,558	4,428,192	2.1
Others of concern[1]	836,100	870,700	1,596,200	1,182,900	8,309,800	4,223,827	6,014,447	42.4
Total	**42,865,300**	**63,907,700**	**71,439,500**	**74,791,900**	**91,920,400**	**94,663,734**	**112,564,131**	**18.9**

NA = Value is zero or not available. (1) "Others in need of intl. protection" are those who have not been reported under other categories but who likely need international protection. Prior to 2018, they were included among "Others of concern." (2) Persons who have returned to their place of origin in that year. (3) Conflict-generated only, of concern to UNHCR.

Refugees and People in a Refugee-Like Situation, 2022

Source: *UNHCR Global Trends*, United Nations High Commissioner for Refugees (UNHCR)

Refugees are persons recognized under the 1951 UN Refugee Convention/1967 Protocol, 1969 OAU (Org. of African Unity) Refugee Convention, the refugee definition in the 1984 Cartagena Declaration as incorporated into national laws, those recognized in accordance with the UNHCR Statute, and persons granted/receiving protection. Persons in a refugee-like situation have not yet had their status ascertained. Only countries hosting 77,000 or more refugees/people in a refugee-like situation are shown; of those countries, only places originating 7,500 or more persons are given, in decreasing order. Data are provisional and as of year-end.

Place of asylum	Origin of most refugees (excl. asylum-seekers with pending cases)	Number
Africa		**7,545,579**
Algeria	Syria, Western Sahara	99,107
Burundi	Dem. Rep. of the Congo	84,636
Cameroon	Nigeria, Central African Republic	473,887
Chad	Sudan, Central African Republic, Cameroon, Nigeria	592,764
Dem. Rep. of the Congo	Central African Republic, Rwanda, South Sudan, Burundi	520,544
Egypt	Syria, Palestinian[1], Sudan, South Sudan, Eritrea	294,632
Ethiopia	South Sudan, Somalia, Eritrea, Sudan	879,598
Kenya	Somalia, South Sudan, Dem. Rep. of the Congo, Ethiopia, Burundi	504,473
Mauritania	Mali	100,981
Niger	Nigeria, Mali	255,307
Nigeria	Cameroon	91,275
Rwanda	Dem. Rep. of the Congo, Burundi	120,753
South Sudan	Sudan, Dem. Rep. of the Congo	308,369
Sudan	South Sudan, Eritrea, Syria, Ethiopia, Central African Republic	1,097,128
Tanzania	Burundi, Dem. Rep. of the Congo	206,229
Uganda	South Sudan, Dem. Rep. of the Congo, Somalia, Burundi, Rwanda, Eritrea	1,463,523
Asia		**12,271,919**
Bangladesh	Myanmar (Burma)	952,384
India	Sri Lanka, China, Myanmar (Burma), Afghanistan	242,835
Iran	Iraq, Afghanistan	3,425,091
Iraq	Syria, Palestinian[1]	273,716
Jordan	Syria, Iraq	697,761
Lebanon	Syria	818,861
Malaysia	Myanmar (Burma)	134,554
Pakistan	Afghanistan	1,743,785
Thailand	Myanmar (Burma)	94,472
Turkey (Türkiye)	Syria, Iraq, Afghanistan	3,568,259
Yemen	Somalia	77,458
Europe		**8,728,098**
Austria	Ukraine, Syria, Afghanistan, Iraq, Somalia, Iran	258,613
Belgium	Ukraine, various/unknown, Syria	151,408
Bulgaria	Ukraine, Syria	176,297
Czechia	Ukraine	435,212
France	Ukraine, Afghanistan, Syria, Russia, Sri Lanka, Dem. Rep. of the Congo, Sudan, Guinea, Turkey (Türkiye), Serbia-Kosovo, Iraq, Côte d'Ivoire, Eritrea, Somalia, China, Albania, Cambodia, Bangladesh, Mali, Mauritania, Vietnam	612,934
Germany	Ukraine, Syria, Afghanistan, Iraq, Eritrea, various/unknown, Turkey (Türkiye), Iran, Somalia, Russia, Nigeria, stateless[2]	2,075,445
Greece	Syria, Afghanistan, Ukraine, Iraq, various/unknown, Palestinian[5]	160,761
Ireland	Ukraine	81,256
Italy	Ukraine, Nigeria, Afghanistan, Pakistan, Mali, Somalia	296,181
Moldova	Ukraine	105,374
Netherlands	Ukraine, Syria, Eritrea, Afghanistan	218,457
Poland	Ukraine	971,129
Romania	Ukraine	105,621
Russia	Ukraine	1,277,672
Slovakia	Ukraine	96,563
Spain	Ukraine, Venezuela, Syria	317,751
Sweden	Syria, Ukraine, Afghanistan, Eritrea, stateless[2], Iraq, Somalia	277,726
Switzerland	Ukraine, Eritrea, Syria, Afghanistan, Turkey (Türkiye)	182,474
United Kingdom	Ukraine, Iran, Eritrea, Syria, Sudan, Afghanistan, Iraq, Pakistan	328,989
Latin America		**292,860**
Mexico	Honduras, Venezuela, El Salvador	95,579
North America and the Caribbean		**507,782**
Canada	Ukraine	140,621
United States	China, El Salvador, Guatemala, Venezuela, Honduras, Haiti, Egypt, Mexico, India, Afghanistan, Syria, Russia, Ethiopia	363,059
Oceania		**66,795**
Total		**29,413,033**

(1) Palestinians under the UNHCR mandate only. (2) Persons not considered nationals by any state under the operation of its laws.

Internally Displaced Persons, 2022

Source: Internal Displacement Monitoring Centre, Norwegian Refugee Council

Internally displaced persons (IDPs) are people who have been forced to move due to conflict or natural disasters but who have not crossed into another country. As such, they are not protected by international refugee law and legally remain under the protection of their home country. Estimates shown are of those displaced by conflict and violence only as of year end; they may comprise only registered IDPs or those displaced a certain area of a country.

Country/territory	Number	Country/territory	Number	Country/territory	Number
Abyei Area[1]	56,000	Guatemala	242,000	Pakistan	21,000
Afghanistan	4,394,000	Haiti	171,000	Palestine[2]	12,000
Armenia	8,400	Honduras	247,000	Papua New Guinea	91,000
Azerbaijan	659,000	India	631,000	Peru	73,000
Bangladesh	427,000	Indonesia	72,000	Philippines	102,000
Benin	1,200	Iraq	1,169,000	Russia	7,500
Bosnia and Herzegovina	91,000	Kazakhstan	120	Senegal	8,400
Brazil	5,600	Kenya	30,000	Serbia	195,000
Burkina Faso	1,882,000	Kosovo	16,000	Sierra Leone	3,000
Burundi	8,500	Kyrgyzstan	4,000	Solomon Islands	1,000
Cameroon	987,000	Libya	135,000	Somalia	3,864,000
Central African Republic	516,000	Madagascar	2,800	South Sudan	1,475,000
Chad	300,000	Mali	380,000	Sri Lanka	12,000
Colombia	4,766,000	Mayotte (France)	8	Sudan	3,553,000
Congo, Dem. Rep. of	5,686,000	Mexico	386,000	Syria	6,865,000
Congo Republic	27,000	Mozambique	1,030,000	Thailand	41,000
Côte d'Ivoire	302,000	Myanmar (Burma)	1,498,000	Togo	2,300
Cyprus	246,000	New Caledonia (France)	150	Turkey (Türkiye)	1,099,000
El Salvador	52,000	Nicaragua	77	Uganda	4,800
Ethiopia	3,852,000	Niger	372,000	Ukraine	5,914,000
Gambia, The	5,600	Nigeria	3,646,000	Yemen	4,523,000
Georgia	308,000	North Macedonia	110	**Total**	**62.5 mil**

(1) Disputed territory between Sudan and South Sudan. (2) In the West Bank, East Jerusalem, and Gaza.

Countries With Highest Mortality Rates by Selected Causes of Death

Source: *World Health Statistics 2023*, World Health Organization (WHO)

(per 100,000 live births or 100,000 population)

Rank	Country	Maternal mortality ratio, 2020	Rank	Country	Suicide mortality rate, 2019	Rank	Country	Mortality rate due to homicide, 2019
1.	South Sudan	1,223	1.	Lesotho	72.4	1.	El Salvador	85.0
2.	Chad	1,063	2.	Guyana	40.3	2.	Honduras	66.9
3.	Nigeria	1,047	3.	Eswatini	29.4	3.	Venezuela	63.6
4.	Central African Rep.	835	4.	South Korea	28.6	4.	Jamaica	50.3
5.	Guinea-Bissau	725	5.	Kiribati	28.3	5.	Lesotho	43.5
6.	Liberia	652	6.	Micronesia, Fed. States	28.2	6.	Trinidad and Tobago	39.4
7.	Somalia	621	7.	Lithuania	26.1	7.	Colombia	38.3
8.	Afghanistan	620	8.	Suriname	25.4	8.	Bahamas, The	38.1
9.	Lesotho	566	9.	Russia	25.1	9.	Belize	37.3
10.	Guinea	553	10.	South Africa	23.5	10.	South Africa	35.9
11.	Congo, Dem. Rep. of	547	11.	Ukraine	21.6	11.	Brazil	32.6
12.	Kenya	530	12.	Belarus	21.2	12.	St. Vincent and the Grenadines	29.4
13.	Benin	523	13.	Uruguay	21.2	13.	Mexico	25.4
14.	Burundi	494	14.	Montenegro	21.0	14.	Guatemala	25.1
15.	Côte d'Ivoire	480	15.	Latvia	20.1	15.	Guyana	24.7
16.	Mauritania	464	16.	Slovenia	19.8	16.	Central African Republic	21.3
17.	Gambia, The	458	17.	Belgium	18.3	17.	Haiti	20.7
18.	Sierra Leone	443	18.	Vanuatu	18.0	18.	St. Lucia	20.2
19.	Niger	441	19.	Mongolia	17.9	19.	Eswatini	18.5
20.	Mali	440	20.	Kazakhstan	17.6	20.	Namibia	18.0
	Global	**223**		**Global**	**9.2**		**Global**	**6.2**

Note: 2020 ranking excl. some countries with small pops.; 2019 rankings excl. countries with a population of less than 90,000.

Global HIV/AIDS Status, 2022

Source: HIV Justice Network, Joint United Nations Programme on HIV/AIDS (UNAIDS)

The annual number of AIDS-related deaths has dropped approximately 68.5% between 2004—when the number of such deaths reached a peak of 2.0 million—and 2022. The number of new infections each year has also decreased (59.4%), from a high of 3.2 million in 1995 to 1.3 million in 2022. The risk of HIV infection remained high and access to services was inadequate for what UNAIDS considers key population groups. Median HIV prevalence in the adult population (ages 15-49) worldwide was 0.7% in 2022, but median prevalence was higher in key populations: sex workers (2.5%), gay men and other men who have sex with men (7.7%), people who inject drugs (5.0%), transgender persons (10.3%), and people in prisons (1.4%). In 2022, about 76% of all people living with HIV were accessing antiretroviral therapy. Laws criminalizing nondisclosure, exposure, or transmission of HIV existed in 96 countries; 35 U.S. states criminalized actions taken by people with HIV through HIV- or STD-specific laws.

An estimated $562.6 billion was spent on the HIV/AIDS epidemic in 2000-15 according to a study published in *The Lancet* in 2018. At year-end 2022, $20.8 billion (in constant 2019 U.S. dollars) was available to low- and middle-income countries in responding to AIDS, short of the $29 billion UNAIDS estimated would be needed in 2025 to end AIDS as a public health threat.

Current and New HIV/AIDS Cases and Deaths by Region, 2022

Source: Joint United Nations Programme on HIV/AIDS (UNAIDS)

Region	Number living with HIV	Percent of world total[1]	New HIV infections	AIDS-related deaths
Asia and the Pacific	6,500,000	16.7%	300,000	150,000
Caribbean	330,000	0.8	16,000	5,600
Eastern and Southern Africa	20,800,000	53.3	500,000	260,000
Eastern Europe and Central Asia[2]	2,000,000	5.1	160,000	48,000
Latin America	2,200,000	5.6	110,000	27,000
Middle East and North Africa	190,000	0.5	17,000	5,300
Western and Central Africa	4,800,000	12.3	160,000	120,000
Western and Central Europe and North America[2]	2,300,000	5.9	58,000	13,000
World[3]	**39,000,000**	**100.0**	**1,300,000**	**630,000**

(1) Population within a region living with HIV as a percentage of population worldwide living with HIV. (2) Numbers do not include estimates for children (aged 0-14 years). (3) Figures may not add up to totals because of rounding.

Drinking Water, Sanitation, and Hygiene, 2022

Source: WHO/UNICEF Joint Monitoring Programme for Water Supply, Sanitation, and Hygiene (JMP)

In 2022, an estimated 91.2% of the world's population had access to at least basic drinking water services, up from 82% in 2000. A gap remained, however, between coverage in urban (96.6%) and rural areas (84.0%). Having basic drinking water service means access to an off-premise improved water source, collecting water from which takes up to 30 min. roundtrip. As of the same year, 80.8% of people worldwide, compared to 56% in 2000, used at least basic sanitation services; 11.0% of the rural population and <1% of the urban population still practiced open defecation. Those without access to improved sanitation facilities, which are designed to prevent contact with human waste, are at increased risk of contracting a variety of infectious and parasitic diseases such as diarrhea, malaria, and hepatitis A.

High-income countries had near-universal (99% or greater) access to at least basic water and sanitation services in 2022. In comparison, while 97.1% of the population of Russia (upper middle income) had access to at least basic drinking water services, only 89.4% had access to at least basic sanitation services. In China (also upper middle income), the figures were 97.6% and 95.9%, respectively.

In 2022, only 75.2% of the world population had access to basic hygiene services at home, specifically a basic handwashing facility with soap and water available.

Lowest Access to Basic Drinking Water Services, 2022

Source: WHO/UNICEF Joint Monitoring Programme for Water Supply, Sanitation, and Hygiene (JMP)

A person who spends up to 30 min. roundtrip collecting water from an off-premise improved water source is said to have basic access to drinking water. Improved water sources protect from outside contamination and include piped water, boreholes or tubewells, dug wells, rainwater, and packaged or delivered water.

(ranked by % of total pop. with at least basic access)

Rank	Country/area	% of pop. with access Total	Rural	Urban	Rank	Country/area	% of pop. with access Total	Rural	Urban
1.	Dem. Rep. of the Congo	35.1%	13.8%	59.3%	16.	Guinea-Bissau	61.8%	52.5%	73.1%
2.	Central African Republic	36.3	27.4	48.1	17.	Zimbabwe	62.3	47.7	92.8
3.	South Sudan	41.2	33.6	70.0	18.	Burundi	62.4	57.7	90.7
4.	Niger	48.9	40.9	88.3	19.	Kenya	62.9	53.3	86.4
5.	Burkina Faso	49.5	34.8	80.9	20.	Mozambique	63.2	48.3	87.3
6.	Papua New Guinea	50.2	44.5	86.9		Australia and New Zealand	>99.0	>99.0	>99.0
7.	Ethiopia	51.5	42.2	83.2		Central and Southern Asia	93.3	91.7	96.0
8.	Eritrea[1]	51.8	27.8	89.7		Eastern and South-Eastern Asia	96.7	93.9	98.4
9.	Chad	52.0	43.8	77.9		Europe and Northern America	98.9	97.3	>99.0
10.	Madagascar	53.5	36.0	79.8		Latin America and the Caribbean	97.6	91.6	>99.0
11.	Angola	57.7	27.8	71.7		Northern Africa and Western Asia	91.9	84.4	96.3
12.	Somalia	58.3	38.6	80.1		Oceania	59.9	50.9	92.8
13.	Uganda	59.3	51.8	80.3		Sub-Saharan Africa	65.0	50.1	85.3
14.	Tanzania	60.8	49.0	81.1		World	91.2	84.0	96.6
15.	Yemen	61.8	51.8	77.2					

(1) 2016 ests.

Lowest Access to Basic Sanitation Services, 2022

Source: WHO/UNICEF Joint Monitoring Programme for Water Supply, Sanitation, and Hygiene (JMP)

Improved sanitation facilities are those designed to hygienically prevent human contact with feces and urine, including sewer or septic system connections, ventilated improved pit latrines, and composting toilets, and are not shared with other households. If human waste is not safely managed on- or off-site, then access to sanitation services is considered basic.

(ranked by % of total pop. with at least basic access)

Rank	Country/area	% of pop. with access Total	Rural	Urban	Rank	Country/area	% of pop. with access Total	Rural	Urban
1.	Ethiopia	9.3%	5.5%	22.3%	16.	Burkina Faso	24.8%	16.6%	42.2%
2.	Eritrea[1]	11.9	5.6	22.0	17.	Guinea-Bissau	27.8	16.2	42.1
3.	Chad	12.9	4.5	39.5	18.	Ghana	28.6	21.4	33.7
4.	Central African Republic	13.8	5.7	24.5	19.	Tanzania	30.6	21.3	46.8
5.	Madagascar	14.8	10.2	21.6	20.	Guinea	31.3	21.7	47.0
6.	South Sudan	16.1	9.3	41.8		Australia and New Zealand	>99.0	NA	NA
7.	Dem. Rep. of the Congo	16.2	11.2	21.8		Central and Southern Asia	76.9	73.2	83.0
8.	Niger	16.4	9.0	52.8		Eastern and South-Eastern Asia	93.8	89.7	96.4
9.	Togo	19.2	9.1	32.1		Europe and Northern America	97.6	93.8	98.7
10.	Papua New Guinea	19.3	14.7	48.8		Latin America and the Caribbean	89.5	74.6	93.3
11.	Benin	19.5	9.6	29.5		Northern Africa and Western Asia	92.9	86.4	96.5
12.	Congo Republic[2]	20.6	6.3	27.2		Oceania	33.3	22.9	69.0
13.	Uganda	21.0	17.9	29.9		Sub-Saharan Africa	34.7	24.3	48.7
14.	Liberia	22.5	9.2	34.3		World	80.8	70.1	88.9
15.	Sierra Leone	22.9	13.9	34.5					

NA = Not available. (1) 2016 ests. (2) 2021 ests.

Foreign Development Aid Donors, 2020-22

Source: Development Assistance Committee (DAC), Organisation for Economic Co-operation and Development (OECD)

The amount of official development assistance (ODA), in the form of grants or loans, each DAC member country disbursed to developing countries is given here. Net ODA is disbursements less repayments on earlier loans. The OECD uses the ODA grant equivalent to better reflect donor effort, with more generous loans having a higher ODA value.

(ranked by size of ODA grant equivalent as % of 2022 gross national income [GNI]; 2022 figures are prelim.)

Rank	Donor	ODA as % of GNI 2022	Net ODA in mil of current U.S. dollars 2022	2021	2020	Rank	Donor	ODA as % of GNI 2022	Net ODA in mil of current U.S. dollars 2022	2021	2020
1.	Luxembourg ..	1.00%	$529.9	$539.4	$452.3	19.	Italy..........	0.32%	$6,520.3	$6,271.8	$4,395.9
2.	Sweden......	0.90	5,455.6	5,934.2	6,348.4	20.	Spain	0.30	3,978.4	3,358.5	2,739.3
3.	Norway......	0.86	5,161.0	4,673.0	4,195.7	21.	Lithuania.....	0.29	197.1	NA	NA
4.	Germany.....	0.83	35,301.5	32,455.6	29,320.4	22.	Hungary	0.28	395.6	435.1	417.9
5.	Denmark.....	0.70	2,850.4	2,913.7	2,640.9	23.	Slovenia	0.27	163.8	116.2	90.7
6.	Netherlands ..	0.67	6,470.7	5,265.9	5,330.0	24.	New Zealand..	0.23	537.6	685.3	529.7
7.	Ireland......	0.64	2,452.0	1,154.9	987.8	25.	Portugal	0.23	421.5	438.8	420.5
8.	Finland	0.58	1,613.5	1,497.6	1,277.9	26.	U.S..........	0.22	55,000.4	47,528.2	35,396.4
9.	Switzerland ..	0.56	4,476.1	3,911.4	3,720.8	27.	Australia	0.19	3,039.6	3,546.4	2,868.8
10.	France......	0.56	17,353.0	16,721.9	16,013.1	28.	South Korea ..	0.17	2,882.7	2,997.9	2,292.8
11.	Poland......	0.51	3,363.0	971.2	812.0	29.	Slovakia	0.15	171.0	155.3	141.2
12.	UK..........	0.51	15,716.1	16,277.8	19,253.4	30.	Greece	0.14	305.4	340.9	325.7
13.	Belgium......	0.45	2,691.0	2,649.2	2,376.4	**Total DAC countries**		0.36	205,978.6	184,791.9	162,557.3
14.	Austria......	0.39	1,842.2	1,492.2	1,321.4	**G7 countries**[1]		0.35	155,900.3	141,278.2	122,910.3
15.	Japan	0.39	16,722.6	15,765.3	13,660.2	**EU institutions**		NA	27,630.9	20,639.1	21,055.9
16.	Canada......	0.37	9,286.4	6,257.7	4,870.9	**Total non-DAC**					
17.	Czechia......	0.36	987.1	366.1	299.1	**countries**[2].......		NA	17,845.2	18,954.8	15,519.4
18.	Iceland......	0.34	93.1	70.8	57.9						

NA = Not applicable/available. (1) Canada, France, Germany, Italy, Japan, the UK, and the U.S. (2) Countries not shown here.

Recipients of U.S. Official Development Assistance, 2020-21

Source: Development Assistance Committee (DAC), Organisation for Economic Co-operation and Development (OECD)

(net flows of official development assistance, in mil of current U.S. dollars; ranked by 2021 numbers)

Rank	Country	2020	2021	Rank	Country	2020	2021
1.	Afghanistan..............	$1,009.47	$1,480.72	12.	Colombia...............	$558.76	$673.18
2.	Ethiopia.................	794.18	1,324.63	13.	Uganda................	642.26	630.78
3.	Jordan..................	1,212.80	1,267.98	14.	Mozambique............	483.14	573.86
4.	Nigeria.................	926.80	912.51	15.	Tanzania...............	605.55	506.86
5.	Yemen..................	703.78	900.57	16.	Somalia................	690.42	469.79
6.	Dem. Rep. of the Congo	778.09	898.85	17.	Iraq...................	533.81	461.33
7.	Syria...................	690.14	801.62	18.	Bangladesh.............	309.57	443.83
8.	South Sudan.............	724.76	799.29	19.	Zambia................	391.79	399.98
9.	Sudan..................	229.78	734.12	20.	Zimbabwe..............	282.37	343.13
10.	Kenya..................	679.42	701.44	21.	Ukraine................	236.30	304.72
11.	South Africa	717.23	697.57	**Total developing countries**		29,673.06	38,229.28

Nuclear Powers of the World

As of Sept. 2023, eight countries were acknowledged nuclear weapons states: the **U.S., UK, France, China, India, Pakistan, Russia, North Korea. Israel** was presumed to have an arsenal.

All of the more than 40 nations with the knowledge or technology to produce nuclear weapons have signed the Nuclear Non-Proliferation Treaty (NPT) with the exception of Israel, India, and Pakistan. After expelling Intl. Atomic Energy Agency (IAEA) inspectors in Dec. 2002, North Korea announced on Jan. 10, 2003, its withdrawal from the NPT effective the following day.

Iran argued for the right to pursue the peaceful application of nuclear technology, but the IAEA maintained the country had violated the NPT. In 2015, the so-called P5+1 (the five permanent members of the UN Security Council plus Germany) signed a Joint Comprehensive Plan of Action (JCPOA) with Iran, which agreed to curb its ability to enrich uranium as well as reduce its current stockpile of the material. Nuclear-related sanctions on Iran were lifted in Jan. 2016, after the IAEA certified the country had implemented key measures. The U.S., under

Pres. Donald Trump, pulled out of the JCPOA in May 2018, and reimposed sanctions that Nov. The other JCPOA states maintained their commitment. In July 2019, Iran resumed enriching uranium, increasing its stockpile beyond what the deal allowed. Under Pres. Joe Biden, the U.S. expressed interest in reviving the agreement on the condition that Iran returned to compliance, with talks still ongoing as of 2023.

North Korea conducted six nuclear tests between 2006 and 2017. In July 2017, it held two intercontinental ballistic missile tests, which appeared to indicate North Korean missiles were capable of reaching the U.S. In response, the UN Security Council unanimously approved new sanctions on North Korea. The country resumed missile testing in May 2019. Although Trump and North Korean leader Kim Jong Un met multiple times in 2018-19, no formal agreement on denuclearization was reached. North Korean state media reported passage of a law in Sept. 2022 making the country's nuclear status "irreversible" and authorizing preemptive nuclear strikes.

Estimated Numbers of Nuclear Weapons by Country, 1945-2023

Source: Hans M. Kristensen, Matt Korda, and Eliana Reynolds, Federation of American Scientists (FAS)

Year	United States	USSR/Russia	United Kingdom	France	China	Israel[1]	India	Pakistan	Total[2]
1945	6	—	—	—	—	—	—	—	6
1950	369	5	—	—	—	—	—	—	374
1960	20,434	1,605	30	—	—	—	—	—	22,069
1970	26,662	11,643	280	36	75	8	—	—	38,696
1980	24,304	30,062	350	250	280	31	—	—	55,246
1990	21,004	37,000	300	505	430	53	—	—	59,239
2000	10,577	21,000	185	470	400	72	—	—	32,632
2010	9,400	12,300	225	300	240	60-80	60-80	70-90	22,400
2020	5,800	6,372	195	290	320	90	150	160	13,410
2023[3]	5,244	5,889	225	290	410	90	164	170	12,512

(1) Israel is widely presumed to have a nuclear stockpile although it has never confirmed nor denied its nuclear status. (2) Numbers may not add up to totals due to rounding and include deployed warheads, those in reserve or in a military stockpile, and retired warheads awaiting dismantlement. (3) As of early 2023, North Korea was estimated to have produced sufficient material for about 50-70 warheads, with approximately 30 assembled for short- and medium-range missiles.

Nuclear Arms Treaties and Negotiations: A Historical Overview

Aug. 5, 1963: Partial (Limited) Test Ban Treaty signed by the UK, U.S., and USSR, went into effect Oct. 10, 1963. Prohibits parties from testing or participating in the testing of nuclear weapons in the atmosphere, in outer space, and under water.

July 1, 1968: Nuclear Non-Proliferation Treaty (NPT) opened to signatures, went into effect Mar. 5, 1970. With the UK, U.S., and USSR as major signers, the parties agree not to help non-nuclear nations get or make nuclear weapons, though such nations can pursue the peaceful application of nuclear energy. On May 11, 1995, parties to the treaty voted to extend it indefinitely. As of Sept. 2023, 191 states were party to the treaty, not including North Korea, which withdrew in 2003. Israel, India, and Pakistan were not signatories.

May 26, 1972: The **Strategic Arms Limitation Talks (SALT I)** led to the signing of two agreements by the U.S. and USSR: the **Treaty on the Limitation of Anti-Ballistic Missile Systems** (or **ABM Treaty**) and an interim agreement. These agreements cap the numbers of intercontinental ballistic missile (ICBM) launchers and submarine-launched ballistic missile (SLBM) launchers.

July 3, 1974: Treaty on the Limitation of Underground Nuclear Weapon Tests (or **Threshold Test Ban Treaty**) signed by the U.S. and USSR. Limits underground testing of nuclear weapons to yields of 150 kilotons or less. On May 28, 1976, U.S. and Russia signed the **Peaceful Nuclear Explosions Treaty**, governing explosions outside weapons test sites. Both treaties entered into force Dec. 11, 1990.

June 18, 1979: Strategic Offensive Arms Limitation Treaty (or **SALT II**) signed by the U.S. and USSR. Limited each side to 2,400 missile launchers and heavy bombers; ceiling to apply until Jan. 1, 1985. Never ratified; superseded by START I.

Dec. 8, 1987: Intermediate-Range Nuclear Forces (INF) Treaty signed by the U.S. and USSR. Eliminated all U.S. and Soviet intermediate- and shorter-range nuclear missiles, the first time a treaty banned an entire category of nuclear weapons. Entered into force June 1, 1988. The treaty lapsed Aug. 2, 2019, after the U.S., citing Russian "noncompliance," gave formal notice of its withdrawal on Feb. 2, 2019, and Russia responded by suspending its participation.

July 31, 1991: Strategic Arms Reduction Treaty (START I) signed by the USSR and U.S. to reduce long-range nuclear forces no later than seven years after the treaty entered into force. This was the first treaty to mandate reductions in so-called strategic nuclear weapons by the superpowers.

With the Soviet Union breakup in Dec. 1991, four former republics became independent nations with strategic nuclear arms: Russia, Ukraine, Kazakhstan, and Belarus. Under the **Lisbon Protocol** of May 1992, Ukraine, Kazakhstan, and Belarus agreed to accede to the NPT as non-nuclear-weapon states, to destroy or transfer their nuclear weapons to Russia, and to ratify START I. START I expired on Dec. 5, 2009.

Jan. 3, 1993: START II signed by the U.S. and Russia, ratified by the two on Jan. 26, 1996, and Apr. 14, 2000, respectively. Called for further reductions in their long-range nuclear arsenals. Both sides withdrew before the treaty went into force.

Sept. 24, 1996: Comprehensive Nuclear-Test-Ban Treaty (CTBT) signed by 71 countries, including the five nuclear-weapons states (China, France, Russia, UK, U.S.). The CTBT bans all nuclear explosions. It is intended to prevent the nuclear powers from developing more advanced weapons while limiting the ability of other states to acquire such devices. As of Sept. 2023, the CTBT had been signed by 186 nations and ratified by 178 of them. It will enter into force only after all Annex 2 states—the 44 states with nuclear capabilities at the time of the treaty's final negotiations—have signed and ratified it. Only 36 have done so to date. Of the remaining Annex 2 countries, five have yet to ratify the CTBT (China, Egypt, Iran, Israel, the U.S.), and three have yet to sign it (India, North Korea, Pakistan).

Dec. 13, 2001: The U.S. announced its intention to withdraw from the **ABM Treaty** in 180 days, arguing that it hindered the government in protecting itself from "future terrorist or rogue state missile attacks." Russia responded by withdrawing from START II, stating that U.S. withdrawal from the ABM Treaty effectively invalidated START II.

May 24, 2002: Strategic Offensive Reductions Treaty (SORT or Moscow Treaty) signed by the U.S. and Russia, entered into force June 1, 2003. Committed both countries to cutting nuclear arsenals to 1,700-2,200 warheads each by Dec. 31, 2012. SORT lapsed upon entry into force of the New START Treaty.

Apr. 8, 2010: New START Treaty signed by the U.S. and Russia, entered into force Feb. 5, 2011. It limits each country's arsenal of deployed strategic nuclear warheads to 1,550. Both countries agreed in Feb. 2021 to a five-year extension. In Feb. 2023, Russia announced the suspension of its participation in the treaty. It said it would continue to observe treaty limits on strategic offensive arms but no longer cooperate with inspections.

Major International Organizations

African Union (AU), inaugurated July 9, 2002, following disbanding of the Organization of African Unity (OAU). Africa's 55 countries make up its members. (Morocco withdrew in 1984 after the OAU admitted Western Sahara [Sahrawi Arab Dem. Rep.], a territory it claimed, but Morocco rejoined in 2017.) **Headquarters:** Addis Ababa, Ethiopia. **Website:** au.int

Asia-Pacific Economic Cooperation (APEC), founded Nov. 1989. Its 21 member economies are Australia, Brunei, Canada, Chile, China, Hong Kong, Indonesia, Japan, Malaysia, Mexico, New Zealand, Papua New Guinea, Peru, Philippines, Russia, Singapore, South Korea, Taiwan, Thailand, the U.S., and Vietnam. **Secretariat:** Singapore. **Website:** www.apec.org

Association of Southeast Asian Nations (ASEAN), formed Aug. 8, 1967. Its 10 members are Brunei, Cambodia, Indonesia, Laos, Malaysia, Myanmar, Philippines, Singapore, Thailand, and Vietnam. **Secretariat:** Jakarta, Indonesia. **Website:** asean.org

The Commonwealth, originally called the British Commonwealth of Nations, then the Commonwealth of Nations, in 1949, is an association of nations and dependencies, most part of the former British Empire. King Charles III, the current British monarch, is the symbolic head of the Commonwealth. The secretary-general is chosen by Commonwealth leaders.

There are 56 independent, sovereign nations in the Commonwealth as of Sept. 2023. Among them are the UK and 14 other nations, known as Commonwealth Realms, that recognize the British monarch as their head of state. **Secretariat:** London, UK. **Website:** thecommonwealth.org

Commonwealth of Independent States (CIS), established in Dec. 1991 as an alliance of former Soviet constituent republics. Its members are Armenia, Azerbaijan, Belarus, Kazakhstan, Kyrgyzstan, Moldova, Russia, Tajikistan, and Uzbekistan; Turkmenistan is an associate member. Georgia left the organization and Ukraine began to withdraw from CIS agreements following fighting with Russia over disputed territory. **Headquarters:** Minsk, Belarus. **Website:** cis.minsk.by

European Union (EU), known as the European Community (EC) until 1993. The Treaty on European Union (Maastricht Treaty) was signed on Feb. 7, 1992 (in effect Nov. 1993). As of Jan. 1, 1993, there has been a single market, with no restrictions on the movement of people, goods, services, and money, within the EU.

The EU has its origins in the European Coal and Steel Community (ECSC), European Economic Community (EEC, or Common Market), and European Atomic Energy Community (Euratom). A merger of the three communities' executives went into effect in 1967. As of Sept. 2023, there were 27 EU members: 11 of the 12 original members (Belgium, Denmark, France, Germany, Greece, Ireland, Italy, Luxembourg, Netherlands, Portugal, Spain); 3 that joined in 1995 (Austria, Finland, Sweden); 10 in 2004 (Cyprus, Czechia, Estonia, Hungary, Latvia, Lithuania, Malta, Poland, Slovakia, Slovenia); 2 in 2007 (Bulgaria, Romania); and 1 in 2013 (Croatia). The euro is the official currency in 20 of these 27 countries. Albania, Bosnia and Herzegovina, Moldova, Montenegro, North Macedonia,

Serbia, Turkey (Türkiye), and Ukraine were candidate countries. The UK, one of the original EU members, withdrew from the organization, Jan. 31, 2020, after UK citizens voted in favor of Brexit in 2016. **De facto capital:** Brussels, Belgium. **Website:** europa.eu

Group of Seven (G7), forum of major industrialized countries. France, Germany, Italy, Japan, the UK, and the U.S. first met in 1975 as the Group of Six. Canada joined in 1976. In 2014, group members boycotted a planned G8 summit in Russia (joined 1998) in condemnation of its annexation of Crimea. The EU is represented at summits. The **Group of Twenty (G20),** which first gathered in 1999, comprises 19 countries and the EU.

International Criminal Police Organization (INTERPOL), created 1923, is the world's largest intergovernmental police organization. There were 195 member nations as of Sept. 2023. **General Secretariat:** Lyon, France. **Website:** www.interpol.int

League of Arab States (Arab League), created Mar. 22, 1945. Its 22 members are Algeria, Bahrain, Comoros, Djibouti, Egypt, Iraq, Jordan, Kuwait, Lebanon, Libya, Mauritania, Morocco, Oman, Palestine (considered an independent state by the League), Qatar, Saudi Arabia, Somalia, Sudan, Syria (membership suspended since 2011), Tunisia, United Arab Emirates, and Yemen. **Headquarters:** Cairo, Egypt. **Website:** www.lasportal.org

North Atlantic Treaty Organization (NATO), created with the signing of what is popularly known as the Washington Treaty Apr. 4, 1949 (in effect Aug. 24, 1949). Its 31 members as of Sept. 2023 are Albania, Belgium, Bulgaria, Canada, Croatia, Czechia, Denmark, Estonia, Finland, France, Germany, Greece, Hungary, Iceland, Italy, Latvia, Lithuania, Luxembourg, Montenegro, Netherlands, North Macedonia, Norway, Poland, Portugal, Romania, Slovakia, Slovenia, Spain, Turkey (Türkiye), UK, and U.S. **Headquarters:** Brussels, Belgium. **Website:** www.nato.int

With the end of the Cold War in the early 1990s, members put greater stress on political action and on creating a force that could rapidly deploy to local crises. A NATO-led multinational force was deployed to help keep the peace in Bosnia and Herzegovina in 1995. In 1999, a force was deployed in Kosovo. NATO's first mission outside Europe was in Afghanistan in 2003.

Organization of American States (OAS), which describes itself as the world's oldest regional organization, was officially formed by the signing of a charter on Apr. 30, 1948. The OAS's 35 members are Antigua and Barbuda, Argentina, The Bahamas, Barbados, Belize, Bolivia, Brazil, Canada, Chile, Colombia, Costa Rica, Cuba, Dominica, Dominican Republic, Ecuador, El Salvador, Grenada, Guatemala, Guyana, Haiti, Honduras, Jamaica, Mexico, Nicaragua, Panama, Paraguay, Peru, St. Kitts and Nevis, St. Lucia, St. Vincent and the Grenadines, Suriname, Trinidad and Tobago, U.S., Uruguay, and Venezuela. **Headquarters:** Washington, DC. **Website:** www.oas.org

Organization for Economic Cooperation and Development (OECD), established Dec. 14, 1960. Its 38 members, as of Sept. 2023, are Australia, Austria, Belgium, Canada, Chile, Colombia, Costa Rica, Czechia, Denmark, Estonia, Finland, France, Germany, Greece, Hungary, Iceland, Ireland, Israel, Italy, Japan, Latvia, Lithuania, Luxembourg, Mexico, Netherlands, New Zealand, Norway, Poland, Portugal, Slovakia, Slovenia, South Korea, Spain, Sweden, Switzerland, Turkey, UK, and the U.S. Brazil, China, India, Indonesia, and South Africa are OECD key partners. **Headquarters:** Paris, France. **Website:** www.oecd.org

Organization of the Petroleum Exporting Countries (OPEC), created Sept. 14, 1960, by Iran, Iraq, Kuwait, Saudi Arabia, and Venezuela. In addition to the founding countries, members as of Sept. 2023 include Algeria, Angola, Congo Republic, Equatorial Guinea, Gabon, Libya, Nigeria, and United Arab Emirates. Indonesia, Qatar, and Ecuador are former members. **Secretariat/headquarters:** Vienna, Austria. **Website:** www.opec.org

Organization for Security and Cooperation in Europe (OSCE), established in 1972 by NATO and Warsaw Pact members. There were 57 member states from Europe, Central Asia, and North America as of Sept. 2023, making it the world's largest regional security organization. **Secretariat:** Vienna, Austria. **Website:** www.osce.org

United Nations

The 78th regular session of the UN General Assembly opened on Sept. 5, 2023, attended by delegates from 193 member states. The UN headquarters is located on 18 acres, considered international territory, in New York, NY.

Proposals to establish an organization for maintaining world peace led to the convening of the United Nations Conference on International Organization in San Francisco, Apr. 25-June 26, 1945, where the UN charter was drawn. It was signed June 26 by 50 nations and on Oct. 15 by Poland. It went into effect Oct. 24, 1945, upon ratification by the permanent members of the Security Council and a majority of the other signatories.

Purposes. To maintain international peace and security; to promote sustained economic growth and sustainable development; to achieve international cooperation in solving economic, social, cultural, and humanitarian problems; to protect human rights; and to advance justice and international law.

Visitors to the UN. Normally, the UN headquarters is open every day except New Year's Day, Good Friday, Eid al-Fitr, Memorial Day, Eid al-Adha, Independence Day, Labor Day, Thanksgiving, and Christmas. It is typically closed to the public during the UN general debate and for meetings of heads of state and government. Guided tours were temporarily suspended in Mar. 2020, when the UN closed its headquarters to the public because of the COVID-19 pandemic.

As of Sept. 2023, the UN offered a one-hour in-person guided tour or a virtual tour with a live guide to groups of up to 20-30 people. Specialty tours with a focus on art, architecture, or Black history, among other subjects, were also available. In addition, groups could book an online briefing with a UN expert. Children under 5 years of age are not permitted on tours; the UN offers a children's tour for ages 5-10. Guided tours at the UN's other headquarters—in Geneva, Switzerland; Vienna, Austria; and Nairobi, Kenya—are also available. For updates, visit the UN website. **Website:** www.un.org/visit

Six Main Organs of the United Nations

General Assembly. The General Assembly comprises representatives from all member nations. Each nation is entitled to one vote. The General Assembly meets in Sept. for an annual session; the Security Council or a majority of UN members can convoke a special session. Decisions on important issues, such as security, require a two-thirds majority of the General Assembly; a simple majority can decide other issues.

The General Assembly must approve the UN budget and apportion expenses among members. A member in arrears can lose its vote if the amount of arrears equals or exceeds the amount of the contributions due for the preceding two full years. **Website:** www.un.org/en/ga/

Security Council. The Security Council has primary responsibility within the UN for maintaining peace and security. It consists of 15 members, five of whom (China, France, Russia, United Kingdom, U.S.) have permanent seats. Ten are elected for two-year terms by the General Assembly. Nonpermanent members with terms expiring Dec. 31, 2023, are Albania, Brazil, Gabon, Ghana, and United Arab Emirates; those with terms expiring Dec. 31, 2024, are Ecuador, Japan, Malta, Mozambique, and Switzerland. Algeria, Guyana, Sierra Leone, Slovenia, and South Korea have been elected to two-year terms starting on Jan. 1, 2024.

Any UN member may participate in Council discussions at its invitation. Decisions on procedural questions are made by an affirmative vote of nine members. On all other matters the affirmative vote of nine members must include the concurring votes of all permanent members (giving them veto power).

The Security Council directs the various peacekeeping forces deployed throughout the world. **Website:** www.un.org/securitycouncil/

Secretariat. The Secretariat is responsible for the UN's day-to-day operations. It is headed by the secretary-general, who is appointed by the General Assembly, on the recommendation of the Security Council, for a five-year, renewable term. The secretary-general reports to the General Assembly and may bring to the attention of the Security Council any matter that threatens international peace. The Secretariat maintained an international staff of 35,762 as of Dec. 31, 2021. **Website:** www.un.org/en/about-us/secretariat

United Nations Secretaries General

Took office	Secretary, nation
1946	Trygve Lie, Norway
1953	Dag Hammarskjöld, Sweden
1961	U Thant, Burma (Myanmar)
1972	Kurt Waldheim, Austria
1982	Javier Pérez de Cuéllar, Peru
1992	Boutros Boutros-Ghali, Egypt
1997	Kofi Annan, Ghana
2007	Ban Ki-moon, South Korea
2017	António Guterres, Portugal

Economic and Social Council. ECOSOC consists of 54 members elected by the General Assembly to overlapping three-year terms. The council is responsible for economic, social, and environmental issues in relation to sustainable development. It conducts multiple substantive sessions throughout the year, meeting with policymakers, parliamentarians, academics, nongovernmental organizations, private-sector representatives, and youth. **Website:** www.un.org/ecosoc/

International Court of Justice (World Court). The International Court of Justice is the principal judicial organ of the UN. The Court has jurisdiction over cases that UN members or parties to the court's statute submit to it. In addition to rendering judgments, the Court issues advisory opinions.

The court's 15 judges are elected to nine-year terms by the General Assembly and the Security Council. No two judges may come from the same nation, and they should represent the world's principal legal systems. Once elected, the judges no longer act as representatives of a government. The Court remains permanently in session, except during vacations. All questions are decided by a majority. The International Court of Justice sits in The Hague, Netherlands. **Website:** www.icj-cij.org

Trusteeship Council. The Trusteeship Council, made up of the five permanent Security Council members, supervised the administration of UN trust territories. All 11 trust territories have since attained their right to self-determination. The Council formally suspended its work on Nov. 1, 1994, with Palau's independence.

The text of the **UN Charter** is online at www.un.org/en/about-us/un-charter/.

Ongoing UN Peacekeeping Missions, 2023

Source: Dept. of Peacekeeping Operations (DPKO), Dept. of Field Support, Dept. of Management; United Nations Secretariat
Unless otherwise noted, numbers are for peacekeeping operations only (not including political and peacebuilding missions) as of May 31, 2023. Year given in graphic is the year each mission started.

Uniformed personnel (troops, police, military observers, and staff officers)	75,384	Approved budget for July 1, 2023-June 30, 2024 (excl. UNTSO and UNMOGIP, financed by UN regular budget, and MINUSMA[1])	$6.1 bil
Countries contributing uniformed personnel	121	Peacekeeping operations since 1948	71
Civilian personnel (as of May 2018 except for MINUSCA, MINUSMA, UNIFIL, UNMISS, UNMOGIP, UNTSO as of 2021):	11,996	Total fatalities in all peace operations since 1948 (as of June 30, 2023)	4,314
Total personnel serving in 12 current peacekeeping operations	88,681	Est. total cost of operations, 1948 to June 30, 2010	$69 bil

Mali MINUSMA 2013-
Western Sahara MINURSO 1991-
Abyei, Sudan UNISFA 2011-
Kosovo UNMIK 1999-
Cyprus UNFICYP 1964-
Lebanon UNIFIL 1978-
Syria (Golan Heights) UNDOF 1974-
India & Pakistan UNMOGIP 1949-
Central African Rep. MINUSCA 2014-
Dem. Rep. of the Congo MONUSCO 2010-
South Sudan UNMISS 2011-
Egypt, Israel, Jordan, Lebanon, & Syria UNTSO 1948-

(1) The UN Security Council June 30, 2023, terminated MINUSMA's mandate. The UN authorized $590 mil in funding to support the mission until all personnel are withdrawn from Mali, by year-end 2023.

Roster of the United Nations

Listed below are the 193 members of the United Nations, with the years in which they were admitted (as of Sept. 2023). Vatican City (Holy See), Kosovo, and China (Taiwan)[1] are not members. Taiwan's repeated bids for UN membership have so far been unsuccessful. Palestine and Vatican City are non-member states of the UN with permanent observer status.

Member	Year	Member	Year	Member	Year	Member	Year
Afghanistan	1946	Dominica	1978	Libya	1955	Saint Vincent and the	
Albania	1955	Dominican Republic	1945	Liechtenstein	1990	Grenadines	1980
Algeria	1962	Ecuador	1945	Lithuania	1991	Samoa	1976
Andorra	1993	Egypt[4]	1945	Luxembourg	1945	San Marino	1992
Angola	1976	El Salvador	1945	Madagascar	1960	São Tomé and Príncipe	1975
Antigua and Barbuda	1981	Equatorial Guinea	1968	Malawi	1964	Saudi Arabia	1945
Argentina	1945	Eritrea	1993	Malaysia[7]	1957	Senegal	1960
Armenia	1992	Estonia	1991	Maldives	1965	Serbia[2,9]	2000
Australia	1945	Ethiopia	1945	Mali	1960	Seychelles	1976
Austria	1955	Fiji	1970	Malta	1964	Sierra Leone	1961
Azerbaijan	1992	Finland	1955	Marshall Islands	1991	Singapore[8]	1965
Bahamas, The	1973	France	1945	Mauritania	1961	Slovakia[3]	1993
Bahrain	1971	Gabon	1960	Mauritius	1968	Slovenia[2]	1992
Bangladesh	1974	Gambia, The	1965	Mexico	1945	Solomon Islands	1978
Barbados	1966	Georgia	1992	Micronesia, Fed. States	1991	Somalia	1960
Belarus	1945	Germany[5]	1973	Moldova	1992	South Africa[11]	1945
Belgium	1945	Ghana	1957	Monaco	1993	South Sudan[12]	2011
Belize	1981	Greece	1945	Mongolia	1961	Spain	1955
Benin	1960	Grenada	1974	Montenegro[2,8]	2006	Sri Lanka	1955
Bhutan	1971	Guatemala	1945	Morocco	1956	Sudan[12]	1956
Bolivia	1945	Guinea	1958	Mozambique	1975	Suriname	1975
Bosnia and		Guinea-Bissau	1974	Myanmar (Burma)	1948	Swaziland	1968
Herzegovina[2]	1992	Guyana	1966	Namibia	1990	Sweden	1946
Botswana	1966	Haiti	1945	Nauru	1999	Switzerland	2002
Brazil	1945	Honduras	1945	Nepal	1955	Syria[3]	1945
Brunei	1984	Hungary	1955	Netherlands	1945	Tajikistan	1992
Bulgaria	1955	Iceland	1946	New Zealand	1945	Tanzania[13]	1961
Burkina Faso	1960	India	1945	Nicaragua	1945	Thailand	1946
Burundi	1962	Indonesia[6]	1950	Niger	1960	Timor-Leste	2002
Cabo Verde	1975	Iran	1945	Nigeria	1960	Togo	1960
Cambodia	1955	Iraq	1945	North Macedonia[2,9]	1993	Tonga	1999
Cameroon	1960	Ireland	1955	Norway	1945	Trinidad and Tobago	1962
Canada	1945	Israel	1949	Oman	1971	Tunisia	1956
Central African Rep.	1960	Italy	1955	Pakistan	1947	Turkey (Türkiye)	1945
Chad	1960	Jamaica	1962	Palau	1994	Turkmenistan	1992
Chile	1945	Japan	1956	Panama	1945	Tuvalu	2000
China[1]	1945	Jordan	1955	Papua New Guinea	1975	Uganda	1962
Colombia	1945	Kazakhstan	1992	Paraguay	1945	Ukraine	1945
Comoros	1975	Kenya	1963	Peru	1945	United Arab Emirates	1971
Congo, Dem. Rep. of	1960	Kiribati	1999	Philippines	1945	United Kingdom	1945
Congo Republic	1960	Korea, North	1991	Poland	1945	United States	1945
Costa Rica	1945	Korea, South	1991	Portugal	1955	Uruguay	1945
Côte d'Ivoire	1960	Kuwait	1963	Qatar	1971	Uzbekistan	1992
Croatia[2]	1992	Kyrgyzstan	1992	Romania	1955	Vanuatu	1981
Cuba	1945	Laos	1955	Russia[10]	1945	Venezuela	1945
Cyprus	1960	Latvia	1991	Rwanda	1962	Vietnam	1977
Czechia[3]	1993	Lebanon	1945	Saint Kitts and Nevis	1983	Yemen[14]	1947
Denmark	1945	Lesotho	1966	Saint Lucia	1979	Zambia	1964
Djibouti	1977	Liberia	1945			Zimbabwe	1980

(1) The General Assembly (GA) voted in 1971 to expel the Chinese government in Taiwan and admit the government in Beijing. (2) The Socialist Federal Republic of Yugoslavia was an original UN member. After four of its six republics (Bosnia and Herzegovina, Croatia, Macedonia, and Slovenia) declared independence in 1991-92, the two remaining republics, Montenegro and Serbia, reconstituted as the Federal Republic of Yugoslavia. They sought to take over the former Yugoslavia's UN seat in 1992 but were expelled a few months later by GA vote. The Federal Republic of Yugoslavia was granted membership in 2000. In 2003, the country changed its name to Serbia and Montenegro. (3) Czechoslovakia, an original UN member from 1945 to 1992, was succeeded by both the Czech Republic and Slovakia in 1993. (4) Egypt and Syria were original UN members. In 1958, Egypt and Syria established the United Arab Republic and continued under a single UN membership. In 1961, Syria resumed separate membership following independence. (5) The Federal Republic of Germany and the German Democratic Republic became UN members in 1973. In 1990, the two formed one sovereign state. (6) Withdrew from the UN in 1965; rejoined in 1966. (7) The Federation of Malaya joined the UN in 1957. In 1963, it changed its name to Malaysia following the accession of Singapore, Sabah, and Sarawak. Singapore became an independent UN member in 1965. (8) After Montenegro declared independence in 2006, the Republic of Serbia continued Serbia and Montenegro's UN membership. Montenegro was admitted to the UN as the Republic of Montenegro the same month. (9) Admitted to the UN under the provisional name of the former Yugoslav Republic of Macedonia. Under the terms of an agreement with Greece in force Feb. 12, 2019, the country changed its name to the Republic of North Macedonia. (10) The USSR was an original UN member. After the USSR's dissolution in 1991, Russia informed the UN it would continue the Soviet Union's membership in the Security Council and all other UN organs with the support of the Commonwealth of Independent States (comprising most of the former Soviet republics). (11) Readmitted in 1994. Its delegation had been suspended from participation in 1974 because of apartheid. (12) The Republic of South Sudan seceded from the Republic of the Sudan in 2011 and was admitted to the UN the same year. (13) Tanganyika (UN member from 1961) and Zanzibar (member from 1963), merged in 1964 to form the United Republic of Tanganyika and Zanzibar, later renamed the United Republic of Tanzania. It continued a single UN membership. (14) The Yemen Arab Republic was admitted in 1947; the People's Democratic Republic of Yemen in 1967. In 1990, the two nations formed the Republic of Yemen.

U.S. Representatives to the United Nations, 1946-2023

The U.S. Permanent Representative to the United Nations is head of the U.S. Mission to the UN in New York. He or she is appointed by the president and confirmed by the Senate. Year given is the year each took office.

Year	Representative	Year	Representative	Year	Representative	Year	Representative
1946	Edward R. Stettinius Jr.	1971	George H. W. Bush	1992	Edward J. Perkins	2005	John R. Bolton
1946	Herschel V. Johnson[1]	1973	John A. Scali	1993	Madeleine K. Albright	2006	Alejandro D. Wolff[1]
1947	Warren R. Austin	1975	Daniel P. Moynihan	1997	Bill Richardson	2007	Zalmay M. Khalilzad
1953	Henry Cabot Lodge Jr.	1976	William W. Scranton	1998	A. Peter Burleigh[1]	2009	Susan E. Rice
1960	James J. Wadsworth	1977	Andrew Young	1999	Richard C. Holbrooke	2013	Samantha Power
1961	Adlai E. Stevenson	1979	Donald McHenry	2001	James B. Cunningham[1]	2017	Nikki R. Haley
1965	Arthur J. Goldberg	1981	Jeane J. Kirkpatrick	2001	John D. Negroponte	2019	Jonathan R. Cohen[1]
1968	George W. Ball	1985	Vernon A. Walters	2004	John C. Danforth	2019	Kelly Craft
1968	James Russell Wiggins	1989	Thomas R. Pickering	2005	Anne W. Patterson[1]	2021	Linda Thomas-Greenfield
1969	Charles W. Yost						

(1) Acting.

International Criminal Court

The International Criminal Court (ICC) was created when 120 nations signed the Rome Statute on July 17, 1998. Its mission is to try individuals accused of genocide, war crimes, and crimes against humanity, which was undertaken in the past by temporary tribunals. The statute came into force on July 1, 2002. As of Sept. 2023, 123 nations were state parties to the Rome Statute of the ICC. China, Russia, and the U.S. are among those countries that have not yet signed or ratified the treaty.

The ICC, unlike the International Court of Justice (World Court), is not part of the UN. It is an independent international agency with its own administration and budget, which is made up of funds from member states and voluntary contributions by other institutions, international groups, individuals, and corporations. It consists of 18 judges elected by state parties to nine-year, nonrenewable terms. An absolute majority of these 18 judges elect 3 from among themselves to serve as president and first and second vice presidents. A Registry handles the nonjudicial aspects of administration. The Office of the Prosecutor reviews, investigates, and prosecutes cases referred to it by a state or by the UN Security Council.

As of Sept. 2023, 31 cases had been brought before the ICC. The Office of the Prosecutor was investigating situations in Afghanistan, Bangladesh/Myanmar (Burma), Burundi, Central African Republic, Côte d'Ivoire, Dem. Rep. of the Congo, Georgia, Kenya, Libya, Mali, Palestine, the Philippines, Sudan (Darfur), Uganda, Ukraine, and Venezuela. The court issued its first-ever conviction in 2012, when it found the warlord Thomas Lubanga Dyilo guilty of war crimes for his use of child soldiers in the Dem. Rep. of the Congo. In Mar. 2023, the ICC issued arrest warrants for Russian pres. Vladimir Putin and another Russian government official for the alleged war crime of unlawful deportation and transfer of children from occupied Ukraine to Russia.

Though jurisdiction is limited to member nations, the ICC is a court of last resort. It may also initiate cases involving non-member nations if it deems the country's authorities have not taken steps to investigate or prosecute a case. The ICC is headquartered in The Hague, Netherlands, though it may sit elsewhere.

Website: www.icc-cpi.int

Geneva Conventions

The Geneva Conventions are four international treaties governing the protection of civilians and medical and religious personnel in times of war, the treatment of prisoners of war, and the care of the wounded and sick in the armed forces. The first convention, covering the sick and wounded in war, was concluded in Geneva, Switzerland, in 1864, at a conference convened by the Swiss government at the urging of the International Committee of the Red Cross. The convention was amended and expanded in 1906. In 1929, two more conventions covering the wounded and prisoners of war were signed. Outrage at the treatment of prisoners and civilians during WWII by some belligerents, notably Germany and Japan, prompted the conclusion, on Aug. 12, 1949, of four new conventions. Three of these restated and strengthened the previous conventions.

The fourth Geneva Convention of 1949 codified general principles of international law governing the treatment of civilians in wartime, with special safeguards for wounded persons, children under 15 years of age, pregnant women, and the elderly. Discrimination on racial, religious, national, or political grounds was forbidden. Torture, collective punishment, unwarranted destruction of property, and forced use of civilians for an occupier's armed forces were prohibited. Also included was a pledge for the humane treatment, adequate feeding, and delivery of supplies to prisoners. Two additional protocols, adopted in June 1977, increased protections for victims of international and non-international armed conflicts (e.g., civil wars). (A third protocol, adopted in 2005, created the Red Crystal emblem for use along with the Red Cross and Red Crescent.)

Nearly all countries have formally accepted all or most international humanitarian law as binding. However, there is no permanent international machinery in place to enforce these treaties.

Genocide

Source: Convention on the Prevention and Punishment of the Crime of Genocide, United Nations Treaty Series 277; Rome Statute of the International Criminal Court (ICC)

The term "genocide" (which combines Greek and Latin roots to mean "murder of a race") was coined by Polish-Jewish lawyer Raphael Lemkin in 1944 to describe the intentional or attempted destruction of a national, ethnic, racial, or religious group. Genocide is defined as killing members of a group, causing serious bodily harm to members of a group, or otherwise attempting to bring about a group's destruction, including efforts to prevent births or transfer children away from a group. Although the legal definition of genocide does not extend to political groups, the term is often used colloquially to refer to large-scale political violence.

The prohibition against genocide is part of customary international law and is codified in the Convention on the Prevention and Punishment of the Crime of Genocide, which entered into force on Jan. 12, 1951. As of Sept. 2023, 153 nations, including the U.S., were parties to it. Genocide is also prohibited by the domestic laws of many nations.

The first modern trials for genocide were conducted by the Allies after WWII. Although the charter of the Nuremberg Tribunal—the international court set up to try Nazi war criminals—did not use the term genocide, its definition of "crimes against humanity" included persecution on racial or religious grounds. More recently, the UN Security Council created ad hoc tribunals to try those responsible for genocide and other serious crimes in former Yugoslavia and in Rwanda. The ICC also has jurisdiction to try perpetrators. Sudanese Pres. Omar Hassan al-Bashir is the first person the ICC has charged with the crime of genocide, for the violence in Darfur against the Fur, Masalit, and Zaghawa people. Bashir was deposed in Apr. 2019 and remained detained in Sudan as of mid-2023. The ICC's first Darfur-related trial, which opened in Apr. 2022 with former Janjaweed commander Ali Muhammad Ali Abd-Al-Rahman (Ali Kushayb) as defendant, was ongoing.

UN investigators recommended in 2018 that Myanmar's top military leaders be tried on charges including genocide of the country's Rohingya population. The ICC in 2019 authorized an investigation into the situation. At least 6,700 Rohingya are estimated to have been killed by armed government forces in Aug.-Sept. 2017.

Examples of Genocides Since 1900

Year	Event	Location	Est. deaths
1915	Extermination of Armenians by the nationalist Young Turks	Turkey/Ottoman Empire	1,000,000+
1930s	Intentional infliction of famine on Ukraine	Soviet Union (Ukraine)	6,000,000-7,000,000
1933-45	Attempted destruction of European Jewry (Holocaust)	Europe	6,000,000
1939-45	Attempted destruction of European Roma	Europe	250,000-500,000
1975-79	Khmer Rouge campaign of extermination under Pol Pot[1]	Cambodia	1,500,000-2,000,000
1981-83	Army and paramilitary killings of indigenous Mayan during civil war	Guatemala	200,000+
1988	Anfal Campaign (named by the Iraqi government) against Iraqi Kurds	Iraq	100,000-200,000
1992-95	Ethnic killings during the breakup of Yugoslavia, chiefly Serbs against Bosnian Muslims (known as Bosniaks)	Bosnia-Herzegovina, Serbia, Croatia	200,000
1994	Hutu massacre of Tutsis	Rwanda	800,000
2003-present	Govt. forces and govt.-backed Arab militia (Janjaweed) attacks on non-Arab southern tribes, mainly Fur, Masalit, Zaghawa[2]	Darfur region, Sudan	300,000-600,000
2014-19	Self-proclaimed Islamic State (ISIS) against Yazidi, Christian, and Shia Muslim population	Iraq, Syria	5,000+

Note: Ests. based on historical evidence. The legal definition of "genocide" does not include politically motivated mass killings. Therefore, instances of mass violence against political or class enemies, such as Josef Stalin's purges of some 20 mil Soviets in the 1930s, and Mao Zedong's Cultural Revolution, which killed several million Chinese, are not included. (1) Though many of the murders committed by the Khmer Rouge regime were politically or class motivated, Nov. 2018, found two senior officials guilty of genocide of Vietnamese in Cambodia and the Cham ethnic group. (2) In 2005, a UN commission concluded that although the "international offenses ... that have been committed in Darfur may be no less serious and heinous than genocide," it did not term the situation a genocide.

NATIONS OF THE WORLD

As of mid-2023, there were **196 nations** in the world. This number includes three nations that are not United Nations (UN) members—Kosovo, Taiwan, and Vatican City (Holy See). Certain regions and territories can be found under the entry for their governing nation. **Sources:** FAOSTAT and AQUASTAT, Food and Agric. Org. of the UN (FAO); Global Health Observatory and Coronavirus (COVID-19) Dashboard, World Health Organization (WHO); Intl. Data Base, U.S. Census Bureau, U.S. Dept. of Commerce; Energy Information Administration, U.S. Dept. of Energy; *International Financial Statistics*, Intl. Monetary Fund (IMF); Joint UN Programme on HIV/AIDS (UNAIDS); ILOSTAT, International Labour Organization; *The Military Balance*, Intl. Inst. for Strategic Studies; *Oil & Gas Journal*, Endeavor Business Media; *International Migrant Stock* and *World Urbanization Prospects*, Population Div., UN Dept. of Economic and Social Affairs; UN Educational, Scientific, and Cultural Org. (UNESCO); UNWTO World Tourism Barometer © World Tourism Org.; U.S. Dept. of State; Wards Intelligence, a div. of Informa; The World Bank; *The World Factbook*, Central Intelligence Agency (CIA); Gina A. Zurlo, ed., *World Religion Database* (Leiden/Boston: Brill, July 2023); World Telecommunication/ICT Indicators Database, Intl. Telecommunication Union; Xe.com.

Note: Because of rounding or incomplete enumeration, percentages may not add up to 100%. FY = Fiscal year. NA = Not available/applicable. Figures are for years noted below unless otherwise indicated within a country's profile. **Population, age distrib.,** and **pop. density** are mid-2023 ests. **Growth** gives the avg. annual percent change in the pop. resulting from **births** and **deaths** at midyear 2023 as well as the flow of migrants into and out of a country. International **migrants,** including foreign-born citizens and refugees, as a percent of the total pop. is for mid-2020. Percent of total pop. living in **urban** areas, as defined by each country, are projections for mid-2023. **Ethnic groups** are given in descending order of size; data are most recent available. **Languages** are ranked with those most widely spoken listed first. **Arable land** is given as percentage of country's land area. Pop. of **capitals** and **cities** are projected ests. for urban agglomerations as of mid-2018 or mid-2023. **Defense budget** and **active troops** are for 2022. Selected **industries** are ranked by descending value of annual output. Selected **chief agric.** products are listed in descending order of importance by annual tonnage. Total renewable **water** resources per inhabitant is for 2020. Reserves of **crude oil** (incl. lease condensate) are as of Jan. 1, 2021; countries without this entry lack reserves. **Electricity prod.** indicates net, not gross, generated in 2021. **Labor force** percentages are latest available; **unemployment** (percentage of total labor force age 15 and older currently available for and seeking work) are 2022 ests. **Monetary unit** exchange rate is as of Aug. 28, 2023. **GDP** and **per capita GDP,** 2022 ests., are based on purchasing power parity exchange rates; **GDP growth** is annual percent change between 2021 and 2022. Value of **imports** and **exports,** calculated on an exchange rate basis, are from 2021; 2019 trade partners are listed in descending order of importance by percentage of total dollar value. **Tourism** is 2021 receipts from intl. visitors; data not available for all countries. **Budget** calculated on an exchange rate basis, not purchasing power parity terms, is 2019 expenditures. **Inflation** is measured by the percent change in the consumer price index (or avg. consumer cost for certain goods and services) between 2021 and 2022. Total length of a country's **railway** network is the latest available. **Motor vehicle** statistics, for cars and comm. vehicles in operation based on registrations, are for 2022. The number of **airports** with paved, usable runways are latest available. Number of **mobile-cellular** telephone subscriptions offering voice communications and active mobile-**broadband** subscriptions are for 2022. Percentage of pop. accessing the **internet,** regardless of device used, are for 2021 or 2022. Current health **expend.** (both government and private) is given as a percentage of GDP in 2020. **Life expect.** is in avg. number of years at birth for persons born in 2023. **Infant mortality** measures the probability of a child dying between birth and exact age 1 in 2023. **Undernourished,** the prevalence of undernourishment, is the proportion of the population in 2020-22 whose habitual food consumption is insufficient for an active, healthy life. **HIV** prevalence is the percentage of a country's pop. of 15- to 49-year-olds living with HIV in 2022. **COVID-19** data were reported to WHO as of Aug. 16, 2023 (cases/deaths) or Aug. 20, 2023 (vaccinations); all figures subject to continuous verification and change. Vaccinated data include those who received a complete primary series of any COVID vaccine. **Education** and **literacy** rate ests. are latest available. Literacy measures the percent of the pop. age 15 and older able to read and write simple statements; some countries define as literate those who have completed certain schooling. Current events as of Oct. 1, 2023.

See pages 489-504 for full-color maps and flags of all nations.

Afghanistan
Islamic Emirate of Afghanistan

People: Population: 39,232,003 (37). **Age distrib.:** <15: 39.8%; 65+: 2.9%. **Growth:** 2.3%. **Migrants:** 0.4%. **Pop. density:** 155.8 per sq mi, 60.2 per sq km. **Urban:** 26.9%. **Ethnic groups:** Pashtun, Tajik, Hazara, Uzbek; smaller numbers of 10 other constitutionally recognized ethnic groups. **Languages:** Afghan Persian or Dari, Pashto (both official); Uzbeki, English, Turkmani, Urdu. **Religions:** Muslim 99.9% (Sunni [official] 89%, Shia 11%).

Geography: Total area: 251,827 sq mi, 652,230 sq km (41); **Land area:** 251,827 sq mi, 652,230 sq km. **Location:** SW Asia, NW of Indian subcontinent. Pakistan on E, S; Iran on W; Turkmenistan, Uzbekistan, Tajikistan on N. NE tip touches China. **Topography:** Landlocked and mountainous, much of it over 4,000 ft above sea level. The Hindu Kush Mts. tower 16,000 ft above Kabul and reach a height of 25,000 ft to the E. Dry climate with extreme temperatures; large desert regions. **Arable land:** 12.0%. **Capital:** Kabul, 4,588,666. **Cities:** Herat, 695,043; Mazar-e Sharif, 624,500; Kandahar, 542,565.

Government: Type: Theocratic; U.S. does not recognize the Taliban govt. **Head of state and govt.:** Taliban leader Haibatullah Akhundzada. **Local divisions:** 34 provinces. **Defense budget:** NA. **Active troops:** 100,000 (Taliban).

Economy: Industries: small-scale prod. of bricks, textiles, soap, furniture, shoes, fertilizer, apparel, food prods. **Chief agric.:** wheat, milk, grapes, vegetables, potatoes, watermelons. **Natural resources:** nat. gas, petroleum, coal, copper, chromite, talc, barites, sulfur, lead, zinc, iron ore, salt, prec./semiprec. stones. **Water:** 1,678 cu m per capita. **Electricity prod.:** 829.1 mil kWh. **Labor force:** agric. 46.0%, industry 18.5%, services 35.5%. **Unemployment** (2020): 11.77%.

Finance: Monetary unit: Afghani (AFN) (82.53 = $1 U.S.). **GDP** (2021): $67.1 bil; **per capita GDP** (2021): $1,674; **GDP growth** (2021): –20.7%. **Imports** (2020): $7.0 bil; (2021) UAE 23%, Pakistan 17%, India 13%, China 9%, Uzbekistan 7%. **Exports** (2020): $1.5 bil (not incl. illicit exports); UAE 45%, Pakistan 24%, India 22%. **Tourism** (2020): $65 mil. **Budget:** $5.3 bil. **Inflation** (2018-19): 2.3%.

Transport: Motor vehicles: 44.7 per 1,000 pop. **Airports:** 29. **Communications: Mobile** (2021): 56.6 per 100 pop. **Broadband** (2021): 18.5 per 100 pop. **Internet** (2021): 18.4%.

Health: Expend. (2021): 16.8%. **Life expect.:** 52.5 male; 55.7 female. **Births:** 34.8 per 1,000 pop. **Deaths:** 12.1 per 1,000 pop. **Infant mortality:** 103.1 per 1,000 pop. **Undernourished:** 30.1%. **HIV:** <0.1%. **COVID-19:** 224,853 cases, 7,942 deaths; rates per 100,000: 577.6 cases, 20.4 deaths. 43.6% vaccinated.

Education: Compulsory: ages 7-15. **Literacy:** 37.3%.

Website: moj.gov.af/en/ or www.state.gov/countries-areas/afghanistan/

Afghanistan, occupying a favored invasion route since antiquity, has been variously known as Ariana or Bactria (in ancient times) and Khorasan (in the Middle Ages). Foreign empires alternated rule with local emirs and kings until the 18th cent., when a unified kingdom was established. In 1973, a military coup ushered in a republic.

Pro-Soviet leftists took power in a bloody 1978 coup. In Dec. 1979 the USSR began a massive airlift into Kabul and backed a new coup, leading to the installation of a more pro-Soviet leader. Soviet forces fanned out over Afghanistan and waged a protracted guerrilla war against Muslim rebels (aided by the U.S.); some 15,000 Soviet troops reportedly died.

A UN-mediated agreement was signed Apr. 14, 1988, providing for withdrawal of Soviet troops, a neutral Afghan state, and repatriation of refugees. Afghan rebels rejected the pact. The Soviets completed their troop withdrawal Feb. 15, 1989; fighting between Afghan rebels and government forces ensued. Communist Pres. Najibullah resigned Apr. 16, 1992, as competing guerrilla forces advanced on Kabul. The rebels achieved power Apr. 28. More than 2 mil Afghans had been killed, and 6 mil had left the country since 1979.

Clashes between moderates and Islamic fundamentalist forces followed the rebel victory. The Taliban, an insurgent radical-Islamist faction, captured Kabul in Sept. 1996 and empowered religious police to enforce strict Islamic codes of dress and behavior.

Victories in the north, Aug. 1998, essentially gave the Taliban control over the entire country. On Aug. 20, 1998, U.S. cruise missiles struck SE of Kabul, hitting facilities the U.S. said were terrorist training camps run by al-Qaeda leader Osama bin Laden.

After the Sept. 11, 2001, attacks on the World Trade Center and Pentagon, the U.S., blaming bin Laden, demanded that the Taliban surrender him and shut down his al-Qaeda terrorist network. When the Taliban refused, the U.S., with British assistance, began bombing Afghanistan Oct. 7, and sent in ground troops as part of Operation Enduring Freedom (OEF).

Supported by the U.S., the opposition Northern Alliance captured Kabul in Nov.; Taliban forces abandoned Kandahar, their last stronghold, to southern tribal fighters Dec. 7. A power-sharing agreement signed by four anti-Taliban factions, including the Northern Alliance, provided for an interim government headed by Hamid Karzai, a Pashtun tribal leader.

A new constitution, approved in Jan. 2004, included protections for women's rights denied under Taliban rule. Karzai won the Oct. 9, 2004, presidential election.

Although the U.S. announced the end of major combat operations in Afghanistan, May 1, 2003, resistance continued. NATO officially assumed control of peacekeeping forces—the Intl. Security Assistance Force (ISAF)—Aug. 11, 2003.

The most intense fighting in more than 4 years erupted Mar. 2006 with a new wave of attacks and other strikes by Taliban insurgents. Operating from sanctuaries in Pakistan, Islamist suicide bombers and Taliban insurgents stepped up their activities, 2007-11. Karzai was sworn in for a second term Nov. 19, 2009.

Ending a decade-long manhunt, U.S. commandos killed bin Laden shortly after midnight May 2, 2011, in Abbottabad, Pakistan. Ayman al-Zawahiri, who helped plan the Sept. 11 and other attacks on the U.S., succeeded bin Laden as head of al-Qaeda.

Between Jan. 2009 and June 2011, the number of U.S. troops in Afghanistan rose from about 36,000 to 101,000, while the number of allied foreign forces under ISAF increased from nearly 32,000 to more than 42,000. The U.S., June 22, 2011, outlined a timetable for drawing down troops and ending their combat role, with a residual force focusing on combating Islamic extremists and training and advising Afghan troops. OEF and ISAF officially ended Dec. 28, 2014; since Oct. 2001, 2,215 U.S. and 1,270 allied troops had been killed. The NATO-led Resolute Support Mission (RSM) to aid Afghan forces began Jan. 1, 2015.

A June 14, 2014, presidential runoff election was marred by allegations of electoral fraud. Ashraf Ghani Ahmadzai was declared the winner Sept. 21. Fighting between government and Taliban forces continued. Beginning in 2014, an affiliate of the Sunni extremist group ISIS was active in eastern Afghanistan. Following the death of his predecessor in a 2016 U.S. drone strike, Haibatullah Akhundzada became head of the Taliban.

A U.S. report estimated that, in late 2018, the government effectively controlled only about half of the country's districts. Ghani won a Sept. 28, 2019, presidential election. U.S. intelligence officials concluded, by early 2020, that Russia had paid bounties to Taliban-linked forces to kill U.S. and allied troops.

Combat, including airstrikes, and terrorist attacks caused high civilian casualties. The UN reported over 26,000 conflict-related civilian deaths, Jan. 2014-June 2021.

Under a U.S.-Taliban bilateral agreement signed Feb. 29, 2020, in return for a Taliban pledge that Afghanistan would not be a base for anti-U.S. terrorism, the U.S. pledged to withdraw its troops (then about 12,000). U.S. Pres. Joe Biden announced, Apr. 14, 2021, that withdrawal of the remaining 2,500-3,500 U.S. troops would begin May 1, to be completed by Sept. Remaining non-U.S. RSM forces also began withdrawing May 1.

Direct Taliban-Afghan government talks began in Qatar, Sept. 12, 2020, but made little progress, and the Taliban stepped up its attacks. With the U.S. withdrawal nearing completion in mid-2021, Taliban offensives rapidly captured provinces and major cities nationwide. Taliban forces entered and effectively took control of Kabul, Aug. 15, and Ghani fled the country.

The U.S. sent thousands of troops to evacuate people from Kabul's airport. By the time U.S. and coalition-partner flights ended Aug. 30 and the last U.S. troops left, about 123,000 civilians had been evacuated, including 6,000 Americans, other foreign nationals, and Afghans who had assisted the U.S. and its allies since 2001. As thousands of Afghans seeking (often unsuccessfully) to leave gathered outside the airport, an ISIS suicide bombing, Aug. 26, resulted in the deaths of 13 U.S. troops and some 170 others.

The new Taliban government severely limited women's rights—including restricting access to education, work opportunities, public places, and travel and imposing dress codes—as well as other freedoms. The U.S. and many other nations did not recognize the Taliban government; foreign aid fell (though some humanitarian aid through NGOs continued). Drought and aid cuts contributed to a humanitarian crisis, aggravated by a prohibition on Afghan women working in NGOs. As of mid-2023, more than 15 mil Afghans faced food insecurity. As of June 30, 2023, the UNHCR estimated that more than 1.6 mil Afghans had become refugees in neighboring countries since Aug. 2021.

A U.S. drone strike, July 31, 2022, killed al-Qaeda leader al-Zawahiri in Kabul.

Albania
Republic of Albania

People: Population: 3,101,621 (135). **Age distrib.:** <15: 17.9%; 65+: 14.6%. **Growth:** 0.2%. **Migrants:** 1.7%. **Pop. density:** 293.2 per sq mi, 113.2 per sq km. **Urban:** 64.6%. **Ethnic groups:** Albanian 82.6%. **Languages:** Albanian (official). **Religions:** Muslim 58.5% (Sunni 54%, Shia 4%), Christian 38.6% (Orthodox 18.6%, Catholic 18.4%), agnostic 2.2%.

Geography: Total area: 11,100 sq mi, 28,748 sq km (141). **Land area:** 10,578 sq mi, 27,398 sq km. **Location:** SE Europe, on SE coast of Adriatic Sea. Greece on S; Montenegro, Kosovo on N; North Macedonia on E. **Topography:** Narrow coastal plain; hills and mountains covered with scrub forest, cut by small E-W rivers. **Arable land:** 21.9%. **Capital:** Tirana, 520,059.

Government: Type: Parliamentary republic. **Head of state:** Pres. Bajram Begaj; b. 1967; in office: July 24, 2022. **Head of govt.:** Prime Min. Edi Rama; b. 1964; in office: Sept. 15, 2013. **Local divisions:** 12 counties. **Defense budget:** $286 mil. **Active troops:** 7,500.

Economy: Industries: food, footwear, apparel, clothing, lumber. **Chief agric.:** milk, maize, tomatoes, potatoes, watermelons, wheat. **Natural resources:** petroleum, nat. gas, coal, bauxite, chromite, copper, iron ore, nickel, salt, timber, hydropower. **Water:** 10,494 cu m per capita. **Crude oil reserves:** 150 mil bbls. **Electricity prod.:** 9.0 bil kWh. **Labor force:** agric. 34.6%, industry 21.6%, services 43.8%. **Unemployment:** 11.8%.

Finance: Monetary unit: Lek (ALL) (101.46 = $1 U.S.). **GDP:** $51.5 bil; **per capita GDP:** $18,552; **GDP growth:** 4.8%. **Imports:** $8.0 bil; Italy 28%, Greece 12%, China 11%, Turkey 9%. **Exports:** $5.6 bil; Italy 45%, Spain 8%, Germany 6%. **Tourism:** $2.3 bil. **Budget:** $4.5 bil. **Inflation:** 6.7%.

Transport: Railways: 263 mi. **Airports:** 3.

Communications: Mobile: 97.9 per 100 pop. **Broadband:** 75.3 per 100 pop. **Internet:** 82.6%.

Health: Expend.: NA. **Life expect.:** 77.0 male; 82.6 female. **Births:** 12.5 per 1,000 pop. **Deaths:** 7.4 per 1,000 pop. **Infant mortality:** 10.5 per 1,000 live births. **Undernourished:** 4.1%. **HIV:** <0.1%. **COVID-19:** 334,090 cases, 3,604 deaths; rates per 100,000: 11,609.2 cases, 125.2 deaths. 44.8% vaccinated.

Education: Compulsory: ages 6-14. **Literacy:** 98.5%.

Website: www.kryeministria.al

Ancient Illyria was conquered by Romans, Slavs, and Turks (15th cent.); the Turks Islamized the population. Independent Albania was proclaimed in 1912. Italy invaded in 1939.

Communist partisans took over in 1944 and allied Albania with the USSR but broke with the USSR in 1960 over de-Stalinization. Billions of dollars in Chinese financial assistance was cut off in 1978 when Albania attacked China's policies. Large-scale purges of officials occurred during the 1970s.

Enver Hoxha, the nation's ruler for four decades, died Apr. 11, 1985. The new regime introduced some liberalization.

Albania's former Communists were routed in elections Mar. 1992, amid economic collapse and social unrest. Sali Berisha was elected as the first non-Communist president since WWII. Berisha's party claimed a landslide victory in disputed parliamentary elections, May 26 and June 2, 1996. Public protests over the collapse of fraudulent investment schemes in Jan. 1997 led to armed rebellion. The UN Security Council, Mar. 28, authorized a 7,000-member force to restore order. Socialists and their allies won parliamentary elections, June 29 and July 6, 1997.

During NATO's air war against Yugoslavia, Mar.-June 1999, Albania hosted some 465,000 Kosovar refugees. A pro-Berisha coalition victory in July 3, 2005, elections ended eight years of Socialist rule. Albania became a full member of NATO Apr. 1, 2009. Socialists won June 23, 2013, parliamentary elections, and Edi Rama became prime min. The Socialists won June 25, 2017, elections; in the campaign, Rama pledged to reduce organized crime and political corruption, key issues for EU membership. Rama's Socialists won Apr. 25, 2021, parliamentary elections. EU membership negotiations began, July 19, 2022.

Algeria
People's Democratic Republic of Algeria

People: Population: 44,758,398 (34). **Age distrib.:** <15: 31.0%; 65+: 6.7%. **Growth:** 1.3%. **Migrants:** 0.6%. **Pop. density:** 48.7 per sq mi, 18.8 per sq km. **Urban:** 75.3%. **Ethnic groups:** Arab-Berber 99%. **Languages:** Arabic (official), French (lingua franca), Berber or Tamazight (official), Berber dialects. **Religions:** Muslim 98.2% (Sunni [official]).

Geography: Total area: 919,595 sq mi, 2,381,740 sq km (10). **Land area:** 919,595 sq mi, 2,381,740 sq km. **Location:** NW Africa, from Medit. Sea into Sahara. Morocco, Western Sahara on W; Mauritania, Mali, Niger on S; Libya, Tunisia on E. **Topography:** The Tell, on the coast, comprises fertile plains 50-100 mi wide with a moderate climate and adequate rain. Two major chains of Atlas Mts., running roughly E-W and reaching 7,000 ft, enclose a dry plateau region. The Sahara lies below. **Arable land:** 3.2%. **Capital:** Algiers, 2,901,810. **Cities:** Oran, 935,947.

Government: Type: Presidential republic. **Head of state:** Pres. Abdelmadjid Tebboune; b. 1945; in office: Dec. 12, 2019. **Head of govt.:** Prime Min. Ayman Benabderrahmane; b. 1966; in office: June 30, 2021. **Local divisions:** 58 provinces. **Defense budget:** $8.9 bil. **Active troops:** 139,000.

Economy: Industries: petroleum, nat. gas, light industries, mining, electrical, petrochemical, food proc. **Chief agric.:** potatoes, wheat, milk, watermelons, barley, onions. **Natural resources:** petroleum, nat. gas, iron ore, phosphates, uranium, lead, zinc. **Water:** 266 cu m per capita. **Crude oil reserves:** 12.2 bil bbls. **Electricity prod.:** 77.5 bil kWh. **Labor force:** agric. 10.3%, industry 31.0%, services 58.6%. **Unemployment:** 11.6%.

Finance: Monetary unit: Dinar (DZD) (136.80 = $1 U.S.). **GDP:** $593.2 bil; **per capita GDP:** $13,210; **GDP growth:** 3.1%. **Imports:** $44.3 bil; China 18%, France 14%, Italy 8%, Spain 8%. **Exports:** $41.8 bil; Italy 13%, France 13%, Spain 12%, U.S. 7%, UK 7%. **Tourism:** $73 mil. **Budget:** $64.7 bil. **Inflation:** 9.3%.

Transport: Railways: 2,498 mi. **Motor vehicles:** 134.4 per 1,000 pop. **Airports:** 67.

Communications: Mobile: 109.2 per 100 pop. **Broadband:** 99.7 per 100 pop. **Internet:** 70.8%.

Health: Expend.: 6.3%. **Life expect.:** 77.0 male; 78.6 female. **Births:** 20.9 per 1,000 pop. **Deaths:** 4.4 per 1,000 pop. **Infant mortality:** 18.8 per 1,000 live births. **Undernourished:** <2.5%. **HIV:** <0.1%. **COVID-19:** 271,852 cases, 6,881 deaths; rates per 100,000: 619.9 cases, 15.7 deaths. 14.8% vaccinated.

Education: Compulsory: ages 6-15. **Literacy:** 81.4%.

Website: www.algerianembassy.org, www.premier-ministre.gov.dz

Earliest known inhabitants were ancestors of Berbers, followed by Phoenicians, Romans, Vandals, and Arabs. Turkey ruled 1518-1830, when France took control. Large-scale European immigration followed. Arab nationalists launched a guerrilla war, 1954, that more than 400,000 French troops were unable to suppress. After French Pres. Charles de Gaulle came to power, 1958, colonial rule ended, nearly all Europeans left, and Algeria declared independence July 5, 1962. Ahmed Ben Bella ruled until 1965, when an army coup installed Col. Houari Boumedienne, a former guerrilla leader who held power until his death in 1978.

Hundreds died in anti-government riots protesting economic hardship, Oct. 1988. The government canceled the Jan. 1992 elections and banned all nonreligious activities at Algeria's 10,000 mosques. Pres. Mohammed Boudiaf was assassinated June 29, 1992. Over the next seven years, Muslim fundamentalists attacked high-ranking officials, security forces, and foreigners; pro-government death squads were active.

Liamine Zeroual won the Nov. 16, 1995, presidential election. A new constitution banning Islamic political parties and increasing the president's powers passed in a Nov. 1996 referendum. Abdelaziz Bouteflika, who became president after a flawed Apr. 15, 1999, election, reconciled with rebels. Bouteflika was reelected Apr. 8, 2004, though opponents charged fraud.

Under a reconciliation plan approved by referendum Sept. 2005, the government in Mar. 2006 began freeing Islamists jailed for their role in the 1990s civil war, which left up to 200,000 people dead and 8,000 "disappeared."

Radical Islamists bombed police stations in Oct. 2006 and Feb. 2007. A group known as al-Qaeda in the Islamic Maghreb (AQIM) carried out terrorist attacks, 2007-08, that killed more than 200 people.

Bouteflika claimed more than 90% of the vote in a 2009 election denounced as fraudulent by opposition parties. During Arab Spring uprisings in early 2011, Bouteflika's government suppressed street protests in Algiers, Feb. 12. The country's governing party, the Natl. Liberation Front (FLN), strengthened its hold on power in May 10, 2012, parliamentary elections that opposition groups called fraudulent.

AQIM members seized the In Amenas gas facility Jan. 16, 2013, holding about 40 foreign workers hostage for 4 days and demanding the release of about 100 Islamist prisoners; 38 hostages died, as well as some 29 militants, as Algerian special forces attempted to liberate the facility.

The 77-year-old Bouteflika, who had suffered a stroke in 2013, won a fourth term as president with 81.5% of the vote in the Apr. 17, 2014, election. The FLN won May 4, 2017, parliamentary elections.

Large-scale protests following the Feb. 2019 announcement that Bouteflika would seek a fifth term led to his forced resignation Apr. 2, 2019. In a Dec. 12, 2019, presidential election, boycotted by many government opponents, FLN candidate Abdelmadjid Tebboune won with 58% of the vote. Following June 12, 2021, parliamentary elections, won by the FLN, Tebboune appointed a new prime minister.

Andorra
Principality of Andorra

People: Population: 85,468 (186). **Age distrib.:** <15: 12.3%; 65+: 19.5%. **Growth:** −0.1%. **Migrants:** 59.0%. **Pop. density:** 473.0 per sq mi, 182.6 per sq km. **Urban:** 87.8%. **Ethnic groups** (by nationality): Andorran 48.3%, Spanish 24.8%, Portuguese 11.2%, French 4.5%. **Languages:** Catalan (official), Castilian, Portuguese, French. **Religions:** Christian 88.4% (Catholic [official] 87.4%), agnostic 8.0%.

Geography: Total area: 181 sq mi, 468 sq km (180); **Land area:** 181 sq mi, 468 sq km. **Location:** SW Europe, in Pyrenees Mts. Spain on S, France on N. **Topography:** High mountains and narrow valleys across country. **Arable land:** 1.6%. **Capital:** Andorra la Vella, 22,614.

Government: Type: Parliamentary democracy. **Heads of state:** President of France and Bishop of Urgell (Spain), as co-princes. **Head of govt.:** Xavier Espot Zamora; in office: May 16, 2019. **Local divisions:** 7 parishes. **Defense budget/active troops:** NA.

Economy: Industries: tourism (skiing), banking, timber, furniture. **Chief agric.:** rye, wheat, barley, oats; sheep, cattle. **Natural resources:** hydropower, mineral water, timber, iron ore, lead. **Water:** 4,085 cu m per capita. **Labor force:** agric. 0.5%, industry 4.4%, services 95.1%. **Unemployment:** NA.

Finance: Monetary unit: Euro (EUR) (0.93 = $1 U.S.). **GDP:** NA; **per capita GDP:** NA; **GDP growth:** 8.8%. **Imports** (2020): $1.7 bil; Spain 71%, France 17%. **Exports** (2020): $1.8 bil; Spain 40%, France 19%, U.S. 11%. **Tourism** (2019): $1.9 bil. **Budget** (2016): $2.1 bil. **Inflation:** NA.

Transport: NA.

Communications: Mobile: 142.2 per 100 pop. **Broadband:** 95.2 per 100 pop. **Internet:** 93.9%.

Health: Expend.: 9.1%. **Life expect.:** 81.4 male; 86.0 female. **Births:** 6.9 per 1,000 pop. **Deaths:** 8.0 per 1,000 pop. **Infant mortality:** 3.4 per 1,000 live births. **Undernourished:** NA. **HIV:**

NA. **COVID-19:** 48,015 cases, 159 deaths; rates per 100,000: 62,143.3 cases, 205.8 deaths. 67.7% vaccinated.
Education: Compulsory: ages 6-15. **Literacy:** 100.0%.
Website: www.govern.ad

France and the bishop of Urgell held joint sovereignty over Andorra from 1278 to 1993. Voters chose to adopt a parliamentary system Mar. 14, 1993, although co-princes remain heads of state. Tourism, especially skiing, and banking are economic mainstays. For years, Andorra served as a tax haven, but it began reforms in 2008 and was removed by the OECD from its list of uncooperative tax havens, May 27, 2009. In Mar. 2015, the government seized control of Banca Privada d'Andorra (BPA) and arrested its chief executive after money laundering accusations. The parliament approved, Nov. 30, 2016, a measure to end, in stages, banking secrecy for foreigners' accounts.

Angola
Republic of Angola

People: Population: 35,981,281 (41). **Age distrib.:** <15: 47.2%; 65+: 2.3%. **Growth:** 3.3%. **Migrants:** 2.0%. **Pop. density:** 74.8 per sq mi, 28.9 per sq km. **Urban:** 68.7%. **Ethnic groups:** Ovimbundu 37%, Kimbundu 25%, Bakongo 13%, mestico (mixed European/native African) 2%. **Languages:** Portuguese (official), Umbundu, Kikongo, Kimbundu, Chokwe, Nhaneca, Nganguela, Fiote. **Religions:** Christian 93.7% (Catholic 57.7%, Protestant 29.2%), ethnic religionist 4.3%.

Geography: Total area: 481,354 sq mi, 1,246,700 sq km (22); **Land area:** 481,354 sq mi, 1,246,700 sq km. **Location:** SW Africa on the Atlantic. Namibia on S, Zambia on E, Dem. Rep. of the Congo on N; Cabinda, an exclave separated by short Atlantic coast of the DRC, borders Rep. of the Congo. **Topography:** Mostly plateau 3,000-5,000 ft above sea level, rising from a narrow coastal strip. Temperate highland area in the W-central region, a desert in S, and a tropical rain forest in Cabinda. **Arable land:** 4.3%. **Capital:** Luanda, 9,292,336. **Cities:** Lubango, 958,548; Cabinda, 904,676.

Government: Type: Presidential republic. **Head of state and govt.:** João Lourenço; b. 1954; in office: Sept. 26, 2017. **Local divisions:** 18 provinces. **Defense budget:** $1.8 bil. **Active troops:** 107,000.

Economy: Industries: petroleum, diamonds, cement, metal prods., fish/food proc. **Chief agric.:** cassava, bananas, maize, sweet potatoes, pineapples, sugarcane. **Natural resources:** petroleum, diamonds, iron ore, phosphates, copper, feldspar, gold, bauxite, uranium. **Water:** 4,515 cu m per capita. **Crude oil reserves:** 7.8 bil bbls. **Electricity prod.:** 16.4 mil kWh. **Labor force:** agric. 58.7%, industry 7.8%, services 33.5%. **Unemployment:** 6.6%.

Finance: Monetary unit: Kwanza (AOA) (835.61 = $1 U.S.). **GDP:** $248.2 bil; **per capita GDP:** $6,974; **GDP growth:** 3.0%. **Imports:** $18.8 bil; China 22%, Portugal 15%, Nigeria 6%, Belgium 6%. **Exports:** $33.7 bil; China 62%, India 10%. **Tourism:** $22 mil. **Budget:** $17.2 bil. **Inflation** (2020-21): 25.8%.

Transport: Railways: 1,716 mi. **Motor vehicles:** 5.8 per 1,000 pop. **Airports:** 32.

Communications: Mobile: 67.4 per 100 pop. **Broadband:** 26.3 per 100 pop. **Internet:** 32.6%.

Health: Expend.: 2.9%. **Life expect.:** 60.4 male; 64.7 female. **Births:** 41.4 per 1,000 pop. **Deaths:** 7.8 per 1,000 pop. **Infant mortality:** 57.2 per 1,000 live births. **Undernourished:** 21.6%. **HIV:** 1.5%. **COVID-19:** 105,384 cases, 1,934 deaths; rates per 100,000: 320.6 cases, 5.9 deaths. 28.5% vaccinated.
Education: Compulsory: ages 6-11. **Literacy:** 72.3%.
Website: www.governo.gov.ao

From the early centuries CE to 1500, Bantu tribes penetrated most of the region. Portuguese came in 1583, allied with the Bakongo kingdom in the north, and developed the slave trade. Large-scale colonization began in the 20th cent., when 400,000 Portuguese immigrated.

A guerrilla war, 1961-75, ended when Portugal granted Angola independence. Fighting then erupted among rival rebel groups, including the Soviet-backed Popular Movement for the Liberation of Angola (MPLA) and the National Union for the Total Independence of Angola (UNITA), aided by the U.S. and South Africa. Cuban troops helped the MPLA win control of most of the country by 1976, although fighting continued. MPLA-UNITA peace accords in 1991 and 1994 failed to hold. The UN estimated that the civil war had claimed some 1 mil lives and left another 2.5 mil people homeless by mid-2001. Government troops killed rebel leader Jonas Savimbi Feb. 22, 2002. UNITA agreed to a truce Apr. 4, 2002. Separatist rebels in oil-rich Cabinda agreed to a cease-fire July 2006.

With proven petroleum reserves estimated at 8-9 bil barrels, Angola is among Africa's leading oil producers. Wealth is extremely unevenly distributed, and corruption has been widespread. The ruling MPLA claimed victory in voting Sept. 2008, in Angola's first parliamentary elections in 16 years. Parliament approved Jan. 21, 2010, a new constitution augmenting the power of MPLA leader José Eduardo dos Santos, Angola's president since 1979. The MPLA won flawed elections, Aug 31, 2012, giving dos Santos another 5-year term. The MPLA won disputed Aug. 23, 2017, elections, and João Lourenço took office as president, Sept. 26. On Nov. 15, Lourenço dismissed as head of the state oil company dos Santos's daughter, Isabel dos Santos, suspected of misappropriating up to $1 bil of government funds. On Jan. 11, 2018, Lourenço removed as head of the country's sovereign wealth fund dos Santos's son, José Filomeno dos Santos; he was sentenced, Aug. 2020, to 5 years in prison for embezzlement.

A new penal code, approved Jan. 23, 2019, decriminalized same-sex relationships and prohibited discrimination based on sexual orientation.

The MPLA was declared, Aug. 29, 2022, the winner by a slim margin of Aug. 24 parliamentary elections. A UNITA challenge was rejected by the Constitutional Court, Sept. 8, giving Lourenço another term as president.

Antigua and Barbuda

People: Population: 101,489 (182). **Age distrib.:** <15: 22.0%; 65+: 10.1%. **Growth:** 1.1%. **Migrants:** 30.0%. **Pop. density:** 593.4 per sq mi, 229.1 per sq km. **Urban:** 24.3%. **Ethnic groups:** African descent 87.3%, mixed 4.7%, Hispanic 2.7%. **Languages:** English (official), Antiguan creole. **Religions:** Christian 92.3% (Protestant 76.6%, Catholic 10.4%), Spiritist 3.6%.

Geography: Total area: 171 sq mi, 443 sq km (Antigua, 108 sq mi, 280 sq km; Barbuda, 62 sq mi, 161 sq km) (183); **Land area:** 171 sq mi, 443 sq km. **Location:** E Caribbean. St. Kitts and Nevis to W, Guadeloupe (Fr.) to S. **Topography:** Mostly low-lying and limestone coral islands. Antigua is mostly hilly with an indented coast; Barbuda is a flat island with a large lagoon on W. **Arable land:** 9.1%. **Capital:** St. John's, 20,764.

Government: Type: Parliamentary democracy under constitutional monarchy. **Head of state:** King Charles III, rep. by Gov.-Gen. Rodney Williams; b. 1947; in office: Aug. 14, 2014. **Head of govt.:** Prime Min. Gaston Browne; b. 1967; in office: June 13, 2014. **Local divisions:** 6 parishes, 2 dependencies. **Defense budget:** $8 mil. **Active troops:** 180.

Economy: Industries: tourism, constr., light mfg. **Chief agric.:** tropical fruit, milk, mangoes/guavas, melons, tomatoes, pineapples. **Natural resources:** negligible. **Water:** 531 cu m per capita. **Electricity prod.:** 350.9 mil kWh. **Labor force:** NA. **Unemployment:** NA.

Finance: Monetary unit: East Caribbean Dollar (XCD) (2.70 = $1 U.S.). **GDP:** $2.4 bil; **per capita GDP:** $25,337; **GDP growth:** 8.5%. **Imports:** $868.8 mil; (2021) U.S. 42%, Poland 25%, China 10%. **Exports:** $749.5 mil; (2021) Suriname 20%, Barbados 17%, Poland 12%, UK 10%, France 7%. **Tourism:** $488 mil. **Budget** (2020): $357 mil. **Inflation:** 7.5%.

Transport: Airports: 2.

Communications: Mobile (2021): 197.4 per 100 pop. **Broadband** (2021): 51.5 per 100 pop. **Internet:** 95.7%.

Health: Expend.: 5.6%. **Life expect.:** 75.9 male; 80.3 female. **Births:** 15.0 per 1,000 pop. **Deaths:** 5.7 per 1,000 pop. **Infant mortality:** 14.0 per 1,000 live births. **Undernourished:** NA. **HIV:** NA. **COVID-19:** 9,106 cases, 146 deaths; rates per 100,000: 9,298.6 cases, 149.1 deaths. 63.7% vaccinated.

Education: Compulsory: ages 5-15. **Literacy:** 99.0%.

Website: ab.gov.ag

Christopher Columbus landed on Antigua in 1493. The British colonized it in 1632. The British-associated state of Antigua achieved independence as Antigua and Barbuda on Nov. 1, 1981. Tourism generally accounts for well over half of GDP. The worldwide recession caused the economy to shrink in 2009-11. With the economy still weak, the opposition Antigua and Barbuda Labour Party (ABLP) won June 12, 2014, parliamentary elections. ABLP leader Gaston Browne became prime minister and supported development projects opposed by environmental groups. Hurricane Irma caused massive damage on Barbuda, Sept. 5-6, 2017.

The ABLP easily retained power in Mar. 21, 2018, elections. With the economy not fully recovered from the sharp decline in tourism, 2020-21, caused by the COVID-19 pandemic and the country dealing with high inflation, the ABLP only narrowly won Jan. 18, 2023, elections.

Argentina
Argentine Republic

People: Population: 46,621,847 (33). **Age distrib.:** <15: 23.5%; 65+: 12.7%. **Growth:** 0.8%. **Migrants:** 5.0%. **Pop. density:** 44.1 per sq mi, 17.0 per sq km. **Urban:** 92.5%. **Ethnic groups:** European (mostly Spanish/Italian descent) and mestizo (mixed European/Amerindian) 97.2%, Amerindian 2.4%. **Languages:** Spanish (official), Italian, English, German, French, Indigenous (Quechua, Guarani, Mapudungun). **Religions:** Christian 88.2% (Catholic [official] 75.7%), agnostic 7.3%, Muslim 2.3%.

Geography: Total area: 1,073,518 sq mi, 2,780,400 sq km (8). **Land area:** 1,056,642 sq mi, 2,736,690 sq km. **Location:** Occupies most of southern S America. Chile on W; Bolivia, Paraguay on N; Brazil, Uruguay on NE. **Topography:** Andean, Central, Misiones, and Southern mountain ranges in W. Aconcagua (22,831 ft) is highest peak in Western Hemisphere. Gran Chaco, heavily wooded plains, are E of Andes in N; fertile, treeless Pampas in the central region. Patagonia, in S, is bleak and arid. Rio de la Plata, an estuary in NE, 170 by 140 mi, is mostly freshwater, from 2,485-mi Paraná and 1,000-mi Uruguay Rivers. **Arable land:** 15.4%. **Capital:** Buenos Aires, 15,490,415. **Cities:** Córdoba, 1,611,651; Rosario, 1,594,096; Mendoza, 1,226,427.

Government: Type: Presidential republic. **Head of state and govt.:** Pres. Alberto Ángel Fernández; b. 1959; in office: Dec. 10, 2019. **Local divisions:** 23 provinces, 1 autonomous city. **Defense budget:** $3.4 bil. **Active troops:** 72,100.

Economy: Industries: food proc., motor vehicles, consumer durables, textiles, chemicals and petrochemicals. **Chief agric.:** maize, soybeans, wheat, sugarcane, milk, barley. **Natural resources:** lead, zinc, tin, copper, iron ore, manganese, petroleum, uranium. **Water:** 19,388 cu m per capita. **Crude oil reserves:** 2.5 bil bbls. **Electricity prod.:** 146.6 bil kWh. **Labor force:** agric. 7.7%, industry 20.0%, services 72.4%. **Unemployment:** 6.5%.

Finance: Monetary unit: Peso (ARS) (349.95 = $1 U.S.). **GDP:** $1.2 tril; **per capita GDP:** $26,505; **GDP growth:** 5.2%. **Imports:** $72.4 bil; Brazil 21%, China 18%, U.S. 14%, Germany 6%. **Exports:** $87.4 bil; Brazil 16%, China 11%, U.S. 7%. **Tourism:** $406 mil. **Budget:** $170.7 bil. **Inflation** (2016-17): 25.7%.

Transport: Railways: 11,101 mi. **Motor vehicles:** 306.2 per 1,000 pop. **Airports:** 161.

Communications: Mobile: 132.4 per 100 pop. **Broadband** (2021): 72.9 per 100 pop. **Internet:** 88.4%.

Health: Expend.: 10.0%. **Life expect.:** 75.5 male; 81.8 female. **Births:** 15.4 per 1,000 pop. **Deaths:** 7.3 per 1,000 pop. **Infant mortality:** 9.1 per 1,000 live births. **Undernourished:** 3.2%. **HIV:** 0.4%. **COVID-19:** 10,044,957 cases, 130,472 deaths; rates per 100,000: 22,225.4 cases, 288.7 deaths. 83.7% vaccinated.

Education: Compulsory: ages 4-17. **Literacy:** 99.0%.

Website: www.argentina.gob.ar

Nomadic Indians roamed the Pampas when Spaniards arrived, 1515-16, led by Juan Díaz de Solís. Nearly all the Indians were killed by the late 19th cent. The colonists won independence, 1816. A long period of disorder ended in a strong centralized government.

Large-scale Italian, German, and Spanish immigration in the decades after 1880 spurred modernization. Social reforms were enacted in the 1920s, but military coups prevailed, 1930-46, until Gen. Juan Perón was elected president.

Perón, with his wife, Eva Duarte (d. 1952), introduced labor reforms but suppressed speech and press freedoms, closed religious schools, and ran the country into debt. A 1955 coup exiled Perón. A series of military and civilian regimes followed. Perón returned in 1973 and was again elected president. He died 10 months later. His wife and vice president, Isabel, succeeded him.

A military junta ousted Isabel Perón in 1976 amid charges of corruption. Under a continuing state of siege, the army conducted a "dirty war" against guerrillas and leftists. An estimated 30,000 people "disappeared."

Argentine troops seized control of the British-held Falkland Islands (Islas Malvinas) on Apr. 2, 1982. The British imposed an air and sea blockade around the Falklands. Fighting began May 1. British troops landed on East Falkland May 21. Argentine troops surrendered, June 14.

Democratic rule returned in 1983. On Dec. 9, 1985, five former junta members were found guilty of murder and human rights abuses during the "dirty war" period. Buenos Aires Mayor Fernando de la Rúa won the presidential election Oct. 24, 1999, but resigned in 2001 after a prolonged recession resulted in debt of more than $130 bil. Congress, Jan. 1, 2002, chose a Peronist, Eduardo Alberto Duhalde, to finish de la Rúa's term. Further economic decline and renewed protests led Duhalde, July 2, to schedule an early presidential election for Mar. 2003; another Peronist, Néstor Kirchner, took office May 25, 2003. A new IMF aid deal, approved Sept. 10, 2003, rescued Argentina from default.

The Supreme Court, June 14, 2005, overturned amnesty laws that had barred prosecution for "dirty war" crimes committed while the military ruled Argentina. In July 2010, Argentina became the first Latin American country to extend full marriage rights to same-sex couples.

Cristina Fernández de Kirchner ran as the Peronist candidate after her husband and was elected president Oct. 28, 2007. She was reelected Oct. 23, 2011. In 2013, special prosecutor Alberto Nisman accused Fernández de Kirchner of interfering with his investigation of Iranian involvement in a 1994 Jewish community center bombing in Buenos Aires that killed 85 people. Nisman was found shot dead in his home, Jan. 18, 2015. A border police investigation concluded, Nov. 2017, that Nisman had been murdered. On Mar. 5, 2018, Fernández de Kirchner was ordered to stand trial on charges of covering up Iranian involvement in the Jewish center bombing, but a court dismissed the case, Oct. 7, 2021.

Buenos Aires Archbishop Jorge Mario Bergoglio was elected pope Mar. 13, 2013; he was the first pope from the Americas. He took the name Francis.

Defeating Peronist candidate Daniel Scioli in a runoff, Mauricio Macri of the center-right Republican Proposal Party was elected president Nov. 22, 2015. Pres. Macri, Sept. 3, 2018, announced austerity measures to stem a budget deficit and a sharp drop in the value of the peso. With economic problems continuing, Peronist Alberto Fernández defeated Macri in the Oct. 27, 2019, presidential election; Cristina Fernández de Kirchner was elected vice president. Argentina's Congress, Dec. 30, 2020, completed legislation legalizing abortion in the first 14 weeks of pregnancy. Fernández de Kirchner was unharmed in a Sept. 1, 2022, assassination attempt. With a victory over France, Dec. 18, 2022, Argentina won the men's World Cup soccer tournament (played in Qatar).

Armenia
Republic of Armenia

People: Population: 2,989,091 (136). **Age distrib.:** <15: 18.0%; 65+: 14.5%. **Growth:** −0.4%. **Migrants:** 6.4%. **Pop. density:** 274.5 per sq mi, 106.0 per sq km. **Urban:** 63.7%. **Ethnic groups:** Armenian 98.1%, Yezidi (Kurd) 1.2%. **Languages:** Armenian (official). **Religions:** Christian 94.6% (Orthodox [official] 81.4%), agnostic 2.7%.

Geography: Total area: 11,484 sq mi, 29,743 sq km (139); **Land area:** 10,889 sq mi, 28,203 sq km. **Location:** SW Asia. Georgia on N, Azerbaijan on E, Iran on S, Turkey on W. **Topography:** Mountainous with many peaks above 10,000 ft. **Arable land:** 15.6%. **Capital:** Yerevan, 1,094,813.

Government: Type: Parliamentary democracy. **Head of state:** Pres. Vahagn Khachaturyan; b. 1959; in office: Mar. 13, 2022. **Head of govt.:** Prime Min. Nikol Pashinyan; b. 1975; in office: Sept. 10, 2021. **Local divisions:** 11 provinces. **Defense budget:** $749 mil. **Active troops:** 42,900.

Economy: Industries: brandy, mining, diamond proc., metal-cutting machine tools, forging/pressing machines, elec. motors, knitted wear. **Chief agric.:** milk, potatoes, grapes, vegetables, tomatoes, watermelons. **Natural resources:** gold, copper, molybdenum, zinc, bauxite. **Water:** 2,622 cu m per capita. **Electricity prod.:** 7.3 bil kWh. **Labor force:** agric. 30.3%, industry 17.5%, services 52.2%. **Unemployment:** 12.6%.

Finance: Monetary unit: Dram (AMD) (384.13 = $1 U.S.). **GDP:** $52.7 bil; **per capita GDP:** $18,942; **GDP growth:** 12.6%. **Imports:** $6.1 bil; Russia 29%, China 10%, Georgia 8%, Iran 6%. **Exports:** $5.0 bil; Russia 22%, Switzerland 20%, China 7%, Bulgaria 6%. **Tourism:** $784 mil. **Budget:** $3.4 bil. **Inflation:** 8.6%.

Transport: Railways: 426 mi. **Airports:** 10.

Communications: Mobile: 135.3 per 100 pop. **Broadband:** 102.0 per 100 pop. **Internet:** 78.6%.

Health: Expend.: 12.2%. **Life expect.:** 73.1 male; 79.9 female. **Births:** 10.8 per 1,000 pop. **Deaths:** 9.5 per 1,000 pop. **Infant mortality:** 11.9 per 1,000 live births. **Undernourished:** <2.5%. **HIV:** 0.3%. **COVID-19:** 449,299 cases, 8,751 deaths; rates per 100,000: 15,162.5 cases, 295.3 deaths. 35.7% vaccinated.

Education: Compulsory: ages 6-17. **Literacy:** 99.8%.

Website: www.gov.am

Ancient Armenia extended into parts of what are now Turkey and Iran. Present-day Armenia was set up as a Soviet republic Apr. 2, 1921. It joined Georgia and Azerbaijan SSRs Mar. 12, 1922, to form the Transcaucasian SFSR, which became part of the USSR Dec. 30, 1922. Armenia became a constituent republic of the USSR Dec. 5, 1936. An earthquake struck Armenia Dec. 7, 1988; approximately 25,000 were killed.

Armenia became an independent state when the USSR disbanded Dec. 26, 1991. Nagorno-Karabakh, an enclave in Azerbaijan with an ethnic Armenian majority, seceded from Azerbaijan in 1988. A 1992-94 war that cost 30,000 lives ended in a cease-fire with Armenian forces in control of Nagorno-Karabakh and adjacent areas. Deadly clashes between Armenian and Azerbaijani forces occurred in 2015-16 in and near Nagorno-Karabakh. After Azerbaijani victories in heavy fighting beginning in Sept. 2020, Armenia agreed, in a Nov. 9 cease-fire, to cede areas in Azerbaijan it had controlled since 1994. A new offensive by Azerbaijan in Sept. 2023 gave it complete control of Nagorno-Karabakh, prompting more than 100,000 ethnic Armenians (most of the Armenian pop.) in the region to flee to Armenia as of Sept. 30.

Voters approved, July 5, 1995, a new constitution increasing presidential powers. Pres. Levon Ter-Petrosian won reelection Sept. 22, 1996, amid claims of fraud. He resigned Feb. 3, 1998, and Robert Kocharian, a nationalist born in Nagorno-Karabakh, won the presidency Mar. 30, 1998. Gunmen stormed Parliament Oct. 27, 1999, killing Prime Min. Vazgen Sarkissian and 7 others. Kocharian won a second term Mar. 5, 2003.

Prime Min. Serzh Sargsyan defeated Ter-Petrosian in a Feb. 19, 2008, presidential election. Armenia did not ratify an Oct. 2009 treaty it had approved with Turkey over the 1915-18 killing of more than 1 mil Armenians by Ottoman Turks, due to renewed friction between the countries in 2010. Sargsyan won reelection Feb. 18, 2013. Constitutional revisions transitioned the government to a parliamentary system as of 2018. Opposition leader Nikol Pashinyan was elected prime min. by parliament May 8. Pashinyan's party won a landslide victory in Dec. 9, 2018, parliamentary elections. Blamed for Armenia's defeat in 2020 fighting against Azerbaijan, Pashinyan resigned Apr. 25, 2021, but retained office after winning June 20 elections; the opposition charged electoral fraud.

Australia
Commonwealth of Australia

People: Population: 26,461,166 (54). **Age distrib.:** <15: 18.4%; 65+: 16.7%. **Growth:** 1.2%. **Migrants:** 30.1%. **Pop. density:** 8.9 per sq mi, 3.4 per sq km. **Urban:** 86.6%. **Ethnic groups:** English 33%, Australian 29.9%, Irish 9.5%, Scottish 8.6%, Chinese 5.5%, Italian 4.4%, German 4%, Indian 3.1%, Australian Aboriginal 2.9%. **Languages:** English, Chinese (Mandarin, Cantonese), Arabic, Vietnamese. **Religions:** Christian 52.8% (Catholic 22.9%, Protestant 22.2%), agnostic 28.6%, atheist 7.4%, Buddhist 3.2%, Muslim 3.1% (Sunni 2%).

Geography: Total area: 2,988,902 sq mi, 7,741,220 sq km (6); **Land area:** 2,966,153 sq mi, 7,682,300 sq km. **Location:** SE of Asia. Surrounded by Indian O. on W and S, Pacific O. (Coral, Tasman Seas) in E. Tasmania lies 150 mi S of Victoria state, across Bass Strait. Nearest are Indonesia, Papua New Guinea on N; Solomons, Fiji, and New Zealand on E. **Topography:** An island continent. The Great Dividing Range along the E coast has Mt. Kosciusko (7,310 ft). The Western Plateau rises to 2,000 ft, with arid areas in the Great Sandy and Great Victoria Deserts. The NW part of Western Australia and Northern Terr. are arid and hot. The NE has heavy rainfall. Jungles in Cape York Peninsula. **Arable land:** 4.1%. **Capital:** Canberra, 472,304. **Cities:** Melbourne, 5,235,407; Sydney, 5,120,894; Brisbane, 2,504,505; Perth, 2,117,997; Adelaide, 1,366,783.

Government: Type: Federal parliamentary democracy under constitutional monarchy. **Head of state:** King Charles III, rep. by Gov.-Gen. David Hurley; b. 1953; in office: July 1, 2019. **Head of govt.:** Prime Min. Anthony Albanese; b. 1963; in office: May 23, 2022. **Local divisions:** 6 states, 2 territories. **Defense budget:** $33.8 bil. **Active troops:** 59,800.

Economy: Industries: mining, industrial and transp. equip., food proc., chemicals, steel. **Chief agric.:** sugarcane, wheat, barley, milk, rapeseed, beef. **Natural resources:** alumina, coal, iron ore, copper, lithium, tin, gold, silver, uranium, nickel, tungsten, rare earth elements, mineral sands, lead, zinc, diamonds, opals, nat. gas, petroleum. **Water:** 19,294 cu m per capita. **Crude oil reserves:** 2.4 bil bbls. **Electricity prod.:** 246.8 bil kWh. **Labor force:** agric. 2.4%, industry 18.8%, services 78.8%. **Unemployment:** 3.7%.

Finance: Monetary unit: Dollar (AUD) (1.56 = $1 U.S.). **GDP:** $1.6 tril; **per capita GDP:** $62,625; **GDP growth:** 3.6%. **Imports:** $298.7 bil; (2021) China 28%, U.S. 10%, Japan 6%. **Exports:** $389.8 bil; (2021) China 40%, Japan 14%, South Korea 9%, India 6%. **Tourism:** $17.0 bil. **Budget:** $532.6 bil. **Inflation:** 6.6%.

Transport: Railways: 22,409 mi. **Motor vehicles:** 751.4 per 1,000 pop. **Airports:** 349.

Communications: Mobile: 107.0 per 100 pop. **Broadband:** 123.7 per 100 pop. **Internet:** 96.2%.

Health: Expend.: 10.6%. **Life expect.:** 81.1 male; 85.5 female. **Births:** 12.2 per 1,000 pop. **Deaths:** 6.8 per 1,000 pop. **Infant mortality:** 3.0 per 1,000 live births. **Undernourished:** <2.5%. **HIV:** NA. **COVID-19:** 11,576,428 cases, 22,696 deaths; rates per 100,000: 45,398.0 cases, 89.0 deaths. 84.8% vaccinated.

Education: Compulsory: ages 6-15. **Literacy:** NA.

Website: www.australia.gov.au

Australia harbors many plant and animal species not found elsewhere, including kangaroos, koalas, platypuses, dingoes (wild dogs), Tasmanian devils, wombats, and barking and frilled lizards.

Aboriginal peoples first reached Australia, from SE Asia, at least 45,000-50,000 years ago and perhaps thousands of years earlier. British Capt. James Cook explored the eastern coast in 1770, when the entire continent and its offshore islands were inhabited by Indigenous peoples. The first European settlers, beginning in 1788, were mostly convicts, soldiers, and government officials. By 1830, Britain had claimed the entire continent, and the immigration of free settlers accelerated. The Commonwealth was proclaimed Jan. 1, 1901. Northern Terr. was granted limited self-rule July 1, 1978.

State/territory, capital	Tot. area (sq mi)	Pop.
New South Wales, Sydney	309,326	8,293,965
Victoria, Melbourne	87,817	6,766,559
Queensland, Brisbane	667,857	5,418,453
Western Australia, Perth	975,685	2,855,594
South Australia, Adelaide	380,048	1,844,616
Tasmania, Hobart	26,410	572,660
Australian Capital Terr., Canberra	910	464,601
Northern Terr., Darwin	520,385	251,654

Note: Estimated pop. as of Mar. 2023. (Source: Australian Bureau of Statistics.)

In a 1967 referendum, Australians voted to change parts of the country's constitution that discriminated against Aboriginal Australians. Racially discriminatory immigration policies ended in 1973, after 3 mil Europeans (half British) had entered since 1945.

Australia is among the top exporters of lamb, wool, and wheat. Major mineral deposits, including coal, have been developed, largely for export. Slumping commodity prices and sluggish exports to China impacted the economy beginning in 2016. By 2019, the government instituted various economic stimulus measures to boost sagging GDP growth.

Australian troops fought in U.S.-led military operations in Afghanistan (beginning 2001) and Iraq (beginning 2003); the last Australian troops left Afghanistan in 2021. Some 2,000 Australian peacekeepers began arriving in the Solomon Isls., July 24, 2003; nearly all were withdrawn by mid-2005. In race riots in Sydney suburbs, Dec. 11-12, 2005, thousands of youths assaulted people of Middle Eastern ancestry, who then retaliated. Australian troops were dispatched, 2006, to suppress disorder in the Solomon Isls. in Apr. and Timor in May. The last Australian troops in Timor returned home on Mar. 27, 2013.

Australian warplanes joined the U.S.-led air campaign in Iraq (2014-18) and Syria (2015-18) against the Sunni extremist group ISIS. About 23,000 refugees fleeing warfare in Syria and Iraq arrived in Australia 2015-17.

The Labor Party's Julia Gillard became, June 24, 2010, Australia's first female prime minister. Downpours from Cyclone Tasha and other storms caused severe flooding in Queensland, Dec. 2010-Jan. 2011. Prime Min. Gillard, Mar. 20, 2013, officially apologized for Australia's forced adoption policy (in effect late 1950s-70s), in which the state took the babies of single, teenage, or "unfit" mothers, often under duress. Labor's Kevin Rudd replaced Gillard June 26, 2013.

The conservatives returned to power after Sept. 7, 2013, elections, making Tony Abbott prime min. Malcolm Turnbull replaced Abbott as prime min., Sept. 15, 2015, after defeating him in a vote for Liberal Party leader. Turnbull's Liberal/National Party coalition won a narrow victory in July 2, 2016, elections. Liberal Scott Morrison replaced Turnbull as prime min., Aug. 24, 2018.

National and state governments instituted travel restrictions and lockdown measures, beginning in 2020, to combat the COVID-19 pandemic; violent anti-vaccination, anti-lockdown protests took place in Melbourne, Sept. 2021. As of Aug. 2023, Australia had recorded nearly 11.6 mil total confirmed COVID-19 cases (15th-highest in the world).

Under a 2021 agreement, elaborated in 2023, Australia would first buy from the U.S. and then build, with U.S. and UK assistance, nuclear-powered submarines, countering China's growing sea power.

May 21, 2022, elections returned Labor to power, with a slim House of Representatives majority; Anthony Albanese became prime min. Australia and New Zealand hosted the FIFA Women's World Cup soccer tournament, July-Aug. 2023.

Australian External Territories

Norfolk Isl., area 14.3 sq mi, pop. (2021 census) 2,188, was taken over, 1914. The soil is very fertile, suitable for citrus, bananas, and coffee. Many of the inhabitants are descended from Pitcairn Islanders who moved to Norfolk in 1856 after the British abandoned an attempted penal colony. Australia offered the island limited home rule in 1979 but revoked its autonomy in 2015. The island's legislative assembly was replaced by an elected regional council in 2016. **Website:** www.norfolkisland.gov.nf

The only inhabitants of **Coral Sea Isls.**, area 2.7 sq mi, are meteorological staff on Willis Isl.

Ashmore and Cartier Isls., area 1.9 sq mi, in the Indian O., came under Australian authority in 1934. **Heard Isl. and McDonald Isls.**, area 159.1 sq mi, are administered by the Australian Antarctic Division.

Cocos (Keeling) Isls. are 27 coral islands in the Indian O. about 1,833 mi NW of Australia. Area 5.4 sq mi; pop. (2021 census) 593. The residents voted to become part of Australia, Apr. 1984. **Website:** www.shire.cc

Christmas Isl., area 52.1 sq mi, pop. (2021 census) 1,692; 230 mi S of Java, was transferred by Britain in 1958. Phosphate mining is the main economic activity, though high-grade phosphate deposits are nearly depleted. **Website:** www.shire.gov.cx

Australian Antarctic Territory was claimed by the UK and then transferred to Australian sovereignty in 1933. It comprises some 2.2 mil sq mi of territory S of 60th parallel S lat. between 45°E and 160°E (not incl. France's Adelie Coast) and between 136°E and 142°E.

Austria
Republic of Austria

People: Population: 8,940,860 (99). **Age distrib.:** <15: 14.1%; 65+: 20.8%. **Growth:** 0.3%. **Migrants:** 19.3%. **Pop. density:** 280.9 per sq mi, 108.4 per sq km. **Urban:** 59.5%. **Ethnic groups** (by birth country): Austrian 80.8%, German 2.6%. **Languages:** German (official), Turkish, Serbian, Croatian (official in one state). **Religions:** Christian 67.0% (Catholic 59.7%), agnostic 21.9%, Muslim 8.1% (Sunni), atheist 2.5%.

Geography: Total area: 32,383 sq mi, 83,871 sq km (112); **Land area:** 31,832 sq mi, 82,445 sq km. **Location:** S Central Europe. Switzerland, Liechtenstein on W; Germany, Czechia on N; Slovakia, Hungary on E; Slovenia, Italy on S. **Topography:** Primarily

mountainous, with the Alps and foothills covering the western and southern provinces. The eastern provinces and Vienna are located in the Danube River Basin. **Arable land:** 16.0%. **Capital:** Vienna, 1,975,271.

Government: Type: Federal parliamentary republic. **Head of state:** Pres. Alexander Van der Bellen; b. 1944; in office: Jan. 26, 2017. **Head of govt.:** Chancellor Karl Nehammer; b. 1972; in office: Dec. 6, 2021. **Local divisions:** 9 states. **Defense budget:** $3.6 bil. **Active troops:** 23,300.

Economy: Industries: constr., machinery, vehicles and parts, food, metals, chemicals, lumber and paper, electronics, tourism. **Chief agric.:** milk, maize, sugar beet, wheat, barley, potatoes. **Natural resources:** oil, coal, lignite, timber, iron ore, copper, zinc, antimony, magnesite, tungsten, graphite, salt, hydropower. **Water:** 8,627 cu m per capita. **Crude oil reserves:** 35 mil bbls. **Electricity prod.:** 64.2 bil kWh. **Labor force:** agric. 3.7%, industry 25.6%, services 70.6%. **Unemployment:** 4.7%.

Finance: Monetary unit: Euro (EUR) (0.93 = $1 U.S.). **GDP:** $614.3 bil; per capita GDP: $67,936; **GDP growth:** 5.0%. **Imports:** $265.8 bil; Germany 39%, Italy 7%. **Exports:** $268.3 bil; Germany 28%, U.S. 7%, Italy 6%. **Tourism:** $9.9 bil. **Budget:** $215.5 bil. **Inflation:** 8.5%.

Transport: Railways: 3,805 mi. **Motor vehicles:** 641.1 per 1,000 pop. **Airports:** 24.

Communications: Mobile: 123.4 per 100 pop. **Broadband:** 113.5 per 100 pop. **Internet:** 93.6%.

Health: Expend. (2021): 12.2%. **Life expect.:** 79.9 male; 85.2 female. **Births:** 9.4 per 1,000 pop. **Deaths:** 9.9 per 1,000 pop. **Infant mortality:** 3.2 per 1,000 live births. **Undernourished:** <2.5%. **HIV:** NA. **COVID-19:** 6,081,287 cases, 22,534 deaths; rates per 100,000: 68,320.9 cases, 253.2 deaths. 74.4% vaccinated.

Education: Compulsory: ages 5-17. **Literacy:** NA.

Website: www.bundeskanzleramt.gv.at

Rome conquered Austrian lands from Celtic tribes around 15 BCE. In 788 the territory was incorporated into Charlemagne's empire. By 1300, the House of Habsburg had gained control; it added vast territories in all parts of Europe to the realm in the next few hundred years.

Austrian dominance of Germany was undermined in the 18th cent. and ended by Prussia by 1866. But the Congress of Vienna, 1815, confirmed Austrian control of a large empire in SE Europe consisting of Germans, Hungarians, Slavs, Italians, and others. The dual Austro-Hungarian monarchy was established in 1867, giving autonomy to Hungary and almost 50 years of peace.

World War I, which started after the June 28, 1914, assassination of Archduke Franz Ferdinand, the Habsburg heir, by a Serbian nationalist, destroyed the empire. By 1918 Austria was reduced to a small republic, with the borders it has today.

Nazi Germany, ruled by the Austrian-born Adolf Hitler, annexed Austria Mar. 13, 1938. The republic was reestablished in 1945, under Allied occupation. Full independence and neutrality were restored in 1955. Austria joined the EU Jan. 1, 1995.

The right-wing, anti-immigrant Austrian Freedom Party (FPO) challenged the dominance of the Social Democratic Party (SPO) beginning in the late 1990s. However, the SPO won parliamentary elections in 2006, 2008, and 2013. Hundreds of thousands of migrants fleeing war and hardship in Syria and elsewhere entered Austria in 2015, many en route to N Europe. About 125,000 migrants applied for asylum in Austria in 2015-16. Government actions in 2016 sharply limited future asylum claims.

Former Green Party leader Alexander Van der Bellen defeated FPO candidate Norbert Hofer in a Dec. 4, 2016, presidential runoff election. The conservative Austrian People's Party (OVP) won Oct. 15, 2017, parliamentary elections; after forming a coalition with the FPO, OVP leader Sebastian Kurz became chancellor Dec. 18. After the coalition collapsed, the OVP won Sept. 29, 2019, elections, and Kurz formed a new coalition with the Green Party. Under investigation for corruption, Kurz announced his resignation, Oct. 9, 2021. The OVP's Karl Nehammer became chancellor Dec. 6, 2021. Van der Bellen won reelection, Oct. 9, 2022.

Azerbaijan
Republic of Azerbaijan

People: Population: 10,420,515 (90). **Age distrib.:** <15: 22.7%; 65+: 8.5%. **Growth:** 0.6%. **Migrants:** 2.5%. **Pop. density:** 326.6 per sq mi, 126.1 per sq km. **Urban:** 57.6%. **Ethnic groups:** over 80 ethnic groups, incl. Azerbaijani 91.6%, Lezghin 2%. **Languages:** Azerbaijani (Azeri) (official), Russian, Armenian. **Religions:** Muslim 96.4% (Shia 66%, Sunni 30%), Christian 2.4% (Orthodox).

Geography: Total area: 33,436 sq mi, 86,600 sq km (111); **Land area:** 31,903 sq mi, 82,629 sq km. **Location:** SW Asia. Russia, Georgia on N; Iran on S; Armenia on W; Caspian Sea on E. **Topography:** The Great Caucasus Mts. in N, Karabakh Upland in W border the Kur-Araz lowland. Arid climate except in subtropical SE. **Arable land:** 25.3%. **Capital:** Baku, 2,432,304.

Government: Type: Presidential republic. **Head of state:** Pres. Ilham Aliyev; b. 1961; in office: Oct. 31, 2003. **Head of govt.:** Prime Min. Ali Asadov; b. 1956; in office: Oct. 8, 2019. **Local divisions:** 66 districts, 11 cities. **Defense budget:** $2.6 bil. **Active troops:** 64,050.

Economy: Industries: petroleum/petroleum prods., nat. gas, oil field equip.; steel, iron ore; cement. **Chief agric.:** milk, wheat, potatoes, barley, tomatoes, watermelons. **Natural resources:** petroleum, nat. gas, iron ore, nonferrous metals, bauxite. **Water:** 3,420 cu m per capita. **Crude oil reserves:** 7 bil bbls. **Electricity prod.:** 26.3 bil kWh. **Labor force:** agric. 34.2%, industry 15.4%, services 50.4%. **Unemployment:** 5.5%.

Finance: Monetary unit: Manat (AZN) (1.70 = $1 U.S.). **GDP:** $180.8 bil; **per capita GDP:** $17,764; **GDP growth:** 4.6%. **Imports:** $16.3 bil; UK 17%, Russia 17%, Turkey 12%, China 6%. **Exports:** $25.5 bil; (2017) Italy 28%, Turkey 15%, Israel 7%. **Tourism:** $313 mil. **Budget:** $16 bil. **Inflation:** 13.9%.

Transport: Railways: 1,830 mi. **Motor vehicles:** 148.1 per 1,000 pop. **Airports:** 30.

Communications: Mobile: 106.9 per 100 pop. **Broadband:** 77.1 per 100 pop. **Internet:** 86.0%.

Health: Expend.: 4.6%. **Life expect.:** 72.4 male; 77.8 female. **Births:** 11.5 per 1,000 pop. **Deaths:** 6.8 per 1,000 pop. **Infant mortality:** 11.9 per 1,000 live births. **Undernourished:** <2.5%. **HIV:** 0.1%. **COVID-19:** 832,044 cases, 10,295 deaths; rates per 100,000: 8,206.2 cases, 101.5 deaths. 47.4% vaccinated.

Education: Compulsory: ages 5-14. **Literacy:** 99.8%.

Website: www.president.az

Azerbaijan was home to Scythian tribes and part of the Roman Empire. Overrun by Turks in the 11th cent. and conquered by Russia in 1806 and 1813, it joined the USSR Dec. 30, 1922, and became a constituent republic in 1936. Azerbaijan gained independence when the Soviet Union disbanded Dec. 26, 1991.

Nagorno-Karabakh, an enclave with a majority population of ethnic Armenians, seceded from Azerbaijan in 1988. A war between mostly Muslim Azerbaijan and mostly Christian Armenia, 1992-94, in which 30,000 died, left Armenia-backed separatists in control of Nagorno-Karabakh; hundreds of thousands of Azeris were expelled from the region. After heavy fighting Sept.-Nov. 2020, Azerbaijan regained control of much of the territory lost in the early 1990s. In a new offensive, Sept. 2023, Azerbaijan regained full control of Nagorno-Karabakh.

Voters approved a new constitution expanding presidential powers, Nov. 12, 1995. Pres. Haydar Aliyev, a pro-Russian former Communist, was reelected Oct. 11, 1998, but international monitors called the vote seriously flawed. His son Ilham Aliyev won a flawed Oct. 15, 2003, presidential election. He responded to violent protests Oct. 16 by arresting hundreds of opposition leaders and their supporters.

The opening May 25, 2005, of the Baku-Tbilisi-Ceyhan pipeline, providing an outlet for Azerbaijan's vast Caspian oil reserves, transformed the nation's economy. Construction began in 2014 on new pipelines to carry natural gas from Caspian Sea deposits in Azerbaijan to Georgia, Turkey, and Europe. An agreement announced July 18, 2022, would significantly increase Azerbaijani gas exports to the EU.

Pres. Ilham Aliyev won flawed 2008, 2013, and 2018 elections.

The European Parliament voted, Sept. 2017, to investigate a so-called Azerbaijani Laundromat scheme, in which almost $3 bil was reportedly sent out of Azerbaijan, including money allegedly paid to European officials to influence policy toward Azerbaijan.

The Bahamas
Commonwealth of The Bahamas

People: Population: 358,508 (173). **Age distrib.:** <15: 21.8%; 65+: 8.2%. **Growth:** 0.8%. **Migrants:** 16.2%. **Pop. density:** 92.8 per sq mi, 35.8 per sq km. **Urban:** 83.6%. **Ethnic groups:** African descent 90.6%, white 4.7%, mixed 2.1%. **Languages:** English (official), Creole (among Haitian immigrants). **Religions:** Christian (official) 92.3% (Protestant 71.1%, Catholic 13.3%), agnostic 4.7%.

Geography: Total area: 5,359 sq mi, 13,880 sq km (156); **Land area:** 3,865 sq mi, 10,010 sq km. **Location:** In Atlantic O., SE of Florida. U.S. is on W, Cuba to SW. **Topography:** Nearly 700 islands (30 inhabited) and over 2,000 cays in the W Atlantic O. extend 760 mi NW to SE. **Arable land:** 0.8%. **Capital:** Nassau, 279,668.

Government: Type: Parliamentary democracy under constitutional monarchy. **Head of state:** King Charles III, rep. by Gov.-Gen. Cynthia A. Pratt; b. 1945; in office: Sept. 1, 2023. **Head of govt.:** Prime Min. Philip Davis; b. 1951; in office: Sept. 18, 2021. **Local divisions:** 31 districts. **Defense budget:** $95 mil. **Active troops:** 1,500.

Economy: Industries: tourism, banking, oil bunkering, maritime, transshipment and logistics, salt, aragonite. **Chief agric.:** sugarcane, grapefruit, vegetables, bananas, tomatoes, poultry. **Natural resources:** salt, aragonite, timber. **Water:** 1,780 cu m per capita. **Electricity prod.:** 2.1 bil kWh. **Labor force:** agric. 3.2%, industry 11.7%, services 85.1%. **Unemployment:** 10.1%.

Finance: Monetary unit: Dollar (BSD) (1.00 = $1 U.S.). **GDP:** $16.6 bil; **per capita GDP:** $40,379; **GDP growth:** 14.4%. **Imports:** $4.9 bil; (2021) U.S. 37%, South Korea 12%, Germany 9%, China 7%, Russia 6%. **Exports:** $3.2 bil; (2021) U.S. 26%, Germany 16%, Singapore 13%, Poland 13%, Thailand 9%. **Tourism:** $2.7 bil. **Budget** (2020): $2.9 bil. **Inflation:** 5.6%.

Transport: Motor vehicles: 394.0 per 1,000 pop. **Airports:** 24.

Communications: Mobile: 98.5 per 100 pop. **Broadband:** 98.5 per 100 pop. **Internet:** 94.3%.

Health: Expend.: 7.6%. **Life expect.:** 74.5 male; 77.9 female. **Births:** 13.1 per 1,000 pop. **Deaths:** 5.7 per 1,000 pop. **Infant mortality:** 9.6 per 1,000 live births. **Undernourished:** NA. **HIV:** 0.9%. **COVID-19:** 38,084 cases, 844 deaths; rates per 100,000: 9,684.6 cases, 214.6 deaths. 42.5% vaccinated.

Education: Compulsory: ages 5-16. **Literacy:** NA.

Website: www.bahamas.gov.bs

Christopher Columbus likely first set foot in the Americas on San Salvador (Watling Isl.) in 1492, when Arawak Indians inhabited the islands. British settlement began in 1647; the islands became a British colony in 1783. Independence was attained July 10, 1973. Tourism and international finance are major industries. Hurricane Dorian, Sept. 1-3, 2019, devastated the northern Bahamas. The COVID-19 pandemic hurt the tourism industry; real GDP fell more than 16% in 2020, before rebounding in 2021. The impact of the pandemic hurt the governing party in Sept. 16, 2021, parliamentary elections; Philip Davis of the opposition Progressive Liberal Party became prime minister after the PLP won 32 of 39 lower house seats.

Bahrain
Kingdom of Bahrain

People: Population: 1,553,886 (151). **Age distrib.:** <15: 18.1%; 65+: 4.0%. **Growth:** 0.8%. **Migrants:** 55.0%. **Pop. density:** 5,295.5 per sq mi, 2,044.6 per sq km. **Urban:** 89.9%. **Ethnic groups:** Bahraini 46%, Asian 45.5%, other Arab 4.7%. **Languages:** Arabic (official), English, Farsi, Urdu. **Religions:** Muslim (official) 82.1% (Shia 53%, Sunni 29%), Christian 11.3%, Hindu 5.6%.

Geography: Total area: 293 sq mi, 760 sq km (174); **Land area:** 293 sq mi, 760 sq km. **Location:** SW Asia, in Persian Gulf. Saudi Arabia on W, Qatar on E. **Topography:** Bahrain Island and several adjacent, smaller islands are flat, hot, and humid with little rain. **Arable land:** 2.7%. **Capital:** Manama, 708,882.

Government: Type: Constitutional monarchy. **Head of state:** King Hamad bin Isa al-Khalifa; b. 1950; in office: as emir Mar. 6, 1999; as king Feb. 14, 2002. **Head of govt.:** Prime Min. Salman bin Hamad al-Khalifa; b. 1969; in office: Nov. 11, 2020. **Local divisions:** 4 governorates. **Defense budget:** $1.4 bil. **Active troops:** 8,200.

Economy: Industries: petroleum proc. and refining, aluminum smelting, iron pelletization, fertilizers, Islamic and offshore banking, insurance. **Chief agric.:** mutton, dates, milk, poultry, tomatoes, fruit. **Natural resources:** oil, nat. gas, fish, pearls. **Water:** 68 cu m per capita. **Crude oil reserves:** 187 mil bbls. **Electricity prod.:** 31.8 bil kWh. **Labor force:** agric. 1.0%, industry 34.9%, services 64.1%. **Unemployment:** 1.4%.

Finance: Monetary unit: Dinar (BHD) (0.38 = $1 U.S.). **GDP:** $90.1 bil; **per capita GDP:** $61,228; **GDP growth:** 4.9%. **Imports** (2018): $27.2 bil; UAE 27%, China 11%, Saudi Arabia 7%. **Exports** (2018): $30.1 bil; UAE 31%, Saudi Arabia 12%, Japan 8%, U.S. 8%. **Tourism:** $1.8 bil. **Budget:** $12.6 bil. **Inflation:** 3.6%.

Transport: Motor vehicles: 464.1 per 1,000 pop. **Airports:** 4.

Communications: Mobile: 145.4 per 100 pop. **Broadband:** 157.8 per 100 pop. **Internet:** 100.0%.

Health: Expend.: 4.7%. **Life expect.:** 77.9 male; 82.5 female. **Births:** 12.3 per 1,000 pop. **Deaths:** 2.8 per 1,000 pop. **Infant mortality:** 10.0 per 1,000 live births. **Undernourished:** NA. **HIV:** NA. **COVID-19:** 696,614 cases, 1,536 deaths; rates per 100,000: 40,939.4 cases, 90.3 deaths. 72.1% vaccinated.

Education: Compulsory: ages 6-14. **Literacy:** 97.5%.

Website: www.bahrain.bh

Long ruled by the Khalifa family, Bahrain was a British protectorate from 1861 to Aug. 15, 1971, when it regained independence. Oil was discovered in 1932. Natural gas output has more than doubled since 1990. A major offshore oil and gas field discovery was announced in Apr. 2018.

Emir Hamad bin Isa al-Khalifa proclaimed himself king Feb. 14, 2002. Local elections in May 2002 marked the first time Bahraini women were allowed to vote and run for office. The monarchy suppressed Arab Spring demonstrations Feb.-Mar. 2011. Protests, however, continued, largely by members of the country's Shiite majority against the mostly Sunni ruling elite. A 2015 Human Rights Watch report accused the government of torturing detained dissidents. Forced labor and sexual exploitation of Asian and African immigrants also gained international attention. Court rulings, 2016-17, ordered the dissolution of leading opposition groups. Crown prince Salman bin Hamad al-Khalifa became prime minister, Nov. 11, 2020.

Bahrain was one of a Saudi-led group of nations that broke diplomatic relations and embargoed trade with Qatar, June 2017-Jan. 2021, alleging Qatari support for terrorist and sectarian groups. Bahrain and Israel signed an agreement, Sept. 15, 2020, to establish diplomatic relations. Bahrain signed a security agreement with the U.S., Sept. 13, 2023.

Bangladesh
People's Republic of Bangladesh

People: Population: 167,184,465 (8). **Age distrib.:** <15: 25.4%; 65+: 7.5%. **Growth:** 0.9%. **Migrants:** 1.3%. **Pop. density:** 3,326.5 per sq mi, 1,284.4 per sq km. **Urban:** 40.5%. **Ethnic groups:**

Bengali 98.9%+. **Languages:** Bangla or Bengali (official). **Religions:** Muslim (official) 88.8% (Sunni), Hindu 9.3%.

Geography: Total area: 57,321 sq mi, 148,460 sq km (92); **Land area:** 50,259 sq mi, 130,170 sq km. **Location:** S Asia, on N bend of Bay of Bengal. India nearly surrounds country on W, N, E; Myanmar on SE. **Topography:** Mostly a low plain cut by the Ganges and Brahmaputra R. and their delta. Alluvial and marshy along the coast. Hilly only in the extreme SE and NE. Its tropical monsoon climate makes country among the world's rainiest. **Arable land:** 62.3%. **Capital:** Dhaka, 23,209,616. **Cities:** Chittagong, 5,379,660.

Government: Type: Parliamentary republic. **Head of state:** Pres. Mohammad Shahabuddin Chuppi; b. 1949; in office: Apr. 24, 2023. **Head of govt.:** Prime Min. Sheikh Hasina; b. 1947; in office: Jan. 6, 2009. **Local divisions:** 8 divisions. **Defense budget:** $4.3 bil. **Active troops:** 163,050.

Economy: Industries: jute, cotton, garments, paper, leather, fertilizer, iron and steel, cement, petroleum prods., tobacco, pharmaceuticals. **Chief agric.:** rice, potatoes, maize, sugarcane, milk, vegetables. **Natural resources:** nat. gas, timber, coal. **Water:** 7,451 cu m per capita. **Crude oil reserves:** 28 mil bbls. **Electricity prod.:** 80.6 bil kWh. **Labor force:** agric. 37.1%, industry 21.7%, services 41.2%. **Unemployment:** 4.7%.

Finance: Monetary unit: Taka (BDT) (109.22 = $1 U.S.). **GDP:** $1.3 tril; **per capita GDP:** $7,395; **GDP growth:** 7.1%. **Imports:** $85.3 bil; China 31%, India 15%. **Exports:** $49.4 bil; U.S. 15%, Germany 14%, UK 8%, Spain 7%, France 7%. **Tourism:** $272 mil. **Budget:** $46.4 bil. **Inflation:** 7.7%.

Transport: Railways: 1,529 mi. **Motor vehicles:** 3.2 per 1,000 pop. **Airports:** 16.

Communications: Mobile: 105.3 per 100 pop. **Broadband:** 51.8 per 100 pop. **Internet:** 38.9%.

Health: Expend.: 2.6%. **Life expect.:** 72.8 male; 77.2 female. **Births:** 17.5 per 1,000 pop. **Deaths:** 5.5 per 1,000 pop. **Infant mortality:** 29.6 per 1,000 live births. **Undernourished:** 11.2%. **HIV:** <0.1%. **COVID-19:** 2,045,159 cases, 29,476 deaths; rates per 100,000: 1,241.8 cases, 17.9 deaths. 85.7% vaccinated.

Education: Compulsory: ages 6-10. **Literacy:** 74.9%.

Website: bangladesh.gov.bd

Muslim invaders conquered the formerly Hindu area in the 12th cent. British rule lasted from the 18th cent. to 1947, when East Bengal became part of Pakistan.

Opposing domination by West Pakistan, the Awami League, based in the East, won control of the National Assembly in 1971. Assembly sessions were postponed; riots broke out. Pakistani troops attacked, Mar. 25; Bangladesh independence was proclaimed the next day. In the ensuing civil war, 1 mil died and 10 mil fled to India. War between India and Pakistan broke out Dec. 3, 1971. Pakistan surrendered in the East on Dec. 16. Mujibur Rahman, known as Sheikh Mujib, became prime min.; he was killed in a coup Aug. 15, 1975.

Army rivals killed Pres. Ziaur Rahman in an unsuccessful coup attempt, May 1981. Vice Pres. Abdus Sattar assumed the presidency but was ousted in a coup led by army chief of staff Gen. H. M. Ershad, Mar. 1982. A parliamentary system of government was adopted in 1991. A cyclone, Apr. 1991, killed over 131,000 people.

Political turmoil led to the resignation, Mar. 1996, of Prime Min. Khaleda Zia, a building near Dhaka that housed garment factories, collapsed Apr. 24, 2013. Sheikh Mujib's daughter, known as Sheikh Hasina, led the country after the June 1996 election. Khaleda Zia returned to power following parliamentary elections, Oct. 1, 2001. Militant Islamist bombings killed more than two dozen people Aug.-Dec. 2005. Bangladeshi economist Muhammad Yunus won the 2006 Nobel Peace Prize for using very small loans (microcredit) to help alleviate the nation's severe poverty.

Amid escalating political violence, Pres. Iajuddin Ahmed declared a state of emergency, Jan. 11, 2007, and a military-backed caretaker government took office. Cyclone Sidr struck Nov. 15, 2007, damaging more than 1.5 mil homes and leaving about 3,400 dead.

The Awami League triumphed in parliamentary elections Dec. 2008, and Sheikh Hasina returned as prime min. Jan. 6, 2009. She remained in office when her party won 2014 and 2018 elections. Her political rival, Khaleda Zia, was convicted, Feb. and Oct. 2018, on embezzlement charges Zia claimed were politically motivated; she was sentenced to a total of 17 years in prison. In 2022-23, the government intensified crackdowns on opposition parties, rights activists, and media ahead of announced Jan. 2024 parliamentary elections.

A garment factory fire Nov. 24, 2012, near Dhaka killed 112 workers. Rana Plaza, a building near Dhaka that housed garment factories, collapsed Apr. 24, 2013, killing more than 1,100 workers in the deadliest garment-industry disaster in world history. The owner of Rana Plaza, Sohel Rana, was among dozens of people charged, in 2016, with murder in connection with the disaster. With the murder case still pending, Sohel Rana was convicted, Aug. 29, 2017, and sentenced to 3 years in prison on corruption charges. After lengthy procedural delays, the murder trial resumed in early 2022.

Security forces in Dhaka, July 1-2, 2015, arrested 12 people said to be affiliated with al-Qaeda. Assassinations of non-Muslims and activists, attributed to Islamist militants, escalated in 2016. In an attack in Dhaka, July 1-2, 2016, for which ISIS claimed responsibility, 20 people, mostly foreigners, held hostage inside a restaurant were killed, as well as 2 police officers and 5 terrorist gunmen.

Beginning in late 2016, recurrent military and vigilante attacks in neighboring Myanmar caused much of the Rohingya population to seek refuge in Bangladesh. Anti-Rohingya violence in Myanmar peaked in Aug.-Sept. 2017, leading hundreds of thousands to flee. As of Aug. 31, 2023, about 963,000 Rohingya refugees were in Bangladesh.

Barbados

People: Population: 303,431 (175). **Age distrib.:** <15: 16.8%; 65+: 15.7%. **Growth:** 0.2%. **Migrants:** 12.1%. **Pop. density:** 1,827.6 per sq mi, 705.7 per sq km. **Urban:** 31.4%. **Ethnic groups:** African descent 92.4%, mixed 3.1%, white 2.7%. **Languages:** English (official), Bajan (English-based Creole). **Religions:** Christian (official) 94.4% (Protestant 78.8%).

Geography: Total area: 166 sq mi, 430 sq km (184); **Land area:** 166 sq mi, 430 sq km. **Location:** In Atlantic O., farthest E of West Indies. Nearest neighbors are St. Lucia and St. Vincent and the Grenadines to the W. **Topography:** Almost completely surrounded by coral reefs. Highest point is Mt. Hillaby (1,102 ft). **Arable land:** 16.3%. **Capital:** Bridgetown, 89,201.

Government: Type: Parliamentary republic. **Head of state:** Pres. Sandra Mason; b. 1949; in office: Nov. 30, 2021. **Head of govt.:** Prime Min. Mia Mottley; b. 1965; in office: May 25, 2018. **Local divisions:** 11 parishes, 1 city. **Defense budget:** $42 mil. **Active troops:** 610.

Economy: Industries: tourism, sugar, light mfg., component assembly for export. **Chief agric.:** sugarcane, poultry, vegetables, milk, eggs, pork. **Natural resources:** petroleum, fish, nat. gas. **Water:** 278 cu m per capita. **Crude oil reserves:** 2 mil bbls. **Electricity prod.:** 1.1 bil kWh. **Labor force:** agric. 2.8%, industry 16.6%, services 80.6%. **Unemployment:** 8.2%.

Finance: Monetary unit: Dollar (BBD) (2.00 = $1 U.S.). **GDP:** $5.0 bil; **per capita GDP:** $17,837; **GDP growth:** 10.0%. **Imports:** $2.1 bil; (2021) U.S. 37%, South Korea 12%, Germany 9%, China 7%, Russia 6%. **Exports:** $357.0 mil; (2021) U.S. 20%, Jamaica 12%, Guyana 8%, Trinidad and Tobago 7%, Italy 6%. **Tourism:** $575 mil. **Budget** (2020): $1.5 bil. **Inflation** (2018-19): 4.1%.

Transport: Motor vehicles: 434.8 per 1,000 pop. **Airports:** 1. **Communications: Mobile:** 114.9 per 100 pop. **Broadband:** 64.8 per 100 pop. **Internet:** 85.8%.

Health: Expend.: 7.2%. **Life expect.:** 76.0 male; 81.6 female. **Births:** 10.7 per 1,000 pop. **Deaths:** 8.0 per 1,000 pop. **Infant mortality:** 9.8 per 1,000 live births. **Undernourished:** <2.5%. **HIV:** 1.0%. **COVID-19:** 109,503 cases, 620 deaths; rates per 100,000: 38,104.6 cases, 215.7 deaths. 53.9% vaccinated.

Education: Compulsory: ages 5-15. **Literacy:** 99.6%.

Website: www.gov.bb

Barbados was probably named by Portuguese sailors in reference to bearded fig trees. An English ship visited in 1605, and English settlers arrived on the uninhabited island in 1627. Enslaved labor was forced to work the sugarcane plantations until slavery was abolished in 1834. Barbados became independent Nov. 30, 1966. Tourism, banking, and manufacturing have surpassed sugarcane in economic importance since the 1990s. Ousting the ruling Democratic Labour Party, the Barbados Labour Party (BLP) won all 30 House of Assembly seats in May 24, 2018, elections, making Mia Mottley the country's first female prime min.

Barbados became a republic, Nov. 30, 2021, ending the role of the British monarch as head of state. Elected by Parliament, Oct. 20, 2021, Sandra Mason became the country's first president. Mottley's BLP again won all 30 seats in Jan. 19, 2022, elections. Barbados's High Court, Dec. 12, 2022, struck down laws criminalizing gay sex.

Belarus
Republic of Belarus

People: Population: 9,383,853 (96). **Age distrib.:** <15: 16.3%; 65+: 17.3%. **Growth:** −0.3%. **Migrants:** 11.3%. **Pop. density:** 119.8 per sq mi, 46.2 per sq km. **Urban:** 80.7%. **Ethnic groups:** Belarusian 83.7%, Russian 8.3%, Polish 3.1%. **Languages:** Russian, Belarusian (both official). **Religions:** Christian 80.1% (Orthodox 65.0%, Catholic 11.6%), agnostic 17.4%, atheist 2.0%.

Geography: Total area: 80,155 sq mi, 207,600 sq km (84); **Land area:** 78,340 sq mi, 202,900 sq km. **Location:** Eastern Europe. Poland on W; Latvia, Lithuania on N; Russia on E; Ukraine on S. **Topography:** Landlocked country consisting mostly of hilly lowland with significant marsh areas in S. **Arable land:** 27.7%. **Capital:** Minsk, 2,057,257.

Government: Type: Presidential republic in name; in fact a dictatorship. **Head of state:** Pres. Aleksandr Lukashenko; b. 1954; in office: July 20, 1994. **Head of govt.:** Prime Min. Roman Golovchenko; b. 1973; in office: June 4, 2020. **Local divisions:** 6 regions, 1 municipality. **Defense budget:** $818 mil. **Active troops:** 47,950.

Economy: Industries: metal-cutting machine tools, tractors, trucks, earthmovers. **Chief agric.:** milk, potatoes, sugar beet, wheat, triticale, barley. **Natural resources:** timber, peat, oil, nat. gas, granite, dolomitic limestone, marl, chalk, sand, gravel, clay.

Water: 6,127 cu m per capita. **Crude oil reserves:** 198 mil bbls. **Electricity prod.:** 43.9 bil kWh. **Labor force:** agric. 8.1%, industry 32.6%, services 59.4%. **Unemployment:** 4.2%.

Finance: Monetary unit: Ruble (BYN) (2.50 = $1 U.S.). **GDP:** $208.0 bil; **per capita GDP:** $22,591; **GDP growth:** –4.7%. **Imports:** $45.5 bil; Russia 57%, China 7%. **Exports:** $49.4 bil; Russia 42%, Ukraine 13%, UK 7%. **Tourism:** $427 mil. **Budget:** $24.2 bil. **Inflation:** 15.2%.

Transport: Railways: 3,435 mi. **Motor vehicles:** 368.3 per 1,000 pop. **Airports:** 33.

Communications: Mobile: 123.4 per 100 pop. **Broadband:** 97.8 per 100 pop. **Internet:** 89.5%.

Health: Expend.: 6.4%. **Life expect.:** 69.6 male; 79.9 female. **Births:** 8.6 per 1,000 pop. **Deaths:** 13.3 per 1,000 pop. **Infant mortality:** 2.1 per 1,000 live births. **Undernourished:** <2.5%. **HIV:** 0.4%. **COVID-19:** 994,037 cases, 7,118 deaths; rates per 100,000: 10,519.7 cases, 75.3 deaths. 66.4% vaccinated.

Education: Compulsory: ages 6-16. **Literacy:** 99.9%.

Website: www.belarus.by

Belarus became a constituent republic of the USSR in 1922. Overrun by German armies in 1941, Belarus was recaptured by Soviet troops in 1944. Following WWII, Belarus increased in area through Soviet annexation of part of NE Poland. Belarus became independent when the Soviet Union disbanded Dec. 26, 1991.

Russia and Belarus signed a pact, Apr. 2, 1996, linking their political and economic systems. Sept. 2021 talks strengthened economic ties.

An authoritarian constitution enacted in Nov. 1996 gave Pres. Aleksandr Lukashenko (elected 1994) vast new powers. He retained office in five flawed elections, 2001-20. Weeks of large-scale protests followed the Aug. 9, 2020, elections; a brutal government response included thousands of arrests and reported torture of prisoners. Leading dissidents were jailed or exiled. Belarus supported Russia's 2022 invasion of Ukraine; Russian ground troops entered N Ukraine from Belarus, and Russian air attacks were launched from Belarus. Lukashenko claimed to have negotiated an end to a June 2023 mutiny in Russia by forces of the mercenary Wagner Group.

Belgium
Kingdom of Belgium

People: Population: 11,913,633 (82). **Age distrib.:** <15: 17.0%; 65+: 19.9%. **Growth:** 0.5%. **Migrants:** 17.3%. **Pop. density:** 1,019.1 per sq mi, 393.5 per sq km. **Urban:** 98.2%. **Ethnic groups:** Belgian 75.2%, Italian 4.1%, Moroccan 3.7%, French 2.4%, Turkish 2%, Dutch 2%. **Languages:** Dutch, French, German (all official). **Religions:** Christian 61.4% (Catholic 58.5%), agnostic 26.3%, Muslim 9.1% (Sunni), atheist 2.3%.

Geography: Total area: 11,787 sq mi, 30,528 sq km (137); **Land area:** 11,690 sq mi, 30,278 sq km. **Location:** Western Europe, on North Sea. France on W and S, Luxembourg on SE, Germany on E, Netherlands on N. **Topography:** Mostly flat; trisected by the Scheldt and Meuse, major commercial rivers. The land becomes hilly and forested in the Ardennes region to the SE. **Arable land:** 28.6%. **Capital:** Brussels, 2,121,992. **Cities:** Antwerpen, 1,057,215.

Government: Type: Federal parliamentary democracy under constitutional monarchy. **Head of state:** King Philippe; b. 1960; in office: July 21, 2013. **Head of govt.:** Prime Min. Alexander De Croo; b. 1975; in office: Oct. 1, 2020. **Local divisions:** 3 regions. **Defense budget:** $5.7 bil. **Active troops:** 23,200.

Economy: Industries: engineering and metal prods., motor vehicle assembly, transp. equip., scientific instruments, processed food/beverages. **Chief agric.:** sugar beet, milk, potatoes, wheat, pork, lettuce. **Natural resources:** constr. materials, silica sand, carbonates. **Water:** 1,579 cu m per capita. **Electricity prod.:** 94.9 bil kWh. **Labor force:** agric. 0.9%, industry 19.4%, services 79.7%. **Unemployment:** 5.6%.

Finance: Monetary unit: Euro (EUR) (0.93 = $1 U.S.). **GDP:** $758.8 bil; **per capita GDP:** $65,027; **GDP growth:** 3.2%. **Imports:** $509.0 bil; Netherlands 16%, Germany 13%, France 10%, U.S. 8%. **Exports:** $515.6 bil; Germany 17%, France 14%, Netherlands 13%, UK 8%, U.S. 6%. **Tourism:** $6.3 bil. **Budget:** $277.5 bil. **Inflation:** 9.6%.

Transport: Railways: 2,238 mi. **Motor vehicles:** 581.5 per 1,000 pop. **Airports:** 26.

Communications: Mobile: 101.9 per 100 pop. **Broadband:** 94.9 per 100 pop. **Internet:** 94.0%.

Health: Expend.: 11.1%. **Life expect.:** 79.5 male; 84.8 female. **Births:** 10.9 per 1,000 pop. **Deaths:** 9.6 per 1,000 pop. **Infant mortality:** 3.2 per 1,000 live births. **Undernourished:** <2.5%. **HIV:** 0.2%. **COVID-19:** 4,804,436 cases, 34,376 deaths; rates per 100,000: 41,696.8 cases, 298.3 deaths. 78.8% vaccinated.

Education: Compulsory: ages 6-17. **Literacy:** NA.

Website: www.belgium.be

Belgium derives its name from the Belgae, the first recorded inhabitants, probably Celts. The land was ruled for 1,800 years by conquerors, including Rome, the Franks, Burgundy, Spain, Austria, and France. After 1815, Belgium was made a part of the Netherlands but became an independent constitutional monarchy in 1830.

King Leopold III surrendered to Germany, May 28, 1940. After WWII, he was forced to abdicate in favor of his son, King Baudouin. Baudouin was succeeded by his brother, Albert II, Aug. 9, 1993. Albert's son Philippe became king July 21, 2013.

The Flemings of northern Belgium speak Dutch, while the Walloons in the south speak French. The language difference is a source of controversy between the two groups. Parliament has passed measures transferring power from the central government to three regions—Wallonia, Flanders, and Brussels. Constitutional changes in 1993 made Belgium a federal state. After elections June 2007, rivalries between Flemings and Walloons created a 9-month political stalemate. June 2010 elections led to a political deadlock that lasted until Dec. 2011. After May 25, 2014, elections, Charles Michel was sworn in as prime min. Oct. 11, heading a center-right coalition government.

Evidence emerged in Nov. 2015 that Islamist extremists living in Belgium planned and took part in terrorist attacks in France, Nov. 13, that killed 130. In Mar. 22, 2016, attacks for which the Sunni extremist group ISIS claimed responsibility, 3 suicide bombers killed 32 others and wounded more than 300 in a Brussels subway station and at the city's airport (6 men were convicted of murder, July 25, 2023, for their roles in the 2016 attacks).

Michel's coalition collapsed, Dec. 2018, over immigration policy; he continued as caretaker prime min. After inconclusive May 26, 2019, elections, Sophie Wilmès became caretaker prime min., Oct. 27—Belgium's first female head of government. A 7-party coalition headed by Prime Min. Alexander De Croo took office Oct. 1, 2020.

Belize

People: Population: 419,137 (170). **Age distrib.:** <15: 28.2%; 65+: 5.4%. **Growth:** 1.6%. **Migrants:** 15.6%. **Pop. density:** 47.6 per sq mi, 18.4 per sq km. **Urban:** 46.6%. **Ethnic groups:** mestizo 52.9%, Creole 25.9%, Maya 11.3%, Garifuna 6.1%, East Indian 3.9%, Mennonite 3.6%. **Languages:** English (official), Spanish, Creole, Maya, German, Garifuna. **Religions:** Christian 92.2% (Catholic 60.7%, Protestant 25.6%), Baha'i 2.5%, Hindu 2.1%.

Geography: Total area: 8,867 sq mi, 22,966 sq km (148); **Land area:** 8,805 sq mi, 22,806 sq km. **Location:** Eastern coast of Central America. Mexico on N, Guatemala on W and S. **Topography:** Swampy lowlands in N, Maya Mts. in S, coral reefs and cays near coast. Tropical climate. **Arable land:** 4.4%. **Capital:** Belmopan, 22,964.

Government: Type: Parliamentary democracy under constitutional monarchy. **Head of state:** King Charles III, rep. by Gov.-Gen. Froyla Tzalam, in office: May 27, 2021. **Head of govt.:** Prime Min. John Briceño; b. 1960; in office: Nov. 12, 2020. **Local divisions:** 6 districts. **Defense budget:** $23 mil. **Active troops:** 1,500.

Economy: Industries: garment prod., food proc., tourism, constr. **Chief agric.:** sugarcane, oranges, bananas, maize, poultry, rice. **Natural resources:** timber, fish, hydropower. **Water:** 54,659 cu m per capita. **Crude oil reserves:** 7 mil bbls. **Electricity prod.:** 644.1 mil kWh. **Labor force:** agric. 21.2%, industry 18.9%, services 59.9%. **Unemployment:** 9.7%.

Finance: Monetary unit: Dollar (BZD) (2.02 = $1 U.S.). **GDP:** $4.6 bil; **per capita GDP:** $11,451; **GDP growth:** 12.1%. **Imports:** $1.3 bil; (2021) U.S. 29%, China 14%, Seychelles 13%, Guatemala 10%, Mexico 9%. **Exports:** $1.0 bil; (2021) U.S. 16%, UK 16%, Guatemala 7%, Italy 6%, Spain 6%. **Tourism:** $374 mil. **Budget:** $656 mil. **Inflation:** 6.3%.

Transport: Motor vehicles: 122.3 per 1,000 pop. **Airports:** 6.

Communications: Mobile (2021): 66.0 per 100 pop. **Broadband** (2021): 44.2 per 100 pop. **Internet:** 62.0%.

Health: Expend.: 6.9%. **Life expect.:** 71.9 male; 75.6 female. **Births:** 18.0 per 1,000 pop. **Deaths:** 5.2 per 1,000 pop. **Infant mortality:** 11.3 per 1,000 live births. **Undernourished:** 4.9%. **HIV:** 1.3%. **COVID-19:** 70,782 cases, 688 deaths; rates per 100,000: 17,801.1 cases, 173.0 deaths. 50.7% vaccinated.

Education: Compulsory: ages 5-12. **Literacy:** NA.

Website: www.belize.gov.bz

Belize (formerly British Honduras) gained independence from Great Britain Sept. 21, 1981. Belize has become a center for drug trafficking between Colombia and the U.S. Ending 12 years of United Democratic Party governance, the People's United Party swept Nov. 11, 2020, elections, making PUP leader John Briceño prime minister.

Benin
Republic of Benin

People: Population: 14,219,908 (74). **Age distrib.:** <15: 45.4%; 65+: 2.5%. **Growth:** 3.3%. **Migrants:** 3.3%. **Pop. density:** 332.9 per sq mi, 128.5 per sq km. **Urban:** 50.1%. **Ethnic groups:** Fon and related 38.4%, Adja/related 15.1%, Yoruba/related 12%, Bariba/related 9.6%, Fulani/related 8.6%, Ottamari/related 6.1%, Yoa-Lokpa/related 4.3%, Dendi/related 2.9%. **Languages:** French (official), Fon, Yom, Yoruba in S; Bariba, Fulfulde in N. **Religions:** Christian 45.6% (Catholic 23.8%, independent 11.6%, Protestant 10.2%), Muslim 27.5% (Sunni), ethnic religionist 26.5%.

Geography: Total area: 43,484 sq mi, 112,622 sq km (100); **Land area:** 42,711 sq mi, 110,622 sq km. **Location:** W Africa on Gulf of Guinea. Togo on W; Burkina Faso, Niger on N; Nigeria on E. **Topography:** Mostly flat and covered with dense vegetation. The coast is hot, humid, and rainy. **Arable land:** 24.8%. **Capital:** Cotonou (seat), 722,139; Porto-Novo (constitutional), 285,328. **Cities:** Abomey-Calavi, 1,252,890.

Government: Type: Presidential republic. **Head of state and govt.:** Pres. Patrice Talon; b. 1958; in office: Apr. 6, 2016. **Local divisions:** 12 departments. **Defense budget:** $394 mil. **Active troops:** 12,300.

Economy: Industries: textiles, food proc., constr. materials, cement. **Chief agric.:** cassava, yams, maize, cotton, oil palm fruit, rice. **Natural resources:** offshore oil, limestone, marble, timber. **Water:** 2,177 cu m per capita. **Crude oil reserves:** 8 mil bbls. **Electricity prod.:** 241.1 mil kWh. **Labor force:** agric. 28.1%, industry 22.5%, services 49.3%. **Unemployment:** 1.7%.

Finance: Monetary unit: CFA Franc (XOF) (606.88 = $1 U.S.). **GDP:** $54.2 bil; **per capita GDP:** $4,056; **GDP growth:** 6.3%. **Imports** (2020): $3.9 bil; China 28%, Thailand 9%, India 8%, Togo 6%. **Exports** (2020): $3.5 bil; Nigeria 25%, Bangladesh 14%, UAE 14%, India 13%, China 8%. **Tourism** (2020): $200 mil. **Budget:** $2.1 bil. **Inflation:** 1.4%.

Transport: Railways: 272 mi. **Motor vehicles:** 3.8 per 1,000 pop. **Airports:** 1.

Communications: Mobile: 109.0 per 100 pop. **Broadband:** 42.2 per 100 pop. **Internet:** 34.0%.

Health: Expend.: 2.6%. **Life expect.:** 60.8 male; 64.6 female. **Births:** 40.7 per 1,000 pop. **Deaths:** 7.8 per 1,000 pop. **Infant mortality:** 54.3 per 1,000 live births. **Undernourished:** 9.9%. **HIV:** 0.8%. **COVID-19:** 28,014 cases, 163 deaths; rates per 100,000: 231.1 cases, 1.3 deaths. 22.6% vaccinated.

Education: Compulsory: ages 6-11. **Literacy:** 45.8%.

Website: www.gouv.bj

The Kingdom of Abomey, rising to power in the 17th cent., came under French domination in the late 19th cent. and was incorporated into French West Africa by 1904. Under the name Dahomey, the country gained independence Aug. 1, 1960; it became Benin in 1975. In the fifth coup since independence, Mathieu (Ahmed) Kérékou took power in 1972; he ruled until 1991, when democracy was restored, and served as elected president 1996-2006.

Patrice Talon won a presidential runoff election Mar. 20, 2016. Rule changes to help Talon loyalists in Apr. 28, 2019, legislative elections, as well as a crackdown on dissent, led to violent protests. With opposition suppressed, Talon won reelection, Apr. 11, 2021, with more than 86% of the vote.

Benin's parliament, Oct. 20, 2021, adopted legislation to legalize abortion in most cases. Parties supporting Talon won more open Jan. 8, 2023, legislative elections; an opposition party gained 28 seats.

Bhutan
Kingdom of Bhutan

People: Population: 876,181 (161). **Age distrib.:** <15: 23.5%; 65+: 6.5%. **Growth:** 1.0%. **Migrants:** 6.9%. **Pop. density:** 59.1 per sq mi, 22.8 per sq km. **Urban:** 44.4%. **Ethnic groups:** Ngalop or Bhote 50%, ethnic Nepali (predom. Lhotshampas) 35%, indigenous or migrant tribes 15%. **Languages:** Sharchopkha, Dzongkha (official), Lhotshamkha. **Religions:** Buddhist (official) 81.4% (Lamaist), Hindu 12.2% (Shaivite 6%, Vaishnavite 6%), ethnic religionist 3.6%, Christian 2.5%.

Geography: Total area: 14,824 sq mi, 38,394 sq km (133); **Land area:** 14,824 sq mi, 38,394 sq km. **Location:** S Asia, in eastern Himalayan Mts. India (Sikkim state) on W and S, China on N. **Topography:** Very high mountains in the N, fertile valleys in the center, and thick forests in the Duar Plain in the S. **Arable land:** 2.5%. **Capital:** Thimphu, 203,297.

Government: Type: Constitutional monarchy. **Head of state:** King Jigme Khesar Namgyel Wangchuck; b. 1980; in office: Dec. 14, 2006. **Head of govt.:** Prime Min. Lotay Tshering; in office: Nov. 7, 2018. **Local divisions:** 20 districts. **Defense budget/active troops:** NA.

Economy: Industries: cement, wood prods., processed fruits, alcoholic beverages, calcium carbide, tourism. **Chief agric.:** milk, rice, maize, potatoes, roots/tubers, oranges. **Natural resources:** timber, hydropower, gypsum, calcium carbonate. **Water:** 101,088 cu m per capita. **Electricity prod.:** 9.0 bil kWh. **Labor force:** agric. 56.0%, industry 10.1%, services 33.9%. **Unemployment:** 3.6%.

Finance: Monetary unit: Ngultrum (BTN) (82.62 = $1 U.S.). **GDP:** $9.4 bil; **per capita GDP** (2021): $12,036; **GDP growth** (2021): 4.1%. **Imports:** $1.0 bil; India 85%. **Exports:** $741.6 mil; India 94%. **Tourism:** $4 mil. **Budget** (2020): $777 mil (nearly one-quarter financed by India's govt.). **Inflation:** 5.6%.

Transport: Airports: 2.

Communications: Mobile: 94.9 per 100 pop. **Broadband:** 94.6 per 100 pop. **Internet:** 85.6%.

Health: Expend.: 4.4%. **Life expect.:** 71.8 male; 74.3 female. **Births:** 15.6 per 1,000 pop. **Deaths:** 6.1 per 1,000 pop. **Infant mortality:** 25.6 per 1,000 live births. **Undernourished:** NA. **HIV:** 0.2%. **COVID-19:** 62,694 cases, 21 deaths; rates per 100,000: 8,125.1 cases, 2.7 deaths. 87.8% vaccinated.

Education: Compulsory: NA. **Literacy:** 71.0%.

Website: www.bhutan.gov.bt

The region came under Tibetan rule in the 16th cent. British influence grew in the 19th cent. A Buddhist monarchy was set up in 1907. After a 1910 treaty, Britain guided Bhutan's external affairs, while the country remained internally self-governing. Upon independence the treaty was revised, 1949, to allow India to assume Britain's role.

Isolated for much of its history, Bhutan has taken steps toward modernization. King Jigme Singye Wangchuck, in power since 1972, stepped down Dec. 14, 2006, in favor of his son, Jigme Khesar Namgyel Wangchuck. Multiparty parliamentary elections took place Mar. 24, 2008. A new constitution, ratified July 18, made Bhutan a democratic constitutional monarchy. The People's Democratic Party won July 13, 2013, parliamentary elections. After the United Party of Bhutan won Oct. 18, 2018, elections, surgeon Lotay Tshering became prime min.

Bolivia
Plurinational State of Bolivia

People: Population: 12,186,079 (79). **Age distrib.:** <15: 29.1%; 65+: 6.8%. **Growth:** 1.1%. **Migrants:** 1.4%. **Pop. density:** 29.1 per sq mi, 11.2 per sq km. **Urban:** 71.2%. **Ethnic groups:** mestizo (mixed white/Amerindian) 68%, Indigenous 20%, white 5%, cholo/chola 2%. **Languages:** Spanish, Quechua, Aymara, Guarani (all official). **Religions:** Christian 92.4% (Catholic 77.9%), ethnic religionist 2.5%, agnostic 2.4%, Baha'i 2.4%.

Geography: Total area: 424,164 sq mi, 1,098,581 sq km (27); **Land area:** 418,265 sq mi, 1,083,301 sq km. **Location:** W central South America, in the Andes Mts. One of two landlocked countries in S America. Peru, Chile on W; Argentina, Paraguay on S; Brazil on E and N. **Topography:** The great central plateau, more than 500 mi long at an elevation of 12,000 ft, lies between two cordilleras having three of the highest peaks in S America. Lake Titicaca, on Peruvian border, is world's highest lake (12,500 ft) navigable by large boats. The E central region has semitropical forests; the llanos, or Amazon-Chaco lowlands, are in E. **Arable land:** 4.5%. **Capital:** La Paz (administrative), 1,935,619; Sucre (constitutional), 277,910. **Cities:** Santa Cruz, 1,820,114; Cochabamba, 1,400,250.

Government: Type: Presidential republic. **Head of state and govt.:** Pres. Luis Alberto Arce Catacora; b. 1963; in office: Nov. 8, 2020. **Local divisions:** 9 departments. **Defense budget:** $481 mil. **Active troops:** 34,100.

Economy: Industries: mining, smelting, electricity, petroleum, food/beverages, handicrafts, clothing, jewelry. **Chief agric.:** sugarcane, soybeans, potatoes, maize, sorghum, rice. **Natural resources:** lithium, tin, nat. gas, petroleum, zinc, tungsten, antimony, silver, iron, lead, gold, timber, hydropower. **Water:** 49,173 cu m per capita. **Crude oil reserves:** 241 mil bbls. **Electricity prod.:** 10.6 bil kWh. **Labor force:** agric. 29.2%, industry 18.5%, services 52.2%. **Unemployment:** 4.4%.

Finance: Monetary unit: Boliviano (BOB) (6.91 = $1 U.S.). **GDP:** $118.4 bil; **per capita GDP:** $9,684; **GDP growth:** 3.1%. **Imports:** $10.8 bil; (2017) Brazil 22%, Chile 15%, China 13%, Peru 11%, Argentina 8%, U.S. 7%. **Exports:** $11.4 bil; Argentina 16%, Brazil 15%, UAE 12%, India 10%, U.S. 6%. **Tourism:** $190 mil. **Budget:** $14.8 bil. **Inflation:** 1.7%.

Transport: Railways: 2,461 mi. **Motor vehicles:** 84.5 per 1,000 pop. **Airports:** 21.

Communications: Mobile (2021): 99.6 per 100 pop. **Broadband** (2021): 86.7 per 100 pop. **Internet:** 66.0%.

Health: Expend.: 7.9%. **Life expect.:** 71.0 male; 74.0 female. **Births:** 18.1 per 1,000 pop. **Deaths:** 6.5 per 1,000 pop. **Infant mortality:** 22.3 per 1,000 live births. **Undernourished:** 19.4%. **HIV:** 0.4%. **COVID-19:** 1,206,420 cases, 22,399 deaths; rates per 100,000: 10,335.1 cases, 191.9 deaths. 53.9% vaccinated.

Education: Compulsory: ages 4-17. **Literacy:** 93.9%.

Website: www.bolivia.gob.bo

The Incas conquered the region's earlier Indian inhabitants in the 13th cent. Spanish colonial rule began in the 1530s and lasted until Aug. 6, 1825. The country is named after independence fighter Simón Bolívar. In a series of wars, Bolivia lost its Pacific coast to Chile, the oil-bearing Chaco to Paraguay, and rubber-growing areas to Brazil, 1879-1935.

Economic unrest, especially among militant mine workers, led to continuing political instability. A reformist government under Victor Paz Estenssoro, 1951-64, nationalized tin mines and attempted to improve conditions for the Indian majority but was overthrown by a military junta. A series of coups and countercoups continued until constitutional government was restored in 1982.

U.S. pressure on the government to reduce production of coca, the raw material for cocaine, led to clashes between police and growers. Gen. Hugo Banzer Suárez, who ruled as a dictator, 1971-78, later governed as president, 1997-2001.

Leftist Juan Evo Morales Ayma won the presidential election, Dec. 2005. Bolivia's first Indigenous president, he nationalized the hydrocarbon sector and launched a land-redistribution program. Voters, Jan. 25, 2009, approved a new constitution strengthening the rights of Bolivia's Indigenous majority. Morales won a second term Dec. 6, 2009. His government nationalized major utility companies in 2012. Morales won reelection Oct. 12, 2014.

After Morales appeared to narrowly win a fourth term in Oct. 20, 2019, elections, large-scale protests and allegations of fraud forced his resignation, Nov. 10; second Senate Vice Pres. Jeanine Áñez Chavez became acting president, Nov. 12, in a process later criticized by the OAS. In a new election, Oct. 18, 2020, Luis Alberto Arce Catacora of Morales's leftist party easily won the presidency. Áñez, who was arrested Mar. 13, 2021, was convicted of assuming the presidency illegally and sentenced to 10 years in prison, June 10, 2022; additional charges were pending. Luis Fernando Camacho, a losing candidate in the 2020 election, was arrested in Dec. 2022 on charges related to Morales's ouster.

Bolivia was severely affected by the COVID-19 pandemic that began in 2020. A WHO study released in May 2022 estimated COVID-related deaths in Bolivia in 2020-21 at about four times the officially reported figure.

Bosnia and Herzegovina

People: Population: 3,807,764 (130). **Age distrib.:** <15: 13.1%; 65+: 17.9%. **Growth:** −0.2%. **Migrants:** 1.1%. **Pop. density:** 192.7 per sq mi, 74.4 per sq km. **Urban:** 50.3%. **Ethnic groups:** Bosniak 50.1%, Serb 30.8%, Croat 15.4%. **Languages:** Bosnian, Serbian, Croatian (all official). **Religions:** Christian 49.5% (Orthodox 37.9%, Catholic 11.3%), Muslim 47.3% (Sunni), agnostic 2.8%.

Geography: Total area: 19,767 sq mi, 51,197 sq km (125); **Land area:** 19,763 sq mi, 51,187 sq km. **Location:** Balkan Peninsula in SE Europe. Serbia, Montenegro on E and SE; Croatia on N and W. **Topography:** Hilly with some mountains. **Arable land:** 19.7%. **Capital:** Sarajevo, 345,549.

Government: Type: Parliamentary republic. **Heads of state:** Collective presidency with rotating leadership every 8 months. **Head of govt.:** Chair of the Council of Ministers Borjana Kristo; b. 1961; in office: Jan. 25, 2023. **Local divisions:** 3 first-order admin. divisions. **Defense budget:** $169 mil. **Active troops:** 10,500.

Economy: Industries: steel, coal, iron ore, lead, zinc, manganese, bauxite, aluminum, motor vehicle assembly, textiles, tobacco prods. **Chief agric.:** maize, milk, vegetables, potatoes, wheat, plums/sloes. **Natural resources:** coal, iron ore, antimony, bauxite, copper, lead, zinc, chromite, cobalt, manganese, nickel, clay, gypsum, salt, sand, timber, hydropower. **Water:** 11,430 cu m per capita. **Electricity prod.:** 17.4 bil kWh. **Labor force:** agric. 11.3%, industry 34.3%, services 54.4%. **Unemployment:** 14.1%.

Finance: Monetary unit: Convertible Mark (BAM) (1.81 = $1 U.S.). **GDP:** $65.9 bil; **per capita GDP:** $20,377; **GDP growth:** 3.9%. **Imports:** $12.7 bil; Croatia 15%, Serbia 13%, Germany 10%, Italy 9%, Slovenia 7%, China 6%. **Exports:** $9.9 bil; Germany 14%, Italy 12%, Croatia 11%, Serbia 11%, Austria 9%, Slovenia 8%. **Tourism:** $973 mil. **Budget:** $8.2 bil. **Inflation:** 14.0%.

Transport: Railways: 600 mi. **Airports:** 7.

Communications: Mobile: 117.9 per 100 pop. **Broadband:** 64.4 per 100 pop. **Internet:** 78.8%.

Health: Expend.: 9.8%. **Life expect.:** 75.3 male; 81.4 female. **Births:** 8.3 per 1,000 pop. **Deaths:** 10.3 per 1,000 pop. **Infant mortality:** 5.1 per 1,000 live births. **Undernourished:** <2.5%. **HIV:** NA. **COVID-19:** 403,061 cases, 16,352 deaths; rates per 100,000: 12,285.4 cases, 498.4 deaths. 25.9% vaccinated.

Education: Compulsory: ages 6-14. **Literacy:** 98.1%.

Website: www.fbihvlada.gov.ba

Bosnia was ruled by Croatian kings c. 958 CE, and by Hungary 1000-1200. It became organized c. 1200 and later took control of Herzegovina. The kingdom disintegrated after 1391, with the southern part becoming the independent duchy of Herzegovina. It was conquered by Turks in 1463 and made a Turkish province. The area was placed under control of Austria-Hungary in 1878 and made part of the province of Bosnia and Herzegovina, which was formally annexed to Austria-Hungary, 1908. Bosnia became a province of Yugoslavia in 1918. It was reunited with Herzegovina as a federated republic under the 1946 Yugoslav constitution.

Bosnia and Herzegovina declared sovereignty Oct. 15, 1991. A referendum for independence was passed Feb. 29, 1992. Ethnic Serbs' opposition to the referendum spurred violent clashes and bombings. The U.S. and EU recognized the republic Apr. 7. Fierce three-way fighting continued between Bosnia's Serbs, Muslims, and Croats. Serb forces engaged in ethnic cleansing, killing thousands of Bosnian Muslims (Bosniaks) and expelling Muslims and other non-Serbs from areas under Bosnian Serb control. Muslims and Croats in Bosnia began a cease-fire Feb. 23, 1994, and signed an accord, Mar. 18, to create a Muslim-Croat confederation in Bosnia. However, by mid-1994, Bosnian Serbs controlled over 70% of the country.

As fighting continued in 1995, the balance of power shifted toward the Muslim-Croat alliance. Massive NATO airstrikes on Bosnian Serb targets beginning Aug. 30 triggered a new round of peace talks. These talks produced an agreement to create autonomous regions within Bosnia, with the Serb region (Republika Srpska) constituting 49% of the country.

A peace agreement was signed in Paris, Dec. 14, 1995, by leaders of Bosnia, Croatia, and Serbia. Some 60,000 NATO troops (about 20,000 from the U.S.) moved in to police the accord. Meanwhile, a UN tribunal—the International Criminal Tribunal for the Former Yugoslavia (ICTY), established in 1993 at The Hague, Netherlands—began bringing charges against suspected war criminals. Elections were held Sept. 14, 1996, for a 3-person collective presidency, for seats in a federal parliament, and for regional offices. In Dec. a revamped NATO Stabilization Force (SFOR) of over 30,000 members (more than 8,000 from the U.S.) received an 18-month mandate, which was later extended.

The ICTY found Radislav Krstic, a Bosnian Serb general, guilty in 2001, in connection with the genocide of thousands of Muslims at Srebrenica in 1995. An EU peacekeeping force (EUFOR), initially with 7,000 members, assumed responsibility from SFOR, Dec. 2, 2004. Accused of complicity in the Srebrenica and other atrocities, former Bosnian Serb leader Radovan Karadzic was convicted, Mar. 24, 2016, by the ICTY of genocide, war crimes, and crimes against humanity; he was ultimately sentenced to life in prison. Gen. Ratko Mladic, the former Bosnian Serb military commander accused of directing the Srebrenica massacre, was convicted by the ICTY, Nov. 22, 2017, of genocide, war crimes, and crimes against humanity and sentenced to life in prison. An ICTY successor tribunal at The Hague convicted, June 30, 2021, two former high-ranking Serbian security officials of abetting war crimes in Bosnia. EUFOR strength in Bosnia was about 1,100 in 2023.

Bosnia ranked among the hardest-hit countries by per capita deaths during the COVID-19 pandemic that began in 2020.

Botswana
Republic of Botswana

People: Population: 2,417,596 (142). **Age distrib.:** <15: 29.2%; 65+: 5.9%. **Growth:** 1.4%. **Migrants:** 4.7%. **Pop. density:** 11.0 per sq mi, 4.3 per sq km. **Urban:** 72.9%. **Ethnic groups:** Tswana or Setswana 79%, Kalanga 11%, Basarwa 3%. **Languages:** Setswana, Sekalanga, Shekgalagadi, English (official). **Religions:** Christian 75.3% (independent 48.9%, Protestant 18.6%), ethnic religionist 23.1%.

Geography: Total area: 224,607 sq mi, 581,730 sq km (48); **Land area:** 218,816 sq mi, 566,730 sq km. **Location:** Southern Africa. Namibia on N and W, Zambia on N, Zimbabwe on NE, South Africa on S. **Topography:** The Kalahari Desert, supporting nomadic peoples and wildlife, spreads over SW. Swamplands and farming areas in N; rolling plains in E where livestock are grazed. **Arable land:** 0.5%. **Capital:** Gaborone, 269,338.

Government: Type: Parliamentary republic. **Head of state and govt.:** Pres. Mokgweetsi Masisi; b. 1962; in office: Apr. 1, 2018. **Local divisions:** 10 districts, 6 town councils. **Defense budget:** $495 mil. **Active troops:** 9,000.

Economy: Industries: diamonds, copper, nickel, salt, soda ash, potash, coal, iron ore, silver. **Chief agric.:** milk, roots/tubers, vegetables, sorghum, beef, game meat. **Natural resources:** diamonds, copper, nickel, salt, soda ash, potash, coal, iron ore, silver. **Water:** 5,205 cu m per capita. **Electricity prod.:** 2.2 bil kWh. **Labor force:** agric. 23.1%, industry 14.7%, services 62.2%. **Unemployment:** 20.7%.

Finance: Monetary unit: Pula (BWP) (13.50 = $1 U.S.). **GDP:** $48.2 bil; **per capita GDP:** $18,323; **GDP growth:** 5.8%. **Imports:** $9.3 bil; South Africa 58%, Namibia 9%, Canada 7%. **Exports:** $7.9 bil; India 21%, Belgium 19%, UAE 19%, South Africa 9%, Israel 7%, Hong Kong 6%. **Tourism** (2020): $211 mil. **Budget** (2020): $6 bil. **Inflation:** 11.7%.

Transport: Railways: 552 mi. **Motor vehicles:** 240.2 per 1,000 pop. **Airports:** 10.

Communications: Mobile: 165.3 per 100 pop. **Broadband:** 108.2 per 100 pop. **Internet:** 73.5%.

Health: Expend.: 6.2%. **Life expect.:** 64.0 male; 68.2 female. **Births:** 20.0 per 1,000 pop. **Deaths:** 9.0 per 1,000 pop. **Infant mortality:** 24.4 per 1,000 live births. **Undernourished:** 22.9%. **HIV:** 16.4%. **COVID-19:** 330,229 cases, 2,800 deaths; rates per 100,000: 14,042.6 cases, 119.1 deaths. 70.7% vaccinated.

Education: Compulsory: NA. **Literacy:** 88.5%.

Website: www.gov.bw

First inhabited by San people, then Bantus, the region became the British protectorate of Bechuanaland in 1886. The country became fully independent Sept. 30, 1966. Mining, especially of diamonds, has contributed to economic growth. Pres. Festus Mogae transferred power Apr. 1, 2008, to Seretse Khama Ian Khama, son of Botswana's independence leader and first president (1966-80), Sir Seretse Khama. Mokgweetsi Eric Masisi became president, Apr. 1, 2018. In power since independence, the Botswana Democratic Party won Oct. 23, 2019, legislative elections—keeping the BDP's Masisi in office.

The High Court, June 11, 2019, struck down 1965 penal code provisions criminalizing same-sex relationships. During the COVID-19 pandemic that began in 2020, Botswana had one of the highest vaccination rates of any African country.

Brazil
Federative Republic of Brazil

People: Population: 218,689,757 (7). **Age distrib.:** <15: 19.8%; 65+: 10.5%. **Growth:** 0.6%. **Migrants:** 0.5%. **Pop. density:** 67.8 per sq mi, 26.2 per sq km. **Urban:** 87.8%. **Ethnic groups:** white

47.7%, mixed 43.1%, Black 7.6%. **Languages:** Portuguese (official). **Religions:** Christian 90.5% (Catholic 63.6%, Protestant 14.4%, independent 12.4%), Spiritist 4.8%, agnostic 2.9%.

Geography: Total area: 3,287,957 sq mi, 8,515,770 sq km (5); **Land area:** 3,227,096 sq mi, 8,358,140 sq km. **Location:** Occupies eastern half of S America. French Guiana, Suriname, Guyana, Venezuela on N; Colombia, Peru, Bolivia, Paraguay on W; Argentina, Uruguay on S. **Topography:** Atlantic coastline stretches 4,603 mi. Heavily wooded Amazon basin covers N half of country. Vast network of navigable rivers. The Amazon R. flows 2,093 mi in Brazil. The NE region is semiarid scrubland, heavily settled and poor. Almost half of pop. resides in S central region. Most major cities are in the narrow coastal belt. Almost the entire country has a tropical or semitropical climate. **Arable land:** 7.0%. **Capital:** Brasília, 4,873,048. **Cities:** São Paulo, 22,619,736; Rio de Janeiro, 13,727,720; Belo Horizonte, 6,247,889.

Government: Type: Federal presidential republic. **Head of state and govt.:** Pres. Luiz Inácio Lula da Silva; b. 1945; in office: Jan. 1, 2023. **Local divisions:** 26 states, 1 federal district. **Defense budget:** $23.0 bil. **Active troops:** 366,500.

Economy: Industries: textiles, shoes, chemicals, cement, lumber, iron ore, tin, steel, aircraft, motor vehicles and parts. **Chief agric.:** sugarcane, soybeans, maize, milk, cassava, oranges. **Natural resources:** alumina, bauxite, beryllium, gold, iron ore, manganese, nickel, niobium, phosphates, platinum, tantalum, tin, rare earth elements, uranium, petroleum. **Water:** 40,680 cu m per capita. **Crude oil reserves:** 12.7 bil bbls. **Electricity prod.:** 662.6 bil kWh. **Labor force:** agric. 9.7%, industry 20.6%, services 69.7%. **Unemployment:** 9.5%.

Finance: Monetary unit: Real (BRL) (4.89 = $1 U.S.). **GDP:** $3.8 tril; **per capita GDP:** $17,822; **GDP growth:** 2.9%. **Imports:** $297.9 bil; China 21%, U.S. 18%, Germany 6%, Argentina 6%. **Exports:** $172.2 bil; China 28%, U.S. 13%. **Tourism** (2020): $2.9 bil. **Budget** (2020): $6173 bil. **Inflation:** 9.3%.

Transport: Railways: 18,548 mi. **Motor vehicles:** 213.5 per 1,000 pop. **Airports:** 698.

Communications: Mobile: 98.9 per 100 pop. **Broadband:** 93.1 per 100 pop. **Internet:** 80.5%.

Health: Expend.: 10.3%. **Life expect.:** 72.6 male; 79.8 female. **Births:** 13.4 per 1,000 pop. **Deaths:** 6.9 per 1,000 pop. **Infant mortality:** 13.1 per 1,000 live births. **Undernourished:** 4.7%. **HIV:** 0.6%. **COVID-19:** 37,717,062 cases, 704,659 deaths; rates per 100,000: 17,744.2 cases, 331.5 deaths. 80.7% vaccinated.

Education: Compulsory: ages 4-17. **Literacy:** 94.3%.

Website: www.brasil.gov.br

Pedro Álvares Cabral, a Portuguese navigator, is generally credited as the first European to reach Brazil, in 1500. The country was thinly settled by various Indigenous groups. Only a few survive today, mostly in the Amazon Basin.

In the next centuries, Portuguese colonists gradually pushed inland, bringing along large numbers of enslaved Africans. (Slavery was not abolished until 1888.) The king of Portugal, fleeing Napoleon's army, moved the seat of government to Brazil in 1808. Brazil thereupon became a kingdom under Dom Joao VI. After Joao VI returned to Portugal, his son Pedro proclaimed Brazil's independence, Sept. 7, 1822, and was crowned emperor. The second emperor, Dom Pedro II, was deposed in 1889, and a republic proclaimed.

A military junta took control in 1930; Getulio Vargas assumed dictatorial power. The military forced him out in 1945. A democratic regime prevailed 1945-64, during which time the capital was moved from Rio de Janeiro to Brasília. Military-backed governments ruled Brazil for the next 20 years. Censorship was imposed, and the opposition was suppressed. Democratic presidential elections held in 1985 brought back civilian rule.

By the 1990s, Brazil had one of the world's largest economies (8th-largest in 2022). Income is unevenly distributed, however, and poverty widespread. Development has destroyed much of the Amazon ecosystem.

A new civil code guaranteeing legal equality for women was enacted Aug. 15, 2001. Luiz Inácio Lula da Silva, a union leader and reformer, won a presidential runoff, Oct. 2002. Brazil's space program launched its first rocket into space Oct. 23, 2004.

Despite political corruption scandals, Lula won a second presidential term, Oct. 2006. The nation reported huge offshore oil finds in 2007-08. Lula's former chief of staff, Dilma Rousseff, won a runoff election Oct. 31, 2010, to become Brazil's first woman president. She narrowly won reelection in an Oct. 26, 2014, runoff.

A Zika virus outbreak and related microcephaly caused 2,952 confirmed microcephaly cases and 369,013 confirmed or suspected Zika infections, 2015-17.

A $3-bil bribery and corruption scandal involving Petrobras (the national oil company), Pres. Rousseff's Workers' Party, and high-level government officials led to the resignations of Petrobras's top executives in Feb. 2015. José Dirceu, Lula's former chief of staff, was sentenced, May 18, 2016, to 23 years in prison for money laundering and other Petrobras-related offenses. Former Pres. Lula was convicted, July 12, 2017, of bribery and money laundering in connection with the Petrobras scandal; Mar. 2021 court rulings essentially overturned his convictions.

As Brazil suffered an economic downturn, the lower house of Congress, Apr. 17, 2016, charged Pres. Rousseff with illegally manipulating the federal budget. Her Senate impeachment trial, Aug. 25-31, ended with her conviction and removal from office. Vice Pres. Michel Temer, a centrist and political rival, succeeded Rousseff. Former lower house speaker Eduardo Cunha was sentenced, Mar. 30, 2017, to more than 15 years in prison following his conviction on Petrobras-related corruption charges. Pres. Temer was charged with corruption in 2017.

Campaigning against corruption, pledging to boost the economy (including through further Amazon development), and promising harsh action against violent crime and an alleged leftist threat, far-right candidate Jair Bolsonaro won an Oct. 28, 2018, presidential runoff election. Amazon deforestation accelerated beginning in 2019 but fell sharply in 2023 after Bolsonaro left office.

Bolsonaro belittled the threat of the COVID-19 pandemic that began in 2020, and his government was slow to respond. Brazil was affected by the pandemic worse than almost any other country. As of Aug. 2023, Brazil had more than 37.7 mil confirmed COVID-19 cases (6th-highest in the world) and over 704,000 recorded deaths (2nd-highest).

Lula narrowly defeated Bolsonaro in an Oct. 30, 2022, presidential runoff election, but Bolsonaro repeatedly claimed voting irregularities. On Jan. 8, 2023, one week after Lula's inauguration, rightist pro-Bolsonaro rioters briefly seized government buildings in Brasília, in an apparent attempt to overturn the election result.

Brunei
Brunei Darussalam

People: Population: 484,991 (168). **Age distrib.:** <15: 21.8%; 65+: 7.1%. **Growth:** 1.4%. **Migrants:** 25.6%. **Pop. density:** 238.6 per sq mi, 92.1 per sq km. **Urban:** 79.1%. **Ethnic groups:** Malay 67.4%, Chinese 9.6%. **Languages:** Malay (Bahasa Melayu) (official), English, Chinese dialects. **Religions:** Muslim 57.1% (Sunni [official]), Christian 12.1%, Buddhist 10.3% (Mahayanist 8%), ethnic religionist 10.1%, Chinese folk-religionist 5.6%, Confucianist 2.1%.

Geography: Total area: 2,226 sq mi, 5,765 sq km (165) **Land area:** 2,033 sq mi, 5,265 sq km. **Location:** SE Asia, on the N coast of the island of Borneo. It is surrounded on its landward side by the Malaysian state of Sarawak. **Topography:** Narrow coastal plain with mountains in E, hilly lowlands in W. Swamps in W and NE. Tropical climate. **Arable land:** 0.8%. **Capital:** Bandar Seri Begawan, 40,781.

Government: Type: Absolute monarchy or sultanate. **Head of state and govt.:** Sultan and Prime Min. Sir Hassanal Bolkiah Mu'izzaddin Waddaulah; b. 1946; in office: Jan. 1, 1984 (sultan since Oct. 5, 1967). **Local divisions:** 4 districts. **Defense budget:** $435 mil. **Active troops:** 7,200.

Economy: Industries: petroleum, petroleum refining, liquefied nat. gas, constr. **Chief agric.:** poultry, eggs, fruit, cassava, bananas, legumes. **Natural resources:** petroleum, nat. gas, timber. **Water:** 19,430 cu m per capita. **Crude oil reserves:** 1.1 bil bbls. **Electricity prod.:** 4.7 bil kWh. **Labor force:** agric. 1.3%, industry 24.3%, services 74.4%. **Unemployment:** 7.2%.

Finance: Monetary unit: Dollar (BND) (1.36 = $1 U.S.). **GDP:** $31.1 bil; **per capita GDP:** $69,275; **GDP growth:** −1.6%. **Imports:** $9.2 bil; Singapore 18%, China 14%, Malaysia 12%. **Exports:** $11.2 bil; Japan 34%, Australia 12%, Singapore 10%, India 8%, Malaysia 8%, Thailand 7%, China 6%. **Tourism** (2020): $16 mil. **Budget** (2020): $3.2 bil. **Inflation:** 3.7%.

Transport: Motor vehicles: 570.4 per 1,000 pop. **Airports:** 1.

Communications: Mobile: 117.8 per 100 pop. **Broadband:** 118.8 per 100 pop. **Internet:** 98.1%.

Health: Expend.: 2.4%. **Life expect.:** 76.3 male; 81.1 female. **Births:** 16.0 per 1,000 pop. **Deaths:** 3.9 per 1,000 pop. **Infant mortality:** 10.3 per 1,000 live births. **Undernourished:** NA. **HIV:** NA. **COVID-19:** 310,379 cases, 163 deaths; rates per 100,000: 70,947.2 cases, 37.3 deaths. 102.1% vaccinated.

Education: Compulsory: ages 6-14. **Literacy:** 97.6%.

Website: www.gov.bn

The Sultanate of Brunei was a powerful state in the early 16th cent., with authority over all of the island of Borneo as well as parts of the Sulu Islands and the Philippines. In 1888, a treaty placed the state under the protection of Great Britain.

Brunei became a fully sovereign and independent state on Jan. 1, 1984. A new penal code based on Islamic law, implemented in stages 2014-19, imposed harsh physical punishments for crimes such as theft, as well as for adultery and gay sex. Brunei outlawed public Christmas celebrations and displays in 2015.

Oil and natural gas account for significant portions of GDP and exports. Brunei's GDP per capita is among the world's highest.

Bulgaria
Republic of Bulgaria

People: Population: 6,827,736 (106). **Age distrib.:** <15: 14.0%; 65+: 20.8%. **Growth:** −0.7%. **Migrants:** 2.7%. **Pop. density:** 163.0 per sq mi, 62.9 per sq km. **Urban:** 76.7%. **Ethnic groups:** Bulgarian

76.9%, Turkish 8%, Romani 4.4%. **Languages:** Bulgarian (official), Turkish, Romani. **Religions:** Christian 83.0% (Orthodox 78.8%), Muslim 13.7% (Sunni), agnostic 2.5%.

Geography: Total area: 42,811 sq mi, 110,879 sq km (103); **Land area:** 41,888 sq mi, 108,489 sq km. **Location:** SE Europe, in E Balkan Peninsula on Black Sea. Romania on N; Serbia, North Macedonia on W; Greece, Turkey on S. **Topography:** The Stara Planina (Balkan) Mts. stretch E-W across the center of country, with the Danubian plain on N, the Rhodope Mts. on SW, and Thracian Plain on SE. **Arable land:** 32.2%. **Capital:** Sofia, 1,288,114.

Government: Type: Parliamentary republic. **Head of state:** Pres. Rumen Radev; b. 1963; in office: Jan. 22, 2017. **Head of govt.:** Prime Min. Nikolay Denkov; b. 1962; in office: June 6, 2023. **Local divisions:** 28 provinces. **Defense budget:** $1.3 bil. **Active troops:** 36,950.

Economy: Industries: electricity, gas, water; food, beverages, tobacco; machinery and equip. **Chief agric.:** wheat, maize, sunflower seed, milk, barley, rapeseed. **Natural resources:** bauxite, copper, lead, zinc, coal, timber. **Water:** 3,065 cu m per capita. **Crude oil reserves:** 15 mil bbls. **Electricity prod.:** 41.5 bil kWh. **Labor force:** agric. 6.3%, industry 30.8%, services 62.9%. **Unemployment:** 4.4%.

Finance: Monetary unit: Lev (BGN) (1.81 = $1 U.S.). **GDP:** $217.1 bil; **per capita GDP:** $33,582; **GDP growth:** 3.4%. **Imports** (2020): $50.1 bil; Germany 11%, Russia 9%, Italy 7%, Romania 7%, Turkey 7%. **Exports:** $51.5 bil; Germany 16%, Romania 8%, Italy 7%, Turkey 7%, Greece 6%. **Tourism:** $2.5 bil. **Budget** (2020): $26.5 bil. **Inflation:** 15.3%.

Transport: Railways: 2,504 mi. **Motor vehicles:** 487.9 per 1,000 pop. **Airports:** 57.

Communications: Mobile: 117.4 per 100 pop. **Broadband:** 115.6 per 100 pop. **Internet:** 79.1%.

Health: Expend.: 8.5%. **Life expect.:** 72.6 male; 79.2 female. **Births:** 8.0 per 1,000 pop. **Deaths:** 14.3 per 1,000 pop. **Infant mortality:** 7.8 per 1,000 live births. **Undernourished:** <2.5%. **HIV:** <0.1%. **COVID-19:** 1,299,201 cases, 38,397 deaths; rates per 100,000: 18,689.6 cases, 552.4 deaths. 30.4% vaccinated.

Education: Compulsory: ages 5-15. **Literacy:** 98.4%.

Website: www.gob.bg

Bulgaria was settled by Slavs in the 6th cent. Turkic Bulgars arrived in the 7th cent., merged with the Slavs, became Christians by the 9th cent., and set up powerful empires in the 10th and 12th cents. Ottomans took over in 1396 and ruled for nearly 500 years.

An 1876 revolt led to an independent kingdom in 1908. Bulgaria expanded after the first Balkan War but lost its Aegean coastline in WWI, when it sided with Germany. Bulgaria joined the Axis in WWII but withdrew in 1944. Communists took power with Soviet aid; the monarchy was abolished Sept. 8, 1946.

On Nov. 10, 1989, Communist Party leader and head of state Todor Zhivkov resigned after 35 years. In Jan. 1990, Parliament voted to revoke the constitutionally guaranteed dominant role of the Communist Party. A new constitution took effect July 13, 1991.

Bulgaria became a full member of NATO, Apr. 2, 2004, and entered the EU, Jan. 1, 2007.

A terrorist blew up a bus carrying Israeli tourists, July 18, 2012, leaving 5 Israelis, the Bulgarian bus driver, and the bomber dead. An investigation ended Feb. 5, 2013, blamed the Muslim militant group Hezbollah, which denied involvement.

Worsening economic conditions in 2012-13 inspired protests that led center-right, pro-EU Prime Min. Boyko Borisov to submit his government's resignation Feb. 20, 2013. After Oct. 5, 2014, elections, Borisov again became prime min. Construction began in 2015 on the second phase of a security fence along the Turkish border, intended to stop Middle Eastern, SW Asian, and African migrants from entering Bulgaria; about 30,000 entered in 2015.

Socialist-backed, pro-Moscow candidate Rumen Radev won Bulgaria's presidential runoff election Nov. 13, 2016. Radev was reelected, Nov. 21, 2021.

Borisov's GERB party won Mar. 26, 2017, parliamentary elections. After inconclusive Apr. 4 and July 11, 2021, parliamentary elections, in which widespread corruption hurt GERB, a new anti-corruption party won Nov. 14 elections. Kiril Petkov became prime min. but resigned, June 27, 2022, after losing a no-confidence vote. After inconclusive Oct. 2, 2022, elections, GERB and the reformist, pro-EU bloc We Continue the Change won the most seats in Apr. 2, 2023, elections and formed a coalition government.

Bulgaria was hard-hit by the COVID-19 pandemic that began in 2020; deaths per 100,000 pop. were among the highest in the world.

Burkina Faso

People: Population: 22,489,126 (60). **Age distrib.:** <15: 42.2%; 65+: 3.2%. **Growth:** 2.5%. **Migrants:** 3.5%. **Pop. density:** 212.7 per sq mi, 82.1 per sq km. **Urban:** 32.5%. **Ethnic groups:** Mossi 52%, Fulani (Peuhl) 8.4%, Gurma 7%, Bobo 4.9%, Gurunsi 4.6%, Senufo 4.5%, Bissa 3.7%, Lobi 2.4%, Dagara 2.4%. **Languages:** Mossi, Fula, Gourmantche, Dyula, Bissa, Gurunsi, French (official). **Religions:** Muslim 56.7% (Sunni), Christian 23.4% (Catholic 15.4%), ethnic religionist 19.3%.

Geography: Total area: 105,869 sq mi, 274,200 sq km (74); **Land area:** 105,715 sq mi, 273,800 sq km. **Location:** W Africa, S of the Sahara. Mali on NW; Niger on NE; Benin, Togo, Ghana, Côte d'Ivoire on S. **Topography:** Landlocked in the savanna region of W Africa. The N is arid, hot, and thinly populated. **Arable land:** 22.3%. **Capital:** Ouagadougou, 3,203,923. **Cities:** Bobo-Dioulasso, 1,128,646.

Government: Type: Presidential republic. **Head of state:** Interim Pres. Ibrahim Traoré; in office: Oct. 6, 2022. **Head of govt.:** Prime Min. Albert Ouedraogo b. 1969; in office: Mar. 3, 2022. **Local divisions:** 13 regions. **Defense budget:** $469 mil. **Active troops:** 7,000.

Economy: Industries: cotton lint, beverages, agric. proc., soap, cigarettes, textiles. **Chief agric.:** sorghum, maize, millet, cotton, cow peas, sugarcane. **Natural resources:** gold, manganese, zinc, limestone, marble, phosphates, pumice, salt. **Water:** 646 cu m per capita. **Electricity prod.:** 1.8 bil kWh. **Labor force:** agric. 73.3%, industry 7.1%, services 19.7%. **Unemployment:** 5.2%.

Finance: Monetary unit: CFA Franc (XOF) (606.88 = $1 U.S.). **GDP:** $57.7 bil; **per capita GDP:** $2,546; **GDP growth:** 1.5%. **Imports** (2020): $4.8 bil; Côte d'Ivoire 15%, China 9%, Ghana 8%, France 8%, India 6%. **Exports** (2020): $5.4 bil; Switzerland 59%, India 21%. **Tourism** (2020): $75 mil. **Budget:** $3.8 bil. **Inflation:** 14.3%.

Transport: Railways: 386 mi. **Motor vehicles:** 20.9 per 1,000 pop. **Airports:** 2.

Communications: Mobile (2021): 111.7 per 100 pop. **Broadband** (2021): 60.9 per 100 pop. **Internet:** 21.6%.

Health: Expend.: 6.7%. **Life expect.:** 62.0 male; 65.7 female. **Births:** 32.7 per 1,000 pop. **Deaths:** 7.5 per 1,000 pop. **Infant mortality:** 48.2 per 1,000 live births. **Undernourished:** 16.2%. **HIV:** 0.6%. **COVID-19:** 22,056 cases, 396 deaths; rates per 100,000: 105.5 cases, 1.9 deaths. 25.0% vaccinated.

Education: Compulsory: ages 6-15. **Literacy:** 46.0%.

Website: www.gouvernement.gov.bf or burkina-usa.org

The Mossi people entered Burkina Faso in the 11th-13th cents. Their kingdoms ruled until they were defeated by the Mali and Songhai empires. French control came by 1896, but Upper Volta (renamed Burkina Faso on Aug. 4, 1984) was not established as a separate territory until 1947. Independence came Aug. 5, 1960. The military seized power in 1980. After a 1987 coup, Blaise Compaoré became sole ruler by 1989. Violent protests in 2014 led to his resignation, Oct. 31. Former center-left Prime Min. Roch Marc Christian Kaboré was elected president, Nov. 29, 2015.

Islamist extremists attacked a café and hotel in Ouagadougou Jan. 15-16, 2016, leaving 30 victims dead. By mid-2019, insurgents allied with Islamist extremists controlled parts of northern and eastern Burkina Faso, and extremist violence subsequently escalated.

Kaboré, who had won reelection Nov. 22, 2020, was ousted in a military coup, Jan. 24, 2022. Coup leader Lt. Col. Paul-Henri Sandaogo Damiba pledged stronger action against insurgents, but attacks by Islamist extremists continued. A coup, Sept. 30-Oct. 2, by military units dissatisfied with the lack of progress against insurgents, led by Capt. Ibrahim Traoré, ousted Damiba. Extremist attacks, as well as alleged atrocities by government forces, continued in 2023. As of Mar. 31, 2023, more than 2 mil people were internally displaced.

Burma

See Myanmar.

Burundi
Republic of Burundi

People: Population: 13,162,952 (77). **Age distrib.:** <15: 42.7%; 65+: 3.3%. **Growth:** 3.6%. **Migrants:** 2.9%. **Pop. density:** 1,327.6 per sq mi, 512.6 per sq km. **Urban:** 14.8%. **Ethnic groups:** Hutu, Tutsi, Twa, Phuthi, South Asian. **Languages:** Kirundi, French (both official). **Religions:** Christian 94.4% (Catholic 64.8%, Protestant 26.2%), ethnic religionist 3.3%, Muslim 2.2% (Sunni).

Geography: Total area: 10,745 sq mi, 27,830 sq km (143); **Land area:** 9,915 sq mi, 25,680 sq km. **Location:** Central Africa. Rwanda on N, Dem. Rep. of the Congo on W, Tanzania on E and S. **Topography:** Mostly grassy highland, with mountains reaching 8,900 ft. The southernmost source of the White Nile is located in Burundi. Lake Tanganyika is the world's second deepest lake (max. depth 4,823 ft). **Arable land:** 49.5%. **Capital:** Bujumbura, 1,206,767; Gitega (political).

Government: Type: Presidential republic. **Head of state and govt.:** Pres. Evariste Ndayishimiye b. 1968; in office: June 18, 2020. **Local divisions:** 18 provinces. **Defense budget:** $67 mil. **Active troops:** 30,050.

Economy: Industries: light consumer goods, cement, assembly of imported components, public works constr., food proc. (fruits). **Chief agric.:** cassava, bananas, sweet potatoes, plantains, beans, vegetables. **Natural resources:** nickel, uranium, rare earth oxides, peat, cobalt, copper, platinum, vanadium, hydropower, niobium, tantalum, gold, tin, tungsten, kaolin, limestone. **Water:** 1,054 cu m per capita. **Electricity prod.:** 358.0 mil kWh. **Labor force:** agric. 85.9%, industry 3.6%, services 10.5%. **Unemployment:** 1.0%.

Finance: Monetary unit: Franc (BIF) (2,830.23 = $1 U.S.). **GDP:** $10.8 bil; **per capita GDP:** $836; **GDP growth:** 1.8%. **Imports** (2018): $905.3 mil; China 14%, Saudi Arabia 14%, India 9%, Kenya 7%, UAE 7%. **Exports** (2018): $285.1 mil; UAE 50%, Dem. Rep. of Congo 7%. **Tourism** (2020): $1 mil. **Budget** (2020): $1.1 bil. **Inflation:** 18.8%.

Transport: Motor vehicles: 7.7 per 1,000 pop. **Airports:** 1.
Communications: Mobile: 58.0 per 100 pop. **Broadband:** 8.7 per 100 pop. **Internet:** 5.8%.
Health: Expend.: 6.5%. **Life expect.:** 65.7 male; 70.0 female. **Births:** 34.9 per 1,000 pop. **Deaths:** 5.9 per 1,000 pop. **Infant mortality:** 36.8 per 1,000 live births. **Undernourished:** NA. **HIV:** 0.9%. **COVID-19:** 54,239 cases, 15 deaths; rates per 100,000: 456.1 cases, 0.1 deaths. 0.3% vaccinated.
Education: Compulsory: NA. **Literacy:** 74.7%.
Website: presidence.gov.bi or www.burundiembassydc-usa.org

The Pygmy Twa people were the first inhabitants, followed by Bantu Hutus, who were conquered in the 16th cent. by the Tutsi, probably from Ethiopia. Germany gained control in 1899. Belgium took over in 1916, successively exercising a League of Nations mandate and UN trusteeship over Ruanda-Urundi (now the two countries of Rwanda and Burundi). Burundi became independent July 1, 1962.

An unsuccessful Hutu rebellion in 1972-73 left 10,000 Tutsi and 150,000 Hutu dead. Over 100,000 Hutu fled to Tanzania and Zaire (now Dem. Rep. of the Congo). In the 1980s, Burundi's Tutsi-dominated regime pledged itself to ethnic reconciliation and democratic reform. In the nation's first democratic presidential election, June 1993, a Hutu, Melchior Ndadaye, was elected. He was killed in an attempted coup, Oct. 21, 1993. At least 150,000 Burundians died in ethnic conflicts over the next three years. Pres. Cyprien Ntaryamira, elected Jan. 1994, and the president of Rwanda were killed when missiles shot down their plane, Apr. 6. The incident sparked massive carnage in Rwanda; violence in Burundi, initially far more limited, intensified in 1995. Ethnic strife continued after a military coup, July 25, 1996. Most warring groups signed a draft peace treaty, Aug. 2000. A power-sharing government headed by Pierre Buyoya was sworn in Nov. 1, 2001, but clashes with rebels continued.

Domitien Ndayizeye, a Hutu, became president Apr. 2003. The UN Security Council authorized, May 2004, a peacekeeping force (ONUB) for Burundi. Approval of a power-sharing constitution by referendum, Feb. 28, 2005, paved the way for local and parliamentary elections. Chosen by parliament, Pierre Nkurunziza, former leader of a Hutu rebel group, became president Aug. 2005. ONUB was succeeded by the UN Integrated Office in Burundi (BINUB), 2007-10, and by the UN Office in Burundi (BNUB), 2011-14, both intended to assist with political transition. Under a reconciliation accord reached Dec. 4, 2008, remaining Hutu rebels began to demobilize. Candidates opposing Nkurunziza dropped out of the June 2010 presidential election, claiming the vote was rigged. The government was accused of ordering extrajudicial killings, 2010-11.

Violent protests began after Nkurunziza's Apr. 2015 decision to seek a constitutionally dubious third term, which he won, July 21, despite a coup attempt. Political violence and harsh government repression continued in Nkurunziza's third term, leading hundreds of thousands to flee the country. Evariste Ndayishimiye, of Nkurunziza's ruling party, won the May 20, 2020, election, which the opposition claimed was rigged. Nkurunziza died June 8, 2020, before the end of his term.

Cabo Verde
Republic of Cabo Verde

People: Population: 603,901 (166). **Age distrib.:** <15: 26.7%; 65+: 6.1%. **Growth:** 1.2%. **Migrants:** 2.8%. **Pop. density:** 387.8 per sq mi, 149.7 per sq km. **Urban:** 68.0%. **Ethnic groups:** Creole (mulatto) 71%, African 28%. **Languages:** Portuguese (official), Crioulo (Portuguese-based Creole). **Religions:** Christian 94.5% (Catholic 83.7%), Muslim 3.0% (Sunni).
Geography: Total area: 1,557 sq mi, 4,033 sq km (167); **Land area:** 1,557 sq mi, 4,033 sq km. **Location:** In Atlantic O., off W tip of Africa. Nearest neighbors are Mauritania, Senegal to E. **Topography:** 15 Cabo Verde islands, volcanic in origin (active crater on Fogo). Landscape is eroded and stark, with vegetation mostly in interior valleys. **Arable land:** 12.4%. **Capital:** Praia, 167,504.
Government: Type: Parliamentary republic. **Head of state:** Pres. José Maria Neves; b. 1960; in office: Nov. 9, 2021. **Head of govt.:** Prime Min. José Ulisses Correia e Silva; b. 1962; in office: Apr. 22, 2016. **Local divisions:** 22 municipalities. **Defense budget:** $12 mil. **Active troops:** 1,200.
Economy: Industries: food and beverages, fish proc., shoes and garments, salt mining, ship repair. **Chief agric.:** sugarcane, tomatoes, bananas, cabbages, coconuts, cassava. **Natural resources:** salt, basalt rock, limestone, kaolin, fish, clay, gypsum. **Water:** 540 cu m per capita. **Electricity prod.:** 456.9 mil kWh. **Labor force:** agric. 11.0%, industry 22.2%, services 66.9%. **Unemployment:** 13.6%.
Finance: Monetary unit: Escudo (CVE) (102.02 = $1 U.S.). **GDP:** $5.4 bil; **per capita GDP:** $9,083; **GDP growth:** 17.7%. **Imports:** $1.1 bil; Portugal 36%, Netherlands 16%, Spain 11%, China 6%. **Exports:** $459.9 mil; Spain 65%, Portugal 14%, Italy 8%. **Tourism:** $146 mil. **Budget:** $619 mil. **Inflation** (2020-21): 1.9%.

Transport: Airports: 9.
Communications: Mobile: 99.2 per 100 pop. **Broadband:** 74.6 per 100 pop. **Internet:** 69.8%.
Health: Expend.: 6.0%. **Life expect.:** 71.7 male; 76.4 female. **Births:** 18.2 per 1,000 pop. **Deaths:** 5.8 per 1,000 pop. **Infant mortality:** 23.0 per 1,000 live births. **Undernourished:** 18.2%. **HIV:** 0.9%. **COVID-19:** 64,230 cases, 415 deaths; rates per 100,000: 11,552.4 cases, 74.6 deaths. 55.5% vaccinated.
Education: Compulsory: ages 6-15. **Literacy:** 90.8%.
Website: www.governo.cv

The first Portuguese colonists landed in 1462; enslaved African workers were brought soon after, and most Cabo Verdeans descend from both groups. Independence for Cabo Verde (known as Cape Verde until Oct. 2013) came July 5, 1975. Remittances from Cabo Verdean emigrants are a major source of income.

The nation's first free presidential election was held Feb. 17, 1991. Jorge Carlos Fonseca, of the center-right MFD party, won a presidential runoff election Aug. 21, 2011; he was reelected, Oct. 2, 2016. José Maria Neves, of the leftist PAICV, won the Oct. 17, 2021, presidential election.

Cambodia
Kingdom of Cambodia

People: Population: 16,891,245 (72). **Age distrib.:** <15: 29.5%; 65+: 5.1%. **Growth:** 1.0%. **Migrants:** 0.5%. **Pop. density:** 247.8 per sq mi, 95.7 per sq km. **Urban:** 25.6%. **Ethnic groups:** Khmer 95.4%, Cham 2.4%. **Languages:** Khmer (official). **Religions:** Buddhist 85.3% (Theravadin 83%), ethnic religionist 4.0%, Christian 2.9%, Chinese folk-religionist 2.6%, agnostic 2.3%, Muslim 1.9% (Sunni).
Geography: Total area: 69,898 sq mi, 181,035 sq km (88); **Land area:** 68,153 sq mi, 176,515 sq km. **Location:** SE Asia, on Indochina Peninsula. Thailand on W and N, Laos on NE, Vietnam on E. **Topography:** The central area, formed by the Mekong R. basin and Tonle Sap Lake, is level. Hills and mountains in SE; long escarpment in NW separates the country from Thailand. **Arable land:** 23.3%. **Capital:** Phnom Penh, 2,281,198.
Government: Type: Parliamentary constitutional monarchy. **Head of state:** King Norodom Sihamoni; b. 1953; in office: Oct. 29, 2004. **Head of govt.:** Prime Min. Hun Manet; b. 1977; in office: Aug. 22, 2023. **Local divisions:** 24 provinces, 1 municipality. **Defense budget:** $1.0 bil. **Active troops:** 124,300.
Economy: Industries: tourism, garments, constr., rice milling, fishing, wood and wood prods., rubber, cement, gem mining, textiles. **Chief agric.:** cassava, rice, maize, vegetables, sugarcane, soybeans. **Natural resources:** oil and gas, timber, gems, iron ore, manganese, phosphates. **Water:** 28,477 cu m per capita. **Electricity prod.:** 8.7 bil kWh. **Labor force:** agric. 38.9%, industry 25.4%, services 35.7%. **Unemployment:** 0.4%.
Finance: Monetary unit: Riel (KHR) (4,148.53 = $1 U.S.). **GDP:** $89.7 bil; **per capita GDP:** $5,349; **GDP growth:** 5.2%. **Imports:** $32.8 bil; China 27%, Thailand 25%, Vietnam 15%, Singapore 8%. **Exports:** $20.1 bil; U.S. 21%, Singapore 8%, Thailand 8%, Germany 7%, Japan 6%. **Tourism:** $184 mil. **Budget:** $6.5 bil. **Inflation:** 5.3%.

Transport: Railways: 399 mi (under restoration). **Airports:** 6.
Communications: Mobile: 116.3 per 100 pop. **Broadband:** 102.0 per 100 pop. **Internet:** 60.2%.
Health: Expend.: 7.5%. **Life expect.:** 69.2 male; 73.0 female. **Births:** 18.8 per 1,000 pop. **Deaths:** 5.7 per 1,000 pop. **Infant mortality:** 28.8 per 1,000 live births. **Undernourished:** 4.8%. **HIV:** 0.5%. **COVID-19:** 138,940 cases, 3,056 deaths; rates per 100,000: 831.0 cases, 18.3 deaths. 87.8% vaccinated.
Education: Compulsory: NA. **Literacy:** 83.9%.
Website: cnv.org.kh

Early kingdoms dating from that of Funan in the 1st cent. CE culminated in the great Khmer empire that flourished from the 9th cent. to the 13th, encompassing present-day Thailand, Cambodia, Laos, and southern Vietnam. The peripheral areas were lost to invading Siamese and Vietnamese. France established a protectorate in 1863. Independence came in 1953.

Prince Norodom Sihanouk, king (1941-55) and head of state from 1960, tried to maintain neutrality during the Vietnam War. The U.S. bombed Cambodia, 1969-73, targeting suspected border sanctuaries of Vietnamese insurgents.

In 1970, pro-U.S. Prem. Lon Nol seized power, demanded removal of 40,000 North Vietnamese troops, and abolished the monarchy. Open war began between Lon Nol's government and Communist Khmer Rouge guerrillas, led by Pol Pot and supported by Vietnam and China. The U.S. provided Lon Nol with military and economic aid.

Khmer Rouge forces captured Phnom Penh Apr. 17, 1975. Cities were depopulated with the stated goal of making Cambodia a classless agrarian society; Cambodians were executed or forced to work on cooperative farms. An estimated 1.7 mil people died in "killing fields" or from other hardships under Khmer Rouge rule, 1975-79.

Border fighting in 1978 developed into a full-fledged Vietnamese invasion. Formation of a Vietnamese-backed government was announced, Jan. 8, 1979, one day after Phnom Penh was seized. Thousands of refugees fled to Thailand; widespread starvation was reported. Vietnamese troops remained in Cambodia until Sept. 1989 to combat resistance from Khmer Rouge guerrillas. Following 1993 UN-sponsored elections, two leading parties agreed to share power in an interim government. On Sept. 21, the National Assembly adopted a constitution reestablishing a monarchy with Sihanouk as king. The Khmer Rouge insurgency weakened and splintered by 1996.

Co-Prime Min. Hun Sen staged a coup July 5, 1997, ousting his rival, Prince Norodom Ranariddh. Pol Pot was denounced by his former comrades at a show trial, July 25, 1997, and sentenced to house arrest; he died Apr. 15, 1998. Sihanouk abdicated because of poor health and was succeeded, Oct. 2004, by his son Norodom Sihamoni. A UN-backed war crimes tribunal convicted a former prison warden known as Duch July 2010 for overseeing the killing and torture of more than 14,000 inmates under the Khmer Rouge.

Hun Sen's Cambodian People's Party (CPP) retained power through a series of flawed elections and repressive policies. The political party of opposition leader Kem Sokha was dissolved in Nov. 2017, and several media outlets were shut down. Trials of more than 100 opposition figures resulted in prison terms, 2021-22. Kem Sokha was convicted of treason and sentenced to 27 years' confinement, Mar. 3, 2023. A new opposition party was barred, May 15, 2023, from participating in July 23 elections swept by the CPP. Hun Sen transferred the premiership, Aug. 22, 2023, to his son Hun Manet but remained CPP head and Senate president.

In recent years, Chinese investment, military, and other aid, and tourism have increased sharply.

Cameroon
Republic of Cameroon

People: Population: 30,135,732 (51). **Age distrib.:** <15: 41.7%; 65+: 3.2%. **Growth:** 2.7%. **Migrants:** 2.2%. **Pop. density:** 165.1 per sq mi, 63.8 per sq km. **Urban:** 59.3%. **Ethnic groups:** Bamileke-Bamu 24.3%, Beti/Bassa, Mbam 21.6%, Biu-Mandara 14.6%, Arab-Choa/Hausa/Kanuri 11%, Adamawa-Ubangi 9.8%, Grassfields 7.7%, Kako, Meka/Pygmy 3.3%, Cotier/Ngoe/Oroko 2.7%. **Languages:** English, French (both official); 24 major African lang. groups. **Religions:** Christian 62.3% (Catholic 29.9%, Protestant 25.5%), Muslim 20.0% (Sunni), ethnic religionist 16.6%.

Geography: Total area: 183,568 sq mi, 475,440 sq km (54); **Land area:** 182,514 sq mi, 472,710 sq km. **Location:** Between W and central Africa. Nigeria on NW; Chad, Central African Rep. on E; Rep. of the Congo, Gabon, Equatorial Guinea on S. **Topography:** Low coastal plain with rain forests in S; plateaus in center lead to forested mountains in W, including Mt. Cameroon (13,435 ft). Grasslands in N, marshes around Lake Chad. **Arable land:** 13.1%. **Capital:** Yaoundé, 4,509,287. **Cities:** Douala, 4,063,200.

Government: Type: Presidential republic. **Head of state:** Pres. Paul Biya; b. 1933; in office: Nov. 6, 1982. **Head of govt.:** Prime Min. Joseph Dion Ngute; b. 1954; in office: Jan. 4, 2019. **Local divisions:** 10 regions. **Defense budget:** $419 mil. **Active troops:** 25,400.

Economy: Industries: petroleum prod./refining, aluminum prod., food proc., light consumer goods, textiles, lumber, ship repair. **Chief agric.:** cassava, plantains, maize, oil palm fruit, taro, sugarcane. **Natural resources:** petroleum, bauxite, iron ore, timber, hydropower. **Water:** 10,666 cu m per capita. **Crude oil reserves:** 200 mil bbls. **Electricity prod.:** 8.0 bil kWh. **Labor force:** agric. 42.6%, industry 15.5%, services 41.9%. **Unemployment:** 4.0%.

Finance: Monetary unit: Central African CFA Franc (XAF) (606.88 = $1 U.S.). **GDP:** $123.0 bil; **per capita GDP:** $4,408; **GDP growth:** 3.5%. **Imports:** $9.0 bil; China 28%, Nigeria 15%, France 9%, Belgium 6%. **Exports:** $7.4 bil; China 17%, Netherlands 14%, Italy 9%, UAE 8%, India 7%, U.S. 6%, Belgium 6%. **Tourism:** $507 mil. **Budget:** $7.4 bil. **Inflation:** 6.2%.

Transport: Railways: 613 mi. **Motor vehicles:** 18.3 per 1,000 pop. **Airports:** 11.

Communications: Mobile: 82.8 per 100 pop. **Broadband:** 28.8 per 100 pop. **Internet:** 45.6%.

Health: Expend.: 3.8%. **Life expect.:** 61.9 male; 65.6 female. **Births:** 35.1 per 1,000 pop. **Deaths:** 7.5 per 1,000 pop. **Infant mortality:** 47.4 per 1,000 live births. **Undernourished:** 6.4%. **HIV:** 2.6%. **COVID-19:** 125,090 cases, 1,974 deaths; rates per 100,000: 471.2 cases, 7.4 deaths. 11.9% vaccinated.

Education: Compulsory: ages 6-11. **Literacy:** 78.2%.

Website: www.spm.gov.cm

Portuguese sailors were the first Europeans to reach Cameroon, in the 15th cent. The European and American slave trade was very active in the area. German control lasted from 1884 to 1916, when France and Britain divided the country. French Cameroon became independent Jan. 1, 1960; one part of British Cameroon joined Nigeria in 1961 while the other part joined Cameroon. Pres. Paul Biya has retained power since 1982 in a series of elections that were boycotted by opposition parties or disputed as fraudulent.

More than a dozen French citizens were kidnapped during 2013, allegedly in retaliation for France's intervention in Mali, by the Nigerian-based jihadist group Boko Haram. Kidnappings and attacks by Boko Haram in northern Cameroon continued in subsequent years. Beginning in 2015, Cameroon troops fought in Nigeria against Islamist-extremist forces; a 2017 Amnesty Intl. report accused the Cameroon military of torturing detainees.

Beginning in late 2016, government forces violently suppressed protesters and fought separatists in Anglophone areas of western Cameroon. As a result of violence in the north and west, more than 1 mil people were internally displaced as of Aug. 31, 2023.

Canada

People: Population: 38,516,736 (38). **Age distrib.:** <15: 15.6%; 65+: 20.5%. **Growth:** 0.7%. **Migrants:** 21.3%. **Pop. density:** 11.0 per sq mi, 4.2 per sq km. **Urban:** 81.9%. **Ethnic groups:** Canadian 15.6%, English 14.7%, Scottish 12.1%, Irish 12.1%, French 11%, German 8.1%, Chinese 4.7%, Italian 4.3%, Indian 3.7%, Ukrainian 3.5%, First Nations 1.7%. **Languages:** English, French (both official). **Religions:** Christian 60.5% (Catholic 42.6%, Protestant 10.0%), agnostic 23.7%, Muslim 4.2% (Sunni), atheist 3.0%, Chinese folk-religionist 2.1%, Buddhist 1.8% (Mahayanist), Hindu 1.4%, Sikh 1.4%.

Geography: Total area: 3,855,103 sq mi, 9,984,670 sq km (2); **Land area:** 3,511,023 sq mi, 9,093,507 sq km. **Location:** Extends 3,426 mi E-W and S from the North Pole to the U.S. **Topography:** Seacoast includes 36,356 mi of mainland and 115,133 mi of islands, including the Arctic islands almost from Greenland to near the Alaskan border. Generally temperate, though varies from freezing winter cold to blistering summer heat. **Arable land:** 4.4%. **Capital:** Ottawa-Gatineau, 1,437,188. **Cities:** Toronto, 6,371,958; Montréal, 4,307,958; Vancouver, 2,657,088; Calgary, 1,639,613; Edmonton, 1,544,448; Québec, 844,249; Winnipeg, 841,108; Halifax, 419,882; Victoria, 397,703.

Government: Type: Federal parliamentary democracy under constitutional monarchy. **Head of state:** King Charles III, rep. by Gov.-Gen. Mary Simon; b. 1947; in office: July 26, 2021. **Head of govt.:** Prime Min. Justin Trudeau; b. 1971; in office: Nov. 4, 2015. **Local divisions:** 10 provinces, 3 territories. **Defense budget:** $24.6 bil. **Active troops:** 66,500.

Economy: Industries: transp. equip., chemicals, minerals, food prods., wood and paper prods., fish prods. **Chief agric.:** wheat, rapeseed, maize, barley, milk, soybeans. **Natural resources:** bauxite, iron ore, nickel, zinc, copper, gold, lead, uranium, rare earth elements, molybdenum, potash, diamonds, silver, fish, timber, wildlife, coal, petroleum, nat. gas. **Water:** 76,890 cu m per capita. **Crude oil reserves:** 170.3 bil bbls. **Electricity prod.:** 625.9 bil kWh. **Labor force:** agric. 1.3%, industry 19.3%, services 79.4%. **Unemployment:** 5.2%.

Finance: Monetary unit: Dollar (CAD) (1.36 = $1 U.S.). **GDP:** $2.3 tril; **per capita GDP:** $58,400; **GDP growth:** 3.4%. **Imports:** $609.3 bil; U.S. 57%, China 11%. **Exports:** $611.1 bil; U.S. 73%. **Tourism:** $13.1 bil. **Budget:** $862.0 bil. **Inflation:** 6.8%.

Transport: Railways: 30,709 mi. **Motor vehicles:** 675.6 per 1,000 pop. **Airports:** 523.

Communications: Mobile: 91.2 per 100 pop. **Broadband:** 86.4 per 100 pop. **Internet:** 92.8%.

Health: Expend. (2021): 11.7%. **Life expect.:** 81.7 male; 86.4 female. **Births:** 10.1 per 1,000 pop. **Deaths:** 8.2 per 1,000 pop. **Infant mortality:** 4.3 per 1,000 live births. **Undernourished:** <2.5%. **HIV:** NA. **COVID-19:** 4,697,504 cases, 53,147 deaths; rates per 100,000: 12,446.3 cases, 140.8 deaths. 83.0% vaccinated.

Education: Compulsory: ages 6-15. **Literacy:** NA.

Website: www.canada.ca

Indigenous people have lived in Canada for at least 12,000 years. Vikings reached and briefly settled in part of Newfoundland in the 10th cent. Italian seaman Giovanni Caboto (a.k.a. John Cabot) claimed parts of the Atlantic coast for England in 1497 and 1498. After French explorer Jacques Cartier reached the Gulf of St. Lawrence in 1534, France pioneered Canadian settlement by Western Europeans, establishing Québec City (1608) and Montréal (1642) and declaring New France a colony in 1663.

Britain acquired Acadia (later Nova Scotia) in 1717 and defeated French forces in Canada to gain control of all of New France by 1763. The French, through the Quebec Act of 1774, retained rights to their language, religion, and civil law. During the American Revolution, many colonials, calling themselves United Empire Loyalists, moved north to Canada. Fur traders and explorers led Canadians of European origin westward across the continent. Sir Alexander Mackenzie reached the Pacific in 1793 and scrawled on a rock, "From Canada by land."

In Upper and Lower Canada (later called Ontario and Quebec) and in the Maritimes, legislative assemblies were formed in the 18th cent. Upper Canada was involved in the War of 1812 between Great Britain and the U.S.

In 1837 political agitation for a more democratic government culminated in rebellions in Upper and Lower Canada and the union of the two into the colony of Canada in 1839. The union lasted until the 1867 British North America Act (now known as the Constitution Act, 1867) launched the Dominion of Canada, consisting of Ontario, Quebec, and the former colonies of Nova Scotia and New Brunswick.

The British North America Act, which was the basis for the country's written constitution, established a federal system of government modeled on the British parliament and cabinet structure under the crown. Canada was proclaimed a self-governing dominion within the British Empire in 1931. The Constitution Act,

Canada's Provinces and Territories

Province/territory	Joined confed.	Tot. area (sq mi)	Population (2022)	Capital	Premier	Party	In office
Alberta	1905	255,541	4,510,891	Edmonton	Danielle Smith	United Cons.	2022
British Columbia	1871	364,764	5,356,284	Victoria	David Eby	New Democratic	2022
Manitoba	1870	250,116	1,413,409	Winnipeg	Wab Kinew	New Democratic	2023
New Brunswick	1867	28,150	809,568	Fredericton	Blaine Higgs	Prog. Cons.	2018
Newfoundland and Labrador	1949	156,453	531,583	St. John's	Andrew Furey	Liberal	2020
Nova Scotia	1867	21,345	1,025,445	Halifax	Tim Houston	Prog. Cons.	2021
Ontario	1867	415,598	15,145,006	Toronto	Doug Ford	Prog. Cons.	2018
Prince Edward Island	1873	2,185	167,188	Charlottetown	Dennis King	Prog. Cons.	2019
Québec	1867	595,391	8,672,185	Québec	François Legault	Coalition Avenir Québec	2018
Saskatchewan	1905	251,366	1,178,422	Regina	Scott Moe	Saskatchewan	2018
Northwest Territories[1]	1871	519,734	44,685	Yellowknife	Caroline Cochrane	Nonpartisan	2019
Nunavut[1,2]	1999	808,185	40,485	Iqaluit	P.J. Akeeagok	Nonpartisan	2021
Yukon[1]	1898	186,272	43,905	Whitehorse	Ranj Pillai	Liberal	2023

Note: Census pop. as of Jan. 1. (Source: Statistics Canada.) (1) Territories also have federally appointed commissioners to represent federal interests. (2) Territory created in 1999 from eastern portion of Northwest Territories.

1982, gave Canada the right to amend its constitution, thereby severing its last legislative link with Britain.

Failure in 1990 of the so-called Meech Lake Accord, which would have assured constitutional protection for Quebec's efforts to preserve its French language and culture, sparked a separatist revival in Quebec. The Charlottetown agreement, calling for constitutional changes, such as recognition of Quebec as a "distinct society" within the Canadian confederation, was defeated by a national referendum Oct. 1992. A Quebec referendum on secession, Oct. 1995, also failed.

On Jan. 7, 1998, the government apologized to Indigenous peoples for 150 years of mistreatment. Nunavut ("Our Land"), carved from the Northwest Territories as a homeland for the Inuit, was established Apr. 1, 1999. A national commission concluded in 2015 that the forced removal, 1883-1996, of thousands of Indigenous children to residential schools (including Roman Catholic and other religious schools), where some students suffered abuse, constituted "cultural genocide"; in mid-2021, the remains of more than 1,000 children were found on the grounds of several former schools.

Same-sex marriage (already permitted in 8 provinces) became legal throughout the country July 2005. Marijuana was legalized nationally for medical purposes in 2001 and for recreational use in 2018.

Twelve years of Liberal Party rule ended when the Conservatives won parliamentary elections, Jan. 23, 2006. Elections Oct. 19, 2015, returned Liberals to power, and Justin Trudeau, son of former Prime Min. Pierre Trudeau, became prime min. After Oct. 21, 2019, and Sept. 20, 2021, elections, Justin Trudeau continued as prime minister, although the Liberals fell short of a majority each time.

The Canadian government approved, Nov. 29, 2016, a major expansion (opposed by environmental groups) of the Trans Mountain pipeline to transport oil from Alberta to British Columbia. Plans to build the Keystone XL pipeline, to carry Alberta oil to the Gulf of Mexico, were abandoned in 2021, after U.S. approval was rescinded.

On Oct. 22, 2014, a terrorist gunman in Ottawa, apparently inspired by the Islamist extremist group ISIS, killed a soldier at the Canadian War Memorial and opened fire in the Parliament building before being shot to death. Canada joined the U.S.-led campaign of airstrikes against ISIS forces in Iraq (2014-16) and Syria (2015-16). Canada resettled, 2015-16, almost 40,000 refugees fleeing Syria's civil war. Following the Aug. 2021 Taliban takeover of Afghanistan, Canada announced, Sept. 27, it would accept 40,000 Afghan refugees. By Aug. 2023, more than 175,000 Ukrainians had arrived in Canada since Russia's Feb. 2022 invasion of Ukraine.

The North American Free Trade Agreement (NAFTA) among Canada, Mexico, and the U.S. went into effect Jan. 1, 1994. A revised agreement—renamed the U.S.-Mexico-Canada Agreement (USMCA)—including auto industry changes and increased U.S. access to the Canadian dairy market, went into effect July 1, 2020.

A Canada-EU trade agreement eliminating almost all tariffs was signed Oct. 30, 2016. Canada signed, Mar. 8, 2018, an 11-nation trans-Pacific trade-liberalization agreement.

The COVID-19 pandemic reached Canada by early 2020. Large-scale protests by truckers and their supporters, Jan.-Feb. 2022, against vaccination requirements and other COVID-19 restrictions, blocked downtown Ottawa as well as Canada-U.S. border crossings, severely disrupting trade.

Canada had its worst wildfire season on record in summer 2023, likely linked to climate change. The fires caused dangerous levels of air pollution across large areas of Canada (and the U.S.). With over 1,000 fires burning nationwide in mid-Aug., Yellowknife, as well as other communities in NWT and British Columbia, were told to evacuate.

Canada accused India of assassinating an India-born, Canadian Sikh community leader in British Columbia June 18, 2023, which India denied.

Central African Republic

People: Population: 5,552,228 (118). **Age distrib.:** <15: 38.8%; 65+: 3.5%. **Growth:** 1.8%. **Migrants:** 1.8%. **Pop. density:** 23.1 per sq mi, 8.9 per sq km. **Urban:** 43.6%. **Ethnic groups:** Baya 28.8%, Banda 22.9%, Mandjia 9.9%, Sara 7.9%, M'Baka-Bantu 7.9%, Arab-Fulani (Peuhl) 6%, Mbum 6%, Ngbanki 5.5%, Zande-Nzakara 3%, other Central African Republic ethnic groups 2%. **Languages:** French (official), Sangho (lingua franca and national lang.), tribal langs. **Religions:** Christian 74.8% (Catholic 38.5%, independent 18.3%, Protestant 18.0%), Muslim 13.9% (Sunni), ethnic religionist 10.3%.

Geography: Total area: 240,535 sq mi, 622,984 sq km (45); **Land area:** 240,535 sq mi, 622,984 sq km. **Location:** Central Africa. **Chad on N, Cameroon on W, Rep. of the Congo and the DRC on S, South Sudan and Sudan on E. Topography:** Mostly rolling plateau, avg. elevation 2,000 ft, with rivers draining S to the Congo and N to Lake Chad. Open, well-watered savanna covers most of area, with an arid area in NE and tropical rain forest in SW. **Arable land:** 2.9%. **Capital:** Bangui, 958,335.

Government: Type: Presidential republic. **Head of state:** Pres. Faustin-Archange Touadéra; b. 1957; in office: Mar. 30, 2016. **Head of govt.:** Prime Min. Félix Moloua; in office: Feb. 7, 2022. **Local divisions:** 14 prefectures, 2 economic prefectures, 1 commune. **Defense budget:** $39 mil. **Active troops:** 9,150.

Economy: Industries: gold and diamond mining, logging, brewing, sugar refining. **Chief agric.:** cassava, yams, groundnuts, taro, bananas, sugarcane. **Natural resources:** diamonds, uranium, timber, gold, oil, hydropower. **Water:** 29,194 cu m per capita. **Electricity prod.:** 151.1 mil kWh. **Labor force:** agric. 68.5%, industry 6.7%, services 24.8%. **Unemployment:** 6.4%.

Finance: Monetary unit: Central African CFA Franc (XAF) (606.88 = $1 U.S.). **GDP:** $5.4 bil; **per capita GDP:** $967; **GDP growth:** 0.0%. **Imports** (2017): $393.1 mil; India 18%, France 12%, U.S. 11%, China 9%, Netherlands 7%, Belgium 7%, Malta 6%. **Exports** (2017): $113.7 mil; China 41%, UAE 19%, France 7%. **Tourism** (2020): $30 mil. **Budget:** $385 mil. **Inflation:** 5.6%.

Transport: Motor vehicles: 1.3 per 1,000 pop. **Airports:** 1.

Communications: Mobile (2021): 33.6 per 100 pop. **Broadband** (2021): 5.2 per 100 pop. **Internet:** 10.6%.

Health: Expend.: 9.4%. **Life expect.:** 54.6 male; 57.3 female. **Births:** 32.4 per 1,000 pop. **Deaths:** 11.5 per 1,000 pop. **Infant mortality:** 81.7 per 1,000 live births. **Undernourished:** 48.7%. **HIV:** 3.4%. **COVID-19:** 15,367 cases, 113 deaths; rates per 100,000: 318.2 cases, 2.3 deaths. 51.5% vaccinated.

Education: Compulsory: ages 6-15. **Literacy:** 37.5%.

Website: www.gouv.cf or www.usrcaembassy.org

Various Bantu peoples migrated through the region for centuries before French control was asserted in the late 19th cent., when the region was named Ubangi-Shari. Independence was attained Aug. 13, 1960.

Pres. Jean-Bedel Bokassa, who seized power in a 1965 military coup, proclaimed himself emperor Dec. 1976. Bokassa's rule was characterized by ruthless authoritarianism. He was ousted in a bloodless coup aided by France, Sept. 20, 1979. In 1981, Gen. André Kolingba became head of state in another bloodless coup. Elections in Aug. and Sept. 1993 led to civilian rule under Pres. Ange-Félix Patassé.

Patassé was ousted Mar. 15, 2003, by rebels under former army chief François Bozizé. Bozizé won a presidential runoff election May 8, 2005, but insurgent activity by Patassé loyalists and others continued in the north. A national peace conference, Dec. 8-20, 2008, enabled the installation of a unity government Jan. 19, 2009. Pres. Bozizé won reelection Jan. 23, 2011, but was ousted when the largely Muslim rebel group Seleka, led by Michel Djotodia, seized the capital Mar. 24, 2013. Bozizé supporters and Christian militias clashed with pro-Djotodia and Muslim fighters, resulting in thousands of deaths. A National Transitional Council elected Catherine

Samba-Panza interim pres. Jan. 20, 2014. France sent peacekeeping troops (2014-16). A UN peacekeeping force (MINUSCA) was authorized Apr. 10, 2014.

Faustin-Archange Touadéra, a Christian, won a UN-supervised presidential runoff election, Feb. 14, 2016. Violence between Muslims and Christians, as well as between rival militias and ethnic groups, continued. The government signed peace agreements with rebel groups Feb. 6 and Apr. 9, 2019. But violence persisted, and rebels at times controlled large areas of the country. Russian mercenaries began, in 2018, assisting CAR troops fighting rebels. Touadéra won reelection, Dec. 27, 2020. A new constitution, approved in a July 30, 2023, referendum boycotted by opposition groups, eliminated presidential term limits.

About 17,000 MINUSCA uniformed personnel were in the CAR as of July 31, 2023. About 515,000 people were internally displaced and 747,000 were refugees in neighboring countries.

Chad
Republic of Chad

People: Population: 18,523,165 (66). **Age distrib.:** <15: 46.2%; 65+: 2.5%. **Growth:** 3.1%. **Migrants:** 3.3%. **Pop. density:** 38.1 per sq mi, 14.7 per sq km. **Urban:** 24.4%. **Ethnic groups:** Sara (Ngambaye/Sara/Madjingaye/Mbaye) 30.5%, Kanembu/Bornu/Buduma 9.8%, Arab 9.7%, Wadai/Maba/Masalit/Mimi 7%, Gorane 5.8%, Masa/Musseye/Musgum 4.9%, Bulala/Medogo/Kuka 3.7%, Marba/Lele/Mesme 3.5%, Mundang 2.7%, Bidiyo/Migaama/Kenga/Dangleat 2.5%, Dadjo/Kibet/Muro 2.4%, Tupuri/Kera 2%, Gabri/Kabalaye/Nanchere/Somrai 2%. **Languages:** French, Arabic (both official); Sara; 120+ langs. and dialects. **Religions:** Muslim 56.9% (Sunni), Christian 35.1% (Catholic 20.0%, Protestant 10.0%), ethnic religionist 7.1%.

Geography: Total area: 495,755 sq mi, 1,284,000 sq km (20); **Land area:** 486,180 sq mi, 1,259,200 sq km. **Location:** Central N Africa. Libya on N; Niger, Nigeria, Cameroon on W; Central African Republic on S; Sudan on E. **Topography:** Wooded savanna, steppe, and desert in the S; part of the Sahara in the N. Southern rivers flow N to Lake Chad, surrounded by marshland. **Arable land:** 4.2%. **Capital:** N'Djaména, 1,592,324.

Government: Type: Presidential republic. **Head of state:** Interim Pres. Mahamat Idriss Déby Itno; b. 1984; in office: Apr. 20, 2021. **Head of govt.:** Prime Min. Saleh Kebzabo; b. 1947; in office: Oct. 12, 2022. **Local divisions:** 23 provinces. **Defense budget:** $259 mil. **Active troops:** 33,250.

Economy: Industries: oil, cotton textiles, brewing, natron (sodium carbonate), soap, cigarettes, constr. materials. **Chief agric.:** sorghum, groundnuts, millet, yams, cereals, sugarcane. **Natural resources:** petroleum, uranium, natron, kaolin, fish, gold, limestone, sand/gravel, salt. **Water:** 2,782 cu m per capita. **Crude oil reserves:** 1.5 bil bbls. **Electricity prod.:** 312.4 mil kWh. **Labor force:** agric. 68.9%, industry 9.7%, services 21.4%. **Unemployment:** 1.4%.

Finance: Monetary unit: Central African CFA Franc (XAF) (606.88 = $1 U.S.). **GDP:** $29.6 bil; **per capita GDP:** $1,668; **GDP growth:** 2.2%. **Imports** (2017): $2.2 bil; China 29%, UAE 16%, France 10%, U.S. 8%. **Exports** (2017): $2.5 bil; China 32%, UAE 21%, India 19%, U.S. 10%, France 6%. **Budget** (2020): $2.1 bil. **Inflation:** 5.8%.

Transport: Airports: 9.

Communications: Mobile: 68.2 per 100 pop. **Broadband:** 7.8 per 100 pop. **Internet:** 17.9%.

Health: Expend.: 5.4%. **Life expect.:** 57.7 male; 61.5 female. **Births:** 39.9 per 1,000 pop. **Deaths:** 9.2 per 1,000 pop. **Infant mortality:** 64.0 per 1,000 live births. **Undernourished:** 31.4%. **HIV:** 1.0%. **COVID-19:** 7,698 cases, 194 deaths; rates per 100,000: 46.9 cases, 1.2 deaths. 29.3% vaccinated.

Education: Compulsory: ages 6-15. **Literacy:** 26.8%.

Website: presidence.td

Chad was the site of Paleolithic and Neolithic cultures before the Sahara Desert formed. A succession of kingdoms and Arab slave traders dominated Chad until France took control around 1900. Independence came Aug. 11, 1960. Northern Muslim rebels fought animist and Christian southern government and French troops from 1966.

Rebel forces led by Hissène Habré captured the capital and forced Pres. Goukouni Oueddei to flee the country in June 1982. In Dec. 1990, a Libyan-supported insurgent group, the Patriotic Salvation Movement, overthrew Habré, who went into exile in Senegal. (Accused of killing and torturing thousands in the 1980s, Habré was convicted in Senegal, May 30, 2016, of crimes against humanity and sentenced to life in prison. Habré died Aug. 24, 2021.)

After approval of a new constitution Mar. 1996, Chad's first multiparty presidential election was held in June and July.

Violence along the Sudan border escalated in 2006, as Sudanese janjaweed militias and Chadian rebels attacked civilians, and Darfur rebels preyed on refugee camps. On Jan. 15, 2010, Chad and Sudan signed an accord aimed at normalizing relations and suppressing cross-border activities by rebel groups. By early 2023, about 400,000 Sudanese refugees were living in Chad, and escalating violence in Sudan beginning in Apr. brought another 418,000 refugees into Chad by mid-Sept.

After Islamist groups took over northern Mali and imposed a repressive regime in late 2012, Chad contributed roughly 2,000 soldiers to aid French, Malian, and other African forces in a military intervention. On Apr. 15, 2013, Chad announced it would begin pulling its troops out of Mali. Beginning in 2015, Chad periodically sent troops into Nigeria to fight Boko Haram Islamist extremists; extremist fighters and suicide bombers staged attacks in Chad.

Pres. Idriss Déby, who won reelection for a sixth term, Apr. 11, 2021, died Apr. 20 from injuries suffered while he was with government troops fighting rebels in northern Chad. His son, Mahamat Idriss Déby, succeeded him. Although elections were promised by Oct. 2022, the interim government, Oct. 1, 2022, delayed them by two years.

Chile
Republic of Chile

People: Population: 18,549,457 (65). **Age distrib.:** <15: 19.3%; 65+: 13.1%. **Growth:** 0.6%. **Migrants:** 8.6%. **Pop. density:** 64.6 per sq mi, 24.9 per sq km. **Urban:** 88.0%. **Ethnic groups:** white and non-Indigenous 88.9%, Mapuche 9.1%. **Languages:** Spanish (official), English, Indigenous. **Religions:** Christian 87.2% (Catholic 60.0%, independent 22.5%), agnostic 9.1%, atheist 2.6%.

Geography: Total area: 291,933 sq mi, 756,102 sq km (37); **Land area:** 287,187 sq mi, 743,812 sq km. **Location:** W coast of southern S America. Peru on N, Bolivia on NE, Argentina on E. **Topography:** Andes Mts., with some of world's highest peaks, on E border; on W is 2,650-mi Pacific coast. Width varies 100-250 mi. Atacama Desert in N. **Arable land:** 1.8%. **Capital:** Santiago, 6,903,392; Valparaíso (legislative seat), 1,008,599.

Government: Type: Presidential republic. **Head of state and govt.:** Pres. Gabriel Boric; b. 1986; in office: Mar. 11, 2022. **Local divisions:** 16 regions. **Defense budget:** $3.8 bil. **Active troops:** 68,500.

Economy: Industries: copper, lithium, other minerals, foodstuffs, fish proc., iron and steel, wood and wood prods., transp. equip., cement. **Chief agric.:** grapes, apples, wheat, sugar beet, milk, potatoes. **Natural resources:** copper, timber, iron ore, nitrates, prec. metals, molybdenum, hydropower. **Water:** 48,287 cu m per capita. **Crude oil reserves:** 150 mil bbls. **Electricity prod.:** 84.7 bil kWh. **Labor force:** agric. 6.6%, industry 23.0%, services 70.4%. **Unemployment:** 7.8%.

Finance: Monetary unit: Peso (CLP) (849.00 = $1 U.S.). **GDP:** $592.2 bil; **per capita GDP:** $30,209; **GDP growth:** 2.4%. **Imports:** $102.1 bil; China 24%, U.S. 20%, Brazil 8%. **Exports:** $100.6 bil; China 32%, U.S. 14%, Japan 9%, South Korea 7%. **Tourism:** $113 mil. **Budget** (2020): $73.2 bil. **Inflation:** 11.6%.

Transport: Railways: 4,525 mi. **Motor vehicles:** 316.4 per 1,000 pop. **Airports:** 90.

Communications: Mobile: 134.7 per 100 pop. **Broadband:** 109.5 per 100 pop. **Internet:** 90.2%.

Health: Expend. (2021): 9.1%. **Life expect.:** 77.0 male; 83.1 female. **Births:** 12.6 per 1,000 pop. **Deaths:** 6.6 per 1,000 pop. **Infant mortality:** 6.4 per 1,000 live births. **Undernourished:** 2.5%. **HIV:** 0.6%. **COVID-19:** 5,289,055 cases, 61,614 deaths; rates per 100,000: 27,667.9 cases, 322.3 deaths. 92.7% vaccinated.

Education: Compulsory: ages 6-17. **Literacy:** 97.0%.

Website: www.gob.cl

Northern Chile was under Inca rule before the Spanish conquest, 1536-40. The southern Araucanian Indians resisted until the late 19th cent. Independence was gained 1810-18 under José de San Martín and Bernardo O'Higgins; the latter, as supreme director 1817-23, sought social and economic reforms until deposed. Chile defeated Peru and Bolivia in 1836-39 and 1879-84, gaining mineral-rich northern land. Chile is the world's largest producer of copper, responsible for more than 25% of the world total; copper exports are a mainstay of the economy.

In 1970, Salvador Allende Gossens, a Marxist, became president. His government improved conditions for the poor, but property seizures by left-wing extremists, poorly planned socialist economic programs, and a destabilization campaign backed by the U.S. led to political and financial chaos. A U.S.-backed military junta seized power Sept. 11, 1973; Allende apparently killed himself. The junta, headed by Gen. Augusto Pinochet Ugarte, implemented plans to privatize the economy and "exterminate Marxism." Repression continued into the 1980s.

In Dec. 1989 voters elected a civilian president. In Mar. 1994, a Chilean human rights group estimated that more than 3,100 people were killed or "disappeared" during Pinochet's rule.

Ricardo Lagos Escobar, Chile's first Socialist president since the 1973 coup, took office Mar. 11, 2000. Michelle Bachelet Jeria, also a Socialist, won a runoff election Jan. 2006 and took office in Mar. as Chile's first woman president.

Billionaire businessman Sebastián Piñera Echenique, a conservative, won a presidential runoff election Jan. 2010. An earthquake and tsunami, Feb. 27, 2010, killed at least 521 people and caused up to $30 bil in property damage. Low wages sparked protests against the Piñera government. Bachelet returned to the presidency after winning a runoff election Dec. 15, 2013. Chile legalized civil unions between same-sex couples, Oct. 22, 2015, and abortion in very limited circumstances, Aug. 2, 2017.

With the Socialists' popularity hurt by a sluggish economy, Piñera returned as president after winning a Dec. 17, 2017, runoff. Pope

Francis, Apr. 11, 2018, apologized for "grave errors" in the handling by Catholic Church officials in Chile of numerous allegations of child sex abuse by clergy. Months of large-scale demonstrations, beginning Oct. 2019, protested economic inequality. A harsh police response resulted in more than 30 deaths and thousands of injuries. Progressive Gabriel Boric defeated a rightist candidate in a Dec. 19, 2021, runoff to become Chile's youngest elected president.

In an Oct. 25, 2020, plebiscite, Chileans voted to rewrite the country's Pinochet-era constitution. However, the new constitution was widely perceived as overly progressive and was voted down in a Sept. 4, 2022, plebiscite. In May 7, 2023, voting, rightists won two-thirds of the seats on a new committee to rewrite the constitution.

Tierra del Fuego is the largest (18,800 sq mi) island in the archipelago of the same name at the southern tip of S America. It was visited 1520 by Magellan and named Land of Fire because of its many Indian bonfires. Part of the island is in Chile, part in Argentina. Punta Arenas, on a mainland peninsula, is the world's southernmost city; Puerto Williams is the southernmost settlement.

China
People's Republic of China

(Statistical data do not include Hong Kong or Macau.)

People: Population: 1,413,142,846 (1). **Age distrib.:** <15: 16.5%; 65+: 14.1%. **Growth:** 0.2%. **Migrants:** 0.1%. **Pop. density:** 392.4 per sq mi, 151.5 per sq km. **Urban:** 64.6%. **Ethnic groups:** Han Chinese 91.1%, ethnic minorities (incl. Zhang, Hui, Manchu, Uighur, Miao, Yi, Tujia, Tibetan, Mongol, Dong, Buyei, Yao, Bai, Korean) 8.9%. **Languages:** Standard Chinese or Mandarin (official; Putonghua, based on Beijing dialect), Yue (Cantonese), Wu (Shanghainese), Minbei (Fuzhou), Minnan (Hokkien-Taiwanese), Xiang, Gan, Hakka dialects. **Religions:** Chinese folk-religionist 31.3%, agnostic 31.3%, Buddhist 16.9% (Mahayanist), Christian 7.7%, atheist 6.3%, ethnic religionist 4.0%, Muslim 1.8% (Sunni).

Geography: Total area: 3,705,407 sq mi, 9,596,960 sq km (4); **Land area:** 3,600,947 sq mi, 9,326,410 sq km. **Location:** Occupies most of the habitable mainland of E Asia. Mongolia on N; Russia on NE and NW; Kazakhstan, Kyrgyzstan, Tajikistan, Afghanistan, Pakistan on W; India, Nepal, Bhutan, Myanmar, Laos, Vietnam on S; North Korea on NE. **Topography:** Two-thirds of territory is mountainous or desert. The Da Xing'an Ling Mts. in N separate Manchuria and Mongolia. Other ranges incl. the Tien Shan in Xinjiang and the Himalayan and Kunlun Mts. in the SW and in Tibet. Three great river systems—the Chang (Yangtze), Huang (Yellow), and Xi—cross the country's eastern half. **Arable land:** 11.6%. **Capital:** Beijing, 21,766,214. **Cities:** Shanghai, 29,210,808; Chongqing, 17,340,704; Guangzhou, Guangdong, 14,284,353; Tianjin, 14,238,643; Shenzhen, 13,072,633; Nanjing, Jiangsu, 9,698,464; Chengdu, 9,653,772; Xi'an, Shaanxi, 8,785,174.

Government: Type: Communist party-led state. **Head of state:** Pres. Xi Jinping; b. 1953; in office: Mar. 14, 2013 (gen. sec. of Communist Party since Nov. 15, 2012). **Head of govt.:** Prem. Li Qiang; b. 1959; in office: Mar. 11, 2023. **Local divisions:** 22 provinces (not incl. Taiwan), 5 autonomous regions, 4 municipalities, special admin. regions of Hong Kong (as of July 1, 1997) and Macau (as of Dec. 20, 1999). **Defense budget:** $242.4 bil. **Active troops:** 2,035,000.

Economy: Industries: mining and ore proc., iron, steel, aluminum, other metals, coal; machine building; armaments; textiles and apparel; petroleum; cement; chemicals; fertilizer; consumer prods.; food proc.; transp. equip.; telecom equip.; comm. space launch vehicles, satellites. **Chief agric.:** maize, rice, vegetables, wheat, sugarcane, potatoes. **Natural resources:** coal, iron ore, helium, petroleum, nat. gas; arsenic, bismuth, cobalt, cadmium, ferrosilicon; aluminum, lead, zinc, rare earth elements, uranium. **Water:** 1,930 cu m per capita. **Crude oil reserves:** 26 bil bbls. **Electricity prod.:** 8.2 tril kWh. **Labor force:** agric. 24.4%, industry 28.2%, services 47.4%. **Unemployment:** 4.9%.

Finance: Monetary unit: Yuan Renminbi (CNY) (7.27 = $1 U.S.). **GDP:** $30.3 tril; **per capita GDP:** $21,476; **GDP growth:** 3.0%. **Imports:** $3.1 tril; South Korea 9%, Japan 8%, Australia 7%, Germany 7%, U.S. 7%, Taiwan 6%. **Exports:** $3.6 tril; U.S. 17%, Hong Kong 10%, Japan 6%. **Tourism:** $11.3 bil. **Budget:** $4.9 tril. **Inflation:** 2.0%.

Transport: Railways: 93,206 mi. **Motor vehicles:** 224.5 per 1,000 pop. **Airports:** 510.

Communications: Mobile: 124.9 per 100 pop. **Broadband:** 107.8 per 100 pop. **Internet:** 75.6%.

Health: Expend.: 5.6%. **Life expect.:** 75.5 male; 81.2 female. **Births:** 9.7 per 1,000 pop. **Deaths:** 7.8 per 1,000 pop. **Infant mortality:** 6.5 per 1,000 live births. **Undernourished:** <2.5%. **HIV:** NA. **COVID-19:** 99,302,177 cases, 121,628 deaths; rates per 100,000: 6,749.3 cases, 8.3 deaths. 87.3% vaccinated.

Education: Compulsory: ages 6-14. **Literacy:** 97.2%.

Website: www.gov.cn

Remains of various humanlike creatures who lived as early as several hundred thousand years ago have been found in many parts of China. Neolithic agricultural settlements dotted the Huang (Yellow) R. basin from about 5000 BCE. Their language, religion, and art were the sources of later Chinese civilization.

Bronze metallurgy reached a peak and Chinese pictographic writing, similar to today's, was in use in the more developed culture of the Shang Dynasty (c. 1766 BCE-c. 1045 BCE), which ruled much of North China.

A succession of dynasties and interdynastic warring kingdoms ruled China for the next 3,000 years. They expanded Chinese political and cultural domination to the south and west, and developed a technologically and culturally advanced society that was unaffected by foreign rule (Mongols in the Yuan Dynasty, 1279-1368, and Manchus in the Qing Dynasty, 1644-1912).

Rebellions in the 19th cent. left tens of millions dead. Russia, Japan, Britain, and other powers exercised political and economic control in large parts of the country. China became a republic in 1912, when the Qing emperor Puyi abdicated following the Wuchang Uprising inspired by Dr. Sun Yat-sen, founder of the Kuomintang (Nationalist) party. By 1928, the Kuomintang, led by Chiang Kai-shek, succeeded in nominal reunification of China. About the same time, a bloody purge of Communists from the ranks of the Kuomintang fomented hostilities.

For over 50 years, 1894-1945, China was involved in conflicts with Japan. In 1895, China ceded Korea, Taiwan, and other areas. On Sept. 18, 1931, Japan seized the Northeastern Provinces (Manchuria) and set up a puppet state called Manchukuo. Taking advantage of Chinese dissension, Japan invaded China proper July 7, 1937. On Nov. 20 the retreating Nationalist government moved its capital to Chongqing (Chungking) from Nanjing (Nanking), which Japanese troops then ravaged Dec. 13.

From 1939 the Sino-Japanese War (1937-45) became part of the broader world conflict. After its defeat in World War II, Japan relinquished China. Within China, conflicts involving the Kuomintang, Communists, and other factions resumed. China came under the domination of Communist armies, 1949-50. The Kuomintang government fled to Taiwan, Dec. 8, 1949.

The People's Republic of China was proclaimed in Beijing (Peking) Oct. 1, 1949, under Mao Zedong. China and the USSR signed a 30-year treaty of "friendship, alliance, and mutual assistance," Feb. 15, 1950. The U.S. refused to recognize the new regime. On Nov. 26, 1950, the People's Republic sent armies into Korea against U.S. troops and forced a stalemate in the Korean War.

Frequent drastic changes in policy and violent factionalism 1949-52 interfered with economic development. In 1957, Mao admitted an estimated 800,000 people had been executed 1949-54; opponents claimed much higher figures. The Great Leap Forward, 1958-60, tried to accelerate economic development through intensive labor on huge new rural communes and emphasis on ideological purity. Many resisted, and the program was largely abandoned.

By the 1960s, relations with the USSR deteriorated, and the USSR canceled aid accords. The Great Proletarian Cultural Revolution, 1965, an attempt to instruct a new generation in revolutionary principles, resulted in massive purges. Millions of urban teenagers were relocated to rural areas. By 1968 the movement had run its course; many purged officials returned to office in subsequent years, and several ideological reforms were gradually weakened.

On Oct. 25, 1971, the UN General Assembly ousted the Taiwan government from the UN and seated the People's Republic. U.S. Pres. Richard Nixon visited China Feb. 21-28, 1972. China and the U.S. opened liaison offices in each other's capitals, May-June 1973. The U.S., Dec. 15, 1978, formally recognized the People's Republic of China as the sole legal government of China; diplomatic relations were established, Jan. 1, 1979.

Mao died Sept. 9, 1976. By 1978, Vice Prem. Deng Xiaoping had consolidated power, succeeding Mao as "paramount leader" of China. The new ruling group modified Maoist policies in education, culture, and industry, and sought better ties with non-Communist countries. By the mid-1980s, China had enacted far-reaching economic reforms, including market-oriented incentives, although close government-industry coordination continued.

Some 100,000 students and workers marched in Beijing to demand political reforms, May 4, 1989. As the unrest spread, martial law was imposed, May 20. Troops entered Beijing, June 3-4, and crushed the pro-democracy protests, as tanks and armored personnel carriers rolled through Tiananmen Square. It is estimated that hundreds and thousands were injured, and hundreds of students and workers were arrested.

Deng Xiaoping died Feb. 19, 1997. Hong Kong reverted to Chinese sovereignty July 1, 1997. Portugal returned Macau to China Dec. 20, 1999.

China, Oct. 15-16, 2003, became the third nation (after the U.S. and USSR) to send a person into space. In Dec. 2013, China became the third nation to reach the moon with a spacecraft that made a soft landing. In 2021, China landed a rover on Mars and sent its first astronauts to a space station in Earth orbit.

China's industries, exports, and energy demand have increased rapidly since the 1980s. China became the world's largest producer and consumer of coal. In part to diversify energy production, China completed construction in 2006 of the world's largest hydroelectric dam, the Three Gorges Dam on the Yangtze R. China announced, Sept. 3, 2016, that it had ratified the 195-nation agreement to limit climate change negotiated in Paris in Dec. 2015. However, in subsequent years, China remained the largest source of greenhouse gas emissions.

An earthquake in Sichuan prov. May 12, 2008, left 69,226 dead and 17,923 missing. The Nobel Peace Prize was awarded Oct. 8, 2010, to Liu Xiaobo, an incarcerated human rights activist; Liu died of cancer in government custody, July 13, 2017. Xi Jinping was chosen Communist Party general secretary, Nov. 15, 2012. In Mar. 2013, the National People's Congress (NPC) elected Xi as president of China and Li Keqiang as premier. They were reelected Mar. 2018. The NPC elected Xi to a third term, Mar. 10, 2023; Xi ally Li Qiang was elected premier by the NPC, Mar. 11.

Western experts Jan.-Feb. 2010 blamed hackers in China for cyberattacks on Google and other firms. Hackers in China were suspected in new attacks on U.S. government computer systems in 2014. The U.S., July 19, 2021, accused China of orchestrating cyberattacks on companies and organizations in the U.S. and around the world.

After double-digit gains for many years since the 1980s, China's GDP growth slowed beginning in 2012. However, by 2014, China's GDP (measured by purchasing power parity) was the largest in the world. Since 2010, China has been the world's largest exporter. Since 2013, partly under the $1-tril Belt and Road Initiative, China has been financing and building infrastructure projects in many developing countries worldwide.

The U.S. accused China in 2017 of unfair trade practices. In 2018-19, the U.S. implemented tariffs on hundreds of billions of dollars' worth of Chinese products; China retaliated with tariffs on U.S. goods. Under a 2020 agreement, the U.S. reduced some tariffs in exchange for Chinese pledges to increase purchases of some U.S. products and take steps to protect U.S. technology and intellectual property. The U.S. trade in goods deficit with China was $382 bil in 2022, down from $418 bil in 2018.

To stem population growth, a requirement that families have a maximum of one child was implemented in 1980. Subsequently, amid concerns about worker shortages and an aging population, the limit was changed to two children by 2016 and three children in 2021.

China has occupied the Paracel Isls., in the South China Sea, since 1974. Taiwan and Vietnam also claim the resource-rich islands. The Spratly Isls. are similarly in dispute with Taiwan, Vietnam, Malaysia, and the Philippines. The international Permanent Court of Arbitration in The Hague, July 12, 2016, rejected China's claim to most of the South China Sea as territorial waters and ruled that China's building of artificial islands—in some cases militarized—in disputed areas violated international law. China had the world's largest navy by 2017.

A new coronavirus, causing the disease COVID-19, emerged in late 2019 in Wuhan; its severity may have been initially concealed, especially by local officials. The origin of the virus was uncertain. By Feb. 2020, the virus was spreading worldwide. As of mid-Aug. 2023, the COVID-19 pandemic had caused about 770 mil confirmed cases globally (over 99 mil in China) and more than 6.9 mil confirmed deaths (over 120,000 in China). Strict lockdown measures, under the Chinese government's "zero COVID" policy, hurt the economy. Large protests against lockdown restrictions took place in many cities, Nov. 2022. By Dec., most restrictions had been eased or eliminated. Sharp spikes in cases and deaths occurred Dec. 2022-Jan. 2023.

Amid heightened Chinese-U.S. tensions, an apparent Chinese spy balloon that had flown across the U.S. was shot down off the U.S. east coast, Feb. 4, 2023.

Autonomous Regions

Guangxi Zhuang is in SE China, bounded on the N by Guizhou and Hunan provinces, E and S by Guangdong, on the SW by Vietnam, and on the W by Yunnan. It produces rice and forest products. Pop. (2020): 50,126,804. Capital: Nanning; pop. (2023 est.) 4,191,891.

Inner Mongolia was organized by the People's Republic in 1947. Its boundaries were later expanded, to an area of 454,600 sq mi, allegedly to dilute the minority Mongol population. Han Chinese greatly outnumber Mongols. China began, Sept. 1, 2020, replacing Mongolian- with Mandarin-language instruction in schools. Pop. (2020) 24,049,155. Capital: Hohhot; pop. (2023 est.) 2,380,636.

Ningxia Hui, in N central China, is about 60,000 sq mi. Pop. (2020) 7,202,654. Capital: Yinchuan; pop. (2023 est.) 1,716,591. The climate is mostly semiarid, with desert areas in the N. The Huang (Yellow) R. furnishes water for irrigation. The majority of the population is Han. The Hui, most of whom follow Islam, constitute about one-third of the population; a crackdown on Muslim practices began in the late 2010s.

Xinjiang Uighur, in Central Asia, is 635,900 sq mi, pop. (2020) 25,852,345 (75% Uighurs, a Turkic Muslim group, with a heavy Han Chinese increase in recent years). Capital: Urumqi; pop. (2023 est.) 4,865,038. It is China's richest region in strategic minerals. In recent decades, China has moved to suppress Uighur cultural and religious practices and to crack down on Uighur separatists. Legislation effective Apr. 1, 2017, placed new restrictions on women wearing face veils in public. Chinese authorities reportedly destroyed mosques, removed children from Uighur families, forced birth control measures on Uighur women, and carried out intensive electronic surveillance of the Uighur population. The number of people sentenced to prison terms began increasing sharply in 2017. In addition, by 2019, an estimated 1-1.5 mil Uighurs had been interned in "re-education" or labor camps; large-scale use of forced labor was reported. China alleged that, by the end of 2019, most camps had been closed, but dissidents and others reported that large numbers of Uighurs subsequently remained in detention. U.S. anti-forced-labor legislation in 2022 essentially barred imports of products with supply chains linked to Xinjiang.

Tibet, 471,700 sq mi, is a thinly populated region of high plateaus and massive mountains, the Himalayas on the S, the Kunluns on the N. Capital: Lhasa. Avg. elevation is 15,000 ft. Jiachan, 15,870 ft, is believed to be the highest inhabited town on Earth. Pop. (2020) 3,648,100 (of whom about 500,000 are Chinese). Millions of Tibetans live in vast adjacent areas that have long been incorporated into China.

China ruled all of Tibet from the 18th cent. Independence came in 1911, but China reasserted control in 1951, and a Communist government was installed in 1953. Serfdom was abolished, but all land remained collectivized. A Tibetan uprising within China in 1956 spread to Lhasa in 1959. The rebellion was crushed by Chinese troops, and Buddhism was almost totally suppressed. The Dalai Lama and 100,000 Tibetans fled to India. Efforts by Chinese authorities to halt peaceful demonstrations by Tibetan monks led to anti-Chinese riots in Lhasa, Mar. 14, 2008—crushed by Chinese government troops. Protests (including about 160 self-immolations since 2009), as well as government repression and coerced assimilation, continued in subsequent years.

Hong Kong

Hong Kong (Xianggang), located at the mouth of the Zhu Jiang (Pearl R.) in SE China, 90 mi S of Guangzhou, was a British dependency from 1842 until July 1, 1997, when it became a Special Administrative Region of China. Its nucleus is Hong Kong Isl., 31 sq mi, occupied by the British in 1841 and formally ceded to them in 1842, on which is located the seat of government. Opposite is Kowloon Peninsula, 3 sq mi, and Stonecutters Isl., added to the territory in 1860. An additional 355 sq mi known as the New Territories, a mainland area and islands, were leased from China, 1898, for 99 years. Area 428 sq mi (total); 414 sq mi (land); pop. (2023 est.) 7,288,167. **Website:** www.gov.hk

Hong Kong is a major trade and banking center. Per capita GDP, over $69,000 in 2022, is among the highest in the world. Principal industries are textiles and apparel, tourism, banking, shipping, and electronics. A majority of tourists are from mainland China.

Hong Kong harbor was long an important British naval station and one of the world's great transshipment ports. The colony often provided refuge for exiles from mainland China. It was occupied by Japan during WWII.

From 1949 to 1962, Hong Kong absorbed more than 1 mil refugees fleeing Communist China. Starting in the 1950s, cheap labor led to a boom in light manufacturing, while liberal tax policies attracted foreign investment. Hong Kong became one of the wealthiest, most productive areas in the Far East. In recent years, manufacturing has been shifting from Hong Kong to mainland China.

With the end of the 99-year lease on the New Territories drawing near, Britain and China signed an agreement, Dec. 19, 1984, under which all of Hong Kong was to be returned to China in 1997; under this agreement Hong Kong was to be allowed to keep its capitalist system for 50 years. Following the transfer of government, Hong Kong retained its currency, the Hong Kong dollar; in recent years, a growing portion of financial transactions use the Chinese renminbi. Cantonese, English, and Mandarin are official languages.

Leung Chunying, with close ties to China, was elected chief executive Mar. 2012 by a committee of about 1,200 members. Large pro-democracy protests took place July-Dec. 2014. Pro-Beijing candidate Carrie Lam was chosen chief executive by the election committee, Mar. 26, 2017. China's foreign ministry stated, June 30, 2017, that the 1984 agreement with Britain no longer had binding force.

Large-scale protests (up to 2 mil people) in 2019 opposed proposed legislation authorizing Hong Kong to extradite suspects to mainland China. Police often used force against sometimes-violent demonstrations. Lam, Sept. 4, withdrew the extradition bill. Protests continued, demanding greater democracy and an investigation of police tactics. The Chinese government enacted a broad Hong Kong security law, in effect as of June 30, 2020, that was used to crack down on speech, peaceful protests, media outlets, and political activists. Mar. 2021 electoral-law changes reduced the number of directly elected seats on Hong Kong's Legislative Council and instituted vetting of candidates for compliance with the 2020 security law. In Dec. 19, 2021, Legislative Council elections marked by low turnout, pro-Beijing candidates won virtually all seats at stake. The election committee, May 8, 2022, chose former security chief John Lee as Hong Kong's new chief executive.

Macau

Macau, area of 11 sq mi, is a peninsula and two small islands at the mouth of the Xi (Pearl) R. in China. It was established as a Portuguese trading colony in 1557. In 1849, Portugal claimed sovereignty over the territory; this claim was accepted by China in an 1887 treaty. Portugal granted broad autonomy in 1976. Under a 1987 agreement, Macau reverted to China Dec. 20, 1999. The

Chinese government guaranteed Macau it would not interfere in its way of life for a period of 50 years. However, pro-democracy candidates were barred from running in Sept. 12, 2021, legislative elections. Tourism, including casino gambling, is a mainstay of the economy; most tourists are from mainland China. Per capita GDP was $55,345 in 2022, a nearly $73,000 drop from 2019, as COVID-19 severely hurt the tourism industry 2020-22. Pop. (2023 est.) 639,971. Website: www.gov.mo

Colombia
Republic of Colombia

People: Population: 49,336,454 (29). **Age distrib.:** <15: 22.5%; 65+: 10.9%. **Growth:** 0.5%. **Migrants:** 3.7%. **Pop. density:** 123.0 per sq mi, 47.5 per sq km. **Urban:** 82.4%. **Ethnic groups:** mestizo and white 87.6%, Afro-Colombian (incl. mulatto, Raizal, Palenquero) 6.8%, Amerindian 4.3%. **Languages:** Spanish (official), 65 Amerindian langs. **Religions:** Christian 94.8% (Catholic [official] 85.8%), agnostic 2.9%.

Geography: Total area: 439,736 sq mi, 1,138,910 sq km (25); **Land area:** 401,044 sq mi, 1,038,700 sq km. **Location:** NW corner of S America. Panama on NW, Ecuador and Peru on S, Brazil and Venezuela on E. **Topography:** Three Andes ranges—Western, Central, and Eastern Cordilleras—run N-S. The eastern range consists mostly of high tablelands. The Magdalena R. rises in the Andes, flows N to Caribbean through a rich alluvial plain. Sparsely settled plains in E are drained by Orinoco and Amazon systems. **Arable land:** 1.8%. **Capital:** Bogotá, 11,507,960. **Cities:** Medellín, 4,102,308; Cali, 2,863,730; Barranquilla, 2,349,400.

Government: Type: Presidential republic. **Head of state and govt.:** Pres. Gustavo Petro; b. 1960; in office: Aug. 7, 2022. **Local divisions:** 32 departments, 1 capital district. **Defense budget:** $6.3 bil. **Active troops:** 255,950.

Economy: Industries: textiles, food proc., oil, clothing and footwear, beverages, chemicals, cement. **Chief agric.:** sugarcane, milk, oil palm fruit, potatoes, rice, bananas. **Natural resources:** petroleum, nat. gas, coal, iron ore, nickel, gold, copper, emeralds, hydropower. **Water:** 46,381 cu m per capita. **Crude oil reserves:** 2 bil bbls. **Electricity prod.:** 80.9 bil kWh. **Labor force:** agric. 15.9%, industry 20.1%, services 63.9%. **Unemployment:** 10.7%.

Finance: Monetary unit: Peso (COP) (4,103.77 = $1 U.S.). **GDP:** $1.1 tril; **per capita GDP:** $20,287; **GDP growth:** 7.5%. **Imports:** $70.8 bil; U.S. 27%, China 20%, Mexico 7%, Brazil 6%. **Exports:** $50.8 bil; U.S. 31%, China 11%, Panama 8%. **Tourism:** $2.7 bil. **Budget:** $103.1 bil. **Inflation:** 10.2%.

Transport: Railways: 1,330 mi. **Motor vehicles:** 114.1 per 1,000 pop. **Airports:** 121.

Communications: Mobile: 155.8 per 100 pop. **Broadband:** 76.2 per 100 pop. **Internet:** 72.8%.

Health: Expend.: 9.0%. **Life expect.:** 71.3 male; 78.7 female. **Births:** 15.1 per 1,000 pop. **Deaths:** 7.8 per 1,000 pop. **Infant mortality:** 11.7 per 1,000 live births. **Undernourished:** 6.6%. **HIV:** 0.5%. **COVID-19:** 6,378,000 cases, 142,961 deaths; rates per 100,000: 12,534.7 cases, 281.0 deaths. 72.8% vaccinated.

Education: Compulsory: ages 5-16. **Literacy:** 95.6%.

Website: id.presidencia.gov.co

Spain subdued the local Indian kingdoms (Funza, Tunja) by the 1530s and ruled Colombia and neighboring areas as New Granada for 300 years. Independence was won by 1819. Venezuela and Ecuador broke away in 1829-30, and Panama withdrew in 1903.

In the 20th and early 21st cents., Colombia was plagued by rural and urban violence. "La Violencia" of 1948-58 claimed 200,000 lives. Guerrilla warfare and terrorist attacks by leftist rebels, including the Revolutionary Armed Forces of Colombia (FARC), began in the 1960s. Violence by right-wing paramilitary groups became widespread by the 1980s. Government activity against drug cartels sparked retaliation killings of politicians and judges. The FARC engaged in drug trafficking and kidnappings for ransom to finance its operations.

Álvaro Uribe Vélez, a hardliner, won a presidential election, May 2002, and launched a new government offensive against the FARC. Uribe won reelection, May 2006. Key political figures were arrested in 2007 on charges of colluding with paramilitary death squads. Former Defense Min. Juan Manuel Santos Calderón won presidential elections, June 2010 and June 2014. A peace accord with the FARC, providing for FARC disarmament and reintegration into civilian life, went into effect Dec. 1, 2016. On Oct. 7, 2016, Santos won the Nobel Peace Prize. On June 27, 2017, about 7,000 FARC rebels finished surrendering weapons, but violence by criminal gangs, former FARC members, and other rebels continued. New ceasefires by some armed groups were announced Sept. 28, 2022, and June 9, 2023. Millions of Colombians were internally displaced by decades of violence; 4.8 million Colombians were conflict-related IDPs as of the end of 2022.

Iván Duque, a conservative, won a June 17, 2018, presidential runoff election. A series of national strikes, Nov.-Dec. 2019, protested government economic policies, failure to fully implement the FARC accord, and killings of Indigenous and other rights activists. Weeks of demonstrations began Apr. 2021, protesting poverty, inequality, and proposed tax hikes. Promising economic changes,

leftist Gustavo Petro won the June 19, 2022, presidential runoff election. Nicolás Petro, the president's son, was charged, July 29, 2023, with money laundering related to drug trafficking.

A ruling by Colombia's Constitutional Court, Feb. 21, 2022, legalized most abortions.

Beginning in 2015, large numbers of Venezuelans fleeing hardship and repression entered Colombia. By early 2023, about 2.5 mil Venezuelans were in Colombia, which granted many of them temporary legal status.

Comoros
Union of the Comoros

People: Population: 888,378 (160). **Age distrib.:** <15: 33.4%; 65+: 4.5%. **Growth:** 1.3%. **Migrants:** 1.4%. **Pop. density:** 1,029.5 per sq mi, 397.5 per sq km. **Urban:** 30.1%. **Ethnic groups:** Antalote, Cafre, Makoa, Oimatsaha, Sakalava. **Languages:** Arabic, French, Shikomoro (Comorian) (similar to Swahili) (all official). **Religions:** Muslim 98.3% (Sunni [official] 98%).

Geography: Total area: 863 sq mi, 2,235 sq km (170); **Land area:** 863 sq mi, 2,235 sq km. **Location:** 3 islands—Grande Comore (Njazidja), Anjouan (Nzwani), and Moheli (Mwali)—in the Mozambique Channel between NW Madagascar and SE Africa. Nearest neighbor is Mozambique on W. **Topography:** Of volcanic origin; an active volcano on Grande Comore. **Arable land:** 34.9%. **Capital:** Moroni, 62,351.

Government: Type: Federal presidential republic. **Head of state and govt.:** Pres. Azali Assoumani; b. 1959; in office: May 26, 2016. **Local divisions:** 3 islands. **Defense budget/active troops:** NA.

Economy: Industries: fishing, tourism, perfume distillation. **Chief agric.:** coconuts, cassava, rice, bananas, pulses, milk. **Natural resources:** fish. **Water:** 1,380 cu m per capita. **Electricity prod.:** 138.3 mil kWh. **Labor force:** agric. 35.0%, industry 20.2%, services 44.9%. **Unemployment:** 8.8%.

Finance: Monetary unit: Franc (KMF) (455.16 = $1 U.S.). **GDP:** $3.2 bil; **per capita GDP:** $3,832; **GDP growth:** 2.4%. **Imports:** $407.0 mil; China 22%, UAE 16%, France 11%, Pakistan 9%, India 6%. **Exports:** $139.6 mil; France 32%, India 23%, Germany 10%, Turkey 9%, Madagascar 7%. **Tourism:** $71 mil. **Budget (2018):** $228 mil. **Inflation** (2016-17): 1.0%.

Transport: Airports: 4.

Communications: Mobile: 100.2 per 100 pop. **Broadband:** 61.5 per 100 pop. **Internet:** 27.3%.

Health: Expend.: 5.3%. **Life expect.:** 65.2 male; 69.9 female. **Births:** 22.1 per 1,000 pop. **Deaths:** 6.5 per 1,000 pop. **Infant mortality:** 56.0 per 1,000 live births. **Undernourished:** 13.5%. **HIV:** <0.1%. **COVID-19:** 9,109 cases, 160 deaths; rates per 100,000: 1,047.5 cases, 18.4 deaths. 45.7% vaccinated.

Education: Compulsory: ages 6-11. **Literacy:** 62.0%.

Website: beit-salam.km

France acquired the islands from Muslim sultans, 1841-1909. The islands were granted internal autonomy in 1961. In a 1974 referendum, all islands favored independence except Mayotte. The Comorian government declared independence July 6, 1975, with Ahmed Abdallah as its president. In a 1976 referendum, Mayotte voted to remain French.

A leftist regime that seized power from Abdallah in 1975 was deposed in a pro-French 1978 coup in which he regained the presidency. In Nov. 1989, Pres. Abdallah was assassinated; soon after, a multiparty system was instituted.

Anjouan and Moheli seceded from the Comoros in 1997. Unrest on Grande Comore culminated in a military coup, Apr. 1999. A constitution adopted in a referendum Dec. 2001 that went into effect the following year reunited Anjouan and Moheli with Grande Comore, granting each a semi-autonomous status and its own president.

Irregularities marred the Apr. 2002 runoff election for national president, won by Azali Assoumani, who led the 1999 coup. Having left office in 2006, Assoumani was again elected president in an Apr. 10, 2016, runoff. After changing the constitution to permit him to run, Assoumani won reelection, Mar. 24, 2019, in voting international observers deemed not credible.

Congo, Democratic Republic of the (DRC)

(The Democratic Republic of the Congo [formerly Zaire], now commonly called the DRC, is also known as Congo-Kinshasa. The Republic of the Congo is also known as Congo [Brazzaville].)

People: Population: 111,859,928 (14). **Age distrib.:** <15: 46.0%; 65+: 2.5%. **Growth:** 3.1%. **Migrants:** 1.1%. **Pop. density:** 127.8 per sq mi, 49.3 per sq km. **Urban:** 47.4%. **Ethnic groups:** 200+ groups, majority Bantu. Four largest groups (Mongo, Luba, Kongo [all Bantu], and Mangbetu-Azande [Hamitic]) 45%. **Languages:** French (official), Lingala (lingua franca trade lang.), Kingwana (Kiswahili or Swahili dialect), Kikongo, Tshiluba. **Religions:** Christian 95.2% (Catholic 52.0%, independent 25.5%, Protestant 17.7%), ethnic religionist 2.3%.

Geography: Total area: 905,355 sq mi, 2,344,858 sq km (11); **Land area:** 875,312 sq mi, 2,267,048 sq km. **Location:** Central Africa. Congo (Brazzaville) on W; Central African Republic, South

Sudan on N; Uganda, Rwanda, Burundi, Tanzania on E; Zambia, Angola on S. **Topography:** Includes the bulk of the Congo R. basin. Central region is a low-lying plateau covered by rain forest. Mountainous terraces in the W, savannas in the S and SE, grasslands toward the N, and the Ruwenzori Mts. on the E. A short strip of territory borders the Atlantic O. **Arable land:** 6.0%. **Capital:** Kinshasa, 16,315,534. **Cities:** Mbuji-Mayi, 2,891,746; Lubumbashi, 2,811,959; Kananga, 1,664,442.

Government: Type: Semi-presidential republic. **Head of state:** Pres. Felix Tshisekedi; b. 1963; in office: Jan. 24, 2019. **Head of govt.:** Prime Min. Jean-Michel Sama Lukonde Kyenge; b. 1977; in office: Feb. 15, 2021. **Local divisions:** 26 provinces. **Defense budget:** $372 mil. **Active troops:** 134,250.

Economy: Industries: mining, mineral proc., consumer prods., metal prods., processed foods and beverages, timber, cement. **Chief agric.:** cassava, plantains, sugarcane, maize, oil palm fruit, rice. **Natural resources:** cobalt, copper, niobium, tantalum, petroleum, diamonds, gold, silver, zinc, manganese, tin, uranium, coal, hydropower, timber. **Water:** 14,325 cu m per capita. **Crude oil reserves:** 180 mil bbls. **Electricity prod.:** 11.0 bil kWh. **Labor force:** agric. 55.3%, industry 10.0%, services 34.7%. **Unemployment:** 5.0%.

Finance: Monetary unit: Franc (CDF) (2,469.13 = $1 U.S.). **GDP:** $132.4 bil; **per capita GDP:** $1,337; **GDP growth:** 8.9%. **Imports:** $22.2 bil; China 29%, South Africa 15%, Zambia 12%. **Exports:** $22.4 bil; China 53%, UAE 11%, Saudi Arabia 6%. **Tourism:** $108 mil. **Budget:** $6.4 bil. **Inflation** (2016-17): 41.5%.

Transport: Railways: 2,490 mi. **Motor vehicles:** 25.3 per 1,000 pop. **Airports:** 26.

Communications: Mobile: 50.3 per 100 pop. **Broadband:** 26.2 per 100 pop. **Internet:** 22.9%.

Health: Expend.: 4.1%. **Life expect.:** 60.4 male; 64.1 female. **Births:** 39.6 per 1,000 pop. **Deaths:** 7.7 per 1,000 pop. **Infant mortality:** 59.1 per 1,000 live births. **Undernourished:** 35.3%. **HIV:** 0.6%. **COVID-19:** 97,697 cases, 1,468 deaths; rates per 100,000: 109.1 cases, 1.6 deaths. 16.1% vaccinated.

Education: Compulsory: ages 6-11. **Literacy:** 80.0%.

Website: www.presidence.cd

The earliest inhabitants of Congo may have been the Pygmies, followed by Bantus from the east and Nilotic people from the north. The large Bantu Bakongo kingdom ruled much of Congo and Angola when Portuguese explorers visited in the 15th cent.

Leopold II, king of the Belgians, formed an international group to exploit the Congo region in 1876. In 1877, British explorer Henry M. Stanley traveled the Congo R, and in 1879, in the service of Leopold II, he returned to help colonize the region. The Conference of Berlin, 1884-85, established the Congo Free State with Leopold as king and chief owner. The colony became known as the Belgian Congo in 1908 when Leopold sold it to the Belgian government. Millions of Congolese rubber plantation workers were exploited and died under brutal European rule between 1880 and 1920. (On June 30, 2020, Belgium's king expressed "deepest regrets for the wounds of the past.")

Belgian and Congolese leaders agreed Jan. 27, 1960, that Congo would become independent. In May 31 elections, Patrice Lumumba's party won a plurality in the National Assembly. The Republic of the Congo was proclaimed June 30. Europeans and others fled widespread violence. The UN Security Council, Aug. 9, called on Belgium to withdraw its troops and sent a UN contingent. Lumumba was dismissed as premier in Sept. and murdered Jan. 17, 1961. The last UN troops left the Congo June 30, 1964.

In late 1965, Gen. Joseph D. Mobutu was named president. He later changed his name to Mobutu Sese Seko and ruled as a dictator. The country became the Democratic Republic of the Congo (1966) and the Republic of Zaire (1971). Under Mobutu, economic decline and government corruption plagued the country.

During 1994, Zaire was inundated with refugees from the massive ethnic bloodshed in Rwanda. Ethnic violence spread to eastern Zaire in 1996. In Oct., militant Hutus, who dominated in the refugee camps, fought rebels (mostly Tutsis) in Zaire, precipitating intervention by government troops. The rebels, led by Gen. Laurent Kabila, moved west across Zaire. On May 17, 1997, Kabila's troops entered Kinshasa, and Mobutu went into exile. The country again became the DRC.

Kabila, who ruled by decree, alienated UN officials, international aid donors, and former allies. Rebels assisted by Rwanda and Uganda threatened Kinshasa in Aug. 1998 but were turned back with help from Angola, Namibia, and Zimbabwe. Rebel groups agreed to a cease-fire, Aug. 31, 1999, but the truce was widely violated. Kabila was assassinated Jan. 16, 2001, and was succeeded by his son Joseph.

The estimated death toll from the civil war and related causes was 3.3 mil through Nov. 2002. By then, Rwanda and Uganda had agreed to pull out their remaining troops. A power-sharing accord signed Apr. 2, 2003, led to the installation of a new DRC government in July. Under a new constitution in effect as of Feb. 18, 2006, a UN peacekeeping force (MONUC), established in 1999, oversaw July 2006 elections. Kabila defeated former rebel leader Jean-Pierre Bemba in a presidential runoff election, Oct. 2006.

Hundreds reportedly died in Kinshasa, Mar. 22-23, 2007, in clashes between security forces and a militia loyal to Bemba. A peace deal with militia groups in eastern DRC, including one led by Tutsi rebel Gen. Laurent Nkunda, was signed Jan. 23, 2008, but Nkunda launched a new offensive Aug. 28; Rwandan authorities arrested him Jan. 2009.

Kabila was reelected, Nov. 28, 2011. A June 2011 study estimated that more than 1,000 women were raped in the DRC every day. The Intl. Criminal Court (ICC) at The Hague convicted Congolese warlord Thomas Lubanga Dyilo Mar. 2012 of war crimes for conscripting child soldiers during the country's civil war. The ICC, May 23, 2014, sentenced rebel leader Germain Katanga to 12 years in prison in connection with a 2003 massacre of more than 200 villagers.

The MONUC peacekeeping mission was reconstituted and renamed MONUSCO as of July 1, 2010. Eleven African nations signed a peace plan Feb. 24, 2013, designed to end the violence in the DRC. Rebel leader Bosco Ntaganda surrendered in Rwanda Mar. 18, 2013, to face charges of war crimes and crimes against humanity; he was convicted by the ICC, July 8, 2019. A peace agreement with the M23 militia group was reached in Dec. 2013. About 8,000 rebels laid down their arms, but other fighters remained active. With Kabila legally required to leave office in Dec. 2016, protests occurred, 2016-17, over government delays in scheduling the next presidential election. After a Dec. 30, 2018, election—in which widespread voting irregularities were reported—Félix Tshisekedi was declared the winner.

Political and ethnic violence continued in eastern DRC, involving various armed rebel groups—including a resurgent M23 (reportedly backed by Rwanda) and an ISIS affiliate. MONUSCO peacekeepers included almost 15,000 uniformed personnel as of July 31, 2023. As of June 2023, almost 6.3 mil Congolese were internally displaced.

A severe Ebola outbreak in eastern DRC began in 2018. By the time the WHO declared the outbreak over, June 25, 2020, there had been 3,470 cases and 2,287 deaths. Although the DRC was affected by the COVID-19 pandemic, only 16% of the pop. had been vaccinated as of Aug. 2023.

Congo, Republic of the

(The Republic of the Congo is also known as Congo [Brazzaville]. The Democratic Republic of the Congo [formerly Zaire], now commonly called the DRC, is also known as Congo-Kinshasa.)

People: Population: 5,677,493 (115). **Age distrib.:** <15: 38.4%; 65+: 4.3%. **Growth:** 2.3%. **Migrants:** 7.0%. **Pop. density:** 43.1 per sq mi, 16.6 per sq km. **Urban:** 69.2%. **Ethnic groups:** Kongo (Bakongo) 40.5%, Teke 16.9%, Mbochi 13.1%, foreigner 8.2%, Sangha 5.6%, Mbere/Mbeti/Kele 4.4%, Punu 4.3%. **Languages:** French (official); French Lingala, Monokutuba (lingua franca trade langs.); many local langs., dialects (Kikongo most widespread). **Religions:** Christian 89.5% (Catholic 66.0%, independent 11.8%, Protestant 11.7%), ethnic religionist 4.9%, agnostic 3.1%.

Geography: Total area: 132,047 sq mi, 342,000 sq km (63); **Land area:** 131,854 sq mi, 341,500 sq km. **Location:** W central Africa. Gabon and Cameroon on W, Central African Republic on N, Dem. Rep. of the Congo on E, Angola on SW. **Topography:** Thick forests across much of country. A coastal plain leads to the fertile Niari Valley. The Congo R. basin consists of flood plains in the lower portion and savanna in the upper. **Arable land:** 1.6%. **Capital:** Brazzaville, 2,637,733. **Cities:** Pointe-Noire, 1,336,387.

Government: Type: Presidential republic. **Head of state:** Pres. Denis Sassou-Nguesso; b. 1943; in office: Oct. 25, 1997. **Head of govt.:** Prime Min. Anatole Collinet Makosso; b. 1965; in office: July 22, 2021. **Local divisions:** 12 departments. **Defense budget:** $264 mil. **Active troops:** 10,000.

Economy: Industries: petroleum extraction, cement, lumber, brewing, sugar, palm oil, soap. **Chief agric.:** cassava, sugarcane, oil palm fruit, cassava leaves, bananas, plantains. **Natural resources:** petroleum, timber, potash, lead, zinc, uranium, copper, phosphates, gold, magnesium, nat. gas, hydropower. **Water:** 150,777 cu m per capita. **Crude oil reserves:** 2.9 bil bbls. **Electricity prod.:** 4.0 bil kWh. **Labor force:** agric. 36.3%, industry 21.2%, services 42.5%. **Unemployment:** 21.8%.

Finance: Monetary unit: Central African CFA Franc (XAF) (606.88 = $1 U.S.). **GDP:** $22.6 bil; **per capita GDP:** $3,791; **GDP growth:** 1.5%. **Imports** (2020): $3.3 bil; China 15%, France 12%, Belgium 6%. **Exports** (2020): $4.7 bil; China 49%, UAE 15%, India 6%. **Tourism** (2020): $4 mil. **Budget:** $2.6 bil. **Inflation:** 3.0%.

Transport: Railways: 317 mi. **Motor vehicles:** 20.1 per 1,000 pop. **Airports:** 8.

Communications: Mobile (2021): 96.8 per 100 pop. **Broadband** (2021): 15.8 per 100 pop. **Internet** (2017): 8.7%.

Health: Expend.: 4.5%. **Life expect.:** 70.8 male; 73.6 female. **Births:** 29.1 per 1,000 pop. **Deaths:** 5.0 per 1,000 pop. **Infant mortality:** 31.4 per 1,000 live births. **Undernourished:** 33.3%. **HIV:** 4.1%. **COVID-19:** 25,196 cases, 389 deaths; rates per 100,000: 456.6 cases, 7.1 deaths. 11.9% vaccinated.

Education: Compulsory: ages 6-15. **Literacy:** 80.6%.

Website: presidence.cg or www.ambacongo-us.org

The Loango kingdom flourished in the 15th cent., as did the Anzico kingdom of the Batekes; by the late 17th cent. they had weakened. By 1885, France controlled the region. The Republic of the Congo gained independence Aug. 15, 1960.

After a 1963 coup, the country adopted a Marxist-Leninist stance. However, France remained a dominant trade partner and source of technical assistance, and French-owned private enterprise retained a major economic role. In 1970, the country was renamed People's Republic of the Congo. Since the 1980s, oil has dominated the economy. In June 2018, the country joined OPEC.

In 1990, Marxism was renounced and opposition parties were legalized. In 1991 the country's name was changed back to Rep. of the Congo. A democratically elected government came into office in 1992. Factional fighting broke out in Brazzaville, June 1997. Troops loyal to former Marxist dictator Denis Sassou-Nguesso took control of the city Oct. 15, 1997; he claimed lopsided victories in 2002 and 2009 presidential elections. After 2015 constitutional changes allowed him to run again, Sassou-Nguesso was reelected Mar. 20, 2016, and Mar. 21, 2021—in the latter case, with almost 90% of the vote after some opposition groups boycotted the election and the main opposition candidate died of COVID-19 on election day.

Costa Rica
Republic of Costa Rica

People: Population: 5,256,612 (123). **Age distrib.:** <15: 19.3%; 65+: 10.6%. **Growth:** 1.0%. **Migrants:** 10.2%. **Pop. density:** 266.6 per sq mi, 102.9 per sq km. **Urban:** 82.6%. **Ethnic groups:** white or mestizo 83.6%, mulatto 6.7%, Indigenous 2.4%. **Languages:** Spanish (official), English. **Religions:** Christian 94.2% (Catholic [official] 75.0%), agnostic 4.2%.

Geography: Total area: 19,730 sq mi, 51,100 sq km (126); **Land area:** 19,714 sq mi, 51,060 sq km. **Location:** Central America. Nicaragua on N, Panama on S. **Topography:** Tropical lowlands by the Caribbean. The interior plateau, at an elevation of about 4,000 ft, is temperate. **Arable land:** 4.8%. **Capital:** San José, 1,461,989.

Government: Type: Presidential republic. **Head of state and govt.:** Pres. Rodrigo Chaves Robles; b. 1961; in office: May 8, 2022. **Local divisions:** 7 provinces. **Defense budget:** $423 mil (paramilitary budget). **Active troops:** No armed forces. 9,950 paramilitary-style police and coast guard only.

Economy: Industries: medical equip., food proc., textiles and clothing, constr. materials, fertilizer, plastic prods. **Chief agric.:** sugarcane, pineapples, bananas, milk, oil palm fruit, fruit. **Natural resources:** hydropower. **Water:** 22,182 cu m per capita. **Electricity prod.:** 12.7 bil kWh. **Labor force:** agric. 17.1%, industry 17.2%, services 65.7%. **Unemployment:** 11.5%.

Finance: Monetary unit: Colon (CRC) (541.75 = $1 U.S.). **GDP:** $129.1 bil; **per capita GDP:** $24,923; **GDP growth:** 4.3%. **Imports:** $22.3 bil; U.S. 41%, China 13%, Mexico 7%. **Exports:** $23.8 bil; U.S. 38%, Netherlands 6%. **Tourism:** $1.6 bil. **Budget:** $14 bil. **Inflation:** 8.3%.

Transport: Railways: 173 mi (some sections rehabilitated after entire network fell into disrepair). **Motor vehicles:** 250.4 per 1,000 pop. **Airports:** 47.

Communications: Mobile: 152.0 per 100 pop. **Broadband:** 96.5 per 100 pop. **Internet:** 82.6%.

Health: Expend.: 7.9%. **Life expect.:** 77.0 male; 82.4 female. **Births:** 10.7 per 1,000 pop. **Deaths:** 5.5 per 1,000 pop. **Infant mortality:** 7.0 per 1,000 live births. **Undernourished:** 3.0%. **HIV:** 0.5%. **COVID-19:** 1,238,883 cases, 9,428 deaths; rates per 100,000: 24,319.9 cases, 185.1 deaths. 85.6% vaccinated.

Education: Compulsory: ages 4-16. **Literacy:** 98.0%.
Website: www.presidencia.gob.cr

Guaymi Indians inhabited the area when Spaniards arrived, 1502. Independence came in 1821. Costa Rica seceded from the Central American Federation in 1838. Since the civil war of 1948-49, free political institutions have been preserved.

Nobel Peace Prize-winner Óscar Arias Sánchez, president 1986-90, won a second term in 2006. In 2010, the ruling party's Laura Chinchilla Miranda became the nation's first female president. The opposition Citizen Action Party (PAC) won 2014 and 2018 presidential elections. Beginning in 2018, Nicaraguans fleeing political violence and repression entered Costa Rica—a total of up to 200,000 by 2023.

The important tourism industry was hurt by travel restrictions and business closures to combat the COVID-19 epidemic, which had spread worldwide by 2020.

Economist and political outsider Rodrigo Chavez won the Apr. 3, 2022, presidential runoff election.

Côte d'Ivoire
Republic of Côte d'Ivoire

People: Population: 29,344,847 (52). **Age distrib.:** <15: 36.6%; 65+: 3.0%. **Growth:** 2.2%. **Migrants:** 9.7%. **Pop. density:** 239.0 per sq mi, 92.3 per sq km. **Urban:** 53.1%. **Ethnic groups:** Akan 28.9%, Voltaique or Gur 16.1%, Northern Mande 14.5%, Kru 8.5%, Southern Mande 6.9%, non-Ivoirian 24.2%. **Languages:** French (official), 60 native dialects (Dioula most widely spoken). **Religions:**

Muslim 43.1% (Sunni), Christian 35.2% (Catholic 18.3%, Protestant 11.9%), ethnic religionist 21.1%.

Geography: Total area: 124,504 sq mi, 322,463 sq km (68); **Land area:** 122,782 sq mi, 318,003 sq km. **Location:** S coast of W Africa. Liberia, Guinea on W; Mali, Burkina Faso on N; Ghana on E. **Topography:** Forests cover W half of country. A sparse inland plain leads to low mountains in NW. **Arable land:** 11.0%. **Capital:** Abidjan (administrative), 5,686,350; Yamoussoukro (official), 231,072.

Government: Type: Presidential republic. **Head of state:** Pres. Alassane Ouattara; b. 1942; in office: Apr. 11, 2011 (sworn in Dec. 4, 2010). **Head of govt.:** Prime Min. Patrick Achi; b. 1955; in office: Apr. 19, 2022. **Local divisions:** 12 districts, 2 autonomous districts. **Defense budget:** $610 mil. **Active troops:** 27,400.

Economy: Industries: foodstuffs, beverages, wood prods., oil refining, gold mining, truck and bus assembly, textiles, fertilizer. **Chief agric.:** yams, cassava, cocoa, oil palm fruit, sugarcane, rice. **Natural resources:** petroleum, nat. gas, diamonds, manganese, iron ore, cobalt, bauxite, copper, gold, nickel, tantalum, silica sand, clay, cocoa beans, coffee, palm oil, hydropower. **Water:** 3,190 cu m per capita. **Crude oil reserves:** 100 mil bbls. **Electricity prod.:** 11.0 bil kWh. **Labor force:** agric. 45.0%, industry 10.8%, services 44.2%. **Unemployment:** 2.6%.

Finance: Monetary unit: CFA Franc (XOF) (606.88 = $1 U.S.). **GDP:** $184.1 bil; **per capita GDP:** $6,538; **GDP growth:** 6.7%. **Imports** (2020): $12.7 bil; China 18%, Nigeria 13%, France 11%. **Exports** (2020): $13.2 bil; Netherlands 10%, U.S. 6%, France 6%. **Tourism** (2020): $166 mil. **Budget:** $10.1 bil. **Inflation:** 5.3%.

Transport: Railways: 410 mi. **Motor vehicles:** 29.8 per 1,000 pop. **Airports:** 7.

Communications: Mobile: 174.0 per 100 pop. **Broadband:** 97.8 per 100 pop. **Internet:** 35.5%.

Health: Expend.: 3.7%. **Life expect.:** 60.5 male; 65.0 female. **Births:** 27.9 per 1,000 pop. **Deaths:** 7.5 per 1,000 pop. **Infant mortality:** 54.0 per 1,000 live births. **Undernourished:** 7.7%. **HIV:** 1.8%. **COVID-19:** 88,338 cases, 835 deaths; rates per 100,000: 334.9 cases, 3.2 deaths. 46.1% vaccinated.

Education: Compulsory: ages 6-15. **Literacy:** 89.9%.
Website: www.gouv.ci

A French protectorate from 1842, Côte d'Ivoire became independent in 1960. The name was officially changed from Ivory Coast, Oct. 1985.

Students and workers protested, Feb. 1990, demanding the ouster of longtime Pres. Félix Houphouët-Boigny. Côte d'Ivoire held its first multiparty presidential election Oct. 1990, which Houphouët-Boigny won. He died Dec. 7, 1993. His successor, Henri Konan Bédié, was reelected Oct. 1995 but ousted in a military coup Dec. 24, 1999. The coup leader, Robert Guéi, lost a presidential vote Oct. 2000 but claimed victory anyway. After mass protests, he fled, and Laurent Gbagbo became president. Guéi was killed in Abidjan Sept. 19, 2002.

Agreement on power sharing was reached in Mar. 2003, and Gbagbo and former rebel leaders declared an end to their war July 5. The country remained divided, however. Rebels held the north and government forces controlled the south. Under a new accord reached Mar. 2007, rebel leader Guillaume Soro became prime minister.

After apparently losing a presidential runoff election, Nov. 28, 2010, to former Prime Min. Alassane Ouattara, Gbagbo clung to power. A violent power struggle followed, claiming several thousand lives and displacing at least 1 mil people. Ouattara loyalists captured Gbagbo in Abidjan, Apr. 2011. After Ouattara took power, Gbagbo supporters were killed and tortured. Ouattara won reelection Oct. 25, 2015. Legislative elections were held and a new constitution approved in 2016. Amid violent clashes over the legality of his candidacy, Ouattara won reelection, Oct. 31, 2020.

The ICC tried Gbagbo for crimes against humanity. He was acquitted, Jan. 15, 2019. His wife, Simone Gbagbo, was sentenced, Mar. 10, 2015, by a Côte d'Ivoire court to 20 years in prison for her role in the violence that followed the 2010 election. (She was released in Aug. 2018.) In attacks, Mar. 13, 2016, for which al-Qaeda in the Islamic Maghreb claimed responsibility, gunmen killed 19 people and wounded more than 30 at three resort hotels in Grand-Bassam.

Croatia
Republic of Croatia

People: Population: 4,169,239 (128). **Age distrib.:** <15: 14.0%; 65+: 22.6%. **Growth:** −0.5%. **Migrants:** 12.9%. **Pop. density:** 192.9 per sq mi, 74.5 per sq km. **Urban:** 58.6%. **Ethnic groups:** Croat 90.4%, Serb 4.4%, other (incl. Bosniak, Hungarian, Slovene, Czech, Romani) 4.4%. **Languages:** Croatian (official). **Religions:** Christian 94.7% (Catholic [official] 86.6%), agnostic 2.4%, Muslim 2.0% (Sunni).

Geography: Total area: 21,851 sq mi, 56,594 sq km (124); **Land area:** 21,612 sq mi, 55,974 sq km. **Location:** SE Europe, on the Balkan Peninsula. Slovenia, Hungary on N; Bosnia and Herzegovina, Serbia, Montenegro on E. **Topography:** Flat plains in NE; highlands, low mts. along Adriatic. **Arable land:** 15.3%. **Capital:** Zagreb, 684,114.

Government: Type: Parliamentary republic. **Head of state:** Pres. Zoran Milanovic; b. 1966; in office: Feb. 18, 2020. **Head of govt.:** Prime Min. Andrej Plenkovic; b. 1970; in office: Oct. 19, 2016. **Local divisions:** 20 counties, 1 city with special county status. **Defense budget:** $1.3 bil. **Active troops:** 16,700.

Economy: Industries: chemicals and plastics, machine tools, fabricated metal, electronics. **Chief agric.:** maize, wheat, sugar beet, milk, barley, soybeans. **Natural resources:** oil, coal, bauxite, iron ore, calcium, gypsum, natural asphalt, silica, mica, clays, salt, hydropower. **Water:** 25,699 cu m per capita. **Crude oil reserves:** 71 mil bbls. **Electricity prod.:** 14.6 bil kWh. **Labor force:** agric. 6.8%, industry 28.8%, services 64.4%. **Unemployment:** 6.7%.

Finance: Monetary unit: Euro (EUR) (0.93 = $1 U.S.). **GDP:** $155.6 bil; **per capita GDP:** $40,380; **GDP growth:** 6.3%. **Imports** (2017): $36.3 bil; Italy 14%, Germany 14%, Slovenia 11%, Hungary 7%, Austria 6%. **Exports:** $35.3 bil; Italy 13%, Germany 13%, Slovenia 10%, Bosnia and Herzegovina 9%, Austria 6%. **Tourism:** $10.8 bil. **Budget:** $211.1 bil. **Inflation:** 10.8%.

Transport: Railways: 1,626 mi. **Motor vehicles:** 495.2 per 1,000 pop. **Airports:** 24.

Communications: Mobile: 111.2 per 100 pop. **Broadband:** 114.5 per 100 pop. **Internet:** 82.1%.

Health: Expend.: 7.8%. **Life expect.:** 74.4 male; 80.8 female. **Births:** 8.6 per 1,000 pop. **Deaths:** 13.0 per 1,000 pop. **Infant mortality:** 8.6 per 1,000 live births. **Undernourished:** <2.5%. **HIV:** <0.1%. **COVID-19:** 1,274,198 cases, 18,290 deaths; rates per 100,000: 31,398.4 cases, 450.7 deaths. 58.2% vaccinated.

Education: Compulsory: ages 7-14. **Literacy:** 99.5%.

Website: vlada.gov.hr

From the 7th cent. the area was inhabited by Croats, a south Slavic people. It was formed into a kingdom under Tomislav in 924, and joined with Hungary in 1102. The Croats became western-ized and separated from Slavs under Austro-Hungarian influence. Croatia united with other Yugoslav areas to proclaim the Kingdom of Serbs, Croats, and Slovenes in 1918. A nominally independent state between 1941 and 1945, it became a constituent republic of Yugoslavia in the 1946 constitution.

On June 25, 1991, Croatia declared independence from Yugo-slavia. Fighting began between ethnic Serbs and Croats. The Serbs gained control of some Croatian territory, but Croatian troops recaptured most of it Aug. 1995. A peace accord was signed in Dec. The last Serb-held enclave, E Slavonia, was returned to Croatia in 1998. Croatia became a full NATO member Apr. 1, 2009. It joined the EU July 1, 2013, and began using the euro as its currency Jan. 1, 2023.

Kolinda Grabar-Kitarovic of the conservative Croatian Demo-cratic Union (HDZ) party won a runoff election, Jan. 11, 2015, to become Croatia's first woman president. Zoran Milanovic of the center-left Social Democratic Party defeated her in a Jan. 5, 2020, presidential runoff.

The HDZ won the most seats in Sept. 11, 2016, parliamentary elections, and party leader Andrej Plenkovic formed a coalition government, Oct. 19. Plenkovic's HDZ increased its number of seats in July 5, 2020, elections.

Beginning Sept. 2015, tens of thousands of Middle Eastern, Asian, and African refugees and other migrants—most trying to reach N Europe—entered Croatia from Serbia. Croatia announced that as of Mar. 9, 2016, it would block virtually all migrants from transiting through the country.

Extreme heat and wildfires, possibly related to climate change, plagued Croatia in summer 2023.

Cuba
Republic of Cuba

People: Population: 10,985,974 (85). **Age distrib.:** <15: 16.4%; 65+: 16.8%. **Growth:** −0.2%. **Migrants:** 0.03%. **Pop. density:** 259.1 per sq mi, 100.0 per sq km. **Urban:** 77.5%. **Ethnic groups:** white 64.1%, mulatto or mixed 26.6%, Black 9.3%. **Languages:** Spanish (official). **Religions:** Christian 62.0% (Catholic 54.9%), Spiritist 17.0%, agnostic 16.3%, atheist 4.1%.

Geography: Total area: 42,803 sq mi, 110,860 sq km (104). **Land area:** 42,402 sq mi, 109,820 sq km. **Location:** In Caribbean, westernmost of West Indies. The Bahamas, U.S. to N; Mexico to W; Jamaica to S; Haiti to E. **Topography:** Coastline is about 2,500 mi. The N coast is steep and rocky, the S coast low and marshy. Low hills and fertile valleys cover more than half the country. Three mountain ranges. **Arable land:** 28.0%. **Capital:** Havana, 2,148,930.

Government: Type: Communist state. **Head of state:** Pres. Miguel Díaz-Canel Bermúdez; b. 1960; in office: Apr. 19, 2018. **Head of govt.:** Prime Min. Manuel Marrero Cruz; b. 1963; in office: Dec. 21, 2019. **Local divisions:** 15 provinces, 1 special municipal-ity. **Defense budget:** NA. **Active troops:** 49,000.

Economy: Industries: petroleum, nickel, cobalt, pharmaceuti-cals, tobacco, constr., steel, cement, agric. machinery, sugar. **Chief agric.:** sugarcane, cassava, vegetables, plantains, sweet potatoes, tomatoes. **Natural resources:** cobalt, nickel, iron ore, chromium, copper, salt, timber, silica, petroleum. **Water:** 3,366 cu m per cap-ita. **Crude oil reserves:** 124 mil bbls. **Electricity prod.:** 19.8 bil

kWh. **Labor force:** agric. 17.7%, industry 17.1%, services 65.2%. **Unemployment:** 1.4%.

Finance: Monetary unit: Peso (CUP) (23.98 = $1 U.S.). **GDP:** NA; **per capita GDP:** NA; **GDP growth** (2021): 1.3%. **Imports** (2017): $11.1 bil; Spain 19%, China 15%, Italy 6%. **Exports** (2017): $2.6 bil; China 38%, Spain 11%. **Tourism:** $404 mil. **Budget** (2017): $64.6 bil. **Inflation** (2016-17): 5.5%.

Transport: Railways: 5,199 mi. **Motor vehicles:** 53.5 per 1,000 pop. **Airports:** 64.

Communications: Mobile: 67.8 per 100 pop. **Broadband:** 42.2 per 100 pop. **Internet:** 71.1%.

Health: Expend.: 12.5%. **Life expect.:** 77.5 male; 82.4 female. **Births:** 10.0 per 1,000 pop. **Deaths:** 9.4 per 1,000 pop. **Infant mortality:** 4.1 per 1,000 live births. **Undernourished:** <2.5%. **HIV:** 0.6%. **COVID-19:** 1,115,064 cases, 8,530 deaths; rates per 100,000: 9,844.6 cases, 75.3 deaths. 88.4% vaccinated.

Education: Compulsory: ages 6-14. **Literacy:** 99.7%.

Website: www.presidencia.gob.cu

Some 50,000 Indigenous people lived in Cuba when Christo-pher Columbus reached it in 1492. Except for British occupation of Havana, 1762-63, Cuba remained Spanish until 1898. A sugar plantation economy, built primarily on enslaved labor, developed from the 18th cent. Sugar remains a leading agricultural product. Spain failed to deliver on rights guaranteed in 1878, prompting a full-scale liberation movement under Jose Martí in 1895.

The Spanish-American War began Apr. 1898, following the Feb. sinking of the USS Maine in Havana harbor. Spain lost the war and gave up all claims to Cuba. U.S. troops withdrew in 1902, but under 1903 and 1934 agreements, the U.S. continued to lease a site at Guantánamo Bay in the SE as a naval base. U.S. and other foreign investors dominated the economy. In 1952, former Pres. Fulgencio Batista established a dictatorship, which grew increasingly harsh and corrupt. Fidel Castro began a rebellion in 1956. Batista fled Jan. 1, 1959, and Castro took power.

Government-instituted economic and social changes failed to restore promised liberties. Opponents were imprisoned or exe-cuted. Some 700,000 Cubans emigrated in the first years after Castro's takeover, mostly to the U.S. By 1960, all banks and indus-trial companies had been nationalized, including over $1-bil worth of U.S.-owned properties, mostly without compensation. U.S. eco-nomic sanctions became a complete trade embargo under leg-islation passed by Congress in 1961. The U.S. broke diplomatic relations with Cuba in Jan. 1961.

In Apr. 1961, some 1,400 Cubans, trained and backed by the U.S. Central Intelligence Agency, unsuccessfully tried to overthrow the regime. On Oct. 22, 1962, U.S. Pres. John F. Kennedy ordered a naval blockade around Cuba and demanded that Soviet-installed nuclear missiles be withdrawn. The crisis ended Oct. 28 when Soviet Prem. Nikita S. Khrushchev agreed to withdraw the missiles; the U.S. pledged not to invade Cuba and removed its own missiles from Turkey.

In 1978 and 1980, the U.S. agreed to accept political prison-ers released by Cuba, some of whom were criminals and mental patients. A 1987 agreement provided for 20,000 Cubans to emi-grate to the U.S. each year. Cuba's support for left-wing regimes and liberation movements in Central America, Africa, and the Caribbean contributed to poor relations with the U.S.

Cuba's economy, hobbled by U.S. sanctions and dependent on aid from other Communist countries, was shaken by the collapse of the Communist bloc in the late 1980s. Anti-government demonstra-tions in Aug. 1994 prompted Castro to loosen emigration restric-tions. A new U.S.-Cuba accord in Sept. ended the exodus of "boat people" after more than 30,000 had left Cuba.

On July 31, 2006, the ailing Fidel Castro yielded power to his 75-year-old brother Raúl. (Fidel Castro, age 90, died Nov. 25, 2016.) The U.S. in 2009 eased restrictions on remittances and fam-ily travel to Cuba. The Cuban government announced, Sept. 2010, economic restructuring plans involving cutting more than 500,000 public jobs. A Communist Party conference, Apr. 2011, approved an expansion of private property rights and private ownership of some small businesses. Legislation to encourage foreign investment was adopted in Mar. 2014.

The U.S., Jan. 11, 2002, began using its naval base at Guantá-namo Bay to detain prisoners captured in Afghanistan and other suspected Islamist fighters or terrorists. The indefinite detention, as well as aggressive interrogation of prisoners in the early 2000s, was criticized by human rights groups. After over 700 prisoner releases to other countries, the detention center held 30 men as of Sept. 30, 2023. A 2023 report by a UN investigator found detention conditions to be "cruel, inhuman, and degrading."

Under Pres. Barack Obama, the U.S. restored full diplomatic relations with Cuba, July 20, 2015. Some travel and economic restrictions were eased. Scheduled U.S. commercial flights to Cuba, suspended since the early 1960s, resumed Aug. 31, 2016. The Trump administration, 2017-20, tightened travel regulations and economic sanctions—some of which were again eased by the Biden administration in 2022.

The U.S. announced, Sept. 29, 2017, the withdrawal of nones-sential personnel from its Havana embassy, after staff and family members developed various medical problems. A U.S. study con-cluded in 2020 that "directed, pulsed radiofrequency energy" could have caused "Havana syndrome" illnesses (which also affected U.S. personnel in other countries), although much uncertainty remained.

Elected by the National Assembly, Miguel Díaz-Canel Bermúdez became head of state Apr. 19, 2018, succeeding Raúl Castro. A new constitution, approved in a Feb. 24, 2019, referendum, created a new office of prime minister. Díaz-Canel succeeded Raúl Castro as Communist Party head in Apr. 2021. Díaz-Canel was reelected president, Apr. 19, 2023.

Large demonstrations in several cities, July 11, 2021, protesting food shortages and other hardships were met with hundreds of arrests and other government measures to suppress dissent. Continuing economic hardship and repression sparked a new upsurge in immigration to the U.S., 2021-23. July 2022 legislation, approved by voters in a Sept. 25 referendum, permitted same-sex couples to marry and adopt children.

Cyprus
Republic of Cyprus

People: Population: 1,308,120 (155). **Age distrib.:** <15: 15.6%; 65+: 14.0%. **Growth:** 1.0%. **Migrants:** 15.8%. **Pop. density:** 366.6 per sq mi, 141.6 per sq km. **Urban:** 67.0%. **Ethnic groups:** Greek 98.8% (Greek-Cypriot citizens in Republic of Cyprus only). **Languages:** Greek, Turkish (both official); English; Romanian; Russian; Bulgarian. **Religions:** Christian 70.1% (Orthodox 66.6%), Muslim 23.1% (Sunni), agnostic 3.8%.

Geography: Total area: 3,572 sq mi, 9,251 sq km (164). **Land area:** 3,568 sq mi, 9,241 sq km. **Location:** Eastern Mediterranean Sea, off Turkish coast. Nearest neighbors are Turkey to N, Syria and Lebanon to E. **Topography:** Two mountain ranges run E-W, separated by a wide, fertile plain. **Arable land:** 10.3%. **Capital:** Nicosia (Lefkosia), 269,469.

Government: Type: Presidential republic. **Head of state and govt.:** Pres. Nikos Christodoulides; b. 1973; in office: Feb. 28, 2023. **Local divisions:** 6 districts. **Defense budget:** $497 mil. **Active troops:** 12,000.

Economy: Industries: tourism, food and beverage proc., cement and gypsum, ship repair and refurb., textiles, light chemicals, metal prods. **Chief agric.:** milk, potatoes, pork, sheep milk, goat milk, barley. **Natural resources:** copper, pyrites, asbestos, gypsum, timber, salt, marble, clay earth pigment. **Water:** 646 cu m per capita. **Electricity prod.:** 4.9 bil kWh. **Labor force:** agric. 2.8%, industry 17.9%, services 79.2%. **Unemployment:** 7.0%.

Finance: Monetary unit: Euro (EUR) (0.93 = $1 U.S.). **GDP:** $45.4 bil; **per capita GDP:** $49,931; **GDP growth:** 5.6%. **Imports:** $23.7 bil; Greece 16%, Italy 10%, Turkey 8%. **Exports:** $24.6 bil; India 9%, Greece 9%, Libya 8%, UK 7%. **Tourism:** $2.1 bil. **Budget:** $10.0 bil. **Inflation:** 8.4%.

Transport: Motor vehicles: 507.1 per 1,000 pop. **Airports:** 13. **Communications: Mobile** (2021): 148.7 per 100 pop. **Broadband** (2021): 81.7 per 100 pop. **Internet:** 89.6%.

Health: Expend.: 8.1%. **Life expect.:** 77.2 male; 82.9 female. **Births:** 10.4 per 1,000 pop. **Deaths:** 7.0 per 1,000 pop. **Infant mortality:** 8.2 per 1,000 live births. **Undernourished:** <2.5%. **HIV:** NA. **COVID-19:** 660,854 cases, 1,364 deaths; rates per 100,000: 74,420.1 cases, 153.6 deaths. 72.5% vaccinated.

Education: Compulsory: ages 5-14. **Literacy:** 99.4%.

Website: www.cyprus.gov.cy

The Ottoman Empire held Cyprus, 1571-1878, until it yielded control to Britain. Agitation for enosis (union) with Greece, which the Turkish minority opposed, increased after WWII and led to violence in 1955-56. In 1959, Britain, Greece, Turkey, and Cypriot leaders approved a plan for an independent republic, with constitutional guarantees for the Turkish minority.

Archbishop Makarios III was elected president, and full independence became final Aug. 16, 1960. Strife between Greek Cypriot and Turkish Cypriot communities prompted the UN to send a peacekeeping force (UNFICYP) in 1964; more than 850 UNFICYP uniformed personnel were in Cyprus as of July 31, 2023.

The Cypriot National Guard, led by officers from the Greek army, seized the government July 15, 1974. On July 20, Turkey invaded the island, and by Aug. 16, Turkish forces had occupied the northeastern 40%. Turkish troops remained in northern Cyprus in 2023.

Turkish Cyprus opened its border with Greek Cyprus Apr. 23, 2003, for the first time since partition. In separate referendums Apr. 2004, 65% of Turkish Cypriot voters accepted a UN-sponsored reunification plan, but 76% of Greek Cypriots rejected it. Still divided, Cyprus became a full member of the EU on May 1, 2004. Greek Cyprus began using the euro as its currency in 2008. The conservative candidate and head of the Democratic Rally party, Nicos Anastasiades, won 2013 and 2018 presidential elections.

In part because Cypriot banks held large amounts of Greek bonds, Cyprus suffered a banking crisis in 2013. A $13 bil bailout package was agreed upon Mar. 5, 2013, by the Intl. Monetary Fund, the European Central Bank, and eurozone countries. Cyprus agreed to stringent banking reforms and economic austerity; large depositors lost some of their money.

Independent Nikos Christodoulides, with center-right backing, won a Feb. 12, 2023, presidential runoff election.

Turkish Republic of Northern Cyprus

A declaration of independence was announced by Turkish-Cypriot leader Rauf Denktash, Nov. 15, 1983. The state, a parliamentary republic with enhanced presidency, is not internationally recognized but has trade relations with some countries. Political moderate Mustafa Akinci won an Apr. 26, 2015, presidential runoff election. New UN-sponsored reunification talks began in June 2015, but after several rounds of negotiations, the UN announced, July 7, 2017, that talks had failed. Akinci was defeated for reelection in an Oct. 18, 2020, presidential runoff by Turkish nationalist Ersin Tatar. An Apr. 2021 UN-sponsored meeting on restarting unification negotiations failed to make progress. Area 1,295 sq mi; pop. (2011 census) 286,257, nearly all ethnically Turkish. Capital: Nicosia (Lefkosia). Local divisions: 5 districts. Active troops: 3,000. Website: www.kktcb.org

Czechia
Czech Republic

(As of May 17, 2016, the country's official short form name in English was Czechia.)

People: Population: 10,706,242 (87). **Age distrib.:** <15: 15.8%; 65+: 20.5%. **Growth:** 0.0%. **Migrants:** 5.1%. **Pop. density:** 359.0 per sq mi, 138.6 per sq km. **Urban:** 74.6%. **Ethnic groups:** Czech 57.3%, Moravian 3.4%. **Languages:** Czech (official). **Religions:** agnostic 57.4%, Christian (official) 35.3% (Catholic 31.0%), atheist 6.4%.

Geography: Total area: 30,451 sq mi, 78,867 sq km (114). **Land area:** 29,825 sq mi, 77,247 sq km. **Location:** E central Europe. Poland on N, Germany on N and W, Austria on S, Slovakia on E and SE. **Topography:** Bohemia, in W, is a plateau surrounded by mountains; Moravia is hilly. **Arable land:** 32.1%. **Capital:** Prague, 1,323,339.

Government: Type: Parliamentary republic. **Head of state:** Pres. Petr Pavel; b. 1961; in office: Mar. 9, 2023. **Head of govt.:** Prime Min. Petr Fiala; b. 1964; in office: Dec. 17, 2021. **Local divisions:** 13 regions, 1 capital city. **Defense budget:** $3.8 bil. **Active troops:** 26,600.

Economy: Industries: motor vehicles, metallurgy, machinery and equip., glass, armaments. **Chief agric.:** wheat, sugar beet, milk, barley, rapeseed, potatoes. **Natural resources:** coal, kaolin, clay, graphite, timber. **Water:** 1,228 cu m per capita. **Crude oil reserves:** 15 mil bbls. **Electricity prod.:** 76.6 bil kWh. **Labor force:** agric. 2.5%, industry 36.9%, services 60.6%. **Unemployment:** 2.4%.

Finance: Monetary unit: Koruna (CZK) (22.35 = $1 U.S.). **GDP:** $525.7 bil; **per capita GDP:** $49,946; **GDP growth:** 2.5%. **Imports:** $196.2 bil; Germany 27%, China 12%, Poland 9%. **Exports:** $204.8 bil; Germany 31%, Slovakia 7%, Poland 6%. **Tourism:** $3.1 bil. **Budget:** $103.2 bil. **Inflation:** 15.1%.

Transport: Railways: 5,933 mi. **Motor vehicles:** 670.6 per 1,000 pop. **Airports:** 41.

Communications: Mobile: 128.4 per 100 pop. **Broadband:** 105.0 per 100 pop. **Internet:** 84.5%.

Health: Expend.: 9.2%. **Life expect.:** 75.1 male; 81.6 female. **Births:** 10.0 per 1,000 pop. **Deaths:** 12.3 per 1,000 pop. **Infant mortality:** 2.6 per 1,000 live births. **Undernourished:** <2.5%. **HIV:** <0.1%. **COVID-19:** 4,643,607 cases, 42,815 deaths; rates per 100,000: 43,422.8 cases, 400.4 deaths. 65.5% vaccinated.

Education: Compulsory: ages 5-14. **Literacy:** 99.0%.

Website: www.vlada.cz

Bohemia and Moravia were part of the Great Moravian Empire in the 9th cent. and later became part of the Holy Roman Empire. Under the kings of Bohemia, Prague in the 14th cent. was the cultural center of Central Europe. Bohemia and Hungary became part of Austria-Hungary.

In 1914-18, Thomas G. Masaryk and Eduard Benes formed a provisional government with the support of Slovak leaders, including Milan Stefanik. They proclaimed the Republic of Czechoslovakia Oct. 28, 1918.

By 1938, Nazi Germany had generated disaffection among German-speaking citizens in Sudetenland and demanded its cession. British Prime Minister Neville Chamberlain signed with Adolf Hitler at Munich, Sept. 30, 1938, an agreement to the cession, with a guarantee of peace by Hitler and Italian dictator Benito Mussolini. Germany occupied Sudetenland Oct. 1-2. Hitler on Mar. 15, 1939, dissolved Czechoslovakia, made protectorates of Bohemia and Moravia, and supported the autonomy of Slovakia, proclaimed independent Mar. 14, 1939.

Soviet troops with some Czechoslovak contingents entered eastern Czechoslovakia in 1944 and reached Prague in May 1945; Benes returned as president. In May 1946 elections, the Communist Party won 38% of the votes. In Feb. 1948, the Communists seized power in advance of scheduled elections. The country was renamed the Czechoslovak Socialist Republic. A harsh Stalinist period followed; all opposition was suppressed.

In Jan. 1968 a liberalization movement spread through Czechoslovakia. Long-time Stalinist ruler Antonin Novotny was deposed; the democrat Slovak Alexander Dubcek succeeded him. On

Aug. 20, troops from the USSR and 4 Warsaw Pact nations invaded Czechoslovakia. Despite demonstrations and riots by students and workers, press censorship was imposed and liberal leaders were ousted. On Apr. 17, 1969, Dubcek resigned as Communist Party leader and was succeeded by Gustav Husak. Censorship was tightened, and the Communist Party expelled a third of its members.

More than 700 leading Czechoslovak intellectuals and former party leaders signed a human rights manifesto in 1977, called Charter 77, prompting a renewed crackdown by the regime.

The police crushed a massive protest in Prague, Nov. 17, 1989. As protesters demanded free elections, the Communist Party leadership resigned Nov. 24; millions went on strike Nov. 27.

On Dec. 10, 1989, the first cabinet in 41 years without a Communist majority took power; Vaclav Havel, playwright and human rights campaigner, was chosen president, Dec. 29. In Mar. 1990 the country was officially renamed the Czech and Slovak Federal Republic. A Slovak-led coalition blocked Havel's bid to win reelection July 1992.

Slovakia declared sovereignty, July 17, 1992. Czech and Slovak leaders agreed, July 23, on a plan for a peaceful division of Czechoslovakia. It split into two separate states—the Czech Republic and Slovakia—Jan. 1, 1993. Havel was elected president of the Czech Republic on Jan. 26. The country became a full member of NATO in 1999.

Vaclav Klaus replaced the retiring Havel, 2003. The nation became a full EU member May 1, 2004.

Center-right parties made a strong showing in May 2010 parliamentary elections. Conservative Milos Zeman was elected president, Jan. 26, 2013; running on an anti-immigration, anti-EU platform, Zeman narrowly won reelection, Jan. 2018.

Billionaire Andrej Babis became prime minister, Dec. 13, 2017, after his new, anti-immigration party ANO won the most seats in Oct. elections. In 2019, Babis resisted calls for his resignation over corruption allegations. The center-right Together bloc, headed by Petr Fiala, narrowly outpolled ANO in Oct. 2021 elections; Fiala formed a coalition government and became prime minister Dec. 17, 2021.

Following Russia's Feb. 2022 invasion of Ukraine, more than 368,000 Ukrainian refugees were in Czechia as of mid-Sept. 2023. Soaring energy costs related to the Ukraine war contributed to high inflation, 2022-23. Pro-Western retired general Petr Pavel defeated Babis in a Jan. 28, 2023, presidential runoff election.

Denmark
Kingdom of Denmark

People: Population: 5,946,984 (113). **Age distrib.:** <15: 16.2%; 65+: 20.6%. **Growth:** 0.4%. **Migrants:** 12.4%. **Pop. density:** 363.0 per sq km, 140.1 per sq km. **Urban:** 88.5%. **Ethnic groups:** Danish (incl. Greenlandic [predom. Inuit] and Faroese) 85.6%, Turkish 1.1%, other (incl. Polish, Syrian, Romanian, German, Iraqi) 13.3%. **Languages:** Danish, Faroese, Greenlandic, English (predominant second lang.). **Religions:** Christian 78.0% (Protestant 75.7%), agnostic 13.5%, Muslim 6.1% (Sunni).

Geography:Total area: 16,639 sq mi, 43,094 sq km (130); **Land area:** 16,384 sq mi, 42,434 sq km. **Location:** Northern Europe, separating North and Baltic Seas. Germany on S, Norway on NW, Sweden on NE. **Topography:** Consists of the Jutland Peninsula and more than 400 islands; flat and gently rolling plains. **Arable land:** 58.9%. **Capital:** Copenhagen, 1,381,005.

Government: Type: Parliamentary constitutional monarchy. **Head of state:** Queen Margrethe II; b. 1940; in office: Jan. 14, 1972. **Head of govt.:** Prime Min. Mette Frederiksen; b. 1977; in office: June 27, 2019. **Local divisions:** 5 regions. **Defense budget:** $5.1 bil. **Active troops:** 15,400.

Economy: Industries: wind turbines, pharmaceuticals, medical equip., shipbuilding and refurb, iron, steel, nonferrous metals, chemicals, food proc., machinery and transp. equip., textiles and clothing. **Chief agric.:** milk, wheat, barley, potatoes, sugar beet, pork. **Natural resources:** petroleum, nat. gas, fish, salt, limestone, chalk, stone, gravel and sand. **Water:** 1,036 cu m per capita. **Crude oil reserves:** 441 mil bbls. **Electricity prod.:** 32.8 bil kWh. **Labor force:** agric. 2.0%, industry 19.3%, services 78.6%. **Unemployment:** 4.2%.

Finance: Monetary unit: Krone (DKK) (6.89 = $1 U.S.). **GDP:** $436.9 bil; **per capita GDP:** $74,005; **GDP growth:** 3.8%. **Imports:** $208.1 bil; (2021) Germany 21%, Sweden 12%, China 9%, Netherlands 8%. **Exports:** $234.3 bil; (2021) Germany 14%, U.S. 10%, Sweden 10%, China 6%. **Tourism:** $4.5 bil. **Budget:** $172.4 bil. **Inflation:** 7.7%.

Transport: Railways: 1,667 mi. **Motor vehicles:** 544.0 per 1,000 pop. **Airports:** 28.

Communications: Mobile: 126.5 per 100 pop. **Broadband:** 142.3 per 100 pop. **Internet:** 97.9%.

Health: Expend. (2021): 10.8%. **Life expect.:** 80.0 male; 83.9 female. **Births:** 11.3 per 1,000 pop. **Deaths:** 9.6 per 1,000 pop. **Infant mortality:** 3.0 per 1,000 live births. **Undernourished:** <2.5%. **HIV:** <0.1%. **COVID-19:** 3,415,091 cases, 8,780 deaths; rates per 100,000: 58,650.7 cases, 150.8 deaths. 80.6% vaccinated. **Education:** Compulsory: ages 6-15. **Literacy:** NA.

Website: denmark.dk

Most of the Viking raiders in the early Middle Ages were Danes. The Danish kingdom was a major power until the 17th cent., when it lost its land in southern Sweden. Norway was separated in 1815, and Schleswig-Holstein in 1864. Northern Schleswig was returned in 1920. Nazi Germany occupied Denmark, Apr. 1940-May 1945, but Danes helped more than 7,200 Jews escape to safety in Sweden, Sept. 1943.

The Danish newspaper Jyllands-Posten published, Sept. 30, 2005, cartoon images of the prophet Muhammad, offensive to Muslims; the caricatures, republished elsewhere, triggered violent protests and a boycott of Danish products in Islamic countries.

After Sept. 2011 parliamentary elections, Helle Thorning-Schmidt of the center-left Social Democrats became Denmark's first female prime min. A bill granting marriage rights to same-sex couples was voted into law, June 7, 2012. In 2014-16, in part as a result of the Syrian refugee crisis, almost 50,000 migrants sought asylum in Denmark. A center-right coalition returned to power in June 2015 elections in which the anti-immigration Danish People's Party won 21% of the vote. Asylum applications fell sharply beginning in 2017. May 2018 legislation banned wearing a face-covering garment such as a burqa or niqab in public. Dec. 2018 legislation required preschool education, including "Danish values" lessons, in largely immigrant areas. After the Social Democrats won June 5, 2019, elections, party leader Mette Frederiksen became prime min. June 2021 legislation allowed Denmark to move asylum seekers to countries outside Europe while their applications were being processed. After the Social Democrats won the most seats in Nov. 1, 2022, elections, Frederiksen formed a broad coalition government with center-right parties.

The **Faroe Islands** in the N Atlantic, about 300 mi NW of the Shetlands, and 850 mi from Denmark proper, 18 inhabited, have an area of 538 sq mi and pop. (2023 est.) of 52,600. They are an administrative division of Denmark, self-governing in most matters. Capital: Tórshavn; pop. (2018 est.) 20,817. Fish is a primary export. **Website:** www.government.fo

Kalaallit Nunaat (Greenland)

Greenland, an island between the North Atlantic and the Arctic Oceans, is separated from the North American continent by Davis Strait and Baffin Bay. Total area is 836,330 sq mi, about 79% of which is ice-capped. Most of the island is a lofty plateau 9,000-10,000 ft in elevation. The average thickness of the cap is 1,000 ft. Scientists point to accelerated melting of Greenland's ice sheet—about 4 tril tons of ice lost 1994-2017, according to a 2021 study—as evidence of global warming. The pop. (2022 est.) was 57,792. Ethnic groups: Greenlandic 89.1%, Danish 7.5%. Under the 1953 Danish constitution, the colony gained representatives in the Folketing (Danish legislature). The Danish parliament, 1978, approved home rule for Greenland, effective May 1, 1979. With home rule, Greenlandic place names came into official use. The name for its capital is Nuuk (2018 est. pop., 18,406), rather than Godthab. Voters approved a new Self-Government Act in Nov. 2008. Per capita GDP was $41,800 (2015 est.). The labor force is distributed as follows: agric. 15.9%, industry 10.1%, services 73.9%. Fish and fish products account for over 90% of exports. Other natural resources include coal, iron ore, lead, zinc, molybdenum, diamonds, gold, platinum, uranium, and hydropower. Website: naalakkersuisut.gl

Djibouti
Republic of Djibouti

People: Population: 976,143 (158). **Age distrib.:** <15: 28.6%; 65+: 4.1%. **Growth:** 1.9%. **Migrants:** 12.1%. **Pop. density:** 109.1 per sq mi, 42.1 per sq km. **Urban:** 78.6%. **Ethnic groups:** Somali 60%, Afar 35%, other (mostly Yemeni Arab, also French, Ethiopian, Italian) 5%. **Languages:** French, Arabic (both official); Somali; Afar. **Religions:** Muslim (official) 97.5% (Sunni).

Geography: Total area: 8,958 sq mi, 23,200 sq km (147); **Land area:** 8,950 sq mi, 23,180 sq km. **Location:** E coast of Africa, separated from Arabian Peninsula by strategically vital strait of Bab el-Mandeb. Eritrea on NW, Ethiopia on W and SW, Somalia on SE. **Topography:** Low coastal plain with mountains behind and an interior plateau. Arid, sandy, and desolate. Hot and dry climate. **Arable land:** 0.1%. **Capital:** Djibouti, 599,504.

Government: Type: Presidential republic. **Head of state:** Pres. Ismail Omar Guelleh; b. 1947; in office: May 8, 1999. **Head of govt.:** Prime Min. Abdoulkader Kamil Mohamed; b. 1951; in office: Apr. 1, 2013. **Local divisions:** 6 districts. **Defense budget:** NA. **Active troops:** 8,450.

Economy: Industries: constr., agric. proc., shipping. **Chief agric.:** vegetables, milk, beef, camel milk, lemons, limes. **Natural resources:** potential geothermal power, gold, clay, granite, limestone, marble, salt, diatomite, gypsum, pumice, petroleum. **Water:** 304 cu m per capita. **Electricity prod.:** 58.2 mil kWh. **Labor force:** agric. 1.2%, industry 6.1%, services 92.7%. **Unemployment:** 27.9%.

Finance: Monetary unit: Franc (DJF) (177.88 = $1 U.S.). **GDP:** $6.6 bil; **per capita GDP:** $5,893; **GDP growth:** 3.0%. **Imports:** $5.5 bil; China 43%, UAE 15%, India 7%. **Exports:** $5.2 bil; Saudi

Arabia 42%, India 15%, China 14%. **Tourism** (2020): $30 mil. **Budget:** $754 mil. **Inflation:** 5.2%.

Transport: Railways: 60 mi (Djibouti segment of Addis Ababa-Djibouti railway). **Airports:** 3.

Communications: Mobile: 46.3 per 100 pop. **Broadband:** 31.5 per 100 pop. **Internet:** 68.9%.

Health: Expend.: 2.0%. **Life expect.:** 63.0 male; 68.3 female. **Births:** 22.0 per 1,000 pop. **Deaths:** 7.1 per 1,000 pop. **Infant mortality:** 46.0 per 1,000 live births. **Undernourished:** 16.8%. **HIV:** NA. **COVID-19:** 15,690 cases, 189 deaths; rates per 100,000: 1,588.1 cases, 19.1 deaths. 35.6% vaccinated.

Education: Compulsory: ages 6-15. **Literacy:** NA.

Website: www.presidence.dj

France gained control of the territory in stages between 1862 and 1900. As French Somaliland, it became an overseas French territory in 1945; in 1967 it was renamed the French Territory of the Afars and the Issas. Ethiopia and Somalia renounced their claims to the area, but each accused the other of trying to gain control. There were clashes between Afars (ethnically related to Ethiopians) and Issas (related to Somalis) in 1976. Immigrants from both countries continued to enter Djibouti until independence on June 27, 1977.

Post-independence economic support has come from France, Arab countries, the U.S., and China. A peace accord Dec. 1994 ended a 3-year Afar rebel uprising. Protests associated with the Arab Spring broke out in late Jan. 2011 demanding the resignation of Pres. Ismail Omar Guelleh. Authorities suppressed the protests. The U.S. announced, May 5, 2014, the signing of a new 20-year lease for its military base in Djibouti. A 460-mi Chinese-built railroad linking Addis Ababa, Ethiopia, with Djibouti City began service Oct. 5, 2016. China opened a naval base in Djibouti, Aug. 1, 2017. Guelleh won a fifth term in Apr. 9, 2021, elections largely boycotted by the opposition.

Dominica
Commonwealth of Dominica

People: Population: 74,656 (188). **Age distrib.:** <15: 20.8%; 65+: 13.4%. **Growth:** 0.02%. **Migrants:** 11.5%. **Pop. density:** 257.5 per sq mi, 99.4 per sq km. **Urban:** 72.0%. **Ethnic groups:** African descent 84.5%, mixed 9%, Indigenous 3.8%. **Languages:** English (official), French patois. **Religions:** Christian 94.0% (Catholic 49.4%, Protestant 41.3%), Spiritist 2.6%, Baha'i 2.0%.

Geography: Total area: 290 sq mi, 751 sq km (175); **Land area:** 290 sq mi, 751 sq km. **Location:** E Caribbean, most northerly Windward Isl. Guadeloupe to N, Martinique to S (both French terr.). **Topography:** Central ridge runs N-S, terminating in cliffs. Volcanic in origin, with numerous thermal springs. **Arable land:** 8.0%. **Capital:** Roseau, 14,942.

Government: Type: Parliamentary republic. **Head of state:** Pres. Sylvanie Burton; in office: Oct. 2, 2023. **Head of govt.:** Prime Min. Roosevelt Skerrit; b. 1972; in office: Jan. 8, 2004. **Local divisions:** 10 parishes. **Defense budget/active troops:** NA.

Economy: Industries: soap, coconut oil, tourism, copra, furniture, cement blocks, shoes. **Chief agric.:** bananas, yams, grapefruit, taro, milk, coconuts. **Natural resources:** timber, hydropower. **Water:** 2,778 cu m per capita. **Electricity prod.:** 171.1 mil kWh. **Labor force:** NA. **Unemployment:** NA.

Finance: Monetary unit: East Caribbean Dollar (XCD) (2.70 = $1 U.S.). **GDP:** $987.3 mil; **per capita** GDP: $13,573; **GDP growth:** 5.9%. **Imports:** $302.0 mil; (2021) U.S. 75%. **Exports:** $105.0 mil; (2021) Saudi Arabia 28%, France 6%. **Tourism:** $16 mil. **Budget** (2021): >$184 mil. **Inflation** (2019-20): −0.7%.

Transport: Airports: 2.

Communications: Mobile (2021): 85.9 per 100 pop. **Broadband** (2021): 67.8 per 100 pop. **Internet:** 80.9%.

Health: Expend.: 5.6%. **Life expect.:** 75.5 male; 81.5 female. **Births:** 13.6 per 1,000 pop. **Deaths:** 8.1 per 1,000 pop. **Infant mortality:** 11.0 per 1,000 live births. **Undernourished:** 6.7%. **HIV:** NA. **COVID-19:** 15,760 cases, 74 deaths; rates per 100,000: 21,891.6 cases, 102.8 deaths. 42.6% vaccinated.

Education: Compulsory: ages 5-16. **Literacy:** NA.

Website: dominica.gov.dm

A British colony since 1805, Dominica was granted self-government in 1967. Independence was achieved Nov. 3, 1978. Hurricanes and other tropical storms periodically devastate the island.

Coups were attempted in 1980 and 1981. Prime Min. Pierre Charles died Jan. 6, 2004, and was succeeded by Roosevelt Skerrit. The COVID-19 pandemic hurt the important tourism industry beginning in 2020. Elected by parliament Sept. 27, 2023, Sylvanie Burton became Dominica's first female president and first head of state of Kalinago (or Carib) descent.

Dominican Republic

People: Population: 10,790,744 (86). **Age distrib.:** <15: 25.9%; 65+: 7.3%. **Growth:** 0.9%. **Migrants:** 5.6%. **Pop. density:** 578.4 per sq mi, 223.3 per sq km. **Urban:** 84.4%. **Ethnic groups:** mixed 70.4% (mestizo/indio 58%, mulatto 12.4%), Black 15.8%, white

13.5%. **Languages:** Spanish (official). **Religions:** Christian 93.9% (Catholic [official] 80.3%), agnostic 3.1%, Spiritist 2.2%.

Geography: Total area: 18,792 sq mi, 48,670 sq km (128); **Land area:** 18,656 sq mi, 48,320 sq km. **Location:** W Indies, sharing isl. of Hispaniola with Haiti on W, Puerto Rico (U.S.) to E. **Topography:** The Cordillera Central range crosses center, rising to over 10,000 ft, highest in the Caribbean. Cibao Valley to N. **Arable land:** 18.5%. **Capital:** Santo Domingo, 3,523,890.

Government: Type: Presidential republic. **Head of state and govt.:** Pres. Luis Rodolfo Abinader Corona; b. 1967; in office: Aug. 16, 2020. **Local divisions:** 10 regions. **Defense budget:** $761 mil. **Active troops:** 56,050.

Economy: Industries: tourism, sugar proc., gold mining, textiles, cement, tobacco. **Chief agric.:** sugarcane, bananas, papayas, rice, plantains, milk. **Natural resources:** nickel, bauxite, gold, silver. **Water:** 2,166 cu m per capita. **Electricity prod.:** 17.6 bil kWh. **Labor force:** agric. 8.3%, industry 20.3%, services 71.4%. **Unemployment:** 7.1%.

Finance: Monetary unit: Peso (DOP) (56.78 = $1 U.S.). **GDP:** $256.4 bil; **per capita** GDP: $22,834; **GDP growth:** 4.9%. **Imports:** $28.5 bil; (2021) U.S. 42%, China 19%. **Exports:** $20.5 bil; (2021) U.S. 51%, Haiti 7%, Switzerland 7%. **Tourism:** $5.7 bil. **Budget:** $14.5 bil. **Inflation:** 8.8%.

Transport: Railways: 308 mi. **Motor vehicles:** 208.3 per 1,000 pop. **Airports:** 16.

Communications: Mobile: 90.4 per 100 pop. **Broadband:** 71.6 per 100 pop. **Internet:** 85.2%.

Health: Expend.: 4.9%. **Life expect.:** 70.3 male; 73.5 female. **Births:** 17.3 per 1,000 pop. **Deaths:** 7.3 per 1,000 pop. **Infant mortality:** 22.7 per 1,000 live births. **Undernourished:** 6.3%. **HIV:** 1.0%. **COVID-19:** 667,048 cases, 4,384 deaths; rates per 100,000: 6,149.1 cases, 40.4 deaths. 56.2% vaccinated.

Education: Compulsory: ages 3-17. **Literacy:** 95.2%.

Website: www.dominicana.gob.do

Carib and Arawak Indians inhabited the island of Hispaniola when Christopher Columbus landed in 1492. The city of Santo Domingo, founded 1496, is the oldest European settlement in the Western Hemisphere.

France took over the western third of the island (now Haiti) in 1697 and Santo Domingo in 1795. Spain returned intermittently 1803-21, as several native republics came and went. Haiti ruled again, 1822-44; Spanish occupation occurred 1861-63. U.S. Marines occupied the country 1916-24.

In 1930, Gen. Rafael Leonidas Trujillo Molina was elected president. The brutal Trujillo era ended with his assassination in 1961. Pres. Joaquín Balaguer, appointed by Trujillo in 1960, resigned under pressure in 1962.

Juan Bosch, elected president in the first free elections in 38 years, was overthrown in 1963. On Apr. 24, 1965, Bosch's followers and others, including a few Communists, launched a revolt. Four days later U.S. Marines intervened against pro-Bosch forces. A provisional government supervised a June 1966 election in which Balaguer defeated Bosch. Balaguer remained in office for most of the next 28 years, but his May 1994 reelection was widely denounced as fraudulent. He called for new elections but did not run, and Leonel Fernández Reyna was elected June 1996. After a presidential election defeat in 2000, Fernández again won the presidency in 2004 and 2008. Fernández ally Danilo Medina Sánchez, of the center-left Dominican Liberation Party (PLD), was elected in 2012 and 2016. In the 2020 presidential election (delayed from May 17 to July 5 by the COVID-19 pandemic), businessman Luis Rodolfo Abinader defeated the PLD candidate.

The Constitutional Court ruled, Sept. 23, 2013, that people born in the Dominican Rep. after 1929 to undocumented immigrant parents were not entitled to citizenship. The decision affected perhaps 200,000 people, most of Haitian descent. May 2014 legislation provided a complex path to citizenship for such people, which most did not complete. In 2015, the government required undocumented immigrants—estimated at more than 500,000, most of them Haitian—to register or face deportation. By the end of 2017, more than 250,000 Haitians had left the country voluntarily or been deported. As undocumented emigration from Haiti, largely to escape violence and hardship, increased in the 2020s, the Dominican Rep. stepped up deportations and began constructing a border wall.

Ecuador
Republic of Ecuador

People: Population: 17,483,326 (70). **Age distrib.:** <15: 27.2%; 65+: 9.0%. **Growth:** 1.1%. **Migrants:** 4.4%. **Pop. density:** 163.6 per sq mi, 63.2 per sq km. **Urban:** 64.8%. **Ethnic groups:** mestizo (mixed Amerindian/white) 71.9%, Montubio 7.4%, Amerindian 7%, white 6.1%, Afroecuadorian 4.3%. **Languages:** Spanish (Castilian) (official), Quechua. **Religions:** Christian 95.0% (Catholic 83.6%), agnostic 3.7%.

Geography: Total area: 109,484 sq mi, 283,561 sq km (73); **Land area:** 106,889 sq mi, 276,841 sq km. **Location:** NW S America, on Pacific coast, astride the equator. Colombia on N,

Peru on E and S. **Topography:** Two Andes ranges run N-S, splitting country into 3 zones: hot, humid lowlands on coast; temperate highlands between ranges; and rainy, tropical lowlands to E. **Arable land:** 4.1%. **Capital:** Quito, 1,956,995. **Cities:** Guayaquil, 3,142,466.

Government: Type: Presidential republic. **Head of state and govt.:** Pres. Guillermo Lasso Mendoza; b. 1955; in office: May 24, 2021. **Local divisions:** 24 provinces. **Defense budget:** $1.6 bil. **Active troops:** 41,250.

Economy: Industries: petroleum, food proc., textiles, wood prods., chemicals. **Chief agric.:** sugarcane, bananas, milk, oil palm fruit, maize, rice. **Natural resources:** petroleum, fish, timber, hydropower. **Water:** 25,075 cu m per capita. **Crude oil reserves:** 8.3 bil bbls. **Electricity prod.:** 32.3 bil kWh. **Labor force:** agric. 32.2%, industry 16.8%, services 51.0%. **Unemployment:** 4.0%.

Finance: Monetary unit: U.S. Dollar (USD) (1.00 = $1 U.S.). **GDP:** $230.8 bil; **per capita GDP:** $12,822; **GDP growth:** 2.9%. **Imports:** $28.6 bil; U.S. 22%, China 18%, Colombia 9%. **Exports:** $29.3 bil; U.S. 30%, China 13%, Panama 8%, Chile 7%. **Tourism:** $1.1 bil. **Budget:** $39.3 bil. **Inflation:** 3.5%.

Transport: Railways: 600 mi. **Motor vehicles:** 101.1 per 1,000 pop. **Airports:** 104.

Communications: Mobile: 97.2 per 100 pop. **Broadband:** 59.4 per 100 pop. **Internet:** 69.7%.

Health: Expend.: 8.5%. **Life expect.:** 69.7 male; 80.4 female. **Births:** 18.0 per 1,000 pop. **Deaths:** 7.1 per 1,000 pop. **Infant mortality:** 11.2 per 1,000 live births. **Undernourished:** 13.9%. **HIV:** 0.4%. **COVID-19:** 1,069,114 cases, 36,042 deaths; rates per 100,000: 6,059.7 cases, 204.3 deaths. 80.7% vaccinated.

Education: Compulsory: ages 3-17. **Literacy:** 94.5%.

Website: www.presidencia.gob.ec

The region, which was the northern Inca empire, was conquered by Spain in 1533. Liberation forces defeated the Spanish May 24, 1822, near Quito. Ecuador became part of the Great Colombia Republic but seceded, May 13, 1830.

Ecuadoran Indigenous peoples, demanding greater rights, staged protests in the 1990s. A border war with Peru flared Jan. 26-Mar. 1, 1995. Elected president, July 1996, Abdalá Bucaram imposed stiff price increases and other austerity measures; the National Assembly, Feb. 1997, dismissed him for "mental incapacity."

Jamil Mahuad Witt won a presidential runoff election July 1998. Opposed by Indian groups and military leaders, he was ousted Jan. 2000, and succeeded by Vice Pres. Gustavo Noboa Bejarano. Noboa enacted a plan introduced by Mahuad to replace the sucre with the U.S. dollar as Ecuador's currency. Lucio Gutiérrez Borbúa, a leader in the 2000 coup, won a presidential runoff Nov. 2002.

Gutiérrez imposed economic austerity measures, purged opponents from the Supreme Court, Dec. 2004, and then dissolved it, Apr. 2005. The National Assembly ousted Gutiérrez Apr. 20. In May 2006, Ecuador took over oil assets belonging to U.S.-based Occidental Petroleum.

Rafael Correa, a left-wing economist, won a presidential runoff vote Nov. 2006. Correa initially boosted development spending and aid to poor families; later, as oil revenue dropped, Ecuador in Dec. 2008 defaulted on part of its $10-bil foreign debt. Correa, reelected Apr. 2009, pressured foreign oil companies in 2010 to increase the government's share of mineral revenues. Correa was reelected Feb. 17, 2013. A 2013 communications law limited press freedom. Lenin Moreno Garces won an Apr. 2, 2017, presidential runoff election. In an Apr. 11, 2021, presidential runoff, businessman Guillermo Lasso Mendoza was elected.

Ecuador granted asylum, Aug. 16, 2012, to Julian Assange, the founder of WikiLeaks. Assange was in Ecuador's UK embassy in London avoiding possible extradition, including to the U.S. in connection with the hacking and publication of classified information. After Ecuador withdrew asylum, Assange was arrested at the embassy, Apr. 11, 2019; legal appeals to block his extradition to the U.S. were still ongoing in Sept. 2023.

Beginning in 2015, large numbers of Venezuelans fleeing economic hardship and repression entered Ecuador. More than 500,000 Venezuelan refugees were in Ecuador as of July 2023.

Following a 2021 court decision, regulations in effect in 2022 permitted abortion in limited circumstances for rape victims.

Drug trafficking and crime by drug gangs has increased sharply in recent years. Facing impeachment on corruption charges, Pres. Lasso dissolved the National Assembly, May 17, 2023. New first-round presidential elections were scheduled for Aug. 20, 2023. Presidential candidate Fernando Villavicencio, outspoken about drug crime and corruption, was shot and killed at a campaign event Aug. 9. After Aug. 20 voting, Luisa Gonzáles, of Correa's party, and businessman Daniel Noboa faced an Oct. 15, 2023, presidential runoff.

Voters, Aug. 20, 2023, approved a referendum measure to block oil drilling in part of the Amazon.

The **Galápagos Islands,** pop. (2020 est.) 33,042, about 600 mi to the W, are the home of giant tortoises and other distinctive animals. The Galápagos are vulnerable to the impacts of climate change. Ecuador announced, Nov. 2, 2021, it would increase by almost 50% the size of a protected marine reserve.

Egypt
Arab Republic of Egypt

People: Population: 109,546,720 (15). **Age distrib.:** <15: 34.4%; 65+: 5.4%. **Growth:** 0.5%. **Migrants:** 1.6%. **Pop. density:** 285.0 per sq mi, 110.0 per sq km. **Urban:** 43.1%. **Ethnic groups** (by nationality): Egyptian 99.7%. **Languages:** Arabic (official), English and French widely understood by educated classes. **Religions:** Muslim 90.4% (Sunni [official]), Christian 9.0% (Orthodox 8.1%).

Geography: Total area: 386,662 sq mi, 1,001,450 sq km (29). **Land area:** 384,345 sq mi, 995,450 sq km. **Location:** NE corner of Africa. Libya on W; Sudan on S; Israel, Gaza Strip on E. **Topography:** Almost entirely desolate and barren with hills and mountains in E and along Nile. Most people live in 550-mi-long Nile Valley. **Arable land:** 3.1%. **Capital:** Cairo, 22,183,201. **Cities:** Alexandria, 5,588,477.

Government: Type: Presidential republic. **Head of state:** Pres. Abdel Fattah al-Sisi; b. 1954; in office: June 8, 2014. **Head of govt.:** Prime Min. Mostafa Madbouly; in office: June 7, 2018. **Local divisions:** 27 governorates. **Defense budget:** $5.2 bil. **Active troops:** 438,500.

Economy: Industries: textiles, food proc., tourism, chemicals, pharmaceuticals, hydrocarbons, constr., cement, metals, light manufactures. **Chief agric.:** sugarcane, sugar beet, wheat, maize, tomatoes, rice. **Natural resources:** petroleum, nat. gas, iron ore, phosphates, manganese, limestone, gypsum, talc, asbestos, lead, rare earth elements, zinc. **Water:** 562 cu m per capita. **Crude oil reserves:** 3.3 bil bbls. **Electricity prod.:** 202.3 bil kWh. **Labor force:** agric. 19.8%, industry 29.1%, services 51.1%. **Unemployment:** 7.0%.

Finance: Monetary unit: Pound (EGP) (30.90 = $1 U.S.). **GDP:** $1.7 tril; **per capita GDP:** $15,091; **GDP growth:** 6.6%. **Imports:** $94.0 bil; (2021) China 18%, Saudi Arabia 9%, U.S. 6%. **Exports:** $58.3 bil; (2021) U.S. 8%, Turkey 7%, Greece 7%, Italy 6%. **Tourism:** $8.9 bil. **Budget:** (2020) $100.3 bil. **Inflation:** 13.9%.

Transport: Railways: 3,160 mi. **Motor vehicles:** 61.3 per 1,000 pop. **Airports:** 72.

Communications: Mobile: 93.2 per 100 pop. **Broadband:** 65.0 per 100 pop. **Internet:** 72.2%.

Health: Expend.: 4.4%. **Life expect.:** 73.5 male; 76.0 female. **Births:** 20.5 per 1,000 pop. **Deaths:** 4.3 per 1,000 pop. **Infant mortality:** 17.3 per 1,000 live births. **Undernourished:** 7.2%. **HIV:** <0.1%. **COVID-19:** 516,023 cases, 24,830 deaths; rates per 100,000: 504.3 cases, 24.3 deaths. 41.4% vaccinated.

Education: Compulsory: ages 6-17. **Literacy:** 73.1%.

Website: www.egypt.gov.eg

Archaeological records of ancient Egyptian civilization date back to 4000 BCE. A unified kingdom arose around 3200 BCE and extended south into Nubia and as far north as Syria. A high culture of rulers and priests was built on an economic base of serfdom, fertile soil, and annual flooding of the Nile.

Imperial decline facilitated conquest by Asian invaders (Hyksos, Assyrians). The last native dynasty fell in 341 BCE to the Persians, who were in turn replaced by Greeks (Alexander and the Ptolemies), Romans, Byzantines, and Arabs, who introduced Islam and the Arabic language. The ancient Egyptian language was preserved only in Coptic Christian liturgy.

Egypt was ruled as part of larger Islamic empires for many centuries. Britain intervened in Egypt in 1882 and ruled the country as a protectorate, 1914-22. A 1936 treaty strengthened Egyptian autonomy, but Britain retained bases in Egypt and a condominium (joint rule with Egypt) over Sudan. When the state of Israel was proclaimed in 1948, Egypt joined other Arab nations invading Israel and was defeated. In 1951 Egypt abrogated the 1936 treaty; Sudan became independent in 1956.

A July 1952 uprising overthrew King Farouk and established a republic. Lt. Col. Gamal Abdel Nasser rose to power, becoming premier in 1954 and president in 1956. Nasser pushed construction of Egypt's Aswan High Dam, completed in 1970.

After guerrilla raids across its border, Israel invaded Egypt's Sinai Peninsula, Oct. 29, 1956. Egypt rejected a cease-fire demand by Britain and France; on Oct. 31 the two nations dropped bombs and on Nov. 5-6 landed forces. Egypt and Israel accepted a UN cease-fire; fighting ended Nov. 7. Full-scale war with Israel broke out again, June 5, 1967; before it ended under a UN cease-fire June 10, Israel had captured Gaza and the Sinai Peninsula and taken control of the E bank of the Suez Canal.

Nasser died Sept. 28, 1970, and was replaced by Vice Pres. Anwar Sadat. In a surprise attack Oct. 6, 1973, Egyptian forces crossed the Suez Canal into the Sinai. (At the same time, Syrian forces attacked Israelis on the Golan Heights.) Israel counterattacked, crossed the canal, and surrounded Suez City. A UN cease-fire took effect Oct. 24. Under an agreement signed Jan. 1974, Israeli forces withdrew from the canal's W bank; limited numbers of Egyptian forces occupied a strip along the E bank. A second accord was signed in 1975, with Israel yielding Sinai oil fields.

Pres. Sadat's surprise visit to Jerusalem, Nov. 1977, opened the prospect of peace with Israel. On Mar. 26, 1979, Egypt and Israel signed a formal peace treaty, ending 30 years of war and establishing diplomatic relations. On Oct. 6, 1981, Muslim extremists within the army assassinated Pres. Sadat, who was succeeded by Hosni Mubarak. Israel returned control of the Sinai to Egypt in Apr. 1982.

Egyptian security forces battled Islamist violence in the 1990s and early 2000s. On Nov. 17, 1997, near Luxor, Muslim extremists killed 58 foreign tourists and 4 Egyptians. Bombs Oct. 7, 2004, in and near Taba, a Sinai tourist site popular with Israelis, killed at least 35 people. Another 88 people were killed in bombings July 23, 2005, at Sharm el Sheikh, a Red Sea resort city. Suicide bombings at the Sinai resort town of Dahab, Apr. 24, 2006, killed at least 18 people; security forces May 9 killed Nasser Khamis al-Mallahi, leader of the group blamed for the Taba, Sharm el Sheikh, and Dahab attacks.

Following 18 days of mass protests in which at least 846 people died in clashes between Arab Spring dissidents and Mubarak loyalists, Mubarak surrendered power Feb. 11, 2011. A transitional military regime prepared for elections. Mubarak was convicted on corruption charges, May 9, 2015, and sentenced to three years in prison. Released, Mar. 24, 2017, from a military hospital, Mubarak died Feb. 25, 2020.

Islamist candidate Mohammed Morsi of the Muslim Brotherhood was declared winner of the presidential election, June 2012. Morsi overhauled the military leadership Aug. 12. On Oct. 8, 2012, he pardoned select political prisoners detained during the Arab Spring uprising. Violent clashes between Morsi supporters and opponents erupted Nov. 23 after Morsi announced an edict interpreted as a power-grab. The proposal of a new Islamist constitution prompted demonstrations throughout Dec.; it passed Dec. 23, 2012.

The military forced Morsi out of office July 3, 2013, and cracked down violently, Aug. 14, on pro-Morsi protesters. More than 600 protesters and at least 40 police officers died in confrontations. The military outlawed the Muslim Brotherhood as a terrorist organization Dec. 25, 2013. Under a new constitution approved in a Jan. 2014 referendum, former Gen. Abdel Fattah al-Sisi, one of the leaders in ousting Morsi, won a May presidential election. Violence between Morsi supporters and security forces continued, causing hundreds of deaths on both sides. Muslim Brotherhood leader Mohamed Badie was sentenced to death June 21, 2014, in connection with July 2013 violence; the sentence was reduced to life in prison Aug. 30, 2014. Morsi was sentenced to 20 years in prison, Apr. 21, 2015, in a trial related to Dec. 2012 street violence. He died, June 17, 2019, after collapsing in court while facing separate espionage charges.

The Sisi government carried out arrests of dissidents and journalists, and it suppressed protests and free expression. Sisi won a new term as president in a Mar. 2018 election from which opposition candidates were essentially barred. Constitutional changes approved in an Apr. 2019 referendum extended the president's term to 6 years and increased presidential power over the judiciary.

Beginning in 2013, Islamist militants battled security forces and seized territory in the northern Sinai. Terrorist attacks occurred at major tourist sites in Luxor and Giza in June 2015. A Russian airliner crashed in the Sinai, Oct. 31, 2015, apparently after a bomb onboard exploded, killing all 224 on board; Sinai Province, an ISIS-affiliated Islamist group, claimed responsibility. Egypt announced, Aug. 4, 2016, that it had killed Sinai Province's leader in an airstrike. A suicide bombing, for which ISIS claimed responsibility, killed about 30 people at a Coptic Christian chapel in Cairo, Dec. 11, 2016. About 75 people were killed in three attacks on Coptic Christians, Apr.-May 2017. Militant attacks killed scores of Egyptian soldiers and police July-Oct. 2017. An attack on a Sufi mosque in the northern Sinai, Nov. 24, 2017, left more than 300 dead. An Egyptian military offensive, launched Feb. 2018, against Islamist militants in the Sinai and other areas somewhat reduced militant attacks.

A WHO May 2022 report estimated about 250,000 excess deaths in Egypt in 2020-21 related to the COVID-19 pandemic, compared with fewer than 25,000 officially reported COVID-19 deaths as of Aug. 2023.

The Suez Canal, 103 mi long, links the Mediterranean and Red Seas. It was built by a French corporation 1859-69, but Britain obtained controlling interest in 1875. On July 26, 1956, Egypt nationalized the canal.

El Salvador
Republic of El Salvador

People: Population: 6,602,370 (108). **Age distrib.:** <15: 25.4%; 65+: 8.2%. **Growth:** 0.5%. **Migrants:** 0.7%. **Pop. density:** 825.3 per sq mi, 318.6 per sq km. **Urban:** 75.4%. **Ethnic groups:** mestizo 86.3%, white 12.7%. **Languages:** Spanish (official), Nawat. **Religions:** Christian 96.2% (Catholic [official] 64.9%, independent 15.9%, Protestant 15.3%), agnostic 3.0%.

Geography: Total area: 8,124 sq mi, 21,041 sq km (150). **Land area:** 8,000 sq mi, 20,721 sq km. **Location:** Central America. Guatemala on N, Honduras on N. **Topography:** A hot Pacific coastal plain in S rises to a cooler plateau and valley region, densely populated. The N is mountainous with many volcanoes. **Arable land:** 34.8%. **Capital:** San Salvador, 1,116,052.

Government: Type: Presidential republic. **Head of state and govt.:** Pres. Nayib Bukele; b. 1981; in office: June 1, 2019. **Local**

divisions: 14 departments. **Defense budget:** $257 mil. **Active troops:** 24,500.

Economy: Industries: food proc., beverages, petroleum, chemicals, fertilizer, textiles, furniture, light metals. **Chief agric.:** sugarcane, maize, milk, poultry, sorghum, beans. **Natural resources:** hydropower, geothermal power, petroleum. **Water:** 4,050 cu m per capita. **Electricity prod.:** 6.6 bil kWh. **Labor force:** agric. 15.2%, industry 23.7%, services 61.0%. **Unemployment:** 3.8%.

Finance: Monetary unit: Colon (SVC) (8.75 = $1 U.S.). **GDP:** $70.3 bil; **per capita GDP:** $11,096; **GDP growth:** 2.6%. **Imports:** $15.8 bil; U.S. 30%, China 14%, Guatemala 13%, Mexico 8%, Honduras 6%. **Exports:** $8.5 bil; U.S. 40%, Guatemala 15%, Honduras 15%, Nicaragua 6%. **Tourism:** $993 mil. **Budget:** $7.3 bil. **Inflation:** 7.2%.

Transport: Railways: 8 mi. **Motor vehicles:** 53.8 per 1,000 pop. **Airports:** 5.

Communications: Mobile: 181.6 per 100 pop. **Broadband:** 74.9 per 100 pop. **Internet:** 62.9%.

Health: Expend.: 9.9%. **Life expect.:** 72.2 male; 79.3 female. **Births:** 17.5 per 1,000 pop. **Deaths:** 5.9 per 1,000 pop. **Infant mortality:** 11.9 per 1,000 live births. **Undernourished:** 7.7%. **HIV:** 0.5%. **COVID-19:** 201,785 cases, 4,230 deaths; rates per 100,000: 3,111.0 cases, 65.2 deaths. 67.7% vaccinated.

Education: Compulsory: ages 1-15. **Literacy:** 90.0%.

Website: www.presidencia.gob.sv

El Salvador became independent of Spain in 1821 and of the Central American Federation in 1839.

After a military coup in 1979, a military-civilian junta failed to quell a rebellion by leftist insurgents, armed by Cuba and Nicaragua. Right-wing death squads killed thousands of suspected leftists in the 1980s. The U.S. supported the government with military aid. After taking the lives of some 75,000 people (with thousands more "disappeared"), the civil war ended Jan. 16, 1992, as the government and leftist rebels signed a peace treaty.

The right-wing ARENA party held the presidency, 1989-2009, and the leftist FMLN, 2009-19. Rejecting both major parties, voters elected Nayib Bukele, who pledged to reduce corruption, in the Feb. 3, 2019, presidential election. Bukele's party and allies won a sweeping victory in Feb. 28, 2021, legislative elections.

Beginning in 2013, tens of thousands of migrants or asylum seekers from El Salvador tried to enter the U.S. from Mexico; many were fleeing widespread gang violence. Amid continuing violence, the Legislative Assembly, Mar. 2022, granted the government emergency powers, including suspension of civil liberties. Subsequently, gang violence dropped sharply; more than 70,000 people had been arrested by mid-2023, amid scores of suspicious deaths in prisons and reports of arbitrary arrests as well as physical abuse.

A Zika virus outbreak, 2015-17, caused more than 11,800 confirmed or suspected cases.

Equatorial Guinea
Republic of Equatorial Guinea

People: Population: 1,737,695 (150). **Age distrib.:** <15: 36.1%; 65+: 4.9%. **Growth:** 3.4%. **Migrants:** 16.4%. **Pop. density:** 160.4 per sq mi, 61.9 per sq km. **Urban:** 74.4%. **Ethnic groups:** Fang 85.7%, Bubi 6.5%, Ndowe 3.6%. **Languages:** Spanish, French, Portuguese (all official); Fang; Bubi. **Religions:** Christian (official) 89.7% (Catholic 83.5%), Muslim 4.1% (Sunni), agnostic 3.4%.

Geography: Total area: 10,831 sq mi, 28,051 sq km (142). **Land area:** 10,831 sq mi, 28,051 sq km. **Location:** Bioko Isl. off W Africa coast in Gulf of Guinea. Rio Muni, mainland enclave, has Gabon on S, Cameroon on E and N. **Topography:** Bioko Isl. consists of 2 volcanic mountains and connecting valley. Rio Muni, with over 90% of area, has coastal plain and low hills. **Arable land:** 1.9%. **Capital:** Malabo, 296,770. **Cities:** Bata, 474,467.

Government: Type: Presidential republic. **Head of state:** Pres. Teodoro Obiang Nguema Mbasogo; b. 1942; in office: Aug. 3, 1979. **Head of govt.:** Prime Min. Manuela Roka Botey; in office: Feb. 1, 2023. **Local divisions:** 8 provinces. **Defense budget:** NA. **Active troops:** 1,450.

Economy: Industries: petroleum, nat. gas, sawmilling. **Chief agric.:** sweet potatoes, cassava, roots/tubers, plantains, oil palm fruit, bananas. **Natural resources:** petroleum, nat. gas, timber, gold, bauxite, diamonds, tantalum, sand and gravel, clay. **Water:** 18,532 cu m per capita. **Crude oil reserves:** 1.1 bil bbls. **Electricity prod.:** 1.4 bil kWh. **Labor force:** agric. 55.5%, industry 13.7%, services 30.7%. **Unemployment:** 8.7%.

Finance: Monetary unit: Central African CFA Franc (XAF) (606.88 = $1 U.S.). **GDP:** $29.1 bil; **per capita GDP:** $17,396; **GDP growth:** 3.1%. **Imports** (2019): $6.2 bil; U.S. 22%, Spain 19%, China 12%, UK 6%. **Exports** (2019): $8.8 bil; China 34%, India 19%, Spain 11%, U.S. 7%. **Budget** (2018): $2.5 bil. **Inflation:** 4.8%.

Transport: Airports: 6.

Communications: Mobile: 53.3 per 100 pop. **Broadband:** 0.9 per 100 pop. **Internet:** 53.9%.

Health: Expend.: 3.8%. **Life expect.:** 61.5 male; 66.1 female. **Births:** 29.5 per 1,000 pop. **Deaths:** 8.9 per 1,000 pop. **Infant mortality:** 77.9 per 1,000 live births. **Undernourished:** NA. **HIV:** 6.7%. **COVID-19:** 17,130 cases, 183 deaths; rates per 100,000: 1,221.0 cases, 13.0 deaths. 15.3% vaccinated.

Education: Compulsory: ages 7-12. **Literacy:** 95.3%.
Website: www.guineaecuatorialpress.com

Fernando Po (now Bioko) Island was reached by Portugal in the late 15th cent. and ceded to Spain in 1778. Independence came Oct. 12, 1968. Anti-Spanish riots erupted in 1969 in Rio Muni province on the mainland.

Masie Nguema Biyogo, a mainlander, became president for life in 1972. His reign, among the most brutal in Africa, left the nation bankrupt; most of the nation's 7,000 Europeans emigrated. He was ousted in a military coup, Aug. 1979. Teodoro Obiang Nguema Mbasogo, leader of the coup, became president. Presidential elections in 1996, 2002, 2009, 2016, and 2022 were seriously flawed.

The economy is dependent on oil exports. As a result of government misuse and embezzlement of oil revenue, poverty remains widespread.

Human Rights Watch reported in 2012 that the regime "tortures and arbitrarily detains" dissidents. The seat of government was officially moved, Feb. 2017, from Malabo (on Bioko) to Ciudad de la Paz on the mainland. Obiang, Jan. 31, 2023, named Manuela Roka Botey the country's first female prime min.

Eritrea
State of Eritrea

People: Population: 6,274,796 (110). **Age distrib.:** <15: 36.3%; 65+: 4.0%. **Growth:** 1.1%. **Migrants:** 0.4%. **Pop. density:** 160.9 per sq mi, 62.1 per sq km. **Urban:** 43.3%. **Ethnic groups:** Tigrinya 50%, Tigre 30%, Saho 4%, Afar 4%, Kunama 4%, Bilen 3%, Hedareb/Beja 2%, Nara 2%. **Languages:** Tigrinya, Arabic, English (all official); Tigre; Kunama; Afar. **Religions:** Muslim 51.1% (Sunni), Christian 46.6% (Orthodox 39.5%).

Geography: Total area: 45,406 sq mi, 117,600 sq km (99); **Land area:** 38,996 sq mi, 101,000 sq km. **Location:** E Africa, on SW coast of Red Sea. Sudan on W, Ethiopia on S, Djibouti on SE. **Topography:** Includes many islands of Dahlak Archipelago. Low coastal plains in S, mountain range with peaks to 9,000 ft in N. **Arable land:** 5.7%. **Capital:** Asmara, 1,072,666.

Government: Type: Presidential republic. **Head of state and govt.:** Pres. Isaias Afwerki; b. 1946; in office: June 8, 1993. **Local divisions:** 6 regions. **Defense budget:** NA. **Active troops:** 301,750.

Economy: Industries: food proc., beverages, clothing and textiles, light mfg., salt, cement. **Chief agric.:** sorghum, milk, vegetables, barley, cereals, pulses. **Natural resources:** gold, potash, zinc, copper, salt, fish. **Water:** 2,063 cu m per capita. **Electricity prod.:** 452.9 mil kWh. **Labor force:** agric. 62.4%, industry 8.6%, services 29.0%. **Unemployment:** 6.6%.

Finance: Monetary unit: Nakfa (ERN) (15.00 = $1 U.S.). **GDP:** NA; **per capita GDP:** NA; **GDP growth:** NA. **Imports** (2017): $1.1 bil; (2017) UAE 14.5%, China 13.2%, Saudi Arabia 13.2%, Italy 12.9%, Turkey 5.6%. **Exports** (2017): $624.3 mil; (2017) China 62%, South Korea 28.3%. **Budget** (2018): $549 mil. **Inflation** (2016-17): 9.0%.

Transport: Railways: 190 mi. **Airports:** 4.

Communications: Mobile (2021): 49.7 per 100 pop. **Broadband:** NA. **Internet:** 21.7%.

Health: Expend.: 4.1%. **Life expect.:** 64.6 male; 69.9 female. **Births:** 26.7 per 1,000 pop. **Deaths:** 6.6 per 1,000 pop. **Infant mortality:** 40.6 per 1,000 live births. **Undernourished:** NA. **HIV:** 0.4%. **COVID-19:** 10,189 cases, 103 deaths; rates per 100,000: 287.3 cases, 2.9 deaths. 0.0% vaccinated.

Education: Compulsory: ages 6-13. **Literacy:** 76.6%.
Website: shabait.com

Eritrea was part of the Ethiopian kingdom of Aksum. It was an Italian colony from 1890 to 1941, when it was captured by the British. Following a period of British and UN supervision, Eritrea was awarded to Ethiopia as part of a federation in 1952. Ethiopia annexed Eritrea as a province in 1962. After a 31-year struggle, Eritrea formally declared its independence May 24, 1993. A constitution was ratified in 1997 but not implemented.

A border war with Ethiopia erupted in June 1998. Although a peace treaty was signed Dec. 12, 2000, border disputes and tensions continued. Agreements signed July 9, 2018, ended the "state of war between Ethiopia and Eritrea" and restored diplomatic relations as well as communications, transportation, and commercial links.

Many thousands have fled repressive conditions and forced labor in Eritrea. Tens of thousands of Eritreans were among migrants reaching or trying to reach Europe, 2014-18. Thousands migrated to Ethiopia after the border reopened in 2018.

Beginning in 2020, Eritrean troops fought in northern Ethiopia, assisting government forces fighting Tigrayan rebels. Eritrean soldiers were widely accused of atrocities against civilians. Months after a Nov. 2022 peace deal between the Ethiopian government and Tigray rebels, Eritrean troops remained in parts of northern Ethiopia.

Estonia
Republic of Estonia

People: Population: 1,202,762 (156). **Age distrib.:** <15: 15.6%; 65+: 22.2%. **Growth:** –0.7%. **Migrants:** 15.0%. **Pop. density:** 73.5 per sq mi, 28.4 per sq km. **Urban:** 69.8%. **Ethnic groups:** Estonian 68.7%, Russian 24.8%. **Languages:** Estonian (official), Russian. **Religions:** agnostic 58.2%, Christian 37.3% (Protestant 19.2%, Orthodox 16.1%), atheist 3.9%.

Geography: Total area: 17,463 sq mi, 45,228 sq km (129); **Land area:** 16,366 sq mi, 42,388 sq km. **Location:** Eastern Europe, bordering Baltic Sea and Gulf of Finland. Russia on E, Latvia on S. **Topography:** Marshy lowland with numerous lakes and swamps. Elongated hills show evidence of former glaciation. More than 800 islands on Baltic coast. **Arable land:** 16.4%. **Capital:** Tallinn, 454,245.

Government: Type: Parliamentary republic. **Head of state:** Pres. Alar Karis; b. 1958; in office: Oct. 11, 2021. **Head of govt.:** Prime Min. Kaja Kallas; b. 1977; in office: Jan. 26, 2021. **Local divisions:** 15 urban municipalities, 64 rural municipalities. **Defense budget:** $830 mil. **Active troops:** 7,200.

Economy: Industries: food, engineering, electronics, wood/wood prods., textiles, information tech., telecom. **Chief agric.:** wheat, milk, barley, rapeseed, rye, oats. **Natural resources:** oil shale, peat, rare earth elements, phosphorite, clay, limestone, sand, dolomite, sea mud. **Water:** 9,654 cu m per capita. **Electricity prod.:** 6.7 bil kWh. **Labor force:** agric. 2.7%, industry 29.0%, services 68.3%. **Unemployment:** 5.9%.

Finance: Monetary unit: Euro (EUR) (0.93 = $1 U.S.). **GDP:** $62.8 bil; **per capita GDP:** $46,697; **GDP growth:** –1.3%. **Imports:** $29.2 bil; (2021) Russia 15%, Finland 10%, Germany 10%, Latvia 7%, Lithuania 6%. **Exports:** $29.1 bil; (2021) Finland 12%, U.S. 9%, Latvia 9%, Sweden 8%, Russia 6%. **Tourism:** $641 mil. **Budget:** $12.3 bil. **Inflation:** 19.4%.

Transport: Railways: 895 mi. **Airports:** 13.

Communications: Mobile: 155.0 per 100 pop. **Broadband:** 209.6 per 100 pop. **Internet:** 91.0%.

Health: Expend. (2021): 7.5%. **Life expect.:** 73.5 male; 82.9 female. **Births:** 8.5 per 1,000 pop. **Deaths:** 13.1 per 1,000 pop. **Infant mortality:** 3.4 per 1,000 live births. **Undernourished:** <2.5%. **HIV:** 0.7%. **COVID-19:** 601,773 cases, 2,901 deaths; rates per 100,000: 45,281.0 cases, 218.3 deaths. 63.2% vaccinated.

Education: Compulsory: ages 7-15. **Literacy:** 99.9%.
Website: www.eesti.ee

Estonia, a province of imperial Russia before World War I, was independent between World Wars I and II. The USSR conquered it in 1940 and incorporated it as the Estonian SSR. Estonia, Aug. 20, 1991, declared independence, which the Soviet Union recognized Sept. 1991. The first free elections in over 50 years were held Sept. 20, 1992. The last occupying Russian troops departed Aug. 31, 1994.

Estonia became a full member of the EU and NATO, 2004, and adopted the euro, 2011. NATO leaders, July 2016, agreed to station troops in Estonia. Following Russia's Feb. 2022 invasion of Ukraine, a June 2022 NATO summit agreed to strengthen forces defending Estonia.

Parliament elected Kersti Kaljulaid, Oct. 3, 2016, to be Estonia's first woman president. The Reform Party's Kaja Kallas became, Jan. 26, 2021, Estonia's first post-Soviet female prime minister. Alar Karis, backed by Kallas, was elected president, Aug. 31, 2021. Kallas's Reform Party won Mar. 5, 2023, elections, and she formed a new coalition government Apr. 12.

Energy-cost spikes related to the war in Ukraine contributed to double-digit inflation in 2022 and Jan.-May 2023.

Eswatini
Kingdom of Eswatini

(King Mswati III announced, Apr. 19, 2018, that he was changing the country's name from Swaziland to "Eswatini" to celebrate the 50th anniversary of its independence.)

People: Population: 1,130,043 (157). **Age distrib.:** <15: 32.2%; 65+: 4.0%. **Growth:** 0.7%. **Migrants:** 2.8%. **Pop. density:** 170.1 per sq mi, 65.7 per sq km. **Urban:** 24.8%. **Ethnic groups:** predom. Swazi; smaller pops. of Zulu, people of European ancestry. **Languages:** English (used in govt.), siSwati (both official). **Religions:** Christian 87.3% (independent 62.9%, Protestant 18.8%), ethnic religionist 9.9%.

Geography: Total area: 6,704 sq mi, 17,364 sq km (154); **Land area:** 6,643 sq mi, 17,204 sq km. **Location:** Southern Africa, near Indian O. coast. South Africa on N, W, S; Mozambique on E. **Topography:** Descends W-E in broad belts, becoming more arid in low veld region, then rising to plateau in E. **Arable land:** 10.3%. **Capital:** Mbabane (administrative), 68,010; Lobamba (legislative).

Government: Type: Absolute monarchy. **Head of state:** King Mswati III; b. 1968; in office: Apr. 25, 1986. **Head of govt.:** Prime Min. Cleopas Sipho Dlamini; b. 1968; in office: July 16, 2021. **Local divisions:** 4 regions. **Defense budget/active troops:** NA.

Economy: Industries: soft drink concentrates, coal, forestry, sugar proc., textiles, apparel. **Chief agric.:** sugarcane, maize, roots/tubers, grapefruit, oranges, milk. **Natural resources:** asbestos, coal, clay, cassiterite, hydropower, forests, small gold/diamond deposits, quarry stone, talc. **Water:** 3,887 cu m per capita. **Electricity prod.:** 744.8 mil kWh. **Labor force:** agric. 12.4%, industry 24.5%, services 63.1%. **Unemployment:** 24.4%.

Finance: Monetary unit: Lilangeni (SZL) (18.56 = $1 U.S.). **GDP:** $13.0 bil; **per capita GDP:** $10,782; **GDP growth:** 3.9%. **Imports:** $2.2 bil; (2017) South Africa 81.6%, China 5.2%. **Exports:** $2.1 bil; (2017) South Africa 94%. **Tourism:** $8 mil. **Budget** (2020): $1.5 bil. **Inflation** (2018-19): 2.6%.

Transport: Railways: 187 mi. **Airports:** 2.

Communications: Mobile: 122.2 per 100 pop. **Broadband:** 113.5 per 100 pop. **Internet:** 58.9%.

Health: Expend.: 6.5%. **Life expect.:** 58.2 male; 62.3 female. **Births:** 22.8 per 1,000 pop. **Deaths:** 9.5 per 1,000 pop. **Infant mortality:** 38.1 per 1,000 live births. **Undernourished:** 11.6%. **HIV:** 25.9%. **COVID-19:** 74,882 cases, 1,427 deaths; rates per 100,000: 6,454.4 cases, 123.0 deaths. 36.8% vaccinated.

Education: Compulsory: ages 6-12. **Literacy:** 89.3%.

Website: www.gov.sz

The royal house of Eswatini traces back 400 years. The Zulus drove the Swazis, a Bantu people, from lands to the N, 1820. Britain and Transvaal (later part of South Africa) later guaranteed their autonomy, and Britain assumed control after 1903. Independence came Sept. 6, 1968. In 1973, the king repealed the constitution and assumed full powers.

A new constitution banning political parties took effect Oct. 13, 1978. Under a revised constitution effective Feb. 8, 2006, non-partisan parliamentary elections were permitted. The pro-democracy People's United Democratic Movement (PU-DEMO) was outlawed as a terrorist group in 2008. Anti-monarchy protests and looting in mid-2021 were suppressed.

In recent decades, Eswatini has suffered from an AIDS epidemic. AIDS-related deaths fell sharply due to antiretroviral therapy, but as of 2021, 27.9% of adults were HIV positive, the highest rate in the world.

Ethiopia
Federal Democratic Republic of Ethiopia

People: Population: 116,462,712 (12). **Age distrib.:** <15: 39.0%; 65+: 3.3%. **Growth:** 2.4%. **Migrants:** 0.9%. **Pop. density:** 275.1 per sq mi, 106.2 per sq km. **Urban:** 23.2%. **Ethnic groups:** Oromo 35.8%, Amhara 24.1%, Somali 7.2%, Tigray 5.7%, Sidama 4.1%, Guragie 2.6%, Welaita 2.3%, Afar 2.2%. **Languages:** Oromo (official in one state); Amharic (official nationally); Somali, Tigrigna (both official in one state each); Sidamo; Wolaytta; Gurage. **Religions:** Christian 60.7% (Orthodox 41.4%, Protestant 16.1%), Muslim 34.2% (Sunni), ethnic religionist 4.9%.

Geography: Total area: 426,373 sq mi, 1,104,300 sq km (26); **Land area:** 423,388 sq mi, 1,096,570 sq km. **Location:** E Africa. Sudan, South Sudan on W; Kenya on S; Somalia, Djibouti on E; Eritrea on N. **Topography:** A central plateau, 6,000-10,000 ft high, rises to mountains near the Great Rift Valley, cutting in from SW. Blue Nile and other rivers cross the plateau, which descends to plains on W and SE. **Arable land:** 14.5%. **Capital:** Addis Ababa, 5,460,591.

Government: Type: Federal parliamentary republic. **Head of state:** Pres. Sahle-Work Zewde; b. 1950; in office: Oct. 25, 2018. **Head of govt.:** Prime Min. Abiy Ahmed; b. 1976; in office: Apr. 2, 2018. **Local divisions:** 11 regional states (ethnically based), 2 chartered cities. **Defense budget:** $1.6 bil. **Active troops:** 503,000.

Economy: Industries: food proc., beverages, textiles, leather, garments, chemicals, metals proc., cement. **Chief agric.:** maize, cereals, wheat, sorghum, milk, barley. **Natural resources:** gold, platinum, copper, potash, nat. gas, hydropower. **Water:** 1,061 cu m per capita. **Crude oil reserves:** 428,000 bbls. **Electricity prod.:** 14.7 bil kWh. **Labor force:** agric. 63.7%, industry 10.2%, services 26.2%. **Unemployment:** 4.0%.

Finance: Monetary unit: Birr (ETB) (55.15 = $1 U.S.). **GDP:** $346.9 bil; **per capita GDP:** $2,812; **GDP growth:** 5.3%. **Imports:** $20.9 bil; China 27%, India 9%, UAE 9%, France 9%, UK 7%. **Exports:** $9.5 bil; China 17%, U.S. 16%, UAE 8%, Saudi Arabia 6%. **Tourism:** $964 mil. **Budget** (2020): $14.0 bil. **Inflation** (2020-21): 26.8%.

Transport: Railways: 409 mi (Ethiopian segment of Addis Ababa-Djibouti railroad). **Motor vehicles:** 2.0 per 1,000 pop. **Airports:** 17.

Communications: Mobile: 56.0 per 100 pop. **Broadband:** 25.7 per 100 pop. **Internet:** 16.7%.

Health: Expend.: 3.5%. **Life expect.:** 64.9 male; 69.4 female. **Births:** 30.1 per 1,000 pop. **Deaths:** 6.0 per 1,000 pop. **Infant mortality:** 33.9 per 1,000 live births. **Undernourished:** 21.9%. **HIV:** 0.8%. **COVID-19:** 500,991 cases, 7,574 deaths; rates per 100,000: 435.8 cases, 6.6 deaths. 38.0% vaccinated.

Education: Compulsory: ages 7-14. **Literacy:** 51.8%.

Website: www.ethiopia.gov.et

Ethiopian culture was influenced by Egypt and Greece. Italy invaded the region in 1880, but Ethiopia maintained its independence until the Italian invasion of 1936. British forces freed the country in 1941.

A series of droughts in the 1970s killed hundreds of thousands. An army mutiny, strikes, and student demonstrations led to the 1974 dethronement of Ethiopia's Emperor, Haile Selassie I, ending his 58-year reign. The ruling junta, known as the Dergue, dissolved

parliament, abolished the monarchy, established a socialist state, redistributed land, curbed the influence of the Coptic Church, and violently suppressed opposition.

The regime, torn by bloody coups, faced uprisings by tribal and political groups aided in part by Sudan and Somalia. In 1978, Soviet advisers and Cuban troops helped defeat Somali forces. Ethiopia and Somalia signed a peace agreement in 1988. A worldwide relief effort began in 1984, as an extended drought precipitated famine; up to 1 mil people died.

The Ethiopian People's Revolutionary Democratic Front (EPRDF) launched a major push against government forces in 1991, prompting Pres. Mengistu Haile Mariam's resignation. The EPRDF set up a transitional government. It won five parliamentary elections, 1995-2015.

Eritrea, a province on the Red Sea, declared its independence May 24, 1993. Fighting along the border with Eritrea, which erupted in 1998, intensified in May 2000. Although a peace treaty was signed Dec. 12, 2000, tensions and border conflicts persisted until a July 9, 2018, accord.

Violent protests by members of the Oromo ethnic group claimed hundreds of lives in 2016. Successive droughts caused severe food shortages in 2015-17, affecting about 18 mil people. Amid continuing ethnic violence in eastern Ethiopia and anti-government protests, Prime Min. Hailemariam Desalegn resigned, Feb. 15, 2018. New Prime Min. Abiy Ahmed, the country's first Oromo leader, implemented some economic and political reforms. For his domestic policies and 2018 peace accord with Eritrea, Abiy was awarded the Nobel Peace Prize, Oct. 11, 2019. However, political repression subsequently increased.

Elected by parliament, Oct. 25, 2018, Sahle-Work Zewde became Ethiopia's first female president.

A Nov. 2020 attack on a military base in the opposition-controlled northern Tigray region led to a large-scale government offensive against the Tigray People's Liberation Front (TPLF). As fighting continued, widespread atrocities against civilians were reported. A TPLF offensive pushed back government troops in mid-2021. By then, hundreds of thousands in Tigray faced famine, as drought plagued the region and the Abiy government reportedly blocked aid shipments. TPLF forces advanced into the neighboring Amhara and Afar regions, before being largely beaten back by government troops and allied militias. After two years of war in which hundreds of thousands died and millions were displaced, negotiations in South Africa produced a Nov. 2, 2022, cease-fire agreement, calling for disarmament of Tigrayan rebels and the free flow of humanitarian aid into Tigray. However, more than 20 mil people nationwide faced food insecurity as of Aug. 2023; some international aid was suspended in 2023 amid reports of large-scale theft of donors' food shipments.

A government crackdown began in May 2022 against a militia it formerly allied with in Amhara, though activists were also swept up. Mid-2022 massacres in the Oromia region were blamed on the rebel Oromo Liberation Army, which denied responsibility. Government-militia fighting in Amhara continued in 2023.

Ethiopia began construction, Apr. 2, 2011, of Africa's largest dam, the Grand Renaissance Dam across the Blue Nile. Power generation began in 2022.

Fiji
Republic of Fiji

People: Population: 947,760 (159). **Age distrib.:** <15: 25.2%; 65+: 8.5%. **Growth:** 0.4%. **Migrants:** 1.6%. **Pop. density:** 134.3 per sq mi, 51.9 per sq km. **Urban:** 58.7%. **Ethnic groups:** iTaukei (predom. Melanesian with Polynesian admixture) 56.8%, Indo-Fijian 37.5%. **Languages:** English, iTaukei, Fiji Hindi (all official). **Religions:** Christian 64.4% (Protestant 41.0%, Catholic 12.1%, independent 11.3%), Hindu 27.1% (Shaivite 10%, Vaishnavite 10%), Muslim 6.2% (Sunni).

Geography: Total area: 7,056 sq mi, 18,274 sq km (152); **Land area:** 7,056 sq mi, 18,274 sq km. Viti Levu, largest island of group, has over half the total land area. **Location:** Western S Pacific O. Nearest neighbors are Vanuatu to W, Tonga to E. **Topography:** 322 isls. (about 110 inhabited), many mountainous, with tropical forests and large fertile areas. **Arable land:** 4.2%. **Capital:** Suva, 178,339. **Cities:** NA.

Government: Type: Parliamentary republic. **Head of state:** Pres. Wiliame Katonivere; b. 1964; in office: Nov. 12, 2021. **Head of govt.:** Prime Min. Sitiveni Rabuka; b. 1948; in office: Dec. 24, 2022. **Local divisions:** 14 provinces, 1 dependency. **Defense budget:** $44 mil. **Active troops:** 4,040.

Economy: Industries: tourism, sugar proc., clothing, copra. **Chief agric.:** sugarcane, cassava, taro, poultry, vegetables, coconuts. **Natural resources:** timber, fish, gold, copper, hydropower. **Water:** 31,848 cu m per capita. **Electricity prod.:** 1.1 bil kWh. **Labor force:** agric. 28.9%, industry 14.7%, services 56.4%. **Unemployment:** 4.3%.

Finance: Monetary unit: Dollar (FJD) (2.27 = $1 U.S.). **GDP:** $13.1 bil; **per capita GDP:** $14,125; **GDP growth:** 16.1%. **Imports:** $2.3 bil; (2017) Singapore 18%, China 13.8%, Australia 13%, New Zealand 11%, France 11%, South Korea 8%. **Exports:** $1.2 bil; U.S.

29%, Australia 14%, New Zealand 7%, Japan 6%, Tonga 6%. **Tourism:** $35 mil. **Budget** (2020): $1.5 bil. **Inflation:** 4.5%.

Transport: Railways: 371 mi. **Motor vehicles:** 152.3 per 1,000 pop. **Airports:** 4.

Communications: Mobile (2021): 107.2 per 100 pop. **Broadband** (2021): 76.1 per 100 pop. **Internet:** 87.7%.

Health: Expend.: 3.7%. **Life expect.:** 71.9 male; 77.3 female. **Births:** 16.3 per 1,000 pop. **Deaths:** 6.4 per 1,000 pop. **Infant mortality:** 9.9 per 1,000 live births. **Undernourished:** 6.6%. **HIV:** 0.3%. **COVID-19:** 69,047 cases, 885 deaths; rates per 100,000: 7,702.3 cases, 98.7 deaths. 71.5% vaccinated.

Education: Compulsory: NA. **Literacy:** 99.1%.

Website: www.fiji.gov.fj

A British colony since 1874, Fiji became independent Oct. 10, 1970. Cultural differences between Indo-Fijians (mostly descendants of contract laborers brought to the islands from India in the 19th cent.) and Indigenous Fijians have led to political tensions. More than 100,000 people of Indian descent left Fiji after a 1987 coup deposed an Indo-Fijian-majority government.

The country's first Indo-Fijian prime minister, Mahendra Chaudhry, and other government officials were taken captive May 19, 2000, by Indigenous Fijian gunmen, culminating in a military takeover, May 29, led by Frank Bainimarama. An interim military-backed government was installed in July 2000. Prime Min. Laisenia Qarase headed an elected civilian government, 2001-06, but was ousted in a military coup Dec. 5, 2006. Bainimarama took office as interim prime min. After a court ruled in 2009 that the 2006 coup was illegal, Fiji's president abrogated the constitution, dissolved the judiciary, and reappointed Bainimarama. He accepted a new draft constitution released Mar. 22, 2013, and he retained office in democratic elections Sept. 17, 2014. Bainimarama's party narrowly won Nov. 18, 2018, elections.

The COVID-19 pandemic severely hurt the important tourism industry in 2020-21.

In Dec. 14, 2022, elections, Bainimarama's party lost its majority. Opposition parties formed a coalition government, and Sitiveni Rabuka became prime minister Dec. 24, 2022. On June 14, 2023, Fiji signed a defense agreement with New Zealand, seen as a move to counter growing Chinese influence in the Pacific.

Finland
Republic of Finland

People: Population: 5,614,571 (116). **Age distrib.:** <15: 16.2%; 65+: 23.2%. **Growth:** 0.2%. **Migrants:** 7.0%. **Pop. density:** 47.9 per sq mi, 18.5 per sq km. **Urban:** 85.8%. **Ethnic groups:** Finnish, Swedish, Russian, Estonian, Romani, Sami. **Languages:** Finnish, Swedish (both official). **Religions:** Christian (official) 76.1% (Protestant 73.7%), agnostic 17.8%, Muslim 3.7% (Sunni), atheist 2.0%.

Geography: Total area: 130,559 sq mi, 338,145 sq km (64). **Land area:** 117,304 sq mi, 303,815 sq km. **Location:** Northern Europe. Norway on N, Swe78den on W, Russia on E. **Topography:** Flat with low hills and many lakes in S and center. The N has mountainous areas 3,000-4,000 ft above sea level. **Arable land:** 7.4%. **Capital:** Helsinki, 1,337,786.

Government: Type: Parliamentary republic. **Head of state:** Pres. Sauli Niinistö b. 1948; in office: Mar. 1, 2012. **Head of govt.:** Prime Min. Petteri Orpo; b. 1969; in office: June 20, 2023. **Local divisions:** 19 regions. **Defense budget:** $5.8 bil. **Active troops:** 19,250.

Economy: Industries: metals/metal prods., electronics, machinery and scientific instruments, shipbuilding, pulp and paper, foodstuffs, chemicals, textiles. **Chief agric.:** milk, barley, oats, wheat, potatoes, sugar beet. **Natural resources:** timber, iron ore, copper, lead, zinc, chromite, nickel, gold, silver, limestone. **Water:** 19,853 cu m per capita. **Electricity prod.:** 69.7 bil kWh. **Labor force:** agric. 4.1%, industry 21.4%, services 74.5%. **Unemployment:** 6.8%.

Finance: Monetary unit: Euro (EUR) (0.93 = $1 U.S.). **GDP:** $328.0 bil; **per capita GDP:** $59,027; **GDP growth:** 2.1%. **Imports:** $116.3 bil; (2021) Germany 16%, Sweden 15%, Russia 11%, China 7%, Netherlands 7%. **Exports:** $116.9 bil; (2021) Germany 13%, Sweden 9%, U.S. 8%, Netherlands 6%, China 6%. **Tourism:** $1.1 bil. **Budget** (2020): $153.6 bil (central govt.). **Inflation:** 7.1%.

Transport: Railways: 3,677 mi. **Motor vehicles:** 569.1 per 1,000 pop. **Airports:** 74.

Communications: Mobile: 128.7 per 100 pop. **Broadband:** 160.4 per 100 pop. **Internet:** 93.0%.

Health: Expend.: 9.6%. **Life expect.:** 79.1 male; 85.0 female. **Births:** 10.3 per 1,000 pop. **Deaths:** 10.4 per 1,000 pop. **Infant mortality:** 2.1 per 1,000 live births. **Undernourished:** <2.5%. **HIV:** NA. **COVID-19:** 1,483,278 cases, 10,138 deaths; rates per 100,000: 26,845.2 cases, 183.5 deaths. 78.7% vaccinated.

Education: Compulsory: ages 7-17. **Literacy:** NA.

Website: valtioneuvosto.fi

Early Finns may have migrated from the Ural region and other areas about 6,000 years ago. Swedish settlers brought the country into Sweden, 1154 to 1809, when Finland became an autonomous grand duchy of the Russian Empire. On Dec. 6, 1917, Finland declared its independence, and in 1919 it became a republic. On Nov. 30, 1939, the Soviet Union invaded, and Finland was forced to cede 16,173 sq mi of territory. After World War II, further cessions were exacted.

Finland entered the EU Jan. 1, 1995. More than 32,000 migrants applied for asylum in Finland in 2015. The government, 2016, announced it would deport rejected applicants and concluded agreements with Russia to reduce border crossings. During 2016, 65% of asylum applications were rejected.

The Social Democratic Party (SDP) won Apr. 14, 2019, parliamentary elections and formed a coalition government. The SDP's Sanna Marin became prime minister, Dec. 10, after her predecessor resigned.

Following Russia's Feb. 2022 invasion of Ukraine, Finland applied to join NATO; it was officially admitted Apr. 4, 2023.

The conservative National Coalition Party won Apr. 2, 2023, elections. Party leader Petteri Orpo formed a coalition government, including the right-wing, anti-immigration Finns Party, and became prime minister June 20, 2023.

Aland, or Ahvenanmaa, an autonomous, Swedish-speaking province, is a group of small islands, 590 sq mi, in the Gulf of Bothnia, 25 mi from Sweden, 15 mi from Finland. Mariehamn is the chief port and seat of government. **Website:** www.aland.ax

France
French Republic

People: Population: 68,521,974 (21). **Age distrib.:** <15: 17.5%; 65+: 21.7%. **Growth:** 0.3%. **Migrants:** 13.1%. **Pop. density:** 277.1 per sq mi, 107.0 per sq km. **Urban:** 81.8%. **Ethnic groups:** Celtic and Latin with Teutonic, Slavic, North African (Algerian, Moroccan, Tunisian), Indochinese, Basque minorities. **Languages:** French (official), declining regional dialects and langs. (Provençal, Breton, Alsatian, Corsican, Catalan, Basque, Flemish, Occitan, Picard). **Religions:** Christian 62.0% (Catholic 57.9%), agnostic 20.9%, Muslim 10.2% (Sunni), atheist 4.5%.

Geography: Total area: 248,573 sq mi, 643,801 sq km (incl. overseas departments) (43). **Land area:** 247,270 sq mi, 640,427 sq km (incl. overseas departments). **Location:** Western Europe, between Atlantic O. and Medit. Sea. Spain, Andorra, Monaco on S; Italy, Switzerland, Germany on E; Luxembourg, Belgium on N. **Topography:** A wide plain covers more than half of the country, in N and W, drained to W by Seine, Loire, Garonne Rivers. The Alps (Mt. Blanc is tallest in W Europe at 15,781 ft), the lower Jura range, and forested Vosges are in E. The Rhone flows from Lake Geneva to Mediterranean. Pyrenees are on SW border. **Arable land:** 32.8%. **Capital:** Paris, 11,208,440. **Cities:** Lyon, 1,761,188; Marseille-Aix-en-Provence, 1,627,549; Lille, 1,079,120; Toulouse, 1,060,460.

Government: Type: Semi-presidential republic. **Head of state:** Pres. Emmanuel Macron; b. 1977; in office: May 14, 2017. **Head of govt.:** Prime Min. Élisabeth Borne; b. 1961; in office: May 17, 2022. **Local divisions:** 13 metropolitan regions, 5 overseas regions. **Defense budget:** $54.4 bil. **Active troops:** 203,250.

Economy: Industries: machinery, chemicals, automobiles, metallurgy, aircraft, electronics, textiles, food proc., tourism. **Chief agric.:** wheat, sugar beet, milk, barley, maize, potatoes. **Natural resources:** coal, iron ore, bauxite, zinc, uranium, antimony, arsenic, potash, feldspar, fluorspar, gypsum, timber, fish. **Water:** 3,233 cu m per capita. **Crude oil reserves:** 62 mil bbls. **Electricity prod.:** 530.4 bil kWh. **Labor force:** agric. 2.5%, industry 19.5%, services 78.0%. **Unemployment:** 7.4%.

Finance: Monetary unit: Euro (EUR) (0.93 = $1 U.S.). **GDP:** $3.8 tril; **per capita GDP:** $55,493; **GDP growth:** 2.6%. **Imports:** $957.7 bil; Germany 18%, Belgium 9%, Italy 9%, Spain 7%, China 7%, Netherlands 6%. **Exports:** $920.9 bil; Germany 14%, U.S. 8%, Italy 7%, Spain 7%, Belgium 7%, UK 7%. **Tourism:** $40.8 bil. **Budget:** $1.5 tril. **Inflation:** 5.2%.

Transport: Railways: 17,311 mi. **Motor vehicles:** 712.4 per 1,000 pop. **Airports:** 294.

Communications: Mobile: 118.8 per 100 pop. **Broadband:** 106.9 per 100 pop. **Internet:** 85.3%.

Health: Expend.: 12.2%. **Life expect.:** 79.7 male; 85.5 female. **Births:** 10.9 per 1,000 pop. **Deaths:** 9.9 per 1,000 pop. **Infant mortality:** 3.1 per 1,000 live births. **Undernourished:** <2.5%. **HIV:** 0.3%. **COVID-19:** 38,997,490 cases, 167,985 deaths; rates per 100,000: 59,959.8 cases, 258.3 deaths. 78.4% vaccinated.

Education: Compulsory: ages 3-15. **Literacy:** NA.

Website: www.gouvernement.fr

Julius Caesar conquered Celtic Gaul 58-51 bce; Romans ruled for 500 years. Under Charlemagne, Frankish rule extended over much of Europe. After his death (in 814), France emerged as one of the successor kingdoms.

The monarchy was overthrown in the French Revolution (1789-93) and succeeded by the First Republic, followed by the First Empire under Napoleon I (1804-15), a monarchy (1814-48), the Second Republic (1848-52), the Second Empire (1852-70), the Third Republic (1871-1946), the Fourth Republic (1946-58), and the Fifth Republic (1958-present).

France suffered severe losses in people and wealth in WWI (1914-18) when it was invaded by Germany. By the Treaty of Versailles, 1919, France exacted return of Alsace and Lorraine, provinces seized by Germany in 1871 after it defeated France in the Franco-Prussian War. During WWII (1939-45), Germany invaded France in May 1940 and signed an armistice with a government based in Vichy. After the Allies liberated France in 1944, Gen. Charles de Gaulle became head of the provisional government, serving until 1946. De Gaulle again became premier in 1958, during a crisis over Algeria, and obtained voter approval for a new constitution, ushering in the Fifth Republic. He then became president.

France withdrew from Indochina in 1954 and from Morocco and Tunisia in 1956. Most of its remaining African territories, including Algeria, were freed 1958-62.

In May 1968, students in Paris and other centers rioted, battled police, and were joined by workers who launched nationwide strikes. De Gaulle resigned from office in Apr. 1969, after losing a nationwide referendum on constitutional reform. Georges Pompidou was elected to succeed him. After Pompidou's death, in 1974, Valery Giscard d'Estaing was elected president; he continued his predecessors' conservative policies.

In 1981, France elected Socialist François Mitterrand president. Under Mitterrand the government nationalized industries and banks. After 1986, however, when rightists won a narrow victory in the National Assembly, France pursued a privatization program, selling many state-owned companies. Mitterrand won a second 7-year term in 1988.

Conservative Jacques Chirac won the presidency in 1995 and was reelected in 2002. A summer 2003 heat wave caused an est. 15,000 deaths. Parliament gave final approval in 2004 to a law barring the wearing of Islamic head scarves and other religious symbols in public schools. A state of emergency was declared Nov. 8, 2005, after 12 days of riots that began in Paris and spread to some 300 French cities and towns; rioters were mainly young immigrants from N and W Africa.

The conservative Nicolas Sarkozy won the 2007 presidential runoff election. Sarkozy responded to the global recession, Dec. 2008, with economic stimulus measures. With France's economy still struggling, the Socialist François Hollande won a presidential runoff over Sarkozy in 2012. Hollande, May 18, 2013, signed a bill that legalized same-sex marriage and allowed gay couples to adopt children.

After forming a new party in 2016, centrist Emmanuel Macron was elected president, May 7, 2017, defeating Marine Le Pen of the far-right National Front (renamed National Rally in 2018) in a runoff. Macron pledged reforms to improve GDP growth and reduce unemployment. After his party won June 2017 parliamentary elections, the government made it easier for many companies to hire, fire, and negotiate terms with workers. Months of large "yellow vest" demonstrations began Nov. 17, 2018, triggered by a fuel-tax increase and expanding to protest economic conditions. Government responses included rolling back the tax increase and raising the minimum wage. Macron again defeated Le Pen (by a narrower margin) in an Apr. 24, 2022, presidential runoff to win a second term. Macron's party and its allies lost their National Assembly majority in June 2022 elections; leftist parties won the second-largest bloc of seats, and the National Rally took 89 seats (a gain of 81). Legislation in 2023 raising the retirement age for many workers (enacted by parliamentary maneuver without a National Assembly vote) sparked months of strikes and demonstrations. Protests and rioting followed the June 27, 2023, fatal shooting by a police officer of a teenager of N African descent after a traffic stop outside Paris.

France took part in the U.S.-led campaign of airstrikes against the Sunni extremist group ISIS in Iraq (beginning 2014) and in Syria (beginning 2015). French troops entered the conflict between government forces in Mali and Islamist militants Jan. 11, 2013. France maintained a counterterrorism force in the region, consisting of more than 5,000 troops in mid-2021. Subsequently, France reduced troop strength, calling for greater international sharing of counterterrorism responsibility and responding to requests from some African governments to withdraw troops.

On Jan. 7, 2015, two Islamist-extremist French gunmen of Algerian descent attacked the Paris offices of the magazine Charlie Hebdo (which had published satirical images of Muhammad), killing 12 people. A third gunman, who claimed loyalty to ISIS, killed 5 people Jan. 8-9. On Nov. 13, 2015, in coordinated attacks in and near Paris for which ISIS claimed responsibility, terrorists killed 130, many in Paris's Bataclan concert hall. In a July 14, 2016, attack ISIS claimed to have inspired, a Tunisian-born French resident drove a truck through a Bastille Day fireworks crowd in Nice, killing 86.

France ratified, June 15, 2016, a global agreement to reduce greenhouse gas emissions negotiated at a UN climate conference in Paris, Dec. 2015. A fire, Apr. 15, 2019, heavily damaged Paris's Notre-Dame Cathedral, largely built in the 12th and 13th cents. June and July 2019 heat waves caused about 1,500 deaths. Extreme heat, linked by many scientists to climate change, again gripped the country in the summers of 2022 and 2023.

France was one of the countries hardest hit, beginning in 2020, by the COVID-19 pandemic, recording about 39 mil total confirmed cases by Aug. 2023—4th-highest in the world. The pandemic had a severe impact on the economy, including the important tourism industry in mainland France, Corsica, and overseas islands.

The island of **Corsica** in the Mediterranean, W of Italy and N of Sardinia, is a territorial collectivity and region of France comprising two departments. It elects 2 senators and 3 deputies to the French Parliament. Area 3,369 sq mi; pop. (2022 est.) 349,465. The capital is Ajaccio, birthplace of Napoleon I. Violence by Corsican separatist groups was common in the 1980s and 1990s. Corsicans rejected, 51%-49%, a limited autonomy plan in a referendum July 6, 2003. **Website:** www.isula.corsica

French Overseas Departments

French Guiana is on the NE coast of South America with Suriname on the W and Brazil on the E and S. Its area is 35,135 sq mi (total), 34,421 sq mi (land); pop. (2022 est.) 294,436. Guiana sends 1 senator and 2 deputies to the French Parliament. Guiana is administered by a prefect and has a Council General of 16 elected members; capital is Cayenne, pop. (2020 est.) 61,645.

The famous penal colony, Devil's Island, was phased out between 1938 and 1951. The European Space Agency helps to maintain a satellite-launching center (est. 1964 by France), in the city of Kourou.

Immense forests of rich timber cover much of the land. Fishing (especially shrimp), forestry, and gold mining are the most important industries. Natural resources include petroleum, kaolin, niobium, tantalum, and clay.

Guadeloupe, in the West Indies' Leeward Isls., consists of two large islands, Basse-Terre and Grande-Terre, separated by the Salt R., plus Marie Galante and the Saintes group to the S and Desirade to the N. A French possession since 1635, the department is represented in the French Parliament; administration consists of a prefect (governor) as well as an elected general and regional councils.

Area of the islands is 525 sq mi; pop. (2022 est.) 372,939, mainly descendants of enslaved people; capital is Basse-Terre (2018 est. pop. 58,397) on Basse-Terre Island. The land is fertile; sugar, rum, and bananas are exported. Tourism is an important industry.

Martinique, the northernmost of the Windward Islands, in the West Indies, has been a possession since 1635, and a department since Mar. 1946. It is represented in the French Parliament by 2 senators and 4 deputies. The island was the birthplace of Napoleon's first wife, Empress Josephine.

It has an area of 425 sq mi (total), 409 sq mi (land); pop. (2022 est.) 350,373, mostly descendants of enslaved laborers. The capital is Fort-de-France; pop. (2018 est.) 79,361. It is a popular tourist destination. The chief exports are rum, bananas, and petroleum products. **Website:** www.collectivitedemartinique.mq

Mayotte, claimed by Comoros and administered by France, voted in 1976 to become a territorial collectivity of France. An island NW of Madagascar, area is 144 sq mi, pop. (2022 est.) 299,348. The capital is Mamoudzou; pop. (2018 est.) 6,180. In a Mar. 29, 2009, referendum, 95% of voters endorsed a plan under which Mayotte became an overseas department of France as of Mar. 31, 2011.

Réunion is a volcanic island in the Indian O. about 420 mi E of Madagascar, and has belonged to France since 1665. Area, 972 sq mi (total), 968 sq mi (land); pop. (2022 est.) 868,846. Capital: Saint-Denis; pop. (2018 est.) 147,209. The chief export is sugar. Tourism contributes to the economy. Réunion elects 5 deputies, 3 senators to the French Parliament. **Website:** regionreunion.com

French Overseas Territorial Authorities

French Polynesia, comprises 130 islands widely scattered among 5 archipelagos in the S Pacific; administered by a Council of Ministers (headed by a president). Territorial Assembly and the Council have headquarters at Papeete (2018 est. pop., 136,005), on Tahiti, one of the Society Islands (which include the Windward Isls. and Leeward Isls.). Two deputies and a senator are elected to the French Parliament.

Other groups are the Marquesas Isls.; the Tuamotu Archipelago; the Gambier Isls.; and the Austral, or Tubuai, Isls.

Total area of the islands administered from Tahiti is 1,609 sq mi (total), 1,478 sq mi (land); pop. (2022 est.) 299,356. Tahiti is mountainous with a productive coastline bearing coconuts, citrus, pineapples, and vanilla. Tourism is the largest industry.

Tahiti was visited by Capt. James Cook in 1769 and by Capt. Bligh in the *Bounty*, 1788-89. Its beauty impressed Herman Melville, Paul Gauguin, and Charles Darwin. A UN General Assembly resolution May 17, 2013, called on France to grant French Polynesia independence. Anti-independence parties won 2013 and 2018 general elections, but a pro-independence party won in 2023.

A 2013-14 Zika virus outbreak affected about 28,000 people. **Website:** www.presidence.pf

St. Pierre and Miquelon became a territorial collectivity in 1985. It consists of two groups of rocky islands near the SW coast of Newfoundland. Fish products are the chief export. The St. Pierre group has an area of 10 sq mi; Miquelon, 83 sq mi. Total pop. (2022 est.) 5,257. Capital: Saint-Pierre, pop. (2018 est.) 5,723. Both Mayotte and St. Pierre and Miquelon elect a deputy and a senator to the French Parliament.

St. Barthélemy and **St. Martin**, both formerly part of Guadeloupe, voted for secession in 2003 and became overseas territorial collectivities in 2007. Both suffered severe damage from Hurricane Irma, Sept. 6, 2017, which caused at least 11 deaths. Total area 10 sq mi and 19 sq mi; total pop. (2022 est.) 7,103 and 32,792 respectively.

The territorial collectivity of **Wallis and Futuna** comprises two island groups in the SW Pacific S of Tuvalu, N of Fiji, and W of Samoa. It became an overseas territory July 29, 1961. The islands have a total area of 55 sq mi and pop. (2022 est.) of 15,891. Alofi, attached to Futuna, is uninhabited. Capital: Mata-Utu; pop. (2018 est.) 1,025. Chief exports are copra, chemicals, and construction materials. A senator and a deputy are elected to the French Parliament.

Overseas Territory and Special Collectivity

The territory of **French Southern and Antarctic Lands** comprises island groups in the Indian O. Area: 2,991 sq mi (total), 2,960 sq mi (land).

The U.S. does not recognize French claim to Adelie Land, an area of about 193,051 sq mi on Antarctica. Adelie, reached 1840, has a 185-mi coastline and tapers 1,240 mi inland to the S Pole. It has a research station. The area includes the Ninnis and Mertz glaciers.

The Indian O. groups are as follows: Kerguelen Archipelago, visited 1772, consists of one large and 300 small islands. The chief is 87 mi long, 74 mi wide, and has Mt. Ross (6,429 ft). Principal research station is Port-aux-Français. There are seals, blue whales, coal, peat, semiprecious stones. Crozet Archipelago, reached 1772, covers 136 sq mi. Eastern Island rises to 6,560 ft. Volcanic Saint Paul, in southern Indian O., has warm springs. Amsterdam Island is nearby; both produce cod and rock lobster. Military garrisons and meteorological stations are located on the Scattered Isls.

The special collectivity of **New Caledonia** and Dependencies is a group of islands in the Pacific O. about 1,115 mi E of Australia and approx. the same distance NW of New Zealand. Dependencies are the Loyalty Isls., Isle of Pines, Belep Archipelago, and Huon Isls.

The largest island, New Caledonia, is 6,530 sq mi. Total area of the territory is 7,172 sq mi (total), 7,056 sq mi (land); pop. (2022 est.) 297,160. The group was acquired by France in 1853.

The territory is administered by a High Commissioner. There is a popularly elected Territorial Congress. Two deputies and two senators are elected to the French Parliament. Capital: Nouméa; pop. (2018 est.) 197,787.

Mining is a key industry. New Caledonia is one of the world's largest nickel producers. Chrome, iron, cobalt, manganese, silver, gold, lead, and copper are also found. Tourism is an important industry.

In 1987, New Caledonian voters chose by referendum to remain within France. French and Melanesians (Kanaks) clashed in 1988. An agreement (the Nouméa Accord) signed May 5, 1998, between France and rival New Caledonian factions specified a 20-year period of shared sovereignty and up to three referenda on independence, 2018-22. On Nov. 4, 2018, and Oct. 4, 2020, referendum voters rejected independence. Independence was rejected a third time in a Dec. 12, 2021, referendum boycotted by pro-independence groups, which had wanted a pandemic-related delay.

Website: gouv.nc

Gabon
Gabonese Republic

People: Population: 2,397,368 (143). **Age distrib.:** <15: 35.0%; 65+: 4.2%. **Growth:** 2.4%. **Migrants:** 18.7%. **Pop. density:** 24.1 per sq mi, 9.3 per sq km. **Urban:** 91.0%. **Ethnic groups:** Gabonese-born 80.1% (incl. Fang, Shira-Punu/Vili, Nzabi-Duma, Mbede-Teke, Myene, Kota-Kele, Okande-Tsogo, Pygmy), Cameroonian 4.6%, Malian 2.4%, Beninese 2.1%, other (incl. Congolese [DRC], Equatorial Guinean, Nigerian) 5.5%. **Languages:** French (official), Fang, Myene, Nzebi, Bapounou/Eschira, Bandjabi. **Religions:** Christian 85.0% (Catholic 57.0%, independent 15.9%, Protestant 12.1%), Muslim 10.1% (Sunni), ethnic religionist 3.2%.

Geography: Total area: 103,347 sq mi, 267,667 sq km (76); **Land area:** 99,486 sq mi, 257,667 sq km. **Location:** Atlantic coast of W central Africa. Equatorial Guinea, Cameroon on N; Rep. of the Congo on E and S. **Topography:** Heavily forested, consisting of coastal lowlands; plateaus in N, E, and S; mountains in N, SE, and center. The Ogooue R. system covers most of Gabon. **Arable land:** 1.3%. **Capital:** Libreville, 869,773.

Government: Type: Presidential republic. **Head of state:** Interim Pres. Brice Oligui Nguema; in office: Sept. 4, 2023. **Head of govt.:** Interim Prime Min. Raymond Ndong Sima; in office: Sept. 7, 2023. **Local divisions:** 9 provinces. **Defense budget:** $280 mil. **Active troops:** 4,700.

Economy: Industries: petroleum extraction and refining; manganese, gold; chemicals, ship repair, food and beverages, textiles. **Chief agric.:** plantains, cassava, sugarcane, yams, taro, vegetables. **Natural resources:** petroleum, nat. gas, diamonds, niobium, manganese, uranium, gold, timber, iron ore, hydropower. **Water:** 74,582 cu m per capita. **Crude oil reserves:** 2 bil bbls. **Electricity prod.:** 2.3 bil kWh. **Labor force:** agric. 29.0%, industry 16.1%, services 54.9%. **Unemployment:** 21.5%.

Finance: Monetary unit: Central African CFA Franc (XAF) (606.88 = $1 U.S.). **GDP:** $39.3 bil; **per capita GDP:** $16,471; **GDP growth:** 3.0%. **Imports** (2019): $5.0 bil; France 22%, China 17%, Belgium 6%, U.S. 6%. **Exports** (2019): $10.8 bil; China 63%. **Budget:** $2.9 bil. **Inflation:** 4.2%.

Transport: Railways: 403 mi. **Airports:** 14.
Communications: Mobile: 125.4 per 100 pop. **Broadband:** 94.4 per 100 pop. **Internet:** 71.7%.
Health: Expend.: 3.4%. **Life expect.:** 68.3 male; 71.8 female. **Births:** 25.9 per 1,000 pop. **Deaths:** 5.6 per 1,000 pop. **Infant mortality:** 27.7 per 1,000 live births. **Undernourished:** 23.0%. **HIV:** 2.9%. **COVID-19:** 48,992 cases, 307 deaths; rates per 100,000: 2,201.2 cases, 13.8 deaths. 11.6% vaccinated.
Education: Compulsory: ages 6-15. **Literacy:** 85.5%.
Website: www.gouvernement.ga

France established control over the region in the second half of the 19th cent. Gabon became independent Aug. 17, 1960. Backed by France, Pres. Albert-Bernard Bongo (later Omar Bongo Ondimba) ruled the country 1967-2009, greatly enriching himself and his family. After he died June 8, 2009, his son Ali Bongo Ondimba claimed victory in a disputed 2009 presidential election. He claimed a disputed reelection victory in 2016. With Bongo out of the country for medical treatment, government forces put down a Jan. 7, 2019, attempted coup.

Gabon has abundant natural resources (including oil), although there is extreme income inequality. Gabon joined the Commonwealth in 2022. After Bongo was declared the winner of a flawed Aug. 26, 2023, presidential election, military officers led by Gen. Brice Oligui Nguema announced, Aug. 30, Bongo's overthrow in a coup.

The Gambia
Republic of The Gambia

People: Population: 2,468,569 (141). **Age distrib.:** <15: 38.9%; 65+: 3.6%. **Growth:** 2.2%. **Migrants:** 8.9%. **Pop. density:** 631.8 per sq mi, 243.9 per sq km. **Urban:** 64.5%. **Ethnic groups:** Mandinka/Jahanka 33.3%, Fulani/Tukulur/Lorobo 18.2%, Wolof 12.9%, Jola/Karoninka 11%, Serahuleh 7.2%, Serer 3.5%, non-Gambian 9.9%. **Languages:** English (official), Mandinka, Wolof, Fula, other Indigenous vernaculars. **Religions:** Muslim 89.6% (Sunni), ethnic religionist 4.5%, Christian 4.5%.

Geography: Total area: 4,363 sq mi, 11,300 sq km (160); **Land area:** 3,907 sq mi, 10,120 sq km. **Location:** Atlantic coast near W tip of Africa. Surrounded on 3 sides by Senegal. **Topography:** Narrow strip of land on each side of lower Gambia R. **Arable land:** 43.5%. **Capital:** Banjul, 481,472.

Government: Type: Presidential republic. **Head of state and govt.:** Pres. Adama Barrow; b. 1965; in office: Jan. 19, 2017. **Local divisions:** 5 regions, 1 city, 1 municipality. **Defense budget:** $14 mil. **Active troops:** 4,100.

Economy: Industries: peanuts, fish, hides, tourism, beverages, agric. machinery assembly. **Chief agric.:** groundnuts, milk, oil palm fruit, millet, sorghum, rice. **Natural resources:** fish, clay, silica sand, titanium, tin, zircon. **Water:** 3,310 cu m per capita. **Electricity prod.:** 307.9 mil kWh. **Labor force:** agric. 48.5%, industry 7.4%, services 44.1%. **Unemployment:** 4.8%.

Finance: Monetary unit: Dalasi (GMD) (60.79 = $1 U.S.). **GDP:** $6.8 bil; **per capita GDP:** $2,510; **GDP growth:** 4.9%. **Imports:** $726.0 mil; China 33%, India 10%. **Exports:** $135.4 mil; (2017) China 38%, India 22%, Mali 7%. **Tourism:** $57 mil. **Budget** (2018): $353 mil. **Inflation:** 11.5%.

Transport: Airports: 1.
Communications: Mobile (2021): 101.4 per 100 pop. **Broadband** (2021): 50.3 per 100 pop. **Internet:** 33.0%.
Health: Expend.: 2.6%. **Life expect.:** 66.3 male; 69.8 female. **Births:** 28.0 per 1,000 pop. **Deaths:** 5.7 per 1,000 pop. **Infant mortality:** 36.4 per 1,000 live births. **Undernourished:** 19.6%. **HIV:** 1.4%. **COVID-19:** 12,626 cases, 372 deaths; rates per 100,000: 522.5 cases, 15.4 deaths. 22.3% vaccinated.
Education: Compulsory: ages 7-15. **Literacy:** 58.1%.
Website: op.gov.gm

The peoples of The Gambia were at one time associated with the West African empires of Ghana, Mali, and Songhai. The area became Britain's first African possession in 1588.

Independence came Feb. 18, 1965; republic status within the Commonwealth was achieved in 1970. The country suffered from severe famine in the 1970s. Senegambia, a confederation with Senegal, lasted from 1982 to 1989.

On July 22, 1994, after 24 years in power, Pres. Dawda K. Jawara was deposed in a bloodless coup by a military officer, Yahya Jammeh. Jammeh barred political activity, detained opponents, and governed by decree. There was a nominal return to constitutional government in 1996. Jammeh won a fourth 5-year term in 2011. After businessman Adama Barrow defeated Jammeh in the Dec. 1, 2016, presidential election, Jammeh rejected the results. Barrow was sworn in, Jan. 19, 2017, in Senegal. Under pressure from ECOWAS and the UN, Jammeh went into exile, Jan. 21, 2017. Barrow won reelection, Dec. 4, 2021.

Georgia

People: Population: 4,936,390 (125). **Age distrib.:** <15: 20.7%; 65+: 16.4%. **Growth:** 0.0%. **Migrants:** 2.0%. **Pop. density:** 183.4 per sq mi, 70.8 per sq km. **Urban:** 60.7%. **Ethnic groups:** Georgian 86.8%, Azeri 6.3%, Armenian 4.5%. **Languages:** Georgian (official), Azeri, Armenian, Abkhaz (official in Abkhazia). **Religions:** Christian 86.2% (Orthodox [official] 83.2%), Muslim 11.1% (Shia 6%, Sunni 5%), agnostic 2.4%.

Geography: Total area: 26,911 sq mi, 69,700 sq km (119). (About 18% is occupied by Russia.) **Land area:** 26,911 sq mi, 69,700 sq km. **Location:** SW Asia, on E coast of Black Sea. Russia on N and NE, Turkey and Armenia on S, Azerbaijan on SE. **Topography:** Main range of Caucasus Mts. in NE separates country from Russia. **Arable land:** 4.5%. **Capital:** Tbilisi, 1,082,245.

Government: Type: Semi-presidential republic. **Head of state:** Pres. Salome Zourabichvili; b. 1952; in office: Dec. 16, 2018. **Head of govt.:** Prime Min. Irakli Garibashvili; b. 1982; in office: Feb. 22, 2021. **Local divisions:** 9 regions, 1 city, 2 autonomous republics. **Defense budget:** $314 mil. **Active troops:** 20,650.

Economy: Industries: steel, machine tools, elec. appliances, mining, chemicals, wood prods., wine. **Chief agric.:** milk, grapes, maize, potatoes, wheat, watermelons. **Natural resources:** timber, hydropower, manganese, iron ore, copper, minor coal/oil deposits. **Water:** 15,875 cu m per capita. **Crude oil reserves:** 35 mil bbls. **Electricity prod.:** 12.6 bil kWh. **Labor force:** agric. 40.4%, industry 13.8%, services 45.8%. **Unemployment:** 11.3%.

Finance: Monetary unit: Lari (GEL) (2.62 = $1 U.S.). **GDP:** $74.7 bil; **per capita GDP:** $20,113; **GDP growth:** 10.1%. **Imports:** $11.2 bil; Turkey 17%, China 11%, Russia 9%, Azerbaijan 6%, U.S. 6%. **Exports:** $8.1 bil; Russia 12%, Azerbaijan 12%, Armenia 9%, Bulgaria 8%, China 6%, Turkey 6%, Ukraine 6%. **Tourism:** $1.2 bil. **Budget:** $5.1 bil. **Inflation:** 11.9%.

Transport: Railways: 847 mi. **Airports:** 18.

Communications: Mobile: 156.1 per 100 pop. **Broadband:** 109.5 per 100 pop. **Internet:** 78.7%.

Health: Expend.: 7.6%. **Life expect.:** 68.3 male; 76.6 female. **Births:** 12.3 per 1,000 pop. **Deaths:** 13.6 per 1,000 pop. **Infant mortality:** 22.6 per 1,000 live births. **Undernourished:** 2.9%. **HIV:** 0.3%. **COVID-19:** 1,850,905 cases, 17,122 deaths; rates per 100,000: 46,398.2 cases, 429.2 deaths. 31.6% vaccinated.

Education: Compulsory: ages 6-14. **Literacy:** 99.6%.

Website: www.gov.ge

The region, which contained the ancient kingdoms of Colchis and Iberia, was Christianized in the 4th cent. and conquered by Arabs in the 8th cent. Annexed by Russia in 1801, Georgia was forcibly incorporated into the USSR in 1922.

Georgia gained independence when the Soviet Union disbanded Dec. 26, 1991. After a power struggle, former Soviet Foreign Min. Eduard A. She ardnadze became president. He survived several coup attempts and won reelection in 1995 and 2000. Parliamentary elections Nov. 2, 2003, denounced as fraudulent sparked massive anti-government protests, causing Shevardnadze to resign Nov. 23. Opposition leader Mikhail Saakashvili won the 2004 presidential election. He survived an apparent assassination attempt along with U.S. Pres. George W. Bush in Tbilisi May 10, 2005. He suppressed an alleged coup plot, Sept. 6, 2006, and cracked down violently on anti-government protests, Nov. 2007. He called early elections, Jan. 2008, which he won. Barred by term limits from seeking reelection in 2013, he left the country. In 2018, he was convicted of abuse of power, and he was imprisoned following his return to Georgia in 2021.

Giorgi Margvelashvili of the recently formed Georgian Dream coalition, which won 2012 parliamentary elections, was elected president Oct. 27, 2013. Constitutional changes that went into effect in 2013 greatly increased the powers of the prime minister. Georgian Dream won Oct. 2016 parliamentary elections. Independent Salome Zurabishvili, backed by Georgian Dream, won a disputed Nov. 28, 2018, presidential election, becoming Georgia's first female president. Georgian Dream won disputed Oct.-Nov. 2020 parliamentary elections. Giorgi Gakharia of Georgian Dream, prime minister since 2019, resigned in Feb. 2021 over plans to arrest opposition leader Nika Melia; Irakli Garibashvili replaced Gakharia.

Georgia has close economic ties with the EU under a 2014 cooperation agreement. It applied for EU membership, Mar. 3, 2022.

After independence, secessionist movements in South Ossetia and Abkhazia, supported by Russia, rejected the Tbilisi government. Open warfare erupted in Aug. 2008 between Georgia and Russia, which dispatched forces to South Ossetia and Abkhazia and attacked key Georgian cities. After a cease-fire signed Aug. 15-16, Russian troops remained in the breakaway regions. Russia, Aug. 2008, formally recognized South Ossetia and Abkhazia's independence; almost all other nations have not.

Germany
Federal Republic of Germany

People: Population: 84,220,184 (18). **Age distrib.:** <15: 13.7%; 65+: 23.3%. **Growth:** −0.1%. **Migrants:** 18.8%. **Pop. density:** 625.6 per sq mi, 241.5 per sq km. **Urban:** 77.8%. **Ethnic groups:** German 86.3%, Turkish 1.8%, Polish 1%, Syrian 1%, Romanian 1%. **Languages:** German (official), Danish, Frisian, Sorbian, Romani (all official minority langs.). **Religions:** Christian 65.1% (Protestant 30.6%, Catholic 29.8%), agnostic 24.4%, Muslim 7.3% (Sunni 6%), atheist 2.7%.

Geography: Total area: 137,847 sq mi, 357,022 sq km (62); **Land area:** 134,623 sq mi, 348,672 sq km. **Location:** Central Europe.

Denmark on N; Netherlands, Belgium, Luxembourg, France on W; Switzerland, Austria on S; Czechia, Poland on E. Topography: Flat in N, hilly in center and W, and mountainous in Bavaria in the S. Chief rivers—Elbe, Weser, Ems, Rhine, and Main—flow toward North Sea; Danube flows toward Black Sea. **Arable land:** 33.4%. **Capital:** Berlin, 3,573,938. **Cities:** Hamburg, 1,787,520; Munich, 1,576,416; Cologne, 1,143,715.

Government: Type: Federal parliamentary republic. **Head of state:** Pres. Frank-Walter Steinmeier; b. 1956; in office: Mar. 22, 2017. **Head of govt.:** Chancellor Olaf Scholz; b. 1958; in office: Dec. 8, 2021. **Local divisions:** 16 states. **Defense budget:** $53.4 bil. **Active troops:** 183,150.

Economy: Industries: iron, steel, coal, cement, chemicals, machinery, vehicles, machine tools, electronics, automobiles, food and beverages. **Chief agric.:** milk, pork, wheat, beef, potatoes, barley. **Natural resources:** coal, lignite, nat. gas, iron ore, copper, nickel, uranium, potash, salt, constr. materials, timber. **Water:** 1,838 cu m per capita. **Crude oil reserves:** 115 mil bbls. **Electricity prod.:** 557.1 bil kWh. **Labor force:** agric. 1.3%, industry 27.6%, services 71.1%. **Unemployment:** 3.0%.

Finance: Monetary unit: Euro (EUR) (0.93 = $1 U.S.). **GDP:** $5.3 tril; **per capita GDP:** $63,150; **GDP growth:** 1.8%. **Imports:** $1.8 tril; (2021) China 10%, Netherlands 10%, Poland 7%, Italy 6%, France 6%. **Exports:** $2.0 tril; (2021) U.S. 9%, China 8%, France 8%, Netherlands 6%, Italy 6%. **Tourism:** $22.2 bil. **Budget (2020):** $1.9 tril. **Inflation:** 6.9%.

Transport: Railways: 24,469 mi. **Motor vehicles:** 629.3 per 1,000 pop. **Airports:** 318.

Communications: Mobile: 125.2 per 100 pop. **Broadband:** 95.5 per 100 pop. **Internet:** 91.6%.

Health: Expend. (2021): 12.8%. **Life expect.:** 79.4 male; 84.2 female. **Births:** 9.0 per 1,000 pop. **Deaths:** 12.0 per 1,000 pop. **Infant mortality:** 3.1 per 1,000 live births. **Undernourished:** <2.5%. **HIV:** NA. **COVID-19:** 38,437,756 cases, 174,979 deaths; rates per 100,000: 46,217.7 cases, 210.4 deaths. 76.4% vaccinated.

Education: Compulsory: ages 6-18. **Literacy:** NA.

Website: www.deutschland.de

Julius Caesar defeated Germanic tribes, 55 and 53 BCE, but Roman expansion north of the Rhine was stopped in 9 CE. Charlemagne, ruler of the Franks, consolidated Saxon, Bavarian, Rhenish, Frankish, and other lands; after him the eastern part became the German Empire. The Thirty Years' War, 1618-48, split Germany into small principalities and kingdoms.

Otto von Bismarck, Prussian chancellor, formed the North German Confederation, 1867. In 1870 Bismarck maneuvered Napoleon III into declaring war. After the quick defeat of France, Bismarck formed the German Empire and on Jan. 18, 1871, in Versailles, proclaimed King Wilhelm I of Prussia the German emperor (Deutscher kaiser).

The German Empire reached its peak before WWI in 1914, with 208,780 sq mi, plus overseas colonies. After losing the war in 1918, Germany ceded Alsace-Lorraine to France, West Prussia and Posen (Poznan) province to Poland, and part of Schleswig to Denmark. It lost all colonies and the ports of Memel and Danzig.

Republic of Germany, 1919-33, adopted the Weimar constitution; met reparation payments and elected Friedrich Ebert and Gen. Paul von Hindenburg presidents.

Third Reich, 1933-45: Adolf Hitler led the National Socialist German Workers' (Nazi) party after WWI. Pres. von Hindenburg named Hitler chancellor in 1933; on Aug. 3, 1934, the day after Hindenburg's death, the cabinet joined the offices of president and chancellor and made Hitler *führer* (leader). Hitler abolished freedom of speech and assembly, and began a long series of persecutions culminating in the murder of millions of Jews and others in the Holocaust.

He repudiated the Versailles treaty and reparations agreements, remilitarized the Rhineland (1936), and annexed Austria (Anschluss, 1938). At Munich he made an agreement with British Prime Min. Neville Chamberlain, which permitted Germany to annex part of Czechoslovakia. He declared war on Poland Sept. 1, 1939, precipitating WWII. With total defeat near, Hitler committed suicide in Berlin Apr. 1945. The victorious Allies voided all acts and annexations of Hitler's Reich.

Germany was sectioned into four zones of occupation, administered by the Allied Powers (U.S., USSR, UK, and France). The USSR took control of many E German states. The territory E of the so-called Oder-Neisse line was assigned to, and later annexed by, Poland. The USSR annexed Northern East Prussia (now Kaliningrad). Greater Berlin, within but not part of the Soviet zone, was administered by the four occupying powers under the Allied Command. In 1948 the USSR withdrew, established its single command in East Berlin, and cut off supplies. The Western Allies utilized a gigantic airlift to bring food to West Berlin, 1948-49.

In 1949, two separate German states were established. The zones administered by the Western Allies became West Germany; the Soviet sector became East Germany. West Berlin was considered a West German enclave, a status the Soviet bloc disputed.

East Germany. The German Democratic Republic (East Germany) was proclaimed in the Soviet sector of Berlin Oct. 7,

1949. It was declared fully sovereign in 1954, but Soviet troops remained.

Coincident with the entrance of West Germany into the European defense community in 1952, the East German government decreed a prohibited zone 3 mi deep along its 600-mi border with West Germany. East Germany also erected a fortified wall dividing Berlin in 1961, after over 3 mil East Germans had fled to the West. The oppressive Communist regime maintained control through the state security police, known as the Stasi.

By the early 1970s, the economy of East Germany was highly industrialized, and the nation was credited with the highest standard of living among Warsaw Pact countries. Growth slowed in the late 1970s because of shortages of natural resources and labor and huge debt. Comparison with the lifestyle in the West caused many young people to emigrate.

In the late 1980s the government firmly resisted following the USSR's policy of openness (glasnost) but was faced with nationwide demonstrations demanding reform. Pres. Erich Honecker, in office since 1976, was forced to resign Oct. 18, 1989. On Nov. 9, the East German government announced its decision to open the border with the West, signaling the end of the Berlin Wall. On Aug. 23, 1990, the East German parliament agreed to reunite with West Germany.

West Germany. The Federal Republic of Germany (West Germany) was proclaimed May 23, 1949, in Bonn. The occupying powers—the U.S., Britain, and France—restored civil status, Sept. 21. The Western Allies ended the state of war with Germany in 1951, while the USSR did so in 1955. The republic became fully independent May 5, 1955. The U.S. maintained military bases.

Dr. Konrad Adenauer, a Christian Democrat, was made chancellor 1949 and was reelected 1953, 1957, and 1961. Willy Brandt, heading a coalition of Social Democrats and Free Democrats, became chancellor 1969 and pursued a policy of Ostpolitik, or rapprochement with East Germany and the USSR. Brandt resigned May 1974 after a spy scandal. Terrorist acts on German soil in the 1970s included activities of the Baader-Meinhof gang, also known as the Red Army Faction, and the murder of Israeli athletes by Palestinian commandos at the Olympic Games in Munich, Sept. 5, 1972.

Helmut Kohl became chancellor in 1982 and led the Christian Democratic Union (CDU) and its Bavarian sister party Christian Social Union (CSU) to victory in 1983 and 1987.

Unified Germany. In May 1990, NATO ministers voted to make the united Germany a full member of NATO and barred the new Germany from having its own nuclear, chemical, or biological weapons. The merger of the two Germanys took place Oct. 3, and the first all-German elections since 1932 were held Dec. 2, with Kohl confirmed as leader of the unified nation. Eastern Germany received over $1 tril in public and private funds from western Germany, 1990-95. In 1991, Berlin again became Germany's official capital; the Bundestag (parliament) relocated from Bonn to Berlin in 1999. The Christian Democrats lost parliamentary elections, Sept. 27, 1998, and Gerhard Schröder, of the Social Democratic Party (SPD), became chancellor. The Christian Democrats, led by Angela Merkel, won a razor-thin plurality in 2005 parliamentary elections, and she became chancellor Nov. 22, heading a "grand coalition" that included the SPD.

Responding to the global recession, the government passed a 50-bil euro economic stimulus plan in early 2009. Merkel led a center-right coalition to victory in 2009 national elections. Merkel led the response to the European debt crisis beginning in late 2009; debtor nations were required to adopt stern austerity measures.

Merkel's Christian Democrats won Sept. 22, 2013, parliamentary elections but fell short of a majority. She formed a new coalition, including the SPD, in Dec.

Germany was the destination in 2015-16 for many migrants reaching Europe after fleeing war or hardship in the Middle East, SW Asia, or Africa; it also received, in 2015, large numbers of migrants from the Balkans. More than 1.2 mil migrants applied for asylum, 2015-16. Germany provided temporary care, set up expedited procedures for asylum applicants, and began repatriating migrants judged not to be refugees. Germany played a key role in negotiating a Mar. 2016 EU-Turkey agreement to stem the flow of migrants to Europe. In an attack for which ISIS claimed responsibility, a Tunisian migrant killed 12 when he stole a truck and drove it into a crowded Berlin outdoor market, Dec. 19, 2016.

Legislation legalizing same-sex marriage was signed into law by Germany's president, July 21, 2017.

Merkel's CDU/CSU won a plurality in Sept. 24, 2017, elections; the far-right, anti-immigration Alternative for Germany (AfD) party won 12.6% of the vote. Merkel reached agreement, Feb. 2018, on a new coalition with the SPD. Far-right protests and rioting in Chemnitz in Aug. included attacks on apparent immigrants.

A study commissioned by the German Catholic Church, released Sept. 2018, found evidence that more than 3,600 children had been sexually abused, 1946-2014, by over 1,600 members of the clergy.

German Defense Min. Ursula von der Leyen became, Dec. 1, 2019, the first woman to head the European Commission.

In Sept. 26, 2021, parliamentary elections, the SPD increased its vote share and outpolled the CDU/CSU, with the Greens and

center-right Free Democrats also increasing their support (AfD won about 10% of the vote). SPD leader Olaf Scholz formed a coalition with the Greens and Free Democrats; he became chancellor Dec. 8.

Heavily dependent on foreign energy imports, Germany joined EU sanctions against Russia over its 2022 invasion of Ukraine. Germany also blocked the opening of a new natural gas pipeline (Nord Stream 2) from Russia, Feb. 22, 2022, and essentially ended Russian oil imports by the end of the year. As of mid-Sept. 2023, over 1 mil Ukrainian refugees were in Germany.

German authorities announced, Dec. 7, 2022, the arrests of 25 far-right extremists, said to be plotting the violent overthrow of the government.

Severely affected by the COVID-19 pandemic, Germany had recorded over 38.4 mil confirmed cases by Aug. 2023, 5th-highest in the world.

Helgoland, an island of 0.66 sq mi in the North Sea, was taken from Denmark by a British naval force in 1807 and ceded to Germany in 1890. The island was surrendered to the UK, May 23, 1945, and returned to then-West Germany, Mar. 1, 1952.

Ghana
Republic of Ghana

People: Population: 33,846,114 (44). **Age distrib.:** <15: 37.7%; 65+: 4.4%. **Growth:** 2.2%. **Migrants:** 1.5%. **Pop. density:** 385.3 per sq mi, 148.8 per sq km. **Urban:** 59.2%. **Ethnic groups:** Akan 45.7%, Mole-Dagbani 18.5%, Ewe 12.8%, Ga-Dangme 7.1%, Gurma 6.4%, Guan 3.2%, Grusi 2.7%, Mande 2%. **Languages:** Asante, Ewe, Fante, Boron (Brong), Dagomba, Dangme, Dagarte (Dagaba), Kokomba, Akyem, Ga, English (official). **Religions:** Christian 73.6% (Protestant 34.6%, independent 22.9%, Catholic 16.2%), Muslim 18.0% (Sunni 12%, Islamic schismatic 7%), ethnic religionist 7.8%.

Geography: Total area: 92,098 sq mi, 238,533 sq km (80); **Land area:** 87,851 sq mi, 227,533 sq km. **Location:** S coast of W Africa. Côte d'Ivoire on W, Burkina Faso on N, Togo on E. **Topography:** Mostly low fertile plains and scrubland, cut by rivers and by the artificial Lake Volta. **Arable land:** 20.7%. **Capital:** Accra, 2,660,072. **Cities:** Kumasi, 3,768,239; Sekondi Takoradi, 1,077,929.

Government: Type: Presidential republic. **Head of state and govt.:** Pres. Nana Addo Dankwa Akufo-Addo; b. 1944; in office: Jan. 7, 2017. **Local divisions:** 16 regions. **Defense budget:** $262 mil. **Active troops:** 15,500.

Economy: Industries: mining, lumbering, light mfg., aluminum smelting, food proc., cement, small comm. shipbuilding. **Chief agric.:** cassava, yams, plantains, maize, oil palm fruit, taro. **Natural resources:** gold, timber, industrial diamonds, bauxite, manganese, fish, rubber, hydropower, petroleum, silver, salt, limestone. **Water:** 1,809 cu m per capita. **Crude oil reserves:** 660 mil bbls. **Electricity prod.:** 20.9 bil kWh. **Labor force:** agric. 39.5%, industry 19.1%, services 41.4%. **Unemployment:** 3.9%.

Finance: Monetary unit: Cedi (GHS) (11.38 = $1 U.S.). **GDP:** $217.5 bil; **per capita GDP:** $6,498; **GDP growth:** 3.2%. **Imports:** $26.0 bil; (2020) China 42%. **Exports:** $23.9 bil; (2020) Switzerland 23%, UAE 12%, China 12%, India 9%. **Tourism:** $567 mil. **Budget** (2018): $14.1 bil. **Inflation:** 31.3%.

Transport: Railways: 588 mi. **Motor vehicles:** 6.7 per 1,000 pop. **Airports:** 7.

Communications: Mobile: 119.6 per 100 pop. **Broadband:** 68.4 per 100 pop. **Internet:** 68.2%.

Health: Expend.: 4.0%. **Life expect.:** 68.1 male; 71.4 female. **Births:** 28.0 per 1,000 pop. **Deaths:** 6.0 per 1,000 pop. **Infant mortality:** 31.9 per 1,000 live births. **Undernourished:** 4.9%. **HIV:** 1.7%. **COVID-19:** 171,653 cases, 1,462 deaths; rates per 100,000: 552.4 cases, 4.7 deaths. 34.7% vaccinated.

Education: Compulsory: ages 4-14. **Literacy:** 80.4%.

Website: www.ghana.gov.gh

Named for an African empire along the Niger R., 400-1240 CE, Ghana was ruled by Britain for 113 years as the Gold Coast. The UN in 1956 approved merger with the British Togoland trust territory. Independence came Mar. 6, 1957, and republic status within the Commonwealth in 1960.

Pres. Kwame Nkrumah built hospitals and schools and promoted development projects but ran the country into debt, jailed opponents, and was accused of corruption. A 1964 referendum gave Nkrumah dictatorial powers and set up a one-party socialist state. A police-army coup overthrew Nkrumah in 1966. Elections were held in 1969, but four other coups occurred in 1972, 1978, 1979, and 1981. A new constitution, allowing multiparty politics, was approved in Apr. 1992. Former coup leader Jerry Rawlings won the 1996 presidential election.

Opposition leader John Agyekum Kufuor won a 2000 runoff vote and was sworn in Jan. 7, 2001, marking Ghana's first peaceful transfer of power from one elected president to another. A major offshore oil and gas find was announced June 2007. Nana Addo Dankwa Akufo-Addo won the Dec. 7, 2016, presidential election and was reelected, Dec. 7, 2020. Akufo-Addo signed, Aug. 2, 2023, legislation abolishing the death penalty for most crimes.

Greece
Hellenic Republic

People: Population: 10,497,595 (89). **Age distrib.:** <15: 14.0%; 65+: 23.3%. **Growth:** –0.3%. **Migrants:** 12.9%. **Pop. density:** 208.1 per sq mi, 80.4 per sq km. **Urban:** 80.7%. **Ethnic groups** (citizenship): Greek 91.6%, Albanian 4.4%. Greece does not collect ethnicity data. **Languages:** Greek (official). **Religions:** Christian 87.5% (Orthodox [official] 85.0%), Muslim 6.6% (Sunni), agnostic 5.1%.

Geography: Total area: 50,949 sq mi, 131,957 sq km (95); **Land area:** 50,443 sq mi, 130,647 sq km. **Location:** S end of Balkan Peninsula in SE Europe. Albania, North Macedonia, Bulgaria on N; Turkey on E. **Topography:** About three-quarters is non-arable, with mountains in all areas incl. N-S Pindus Mts. Heavily indented coastline is 9,385 mi long. About 2,000 islands, only 169 inhabited, among them Crete, Rhodes, Milos, Kerkira (Corfu), Chios, Lesbos, Samos, Euboea, Delos, Mykonos. **Arable land:** 16.5%. **Capital:** Athens, 3,154,463. **Cities:** Thessaloniki, 814,524.

Government: Type: Parliamentary republic. **Head of state:** Pres. Katerina Sakellaropoulou; b. 1956; in office: Mar. 13, 2020. **Head of govt.:** Prime Min. Kyriakos Mitsotakis; b. 1968; in office: July 8, 2019. **Local divisions:** 13 regions, 1 autonomous monastic state. **Defense budget:** $7.9 bil. **Active troops:** 132,200.

Economy: Industries: tourism, food and tobacco proc., textiles, chemicals, metal prods. **Chief agric.:** maize, olives, wheat, milk, peaches/nectarines, oranges. **Natural resources:** lignite, petroleum, iron ore, bauxite, lead, zinc, nickel, magnesite, marble, salt. **Water:** 6,562 cu m per capita. **Crude oil reserves:** 10 mil bbls. **Electricity prod.:** 52.5 bil kWh. **Labor force:** agric. 11.4%, industry 15.3%, services 73.4%. **Unemployment:** 12.2%.

Finance: Monetary unit: Euro (EUR) (0.93 = $1 U.S.). **GDP:** $389.2 bil; **per capita GDP:** $36,835; **GDP growth:** 5.9%. **Imports:** $103.5 bil; Germany 11%, China 9%, Italy 8%, Iraq 7%, Russia 6%. **Exports:** $87.5 bil; Italy 10%, Germany 7%. **Tourism:** $12.4 bil. **Budget:** $97.3 bil. **Inflation:** 9.6%.

Transport: Railways: 1,457 mi. **Motor vehicles:** 677.7 per 1,000 pop. **Airports:** 68.

Communications: Mobile: 109.1 per 100 pop. **Broadband:** 95.2 per 100 pop. **Internet:** 83.2%.

Health: Expend.: 9.5%. **Life expect.:** 79.2 male; 84.4 female. **Births:** 7.5 per 1,000 pop. **Deaths:** 12.0 per 1,000 pop. **Infant mortality:** 3.5 per 1,000 live births. **Undernourished:** <2.5%. **HIV:** 0.2%. **COVID-19:** 5,352,647 cases, 37,311 deaths; rates per 100,000: 49,938.1 cases, 348.1 deaths. 74.0% vaccinated.

Education: Compulsory: ages 5-14. **Literacy:** 97.9%.

Website: primeminister.gr

The achievements of ancient Greece in art, architecture, science, mathematics, philosophy, drama, literature, and democracy became legacies for succeeding ages. Greece reached the height of its power, particularly in the Athenian city-state, in the 5th cent. BCE. Greece fell under Roman rule in the 2nd and 1st cents. BCE. In the 4th cent. CE, it became part of the Byzantine Empire and, after the fall of Constantinople to the Turks in 1453, part of the Ottoman Empire.

Greece won its war of independence from Turkey, 1821-29, and became a kingdom. A republic was established 1924; the monarchy was restored, 1935. In Oct. 1940, Greece rejected an ultimatum from Italy, but the country was defeated and occupied by German, Italian, and Bulgarian forces. By the end of 1944 the invaders withdrew. Communist resistance forces were overcome by Royalist and British troops. A plebiscite restored the monarchy.

Communists waged guerrilla war 1947-49 against the government but were defeated with the aid of the U.S. A period of reconstruction and rapid development followed, mainly with conservative governments under Prem. Constantine Karamanlis. The Center Union, led by Georgios Papandreou, won elections in 1963 and 1964, but King Constantine forced Papandreou to resign. A period of political maneuvers ended with Col. George Papadopoulos's military takeover Apr. 1967. King Constantine tried to reverse the consolidation of the harsh dictatorship, Dec. 1967, but failed and fled to Italy. Papadopoulos was ousted Nov. 1973.

Greek army officers serving in the Cyprus National Guard staged a coup on the island July 15, 1974. Turkey invaded Cyprus a week later, precipitating the collapse of the Greek junta. Democratic government returned, and in 1975 the monarchy was abolished.

The 1981 electoral victory of the Panhellenic Socialist Movement (Pasok) of Andreas Papandreou (Georgios's son) substantially changed Greece's internal and external policies. A scandal contributed to the 1989 defeat of the Socialists at the polls. Papandreou, who was acquitted Jan. 1992 of corruption charges, led the Socialists to a comeback victory in 1993 general elections. The Socialists retained power in 1996 and 2000 elections.

The conservative New Democracy (ND) party won 2004 parliamentary elections, and Konstantinos (Costas) Karamanlis became prime min. Beset by scandals and an ailing economy, Karamanlis called early elections for Oct. 4, 2009, won by Pasok under the leadership of the U.S.-born George A. Papandreou (Andreas's son). The IMF and eurozone countries agreed in 2010 on a 110-bil euro loan package to prevent Greece from defaulting on its debt; in return, Greek leaders implemented an austerity plan. As the debt crisis continued, parliament passed, amid violent anti-austerity

protests, new austerity measures, Feb. 2012, to obtain a second, 130-bil euro bailout in Mar. The conservative, pro-bailout Antonis Samaras of ND became prime min., June 2012. Recession and austerity measures, 2007-13, caused Greece's GDP to shrink by 26%. In 2014, 36% of people lived below the poverty line.

Campaigning against austerity, the leftist Syriza party won Jan. 25, 2015, elections. Syriza's Alexis Tsipras became prime min. In a July 5 referendum, Greek voters decisively rejected further austerity. However, negotiations after the referendum produced an 86-bil euro third bailout agreement with tough austerity terms. As austerity measures were implemented, unemployment was over 20% in 2016 and 2017. After negotiating extended debt repayment, Greece exited the bailout program, Aug. 20, 2018. Syriza lost July 7, 2019, elections to ND, and Kyriakos Mitsotakis became prime min. Elected by parliament, Jan. 22, 2020, Katerina Sakellaropoulou took office, Mar. 13, as Greece's first woman president. ND won June 25, 2023, elections, giving Mitsotakis a second term as prime min.

In 2015, more than 861,000 migrants from the Middle East, SW Asia, and Africa trying to reach the EU arrived in Greece. A 2016 EU-Turkey agreement reduced the number of undocumented migrants reaching Greece, but more than 407,000 arrived from 2016 to mid-Sept. 2023. Most migrants tried to continue to N Europe. About 67,000 refugees registered with the UNHCR were in Greece as of mid-2023. Greece has been accused in recent years of forcibly preventing migrants from entering the country and of forcing out some who had arrived. Hundreds died, June 14, 2023, when an overcrowded boat carrying migrants sank near the Greek coast, prompting questions about the assistance provided by the Greek Coast Guard.

Severe summer heat waves and associated widespread wildfires, 2021-23, were likely related to climate change. Torrential rainstorms, Sept. 2023, caused extensive damage in agricultural areas.

Grenada

People: Population: 114,299 (180). **Age distrib.:** <15: 22.2%; 65+: 12.3%. **Growth:** 0.3%. **Migrants:** 6.4%. **Pop. density:** 860.6 per sq mi, 332.3 per sq km. **Urban:** 37.1%. **Ethnic groups:** African descent 82.4%, mixed 13.3%, East Indian 2.2%. **Languages:** English (official), French patois. **Religions:** Christian 96.3% (Catholic 49.6%, Protestant 40.1%).

Geography: Total area: 133 sq mi, 344 sq km (186). **Land area:** 133 sq mi, 344 sq km. **Location:** In Caribbean, 90 mi N of Venezuela. Trinidad and Tobago to S, St. Vincent and the Grenadines to N. **Topography:** Main island is mountainous. Country also comprises Carriacou and Petit Martinique Isls. **Arable land:** 8.8%. **Capital:** St. George's, 39,297.

Government: Type: Parliamentary democracy under constitutional monarchy. **Head of state:** King Charles III, rep. by Gov.-Gen. Cécile La Grenade; b. 1952; in office: May 7, 2013. **Head of govt.:** Prime Min. Dickon Mitchell; b. 1978; in office: June 24, 2022. **Local divisions:** 6 parishes, 1 dependency. **Defense budget/active troops:** NA.

Economy: Industries: food and beverages, textiles, light assembly operations, tourism, constr., education, call-center operations. **Chief agric.:** bananas, watermelons, sweet potatoes, sugarcane, tomatoes, plantains. **Natural resources:** timber, tropical fruit. **Water:** 1,777 cu m per capita. **Electricity prod.:** 217.2 mil kWh. **Labor force:** agric. 11%, industry 20%, services 69%. **Unemployment:** NA.

Finance: Monetary unit: East Caribbean Dollar (XCD) (2.70 = $1 U.S.). **GDP:** $2.1 bil; **per capita GDP:** $16,987; **GDP growth:** 5.8%. **Imports:** $650.0 mil; (2021) U.S. 35%, Trinidad and Tobago 17%, Cayman Islands 8%. **Exports:** $393.8 mil; (2021) U.S. 30%, St. Vincent and the Grenadines 12%, France 7%. **Tourism:** $63 mil. **Budget:** $263 mil. **Inflation:** 2.6%.

Transport: Airports: 3.

Communications: Mobile (2021): 81.1 per 100 pop. **Broadband** (2021): 76.6 per 100 pop. **Internet:** 77.8%.

Health: Expend.: 5.8%. **Life expect.:** 73.4 male; 78.8 female. **Births:** 13.6 per 1,000 pop. **Deaths:** 8.3 per 1,000 pop. **Infant mortality:** 9.2 per 1,000 live births. **Undernourished:** NA. **HIV:** NA. **COVID-19:** 19,693 cases, 238 deaths; rates per 100,000: 17,501.3 cases, 211.5 deaths. 34.7% vaccinated.

Education: Compulsory: ages 5-16. **Literacy:** 98.6%.

Website: www.gov.gd

Christopher Columbus sighted Grenada in 1498. The first European settlers were French, 1650. The island was held alternately by France and England until final British occupation, 1784. Grenada became fully independent Feb. 7, 1974, during a general strike.

On Oct. 14, 1983, a military coup ousted Prime Min. Maurice Bishop, who was executed Oct. 19. A largely U.S. force invaded Grenada, Oct. 25. Resistance from the Grenadian army and Cuban advisors was quickly overcome, and U.S. troops left Grenada in June 1985.

Hurricane Ivan slammed into Grenada, Sept. 7, 2004, killing 39 and damaging an estimated 90% of the buildings. The center-right New National Party (NNP) won 2013 and 2018 legislative elections. In June 23, 2022, elections, the center-left National Democratic

Congress (NDC) defeated the NNP. The NDC's Dickon Mitchell became prime min., June 24, 2022.

Guatemala
Republic of Guatemala

People: Population: 17,980,803 (69). **Age distrib.:** <15: 32.0%; 65+: 5.2%. **Growth:** 1.5%. **Migrants:** 0.5%. **Pop. density:** 434.6 per sq mi, 167.8 per sq km. **Urban:** 53.1%. **Ethnic groups:** mestizo or Ladino (mixed Amerindian/Spanish) 56%, Maya 41.7%. **Languages:** Spanish (official), Maya langs. (incl. Q'eqchi', K'iche, Mam, Kaqchikel). **Religions:** Christian 97.1% (Catholic [official] 65.5%, Protestant 19.1%, independent 11.3%).

Geography: Total area: 42,042 sq mi, 108,889 sq km (105); **Land area:** 41,374 sq mi, 107,159 sq km. **Location:** Central America. Mexico on N and W, El Salvador on S, Honduras and Belize on E. **Topography:** Central highland and mountain areas bordered by a narrow Pacific coast and lowlands and fertile river valleys on the Caribbean. Numerous volcanoes in S, more than half a dozen over 11,000 ft. **Arable land:** 14.5%. **Capital:** Guatemala City, 3,095,099.

Government: Type: Presidential republic. **Head of state and govt.:** Pres. Alejandro Giammattei; b. 1956; in office: Jan. 14, 2020. **Local divisions:** 22 departments. **Defense budget:** $400 mil. **Active troops:** 18,050.

Economy: Industries: sugar, textiles/clothing, furniture, chemicals, petroleum, metals, rubber, tourism. **Chief agric.:** sugarcane, bananas, oil palm fruit, maize, melons, potatoes. **Natural resources:** petroleum, nickel, rare woods, fish, chicle, hydropower. **Water:** 7,140 cu m per capita. **Crude oil reserves:** 86 mil bbls. **Electricity prod.:** 14.4 bil kWh. **Labor force:** agric. 29.2%, industry 22.1%, services 48.8%. **Unemployment:** 2.6%.

Finance: Monetary unit: Quetzal (GTQ) (7.86 = $1 U.S.). **GDP:** $187.8 bil; **per capita GDP:** $10,818; **GDP growth:** 4.1%. **Imports:** $27.4 bil; U.S. 36%, China 12%, Mexico 11%. **Exports:** $15.3 bil; U.S. 33%, El Salvador 12%, Honduras 8%. **Tourism:** $388 mil. **Budget:** $10.4 bil. **Inflation:** 6.9%.

Transport: Railways: 497 mi (rail service suspended in 2007). **Motor vehicles:** 144.8 per 1,000 pop. **Airports:** 16.

Communications: Mobile: 115.2 per 100 pop. **Broadband** (2021): 17.0 per 100 pop. **Internet:** 50.8%.

Health: Expend.: 6.5%. **Life expect.:** 71.2 male; 75.3 female. **Births:** 21.9 per 1,000 pop. **Deaths:** 4.9 per 1,000 pop. **Infant mortality:** 25.6 per 1,000 live births. **Undernourished:** 13.3%. **HIV:** 0.2%. **COVID-19:** 1,271,061 cases, 20,235 deaths; rates per 100,000: 7,094.7 cases, 112.9 deaths. 39.8% vaccinated.

Education: Compulsory: through age 16. **Literacy:** 83.4%.

Website: guatemala.gob.gt or www.presidencia.gob.gt

A Mayan Indian empire flourished in present-day Guatemala for over 1,000 years before Spaniards came. Guatemala was a Spanish colony 1524-1821. A republic was established in 1839.

In 1954, the U.S. Central Intelligence Agency engineered the overthrow of elected Pres. Jacobo Arbenz Guzmán, a left-wing reformer. Since then, the country has experienced a variety of military and civilian governments and periods of insurgency, repression, paramilitary violence, and civil war.

The Guatemalan government and leftist rebels signed a peace accord Dec. 29, 1996. During more than 35 years of armed conflict, some 200,000 people were killed or "disappeared"; most casualties were attributed to the government and its paramilitary allies. Gen. Efraín Ríos Montt, dictator in 1982-83, was found guilty of genocide May 10, 2013, but the Constitutional Court overturned his conviction May 20; Ríos Montt died, Apr. 1, 2018, during a retrial.

Former Pres. Alfonso Portillo was extradited to the U.S. May 24, 2013, and pleaded guilty to money laundering, Mar. 18, 2014. Drug trafficking, arms smuggling, police corruption, and gang violence posed threats to national stability. Hundreds of thousands of Guatemalans were among the asylum seekers and other migrants detained trying to enter the U.S. from Mexico 2013-23.

Vice Pres. Roxana Baldetti resigned, May 2015, and was convicted on fraud charges, Oct. 9, 2018. Following large-scale protests, Pres. Otto Pérez Molina resigned Sept. 2, 2015, amid corruption allegations. Pérez Molina and Baldetti were convicted on corruption charges, Dec. 7, 2022.

Former comedian Jimmy Ernesto Morales Cabrera won a runoff election for president, Oct. 25, 2015. Under investigation by a UN-sponsored anti-corruption panel, Morales, 2018-19, took steps to block the panel's work. Conservative Alejandro Giammattei won an Aug. 11, 2019, presidential runoff election. Amid a crackdown on independent journalists and judges, several opposition candidates were disqualified from the 2023 presidential election. However, Bernardo Arévalo, running on an anti-corruption platform, defeated conservative Sandra Torres in an Aug. 20 runoff.

Guinea
Republic of Guinea

People: Population: 13,607,249 (75). **Age distrib.:** <15: 41.0%; 65+: 4.0%. **Growth:** 2.8%. **Migrants:** 0.9%. **Pop. density:** 143.4 per sq mi, 55.4 per sq km. **Urban:** 38.1%. **Ethnic groups:** Fulani (Peuhl) 33.4%, Malinke 29.4%, Susu 21.2%, Guerze 7.8%, Kissi 6.2%. **Languages:** French (official), ethnic group-specific langs. **Religions:** Muslim 87.4% (Sunni), ethnic religionist 8.9%, Christian 3.4%.

Geography: Total area: 94,926 sq mi, 245,857 sq km (77); **Land area:** 94,872 sq mi, 245,717 sq km. **Location:** Atlantic coast of W Africa. Guinea-Bissau, Senegal, Mali on N; Côte d'Ivoire on E; Liberia, Sierra Leone on S. **Topography:** Narrow coastal belt leads to mountainous middle region, source of the Gambia, Senegal, and Niger R. Upper Guinea, farther inland, is cooler upland. The SE is forested. **Arable land:** 12.6%. **Capital:** Conakry, 2,110,937.

Government: Type: Presidential republic. **Head of state:** Pres. Mamady Doumbouya; b. 1980; in office: Oct. 1, 2021. **Head of govt.:** Prime Min. Bernard Gomou; in office: Aug. 20, 2022. **Local divisions:** 7 administrative regions, 1 governorate. **Defense budget:** $327 mil. **Active troops:** 9,700.

Economy: Industries: bauxite, gold, diamonds, iron ore; light mfg.; agric. proc. **Chief agric.:** rice, cassava, groundnuts, maize, oil palm fruit, fonio. **Natural resources:** bauxite, iron ore, diamonds, gold, uranium, hydropower, fish, salt. **Water:** 17,209 cu m per capita. **Electricity prod.:** 2.8 bil kWh. **Labor force:** agric. 59.2%, industry 7.0%, services 33.8%. **Unemployment:** 5.7%.

Finance: Monetary unit: Franc (GNF) (8,567.17 = $1 U.S.). **GDP:** $44.2 bil; **per capita GDP:** $3,187; **GDP growth:** 4.7%. **Imports:** $5.4 bil; China 39%, India 8%, Netherlands 6%. **Exports:** $10.3 bil; UAE 39%, China 36%, India 6%. **Tourism:** $13 mil. **Budget:** $2.0 bil. **Inflation:** 10.5%.

Transport: Railways: 675 mi. **Airports:** 4.

Communications: Mobile (2021): 101.9 per 100 pop. **Broadband** (2021): 23.4 per 100 pop. **Internet:** 34.7%.

Health: Expend.: 4.0%. **Life expect.:** 62.4 male; 66.2 female. **Births:** 35.5 per 1,000 pop. **Deaths:** 8.0 per 1,000 pop. **Infant mortality:** 48.3 per 1,000 live births. **Undernourished:** 12.9%. **HIV:** 1.4%. **COVID-19:** 38,563 cases, 468 deaths; rates per 100,000: 293.6 cases, 3.6 deaths. 36.0% vaccinated.

Education: Compulsory: ages 7-12. **Literacy:** 45.3%.

Website: www.primature.gov.gn

Guinea, a French colony, attained independence Oct. 2, 1958. Sékou Touré, Guinea's first president (1958-84), turned to Communist nations for support and set up a one-party state. Thousands of opponents were jailed and tortured, and many were killed in the 1970s after an unsuccessful Portuguese invasion.

The military took control in a bloodless coup after the Mar. 1984 death of Touré. A new constitution was approved in 1991, but movement toward democracy was slow. Gen. Lansana Conté, the incumbent, won a long-awaited presidential election in Dec. 1993, which outside monitors called flawed. Conté won reelection in 1998.

Major opposition parties boycotted the 2003 presidential election, in which the ailing Conté won 95.6% of the vote. More than 120 died in Jan.-Feb. 2007 strikes and protests that pressured Conté to name a new prime min.; protests followed Prime Min. Lansana Kouyate's ouster by Conté in May 2008. After Conté's death Dec. 22, a military junta took power. More than 150 people were reportedly killed Sept. 28, 2009, when Guinean troops fired into a crowd of about 50,000 anti-government protesters in Conakry. After an assassination attempt Dec. 3, 2009, by a former aide left Pres. Moussa Dadis Camara seriously wounded, Vice Pres. Sékouba Konaté became interim head of state.

Presidential elections June-Nov. 2010 brought a civilian government headed by Alpha Condé to power. He won reelection, Oct. 11, 2015. A new constitution, approved in a Mar. 22, 2020, referendum boycotted by the opposition, permitted Condé to seek a third term. He won a disputed Oct. 18, 2020, election. Demonstrations before and after election day left dozens dead. Condé was ousted in a Sept. 5, 2021, military coup led by Col. Mamady Doumbouya, who suspended the constitution and set up a transitional government.

The largest known outbreak of Ebola virus disease (EVD) began in Guinea in Dec. 2013 and spread rapidly to Liberia and Sierra Leone. By mid-2016, the WHO had recorded 28,616 EVD cases in the 3 countries (including 3,814 in Guinea) and 11,310 deaths (2,544 in Guinea).

Guinea-Bissau
Republic of Guinea-Bissau

People: Population: 2,078,820 (147). **Age distrib.:** <15: 42.5%; 65+: 3.1%. **Growth:** 2.5%. **Migrants:** 0.9%. **Pop. density:** 191.5 per sq mi, 73.9 per sq km. **Urban:** 45.5%. **Ethnic groups:** Balanta 30%, Fulani 30%, Manjaco 14%, Mandinga 13%, Papel 7%. **Languages:** Portuguese-based Creole, Portuguese (official), Pular, Mandingo. **Religions:** Muslim 45.8% (Sunni), ethnic religionist 39.7%, Christian 13.3% (Catholic 9.4%).

Geography: Total area: 13,948 sq mi, 36,125 sq km (134); **Land area:** 10,857 sq mi, 28,120 sq km. **Location:** Atlantic coast of W Africa. Senegal on N, Guinea on E and S. **Topography:** A swampy coastal plain covers most of country. Low savanna region to E. **Arable land:** 10.7%. **Capital:** Bissau, 664,446.

Government: Type: Semi-presidential republic. **Head of state:** Pres. Umaro Cissoko Embaló; b. 1972; in office: Feb. 27, 2020. **Head of govt.:** Prime Min. Geraldo Martins; in office: June 4, 2023. **Local divisions:** 9 regions. **Defense budget:** NA. **Active troops:** 4,450.

Economy: Industries: agric. prods. proc., beer, soft drinks. **Chief agric.:** rice, cashew nuts, roots/tubers, oil palm fruit, plantains, cassava. **Natural resources:** fish, timber, phosphates, bauxite, clay, granite, limestone. **Water:** 15,955 cu m per capita. **Electricity prod.:** 82.5 mil kWh. **Labor force:** agric. 50.3%, industry 10.5%, services 39.2%. **Unemployment:** 3.6%.

Finance: Monetary unit: CFA Franc (XOF) (606.88 = $1 U.S.). **GDP:** $4.6 bil; **per capita GDP:** $2,190; **GDP growth:** 3.5%. **Imports** (2020): $439.0 mil; Portugal 31%, Senegal 20%, China 10%, Netherlands 7%, Pakistan 7%. **Exports** (2020): $232.5 mil; India 50%, Belgium 28%, Côte d'Ivoire 8%. **Tourism** (2020): $3 mil. **Budget:** $278 mil. **Inflation:** 9.4%.

Transport: Airports: 2.
Communications: Mobile: 125.9 per 100 pop. **Broadband:** 62.5 per 100 pop. **Internet:** 35.2%.

Health: Expend.: 8.4%. **Life expect.:** 61.8 male; 66.4 female. **Births:** 36.3 per 1,000 pop. **Deaths:** 7.3 per 1,000 pop. **Infant mortality:** 47.7 per 1,000 live births. **Undernourished:** 37.9%. **HIV:** 2.4%. **COVID-19:** 9,614 cases, 177 deaths; rates per 100,000: 488.5 cases, 9.0 deaths. 27.1% vaccinated.

Education: Compulsory: ages 6-14. **Literacy:** 52.9%.
Website: www.gov.gw

Portuguese mariners explored the area in the mid-15th cent.; the slave trade flourished in the 17th and 18th cents., and colonization began in the 19th. Independence came Sept. 10, 1974, ending 13 years of guerrilla warfare against the Portuguese regime.

A Nov. 1980 coup gave army chief João Bernardo Vieira absolute power. Multiparty elections were held in 1994. A 1998 army uprising triggered a civil war; rebel troops ousted Vieira on May 7, 1999.

Civilian rule returned with 1999-2000 elections, but top military officers staged a coup Sept. 14, 2003. Vieira won a presidential runoff election, July 24, 2005. A group of soldiers murdered Vieira, Mar. 2, 2009. In the 2009 presidential election, the ruling party (PAIGC) candidate, Malam Bacai Sanhá, won a runoff vote July 26. He died Jan. 9, 2012. A coup was staged, Apr. 12, 2012. Drug trafficking increased substantially, with the support of the military. José Mário Vaz of the PAIGC won a May 18, 2014, presidential runoff. In a Dec. 29, 2019, presidential runoff, Umaro Sissoco Embaló defeated the candidate of the PAIGC, which disputed the result. Forces loyal to Embaló put down a coup attempt, Feb. 1, 2022. Accusing legislators of corruption, Embaló dissolved parliament, May 16, 2022. New elections, June 4, 2023, were won by a coalition headed by the PAIGC; Geraldo Martins of the PAIGC became prime min.

Guyana
Cooperative Republic of Guyana

People: Population: 791,739 (162). **Age distrib.:** <15: 23.7%; 65+: 7.9%. **Growth:** 0.3%. **Migrants:** 4.0%. **Pop. density:** 10.4 per sq mi, 4.0 per sq km. **Urban:** 27.2%. **Ethnic groups:** East Indian 39.8%, African descent 29.3%, mixed 19.9%, Amerindian 10.5%. **Languages:** English (official), Guyanese Creole, Amerindian langs., Indian langs., Chinese. **Religions:** Christian 54.6% (Protestant 34.2%, independent 11.7%), Hindu 30.2% (Saktist 14%, Vaishnavite 8%, Shaivite 8%), Muslim 7.9% (Sunni), ethnic religionist 2.1%.

Geography: Total area: 83,000 sq mi, 214,969 sq km (83); **Land area:** 76,004 sq mi, 196,849 sq km. **Location:** N coast of S America. Venezuela on W, Brazil on S, Suriname on E. **Topography:** Dense tropical forests cover much of land. A grassy savanna divides it from flat coastal area, where 90% of the pop. lives, with its rich alluvial soil. **Arable land:** 2.1%. **Capital:** Georgetown, 109,934.

Government: Type: Parliamentary republic. **Head of state and govt.:** Pres. Mohammed Irfaan Ali; b. 1980; in office: Aug. 2, 2020. **Local divisions:** 10 regions. **Defense budget:** $85 mil. **Active troops:** 3,400.

Economy: Industries: bauxite, sugar, rice milling, timber, textiles, gold mining. **Chief agric.:** rice, sugarcane, coconuts, pumpkins, squash, gourds. **Natural resources:** bauxite, gold, diamonds, hardwood timber, shrimp, fish. **Water:** 344,542 cu m per capita. **Electricity prod.:** 1.2 bil kWh. **Labor force:** agric. 13.1%, industry 25.4%, services 61.5%. **Unemployment:** 12.4%.

Finance: Monetary unit: Dollar (GYD) (209.04 = $1 U.S.). **GDP:** $32.9 bil; **per capita GDP:** $40,642; **GDP growth:** 57.8%. **Imports:** $6.6 bil; (2021) Singapore 33%, U.S. 19%, Trinidad and Tobago 12%, China 8%. **Exports:** $4.6 bil; (2021) U.S. 40%, Singapore 14%, UAE 6%, UK 6%, Barbados 6%. **Tourism:** $26 mil. **Budget:** $1.5 bil. **Inflation:** 6.1%.

Transport: Motor vehicles: 137.9 per 1,000 pop. **Airports:** 11.
Communications: Mobile (2021): 106.4 per 100 pop. **Broadband** (2021): 33.8 per 100 pop. **Internet:** 84.8%.

Health: Expend.: 5.5%. **Life expect.:** 70.3 male; 74.1 female. **Births:** 16.7 per 1,000 pop. **Deaths:** 7.0 per 1,000 pop. **Infant mortality:** 21.6 per 1,000 live births. **Undernourished:** <2.5%. **HIV:** 1.5%. **COVID-19:** 73,385 cases, 1,299 deaths; rates per 100,000: 9,330.0 cases, 165.2 deaths. 48.6% vaccinated.

Education: Compulsory: ages 6-11. **Literacy:** 88.9%.
Website: parliament.gov.gy

Guyana became a Dutch possession in the 17th cent., but sovereignty passed to Britain in 1815. Indentured servants from India soon outnumbered the enslaved African population. Guyana became independent May 26, 1966.

The Port Kaituma ambush of U.S. Rep. Leo J. Ryan and others investigating mistreatment of American followers of the Rev. Jim Jones's Peoples Temple cult triggered a mass suicide-execution of more than 900 at their commune in Jonestown, Nov. 18, 1978.

An Oct. 1992 election victory began more than two decades of People's Progressive Party/Civic (PPP/C) governance. An opposition coalition won May 11, 2015, elections, and coalition leader David Granger became president, May 16. Major offshore oil discoveries were announced in 2015-19. A Mar. 2, 2020, election returned the PPP/C to power.

Haiti
Republic of Haiti

People: Population: 11,470,261 (83). **Age distrib.:** <15: 30.9%; 65+: 4.2%. **Growth:** 1.2%. **Migrants:** 0.2%. **Pop. density:** 1,077.9 per sq mi, 416.2 per sq km. **Urban:** 59.7%. **Ethnic groups:** Black 95%, mixed and white 5%. **Languages:** French, Creole (both official). **Religions:** Christian 93.8% (Catholic [official] 66.5%, Protestant 19.8%), agnostic 3.2%, Spiritist 2.7%.

Geography: Total area: 10,714 sq mi, 27,750 sq km (144); **Land area:** 10,641 sq mi, 27,560 sq km. **Location:** In Caribbean; occupies western third of isl. of Hispaniola. Dominican Republic on E, Cuba to W. **Topography:** About two-thirds is mountainous. Much of rest is semiarid. Coastal areas are warm and moist. **Arable land:** 36.5%. **Capital:** Port-au-Prince, 2,987,455.

Government: Type: Semi-presidential republic. **Head of govt.:** Prime Min. Ariel Henry; b. 1949; in office: July 20, 2021. Henry also assumed duties as acting head of state until election can be held. **Local divisions:** 10 departments. **Defense budget:** $14 mil. **Active troops:** 700.

Economy: Industries: textiles, sugar refining, flour milling, cement, light assembly using imported parts. **Chief agric.:** sugarcane, cassava, mangoes/guavas, plantains, bananas, yams. **Natural resources:** bauxite, copper, calcium carbonate, gold, marble, hydropower. **Water:** 1,230 cu m per capita. **Electricity prod.:** 990.3 mil kWh. **Labor force:** agric. 45.6%, industry 12.4%, services 42.0%. **Unemployment:** 14.8%.

Finance: Monetary unit: Gourde (HTG) (136.09 = $1 U.S.). **GDP:** $38.3 bil; **per capita GDP:** $3,305; **GDP growth:** −1.7%. **Imports:** $5.2 bil; (2021) U.S. 26%, Dominican Republic 23%, China 19%. **Exports:** $1.2 bil; (2021) U.S. 83%. **Tourism:** $80 mil. **Budget** (2020): $1.5 bil. **Inflation:** 34.0%.

Transport: Motor vehicles: 9.7 per 1,000 pop. **Airports:** 4.
Communications: Mobile (2021): 63.9 per 100 pop. **Broadband** (2021): 28.2 per 100 pop. **Internet:** 38.9%.

Health: Expend.: 3.2%. **Life expect.:** 63.0 male; 66.7 female. **Births:** 21.5 per 1,000 pop. **Deaths:** 7.7 per 1,000 pop. **Infant mortality:** 38.8 per 1,000 live births. **Undernourished:** 45.0%. **HIV:** 1.7%. **COVID-19:** 34,301 cases, 860 deaths; rates per 100,000: 300.8 cases, 7.5 deaths. 3.1% vaccinated.

Education: Compulsory: ages 6-11. **Literacy:** 61.7%.
Website: www.primature.gouv.ht or www.haiti.org

Haiti, visited by Christopher Columbus in 1492 and a French colony from 1697, attained its independence, 1804, following a rebellion led by formerly enslaved Toussaint L'Ouverture. After a period of political violence, the U.S. occupied the country 1915-34.

François Duvalier, known as Papa Doc, was elected president in 1957; in 1964 he was named president for life. Upon his death in 1971, he was succeeded by his son, Jean Claude Duvalier, known as Baby Doc. Following weeks of unrest, Jean Claude fled Haiti aboard a U.S. Air Force jet Feb. 7, 1986. His departure ended the Duvalier family's brutal 28-year dictatorship, but political violence, corruption, poverty, AIDS, and other health problems have continued to plague Haiti.

Jean-Bertrand Aristide was elected president in 1990, but the military arrested and expelled him from the country in Sept. 1991. Tens of thousands of Haitian refugees tried to enter the U.S. in the early 1990s.

The UN authorized in 1994 an invasion of Haiti by a U.S.-led multinational force. A full-scale invasion was averted, Sept. 18, when military leaders agreed to step down. Aristide was restored to office Oct. 15. A UN peacekeeping force exercised responsibility in Haiti from 1995 to 1997. Aristide transferred power to his elected successor, René Préval, in 1996.

Aristide won the 2000 presidency in an election boycotted by opposition groups. An armed uprising in early 2004 and pressure from France and the U.S. toppled Aristide, who went into exile Feb. 29. A U.S.-led contingent, sent in after the upheaval, yielded authority June 1, 2004, to a UN stabilization force (MINUSTAH). MINUSTAH's mission ended Oct. 15, 2017.

Préval was again elected president in 2006. Skyrocketing prices for food imports sparked riots and mass protests in Apr. 2008. A succession of hurricanes and tropical storms, Aug.-Sept. 2008, left more than 550 Haitians dead and up to 1 mil homeless.

An earthquake Jan. 12, 2010, near Port-au-Prince caused cataclysmic damage. More than 220,000 people were killed, at least 300,000 were injured, and more than 1.5 mil were left homeless. In the following years, rebuilding proceeded slowly. A severe cholera epidemic began soon after the 2010 earthquake; through 2018, about 820,000 total cases had been reported and almost 9,800 people had died. The UN publicly acknowledged responsibility for the epidemic Dec. 1, 2016.

Michel Martelly, an entertainer, won a Mar. 20, 2011, presidential runoff election. After allegations of widespread fraud in the Oct. 25, 2015, first-round election for a new president, an electoral commission ruled that the balloting should be held again. The Nov. 20, 2016, re-vote was won by businessman Jovenel Moise. Protests against corruption and economic hardship occurred in 2019. Gang violence and anti-government protests plagued Haiti in early 2021.

Pres. Moise was assassinated, July 7, 2021, apparently by Colombian mercenaries. On July 20, 2021, Ariel Henry, designated by Moise shortly before the assassination to become prime minister, took office as prime minister and acting president. A powerful earthquake, Aug. 14, 2021, in SW Haiti killed more than 2,200 and caused widespread damage and suffering. Gang violence and kidnappings for ransom intensified in late 2021 and continued in 2022-23, accompanied by retaliatory violence against gang members. Severe food shortages afflicted millions of Haitians. A dual Haitian-Chilean citizen, charged in the U.S. with helping plan and finance the plot against Moise, pleaded guilty, Mar. 24, 2023. A retired Colombian army officer, facing a U.S. trial, pleaded guilty, Sept. 7, to supporting the assassination plot. The UN approved, Oct. 2, 2023, a Kenya-led mission in which Kenyan and other nations' security forces would work to reduce violence in Haiti.

Honduras
Republic of Honduras

People: Population: 9,571,352 (95). **Age distrib.:** <15: 29.1%; 65+: 5.5%. **Growth:** 1.2%. **Migrants:** 0.4%. **Pop. density:** 221.6 per sq mi, 85.5 per sq km. **Urban:** 60.2%. **Ethnic groups:** mestizo (mixed Amerindian/European) 90%, Amerindian 7%, African descent 2%. **Languages:** Spanish (official), Amerindian dialects. **Religions:** Christian 95.6% (Catholic [official] 70.3%, Protestant 17.3%), agnostic 2.2%.

Geography: Total area: 43,278 sq mi, 112,090 sq km (101); **Land area:** 43,201 sq mi, 111,890 sq km. **Location:** Central America. Guatemala on W; El Salvador, Nicaragua on S. **Topography:** Caribbean coast is 500 mi long. Pacific coast, on Gulf of Fonseca, is 40 mi long. Mountainous with wide fertile valleys and rich forests. **Arable land:** 9.1%. **Capital:** Tegucigalpa, 1,568,025.

Government: Type: Presidential republic. **Head of state and govt.:** Pres. Iris Xiomara Castro de Zelaya; b. 1959; in office: Jan. 27, 2022. **Local divisions:** 18 departments. **Defense budget:** $371 mil. **Active troops:** 14,950.

Economy: Industries: sugar proc., coffee, woven and knit apparel, wood prods., cigars. **Chief agric.:** sugarcane, oil palm fruit, milk, bananas, maize, coffee. **Natural resources:** timber, gold, silver, copper, lead, zinc, iron ore, antimony, coal, fish, hydropower. **Water:** 9,305 cu m per capita. **Electricity prod.:** 12.0 bil kWh. **Labor force:** agric. 24.8%, industry 23.3%, services 51.9%. **Unemployment:** 7.1%.

Finance: Monetary unit: Lempira (HNL) (24.62 = $1 U.S.). **GDP:** $70.3 bil; **per capita GDP:** $6,741; **GDP growth:** 4.0%. **Imports:** $14.5 bil; U.S. 42%, China 10%, Guatemala 8%, El Salvador 8%, Mexico 6%. **Exports:** $7.9 bil; U.S. 53%, El Salvador 8%. **Tourism:** $303 mil. **Budget:** $6.5 bil. **Inflation:** 9.1%.

Transport: Railways: 434 mi. **Motor vehicles:** 23.8 per 1,000 pop. **Airports:** 13.

Communications: Mobile: 76.1 per 100 pop. **Broadband:** 49.6 per 100 pop. **Internet:** 48.1%.

Health: Expend. (2021): 9.1%. **Life expect.:** 68.4 male; 75.5 female. **Births:** 20.2 per 1,000 pop. **Deaths:** 5.9 per 1,000 pop. **Infant mortality:** 15.4 per 1,000 live births. **Undernourished:** 18.7%. **HIV:** 0.2%. **COVID-19:** 474,566 cases, 11,127 deaths; rates per 100,000: 4,791.4 cases, 112.3 deaths. 58.1% vaccinated.

Education: Compulsory: ages 5-16. **Literacy:** 88.5%.

Website: www.presidencia.gob.hn

Mayan civilization flourished in Honduras in the 1st millennium CE. Columbus arrived in 1502. Honduras became independent after freeing itself from Spain, 1821, and from the Fed. of Central America, 1838.

In 1975, the army ousted Gen. Oswaldo Lopez Arellano, president for most of the time since 1963, over charges of pervasive bribery by United Brands Co. of the U.S. An elected civilian government took power in 1982.

Hurricane Mitch, Oct. 1998, killed at least 5,600.

Juan Orlando Hernández of the conservative National Party won the Nov. 2013 presidential election. He won reelection, Nov. 26, 2017.

Honduras has become a transshipment point for illegal drugs being smuggled to the U.S. Pres. Hernández's brother was convicted in the U.S., Oct. 18, 2019, of drug-related crimes. Drug-gang violence contributed to an increase in Hondurans trying to enter the U.S. along the Mexican border, 2013-23. A government-declared state of emergency, beginning Dec. 2022, to counter gang violence suspended some constitutional rights.

In Mar. 2016, environmental activist Berta Cáceres was shot to death, a murder apparently ordered by a company facing delays on a dam project. The NGO Global Witness estimated in mid-2017 that more than 120 environmental activists or opponents of land seizures for development had been killed since 2009.

Leftist Xiomara Castro won the Nov. 28, 2021, election to become Honduras's first woman president. Former Pres. Hernández was extradited to the U.S., Apr. 21, 2022, to face drug charges. The government announced, Mar. 25, 2023, that Honduras was switching diplomatic relations from Taiwan to the People's Republic of China.

Hungary

People: Population: 9,670,009 (94). **Age distrib.:** <15: 14.6%; 65+: 21.3%. **Growth:** −0.3%. **Migrants:** 6.1%. **Pop. density:** 279.5 per sq mi, 107.9 per sq km. **Urban:** 72.9%. **Ethnic groups:** Hungarian 85.6%, Romani 3.2% (probable undercount; may be 5%-10% of pop.). **Languages:** Hungarian (official), English, German. **Religions:** Christian 87.3% (Catholic 57.9%, Protestant 25.9%), agnostic 7.6%, atheist 4.0%.

Geography: Total area: 35,918 sq mi, 93,028 sq km (108); **Land area:** 34,598 sq mi, 89,608 sq km. **Location:** E central Europe. Ukraine, Slovakia on N; Austria on W; Slovenia, Croatia, Serbia on S; Romania on E. **Topography:** Danube R. forms Slovak border in NW, then swings S to bisect country. Eastern half of country is mainly a great fertile plain, the Alfold. Hilly in W and N. **Arable land:** 45.4%. **Capital:** Budapest, 1,778,052.

Government: Type: Parliamentary republic. **Head of state:** Pres. Katalin Novák; b. 1977; in office: May 10, 2022. **Head of govt.:** Prime Min. Viktor Orbán; b. 1963; in office: May 29, 2010. **Local divisions:** 19 counties, 23 cities with county rights, 1 capital city. **Defense budget:** $3.0 bil. **Active troops:** 32,150.

Economy: Industries: mining, metallurgy, constr. materials, processed foods, textiles, chemicals (espec. pharmaceuticals), motor vehicles. **Chief agric.:** maize, wheat, milk, sunflower seed, barley, rapeseed. **Natural resources:** bauxite, coal, nat. gas. **Water:** 10,766 cu m per capita. **Crude oil reserves:** 12 mil bbls. **Electricity prod.:** 34.2 bil kWh. **Labor force:** agric. 4.4%, industry 31.4%, services 64.2%. **Unemployment:** 3.4%.

Finance: Monetary unit: Forint (HUF) (355.03 = $1 U.S.). **GDP:** $405.8 bil; **per capita GDP:** $41,907; **GDP growth:** 4.6%. **Imports:** $147.6 bil; Germany 25%, China 6%, Poland 6%, Austria 6%. **Exports:** $148.2 bil; Germany 27%. **Tourism:** $4.1 bil. **Budget:** $74.1 bil. **Inflation:** 14.6%.

Transport: Railways: 4,776 mi. **Motor vehicles:** 471.7 per 1,000 pop. **Airports:** 20.

Communications: Mobile: 104.1 per 100 pop. **Broadband:** 81.6 per 100 pop. **Internet:** 90.5%.

Health: Expend.: 7.3%. **Life expect.:** 72.1 male; 78.7 female. **Births:** 9.2 per 1,000 pop. **Deaths:** 15.0 per 1,000 pop. **Infant mortality:** 4.8 per 1,000 live births. **Undernourished:** <2.5%. **HIV:** NA. **COVID-19:** 2,203,356 cases, 48,801 deaths; rates per 100,000: 22,553.4 cases, 499.5 deaths. 63.5% vaccinated.

Education: Compulsory: ages 4-16. **Literacy:** 99.1%.

Website: kormany.hu

Earliest settlers, chiefly Slav and Germanic, were overrun by Magyars from the east. Stephen I (997-1038) was made king by Pope Sylvester II in 1000 CE. The country suffered repeated Turkish invasions in the 15th-17th cents. After the Turks were defeated, 1686-97, Austria dominated, but Hungary obtained concessions, and regained internal independence in 1867 under a dual monarchy with the emperor of Austria. Defeated with the Central Powers at the end of WWI in 1918, Hungary lost Transylvania to Romania, Croatia and Bacska to Yugoslavia, and Slovakia and Carpatho-Ruthenia to Czechoslovakia. All had large Hungarian minorities. A republic under Michael Karolyi and a Bolshevist revolt under Bela Kun were followed by a vote for a monarchy in 1920 with Adm. Nicholas Horthy as regent.

Hungary allied with Germany before WWII and was allowed to annex, 1938-41, most of its lost territories. Russian troops captured the country, 1944-45. Hungary returned to its borders of 1937.

A republic was declared Feb. 1, 1946. In 1947 a hard-line Communist, pro-Soviet government was installed. Demonstrations against Communist rule developed into open revolt in 1956. Soviet forces launched a massive attack Nov. 4 against Budapest. About 200,000 persons fled the country. Thousands were arrested and executed.

Major economic reforms were launched early in 1968, switching from a central planning system to one based on market forces and profit. In 1989 Parliament legalized freedom of assembly and association as Hungary shifted away from Communism. In Oct. the Communist Party was formally dissolved. The last Soviet troops left June 19, 1991. Hungary became a full member of NATO in 1999 and of the EU in 2004.

The center-right Fidesz party ousted the Socialists in 2010 parliamentary elections, and Viktor Orbán became prime min.

A fiscally and socially conservative constitution went into force Jan. 1, 2012. Fidesz won Apr. 6, 2014, elections.

Hungary was a major transit route in 2015 for migrants from the Balkans, SW Asia, the Middle East, and Africa trying to reach N Europe; more than 411,000 migrants entered or tried to enter Hungary by the end of Oct., when Hungary completed more than 300 mi of security fencing along its southern border. The government refused to participate in a 2015 EU refugee resettlement program.

After an anti-immigration campaign, Fidesz increased its majority in Apr. 8, 2018, voting. The EU in 2018 began consideration of disciplinary measures against Hungary, in part over limits on press and other freedoms. Dec. 2018 Hungarian legislation limited judicial independence. Legislation in 2020 and 2021 repealed legal rights of transgender people and restricted information about gay people in educational materials or media for minors. The EU, in 2021, began withholding grant payments to Hungary.

Elected by parliament, Mar. 10, 2022, Fidesz's Katalin Novák became Hungary's first woman president. Benefitting from gerrymandering and media control, Fidesz won Apr. 3, 2022, elections. Citing Russia's Feb. 2022 invasion of Ukraine, Orbán declared a state of emergency, May 24, expanding his powers. High inflation plagued the economy in 2022-23.

Iceland

People: Population: 360,872 (172). **Age distrib.:** <15: 20.0%; 65+: 16.6%. **Growth:** 0.9%. **Migrants:** 19.2%. **Pop. density:** 9.3 per sq mi, 3.6 per sq km. **Urban:** 94.0%. **Ethnic groups** (by birth country): Icelandic 81.3%, Polish 5.6%. **Languages:** Icelandic, English, Nordic langs., German. **Religions:** Christian 91.6% (Protestant 79.6%), agnostic 5.7%.

Geography: Total area: 39,769 sq mi, 103,000 sq km (106). **Land area:** 38,707 sq mi, 100,250 sq km. **Location:** Isl. at N end of Atlantic O. Nearest neighbor is Greenland (Den.) to W. **Topography:** Recent volcanic origin. Three-quarters of surface is wasteland: glaciers, lakes, a lava desert, geysers, and hot springs. The climate is moderated by the Gulf Stream. **Arable land:** 1.2%. **Capital:** Reykjavik, 216,364.

Government: Type: Unitary parliamentary republic. **Head of state:** Pres. Gudni Thorlacius Johannesson; b. 1968; in office: Aug. 1, 2016. **Head of govt.:** Prime Min. Katrin Jakobsdottir; b. 1976; in office: Nov. 30, 2017. **Local divisions:** 64 municipalities. **Defense budget:** $42 mil (Coast Guard budget). **Active troops:** No armed forces; 250 Coast Guard. Relies on NATO allies for air policing and defense.

Economy: Industries: tourism, fish proc., aluminum smelting, geothermal power, hydropower, medical/pharmaceutical prods. **Chief agric.:** milk, mutton, poultry, potatoes, barley, pork. **Natural resources:** fish, hydropower, geothermal power, diatomite. **Water:** 498,179 cu m per capita. **Electricity prod.:** 19.3 bil kWh. **Labor force:** agric. 4.0%, industry 18.8%, services 77.1%. **Unemployment:** 3.8%.

Finance: Monetary unit: Krona (ISK) (131.65 = $1 U.S.). **GDP:** $26.4 bil; **per capita GDP:** $69,081; **GDP growth:** 6.4%. **Imports:** $10.2 bil; (2021) Norway 11%, Denmark 10%, Netherlands 9%, Germany 9%, China 7%. **Exports:** $9.8 bil; (2021) Netherlands 24%, Spain 10%, Germany 10%, UK 9%, U.S. 7%. **Tourism:** $1.3 bil. **Budget** (2018): $11.5 bil. **Inflation:** 8.3%.

Transport: Motor vehicles: 923.4 per 1,000 pop. **Airports:** 7. **Communications: Mobile:** 122.5 per 100 pop. **Broadband:** 126.1 per 100 pop. **Internet:** 99.7%.

Health: Expend. (2021): 9.7%. **Life expect.:** 81.6 male; 86.2 female. **Births:** 12.8 per 1,000 pop. **Deaths:** 6.6 per 1,000 pop. **Infant mortality:** 1.6 per 1,000 live births. **Undernourished:** <2.5%. **HIV:** 0.1%. **COVID-19:** 208,845 cases, 186 deaths; rates per 100,000: 57,353.9 cases, 51.1 deaths. 79.2% vaccinated.

Education: Compulsory: ages 6-15. **Literacy:** NA.

Website: www.government.is

Iceland was an independent republic from 930 to 1262, when it joined with Norway. Its language has maintained its purity for 1,000 years. The Althing, or assembly, established in 930, is the world's oldest surviving parliament. Danish rule lasted 1380-1918; the last ties with the Danish crown were severed in 1944.

Iceland's banking system and currency collapsed amid the global financial crisis in Oct. 2008. More than $10 bil in loans from the IMF and European governments restored financial stability; austerity measures were imposed, and the nation entered a deep recession. An Apr. 2010 eruption of the Eyjafjallajökull volcano disrupted European air traffic. Following Oct. 28, 2017, elections, Katrin Jakobsdottir of the Left-Green Movement became prime min., forming a coalition with center-right parties. The parties in Jakobsdottir's coalition won a majority in Sept. 25, 2021, elections.

Iceland's glaciers have been shrinking, an apparent effect of climate change.

India
Republic of India

People: Population: 1,399,179,585 (2). **Age distrib.:** <15: 24.8%; 65+: 6.8%. **Growth:** 0.7%. **Migrants:** 0.4%. **Pop. density:** 1,218.8 per sq mi, 470.6 per sq km. **Urban:** 36.4%. **Ethnic groups:** Indo-Aryan 72%, Dravidian 25%. **Languages:** Hindi (most widely spoken); 22 other official langs. (incl. Bengali, Marathi, Telugu, Tamil, Gujarati, Urdu); English (subsidiary official lang.; most important for natl., political, commercial communication); Hindustani (variant of Hindi/Urdu widely spoken throughout N). **Religions:** Hindu 71.7% (Vaishnavite 27%, Shaivite 26%, Saktist 19%), Muslim 15.1% (Sunni), Christian 5.1%, ethnic religionist 3.6%, Sikh 1.8%, agnostic 1.2%.

Geography: Total area: 1,269,219 sq mi, 3,287,263 sq km (7). **Land area:** 1,147,956 sq mi, 2,973,193 sq km. **Location:** Occupies most of Indian subcontinent in S Asia. Pakistan on W; China, Nepal, Bhutan on N; Myanmar, Bangladesh on E. **Topography:** The Himalayan Mts., highest in world, stretch across northern borders. The Ganges Plain below is among the world's most densely populated regions. The climate varies from tropical heat in S to near-Arctic cold in N. Rajasthan Desert in NW. NE Assam Hills get 400 in. of rain a year. **Arable land:** 51.9%. **Capital:** Delhi, 32,941,309. **Cities:** Mumbai (Bombay), 21,296,517; Kolkata (Calcutta), 15,332,793; Bangalore, 13,607,800; Chennai (Madras), 11,776,147; Hyderabad, 10,801,163; Ahmadabad, 8,650,605; Surat, 8,064,949; Pune (Poona), 7,166,374.

Government: Type: Federal parliamentary republic. **Head of state:** Pres. Droupadi Murmu; b. 1958; in office: July 25, 2022. **Head of govt.:** Prime Min. Narendra Modi; b. 1950; in office: May 26, 2014. **Local divisions:** 28 states, 8 union territories. **Defense budget:** $66.6 bil. **Active troops:** 1,463,700.

Economy: Industries: textiles, chemicals, food proc., steel, transp. equip., cement, mining, petroleum, machinery, software, pharmaceuticals. **Chief agric.:** sugarcane, rice, wheat, buffalo milk, milk, potatoes. **Natural resources:** coal, antimony, iron ore, lead, manganese, mica, bauxite, rare earth elements, titanium ore, chromite, nat. gas, diamonds, petroleum, limestone. **Water:** 1,385 cu m per capita. **Crude oil reserves:** 4.6 bil bbls. **Electricity prod.:** 1.7 tril kWh. **Labor force:** agric. 44.0%, industry 25.3%, services 30.7%. **Unemployment:** 7.3%.

Finance: Monetary unit: Rupee (INR) (82.62 = $1 U.S.). **GDP:** $11.9 tril; **per capita GDP:** $8,379; **GDP growth:** 7.0%. **Imports:** $717.1 bil; China 15%, U.S. 7%, UAE 6%. **Exports:** $643.1 bil; U.S. 17%, UAE 9%. **Tourism:** $8.8 bil. **Budget** (2020): $818.9 bil. **Inflation:** 6.7%.

Transport: Railways: 40,733 mi. **Motor vehicles:** 58.9 per 1,000 pop. **Airports:** 253.

Communications: Mobile: 80.6 per 100 pop. **Broadband:** 56.5 per 100 pop. **Internet:** 46.3%.

Health: Expend.: 3.0%. **Life expect.:** 66.0 male; 69.6 female. **Births:** 16.5 per 1,000 pop. **Deaths:** 9.7 per 1,000 pop. **Infant mortality:** 30.4 per 1,000 live births. **Undernourished:** 16.6%. **HIV:** 0.2%. **COVID-19:** 44,996,599 cases, 531,925 deaths; rates per 100,000: 3,260.6 cases, 38.5 deaths. 69.0% vaccinated.

Education: Compulsory: ages 6-13. **Literacy:** 74.4%.

Website: www.india.gov.in

India has one of the oldest civilizations in the world. Excavations trace the Indus Valley civilization back for at least 5,000 years. Paintings in the mountain caves of Ajanta, richly carved temples, the Taj Mahal in Agra, and the Kutab Minar in Delhi are among treasured relics of the past.

Aryan tribes, speaking Sanskrit, invaded from the NW around 1500 BCE. Asoka ruled most of the Indian subcontinent in the 3rd cent. BCE and established Buddhism. But Hinduism revived and eventually predominated. Under the Guptas, 4th-6th cent. CE, science, literature, and the arts enjoyed a golden age. Arab invaders established a Muslim foothold in the west in the 8th cent., and Turkish Muslims gained control of North India by 1200. The Mughal emperors ruled 1526-1857.

Vasco da Gama established Portuguese trading posts 1498-1503. The Dutch followed. The British East India Co. sent Capt. William Hawkins, 1609, to get concessions from the Mughal emperor for spices and textiles. Operating as the East India Co., the British gained control of most of India. The British parliament assumed political direction; under Lord Bentinck, 1828-35, rule by rajahs (princes) was curbed. After the Sepoy troops mutinied, 1857-58, the British supported the native rulers.

Nationalism grew after WWI. The Indian National Congress and the Muslim League demanded constitutional reform. A leader emerged in Mohandas K. Gandhi (called Mahatma, or Great Soul) (b. Oct. 2, 1869), who advocated self-rule, nonviolence, and an end to caste discrimination against "untouchables." In 1930 he launched a program of civil disobedience, boycotting British goods and rejecting taxes without representation. He was assassinated Jan. 30, 1948.

In 1935, Britain gave India a constitution providing a bicameral federal congress. Muhammad Ali Jinnah, head of the Muslim League, sought creation of a Muslim nation, Pakistan.

The British government partitioned British India into the dominions of India and Pakistan. India became a member of the UN in 1945, a self-governing member of the Commonwealth in 1947, and a democratic republic, Jan. 26, 1950. More than 12 mil Hindu and Muslim refugees crossed the India-Pakistan borders in 1947; about 200,000 were killed in communal fighting.

After Pakistan troops began attacks on Bengali separatists in East Pakistan, Mar. 25, 1971, some 10 mil refugees fled to India. India and Pakistan went to war Dec. 3, 1971, on both the east and west fronts. Pakistan troops, Dec. 16, surrendered in the east, which became Bangladesh; Pakistan agreed to a cease-fire in the west Dec. 17.

Indira Gandhi, India's prime minister since Jan. 1966, invoked emergency powers in June 1975. Thousands of opponents were arrested and press censorship imposed. These and other actions, including population control through forced vasectomies, were widely resented. Opposition parties, united in the Janata coalition, won the 1977 elections.

Gandhi became prime minister for the second time in 1980. She was assassinated by two of her Sikh bodyguards Oct. 31, 1984, in response to the government suppression in June 1984 of a Sikh uprising in Punjab, which included an assault on the Golden Temple at Amritsar, the holiest Sikh shrine. Widespread rioting followed the assassination; thousands of Sikhs were killed and some 50,000 left homeless. Rajiv, India Gandhi's son, replaced her as prime min. A gas leak at a Union Carbide chemical plant in Bhopal, Dec. 1984, eventually killed some 14,000 people.

Many died in religious, ethnic, and political conflicts during the late 1980s and early '90s. To suppress the Sikh insurgency in Punjab, Indian government troops attacked the Golden Temple again in 1988. Rajiv Gandhi, swept from office in 1989, was assassinated May 21, 1991. Nationwide riots followed the destruction of a 16th-cent. mosque in Ayodhya by Hindu militants in Dec. 1992. Ethnic clashes in Assam, in NE India, killed thousands in Feb. 1993. Bombs jolted Mumbai and Kolkata, Mar. 12-19, killing over 300.

India conducted a series of nuclear tests in mid-May 1998, raising tensions with Pakistan. India blamed Pakistani-sponsored terrorist groups for an Oct. 1, 2001, suicide attack on the state legislature in Jammu and Kashmir (see below), in which at least 40 people died, and a Dec. 13 assault on the Indian parliament in New Delhi that left 13 people dead. Hindu-Muslim clashes in Gujarat Feb.-Mar. 2002 claimed more than 1,000 lives.

The Congress Party won the most seats in 2004 parliamentary elections.

The Indian Ocean tsunami of Dec. 26, 2004, left more than 16,000 people dead and over 647,000 displaced in India. Islamic extremists set off 7 bombs on commuter trains in Mumbai, July 11, 2006, killing some 200 people.

Chandrayaan-1, India's first lunar survey mission, was launched into space Oct. 22, 2008. *Chandrayaan-3* was the first mission from any nation to make a soft landing, Aug. 23, 2023, in the Moon's south polar region.

Ten Pakistanis linked to a Kashmir militant group stormed several sites in Mumbai, Nov. 2008, killing 163 people.

In 2009 parliamentary elections, the United Progressive Alliance, headed by the Congress Party, gained a resounding victory. Electricity blackouts July 30-31, 2012, left 670 mil people without power.

Several rapes in New Delhi in Nov.-Dec. 2012 prompted protests for their mishandling by police and government inaction. Tougher laws against sexual violence were passed Feb. 4, 2013. The Hindu nationalist Bharatiya Janata party (BJP) won a large majority in Apr.-May 2014 parliamentary elections; Narendra Modi became prime min.

Development of high-tech industries has propelled rapid economic growth in most years since the 1990s; hundreds of millions have emerged from extreme poverty, although distribution of wealth remains highly uneven. Since 2011, India has had the world's third-largest GDP. To combat climate change, the government released a plan, Oct. 1, 2015, for reducing the rate of growth in India's carbon emissions.

The Supreme Court, Sept. 6, 2018, struck down a 19th-cent. law that made consensual gay sex a criminal offense. The BJP increased its majority in Apr.-May 2019 elections. A check of citizenship status in Assam produced a list, released Aug. 31, 2019, of 1.9 mil people, mostly Muslim ethnic Bengalis, judged to be non-citizens and subject to deportation. Dec. 2019 legislation facilitating citizenship provoked Muslims. On Aug. 5, 2020, Modi participated in a groundbreaking ceremony for a Hindu temple on the site of the destroyed Ayodhya mosque. Anti-Muslim violence increased in the early 2020s.

A Sept. 22, 2021, Supreme Court ruling opened India's elite military academy to women. In one of the country's worst rail disasters, more than 290 people died in a multi-train accident, June 2, 2023, in the eastern state of Odisha. In the northeastern state of Manipur, ethnic violence beginning in May 2023 left about 200 dead by Sept. and displaced tens of thousands.

Severe heatwaves, likely related to climate change, gripped northern India in the 2020s.

The COVID-19 pandemic that began in 2020 impacted India more severely than almost any other country. Spikes in new cases at times overwhelmed the health care system. By Aug. 2023, India had recorded about 45 mil confirmed cases (3rd-highest in the world). A WHO report released in May 2022 estimated that India had more than 4.7 mil excess deaths in 2020-21 associated with COVID-19.

According to UN estimates, India's population surpassed China's in 2023, making India the world's most populous nation.

Sikkim, bordered by Tibet, Bhutan, and Nepal, formerly British protected, became a protectorate of India in 1950. Area 2,740 sq mi; pop. (2011 census) 610,577; capital is Gangtok. In Sept. 1974, India's parliament voted to make Sikkim an associate Indian state, absorbing it into India.

Kashmir is a predominantly Muslim region in the NW that borders India, Pakistan, Afghanistan, and China. Muslim rule of the previously Hindu kingdom began in 1341; after almost 200 years under the Mughals, the area was incorporated into British India in 1846. Fighting broke out in the region between India and Pakistan in 1947 following independence from Britain. A cease-fire was negotiated by the UN Jan. 1, 1949; it gave Pakistan control of one-third of the area as Azad Kashmir, in the W and NW, and India the remaining two-thirds, as the Indian state of Jammu and Kashmir. Area 39,146 sq mi; pop. (2011 census) 12,541,302. Capitals: Srinagar (summer), pop. (2023 est.) 1,698,277; Jammu (winter), pop. (2023 est.) 726,618. Fighting in the area resumed during 1965 and 1971. China occupied about 14,000 sq mi in the Ladakh district after a war with India in 1962. India separated Ladakh from Jammu and Kashmir in 2019. On June 15, 2020, at least 20 Indian soldiers were killed in fighting with Chinese troops in a disputed border area of Ladakh.

Since 1989, Indian security forces in Jammu and Kashmir have battled Islamic separatist fighters. India has charged Pakistan with aiding the separatists. A cease-fire between Indian and Pakistani troops along the line of control took effect Nov. 2003. Some breaches occurred, and fighting between Indian forces and Islamic militants has continued. After a period of intense cross-border shelling, India and Pakistan agreed on a new cease-fire, May 29, 2018. More than 40 Indian paramilitary troops in Kashmir were killed in a terrorist bombing, Feb. 14, 2019. India and Pakistan, Feb. 25, 2021, recommitted to uphold a cease-fire. Estimates of conflict-related deaths since 1989 range from 40,000 to over 80,000.

The Indian government revoked statehood for Jammu and Kashmir, effective Oct. 31, 2019, to create two federally administered territories; India increased security forces and reportedly detained thousands.

France, 1952-54, peacefully yielded to India its five colonies, former French India: Pondicherry, Karikal, Mahe, and Yanaon were merged to become Pondicherry, now Puducherry, area 185 sq mi; pop. (2011 census) 1,247,953. The colony of Chandernagor was incorporated into the state of West Bengal.

Indonesia
Republic of Indonesia

People: Population: 279,476,346 (4). **Age distrib.:** <15: 24.2%; 65+: 7.7%. **Growth:** 0.8%. **Migrants:** 0.1%. **Pop. density:** 399.6 per sq mi, 154.3 per sq km. **Urban:** 58.6%. **Ethnic groups:** Javanese 40.1%, Sundanese 15.5%, Malay 3.7%, Batak 3.6%, Madurese 3%, Betawi 2.9%, Minangkabau 2.7%, Buginese 2.7%, Bantenese 2%. **Languages:** Bahasa Indonesia (official; modified form of Malay), English, Dutch, local dialects (Javanese most widely spoken). **Religions:** Muslim 79.6% (Sunni), Christian 12.3%, ethnic religionist 2.0%.

Geography: Total area: 735,358 sq mi, 1,904,569 sq km (14); **Land area:** 699,451 sq mi, 1,811,569 sq km. **Location:** Archipelago SE of Asian mainland along the equator. Malaysia on N, Papua New Guinea on E, Timor-Leste on S. **Topography:** Comprises 17,508 islands (about 6,000 inhabited), incl. Java, Sumatra, Kalimantan (most of Borneo), Sulawesi (Celebes), and West Irian (Irian Jaya, the W half of New Guinea). Also Bangka, billiton, Madura, Bali, Timor. Cooler climate in mountains and plateaus on the major isls.; tropical lowlands. **Arable land:** 13.9%. **Capital:** Jakarta, 11,248,839 (new capital of Nusantara is expected to be established in Aug. 2024). **Cities:** Bekasi, 3,729,351; Surabaya, 3,044,413; Depok, 3,041,229; Bandung, 2,674,000; Tangerang, 2,514,077.

Government: Type: Presidential republic. **Head of state and govt.:** Pres. Joko Widodo; b. 1961; in office: Oct. 20, 2014. **Local divisions:** 35 provinces, 1 autonomous province, 1 special region, 1 national capital district. **Defense budget:** $9.1 bil. **Active troops:** 395,500.

Economy: Industries: petroleum and nat. gas, textiles, automotive, elec. appliances, apparel, footwear, mining, cement, medical instruments and appliances. **Chief agric.:** oil palm fruit, rice, maize, sugarcane, coconuts, cassava. **Natural resources:** petroleum, tin, nat. gas, nickel, timber, bauxite, copper, coal, gold, silver. **Water:** 7,380 cu m per capita. **Crude oil reserves:** 2.5 bil bbls. **Electricity prod.:** 306.6 bil kWh. **Labor force:** agric. 29.0%, industry 21.8%, services 49.3%. **Unemployment:** 3.6%.

Finance: Monetary unit: Rupiah (IDR) (15,258.19 = $1 U.S.). **GDP:** $4.0 tril; **per capita GDP:** $14,653; **GDP growth:** 5.3%. **Imports:** $217.7 bil; China 27%, Singapore 12%, Japan 8%. **Exports:** $246.9 bil; China 15%, U.S. 10%, Japan 9%, Singapore 8%, India 7%. **Tourism:** $521 mil. **Budget** (2020): $193.0 bil. **Inflation:** 4.2%.

Transport: Railways: 5,070 mi (only partly operational). **Motor vehicles:** 82.7 per 1,000 pop. **Airports:** 186.

Communications: Mobile: 114.9 per 100 pop. **Broadband:** 91.1 per 100 pop. **Internet:** 66.5%.

Health: Expend.: 3.4%. **Life expect.:** 71.1 male; 75.7 female. **Births:** 15.1 per 1,000 pop. **Deaths:** 6.8 per 1,000 pop. **Infant mortality:** 19.3 per 1,000 live births. **Undernourished:** 5.9%. **HIV:** 0.3%. **COVID-19:** 6,813,095 cases, 161,916 deaths; rates per 100,000: 2,490.9 cases, 59.2 deaths. 63.9% vaccinated.

Education: Compulsory: ages 7-15. **Literacy:** 96.0%.

Website: www.indonesia.go.id

Hindu and Buddhist civilization from India reached Indonesia nearly 2,000 years ago, taking root especially in Java. Islam spread along the maritime trade routes in the 15th cent. and became predominant by the 16th cent. The Dutch replaced the Portuguese as the area's most important European trade power in the 17th cent., securing territorial control over Java by 1750. The other islands were subdued in the early 20th cent.

Following Japanese occupation, 1942-45, nationalists led by Sukarno and Hatta declared independence. The Netherlands ceded sovereignty in 1949. A republic was declared, Aug. 17, 1950, with Sukarno as president.

Irian Jaya, on New Guinea, remained under Dutch control but was transferred by the UN to Indonesia in 1963; it became the provinces of Papua and West Papua in the early 2000s. Pro-independence protests and an armed separatist movement were met by a harsh government crackdown in the late 2010s and early 2020s, including allegations of atrocities against civilians. Tens of thousands were displaced.

Sukarno suspended parliament in 1960 and was named president for life in 1963. He made close alliances with Communist governments. In Sept. 1965 an attempted coup was successfully put down, but Sukarno was forced to cede power to the army, led by Gen. Suharto. The regime blamed the coup on the Communist Party; more than 300,000 alleged Communists were killed in army-initiated massacres.

Parliament reelected Suharto to a seventh consecutive presidential term in 1998, as a severe economic downturn focused public anger on nepotism, cronyism, and corruption in the Suharto regime. Suharto resigned May 21, 1998. Abdurrahman Wahid, leader of Indonesia's largest Muslim organization, was elected president in 1999. In Aug. 2000, under pressure from the legislature, he agreed to share power with Vice Pres. Megawati Sukarnoputri, the daughter of the late Pres. Sukarno. Charging Wahid with incompetence and corruption, the legislature ousted him July 23, 2001, and Megawati became Indonesia's first woman president.

Clashes between Muslims and Christians in the Maluku (Molucca) Isls., 1999-2002, claimed about 5,000 lives. East Timor, a former Portuguese colony that Indonesia invaded in Dec. 1975 and controlled until Oct. 1999, became a fully independent country May 20, 2002, as Timor-Leste.

Separatists in Aceh, NW Sumatra, fought government troops, 1980s-2000s. A peace agreement granting Aceh greater autonomy was signed Aug. 15, 2005. Aceh adopted a strict penal code based on sharia law and sometimes enforced by vigilantes; prohibited conduct was punished by public canings.

Investigators blamed Islamic terrorists for bombings that killed 202 people, mostly foreign tourists, at nightclubs in Bali, Oct. 12, 2002, and 12 people at a Marriott hotel in Jakarta, Aug. 5, 2003. Susilo Bambang Yudhoyono, a retired general, defeated Megawati in a 2004 direct presidential runoff vote.

A massive earthquake off NW Sumatra, Dec. 26, 2004, triggered tsunamis that wreaked havoc in the Indian Ocean region. The death toll in Indonesia alone exceeded 165,000.

Pres. Yudhoyono won a second 5-year term July 8, 2009.

The General Elections Commission, July 22, 2014, declared populist Jakarta governor Joko Widodo the presidential election winner. All 162 people aboard an AirAsia Indonesia flight were killed, Dec. 28, 2014, when the plane crashed into the Java Sea near Borneo.

Assaults by terrorist gunmen and bombers in Jakarta, Jan. 14, 2016, left 8 dead, including 4 attackers; ISIS claimed responsibility. A series of ISIS-inspired suicide bombings at churches and attacks on police, May 2018, left 13 victims dead.

Rainforest destruction and air pollution from fires to clear areas for agriculture have been major environmental problems in recent years.

All 189 on board an Indonesian Lion Air flight were killed, Oct. 29, 2018, when the Boeing 737 Max 8 plane crashed shortly after takeoff from Jakarta.

Pres. Widodo won reelection in Apr. 17, 2019, voting.

In Malang, more than 130 people died after police fired tear gas at unruly soccer fans, Oct. 1, 2022, touching off panic and stampedes. Dec. 2022 penal code revisions criminalized extramarital sex and limited free expression.

The COVID-19 pandemic that began in 2020 had a devastating impact in Indonesia. A 2022 WHO report estimated more than 1 mil excess deaths in Indonesia in 2020-21, far exceeding the recorded death toll from COVID-19.

Iran
Islamic Republic of Iran

People: Population: 87,590,873 (17). **Age distrib.:** <15: 23.5%; 65+: 6.7%. **Growth:** 0.9%. **Migrants:** 3.3%. **Pop. density:** 148.1 per sq mi, 57.2 per sq km. **Urban:** 77.3%. **Ethnic groups:** Persian, Azeri, Kurd, Lur, Baloch, Arab, Turkmen, Turkic tribes. **Languages:** Persian Farsi (official), Azeri and other Turkic dialects, Kurdish, Gilaki and Mazandarani, Luri, Balochi, Arabic. **Religions:** Muslim 98.5% (Shia [official] 81%, Sunni 17%).

Geography: Total area: 636,372 sq mi, 1,648,195 sq km (17). **Land area:** 591,352 sq mi, 1,531,595 sq km. **Location:** Between the Middle East and S Asia. Iraq, Turkey on W; Armenia, Azerbaijan, Turkmenistan on N; Afghanistan, Pakistan on E. **Topography:** Interior highlands and plains surrounded by high mountains, up to 18,000 ft. Large salt deserts cover much of area; some oases and forests. Most of pop. inhabits N and NW. **Arable land:** 9.7%. **Capital:** Tehran, 9,499,781. **Cities:** Mashhad, 3,367,852; Esfahan, 2,258,396; Shiraz, 1,720,954; Tabriz, 1,660,737; Karaj, 1,593,608.

Government: Type: Theocratic republic. **Religious head:** Ayatollah Sayyed Ali Khamenei; b. 1939; in office: June 4, 1989. **Head of state and govt.:** Pres. Ebrahim Raisi; b. 1960; in office: Aug. 5, 2021. **Local divisions:** 31 provinces. **Defense budget:** $44.0 bil. **Active troops:** 610,000.

Economy: Industries: petroleum, petrochemicals, gas, fertilizer, caustic soda, textiles, cement and other constr. materials. **Chief agric.:** wheat, sugarcane, milk, sugar beet, tomatoes, barley. **Natural resources:** petroleum, nat. gas, coal, chromium, copper, iron ore, lead, manganese, zinc, sulfur. **Water:** 1,632 cu m per capita. **Crude oil reserves:** 208.6 bil bbls. **Electricity prod.:** 340.9 bil kWh. **Labor force:** agric. 16.3%, industry 34.4%, services 49.4%. **Unemployment:** 11.0%.

Finance: Monetary unit: Rial (IRR) (42,135.33 = $1 U.S.). **GDP:** $1.6 tril; per capita GDP: $18,075; **GDP growth:** 2.7%. **Imports** (2017): $76.4 bil; China 28%, UAE 20%, India 11%, Turkey 7%, Brazil 6%. **Exports** (2017): $101.4 bil; China 48%, India 12%, South Korea 8%, Turkey 6%. **Budget:** $90.2 bil. **Inflation** (2020-21): 43.4%.

Transport: Railways: 5,271 mi. **Motor vehicles:** 82.8 per 1,000 pop. **Airports:** 140.

Communications: Mobile: 164.5 per 100 pop. **Broadband:** 115.6 per 100 pop. **Internet:** 78.6%.

Health: Expend.: 5.3%. **Life expect.:** 74.1 male; 76.9 female. **Births:** 14.8 per 1,000 pop. **Deaths:** 5.2 per 1,000 pop. **Infant mortality:** 14.6 per 1,000 live births. **Undernourished:** 6.1%. **HIV:** <0.1%. **COVID-19:** 7,613,468 cases, 146,321 deaths; rates per 100,000: 9,064.4 cases, 174.2 deaths. 69.7% vaccinated.

Education: Compulsory: ages 6-14. **Literacy:** 88.7%.

Website: www.president.ir

Ancestors of inhabitants of Iran, formerly known as Persia, came from the east during the second millennium BCE; they were an Indo-European group related to the Aryans of India. In 549 BCE, Cyrus the Great united the Medes and Persians in the Persian Empire; he conquered Babylonia in 538 BCE, and restored Jerusalem to the Jews. Alexander the Great conquered Persia in 333 BCE, but Persians regained independence in the next century under the Parthians, themselves succeeded by Sassanian Persians in 226 CE. Arabs brought Islam to Persia in the 7th cent., replacing the indigenous Zoroastrian faith. After Persian political and cultural autonomy was reasserted in the 9th cent., arts and sciences flourished.

Turks and Mongols ruled Persia in turn from the 11th cent. to 1502, when Ismael I established the Iranian Safavid dynasty and made Shiite Islam the official religion. The dynasty lasted until 1722. The British and Russian empires vied for influence in the 19th cent.; Britain severed Afghanistan from Iran in 1857.

Reza Khan, a military officer, became prime min., 1923, and shah in 1925. He began modernization, curbed foreign influence, and officially changed the country's name from Persia to Iran in 1935. Fearing the shah's Axis sympathies, British and Soviet troops forced him to abdicate, 1941; he was succeeded by his son, Mohammad Reza Pahlavi. The U.S. Central Intelligence Agency had a major role in the ouster, 1953, of Prime Min. Muhammad Mossadegh, who had nationalized the oil industry.

With U.S. backing, the shah brought economic and social change to Iran (White Revolution), but repression of opposition groups grew severe. Violent protests in 1978 eventually forced the shah to depart, Jan. 16, 1979 (he died in Egypt, July 27, 1980). Forces loyal to Shiite leader Ayatollah Ruhollah Khomeini defeated government troops, Feb 11, 1979. Khomeini established an Islamic theocracy.

Iranian militants seized the U.S. embassy in Tehran Nov. 4, 1979, and took hostages, including 62 Americans. Despite international condemnations and U.S. efforts, including an abortive Apr. 1980 rescue attempt, the crisis continued until Jan. 20, 1981, when an accord, involving the release of frozen Iranian assets, was reached.

War between Iran and Iraq, 1980-88, killed hundreds of thousands. In Nov. 1986 it became known that the U.S., which had generally sided with Iraq during the war, had secretly shipped arms to Iran to gain help in obtaining the release of U.S. hostages held in Lebanon.

A U.S. Navy warship shot down an Iranian airliner, July 3, 1988, after mistaking it for an F-14 fighter jet; all 290 aboard died.

An earthquake struck northern Iran June 21, 1990, killing more than 45,000 and leaving 400,000 homeless. Some 1 mil Kurdish refugees fled from Iraq to Iran following the Persian Gulf War of 1991. To curb Iran's alleged support for international terrorism, the U.S. in 1996 authorized sanctions on foreign companies that invested there.

An earthquake Dec. 26, 2003, in Bam, SE Iran, killed about 26,000 people.

The religiously conservative mayor of Tehran, Mahmoud Ahmadinejad, defeated former Pres. Hashemi Rafsanjani in a 2005 runoff election. U.S. Pres. George W. Bush's administration accused Iran of seeking to build nuclear weapons, aiding Shiite militias opposing government forces in the U.S.-led war in Iraq (2003-11), and supplying rockets to Hezbollah fighters in Lebanon for use against Israel.

Seeking to halt Iran's uranium-enrichment program, the UN Security Council imposed sanctions, 2006-07.

Ahmadinejad won the 2009 presidential election. His main opponent claimed the vote count was fraudulent. Huge post-election protests were crushed. Tensions with the U.S. and European governments were heightened in 2009 by disclosures that Iran had been secretly enriching uranium and by Iranian tests of medium-range missiles.

The UN and U.S. toughened sanctions, June-July 2010. Iran accused Israel, the U.S., and other Western powers of carrying out cyberattacks against the country's nuclear facilities and of assassinating Iranian scientists. Iran announced, Jan. 2012, it was enriching uranium at its underground Fordo nuclear facility.

The moderate cleric Hassan Rouhani was elected president June 14, 2013. An agreement—signed July 14, 2015, by the U.S., UK, France, Germany, Russia, China, Iran, and the EU—required Iran to limit and partly dismantle its nuclear program and submit to international inspections in return for the lifting of most sanctions. Rouhani won reelection as president, May 19, 2017. Large-scale protests, mainly against poor economic conditions, occurred in dozens of cities around Iran, Dec. 2017-Jan. 2018, until suppressed by forces of the Islamic Revolutionary Guard Corps (IRGC). Pres. Donald Trump announced, May 8, 2018, that the U.S. would withdraw from the 2015 nuclear agreement and reimpose U.S. sanctions. Beginning in July 2019, Iran took nuclear program actions in violation of the 2015 accord.

The U.S. blamed Iran for 2019 attacks on oil tankers in the Persian Gulf region. Attacks continued in subsequent years.

Playing a role in regional conflicts, Iran supported the Syrian government in its civil war, beginning 2012, and Shiite militia forces in Iraq, beginning 2014. The U.S. and Saudi Arabia blamed Iran for Sept. 14, 2019, drone and cruise missile strikes on two Saudi oil facilities; Iranian-backed Houthi rebels in Yemen had claimed responsibility. Widespread demonstrations protesting economic conditions were suppressed, Nov. 2019; up to 1,500 protesters may have been killed.

A U.S. drone strike in Iraq, Jan. 3, 2020, killed IRGC general Qassem Soleimani, in charge of the corps' foreign operations. Iran, Jan. 7, fired missiles at two Iraqi military bases housing U.S. troops. On Jan. 8, Iran mistakenly shot down a Ukrainian airliner shortly after its takeoff from Tehran, killing all 176 onboard.

An explosion and fire caused extensive damage, July 2, 2020, at a key Iranian nuclear facility; Israeli sabotage was suspected. Similar disasters occurred, 2020-21, at Iranian industrial, nuclear, and infrastructure sites or aboard warships. A leading Iranian nuclear scientist was assassinated, Nov. 27, 2020.

Iran was hard-hit by the COVID-19 pandemic that began in 2020; health care facilities were at times severely strained.

In an election marked by low turnout, hardliner Ebrahim Raisi was elected president, June 18, 2021.

The death in custody, Sept. 16, 2022, of a woman arrested for a dress-code violation sparked nationwide, sometimes violent protests, met with a lethal response by security forces. As protests continued in 2023, thousands of schoolgirls were victims of poisoning attacks early in the year. Iran's parliament approved, Sept. 20, 2023, legislation toughening penalties for dress-code violations.

After Chinese-mediated talks, Iran and Saudi Arabia announced, Mar. 10, 2023, they would restore diplomatic relations (severed in 2016). Following lengthy negotiations, Iran released, Sept. 18, 2023, 5 imprisoned Americans; the U.S. unfroze $6 bil of Iranian assets, to be used for humanitarian purposes, and dropped sanctions-related charges against 5 Iranians.

Iraq
Republic of Iraq

People: Population: 41,266,109 (36). **Age distrib.:** <15: 35.2%; 65+: 3.6%. **Growth:** 1.9%. **Migrants:** 0.9%. **Pop. density:** 244.4 per sq mi, 94.4 per sq km. **Urban:** 71.6%. **Ethnic groups:** Arab 75%-80%, Kurdish 15%-20%, other (incl. Turkmen, Yezidi, Shabak, Kaka'i) 5%. **Languages:** Arabic, Kurdish (both official); Turkmen, Syriac. **Religions:** Muslim (official) 97.7% (Shia 62%, Sunni 35%).

Geography: Total area: 169,235 sq mi, 438,317 sq km (58); **Land area:** 168,868 sq mi, 437,367 sq km. **Location:** Middle East, occupying most of historic Mesopotamia. Jordan, Syria on W; Turkey on N; Iran on E; Kuwait, Saudi Arabia on S. **Topography:** Mostly an alluvial plain, including the Tigris and Euphrates Rivers, descending from mountains in N to desert in SW. Persian Gulf region is marshland. **Arable land:** 11.4%. **Capital:** Baghdad, 7,711,305. **Cities:** Mosul, 1,792,020; Basra, 1,448,124; Kirkuk, 1,074,884.

Government: Type: Federal parliamentary republic. **Head of state:** Pres. Abdul Latif Rashid; b. 1944; in office Oct. 13, 2022. **Head of govt.:** Prime Min. Mohammed Shia al-Sudani; b. 1970; in office: Oct. 27, 2022. **Local divisions:** 18 governorates (3 administered by Kurdistan Regional Govt.). **Defense budget:** $8.7 bil. **Active troops:** 193,000.

Economy: Industries: petroleum, chemicals, textiles, leather, constr. materials, food proc., fertilizer, metal fabrication/proc. **Chief agric.:** wheat, barley, dates, tomatoes, rice, maize. **Natural resources:** petroleum, nat. gas, phosphates, sulfur. **Water:** 2,234 cu m per capita. **Crude oil reserves:** 145 bil bbls. **Electricity prod.:** 97.3 bil kWh. **Labor force:** agric. 19.8%, industry 21.3%, services 58.9%. **Unemployment:** 15.5%.

Finance: Monetary unit: Dinar (IQD) (1,309.39 = $1 U.S.). **GDP:** $483.3 bil; **per capita GDP:** $10,862; **GDP growth:** 7.0%. **Imports:** $50.7 bil; UAE 28%, Turkey 21%, China 19%. **Exports:** $78.3 bil; China 26%, India 24%, South Korea 9%, U.S. 8%, Italy 6%, Greece 6%. **Tourism:** $2.0 bil. **Budget** (2020): $85.5 bil. **Inflation:** 5.0%.

Transport: Railways: 1,412 mi. **Motor vehicles:** 72.9 per 1,000 pop. **Airports:** 72.

Communications: Mobile: 98.2 per 100 pop. **Broadband:** 46.2 per 100 pop. **Internet:** 78.7%.

Health: Expend.: 5.1%. **Life expect.:** 71.6 male; 75.4 female. **Births:** 24.2 per 1,000 pop. **Deaths:** 3.9 per 1,000 pop. **Infant mortality:** 19.2 per 1,000 live births. **Undernourished:** 16.3%. **HIV:** <0.1%. **COVID-19:** 2,465,545 cases, 25,375 deaths; rates per 100,000: 6,129.8 cases, 63.1 deaths. 19.8% vaccinated.

Education: Compulsory: ages 6-11. **Literacy:** 85.6%.

Website: www.pmo.iq

The Tigris-Euphrates valley, formerly called Mesopotamia, was the site of one of the earliest civilizations in the world. Mesopotamia ceased to be a separate entity after Persian, Greek, and Arab conquests. The Arabs founded Baghdad, from where the caliph ruled a vast Islamic empire in the 8th and 9th cents. Mongol and Turkish conquests led to a decline in the region's population, economy, cultural life, and irrigation system.

Britain secured a League of Nations mandate over Iraq after WWI. Independence under a king came in 1932. Rebellious army officers killed King Faisal II, July 1958, and established a leftist, pan-Arab republic. The Baath Arab Socialist Party increasingly dominated successive regimes. A Baath leader, Saddam Hussein, became president in 1979. He ruled as a dictator for more than two decades, repressing Iraq's Kurds and Shiites. Israeli planes destroyed a nuclear reactor near Baghdad in 1981, claiming it could be used to produce nuclear weapons.

After skirmishing intermittently for 10 months, Iraq and Iran entered into open warfare on Sept. 22, 1980. Iran repulsed early Iraqi advances, producing a long and costly stalemate; hundreds of thousands of Iraqis lost their lives during the 8-year conflict. Saddam used poison gas against Iraqi Kurds in 1988, killing more than 5,000 people in Halabja, the first mass use of poison gas against civilians since the Holocaust.

Iraq invaded Kuwait in 1990. Backed by the UN, a U.S.-led coalition launched air and missile attacks on Iraq, Jan. 16, 1991, and began a ground attack to retake Kuwait Feb. 23. Iraqi forces were defeated in four days. Some 175,000 Iraqis were taken prisoner, and Iraqi casualties were estimated at over 85,000. As part of the cease-fire agreement, Iraq agreed to scrap all poison gas and germ weapons and allow UN observers to inspect the sites.

Iraq cooperation with UN weapons inspection teams was intermittent throughout the 1990s. Standoffs over inspections culminated in intensive U.S. and British aerial bombardment of Iraqi military targets, Dec. 16-19, 1998. After two years of sporadic activity, U.S. and British warplanes struck sites near Baghdad mid-Feb. 2001.

Despite opposition from some countries, including France, Germany, and Russia, a U.S.-led coalition invaded Iraq Mar. 19, 2003. By Apr. 6 the British controlled Basra and other areas in the south, and the U.S. entered Baghdad Apr. 7. Saddam disappeared, the Iraqi government collapsed, and most of Iraq's armed forces dissolved into the civilian population. On May 1, U.S. Pres. George W. Bush declared the end of major combat. Searches failed to find chemical, biological, or nuclear weapons that the U.S. and other countries claimed Iraq had stockpiled.

The U.S.-led Coalition Provisional Authority was unable to maintain order following Saddam's fall. Reconstruction efforts were hampered by guerrilla attacks from Baath remnants, Islamic extremists, and others. U.S. troops killed two of Saddam's sons, Uday and Qusay, July 22, 2003, in Mosul. Saddam Hussein was captured in an underground hideout mid-Dec. 2003; tried and convicted for committing crimes against humanity in the 1980s, he was executed Dec. 30, 2006.

Photographs released in Apr. 2004 showed instances of physical abuse and sexual humiliation of Iraqi inmates by U.S. military personnel at Baghdad's Abu Ghraib prison in 2003.

On June 28, 2004, U.S. authorities transferred sovereignty to a transitional Iraqi government. Despite insurgent threats, an estimated 8 mil people in Iraq, mostly Shiites and Kurds, cast ballots Jan. 30, 2005, for a transitional national assembly. Insurgents launched new waves of attacks. Rumors of a suicide bomber set off a stampede by Shiite pilgrims in northern Baghdad Aug. 31, killing close to 1,000 people. The U.S. blamed Jordanian militant Abu Musab al-Zarqawi, leader of al-Qaeda in Iraq, for directing a series of kidnappings, beheadings, and suicide bombings. He was killed by a U.S. airstrike, June 2006.

A new government elected in legislative elections Dec. 15, 2005, was installed May 20, 2006, headed by Shiite leader Nouri Kamel al-Maliki. The Iraqi civilian death toll averaged more than 2,800 per month in 2006.

A 2007 "surge" elevated U.S. troop strength from 132,000 in Jan. to 171,000 in Oct. Military and civilian casualties began dropping after mid-2007. A cease-fire by Shiite militias and a shift by Sunni clan leaders against al-Qaeda in Iraq contributed to the reduction in violence.

A Nov. 2008 agreement called for all U.S. forces to leave Iraq by Dec. 31, 2011. Inconclusive legislative elections were held Mar. 7, 2010. On Aug. 31, Pres. Barack Obama formally declared an end to the U.S. combat role, and Operation Iraqi Freedom was succeeded by Operation New Dawn. More than 9 months of political deadlock ended when Prime Min. Maliki was sworn in for a second term Dec. 21.

U.S. troops completed their withdrawal from Iraq Dec. 15, 2011. From Mar. 2003 through Dec. 2011, more than 4,500 U.S. service members died in operations in Iraq; another 32,000 were wounded. British troop losses totaled 179; other allies, 139. More than 115,000 Iraqi civilians and over 10,000 police and security forces were killed. U.S. budgeted costs of the Iraq war exceeded $820 bil for the 2003-12 period.

Tensions manifested between Sunnis and Shiites after the U.S. departure. The Sunni insurgent group al-Qaeda in Iraq was blamed for ongoing violence. About 25,000 civilians were killed, 2012-14.

In parliamentary elections Apr. 30, 2014, Maliki's coalition won the largest bloc of seats. Shiite Haider al-Abadi, of Maliki's Dawa Party, became prime min. Sept. 8.

In Dec. 2013, the Sunni extremist Islamic State in Iraq and Syria (ISIS) began crossing from Syria into Iraq and seizing territory. The ISIS offensive intensified beginning in June 2014. The group took control of large areas of northern and central Iraq, including the cities of Mosul (Iraq's second-largest) and Tikrit, where ISIS killed 1,700 captured Shiite soldiers. ISIS imposed Islamic law, with harsh punishments, in areas it controlled while suppressing, killing, and sexually assaulting civilians who were non-Sunni Muslims or members of the Yazidi sect and other religious minorities. (Nadia Murad, a Yazidi sexual assault survivor, shared the 2018 Nobel Peace Prize for her activism against sexual violence in war.) The U.S., later joined by other nations, began, Aug. 8, 2014, airstrikes against ISIS targets; the U.S. provided military aid, including ground troops (beginning in 2014), to Iraqi government forces and Kurdish fighters opposing ISIS.

Forces fighting ISIS in 2015-17 included government troops, Shiite militias (often backed by Iran), Sunni tribal militias, and Kurdish troops. Kurdish fighters made gains in northern Iraq, and government and Shiite forces completed recapturing Tikrit, Apr. 1, 2015. Abadi proclaimed the recapture of Mosul, July 9, 2017, and announced, Dec. 9, that all ISIS territory in Iraq had been retaken. However, thousands of ISIS fighters remained in the country, attacking civilians and security forces.

In a Sept. 25, 2017, referendum, called by the Kurdistan Regional Government—but deemed illegal by the Iraqi government—92.7% of participants voted for Kurdistan's independence from Iraq. Iraqi government and Shiite-militia forces responded by driving Kurdish troops from territory outside the Kurdistan autonomous region that the Kurds had occupied during the fight against ISIS.

The U.S. deactivated, Apr. 30, 2018, its land forces command in Baghdad, but more than 5,000 U.S. troops remained in Iraq—reduced to about 2,500 by late 2020. Combat missions by U.S. troops were officially ended in 2021.

Following May 12, 2018, parliamentary elections, on Oct. 2, 2018, parliament elected Kurdish politician Barham Salih as president, and Shiite consensus candidate Adel Abdul Mahdi was designated prime min. After protests against economic conditions, corruption, and Iranian influence—in which hundreds were killed by security forces—the prime min. resigned, Nov. 29, 2019. Protests continued into 2020. Iran-backed militia forces attacked the U.S. embassy in Baghdad, Dec. 31, 2019. Mustafa al-Kadhimi became prime min., May 7, 2020.

In Oct. 10, 2021, parliamentary elections, the Sadrist Movement of Shiite leader Muqtada al-Sadr won the largest bloc of seats. Political disputes blocked formation of a new government, and pro-Sadr demonstrators clashed violently with security forces and pro-Iran Shiite militias. A new government was approved by parliament Oct. 27, 2022; Mohammed Shia al-Sudani became prime minister, heading a coalition of pro-Iran groups. Kurdish politician Abdul Latif Rashid was elected president by parliament, Oct. 13, 2022.

At least 119 died when fire swept through a building, near Mosul, Sept. 26, 2023, crowded with people celebrating a wedding.

Ireland

People: Population: 5,323,991 (122). **Age distrib.:** <15: 19.0%; 65+: 15.5%. **Growth:** 0.9%. **Migrants:** 17.6%. **Pop. density:** 200.2 per sq mi, 77.3 per sq km. **Urban:** 64.5%. **Ethnic groups:** Irish 82.2%, other white 9.5%, Asian 2.1%. **Languages:** English (official; generally used), Irish (Gaelic or Gaeilge) (official; spoken mainly along W coast). **Religions:** Christian 90.2% (Catholic 84.6%), agnostic 7.4%, Muslim 1.6% (Sunni).

Geography: Total area: 27,133 sq mi, 70,273 sq km (118); **Land area:** 26,596 sq mi, 68,883 sq km. **Location:** Atlantic O. just W of Great Britain. Northern Ireland (UK) on E. **Topography:** Central plateau surrounded by isolated groups of hills and mountains. Heavily indented Atlantic coastline. **Arable land:** 6.3%. **Capital:** Dublin, 1,270,172.

Government: Type: Parliamentary republic. **Head of state:** Pres. Michael D. Higgins; b. 1941; in office: Nov. 11, 2011. **Head of govt.:** Prime Min. Leo Varadkar; b. 1979; in office: Dec. 17, 2022. **Local divisions:** 28 counties, 3 cities. **Defense budget:** $1.2 bil. **Active troops:** 8,200.

Economy: Industries: pharmaceuticals, chemicals, computer hardware and software, food prods., beverages and brewing, medical devices. **Chief agric.:** milk, barley, beef, wheat, potatoes, pork. **Natural resources:** nat. gas, peat, copper, lead, zinc, silver, barite, gypsum, limestone, dolomite. **Water:** 10,531 cu m per capita. **Electricity prod.:** 33.6 bil kWh. **Labor force:** agric. 4.5%, industry 18.8%, services 76.7%. **Unemployment:** 4.4%.

Finance: Monetary unit: Euro (EUR) (0.93 = $1 U.S.). **GDP:** $645.6 bil; **per capita GDP:** $126,905; **GDP growth:** 12.0%. **Imports:** $477.5 bil; UK 31%, U.S. 16%, Germany 10%. **Exports:** $677.0 bil; U.S. 28%, Belgium 10%, Germany 10%, UK 9%. **Tourism:** $2.7 bil. **Budget:** $97.7 bil. **Inflation:** 7.8%.

Transport: Railways: 1,049 mi. **Motor vehicles:** 534.1 per 1,000 pop. **Airports:** 16.

Communications: Mobile: 113.3 per 100 pop. **Broadband:** 118.1 per 100 pop. **Internet:** 95.2%.

Health: Expend. (2021): 6.7%. **Life expect.:** 80.5 male; 84.1 female. **Births:** 11.3 per 1,000 pop. **Deaths:** 7.1 per 1,000 pop. **Infant mortality:** 3.2 per 1,000 live births. **Undernourished:** <2.5%. **HIV:** NA. **COVID-19:** 1,716,606 cases, 9,148 deaths; rates per 100,000: 34,578.0 cases, 184.3 deaths. 80.3% vaccinated.

Education: Compulsory: ages 6-15. **Literacy:** NA.

Website: www.gov.ie

Celtic tribes invaded the islands about the 4th cent. bce; their Gaelic culture and literature flourished in the 5th cent. ce, the same century in which St. Patrick converted the Irish to Christianity. Norse invasions began in the 8th cent., ending with defeat of the Danes by the Irish King Brian Boru in 1014. English invasions started in the 12th cent. For over 700 years the Anglo-Irish struggle continued with bitter rebellions and savage repressions. In the Irish Potato Famine, failure of the staple potato crop, 1845-49, caused 1 mil deaths from starvation and related diseases; up to 2 mil people emigrated, many to the U.S.

The Easter Monday Rebellion in 1916 failed but was followed by guerrilla warfare and harsh reprisals by British troops called the Black and Tans. The Dail Eireann (Irish parliament) reaffirmed independence in Jan. 1919. The British offered dominion status to Ulster (6 counties) and southern Ireland (26 counties) Dec. 1921. The constitution of the Irish Free State, a British dominion, was adopted Dec. 11, 1922. Northern Ireland remained part of the UK (see United Kingdom—Northern Ireland).

A new constitution adopted by plebiscite came into operation Dec. 29, 1937. It declared the name of the state Eire in the Irish language (Ireland in the English) and declared it a sovereign democratic state. On Dec. 21, 1948, the country was declared a republic rather than a dominion and withdrew from the Commonwealth. The British Parliament recognized both actions, 1949, but the six northeastern counties remained in the UK.

Irish governments have favored peaceful unification of all Ireland and cooperated with Britain against terrorist groups. After negotiators in Northern Ireland approved a peace settlement on Good Friday, Apr. 10, 1998, voters in the Irish Republic endorsed the accord, on May 22, and the Irish gave up their constitution's territorial claims on the north.

Expansion of educational opportunities and foreign investment in high-tech industries in the 1990s boosted Ireland's prosperity. In 1990, Mary Robinson became Ireland's first woman president.

Responding to allegations of child sex abuse by Catholic clergy in Ireland, Pope Benedict XVI issued a public apology to victims and their families Mar. 2010.

After a 2008-10 financial crisis, the EU approved an 85-bil euro emergency loan package that obligated Ireland to impose unpopular austerity measures. Fianna Fáil, the party that had dominated Irish politics since the 1930s, was defeated in Feb. 2011 elections, and Enda Kenny of the center-right Fine Gael became prime minister. Leo Varadkar of Fine Gael succeeded Kenny, June 14, 2017. Inconclusive Feb. 8, 2020, elections saw the nationalist Sinn Féin party make gains. On June 27, a coalition government of Fianna Fáil, Fine Gael, and the Green Party took office, initially headed by Fianna Fáil's Micheál Martin; in a pre-agreed rotation, he was succeeded by Varadkar Dec. 17, 2022.

In a national referendum, May 22, 2015, voters legalized same-sex marriage. In a May 25, 2018, referendum, voters essentially legalized almost all abortions.

Israel
State of Israel

People: Population: 9,043,387 (98). **Age distrib.:** <15: 27.6%; 65+: 12.1%. **Growth:** 1.4%. **Migrants:** 22.6%. **Pop. density:** 1,089.6 per sq mi, 420.7 per sq km. **Urban:** 92.9%. **Ethnic groups:** Jewish 74% (Israel-born 78.7%, Europe/America/Oceania-born 14.8%, Africa-born 4.2%, Asia-born 2.3%), Arab 21.1%. **Languages:** Hebrew (official), Arabic, English. **Religions:** Jewish (official) 70.8%, Muslim 20.6% (Sunni), agnostic 5.4%, Christian 2.0%.
Geography: Total area: 8,470 sq mi, 21,937 sq km (149); **Land area:** 8,300 sq mi, 21,497 sq km. **Location:** Middle East, on E end of Mediterranean Sea. Lebanon on N; Syria, West Bank, Jordan on E; Gaza Strip, Egypt on W. **Topography:** The Mediterranean coastal plain is fertile and well-watered. Judean Plateau in center. Semi-desert Negev region extends to apex at head of Gulf of Aqaba. The E border drops sharply into the Jordan Rift Valley, which incl. Lake Tiberias (Sea of Galilee) and the Dead Sea (1,339 ft below sea level), lowest point in Asia. **Arable land:** 17.4%.
Capital: Jerusalem, 969,804. **Cities:** Tel Aviv-Yafo, 4,420,855; Haifa, 1,174,429.
Government: Type: Parliamentary democracy. **Head of state:** Pres. Isaac Herzog; b. 1960; in office: July 7, 2021. **Head of govt.:** Prime Min. Benjamin Netanyahu; b. 1949; in office: Dec. 29, 2022. **Local divisions:** 6 districts. **Defense budget:** $19.4 bil. **Active troops:** 169,500.
Economy: Industries: high-tech prods. (incl. aviation, communications, computer-aided design and manufactures, medical electronics, fiber optics), wood and paper prods. **Chief agric.:** milk, potatoes, poultry, tomatoes, carrots, turnips. **Natural resources:** timber, potash, copper ore, nat. gas, phosphate rock, magnesium bromide, clays, sand. **Water:** 206 cu m per capita. **Crude oil reserves:** 13 mil bbls. **Electricity prod.:** 73.1 bil kWh. **Labor force:** agric. 0.9%, industry 17.0%, services 82.1%. **Unemployment:** 3.5%.
Finance: Monetary unit: Shekel (ILS) (3.80 = $1 U.S.). **GDP:** $472.8 bil; **per capita GDP:** $49,509; **GDP growth:** 6.5%. **Imports:** $124.6 bil; (2020) U.S. 12%, China 11%, Germany 7.5%, Switzerland 7%, Turkey 6%. **Exports:** $143.9 bil; (2021) U.S. 27%, China 8% (approx. 6% of exports to Gaza Strip and the West Bank). **Tourism:** $2.2 bil. **Budget:** $154.9 bil. **Inflation:** 4.4%.
Transport: Railways: 930 mi. **Motor vehicles:** 419.4 per 1,000 pop. **Airports:** 33.
Communications: Mobile: 152.2 per 100 pop. **Broadband** (2021): 123.6 per 100 pop. **Internet:** 90.3%.
Health: Expend.: 8.3%. **Life expect.:** 80.2 male; 84.3 female. **Births:** 19.3 per 1,000 pop. **Deaths:** 5.6 per 1,000 pop. **Infant mortality:** 3.0 per 1,000 live births. **Undernourished:** <2.5%. **HIV:** NA. **COVID-19:** 4,833,089 cases, 12,625 deaths; rates per 100,000: 55,838.1 cases, 145.9 deaths. 71.7% vaccinated.
Education: Compulsory: ages 3-17. **Literacy:** 97.8%.
Website: www.gov.il

Occupying the southwest corner of the ancient Fertile Crescent, Israel contains some of the oldest known evidence of agriculture and of primitive town life. The Hebrews probably arrived early in the 2nd millennium BCE. Under King David and his successors (c. 1000 BCE-597 BCE), Judaism was developed and secured. After conquest by Babylonians, Persians, and Greeks, an independent Jewish kingdom was revived, 168 BCE, but Rome took over in the next century, suppressed Jewish revolts in 70 CE and 135 CE, and renamed Judea Palestine, after the earlier coastal inhabitants, the Philistines.

Arab invaders conquered Palestine in 636. The Arabic language and Islam prevailed within a few centuries, but a Jewish minority remained. The land was ruled from the 11th cent. as a part of non-Arab empires (Seljuks, Mamluks, and Ottomans (with a Crusader interval, 1098-1291).

After four centuries of Ottoman rule, the land was taken in 1917 by Britain, which pledged in the Balfour Declaration to support a Jewish homeland there. In 1920 a British Palestine Mandate was recognized; in 1922 the land east of the Jordan R. was detached.

Jewish immigration, begun in the late 19th cent., swelled in the 1930s and 1940s with refugees from Nazi Germany and survivors of the Holocaust; heavy Arab immigration from Syria and Lebanon also occurred. Arab opposition to Jewish immigration turned violent in 1920, 1921, 1929, and 1936. The UN General Assembly voted in 1947 to partition Palestine into an Arab and a Jewish state. Britain withdrew in May 1948.

Israel was declared independent May 14, 1948; Arabs rejected partition. Egypt, Jordan, Syria, Lebanon, Iraq, and Saudi Arabia invaded but failed to destroy the Jewish state, which gained territory. Separate armistices with the Arab nations were signed in

1949; Jordan occupied the West Bank, Egypt occupied Gaza. Neither granted Palestinian autonomy.

After persistent terrorist raids, Israel invaded Egypt's Sinai, Oct. 29, 1956, aided briefly by British and French forces. A UN cease-fire was arranged Nov. 6.

An uneasy truce between Israel and the Arab countries lasted until 1967, when Egypt reoccupied the Gaza Strip and closed the Gulf of Aqaba to Israeli shipping. In the Six-Day War, starting June 5, the Israelis took the Gaza Strip, occupied the Sinai Peninsula to the Suez Canal, and captured East Jerusalem, Syria's Golan Heights, and Jordan's West Bank.

Egypt and Syria attacked Israel, Oct. 6, 1973 (Yom Kippur, the most solemn day in the Jewish calendar). Israel counterattacked, driving the Syrians back, and crossed the Suez Canal. A cease-fire took effect Oct. 24 and a UN peacekeeping force arrived. Under a 1974 disengagement agreement, Israel withdrew from the canal's west bank. Israeli forces raided Entebbe, Uganda, in 1976 and rescued 103 hostages who had been seized by Arab and German terrorists.

Israel's prime ministers, including David Ben-Gurion, Golda Meir, and Yitzhak Rabin, pursued a moderate socialist program, 1948-77. In 1977, the conservative opposition, led by Menachem Begin, was voted into office for the first time. Egypt's Pres. Anwar al-Sadat visited Jerusalem in 1977, and on Mar. 26, 1979, Egypt and Israel signed a formal peace treaty, ending 30 years of war. Israel returned the Sinai to Egypt in 1982.

Israeli forces invaded Lebanon, June 6, 1982, to destroy Palestine Liberation Organization (PLO) strongholds. After massive Israeli bombing of West Beirut, the PLO agreed to evacuate the city. Israeli troops entered West Beirut Sept. 14. Israel drew widespread condemnation when Lebanese Christian forces, Sept. 16, entered two West Beirut refugee camps and slaughtered hundreds of Palestinians.

In 1989, violence escalated over the Israeli military occupation of the West Bank and Gaza Strip. In a series of uprisings known as the first intifada, Palestinian protesters defied Israeli troops, who forcibly retaliated.

Ongoing peace talks led to historic agreements between Israel and the PLO, Sept. 1993. The PLO recognized Israel's right to exist; Israel recognized the PLO as the Palestinians' representative. The two sides then signed, Sept. 13, an agreement (known as the Oslo Accord) for limited Palestinian self-rule in the West Bank and Gaza. A follow-up Sept. 1995 agreement (Oslo II) essentially divided the West Bank into areas under Israeli or Palestinian control. Israel and Jordan signed, July 25, 1994, in Washington, DC, a declaration ending their 46-year state of war.

On Nov. 4, 1995, an Orthodox Jewish Israeli assassinated Labor Party Prime Min. Yitzhak Rabin in Tel Aviv. Support for Rabin's successor, Shimon Peres, was shaken by a series of suicide bombings and rocket attacks by Islamic militants. Emphasizing security issues, the candidate of the conservative Likud bloc, Benjamin Netanyahu, was elected prime minister on May 29, 1996.

Under an interim accord signed by Netanyahu and PLO leader Yasir Arafat, Oct. 23, 1998, Israel agreed to yield more West Bank territory to the Palestinians, in exchange for new security guarantees. After May 1999 elections, the Labor Party's Ehud Barak replaced Netanyahu as prime minister.

Israel pulled virtually all its troops out of southern Lebanon in May 2000. Marathon summit talks in the U.S. between Barak and Arafat, July 11-25, failed. A second intifada began in late Sept. in Israel and the Palestinian territories. Barak called new elections for prime minister but lost Feb. 2001 to Ariel Sharon, a hardliner. The bloodshed intensified during the summer, as Palestinian suicide bombers attacked Israeli civilians, and Israel struck at Palestinian-controlled territory attempting to assassinate suspected terrorists.

Israel launched a major West Bank offensive Mar. 29, 2002, two days after a suicide bomber killed 26 Israeli Jews at a Passover celebration in Netanya. Palestinian-Israeli violence in the West Bank has flared periodically in subsequent years.

Sharon's decision to pull all Israeli settlers and troops out of Gaza was approved by the cabinet Feb. 2005. Sharon and Deputy Prime Min. Ehud Olmert then formed the centrist Kadima Party. Sharon suffered a massive stroke Jan. 4, 2006. Olmert became prime minister, led Kadima to victory in Mar. elections, and formed a broad coalition government.

Clashes in mid-2006 along the Gaza and Lebanon borders rapidly escalated into full-scale war. By Aug. 14, a UN-sponsored cease-fire had taken hold. Olmert, targeted in multiple corruption inquiries, announced his resignation July 30, 2008. (He was convicted on bribery charges, 2014 and 2015.) After a campaign overshadowed by a three-week war between Israel and Hamas in Gaza, both Kadima and Likud fell far short of a majority in Feb. 2009 elections. On Mar. 31, Netanyahu became prime min. for a second time.

Israel's relations with allies were strained when the Israeli government announced in Mar. 2010 that it would build 1,600 homes in Ramat Shlomo (a Jewish settlement in mostly Arab East Jerusalem) and when 10 Turkish pro-Palestinian activists died as a result of clashes with Israeli commandos May 31 on board the Mavi Marmara, part of a flotilla seeking to break Israel's blockade of Gaza.

SCIENCE & TECHNOLOGY

STEP BY STEP Gert-Jan Oskam, a Dutch man paralyzed below the waist by a spinal cord injury for over a decade, regained the ability to walk via implanted electrodes; researchers announced the breakthrough in *Nature*, May 24, 2023.

BIG ISLAND ERUPTION For the first time in nearly four decades, the world's biggest active volcano, Mauna Loa on the island of Hawaii, erupted in late 2022.

WATCH THIS SPACE Canadian Space Agency astronaut Jeremy Hansen and NASA astronauts Victor Glover, Reid Wiseman, and Christina Koch were expected to crew *Artemis II*, NASA's 10-day mission around the moon, in Nov. 2024.

LOST AT SEA The submersible *Titan* June 18, 2023, lost contact just 1 hour, 45 minutes after commencing its dive in the North Atlantic to the wreckage of the *Titanic*; a massive international search was launched but all five aboard were killed.

SPORTS

MOST VALUABLE MAHOMES QB Patrick Mahomes threw three touchdown passes and ran for 44 yards in Kansas City's 38-35 Super Bowl win over Philadelphia, Feb. 12, 2023.

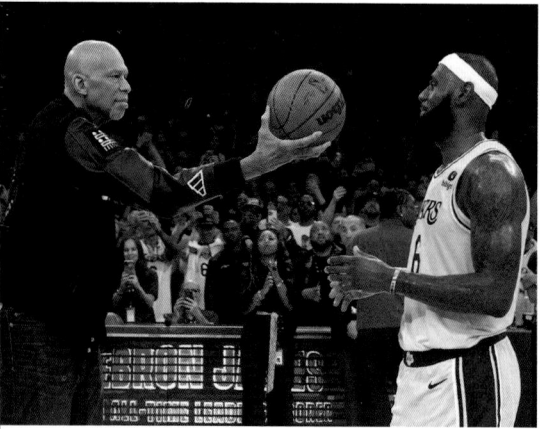

PASSING THE BALL With his 38,388th point, LeBron James claimed the all-time NBA points record from fellow Laker star Kareem Abdul-Jabbar on Feb. 7, 2023, in Los Angeles.

TWO IN A ROW Bulldogs quarterback Stetson Bennett IV was credited with six touchdowns in Georgia's thrashing of TCU, 65-7, in the CFP Championship Game Jan. 9, 2023.

WORLD CUP HERO Playing in his fifth FIFA World Cup, superstar Lionel Messi finally claimed victory as Argentina defeated France Dec. 18, 2022, in Lusail City, Qatar.

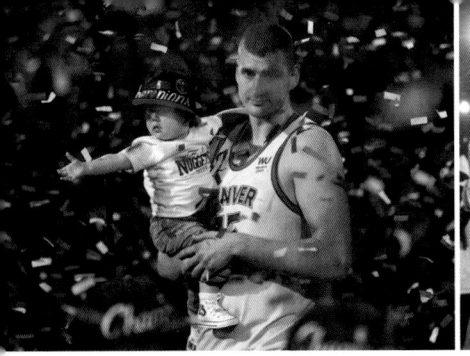

MILE-HIGH WINNERS Finals MVP Nikola Jokić and the Denver Nuggets celebrated a five-game victory over Miami in the 2023 NBA Finals June 12, 2023.

FIRST TIME CHAMPS Spain's Olga Carmona scored the deciding goal to claim victory over England in the FIFA Women's World Cup Final in Sydney, Australia, Aug. 20, 2023.

CONN ARTIST Final Four most outstanding player Adama Sanogo helped UConn claim their fifth NCAA men's basketball title in 25 years Apr. 3, 2023, defeating the San Diego St. Aztecs, 76-59.

HEAVEN SENT LSU junior Angel Reese was named most outstanding player after leading the Tigers to victory over Iowa, 102-85, in the NCAA women's basketball title game Apr. 2, 2023.

BET ON BLACK (AND GOLD) Jonathan Marchessault and the Vegas Golden Knights walloped the Florida Panthers 9-3 in Game 5 June 13, 2023, to claim the Stanley Cup Final win.

ARTS

TOY STORY Starring Ryan Gosling and Margot Robbie, *Barbie* became the highest grossing film of 2023, raking in $162 million in its opening weekend alone.

CURTAIN CALL After 13,981 performances, Andrew Lloyd Webber's *The Phantom of the Opera* ended its historic Broadway run Apr. 16, 2023.

JUGGLING OSCARS *Everything Everywhere All at Once*, directed and written by Daniel Kwan and Daniel Scheinert, all but swept the 2023 Academy Awards Mar. 12, 2023, claiming prizes for best picture, director, original screenplay, actress, supporting actor and actress, and film editing.

STARRY NIGHTS Beyoncé and Taylor Swift each launched major concert tours in 2023, selling out stadiums despite high ticket prices and stunning fans with their elaborate multihour stage shows.

PEOPLE

HOST WITH THE MOST *Wheel of Fortune* producers announced June 27, 2023, that go-to radio and TV host Ryan Seacrest would take over for Pat Sajak, who was retiring from the daily game show after over four decades.

WORKERS UNITE SAG-AFTRA Pres. Fran Drescher, best known as star of the 1990s sitcom *The Nanny*, announced July 13, 2023, that the actors' union would join striking Hollywood writers, effectively shutting down the industry.

A ROYAL WELCOME The UK's Prince Harry sold more than 1.43 million copies of his highly anticipated memoir *Spare* Jan. 10, 2023, its first day on bookstore shelves.

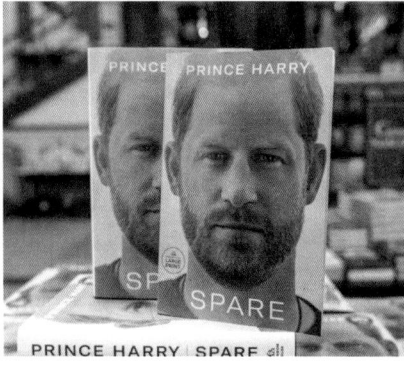

ROCK HEAD The Rock & Roll Hall of Fame board voted out its longtime champion and cofounder, *Rolling Stone* founding editor Jann Wenner (pictured here between two former Beatles), Sept. 16, 2023, over sexist and racist remarks.

797

KIRSTIE ALLEY
Jan. 12, 1951-Dec. 5, 2022

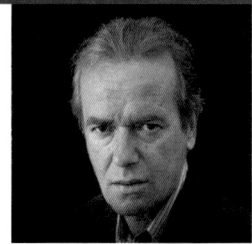

MARTIN AMIS
Aug. 25, 1949-May 19, 2023

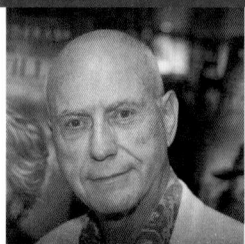

ALAN ARKIN
Mar. 26, 1934-June 29, 2023

BURT BACHARACH
May 12, 1928-Feb. 8, 2023

BOB BARKER
Dec. 12, 1923-Aug. 26, 2023

JEFF BECK
June 24, 1944-Jan. 10, 2023

HARRY BELAFONTE
Mar. 1, 1927-Apr. 25, 2023

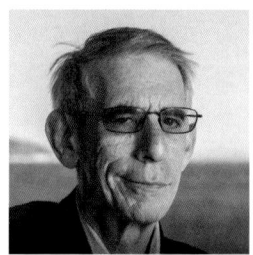

RICHARD BELZER
Aug. 4, 1944-Feb. 19, 2023

POPE BENEDICT XVI
Apr. 16, 1927-Dec. 31, 2022

TONY BENNETT
Aug. 3, 1926-July 21, 2023

JIM BROWN
Feb. 17, 1936-May 18, 2023

JIMMY BUFFETT
Dec. 25, 1946-Sept. 1, 2023

DICK BUTKUS
Dec. 9, 1942-Oct. 5, 2023

IRENE CARA
Mar. 18, 1959-Nov. 25, 2022

DAVID CROSBY
Aug. 14, 1941-Jan. 18, 2023

GLENDA JACKSON
May 9, 1936-June 15, 2023

GORDON LIGHTFOOT
Nov. 17, 1938-May 1, 2023

GINA LOLLOBRIGIDA
July 4, 1927-Jan. 16, 2023

DAVID McCALLUM
Sept. 19, 1933-Sept. 25, 2023

CORMAC McCARTHY
July 20, 1933-June 13, 2023

CHRISTINE McVIE
July 12, 1943-Nov. 30, 2022

SINEAD O'CONNOR
Dec. 8, 1966-July 26, 2023

PELÉ
Oct. 23, 1940-Dec. 29, 2022

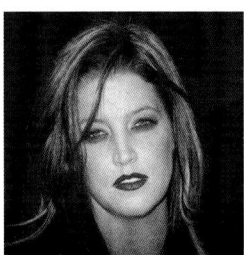

LISA MARIE PRESLEY
Feb. 1, 1968-Jan. 12, 2023

FAREWELL

WILLIS REED
June 25, 1942-Mar. 21, 2023

PAUL REUBENS
Aug. 27, 1952-July 30, 2023

PAT ROBERTSON
Mar. 22, 1930-June 8, 2023

BROOKS ROBINSON
May 18, 1937-Sept. 26, 2023

WAYNE SHORTER
Aug. 25, 1933-Mar. 2, 2023

SUZANNE SOMERS
Oct. 16, 1946-Oct. 15, 2023

JERRY SPRINGER
Feb. 13, 1944-Apr. 27, 2023

TINA TURNER
Nov. 26, 1939-May 24, 2023

BARBARA WALTERS
Sept. 25, 1929-Dec. 30, 2022

RAQUEL WELCH
Sept. 5, 1940-Feb. 15, 2023

CINDY WILLIAMS
Aug. 22, 1947-Jan. 25, 2023

TREAT WILLIAMS
Dec. 1, 1951-June 12, 2023

Netanyahu's right-wing Likud-Yisrael Beitenu political bloc narrowly won Jan. 22, 2013, parliamentary elections. After Mar. 17, 2015, elections, Netanyahu assembled a new coalition government.

Conflict between Israel and Hamas escalated in 2014. Rocket attacks from Gaza into Israel increased beginning in June. Israel launched air and artillery attacks on targets in Gaza, and Israeli ground forces entered Gaza July 17, in part to destroy tunnels used to infiltrate fighters into Israel. Israeli ground and air attacks caused high civilian casualties. Israel pulled out ground troops Aug. 5. A cease-fire was agreed Aug. 26.

Tensions between Iran and Israel have grown over Iran's nuclear and missile programs, which Israel sees as existential threats, as well as over Iranian support for regional anti-Israel militias and governments. Israeli airstrikes have targeted Iranian military assets or Iranian-backed forces in Syria, Iraq, and Lebanon.

On May 14, 2018, the U.S. officially moved its embassy from Tel Aviv, where most embassies are located, to Jerusalem. A proclamation signed Mar. 25, 2019, by U.S. Pres. Donald Trump recognized Israeli sovereignty over the Golan Heights.

Controversial July 2018 legislation declared that "the Jewish people … have an exclusive right to national self-determination" in Israel. With Netanyahu plagued by corruption scandals, Likud finished in a virtual tie with the centrist opposition Blue and White alliance, led by Benny Gantz, in Apr. 9 and Sept. 17, 2019, elections. After a third election, Mar. 2, 2020, produced a similar stalemate, Netanyahu and Gantz reached a power-sharing agreement, with Netanyahu initially continuing as prime minister. Netanyahu had been formally indicted, Jan. 28, 2020, on bribery, fraud, and breach of trust charges. The Netanyahu-Gantz coalition collapsed, Dec. 22, 2020. Following a fourth inconclusive election, Mar. 23, 2021, rightist Naftali Bennett became prime minister, June 13, initially heading a diverse 8-party coalition.

The U.S., Israel, and the United Arab Emirates announced, Aug. 13, 2020, that Israel and the UAE would normalize relations; Israel agreed to suspend plans to annex portions of the West Bank. Israel, Bahrain, and the U.S. announced, Sept. 11, that Israel and Bahrain would establish diplomatic ties.

Renewed heavy fighting between Hamas and Israel occurred May 2021—and between Islamic Jihad in Gaza and Israel Aug. 2022 and May 2023. Deadly clashes between Palestinians and Israeli security forces in the West Bank intensified in 2022—and again in 2023 (as well as attacks on Israeli civilians), amid more aggressive actions by security forces and militant Israeli settlers.

Bennett's coalition collapsed, June 2022. A right-wing coalition headed by Likud won new elections, Nov. 1, and Netanyahu again became prime minister, Dec. 29, 2022. Government plans to limit the powers and independence of the judiciary sparked months of large-scale demonstrations and strikes in 2023; legislation narrowing judicial review won final passage July 24, 2023.

More than 1,400 Israelis were killed in an unprecedented, highly coordinated attack by Hamas launched from Gaza Oct. 7, 2023. Israel declared war on Hamas, cut off electricity and supply lines to Gaza, and launched air and artillery strikes, killing an est. 5,000 Palestinians by Oct. 23, 2023.

Palestinian Territories

The Palestinian territories comprise the Gaza Strip, often called Gaza, and the West Bank, both occupied by Israel in 1967. Since 1996 the Palestinian Authority has been responsible for civil government in the territories. Elected president Jan. 20, 1996, PLO leader Yasir Arafat headed the Palestinian Authority until his death Nov. 11, 2004. Mahmoud Abbas, of the PLO's Fatah faction, was elected president Jan. 2005. A victory by Hamas militants in Jan. 2006 legislative elections led to a power struggle with Abbas. In bitter fighting, Hamas ousted Fatah from Gaza, June 2007, but Abbas retained power in the West Bank. As of 2023, Gaza remained largely in Hamas control.

The UN General Assembly voted, Nov. 29, 2012, to make Palestine a non-member observer state. Speaking at the UN Sept. 30, 2015, Abbas said the Palestinian Authority would no longer be bound by the Oslo Accords, which he alleged Israel had violated.

The **Gaza Strip** extends NE from the Sinai Peninsula for 25 mi, with the Mediterranean Sea to the W and Israel to the E. Nearly all the inhabitants are Palestinian Arabs. Area 139 sq mi; pop. (2023 est.) 2,037,744. Hamas's security force, the Izz al-Din al-Qassam Brigades, numbers 15,000-20,000.

Israel captured Gaza from Egypt in the 1967 war. It remained under Israeli occupation until May 1994, when the Israeli Defense Forces largely withdrew. Agreements between Israel and the PLO in 1993 and 1994 provided for interim self-rule in Gaza, but Israel retained control over security. Israel forcibly evacuated all 9,000 Jewish settlers from Gaza by Aug. 22, 2005, and the last remaining Israeli soldiers pulled out Sept. 12. Israel established a fortified barrier on its Gaza border to block Palestinian infiltrators.

After the Hamas takeover, Israel declared Gaza a "hostile entity," Sept. 19, 2007, and intensified military and economic pressures. Hamas thwarted an Israeli blockade, Jan. 2008, blowing up part of the border wall between Gaza and Egypt. Retaliating for Hamas

rocket and mortar attacks, Israel launched an aerial assault and ground offensive in Gaza, Dec. 2008-Jan. 2009. After the *Mavi Marmara* incident, Israel June 2010 eased some restrictions on the flow of goods to Gaza. Egypt's new Islamist govt. lifted the blockade along its Gaza border May 28, 2011. However, Egypt's subsequent military government re-closed the border in 2013 and sought to destroy tunnels dug by Hamas to bring military and other equipment into Gaza. Egypt opened the Gaza border intermittently beginning in 2015.

Members of the Israeli Air Force, Oct. 31, 2012, assassinated Hamas's military chief, Ahmed al-Jabari, in the Gaza Strip. In 2017, Israel began building a below-ground barrier on the Gaza border in an effort to block Hamas tunneling. Large-scale, sometimes violent protests occurred, Mar.-May 2018, on the Gaza side of the Israeli border wall, accompanied by attempts to storm the wall and firing across the border into Israel; more than 100 protesters were killed by Israeli security forces. Cross-border violence subsequently flared again periodically.

The **West Bank** is located W of the Jordan R. and Dead Sea, bounded by Jordan on the E and by Israel on the N, W, and S. The Palestinian Authority administers several major cities, but Israel retains control over much land, including Jewish settlements. Total area 2,263 sq mi, land area 2,178 sq mi; pop. (2023 est.) 3,050,760. The Palestinian Authority's National Security Force is a paramilitary organization of about 10,000 that maintains internal security in the West Bank.

In June 2002 the Israeli government began building a controversial security barrier in the West Bank to restrict Palestinian access to Israel and reduce infiltration by suicide bombers. In a nonbinding ruling, July 9, 2004, the World Court said the barrier violated international law. Israel has continued to allow the expansion of Jewish settlements—accelerated by the Netanyahu government in 2023. By 2023, more than 500,000 Jewish settlers were living in the West Bank (not including about 340,000 in East Jerusalem, which Israel annexed in 1967).

Italy
Italian Republic

People: Population: 61,021,855 (24). **Age distrib.:** <15: 12.1%; 65+: 23.3%. **Growth:** –0.1%. **Migrants:** 10.6%. **Pop. density:** 537.3 per sq mi, 207.5 per sq km. **Urban:** 72.0%. **Ethnic groups:** Italian (incl. small clusters of German-, French-, and Slovene-Italians in N; Albanian- and Greek-Italians in S). **Languages:** Italian (official), German, French, Slovene. **Religions:** Christian 75.7% (Catholic [official] 71.2%), agnostic 13.1%, Muslim 6.2% (Sunni), atheist 3.9%.

Geography: Total area: 116,348 sq mi, 301,340 sq km (71). **Land area:** 113,568 sq mi, 294,140 sq km. **Location:** Southern Europe, jutting into Mediterranean Sea. France on W; Switzerland, Austria on N; Slovenia on E. **Topography:** Long boot-shaped peninsula, with Apennine Mts. running SE its length, from the Alps into Mediterranean, with islands of Sicily and Sardinia offshore. The alluvial Po Valley drains most of N. Rest of the country is rugged and mountainous, except for intermittent coastal plains like the Campania S of Rome. **Arable land:** 24.3%. **Capital:** Rome, 4,315,671. **Cities:** Milan, 3,154,570; Naples, 2,179,384; Turin, 1,801,944.

Government: Type: Parliamentary republic. **Head of state:** Pres. Sergio Mattarella; b. 1941; in office: Feb. 3, 2015. **Head of govt.:** Prime Min. Giorgia Meloni; b. 1977; in office: Oct. 22, 2022. **Local divisions:** 20 regions (5 autonomous). **Defense budget:** $31.1 bil. **Active troops:** 161,050.

Economy: Industries: tourism, machinery, iron and steel, chemicals, food proc., textiles, motor vehicles, clothing, footwear. **Chief agric.:** milk, grapes, wheat, maize, tomatoes, apples. **Natural resources:** coal, antimony, mercury, zinc, potash, marble, barite, asbestos, pumice, fluorspar, feldspar, pyrite (sulfur), nat. gas/crude oil reserves, fish. **Water:** 3,164 cu m per capita. **Crude oil reserves:** 498 mil bbls. **Electricity prod.:** 274.2 bil kWh. **Labor force:** agric. 4.1%, industry 26.6%, services 69.3%. **Unemployment:** 8.1%.

Finance: Monetary unit: Euro (EUR) (0.93 = $1 U.S.). **GDP:** $3.1 tril; **per capita GDP:** $51,865; **GDP growth:** 3.7%. **Imports:** $637.9 bil; Germany 16%, France 9%, China 7%. **Exports:** $687.9 bil; Germany 12%, France 11%, U.S. 10%. **Tourism:** $25.2 bil. **Budget** (2020): $1.1 tril. **Inflation:** 8.2%.

Transport: Railways: 11,480 mi. **Motor vehicles:** 747.8 per 1,000 pop. **Airports:** 98.

Communications: Mobile: 133.0 per 100 pop. **Broadband:** 96.4 per 100 pop. **Internet:** 85.1%.

Health: Expend. (2021): 9.5%. **Life expect.:** 80.5 male; 85.3 female. **Births:** 7.0 per 1,000 pop. **Deaths:** 11.3 per 1,000 pop. **Infant mortality:** 3.1 per 1,000 live births. **Undernourished:** <2.5%. **HIV:** 0.2%. **COVID-19:** 25,929,238 cases, 191,167 deaths; rates per 100,000: 43,475.2 cases, 320.5 deaths. 83.8% vaccinated.

Education: Compulsory: ages 6-17. **Literacy:** 99.4%.

Website: www.governo.it

Rome emerged as the major power in Italy after 500 BCE, dominating the Etruscans to the north and Greeks to the south. Under the Empire, which lasted until the 5th cent. CE, Rome ruled most of Western Europe, the Balkans, the Middle East, and North Africa.

After Rome fell, Italy became a patchwork of kingdoms, principalities, and city-states until reunified, 1870.

The Fascist leader Benito Mussolini came to power, 1922, and aligned Italy with Nazi Germany in WWII. After Fascism was overthrown in 1943, Italy declared war on Germany and Japan and contributed to the Allied victory. It surrendered conquered lands and lost its colonies. Mussolini was killed by partisans Apr. 28, 1945. Victor Emmanuel III abdicated May 9, 1946; his son Humbert II was king until June 10, when Italy became a republic after a referendum, June 2-3. In the postwar decades, Italy had a succession of short-lived governments.

Christian Democratic leader and former Prime Min. Aldo Moro was abducted and murdered in 1978 by Red Brigade terrorists. A wave of left-wing political violence continued into the 1980s.

In Mar. 1994 voting, right-wing parties won a majority, dislodging Italy's long-powerful Christian Democratic Party. Italy led a 7,000-member peacekeeping force in Albania, Apr.-Aug. 1997.

Supporters of Silvio Berlusconi, a multibillionaire media magnate, won the 2001 parliamentary elections. Berlusconi backed American-led military operations in Afghanistan (2001) and Iraq (2003). The last Italian troops left Afghanistan in 2021.

Berlusconi lost 2006 parliamentary elections but returned at the head of a center-right coalition after Apr. 2008 elections. Sluggish economic growth and rising public debt raised investors' concerns about Italy's financial stability. Berlusconi resigned Nov. 12, 2011, but Italy's economic problems worsened. After Feb. 25, 2013, elections, a coalition government was announced Apr. 27, 2013, led by the center-left Democratic Party (PD). Berlusconi was convicted in 2012 of tax fraud and in 2015 of bribing a senator. Legalization of civil unions between same-sex couples won final parliamentary approval, May 11, 2016.

About 625,000 African, Middle Eastern, and SW Asian migrants fleeing violence and economic hardship crossed the Mediterranean from North Africa (mainly Libya) to Italy, 2014-17. More than 13,000 died trying to make the crossing. Beginning in 2017, Italy (and the EU) worked with various Libyan authorities to reduce migrant crossings. However, the pace of crossings increased again in 2021 (over 67,000 migrant arrivals; over 1,500 deaths) and 2022 (over 105,000 arrivals; more than 1,450 deaths). In 2023, more than 130,000 migrants had arrived by Oct. 1.

In Mar. 4, 2018, elections, the populist Five Star Movement (M5S) and the anti-immigration League made strong showings. A League-M5S coalition government took office June 1, 2018. With League-M5S disputes increasing and the economy stagnant, the government resigned, Aug. 20, 2019. M5S and the PD agreed, Aug. 28, to form a new coalition. Prime Min. Giuseppe Conte resigned, Jan. 26, 2021, after losing support largely over response to the COVID-19 pandemic. Mario Draghi became prime minister Feb. 13 but defections from his coalition forced Draghi to resign, July 21, 2022. In Sept. 25, 2022, elections, a rightist, anti-immigration coalition won a majority of seats—led by the Brothers of Italy party of Giorgia Meloni. She became, Oct. 22, 2022, Italy's first female prime minister, heading a government that also included the League and Berlusconi's Forza Italia party (Berlusconi died June 12, 2023).

Italy was one of the first European countries severely impacted, in early 2020, by COVID-19. Health care facilities were strained, and GDP fell 9% in 2020. Severe heat waves in the 2020s were likely related to climate change.

Sicily, 9,927 sq mi, pop. (2014 est.) 5,094,937, is an island 180 by 120 mi, seat of an autonomous region that embraces the island of Pantelleria, 32 sq mi, and the Lipari group, 44 sq mi, including two active volcanoes: Vulcano (1,637 ft) and Stromboli (3,031 ft). From prehistoric times Sicily has been settled by various peoples; a Greek state had its capital at Syracuse. Rome took Sicily from Carthage 215 BCE. Mt. Etna, a 10,925-ft active volcano, is its tallest peak.

Sardinia, 9,301 sq mi, pop. (2014 est.) 1,663,859, lies in the Mediterranean, 115 mi W of Italy and 7½ mi S of Corsica. It is 160 mi long, 68 mi wide, and mountainous. Mining, historically important, has declined in recent decades, and tourism has increased. In 1720, Sardinia was added to the possessions of the Dukes of Savoy in Piedmont and Savoy to form the Kingdom of Sardinia. Elba, 86 sq mi, lies 6 mi W of Tuscany. Napoleon I lived in exile on Elba 1814-15.

Jamaica

People: Population: 2,820,982 (137). **Age distrib.:** <15: 24.1%; 65+: 10.1%. **Growth:** 0.1%. **Migrants:** 0.8%. **Pop. density:** 674.6 per sq mi, 260.5 per sq km. **Urban:** 57.4%. **Ethnic groups:** Black 92.1%, mixed 6.1%. **Languages:** English, Jamaican patois. **Religions:** Christian 84.8% (Protestant 61.5%, independent 18.3%), Spiritist 9.7%, agnostic 4.3%.

Geography: Total area: 4,244 sq mi, 10,991 sq km (161); **Land area:** 4,182 sq mi, 10,831 sq km. **Location:** W Indies. Cuba to N, Haiti to E. **Topography:** Four-fifths of country is covered by mountains. **Arable land:** 11.1%. **Capital:** Kingston, 597,124.

Government: Type: Parliamentary democracy under constitutional monarchy. **Head of state:** King Charles III, rep. by Gov.-Gen. Patrick Allen; b. 1951; in office: Feb. 26, 2009. **Head of govt.:** Prime Min. Andrew Holness; b. 1972; in office: Mar. 3, 2016. **Local divisions:** 14 parishes. **Defense budget:** $204 mil. **Active troops:** 5,950.

Economy: Industries: agriculture, mining, manufacture, constr., financial and insurance services, tourism, telecom. **Chief agric.:** sugarcane, goat milk, yams, poultry, coconuts, oranges. **Natural resources:** bauxite, alumina, gypsum, limestone. **Water:** 3,655 cu m per capita. **Electricity prod.:** 4.3 bil kWh. **Labor force:** agric. 15.5%, industry 16.2%, services 68.3%. **Unemployment:** 6.0%.

Finance: Monetary unit: Dollar (JMD) (155.36 = $1 U.S.). **GDP:** $33.4 bil; **per capita GDP:** $11,822; **GDP growth:** 4.2%. **Imports:** $7.4 bil; (2021) U.S. 35%, China 13%. **Exports:** $4.4 bil; (2021) U.S. 46%, Netherlands 9%, Canada 6%. **Tourism:** $2.1 bil. **Budget** (2020): $4.6 bil. **Inflation:** 10.4%.

Transport: Motor vehicles: 78.8 per 1,000 pop. **Airports:** 11.

Communications: Mobile: 106.2 per 100 pop. **Broadband:** 66.7 per 100 pop. **Internet:** 82.4%.

Health: Expend.: 6.6%. **Life expect.:** 74.3 male; 77.9 female. **Births:** 15.8 per 1,000 pop. **Deaths:** 7.4 per 1,000 pop. **Infant mortality:** 10.9 per 1,000 live births. **Undernourished:** 8.3%. **HIV:** 1.3%. **COVID-19:** 155,860 cases, 3,596 deaths; rates per 100,000: 5,263.5 cases, 121.4 deaths. 25.6% vaccinated.

Education: Compulsory: ages 6-11. **Literacy:** 88.7%.

Website: jis.gov.jm

Jamaica was visited by Christopher Columbus, 1494, and ruled by Spain (under whom Arawak Indians died out) until seized by Britain, 1655. Use of enslaved African labor, begun by the Spanish, expanded significantly under British rule. Jamaica won independence Aug. 6, 1962. The island's rich musical innovations include ska and reggae. Rastafarianism is an influential religious movement.

In 1976, Jamaica's socialist government acquired 50% ownership of U.S. and Canadian companies' bauxite mines. Rudimentary welfare state measures were passed. Relations with the U.S. improved in the 1980s when Jamaican politics entered a more conservative phase.

Portia Simpson-Miller of the People's National Party (PNP) became Jamaica's first female prime min., Mar. 30, 2006. The Jamaica Labour Party (JLP) won Sept. 3, 2007, elections. While trying to arrest alleged gang leader Christopher (Dudus) Coke, police and soldiers clashed with residents in a section of Kingston in May 2010, leaving 76 people dead. Coke pleaded guilty in the U.S. to racketeering charges in 2011. The PNP won Dec. 2011 elections; Simpson-Miller again became prime min. After she implemented unpopular austerity measures to obtain IMF aid, the JLP won Feb. 25, 2016, elections; Andrew Holness became prime min. The JLP won Sept. 3, 2020, elections.

Japan

People: Population: 123,719,238 (11). **Age distrib.:** <15: 12.3%; 65+: 29.2%. **Growth:** -0.4%. **Migrants:** 2.2%. **Pop. density:** 879.1 per sq mi, 339.4 per sq km. **Urban:** 92.0%. **Ethnic groups** (by nationality): Japanese 97.9%. **Languages:** Japanese. **Religions:** Buddhist 56.2% (Mahayanist), new religionist 25.6%, agnostic 10.4%, atheist 2.9%, Shintoist 2.2%, Christian 2.2%.

Geography: Total area: 145,914 sq mi, 377,915 sq km (61); **Land area:** 140,728 sq mi, 364,485 sq km. Consists of 4 main islands: Honshu ("mainland"), 87,805 sq mi; Hokkaido, 30,144 sq mi; Kyushu, 14,114 sq mi; Shikoku, 7,049 sq mi. **Location:** Archipelago off E coast of Asia. Russia to N, N. Korea and S. Korea to W. **Topography:** Deeply indented coast. The northern islands are continuation of the Sakhalin Mts. China's Kunlun range continues into southern islands. The ranges meet in Japanese Alps. Group of mostly extinct or inactive volcanoes, incl. Mt. Fuji (Fujiyama) (12,388 ft), cross Honshu E-W in a vast transverse fissure. **Arable land:** 11.2%. **Capital:** Tokyo, 37,194,105. **Cities:** Kinki MMA (Osaka), 19,013,434; Chukyo MMA (Nagoya), 9,569,328; Kitakyushu-Fukuoka MMA, 5,490,271.

Government: Type: Parliamentary constitutional monarchy. **Head of state:** Emperor Naruhito; b. 1960; in office: May 1, 2019. **Head of govt.:** Prime Min. Fumio Kishida; b. 1957; in office Oct. 4, 2021. **Local divisions:** 47 prefectures. **Defense budget:** $48.1 bil. **Active troops:** 247,150.

Economy: Industries: motor vehicles, electronic equip., machine tools, steel and nonferrous metals, ships, chemicals. **Chief agric.:** rice, milk, sugar beet, vegetables, eggs, poultry. **Natural resources:** negligible mineral resources, fish. **Water:** 3,400 cu m per capita. **Crude oil reserves:** 44 mil bbls. **Electricity prod.:** 954.9 bil kWh. **Labor force:** agric. 3.2%, industry 23.7%, services 73.1%. **Unemployment:** 2.6%.

Finance: Monetary unit: Yen (JPY) (146.41 = $1 U.S.). **GDP:** $5.7 tril; **per capita GDP:** $45,573; **GDP growth:** 1.0%. **Imports:** $941.7 bil; (2021) China 24%, U.S. 10%, Australia 7%. **Exports:**

$919.2 bil; (2021) China 21%, U.S. 18%, South Korea 7%, Taiwan 7%. **Tourism:** $4.7 bil. **Budget** (2021): $1.9 tril. **Inflation:** 2.5%.

Transport: Railways: 16,970 mi. **Motor vehicles:** 632.6 per 1,000 pop. **Airports:** 142.

Communications: Mobile: 167.5 per 100 pop. **Broadband:** 234.4 per 100 pop. **Internet:** 82.9%.

Health: Expend.: 10.9%. **Life expect.:** 82.1 male; 88.1 female. **Births:** 6.9 per 1,000 pop. **Deaths:** 11.7 per 1,000 pop. **Infant mortality:** 1.9 per 1,000 live births. **Undernourished:** 3.2%. **HIV:** NA. **COVID-19:** 33,803,572 cases, 74,694 deaths; rates per 100,000: 26,727.2 cases, 59.1 deaths. 81.8% vaccinated.

Education: Compulsory: ages 6-14. **Literacy:** NA.

Website: www.japan.go.jp

According to Japanese legend, the empire was founded by Emperor Jimmu, 660 BCE, but earliest records of a unified Japan date from 1,000 years later. Chinese influence was strong in the formation of Japanese civilization. Buddhism was introduced before the 6th cent. CE.

A feudal system, with locally powerful noble families and their samurai warrior retainers, dominated from 1192. Central power was held by successive families of shoguns (military dictators), 1192-1867, until recovered by Emperor Meiji, 1868. The Portuguese and Dutch had minor trade with Japan in the 16th and 17th cents.; U.S. Commodore Matthew C. Perry opened the country to U.S. trade in a treaty ratified 1854. Industrialization began in the late 19th cent. Military conflicts won Taiwan from China, 1894-95, and the southern half of Sakhalin from Russia, 1904-05. Japan annexed Korea, 1910.

In WWI Japan ousted Germany from Shandong in China and took over German Pacific islands. Japan took Manchuria in 1931 and launched full-scale war in China in 1937. In WWII, Japan attacked Pearl Harbor, Dec. 7, 1941, launching war with the U.S. The U.S. dropped atomic bombs on Hiroshima, Aug. 6, and Nagasaki, Aug. 9, 1945. Japan surrendered Aug. 14.

In a new constitution adopted May 3, 1947, Japan renounced the right to wage war; the emperor renounced claims to divinity; and the Diet became the sole lawmaking authority. The U.S. and 48 other non-Communist nations signed a peace treaty with Japan on Sept. 8, 1951; on the same day, the U.S. signed a bilateral defense agreement with Japan. The peace treaty restored Japan's sovereignty effective Apr. 28, 1952.

Rebuilding after WWII, Japan emerged as one of the most powerful economies in the world.

In 1968, the U.S. returned control of the Bonin Isls., Volcano Isls. (including Iwo Jima), and Marcus Isls to Japan. In 1972, the U.S. returned Okinawa, the other Ryukyu Isls., and the Daito Isls., but the U.S. continued to maintain military bases on Okinawa.

The Liberal Democratic Party (LDP) governed Japan from the mid-1950s through early 1990s. In 1994, Tomiichi Murayama became Japan's first Socialist premier since 1947-48. With the country mired in a lengthy recession, the LDP regained power in 1996.

For the first time since WWII, Japan sent troops to an overseas war zone, when about 600 noncombat troops served in Iraq Feb. 2004-July 2006. Legislation formalizing a new constitutional interpretation allowing the military to take offensive action to aid an ally, such as the U.S., won final passage Sept. 19, 2015.

The 2008-09 global recession hit Japan hard, prompting a series of economic stimulus plans. The LDP suffered a crushing defeat in 2009 parliamentary elections, won by the opposition Democratic Party of Japan (DPJ).

A 9.0 magnitude earthquake and tsunami off Japan's east coast Mar. 11, 2011, left almost 21,000 people dead. The Fukushima Daiichi nuclear power plant experienced meltdowns, spewing radiation over a large area. (On Aug. 24, 2023, despite opposition in nearby countries and the fishing industry, Japan began releasing into the sea treated wastewater used to cool nuclear fuel rods.)

Elections swept LDP candidates into office in Dec. 2012, and former Prime Min. Shinzo Abe became prime minister. Abe's LDP won Dec. 14, 2014, and Oct. 22, 2017, elections.

Japan signed, Mar. 8, 2018, an 11-nation trans-Pacific trade pact. Japan and the EU signed, July 17, 2018, a trade liberalization agreement.

Emperor Akihito, 85, abdicated, Apr. 30, 2019; he was succeeded, May 1, by his son Naruhito. Abe announced, Aug. 28, 2020, that he would resign because of ill health. The LDP's Yoshihide Suga became prime minister Sept. 16.

The COVID-19 pandemic reached Japan by Jan. 2020. The 2020 Summer Olympics in Tokyo were delayed until 2021; Japan barred virtually all spectators. Prime Min. Suga, facing declining popularity over handling of the COVID-19 pandemic, announced, Sept. 3, 2021, he would resign. Former foreign min. Fumio Kishida became prime minister, Oct. 4, 2021, and led the LDP to victory in Oct. 31 elections.

Former Prime Min. Abe was shot to death, July 8, 2022, at a political rally; LDP ties to the Unification Church was the assassin's apparent motivation. Enhanced Japan-U.S.-South Korea security cooperation was agreed to, Aug. 18, 2023, at a summit meeting in the U.S.

Jordan
Hashemite Kingdom of Jordan

People: Population: 11,086,716 (84). **Age distrib.:** <15: 31.4%; 65+: 4.0%. **Growth:** 0.8%. **Migrants:** 33.9%. **Pop. density:** 323.4 per sq mi, 124.8 per sq km. **Urban:** 92.0%. **Ethnic groups** (by nationality): Jordanian 69.3%, Syrian 13.3%, Palestinian 6.7%, Egyptian 6.7%. **Languages:** Arabic (official), English (widely understood among upper/middle classes). **Religions:** Muslim 95.4% (Sunni [official] 93%), agnostic 2.5%.

Geography: Total area: 34,495 sq mi, 89,342 sq km (110); **Land area:** 34,287 sq mi, 88,802 sq km. **Location:** Middle East. Israel, West Bank on W; Saudi Arabia on S; Iraq on E; Syria on N. **Topography:** Mostly arid. Fertile areas in W. Only port is on short Aqaba Gulf coast. Country shares Dead Sea (1,339 ft below sea level) with Israel. **Arable land:** 2.2%. **Capital:** Amman, 2,232,240.

Government: Type: Parliamentary constitutional monarchy. **Head of state:** King Abdullah II; b. 1962; in office: Feb. 7, 1999. **Head of govt.:** Prime Min. Bisher Al Khasawneh; b. 1969; in office: Oct. 7, 2020. **Local divisions:** 12 governorates. **Defense budget:** $1.9 bil. **Active troops:** 100,500.

Economy: Industries: tourism, information tech., clothing, fertilizer, potash, phosphate mining, pharmaceuticals. **Chief agric.:** tomatoes, poultry, olives, milk, potatoes, cucumbers. **Natural resources:** phosphates, potash, shale oil. **Water:** 92 cu m per capita. **Crude oil reserves:** 1 mil bbls. **Electricity prod.:** 21.9 bil kWh. **Labor force:** agric. 3.2%, industry 17.6%, services 79.1%. **Unemployment:** 17.9%.

Finance: Monetary unit: Dinar (JOD) (0.71 = $1 U.S.). **GDP:** $124.2 bil; **per capita GDP:** $11,003; **GDP growth:** 2.5%. **Imports:** $23.4 bil; (2021) China 17%, Saudi Arabia 14%, UAE 11%. **Exports:** $13.9 bil; (2021) U.S. 26%, India 13%, Saudi Arabia 11%. **Tourism:** $2.7 bil. **Budget:** $13.5 bil. **Inflation:** 4.2%.

Transport: Railways: 316 mi. **Motor vehicles:** 164.3 per 1,000 pop. **Airports:** 16.

Communications: Mobile: 67.6 per 100 pop. **Broadband:** 67.6 per 100 pop. **Internet:** 86.0%.

Health: Expend.: 7.5%. **Life expect.:** 74.8 male; 77.8 female. **Births:** 22.4 per 1,000 pop. **Deaths:** 3.5 per 1,000 pop. **Infant mortality:** 13.6 per 1,000 live births. **Undernourished:** NA. **HIV:** <0.1%. **COVID-19:** 1,746,997 cases, 14,122 deaths; rates per 100,000: 17,122.2 cases, 138.4 deaths. 44.7% vaccinated.

Education: Compulsory: ages 6-15. **Literacy:** 98.4%.

Website: portal.jordan.gov.jo

From ancient times to 1922 the lands to the east of the Jordan R. were culturally and politically united with the lands to the W. Arabs conquered the area in the 7th cent.; the Ottomans took control in the 16th. Britain's 1920 Palestine Mandate covered both sides of the Jordan. In 1921, Abdullah, son of the ruler of Hejaz in Arabia, was installed by Britain as emir of an autonomous Transjordan, covering two-thirds of Palestine. An independent kingdom was proclaimed, 1946.

During the 1948 Arab-Israeli war, the West Bank and East Jerusalem were added to the kingdom, which changed its name to Jordan. These territories were lost to Israel in 1967, which swelled the number of Arab refugees on the East Bank.

Jordan and Israel signed a peace treaty, Oct. 26, 1994. King Hussein died Feb. 7, 1999, ending a nearly 47-year reign; his eldest son assumed the throne as Abdullah II. The king responded to Arab Spring protests, 2011-12, by somewhat liberalizing parliamentary election laws.

In 2014, Jordan joined the U.S.-led military campaign against ISIS in Syria and Iraq. More than 655,000 Syrians fleeing civil war were living in Jordan as of Aug. 31, 2023.

Two aides to Abdullah II's half-brother Prince Hamzah were sentenced in July 2021 to 15 years in prison for conspiring with Hamzah to make him ruler of Jordan.

Kazakhstan
Republic of Kazakhstan

People: Population: 19,543,464 (64). **Age distrib.:** <15: 27.9%; 65+: 9.3%. **Growth:** 0.7%. **Migrants:** 19.9%. **Pop. density:** 18.7 per sq mi, 7.2 per sq km. **Urban:** 58.2%. **Ethnic groups:** Kazakh (Qazaq) 69.6%, Russian 17.9%, Uzbek 3.3%. **Languages:** Kazakh or Qazaq, Russian (both official). **Religions:** Muslim 72.2% (Sunni), Christian 24.7% (Orthodox 22.9%), agnostic 2.3%.

Geography: Total area: 1,052,090 sq mi, 2,724,900 sq km (9); **Land area:** 1,042,360 sq mi, 2,699,700 sq km. **Location:** Central Asia. Russia on N; China on E; Kyrgyzstan, Uzbekistan, Turkmenistan on S. **Topography:** Extends from lower reaches of Volga in Europe to Altay Mts. on Chinese border. **Arable land:** 11.0%. **Capital:** Astana, 1,291,280. **Cities:** Almaty, 1,987,301; Shimkent, 1,155,073.

Government: Type: Presidential republic. **Head of state:** Pres. Kassym-Jomart Tokayev; b. 1953; in office: Mar. 20, 2019. **Head of govt.:** Prime Min. Alikhan Smailov; b. 1972; in office: Jan. 11, 2022.

Local divisions: 17 provinces, 4 cities. **Defense budget:** $1.9 bil. **Active troops:** 39,000.

Economy: Industries: oil, coal, iron ore, manganese, chromite, lead, zinc, copper, titanium, bauxite, gold, silver, phosphates, sulfur, uranium. **Chief agric.:** wheat, milk, potatoes, barley, watermelons, melons. **Natural resources:** petroleum, nat. gas, coal, iron ore, manganese, chrome ore, nickel, cobalt, copper, molybdenum, lead, zinc, bauxite, gold, uranium. **Water:** 5,774 cu m per capita. **Crude oil reserves:** 30 bil bbls. **Electricity prod.:** 104.5 bil kWh. **Labor force:** agric. 15.0%, industry 21.2%, services 63.8%. **Unemployment:** 5.0%.

Finance: Monetary unit: Tenge (KZT) (463.77 = $1 U.S.). **GDP:** $604.6 bil; **per capita GDP:** $30,810; **GDP growth:** 3.2%. **Imports:** $49.2 bil; Russia 34%, China 24%. **Exports:** $66.1 bil; China 13%, Italy 12%, Russia 10%, Netherlands 7%, France 6%. **Tourism:** $535 mil. **Budget (2020):** $42.0 bil. **Inflation** (2020-21): 8.0%.

Transport: Railways: 10,337 mi. **Airports:** 63.

Communications: Mobile: 130.4 per 100 pop. **Broadband:** 94.5 per 100 pop. **Internet:** 92.3%.

Health: Expend.: 3.8%. **Life expect.:** 68.7 male; 77.7 female. **Births:** 17.6 per 1,000 pop. **Deaths:** 8.2 per 1,000 pop. **Infant mortality:** 8.1 per 1,000 live births. **Undernourished:** <2.5%. **HIV:** NA. **COVID-19:** 1,502,857 cases, 19,072 deaths; rates per 100,000: 8,003.8 cases, 101.6 deaths. 68.1% vaccinated.

Education: Compulsory: ag 3 6-14. **Literacy:** 99.8%.

Website: egov.kz

The region came under the Mongols' rule in the 13th cent. and gradually came under Russian rule, 1730-1853. It was admitted to the USSR as a constituent republic in 1936.

Kazakhstan became independent when the Soviet Union dissolved Dec. 26, 1991. The Communist Party chief, Nursultan Nazarbayev, was elected president unopposed. Dissent was suppressed. Nazarbayev encouraged Western investment in the oil industry, helping the economy. Regular production began, Oct. 2016, at the large Kashagan oil field in the Caspian Sea.

Kazakhstan agreed, Feb. 1994, to dismantle nuclear missiles. Private land ownership was legalized Dec. 1995.

Pres. Nazarbayev was reelected in 1999, 2005, 2011, and 2015. His Nur Otan party won 2016 and 2021 parliamentary elections. Nazarbayev resigned, Mar. 20, 2019, retaining influence as "first president." Kassym-Jomart Tokayev of Nur Otan became acting president and won a June 9, 2019, presidential election.

Sparked by a rise in fuel prices, violent protests over economic conditions and corruption—and a harsh crackdown by security forces—left over 230 dead in Jan. 2022. In a June 5 referendum, voters approved constitutional changes including limits on the official powers of former Pres. Nazarbayev. Tokayev was reelected, Nov. 20, 2022. The ruling party, renamed from Nur Otan to Amanat in 2022, dominated Mar. 19, 2023, parliamentary elections.

Kenya
Republic of Kenya

People: Population: 57,052,004 (27). **Age distrib.:** <15: 36.5%; 65+: 3.3%. **Growth:** 2.1%. **Migrants:** 2.0%. **Pop. density:** 259.6 per sq mi, 100.2 per sq km. **Urban:** 29.5%. **Ethnic groups:** Kikuyu 17.1%, Luhya 14.3%, Kalenjin 13.4%, Luo 10.7%, Kamba 9.8%, Somali 5.8%, Kisii 5.7%, Mijikenda 5.2%, Meru 4.2%, Maasai 2.5%, Turkana 2.1%. **Languages:** English, Kiswahili (both official); numerous Indigenous langs. **Religions:** Christian 82.2% (Protestant 45.0%, Catholic 21.1%, independent 15.5%), ethnic religionist 8.0%, Muslim 7.9% (Sunni).

Geography: Total area: 224,081 sq mi, 580,367 sq km (49); **Land area:** 219,746 sq mi, 569,140 sq km. **Location:** E Africa, on coast of Indian O. Uganda on W, Tanzania on S, Somalia on E, Ethiopia on N, South Sudan on NW. **Topography:** Northern three-fifths of country is arid. A low coastal area and a plateau 3,000-10,000-ft high is in S. The Great Rift Valley enters the country N-S, flanked by high mountains. **Arable land:** 10.2%. **Capital:** Nairobi, 5,325,160. **Cities:** Mombasa, 1,440,396.

Government: Type: Presidential republic. **Head of state and govt.:** Pres. William Ruto; b. 1966; in office: Sept. 13, 2022. **Local divisions:** 47 counties. **Defense budget:** $1.3 bil. **Active troops:** 24,100.

Economy: Industries: small-scale consumer goods (plastic, furniture, batteries), agric. prods., horticulture, oil refining, aluminum, steel, lead, cement, comm. ship repair. **Chief agric.:** milk, tea, beef, maize, sugarcane, tomatoes. **Natural resources:** limestone, soda ash, salt, gems, fluorspar, zinc, diatomite, gypsum, wildlife, hydropower. **Water:** 571 cu m per capita. **Electricity prod.:** 11.8 bil kWh. **Labor force:** agric. 33.0%, industry 15.7%, services 51.2%. **Unemployment:** 5.5%.

Finance: Monetary unit: Shilling (KES) (145.20 = $1 U.S.). **GDP:** $311.4 bil; **per capita GDP:** $5,764; **GDP growth:** 4.8%. **Imports:** $21.9 bil; (2020) China 27%, India 11%, UAE 7%. **Exports:** $11.8 bil; (2020) Uganda 14%, Pakistan 8%, Netherlands 8%, U.S. 8%, UK 7%. **Tourism:** $843 mil. **Budget:** $24.3 bil. **Inflation:** 7.7%.

Transport: Railways: 2,373 mi. **Motor vehicles:** 35.9 per 1,000 pop. **Airports:** 16.

Communications: Mobile: 121.7 per 100 pop. **Broadband:** 59.0 per 100 pop. **Internet:** 28.8%.

Health: Expend.: 4.3%. **Life expect.:** 68.3 male; 71.8 female. **Births:** 26.0 per 1,000 pop. **Deaths:** 5.0 per 1,000 pop. **Infant mortality:** 26.9 per 1,000 live births. **Undernourished:** 27.8%. **HIV:** 3.7%. **COVID-19:** 343,955 cases, 5,689 deaths; rates per 100,000: 639.7 cases, 10.6 deaths. 20.6% vaccinated.

Education: Compulsory: ages 6-17. **Literacy:** 82.6%.

Website: www.president.go.ke

Arab colonies exported spices and slaves from the Kenya coast as early as the 8th cent. Britain obtained control in the 19th cent. Kenya won independence Dec. 12, 1963, four years after the end of the violent Mau Mau uprising. Jomo Kenyatta, the country's leader since independence, died Aug. 22, 1978. He was succeeded by his vice president, Daniel arap Moi.

Tribal clashes in the western provinces in the 1990s claimed thousands of lives. Pres. Moi won a fourth term in Dec. 1997, in an election plagued by irregularities. A truck bomb explosion at the U.S. embassy in Nairobi, Aug. 7, 1998, killed more than 200 people and injured about 5,000. The U.S. blamed the attack on al-Qaeda.

Pres. Moi succeeded, Dec. 2002, by Mwai Kibaki of the opposition Democratic Party. After a disputed election Dec. 2007, Kenya's electoral commission declared Kibaki the winner over challenger Raila Odinga. Weeks of factional violence followed, leaving some 1,500 people dead and 600,000 displaced. Uhuru Kenyatta (Jomo Kenyatta's son) was declared, Mar. 10, 2013, the winner over Odinga in the Mar. 4 presidential election, amid accusations of vote-rigging. On Aug. 11, 2017, Kenyatta was again declared the victor over Odinga in Aug. 8 presidential voting; Odinga charged electoral fraud. After the Supreme Court, Sept. 1, nullified the result, Kenyatta won an Oct. 26 re-vote boycotted by Odinga.

Kenya sent troops into Somalia in 2011 (they joined with an African Union force in 2012) to combat the Somali Islamist extremist group al-Shabab. Al-Shabab carried out a series of deadly terrorist attacks in Kenya. An Apr. 2, 2015, attack on Garissa Univ. College killed 148. About 329,000 Somali refugees and asylum seekers were living in Kenya as of Aug. 31, 2023 (in the mid-2010s, tens of thousands were repatriated to Somalia, amid allegations of forced returns).

Years of drought left millions of Kenyans facing food insecurity in 2022.

Vice Pres. William Ruto, with 50.5% of the vote, was declared the winner over Odinga in the Aug. 9, 2022, presidential election. Rejecting a challenge by Odinga, the Supreme Court, Sept. 5, upheld the election result. Soaring prices and tax increases sparked violent protests (over 30 dead) in July 2023.

Kenya agreed to lead and contribute forces to a multinational security mission (approved by the UN, Oct. 2, 2023) intended to reduce violence in Haiti.

Kiribati
Republic of Kiribati

People: Population: 115,372 (179). **Age distrib.:** <15: 27.1%; 65+: 5.2%. **Growth:** 1.0%. **Migrants:** 2.6%. **Pop. density:** 368.4 per sq mi, 142.3 per sq km. **Urban:** 57.8%. **Ethnic groups:** I-Kiribati 95.8%, I-Kiribati/mixed 3.8%. **Languages:** Gilbertese, English (official). **Religions:** Christian 96.8% (Catholic 44.8%, Protestant 36.2%, independent 15.7%), Baha'i 2.5%.

Geography: Total area: 313 sq mi, 811 sq km (173); **Land area:** 313 sq mi, 811 sq km. **Location:** 33 atolls (Gilbert, Line, and Phoenix Isls.) in mid-Pacific scattered over an area of about 1.35 mil sq mi around the point where the International Date Line formerly crossed the Equator. The Date Line was moved in 1997 to follow Kiribati's E border. Nearest neighbors are Nauru to SW, Tuvalu and Tokelau Isls. (N.Z.) to S. **Topography:** Except Banaba (Ocean) Isl., all are low-lying, with soil of coral sand and rock fragments, and erratic rainfall. **Arable land:** 2.5%. **Capital:** Tarawa, 64,011.

Government: Type: Presidential republic. **Head of state and govt.:** Pres. Taneti Maamau; b. 1960; in office: Mar. 11, 2016. **Local divisions:** 3 geographical units (no first-order admin. divisions). **Defense budget/active troops:** NA.

Economy: Industries: fishing, handicrafts. **Chief agric.:** coconuts, roots/tubers, bananas, vegetables, taro, tropical fruit. **Natural resources:** phosphate (prod. discontinued in 1979), coconuts, fish. **Water:** 0. **Electricity prod.:** 33.8 mil kWh. **Labor force:** agric. 15.0%, industry 10.0%, services 75.0%. **Unemployment:** NA.

Finance: Monetary unit: Australian Dollar (AUD) (1.56 = $1 U.S.). **GDP:** $310.3 mil; **per capita GDP:** $2,365; **GDP growth:** 1.6%. **Imports:** $202.0 mil; China 20%, Fiji 19%, Australia 12%, Taiwan 11%, South Korea 11%, New Zealand 7%. **Exports:** $10.8 mil; Thailand 53%, Philippines 17%, South Korea 10%, Japan 9%. **Tourism (2020):** $0.03 mil. **Budget** (2017): $205 mil. **Inflation** (2018-19): −1.8%.

Transport: Airports: 4.

Communications: Mobile: 48.8 per 100 pop. **Broadband:** 47.3 per 100 pop. **Internet:** 53.6%.

Health: Expend.: 11.6%. **Life expect.:** 65.6 male; 71.0 female. **Births:** 19.9 per 1,000 pop. **Deaths:** 6.9 per 1,000 pop. **Infant**

mortality: 32.2 per 1,000 live births. **Undernourished:** 12.1%. **HIV:** NA. **COVID-19:** 5,085 cases, 24 deaths; rates per 100,000: 4,257.0 cases, 20.1 deaths. 68.2% vaccinated.

Education: Compulsory: ages 6-14. **Literacy:** NA.

Website: www.president.gov.ki

A British protectorate since 1892, the Gilbert and Ellice Islands colony was completed with the inclusion of the Phoenix Islands, 1937. Tarawa Atoll was the scene of some of the fiercest fighting in the Pacific during WWII.

Self-rule was granted 1971; the Ellice Islands separated from the colony in 1975 and became independent Tuvalu, 1978. Kiribati (pronounced *Kiribass*) independence was attained July 12, 1979. Kiribati's land area is shrinking as a result of rising sea levels; in 2014, the government began buying land in Fiji for agriculture and possible future resettlement.

Opposition candidate Taneti Maamau won the Mar. 9, 2016, presidential election. With Chinese investment increasing, Kiribati broke relations with Taiwan, Sept. 20, 2019. Maamau won a second term as president, June 22, 2020.

Korea, North
Democratic People's Republic of Korea

People: Population: 26,072,217 (55). **Age distrib.:** <15: 19.9%; 65+: 11.0%. **Growth:** 0.4%. **Migrants:** 0.2%. **Pop. density:** 560.8 per sq mi, 216.5 per sq km. **Urban:** 63.2%. **Ethnic groups:** racially homogeneous; small Chinese community, a few ethnic Japanese. **Languages:** Korean. **Religions:** agnostic 58.5%, atheist 15.1%, new religionist 12.6%, ethnic religionist 11.9%.

Geography: Total area: 46,540 sq mi, 120,538 sq km (97); **Land area:** 46,490 sq mi, 120,408 sq km. **Location:** Northern E Asia. China and Russia on N, S. Korea on S. **Topography:** Mountains and hills cover nearly entire country, with narrow valleys and small plains in between. N and E coasts are most rugged areas. **Arable land:** 19.1%. **Capital:** P'yongyang, 3,157,538.

Government: Type: Dictatorship, single-party state. **Head of state:** State Affairs Commission Pres. Kim Jong Un; b. 1983; officially assumed post Dec. 17, 2011. **Head of govt.:** Supreme People's Assembly Pres. Choe Ryong Hae; in office: Apr. 11, 2019. **Local divisions:** 9 provinces, 4 special administration cities. **Defense budget:** NA. **Active troops:** 1,280,000.

Economy: Industries: military prods.; machine building, elec. power, chemicals; mining, metallurgy; textiles, food proc.; tourism. **Chief agric.:** rice, maize, vegetables, apples, potatoes, cabbages. **Natural resources:** coal, iron ore, limestone, magnesite, graphite, copper, zinc, lead, prec. metals, hydropower. **Water:** 2,993 cu m per capita. **Electricity prod.:** 14.5 bil kWh. **Labor force:** agric. 43.5%, industry 14.2%, services 42.3%. **Unemployment:** 3.0%.

Finance: Monetary unit: Won (KPW) (900.00 = $1 U.S.). **GDP:** NA; **per capita GDP:** NA; **GDP growth:** NA. **Imports** (2018): $2.3 bil; China 96%. **Exports** (2017): $4.6 bil; China 67%, Suriname 6%. **Budget** (2007): $3.3 bil. **Inflation:** NA.

Transport: Railways: 4,620 mi. **Airports:** 39.

Communications: Mobile (2021): 23.1 per 100 pop. **Broadband** (2021): 23.1 per 100 pop. **Internet:** NA.

Health: Expend.: NA. **Life expect.:** 69.5 male; 76.5 female. **Births:** 13.4 per 1,000 pop. **Deaths:** 9.5 per 1,000 pop. **Infant mortality:** 16.2 per 1,000 live births. **Undernourished:** 45.5%. **HIV:** NA. **COVID-19:** NA.

Education: Compulsory: ages 6-17. **Literacy:** 100.0%.

Permanent UN mission: 820 Second Ave., 13th Fl., New York, NY 10017; (212) 972-3105.

Website: naenara.com.kp

The Democratic People's Republic of Korea was founded May 1, 1948, in the zone occupied by Russia after WWII. Its armies tried to conquer the south, 1950. After three years of fighting, with Chinese and U.S. intervention, a cease-fire was proclaimed. A demilitarized zone (DMZ) was established, straddling the cease-fire line.

For the next four decades, a hard-line Communist regime headed by Kim Il Sung kept tight control over the nation's political, economic, and cultural life. The nation used its mineral and hydroelectric resources to develop its military strength. By the early 1990s, North Korea was widely believed to be developing nuclear weapons. The U.S. and North Korea signed an agreement, Oct. 21, 1994, providing for phased dismantling of North Korea's nuclear development program in return for U.S. energy aid and improved ties with the U.S.

Kim Il Sung died July 8, 1994. He was succeeded by his son, Kim Jong Il. Defections by high officials, a deteriorating economy, and severe food shortages plagued North Korea, beginning in the late 1990s. North Korea and Japan agreed to normalize relations in a Sept. 2002 summit.

In Oct. 2002, North Korea admitted to pursuing a secret nuclear weapons program in violation of past agreements. During 2003-09, as six-nation talks sponsored by China sought to resolve the nuclear issue, North Korea alternately stopped and resumed its nuclear program. North Korea conducted its first nuclear explosion Oct. 9, 2006.

In Apr.-May 2009, North Korea suspended participation in the six-nation talks, expelled IAEA inspectors, tested multiple missiles,

and exploded a nuclear device underground. The UN Security Council June 12 toughened sanctions on North Korea.

Kim Jong Il died Dec. 17, 2011. He was succeeded by his son Kim Jong Un. In Dec. 2013, Kim Jong Un ordered the execution of his politically powerful uncle, Jang Song Thaek.

North Korea conducted a nuclear test Feb. 10, 2013, and it negated, Mar. 11, 2013, the cease-fire agreement with the South that ended the Korean War. It conducted numerous short- and medium-range missile tests 2013-15. North Korea was apparently responsible for cyberattacks on Sony Pictures Entertainment, Nov. 2014, related to a comedy film about Kim Jong Un. North Korea conducted its fourth nuclear weapons test on Jan. 6, 2016, and its fifth on Sept. 9. North Korea continued missile tests, 2016-17, including its first ICBM launch, July 4, 2017. U.S. and UN sanctions were strengthened in 2016 and again in 2017. North Korea conducted its sixth nuclear test, Sept. 3, 2017.

On Apr. 27, 2018, Kim Jong Un met in the DMZ with South Korean Pres. Moon Jae-in. They agreed to work toward a peace treaty and denuclearization of the Korean Peninsula. North Korea said it destroyed, May 24, its nuclear test site. At a June 12 summit meeting in Singapore with U.S. Pres. Donald Trump, Kim again made a general denuclearization pledge. However, U.S. officials, and an Aug. 2018 UN report, concluded that North Korea was continuing its nuclear and missile programs. Two Trump-Kim summits in 2019 produced no progress. Beginning May 2019, North Korea fired a number of short-range missiles, its first missile tests since 2017. Tests of various types of missiles continued in 2020-23.

North Korea initially maintained it had no cases of COVID-19, which began spreading worldwide in early 2020. Protective measures, such as closing the border in 2020 with key trading partner China, contributed to a severe economic crisis; some imports from China resumed in early 2022. In May 2022, North Korea acknowledged for the first time that COVID-19 was spreading in the country. Millions of cases had likely occurred by the time Kim Jong Un declared victory over COVID-19 on Aug. 11; the claim met with widespread international skepticism.

Korea, South
Republic of Korea

People: Population: 51,966,948 (28). **Age distrib.:** <15: 11.5%; 65+: 18.4%. **Growth:** 0.2%. **Migrants:** 3.4%. **Pop. density:** 1,388.7 per sq mi, 536.2 per sq km. **Urban:** 81.5%. **Ethnic groups:** homogeneous. **Languages:** Korean, English (widely taught). **Religions:** Christian 32.7% (independent 13.5%, Protestant 12.6%), Buddhist 24.8% (Mahayanist), ethnic religionist 15.3%, new religionist 14.4%, Confucianist 10.8%.

Geography: Total area: 38,502 sq mi, 99,720 sq km (107); **Land area:** 37,421 sq mi, 96,920 sq km. **Location:** Northern E Asia. N. Korea on N. **Topography:** Mountainous, with a rugged E coast. W and S coasts are deeply indented, with many islands and harbors. **Arable land:** 13.8%. **Capital:** Seoul, 9,988,049; Sejong (administrative capital for some of govt.). **Cities:** Busan, 3,471,949; Incheon, 2,848,557; Daegu, 2,180,997; Daejeon, 1,577,436; Gwangju, 1,529,472.

Government: Type: Presidential republic. **Head of state and govt.:** Pres. Yoon Suk-yeol; b. 1960; in office: May 10, 2022. **Local divisions:** 9 provinces, 6 metropolitan cities, 1 special city, 1 special self-governing city. **Defense budget:** $43.0 bil. **Active troops:** 555,000.

Economy: Industries: electronics, telecom, auto prod., chemicals, shipbuilding, steel. **Chief agric.:** rice, vegetables, cabbages, milk, onions, pork. **Natural resources:** coal, tungsten, graphite, molybdenum, lead. **Water:** 1,359 cu m per capita. **Electricity prod.:** 587.3 bil kWh. **Labor force:** agric. 5.3%, industry 24.6%, services 70.0%. **Unemployment:** 2.8%.

Finance: Monetary unit: Won (KRW) (1,324.37 = $1 U.S.). **GDP:** $2.6 tril; **per capita GDP:** $50,070; **GDP growth:** 2.6%. **Imports:** $698.1 bil; (2021) China 24%, US 12%, Japan 9%. **Exports:** $771.2 bil; (2021) China 24%, US 15%, Vietnam 9%, Hong Kong 6%. **Tourism:** $10.5 bil. **Budget:** $372.4 bil. **Inflation:** 5.1%.

Transport: Railways: 2,472 mi. **Motor vehicles:** 498.8 per 1,000 pop. **Airports:** 71.

Communications: Mobile: 148.6 per 100 pop. **Broadband:** 120.1 per 100 pop. **Internet:** 97.2%.

Health: Expend.: 8.4%. **Life expect.:** 80.1 male; 86.4 female. **Births:** 7.0 per 1,000 pop. **Deaths:** 7.3 per 1,000 pop. **Infant mortality:** 2.8 per 1,000 live births. **Undernourished:** <2.5%. **HIV:** NA. **COVID-19:** 33,897,537 cases, 35,557 deaths; rates per 100,000: 66,116.8 cases, 69.4 deaths. 86.4% vaccinated.

Education: Compulsory: ages 6-14. **Literacy:** 98.8%.

Website: www.korea.net

The recorded history of Korea, once called the Hermit Kingdom, dates back to the 1st cent. BCE. It was united in a kingdom under the Silla Dynasty, 668 CE. It was at times associated with the Chinese empire; the treaty that concluded the Sino-Japanese war of 1894-95 recognized Korea's complete independence. In 1910 Japan forcibly annexed Korea, controlling it until 1945. (Japan's exploitation of forced labor and "comfort women" while it occupied Korea strained Japanese-South Korean relations in subsequent decades.)

At the Potsdam conference, July 1945, near the end of WWII, the 38th parallel was designated as the line dividing Soviet (north) and U.S. (south) occupation zones. Soviet and U.S. troops entered Korea.

The South Koreans formed the Republic of Korea in May 1948. Dr. Syngman Rhee was chosen president. A separate, Communist regime was formed in the North; its army (later aided by Chinese troops) attacked the south in June 1950, initiating the Korean War. UN troops, largely U.S. and under U.S. command, supported South Korea in the war, which ended in an armistice (July 1953) leaving Korea divided by a demilitarized zone (DMZ) along the 38th parallel. The U.S. kept troops in South Korea (about 28,500 in 2023).

Rhee's authoritarian rule became increasingly unpopular, forcing his resignation Apr. 26, 1960. In an army coup May 16, 1961, Gen. Park Chung-hee became chairman of a ruling junta. First elected president, 1963, Park was assassinated by the chief of the Korean intelligence agency, Oct. 26, 1979.

In May 1980, Gen. Chun Doo-hwan, head of military intelligence, ordered the brutal suppression of pro-democracy demonstrations in Kwangju. Chun became president, Aug. 27, 1980. On July 1, 1987, following anti-government protests, Chun agreed to democratic reforms. In Dec., Roh Tae-woo, a longtime ally of Chun's, was elected president.

Pres. Kim Young-sam took office in 1993. Convicted of mutiny, treason, and corruption, Chun was sentenced to death by a Seoul court, Aug. 26, 1996, for his role in the 1979 coup and 1980 Kwangju massacre; Roh received a 225-year prison sentence. Kim Dae-jung, a longtime dissident, won the presidential election Dec. 18, 1997. Chun and Roh were released and pardoned Dec. 22.

For seeking improved relations with North Korea, Kim Dae-jung was named, Oct. 13, 2000, winner of the Nobel Peace Prize. Roh Moo-hyun won the 2002 presidential election.

The IAEA, Sept. 2, 2004, said South Korea had acknowledged having secretly processed a small amount of uranium to near weapons-grade level in 2000 (North Korea, 2006-17, conducted 6 nuclear weapons tests).

Conservative Park Geun-hye became South Korea's first female president in Dec. 19, 2012, elections. Pres. Park was impeached for corruption by the National Assembly, Dec. 9, 2016, and removed from office, Mar. 10, 2017. A criminal trial ended, Apr. 6, 2018, in a conviction and prison sentence; she was pardoned and released in Dec. 2021.

Following a series of North Korean missile tests, a U.S.-South Korean agreement to deploy an advanced U.S. missile defense system known as THAAD in South Korea was announced July 8, 2016.

Moon Jae-in of the Democratic Party (DP), who campaigned on a policy of diplomatic engagement with North Korea, won the May 9, 2017, presidential election. Moon met with North Korean leader Kim Jong Un in the DMZ, Apr. 27, 2018, but North-South tensions subsequently increased.

A U.S.-South Korea trade liberalization agreement went into effect Mar. 15, 2012. Revisions signed Sept. 24, 2018, were aimed in part at increasing U.S. auto exports.

After a Constitutional Court decision, abortion was decriminalized as of Jan. 1, 2021. Amid economic problems and a lack of results from engagement with North Korea, conservative Yoon Suk-yeol narrowly defeated the DP candidate in the Mar. 9, 2022, presidential election. Concerned by aggressive Chinese and North Korean military actions, the Yoon government sought improved relations with Japan; at an Aug. 2023 summit meeting, South Korea, the U.S., and Japan agreed to increase security cooperation.

South Korea was affected by late Jan. 2020 by the COVID-19 pandemic. Total confirmed cases by Aug. 2023 were 7th-highest in the world.

Kosovo
Republic of Kosovo

People: Population: 1,964,327 (148). **Age distrib.:** <15: 23.1%; 65+: 8.2%. **Growth:** 0.6%. **Migrants:** NA. **Pop. density:** 467.3 per sq mi, 180.4 per sq km. **Urban:** NA. **Ethnic groups:** Albanian 92.9%, Bosniak 1.6%, Serb 1.5%. **Languages:** Albanian, Serbian (both official); Bosnian. **Religions:** Muslim 92.6% (Sunni), Christian 6.3%.

Geography: Total area: 4,203 sq mi, 10,887 sq km (162); **Land area:** 4,203 sq mi, 10,887 sq km. **Location:** SE Europe. Serbia on N, Montenegro on NW, Albania on SW, North Macedonia on SE. **Topography:** Low flood basins surrounded by several high mountain ranges. **Arable land:** 27.4%. **Capital:** Pristina.

Government: Type: Parliamentary republic. **Head of state:** Pres. Vjosa Osmani; b. 1982; in office: Apr. 4, 2021. **Head of govt.:** Prime Min. Albin Kurti; b. 1975; in office: Mar. 22, 2021. **Local divisions:** 38 municipalities. **Defense budget:** NA. **Active troops:** 2,500 Kosovo Security Force (nonmilitary) only.

Economy: Industries: mineral mining, constr. materials, base metals, leather, machinery, appliances, foodstuffs and beverages. **Chief agric.:** wheat, corn, berries; dairy, livestock; fish. **Natural resources:** nickel, lead, zinc, magnesium, lignite, kaolin, chrome,

bauxite. **Water:** NA. **Electricity prod.:** 6.3 bil kWh. **Labor force:** agric. 4.4%, industry 17.4%, services 78.2%. **Unemployment:** NA.

Finance: Monetary unit: Euro (EUR) (0.93 = $1 U.S.). **GDP:** $25.9 bil; **per capita GDP:** $14,723; **GDP growth:** 3.5%. **Imports:** $6.1 bil; (2021) Germany 13%, Turkey 13%, China 10%, Serbia 7%, Italy 6%. **Exports:** $3.1 bil; (2021) U.S. 16%, Albania 15%, North Macedonia 12%, Germany 8%, Italy 8%. **Budget** (2020): $2.5 bil. **Inflation:** 11.6%.

Transport: Railways: 272 mi. **Airports:** 3.

Communications: Mobile: NA. **Broadband:** NA. **Internet** (2018): 89.4%.

Health: Expend.: NA. **Life expect.:** 69.9 male; 74.5 female. **Births:** 14.6 per 1,000 pop. **Deaths:** 7.7 per 1,000 pop. **Infant mortality:** 24.9 per 1,000 live births. **Undernourished:** NA. **HIV:** NA. **COVID-19:** 273,923 cases, 3,209 deaths; rates per 100,000: 15,254.7 cases, 178.7 deaths. 46.3% vaccinated.

Education: Compulsory: ages 6-14. **Literacy:** NA.

Website: www.rks-gov.net

Kosovo was part of the Roman and Byzantine empires before Serbs, a Slavic people, took control in the Middle Ages. After Ottoman Turks defeated Serb forces, 1389, Kosovo's population became predominantly Muslim and Kosovar (ethnic Albanian). Serbia regained control in the First Balkan War (1912-13). Kosovo entered the Kingdom of Serbs, Croats, and Slovenes as part of Serbia after World War I and became an autonomous province of Serbia, a constituent republic of Yugoslavia, after World War II.

Revoking provincial autonomy, Serbia began ruling Kosovo by force in 1989. Albanian secessionists proclaimed an independent Republic of Kosovo in July 1990. As Yugoslavia collapsed, the republics of Serbia (incl. Kosovo) and Montenegro proclaimed a new Federal Republic of Yugoslavia, 1992. Guerrilla attacks by the Kosovo Liberation Army (KLA) in 1997 brought a ferocious counter-offensive by Serbian authorities.

Fearful that the Serbs were employing "ethnic cleansing" tactics, NATO launched an air war against Yugoslavia, Mar.-June 1999; the Serbs retaliated by terrorizing the Kosovars. Hundreds of thousands fled, mostly to Albania and Macedonia (now North Macedonia). A 50,000-member multinational force (KFOR) entered Kosovo in June, and most refugees returned by Sept. 1, 1999.

From June 1999, Kosovo was administered by a UN mission (UNMIK). Kosovo declared independence, Feb. 17, 2008. More than 100 nations, including the U.S. and most EU members, have recognized Kosovo; Serbia and Russia have not.

An EU special prosecutor reported, July 29, 2014, evidence of ethnic cleansing against Serbs by the KLA in the late 1990s. Prime Min. Hashim Thaçi, who headed the KLA at that time, had denied any wrongdoing. Thaçi was replaced as prime min., Dec. 9, 2014. Parliament elected Thaçi president of Kosovo, Feb. 26, 2016. An indictment against Thaçi for war crimes was announced June 24, 2020; he resigned Nov. 5. Parliament speaker Vjosa Osmani became acting head of state and was elected president by parliament, Apr. 4, 2021. After his party swept Feb. 14, 2021, parliamentary elections, Albin Kurti became prime minister.

Tensions between ethnic Serbs and Albanians in northern Kosovo remained high, prompting KFOR to increase its troop strength in 2023 (about 4,500 by midyear). Ethnic Serb gunmen battled police in northern Kosovo, Sept. 24, 2023, leaving 4 people dead.

Kuwait
State of Kuwait

People: Population: 3,103,580 (134). **Age distrib.:** <15: 23.3%; 65+: 3.4%. **Growth:** 1.1%. **Migrants:** 72.8%. **Pop. density:** 451.1 per sq mi, 174.2 per sq km. **Urban:** 100.0%. **Ethnic groups:** Asian 40.3%, Kuwaiti 30.4%, other Arab 27.4%. **Languages:** Arabic (official), English (widely spoken). **Religions:** Muslim (official) 82.4% (Sunni 66%, Shia 17%), Christian 12.1%, Hindu 3.9%.

Geography: Total area: 6,880 sq mi, 17,818 sq km (153). **Land area:** 6,880 sq mi, 17,818 sq km. **Location:** Middle East, at N end of Persian Gulf. Iraq on N, Saudi Arabia on S. **Topography:** Flat, very dry, and extremely hot. **Arable land:** 0.4%. **Capital:** Kuwait City, 3,297,759.

Government: Type: Constitutional monarchy (emirate). **Head of state:** Emir Nawaf al-Ahmad al-Jabir al-Sabah; b. 1937; in office: Sept. 30, 2020. **Head of govt.:** Prime Min. Sheikh Ahmad Al-Nawaf Al-Ahmad al-Sabah; in office: Mar. 5, 2023. **Local divisions:** 6 governorates. **Defense budget:** $9.2 bil. **Active troops:** 17,500.

Economy: Industries: petroleum, petrochemicals, cement, shipbuilding and repair, water desalination, food proc., constr. materials. **Chief agric.:** eggs, dates, tomatoes, cucumbers, poultry, milk. **Natural resources:** petroleum, fish, shrimp, nat. gas. **Water:** 5 cu m per capita. **Crude oil reserves:** 101.5 bil bbls (incl. half of Neutral Zone reserves with Saudi Arabia). **Electricity prod.:** 71.2 bil kWh. **Labor force:** agric. 2.0%, industry 25.3%, services 72.7%. **Unemployment:** 2.5%.

Finance: Monetary unit: Dinar (KWD) (0.31 = $1 U.S.). **GDP:** $247.8 bil; **per capita GDP:** $58,056; **GDP growth:** 8.2%. **Imports:** $49.0 bil; China 14%, UAE 12%, U.S. 10%, Saudi Arabia 6%, Japan 6%. **Exports:** $77.1 bil; China 20%, South Korea 16%, India 15%,

Japan 10%, Taiwan 6%. **Tourism:** $470 mil. **Budget:** $72.0 bil. **Inflation:** 4.0%.

Transport: Motor vehicles: 774.4 per 1,000 pop. **Airports:** 4.
Communications: Mobile: 181.0 per 100 pop. **Broadband:** 151.5 per 100 pop. **Internet:** 99.7%.
Health: Expend.: 6.3%. **Life expect.:** 77.9 male; 80.9 female. **Births:** 17.7 per 1,000 pop. **Deaths:** 2.3 per 1,000 pop. **Infant mortality:** 7.3 per 1,000 live births. **Undernourished:** <2.5%. **HIV:** <0.1%. **COVID-19:** 666,081 cases, 2,570 deaths; rates per 100,000: 15,597.0 cases, 60.2 deaths. 78.4% vaccinated.
Education: Compulsory: ages 6-14. **Literacy:** 96.5%.
Website: www.pm.gov.kw

Kuwait is ruled by the Sabah dynasty, founded 1759. Britain ran foreign relations and defense from 1899 until independence in 1961. More than two-thirds of the population is non-Kuwaiti, including many Palestinians and non-Arab Asians, and cannot vote.

Oil exports provide most of Kuwait's income. Oil pays for free medical care and education for citizens. There is no income tax. Government efforts to diversify the economy proceeded slowly.

Kuwait was attacked and overrun by Iraqi forces Aug. 1990. In Operation Desert Storm a U.S.-led coalition began bombing Iraq and Iraqi forces in Kuwait, Jan. 1991, then launched a ground assault Feb. 23. By Feb. 27, Iraqi forces were routed and Kuwait liberated.

Political rights were extended to women, May 16, 2005; the first female cabinet member was appointed June 12. A suicide bomber killed 27 people and wounded more than 200 at a Shiite mosque, June 26, 2015; an ISIS-affiliated Sunni extremist group claimed responsibility.

Sheikh Sabah al-Ahmad al-Jabir al-Sabah, emir for 14 years, died Sept. 29, 2020. He was succeeded by his half-brother, Sheikh Nawaf al-Ahmad al-Jabir al-Sabah. The new emir's half-brother, Crown Prince Sheikh Meshal al-Ahmad al-Sabah, assumed most of the emir's responsibilities in Nov. 2021. After Sept. 29, 2022, legislative elections (in which Islamists and other opposition candidates made gains) were annulled, new elections, June 6, 2023, produced a somewhat more pro-government legislature.

Kyrgyzstan
Kyrgyz Republic

People: Population: 6,122,781 (111). **Age distrib.:** <15: 29.5%; 65+: 6.6%. **Growth:** 0.8%. **Migrants:** 3.1%. **Pop. density:** 82.7 per sq mi, 31.9 per sq km. **Urban:** 37.8%. **Ethnic groups:** Kyrgyz 73.8%, Uzbek 14.8%, Russian 5.1%, other (incl. Uyghur, Tajik, Turk, Kazakh, Tatar, Ukrainian, Korean, German) 5.2%. **Languages:** Kyrgyz, Russian (both official); Uzbek. **Religions:** Muslim 89.3% (Sunni), agnostic 5.2%, Christian 3.8%.
Geography: Total area: 77,202 sq mi, 199,951 sq km (85); **Land area:** 74,055 sq mi, 191,801 sq km. **Location:** Central Asia. Kazakhstan on N, China on E, Uzbekistan on W, Tajikistan on S. **Topography:** Landlocked country nearly covered by Tien Shan and Pamir Mts.; avg. elevation 9,020 ft. Issyk-Kul, a large salt lake in NE, is 1 mi above sea level. **Arable land:** 6.7%. **Capital:** Bishkek, 1,104,742.
Government: Type: Parliamentary republic. **Head of state and govt.:** Pres. Sadyr Japarov; b. 1968; in office: Jan. 28, 2021. **Local divisions:** 7 provinces, 2 cities. **Defense budget:** NA. **Active troops:** 10,900.
Economy: Industries: small machinery, textiles, food proc., cement, shoes, lumber, refrigerators, furniture, elec. motors. **Chief agric.:** milk, potatoes, sugar beet, maize, wheat, barley. **Natural resources:** hydropower, gold, rare earth metals, coal, oil, nat. gas, nepheline, mercury, bismuth, lead, zinc. **Water:** 3,620 cu m per capita. **Crude oil reserves:** 40 mil bbls. **Electricity prod.:** 14.5 bil kWh. **Labor force:** agric. 16.6%, industry 26.9%, services 56.6%. **Unemployment:** 4.6%.
Finance: Monetary unit: Som (KGS) (88.25 = $1 U.S.). **GDP:** $41.7 bil; **per capita GDP:** $6,133; **GDP growth:** 7.0%. **Imports:** $5.9 bil; China 53%, Russia 17%, Kazakhstan 7%, Uzbekistan 7%. **Exports:** $3.4 bil; UK 56%, Kazakhstan 13%, Russia 13%. **Tourism:** $207 mil. **Budget:** $2.9 bil. **Inflation:** 13.9%.
Transport: Railways: 263 mi. **Airports:** 18.
Communications: Mobile (2021): 130.4 per 100 pop. **Broadband** (2021): 119.3 per 100 pop. **Internet:** 77.9%.
Health: Expend.: 5.3%. **Life expect.:** 68.6 male; 77.0 female. **Births:** 19.1 per 1,000 pop. **Deaths:** 6.1 per 1,000 pop. **Infant mortality:** 25.1 per 1,000 live births. **Undernourished:** 4.8%. **HIV:** 0.3%. **COVID-19:** 87,925 cases, 1,024 deaths; rates per 100,000: 1,347.7 cases, 15.7 deaths. 20.4% vaccinated.
Education: Compulsory: ages 6-15. **Literacy:** 99.6%.
Website: www.gov.kg

The region was inhabited around the 13th cent. by the Kyrgyz. It was annexed to Russia, 1864, and became a constituent republic of the USSR in 1936. Kyrgyzstan declared independence Aug. 31, 1991, ahead of the USSR disbanding Dec. 26, 1991.

In power since 1990, Pres. Askar Akayev won a third 5-year term in the 2000 election. Fraud by Akayev loyalists in parliamentary elections Feb.-Mar. 2005 sparked protests. Akayev fled the country, Mar. 24, and formally resigned, Apr. 4. His interim successor, former Prime Min. Kurmanbek Bakiyev, a leader of the "tulip revolution,"

won the 2005 presidential vote. He was reelected, 2009, but was ousted by opposition parties Apr. 7, 2010.

Fighting in mid-June 2010 between majority Kyrgyz and minority Uzbeks in the southern cities of Osh and Jalalabad claimed up to 2,000 lives. Former Prime Min. Sooronbay Jeenbekov won the Oct. 15, 2017, presidential election. Violent protests against alleged widespread fraud followed Oct. 4, 2020, parliamentary elections. The results, favoring parties supporting Pres. Jeenbekov, were annulled, and Jeenbekov resigned Oct. 15. Sadyr Japarov, until recently jailed for abducting a political rival, succeeded Jeenbekov and won a landslide victory in a Jan. 10, 2021, presidential election. A new constitution approved in an Apr. 11, 2021, referendum gave Kyrgyzstan a presidential rather than parliamentary system of government. Kyrgyzstan-Tajikistan fighting in a disputed border region flared in Apr. 2021 and again in Sept. 2022.

Laos
Lao People's Democratic Republic

People: Population: 7,852,377 (103). **Age distrib.:** <15: 30.6%; 65+: 4.6%. **Growth:** 1.3%. **Migrants:** 0.7%. **Pop. density:** 88.1 per sq mi, 34.0 per sq km. **Urban:** 38.2%. **Ethnic groups:** Lao 53.2%, Khmou 11%, Hmong 9.2%, Phouthay 3.4%, Tai 3.1%, Makong 2.5%, Katong 2.2%, Lue 2%. **Languages:** Lao (official), French, English, ethnic langs. **Religions:** Buddhist 54.6% (Theravadin), ethnic religionist 40.4%, Christian 2.8%.
Geography: Total area: 91,429 sq mi, 236,800 sq km (82); **Land area:** 89,112 sq mi, 230,800 sq km. **Location:** Indochina Peninsula in SE Asia. Myanmar, China on N; Vietnam on E; Cambodia on S; Thailand on W. **Topography:** Landlocked, dominated by jungle. Mountains along E border are source of E-W rivers. Mekong R. defines most of W border. **Arable land:** 5.3%. **Capital:** Vientiane, 721,199.
Government: Type: Communist state. **Head of state:** Pres. Thongloun Sisoulith; b. 1945; in office: Mar. 22, 2021. **Head of govt.:** Prime Min. Sonxai Siphandon; in office: Dec. 30, 2022. **Local divisions:** 17 provinces, 1 prefecture. **Defense budget:** NA. **Active troops:** 29,100.
Economy: Industries: mining, timber, elec. power, agric. proc., rubber, constr., garments. **Chief agric.:** rice, roots/tubers, cassava, sugarcane, vegetables, bananas. **Natural resources:** timber, hydropower, gypsum, tin, gold, gems. **Water:** 45,838 cu m per capita. **Electricity prod.:** 40.0 bil kWh. **Labor force:** agric. 58.1%, industry 10.8%, services 31.1%. **Unemployment:** 2.6%.
Finance: Monetary unit: Kip (LAK) (19,516.74 = $1 U.S.). **GDP:** $70.7 bil; **per capita GDP:** $9,384; **GDP growth:** 2.7%. **Imports:** $6.5 bil; Thailand 53%, China 26%, Vietnam 10%. **Exports:** $7.8 bil; Thailand 36%, China 28%, Vietnam 16%. **Tourism:** $1 mil. **Budget:** $3.8 bil. **Inflation:** 23.0%.
Transport: Railways: 262 mi. **Airports:** 8.
Communications: Mobile (2021): 65.0 per 100 pop. **Broadband** (2021): 56.4 per 100 pop. **Internet:** 62.0%.
Health: Expend.: 2.7%. **Life expect.:** 67.0 male; 70.3 female. **Births:** 20.4 per 1,000 pop. **Deaths:** 6.3 per 1,000 pop. **Infant mortality:** 36.6 per 1,000 live births. **Undernourished:** 4.7%. **HIV:** 0.4%. **COVID-19:** 218,793 cases, 671 deaths; rates per 100,000: 3,007.2 cases, 9.2 deaths. 78.2% vaccinated.
Education: Compulsory: ages 6-14. **Literacy:** 87.1%.
Website: na.gov.la

Laos became a French protectorate in 1893, but regained independence as a constitutional monarchy July 19, 1949. Conflicts among neutralist, Communist, and conservative factions created a chaotic political situation. Armed conflict increased after 1960.

The three factions formed a coalition government in June 1962 with neutralist Prince Souvanna Phouma as premier. A 14-nation conference in Geneva signed agreements, 1962, guaranteeing independence. By 1964 the leftist Pathet Lao had withdrawn from the coalition, and, with aid from North Vietnamese troops, renewed attacks. During the Vietnam War, U.S. planes (1964-73) dropped more than 2 mil tons of bombs on targets in Laos, principally the Ho Chi Minh trail, a supply line from North Vietnam to Communist forces in Laos, South Vietnam, and Cambodia. (Beginning in the 1990s, the U.S., other nations, and the UN provided aid to dismantle unexploded bombs.)

After Pathet Lao military gains in Laos, Souvanna Phouma, May 1975, ordered government troops to cease fighting; the Pathet Lao took control. The Lao People's Democratic Republic was proclaimed Dec. 3, 1975.

From the mid-1970s through the 1980s, Laos relied on Vietnam for military and financial aid. After easing its finance laws in 1988, Laos attracted investment from Thailand, China, South Korea, the U.S., and other nations. Laos was admitted to the Assn. of SE Asian Nations in 1997. The U.S. Congress approved normalization of trade with Laos in 2004.

Despite environmental and safety concerns, since the 1990s, dozens of dams have been built or planned on Mekong R. tributaries, providing hydroelectricity for domestic use and export. A dam collapse, July 23, 2018, killed at least 35.

Latvia
Republic of Latvia

People: Population: 1,821,750 (149). **Age distrib.:** <15: 14.9%; 65+: 21.7%. **Growth:** −1.1%. **Migrants:** 12.7%. **Pop. density:** 75.8 per sq mi, 29.3 per sq km. **Urban:** 68.7%. **Ethnic groups:** Latvian 62.7%, Russian 24.5%, Belarusian 3.1%, Ukrainian 2.2%, Polish 2%. **Languages:** Latvian (official), Russian. **Religions:** Christian 83.2% (Protestant 37.5%, Catholic 23.2%, Orthodox 21.9%), agnostic 12.9%, atheist 3.2%.

Geography: Total area: 24,938 sq mi, 64,589 sq km (122); **Land area:** 24,034 sq mi, 62,249 sq km. **Location:** E Europe, on Baltic Sea. Estonia on N; Russia on E; Belarus, Lithuania on S. **Topography:** Lowland with numerous lakes, marshes, and peat bogs. Principal river is W. Dvina (Daugava). Glacial hills in E. **Arable land:** 21.9%. **Capital:** Riga, 621,369.

Government: Type: Parliamentary republic. **Head of state:** Pres. Edgars Rinkevics; b. 1973; in office, July 8, 2023. **Head of govt.:** Evika Silina; b. 1975; in office, Sept. 15, 2023. **Local divisions:** 36 municipalities, 7 state cities. **Defense budget:** $852 mil. **Active troops:** 6,600.

Economy: Industries: processed foods, processed wood prods., textiles, processed metals, pharmaceuticals, railroad cars, synthetic fibers. **Chief agric.:** wheat, milk, rapeseed, barley, oats, potatoes. **Natural resources:** peat, limestone, dolomite, amber, hydropower, timber. **Water:** 18,524 cu m per capita. **Electricity prod.:** 5.5 bil kWh. **Labor force:** agric. 6.8%, industry 23.5%, services 69.6%. **Unemployment:** 6.4%.

Finance: Monetary unit: Euro (EUR) (0.93 = $1 U.S.). **GDP:** $75.3 bil; **per capita GDP:** $39,956; **GDP growth:** 2.0%. **Imports:** $26.6 bil; (2021) Lithuania 15%, Russia 14%, Germany 9%, Poland 8%, Estonia 8%. **Exports:** $25.2 bil; (2021) Lithuania 17%, Estonia 9%, UK 8%, Germany 7%, Russia 7%. **Tourism:** $753 mil. **Budget** (2020): $14.2 bil. **Inflation:** 17.3%.

Transport: Railways: 1,377 mi. **Motor vehicles:** 472.8 per 1,000 pop. **Airports:** 18.

Communications: Mobile: 117.1 per 100 pop. **Broadband:** 120.1 per 100 pop. **Internet:** 91.0%.

Health: Expend.: 7.4%. **Life expect.:** 71.8 male; 80.8 female. **Births:** 8.5 per 1,000 pop. **Deaths:** 14.7 per 1,000 pop. **Infant mortality:** 4.8 per 1,000 live births. **Undernourished:** <2.5%. **HIV:** 0.7%. **COVID-19:** 975,826 cases, 7,374 deaths; rates per 100,000: 51,152.6 cases, 386.5 deaths. 69.6% vaccinated.

Education: Compulsory: ages 5-15. **Literacy:** 99.9%.

Website: www.mk.gov.lv

Prior to 1918, Latvia was occupied by the Russians and Germans. It was an independent republic, 1918-39. The Aug. 1939 Soviet-German agreement assigned Latvia to the Soviet sphere of influence. It was officially absorbed by the USSR in 1940. It was overrun by the German army in 1941, but retaken in 1945.

Latvia declared independence, Aug. 21, 1991. The last Russian troops in Latvia withdrew by Aug. 31, 1994. Responding to international pressure, Latvian voters, 1998, eased citizenship laws that had discriminated against some 500,000 ethnic Russians. Latvia joined the EU and NATO in 2004. It began using the euro as its currency Jan. 1, 2014.

After more than 50 people died, Nov. 21, 2013, in a Riga supermarket roof collapse, Prime Min. Valdis Dombrovskis (of the center-right Unity Party) resigned. Laimdota Straujuma became Latvia's first woman prime min., Jan. 22, 2014. She resigned, Dec. 7, 2015, after agreeing to an unpopular EU refugee resettlement program. NATO announced, Feb. 5, 2016, it would station troops in Latvia to deter Russian aggression. After money-laundering scandals, populist parties did well in inconclusive Oct. 6, 2018, elections. Krisjanis Karins of New Unity formed a coalition and became prime min., Jan. 23, 2019. Following Russia's Feb. 2022 invasion of Ukraine, a June 2022 NATO summit pledged to increase troops defending Latvia. High inflation, related to the Ukraine war, plagued the economy in 2022-23. New Unity won the most votes in Oct. 1, 2022, elections. Elected by parliament, May 31, 2023, Edgars Rinkevics became Latvia's first openly gay president. Disputes within his coalition led Karins to resign, Aug. 17, 2023. Evika Silina of New Unity became prime min. in Sept.

Lebanon
Lebanese Republic

People: Population: 5,331,203 (121). **Age distrib.:** <15: 19.2%; 65+: 9.1%. **Growth:** 0.6%. **Migrants:** 25.1%. **Pop. density:** 1,349.7 per sq mi, 521.1 per sq km. **Urban:** 89.4%. **Ethnic groups:** Arab 95%, Armenian 4%. (Many Christian Lebanese identify not as Arab but as Phoenician, descendants of ancient Canaanites.) **Languages:** Arabic (official), French, English, Armenian. **Religions:** Muslim 60.0% (Shia 28%, Sunni 27%, Islamic schismatic 5%), Christian 33.8% (Catholic 27.5%), agnostic 3.0%, Buddhist 2.0% (Theravadin).

Geography: Total area: 4,015 sq mi, 10,400 sq km (163) **Land area:** 3,950 sq mi, 10,230 sq km. **Location:** Middle East, on E end of Mediterranean Sea. Syria on E, Israel on S. **Topography:** Narrow coastal strip. Two N-S mountain ranges enclose the fertile Beqaa Valley. The Litani R. runs S through the valley. **Arable land:** 13.6%. **Capital:** Beirut, 2,421,354.

Government: Type: Parliamentary republic. **Head of state:** Vacant. **Head of govt.:** Caretaker Prime Min. Najib Mikati; b. 1955; in office: Sept. 10, 2021. **Local divisions:** 8 governorates. **Defense budget:** NA. **Active troops:** 60,000.

Economy: Industries: banking, tourism, real estate and constr., food proc., wine, jewelry, cement, textiles, mineral and chem. prods., wood and furniture prods. **Chief agric.:** potatoes, milk, tomatoes, apples, oranges, olives. **Natural resources:** limestone, iron ore, salt, water (surplus in a water-deficit region). **Water:** 660 cu m per capita. **Electricity prod.:** 20.6 bil kWh. **Labor force:** agric. 3.8%, industry 20.8%, services 75.4%. **Unemployment:** 12.6%.

Finance: Monetary unit: Pound (LBP) (15,002.37 = $1 U.S.). **GDP (2021):** $80.1 bil; **per capita GDP (2021):** $14,331; **GDP growth** (2021): −7.0%. **Imports:** $17.4 bil; UAE 11%, China 10%, Italy 8%, Greece 8%, Turkey 7%, U.S. 6%. **Exports:** $10.1 bil; Switzerland 27%, UAE 15%, South Korea 11%, Saudi Arabia 7%, Kuwait 6%. **Tourism:** $3.1 bil. **Budget:** $16.6 bil. **Inflation** (2020-21): 154.8%.

Transport: Railways: 249 mi (unusable due to damage from fighting). **Motor vehicles:** 195.6 per 1,000 pop. **Airports:** 5.

Communications: Mobile (2021): 76.7 per 100 pop. **Broadband** (2021): 77.8 per 100 pop. **Internet:** 86.6%.

Health: Expend.: 8.0%. **Life expect.:** 77.6 male; 80.5 female. **Births:** 12.9 per 1,000 pop. **Deaths:** 5.6 per 1,000 pop. **Infant mortality:** 6.9 per 1,000 live births. **Undernourished:** NA. **HIV:** <0.1%. **COVID-19:** 1,239,904 cases, 10,947 deaths; rates per 100,000: 18,165.9 cases, 160.4 deaths. 35.4% vaccinated.

Education: Compulsory: ages 6-15. **Literacy:** 95.3%.

Website: www.pcm.gov.lb or www.presidency.gov.lb

Formed from five former Turkish Empire districts, Lebanon became independent Sept. 1, 1920, and was administered under French mandate 1920-41. French troops withdrew in 1946.

Under the 1943 National Covenant, all public positions were divided among the various religious communities, with Christians in the majority. By the 1970s, Muslims became the majority and demanded a larger political and economic role.

U.S. Marines intervened, May-Oct. 1958, during a Syrian-aided revolt. Continued raids against Israeli civilians, 1970-75, brought Israeli retaliation in southern Lebanon.

An estimated 60,000 were killed in a 1975-76 civil war. Palestinian units and leftist Muslims fought against Maronite militia (the Phalange) and other Christians. Several Arab countries provided support to various factions, while Israel aided Christian forces. Syria, which intervened in 1976 to fight Palestinian groups, largely policed a cease-fire.

Israeli forces invaded Lebanon June 6, 1982, attacking strongholds of the Palestine Liberation Organization (PLO). Israeli and Syrian forces engaged in the Bekaa Valley. On Aug. 21, the PLO evacuated W Beirut after massive Israeli bombings. Israeli troops entered W Beirut following the Sept. 14 assassination of newly elected Lebanese Pres. Bashir Gemayel. On Sept. 16, 1982, Lebanese Christian troops entered the Sabra and Shatila refugee camps and massacred hundreds of Palestinian civilians. An agreement May 17, 1983, between Lebanon, Israel, and the U.S. (but not Syria) provided for the withdrawal of Israeli troops; at least 30,000 Syrian troops remained in Lebanon, and Israel held onto a "security zone" in the south.

In 1983, some 50 people were killed in an explosion at the U.S. embassy, Apr. 18; 241 U.S. service members and 58 French soldiers died in separate Islamist suicide attacks, Oct. 23. The 1980s witnessed kidnappings of U.S., British, French, and Soviet citizens by Islamic militants.

A treaty signed May 22, 1991, between Lebanon and Syria recognized Lebanon as a separate state for the first time since 1943.

Israeli forces conducted air raids and artillery strikes against guerrilla bases and villages in southern Lebanon, causing over 200,000 to flee their homes July 25-29, 1993. Some 500,000 civilians fled in Apr. 1996 when Israel struck suspected guerrilla bases in the south. The economy revived in the 1990s, but Syria continued to dominate Lebanon's political affairs. Israel withdrew virtually all its troops from southern Lebanon by May 2000, leaving Hezbollah, an Iranian-backed Shiite Muslim guerrilla group, in control of much of the region.

Rafik al-Hariri, a former prime min. (1992-98, 2000-04), was killed by a truck bomb, Feb. 14, 2005. Many Lebanese blamed Syria or Hezbollah. As anti-Syrian protests mounted, Syrian troops left Lebanon. A Hezbollah official was convicted in absentia by a UN tribunal, Aug. 18, 2020, of conspiracy in connection with the bombing.

Beginning July 2006, Hezbollah bombarded northern Israel with thousands of rockets, and Israeli air and ground forces assaulted suspected Hezbollah strongholds in southern Lebanon and southern Beirut. A UN-sponsored cease-fire took hold, Aug. 14, 2006. To enforce the truce, thousands of Lebanese troops moved into southern Lebanon, and the small UN force already in Lebanon (UNIFIL) was expanded. UNIFIL had about 10,000 uniformed personnel in Lebanon as of Aug. 30, 2023.

A 2008 power-sharing accord between the government and Hezbollah eased factional violence and paved the way for Gen.

Michel Suleiman to become president, ending an 18-month stalemate. Factional disputes in parliament led to a lengthy delay in electing a successor when Suleiman's term expired in May 2014. Maronite Christian Michel Aoun, after gaining the support of Hezbollah, was elected president Oct. 31, 2016. Saad al-Hariri, a Sunni Muslim, became prime min., Dec. 18, 2016. Hezbollah and allied Shiite parties made gains in May 6, 2018, parliamentary elections.

The Syrian civil war, in which Hezbollah fighters supported Syria's government (dominated by followers of the Alawite sect of Shiite Islam) and many opposition fighters were Sunni Muslims, spilled over into Lebanon beginning in 2012. As of June 30, 2023, about 795,000 Syrian refugees were in Lebanon.

Months of protests against deteriorating economic conditions began in Oct. 2019. Prime Min. Hariri resigned, Oct. 29. Hassan Diab replaced him, Jan. 21, 2020. The economic crisis deepened in the following months.

A massive explosion in Beirut, Aug. 4, 2020, at a warehouse storing dangerous chemicals caused more than 200 deaths and about 6,500 injuries and displaced 300,000. Protests against government corruption and inefficiency followed, and the country's economic crisis continued to worsen. Diab resigned Aug. 10, 2020. Entrepreneur and former Prime Min. Najib Mikati formed a new government and became prime minister Sept. 10, 2021. After May 15, 2022, elections, Mikati became caretaker prime minister, as negotiations to form a new government proceeded. When Pres. Aoun's term ended, Oct. 2022, parliamentary deadlocks delayed the selection of a successor.

Lesotho
Kingdom of Lesotho

People: Population: 2,210,646 (144). **Age distrib.:** <15: 32.4%; 65+: 5.4%. **Growth:** 0.8%. **Migrants:** 0.6%. **Pop. density:** 188.6 per sq mi, 72.8 per sq km. **Urban:** 30.4%. **Ethnic groups:** Sotho 99.7%. **Languages:** Sesotho, English (both official); Phuti; Zulu; Xhosa. **Religions:** Christian 92.9% (Catholic 51.8%, Protestant 31.6%), ethnic religionist 5.6%.

Geography: Total area: 11,720 sq mi, 30,355 sq km (138); **Land area:** 11,720 sq mi, 30,355 sq km. **Location:** Southern Africa. Completely surrounded by South Africa. **Topography:** Landlocked and mountainous, 5,000 to 11,000 ft in elevation. **Arable land:** 14.1%. **Capital:** Maseru, 201,851.

Government: Type: Parliamentary constitutional monarchy. **Head of state:** King Letsie III; b. 1963; in office: Feb. 7, 1996. **Head of govt.:** Prime Min. Ntsokoane Samuel Matekane; in office: Oct. 28, 2022. **Local divisions:** 10 districts. **Defense budget:** $40 mil. **Active troops:** 2,000.

Economy: Industries: food, beverages, textiles, apparel assembly, handicrafts, constr., tourism. **Chief agric.:** milk, potatoes, maize, vegetables, fruit, beef. **Natural resources:** water, diamonds, sand, clay, building stone. **Water:** 1,411 cu m per capita. **Electricity prod.:** 501.2 mil kWh. **Labor force:** agric. 30.0%, industry 34.9%, services 35.1%. **Unemployment:** 18.0%.

Finance: Monetary unit: Loti (LSL) (18.56 = $1 U.S.). **GDP:** $6.2 bil; **per capita GDP:** $2,695; **GDP growth:** 0.6%. **Imports:** $2.2 bil; South Africa 85%. **Exports:** $1.1 bil; U.S. 29%, Belgium 26%, South Africa 25%, Switzerland 6%. **Tourism:** $8 mil. **Budget (2020):** $1.2 bil. **Inflation:** 8.3%.

Transport: Airports: 3.
Communications: Mobile: 67.5 per 100 pop. **Broadband:** 67.1 per 100 pop. **Internet:** 48.0%.
Health: Expend.: 11.8%. **Life expect.:** 57.9 male; 62.0 female. **Births:** 23.0 per 1,000 pop. **Deaths:** 10.9 per 1,000 pop. **Infant mortality:** 47.0 per 1,000 live births. **Undernourished:** 46.0%. **HIV:** 19.3%. **COVID-19:** 34,490 cases, 706 deaths; rates per 100,000: 1,610.0 cases, 33.0 deaths. 43.8% vaccinated.
Education: Compulsory: ages 6-12. **Literacy:** 81.0%.
Website: www.gov.ls

Lesotho (once called Basutoland) became a British protectorate in 1868. Independence came Oct. 4, 1966. Livestock raising is a major industry; textiles, clothing, and diamonds are leading exports. Cultivation of marijuana is a significant source of income.

Letsie III became king Nov. 12, 1990. In Mar. 1993, Ntsu Mokhehle, a civilian, was elected prime minister, ending 23 years of military rule. After a series of violent disturbances, the king dismissed the Mokhehle government Aug. 17, 1994; constitutional rule was restored Sept. 14.

Letsie abdicated Jan. 25, 1995. King Moshoeshoe died, Jan. 15, 1996, and Letsie returned to power Feb. 7. After parliamentary elections May 26, 2012, the left-leaning Thomas Motsoahae Thabane became prime min. He fled to South Africa, Aug.-Sept. 2014, when units of the military attacked police forces loyal to Thabane. June 3, 2017, elections returned Thabane to office. He resigned May 19, 2020, after allegations he was involved in the 2017 murder of his wife. Finance Min. Moeketsi Majoro became prime min. May 20.

Lesotho suffered a spike in COVID-19 cases with the emergence of the Omicron variant in late 2021-early 2022. After his party won the most seats in Oct. 7, 2022, elections, Samuel Matekane became prime min. Oct. 28, 2022.

Liberia
Republic of Liberia

People: Population: 5,506,280 (119). **Age distrib.:** <15: 39.3%; 65+: 3.2%. **Growth:** 2.7%. **Migrants:** 1.7%. **Pop. density:** 148.1 per sq mi, 57.2 per sq km. **Urban:** 53.6%. **Ethnic groups:** Kpelle 20.3%, Bassa 13.4%, Grebo 10%, Gio 8%, Mano 7.9%, Kru 6%, Lorma 5.1%, Kissi 4.8%, Gola 4.4%, Krahn 4%, Vai 4%, Mandingo 3.2%, Gbandi 3%. **Languages:** English (official), about 20 ethnic-group langs. **Religions:** Christian 41.5% (Protestant 18.3%, independent 13.4%), ethnic religionist 39.9%, Muslim 16.4% (Sunni).

Geography: Total area: 43,000 sq mi, 111,369 sq km (102); **Land area:** 37,189 sq mi, 96,320 sq km. **Location:** SW coast of W Africa. Sierra Leone on W, Guinea on N, Côte d'Ivoire on E. **Topography:** Marshy Atlantic coastline rises to low mountains and plateaus in forested interior. Six major rivers flow in parallel courses to the ocean. **Arable land:** 5.2%. **Capital:** Monrovia, 1,678,020.

Government: Type: Presidential republic. **Head of state and govt.:** Pres. George Weah; b. 1966; in office: Jan. 22, 2018. **Local divisions:** 15 counties. **Defense budget:** $19 mil. **Active troops:** 2,010.

Economy: Industries: mining, rubber and palm oil proc., diamonds. **Chief agric.:** cassava, sugarcane, oil palm fruit, rice, bananas, vegetables. **Natural resources:** iron ore, timber, diamonds, gold, hydropower. **Water:** 45,871 cu m per capita. **Electricity prod.:** 920.2 mil kWh. **Labor force:** agric. 40.6%, industry 8.1%, services 51.3%. **Unemployment:** 3.6%.

Finance: Monetary unit: Dollar (LRD) (187.09 = $1 U.S.). **GDP:** $9.1 bil; **per capita GDP:** $1,725; **GDP growth:** 4.8%. **Imports (2019):** $1.2 bil; China 41%, Japan 21%, South Korea 18%. **Exports (2019):** $554.0 mil; Guyana 32%, Poland 10%, Switzerland 8%, Japan 7%. **Tourism (2019):** $2 mil. **Budget:** $6 mil. **Inflation (2017-18):** 23.6%.

Transport: Railways: 267 mi (mostly inoperable due to damage from fighting). **Motor vehicles:** 17.6 per 1,000 pop. **Airports:** 2.
Communications: Mobile (2021): 31.8 per 100 pop. **Broadband (2021):** 6.6 per 100 pop. **Internet:** 33.6%.
Health: Expend.: 9.5%. **Life expect.:** 59.7 male; 63.0 female. **Births:** 33.0 per 1,000 pop. **Deaths:** 8.5 per 1,000 pop. **Infant mortality:** 56.1 per 1,000 live births. **Undernourished:** 38.4%. **HIV:** 1.0%. **COVID-19:** 8,090 cases, 294 deaths; rates per 100,000: 160.0 cases, 5.8 deaths. 73.8% vaccinated.
Education: Compulsory: ages 6-11. **Literacy:** 48.3%.
Website: www.emansion.gov.lr

Liberia was founded in 1822 by freed Black slaves from the U.S. who settled at Monrovia with the aid of colonization societies. It became a republic July 26, 1847, with a constitution modeled on that of the U.S. Descendants of freed slaves dominated politics for much of the 19th and 20th cents.

Under Pres. William V. S. Tubman, Liberia was a founding member of the UN in 1945. Tubman died in 1971 and was succeeded by his vice president, William R. Tolbert Jr. Charging rampant corruption, an Army Redemption Council of enlisted men staged a bloody predawn coup, Apr. 12, 1980, killing Pres. Tolbert and installing Sgt. Samuel Doe, an Indigenous African, as head of state. In 1985, Doe was chosen president in a disputed election.

A civil war began Dec. 1989. In Sept. 1990, Pres. Doe was executed. Despite the introduction of a multinational peacekeeping force, the conflict intensified. Factional fighting devastated Monrovia in Apr. 1996. Ruth Perry became modern Africa's first female head of state Sept. 3, 1996, leading a transitional government. By then, the civil war had claimed more than 150,000 lives.

Former rebel leader Charles Taylor was elected president July 1997. The UN imposed sanctions in 2001, to punish Liberia for aiding an insurgency in Sierra Leone.

A UN-sponsored war crimes tribunal indicted Taylor, June 2003, for his role in the Sierra Leone conflict. With Liberian rebels threatening Monrovia, Taylor resigned Aug. 11 and went into exile. The UN authorized a 15,000-member peacekeeping force (UNMIL) Sept. 19. (UNMIL officially ended Mar. 30, 2018.) A businessman, Charles Gyude Bryant, was sworn in Oct. 14, 2003, to head a power-sharing interim government. Ellen Johnson-Sirleaf won presidential elections in 2005 and 2011, and shared the 2011 Nobel Peace Prize. Charles Taylor was convicted at The Hague in 2012 of aiding and abetting war crimes and crimes against humanity, and sentenced to 50 years in prison. Former soccer star George Weah succeeded Johnson-Sirleaf after winning a Dec. 26, 2017, presidential runoff election.

Liberia was seriously affected, 2014-16, by an Ebola virus epidemic; the WHO reported a total of 10,675 Liberian cases, which caused 4,809 deaths. The country was affected by the COVID-19 pandemic beginning in 2020.

Libya
State of Libya

People: Population: 7,252,573 (105). **Age distrib.:** <15: 32.8%; 65+: 4.4%. **Growth:** 1.5%. **Migrants:** 12.0%. **Pop. density:** 10.7 per sq mi, 4.1 per sq km. **Urban:** 81.6%. **Ethnic groups:** Berber and Arab 97%, other (incl. Egyptian, Greek, Indian, Italian, Maltese, Pakistani, Tunisian, Turkish) 3%. **Languages:** Arabic (official), Italian, English, Berber. **Religions:** Muslim 99.0% (Sunni [official] 94%, Islamic schismatic 5%).

Geography: Total area: 679,362 sq mi, 1,759,540 sq km (16); **Land area:** 679,362 sq mi, 1,759,540 sq km. **Location:** Mediterranean coast of N Africa. Tunisia, Algeria on W; Niger, Chad on S; Sudan, Egypt on E. **Topography:** Desert and semidesert regions cover 92% of land with low mountains in N, higher mountains in S, and a narrow coastal zone. **Arable land:** 1.0%. **Capital:** Tripoli, 1,183,292. **Cities:** Misratah, 984,193; Banghazi, 859,209.

Government: Type: In transition. **Head of state:** Pres. Mohammed Al Menfi; b. 1976; in office: Feb. 5, 2021. **Head of govt.:** Prime Min. Abdul Hamid Dbeibeh; b. 1959; in office: Feb. 5, 2021. **Local divisions:** 22 governorates. **Defense budget/active troops:** NA.

Economy: Industries: petroleum, petrochemicals, aluminum, iron and steel, food proc., textiles, handicrafts, cement. **Chief agric.:** potatoes, watermelons, tomatoes, onions, dates, milk. **Natural resources:** petroleum, nat. gas, gypsum. **Water:** 102 cu m per capita. **Crude oil reserves:** 48.4 bil bbls. **Electricity prod.:** 32.0 bil kWh. **Labor force:** agric. 16.3%, industry 19.3%, services 64.4%. **Unemployment:** 20.7%.

Finance: Monetary unit: Dinar (LYD) (4.82 = $1 U.S.). **GDP:** $159.2 bil; **per capita GDP:** $23,375; **GDP growth:** –1.2%. **Imports** (2020): $14.3 bil; China 16%, Turkey 14%, Italy 9%, UAE 9%. **Exports** (2020): $9.5 bil; Italy 18%, China 16%, Germany 15%, Spain 15%, UAE 6%, France 6%. **Budget:** $37.5 bil. **Inflation** (2016-17): 28.5%.

Transport: Motor vehicles: 558.4 per 1,000 pop. **Airports:** 68. **Communications: Mobile:** 204.6 per 100 pop. **Broadband:** 125.6 per 100 pop. **Internet:** 21.8%.

Health: Expend.: NA. **Life expect.:** 75.2 male; 79.8 female. **Births:** 20.9 per 1,000 pop. **Deaths:** 3.5 per 1,000 pop. **Infant mortality:** 11.0 per 1,000 live births. **Undernourished:** 8.4%. **HIV:** 0.2%. **COVID-19:** 507,266 cases, 6,437 deaths; rates per 100,000: 7,382.4 cases, 93.7 deaths. 18.0% vaccinated.

Education: Compulsory: ages 6-14. **Literacy:** 91.0%.

Website: pm.gov.ly or www.embassyoflibyadc.org

First settled by Berbers, Libya was ruled in succession by Carthage, Rome, the Vandals, and the Ottomans. Italy ruled from 1912, and Britain and France after WWII. Libya became an independent constitutional monarchy Jan. 2, 1952. In 1969 a junta led by Col. Muammar al-Qaddafi seized power.

Under Qaddafi's dictatorship, dissent was suppressed and wars were waged with Egypt and Chad. During the 1980s, Libya was accused of promoting terrorism, such as the Apr. 5, 1986, bombing of a West Berlin nightclub, which killed 3, including a U.S. serviceman. The U.S. attacked what it called "terrorist-related targets" in Libya, Apr. 14, including Qaddafi's barracks.

Libyan agents were accused of planting bombs that blew up Pan Am Flight 103 over Lockerbie, Scotland, killing 270 people Dec. 21, 1988, and French UTA Flight 772 over Niger, killing 170 people Sept. 19, 1989.

Libya agreed in 2003 to renounce terrorism and settle compensation cases for the families of the Lockerbie and UTA bombing victims. The UN lifted sanctions in Sept., and in Dec., Libya renounced nuclear, chemical, and biological weapons and long-range missiles.

Arab Spring rebels fought Qaddafi's forces throughout the spring of 2011. With diplomatic backing from the Arab League and the UN, NATO forces imposed an arms embargo and no-fly zone against Qaddafi. Aided by NATO, rebels took control of Tripoli Aug. 23, 2011. Rebels killed Qaddafi Oct. 20, 2011. Ansar al-Shariah terrorists attacked the U.S. consulate and a CIA base in Benghazi Sept. 11, 2012, killing Ambassador J. Christopher Stephens and three other Americans.

As violence between Islamists, rival militia groups, and pro-government forces continued, parliamentary elections were held June 25, 2014. The new parliament met in Tobruk because of Islamist militia control of Tripoli. A UN-backed Government of National Accord (GNA), formed in Jan. 2016, largely took control in Tripoli, but was not recognized by the Tobruk government. ISIS seized territory in Libya by early 2016. An offensive by pro-GNA and other militia forces, aided by the U.S., had retaken most ISIS territory by Dec. 2016. By mid-2017, forces led by former Libyan army Gen. Khalifa Haftar gained control of eastern Libya.

Haftar's forces began, Apr. 2019, an offensive toward Tripoli; they were supported by Russian military aid but ended their unsuccessful offensive June 2020. The GNA forces, plus various militias and other armed groups that opposed Haftar, received Turkish military support. UN-sponsored talks produced a cease-fire, Oct. 23, 2020, followed by agreement, Feb. 5, 2021, on a new interim government in Tripoli charged with preparing for nationwide elections. However, planned Dec. 2021 elections were postponed, and disagreements and conflict between rival groups continued in 2022 and 2023.

Beginning in 2014, Libya was a major transit route for African, Asian, and other migrants trying to reach Europe. By mid-2017, efforts by Italy and other EU nations reduced migrant crossings of the Mediterranean, but crossing attempts increased again in 2021-23. By early 2023, more than 700,000 migrants from dozens of countries were estimated to be in Libya. Thousands of migrants intercepted at sea were in Libyan detention centers, where they often faced harsh conditions.

Torrential rains, Sept. 2023, in NE Libya caused two dams in poor repair to collapse and led to catastrophic flooding in and near the coastal city of Derna. Thousands died, and tens of thousands were displaced.

Liechtenstein
Principality of Liechtenstein

People: Population: 39,993 (190). **Age distrib.:** <15: 15.3%; 65+: 20.4%. **Growth:** 0.7%. **Migrants:** 67.9%. **Pop. density:** 647.4 per sq mi, 250.0 per sq km. **Urban:** 14.6%. **Ethnic groups** (by nationality): Liechtensteiner 65.6%, Swiss 9.6%, Austrian 5.8%, German 4.5%, Italian 3.1%. **Languages:** German (official). **Religions:** Christian 86.8% (Catholic [official] 73.5%, Protestant 11.2%), Muslim 7.4% (Sunni), agnostic 5.5%.

Geography: Total area: 62 sq mi, 160 sq km (191); **Land area:** 62 sq mi, 160 sq km. **Location:** Central Europe, in Alps. Switzerland on W, Austria on E. **Topography:** Rhine Valley occupies one-third of country, Alps in the rest. **Arable land:** 10.8%. **Capital:** Vaduz, 5,470.

Government: Type: Constitutional monarchy. **Head of state:** Prince Hans-Adam II; b. 1945; in office: Nov. 13, 1989. **Head of govt.:** Prime Min. Daniel Risch; b. 1978; in office: Mar. 25, 2021. **Local divisions:** 11 communes. **Defense budget/active troops:** NA.

Economy: Industries: electronics, metal mfg., dental prods., ceramics, pharmaceuticals, food prods., precision instruments, tourism, optical instruments. **Chief agric.:** wheat, barley, corn, potatoes; livestock, dairy prods. **Natural resources:** hydroelectric potential. **Water:** 0. **Labor force:** agric. 0.8%, industry 36.9%, services 62.3%. **Unemployment:** NA.

Finance: Monetary unit: Swiss Franc (CHF) (0.88 = $1 U.S.). **GDP:** NA; **per capita GDP:** NA; **GDP growth:** NA. **Imports** (2014): $2.2 bil. **Exports** (2015): $3.2 bil. Data excl. trade with Switzerland. **Budget** (2011): $890.4 mil. **Inflation** (2015-16): –0.4%.

Transport: Railways: 6 mi (owned by Austrian Railway System). **Communications: Mobile:** 126.3 per 100 pop. **Broadband:** 123.3 per 100 pop. **Internet:** 95.6%.

Health: Expend.: NA. **Life expect.:** 80.5 male; 85.6 female. **Births:** 10.3 per 1,000 pop. **Deaths:** 8.1 per 1,000 pop. **Infant mortality:** 4.0 per 1,000 live births. **Undernourished:** NA. **HIV:** NA. **COVID-19:** 21,474 cases, 87 deaths; rates per 100,000: 55,421.1 cases, 224.5 deaths. 68.0% vaccinated.

Education: Compulsory: ages 6-14. **Literacy:** NA.

Website: www.liechtenstein.li

Liechtenstein became sovereign in 1806. It is united with Switzerland by a customs and monetary union. Many workers commute daily from Austria, Switzerland, and Germany.

On Aug. 15, 2004, Prince Hans-Adam II assigned day-to-day responsibilities to his son, Crown Prince Alois. Long a tax haven, Liechtenstein took steps, 2008-13, to ease banking secrecy laws.

Lithuania
Republic of Lithuania

People: Population: 2,655,755 (139). **Age distrib.:** <15: 15.3%; 65+: 21.6%. **Growth:** –1.0%. **Migrants:** 5.3%. **Pop. density:** 109.7 per sq mi, 42.4 per sq km. **Urban:** 68.7%. **Ethnic groups:** Lithuanian 84.6%, Polish 6.5%, Russian 5%. **Languages:** Lithuanian (official), Russian, Polish. **Religions:** Christian 89.7% (Catholic 80.9%), agnostic 9.3%.

Geography: Total area: 25,212 sq mi, 65,300 sq km (121); **Land area:** 24,201 sq mi, 62,680 sq km. **Location:** Eastern Europe, on SE coast of Baltic. Latvia on N; Belarus on E, S; Poland, Russia on W. **Topography:** Lowland with hills in W and S. Many small lakes and rivers with marshes espec. in N and W. **Arable land:** 36.4%. **Capital:** Vilnius, 541,275.

Government: Type: Semi-presidential republic. **Head of state:** Gitanas Nauseda; b. 1964; in office: July 12, 2019. **Head of govt.:** Prime Min. Ingrida Simonyte; b. 1974; in office: Dec. 11, 2020. **Local divisions:** 60 municipalities. **Defense budget:** $1.6 bil. **Active troops:** 23,000.

Economy: Industries: metal-cutting machine tools, elec. motors, TVs, refrigerators and freezers, petroleum refining, ship-building, furniture. **Chief agric.:** wheat, milk, sugar beet, rapeseed, barley, triticale. **Natural resources:** peat, amber. **Water:** 9,000 cu m per capita. **Crude oil reserves:** 12 mil bbls. **Electricity prod.:** 3.7 bil kWh. **Labor force:** agric. 5.3%, industry 26.3%, services 68.4%. **Unemployment:** 5.6%.

Finance: Monetary unit: Euro (EUR) (0.93 = $1 U.S.). **GDP:** $137.1 bil; **per capita GDP:** $48,397; **GDP growth:** 1.9%. **Imports:** $50.4 bil; (2021) Poland 12%, Germany 12%, Russia 11%, Latvia 8%. **Exports:** $53.4 bil; (2021) Russia 10%, Latvia 9%, Germany 8%, Poland 7%, U.S. 6%. **Tourism:** $590 mil. **Budget:** $18.5 bil. **Inflation:** 19.7%.

Transport: Railways: 1,187 mi. **Motor vehicles:** 614.9 per 1,000 pop. **Airports:** 22.

Communications: Mobile: 139.1 per 100 pop. **Broadband:** 133.3 per 100 pop. **Internet:** 87.7%.

Health: Expend. (2021): 7.9%. **Life expect.:** 70.6 male; 81.6 female. **Births:** 9.1 per 1,000 pop. **Deaths:** 15.2 per 1,000 pop. **Infant mortality:** 3.6 per 1,000 live births. **Undernourished:** <2.5%. **HIV:** 0.2%. **COVID-19:** 1,322,440 cases, 9,695 deaths; rates per 100,000: 47,329.9 cases, 347.0 deaths. 68.0% vaccinated.

Education: Compulsory: ages 6-16. **Literacy:** 99.8%.

Website: lrvk.lrv.lt

Lithuania, briefly occupied by the German army, 1914-18, was annexed by the Soviet Union until 1919. In 1939 it rejoined the Soviet sphere of influence and was annexed by the USSR Aug. 3, 1940.

Lithuania declared its independence Mar. 11, 1990; independence was ratified by the Soviet Union Sept. 1991. The country became a full member of NATO and the EU in 2004; it began using the euro as its currency, Jan. 1, 2015. Independent Gitanas Nauseda won a presidential runoff election, May 26, 2019. With COVID-19 cases spiking and the economy faltering, center-right parties won Oct. 2020 parliamentary elections. Ingrida Simonyte of Homeland Union became prime minister, Nov. 24, ending center-left governance.

NATO, which first stationed troops in Lithuania in 2017, decided at a June 2022 summit meeting (following Russia's Feb. 2022 invasion of Ukraine) to increase troop strength defending Lithuania.

Luxembourg
Grand Duchy of Luxembourg

People: Population: 660,924 (164). **Age distrib.:** <15: 16.7%; 65+: 15.9%. **Growth:** 1.6%. **Migrants:** 47.6%. **Pop. density:** 661.9 per sq mi, 255.6 per sq km. **Urban:** 92.1%. **Ethnic groups** (by nationality): Luxembourger 52.9%, Portuguese 14.5%, French 7.6%, Italian 3.7%, Belgian 3%, German 2%. **Languages:** Luxembourgish (national lang.), French, German (all official admin. and judicial langs.); Portuguese; Italian; English. **Religions:** Christian 73.6% (Catholic 70.9%), agnostic 20.9%, Muslim 3.5% (Sunni).

Geography: Total area: 998 sq mi, 2,586 sq km (169); **Land area:** 998 sq mi, 2,586 sq km. **Location:** Western Europe. Belgium on W, France on S, Germany on E. **Topography:** Heavy forests (Ardennes) cover N. Low, open plateau in S. **Arable land:** 24.3%. **Capital:** Luxembourg, 119,752.

Government: Type: Constitutional monarchy. **Head of state:** Grand Duke Henri; b. 1955; in office: Oct. 7, 2000. **Head of govt.:** Prime Min. Xavier Bettel; b. 1973; in office: Dec. 4, 2013. **Local divisions:** 12 cantons. **Defense budget:** $444 mil. **Active troops:** 410.

Economy: Industries: banking and financial services, constr., real estate services, iron, metals, steel, information tech., telecom, cargo transp. and logistics. **Chief agric.:** milk, wheat, barley, triticale, potatoes, pork. **Natural resources:** iron ore (no longer exploited). **Water:** 5,591 cu m per capita. **Electricity prod.:** 920.8 mil kWh. **Labor force:** agric. 1.1%, industry 9.4%, services 89.5%. **Unemployment:** 4.7%.

Finance: Monetary unit: Euro (EUR) (0.93 = $1 U.S.). **GDP:** $92.5 bil; **per capita GDP:** $142,214; **GDP growth:** 1.5%. **Imports:** $148.2 bil; Belgium 27%, Germany 24%, France 11%. **Exports:** $177.8 bil; Germany 23%, France 13%, Belgium 12%, Netherlands 6%. **Tourism:** $5.5 bil. **Budget:** $30.0 bil. **Inflation:** 6.3%.

Transport: Railways: 168 mi. **Motor vehicles:** 777.9 per 1,000 pop. **Airports:** 1.

Communications: Mobile (2021): 137.1 per 100 pop. **Broadband** (2021): 115.0 per 100 pop. **Internet:** 98.2%.

Health: Expend. (2021): 5.4%. **Life expect.:** 80.7 male; 85.8 female. **Births:** 11.6 per 1,000 pop. **Deaths:** 7.2 per 1,000 pop. **Infant mortality:** 3.2 per 1,000 live births. **Undernourished:** <2.5%. **HIV:** 0.2%. **COVID-19:** 383,075 cases, 1,000 deaths; rates per 100,000: 61,183.5 cases, 159.7 deaths. 71.7% vaccinated.

Education: Compulsory: ages 4-15. **Literacy:** NA.

Website: gouvernement.lu

Luxembourg, founded about 963, was ruled by Burgundy, Spain, Austria, and France from 1448 to 1815. It left the Germanic Confederation in 1866. Overrun by Germany in two world wars, Luxembourg ended its neutrality in 1948, when a customs union with Belgium and the Netherlands was adopted. Luxembourg was one of 12 founding members of NATO in 1949 and one of six founding members (1951) of what became the European Union.

After Oct. 20, 2013, elections, the Democratic Party's Xavier Bettel formed a center-left coalition. Same-sex marriage was legalized in 2014. Bettel, May 15, 2015, became the first EU government head to marry a same-sex partner. Bettel's coalition retained power in Oct. 14, 2018, elections.

To reduce traffic, the government made public transportation free as of Mar. 1, 2020.

Madagascar
Republic of Madagascar

People: Population: 28,812,195 (53). **Age distrib.:** <15: 37.5%; 65+: 3.8%. **Growth:** 2.2%. **Migrants:** 0.1%. **Pop. density:** 128.3 per sq mi, 49.5 per sq km. **Urban:** 40.6%. **Ethnic groups:** Malayo-Indonesian (Merina and related Betsileo), Cotiers (mixed African/

Malayo-Indonesian/Arab ancestry), French, Indian, Creole, Comoran. **Languages:** Malagasy, French (both official); English. **Religions:** Christian 59.5% (Protestant 29.9%, Catholic 24.9%), ethnic religionist 37.8%, Muslim 2.1% (Sunni).

Geography: Total area: 226,658 sq mi, 587,041 sq km (47); **Land area:** 224,534 sq mi, 581,540 sq km. **Location:** In Indian O., off SE coast of Africa. Comoro Isls. to NW, Mozambique to W. **Topography:** Humid coastal strip in E, fertile valleys in mountainous center plateau region, and a wider coastal strip on W. **Arable land:** 5.2%. **Capital:** Antananarivo, 3,872,264.

Government: Type: Semi-presidential republic. **Head of state:** Pres. Andry Rajoelina; b. 1974; in office: Jan. 19, 2019. **Head of govt.:** Prime Min. Christian Ntsay; b. 1961; in office: June 6, 2018. **Local divisions:** 6 provinces. **Defense budget:** $102 mil. **Active troops:** 13,500.

Economy: Industries: meat proc., seafood, soap, beer, leather, sugar, textiles, glassware, cement, auto assembly. **Chief agric.:** rice, sugarcane, cassava, sweet potatoes, milk, vegetables. **Natural resources:** graphite, chromite, coal, bauxite, rare earth elements, salt, quartz, tar sands, semiprec. stones, mica, fish, hydropower. **Water:** 12,170 cu m per capita. **Electricity prod.:** 2.1 bil kWh. **Labor force:** agric. 73.9%, industry 10.4%, services 15.7%. **Unemployment:** 2.1%.

Finance: Monetary unit: Ariary (MGA) (4,529.09 = $1 U.S.). **GDP:** $52.5 bil; **per capita GDP:** $1,774; **GDP growth:** 3.8%. **Imports:** $4.8 bil; China 24%, France 11%, UAE 9%, India 7%. **Exports:** $3.3 bil; U.S. 19%, France 18%, UAE 7%, China 6%, Japan 6%. **Tourism:** $93 mil. **Budget** (2022): $2.1 bil. **Inflation:** 8.2%.

Transport: Railways: 519 mi. **Motor vehicles:** 15.5 per 1,000 pop. **Airports:** 26.

Communications: Mobile: 70.2 per 100 pop. **Broadband:** 23.7 per 100 pop. **Internet:** 19.7%.

Health: Expend.: 3.9%. **Life expect.:** 67.1 male; 69.9 female. **Births:** 28.1 per 1,000 pop. **Deaths:** 5.9 per 1,000 pop. **Infant mortality:** 38.3 per 1,000 live births. **Undernourished:** 51.0%. **HIV:** 0.4%. **COVID-19:** 68,319 cases, 1,425 deaths; rates per 100,000: 246.7 cases, 5.1 deaths. 9.5% vaccinated.

Education: Compulsory: ages 6-10. **Literacy:** 77.3%.

Website: www.primature.gov.mg

Madagascar was settled 2,000 years ago by Malayan-Indonesian people, whose descendants still predominate. A unified kingdom ruled in the 18th and 19th cent. The island became a French protectorate, 1885, and a colony, 1896. Independence came June 26, 1960.

Discontent with inflation and French domination led to a coup in 1972. The new regime nationalized French-owned financial interests, closed French bases and a U.S. space-tracking station, and obtained Chinese aid. The government conducted a program of arrests, expulsion of foreigners, and repression of strikes in 1979.

In 1990, Madagascar ended a ban on multiparty politics that had existed since 1975. A 1993 presidential election ended the 17-year rule of Adm. Didier Ratsiraka.

Marc Ravalomanana won 2001 and 2006 presidential elections. A power struggle between Ravalomanana and the military-backed Andry Rajoelina led to Rajoelina's installation as head of a transitional regime, Mar. 17, 2009. Presidential elections in 2013 were won by Hery Rajaonarimampianina. Rajoelina defeated Ravalomanana in a disputed Dec. 19, 2018, presidential runoff.

The government attempted to limit media coverage of the COVID-19 pandemic that began in 2020. Years of drought, compounded by severe cyclone damage in early 2023, left more than 2 mil people in need of food and livelihood assistance.

Malawi
Republic of Malawi

People: Population: 21,279,597 (62). **Age distrib.:** <15: 38.5%; 65+: 3.8%. **Growth:** 2.3%. **Migrants:** 1.0%. **Pop. density:** 585.8 per sq mi, 226.2 per sq km. **Urban:** 18.3%. **Ethnic groups:** Chewa 34.3%, Lomwe 18.8%, Yao 13.2%, Ngoni 10.4%, Tumbuka 9.2%, Sena 3.8%, Mang'anja 3.2%. **Languages:** English (official), Chewa (common), Lambya, Lomwe, Ngoni, Nkhonde. **Religions:** Christian 80.1% (Protestant 36.6%, Catholic 32.1%, independent 11.4%), Muslim 14.5% (Sunni), ethnic religionist 4.6%.

Geography: Total area: 45,747 sq mi, 118,484 sq km (98); **Land area:** 36,324 sq mi, 94,080 sq km. **Location:** SE Africa. Zambia on W, Mozambique on S and E, Tanzania on N. **Topography:** 560 mi N-S along Lake Nyasa (Lake Malawi), most of which belongs to Malawi. High plateaus and mountains line the Rift Valley along length of nation. **Arable land:** 42.4%. **Capital:** Lilongwe, 1,276,316. **Cities:** Blantyre-Limbe, 1,030,975.

Government: Type: Presidential republic. **Head of state and govt.:** Pres. Lazarus Chakwera; b. 1955; in office: June 28, 2020. **Local divisions:** 28 districts. **Defense budget:** $75 mil. **Active troops:** 10,700.

Economy: Industries: tobacco, tea, sugar, sawmill prods., cement, consumer goods. **Chief agric.:** sweet potatoes, cassava, sugarcane, maize, mangoes/guavas, potatoes. **Natural resources:** limestone; hydropower; unexploited deposits of uranium, coal, bauxite. **Water:** 903 cu m per capita. **Electricity prod.:** 1.4 bil kWh.

Labor force: agric. 61.9%, industry 8.1%, services 30.0%. **Unemployment:** 5.6%.

Finance: Monetary unit: Kwacha (MWK) (1,077.24 = $1 U.S.). **GDP:** $35.3 bil; **per capita GDP:** $1,732; **GDP growth:** 0.9%. **Imports:** $3.6 bil; South Africa 17%, China 16%, UAE 9%, India 9%, UK 8%. **Exports:** $1.5 bil; Belgium 16%, U.S. 8%, Egypt 7%, South Africa 6%, Germany 6%. **Tourism** (2020): $26 mil. **Budget:** $2.1 bil. **Inflation:** 21.0%.

Transport: Railways: 477 mi. **Motor vehicles:** 2.5 per 1,000 pop. **Airports:** 7.

Communications: Mobile: 60.1 per 100 pop. **Broadband:** 38.7 per 100 pop. **Internet:** 24.4%.

Health: Expend.: 5.4%. **Life expect.:** 69.6 male; 75.9 female. **Births:** 27.3 per 1,000 pop. **Deaths:** 4.5 per 1,000 pop. **Infant mortality:** 32.7 per 1,000 live births. **Undernourished:** 17.8%. **HIV:** 7.1%. **COVID-19:** 88,835 cases, 2,686 deaths; rates per 100,000: 464.4 cases, 14.0 deaths. 22.1% vaccinated.

Education: Compulsory: ages 6-13. **Literacy:** 67.3%.

Website: www.malawi.gov.mw

Bantus came to the land in the 16th cent., Arab slavers in the 19th. The area became the British protectorate Nyasaland in 1891. It became independent July 6, 1964, and a republic in 1966. After three decades as a one-party state, Malawi adopted a new constitution and held multiparty elections, 1994.

Ruling-party candidate Bingu wa Mutharika won a disputed 2004 presidential election. He won reelection May 2009. Joyce Banda became Malawi's first female pres. after the death of Mutharika Apr. 5, 2012. In May 20-22, 2014, presidential elections, Peter Mutharika (the former president's brother) was declared the winner. Drought affected up to 8 mil in 2016. After Peter Mutharika appeared to narrowly win reelection, May 21, 2019, opposition candidate Lazarus Chakwera claimed voting irregularities, and the Constitutional Court, Feb. 3, 2020, annulled the result. Chakwera won a June 23 re-vote.

Affected by the COVID-19 pandemic that began in 2020, Malawi experienced widespread vaccine resistance. The country's worst known cholera outbreak began in Mar. 2022; nearly 2,000 died before the outbreak was brought under control in mid-2023. More than 1,000 died when Cyclone Freddy struck Malawi in Mar. 2023.

Malaysia

People: Population: 34,219,975 (43). **Age distrib.:** <15: 22.5%; 65+: 8.1%. **Growth:** 1.0%. **Migrants:** 10.7%. **Pop. density:** 269.7 per sq mi, 104.1 per sq km. **Urban:** 78.7%. **Ethnic groups:** Bumiputera 62.5% (Malays and Indigenous, incl. Orang Asli, Dayak, Anak Negeri), Chinese 20.6%, non-citizen 9.8%, Indian 6.2%. **Languages:** Bahasa Malaysia (official), English, Chinese, Tamil, Telugu, Malayalam, Panjabi, Thai. **Religions:** Muslim 55.8% (Sunni [official]), Chinese folk-religionist 18.6%, Christian 9.2%, Hindu 6.4%, Buddhist 5.4% (Mahayanist), ethnic religionist 3.3%.

Geography: Total area: 127,355 sq mi, 329,847 sq km (66); **Land area:** 126,895 sq mi, 328,657 sq km. **Location:** SE tip of Asia, plus N coast of the island of Borneo. Thailand, Brunei on N; Indonesia on S. **Topography:** Most of W is covered by tropical jungle, including a central mountain range that runs N-S through the peninsula. Marshy W coast, sandy E coast. Wide swampy coastal plain with interior jungles and mountains in E. **Arable land:** 2.5%.

Capital: Kuala Lumpur, 8,621,724; Putrajaya (administrative). **Cities:** Johor Bahru, 1,086,214.

Government: Type: Federal parliamentary constitutional monarchy. **Head of state:** King Sultan Abdullah Sultan Ahmad Shah; b. 1959; in office: Jan. 24, 2019. **Head of govt.:** Prime Min. Anwar Ibrahim; in office: Nov. 24, 2022. **Local divisions:** 13 states, 1 federal territory. **Defense budget:** $4.1 bil. **Active troops:** 113,000.

Economy: Industries: rubber and palm oil proc. and mfg., petroleum and nat. gas, light mfg., pharmaceuticals, medical tech., logging. **Chief agric.:** oil palm fruit, rice, poultry, eggs, vegetables, rubber. **Natural resources:** tin, petroleum, timber, copper, iron ore, nat. gas, bauxite. **Water:** 17,920 cu m per capita. **Crude oil reserves:** 3.6 bil bbls. **Electricity prod.:** 165.0 bil kWh. **Labor force:** agric. 9.6%, industry 28.3%, services 62.1%. **Unemployment:** 3.7%.

Finance: Monetary unit: Ringgit (MYR) (4.65 = $1 U.S.). **GDP:** $1.1 tril; **per capita GDP:** $33,434; **GDP growth:** 8.7%. **Imports:** $230.2 bil; (2021) China 29%, Singapore 11%, Japan 6%, US 6%, Taiwan 6%. **Exports:** $256.7 bil; (2021) Singapore 15%, China 14%, U.S. 13%, Hong Kong 6%, Japan 6%. **Tourism:** $77 mil. **Budget:** $85.9 bil. **Inflation:** 3.4%.

Transport: Railways: 1,150 mi. **Motor vehicles:** 533.5 per 1,000 pop. **Airports:** 39.

Communications: Mobile: 141.3 per 100 pop. **Broadband:** 127.4 per 100 pop. **Internet:** 97.4%.

Health: Expend.: 4.1%. **Life expect.:** 74.8 male; 78.1 female. **Births:** 14.4 per 1,000 pop. **Deaths:** 5.7 per 1,000 pop. **Infant mortality:** 6.5 per 1,000 live births. **Undernourished:** 2.7%. **HIV:** 0.3%. **COVID-19:** 5,125,089 cases, 37,187 deaths; rates per 100,000: 15,834.8 cases, 114.9 deaths. 85.1% vaccinated.

Education: Compulsory: ages 6-11. **Literacy:** 95.0%.

Website: www.malaysia.gov.my

European traders visited in the 16th cent.; Britain established control in 1867. Malaysia was created Sept. 16, 1963. It included Malaya (which gained independence in 1957 after the suppression of Communist rebels), plus the formerly British Singapore, Sabah (N Borneo), and Sarawak (NW Borneo). Singapore was separated in 1965.

Malaysia has abundant natural resources, though rainforest destruction has become a major environmental problem. Work on a federal administrative center at Putrajaya, south of Kuala Lumpur, was completed in 1999.

National Front leader Najib Razak took over the premiership in 2009. In a close election (deemed fraudulent by the opposition), May 5, 2013, the governing coalition was returned to power.

A Malaysia Airlines flight, carrying 239 passengers and crew, lost contact with air traffic control Mar. 8, 2014, and was presumed lost in the Indian Ocean. On July 17, 2014, a Malaysia Airlines flight from Amsterdam to Kuala Lumpur was shot down over separatist-controlled eastern Ukraine; all 298 people onboard were killed.

A security law enacted Dec. 3, 2015, gave the Malaysian government sweeping powers to conduct surveillance and searches and to suppress protests.

Beginning in 2015, Malaysian authorities (and other countries) investigated possible misappropriation of more than $4.5 bil from a government development fund (1MDB), including up to $1 bil in transfers to bank accounts controlled by Prime Min. Najib. After the National Front lost May 9, 2018, elections and new Prime Min. Mahathir Mohamad took office, Najib was charged, in 2018, with dozens of corruption-related offenses. He was convicted, July 28, 2020, on 7 corruption counts. With his coalition fracturing, Mahathir resigned, Feb. 24, 2020. Muhyiddin Yassin, backed by Najib's party, became prime minister Mar. 1. Criticized for his handling of the COVID-19 pandemic, Muhyiddin resigned Aug. 16, 2021. Ismail Sabri Yaakob, of Najib's party, became prime minister Aug. 21.

After losing appeals of his 2020 conviction, Najib was imprisoned, Aug. 23, 2022. A progressive coalition headed by Anwar Ibrahim won the most seats in Nov. 19, 2022, elections, and he became prime minister.

Maldives
Republic of Maldives

People: Population: 389,568 (171). **Age distrib.:** <15: 22.3%; 65+: 5.8%. **Growth:** −0.2%. **Migrants:** 13.0%. **Pop. density:** 3,385.8 per sq mi, 1,307.3 per sq km. **Urban:** 42.0%. **Ethnic groups:** homogeneous mix of Sinhalese, Dravidian, Arab, Australasian, African. **Languages:** Dhivehi (official), English (spoken by most govt. officials). **Religions:** Muslim 98.8% (Sunni [official]).

Geography: Total area: 115 sq mi, 298 sq km (188); **Land area:** 115 sq mi, 298 sq km. **Location:** In Indian O. Nearest neighbor is India to NE. **Topography:** 19 atolls with 1,190 islands, 200 inhabited. None of the islands are over 5 sq mi in area; all are nearly flat. **Arable land:** 13.0%. **Capital:** Male, 176,851.

Government: Type: Presidential republic. **Head of state and govt.:** Pres. Ibrahim Mohamed Solih; b. 1962; in office: Nov. 17, 2018. **Local divisions:** 21 admin. atolls. **Defense budget:** $101 mil. **Active troops:** 4,000.

Economy: Industries: tourism, fish proc., shipping, boat building, coconut proc., woven mats, rope. **Chief agric.:** papayas, vegetables, roots/tubers, nuts, fruit. **Natural resources:** fish. **Water:** 56 cu m per capita. **Electricity prod.:** 662.0 mil kWh. **Labor force:** agric. 10.5%, industry 26.4%, services 63.1%. **Unemployment:** 4.9%.

Finance: Monetary unit: Rufiyaa (MVR) (15.42 = $1 U.S.). **GDP:** $13.0 bil; **per capita GDP:** $24,772; **GDP growth:** 12.3%. **Imports:** $3.5 bil; UAE 24%, China 16%, Singapore 14%, India 11%, Malaysia 6%. **Exports:** $4.0 bil; Thailand 24%, U.S. 13%, China 12%, France 11%, Germany 11%. **Tourism:** $3.5 bil. **Budget** (2020): $1.8 bil. **Inflation:** 2.3%.

Transport: Airports: 7.

Communications: Mobile: 136.5 per 100 pop. **Broadband:** 53.6 per 100 pop. **Internet:** 85.8%.

Health: Expend.: 11.3%. **Life expect.:** 74.8 male; 79.7 female. **Births:** 15.3 per 1,000 pop. **Deaths:** 4.2 per 1,000 pop. **Infant mortality:** 25.0 per 1,000 live births. **Undernourished:** NA. **HIV:** <0.1%. **COVID-19:** 186,694 cases, 316 deaths; rates per 100,000: 34,538.2 cases, 58.5 deaths. 71.3% vaccinated.

Education: Compulsory: ages 6-12. **Literacy:** 97.9%.

Website: presidency.gov.mv

A British protectorate since 1887, the nation achieved independence July 26, 1965; long a sultanate, the Maldives became a republic in 1968. Rising sea levels threaten the island nation. The Indian Ocean tsunami of Dec. 26, 2004, killed at least 82 people in the Maldives.

Pres. Maumoon Abdul Gayoom, in office 1978-2008, lost a 2008 runoff election to pro-democracy leader and former political prisoner Mohamed (Anni) Nasheed. Following protests over the arrest of a judge, Nasheed resigned Feb. 2012. Abdulla Yameen Abdul Gayoom (the former president's half-brother) won a Nov. 16, 2013, presidential runoff. Nasheed, convicted in 2015 on terrorism charges, later received political asylum in the UK. In 2017, the government detained political opponents. Opposition candidate Ibrahim Mohamed Solih defeated Yameen in the Sept. 23, 2018, presidential election. Nasheed returned to the Maldives, Nov. 1, 2018. Solih's party won Apr. 6, 2019, parliamentary elections. Nasheed was severely injured in an assassination attempt, May 6, 2021. Yameen was convicted on corruption charges, Dec. 25, 2022. Mohamed Muizzu, of Yameen's party, defeated Solih in a Sept. 30, 2023, presidential runoff election.

Mali
Republic of Mali

People: Population: 21,359,722 (61). **Age distrib.:** <15: 47.1%; 65+: 3.1%. **Growth:** 2.9%. **Migrants:** 2.4%. **Pop. density:** 45.3 per sq mi, 17.5 per sq km. **Urban:** 46.2%. **Ethnic groups:** Bambara 33.3%, Fulani (Peuhl) 13.3%, Sarakole/Soninke/Marka 9.8%, Senufo/Manianka 9.6%, Malinke 8.8%, Dogon 8.7%, Sonrai 5.9%, Bobo 2.1%. **Languages:** Bambara (official), French, Peuhl/Foulfoulbe/Fulani, Dogon, Maraka/Soninke, Malinke, Sonrhai/Djerma, Minianka, Tamacheq. **Religions:** Muslim 89.3% (Sunni), ethnic religionist 8.4%, Christian 2.2%.

Geography: Total area: 478,841 sq mi, 1,240,192 sq km (23); **Land area:** 471,118 sq mi, 1,220,190 sq km. **Location:** W Africa. Mauritania, Senegal on W; Guinea, Côte d'Ivoire, Burkina Faso on S; Niger on E; Algeria on N. **Topography:** Landlocked grassy plain in upper basins of the Senegal and Niger R., extending N into the Sahara. **Arable land:** 6.8%. **Capital:** Bamako, 2,929,373.

Government: Type: Semi-presidential republic. **Head of state:** Transitional Pres. Assimi Goïta; b. c. 1983; in office: June 7, 2021. **Head of govt.:** Transitional Prime Min. Choguel Kokalla Maiga; b. 1958; in office: June 7, 2021. **Local divisions:** 10 regions, 1 district. **Defense budget:** $831 mil. **Active troops:** 21,000.

Economy: Industries: food proc., constr., phosphate and gold mining. **Chief agric.:** maize, rice, millet, sorghum, mangoes/guavas, cotton. **Natural resources:** gold, phosphates, kaolin, salt, limestone, uranium, gypsum, granite, hydropower. **Water:** 5,926 cu m per capita. **Electricity prod.:** 3.4 bil kWh. **Labor force:** agric. 67.7%, industry 10.0%, services 22.3%. **Unemployment:** 2.8%.

Finance: Monetary unit: CFA Franc (XOF) (606.88 = $1 U.S.). **GDP:** $56.9 bil; **per capita GDP:** $2,517; **GDP growth:** 3.7%. **Imports** (2020): $6.3 bil; Senegal 23%, Côte d'Ivoire 15%, China 11%, France 9%. **Exports** (2020): $5.2 bil; UAE 66%, Switzerland 26%. **Tourism** (2020): $82 mil. **Budget** (2018): $3.5 bil. **Inflation** (2020-21): 3.9%.

Transport: Railways: 368 mi. **Motor vehicles:** 2.0 per 1,000 pop. **Airports:** 8.

Communications: Mobile: 114.5 per 100 pop. **Broadband:** 58.5 per 100 pop. **Internet:** 34.5%.

Health: Expend.: 4.3%. **Life expect.:** 60.6 male; 65.1 female. **Births:** 40.5 per 1,000 pop. **Deaths:** 8.3 per 1,000 pop. **Infant mortality:** 59.0 per 1,000 live births. **Undernourished:** 12.8%. **HIV:** 0.9%. **COVID-19:** 33,151 cases, 743 deaths; rates per 100,000: 163.7 cases, 3.7 deaths. 17.9% vaccinated.

Education: Compulsory: ages 7-15. **Literacy:** 30.8%.

Website: primature.ml

Until the 15th cent. the area was part of the great Mali Empire. Timbuktu (Tombouctou) was a center of Islamic study. French rule was secured, 1898. The Sudanese Rep. and Senegal became independent as the Mali Federation in 1960, but Senegal withdrew, and the Sudanese Rep. was renamed Mali.

A coup toppled a socialist regime led, 1960-68, by Pres. Modibo Keita. Famine struck in 1973-74, killing as many as 100,000 people. The military, Mar. 1991, overthrew Pres. Moussa Traoré, who had ruled since 1968. The government and a Tuareg rebel group signed a peace accord in 1994, but Taureg separatists remained active in the north.

Amadou Toumani Touré, who led the 1991 coup, was elected president in 2002 and reelected 2007. After a Mar. 2012 coup, Islamist rebels, allied with Taureg groups, seized control of the country's north. In Jan. 2013, France and West African regional forces entered the fight against the Islamists, who were pushed out of most areas they had seized. The UN Stabilization Mission in Mali (MINUSMA) was approved Apr. 25, 2013. Ibrahim Boubacar Keita was elected president Aug. 11, 2013. Attacks by Taureg rebels and fights against Islamists continued in 2014 and early 2015. A new peace agreement with Taureg fighters was signed mid-2015, but violence continued. Islamists linked to al-Qaeda and ISIS remained active. Violence in central Mali left hundreds dead in 2019.

Beginning in June 2020, large-scale demonstrations protested corruption, economic conditions, and disputed Mar.-Apr. parliamentary elections. Keita and his prime minister, Boubou Cissé, were ousted, Aug. 18, 2020, in a military coup led by Col. Assimi Goïta. On May 24, 2021, Goïta ousted civilian transitional leaders, and he became transitional president June 7.

Fighting throughout the country persisted in 2022 and 2023, and Islamist extremists increased their control of territory in the north. Its relations with the Goïta government strained, France withdrew its troops from Mali in 2022. By 2022, Russian merce-naries were fighting alongside government troops. Following a Mali government request, the UN Security Council voted, June 30, 2023, to end the MINUSMA mission by year-end.

Malta
Republic of Malta

People: Population: 467,138 (169). **Age distrib.:** <15: 14.5%; 65+: 22.6%. **Growth:** 0.6%. **Migrants:** 26.0%. **Pop. density:** 3,828.7 per sq mi, 1,478.3 per sq km. **Urban:** 94.9%. **Ethnic groups:** Maltese (descendants of ancient Carthaginians and Phoenicians with Italian, other Mediterranean stock). **Languages:** Maltese, English (both official). **Religions:** Christian 94.7% (Catholic [official] 92.7%), Muslim 3.0% (Sunni).

Geography: Total area: 122 sq mi, 316 sq km (187); **Land area:** 122 sq mi, 316 sq km. Island of Malta is 95 sq mi. Gozo, 26 sq mi, and Comino, 1 sq mi, are other islands in group. **Location:** Center of Mediterranean Sea. Nearest neighbor is Italy to N. **Topography:** Heavily indented coastline. Low hills cover interior. **Arable land:** 24.4%. **Capital:** Valletta, 212,768.

Government: Type: Parliamentary republic. **Head of state:** Pres. George Vella; b. 1942; in office: Apr. 4, 2019. **Head of govt.:** Prime Min. Robert Abela; b. 1977; in office: Jan. 13, 2020. **Local divisions:** 68 localities. **Defense budget:** $87 mil. **Active troops:** 1,700.

Economy: Industries: tourism, electronics, shipbuilding and repair, constr., food and beverages, pharmaceuticals, footwear. **Chief agric.:** milk, tomatoes, potatoes, onions, cauliflowers, broccoli. **Natural resources:** limestone, salt. **Water:** 114 cu m per capita. **Electricity prod.:** 2.1 bil kWh. **Labor force:** agric. 0.9%, industry 17.9%, services 81.3%. **Unemployment:** 2.8%.

Finance: Monetary unit: Euro (EUR) (0.93 = $1 U.S.). **GDP:** $29.3 bil; **per capita GDP:** $55,928; **GDP growth:** 6.9%. **Imports:** $21.4 bil; Russia 22%, Italy 12%, UK 11%, Germany 6%. **Exports:** $22.1 bil; Germany 12%, France 9%, Italy 9%. **Tourism** (2020): $780 mil. **Budget:** $5.6 bil. **Inflation:** 6.2%.

Transport: Motor vehicles: 808.2 per 1,000 pop. **Airports:** 1.

Communications: Mobile: 131.6 per 100 pop. **Broadband:** 108.5 per 100 pop. **Internet:** 91.5%.

Health: Expend.: 10.8%. **Life expect.:** 81.3 male; 85.6 female. **Births:** 9.6 per 1,000 pop. **Deaths:** 8.6 per 1,000 pop. **Infant mortality:** 4.5 per 1,000 live births. **Undernourished:** 4.6%. **HIV:** 0.2%. **COVID-19:** 119,574 cases, 873 deaths; rates per 100,000: 23,237.9 cases, 169.7 deaths. 85.4% vaccinated.

Education: Compulsory: ages 5-15. **Literacy:** 94.9%.

Website: www.gov.mt

Malta was ruled by Phoenicians, Romans, Arabs, Normans, the Knights of Malta, France, and Britain (since 1814). It became independent Sept. 21, 1964, and a republic in 1974.

Malta became a full member of the EU May 1, 2004. Same-sex marriage was legalized in 2017.

The Labour Party won June 3, 2017, elections, called early by Prime Min. Joseph Muscat in the face of corruption allegations. Daphne Caruana Galizia, a journalist reporting on corruption, was killed by a car bomb, Oct. 16, 2017. Labour's Robert Abela replaced Muscat in Jan. 2020. Labour won Mar. 26, 2022, elections.

Marshall Islands
Republic of the Marshall Islands

People: Population: 80,966 (187). **Age distrib.:** <15: 30.7%; 65+: 5.5%. **Growth:** 1.3%. **Migrants:** 5.6%. **Pop. density:** 1,158.6 per sq mi, 447.3 per sq km. **Urban:** 78.9%. **Ethnic groups:** Marshallese 95.6%. **Languages:** Marshallese, English (both official). **Religions:** Christian 94.8% (Protestant 71.0%, independent 15.4%), Baha'i 2.9%.

Geography: Total area: 70 sq mi, 181 sq km (190); **Land area:** 70 sq mi, 181 sq km. **Location:** In N Pacific O.; made up of two 800-mi-long island chains, including atolls of Bikini, Enewetak, Kwajalein, Majuro, Rongelap, and Utirik. Nearest neighbors are Micronesia to W, Nauru and Kiribati to S. **Topography:** Low coral limestone and sand islands. **Arable land:** 2.8%. **Capital:** Majuro, 30,661.

Government: Type: Mixed presidential-parliamentary system in free association with U.S. **Head of state and govt.:** Pres. David Kabua; b. 1951; in office: Jan. 13, 2020. **Local divisions:** 24 municipalities. **Defense budget/active troops:** NA.

Economy: Industries: copra, tuna proc., tourism, craft items. **Chief agric.:** coconuts. **Natural resources:** coconut prods., marine prods., deep-seabed minerals. **Water:** 0. **Labor force:** agric. 11.0%, industry 16.3%, services 72.7%. **Unemployment:** NA.

Finance: Monetary unit: U.S. Dollar (USD) (1.00 = $1 U.S.). **GDP:** $300.5 mil; **per capita GDP:** $7,228; **GDP growth:** 1.5%. **Imports** (2020): $171.2 mil; South Korea 39%, China 27%, Japan 15%. **Exports** (2020): $76.7 mil; Poland 28%, Denmark 19%, South Korea 13%, Indonesia 10%, Cyprus 6%. **Tourism** (2020): $4 mil. **Budget:** $153 mil. **Inflation** (2016-17): 0%.

Transport: Airports: 4.

Communications: Mobile (2021): 38.0 per 100 pop. **Broadband:** NA. **Internet** (2017): 38.7%.

Health: Expend.: 13.0%. **Life expect.:** 72.7 male; 77.3 female. **Births:** 21.6 per 1,000 pop. **Deaths:** 4.3 per 1,000 pop. **Infant mortality:** 21.1 per 1,000 live births. **Undernourished:** NA. **HIV:** NA. **COVID-19:** 16,098 cases, 17 deaths; rates per 100,000: 27,195.3 cases, 28.7 deaths. 68.7% vaccinated.

Education: Compulsory: ages 5-17. **Literacy:** 98.3%.
Website: rmiparliament.org

The Marshall Islands were a German possession until WWI and were administered by Japan between the World Wars. After WWII, they were administered by the U.S. During 1946-58, Bikini and Enewetak Atolls were used as test sites for U.S. nuclear weapons.

A Compact of Free Association (COFA), ratified by the U.S. in 1986, gave the islands their independence; the U.S. agreed to provide financial aid to the islands, maintain their defense, and compensate victims of nuclear testing. The COFA was amended in 2003, including an extension of financial aid through 2023.

Elected by parliament, Jan. 27, 2016, Hilda Heine became the country's first female president. David Kabua replaced her in Jan. 2020. The Marshall Islands is vulnerable to rising sea levels resulting from climate change.

Mauritania
Islamic Republic of Mauritania

People: Population: 4,244,878 (127). **Age distrib.:** <15: 36.1%; 65+: 4.3%. **Growth:** 2.0%. **Migrants:** 3.9%. **Pop. density:** 10.7 per sq mi, 4.1 per sq km. **Urban:** 57.7%. **Ethnic groups:** Black Moor (Haratine—Arab-speaking descendants of African origin who are or were enslaved by white Moors) 40%, white Moor (Arab-Berber descent, known as Beydane) 30%, Sub-Saharan Mauritanian (non-Arabic speaking) 30%. **Languages:** Arabic (official and national); Pular, Soninke, Wolof (all national langs.); French. **Religions:** Muslim 99.3% (Sunni [official]).

Geography: Total area: 397,955 sq mi, 1,030,700 sq km (28); **Land area:** 397,955 sq mi, 1,030,700 sq km. **Location:** NW Africa. Western Sahara on N; Algeria, Mali on E; Senegal on S. **Topography:** Fertile Senegal R. valley in S gives way to wide central region of sandy plains and scrub trees. N is arid and extends into the Sahara. **Arable land:** 0.4%. **Capital:** Nouakchott, 1,491,958.

Government: Type: Presidential republic. **Head of state:** Pres. Mohamed Cheikh El Ghazouani; b. 1956; in office: Aug. 1, 2019. **Head of govt.:** Prime Min. Mohamed Ould Bilal; b. 1963; in office: Aug. 6, 2020. **Local divisions:** 15 regions. **Defense budget:** $229 mil. **Active troops:** 15,850.

Economy: Industries: fish proc., oil prod., mining. **Chief agric.:** rice, milk, goat milk, sheep milk, sorghum, mutton. **Natural resources:** iron ore, gypsum, copper, phosphate, diamonds, gold, oil, fish. **Water:** 2,452 cu m per capita. **Crude oil reserves:** 20 mil bbls. **Electricity prod.:** 1.9 bil kWh. **Labor force:** agric. 29.5%, industry 18.9%; services 51.7%. **Unemployment:** 11.1%.

Finance: Monetary unit: Ouguiya (MRU) (38.18 = $1 U.S.). **GDP:** $30.4 bil; **per capita GDP:** $6,424; **GDP growth:** 5.2%. **Imports:** $4.3 bil; China 26%, France 6%, Spain 6%, Morocco 6%. **Exports:** $3.2 bil; China 32%, Switzerland 13%, Spain 9%, Japan 9%. **Tourism:** $4 mil. **Budget:** $1.4 bil. **Inflation:** 9.5%.

Transport: Railways: 452 mi. **Motor vehicles:** 9.4 per 1,000 pop. **Airports:** 9.

Communications: Mobile: 113.1 per 100 pop. **Broadband:** 61.5 per 100 pop. **Internet:** 58.8%.

Health: Expend.: 3.4%. **Life expect.:** 63.1 male; 68.1 female. **Births:** 27.6 per 1,000 pop. **Deaths:** 7.3 per 1,000 pop. **Infant mortality:** 50.0 per 1,000 live births. **Undernourished:** 8.7%. **HIV:** 0.3%. **COVID-19:** 63,714 cases, 997 deaths; rates per 100,000: 1,370.3 cases, 21.4 deaths. 33.1% vaccinated.

Education: Compulsory: ages 6-14. **Literacy:** 67.0%.
Website: primature.gov.mr

A French protectorate from 1903, Mauritania became independent Nov. 28, 1960. It annexed the south of former Spanish Sahara (now Morocco-claimed Western Sahara) in 1976 but renounced its claim to the region after signing a peace treaty with the Saharan guerrillas of the Polisario Front, 1979.

Up to 10,000 people tried to emigrate in handmade boats to Spain's Canary Islands Jan.-June 2006; more than 1,700 died. After decades of military rule, civilian rule was restored, 2006-07, but a 2008 military coup toppled the elected government. The coup leader, Gen. Mohamed Ould Abdel Aziz, won disputed presidential elections in 2009 and 2014. Mohamed Ould Ghazouani, backed by Aziz, won a disputed June 22, 2019, presidential election. Amid corruption allegations, Ghazouani named a new prime minister, Aug. 6, 2020.

In 2013, U.S. troops began training and equipping Mauritanian counterterrorism forces combatting Islamic extremists. In 2017, Mauritania and four other nations created the anti-terrorism G5 Sahel Cross-Border Joint Force.

Major oil finds have recently been developed. Slavery, though repeatedly abolished, continues to exist in Mauritania.

More than 100,000 refugees fleeing violence in neighboring Mali were in Mauritania as of July 31, 2023.

Mauritius
Republic of Mauritius

People: Population: 1,309,448 (154). **Age distrib.:** <15: 15.3%; 65+: 13.4%. **Growth:** 0.1%. **Migrants:** 2.3%. **Pop. density:** 1,670.7 per sq mi, 645.0 per sq km. **Urban:** 40.9%. **Ethnic groups:** Indo-Mauritian (approx. two-thirds of pop.), Creole, Sino-Mauritian, Franco-Mauritian. **Languages:** Creole, Bhojpuri, French, English (one of two official langs. of National Assembly). **Religions:** Hindu 42.5% (Shaivite 15%, Vaishnavite 14%, Saktist 14%), Christian 33.0% (Catholic 21.2%, Protestant 10.9%), Muslim 16.7% (Sunni 13%), agnostic 2.8%, Baha'i 1.0%.

Geography: Total area: 788 sq mi, 2,040 sq km (171); **Land area:** 784 sq mi, 2,030 sq km. **Location:** In Indian O., 500 mi E of Madagascar, its nearest neighbor. **Topography:** A volcanic island nearly surrounded by coral reefs. A central plateau is encircled by peaks. **Arable land:** 37.6%. **Capital:** Port Louis, 149,365.

Government: Type: Parliamentary republic. **Head of state:** Pres. Prithvirajsing Roopun; b. 1959; in office: Dec. 2, 2019. **Head of govt.:** Prime Min. Pravind Jugnauth; b. 1961; in office: Jan. 23, 2017. **Local divisions:** 9 districts, 3 dependencies. **Defense budget:** $230 mil. **Active troops:** No standing armed forces; 2,550 paramilitary. Special Mobile Force (part of police) and coast guard provide security.

Economy: Industries: food proc. (largely sugar milling), textiles, clothing, mining, chemicals, metal prods. **Chief agric.:** sugarcane, poultry, pumpkins, gourds, potatoes, eggs. **Natural resources:** fish. **Water:** 2,163 cu m per capita. **Electricity prod.:** 2.9 bil kWh. **Labor force:** agric. 5.1%, industry 23.6%, services 71.2%. **Unemployment:** 7.2%.

Finance: Monetary unit: Rupee (MUR) (45.63 = $1 U.S.). **GDP:** $34.0 bil; **per capita GDP:** $26,906; **GDP growth:** 8.7%. **Imports:** $6.1 bil; China 15%, India 13%, France 10%, South Africa 8%, UAE 7%. **Exports:** $3.2 bil; France 10%, South Africa 10%, U.S. 10%, UK 8%, Zambia 7%, Madagascar 6%. **Tourism:** $366 mil. **Budget** (2020): $3.7 bil. **Inflation:** 10.8%.

Transport: Motor vehicles: 271.3 per 1,000 pop. **Airports:** 2.

Communications: Mobile: 161.4 per 100 pop. **Broadband:** 117.3 per 100 pop. **Internet:** 67.6%.

Health: Expend.: 6.7%. **Life expect.:** 72.3 male; 78.1 female. **Births:** 9.8 per 1,000 pop. **Deaths:** 9.0 per 1,000 pop. **Infant mortality:** 11.8 per 1,000 live births. **Undernourished:** 6.8%. **HIV:** NA. **COVID-19:** 309,019 cases, 1,053 deaths; rates per 100,000: 24,298.4 cases, 82.8 deaths. 85.6% vaccinated.

Education: Compulsory: ages 5-15. **Literacy:** 92.2%.
Website: govmu.org

Mauritius was uninhabited when settled in 1638 by the Dutch, who introduced sugarcane. France took over in 1721, bringing African slaves. Britain ruled from 1810, bringing Indian workers. Mauritius became independent, Mar. 12, 1968, and a republic, Mar. 12, 1992.

Prime Min. Pravind Jugnauth's party won Nov. 7, 2019, legislative elections. An oil tanker ran aground off the SE coast, July 25, 2020, spilling 1,000 tons of fuel.

Mexico
United Mexican States

People: Population: 129,875,529 (10). **Age distrib.:** <15: 23.8%; 65+: 8.0%. **Growth:** 0.6%. **Migrants:** 0.9%. **Pop. density:** 173.0 per sq mi, 66.8 per sq km. **Urban:** 81.6%. **Ethnic groups:** mestizo (Amerindian-Spanish) 62%, predom. Amerindian 21%, Amerindian 7%. **Languages:** Spanish, Indigenous langs. (incl. Mayan, Nahuatl). **Religions:** Christian 95.5% (Catholic 84.4%), agnostic 3.1%.

Geography: Total area: 758,449 sq mi, 1,964,375 sq km (13); **Land area:** 750,561 sq mi, 1,943,945 sq km. **Location:** Southern N America. U.S. on N, Guatemala and Belize on S. **Topography:** The Sierra Madre Occidental Mts. run NW-SE near the W coast; the Sierra Madre Oriental Mts. are near Gulf of Mexico. They join S of Mexico City. In between lies a dry central plateau (5,000-8,000 ft) with temperate vegetation. Coastal lowlands are tropical. About 45% of land is arid. **Arable land:** 10.3%. **Capital:** Mexico City, 22,281,442. **Cities:** Guadalajara, 5,419,880; Monterrey, 5,116,647; Puebla, 3,344,761; Toluca de Lerdo, 2,626,368; Tijuana, 2,259,787.

Government: Type: Federal presidential republic. **Head of state and govt.:** Pres. Andrés Manuel López Obrador; b. 1953; in office: Dec. 1, 2018. **Local divisions:** 32 states. **Defense budget:** $5.7 bil. **Active troops:** 216,000.

Economy: Industries: food/beverages, tobacco, chemicals, iron and steel, petroleum, mining, textiles, clothing, motor vehicles. **Chief agric.:** sugarcane, maize, milk, oranges, sorghum, tomatoes. **Natural resources:** petroleum, silver, antimony, copper, gold, lead, zinc, nat. gas, timber. **Water:** 3,582 cu m per capita. **Crude oil reserves:** 5.8 bil bbls. **Electricity prod.:** 337.0 bil kWh. **Labor force:** agric. 12.3%, industry 25.6%, services 62.0%. **Unemployment:** 3.3%.

Finance: Monetary unit: Peso (MXN) (16.72 = $1 U.S.). **GDP:** $2.7 tril; **per capita GDP:** $21,512; **GDP growth:** 3.1%. **Imports:** $544.8 bil; U.S. 54%, China 14%. **Exports:** $522.2 bil; U.S. 75%. **Tourism:** $19.8 bil. **Budget** (2020): $313.4 bil. **Inflation:** 3.4%.

Transport: Railways: 14,533 mi. **Motor vehicles:** 347.7 per 1,000 pop. **Airports:** 243.

Communications: Mobile: 100.3 per 100 pop. **Broadband:** 87.9 per 100 pop. **Internet:** 70.0%.

Health: Expend.: 6.2%. **Life expect.:** 70.3 male; 76.8 female. **Births:** 14.0 per 1,000 pop. **Deaths:** 7.1 per 1,000 pop. **Infant**

mortality: 12.0 per 1,000 live births. **Undernourished:** <2.5%. **HIV:** 0.4%. **COVID-19:** 7,633,355 cases, 334,336 deaths; rates per 100,000: 5,920.4 cases, 259.3 deaths. 63.1% vaccinated.
Education: Compulsory: ages 4-17. **Literacy:** 95.3%.
Website: www.gob.mx

Mexico was the site of advanced civilizations. The Mayans, an agricultural people, moved up from Yucatan, built huge stone pyramids, and invented a calendar. The Toltecs were overcome by the Aztecs, who founded Tenochtitlan 1325 ce, now Mexico City. Hernán Cortés, Spanish conquistador, destroyed the Aztec empire, 1519-21. After three centuries of Spanish rule the people revolted, beginning in 1810. Spain recognized Mexican independence, 1821. A republic was declared in 1823.

Mexican territory extended into the present-day United States. Texas established a republic in 1836, and Mexico lost California and most of the SW in the U.S.-Mexican War, 1846-48.

The French supported an Austrian archduke on the Mexican throne as Maximilian I, 1864-67. He was deposed in an uprising led by Benito Juárez. Dictatorial rule by Porfirio Díaz, president 1877-80, 1884-1911, led to a period of rebellion and factional fighting. A new constitution in 1917 brought reform.

The Institutional Revolutionary Party (PRI) dominated politics from 1929 until the late 1990s. Gains in agriculture, industry, and social services were achieved, but poverty remained widespread. Vast oil reserves were discovered, 1970s-80s. About 10,000 people died when a magnitude 8.0 earthquake struck near Mexico City, Sept. 19, 1985.

The National Action Party won the 2000 and 2006 presidential elections. Despite a government crackdown on drug cartels, drug-related violence intensified. Enrique Peña Nieto (PRI) won the 2012 presidential election. Notorious drug cartel leader Joaquín Guzmán Loera, known as El Chapo, was extradited to the U.S., Jan. 19, 2017, and convicted, Feb. 12, 2019, of drug trafficking.

Vowing to reduce violence and corruption and to combat poverty, leftist Andrés Manuel López Obrador of the Moreno Party easily won the July 1, 2018, presidential election. However, drug cartel and other violence, including killings of journalists, continued; by 2023, tens of thousands had been murdered or "disappeared" since López Obrador took office.

A Supreme Court decision, June 3, 2015, in effect legalized same-sex marriage nationwide. The Court held, Sept. 6, 2023, that federal laws criminalizing abortion were unconstitutional, making abortion legal nationwide at least in federal health care facilities; at the time of the ruling, abortion was legal under state law in 12 of the country's 32 states.

The North American Free Trade Agreement (NAFTA) with the U.S. and Canada took effect Jan. 1, 1994. A revised pact—renamed the U.S.-Mexico-Canada Agreement (USMCA)—came into force July 1, 2020. It strengthened labor and environmental provisions.

With hundreds of thousands of Central American asylum-seekers and other migrants crossing from Mexico into the U.S. in 2019, Mexico agreed, June 7, to increase troops at its southern border with Guatemala. By 2021, under a 2019 U.S. policy, tens of thousands of asylum seekers were forced to wait in Mexico, often in harsh conditions, while their U.S. cases were pending. The U.S. "wait in Mexico" policy ended in 2022. Border crossings (including people from throughout the Americas and elsewhere) were at historically high levels in 2022 and during many months in 2023.

Hard-hit by the COVID-19 pandemic, Mexico recorded over 334,000 deaths by Aug. 2023, though deaths may have been much higher; a May 2022 WHO report estimated excess deaths related to the COVID-19 pandemic in 2020-21 were twice the official tally.

Micronesia, Fed. States of
Federated States of Micronesia

People: Population: 100,319 (184). **Age distrib.:** <15: 27.4%; 65+: 5.5%. **Growth:** −0.7%. **Migrants:** 2.5%. **Pop. density:** 370.1 per sq mi, 142.9 per sq km. **Urban:** 23.4%. **Ethnic groups:** Chuukese/Mortlockese 49.3%, Pohnpeian 29.8%, Kosraean 6.3%, Yapese 5.7%, Yap outer islander 5.1%. **Languages:** English (official), Chuukese, Kosrean, Pohnpeian, Yapese, Ulithian, Woleaian, Nukuoro, Kapingamarangi. **Religions:** Christian 95.0% (Catholic 50.1%, Protestant 37.9%), ethnic religionist 2.5%.
Geography: Total area: 271 sq mi, 702 sq km (178); **Land area:** 271 sq mi, 702 sq km. **Location:** Consists of 607 islands in four major island groups in W Pacific O. **Topography:** Mountainous islands and coral atolls; volcanic outcroppings on Pohnpei, Kosrae, and Truk. **Tropical climate. Arable land:** 2.9%. **Capital:** Palikir, 6,996.
Government: Type: Federal republic in free association with U.S. **Head of state and govt.:** Pres. Wesley W. Simina; b. 1961; in office: May 12, 2023. **Local divisions:** 4 states. **Defense budget/ active troops:** NA.
Economy: Industries: tourism, constr., specialized aquaculture, craft items. **Chief agric.:** coconuts, cassava, vegetables, sweet potatoes, bananas, pork. **Natural resources:** timber, marine prods., deep-seabed minerals, phosphate. **Water:** 0. **Labor force:** agric. 0.9%, industry 5.2%, services 93.9%. **Unemployment:** NA.

Finance: Monetary unit: U.S. Dollar (USD) (1.00 = $1 U.S.). **GDP:** $440.1 mil; **per capita GDP:** $3,855; **GDP growth:** −0.6%. **Imports** (2013): $258.5 mil; U.S. 32%, China 16%, Japan 14%, Taiwan 9%, Philippines 6%, South Korea 6%. **Exports** (2013): $88.3 mil; Thailand 73%, Japan 10%, China 9%. **Budget** (2018): $223 mil. **Inflation:** 5.4%.
Transport: Airports: 6.
Communications: Mobile (2021): 19.4 per 100 pop. **Broadband:** NA. **Internet:** 40.4%.
Health: Expend.: 11.6%. **Life expect.:** 72.6 male; 76.9 female. **Births:** 18.1 per 1,000 pop. **Deaths:** 4.2 per 1,000 pop. **Infant mortality:** 21.4 per 1,000 live births. **Undernourished:** NA. **HIV:** NA. **COVID-19:** 26,530 cases, 65 deaths; rates per 100,000: 23,065.0 cases, 56.5 deaths. 70.3% vaccinated.
Education: Compulsory: ages 6-13. **Literacy:** NA.
Website: gov.fm

Micronesia, formerly known as the Caroline Islands, was ruled successively by Spain, Germany, Japan, and the U.S. The nation gained independence under a Compact of Free Association (COFA) with the U.S., Nov. 1986. Micronesia is vulnerable to rising sea levels linked to climate change. Amid U.S. efforts to counter Chinese influence in the Pacific, the U.S. and Micronesia signed agreements in 2023 to extend U.S. financial aid under COFA.

Moldova
Republic of Moldova

People: Population: 3,250,532 (133). **Age distrib.:** <15: 15.1%; 65+: 14.5%. **Growth:** −1.1%. **Migrants:** 2.6%. **Pop. density:** 256.0 per sq mi, 98.8 per sq km. **Urban:** 43.4%. **Ethnic groups:** Moldovan 75.1%, Romanian 7%, Ukrainian 6.6%, Gagauz 4.6%, Russian 4.1%. **Languages:** Moldovan/Romanian (official), Russian, Gagauz, Ukrainian. **Religions:** Christian 97.7% (Orthodox [official] 94.5%).
Geography: Total area: 13,070 sq mi, 33,851 sq km (136); **Land area:** 12,699 sq mi, 32,891 sq km. **Location:** Eastern Europe. Romania on W; Ukraine on N, E, and S. **Topography:** Landlocked; mainly hilly plains with steppelands in S near Black Sea. **Arable land:** 51.9%. **Capital:** Chisinau, 487,707.
Government: Type: Parliamentary republic. **Head of state:** Pres. Maia Sandu; b. 1972; in office: Dec. 24, 2020. **Head of govt.:** Prime Min. Dorin Recean; b. 1974; in office: Feb. 16, 2023. **Local divisions:** 32 raions, 3 municipalities, 2 territorial units (1 autonomous). **Defense budget:** $46 mil. **Active troops:** 5,150.
Economy: Industries: sugar proc., vegetable oil, food proc., agric. machinery, foundry equip., refrigerators and freezers. **Chief agric.:** maize, wheat, sunflower seed, grapes, apples, sugar beet. **Natural resources:** lignite, phosphorites, gypsum, limestone. **Water:** 3,042 cu m per capita. **Electricity prod.:** 6.7 bil kWh. **Labor force:** agric. 37.6%, industry 16.5%, services 45.9%. **Unemployment:** 2.3%.
Finance: Monetary unit: Leu (MDL) (17.83 = $1 U.S.). **GDP:** $39.5 bil; **per capita GDP:** $15,238; **GDP growth:** −5.9%. **Imports:** $7.9 bil; Romania 20%, Russia 10%, Ukraine 9%, Germany 8%, China 7%, Turkey 6%, Italy 6%. **Exports:** $4.2 bil; Romania 27%, Russia 9%, Italy 9%, Germany 9%, Turkey 6%. **Tourism:** $419 mil. **Budget:** $3.8 bil. **Inflation:** 28.7%.
Transport: Railways: 728 mi. **Airports:** 5.
Communications: Mobile: 127.4 per 100 pop. **Broadband:** 90.4 per 100 pop. **Internet:** 61.3%.
Health: Expend.: 6.8%. **Life expect.:** 65.8 male; 73.9 female. **Births:** 8.6 per 1,000 pop. **Deaths:** 14.4 per 1,000 pop. **Infant mortality:** 14.1 per 1,000 live births. **Undernourished:** <2.5%. **HIV:** 0.9%. **COVID-19:** 620,927 cases, 12,125 deaths; rates per 100,000: 15,392.5 cases, 300.6 deaths. 35.2% vaccinated.
Education: Compulsory: ages 6-18. **Literacy:** 99.6%.
Website: moldova.md

In 1918, Romania annexed Bessarabia, west of the Dniester (Nistru) R. In 1924, the Soviet Union established the Moldavian Autonomous Soviet Socialist Republic on the eastern bank of the river (Trans-Dniester region, or Transnistria). It was merged with the Romanian-speaking districts of Bessarabia in 1940 to form the Moldavian SSR. During WWII, Romania, allied with Germany, occupied the area. It was recaptured by the USSR in 1944. Moldova declared independence Aug. 27, 1991, prior to the dissolution of the USSR Dec. 26, 1991.

Fighting erupted Mar. 1992 in Transnistria between Moldovan security forces and Slavic separatists—including ethnic Russians. Defying the Moldovan government, voters in the breakaway Transnistria held legislative elections and approved a separatist constitution in 1995. A peace accord with Transnistria separatists was signed in Moscow in 1997. In a 2006 referendum, Transnistria voters overwhelmingly supported independence from Moldova and eventual union with Russia. About 1,500 Russian troops were in Transnistria in 2023.

Pro-Western parties won Moldova's parliamentary elections in 2009, 2010, and 2014. In Moldova's first direct presidential election, pro-Russian candidate Igor Dodon won a Nov. 13, 2016, runoff. Following Feb. 24, 2019, parliamentary elections, pro-EU Maia Sandu became prime min. in June, but she lost a no-confidence vote in Nov. Sandu defeated Dodon in a Nov. 15, 2020, runoff to become Moldova's first woman president. Sandu's party swept July 11, 2021, parliamentary elections. The EU, June 23, 2022, officially made Moldova a candidate for membership.

In the wake of Russia's Feb. 2022 invasion of Ukraine, Moldova hosted about 117,000 Ukrainian refugees as of mid-Sept. 2023. After high inflation and energy shortages related to the Ukraine war sparked protests, pro-EU politician Dorin Recean replaced Natalia Gavrilita as prime minister, Feb. 16, 2023.

Monaco
Principality of Monaco

People: Population: 31,597 (192). **Age distrib.:** <15: 9.4%; 65+: 36.2%. **Growth:** 0.7%. **Migrants:** 67.8%. **Pop. density:** 40,917.9 per sq mi, 15,798.5 per sq km. **Urban:** 100.0%. **Ethnic groups** (by birth country): Monegasque 32.1%, French 19.9%, Italian 15.3%, British 5%, Belgian 2.3%, Swiss 2%. **Languages:** French (official), English, Italian, Monegasque. **Religions:** Christian 84.8% (Catholic [official] 82.0%), agnostic 10.9%, atheist 2.1%, Jewish 1.5%.

Geography: Total area: 0.77 sq mi, 2 sq km (195); **Land area:** 0.77 sq mi, 2 sq km. **Location:** NW Mediterranean coast. France to W, N, and E. **Topography:** Principality rises from port up to Monaco-Ville on a high promontory. **Arable land:** 0%. **Capital:** Monaco.

Government: Type: Constitutional monarchy. **Head of state:** Prince Albert II; b. 1958; in office: Apr. 6, 2005. **Head of govt.:** Min. of State Pierre Dartout; b. 1954; in office: Sept. 1, 2020. **Local divisions:** no first-order admin. divisions. **Defense budget/active troops:** NA.

Economy: Industries: banking, insurance, tourism, constr. **Chief agric.:** none. **Natural resources:** none. **Water:** NA. **Labor force:** agric. 0%, industry 16.1%, services 83.9%. **Unemployment:** NA.

Finance: Monetary unit: Euro (EUR) (0.93 = $1 U.S.). **GDP:** NA; **per capita GDP:** NA; **GDP growth** (2021): 21.6%. **Imports** (2017): $1.4 bil; (2021) Italy, Switzerland, UK, Germany, China. **Exports** (2017): $964.6 mil; (2021) Italy, Switzerland, Germany, Belgium, Spain. **Budget** (2011): $953.6 mil. **Inflation:** NA.

Transport: Railways: Only one railway station; France operates service in Monaco.

Communications: Mobile: 106.8 per 100 pop. **Broadband:** 103.4 per 100 pop. **Internet:** 86.1%.

Health: Expend.: 1.7%. **Life expect.:** 85.8 male; 93.6 female. **Births:** 6.6 per 1,000 pop. **Deaths:** 10.9 per 1,000 pop. **Infant mortality:** 1.8 per 1,000 live births. **Undernourished:** NA. **HIV:** NA. **COVID-19:** 16,881 cases, 67 deaths; rates per 100,000: 43,015.5 cases, 170.7 deaths. 68.0% vaccinated.

Education: Compulsory: ages 6-16. **Literacy:** NA.
Website: www.gouv.mc

Monaco has belonged to the House of Grimaldi almost continuously since 1297. It was annexed by France in 1793 and was placed under the protectorate of Sardinia in 1815. An 1861 treaty restored independence. The Prince of Monaco was an absolute ruler until the 1911 constitution. Monaco is noted for its climate, scenery, casinos, and Formula One Grand Prix auto race. The country is a tourist destination and tax haven for the wealthy. Prince Rainier III, ruler from 1949, died in 2005 and was succeeded by his son, Albert II.

Mongolia

People: Population: 3,255,468 (132). **Age distrib.:** <15: 26.2%; 65+: 5.6%. **Growth:** 0.8%. **Migrants:** 0.7%. **Pop. density:** 5.4 per sq mi, 2.1 per sq km. **Urban:** 69.1%. **Ethnic groups:** Khalkh 83.8%, Kazak 3.8%, Durvud 2.6%, Bayad 2%. **Languages:** Mongolian (official) (Khalkha dialect predom.), Turkic, Russian. **Religions:** Buddhist 59.8% (Lamaist), ethnic religionist 18.2%, agnostic 12.9%, Muslim 5.0% (Sunni), Christian 2.0%.

Geography: Total area: 603,909 sq mi, 1,564,116 sq km (18); **Land area:** 599,831 sq mi, 1,553,556 sq km. **Location:** E Central Asia. Russia on N, China on E, W, and S. **Topography:** Mostly high plateau with mountains, salt lakes, and vast grasslands. Gobi Desert in S. **Arable land:** 0.9%. **Capital:** Ulaanbaatar, 1,672,627.

Government: Type: Semi-presidential republic. **Head of state:** Pres. Ukhnaa Khurelsukh; b. 1968; in office: June 5, 2021. **Head of govt.:** Prime. Min. Luvsannamsrain Oyun-Erdene; b. 1980; in office: Jan. 27, 2021. **Local divisions:** 21 provinces, 1 municipality. **Defense budget:** $90 mil. **Active troops:** 9,700.

Economy: Industries: constr. and constr. materials, mining, oil, food and beverages, animal prods. proc., cashmere and natural fiber mfg. **Chief agric.:** milk, wheat, goat milk, potatoes, mutton, sheep milk. **Natural resources:** oil, coal, copper, molybdenum, tungsten, phosphates, tin, nickel, zinc, fluorspar, gold, silver, iron. **Water:** 10,615 cu m per capita. **Electricity prod.:** 7.1 bil kWh. **Labor force:** agric. 24.3%, industry 20.9%, services 54.8%. **Unemployment:** 8.2%.

Finance: Monetary unit: Tughrik (MNT) (4375.90 = $1 U.S.). **GDP:** $48.4 bil; **per capita GDP:** $14,230; **GDP growth:** 4.8%. **Imports** (2020): $7.3 bil; China 31%, Russia 29%, Japan 10%. **Exports** (2020): $7.6 bil; China 81%, Switzerland 9%. **Tourism:** $21 mil. **Budget** (2020): $5.0 bil. **Inflation:** 15.2%.

Transport: Railways: 1,128 mi. **Airports:** 15.
Communications: Mobile: 142.3 per 100 pop. **Broadband:** 117.6 per 100 pop. **Internet:** 81.6%.

Health: Expend.: 4.9%. **Life expect.:** 67.5 male; 76.0 female. **Births:** 15.4 per 1,000 pop. **Deaths:** 6.3 per 1,000 pop. **Infant mortality:** 19.8 per 1,000 live births. **Undernourished:** 8.0%. **HIV:** <0.1%. **COVID-19:** 1,010,975 cases, 2,284 deaths; rates per 100,000: 30,838.5 cases, 69.7 deaths. 66.7% vaccinated.

Education: Compulsory: ages 6-17. **Literacy:** 99.2%.
Website: zasag.mn

Mongolia reached the zenith of its power in the 13th cent. when Genghis Khan and his successors conquered all of China and extended their influence as far west as Hungary and Poland. In later centuries, the empire dissolved, and Mongolia became a province of China.

With the advent of the 1911 Chinese revolution, Mongolia, with Russian backing, declared its independence. A Communist regime was established, 1921. The Mongolian People's Revolutionary Party (MPRP) yielded its monopoly on power, 1990. A new constitution took effect, 1992.

Riots followed 2008 parliamentary elections, won by the ruling MPRP (renamed the Mongolian People's Party, or MPP, in 2010). The Democratic Party (DP) won the 2009 presidential election and 2012 legislative elections. With the economy slumping, the MPP won June 29, 2016, parliamentary elections. The IMF approved a $5.5-bil bailout package, May 24, 2017. The MPP won June 24, 2020, legislative elections. Following protests over the government's response to the COVID-19 pandemic, Prime Min. Ukhnaa Khurelsukh (of the MPP) resigned, Jan. 21, 2021. Luvsannamsrai Oyun-Erdene became prime minister, Jan. 27, and Khurelsukh won the June 9 presidential election.

Montenegro

People: Population: 602,445 (167). **Age distrib.:** <15: 17.9%; 65+: 17.4%. **Growth:** −0.4%. **Migrants:** 11.3%. **Pop. density:** 116.0 per sq mi, 44.8 per sq km. **Urban:** 68.5%. **Ethnic groups:** Montenegrin 45%, Serbian 28.7%, Bosniak 8.7%, Albanian 4.9%, Muslim 3.3%. **Languages:** Serbian, Montenegrin (official), Bosnian, Albanian, Serbo-Croat. **Religions:** Christian 79.8% (Orthodox 71.1%), Muslim 17.5% (Sunni), agnostic 2.4%.

Geography: Total area: 5,333 sq mi, 13,812 sq km (157); **Land area:** 5,194 sq mi, 13,452 sq km. **Location:** Balkan Peninsula in SE Europe. Bosnia and Herzegovina on N and W, Serbia on E, Albania on SE, Croatia on W. **Topography:** Mostly rugged and mountainous, with few arable regions, mostly along the Zeta R. Highly indented narrow coastline. **Arable land:** 0.7%. **Capital:** Podgorica, 177,177.

Government: Type: Parliamentary republic. **Head of state:** Pres. Jakov Milatovic; b. 1986; in office: May 20, 2023. **Head of govt.:** Prime. Min. Dritan Abazovic; b. 1985; in office: Apr. 28, 2022. **Local divisions:** 25 municipalities. **Defense budget:** $100 mil. **Active troops:** 2,350.

Economy: Industries: steelmaking, aluminum, agric. proc., consumer goods, tourism. **Chief agric.:** milk, potatoes, grapes, vegetables, tomatoes, watermelons. **Natural resources:** bauxite, hydroelectricity. **Water:** NA. **Electricity prod.:** 3.3 bil kWh. **Labor force:** agric. 7.4%, industry 18.8%, services 73.8%. **Unemployment:** 15.4%.

Finance: Monetary unit: Euro (EUR) (0.93 = $1 U.S.). **GDP:** $16.6 bil; **per capita GDP:** $26,984; **GDP growth:** 6.1%. **Imports:** $3.6 bil; Serbia 30%, Bosnia and Herzegovina 8%, Croatia 8%, Italy 6%, Greece 6%. **Exports:** $2.5 bil; Serbia 17%, Hungary 15%, China 11%, Russia 7%, Bosnia and Herzegovina 6%, Germany 6%. **Tourism:** $896 mil. **Budget** (2020): $2.6 bil. **Inflation:** 13.0%.

Transport: Railways: 155 mi. **Airports:** 5.
Communications: Mobile: 203.2 per 100 pop. **Broadband:** 102.5 per 100 pop. **Internet:** 88.2%.

Health: Expend.: 11.4%. **Life expect.:** 75.6 male; 80.5 female. **Births:** 11.0 per 1,000 pop. **Deaths:** 10.3 per 1,000 pop. **Infant mortality:** 3.2 per 1,000 live births. **Undernourished:** <2.5%. **HIV:** 0.1%. **COVID-19:** 251,133 cases, 2,654 deaths; rates per 100,000: 39,985.4 cases, 422.6 deaths. 40.1% vaccinated.

Education: Compulsory: ages 6-14. **Literacy:** 99.0%.
Website: www.gov.me

Part of the medieval Serbian Kingdom, Montenegro preserved its autonomy for centuries because of its mountainous terrain. After WWI, it was part of the Kingdom of Serbs, Croats, and Slovenes, later renamed Yugoslavia. Italian forces occupied parts of Montenegro during WWII. In 1945, with the establishment of a federal Yugoslavia under Communist rule, Montenegro became one of six constituent republics.

In Apr. 1992, after four other republics had declared independence, Montenegro and Serbia became the Federal Republic of Yugoslavia. On June 3, 2006, Montenegro declared independence. The governing, pro-Western Democratic Party of Socialists (DPS) won the most seats in Oct. 16, 2016, parliamentary elections. Montenegro became a member of NATO, June 5, 2017. The DPS's Milo Djukanovic won the Apr. 15, 2018, presidential election. Parliament legalized same-sex partnerships, July 1, 2020. In Aug. 30, 2020, parliamentary elections, a coalition of opposition parties won a slim majority, but Prime Min. Zdravko Krivokapic lost a no-confidence vote, Feb. 4, 2022.

Pro-EU Dritan Abazovic became prime minister, Apr. 28, but lost a no-confidence vote, Aug. 20. In new parliamentary elections, June 11, 2023, the Europe Now Movement (PES) won the most votes, and Milojko Spajic of PES worked to form a coalition government.

Jakov Milatovic of PES defeated Djukanovic in an Apr. 2, 2023, presidential runoff election.

Morocco
Kingdom of Morocco

People: Population: 37,067,420 (40). **Age distrib.:** <15: 26.0%; 65+: 8.1%. **Growth:** 0.9%. **Migrants:** 0.3%. **Pop. density:** 134.0 per sq mi, 51.7 per sq km. **Urban:** 65.1%. **Ethnic groups:** Arab-Berber 99%. **Languages:** Arabic (official), Berber langs. (incl. Tamazight [official]), French (lang. of business, govt., diplomacy). **Religions:** Muslim 99.7% (Sunni [official]).

Geography: Total area: 276,662 sq mi, 716,550 sq km (39); **Land area:** 276,565 sq mi, 716,300 sq km. Total/land area incl. Western Sahara (102,703 sq mi, 266,000 sq km). **Location:** NW coast of Africa. Western Sahara on S, Algeria on E, Spain to N. **Topography:** Five natural regions: mountain ranges (Riff in N, Middle Atlas, Upper Atlas, and Anti-Atlas); rich plains in W; alluvial plains in SW; well-cultivated plateaus in center; pre-Sahara arid zone extending from SE. **Arable land:** 16.8%. **Capital:** Casablanca, 3,892,837. **Cities:** Rabat, 1,959,388; Tanger, 1,314,178; Fès, 1,290,039; Marrakech, 1,049,690.

Government: Type: Parliamentary constitutional monarchy. **Head of state:** King Mohammed VI; b. 1963; in office: July 30, 1999. **Head of govt.:** Prime Min. Aziz Akhannouch; b. 1961; in office: Oct. 7, 2021. **Local divisions:** 11 regions (not incl. 12th claimed region that lies within territory of disputed Western Sahara). **Defense budget:** $6.4 bil. **Active troops:** 195,800.

Economy: Industries: automotive parts, phosphate mining and proc., aerospace, food proc., leather goods. **Chief agric.:** wheat, sugar beet, milk, potatoes, olives, tangerines/mandarins. **Natural resources:** phosphates, iron ore, manganese, lead, zinc, fish, salt. **Water:** 786 cu m per capita. **Crude oil reserves:** 684,000 bbls. **Electricity prod.:** 41.2 bil kWh. **Labor force:** agric. 34.6%, industry 22.8%, services 42.6%. **Unemployment:** 10.5%.

Finance: Monetary unit: Dirham (MAD) (10.14 = $1 U.S.). **GDP:** $362.0 bil; **per capita GDP:** $9,519; **GDP growth:** 1.1%. **Imports:** $60.0 bil; Spain 19%, France 11%, China 9%, U.S. 7%. **Exports:** $47.1 bil; (2021) Spain 20%, France 19%. **Tourism:** $3.8 bil. **Budget:** $35.6 bil. **Inflation:** 6.7%.

Transport: Railways: 1,284 mi. **Motor vehicles:** 138.2 per 1,000 pop. **Airports:** 36.

Communications: Mobile (2021): 137.5 per 100 pop. **Broadband** (2021): 82.0 per 100 pop. **Internet:** 88.1%.

Health: Expend.: 6.0%. **Life expect.:** 72.3 male; 75.7 female. **Births:** 17.1 per 1,000 pop. **Deaths:** 6.6 per 1,000 pop. **Infant mortality:** 18.7 per 1,000 live births. **Undernourished:** 6.3%. **HIV:** <0.1%. **COVID-19:** 1,275,394 cases, 16,297 deaths; rates per 100,000: 3,455.4 cases, 44.2 deaths. 63.7% vaccinated.

Education: Compulsory: ages 6-14. **Literacy:** 75.9%.

Website: www.egov.ma

Berbers were the region's original inhabitants, followed by Carthaginians and Romans. Arabs conquered it in 683. In the 11th and 12th cents., a Berber empire ruled all NW Africa and most of Spain from Morocco.

Part of Morocco came under Spanish rule in the 19th cent.; France controlled the rest in the early 20th cent. Tribal uprisings lasted from 1911 to 1933. Independence was achieved Mar. 2, 1956. Tangier, an internationalized seaport, was incorporated into Morocco, 1956. Ifni, a Spanish enclave, was ceded in 1969.

King Hassan II assumed the throne in 1961, reigning until his death in 1999; he was succeeded by his eldest son. A bicameral legislature was established in 1997.

Five terrorist attacks, linked to al-Qaeda, in Casablanca May 16, 2003, left 45 dead. Following a series of suicide bombings in 2007, the government stepped up its campaign against militant Islamists. After Arab Spring street demonstrations Feb.-Mar. 2011, the monarchy implemented modest constitutional reforms. Throughout 2011, Moroccans staged protests over persistent unemployment, alleged unjust detentions, and lack of free speech. The moderate Islamist Justice and Development Party (PJD) won a plurality in Oct. 7, 2016, parliamentary elections. Large protests in the impoverished Rif region, 2017-18, prompted a harsh response by security forces. Morocco completed, Dec. 2018, one of the world's largest concentrated solar power complexes. Morocco and Israel agreed, Dec. 10, 2020, to establish diplomatic relations. The National Rally of Independents (RNI) party won Sept. 8, 2021, parliamentary elections; the RNI's Aziz Akhannouch became prime minister. An earthquake near Marrakesh, Sept. 8, 2023, left more than 2,900 dead.

Western Sahara

Western Sahara, formerly the protectorate of Spanish Sahara, is bounded on the N by Morocco, the NE by Algeria, the E and S by Mauritania, and the W by the Atlantic O. Phosphates are the major resource. Pop. (2021 est.) 668,862. Capital is Laayoune; pop. (2018 est.) 232,388.

Spain withdrew in Feb. 1976. On Apr. 14, 1976, Morocco annexed over 70,000 sq mi, with the remainder annexed by Mauritania. The Polisario Front guerrilla movement, which proclaimed the region independent Feb. 27, launched attacks with Algerian support. After Mauritania signed a treaty with Polisario Aug. 5, 1979, Morocco occupied Mauritania's portion of Western Sahara.

After years of bitter fighting, Morocco controlled the main urban areas, and Polisario vast, sparsely populated desert areas. The two sides implemented a cease-fire in 1991, when a UN peacekeeping force (MINURSO) was established with a mandate to prepare for a referendum on self-determination. Following military clashes, Polisario ended the cease-fire Nov. 14, 2020. Pres. Donald Trump announced Dec. 10, 2020, the U.S. would recognize Morocco's claim to Western Sahara—the U.S. was the first country to do so officially—as part of a deal in which Morocco would normalize relations with Israel. MINURSO had about 200 military personnel in Western Sahara as of July 31, 2023; a referendum had still not been held.

Mozambique
Republic of Mozambique

People: Population: 32,513,805 (45). **Age distrib.:** <15: 45.0%; 65+: 2.9%. **Growth:** 2.5%. **Migrants:** 1.1%. **Pop. density:** 107.1 per sq mi, 41.3 per sq km. **Urban:** 38.8%. **Ethnic groups:** African (incl. Makhuwa, Tsonga, Lomwe, Sena) 99%. **Languages:** Makhuwa, Portuguese (official), Tsonga, Nyanja, Sena, Lomwe, Chuwabo, Ndau, Tswa, other Mozambican langs. **Religions:** Christian 56.6% (Catholic 24.7%, Protestant 16.0%, independent 15.8%), ethnic religionist 24.9%, Muslim 17.9% (Sunni).

Geography: Total area: 308,642 sq mi, 799,380 sq km (34); **Land area:** 303,623 sq mi, 786,380 sq km. **Location:** SE coast of Africa. Tanzania on N; Malawi, Zambia, Zimbabwe on W; South Africa, Eswatini on S. **Topography:** Coastal lowlands comprise nearly half the country with plateaus rising in steps to mountains along western border. **Arable land:** 7.2%. **Capital:** Matola, 1,852,405. **Cities:** Maputo, 1,162,793

Government: Type: Presidential republic. **Head of state:** Pres. Filipe Jacinto Nyusi; b. 1959; in office: Jan. 15, 2015. **Head of govt.:** Prime Min. Adriano Afonso Maleiane; in office: Mar. 3, 2022. **Local divisions:** 10 provinces, 1 city. **Defense budget:** $145 mil. **Active troops:** 11,200.

Economy: Industries: aluminum, petroleum prods., chemicals, textiles, cement, glass, asbestos, tobacco, food, beverages. **Chief agric.:** sugarcane, cassava, maize, milk, bananas, tomatoes. **Natural resources:** coal, titanium, nat. gas, hydropower, tantalum, graphite. **Water:** 6,946 cu m per capita. **Electricity prod.:** 19.9 bil kWh. **Labor force:** agric. 70.3%, industry 9.3%, services 20.5%. **Unemployment:** 3.9%.

Finance: Monetary unit: Metical (MZN) (63.84 = $1 U.S.). **GDP:** $48.4 bil; **per capita GDP:** $1,468; **GDP growth:** 4.1%. **Imports:** $10.4 bil; South Africa 31%, India 18%, China 17%. **Exports:** $6.4 bil; South Africa 16%, India 13%, China 12%, Italy 7%. **Tourism:** $127 mil. **Budget:** $4.6 bil. **Inflation:** 10.3%.

Transport: Railways: 2,975 mi. **Motor vehicles:** 3.9 per 1,000 pop. **Airports:** 21.

Communications: Mobile: 42.1 per 100 pop. **Broadband:** 20.8 per 100 pop. **Internet:** 17.4%.

Health: Expend.: 7.6%. **Life expect.:** 56.4 male; 59.0 female. **Births:** 36.9 per 1,000 pop. **Deaths:** 9.9 per 1,000 pop. **Infant mortality:** 59.8 per 1,000 live births. **Undernourished:** 30.5%. **HIV:** 11.6%. **COVID-19:** 233,417 cases, 2,243 deaths; rates per 100,000: 746.8 cases, 7.2 deaths. 68.2% vaccinated.

Education: Compulsory: NA. **Literacy:** 63.4%.

Website: www.portaldogoverno.gov.mz

The first Portuguese post on the Mozambique coast was established in 1505 on the trade route to Asia. Mozambique became independent June 25, 1975, after a 10-year war against Portuguese rule led by Frelimo (Front for the Liberation of Mozambique).

The Frelimo government, headed by Pres. Samora Machel, transitioned to a Communist system. Most of the country's whites emigrated. In the 1980s, severe drought and civil war caused famine and heavy loss of life. Pres. Machel was killed in a plane crash, Oct. 19, 1986. Frelimo formally abandoned Marxist-Leninism in 1989, and a new constitution, effective Nov. 30, 1990, established multiparty elections and a free-market economy.

A 1992 peace agreement ended 15 years of hostilities (up to 1 mil killed) between the government and the Mozambique National Resistance (Renamo), which became the main opposition party. Repatriation of 1.7 mil Mozambican refugees ended June 1995.

Frelimo retained power under Pres. Joaquim Chissano (1986-2005) and Pres. Armando Guebuza (2005-15). Filipe Jacinto Nyusi of Frelimo won the Oct. 15, 2014, presidential election. Clashes began in 2013 between government forces and Renamo, which challenged 2014 election results. A truce beginning Dec. 2016 paved the way for May 2018 constitutional amendments decentralizing political power. Cyclone Idai, Mar. 2019, killed more than 600 and displaced hundreds of thousands. Nyusi was reelected Oct. 15, 2019.

Natural gas reserves are estimated at more than 100 tril cu ft (third-largest in Africa). Beginning Oct. 2017, Islamist militants staged a series of attacks in the gas-rich northern Cabo Delgado region. Violence escalated in 2020-21. By mid-2021, Rwandan and other African forces were aiding Mozambican troops. Islamist attacks continued in 2022-23. The UNHCR estimated that, as of June 30, 2023, more than 834,000 people in northern Mozambique were internally displaced by the conflict.

Myanmar
(Burma)
Union of Myanmar

People: Population: 57,970,293 (26). **Age distrib.:** <15: 24.8%; 65+: 6.8%. **Growth:** 0.8%. **Migrants:** 0.1%. **Pop. density:** 229.7 per sq mi, 88.7 per sq km. **Urban:** 32.1%. **Ethnic groups:** Burman (Bamar) 68%, Shan 9%, Karen 7%, Rakhine 4%, Chinese 3%, Indian 2%, Mon 2%. **Languages:** Burmese (official). **Religions:** Buddhist (official) 76.0% (Theravadin), ethnic religionist 8.2%, Christian 8.1%, Muslim 3.6% (Sunni).

Geography: Total area: 261,228 sq mi, 676,578 sq km (40); **Land area:** 252,321 sq mi, 653,508 sq km. **Location:** Between S and SE Asia, on Bay of Bengal. Bangladesh, India on W; China, Laos, Thailand on E. **Topography:** Surrounding mountains on W, N, and E. Dense forests cover much of nation. N-S rivers provide habitable valleys, espec. the Irrawaddy, navigable for 900 mi. Tropical monsoon climate. **Arable land:** 16.8%. **Capital:** Nay Pyi Taw (administrative), 722,836. **Cities:** Yangon, 5,610,241; Mandalay, 1,531,860.

Government: Type: Previously parliamentary republic. **Head of state and govt.:** Prime Min. Senior Gen. Min Aung Hlaing (self-appointed head of a "caretaker govt." set up by the military); b. 1956; in office: Aug. 1, 2021. **Local divisions:** 7 regions, 7 states, 1 union territory. **Defense budget:** $1.9 bil. **Active troops:** 356,000.

Economy: Industries: agric. proc.; wood/wood prods.; copper, tin, tungsten, iron; cement, constr. materials; pharmaceuticals; fertilizer. **Chief agric.:** rice, sugarcane, beans, vegetables, milk, maize. **Natural resources:** petroleum, timber, tin, antimony, zinc, copper, tungsten, lead, coal, marble, limestone, prec. stones, nat. gas, hydropower. **Water:** 21,463 cu m per capita. **Crude oil reserves:** 139 mil bbls. **Electricity prod.:** 22.4 bil kWh. **Labor force:** agric. 46.5%, industry 18.6%, services 35.0%. **Unemployment (2020):** 1.5%.

Finance: Monetary unit: Kyat (MMK) (2,098.44 = $1 U.S.). **GDP:** $263.9 bil; **per capita GDP:** $4,870; **GDP growth:** 3.0%. **Imports** (2019): $17.4 bil; China 43%, Thailand 15%, Singapore 12%. **Exports** (2019): $17.5 bil; China 24%, Thailand 24%, Japan 7%. Import/export figures are underestimates due to smuggling. **Tourism** (2019): $2.5 bil. **Budget** (2020): $18 bil. **Inflation** (2018-19): 8.8%.

Transport: Railways: 3,126 mi. **Motor vehicles:** 0.9 per 1,000 pop. **Airports:** 36.

Communications: Mobile: 106.7 per 100 pop. **Broadband:** 97.1 per 100 pop. **Internet:** 44.0%.

Health: Expend.: 4.6%. **Life expect.:** 68.1 male; 71.6 female. **Births:** 16.1 per 1,000 pop. **Deaths:** 7.4 per 1,000 pop. **Infant mortality:** 33.4 per 1,000 live births. **Undernourished:** 3.8%. **HIV:** 0.9%. **COVID-19:** 641,148 cases, 19,494 deaths; rates per 100,000: 1,178.4 cases, 35.8 deaths. 64.7% vaccinated.

Education: Compulsory: ages 5-9. **Literacy:** 89.1%.

Website: www.myanmar.gov.mm

The Burmese arrived from Tibet before the 9th cent., displacing earlier cultures, and a Buddhist monarchy was established by the 11th cent. Burma was conquered by China's Mongol dynasty in 1272, then ruled by the Shan people as a Chinese tributary until the 16th cent. Britain subjugated Burma in three wars, 1824-84, and ruled the country as part of India until 1937, when Burma became self-governing. Full independence was achieved Jan. 4, 1948.

Gen. Ne Win dominated politics from 1962 to 1988, first as military ruler, then as constitutional president, advancing policies that increased economic socialization and international isolation. Ne Win resigned July 1988, following antigovernment riots. In Sept., the military seized power, under Gen. Saw Maung. In 1989 the country's name was changed to Myanmar.

Although the main opposition party won a decisive victory in 1990 multiparty elections, the military refused to surrender power. A key opposition leader, Aung San Suu Kyi, was held under house arrest, 1989-95, 2000-02, and 2003-10.

In late Sept. 2007, thousands of Buddhist monks led mass protests in Yangon; security forces cracked down by raiding monasteries, arresting monks, and firing on demonstrators. Cyclone Nargis, May 2-3, 2008, killed more than 138,000.

Suu Kyi's National League for Democracy (NLD) won 43 of 45 parliamentary seats in an Apr. 1, 2012, election, and Suu Kyi traveled to Oslo, Norway, to accept the Nobel Peace Prize (awarded in 1991). The NLD won Nov. 8, 2015, parliamentary elections. NLD candidates were elected president by the parliament, 2016 and 2018. Suu Kyi, constitutionally barred from the presidency, assumed the newly created post of state counsellor, Apr. 6, 2016, becoming the country's de facto leader. The NLD swept Nov. 8, 2020, parliamentary elections.

A military coup, Feb. 1, 2021, ousted the civilian government. Suu Kyi and other NLD leaders were arrested (Suu Kyi was subsequently convicted of various offenses), and Nov. 2020 election

results were annulled. Protests against the coup were met with a deadly crackdown. At least hundreds of protesters were killed. Thousands were arrested; hundreds were estimated to have died in detention, and others were tortured. The first executions of pro-democracy activists occurred July 2022. Opponents of the coup began an armed rebellion against the military regime. As a result of the rebellion and various ethnic conflicts, more than 1.9 mil people in Myanmar were internally displaced as of July 31, 2023.

Violence against Rohingya Muslims, in Rakhine state in the W, intensified beginning in 2012. Almost all of Myanmar's Rohingya are not recognized as citizens by the government. Almost 100,000 Rohingya fled by boat, 2014-15, seeking asylum. Attacks by the military beginning in Oct. 2016 caused about 75,000 Rohingya to flee to Bangladesh. New military and vigilante attacks on Rohingya in which at least 10,000 were killed led almost three-quarters of a million Rohingya to flee to Bangladesh beginning in Aug. 2017. A UN official reported, July 2019, that about 128,000 Rohingya in Myanmar were confined to "concentration camps." As of Aug. 31, 2023, Bangladesh hosted about 963,000 Rohingya refugees.

Namibia
Republic of Namibia

People: Population: 2,777,232 (138). **Age distrib.:** <15: 34.5%; 65+: 3.9%. **Growth:** 1.8%. **Migrants:** 4.3%. **Pop. density:** 8.7 per sq mi, 3.4 per sq km. **Urban:** 54.9%. **Ethnic groups:** Ovambo 50%, Kavangos 9%, Herero 7%, Damara 7%, mixed European and African ancestry 6.5%, European 6%, Nama 5%, Caprivian 4%, San 3%, Baster 2%. **Languages:** Oshiwambo langs., Nama/Damara, Kavango langs., Afrikaans (common), Herero langs., Zambezi langs., English (official). **Religions:** Christian 91.5% (Protestant 63.7%, Catholic 17.7%), ethnic religionist 4.9%, agnostic 2.7%.

Geography: Total area: 318,261 sq mi, 824,292 sq km (33); **Land area:** 317,874 sq mi, 823,290 sq km. **Location:** Southern Africa on Atlantic coast. Angola on N; Botswana, Zambia on E; South Africa on S. **Topography:** Three distinct regions incl. Namib Desert along the Atlantic, a mountainous central plateau with woodland savanna, and Kalahari Desert in E. True forests found in NE. Four rivers but little other surface water. **Arable land:** 1.0%. **Capital:** Windhoek, 477,267.

Government: Type: Presidential republic. **Head of state and govt.:** Pres. Hage Geingob; b. 1941; in office: Mar. 21, 2015. **Local divisions:** 14 regions. **Defense budget:** $363 mil. **Active troops:** 9,900.

Economy: Industries: meatpacking, fish proc., dairy prods., pasta, beverages, mining. **Chief agric.:** beef, milk, grapes, millet, maize. **Natural resources:** diamonds, copper, uranium, gold, silver, lead, tin, lithium, cadmium, tungsten, zinc, salt, hydropower, fish. **Water:** 15,707 cu m per capita. **Electricity prod.:** 1.6 bil kWh. **Labor force:** agric. 22.1%, industry 16.4%, services 61.5%. **Unemployment:** 20.8%.

Finance: Monetary unit: Dollar (NAD) (18.56 = $1 U.S.). **GDP:** $28.8 bil; **per capita GDP:** $11,206; **GDP growth:** 4.6%. **Imports:** $6.1 bil; (2020) South Africa 40%, Zambia 20%, Dem. Rep. of the Congo 6%. **Exports:** $4.0 bil; (2020) China 29%, South Africa 20%, Botswana 8%, Belgium 6%. **Tourism:** $137 mil. **Budget:** $4.7 bil. **Inflation:** 6.1%.

Transport: Railways: 1,633 mi. **Motor vehicles:** 140.2 per 1,000 pop. **Airports:** 19.

Communications: Mobile: 113.2 per 100 pop. **Broadband:** 77.4 per 100 pop. **Internet:** 53.0%.

Health: Expend.: 8.9%. **Life expect.:** 62.1 male; 65.4 female. **Births:** 24.6 per 1,000 pop. **Deaths:** 8.1 per 1,000 pop. **Infant mortality:** 28.7 per 1,000 live births. **Undernourished:** 17.1%. **HIV:** 11.0%. **COVID-19:** 171,998 cases, 4,098 deaths; rates per 100,000: 6,769.2 cases, 161.3 deaths. 21.6% vaccinated.

Education: Compulsory: ages 7-13. **Literacy:** 92.3%.

Website: www.gov.na

Namibia was declared a German protectorate in 1890 and officially called South-West Africa. German troops putting down a rebellion killed tens of thousands of Herero and Nama people, 1904-08 (Germany, in 2021, acknowledged the "genocide"). South Africa seized the territory in 1915 during WWI. In 1966, the Marxist South-West Africa People's Organization (SWAPO) launched a guerrilla war for independence, aided by Angola and Cuba. The UN General Assembly named the area Namibia in 1968.

A 1988 U.S.-mediated agreement ended South African administration. A constitution providing for multiparty government was adopted Feb. 9, 1990, and Namibia gained independence Mar. 21. Walvis Bay, the principal deepwater port, was returned to Namibia by South Africa in 1994.

SWAPO, the leading political group since independence, won Nov. 2019 presidential and parliamentary elections but saw its vote decline amid a corruption scandal and a slumping economy.

Nauru
Republic of Nauru

People: Population: 9,852 (195). **Age distrib.:** <15: 30.1%; 65+: 4.2%. **Growth:** 0.4%. **Migrants:** 20.3%. **Pop. density:** 1,215.1 per sq mi, 469.1 per sq km. **Urban:** 100.0%. **Ethnic groups:** Nauruan 94.6%, I-Kiribati 2.2%. **Languages:** Nauruan (official), English (used in govt. and commerce). **Religions:** Christian 73.2% (Protestant 42.2%, Catholic 24.3%), Chinese folk-religionist 10.9%, Baha'i 9.8%, agnostic 4.6%.

Geography: Total area: 8.1 sq mi, 21 sq km (194); **Land area:** 8.1 sq mi, 21 sq km. **Location:** In W Pacific O. just S of equator. Nearest neighbor is Kiribati to E. **Topography:** Mostly a plateau bearing high-grade phosphate deposits, surrounded by a sandy shore and coral reef in concentric rings. **Arable land:** 0%. **Capital:** Nauru, 11,312.

Government: Type: Parliamentary republic. **Head of state and govt.:** Pres. Russ Kun; b. 1975; in office: Sept. 29, 2022. **Local divisions:** 14 districts. **Defense budget/active troops:** NA.

Economy: Industries: phosphate mining, offshore banking, coconut prods. **Chief agric.:** coconuts, tropical fruit, vegetables, pork, eggs, pig offals. **Natural resources:** phosphates, fish. **Water:** 924 cu m per capita. **Electricity prod.:** 42.0 mil kWh. **Labor force:** Most employed in phosphate mining, public admin., education, and transportation. **Unemployment:** NA.

Finance: Monetary unit: Australian Dollar (AUD) (1.56 = $1 U.S.). **GDP:** $166.2 mil; **per capita GDP:** $13,118; **GDP growth:** 2.4%. **Imports** (2018): $94.8 mil; Taiwan 52%, Australia 28%. **Exports** (2018): $31.1 mil; Thailand 34%, Australia 16%, U.S. 13%, South Korea 10%, Philippines 9%, Japan 7%. **Budget** (2020): $158 mil. **Inflation** (2016-17): 5.1%.

Transport: Airports: 1.

Communications: Mobile (2021): 79.9 per 100 pop. **Broadband** (2021): 32.0 per 100 pop. **Internet:** 83.9%.

Health: Expend.: 12.0%. **Life expect.:** 64.7 male; 72.0 female. **Births:** 20.7 per 1,000 pop. **Deaths:** 6.4 per 1,000 pop. **Infant mortality:** 7.7 per 1,000 live births. **Undernourished:** NA. **HIV:** NA. **COVID-19:** 5,393 cases, 1 death; rates per 100,000: 49,778.5 cases, 9.2 deaths. 104.7% vaccinated.

Education: Compulsory: ages 4-17. **Literacy:** NA.
Website: naurugov.nr

The British reached the island in 1798, but it was annexed to the German Empire in 1886. After WWI, Australia administered Nauru under a League of Nations mandate. Japan occupied the island during WWII. In 1947 Nauru was made a UN trust territory, administered by Australia. It became an independent republic Jan. 31, 1968.

Phosphate exports provided Nauru with high per capita revenues. Phosphate reserves, however, are nearly depleted, and environmental damage from strip mining has been severe. Rising sea levels linked to global climate change have eroded Nauru's coastline.

A 2012 Amnesty Intl. report found inhumane living conditions at Australia's detention center on Nauru for migrants intercepted trying to enter Australia by boat. An Australian government report, released Mar. 20, 2015, confirmed abuse of detainees by staff. After hundreds of refugees had left Nauru for resettlement in the U.S. or other countries, hundreds had been returned to their country of origin, and hundreds were moved to Australia for medical treatment or temporary detention, by mid-2023 no refugees remained in the Nauru detention center. However, the detention center remained officially open for potential future refugees.

Nepal

People: Population: 30,899,443 (49). **Age distrib.:** <15: 26.3%; 65+: 6.2%. **Growth:** 0.7%. **Migrants:** 1.7%. **Pop. density:** 558.3 per sq mi, 215.6 per sq km. **Urban:** 21.9%. **Ethnic groups:** Chhettri 16.5%, Brahman-Hill 11.3%, Magar 6.9%, Tharu 6.2%, Tamang 5.6%, Bishwokarma 5%, Musalman 4.9%, Newar 4.6%, Yadav 4.2%, Rai 2.2%. **Languages:** Nepali (official), Maithali, Bhojpuri, Tharu, Tamang, Bajjika (123 langs. reported as mother tongue in 2021 census). **Religions:** Hindu 65.1% (Shaivite 30%, Vaishnavite 29%), ethnic religionist 13.0%, Buddhist 12.2% (Lamaist 11%), Christian 4.8%, Muslim 4.3% (Sunni).

Geography: Total area: 56,827 sq mi, 147,181 sq km (93); **Land area:** 55,348 sq mi, 143,351 sq km. **Location:** Astride Himalaya Mts. China on N, India on S. **Topography:** The Himalayas across the N, hill country with fertile valleys across the center. S border region is part of flat, subtropical Ganges Plain. **Arable land:** 14.7%. **Capital:** Kathmandu, 1,571,010.

Government: Type: Federal parliamentary republic. **Head of state:** Pres. Ram Chandra Poudel; b. 1944; in office: Mar. 13, 2023. **Head of govt.:** Prime Min. Pushpa Kamal Dahal; b. 1954; in office: Dec. 26, 2022. **Local divisions:** 7 provinces. **Defense budget:** $421 mil. **Active troops:** 96,600.

Economy: Industries: tourism, carpets, textiles; small rice, jute, sugar, oilseed mills; cigarettes, cement/brick prod. **Chief agric.:** rice, vegetables, sugarcane, potatoes, maize, wheat. **Natural resources:** quartz, water, timber, hydropower; small deposits of lignite, copper, cobalt, iron ore. **Water:** 7,214 cu m per capita. **Electricity prod.:** 6.1 bil kWh. **Labor force:** agric. 62.3%, industry 16.1%, services 21.6%. **Unemployment:** 11.1%.

Finance: Monetary unit: Rupee (NPR) (132.26 = $1 U.S.). **GDP:** $144.3 bil; **per capita GDP:** $4,725; **GDP growth:** 5.6%. **Imports:**

$17.0 bil; India 70%, China 15%. **Exports:** $2.5 bil; India 68%, U.S. 10%. **Tourism:** $120 mil. **Budget** (2020): $9.0 bil. **Inflation:** 7.7%.

Transport: Railways: 37 mi. **Airports:** 11.

Communications: Mobile (2021): 127.2 per 100 pop. **Broadband** (2021): 59.6 per 100 pop. **Internet:** 51.6%.

Health: Expend.: 5.2%. **Life expect.:** 72.0 male; 73.4 female. **Births:** 17.3 per 1,000 pop. **Deaths:** 5.6 per 1,000 pop. **Infant mortality:** 24.6 per 1,000 live births. **Undernourished:** 5.4%. **HIV:** 0.1%. **COVID-19:** 1,003,417 cases, 12,031 deaths; rates per 100,000: 3,443.8 cases, 41.3 deaths. 83.7% vaccinated.

Education: Compulsory: ages 4-12. **Literacy:** 71.2%.
Website: nepal.gov.np

Nepal was originally a group of principalities, with the Gurkha principality becoming dominant about 1769. In 1951 King Tribhubana Bir Bikram, member of the Shah family, ended the system of rule by hereditary premiers of the Ranas family, who had kept the kings virtual prisoners, and established a cabinet system of government. Polygamy, child marriage, and the caste system were officially abolished in 1963. Political parties were legalized in 1990.

Nine members of Nepal's royal family, including King Birendra, died in a June 1, 2001, massacre. The killings were blamed on a 10th family member, Crown Prince Dipendra, who reportedly killed himself, allowing Birendra's brother Gyanendra Bir Bikram Shah Dev to take the throne.

Citing a Maoist insurgency, King Gyanendra assumed absolute authority, Feb. 1, 2005, but after protests, he agreed, Apr. 24, 2006, to reinstate parliament. A new government signed a peace accord with Maoist rebels Nov. 21 ending a decade-long civil war that claimed 13,000 lives. Maoists joined an interim parliament and cabinet in 2007. A constituent assembly voted May 2008 to abolish the monarchy and make Nepal a republic.

A new constitution, establishing a federal system with seven states, was adopted Sept. 20, 2015. Khadga Prasad Sharma Oli, leader of a non-Maoist Communist party, was elected prime min. by parliament, Oct. 11, 2015. Bidhya Devi Bhandari (of Oli's party) was elected by parliament, Oct. 28, 2015, as Nepal's first female president. Oli, facing a no-confidence vote, announced his resignation, July 23, 2016. A coalition of Communist parties won late 2017 legislative elections, and Oli returned as prime min., Feb. 15, 2018. After Oli lost support within his coalition, opposition leader Sher Bahadur Deuba became prime minister July 13, 2021. Following inconclusive Nov. 20, 2022, elections, former Maoist guerrilla Pushpa Kamal Dahal became prime minister Dec. 26, heading a coalition government. Ram Chandra Poudel, backed by Dahal, became president Mar. 13, 2023.

A magnitude 7.8 earthquake near Kathmandu, Apr. 25, 2015, displaced 2.8 mil. Historic temples were heavily damaged. After a second quake, May 12, 2015, the combined death toll exceeded 8,600.

Nepal did not permit climbing on Mount Everest in the 2020 season because of the COVID-19 pandemic. Crowding and unfavorable weather (perhaps related to climate change) contributed to an especially high death toll on Everest in 2023.

Netherlands
Kingdom of the Netherlands

People: Population: 17,463,930 (71). **Age distrib.:** <15: 15.2%; 65+: 20.4%. **Growth:** 0.4%. **Migrants:** 13.8%. **Pop. density:** 1,334.5 per sq mi, 515.3 per sq km. **Urban:** 93.2%. **Ethnic groups:** Dutch 75.4%, EU (excl. Dutch) 6.4%, Turkish 2.4%, Moroccan 2.4%, Surinamese 2.1%, Indonesian 2%. **Languages:** Dutch (official). **Religions:** Christian 52.9% (Catholic 30.1%, Protestant 19.6%), agnostic 33.7%, Muslim 7.9% (Sunni), atheist 3.0%.

Geography: Total area: 16,040 sq mi, 41,543 sq km (131); **Land area:** 13,086 sq mi, 33,893 sq km. **Location:** NW Europe on North Sea. Germany on E, Belgium on S. **Topography:** Land is flat with avg. elevation of 37 ft above sea level; much of land reclaimed and protected by some 1,500 mi of dikes. **Arable land:** 29.8%. **Capital:** Amsterdam, 1,174,025; s-Gravenhage (The Hague) (seat), 714,904. **Cities:** Rotterdam, 1,018,012.

Government: Type: Parliamentary constitutional monarchy. **Head of state:** King Willem-Alexander; b. 1967; in office: Apr. 30, 2013. **Head of govt.:** Prime Min. Mark Rutte; b. 1967; in office: Oct. 14, 2010. **Local divisions:** 12 provinces, 3 public entities. **Defense budget:** $15.2 bil. **Active troops:** 33,600.

Economy: Industries: agroindustries, metal/engineering prods., elec. machinery/equip., chemicals. **Chief agric.:** milk, potatoes, sugar beet, pork, onions, wheat. **Natural resources:** nat. gas, petroleum, peat, limestone, salt, sand and gravel. **Water:** 5,311 cu m per capita. **Crude oil reserves:** 138 mil bbls. **Electricity prod.:** 117.4 bil kWh. **Labor force:** agric. 2.3%, industry 13.9%, services 83.8%. **Unemployment:** 3.5%.

Finance: Monetary unit: Euro (EUR) (0.93 = $1 U.S.). **GDP:** $1.2 tril; **per capita GDP:** $69,577; **GDP growth:** 4.5%. **Imports:** $735.7 bil; Germany 15%, China 11%, Belgium 9%, U.S. 8%, Russia 7%. **Exports:** $839.6 bil; Germany 20%, Belgium 12%, UK 9%, France 7%. **Tourism:** $9.4 bil. **Budget:** $374.2 bil. **Inflation:** 10.0%.

Transport: Railways: 1,898 mi. **Motor vehicles:** 580.5 per 1,000 pop. **Airports:** 23.

Communications: Mobile: 118.1 per 100 pop. **Broadband:** 123.3 per 100 pop. **Internet:** 92.5%.

Health: Expend. (2021): 11.2%. **Life expect.:** 80.1 male; 83.3 female. **Births:** 10.5 per 1,000 pop. **Deaths:** 9.7 per 1,000 pop. **Infant mortality:** 3.7 per 1,000 live births. **Undernourished:** <2.5%. **HIV:** NA. **COVID-19:** 8,616,766 cases, 22,986 deaths; rates per 100,000: 49,500.1 cases, 132.0 deaths. 68.0% vaccinated.

Education: Compulsory: ages 5-17. **Literacy:** NA.

Website: www.government.nl

Julius Caesar conquered the region in 55 BCE, when it was inhabited by Celtic and Germanic tribes. After the empire of Charlemagne fell apart, the Netherlands (Holland, Belgium, Flanders) split among counts, dukes, and bishops, passed to Burgundy and thence to Spain. William the Silent, prince of Orange, led a confederation of the northern provinces, called Estates, in the Union of Utrecht, 1579; in 1581 they repudiated allegiance to Spain. The rise of the Dutch republic to naval, economic, and artistic eminence came in the 17th cent.

After a period of French hegemony, 1795-1813, the Congress of Vienna in 1815 formed a kingdom of the Netherlands, including Belgium, under William I. In 1830, Belgium seceded.

The Netherlands maintained its neutrality in WWI but was invaded during WWII and occupied by Germany, 1940-45. In 1949, after several years of fighting, the Netherlands granted independence to Indonesia.

On Apr. 30, 2009, an attempt to assassinate Queen Beatrix failed (but left 8 dead). Beatrix, 75, abdicated the throne to her son, Willem-Alexander, Apr. 30, 2013. A Malaysia Airlines flight from Amsterdam to Kuala Lumpur was shot down over eastern Ukraine, July 17, 2014; nearly 200 Dutch passport holders were among 298 killed.

Prime Min. Mark Rutte's center-right People's Party won Mar. 15, 2017, parliamentary elections, holding off a challenge from the anti-Islamic, right-wing Freedom Party. Rutte resigned, Jan. 15, 2021, over a government-benefits scandal, but his party won Mar. 17 elections. After months of negotiations, a new coalition government headed by Rutte was sworn in Jan. 10, 2022. Rutte's coalition collapsed in July 2023 in a dispute about immigration policy; new elections were scheduled for Nov. 22.

On July 1, 2023, the 150th anniversary of the abolition of slavery in the Netherlands' American possessions, King Willem-Alexander apologized for the Dutch role in bringing enslaved Africans to the Americas and keeping them in bondage.

Dutch Dependencies

Constitutional changes effective Oct. 10, 2010, dissolved the political entity known as the Netherlands Antilles. Curaçao (area 171 sq mi), an island near the coast of Venezuela, and Sint Maarten (13 sq mi), occupying the southern one-third of the island of St. Martin, SE of Puerto Rico, were elevated to the status of autonomous countries. Bonaire, Saba, and Sint Eustatius became special municipalities. Sint Maarten suffered extensive damage from Hurricane Luis, Sept. 1995, and Hurricane Irma, Sept. 2017. Pop. of Curaçao, 152,849 (2023 est.); that of its capital, Willemstad, 144,037 (2018 est.). Sint Maarten, pop. 45,677 (2023 est.); capital is Philipsburg. Principal industries: Curaçao, tourism, petroleum refining and transshipment, light mfg.; Sint Maarten, tourism, light industry. International tourism receipts were $682 mil (2019) for Curaçao, $703 mil (2019) for Sint Maarten. Per capita GDP of Sint Maarten was $36,191 (2018), Curaçao, $20,681 (2020). **Websites:** gobiernu.cw (Curaçao); www.sintmaartengov.org (Sint Maarten)

Aruba, about 26 mi west of Curaçao, was separated from the Netherlands Antilles on Jan. 1, 1986; it is an autonomous component of the Netherlands, with a status similar to Curaçao and Sint Maarten. Area: 69 sq mi; pop. (2023 est.) 123,702. Capital: Oranjestad; pop. (2018 est.) 29,877. Chief industries are tourism, petroleum transshipment facilities, banking. **Website:** www.kabga.aw

New Zealand

People: Population: 5,109,702 (124). **Age distrib.:** <15: 19.2%; 65+: 16.5%. **Growth:** 1.1%. **Migrants:** 28.7%. **Pop. density:** 50.0 per sq mi, 19.3 per sq km. **Urban:** 87.0%. **Ethnic groups:** European 64.1%, Maori 16.5%, Chinese 4.9%, Indian 4.7%, Samoan 3.9%. **Languages:** English (de facto official), Maori (de jure official), Samoan, Northern Chinese. **Religions:** Christian 52.4% (Protestant 31.0%, Catholic 12.8%), agnostic 36.2%, Buddhist 3.5% (Mahayanist), Hindu 2.3%, Muslim 1.8% (Sunni), atheist 1.4%.

Geography: Total area: 103,799 sq mi, 268,838 sq km (75); **Land area:** 102,138 sq mi, 264,537 sq km. **Location:** SW Pacific O. Nearest neighbors are Australia to W, Fiji and Tonga to N. **Topography:** Two main islands (North and South Isls.) are hilly and mountainous. The E coasts consist of fertile plains, incl. Canterbury Plains on South Isl. Volcanic plateau in center of North Isl. Glaciers and 15 peaks over 10,000 ft on South Isl. **Arable land:** 2.3%. **Capital:** Wellington, 421,624. **Cities:** Auckland, 1,673,220.

Government: Type: Parliamentary democracy under constitutional monarchy. **Head of state:** King Charles III, rep. by Gov.-Gen. Cindy Kiro; b. 1958; in office: Oct. 21, 2021. **Head of govt.:** Prime Min. Chris Hipkins; b. 1978; in office: Jan. 25, 2023. **Local divisions:** 16 regions, 1 territory. **Defense budget:** $3.4 bil. **Active troops:** 9,200.

Economy: Industries: agric., forestry, fishing, logs and wood articles, mfg., mining, constr., financial services, real estate services, tourism. **Chief agric.:** milk, beef, kiwi fruit, apples, potatoes, mutton. **Natural resources:** nat. gas, iron ore, sand, coal, timber, hydropower, gold, limestone. **Water:** 67,811 cu m per capita. **Crude oil reserves:** 41 mil bbls. **Electricity prod.:** 43.4 bil kWh. **Labor force:** agric. 6.1%, industry 20.0%, services 73.9%. **Unemployment:** 3.3%.

Finance: Monetary unit: Dollar (NZD) (1.69 = $1 U.S.). **GDP:** $266.3 bil; **per capita GDP:** $51,967; **GDP growth:** 2.2%. **Imports:** $62.9 bil; China 18%, Australia 15%, U.S. 9%, Japan 6%. **Exports:** $54.8 bil; China 28%, Australia 14%, U.S. 9%, Japan 6%. **Tourism:** $2.9 bil. **Budget** (2020): $88.6 bil. **Inflation:** 7.2%.

Transport: Railways: 2,565 mi. **Motor vehicles:** 889.4 per 1,000 pop. **Airports:** 39.

Communications: Mobile: 114.7 per 100 pop. **Broadband:** 96.2 per 100 pop. **Internet:** 95.9%.

Health: Expend.: 10.0%. **Life expect.:** 81.0 male; 84.6 female. **Births:** 12.7 per 1,000 pop. **Deaths:** 6.9 per 1,000 pop. **Infant mortality:** 3.4 per 1,000 live births. **Undernourished:** <2.5%. **HIV:** <0.1%. **COVID-19:** 2,368,831 cases, 3,249 deaths; rates per 100,000: 49,123.1 cases, 67.4 deaths. 84.7% vaccinated.

Education: Compulsory: ages 6-15. **Literacy:** NA.

Website: www.govt.nz

New Zealand comprises North Island, 43,911 sq mi; South Island, 58,084 sq mi; Stewart Island, 649 sq mi; Chatham Isls., 373 sq mi; and several groups of smaller islands. The Maori, a Polynesian group from the eastern Pacific, reached New Zealand before and during the 14th cent. The first European to sight New Zealand was Dutch navigator Abel Janszoon Tasman. The Maori refused to allow him to land. British Capt. James Cook explored the coasts, 1769-70.

British sovereignty was proclaimed and Maori land rights were recognized in the Treaty of Waitangi, 1840, with organized British settlement beginning the same year. Representative institutions were granted in 1853. The Maori Wars, or New Zealand Wars, ended in 1870 with British victory. The colony became a dominion in 1907 and gained full independence in 1947.

A progressive tradition in politics began in the 19th cent. Much of the nation's economy has been deregulated since the 1980s. Jenny Shipley of the National Party became the nation's first female prime min., Dec. 8, 1997. The Labour Party won 1999 elections.

A measure establishing a supreme court and ending appeals to the UK Privy Council passed Oct. 14, 2003. A major settlement of Maori land claims was signed June 25, 2008.

A Christchurch earthquake, Feb. 22, 2011, killed 181 people and caused extensive damage. Parliament legalized same-sex marriage Apr. 17, 2013.

After the National Party (in office since 2008) fell short of a majority in Sept. 23, 2017, elections, Labour Party head Jacinda Ardern formed a coalition government.

A gunman killed 51 in attacks at two Christchurch-area mosques, Mar. 15, 2019. Parliament, Apr. 10, outlawed many types of semi-automatic weapons. Mar. 2020 legislation legalized most abortions. Labour won 2020 elections.

New Zealand at times used strict lockdown measures and vaccine mandates to counter the COVID-19 pandemic that began in 2020; some measures were met with violent protests. Ardern announced, Jan. 19, 2023, that she would resign as prime minister; Labour's Chris Hipkins succeeded her Jan. 25. Australia and New Zealand hosted the FIFA Women's World Cup soccer tournament, July-Aug. 2023.

In 1965, the **Cook Islands** (area: 91 sq mi; 2023 est. pop.: 7,939), halfway between New Zealand and Hawaii, became self-governing. Capital: Rarotonga, pop. 13,067 (2018 est.). New Zealand retained responsibility for defense and foreign affairs. **Niue** (area: 100 sq mi; 2022 est. pop.: 2,000) attained the same status in 1974; capital: Alofi, pop. 727 (2018 est.). It lies about 675 mi W of Cook Isls. The U.S. announced, Sept. 25, 2023, it would establish diplomatic relations with the Cook Islands and Niue. **Tokelau** (area: 4.6 sq mi; 2019 est. pop.: 1,647) comprises three atolls 300 mi N of Samoa. Referendums in 2006 and 2007 on Tokelau self-government failed to gain the required two-third majority. **Ross Dependency,** administered by New Zealand since 1923, comprises 160,000 sq mi of Antarctic territory. **Websites:** www.cookislands.gov.ck; www.gov.nu; www.tokelau.org.nz

Nicaragua
Republic of Nicaragua

People: Population: 6,359,689 (109). **Age distrib.:** <15: 25.5%; 65+: 5.8%. **Growth:** 0.9%. **Migrants:** 0.6%. **Pop. density:** 137.3 per sq mi, 53.0 per sq km. **Urban:** 59.8%. **Ethnic groups:** mestizo (mixed Amerindian/white) 69%, white 17%, Black 9%, Amerindian 5%. **Languages:** Spanish (official), Miskito, Mestizo on Carib. coast. **Religions:** Christian 94.9% (Catholic 68.6%, Protestant 19.1%), agnostic 2.8%.

Geography: Total area: 50,336 sq mi, 130,370 sq km (96); **Land area:** 46,328 sq mi, 119,990 sq km. **Location:** Central America. Honduras on N, Costa Rica on S. **Topography:** Both Caribbean and Pacific coasts are over 200 mi long. Cordillera Mts., with many volcanic peaks, run NW-SE through middle of country. **Arable land:** 12.5%. **Capital:** Managua, 1,094,510.

Government: Type: Presidential republic. **Head of state and govt.:** Pres. Daniel Ortega Saavedra; b. 1945; in office: Jan. 10, 2007. **Local divisions:** 15 departments, 2 autonomous regions. **Defense budget:** $85 mil. **Active troops:** 12,000.

Economy: Industries: food proc., chemicals, machinery and metal prods., knit and woven apparel, petroleum refining/distrib. **Chief agric.:** sugarcane, milk, rice, maize, plantains, groundnuts. **Natural resources:** gold, silver, copper, tungsten, lead, zinc, timber, fish. **Water:** 24,835 cu m per capita. **Electricity prod.:** 4.6 bil kWh. **Labor force:** agric. 28.7%, industry 18.4%, services 52.9%. **Unemployment:** 5.6%.

Finance: Monetary unit: Cordoba (NIO) (36.59 = $1 U.S.). **GDP:** $47.8 bil; **per capita GDP:** $6,875; **GDP growth:** 3.8%. **Imports:** $8.3 bil; U.S. 27%, Mexico 12%, China 11%, Guatemala 9%, Costa Rica 7%, El Salvador 6%, Honduras 6%. **Exports:** $6.6 bil; U.S. 60%. **Tourism:** $184 mil. **Budget:** $3.5 bil. **Inflation:** 10.5%.

Transport: Motor vehicles: 73.4 per 1,000 pop. **Airports:** 12. **Communications: Mobile** (2021): 97.1 per 100 pop. **Broadband** (2021): 62.8 per 100 pop. **Internet:** 57.1%.

Health: Expend.: 8.6%. **Life expect.:** 73.0 male; 76.2 female. **Births:** 16.6 per 1,000 pop. **Deaths:** 5.1 per 1,000 pop. **Infant mortality:** 14.7 per 1,000 live births. **Undernourished:** 17.8%. **HIV:** 0.3%. **COVID-19:** 15,984 cases, 245 deaths; rates per 100,000: 241.3 cases, 3.7 deaths. 92.3% vaccinated.

Education: Compulsory: ages 5-11. **Literacy:** 82.6%. **Website:** www.asamblea.gob.ni

Nicaragua, inhabited by various Indian tribes, was conquered by Spain in 1552. After gaining independence from Spain, 1821, Nicaragua was united for a short period with Mexico, then with the United Provinces of Central America, before becoming an independent republic, 1838. U.S. Marines occupied the country at times in the early 20th cent., the last time from 1926 to 1933.

Gen. Anastasio Somoza Debayle held the presidency 1967-72, 1974-79. Martial law was imposed in Dec. 1974, after officials were kidnapped by Marxist Sandinista guerrillas. Nationwide strikes touched off a civil war, 1978, which ended when Somoza fled Nicaragua and the Sandinistas took control of Managua, July 1979. Somoza was assassinated in Paraguay, Sept. 17, 1980.

Relations with the U.S. were strained as a result of Nicaragua's aid to leftist guerrillas in El Salvador and U.S. backing of anti-Sandinista contra guerrilla groups, which fought the Sandinista government throughout the 1980s. In 1985 the U.S. House rejected Pres. Ronald Reagan's request for military aid to the contras. The U.S. later secretly diverted funds to the contras.

In a stunning upset, Violeta Barrios de Chamorro defeated Sandinista leader Daniel Ortega Saavedra in national elections, Feb. 25, 1990. Conservative candidates won the 1996 and 2001 presidential elections. Drought and a drop in coffee prices precipitated an economic crisis in 2001.

Ortega won the Nov. 2006 presidential election. He was reelected Nov. 6, 2011, and Nov. 6, 2016. In 2016, Rosario Murillo Zambrana, Ortega's wife, was elected vice president.

Months of protests, beginning Apr. 2018, against government policies and authoritarian rule resulted in hundreds of deaths, most at the hands of security forces or allied paramilitary groups. Hundreds were arrested, some reportedly tortured in detention. By early 2021, more than 100,000 Nicaraguans had fled the country. In the months leading up to the Nov. 7, 2021, presidential election, opposition leaders, activists, and critics of the government were arrested; Ortega and Murillo were reelected. The government continued its crackdown on dissent in 2022-23, including arresting Catholic clerics and shutting down church media outlets. Nicaraguans continued to leave for other countries—a total of about 200,000 to Costa Rica alone by 2023.

Seeking Chinese aid, Nicaragua established diplomatic relations with China, Dec. 10, 2021, breaking ties with Taiwan.

Niger
Republic of Niger

People: Population: 25,396,840 (56). **Age distrib.:** <15: 49.7%; 65+: 2.7%. **Growth:** 3.7%. **Migrants:** 1.4%. **Pop. density:** 51.9 per sq mi, 20.0 per sq km. **Urban:** 17.1%. **Ethnic groups:** Hausa 53.1%, Zarma/Songhai 21.2%, Tuareg 11%, Fulani (Peuhl) 6.5%, Kanuri 5.9%. **Languages:** French (official), Hausa, Djerma. **Religions:** Muslim 96.7% (Sunni), ethnic religionist 3.0%.

Geography: Total area: 489,191 sq mi, 1,267,000 sq km (21); **Land area:** 489,076 sq mi, 1,266,700 sq km. **Location:** Interior of N Africa. Libya, Algeria on N; Mali, Burkina Faso on W; Benin, Nigeria on S; Chad on E. **Topography:** Mostly arid desert and mountains. Narrow savanna in S and Niger R. basin in the SW. **Arable land:** 14.0%. **Capital:** Niamey, 1,437,233.

Government: Type: Semi-presidential republic. **Head of state:** Pres. Mohamed Bazoum; b. 1960; in office: Apr. 2, 2021. **Head of**

govt.: Prime Min. Mahamadou Ouhoumoudou; b. 1952; in office: Apr. 3, 2021. **Local divisions:** 7 regions, 1 capital district. **Defense budget:** $244 mil. **Active troops:** 33,100.

Economy: Industries: uranium mining, petroleum, cement, brick, soap, textiles, food proc., chemicals, slaughterhouses. **Chief agric.:** millet, cow peas, sorghum, onions, milk, groundnuts. **Natural resources:** uranium, coal, iron ore, tin, phosphates, gold, molybdenum, gypsum, salt, petroleum. **Water:** 1,407 cu m per capita. **Crude oil reserves:** 150 mil bbls. **Electricity prod.:** 450.9 mil kWh. **Labor force:** agric. 70.7%, industry 7.6%, services 21.7%. **Unemployment:** 0.5%.

Finance: Monetary unit: CFA Franc (XOF) (606.88 = $1 U.S.). **GDP:** $39.4 bil; **per capita GDP:** $1,505; **GDP growth:** 11.5%. **Imports** (2020): $3.5 bil; China 19%, France 9%, UAE 7%, Côte d'Ivoire 6%, India 6%. **Exports** (2020): $1.3 bil; UAE 54%, China 25%, France 7%. **Tourism** (2020): $85 mil. **Budget:** $2.8 bil. **Inflation:** 4.2%.

Transport: Motor vehicles: 15.0 per 1,000 pop. **Airports:** 10. **Communications: Mobile** (2021): 56.4 per 100 pop. **Broadband** (2021): 5.5 per 100 pop. **Internet:** 22.2%.

Health: Expend.: 6.2%. **Life expect.:** 58.9 male; 62.1 female. **Births:** 46.9 per 1,000 pop. **Deaths:** 9.7 per 1,000 pop. **Infant mortality:** 65.5 per 1,000 live births. **Undernourished:** 16.1%. **HIV:** 0.2%. **COVID-19:** 9,515 cases, 315 deaths; rates per 100,000: 39.3 cases, 1.3 deaths. 22.7% vaccinated.

Education: Compulsory: NA. **Literacy:** 37.3%. **Website:** www.gouv.ne

Niger was part of ancient and medieval African empires. European explorers reached the area in the late 18th cent. The French colony of Niger was established 1900-22 after the defeat of Tuareg fighters, who had invaded the area from the north a century before. The country became independent Aug. 3, 1960.

In 1993, Niger held its first free and open elections since independence. A peace accord Apr. 24, 1995, ended a Tuareg rebellion that began in 1990. After a coup, Jan. 27, 1996, the military retained control. Oct.-Nov. 1999 elections, under a new constitution, restored civilian rule.

Popularly elected in 1999 and 2004, Pres. Mamadou Tandja invoked emergency powers in 2009 to remain in office. He was overthrown by a military junta Feb. 18, 2010. Civilian rule returned following 2011 elections. Pres. Mahamadou Issoufou won reelection in 2016. Mohamed Bazoum, of Issoufou's party, won a Feb. 21, 2021, presidential runoff.

Beginning in Feb. 2015, the Nigeria-based Islamist extremist group Boko Haram staged attacks in southern Niger. Islamist extremists based in Mali staged attacks in W Niger; an attack by ISIS-affiliated militants, Oct. 4, 2017, killed 9, including 4 U.S. special operations troops. As Islamist violence increased in 2023, by Aug. 31, Niger had more than 335,000 internally displaced persons.

A military coup led by Gen. Abdourahamane Tchiani overthrew Pres. Bazoum, July 26, 2023. Coup leaders demanded that France withdraw its troops from Niger, which France agreed to in Sept.; the U.S. concentrated its troops in Niger at a counterterrorism base in the north.

Nigeria
Federal Republic of Nigeria

People: Population: 230,842,743 (6). **Age distrib.:** <15: 40.7%; 65+: 3.4%. **Growth:** 2.5%. **Migrants:** 0.6%. **Pop. density:** 656.5 per sq mi, 253.5 per sq km. **Urban:** 54.3%. **Ethnic groups:** More than 250 ethnic groups, incl. Hausa 30%, Yoruba 15.5%, Igbo (Ibo) 15.2%, Fulani 6%, Tiv 2.4%, Kanuri/Beriberi 2.4%. **Languages:** English (official), Hausa, Yoruba, Igbo (Ibo), Fulani, 500+ indigenous langs. **Religions:** Muslim 46.8% (Sunni), Christian 46.3% (Protestant 24.2%, independent 11.5%, Catholic 10.6%), ethnic religionist 6.5%.

Geography: Total area: 356,669 sq mi, 923,768 sq km (31); **Land area:** 351,649 sq mi, 910,768 sq km. **Location:** S coast of W Africa. Benin on W, Niger on N, Chad and Cameroon on E. **Topography:** 4 E-W regions: a coastal mangrove swamp, a tropical rain forest, a plateau of savanna and open woodland, and semi-desert in N. **Arable land:** 40.5%. **Capital:** Lagos, 15,945,912. **Cities:** Kano, 4,348,481; Ibadan, 3,874,908; Abuja, 3,839,646; Port Harcourt, 3,480,101.

Government: Type: Federal presidential republic. **Head of state and govt.:** Pres. Bola Ahmed Adekunle Tinubu; b. 1952; in office: May 29, 2023. **Local divisions:** 36 states, 1 territory. **Defense budget:** $2.8 bil. **Active troops:** 143,000.

Economy: Industries: crude oil, coal, tin, columbite; rubber prods.; wood; hides/skins, textiles, cement and other constr. materials. **Chief agric.:** cassava, yams, maize, oil palm fruit, rice, vegetables. **Natural resources:** nat. gas, petroleum, tin, iron ore, coal, limestone, niobium, lead, zinc. **Water:** 1,388 cu m per capita. **Crude oil reserves:** 36.9 bil bbls. **Electricity prod.:** 31.5 bil kWh. **Labor force:** agric. 35.2%, industry 12.7%, services 52.1%. **Unemployment:** 5.8%.

Finance: Monetary unit: Naira (NGN) (773.47 = $1 U.S.). **GDP:** $1.3 tril; **per capita GDP:** $5,860; **GDP growth:** 3.3%. **Imports:** $66.1 bil; China 30%, Netherlands 11%, U.S. 6%. **Exports** (2017):

$44.5 bil; (2021) India 16%, Spain 12%, U.S. 6%, France 6%. **Tourism:** $256 mil. **Budget:** $59.9 bil. **Inflation:** 18.8%.

Transport: Railways: 2,360 mi (majority in severe disrepair). **Motor vehicles:** 9.4 per 1,000 pop. **Airports:** 40.

Communications: Mobile: 101.7 per 100 pop. **Broadband:** 41.4 per 100 pop. **Internet:** 55.4%.

Health: Expend.: 3.4%. **Life expect.:** 59.9 male; 63.8 female. **Births:** 34.0 per 1,000 pop. **Deaths:** 8.5 per 1,000 pop. **Infant mortality:** 55.2 per 1,000 live births. **Undernourished:** 15.9%. **HIV:** NA. **COVID-19:** 266,675 cases, 3,155 deaths; rates per 100,000: 129.4 cases, 1.5 deaths. 37.8% vaccinated.

Education: Compulsory: ages 6-14. **Literacy:** 62.0%.

Website: nigeria.gov.ng

Early cultures in Nigeria date back to at least 700 BCE. From the 12th to the 14th cent., more advanced cultures developed in the Yoruba area, at Ife, and in the north, where Muslim influence prevailed. Portuguese and British slavers appeared in the 15th-16th cent. Britain seized Lagos, 1861, and gradually extended control inland until 1900. Nigeria became independent Oct. 1, 1960, and a republic Oct. 1, 1963.

On May 30, 1967, the Eastern Region seceded, proclaiming itself the Republic of Biafra, plunging the country into civil war. Casualties were estimated at over 1 mil, including many Biafrans (mostly Igbos) who died of starvation despite international relief efforts. The secessionists capitulated Jan. 12, 1970.

Nigeria emerged as one of the world's leading oil exporters in the 1970s, but much of the revenue has been squandered through corruption and mismanagement. Oil spills have polluted much of the Niger Delta region.

After 13 years of military rule, the nation made a peaceful return to civilian government Oct. 1979. Military rule resumed Dec. 31, 1983. A coup brought Gen. Sani Abacha to power in 1993. His brutal rule ended June 8, 1998, when he died of an apparent heart attack. Olusegun Obasanjo won a presidential election Feb. 27, 1999, to lead a civilian government.

The imposition of strict Islamic law in northern states led to clashes, Jan.-Mar. 2000, in which at least 300 people died. Fighting between Muslims and Christians in the early 2000s claimed hundreds of lives. Vice Pres. Goodluck Jonathan, a southern Christian, became president in 2010 when his predecessor died. Jonathan won reelection Apr. 16, 2011, over Muhammadu Buhari, a northern-based Muslim.

Boko Haram, a radical Islamist group based in NE Nigeria seeking to establish an Islamist state, began terrorist attacks in 2009 against government forces and civilian targets. The group gained control of a large area in the NE and terrorist attacks escalated, 2013-15. Boko Haram split, in 2016, into ISIS-affiliated and non-affiliated factions.

Vowing tougher action against Boko Haram, Buhari defeated Jonathan in the Mar. 28-29, 2015, presidential election. Subsequent government offensives retook much of the territory Boko Haram had seized, but Boko Haram forces, including the ISIS-affiliated militants, continued to control areas of NE Nigeria and stage deadly attacks against civilians and security forces in the NE and elsewhere in the country, 2016-23.

Amid ongoing Islamist, as well as other religious and ethnic violence (including in Biafra), Buhari won reelection, Feb. 23, 2019. Boko Haram leader Abubakar Shekau died, May 2021, in a conflict with ISIS-affiliated fighters, as the ISIS forces became the dominant extremist group in the NE.

Islamist extremists, as well as other groups apparently seeking ransom, have kidnapped thousands of Nigerians and foreigners since 2014, including a number of mass abductions of schoolchildren.

The Council on Foreign Relations estimated that, as of July 1, 2023, more than 98,000 people had been killed since 2011 as a result of Islamist extremist attacks, clashes with security forces, and actions by other armed groups. The UNHCR estimated that, as of Aug. 31, 2023, more than 355,000 Nigerian refugees were in Niger, Cameroon, or Chad; almost 2.4 mil Nigerians were internally displaced.

Bola Tinubu (of Buhari's party) was declared the winner of the Feb. 25, 2023, presidential election; opposition candidates disputed the result, charging widespread voting irregularities.

A WHO study released in May 2022 estimated 186,000 excess deaths in Nigeria related to the COVID-19 pandemic in 2020-21, exceeding the reported death tally by many tens of thousands.

North Macedonia
Republic of North Macedonia

(Under the Prespa Agreement, in force as of Feb. 12, 2019, Macedonia and Greece agreed to recognize the former under the name North Macedonia, ending a longstanding regional dispute.)

People: Population: 2,133,410 (145). **Age distrib.:** <15: 16.1%; 65+: 15.3%. **Growth:** 0.1%. **Migrants:** 6.3%. **Pop. density:** 217.3 per sq mi, 83.9 per sq km. **Urban:** 59.5%. **Ethnic groups:** Macedonian 58.4%, Albanian 24.3%, Turkish 3.9%, Romani 2.5% (usu. underestimated and may be 6.5%-13% of pop.). **Languages:** Macedonian, Albanian (both official); Turkish; minority langs (incl. Romani, Aromanian, Serbian) co-official in certain municipalities.

Religions: Christian 64.4% (Orthodox [official] 62.6%), Muslim 32.8% (Sunni), agnostic 2.5%.

Geography: Total area: 9,928 sq mi, 25,713 sq km (146); **Land area:** 9,820 sq mi, 25,433 sq km. **Location:** SE Europe. Bulgaria on E, Greece on S, Albania on W, Serbia on N. **Topography:** Landlocked, mostly mountainous with deep river valleys, 3 large lakes. Country is bisected by Vardar R. **Arable land:** 16.5%. **Capital:** Skopje, 611,107.

Government: Type: Parliamentary republic. **Head of state:** Pres. Stevo Pendarovski; b. 1963; in office: May 12, 2019. **Head of govt.:** Prime Min. Dimitar Kovacevski; b. 1974; in office: Jan. 16, 2022. **Local divisions:** 70 municipalities, 1 city. **Defense budget:** $229 mil. **Active troops:** 8,000.

Economy: Industries: food proc., beverages, textiles, chemicals, iron, steel, cement, energy, pharmaceuticals. **Chief agric.:** milk, grapes, wheat, potatoes, green chillies/peppers, cabbages. **Natural resources:** iron ore, copper, lead, zinc, chromite, manganese, nickel, tungsten, gold, silver, asbestos, gypsum, timber. **Water:** 3,072 cu m per capita. **Electricity prod.:** 5.2 bil kWh. **Labor force:** agric. 10.8%, industry 30.8%, services 58.4%. **Unemployment:** 15.1%.

Finance: Monetary unit: Denar (MKD) (56.89 = $1 U.S.). **GDP:** $41.5 bil; **per capita GDP:** $20,162; **GDP growth:** 2.1%. **Imports:** $11.4 bil; UK 14%, Germany 14%, Greece 8%, Serbia 8%. **Exports:** $9.2 bil; Germany 45%, Serbia 8%. **Tourism:** $385 mil. **Budget** (2020): $4.5 bil. **Inflation:** 14.2%.

Transport: Railways: 434 mi. **Airports:** 8.

Communications: Mobile: 97.8 per 100 pop. **Broadband:** 75.6 per 100 pop. **Internet:** 83.0%.

Health: Expend.: 7.9%. **Life expect.:** 75.0 male; 79.3 female. **Births:** 10.3 per 1,000 pop. **Deaths:** 9.6 per 1,000 pop. **Infant mortality:** 7.2 per 1,000 live births. **Undernourished:** 3.6%. **HIV:** <0.1%. **COVID-19:** 348,374 cases, 9,941 deaths; rates per 100,000: 16,721.6 cases, 477.2 deaths. 39.9% vaccinated.

Education: Compulsory: ages 6-18. **Literacy:** 98.4%.

Website: www.vlada.mk

Muslim Turks ruled present-day North Macedonia from 1389 to 1912. In 1913, the area was incorporated into Serbia, which in 1918 became part of the Kingdom of Serbs, Croats, and Slovenes (later Yugoslavia). In 1946, the area, then called Macedonia, became a constituent republic of Yugoslavia.

Macedonia declared its independence Sept. 8, 1991, and was admitted to the UN in 1993. For decades, Greece, objecting to Macedonia's use of what it considered a Hellenic name, blocked Macedonia's bids to join NATO and the EU.

Ethnic Albanian guerrillas launched an offensive Mar. 2001 in NW Macedonia. An accord signed Aug. 13 paved the way for a NATO peacekeeping force. A law broadening the rights of ethnic Albanians was enacted Jan. 2002.

In 2015 and early 2016, tens of thousands of migrants from the Middle East and SW Asia who landed in Greece tried to cross Macedonia on their way to N Europe. After building border fencing and taking other steps to restrict access, Macedonia announced, Mar. 9, 2016, that its border with Greece was closed to migrants.

After a government wiretapping and corruption scandal, conservative Prime Min. Nikola Gruevski resigned Jan. 15, 2016. Following parliamentary elections in Dec. 2016, Social Democrat Zoran Zaev formed a coalition and became prime min. May 31, 2017. Macedonia and Greece reached an agreement, effective as of Feb. 12, 2019, for the former to change its name to North Macedonia. Pro-EU, pro-NATO candidate Stevo Pendarovski won a May 5 presidential runoff election. North Macedonia joined NATO Mar. 27, 2020. Zaev resigned Dec. 23, 2021, following his party's losses in municipal elections. Social Democrat Dimitar Kovacevski became prime min., Jan. 16, 2022.

Norway
Kingdom of Norway

People: Population: 5,597,924 (117). **Age distrib.:** <15: 16.6%; 65+: 18.9%. **Growth:** 0.8%. **Migrants:** 15.7%. **Pop. density:** 47.6 per sq mi, 18.4 per sq km. **Urban:** 84.0%. **Ethnic groups:** Norwegian (incl. Sami) 81.5%, other European 8.9%. **Languages:** Bokmal Norwegian, Nynorsk Norwegian (both official); Sami (official in some areas). **Religions:** Christian 83.9% (Protestant 78.0%), agnostic 7.5%, Muslim 6.7% (Sunni).

Geography: Total area: 125,021 sq mi, 323,802 sq km (67); **Land area:** 117,484 sq mi, 304,282 sq km. **Location:** W part of Scandinavian peninsula in NW Europe (extends farther N than any European land). Sweden, Finland, Russia on E. **Topography:** Highly indented coast lined with tens of thousands of islands. Mountains and plateaus cover most of country, which is only 33% forested. **Arable land:** 2.2%. **Capital:** Oslo, 1,085,992.

Government: Type: Parliamentary constitutional monarchy. **Head of state:** King Harald V; b. 1937; in office: Jan. 17, 1991. **Head of govt.:** Prime Min. Jonas Gahr Store; b. 1960; in office: Oct. 14, 2021. **Local divisions:** 11 counties. **Defense budget:** $7.4 bil. **Active troops:** 25,400.

Economy: Industries: petroleum and gas, shipping, fishing, aquaculture, food proc., shipbuilding, pulp/paper prods.

Chief agric.: milk, barley, wheat, potatoes, oats, pork. **Natural resources:** petroleum, nat. gas, iron ore, copper, lead, zinc, titanium, pyrites, nickel, fish, timber, hydropower. **Water:** 72,493 cu m per capita. **Crude oil reserves:** 8.1 bil bbls. **Electricity prod.:** 157.5 bil kWh. **Labor force:** agric. 2.3%, industry 19.2%, services 78.5%. **Unemployment:** 3.2%.

Finance: Monetary unit: Krone (NOK) (10.72 = $1 U.S.). **GDP:** $627.0 bil; **per capita GDP:** $114,899; **GDP growth:** 3.3%. **Imports:** $140.4 bil; (2021) Sweden 18%, Germany 12%, China 10%, Denmark 6%. **Exports:** $199.1 bil; (2021) UK 21%, Germany 19%, Sweden 8%, Netherlands 7%, China 6%. **Tourism:** $1.9 bil. **Budget** (2020): $210.5 bil. **Inflation:** 5.8%.

Transport: Railways: 2,391 mi. **Motor vehicles:** 644.6 per 1,000 pop. **Airports:** 67.

Communications: Mobile: 110.7 per 100 pop. **Broadband:** 98.3 per 100 pop. **Internet:** 99.0%.

Health: Expend. (2021): 10.1%. **Life expect.:** 81.4 male; 84.7 female. **Births:** 10.4 per 1,000 pop. **Deaths:** 8.2 per 1,000 pop. **Infant mortality:** 1.8 per 1,000 live births. **Undernourished:** <2.5%. **HIV:** NA. **COVID-19:** 1,486,695 cases, 5,621 deaths; rates per 100,000: 27,697.7 cases, 104.7 deaths. 74.9% vaccinated.

Education: Compulsory: ages 6-15. **Literacy:** NA.

Website: www.regjeringen.no

The first ruler of Norway was Harald the Fairhaired, who came to power in 872 CE. Between 800 and 1000, Norway's Vikings raided and occupied widely dispersed parts of Europe. The country was united with Denmark, 1381-1814, and with Sweden, 1814-1905. In 1905, the country became independent with Prince Charles of Denmark as king.

Norway remained neutral during WWI. In WWII, Germany attacked Norway Apr. 9, 1940, and held it until liberation May 8, 1945. The country abandoned its neutrality after the war and joined NATO. In a referendum Nov. 28, 1994, Norwegian voters rejected European Union membership.

Norway has one of the highest living standards in the world. Hydropower accounts for more than 90% of electricity production. In the early 2000s, the country became a leading producer and exporter of oil and natural gas, with extensive reserves in the North Sea. Norway used oil and gas revenue to build up the world's largest sovereign wealth fund (about $1.4 tril as of Sept. 2023).

A right-wing extremist, Anders Behring Breivik, confessed to killing 8 people with a car bomb in central Oslo and murdering 69 at a camp sponsored by the Labor Party's youth wing July 22, 2011. Parliament, June 18, 2013, made military service compulsory for women as well as men. Rightist and anti-immigration parties won the most seats in Sept. 9, 2013, elections; Conservative Party leader Erna Solberg became prime min. In 2015, about 31,000 migrants from the Middle East, SW Asia, and Africa applied for asylum. Solberg's coalition won 2017 elections. After a campaign in which climate change was a key issue, Labor won the most seats in Sept. 13, 2021, elections; party leader Jonas Gahr Store became prime minister Oct. 14.

Svalbard is a group of mountainous islands in the Arctic O., area 23,956 sq mi, pop. (2021 est.) 2,926. The largest, Spitsbergen (formerly called West Spitsbergen), 14,546 sq mi, seat of the governor, is about 370 mi N of Norway. By the 1920 Svalbard Treaty (in force 1925), major European powers recognized Norway's sovereignty over the archipelago.

Jan Mayen, area 146 sq mi, is a volcanic island located about 565 mi W-NW of Norway; it was annexed in 1929. The only people on Jan Mayen are military personnel and researchers. Norway operates a research station on volcanic Bouvet Isl. (annexed 1930), area 19 sq mi, in the South Atlantic O., about midway between South Africa and Antarctica.

Oman
Sultanate of Oman

People: Population: 3,833,465 (129). **Age distrib.:** <15: 29.9%; 65+: 4.0%. **Growth:** 1.8%. **Migrants:** 46.5%. **Pop. density:** 32.1 per sq mi, 12.4 per sq km. **Urban:** 88.4%. **Ethnic groups:** Arab, Baluchi, South Asian (Indian, Pakistani, Sri Lankan, Bangladeshi), African. **Languages:** Arabic (official), English, Baluchi, Swahili, Urdu, Indian dialects. **Religions:** Muslim (official) 90.0% (Sunni 48%, Islamic schismatic 36%), Hindu 5.0%, Christian 3.6%.

Geography: Total area: 119,499 sq mi, 309,500 sq km (70). **Land area:** 119,499 sq mi, 309,500 sq km. **Location:** SE coast of Arabian peninsula. United Arab Emirates, Saudi Arabia, Yemen on W. **Topography:** A narrow coastal plain, a range of barren mountains reaching 9,900 ft, and a wide, stony, mostly waterless plateau, avg. elevation 1,000 ft. An exclave at the tip of the Musandam peninsula controls access to the Persian Gulf. **Arable land:** 0.3%. **Capital:** Muscat, 1,650,319.

Government: Type: Absolute monarchy. **Head of state and govt.:** Sultan and Prime Min. Haitham bin Tariq bin Taimur al-Said; b. 1954; in office: Jan. 11, 2020. **Local divisions:** 11 governorates. **Defense budget:** $6.4 bil. **Active troops:** 42,600.

Economy: Industries: crude oil prod. and refining, nat. and liquefied nat. gas prod., constr., cement, copper, steel, chemicals, optic fiber. **Chief agric.:** dates, tomatoes, vegetables, goat milk,

milk, cucumbers. **Natural resources:** petroleum, copper, asbestos, marble, limestone, chromium, gypsum, nat. gas. **Water:** 274 cu m per capita. **Crude oil reserves:** 5.4 bil bbls. **Electricity prod.:** 36.6 bil kWh. **Labor force:** agric. 4.1%, industry 48.3%, services 47.6%. **Unemployment:** 2.3%.

Finance: Monetary unit: Rial (OMR) (0.38 = $1 U.S.). **GDP:** $190.9 bil; **per capita GDP:** $41,724; **GDP growth:** 4.3%. **Imports:** $36.5 bil; UAE 36%, China 10%, Japan 7%, India 7%. **Exports:** $46.3 bil; China 46%, India 8%, Japan 6%, South Korea 6%, UAE 6%. **Tourism:** $362 mil. **Budget** (2018): $36.0 bil. **Inflation:** 2.8%.

Transport: Motor vehicles: 401.7 per 1,000 pop. **Airports:** 13.

Communications: Mobile (2021): 135.1 per 100 pop. **Broadband** (2021): 112.6 per 100 pop. **Internet:** 96.4%.

Health: Expend.: 5.3%. **Life expect.:** 75.2 male; 79.2 female. **Births:** 21.6 per 1,000 pop. **Deaths:** 3.2 per 1,000 pop. **Infant mortality:** 14.2 per 1,000 live births. **Undernourished:** 2.8%. **HIV:** <0.1%. **COVID-19:** 399,449 cases, 4,628 deaths; rates per 100,000: 7,822.2 cases, 90.6 deaths. 59.7% vaccinated.

Education: Compulsory: ages 6-15. **Literacy:** 95.7%.

Website: www.oman.om

Oman was originally called Muscat and Oman. A long history of rule by other lands, including Portugal in the 16th cent., ended with the ouster of the Persians in 1744. By the early 19th cent., Muscat and Oman controlled much of the Persian and Pakistan coasts.

British influence was confirmed in a 1951 treaty, and Britain helped suppress an uprising by interior tribes in the 1950s.

On July 23, 1970, Sultan Qaboos bin Said al-Said became ruler. He changed the nation's name to Sultanate of Oman. Petroleum and natural gas are major sources of income. Oman has strong ties to the U.S. but also favorable relations with Iran. After Arab Spring protests Feb. 2011, Sultan Qaboos expanded the powers of the lower house of parliament, Oct. 20, 2011. Sultan Qaboos died, Jan. 10, 2020; he was succeeded the next day by his cousin Haitham bin Tariq al-Said.

Pakistan
Islamic Republic of Pakistan

People: Population: 247,653,551 (5). **Age distrib.:** <15: 34.8%; 65+: 4.8%. **Growth:** 1.9%. **Migrants:** 1.5%. **Pop. density:** 832.1 per sq mi, 321.3 per sq km. **Urban:** 38.0%. **Ethnic groups:** Punjabi 44.7%, Pashtun (Pathan) 15.4%, Sindhi 14.1%, Saraiki 8.4%, Muhajir 7.6%, Balochi 3.6%. **Languages:** Punjabi, Pashto or Pashtu, Sindhi, Saraiki, Urdu (official), Balochi, Hindko, English (official; lingua franca of elite and most govt. ministries). **Religions:** Muslim (official) 96.7% (Sunni 84%, Shia 10%), Christian 1.8%, Hindu 1.2%.

Geography: Total area: 307,374 sq mi, 796,095 sq km (35). **Land area:** 297,637 sq mi, 770,875 sq km. **Location:** W part of S Asia. Iran on W, Afghanistan and China on N, India on E. **Topography:** The Indus R. rises in the Hindu Kush and Himalaya Mts. in the N, then flows 1,000 mi into Arabian Sea. Thar Desert, Eastern Plains flank Indus Valley. **Arable land:** 39.6%. **Capital:** Islamabad, 1,232,447. **Cities:** Karachi, 17,236,230; Lahore, 13,979,390; Faisalabad, 3,710,845; Gujranwala, 2,415,416; Peshawar, 2,411,785; Rawalpindi, 2,377,325; Multan, 2,154,600.

Government: Type: Federal parliamentary republic. **Head of state:** Pres. Arif Alvi; b. 1949; in office: Sept. 9, 2018. **Head of govt.:** Prime Min. Anwaar-ul-Haq Kakar; in office: Aug. 14, 2023. **Local divisions:** 4 provinces, 1 capital territory, 2 admin. entities (Azad Kashmir and Gilgit-Baltistan) in Pakistan-administered part of disputed region. **Defense budget:** $9.8 bil. **Active troops:** 651,800.

Economy: Industries: textiles and apparel, food proc., pharmaceuticals, surgical instruments, constr. materials, paper prods., fertilizer, shrimp. **Chief agric.:** sugarcane, buffalo milk, wheat, milk, rice, maize. **Natural resources:** nat. gas, limited petroleum, poor quality coal, iron ore, copper, salt, limestone. **Water:** 1,117 cu m per capita. **Crude oil reserves:** 540 mil bbls. **Electricity prod.:** 150.2 bil kWh. **Labor force:** agric. 37.5%, industry 25.2%, services 37.3%. **Unemployment:** 6.4%.

Finance: Monetary unit: Rupee (PKR) (303.12 = $1 U.S.). **GDP:** $1.5 tril; **per capita GDP:** $6,437; **GDP growth:** 6.2%. **Imports:** $76.4 bil; China 28%, UAE 11%. **Exports:** $35.6 bil; U.S. 14%, China 8%, Germany 7%, UK 6%. **Tourism:** $559 mil. **Budget** (2020): $59.6 bil. **Inflation:** 19.9%.

Transport: Railways: 7,383 mi. **Motor vehicles:** 20.1 per 1,000 pop. **Airports:** 108.

Communications: Mobile: 81.7 per 100 pop. **Broadband:** 51.5 per 100 pop. **Internet:** 21.0%.

Health: Expend.: 3.0%. **Life expect.:** 67.9 male; 72.1 female. **Births:** 26.0 per 1,000 pop. **Deaths:** 5.9 per 1,000 pop. **Infant mortality:** 52.7 per 1,000 live births. **Undernourished:** 18.5%. **HIV:** 0.2%. **COVID-19:** 1,580,631 cases, 30,656 deaths; rates per 100,000: 715.6 cases, 13.9 deaths. 63.6% vaccinated.

Education: Compulsory: ages 5-16. **Literacy:** 58.0%.

Website: pakistan.gov.pk

Pakistan shares the 5,000-year history of the India-Pakistan subcontinent. At present-day Harappa and Mohenjo Daro, the Indus Valley civilization, with large cities and elaborate irrigation systems, flourished c. 4,000-2,500 BCE. Aryan invaders from the northwest conquered the region around 1,500 BCE, forging the Vedic civilization that dominated the region for over a thousand years. The first Arab invasion, 712 CE, introduced Islam. Present-day Pakistan and India were part of the Mughal Empire from 1526 to 1857. Muslim power faded by the end of the 19th cent. as the British gained control.

Muhammad Ali Jinnah (1876-1948) was the principal architect of Pakistan. When the British withdrew, Aug. 14, 1947, two largely Islamic regions of British India acquired self-government as Pakistan, with dominion status in the Commonwealth. Pakistan consisted of West Pakistan and East Pakistan, nearly 1,000 mi apart on opposite sides of India. Kashmir, a predominantly Muslim region divided between Pakistan and India, has remained a source of conflict between the two countries.

Rioting and strikes broke out in the East after Pakistan's government, Mar. 1, 1971, postponed the constituent assembly, dominated by supporters of regional autonomy for East Pakistan. Armed conflict between East and West lasted from Mar. to Dec. 1971, with India siding with Easterners, who proclaimed the independent nation of Bangladesh. Thousands were killed, and some 10 mil Easterners fled to India. Full-scale war erupted between India and Pakistan. A day after Pakistan troops in the East surrendered, Pakistan agreed to a cease-fire in the West Dec. 17, 1971. On July 3, 1972, Pakistan and India signed a pact providing for troop withdrawals.

Zulfikar Ali Bhutto, who became president in 1971 and prime min. in 1973, was overthrown in a military coup July 1977. Convicted of complicity in a 1974 political murder, he was executed Apr. 4, 1979.

Millions of Afghan refugees entered Pakistan after the USSR invaded Afghanistan Dec. 1979, after U.S.-led forces began fighting the Taliban in Afghanistan in 2001, and after the Taliban regained control in Afghanistan in 2021. Although millions of refugees were repatriated, more than 1.7 mil Afghan refugees were estimated to be living in Pakistan in 2023. Pakistan announced, Oct. 2023, that all undocumented immigrants had to leave the country by Nov. 1 or face deportation.

Pres. Mohammad Zia ul-Haq was killed when his plane exploded in Aug. 1988. Following Nov. elections, Benazir Bhutto, daughter of Zulfikar Ali Bhutto, became prime min. and the first elected woman leader of a Muslim nation. She was accused of corruption and dismissed by the president, Aug. 1990. Bhutto returned to power Oct. 1993 but was dismissed Nov. 1996 amid further corruption charges. Responding to India's nuclear weapons tests, Pakistan conducted its own tests in 1998.

Prime Min. Nawaz Sharif fired, Oct. 1999, army chief Gen. Pervez Musharraf, whose supporters staged a bloodless coup. Musharraf assumed the presidency June 20, 2001. Following the Sept. 11, 2001, terrorist attacks on the U.S., Pres. Musharraf pledged cooperation with the U.S. in fighting Taliban and al-Qaeda militants within Pakistan and in neighboring Afghanistan. An earthquake that rocked Pakistan and the Pakistani-held region of Kashmir Oct. 8, 2005, killed about 80,000 people.

More than 140 people died Oct. 18, 2007, when suicide bombers struck Benazir Bhutto's convoy upon her return from more than eight years in exile. Musharraf, who had won the Oct. 6 presidential election, gave up his army post Nov. 25 and was sworn in as civilian president the next day. Bhutto was assassinated Dec. 27, 2007, after a rally in Rawalpindi.

Headed by Bhutto's widower, Asif Ali Zardari, the Pakistan Peoples Party led in parliamentary elections Feb. 18, 2008. Musharraf resigned Aug. 18 under threat of impeachment, and Zardari became president Sept. 9. Amid deteriorating security, U.S. and Pakistani forces clashed with the Taliban near the Afghan border, and Islamists carried out new suicide attacks. A 2009 government offensive against the Taliban in the strategic Swat Valley displaced nearly 2 mil civilians. Catastrophic floods and monsoon rains, July-Aug. 2010, inundated one-fifth of Pakistan, leaving more than 1,750 people dead and displacing up to 20 mil.

On May 2, 2011, U.S. commandos killed al-Qaeda leader Osama bin Laden in Abbottabad. The raid was carried out without prior warning to Pakistan; the U.S. suspected some Pakistani military and other officials of covert links and assistance to Islamist extremist groups such as the Taliban and al-Qaeda.

On Oct. 9, 2012, 15-year-old Malala Yousafzai, who advocated for education rights for girls in Pakistan, was shot by the Taliban, sparking worldwide outrage. After treatment at a British hospital, she resumed her advocacy, for which she shared the 2014 Nobel Peace Prize. A terrorist attack on a Peshawar school, Dec. 16, 2014, left about 150 dead. In 2007-14, an estimated 7,500 people died in terrorist attacks. Fighting between Pakistani forces and Islamic extremists resulted in more than 17,000 fatalities, 2007-14.

Musharraf, charged with treason in 2014, was convicted in absentia, Dec. 2019. He had been allowed to leave the country in 2016. Former Prime Min. Nawaz Sharif was returned to office in May 11, 2013, elections. With Sharif accused of corruption, a Supreme Court ruling, July 28, 2017, forced him to step down as prime min. Sharif was convicted on corruption charges, July and Dec. 2018; he was allowed to leave the country Nov. 2019.

A July 13, 2018, Islamist extremist suicide bombing in Mastung left at least 149 dead.

The party of former cricket star Imran Khan, the Pakistan Movement for Justice, with apparent backing from the military, won the most seats in July 25, 2018, parliamentary elections; Khan became prime min. Aug. 18. Arif Alvi, from Khan's party, was elected president Sept. 4, 2018. Hurt by economic problems and a loss of military support, Khan lost a no-confidence vote and was removed from office, Apr. 10, 2022. Shehbaz Sharif (brother of Nawaz Sharif) became prime minister, Apr. 11.

Following the 2021 Taliban victory in Afghanistan, attacks increased sharply in Pakistan by Islamist militants apparently using sanctuaries in eastern Afghanistan. Unusually heavy monsoon rains, perhaps related to climate change, beginning in June 2022 caused flooding that inundated one-third of the country and killed over 1,700; more than 33 mil people were displaced.

A WHO study released in May 2022 estimated 230,000 excess deaths in Pakistan related to the COVID-19 pandemic in 2020-21, eight times higher than the recorded tally.

Facing charges in multiple court cases, former Prime Min. Kahn was convicted in one case, Aug. 5, 2023, but appealed. Shehbaz Sharif was replaced, Aug. 14, 2023, by a caretaker prime minister to prepare for new elections.

Palau
Republic of Palau

People: Population: 21,779 (193). **Age distrib.:** <15: 17.5%; 65+: 10.7%. **Growth:** 0.4%. **Migrants:** 28.1%. **Pop. density:** 122.9 per sq mi, 47.4 per sq km. **Urban:** 82.4%. **Ethnic groups:** Palauan (Micronesian with Malayan/Melanesian admixtures) 70.6%, Asian 26.5%. **Languages:** Palauan (official on most islands), English (official), Filipino. **Religions:** Christian 91.3% (Catholic 44.6%, Protestant 33.5%, independent 13.1%), agnostic 2.7%, Muslim 2.6% (Sunni).

Geography: Total area: 177 sq mi, 459 sq km (181); **Land area:** 177 sq mi, 459 sq km. **Location:** Archipelago (26 islands, more than 300 islets) in W Pacific O., about 530 mi SE of the Philippines. Micronesia to E, Indonesia to S. **Topography:** A mountainous main island and low coral atolls, usually fringed with large barrier reefs. **Arable land:** 0.7%. **Capital:** Ngerulmud.

Government: Type: Presidential republic in free association with U.S. **Head of state and govt.:** Pres. Surangel Whipps Jr.; b. 1968; in office: Jan. 21, 2021. **Local divisions:** 16 states. **Defense budget/active troops:** NA.

Economy: Industries: tourism, fishing, subsistence agriculture. **Chief agric.:** coconuts, cassava, sweet potatoes; fish, pigs, chickens. **Natural resources:** forests, minerals (espec. gold), marine prods., deep-seabed minerals. **Water:** 0. **Labor force:** agric. 1.2%, industry 12.4%, services 86.4%. **Unemployment:** NA.

Finance: Monetary unit: US Dollar (USD) (1.00 = $1 U.S.). **GDP** (2021): $274.2 mil; **per capita GDP** (2021): $15,212; **GDP growth** (2021): -13.3%. **Imports:** $180.4 mil; South Korea 19%, China 18%, Taiwan 17%, U.S. 17%, Japan 16%. **Exports:** $12.1 mil; Japan 70%, South Korea 15%, U.S. 7%. **Tourism:** $6 mil. **Budget:** $121 mil. **Inflation:** 12.4%.

Transport: Airports: 1.

Communications: Mobile: 132.9 per 100 pop. **Broadband:** NA. **Internet:** NA.

Health: Expend.: 18.4%. **Life expect.:** 71.8 male; 78.2 female. **Births:** 11.6 per 1,000 pop. **Deaths:** 8.3 per 1,000 pop. **Infant mortality:** 11.0 per 1,000 live births. **Undernourished:** NA. **HIV:** NA. **COVID-19:** 6,197 cases, 9 deaths; rates per 100,000: 34,252.7 cases, 49.7 deaths. 101.0% vaccinated.

Education: Compulsory: ages 6-17. **Literacy:** 96.6%.

Website: www.palaugov.pw

Spain acquired the Palau Islands, 1886, and sold them to Germany, 1899. Japan seized them in 1914. U.S. forces occupied the islands in 1944; in 1947, they became part of a U.S.-administered UN trust territory. In 1981, Palau became an autonomous republic. It ratified a Compact of Free Association (COFA) with the U.S. in 1993 and became independent Oct. 1, 1994. Oct. 2015 legislation created a 193,000 sq mi marine sanctuary. Agreements signed in 2018 and 2023 extended U.S. financial aid to Palau under the COFA.

Palau is vulnerable to rising sea levels and stronger storms resulting from climate change.

Panama
Republic of Panama

People: Population: 4,404,108 (126). **Age distrib.:** <15: 25.2%; 65+: 9.9%. **Growth:** 1.5%. **Migrants:** 7.3%. **Pop. density:** 153.4 per sq mi, 59.2 per sq km. **Urban:** 69.5%. **Ethnic groups:** mestizo (mixed Amerindian/white) 65%, Native American (incl. Ngabe, Kuna) 12.3%, Black or African descent 9.2%, mulatto 6.8%, white 6.7%. **Languages:** Spanish (official), Indigenous langs. **Religions:** Christian 90.0% (Catholic 72.5%, Protestant 11.1%), agnostic 4.0%.

Geography: Total area: 29,120 sq mi, 75,420 sq km (116); **Land area:** 28,703 sq mi, 74,340 sq km. **Location:** Central America. Costa Rica on W, Colombia on E. **Topography:** Two mountain ranges run length of isthmus. Tropical rain forests cover the Caribbean coast and E. **Arable land:** 7.6%. **Capital:** Panama City, 1,976,866.

Government: Type: Presidential republic. **Head of state and govt.:** Pres. Laurentino "Nito" Cortizo; b. 1953; in office: July 1, 2019. **Local divisions:** 10 provinces, 4 Indigenous regions. **Defense budget:** $870 mil. **Active troops:** No armed forces. 27,700 paramilitary only.

Economy: Industries: constr., brewing, cement/other constr. materials, sugar milling. **Chief agric.:** sugarcane, bananas, rice, poultry, milk, plantains. **Natural resources:** copper, mahogany forests, shrimp, hydropower. **Water:** 32,285 cu m per capita. **Electricity prod.:** 11.2 bil kWh. **Labor force:** agric. 15.7%, industry 16.8%, services 67.5%. **Unemployment:** 8.8%.

Finance: Monetary unit: Balboa (PAB) (1.00 = $1 U.S.). **GDP:** $173.2 bil; **per capita GDP:** $39,280; **GDP growth:** 10.8%. **Imports:** $24.6 bil; China 21%, U.S. 19%, Japan 16%, Colombia 6%. **Exports:** $27.2 bil; Ecuador 20%, Guatemala 14%, China 8%, U.S. 6%, Netherlands 6%. Incl. Colón Free Trade Zone. **Tourism:** $2.1 bil. **Budget** (2020): $15.1 bil. **Inflation:** 2.9%.

Transport: Railways: 48 mi. **Motor vehicles:** 211.5 per 1,000 pop. **Airports:** 57.

Communications: Mobile: 156.3 per 100 pop. **Broadband:** 96.8 per 100 pop. **Internet:** 67.5%.

Health: Expend.: 9.7%. **Life expect.:** 75.6 male; 81.5 female. **Births:** 17.7 per 1,000 pop. **Deaths:** 5.9 per 1,000 pop. **Infant mortality:** 15.3 per 1,000 live births. **Undernourished:** 5.3%. **HIV:** 1.0%. **COVID-19:** 1,047,321 cases, 8,652 deaths; rates per 100,000: 24,272.9 cases, 200.5 deaths. 73.6% vaccinated.

Education: Compulsory: ages 4-14. **Literacy:** 95.7%.

Website: www.presidencia.gob.pa

The coast of Panama was sighted by Rodrigo de Bastidas, sailing with Columbus for Spain in 1501, and was visited by Columbus in 1502. Vasco Núñez de Balboa crossed the isthmus and "discovered" the Pacific Ocean, Sept. 13, 1513. Spanish colonies were ravaged by Francis Drake, 1572-95, and Henry Morgan, 1668-71. Morgan destroyed the old city of Panama, which was founded in 1519. Freed from Spain, Panama joined Colombia in 1821.

Panama declared independence from Colombia Nov. 3, 1903, and granted control of the Canal Zone to the U.S. Feb. 26, 1904. The U.S.-built Panama Canal opened Aug. 15, 1914. A 1978 treaty provided for its gradual return to Panama—completed Dec. 31, 1999. A $5.3-bil canal expansion was approved by referendum Oct. 22, 2006. The first ship crossed the new wider channel June 26, 2016.

Pres. Eric Arturo Delvalle was ousted by the National Assembly, Feb. 26, 1988, after he tried to fire Gen. Manuel Antonio Noriega, who was under a U.S. indictment on drug charges. U.S. troops invaded Panama Dec. 20, 1989, and Noriega surrendered Jan. 3, 1990. He spent two decades in a U.S. prison. While serving a 20-year sentence in Panama, Noriega died May 29, 2017.

Information published beginning Apr. 3, 2016, from "Panama Papers" documents—leaked from a Panama City law firm—linked public officials and others in various countries to offshore bank accounts and companies created to conceal wealth or avoid taxes. Vowing to fight corruption, Laurentino Cortizo of the Democratic Revolutionary Party narrowly won the May 5, 2019, presidential election.

In the 2020s, hundreds of thousands of migrants heading north from South America transited Panama, including the remote Darién Gap region, en route to the U.S.

Papua New Guinea
Independent State of Papua New Guinea

People: Population: 9,819,350 (93). **Age distrib.:** <15: 37.3%; 65+: 3.9%. **Growth:** 2.3%. **Migrants:** 0.3%. **Pop. density:** 56.2 per sq mi, 21.7 per sq km. **Urban:** 13.7%. **Ethnic groups:** Melanesian, Papuan, Negrito, Micronesian, Polynesian. **Languages:** Tok Pisin, English, Hiri Motu (all official); some 839 Indigenous langs. (many spoken by fewer than 1,000). **Religions:** Christian (official) 95.3% (Protestant 57.4%, Catholic 32.0%), ethnic religionist 2.9%.

Geography: Total area: 178,704 sq mi, 462,840 sq km (57); **Land area:** 174,850 sq mi, 452,860 sq km. **Location:** SE Asia; E half of island of New Guinea and about 600 nearby islands. Indonesia on W, Australia on S. **Topography:** Thickly forested mountains cover much of center, with lowlands along the coasts. Incl. some islands of Bismarck and Solomon groups, such as Admiralty Isls., New Ireland, New Britain, and Bougainville. **Arable land:** 0.7%. **Capital:** Port Moresby, 409,831.

Government: Type: Parliamentary democracy under constitutional monarchy. **Head of state:** King Charles III, rep. by Gov.-Gen. Bob Dadae; in office: Feb. 28, 2017. **Head of govt.:** Prime Min. James Marape; in office: May 30, 2019. **Local divisions:** 20 provinces, 1 autonomous region, 1 district. **Defense budget:** $99 mil. **Active troops:** 4,000.

Economy: Industries: copra crushing, palm oil proc., plywood prod., wood chip prod., mining, crude oil/petroleum prods. **Chief agric.:** oil palm fruit, bananas, coconuts, fruit, sweet potatoes, game meat. **Natural resources:** gold, copper, silver, nat. gas, timber, oil, fish. **Water:** 89,527 cu m per capita. **Crude oil reserves:** 160 mil bbls. **Electricity prod.:** 4.9 bil kWh. **Labor force:** agric. 17.2%, industry 9.9%, services 72.9%. **Unemployment:** 2.8%.

Finance: Monetary unit: Kina (PGK) (3.61 = $1 U.S.). **GDP:** $45.1 bil; **per capita GDP:** $4,447; **GDP growth:** 4.6%. **Imports** (2018): $4.8 bil; (2021) Australia 27%, China 25%, Singapore 13%, Malaysia 8%, Indonesia 5%. **Exports** (2018): $10.6 bil; (2021) Japan 25%, China 25%, Australia 16%, Taiwan 6%, South Korea 6%. **Tourism:** $1 mil. **Budget:** $5.1 bil. **Inflation** (2020-21): 4.5%.

Transport: Motor vehicles: 17.5 per 1,000 pop. **Airports:** 21.

Communications: Mobile (2021): 48.4 per 100 pop. **Broadband** (2021): 11.1 per 100 pop. **Internet:** 32.1%.

Health: Expend.: 2.5%. **Life expect.:** 68.0 male; 71.5 female. **Births:** 28.5 per 1,000 pop. **Deaths:** 5.5 per 1,000 pop. **Infant mortality:** 32.8 per 1,000 live births. **Undernourished:** 23.4%. **HIV:** 1.0%. **COVID-19:** 46,864 cases, 670 deaths; rates per 100,000: 523.8 cases, 7.5 deaths. 3.7% vaccinated.

Education: Compulsory: NA. **Literacy:** 64.2%.

Website: www.pm.gov.pg

Human remains dating back at least 10,000 years have been found in the interior of New Guinea. European colonization began in the 19th cent., when the Dutch took control of the island's western half (now part of Indonesia). The southern half of eastern New Guinea was claimed by Britain in 1884 and transferred to Australia in 1905. Germany claimed the northern half in 1884, but Australia captured it in WWI. Self-government was achieved Dec. 1, 1973, and independence Sept. 16, 1975.

Secessionist rebels clashed with government forces on Bougainville 1988-97, claiming some 20,000 lives. A Bougainville autonomy agreement was signed Aug. 30, 2001. In a late-2019 nonbinding referendum, 98% of Bougainville voters favored independence. Independence advocate and former rebel leader Ishmael Toroama was elected president of Bougainville in Sept. 2020.

Sir Michael Somare, the nation's first prime min. (1975-80, 1982-85), regained the office in 2002. Somare took indefinite medical leave Apr. 2011. After June-July 2012 parliamentary elections, Peter O'Neill served as prime minister. Losing support over economic conditions and corruption, O'Neill resigned, May 26, 2019. James Marape was elected prime minister by parliament, May 30, 2019. After July 2022 elections marred by violence (at least 50 deaths) and apparent fraud, Marape was reelected by parliament, Aug. 9. Continuing violence, 2022-23, caused scores of additional deaths and displaced tens of thousands.

The Supreme Court, Apr. 26, 2016, ruled illegal Australia's detention center on Manus Island for migrants intercepted trying to reach Australia by boat. The center, where detainees endured harsh living conditions, was closed Oct. 31, 2017. Approximately 600 detainees, all male, were relocated. After most detainees had gone to the U.S. or other countries, about 70 remained in Papua New Guinea as of Sept. 2023.

The country has extensive energy resources. Shipments of liquefied natural gas through a new processing and shipping facility near Port Moresby began in May 2014. To counter growing Chinese influence in the Pacific, Papua New Guinea and the U.S. signed a new defense agreement, May 22, 2023.

Paraguay
Republic of Paraguay

People: Population: 7,439,863 (104). **Age distrib.:** <15: 22.4%; 65+: 9.1%. **Growth:** 1.1%. **Migrants:** 2.4%. **Pop. density:** 48.5 per sq mi, 18.7 per sq km. **Urban:** 63.1%. **Ethnic groups:** mestizo (mixed Spanish/Amerindian) 95%. **Languages:** Spanish, Guaraní (both official). **Religions:** Christian 95.1% (Catholic [official] 84.4%), agnostic 2.0%, ethnic religionist 2.0%.

Geography: Total area: 157,048 sq mi, 406,752 sq km (59); **Land area:** 153,399 sq mi, 397,302 sq km. **Location:** Landlocked country in central S America. Bolivia on N, Argentina on S, Brazil on E. **Topography:** Paraguay R. bisects country. Fertile plains, wooded slopes, grasslands to E. Gran Chaco plain, with marshes and scrub trees, to W. Extreme W is arid. **Arable land:** 11.9%. **Capital:** Asunción, 3,510,511.

Government: Type: Presidential republic. **Head of state and govt.:** Pres. Santiago Peña Palacios; b. 1978; in office: Aug. 15, 2023. **Local divisions:** 17 departments, 1 capital city. **Defense budget:** $276 mil. **Active troops:** 13,950.

Economy: Industries: sugar proc., cement, textiles, beverages, wood prods., steel. **Chief agric.:** soybeans, sugarcane, maize, cassava, wheat, rice. **Natural resources:** hydropower, timber, iron ore, manganese, limestone. **Water:** 54,366 cu m per capita. **Electricity prod.:** 40.0 bil kWh. **Labor force:** agric. 19.7%, industry 19.5%, services 60.8%. **Unemployment:** 6.9%.

Finance: Monetary unit: Guarani (PYG) (7,290.82 = $1 U.S.). **GDP:** $108.3 bil; **per capita GDP:** $15,977; **GDP growth:** 0.1%. **Imports:** $13.5 bil; Brazil 24%, U.S. 22%, China 17%, Argentina 10%. **Exports:** $14.2 bil; Brazil 32%, Argentina 22%, Chile 8%, Russia 8%. **Tourism:** $84 mil. **Budget:** $8.7 bil. **Inflation:** 9.8%.

Transport: Railways: 19 mi. **Motor vehicles:** 182.1 per 1,000 pop. **Airports:** 15.

Communications: Mobile: 127.7 per 100 pop. **Broadband:** 70.9 per 100 pop. **Internet:** 76.3%.

Health: Expend.: 7.6%. **Life expect.:** 76.0 male; 81.4 female. **Births:** 16.2 per 1,000 pop. **Deaths:** 4.9 per 1,000 pop. **Infant**

mortality: 22.6 per 1,000 live births. **Undernourished:** 4.2%. **HIV:** 0.5%. **COVID-19:** 735,759 cases, 19,961 deaths; rates per 100,000: 10,315.5 cases, 279.9 deaths. 49.7% vaccinated.

Education: Compulsory: ages 5-17. **Literacy:** 94.5%.

Website: www.presidencia.gov.py

Guaraní Indians preceded Europeans in Paraguay, which was visited by Sebastian Cabot in 1527 and became a Spanish possession in 1535. Paraguay gained independence from Spain in 1811. It lost half its population and much of its territory to Brazil, Uruguay, and Argentina in the War of the Triple Alliance, 1865-70. Large areas were won from Bolivia in the Chaco War, 1932-35. Gen. Alfredo Stroessner held the presidency 1954-89, until his ouster in a military coup.

Power struggles ensued between civilian and military leaders, 1993-97. The assassination of Vice Pres. Luis María Argaña, Mar. 23, 1999, was widely attributed to Pres. Raúl Cubas Grau and triggered protests and an impeachment vote; Cubas resigned Mar. 28. An attempted military coup was suppressed May 18, 2000.

Nicanor Duarte Frutos of the conservative Colorado Party won the presidency, Apr. 27, 2003.

Paraguayan authorities blamed a leftist group for the Sept. 2004 kidnapping and subsequent murder of Cecilia Cubas, daughter of former Pres. Cubas. Fernando Lugo, a former Catholic cleric known as the "bishop of the poor," won a presidential election Apr. 20, 2008, ending over six decades of Colorado rule. On June 22, 2012, Lugo was removed from office after his handling of a dispute between landless peasants and police left 17 dead June 15. Colorado candidates won the presidency in 2013 and 2018 elections. Santiago Peña of the Colorado Party won the Apr. 30, 2023, presidential election.

Peru
Republic of Peru

People: Population: 32,440,172 (46). **Age distrib.:** <15: 26.0%; 65+: 8.0%. **Growth:** 0.5%. **Migrants:** 3.7%. **Pop. density:** 65.6 per sq mi, 25.3 per sq km. **Urban:** 78.9%. **Ethnic groups:** mestizo (mixed Amerindian/white) 60.2%, Amerindian 25.8%, white 5.9%, African descent 3.6%. **Languages:** Spanish, Quechua, Aymara (all official). **Religions:** Christian 96.4% (Catholic [official] 84.0%).

Geography: Total area: 496,225 sq mi, 1,285,216 sq km (19); **Land area:** 494,209 sq mi, 1,279,996 sq km. **Location:** Pacific coast of S America. Ecuador, Colombia on N; Brazil, Bolivia on E; Chile on S. **Topography:** An arid coastal strip, 10-100 mi wide. The Andes cover one-quarter of land area. The uplands are well-watered, as are the eastern slopes reaching the Amazon Basin, which covers half of country. **Arable land:** 3.4%. **Capital:** Lima, 11,204,382. **Cities:** Arequipa, 958,998.

Government: Type: Presidential republic. **Head of state and govt.** Pres. Dina Boluarte; b. 1962; in office: Dec. 7, 2022. **Local divisions:** 25 regions, 1 province. **Defense budget:** $1.7 bil. **Active troops:** 81,000.

Economy: Industries: mining/efining of minerals; steel, metal fabrication; petroleum extraction/refining, nat. gas and nat. gas liquefaction; fishing/fish proc., cement, glass, textiles. **Chief agric.:** sugarcane, potatoes, rice, plantains, milk, poultry. **Natural resources:** copper, silver, gold, petroleum, timber, fish, iron ore, coal, phosphate, potash, hydropower, nat. gas. **Water:** 57,012 cu m per capita. **Crude oil reserves:** 859 mil bbls. **Electricity prod.:** 58.1 bil kWh. **Labor force:** agric. 27.9%, industry 17.0%, services 55.1%. **Unemployment:** 3.7%.

Finance: Monetary unit: Sol (PEN) (3.70 = $1 U.S.). **GDP:** $512.4 bil; **per capita GDP:** $15,048; **GDP growth:** 2.7%. **Imports:** $58.6 bil; China 24%, U.S. 22%, Brazil 6%. **Exports:** $66.1 bil; China 29%, U.S. 12%. **Tourism:** $688 mil. **Budget:** $49.1 bil. **Inflation:** 8.3%.

Transport: Railways: 1,152 mi. **Motor vehicles:** 78.6 per 1,000 pop. **Airports:** 59.

Communications: Mobile: 122.0 per 100 pop. **Broadband:** 85.3 per 100 pop. **Internet:** 74.7%.

Health: Expend.: 6.3%. **Life expect.:** 65.4 male; 72.7 female. **Births:** 17.0 per 1,000 pop. **Deaths:** 11.0 per 1,000 pop. **Infant mortality:** 10.8 per 1,000 live births. **Undernourished:** 7.0%. **HIV:** 0.4%. **COVID-19:** 4,517,034 cases, 221,364 deaths; rates per 100,000: 13,699.7 cases, 671.4 deaths. 86.9% vaccinated.

Education: Compulsory: ages 3-16. **Literacy:** 94.5%.

Website: www.peru.gob.pe

The powerful Inca Empire had its seat at Cuzco in the Andes and covered much of western S America. A civil war had weakened the empire when Spaniard Francisco Pizarro began raiding Peru for its wealth, 1532. In 1533 he executed the Inca ruler, Atahualpa, and enslaved the people.

José de San Martin captured Lima from the Spanish in 1821; Simón Bolívar routed Spanish forces in 1824, and for much of the 19th cent., the country was governed by military leaders. Chile defeated Peru in the War of the Pacific, 1879-83. Right-wing groups allied with the military and the leftist APRA party vied for power in the first half of the 20th cent.

Peru returned to democratic leadership in 1980 but was plagued by economic problems and by leftist Shining Path (Sendero Luminoso) guerrillas. Conflict between guerrillas and government troops, 1980-2000, killed more than 69,000.

Elected president in June 1990, Alberto Fujimori dissolved Congress, suspended parts of the constitution, and initiated press censorship, Apr. 1992. The leader of Shining Path was captured Sept. 12. Fujimori won reelection in 1995 and 2000, but his repressive antiterrorism tactics drew international criticism. Scandals involving a top aide led Fujimori to leave office, Nov. 2000. He was convicted, 2007-15, on various charges.

In a presidential runoff election June 5, 2011, leftist Ollanta Humala Tasso defeated Keiko Fujimori, daughter of the former president. Pedro Pablo Kuczynski defeated Keiko Fujimori, June 5, 2016. Facing impeachment over a corruption scandal, Kuczynski resigned and was replaced, Mar. 2018, by Vice Pres. Martín Vizcarra. Accused of corruption, Vizcarra was impeached by Congress, Nov. 9, 2020.

In a June 6, 2021, presidential runoff, leftist José Pedro Castillo Terrones narrowly defeated Keiko Fujimori. Corruption scandals and protests over rising prices marred Castillo's administration. Castillo was removed from office and arrested, Dec. 7, 2022, after an unsuccessful attempt to dissolve Congress to avoid impeachment; First Vice Pres. Dina Boluarte became Peru's first female head of state. Castillo's arrest touched off sometimes-violent protests, met with a lethal response by security forces that left dozens dead.

As of Aug. 2023, more than 1.5 mil Venezuelan migrants were in Peru, having fled economic hardship and repression.

In the early 2020s, Peru was one of the worst affected countries in Latin America by the COVID-19 pandemic, which at times severely strained the health care system.

Philippines
Republic of the Philippines

People: Population: 116,434,200 (13). **Age distrib.:** <15: 30.5%; 65+: 5.4%. **Growth:** 1.6%. **Migrants:** 0.2%. **Pop. density:** 1,011.4 per sq mi, 390.5 per sq km. **Urban:** 48.3%. **Ethnic groups:** Tagalog 24.4%, Bisaya/Binisaya 11.4%, Cebuano 9.9%, Ilocano 8.8%, Hiligaynon/Ilonggo 8.4%, Bikol/Bicol 6.8%, Waray 4%. **Languages:** Filipino, English (both official); 8 major dialects (incl. Tagalog). **Religions:** Christian 90.7% (Catholic 69.4%, independent 16.1%), Muslim 5.5% (Sunni), ethnic religionist 2.2%.

Geography: Total area: 115,831 sq mi, 300,000 sq km (72); **Land area:** 115,124 sq mi, 298,170 sq km. **Location:** Archipelago in SE Asia. Malaysia, Indonesia on S; Taiwan on N. **Topography:** Comprises some 7,107 islands stretching 1,100 mi N-S. About 95% of area and pop. are on 11 largest islands, which are mountainous, except for the heavily indented coastlines and central plain on Luzon. **Arable land:** 18.7%. **Capital:** Manila, 14,667,089. **Cities:** Davao City, 1,949,400; Cebu City, 1,024,946.

Government: Type: Presidential republic. **Head of state and govt.:** Pres. Ferdinand "Bongbong" Romualdez Marcos Jr.; b. 1957; in office: June 30, 2022. **Local divisions:** 81 provinces, 38 chartered cities. **Defense budget:** $5.5 bil. **Active troops:** 145,300.

Economy: Industries: semiconductors and electronics assembly, business process outsourcing, food/beverage mfg., constr. **Chief agric.:** sugarcane, rice, coconuts, maize, bananas, vegetables. **Natural resources:** timber, petroleum, nickel, cobalt, silver, gold, salt, copper. **Water:** 4,371 cu m per capita. **Crude oil reserves:** 139 mil bbls. **Electricity prod.:** 108.2 bil kWh. **Labor force:** agric. 24.3%, industry 18.7%, services 57.0%. **Unemployment:** 2.2%.

Finance: Monetary unit: Peso (PHP) (56.67 = $1 U.S.). **GDP:** $1.2 tril; **per capita GDP:** $10,133; **GDP growth:** 7.6%. **Imports:** $126.5 bil; China 29%, Japan 8%, South Korea 7%, U.S. 6%, Singapore 6%, Indonesia 6%. **Exports:** $87.8 bil; China 16%, U.S. 15%, Japan 13%, Hong Kong 12%, Singapore 7%. **Tourism:** $600 mil. **Budget (2020):** $91.0 bil. **Inflation:** 5.8%.

Transport: Railways: 48 mi. **Motor vehicles:** 46.7 per 1,000 pop. **Airports:** 89.

Communications: Mobile: 144.0 per 100 pop. **Broadband:** 69.8 per 100 pop. **Internet:** 52.7%.

Health: Expend. (2021): 5.6%. **Life expect.:** 67.0 male; 74.2 female. **Births:** 22.2 per 1,000 pop. **Deaths:** 6.3 per 1,000 pop. **Infant mortality:** 22.1 per 1,000 live births. **Undernourished:** 5.2%. **HIV:** 0.3%. **COVID-19:** 4,173,631 cases, 66,646 deaths; rates per 100,000: 3,808.7 cases, 60.8 deaths. 71.6% vaccinated.

Education: Compulsory: ages 5-17. **Literacy:** 96.3%.

Website: www.gov.ph

Originally inhabited by Malay peoples, the archipelago was visited by Magellan, 1521. The Spanish founded Manila, 1571. Spain ceded the islands, named for King Philip II of Spain, to the U.S. for $20 mil, 1898, following the Spanish-American War. U.S. troops suppressed a guerrilla uprising in a brutal war, 1899-1905. Japan attacked the Philippines Dec. 8, 1941, and occupied the islands during WWII. Independence was proclaimed, July 4, 1946. A republic was established.

The repressive and corrupt regime of Pres. Ferdinand Marcos and his wife, Imelda, was in place 1965-86. The assassination of prominent opposition leader Benigno S. Aquino Jr., Aug. 21, 1983, sparked calls for Marcos's resignation. Marcos defeated Corazon

Aquino, widow of the slain opposition leader, Feb. 16, 1986, in an allegedly fraudulent election. Mass protests and international pressure forced Marcos to flee the country Feb. 25, and Aquino became president.

Her government was plagued by a weak economy, widespread poverty, and Communist and Muslim insurgencies. Fidel Ramos won the May 1992 presidential election. A treaty with Muslim separatist guerrillas providing for expansion and development of an autonomous Muslim region on Mindanao, in the southern Philippines, was signed Sept. 2, 1996.

Joseph (Erap) Estrada, a former movie actor, won the presidential election, May 11, 1998, but was impeached on bribery and corruption charges Nov. 13, 2000. Vice Pres. Gloria Macapagal Arroyo became president Jan. 20, 2001, and won reelection May 10, 2004. After Estrada was convicted in 2007 of taking more than $85 mil in bribes and kickbacks while in office, then pardoned, Benigno "NoyNoy" Aquino III, the son of former Pres. Aquino, defeated Estrada in the May 10, 2010, presidential election.

The government, 2012 and 2014, signed new peace and autonomy deals with Muslim rebels on Mindanao; violence had persisted after the 1996 accord. However, the Abu Sayyaf Islamist guerrilla group and the rebel group Maute, both of which claimed allegiance to ISIS, continued to stage attacks.

Typhoon Haiyan, Nov. 8, 2013, killed more than 6,200 people and displaced over 4 mil.

Vowing a tough crackdown on drug crime, Rodrigo Duterte was elected president, May 9, 2016. The death toll in the war on drugs, largely from extrajudicial killings by police or vigilantes, was estimated as high as 30,000 by 2021.

Muslim rebels held part of the city of Marawi, May-Oct. 2017. Legislation to implement the 2014 autonomy agreement was signed in July 2018. Jan. 21 and Feb. 6, 2019, referenda in the south endorsed a new Bangsamoro autonomous region, although extremist attacks continued. Duterte signed, July 3, 2020, an antiterrorism bill giving security forces sweeping powers. Prosecuted in the Philippines, journalist Maria Ressa shared the 2021 Nobel Peace Prize.

Ferdinand "Bongbong" Marcos Jr., the former dictator's son, easily won the May 9, 2022, presidential election. Sara Duterte, the outgoing president's daughter, was elected vice president.

The Philippines was severely affected by the COVID-19 pandemic that began in 2020. Schools fully reopened in Aug. 2022 after more than two years of pandemic shutdown.

Amid concerns about growing Chinese power and aggression in the South China Sea, the Philippines and U.S. announced, Feb. 2023, an agreement giving the U.S. increased access to military bases in the Philippines.

Poland
Republic of Poland

People: Population: 37,991,766 (39). **Age distrib.:** <15: 14.3%; 65+: 19.3%. **Growth:** −0.3%. **Migrants:** 2.2%. **Pop. density:** 323.4 per sq mi, 124.9 per sq km. **Urban:** 60.2%. **Ethnic groups:** Polish 96.9%. **Languages:** Polish (official). **Religions:** Christian 96.0% (Catholic 93.3%), agnostic 3.6%.

Geography: Total area: 120,728 sq mi, 312,685 sq km (69); **Land area:** 117,474 sq mi, 304,255 sq km. **Location:** On Baltic Sea in E central Europe. Germany on W; Czechia, Slovakia on S; Lithuania, Belarus, Ukraine on E; Russia on N. **Topography:** Mostly lowlands forming part of the Northern European Plain. The Carpathian Mts. along S border rise to 8,200 ft. **Arable land:** 36.2%. **Capital:** Warsaw, 1,797,516. **Cities:** Cracow, 769,417.

Government: Type: Parliamentary republic. **Head of state:** Pres. Andrzej Duda; b. 1972; in office: Aug. 6, 2015. **Head of govt.:** Prime Min. Mateusz Morawiecki; b. 1968; in office: Dec. 11, 2017. **Local divisions:** 16 provinces. **Defense budget:** $13.4 bil. **Active troops:** 114,050.

Economy: Industries: machine building, iron and steel, coal mining, chemicals, shipbuilding, food proc., glass, beverages, textiles. **Chief agric.:** milk, sugar beet, wheat, potatoes, triticale, maize. **Natural resources:** coal, sulfur, copper, nat. gas, silver, lead, salt, amber. **Water:** 1,599 cu m per capita. **Crude oil reserves:** 113 mil bbls. **Electricity prod.:** 166.6 bil kWh. **Labor force:** agric. 8.4%, industry 30.9%, services 60.7%. **Unemployment:** 2.6%.

Finance: Monetary unit: Zloty (PLN) (4.14 = $1 U.S.). **GDP:** $1.6 tril; **per capita GDP:** $43,269; **GDP growth:** 4.9%. **Imports:** $380.7 bil; (2020) Germany 25%, China 12%. **Exports:** $411.6 bil; (2020) Germany 28%, UK 6%, Czechia 6%, France 6%. **Tourism:** $9.1 bil. **Budget:** $248.9 bil. **Inflation:** 14.4%.

Transport: Railways: 12,093 mi. **Motor vehicles:** 803.9 per 1,000 pop. **Airports:** 87.

Communications: Mobile: 131.9 per 100 pop. **Broadband:** 192.1 per 100 pop. **Internet:** 86.9%.

Health: Expend. (2021): 6.6%. **Life expect.:** 71.7 male; 80.0 female. **Births:** 8.7 per 1,000 pop. **Deaths:** 12.9 per 1,000 pop. **Infant mortality:** 5.1 per 1,000 live births. **Undernourished:** <2.5%. **HIV:** NA. **COVID-19:** 6,518,400 cases, 119,636 deaths; rates per 100,000: 17,172.6 cases, 315.2 deaths. 60.3% vaccinated.

Education: Compulsory: ages 6-15. **Literacy:** 99.8%.
Website: www.gov.pl

Slavic tribes in the area were converted to Latin Christianity in the 10th cent. Poland was a great power from the 14th to the 17th cent. In three partitions (1772, 1793, 1795) it was apportioned among Prussia, Russia, and Austria. Overrun by the Austro-German armies in WWI, it declared its independence on Nov. 11, 1918, and was recognized as independent by the Treaty of Versailles, June 28, 1919. Large territories to the east were taken in a war with Russia, 1921.

Germany and the USSR invaded Poland Sept. 1939 and divided the country. During the war, Nazis killed some 6 mil Polish citizens, half of them Jews. (Controversial 2018 legislation outlawed attributing to Poland any role in Nazi atrocities.) In compensation for territory ceded to the USSR when WWII ended, Poland received German territory comprising Silesia, Pomerania, West Prussia, and part of East Prussia. Communists, who aligned themselves with the USSR, dominated the 1947 election.

In 12 years of rule by Stalinists, large estates were abolished, industries nationalized, schools secularized, and Roman Catholic prelates jailed. Farm production fell off. Harsh working conditions caused a riot in Poznan, June 28-29, 1956. A new Politburo, committed to a more independent Polish Communism, was named Oct. 1956. Collectivization of farms was ended and religious liberty increased.

After worker riots over price rises and new wage rules, 1970, the rules were dropped and price rises revoked.

Independent trade union Solidarity gained strength in the 1980s. Led by Lech Walesa, Solidarity helped to win political and economic reforms, including free elections, in an Apr. 5, 1989, accord. Candidates endorsed by Solidarity swept the parliamentary elections, June 4. Walesa became president Dec. 22, 1990.

Policies to transform the economy into a free-market system led to inflation, unemployment, and a return to the political left in 1993 parliamentary elections. A former Communist, Aleksander Kwasniewski, succeeded Walesa as president, 1995. Poland became a full member of NATO, Mar. 12, 1999, and entered the European Union May 1, 2004.

Andrzej Duda of the conservative Law and Justice (PiS) party won a May 24, 2015, presidential runoff. PiS won Oct. 25, 2015, parliamentary elections. Beginning in 2015, PiS governments resisted EU resettlement programs for non-European migrants entering the EU. July 2017 legislation allowing the justice minister to appoint judges drew EU criticism as a threat to judicial independence. Legislation effective July 2018 to force the retirement of some Supreme Court judges prompted widespread protests. PiS won a slim majority in Oct. 13, 2019, parliamentary elections. Duda narrowly won reelection, July 12, 2020. Following an Oct. 2020 court ruling, and despite massive protests, a ban on almost all abortions went into effect Jan. 27, 2021. The EU, in 2021, began withholding some grant funding to Poland, and the top EU court ruled, June 5, 2023, that some of Poland's judiciary changes violated EU law.

NATO increased troop strength in Poland in response to Russia's Feb. 2022 invasion of Ukraine. Poland provided weaponry and was a transshipment point for other military aid to Ukraine, but Polish-Ukrainian relations cooled in Sept. 2023 amid a dispute over Ukrainian grain imports. As of mid-Sept. 2023, Poland hosted about 960,000 Ukrainian refugees.

Portugal
Portuguese Republic

People: Population: 10,223,150 (91). **Age distrib.:** <15: 12.9%; 65+: 22.0%. **Growth:** −0.2%. **Migrants:** 9.8%. **Pop. density:** 289.5 per sq mi, 111.8 per sq km. **Urban:** 67.9%. **Ethnic groups:** Portuguese 95%; citizens from Portugal's former colonies and other foreign born 5%. **Languages:** Portuguese, Mirandese (both official). **Religions:** Christian 88.8% (Catholic 83.0%), agnostic 7.8%.

Geography: Total area: 35,556 sq mi, 92,090 sq km (109); **Land area:** 35,317 sq mi, 91,470 sq km. **Location:** SW extreme of Europe. Spain on N, E. **Topography:** Tajus R. bisects country NE-SW. N is cool and rainy, mountainous. S is drier, with warm climate and rolling plains. **Arable land:** 10.5%. **Capital:** Lisbon, 3,000,536. **Cities:** Porto, 1,324,652.

Government: Type: Semi-presidential republic. **Head of state:** Pres. Marcelo Rebelo de Sousa; b. 1948; in office: Mar. 9, 2016. **Head of govt.:** Prime Min. António Costa; b. 1961; in office: Nov. 24, 2015. **Local divisions:** 18 districts, 2 autonomous regions. **Defense budget:** $2.6 bil. **Active troops:** 26,700.

Economy: Industries: textiles, clothing, footwear, wood and cork, paper and pulp, chemicals, fuels and lubricants, automobiles/auto parts, base metals. **Chief agric.:** milk, tomatoes, olives, grapes, maize, potatoes. **Natural resources:** fish, forests (cork), iron ore, copper, zinc, tin, tungsten, silver, gold, uranium, marble, clay, gypsum, salt, hydropower. **Water:** 7,591 cu m per capita. **Electricity prod.:** 47.5 bil kWh. **Labor force:** agric. 5.2%, industry 23.9%, services 70.9%. **Unemployment:** 5.8%.

Finance: Monetary unit: Euro (EUR) (0.93 = $1 U.S.). **GDP:** $430.2 bil; **per capita GDP:** $41,452; **GDP growth:** 6.7%. **Imports:**

$112.4 bil; (2021) Spain 31%, Germany 12%, France 6%. **Exports:** $105.6 bil; (2021) Spain 26%, France 12%, Germany 12%, U.S. 6%. **Tourism:** $11.9 bil. **Budget:** $101.9 bil. **Inflation:** 7.8%.
Transport: Railways: 1,570 mi. **Motor vehicles:** 670.0 per 1,000 pop. **Airports:** 43.
Communications: Mobile: 124.5 per 100 pop. **Broadband:** 95.7 per 100 pop. **Internet:** 84.5%.
Health: Expend. (2021): 11.2%. **Life expect.:** 78.6 male; 85.0 female. **Births:** 8.0 per 1,000 pop. **Deaths:** 10.9 per 1,000 pop. **Infant mortality:** 2.5 per 1,000 live births. **Undernourished:** <2.5%. **HIV:** 0.5%. **COVID-19:** 5,601,153 cases, 27,094 deaths; rates per 100,000: 54,401.7 cases, 263.2 deaths. 86.0% vaccinated.
Education: Compulsory: ages 6-17. **Literacy:** 96.8%.
Website: www.portugal.gov.pt

Portugal, an independent state since the 12th cent., was a kingdom until a 1910 revolution drove out King Manoel II and a republic was proclaimed. Beginning in 1932, Prime Min. Antonio de Oliveira Salazar headed a repressive government. Illness forced his retirement in Sept. 1968.

On Apr. 25, 1974, a military junta led by Gen. Antonio de Spinola seized the government; Spinola became president. The new government granted independence to Guinea-Bissau, Mozambique, Cabo Verde, Angola, and São Tomé and Príncipe.

With the economy lagging, the Socialists won 2005 and 2009 parliamentary elections. After Portugal was given a 78-bil euro bailout package from international lenders to avert default, the center-right Social Democratic Party won parliamentary elections June 2011. Austerity cuts caused widespread protests in Nov. 2012. After parliamentary elections Oct. 4, 2015, Socialist António Costa became prime min., Nov. 24, leading an anti-austerity leftist coalition. Costa retained office after the Socialists won the most seats in Oct. 6, 2019, elections and gained an outright majority in Jan. 30, 2022, voting.

In recent years, Portugal has experienced extreme heat, drought, and wildfires likely related to climate change.

Azores Isls., in the Atlantic, 740 mi W of Portugal, have an area of 868 sq mi and a pop. (2014 est.) of 246,353. A 1951 agreement gave the U.S. the rights to use defense facilities in the Azores. The **Madeira Isls.,** 350 mi off the NW coast of Africa, have an area of 306 sq mi and a pop. (2014 est.) of 258,686. Both groups were offered partial autonomy in 1976.

Qatar
State of Qatar

People: Population: 2,532,104 (140). **Age distrib.:** <15: 13.1%; 65+: 1.4%. **Growth:** 0.9%. **Migrants:** 77.3%. **Pop. density:** 566.0 per sq mi, 218.5 per sq km. **Urban:** 99.4%. **Ethnic groups:** non-Qatari 88.4%, Qatari 11.6%. **Languages:** Arabic (official), English. **Religions:** Muslim 79.4% (Sunni [official] 67%, Shia 12%), Christian 13.6% (Catholic 12.2%), Hindu 3.0%, agnostic 2.1%.
Geography: Total area: 4,473 sq mi, 11,586 sq km (159); **Land area:** 4,473 sq mi, 11,586 sq km. **Location:** Middle East, occupying peninsula on W coast of Persian Gulf. Saudi Arabia on S. **Topography:** Mostly flat desert with some limestone ridges; scarce vegetation. **Arable land:** 1.8%. **Capital:** Doha, 658,344. **Cities:** Ar-Rayyan, 798,382.
Government: Type: Absolute monarchy. **Head of state:** Sheikh Tamim bin Hamad al-Thani; b. 1980; in office: June 25, 2013. **Head of govt.:** Prime Min. Muhammad bin Abd al-Rahman Al Thani; b. 1980; in office: Mar. 7, 2023. **Local divisions:** 8 municipalities. **Defense budget:** $8.4 bil. **Active troops:** 16,500.
Economy: Industries: liquefied nat. gas, crude oil prod./refining, ammonia, fertilizer, petrochemicals, steel reinforcing bars. **Chief agric.:** tomatoes, dates, camel milk, sheep milk, goat milk, pumpkins/gourds. **Natural resources:** petroleum, fish, nat. gas. **Water:** 20 cu m per capita. **Crude oil reserves:** 25.2 bil bbls. **Electricity prod.:** 47.5 bil kWh. **Labor force:** agric. 1.2%, industry 54.0%, services 44.8%. **Unemployment:** 0.1%.
Finance: Monetary unit: Riyal (QAR) (3.64 = $1 U.S.). **GDP:** $309.0 bil; **per capita GDP:** $114,648; **GDP growth:** 4.8%. **Imports:** $61.2 bil; U.S. 15%, France 13%, UK 9%, China 9%. **Exports:** $105.5 bil; Japan 17%, South Korea 16%, India 14%, China 13%, Singapore 7%. **Tourism:** $4.3 bil. **Budget:** $57.3 bil. **Inflation:** 5.0%.
Transport: Motor vehicles: 769.8 per 1,000 pop. **Airports:** 4.
Communications: Mobile: 174.1 per 100 pop. **Broadband:** 174.0 per 100 pop. **Internet:** 100.0%.
Health: Expend.: 4.2%. **Life expect.:** 77.9 male; 82.2 female. **Births:** 9.3 per 1,000 pop. **Deaths:** 1.4 per 1,000 pop. **Infant mortality:** 6.5 per 1,000 live births. **Undernourished:** NA. **HIV:** <0.1%. **COVID-19:** 514,524 cases, 690 deaths; rates per 100,000: 17,858.9 cases, 24.0 deaths. 99.0% vaccinated.
Education: Compulsory: ages 6-17. **Literacy:** 93.5%.
Website: hukoomi.gov.qa

Qatar was under Bahrain's control until the Ottoman Turks took power, 1872 to 1915. In a treaty signed 1916, Qatar gave Great Britain responsibility for its defense and foreign relations. Qatar declared itself independent, Sept. 1, 1971. In municipal elections held Mar. 8, 1999, women participated for the first time as candidates and

voters. Qatar's emir, Sheikh Hamad bin Khalifa al-Thani, abdicated in favor of his son, Sheikh Tamim bin Hamad al-Thani, June 25, 2013. A major producer and exporter of oil and natural gas, Qatar is one of the world's wealthiest nations per capita.

Since the early 2000s, Qatar has hosted U.S. military facilities and forces. Beginning June 5, 2017, a Saudi-led group of Arab nations, alleging Qatari support for terrorist and sectarian groups, broke diplomatic relations with Qatar and imposed a travel and trade ban. On Aug. 24, Qatar restored full diplomatic relations with Iran (severed in 2016). A member of OPEC since 1961, Qatar left the organization Jan. 1, 2019. An agreement to end the Saudi-led boycott was signed Jan. 5, 2021. Qatar held its first elections, Oct. 2, 2021, for some members of a national advisory council.

Qatar hosted the men's World Cup soccer tournament, Nov.-Dec. 2022. The host country was widely criticized for exploitation and abuse of migrant workers in World Cup-related construction and service jobs.

Romania

People: Population: 18,326,327 (68). **Age distrib.:** <15: 15.6%; 65+: 22.2%. **Growth:** −1.0%. **Migrants:** 3.7%. **Pop. density:** 206.5 per sq mi, 79.7 per sq km. **Urban:** 54.7%. **Ethnic groups:** Romanian 89.3%, Hungarian 6%, Romani 3.4% (usu. underestimated in official data; Romani may be up to 5%-11% of pop.). **Languages:** Romanian (official), Hungarian. **Religions:** Christian 98.7% (Orthodox 80.8%, Protestant 10.1%).
Geography: Total area: 92,043 sq mi, 238,391 sq km (81); **Land area:** 88,761 sq mi, 229,891 sq km. **Location:** SE Europe, on the Black Sea. Moldova on E, Ukraine on N, Hungary and Serbia on W, Bulgaria on S. **Topography:** The Carpathian Mts. surround the N central Transylvanian plateau. The lower reaches of the Danube river system flow through plains S and E of the mountains. **Arable land:** 37.3%. **Capital:** Bucharest, 1,776,385.
Government: Type: Semi-presidential republic. **Head of state:** Pres. Klaus Iohannis; b. 1959; in office: Dec. 21, 2014. **Head of govt.:** Prime Min. Ion-Marcel Ciolacu; in office: June 15, 2023. **Local divisions:** 41 counties, 1 municipality. **Defense budget:** $5.2 bil. **Active troops:** 71,500.
Economy: Industries: elec. machinery/equip., auto assembly, textiles/footwear, light machinery, metallurgy, chemicals, food proc. **Chief agric.:** maize, wheat, milk, sunflower seed, potatoes, barley. **Natural resources:** petroleum, timber, nat. gas, coal, iron ore, salt, hydropower. **Water:** 11,021 cu m per capita. **Crude oil reserves:** 600 mil bbls. **Electricity prod.:** 55.0 bil kWh. **Labor force:** agric. 18.6%, industry 30.4%, services 51.0%. **Unemployment:** 5.4%.
Finance: Monetary unit: Leu (RON) (4.57 = $1 U.S.). **GDP:** $794.1 bil; **per capita GDP:** $41,888; **GDP growth:** 4.8%. **Imports:** $132.1 bil; Germany 19%, Italy 9%, Hungary 7%, Poland 6%. **Exports:** $115.9 bil; Germany 22%, Italy 10%, France 7%. **Tourism:** $3.3 bil. **Budget:** $83.6 bil. **Inflation:** 13.8%.
Transport: Railways: 6,604 mi. **Motor vehicles:** 484.9 per 1,000 pop. **Airports:** 26.
Communications: Mobile: 118.1 per 100 pop. **Broadband:** 93.6 per 100 pop. **Internet:** 85.5%.
Health: Expend.: 6.3%. **Life expect.:** 72.9 male; 80.0 female. **Births:** 8.6 per 1,000 pop. **Deaths:** 14.9 per 1,000 pop. **Infant mortality:** 5.7 per 1,000 live births. **Undernourished:** <2.5%. **HIV:** 0.1%. **COVID-19:** 3,411,957 cases, 68,262 deaths; rates per 100,000: 17,652.2 cases, 353.2 deaths. 42.8% vaccinated.
Education: Compulsory: ages 7-16. **Literacy:** 98.9%.
Website: www.gov.ro

Romania's earliest known people merged with invading Proto-Thracians, preceding by centuries the Dacians. Rome occupied the Dacian kingdom, 106-271 CE; people and language were Romanized. The Turkey-dominated principalities of Wallachia and Moldavia were united in 1859, became Romania in 1861, and gained recognition as an independent kingdom, 1881.

After WWI, Romania acquired Bessarabia, Bukovina, Transylvania, and Banat. In 1940 it ceded Bessarabia and Northern Bukovina to the USSR, part of southern Dobrudja to Bulgaria, and northern Transylvania to Hungary. In 1941, Prem. Marshal Ion Antonescu led Romania in support of Germany against the USSR. He was overthrown in 1944, and Romania joined the Allies. After occupation by Soviet troops, a People's Republic was proclaimed, Dec. 30, 1947.

The domestic policies of Nicolae Ceausescu (in power 1965) were repressive. All industry was state-owned, and state farms and cooperatives owned almost all arable land. Ceausescu's security forces fired on anti-government demonstrators, Dec. 1989, killing hundreds, but when the army sided with the protesters, his regime fell. Ceausescu and his wife were executed Dec. 25, 1989.

A new constitution providing for a multiparty system took effect Dec. 8, 1991. Many state-owned companies were privatized in 1996. Romania became a full NATO member in 2004. It entered the European Union Jan. 1, 2007.

The Social Democratic Party's (PSD) Victor-Viorel Ponta became prime min. May 7, 2012. He ran for president in 2014 but lost the runoff to centrist Klaus Iohannis. Large protests over government incompetence led to Ponta's resignation, Nov. 4, 2015. The PSD's Viorica Dancila became Romania's first female prime min. Jan. 29, 2018. After Dancila, Oct. 10, 2019, lost a no-confidence vote, Ludovic Orban of the center-right National Liberal Party (PNL) became prime min., Nov. 4. Iohannis won reelection in a Nov. 24 presidential runoff (defeating Dancila). After Dec. 6, 2020, parliamentary elections, Nicolae Ciuca of the PNL became prime min., Nov. 25, 2021, heading a broad coalition with the PSD; as agreed, in June 2023, Ciuca resigned and was replaced by the PSD's Marcel Ciolacu.

Russia
Russian Federation

People: Population: 141,698,923 (9). **Age distrib.:** <15: 16.8%; 65+: 17.2%. **Growth:** −0.2%. **Migrants:** 8.0%. **Pop. density:** 22.4 per sq mi, 8.7 per sq km. **Urban:** 75.3%. **Ethnic groups:** Russian 77.7%, Tatar 3.7%. **Languages:** Russian (official), Tatar. **Religions:** Christian 82.5% (Orthodox 79.5%), Muslim 12.8% (Sunni), agnostic 3.2%.

Geography: Total area: 6,601,668 sq mi, 17,098,242 sq km (1); **Land area:** 6,323,482 sq mi, 16,377,742 sq km, about 76% of total area of the former USSR and the largest country in the world. **Location:** Stretches from Eastern Europe across N Asia to the Pacific O. Finland, Norway, Estonia, Latvia, Belarus, Ukraine on W; Georgia, Azerbaijan, Kazakhstan, China, Mongolia, N. Korea on S; Kaliningrad exclave bordered by Poland on the S, Lithuania on the N and E. **Topography:** Every type of climate except distinctly tropical. European portion is low plain, grassy in S, wooded in N, with Ural Mts. on E and Caucasus Mts. on S. Urals stretch N-S for 2,500 mi. Asiatic portion is vast plain, with mountains on S and in E; tundra covers extreme N with forest belt below; plains, marshes in W, desert in SW. **Arable land:** 7.4%. **Capital:** Moscow, 12,680,389. **Cities:** Saint Petersburg, 5,561,294; Novosibirsk, 1,694,765; Yekaterinburg, 1,527,728; Kazan, 1,291,884; Nizhniy Novgorod, 1,251,332; Chelyabinsk, 1,240,926.

Government: Type: Semi-presidential republic. **Head of state:** Pres. Vladimir Putin; b. 1952; in office: May 7, 2012. **Head of govt.:** Prime Min. Mikhail Mishustin; b. 1966; in office: Jan. 16, 2020. **Local divisions:** 46 provinces (oblasts), 21 republics, 4 autonomous okrugs, 9 krays, 2 federal cities, 1 autonomous oblast. **Defense budget:** $66.9 bil. **Active troops:** 1,190,000.

Economy: Industries: coal, oil, gas, chemicals, metals; machine building; defense (incl. radar, missile prod.); shipbuilding; road, rail transp. equip.; communications equip.; agric. machinery, tractors, constr. equip. **Chief agric.:** wheat, sugar beet, milk, potatoes, barley, sunflower seed. **Natural resources:** oil, nat. gas, coal, minerals, bauxite, rare earth elements, timber. Climate, terrain, and distance are obstacles to resource exploitation. **Water:** 31,010 cu m per capita. **Crude oil reserves:** 80 bil bbls. **Electricity prod.:** 1.1 tril kWh. **Labor force:** agric. 5.8%, industry 26.9%, services 67.3%. **Unemployment** (2021): 4.7%.

Finance: Monetary unit: Ruble (RUB) (95.59 = $1 U.S.). **GDP:** $5.3 tril; **per capita GDP:** $36,485; **GDP growth:** −2.1%. **Imports:** $379.9 bil; China 20%, Germany 13%, Belarus 6%. **Exports:** $550.0 bil; China 14%, Netherlands 10%. **Tourism:** $4.0 bil. **Budget:** $571.5 bil. **Inflation** (2020-21): 6.7%.

Transport: Railways: 53,124 mi. **Motor vehicles:** 484.2 per 1,000 pop. **Airports:** 594.

Communications: Mobile (2021): 169.0 per 100 pop. **Broadband** (2021): 107.6 per 100 pop. **Internet:** 90.4%.

Health: Expend.: 7.6%. **Life expect.:** 67.2 male; 77.2 female. **Births:** 8.5 per 1,000 pop. **Deaths:** 14.1 per 1,000 pop. **Infant mortality:** 6.6 per 1,000 live births. **Undernourished:** <2.5%. **HIV:** NA. **COVID-19:** 22,983,150 cases, 399,938 deaths; rates per 100,000: 15,749.0 cases, 274.1 deaths. 54.9% vaccinated.

Education: Compulsory: ages 7-17. **Literacy:** 99.7%.

Website: government.ru

Slavic tribes began migrating into present-day Russia from the W in the 5th cent. Scandinavian chieftains controlled much of today's western Russia beginning in the 9th cent. In the 13th cent., Mongols overran the area. Under the grand dukes and princes of Muscovy, or Moscow, Mongol control was ended by 1480. Ivan the Terrible was proclaimed Tsar of Russia, 1547. Peter the Great (1682-1725) extended the domain and, in 1721, founded the Russian empire. Western ideas and the beginnings of modernization spread through the empire in the 19th and early 20th cent.

Military reverses in the 1905 war with Japan and in WWI led to the breakdown of the Tsarist regime. The 1917 Revolution began in Mar. with a series of sporadic strikes for higher wages by factory workers. A provisional democratic government under Prince Georgi Lvov was established but a second provisional government, under Alexander Kerensky, followed in May. Vladimir Ilyich Lenin, Nov. 7, overthrew the Kerensky government and the freely elected Constituent Assembly in a Communist coup.

Soviet Union. Lenin's death Jan. 21, 1924, led to an internal power struggle won by Joseph Stalin. His brutal tactics, including purge trials, mass executions, and exile to work camps, resulted in millions of deaths.

Despite a Germany-USSR non-aggression pact signed in Aug. 1939, Germany invaded the Soviet Union, June 1941. Russian winter counterthrusts, 1941-42 and 1942-43; victory at Stalingrad (now

Volgograd), Feb. 2, 1943 (2 mil total casualties); and resistance to the siege of Leningrad (now St. Petersburg) stopped the German advance. Russian armies drove the Germans from Eastern Europe and the Balkans in the next two years.

After WWII, Communists took over in countries throughout the region, extending the Soviet sphere of influence. The USSR and the U.S., the world's leading nuclear superpowers, became Cold War rivals. After Stalin died, Mar. 5, 1953, Nikita Khrushchev gained power and denounced Stalin, 1956, beginning "de-Stalinization."

Under Khrushchev the open antagonism of Poles and Hungarians toward Moscow's domination was suppressed in 1956. He aided the Cuban revolution under Fidel Castro but withdrew Soviet missiles from Cuba during a confrontation with U.S. Pres. John Kennedy, Sept.-Oct. 1962. Khrushchev was deposed, Oct. 1964, and replaced by Leonid I. Brezhnev. In Aug. 1968, Soviet forces invaded Czechoslovakia, crushing liberalization there.

Massive Soviet military aid to North Vietnam in the late 1960s and early 1970s helped ensure Communist victories throughout Indochina. In Dec. 1979, Soviet forces entered Afghanistan to support a pro-Soviet regime against U.S.-supported Muslim resistance fighters. In Apr. 1988, the Soviets agreed to withdraw their troops, ending a futile 8-year war.

Mikhail Gorbachev was chosen Communist Party gen. sec., Mar. 1985. In 1987 he initiated a program of political and economic reforms through openness (*glasnost*) and restructuring (*perestroika*). Gorbachev faced economic problems as well as ethnic and nationalist unrest in the republics. A coup by Communist hardliners Aug. 1991 was foiled with help from Russian Republic Pres. Boris Yeltsin. On Aug. 24, Gorbachev resigned as leader of the Communist Party. Several republics declared their independence. On Aug. 29, the Soviet Parliament voted to suspend all activities of the Communist Party. The Soviet Union officially broke up Dec. 26, 1991.

Russian Federation. Under Pres. Yeltsin, Russia took steps toward privatization, which caused inflation and a severe economic downturn. In June 1992, Yeltsin and U.S. Pres. George H. W. Bush agreed to massive arms reductions. In a referendum Dec. 12, 1993, a new constitution was approved. Russian troops fought rebels in the breakaway republic of Chechnya Dec. 1994-Aug. 1996, when a peace accord temporarily ended the conflict. Yeltsin was reelected in 1996.

An Aug. 1999 operation to suppress Islamic rebels in the republic of Dagestan reignited the war in neighboring Chechnya, where Russia launched a full-scale assault. Yeltsin unexpectedly resigned Dec. 31, 1999, naming Prime Min. Vladimir Putin as his interim successor. Putin won presidential elections Mar. 2000 and Mar. 2004. Putin's allies won legislative elections, Dec. 2003.

After Chechen rebels, Sept. 1, 2004, seized control of a school in Beslan, North Ossetia, Russian troops stormed the school Sept. 3; more than 330 people, including 186 children, died. Putin cited the terrorist threat Sept. 13 in proposing a government overhaul that tightened his control over parliament and regional officeholders. Russian forces killed Chechen rebel leader Aslan Maskhadov, Mar. 8, 2005, and Chechen guerrilla leader Shamil Basayev, organizer of the Beslan attack, July 10, 2006.

Constitutionally barred from seeking another term, Pres. Putin backed his protégé Prime Min. Dmitri Medvedev, who won the presidential election Mar. 2, 2008. Medvedev named Putin as prime min. A long-simmering conflict with Georgia erupted into open warfare Aug. 7-16. Russian troops supported secessionists in the enclaves of South Ossetia and Abkhazia, which Russia recognized as independent, Aug. 26, 2008.

Russia declared, Apr. 16, 2009, that it had ended counterterrorism operations in Chechnya; from June through Aug., there was an upsurge of insurgent violence in Chechnya and neighboring Dagestan and Ingushetia. Suicide bombers from Dagestan struck two Moscow subway stations Mar. 29, 2010, killing 40 people.

Medvedev and U.S. Pres. Barack Obama, Apr. 8, 2010, signed a nuclear arms reduction treaty known as New START. Putin won the Mar. 4, 2012, presidential election, though there were claims of fraud. Putin signed a law, June 30, 2013, effectively making it illegal to advocate publicly for gay rights. Persecution of LBGTQ people increased in subsequent years. A 2020 constitutional amendment defined marriage as only between a man and a woman.

After Ukraine's pro-Russian president was removed from office Feb. 22, 2014, Russia sent troops into Ukraine's Crimean Peninsula and annexed Crimea Mar. 18. Russia also provided military support to pro-Russian separatists in eastern Ukraine beginning in Apr. 2014.

Russia supported Pres. Bashar al-Assad in Syria's civil war beginning in 2011. Russian airstrikes, starting in 2015, against various rebel forces, including ISIS, and rebel-held areas caused high civilian casualties. An ISIS-affiliated group claimed responsibility for planting a bomb on a Russian airliner that crashed in Egypt, Oct. 31, 2015, killing all 224 onboard.

Putin's United Russia party won Sept. 18, 2016, parliamentary elections. With the media tightly controlled and amid allegations of fraud, Putin won a new 6-year term as president, Mar. 18, 2018; leading dissident Aleksei Navalny was barred from running. Constitutional changes approved in 2020 allowed Putin to serve two more 6-year terms as president after his current term expires in 2024.

U.S. government security agencies concluded in Dec. 2016 that Russia attempted to interfere in the 2016 U.S. presidential election, apparently to assist the candidacy of Donald Trump, using tactics including cyberattacks and manipulation of social media. U.S. officials concluded that Russian interference occurred in the 2018 and 2020 elections as well. The U.S. State Dept. estimated in Sept. 2022 that Russia had spent at least $300 mil since 2014 to influence politics in more than two dozen countries around the world.

Russian agents were apparently responsible for the poisoning, in the UK in Mar. 2018, of a former Russian intelligence officer. Navalny was apparently poisoned, Aug. 20, 2020; he was arrested, Jan. 17, 2021, and subsequently sentenced to decades in prison on various charges.

Beginning in 2014, the U.S. accused Russia of violating the 1987 Intermediate-Range Nuclear Forces (INF) Treaty. The U.S. withdrew from the INF treaty Aug. 2, 2019. A 5-year extension, agreed to by Russia and the U.S., of the New START treaty went into effect Feb. 2021, but Putin announced, Feb. 21, 2023, that Russia would suspend participation.

Putin's party swept Sept. 2021 parliamentary elections. Opposition leaders charged fraud.

On Feb. 24, 2022, Russia launched a large-scale invasion of Ukraine from the north, east, and south. The U.S., the EU, and other nations imposed sanctions that hurt the Russian economy. The initial northern attack faltered, but Russia gained control of extensive areas of eastern and southern Ukraine, which Ukrainian counteroffensives sought to reclaim. Russian attacks caused high Ukrainian civilian casualties, and Russian troops were accused of war crimes. After sham referenda in Russian-controlled parts of four eastern and southern Ukrainian provinces, Putin signed legislation, Oct. 5, 2022, to annex the four regions. With the war continuing, U.S. estimates put the number of Russian casualties at almost 300,000 (incl. 120,000 dead and at least 170,000 injured) by Aug. 2023. In 2023, Ukraine increasingly launched drone and other attacks against targets in Russia.

On June 23-24, 2023, mercenaries in the Wagner Group (which had been fighting in Ukraine), led by Yevgeny Prigozhin, mutinied—seizing a military headquarters in Rostov-on-Don and advancing toward Moscow—before withdrawing, reportedly after mediation by Belarus. Prigozhin died, Aug. 23, 2023, when his plane apparently exploded midflight.

Russia was one of the world's most severely affected countries by the COVID-19 pandemic. A May 2022 WHO report estimated 1 mil excess COVID-related deaths in Russia in 2020-21, more than triple its reported number.

Rwanda
Republic of Rwanda

People: Population: 13,400,541 (76). **Age distrib.:** <15: 37.9%; 65+: 3.0%. **Growth:** 1.7%. **Migrants:** 4.0%. **Pop. density:** 1,407.0 per sq mi, 543.2 per sq km. **Urban:** 17.9%. **Ethnic groups:** Hutu, Tutsi, Twa. **Languages:** Kinyarwanda (universal Bantu vernacular), French, English, Swahili/Kiswahili (all official). **Religions:** Christian 91.7% (Catholic 44.3%, Protestant 35.0%, independent 12.5%), Muslim 5.3% (Sunni), ethnic religionist 2.5%.

Geography: Total area: 10,169 sq mi, 26,338 sq km (145); **Land area:** 9,524 sq mi, 24,668 sq km. **Location:** E central Africa. Uganda on N, Dem. Rep. of the Congo on W, Burundi on S, Tanzania on E. **Topography:** Grassy uplands and hills cover most of country, with chain of volcanoes in NW. Nile R. source is in headwaters of the Kagera (Akagera) R. **Arable land:** 51.4%. **Capital:** Kigali, 1,247,551.

Government: Type: Presidential republic. **Head of state:** Pres. Paul Kagame; b. 1957; in office: Apr. 22, 2000 (de facto from Mar. 24). **Head of govt.:** Prime Min. Edouard Ngirente; b. 1973; in office: Aug. 30, 2017. **Local divisions:** 4 provinces, 1 city. **Defense budget:** $169 mil. **Active troops:** 33,000.

Economy: Industries: cement, agric. prods., small-scale beverages, soap, furniture, shoes, plastic goods, textiles, cigarettes. **Chief agric.:** bananas, sweet potatoes, cassava, potatoes, plantains, beans. **Natural resources:** gold, tin ore, tungsten ore, methane, hydropower. **Water:** 1,027 cu m per capita. **Electricity prod.:** 854.7 mil kWh. **Labor force:** agric. 54.7%, industry 18.7%, services 26.7%. **Unemployment:** 13.0%.

Finance: Monetary unit: Franc (RWF) (1,187.48 = $1 U.S.). **GDP:** $38.5 bil; **per capita GDP:** $2,792; **GDP growth:** 8.2%. **Imports:** $3.9 bil; China 17%, Kenya 10%, Tanzania 9%, UAE 9%, India 7%. **Exports:** $2.1 bil; UAE 35%, Dem. Rep. of the Congo 28%. **Tourism:** $150 mil. **Budget:** $2.9 bil. **Inflation:** 17.7%.

Transport: Airports: 4.

Communications: Mobile: 79.9 per 100 pop. **Broadband:** 60.1 per 100 pop. **Internet:** 30.5%.

Health: Expend.: 7.3%. **Life expect.:** 64.2 male; 68.2 female. **Births:** 25.7 per 1,000 pop. **Deaths:** 5.8 per 1,000 pop. **Infant mortality:** 25.6 per 1,000 live births. **Undernourished:** 31.6%. **HIV:** 2.3%. **COVID-19:** 133,194 cases, 1,468 deaths; rates per 100,000: 1,028.3 cases, 11.3 deaths. 80.3% vaccinated.

Education: Compulsory: ages 7-12. **Literacy:** 75.9%.
Website: www.gov.rw

For centuries, the Tutsi dominated the Hutu majority. A civil war broke out in 1959 and Tutsi power was ended. Many Tutsi went into exile. Rwanda, which had been part of the Belgian UN trusteeship of Rwanda-Urundi, became independent July 1, 1962.

A large-scale massacre of Tutsi occurred in 1963. Hutu rivalries led to a bloodless coup July 1973 in which Hutu army officer Juvénal Habyarimana took power. After an invasion and coup attempt by Tutsi exiles in 1990, a multiparty democracy was established.

Renewed ethnic strife led to an Aug. 1993 peace accord between the government and rebels of the Tutsi-led Rwandan Patriotic Front (RPF). But after Habyarimana and Burundi Pres. Cyprien Ntaryamira were killed Apr. 6, 1994, in a suspicious plane crash, violence broke out. More than 1 mil may have died in massacres, mostly of Tutsi by Hutu militias, and in civil warfare as the RPF sought power. About 2 mil Tutsi and Hutu fled to camps in Zaire (now Dem. Rep. of the Congo, or DRC) and other countries; many died of disease. French troops under a UN mandate temporarily moved into SW Rwanda June 23 to establish a safe zone. The RPF claimed victory, installing a government led by a moderate Hutu president in July. More than 1 mil refugees, mostly Hutu, returned to Rwanda in Nov.-Dec. 1996.

Former Prime Min. Jean Kambanda pleaded guilty to genocide, May 1, 1998, before the UN-backed Intl. Criminal Tribunal for Rwanda (ICTR); he received a life sentence Sept. 4, 1998. RPF leader Maj. Gen. Paul Kagame became Rwanda's first Tutsi president Apr. 22, 2000.

Rwandans approved a new constitution, May 26, 2003, and reelected Pres. Kagame, Aug. 25. Rwanda cut diplomatic ties with France Nov. 24, 2006, after a French judge linked Kagame to the 1994 deaths of Habyarimana and Ntaryamira. The country restored relations with France, Nov. 2009, the same month Rwanda joined the Commonwealth. Accused of being one of the architects of the 1994 genocide, Col. Theoneste Bagosora was convicted and sentenced to prison by the ICTR, Dec. 18, 2008. A Rwandan court Jan. 20, 2009, sentenced former Justice Min. Agnes Ntamabyariro to life in prison for her role in inciting the massacres. Up to 4,000 Rwandan troops fought that month alongside Congolese forces against Hutu militias in eastern DRC. After a campaign criticized as repressive by human rights groups, Pres. Kagame won reelection Aug. 9, 2010.

An Oct. 17, 2012, UN report found that the Rwanda military was backing a rebellion (2012-13) by the mostly-Tutsi M23 group in the DRC. Shortly before the ICTR ceased operations, Dec. 31, 2015, one of its most-wanted fugitives, Ladislas Ntaganzwa, was arrested by Interpol in the DRC. His genocide trial in Rwanda ended in a conviction and life sentence, May 28, 2020. Suppressing political opposition, Kagame won—with almost 99% of the vote—a new term as president in an Aug. 4, 2017, election.

Dissident Paul Rusesabagina, whose protection of over 1,200 Tutsi from the 1994 genocide was dramatized in the film Hotel Rwanda, was arrested, Aug. 2020, on terrorism charges. He was convicted and sentenced to 25 years in prison, Sept. 20, 2021. After widespread criticism of Rwanda's actions, the sentence was commuted and Rusesabagina was released, Mar. 24, 2023.

Saint Kitts and Nevis
Federation of Saint Kitts and Nevis

People: Population: 54,817 (189). **Age distrib.:** <15: 19.4%; 65+: 12.1%. **Growth:** 0.6%. **Migrants:** 14.5%. **Pop. density:** 548.0 per sq mi, 210.0 per sq km. **Urban:** 31.1%. **Ethnic groups:** African descent 92.5%, mixed 3%, white 2.1%. **Languages:** English (official). **Religions:** Christian 93.7% (Protestant 76.6%), agnostic 2.0%.

Geography: Total area: 101 sq mi, 261 sq km (189); **Land area:** 101 sq mi, 261 sq km. **Location:** At the part of the Leeward group of Lesser Antilles in E Caribbean Sea. Antigua and Barbuda to E. **Topography:** Forested volcanic slopes on St. Kitts; beaches rising to central peak on Nevis. Tropical climate moderated by sea breezes. **Arable land:** 19.2%. **Capital:** Basseterre, 14,434.

Government: Type: Federal parliamentary democracy under constitutional monarchy. **Head of state:** King Charles III, rep. by Gov.-Gen. Marcella Liburd; in office: Feb. 1, 2023. **Head of govt.:** Prime Min. Terrance Drew; in office: Aug. 6, 2022. **Local divisions:** 14 parishes. **Defense budget/active troops:** NA.

Economy: Industries: tourism, cotton, salt, copra, clothing, footwear, beverages. **Chief agric.:** coconuts, tropical fruit, roots/tubers, vegetables, sweet potatoes, pulses. **Water:** 451 cu m per capita. **Electricity prod.:** 215.9 mil kWh. **Labor force:** NA. **Unemployment:** NA.

Finance: Monetary unit: East Caribbean Dollar (XCD) (2.70 = $1 U.S.). **GDP:** $1.6 bil; **per capita GDP:** $34,052; **GDP growth:** 9.0%. **Imports:** $441.2 mil; (2021) U.S. 50%, Trinidad and Tobago 10%. **Exports:** $408.5 mil; (2021) U.S. 56%, Italy 19%. **Tourism:** $29 mil. **Budget** (2020): $324 mil. **Inflation:** 2.7%.

Transport: Railways: 31 mi. **Airports:** 2.

Communications: Mobile (2021): 119.1 per 100 pop. **Broadband** (2021): 101.7 per 100 pop. **Internet:** 79.5%.

Health: Expend.: 5.4%. **Life expect.:** 74.9 male; 79.8 female. **Births:** 12.1 per 1,000 pop. **Deaths:** 7.3 per 1,000 pop. **Infant mortality:** 8.2 per 1,000 live births. **Undernourished:** NA. **HIV:** NA. **COVID-19:** 6,607 cases, 46 deaths; rates per 100,000: 12,421.0 cases, 86.5 deaths. 50.8% vaccinated.

Education: Compulsory: ages 5-16. **Literacy:** NA.

Website: www.gov.kn

St. Kitts (formerly St. Christopher; known by Indigenous peoples as Liamuiga) and Nevis were reached by Columbus in 1493. They were settled by Britain in 1623 (ownership was disputed with France until 1713). The colony achieved self-government in 1967, becoming independent, Sept. 19, 1983. Twenty years of Labour Party governments ended when an opposition coalition won Feb. 16, 2015, legislative elections. The coalition won June 5, 2020, elections, but Aug. 5, 2022, elections returned Labour to power.

Saint Lucia

People: Population: 167,591 (178). **Age distrib.:** <15: 18.2%; 65+: 14.8%. **Growth:** 0.3%. **Migrants:** 4.5%. **Pop. density:** 716.3 per sq mi, 276.6 per sq km. **Urban:** 19.2%. **Ethnic groups:** Black/African descent 85.3%, mixed 10.9%, East Indian 2.2%. **Languages:** English (official), Saint Lucian Creole. **Religions:** Christian 95.5% (Catholic 69.1%, Protestant 23.1%).

Geography: Total area: 238 sq mi, 616 sq km (179); **Land area:** 234 sq mi, 606 sq km. **Location:** E Caribbean, second largest of Windward Isls. Martinique (Fr.) to N, St. Vincent to S. **Topography:** Mountainous, volcanic in origin; Soufrière Volcanic Centre in S. Wooded mountains run N-S. **Arable land:** 4.4%. **Capital:** Castries, 22,258.

Government: Type: Parliamentary democracy under constitutional monarchy. **Head of state:** King Charles III, rep. by Acting Gov.-Gen. Errol Charles, in office: Nov. 11, 2021. **Head of govt.:** Prime Min. Philip J. Pierre; in office: July 28, 2021. **Local divisions:** 10 districts. **Defense budget/active troops:** NA.

Economy: Industries: tourism, clothing, electronic components assembly, beverages, corrugated cardboard boxes, lime proc. **Chief agric.:** bananas, coconuts, fruit, tropical fruit, plantains, roots/tubers. **Natural resources:** forests, sandy beaches, pumice, mineral springs. **Water:** 1,634 cu m per capita. **Electricity prod.:** 353.6 mil kWh. **Labor force:** agric. 10.5%, industry 15.9%, services 73.6%. **Unemployment:** 17.4%.

Finance: Monetary unit: East Caribbean Dollar (XCD) (2.70 = $1 U.S.). **GDP:** $3.2 bil; **per capita GDP:** $17,756; **GDP growth:** 15.4%. **Imports:** $846.5 mil; (2021) Brazil 64%, U.S. 14%, Russia 8%, Colombia 7%. **Exports:** $890.7 mil; (2021) Brazil 98%. **Tourism:** $776 mil. **Budget (2020):** $516 mil. **Inflation:** 6.4%.

Transport: Airports: 2.

Communications: Mobile (2021): 95.6 per 100 pop. **Broadband** (2021): 51.8 per 100 pop. **Internet:** 78.1%.

Health: Expend.: 6.7%. **Life expect.:** 76.5 male; 82.1 female. **Births:** 11.7 per 1,000 pop. **Deaths:** 8.2 per 1,000 pop. **Infant mortality:** 11.8 per 1,000 live births. **Undernourished:** NA. **HIV:** NA. **COVID-19:** 30,052 cases, 409 deaths; rates per 100,000: 16,365.8 cases, 222.7 deaths. 29.9% vaccinated.

Education: Compulsory: ages 5-14. **Literacy:** NA.

Website: www.govt.lc

St. Lucia, ceded to Britain by France with the Treaty of Paris, 1814, gained independence Feb. 22, 1979. The conservative United Workers Party (UWP) defeated the governing St. Lucia Labor Party (SLP) in June 6, 2016, elections. The SLP returned to power following July 26, 2021, elections.

The COVID-19 pandemic severely hurt the important tourism industry. GDP began recovering in 2021 after a 20% drop in 2020.

Saint Vincent and the Grenadines

People: Population: 100,804 (183). **Age distrib.:** <15: 19.0%; 65+: 12.4%. **Growth:** –0.2%. **Migrants:** 4.3%. **Pop. density:** 671.2 per sq mi, 259.1 per sq km. **Urban:** 54.3%. **Ethnic groups:** African descent 71.2%, mixed 23%, Indigenous 3%. **Languages:** English, Vincentian Creole English, French patois. **Religions:** Christian 88.4% (Protestant 59.8%, independent 22.9%), Hindu 3.4%, agnostic 2.5%.

Geography: Total area: 150 sq mi, 389 sq km (185); **Land area:** 150 sq mi, 389 sq km. **Location:** E Caribbean; St. Vincent (133 sq mi) and the northern islets of the Grenadines form a part of Windward chain. St. Lucia to N, Barbados to E, Grenada to S. **Topography:** St. Vincent is volcanic, with a ridge of thickly wooded mountains running its length. **Arable land:** 5.1%. **Capital:** Kingstown, 26,636.

Government: Type: Parliamentary democracy under constitutional monarchy. **Head of state:** King Charles III, rep. by Gov.-Gen. Susan Dougan; in office: Aug. 1, 2019. **Head of govt.:** Prime Min. Ralph Gonsalves; b. 1946; in office: Mar. 29, 2001. **Local divisions:** 6 parishes. **Defense budget/active troops:** NA.

Economy: Industries: tourism, food proc., cement, furniture, clothing, starch. **Chief agric.:** bananas, sugarcane, roots/tubers, plantains, vegetables, fruit. **Natural resources:** hydropower. **Water:** 901 cu m per capita. **Electricity prod.:** 164.2 mil

kWh. **Labor force:** agric. 10.3%, industry 20.6%, services 69.1%. **Unemployment:** 19.0%.

Finance: Monetary unit: East Caribbean Dollar (XCD) (2.70 = $1 U.S.). **GDP:** $1.8 bil; **per capita GDP:** $17,207; **GDP growth:** 5.0%. **Imports:** $415.7 mil; (2021) U.S. 29%, Netherlands 15%, Trinidad and Tobago 10%, China 8%. **Exports:** $125.8 mil; (2021) Netherlands 45%, India 9%, U.S. 6%. **Tourism:** $36 mil. **Budget (2020):** $288 mil. **Inflation:** 5.7%.

Transport: Airports: 5.

Communications: Mobile: 100.5 per 100 pop. **Broadband** (2021): 93.3 per 100 pop. **Internet:** 84.9%.

Health: Expend.: 4.8%. **Life expect.:** 74.9 male; 79.0 female. **Births:** 12.1 per 1,000 pop. **Deaths:** 7.6 per 1,000 pop. **Infant mortality:** 12.6 per 1,000 live births. **Undernourished:** 3.1%. **HIV:** NA. **COVID-19:** 9,631 cases, 124 deaths; rates per 100,000: 8,681.3 cases, 111.8 deaths. 28.5% vaccinated.

Education: Compulsory: ages 5-16. **Literacy:** NA.

Website: www.gov.vc

St. Vincent received its name because of the unsupported belief that Christopher Columbus landed there on Jan. 22, 1498 (St. Vincent's Day). Britain and France laid claim to the island in the 17th and 18th cent.; the Treaty of Versailles, 1783, ceded it to Britain. Independence came Oct. 27, 1979.

Samoa
Independent State of Samoa

People: Population: 207,501 (177). **Age distrib.:** <15: 27.3%; 65+: 6.9%. **Growth:** 0.6%. **Migrants:** 2.0%. **Pop. density:** 190.5 per sq mi, 73.6 per sq km. **Urban:** 17.5%. **Ethnic groups** (by citizenship): Samoan 96%, Samoan/New Zealander 2%. **Languages:** Samoan (Polynesian), English (both official). **Religions:** Christian (official) 98.8% (Protestant 49.4%, independent 33.3%, Catholic 16.1%).

Geography: Total area: 1,093 sq mi, 2,831 sq km (168); **Land area:** 1,089 sq mi, 2,821 sq km. **Location:** S Pacific O. Nearest neighbors are Fiji to SW, Tonga to S. **Topography:** Main islands, Savaii (659 sq mi) and Upolu (432 sq mi), both ruggedly mountainous. Small islands of Manono and Apolima. **Arable land:** 4.1%. **Capital:** Apia, 36,066.

Government: Type: Parliamentary republic. **Head of state:** Tuimaleali'ifano Va'aletoa Sualauvi II; b. 1947; in office: July 21, 2017. **Head of govt.:** Prime Min. Fiame Naomi Mata'afa; b. 1957; in office: July 28, 2021. **Local divisions:** 11 districts. **Defense budget/active troops:** NA.

Economy: Industries: food proc., building materials, auto parts. **Chief agric.:** coconuts, taro, bananas, yams, tropical fruit, pineapples. **Natural resources:** hardwood forests, fish, hydropower. **Water:** 0. **Electricity prod.:** 178.0 mil kWh. **Labor force:** agric. 24.1%, industry 16.5%, services 59.4%. **Unemployment:** 10.3%.

Finance: Monetary unit: Tala (WST) (2.74 = $1 U.S.). **GDP:** $1.3 bil; **per capita GDP:** $6,041; **GDP growth:** –6.0%. **Imports** (2020): $376.8 mil; (2021) New Zealand 24%, China 19%, Singapore 11%, U.S. 8%, Australia 7%. **Exports:** $97.8 mil; (2021) U.S. 20%, New Zealand 16%, American Samoa 11%, Brazil 8%, Australia 7%. **Tourism** (2020): $24 mil. **Budget (2020):** $263 mil. **Inflation:** 11.0%.

Transport: Airports: 1.

Communications: Mobile: 60.4 per 100 pop. **Broadband:** 33.6 per 100 pop. **Internet:** 78.2%.

Health: Expend.: 5.3%. **Life expect.:** 72.6 male; 78.5 female. **Births:** 19.0 per 1,000 pop. **Deaths:** 5.4 per 1,000 pop. **Infant mortality:** 17.8 per 1,000 live births. **Undernourished:** 4.6%. **HIV:** NA. **COVID-19:** 16,778 cases, 31 deaths; rates per 100,000: 8,456.1 cases, 15.6 deaths. 89.7% vaccinated.

Education: Compulsory: ages 5-12. **Literacy:** 99.1%.

Website: www.samoagovt.ws

Samoa (formerly Western Samoa) was a German colony, 1899 to 1914, when New Zealand landed troops and took over. It became a New Zealand mandate under the League of Nations and, in 1945, a New Zealand UN Trusteeship. An elected local government took office in Oct. 1959, and the country became fully independent Jan. 1, 1962. In 2011, Samoa moved west of the Intl. Date Line to reduce time differences with Australia and New Zealand. A new party headed by Fiame Naomi Mata'afa defeated the party of Prime Min. Tuila'epa Sailele Malielegaoi (in office more than two decades) in Apr. 9, 2021, elections. After a constitutional crisis in which Tuila'epa refused to concede, Fiame became Samoa's first female prime minister. Samoa and China signed a cooperation agreement, May 28, 2022.

San Marino
Republic of San Marino

People: Population: 34,892 (191). **Age distrib.:** <15: 14.3%; 65+: 21.1%. **Growth:** 0.6%. **Migrants:** 16.3%. **Pop. density:** 1,481.5 per sq mi, 572.0 per sq km. **Urban:** 97.8%. **Ethnic groups:**

Sammarinese, Italian. **Languages:** Italian. **Religions:** Christian 91.2% (Catholic), agnostic 5.8%.

Geography: Total area: 24 sq mi, 61 sq km (192); **Land area:** 24 sq mi, 61 sq km. **Location:** Completely surrounded by Italy, in N center of that country, near Adriatic coast. **Topography:** On slopes of Mt. Titano. **Arable land:** 33.1%. **Capital:** San Marino, 4,465.

Government: Type: Parliamentary republic. **Heads of state:** Two captains regent, elected by parliament from among its members, to 6-month term. **Head of govt.:** Sec. of State for Foreign and Political Affairs Luca Beccari; b. 1974; in office: Jan. 8, 2020. **Local divisions:** 9 municipalities. **Defense budget/active troops:** NA.

Economy: Industries: tourism, banking, textiles, electronics, ceramics, cement, wine. **Chief agric.:** wheat, grapes, corn; cattle, pigs, horses. **Natural resources:** building stone. **Water:** NA. **Labor force:** agric. 0.2%, industry 33.5%, services 66.3%. **Unemployment:** NA.

Finance: Monetary unit: Euro (EUR) (0.93 = $1 U.S.). **GDP (2021):** $2.3 bil; **per capita GDP (2021):** $67,983; **GDP growth (2021):** 8.5%. **Imports** (2011): $2.6 bil; Germany 21%, Italy 13%, Poland 10%, France 7%, Spain 7%, Belgium 6%, Romania 6%. **Exports** (2011): $3.8 bil; Romania 10%, France 9%, Germany 8%, U.S. 8%, Austria 6%, Brazil 6%, Poland 6%, Russia 6%. **Budget:** $363 mil. **Inflation** (2016-17): 1.1%.

Transport: NA.

Communications: Mobile: 121.8 per 100 pop. **Broadband:** 136.7 per 100 pop. **Internet:** 74.9%.

Health: Expend.: 8.7%. **Life expect.:** 81.5 male; 86.8 female. **Births:** 8.9 per 1,000 pop. **Deaths:** 8.8 per 1,000 pop. **Infant mortality:** 6.4 per 1,000 live births. **Undernourished:** NA. **HIV:** NA. **COVID-19:** 24,382 cases, 125 deaths; rates per 100,000: 71,842.8 cases, 368.3 deaths. 70.0% vaccinated.

Education: Compulsory: ages 6-15. **Literacy:** 99.9%.

Website: www.gov.sm

San Marino, founded in the 4th cent., claims to be the world's oldest republic. It has a treaty of friendship with Italy. The Sammarinese Christian Democratic Party (PDCS) won 2019 parliamentary elections. In a Sept. 26, 2021, referendum, voters approved legalizing abortion in the first 12 weeks of pregnancy.

São Tomé and Príncipe
Democratic Republic of São Tomé and Príncipe

People: Population: 220,372 (176). **Age distrib.:** <15: 37.2%; 65+: 3.2%. **Growth:** 1.5%. **Migrants:** 1.0%. **Pop. density:** 592.1 per sq mi, 228.6 per sq km. **Urban:** 76.4%. **Ethnic groups:** mestico, angolares (descendants of Angolan slaves), forros (descendants of freed slaves), servicais (contract laborers fr. Angola, Mozambique, Cabo Verde), tongas (children of servicais born on the islands), Europeans (primarily Portuguese), Asians (mostly Chinese). **Languages:** Portuguese (official), Forro, Cabo Verdian, French, Angolar, English. **Religions:** Christian 96.1% (Catholic 71.8%, independent 15.9%), Baha'i 2.2%.

Geography: Total area: 372 sq mi, 964 sq km (172); **Land area:** 372 sq mi, 964 sq km. **Location:** Gulf of Guinea about 125 mi off W central Africa. Gabon, Equatorial Guinea to E. **Topography:** Part of an extinct volcano chain; lush forests and croplands. **Arable land:** 4.2%. **Capital:** São Tomé, 80,099.

Government: Type: Semi-presidential republic. **Head of state:** Pres. Carlos Vila Nova; b. 1956; in office: Oct. 2, 2021. **Head of govt.:** Prime Min. Patrice Trovoada; b. 1962; in office: Nov. 11, 2022. **Local divisions:** 6 districts, 1 autonomous region. **Defense budget/active troops:** NA.

Economy: Industries: light constr., textiles, soap, beer, fish proc., timber. **Chief agric.:** plantains, oil palm fruit, coconuts, taro, bananas, fruit. **Natural resources:** fish, hydropower. **Water:** 9,947 cu m per capita. **Electricity prod.:** 100.5 mil kWh. **Labor force:** agric. 18.0%, industry 20.2%, services 61.7%. **Unemployment:** 15.3%.

Finance: Monetary unit: Dobra (STN) (22.72 = $1 U.S.). **GDP:** $1.1 bil; **per capita GDP:** $4,738; **GDP growth:** 0.9%. **Imports:** $201.1 mil; Portugal 41%, Angola 17%, China 8%. **Exports:** $75.3 mil; Singapore 30%, Switzerland 24%, France 11%, Poland 7%, Belgium 7%. **Tourism:** $30 mil. **Budget:** $102 mil. **Inflation:** 18.0%.

Transport: Airports: 2.

Communications: Mobile: 86.8 per 100 pop. **Broadband:** 40.8 per 100 pop. **Internet:** 51.2%.

Health: Expend.: 4.9%. **Life expect.:** 65.7 male; 69.1 female. **Births:** 27.4 per 1,000 pop. **Deaths:** 6.1 per 1,000 pop. **Infant mortality:** 43.5 per 1,000 live births. **Undernourished:** 13.1%. **HIV:** 0.4%. **COVID-19:** 6,589 cases, 80 deaths; rates per 100,000: 3,006.5 cases, 36.5 deaths. 51.1% vaccinated.

Education: Compulsory: ages 6-11. **Literacy:** 93.8%.

Website: www.parlamento.st

The Portuguese reached the islands in 1471 and brought the first inhabitants—convicts and exiled Jews. Sugarcane planting was replaced by the slave trade as the chief economic activity until coffee and cocoa were introduced in the 19th cent.

Portugal agreed, 1974, to turn the colony over to the Gabon-based Movement for the Liberation of São Tomé and Príncipe; its East German-trained leader, Manuel Pinto da Costa, became the country's first president. Independence came July 12, 1975. Democratic reforms were instituted in 1987.

The country, one of the world's poorest, has sought to develop oil deposits in the Gulf of Guinea and tourism. Seeking aid and investment, São Tomé broke diplomatic ties with Taiwan and established relations with China, Dec. 2016. Carlos Vila Nova of the Independent Democratic Action (ADI) party won a Sept. 5, 2021, presidential runoff election. The ADI, formerly in opposition, won the most votes in Sept. 25, 2022, parliamentary elections. The ADI's Patrice Trovoada, who became prime minister Nov. 11, announced Nov. 25 that a coup had been thwarted.

Saudi Arabia
Kingdom of Saudi Arabia

People: Population: 35,939,806 (42). **Age distrib.:** <15: 23.5%; 65+: 4.2%. **Growth:** 1.7%. **Migrants:** 38.6%. **Pop. density:** 43.3 per sq mi, 16.7 per sq km. **Urban:** 85.0%. **Ethnic groups:** Arab 90%, Afro-Asian 10%. **Languages:** Arabic (official). **Religions:** Muslim 90.3% (Sunni [official] 81%, Shia 9%), Christian 6.0% (Catholic), Hindu 2.0%.

Geography: Total area: 830,000 sq mi, 2,149,690 sq km (12); **Land area:** 830,000 sq mi, 2,149,690 sq km. **Location:** Occupies most of Arabian Peninsula in Middle East. Kuwait, Iraq, Jordan on N; Yemen, Oman on S; UAE, Qatar on E. **Topography:** Bordered by Red Sea on W. Highlands in W slope as barren desert to the Persian Gulf on E. **Arable land:** 1.6%. **Capital:** Riyadh, 7,682,430. **Cities:** Jiddah, 4,862,941; Mecca, 2,149,928; Medina, 1,572,571; Ad-Dammam, 1,329,291.

Government: Type: Absolute monarchy. **Head of state:** King Salman bin Abdul Aziz; b. 1924; in office: Jan. 23, 2015. **Head of govt.:** Mohammed bin Salman; b. 1985; in office: Sept. 27, 2022. **Local divisions:** 13 regions. **Defense budget:** $45.6 bil. **Active troops:** 257,000.

Economy: Industries: crude oil prod., petroleum refining, basic petrochemicals, ammonia, industrial gases, caustic soda, cement, fertilizer. **Chief agric.:** milk, dates, poultry, fruit, watermelons, barley. **Natural resources:** petroleum, nat. gas, iron ore, gold, copper. **Water:** 69 cu m per capita. **Crude oil reserves:** 258.6 bil bbls (incl. half of Neutral Zone reserves with Kuwait). **Electricity prod.:** 366.7 bil kWh. **Labor force:** agric. 2.7%, industry 20.0%, services 77.3%. **Unemployment:** 5.6%.

Finance: Monetary unit: Riyal (SAR) (3.75 = $1 U.S.). **GDP:** $2.2 tril; **per capita GDP:** $59,065; **GDP growth:** 8.7%. **Imports:** $213.0 bil; China 18%, UAE 12%, U.S. 9%. **Exports:** $286.5 bil; China 20%, India 11%, Japan 11%, South Korea 9%. **Tourism:** $3.8 bil. **Budget:** $282.4 bil. **Inflation:** 2.5%.

Transport: Railways: 3,362 mi. **Motor vehicles:** 277.1 per 1,000 pop. **Airports:** 82.

Communications: Mobile: 132.4 per 100 pop. **Broadband:** 126.0 per 100 pop. **Internet:** 100.0%.

Health: Expend. (2018): 5.5%. **Life expect.:** 75.3 male; 78.6 female. **Births:** 13.9 per 1,000 pop. **Deaths:** 3.5 per 1,000 pop. **Infant mortality:** 12.0 per 1,000 live births. **Undernourished:** 3.8%. **HIV:** <0.1%. **COVID-19:** 841,469 cases, 9,646 deaths; rates per 100,000: 2,417.1 cases, 27.7 deaths. 73.1% vaccinated.

Education: Compulsory: ages 6-14. **Literacy:** 97.6%.

Website: www.my.gov.sa

Arabia was divided among numerous warring groups and small kingdoms before Muhammad united it in the early 7th cent. His successors conquered the entire Middle East and North Africa, bringing Islam and the Arabic language. But Arabia soon returned to its former status.

Nejd, in central Arabia, long an independent state and center of the Wahhabi sect, fell under Turkish rule in the 18th cent. Ibn Saud, founder of the Saudi dynasty, overthrew the Turks, 1913. He captured Hasa, a Turkish province in eastern Arabia, also 1913; the Hejaz region in western Arabia, 1925; and most of Asir, in SW Arabia, by 1926. The discovery of oil in the 1930s transformed the nation. The Hejaz contains the holy cities of Islam—Medina and Mecca.

Ibn Saud reigned until his death, Nov. 1953. Subsequent kings as of mid-2023 have been his sons. King Salman, June 21, 2017, named as crown prince (heir to the throne) his son Mohammed bin Salman. Known as MBS, the crown prince took on increasing responsibilities. He became Saudi Arabia's prime minister Sept. 27, 2022.

The Islamic religious code is the law of the land. Alcohol and public entertainments are restricted. Dissent is repressed.

Saudi Arabia has often allied itself with and purchased arms from the U.S. and other Western nations. Saudi units, nevertheless, fought against Western ally Israel in the 1948 and 1973 Arab-Israeli wars. Saudi Arabia played a leading role in the 1973-74 Arab oil embargo against the U.S. and other nations.

After Iraq invaded Kuwait, Aug. 2, 1990, Saudi Arabia accepted the Kuwait royal family and more than 400,000 Kuwaiti refugees. Western and Arab troops also deployed on Saudi soil before and during the 1991 Persian Gulf War.

When 15 of the 19 al-Qaeda hijackers who carried out the Sept. 11, 2001, attacks on the U.S. were found to be Saudi, some in the U.S. blamed the Saudi government for allowing Muslim extremism to flourish in Saudi Arabia.

In 2012, Saudi women competed in the Olympics for the first time. A royal decree, Jan. 11, 2013, permitted women to hold 30 of the 150 seats on the government's advisory Shura council. Women were allowed to vote and run for office in municipal elections for the first time in 2015. The male guardianship system that subordinated women was loosened in the late 2010s. A royal decree, effective June 24, 2018, made it legal for women to drive. Decrees issued Aug. 2, 2019, gave women the rights to obtain passports and travel freely, as well as increasing rights in employment and family matters.

Middle East Respiratory Syndrome (MERS), a disease caused by a coronavirus, was first recognized in Saudi Arabia in 2012 and had spread to 26 other countries as of mid-2023, causing more than 2,600 cases and over 900 deaths.

Beginning in 2014, Saudi warplanes participated in U.S.-led airstrikes against ISIS in Syria. ISIS staged terrorist attacks inside Saudi Arabia in 2014 and subsequent years.

Saudi Arabia led a coalition of Sunni nations that began airstrikes, Mar. 25, 2015, and took other military action against Iran-backed Shiite Houthi rebels in Yemen, causing high civilian casualties. Rebels launched drone and missile strikes on targets in Saudi Arabia and claimed credit for attacks, Sept. 14, 2019, on two major oil installations; Saudi Arabia blamed Iran for the Sept. 14 attacks. A truce in Yemen beginning Apr. 2, 2022, significantly reduced violence.

King Salman announced, Apr. 25, 2016, a plan for economic diversification and privatization by the year 2030. In what was said to be a government anti-corruption campaign, hundreds of business leaders and royal family members were detained, Nov. 2017-Jan. 2018, and more than $100 bil in assets taken.

Saudi dissident and journalist Jamal Khashoggi was killed, Oct. 2, 2018, inside the Saudi consulate in Istanbul, Turkey. A CIA assessment concluded with "high confidence" in Nov. 2018 that MBS ordered the killing.

The Saudi-backed LIV Golf tour, widely perceived as intended to boost Saudi Arabia's international image, launched in 2022; men's pro golfers received multimillion-dollar guaranteed fees to join the tour. A potential merger of LIV and the PGA Tour was announced June 6, 2023.

To combat COVID-19 spread, Saudi Arabia barred foreign residents (usually numbering over 2 mil) from making the hajj, or pilgrimage, to Mecca in 2020 and 2021. The 2022 hajj was limited to 1 mil fully vaccinated pilgrims. Restrictions were lifted in 2023.

Saudi Arabia and Iran announced, Mar. 10, 2023, an agreement to restore diplomatic relations, severed by Saudi Arabia in 2016. A Human Rights Watch report, issued Aug. 21, 2023, accused Saudi border guards of systematically killing or maiming Ethiopian and other East African migrants trying to enter the kingdom through Yemen.

Senegal
Republic of Senegal

People: Population: 18,384,660 (67). **Age distrib.:** <15: 41.2%; 65+: 3.3%. **Growth:** 2.5%. **Migrants:** 1.6%. **Pop. density:** 247.3 per sq mi, 95.5 per sq km. **Urban:** 49.6%. **Ethnic groups:** Wolof 39.7%, Pular 27.5%, Serer 16%, Mandinka 4.9%, Jola 4.2%, Soninke 2.4%, other (incl. Europeans, persons of Lebanese descent) 5.4%. **Languages:** French (official), Wolof, Pular, Jola, Mandinka, Serer, Soninke. **Religions:** Muslim 91.6% (Sunni), Christian 5.0% (Catholic), ethnic religionist 3.0%.

Geography: Total area: 75,955 sq mi, 196,722 sq km (86); **Land area:** 74,336 sq mi, 192,530 sq km. **Location:** W extreme of Africa. Mauritania on N, Mali on E, Guinea and Guinea-Bissau on S; surrounds The Gambia on three sides. **Topography:** Mostly low rolling plains, rising somewhat in SE. Swamp and jungles in SW. **Arable land:** 19.9%. **Capital:** Dakar, 3,429,536.

Government: Type: Presidential republic. **Head of state:** Pres. Macky Sall; b. 1961; in office: Apr. 2, 2012. **Head of govt.:** Prime Min. Amadou Ba; b. 1961; in office: Sept. 17, 2022. **Local divisions:** 14 regions. **Defense budget:** $423 mil. **Active troops:** 13,600.

Economy: Industries: agric. and fish proc., phosphate mining, fertilizer prod., petroleum refining, zircon and gold mining, constr. materials, ship constr./repair. **Chief agric.:** groundnuts, watermelons, rice, sugarcane, cassava, millet. **Natural resources:** fish, phosphates, iron ore. **Water:** 2,327 cu m per capita. **Electricity prod.:** 5.6 bil kWh. **Labor force:** agric. 21.6%, industry 22.6%, services 55.8%. **Unemployment:** 3.4%.

Finance: Monetary unit: CFA Franc (XOF) (606.88 = $1 U.S.). **GDP:** $72.9 bil; **per capita GDP:** $4,209; **GDP growth:** 4.2%. **Imports** (2018): $9.0 bil; China 17%, France 11%, Belgium 7%, Russia 7%, Netherlands 7%. **Exports** (2018): $5.3 bil; Mali 22%, Switzerland 14%, India 9%, China 7%. **Budget:** $5.7 bil. **Inflation:** 9.7%.

Transport: Railways: 563 mi. **Airports:** 9.

Communications: Mobile: 120.4 per 100 pop. **Broadband:** 98.0 per 100 pop. **Internet:** 58.1%.

Health: Expend.: 5.2%. **Life expect.:** 68.5 male; 72.1 female. **Births:** 30.8 per 1,000 pop. **Deaths:** 5.0 per 1,000 pop. **Infant mortality:** 31.8 per 1,000 live births. **Undernourished:** 5.7%. **HIV:** 0.3%. **COVID-19:** 89,014 cases, 1,971 deaths; rates per 100,000: 531.6 cases, 11.8 deaths. 9.0% vaccinated.

Education: Compulsory: ages 6-16. **Literacy:** 56.3%.

Website: www.sec.gouv.sn

Portuguese settlers arrived in the 15th cent., but French control grew from the 17th cent. The last independent Muslim state was subdued in 1893. Senegal became an independent republic Aug. 20, 1960, but French political and economic influence remained strong. Senegambia, 1982-89, was a loose confederation of Senegal and The Gambia.

Forty years of Socialist Party rule ended when Abdoulaye Wade won a presidential runoff election, Mar. 19, 2000. A Senegalese ferry capsized Sept. 26, 2002, killing at least 1,863 people. Wade lost his bid for a third term Mar. 26, 2012, to Macky Sall. After a campaign marred by violence, Sall's coalition won July 30, 2017, legislative elections. Sall won the Feb. 24, 2019, presidential election; leading opposition candidates were barred. Sall's coalition put together a one-seat majority after July 31, 2022, legislative elections.

Opposition leader Ousmane Sonko was convicted, June 1, 2023, on a charge of corrupting youth, touching off protests that left at least 16 dead. The government dissolved Sonko's party, July 31, as he faced new charges related to the protests.

Serbia
Republic of Serbia

People: Population: 6,693,375 (107). **Age distrib.:** <15: 14.5%; 65+: 19.7%. **Growth:** −0.6%. **Migrants:** 9.4%. **Pop. density:** 223.8 per sq mi, 86.4 per sq km. **Urban:** 57.1% (incl. Kosovo). **Ethnic groups:** Serb 83.3%, Hungarian 3.5%, Romani 2.1% (usu. underestimated; may be up to 5%-11% of pop.), Bosniak 2%. **Languages:** Serbian (official), Hungarian. **Religions:** Christian 90.5% (Orthodox 82.7%), Muslim 7.3% (Sunni).

Geography: Total area: 29,913 sq mi, 77,474 sq km (115); **Land area:** 29,913 sq mi, 77,474 sq km. **Location:** Balkan Peninsula in SE Europe. Croatia, Bosnia and Herzegovina on W; Hungary on N; Romania, Bulgaria on E; Montenegro, Albania, North Macedonia on S. **Topography:** Terrain varies widely—fertile plains drained by Danube, other rivers in N; limestone basins in E; mountains, hills in SE. **Arable land:** 31.1%. **Capital:** Belgrade, 1,408,144.

Government: Type: Parliamentary republic. **Head of state:** Pres. Aleksandar Vucic; b. 1970; in office: May 31, 2017. **Head of govt.:** Prime Min. Ana Brnabic; b. 1975; in office: June 29, 2017. **Local divisions:** 117 municipalities, 28 cities (of which 37 municipalities and 8 cities comprise the autonomous province of Vojvodina). **Defense budget:** $1.2 bil. **Active troops:** 28,150.

Economy: Industries: automobiles, base metals, furniture, food proc., machinery, chemicals, sugar, tires. **Chief agric.:** maize, wheat, sugar beet, milk, sunflower seed, potatoes. **Natural resources:** oil, gas, coal, iron ore, copper, zinc, antimony, chromite, gold, silver, magnesium, pyrite, limestone, marble, salt. **Water:** 18,564 cu m per capita. **Crude oil reserves:** 78 mil bbls. **Electricity prod.:** 34.8 bil kWh. **Labor force:** agric. 13.9%, industry 28.9%, services 57.1%. **Unemployment:** 9.5%.

Finance: Monetary unit: Dinar (RSD) (108.47 = $1 U.S.). **GDP:** $161.6 bil; **per capita GDP:** $23,911; **GDP growth:** 2.3%. **Imports:** $39.0 bil; Germany 13%, Russia 9%, Italy 8%, Hungary 6%. **Exports:** $33.7 bil; Germany 12%, Italy 10%, Bosnia and Herzegovina 7%, Romania 6%. **Tourism:** $1.9 bil. **Budget** (2020): $25.7 bil (central and local govts.). **Inflation:** 12.0%.

Transport: Railways: 2,071 mi. **Motor vehicles:** 391.1 per 1,000 pop. **Airports:** 10.

Communications: Mobile (2021): 123.7 per 100 pop. **Broadband** (2021): 103.6 per 100 pop. **Internet:** 83.5%.

Health: Expend.: 8.7%. **Life expect.:** 72.5 male; 77.9 female. **Births:** 8.9 per 1,000 pop. **Deaths:** 15.1 per 1,000 pop. **Infant mortality:** 4.6 per 1,000 live births. **Undernourished:** <2.5%. **HIV:** <0.1%. **COVID-19:** 2,545,186 cases, 18,057 deaths; rates per 100,000: 36,744.5 cases, 260.7 deaths. 45.6% vaccinated.

Education: Compulsory: ages 7-14. **Literacy:** 99.5%.

Website: www.srbija.gov.rs

Serbia was a vassal principality of Turkey from 1389 to 1878, when the Treaty of Berlin established it as an independent kingdom. After the Balkan wars, Serbia annexed Old Serbia and Macedonia, 1913.

When the Austro-Hungarian empire collapsed after WWI, the Kingdom of Serbs, Croats, and Slovenes—Yugoslavia after 1929—was formed from the provinces of Croatia, Dalmatia, Bosnia, Herzegovina, Slovenia, Vojvodina, and the independent state of Montenegro.

After Nazi Germany's occupation 1941-45, Yugoslavia became a federal republic, headed by Josip Broz, a Communist, known as Marshal Tito. He rejected Stalin's dictatorship and accepted economic and military aid from the West. After Tito died in 1980, Yugoslavia held together for a decade before breaking apart. During 1991-95, Serbia, under Pres. Slobodan Milosevic, supported ethnic Serb fighters in Croatia and in Bosnia and Herzegovina, which had declared independence. The republics of Serbia and Montenegro proclaimed a new Federal Republic of Yugoslavia, Apr. 17, 1992. The UN imposed sanctions on the newly reconstituted Yugoslavia to end the bloodshed in Bosnia.

A peace agreement was reached in 1995. A UN-backed war crimes tribunal began in May 1996 to try suspects from the former Yugoslavia. Barred from running for a third term as Serbian president, Milosevic had himself inaugurated as president of Yugoslavia, July 23, 1997.

Serbian efforts to suppress a secessionist movement in Kosovo led in Mar.-June 1999 to a war with the U.S. and its NATO allies; they accused Milosevic of pursuing a policy of ethnic cleansing against the predominantly Muslim Kosovars (ethnic Albanians). NATO stationed a multinational force in Kosovo, which was placed under UN administration.

Milosevic initially refused to accept defeat by opposition leader Vojislav Kostunica in a 2000 presidential election but resigned Oct. 6 after mass demonstrations. After surrendering to Serbian authorities Apr. 1, 2001, Milosevic was extradited June 28 to The Hague, Netherlands, where a UN tribunal had indicted him for war crimes. He was found dead in prison Mar. 11, 2006, before his trial was completed.

A pact to reconstitute Yugoslavia as a new union of Serbia and Montenegro took effect Feb. 4, 2003. Zoran Djindjic, premier of the Republic of Serbia, was assassinated Mar. 12 in Belgrade, triggering a roundup of more than 4,500 people associated with organized crime and the Milosevic regime. Montenegrins voted for separation in a referendum May 21, 2006, and Montenegro became an independent republic June 3.

Kosovo declared independence from Serbia Feb. 17, 2008, but Serbia refused to recognize the new country. Following parliamentary elections in Serbia May 11, a pro-Western government took office. To meet a requirement for future EU membership, Serbia arrested, in 2008, former Bosnian Serb leader Radovan Karadzic; he was convicted at The Hague of genocide and crimes against humanity, Mar. 24, 2016. Serbia's parliament passed a resolution Mar. 31, 2010, apologizing for the 1995 massacre of 8,000 Bosniaks (primarily Muslim ethnic group) by Bosnian Serbs at Srebrenica. Ratko Mladic, the former Bosnian Serb military commander accused of directing the Srebrenica massacre, was arrested in Serbia, May 2011, and sent to The Hague; he was convicted, Nov. 22, 2017, of genocide, war crimes, and crimes against humanity. Aleksandar Vucic, an advocate of EU membership and also close ties to Russia, became prime min. following Mar. 16, 2014, elections.

An estimated 900,000 refugees and other migrants, largely from the Middle East and SW Asia, passed through Serbia in 2015 and early 2016, most en route to N Europe. The government essentially closed Serbia's borders Mar. 9, 2016.

Vucic was elected president, Apr. 2, 2017. Ana Brnabic took office, June 29, as Serbia's first female prime min. Months of anti-Vucic demonstrations began in late 2018, protesting authoritarian policies and control of the media. In June 21, 2020, parliamentary elections boycotted by leading opposition parties, Vucic's coalition won a landslide victory. Vucic won reelection, Apr. 3, 2022, and his coalition won parliamentary elections.

Two mass shootings in early May 2023 that left 18 dead prompted large-scale protests.

Vojvodina (8,304 sq mi) is a nominally autonomous province in northern Serbia with a pop. (2011 census) of 1,931,809, mostly Serbian. The capital is Novi Sad. **Website:** www.vojvodina.gov.rs

Seychelles
Republic of Seychelles

People: Population: 97,617 (185). **Age distrib.:** <15: 18.0%; 65+: 9.5%. **Growth:** 0.6%. **Migrants:** 13.3%. **Pop. density:** 555.7 per sq mi, 214.5 per sq km. **Urban:** 58.8%. **Ethnic groups:** predominantly creole (mainly East African/Malagasy heritage); also French, Indian, Chinese, Arab pops. **Languages:** Seychellois Creole, English, French (all official). **Religions:** Christian 94.4% (Catholic 82.8%, Protestant 10.5%), agnostic 2.4%.

Geography: Total area: 176 sq mi, 455 sq km (182); **Land area:** 176 sq mi, 455 sq km. **Location:** In Indian O. 700 mi NE of Madagascar. Nearest neighbors are Madagascar and Somalia on NW. **Topography:** Archipelago of over 116 islands. One group is composed of coral; the Mahe group of isls., predominantly mountainous, is granite. **Arable land:** 0.3%. **Capital:** Victoria, 28,091.

Government: Type: Presidential republic. **Head of state and govt.:** Pres. Wavel Ramkalawan; b. 1961; in office: Oct. 26, 2020. **Local divisions:** 27 admin. districts. **Defense budget:** NA. **Active troops:** 420.

Economy: Industries: fishing, tourism, beverages. **Chief agric.:** coconuts, vegetables, bananas, fruit, eggs, poultry. **Natural resources:** fish, coconuts, cinnamon trees. **Water:** 0. **Electricity prod.:** 643.2 mil kWh. **Labor force:** NA. **Unemployment:** NA.

Finance: Monetary unit: Rupee (SCR) (13.62 = $1 U.S.). **GDP:** $3.5 bil; **per capita GDP:** $35,228; **GDP growth:** 8.8%. **Imports:** $1.8 bil; UAE 21%, Qatar 13%, British Virgin Islands 7%, Germany 6%, France 6%. **Exports:** $1.8 bil; UAE 17%, UK 13%, France 12%, British Virgin Islands 11%, Zambia 9%. **Tourism:** $588 mil. **Budget:** $586 mil. **Inflation** (2019-20): 8.3%.

Transport: Airports: 7.

Communications: Mobile: 191.5 per 100 pop. **Broadband:** 99.2 per 100 pop. **Internet:** 81.6%.

Health: Expend.: 6.4%. **Life expect.:** 72.0 male; 80.9 female. **Births:** 12.1 per 1,000 pop. **Deaths:** 6.9 per 1,000 pop. **Infant mortality:** 10.4 per 1,000 live births. **Undernourished:** 4.3%. **HIV:** NA. **COVID-19:** 50,937 cases, 172 deaths; rates per 100,000: 51,793.1 cases, 174.9 deaths. 85.0% vaccinated.

Education: Compulsory: ages 6-15. **Literacy:** 96.2%.

Website: www.egov.sc

The islands were occupied by France in 1768 and seized by Britain in 1794. Seychelles declared independence June 29, 1976. Tourism, a major driver of economic growth, was hurt by the COVID-19 pandemic in 2020, before rebounding in 2021.

The country's first president was ousted in a 1977 coup by socialist leader France Albert René. A 1993 constitution provided for a multiparty state. René resigned in 2004. Vice Pres. James Michel succeeded him and won 2006, 2011, and 2015 elections. After Michel resigned in 2016, Vice Pres. Danny Faure became president. Opposition candidate Wavel Ramkalawan defeated Faure in the Oct. 2020 presidential election, ending more than four decades of rule by Faure's party.

Sierra Leone
Republic of Sierra Leone

People: Population: 8,908,040 (100). **Age distrib.:** <15: 40.5%; 65+: 2.6%. **Growth:** 2.4%. **Migrants:** 0.7%. **Pop. density:** 322.1 per sq mi, 124.4 per sq km. **Urban:** 44.3%. **Ethnic groups:** Temne 35.4%, Mende 30.8%, Limba 8.8%, Kono 4.3%, Korankoh 4%, Fullah 3.8%, Mandingo 2.8%, Loko 2%. **Languages:** English (official), Mende (principal vernacular in S), Temne (principal vernacular in N), Krio (English-based Creole, a lingua franca). **Religions:** Muslim 67.1% (Sunni), ethnic religionist 19.9%, Christian 11.3%.

Geography: Total area: 27,699 sq mi, 71,740 sq km (117); **Land area:** 27,653 sq mi, 71,620 sq km. **Location:** W coast of W Africa. Guinea on N and E, Liberia on S. **Topography:** Mangrove swamps in heavily indented, 210-mi coastline. Wooded hills rise to a plateau and mountains in E. **Arable land:** 21.9%. **Capital:** Freetown, 1,309,168.

Government: Type: Presidential republic. **Head of state and govt.:** Pres. Julius Maada Bio; b. 1964; in office: Apr. 4, 2018. **Local divisions:** 4 provinces, 1 area. **Defense budget:** $26 mil. **Active troops:** 8,500.

Economy: Industries: diamond mining, iron ore, rutile and bauxite mining, small-scale mfg. (beverages, textiles, footwear). **Chief agric.:** cassava, rice, vegetables, oil palm fruit, sweet potatoes, milk. **Natural resources:** diamonds, titanium ore, bauxite, iron ore, gold, chromite. **Water:** 20,058 cu m per capita. **Electricity prod.:** 207.9 mil kWh. **Labor force:** agric. 42.7%, industry 11.9%, services 45.4%. **Unemployment:** 3.6%.

Finance: Monetary unit: Leone (SLE) (22.27 = $1 U.S.). **GDP:** $16.6 bil; **per capita GDP:** $1,931; **GDP growth:** 3.5%. **Imports** (2020): $1.4 bil; China 27%, India 11%, U.S. 6%. **Exports** (2020): $701.0 mil; Belgium 26%, China 25%, Romania 9%, UAE 6%. **Tourism** (2020): $39 mil. **Budget:** $867 mil. **Inflation:** 27.2%.

Transport: Motor vehicles: 5.1 per 1,000 pop. **Airports:** 1.

Communications: Mobile (2021): 97.7 per 100 pop. **Broadband** (2021): 21.2 per 100 pop. **Internet** (2020): 18.0%.

Health: Expend.: 8.8%. **Life expect.:** 57.5 male; 60.7 female. **Births:** 31.5 per 1,000 pop. **Deaths:** 9.1 per 1,000 pop. **Infant mortality:** 72.3 per 1,000 live births. **Undernourished:** 27.8%. **HIV:** 1.4%. **COVID-19:** 7,762 cases, 125 deaths; rates per 100,000: 97.3 cases, 1.6 deaths. 62.2% vaccinated.

Education: Compulsory: ages 6-14. **Literacy:** 47.7%.

Website: statehouse.gov.sl

The British founded Freetown, 1787, as a haven for freed slaves. Full independence arrived Apr. 27, 1961. A one-party state was established by referendum in 1978.

Mutinous soldiers ousted Pres. Joseph Momoh, Apr. 30, 1992. A coup, Jan. 16, 1996, paved the way for multiparty elections and a return to civilian rule. A peace accord, signed Nov. 30 with the Revolutionary United Front (RUF), brought a temporary halt to a civil war that had claimed over 10,000 lives in five years.

After a May 25, 1997, coup, Nigeria's military restored Pres. Ahmad Tejan Kabbah to power on Mar. 10, 1998, but RUF rebels mounted a guerrilla counteroffensive, killing thousands of civilians and mutilating thousands more. A power-sharing agreement between the Kabbah government and the RUF, July 1999, collapsed in early May 2000, but rebel leader Foday Sankoh was captured in Freetown, May 17. Government and rebel leaders declared an official end to the war Jan. 18, 2002; more than 50,000 people had died in the conflict. Kabbah won the May 14, 2002, presidential election.

Opposition leader Ernest Bai Koroma won a presidential runoff vote, Sept. 8, 2007. A 2012 cholera epidemic caused about 23,000 cases and 300 deaths. Koroma won reelection Nov. 17, 2012. An Ebola virus epidemic caused 14,124 cases and 3,956 deaths in Sierra Leone, 2013-16. After a campaign marred by violence, Julius Maada Bio, a leader of the 1992 mutiny and 1996 coup, was declared the winner, Apr. 4, 2018, of a presidential runoff election. On Feb. 7, 2019, Bio declared a national emergency in response to the high incidence of rape and other sexual violence against women. Parliament voted, July 23, 2021, to abolish capital punishment. Soaring inflation in 2022 led to violent protests in Aug. 2022, met with a deadly government response. Amid a continuing economic crisis, Bio was declared the winner of the June 24, 2023, presidential election; the opposition and international observers charged irregularities in vote counting.

Singapore
Republic of Singapore

People: Population: 5,975,383 (112). **Age distrib.:** <15: 14.8%; 65+: 13.7%. **Growth:** 0.9%. **Migrants:** 43.1%. **Pop. density:** 21,822.0 per sq mi, 8,425.5 per sq km. **Urban:** 100.0%. **Ethnic groups:** Chinese 74.2%, Malay 13.7%, Indian 8.9%, other (incl. Eurasian, Caucasian, Japanese, Filipino, Vietnamese) 3.2%. **Languages:** English, Mandarin, Malay, Tamil (all official); other Chinese dialects (incl. Hokkien, Cantonese, Teochew, Hakka). **Religions:** Chinese folk-religionist 35.5%, Christian 21.6%, Muslim 15.5% (Sunni), Buddhist 15.4% (Mahayanist 14%), Hindu 5.1% (Shaivite 3%, Vaishnavite 2%), agnostic 4.9%.
Geography: Total area: 278 sq mi, 719 sq km (177); **Land area:** 274 sq mi, 709 sq km. **Location:** Off tip of Malayan Peninsula in SE Asia. Nearest neighbors are Malaysia on N, Indonesia on S. **Topography:** Flat, formerly swampy island with 40 nearby islets. **Arable land:** 0.8%. **Capital:** Singapore, 6,080,859.
Government: Type: Parliamentary republic. **Head of state:** Pres. Tharman Shanmugaratnam; in office: Sept. 14, 2023. **Head of govt.:** Prime Min. Lee Hsien Loong; b. 1952; in office: Aug. 12, 2004. **Local divisions:** no first-order admin. divisions. **Defense budget:** $11.9 bil. **Active troops:** 51,000.
Economy: Industries: electronics, chemicals, financial services, oil drilling equip., petroleum refining, biomedical prods., scientific instruments. **Chief agric.:** poultry, eggs, vegetables, pork, duck meat, spinach. **Natural resources:** fish, deepwater ports. **Water:** 103 cu m per capita. **Electricity prod.:** 53.5 bil kWh. **Labor force:** agric. 0.3%, industry 14.4%, services 85.3%. **Unemployment:** 2.8%.
Finance: Monetary unit: Dollar (SGD) (1.36 = $1 U.S.). **GDP:** $719.1 bil; **per capita GDP:** $127,565; **GDP growth:** 3.6%. **Imports:** $609.3 bil; China 16%, Malaysia 11%, U.S. 9%, Taiwan 7%. **Exports:** $733.8 bil; China 15%, Hong Kong 13%, Malaysia 9%, U.S. 8%, Indonesia 7%. **Tourism:** $3.8 bil. **Budget (2020):** $90.3 bil (operational and development expenditures). **Inflation:** 6.1%.
Transport: Motor vehicles: 144.1 per 1,000 pop. **Airports:** 9.
Communications: Mobile: 156.5 per 100 pop. **Broadband:** 156.5 per 100 pop. **Internet:** 96.0%.
Health: Expend.: 6.1%. **Life expect.:** 83.8 male; 89.3 female. **Births:** 8.9 per 1,000 pop. **Deaths:** 4.2 per 1,000 pop. **Infant mortality:** 1.5 per 1,000 live births. **Undernourished:** NA. **HIV:** NA. **COVID-19:** 2,548,327 cases, 1,872 deaths; rates per 100,000: 43,558.6 cases, 32.0 deaths. 89.7% vaccinated.
Education: Compulsory: ages 6-11. **Literacy:** 97.1%.
Website: www.gov.sg
Founded in 1819 by Sir Thomas Stamford Raffles, Singapore was a British colony until 1959, when it became autonomous within the Commonwealth. On Sept. 16, 1963, it joined with Malaya, Sarawak, and Sabah to form the Federation of Malaysia. Tensions between Malays, dominant in the federation, and ethnic Chinese, dominant in Singapore, led to an accord under which Singapore became a separate nation, Aug. 9, 1965.
Singapore is a major port and manufacturing, banking, and commerce center. Asian immigrant workers hold many low-paying jobs. The government, dominated by the People's Action Party (PAP), has taken strong actions to keep order and suppress dissent.
Singapore's first prime min., Lee Kuan Yew (in office 1959-90), credited with building the country's strong economy, died Mar. 23, 2015. His son, Lee Hsien Loong, took office as prime min., Aug. 12, 2004. Halimah Yacob became Singapore's first female president, Sept. 14, 2017.
Nov. 2022 legislation decriminalized consensual sex between men. Tharman Shanmugaratnam, a former PAP member, won the Sept. 1, 2023, presidential election.

Slovakia
Slovak Republic

People: Population: 5,425,319 (120). **Age distrib.:** <15: 15.4%; 65+: 17.8%. **Growth:** –0.1%. **Migrants:** 3.6%. **Pop. density:** 292.1 per sq mi, 112.8 per sq km. **Urban:** 54.0%. **Ethnic groups** (by nationality): Slovak 83.8%, Hungarian 7.8%, Romani 1.2% (usu. underestimated and may be 7%-11% of pop.). **Languages:** Slovak (official), Hungarian. **Religions:** Christian 84.9% (Catholic 75.3%), agnostic 12.2%, atheist 2.9%.
Geography: Total area: 18,933 sq mi, 49,035 sq km (127); **Land area:** 18,573 sq mi, 48,105 sq km. **Location:** E central Europe. Poland on N, Hungary on S, Austria and Czechia on W, Ukraine on E. **Topography:** Carpathian Mts. in N, fertile Danube plain in S. **Arable land:** 27.6%. **Capital:** Bratislava, 440,787.

Government: Type: Parliamentary republic. **Head of state:** Pres. Zuzana Caputova; b. 1973; in office: June 15, 2019. **Head of govt.:** Prime Min. L'udovít Ódor; b. 1976; in office: May 15, 2023. **Local divisions:** 8 regions. **Defense budget:** $2.0 bil. **Active troops:** 17,950.
Economy: Industries: automobiles; metal and metal prods.; electricity, gas, coke, oil, nuclear fuel; chemicals, synthetic fibers, wood and paper prods.; machinery. **Chief agric.:** wheat, maize, sugar beet, milk, barley, rapeseed. **Natural resources:** lignite, iron ore, copper and manganese ore, salt. **Water:** 9,176 cu m per capita. **Crude oil reserves:** 9 mil bbls. **Electricity prod.:** 27.2 bil kWh. **Labor force:** agric. 2.5%, industry 36.7%, services 60.8%. **Unemployment:** 6.1%.
Finance: Monetary unit: Euro (EUR) (0.93 = $1 U.S.). **GDP:** $203.5 bil; **per capita GDP:** $37,460; **GDP growth:** 1.7%. **Imports:** $107.4 bil; Germany 18%, Czechia 18%, Poland 8%, Hungary 7%. **Exports:** $107.4 bil; Germany 22%, Czechia 11%, Poland 7%, France 7%, Hungary 6%. **Tourism:** $1.1 bil. **Budget:** $44.9 bil. **Inflation:** 12.8%.
Transport: Railways: 2,254 mi. **Motor vehicles:** 531.3 per 1,000 pop. **Airports:** 19.
Communications: Mobile: 131.9 per 100 pop. **Broadband:** 86.7 per 100 pop. **Internet:** 88.9%.
Health: Expend.: 7.2%. **Life expect.:** 73.1 male; 80.4 female. **Births:** 10.3 per 1,000 pop. **Deaths:** 11.5 per 1,000 pop. **Infant mortality:** 5.3 per 1,000 live births. **Undernourished:** 2.8%. **HIV:** <0.1%. **COVID-19:** 1,866,857 cases, 21,167 deaths; rates per 100,000: 34,204.8 cases, 387.8 deaths. 51.4% vaccinated.
Education: Compulsory: ages 5-15. **Literacy:** NA.
Website: www.government.gov.sk
Settled by Illyrian, Celtic, and Germanic peoples, Slovakia was incorporated into Great Moravia in the 9th cent. It became part of Hungary in the 11th cent. Overrun by Czech Hussites in the 15th cent., it was restored to Hungarian rule in 1526. After WWI, the Slovaks joined the Czechs of Bohemia to form the Republic of Czechoslovakia, Oct. 28, 1918.
Germany invaded Czechoslovakia, 1939, and declared Slovakia independent. Slovakia rejoined Czechoslovakia in 1945. Czechoslovakia split into two separate states—the Czech Republic and Slovakia—on Jan. 1, 1993.
Slovakia joined the EU and NATO in 2004. After a corruption scandal, Peter Pellegrini, then of the social-democratic Smer party, replaced Prime Min. Robert Fico (also of Smer), Mar. 22, 2018. Anti-corruption activist Zuzana Caputová won a Mar. 30, 2019, runoff election to become Slovakia's first female president. The center-right Ordinary People (OP) party won Feb. 29, 2020, legislative elections and governed until mid-2023. In Sept. 30, 2023, elections, Smer (led by Fico, who campaigned on pro-Russia positions) gained the most seats, but short of a majority, followed by the pro-Western Progressive Slovakia party. Negotiations began to form a coalition government.

Slovenia
Republic of Slovenia

People: Population: 2,099,790 (146). **Age distrib.:** <15: 14.5%; 65+: 22.7%. **Growth:** –0.1%. **Migrants:** 13.4%. **Pop. density:** 269.9 per sq mi, 104.2 per sq km. **Urban:** 56.1%. **Ethnic groups:** Slovene 83.1%, Serb 2%. **Languages:** Slovene (official), Croatian; Hungarian, Italian official in certain municipalities. **Religions:** Christian 81.7% (Catholic 76.3%), agnostic 11.3%, Muslim 4.1% (Sunni), atheist 2.8%.
Geography: Total area: 7,827 sq mi, 20,273 sq km (151); **Land area:** 7,780 sq mi, 20,151 sq km. **Location:** SE Europe. Italy on W, Austria on N, Hungary on NE, Croatia on SE, S. **Topography:** Mostly hilly; more than half forested. **Arable land:** 9.0%. **Capital:** Ljubljana, 286,491.
Government: Type: Parliamentary republic. **Head of state:** Pres. Natasa Pirc Musar; b. 1968; in office: Dec. 23, 2023. **Head of govt.:** Prime Min. Robert Golob; b. 1967; in office: June 1, 2022. **Local divisions:** 200 municipalities, 12 urban municipalities. **Defense budget:** $883 mil. **Active troops:** 6,400.
Economy: Industries: ferrous metallurgy and aluminum prods.; lead and zinc smelting, electronics (incl. military), trucks, automobiles, elec. power equip., wood prods. **Chief agric.:** milk, maize, wheat, grapes, barley, potatoes. **Natural resources:** lignite, lead, zinc, building stone, hydropower, forests. **Water:** 15,330 cu m per capita. **Electricity prod.:** 14.9 bil kWh. **Labor force:** agric. 4.1%, industry 30.0%, services 65.9%. **Unemployment:** 4.2%.
Finance: Monetary unit: Euro (EUR) (0.93 = $1 U.S.). **GDP:** $105.5 bil; **per capita GDP:** $50,032; **GDP growth:** 5.4%. **Imports:** $47.7 bil; Germany 14%, Italy 12%, Austria 8%, Switzerland 8%, China 7%. **Exports:** $51.6 bil; Germany 18%, Italy 11%, Croatia 8%, Austria 7%. **Tourism:** $2.0 bil. **Budget:** $23.5 bil. **Inflation:** 8.8%.
Transport: Railways: 750 mi. **Motor vehicles:** 643.4 per 1,000 pop. **Airports:** 9.
Communications: Mobile: 126.2 per 100 pop. **Broadband:** 96.0 per 100 pop. **Internet:** 88.9%.

Health: Expend. (2021): 9.2%. **Life expect.:** 79.2 male; 85.0 female. **Births:** 8.1 per 1,000 pop. **Deaths:** 10.5 per 1,000 pop. **Infant mortality:** 1.5 per 1,000 live births. **Undernourished:** <2.5%. **HIV:** <0.1%. **COVID-19:** 1,344,668 cases, 9,431 deaths; rates per 100,000: 64,158.3 cases, 450.0 deaths. 56.6% vaccinated.

Education: Compulsory: ages 6-14. **Literacy:** 99.7%.

Website: www.gov.si

The Slovenes settled in their current territory during the 6th to 8th cent. They fell under German domination in the 9th cent. After 1848, the Slovenes, divided among several Austrian provinces, began their struggle for unification. In 1918 a majority of Slovenes became part of the Kingdom of Serbs, Croats, and Slovenes, later renamed Yugoslavia.

Slovenia declared independence June 25, 1991; attained full membership in the EU and NATO in 2004; and adopted the euro Jan. 1, 2007. About 474,000 migrants (many from the Middle East and SW Asia) entered Slovenia Oct. 1, 2015-Mar. 8, 2016; Slovenia, Mar. 8, essentially closed its border to migrants. The rightist, anti-immigration Slovenian Democratic Party (SDS) won the most seats in June 3, 2018, National Assembly elections. Five center-left parties formed a coalition minority government but couldn't pass legislation. Janez Jansa of SDS became prime minister, Mar. 13, 2020. The environmentalist, pro-democracy Freedom Movement (GS) outpolled the SDS in Apr. 24, 2022, elections; Robert Golob of GS became prime minister, heading a center-left coalition government. Independent Natasa Pirc Musar, backed by Golob, defeated the SDS candidate in a Nov. 13, 2022, runoff to become Slovenia's first woman president.

Solomon Islands

People: Population: 714,766 (163). **Age distrib.:** <15: 31.1%; 65+: 5.1%. **Growth:** 1.7%. **Migrants:** 0.4%. **Pop. density:** 66.1 per sq mi, 25.5 per sq km. **Urban:** 26.0%. **Ethnic groups:** Melanesian 95.3%, Polynesian 3.1%. **Languages:** Melanesian pidgin (lingua franca in much of country), English (official), 120 Indigenous langs. **Religions:** Christian 95.3% (Protestant 68.2%, Catholic 20.5%), ethnic religionist 3.1%.

Geography: Total area: 11,157 sq mi, 28,896 sq km (140); **Land area:** 10,805 sq mi, 27,986 sq km. **Location:** Melanesian Archipelago in W Pacific O. Nearest neighbor is Papua New Guinea to W. **Topography:** 10 large volcanic, rugged islands; 4 groups of smaller islands. **Arable land:** 0.8%. **Capital:** Honiara, 81,801.

Government: Type: Parliamentary democracy under constitutional monarchy. **Head of state:** King Charles III, rep. by Gov.-Gen. David Vunagi; in office: July 7, 2019. **Head of govt.:** Prime Min. Manasseh Sogavare; b. 1955; in office: Apr. 24, 2019. **Local divisions:** 9 provinces, 1 city. **Defense budget/active troops:** NA.

Economy: Industrio: fioh (tuna), mining, timber. **Chief agric.:** oil palm fruit, sweet potatoes, coconuts, taro, yams, fruit. **Natural resources:** fish, forests, gold, bauxite, phosphates, lead, zinc, nickel. **Water:** 65,076 cu m per capita. **Electricity prod.:** 115.4 mil kWh. **Labor force:** agric. 38.0%, industry 10.9%, services 51.1%. **Unemployment:** 1.5%.

Finance: Monetary unit: Dollar (SBD) (8.45 = $1 U.S.). **GDP:** $1.9 bil; **per capita GDP:** $2,654; **GDP growth:** –4.1%. **Imports:** $619.5 mil; China 24%, Australia 13%, South Korea 12%, Singapore 12%, Malaysia 10%. **Exports:** $413.7 mil; China 65%, Italy 9%, India 6%. **Tourism** (2020): $6 mil. **Budget:** $537 mil. **Inflation:** 5.5%.

Transport: Airports: 1.

Communications: Mobile (2021): 67.0 per 100 pop. **Broadband** (2021): 18.1 per 100 pop. **Internet:** 36.1%.

Health: Expend.: 4.4%. **Life expect.:** 74.3 male; 79.7 female. **Births:** 22.3 per 1,000 pop. **Deaths:** 4.0 per 1,000 pop. **Infant mortality:** 19.5 per 1,000 live births. **Undernourished:** 19.0%. **HIV:** NA. **COVID-19:** 21,611 cases, 153 deaths; rates per 100,000: 3,146.2 cases, 22.3 deaths. 37.0% vaccinated.

Education: Compulsory: NA. **Literacy:** NA.

Website: www.parliament.gov.sb

The Solomon Isls. were inhabited by Melanesians. Britain established a protectorate in the 1890s over most of the group. The islands, including Guadalcanal, saw major WWII battles. They achieved self-government, Jan. 2, 1976, and formal independence, July 7, 1978.

To restore order after years of factional violence, an Australian-led regional security force (RAMSI) arrived in July 2003.

Former prime min. Manasseh Sogavare (2000-01, 2006-07) again became head of government following Nov. 19, 2014, parliamentary elections. RAMSI formally ended June 2017. Sogavare, Nov. 6, 2017, lost a no-confidence vote, but he returned as prime minister after Apr. 3, 2019, elections.

Seeking Chinese aid, the government in 2019 switched diplomatic relations from Taiwan to China. A security agreement with China was signed in 2022. Parliament, Sept. 8, 2022, approved a constitutional amendment postponing 2023 elections. The U.S., in 2023, reopened an embassy in the Solomon Islands, ending a 30-year absence. Visiting China in July 2023, Sogavare signed police cooperation and other agreements.

Somalia
Federal Republic of Somalia

People: Population: 12,693,796 (78). **Age distrib.:** <15: 41.5%; 65+: 2.7%. **Growth:** 2.5%. **Migrants:** 0.4%. **Pop. density:** 52.4 per sq mi, 20.2 per sq km. **Urban:** 47.9%. **Ethnic groups:** Somali 85%, Bantu and other non-Somali 15%. **Languages:** Somali, Arabic (both official); Italian; English. **Religions:** Muslim 99.9% (Sunni [official] 98%).

Geography: Total area: 246,201 sq mi, 637,657 sq km (44); **Land area:** 242,216 sq mi, 627,337 sq km. **Location:** Eastern horn of Africa. Djibouti, Ethiopia, Kenya on W. **Topography:** Coastline extends for 1,700 mi. Hills cover the N; center and S are flat. **Arable land:** 1.8%. **Capital:** Mogadishu, 2,610,483. **Cities:** Hargeysa, 1,127,198.

Government: Type: Federal parliamentary republic. **Head of state:** Pres. Hassan Sheikh Mohamud; b. 1955; in office: May 23, 2022. **Head of govt.:** Prime Min. Hamza Abdi Barre; in office: June 25, 2022. **Local divisions:** 18 regions. **Defense budget:** NA. **Active troops:** 13,900.

Economy: Industries: light industries incl. sugar refining, textiles, wireless communication. **Chief agric.:** camel milk, milk, sheep milk, goat milk, sugarcane, fruit. **Natural resources:** uranium, largely unexploited reserves of iron ore, tin, gypsum, bauxite, copper, salt, nat. gas. **Water:** 925 cu m per capita. **Electricity prod.:** 407.9 mil kWh. **Labor force:** agric. 26.3%, industry 17.7%, services 56.0%. **Unemployment:** 20.0%.

Finance: Monetary unit: Shilling (SOS) (558.56 = $1 U.S.). **GDP:** $24.0 bil; **per capita GDP:** $1,364; **GDP growth:** 4.8%. **Imports** (2018): $94.4 bil; UAE 32%, China 20%, India 17%, Turkey 7%. **Exports** (2014): $819.0 mil; UAE 47%, Saudi Arabia 19%. **Budget** (2014): $151.1 mil. **Inflation** (2016-17): 1.5%.

Transport: Airports: 8.

Communications: Mobile: 50.3 per 100 pop. **Broadband:** 2.5 per 100 pop. **Internet** (2017): 2.0%.

Health: Expend.: NA. **Life expect.:** 53.8 male; 58.6 female. **Births:** 37.7 per 1,000 pop. **Deaths:** 11.4 per 1,000 pop. **Infant mortality:** 85.1 per 1,000 live births. **Undernourished:** 48.7%. **HIV:** NA. **COVID-19:** 27,334 cases, 1,361 deaths; rates per 100,000: 172.0 cases, 8.6 deaths. 48.2% vaccinated.

Education: Compulsory: NA. **Literacy:** NA.

Website: villasomalia.gov.so

British Somaliland (present-day N Somalia) was formed in the 19th cent., as was Italian Somaliland (now central and S Somalia). Italy lost its African colonies in WWII. British Somaliland gained independence, June 26, 1960, and by prearrangement, merged, July 1, with the UN Trust Territory of Somalia to create the independent Somali Republic.

On Oct. 15, 1969, Somalia's first civilian president, Abdirashid Ali Sharmarke, was assassinated. Six days later, Maj. Gen. Muhammad Siad Barre led a military coup. In 1970, he declared the country a socialist state.

Somalia has laid claim to Ogaden, the huge eastern region of Ethiopia, peopled mostly by Somalis. Some 11,000 Cuban troops with Soviet arms defeated Somali army troops and ethnic Somali rebels in Ethiopia, 1978. Guerrilla fighting in Ogaden continued until 1988, when a peace agreement was reached with Ethiopia.

Fighting in Mogadishu led Siad Barre to flee the capital, Jan. 1991. Fighting between rival factions caused 40,000 casualties, 1991-92, and by mid-1992, the civil war, drought, and banditry combined to produce a famine that threatened some 1.5 mil people.

U.S. troops and the UN worked to safeguard food delivery, 1991-93, resulting in significant U.S. and other casualties; a failed mission Oct. 3-4, 1993, left 18 U.S. troops and more than 500 Somalis dead. The U.S. withdrew its peacekeeping forces Mar. 25, 1994.

When the last UN troops pulled out, Mar. 3, 1995, armed factions controlled different regions. A peace deal Jan. 29, 2004, led to the Aug. 22 inauguration of a transitional parliament, Somalia's first legislature in 13 years. Meeting in Nairobi, Kenya, the parliament chose Abdullahi Yusuf Ahmed as president. On June 5, 2005, an Islamist militia took over Mogadishu. Islamists held much of the central and southern regions.

With aid from Ethiopian troops, transitional govt. forces recaptured Mogadishu in Dec. 2006. The UN Security Council authorized, Feb. 20, 2007, an African Union peacekeeping mission to Somalia (AMISOM). An upsurge of fighting in Mogadishu, Feb.-Apr., killed hundreds of people and caused 350,000 to flee. Bombings and kidnappings escalated in 2007-08; many of the attacks on transitional authorities and their allies were blamed on al-Shabab, an al-Qaeda ally.

After Pres. Yusuf resigned Dec. 29, 2008, the transitional parliament, meeting in Djibouti Jan. 31, 2009, elected a moderate Islamist, Sheikh Sharif Sheikh Ahmed. Meanwhile, pirates carried out more than 200 attacks off the Horn of Africa in 2009. Pirates and Islamist insurgents continued to disrupt famine relief efforts in 2010-11. Pressured by AMISOM forces, al-Shabab pulled out of Mogadishu, Aug. 6, 2011, but continued to control much of southern Somalia. A caretaker government was sworn in Aug. 20, 2012, and the new parliament elected Hassan Sheikh Mohamud president Sept. 10. Bombings and other attacks by al-Shabab, in Mogadishu and elsewhere, continued. AMISOM and Somali forces had pushed al-Shabab out of major towns by mid-2015. However, the group's terrorist attacks continued, and it retook territory in subsequent years.

Delayed by violence, late 2016 indirect elections resulted in the seating of a new bicameral parliament Dec. 27. Parliament, Feb. 8, 2017, elected former Prime Min. Mohamed Abdullahi Mohamed (2010-11) as Somalia's president. He pledged stronger action against Islamist militants, but further deadly al-Shabab attacks occurred. A truck bombing in Mogadishu, Oct. 14, 2017, killed more than 500. Combat and terrorist attacks continued, 2018-23. Al-Shabab car bombings in Mogadishu, Oct. 29, 2022, left more than 100 dead.

U.S. forces assisted Somali government forces and AMISOM troops. AMISOM had about 19,000 troops in Somalia on Apr. 1, 2022, when its mission officially ended. It was replaced by the African Union Transition Mission in Somalia (ATMIS), under which Somali government forces would, over time, take the lead role in fighting al-Shabab.

Delayed indirect legislative elections were completed Apr. 2022, and on May 15, Hassan Sheikh Mohamud was again elected president by legislators. Ongoing drought and warfare left millions of Somalis facing food insecurity in 2022. Heavy rains and flooding in central Somalia, May 2023, displaced more than 245,000.

South Africa
Republic of South Africa

People: Population: 58,048,332 (25). **Age distrib.:** <15: 27.4%; 65+: 7.3%. **Growth:** 0.9%. **Migrants:** 4.8%. **Pop. density:** 123.8 per sq mi, 47.8 per sq km. **Urban:** 68.8%. **Ethnic groups:** Black African 80.9%, colored (South African term for persons of mixed-race ancestry) 8.8%, white 7.8%, Indian/Asian 2.6%. **Languages:** isiZulu, isiXhosa, Afrikaans, Sepedi, Setswana, English, Sesotho, Xitsonga, siSwati, Tshivenda, isiNdebele (all official). **Religions:** Christian 81.6% (independent 47.6%, Protestant 26.6%), ethnic religionist 6.8%, agnostic 5.9%, Hindu 2.4%.

Geography: Total area: 470,693 sq mi, 1,219,090 sq km (24); **Land area:** 468,909 sq mi, 1,214,470 sq km. **Location:** Southern extreme of Africa. Namibia, Botswana, Zimbabwe on N; Mozambique, Eswatini on E; surrounds Lesotho. **Topography:** Large interior plateau reaches close to the country's 1,739-mi coastline. Few major rivers or lakes. Rainfall is sparse in W, more plentiful in E. **Arable land:** 9.9%. **Capital:** Cape Town (legislative), 4,890,280; Pretoria (administrative), 2,818,100; Bloemfontein (judicial), 598,383. **Cities:** Johannesburg, 6,198,016; Ekurhuleni, 4,118,327; Durban (Ethekwini), 3,228,003.

Government: Type: Parliamentary republic. **Head of state and govt.:** Pres. Cyril Ramaphosa; b. 1952; in office: Feb. 15, 2018. **Local divisions:** 9 provinces. **Defense budget:** $3.1 bil. **Active troops:** 74,000.

Economy: Industries: mining (platinum, gold, chromium), auto assembly, metalworking, machinery, textiles, iron and steel, chemicals, fertilizer, foodstuffs. **Chief agric.:** sugarcane, maize, milk, potatoes, grapes, poultry. **Natural resources:** gold, chromium, antimony, coal, iron ore, manganese, nickel, phosphates, tin, rare earth elements, uranium, gem diamonds, platinum, copper, vanadium, salt, nat. gas. **Water:** 866 cu m per capita. **Crude oil reserves:** 15 mil bbls. **Electricity prod.:** 221.5 bil kWh. **Labor force:** agric. 21.3%, industry 17.3%, services 61.4%. **Unemployment:** 29.8%.

Finance: Monetary unit: Rand (ZAR) (18.56 = $1 U.S.). **GDP:** $952.6 bil; **per capita GDP:** $15,905; **GDP growth:** 2.0%. **Imports:** $104.8 bil; China 18%, Germany 11%, U.S. 6%. **Exports:** $130.9 bil; China 15%, UK 8%, Germany 7%, U.S. 6%, India 5%. **Tourism:** $2.1 bil. **Budget** (2020): $121.2 bil. **Inflation:** 7.0%.

Transport: Railways: 13,040 mi. **Motor vehicles:** 282.0 per 1,000 pop. **Airports:** 130.

Communications: Mobile: 167.4 per 100 pop. **Broadband:** 135.1 per 100 pop. **Internet:** 72.3%.

Health: Expend.: 8.6%. **Life expect.:** 69.4 male; 72.6 female. **Births:** 18.3 per 1,000 pop. **Deaths:** 7.2 per 1,000 pop. **Infant mortality:** 24.4 per 1,000 live births. **Undernourished:** 7.9%. **HIV:** 17.8%. **COVID-19:** 4,072,533 cases, 102,595 deaths; rates per 100,000: 6,866.7 cases, 173.0 deaths. 35.5% vaccinated.

Education: Compulsory: ages 7-15. **Literacy:** 95.0%.

Website: www.gov.za

San and KhoiKhoi people were the original inhabitants. Bantus, including Zulu, Xhosa, Swazi, and Sotho, occupied the area from northeastern to southern South Africa before the 17th cent.

The Dutch settled the Cape of Good Hope area, beginning in the 17th cent. Britain seized the Cape, 1806. Many Dutch trekked north and founded two republics, Transvaal and Orange Free State. Diamonds were discovered, 1867, and gold, 1886. The Dutch (Boers) resented encroachments by the British and others; the Anglo-Boer War followed, 1899-1902. Britain won and created, May 31, 1910, the Union of South Africa, incorporating two British colonies (Cape and Natal) with Transvaal and Orange Free State. After a referendum, the Union became the Republic of South Africa, May 31, 1961, and withdrew from the Commonwealth (it rejoined in 1994).

Daniel Malan's National Party, elected in 1948, made the policy of separate development of the races, or apartheid, official. Under apartheid, the majority-Black population was restricted to living and working in designated areas, attended separate schools, could hold only certain jobs, and were paid less than whites for similar work. Only whites could vote or run for public office. Persons of Asian Indian ancestry and those of mixed race ("coloureds") had limited political rights.

Protests against apartheid were suppressed. At Sharpeville on Mar. 21, 1960, government troops killed 69 Black protesters. At least 600 persons, mostly Bantus, were killed in 1976 anti-apartheid riots. In 1986, Nobel Peace Prize winner Bishop Desmond Tutu called for Western nations to apply sanctions against South Africa to force an end to apartheid. On May 19, 1986, South Africa attacked guerrilla strongholds of the anti-apartheid African National Congress (ANC) in neighboring countries.

Some 2 mil South African Black workers staged a strike, June 6-8, 1988. Pres. P. W. Botha, head of the government since 1978, resigned Aug. 14, 1989, and was replaced by F. W. de Klerk. In 1990 the government lifted its ban on the ANC. Anti-apartheid leader Nelson Mandela was freed Feb. 11 after more than 27 years in prison.

In 1993 negotiators agreed on basic principles for a new democratic constitution, and Mandela and de Klerk shared the Nobel Peace Prize. South Africa's partially self-governing Black territories, or "homelands," were incorporated into a national system of nine provinces. The ANC won elections Apr. 26-29, 1994, making Mandela president. The predominantly-Zulu Inkatha Freedom Party won control of the legislature in a mainly Zulu province. By then, fighting between the ANC and Inkatha had killed more than 14,000 people in the Zulu region.

A post-apartheid constitution became law Dec. 10, 1996. The ANC won elections, June 2, 1999, and ANC leader Thabo Mbeki became president. South Africa, Nov. 30, 2006, became the first African country to legalize same-sex marriage.

Mbeki's former deputy president, Jacob Zuma, became president after Apr. 22, 2009, elections. Despite corruption charges, Zuma was reelected president by the National Assembly, May 21, 2014. With the economy weak and claims of corruption continuing, Zuma resigned Feb. 14, 2018. The ANC's Cyril Ramaphosa replaced him. The ANC retained a parliamentary majority in May 8, 2019, elections, and the National Assembly reelected Ramaphosa president, May 22, 2019. The jailing, July 7, 2021, of former Pres. Zuma for failing to cooperate with a corruption inquiry triggered violent protests and looting that left hundreds dead.

In the early 2020s, South Africa was the African country hit hardest by the COVID-19 pandemic, in terms of both total confirmed cases and total confirmed deaths.

At least 77 people died after fire gutted an illegally occupied, overcrowded, and unsafe building in Johannesburg, Aug. 31, 2023.

South Sudan
Republic of South Sudan

People: Population: 12,118,379 (80). **Age distrib.:** <15: 41.9%; 65+: 2.6%. **Growth:** 4.8%. **Migrants:** 7.9%. **Pop. density:** 49.7 per sq mi, 19.2 per sq km. **Urban:** 21.2%. **Ethnic groups:** Dinka (Jieng) 35%-40%, Nuer (Naath) approx. 15%, Shilluk (Chollo), Azande, Bari, Kakwa, Kuku, Murle, Mandari, Didinga. **Languages:** English (official), Arabic (incl. Juba, Sudanese variants), ethnic langs. **Religions:** Christian 61.3% (Catholic 38.3%, Protestant 21.9%), ethnic religionist 31.0%, Muslim 7.1% (Sunni).

Geography: Total area: 248,777 sq mi, 644,329 sq km (42). **Location:** NE Africa. Sudan on N, Uganda and Kenya on S, Ethiopia on E, Central African Rep. and Dem. Rep. of the Congo on W. **Topography:** The White Nile R. flows N through center of country and feeds the Sudd, a swampy area occupying more than 15% of the country's center; it is one of the world's largest wetlands. **Arable land:** 3.8%. **Capital:** Juba, 459,342.

Government: Type: Presidential republic. **Head of state and govt.:** Pres. Salva Kiir Mayardit; b. 1951; in office: July 9, 2011. **Local divisions:** 10 states. **Defense budget:** $64 mil. **Active troops:** 53,000.

Economy: Chief agric.: milk, sorghum, vegetables, cassava, goat milk, fruit. **Natural resources:** hydropower, gold, diamonds, petroleum, hardwoods, limestone, iron ore, copper, chromium ore, zinc, tungsten, mica, silver. **Water:** 4,422 cu m per capita. **Electricity prod.:** 569.3 mil kWh. **Labor force:** agric. 62.1%, industry 13.1%, services 24.7%. **Unemployment:** 13.0%.

Finance: Monetary unit: Pound (SSP) (1,008.43 = $1 U.S.). **GDP:** NA; **per capita GDP:** NA; **GDP growth:** NA. **Imports:** $4.0 bil; UAE 37%, Kenya 18%, China 18%. **Exports:** $4.7 bil; China 88%. **Budget:** $1.9 bil. **Inflation:** −6.7%.

Transport: Railways: 154 mi. **Airports:** 4.

Communications: Mobile: 30.0 per 100 pop. **Broadband:** 7.0 per 100 pop. **Internet** (2020): 6.5%.

Health: Expend.: 5.3%. **Life expect.:** 57.9 male; 61.6 female. **Births:** 37.1 per 1,000 pop. **Deaths:** 9.2 per 1,000 pop. **Infant mortality:** 61.6 per 1,000 live births. **Undernourished:** 21.4%. **HIV:** 1.9%. **COVID-19:** 18,368 cases, 138 deaths; rates per 100,000: 164.1 cases, 1.2 deaths. 37.7% vaccinated.

Education: Compulsory: ages 6-13. **Literacy:** 34.5%.

Website: www.eservices.gov.ss

South Sudan was a region of the Republic of the Sudan when that country became independent in 1956. Northerners (mostly Arab Muslims) dominated, while southerners (mostly Black Africans who practiced Christianity or traditional religions) were marginalized. Southern rebels waged war against the north, 1955-72, until an agreement was reached offering regional self-government for the south. Oil was discovered in the south in 1978.

Civil war broke out again in 1983. Fighting and related famine cost an estimated 2 mil lives and displaced millions of southerners. A peace accord was signed in 2005. A power-sharing agreement allowed for an independence referendum.

Almost 99% of southern Sudanese who voted in the referendum, Jan. 9-15, 2011, supported secession. The UN Security Council, July 8, authorized a peacekeeping force (UNMISS) for the area. South Sudan attained full independence July 9, 2011.

Pres. Salva Kiir fired Vice Pres. Riek Machar, July 23, 2013. Heavy fighting broke out in Juba in Dec. 2013 between government troops and rebels led by Machar. Forces of Kiir and Machar (who belong to different ethnic groups) battled throughout the country in 2014-15. Kiir and Machar signed a peace accord Aug. 2015. Renewed heavy fighting began July 7, 2016. A new peace agreement was signed Sept. 12, 2018. A U.S.-funded study reported, Sept. 26, 2018, that South Sudan's civil war had caused about 383,000 "excess deaths" since late 2013. After Kiir and Machar agreed in Feb. 2020 on a new transitional government, leading to national elections, Machar was sworn in as first vice president Feb. 22. However, some violence continued. As of Aug. 31, 2023, more than 2.25 mil South Sudanese were internally displaced. About 2.3 mil were refugees in neighboring countries in mid-2023. As of July 31, 2023, UNMISS had more than 15,000 uniformed personnel in South Sudan. Millions of South Sudanese faced hunger in 2023 as a result of drought, floods, and food shortages related to the war in Ukraine.

Spain
Kingdom of Spain

People: Population: 47,222,613 (32). **Age distrib.:** <15: 13.4%; 65+: 20.5%. **Growth:** 0.1%. **Migrants:** 14.6%. **Pop. density:** 245.1 per sq mi, 94.6 per sq km. **Urban:** 81.6%. **Ethnic groups** (by birth country): Spanish 84.8%. **Languages:** Castilian Spanish (official); Catalan, Galician, Basque (all official in areas). **Religions:** Christian 85.0% (Catholic [official] 81.7%), agnostic 9.6%, Muslim 3.4% (Sunni).

Geography: Total area: 195,124 sq mi, 505,370 sq km (52); **Land area:** 192,657 sq mi, 498,980 sq km. **Location:** SW Europe. Portugal on W; France, Andorra on N; Morocco to S. **Topography:** High, arid plateau broken by mountain ranges and river valleys in interior. The NW is heavily watered, the S has lowlands and a Medit. climate. **Arable land:** 23.1%. **Capital:** Madrid, 6,751,374. **Cities:** Barcelona, 5,687,356.

Government: Type: Parliamentary constitutional monarchy. **Head of state:** King Felipe VI; b. 1968; in office: June 19, 2014. **Head of govt.:** Pres. Pedro Sánchez Pérez-Castejón; b. 1972; in office: June 2, 2018. **Local divisions:** 17 autonomous communities, 2 autonomous cities. **Defense budget:** $14.7 bil. **Active troops:** 124,150.

Economy: Industries: textiles/apparel (incl. footwear), food/beverages, metals/metal manufactures, chemicals, shipbuilding, automobiles, machine tools, tourism. **Chief agric.:** barley, milk, wheat, olives, grapes, tomatoes. **Natural resources:** coal, lignite, iron ore, copper, lead, zinc, uranium, tungsten, mercury, pyrites, magnesite, fluorspar, gypsum, sepiolite, kaolin, potash, hydropower. **Water:** 2,385 cu m per capita. **Crude oil reserves:** 150 mil bbls. **Electricity prod.:** 259.4 bil kWh. **Labor force:** agric. 4.1%, industry 20.2%, services 75.8%. **Unemployment:** 13.0%.

Finance: Monetary unit: Euro (EUR) (0.93 = $1 U.S.). **GDP:** $2.2 tril; **per capita GDP:** $45,825; **GDP growth:** 5.5%. **Imports:** $476.7 bil; Germany 13%, France 11%, China 8%, Italy 7%. **Exports:** $497.9 bil; France 15%, Germany 11%, Italy 8%, Portugal 8%, UK 7%. **Tourism:** $34.5 bil. **Budget:** $586.0 bil. **Inflation:** 8.4%.

Transport: Railways: 9,624 mi. **Motor vehicles:** 639.2 per 1,000 pop. **Airports:** 102.

Communications: Mobile: 124.1 per 100 pop. **Broadband:** 110.0 per 100 pop. **Internet:** 94.5%.

Health: Expend.: 10.7%. **Life expect.:** 80.1 male; 85.6 female. **Births:** 7.1 per 1,000 pop. **Deaths:** 10.1 per 1,000 pop. **Infant mortality:** 2.4 per 1,000 live births. **Undernourished:** <2.5%. **HIV:** 0.2%. **COVID-19:** 13,980,340 cases, 121,852 deaths; rates per 100,000: 29,536.4 cases, 257.4 deaths. 79.0% vaccinated.

Education: Compulsory: ages 6-15. **Literacy:** 98.6%.

Website: www.lamoncloa.gob.es

Settled by Iberians, Basques, and Celts, Spain was successively ruled (wholly or in part) by Carthage, Rome, and the Visigoths. Muslims invaded Iberia from N Africa in 711. Reconquest of the peninsula by Christians from the N laid the foundations of modern Spain. In 1469 the kingdoms of Aragon and Castile were united by the marriage of Ferdinand II and Isabella I. Moorish rule ended with the fall of Granada, 1492, the year Spain's large Jewish community was expelled.

Spain established a colonial empire after Columbus's 1492 "discovery" of America. Cortés conquered Mexico, and Pizarro conquered Peru. Spain lost most of its American colonies in the early 19th cent. and Cuba, the Philippines, and Puerto Rico in the Spanish-American War, 1898.

Primo de Rivera became dictator, 1923. King Alfonso XIII revoked the dictatorship, 1930, but was forced into exile in 1931. A republic was proclaimed, which disestablished the church, curtailed its privileges, and secularized education. A Popular Front of socialists, Communists, republicans, and anarchists governed 1936-39.

Army officers under Francisco Franco revolted, 1936. Some 500,000 to 1 mil died in the Spanish Civil War before Franco's Nationalist forces won a complete victory Apr. 1, 1939. Franco ruled as a dictator. Spain was officially neutral in WWII but had cordial relations with Nazi Germany for most of the war.

After Franco's death, Nov. 20, 1975, Prince Juan Carlos became king. In free elections, June 1977, moderates and democratic socialists won the most votes. The king thwarted a 1981 coup attempt by right-wing military officers. The Socialist Workers' Party (PSOE), under Felipe González Márquez, won four consecutive general elections, 1982-93, but lost to a coalition of conservative and regional parties, 1996.

Islamic extremists bombed four commuter trains in central Madrid, Mar. 11, 2004, killing 191 people. The PSOE won elections three days later. Spain legalized same-sex marriage in 2005.

Spain's economy suffered during the worldwide financial crisis that began in 2008; in May 2010, as the budget deficit mounted, the government introduced austerity measures to reassure international lenders. Mariano Rajoy's conservative Popular Party (PP) won Nov. 2011 elections. Spain received a 100-bil euro EU bailout for its ailing banks in 2012. Spain's unemployment rate surpassed 26% in 2013. GDP began growing in 2014, after five years of decline.

Juan Carlos abdicated in favor of his son, who became King Felipe VI, June 19, 2014. Hurt by corruption scandals, the PP lost support in Dec. 20, 2015, and June 26, 2016, legislative elections, but Rajoy formed a minority govt., Oct. 31, 2016.

In one of a series of events linked by police to an Islamist extremist cell in Catalonia, 14 people were killed and more than 100 injured in Barcelona, Aug. 17, 2017, when a terrorist drove a van through a crowded pedestrian area.

Rajoy lost a no-confidence vote, June 1, 2018; the PSOE's Pedro Sánchez became prime min. After Apr. 28 and Nov. 10, 2019, elections, Sánchez formed a new coalition minority government, Jan. 7, 2020.

Spain was the European entry point for almost 215,000 African and Middle Eastern migrants (most arriving by boat), 2018-22. More than 35,000 arrived, Jan. to mid-Sept. 2023 (over half reaching the Canary Isls.). Thousands died attempting dangerous sea crossings.

Spain (incl. the Canary Isls.) experienced extreme summer heat, drought, and wildfires in 2022 and 2023, a possible impact of climate change.

July 23, 2023, elections were inconclusive. The PP won more seats than Sánchez's PSOE, but both fell short of a majority.

With a 1-0 victory over England, Aug. 20, 2023, Spain won the FIFA Women's World Cup soccer tournament. The head of Spain's soccer federation, provisionally suspended by FIFA and facing a possible criminal charge for apparently forcibly kissing a player after the game, resigned Sept. 10.

Catalonia and the **Basque Country** were granted autonomy, Jan. 1980, following approval in referendums. But Basque extremists pushed for independence. The Basque separatist group ETA carried out bombings that killed about 830 since 1968. ETA declared a unilateral cease-fire in 2011 and said in 2018 that it was disbanding. In Catalonia, voters approved expanded home-rule, June 18, 2006.

Separatist parties won Catalonia's regional parliamentary elections Sept. 27, 2015. Catalonia scheduled a separation referendum for Oct. 1, 2017, but Spanish authorities took steps to interfere with balloting. After the regional parliament, Oct. 27, voted to declare independence, the national government dissolved the parliament and removed pro-independence regional president Carles Puigdemont from office. In new regional parliamentary elections, Dec. 21, separatists again won a majority.

In Feb. 14, 2021, elections, pro-independence parties won a majority. Regional president Pere Aragones called for negotiations with the Spanish govt. Website: web.gencat.cat

The **Balearic Isls.** in the W Mediterranean, 1,927 sq mi, is an autonomous community of Spain; they include Majorca (Mallorca; capital Palma de Mallorca), Minorca, Cabrera, Ibiza, and Formentera. The **Canary** Isls., 2,807 sq mi, an autonomous community in the Atlantic W of Morocco, includes the islands of Tenerife, La Palma, La Gomera, El Hierro, Gran Canaria, Fuerteventura, and Lanzarote; Las Palmas and Santa Cruz are thriving ports.

Ceuta and **Melilla**, small Spanish enclaves on Morocco's Mediterranean coast, gained limited autonomy in Sept. 1994. In 2014-23, thousands of African and Middle Eastern migrants crossed the borders between Morocco and the enclaves.

Spain has sought the return of **Gibraltar**, in British hands since 1704.

Sri Lanka
Democratic Socialist Republic of Sri Lanka

People: Population: 23,326,272 (58). **Age distrib.:** <15: 23.0%; 65+: 12.1%. **Growth:** 0.6%. **Migrants:** 0.2%. **Pop. density:** 934.8 per sq mi, 360.9 per sq km. **Urban:** 19.2%. **Ethnic groups:** Sinhalese 74.9%, Sri Lankan Tamil 11.2%, Sri Lankan Moor 9.2%, Indian Tamil 4.2%. **Languages:** Sinhala, Tamil (both official and national); English (commonly used in govt.). **Religions:** Buddhist (official) 67.8% (Theravada), Hindu 12.9% (Shaivite 9%), Christian 9.4%, Muslim 9.2% (Sunni).

Geography: Total area: 25,332 sq mi, 65,610 sq km (120); **Land area:** 24,954 sq mi, 64,630 sq km. **Location:** Indian O. off SE coast of India. **Topography:** Coastal area and N half are flat; S central area is hilly and mountainous. **Arable land:** 22.2%. **Capital:** Colombo (commercial), 632,543; Sri Jayewardenepura Kotte (legislative), 103,248.

Government: Type: Presidential republic. **Head of state and govt.:** Pres. Ranil Wickremesinghe; b. 1949; in office: July 20, 2022. **Local divisions:** 9 provinces. **Defense budget:** $1.2 bil. **Active troops:** 255,000.

Economy: Industries: rubber, tea, coconuts, tobacco and other agric. commodities; telecom, insurance, banking; tourism, shipping; clothing, textiles; cement, petroleum refining. **Chief agric.:** rice, coconuts, sugarcane, plantains, milk, tea. **Natural resources:** limestone, graphite, mineral sands, gems, phosphates, clay, hydropower. **Water:** 2,466 cu m per capita. **Electricity prod.:** 16.4 bil kWh. **Labor force:** agric. 25.7%, industry 27.9%, services 46.4%. **Unemployment:** 6.7%.

Finance: Monetary unit: Rupee (LKR) (323.73 = $1 U.S.). **GDP:** $319.5 bil; **per capita GDP:** $14,405; **GDP growth:** –7.8%. **Imports** (2020): $18.3 bil; India 24%, China 23%, Singapore 7%, UAE 6%. **Exports** (2020): $13.1 bil; U.S. 24%, India 8%, UK 7%, Germany 7%. **Tourism:** $507 mil. **Budget:** $17.5 bil. **Inflation:** 49.7%.

Transport: Railways: 971 mi. **Motor vehicles:** 68.8 per 1,000 pop. **Airports:** 11.

Communications: Mobile: 143.1 per 100 pop. **Broadband:** 75.0 per 100 pop. **Internet:** 44.5%.

Health: Expend.: 4.1%. **Life expect.:** 73.6 male; 79.8 female. **Births:** 14.6 per 1,000 pop. **Deaths:** 7.4 per 1,000 pop. **Infant mortality:** 6.8 per 1,000 live births. **Undernourished:** 5.3%. **HIV:** <0.1%. **COVID-19:** 672,575 cases, 16,882 deaths; rates per 100,000: 3,140.9 cases, 78.8 deaths. 68.9% vaccinated.

Education: Compulsory: ages 5-15. **Literacy:** 92.4%.

Website: www.gov.lk

The island was known to the ancient world as Taprobane (Greek for copper-colored) and later as Serendip (from Arabic). Colonists from N India subdued the Indigenous Veddahs about 543 BCE; their descendants, the Buddhist Sinhalese, still form most of the population. Hindu descendants of Tamil immigrants from S India are the largest minority ethnic group.

Parts were occupied by the Portuguese in 1505 and the Dutch in 1658. The British seized the island in 1796. It became an independent member of the Commonwealth as Ceylon in 1948 before changing its name to Sri Lanka May 22, 1972.

Prime Min. Solomon W. R. D. Bandaranaike was assassinated Sept. 25, 1959. His widow, Sirimavo Bandaranaike, served as prime min. 1960-65, 1970-77, 1994-2000. In the 1970s, thousands of ultra-leftists were executed, while massive land reform and nationalization of foreign-owned plantations took place.

Tensions between Sinhalese and Tamil separatists erupted in the early 1980s and turned into a 20-year civil war that killed more than 60,000; another 20,000, mostly young Tamils, "disappeared" while in government custody. Pres. Ranasinghe Premadasa was assassinated May 1, 1993, by a Tamil rebel. A truce intended to bring an end to the civil war was signed Feb. 22, 2002.

More than 31,000 died in the Dec. 26, 2004, Indian Ocean tsunami. Prime Min. Mahinda Rajapaksa won the 2005 presidential election and was reelected in 2010. Thousands died during more than three years of fighting among government forces, paramilitary groups, and Tamil rebels beginning in Dec. 2005. Tamil leader Vellupillai Prabhakaran was killed May 18-19, 2009, and Pres. Rajapaksa formally declared victory. Maithripala Sirisena defeated Rajapaksa in the Jan. 8, 2015, presidential election.

Loans and investments from China have financed large infrastructure projects in recent years. More than 250 died Easter Sunday, Apr. 21, 2019, in suicide bombings at churches and other sites carried out by Islamist extremists. Gotabaya Rajapaksa, brother of the former president, won the Nov. 16, 2019, presidential election. He named Mahinda Rajapaksa prime min.

Amid a financial crisis and violent protests against widespread shortages and mismanagement of the economy, Mahinda Rajapaksa resigned, May 9, 2022, and was replaced as prime min., May 12, by Ranil Wickremesinghe. As protests intensified, Gotabaya Rajapaksa resigned, July 14. Wickremesinghe, July 20, was elected president by parliament. He declared a state of emergency and cracked down on protesters and their leaders. Sri Lanka, which defaulted on debt payments in 2022, obtained a $3-bil IMF bailout in Mar. 2023.

Sudan
Republic of the Sudan

People: Population: 49,197,555 (30). **Age distrib.:** <15: 40.5%; 65+: 3.2%. **Growth:** 2.6%. **Migrants:** 3.1%. **Pop. density:** 73.6 per sq mi, 28.4 per sq km. **Urban:** 36.3%. **Ethnic groups:** over 500 ethnic groups, incl. Sudanese Arab (approx. 70%), Fur, Beja, Nuba, Ingessana. **Languages:** Arabic, English (both official); Nubian; Ta Bedawie; Fur. **Religions:** Muslim (official) 92.4% (Sunni), Christian 4.2%, ethnic religionist 2.3%.

Geography: Total area: 718,723 sq mi, 1,861,484 sq km (15); **Land area:** 668,602 sq mi, 1,731,671 sq km. **Location:** E end of Sahara desert zone. Egypt on N; Libya, Chad, Central African Republic on W; South Sudan on S; Ethiopia, Eritrea on E. **Topography:** The N consists of Libyan Desert in W and the mountainous Nubia Desert in E, with narrow Nile Valley between. Large rainy areas with fields, pastures, and forests in center. The S has rich soil, heavy rain. **Arable land:** 11.2%. **Capital:** Khartoum, 6,344,348. **Cities:** Nyala, 1,056,952.

Government: Type: Presidential republic. **Head of state:** Sovereign Council Chair Gen. Abdel Fattah al-Burhan; b. 1960; in office: Aug. 21, 2019. **Head of govt.:** Acting Prime Min. Osman Hussein; in office: Jan. 19, 2022. **Local divisions:** 18 states. **Defense budget:** NA. **Active troops:** 104,300.

Economy: Industries: oil, cotton ginning, textiles, cement, edible oils, sugar, soap distilling, shoes, petroleum refining, pharmaceuticals, armaments. **Chief agric.:** sugarcane, sorghum, milk, groundnuts, onions, sesame seed. **Natural resources:** petroleum; small reserves of iron ore, copper, chromium ore, zinc, tungsten, mica, silver, gold; hydropower. **Water:** 862 cu m per capita. **Crude oil reserves:** 5 bil bbls. **Electricity prod.:** 16.6 bil kWh. **Labor force:** agric. 40.6%, industry 14.6%, services 44.8%. **Unemployment:** 18.7%.

Finance: Monetary unit: Pound (SDG) (593.80 = $1 U.S.). **GDP:** $197.6 bil; **per capita GDP:** $4,216; **GDP growth:** –1.0%. **Imports:** $9.8 bil; China 31%, India 14%, UAE 11%, Egypt 6%. **Exports:** $5.9 bil; UAE 31%, China 19%, Saudi Arabia 14%, India 12%. **Tourism:** $1.1 bil. **Budget:** $8.3 bil. **Inflation:** 138.8%.

Transport: Railways: 4,506 mi. **Motor vehicles:** 3.3 per 1,000 pop. **Airports:** 17.

Communications: Mobile: 74.0 per 100 pop. **Broadband:** 47.6 per 100 pop. **Internet** (2020): 28.4%.

Health: Expend.: 3.0%. **Life expect.:** 65.2 male; 69.8 female. **Births:** 33.3 per 1,000 pop. **Deaths:** 6.2 per 1,000 pop. **Infant mortality:** 41.4 per 1,000 live births. **Undernourished:** 11.9%. **HIV:** 0.1%. **COVID-19:** 63,993 cases, 5,046 deaths; rates per 100,000: 145.9 cases, 11.5 deaths. 30.6% vaccinated.

Education: Compulsory: ages 6-13. **Literacy:** 60.7%.

Website: www.presidency.gov.sd

Northern Sudan, ancient Nubia, was settled by Egyptians in antiquity. The population was converted to Coptic Christianity in the 6th cent. Arab conquests brought Islam to the area in the 15th cent. In the 1820s, Egypt took over Sudan. In the 1880s, Muhammad Ahmad, who called himself the Mahdi (leader of the faithful), and his followers, the dervishes, led a revolution. An Anglo-Egyptian force crushed the Mahdi's successors, 1898.

Sudan gained independence Jan. 1, 1956. In 1969, a Revolutionary Council took power, led by authoritarian Pres. Gaafar al-Nimeiry. He was overthrown, Apr. 6, 1985. Sudan held democratic elections in 1986. Brig. Omar Hassan Ahmad al-Bashir staged a coup, June 30, 1989. He became president in 1993.

During 1955-72 and 1983-2005, rebels in the south (primarily Christians and followers of traditional religions) fought against government domination by mostly Arab-Muslim northern Sudan. War and famine cost an estimated 2 mil lives. An accord largely ended the rebellion Jan. 9, 2005, but violence continued.

A rebellion in the Darfur region of western Sudan caused a new crisis, 2003-11. Marauding Arab militias, the janjaweed, reportedly acting in collusion with Sudanese government troops, looted and burned homes in Darfur. More than 7,000 African Union (AU) peacekeepers were ineffectual. By Sept. 2009, the Darfur war had killed about 300,000 people and displaced another 2.7 mil.

After southern Sudanese voted overwhelmingly for secession, Jan. 9-15, 2011, South Sudan attained full independence July 9. Conflict in Darfur flared up again in 2014-16. A UN-AU peacekeeping mission in Darfur (UNAMID) was established. The government signed a peace agreement, Oct. 3, 2020, with some Darfur and southern rebel groups. The UNAMID mission ended Dec. 31, 2020, but violence in Darfur persisted.

After months of deadly protests triggered by economic hardship, Bashir was ousted in a military coup, Apr. 11, 2019. Protests continued, demanding civilian rule. An agreement signed Aug. 17, 2019, by military and protest leaders provided for a power-sharing transition government, followed by a democratically elected government.

In an Oct. 25, 2021, coup led by transition government head Gen. Abdel Fattah al-Burhan, the military essentially seized full power. In the following months, security forces cracked down violently on anti-coup protesters.

Fierce fighting in and around Khartoum began Apr. 15, 2023, between the Sudanese armed forces and the formerly allied paramilitary Rapid Support Forces (RSF). The fighting, causing high civilian casualties, quickly spread to western Sudan, including Darfur, and to southern Sudan. As of late Sept., more than 812,000 Sudanese who had fled since fighting began were refugees in neighboring countries; over 4.2 mil people were internally displaced.

Suriname
Republic of Suriname

People: Population: 639,759 (165). **Age distrib.:** <15: 22.8%; 65+: 7.3%. **Growth:** 1.1%. **Migrants:** 8.1%. **Pop. density:** 10.6 per sq mi, 4.1 per sq km. **Urban:** 66.4%. **Ethnic groups:** Hindustani or East Indian (descended fr. 19th-cent. emigrants fr. northern India) 27.4%, Maroon (descendants of escaped African slaves) 21.7%, Creole (mixed white/Black) 15.7%, Javanese 13.7%, mixed 13.4%. **Languages:** Dutch (official), English (widely spoken), Sranang Tongo (Surinamese), Caribbean Hindustani, Javanese. **Religions:** Christian 52.0% (Catholic 31.3%, Protestant 15.4%), Hindu 20.3% (Vaishnavite 7%, Saktist 7%, Shaivite 7%), Muslim 15.5% (Sunni), agnostic 4.9%, Spiritist 2.8%.

Geography: Total area: 63,251 sq mi, 163,820 sq km (90); **Land area:** 60,232 sq mi, 156,000 sq km. **Location:** N shore of S America. Guyana on W, Brazil on S, French Guiana on E. **Topography:** Flat Atlantic coast, where dikes permit agriculture. Inland is forest belt. Hills cover three-fourths of country in S. **Arable land:** 0.4%. **Capital:** Paramaribo, 239,457.

Government: Type: Presidential republic. **Head of state and govt.:** Pres. Chandrikapersad Santokhi; b. 1959; in office: July 16, 2020. **Local divisions:** 10 districts. **Defense budget:** NA. **Active troops:** 1,840.

Economy: Industries: gold mining, oil, lumber, food proc., fishing. **Chief agric.:** rice, sugarcane, bananas, oranges, vegetables, plantains. **Natural resources:** timber, hydropower, fish, kaolin, shrimp, bauxite, gold; small amounts of nickel, copper, platinum, iron ore. **Water:** 168,760 cu m per capita. **Crude oil reserves:** 89 mil bbls. **Electricity prod.:** 2.0 bil kWh. **Labor force:** agric. 7.9%, industry 26.6%, services 65.5%. **Unemployment:** 8.6%.

Finance: Monetary unit: Dollar (SRD) (38.34 = $1 U.S.). **GDP:** $10.9 bil; **per capita GDP:** $17,620; **GDP growth:** 1.9%. **Imports:** $1.9 bil; (2021) U.S. 19%, China 16%, Netherlands 15%, Trinidad and Tobago 8%. **Exports:** $2.3 bil; (2021) Switzerland 51%, UAE 22%, Belgium 6%. **Tourism:** $13 mil. **Budget:** $1.6 bil. **Inflation:** 52.5%.

Transport: Motor vehicles: 301.4 per 1,000 pop. **Airports:** 6. **Communications: Mobile:** 150.3 per 100 pop. **Broadband:** 124.3 per 100 pop. **Internet:** 65.9%.

Health: Expend.: 6.8%. **Life expect.:** 68.9 male; 76.5 female. **Births:** 15.2 per 1,000 pop. **Deaths:** 6.6 per 1,000 pop. **Infant mortality:** 29.9 per 1,000 live births. **Undernourished:** 9.0%. **HIV:** 1.6%. **COVID-19:** 82,588 cases, 1,408 deaths; rates per 100,000: 14,078.3 cases, 240.0 deaths. 40.6% vaccinated.

Education: Compulsory: ages 7-12. **Literacy:** 95.0%.

Website: www.gov.sr or www.surinameembassy.org

The Netherlands acquired Suriname in 1667 from Britain. The 1954 Dutch constitution raised the colony to a level of equality with the Netherlands. Independence was granted Nov. 25, 1975; some 40% of the population (mostly E Indians, who opposed independence) immigrated to the Netherlands.

Désiré "Dési" Bouterse, who masterminded coups in 1982 and 1990, was elected president by the National Assembly, July 19, 2010. Bouterse had been convicted in absentia in the Netherlands, 1999, for drug trafficking. Named by the U.S. as a transshipment point for cocaine, Suriname agreed in 2012 to improve shipping inspections. Bouterse's son Dino pleaded guilty in the U.S., Aug. 29, 2014, to drug trafficking and terrorism charges. Bouterse was reelected by the National Assembly, July 14, 2015. He was convicted, in Surname Nov. 29, 2019, of murder in connection with the 1982 coup; he appealed. Following an opposition victory in May 25, 2020, elections, the new National Assembly elected Chandrikapersad Santokhi president, July 13.

Suriname was affected, 2015-17, by a Zika virus outbreak (about 3,500 cases).

Sweden
Kingdom of Sweden

People: Population: 10,536,338 (88). **Age distrib.:** <15: 17.3%; 65+: 20.7%. **Growth:** 0.5%. **Migrants:** 19.8%. **Pop. density:** 66.5 per sq mi, 25.7 per sq km. **Urban:** 88.7%. **Ethnic groups** (by birth country): Swedish 80.3%, Syrian 1.9%, Iraqi 1.4%, Finnish 1.4%, Indigenous Sami. **Languages:** Swedish (official). **Religions:** Christian 56.0% (Protestant 52.8%), agnostic 21.7%, atheist 11.8%, Muslim 9.3% (Sunni 7%).

Geography: Total area: 173,860 sq mi, 450,295 sq km (56); **Land area:** 158,431 sq mi, 410,335 sq km. **Location:** Scandinavian Peninsula in N Europe. Norway on W, Denmark on S (across Kattegat strait), Finland on E. **Topography:** Mountains along NW border cover 25% of Sweden. Flat or rolling terrain with several large lakes across central and southern areas. **Arable land:** 6.2%. **Capital:** Stockholm, 1,700,066.

Government: Type: Parliamentary constitutional monarchy. **Head of state:** King Carl XVI Gustaf; b. 1946; in office: Sept. 15, 1973. **Head of govt.:** Prime Min. Ulf Kristersson; b. 1963; in office: Oct. 18, 2022. **Local divisions:** 21 counties. **Defense budget:** $8.1 bil. **Active troops:** 14,600.

Economy: Industries: iron and steel, precision equip. (bearings, radio/phone parts, armaments), wood pulp and paper prods., processed foods, motor vehicles. **Chief agric.:** wheat, milk, sugar beet, barley, potatoes, oats. **Natural resources:** iron ore, copper, lead, zinc, gold, silver, tungsten, uranium, arsenic, feldspar, timber, hydropower. **Water:** 17,229 cu m per capita. **Electricity prod.:** 165.3 bil kWh. **Labor force:** agric. 2.0%, industry 18.2%, services 79.9%. **Unemployment:** 7.4%.

Finance: Monetary unit: Krona (SEK) (11.00 = $1 U.S.). **GDP:** $677.2 bil; **per capita GDP:** $64,578; **GDP growth:** 2.6%. **Imports:** $263.3 bil; (2021) Germany 18%, Netherlands 9%, Norway 8%, China 7%, Denmark 7%. **Exports:** $290.8 bil; (2021) Germany 10%, Norway 9%, U.S. 8%, Denmark 8%, Finland 6%. **Tourism:** $6.1 bil. **Budget:** $256.5 bil. **Inflation:** 8.4%.

Transport: Railways: 6,779 mi. **Motor vehicles:** 542.7 per 1,000 pop. **Airports:** 149.

Communications: Mobile: 125.1 per 100 pop. **Broadband:** 128.3 per 100 pop. **Internet:** 95.0%.

Health: Expend. (2021): 11.3%. **Life expect.:** 81.1 male; 84.7 female. **Births:** 10.8 per 1,000 pop. **Deaths:** 9.5 per 1,000 pop. **Infant mortality:** 2.3 per 1,000 live births. **Undernourished:** <2.5%. **HIV:** NA. **COVID-19:** 2,713,674 cases, 24,676 deaths; rates per 100,000: 26,276.0 cases, 238.9 deaths. 70.2% vaccinated.

Education: Compulsory: ages 6-15. **Literacy:** NA.

Website: sweden.se

The Swedes have lived in present-day Sweden for at least 5,000 years. Gothic tribes from Sweden played a major role in the disintegration of the Roman Empire. Swedish chieftains controlled much of present-day western Russia and Ukraine in the 9th cent. The Swedes were Christianized from the 11th cent., and a strong centralized monarchy developed. The Riksdag, the first European parliament to represent all classes of society, was first called in 1435.

A revolt led by Gustavus I in 1521-23 freed Sweden from Danish rule (dating from 1397); he built up the government and military and established the Lutheran Church. In the 17th cent. Sweden was a major European power, gaining most of the Baltic seacoast. The Napoleonic wars, 1799-1815, in which Sweden acquired Norway (it became independent 1905), were the last in which Sweden participated.

The Social Democratic Party (SAP) has governed Sweden for most of the period since World War II. Prime Min. Olof Palme was shot to death in Stockholm, Feb. 28, 1986. Sweden entered the EU, Jan. 1, 1995. A center-right alliance defeated the SAP in 2006 and 2010 parliamentary elections. Parliament voted Apr. 1, 2009, to legalize same-sex marriage. The SAP won Sept. 14, 2014, elections, in which the right-wing, anti-immigration Sweden Democrats (SD) won 49 seats.

About 238,000 migrants, mostly from the Middle East, SW Asia, and Africa, applied for asylum in Sweden in 2015-18. Legislation tightening asylum rules was enacted June 21, 2016. Of applications decided, 2015-18, about 50% were approved.

In Sept. 9, 2018, elections, an SAP-led coalition fell short of a majority but retained power; the SD won 62 seats. As the COVID-19 pandemic spread in 2020, Sweden's government resisted strict lockdowns to combat transmission. In Nov. 2021, the SAP's Magdalena Andersson became Sweden's first female prime min. In Sept. 11, 2022, elections center-right parties, including the SD (which won 73 seats and over 20% of the vote), narrowly defeated the SAP-led coalition. The Moderate Party's Ulf Kristersson formed a coalition government that officially did not include the SD but would rely on SD support in parliament.

Following Russia's Feb. 2022 invasion of Ukraine, Sweden applied to join NATO, May 18, 2022.

Switzerland
Swiss Confederation

People: Population: 8,563,760 (102). **Age distrib.:** <15: 15.1%; 65+: 20.0%. **Growth:** 0.6%. **Migrants:** 28.8%. **Pop. density:** 554.5 per sq mi, 214.1 per sq km. **Urban:** 74.2%. **Ethnic groups** (by birth country): Swiss 69.2%, German 4.2%, Italian 3.2%, Portuguese 2.5%, French 2.1%. **Languages:** German, French, Italian, Romansch (all official); English; Portuguese; Albanian; Serbo-Croatian; Spanish. **Religions:** Christian 73.5% (Catholic 39.6%, Protestant 29.5%), agnostic 17.0%, Muslim 6.8% (Sunni).

Geography: Total area: 15,937 sq mi, 41,277 sq km (132); **Land area:** 15,443 sq mi, 39,997 sq km. **Location:** In Alps Mts. in central Europe. France on W; Italy on S; Liechtenstein, Austria on E; Germany on N. **Topography:** The Alps cover 60% of land area; the Jura, near France, 10%. The midlands run NE-SW in-between. **Arable land:** 10.0%. **Capital:** Bern, 440,889. **Cities:** Zurich, 1,431,538.

Government: Type: Federal republic (formally a confederation). **Head of state and govt.:** President chosen on rotating basis from among 7-member Federal Council for 1-year term. **Local divisions:** 26 cantons. **Defense budget:** $5.6 bil. **Active troops:** 19,550.

Economy: Industries: machinery, chemicals, watches, textiles, precision instruments, tourism, banking, insurance. **Chief agric.:** milk, sugar beet, wheat, potatoes, pork, barley. **Natural resources:** timber, salt. **Water:** 6,182 cu m per capita. **Electricity prod.:** 59.5 bil kWh. **Labor force:** agric. 2.2%, industry 19.9%, services 77.9%. **Unemployment:** 4.2%.

Finance: Monetary unit: Franc (CHF) (0.88 = $1 U.S.). **GDP:** $733.1 bil; **per capita GDP:** $83,598; **GDP growth:** 2.1%. **Imports:** $480.5 bil; Germany 21%, Italy 8%, France 6%, U.S. 6%. **Exports:** $571.4 bil; Germany 16%, U.S. 14%, UK 8%, China 7%, France 6%, India 6%. **Tourism:** $11.0 bil. **Budget** (2018): $230.4 bil (federal, cantonal, and municipal). **Inflation:** 2.8%.

Transport: Railways: 3,291 mi. **Motor vehicles:** 639.5 per 1,000 pop. **Airports:** 40.

Communications: Mobile: 119.6 per 100 pop. **Broadband:** 100.8 per 100 pop. **Internet:** 95.6%.

Health: Expend.: 11.8%. **Life expect.:** 81.9 male; 85.8 female. **Births:** 10.2 per 1,000 pop. **Deaths:** 8.4 per 1,000 pop. **Infant mortality:** 3.0 per 1,000 live births. **Undernourished:** <2.5%. **HIV:** NA. **COVID-19:** 4,408,474 cases, 14,034 deaths; rates per 100,000: 50,937.8 cases, 162.2 deaths. 65.8% vaccinated.

Education: Compulsory: ages 5-15. **Literacy:** NA.

Website: www.ch.ch

Switzerland, the former Roman province of Helvetia, traces its modern history to 1291, when three cantons created a defensive league. Other cantons were subsequently admitted to the Swiss Confederation, which obtained its independence from the Holy Roman Empire through the Peace of Westphalia (1648). The cantons were joined under a federal constitution in 1848.

Switzerland has maintained an armed neutrality since 1815 and has not been involved in a foreign war since 1515. It is the seat of many UN and other international agencies but only became a full UN member on Sept. 10, 2002.

Switzerland is a world banking center. The government announced, Mar. 1997, a $4.7-bil fund to compensate victims of the Nazi Holocaust and other catastrophes. Swiss banks agreed Aug. 12, 1998, to pay $1.25 bil in reparations. A June 2002 referendum decriminalized abortion. Referenda in 2005 harmonized many policies with the EU.

In a Nov. 2009 referendum, voters approved a constitutional ban on construction of new minarets on mosques. A Mar. 2021 referendum banned face coverings such as a burqa in public.

Switzerland officially opened the 35-mi Gotthard Base Tunnel, the world's longest railway tunnel, June 1, 2016. In a May 19, 2019, referendum, voters approved stricter gun controls. Dec. 18, 2020, legislation legalized same-sex marriage, ratified by voters in a Sept. 26, 2021, referendum. UBS, Switzerland's largest bank, agreed in Mar. 2023 to acquire its scandal-plagued rival Credit Suisse.

In recent years, glaciers in the Swiss Alps have been shrinking as a result of climate change—including a 10% total volume loss in the hot summers of 2022 and 2023.

Syria
Syrian Arab Republic

People: Population: 22,933,531 (59). **Age distrib.:** <15: 33.3%; 65+: 4.1%. **Growth:** 6.4%. **Migrants:** 5.0%. **Pop. density:** 319.5 per sq mi, 123.4 per sq km. **Urban:** 57.4%. **Ethnic groups:** Arab 50%, Alawite 15%, Kurd 10%, Levantine 10%, other (incl. Druze, Ismaili, Imami, Nusairi, Assyrian, Turkoman, Armenian) 15%. **Languages:** Arabic (official), Kurdish, Armenian, Aramaic, Circassian, French, English. **Religions:** Muslim (official) 95.6% (Sunni 81%, Shia 14%), Christian 2.5%.

Geography: Total area: 72,370 sq mi, 187,437 sq km (87); **Land area:** 71,771 sq mi, 185,887 sq km. (500 sq mi of area is occupied by Israel.) **Location:** Middle East, at E end of Medit. Sea. Lebanon, Israel on W; Jordan on S; Iraq on E; Turkey on N. **Topography:** A short Medit. coastline stretches E and S with fertile lowlands and plains, alternating with mountains and large desert areas. **Arable land:** 25.4%. **Capital:** Damascus, 2,584,771. **Cities:** Aleppo, 2,203,025; Homs, 1,443,429.

Government: Type: Presidential republic; highly authoritarian regime. **Head of state:** Pres. Bashar al-Assad; b. 1965; in office: July 17, 2000. **Head of govt.:** Prime Min. Hussein Arnous; b. 1953; in office: Aug. 31, 2020. **Local divisions:** 14 provinces. **Defense budget:** NA. **Active troops:** 169,000. (Est. 50,000 Syrian Democratic Forces in territory where govt. does not exercise effective control.)

Economy: Industries: petroleum, textiles, food proc., beverages, tobacco, phosphate rock mining, cement. **Chief agric.:** wheat, barley, milk, olives, tomatoes, oranges. **Natural resources:** petroleum, phosphates, chrome and manganese ores, asphalt, iron ore, rock salt, marble, gypsum, hydropower. **Water:** 960 cu m per capita. **Crude oil reserves:** 2.5 bil bbls. **Electricity prod.:** 16.8 bil kWh. **Labor force:** agric. 12.5%, industry 22.2%, services 65.4%. **Unemployment:** 9.6%.

Finance: Monetary unit: Pound (SYP) (13,001.62 = $1 U.S.). **GDP:** NA; **per capita GDP:** NA; **GDP growth** (2020): –3.9%. **Imports**

(2017): $6.3 bil; Turkey 27%, China 22%, UAE 14%. **Exports** (2017): $1.9 bil; Saudi Arabia 23%, Turkey 18%, Egypt 14%, UAE 8%, Jordan 7%. **Budget** (2017): $3.2 bil. **Inflation** (2016-17): 28.1%.

Transport: Railways: 1,275 mi. **Motor vehicles:** 154.7 per 1,000 pop. **Airports:** 29.

Communications: Mobile (2021): 79.7 per 100 pop. **Broadband** (2021): 17.4 per 100 pop. **Internet** (2020): 35.8%.

Health: Expend.: NA. **Life expect.:** 73.1 male; 76.1 female. **Births:** 22.2 per 1,000 pop. **Deaths:** 4.1 per 1,000 pop. **Infant mortality:** 15.5 per 1,000 live births. **Undernourished:** 27.8%. **HIV:** <0.1%. **COVID-19:** 57,423 cases, 3,163 deaths; rates per 100,000: 328.1 cases, 18.1 deaths. 13.5% vaccinated.

Education: Compulsory: ages 6-14. **Literacy:** 86.4%.

Website: www.egov.sy

Syria was the center of the Seleucid Empire but later was absorbed into the Roman and Arab empires. Ottoman rule prevailed for four cents., until the end of WWI.

The state of Syria was formed from former Turkish districts, separated by the Treaty of Sevres, 1920, and divided into the states of Syria and Greater Lebanon. Both were administered under a French League of Nations mandate, 1920-41. The occupying French proclaimed Syria a republic Sept. 16, 1941; independence came Apr. 17, 1946. Syria joined the Arab invasion of Israel in 1948.

Syria belonged to the United Arab Republic from Feb. 1958 to Sept. 1961. The Socialist Baath party seized power Mar. 1963 and became the only legal party. The Alawite minority has dominated the government (Alawism is a sect of Shiite Islam).

In the June 1967 Arab-Israeli war, Israel seized and occupied the Golan Heights, from which Syria had shelled Israeli settlements. On Oct. 6, 1973, Syria and Egypt attacked Israel but failed to recapture the Golan Heights. Syrian troops entered Lebanon in 1976, during the Lebanese civil war, and remained a strong presence in the country. Syria sided with Iran during the Iran-Iraq War, 1980-88.

Thousands died in the city of Hama Feb. 1982 when government forces crushed a Muslim Brotherhood uprising. Following Israel's invasion of Lebanon, June 6, 1982, Israeli planes destroyed Syrian planes and antiaircraft missile batteries in the Bekaa Valley, June 9.

Hafez al-Assad, president of Syria since 1971, died June 10, 2000, and was succeeded by his son Bashar al-Assad. Syria aided fighters of the Lebanon-based Shiite group Hezbollah in their conflict with Israel and gave about 180,000 Lebanese temporary refuge when Israeli forces targeted Hezbollah, July-Aug. 2006. On Sept. 6, 2007, Israel bombed a secret site in N Syria where the Israelis believed Syria and North Korea were developing a nuclear facility; both countries denied the claim.

The Assad regime used troops and tanks during Arab Spring demonstrations in Mar. 2011, but the confrontations escalated into outright rebellion. A number of armed opposition groups fought Assad's forces and each other for control of territory. Hezbollah forces fought on the side of the Assad government, which was also backed by Iran.

International intelligence communities announced, May 2013, increasing evidence that Assad's forces had used chemical and biological weapons. A chemical attack on an opposition-controlled Damascus suburb Aug. 21, 2013, killed more than 1,400. Russian and U.S. negotiators reached an agreement with Syria requiring the Assad government to relinquish chemical weapons. The last known covered chemical weapons were believed to have been removed June 23, 2014. Assad's forces continued using chlorine gas (not covered by the 2013 agreement). Syrian aircraft dropped chemical weapons prohibited by the 2013 agreement on a rebel-held town, Apr. 4, 2017; the U.S., Apr. 6, launched a cruise missile attack on the air base used by the planes. Israeli warplanes reportedly attacked, Sept. 7, 2017, Syrian military sites producing chemical weapons and missiles. An apparent chemical attack, Apr. 7, 2018, that killed dozens in a then-rebel-held area east of Damascus prompted U.S., UK, and French retaliatory airstrikes, Apr. 13.

By summer 2014, the Sunni extremist group ISIS (Islamic State in Iraq and Syria) controlled large areas in eastern and northern Syria. The night of Sept. 22-23, 2014, the U.S. began a campaign of airstrikes against ISIS and other Islamist extremist groups in Syria, supported by several Middle East countries and European and other allies. Russia, which backed Assad, sent warplanes and troops to Syria in Sept. 2015 and began its own air campaign, Sept. 30, against anti-government forces. Heavy Russian airstrikes helped the Assad regime regain control of large areas, 2016-18, often with high civilian casualties. Syrian Kurdish and other rebel groups making up the Syrian Democratic Forces (SDF), with support from U.S. airstrikes and special operations troops, retook territory in northern and eastern Syria from ISIS, 2015-17, including Raqqa (ISIS's self-proclaimed capital), Oct. 2017. The SDF said it captured the last ISIS-controlled area in Mar. 2019, although ISIS continued to stage attacks. ISIS leader Abu Bakr al-Baghdadi died (an apparent suicide) in a U.S. raid on his N Syria compound, Oct. 26, 2019. Three subsequent ISIS leaders were killed in Syria, 2022-23.

The U.S., in early 2019, announced plans to reduce its ground troops in Syria (about 900 remained in 2023).

Beginning in 2016, Turkish troops and groups aligned with them attacked Syrian Kurdish forces and tried to limit Kurdish-controlled areas in northern Syria. When the U.S., Oct. 2019, pulled back troops in northern Syria, Turkish and allied forces launched a new attack on the SDF, displacing tens of thousands of people and shrinking Kurdish-controlled territory.

By 2019, non-Kurdish rebels had largely retreated to Idlib Province in NW Syria; a Syrian government offensive, supported by Russian airstrikes, began Apr. 2019; Turkish troops supported some Idlib rebel groups. A Mar. 2020 cease-fire reduced violence somewhat.

Estimates of the total death toll in Syria's civil war since Mar. 2011 varied widely; the Syrian Observatory for Human Rights issued an overall estimate of more than 613,000, including 503,000 it said it had documented as of Mar. 2023. The UNHCR reported the number of Syrian refugees in Turkey, the Middle East, and North Africa at more than 5.2 mil as of mid-Sept. 2023. More than 1 mil Syrians had applied for asylum in Europe. About 6.8 mil people were displaced within Syria in 2023 according to UNHCR estimates.

A powerful earthquake centered in south-central Turkey, Feb. 6, 2023, plus aftershocks, caused massive damage in northern Syria. More than 8,400 died in Syria, and the Assad government apparently blocked some aid shipments to rebel-held areas already suffering from shortages of food, shelter, and medical facilities.

The Arab League agreed, May 7, 2023, to readmit Syria (expelled in 2011).

The removal of fuel subsidies, Aug. 2023, sparked demonstrations, largely in southern Syria, protesting economic hardship and calling of Assad's ouster.

Taiwan

People: Population: 23,588,613 (57). **Age distrib.:** <15: 12.2%; 65+: 18.1%. **Growth:** 0.03%. **Migrants:** NA. **Pop. density:** 1,893.8 per sq mi, 731.2 per sq km. **Urban:** 80.1%. **Ethnic groups:** Han Chinese (incl. Holo [approx. 70% of pop.], Hakka, other groups originating in mainland China) 95%+, Indigenous Malayo-Polynesian peoples 2.3%. **Languages:** Mandarin (official), Min Nan, Hakka dialects, about 16 Indigenous langs. **Religions:** Chinese folk-religionist 42.0%, Buddhist 26.7% (Mahayanist), Daoist 12.9%, new religionist 6.8%, Christian 6.3%, agnostic 4.4%.

Geography: Total area: 13,892 sq mi, 35,980 sq km (135). **Land area:** 12,456 sq mi, 32,260 sq km. **Location:** Off SE coast of China, between E & S China Seas. **Topography:** A mountain range forms backbone of island. The eastern half is very steep and craggy; western slope is flat, fertile, and well cultivated. **Arable land:** 16.9%. **Capital:** Taibei, 2,754,196. **Cities:** Xinbei, 4,504,147; Taoyuan, 2,318,850; Gaoxiong, 1,552,899; Taizhong, 1,369,066.

Government: Type: Semi-presidential republic. **Head of state:** Pres. Tsai Ing-wen; b. 1956; in office: May 20, 2016. **Head of govt.:** Prem. Chen Chien-jen; in office: Jan. 25, 2023. **Local divisions:** 13 counties, 3 cities, 6 special municipalities. **Defense budget:** $16.2 bil. **Active troops:** 169,000.

Economy: Industries: electronics, communications and information tech. prods., petroleum refining, chemicals, textiles, iron and steel, machinery, cement, food proc. **Chief agric.:** rice, vegetables, pork, cabbages, poultry, sugarcane. **Natural resources:** coal, nat. gas, limestone, marble, asbestos. **Water:** NA. **Crude oil reserves:** 2 mil bbls. **Electricity prod.:** 287.0 bil kWh. **Labor force:** agric. 4.8%, industry 36.6%, services 58.6%. **Unemployment:** 3.9%.

Finance: Monetary unit: New Dollar (TWD) (31.91 = $1 U.S.). **GDP:** NA; **per capita GDP:** NA; **GDP growth:** NA. **Imports** (2019): $308.7 bil; China 21%, Japan 16%, U.S. 11%, South Korea 6%. **Exports** (2019): $388.5 bil; China 26%, U.S. 14%, Hong Kong 12%, Japan 7%, Singapore 7%. **Tourism:** $744 mil. **Budget:** $105.8 bil. **Inflation** (2018-19): 0.5%.

Transport: Railways: 1,002 mi. **Motor vehicles:** 360.2 per 1,000 pop. **Airports:** 35.

Communications: Mobile: 126.6 per 100 pop. **Broadband:** 118.7 per 100 pop. **Internet:** 86.3%.

Health: Expend.: NA. **Life expect.:** 78.4 male; 84.5 female. **Births:** 7.3 per 1,000 pop. **Deaths:** 8.0 per 1,000 pop. **Infant mortality:** 3.9 per 1,000 live births. **Undernourished:** 3.0%. **HIV:** NA. **COVID-19:** 10,241,520 cases, 17,667 deaths; rates per 100,000: 43,865.8 cases, 75.7 deaths. 89.0% vaccinated.

Education: Compulsory: ages 6-15. **Literacy:** 98.5%.

Website: www.taiwan.gov.tw

Large-scale immigration from China began in the 17th cent. The island came under mainland control after an interval of Dutch rule, 1620-62. Japan ruled Taiwan (also called Formosa), 1895-1945. The Kuomintang (Chinese Nationalist Party) government fled to Taiwan in 1949 and established the Republic of China under Chiang Kai-shek, who ruled until his death in 1975. The U.S. provided military aid to deter a Communist invasion.

In 1971, the UN expelled Taiwan and recognized the mainland government. The U.S. acknowledged the People's Republic of China, Dec. 15, 1978, and severed diplomatic relations with Taiwan. The U.S. and Taiwan have maintained strong economic, defense, and unofficial ties. After opportunities for Chinese aid and investment led a number of countries to break relations in the 2010s and 2020s, Taiwan maintained diplomatic ties with 13 countries as of Sept. 30, 2023.

Land reform, government planning, U.S. aid and investment, and free universal education brought advances in industry, agriculture, and living standards. In 1987 martial law was lifted after 38 years, and in 1991 more than four decades of emergency rule ended. Taiwan held its first direct presidential election Mar. 23, 1996.

Five decades of Kuomintang rule ended when Chen Shui-bian, leader of the pro-independence Democratic Progressive Party (DPP), won the Mar. 2000 presidential election. Chen was wounded in an apparent assassination attempt Mar. 19, 2004, one day before he won a second term as president. Promising increased cooperation with China, Kuomintang candidate Ma Ying-jeou won the 2008 and 2012 presidential elections.

The People's Republic considers Taiwan a rebel province of the mainland; in 1991, the Kuomintang dropped its claim to be the sole government of both. The first formal talks between Taiwan and China were held Feb. 11, 2014. Concern over recent Kuomintang pro-China policies helped the DPP win the Jan. 16, 2016, presidential election; Tsai Ingwen became Taiwan's first female president. She was reelected, Jan. 11, 2020.

In accordance with a Constitutional Court ruling, legislation legalizing same-sex marriage went into effect May 24, 2019.

Objecting to an Aug. 2022 visit to Taiwan by U.S. House Speaker Nancy Pelosi, China staged large-scale military exercises near Taiwan. Chinese military shows of force near Taiwan increased in 2023. As of Jan. 1, 2024, Taiwan planned to increase the length of compulsory military service for young men.

The Penghu Isls. (Pescadores), 49 sq mi, pop. (2011 est.) 96,597, lie between Taiwan and the mainland. Kinmen, fmr. Quemoy, pop. (2011 est.) 99,691, and Matsu, pop. (2011 est.) 10,106, lie just off the mainland.

Tajikistan
Republic of Tajikistan

People: Population: 9,245,937 (97). **Age distrib.:** <15: 37.1%; 65+: 3.7%. **Growth:** 1.4%. **Migrants:** 2.9%. **Pop. density:** 169.2 per sq mi, 65.3 per sq km. **Urban:** 28.2%. **Ethnic groups:** Tajik 84.3% (incl. Pamiri, Yagnobi), Uzbek 13.8%, other (incl. Kyrgyz, Russian, Turkmen, Tatar, Arab) 2%. **Languages:** Tajik (official), Uzbek, Russian (used in govt. and business). **Religions:** Muslim 98.2% (Sunni [official] 88%, Shia 10%).

Geography: Total area: 55,637 sq mi, 144,100 sq km (94). **Land area:** 54,637 sq mi, 141,510 sq km. **Location:** Central Asia. Uzbekistan on N and W, Kyrgyzstan on N, China on E, Afghanistan on S. **Topography:** Mountainous; contains the Pamirs, Trans-Alai mountain system. **Arable land:** 6.0%. **Capital:** Dushanbe, 986,899.

Government: Type: Presidential republic. **Head of state:** Pres. Emomali Rahmon; b. 1952; in office: Nov. 6, 1994. **Head of govt.:** Prime Min. Qohir Rasulzoda; b. 1961; in office: Nov. 23, 2013. **Local divisions:** 2 provinces, 1 autonomous province, 1 capital region, 1 area (Districts Under Republican Admin.). **Defense budget:** $107 mil. **Active troops:** 8,800.

Economy: Industries: aluminum, cement, coal, gold, silver. **Chief agric.:** milk, potatoes, wheat, watermelons, onions, tomatoes. **Natural resources:** hydropower, petroleum, uranium, mercury, brown coal, lead, zinc, antimony, tungsten, silver, gold. **Water:** 2,297 cu m per capita. **Crude oil reserves:** 12 mil bbls. **Electricity prod.:** 19.7 bil kWh. **Labor force:** agric. 42.6%, industry 20.1%, services 37.3%. **Unemployment:** 7.8%.

Finance: Monetary unit: Somoni (TJS) (10.98 = $1 U.S.). **GDP:** $48.6 bil; **per capita GDP:** $4,885; **GDP growth:** 8.0%. **Imports:** $4.3 bil; China 40%, Russia 38%, Kazakhstan 19%. **Exports:** $2.2 bil; Turkey 24%, Switzerland 22%, Uzbekistan 16%, Kazakhstan 12%, China 10%. **Tourism:** $11 mil. **Budget:** $2.4 bil. **Inflation** (2018-19): 7.7%.

Transport: Railways: 423 mi. **Airports:** 17.

Communications: Mobile (2021): 118.8 per 100 pop. **Broadband** (2021): 24.3 per 100 pop. **Internet** (2017): 22.0%.

Health: Expend.: 8.2%. **Life expect.:** 69.2 male; 73.1 female. **Births:** 26.4 per 1,000 pop. **Deaths:** 4.9 per 1,000 pop. **Infant mortality:** 23.1 per 1,000 live births. **Undernourished:** 9.3%. **HIV:** 0.2%. **COVID-19:** 17,786 cases, 125 deaths; rates per 100,000: 186.5 cases, 1.3 deaths. 53.0% vaccinated.

Education: Compulsory: ages 7-15. **Literacy:** 99.8%.

Website: www.president.tj

Societies were settled in the region from about 3000 bce. Invaders have included Iranians, Arabs (who converted the population to Islam), Mongols, Uzbeks, Afghans, and Russians. The USSR gained control 1918-25, making the region a part of the Uzbek SSR until the Tajik SSR was proclaimed, 1929.

Tajikistan declared independence Sept. 9, 1991. Factional fighting led to the installation of a pro-Communist regime, Jan. 1993. A new constitution establishing a presidential system was approved by referendum in 1994.

About 55,000 died in clashes between Muslim rebels and loyalist troops (supported by Russia) by mid-1997. Pres. Emomali Rakhmonov, first elected in 1994, won a Nov. 1999 election called a farce by human-rights observers. Leading opposition groups boycotted the Nov. 2006 election, again won by Rakhmonov (who changed his name to Rahmon in 2007). He won reelection in Nov. 2013 and Oct. 2020.

Poverty and corruption are widespread in Tajikistan. After rebels murdered a Tajik general, July 21, 2012, the army killed about 30 militants, July 24. A former warlord surrendered, Aug. 13, in exchange for a troop withdrawal. In the 2010s, an est. 1,300 Tajiks joined ISIS forces in Syria and Iraq. In an assault claimed by ISIS, four Western tourists were killed in Tajikistan, July 29, 2018. Islamist militant prison riots, Nov. 2018 and May 2019, left at least 55 dead. Apr. 2021 fighting in a disputed area of the border with Kyrgyzstan killed about 40; fighting erupted again in Sept. 2022. Dozens died, 2021-22, when security forces cracked down violently on rights demonstrators in an area of eastern Tajikistan populated largely by the Pamiri minority.

Tanzania
United Republic of Tanzania

People: Population: 65,642,682 (23). **Age distrib.:** <15: 41.5%; 65+: 3.4%. **Growth:** 2.7%. **Migrants:** 0.7%. **Pop. density:** 191.9 per sq mi, 74.1 per sq km. **Urban:** 37.4%. **Ethnic groups:** African 99% (of which 95% are Bantu consisting of 130+ tribes); Arab, African, mixed Arab/African on Zanzibar. **Languages:** Kiswahili or Swahili, English (primary lang. of commerce, admin., higher ed.) (both official); Arabic (widely spoken in Zanzibar). **Religions:** Christian 55.9% (Protestant 27.7%, Catholic 26.1%), Muslim 32.6% (Sunni), ethnic religionist 9.7%.

Geography: Total area: 365,755 sq mi, 947,300 sq km (30); **Land area:** 342,009 sq mi, 885,800 sq km. **Location:** Coast of E Africa. Kenya, Uganda on N; Rwanda, Burundi, Dem. Rep. of the Congo on W; Zambia, Malawi, Mozambique on S. **Topography:** Hot, arid central plateau surrounded by lake region in W. Temperate highlands in N and S; coastal plains. Mt. Kilimanjaro (19,341 ft) is highest in Africa. **Arable land:** 15.2%. **Capital:** Dar es Salaam (de facto), 7,775,865; Dodoma (legislative), 261,645. **Cities:** Mwanza, 1,310,754.

Government: Type: Presidential republic. **Head of state and govt.:** Pres. Samia Suluhu Hassan; b. 1960; in office: Mar. 19, 2021. **Local divisions:** 31 regions. **Defense budget:** $943 mil. **Active troops:** 27,000.

Economy: Industries: agric. proc.; mining; salt, soda ash; cement, oil refining, shoes, apparel, wood prods., fertilizer. **Chief agric.:** cassava, maize, sweet potatoes, sugarcane, rice, bananas. **Natural resources:** hydropower, tin, phosphates, iron ore, coal, diamonds, gems, gold, nat. gas, nickel. **Water:** 1,612 cu m per capita. **Electricity prod.:** 8.2 bil kWh. **Labor force:** agric. 64.3%, industry 7.2%, services 28.5%. **Unemployment:** 2.8%.

Finance: Monetary unit: Shilling (TZS) (2,499.47 = $1 U.S.). **GDP:** $196.6 bil; **per capita GDP:** $3,097; **GDP growth:** 4.6%. **Imports:** $9.2 bil; (2020) China 34%, Dem. Rep. of the Congo 14%, India 12%, UAE 6%. **Exports:** (2020) $8.6 bil; (2020) India 15%, UAE 15%, Switzerland 14%, Uganda 12%, China 7%. **Tourism:** $1.4 bil. **Budget:** $10.0 bil. **Inflation:** 4.4%.

Transport: Railways: 2,546 mi. **Motor vehicles:** 2.1 per 1,000 pop. **Airports:** 10.

Communications: Mobile: 91.9 per 100 pop. **Broadband:** 28.6 per 100 pop. **Internet:** 31.6%.

Health: Expend.: 3.7%. **Life expect.:** 68.7 male; 72.3 female. **Births:** 32.9 per 1,000 pop. **Deaths:** 5.0 per 1,000 pop. **Infant mortality:** 30.3 per 1,000 live births. **Undernourished:** 23.5%. **HIV:** 4.3%. **COVID-19:** 43,078 cases, 846 deaths; rates per 100,000: 72.1 cases, 1.4 deaths. 53.8% vaccinated.

Education: Compulsory: ages 7-13. **Literacy:** 81.8%.

Website: www.tanzania.go.tz

Arab colonization and slaving in Tanganyika began in the 8th cent.; Portuguese sailors explored the coast around 1500. Other Europeans followed.

In 1885 Germany established German East Africa, of which Tanganyika formed the bulk. Under Britain, it became a League of Nations mandate and after 1946, a UN trust territory. It became independent, Dec. 9, 1961, and a republic within the Commonwealth a year later.

Zanzibar, area 640 sq mi, lies 23 mi off mainland Tanzania. The island of Pemba, area 380 sq mi, is 25 mi to the NE. Ethnic groups in Zanzibar include Arabs and Africans. Zanzibar and Pemba are major producers of cloves and clove oil.

Zanzibar was for centuries the center for Arab slave traders. Portugal ruled the region for two centuries until ousted by Arabs around 1700. Zanzibar became a British Protectorate in 1890; independence came Dec. 10, 1963. Revolutionary forces overthrew the Sultan, Jan. 12, 1964. The new government ousted Western diplomats and journalists, slaughtered thousands of Arabs, and nationalized farms.

The Republic of Tanganyika and the Republic of Zanzibar joined to form the United Republic of Tanzania, Apr. 26, 1964. Zanzibar retains internal self-government.

Until resigning as president in 1985, Julius K. Nyerere, a former Tanganyikan independence leader, dominated Tanzania's single-party government, which emphasized government planning and economic control. A multiparty system was established in 1992, and the economy was privatized in the 1990s.

A bomb at the U.S. embassy in Dar es Salaam, Aug. 7, 1998, killed 11 and injured at least 70. The U.S. blamed the attack on Islamic terrorists associated with Osama bin Laden.

John Magufuli, of the ruling party, won the Oct. 25, 2015, presidential election. Magufuli suppressed press freedom and political opposition. He won a second term in an Oct. 28, 2020, election dismissed as fraudulent by the opposition. Magufuli denied (despite widespread evidence) the COVID-19 pandemic was a problem in Tanzania and limited cooperation with the WHO.

Magufuli died Mar. 17, 2021. Vice Pres. Samia Suluhu Hassan became Tanzania's first woman president. She encouraged COVID-19 vaccination and somewhat eased restrictions on journalists.

Large natural gas deposits (57 tril cu ft) have been discovered in recent years.

Thailand
Kingdom of Thailand

People: Population: 69,794,997 (20). **Age distrib.:** <15: 16.0%; 65+: 14.5%. **Growth:** 0.2%. **Migrants:** 5.2%. **Pop. density:** 353.8 per sq mi, 136.6 per sq km. **Urban:** 53.6%. **Ethnic groups** (by nationality): Thai 97.5%. **Languages:** Thai (official), English (secondary lang. of elite). **Religions:** Buddhist (official) 86.6% (Theravadin 79%), Muslim 6.1% (Sunni), ethnic religionist 2.2%.

Geography: Total area: 198,117 sq mi, 513,120 sq km (51); **Land area:** 197,256 sq mi, 510,890 sq km. **Location:** On Indochinese and Malayan peninsulas in SE Asia. Myanmar on W and N, Laos on N, Cambodia on E, Malaysia on S. **Topography:** A plateau dominates NE third of Thailand, dropping to fertile alluvial valley of Chao Phraya R. in center. Forested mountains with narrow fertile valleys in N. Rain forests cover S peninsula region. **Arable land:** 33.6%. **Capital:** Krung Thep (Bangkok), 11,069,982. **Cities:** Chon Buri, 1,454,222; Samut Prakan, 1,358,871; Chiang Mai, 1,213,348.

Government: Type: Constitutional monarchy. **Head of state:** King Vajiralongkorn; b. 1952; in office: Dec. 1, 2016. **Head of govt.:** Prime Min. Srettha Thavisin; b. 1962; in office: Sept. 5, 2023. **Local divisions:** 76 provinces, 1 municipality. **Defense budget:** $6.2 bil. **Active troops:** 360,850.

Economy: Industries: tourism, textiles and garments, agric. proc., beverages, tobacco, cement, light mfg. (jewelry, elec. appliances, computers and parts, integrated circuits, furniture. **Chief agric.:** sugarcane, cassava, rice, oil palm fruit, rubber, maize. **Natural resources:** tin, rubber, nat. gas, tungsten, tantalum, timber, lead, fish, gypsum, lignite, fluorite. **Water:** 6,284 cu m per capita. **Crude oil reserves:** 253 mil bbls. **Electricity prod.:** 186.9 bil kWh. **Labor force:** agric. 31.6%, industry 22.5%, services 45.9%. **Unemployment:** 0.9%.

Finance: Monetary unit: Baht (THB) (35.19 = $1 U.S.). **GDP:** $1.5 tril; **per capita GDP:** $20,672; **GDP growth:** 2.6%. **Imports:** $295.8 bil; China 22%, Japan 14%, U.S. 7%, Malaysia 6%. **Exports:** $296.0 bil; U.S. 13%, China 12%, Japan 10%. **Tourism:** $5.1 bil. **Budget:** (2020) $128.6 bil. **Inflation:** 6.1%.

Transport: Railways: 2,564 mi. **Motor vehicles:** 269.6 per 1,000 pop. **Airports:** 63.

Communications: Mobile: 176.3 per 100 pop. **Broadband:** 121.8 per 100 pop. **Internet:** 88.0%.

Health: Expend.: 4.4%. **Life expect.:** 74.9 male; 81.1 female. **Births:** 10.0 per 1,000 pop. **Deaths:** 7.9 per 1,000 pop. **Infant mortality:** 6.4 per 1,000 live births. **Undernourished:** 5.2%. **HIV:** 1.1%. **COVID-19:** 4,756,150 cases, 34,453 deaths; rates per 100,000: 6,814.0 cases, 49.4 deaths. 77.6% vaccinated.

Education: Compulsory: ages 6-14. **Literacy:** 94.1%.

Website: www.soc.go.th

Thais began migrating from southern China during the 11th cent. and established a unified Thai kingdom, 1350. Known as Siam until 1939, Thailand is the only country in SE Asia never colonized by Europeans. King Mongkut and his son King Chulalongkorn, ruling successively from 1851 to 1910, modernized the country and signed trade treaties with Britain and France. A bloodless revolution in 1932 limited the monarchy. Thailand was an ally of Japan during WWII and of the U.S. during the postwar period. For decades, the military had a dominant role in governing the country.

By the end of the 1990s, according to UN estimates, more than 750,000 people in Thailand had HIV/AIDS, with 143,000 new infections in 1991 alone. A nationwide prevention campaign reduced the number of new HIV infections.

Beginning in 2004, security forces tried to suppress a Muslim insurgency in southern Thailand. By 2023, more than 7,300 people, mostly civilians, had been killed. Peace talks resumed in 2022 and continued sporadically in 2023.

Following elections in Jan. 2001, Thaksin Shinawatra became prime min. A military junta took power in a bloodless coup Sept. 19, 2006. Thaksin supporters won Dec. 2007 elections, and Samak Sundaravej became prime min. after civilian rule was restored Jan. 22, 2008. Thailand's Constitutional Court ousted Samak in Sept., and Thaksin's brother-in-law Somchai Wongsawat became prime min. Sept. 18. But a Constitutional Court ruling, Dec. 2, barred him from politics.

On Feb. 26, 2010, Thailand's Supreme Court ordered the seizure of about $1.4 bil of Thaksin's family assets. After Thaksin supporters, known as Red Shirts, staged mass rallies and began to build a fortified compound in Bangkok, a crackdown by Thai security forces May 14-19, 2010, left more than 90 people dead. Thaksin's sister, Yingluck Shinawatra, became Thailand's first female prime min. after parliamentary elections July 3, 2011. On May 7, 2014, she was removed from office by the Constitutional Court, and the military seized power in a May 22 coup. An interim legislature, with a majority of military members, named coup leader Gen. Prayut Chan-ocha as prime min. in Aug. 2014.

A 2015 investigation resulted in charges against more than 100, including government and military officials, for involvement in human trafficking of migrants from Myanmar and Bangladesh. More than 60 traffickers were convicted, July 19, 2017.

In an Aug. 7, 2016, referendum (opposition campaigning had been barred), voters approved a military-drafted new constitution and a companion measure giving the military a strong role in selecting prime ministers after a return to civilian rule.

King Bhumibol, monarch since June 1946, died Oct. 13, 2016; crown prince Maha Vajiralongkorn succeeded him Dec. 1.

Following disputed Mar. 24, 2019, legislative elections, the National Assembly, June 5, elected Prayut to remain prime min. Months of large student-led protests, 2020-21, demanded political reforms; hundreds were arrested. In May 14, 2023, lower-house elections, opposition parties—led by Move Forward and Pheu Thai (Thaksin's party)—won a majority of seats. After the largely military-appointed Senate blocked Move Forward's reformist leader from becoming prime minister, businessman Srettha Thavisin of Pheu Thai gained military backing and was elected prime minister by the National Assembly Aug. 22, 2023.

Timor-Leste
Democratic Republic of Timor-Leste

People: Population: 1,476,042 (152). **Age distrib.:** <15: 39.0%; 65+: 4.3%. **Growth:** 2.1%. **Migrants:** 0.6%. **Pop. density:** 257.0 per sq mi, 99.2 per sq km. **Urban:** 32.5%. **Ethnic groups:** Austronesian (Malayo-Polynesian), Melanesian-Papuan, small Chinese minority. **Languages:** Tetun Prasa, Portuguese (both official); Indonesian, English (working langs.); about 32 Indigenous langs.
Religions: Christian 87.6% (Catholic 82.7%), ethnic religionist 7.1%, Muslim 4.2% (Sunni).

Geography: Total area: 5,743 sq mi, 14,874 sq km (155); **Land area:** 5,743 sq mi, 14,874 sq km. **Location:** E half of Timor Isl. in SW Pacific O. Indonesia on W half of island. **Topography:** Rugged terrain, rising to 9,721 ft at Mt. Ramelau. **Arable land:** 7.5%. **Capital:** Dili, 281,135.

Government: Type: Semi-presidential republic. **Head of state:** Pres. José Ramos-Horta; b. 1949; in office: May 20, 2022. **Head of govt.:** Prime Min. Kay Rala Xanana Gusmao; b. 1946; in office: July 1, 2023. **Local divisions:** 12 municipalities, 1 special admin. region. **Defense budget:** $44 mil. **Active troops:** 2,280.

Economy: Industries: printing, soap mfg., handicrafts, woven cloth. **Chief agric.:** rice, maize, vegetables, coffee, roots/tubers. **Natural resources:** gold, petroleum, nat. gas, manganese, marble. **Water:** 6,231 cu m per capita. **Electricity prod.:** 536.8 mil kWh. **Labor force:** agric. 41.6%, industry 14.4%, services 44.0%. **Unemployment:** 4.9%.

Finance: Monetary unit: U.S. Dollar (USD) (1.00 = $1 U.S.). **GDP:** $6.5 bil; **per capita GDP:** $4,828; **GDP growth:** –17.5%. **Imports:** $1.5 bil; Indonesia 39%, China 27%, Singapore 10%. **Exports:** $2.3 bil; Singapore 51%, China 20%, Japan 9%, Indonesia 6%. **Tourism:** $12 mil. **Budget:** $1.4 bil. **Inflation** (2018-19): 1.0%.

Transport: Airports: 2.

Communications: Mobile: 110.4 per 100 pop. **Broadband:** 29.9 per 100 pop. **Internet:** 39.5%.

Health: Expend.: 9.9%. **Life expect.:** 68.6 male; 72.0 female. **Births:** 30.4 per 1,000 pop. **Deaths:** 5.6 per 1,000 pop. **Infant mortality:** 32.9 per 1,000 live births. **Undernourished:** 22.3%. **HIV:** 0.2%. **COVID-19:** 23,460 cases, 138 deaths; rates per 100,000: 1,779.4 cases, 10.5 deaths. 60.6% vaccinated.

Education: Compulsory: ages 6-14. **Literacy:** 69.9%.

Website: timor-leste.gov.tl

The collapse of Portuguese rule in East Timor led to factional fighting, Aug. 1975, and an invasion by Indonesia in Dec. Indonesia annexed East Timor in 1976. In over two decades, some 200,000 Timorese died due to civil war, famine, and persecution by Indonesian authorities. In a referendum held Aug. 1999 under UN auspices,

Timorese voted overwhelmingly for independence but were then terrorized by pro-Indonesian militias. An international peacekeeping force entered in Sept.; a UN interim administration formally took command Oct. 26, 1999. Pro-independence forces won elections for a constituent assembly Aug. 2001. Xanana Gusmão, a former guerrilla leader, won the presidential election Apr. 2002. As Timor-Leste, the territory became independent May 20.

José Ramos-Horta, a Nobel Peace Prize laureate, won a presidential runoff vote May 2007. Ramos-Horta chose Gusmão as prime min. Gusmão-supported independent Taur Matan Ruak became president in a May 2012 runoff election. Gusmão's CNRT party won July parliamentary elections. The UN peacekeeping mission ended Dec. 31, 2012.

Beginning in 2005, much of East Timor's budget consisted of revenue from offshore oil and natural gas deposits. Lower oil prices beginning in 2014, as well as depletion of oil fields and costly infrastructure projects, hurt the economy. Gusmão resigned Feb. 6, 2015, and was replaced as prime min. by a member of the Fretilin party. Fretilin's Francisco Guterres won the Mar. 20, 2017, presidential election. A coalition including the CNRT won parliamentary elections, May 12, 2018; Taur Matan Ruak became prime min.

Timor-Leste and Australia signed a treaty, Mar. 6, 2018, establishing the boundary between them in an oil- and gas-rich area of the Timor Sea. Ramos-Horta again became president after defeating Guterres in an Apr. 2022 runoff election. The CNRT won May 21, 2023, parliamentary elections, and Gusmão again became prime min.

Togo
Togolese Republic

People: Population: 8,703,961 (101). **Age distrib.:** <15: 39.0%; 65+: 4.3%. **Growth:** 2.4%. **Migrants:** 3.4%. **Pop. density:** 414.5 per sq mi, 160.0 per sq km. **Urban:** 44.5%. **Ethnic groups:** Adja-Ewe/Mina 42.4%, Kabye/Tem 25.9%, Para-Gourma/Akan 17.1%, Akposso/Akebu 4.1% (est. 37 ethnic groups total). **Languages:** French (official, lang. of commerce), Ewe and Mina (in S), Kabye and Dagomba (in N). **Religions:** Christian 48.1% (Catholic 30.1%, Protestant 14.4%), ethnic religionist 32.5%, Muslim 18.7% (Sunni).

Geography: Total area: 21,925 sq mi, 56,785 sq km (123); **Land area:** 20,998 sq mi, 54,385 sq km. **Location:** S coast of W Africa. Ghana on W, Burkina Faso on N, Benin on E. **Topography:** Hills running SW-NE split Togo into two savanna plains regions. **Arable land:** 48.7%. **Capital:** Lomé, 1,981,615.

Government: Type: Presidential republic. **Head of state:** Pres. Faure Gnassingbé b. 1966; in office: May 4, 2005. **Head of govt.:** Prime Min. Victoire Tomegah-Dogbé b. 1959; in office: Sept. 28, 2020. **Local divisions:** 5 regions. **Defense budget:** $173 mil. **Active troops:** 13,450.

Economy: Industries: phosphate mining, agric. proc., cement, handicrafts, textiles, beverages. **Chief agric.:** cassava, maize, yams, sorghum, beans, oil palm fruit. **Natural resources:** phosphates, limestone, marble. **Water:** 1,776 cu m per capita. **Electricity prod.:** 625.1 mil kWh. **Labor force:** agric. 30.9%, industry 20.4%, services 48.7%. **Unemployment:** 4.1%.

Finance: Monetary unit: CFA Franc (XOF) (606.88 = $1 U.S.). **GDP:** $23.1 bil; **per capita GDP:** $2,608; **GDP growth:** 5.8%. **Imports** (2020): $2.4 bil; China 18%, South Korea 13%, India 11%, Belgium 10%, Netherlands 8%. **Exports** (2020): $1.7 bil; India 16%, Benin 15%, Burkina Faso 6%, France 6%. **Tourism** (2020): $77 mil. **Budget:** $1.2 bil. **Inflation:** 8.0%.

Transport: Railways: 353 mi. **Motor vehicles:** 32.4 per 1,000 pop. **Airports:** 2.

Communications: Mobile: 74.2 per 100 pop. **Broadband:** 38.0 per 100 pop. **Internet:** 35.0%.

Health: Expend.: 6.0%. **Life expect.:** 69.1 male; 74.4 female. **Births:** 31.4 per 1,000 pop. **Deaths:** 5.2 per 1,000 pop. **Infant mortality:** 39.8 per 1,000 live births. **Undernourished:** 17.4%. **HIV:** 1.7%. **COVID-19:** 39,513 cases, 290 deaths; rates per 100,000: 477.3 cases, 3.5 deaths. 18.8% vaccinated.

Education: Compulsory: ages 6-15. **Literacy:** 66.5%.

Website: primature.gouv.tg

Togoland was administered by Germany and then by France and Britain. The French sector became the republic of Togo Apr. 27, 1960. In office since 1967, Pres. Gnassingbé Eyadéma was Africa's longest-serving head of state until his death Feb. 5, 2005. His son, Faure Gnassingbé, was installed as president and won an Apr. 24 election. Opposition parties disputed the result, and protests led to violent clashes in Lomé.

Former Defense Min. Kpatcha Gnassingbé, the president's brother, was arrested Apr. 12, 2009, and accused of plotting a coup. Pres. Gnassingbé won reelection Mar. 4, 2010. Anti-government protests led prime Min. Gilbert Fossoun Houngbo to resign, July 13, 2012. Pres. Gnassingbé won a third term in disputed Apr. 25, 2015, elections. More than a dozen people died and dozens were injured in anti-government protests, beginning Aug. 2017. Gnassingbé's party won Dec. 20, 2018, legislative elections, and Gnassingbé won a new term as president, Feb. 22, 2020. Victoire Tomegah-Dogbé became Togo's first woman prime minister, Sept. 28, 2020. Togo joined the Commonwealth in 2022.

Tonga
Kingdom of Tonga

People: Population: 105,221 (181). **Age distrib.:** <15: 29.9%; 65+: 7.3%. **Growth:** –0.3%. **Migrants:** 3.5%. **Pop. density:** 380.1 per sq mi, 146.8 per sq km. **Urban:** 23.2%. **Ethnic groups:** Tongan 96.5%, other (incl. European, Fijian, Samoan, Indian, Chinese, other Pacific Islander, other Asian) 3.5%. **Languages:** Tongan.
Religions: Christian 95.5% (independent 55.9%, Protestant 30.3%), Baha'i 3.8%.
Geography: Total area: 288 sq mi, 747 sq km (176); **Land area:** 277 sq mi, 717 sq km. **Location:** Western S Pacific O. Nearest neighbors are Fiji to NW, Samoa to NE. **Topography:** Comprises 170 volcanic and coral islands, 36 inhabited. **Arable land:** 27.8%. **Capital:** Nuku'alofa, 22,904.
Government: Type: Constitutional monarchy. **Head of state:** King Tupou VI; b. 1959; in office: Mar. 18, 2012. **Head of govt.:** Prime Min. Siaosi Sovaleni; b. 1970; in office: Dec. 27, 2021. **Local divisions:** 5 island divisions. **Defense budget:** $8 mil. **Active troops:** 600.
Economy: Industries: tourism, constr., fishing. **Chief agric.:** coconuts, gourds, cassava, sweet potatoes, vegetables, yams. **Natural resources:** fish. **Water:** 0. **Electricity prod.:** 77.9 mil kWh. **Labor force:** agric. 30.4%, industry 26.9%, services 42.7%. **Unemployment:** 3.0%.
Finance: Monetary unit: Pa'anga (TOP) (2.39 = $1 U.S.). **GDP** (2021): $718.6 mil; **per capita GDP** (2021): $6,779; **GDP growth** (2021): –2.7%. **Imports:** $285.7 mil; Fiji 29%, New Zealand 23%, China 14%, U.S. 8%, Australia 6%, Japan 6%. **Exports:** $58.7 mil; U.S. 38%, South Korea 18%, Australia 14%, New Zealand 14%, Japan 6%. **Tourism:** $9 mil. **Budget:** $196 mil. **Inflation:** 11.0%.
Transport: Airports: 1.
Communications: Mobile (2021): 60.7 per 100 pop. **Broadband** (2021): 60.7 per 100 pop. **Internet:** 71.6%.
Health: Expend.: 5.3%. **Life expect.:** 76.1 male; 79.5 female. **Births:** 20.0 per 1,000 pop. **Deaths:** 5.0 per 1,000 pop. **Infant mortality:** 12.1 per 1,000 live births. **Undernourished:** NA. **HIV:** NA. **COVID-19:** 16,821 cases, 12 deaths; rates per 100,000: 15,914.7 cases, 11.4 deaths. 73.2% vaccinated.
Education: Compulsory: ages 4-18. **Literacy:** 99.4%.
Website: www.gov.to
First inhabited by ancestors of Polynesians c. 2000 BCE, Tonga was visited by the Dutch in the early 17th cent. and by British explorer James Cook in the 1770s. A series of civil wars ended, 1845, with establishment of the Tupou dynasty. In 1900, Tonga became a British protectorate. Tonga gained independence June 1970 and joined the Commonwealth. Elections in Nov. 2010 made the country its first democratically elected parliament. George Tupou VI became king Mar. 18, 2012.
In recent years, Tonga has relied on borrowing from China to fund development projects. The U.S., in 2023, opened an embassy in Tonga.

Trinidad and Tobago
Republic of Trinidad and Tobago

People: Population: 1,407,460 (153). **Age distrib.:** <15: 19.0%; 65+: 13.6%. **Growth:** 0.1%. **Migrants:** 5.6%. **Pop. density:** 710.9 per sq mi, 274.5 per sq km. **Urban:** 53.4%. **Ethnic groups:** East Indian 35.4%, African descent 34.2%, mixed-other 15.3%, mixed African/East Indian 7.7%. **Languages:** English (official), Trinidadian Creole English, Tobagonian Creole English, Caribbean Hindustani, Trinidadian Creole French, Spanish, Chinese. **Religions:** Christian 64.2% (Catholic 27.0%, Protestant 25.3%, independent 11.1%), Hindu 23.6% (Saktist 9%, Shaivite 8%, Vaishnavite 7%), Muslim 6.4% (Sunni), agnostic 2.3%.
Geography: Total area: 1,980 sq mi, 5,128 sq km (166); **Land area:** 1,980 sq mi, 5,128 sq km. **Location:** In Caribbean, off E coast of Venezuela. **Topography:** Three low mountain ranges cross Trinidad E-W, with a well-watered plain between N and central ranges. Parts of E and W coasts are swamps. Tobago, 116 sq mi, lies 20 mi NE. **Arable land:** 4.9%. **Capital:** Port of Spain, 545,045.
Government: Type: Parliamentary republic. **Head of state:** Pres. Christine Kangaloo; b. 1961; in office: Mar. 20, 2023. **Head of govt.:** Prime Min. Keith Rowley; b. 1949; in office: Sept. 9, 2015. **Local divisions:** 9 regions, 3 boroughs, 2 cities, 1 ward. **Defense budget:** $838 mil. **Active troops:** 4,650.
Economy: Industries: petroleum and petroleum prods., liquefied nat. gas, methanol, ammonia, urea, steel prods., beverages. **Chief agric.:** poultry, fruit, coconuts, citrus fruit, milk, plantains. **Natural resources:** petroleum, nat. gas, asphalt. **Water:** 2,744 cu m per capita. **Crude oil reserves:** 243 mil bbls. **Electricity prod.:** 8.7 bil kWh. **Labor force:** agric. 3.0%, industry 26.4%, services 70.6%. **Unemployment:** 4.0%.
Finance: Monetary unit: Dollar (TTD) (6.80 = $1 U.S.). **GDP:** $42.5 bil; **per capita GDP:** $27,778; **GDP growth:** 2.5%. **Imports:** $8.6 bil; (2021) U.S. 37%, China 9%, Mexico 6%. **Exports:** $11.5 bil; (2021) U.S. 37%, Guyana 6%. **Tourism:** $55 mil. **Budget** (2020): $7.5 bil. **Inflation:** 5.8%.
Transport: Motor vehicles: 330.4 per 1,000 pop. **Airports:** 2.
Communications: Mobile: 130.6 per 100 pop. **Broadband** (2021): 40.3 per 100 pop. **Internet:** 79.0%.
Health: Expend.: 7.3%. **Life expect.:** 74.3 male; 78.2 female. **Births:** 10.6 per 1,000 pop. **Deaths:** 8.5 per 1,000 pop. **Infant mortality:** 15.4 per 1,000 live births. **Undernourished:** 12.2%. **HIV:** 1.0%. **COVID-19:** 191,496 cases, 4,390 deaths; rates per 100,000: 13,683.3 cases, 313.7 deaths. 51.4% vaccinated.
Education: Compulsory: ages 5-11. **Literacy:** 99.0%.
Website: www.ttconnect.gov.tt
Christopher Columbus sighted Trinidad in 1498. It became a British possession in 1802; in the 1800s tens of thousands of indentured servants and their families were brought from India to work in agriculture. Trinidad and Tobago won independence Aug. 31, 1962. It became a republic in 1976. The nation, among the most prosperous in the Caribbean, produces oil and natural gas. In recent years, drug-related crime and other violent crime, especially against women, has increased.
Basdeo Panday was the nation's first prime min. of Indian ancestry (1995-2001). The country's first female prime min., Kamla Persad-Bissessar, took office May 26, 2010. After Sept. 7, 2015, elections, Keith Rowley of the People's National Movement (PNM) became prime min. On Mar. 19, 2018, Paula-Mae Weekes became Trinidad's first female president. The PNM narrowly won Aug. 10, 2020, elections. Christine Kangaloo succeeded Weekes as president, Mar. 20, 2023.

Tunisia
Republic of Tunisia

People: Population: 11,976,182 (81). **Age distrib.:** <15: 24.8%; 65+: 10.0%. **Growth:** 0.6%. **Migrants:** 0.5%. **Pop. density:** 199.7 per sq mi, 77.1 per sq km. **Urban:** 70.5%. **Ethnic groups:** Arab 98%. **Languages:** Arabic (official), French (used in commerce); Berber (Tamazight). **Religions:** Muslim (official) 99.5% (Sunni 98%).
Geography: Total area: 63,170 sq mi, 163,610 sq km (91); **Land area:** 59,985 sq mi, 155,360 sq km. **Location:** N coast of Africa. Algeria on W, Libya on E. **Topography:** The N is wooded and fertile. Grazing lands and orchards are in central coastal plains. The S is arid, approaching Sahara Desert. **Arable land:** 18.2%. **Capital:** Tunis, 2,475,446.
Government: Type: Parliamentary republic. **Head of state:** Pres. Kais Saied; b. 1958; in office: Oct. 23, 2019. **Head of govt.:** Prime Min. Ahmed Hachani; b. 1956; in office: Aug. 1, 2023. **Local divisions:** 24 governorates. **Defense budget:** $1.3 bil. **Active troops:** 35,800.
Economy: Industries: petroleum, mining, tourism, textiles, footwear, agribusiness, beverages. **Chief agric.:** wheat, milk, tomatoes, barley, olives, watermelons. **Natural resources:** petroleum, phosphates, iron ore, lead, zinc, salt. **Water:** 390 cu m per capita. **Crude oil reserves:** 425 mil bbls. **Electricity prod.:** 20.9 bil kWh. **Labor force:** agric. 13.9%, industry 34.2%, services 51.9%. **Unemployment:** 16.1%.
Finance: Monetary unit: Dinar (TND) (3.11 = $1 U.S.). **GDP:** $154.3 bil; **per capita GDP:** $12,490; **GDP growth:** 2.5%. **Imports:** $24.3 bil; France 17%, Italy 16%, Germany 8%, China 8%, Algeria 7%. **Exports:** $19.7 bil; France 29%, Italy 17%, Germany 13%. **Tourism:** $1.0 bil. **Budget:** $12.4 bil. **Inflation:** 8.3%.
Transport: Railways: 1,350 mi (only partly operational). **Motor vehicles:** 181.1 per 1,000 pop. **Airports:** 15.
Communications: Mobile: 129.3 per 100 pop. **Broadband:** 85.8 per 100 pop. **Internet:** 79.0%.
Health: Expend.: 6.3%. **Life expect.:** 75.4 male; 78.8 female. **Births:** 14.1 per 1,000 pop. **Deaths:** 6.4 per 1,000 pop. **Infant mortality:** 11.6 per 1,000 live births. **Undernourished:** 3.0%. **HIV:** <0.1%. **COVID-19:** 1,153,361 cases, 29,423 deaths; rates per 100,000: 9,758.8 cases, 249.0 deaths. 54.2% vaccinated.
Education: Compulsory: ages 6-14. **Literacy:** 82.7%.
Website: www.tunisie.gov.tn or www.pm.gov.tn
Site of ancient Carthage and a former Barbary state under the suzerainty of Turkey, Tunisia became a protectorate of France, May 12, 1881. The nation became independent Mar. 20, 1956, and ended the monarchy the following year. Habib Bourguiba, an independence leader, served as president until 1987, when he was deposed by his prime min., Zine al-Abidine Ben Ali, who then won five presidential elections, 1989-2009, all tightly controlled.
Arab Spring protests, which began Dec. 2010, ousted Ben Ali, Jan. 14, 2011. The moderate Islamist Ennahda party won Oct. 2011 elections but failed to institute promised reforms. The secular Nida Tunis party won 2014 legislative and presidential elections.
Three Islamist extremist gunmen attacked a museum in Tunis, Mar. 18, 2015, killing 22. A gunman killed 38 foreign tourists at a resort hotel in Sousse, June 26; ISIS claimed responsibility.
July 2017 legislation gave women greater protection from abuse and sexual harassment.
In an Oct. 13, 2019, presidential runoff, law professor Kais Saied, an independent, won election. A decade-long weak economy was aggravated, beginning in 2020, by the impact of the COVID-19

pandemic. On July 25, 2021, Pres. Saied took on expanded powers. He announced, Sept. 22, increased powers to rule by decree, and he dissolved the legislature, Mar. 30, 2022. In a July 25 referendum boycotted by the opposition, a new constitution was approved centralizing power in the presidency. Most parties and voters boycotted Dec. 2022-Jan. 2023 elections for a new parliament. In early 2023, amid a continuing economic crisis, dozens of opposition figures were arrested.

In recent years, a growing number of African and other migrants trying to reach Europe by boat have embarked from Tunisia. Under a Tunisia-EU agreement announced July 16, 2023, Tunisia would crack down on migrants and people smugglers in exchange for badly needed economic aid.

Turkey (Türkiye)
Republic of Turkey

(As of June 1, 2022, the country formally changed its name to Türkiye [tur-KEE-yeh], using the Turkish-language spelling.)

People: Population: 83,593,483 (19). **Age distrib.:** <15: 22.1%; 65+: 9.3%. **Growth:** 0.6%. **Migrants:** 7.2%. **Pop. density:** 281.3 per sq mi, 108.6 per sq km. **Urban:** 77.5%. **Ethnic groups:** Turkish 70%-75%, Kurdish 19%. **Languages:** Turkish (official), Kurdish. **Religions:** Muslim 98.3% (Sunni 83%, Shia 15%).

Geography: Total area: 302,535 sq mi, 783,562 sq km (36); **Land area:** 297,157 sq mi, 769,632 sq km. **Location:** Asia Minor, stretching onto continental Europe; borders on Medit. and Black Seas. Bulgaria, Greece on W; Georgia, Armenia on N; Iran on E; Iraq, Syria on S. **Topography:** Center has wide plateaus with hot, dry summers and cold winters. High mountains ring the interior on all but W, with more than 20 peaks over 10,000 ft. Rolling plains in W; mild, fertile coastal plains in S and W. **Arable land:** 25.8%. **Capital:** Ankara, 5,397,098. **Cities:** Istanbul, 15,847,768; Izmir, 3,088,414; Bursa, 2,086,325; Adana, 1,835,895.

Government: Type: Presidential republic. **Head of state and govt.:** Pres. Recep Tayyip Erdogan; b. 1954; in office: Aug. 28, 2014. (The position of prime minister was eliminated in June 2018.) **Local divisions:** 81 provinces. **Defense budget:** $6.2 bil. **Active troops:** 355,200.

Economy: Industries: textiles, food proc., automobiles, electronics, mining, steel, petroleum, constr., lumber, paper. **Chief agric.:** milk, wheat, sugar beet, tomatoes, barley, maize. **Natural resources:** coal, iron ore, copper, chromium, antimony, mercury, gold, barite, borate, strontium, emery, feldspar, limestone, magnesite, marble, perlite, pumice, pyrites (sulfur), clay, hydropower. **Water:** 2,509 cu m per capita. **Crude oil reserves:** 366 mil bbls. **Electricity prod.:** 317.1 bil kWh. **Labor force:** agric. 17.1%, industry 26.5%, services 56.3%. **Unemployment:** 10.0%.

Finance: Monetary unit: Lira (TRY) (26.56 = $1 U.S.). **GDP:** $3.2 tril; **por capita GDP:** $37,274; **GDP growth:** 5.0%. **Imports:** $285.6 bil; Germany 11%, China 9%, Russia 9%. **Exports:** $282.9 bil; Germany 9%, UK 6%. **Tourism:** $26.6 bil. **Budget** (2020): $249.3 bil. **Inflation:** 72.3%.

Transport: Railways: 7,144 mi. **Motor vehicles:** 242.8 per 1,000 pop. **Airports:** 91.

Communications: Mobile: 105.8 per 100 pop. **Broadband:** 84.0 per 100 pop. **Internet:** 83.4%.

Health: Expend.: 4.6%. **Life expect.:** 74.1 male; 78.9 female. **Births:** 14.0 per 1,000 pop. **Deaths:** 6.1 per 1,000 pop. **Infant mortality:** 18.9 per 1,000 live births. **Undernourished:** <2.5%. **HIV:** NA. **COVID-19:** 17,004,677 cases, 101,419 deaths; rates per 100,000: 20,162.3 cases, 120.3 deaths. 59.8% vaccinated.

Education: Compulsory: ages 6-17. **Literacy:** 96.7%.

Website: www.tccb.gov.tr

Ancient inhabitants of Turkey were among the world's first agriculturalists. Such civilizations as the Hittite, Phrygian, and Lydian flourished in Asiatic Turkey (Asia Minor), as did much of Greek civilization. After the fall of Rome in the 5th cent., Constantinople (now Istanbul) was the capital of the Byzantine Empire for 1,000 years. It fell in 1453 to Ottoman Turks, who ruled a vast empire for over 400 years.

Just before WWI, Turkey, or the Ottoman Empire, ruled what is now Syria, Lebanon, Iraq, Jordan, Israel, Saudi Arabia, Yemen, and islands in the Aegean Sea. Turkey joined Germany and Austria in WWI, and its defeat resulted in the loss of territory and the fall of the sultanate. A secular republic was established Oct. 29, 1923. The first pres., Mustafa Kemal (later Kemal Ataturk), led Turkey until his death in 1938.

Turkey kept neutral during most of WWII. The country became a full member of NATO in 1952. Military coups overthrew civilian governments in 1960 and 1980. Turkey invaded nearby Cyprus July 20, 1974, to prevent that country from uniting with Greece, and Cyprus was divided into Greek and Turkish zones.

Turkey joined the U.S.-led force that ousted Iraq from Kuwait, 1991. Millions of Iraqi Kurdish refugees fled to Turkey's SE border region after the war. Turkish offensives in Kurdish areas of Turkey caused heavy casualties among separatist guerrillas and civilians. Kurdish militants raided Turkish diplomatic missions in some 25 Western European cities, June 24, 1993.

Tansu Ciller became Turkey's first woman prime min. July 5, 1993. The Islamic Welfare Party gained strength in the 1990s, and

in June 1996, a coalition with Ciller's True Path Party was formed. The pro-Islamic government resigned June 18, 1997, under pressure from the military, which stepped up its campaign against Islamic fundamentalism in 1998.

Kurdish rebel leader Abdullah Öcalan was captured Feb. 15, 1999, and convicted of terrorism June 29. His organization, the Kurdistan Workers' Party (PKK), announced in 1999 that it would abandon its 14-year-old insurgency. Violence continued at a lower level, however.

Earthquakes in Apr. and Nov. 1999 killed over 17,000 people. The Islamic Justice and Development Party (AKP) led by Recep Tayyip Erdogan won Nov. 3, 2002, parliamentary elections. Erdogan became prime min., May 14, 2003. His party scored a landslide win in 2007 parliamentary elections.

Erdogan won on Aug. 10, 2014, election to become Turkey's first popularly elected president. In an Apr. 16, 2017, referendum, accompanied by allegations of irregularities, voters narrowly approved constitutional amendments strengthening the president's powers and abolishing the post of prime minister after the next elections. Erdogan won the June 24, 2018, presidential election; the AKP won parliamentary elections the same day.

During Syria's civil war (2011-), Turkey became a haven for Syrian refugees (almost 3.3 mil as of mid-Sept. 2023). Turkey was also a major transit route for hundreds of thousands of Syrian and other migrants trying to reach Europe. Under a Turkey-EU agreement, effective Mar. 20, 2016, Turkey pledged, in return for EU aid, to crack down on smugglers ferrying migrants to Greece. Migrant crossings decreased.

Turkish government forces launched a new offensive against the PKK in SE Turkey, beginning in mid-2015, and Kurdish extremists staged terrorist attacks in Turkish cities, as well as attacks on government troops. Turkey began airstrikes, July 24, 2015, against PKK strongholds in N Iraq and later launched attacks on Syrian Kurdish fighters said to be affiliated with the PKK. Turkish ground troops fought in Syria beginning in 2016, mainly to limit areas controlled by Syrian Kurds (allied with the U.S. in fighting ISIS in Syria). After the U.S., Oct. 2019, pulled back troops from N Syria, a new offensive by Turkish and allied Syrian militia forces drove Syrian Kurdish fighters out of areas near the Turkish border.

Terrorist attacks within Turkey attributed to ISIS included suicide bombings at Istanbul's main airport, June 28, 2016, that killed at least 45. On Aug. 20, a suicide bomber killed at least 54 at a wedding in SE Turkey.

A coup attempt against Erdogan by elements of the military, July 15-16, 2016, was put down by loyal military units. The government blamed the coup on Muslim cleric Fethullah Gülen, living in the U.S. The abortive coup left at least 240 dead, and some 50,000 soldiers, government officials, and civilians (including journalists) were detained. Intensifying an ongoing crackdown on dissent, the government closed more than 100 media outlets and fired or suspended tens of thousands of judges, government officials, and teachers. July 2020 legislation increased government control of social media platforms in Turkey.

Tensions in U.S.-Turkish relations, along with economic problems, contributed to a sharp drop in the lira's value, 2018-19. Under a July 2020 decree issued by Erdogan, Istanbul's Hagia Sophia-built as a Christian church in the 6th cent., used as a mosque 1453-1934, and a museum since 1934-once again was converted to a mosque.

A continuing weak economy and currency were aggravated by high inflation in 2022-23. The COVID-19 pandemic also hurt the economy. (Turkey's total confirmed COVID-19 cases of 17 mil was 12th highest in the world as of Aug. 2023.)

A powerful Feb. 6, 2023, earthquake in south-central Turkey, plus aftershocks, killed over 50,000 and caused widespread destruction. Taking advantage of tightly controlled media, Erdogan narrowly won a new term as president in a May 28, 2023, runoff. The AKP and allied parties won a majority in parliamentary elections the same month.

Turkmenistan

People: Population: 5,690,818 (114). **Age distrib.:** <15: 24.6%; 65+: 6.5%. **Growth:** 1.0%. **Migrants:** 3.2%. **Pop. density:** 31.4 per sq mi, 12.1 per sq km. **Urban:** 54.0%. **Ethnic groups:** Turkmen 85%, Uzbek 5%, Russian 4%. **Languages:** Turkmen (official), Russian, Uzbek. **Religions:** Muslim (official) 97.0% (Sunni 96%).

Geography: Total area: 188,456 sq mi, 488,100 sq km (53); **Land area:** 181,441 sq mi, 469,930 sq km. **Location:** Central Asia. Kazakhstan on N; Uzbekistan on N and E; Afghanistan, Iran on S. **Topography:** Kara Kum Desert occupies 80% of country. Bordered on W by Caspian Sea. **Arable land:** 4.1%. **Capital:** Ashgabat, 902,353.

Government: Type: Presidential republic; authoritarian. **Head of state and govt.:** Pres. Serdar Berdimuhamedov; b. 1981; in office: Mar. 19, 2022. **Local divisions:** 5 provinces, 1 independent city. **Defense budget:** NA. **Active troops:** 36,500.

Economy: Industries: nat. gas, oil, petroleum prods., textiles, food proc. **Chief agric.:** milk, wheat, cotton, tomatoes, potatoes, watermelons. **Natural resources:** petroleum, nat. gas, sulfur, salt.

Water: 4,106 cu m per capita. **Crude oil reserves:** 600 mil bbls. **Electricity prod.:** 21.4 bil kWh. **Labor force:** agric. 22.3%, industry 34.2%, services 43.4%. **Unemployment:** 5.0%.

Finance: Monetary unit: Manat (TMT) (3.49 = $1 U.S.). **GDP** (2019): $96.2 bil; **per capita GDP** (2019): $15,629; **GDP growth** (2020): –3.4%. **Imports** (2017): $4.6 bil; Turkey 25%, Russia 18%, China 14%, Germany 6%. **Exports** (2017): $7.5 bil; China 82%. **Budget:** $6.1 bil. **Inflation** (2016-17): 8.0%.

Transport: Railways: 3,177 mi. **Airports:** 21.

Communications: Mobile (2021): 98.6 per 100 pop. **Broadband** (2021): 13.9 per 100 pop. **Internet** (2021): 21.3%.

Health: Expend.: 5.7%. **Life expect.:** 69.1 male; 75.3 female. **Births:** 17.2 per 1,000 pop. **Deaths:** 6.0 per 1,000 pop. **Infant mortality:** 36.7 per 1,000 live births. **Undernourished:** 5.7%. **HIV:** NA. **COVID-19:** 0 cases, 0 deaths. 53.0% vaccinated.

Education: Compulsory: ages 6-17. **Literacy:** 99.7%.

Website: turkmenistan.gov.tm

The region has been inhabited by Turkic peoples since the 10th cent. It became part of Russian Turkestan in 1881, and a constituent republic of the USSR in 1925. Turkmenistan declared independence Oct. 27, 1991, and became an independent state when the USSR disbanded Dec. 26, 1991.

Turkmenistan has extensive natural gas reserves and also oil reserves. Political power centers on the former Communist Party apparatus and authoritarian leadership. Gurbanguly Berdymukhammedov won the Feb. 2007 presidential election, considered fraudulent by international observers. He was reelected with 97% of the vote in 2012 and 98% in 2017. After the president announced in Feb. 2022 he would step down, his son, Serdar Berdymukhammedov, was declared the winner of the Mar. 12 election.

Tuvalu

People: Population: 11,639 (194). **Age distrib.:** <15: 29.3%; 65+: 7.4%. **Growth:** 0.8%. **Migrants:** 2.0%. **Pop. density:** 1,159.4 per sq mi, 447.7 per sq km. **Urban:** 66.2%. **Ethnic groups:** Tuvaluan 97%, Tuvaluan/I-Kiribati 1.6%. **Languages:** Tuvaluan, English (both official); Samoan. **Religions:** Christian 95.0% (Protestant [official] 85.6%), agnostic 2.8%.

Geography: Total area: 10 sq mi, 26 sq km (193). **Land area:** 10 sq mi, 26 sq km. **Location:** 9 islands forming NW-SE chain 360 mi long in SW Pacific O. Nearest neighbors are Kiribati to NE, Fiji to S. **Topography:** All low-lying atolls, no more than 15 ft above sea level, composed of coral reefs. **Arable land:** 0%. **Capital:** Funafuti, 7,042.

Government: Type: Parliamentary democracy under constitutional monarchy. **Head of state:** King Charles III, rep. by Gov.-Gen. Tofiga Falani; in office: Sept. 28, 2021. **Head of govt.:** Prime Min. Kausea Natano; b. 1957; in office: Sept. 19, 2019. **Local divisions:** 7 island councils, 1 town council. **Defense budget/active troops:** NA.

Economy: Industries: fishing. **Chief agric.:** coconuts, vegetables, tropical fruit, bananas, roots/tubers, pork. **Natural resources:** fish, coconuts. **Water:** 0. **Labor force:** Most make living through exploitation of the sea, reefs, and atolls and through overseas remittances. **Unemployment:** NA.

Finance: Monetary unit: Tuvaluan Dollar (TVD), equivalent to the Australian Dollar (AUD) (1.56 = $1 U.S.). **GDP:** $61.3 mil; **per capita GDP:** $5,421; **GDP growth:** 0.7%. **Imports:** $51.2 mil; China 32%, Japan 29%, Fiji 23%, New Zealand 6%. **Exports:** $2.7 mil; Thailand 50%, Indonesia 40%. **Tourism** (2019): $8 mil. **Budget:** $88 mil. **Inflation** (2016-17): 4.1%.

Transport: NA.

Communications: Mobile (2021): 80.3 per 100 pop. **Broadband:** NA. **Internet:** 71.6%.

Health: Expend.: 21.5%. **Life expect.:** 66.3 male; 71.3 female. **Births:** 22.3 per 1,000 pop. **Deaths:** 7.9 per 1,000 pop. **Infant mortality:** 28.3 per 1,000 live births. **Undernourished:** NA. **HIV:** NA. **COVID-19:** 2,943 cases, 1 death; rates per 100,000: 24,957.6 cases, 8.5 deaths. 80.6% vaccinated.

Education: Compulsory: ages 6-13. **Literacy:** NA.

Website: dfa.gov.tv

The Ellice Islands separated from the British Gilbert and Ellice Islands Colony in 1975 and became Tuvalu; independence came Oct. 1, 1978. In 2000, Tuvalu joined the United Nations. Following Sept. 9, 2019, elections, the legislature elected Kausea Natano prime minister, Sept. 19. Rising sea levels due to climate change are threatening to submerge the tiny island nation. To dramatize the crisis, Tuvalu's foreign min. addressed a Nov. 2021 climate conference by video, standing in knee-deep water on what he said was formerly dry land.

Uganda
Republic of Uganda

People: Population: 47,729,952 (31). **Age distrib.:** <15: 47.3%; 65+: 2.4%. **Growth:** 3.2%. **Migrants:** 3.8%. **Pop. density:** 627.2 per sq mi, 242.2 per sq km. **Urban:** 26.8%. **Ethnic groups:** Baganda 16.5%, Banyankole 9.6%, Basoga 8.8%, Bakiga 7.1%, Iteso 7%, Langi 6.3%, Bagisu 4.9%, Acholi 4.4%, Lugbara 3.3%. **Languages:** English, Swahili (both official); Ganda or Luganda

(most widely used Niger-Congo lang.). **Religions:** Christian 84.4% (Catholic 40.9%, Protestant 40.9%), Muslim 12.2% (Sunni).

Geography: Total area: 93,065 sq mi, 241,038 sq km (79); **Land area:** 76,101 sq mi, 197,100 sq km. **Location:** E Central Africa. South Sudan on N, Dem. Rep. of the Congo on W, Rwanda and Tanzania on S, Kenya on E. **Topography:** Mostly high plateau 3,000-6,000 ft high, with Ruwenzori Range in W (Mt. Margherita, 16,765 ft), volcanoes in SW. NE is arid, W and SW rainy. Lakes Victoria, Edward, Albert form much of borders. **Arable land:** 34.4%. **Capital:** Kampala, 3,846,102.

Government: Type: Presidential republic. **Head of state and govt.:** Pres. Yoweri Kaguta Museveni; b. 1944; in office: Jan. 29, 1986. **Local divisions:** 134 districts, 1 capital city. **Defense budget:** $1.1 bil. **Active troops:** 45,000.

Economy: Industries: sugar proc., brewing, tobacco, cotton textiles, cement, steel prod. **Chief agric.:** sugarcane, plantains, cassava, maize, sweet potatoes, milk. **Natural resources:** copper, cobalt, hydropower, limestone, salt, gold. **Water:** 1,314 cu m per capita. **Crude oil reserves:** 2.5 bil bbls. **Electricity prod.:** 4.4 bil kWh. **Labor force:** agric. 62.9%, industry 9.5%, services 27.6%. **Unemployment:** 4.3%.

Finance: Monetary unit: Shilling (UGX) (3,702.67 = $1 U.S.). **GDP:** $127.3 bil; **per capita GDP:** $2,694; **GDP growth:** 4.7%. **Imports:** $10.7 bil; China 19%, India 17%, Kenya 16%, UAE 7%. **Exports:** $6.2 bil; UAE 58%, Kenya 9%. **Tourism:** $927 mil. **Budget:** $6.9 bil. **Inflation:** 7.2%.

Transport: Railways: 773 mi. **Motor vehicles:** 13.7 per 1,000 pop. **Airports:** 5.

Communications: Mobile: 70.0 per 100 pop. **Broadband:** 54.4 per 100 pop. **Internet:** 10.3%.

Health: Expend.: 4.0%. **Life expect.:** 67.1 male; 71.6 female. **Births:** 40.3 per 1,000 pop. **Deaths:** 4.9 per 1,000 pop. **Infant mortality:** 29.4 per 1,000 live births. **Undernourished:** 31.6%. **HIV:** 5.1%. **COVID-19:** 171,729 cases, 3,632 deaths; rates per 100,000: 375.4 cases, 7.9 deaths. 28.6% vaccinated.

Education: Compulsory: ages 6-12. **Literacy:** 79.0%.

Website: www.gou.go.ug

Britain obtained a protectorate over Uganda in 1894. The country became independent Oct. 9, 1962, and a republic within the Commonwealth a year later. In 1967, the traditional kingdoms, including the powerful Buganda state, were abolished.

Gen. Idi Amin seized power from Prime Min. Milton Obote in 1971. During his 8-year dictatorship, he was responsible for the deaths of up to 300,000 of his opponents. In 1972 he expelled nearly all of Uganda's 45,000 Asians. Tanzanian troops and Ugandan exiles and rebels ousted Amin, Apr. 11, 1979.

Obote, president from Dec. 1980, was ousted in a military coup July 1985. Guerrilla war and rampant human rights abuses had plagued Uganda under Obote's regime.

Yoweri Museveni took power in Jan. 1986. In 1993 the Buganda and other traditional monarchies were restored for ceremonial purposes. Uganda helped Laurent Kabila seize power in the Dem. Rep. of the Congo (DRC; formerly Zaire) in 1997 but sent troops in 1998 to aid insurgents seeking his ouster. A withdrawal accord was signed Sept. 2002.

Pres. Museveni won flawed 2001, 2006, 2011, and 2016 elections. Opposition politicians were arrested, Aug. 2018; anti-government protests were violently suppressed. Museveni was declared the winner of the Jan. 14, 2021, presidential election. His main opponent, Robert Kyagulanyi (a former entertainer known as Bobi Wine) charged fraud. Hundreds of Wine's supporters were arrested and beaten.

The rebel Lord's Resistance Army (LRA), led by Joseph Kony, began an insurgency against the Museveni government in 1986 and abducted tens of thousands of children to serve as soldiers and sex slaves. According to UN estimates, the LRA, 1987-2012, killed more than 100,000 people and displaced some 2.5 mil in Uganda and neighboring countries. Peace talks began in 2006, and LRA violence in Uganda diminished. A cease-fire accord was signed Feb. 23, 2008.

In 2007, Uganda began supplying troops to the African Union's peacekeeping force in Somalia. Suicide bombings July 11, 2010, killed 76 people in Kampala; al-Shabaab, a Somali al-Qaeda-linked Islamist group, claimed responsibility. In recent years, the DRC-based, ISIS-affiliated Allied Democratic Forces has staged attacks in Uganda; a June 16, 2023, attack on a school left at least 41 dead.

The UNHCR estimated that, as of July 31, 2023, Uganda hosted almost 1.58 mil refugees and asylum seekers, including over 891,000 from South Sudan and 498,000 from the DRC.

Legislation signed by Museveni May 29, 2023, toughened penalties for homosexuality (already illegal), including life imprisonment for engaging in gay sex—and the death penalty in some cases.

Ukraine

People: Population: 43,306,477 (35). **Age distrib.:** <15: 11.9%; 65+: 20.0%. **Growth:** –0.5%. **Migrants:** 11.4%. **Pop. density:** 193.6 per sq mi, 74.8 per sq km. **Urban:** 70.1% (incl. Crimea). **Ethnic groups:** Ukrainian 77.8%, Russian 17.3%. **Languages:** Ukrainian (official), Russian (regional lang.). **Religions:** Christian 86.5%

(Orthodox 71.1%, Catholic 11.5%), agnostic 9.7%, atheist 2.1%, Muslim 1.5% (Sunni).

Geography: Total area: 233,032 sq mi, 603,550 sq km (about 7.1% was occupied by Russia as of Sept. 2023) (46); **Land area:** 223,681 sq mi, 579,330 sq km. **Location:** Eastern Europe. Belarus on N; Russia on NE and E; Moldova, Romania on SW; Hungary, Slovakia, Poland on W. **Topography:** Part of E European plain with arable black soil. Carpathians in the SW, Crimean chain in the S. **Arable land:** 56.8%. **Capital:** Kiev, 3,016,789. **Cities:** Kharkiv, 1,421,052; Odesa, 1,007,716.

Government: Type: Semi-presidential republic. **Head of state:** Pres. Volodymyr Zelenskyy; b. 1978; in office: May 20, 2019. **Head of govt.:** Prime Min. Denys Shmyhal; b. 1975; in office: Mar. 4, 2020. **Local divisions:** 24 provinces, 1 autonomous republic, 2 municipalities. **Defense budget:** $3.5 bil. **Active troops:** 688,000.

Economy: Industries: coal, elec. power, metals, machinery and transp. equip., chemicals. **Chief agric.:** maize, wheat, potatoes, sunflower seed, sugar beet, milk. **Natural resources:** iron ore, coal, manganese, nat. gas, oil, salt, sulfur, graphite, titanium, magnesium, kaolin, nickel, mercury, timber. **Water:** 4,008 cu m per capita. **Crude oil reserves:** 395 mil bbls. **Electricity prod.:** 150.0 bil kWh. **Labor force:** agric. 14.7%, industry 24.5%, services 60.9%. **Unemployment** (2021): 9.8%.

Finance: Monetary unit: Hryvnia (UAH) (36.86 = $1 U.S.). **GDP:** $448.6 bil; **per capita GDP:** $12,671; **GDP growth:** −29.1%. **Imports:** $84.2 bil; China 13%, Russia 12%, Germany 10%, Poland 9%, Belarus 7%. **Exports:** $81.5 bil; Russia 9%, China 8%, Germany 6%, Poland 6%. **Tourism:** $950 mil. **Budget:** $63.7 bil (planned and consolidated). **Inflation:** 20.2%.

Transport: Railways: 13,504 mi. **Motor vehicles:** 294.7 per 1,000 pop. **Airports:** 108.

Communications: Mobile (2021): 135.0 per 100 pop. **Broadband** (2021): 80.1 per 100 pop. **Internet:** 79.2%.

Health: Expend.: 7.6%. **Life expect.:** 64.5 male; 75.4 female. **Births:** 5.8 per 1,000 pop. **Deaths:** 19.8 per 1,000 pop. **Infant mortality:** 9.0 per 1,000 live births. **Undernourished:** 4.8%. **HIV:** NA. **COVID-19:** 5,518,385 cases, 109,904 deaths; rates per 100,000: 12,618.1 cases, 251.3 deaths. 34.8% vaccinated.

Education: Compulsory: ages 6-16. **Literacy:** 100.0%.

Website: www.kmu.gov.ua

Ukrainians' Slavic ancestors inhabited the region well before the 1st cent. CE. In the 9th cent., the princes of Kyiv established a strong state called Kyivan Rus, which included much of present-day Ukraine. Internal conflicts led to the disintegration of the Ukrainian state by the 13th cent. Mongol rule was supplanted by Poland and Lithuania in the 14th and 15th cent. The N Black Sea coast and Crimea came under Turkish control in 1478. Ukrainian Cossacks, starting in the late 16th cent., rebelled against the occupiers of Ukraine: Russia, Poland, and Turkey.

An independent Ukrainian National Republic was proclaimed on Jan. 22, 1918. But in 1921, Ukraine's neighbors occupied and divided Ukrainian territory. In 1922, Ukraine became a constituent republic of the USSR. In 1932-33, the Soviet government engineered a famine in eastern Ukraine, and 6-7 mil Ukrainians died. During WWII the Ukrainian nationalist underground fought Nazi and Soviet forces. Over 5 mil Ukrainians died in the war. The reoccupation of Ukraine by Soviet troops in 1944 brought a renewed wave of repression.

The world's worst nuclear power plant disaster occurred in Chernobyl, Ukraine, in Apr. 1986; many thousands were killed or disabled as a result of the radiation leak.

Ukrainian independence was restored, Dec. 1991, with the Soviet Union's dissolution. Following a 1994 accord with Russia and the U.S., Ukraine's large nuclear arsenal was transferred to Russia for destruction.

Russian-backed Prime Min. Viktor Yanukovych was declared the winner in Nov. of the 2004 presidential election. Massive protests (the Orange Revolution) forced an election rerun, Dec. 26, won by Viktor Yushchenko. Yanukovych was the winner in the Feb. 2010 presidential election.

Large anti-Yanukovych protests began in Nov. 2013, following his decision not to sign a free trade pact with the EU. Parliament removed Yanukovych from office, Feb. 22, 2014. Pro-EU candidate Petro Poroshenko won a May 25, 2014, presidential election. The EU agreement was completed Sept. 16.

Hurt by corruption and a weak economy, Poroshenko lost an Apr. 21, 2019, presidential runoff election to entertainer and businessman Volodymyr Zelenskyy. Zelenskyy's party won July 21, 2019, parliamentary elections.

Russian forces entered Crimea in Mar. 2014, and Russia annexed the region Mar. 18. Fighting began in Apr. 2014 in eastern Ukraine between Ukrainian forces and pro-Russian separatists, aided by Russia. A missile shot down a Malaysian airliner over separatist-controlled eastern Ukraine, July 17, 2014, killing all 298 on board.

On Feb. 24, 2022, Russia launched a large-scale invasion of Ukraine from the north, east, and south. The U.S., as well as many European and other nations, provided extensive military aid to Ukraine, which defeated an initial Russian advance toward Kyiv. By Aug. 2022, Russia controlled large portions of eastern and southern

Ukraine; after sham referenda in four partially occupied provinces, Russia annexed them in Oct. Ukrainian counteroffensives in fall 2022 and beginning in late spring 2023 recaptured some territory in the east and south. The U.S., Aug. 2023, estimated Ukraine's combat casualties as perhaps 70,000 killed and 100,000-120,000 wounded.

Russian missiles and artillery repeatedly attacked civilian targets, causing widespread destruction and high civilian casualties, and there was evidence that Russian troops committed war crimes. As of May 2023, more than 5 mil Ukrainians were internally displaced. The UNHCR estimated, as of mid-Sept. 2023, that about 4.9 mil Ukrainians were refugees in European or other nations (excluding Russia and Belarus); Russia was believed to have forcibly deported large numbers of Ukrainians.

United Arab Emirates

People: Population: 9,973,449 (92). **Age distrib.:** <15: 16.2%; 65+: 2.0%. **Growth:** 0.6%. **Migrants:** 88.1%. **Pop. density:** 309.0 per sq mi, 119.3 per sq km. **Urban:** 87.8%. **Ethnic groups:** South Asian 59.4% (incl. Indian 38.2%, Bangladeshi 9.5%, Pakistani 9.4%), Emirati 11.6%, Egyptian 10.2%, Filipino 6.1%. **Languages:** Arabic (official), English, Hindi, Malayam, Urdu, Pashto, Tagalog, Persian. **Religions:** Muslim 78.3% (Sunni [official] 67%, Shia 7%, Islamic schismatic 4%), Christian 11.0% (Catholic 9.7%), Hindu 6.3%.

Geography: Total area: 32,278 sq mi, 83,600 sq km (113); **Land area:** 32,278 sq mi, 83,600 sq km. **Location:** Middle East, on S shore of the Persian Gulf. Saudi Arabia on W and S, Oman on E. **Topography:** A barren, flat coastal plain gives way to uninhabited sand dunes on S. Hajar Mts. in E. **Arable land:** 0.7%. **Capital:** Abu Dhabi, 1,566,999. **Cities:** Dubai, 3,007,583; Sharjah, 1,830,858.

Government: Type: Federation of monarchies. **Head of state:** Pres. Sheikh Mohamed bin Zayed al Nahyan; b. 1961; in office: May 14, 2022. **Head of govt.:** Prime Min. Sheikh Muhammad bin Rashid al-Maktum; b. 1949; in office: Jan. 5, 2006. **Local divisions:** 7 emirates: Abu Dhabi, Ajman, Dubai, Fujaira, Ras al-Khaimah, Sharjah, Umm al-Qaiwain. **Defense budget:** $20.4 bil. **Active troops:** 63,000.

Economy: Industries: petroleum and petrochemicals, fishing, aluminum, cement, fertilizer, comm. ship repair, constr. materials. **Chief agric.:** dates, cucumbers, tomatoes, goat meat, eggs, milk. **Natural resources:** petroleum, nat. gas. **Water:** 15 cu m per capita. **Crude oil reserves:** 97.8 bil bbls. **Electricity prod.:** 135.6 bil kWh. **Labor force:** agric. 1.7%, industry 27.2%, services 71.1%. **Unemployment:** 2.8%.

Finance: Monetary unit: Dirham (AED) (3.67 = $1 U.S.). **GDP:** $828.3 bil; **per capita GDP:** $87,729; **GDP growth:** 7.4%. **Imports** (2017): $229.2 bil; China 15%, India 12%, U.S. 7%. **Exports** (2017): $308.5 bil; India 11%, Japan 10%, Saudi Arabia 7%, Switzerland 6%, China 6%, Iraq 6%. **Tourism:** $34.4 bil. **Budget:** $127.3 bil (excl. emirate-level spending in Abu Dhabi and Dubai). **Inflation:** 4.8%.

Transport: Motor vehicles: 406.1 per 1,000 pop. **Airports:** 25.

Communications: Mobile: 212.2 per 100 pop. **Broadband:** 234.9 per 100 pop. **Internet:** 100.0%.

Health: Expend.: 5.7%. **Life expect.:** 78.4 male; 81.2 female. **Births:** 10.8 per 1,000 pop. **Deaths:** 1.6 per 1,000 pop. **Infant mortality:** 5.1 per 1,000 live births. **Undernourished:** <2.5%. **HIV:** <0.1%. **COVID-19:** 1,067,030 cases, 2,349 deaths; rates per 100,000: 10,788.5 cases, 23.8 deaths. 99.0% vaccinated.

Education: Compulsory: ages 6-17. **Literacy:** 98.1%.

Website: u.ae

The 7 "Trucial Sheikdoms" gave Britain control of defense and foreign relations in the 19th cent. They merged to become an independent state Dec. 2, 1971. Oil revenues have made the UAE one of the world's wealthiest countries. Banking, construction, and tourism have also become economically important.

In Mar. 2015, the UAE joined a Saudi-led coalition conducting military operations against Shiite Houthi rebels in Yemen's civil war. A Houthi drone and missile attack on fuel tankers in Abu Dhabi killed 3, Jan. 17, 2022. A truce beginning in 2022 reduced violence in Yemen's civil war.

The UAE and Israel signed an agreement, Sept. 15, 2020, to normalize relations.

Sheikh Khalifa bin Zayed al Nahyan, president since 2004, died May 13, 2022. He was succeeded, May 14, by his half-brother Sheikh Mohamed bin Zayed al Nahyan.

United Kingdom
United Kingdom of Great Britain and Northern Ireland

People: Population: 68,138,484 (22). **Age distrib.:** <15: 16.9%; 65+: 19.1%. **Growth:** 0.5%. **Migrants:** 13.8%. **Pop. density:** 729.5 per sq mi, 281.6 per sq km. **Urban:** 84.6%. **Ethnic groups:** white 87.2%, Black/African/Caribbean/Black British 3%, Asian/Asian British: Indian 2.3%. **Languages:** English; Scots, Scottish Gaelic, Welsh, Irish (all recognized regional langs.). **Religions:** Christian 65.0% (Protestant 46.6%, Catholic 11.9%), agnostic 23.1%, Muslim 7.2% (Sunni).

Geography: Total area: 94,058 sq mi, 243,610 sq km (78); **Land area:** 93,410 sq mi, 241,930 sq km. **Location:** Off NW coast of Europe, across English Channel, Strait of Dover, North Sea. Ireland to W, France to SE. **Topography:** England is mostly rolling land, rising to Uplands of southern Scotland. Lowlands in center of Scotland, granite highlands in N. British Isles have milder climate than N Europe due to Gulf Stream and ample rainfall. Severn, 220 mi, and Thames, 215 mi, are longest rivers. **Arable land:** 24.8%. **Capital:** London, 9,648,110. **Cities:** Manchester, 2,791,005; Birmingham (West Midlands), 2,665,100; West Yorkshire, 1,928,661; Glasgow, 1,698,088; Southampton/Portsmouth (South Hampshire), 951,531; Liverpool, 917,032; Newcastle upon Tyne, 823,431; Nottingham, 806,757; Sheffield, 745,876; Bristol, 707,412; Belfast, 643,005; Edinburgh, 553,569; Cardiff, 488,153.

Government: Type: Parliamentary constitutional monarchy. **Head of state:** King Charles III, b. 1948; in office: Sept. 8, 2022. **Head of govt.:** Prime Min. Rishi Sunak; b. 1980; in office: Oct. 25, 2022. **Local divisions:** 229 local authorities (England: 152; Wales: 22; Scotland: 32; Northern Ireland: 11; 12 other dependent areas). **Defense budget:** $70.0 bil. **Active troops:** 150,350.

Economy: Industries: machine tools, elec. power equip., automation equip., railroad equip., shipbuilding, aircraft, motor vehicles and parts, electronics and communications equip. **Chief agric.:** wheat, milk, barley, sugar beet, potatoes, rapeseed. **Natural resources:** coal, petroleum, nat. gas, iron ore, lead, zinc, gold, tin, limestone, salt, clay, chalk, gypsum, potash, silica sand, slate. **Water:** 2,165 cu m per capita. **Crude oil reserves:** 2.5 bil bbls. **Electricity prod.:** 288.6 bil kWh. **Labor force:** agric. 1.0%, industry 18.0%, services 81.0%. **Unemployment:** 3.6%.

Finance: Monetary unit: Pound (GBP) (0.79 = $1 U.S.). **GDP:** $3.7 tril; **per capita GDP:** $54,603; **GDP growth:** 4.1%. **Imports:** $898.7 bil; (2021) China 13%, Germany 11%, U.S. 8%, Netherlands 6%, Norway 5%. **Exports:** $874.5 bil; (2021) U.S. 13%, Germany 9%, Netherlands 8%, Ireland 7%, Switzerland 6%. **Tourism:** $33.1 bil. **Budget** (2020): $1.4 tril. **Inflation:** 7.9%.

Transport: Railways: 10,184 mi. **Motor vehicles:** 600.7 per 1,000 pop. **Airports:** 271.

Communications: Mobile: 120.8 per 100 pop. **Broadband:** 115.1 per 100 pop. **Internet:** 96.7%.

Health: Expend. (2021): 11.9%. **Life expect.:** 80.0 male; 84.2 female. **Births:** 10.8 per 1,000 pop. **Deaths:** 9.1 per 1,000 pop. **Infant mortality:** 3.8 per 1,000 live births. **Undernourished:** <2.5%. **HIV:** NA. **COVID-19:** 24,671,491 cases, 228,707 deaths; rates per 100,000: 36,342.5 cases, 336.9 deaths. 75.4% vaccinated.

Education: Compulsory: ages 5-15. **Literacy:** NA.
Website: www.gov.uk

The United Kingdom of Great Britain and Northern Ireland comprises England, Wales, Scotland, and Northern Ireland.

Royal Family. Since 1901, ruling sovereigns have been members of the House of Windsor. Elizabeth II (b. Apr. 21, 1926) succeeded King George VI to the throne Feb. 6, 1952. Elizabeth II, who became Britain's longest-reigning monarch in 2015, died Sept. 8, 2022.

Charles Philip Arthur George (b. Nov. 14, 1948), Elizabeth II's eldest son, immediately succeeded her as King Charles III (coronation: May 6, 2023). His second wife, Camilla (married Apr. 9, 2005), became Queen. (Charles's first wife, Diana—married 1981, divorced 1996—died in a car crash in Paris, Aug. 31, 1997.)

Charles III's first son, William Philip Arthur Louis (b. June 21, 1982), is the Prince of Wales and heir apparent. William married Catherine (Kate) Middleton, Apr. 29, 2011. Their son George Alexander Louis (b. July 22, 2013) is second in line to the throne; Charlotte Elizabeth Diana (b. May 2, 2015) is third; Louis Arthur Charles (b. Apr. 23, 2018) is fourth. On May 19, 2018, King Charles's younger son, Henry Charles Albert David (Harry, b. Sept. 15, 1984; fifth in line) married American actor Meghan Markle. Their son Archie Harrison was born May 6, 2019; daughter Lilibet Diana was born June 4, 2021. Harry and Meghan withdrew from official duties as of Mar. 31, 2020. Prince Andrew, younger brother of Charles III, stepped back from official duties Nov. 20, 2019, following allegations related to his friendship with convicted sex offender Jeffrey Epstein.

Parliament is the UK's legislative body, with certain powers over dependent units. It consists of two houses. The House of Commons has 650 members, elected by direct ballot and divided as follows: England, 533; Wales, 40; Scotland, 59; Northern Ireland, 18. The House of Lords (Sept. 2023) comprised 778 members: 87 hereditary peers, 666 life peers, and 25 archbishops and bishops of the Church of England.

Resources and Industries. Great Britain is a global trade and financial services center. Service industries account for about four-fifths of GDP; industry for most of the rest; agriculture for less than 1%. Manufacturing, historically important since the Industrial Revolution, has declined in economic significance, while finance, centered in London, has grown in importance. Coal production, also historically important, has declined by more than 90% since 1970. Large oil and gas fields in the North Sea began commercial production in 1975, but proved reserves and production were declining in the 21st cent. Large offshore wind farms have been constructed in the North Sea.

Religion and Education. The Church of England is Protestant Episcopal. The monarch is its temporal head. There are two provinces, Canterbury and York, each headed by an archbishop. Westminster Abbey (1050-1760) is the site of coronations and the tombs of Elizabeth I, Mary, Queen of Scots, kings, poets, and the Unknown Warrior (buried Nov. 11, 1920). Celebrated British universities Oxford and Cambridge each date to the 13th cent.

History. Britain was separated from the European continent at least 200,000 years ago by catastrophic flooding that created the English Channel. Migrants across the Channel included the Celts, who arrived 2,500 to 3,000 years ago. Their language survives in Welsh and Gaelic enclaves.

England was part of the Roman Empire 43-410 CE, after which waves of Jutes, Angles, and Saxons arrived from German lands, followed by Danish raiders from the 8th through 11th cent. French-speaking Normans arrived in 1066, uniting the country with their dominions in France.

Opposition by nobles to royal authority forced King John to agree to the Magna Carta in 1215, a guarantee of rights and the rule of law. In the ensuing decades, the foundations of the parliamentary system were laid.

English dynastic claims to large parts of France led to the Hundred Years War, 1338-1453, an unsuccessful campaign. A long civil war, the War of the Roses, 1455-85, ended with the establishment of the Tudor monarchy. The economy prospered over long periods of domestic peace unmatched in continental Europe. The Church of England separated from the authority of the pope, 1534.

During the reign of Queen Elizabeth I, 1558-1603, England became a major naval power, leading to the founding of colonies in the New World and the expansion of trade with Europe and Asia. Scotland and England shared a single monarch after James VI of Scotland was crowned James I of England in 1603.

A struggle between Parliament and the Stuart kings led to a civil war, 1642-49, and the establishment of a republic under the Puritan Oliver Cromwell. The monarchy was restored in 1660, but the Glorious Revolution of 1688 confirmed the sovereignty of Parliament: a Bill of Rights was granted 1689. Scotland was united with England after the ratification of the Articles of Union of Scotland and England, May 1707.

Technological and entrepreneurial innovations led to the Industrial Revolution in the 18th cent. The 13 N American colonies were lost but replaced by growing empires in Canada, India, Australia, and elsewhere. Britain's role in the defeat of Napoleon, 1815, strengthened its position as the leading world power.

The limited extension of voting rights in 1832, 1867, and 1884; the formation of trade unions; and the development of universal public education were among the social changes that accompanied the spread of industrialization and urbanization in the 19th cent. (Men gained full voting rights in 1918 and women in 1928.) Large parts of Africa and Asia were added to the empire during the reign of Queen Victoria, 1837-1901.

Though victorious in WWI, Britain suffered huge casualties and economic dislocation. Ireland became independent in 1921, and independence movements became active in India and other colonies. The country suffered major bombing damage in WWII but rallied behind Prime Min. Winston Churchill and held off Germany until Allied victory was achieved, 1945.

In the postwar period, Britain lost its world leadership position to other powers. Labour governments nationalized some basic industries and expanded social welfare programs. In 1973, the UK joined the European Economic Community, which became the European Union (EU). Prime Min. Margaret Thatcher's Conservative governments, 1979-90, fostered private enterprise and began denationalization of key industries. The Channel Tunnel linking Britain to the Continent was opened May 6, 1994.

After the Sept. 11 attacks on the U.S., the UK participated, beginning in 2001, in the Afghanistan war; the last British troops left in 2021. Labour Prime Min. Tony Blair committed British troops to the 2003 U.S.-led invasion of Iraq. UK forces, which numbered 46,000 at the height of combat operations, almost entirely pulled out by mid-2009.

Suicide bombings on 3 London underground trains and a bus, July 7, 2005, left 56 people dead.

Legislation in 2005 established a Supreme Court, to replace the House of Lords as the UK's highest court. Blair, who had won three elections, was succeeded by Labour's Gordon Brown, June 2007.

In the wake of Britain's deepest recession since WWII, voters rejected the Labour Party in May 2010 elections. Conservative Prime Min. David Cameron responded to the fiscal crisis with austerity measures. Parliament voted in favor of same-sex marriage July 16, 2013. The Conservatives won May 7, 2015, elections. Tens of thousands of migrants to Europe from Africa, the Middle East, and SW Asia in 2015 tried to enter Britain. Anti-immigrant sentiment, including concerns about immigration from elsewhere in the EU, contributed to a 51.9%-48.1% referendum vote, June 23, 2016, favoring Britain's exit from the EU ("Brexit"). Conservative Theresa May replaced Cameron, July 13.

A suicide bomber apparently with ISIS connections killed 22 victims and injured more than 100 at a concert in Manchester,

May 22, 2017. In London, June 3, three attackers fatally ran down with a van or stabbed 8 victims; ISIS claimed responsibility.

Prime Min. May and EU leaders completed, Nov. 2018, a separation agreement, but Parliament, Jan.-Mar. 2019, rejected it three times. Conservative Boris Johnson, a Brexit hardliner, replaced May as prime min., July 24, 2019, and negotiated a revised EU agreement. It included a provision ("the Northern Ireland protocol") that kept Northern Ireland largely aligned with EU policies, to prevent a "hard" border between Northern Ireland and the Irish Republic (an EU member), while requiring customs checks between Britain and Northern Ireland. Campaigning to "get Brexit done," Johnson and the Conservatives won a sweeping victory in Dec. 12 election. Britain formally exited the EU Jan. 31, 2020. A UK-EU agreement ("the Windsor framework"), significantly modifying the Northern Ireland protocol and reducing customs checks of goods entering Northern Ireland from the rest of the UK, was adopted in Mar. 2023.

Britain was one of the hardest-hit countries by the COVID-19 pandemic that began in 2020. Total confirmed cases by Aug. 2023 exceeded 24.6 mil (10th-highest in the world); over 228,000 had died. By the end of 2021, GDP had largely recovered from a pandemic-related 2020 decline of over 9%, but stagnant growth, soaring inflation, and high interest rates to counter inflation plagued the economy in 2022-23.

Facing declining popularity and a revolt in the Conservative Party (including over being fined for violating his own government's COVID-19 restrictions), Johnson announced, July 7, 2022, that he would step down. Liz Truss, the foreign sec., became Conservative Party leader Sept. 5 and prime min. Sept. 6, 2022, but stepped down after just 45 days, amid a financial and political crisis. Former Chancellor of the Exchequer Rishi Sunak became Conservative Party leader Oct. 24 and prime min. Oct. 25, 2022.

With migrant crossings of the English Channel to the UK increasing in the 2020s, the UK announced in Apr. 2022 an agreement to deport migrants to Rwanda (which would receive British aid). Court challenges delayed implementation.

The UK experienced severe heat waves in summer 2022, including the highest temperature ever recorded in the country: 40.3°C (104.5°F) on July 19. June 2023 was the hottest June ever recorded.

When Cyprus gained independence, the UK retained the sovereign base areas of Akrotiri (47 sq mi) and Dhekelia (51 sq mi) on the island.

Wales

The Principality of Wales in western Britain has an area of 8,019 sq mi and a population (2021 census) of 3,107,500. Cardiff is the capital, pop. (2022 est.) 484,591.

The creation of a 60-seat elected Welsh assembly with limited powers passed by a thin margin in a Sept. 18, 1997, referendum.

Early Anglo-Saxon invaders drove Celtic peoples into the mountains of Wales, where they developed a distinct nationality. Members of the ruling house of Gwynedd in the 13th cent. fought England but were crushed, 1283. Edward of Caernarvon, son of Edward I of England, was created Prince of Wales, 1301. **Website:** gov.wales

Scotland

Scotland occupies the northern 37% of the main British island, and the Hebrides, Orkney, Shetland, and smaller islands. Length 275 mi, breadth approx. 150 mi, area 30,414 sq mi, pop. (2020 est.) 5,466,000.

The Lowlands, a belt of land approx. 60 mi wide from the Firth of Clyde to the Firth of Forth, divide the farming region of the Southern Uplands from the granite Highlands of the N; they contain 75% of the population and most of the industry. The Highlands, famous for hunting and fishing, have been opened to industry by many hydroelectric power stations.

Edinburgh, pop. (2022 est.) 548,206, is the capital. Glasgow, pop. (2023 est.) 1,698,088, is Scotland's major port and shipbuilding center and has developed a services-based economy in the 21st cent., including financial services, health care, and engineering. Aberdeen, pop. (2019 est.) 228,670, is a major port and center of granite, fish-processing, and North Sea oil industries. Dundee, pop. (2019 est.) 149,320, NE of Edinburgh, is an industrial and fish-processing center.

History. Scotland was called Caledonia by the Romans who battled early Celtic tribes and occupied southern areas from the 1st to the 4th cent. Missionaries from England introduced Christianity in the 4th cent.; St. Columba, an Irish monk, converted most of Scotland in the 6th cent.

The Kingdom of Scotland was founded in 1018. William Wallace and Robert Bruce both defeated English armies 1297 and 1314, respectively. In 1603, James VI of Scotland, son of Mary, Queen of Scots, succeeded to the English throne as James I, and effected the Union of the Crowns. In 1707 Scotland received representation in the British Parliament. A 1997 proposal to create a regional legislature passed by a landslide; the Scottish Parliament has limited taxing authority and autonomy in areas such as education and

social welfare. In 2011 elections for the 129-seat parliament, the pro-independence Scottish National Party (SNP) won a majority. In a referendum on independence Sept. 18, 2014, 55% of Scottish voters opposed separating from the UK. The SNP remained in power but narrowly fell short of a majority in 2016 and 2021 parliamentary elections.

Memorials of Robert Burns, Sir Walter Scott, John Knox, and Mary, Queen of Scots, draw many tourists, as do the beauties of the Trossachs, Loch Katrine, Loch Lomond, and abbey ruins.

Industries. Engineering products are a key industry, with growing emphasis on office machinery, autos, electronics, and other consumer goods. Support industries for offshore energy production (oil, gas, and wind turbines) have grown in recent decades.

Scotland produces fine woolens, worsteds, tweeds, silks, fine linens, and jute. It is known for its special breeds of cattle and sheep. Commercial fishing is an important industry. Whisky is a major export.

The Hebrides are a group of about 500 islands, 100 inhabited, off the W coast. The **Inner Hebrides** include Skye, Mull, and Iona, the last famous for the arrival of St. Columba, 563 CE. The **Outer Hebrides** include Lewis and Harris. Industries include sheep raising and weaving. The approx. 70 **Orkney Isls.** are to the NE. The capital is Kirkwall, on Pomona Isl. Fish curing, sheep raising, and weaving are occupations. NE of Orkney are the 200 **Shetland Isls.**, 24 inhabited, home of Shetland ponies. Orkney and Shetland are centers for the North Sea oil industry. **Website:** www.gov.scot

Northern Ireland

Northern Ireland was constituted in 1920 from 6 of the 9 counties of Ulster, the NE corner of Ireland. Area 5,452 sq mi, pop. (2021 census) 1,903,100. Capital and chief industrial center, Belfast, pop. (2023 est.) 643,005.

Industries. Shipbuilding, including large tankers, has long been an important industry, centered in Belfast, the largest port. Linen is manufactured, along with apparel, rope, and twine. Growing diversification has added engineering products, synthetic fibers, and electronics. Major farm products include livestock, poultry, potatoes, and dairy foods.

Government and History. An act of the British Parliament, 1920, divided Northern from Southern Ireland, each with a parliament and government. When Ireland became a dominion, 1921, and later a republic, Northern Ireland chose to remain a part of the UK.

During 1968-69, Roman Catholics, then a smaller portion of the pop. than Protestants, claimed discrimination in voting rights, housing, and employment. Violence and terrorism intensified, involving branches of the Irish Republican Army (IRA; outlawed in the Irish Republic), Protestant groups, police, and British troops. Between 1969 and 2001, more than 3,500 were killed in sectarian violence in Northern Ireland, Ireland, England, and elsewhere. For most of this period, Britain imposed direct rule.

A settlement reached on Good Friday, Apr. 10, 1998, and approved May 22 by voters in Northern Ireland and the Irish Republic, restored home rule and election of a 108-member assembly with safeguards for the rights of different communities. Both Ireland and Great Britain agreed to relinquish constitutional claims on Northern Ireland. IRA dissidents detonated a bomb at Omagh Aug. 15 that killed 29 people and injured over 330.

London transferred authority to a Northern Ireland power-sharing government in 1999. The IRA July 2005 renounced violence; Britain reduced its military presence. A dispute between the pro-UK Democratic Unionist Party (DUP) and the Irish nationalist party Sinn Féin caused the government to collapse in Jan. 2017. After inconclusive Mar. 2017 elections for the Northern Ireland assembly, a new power-sharing government was not formed until Jan. 2020. Same-sex marriage and most abortions became legal in Northern Ireland in 2020. Sinn Féin won the largest bloc of seats in May 5, 2022, elections for the Northern Ireland assembly; the DUP, which finished second, delayed the formation of a new power-sharing government, first seeking changes to the Northern Ireland protocol—and in 2023 questioning the Windsor framework as well.

Religion and Education. According to the 2021 census, the population of Northern Ireland was about 42.3% Catholic, 37.4% Protestant and other Christian, 1.3% other non-Christian religions, 17.4% no religion, and 1.6% not stated. Education is compulsory between the ages of 4 and 16 years. **Website:** www.northernireland.gov.uk

Channel Islands

The Channel Islands, area 75 sq mi, off the NW coast of France, the only parts of the former Dukedom of Normandy belonging to England, are Jersey, Guernsey, and the dependencies of Guernsey—Alderney, Brecqhou, Herm, Jethou, Lihou, and Sark. The Bailiwicks of **Jersey**, area 45 sq mi, pop. (2021 census) 103,267, capital St. Helier (2018 est. pop., 34,386), and **Guernsey**, area 30 sq mi, pop. (2021 census) 63,448, capital St. Peter Port (2018 est. pop., 16,271), have separate legal existences and lieutenant governors named by the Crown. The islands were the only British soil occupied by German troops in WWII. **Websites:** www.gov.je; www.gov.gg

Isle of Man

The Isle of Man, area 221 sq mi, pop. (2021 census) 84,640, is in the Irish Sea, 20 mi from Scotland, 30 mi from Cumberland. It is rich in lead and iron. The island has its own laws and a lieutenant governor appointed by the Crown. The Tynwald (legislature) consists of the Legislative Council, partly elected, and House of Keys, elected. Capital: Douglas; pop. (2021 census) 26,677. Leading employment sectors in 2016 were professional, education, medical, and scientific services 22.6%; insurance, banking, finance, and business services 20.9%; and misc. services 9.3%. Man is famous for the Manx tailless cat. **Website:** www.gov.im

Gibraltar

A dependency on the S coast of Spain, Gibraltar guards the entrance to the Mediterranean. Known as the Rock, Gibraltar has been in British possession since 1704. It is 3 mi long and 0.75 mi wide (total area, 2.25 sq mi) and reaches a max. elevation of 1,396 ft. A narrow isthmus connects it with the rest of the Iberian Peninsula. Pop. (2022 est.) 29,573.

Gibraltar has historically been—and remains—an object of contention between Britain and Spain. In 1967, residents voted almost unanimously to remain under British rule. A 1969 constitution increased Gibraltarian control of domestic affairs. Voters rejected a plan for the UK and Spain to share sovereignty, Nov. 7, 2002. Residents approved a new constitution Nov. 30, 2006. **Website:** www.gibraltar.gov.gi

British West Indies

A number of the Leeward Isls. are self-governing British possessions. Universal suffrage was instituted 1951-54; ministerial systems were set up 1956-60.

The Leeward Isls. associated with the UK are **Montserrat**, area 39 sq mi, pop. (2022 est.) 5,414. Brades Estate (2018 est. pop., 472) is de facto capital after Plymouth was abandoned in 1997 due to volcanic activity. The **British Virgin Isls.**, 58 sq mi, pop. (2022 est.) 38,632, capital Road Town (2018 est. pop., 15,137); and **Anguilla**, 35 sq mi, pop. (2022 est.) 18,741, capital The Valley (2018 est. pop., 1,402). Montserrat was devastated by the Soufrière Hills volcano, which began erupting July 18, 1995.

The three **Cayman Isls.**, a dependency, lie S of Cuba, NW of Jamaica. Pop. (2022 est.) 64,309, most of it on Grand Cayman. It is a free port; in the 1970s Grand Cayman became a tax-free refuge for foreign funds and branches of many Western banks were opened there. International tourism receipts in 2019 were $919 mil. Total area 102 sq mi. Capital: George Town; pop. (2018 est.) 34,875.

The **Turks and Caicos Isls.** are a dependency at the SE end of the Bahama Islands. Of about 40 islands, only 8 are inhabited; area 366 sq mi, pop. (2022 est.) 58,286; capital Cockburn Town (Grand Turk), pop. 5,447 (2018 est.). Salt, shellfish, and conch shells are the main exports.

In Sept. 2017, Anguilla, the British Virgin Isls., and the Turks and Caicos Isls. suffered severe damage from Hurricane Irma. Hurricane Maria further damaged the Turks and Caicos Isls.

Bermuda

Bermuda is a British dependency governed by a royal governor and an assembly, dating from 1620, the oldest legislative body among British dependencies. It is a group of about 150 small islands of coral formation, 20 inhabited, comprising 21 sq mi in the western Atlantic, 580 mi E of N. Carolina. Pop. (2022 est.) 72,337 (about 54% of African descent). Pop. density is high. Capital: Hamilton; pop. (2018 est.) 10,073.

Tourism is the major industry; tourism receipts in 2019 were $600 mil. Bermuda is also a haven for the offshore insurance industry. Exports include petroleum products, medicine. GDP per capita in 2016 was $99,400. In a referendum Aug. 15, 1995, voters rejected independence by nearly a 3-to-1 majority. **Website:** www.gov.bm

South Atlantic Territories

The **Falkland Isls.**, a dependency, lie 300 mi E of the Strait of Magellan at the southern end of S America.

The Falklands include 2 large islands and about 200 smaller ones, area 4,700 sq mi, pop. (2016 est.) 3,198. Capital Stanley, pop. (2018 est.) 2,269. The licensing of foreign fishing vessels is a major source of revenue. Fishing, tourism, and sheep farming are main industries; wool is the leading export. There are indications of large oil and gas deposits. Argentina claims the islands as Islas Malvinas; 97% of inhabitants are of British origin. Argentina invaded the islands Apr. 2, 1982. A British military task force sent to the area forced an Argentine surrender at Port Stanley, June 14, 1982. **Website:** www.falklands.gov.fk

British Antarctic Territory, S of 60° S lat., formerly a dependency of the Falkland Isls., was made a separate colony in 1962 and includes the South Shetland Isls., the South Orkney Isls., and the Antarctic Peninsula. A chain of meteorological stations is maintained.

South Georgia and the **South Sandwich Isls.**, formerly administered by the Falklands Isls., became a separate dependency in 1985. Total area of 1,507 sq mi. South Georgia, with no permanent population, is about 800 mi SE of the Falklands; the South Sandwich Isls. are uninhabited, about 470 mi SE of South Georgia. **Website:** www.gov.gs

St. Helena, an island 1,200 mi off the W coast of Africa and 1,800 mi E of S America, 47 sq mi. Total area of St. Helena, Ascension, and Tristan da Cunha is 152 sq mi; total pop. (2022 est.) 7,925. Construction, crafts, fishing are chief industries. After Napoleon Bonaparte was defeated at Waterloo the Allies exiled him to St. Helena, where he lived from Oct. 16, 1815, to his death, May 5, 1821. Capital: Jamestown; pop. (2018 est.) 603. **Website:** www.sainthelena.gov.sh

Tristan da Cunha is the principal island, area 38 sq mi, in a group of islands of volcanic origin, total area 71 sq mi, halfway between the Cape of Good Hope and S America. The islands are part of the British overseas territory of St. Helena, Ascension, and Tristan da Cunha.

Ascension is an island of volcanic origin, 34 sq mi in area, 700 mi NW of St. Helena. It is part of the British overseas territory of St. Helena, Ascension, and Tristan da Cunha. It is a communications relay center for Britain and has a U.S. satellite tracking center. The island is noted for sea turtles. **Website:** www.ascension.gov.ac

British Indian Ocean Territory (BIOT)

Formed Nov. 1965, with islands formerly dependencies of Mauritius (the Chagos Archipelago, including Diego Garcia) or Seychelles (Aldabra, Farquhar, and Des Roches—later transferred back to Seychelles). Total area 21,004 sq mi, land area 23 sq mi. The Chagos civilian population was removed by the UK by the 1970s to make way for expansion of the U.S. military base on Diego Garcia. The UK has opposed islanders' efforts to return home. A UN court advisory opinion (2019) and UN maritime court decision (2021) found UK control of the Chagos illegal.

Pacific Ocean Territories

Pitcairn Isl. is in the Pacific, halfway between S America and Australia. The island was reached in 1767 by British sea captain Philip Carteret but was not inhabited until 23 years later when the mutineers of the *Bounty* landed there. Pop. (2021 est.) 50; descendants of mutineers and their Tahitian wives. It is administered by a British High Commissioner in New Zealand and a local Council. The uninhabited islands of Henderson, Ducie, and Oeno are in the Pitcairn group, area 18 sq mi. **Website:** www.government.pn

United States
United States of America

(Figures for U.S. may differ elsewhere in The World Almanac.*)*
People: Population: 339,665,118 (3). **Age distrib.:** <15: 18.2%; 65+: 18.1%. **Growth:** 0.7%. **Migrants:** 15.3%. **Pop. density:** 96.2 per sq mi, 37.1 per sq km. **Urban:** 83.3%. **Ethnic groups:** white 61.6%, Black 12.4%, Asian 6%. An est. 18.7% of pop. is Hispanic (any race). **Languages:** English, Spanish; Hawaiian official in Hawaii, 20 Indigenous langs. official in Alaska. No official natl. lang. **Religions:** Christian 72.4% (Catholic 26.7%, independent 23.4%, Protestant 19.6%), agnostic 17.7%, atheist 3.5%, Jewish 1.6%, Muslim 1.6% (Sunni), Buddhist 1.4% (Mahayanist).

Geography: Total area: 3,796,742 sq mi, 9,833,517 sq km (3); **Land area:** 3,531,905 sq mi, 9,147,593 sq km. (Area is for 50 states and DC only.) **Location:** Primarily N America. Canada on N, Mexico on S; Pacific on W, Atlantic on E. **Topography:** Vast central plain, mountains in W, hills and low mountains in E. **Arable land:** 17.2%. **Capital:** Washington, DC, 5,490,080.

Government: Type: Constitutional federal republic. **Head of state and govt.:** Pres. Joseph R. Biden Jr.; b. 1942; in office: Jan. 20, 2021. **Local divisions:** 50 states, 1 district. **Defense budget:** $766.6 bil. **Active troops:** 1,359,600.

Economy: Industries: petroleum, steel, motor vehicles, aerospace, telecom, chemicals, electronics, food proc., consumer goods, lumber, mining. **Chief agric.:** maize, milk, soybeans, wheat, sugarcane, sugar beet. **Natural resources:** coal, copper, lead, molybdenum, phosphates, rare earth elements, uranium, bauxite, gold, iron, mercury, nickel, potash, silver, tungsten, zinc, petroleum, nat. gas, timber. **Water:** 9,272 cu m per capita. **Crude oil reserves** (2020): 47.1 bil bbls. **Electricity prod.:** 4.2 tril kWh. **Labor force:** agric. 1.7%, industry 19.2%, services 79.2%. **Unemployment:** 3.6%.

Finance: Monetary unit: Dollar (USD) (1.00 = $1 U.S.). **GDP:** $25.5 tril; **per capita GDP:** $76,399; **GDP growth:** 2.1%. **Imports:** $3.4 tril; (2021) China 19%, Mexico 13%, Canada 13%. **Exports:**

$2.6 tril; (2021) Canada 16%, Mexico 15%, China 9%. **Tourism:** $70.2 bil. **Budget:** $7.6 tril. **Inflation:** 8.0%.

Transport: Railways: 182,412 mi. **Motor vehicles:** 905.0 per 1,000 pop. **Airports:** 5,054.

Communications: Mobile: 110.2 per 100 pop. **Broadband:** 173.5 per 100 pop. **Internet:** 91.8%.

Health: Expend.: 18.8%. **Life expect.:** 78.5 male; 82.9 female. **Births:** 12.2 per 1,000 pop. **Deaths:** 8.4 per 1,000 pop. **Infant mortality:** 5.1 per 1,000 live births. **Undernourished:** <2.5%. **HIV:** NA. **COVID-19:** 103,436,829 cases, 1,127,152 deaths; rates per 100,000: 31,249.5 cases, 340.5 deaths. 68.9% vaccinated.

Education: Compulsory: ages 6-17. **Literacy:** NA.

Website: www.usa.gov

See also U.S. History chapter; Chronology of the Year's Events.

Uruguay
Oriental Republic of Uruguay

People: Population: 3,416,264 (131). **Age distrib.:** <15: 19.0%; 65+: 15.4%. **Growth:** 0.3%. **Migrants:** 3.1%. **Pop. density:** 50.6 per sq mi, 19.5 per sq km. **Urban:** 95.8%. **Ethnic groups:** white 87.7%, Black 4.6%, Indigenous 2.4%. **Languages:** Spanish (official). **Religions:** Christian 62.8% (Catholic 51.4%), agnostic 29.2%, atheist 7.0%.

Geography: Total area: 68,037 sq mi, 176,215 sq km (89); **Land area:** 67,574 sq mi, 175,015 sq km. **Location:** Southern S America, on Atlantic O. Argentina on W, Brazil on N. **Topography:** Rolling, grassy plains and hills, well-watered by rivers flowing W to Uruguay R. **Arable land:** 11.6%. **Capital:** Montevideo, 1,774,396.

Government: Type: Presidential republic. **Head of state and govt.:** Pres. Luis Alberto Lacalle Pou; b. 1973; in office: Mar. 1, 2020. **Local divisions:** 19 departments. **Defense budget:** $546 mil. **Active troops:** 21,100.

Economy: Industries: food proc., elec. machinery, transp. equip., petroleum prods., textiles, chemicals, beverages. **Chief agric.:** soybeans, milk, rice, maize, wheat, barley. **Natural resources:** hydropower, minor minerals, fish. **Water:** 49,572 cu m per capita. **Electricity prod.:** 15.8 bil kWh. **Labor force:** agric. 8.4%, industry 18.9%, services 72.6%. **Unemployment:** 7.8%.

Finance: Monetary unit: Peso (UYU) (37.72 = $1 U.S.). **GDP:** $98.7 bil; **per capita GDP:** $28,842; **GDP growth:** 4.9%. **Imports:** $15.1 bil; Brazil 25%, China 15%, U.S. 11%, Argentina 11%. **Exports:** $18.8 bil; China 29%, Brazil 12%. **Tourism:** $541 mil. **Budget (2020):** $17.6 bil. **Inflation:** 9.1%.

Transport: Railways: 1,040 mi (operational; govt. claims 1,840 mi total length). **Motor vehicles:** 396.4 per 1,000 pop. **Airports:** 11.

Communications: Mobile: 138.5 per 100 pop. **Broadband:** 115.8 per 100 pop. **Internet:** 89.9%.

Health: Expend.: 9.2%. **Life expect.:** 75.6 male; 81.9 female. **Births:** 12.7 per 1,000 pop. **Deaths:** 9.1 per 1,000 pop. **Infant mortality:** 8.1 per 1,000 live births. **Undernourished:** <2.5%. **HIV:** 0.6%. **COVID-19:** 1,038,774 cases, 7,634 deaths; rates per 100,000: 29,903.7 cases, 219.8 deaths. 83.6% vaccinated.

Education: Compulsory: ages 4-17. **Literacy:** 98.8%.

Website: www.gub.uy

Spanish settlers began to supplant the Indigenous Charrua Indians in 1624. Uruguay was attached to the Spanish Viceroyalty of Rio de la Plata in the 18th cent. Rebels fought against Spain beginning in 1810, with independence declared Aug. 25, 1825. To suppress Tupamaro guerrilla activities, a repressive military regime took power in 1973. Constitutional government was restored in 1985.

Same-sex marriage and marijuana use were legalized in 2013.

José (Pepe) Mujica, a former guerrilla, transformed his Marxist Tupamaro movement into a mainstream political party. Tabaré Vázquez, the candidate of Mujica's Broad Front coalition, won a presidential runoff election, Nov. 30, 2014. Conservative Luis Lacalle Pou narrowly defeated the Broad Front candidate in a Nov. 24, 2019, runoff.

Uzbekistan
Republic of Uzbekistan

People: Population: 31,360,836 (48). **Age distrib.:** <15: 29.7%; 65+: 6.4%. **Growth:** 0.8%. **Migrants:** 3.5%. **Pop. density:** 190.9 per sq mi, 73.7 per sq km. **Urban:** 50.5%. **Ethnic groups:** Uzbek 83.8%, Tajik 4.8%, Kazakh 2.5%, Russian 2.3%, Karakalpak 2.2%. **Languages:** Uzbek (official), Russian, Tajik. **Religions:** Muslim (official) 96.3% (Sunni).

Geography: Total area: 172,742 sq mi, 447,400 sq km (57); **Land area:** 164,248 sq mi, 425,400 sq km. **Location:** Central Asia. Kazakhstan on N and W; Kyrgyzstan, Tajikistan on E; Afghanistan, Turkmenistan on S. **Topography:** Mostly plains and desert. **Arable land:** 9.1%. **Capital:** Tashkent, 2,603,243.

Government: Type: Presidential republic; highly authoritarian. **Head of state:** Pres. Shavkat Mirziyoyev; b. 1957; in office: Sept. 8, 2016. **Head of govt.:** Prime Min. Abdulla Aripov; b. 1961; in office: Dec. 14, 2016. **Local divisions:** 12 provinces, 1 autonomous republic, 1 city. **Defense budget:** NA. **Active troops:** 48,000.

Economy: Industries: textiles, food proc., machine building, metallurgy, mining, hydrocarbon extraction, chemicals. **Chief agric.:** milk, wheat, potatoes, carrots/turnips, cotton, tomatoes. **Natural resources:** nat. gas, petroleum, coal, gold, uranium, silver, copper, lead, zinc, tungsten, molybdenum. **Water:** 1,460 cu m per capita. **Crude oil reserves:** 594 mil bbls. **Electricity prod.:** 59.2 bil kWh. **Labor force:** agric. 23.9%, industry 25.4%, services 50.6%. **Unemployment:** 6.0%.

Finance: Monetary unit: Som (UZS) (12,055.23 = $1 U.S.). **GDP:** $339.8 bil; **per capita GDP:** $9,533; **GDP growth:** 5.7%. **Imports:** $27.8 bil; China 23%, Russia 18%, South Korea 11%, Kazakhstan 9%, Turkey 6%. **Exports:** $16.4 bil; Switzerland 19%, UK 17%, Russia 15%, China 14%, Kazakhstan 9%, Turkey 8%. **Tourism:** $553 mil. **Budget:** $16.3 bil. **Inflation:** 11.5%.

Transport: Railways: 2,884 mi. **Motor vehicles:** 81.7 per 1,000 pop. **Airports:** 33.

Communications: Mobile: 103.1 per 100 pop. **Broadband:** 103.8 per 100 pop. **Internet:** 76.6%.

Health: Expend.: 6.7%. **Life expect.:** 73.2 male; 78.6 female. **Births:** 22.2 per 1,000 pop. **Deaths:** 5.2 per 1,000 pop. **Infant mortality:** 18.9 per 1,000 live births. **Undernourished:** <2.5%. **HIV:** NA. **COVID-19:** 171,887 cases, 1,016 deaths; rates per 100,000: 513.6 cases, 3.0 deaths. 53.8% vaccinated.

Education: Compulsory: ages 7-18. **Literacy:** 100.0%.

Website: www.gov.uz

The region was overrun by the Mongols under Genghis Khan in 1220. In the 14th cent., Uzbekistan became the center of a native Timurid empire. In later centuries Muslim feudal states emerged. Russian military conquest began in the 19th cent. The Uzbek SSR became a Soviet republic in 1925.

Uzbekistan gained independence when the Soviet Union disbanded Dec. 26, 1991, and was led by the authoritarian government of a former Communist, Islam A. Karimov.

Attacks by Islamic militants, Mar.-July 2004, killed more than 50 people. In June 2004, Russia's OAO Lukoil signed a $1-bil deal to develop Uzbekistan's natural gas fields.

After armed dissidents at Andizhan attacked government buildings and freed hundreds of prisoners, May 2005, security forces killed many rebels and unarmed demonstrators. Karimov then launched a general crackdown on human rights activists.

Karimov remained in office following the expiration of his presidential term Jan. 22, 2007, despite a two-term constitutional limit. He won a third term Dec. 23 (88.1% of the vote) and a fourth term, Mar. 29, 2015 (90.4%). The government announced, Sept. 2, 2016, that Karimov had died. Prime Min. Shavkat Mirziyoyev became interim president and won a flawed Dec. 4 presidential election. Mirziyoyev took steps to reduce repression, including freeing some jailed dissidents and reducing forced labor in the cotton harvests. Mirziyoyev won an Oct. 24, 2021, presidential election from which several opposition candidates were barred. Constitutional changes approved in an Apr. 30, 2023, referendum would allow Mirziyoyev to serve two more 7-year terms as president after his current term expires in 2026.

Vanuatu
Republic of Vanuatu

People: Population: 313,046 (174). **Age distrib.:** <15: 31.7%; 65+: 4.9%. **Growth:** 1.6%. **Migrants:** 1.1%. **Pop. density:** 66.5 per sq mi, 25.7 per sq km. **Urban:** 26.0%. **Ethnic groups:** Ni-Vanuatu 99%. **Languages:** 100+ local langs.; Bislama (creole), English, French (all official). **Religions:** Christian (official) 93.8% (Protestant 74.2%, Catholic 10.0%), ethnic religionist 4.2%.

Geography: Total area: 4,706 sq mi, 12,189 sq km (158); **Land area:** 4,706 sq mi, 12,189 sq km. **Location:** More than 80 islands (about 65 inhabited) in SW Pacific, 1,200 mi NE of Brisbane, Australia. Fiji to E, Solomon Isls. to NW. **Topography:** Dense forest with narrow coastal strips of cultivated land. **Arable land:** 1.6%. **Capital:** Port Vila, 52,690.

Government: Type: Parliamentary republic. **Head of state:** Pres. Nikenike Vurobaravu; b. 1964; in office: July 23, 2022. **Head of govt.:** Prime Min. Sato Kilman; b. 1957; in office: Sept. 4, 2023. **Local divisions:** 6 provinces. **Defense budget/active troops:** NA.

Economy: Industries: food and fish freezing, wood proc., meat canning. **Chief agric.:** coconuts, roots/tubers, bananas, vegetables, pork, fruit. **Natural resources:** manganese, hardwood forests, fish. **Water:** 32,558 cu m per capita. **Electricity prod.:** 71.7 mil kWh. **Labor force:** agric. 48.0%, industry 8.5%, services 43.5%. **Unemployment:** 2.1%.

Finance: Monetary unit: Vatu (VUV) (121.72 = $1 U.S.). **GDP:** $1.1 bil; **per capita GDP:** $3,289; **GDP growth:** 1.8%. **Imports:** $495.9 mil; China 29%, Australia 18%, New Zealand 11%, Fiji 11%. **Exports:** $88.8 mil; Japan 33%, Thailand 13%, Mauritania 13%, South Korea 11%, China 9%, Fiji 7%. **Tourism:** $2 mil. **Budget:** $355 mil. **Inflation (2020-21):** 2.3%.

Transport: Motor vehicles: 58.1 per 1,000 pop. **Airports:** 3.

Communications: Mobile: 78.2 per 100 pop. **Broadband:** 324.8 per 100 pop. **Internet:** 66.3%.

Health: Expend.: 4.0%. **Life expect.:** 73.7 male; 77.2 female. **Births:** 21.2 per 1,000 pop. **Deaths:** 4.0 per 1,000 pop. **Infant mortality:** 14.0 per 1,000 live births. **Undernourished:** 9.5%. **HIV:** NA. **COVID-19:** 12,019 cases, 14 deaths; rates per 100,000: 3,913.1 cases, 4.6 deaths. 52.8% vaccinated.

Education: Compulsory: NA. **Literacy:** 89.1%.

Website: www.gov.vu

The Anglo-French condominium of the New Hebrides, administered jointly since 1906, became the independent Republic of Vanuatu on July 30, 1980. Cyclone Pam, Mar. 13-14, 2015, destroyed 96% of crops and left 166,000 people in need of aid. The COVID-19 pandemic hurt tourism revenue, 2020-21. Following Oct. 13, 2022, elections, Alatoi Ishmael Kalsakau formed a coalition government. After he lost a no-confidence vote, Meltek Sato Kilman Livtuvanu replaced him as prime minister Sept. 4, 2023. Kilman lost his parliamentary majority by a month later and faced an Oct. 6 no-confidence vote.

Vanuatu is vulnerable to climate change effects such as rising sea levels and stronger storms.

Vatican City
The Holy See (Vatican City State)

People: Population (2022): 1,000 (196). **Migrants:** 100.0%. **Pop. density** (2022): 5,886.3 per sq mi, 2,272.7 per sq km. **Urban:** 100.00%. **Ethnic groups:** Italian, Swiss, Argentinian, other nationalities. **Languages:** Italian, Latin, French. **Religions:** Christian 100.0% (Catholic [official]).

Geography: Total area: 0.17 sq mi, 0.44 sq km (196); **Land area:** 0.17 sq mi, 0.44 sq km. **Location:** Within the city of Rome, completely surrounded by Italy. **Arable land:** 0%. **Capital:** Vatican City, 801.

Government: Ecclesiastical elective monarchy; self-described as "absolute monarchy."

Economy: Industries: printing; coin, medal, postage stamp prod.; mosaics, staff uniforms; worldwide banking, financial activities. **Water:** 0. **Labor force:** Essentially services with small amount of industry; nearly all dignitaries, priests, nuns, guards, and approx. 3,000 lay workers live outside the Vatican.

Finance: Monetary unit: Euro (EUR) (0.93 = $1 U.S.). **GDP:** NA; **per capita GDP:** NA; **GDP growth:** NA. **Budget** (2013): $348 mil.

Communications: Internet: 74.9%.

Health: COVID-19: 26 cases; rates per 100,000: 3,213.8 cases.

Apostolic Nunciature: 3339 Massachusetts Ave. NW 20008; 333-7171.

Website: www.vatican.va or www.vaticanstate.va

The popes for many centuries, with brief interruptions, held temporal sovereignty over mid-Italy (the so-called Papal States), comprising an area of some 16,000 sq mi, with a population in the 19th cent. of more than 3 mil. This territory was incorporated in the new Kingdom of Italy (1861), the sovereignty of the pope being confined to the palaces of the Vatican and the Lateran in Rome and the villa of Castel Gandolfo, by an Italian law, May 13, 1871.

A Treaty of Conciliation, a concordat, and a financial convention with Italy were signed Feb. 11, 1929. They established the independent state of Vatican City and gave the Roman Catholic Church special status in Italy. The treaty was incorporated into Italy's Constitution in 1947. Italy and the Vatican signed an agreement in 1984 eliminating Roman Catholicism as the state religion and ending required religious education in Italian schools.

Vatican City includes the Basilica of Saint Peter, the Vatican Palace and Museum, the Vatican gardens, and neighboring buildings; 13 buildings in Rome, outside the boundaries, enjoy extraterritorial rights. The legal system is based on the code of canon law, the apostolic constitutions, and laws especially promulgated for Vatican City by the pope.

Pope Benedict XVI, elected Apr. 19, 2005, became, Feb. 28, 2013, the first pontiff to resign since 1415 (Benedict died Dec. 31, 2022). Cardinal Jorge Mario Bergoglio, from Argentina, was elected Mar. 13, taking the name Francis. He became the first Latin American and first Jesuit pope.

Cardinal George Pell, prefect of the Vatican's Secretariat for the Economy, was convicted in Australia in 2018 of child sex abuse; his conviction was overturned on appeal, Apr. 7, 2020. Former cardinal and archbishop of Washington, DC, Theodore McCarrick was defrocked by the Vatican, Feb. 2019, for sexual abuse of minors. A May 9, 2019, papal edict required priests and nuns to report to church authorities sexual abuse or attempted cover-ups. A new constitution, 2022, somewhat strengthened the role of women and increased protections against sexual abuse.

Venezuela
Bolivarian Republic of Venezuela

People: Population: 30,518,260 (50). **Age distrib.:** <15: 25.1%; 65+: 8.9%. **Growth:** 2.4%. **Migrants:** 4.7%. **Pop. density:** 89.6 per sq mi, 34.6 per sq km. **Urban:** 88.4%. **Ethnic groups:** Spanish, Italian, Portuguese, Arab, German, African, Indigenous. **Languages:** Spanish (official), Indigenous dialects. **Religions:** Christian 91.0% (Catholic [official] 77.8%), agnostic 5.6%.

Geography: Total area: 352,144 sq mi, 912,050 sq km (32); **Land area:** 340,561 sq mi, 882,050 sq km. **Location:** Carib. coast of S America. Colombia on W, Brazil on S, Guyana on E. **Topography:** Plains, called llanos, extend between Andes Mts. and Orinoco Delta. Orinoco stretches 1,600 mi and drains 80% of country. **Arable land:** 2.9%. **Capital:** Caracas, 2,972,145. **Cities:** Maracaibo, 2,367,626; Valencia, 1,983,445; Barquisimeto, 1,254,192.

Government: Type: Federal presidential republic. **Head of state and govt.:** Pres. Nicolás Maduro Moros; b. 1962; in office: Apr. 19, 2013. (The U.S. does not recognize Maduro; an interim govt. led by National Assembly leader Juan Guaidó was dissolved in Dec. 2022.) **Local divisions:** 23 states, 1 capital district, 1 federal dependency (with 11 federally controlled island groups). **Defense budget:** NA. **Active troops:** 123,000.

Economy: Industries: agric. prods., livestock, raw materials, machinery and equip., transp. equip., constr. materials, medical equip., pharmaceuticals. **Chief agric.:** sugarcane, maize, milk, rice, plantains, bananas. **Natural resources:** petroleum, nat. gas, iron ore, gold, bauxite, hydropower, diamonds. **Water:** 46,596 cu m per capita. **Crude oil reserves:** 303.8 bil bbls. **Electricity prod.:** 94.7 bil kWh. **Labor force:** agric. 13.1%, industry 17.5%, services 69.4%. **Unemployment:** 5.3%.

Finance: Monetary unit: Bolivar (VES) (32.23 = $1 U.S.). **GDP:** NA; **per capita GDP:** NA; **GDP growth:** NA. **Imports** (2018): $18.4 bil; China 28%, U.S. 22%, Brazil 8%, Spain 6%, Mexico 6%. **Exports** (2018): $83.4 bil; India 34%, China 28%, U.S. 12%, Spain 6%. **Budget** (2017): $76 mil. **Inflation** (2018-19): 146,101.7%.

Transport: Railways: 278 mi. **Motor vehicles:** 133.5 per 1,000 pop. **Airports:** 127.

Communications: Mobile: 63.4 per 100 pop. **Broadband:** 48.8 per 100 pop. **Internet** (2017): 61.6%.

Health: Expend.: 3.8%. **Life expect.:** 71.2 male; 77.5 female. **Births:** 17.0 per 1,000 pop. **Deaths:** 6.6 per 1,000 pop. **Infant mortality:** 14.1 per 1,000 live births. **Undernourished:** 17.9%. **HIV:** 0.5%. **COVID-19:** 552,695 cases, 5,856 deaths; rates per 100,000: 1,943.6 cases, 20.6 deaths. 50.2% vaccinated.

Education: Compulsory: NA. **Literacy:** 97.5%.

Website: www.state.gov/countries-areas/venezuela/

Columbus first set foot on the South American continent on the peninsula of Paria, Aug. 1498. Alonso de Ojeda, 1499, called the land Venezuela, or Little Venice, because the native people had houses on stilts. Spanish colonialists dominated Venezuela until Simón Bolívar's victory near Carabobo in June 1821. The republic was formed after secession from the Colombian Federation in 1830. Military strongmen ruled Venezuela for much of its history. Beginning in 1959, the country had democratically elected governments.

Venezuela has the world's largest crude oil reserves, and the economy in recent decades has been heavily dependent on oil revenues. The government, Jan. 1, 1976, nationalized the oil industry. The country also has large reserves of natural gas.

Two attempted coups were thwarted by loyalist troops in Feb. and Nov. 1992. Coup leader Hugo Chávez, who ran as a populist, was elected president Dec. 1998. That month, voters approved a new constitution greatly increasing his powers.

Popular among the poor, Chávez alienated middle- and upperclass Venezuelans with economic and political reforms, and his foreign policy antagonized the U.S. With the economy surging, he won the Dec. 2006 presidential election. Suffering from cancer, Chávez won reelection, Oct. 7, 2012. He died Mar. 5, 2013, before he could be sworn in. Vice Pres. Nicolás Maduro Moros won a narrow victory in Apr. 14, 2013, elections.

With the economy hurt by low oil prices, declining oil production, and tight currency and price controls, GDP declined sharply beginning in 2014 and inflation soared. Shortages of food, medicine, and other goods were widespread. A political crisis intensified economic problems. Beginning in 2015, millions of Venezuelans emigrated, largely to other South American nations and to the U.S.

Large anti-Maduro protests, Feb.-June 2014, were met with a harsh crackdown. An opposition coalition won Dec. 6, 2015, National Assembly elections, but the Supreme Court often overturned legislation. Looting and sometimes violent demonstrations were widespread in 2016-17. In a flawed election, May 20, 2018, Maduro won a new term as president. The National Assembly, Jan. 15, 2019, declared Maduro's presidency illegitimate. National Assembly head Juan Guaidó, Jan. 23, 2019, declared himself interim president. Dozens of countries, including the U.S., recognized Guaidó, but Maduro clung to power. The military cracked down on protesters. UN reports in 2019 and 2020 concluded that detainees were being tortured and that security forces and death squads had committed thousands of extrajudicial killings. Pro-Maduro candidates swept Dec. 6, 2020, National Assembly elections boycotted by the opposition. The COVID-19 pandemic that began in 2020 added to the country's suffering.

With Maduro apparently entrenched in power, opposition groups voted in Dec. 2022 to dissolve the interim government that Guaidó had headed.

The economy somewhat stabilized in the early 2020s and GDP growth returned, but extreme poverty and deprivation remained widespread. By May 2023, more than 7.2 mil Venezuelans were migrants, refugees, or asylum seekers worldwide.

Vietnam
Socialist Republic of Vietnam

People: Population: 104,799,174 (16). **Age distrib.:** <15: 23.4%; 65+: 7.9%. **Growth:** 0.9%. **Migrants:** 0.1%. **Pop. density:** 875.4 per sq mi, 338.0 per sq km. **Urban:** 39.5%. **Ethnic groups:** Kinh (Viet) 85.3% (54 total ethnic groups recognized). **Languages:** Vietnamese (official), English, French, Chinese, Khmer. **Religions:** Buddhist 49.3% (Mahayanist 48%), agnostic 12.0%, new religionist 10.9%, ethnic religionist 10.3%, Christian 9.8%, atheist 6.0%.

Geography: Total area: 127,881 sq mi, 331,210 sq km (65); **Land area:** 119,719 sq mi, 310,070 sq km. **Location:** SE Asia, on E coast of Indochinese Peninsula. China on N; Laos, Cambodia on W. **Topography:** Long and narrow, with 1,400-mi coast. Densely settled Red R. Valley in N; narrow coastal plains in center; wide, often marshy Mekong R. Delta in S. Semi-arid plateaus and barren mountains, with some stretches of tropical rain forest, in rest of country. **Arable land:** 21.7%. **Capital:** Hà Noi, 5,253,385. **Cities:** Thành Pho Ho Chí Minh (Ho Chi Minh City), 9,320,866; Can Tho, 1,865,172; Hai Phòng, 1,422,974; Da Nang, 1,220,634.

Government: Type: Communist state. **Head of state:** Pres. Vo Van Thuong; b. 1970; in office: Mar. 2, 2023. **Head of govt.:** Prime Min. Pham Minh Chinh; b. 1958; in office: Apr. 5, 2021. **Local divisions:** 58 provinces, 5 municipalities. **Defense budget:** $6.0 bil. **Active troops:** 482,000.

Economy: Industries: food proc., garments, shoes, machine-building, mining, coal, steel, cement, chemical fertilizer. **Chief agric.:** rice, vegetables, sugarcane, cassava, maize, pork. **Natural resources:** antimony, phosphates, coal, manganese, rare earth elements, bauxite, chromate, offshore oil/gas deposits, timber, hydropower. **Water:** 9,083 cu m per capita. **Crude oil reserves:** 4.4 bil bbls. **Electricity prod.:** 243.8 bil kWh. **Labor force:** agric. 29.0%, industry 33.1%, services 37.8%. **Unemployment:** 1.9%.

Finance: Monetary unit: Dong (VND) (24,045.70 = $1 U.S.). **GDP:** $1.3 tril; **per capita GDP:** $13,457; **GDP growth:** 8.0%. **Imports:** $338.0 bil; (2021) China 39%, South Korea 17%, Japan 5%. **Exports:** $340.0 bil; (2021) U.S. 28%, China 17%, South Korea 6%, Japan 6%. **Tourism:** $149 mil. **Budget:** $75.8 bil. **Inflation:** 3.2%.

Transport: Railways: 1,616 mi. **Motor vehicles:** 6.9 per 1,000 pop. **Airports:** 38.

Communications: Mobile: 140.0 per 100 pop. **Broadband:** 96.9 per 100 pop. **Internet:** 78.6%.

Health: Expend.: 4.7%. **Life expect.:** 73.2 male; 78.6 female. **Births:** 15.3 per 1,000 pop. **Deaths:** 5.8 per 1,000 pop. **Infant mortality:** 14.4 per 1,000 live births. **Undernourished:** 5.0%. **HIV:** 0.3%. **COVID-19:** 11,622,404 cases, 43,206 deaths; rates per 100,000: 11,940.2 cases, 44.4 deaths. 88.3% vaccinated.

Education: Compulsory: ages 5-14. **Literacy:** 95.8%.

Website: vietnam.gov.vn

Settled by Viets from central China, Vietnam was held by China, 111 BCE-939 CE, and was a vassal state during subsequent periods. Conquest by France began in 1858 and ended in 1884 with the protectorates of Tonkin and Annam in the N and the colony of Cochin-China in the S.

Japan occupied Vietnam in 1940. Several groups formed the Vietminh (Independence) League, headed by Communist guerrilla leader Ho Chi Minh. In Aug. 1945, the Vietminh forced out Bao Dai, former emperor of Annam and head of a Japan-sponsored regime. France, seeking to reestablish colonial control, unsuccessfully battled Communist and nationalist forces, 1946-54.

Separate states formed in N. and S. Vietnam, with Communists under Ho Chi Minh (backed by Russia and China) controlling N. Vietnam and a non-Communist government (backed by the U.S.) controlling S. Vietnam. N. Vietnam aided Vietcong guerrillas who sought to take over S. Vietnam. U.S. troops and the S. Vietnamese army fought N. Vietnamese and Vietcong forces, including in border areas of Laos and Cambodia. Combat deaths: U.S. 47,434 (Aug. 4, 1964-Jan. 27, 1973); S. Vietnam more than 200,000; other allied forces 5,225. Total U.S. fatalities exceeded 58,000. Vietnamese civilian casualties were more than 1 mil. The war displaced more than 6.5 mil in S. Vietnam.

A never-implemented cease-fire agreement was signed in Paris Jan. 27, 1973, by the U.S., N. and S. Vietnam, and the Vietcong. The last U.S. troops left Vietnam Mar. 27, 1973. S. Vietnam surrendered Apr. 30, 1975. N. Vietnam assumed control. The country was officially reunited July 2, 1976.

Heavy fighting with Cambodia took place, 1977-80. Reacting to Vietnam's 1979 invasion of Cambodia, China attacked four Vietnamese border provinces, Feb. 1979.

Vietnam announced in 1987 reforms aimed at reducing central control of the economy. The U.S. ended, Feb. 1994, a 19-year embargo on trade with Vietnam, and it extended full diplomatic recognition to Vietnam July 11, 1995. The U.S. lifted in 2016 its embargo on lethal arms sales to Vietnam.

As part of an anti-corruption campaign, Vietnam's president resigned in Jan. 2023, and the Communist Party-controlled National Assembly replaced him in Mar. 2023. During a Sept. 2023 visit to Vietnam by U.S. Pres. Joe Biden, the two nations completed a strategic partnership agreement.

Yemen
Republic of Yemen

People: Population: 31,565,602 (47). **Age distrib.:** <15: 35.1%; 65+: 3.3%. **Migrants:** 1.3%. **Pop. density:** 154.8 per sq mi, 59.8 per sq km. **Urban:** 39.8%. **Ethnic groups:** predom. Arab; also Afro-Arab, South Asian, European. **Languages:** Arabic (official). **Religions:** Muslim (official) 99.2% (Shia 55%, Sunni 44%).

Geography: Total area: 203,850 sq mi, 527,968 sq km (50); **Land area:** 203,850 sq mi, 527,968 sq km. **Location:** Middle East, on S coast of the Arabian Peninsula. Saudi Arabia on N, Oman on E. **Topography:** Sandy coastal strip; well-watered fertile mountains in interior. **Arable land:** 2.2%. **Capital:** Sana'a; 3,292,497. **Cities:** Aden, 1,079,670.

Government: Type: In transition. **Head of state and govt.:** Presidential Council Chair Rashad Mohammed Al-Alimi; in office: Apr. 19, 2022. **Local divisions:** 22 governorates. **Defense budget:** NA. **Active troops:** 40,000. (20,000 insurgent forces, incl. Houthi and tribes, in territory where govt. does not exercise effective control.)

Economy: Industries: crude oil prod. and petroleum refining; small-scale prod. of cotton textiles, leather goods; food proc.; handicrafts; aluminum prods. **Chief agric.:** mangoes/guavas, potatoes, sorghum, onions, milk, poultry. **Natural resources:** petroleum; fish; rock salt; marble; small deposits of coal, gold, lead, nickel, copper. **Water:** 70 cu m per capita. **Crude oil reserves:** 3 bil bbls. **Electricity prod.:** 3.5 bil kWh. **Labor force:** agric. 28.1%, industry 11.7%, services 60.2%. **Unemployment:** 13.6%.

Finance: Monetary unit: Rial (YER) (250.24 = $1 U.S.). **GDP:** NA; **per capita GDP:** NA; **GDP growth** (2018): 0.8%. **Imports** (2017): $4.1 bil; China 25%, Turkey 10%, UAE 9%, Saudi Arabia 8%, India 7%. **Exports** (2017): $384.5 mil; China 53%, Saudi Arabia 10%, UAE 7%. **Budget:** $3.6 bil. **Inflation** (2016-17): 24.7%.

Transport: Motor vehicles: 35.0 per 1,000 pop. **Airports:** 17.

Communications: Mobile (2021): 46.0 per 100 pop. **Broadband** (2021): 5.0 per 100 pop. **Internet** (2017): 26.7%.

Health: Expend.: NA. **Life expect.:** 65.5 male; 70.3 female. **Births:** 24.1 per 1,000 pop. **Deaths:** 5.5 per 1,000 pop. **Infant mortality:** 45.5 per 1,000 live births. **Undernourished:** 34.5%. **HIV:** <0.1%. **COVID-19:** 11,945 cases, 2,159 deaths; rates per 100,000: 40.0 cases, 7.2 deaths. 2.7% vaccinated.

Education: Compulsory: ages 6-14. **Literacy:** 70.1%.

Website: www.yemen.gov.ye or www.yemenembassy.org

Yemen's territory once was part of the ancient biblical Kingdom of Sheba, or Saba. Yemen became independent in 1918, after centuries of Ottoman Turkish rule.

Imam Yahya ibn Muhammad ruled, 1904-48, and after his assassination was succeeded by his son, Imam Ahmed, 1948-62. Army officers headed by Brig. Gen. Abdullah al-Salal declared the country the Yemen Arab Republic, Sept. 1962. Ahmed's heir, the Imam Mohamad al-Badr, fled to the mountains where tribesmen joined royalist forces, aided by the Saudi monarchy. Fighting between royalists and republicans killed about 150,000 people until hostilities ended in 1970.

South Yemen, formed from the British colony of Aden and British protectorate of South Arabia, became independent Nov. 1967. A Marxist state and a Soviet ally, it took the name People's Democratic Republic of Yemen in 1970. More than 300,000 Yemenis fled from the S to the N after independence, contributing to two decades of hostility between the two states.

The two countries were formally united May 21, 1990, but regional clan-based rivalries led to full-scale civil war in 1994. Northern troops captured the former southern capital of Aden in July.

While on a refueling stop in Aden, Oct. 12, 2000, the destroyer USS Cole was bombed, killing 17 Americans; the U.S. blamed the attack on al-Qaeda terrorists.

Clashes beginning in June 2004 between Yemeni government forces and Shiite rebels led by an anti-U.S. cleric, Hussein al-Houthi, left more than 200 people dead. The government announced Sept. 10 that Yemeni troops had killed al-Houthi.

During 2007-10, Shiite rebels in the northwest, secessionists in the south, Sunni militants in the east affiliated with al-Qaeda in the Arabian Peninsula (AQAP), and pirates in coastal waters challenged Yemeni government authority. Pres. Ali Abdullah Saleh was severely wounded June 3, 2011, in a rocket attack. Vice Pres. Abd Rabbuh Mansur Hadi became acting president and won an uncontested Feb. 2012 election. Anwar al-Awlaki, a U.S. citizen and radical Muslim cleric linked to several plots against the U.S., was killed Sept. 30, 2011, by a U.S. missile in northern Yemen.

Shiite rebels known as Houthis took over Sanaa in Sept. 2014 and gained control of much of western Yemen. A coalition of Sunni nations led by Saudi Arabia, which backed Hadi, began, Mar. 25, 2015, airstrikes against Houthi fighters and Houthi-controlled areas. The U.S. provided weaponry and logistical support (ended in 2021).

UAE ground troops aided forces combating Houthi rebels. Airstrikes (including bombings of hospitals, markets, and schoolchildren) and other fighting caused high civilian casualties. Houthi rebels were aided by Iran. AQAP was active in southern Yemen, and the Sunni extremist group ISIS staged attacks. Houthi forces launched missile and drone attacks on targets in Saudi Arabia and the UAE. Heavy fighting between Houthi and government forces continued through early 2022. A UN-mediated cease-fire went into effect Apr. 2, 2022. Hadi transferred power, in Apr. 2022, to an 8-member Presidential Council. Although the cease-fire expired, Oct. 2, 2022, negotiations—and a lull in fighting—continued in 2023.

By the beginning of 2022, the UN estimated total deaths in Yemen's civil war since 2014 at 377,000, including 154,000 resulting from combat and other violence and 223,000 from indirect causes such as famine. As of Mar. 2023, more than 4.5 mil people were internally displaced, and over 21 mil needed humanitarian assistance. A cholera epidemic that began in late 2016 caused millions of cases and thousands of deaths; new cases declined in 2022, but the epidemic continued in 2023. The impact of the COVID-19 pandemic on Yemen, with a decimated health care system, was difficult to assess.

Zambia
Republic of Zambia

People: Population: 20,216,029 (63). **Age distrib.:** <15: 42.5%; 65+: 2.7%. **Growth:** 2.9%. **Migrants:** 1.0%. **Pop. density:** 70.4 per sq mi, 27.2 per sq km. **Urban:** 46.3%. **Ethnic groups:** Bemba 21%, Tonga 13.6%, Chewa 7.4%, Lozi 5.7%, Nsenga 5.3%, Tumbuka 4.4%, Ngoni 4%, Lala 3.1%, Kaonde 2.9%, Namwanga 2.8%, Lunda (northwestern) 2.6%, Mambwe 2.5%, Luvale 2.2%, Lamba 2.1%. **Languages:** Bantu langs. (incl. Bemba, Nyanja, Tonga, Lozi, Chewa, Nsenga, Tumbuka); English (official). **Religions:** Christian (official) 86.1% (Protestant 35.6%, Catholic 34.1%, independent 16.5%), ethnic religionist 10.5%.

Geography: Total area: 290,587 sq mi, 752,618 sq km (38); **Land area:** 287,028 sq mi, 743,398 sq km. **Location:** S central Africa. Dem. Rep. of the Congo on N; Tanzania, Malawi, Mozambique on E; Zimbabwe, Namibia on S; Angola on W. **Topography:** Mostly high plateau with thick forests, drained by several important rivers including the Zambezi. **Arable land:** 5.1%. **Capital:** Lusaka, 3,181,250.

Government: Type: Presidential republic. **Head of state and govt.:** Pres. Hakainde Hichilema; b. 1962; in office: Aug. 24, 2021. **Local divisions:** 10 provinces. **Defense budget:** $444 mil. **Active troops:** 15,100.

Economy: Industries: copper mining and proc., emerald mining, constr., foodstuffs, beverages, chemicals, textiles, fertilizer, horticulture. **Chief agric.:** sugarcane, cassava, maize, milk, vegetables, soybeans. **Natural resources:** copper, cobalt, zinc, lead, coal, emeralds, gold, silver, uranium, hydropower. **Water:** 5,701 cu m per capita. **Electricity prod.:** 17.7 bil kWh. **Labor force:** agric. 58.7%, industry 8.8%; services 32.5%. **Unemployment:** 6.1%.

Finance: Monetary unit: Kwacha (ZMW) (19.84 = $1 U.S.). **GDP:** $78.0 bil; **per capita GDP:** $3,894; **GDP growth:** 4.7%. **Imports:** $7.7 bil; (2020) South Africa 31%, China 16%, UAE 9%, Dem. Rep. of the Congo 6%. **Exports:** $11.7 bil; (2020) Switzerland 32%, China 14%, Namibia 12%, Dem. Rep. of the Congo 9%, Singapore 8%. **Tourism:** $393 mil. **Budget:** $7.0 bil. **Inflation:** 11.0%.

Transport: Railways: 1,942 mi (incl. 1,156 mi of Tanzania-Zambia Railway Authority). **Motor vehicles:** 24.2 per 1,000 pop. **Airports:** 8. **Communications: Mobile:** 99.1 per 100 pop. **Broadband:** 55.3 per 100 pop. **Internet:** 21.2%.

Health: Expend.: 5.6%. **Life expect.:** 64.9 male; 68.4 female. **Births:** 34.5 per 1,000 pop. **Deaths:** 6.0 per 1,000 pop. **Infant mortality:** 36.3 per 1,000 live births. **Undernourished:** 29.8%. **HIV:** 10.8%. **COVID-19:** 349,287 cases, 4,069 deaths; rates per 100,000: 1,900.0 cases, 22.1 deaths. 49.8% vaccinated.

Education: Compulsory: ages 7-13. **Literacy:** 87.5%.

Website: www.parliament.gov.zm

Ruled by the British as Northern Rhodesia, the country became the independent republic of Zambia within the Commonwealth Oct. 24, 1964. Independence leader Kenneth Kaunda governed as president, 1964-91. A Zambian government corporation in 1970 took over 51% of two foreign-owned copper-mining companies. Privately held land and other enterprises were nationalized in 1975. In the 1980s and 1990s, lowered copper prices hurt the economy and severe drought caused famine.

Oct. 1991 elections brought an end to Kaunda's one-party rule. The new government sought to sell state enterprises, including the copper industry. Pres. Frederick Chiluba won reelection Nov. 1996. In 2001, Chiluba endorsed Levy Patrick Mwanawasa, who won a disputed Dec. election. Food shortages threatened more than 2 mil Zambians in 2002. Mwanawasa won a second term in 2006.

Pres. Mwanawasa died Aug. 19, 2008. Vice Pres. Rupiah Banda became acting pres. He narrowly won the presidency in the Oct. 2008 election but lost to opposition leader Michael Sata Sept. 2011. Sata died in office, Oct. 28, 2014. Edgar Lungu of Sata's

Patriotic Front party narrowly won a Jan. 2015 special election. Lungu narrowly won a new term in Aug. 11, 2016, elections that his main opponent claimed was marred by fraud. Several European countries suspended aid payments, Sept. 2018, after allegations of government corruption and embezzlement of aid money. With inflation and unemployment high, Hakainde Hichilema defeated Lunga in the Aug. 12, 2021, presidential election.

The country has made progress in treating HIV/AIDS, but in 2021, 11% of Zambians ages 15+ were HIV positive.

Zimbabwe
Republic of Zimbabwe

People: Population: 15,418,674 (73). **Age distrib.:** <15: 38.5%; 65+: 3.9%. **Growth:** 2.0%. **Migrants:** 2.8%. **Pop. density:** 103.2 per sq mi, 39.9 per sq km. **Urban:** 32.5%. **Ethnic groups:** African (predom. Shona; Ndebele is second-largest ethnic group) 99.4%. **Languages:** Shona, Ndebele (both official and most widely spoken); English (official, used in business), 13 official minority langs. **Religions:** Christian 80.2% (independent 34.5%, Protestant 34.5%, Catholic 11.1%), ethnic religionist 17.1%.

Geography: Total area: 150,872 sq mi, 390,757 sq km (60); **Land area:** 149,362 sq mi, 386,847 sq km. **Location:** Southern Africa. Zambia on N, Botswana on W, South Africa on S, Mozambique on E. **Topography:** High plateau rising to mountains on E border, sloping down on other borders. **Arable land:** 10.3%. **Capital:** Harare, 1,578,128.

Government: Type: Presidential republic. **Head of state and govt.:** Pres. Emmerson Mnangagwa; b. 1942; in office: Nov. 24, 2017. **Local divisions:** 8 provinces, 2 cities with provincial status. **Defense budget:** $751 mil. **Active troops:** 29,000.

Economy: Industries: mining, steel, wood prods., cement, chemicals, fertilizer, clothing/footwear, foodstuffs, beverages. **Chief agric.:** sugarcane, maize, milk, tobacco, cassava, vegetables. **Natural resources:** coal, chromium ore, asbestos, gold, nickel, copper, iron ore, vanadium, lithium, tin, platinum group metals. **Water:** 1,346 cu m per capita. **Electricity prod.:** 8.0 bil kWh. **Labor force:** agric. 61.6%, industry 11.6%, services 26.7%. **Unemployment:** 7.9%.

Finance: Monetary unit: Dollar (ZWD) (361.90 = $1 U.S.). **GDP:** $41.3 bil; **per capita GDP:** $2,531; **GDP growth:** 3.4%. **Imports** (2020): $5.5 bil; South Africa 41%, Singapore 23%, China 8%. **Exports** (2020): $5.3 bil; UAE 40%, South Africa 23%, Mozambique 9%. **Tourism** (2020): $63 mil. **Budget** (2018): $23 mil. **Inflation:** 104.7%.

Transport: Railways: 2,129 mi. **Motor vehicles:** 50.6 per 1,000 pop. **Airports:** 17.

Communications: Mobile: 87.6 per 100 pop. **Broadband:** 59.6 per 100 pop. **Internet:** 34.8%.

Health: Expend.: 3.4%. **Life expect.:** 65.2 male; 68.5 female. **Births:** 29.4 per 1,000 pop. **Deaths:** 6.7 per 1,000 pop. **Infant mortality:** 34.0 per 1,000 live births. **Undernourished:** 38.4%. **HIV:** 11.0%. **COVID-19:** 265,716 cases, 5,713 deaths; rates per 100,000: 1,787.8 cases, 38.4 deaths. 38.0% vaccinated.

Education: Compulsory: ages 6-12. **Literacy:** 89.7%.

Website: www.zim.gov.zw

Britain took over the area as Southern Rhodesia in 1923 from the British South Africa Co. (which, under Cecil Rhodes, had conquered it by 1897) and granted internal self-government. A 1961 constitution restricted voting to keep whites in power.

On Nov. 11, 1965, Prime Min. Ian D. Smith unilaterally declared independence. Britain termed the act illegal and demanded that the country (known as Rhodesia until 1980) enfranchise the Black African majority. The UN imposed sanctions, and Black nationalists launched guerrilla attacks.

After the country held its first universal-franchise election, Apr. 21, 1979, all parties accepted a cease-fire, Dec. 5. The country changed its name to Zimbabwe upon independence, Apr. 18, 1980. Robert Mugabe, the nation's first prime min., became executive president in 1987. From the late 1990s, Mugabe's rule became increasingly repressive. A land redistribution campaign triggered violent attacks in Apr. 2000 against some white farmers (white landowners had controlled 70% of the land). Production of corn, the nation's food staple, subsequently declined sharply. Mugabe, relying on fraud and intimidation, won the Mar. 9-11, 2002, presidential election. During 2006-08, inflation soared to a yearly rate of more than 100,000%.

Mugabe clung to power after a widely discredited 2008 presidential election and intensified a crackdown on dissidents. Mugabe won the July 31, 2013, presidential election.

Drought caused food shortages in 2016. Police suppressed strikes and demonstrations protesting economic conditions. Mugabe lost the support of the military and his ZANU-PF party, and he resigned, Nov. 21, 2017. Vice Pres. Emmerson Mnangagwa became president, Nov. 24, and narrowly won a disputed July 30, 2018, presidential election. Security forces cracked down violently after Jan. 2019 protests and looting, triggered by food and fuel shortages. Economic hardship and repression continued in 2020-23. Mnangagwa won a disputed Aug. 23-24, 2023, presidential election criticized by international observers.

WORLD ALMANAC EDITORS' PICKS: MOST UNBREAKABLE RECORDS IN SPORTS

Secretariat's 50-year-old all-time record of 2:24.00 for the 1½-mile dirt course at Belmont is considered one of the most unbreakable records in sports. Here are some of our other favorites, accomplished by human athletes.

Cy Young: 511 Wins, 749 Complete Games

There's a reason baseball's most prestigious pitching award is named after the pre-eminent hurler of the dead ball era. Over a 22-year career beginning in 1890, Young started 815 games and completed 749 of them, won 511 times, and logged more than 7,000 innings. All four of those marks remain all-time records more than a century later. The only question is which is the most unbreakable. Walter Johnson is second on the all-time wins list with 417 wins but the closest anyone has come in the 21st century is Greg Maddux, who won 355 games over 23 years. Pud Galvin is second on the all-time complete games list, but still more than 100 games behind Young, who averaged 30 a year. The last player to register more than 10 complete games in a season was James Shields, who had 11 in 2011. In today's statistics-driven era, the likelihood of Young's records being broken is even more remote.

Johnny Vander Meer: Back-to-Back No-Hitters

Johnny Vander Meer had a so-so career record of 119-121, but for a five-day stretch in 1938, he was quite literally unhittable. The Cincinnati southpaw threw a no-hitter against the Boston Bees on June 11, then did the same to the Brooklyn Dodgers four days later, in the first-ever night game at Ebbets Field. Vander Meer was far from perfect in either game. He walked three Bees in the first game and eight Dodgers in the second, concluding the Brooklyn game precariously by loading the bases before securing the final out. Other pitchers have thrown more no-hitters, but to surpass Vander Meer's record, a player would have to toss three straight complete games without giving up a single hit. Given how few starting pitchers today are allowed to throw more than seven innings, the likelihood of that happening declines every year.

Wilt Chamberlain: 100-Point Game

Wilt Chamberlain's 100-point game could hardly have been less auspicious in the offing. The Mar. 2, 1962, contest was held not on the Warriors' home court in Philadelphia, but at an arena in Hershey, PA. Attended by just 4,124 fans, there were no TV cameras and few photographers, one of whom—Paul Vathis from the Associated Press—took the iconic black-and-white shot of Chamberlain holding a piece of paper with the number 100 written on it, the idea of Warriors statistician and public relations director Harvey Pollack. But the lack of hype surrounding Chamberlain's historic achievement makes it no less impressive. Chamberlain played all 48 minutes of the 169-147 game against the NY Knicks, going 36 for 63 from the floor and 28 for 32 from the line shooting underhanded. Chamberlain scored 60 or more points on 15 different occasions that season, averaging 50.4 points per game for the year, another seemingly invulnerable mark. No NBA player has come anywhere close to matching the Big Dipper's 100 points, even aided by the three-point line adopted in 1979. Kobe Bryant's 81-point outburst against the Toronto Raptors on Jan. 22, 2006, is a distant second.

Isner-Mahut: Wimbledon Marathon

There was no reason to expect anything out of the ordinary when France's Nicolas Mahut squared off against American John Isner in the first round of Wimbledon on June 22, 2010. Mahut was a qualifier, and Isner, the 23rd seed, wasn't much more heralded. The contest was held on Court 18, as far from Centre Court as is possible for match play. Even when the match was suspended because of darkness after the fourth set, the contest seemed unexceptional. The fifth set, however, was incomparable. At the time, Wimbledon rules did not permit fifth-set tiebreakers, requiring a win by two games. That proved elusive, as the two men battled for seven more hours and 118 more games before play was adjourned a second time due to darkness. The on-court scoreboard stopped being useful at 47-47 because it hadn't been programmed to go any higher. On the third day of play,

Isner finally broke through to win the set, 70-68, and thus the match, 6-4, 3-6, 6-7 (7), 7-6 (3). The 11-hour, 5-minute match will probably never be equaled now that Grand Slam rules permit fifth-set tiebreakers.

Brett Favre: 336 Interceptions

More than a decade after his 20-year career came to an end, Brett Favre continues to hold two records that many football fans consider unbreakable: a consecutive QB-starts streak of 321 games (including playoffs) and a career total 336 interceptions. Of the two, the latter seems more impregnable. Conceivably, some future Tom Brady might play well into his 40s and never miss a start. But the likelihood of any player holding down a starting job while averaging more than one interception per game seems extremely low in 2023 and beyond. George Blanda, who played 26 seasons, is second on the all-time interception list with 277; the recently retired Brady finished his 23-year career with just 212. And the active leader at the end of the 2022 season, Matt Ryan, had exactly half of Favre's total (183 after the 2022 season). At that pace, the 38-year-old Ryan would have to play more than a dozen more years to surpass Favre.

Michael Phelps: 23 Olympic Gold Medals

In 1972, American swimmer Mark Spitz set a record by winning seven gold medals in a single Olympics, each in world-record time. Then came Michael Phelps. The Baltimore Bullet nearly matched Spitz's achievement in 2004, when he won six gold and two bronze medals. In 2008, he was even better, sweeping all eight events in which he competed and setting world records in seven of them. That performance both surpassed Spitz's single-Olympics haul and gave Phelps more gold medals than any Olympian in any sport. He continued his streak of excellence at the 2012 Games—"just" four gold medals and two silver—and took a victory lap in 2016, winning five golds and one silver at the age of 31. His total medal count of 23 gold, three silver, and two bronze medals make him the most decorated Olympian ever.

UConn Women's Basketball: 111 Straight Wins

Univ. of Connecticut coach Geno Auriemma is no stranger to perfection. His women's Huskies teams completed undefeated seasons in 1995, 2002, 2009, 2010, 2014, and 2016. From 2008-10, UConn reeled off 90 consecutive wins, besting the all-time record of 88, set by UCLA's John Wooden's men's teams in 1971-74. Beginning just four years later, Auriemma outdid himself. After an overtime defeat to Stanford on Nov. 17, 2014, the Huskies didn't lose again until Mar. 31, 2017, when Mississippi State upset them (again in overtime) in the Final Four. All but three of those 111 wins were by double-digit margins, and 61 of them were by 40 points or more. Led by three-time Naismith Trophy winner Breanna Stewart, UConn won two national championships during the streak, completing a run of four straight titles.

Simone Biles: 23 World Championships

For more than 50 years, no woman won more than the nine World Gymnastics Championships captured by the Soviet Union's legendary Laryssa Latynina in the 1950s and 1960s. Romania's Gina Gogean equaled the record in 1997, as did Russia's Svetlana Khorkina six years later, but neither woman surpassed it. In 2015, however, Simone Biles blew past all three of these gymnastic giants. Biles had already placed first in two events in 2013, and in 2014 she captured gold in the balance beam, floor exercises, all-around, and team competition. She repeated that feat in 2015, giving her 10 titles, but that was only the beginning. Biles returned to the World Championships in 2018. At the age of 21, she added four more gold medals to her resume, and five more in 2019 for a total of 19. Even after a two-year break, Biles came back to claim four more championships at the age of 26 in 2023. Her total world champion medal haul of 30 is also an all-time high for both male and female gymnasts, and this doesn't even include her Olympic tally of four gold, one silver, and two bronze medals.

OLYMPIC GAMES

General Olympic Information

The modern Olympic Games, first held in Athens, Greece, in 1896, were the result of efforts by Baron Pierre de Coubertin, a French educator, to promote interest in education and culture and to foster better international understanding through love of athletics. His inspiration was the ancient Greek Olympic Games, most notable of the four Panhellenic celebrations. The games were combined patriotic, religious, and athletic festivals held every four years. The first such recorded festival was held in 776 BCE, when the Greeks began to keep their calendar by "Olympiads," or four-year spans between the games.

Coubertin enlisted 14 nations to send athletes to the first modern Olympics. Now athletes from more than 200 nations and territories compete in the Summer Olympics. The Winter Olympic Games, started in 1924, draw competitors from about 90 countries and territories.

Symbol: Five rings or circles, linked to represent the sporting friendship of all peoples. They also symbolize five geographic areas—Africa, America, Asia, Australia, and Europe. Each ring is a different color—blue, yellow, black, green, and red—which, with the color white, represent the colors of the world's flags.

Flag: The five-ring symbol on a plain white background.

Creed: "The most important thing in the Olympic Games is not to win but to take part, just as the most important thing in life is not the triumph but the struggle. The essential thing is not to have conquered but to have fought well."

Motto: Citius, Altius, Fortius. ("Faster, higher, stronger" in Latin.) Updated in 2021 to "Citius, Altius, Fortius – Communiter" ("Faster, higher, stronger – together").

Oath: "In the name of all the competitors I promise that we shall take part in these Olympic Games, respecting and abiding by the rules which govern them, committing ourselves to a sport without doping and without drugs, in the true spirit of sportsmanship, for the glory of sport and the honor of our teams."

Flame: The modern version of the flame was adopted in 1936. The torch used to kindle it is first lit by the sun's rays in Olympia, Greece, then carried to the site of the Games by relays of runners. Ships and planes are used when necessary.

Winter Olympic Games Sites, 1924-2026

1924	Chamonix, France	1956	Cortina d'Ampezzo, Italy	1980	Lake Placid, NY, U.S.	2006	Turin, Italy
1928	St. Moritz, Switzerland	1960	Squaw Valley, CA, U.S.	1984	Sarajevo, Yugoslavia	2010	Vancouver, BC, Can.
1932	Lake Placid, NY, U.S.	1964	Innsbruck, Austria	1988	Calgary, AB, Canada	2014	Sochi, Russia
1936	Garmisch-Partenkirchen, Germany	1968	Grenoble, France	1992	Albertville, France	2018	Pyeongchang, South Korea
1948	St. Moritz, Switzerland	1972	Sapporo, Japan	1994	Lillehammer, Norway	2022	Beijing, China
1952	Oslo, Norway	1976	Innsbruck, Austria	1998	Nagano, Japan	2026	Milan-Cortina, Italy
				2002	Salt Lake City, UT, U.S.		

Summer Olympic Games Sites, 1896-2032

1896	Athens, Greece	1932	Los Angeles, CA, U.S.	1972	Munich, W. Germany	2004	Athens, Greece
1900	Paris, France	1936	Berlin, Germany	1976	Montréal, QC, Canada	2008	Beijing, China
1904	St. Louis, MO, U.S.	1948	London, England, UK	1980	Moscow, USSR	2012	London, England, UK
1906	Athens, Greece*	1952	Helsinki, Finland	1984	Los Angeles, CA, U.S.	2016	Rio de Janeiro, Brazil
1908	London, England, UK	1956	Melbourne, Australia	1988	Seoul, South Korea	2020	Tokyo, Japan
1912	Stockholm, Sweden	1960	Rome, Italy	1992	Barcelona, Spain	2024	Paris, France
1920	Antwerp, Belgium	1964	Tokyo, Japan	1996	Atlanta, GA, U.S.	2028	Los Angeles, CA, U.S.
1924	Paris, France	1968	Mexico City, Mexico	2000	Sydney, Australia	2032	Brisbane, Australia
1928	Amsterdam, Netherlands						

* = Games not recognized by International Olympic Committee. **Note:** Games VI (1916), XII (1940), and XIII (1944) were not celebrated.

2024 Summer Olympic Games: Preview
Paris, France, July 26-Aug. 11, 2024

The XXXIII Olympic Summer Games are scheduled to take place in Paris, France, in July-Aug. 2024, marking the centenary of the Games hosted by Paris, in 1924. Along with London, England, it will be only the second city to host the summer games three times. Competitions in 329 medal events will include one new event, breaking, the competitive name for breakdancing. While most events will be held in venues in and around Paris, some football (soccer) games will be hosted in six other cities (Bordeaux, Décines-Charpieu, Marseille, Nantes, Nice, and Saint-Étienne); sailing events will be hosted in Marseille; and the territory of French Polynesia, in the South Pacific Ocean, will host surfing events.

2020 Summer Olympic Games
Tokyo, Japan, July 23-Aug. 8, 2021

The second Summer Olympic Games held in Japan set a record for number of athletes (11,656) participating, from 206 nations (including a team composed of refugees). Forty-two venues hosted 339 events in 33 different sports. The International Olympic Committee added four sports to the games: karate, surfing, skateboarding, and sport climbing; baseball and softball were re-introduced.

Originally scheduled to be held July 24-Aug. 9, 2020, the Games were postponed by one year because of the coronavirus pandemic (the event retained the "Tokyo 2020" name for branding and marketing purposes). The Games were played under unprecedented conditions, with no public spectators permitted due to the state of emergency in the Tokyo area. Athletes could arrive no sooner than five days before their competition, and needed to depart within 48 hours after completion. Daily testing occurred and, as of mid-Aug., a total of 533 accredited personnel tested positive for coronavirus during the course of the Games.

U.S. swimmer Caeleb Dressel won five gold medals and set two world records. Fellow U.S. swimmer Katie Ledecky continued her winning streak, earning two golds and two silvers, making her the most decorated U.S. woman athlete of the games. U.S. runner Allyson Felix became the most decorated track and field Olympian in U.S. history by winning her 11th career medal. U.S. gymnast Simone Biles, the 2016 all-around gold medalist, withdrew from four finals to focus on her safety and mental health. She went on to win a silver medal in the team event and a bronze medal on balance beam. Her teammate, gymnast Sunisa Lee, became the first Asian American to win gold in the all-around final; the U.S. women took silver in the team event. Both U.S. basketball teams continued to dominate with the women winning gold for the seventh Olympics in a row, and the men their fourth in a row.

Ahmed Hafnaoui, an 18-year-old swimmer from Tunisia, pulled off an upset win in the 400-m freestyle swimming event. Host country Japan performed well in the new sport of skateboarding, winning gold in three out of four events, as well as one silver and one bronze.

San Marino, which has participated in the games since 1960, became the smallest country in the world to win their first Olympic medals. Russian athletes competed as the Russian Olympic Committee (ROC) as a result of a punishment by the World Anti-Doping Agency for a state-sponsored doping program in Russia.

2020 Summer Olympic Games: Final Medal Standings
(G = Gold, S = Silver, B = Bronze, T = Total medals)

Country	G	S	B	T	Country	G	S	B	T	Country	G	S	B	T
United States ..	39	41	33	113	Kazakhstan....	0	0	8	8	Kyrgyzstan	0	2	1	3
China	38	32	18	88	Iran	3	2	2	7	Argentina	0	1	2	3
Russian Olympic					Belgium.......	3	1	3	7	San Marino....	0	1	2	3
Committee...	20	28	23	71	Belarus.......	1	3	3	7	Bahamas	2	0	0	2
Great Britain ...	22	21	22	65	India	1	2	4	7	Kosovo	2	0	0	2
Japan	27	14	17	58	Austria	1	1	5	7	Tunisia	1	1	0	2
Australia	17	7	22	46	Azerbaijan	0	3	4	7	Estonia	1	0	1	2
Italy..........	10	10	20	40	Bulgaria	3	1	2	6	Fiji...........	1	0	1	2
Germany......	10	11	16	37	Hong Kong	1	2	3	6	Latvia	1	0	1	2
Netherlands ...	10	12	14	36	Egypt	1	1	4	6	Thailand	1	0	1	2
France........	10	12	11	33	Slovenia	3	1	1	5	Jordan........	0	1	1	2
Canada.......	7	6	11	24	Uzbekistan	3	0	2	5	Malaysia	0	1	1	2
Brazil.........	7	6	8	21	Indonesia	1	1	3	5	Nigeria	0	1	1	2
New Zealand ..	7	6	7	20	Colombia	0	4	1	5	Finland	0	0	2	2
Hungary	6	7	7	20	Dominican					Bermuda	1	0	0	1
South Korea ...	6	4	10	20	Republic ...	0	3	2	5	Morocco......	1	0	0	1
Ukraine.......	1	6	12	19	Greece	2	1	1	4	Puerto Rico....	1	0	0	1
Spain	3	8	6	17	Uganda.......	2	1	1	4	Bahrain	0	1	0	1
Cuba.........	7	3	5	15	Ireland	2	0	2	4	Saudi Arabia ..	0	1	0	1
Poland	4	5	5	14	Israel	2	0	2	4	Lithuania	0	1	0	1
Switzerland....	3	4	6	13	Romania	1	3	0	4	North				
Turkey........	2	2	9	13	Venezuela	1	3	0	4	Macedonia ..	0	1	0	1
Taiwan	2	4	6	12	Philippines	1	2	1	4	Namibia	0	1	0	1
Czech Republic	4	4	3	11	Slovakia	1	2	1	4	Turkmenistan .	0	1	0	1
Denmark......	3	4	4	11	Ethiopia	1	1	2	4	Botswana	0	0	1	1
Kenya........	4	4	2	10	Portugal	1	1	2	4	Burkina Faso ..	0	0	1	1
Jamaica	4	1	4	9	Armenia	0	2	2	4	Côte d'Ivoire ..	0	0	1	1
Sweden.......	3	6	0	9	Mongolia	0	1	3	4	Ghana........	0	0	1	1
Serbia........	3	1	5	9	Mexico	0	0	4	4	Grenada	0	0	1	1
Norway	4	2	2	8	Ecuador	2	1	0	3	Kuwait........	0	0	1	1
Croatia	3	3	2	8	Qatar.........	2	0	1	3	Moldova	0	0	1	1
Georgia.......	2	5	1	8	South Africa ...	1	2	0	3	Syria.........	0	0	1	1

Summer Olympic Games Champions, 1896-2020
* = Olympic record; (w) wind-aided; times are shown in hour:minute:sec.

The 1980 games were boycotted by 62 nations, including the U.S. The 1984 games were boycotted by the USSR and most Eastern bloc nations. East and West Germany competed separately, 1968-88. The 1992 Unified Team consisted of 12 former Soviet republics. The 1992 Independent Olympic Participants (IOP) were from Serbia, Montenegro, and Macedonia. In the 2020 Games, Russian athletes competed as Russian Olympic Committee (ROC).

Not all sports are listed here, and many events are omitted, even within listed sports, particularly if the event has not been held in more recent Games. Point systems for scoring events have changed many times. Points shown are those under the point system in use at the time.

Basketball

Men

1936	United States, Canada, Mexico	1996	United States, Yugoslavia, Lithuania	1992	Unified Team, China, United States	
1948	United States, France, Brazil	2000	United States, France, Lithuania	1996	United States, Brazil, Australia	
1952	United States, USSR, Uruguay	2004	Argentina, Italy, United States	2000	United States, Australia, Brazil	
1956	United States, USSR, Uruguay	2008	United States, Spain, Argentina	2004	United States, Australia, Russia	
1960	United States, USSR, Brazil	2012	United States, Spain, Russia	2008	United States, Australia, Russia	
1964	United States, USSR, Brazil	2016	United States, Serbia, Spain	2012	United States, France, Australia	
1968	United States, Yugoslavia, USSR	2020	United States, France, Australia	2016	United States, Spain, Serbia	
1972	USSR, United States, Cuba			2020	United States, Japan, France	
1976	United States, Yugoslavia, USSR		**Women**			

Women

3 x 3 Men	
2020	Latvia, ROC, Serbia

1980 — Yugoslavia, Italy, USSR
1984 — United States, Spain, Yugoslavia
1988 — USSR, Yugoslavia, United States
1992 — United States, Croatia, Lithuania

Women
1976 — USSR, United States, Bulgaria
1980 — USSR, Bulgaria, Yugoslavia
1984 — USSR, Bulgaria, South Korea, China
1988 — United States, Yugoslavia, USSR

3 x 3 Women
2020 — United States, ROC, China

Boxing—Men
Weight class limits have changed many times since the first Olympic boxing events were held in 1904. The limits shown were used in the 2020 Olympic Games. The Super Heavyweight class was known as Heavyweight 1904-80.

Lt. Flyweight (49 kg/108 lbs)

1968	Francisco Rodriguez, Venezuela
1972	Gyorgy Gedo, Hungary
1976	Jorge Hernandez, Cuba
1980	Shamil Sabyrov, USSR
1984	Paul Gonzalez, United States
1988	Ivailo Hristov, Bulgaria
1992	Rogelio Marcelo, Cuba
1996	Daniel Petrov, Bulgaria
2000	Brahim Asloum, France
2004	Yan Bhartelemy Varela, Cuba
2008	Zou Shiming, China
2012	Zou Shiming, China
2016	Hasanboy Dusmatov, Uzbekistan

Flyweight (52 kg/115 lbs)

1904	George Finnegan, United States
1920	Frank Di Gennara, United States
1924	Fidel LaBarba, United States
1928	Antal Kocsis, Hungary
1932	Istvan Enekes, Hungary
1936	Willi Kaiser, Germany
1948	Pascual Perez, Argentina
1952	Nathan Brooks, United States
1956	Terence Spinks, Great Britain
1960	Gyula Török, Hungary
1964	Fernando Atzori, Italy
1968	Ricardo Delgado, Mexico
1972	Georgi Kostadinov, Bulgaria

Flyweight (52 kg/115 lbs)

1976	Leo Randolph, United States
1980	Peter Lesov, Bulgaria
1984	Steve McCrory, United States
1988	Kim Kwang-sun, S. Korea
1992	Choi Chol Su, N. Korea
1996	Maikro Romero, Cuba
2000	Wijan Ponlid, Thailand
2004	Yuriorkis Gamboa Toledano, Cuba
2008	Somjit Jongjohor, Thailand
2012	Robeisy Ramírez, Cuba
2016	Shakhobidin Zoirov, Uzbekistan
2020	Galal Yafai, Great Britain

Bantamweight (56 kg/123 lbs)

1904	Oliver Kirk, United States
1908	A. Henry Thomas, Great Britain
1920	Clarence Walker, South Africa
1924	William Smith, South Africa
1928	Vittorio Tamagnini, Italy
1932	Horace Gwynne, Canada
1936	Ulderico Sergo, Italy
1948	Tibor Csik, Hungary
1952	Pentti Hamalainen, Finland
1956	Wolfgang Behrendt, E. Germany
1960	Oleg Grigoryev, USSR
1964	Takao Sakurai, Japan
1968	Valery Sokolov, USSR
1972	Orlando Martinez, Cuba
1976	Gu Yong Ju, N. Korea
1980	Juan Hernandez, Cuba
1984	Maurizio Stecca, Italy
1988	Kennedy McKinney, United States
1992	Joel Casamayor, Cuba
1996	Istvan Kovacs, Hungary
2000	Guillermo Rigondeaux, Cuba
2004	Guillermo Rigondeaux, Cuba
2008	Badar-Uugan Enkhbat, Mongolia
2012	Luke Campbell, Great Britain
2016	Robeisy Ramírez, Cuba

Featherweight (57 kg/126 lbs)

1904	Oliver Kirk, United States
1908	Richard Gunn, Great Britain
1920	Paul Fritsch, France
1924	John Fields, United States
1928	Lambertus van Klaveren, Netherlands
1932	Carmelo Robledo, Argentina
1936	Oscar Casanovas, Argentina
1948	Ernesto Formenti, Italy
1952	Jan Zachara, Czechoslovakia
1956	Vladimir Safronov, USSR
1960	Francesco Musso, Italy
1964	Stanislav Stephashkin, USSR
1968	Antonio Roldan, Mexico
1972	Boris Kousnetsov, USSR
1976	Angel Herrera, Cuba
1980	Rudi Fink, E. Germany
1984	Meldrick Taylor, United States
1988	Giovanni Parisi, Italy
1992	Andreas Tews, Germany
1996	Somluck Kamsing, Thailand
2000	Bekzat Sattarkhanov, Kazakhstan
2004	Alexey Tishchenko, Russia
2008	Vasyl Lomachenko, Ukraine
2020	Albert Batyrgaziev, ROC

Lightweight (63 kg/139 lbs)

1904	Harry Spanger, United States
1908	Frederick Grace, Great Britain
1920	Samuel Mosberg, United States
1924	Hans Nielsen, Denmark
1928	Carlo Orlandi, Italy
1932	Lawrence Stevens, South Africa
1936	Imre Harangi, Hungary
1948	Gerald Dreyer, South Africa
1952	Aureliano Bolognesi, Italy
1956	Richard McTaggart, Great Britain
1960	Kazimierz Pazdzior, Poland
1964	Jozef Grudzien, Poland
1968	Ronald Harris, United States
1972	Jan Szczepanski, Poland
1976	Howard Davis, United States
1980	Angel Herrera, Cuba
1984	Pernell Whitaker, United States
1988	Andreas Zülow, E. Germany
1992	Oscar De La Hoya, United States
1996	Hocine Soltani, Algeria
2000	Mario Kindelan, Cuba
2004	Mario Kindelan, Cuba
2008	Alexey Tishchenko, Russia
2012	Vasyl Lomachenko, Ukraine

Lightweight (63 kg/139 lbs)

2016	Robson Conceição, Brazil
2020	Andy Cruz, Cuba

Lt. Welterweight (64 kg/141 lbs)

1952	Charles Adkins, United States
1956	Vladimir Yengibaryan, USSR
1960	Bohumil Nemecek, Czechoslovakia
1964	Jerzy Kulej, Poland
1968	Jerzy Kulej, Poland
1972	Ray Seales, United States
1976	Ray Leonard, United States
1980	Patrizio Oliva, Italy
1984	Jerry Page, United States
1988	Viatcheslav Janovski, USSR
1992	Hector Vinent, Cuba
1996	Hector Vinent, Cuba
2000	Mahamadkadyz Abdullaev, Uzbekistan
2004	Manus Boonjumnong, Thailand
2008	Felix Diaz, Dominican Republic
2012	Roniel Iglesias, Cuba
2016	Fazliddin Gaibnazarov, Uzbekistan

Welterweight (69 kg/152 lbs)

1904	Albert Young, United States
1920	Albert Schneider, Canada
1924	Jean Delarge, Belgium
1928	Edward Morgan, New Zealand
1932	Edward Flynn, United States
1936	Sten Suvio, Finland
1948	Julius Torma, Czechoslovakia
1952	Zygmunt Chychla, Poland
1956	Nicolae Linca, Romania
1960	Giovanni Benvenuti, Italy
1964	Marian Kasprzyk, Poland
1968	Manfred Wolke, E. Germany
1972	Emilio Correa, Cuba
1976	Jochen Bachfeld, E. Germany
1980	Andres Aldama, Cuba
1984	Mark Breland, United States
1988	Robert Wangila, Kenya
1992	Michael Carruth, Ireland
1996	Oleg Saitov, Russia
2000	Oleg Saitov, Russia
2004	Bakhtiyar Artayev, Kazakhstan
2008	Bakhyt Sarsekbayev, Kazakhstan
2012	Serik Sapiyev, Kazakhstan
2016	Daniyar Yeleussinov, Kazakhstan
2020	Roniel Iglesias, Cuba

Lt. Middleweight (71 kg/156 lbs)

1952	Laszlo Papp, Hungary
1956	Laszlo Papp, Hungary
1960	Wilbert McClure, United States
1964	Boris Lagutin, USSR
1968	Boris Lagutin, USSR
1972	Dieter Kottysch, W. Germany
1976	Jerzy Rybicki, Poland
1980	Armando Martinez, Cuba
1984	Frank Tate, United States
1988	Park Si-hun, S. Korea
1992	Juan Lemus, Cuba
1996	David Reid, United States
2000	Yermakhan Ibraimov, Kazakhstan

Middleweight (75 kg/165 lbs)

1904	Charles Mayer, United States
1908	John Douglas, Great Britain
1920	Harry Mallin, Great Britain
1924	Harry Mallin, Great Britain
1928	Piero Toscani, Italy
1932	Carmen Barth, United States
1936	Jean Despeaux, France
1948	Laszlo Papp, Hungary
1952	Floyd Patterson, United States
1956	Gennady Schatkov, USSR
1960	Edward Crook, United States
1964	Valery Popenchenko, USSR
1968	Christopher Finnegan, Great Britain
1972	Vyacheslav Lemechev, USSR
1976	Michael Spinks, United States

Middleweight (75 kg/165 lbs)

1980	Jose Gomez, Cuba
1984	Shin Joon-sup, S. Korea
1988	Henry Maske, E. Germany
1992	Ariel Hernandez, Cuba
1996	Ariel Hernandez, Cuba
2000	Jorge Gutierrez, Cuba
2004	Gaydarbek Gaydarbekov, Russia
2008	James Degale, Great Britain
2012	Ryota Murata, Japan
2016	Arlen López, Cuba
2020	Hebert Conceição, Brazil

Lt. Heavyweight (81 kg/179 lbs)

1920	Edward Eagan, United States
1924	Harry Mitchell, Great Britain
1928	Victor Avendaño, Argentina
1932	David Carstens, South Africa
1936	Roger Michelot, France
1948	George Hunter, South Africa
1952	Norvel Lee, United States
1956	James Boyd, United States
1960	Cassius Clay, United States
1964	Cosimo Pinto, Italy
1968	Dan Poznyak, USSR
1972	Mate Parlov, Yugoslavia
1976	Leon Spinks, United States
1980	Slobodan Kacar, Yugoslavia
1984	Anton Josipovic, Yugoslavia
1988	Andrew Maynard, United States
1992	Torsten May, Germany
1996	Vassili Jirov, Kazakhstan
2000	Alexander Lebziak, Russia
2004	Andre Ward, United States
2008	Zhang Xiaoping, China
2012	Yegor Mekhontsev, Russia
2016	Julio César la Cruz, Cuba
2020	Arlen López, Cuba

Heavyweight (91 kg/201 lbs)

1984	Henry Tillman, United States
1988	Ray Mercer, United States
1992	Felix Savon, Cuba
1996	Felix Savon, Cuba
2000	Felix Savon, Cuba
2004	Odlanier Solis Fonte, Cuba
2008	Rakhim Chakhkiev, Russia
2012	Oleksandr Usik, Ukraine
2016	Evgeny Tishchenko, Russia
2020	Julio César la Cruz, Cuba

Super Heavyweight (91+ kg/201+ lbs)

1904	Samuel Berger, United States
1908	Albert Oldham, Great Britain
1920	Ronald Rawson, Great Britain
1924	Otto von Porat, Norway
1928	Arturo Rodriguez Jurado, Argentina
1932	Santiago Lovell, Argentina
1936	Herbert Runge, Germany
1948	Rafael Iglesias, Argentina
1952	H. Edward Sanders, United States
1956	T. Peter Rademacher, United States
1960	Franco De Piccoli, Italy
1964	Joe Frazier, United States
1968	George Foreman, United States
1972	Teofilo Stevenson, Cuba
1976	Teofilo Stevenson, Cuba
1980	Teofilo Stevenson, Cuba
1984	Tyrell Biggs, United States
1988	Lennox Lewis, Canada
1992	Roberto Balado, Cuba
1996	Vladimir Klitchko, Ukraine
2000	Audley Harrison, Great Britain
2004	Alexander Povetkin, Russia
2008	Roberto Cammarelle, Italy
2012	Anthony Joshua, Great Britain
2016	Tony Yoka, France
2020	Bakhodir Jalolov, Uzbekistan

Boxing—Women

Flyweight (51 kg/112 lbs)

2012	Nicola Adams, Great Britain
2016	Nicola Adams, Great Britain
2020	Stoyka Krasteva, Bulgaria

Featherweight (57 kg/126 lbs)

2020	Sena Irie, Japan

Lightweight (60 kg/132 lbs)

2012	Katie Taylor, Ireland
2016	Estelle Mossely, France
2020	Kellie Harrington, Ireland

Welterweight (69 kg/152 lbs)

2020	Busenaz Sürmeneli, Turkey

Middleweight (75 kg/165 lbs)

2012	Claressa Shields, United States
2016	Claressa Shields, United States
2020	Lauren Price, Great Britain

Gymnastics—Men

Floor Exercise

1932	István Pelle, Hungary
1936	Georges Miez, Switzerland
1948	Ferenc Pataki, Hungary
1952	William Thoresson, Sweden
1956	Valentin Muratov, USSR
1960	Nobuyuki Aihara, Japan
1964	Franco Menichelli, Italy
1968	Sawao Kato, Japan
1972	Nikolay Andrianov, USSR
1976	Nikolay Andrianov, USSR
1980	Roland Brückner, E. Germany
1984	Li Ning, China
1988	Sergei Kharkov, USSR
1992	Li Xiaoshuang, China
1996	Ioannis Melissanidis, Greece
2000	Igors Vihrovs, Latvia
2004	Kyle Shewfelt, Canada
2008	Zou Kai, China
2012	Zou Kai, China
2016	Max Whitlock, Great Britain
2020	Artem Dolgopyat, Israel

Horizontal Bar

1896	Hermann Weingärtner, Germany
1904	Anton Heida, United States;
	Edward Hennig, United States (tie)
1924	Leon Stukelj, Yugoslavia
1928	Georges Miez, Switzerland
1932	Dallas Denver Bixler, United States
1936	Aleksanteri Saarvala, Finland
1948	Josef Stalder, Switzerland
1952	Jakob "Jack" Günthard, Switzerland
1956	Takashi Ono, Japan
1960	Takashi Ono, Japan
1964	Boris Shakhlin, USSR
1968	Akinori Nakayama, Japan;
	Mikhail Voronin, USSR (tie)
1972	Mitsuo Tsukahara, Japan
1976	Mitsuo Tsukahara, Japan
1980	Stoyan Deltchev, Bulgaria
1984	Shinji Morisue, Japan
1988	Vladimir Artemov, USSR;
	Valeri Liukin, USSR (tie)
1992	Trent Dimas, United States
1996	Andreas Wecker, Germany
2000	Alexei Nemov, Russia
2004	Igor Cassina, Italy
2008	Zou Kai, China
2012	Epke Zonderland, Netherlands
2016	Fabian Hambüchen, Germany
2020	Daiki Hashimoto, Japan

Individual All-Around

1900	Gustave Sandras, France
1904	Julius Lenhart, United States
1908	G. Alberto Braglia, Italy
1912	G. Alberto Braglia, Italy
1920	Giorgio Zampori, Italy
1924	Leon Stukelj, Yugoslavia
1928	Georges Miez, Switzerland
1932	Romeo Neri, Italy
1936	Karl-Alfred Schwarzmann, Germany
1948	Veikko Huhtanen, Finland
1952	Viktor Ivanovich Chukarin, USSR
1956	Viktor Ivanovich Chukarin, USSR
1960	Boris Shakhlin, USSR
1964	Yukio Endo, Japan
1968	Sawao Kato, Japan
1972	Sawao Kato, Japan
1976	Nikolay Andrianov, USSR
1980	Aleksandr Dityatin, USSR
1984	Koji Gushiken, Japan
1988	Vladimir Artemov, USSR
1992	Vitaly Scherbo, Unified Team (Belarus)
1996	Li Xiaoshuang, China
2000	Alexei Nemov, Russia
2004	Paul Hamm, United States
2008	Yang Wei, China
2012	Kohei Uchimura, Japan
2016	Kohei Uchimura, Japan
2020	Daiki Hashimoto, Japan

Parallel Bars

1896	Alfred Flatow, Germany
1904	George Eyser, United States
1924	August Güttinger, Switzerland
1928	Ladislav Vacha, Czechoslovakia
1932	Romeo Neri, Italy
1936	Konrad Frey, Germany
1948	Michael Reusch, Switzerland
1952	Hans Eugster, Switzerland
1956	Viktor Ivanovich Chukarin, USSR
1960	Boris Shakhlin, USSR
1964	Yukio Endo, Japan
1968	Akinori Nakayama, Japan
1972	Sawao Kato, Japan
1976	Sawao Kato, Japan
1980	Aleksandr Tkachev, USSR
1984	Bart Conner, United States
1988	Vladimir Artemov, USSR
1992	Vitaly Scherbo, Unified Team (Belarus)
1996	Roustam Sharipov, Ukraine
2000	Li Xiaopeng, China
2004	Valeri Goncharov, Ukraine
2008	Li Xiaopeng, China
2012	Feng Zhe, China
2016	Oleg Verniaiev, Ukraine
2020	Zou Jingyuan, China

Pommel Horse

1896	Louis Zutter, Switzerland
1904	Anton Heida, United States
1924	Josef Wilhelm, Switzerland
1928	Hermann Hänggi, Switzerland
1932	István Pelle, Hungary
1936	Konrad Frey, Germany
1948	Paavo Johannes Aaltonen, Finland; Veikko Huhtanen, Finland; Heikki Savolainen, Finland (tie)
1952	Viktor Ivanovich Chukarin, USSR
1956	Boris Shakhlin, USSR
1960	Eugen Georg Oskar Ekman, Finland; Boris Shakhlin, USSR (tie)
1964	Miroslav Cerar, Yugoslavia
1968	Miroslav Cerar, Yugoslavia
1972	Viktor Klimenko, USSR
1976	Zoltan Magyar, Hungary
1980	Zoltan Magyar, Hungary
1984	Li Ning, China; Peter Glen Vidmar, United States (tie)
1988	Dmitri Bilozerchev, USSR; Zsolt Borkai, Hungary; Lubomir Geraskov, Bulgaria (tie)
1992	Pae Gil Su, N. Korea; Vitaly Scherbo, Unified Team (Belarus) (tie)
1996	Li Donghua, Switzerland
2000	Marius Daniel Urzica, Romania
2004	Teng Haibin, China
2008	Xiao Qin, China
2012	Krisztián Berki, Hungary
2016	Max Whitlock, Great Britain
2020	Max Whitlock, Great Britain

Rings

1896	Ioannis Mitropoulos, Greece
1904	Hermann Glass, United States
1924	Francesco Martino, Italy
1928	Leon Stukelj, Yugoslavia
1932	George Gulack, United States
1936	Alois Hudec, Czechoslovakia
1948	Karl Frei, Switzerland
1952	Grant Shaginyan, USSR
1956	Albert Azaryan, USSR
1960	Albert Azaryan, USSR
1964	Takuji Hayata, Japan
1968	Akinori Nakayama, Japan

Rings

1972	Akinori Nakayama, Japan
1976	Nikolay Andrianov, USSR
1980	Aleksandr Dityatin, USSR
1984	Koji Gushiken, Japan; Li Ning, China (tie)
1988	Holger Behrendt, E. Germany; Dmitri Bilozerchev, USSR (tie)
1992	Vitaly Scherbo, Unified Team (Belarus)
1996	Juri Chechi, Italy
2000	Szilveszter Csollany, Hungary
2004	Dimosthenis Tampakos, Greece
2008	Chen Yibing, China
2012	Arthur Zanetti, Brazil
2016	Eleftherios Petrounias, Greece
2020	Liu Yang, China

Team Competition

1904	United States, United States, United States
1908	Sweden, Norway, Finland
1912	Italy, Hungary, Great Britain
1920	Italy, Belgium, France
1924	Italy, France, Switzerland
1928	Switzerland, Czechoslovakia, Yugoslavia
1932	Italy, United States, Finland
1936	Germany, Switzerland, Finland
1948	Finland, Switzerland, Hungary
1952	USSR, Switzerland, Finland
1956	USSR, Japan, Finland
1960	Japan, USSR, Italy
1964	Japan, USSR, Unified Team of Germany
1968	Japan, USSR, E. Germany
1972	Japan, USSR, E. Germany
1976	Japan, USSR, E. Germany
1980	USSR, E. Germany, Hungary
1984	United States, China, Japan
1988	USSR, E. Germany, Japan
1992	Unified Team, China, Japan
1996	Russia, China, Ukraine
2000	China, Ukraine, Russia
2004	Japan, United States, Romania
2008	China, Japan, United States
2012	China, Japan, Great Britain
2016	Japan, Russia, China
2020	ROC, Japan, China

Vault

1896	Carl Schuhmann, Germany
1904	George Eyser, United States; Anton Heida, United States (tie)
1924	Frank Kriz, United States
1928	Eugen Mack, Switzerland
1932	Savino Guglielmetti, Italy
1936	Karl-Alfred Schwarzmann, Germany
1948	Paavo Johannes Aaltonen, Finland
1952	Viktor Ivanovich Chukarin, USSR
1956	Helmut Bantz, Unified Team of Germany; Valentin Muratov, USSR (tie)
1960	Takashi Ono, Japan; Boris Shakhlin, USSR (tie)
1964	Haruhiro Yamashita, Japan
1968	Mikhail Voronin, USSR
1972	Klaus Köste, E. Germany
1976	Nikolay Andrianov, USSR
1980	Nikolay Andrianov, USSR
1984	Lou Yun, China
1988	Lou Yun, China
1992	Vitaly Scherbo, Unified Team (Belarus)
1996	Alexei Nemov, Russia
2000	Gervasio Deferr, Spain
2004	Gervasio Deferr, Spain
2008	Leszek Blanik, Poland
2012	Yang Hak-seon, South Korea
2016	Ri Se Gwang, North Korea
2020	Shin Jeahwan, South Korea

Individual All-Around

2016	Kohei Uchimura, Japan
2020	Daiki Hashimoto, Japan

Gymnastics—Women

Balance Beam
1952 Nina Bocharova, USSR
1956 Agnes Keleti, Hungary
1960 Eva Vechtova-Bosakova, Czechoslovakia
1964 Vera Caslavska, Czechoslovakia
1968 Natalya Kuchinskaya, USSR
1972 Olga Korbut, USSR
1976 Nadia Comaneci, Romania
1980 Nadia Comaneci, Romania
1984 Ecaterina Szabo, Romania; Simona Pauca, Romania (tie)
1988 Daniela Silivas, Romania
1992 Tatiana Lyssenko, Unified Team (Ukraine)
1996 Shannon Miller, United States
2000 Liu Xuan, China
2004 Catalina Ponor, Romania
2008 Shawn Johnson, United States
2012 Deng Linlin, China
2016 Sanne Wevers, Netherlands
2020 Guan Chenchen, China

Floor Exercise
1952 Agnes Keleti, Hungary
1956 Agnes Keleti, Hungary; Larisa Latynina, USSR (tie)
1960 Larisa Latynina, USSR
1964 Larisa Latynina, USSR
1968 Vera Caslavska, Czechoslovakia; Larisa Petrik, USSR (tie)
1972 Olga Korbut, USSR
1976 Nelli Kim, USSR
1980 Nelli Kim, USSR; Nadia Comaneci, Romania (tie)
1984 Ecaterina Szabo, Romania
1988 Daniela Silivas, Romania
1992 Lavinia Milosovici, Romania
1996 Lilia Podkopayeva, Ukraine
2000 Elena Zamolodchikova, Russia
2004 Catalina Ponor, Romania
2008 Sandra Izbasa, Romania
2012 Aly Raisman, United States
2016 Simone Biles, United States
2020 Jade Carey, United States

Individual All-Around
1952 Mariya Gorokhovskaya, USSR
1956 Larisa Latynina, USSR
1960 Larisa Latynina, USSR
1964 Vera Caslavska, Czechoslovakia
1968 Vera Caslavska, Czechoslovakia
1972 Lyudmila Turischeva, USSR
1976 Nadia Comaneci, Romania
1980 Elena Davydova, USSR
1984 Mary-Lou Retton, United States
1988 Elena Shushunova, USSR
1992 Tatiana Gutsu, Unified Team (Ukraine)
1996 Lilia Podkopayeva, Ukraine
2000 Simona Amanar, Romania
2004 Carly Patterson, United States
2008 Nastia Liukin, United States
2012 Gabby Douglas, United States
2016 Simone Biles, United States
2020 Sunisa Lee, United States

Team Competition
1928 Netherlands, Italy, Great Britain
1936 Germany, Czechoslovakia, Hungary
1948 Czechoslovakia, Hungary, United States
1952 USSR, Hungary, Czechoslovakia
1956 USSR, Hungary, Romania
1960 USSR, Czechoslovakia, Romania
1964 USSR, Czechoslovakia, Japan
1968 USSR, Czechoslovakia, E. Germany
1972 USSR, E. Germany, Hungary
1976 USSR, Romania, E. Germany
1980 USSR, Romania, E. Germany
1984 Romania, United States, China
1988 USSR, Romania, E. Germany
1992 Unified Team, Romania, United States
1996 United States, Russia, Romania
2000 Romania, Russia, United States
2004 Romania, United States, Russia
2008 China, United States, Romania
2012 United States, Russia, Romania

Team Competition
2016 United States, Russia, China
2020 ROC, United States, Great Britain

Uneven Bars
1952 Margit Korondi, Hungary
1956 Agnes Keleti, Hungary
1960 Polina Astakhova, USSR
1964 Polina Astakhova, USSR
1968 Vera Caslavska, Czechoslovakia
1972 Karin Janz, E. Germany
1976 Nadia Comaneci, Romania
1980 Maxi Gnauck, E. Germany
1984 Julianne McNamara, United States; Yan-Hong Ma, China (tie)
1988 Daniela Silivas, Romania
1992 Lu Li, China
1996 Svetlana Khorkina, Russia
2000 Svetlana Khorkina, Russia
2004 Emilie LePennec, France
2008 He Kexin, China
2012 Aliya Mustafina, Russia
2016 Aliya Mustafina, Russia
2020 Nina Derwael, Belgium

Vault
1952 Ekaterina Kalinchuk, USSR
1956 Larisa Latynina, USSR
1960 Margarita Nikolaeva, USSR
1964 Vera Caslavska, Czechoslovakia
1968 Vera Caslavska, Czechoslovakia
1972 Karin Janz, E. Germany
1976 Nelli Kim, USSR
1980 Natalia Shaposhnikova, USSR
1984 Ecaterina Szabo, Romania
1988 Svetlana Boginskaya, USSR
1992 Henrietta Onodi, Hungary; Lavinia Milosovici, Romania (tie)
1996 Simona Amanar, Romania
2000 Elena Zamolodchikova, Russia
2004 Monica Rosu, Romania
2008 Hong Un Jong, N. Korea
2012 Sandra Izbaşa, Romania
2016 Simone Biles, United States
2020 Rebeca Andrade, Brazil

Soccer

Men
1900 Great Britain, France, Belgium
1904 Canada, United States, United States
1908 Great Britain, Denmark, Netherlands
1912 Great Britain, Denmark, Netherlands
1920 Belgium, Spain, Netherlands
1924 Uruguay, Switzerland, Sweden
1928 Uruguay, Argentina, Italy
1936 Italy, Austria, Norway
1948 Sweden, Yugoslavia, Denmark
1952 Hungary, Yugoslavia, Sweden
1956 USSR, Yugoslavia, Bulgaria
1960 Yugoslavia, Denmark, Hungary

Men
1964 Hungary, Czechoslovakia, Unified Team of Germany
1968 Hungary, Bulgaria, Japan
1972 Poland; Hungary; USSR, E. Germany (tie for bronze)
1976 E. Germany, Poland, USSR
1980 Czechoslovakia, E. Germany, USSR
1984 France, Brazil, Yugoslavia
1988 USSR, Brazil, W. Germany
1992 Spain, Poland, Ghana
1996 Nigeria, Argentina, Brazil
2000 Cameroon, Spain, Chile

Men
2004 Argentina, Paraguay, Italy
2008 Argentina, Nigeria, Brazil
2012 Mexico, Brazil, South Korea
2016 Brazil, Germany, Nigeria
2020 Brazil, Spain, Mexico

Women
1996 United States, China, Norway
2000 Norway, United States, Germany
2004 United States, Brazil, Germany
2008 United States, Brazil, Germany
2012 United States, Japan, Canada
2016 Germany, Sweden, Canada
2020 Canada, Sweden, United States

Swimming and Diving—Men

50-Meter Freestyle	Time
1988 Matt Biondi, United States	0:22.14
1992 Aleksandr Popov, Unified Team (Rus.)	0:21.91
1996 Aleksandr Popov, Russia	0:22.13
2000 Anthony Ervin, United States	0:21.98
Gary Hall Jr., United States (tie)	0:21.98
2004 Gary Hall Jr., United States	0:21.93
2008 Cesar Cielo Filho, Brazil	0:21.30
2012 Florent Manaudou, France	0:21.34
2016 Anthony Ervin, United States	0:21.40
2020 Caeleb Dressel, United States	0:21.07*

100-Meter Freestyle	Time
1896 Alfred Hajos, Hungary	1:22.2
1904 Zoltan de Halmay, Hungary (100 yds)	1:02.8
1908 Charles Daniels, United States	1:05.6
1912 Duke P. Kahanamoku, United States	1:03.4
1920 Duke P. Kahanamoku, United States	1:01.4
1924 Johnny Weissmuller, United States	0:59.0
1928 Johnny Weissmuller, United States	0:58.6
1932 Yasuji Miyazaki, Japan	0:58.2
1936 Ferenc Csik, Hungary	0:57.6

100-Meter Freestyle	Time
1948 Wally Ris, United States	0:57.3
1952 Clarke Scholes, United States	0:57.4
1956 Jon Henricks, Australia	0:55.4
1960 John Devitt, Australia	0:55.2
1964 Don Schollander, United States	0:53.4
1968 Mike Wenden, Australia	0:52.2
1972 Mark Spitz, United States	0:51.22
1976 Jim Montgomery, United States	0:49.99
1980 Jorg Woithe, E. Germany	0:50.40
1984 Ambrose "Rowdy" Gaines, United States	0:49.80
1988 Matt Biondi, United States	0:48.63
1992 Aleksandr Popov, Unified Team (Rus.)	0:49.02
1996 Aleksandr Popov, Russia	0:48.74
2000 Pieter van den Hoogenband, Netherlands	0:48.30
2004 Pieter van den Hoogenband, Netherlands	0:48.17
2008 Alain Bernard, France	0:47.21
2012 Nathan Adrian, United States	0:47.52
2016 Kyle Chalmers, Australia	0:47.58
2020 Caeleb Dressel, United States	0:47.02*

200-Meter Freestyle		Time
1968	Mike Wenden, Australia	1:55.2
1972	Mark Spitz, United States	1:52.78
1976	Bruce Furniss, United States	1:50.29
1980	Sergei Kopliakov, USSR	1:49.81
1984	Michael Gross, W. Germany	1:47.44
1988	Duncan Armstrong, Australia	1:47.25
1992	Yevgeny Sadovyi, Unified Team (Rus.)	1:46.70
1996	Danyon Loader, New Zealand	1:47.63
2000	Pieter van den Hoogenband, Netherlands	1:45.35
2004	Ian Thorpe, Australia	1:44.71
2008	Michael Phelps, United States	1:42.96*
2012	Yannick Agnel, France	1:43.14
2016	Sun Yang, China	1:44.65
2020	Thomas Dean, Great Britain	1:44.22

400-Meter Freestyle		Time
1904	C. M. Daniels, United States (440 yds)	6:16.2
1908	Henry Taylor, Great Britain	5:36.8
1912	George Hodgson, Canada	5:24.4
1920	Norman Ross, United States	5:26.8
1924	Johnny Weissmuller, United States	5:04.2
1928	Albert Zorilla, Argentina	5:01.6
1932	Clarence Crabbe, United States	4:48.4
1936	Jack Medica, United States	4:44.5
1948	William Smith, United States	4:41.0
1952	Jean Boiteux, France	4:30.7
1956	Murray Rose, Australia	4:27.3
1960	Murray Rose, Australia	4:18.3
1964	Don Schollander, United States	4:12.2
1968	Mike Burton, United States	4:09.0
1972	Brad Cooper, Australia	4:00.27
1976	Brian Goodell, United States	3:51.93
1980	Vladimir Salnikov, USSR	3:51.31
1984	George DiCarlo, United States	3:51.23
1988	Uwe Dassler, E. Germany	3:46.95
1992	Yevgeny Sadovyi, Unified Team (Rus.)	3:45.00
1996	Danyon Loader, New Zealand	3:47.97
2000	Ian Thorpe, Australia	3:40.59
2004	Ian Thorpe, Australia	3:43.10
2008	Park Tae-hwan, S. Korea	3:41.86
2012	Sun Yang, China	3:40.14*
2016	Mack Horton, Australia	3:41.55
2020	Ahmed Hafnaoui, Tunisia	3:43.36

800-Meter Freestyle		Time
2020	Robert Finke, United States	7:41.87

1500-Meter Freestyle		Time
1908	Henry Taylor, Great Britain	22:48.4
1912	George Hodgson, Canada	22:00.0
1920	Norman Ross, United States	22:23.2
1924	Andrew Charlton, Australia	20:06.6
1928	Arne Borg, Sweden	19:51.8
1932	Kusuo Kitamura, Japan	19:12.4
1936	Noboru Terada, Japan	19:13.7
1948	James McLane, United States	19:18.5
1952	Ford Konno, United States	18:30.3
1956	Murray Rose, Australia	17:58.9
1960	John Konrads, Australia	17:19.6
1964	Robert Windle, Australia	17:01.7
1968	Mike Burton, United States	16:38.9
1972	Mike Burton, United States	15:52.58
1976	Brian Goodell, United States	15:02.40
1980	Vladimir Salnikov, USSR	14:58.27
1984	Michael O'Brien, United States	15:05.20
1988	Vladimir Salnikov, USSR	15:00.40
1992	Kieren Perkins, Australia	14:43.48
1996	Kieren Perkins, Australia	14:56.40
2000	Grant Hackett, Australia	14:48.33
2004	Grant Hackett, Australia	14:43.40
2008	Oussama Mellouli, Tunisia	14:40.84
2012	Sun Yang, China	14:31.02*
2016	Gregorio Paltrinieri, Italy	14:34.57
2020	Robert Finke, United States	14:39.65

100-Meter Backstroke		Time
1904	Walter Brack, Germany (100 yds)	1:16.8
1908	Arno Bieberstein, Germany	1:24.6
1912	Harry Hebner, United States	1:21.2
1920	Warren Kealoha, United States	1:15.2
1924	Warren Kealoha, United States	1:13.2
1928	George Kojac, United States	1:08.2
1932	Masaji Kiyokawa, Japan	1:08.6
1936	Adolph Kiefer, United States	1:05.9
1948	Allen Stack, United States	1:06.4
1952	Yoshi Oyakawa, United States	1:05.4
1956	David Theile, Australia	1:02.2
1960	David Theile, Australia	1:01.9

100-Meter Backstroke		Time
1968	Roland Matthes, E. Germany	0:58.7
1972	Roland Matthes, E. Germany	0:56.58
1976	John Naber, United States	0:55.49
1980	Bengt Baron, Sweden	0:56.33
1984	Rick Carey, United States	0:55.79
1988	Daichi Suzuki, Japan	0:55.05
1992	Mark Tewksbury, Canada	0:53.98
1996	Jeff Rouse, United States	0:54.10
2000	Lenny Krayzelburg, United States	0:53.72
2004	Aaron Peirsol, United States	0:54.06
2008	Aaron Peirsol, United States	0:52.54
2012	Matt Grevers, United States	0:52.16
2016	Ryan Murphy, United States	0:51.97*
2020	Evgeny Rylov, ROC	0:51.98

200-Meter Backstroke		Time
1964	Jed Graef, United States	2:10.3
1968	Roland Matthes, E. Germany	2:09.6
1972	Roland Matthes, E. Germany	2:02.82
1976	John Naber, United States	1:59.19
1980	Sandor Wladar, Hungary	2:01.93
1984	Rick Carey, United States	2:00.23
1988	Igor Polyanski, USSR	1:59.37
1992	Martin Lopez-Zubero, Spain	1:58.47
1996	Brad Bridgewater, United States	1:58.54
2000	Lenny Krayzelburg, United States	1:56.76
2004	Aaron Peirsol, United States	1:54.95
2008	Ryan Lochte, United States	1:53.94
2012	Tyler Clary, United States	1:53.41
2016	Ryan Murphy, United States	1:53.62
2020	Evgeny Rylov, ROC	1:53.27*

100-Meter Breaststroke		Time
1968	Don McKenzie, United States	1:07.79
1972	Nobutaka Taguchi, Japan	1:04.94
1976	John Hencken, United States	1:03.11
1980	Duncan Goodhew, Great Britain	1:03.44
1984	Steve Lundquist, United States	1:01.65
1988	Adrian Moorhouse, Great Britain	1:02.04
1992	Nelson Diebel, United States	1:01.50
1996	Fred Deburghgraeve, Belgium	1:00.60
2000	Domenico Fioravanti, Italy	1:00.46
2004	Kosuke Kitajima, Japan	1:00.08
2008	Kosuke Kitajima, Japan	0:58.91
2012	Cameron van der Burgh, South Africa	0:58.46
2016	Adam Peaty, Great Britain	0:57.13*
2020	Adam Peaty, Great Britain	0:57.37

200-Meter Breaststroke		Time
1908	Frodoriok Holman, Groat Britain	3:09.2
1912	Walter Bathe, Germany	3:01.8
1920	Hakan Malmrot, Sweden	3:04.4
1924	Robert Skelton, United States	2:56.6
1928	Yoshiyuki Tsuruta, Japan	2:48.8
1932	Yoshiyuki Tsuruta, Japan	2:45.4
1936	Tetsuo Hamuro, Japan	2:41.5
1948	Joseph Verdeur, United States	2:39.3
1952	John Davies, Australia	2:34.4
1956	Masura Furukawa, Japan	2:34.7
1960	William Mulliken, United States	2:37.4
1964	Ian O'Brien, Australia	2:27.8
1968	Felipe Muñoz, Mexico	2:28.7
1972	John Hencken, United States	2:21.55
1976	David Wilkie, Great Britain	2:15.11
1980	Robertas Zhulpa, USSR	2:15.85
1984	Victor Davis, Canada	2:13.34
1988	Jozsef Szabo, Hungary	2:13.52
1992	Mike Barrowman, United States	2:10.16
1996	Norbert Rozsa, Hungary	2:12.57
2000	Domenico Fioravanti, Italy	2:10.87
2004	Kosuke Kitajima, Japan	2:09.44
2008	Kosuke Kitajima, Japan	2:07.64
2012	Dániel Gyurta, Hungary	2:07.28
2016	Dmitriy Balandin, Kazakhstan	2:07.46
2020	Izaac Stubblety-Cook, Australia	2:06.38*

100-Meter Butterfly		Time
1968	Doug Russell, United States	0:55.9
1972	Mark Spitz, United States	0:54.27
1976	Matt Vogel, United States	0:54.35
1980	Par Arvidsson, Sweden	0:54.92
1984	Michael Gross, W. Germany	0:53.08
1988	Anthony Nesty, Suriname	0:53.00
1992	Pablo Morales, United States	0:53.32
1996	Denis Pankratov, Russia	0:52.27
2000	Lars Froelander, Sweden	0:52.00
2004	Michael Phelps, United States	0:51.25
2008	Michael Phelps, United States	0:50.58
2012	Michael Phelps, United States	0:51.21
2016	Joseph Schooling, Singapore	0:50.39
2020	Caeleb Dressel, United States	0:49.45*

200-Meter Butterfly

Year	Champion	Time
1956	William Yorzyk, United States	2:19.3
1960	Michael Troy, United States	2:12.8
1964	Kevin J. Berry, Australia	2:06.6
1968	Carl Robie, United States	2:08.7
1972	Mark Spitz, United States	2:00.70
1976	Mike Bruner, United States	1:59.23
1980	Sergei Fesenko, USSR	1:59.76
1984	Jon Sieben, Australia	1:57.04
1988	Michael Gross, W. Germany	1:56.94
1992	Mel Stewart, United States	1:56.26
1996	Denis Pankratov, Russia	1:56.51
2000	Tom Malchow, United States	1:55.35
2004	Michael Phelps, United States	1:54.04
2008	Michael Phelps, United States	1:52.03
2012	Chad le Clos, South Africa	1:52.96
2016	Michael Phelps, United States	1:53.36
2020	Kristóf Milák, Hungary	1:51.25*

200-Meter Individual Medley

Year	Champion	Time
1968	Charles Hickcox, United States	2:12.0
1972	Gunnar Larsson, Sweden	2:07.17
1984	Alex Baumann, Canada	2:01.42
1988	Tamas Darnyi, Hungary	2:00.17
1992	Tamas Darnyi, Hungary	2:00.76
1996	Attila Czene, Hungary	1:59.91
2000	Massimiliano Rosolino, Italy	1:58.98
2004	Michael Phelps, United States	1:57.14
2008	Michael Phelps, United States	1:54.23*
2012	Michael Phelps, United States	1:54.27
2016	Michael Phelps, United States	1:54.66
2020	Wang Shun, China	1:55.00

400-Meter Individual Medley

Year	Champion	Time
1964	Dick Roth, United States	4:45.4
1968	Charles Hickcox, United States	4:48.4
1972	Gunnar Larsson, Sweden	4:31.98
1976	Rod Strachan, United States	4:23.68
1980	Aleksandr Sidorenko, USSR	4:22.89
1984	Alex Baumann, Canada	4:17.41
1988	Tamas Darnyi, Hungary	4:14.75
1992	Tamas Darnyi, Hungary	4:14.23
1996	Tom Dolan, United States	4:14.90
2000	Tom Dolan, United States	4:11.76
2004	Michael Phelps, United States	4:08.26
2008	Michael Phelps, United States	4:03.84*
2012	Ryan Lochte, United States	4:05.18
2016	Kosuke Hagino, Japan	4:06.05
2020	Chase Kalisz, United States	4:09.42

4x100-Meter Freestyle Relay

Year	Champion	Time
1964	United States	3:31.2
1968	United States	3:31.7
1972	United States	3:26.42
1984	United States	3:19.03
1988	United States	3:16.53
1992	United States	3:16.74
1996	United States	3:15.41
2000	Australia	3:13.67
2004	South Africa	3:13.17
2008	United States	3:08.24*
2012	France	3:09.93
2016	United States	3:09.92
2020	United States	3:08.97

4x200-Meter Freestyle Relay

Year	Champion	Time
1908	Great Britain	10:55.6
1912	Australasia (Australia and New Zealand)	10:11.6
1920	United States	10:04.4
1924	United States	9:53.4
1928	United States	9:36.2
1932	Japan	8:58.4
1936	Japan	8:51.5
1948	United States	8:46.0
1952	United States	8:31.1
1956	Australia	8:23.6
1960	United States	8:10.2
1964	United States	7:52.1
1968	United States	7:52.33
1972	United States	7:35.78
1976	United States	7:23.22
1980	USSR	7:23.50
1984	United States	7:15.69
1988	United States	7:12.51
1992	Unified Team	7:11.95
1996	United States	7:14.84
2000	Australia	7:07.05
2004	United States	7:07.33
2008	United States	6:58.56*
2012	United States	6:59.70
2016	United States	7:00.66
2020	Great Britain	6:58.58

4x100-Meter Medley Relay

Year	Champion	Time
1960	United States	4:05.4
1964	United States	3:58.4
1968	United States	3:54.9
1972	United States	3:48.16
1976	United States	3:42.22
1980	Australia	3:45.70
1984	United States	3:39.30
1988	United States	3:36.93
1992	United States	3:36.93
1996	United States	3:34.84
2000	United States	3:33.73
2004	United States	3:30.68
2008	United States	3:29.34
2012	United States	3:29.35
2016	United States	3:27.95
2020	United States	3:26.78*

10-Kilometer Marathon

Year	Champion	Time
2008	Maarten van der Weijden, Netherlands	1:51:51.6
2012	Oussama Mellouli, Tunisia	1:49:55.1
2016	Ferry Weertman, Netherlands	1:52:59.8
2020	Florian Wellbrock, Germany	1:48:33.7

Platform Diving

Year	Champion	Points
1904	Dr. G. E. Sheldon, United States	112.75
1908	Hjalmar Johansson, Sweden	183.75
1912	Erik Adlerz, Sweden	73.94
1920	Clarence Pinkston, United States	100.67
1924	Albert White, United States	97.46
1928	Pete Desjardins, United States	98.74
1932	Harold Smith, United States	124.80
1936	Marshall Wayne, United States	113.58
1948	Sammy Lee, United States	130.05
1952	Sammy Lee, United States	156.28
1956	Joaquin Capilla, Mexico	152.44
1960	Robert Webster, United States	165.56
1964	Robert Webster, United States	148.58
1968	Klaus Dibiasi, Italy	164.18
1972	Klaus Dibiasi, Italy	504.12
1976	Klaus Dibiasi, Italy	600.51
1980	Falk Hoffmann, E. Germany	835.65
1984	Greg Louganis, United States	710.91
1988	Greg Louganis, United States	638.61
1992	Sun Shuwei, China	677.31
1996	Dmitri Sautin, Russia	692.34
2000	Tian Liang, China	724.53
2004	Hu Jia, China	748.08
2008	Matthew Mitcham, Australia	537.95
2012	David Boudia, United States	568.65
2016	Chen Aisen, China	545.35
2020	Cao Yuan, China	582.35

Springboard Diving

Year	Champion	Points
1908	Albert Zurner, Germany	85.50
1912	Paul Guenther, Germany	79.23
1920	Louis Kuehn, United States	675.40
1924	Albert White, United States	97.46
1928	Pete Desjardins, United States	185.04
1932	Michael Galitzen, United States	161.38
1936	Richard Degener, United States	163.57
1948	Bruce Harlan, United States	163.64
1952	David Browning, United States	205.29
1956	Robert Clotworthy, United States	159.56
1960	Gary Tobian, United States	170.00
1964	Kenneth Sitzberger, United States	159.90
1968	Bernie Wrightson, United States	170.15
1972	Vladimir Vasin, USSR	594.09
1976	Phil Boggs, United States	619.52
1980	Aleksandr Portnov, USSR	905.02
1984	Greg Louganis, United States	754.41
1988	Greg Louganis, United States	730.80
1992	Mark Lenzi, United States	676.53
1996	Xiong Ni, China	701.46
2000	Xiong Ni, China	708.72
2004	Peng Bo, China	787.30
2008	He Chong, China	572.90
2012	Ilya Zakharov, Russia	555.90
2016	Cao Yuan, China	547.60
2020	Xie Siyi, China	558.75

Synchronized Platform Diving

Year	Champion	Points
2004	Tian Liang & Yang Jinghui, China	383.88
2008	Lin Yue & Huo Liang, China	468.18
2012	Cao Yuan & Zhang Yanquan, China	486.78
2016	Chen Aisen & Lin Yue, China	496.98
2020	Tom Daley & Matty Lee, Great Britain	471.81

Synchronized Springboard Diving

Year	Champion	Points
2004	Nikolaos Siranidis & Thomas Bimis, Greece	353.34
2008	Wang Feng & Qin Kai, China	469.08
2012	Luo Yutong & Qin Kai, China	477.00
2016	Jack Laugher & Chris Mears, Great Britain	454.32
2020	Xie Siyi & Wang Zongyuan, China	467.82

Swimming and Diving—Women

50-Meter Freestyle		Time
1988	Kristin Otto, E. Germany	0:25.49
1992	Yang Wenyi, China	0:24.76
1996	Amy Van Dyken, United States	0:24.87
2000	Inge de Bruijn, Netherlands	0:24.32
2004	Inge de Bruijn, Netherlands	0:24.58
2008	Britta Steffen, Germany	0:24.06
2012	Ranomi Kromowidjojo, Netherlands	0:24.05
2016	Pernille Blume, Denmark	0:24.07
2020	Emma McKeon, Australia	0:23.81*

100-Meter Freestyle		Time
1912	Fanny Durack, Australia	1:22.2
1920	Ethelda Bleibtrey, United States	1:13.6
1924	Ethel Lackie, United States	1:12.4
1928	Albina Osipowich, United States	1:11.0
1932	Helene Madison, United States	1:06.8
1936	Hendrika Mastenbroek, Netherlands	1:05.9
1948	Greta Andersen, Denmark	1:06.3
1952	Katalin Szoke, Hungary	1:06.8
1956	Dawn Fraser, Australia	1:02.0
1960	Dawn Fraser, Australia	1:01.2
1964	Dawn Fraser, Australia	0:59.5
1968	Jan Henne, United States	1:00.0
1972	Sandra Neilson, United States	0:58.59
1976	Kornelia Ender, E. Germany	0:55.65
1980	Barbara Krause, E. Germany	0:54.79
1984	Carrie Steinseifer, United States (tie)	0:55.92
	Nancy Hogshead, United States (tie)	0:55.92
1988	Kristin Otto, E. Germany	0:54.93
1992	Zhuang Yong, China	0:54.64
1996	Li Jingyi, China	0:54.50
2000	Inge de Bruijn, Netherlands	0:53.83
2004	Jodie Henry, Australia	0:53.84
2008	Britta Steffen, Germany	0:53.12
2012	Ranomi Kromowidjojo, Netherlands	0:53.00
2016	Simone Manuel, United States	0:52.70
	Penny Oleksiak, Canada (tie)	0:52.70
2020	Emma McKeon, Australia	0:51.96*

200-Meter Freestyle		Time
1968	Debbie Meyer, United States	2:10.5
1972	Shane Gould, Australia	2:03.56
1976	Kornelia Ender, E. Germany	1:59.26
1980	Barbara Krause, E. Germany	1:58.33
1984	Mary Wayte, United States	1:59.23
1988	Heike Friedrich, E. Germany	1:57.65
1992	Nicole Haislett, United States	1:57.90
1996	Claudia Poll, Costa Rica	1:58.16
2000	Susan O'Neill, Australia	1:58.24
2004	Camelia Potec, Romania	1:58.03
2008	Federica Pellegrini, Italy	1:54.82
2012	Allison Schmitt, United States	1:53.61
2016	Katie Ledecky, United States	1:53.73
2020	Ariarne Titmus, Australia	1:53.50*

400-Meter Freestyle		Time
1924	Martha Norelius, United States	6:02.2
1928	Martha Norelius, United States	5:42.8
1932	Helene Madison, United States	5:28.5
1936	Hendrika Mastenbroek, Netherlands	5:26.4
1948	Ann Curtis, United States	5:17.8
1952	Valerie Gyenge, Hungary	5:12.1
1956	Lorraine Crapp, Australia	4:54.6
1960	Chris von Saltza, United States	4:50.6
1964	Virginia Duenkel, United States	4:43.3
1968	Debbie Meyer, United States	4:31.8
1972	Shane Gould, Australia	4:19.44
1976	Petra Thuemer, E. Germany	4:09.89
1980	Ines Diers, E. Germany	4:08.76
1984	Tiffany Cohen, United States	4:07.10
1988	Janet Evans, United States	4:03.85
1992	Dagmar Hase, Germany	4:07.18
1996	Michelle Smith, Ireland	4:07.25
2000	Brooke Bennett, United States	4:05.80
2004	Laure Manaudou, France	4:05.34
2008	Rebecca Adlington, Great Britain	4:03.22
2012	Camille Muffat, France	4:01.45
2016	Katie Ledecky, United States	3:56.46*
2020	Ariarne Titmus, Australia	3:56.69

800-Meter Freestyle		Time
1968	Debbie Meyer, United States	9:24.0
1972	Keena Rothhammer, United States	8:53.68
1976	Petra Thuemer, E. Germany	8:37.14
1980	Michelle Ford, Australia	8:28.90
1984	Tiffany Cohen, United States	8:24.95
1988	Janet Evans, United States	8:20.20
1992	Janet Evans, United States	8:25.52
1996	Brooke Bennett, United States	8:27.89
2000	Brooke Bennett, United States	8:19.67
2004	Ai Shibata, Japan	8:24.54
2008	Rebecca Adlington, Great Britain	8:14.10
2012	Katie Ledecky, United States	8:14.63
2016	Katie Ledecky, United States	8:04.79*
2020	Katie Ledecky, United States	8:12.57

1500-Meter Freestyle		Time
2020	Katie Ledecky, United States	15:37.34

100-Meter Backstroke		Time
1924	Sybil Bauer, United States	1:23.2
1928	Marie Braun, Netherlands	1:22.0
1932	Eleanor Holm, United States	1:19.4
1936	Dina Senff, Netherlands	1:18.9
1948	Karen Harup, Denmark	1:14.4
1952	Joan Harrison, South Africa	1:14.3
1956	Judy Grinham, Great Britain	1:12.9
1960	Lynn Burke, United States	1:09.3
1964	Cathy Ferguson, United States	1:07.7
1968	Kaye Hall, United States	1:06.2
1972	Melissa Belote, United States	1:05.78
1976	Ulrike Richter, E. Germany	1:01.83
1980	Rica Reinisch, E. Germany	1:00.86
1984	Theresa Andrews, United States	1:02.55
1988	Kristin Otto, E. Germany	1:00.89
1992	Krisztina Egerszegi, Hungary	1:00.68
1996	Beth Botsford, United States	1:01.19
2000	Diana Mocanu, Romania	1:00.21
2004	Natalie Coughlin, United States	1:00.37
2008	Natalie Coughlin, United States	0:58.96
2012	Missy Franklin, United States	0:58.33
2016	Katinka Hosszú, Hungary	0:58.45
2020	Kaylee McKeown, Australia	0:57.47*

200-Meter Backstroke		Time
1968	Lillian "Pokey" Watson, United States	2:24.8
1972	Melissa Belote, United States	2:19.19
1976	Ulrike Richter, E. Germany	2:13.43
1980	Rica Reinisch, E. Germany	2:11.77
1984	Jolanda de Rover, Netherlands	2:12.38
1988	Krisztina Egerszegi, Hungary	2:09.29
1992	Krisztina Egerszegi, Hungary	2:07.06
1996	Krisztina Egerszegi, Hungary	2:07.83
2000	Diana Mocanu, Romania	2:08.16
2004	Kirsty Coventry, Zimbabwe	2:09.19
2008	Kirsty Coventry, Zimbabwe	2:05.24
2012	Missy Franklin, United States	2:04.06*
2016	Maya DiRado, United States	2:05.99
2020	Kaylee McKeown, Australia	2:04.68

100-Meter Breaststroke		Time
1968	Djurdjica Bjedov, Yugoslavia	1:15.8
1972	Cathy Carr, United States	1:13.58
1976	Hannelore Anke, E. Germany	1:11.16
1980	Ute Geweniger, E. Germany	1:10.22
1984	Petra Van Staveren, Netherlands	1:09.88
1988	Tania Dangalakova, Bulgaria	1:07.95
1992	Yelena Rudkovskaya, Unified Team (Belarus)	1:08.00
1996	Penny Heyns, South Africa	1:07.73
2000	Megan Quann, United States	1:07.05
2004	Luo Xuejuan, China	1:06.64
2008	Leisel Jones, Australia	1:05.17
2012	Ruta Meilutyte, Lithuania	1:05.47
2016	Lilly King, United States	1:04.93*
2020	Lydia Jacoby, United States	1:04.95

200-Meter Breaststroke		Time
1924	Lucy Morton, Great Britain	3:33.2
1928	Hilde Schrader, Germany	3:12.6
1932	Clare Dennis, Australia	3:06.3
1936	Hideko Maehata, Japan	3:03.6
1948	Nelly Van Vliet, Netherlands	2:57.2
1952	Eva Szekely, Hungary	2:51.7
1956	Ursula Happe, Germany	2:53.1
1960	Anita Lonsbrough, Great Britain	2:49.5
1964	Galina Prozumenshchikova, USSR	2:46.4
1968	Sharon Wichman, United States	2:44.4
1972	Beverly Whitfield, Australia	2:41.71
1976	Marina Koshevaia, USSR	2:33.35
1980	Lina Kachushite, USSR	2:29.54
1984	Anne Ottenbrite, Canada	2:30.38
1988	Silke Hoerner, E. Germany	2:26.71
1992	Kyoko Iwasaki, Japan	2:26.65
1996	Penny Heyns, South Africa	2:25.41

200-Meter Breaststroke

Year	Champion	Time
2000	Agnes Kovacs, Hungary	2:24.35
2004	Amanda Beard, United States	2:23.37
2008	Rebecca Soni, United States	2:20.22
2012	Rebecca Soni, United States	2:19.59
2016	Rie Kaneto, Japan	2:20.30
2020	Tatjana Schoenmaker, South Africa	2:18.95*

100-Meter Butterfly

Year	Champion	Time
1956	Shelley Mann, United States	1:11.0
1960	Carolyn Schuler, United States	1:09.5
1964	Sharon Stouder, United States	1:04.7
1968	Lynn McClements, Australia	1:05.5
1972	Mayumi Aoki, Japan	1:03.34
1976	Kornelia Ender, E. Germany	1:00.13
1980	Caren Metschuck, E. Germany	1:00.42
1984	Mary T. Meagher, United States	0:59.26
1988	Kristin Otto, E. Germany	0:59.00
1992	Qian Hong, China	0:58.62
1996	Amy Van Dyken, United States	0:59.13
2000	Inge de Bruijn, Netherlands	0:56.61
2004	Petria Thomas, Australia	0:57.72
2008	Lisbeth Trickett, Australia	0:56.73
2012	Dana Vollmer, United States	0:55.98
2016	Sarah Sjöström, Sweden	0:55.48*
2020	Maggie MacNeil, Canada	0:55.59

200-Meter Butterfly

Year	Champion	Time
1968	Ada Kok, Netherlands	2:24.7
1972	Karen Moe, United States	2:15.57
1976	Andrea Pollack, E. Germany	2:11.41
1980	Ines Geissler, E. Germany	2:10.44
1984	Mary T. Meagher, United States	2:06.90
1988	Kathleen Nord, E. Germany	2:09.51
1992	Summer Sanders, United States	2:08.67
1996	Susan O'Neill, Australia	2:07.76
2000	Misty Hyman, United States	2:05.88
2004	Otylia Jedrzejczak, Poland	2:06.05
2008	Liu Zige, China	2:04.18
2012	Jiao Liuyang, China	2:04.06
2016	Mireia Belmonte, Spain	2:04.85
2020	Zhang Yufei, China	2:03.86*

200-Meter Individual Medley

Year	Champion	Time
1968	Claudia Kolb, United States	2:24.7
1972	Shane Gould, Australia	2:23.07
1984	Tracy Caulkins, United States	2:12.64
1988	Daniela Hunger, E. Germany	2:12.59
1992	Lin Li, China	2:11.65
1996	Michelle Smith, Ireland	2:13.93
2000	Yana Klochkova, Ukraine	2:10.68
2004	Yana Klochkova, Ukraine	2:11.14
2008	Stephanie Rice, Australia	2:08.45
2012	Ye Shiwen, China	2:07.57
2016	Katinka Hosszú, Hungary	2:06.58*
2020	Yui Ohashi, Japan	2:08.52

400-Meter Individual Medley

Year	Champion	Time
1964	Donna de Varona, United States	5:18.7
1968	Claudia Kolb, United States	5:08.5
1972	Gail Neall, Australia	5:02.97
1976	Ulrike Tauber, E. Germany	4:42.77
1980	Petra Schneider, E. Germany	4:36.29
1984	Tracy Caulkins, United States	4:39.24
1988	Janet Evans, United States	4:37.76
1992	Krisztina Egerszegi, Hungary	4:36.54
1996	Michelle Smith, Ireland	4:39.18
2000	Yana Klochkova, Ukraine	4:33.59
2004	Yana Klochkova, Ukraine	4:34.83
2008	Stephanie Rice, Australia	4:29.45
2012	Ye Shiwen, China	4:28.43
2016	Katinka Hosszú, Hungary	4:26.36*
2020	Yui Ohashi, Japan	4:32.08

4x100-Meter Freestyle Relay

Year	Champion	Time
1912	Great Britain	5:52.8
1920	United States	5:11.6
1924	United States	4:58.8
1928	United States	4:47.6
1932	United States	4:38.0
1936	Netherlands	4:36.0
1948	United States	4:29.2
1952	Hungary	4:24.4
1956	Australia	4:17.1
1960	United States	4:08.9
1964	United States	4:03.8
1968	United States	4:02.5
1972	United States	3:55.19
1976	United States	3:44.82

4x100-Meter Freestyle Relay

Year	Champion	Time
1980	East Germany	3:42.71
1984	United States	3:43.43
1988	East Germany	3:40.63
1992	United States	3:39.46
1996	United States	3:39.29
2000	United States	3:36.61
2004	Australia	3:35.94
2008	Netherlands	3:33.76
2012	Australia	3:33.15
2016	Australia	3:30.65
2020	Australia	3:29.69*

4x200-Meter Freestyle Relay

Year	Champion	Time
1996	United States	7:59.87
2000	United States	7:57.80
2004	United States	7:53.42
2008	Australia	7:44.31
2012	United States	7:42.92
2016	United States	7:43.03
2020	China	7:40.33*

4x100-Meter Medley Relay

Year	Champion	Time
1960	United States	4:41.1
1964	United States	4:33.9
1968	United States	4:28.3
1972	United States	4:20.75
1976	East Germany	4:07.95
1980	East Germany	4:06.67
1984	United States	4:08.34
1988	East Germany	4:03.74
1992	United States	4:02.54
1996	United States	4:02.88
2000	United States	3:58.30
2004	Australia	3:57.32
2008	Australia	3:52.69
2012	United States	3:52.05
2016	United States	3:53.13
2020	Australia	3:51.60*

10-Kilometer Marathon

Year	Champion	Time
2008	Larisa Ilchenko, Russia	1:59:27.7
2012	Éva Risztov, Hungary	1:57:38.2
2016	Sharon van Rouwendaal, Netherlands	1:56:32.1
2020	Ana Marcela Cunha, Brazil	1:59:30.8

Platform Diving

Year	Champion	Points
1912	Greta Johansson, Sweden	39.90
1920	Stefani Fryland-Clausen, Denmark	34.60
1924	Caroline Smith, United States	33.20
1928	Elizabeth B. Pinkston, United States	31.60
1932	Dorothy Poynton, United States	40.26
1936	Dorothy Poynton Hill, United States	33.93
1948	Victoria M. Draves, United States	68.87
1952	Patricia McCormick, United States	79.37
1956	Patricia McCormick, United States	84.85
1960	Ingrid Kramer, Germany	91.28
1964	Lesley Bush, United States	99.80
1968	Milena Duchkova, Czechoslovakia	109.59
1972	Ulrika Knape, Sweden	390.00
1976	Elena Vaytsekhouskaya, USSR	406.59
1980	Martina Jaschke, E. Germany	596.25
1984	Zhou Jihong, China	435.51
1988	Xu Yanmei, China	445.20
1992	Fu Mingxia, China	461.43
1996	Fu Mingxia, China	521.58
2000	Laura Wilkinson, United States	543.75
2004	Chantelle Newbery, Australia	590.31
2008	Chen Ruolin, China	447.70
2012	Chen Ruolin, China	422.30
2016	Ren Qian, China	439.25
2020	Quan Hongchan, China	466.20

Springboard Diving

Year	Champion	Points
1920	Aileen Riggin, United States	539.90
1924	Elizabeth Becker, United States	474.50
1928	Helen Meany, United States	78.62
1932	Georgia Coleman, United States	87.52
1936	Marjorie Gestring, United States	89.27
1948	Victoria M. Draves, United States	108.74
1952	Patricia McCormick, United States	147.30
1956	Patricia McCormick, United States	142.36
1960	Ingrid Kramer, Germany	155.81
1964	Ingrid Engel-Kramer, Germany	145.00
1968	Sue Gossick, United States	150.77
1972	Micki King, United States	450.03

	Springboard Diving	Points
1976	Jenni Chandler, United States	506.19
1980	Irina Kalinina, USSR	725.91
1984	Sylvie Bernier, Canada	530.70
1988	Gao Min, China	580.23
1992	Gao Min, China	572.40
1996	Fu Mingxia, China	547.68
2000	Fu Mingxia, China	609.42
2004	Guo Jingjing, China	633.15
2008	Guo Jingjing, China	415.35
2012	Wu Minxia, China	414.00
2016	Shi Tingmao, China	406.05
2020	Shi Tingmao, China	383.50

	Synchronized Platform Diving	Points
2004	Lao Lishi & Li Ting, China	352.14
2008	Wang Xin & Chen Ruolin, China	363.54
2012	Chen Ruolin & Wang Hao, China	368.40
2016	Chen Ruolin & Liu Huixia, China	354.00
2020	Chen Yuxi & Zhang Jiaqi, China	363.78

	Synchronized Springboard Diving	Points
2004	Wu Minxia & Guo Jingjing, China	336.90
2008	Guo Jingjing & Wu Minxia, China	343.50
2012	He Zi & Wu Minxia, China	346.20
2016	Wu Minxia & Shi Tingmao, China	345.60
2020	Shi Tingmao & Wang Han, China	326.40

Swimming—Mixed

	4x100-Meter Medley Relay	Time
2020	Great Britain	3:37.58*

Tennis

Men's Singles

1896	John Boland, Great Britain
1900	Hugh Lawrence Doherty, Great Britain
1904	Beals Wright, United States
1908	Josiah George Ritchie, Great Britain
1912	Charles Lyndhurst Winslow, South Africa
1920	Louis Raymond, South Africa
1924	Vincent Richards, United States
1988	Miloslav Mecir, Czechoslovakia
1992	Marc Rosset, Switzerland
1996	Andre Agassi, United States
2000	Yevgeny Kafelnikov, Russia
2004	Nicolas Massu, Chile
2008	Rafael Nadal, Spain
2012	Andy Murray, Great Britain
2016	Andy Murray, Great Britain
2020	Alexander Zverev, Germany

Women's Singles

1900	Charlotte Cooper, Great Britain
1908	Dorothy Katherine Chambers, Great Britain
1912	Marguerite Broquedis, France
1920	Suzanne Lenglen, France
1924	Helen Wills, United States
1988	Steffi Graf, W. Germany
1992	Jennifer Capriati, United States
1996	Lindsay Davenport, United States
2000	Venus Williams, United States
2004	Justine Henin-Hardenne, Belgium
2008	Elena Dementieva, Russia
2012	Serena Williams, United States
2016	Monica Puig, Puerto Rico
2020	Belinda Bencic, Switzerland

Men's Doubles

1896	John Boland, Great Britain & Friedrick Traun, Germany
1900	Hugh Lawrence Doherty & Reginald Frank Doherty, Great Britain
1904	Edgar Leonard & Beals Wright, U.S.
1908	George Whiteside Hillyard & Reginald Frank Doherty, Great Britain
1912	Harry Austin Kitson & Charles Lyndhurst Winslow, South Africa
1920	Noel Turnbull & Maxwell Woosnam, Great Britain
1924	Vincent Richards & Francis Townsend Hunter, U.S.
1988	Kenneth Flach & Robert A. Seguso, United States
1992	Boris Becker & Michael Stich, Germany
1996	Mark Woodforde & Todd Woodbridge, Australia
2000	Sebastien Lareau & Daniel Nestor, Canada
2004	Fernando Gonzales & Nicolas Massu, Chile
2008	Roger Federer & Stanislas Wawrinka, Switzerland
2012	Mike Bryan & Bob Bryan, United States
2016	Marc López & Rafael Nadal, Spain
2020	Nikola Mektić & Mate Pavić, Croatia

Women's Doubles

1920	Winifred Margaret McNair & Kathleen McKane, Great Britain
1924	Hazel Virginia Wightman & Helen Wills, United States
1988	Pam Shriver & Zina Garrison, United States
1992	Gigi Fernandez & Mary Joe Fernandez, United States
1996	Gigi Fernandez & Mary Joe Fernandez, United States
2000	Venus Williams & Serena Williams, United States
2004	Ting Li & Tian Tian Sun, China
2008	Serena Williams & Venus Williams, United States
2012	Serena Williams & Venus Williams, United States
2016	Ekaterina Makarova & Elena Vesnina, Russia
2020	Barbora Krejčíková & Kateřina Siniaková, Czech Republic

Mixed Doubles

2012	Victoria Azarenka & Max Mirnyi, Belarus
2016	Bethanie Mattek-Sands & Jack Sock, United States
2020	Anastasia Pavlyuchenkova & Andrey Rublev, ROC

Track and Field—Men

	100-Meter Run	Time
1896	Thomas Burke, United States	0:12.0
1900	Francis Jarvis, United States	0:11.0
1904	Archie Hahn, United States	0:11.0
1908	Reginald Walker, South Africa	0:10.8
1912	Ralph Craig, United States	0:10.8
1920	Charles Paddock, United States	0:10.8
1924	Harold Abrahams, Great Britain	0:10.6
1928	Percy Williams, Canada	0:10.8
1932	Eddie Tolan, United States	0:10.3
1936	Jesse Owens, United States	0:10.3
1948	Harrison Dillard, United States	0:10.3
1952	Lindy Remigino, United States	0:10.4
1956	Bobby Morrow, United States	0:10.5
1960	Armin Hary, Germany	0:10.2
1964	Bob Hayes, United States	0:10.0
1968	Jim Hines, United States	0:09.95
1972	Valery Borzov, USSR	0:10.14
1976	Hasely Crawford, Trinidad and Tobago	0:10.06
1980	Allan Wells, Great Britain	0:10.25
1984	Carl Lewis, United States	0:09.99

	100-Meter Run	Time
1988	Carl Lewis, United States	0:09.92
1992	Linford Christie, Great Britain	0:09.96
1996	Donovan Bailey, Canada	0:09.84
2000	Maurice Greene, United States	0:09.87
2004	Justin Gatlin, United States	0:09.85
2008	Usain Bolt, Jamaica	0:09.69
2012	Usain Bolt, Jamaica	0:09.63*
2016	Usain Bolt, Jamaica	0:09.81
2020	Marcell Jacobs, Italy	0:09.80

	200-Meter Run	Time
1900	Walter Tewksbury, United States	0:22.2
1904	Archie Hahn, United States	0:21.6
1908	Robert Kerr, Canada	0:22.6
1912	Ralph Craig, United States	0:21.7
1920	Allan Woodring, United States	0:22.0
1924	Jackson Scholz, United States	0:21.6
1928	Percy Williams, Canada	0:21.8
1932	Eddie Tolan, United States	0:21.2
1936	Jesse Owens, United States	0:20.7
1948	Mel Patton, United States	0:21.1

200-Meter Run	Time
1952 Andrew Stanfield, United States	0:20.7
1956 Bobby Morrow, United States	0:20.6
1960 Livio Berruti, Italy	0:20.5
1964 Henry Carr, United States	0:20.3
1968 Tommie Smith, United States	0:19.83
1972 Valery Borzov, USSR	0:20.00
1976 Donald Quarrie, Jamaica	0:20.23
1980 Pietro Mennea, Italy	0:20.19
1984 Carl Lewis, United States	0:19.80
1988 Joe DeLoach, United States	0:19.75
1992 Mike Marsh, United States	0:20.01
1996 Michael Johnson, United States	0:19.32
2000 Konstantinos Kenteris, Greece	0:20.09
2004 Shawn Crawford, United States	0:19.79
2008 Usain Bolt, Jamaica	0:19.30*
2012 Usain Bolt, Jamaica	0:19.32
2016 Usain Bolt, Jamaica	0:19.78
2020 Andre De Grasse, Canada	0:19.62

400-Meter Run	Time
1896 Thomas Burke, United States	0:54.2
1900 Maxwell Long, United States	0:49.4
1904 Harry Hillman, United States	0:49.2
1908 Wyndham Halswelle, Gr. Brit. (walkover)	0:50.0
1912 Charles Reidpath, United States	0:48.2
1920 Bevil Rudd, South Africa	0:49.6
1924 Eric Liddell, Great Britain	0:47.6
1928 Ray Barbuti, United States	0:47.8
1932 William Carr, United States	0:46.2
1936 Archie Williams, United States	0:46.5
1948 Arthur Wint, Jamaica	0:46.2
1952 George Rhoden, Jamaica	0:45.9
1956 Charles Jenkins, United States	0:46.7
1960 Otis Davis, United States	0:44.9
1964 Michael Larrabee, United States	0:45.1
1968 Lee Evans, United States	0:43.86
1972 Vincent Matthews, United States	0:44.66
1976 Alberto Juantorena, Cuba	0:44.26
1980 Viktor Markin, USSR	0:44.60
1984 Alonzo Babers, United States	0:44.27
1988 Steve Lewis, United States	0:43.87
1992 Quincy Watts, United States	0:43.50
1996 Michael Johnson, United States	0:43.49
2000 Michael Johnson, United States	0:43.84
2004 Jeremy Wariner, United States	0:44.00
2008 LaShawn Merritt, United States	0:43.75
2012 Kirani James, Grenada	0:43.94
2016 Wayde van Niekerk, South Africa	0:43.03*
2020 Steven Gardiner, Bahamas	0:43.85

800-Meter Run	Time
1896 Edwin Flack, Australia	2:11.0
1900 Alfred Tysoe, Great Britain	2:01.2
1904 James Lightbody, United States	1:56.0
1908 Mel Sheppard, United States	1:52.8
1912 James "Ted" Meredith, United States	1:51.9
1920 Albert Hill, Great Britain	1:53.4
1924 Douglas Lowe, Great Britain	1:52.4
1928 Douglas Lowe, Great Britain	1:51.8
1932 Thomas Hampson, Great Britain	1:49.8
1936 John Woodruff, United States	1:52.9
1948 Mal Whitfield, United States	1:49.2
1952 Mal Whitfield, United States	1:49.2
1956 Tom Courtney, United States	1:47.7
1960 Peter Snell, New Zealand	1:46.3
1964 Peter Snell, New Zealand	1:45.1
1968 Ralph Doubell, Australia	1:44.3
1972 Dave Wottle, United States	1:45.9
1976 Alberto Juantorena, Cuba	1:43.50
1980 Steve Ovett, Great Britain	1:45.40
1984 Joaquim Cruz, Brazil	1:43.00
1988 Paul Ereng, Kenya	1:43.45
1992 William Tanui, Kenya	1:43.66
1996 Vebjørn Rodal, Norway	1:42.58
2000 Nils Schumann, Germany	1:45.08
2004 Yuriy Borzakovskiy, Russia	1:44.45
2008 Wilfred Bungei, Kenya	1:44.65
2012 David Lekuta Rudisha, Kenya	1:40.91*
2016 David Lekuta Rudisha, Kenya	1:42.15
2020 Emmanuel Korir, Kenya	1:45.06

1500-Meter Run	Time
1896 Edwin Flack, Australia	4:33.2
1900 Charles Bennett, Great Britain	4:06.2
1904 James Lightbody, United States	4:05.4
1908 Mel Sheppard, United States	4:03.4
1912 Arnold Jackson, Great Britain	3:56.8
1920 Albert Hill, Great Britain	4:01.8
1924 Paavo Nurmi, Finland	3:53.6
1928 Harry Larva, Finland	3:53.2
1932 Luigi Beccali, Italy	3:51.2
1936 Jack Lovelock, New Zealand	3:47.8
1948 Henry Eriksson, Sweden	3:49.8
1952 Joseph Barthel, Luxembourg	3:45.2
1956 Ron Delany, Ireland	3:41.2
1960 Herb Elliott, Australia	3:35.6
1964 Peter Snell, New Zealand	3:38.1
1968 Kipchoge Keino, Kenya	3:34.91
1972 Pekka Vasala, Finland	3:36.33
1976 John Walker, New Zealand	3:39.17
1980 Sebastian Coe, Great Britain	3:38.4
1984 Sebastian Coe, Great Britain	3:32.53
1988 Peter Rono, Kenya	3:35.96
1992 Fermin Cacho Ruiz, Spain	3:40.12
1996 Noureddine Morceli, Algeria	3:35.78
2000 Noah Ngeny, Kenya	3:32.07
2004 Hicham El Guerrouj, Morocco	3:34.18
2008 Asbel Kiprop, Kenya[1]	3:33.11
2012 Taoufik Makhloufi, Algeria	3:34.08
2016 Matthew Centrowitz, United States	3:50.00
2020 Jakob Ingebrigtsen, Norway	3:28.32*

(1) Originally won by Rashid Ramzi, Bahrain, who was stripped of the gold in 2009 due to doping.

3000-Meter Steeplechase	Time
1920 Percy Hodge, Great Britain	10:00.4
1924 Ville Ritola, Finland	9:33.6
1928 Toivo Loukola, Finland	9:21.8
1932 Volmari Iso-Hollo, Finland (about 3,450 m; extra lap by error)	10:33.4
1936 Volmari Iso-Hollo, Finland	9:03.8
1948 Tore Sjöstrand, Sweden	9:04.6
1952 Horace Ashenfelter, United States	8:45.4
1956 Chris Brasher, Great Britain	8:41.2
1960 Zdzislaw Krzyszkowiak, Poland	8:34.2
1964 Gaston Roelants, Belgium	8:30.8
1968 Amos Biwott, Kenya	8:51.0
1972 Kipchoge Keino, Kenya	8:23.64
1976 Anders Garderud, Sweden	8:08.02
1980 Bronislaw Malinowski, Poland	8:09.7
1984 Julius Korir, Kenya	8:11.80
1988 Julius Kariuki, Kenya	8:05.51
1992 Matthew Birir, Kenya	8:08.84
1996 Joseph Keter, Kenya	8:07.12
2000 Reuben Kosgei, Kenya	8:21.43
2004 Ezekiel Kemboi, Kenya	8:05.81
2008 Brimin Kiprop Kirpruto, Kenya	8:10.34
2012 Ezekiel Kemboi, Kenya	8:18.56
2016 Conseslus Kipruto, Kenya	8:03.28*
2020 Soufiane El Bakkali. Morocco	8:08.90

5000-Meter Run	Time
1912 Hannes Kolehmainen, Finland	14:36.6
1920 Joseph Guillemot, France	14:55.6
1924 Paavo Nurmi, Finland	14:31.2
1928 Ville Ritola, Finland	14:38.0
1932 Lauri Lehtinen, Finland	14:30.0
1936 Gunnar Höckert, Finland	14:22.2
1948 Gaston Reiff, Belgium	14:17.6
1952 Emil Zatopek, Czechoslovakia	14:06.6
1956 Vladimir Kuts, USSR	13:39.6
1960 Murray Halberg, New Zealand	13:43.4
1964 Bob Schul, United States	13:48.8
1968 Mohamed Gammoudi, Tunisia	14:05.0
1972 Lasse Viren, Finland	13:26.4
1976 Lasse Viren, Finland	13:24.76
1980 Miruts Yifter, Ethiopia	13:20.91
1984 Said Aouita, Morocco	13:05.59
1988 John Ngugi, Kenya	13:11.70
1992 Dieter Baumann, Germany	13:12.52
1996 Venuste Niyongabo, Burundi	13:07.96
2000 Million Wolde, Ethiopia	13:35.49
2004 Hicham El Guerrouj, Morocco	13:14.39
2008 Kenenisa Bekele, Ethiopia	12:57.82*
2012 Mo Farah, Great Britain	13:41.66
2016 Mo Farah, Great Britain	13:03.30
2020 Joshua Cheptegei, Uganda	12:58.15

10,000-Meter Run	Time
1912 Hannes Kolehmainen, Finland	31:20.8
1920 Paavo Nurmi, Finland	31:45.8
1924 Ville Ritola, Finland	30:23.2
1928 Paavo Nurmi, Finland	30:18.8
1932 Janusz Kusocinski, Poland	30:11.4
1936 Ilmari Salminen, Finland	30:15.4
1948 Emil Zatopek, Czechoslovakia	29:59.6
1952 Emil Zatopek, Czechoslovakia	29:17.0
1956 Vladimir Kuts, USSR	28:45.6
1960 Pyotr Bolotnikov, USSR	28:32.2
1964 Billy Mills, United States	28:24.4
1968 Naftali Temu, Kenya	29:27.4
1972 Lasse Viren, Finland	27:38.4
1976 Lasse Viren, Finland	27:40.38
1980 Miruts Yifter, Ethiopia	27:42.7
1984 Alberto Cova, Italy	27:47.54
1988 Brahim Boutayeb, Morocco	27:21.46
1992 Khalid Skah, Morocco	27:46.70
1996 Haile Gebrselassie, Ethiopia	27:07.34
2000 Haile Gebrselassie, Ethiopia	27:18.20
2004 Kenenisa Bekele, Ethiopia	27:05.10
2008 Kenenisa Bekele, Ethiopia	27:01.17*
2012 Mo Farah, Great Britain	27:30.42
2016 Mo Farah, Great Britain	27:05.17
2020 Selemon Barega, Ethiopia	27:43.22

Marathon	Time
1896 Spyridon Louis, Greece	2:58:50
1900 Michel Theato, France	2:59:45.0
1904 Thomas Hicks, United States	3:28:53.0
1908 John Hayes, United States	2:55:18.4
1912 Kenneth McArthur, South Africa	2:36:54.8
1920 Hannes Kolehmainen, Finland	2:32:35.8
1924 Albin Stenroos, Finland	2:41:22.6
1928 Boughera El Ouafi, France	2:32.57
1932 Juan Zabala, Argentina	2:31:36
1936 Kee-chung Sohn, Japan[1]	2:29:19.2
1948 Delfo Cabrera, Argentina	2:34:51.6
1952 Emil Zatopek, Czechoslovakia	2:23:03.2
1956 Alain Mimoun, France	2:25:00.0
1960 Abebe Bikila, Ethiopia	2:15:16.2
1964 Abebe Bikila, Ethiopia	2:12:11.2
1968 Mamo Wolde, Ethiopia	2:20:26.4
1972 Frank Shorter, United States	2:12:19.8
1976 Waldemar Cierpinski, E. Germany	2:09:55.0
1980 Waldemar Cierpinski, E. Germany	2:11:03.0
1984 Carlos Lopes, Portugal	2:09:21
1988 Gelindo Bordin, Italy	2:10:32
1992 Hwang Young-cho, S. Korea	2:13:23
1996 Josia Thugwane, South Africa	2:12:36
2000 Gezahegne Abera, Ethiopia	2:10:11
2004 Stefano Baldini, Italy	2:10:55
2008 Samuel Kamau Wanjiru, Kenya	2:06:32*
2012 Stephen Kiprotich, Uganda	2:08:01
2016 Eliud Kipchoge, Kenya	2:08:44
2020 Eliud Kipchoge, Kenya	2:08:38

(1) Korean runner who competed under Japanese name Kitei Son.

4x100-Meter Relay	Time
1912 Great Britain	0:42.4
1920 United States	0:42.2
1924 United States	0:41.0
1928 United States	0:41.0
1932 United States	0:40.0
1936 United States	0:39.8
1948 United States	0:40.6
1952 United States	0:40.1
1956 United States	0:39.5
1960 Germany (U.S. disqualified)	0:39.5
1964 United States	0:39.0
1968 United States	0:38.24
1972 United States	0:38.19
1976 United States	0:38.33
1980 USSR	0:38.26
1984 United States	0:37.83
1988 USSR (U.S. disqualified)	0:38.19
1992 United States	0:37.40
1996 Canada	0:37.69
2000 United States	0:37.61
2004 Great Britain	0:38.07
2008 Trinidad and Tobago[1]	0:38.06
2012 Jamaica	0:36.84*
2016 Jamaica	0:37.27
2020 Italy	0:37.50

(1) Due to team member Nesta Carter's doping, Jamaica was stripped of the victory in 2017.

4x400-Meter Relay	Time
1908 United States	3:29.4
1912 United States	3:16.6
1920 Great Britain	3:22.2
1924 United States	3:16.0
1928 United States	3:14.2
1932 United States	3:08.2
1936 Great Britain	3:09.0
1948 United States	3:10.4
1952 Jamaica	3:03.9
1956 United States	3:04.8
1960 United States	3:02.2
1964 United States	3:00.7
1968 United States	2:56.16
1972 Kenya	2:59.8
1976 United States	2:58.65
1980 USSR	3:01.1
1984 United States	2:57.91
1988 United States	2:56.16
1992 United States	2:55.74
1996 United States	2:55.99
2000 Nigeria[1]	2:58.68
2004 United States	2:55.91
2008 United States	2:55.39*
2012 The Bahamas	2:56.72
2016 United States	2:57.30
2020 United States	2:55.70

(1) The U.S. was stripped of the medal in 2012 after team member Antonio Pettigrew admitted to doping.

20-Kilometer Walk	Time
1956 Leonid Spirin, USSR	1:31:27.4
1960 Vladimir Golubnichy, USSR	1:34:07.2
1964 Kenneth Matthews, Great Britain	1:29:34.0
1968 Vladimir Golubnichy, USSR	1:33:58.4
1972 Peter Frenkel, E. Germany	1:26:42.4
1976 Daniel Bautista, Mexico	1:24:40.6
1980 Maurizio Damilano, Italy	1:23:35.5
1984 Ernesto Canto, Mexico	1:23:13
1988 Jozef Pribilinec, Czechoslovakia	1:19.57
1992 Daniel Plaza Montero, Spain	1:21:45
1996 Jefferson Perez, Ecuador	1:20:07
2000 Robert Korzeniowski, Poland	1:18:59
2004 Ivano Brugnetti, Italy	1:19:40
2008 Valeriy Borchin, Russia	1:19:01
2012 Chen Ding, China	1:18:46*
2016 Wang Zhen, China	1:19:14
2020 Massimo Stano, Italy	1:21:05

50-Kilometer Walk	Time
1932 Thomas "Tommy" Green, Great Britain	4:50.10
1936 Harold Whitlock, Great Britain	4:30:41.4
1948 John Ljunggren, Sweden	4:41.52
1952 Giuseppe Dordoni, Italy	4:28:07.8
1956 Norman Read, New Zealand	4:30:42.8
1960 Donald Thompson, Great Britain	4:25:30
1964 Abdon Pamich, Italy	4:11:12.4
1968 Christoph Höhne, E. Germany	4:20:13.6
1972 Bernd Kannenberg, W. Germany	3:56:11.6
1980 Hartwig Gauder, E. Germany	3:49:24.0
1984 Raúl González, Mexico	3:47:26
1988 Vyacheslav Ivanenko, USSR	3:38.29
1992 Andrey Perlov, Unified Team (Rus.)	3:50:13
1996 Robert Korzeniowski, Poland	3:43:30
2000 Robert Korzeniowski, Poland	3:42:22
2004 Robert Korzeniowski, Poland	3:38:46
2008 Alex Schwazer, Italy	3:37:09
2012 Jared Tallent, Australia[1]	3:36:53*
2016 Matej Tóth, Slovakia	3:40:58
2020 Dawid Tomala, Poland	3:50:08

(1) Russia's Sergey Kirdyapkin was stripped of the gold medal in 2016 for doping.

110-Meter Hurdles	Time
1896 Thomas Curtis, United States	0:17.6
1900 Alvin Kraenzlein, United States	0:15.4
1904 Frederick Schule, United States	0:16.0
1908 Forrest Smithson, United States	0:15.0
1912 Frederick Kelly, United States	0:15.1
1920 Earl Thomson, Canada	0:14.8
1924 Daniel Kinsey, United States	0:15.0
1928 Sydney Atkinson, South Africa	0:14.8
1932 George Saling, United States	0:14.6
1936 Forrest Towns, United States	0:14.2
1948 William Porter, United States	0:13.9
1952 Harrison Dillard, United States	0:13.7
1956 Lee Calhoun, United States	0:13.5

110-Meter Hurdles

Year	Athlete	Time
1960	Lee Calhoun, United States	0:13.8
1964	Hayes Jones, United States	0:13.6
1968	Willie Davenport, United States	0:13.33
1972	Rod Milburn, United States	0:13.24
1976	Guy Drut, France	0:13:30
1980	Thomas Munkelt, E. Germany	0:13.39
1984	Roger Kingdom, United States	0:13.20
1988	Roger Kingdom, United States	0:12.98
1992	Mark McKoy, Canada	0:13.12
1996	Allen Johnson, United States	0:12.95
2000	Anier Garcia, Cuba	0:13.00
2004	Liu Xiang, China	0:12.91*
2008	Dayron Robles, Cuba	0:12.93
2012	Aries Merritt, United States	0:12.92
2016	Omar McLeod, Jamaica	0:13.05
2020	Hansle Parchment, Jamaica	0:13.04

400-Meter Hurdles

Year	Athlete	Time
1900	Walter Tewksbury, United States	0:57.6
1904	Harry Hillman, United States	0:53.0
1908	Charles Bacon, United States	0:55.0
1920	Frank Loomis, United States	0:54.0
1924	F. Morgan Taylor, United States	0:52.6
1928	David, Lord Burghley, Great Britain	0:53.4
1932	Bob Tisdall, Ireland	0:51.7
1936	Glenn Hardin, United States	0:52.4
1948	Roy Cochran, United States	0:51.1
1952	Charles Moore, United States	0:50.8
1956	Glenn Davis, United States	0:50.1
1960	Glenn Davis, United States	0:49.3
1964	Rex Cawley, United States	0:49.6
1968	David Hemery, Great Britain	0:48.12
1972	John Akii-Bua, Uganda	0:47.82
1976	Edwin Moses, United States	0:47.64
1980	Volker Beck, E. Germany	0:48.70
1984	Edwin Moses, United States	0:47.75
1988	Andre Phillips, United States	0:47.19
1992	Kevin Young, United States	0:46.78
1996	Derrick Adkins, United States	0:47.54
2000	Angelo Taylor, United States	0:47.50
2004	Félix Sánchez, Dominican Republic	0:47.63
2008	Angelo Taylor, United States	0:47.25
2012	Félix Sánchez, Dominican Republic	0:47.63
2016	Kerron Clement, United States	0:47.73
2020	Karsten Warholm, Norway	0:45.94*

Note: Event not held in 1912.

Discus Throw

Year	Athlete	Dist.	
1896	Robert Garrett, United States	29.15m	(95' 7")
1900	Rudolf Bauer, Hungary	36.04m	(118' 3")
1904	Martin Sheridan, United States	39.28m	(128' 10")
1908	Martin Sheridan, United States	40.89m	(134' 1")
1912	Armas Taipale, Finland	45.21m	(148' 3")
1920	Elmer Niklander, Finland	44.68m	(146' 7")
1924	Clarence "Bud" Houser, U.S.	46.15m	(151' 4")
1928	Clarence "Bud" Houser, U.S.	47.32m	(155' 3")
1932	John Anderson, United States	49.49m	(162' 4")
1936	Ken Carpenter, United States	50.48m	(165' 7")
1948	Adolfo Consolini, Italy	52.78m	(173' 2")
1952	Sim Iness, United States	55.03m	(180' 6")
1956	Al Oerter, United States	56.36m	(184' 11")
1960	Al Oerter, United States	59.18m	(194' 2")
1964	Al Oerter, United States	61.00m	(200' 1")
1968	Al Oerter, United States	64.78m	(212' 6")
1972	Ludvik Danek, Czechoslovakia	64.40m	(211' 3")
1976	Mac Wilkins, United States	67.50m	(221' 5")
1980	Viktor Rashchupkin, USSR	66.64m	(218' 8")
1984	Rolf Danneberg, W. Germany	66.60m	(218' 6")
1988	Jürgen Schult, E. Germany	68.82m	(225' 9")
1992	Romas Ubartas, Lithuania	65.12m	(213' 8")
1996	Lars Riedel, Germany	69.40m	(227' 8")
2000	Virgilijus Alekna, Lithuania	69.30m	(227' 4")
2004	Virgilijus Alekna, Lithuania	69.89m	(228' 9¾")*
2008	Gerd Kanter, Estonia	68.82m	(225' 9½")
2012	Robert Harting, Germany	68.27m	(224')
2016	Christoph Harting, Germany	68.37m	(224' 3¾")
2020	Daniel Ståhl, Sweden	68.90m	(226' ½")

Hammer Throw

Year	Athlete	Dist.	
1900	John Flanagan, United States	49.73m	(163' 1")
1904	John Flanagan, United States	51.23m	(168' 1")
1908	John Flanagan, United States	51.92m	(170' 4")
1912	Matt McGrath, United States	54.74m	(179' 7")
1920	Pat Ryan, United States	52.875m	(173' 5¾")
1924	Fred Tootell, United States	53.295m	(174' 10")
1928	Patrick O'Callaghan, Ireland	51.39m	(168' 7")
1932	Patrick O'Callaghan, Ireland	53.92m	(176' 11")
1936	Karl Hein, Germany	56.49m	(185' 4")

Hammer Throw

Year	Athlete	Dist.	
1948	Imre Németh, Hungary	56.07m	(183' 11½")
1952	József Csérmák, Hungary	60.34m	(197' 11")
1956	Harold Connolly, United States	63.19m	(207' 3")
1960	Vasily Rudenkov, USSR	67.10m	(202' 0")
1964	Romuald Klim, USSR	69.74m	(228' 10")
1968	Gyula Zsivótzky, Hungary	73.36m	(240' 8")
1972	Anatoly Bondarchuk, USSR	75.50m	(247' 8")
1976	Yuri Sedykh, USSR	77.52m	(254' 4")
1980	Yuri Sedykh, USSR	81.80m	(268' 4")
1984	Juha Tiainen, Finland	78.08m	(256' 2")
1988	Sergei Litvinov, USSR	84.80m	(278' 2")*
1992	Andrey Abduvaliyev, Unified Team	82.54m	(270' 9")
1996	Balázs Kiss, Hungary	81.24m	(266' 6")
2000	Szymon Ziolkowski, Poland	80.02m	(262' 6")
2004	Koji Murofushi, Japan	82.91m	(272')
2008	Primoz Kozmus, Slovenia	82.02m	(269' 1")
2012	Krisztián Pars, Hungary	80.59m	(264' 5")
2016	Dilshod Nazarov, Tajikistan	78.68m	(258' 1¾")
2020	Wojciech Nowicki, Poland	82.52m	(270' 8¾")

High Jump

Year	Athlete	Height	
1896	Ellery Clark, United States	1.81m	(5' 11¼")
1900	Irving Baxter, United States	1.90m	(6' 2¾")
1904	Samuel Jones, United States	1.80m	(5' 11")
1908	Harry Porter, United States	1.90m	(6' 2¾")
1912	Alma Richards, United States	1.93m	(6' 4")
1920	Richmond Landon, United States	1.94m	(6' 4¼")
1924	Harold Osborn, United States	1.98m	(6' 6")
1928	Robert "Bob" King, United States	1.94m	(6' 4¼")
1932	Duncan McNaughton, Canada	1.97m	(6' 5½")
1936	Cornelius Johnson, United States	2.03m	(6' 8")
1948	John Winter, Australia	1.98m	(6' 6")
1952	Walter Davis, United States	2.04m	(6' 8¼")
1956	Charles Dumas, United States	2.12m	(6' 11½")
1960	Robert Shavlakadze, USSR	2.16m	(7' 1")
1964	Valery Brumel, USSR	2.18m	(7' 1¾")
1968	Dick Fosbury, United States	2.24m	(7' 4¼")
1972	Jüri Tarmak, USSR	2.23m	(7' 3¾")
1976	Jacek Wszola, Poland	2.25m	(7' 4½")
1980	Gerd Wessig, E. Germany	2.36m	(7' 8¾")
1984	Dietmar Mögenburg, W. Germany	2.35m	(7' 8½")
1988	Gennadi Avdeyenko, USSR	2.38m	(7' 9¾")
1992	Javier Sotomayor, Cuba	2.34m	(7' 8")
1996	Charles Austin, United States	2.39m	(7' 10")*
2000	Sergey Klyugin, Russia	2.35m	(7' 8½")
2004	Stefan Holm, Sweden	2.36m	(7' 8¾")
2008	Andrey Silnov, Russia	2.36m	(7' 8¾")
2012	Erik Kynard, United States[1]	2.33m	(7' 7¾")
2016	Derek Drouin, Canada	2.38m	(7' 9¾")
2020	Mutaz Essa Barshim, Qatar & Gianmarco Tamberi, Italy (tie).	2.37m	(7' 9¼")

(1) Ivan Ukhov, Russia, was stripped of the gold medal in 2019 due to doping.

Javelin Throw

Year	Athlete	Dist.	
1908	Eric Lemming, Sweden	54.82m	(179' 10")
1912	Eric Lemming, Sweden	60.64m	(198' 11")
1920	Jonni Myyrä, Finland	65.78m	(215' 9¾")
1924	Jonni Myyrä, Finland	62.96m	(206' 7")
1928	Erik Lundkvist, Sweden	66.60m	(218' 6")
1932	Matti Järvinen, Finland	72.71m	(238' 6½")
1936	Gerhard Stöck, Germany	71.84m	(235' 8")
1948	Kaj Tapio Rautavaara, Finland	69.77m	(228' 11")
1952	Cy Young, United States	73.78m	(242' 1")
1956	Egil Danielsen, Norway	85.71m	(281' 2½")
1960	Viktor Tsybulenko, USSR	84.64m	(277' 8")
1964	Pauli Nevala, Finland	82.66m	(271' 2")
1968	Janis Lusis, USSR	90.10m	(295' 7")
1972	Klaus Wolfermann, W. Germany	90.48m	(296' 10")
1976	Miklós Németh, Hungary	94.58m	(310' 4")
1980	Dainis Kula, USSR	91.20m	(299' 2")
1984	Arto Härkönen, Finland	86.76m	(284' 8")
1988	Tapio Korjus, Finland	84.28m	(276' 6")
1992	Jan Zelezny, Czechoslovakia	89.66m	(294' 2")
1996	Jan Zelezny, Czech Republic	88.16m	(289' 3")
2000	Jan Zelezny, Czech Republic	90.17m	(295' 9½")
2004	Andreas Thorkildsen, Norway	86.50m	(283' 10")
2008	Andreas Thorkildsen, Norway	90.57m	(297' 1¾")
2012	Keshorn Walcott, Trinidad & Tobago	84.58m	(277' 6")
2016	Thomas Röhler, Germany	90.30m	(296' 6")

Javelin Throw

		Dist.
2020	Neeraj Chopra, India	87.58m (287' 4")

Long Jump

		Dist.
1896	Ellery Clark, United States	6.35m (20' 10")
1900	Alvin Kraenzlein, United States	7.18m (23' 6¾")
1904	Meyer Prinstein, United States	7.34m (24' 1")
1908	Frank Irons, United States	7.48m (24' 6½")
1912	Albert Gutterson, United States	7.60m (24' 11¼")
1920	William Petersson, Sweden	7.15m (23' 5½")
1924	William DeHart Hubbard, U.S.	7.45m (24' 5¼")
1928	Ed Hamm, United States	7.73m (25' 4½")
1932	Edward Gordon, United States	7.64m (25' ¾")
1936	Jesse Owens, United States	8.06m (26' 5½")
1948	Willie Steele, United States	7.82m (25' 8")
1952	Jerome Biffle, United States	7.57m (24' 10")
1956	Gregory Bell, United States	7.83m (25' 8¼")
1960	Ralph Boston, United States	8.12m (26' 7¾")
1964	Lynn Davies, Great Britain	8.07m (26' 5¾")
1968	Bob Beamon, United States	8.90m (29' 2½")*
1972	Randy Williams, United States	8.24m (27' ½")
1976	Arnie Robinson, United States	8.35m (27' 4¾")
1980	Lutz Dombrowski, E. Germany	8.54m (28' ¼")
1984	Carl Lewis, United States	8.54m (28' ¼")
1988	Carl Lewis, United States	8.72m (28' 7½")
1992	Carl Lewis, United States	8.67m (28' 5½")
1996	Carl Lewis, United States	8.50m (27' 10¾")
2000	Ivan Pedroso, Cuba	8.55m (28' ¾")
2004	Dwight Phillips, United States.	8.59m (28' 2¼")
2008	Irving Saladino, Panama	8.34m (27' 4¼")
2012	Greg Rutherford, Great Britain	8.31m (27' 3¼")
2016	Jeff Henderson, United States	8.38m (27' 6")
2020	Miltiadis Tentoglou, Greece.	8.41m (27' 7")

Pole Vault

		Height
1896	William Welles Hoyt, United States .	3.30m (10' 10")
1900	Irving Baxter, United States	3.30m (10' 10")
1904	Charles Dvorak, United States	3.50m (11' 6")
1908	Edward Cooke, United States	3.71m (12' 2")
	Alfred Gilbert, United States (tie) . .	3.71m (12' 2")
1912	Harry Stoddard Babcock, U.S.	3.95m (12' 11½")
1920	Frank Foss, United States	4.09m (13' 5")
1924	Lee Barnes, United States	3.95m (12' 11½")
1928	Sabin Carr, United States	4.20m (13' 9¼")
1932	Bill Miller, United States	4.31m (14' 1¾")
1936	Earle Meadows, United States	4.35m (14' 3¼")
1948	Guinn Smith, United States	4.30m (14' 1¼")
1952	Robert Richards, United States	4.55m (14' 11¼")
1956	Robert Richards, United States	4.56m (14' 11½")
1960	Don Bragg, United States	4.70m (15' 5")
1964	Fred Hansen, United States	5.10m (16' 8¾")
1968	Bob Seagren, United States	5.40m (17' 8½")
1972	Wolfgang Nordwig, E. Germany	5.50m (18' ½")
1976	Tadeusz Slusarski, Poland	5.50m (18' ½")
1980	Wladyslaw Kozakiewicz, Poland . . .	5.78m (18' 11½")
1984	Pierre Quinon, France	5.75m (18' 10¼")
1988	Sergei Bubka, USSR	5.90m (19' 4¼")
1992	Maksim Tarasov, Unified Team	
	(Rus.)	5.80m (19' ¼")
1996	Jean Galfione, France	5.92m (19' 5")
2000	Nick Hysong, United States	5.90m (19' 4¼")
2004	Timothy Mack, United States	5.95m (19' 6¼")
2008	Steve Hooker, Australia	5.96m (19' 6¾")
2012	Renaud Lavillenie, France	5.97m (19' 7")
2016	Thiago Braz, Brazil	6.03m (19' 9½")*
2020	Armand Duplantis, Sweden	6.02m (19' 9¼")

Shot Put

		Dist.
1896	Robert Garrett, United States.	11.22m (36' 9¾")
1900	Richard Sheldon, United States	14.10m (46' 3¼")
1904	Ralph Rose, United States	14.81m (48' 7")
1908	Ralph Rose, United States	14.21m (46' 7½")
1912	Pat McDonald, United States	15.34m (50' 4")
1920	Ville Pörhölä, Finland	14.81m (48' 7¼")
1924	Clarence "Bud" Houser,	
	United States	14.99m (49' 2¼")
1928	John Kuck, United States	15.87m (52' ¾")
1932	Leo Sexton, United States	16.00m (52' 6")
1936	Hans Woellke, Germany.	16.20m (53' 1¾")
1948	Wilbur Thompson, United States . . .	17.12m (56' 2")
1952	W. Parry O'Brien, United States . . .	17.41m (57' 1½")
1956	W. Parry O'Brien, United States . . .	18.57m (60' 11¼")

Shot Put

		Dist.
1960	Bill Nieder, United States	19.68m (64' 6¾")
1964	Dallas Long, United States.	20.33m (66' 8½")
1968	Randy Matson, United States.	20.54m (67' 4¾")
1972	Wladyslaw Komar, Poland	21.18m (69' 6")
1976	Udo Beyer, E. Germany	21.05m (69' ¾")
1980	Vladimir Kiselyov, USSR	21.35m (70' ½")
1984	Alessandro Andrei, Italy	21.26m (69' 9")
1988	Ulf Timmermann, E. Germany	22.47m (73' 8¾")
1992	Michael Stulce, United States	21.70m (71' 2½")
1996	Randy Barnes, United States	21.62m (70' 11¼")
2000	Arsi Harju, Finland	21.29m (69' 10¼")
2004	Adam Nelson, United States[1]	21.16m (69' 5¼")
2008	Tomasz Majewski, Poland	21.51m (70' 6¾")
2012	Tomasz Majewski, Poland	21.89m (71' 9¾")
2016	Ryan Crouser, United States	22.52m (73' 10½")
2020	Ryan Crouser, United States	23.30m (76' 5¼")*

(1) Yuriy Bilonog, Ukraine, was stripped of the gold medal in 2012 due to doping.

Triple Jump

		Dist.
1896	James Connolly, United States	13.71m (44' 11¾")
1900	Meyer Prinstein, United States.	14.47m (47' 5¾")
1904	Meyer Prinstein, United States.	14.35m (47' 1")
1908	Tim Ahearne, Gr. Brit.-Ireland	14.92m (48' 11½")
1912	Gustaf Lindblom, Sweden	14.76m (48' 5")
1920	Vilho Tuulos, Finland	14.505m (47' 7")
1924	Anthony Winter, Australia.	15.525m (50' 11¼")
1928	Mikio Oda, Japan	15.21m (49' 11")
1932	Chuhei Nambu, Japan	15.72m (51' 7")
1936	Naoto Tajima, Japan	16.00m (52' 6")
1948	Arne Ahman, Sweden.	15.40m (50' 6¼")
1952	Adhemar Ferreira da Silva, Brazil. . .	16.22m (53' 2¾")
1956	Adhemar Ferreira da Silva, Brazil. . .	16.35m (53' 7¾")
1960	Jozef Schmidt, Poland	16.81m (55' 1½")
1964	Jozef Schmidt, Poland	16.85m (55' 3½")
1968	Viktor Saneyev, USSR	17.39m (57' ¾")
1972	Viktor Saneyev, USSR	17.35m (56' 11¼")
1976	Viktor Saneyev, USSR	17.29m (56' 8¾")
1980	Jaak Uudmäe, USSR	17.35m (56' 11")
1984	Al Joyner, United States.	17.26m (56' 7½")
1988	Khristo Markov, Bulgaria	17.61m (57' 9½")
1992	Mike Conley, United States	18.17m (59' 7½")(w)
1996	Kenny Harrison, United States	18.09m (59' 4¼")*
2000	Jonathan Edwards, Great Britain . . .	17.71m (58' 1¼")
2004	Christian Olsson, Sweden	17.79m (58' 4½")
2008	Nelson Evora, Portugal.	17.67m (57' 11¾")
2012	Christian Taylor, United States.	17.81m (58' 5¼")
2016	Christian Taylor, United States.	17.86m (58' 7¼")
2020	Pedro Pichardo, Portugal	17.98m (58' 11¾")

Decathlon

		Points
1904	Thomas F. Kiely, Ireland.	6,036
1912	Jim Thorpe, United States[1].	8,412.995
1920	Helge Lovland, Norway	6,804.355
1924	Harold Osborn, United States.	7,710.775
1928	Paavo Yrjölä, Finland	8,053.29
1932	James Bausch, United States	8,462.23
1936	Glenn Morris, United States	7,900
1948	Robert Mathias, United States	7,139
1952	Robert Mathias, United States	7,887
1956	Milton Campbell, United States	7,937
1960	Rafer Johnson, United States	8,392
1964	Willi Holdorf, Germany	7,887
1968	Bill Toomey, United States.	8,193
1972	Nikolai Avilov, USSR	8,454
1976	Bruce Jenner, United States.	8,618
1980	Daley Thompson, Great Britain	8,495
1984	Daley Thompson, Great Britain	8,797
1988	Christian Schenk, E. Germany	8,488
1992	Robert Zmelik, Czechoslovakia	8,611
1996	Dan O'Brien, United States	8,824
2000	Erki Nool, Estonia.	8,641
2004	Roman Sebrle, Czech Republic	8,893
2008	Bryan Clay, United States	8,791
2012	Ashton Eaton, United States	8,869
2016	Ashton Eaton, United States	8,893
2020	Damian Warner, Canada	9,018*

Note: Event not held in 1908. (1) Thorpe had been stripped of his medal for playing pro baseball prior to the Olympics. The Intl. Olympic Committee in 1982 posthumously restored him as co-champion, and in 2022 named him the sole gold medal winner in both pentathlon and decathlon.

Track and Field—Women

100-Meter Run

Year	Winner	Time
1928	Elizabeth Robinson, United States	0:12.2
1932	Stella Walsh, Poland	0:11.9
1936	Helen Stephens, United States	0:11.5
1948	Fanny Blankers-Koen, Netherlands	0:11.9
1952	Marjorie Jackson, Australia	0:11.5
1956	Betty Cuthbert, Australia	0:11.5
1960	Wilma Rudolph, United States	0:11.0
1964	Wyomia Tyus, United States	0:11.4
1968	Wyomia Tyus, United States	0:11.08
1972	Renate Stecher, E. Germany	0:11.07
1976	Annegret Richter, W. Germany	0:11.08
1980	Lyudmila Kondratyeva, USSR	0:11.06
1984	Evelyn Ashford, United States	0:10.97
1988	Florence Griffith-Joyner, United States	0:10.54
1992	Gail Devers, United States	0:10.82
1996	Gail Devers, United States	0:10.94
2000	No winner[1]	NA
2004	Yuliya Nesterenko, Belarus	0:10.93
2008	Shelly-Ann Fraser, Jamaica	0:10.78
2012	Shelly-Ann Fraser-Pryce, Jamaica	0:10.75
2016	Elaine Thompson, Jamaica	0:10.71
2020	Elaine Thompson-Herah, Jamaica	0:10.61*

(1) Marion Jones, U.S., was stripped of her gold medal in 2007 due to doping; the Intl. Olympic Committee declined to award the medal to the runner-up, who was also suspected of doping.

200-Meter Run

Year	Winner	Time
1948	Fanny Blankers-Koen, Netherlands	0:24.4
1952	Marjorie Jackson, Australia	0:23.7
1956	Betty Cuthbert, Australia	0:23.4
1960	Wilma Rudolph, United States	0:24.0
1964	Edith McGuire, United States	0:23.0
1968	Irena Szewinska, Poland	0:22.5
1972	Renate Stecher, E. Germany	0:22.40
1976	Bärbel Eckert, E. Germany	0:22.37
1980	Bärbel Wöckel, E. Germany	0:22.03
1984	Valerie Brisco-Hooks, United States	0:21.81
1988	Florence Griffith-Joyner, United States	0:21.34*
1992	Gwen Torrence, United States	0:21.81
1996	Marie-Jose Perec, France	0:22.12
2000	Pauline Davis-Thompson, The Bahamas[1]	0:22.27
2004	Veronica Campbell, Jamaica	0:22.05
2008	Veronica Campbell-Brown, Jamaica	0:21.74
2012	Allyson Felix, United States	0:21.88
2016	Elaine Thompson, Jamaica	0:21.78
2020	Elaine Thompson-Herah, Jamaica	0:21.53

(1) Originally won by Marion Jones, U.S., who was stripped of the gold in 2007 due to doping.

400-Meter Run

Year	Winner	Time
1964	Betty Cuthbert, Australia	0:52.0
1968	Colette Besson, France	0:52.0
1972	Monika Zehrt, E. Germany	0:51.08
1976	Irena Szewinska, Poland	0:49.29
1980	Marita Koch, E. Germany	0:48.88
1984	Valerie Brisco-Hooks, United States	0:48.83
1988	Olga Bryzgina, USSR	0:48.65
1992	Marie-Jose Perec, France	0:48.83
1996	Marie-Jose Perec, France	0:48.25*
2000	Cathy Freeman, Australia	0:49.11
2004	Tonique Williams-Darling, The Bahamas	0:49.41
2008	Christine Ohuruogu, Great Britain	0:49.62
2012	Sanya Richards-Ross, United States	0:49.55
2016	Shaunae Miller, The Bahamas	0:49.44
2020	Shaunae Miller-Uibo, The Bahamas	0:48.36

800-Meter Run

Year	Winner	Time
1928	Lina Radke, Germany	2:16.8
1960	Lyudmila Shevtsova, USSR	2:04.3
1964	Ann Packer, Great Britain	2:01.1
1968	Madeline Manning, United States	2:00.9
1972	Hildegard Falck, W. Germany	1:58.55
1976	Tatyana Kazankina, USSR	1:54.94
1980	Nadezhda Olizarenko, USSR	1:53.43*
1984	Doina Melinte, Romania	1:57.60
1988	Sigrun Wodars, E. Germany	1:56.10
1992	Ellen Van Langen, Netherlands	1:55.54
1996	Svetlana Masterkova, Russia	1:57.73
2000	Maria Mutola, Mozambique	1:56.15

800-Meter Run

Year	Winner	Time
2004	Kelly Holmes, Great Britain	1:56.38
2008	Pamela Jelimo, Kenya	1:54.87
2012	Caster Semenya, South Africa[1]	1:57.23
2016	Caster Semenya, South Africa	1:55.28
2020	Athing Mu, United States	1:55.21

(1) Russia's Mariya Savinova was stripped of the gold medal for doping.

1500-Meter Run

Year	Winner	Time
1972	Lyudmila Bragina, USSR	4:01.04
1976	Tatyana Kazankina, USSR	4:05.48
1980	Tatyana Kazankina, USSR	3:56.06
1984	Gabriella Dorio, Italy	4:03.25
1988	Paula Ivan, Romania	3:53.96
1992	Hassiba Boulmerka, Algeria	3:55.30
1996	Svetlana Masterkova, Russia	4:00.83
2000	Nouria Merah-Benida, Algeria	4:05.10
2004	Kelly Holmes, Great Britain	3:57.90
2008	Nancy Jebet Langat, Kenya	4:00.23
2012	Gamze Bulut, Turkey[1]	4:10.40
2016	Faith Chepngetich Kipyegon, Kenya	4:08.92
2020	Faith Chepngetich Kipyegon, Kenya	3:53.11*

(1) Turkey's Asli Cakir Alpetkin was stripped of the gold medal for doping.

3000-Meter Run

Year	Winner	Time
1984	Maricica Puica, Romania	8:35.96
1988	Tatyana Samolenko, USSR	8:26.53*
1992	Elena Romanova, Unified Team (Rus.)	8:46.04

3000-Meter Steeplechase

Year	Winner	Time
2008	Gulnara Galkina-Samitova, Russia	8:58.81*
2012	Habiba Ghribi, Tunisia[1]	9:08.37
2016	Ruth Jebet, Bahrain	8:59.75
2020	Peruth Chemutai, Uganda	9:01.45

(1) Russia's Yuliya Zaripova was stripped of the gold medal in 2016 for doping.

5000-Meter Run

Year	Winner	Time
1996	Wang Junxia, China	14:59.88
2000	Gabriela Szabo, Romania	14:40.79
2004	Meseret Defar, Ethiopia	14:45.65
2008	Tirunesh Dibaba, Ethiopia	15:41.40
2012	Meseret Defar, Ethiopia	15:04.25
2016	Vivian Cheruiyot, Kenya	14:26.17*
2020	Sifan Hassan, Netherlands	14:36.79

10,000-Meter Run

Year	Winner	Time
1988	Olga Bondarenko, USSR	31:05.21
1992	Derartu Tulu, Ethiopia	31:06.02
1996	Fernanda Ribeiro, Portugal	31:01.63
2000	Derartu Tulu, Ethiopia	30:17.49
2004	Xing Huina, China	30:24.36
2008	Tirunesh Dibaba, Ethiopia	29:54.66
2012	Tirunesh Dibaba, Ethiopia	30:20.75
2016	Almaz Ayana, Ethiopia	29:17.45*
2020	Sifan Hassan, Netherlands	29:55.32

Marathon

Year	Winner	Time
1984	Joan Benoit, United States	2:24:52
1988	Rosa Mota, Portugal	2:25:40
1992	Valentina Yegorova, Unified Team (Rus.)	2:32:41
1996	Fatuma Roba, Ethiopia	2:26:05
2000	Naoko Takahashi, Japan	2:23:14
2004	Mizuki Noguchi, Japan	2:26:20
2008	Constantina Tomescu, Romania	2:26:44
2012	Tiki Gelana, Ethiopia	2:23:07*
2016	Jemima Jelagat Sumgong, Kenya	2:24:04
2020	Peres Jepchirchir, Kenya	2:27:20

4x100-Meter Relay

Year	Winner	Time
1928	Canada	0:48.4
1932	United States	0:46.9
1936	United States	0:46.9
1948	Netherlands	0:47.5
1952	United States	0:45.9
1956	Australia	0:44.5
1960	United States	0:44.5
1964	Poland	0:43.6
1968	United States	0:42.8
1972	West Germany	0:42.81

4x100-Meter Relay

Year	Team	Time
1976	East Germany	0:42.55
1980	East Germany	0:41.60
1984	United States	0:41.65
1988	United States	0:41.98
1992	United States	0:42.11
1996	United States	0:41.95
2000	The Bahamas	0:41.95
2004	Jamaica	0:41.73
2008	Russia	0:42.31
2012	United States	0:40.82*
2016	United States	0:41.01
2020	Jamaica	0:41.02

4x400-Meter Relay

Year	Team	Time
1972	East Germany	3:23.0
1976	East Germany	3:19.23
1980	USSR	3:20.2
1984	United States	3:18.29
1988	USSR	3:15.18*
1992	Unified Team	3:20.20
1996	United States	3:20.91
2000	United States[1]	3:22.62
2004	United States[2]	3:19.01
2008	United States	3:18.54
2012	United States	3:16.87
2016	United States	3:19.06
2020	United States	3:16.85

(1) Due to team member Marion Jones's doping, the U.S. was stripped of the victory in 2008. Jones's teammates won an appeal in 2010 to have their medals restored. (2) Team member Crystal Cox was stripped of her gold medal in 2012 due to doping.

20-Kilometer Walk

Year	Athlete	Time
2000	Wang Liping, China	1:29:05
2004	Athanasia Tsoumeleka, Greece	1:29:12
2008	Olga Kaniskina, Russia	1:26:31
2012	Shijie Qieyang, China[1]	1:25:16
2016	Liu Hong, China	1:28:35
2020	Antonella Palmisano, Italy	1:29:12

(1) Russia's Elena Lashmanova was stripped of the gold medal for doping in 2022.

100-Meter Hurdles

Year	Athlete	Time
1972	Annelie Ehrhardt, E. Germany	0:12.59
1976	Johanna Schaller, E. Germany	0:12.77
1980	Vera Komisova, USSR	0:12.56
1984	Benita Fitzgerald-Brown, United States	0:12.84
1988	Yordanka Donkova, Bulgaria	0:12.38
1992	Paraskevi Patoulidou, Greece	0:12.64
1996	Ludmila Engquist, Sweden	0:12.58
2000	Olga Shishigina, Kazakhstan	0:12.65
2004	Joanna Hayes, United States	0:12.37
2008	Dawn Harper, United States	0:12.54
2012	Sally Pearson, Australia	0:12.35*
2016	Brianna Rollins, United States	0:12.48
2020	Jasmine Camacho-Quinn, Puerto Rico	0:12.37

400-Meter Hurdles

Year	Athlete	Time
1984	Nawal El Moutawakel, Morocco	0:54.61
1988	Debra Flintoff-King, Australia	0:53.17
1992	Sally Gunnell, Great Britain	0:53.23
1996	Deon Hemmings, Jamaica	0:52.82
2000	Irina Privalova, Russia	0:53.02
2004	Faní Halkia, Greece	0:52.82
2008	Melaine Walker, Jamaica	0:52.64
2012	Natalya Antyukh, Russia	0:52.70
2016	Dalilah Muhammad, United States	0:53.13
2020	Sydney McLaughlin, United States	0:51.46*

Discus Throw

Year	Athlete	Dist.	
1928	Halina Konopacka, Poland	39.62m	(130' 0")
1932	Lillian Copeland, United States	40.58m	(133' 2")
1936	Gisela Mauermayer, Germany	47.63m	(156' 3")
1948	Micheline Ostermeyer, France	41.92m	(137' 6")
1952	Nina Ponomareva, USSR	51.42m	(168' 8")
1956	Olga Fikotová, Czechoslovakia	53.69m	(176' 1¾")
1960	Nina Ponomareva, USSR	55.10m	(180' 9")
1964	Tamara Press, USSR	57.27m	(187' 10¾")
1968	Lia Manoliu, Romania	58.28m	(191' 2")
1972	Faina Melnik, USSR	66.62m	(218' 7")
1976	Evelin Jahl, E. Germany	69.00m	(226' 4")
1980	Evelin Jahl, E. Germany	69.96m	(229' 6")
1984	Ria Stalman, Netherlands	65.36m	(214' 5")
1988	Martina Hellmann, E. Germany	72.30m	(237' 2")*
1992	Maritza Martén, Cuba	70.06m	(229' 10")

Discus Throw

Year	Athlete	Dist.	
1996	Ilke Wyludda, Germany	69.66m	(228' 6")
2000	Ellina Zvereva, Belarus	68.40m	(224' 5")
2004	Natalya Sadova, Russia	67.02m	(219' 8¾")
2008	Stephanie Brown Trafton, U.S.	64.74m	(212' 4¾")
2012	Sandra Perkovic, Croatia	69.11m	(226' 9")
2016	Sandra Perkovic, Croatia	69.21m	(227' ¾")
2020	Valarie Allman, United States	68.98m	(226' 3¾")

Hammer Throw

Year	Athlete	Dist.	
2000	Kamila Skolimowska, Poland	71.16m	(233' 5¾")
2004	Olga Kuzenkova, Russia	75.02m	(246' 1")
2008	Yipsi Moreno, Cuba[1]	75.20m	(246' 8¾")
2012	Anita Wlodarczyk, Poland[2]	77.60m	(254' 7")
2016	Anita Wlodarczyk, Poland	82.29m	(269' 11¾")
2020	Anita Wlodarczyk, Poland	78.48m	(257' 5¾")

(1) Belarus's Aksana Miankova was stripped of the gold medal for doping in 2016. (2) Russia's Tatyana Lysenko was stripped of the gold medal for doping in 2016.

High Jump

Year	Athlete	Height	
1928	Ethel Catherwood, Canada	1.59m	(5' 2½")
1932	Jean Shiley, United States	1.67m	(5' 5½")
1936	Ibolya Csák, Hungary	1.60m	(5' 3")
1948	Alice Coachman, United States	1.68m	(5' 6")
1952	Esther Brand, South Africa	1.67m	(5' 5¾")
1956	Mildred McDaniel, United States	1.76m	(5' 9¼")
1960	Iolanda Balas, Romania	1.85m	(6' ¾")
1964	Iolanda Balas, Romania	1.90m	(6' 2¾")
1968	Miloslava Rezková, Czech.	1.82m	(5' 11½")
1972	Ulrike Meyfarth, W. Germany	1.92m	(6' 3½")
1976	Rosemarie Ackermann, E. Germany	1.93m	(6' 4")
1980	Sara Simeoni, Italy	1.97m	(6' 5½")
1984	Ulrike Meyfarth, W. Germany	2.02m	(6' 7½")
1988	Louise Ritter, United States	2.03m	(6' 8")
1992	Heike Henkel, Germany	2.02m	(6' 7½")
1996	Stefka Kostadinova, Bulgaria	2.05m	(6' 8¾")
2000	Yelena Yelesina, Russia	2.01m	(6' 7")
2004	Yelena Slesarenko, Russia	2.06m	(6' 9")*
2008	Tia Hellebaut, Belgium	2.05m	(6' 8¾")
2012	Anna Chicherova, Russia	2.05m	(6' 8¾")
2016	Ruth Beitia, Spain	1.97m	(6' 5½")
2020	Mariya Lasitskene, ROC	2.04m	(6' 8¼")

Javelin Throw

Year	Athlete	Dist.	
1932	"Babe" Didrikson, United States	43.68m	(143' 4")
1936	Tilly Fleischer, Germany	45.18m	(148' 3")
1948	Herma Bauma, Austria	45.57m	(149' 6")
1952	Dana Zátopková, Czechoslovakia	50.47m	(165' 7")
1956	Inese Jaunzeme, USSR	53.86m	(176' 8")
1960	Elvira Ozolina, USSR	55.98m	(183' 8")
1964	Mihaela Penes, Romania	60.54m	(198' 7")
1968	Angéla Németh, Hungary	60.36m	(198' 0")
1972	Ruth Fuchs, E. Germany	63.88m	(209' 7")
1976	Ruth Fuchs, E. Germany	65.94m	(216' 4")
1980	Maria Colón, Cuba	68.40m	(224' 5")
1984	Tessa Sanderson, Great Britain	69.56m	(228' 2")
1988	Petra Felke, E. Germany	74.68m	(245' 0")
1992	Silke Renk, Germany	68.34m	(224' 2")
1996	Heli Rantanen, Finland	67.94m	(222' 11")
2000	Trine Hattestad, Norway	68.91m	(226' 1")
2004	Osleidys Menendez, Cuba	71.53m	(234' 8")*
2008	Barbora Spotáková, Czech Republic	71.42m	(234' ¾")
2012	Barbora Spotáková, Czech Republic	69.55m	(228' 2¼")
2016	Sara Kolak, Croatia	66.18m	(217' 1½")
2020	Liu Shiying, China	66.34m	(217' 7¾")

Note: New records were kept after javelin was modified in 1999.

Long Jump

Year	Athlete	Dist.	
1948	Olga Gyarmati, Hungary	5.69m	(18' 8")
1952	Yvette Williams, New Zealand	6.24m	(20' 5¼")
1956	Elzbieta Krzesinska, Poland	6.35m	(20' 10")
1960	Vera Krepkina, USSR	6.37m	(20' 10¾")
1964	Mary Rand, Great Britain	6.76m	(22' 2¼")
1968	Viorica Viscopoleanu, Romania	6.82m	(22' 4½")
1972	Heidemarie Rosendahl, W. Germany	6.78m	(22' 3")
1976	Angela Voigt, E. Germany	6.72m	(22' ¾")
1980	Tatyana Kolpakova, USSR	7.06m	(23' 2")
1984	Anisoara Cusmir-Stanciu, Romania	6.96m	(22' 10")
1988	Jackie Joyner-Kersee, United States	7.40m	(24' 3½")*
1992	Heike Drechsler, Germany	7.14m	(23' 5¼")
1996	Chioma Ajunwa, Nigeria	7.12m	(23' 4¼")
2000	Heike Drechsler, Germany	6.99m	(22' 11¼")
2004	Tatyana Lebedeva, Russia	7.07m	(23' 2½")
2008	Maurren Higa Maggi, Brazil	7.04m	(23' 1¼")
2012	Brittney Reese, United States	7.12m	(23' 4¼")

	Long Jump	**Dist.**
2016	Tianna Bartoletta, United States	7.17m (23' 6¼")
2020	Malaika Mihambo, Germany	7.00m (22' 11½")

	Pole Vault	**Height**
2000	Stacy Dragila, United States	4.60m (15' 1")
2004	Elena Isinbayeva, Russia	4.91m (16' 1¼")
2008	Elena Isinbayeva, Russia	5.05m (16' 6¾")
2012	Jennifer Suhr, United States	4.75m (15' 7")
2016	Ekateríni Stefanídi, Greece	4.85m (15' 11")
2020	Katie Nageotte, United States	4.90m (16' 1")

	Shot Put	**Dist.**
1948	Micheline Ostermeyer, France	13.75m (45' 1½")
1952	Galina Zybina, USSR	15.28m (50' 1½")
1956	Tamara Tyshkevich, USSR	16.59m (54' 5¼")
1960	Tamara Press, USSR	17.32m (56' 10")
1964	Tamara Press, USSR	18.14m (59' 6¼")
1968	Margitta Gummel, E. Germany	19.61m (64' 4")
1972	Nadezhda Chizhova, USSR	21.03m (69' 0")
1976	Ivanka Khristova, Bulgaria	21.16m (69' 5¼")
1980	Ilona Slupianek, E. Germany	22.41m (73' 6¼")*
1984	Claudia Losch, W. Germany	20.48m (67' 2")
1988	Natalya Lisovskaya, USSR	22.24m (72' 11¾")
1992	Svetlana Krivelyova, Unified Team	21.06m (69' 1¼")
1996	Astrid Kumbernuss, Germany	20.56m (67' 5½")
2000	Yanina Karolchik, Belarus	20.56m (67' 5½")
2004	Yumileidi Cumbá, Cuba	19.59m (64' 3¼")

	Shot Put	**Dist.**
2008	Valerie Vili, New Zealand	20.56m (67' 5½")
2012	Valerie Adams, New Zealand	20.70m (67' 11")
2016	Michelle Carter, United States	20.63m (67' 8¼")
2020	Gong Lijiao, China	20.58m (67' 6¼")

	Triple Jump	**Dist.**
1996	Inessa Kravets, Ukraine	15.33m (50' 3½")
2000	Tereza Marinova, Bulgaria	15.20m (49' 10½")
2004	Francoise Mbango Etone, Cameroon	15.30m (50' 2¼")
2008	Francoise Mbango Etone, Cameroon	15.39m (50' 6")
2012	Olga Rypakova, Kazakhstan	14.98m (49' 1¾")
2016	Caterine Ibargüen, Colombia	15.17m (49' 9¼")
2020	Yulimar Rojas, Venezuela	15.67m (51' 5")*

	Heptathlon	**Points**
1984	Glynis Nunn, Australia	6,390
1988	Jackie Joyner-Kersee, United States	7,291*
1992	Jackie Joyner-Kersee, United States	7,044
1996	Ghada Shouaa, Syria	6,780
2000	Denise Lewis, Great Britain	6,584
2004	Carolina Klüft, Sweden	6,952
2008	Natallia Dobrynska, Ukraine	6,733
2012	Jessica Ennis, Great Britain	6,955
2016	Nafissatou Thiam, Belgium	6,810
2020	Nafissatou Thiam, Belgium	6,791

Track and Field—Mixed

	4x400-Meter Relay	
2020	Poland	3:09.87*

2022 Winter Olympic Games
Beijing, China, Feb. 4-20, 2022

Nearly, 3,000 (2,871) athletes representing 91 nations met in Beijing, China, to compete in a record 109 events in 15 disciplines during the XXIV Olympic Winter Games Feb. 4-20, 2022. These were the second Games held during the worldwide COVID-19 pandemic. China was hosting the Games for the first time since the 2008 Summer Games, repurposing five of the seven structures created for those games. Norway once again dominated the Games with 37 medals, including 16 gold, to top the final medal count, followed by Russian Olympic Committee athletes (32 medals, 6 gold), Germany (27, 12), Canada (26, 4), and the U.S. (25, 8).

The human rights violations and the Uyghur genocide of the host country China caused several countries, including the U.S. and the United Kingdom, to conduct a diplomatic boycott, refusing to send any official representation to the Games. China's close ally, North Korea, did not attend the Games, citing the pandemic and "hostile forces," but the Intl. Olympic Committee (IOC) had already suspended the country. The IOC ruling barring Russia from competing due a state-sponsored doping scandal was still in effect, but Russian athletes were granted exemptions to compete under the designation Russian Olympic Committee (ROC).

At 18, American-born Eileen Gu, competing for China, became the youngest Olympic champion in freestyle skiing, winning gold in the halfpipe and big air, and silver in slopestyle. Sui Wenjing and Han Cong of China won gold in the figure skating pairs competition; they were the 2018 silver medalists. Germany swept the two-man bobsled competition by winning gold, silver, and bronze. The controversial decision by the Court of Arbitration for Sport to allow 15-year-old ROC athlete Kamila Valieva to skate after a delayed report for testing positive for a banned substance in Dec. 2021, left in question the ROC's earlier victory in the figure skating team event; no medals were awarded for this competition pending a resolution. Favored to win the women's singles event, Valieva failed to medal.

Three-time world champion U.S. figure skater Nathan Chen performed five clean quadruple jumps on his way to winning gold in men's singles. U.S. snowboarder Lindsey Jacobellis, a 36-year-old veteran of four previous Olympic Games, won gold and her first Olympic medal since 2006 with 40-year-old teammate Nick Baumgartner in mixed team snowboard cross. American speed skater Erin Jackson won gold in the women's 500-m speed skating event, becoming the first Black woman to medal in Olympic speed skating. After finishing fourth in the snowboard halfpipe, five-time Olympian Shaun White announced his retirement.

Seven new medal events were introduced in 2022: men's and women's big air freestyle; women's monobob; mixed relay in short-track speed skating; and mixed team competitions in freestyle skiing aerials, ski jumping, and snowboard cross.

2022 Winter Olympic Games: Final Medal Standings
(G = Gold, S = Silver, B = Bronze, T = Total medals)

Country	G	S	B	T	Country	G	S	B	T	Country	G	S	B	T
Norway	16	8	13	37	Italy	2	7	8	17	Great Britain	1	1	0	2
Russian Olympic Committee	6	12	14	32	China	9	4	2	15	Belgium	1	0	1	2
					Switzerland	7	2	5	14	Czech Republic	1	0	1	2
Germany	12	10	5	27	France	5	7	2	14	Slovakia	1	0	1	2
Canada	4	8	14	26	South Korea	2	5	2	9	Belarus	0	2	0	2
United States	8	10	7	25	Finland	2	2	4	8	Spain	0	1	0	1
Sweden	8	5	5	18	Slovenia	2	3	2	7	Ukraine	0	1	0	1
Austria	7	7	4	18	Australia	1	2	1	4	Estonia	0	0	1	1
Japan	3	6	9	18	New Zealand	2	1	0	3	Latvia	0	0	1	1
Netherlands	8	5	4	17	Hungary	2	0	2	3	Poland	0	0	1	1

Winter Olympic Games Champions, 1924-2022

East and West Germany competed separately, 1968-88. In 1992, the Unified Team represented the former Soviet republics of Russia, Ukraine, Belarus, Kazakhstan, and Uzbekistan. In 2018, Russian athletes competed under the designation Olympic Athlete(s) from Russia (OAR); in 2022, Russian athletes competed under the designation Russian Olympic Committee (ROC); Russia was banned from competition due to a state-sponsored doping scandal. Not all sports are listed here, and many events are omitted. Point systems used for scoring have changed many times; those shown are of the point system in use at those Games. Times are shown in hour:minute:sec.

Alpine Skiing

Team

2018	Switzerland, Austria, Norway
2022	Austria, Germany, Norway

Men's Downhill

		Time
1948	Henri Oreiller, France	2:55.0
1952	Zeno Colo, Italy	2:30.8
1956	Toni Sailer, Austria	2:52.2
1960	Jean Vuarnet, France	2:06.0
1964	Egon Zimmermann, Austria	2:18.16
1968	Jean-Claude Killy, France	1:59.85
1972	Bernhard Russi, Switzerland	1:51.43
1976	Franz Klammer, Austria	1:45.73
1980	Leonhard Stock, Austria	1:45.50
1984	Bill Johnson, United States	1:45.59
1988	Pirmin Zurbriggen, Switzerland	1:59.63
1992	Patrick Ortlieb, Austria	1:50.37
1994	Tommy Moe, United States	1:45.75
1998	Jean-Luc Cretier, France	1:50.11
2002	Fritz Strobl, Austria	1:39.13
2006	Antoine Deneriaz, France	1:48.80
2010	Didier Defago, Switzerland	1:54.31
2014	Matthias Mayer, Austria	2:06.23
2018	Aksel Lund Svindal, Norway	1:40.25
2022	Beat Feuz, Switzerland	1:42.69

Men's Giant Slalom

		Time
1952	Stein Eriksen, Norway	2:25.0
1956	Toni Sailer, Austria	3:00.1
1960	Roger Staub, Switzerland	1:48.3
1964	François Bonlieu, France	1:46.71
1968	Jean-Claude Killy, France	3:29.28
1972	Gustavo Thoeni, Italy	3:09.62
1976	Heini Hemmi, Switzerland	3:26.97
1980	Ingemar Stenmark, Sweden	2:40.74
1984	Max Julen, Switzerland	2:41.18
1988	Alberto Tomba, Italy	2:06.37
1992	Alberto Tomba, Italy	2:06.98
1994	Markus Wasmeier, Germany	2:52.46
1998	Hermann Maier, Austria	2:38.51
2002	Stephan Eberharter, Austria	2:23.28
2006	Benjamin Raich, Austria	2:35.00
2010	Carlo Janka, Switzerland	2:37.83
2014	Ted Ligety, United States	2:45.29
2018	Marcel Hirscher, Austria	2:18.04
2022	Marco Odermatt Switzerland	2:09.35

Men's Slalom

		Time
1948	Edi Reinalter, Switzerland	2:10.3
1952	Othmar Schneider, Austria	2:00.0
1956	Toni Sailer, Austria	3:14.7
1960	Ernst Hinterseer, Austria	2:08.9
1964	Josef Stiegler, Austria	2:11.13
1968	Jean-Claude Killy, France	1:39.73
1972	Francisco Fernandez-Ochoa, Spain	1:49.27
1976	Piero Gros, Italy	2:03.29
1980	Ingemar Stenmark, Sweden	1:44.26
1984	Phil Mahre, United States	1:39.41
1988	Alberto Tomba, Italy	1:39.47
1992	Finn Christian Jagge, Norway	1:44.39
1994	Thomas Stangassinger, Austria	2:02.02
1998	Hans-Petter Buraas, Norway	1:49.31
2002	Jean-Pierre Vidal, France	1:41.06
2006	Benjamin Raich, Austria	1:43.14
2010	Giuliano Razzoli, Italy	1:39.32
2014	Mario Matt, Austria	1:41.84
2018	Andre Myhrer, Sweden	1:38.99
2022	Clément Noël, France	1:44.09

Men's Combined

		Time
1936	Franz Pfnür, Germany	99.25 (pts.)
1948	Henri Oreiller, France	3.27 (pts.)
1988	Hubert Strolz, Austria	36.55 (pts.)
1992	Josef Polig, Italy	14.58 (pts.)
1994	Lasse Kjus, Norway	3:17.53
1998	Mario Reiter, Austria	3:08.06
2002	Kjetil André Aamodt, Norway	3:17.56
2006	Ted Ligety, United States	3:09.35
2010	Bode Miller, United States	2:44.92
2014	Sandro Viletta, Switzerland	2:45.20
2018	Marcel Hirscher, Austria	2:06.52
2022	Johannes Strolz, Austria	2:31.43

Men's Super Giant Slalom

		Time
1988	Franck Piccard, France	1:39.66
1992	Kjetil André Aamodt, Norway	1:13.04
1994	Markus Wasmeier, Germany	1:32.53
1998	Hermann Maier, Austria	1:34.82
2002	Kjetil André Aamodt, Norway	1:21.58
2006	Kjetil André Aamodt, Norway	1:30.65
2010	Aksel Lund Svindal, Norway	1:30.34
2014	Kjetil Jansrud, Norway	1:18.14
2018	Matthias Mayer, Austria	1:24.44
2022	Matthias Mayer, Austria	1:19.94

Women's Downhill

		Time
1948	Hedi Schlunegger, Switzerland	2:28.3
1952	Trude Beiser-Jochum, Austria	1:47.1
1956	Madeleine Berthod, Switzerland	1:40.7
1960	Heidi Biebl, Germany	1:37.6
1964	Christl Haas, Austria	1:55.39
1968	Olga Pall, Austria	1:40.87
1972	Marie-Theres Nadig, Switzerland	1:36.68
1976	Rosi Mittermaier, W. Germany	1:46.16
1980	Annemarie Moser-Proell, Austria	1:37.52
1984	Michela Figini, Switzerland	1:13.36
1988	Marina Kiehl, W. Germany	1:25.86
1992	Kerrin Lee-Gartner, Canada	1:52.55
1994	Katja Seizinger, Germany	1:35.93
1998	Katja Seizinger, Germany	1:28.89
2002	Carole Montillet, France	1:39.56
2006	Michaela Dorfmeister, Austria	1:56.49
2010	Lindsey Vonn, United States	1:44.19
2014	Tina Maze, Slovenia	1:41.57
	Dominique Gisin, Switzerland (tie)	1:41.57
2018	Sofia Goggia, Italy	1:39.22
2022	Corinne Suter, Switzerland	1:31.87

Women's Giant Slalom

		Time
1952	Andrea Mead Lawrence, United States	2:06.8
1956	Ossi Reichert, Germany	1:56.5
1960	Yvonne Ruegg, Switzerland	1:39.9
1964	Marielle Goitschel, France	1:52.24
1968	Nancy Greene, Canada	1:51.97
1972	Marie-Theres Nadig, Switzerland	1:29.90
1976	Kathy Kreiner, Canada	1:29.13
1980	Hanni Wenzel, Liechtenstein	2:41.66
1984	Debbie Armstrong, United States	2:20.98
1988	Vreni Schneider, Switzerland	2:06.49
1992	Pernilla Wiberg, Sweden	2:12.74
1994	Deborah Compagnoni, Italy	2:30.97
1998	Deborah Compagnoni, Italy	2:50.59
2002	Janica Kostelic, Croatia	2:30.01
2006	Julia Mancuso, United States	2:09.19
2010	Viktoria Rebensburg, Germany	2:27.11
2014	Tina Maze, Slovenia	2:36.87
2018	Mikaela Shiffrin, United States	2:20.02
2022	Sara Hector, Sweden	1:55.69

Note: Beginning in 1980, the event time combined two runs.

Women's Slalom

		Time
1948	Gretchen Fraser, United States	1:57.2
1952	Andrea Mead Lawrence, United States	2:10.6
1956	Renee Colliard, Switzerland	1:52.3
1960	Anne Heggtveit, Canada	1:49.6
1964	Christine Goitschel, France	1:29.86
1968	Marielle Goitschel, France	1:25.86
1972	Barbara Ann Cochran, United States	1:31.24
1976	Rosi Mittermaier, W. Germany	1:30.54
1980	Hanni Wenzel, Liechtenstein	1:25.09
1984	Paoletta Magoni, Italy	1:36.47
1988	Vreni Schneider, Switzerland	1:36.69
1992	Petra Kronberger, Austria	1:32.68
1994	Vreni Schneider, Switzerland	1:56.01
1998	Hilde Gerg, Germany	1:32.40
2002	Janica Kostelic, Croatia	1:46.10
2006	Anja Paerson, Sweden	1:29.04
2010	Maria Riesch, Germany	1:42.89
2014	Mikaela Shiffrin, United States	1:44.54
2018	Frida Hansdotter, Sweden	1:38.63
2022	Petra Vlhová, Slovakia	1:44.98

Women's Combined

		Time
1936	Christl Cranz, Germany	97.06 (pts.)
1948	Trude Beiser-Jochum, Austria	6.58 (pts.)
1988	Anita Wachter, Austria	29.25 (pts.)
1992	Petra Kronberger, Austria	2.55 (pts.)
1994	Pernilla Wiberg, Sweden	3:05.16

Women's Combined		Time
1998	Katja Seizinger, Germany	2:40.74
2002	Janica Kostelic, Croatia	2:43.28
2006	Janica Kostelic, Croatia	2:51.08
2010	Maria Riesch, Germany	2:09.14
2014	Maria Hoefl-Riesch, Germany	2:34.62
2018	Michelle Gisin, Switzerland	2:20.90
2022	Michelle Gisin, Switzerland	2:25.67

Note: In 2010, a one-day super combined event replaced the traditional two-day combined event.

Women's Super Giant Slalom		Time
1988	Sigrid Wolf, Austria	1:19.03
1992	Deborah Compagnoni, Italy	1:21.22
1994	Diann Roffe (Steinrotter), United States	1:22.15
1998	Picabo Street, United States	1:18.02
2002	Daniela Ceccarelli, Italy	1:13.59
2006	Michaela Dorfmeister, Austria	1:32.47
2010	Andrea Fischbacher, Austria	1:20.14
2014	Anna Fenninger, Austria	1:25.52
2018	Ester Ledecká, Czech Republic	1:21.11
2022	Lara Gut-Behrami, Switzerland	1:13.51

Bobsled
(Driver/pilot in parentheses.)

Two-Man Bobsled		Time
1932	United States (Hubert Stevens)	8:14.74
1936	United States (Ivan Brown)	5:29.29
1948	Switzerland (Felix Endrich)	5:29.20
1952	Germany (Andreas Ostler)	5:24.54
1956	Italy (Dalla Costa)	5:30.14
1964	Great Britain (Anthony Nash)	4:21.90
1968	Italy (Eugenio Monti)	4:41.54
1972	W. Germany (Wolfgang Zimmerer)	4:57.07
1976	E. Germany (Meinhard Nehmer)	3:44.42
1980	Switzerland (Erich Schaerer)	4:09.36
1984	E. Germany (Wolfgang Hoppe)	3:25.56
1988	USSR (Janis Kipours)	3:54.19
1992	Switzerland (Gustav Weber)	4:03.26
1994	Switzerland (Gustav Weber)	3:30.81
1998	Canada (Pierre Lueders)	3:37.24
	Italy (Guenther Huber) (tie)	3:37.24
2002	Germany II (Christoph Langen)	3:10.11
2006	Germany (Andre Lange)	3:43.38
2010	Germany (Andre Lange)	3:26.65
2014	Switzerland (Beat Hefti)[1]	3:46.05
2018	Canada (Justin Kripps)	3:16.86
	Germany (Francesco Friedrich) (tie)	3:16.86
2022	Germany (Francesco Friedrich)	3:56.89

Four-Man Bobsled		Time
1924	Switzerland (Eduard Scherrer)	5:45.54
1928	United States (William Fiske) (5-man)	3:20.50
1932	United States (William Fiske)	7:53.68
1936	Switzerland (Pierre Musy)	5:19.85
1948	United States (Francis Tyler)	5:20.10
1952	Germany (Andreas Ostler)	5:07.84
1956	Switzerland (Franz Kapus)	5:10.44
1964	Canada (Victor Emery)	4:14.46
1968	Italy (Eugenio Monti) (2 heats)	2:17.39
1972	Switzerland (Jean Wicki)	4:43.07
1976	E. Germany (Meinhard Nehmer)	3:40.43
1980	E. Germany (Meinhard Nehmer)	3:59.92
1984	E. Germany (Wolfgang Hoppe)	3:20.22
1988	Switzerland (Ekkehard Fasser)	3:47.51
1992	Austria (Ingo Appelt)	3:53.90
1994	Germany (Wolfgang Hoppe)	3:27.28
1998	Germany II (Christoph Langen)	2:39.41
2002	Germany II (Andre Lange)	3:07.51
2006	Germany (Andre Lange)	3:40.42
2010	United States (Steven Holcomb)	3:24.46
2014	Latvia (Oskars Melbardis)[1]	3:40.69
2018	Germany (Francesco Friedrich)	3:15.85
2022	Germany (Francesco Friedrich)	3:54.30

Two-Woman Bobsled		Time
2002	United States II (Jill Bakken)	1:37.76
2006	Germany (Sandra Kiriasis)	3:49.98
2010	Canada (Kaillie Humphries)	3:32.28
2014	Canada (Kaillie Humphries)	3:50.61
2018	Germany (Mariama Jamanka)	3:22.45
2022	Germany (Laura Nolte)	4:03.96

(1) Awarded gold after Russia's Alexander Zubkov was stripped of medals in both events due to doping.

Women's Monobob		Time
2022	Kaillie Humphries, United States	4:19.27

Cross-Country Skiing

Men's Individual Sprint		Time
2002	Tor Arne Hetland, Norway (1.5 km)	2:56.9
2006	Bjoern Lind, Sweden (1.3 km)	2:26.5

Men's Individual Sprint		Time
2010	Nikita Kriukov, Russia	3:36.3
2014	Ola Vigen Hattestad, Norway	3:38.39
2018	Johannes Hoesflot Klaebo, Norway	3:05.75
2022	Johannes Hoesflot Klaebo, Norway	2:58.06

Men's 10 Kilometers		Time
1992	Vegard Ulvang, Norway	27:36.0
1994	Bjoern Daehlie, Norway	24:20.1
1998	Bjoern Daehlie, Norway	27:24.5

Men's 15 Kilometers		Time
1924	Thorleif Haug, Norway	1:14:31
1928	Johan Grottumsbraaten, Norway	1:37:01
1932	Sven Utterstrom, Sweden	1:23:07
1936	Erik-August Larsson, Sweden	1:14:38
1948	Martin Lundstrom, Sweden	1:13:50
1952	Hallgeir Brenden, Norway	1:01:34
1956	Hallgeir Brenden, Norway	0:49:39.0
1960	Haakon Brusveen, Norway	0:51:55.5
1964	Eero Maentyranta, Finland	0:50:54.1
1968	Harald Groenningen, Norway	0:47:54.2
1972	Sven-Ake Lundback, Sweden	0:45:28.24
1976	Nikolai Balukov, USSR	0:43:58.47
1980	Thomas Wassberg, Sweden	0:41:57.63
1984	Gunde Svan, Sweden	0:41:25.6
1988	Mikhail Deviatiarov, USSR	0:41:18.9
1992	Bjoern Daehlie, Norway	0:38:01.9
1994	Bjoern Daehlie, Norway	0:35:48.8
1998	Thomas Alsgaard, Norway	1:07:01.7
2002	Andrus Veerpalu, Estonia	0:37:07.4
2006	Andrus Veerpalu, Estonia	0:38:01.3
2010	Dario Cologna, Switzerland	0:33:36.3
2014	Dario Cologna, Switzerland	0:38:29.7
2018	Dario Cologna, Switzerland	0:33:43.9
2022	Iivo Niskanen, Finland	0:37:54.8

Note: Approx. 18-km course 1924-52.

Men's 30-Kilometer		Time
1956	Veikko Hakulinen, Finland	1:44:06.0
1960	Sixten Jernberg, Sweden	1:51:03.9
1964	Eero Maentyranta, Finland	1:30:50.7
1968	Franco Nones, Italy	1:35:39.2
1972	Vyacheslav Vedenine, USSR	1:36:31.15
1976	Sergei Saveliev, USSR	1:30:29.38
1980	Nikolai Zimyatov, USSR	1:27:02.80
1984	Nikolai Zimyatov, USSR	1:28:56.3
1988	Aleksei Prokourorov, USSR	1:24:26.3
1992	Vegard Ulvang, Norway	1:22:27.8
1994	Thomas Alsgaard, Norway	1:12:26.4
1998	Mika Myllylae, Finland	1:33:55.8
2002	Christian Hoffmann, Austria[1]	1:11:31.0
2006	Eugeni Dementiev, Russia	1:17:00.8
2010	Marcus Hellner, Sweden	1:15:11.4
2022	Alexander Bolshunov, ROC	1:16:09.8

(1) Awarded gold after Johann Muehlegg of Spain was stripped of gold for a drug offense.

Men's Skiathlon		Time
2014	Dario Cologna, Switzerland	1:08:15.4
2018	Simen Hegstad Krüger, Norway	1:16:20.0
2022	Alexander Bolshunov, ROC	1:16:09.8

Men's 50-Kilometer		Time
1924	Thorleif Haug, Norway	3:44:32.0
1928	Per Erik Hedlund, Sweden	4:52:03.0
1932	Veli Saarinen, Finland	4:28:00.0
1936	Elis Wiklund, Sweden	3:30:11.0
1948	Nils Karlsson, Sweden	3:47:48.0
1952	Veikko Hakulinen, Finland	3:33:33.0
1956	Sixten Jernberg, Sweden	2:50:27.0
1960	Kalevi Hamalainen, Finland	2:59:06.3
1964	Sixten Jernberg, Sweden	2:43:52.6
1968	Ole Ellefsaeter, Norway	2:28:45.8
1972	Paal Tyldum, Norway	2:43:14.75
1976	Ivar Formo, Norway	2:37:30.05
1980	Nikolai Zimyatov, USSR	2:27:24.60
1984	Thomas Wassberg, Sweden	2:15:55.8
1988	Gunde Svan, Sweden	2:04:30.9
1992	Bjoern Daehlie, Norway	2:03:41.5
1994	Vladimir Smirnov, Kazakhstan	2:07:20.3
1998	Bjoern Daehlie, Norway	2:05:08.2
2002	Mikhail Ivanov, Russia	2:06:20.8
2006	Giorgio di Centa, Italy	2:06:11.8
2010	Petter Northug, Norway	2:05:35.5
2014	Alexander Legkov, Russia	1:46:55.2
2018	Iivo Niskanen, Finland	2:08:22.1
2022*	Alexander Bolshunov, ROC	1:11:32.7

* = Shortened to 28.4 km due to weather.

Men's 4x10-Kilometer Relay		Time
1936	Finland, Norway, Sweden	2:41:33.0
1948	Sweden, Finland, Norway	2:32:08.0

Men's 4x10-Kilometer Relay

Year		Time
1952	Finland, Norway, Sweden	2:20:16.0
1956	USSR, Finland, Sweden	2:15:30.0
1960	Finland, Norway, USSR	2:18:45.6
1964	Sweden, Finland, USSR	2:18:34.6
1968	Norway, Sweden, Finland	2:08:33.5
1972	USSR, Norway, Switzerland	2:04:47.94
1976	Finland, Norway, USSR	2:07:59.72
1980	USSR, Norway, Finland	1:57:03.46
1984	Sweden, USSR, Finland	1:55:06.30
1988	Sweden, USSR, Czechoslovakia	1:43:58.60
1992	Norway, Italy, Finland	1:39:26.00
1994	Italy, Norway, Finland	1:41:15.00
1998	Norway, Italy, Finland	1:40:55.70
2002	Norway, Italy, Germany	1:32:45.5
2006	Italy, Germany, Sweden	1:43:45.7
2010	Sweden, Norway, Czech Republic	1:45:05.4
2014	Sweden, Russia, France	1:28:42.0
2018	Norway, OAR, France	1:33:04.9
2022	ROC, Norway, France	1:54:50.7

Men's Team Sprint

Year		Time
2006	Bjoern Lind & Thobias Fredriksson, Sweden	17:02.9
2010	Oeystein Pettersen & Petter Northug, Norway	19:01.0
2014	Sami Jauhojaervi & Iivo Niskanen, Finland	23:14.89
2018	Martin Johnsrud Sundby & Johannes Hoesflot Klaebo, Norway	15:56.26
2022	Erik Valnes & Johannes Hoesflot Klaebo, Norway	19:22.99

Women's Individual Sprint

Year		Time
2002	Julia Tchepalova, Russia (1.5 km)	3:10.6
2006	Chandra Crawford, Canada (1.1 km)	2:12.3
2010	Marit Bjoergen, Norway	3:39.2
2014	Maiken Caspersen Falla, Norway	2:35.49
2018	Stina Nilsson, Sweden	3:03.84
2022	Jonna Sundling, Sweden	3:09.68

Women's 5 Kilometers

Year		Time
1964	Claudia Boyarskikh, USSR	17:50.5
1968	Toini Gustafsson, Sweden	16:45.2
1972	Galina Koulacova, USSR	17:00.50
1976	Helena Takalo, Finland	15:48.69
1980	Raisa Smetanina, USSR	15:06.92
1984	Marja-Liisa Hamalainen, Finland	17:04.0
1988	Marjo Matikainen, Finland	15:04.0
1992	Marjut Lukkarinen, Finland	14:13.8
1994	Lyubov Yegorova, Russia	14:08.8
1998	Larissa Lazutina, Russia	17:37.9
2002	Beckie Scott, Canada[1]	25:09.9

(1) Awarded gold after Olga Danilova of Russia was stripped of gold and Larissa Lazutina of Russia was stripped of silver for drug offenses.

Women's 10 Kilometers

Year		Time
1952	Lydia Wideman, Finland	41:40.0
1956	Lyubov Kosyreva, USSR	38:11.0
1960	Maria Gusakova, USSR	39:46.6
1964	Claudia Boyarskikh, USSR	40:24.3
1968	Toini Gustafsson, Sweden	36:46.5
1972	Galina Koulacova, USSR	34:17.82
1976	Raisa Smetanina, USSR	30:13.41
1980	Barbara Petzold, E. Germany	30:31.54
1984	Marja-Liisa Hamalainen, Finland	31:44.2
1988	Vida Ventsene, USSR	30:08.3
1992	Lyubov Yegorova, Unified Team (Rus.)	25:53.7
1994	Lyubov Yegorova, Russia	27:30.1
1998	Larissa Lazutina, Russia	46:06.9
2002	Bente Skari, Norway	28:05.6
2006	Kristina Smigun, Estonia	27:51.4
2010	Charlotte Kalla, Sweden	24:58.4
2014	Justyna Kowalczyk, Poland	28:17.8
2018	Ragnhild Haga, Norway	25:00.5
2022	Therese Johaug, Norway	28:06.3

Women's 15-Kilometer

Year		Time
1992	Lyubov Yegorova, Unified Team (Rus.)	42:20.8
1994	Manuela Di Centa, Italy	39:44.5
1998	Olga Danilova, Russia	46:55.4
2002	Stefania Belmondo, Italy	39:54.4
2006	Kristina Smigun, Estonia	42:48.7
2010	Marit Bjoergen, Norway	39:58.1

Women's Skiathlon

Year		Time
2014	Marit Bjoergen, Norway	38:33.6
2018	Charlotte Kalla, Sweden	40:44.9
2022	Therese Johaug, Norway	44:13.7

Women's 30-Kilometer

Year		Time
1992	Stefania Belmondo, Italy	1:22:30.1
1994	Manuela Di Centa, Italy	1:25:41.6
1998	Julia Tchepalova, Russia	1:22:01.5
2002	Gabriela Paruzzi, Italy	1:30:57.1
2006	Katerina Neumannova, Czech Republic	1:22:25.4
2010	Justyna Kowalczyk, Poland	1:30:33.7
2014	Marit Bjoergen, Norway	1:11:05.2
2018	Marit Bjoergen, Norway	1:22:17.6
2022	Therese Johaug, Norway	1:24:54.0

Women's 4x5-Kilometer Relay

Year		Time
1956	Finland, USSR, Sweden (3x5-km)	1:09:01.0
1960	USSR, Sweden, Finland (3x5-km)	1:04:21.4
1964	USSR, Sweden, Finland (3x5-km)	0:59:20.2
1968	Norway, Sweden, USSR (3x5-km)	0:57:30.0
1972	USSR, Finland, Norway (3x5-km)	0:48:46.15
1976	USSR, Finland, E. Germany	1:07:49.75
1980	E. Germany, USSR, Norway	1:02:11.1
1984	Norway, Czechoslovakia, Finland	1:06:49.7
1988	USSR, Norway, Finland	0:59:51.1
1992	Unified Team, Norway, Italy	0:59:34.8
1994	Russia, Norway, Italy	0:57:12.5
1998	Russia, Norway, Italy	0:55:13.5
2002	Germany, Norway, Switzerland	0:49:30.6
2006	Russia, Germany, Italy	0:54:47.7
2010	Norway, Germany, Finland	0:55:19.5
2014	Sweden, Finland, Germany	0:53:02.7
2018	Norway, Sweden, OAR	0:51:24.3
2022	ROC, Germany, Sweden	0:53:41.0

Women's Team Sprint

Year		Time
2006	Lina Andersson & Anna Dahlberg, Sweden	16:36.9
2010	Evi Sachenbacher-Stehle & Claudia Nystad, Germany	18:03.7
2014	Marit Bjoergen & Ingvild Flugstad Oestberg, Norway	16:04.05
2018	Kikkan Randall & Jessie Diggins, United States	15:56.47
2022	Katharina Hennig & Victoria Carl, Germany	22:09.85

Curling

Men

1998	Switzerland, Canada, Norway
2002	Norway, Canada, Switzerland
2006	Canada, Finland, United States
2010	Canada, Norway, Switzerland
2014	Canada, Great Britain, Sweden
2018	United States, Sweden, Switzerland
2022	Sweden, Great Britain, Canada

Women

1998	Canada, Denmark, Sweden
2002	Britain, Switzerland, Canada
2006	Sweden, Switzerland, Canada
2010	Sweden, Canada, China
2014	Canada, Sweden, Great Britain
2018	Sweden, S. Korea, Japan
2022	Great Britain, Japan, Sweden

Mixed

2018	Canada, Switzerland, Norway
2022	Italy, Norway, Sweden

Figure Skating

Men's Singles

1908[1]	Ulrich Salchow, Sweden
1920[1]	Gillis Grafstrom, Sweden
1924	Gillis Grafstrom, Sweden
1928	Gillis Grafstrom, Sweden
1932	Karl Schaefer, Austria
1936	Karl Schaefer, Austria
1948	Richard Button, United States
1952	Richard Button, United States
1956	Hayes Alan Jenkins, United States
1960	David W. Jenkins, United States
1964	Manfred Schnelldorfer, Germany
1968	Wolfgang Schwartz, Austria
1972	Ondrej Nepela, Czechoslovakia
1976	John Curry, Great Britain
1980	Robin Cousins, Great Britain
1984	Scott Hamilton, United States
1988	Brian Boitano, United States
1992	Viktor Petrenko, Unified Team (Ukr.)
1994	Aleksei Urmanov, Russia
1998	Ilya Kulik, Russia
2002	Alexei Yagudin, Russia
2006	Yevgeny Plushenko, Russia
2010	Evan Lysacek, United States
2014	Yuzuru Hanyu, Japan
2018	Yuzuru Hanyu, Japan
2022	Nathan Chen, United States

(1) Event held during Summer Olympic Games.

Women's Singles

1908[1]	Madge Syers, Great Britain
1920[1]	Magda Julin-Mauroy, Sweden
1924	Herma von Szabo-Planck, Austria
1928	Sonja Henie, Norway
1932	Sonja Henie, Norway
1936	Sonja Henie, Norway
1948	Barbara Ann Scott, Canada
1952	Jeanette Altwegg, Great Britain

Women's Singles

1956	Tenley Albright, United States
1960	Carol Heiss, United States
1964	Sjoukje Dijkstra, Netherlands
1968	Peggy Fleming, United States
1972	Beatrix Schuba, Austria
1976	Dorothy Hamill, United States
1980	Anett Poetzsch, E. Germany
1984	Katarina Witt, E. Germany
1988	Katarina Witt, E. Germany
1992	Kristi Yamaguchi, United States
1994	Oksana Baiul, Ukraine
1998	Tara Lipinski, United States
2002	Sarah Hughes, United States
2006	Shizuka Arakawa, Japan
2010	Kim Yu-na, South Korea
2014	Adelina Sotnikova, Russia
2018	Alina Zagitova, OAR
2022	Anna Shcherbakova, ROC

(1) Event held during Summer Olympic Games.

Pairs

1908[1]	Anna Hubler & Heinrich Burger, Germany
1920[1]	Ludovika Jakobsson & Walter Jakobsson, Finland
1924	Helene Engelman & Alfred Berger, Austria
1928	Andree Joly & Pierre Brunet, France
1932	Andree Joly & Pierre Brunet, France
1936	Maxi Herber & Ernst Baier, Germany
1948	Micheline Lannoy & Pierre Baugniet, Belgium
1952	Ria Falk & Paul Falk, Germany
1956	Elisabeth Schwartz & Kurt Oppelt, Austria
1964	Ludmila Beloussova & Oleg Protopopov, USSR
1968	Ludmila Beloussova & Oleg Protopopov, USSR
1972	Irina Rodnina & Alexei Ulanov, USSR
1976	Irina Rodnina & Aleksandr Zaitzev, USSR
1980	Irina Rodnina & Aleksandr Zaitzev, USSR
1984	Elena Valova & Oleg Vassiliev, USSR
1988	Ekaterina Gordeeva & Sergei Grinkov, USSR
1992	Natalia Mishkutienok & Artur Dimitriev, Unified Team (Rus.)
1994	Ekaterina Gordeeva & Sergei Grinkov, Russia
1998	Oksana Kazakova & Artur Dmitriev, Russia
2002	Elena Berezhnaya & Anton Sikharulidze, Russia; Jamie Salé & David Pelletier, Canada (tie)
2006	Tatyana Totmianina & Maxim Marinin, Russia
2010	Shen Xue & Zhao Hongbo, China
2014	Tatiana Volosozhar & Maxim Trankov, Russia
2018	Aljona Savchenko & Bruno Massot, Germany
2022	Sui Wenjing & Han Cong, China

(1) Event held during Summer Olympic Games.

Ice Dancing

1976	Ludmila Pakhomova & Aleksandr Gorschkov, USSR
1980	Natalya Linichuk & Gennadi Karponosov, USSR
1984	Jayne Torvill & Christopher Dean, Great Britain
1988	Natalia Bestemianova & Andrei Bukin, USSR
1992	Marina Klimova & Sergei Ponomarenko, Unified Team (Rus.)
1994	Pasha Grishuk & Evgeny Platov, Russia
1998	Pasha Grishuk & Evgeny Platov, Russia
2002	Marina Anissina & Gwendal Peizerat, France
2006	Tatyana Navka & Roman Kostomarov, Russia
2010	Tessa Virtue & Scott Moir, Canada
2014	Meryl Davis & Charlie White, United States
2018	Tessa Virtue & Scott Moir, Canada
2022	Gabriella Papadakis & Guillaume Cizeron, France

Mixed Team

2014	Russia, Canada, United States
2018	Canada, OAR, United States
2022[1]	ROC, United States, Japan

(1) Medals not awarded pending a continuing investigation into a positive drug test for an ROC athlete.

Freestyle Skiing

Men's Aerials

		Points
1994	Andreas Schoenbaechler, Switzerland	234.67
1998	Eric Bergoust, United States	255.64
2002	Ales Valenta, Czech Republic	257.02
2006	Xiaopeng Han, China	250.77
2010	Alexei Grishin, Belarus	248.41
2014	Anton Kushnir, Belarus	134.50
2018	Oleksandr Abramenko, Ukraine	128.51
2022	Qi Guangpu, China	129.00

Men's Big Air

		Points
2022	Birk Ruud, Norway	187.75

Men's Moguls

		Points
1992	Edgar Grospiron, France	25.81
1994	Jean-Luc Brassard, Canada	27.24
1998	Jonny Moseley, United States	26.93
2002	Janne Lahtela, Finland	27.97
2006	Dale Begg-Smith, Australia	26.77
2010	Alex Bilodeau, Canada	26.75

Men's Moguls

		Points
2014	Alex Bilodeau, Canada	26.31
2018	Mikaël Kingsbury, Canada	86.63
2022	Walter Wallberg, Sweden	83.23

Men's Ski Cross

2010	Michael Schmid, Switzerland
2014	Jean Frederic Chapuis, France
2018	Brady Leman, Canada
2022	Ryan Regez, Switzerland

Men's Ski Halfpipe

		Points
2014	David Wise, United States	92.00
2018	David Wise, United States	97.20
2022	Nico Porteous, New Zealand	93.00

Men's Ski Slopestyle

		Points
2014	Joss Christensen, United States	95.80
2018	Oystein Braaten, Norway	95.00
2022	Alexander Hall, United States	90.01

Women's Aerials

		Points
1994	Lina Tcherjazova, Uzbekistan	166.84
1998	Nikki Stone, United States	193.00
2002	Alisa Camplin, Australia	193.47
2006	Evelyne Leu, Switzerland	202.55
2010	Lydia Lassila, Australia	214.74
2014	Alla Tsuper, Belarus	98.01
2018	Hanna Huskova, Belarus	96.14
2022	Xu Mengtao, China	108.61

Women's Big Air

		Points
2022	Eileen Gu, China	188.25

Women's Moguls

		Points
1992	Donna Weinbrecht, United States	23.69
1994	Stine Lise Hattestad, Norway	25.97
1998	Tae Satoya, Japan	25.06
2002	Kari Traa, Norway	25.94
2006	Jennifer Heil, Canada	26.50
2010	Hannah Kearney, United States	26.63
2014	Justine Dufour-Lapointe, Canada	22.44
2018	Perrine Laffont, France	78.65
2022	Jakara Anthony, Australia	83.09

Women's Ski Cross

2010	Ashleigh McIvor, Canada
2014	Marielle Thompson, Canada
2018	Kelsey Serwa, Canada
2022	Sandra Naeslund, Sweden

Women's Ski Halfpipe

		Points
2014	Maddie Bowman, United States	89.00
2018	Cassie Sharpe, Canada	95.80
2022	Eileen Gu, China	95.25

Women's Ski Slopestyle

		Points
2014	Dara Howell, Canada	94.20
2018	Sarah Höfflin, Switzerland	91.20
2022	Mathilde Gremaud, Switzerland	86.56

Mixed Team Aerials

		Points
2022	United States, China, Canada	338.34

Ice Hockey

Men

1920[1]	Canada, United States, Czechoslovakia
1924	Canada, United States, Great Britain
1928	Canada, Sweden, Switzerland
1932	Canada, United States, Germany
1936	Great Britain, Canada, United States
1948	Canada, Czechoslovakia, Switzerland
1952	Canada, United States, Sweden
1956	USSR, United States, Canada
1960	United States, Canada, USSR
1964	USSR, Sweden, Czechoslovakia
1968	USSR, Czechoslovakia, Canada
1972	USSR, United States, Czechoslovakia
1976	USSR, Czechoslovakia, W. Germany
1980	United States, USSR, Sweden
1984	USSR, Czechoslovakia, Sweden
1988	USSR, Finland, Sweden
1992	Unified Team, Canada, Czechoslovakia
1994	Sweden, Canada, Finland
1998	Czech Republic, Russia, Finland
2002	Canada, United States, Russia
2006	Sweden, Finland, Czech Republic
2010	Canada, United States, Finland
2014	Canada, Sweden, Finland
2018	OAR, Germany, Canada
2022	Finland, ROC, Slovakia

(1) Event held during Summer Olympic Games.

Women

1998	United States, Canada, Finland
2002	Canada, United States, Sweden

Women

2006	Canada, Sweden, United States
2010	Canada, United States, Finland
2014	Canada, United States, Switzerland
2018	United States, Canada, Finland
2022	Canada, United States, Finland

Luge

Men's Singles

		Time
1964	Thomas Keohler, E. Germany	3:27.77
1968	Manfred Schmid, Austria	2:52.48
1972	Wolfgang Scheidel, E. Germany	3:27.58
1976	Detlef Guenther, E. Germany	3:27.688
1980	Bernhard Glass, E. Germany	2:54.796
1984	Paul Hildgartner, Italy	3:04.258
1988	Jens Mueller, E. Germany	3:05.548
1992	Georg Hackl, Germany	3:02.363
1994	Georg Hackl, Germany	3:21.571
1998	Georg Hackl, Germany	3:18.436
2002	Armin Zoeggeler, Italy	2:57.941
2006	Armin Zoeggeler, Italy	3:26.088
2010	Felix Loch, Germany	3:13.085
2014	Felix Loch, Germany	3:27.526
2018	David Gleirscher, Austria	3:10.702
2022	Johannes Ludwig, Germany	3:48.735

Men's Doubles

		Time
1964	Austria	1:41.62
1968	E. Germany	1:35.85
1972	Italy, E. Germany (tie)	1:28.35
1976	E. Germany	1:25.604
1980	E. Germany	1:19.331
1984	W. Germany	1:23.620
1988	E. Germany	1:31.940
1992	Germany	1:32.053
1994	Italy	1:36.720
1998	Germany	1:41.105
2002	Germany	1:26.082
2006	Austria	1:34.497
2010	Austria	1:22.705
2014	Germany	1:38.933
2018	Germany	1:31.697
2022	Germany	1:56.554

Women's Singles

		Time
1964	Ortun Enderlein, Germany	3:24.67
1968	Erica Lechner, Italy	2:28.66
1972	Anna M. Muller, E. Germany	2:59.18
1976	Margit Schumann, E. Germany	2:50.621
1980	Vera Zozulya, USSR	2:36.537
1984	Steffi Martin, E. Germany	2:46.570
1988	Steffi (Martin) Walter, E. Germany	3:03.973
1992	Doris Neuner, Austria	3:06.696
1994	Gerda Weissensteiner, Italy	3:15.517
1998	Silke Kraushaar, Germany	3:23.779
2002	Sylke Otto, Germany	2:52.464
2006	Sylke Otto, Germany	3:07.979
2010	Tatjana Huefner, Germany	2:46.524
2014	Natalie Geisenberger, Germany	3:19.768
2018	Natalie Geisenberger, Germany	3:05.232
2022	Natalie Geisenberger, Germany	3:53.454

Mixed Team Relay

		Time
2014	Germany, Russia, Latvia	2:45.649
2018	Germany, Canada, Austria	2:24.517
2022	Germany, Austria, Latvia	3:03.406

Ski Jumping

Men's Normal Hill

		Points
1964	Veikko Kankkonen, Finland	229.9
1968	Jiri Raska, Czechoslovakia	216.5
1972	Yukio Kasaya, Japan	244.2
1976	Hans-Georg Aschenbach, E. Germany	252.0
1980	Toni Innauer, Austria	266.3
1984	Jens Weissflog, E. Germany	215.2
1988	Matti Nykaenen, Finland	230.5
1992	Ernst Vettori, Austria	222.8
1994	Espen Bredesen, Norway	282.0
1998	Jani Soininen, Finland	234.5
2002	Simon Ammann, Switzerland	269.0
2006	Lars Bystoel, Norway	266.5
2010	Simon Ammann, Switzerland	276.5
2014	Kamil Stoch, Poland	278.0
2018	Andreas Wellinger, Germany	259.3
2022	Ryoyu Kobayashi, Japan	275.0

Men's Large Hill

		Points
1924	Jacob Tullin Thams, Norway	18.960
1928	Alfred Andersen, Norway	19.208
1932	Birger Ruud, Norway	228.1
1936	Birger Ruud, Norway	232.0
1948	Petter Hugsted, Norway	228.1
1952	Arnfinn Bergmann, Norway	226.0
1956	Antti Hyvarinen, Finland	227.0

Men's Large Hill

		Points
1960	Helmut Recknagel, E. Germany	227.2
1964	Toralf Engan, Norway	230.7
1968	Vladimir Beloussov, USSR	231.3
1972	Wojciech Fortuna, Poland	219.9
1976	Karl Schnabl, Austria	234.8
1980	Jouko Tormanen, Finland	271.0
1984	Matti Nykaenen, Finland	231.2
1988	Matti Nykaenen, Finland	224.0
1992	Toni Nieminen, Finland	239.5
1994	Jens Weissflog, Germany	274.5
1998	Kazuyoshi Funaki, Japan	272.3
2002	Simon Ammann, Switzerland	281.4
2006	Thomas Morgenstern, Austria	276.9
2010	Simon Ammann, Switzerland	283.6
2014	Kamil Stoch, Poland	278.7
2018	Kamil Stoch, Poland	285.7
2022	Marius Lindvik, Norway	296.1

Men's Team

		Points
1988	Finland, Yugoslavia, Norway	634.4
1992	Finland, Austria, Czechoslovakia	644.4
1994	Germany, Japan, Austria	970.1
1998	Japan, Germany, Austria	933.0
2002	Germany, Finland, Slovenia	974.1
2006	Austria, Finland, Norway	984.0
2010	Austria, Germany, Norway	1,107.9
2014	Germany, Austria, Japan	1,041.1
2018	Norway, Germany, Poland	1,098.5
2022	Austria, Slovenia, Germany	942.7

Women's Normal Hill

		Points
2014	Carina Vogt, Germany	247.4
2018	Maren Lundby, Norway	264.6
2022	Ursa Bogataj, Slovenia	239.0

Mixed Team

		Points
2022	Slovenia, ROC, Canada	1,001.5

Snowboarding

Men's Big Air

		Points
2018	Sebastien Toutant, Canada	174.25
2022	Su Yiming, China	182.50

Men's Halfpipe

		Points
1998	Gian Simmen, Switzerland	85.2
2002	Ross Powers, United States	46.1
2006	Shaun White, United States	46.8
2010	Shaun White, United States	48.4
2014	Iouri Podladtchikov, Switzerland	94.75
2018	Shaun White, United States	97.75
2022	Ayumu Hirano, Japan	96.0

Men's Parallel Giant Slalom

1998	Ross Rebagliati, Canada
2002	Philipp Schoch, Switzerland
2006	Philipp Schoch, Switzerland
2010	Jasey Jay Anderson, Canada
2014	Vic Wild, Russia
2018	Nevin Galmarini, Switzerland
2022	Benjamin Karl, Austria

Note: In 2002, the Giant Slalom became the Parallel Giant Slalom.

Men's Parallel Slalom

2014	Vic Wild, Russia

Men's Slopestyle

		Points
2014	Sage Kotsenburg, United States	93.50
2018	Red Gerard, United States	87.16
2022	Max Parrot, Canada	90.96

Men's Snowboard Cross

2006	Seth Wescott, United States
2010	Seth Wescott, United States
2014	Pierre Vaultier, France
2018	Pierre Vaultier, France
2022	Alessandro Haemmerle, Austria

Women's Big Air

		Points
2018	Anna Gasser, Austria	185.00
2022	Anna Gasser, Austria	185.50

Women's Halfpipe

		Points
1998	Nicola Thost, Germany	74.6
2002	Kelly Clark, United States	47.9
2006	Hannah Teter, United States	46.4
2010	Torah Bright, Australia	45.0
2014	Kaitlyn Farrington, United States	91.75
2018	Chloe Kim, United States	98.25
2022	Chloe Kim, United States	94.0

Women's Parallel Giant Slalom

1998	Karine Ruby, France
2002	Isabelle Blanc, France

Women's Parallel Giant Slalom

2006	Daniela Meuli, Switzerland
2010	Nicolien Sauerbreij, Netherlands
2014	Patrizia Kummer, Switzerland
2018	Ester Ledecká, Czech Republic
2022	Ester Ledecká, Czech Republic

Note: In 2002, the Giant Slalom became the Parallel Giant Slalom.

Women's Parallel Slalom

2014	Julia Dujmovits, Austria

Women's Slopestyle

		Points
2014	Jamie Anderson, United States	95.25
2018	Jamie Anderson, United States	83.00
2022	Zoi Sadowski-Synnott, New Zealand	92.88

Women's Snowboard Cross

2006	Tanja Frieden, Switzerland
2010	Maelle Ricker, Canada
2014	Eva Samková, Czech Republic
2018	Michela Moioli, Italy
2022	Lindsey Jacobellis, United States

Mixed Team Snowboard Cross

2022	United States, Italy, Canada

Speed Skating

* = Olympic record

Men's 500 Meters

		Time
1924	Charles Jewtraw, United States	0:44.0
1928	C. Thunberg, Finland; B. Evensen, Norway (tie)	0:43.4
1932	John A. Shea, United States	0:43.4
1936	Ivar Ballangrud, Norway	0:43.4
1948	Finn Helgesen, Norway	0:43.1
1952	Kenneth Henry, United States	0:43.2
1956	Evgeniy Grishin, USSR	0:40.2
1960	Evgeniy Grishin, USSR	0:40.2
1964	Terry McDermott, United States	0:40.1
1968	Erhard Keller, W. Germany	0:40.3
1972	Erhard Keller, W. Germany	0:39.44
1976	Evgeny Kulikov, USSR	0:39.17
1980	Eric Heiden, United States	0:38.03
1984	Sergei Fokichev, USSR	0:38.19
1988	Uwe-Jens Mey, E. Germany	0:36.45
1992	Uwe-Jens Mey, Germany	0:37.14
1994	Aleksandr Golubev, Russia	0:36.33
1998	Hiroyasu Shimizu, Japan	0:35.59
2002	Casey FitzRandolph, United States	0:34.42
2006	Joey Cheek, United States	0:34.82
2010	Mo Tae-bum, S. Korea	0:69.82
2014	Michel Mulder, Netherlands	0:69.312
2018	Havard Lorentzen, Norway	0:34.41
2022	Gao Tingyu, China	0.34.32*

Note: In 2010 and 2014, results include the total of two 500-km race times.

Men's 1000 Meters

		Time
1976	Peter Mueller, United States	1:19.32
1980	Eric Heiden, United States	1:15.18
1984	Gaetan Boucher, Canada	1:15.80
1988	Nikolai Guiliaev, USSR	1:13.03
1992	Olaf Zinke, Germany	1:14.85
1994	Dan Jansen, United States	1:12.43
1998	Ids Postma, Netherlands	1:10.64
2002	Gerard van Velde, Netherlands	1:07.18*
2006	Shani Davis, United States	1:08.89
2010	Shani Davis, United States	1:08.94
2014	Stefan Groothuis, Netherlands	1:08.39
2018	Kjeld Nuis, Netherlands	1:07.95
2022	Thomas Krol, Netherlands	1:07.92

Men's 1500 Meters

		Time
1924	Clas Thunberg, Finland	2:20.8
1928	Clas Thunberg, Finland	2:21.1
1932	John A. Shea, United States	2:57.5
1936	Charles Mathiesen, Norway	2:19.2
1948	Sverre Farstad, Norway	2:17.6
1952	Hjalmar Andersen, Norway	2:20.4
1956	Y. Grishin, USSR; Y. Mikhailov, USSR (tie)	2:08.6
1960	R. Aas, Norway; Y. Grishin, USSR (tie)	2:10.4
1964	Ants Anston, USSR	2:10.3
1968	Cornelis Verkerk, Netherlands	2:03.4
1972	Ard Schenk, Netherlands	2:02.96
1976	Jan Egil Storholt, Norway	1:59.38
1980	Eric Heiden, United States	1:55.44
1984	Gaetan Boucher, Canada	1:58.36
1988	Andre Hoffmann, E. Germany	1:52.06
1992	Johann Koss, Norway	1:54.81
1994	Johann Koss, Norway	1:51.29
1998	Aadne Sondral, Norway	1:47.87
2002	Derek Parra, United States	1:43.95
2006	Enrico Fabris, Italy	1:45.97
2010	Mark Tuitert, Netherlands	1:45.57
2014	Zbigniew Brodka, Poland	1:45.006

Men's 1500 Meters

		Time
2018	Kjeld Nuis, Netherlands	1:44.01
2022	Kjeld Nuis, Netherlands	1:43.21*

Men's 5000 Meters

		Time
1924	Clas Thunberg, Finland	8:39.0
1928	Ivar Ballangrud, Norway	8:50.5
1932	Irving Jaffee, United States	9:40.8
1936	Ivar Ballangrud, Norway	8:19.6
1948	Reidar Liaklev, Norway	8:29.4
1952	Hjalmar Andersen, Norway	8:10.6
1956	Boris Shilkov, USSR	7:48.7
1960	Viktor Kosichkin, USSR	7:51.3
1964	Knut Johannesen, Norway	7:38.4
1968	F. Anton Maier, Norway	7:22.4
1972	Ard Schenk, Netherlands	7:23.61
1976	Sten Stensen, Norway	7:24.48
1980	Eric Heiden, United States	7:02.29
1984	Tomas Gustafson, Sweden	7:12.28
1988	Tomas Gustafson, Sweden	6:44.63
1992	Geir Karlstad, Norway	6:59.97
1994	Johann Koss, Norway	6:34.96
1998	Gianni Romme, Netherlands	6:22.20
2002	Jochem Uytdehaage, Netherlands	6:14.66
2006	Chad Hedrick, United States	6:14.68
2010	Sven Kramer, Netherlands	6:14.60
2014	Sven Kramer, Netherlands	6:10.76
2018	Sven Kramer, Netherlands	6:09.76
2022	Nils van der Poel, Sweden	6:08.84*

Men's 10,000 Meters

		Time
1924	Julius Skutnabb, Finland	18:04.8
1928	Event not held because of thawing of ice	
1932	Irving Jaffee, United States	19:13.6
1936	Ivar Ballangrud, Norway	17:24.3
1948	Ake Seyffarth, Sweden	17:26.3
1952	Hjalmar Andersen, Norway	16:45.8
1956	Sigvard Ericsson, Sweden	16:35.9
1960	Knut Johannesen, Norway	15:46.6
1964	Jonny Nilsson, Sweden	15:50.1
1968	Jonny Hoeglin, Sweden	15:23.6
1972	Ard Schenk, Netherlands	15:01.35
1976	Piet Kleine, Netherlands	14:50.59
1980	Eric Heiden, United States	14:28.13
1984	Igor Malkov, USSR	14:39.90
1988	Tomas Gustafson, Sweden	13:48.20
1992	Bart Veldkamp, Netherlands	14:12.12
1994	Johann Koss, Norway	13:30.55
1998	Gianni Romme, Netherlands	13:15.33
2002	Jochem Uytdehaage, Netherlands	12:58.92
2006	Bob de Jong, Netherlands	13:01.57
2010	Lee Seung-hoon, S. Korea	12:58.55
2014	Jorrit Bergsma, Netherlands	12:44.45
2018	Ted-Jan Bloemen, Canada	12:39.77
2022	Nils van der Poel, Sweden	12:30.74*

Men's Mass Start

2018	Lee Seung-hoon, S. Korea
2022	Bart Swings, Belgium

Men's Team Pursuit

		Time
2006	Italy, Canada, Netherlands	3:44.46
2010	Canada, United States, Netherlands	3:41.37
2014	Netherlands, S. Korea, Poland	3:37.71
2018	Norway, S. Korea, Netherlands	3:37.32
2022	Norway, ROC, United States	3:38.08

Women's 500 Meters

		Time
1960	Helga Haase, Germany	0:45.9
1964	Lydia Skoblikova, USSR	0:45.0
1968	Ludmila Titova, USSR	0:46.1
1972	Anne Henning, United States	0:43.33
1976	Sheila Young, United States	0:42.76
1980	Karin Enke, E. Germany	0:41.78
1984	Christa Rothenburger, E. Germany	0:41.02
1988	Bonnie Blair, United States	0:39.10
1992	Bonnie Blair, United States	0:40.33
1994	Bonnie Blair, United States	0:39.25
1998	Catriona Le May Doan, Canada	0:38.21
2002	Catriona Le May Doan, Canada	0:37.30
2006	Svetlana Zhurova, Russia	0:38.23
2010	Lee Sang-hwa, S. Korea	0:76.09
2014	Lee Sang-hwa, S. Korea	0:74.70
2018	Nao Kodaira, Japan	0:36.94*
2022	Erin Jackson, United States	0.37.04

Note: In 2010 and 2014, results include the total of two 500-km race times.

Women's 1000 Meters

		Time
1960	Klara Guseva, USSR	1:34.1
1964	Lydia Skoblikova, USSR	1:33.2
1968	Carolina Geijssen, Netherlands	1:32.6
1972	Monika Pflug, W. Germany	1:31.40
1976	Tatiana Averina, USSR	1:28.43
1980	Natalya Petruseva, USSR	1:24.10
1984	Karin Enke, E. Germany	1:21.61
1988	Christa Rothenburger, E. Germany	1:17.65

Women's 1000 Meters		Time
1992	Bonnie Blair, United States	1:21.90
1994	Bonnie Blair, United States	1:18.74
1998	Marianne Timmer, Netherlands	1:16.51
2002	Chris Witty, United States	1:13.83
2006	Marianne Timmer, Netherlands	1:16.05
2010	Christine Nesbitt, Canada	1:16.56
2014	Zhang Hong, China	1:14.02
2018	Jorien ter Mors, Netherlands	1:13.56
2022	Miho Takagi, Japan	1:13.19*

Women's 1500 Meters		Time
1960	Lydia Skoblikova, USSR	2:52.2
1964	Lydia Skoblikova, USSR	2:22.6
1968	Kaija Mustonen, Finland	2:22.4
1972	Dianne Holum, United States	2:20.85
1976	Galina Stepanskaya, USSR	2:16.58
1980	Anne Borckink, Netherlands	2:10.95
1984	Karin Enke, E. Germany	2:03.42
1988	Yvonne van Gennip, Netherlands	2:00.68
1992	Jacqueline Boerner, Germany	2:05.87
1994	Emese Hunyady, Austria	2:02.19
1998	Marianne Timmer, Netherlands	1:57.58
2002	Anni Friesinger, Germany	1:54.02
2006	Cindy Klassen, Canada	1:55.27
2010	Ireen Wüst, Netherlands	1:56.89
2014	Jorien ter Mors, Netherlands	1:53.51
2018	Ireen Wüst, Netherlands	1:54.35
2022	Ireen Wüst, Netherlands	1:53.28*

Women's 3000 Meters		Time
1960	Lydia Skoblikova, USSR	5:14.3
1964	Lydia Skoblikova, USSR	5:14.9
1968	Johanna Schut, Netherlands	4:56.2
1972	Christina Baas-Kaiser, Netherlands	4:52.14
1976	Tatiana Averina, USSR	4:45.19
1980	Bjoerg Eva Jensen, Norway	4:32.13
1984	Andrea Schoene, E. Germany	4:24.79
1988	Yvonne van Gennip, Netherlands	4:11.94
1992	Gunda Niemann, Germany	4:19.90
1994	Svetlana Bazhanova, Russia	4:17.43
1998	Gunda Niemann-Stirnemann, Germany	4:07.29
2002	Claudia Pechstein, Germany	3:57.70
2006	Ireen Wüst, Netherlands	4:02.43
2010	Martina Sablikova, Czech Republic	4:02.53
2014	Ireen Wüst, Netherlands	4:00.34
2018	Carlijn Achtereekte, Netherlands	3:59.21
2022	Irene Schouten, Netherlands	3:56.93*

Women's 5000 Meters		Time
1988	Yvonne van Gennip, Netherlands	7:14.13
1992	Gunda Niemann, Germany	7:31.57
1994	Claudia Pechstein, Germany	7:14.37
1998	Claudia Pechstein, Germany	6:59.61
2002	Claudia Pechstein, Germany	6:46.91
2006	Clara Hughes, Canada	6:59.07
2010	Martina Sablikova, Czech Republic	6:50.91
2014	Martina Sablikova, Czech Republic	6:51.54
2018	Esmee Visser, Netherlands	6:50.23
2022	Irene Schouten, Netherlands	6:43.51*

Women's Mass Start		
2018	Nana Takagi, Japan	
2022	Irene Schouten, Netherlands	

Women's Team Pursuit		Time
2006	Germany, Canada, Russia	3:01.25
2010	Germany, Japan, Poland	3:02.82
2014	Netherlands, Poland, Russia	2:58.05
2018	Japan, Netherlands, United States	2:53.89
2022	Canada, Japan, Netherlands	2:53.44*

Speed Skating (Short Track)

*= Olympic record

Men's 500 Meters		Time
1998	Takafumi Nishitani, Japan	0:42.862
2002	Marc Gagnon, Canada	0:41.802

		Time
2006	Apolo Anton Ohno, United States	0:41.935
2010	Charles Hamelin, Canada	0:40.981
2014	Victor An, Russia	0:41.312
2018	Wu Dajing, China	0:39.584*
2022	Shaoang Liu, Hungary	0:40.388

Men's 1000 Meters		Time
1992	Kim Ki-hoon, S. Korea	1:30.76
1994	Kim Ki-hoon, S. Korea	1:34.57
1998	Kim Dong-sung, S. Korea	1:32.375
2002	Steven Bradbury, Australia	1:29.109
2006	Ahn Hyun-soo, S. Korea	1:26.739
2010	Lee Jung-su, S. Korea	1:23.747
2014	Victor An, Russia	1:25.325
2018	Samuel Girard, Canada	1:24.650
2022	Ren Ziwei, China	1:26.768

Men's 1500 Meters		Time
2002	Apolo Anton Ohno, United States	2:18.541
2006	Ahn Hyun-soo, S. Korea	2:25.341
2010	Lee Jung-su, S. Korea	2:17.611
2014	Charles Hamelin, Canada	2:14.985
2018	Lim Hyo-jun, S. Korea	2:10.485
2022	Hwang Dae-heon, S. Korea	2:09.219

Men's 5000-Meter Relay		Time
1992	S. Korea, Canada, Japan	7:14.02
1994	Italy, United States, Australia	7:11.74
1998	Canada, S. Korea, China	7:06.075
2002	Canada, Italy, China	6:51.579
2006	S. Korea, Canada, United States	6:43.376
2010	Canada, S. Korea, United States	6:44.224
2014	Russia, United States, China	6:42.100
2018	Hungary, China, Canada	6:31.971*
2022	Canada, S. Korea, Italy	6:41.257

Women's 500 Meters		Time
1992	Cathy Turner, United States	0:47.04
1994	Cathy Turner, United States	0:45.98
1998	Annie Perreault, Canada	0:46.568
2002	Yang Yang (A), China	0:44.187
2006	Wang Meng, China	0:44.345
2010	Wang Meng, China	0:43.048
2014	Li Jianrou, China	0:45.263
2018	Arianna Fontana, Italy	0:42.569
2022	Arianna Fontana, Italy	0:42.488

Women's 1000 Meters		Time
1998	Chun Lee-kyung, S. Korea	1:42.776
2002	Yang Yang (A), China	1:36.391
2006	Jin Sun-yu, S. Korea	1:32.859
2010	Wang Meng, China	1:29.213
2014	Park Seung-hi, S. Korea	1:30.761
2018	Suzanne Schulting, Netherlands	1:29.778
2022	Suzanne Schulting, Netherlands	1:28.391

Women's 1500 Meters		Time
2002	Ko Gi-hyun, S. Korea	2:31.581
2006	Jin Sun-yu, S. Korea	2:23.494
2010	Zhou Yang, China	2:16.993
2014	Zhou Yang, China	2:19.140
2018	Choi Min-jeong, S. Korea	2:24.948
2022	Choi Min-jeong, S. Korea	2:17.789

Women's 3000-Meter Relay		Time
1992	Canada, United States, Unified Team	4:36.62
1994	S. Korea, Canada, United States	4:26.64
1998	S. Korea, China, Canada	4:16.26
2002	S. Korea, China, Canada	4:12.793
2006	S. Korea, Canada, Italy	4:17.040
2010	China, Canada, United States	4:06.610*
2014	S. Korea, Canada, Italy	4:09.498
2018	S. Korea, Italy, Netherlands	4:07.361
2022	Netherlands, S. Korea, China	4:03.409*

Mixed 2000-Meter Relay		Time
2022	China, Italy, Hungary	2:37.348

Paralympic Games
Mar. 4-13, 2022

More than 550 athletes from 46 countries, participating in 78 events across six sports, met at the XIII Paralympic Winter Games, held Mar. 4-13, 2022, in Beijing, China. The International Paralympic Committee on Mar. 3, 2022, banned Russian and Belarusian athletes from competing in the games, due to Russia's invasion of Ukraine on Feb. 24, 2022. The host country, China, which had previously only won one gold medal, surpassed all expectations by winning 61 medals, 18 of them gold. Ukraine came in second with 29 medals (11 gold). Other leading winners included Canada with 25 medals (8 gold), the United States with 20 (6 gold), and Germany with 19 (4 gold). The XVI Paralympic Summer Games were held Aug. 24-Sept. 5, 2021, in Tokyo, Japan. More than 4,400 athletes from 162 countries participated. Medals were awarded in 22 sports. China claimed 207 total medals, including 96 gold, outpacing Great Britain (124), athletes representing the Russian Paralympic Committee (118), and the United States (104). The 2024 Summer Paralympics were expected to be held in Aug.-Sept. in Paris, France.

The first Olympic Games for athletes with an impairment were held in Rome after the 1960 Summer Olympics; use of the name "paralympic" began with the 1964 games in Tokyo. The Paralympics are held by the Olympic host country in the same year and usually the same city and venue or venues. In 1976, the first Winter Paralympics were held in Ornskoldsvik, Sweden.

COLLEGE SPORTS

COLLEGE FOOTBALL

2022 CFP Championship: Undefeated Georgia Dominates TCU

The Univ. of Georgia Bulldogs walloped the Texas Christian Univ. Horned Frogs, 65-7, winning their second consecutive title Jan. 9, 2023. Led by quarterback Stetson Bennett IV, who was credited with six touchdowns in the romp at SoFi Stadium in Inglewood, CA, the Bulldogs wrapped up an undefeated season with the most points and the most lopsided margin of victory ever in a BCS or CFP title game. Georgia's defense squashed the Horned Frogs, who averaged 474.1 yards per game going into the championship matchup, holding them to just 188 yards and one TD. Georgia head coach Kirby Smart was the first to win back-to-back titles since his former mentor Nick Saban at Alabama in 2011-12.

2022 College Football Final Rankings

College Football Playoff Rankings		Associated Press Poll		USA Today Coaches Poll	
Rank, team	**Rank, team**	**Rank, team**	**Rank, team**	**Rank, team**	**Rank, team**
1. Georgia	14. Oregon St.	1. Georgia	14. Kansas St.	1. Georgia	14. Kansas St.
2. Michigan	15. Oregon	2. TCU	15. Oregon	2. TCU	15. LSU
3. TCU	16. Tulane	3. Michigan	16. LSU	3. Michigan	16. Oregon
4. Ohio St.	17. LSU	4. Ohio St.	17. Oregon St.	4. Ohio St.	17. Oregon St.
5. Alabama	18. UCLA	5. Alabama	18. Notre Dame	5. Alabama	18. Notre Dame
6. Tennessee	19. South Carolina	6. Tennessee	19. Troy	6. Tennessee	19. Mississippi St.
7. Clemson	20. Texas	7. Penn St.	20. Mississippi St.	7. Penn St.	20. Troy
8. Utah	21. Notre Dame	8. Washington	21. UCLA	8. Washington	21. UCLA
9. Kansas St.	22. Mississippi St.	9. Tulane	22. Pittsburgh	9. Tulane	22. Pittsburgh
10. USC	23. NC St.	10. Utah	23. South Carolina	10. Florida St.	23. South Carolina
11. Penn St.	24. Troy	11. Florida St.	24. Fresno St.	11. Utah	24. Fresno St.
12. Washington	25. UT San Antonio	12. USC	25. Texas	12. Clemson	25. Texas
13. Florida St.		13. Clemson		13. USC	

Note: College Football Playoff ranking is through games Dec. 3, 2022. Final AP poll and Coaches poll include games through Jan. 9, 2023 (after all bowls and championship game).

National College Football Championship Game Results, 1998-2022

The Bowl Championship Series (BCS) National Championship game (BCS ranked No. 1 vs. BCS No. 2) determined the NCAA's Football Bowl Subdivision (Div. I-A) champion in 1998-2013. The College Football Playoff (CFP) replaced the BCS at the end of the 2014 regular season. The four-team CFP consists of a semifinal round (rotating among the following six bowl games: Sugar, Rose, Orange, Cotton, Peach, and Fiesta) and a championship game played on a Monday night. A committee ranks 25 teams for the playoffs and selected other bowl games, using guidelines that include strength of schedule, head-to-head results, and won-loss records; preference is given to conference champions. Years shown here are for regular season, not year in which championship was played.

Year	Result	Year	Result	Year	Result
1998	Tennessee 23, Florida St. 16	2007	LSU 38, Ohio St. 24	2015	Alabama 45, Clemson 40
1999	Florida St. 46, Virginia Tech 29	2008	Florida 24, Oklahoma 14	2016	Clemson 35, Alabama 31
2000	Oklahoma 13, Florida St. 2	2009	Alabama 37, Texas 21	2017	Alabama 26, Georgia 23 (OT)
2001	Miami (FL) 37, Nebraska 14	2010	Auburn 22, Oregon 19	2018	Clemson 44, Alabama 16
2002	Ohio St. 31, Miami (FL) 24	2011	Alabama 21, LSU 0	2019	LSU 42, Clemson 25
2003[1]	LSU 21, Oklahoma 14	2012	Alabama 42, Notre Dame 14	2020	Alabama 52, Ohio St. 24
2004[2]	USC 55, Oklahoma 19	2013	Florida St. 34, Auburn 31	2021	Georgia 33, Alabama 18
2005	Texas 41, USC 38	2014	Ohio St. 42, Oregon 20	2022	Georgia 65, TCU 7
2006	Florida 41, Ohio St. 14				

(1) AP named USC No. 1 in its final poll despite its not appearing in the BCS No. 1 vs. No. 2 matchup. (2) The BCS's Presidential Oversight Committee vacated USC's 2004 championship due to rules violations.

National College Football Champions, 1936-1997

Unofficial champion(s), as selected by the AP poll of writers and a separate poll of coaches. Where the polls disagreed, both teams are listed with the AP winner first. The AP poll started in 1936, the coaches poll in 1950.

Year	Champion(s)	Year	Champion(s)	Year	Champion(s)	Year	Champion(s)	Year	Champion(s)
1936	Minnesota	1949	Notre Dame	1962	USC	1974	Oklahoma/USC	1986	Penn St.
1937	Pittsburgh	1950	Oklahoma	1963	Texas	1975	Oklahoma	1987	Miami (FL)
1938	Texas Christian	1951	Tennessee	1964	Alabama	1976	Pittsburgh	1988	Notre Dame
1939	Texas A&M	1952	Michigan St.	1965	Alabama/Mich. St.	1977	Notre Dame	1989	Miami (FL)
1940	Minnesota	1953	Maryland	1966	Notre Dame	1978	Alabama/USC	1990	Colorado/GA Tech
1941	Minnesota	1954	Ohio St./UCLA	1967	USC	1979	Alabama	1991	Miami (FL)/Wash.
1942	Ohio St.	1955	Oklahoma	1968	Ohio St.	1980	Georgia	1992	Alabama
1943	Notre Dame	1956	Oklahoma	1969	Texas	1981	Clemson	1993	Florida St.
1944	Army	1957	Auburn/Ohio St.	1970	Nebraska/Texas	1982	Penn St.	1994	Nebraska
1945	Army	1958	LSU	1971	Nebraska	1983	Miami (FL)	1995	Nebraska
1946	Notre Dame	1959	Syracuse	1972	USC	1984	Brigham Young	1996	Florida
1947	Notre Dame	1960	Minnesota	1973	Notre Dame/	1985	Oklahoma	1997	Mich./Nebraska
1948	Michigan	1961	Alabama		Alabama				

Results of Major Bowl Games

Date indicates year the game was played; bowl games are generally played in late Dec. or early Jan. CFP = College Football Playoff semifinal game.

Rose Bowl Results, 1902-2023

1902	(Jan.) Michigan 49, Stanford 0	1928	Stanford 7, Pittsburgh 6	1941	Stanford 21, Nebraska 13
1916	Washington St. 14, Brown 0	1929	Georgia Tech 8, California 7	1942	Oregon St. 20, Duke 16
1917	Oregon 14, Pennsylvania 0	1930	USC 47, Pittsburgh 14	1943	Georgia 9, UCLA 0
1918-19	Service teams	1931	Alabama 24, Washington St. 0	1944	USC 29, Washington 0
1920	Harvard 7, Oregon 6	1932	USC 21, Tulane 12	1945	USC 25, Tennessee 0
1921	California 28, Ohio St. 0	1933	USC 35, Pittsburgh 0	1946	Alabama 34, USC 14
1922	Washington & Jefferson 0, California 0	1934	Columbia 7, Stanford 0	1947	Illinois 45, UCLA 14
		1935	Alabama 29, Stanford 13	1948	Michigan 49, USC 0
1923	USC 14, Penn St. 3	1936	Stanford 7, SMU 0	1949	Northwestern 20, California 14
1924	Navy 14, Washington 14	1937	Pittsburgh 21, Washington 0	1950	Ohio St. 17, California 14
1925	Notre Dame 27, Stanford 10	1938	California 13, Alabama 0	1951	Michigan 14, California 6
1926	Alabama 20, Washington 19	1939	USC 7, Duke 3	1952	Illinois 40, Stanford 7
1927	Alabama 7, Stanford 7	1940	USC 14, Tennessee 0	1953	USC 7, Wisconsin 0

1954 Michigan St. 28, UCLA 20	1978 Washington 27, Michigan 20	2002 Miami (FL) 37, Nebraska 14
1955 Ohio St. 20, USC 7	1979 USC 17, Michigan 10	2003 Oklahoma 34, Washington St. 14
1956 Michigan St. 17, UCLA 14	1980 USC 17, Ohio St. 16	2004 USC 28, Michigan 14
1957 Iowa 35, Oregon St. 19	1981 Michigan 23, Washington 6	2005 Texas 38, Michigan 37
1958 Ohio St. 10, Oregon 7	1982 Washington 28, Iowa 0	2006 Texas 41, USC 38
1959 Iowa 38, California 12	1983 UCLA 24, Michigan 14	2007 USC 32, Michigan 18
1960 Washington 44, Wisconsin 8	1984 UCLA 45, Illinois 9	2008 USC 49, Illinois 17
1961 Washington 17, Minnesota 7	1985 USC 20, Ohio St. 17	2009 USC 38, Penn St. 24
1962 Minnesota 21, UCLA 3	1986 UCLA 45, Iowa 28	2010 Ohio St. 26, Oregon 17
1963 USC 42, Wisconsin 37	1987 Arizona St. 22, Michigan 15	2011 TCU 21, Wisconsin 19
1964 Illinois 17, Washington 7	1988 Michigan St. 20, USC 17	2012 Oregon 45, Wisconsin 38
1965 Michigan 34, Oregon St. 7	1989 Michigan 22, USC 14	2013 Stanford 20, Wisconsin 14
1966 UCLA 14, Michigan St. 12	1990 USC 17, Michigan 10	2014 Michigan St. 24, Stanford 20
1967 Purdue 14, USC 13	1991 Washington 46, Iowa 34	2015 Oregon 59, Florida St. 20 (CFP)
1968 USC 14, Indiana 3	1992 Washington 34, Michigan 14	2016 Stanford 45, Iowa 16
1969 Ohio St. 27, USC 16	1993 Michigan 38, Washington 31	2017 USC 52, Penn St. 49
1970 USC 10, Michigan 3	1994 Wisconsin 21, UCLA 16	2018 Georgia 54, Oklahoma 48
1971 Stanford 27, Ohio St. 17	1995 Penn St. 38, Oregon 20	(2 OT)(CFP)
1972 Stanford 13, Michigan 12	1996 USC 41, Northwestern 32	
1973 USC 42, Ohio St. 17	1997 Ohio St. 20, Arizona St. 17	2019 Ohio St. 28, Washington 23
1974 Ohio St. 42, USC 21	1998 Michigan 21, Washington St. 16	2020 Oregon 28, Wisconsin 27
1975 USC 18, Ohio St. 17	1999 Wisconsin 38, UCLA 31	2021 Alabama 31, Notre Dame 14 (CFP)
1976 UCLA 23, Ohio St. 10	2000 Wisconsin 17, Stanford 9	2022 Ohio St. 48, Utah 45
1977 USC 14, Michigan 6	2001 Washington 34, Purdue 24	2023 Penn St. 35, Utah 21

Orange Bowl Results, 1935-2022

1935 (Jan.) Bucknell 26, Miami (FL) 0	1966 Alabama 39, Nebraska 28	1996 (Dec.) Nebraska 41, Virginia Tech 21
1936 Catholic 20, Mississippi 19	1967 Florida 27, Georgia Tech 12	1998 (Jan.) Nebraska 42, Tennessee 17
1937 Duquesne 13, Mississippi St. 12	1968 Oklahoma 26, Tennessee 24	1999 Florida 31, Syracuse 10
1938 Auburn 6, Michigan St. 0	1969 Penn St. 15, Kansas 14	2000 Michigan 35, Alabama 34 (OT)
1939 Tennessee 17, Oklahoma 0	1970 Penn St. 10, Missouri 3	2001 Oklahoma 13, Florida St. 2
1940 Georgia Tech 21, Missouri 7	1971 Nebraska 17, LSU 12	2002 Florida 56, Maryland 23
1941 Mississippi St. 14, Georgetown 7	1972 Nebraska 38, Alabama 6	2003 USC 38, Iowa 17
1942 Georgia 40, TCU 26	1973 Nebraska 40, Notre Dame 6	2004 Miami (FL) 16, Florida St. 14
1943 Alabama 37, Boston College 21	1974 Penn St. 16, LSU 9	2005 USC 55, Oklahoma 19
1944 LSU 19, Texas A&M 14	1975 Notre Dame 13, Alabama 11	2006 Penn St. 26, Florida St. 23 (3 OT)
1945 Tulsa 26, Georgia Tech 12	1976 Oklahoma 14, Michigan 6	2007 Louisville 24, Wake Forest 13
1946 Miami (FL) 13, Holy Cross 6	1977 Ohio St. 27, Colorado 10	2008 Kansas 24, Virginia Tech 21
1947 Rice 8, Tennessee 0	1978 Arkansas 31, Oklahoma 6	2009 Virginia Tech 20, Cincinnati 7
1948 Georgia Tech 20, Kansas 14	1979 Oklahoma 31, Nebraska 24	2010 Iowa 24, Georgia Tech 14
1949 Texas 41, Georgia 28	1980 Oklahoma 24, Florida St. 7	2011 Stanford 40, Virginia Tech 12
1950 Santa Clara 21, Kentucky 13	1981 Oklahoma 18, Florida St. 17	2012 West Virginia 70, Clemson 33
1951 Clemson 15, Miami (FL) 14	1982 Clemson 22, Nebraska 15	2013 Florida St. 31, Northern Illinois 10
1952 Georgia Tech 17, Baylor 14	1983 Nebraska 21, LSU 20	2014 Clemson 40, Ohio St. 35
1953 Alabama 61, Syracuse 6	1984 Miami (FL) 31, Nebraska 30	2014 (Dec.) Georgia Tech 49,
1954 Oklahoma 7, Maryland 0	1985 Washington 28, Oklahoma 17	Mississippi St. 34
1955 Duke 34, Nebraska 7	1986 Oklahoma 25, Penn St. 10	2015 Clemson 37, Oklahoma 17 (CFP)
1956 Oklahoma 20, Maryland 6	1987 Oklahoma 42, Arkansas 8	2016 Florida St. 33, Michigan 32
1957 Colorado 27, Clemson 21	1988 Miami (FL) 20, Oklahoma 14	2017 Wisconsin 34, Miami (FL) 24
1958 Oklahoma 48, Duke 21	1989 Miami (FL) 23, Nebraska 3	2018 Alabama 45, Oklahoma 34 (CFP)
1959 Oklahoma 21, Syracuse 6	1990 Notre Dame 21, Colorado 6	2019 Florida 36, Virginia 28
1960 Georgia 14, Missouri 0	1991 Colorado 10, Notre Dame 9	2021 (Jan.) Texas A&M 41,
1961 Missouri 21, Navy 14	1992 Miami (FL) 22, Nebraska 0	North Carolina 27
1962 LSU 25, Colorado 7	1993 Florida St. 27, Nebraska 14	2021 (Dec.) Georgia 34, Michigan 11
1963 Alabama 17, Oklahoma 0	1994 Florida St. 18, Nebraska 16	(CFP)
1964 Nebraska 13, Auburn 7	1995 Nebraska 24, Miami (FL) 17	2022 Tennessee 31, Clemson 14
1965 Texas 21, Alabama 17	1996 Florida St. 31, Notre Dame 26	

Sugar Bowl Results, 1935-2022

1935 (Jan.) Tulane 20, Temple 14	1964 Alabama 12, Mississippi 7	1994 Florida 41, West Virginia 7
1936 TCU 3, LSU 2	1965 LSU 13, Syracuse 10	1995 Florida St. 23, Florida 17
1937 Santa Clara 21, LSU 14	1966 Missouri 20, Florida 18	1995 (Dec.) Virginia Tech 28, Texas 10
1938 Santa Clara 6, LSU 0	1967 Alabama 34, Nebraska 7	1997 (Jan.) Florida 52, Florida St. 20
1939 TCU 15, Carnegie Tech 7	1968 LSU 20, Wyoming 13	1998 Florida St. 31, Ohio St. 14
1940 Texas A&M 14, Tulane 13	1969 Arkansas 16, Georgia 2	1999 Ohio St. 24, Texas A&M 14
1941 Boston College 19, Tennessee 13	1970 Mississippi 27, Arkansas 22	2000 Florida St. 46, Virginia Tech 29
1942 Fordham 2, Missouri 0	1971 Tennessee 34, Air Force 13	2001 Miami (FL) 37, Florida 20
1943 Tennessee 14, Tulsa 7	1972 Oklahoma 40, Auburn 22	2002 LSU 47, Illinois 34
1944 Georgia Tech 20, Tulsa 18	1972 (Dec.) Oklahoma 14, Penn St. 0	2003 Georgia 26, Florida St. 13
1945 Duke 29, Alabama 26	1973 Notre Dame 24, Alabama 23	2004 LSU 21, Oklahoma 14
1946 Oklahoma A&M 33,	1974 Nebraska 13, Florida 10	2005 Auburn 16, Virginia Tech 13
St. Mary's (CA) 13	1975 Alabama 13, Penn St. 6	2006 West Virginia 38, Georgia 35
1947 Georgia 20, N. Carolina 10	1977 (Jan.) Pittsburgh 27, Georgia 3	2007 LSU 41, Notre Dame 14
1948 Texas 27, Alabama 7	1978 Alabama 35, Ohio St. 6	2008 Georgia 41, Hawaii 10
1949 Oklahoma 14, N. Carolina 6	1979 Alabama 14, Penn St. 7	2009 Utah 31, Alabama 17
1950 Oklahoma 35, LSU 0	1980 Alabama 24, Arkansas 9	2010 Florida 51, Cincinnati 24
1951 Kentucky 13, Oklahoma 7	1981 Georgia 17, Notre Dame 10	2011 Ohio St. 31, Arkansas 26
1952 Maryland 28, Tennessee 13	1982 Pittsburgh 24, Georgia 20	2012 Michigan 23, Virginia Tech 20
1953 Georgia Tech 24, Mississippi 7	1983 Penn St. 27, Georgia 23	2013 Louisville 33, Florida 23
1954 Georgia Tech 42, West Virginia 19	1984 Auburn 9, Michigan 7	2014 Oklahoma 45, Alabama 31
1955 Navy 21, Mississippi 0	1985 Nebraska 28, LSU 10	2015 Ohio St. 42, Alabama 35 (CFP)
1956 Georgia Tech 7, Pittsburgh 0	1986 Tennessee 35, Miami (FL) 7	2016 Mississippi 48, Oklahoma St. 20
1957 Baylor 13, Tennessee 7	1987 Nebraska 30, LSU 15	2017 Oklahoma 35, Auburn 19
1958 Mississippi 39, Texas 7	1988 Syracuse 16, Auburn 16	2018 Alabama 24, Clemson 6 (CFP)
1959 LSU 7, Clemson 0	1989 Florida St. 13, Auburn 7	2019 Texas 28, Georgia 21
1960 Mississippi 21, LSU 0	1990 Miami (FL) 33, Alabama 25	2020 Georgia 26, Baylor 14
1961 Mississippi 14, Rice 6	1991 Tennessee 23, Virginia 22	2021 Ohio St. 49, Clemson 28 (CFP)
1962 Alabama 10, Arkansas 3	1992 Notre Dame 39, Florida 28	2022 (Jan.) Baylor 21, Mississippi 7
1963 Mississippi 17, Arkansas 13	1993 Alabama 34, Miami (FL) 13	2022 (Dec.) Alabama 45, Kansas St. 20

Cotton Bowl Results, 1937-2023

1937	(Jan.) TCU 16, Marquette 6	1966	(Dec.) Georgia 24, SMU 9	1997	Brigham Young 19, Kansas St. 15
1938	Rice 28, Colorado 14	1968	(Jan.) Texas A&M 20, Alabama 16	1998	UCLA 29, Texas A&M 23
1939	St. Mary's 20, Texas Tech 13	1969	Texas 36, Tennessee 13	1999	Texas 38, Mississippi St. 11
1940	Clemson 6, Boston College 3	1970	Texas 21, Notre Dame 17	2000	Arkansas 27, Texas 6
1941	Texas A&M 13, Fordham 12	1971	Notre Dame 24, Texas 11	2001	Kansas St. 35, Tennessee 21
1942	Alabama 29, Texas A&M 21	1972	Penn St. 30, Texas 6	2002	Oklahoma 10, Arkansas 3
1943	Texas 14, Georgia Tech 7	1973	Texas 17, Alabama 13	2003	Texas 35, LSU 20
1944	Randolph Field 7, Texas 7	1974	Nebraska 19, Texas 3	2004	Mississippi 31, Oklahoma St. 28
1945	Oklahoma A&M 34, TCU 0	1975	Penn St. 41, Baylor 20	2005	Tennessee 38, Texas A&M 7
1946	Texas 40, Missouri 27	1976	Arkansas 31, Georgia 10	2006	Alabama 13, Texas Tech 10
1947	Arkansas 0, LSU 0	1977	Houston 30, Maryland 21	2007	Auburn 17, Nebraska 14
1948	SMU 13, Penn St. 13	1978	Notre Dame 38, Texas 10	2008	Missouri 38, Arkansas 7
1949	SMU 21, Oregon 13	1979	Notre Dame 35, Houston 34	2009	Mississippi 47, Texas Tech 34
1950	Rice 27, N. Carolina 13	1980	Houston 17, Nebraska 14	2010	Mississippi 21, Oklahoma St. 7
1951	Tennessee 20, Texas 14	1981	Alabama 30, Baylor 2	2011	LSU 41, Texas A&M 24
1952	Kentucky 20, TCU 7	1982	Texas 14, Alabama 12	2012	Arkansas 29, Kansas St. 16
1953	Texas 16, Tennessee 0	1983	SMU 7, Pittsburgh 3	2013	Texas A&M 41, Oklahoma 13
1954	Rice 28, Alabama 6	1984	Georgia 10, Texas 9	2014	Missouri 41, Oklahoma St. 31
1955	Georgia Tech 14, Arkansas 6	1985	Boston College 45, Houston 28	2015	Michigan St. 42, Baylor 41
1956	Mississippi 14, TCU 13	1986	Texas A&M 36, Auburn 16	2015	(Dec.) Alabama 38, Michigan
1957	TCU 28, Syracuse 27	1987	Ohio St. 28, Texas A&M 12		St. 0 (CFP)
1958	Navy 20, Rice 7	1988	Texas A&M 35, Notre Dame 10	2017	(Jan.) Wisconsin 24,
1959	TCU 0, Air Force 0	1989	UCLA 17, Arkansas 3		W. Michigan 16
1960	Syracuse 23, Texas 14	1990	Tennessee 31, Arkansas 27	2017	(Dec.) Ohio St. 24, USC 7
1961	Duke 7, Arkansas 6	1991	Miami (FL) 46, Texas 3	2018	Clemson 30, Notre Dame 3 (CFP)
1962	Texas 12, Mississippi 7	1992	Florida St. 10, Texas A&M 2	2019	Penn St. 53, Memphis 39
1963	LSU 13, Texas 0	1993	Notre Dame 28, Texas A&M 3	2020	Oklahoma 55, Florida 20
1964	Texas 28, Navy 6	1994	Notre Dame 24, Texas A&M 21	2021	Alabama 27, Cincinnati 6 (CFP)
1965	Arkansas 10, Nebraska 7	1995	USC 55, Texas Tech 14	2023	(Jan.) Tulane 46, USC 45
1966	LSU 14, Arkansas 7	1996	Colorado 38, Oregon 6		

Peach Bowl Results, 1968-2022

1968	(Dec.) LSU 31, Florida St. 27	1986	Virginia Tech 25,	2004	(Dec.) Miami (FL) 27, Florida 10
1969	West Virginia 14, S. Carolina 3		N. Carolina St. 24	2005	LSU 40, Miami (FL) 3
1970	Arizona St. 48, N. Carolina 26	1988	(Jan.) Tennessee 27, Indiana 22	2006	Georgia 31, Virginia Tech 24
1971	Mississippi 41, Georgia Tech 18	1988	(Dec.) N. Carolina St. 28, Iowa 23	2007	Auburn 23, Clemson 20 (OT)
1972	N. Carolina St. 49,	1989	Syracuse 19, Georgia 18	2008	LSU 38, Georgia Tech 3
	West Virginia 13	1990	Auburn 27, Indiana 23	2009	Virginia Tech 37, Tennessee 14
1973	Georgia 17, Maryland 16	1992	(Jan.) E. Carolina 37, N. Carolina	2010	Florida St. 26, S. Carolina 17
1974	Vanderbilt 6, Texas Tech 6		St. 34	2011	Auburn 43, Virginia 24
1975	West Virginia 13,	1993	N. Carolina 21, Mississippi St. 17	2012	Clemson 25, LSU 24
	N. Carolina St. 10	1993	(Dec.) Clemson 14, Kentucky 13	2013	Texas A&M 52, Duke 48
1976	Kentucky 21, N. Carolina 0	1995	(Jan.) N. Carolina St. 28,	2014	TCU 42, Mississippi 3
1977	N. Carolina St. 24, Iowa St. 14		Mississippi St. 24	2015	Houston 38, Florida St. 24
1978	Purdue 41, Georgia Tech 21	1995	(Dec.) Virginia 34, Georgia 27	2016	Alabama 24, Washington 7 (CFP)
1979	Baylor 24, Clemson 18	1996	LSU 10, Clemson 7	2018	(Jan.) Central Florida 34,
1981	(Jan.) Miami (FL) 20, Virginia	1998	(Jan.) Auburn 21, Clemson 17		Auburn 27
	Tech 10	1998	(Dec.) Georgia 35, Virginia 33	2018	(Dec.) Florida 41, Michigan 15
1981	(Dec.) West Virginia 26, Florida 6	1999	Mississippi St. 17, Clemson 7	2019	LSU 63, Oklahoma 28 (CFP)
1982	Iowa 28, Tennessee 22	2000	LSU 28, Georgia Tech 14	2021	(Jan.) Georgia 24, Cincinnati 21
1983	Florida St. 28, N. Carolina 3	2001	N. Carolina 16, Auburn 10	2021	(Dec.) Michigan St. 31,
1984	Virginia 27, Purdue 22	2002	Maryland 30, Tennessee 3		Pittsburgh 21
1985	Army 31, Illinois 29	2004	(Jan.) Clemson 27, Tennessee 14	2022	Georgia 42, Ohio St. 41 (CFP)

Fiesta Bowl Results, 1971-2022

1971	(Dec.) Arizona St. 45,	1990	Florida St. 41, Nebraska 17	2008	West Virginia 48, Oklahoma 28
	Florida St. 38	1991	Louisville 34, Alabama 7	2009	Texas 24, Ohio St. 21
1972	Arizona St. 49, Missouri 35	1992	Penn St. 42, Tennessee 17	2010	Boise St. 17, TCU 10
1973	Arizona St. 28, Pittsburgh 7	1993	Syracuse 26, Colorado 22	2011	Oklahoma 48, Connecticut 20
1974	Oklahoma St. 16,	1994	Arizona 29, Miami (FL) 0	2012	Oklahoma St. 41, Stanford 38 (OT)
	Brigham Young 6	1995	Colorado 41, Notre Dame 24	2013	Oregon 35, Kansas St. 17
1975	Arizona St. 17, Nebraska 14	1996	Nebraska 62, Florida 24	2014	UCF 52, Baylor 42
1976	Oklahoma 41, Wyoming 7	1997	Penn St. 38, Texas 15	2014	(Dec.) Boise St. 38, Arizona 30
1977	Penn St. 42, Arizona St. 30	1997	(Dec.) Kansas St. 35,	2016	(Jan.) Ohio St. 44, Notre Dame 28
1978	UCLA 10, Arkansas 10		Syracuse 18	2016	(Dec.) Clemson 31, Ohio St. 0
1979	Pittsburgh 16, Arizona 10	1999	(Jan.) Tennessee 23,		(CFP)
1980	Penn St. 31, Ohio St. 19		Florida St. 16	2017	Penn St. 35, Washington 28
1982	(Jan.) Penn St. 26, USC 10	2000	Nebraska 31, Tennessee 21	2019	(Jan.) LSU 40, UCF 32
1983	Arizona St. 32, Oklahoma 21	2001	Oregon St. 41, Notre Dame 9	2019	(Dec.) Clemson 29, Ohio St. 23
1984	Ohio St. 28, Pittsburgh 23	2002	Oregon 38, Colorado 16		(CFP)
1985	UCLA 39, Miami (FL) 37	2003	Ohio St. 31, Miami (FL) 24 (2 OT)	2021	Iowa St. 34, Oregon 17
1986	Michigan 27, Nebraska 23	2004	Ohio St. 35, Kansas St. 28	2022	(Jan.) Oklahoma St. 37, Notre
1987	Penn St. 14, Miami (FL) 10	2005	Utah 35, Pittsburgh 7		Dame 35
1988	Florida St. 31, Nebraska 28	2006	Ohio St. 34, Notre Dame 20	2022	(Dec.) TCU 51, Michigan 45
1989	Notre Dame 34, West Virginia 21	2007	Boise St. 43, Oklahoma 42 (OT)		(CFP)

All-Time NCAA Bowl Subdivision (FBS) Statistical Leaders

Career Rushing Yards

Player, team	Yrs	Carries	Yds	Avg
Donnel Pumphrey, San Diego St.	2013-16	1,059	6,405	6.05
Ron Dayne, Wisconsin	1996-99	1,115	6,397	5.74
Ricky Williams, Texas	1995-98	1,011	6,279	6.21
Jonathan Taylor, Wisconsin	2017-19	926	6,174	6.67
Tony Dorsett, Pittsburgh	1973-76	1,074	6,082	5.66
DeAngelo Williams, Memphis	2002-05	969	6,026	6.22
Royce Freeman, Oregon	2014-17	947	5,621	5.94
Charles White, USC	1976-79	1,023	5,598	5.47
Travis Prentice, Miami (OH)	1996-99	1,138	5,596	4.92
Cedric Benson, Texas	2001-04	1,112	5,540	4.98

Career Passing Yards

Player, team	Yrs	Comp/att	Yds
Case Keenum, Houston	2007-11	1,546/2,229	19,217
Timmy Chang, Hawaii	2000-04	1,388/2,436	17,072
Landry Jones, Oklahoma	2009-12	1,388/2,183	16,646
Graham Harrell, Texas Tech	2005-08	1,403/2,010	15,793
Ty Detmer, BYU	1988-91	958/1,530	15,031
Kellen Moore, Boise St.	2008-11	1,157/1,658	14,667
Baker Mayfield, Texas Tech/Oklahoma	'15-'17	1,026/1,497	14,607
Luke Falk, Washington St.	2013-17	1,404/2,055	14,486
Colt Brennan, Hawaii	2005-07	1,115/1,584	14,193
Rakeem Cato, Marshall	2011-14	1,153/1,838	14,079

Career Receiving Yards

Player, team	Yrs	Rec	Yds	Yds/G
Corey Davis, W. Michigan	2013-16	332	5,285	105.7
Trevor Insley, Nevada	1996-99	298	5,005	113.8
Ryan Broyles, Oklahoma	2008-11	349	4,586	95.5
Justin Hardy, E. Carolina	2011-14	387	4,541	92.7
Marcus Harris, Wyoming	1993-96	259	4,518	98.2
James Washington, Oklahoma St.	2014-17	225	4,467	85.9
Rashaun Woods, Oklahoma St.	2000-03	293	4,414	92.0
Ryan Yarborough, Wyoming	1990-93	229	4,357	94.7
Troy Edwards, Louisiana Tech	1996-98	280	4,352	128.0
Aaron Turner, Pacific	1989-92	266	4,345	98.8

Career Rushing Yards/Game (min. 2,500 yds)

Player, team	Yrs	Carries	Yds	Avg/game
Ed Marinaro, Cornell	1969-71	918	4,715	174.6
O.J. Simpson, USC	1967-68	621	3,124	164.4
Herschel Walker, Georgia	1980-82	994	5,259	159.4
Garrett Wolfe, N. Illinois	2004-06	807	5,164	156.5
LeShon Johnson, N. Illinois	1992-93	592	3,314	150.6
Jonathan Taylor, Wisconsin	2017-19	926	6,174	150.6
Ron Dayne, Wisconsin	1996-99	1,115	6,397	148.8
Marshall Faulk, San Diego St.	1991-93	766	4,589	148.0
George Jones, San Diego St.	1995-96	486	2,810	147.9
Tony Dorsett, Pittsburgh	1973-76	1,074	6,082	141.4
Troy Davis, Iowa St.	1994-96	782	4,382	141.4

Note: As of end of 2022 season. Prior to 2002, postseason games were not included in NCAA final football statistics or records. All postseason games were included for the 2002 season and thereafter. Career rushing yards per game rankings do not include active players.

All-Time NCAA Bowl Subdivision (FBS) Team Won-Lost Records

Team	Years	W	L	T	Total games	Pct.
Ohio St.*	133	953	331	53	1,337	0.733
Alabama*	128	953	335	43	1,331	0.732
Michigan	143	989	353	36	1,378	0.731
Notre Dame*	133	938	334	42	1,314	0.730
Boise St.	55	482	181	2	665	0.726
Oklahoma	128	934	338	53	1,325	0.725
Texas	130	936	390	33	1,359	0.701
USC*	129	867	363	54	1,284	0.696
Penn St.	136	920	406	41	1,367	0.688
Nebraska	133	912	417	40	1,369	0.681
Tennessee*	126	856	410	53	1,330	0.669
Florida St.*	76	568	280	17	865	0.666
Georgia	129	868	428	54	1,350	0.663
LSU	129	833	431	47	1,311	0.653
Appalachian St.	93	655	349	29	1,033	0.648
Miami (FL)	97	656	382	19	1,057	0.630
Florida	116	753	438	40	1,231	0.628
Auburn	130	793	464	47	1,304	0.626
Ga. Southern*	59	412	246	10	668	0.624
Clemson	127	789	468	45	1,302	0.623
Washington	133	761	465	50	1,276	0.616
Texas A&M	128	771	498	48	1,317	0.604
Arizona St.	110	635	415	24	1,074	0.602
Virginia Tech	129	765	499	46	1,310	0.602
Michigan St.	126	726	479	44	1,249	0.599
Utah	129	711	477	31	1,219	0.596
Miami (OH)	134	713	481	44	1,238	0.594
West Virginia	130	772	522	45	1,339	0.593
Central Mich.	122	642	443	36	1,121	0.589
Western Ky.	104	607	421	30	1,058	0.588
Fresno St.	101	636	442	27	1,105	0.588
Wisconsin	134	735	512	53	1,300	0.586
UCLA	104	629	441	37	1,107	0.586
BYU	98	611	436	26	1,073	0.582

* = Record adjusted by action of the NCAA Committee on Infractions. **Note:** As of end of 2022 season. Includes records as senior college only. Bowl and playoff games are included, and each tie game is computed as half won and half lost. Teams must have been in Div. I for at least 25 years to qualify. Tiebreaker rule began with 1996 season.

Heisman Trophy Winners, 1935-2022

The Heisman Memorial Trophy is awarded annually to the nation's outstanding college football player by the Downtown Athletic Club.

Year	Winner, school, position	Year	Winner, school, position	Year	Winner, school, position
1935	Jay Berwanger, Chicago, HB	1965	Mike Garrett, USC, HB	1994	Rashaan Salaam, Colorado, RB
1936	Larry Kelley, Yale, E	1966	Steve Spurrier, Florida, QB	1995	Eddie George, Ohio St., RB
1937	Clinton Frank, Yale, HB	1967	Gary Beban, UCLA, QB	1996	Danny Wuerffel, Florida, QB
1938	David O'Brien, Texas Christian, QB	1968	O.J. Simpson, USC, RB	1997	Charles Woodson, Michigan, CB
1939	Nile Kinnick, Iowa, HB	1969	Steve Owens, Oklahoma, RB	1998	Ricky Williams, Texas, RB
1940	Tom Harmon, Michigan, HB	1970	Jim Plunkett, Stanford, QB	1999	Ron Dayne, Wisconsin, RB
1941	Bruce Smith, Minnesota, HB	1971	Pat Sullivan, Auburn, QB	2000	Chris Weinke, Florida St., QB
1942	Frank Sinkwich, Georgia, HB	1972	Johnny Rodgers, Nebraska, RB-WR	2001	Eric Crouch, Nebraska, QB
1943	Angelo Bertelli, Notre Dame, QB	1973	John Cappelletti, Penn St., RB	2002	Carson Palmer, USC, QB
1944	Leslie Horvath, Ohio St., QB	1974	Archie Griffin, Ohio St., RB	2003	Jason White, Oklahoma, QB
1945	Felix Blanchard, Army, FB	1975	Archie Griffin, Ohio St., RB	2004	Matt Leinart, USC, QB
1946	Glenn Davis, Army, HB	1976	Tony Dorsett, Pittsburgh, RB	2005	Reggie Bush, USC, RB[1]
1947	John Lujack, Notre Dame, QB	1977	Earl Campbell, Texas, RB	2006	Troy Smith, Ohio St., QB
1948	Doak Walker, SMU, HB	1978	Billy Sims, Oklahoma, RB	2007	Tim Tebow, Florida, QB
1949	Leon Hart, Notre Dame, E	1979	Charles White, USC, RB	2008	Sam Bradford, Oklahoma, QB
1950	Vic Janowicz, Ohio St., HB	1980	George Rogers, S. Carolina, RB	2009	Mark Ingram, Alabama, RB
1951	Richard Kazmaier, Princeton, HB	1981	Marcus Allen, USC, RB	2010	Cam Newton, Auburn, QB
1952	Billy Vessels, Oklahoma, HB	1982	Herschel Walker, Georgia, RB	2011	Robert Griffin III, Baylor, QB
1953	John Lattner, Notre Dame, HB	1983	Mike Rozier, Nebraska, RB	2012	Johnny Manziel, Texas A&M, QB
1954	Alan Ameche, Wisconsin, FB	1984	Doug Flutie, Boston College, QB	2013	Jameis Winston, Florida St., QB
1955	Howard Cassady, Ohio St., HB	1985	Bo Jackson, Auburn, RB	2014	Marcus Mariota, Oregon, QB
1956	Paul Hornung, Notre Dame, QB	1986	Vinny Testaverde, Miami (FL), QB	2015	Derrick Henry, Alabama, RB
1957	John Crow, Texas A&M, HB	1987	Tim Brown, Notre Dame, WR	2016	Lamar Jackson, Louisville, QB
1958	Pete Dawkins, Army, HB	1988	Barry Sanders, Oklahoma St., RB	2017	Baker Mayfield, Oklahoma, QB
1959	Billy Cannon, LSU, HB	1989	Andre Ware, Houston, QB	2018	Kyler Murray, Oklahoma, QB
1960	Joe Bellino, Navy, HB	1990	Ty Detmer, BYU, QB	2019	Joe Burrow, LSU, QB
1961	Ernest Davis, Syracuse, HB	1991	Desmond Howard, Michigan, WR	2020	DeVonta Smith, Alabama, WR
1962	Terry Baker, Oregon St., QB	1992	Gino Torretta, Miami (FL), QB	2021	Bryce Young, Alabama, QB
1963	Roger Staubach, Navy, QB	1993	Charlie Ward, Florida St., QB	2022	Caleb Williams, USC, QB
1964	John Huarte, Notre Dame, QB				

(1) Bush forfeited the trophy voluntarily Sept. 14, 2010, following revelations of NCAA rules violations while Bush was at USC.

College Football Coach of the Year, 1957-2022

The Coach of the Year has been selected by the American Football Coaches Assn. (AFCA) since 1935 as well as the Football Writers Assn. of America (FWAA) since 1957. When polls disagree, both winners are indicated.

1957 Woody Hayes, Ohio St.	1978 Joe Paterno, Penn St.	2003 Pete Carroll, USC (AFCA);
1958 Paul Dietzel, LSU	1979 Earle Bruce, Ohio St.	Nick Saban, LSU (FWAA)
1959 Ben Schwartzwalder, Syracuse	1980 Vince Dooley, Georgia	2004 Tommy Tuberville, Auburn (AFCA);
1960 Murray Warmath, Minnesota	1981 Danny Ford, Clemson	Urban Meyer, Utah (FWAA)
1961 Paul "Bear" Bryant, Alabama (AFCA);	1982 Joe Paterno, Penn St.	2005 Joe Paterno, Penn St. (AFCA);
Darrell Royal, Texas (FWAA)	1983 Ken Hatfield, Air Force (AFCA);	Charlie Weis, Notre Dame (FWAA)
1962 John McKay, USC	Howard Schnellenberger,	2006 Jim Grobe, Wake Forest (AFCA);
1963 Darrell Royal, Texas	Miami (FL) (FWAA)	Greg Schiano, Rutgers (FWAA)
1964 Ara Parseghian, Notre Dame &	1984 LaVell Edwards, Brigham Young	2007 Mark Mangino, Kansas
Frank Broyles, Arkansas (AFCA);	1985 Fisher De Berry, Air Force	2008 Kyle Whittingham, Utah (AFCA);
Ara Parseghian, Notre Dame (FWAA)	1986 Joe Paterno, Penn St.	Nick Saban, Alabama (FWAA)
1965 Tommy Prothro, UCLA (AFCA);	1987 Dick MacPherson, Syracuse	2009 Gary Patterson, TCU
Duffy Daugherty, Mich. St. (FWAA)	1988 Don Nehlen, W. Virginia (AFCA);	2010 Chip Kelly, Oregon
1966 Tom Cahill, Army	Lou Holtz, Notre Dame (FWAA)	2011 Les Miles, LSU (AFCA);
1967 John Pont, Indiana	1989 Bill McCartney, Colorado	Mike Gundy, Oklahoma St. (FWAA)
1968 Joe Paterno, Penn St. (AFCA);	1990 Bobby Ross, Georgia Tech	2012 Brian Kelly, Notre Dame
Woody Hayes, Ohio St. (FWAA)	1991 Don James, Washington	2013 David Cutcliffe, Duke (AFCA);
1969 Bo Schembechler, Michigan	1992 Gene Stallings, Alabama	Gus Malzahn, Auburn (FWAA)
1970 Charles McClendon, LSU &	1993 Barry Alvarez, Wisconsin (AFCA);	2014 Gary Patterson, TCU
Darrell Royal, Texas (AFCA);	Terry Bowden, Auburn (FWAA)	2015 Dabo Swinney, Clemson (AFCA);
Alex Agase, Northwestern (FWAA)	1994 Tom Osborne, Nebraska (AFCA);	Kirk Ferentz, Iowa (FWAA)
1971 Paul "Bear" Bryant, Alabama (AFCA);	Rich Brooks, Oregon (FWAA)	2016 Mike MacIntyre, Colorado
Bob Devaney, Nebraska (FWAA)	1995 Gary Barnett, Northwestern	2017 Scott Frost, UCF
1972 John McKay, USC	1996 Bruce Snyder, Arizona St.	2018 Mike Leach, Washington St. (AFCA);
1973 Paul "Bear" Bryant, Alabama (AFCA);	1997 Mike Price, Washington St.	Bill Clark, UAB (FWAA)
Johnny Majors, Pittsburgh (FWAA)	1998 Phillip Fulmer, Tennessee	2019 Ed Orgeron, LSU
1974 Grant Teaff, Baylor	1999 Frank Beamer, Virginia Tech	2020 Tom Allen, Indiana (AFCA);
1975 Frank Kush, Arizona St. (AFCA);	2000 Bob Stoops, Oklahoma	Jamey Chadwell, Coastal Carolina
Woody Hayes, Ohio St. (FWAA)	2001 Larry Coker, Miami (FL) &	(FWAA)
1976 Johnny Majors, Pittsburgh	Ralph Friedgen, Maryland (AFCA);	2021 Luke Fickell, Cincinnati
1977 Don James, Washington (AFCA);	Ralph Friedgen, Maryland (FWAA)	2022 Sonny Dykes, TCU
Lou Holtz, Arkansas (FWAA)	2002 Jim Tressel, Ohio St.	

COLLEGE BASKETBALL
2023 NCAA Men's Basketball: UConn Dominates San Diego St.

The Univ. of Connecticut Huskies claimed their fifth NCAA men's basketball title in 25 years Apr. 3, 2023, defeating the San Diego St. Aztecs, 76-59, at NRG Stadium in Houston, TX. Huskies junior Adama Sanogo scored 17 points with 10 rebounds and was named the most outstanding player of the Final Four. The tournament saw an unusual spate of upsets, with 16-seed Fairleigh Dickinson eliminating No. 1-seed Purdue in the first round, and no team seeded higher than No. 4 appearing in the Final Four.

NCAA Men's Basketball Division I Champions, 1939-2023
No tournament was held in 2020 due to the COVID-19 pandemic.

Year	Champion	Final opponent	Score	Most outstanding player	Winning coach	Site
1939	Oregon	Ohio St.	46-33	Jimmy Hull, Ohio St.	Howard Hobson	Evanston, IL
1940	Indiana	Kansas	60-42	Marv Huffman, Indiana	Branch McCracken	Kansas City, MO
1941	Wisconsin	Washington St.	39-34	John Kotz, Wisconsin	Bud Foster	Kansas City, MO
1942	Stanford	Dartmouth	53-38	Howie Dallmar, Stanford	Everett Dean	Kansas City, MO
1943	Wyoming	Georgetown	46-34	Ken Sailors, Wyoming	Everett Shelton	New York, NY
1944	Utah	Dartmouth	42-40[1]	Arnold Ferrin, Utah	Vadal Peterson	New York, NY
1945	Oklahoma St.[2]	NYU	49-45	Bob Kurland, Oklahoma St.	Henry Iba	New York, NY
1946	Oklahoma St.[2]	North Carolina	43-40	Bob Kurland, Oklahoma St.	Henry Iba	New York, NY
1947	Holy Cross	Oklahoma	58-47	George Kaftan, Holy Cross	Alvin Julian	New York, NY
1948	Kentucky	Baylor	58-42	Alex Groza, Kentucky	Adolph Rupp	New York, NY
1949	Kentucky	Oklahoma St.	46-36	Alex Groza, Kentucky	Adolph Rupp	Seattle, WA
1950	CCNY	Bradley	71-68	Irwin Dambrot, CCNY	Nat Holman	New York, NY
1951	Kentucky	Kansas St.	68-58	Bill Spivey, Kentucky	Adolph Rupp	Minneapolis, MN
1952	Kansas	St. John's (NY)	80-63	Clyde Lovellette, Kansas	Forrest Allen	Seattle, WA
1953	Indiana	Kansas	69-68	B. H. Born, Kansas	Branch McCracken	Kansas City, MO
1954	La Salle	Bradley	92-76	Tom Gola, La Salle	Kenneth Loeffler	Kansas City, MO
1955	San Francisco	La Salle	77-63	Bill Russell, San Francisco	Phil Woolpert	Kansas City, MO
1956	San Francisco	Iowa	83-71	Hal Lear, Temple	Phil Woolpert	Evanston, IL
1957	North Carolina	Kansas	54-53[1]	Wilt Chamberlain, Kansas	Frank McGuire	Kansas City, MO
1958	Kentucky	Seattle	84-72	Elgin Baylor, Seattle	Adolph Rupp	Louisville, KY
1959	California	West Virginia	71-70	Jerry West, West Virginia	Pete Newell	Louisville, KY
1960	Ohio St.	California	75-55	Jerry Lucas, Ohio St.	Fred Taylor	San Francisco, CA
1961	Cincinnati	Ohio St.	70-65[1]	Jerry Lucas, Ohio St.	Edwin Jucker	Kansas City, MO
1962	Cincinnati	Ohio St.	71-59	Paul Hogue, Cincinnati	Edwin Jucker	Louisville, KY
1963	Loyola (IL)	Cincinnati	60-58[1]	Art Heyman, Duke	George Ireland	Louisville, KY
1964	UCLA	Duke	98-83	Walt Hazzard, UCLA	John Wooden	Kansas City, MO
1965	UCLA	Michigan	91-80	Bill Bradley, Princeton	John Wooden	Portland, OR
1966	UTEP[3]	Kentucky	72-65	Jerry Chambers, Utah	Don Haskins	College Park, MD
1967	UCLA	Dayton	79-64	Lew Alcindor[4], UCLA	John Wooden	Louisville, KY
1968	UCLA	North Carolina	78-55	Lew Alcindor[4], UCLA	John Wooden	Los Angeles, CA
1969	UCLA	Purdue	92-72	Lew Alcindor[4], UCLA	John Wooden	Louisville, KY
1970	UCLA	Jacksonville	80-69	Sidney Wicks, UCLA	John Wooden	College Park, MD
1971	UCLA	Villanova*	68-62	Howard Porter, Villanova*	John Wooden	Houston, TX
1972	UCLA	Florida St.	81-76	Bill Walton, UCLA	John Wooden	Los Angeles, CA
1973	UCLA	Memphis[5]	87-66	Bill Walton, UCLA	John Wooden	St. Louis, MO
1974	North Carolina St.	Marquette	76-64	David Thompson, NC State	Norm Sloan	Greensboro, NC
1975	UCLA	Kentucky	92-85	Richard Washington, UCLA	John Wooden	San Diego, CA
1976	Indiana	Michigan	86-68	Kent Benson, Indiana	Bob Knight	Philadelphia, PA

Year	Champion	Final opponent	Score	Most outstanding player	Winning coach	Site
1977	Marquette	North Carolina	67-59	Butch Lee, Marquette	Al McGuire	Atlanta, GA
1978	Kentucky	Duke	94-88	Jack Givens, Kentucky	Joe Hall	St. Louis, MO
1979	Michigan St.	Indiana St.	75-64	Magic Johnson, Michigan St.	Jud Heathcote	Salt Lake City, UT
1980	Louisville	UCLA*	59-54	Darrell Griffith, Louisville	Denny Crum	Indianapolis, IN
1981	Indiana	North Carolina	63-50	Isiah Thomas, Indiana	Bob Knight	Philadelphia, PA
1982	North Carolina	Georgetown	63-62	James Worthy, N. Carolina	Dean Smith	New Orleans, LA
1983	North Carolina St.	Houston	54-52	Hakeem Olajuwon, Houston	Jim Valvano	Albuquerque, NM
1984	Georgetown	Houston	84-75	Patrick Ewing, Georgetown	John Thompson	Seattle, WA
1985	Villanova	Georgetown	66-64	Ed Pinckney, Villanova	Rollie Massimino	Lexington, KY
1986	Louisville	Duke	72-69	Pervis Ellison, Louisville	Denny Crum	Dallas, TX
1987	Indiana	Syracuse	74-73	Keith Smart, Indiana	Bob Knight	New Orleans, LA
1988	Kansas	Oklahoma	83-79	Danny Manning, Kansas	Larry Brown	Kansas City, MO
1989	Michigan	Seton Hall	80-79[1]	Glen Rice, Michigan	Steve Fisher	Seattle, WA
1990	UNLV	Duke	103-73	Anderson Hunt, UNLV	Jerry Tarkanian	Denver, CO
1991	Duke	Kansas	72-65	Christian Laettner, Duke	Mike Krzyzewski	Indianapolis, IN
1992	Duke	Michigan	71-51	Bobby Hurley, Duke	Mike Krzyzewski	Minneapolis, MN
1993	North Carolina	Michigan	77-71	Donald Williams, N. Carolina	Dean Smith	New Orleans, LA
1994	Arkansas	Duke	76-72	Corliss Williamson, Arkansas	Nolan Richardson	Charlotte, NC
1995	UCLA	Arkansas	89-78	Ed O'Bannon, UCLA	Jim Harrick	Seattle, WA
1996	Kentucky	Syracuse	76-67	Tony Delk, Kentucky	Rick Pitino	E. Rutherford, NJ
1997	Arizona	Kentucky	84-79[1]	Miles Simon, Arizona	Lute Olson	Indianapolis, IN
1998	Kentucky	Utah	78-69	Jeff Sheppard, Kentucky	Tubby Smith	San Antonio, TX
1999	Connecticut	Duke	77-74	Richard Hamilton, Connecticut	Jim Calhoun	St. Petersburg, FL
2000	Michigan St.	Florida	89-76	Mateen Cleaves, Michigan St.	Tom Izzo	Indianapolis, IN
2001	Duke	Arizona	82-72	Shane Battier, Duke	Mike Krzyzewski	Minneapolis, MN
2002	Maryland	Indiana	64-52	Juan Dixon, Maryland	Gary Williams	Atlanta, GA
2003	Syracuse	Kansas	81-78	Carmelo Anthony, Syracuse	Jim Boeheim	New Orleans, LA
2004	Connecticut	Georgia Tech	82-73	Emeka Okafor, Connecticut	Jim Calhoun	San Antonio, TX
2005	North Carolina	Illinois	75-70	Sean May, N. Carolina	Roy Williams	St. Louis, MO
2006	Florida	UCLA	73-57	Joakim Noah, Florida	Billy Donovan	Indianapolis, IN
2007	Florida	Ohio St.	84-75	Corey Brewer, Florida	Billy Donovan	Atlanta, GA
2008	Kansas	Memphis	75-68[1]	Mario Chalmers, Kansas	Bill Self	San Antonio, TX
2009	North Carolina	Michigan St.	89-72	Wayne Ellington, N. Carolina	Roy Williams	Detroit, MI
2010	Duke	Butler	61-59	Kyle Singler, Duke	Mike Krzyzewski	Indianapolis, IN
2011	Connecticut	Butler	53-41	Kemba Walker, Connecticut	Jim Calhoun	Houston, TX
2012	Kentucky	Kansas	67-59	Anthony Davis, Kentucky	John Calipari	New Orleans, LA
2013[6]	Louisville	Michigan	82-76	Luke Hancock, Louisville	Rick Pitino	Atlanta, GA
2014	Connecticut	Kentucky	60-54	Shabazz Napier, Connecticut	Kevin Ollie	Arlington, TX
2015	Duke	Wisconsin	68-63	Tyus Jones, Duke	Mike Krzyzewski	Indianapolis, IN
2016	Villanova	North Carolina	77-74	Ryan Arcidiacono, Villanova	Jay Wright	Houston, TX
2017	North Carolina	Gonzaga	71-65	Joel Berry II, N. Carolina	Roy Williams	Glendale, AZ
2018	Villanova	Michigan	79-62	Donte DiVincenzo, Villanova	Jay Wright	San Antonio, TX
2019	Virginia	Texas Tech	85-77[1]	Kyle Guy, Virginia	Tony Bennett	Minneapolis, MN
2021	Baylor	Gonzaga	86-70	Jared Butler, Baylor	Scott Drew	Indianapolis, IN
2022	Kansas	North Carolina	72-69	Ochai Agbaji, Kansas	Bill Self	New Orleans, LA
2023	Connecticut	San Diego St.	76-59	Adama Sanogo, Connecticut	Dan Hurley	Houston, TX

* = Declared ineligible after the tournament. (1) Overtime. (2) Then known as Oklahoma A&M. (3) Then known as Texas Western. (4) Changed name to Kareem Abdul-Jabbar in 1971. (5) Then known as Memphis State. (6) Title vacated by the NCAA Committee on Infractions in 2018.

All-Time Winningest Men's NCAA Division I Basketball Teams

Team	Yrs	Won	Lost	Pct.	Team	Yrs	Won	Lost	Pct.	Team	Yrs	Won	Lost	Pct.
Kentucky	120	2,375	748	0.760	Louisville	109	1,776	987	0.643	UAB	45	913	536	0.630
N. Carolina . .	113	2,343	852	0.733	Notre Dame . .	120	1,950	1,089	0.642	Weber St.	61	1,129	666	0.629
Kansas.	125	2,385	885	0.729	Arkansas. . . .	100	1,783	997	0.641	Missouri St . . .	111	1,743	1,041	0.626
Duke	118	2,273	920	0.712	Illinois	118	1,878	1,052	0.641	Texas	117	1,879	1,126	0.625
UCLA	104	1,986	888	0.691	Connecticut. . .	120	1,800	1,012	0.640	BYU	121	1,869	1,134	0.622
UNLV	65	1,328	614	0.684	Cincinnati . . .	122	1,889	1,064	0.640	Marquette	107	1,713	1,052	0.620
Syracuse . . .	122	1,973	964	0.672	St. John's (NY)	119	1,922	1,085	0.639	Alabama	110	1,767	1,087	0.619
Arizona	118	1,912	977	0.662	Purdue	125	1,895	1,075	0.638	Princeton	122	1,806	1,120	0.617
W. Kentucky . .	109	1,872	973	0.658	Utah	115	1,875	1,067	0.637	NC St.	111	1,805	1,121	0.617
Villanova	103	1,864	973	0.657	Temple	127	1,978	1,135	0.635	West Virginia . .	114	1,846	1,152	0.616
VCU	53	1,051	554	0.655	Indiana	123	1,913	1,102	0.634	Penn	122	1,836	1,151	0.615
Murray St. . . .	98	1,724	934	0.649	Memphis	102	1,653	955	0.634					

Note: Winningest teams by percentage. Minimum 25 years as Div. I program.

National Invitation Tournament Champions, 1938-2023

The National Invitation Tournament (NIT), first played in 1938, is the oldest U.S. basketball tournament. The first National Collegiate Athletic Association (NCAA) national championship tournament was played one year later. In 2005, the NCAA purchased the NIT from the five New York City-area colleges that had run it. No tournament was held in 2020 in response to the COVID-19 outbreak.

Year	Champion	Year	Champion	Year	Champion	Year	Champion	Year	Champion
1938	Temple	1956	Louisville	1973	Virginia Tech	1990	Vanderbilt	2007	West Virginia
1939	Long Island Univ.	1957	Bradley	1974	Purdue	1991	Stanford	2008	Ohio State
1940	Colorado	1958	Xavier (OH)	1975	Princeton	1992	Virginia	2009	Penn State
1941	Long Island Univ.	1959	St. John's (NY)	1976	Kentucky	1993	Minnesota	2010	Dayton
1942	West Virginia	1960	Bradley	1977	St. Bonaventure	1994	Villanova	2011	Wichita State
1943	St. John's (NY)	1961	Providence	1978	Texas	1995	Virginia Tech	2012	Stanford
1944	St. John's (NY)	1962	Dayton	1979	Indiana	1996	Nebraska	2013	Baylor
1945	DePaul	1963	Providence	1980	Virginia	1997	Michigan	2014	Minnesota
1946	Kentucky	1964	Bradley	1981	Tulsa	1998	Minnesota	2015	Stanford
1947	Utah	1965	St. John's (NY)	1982	Bradley	1999	California	2016	George Washington
1948	St. Louis	1966	Brigham Young	1983	Fresno State	2000	Wake Forest		
1949	San Francisco	1967	Southern Illinois	1984	Michigan	2001	Tulsa	2017	TCU
1950	CCNY	1968	Dayton	1985	UCLA	2002	Memphis	2018	Penn State
1951	Brigham Young	1969	Temple	1986	Ohio State	2003	St. John's (NY)	2019	Texas
1952	La Salle	1970	Marquette	1987	Southern Miss	2004	Michigan	2021	Memphis
1953	Seton Hall	1971	North Carolina	1988	Connecticut	2005	South Carolina	2022	Xavier
1954	Holy Cross	1972	Maryland	1989	St. John's (NY)	2006	South Carolina	2023	North Texas
1955	Duquesne								

2023 Men's NCAA Basketball Tournament

SOUTH

(1) Alabama 96
(16) TX A&M-Corpus Christi 75 — Alabama 73
(8) Maryland 67
(9) West Virginia 65 — Maryland 51
Alabama 64
(5) San Diego St. 63
(12) Coll. of Charleston 57 — San Diego St. 75
(4) Virginia 67
(13) Furman 68 — Furman 52
San Diego St. 71
San Diego St. 57
(6) Creighton 72
(11) NC State 63 — Creighton 85
(3) Baylor 74
(14) UC Santa Barbara 56 — Baylor 76
Creighton 86
San Diego St. 72
(7) Missouri 76
(10) Utah St. 65 — Missouri 63
(2) Arizona 55
(15) Princeton 59 — Princeton 78
Princeton 75
Creighton 56

EAST

(1) Purdue 58
(16) Fairleigh Dickinson 63 — Fairleigh Dickinson 70
(8) Memphis 65
(9) Florida Atlantic 66 — Florida Atlantic 78
Florida Atlantic 62
(5) Duke 74
(12) Oral Roberts 51 — Duke 52
(4) Tennessee 58
(13) Louisiana 55 — Tennessee 65
Tennessee 55
Florida Atlantic 79
(6) Kentucky 61
(11) Providence 53 — Kentucky 69
(3) Kansas St. 77
(14) Montana St. 65 — Kansas St. 75
Kansas St. 98 (OT)
Florida Atlantic 71
(7) Michigan St. 72
(10) USC 62 — Michigan St. 69
(2) Marquette 78
(15) Vermont 61 — Marquette 60
Michigan St. 93
Kansas St. 76

San Diego St. 59
Connecticut 76

MIDWEST

(1) Houston 63
(16) N. Kentucky 52 — Houston 81
(8) Iowa 75
(9) Auburn 83 — Auburn 64
Houston 75
(5) Miami (FL) 63
(12) Drake 56 — Miami (FL) 85
(4) Indiana 71
(13) Kent St. 60 — Indiana 69
Miami (FL) 89
Miami (FL) 88
(6) Iowa St. 41
(11) Pittsburgh 59 — Pittsburgh 73
(3) Xavier 72
(14) Kennesaw St. 67 — Xavier 84
Xavier 71
Miami (FL) 59
(7) Texas A&M 59
(10) Penn St. 76 — Penn St. 66
(2) Texas 81
(15) Colgate 61 — Texas 71
Texas 83
Texas 81

WEST

(1) Kansas 96
(16) Howard 68 — Kansas 71
(8) Arkansas 73
(9) Illinois 63 — Arkansas 72
Arkansas 65
(5) St. Mary's 63
(12) Virginia Commonwealth 51 — St. Mary's 55
(4) Connecticut 87
(13) Iona 63 — Connecticut 70
Connecticut 88
Connecticut 82
(6) TCU 72
(11) Arizona St. 70 — TCU 81
(3) Gonzaga 82
(14) Grand Canyon 70 — Gonzaga 84
Gonzaga 79
Connecticut 72
(7) Northwestern 75
(10) Boise St. 67 — Northwestern 63
(2) UCLA 86
(15) UNC Asheville 53 — UCLA 68
UCLA 76
Gonzaga 54

NCAA Men's Basketball Division I All-Time Leaders

Season points

Player, school (season)	G	FG	3-FG	FT	PTS
Pete Maravich, LSU (1970)	31	522	NA	337	1,381
Elvin Hayes, Houston (1968)	33	519	NA	176	1,214
Frank Selvy, Furman (1954)	29	427	NA	355	1,209
Pete Maravich, LSU (1969)	26	433	NA	282	1,148
Pete Maravich, LSU (1968)	26	432	NA	274	1,138
Bo Kimble, Loyola Marymount (1990)	32	404	92	231	1,131
Hersey Hawkins, Bradley (1988)	31	377	87	284	1,125
Austin Carr, Notre Dame (1970)	29	444	NA	218	1,106
Austin Carr, Notre Dame (1971)	29	430	NA	241	1,101
Otis Birdsong, Houston (1977)	36	452	NA	186	1,090

Career points

Player, school (seasons)	G	FG	3-FG	FT	PTS
Pete Maravich, LSU (1968-70)	83	1,387	NA	893	3,667
Antoine Davis, Detroit Mercy (2018-23)	144	1,219	588	638	3,664
Freeman Williams, Portland St. (1975-78)	106	1,369	NA	511	3,249
Chris Clemons, Campbell (2016-19)	130	1,024	444	733	3,225
Lionel Simmons, La Salle (1987-90)	131	1,244	56	673	3,217
Alphonso Ford, Mississippi Valley St. (1990-93)	109	1,121	333	590	3,165
Doug McDermott, Creighton (2011-14)	145	1,141	274	594	3,150
Mike Daum, South Dakota St. (2016-19)	137	1,005	271	786	3,067
Harry Kelly, Texas Southern (1980-83)	110	1,234	NA	598	3,066
Keydren Clark, St. Peter's (2003-06)	118	967	435	689	3,058

NA = Not available.

Season points per game

Player, school (season)	G	FG	FT	PTS	PPG
Pete Maravich, LSU (1970)	31	522	337	1,381	44.5
Pete Maravich, LSU (1969)	26	433	282	1,148	44.2
Pete Maravich, LSU (1968)	26	432	274	1,138	43.8
Frank Selvy, Furman (1954)	29	427	355	1,209	41.7
Johnny Neumann, Mississippi (1971)	23	366	191	923	40.1
Freeman Williams, Portland St. (1977)	26	417	176	1,010	38.8
Billy McGill, Utah (1962)	26	394	221	1,009	38.8
Calvin Murphy, Niagara (1968)	24	337	242	916	38.2
Austin Carr, Notre Dame (1970)	29	444	218	1,106	38.1
Austin Carr, Notre Dame (1971)	29	430	241	1,101	38.0

Career points per game

Player, school (seasons)	G	FG	FT	PTS	PPG
Pete Maravich, LSU (1968-70)	83	1,387	893	3,667	44.2
Austin Carr, Notre Dame (1969-71)	74	1,017	526	2,560	34.6
Oscar Robertson, Cincinnati (1958-60)	88	1,052	869	2,973	33.8
Calvin Murphy, Niagara (1968-70)	77	947	654	2,548	33.1
Bo Lamar, La.-Lafayette (1972-73)	57	768	326	1,862	32.7
Frank Selvy, Furman (1952-54)	78	922	694	2,538	32.5
Rick Mount, Purdue (1968-70)	72	910	503	2,323	32.3
Darrell Floyd, Furman (1954-56)	71	868	545	2,281	32.1
Nick Werkman, Seton Hall (1962-64)	71	812	649	2,273	32.0
Willie Humes, Idaho St. (1970-71)	48	565	380	1,510	31.5

John R. Wooden Award Winners, 1977-2023

Awarded to the nation's outstanding men's college basketball player by the Los Angeles Athletic Club since 1977; awarded under the same name to women since 2004.

Year	Player, school
1977	Marques Johnson, UCLA
1978	Phil Ford, North Carolina
1979	Larry Bird, Indiana State
1980	Darrell Griffith, Louisville
1981	Danny Ainge, Brigham Young
1982	Ralph Sampson, Virginia
1983	Ralph Sampson, Virginia
1984	Michael Jordan, North Carolina
1985	Chris Mullin, St. John's (NY)
1986	Walter Berry, St. John's (NY)
1987	David Robinson, Navy
1988	Danny Manning, Kansas
1989	Sean Elliott, Arizona
1990	Lionel Simmons, La Salle
1991	Larry Johnson, UNLV
1992	Christian Laettner, Duke
1993	Calbert Cheaney, Indiana
1994	Glenn Robinson, Purdue
1995	Ed O'Bannon, UCLA
1996	Marcus Camby, Massachusetts
1997	Tim Duncan, Wake Forest
1998	Antawn Jamison, North Carolina
1999	Elton Brand, Duke
2000	Kenyon Martin, Cincinnati
2001	Shane Battier, Duke
2002	Jay Williams, Duke
2003	T. J. Ford, Texas
2004	(M) Jameer Nelson, St. Joseph's
	(W) Alana Beard, Duke
2005	(M) Andrew Bogut, Utah
	(W) Seimone Augustus, LSU
2006	(M) J. J. Redick, Duke
	(W) Seimone Augustus, LSU
2007	(M) Kevin Durant, Texas
	(W) Candace Parker, Tennessee
2008	(M) Tyler Hansbrough, N. Carolina
	(W) Candace Parker, Tennessee
2009	(M) Blake Griffin, Oklahoma
	(W) Maya Moore, Connecticut
2010	(M) Evan Turner, Ohio State
	(W) Tina Charles, Connecticut
2011	(M) Jimmer Fredette, Brigham Young
	(W) Maya Moore, Connecticut
2012	(M) Anthony Davis, Kentucky
	(W) Brittney Griner, Baylor
2013	(M) Trey Burke, Michigan
	(W) Brittney Griner, Baylor
2014	(M) Doug McDermott, Creighton
	(W) Chiney Ogwumike, Stanford
2015	(M) Frank Kaminsky, Wisconsin
	(W) Breanna Stewart, Connecticut
2016	(M) Buddy Hield, Oklahoma
	(W) Breanna Stewart, Connecticut
2017	(M) Frank Mason III, Kansas
	(W) Kelsey Plum, Washington
2018	(M) Jalen Brunson, Villanova
	(W) A'ja Wilson, South Carolina
2019	(M) Zion Williamson, Duke
	(W) Sabrina Ionescu, Oregon
2020	(M) Obi Toppin, Dayton
	(W) Sabrina Ionescu, Oregon
2021	(M) Luka Garza, Iowa
	(W) Paige Bueckers, Connecticut
2022	(M) Oscar Tshiebwe, Kentucky
	(W) Aliyah Boston, South Carolina
2023	(M) Zach Edey, Purdue
	(W) Caitlin Clark, Iowa

Naismith Coach of the Year, 1987-2023

Year	Men's coach, school	Women's coach, school
1987	Bob Knight, Indiana	Pat Summitt, Tennessee
1988	Larry Brown, Kansas	Leon Barmore, Louisiana Tech
1989	Mike Krzyzewski, Duke	Pat Summitt, Tennessee
1990	Bobby Cremins, Georgia Tech	Tara VanDerveer, Stanford
1991	Randy Ayers, Ohio St.	Debbie Ryan, Virginia
1992	Mike Krzyzewski, Duke	Chris Weller, Maryland
1993	Dean Smith, North Carolina	Vivian Stringer, Iowa
1994	Nolan Richardson, Arkansas	Pat Summitt, Tennessee
1995	Jim Harrick, UCLA	Geno Auriemma, UConn
1996	John Calipari, UMass	Andy Landers, Georgia
1997	Roy Williams, Kansas	Geno Auriemma, UConn
1998	Bill Guthridge, North Carolina	Pat Summitt, Tennessee
1999	Mike Krzyzewski, Duke	Carolyn Peck, Purdue
2000	Mike Montgomery, Stanford	Geno Auriemma, UConn
2001	Rod Barnes, Mississippi	Muffet McGraw, Notre Dame
2002	Ben Howland, Pittsburgh	Geno Auriemma, UConn
2003	Tubby Smith, Kentucky	Gail Goestenkors, Duke
2004	Phil Martelli, St. Joseph's	Pat Summitt, Tennessee
2005	Bruce Weber, Illinois	Pokey Chatman, LSU
2006	Jay Wright, Villanova	Sylvia Hatchell, North Carolina
2007	Tony Bennett, Washington St.	Gail Goestenkors, Duke
2008	John Calipari, Memphis	Geno Auriemma, UConn
2009	Jamie Dixon, Pittsburgh	Geno Auriemma, UConn
2010	Jim Boeheim, Syracuse	Connie Yori, Nebraska
2011	Steve Fisher, San Diego St.	Tara VanDerveer, Stanford
2012	Bill Self, Kansas	Kim Mulkey, Baylor
2013	Jim Larrañaga, Miami (FL)	Muffet McGraw, Notre Dame
2014	Gregg Marshall, Wichita St.	Muffet McGraw, Notre Dame
2015	John Calipari, Kentucky	Courtney Banghart, Princeton
2016	Jay Wright, Villanova	Geno Auriemma, UConn
2017	Mark Few, Gonzaga	Geno Auriemma, UConn
2018	Tony Bennett, Virginia	Vic Schaefer, Mississippi St.
2019	Rick Barnes, Tennessee	Lisa Bluder, Iowa
2020	Anthony Grant, Dayton	Dawn Staley, South Carolina
2021	Mark Few, Gonzaga	Tara VanDerveer, Stanford
2022	Ed Cooley, Providence	Dawn Staley, South Carolina
2023	Jerome Tang, Kansas St.	Dawn Staley, South Carolina

2023 Women's NCAA Basketball Tournament

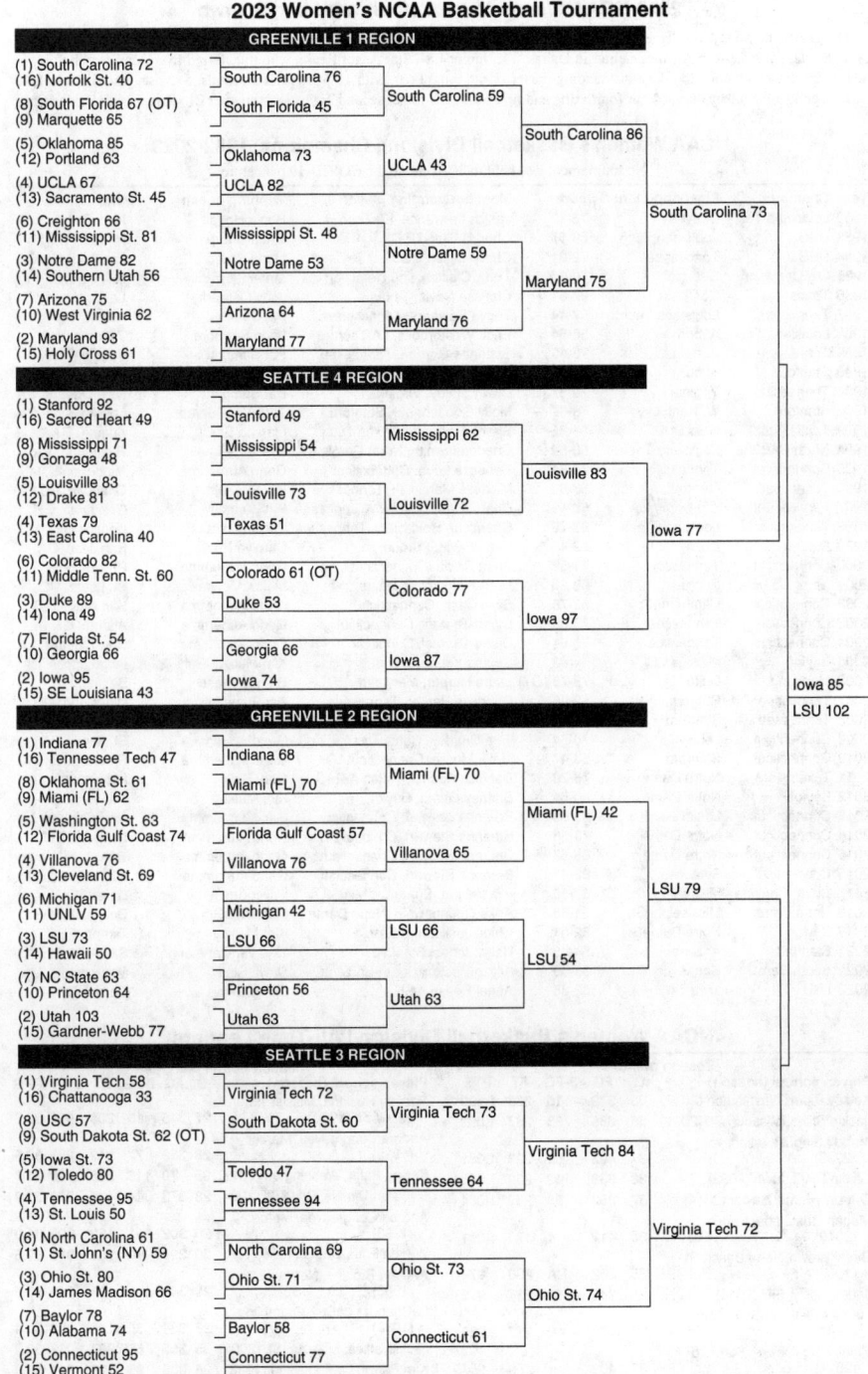

GREENVILLE 1 REGION

(1) South Carolina 72
(16) Norfolk St. 40
— South Carolina 76
(8) South Florida 67 (OT)
(9) Marquette 65
— South Florida 45
— South Carolina 59
(5) Oklahoma 85
(12) Portland 63
— Oklahoma 73
(4) UCLA 67
(13) Sacramento St. 45
— UCLA 82
— UCLA 43
— South Carolina 86
(6) Creighton 66
(11) Mississippi St. 81
— Mississippi St. 48
(3) Notre Dame 82
(14) Southern Utah 56
— Notre Dame 53
— Notre Dame 59
(7) Arizona 75
(10) West Virginia 62
— Arizona 64
(2) Maryland 93
(15) Holy Cross 61
— Maryland 77
— Maryland 76
— Maryland 75
— South Carolina 73

SEATTLE 4 REGION

(1) Stanford 92
(16) Sacred Heart 49
— Stanford 49
(8) Mississippi 71
(9) Gonzaga 48
— Mississippi 54
— Mississippi 62
(5) Louisville 83
(12) Drake 81
— Louisville 73
(4) Texas 79
(13) East Carolina 40
— Texas 51
— Louisville 72
— Louisville 83
(6) Colorado 82
(11) Middle Tenn. St. 60
— Colorado 61 (OT)
(3) Duke 89
(14) Iona 49
— Duke 53
— Colorado 77
(7) Florida St. 54
(10) Georgia 66
— Georgia 66
(2) Iowa 95
(15) SE Louisiana 43
— Iowa 74
— Iowa 87
— Iowa 97
— Iowa 77

GREENVILLE 2 REGION

(1) Indiana 77
(16) Tennessee Tech 47
— Indiana 68
(8) Oklahoma St. 61
(9) Miami (FL) 62
— Miami (FL) 70
— Miami (FL) 70
(5) Washington St. 63
(12) Florida Gulf Coast 74
— Florida Gulf Coast 57
(4) Villanova 76
(13) Cleveland St. 69
— Villanova 76
— Villanova 65
— Miami (FL) 42
(6) Michigan 71
(11) UNLV 59
— Michigan 42
(3) LSU 73
(14) Hawaii 50
— LSU 66
— LSU 66
(7) NC State 63
(10) Princeton 64
— Princeton 56
(2) Utah 103
(15) Gardner-Webb 77
— Utah 63
— Utah 63
— LSU 54
— LSU 79

SEATTLE 3 REGION

(1) Virginia Tech 58
(16) Chattanooga 33
— Virginia Tech 72
(8) USC 57
(9) South Dakota St. 62 (OT)
— South Dakota St. 60
— Virginia Tech 73
(5) Iowa St. 73
(12) Toledo 80
— Toledo 47
(4) Tennessee 95
(13) St. Louis 50
— Tennessee 94
— Tennessee 64
— Virginia Tech 84
(6) North Carolina 61
(11) St. John's (NY) 59
— North Carolina 69
(3) Ohio St. 80
(14) James Madison 66
— Ohio St. 71
— Ohio St. 73
(7) Baylor 78
(10) Alabama 74
— Baylor 58
(2) Connecticut 95
(15) Vermont 52
— Connecticut 77
— Connecticut 61
— Ohio St. 74
— Virginia Tech 72

Iowa 85
LSU 102

2023 NCAA Women's Basketball: LSU Limits Iowa

The Louisiana State Univ. Tigers claimed the women's NCAA basketball title, defeating the Univ. of Iowa Hawkeyes, 102-85, Apr. 2, 2023, at American Airlines Center in Dallas, TX. Junior LSU star Angel Reese, who transferred from Maryland before the season began, was named the most outstanding player of the Final Four, with 15 points, 10 rebounds, 5 assists, and 3 steals. LSU head coach Kim Mulkey claimed her fourth title and first with LSU in her second Tigers season, after 21 seasons with Baylor Univ.

NCAA Women's Basketball Division I Champions, 1982-2023

No tournament was held in 2020 due to the COVID-19 pandemic.

Year	Champion	Final opponent	Score	Most outstanding player	Winning coach	Site
1982	Louisiana Tech	Cheyney	76-62	Janice Lawrence, LA Tech	Sonja Hogg	Norfolk, VA
1983	USC	Louisiana Tech	69-67	Cheryl Miller, USC	Linda Sharp	Norfolk, VA
1984	USC	Tennessee	72-61	Cheryl Miller, USC	Linda Sharp	Los Angeles, CA
1985	Old Dominion	Georgia	70-65	Tracy Claxton, Old Dominion	Marianne Stanley	Austin, TX
1986	Texas	USC	97-81	Clarissa Davis, Texas	Jody Conradt	Lexington, KY
1987	Tennessee	Louisiana Tech	67-44	Tonya Edwards, Tennessee	Pat Summitt	Austin, TX
1988	Louisiana Tech	Auburn	56-54	Erica Westbrooks, LA Tech	Leon Barmore	Tacoma, WA
1989	Tennessee	Auburn	76-60	Bridgette Gordon, Tennessee	Pat Summitt	Tacoma, WA
1990	Stanford	Auburn	88-81	Jennifer Azzi, Stanford	Tara VanDerveer	Knoxville, TN
1991	Tennessee	Virginia	70-67 (OT)	Dawn Staley, Virginia	Pat Summitt	New Orleans, LA
1992	Stanford	W. Kentucky	78-62	Molly Goodenbour, Stanford	Tara VanDerveer	Los Angeles, CA
1993	Texas Tech	Ohio St.	84-82	Sheryl Swoopes, Texas Tech	Marsha Sharp	Atlanta, GA
1994	North Carolina	Louisiana Tech	60-59	Charlotte Smith, North Carolina	Sylvia Hatchell	Richmond, VA
1995	Connecticut	Tennessee	70-64	Rebecca Lobo, Connecticut	Geno Auriemma	Minneapolis, MN
1996	Tennessee	Georgia	83-65	Michelle Marciniak, Tennessee	Pat Summitt	Charlotte, NC
1997	Tennessee	Old Dominion	68-59	Chamique Holdsclaw, Tennessee	Pat Summitt	Cincinnati, OH
1998	Tennessee	Louisiana Tech	93-75	Chamique Holdsclaw, Tennessee	Pat Summitt	Kansas City, MO
1999	Purdue	Duke	62-45	Ukari Figgs, Purdue	Carolyn Peck	San Jose, CA
2000	Connecticut	Tennessee	71-52	Shea Ralph, Connecticut	Geno Auriemma	Philadelphia, PA
2001	Notre Dame	Purdue	68-66	Ruth Riley, Notre Dame	Muffet McGraw	St. Louis, MO
2002	Connecticut	Oklahoma	82-70	Swin Cash, Connecticut	Geno Auriemma	San Antonio, TX
2003	Connecticut	Tennessee	73-68	Diana Taurasi, Connecticut	Geno Auriemma	Atlanta, GA
2004	Connecticut	Tennessee	70-61	Diana Taurasi, Connecticut	Geno Auriemma	New Orleans, LA
2005	Baylor	Michigan St.	84-62	Sophia Young, Baylor	Kim Mulkey-Robertson	Indianapolis, IN
2006	Maryland	Duke	78-75 (OT)	Laura Harper, Maryland	Brenda Frese	Boston, MA
2007	Tennessee	Rutgers	59-46	Candace Parker, Tennessee	Pat Summitt	Cleveland, OH
2008	Tennessee	Stanford	64-48	Candace Parker, Tennessee	Pat Summitt	Tampa Bay, FL
2009	Connecticut	Louisville	76-54	Tina Charles, Connecticut	Geno Auriemma	St. Louis, MO
2010	Connecticut	Stanford	53-47	Maya Moore, Connecticut	Geno Auriemma	San Antonio, TX
2011	Texas A&M	Notre Dame	76-70	Danielle Adams, Texas A&M	Gary Blair	Indianapolis, IN
2012	Baylor	Notre Dame	80-61	Brittney Griner, Baylor	Kim Mulkey	Denver, CO
2013	Connecticut	Louisville	93-60	Breanna Stewart, Connecticut	Geno Auriemma	New Orleans, LA
2014	Connecticut	Notre Dame	79-58	Breanna Stewart, Connecticut	Geno Auriemma	Nashville, TN
2015	Connecticut	Notre Dame	63-53	Breanna Stewart, Connecticut	Geno Auriemma	Tampa, FL
2016	Connecticut	Syracuse	82-51	Breanna Stewart, Connecticut	Geno Auriemma	Indianapolis, IN
2017	South Carolina	Mississippi St.	67-55	A'ja Wilson, South Carolina	Dawn Staley	Dallas, TX
2018	Notre Dame	Mississippi St.	61-58	Arike Ogunbowale, Notre Dame	Muffet McGraw	Columbus, OH
2019	Baylor	Notre Dame	82-81	Chloe Jackson, Baylor	Kim Mulkey	Tampa, FL
2021	Stanford	Arizona	54-53	Haley Jones, Stanford	Tara VanDerveer	San Antonio, TX
2022	South Carolina	Connecticut	64-49	Aliyah Boston, South Carolina	Dawn Staley	Minneapolis, MN
2023	LSU	Iowa	102-85	Angel Reese, LSU	Kim Mulkey	Dallas, TX

NCAA Women's Basketball Division I All-Time Leaders

Season points						Season points per game						
Player, school (season)	G	FG	3-FG	FT	PTS	Player, school (season)	G	FG	3-FG	FT	PTS	PPG
Kelsey Plum, Washington (2017)	35	379	115	236	1,109	Patricia Hoskins, Mississippi Valley St. (1989)	27	345	13	205	908	33.6
Jackie Stiles, Missouri St. (2001)	35	365	65	267	1,062	Andrea Congreaves, Mercer (1992)	28	353	77	142	925	33.0
Maddy Siegrist, Villanova (2023)	37	403	52	223	1,081	Kelsey Plum, Washington (2017)	35	379	115	236	1,109	31.7
Caitlin Clark, Iowa (2023)	38	338	140	239	1,055	Deborah Temple, Delta St. (1984)	28	373	NA	127	873	31.2
Odyssey Sims, Baylor (2014)	37	362	98	232	1,054	Andrea Congreaves, Mercer (1993)	26	302	51	150	805	31.0
Megan Gustafson, Iowa (2019)	36	412	1	176	1,001	Wanda Ford, Drake (1986)	30	390	NA	139	919	30.6
Cindy Brown, Long Beach St. (1987)	35	362	NA	250	974	Anucha Browne, Northwestern (1985)	28	341	NA	173	855	30.5
Jerica Coley, FIU (2014)	33	345	51	231	972	LeChandra LeDay, Grambling (1988)	28	334	36	146	850	30.4
Genia Miller, Cal St. Fullerton (1991)	33	376	0	217	969	Jackie Stiles, Missouri St. (2001)	35	365	65	267	1,062	30.3
Chiney Ogwumike, Stanford (2014)	37	402	4	159	967	Kim Perrot, La.-Lafayette (1990)	28	309	95	128	841	30.0

Career points

Player, school (seasons)	G	FG	3-FG	FT	PTS
Kelsey Plum, Washington (2014-17)	139	1,136	343	912	3,527
Kelsey Mitchell, Ohio St. (2015-18)	139	1,120	497	665	3,402
Jackie Stiles, Missouri St. (1998-2001)	129	1,160	221	852	3,393
Brittney Griner, Baylor (2010-13)	148	1,247	2	787	3,283
Patricia Hoskins, Mississippi Valley St. (1986-89)	110	1,196	24	706	3,122
Lorri Bauman, Drake (1981-84)	120	1,104	NA	907	3,115
Jerica Coley, FIU (2011-14)	131	1,099	160	749	3,107
Rachel Banham, Minnesota (2012-16)	144	1,081	354	577	3,093
Ashley Joens, Iowa St. (2018-23)	158	988	344	740	3,060
Elena Delle Donne, Delaware (2010-13)	114	1,030	206	773	3,039
Maya Moore, Connecticut (2008-11)	154	1,171	311	383	3,036

Career points per game

Player, school (seasons)	G	FG	3-FG	FT	PTS	PPG
Patricia Hoskins, Mississippi Valley St. (1986-89)	110	1,196	24	706	3,122	28.4
Caitlin Clark, Iowa (2020-23)	100	890	347	590	2,717	27.2
Sandra Hodge, New Orleans (1981-84)	107	1,194	NA	472	2,860	26.7
Elena Delle Donne, Delaware (2010-13)	114	1,030	206	773	3,039	26.7
Jackie Stiles, Missouri St. (1998-2001)	129	1,160	221	852	3,393	26.3
Lorri Bauman, Drake (1981-84)	120	1,104	NA	907	3,115	26.0
Andrea Congreaves, Mercer (1990-93)	108	1,107	153	429	2,796	25.9
Cindy Blodgett, Maine (1995-98)	118	1,055	219	676	3,005	25.5
Valorie Whiteside, Appalachian St. (1985-88)	116	1,153	0	638	2,944	25.4
Kelsey Plum, Washington (2014-17)	139	1,136	343	912	3,527	25.4

NA = Not available. **Note:** Career leaders played at least three seasons (in a four-year career) or two (in a three-season career) since official NCAA record-keeping began (1981-82).

Wade Trophy Winners, 1978-2023

Awarded by the National Assn. for Girls and Women in Sport and the Women's Basketball Coaches Assn. (WBCA) to the best college women's basketball player in terms of character, leadership, and player performance.

Year	Player, school	Year	Player, school	Year	Player, school
1978	Carol Blazejowski, Montclair St.	1994	Carol Ann Shudlick, Minnesota	2009	Maya Moore, Connecticut
1979	Nancy Lieberman, Old Dominion	1995	Rebecca Lobo, Connecticut	2010	Maya Moore, Connecticut
1980	Nancy Lieberman, Old Dominion	1996	Jennifer Rizzotti, Connecticut	2011	Maya Moore, Connecticut
1981	Lynette Woodard, Kansas	1997	DeLisha Milton, Florida	2012	Brittney Griner, Baylor
1982	Pam Kelly, Louisiana Tech	1998	Ticha Penicheiro, Old Dominion	2013	Brittney Griner, Baylor
1983	LaTaunya Pollard, Long Beach St.	1999	Stephanie White-McCarty, Purdue	2014	Odyssey Sims, Baylor
1984	Janice Lawrence, Louisiana Tech	2000	Edwina Brown, Texas	2015	Breanna Stewart, Connecticut
1985	Cheryl Miller, USC	2001	Jackie Stiles, Missouri St.	2016	Breanna Stewart, Connecticut
1986	Kamie Ethridge, Texas	2002	Sue Bird, Connecticut	2017	Kelsey Plum, Washington
1987	Shelly Pennefeather, Villanova	2003	Diana Taurasi, Connecticut	2018	A'ja Wilson, South Carolina
1988	Teresa Weatherspoon, Louisiana Tech	2004	Alana Beard, Duke	2019	Sabrina Ionescu, Oregon
1989	Clarissa Davis, Texas	2005	Seimone Augustus, LSU	2020	Sabrina Ionescu, Oregon
1990	Jennifer Azzi, Stanford	2006	Seimone Augustus, LSU	2021	NaLyssa Smith, Baylor
1991	Daedra Charles, Tennessee	2007	Candace Parker, Tennessee	2022	Aliyah Boston, South Carolina
1992	Susan Robinson, Penn St.	2008	Candice Wiggins, Stanford	2023	Caitlin Clark, Iowa
1993	Karen Jennings, Nebraska				

NCAA Men's Baseball Division I Champions, 1947-2023

Year	Champion	Year	Champion	Year	Champion	Year	Champion	Year	Champion
1947	California	1963	USC	1979	Cal St. Fullerton	1994	Oklahoma	2009	LSU
1948	USC	1964	Minnesota	1980	Arizona	1995	Cal St. Fullerton	2010	South Carolina
1949	Texas	1965	Arizona St.	1981	Arizona St.	1996	LSU	2011	South Carolina
1950	Texas	1966	Ohio St.	1982	Miami (FL)	1997	LSU	2012	Arizona
1951	Oklahoma	1967	Arizona St.	1983	Texas	1998	USC	2013	UCLA
1952	Holy Cross	1968	USC	1984	Cal St. Fullerton	1999	Miami (FL)	2014	Vanderbilt
1953	Michigan	1969	Arizona St.	1985	Miami (FL)	2000	LSU	2015	Virginia
1954	Missouri	1970	USC	1986	Arizona	2001	Miami (FL)	2016	Coastal Carolina
1955	Wake Forest	1971	USC	1987	Stanford	2002	Texas	2017	Florida
1956	Minnesota	1972	USC	1988	Stanford	2003	Rice	2018	Oregon St.
1957	California	1973	USC	1989	Wichita St.	2004	Cal St. Fullerton	2019	Vanderbilt
1958	USC	1974	USC	1990	Georgia	2005	Texas	2020	No champion
1959	Oklahoma St.	1975	Texas	1991	LSU	2006	Oregon St.	2021	Mississippi St.
1960	Minnesota	1976	Arizona	1992	Pepperdine	2007	Oregon St.	2022	Mississippi
1961	USC	1977	Arizona St.	1993	LSU	2008	Fresno St.	2023	LSU
1962	Michigan	1978	USC						

NCAA Women's Softball Division I Champions, 1982-2023

Year	Champion	Year	Champion	Year	Champion	Year	Champion	Year	Champion
1982	UCLA	1991	Arizona	2000	Oklahoma	2008	Arizona St.	2016	Oklahoma
1983	Texas A&M	1992	UCLA	2001	Arizona	2009	Washington	2017	Oklahoma
1984	UCLA	1993	Arizona	2002	California	2010	UCLA	2018	Florida St.
1985	UCLA	1994	Arizona	2003	UCLA	2011	Arizona St.	2019	UCLA
1986	Cal St. Fullerton	1995	UCLA	2004	UCLA	2012	Alabama	2020	No champion
1987	Texas A&M	1996	Arizona	2005	Michigan	2013	Oklahoma	2021	Oklahoma
1988	UCLA	1997	Arizona	2006	Arizona	2014	Florida	2022	Oklahoma
1989	UCLA	1998	Fresno St.	2007	Arizona	2015	Florida	2023	Oklahoma
1990	UCLA	1999	UCLA						

NCAA Men's Hockey Division I Champions, 1948-2023

Year	Champion	Year	Champion	Year	Champion	Year	Champion	Year	Champion
1948	Michigan	1964	Michigan	1980	North Dakota	1995	Boston Univ.	2010	Boston College
1949	Boston College	1965	Michigan Tech	1981	Wisconsin	1996	Michigan	2011	Minnesota Duluth
1950	Colorado College	1966	Michigan St.	1982	North Dakota	1997	North Dakota	2012	Boston College
1951	Michigan	1967	Cornell	1983	Wisconsin	1998	Michigan	2013	Yale
1952	Michigan	1968	Denver	1984	Bowling Green	1999	Maine	2014	Union College
1953	Michigan	1969	Denver	1985	Rensselaer	2000	North Dakota	2015	Providence
1954	Rensselaer	1970	Cornell	1986	Michigan St.	2001	Boston College	2016	North Dakota
1955	Michigan	1971	Boston Univ.	1987	North Dakota	2002	Minnesota	2017	Denver
1956	Michigan	1972	Boston Univ.	1988	Lake Superior St.	2003	Minnesota	2018	Minnesota Duluth
1957	Colorado College	1973	Wisconsin	1989	Harvard	2004	Denver	2019	Minnesota Duluth
1958	Denver	1974	Minnesota	1990	Wisconsin	2005	Denver	2020	No champion
1959	North Dakota	1975	Michigan Tech	1991	North Michigan	2006	Wisconsin	2021	Massachusetts
1960	Denver	1976	Minnesota	1992	Lake Superior St.	2007	Michigan St.	2022	Denver
1961	Denver	1977	Wisconsin	1993	Maine	2008	Boston College	2023	Quinnipiac
1962	Michigan Tech	1978	Boston Univ.	1994	Lake Superior St.	2009	Boston Univ.		
1963	North Dakota	1979	Minnesota						

NCAA Women's Hockey Champions, 2001-23

Year	Champion	Year	Champion	Year	Champion	Year	Champion	Year	Champion
2001	Minnesota Duluth	2006	Wisconsin	2011	Wisconsin	2016	Minnesota	2020	No champion
2002	Minnesota Duluth	2007	Wisconsin	2012	Minnesota	2017	Clarkson	2021	Wisconsin
2003	Minnesota Duluth	2008	Minnesota Duluth	2013	Minnesota	2018	Clarkson	2022	Ohio St.
2004	Minnesota	2009	Wisconsin	2014	Clarkson	2019	Wisconsin	2023	Wisconsin
2005	Minnesota	2010	Minnesota Duluth	2015	Minnesota				

NCAA Division I Lacrosse Champions, 1982-2023

Year	Men	Women	Year	Men	Women	Year	Men	Women
1982	North Carolina	Massachusetts	1996	Princeton	Maryland	2010	Duke	Maryland
1983	Syracuse	Delaware	1997	Princeton	Maryland	2011	Virginia	Northwestern
1984	Johns Hopkins	Temple	1998	Princeton	Maryland	2012	Loyola (MD)	Northwestern
1985	Johns Hopkins	New Hampshire	1999	Virginia	Maryland	2013	Duke	North Carolina
1986	North Carolina	Maryland	2000	Syracuse	Maryland	2014	Duke	Maryland
1987	Johns Hopkins	Penn St.	2001	Princeton	Maryland	2015	Denver	Maryland
1988	Syracuse	Temple	2002	Syracuse	Princeton	2016	North Carolina	North Carolina
1989	Syracuse	Penn St.	2003	Virginia	Princeton	2017	Maryland	Maryland
1990	Syracuse[1]	Harvard	2004	Syracuse	Virginia	2018	Yale	James Madison
1991	North Carolina	Virginia	2005	Johns Hopkins	Northwestern	2019	Virginia	Maryland
1992	Princeton	Maryland	2006	Virginia	Northwestern	2020	No champion	No champion
1993	Syracuse	Virginia	2007	Johns Hopkins	Northwestern	2021	Virginia	Boston Coll.
1994	Princeton	Princeton	2008	Syracuse	Northwestern	2022	Maryland	North Carolina
1995	Syracuse	Maryland	2009	Syracuse	Northwestern	2023	Notre Dame	Northwestern

Note: NCAA Championships began in 1971 for men, in 1982 for women. (1) Vacated due to an NCAA rules violation.

NCAA Division I Soccer Champions, 1982-2022

Year	Men	Women	Year	Men	Women	Year	Men	Women
1982	Indiana	North Carolina	1995	Wisconsin	Notre Dame	2009	Virginia	North Carolina
1983	Indiana	North Carolina	1996	St. John's (NY)	North Carolina	2010	Akron	Notre Dame
1984	Clemson	North Carolina	1997	UCLA	North Carolina	2011	North Carolina	Stanford
1985	UCLA	George Mason	1998	Indiana	Florida	2012	Indiana	North Carolina
1986	Duke	North Carolina	1999	Indiana	North Carolina	2013	Notre Dame	UCLA
1987	Clemson	North Carolina	2000	Connecticut	North Carolina	2014	Virginia	Florida St.
1988	Indiana	North Carolina	2001	North Carolina	Santa Clara	2015	Stanford	Penn St.
1989	Santa Clara;		2002	UCLA	Portland	2016	Stanford	USC
	Virginia (tie)	North Carolina	2003	Indiana	North Carolina	2017	Stanford	Stanford
1990	UCLA	North Carolina	2004	Indiana	Notre Dame	2018	Maryland	Florida St.
1991	Virginia	North Carolina	2005	Maryland	Portland	2019	Georgetown	Stanford
1992	Virginia	North Carolina	2006	UC Santa Barbara	North Carolina	2020	Marshall	Santa Clara
1993	Virginia	North Carolina	2007	Wake Forest	USC	2021	Clemson	Florida St.
1994	Virginia	North Carolina	2008	Maryland	North Carolina	2022	Syracuse	UCLA

Note: NCAA Championships began in 1959 for men, in 1982 for women.

NCAA Division I Wrestling Champions, 1964-2023

Year	Champion	Year	Champion	Year	Champion	Year	Champion	Year	Champion
1964	Oklahoma St.	1976	Iowa	1988	Arizona St.	2000	Iowa	2012	Penn St.
1965	Iowa St.	1977	Iowa St.	1989	Oklahoma St.	2001	Minnesota	2013	Penn St.
1966	Oklahoma St.	1978	Iowa	1990	Oklahoma St.	2002	Minnesota	2014	Penn St.
1967	Michigan St.	1979	Iowa	1991	Iowa	2003	Oklahoma St.	2015	Ohio St.
1968	Oklahoma St.	1980	Iowa	1992	Iowa	2004	Oklahoma St.	2016	Penn St.
1969	Iowa St.	1981	Iowa	1993	Iowa	2005	Oklahoma St.	2017	Penn St.
1970	Iowa St.	1982	Iowa	1994	Oklahoma St.	2006	Oklahoma St.	2018	Penn St.
1971	Oklahoma St.	1983	Iowa	1995	Iowa	2007	Minnesota	2019	Penn St.
1972	Iowa St.	1984	Iowa	1996	Iowa	2008	Iowa	2020	No champion
1973	Iowa St.	1985	Iowa	1997	Iowa	2009	Iowa	2021	Iowa
1974	Oklahoma	1986	Iowa	1998	Iowa	2010	Iowa	2022	Penn St.
1975	Iowa	1987	Iowa St.	1999	Iowa	2011	Penn St.	2023	Penn St.

Selected NCAA Division I Teams

(Conferences and coaches listed are as of July 2023.)

Team	Nickname	Team colors	Conference	Basketball coach	Football coach
Air Force	Falcons	Blue & silver	Mountain West	Joe Scott	Troy Calhoun
Akron	Zips	Blue & gold	Mid-American	John Groce	Joe Moorhead
Alabama	Crimson Tide	Crimson & white	Southeastern	Nate Oats	Nick Saban
Appalachian State	Mountaineers	Black & gold	Sun Belt	Dustin Kerns	Shawn Clark
Arizona	Wildcats	Cardinal & navy	Pac-12	Tommy Lloyd	Jedd Fisch
Arizona State	Sun Devils	Maroon & gold	Pac-12	Bobby Hurley	Kenny Dillingham
Arkansas	Razorbacks	Cardinal & white	Southeastern	Eric Musselman	Sam Pittman
Arkansas State	Red Wolves	Scarlet & black	Sun Belt	Bryan Hodgson	Butch Jones
Army	Black Knights	Black, gold, & gray	Patriot League[2]	Kevin Kuwik	Jeff Monken
Auburn	Tigers	Burnt orange & navy blue	Southeastern	Bruce Pearl	Hugh Freeze
Ball State	Cardinals	Cardinal & white	Mid-American	Michael Lewis	Mike Neu
Baylor	Bears	Green & gold	Big 12	Scott Drew	Dave Aranda
Boise State	Broncos	Blue & orange	Mountain West	Leon Rice	Andy Avalos
Boston College	Eagles	Maroon & gold	Atlantic Coast	Earl Grant	Jeff Hafley
Bowling Green	Falcons	Orange & brown	Mid-American	Todd Simon	Scot Loeffler
Brigham Young (BYU)	Cougars	Blue & white	Big 12	Mark Pope	Kalani Sitake
Brown*	Bears	Brown, red, & white	Ivy League	Mike Martin	James Perry
Butler	Bulldogs	Blue & white	Pioneer League[1]	Thad Matta	Mike Uremovich
California	Golden Bears	Blue & gold	Pac-12	Mark Madsen	Justin Wilcox
Central Michigan	Chippewas	Maroon & gold	Mid-American	Tony Barbee	Jim McElwain
Cincinnati	Bearcats	Red & black	Big 12	Wes Miller	Scott Satterfield
Citadel*	Bulldogs	Citadel blue & white	Southern	Ed Conroy	Maurice Drayton
Clemson	Tigers	Tiger orange & regalia	Atlantic Coast	Brad Brownell	Dabo Swinney
Colgate*	Raiders	Maroon, gray, & white	Patriot League	Matt Langel	Stan Dakosty
Colorado	Buffaloes	Silver, black, & gold	Pac-12	Tad Boyle	Deion Sanders
Colorado State	Rams	Green & gold	Mountain West	Niko Medved	Jay Norvell
Columbia*	Lions	Columbia blue & white	Ivy League	Jim Engles	Al Bagnoli
Connecticut	Huskies	National flag blue & white	Big East[2]	Dan Hurley	Jim L. Mora
Cornell*	Big Red	Carnelian red & white	Ivy League	Brian Earl	David Archer
Dartmouth*	Big Green	Dartmouth green & white	Ivy League	David McLaughlin	Sammy McCorkle
Delaware*	Blue Hens	Blue & gold	Coastal Athletic	Martin Ingelsby	Ryan Carty
Duke	Blue Devils	Duke blue & white	Atlantic Coast	Jon Scheyer	Mike Elko
East Carolina	Pirates	Purple & gold	American Athletic	Michael Schwartz	Mike Houston
Eastern Illinois*	Panthers	Blue & gray	Ohio Valley	Marty Simmons	Chris Wilkerson
Eastern Kentucky*	Colonels	Maroon & white	United Athletic[1]	A. W. Hamilton	Walt Wells
Eastern Michigan	Eagles	Green & white	Mid-American	Stan Heath	Chris Creighton
Eastern Washington*	Eagles	Red & white	Big Sky	David Riley	Aaron Best
Florida	Gators	Orange & blue	Southeastern	Todd Golden	Billy Napier
Florida A&M*	Rattlers	Orange & green	Southwestern Athletic	Robert McCullum	Willie Simmons
Florida State	Seminoles	Garnet & gold	Atlantic Coast	Leonard Hamilton	Mike Norvell
Fresno State	Bulldogs	Red & blue	Mountain West	Justin Hutson	Jeff Tedford
Furman*	Paladins	Purple & white	Southern	Bob Richey	Clay Hendrix
Georgia	Bulldogs	Red & black	Southeastern	Mike White	Kirby Smart
Georgia Southern	Eagles	Blue & white	Sun Belt	Charlie Henry	Clay Helton
Georgia Tech	Yellow Jackets	Old gold & white	Atlantic Coast	Damon Stoudamire	Brent Key
Gonzaga*	Bulldogs, Zags	Navy blue, white, & red	West Coast	Mark Few	Does not compete
Harvard*	Crimson	Crimson, black, & white	Ivy League	Tommy Amaker	Tim Murphy
Hawaii	Rainbow Warriors	Green, black, white, silver	Mountain West[1]	Eran Ganot	Timmy Chang
Holy Cross*	Crusaders	Royal purple	Patriot League	Dave Paulsen	Bob Chesney
Houston	Cougars	Scarlet & white	Big 12	Kelvin Sampson	Dana Holgorsen
Howard*	Bison	Blue & white	Mid-Eastern Athletic	Kenny Blakeney	Larry Scott
Idaho*	Vandals	Silver & vandal gold	Big Sky	Alex Pribble	Jason Eck
Illinois	Fighting Illini	Orange & blue	Big Ten	Brad Underwood	Bret Bielema
Illinois State*	Redbirds	Red & white	Missouri Valley	Ryan Pedon	Brock Spack
Indiana	Hoosiers	Cream & crimson	Big Ten	Mike Woodson	Tom Allen
Indiana State*	Sycamores	Royal blue & white	Missouri Valley	Josh Schertz	Curt Mallory
Iowa	Hawkeyes	Black & gold	Big Ten	Fran McCaffery	Kirk Ferentz
Iowa State	Cyclones	Cardinal & gold	Big 12	T. J. Otzelberger	Matt Campbell
Jackson State*	Tigers	Blue & white	Southwestern Athletic	Mo Williams	T. C. Taylor
James Madison*	Dukes	Purple & gold	Sun Belt	Mark Byington	Curt Cignetti
Kansas	Jayhawks	Crimson & blue	Big 12	Bill Self	Lance Leipold
Kansas State	Wildcats	Purple & white	Big 12	Jerome Tang	Chris Klieman
Kent State	Golden Flashes	Navy blue & gold	Mid-American	Rob Senderoff	Kenni Burns
Kentucky	Wildcats	Blue & white	Southeastern	John Calipari	Mark Stoops
Lafayette*	Leopards	Maroon & white	Patriot League	Mike McGarvey	John Troxell
Lehigh*	Mountain Hawks	Brown & white	Patriot League	Brett Reed	Kevin Cahill
Liberty	Flames	Red, white, & blue	Conference USA	Ritchie McKay	Jamey Chadwell
Louisiana State (LSU)	Fighting Tigers	Purple & gold	Southeastern	Matt McMahon	Brian Kelly
Louisiana Tech	Bulldogs	Red & blue	Conference USA	Talvin Hester	Sonny Cumbie
Louisiana-Lafayette	Ragin' Cajuns	Vermilion & white	Sun Belt	Bob Marlin	Michael Desormeaux
Louisiana-Monroe	Warhawks	Maroon & gold	Sun Belt	Keith Richard	Terry Bowden
Louisville	Cardinals	Red & black	Atlantic Coast	Kenny Payne	Jeff Brohm
Maine*	Black Bears	Blue & white	Coastal Athletic[1]	Chris Markwood	Jordan Stevens
Marquette	Golden Eagles	Blue & gold	Big East	Shaka Smart	Does not compete
Marshall	Thundering Herd	Kelly green & white	Sun Belt	Dan D'Antoni	Charles Huff
Maryland	Terrapins	Red, white, black, gold	Big Ten	Kevin Willard	Michael Locksley
Massachusetts	Minutemen	Maroon & white	Independent[1]	Frank Martin	Don Brown
Memphis	Tigers	Blue & gray	American Athletic	Anfernee "Penny" Hardaway	Ryan Silverfield
Miami (Florida)	Hurricanes	Orange & green	Atlantic Coast	Jim Larrañaga	Mario Cristobal
Miami (Ohio)	RedHawks	Red & white	Mid-American	Travis Steele	Chuck Martin
Michigan	Wolverines	Maize & blue	Big Ten	Juwan Howard	Jim Harbaugh
Michigan State	Spartans	Green & white	Big Ten	Tom Izzo	Harlon Barnett
Mid. Tennessee State	Blue Raiders	Royal blue & white	Conference USA	Nick McDevitt	Rick Stockstill
Minnesota	Golden Gophers	Maroon & gold	Big Ten	Ben Johnson	P. J. Fleck

Team	Nickname	Team colors	Conference	Basketball coach	Football coach
Mississippi (Ole Miss)	Rebels	Cardinal red & navy blue	Southeastern	Chris Beard	Lane Kiffin
Mississippi State	Bulldogs	Maroon & white	Southeastern	Chris Jans	Zach Arnett
Missouri	Tigers	Old gold & black	Southeastern	Dennis Gates	Eliah Drinkwitz
Montana*	Grizzlies	Maroon & silver	Big Sky	Travis DeCuire	Bobby Hauck
Montana State*	Bobcats	Blue & gold	Big Sky	Matt Logie	Brent Vigen
Morgan State*	Bears	Blue & orange	Mid-Eastern Athletic	Kevin Broadus	Damon Wilson
Murray State*	Racers	Navy & gold	Missouri Valley	Steve Prohm	Dean Hood
Navy	Midshipmen	Navy blue & gold	American Athletic[1]	Ed DeChellis	Brian Newberry
Nebraska	Cornhuskers	Scarlet & cream	Big Ten	Fred Hoiberg	Matt Rhule
Nevada	Wolf Pack	Silver & blue	Mountain West	Steve Alford	Ken Wilson
Nevada-Las Vegas (UNLV)	Rebels	Scarlet & gray	Mountain West	Kevin Kruger	Barry Odom
New Hampshire*	Wildcats	Blue & white	Coastal Athletic[1]	Nathan Davis	Rick Santos
New Mexico	Lobos	Cherry & silver	Mountain West	Richard Pitino	Danny Gonzales
New Mexico State	Aggies	Crimson & white	Conference USA	Jason Hooten	Jerry Kill
Nicholls State*	Colonels	Red & gray	Southland	Austin Claunch	Tim Rebowe
North Carolina	Tar Heels	Carolina blue & white	Atlantic Coast	Hubert Davis	Mack Brown
North Carolina State	Wolfpack	Red & white	Atlantic Coast	Kevin Keatts	Dave Doeren
North Texas	Mean Green	Green & white	American Athletic	Ross Hodge	Eric Morris
Northern Illinois	Huskies	Cardinal & black	Mid-American	Rashon Burno	Thomas Hammock
Northern Iowa*	Panthers	Purple & old gold	Missouri Valley	Ben Jacobson	Mark Farley
Northwestern	Wildcats	Purple	Big Ten	Chris Collins	David Braun
Northwestern State*	Demons	Purple, white, & orange	Southland	Rick Cabrera	Brad Laird
Notre Dame	Fighting Irish	Blue & gold	Independent[1]	Micah Shrewsberry	Marcus Freeman
Ohio	Bobcats	Hunter green & white	Mid-American	Jeff Boals	Tim Albin
Ohio State	Buckeyes	Scarlet & gray	Big Ten	Chris Holtmann	Ryan Day
Oklahoma	Sooners	Crimson & cream	Big 12	Porter Moser	Brent Venables
Oklahoma State	Cowboys	Orange & black	Big 12	Mike Boynton Jr.	Mike Gundy
Oregon	Ducks	Green & yellow	Pac-12	Dana Altman	Dan Lanning
Oregon State	Beavers	Orange & black	Pac-12	Wayne Tinkle	Jonathan Smith
Penn State	Nittany Lions	Blue & white	Big Ten	Mike Rhoades	James Franklin
Pennsylvania*	Quakers	Red & blue	Ivy League	Steve Donahue	Ray Priore
Pittsburgh	Panthers	Gold & blue	Atlantic Coast	Jeff Capel	Pat Narduzzi
Princeton*	Tigers	Orange & black	Ivy League	Mitch Henderson	Bob Surace
Purdue	Boilermakers	Old gold & black	Big Ten	Matt Painter	Ryan Walters
Rice	Owls	Blue & gray	American Athletic	Scott Pera	Mike Bloomgren
Richmond*	Spiders	Red & blue	Coastal Athletic[1]	Chris Mooney	Russ Huesman
Rutgers	Scarlet Knights	Scarlet	Big Ten	Steve Pikiell	Greg Schiano
Sam Houston State	Bearkats	Orange & white	Conference USA	Chris Mudge	K. C. Keeler
San Diego State	Aztecs	Scarlet & black	Mountain West	Brian Dutcher	Brady Hoke
San Jose State	Spartans	Gold, white, & blue	Mountain West	Tim Miles	Brent Brennan
South Carolina	Gamecocks	Garnet & black	Southeastern	Lamont Paris	Shane Beamer
South Carolina State*	Bulldogs	Garnet & blue	Mid-Eastern Athletic	Erik Martin	Oliver Pough
South Florida	Bulls	Green & gold	American Athletic	Amir Abdur-Rahim	Alex Golesh
Southeast Missouri State*	Redhawks	Red, black, & white	Ohio Valley	Brad Korn	Tom Matukewicz
Southern California (USC)	Trojans	Cardinal & gold	Pac-12	Andy Enfield	Lincoln Riley
Southern Illinois*	Salukis	Maroon & white	Missouri Valley	Bryan Mullins	Nick Hill
Southern Methodist (SMU)	Mustangs	Red & blue	American Athletic	Rob Lanier	Rhett Lashlee
Southern Mississippi	Golden Eagles	Black & gold	Sun Belt[1]	Jay Ladner	Will Hall
Stanford	Cardinal	Cardinal & white	Pac-12	Jerod Haase	Troy Taylor
Stephen F. Austin*	Lumberjacks	Purple & white	United Athletic[1]	Kyle Keller	Colby Carthel
Syracuse	Orange	Orange	Atlantic Coast	Adrian Autry	Dino Babers
Temple	Owls	Cherry & white	American Athletic	Adam Fisher	Stan Drayton
Tennessee	Volunteers	Orange & white	Southeastern	Rick Barnes	Josh Heupel
Tennessee State*	Tigers	Reflex blue & white	Ohio Valley	Brian Collins	Eddie George
Tennessee Tech*	Golden Eagles	Purple & gold	Ohio Valley	John Pelphrey	Dewayne Alexander
Texas	Longhorns	Burnt orange & white	Big 12	Rodney Terry	Steve Sarkisian
Texas A&M	Aggies	Maroon & white	Southeastern	Buzz Williams	Jimbo Fisher
Texas Christian (TCU)	Horned Frogs	Purple & white	Big 12	Jamie Dixon	Sonny Dykes
Texas Southern*	Tigers	Maroon & gray	Southwestern Athletic	Johnny Jones	Clarence McKinney
Texas State	Bobcats	Maroon & gold	Sun Belt	Terrence Johnson	G. J. Kinne
Texas Tech	Red Raiders	Scarlet & black	Big 12	Grant McCasland	Joey McGuire
Toledo	Rockets	Midnight blue & gold	Mid-American	Tod Kowalczyk	Jason Candle
Troy	Trojans	Cardinal, silver, & black	Sun Belt	Scott Cross	Jon Sumrall
Tulane	Green Wave	Olive green & blue	American Athletic	Ron Hunter	Willie Fritz
Tulsa	Golden Hurricane	Old gold, royal blue, & crimson	American Athletic	Eric Konkol	Kevin Wilson
UCLA	Bruins	Blue & gold	Pac-12	Mick Cronin	Chip Kelly
Utah	Utes	Red & white	Pac-12	Craig Smith	Kyle Whittingham
Utah State	Aggies	Navy blue, pewter, & white	Mountain West	Danny Sprinkle	Blake Anderson
UTEP (Texas-El Paso)	Miners	Dark blue, orange, & silver	Conference USA	Joe Golding	Dana Dimel
Vanderbilt	Commodores	Black & gold	Southeastern	Jerry Stackhouse	Clark Lea
Villanova*	Wildcats	Blue & white	Coastal Athletic[1]	Kyle Neptune	Mark Ferrante
Virginia	Cavaliers	Orange & blue	Atlantic Coast	Tony Bennett	Tony Elliott
Virginia Tech	Hokies	Chicago maroon & burnt orange	Atlantic Coast	Mike Young	Brent Pry
Wake Forest	Demon Deacons	Old gold & black	Atlantic Coast	Steve Forbes	Dave Clawson
Washington	Huskies	Purple & gold	Pac-12	Mike Hopkins	Kalen DeBoer
Washington State	Cougars	Crimson & gray	Pac-12	Kyle Smith	Jake Dickert
Weber State*	Wildcats	Purple & white	Big Sky	Eric Duft	Mickey Mental
West Virginia	Mountaineers	Old gold & blue	Big 12	Josh Eilert	Neal Brown
Western Illinois*	Leathernecks	Purple & gold	Missouri Valley[1]	Chad Boudreau	Myers Hendrickson
Western Kentucky	Hilltoppers	Red & white	Conference USA	Steve Lutz	Tyson Helton
Western Michigan	Broncos	Brown & gold	Mid-American	Dwayne Stephens	Lance Taylor
Wisconsin	Badgers	Cardinal & white	Big Ten	Greg Gard	Luke Fickell
Wyoming	Cowboys	Brown & gold	Mountain West	Jeff Linder	Craig Bohl
Yale*	Elis, Bulldogs	Yale blue & white	Ivy League	James Jones	Tony Reno
Youngstown State*	Penguins	Red & white	Missouri Valley[1]	Jerrod Calhoun	Doug Phillips

* = Football Championship Subdivision (FCS) team (formerly known as I-AA). (1) Team competes in conference listed in football but not in basketball. (2) Team competes in conference listed in basketball but not in football.

FOOTBALL

NFL 2022: Mahomes Leads Chiefs to Super Bowl Victory Over Eagles

The Kansas City Chiefs overcame a 10-point halftime deficit to beat the Philadelphia Eagles in Super Bowl LVII, 38-35, at State Farm Stadium in Glendale, AZ, Feb. 12, 2023. With only 8 seconds left in the game, Chiefs kicker Harrison Butker kicked a 27-yard field goal to secure the victory.

Super Bowl LVII featured a matchup of the top-seeded teams in the AFC and NFC, as the Chiefs and Eagles both notched 14-3 regular-season records, led by their respective star quarterbacks Patrick Mahomes and Jalen Hurts.

Mahomes, who threw three touchdown passes and ran for 44 yards, was named the Super Bowl MVP. He played exceptionally despite suffering a serious ankle sprain during the Chiefs' win against the Jacksonville Jaguars in the AFC Divisional Playoffs. Mahomes also was named the NFL's 2022 Most Valuable Player, becoming the first player to win both honors in the same season since Kurt Warner in 1999. Mahomes previously was named NFL MVP in 2018 and Super Bowl MVP in 2020.

The 2022 regular season again featured the 17-game, 18-week schedule that the NFL introduced in 2021. During the first quarter of a Week 17 game between two AFC division leaders, the Buffalo Bills and the Cincinnati Bengals, Bills safety Damar Hamlin was hit in the chest while making a tackle and went into cardiac arrest. The 24-year-old was revived on the field and taken to a hospital, but the game was postponed and later canceled, which meant that the Bills and Bengals each played only 16 regular-season games.

Hamlin was initially listed in critical condition, but he recovered and, in Apr. 2023, announced plans to make an NFL comeback. Meanwhile, the Bills and Bengals met again in the AFC Divisional Playoffs, with Cincinnati defeating Buffalo 27-10 in their second-round game.

The Jaguars went from an NFL-worst 3-14 record in 2021 to winning their first division title since 2017. Led by quarterback Trevor Lawrence—the top pick in the 2021 NFL draft—the team ended the regular season on a five-game winning streak, finishing 9-8. Jacksonville lost to Kansas City in the Divisional Playoffs. The AFC Championship Game featured a rematch of 2021's title-game participants, the Chiefs and the Bengals, with the opposite result, as K.C. beat Cincinnati 23-20.

In the NFC, Tom Brady, widely considered the greatest quarterback of all time, officially retired at the end of the 2022 season. The Tampa Bay Buccaneers star had previously announced his retirement after the 2021 season but changed his mind. In 2022, Brady's Bucs finished first in the South Division, albeit with a disappointing 8-9 record, and were defeated by the Dallas Cowboys 31-14 in the first round of the playoffs. At age 45, Brady broke his own NFL single-season record for pass completions, set in 2021 with 485, with 490. He also extended his NFL career records for most touchdown passes (649), passes completed (7,753), and passing yards (89,214).

The New York Giants made the playoffs for the first time since 2016, going 9-7-1 and securing a wild card berth. The Giants upset the NFC North Division winners Minnesota Vikings 31-24, before being trounced by the Eagles, 38-7.

The Eagles dominated the San Francisco 49ers in the NFC Championship Game, 31-7. The 49ers, who ended the regular season on a 10-game winning streak, were hampered by injuries in the title game. Rookie QB Brock Purdy suffered an elbow injury in the first quarter and was unable to pass effectively when he returned later in the game.

NFL Playoff Results, 2022-23

AFC Wild Card Games: Jacksonville 31, L.A. Chargers 30; Buffalo 34, Miami 31; Cincinnati 24, Baltimore 17.
NFC Wild Card Games: San Francisco 41, Seattle 23; NY Giants 31, Minnesota 24; Dallas 31, Tampa Bay 14.
AFC Divisional Playoff Games: Kansas City 27, Jacksonville 20; Cincinnati 27, Buffalo 10.

NFC Divisional Playoff Games: Philadelphia 38, NY Giants 7; San Francisco 19, Dallas 12.
AFC Championship Game: Kansas City 23, Cincinnati 20.
NFC Championship Game: Philadelphia 31, San Francisco 7.
Super Bowl LVII: Kansas City 38, Philadelphia 35.

Super Bowl LVII: Kansas City 38, Philadelphia 35

The Kansas City Chiefs rallied from a 10-point halftime deficit to defeat the Philadelphia Eagles in Super Bowl LVII, 38-35, at State Farm Stadium in Glendale, AZ, on Feb. 12, 2023. The Chiefs' Harrison Butker kicked a 27-yard field goal with just 8 seconds left to break a 35-35 tie and ice the game for Kansas City.

The game marked the Chiefs' second win and third appearance at the Super Bowl in the past four years. The team had defeated the San Francisco 49ers in Super Bowl LIV in 2020 and lost to the Tampa Bay Buccaneers in Super Bowl LV in 2021. Kansas City also previously lost Super Bowl I and won Super Bowl IV.

Patrick Mahomes was named Super Bowl MVP; he completed 21 of 27 passes for 182 yards, threw for three TDs, and ran for 44 yards. In a losing cause, Eagles QB Jalen Hurts tied the Super Bowl record for most rushing TDs (3) and most points scored (20). He also set the record for most rushing yards by a QB (70).

Kansas City's Travis Kelce and brother Jason Kelce, the Eagles' center, made history by becoming the first siblings to play against each other in a Super Bowl. The Eagles' 35 points were the most ever scored by a losing team in a Super Bowl.

Philadelphia drew first blood when Hurts ran for a 1-yard TD 4:51 into the first quarter. The Chiefs countered with an 18-yard TD pass from Mahomes to tight end Travis Kelce. Early in the second quarter, Philadelphia took a 14-7 lead after Hurts threw a 45-yard pass to A.J. Brown. Kansas City evened the game at 14 when linebacker Nick Bolton returned a fumble 36 yards for a TD. Philadelphia then scored 10 unanswered points; the score was 24-14 at halftime.

The Chiefs scored first in the second half, then took their first lead in the fourth quarter, 28-27, after Mahomes connected with Kadarius Toney for a 5-yard TD pass. Toney minutes later had a Super Bowl-record 65-yard punt return that set up another TD, increasing the Chiefs' lead to 35-27. With 5:15 left in the game, Hurts singlehandedly tied the score at 35 thanks to his third rushing TD of the game, followed by a successful 2-point conversion. Then the Chiefs drove the ball down to the Eagles' 2-yard line, setting up Butker's game-winning field goal.

Quarters

Team	1	2	3	4	Final
Kansas City	7	7	7	17	38
Philadelphia	7	17	3	8	35

Total attendance: 67,827
Game length: 3:31

Team Statistics

	Kansas City	Philadelphia
First downs	21	25
Total net yards	340	417
Rushes-yards	26-158	32-115
Passing yards, net	182	302
Punt returns-yards	2-77	2-35
Kickoff returns-yards	0-0	1-11
Interception returns-yards	0-0	0-0
Field goals made-attempts	1-2	2-2
Pass attempts-completions-interceptions	27-21-0	38-27-0
Sacked-yards lost	0-0	2-2
Punts-average	2-49.0	2-47.5
Fumbles-lost	1-0	2-1
Penalties-yards	3-14	6-33
Time of possession	24:13	35:47

Scoring

Philadelphia: Jalen Hurts, 1-yard run (Jake Elliott PAT)
Kansas City: Travis Kelce, 18-yard pass from Patrick Mahomes (Harrison Butker PAT)
Philadelphia: A.J. Brown, 45-yard pass from Hurts (Elliott PAT)
Kansas City: Nick Bolton, 36-yard fumble recovery (Butker PAT)
Philadelphia: Hurts, 4-yard run (Elliott PAT)
Philadelphia: Elliott, 35-yard field goal
Kansas City: Isiah Pacheco, 1-yard run (Butker PAT)
Philadelphia: Elliott, 33-yard field goal
Kansas City: Kadarius Toney, 5-yard pass from Mahomes (Butker PAT)
Kansas City: Skyy Moore, 4-yard pass from Mahomes (Butker PAT)
Philadelphia: Hurts, 2-yard run (Hurts, 2-point run)
Kansas City: Butker, 27-yard field goal

Individual Statistics

Rushing
Kansas City: Pacheco, 15-76, 1 TD; Mahomes, 6-44; Jerick McKinnon, 4-34; Moore, 1-4.
Philadelphia: Hurts, 15-70, 3 TD; Kenneth Gainwell, 7-21; Miles Sanders, 7-16; Boston Scott, 3-8.

Passing
Kansas City: Mahomes, 21-27, 182 yards, 3 TD, 0 int.
Philadelphia: Hurts, 27-38, 304 yards, 1 TD, 0 int.

Receiving
Kansas City: JuJu Smith-Schuster, 7-53; T. Kelce, 6-81, 1 TD; McKinnon, 3-15; Justin Watson, 2-18; Noah Gray, 1-6; Toney, 1-5, 1 TD; Moore, 1-4, 1 TD.
Philadelphia: DeVonta Smith, 7-100; Brown, 6-96, 1 TD; Dallas Goedert, 6-60; Gainwell, 4-20; Zach Pascal, 2-11; Scott, 1-9; Quez Watkins, 1-8.

NFL Final Standings, 2022

(playoff seeding in parentheses; * = wild card qualifier for playoffs)

AMERICAN FOOTBALL CONFERENCE

East Division	W	L	T	Pct	PF	PA	Div
Buffalo (2)	13	3	0	0.813	455	286	4-2
Miami* (5)	9	8	0	0.529	397	399	3-3
New England	8	9	0	0.471	364	347	3-3
NY Jets	7	10	0	0.412	296	316	2-4
North Division							
Cincinnati (3)	12	4	0	0.750	418	322	3-3
Baltimore* (6)	10	7	0	0.588	350	315	3-3
Pittsburgh	9	8	0	0.529	308	346	3-3
Cleveland	7	10	0	0.412	361	381	3-3
South Division							
Jacksonville (4)	9	8	0	0.529	404	350	4-2
Tennessee	7	10	0	0.412	298	359	3-3
Indianapolis	4	12	1	0.265	289	427	1-4-1
Houston	3	13	1	0.206	289	420	3-2-1
West Division							
Kansas City (1)	14	3	0	0.824	496	369	6-0
L.A. Chargers* (5)	10	7	0	0.588	391	384	2-4
Las Vegas	6	11	0	0.353	395	418	3-3
Denver	5	12	0	0.294	287	359	1-5

NATIONAL FOOTBALL CONFERENCE

East Division	W	L	T	Pct	PF	PA	Div
Philadelphia (1)	14	3	0	0.824	477	344	4-2
Dallas* (5)	12	5	0	0.706	467	342	4-2
NY Giants* (6)	9	7	1	0.559	365	371	1-4-1
Washington	8	8	1	0.500	321	343	2-3-1
North Division							
Minnesota (3)	13	4	0	0.765	424	427	4-2
Detroit	9	8	0	0.529	453	427	5-1
Green Bay	8	9	0	0.471	370	371	3-3
Chicago	3	14	0	0.176	326	463	0-6
South Division							
Tampa Bay (4)	8	9	0	0.471	313	358	4-2
Carolina	7	10	0	0.412	347	374	4-2
New Orleans	7	10	0	0.412	330	345	2-4
Atlanta	7	10	0	0.412	365	386	2-4
West Division							
San Francisco (2)	13	4	0	0.765	450	277	6-0
Seattle* (7)	9	8	0	0.529	407	401	4-2
L.A. Rams	5	12	0	0.294	307	384	1-5
Arizona	4	13	0	0.235	340	449	1-5

Note: Buffalo and Cincinnati each played only 16 regular-season games; the teams' Jan. 2, 2023, matchup was postponed—and subsequently canceled—due to a mid-game injury to Bills safety Damar Hamlin.

NFL Individual Leaders: American Football Conference, 2022

(* = rookie)

PASSING

Player, team	Att	Comp	Pct comp	Yds	Yds/Att	Long	TD	Pct TD	Int	Rating
Tua Tagovailoa, Miami	400	259	64.8	3,548	8.9	84	25	6.3	8	105.5
Patrick Mahomes, Kansas City	648	435	67.1	5,250	8.1	67	41	6.3	12	105.2
Joe Burrow, Cincinnati	606	414	68.3	4,475	7.4	60	35	5.8	12	100.8
Josh Allen, Buffalo	567	359	63.3	4,283	7.6	98	35	6.2	14	96.6
Trevor Lawrence, Jacksonville	584	387	66.3	4,113	7.0	59	25	4.3	8	95.2
Ryan Tannehill, Tennessee	325	212	65.2	2,536	7.8	69	13	4.0	6	94.6
Justin Herbert, L.A. Chargers	699	477	68.2	4,739	6.8	55	25	3.6	10	93.2
Lamar Jackson, Baltimore	326	203	62.3	2,242	6.9	75	17	5.2	7	91.1
Jacoby Brissett, Cleveland	369	236	64.0	2,608	7.1	55	12	3.3	6	88.9
Derek Carr, Las Vegas	502	305	60.8	3,522	7.0	60	24	4.8	14	86.3
Mac Jones, New England	442	288	65.2	2,997	6.8	48	14	3.2	11	84.8
Russell Wilson, Denver	483	292	60.5	3,524	7.3	67	16	3.3	11	84.4
Matt Ryan, Indianapolis	461	309	67.0	3,057	6.6	45	14	3.0	13	83.9
Davis Mills, Houston	479	292	61.0	3,118	6.5	58	17	3.5	15	78.8
*Kenny Pickett, Pittsburgh	389	245	63.0	2,404	6.2	57	7	1.8	9	76.7
Zach Wilson, NY Jets	242	132	54.6	1,688	7.0	79	6	2.5	7	72.8

RUSHING YARDS

Player, team	Yds	Att	Avg	Long	TD
Josh Jacobs, Las Vegas	1,653	340	4.9	86T	12
Derrick Henry, Tennessee	1,538	349	4.4	56	13
Nick Chubb, Cleveland	1,525	302	5.1	41T	12
*Travis Etienne Jr., Jacksonville	1,125	220	5.1	62T	5
Rhamondre Stevenson, New England	1,040	210	5.0	49	5
Najee Harris, Pittsburgh	1,034	272	3.8	36	7
*Dameon Pierce, Houston	939	220	4.3	75T	4
Austin Ekeler, L.A. Chargers	915	204	4.5	72T	13
Raheem Mostert, Miami	891	181	4.9	67	3
Jonathan Taylor, Indianapolis	861	192	4.5	66T	4

RECEPTIONS

Player, team	Rec	Yds	Avg	Long	TD
Tyreek Hill, Miami	119	1,710	14.4	64	7
Travis Kelce, Kansas City	110	1,338	12.2	52	12
Stefon Diggs, Buffalo	108	1,429	13.2	53T	11
Austin Ekeler, L.A. Chargers	107	722	6.7	23	5
Davante Adams, Las Vegas	100	1,516	15.2	60T	14
Michael Pittman, Indianapolis	99	925	9.3	28	4
Ja'Marr Chase, Cincinnati	87	1,046	12.0	60T	9
Diontae Johnson, Pittsburgh	86	882	10.3	37	0
Christian Kirk, Jacksonville	84	1,108	13.2	49	8
*Garrett Wilson, NY Jets	83	1,103	13.3	60	4

SCORING—KICKERS

Player, team	PAT	FG	Long	Pts
Justin Tucker, Baltimore	31	37	58	142
Daniel Carlson, Las Vegas	35	34	57	137
Tyler Bass, Buffalo	48	27	56	129
Nick Folk, New England	32	32	54	128
Riley Patterson, Jacksonville	36	30	53	126
Jason Sanders, Miami	41	26	55	119
Greg Zuerlein, NY Jets	28	30	60	118
Evan McPherson, Cincinnati	40	24	59	112
Ka'imi Fairbairn, Houston	24	29	56	111
Chase McLaughlin, Indianapolis	21	30	54	111

SCORING—NON-KICKERS

Player, team	TD	Rush	Rec	2-Pt	Pts
Austin Ekeler, L.A. Chargers	18	13	5	0	108
Davante Adams, Las Vegas	14	0	14	0	84
Nick Chubb, Cleveland	13	12	1	1	80
Derrick Henry, Tennessee	13	13	0	0	78
Travis Kelce, Kansas City	12	0	12	1	74
Josh Jacobs, Las Vegas	12	12	0	0	72
Stefon Diggs, Buffalo	11	0	11	0	66
Jerick McKinnon, Kansas City	10	1	9	1	62
Najee Harris, Pittsburgh	10	7	3	0	60

(Three players tied with 54 points)

INTERCEPTIONS

Player, team	No.	Yds	Avg	Long	TD
Minkah Fitzpatrick, Pittsburgh	6	94	15.7	34	1
Justin Simmons, Denver	6	51	8.5	23	0
*Jalen Pitre, Houston	5	57	11.4	29	0

(10 players tied with 4)

KICKOFF RETURNS

Player, team	No.	Yds	Avg	Long	TD
*Dallis Flowers, Indianapolis	23	715	31.1	89	0
*Jerome, Ford Cleveland	30	723	24.1	48	0
*Marcus Jones, New England	27	645	23.9	46	0
Braxton Berrios, NY Jets	26	600	23.1	42	0
Ameer Abdullah, Las Vegas	26	543	20.9	33	0
*Isiah Pacheco, Kansas City	29	597	20.6	48	0
Raheem Mostert, Miami	25	502	20.1	31	0
DeAndre Carter, L.A. Chargers	26	497	19.1	33	0

PUNTING

Player, team	No.	Yds	Long	Avg
*Ryan Stonehouse, Tennessee	90	4,779	74	53.1
Tommy Townsend, Kansas City	53	2,672	76	50.4
Logan Cooke, Jacksonville	58	2,862	70	49.3
A.J. Cole III, Las Vegas	59	2,884	67	48.9
Corey Bojorquez, Cleveland	61	2,959	76	48.5
Cameron Johnston, Houston	88	4,229	67	48.1
Sam Martin, Buffalo	46	2,146	67	47.7
Braden Mann, NY Jets	83	3,889	72	46.9

PUNTING (cont.)

Player, team	No.	Yds	Long	Avg
Corliss Waitman, Denver	96	4,470	59	46.6
Thomas Morstead, Miami	61	2,828	66	46.4

PUNT RETURNS

Player, team	No.	Yds	Avg	Long	TD
*Marcus Jones, New England	29	362	12.5	84T	1
DeAndre Carter, L.A. Chargers	29	339	11.7	28	0
Trent Taylor, Cincinnati	33	340	10.3	27	0
Nyheim Hines, Indianapolis/ Buffalo	27	264	9.8	28	0
Desmond King, Houston	33	309	9.4	31	0
*Montrell Washington, Denver	32	271	8.5	30	0
Jamal Agnew, Jacksonville	25	205	8.2	22	0

SACKS

Player, team	No.
Myles Garrett, Cleveland	16.0
Chris Jones, Kansas City	15.5
Matt Judon, New England	15.5
Alex Highsmith, Pittsburgh	14.5
Maxx Crosby, Las Vegas	12.5
Quinnen Williams, NY Jets	12.0
Josh Uche, New England	11.5
Cameron Heyward, Pittsburgh	10.5

NFL Individual Leaders: National Football Conference, 2022
(* = rookie)

PASSING

Player, team	Att	Comp	Pct comp	Yds	Yds/Att	Long	TD	Pct TD	Int	Rating
Jimmy Garoppolo, San Francisco	308	207	67.2	2,437	7.9	57	16	5.2	4	103.0
Jalen Hurts, Philadelphia	460	306	66.5	3,701	8.0	68	22	4.8	6	101.6
Geno Smith, Seattle	572	399	69.8	4,282	7.5	54	30	5.2	11	100.9
Jared Goff, Detroit	587	382	65.1	4,438	7.6	81	29	4.9	7	99.3
Andy Dalton, New Orleans	378	252	66.7	2,871	7.6	64	18	4.8	9	95.2
Daniel Jones, NY Giants	472	317	67.2	3,205	6.8	65	15	3.2	5	92.5
Kirk Cousins, Minnesota	643	424	65.9	4,547	7.1	66	29	4.5	14	92.5
Dak Prescott, Dallas	394	261	66.2	2,860	7.3	68	23	5.8	15	91.1
Aaron Rodgers, Green Bay	542	350	64.6	3,695	6.8	58	26	4.8	12	91.1
Tom Brady, Tampa Bay	733	490	66.8	4,694	6.4	63	25	3.4	9	90.7
Taylor Heinicke, Washington	259	161	62.2	1,859	7.2	61	12	4.6	6	89.6
Marcus Mariota, Atlanta	300	184	61.3	2,219	7.4	75	15	5.0	9	88.2
Matthew Stafford, L.A. Rams	303	206	68.0	2,087	6.9	75	10	3.3	8	87.4
Kyler Murray, Arizona	390	259	66.4	2,368	6.1	38	14	3.6	7	87.2
Justin Fields, Chicago	318	192	60.4	2,242	7.0	56	17	5.3	11	85.2
Carson Wentz, Washington	276	172	62.3	1,755	6.4	75	11	4.0	9	80.2
Baker Mayfield, Carolina/L.A. Rams	335	201	60.0	2,163	6.5	75	10	3.0	8	79.0

RUSHING YARDS

Player, team	Yds	Att	Avg	Long	TD
Saquon Barkley, NY Giants	1,312	295	4.4	68	10
Miles Sanders, Philadelphia	1,269	259	4.9	40T	11
Dalvin Cook, Minnesota	1,173	264	4.4	81T	8
Justin Fields, Chicago	1,143	160	7.1	67T	8
Christian McCaffrey, San Francisco/Carolina	1,139	244	4.7	49	8
Aaron Jones, Green Bay	1,121	213	5.3	36	2
Jamaal Williams, Detroit	1,066	262	4.1	58	17
*Kenneth Walker III, Seattle	1,050	228	4.6	74T	9
*Tyler Allgeier, Atlanta	1,035	210	4.9	44	3
Tony Pollard, Dallas	1,007	193	5.2	57T	9

RECEPTIONS

Player, team	Rec	Yds	Avg	Long	TD
Justin Jefferson, Minnesota	128	1,809	14.1	64	8
CeeDee Lamb, Dallas	107	1,359	12.7	39	9
Amon-Ra St. Brown, Detroit	106	1,161	11.0	49	6
Chris Godwin, Tampa Bay	104	1,023	9.8	44	3
DeVonta Smith, Philadelphia	95	1,196	12.6	45	7
D.K. Metcalf, Seattle	90	1,048	11.6	54	6
A.J. Brown, Philadelphia	88	1,496	17.0	78T	11
T.J. Hockenson, Detroit/Minnesota	86	914	10.6	81	6
Christian McCaffrey, San Francisco/Carolina	85	741	8.7	49	5
Tyler Lockett, Seattle	84	1,033	12.3	40T	9

SCORING—KICKERS

Player, team	PAT	FG	Long	Pts
Jason Myers, Seattle	41	34	56	143
Brett Maher, Dallas	50	29	60	137
Robbie Gould, San Francisco	50	27	51	131
Younghoe Koo, Atlanta	33	32	54	129
Eddy Pineiro, Carolina	30	33	54	129
Graham Gano, NY Giants	32	29	57	119
Greg Joseph, Minnesota	40	26	61	118
Ryan Succop, Tampa Bay	24	31	54	117
Matt Gay, L.A. Rams	31	28	58	115
Mason Crosby, Green Bay	37	25	56	112

SCORING—NON-KICKERS

Player, team	TD	Rush	Rec	2-Pt	Pts
Jamaal Williams, Detroit	17	17	0	1	104
Jalen Hurts, Philadelphia	13	13	0	2	82
Christian McCaffrey, San Francisco/Carolina	13	8	5	0	78
Ezekiel Elliott, Dallas	12	12	0	0	72
Tony Pollard, Dallas	12	9	3	0	72
A.J. Brown, Philadelphia	11	0	11	0	66
George Kittle, San Francisco	11	0	11	0	66
Miles Sanders, Philadelphia	11	11	0	0	66
Saquon Barkley, NY Giants	10	10	0	1	62
Dalvin Cook, Minnesota	10	8	2	0	60

INTERCEPTIONS

Player, team	No.	Yds	Avg	Long	TD
C.J. Gardner-Johnson, Philadelphia	6	54	9.0	25	0
*Tariq Woolen, Seattle	6	47	7.8	40T	1
Jaire Alexander, Green Bay	5	59	11.8	29	0
*DaRon Bland, Dallas	5	19	3.8	15	0
Tashaun Gipson, San Francisco	5	141	28.2	54	0
Patrick Peterson, Minnesota	5	92	18.4	39	0
Harrison Smith, Minnesota	5	58	11.6	35	0

KICKOFF RETURNS

Player, team	No.	Yds	Avg	Long	TD
Keisean Nixon, Green Bay	35	1,009	28.8	105T	1
*Velus Jones Jr., Chicago	22	607	27.6	63	0
Justin Jackson, Detroit	23	613	26.7	42	0
Kene Nwangwu, Minnesota	35	920	26.3	97T	1
Ray-Ray McCloud, San Francisco	26	599	23.0	39	0
Gary Brightwell, NY Giants	26	555	21.3	47	0
Brandon Powell, L.A. Rams	30	605	20.2	34	0

PUNTING

Player, team	No.	Yds	Long	Avg
*Jake Camarda, Tampa Bay	79	3,859	74	48.8
Jack Fox, Detroit	52	2,525	66	48.6
Michael Dickson, Seattle	66	3,199	68	48.5
Johnny Hekker, Carolina	81	3,925	68	48.5
Bryan Anger, Dallas	68	3,291	83	48.4
Riley Dixon, L.A. Rams	73	3,434	67	48.4
*Ryan Wright, Minnesota	74	3,457	73	47.4
Andy Lee, Arizona	68	3,157	65	47.1
Tress Way, Washington	83	3,885	68	46.8
Jamie Gillan, NY Giants	75	3,463	69	46.8

PUNT RETURNS

Player, team	No.	Yds	Avg	Long	TD
Ray-Ray McCloud, San Francisco	33	356	10.8	35	0
Jaelon Darden, Cleveland/Tampa Bay	33	345	10.4	24	0
*KaVontae Turpin, Dallas	29	303	10.4	52	0
*Britain Covey, Philadelphia	33	308	9.3	27	0
Dax Milne, Washington	30	311	7.8	19	0
Brandon Powell, L.A. Rams	24	177	7.4	22	0
Richie James, NY Giants	24	174	7.2	23	0

SACKS

Player, team	No.
Nick Bosa, San Francisco	18.5
Haason Reddick, Philadelphia	16.0
Micah Parsons, Dallas	13.5
Brian Burns, Carolina	12.5
J.J. Watt, Arizona	12.5
Daron Payne, Washington	11.5
Brandon Graham, Philadelphia	11.0
Javon Hargrave, Philadelphia	11.0
Josh Sweat, Philadelphia	11.0

Super Bowl, 1967-2023

The Super Bowl was created as a condition of the merger between the American Football League (AFL, formed in 1959) and National Football League (NFL, formed in 1920). Announced June 8, 1966, the merger agreement stipulated that the leagues would play separate regular season schedules through the 1969 season but meet after each in an AFL-NFL Championship Game, unofficially dubbed the Super Bowl. The first Super Bowl, played at the Memorial Coliseum in Los Angeles on Jan. 15, 1967, did not sell out, unlike every Super Bowl game since. Each player on the victorious Green Bay Packers earned $15,000 for the win; the defeated Kansas City Chiefs each collected $7,500.

No.	Year	Winner	Opponent	Winning coach	Site
I	1967	*Green Bay Packers, 35	Kansas City Chiefs, 10	Vince Lombardi	Memorial Coliseum, Los Angeles, CA
II	1968	Green Bay Packers, 33	*Oakland Raiders, 14	Vince Lombardi	Orange Bowl, Miami, FL
III	1969	*NY Jets, 16	Baltimore Colts, 7	Weeb Ewbank	Orange Bowl, Miami, FL
IV	1970	Kansas City Chiefs, 23	*Minnesota Vikings, 7	Hank Stram	Tulane Stadium, New Orleans, LA
V	1971	Baltimore Colts, 16	*Dallas Cowboys, 13	Don McCafferty	Orange Bowl, Miami, FL
VI	1972	Dallas Cowboys, 24	*Miami Dolphins, 3	Tom Landry	Tulane Stadium, New Orleans, LA
VII	1973	*Miami Dolphins, 14	Washington Redskins, 7	Don Shula	Memorial Coliseum, Los Angeles, CA
VIII	1974	*Miami Dolphins, 24	Minnesota Vikings, 7	Don Shula	Rice Stadium, Houston, TX
IX	1975	*Pittsburgh Steelers, 16	Minnesota Vikings, 6	Chuck Noll	Tulane Stadium, New Orleans, LA
X	1976	Pittsburgh Steelers, 21	*Dallas Cowboys, 17	Chuck Noll	Orange Bowl, Miami, FL
XI	1977	*Oakland Raiders, 32	Minnesota Vikings, 14	John Madden	Rose Bowl, Pasadena, CA
XII	1978	*Dallas Cowboys, 27	Denver Broncos, 10	Tom Landry	Superdome, New Orleans, LA
XIII	1979	Pittsburgh Steelers, 35	*Dallas Cowboys, 31	Chuck Noll	Orange Bowl, Miami, FL
XIV	1980	Pittsburgh Steelers, 31	*L.A. Rams, 19	Chuck Noll	Rose Bowl, Pasadena, CA
XV	1981	Oakland Raiders, 27	*Philadelphia Eagles, 10	Tom Flores	Superdome, New Orleans, LA
XVI	1982	*San Francisco 49ers, 26	Cincinnati Bengals, 21	Bill Walsh	Silverdome, Pontiac, MI
XVII	1983	Washington Redskins, 27	*Miami Dolphins, 17	Joe Gibbs	Rose Bowl, Pasadena, CA
XVIII	1984	*L.A. Raiders, 38	Washington Redskins, 9	Tom Flores	Tampa Stadium, Tampa, FL
XIX	1985	*San Francisco 49ers, 38	Miami Dolphins, 16	Bill Walsh	Stanford Stadium, Stanford, CA
XX	1986	*Chicago Bears, 46	New England Patriots, 10	Mike Ditka	Superdome, New Orleans, LA
XXI	1987	NY Giants, 39	*Denver Broncos, 20	Bill Parcells	Rose Bowl, Pasadena, CA
XXII	1988	*Washington Redskins, 42	Denver Broncos, 10	Joe Gibbs	Jack Murphy Stadium, San Diego, CA
XXIII	1989	*San Francisco 49ers, 20	Cincinnati Bengals, 16	Bill Walsh	Joe Robbie Stadium, Miami, FL
XXIV	1990	San Francisco 49ers, 55	*Denver Broncos, 10	George Seifert	Superdome, New Orleans, LA
XXV	1991	NY Giants, 20	*Buffalo Bills, 19	Bill Parcells	Tampa Stadium, Tampa, FL
XXVI	1992	*Washington Redskins, 37	Buffalo Bills, 24	Joe Gibbs	Metrodome, Minneapolis, MN
XXVII	1993	Dallas Cowboys, 52	*Buffalo Bills, 17	Jimmy Johnson	Rose Bowl, Pasadena, CA
XXVIII	1994	*Dallas Cowboys, 30	Buffalo Bills, 13	Jimmy Johnson	Georgia Dome, Atlanta, GA
XXIX	1995	*San Francisco 49ers, 49	San Diego Chargers, 26	George Seifert	Joe Robbie Stadium, Miami, FL
XXX	1996	*Dallas Cowboys, 27	Pittsburgh Steelers, 17	Barry Switzer	Sun Devil Stadium, Tempe, AZ
XXXI	1997	Green Bay Packers, 35	*New England Patriots, 21	Mike Holmgren	Superdome, New Orleans, LA
XXXII	1998	Denver Broncos, 31	*Green Bay Packers, 24	Mike Shanahan	Qualcomm Stadium, San Diego, CA
XXXIII	1999	Denver Broncos, 34	*Atlanta Falcons, 19	Mike Shanahan	Pro Player Stadium, Miami, FL
XXXIV	2000	*St. Louis Rams, 23	Tennessee Titans, 16	Dick Vermeil	Georgia Dome, Atlanta, GA
XXXV	2001	Baltimore Ravens, 34	*NY Giants, 7	Brian Billick	Raymond James Stadium, Tampa, FL
XXXVI	2002	New England Patriots, 20	*St. Louis Rams, 17	Bill Belichick	Superdome, New Orleans, LA
XXXVII	2003	*Tampa Bay Buccaneers, 48	Oakland Raiders, 21	Jon Gruden	Qualcomm Stadium, San Diego, CA
XXXVIII	2004	New England Patriots, 32	*Carolina Panthers, 29	Bill Belichick	Reliant Stadium, Houston, TX
XXXIX	2005	New England Patriots, 24	*Philadelphia Eagles, 21	Bill Belichick	Alltel Stadium, Jacksonville, FL
XL	2006	Pittsburgh Steelers, 21	*Seattle Seahawks, 10	Bill Cowher	Ford Field, Detroit, MI
XLI	2007	Indianapolis Colts, 29	*Chicago Bears, 17	Tony Dungy	Dolphin Stadium, Miami Gardens, FL
XLII	2008	*NY Giants, 17	New England Patriots, 14	Tom Coughlin	Univ. of Phoenix Stadium, Glendale, AZ
XLIII	2009	Pittsburgh Steelers, 27	**Arizona Cardinals, 23	Mike Tomlin	Raymond James Stadium, Tampa, FL
XLIV	2010	*New Orleans Saints, 31	Indianapolis Colts, 17	Sean Payton	Sun Life Stadium, Miami Gardens, FL
XLV	2011	**Green Bay Packers, 31	Pittsburgh Steelers, 25	Mike McCarthy	Cowboys Stadium, Arlington, TX
XLVI	2012	NY Giants, 21	**New England Patriots, 17	Tom Coughlin	Lucas Oil Stadium, Indianapolis, IN
XLVII	2013	**Baltimore Ravens, 34	San Francisco 49ers, 31	John Harbaugh	Mercedes-Benz Superdome, New Orleans, LA
XLVIII	2014	Seattle Seahawks, 43	Denver Broncos, 8	Pete Carroll	MetLife Stadium, East Rutherford, NJ
XLIX	2015	New England Patriots, 28	**Seattle Seahawks, 24	Bill Belichick	Univ. of Phoenix Stadium, Glendale, AZ
50 (L)	2016	Denver Broncos, 24	**Carolina Panthers, 10	Gary Kubiak	Levi's Stadium, Santa Clara, CA
LI	2017	New England Patriots, 34 (OT)	**Atlanta Falcons, 28	Bill Belichick	NRG Stadium, Houston, TX
LII	2018	Philadelphia Eagles, 41	**New England Patriots, 33	Doug Pederson	U.S. Bank Stadium, Minneapolis, MN
LIII	2019	New England Patriots, 13	**L.A. Rams, 3	Bill Belichick	Mercedes-Benz Stadium, Atlanta, GA
LIV	2020	Kansas City Chiefs, 31	**San Francisco 49ers, 20	Andy Reid	Hard Rock Stadium, Miami Gardens, FL
LV	2021	Tampa Bay Buccaneers, 31	**Kansas City Chiefs, 9	Bruce Arians	Raymond James Stadium, Tampa, FL
LVI	2022	L.A. Rams, 23	**Cincinnati Bengals, 20	Sean McVay	SoFi Stadium, Inglewood, CA
LVII	2023	**Kansas City Chiefs, 38	Philadelphia Eagles, 35	Andy Reid	State Farm Stadium, Glendale, AZ

* = Team won the coin toss and elected to receive. ** = Team won the coin toss and elected to receive in the second half. OT = Overtime.

Super Bowl Sites, 2024-26

No.	Site	Date	No.	Site	Date
LVIII	Allegiant Stadium, Las Vegas, NV	Feb. 11, 2024	LX	Levi's Stadium, Santa Clara, CA	Feb. 8, 2026
LVIX	Caesars Superdome, New Orleans, LA	Feb. 9, 2025			

Super Bowl MVPs, 1967-2023

Year	Most valuable player, team	Year	Most valuable player, team	Year	Most valuable player, team
1967	Bart Starr, Green Bay	1986	Richard Dent, Chicago	2005	Deion Branch, New England
1968	Bart Starr, Green Bay	1987	Phil Simms, NY Giants	2006	Hines Ward, Pittsburgh
1969	Joe Namath, NY Jets	1988	Doug Williams, Washington	2007	Peyton Manning, Indianapolis
1970	Len Dawson, Kansas City	1989	Jerry Rice, San Francisco	2008	Eli Manning, NY Giants
1971	Chuck Howley, Dallas	1990	Joe Montana, San Francisco	2009	Santonio Holmes, Pittsburgh
1972	Roger Staubach, Dallas	1991	Ottis Anderson, NY Giants	2010	Drew Brees, New Orleans
1973	Jake Scott, Miami	1992	Mark Rypien, Washington	2011	Aaron Rodgers, Green Bay
1974	Larry Csonka, Miami	1993	Troy Aikman, Dallas	2012	Eli Manning, NY Giants
1975	Franco Harris, Pittsburgh	1994	Emmitt Smith, Dallas	2013	Joe Flacco, Baltimore
1976	Lynn Swann, Pittsburgh	1995	Steve Young, San Francisco	2014	Malcolm Smith, Seattle
1977	Fred Biletnikoff, Oakland	1996	Larry Brown, Dallas	2015	Tom Brady, New England
1978	Randy White, Harvey Martin; Dallas	1997	Desmond Howard, Green Bay	2016	Von Miller, Denver
1979	Terry Bradshaw, Pittsburgh	1998	Terrell Davis, Denver	2017	Tom Brady, New England
1980	Terry Bradshaw, Pittsburgh	1999	John Elway, Denver	2018	Nick Foles, Philadelphia
1981	Jim Plunkett, Oakland	2000	Kurt Warner, St. Louis	2019	Julian Edelman, New England
1982	Joe Montana, San Francisco	2001	Ray Lewis, Baltimore	2020	Patrick Mahomes, Kansas City
1983	John Riggins, Washington	2002	Tom Brady, New England	2021	Tom Brady, Tampa Bay
1984	Marcus Allen, L.A. Raiders	2003	Dexter Jackson, Tampa Bay	2022	Cooper Kupp, L.A. Rams
1985	Joe Montana, San Francisco	2004	Tom Brady, New England	2023	Patrick Mahomes, Kansas City

Super Bowl Single-Game Statistical Leaders

PASSING YARDS

Player, team	Year	Att/comp	Yds	TD
Tom Brady, New England	2018	48/28	505	3
Tom Brady, New England	2017	62/43	466	2
Kurt Warner, St. Louis	2000	45/24	414	2
Kurt Warner, Arizona	2009	43/31	377	3
Nick Foles, Philadelphia	2018	43/28	373	3
Kurt Warner, St. Louis	2002	44/28	365	1
Donovon McNabb, Philadelphia	2005	51/30	357	3
Joe Montana, San Francisco	1989	36/23	357	2

PASSING TOUCHDOWNS

Player, team	Year	Att/comp	Yds	TD
Steve Young, San Francisco	1995	36/24	325	6
Joe Montana, San Francisco	1990	29/22	297	5
Tom Brady, New England	2015	50/37	328	4
Troy Aikman, Dallas	1993	30/22	273	4
Doug Williams, Washington	1988	29/18	340	4
Terry Bradshaw, Pittsburgh	1979	30/17	318	4

RECEIVING YARDS

Player, team	Year	Rec	Yds	TD
Jerry Rice, San Francisco	1989	11	215	1
Ricky Sanders, Washington	1988	9	193	2
Isaac Bruce, St. Louis	2000	6	162	1

RUSHING YARDS

Player, team	Year	Att	Yds	TD
Timmy Smith, Washington	1988	22	204	2
Marcus Allen, L.A. Raiders	1984	20	191	2
John Riggins, Washington	1983	38	166	1

SCORING

Player, team	Year	Pts	
Jalen Hurts, Philadelphia	2023	20	(3 TDs, 1 2-pt)
James White, New England	2017	20	(3 TDs, 1 2-pt)
Terrell Davis, Denver	1998	18	(3 TDs)
Jerry Rice, San Francisco	1995	18	(3 TDs)
Ricky Watters, San Francisco	1995	18	(3 TDs)
Jerry Rice, San Francisco	1990	18	(3 TDs)
Roger Craig, San Francisco	1985	18	(3 TDs)
Don Chandler, Green Bay	1968	15	(4 FGs, 3 PATs)
Kevin Butler, Chicago Bears	1986	14	(3 FGs, 5 PATs)
Ray Wersching, San Francisco	1982	14	(4 FGs, 2 PATs)

First-Round Selections in the 2023 NFL Draft

Held Apr. 27-29, 2023.

Team	Player	Pos.	College
1. Carolina Panthers[1]	Bryce Young	QB	Alabama
2. Houston Texans	C.J. Stroud	QB	Ohio St.
3. Houston Texans[2]	Will Anderson Jr.	LB	Alabama
4. Indianapolis Colts	Anthony Richardson	QB	Florida
5. Seattle Seahawks[3]	Devon Witherspoon	CB	Illinois
6. Arizona Cardinals[4]	Paris Johnson Jr.	OT	Ohio St.
7. Las Vegas Raiders	Tyree Wilson	DE	Texas Tech
8. Atlanta Falcons	Bijan Robinson	RB	Texas
9. Philadelphia Eagles[5]	Jalen Carter	DT	Georgia
10. Chicago Bears[6]	Darnell Wright	OT	Tennessee
11. Tennessee Titans	Peter Skoronski	OT	Northwestern
12. Detroit Lions[7]	Jahmyr Gibbs	RB	Alabama
13. Green Bay Packers[8]	Lukas Van Ness	DE	Iowa
14. Pittsburgh Steelers[9]	Broderick Jones	OT	Georgia
15. NY Jets[10]	Will McDonald IV	LB	Iowa St.
16. Washington Commanders	Emmanuel Forbes	CB	Mississippi St.
17. New England Patriots[11]	Christian Gonzalez	CB	Oregon
18. Detroit Lions	Jack Campbell	LB	Iowa
19. Tampa Bay Buccaneers	Calijah Kancey	DT	Pittsburgh
20. Seattle Seahawks	Jaxon Smith-Njigba	WR	Ohio St.
21. L.A. Chargers	Quentin Johnston	WR	TCU
22. Baltimore Ravens	Zay Flowers	WR	Boston Coll.
23. Minnesota Vikings	Jordan Addison	WR	USC
24. NY Giants[12]	Deonte Banks	CB	Maryland
25. Buffalo Bills[13]	Dalton Kincaid	TE	Utah
26. Dallas Cowboys	Mazi Smith	DT	Michigan
27. Jacksonville Jaguars[14]	Anton Harrison	OT	Oklahoma
28. Cincinnati Bengals	Myles Murphy	DE	Clemson
29. New Orleans Saints[15]	Bryan Bresee	DT	Clemson
30. Philadelphia Eagles	Nolan Smith	LB	Georgia
31. Kansas City Chiefs	Felix Anudike-Uzomah	DE	Kansas St.

(1) From Chicago. (2) From Arizona. (3) From Denver. (4) From Detroit via L.A. Rams. (5) From Chicago via Carolina. (6) From Philadelphia via New Orleans. (7) From Arizona via Houston and Cleveland. (8) From NY Jets. (9) From New England. (10) From Green Bay. (11) From Pittsburgh. (12) From Jacksonville. (13) From Jacksonville via NY Giants. (14) From Buffalo. (15) From San Francisco via Miami and Denver.

Number One NFL Draft Choices, 1980-2023

Year	Team	Player, pos., college	Year	Team	Player, pos., college
1980	Detroit	Billy Sims, RB, Oklahoma	2002	Houston	David Carr, QB, Fresno St.
1981	New Orleans	George Rogers, RB, South Carolina	2003	Cincinnati	Carson Palmer, QB, USC
1982	New England	Kenneth Sims, DT, Texas	2004	San Diego	Eli Manning, QB, Mississippi
1983	Baltimore Colts	John Elway, QB, Stanford	2005	San Francisco	Alex D. Smith, QB, Utah
1984	New England	Irving Fryar, WR, Nebraska	2006	Houston	Mario Williams, DE, NC State
1985	Buffalo	Bruce Smith, DE, Virginia Tech	2007	Oakland	JaMarcus Russell, QB, LSU
1986	Tampa Bay	Bo Jackson, RB, Auburn	2008	Miami	Jake Long, OT, Michigan
1987	Tampa Bay	Vinny Testaverde, QB, Miami (FL)	2009	Detroit	Matthew Stafford, QB, Georgia
1988	Atlanta	Aundray Bruce, LB, Auburn	2010	St. Louis	Sam Bradford, QB, Oklahoma
1989	Dallas	Troy Aikman, QB, UCLA	2011	Carolina	Cam Newton, QB, Auburn
1990	Indianapolis	Jeff George, QB, Illinois	2012	Indianapolis	Andrew Luck, QB, Stanford
1991	Dallas	Russell Maryland, DL, Miami (FL)	2013	Kansas City	Eric Fisher, OT, Central Michigan
1992	Indianapolis	Steve Emtman, DL, Washington	2014	Houston	Jadeveon Clowney, DE, South Carolina
1993	New England	Drew Bledsoe, QB, Washington St.	2015	Tampa Bay	Jameis Winston, QB, Florida St.
1994	Cincinnati	Dan Wilkinson, DT, Ohio St.	2016	L.A. Rams	Jared Goff, QB, California
1995	Cincinnati	Ki-Jana Carter, RB, Penn St.	2017	Cleveland	Myles Garrett, DE, Texas A&M
1996	NY Jets	Keyshawn Johnson, WR, USC	2018	Cleveland	Baker Mayfield, QB, Oklahoma
1997	St. Louis	Orlando Pace, OT, Ohio St.	2019	Arizona	Kyler Murray, QB, Oklahoma
1998	Indianapolis	Peyton Manning, QB, Tennessee	2020	Cincinnati	Joe Burrow, QB, LSU
1999	Cleveland	Tim Couch, QB, Kentucky	2021	Jacksonville	Trevor Lawrence, QB, Clemson
2000	Cleveland	Courtney Brown, DE, Penn St.	2022	Jacksonville	Travon Walker, DE, Georgia
2001	Atlanta	Michael Vick, QB, Virginia Tech	2023	Carolina	Bryce Young, QB, Alabama

American Football League Champions, 1960-69

Year	Eastern (W-L-T)	Western (W-L-T)	Championship
1960	Houston Oilers (10-4-0)	L.A. Chargers (10-4-0)	Houston 24, L.A. 16
1961	Houston Oilers (10-3-1)	San Diego Chargers (12-2-0)	Houston 10, San Diego 3
1962	Houston Oilers (11-3-0)	Dallas Texans (11-3-0)	Dallas 20, Houston 17 (2 OT)
1963	Boston Patriots (7-6-1)[1]	San Diego Chargers (11-3-0)	San Diego 51, Boston 10
1964	Buffalo Bills (12-2-0)	San Diego Chargers (8-5-1)	Buffalo 20, San Diego 7
1965	Buffalo Bills (10-3-1)	San Diego Chargers (9-2-3)	Buffalo 23, San Diego 0
1966	Buffalo Bills (9-4-1)	Kansas City Chiefs (11-2-1)	Kansas City 31, Buffalo 7
1967	Houston Oilers (9-4-1)	Oakland Raiders (13-1-0)	Oakland 40, Houston 7
1968	NY Jets (11-3-0)	Oakland Raiders (12-2-0)[2]	NY Jets 27, Oakland 23
1969	NY Jets (10-4-0)	Kansas City Chiefs (11-3-0)	Kansas City 17, Oakland 7[3]

(1) Defeated conference champion Buffalo Bills in divisional playoff. (2) Defeated conference champion Kansas City Chiefs in divisional playoff. (3) Kansas City Chiefs defeated NY Jets, and Oakland Raiders defeated Houston Oilers in divisional playoffs.

National Football League Champions, 1933-69

Year	Eastern (W-L-T)	Western (W-L-T)	Championship
1933	NY Giants (11-3-0)	Chicago Bears (10-2-1)	Chicago Bears 23, NY Giants 21
1934	NY Giants (8-5-0)	Chicago Bears (13-0-0)	NY Giants 30, Chicago Bears 13
1935	NY Giants (9-3-0)	Detroit Lions (7-3-2)	Detroit 26, NY Giants 7
1936	Boston Redskins (7-5-0)	Green Bay Packers (10-1-1)	Green Bay 21, Boston 6
1937	Washington Redskins (8-3-0)	Chicago Bears (9-1-1)	Washington 28, Chicago Bears 21
1938	NY Giants (8-2-1)	Green Bay Packers (8-3-0)	NY Giants 23, Green Bay 17
1939	NY Giants (9-1-1)	Green Bay Packers (9-2-0)	Green Bay 27, NY Giants 0
1940	Washington Redskins (9-2-0)	Chicago Bears (8-3-0)	Chicago Bears 73, Washington 0
1941	NY Giants (8-3-0)	Chicago Bears (10-1-0)[1]	Chicago Bears 37, NY Giants 9
1942	Washington Redskins (10-1-0)	Chicago Bears (11-0-0)	Washington 14, Chicago Bears 6
1943	Washington Redskins (6-3-1)[1]	Chicago Bears (8-1-1)	Chicago Bears, 41, Washington 21
1944	NY Giants (8-1-1)	Green Bay Packers (8-2-0)	Green Bay 14, NY Giants 7
1945	Washington Redskins (8-2-0)	Cleveland Rams (9-1-0)	Cleveland Rams 15, Washington 14
1946	NY Giants (7-3-1)	Chicago Bears (8-2-1)	Chicago Bears 24, NY Giants 14
1947	Philadelphia Eagles (8-4-0)[1]	Chicago Cardinals (9-3-0)	Chicago Cardinals 28, Philadelphia 21
1948	Philadelphia Eagles (9-2-1)	Chicago Cardinals (11-1-0)	Philadelphia 7, Chicago Cardinals 0
1949	Philadelphia Eagles (8-2-2)	L.A. Rams (8-2-2)	Philadelphia 14, L.A. Rams 0
1950	Cleveland Browns (10-2-0)[1]	L.A. Rams (9-3-0)[1]	Cleveland Browns 30, L.A. Rams 28
1951	Cleveland Browns (11-1-0)	L.A. Rams (8-4-0)	L.A. Rams 24, Cleveland Browns 17
1952	Cleveland Browns (8-4-0)	Detroit Lions (9-3-0)[1]	Detroit 17, Cleveland Browns 7
1953	Cleveland Browns (11-1-0)	Detroit Lions (10-2-0)	Detroit 17, Cleveland Browns 16
1954	Cleveland Browns (9-3-0)	Detroit Lions (9-2-1)	Cleveland Browns 56, Detroit 10
1955	Cleveland Browns (9-2-1)	L.A. Rams (8-3-1)	Cleveland Browns 38, L.A. Rams 14
1956	NY Giants (8-3-1)	Chicago Bears (9-2-1)	NY Giants 47, Chicago Bears 7
1957	Cleveland Browns (9-2-1)	Detroit Lions (8-4-0)[1]	Detroit 59, Cleveland Browns 14
1958	NY Giants (9-3-0)[1]	Baltimore Colts (9-3-0)	Baltimore 23, NY Giants 17[2]
1959	NY Giants (10-2-0)	Baltimore Colts (9-3-0)	Baltimore 31, NY Giants 16
1960	Philadelphia Eagles (10-2-0)	Green Bay Packers (8-4-0)	Philadelphia 17, Green Bay 13
1961	NY Giants (10-3-1)	Green Bay Packers (11-3-0)	Green Bay 37, NY Giants 0
1962	NY Giants (12-2-0)	Green Bay Packers (13-1-0)	Green Bay 16, NY Giants 7
1963	NY Giants (11-3-0)	Chicago Bears (11-1-2)	Chicago 14, NY Giants 10
1964	Cleveland Browns (10-3-1)	Baltimore Colts (12-2-0)	Cleveland Browns 27, Baltimore 0
1965	Cleveland Browns (11-3-0)	Green Bay Packers (10-3-1)[1]	Green Bay 23, Cleveland Browns 12
1966	Dallas Cowboys (10-3-1)	Green Bay Packers (12-2-0)	Green Bay 34, Dallas 27
1967	Dallas Cowboys (9-5-0)	Green Bay Packers (9-4-1)	Green Bay 21, Dallas 17
1968	Cleveland Browns (10-4-0)	Baltimore Colts (13-1-0)	Baltimore 34, Cleveland Browns 0
1969	Cleveland Browns (10-3-1)	Minnesota Vikings (12-2-0)	Minnesota 27, Cleveland Browns 7

Note: Conference title games preceded NFL Championship from 1967-69. (1) Won divisional or conference playoff. (2) Won at 8:15 of sudden death overtime period.

NFL Divisional Champions and Wild Cards, 1970-95

The American Football League and National Football League officially merged in 1966. At the beginning of the 1970 season, the two leagues became the AFC and NFC conferences in the new NFL. Regular-season (W-L-T) records are in parentheses.

AMERICAN FOOTBALL CONFERENCE

Year	Eastern	Central	Western	Wild card
1970	Baltimore Colts (11-2-1)	Cincinnati Bengals (8-6-0)	Oakland Raiders (8-4-2)	Miami Dolphins (10-4-0)
1971	Miami Dolphins (10-3-1)	Cleveland Browns (9-5-0)	Kansas City Chiefs (10-3-1)	Baltimore Colts (10-4-0)
1972	Miami Dolphins (14-0-0)	Pittsburgh Steelers (11-3-0)	Oakland Raiders (10-3-1)	Cleveland Browns (10-4-0)
1973	Miami Dolphins (12-2-0)	Cincinnati Bengals (10-4-0)	Oakland Raiders (9-4-1)	Pittsburgh Steelers (10-4-0)
1974	Miami Dolphins (11-3-0)	Pittsburgh Steelers (10-3-1)	Oakland Raiders (12-2-0)	Buffalo Bills (9-5-0)
1975	Baltimore Colts (10-4-0)	Pittsburgh Steelers (12-2-0)	Oakland Raiders (11-3-0)	Cincinnati Bengals (11-3-0)
1976	Baltimore Colts (11-3-0)	Pittsburgh Steelers (10-4-0)	Oakland Raiders (13-1-0)	New England Patriots (11-3-0)
1977	Baltimore Colts (10-4-0)	Pittsburgh Steelers (9-5-0)	Denver Broncos (12-2-0)	Oakland Raiders (11-3-0)
1978	New England Patriots (11-5-0)	Pittsburgh Steelers (14-2-0)	Denver Broncos (10-6-0)	Houston Oilers (10-6-0) Miami Dolphins (11-5-0)
1979	Miami Dolphins (10-6-0)	Pittsburgh Steelers (12-4-0)	San Diego Chargers (12-4-0)	Houston Oilers (11-5-0) Denver Broncos (10-6-0)
1980	Buffalo Bills (11-5-0)	Cleveland Browns (11-5-0)	San Diego Chargers (11-5-0)	Houston Oilers (11-5-0) Oakland Raiders (11-5-0)
1981	Miami Dolphins (11-4-1)	Cincinnati Bengals (12-4-0)	San Diego Chargers (10-6-0)	Buffalo Bills (10-6-0) NY Jets (10-5-1)
1982	Strike abbreviated season. See note.			
1983	Miami Dolphins (12-4-0)	Pittsburgh Steelers (10-6-0)	L.A. Raiders (12-4-0)	Denver Broncos (9-7-0) Seattle Seahawks (9-7-0)
1984	Miami Dolphins (14-2-0)	Pittsburgh Steelers (9-7-0)	Denver Broncos (13-3-0)	L.A. Raiders (11-5-0) Seattle Seahawks (12-4-0)
1985	Miami Dolphins (12-4-0)	Cleveland Browns (8-8-0)	L.A. Raiders (12-4-0)	New England Patriots (11-5-0) NY Jets (11-5-0)
1986	New England Patriots (11-5-0)	Cleveland Browns (12-4-0)	Denver Broncos (11-5-0)	Kansas City Chiefs (10-6-0) NY Jets (10-6-0)
1987	Indianapolis Colts (9-6-0)	Cleveland Browns (10-5-0)	Denver Broncos (10-4-1)	Houston Oilers (9-6-0) Seattle Seahawks (9-6-0)
1988	Buffalo Bills (12-4-0)	Cincinnati Bengals (12-4-0)	Seattle Seahawks (9-7-0)	Cleveland Browns (10-6-0) Houston Oilers (10-6-0)
1989	Buffalo Bills (9-7-0)	Cleveland Browns (9-6-1)	Denver Broncos (11-5-0)	Houston Oilers (9-7-0) Pittsburgh Steelers (9-7-0)
1990	Buffalo Bills (13-3-0)	Cincinnati Bengals (9-7-0)	L.A. Raiders (12-4-0)	Houston Oilers (9-7-0) Kansas City Chiefs (11-5-0) Miami Dolphins (12-4-0)
1991	Buffalo Bills (13-3-0)	Houston Oilers (11-5-0)	Denver Broncos (12-4-0)	Kansas City Chiefs (10-6-0) L.A. Raiders (9-7-0) NY Jets (8-8-0)
1992	Miami Dolphins (11-5-0)	Pittsburgh Steelers (11-5-0)	San Diego Chargers (11-5-0)	Buffalo Bills (11-5-0) Houston Oilers (10-6-0) Kansas City Chiefs (10-6-0)
1993	Buffalo Bills (12-4-0)	Houston Oilers (12-4-0)	Kansas City Chiefs (11-5-0)	Denver Broncos (9-7-0) L.A. Raiders (10-6-0) Pittsburgh Steelers (9-7-0)
1994	Miami Dolphins (10-6-0)	Pittsburgh Steelers (12-4-0)	San Diego Chargers (11-5-0)	Cleveland Browns (11-5-0) Kansas City Chiefs (9-7-0) New England Patriots (10-6-0)
1995	Buffalo Bills (10-6-0)	Pittsburgh Steelers (11-5-0)	Kansas City Chiefs (13-3-0)	Miami Dolphins (9-7-0) Indianapolis Colts (9-7-0) San Diego Chargers (9-7-0)

NATIONAL FOOTBALL CONFERENCE

Year	Eastern	Central	Western	Wild card
1970	Dallas Cowboys (10-4-0)	Minnesota Vikings (12-2-0)	San Francisco 49ers (10-3-1)	Detroit Lions (10-4-0)
1971	Dallas Cowboys (11-3-0)	Minnesota Vikings (11-3-0)	San Francisco 49ers (9-5-0)	Washington Redskins (9-4-1)
1972	Washington Redskins (11-3-0)	Green Bay Packers (10-4-0)	San Francisco 49ers (8-5-1)	Dallas Cowboys (10-4-0)
1973	Dallas Cowboys (10-4-0)	Minnesota Vikings (12-2-0)	L.A. Rams (12-2-0)	Washington Redskins (10-4-0)
1974	St. Louis Cardinals (10-4-0)	Minnesota Vikings (10-4-0)	L.A. Rams (10-4-0)	Washington Redskins (10-4-0)
1975	St. Louis Cardinals (11-3-0)	Minnesota Vikings (12-2-0)	L.A. Rams (12-2-0)	Dallas Cowboys (10-4-0)
1976	Dallas Cowboys (11-3-0)	Minnesota Vikings (11-2-1)	L.A. Rams (10-3-1)	Washington Redskins (10-4-0)
1977	Dallas Cowboys (12-2-0)	Minnesota Vikings (9-5-0)	L.A. Rams (10-4-0)	Chicago Bears (9-5-0)
1978	Dallas Cowboys (12-4-0)	Minnesota Vikings (8-7-1)	L.A. Rams (12-4-0)	Atlanta Falcons (9-7-0) Philadelphia Eagles (9-7-0)
1979	Dallas Cowboys (11-5-0)	Tampa Bay Buccaneers (10-6-0)	L.A. Rams (9-7-0)	Chicago Bears (10-6-0) Philadelphia Eagles (11-5-0)
1980	Philadelphia Eagles (12-4-0)	Minnesota Vikings (9-7-0)	Atlanta Falcons (12-4-0)	Dallas Cowboys (12-4-0) L.A. Rams (11-5-0)

Year	Eastern	Central	Western	Wild card
1981	Dallas Cowboys (12-4-0)	Tampa Bay Buccaneers (9-7-0)	San Francisco 49ers (13-3-0)	NY Giants (9-7-0) Philadelphia Eagles (10-6-0)
1982	Strike abbreviated season. See note.			
1983	Washington Redskins (14-2-0)	Detroit Lions (9-7-0)	San Francisco 49ers (10-6-0)	Dallas Cowboys (12-4-0) L.A. Rams (9-7-0)
1984	Washington Redskins (11-5-0)	Chicago Bears (10-6-0)	San Francisco 49ers (15-1-0)	L.A. Rams (10-6-0) NY Giants (9-7-0)
1985	Dallas Cowboys (10-6-0)	Chicago Bears (15-1-0)	L.A. Rams (11-5-0)	NY Giants (10-6-0) San Francisco 49ers (10-6-0)
1986	NY Giants (14-2-0)	Chicago Bears (14-2-0)	San Francisco 49ers (10-5-1)	L.A. Rams (10-6-0) Washington Redskins (12-4-0)
1987	Washington Redskins (11-4-0)	Chicago Bears (11-4-0)	San Francisco 49ers (13-2-0)	Minnesota Vikings (8-7-0) New Orleans Saints (12-3-0)
1988	Philadelphia Eagles (10-6-0)	Chicago Bears (12-4-0)	San Francisco 49ers (10-6-0)	L.A. Rams (10-6-0) Minnesota Vikings (11-5-0)
1989	NY Giants (12-4-0)	Minnesota Vikings (10-6-0)	San Francisco 49ers (14-2-0)	L.A. Rams (11-5-0) Philadelphia Eagles (11-5-0)
1990	NY Giants (13-3-0)	Chicago Bears (11-5-0)	San Francisco 49ers (14-2-0)	New Orleans Saints (8-8-0) Philadelphia Eagles (10-6-0) Washington Redskins (10-6-0)
1991	Washington Redskins (14-2-0)	Detroit Lions (12-4-0)	New Orleans Saints (11-5-0)	Atlanta Falcons (10-6-0) Chicago Bears (11-5-0) Dallas Cowboys (11-5-0)
1992	Dallas Cowboys (13-3-0)	Minnesota Vikings (11-5-0)	San Francisco 49ers (14-2-0)	New Orleans Saints (12-4-0) Philadelphia Eagles (11-5-0) Washington Redskins (9-7-0)
1993	Dallas Cowboys (12-4-0)	Detroit Lions (10-6-0)	San Francisco 49ers (10-6-0)	Green Bay Packers (9-7-0) Minnesota Vikings (9-7-0) NY Giants (11-5-0)
1994	Dallas Cowboys (12-4-0)	Minnesota Vikings (10-6-0)	San Francisco 49ers (13-3-0)	Chicago Bears (9-7-0) Detroit Lions (9-7-0) Green Bay Packers (9-7-0)
1995	Dallas Cowboys (12-4-0)	Green Bay Packers (11-5-0)	San Francisco 49ers (11-5-0)	Philadelphia Eagles (10-6-0) Detroit Lions (10-6-0) Atlanta Falcons (9-7-0)

Note: A strike shortened the 1982 season from 16 to 9 games. The top eight teams in each conference played in a tournament to determine the conference champion.

NFL Division Winners and Playoff Results, 1996-2022

Year	Conference	Division	Winner (W-L-T)	Playoffs[1]	Year
1996	American	Eastern	New England Patriots (11-5-0)	Jacksonville* 30, Denver 27	1996
		Central	Pittsburgh Steelers (10-6-0)	New England 28, Pittsburgh 3	
		Western	Denver Broncos (13-3-0)	New England 20, Jacksonville* 6	
	National	Eastern	Dallas Cowboys (10-6-0)	Green Bay 35, San Francisco* 14	
		Central	Green Bay Packers (13-3-0)	Carolina 26, Dallas 17	
		Western	Carolina Panthers (12-4-0)	Green Bay 30, Carolina 13	
1997	American	Eastern	New England Patriots (10-6-0)	Pittsburgh 7, New England 6	1997
		Central	Pittsburgh Steelers (11-5-0)	Denver* 14, Kansas City 10	
		Western	Kansas City Chiefs (13-3-0)	Denver* 24, Pittsburgh 21	
	National	Eastern	NY Giants (10-5-1)	San Francisco 38, Minnesota* 22	
		Central	Green Bay Packers (13-3-0)	Green Bay 21, Tampa Bay* 7	
		Western	San Francisco 49ers (13-3-0)	Green Bay 23, San Francisco 10	
1998	American	Eastern	NY Jets (12-4-0)	Denver 38, Miami* 3	1998
		Central	Jacksonville Jaguars (11-5-0)	NY Jets 34, Jacksonville 24	
		Western	Denver Broncos (14-2-0)	Denver 23, NY Jets 10	
	National	Eastern	Dallas Cowboys (10-6-0)	Atlanta 20, San Francisco* 18	
		Central	Minnesota Vikings (15-1-0)	Minnesota 41, Arizona* 21	
		Western	Atlanta Falcons (14-2-0)	Atlanta 30, Minnesota 27 (OT)	
1999	American	Eastern	Indianapolis Colts (13-3-0)	Jacksonville 62, Miami* 7	1999
		Central	Jacksonville Jaguars (14-2-0)	Tennessee* 19, Indianapolis 16	
		Western	Seattle Seahawks (9-7-0)	Tennessee* 33, Jacksonville 14	
	National	Eastern	Washington Redskins (10-6-0)	Tampa Bay 14, Washington 13	
		Central	Tampa Bay Buccaneers (11-5-0)	St. Louis 49, Minnesota* 37	
		Western	St. Louis Rams (13-3-0)	St. Louis 11, Tampa Bay 6	
2000	American	Eastern	Miami Dolphins (11-5-0)	Oakland 27, Miami 0	2000
		Central	Tennessee Titans (13-3-0)	Baltimore* 24, Tennessee 10	
		Western	Oakland Raiders (12-4-0)	Baltimore* 16, Oakland 3	
	National	Eastern	NY Giants (12-4-0)	Minnesota 34, New Orleans 16	
		Central	Minnesota Vikings (11-5-0)	NY Giants 20, Philadelphia* 10	
		Western	New Orleans Saints (10-6-0)	NY Giants 41, Minnesota 0	

Year	Conference	Division	Winner (W-L-T)	Playoffs[1]	Year
2001	American	Eastern	New England Patriots (11-5-0)	New England 16, Oakland 13 (OT)	2001
		Central	Pittsburgh Steelers (13-3-0)	Pittsburgh 27, Baltimore* 10	
		Western	Oakland Raiders (10-6-0)	New England 24, Pittsburgh 17	
	National	Eastern	Philadelphia Eagles (11-5-0)	Philadelphia 33, Chicago 19	
		Central	Chicago Bears (13-3-0)	St. Louis 45, Green Bay* 17	
		Western	St. Louis Rams (14-2-0)	St. Louis 29, Philadelphia 24	
2002	American	East	NY Jets (9-7-0)		2002
		North	Pittsburgh Steelers (10-5-1)	Oakland 30, NY Jets 10	
		South	Tennessee Titans (11-5-0)	Tennessee 34, Pittsburgh 31 (OT)	
		West	Oakland Raiders (11-5-0)	Oakland 41, Tennessee 24	
	National	East	Philadelphia Eagles (12-4-0)		
		North	Green Bay Packers (12-4-0)	Philadelphia 20, Atlanta* 6	
		South	Tampa Bay Buccaneers (12-4-0)	Tampa Bay 31, San Francisco 6	
		West	San Francisco 49ers (10-6-0)	Tampa Bay 27, Philadelphia 10	
2003	American	East	New England Patriots (14-2-0)		2003
		North	Baltimore Ravens (10-6-0)	Indianapolis 38, Kansas City 31	
		South	Indianapolis Colts (12-4-0)	New England 17, Tennessee* 14	
		West	Kansas City Chiefs (13-3-0)	New England 24, Indianapolis 14	
	National	East	Philadelphia Eagles (12-4-0)		
		North	Green Bay Packers (10-6-0)	Carolina 29, St. Louis 23 (2 OT)	
		South	Carolina Panthers (11-5-0)	Philadelphia 20, Green Bay 17 (OT)	
		West	St. Louis Rams (12-4-0)	Carolina 14, Philadelphia 3	
2004	American	East	New England Patriots (14-2-0)		2004
		North	Pittsburgh Steelers (15-1-0)	Pittsburgh 20, NY Jets* 17 (OT)	
		South	Indianapolis Colts (12-4-0)	New England 20, Indianapolis 3	
		West	San Diego Chargers (12-4-0)	New England 41, Pittsburgh 27	
	National	East	Philadelphia Eagles (13-3-0)		
		North	Green Bay Packers (10-6-0)	Atlanta 47, St. Louis* 17	
		South	Atlanta Falcons (11-5-0)	Philadelphia 27, Minnesota* 14	
		West	Seattle Seahawks (9-7-0)	Philadelphia 27, Atlanta 10	
2005	American	East	New England Patriots (10-6-0)		2005
		North	Cincinnati Bengals (11-5-0)	Denver 27, New England 13	
		South	Indianapolis Colts (14-2-0)	Pittsburgh* 21, Indianapolis 18	
		West	Denver Broncos (13-3-0)	Pittsburgh* 34, Denver 17	
	National	East	NY Giants (11-5-0)		
		North	Chicago Bears (11-5-0)	Seattle 20, Washington* 10	
		South	Tampa Bay Buccaneers (11-5-0)	Carolina* 29, Chicago 21	
		West	Seattle Seahawks (13-3-0)	Seattle 34, Carolina* 14	
2006	American	East	New England Patriots (12-4-0)		2006
		North	Baltimore Ravens (13-3-0)	Indianapolis 15, Baltimore 6	
		South	Indianapolis Colts (12-4-0)	New England 24, San Diego 21	
		West	San Diego Chargers (14-2-0)	Indianapolis 38, New England 34	
	National	East	Philadelphia Eagles (10-6-0)		
		North	Chicago Bears (13-3-0)	New Orleans 27, Philadelphia 24	
		South	New Orleans Saints (10-6-0)	Chicago 27, Seattle 24 (OT)	
		West	Seattle Seahawks (9-7-0)	Chicago 39, New Orleans 14	
2007	American	East	New England Patriots (16-0-0)		2007
		North	Pittsburgh Steelers (10-6-0)	New England 31, Jacksonville* 20	
		South	Indianapolis Colts (13-3-0)	San Diego 28, Indianapolis 24	
		West	San Diego Chargers (11-5-0)	New England 21, San Diego 12	
	National	East	Dallas Cowboys (13-3-0)		
		North	Green Bay Packers (13-3-0)	Green Bay 42, Seattle 20	
		South	Tampa Bay Buccaneers (9-7-0)	NY Giants* 21, Dallas 17	
		West	Seattle Seahawks (10-6-0)	NY Giants* 23, Green Bay 20 (OT)	
2008	American	East	Miami Dolphins (11-5-0)		2008
		North	Pittsburgh Steelers (12-4-0)	Baltimore* 13, Tennessee 10	
		South	Tennessee Titans (13-3-0)	Pittsburgh 35, San Diego 24	
		West	San Diego Chargers (8-8-0)	Pittsburgh 23, Baltimore* 14	
	National	East	NY Giants (12-4-0)		
		North	Minnesota Vikings (10-6-0)	Arizona 33, Carolina 13	
		South	Carolina Panthers (12-4-0)	Philadelphia* 23, NY Giants 11	
		West	Arizona Cardinals (9-7-0)	Arizona 32, Philadelphia* 25	
2009	American	East	New England Patriots (10-6-0)		2009
		North	Cincinnati Bengals (10-6-0)	Indianapolis 20, Baltimore* 3	
		South	Indianapolis Colts (14-2-0)	NY Jets* 17, San Diego 14	
		West	San Diego Chargers (13-3-0)	Indianapolis 30, NY Jets* 17	
	National	East	Dallas Cowboys (11-5-0)		
		North	Minnesota Vikings (12-4-0)	New Orleans 45, Arizona 14	
		South	New Orleans Saints (13-3-0)	Minnesota 34, Dallas 3	
		West	Arizona Cardinals (10-6-0)	New Orleans 31, Minnesota 28 (OT)	
2010	American	East	New England Patriots (14-2-0)		2010
		North	Pittsburgh Steelers (12-4-0)	Pittsburgh 31, Baltimore* 24	
		South	Indianapolis Colts (10-6-0)	NY Jets* 28, New England 21	
		West	Kansas City Chiefs (10-6-0)	Pittsburgh 24, NY Jets* 19	
	National	East	Philadelphia Eagles (10-6-0)		
		North	Chicago Bears (11-5-0)	Green Bay* 48, Atlanta 21	
		South	Atlanta Falcons (13-3-0)	Chicago 35, Seattle 24	
		West	Seattle Seahawks (7-9-0)	Green Bay* 21, Chicago 14	

Year	Conference	Division	Winner (W-L-T)	Playoffs[1]	Year
2011	American	East	New England Patriots (13-3-0)		2011
		North	Baltimore Ravens (12-4-0)	New England 45, Denver 10	
		South	Houston Texans (10-6-0)	Baltimore 20, Houston 13	
		West	Denver Broncos (8-8-0)	New England 23, Baltimore 20	
	National	East	NY Giants (9-7-0)		
		North	Green Bay Packers (15-1-0)	San Francisco 36, New Orleans 32	
		South	New Orleans Saints (13-3-0)	NY Giants 37, Green Bay 20	
		West	San Francisco 49ers (13-3-0)	NY Giants 20, San Francisco 17 (OT)	
2012	American	East	New England Patriots (12-4-0)		2012
		North	Baltimore Ravens (10-6-0)	Baltimore 38, Denver 35 (2 OT)	
		South	Houston Texans (12-4-0)	New England 41, Houston 28	
		West	Denver Broncos (13-3-0)	Baltimore 28, New England 13	
	National	East	Washington Redskins (10-6-0)		
		North	Green Bay Packers (11-5-0)	San Francisco 45, Green Bay 31	
		South	Atlanta Falcons (13-3-0)	Atlanta 30, Seattle* 28	
		West	San Francisco 49ers (11-4-1)	San Francisco 28, Atlanta 24	
2013	American	East	New England Patriots (12-4-0)		2013
		North	Cincinnati Bengals (11-5-0)	New England 43, Indianapolis 22	
		South	Indianapolis Colts (11-5-0)	Denver 24, San Diego* 17	
		West	Denver Broncos (13-3-0)	Denver 26, New England 16	
	National	East	Philadelphia Eagles (10-6-0)		
		North	Green Bay Packers (8-7-1)	Seattle 23, New Orleans* 15	
		South	Carolina Panthers (12-4-0)	San Francisco* 23, Carolina 10	
		West	Seattle Seahawks (13-3-0)	Seattle 23, San Francisco* 17	
2014	American	East	New England Patriots (12-4-0)		2014
		North	Pittsburgh Steelers (11-5-0)	New England 35, Baltimore* 31	
		South	Indianapolis Colts (11-5-0)	Indianapolis 24, Denver 13	
		West	Denver Broncos (12-4-0)	New England 45, Indianapolis 7	
	National	East	Dallas Cowboys (12-4-0)		
		North	Green Bay Packers (12-4-0)	Seattle 31, Carolina 17	
		South	Carolina Panthers (7-8-1)	Green Bay 26, Dallas 21	
		West	Seattle Seahawks (12-4-0)	Seattle 28, Green Bay 22 (OT)	
2015	American	East	New England Patriots (12-4-0)		2015
		North	Cincinnati Bengals (12-4-0)	New England 27, Kansas City* 20	
		South	Houston Texans (9-7-0)	Denver 23, Pittsburgh* 16	
		West	Denver Broncos (12-4-0)	Denver 20, New England 18	
	National	East	Washington Redskins (9-7-0)		
		North	Minnesota Vikings (11-5-0)	Arizona 26, Green Bay* 20 (OT)	
		South	Carolina Panthers (15-1-0)	Carolina 31, Seattle* 24	
		West	Arizona Cardinals (13-3-0)	Carolina 49, Arizona 15	
2016	American	East	New England Patriots (14-2-0)		2016
		North	Pittsburgh Steelers (11-5-0)	New England 34, Houston 16	
		South	Houston Texans (9-7-0)	Pittsburgh 18, Kansas City 16	
		West	Kansas City Chiefs (12-4-0)	New England 36, Pittsburgh 17	
	National	East	Dallas Cowboys (13-3-0)		
		North	Green Bay Packers (10-6-0)	Atlanta 36, Seattle 20	
		South	Atlanta Falcons (11-5-0)	Green Bay 34, Dallas 31	
		West	Seattle Seahawks (10-5-1)	Atlanta 44, Green Bay 21	
2017	American	East	New England Patriots (13-3-0)		2017
		North	Pittsburgh Steelers (13-3-0)	New England 35, Tennessee* 14	
		South	Jacksonville Jaguars (10-6-0)	Jacksonville 45, Pittsburgh 42	
		West	Kansas City Chiefs (10-6-0)	New England 24, Jacksonville 20	
	National	East	Philadelphia Eagles (13-3-0)		
		North	Minnesota Vikings (13-3-0)	Philadelphia 15, Atlanta* 10	
		South	New Orleans Saints (11-5-0)	Minnesota 29, New Orleans 24	
		West	Los Angeles Rams (11-5-0)	Philadelphia 38, Minnesota 7	
2018	American	East	New England Patriots (11-5-0)		2018
		North	Baltimore Ravens (10-6-0)	Kansas City 31, Indianapolis* 13	
		South	Houston Texans (11-5-0)	New England 41, L.A. Chargers* 28	
		West	Kansas City Chiefs (12-4-0)	New England 37, Kansas City 31 (OT)	
	National	East	Dallas Cowboys (10-6-0)		
		North	Chicago Bears (12-4-0)	L.A. Rams 30, Dallas 22	
		South	New Orleans Saints (13-3-0)	New Orleans 20, Philadelphia* 14	
		West	L.A. Rams (13-3-0)	L.A. Rams 26, New Orleans 23 (OT)	
2019	American	East	New England Patriots (12-4-0)		2019
		North	Baltimore Ravens (14-2-0)	Tennessee* 28, Baltimore 12	
		South	Houston Texans (10-6-0)	Kansas City 51, Houston 31	
		West	Kansas City Chiefs (12-4-0)	Kansas City 35, Tennessee* 24	
	National	East	Philadelphia Eagles (9-7-0)		
		North	Green Bay Packers (13-3-0)	San Francisco 27, Minnesota* 10	
		South	New Orleans Saints (13-3-0)	Green Bay 28, Seattle* 23	
		West	San Francisco 49ers (13-3-0)	San Francisco 37, Green Bay 20	
2020	American	East	Buffalo Bills (13-3-0)		2020
		North	Pittsburgh Steelers (12-4-0)	Buffalo 17, Baltimore* 3	
		South	Tennessee Titans (11-5-0)	Kansas City 22, Cleveland* 17	
		West	Kansas City Chiefs (14-2-0)	Kansas City 38, Buffalo 24	
	National	East	Washington (7-9-0)		
		North	Green Bay Packers (13-3-0)	Green Bay 32, L.A. Rams 18	
		South	New Orleans Saints (12-4-0)	Tampa Bay* 30, New Orleans 20	
		West	Seattle Seahawks (12-4-0)	Tampa Bay* 31, Green Bay 26	
2021	American	East	Buffalo Bills (11-6-0)		2021
		North	Cincinnati Bengals (10-7-0)	Cincinnati 19, Tennessee 16	
		South	Tennessee Titans (12-5-0)	Kansas City 42, Buffalo 36 (OT)	
		West	Kansas City Chiefs (12-5-0)	Cincinnati 27, Kansas City 24 (OT)	
	National	East	Dallas Cowboys (12-5-0)		
		North	Green Bay Packers (13-4-0)	San Francisco* 13, Green Bay 10	
		South	Tampa Bay Buccaneers (13-4-0)	L.A. Rams 30, Tampa Bay 27	
		West	L.A. Rams (12-5-0)	L.A. Rams 20, San Francisco* 17	
2022	American	East	Buffalo Bills (13-3-0)		2022
		North	Cincinnati Bengals (12-4-0)	Kansas City 27, Jacksonville 20	
		South	Jacksonville Jaguars (9-8-0)	Cincinnati 27, Buffalo 10	
		West	Kansas City Chiefs (14-3-0)	Kansas City 23, Cincinnati 20	
	National	East	Philadelphia Eagles (14-3-0)		
		North	Minnesota Vikings (13-4-0)	Philadelphia 38, NY Giants* 7	
		South	Tampa Bay Buccaneers (8-9-0)	San Francisco 19, Dallas* 12	
		West	San Francisco 49ers (13-4-0)	Philadelphia 31, San Francisco 7	

* = Wild card team. (1) Only the final two conference playoff rounds are shown.

American Football Conference Leaders, 1960-2022
(American Football League, 1960-69)

PASSING (BASED ON QB RATING POINTS)

Player, team	Rating	Att	Comp	Yds	TD	Year
Jack Kemp, L.A. Chargers	NA	406	211	3,018	20	1960
George Blanda, Houston Oilers	NA	362	187	3,330	36	1961
Len Dawson, Dallas Texans	NA	310	189	2,759	29	1962
Tobin Rote, San Diego	NA	286	170	2,510	20	1963
Len Dawson, Kansas City	NA	354	199	2,879	30	1964
John Hadl, San Diego	NA	348	174	2,798	20	1965
Len Dawson, Kansas City	NA	284	159	2,527	26	1966
Daryle Lamonica, Oakland	NA	425	220	3,228	30	1967
Len Dawson, Kansas City	NA	224	131	2,109	17	1968
Greg Cook, Cincinnati	NA	197	106	1,854	15	1969
Daryle Lamonica, Oakland	NA	356	179	2,516	22	1970
Bob Griese, Miami	NA	263	145	2,089	19	1971
Earl Morrall, Miami	NA	150	83	1,360	11	1972
Ken Stabler, Oakland	88.3	260	163	1,997	14	1973
Ken Anderson, Cincinnati	95.7	328	213	2,667	18	1974
Ken Anderson, Cincinnati	93.9	377	228	3,169	21	1975
Ken Stabler, Oakland	103.4	291	194	2,737	27	1976
Bob Griese, Miami	87.8	307	180	2,252	22	1977
Terry Bradshaw, Pittsburgh	84.7	368	207	2,915	28	1978
Dan Fouts, San Diego	82.6	530	332	4,082	24	1979
Brian Sipe, Cleveland	91.4	554	337	4,132	30	1980
Ken Anderson, Cincinnati	98.4	479	300	3,754	29	1981
Ken Anderson, Cincinnati	95.3	309	218	2,495	12	1982
Dan Marino, Miami	96.0	296	173	2,210	20	1983
Dan Marino, Miami	108.9	564	362	5,084	48	1984
Ken O'Brien, NY Jets	96.2	488	297	3,888	25	1985
Dan Marino, Miami	92.5	623	378	4,746	44	1986
Bernie Kosar, Cleveland	95.4	389	241	3,033	22	1987
Boomer Esiason, Cincinnati	97.4	388	223	3,572	28	1988
Boomer Esiason, Cincinnati	92.1	455	258	3,525	28	1989
Jim Kelly, Buffalo	101.2	346	219	2,829	24	1990
Jim Kelly, Buffalo	97.6	474	304	3,844	33	1991
Warren Moon, Houston Oilers	89.3	346	224	2,521	18	1992
John Elway, Denver	92.8	551	348	4,030	25	1993
Dan Marino, Miami	89.2	615	385	4,453	30	1994
Jim Harbaugh, Indianapolis	100.7	314	200	2,575	17	1995
John Elway, Denver	89.2	466	287	3,328	26	1996
Mark Brunell, Jacksonville	91.2	435	264	3,281	18	1997
Vinny Testaverde, NY Jets	101.6	421	259	3,256	29	1998
Peyton Manning, Indianapolis	90.7	533	331	4,135	26	1999
Brian Griese, Denver	102.9	336	216	2,688	19	2000
Rich Gannon, Oakland	95.5	549	361	3,828	27	2001
Chad Pennington, NY Jets	104.2	399	275	3,120	22	2002
Steve McNair, Tennessee	100.4	400	250	3,215	24	2003
Peyton Manning, Indianapolis	121.1	497	336	4,557	49	2004
Peyton Manning, Indianapolis	104.1	453	305	3,747	28	2005
Peyton Manning, Indianapolis	101.0	557	362	4,397	31	2006
Tom Brady, New England	117.2	578	398	4,806	50	2007
Philip Rivers, San Diego	105.5	478	312	4,009	34	2008
Philip Rivers, San Diego	104.4	486	317	4,254	28	2009
Tom Brady, New England	111.0	492	324	3,900	36	2010
Tom Brady, New England	105.6	611	401	5,235	39	2011
Peyton Manning, Denver	105.8	583	400	4,659	37	2012
Peyton Manning, Denver	115.1	659	450	5,477	55	2013
Ben Roethlisberger, Pittsburgh	103.3	608	408	4,952	32	2014
Andy Dalton, Cincinnati	106.2	386	255	3,250	25	2015
Tom Brady, New England	112.2	432	291	3,554	28	2016
Alex Smith, Kansas City	104.7	505	341	4,042	26	2017
Patrick Mahomes, Kansas City	113.8	580	383	5,097	50	2018
Ryan Tannehill, Tennessee	117.5	286	201	2,742	22	2019
Deshaun Watson, Houston	112.4	544	382	4,823	33	2020
Joe Burrow, Cincinnati	108.3	520	366	4,611	34	2021
Tua Tagovailoa, Miami	105.5	400	259	3,548	25	2022

RECEPTIONS

Year	Player, team	Rec	Yds	TD
1960	Lionel Taylor, Denver	92	1,235	12
1961	Lionel Taylor, Denver	100	1,176	4
1962	Lionel Taylor, Denver	77	908	4
1963	Lionel Taylor, Denver	78	1,101	10
1964	Charley Hennigan, Houston Oilers	101	1,546	8
1965	Lionel Taylor, Denver	85	1,131	6
1966	Lance Alworth, San Diego	73	1,383	13
1967	George Sauer, NY Jets	75	1,189	6
1968	Lance Alworth, San Diego	68	1,312	10
1969	Lance Alworth, San Diego	64	1,003	4
1970	Marlin Briscoe, Buffalo	57	1,036	8
1971	Fred Biletnikoff, Oakland	61	929	9
1972	Fred Biletnikoff, Oakland	58	802	7
1973	Fred Willis, Houston Oilers	57	371	1
1974	Lydell Mitchell, Baltimore Colts	72	544	2
1975	Reggie Rucker, Cleveland	60	770	3
	Lydell Mitchell, Baltimore Colts	60	544	4
1976	MacArthur Lane, Kansas City	66	686	1
1977	Lydell Mitchell, Baltimore Colts	71	620	4
1978	Steve Largent, Seattle	71	1,168	8
1979	Joe Washington, Baltimore Colts	82	750	3
1980	Kellen Winslow, San Diego	89	1,290	9
1981	Kellen Winslow, San Diego	88	1,075	10
1982	Kellen Winslow, San Diego	54	721	6
1983	Todd Christensen, L.A. Raiders	92	1,247	12
1984	Ozzie Newsome, Cleveland	89	1,001	5
1985	Lionel James, San Diego	86	1,027	6
1986	Todd Christensen, L.A. Raiders	95	1,153	8
1987	Al Toon, NY Jets	68	976	5
1988	Al Toon, NY Jets	93	1,067	5
1989	Andre Reed, Buffalo	88	1,312	9
1990	Haywood Jeffires, Houston Oilers	74	1,048	8
	Drew Hill, Houston Oilers	74	1,019	5
1991	Haywood Jeffires, Houston Oilers	100	1,181	7
1992	Haywood Jeffires, Houston Oilers	90	913	9
1993	Reggie Langhorne, Indianapolis	85	1,038	3
1994	Ben Coates, New England	96	1,174	7
1995	Carl Pickens, Cincinnati	99	1,234	17
1996	Carl Pickens, Cincinnati	100	1,180	12
1997	Tim Brown, Oakland	104	1,408	5
1998	O.J. McDuffie, Miami	90	1,050	7
1999	Jimmy Smith, Jacksonville	116	1,636	6
2000	Marvin Harrison, Indianapolis	102	1,413	14
2001	Rod Smith, Denver	113	1,343	11
2002	Marvin Harrison, Indianapolis	143	1,722	11
2003	LaDainian Tomlinson, San Diego	100	725	4
2004	Tony Gonzalez, Kansas City	102	1,258	7
2005	Chad Johnson, Cincinnati	97	1,432	9
2006	Andre Johnson, Houston	103	1,147	5
2007	Wes Welker, New England	112	1,175	8
	T.J. Houshmandzadeh, Cincinnati	112	1,143	12
2008	Andre Johnson, Houston	115	1,575	8
2009	Wes Welker, New England	123	1,348	4
2010	Reggie Wayne, Indianapolis	111	1,355	6
2011	Wes Welker, New England	122	1,569	9
2012	Wes Welker, New England	118	1,354	6
2013	Antonio Brown, Pittsburgh	110	1,499	8
2014	Antonio Brown, Pittsburgh	129	1,698	13
2015	Antonio Brown, Pittsburgh	136	1,834	10
2016	Antonio Brown, Pittsburgh	106	1,284	12
2017	Jarvis Landry, Miami	112	987	9
2018	DeAndre Hopkins, Houston	115	1,572	11
2019	Keenan Allen, L.A. Chargers	104	1,199	6
	DeAndre Hopkins, Houston	104	1,165	7
2020	Stefon Diggs, Buffalo	127	1,535	8
2021	Tyreek Hill, Kansas City	111	1,239	9
2022	Tyreek Hill, Miami	119	1,710	7

SCORING

Player, team	TD	XPM	FGM	Pts	Year
Gene Mingo, Denver	6	33	18	123	1960
Gino Cappelletti, Boston	8	48	17	147	1961
Gene Mingo, Denver	4	32	27	137	1962
Gino Cappelletti, Boston	2	35	22	113	1963
Gino Cappelletti, Boston	7	36	25	155	1964
Gino Cappelletti, Boston	9	27	17	132	1965
Gino Cappelletti, Boston	6	35	16	119	1966
George Blanda, Oakland	0	56	20	116	1967
Jim Turner, NY Jets	0	43	34	145	1968

RUSHING YARDS

Year	Player, team	Yds	Att	TD
1960	Abner Haynes, Dallas Texans	875	156	9
1961	Billy Cannon, Houston Oilers	948	200	6
1962	Cookie Gilchrist, Buffalo	1,096	214	13
1963	Clem Daniels, Oakland	1,099	215	3
1964	Cookie Gilchrist, Buffalo	981	230	6
1965	Paul Lowe, San Diego	1,121	222	7
1966	Jim Nance, Boston	1,458	299	11
1967	Jim Nance, Boston	1,216	269	7
1968	Paul Robinson, Cincinnati	1,023	238	8

| SCORING | | | | | | RUSHING YARDS | | | |
Player, team	TD	XPM	FGM	Pts	Year	Player, team	Yds	Att	TD
Jim Turner, NY Jets	0	33	32	129	1969	Dickie Post, San Diego	873	182	6
Jan Stenerud, Kansas City	0	26	30	116	1970	Floyd Little, Denver	901	209	3
Garo Yepremian, Miami	0	33	28	117	1971	Floyd Little, Denver	1,133	284	6
Bobby Howfield, NY Jets	0	40	27	121	1972	O.J. Simpson, Buffalo	1,251	292	6
Roy Gerela, Pittsburgh	0	36	29	123	1973	O.J. Simpson, Buffalo	2,003	332	12
Roy Gerela, Pittsburgh	0	33	20	93	1974	Otis Armstrong, Denver	1,407	263	9
O.J. Simpson, Buffalo	23	0	0	138	1975	O.J. Simpson, Buffalo	1,817	329	16
Toni Linhart, Baltimore Colts	0	49	20	109	1976	O.J. Simpson, Buffalo	1,503	290	8
Errol Mann, Oakland	0	39	20	99	1977	Mark van Eeghen, Oakland	1,273	324	7
Pat Leahy, NY Jets	0	41	22	107	1978	Earl Campbell, Houston Oilers	1,450	302	13
John Smith, New England	0	46	23	115	1979	Earl Campbell, Houston Oilers	1,697	368	19
John Smith, New England	0	51	26	129	1980	Earl Campbell, Houston Oilers	1,934	373	13
Jim Breech, Cincinnati	0	49	22	115	1981	Earl Campbell, Houston Oilers	1,376	361	10
Nick Lowery, Kansas City	0	37	26	115	1982	Freeman McNeil, NY Jets	786	151	6
Marcus Allen, L.A. Raiders	14	0	0	84					
Gary Anderson, Pittsburgh	0	38	27	119	1983	Curt Warner, Seattle	1,449	335	13
Gary Anderson, Pittsburgh	0	45	24	117	1984	Earnest Jackson, San Diego	1,179	296	8
Gary Anderson, Pittsburgh	0	40	33	139	1985	Marcus Allen, L.A. Raiders	1,759	380	11
Tony Franklin, New England	0	44	32	140	1986	Curt Warner, Seattle	1,481	319	13
Jim Breech, Cincinnati	0	25	24	97	1987	Eric Dickerson, L.A. Rams-Ind.	1,288*	283	6
Scott Norwood, Buffalo	0	33	32	129	1988	Eric Dickerson, Indianapolis	1,659	388	14
David Treadwell, Denver	0	39	27	120	1989	Christian Okoye, Kansas City	1,480	370	12
Nick Lowery, Kansas City	0	37	34	139	1990	Thurman Thomas, Buffalo	1,297	271	11
Pete Stoyanovich, Miami	0	28	31	121	1991	Thurman Thomas, Buffalo	1,407	288	7
Pete Stoyanovich, Miami	0	34	30	124	1992	Barry Foster, Pittsburgh	1,690	390	11
Jeff Jaeger, L.A. Raiders	0	27	35	132	1993	Thurman Thomas, Buffalo	1,315	355	6
John Carney, San Diego	0	33	34	135	1994	Chris Warren, Seattle	1,545	333	9
Norm Johnson, Pittsburgh	0	39	34	141	1995	Curtis Martin, New England	1,487	368	14
Cary Blanchard, Indianapolis	0	27	36	135	1996	Terrell Davis, Denver	1,538	345	13
Mike Hollis, Jacksonville	0	41	31	134	1997	Terrell Davis, Denver	1,750	369	15
Steve Christie, Buffalo	0	41	33	140	1998	Terrell Davis, Denver	2,008	392	21
Mike Vanderjagt, Indianapolis	0	43	34	145	1999	Edgerrin James, Indianapolis	1,553	369	13
Matt Stover, Baltimore	0	30	35	135	2000	Edgerrin James, Indianapolis	1,709	387	13
Mike Vanderjagt, Indianapolis	0	41	28	125	2001	Priest Holmes, Kansas City	1,555	327	8
Priest Holmes, Kansas City	24	0	0	144	2002	Ricky Williams, Miami	1,853	383	16
Priest Holmes, Kansas City	27	0	0	162	2003	Jamal Lewis, Baltimore	2,066	387	14
Adam Vinatieri, New England	0	48	31	141	2004	Curtis Martin, NY Jets	1,697	371	12
Shayne Graham, Cincinnati	0	47	28	131	2005	Larry Johnson, Kansas City	1,750	336	20
LaDainian Tomlinson, San Diego	31	0	0	186	2006	LaDainian Tomlinson, San Diego	1,815	348	28
Randy Moss, New England	23	0	0	138	2007	LaDainian Tomlinson, San Diego	1,474	315	15
Stephen Gostkowski, New England	0	40	36	148	2008	Thomas Jones, NY Jets	1,312	290	13
Nate Kaeding, San Diego	0	50	32	146	2009	Chris Johnson, Tennessee	2,006	358	14
Sebastian Janikowski, Oakland	0	43	33	142	2010	Arian Foster, Houston	1,616	327	16
Stephen Gostkowski, New England	0	59	28	143	2011	Maurice Jones-Drew, Jacksonville	1,606	343	8
Stephen Gostkowski, New England	0	66	29	153	2012	Jamaal Charles, Kansas City	1,509	285	5
Stephen Gostkowski, New England	0	44	38	158	2013	Jamaal Charles, Kansas City	1,287	259	12
Stephen Gostkowski, New England	0	51	35	156	2014	Le'Veon Bell, Pittsburgh	1,361	290	8
Stephen Gostkowski, New England	0	52	33	151	2015	Chris Ivory, NY Jets	1,070	247	7
Justin Tucker, Baltimore	0	27	38	141	2016	DeMarco Murray, Tennessee	1,287	293	9
Stephen Gostkowski, New England	0	45	37	156	2017	Kareem Hunt, Kansas City	1,327	272	8
Ka'imi Fairbairn, Houston	0	39	37	150	2018	Joe Mixon, Cincinnati	1,168	237	8
Harrison Butker, Kansas City	0	45	34	147	2019	Derrick Henry, Tennessee	1,540	303	16
Daniel Carlson, Las Vegas	0	45	33	144	2020	Derrick Henry, Tennessee	2,027	378	17
Jason Sanders, Miami	0	36	36	144					
Daniel Carlson, Las Vegas	0	30	40	150	2021	Jonathan Taylor, Indianapolis	1,811	332	18
Nick Folk, New England	0	42	36	150					
Justin Tucker, Baltimore	0	31	37	142	2022	Josh Jacobs, Las Vegas	1,653	340	12

* = Includes 277 yards after being traded to NFC; 1,011 yards led AFC. NA = Not applicable/available. **Note:** Passer ratings for years prior to 1973 were determined by different measures and are not directly comparable to current passer ratings.

National Football Conference Leaders, 1960-2022

(National Football League, 1960-69)

| PASSING (BASED ON QB RATING POINTS) | | | | | | RECEPTIONS | | | |
Player, team	Rating	Att	Comp	Yds	TD	Year	Player, team	Rec	Yds	TD
Milt Plum, Cleveland	NA	250	151	2,297	21	1960	Raymond Berry, Baltimore Colts	74	1,298	10
Milt Plum, Cleveland	NA	302	177	2,416	18	1961	Jim Phillips, L.A. Rams	78	1,092	5
Bart Starr, Green Bay	NA	285	178	2,438	12	1962	Bobby Mitchell, Washington	72	1,384	11
Y. A. Tittle, NY Giants	NA	367	221	3,145	36	1963	Bobby Joe Conrad, St. Louis Cardinals	73	967	10
Bart Starr, Green Bay	NA	272	163	2,144	15	1964	Johnny Morris, Chicago	93	1,200	10
Rudy Bukich, Chicago	NA	312	176	2,641	20	1965	Dave Parks, San Francisco	80	1,344	12
Bart Starr, Green Bay	NA	251	156	2,257	14	1966	Charley Taylor, Washington	72	1,119	12
Sonny Jurgensen, Washington	NA	508	288	3,747	31	1967	Charley Taylor, Washington	70	990	9
Earl Morrall, Baltimore Colts	NA	317	182	2,909	26	1968	Clifton McNeil, San Francisco	71	994	7
Sonny Jurgensen, Washington	NA	442	274	3,102	22	1969	Dan Abramowicz, New Orleans	73	1,015	7
John Brodie, San Francisco	NA	378	223	2,941	24	1970	Dick Gordon, Chicago	71	1,026	13
Roger Staubach, Dallas	NA	211	126	1,882	15	1971	Bob Tucker, NY Giants	59	791	4
Norm Snead, NY Giants	NA	325	196	2,307	17	1972	Harold Jackson, Philadelphia	62	1,048	4
Roger Staubach, Dallas	94.6	286	179	2,428	23	1973	Harold Carmichael, Philadelphia	67	1,116	9
Sonny Jurgensen, Washington	94.5	167	107	1,185	11	1974	Charles Young, Philadelphia	63	696	3

PASSING (BASED ON QB RATING POINTS)

Player, team	Rating	Att	Comp	Yds	TD
Fran Tarkenton, Minnesota	91.8	425	273	2,994	25
James Harris, L.A. Rams	89.6	158	91	1,460	8
Roger Staubach, Dallas	87.0	361	210	2,620	18
Roger Staubach, Dallas	84.9	413	231	3,190	25
Roger Staubach, Dallas	92.3	461	267	3,586	27
Ron Jaworski, Philadelphia	91.0	451	257	3,529	27
Joe Montana, San Francisco	88.4	488	311	3,565	19
Joe Theismann, Washington	91.3	252	161	2,033	13
Steve Bartkowski, Atlanta	97.6	432	274	3,167	22
Joe Montana, San Francisco	102.9	432	279	3,630	28
Joe Montana, San Francisco	91.3	494	303	3,653	27
Tommy Kramer, Minnesota	92.6	372	208	3,000	24
Joe Montana, San Francisco	102.1	398	266	3,054	31
Wade Wilson, Minnesota	91.5	332	204	2,746	15
Joe Montana, San Francisco	112.4	386	271	3,521	26
Phil Simms, NY Giants	92.7	311	184	2,284	15
Steve Young, San Francisco	101.8	279	180	2,517	17
Steve Young, San Francisco	107.0	402	268	3,465	25
Steve Young, San Francisco	101.5	462	314	4,023	29
Steve Young, San Francisco	112.8	461	324	3,969	35
Brett Favre, Green Bay	99.5	570	359	4,413	38
Steve Young, San Francisco	97.2	316	214	2,410	14
Steve Young, San Francisco	104.7	356	241	3,029	19
Randall Cunningham, Minnesota	106.0	425	259	3,704	34
Kurt Warner, St. Louis	109.2	499	325	4,353	41
Trent Green, St. Louis	101.8	240	145	2,063	16
Kurt Warner, St. Louis	101.4	546	375	4,830	36
Brad Johnson, Tampa Bay	92.9	451	281	3,049	22
Daunte Culpepper, Minnesota	96.4	454	295	3,479	25
Daunte Culpepper, Minnesota	110.9	548	379	4,717	39
Matt Hasselbeck, Seattle	98.2	449	294	3,459	24
Drew Brees, New Orleans	96.2	554	356	4,418	26
Tony Romo, Dallas	97.4	520	335	4,211	36
Kurt Warner, Arizona	96.9	598	401	4,583	30
Drew Brees, New Orleans	109.6	514	363	4,388	34
Aaron Rodgers, Green Bay	101.2	475	312	3,922	28
Aaron Rodgers, Green Bay	122.5	502	343	4,643	45
Aaron Rodgers, Green Bay	108.0	552	371	4,295	39
Nick Foles, Philadelphia	119.2	317	203	2,891	27
Tony Romo, Dallas	113.2	435	304	3,705	34
Russell Wilson, Seattle	110.1	483	329	4,024	34
Matt Ryan, Atlanta	117.1	534	373	4,944	38
Drew Brees, New Orleans	103.9	536	386	4,334	23
Drew Brees, New Orleans	115.7	489	364	3,992	32
Drew Brees, New Orleans	116.3	378	281	2,979	27
Aaron Rodgers, Green Bay	121.5	526	372	4,299	48
Aaron Rodgers, Green Bay	111.9	531	366	4,115	37
Jimmy Garoppolo, San Francisco	103.0	308	207	2,437	16

RECEPTIONS

Year	Player, team	Rec	Yds	TD
1975	Chuck Foreman, Minnesota	73	691	9
1976	Drew Pearson, Minnesota	58	806	6
1977	Ahmad Rashad, Minnesota	51	681	2
1978	Rickey Young, Minnesota	88	704	5
1979	Ahmad Rashad, Minnesota	80	1,156	9
1980	Earl Cooper, San Francisco	83	567	4
1981	Dwight Clark, San Francisco	85	1,105	4
1982	Dwight Clark, San Francisco	60	913	5
1983	Roy Green, St. Louis Cardinals	78	1,227	14
	Charlie Brown, Washington	78	1,225	8
	Earnest Gray, NY Giants	78	1,139	5
1984	Art Monk, Washington	106	1,372	7
1985	Roger Craig, San Francisco	92	1,016	6
1986	Jerry Rice, San Francisco	86	1,570	15
1987	J. T. Smith, St. Louis Cardinals	91	1,117	8
1988	Henry Ellard, L.A. Rams	86	1,414	10
1989	Sterling Sharpe, Green Bay	90	1,423	12
1990	Jerry Rice, San Francisco	100	1,502	13
1991	Michael Irvin, Dallas	93	1,523	8
1992	Sterling Sharpe, Green Bay	108	1,461	13
1993	Sterling Sharpe, Green Bay	112	1,274	11
1994	Cris Carter, Minnesota	122	1,256	7
1995	Herman Moore, Detroit	123	1,686	14
1996	Jerry Rice, San Francisco	108	1,254	8
1997	Herman Moore, Detroit	104	1,293	8
1998	Frank Sanders, Arizona	89	1,145	3
1999	Muhsin Muhammad, Carolina	96	1,253	8
2000	Muhsin Muhammad, Carolina	102	1,183	6
2001	Keyshawn Johnson, Tampa Bay	106	1,266	1
2002	Randy Moss, Minnesota	106	1,347	7
2003	Torry Holt, St. Louis	117	1,696	12
2004	Joe Horn, New Orleans	94	1,399	11
	Torry Holt, St. Louis	94	1,372	10
2005	Steve Smith, Carolina	103	1,563	12
	Larry Fitzgerald, Arizona	103	1,409	10
2006	Mike Furrey, Detroit	98	1,086	6
2007	Larry Fitzgerald, Arizona	100	1,409	10
2008	Larry Fitzgerald, Arizona	96	1,431	12
2009	Steve Smith, NY Giants	107	1,220	7
2010	Roddy White, Atlanta	115	1,389	10
2011	Roddy White, Atlanta	100	1,296	8
2012	Calvin Johnson, Detroit	122	1,964	5
2013	Pierre Garcon, Washington	113	1,346	5
2014	Julio Jones, Atlanta	104	1,593	6
2015	Julio Jones, Atlanta	136	1,871	8
2016	Larry Fitzgerald, Arizona	107	1,023	6
2017	Larry Fitzgerald, Arizona	109	1,156	6
2018	Michael Thomas, New Orleans	125	1,405	9
2019	Michael Thomas, New Orleans	149	1,725	9
2020	DeAndre Hopkins, Arizona	115	1,407	6
	Davante Adams, Green Bay	115	1,374	18
2021	Cooper Kupp, L.A. Rams	145	1,947	16
2022	Justin Jefferson, Minnesota	128	1,809	8

SCORING

Player, team	TD	XPM	FGM	Pts	Year
Paul Hornung, Green Bay	15	41	15	176	1960
Paul Hornung, Green Bay	10	41	15	146	1961
Jim Taylor, Green Bay	19	0	0	114	1962
Don Chandler, NY Giants	0	52	18	106	1963
Lenny Moore, Baltimore Colts	20	0	0	120	1964
Gale Sayers, Chicago	22	0	0	132	1965
Bruce Gossett, L.A. Rams	0	29	28	113	1966
Jim Bakken, St. Louis Cardinals	0	36	27	117	1967
Leroy Kelly, Cleveland	20	0	0	120	1968
Fred Cox, Minnesota	0	43	26	121	1969
Fred Cox, Minnesota	0	35	30	125	1970
Curt Knight, Washington	0	27	29	114	1971
Chester Marcol, Green Bay	0	29	33	128	1972
David Ray, L.A. Rams	0	40	30	130	1973
Chester Marcol, Green Bay	0	19	25	94	1974
Chuck Foreman, Minnesota	22	0	0	132	1975
Mark Moseley, Washington	0	31	22	97	1976
Walter Payton, Chicago	16	0	0	96	1977
Frank Corral, L.A. Rams	0	31	29	118	1978
Mark Moseley, Washington	0	39	25	114	1979
Ed Murray, Detroit	0	35	27	116	1980
Ed Murray, Detroit	0	46	25	121	1981
Rafael Septien, Dallas	0	40	27	121	
Wendell Tyler, L.A. Rams	13	0	0	78	1982
Mark Moseley, Washington	0	62	33	161	1983

RUSHING YARDS

Player, team	Yds	Att	TD
Jim Brown, Cleveland	1,257	215	9
Jim Brown, Cleveland	1,408	305	8
Jim Taylor, Green Bay	1,474	272	19
Jim Brown, Cleveland	1,863	291	12
Jim Brown, Cleveland	1,446	280	7
Jim Brown, Cleveland	1,544	289	17
Gale Sayers, Chicago	1,231	229	8
Leroy Kelly, Cleveland	1,205	235	11
Leroy Kelly, Cleveland	1,239	248	16
Gale Sayers, Chicago	1,032	236	8
Larry Brown, Washington	1,125	237	5
John Brockington, Green Bay	1,105	216	4
Larry Brown, Washington	1,216	285	8
John Brockington, Green Bay	1,144	265	3
Lawrence McCutcheon, L.A. Rams	1,109	236	3
Jim Otis, St. Louis Cardinals	1,076	269	5
Walter Payton, Chicago	1,390	311	13
Walter Payton, Chicago	1,852	339	14
Walter Payton, Chicago	1,395	333	11
Walter Payton, Chicago	1,610	369	14
Walter Payton, Chicago	1,460	317	6
George Rogers, New Orleans	1,674	378	13
Tony Dorsett, Dallas	745	177	5
Eric Dickerson, L.A. Rams	1,808	390	18

SCORING

Player, team	TD	XPM	FGM	Pts
Ray Wersching, San Francisco	0	56	25	131
Kevin Butler, Chicago	0	51	31	144
Kevin Butler, Chicago	0	36	28	120
Jerry Rice, San Francisco	23	0	0	138
Mike Cofer, San Francisco	0	40	27	121
Mike Cofer, San Francisco	0	49	29	136
Chip Lohmiller, Washington	0	41	30	131
Chip Lohmiller, Washington	0	56	31	149
Morten Andersen, New Orleans	0	33	29	120
Chip Lohmiller, Washington	0	30	30	120
Jason Hanson, Detroit	0	28	34	130
Fuad Reveiz, Minnesota	0	30	34	132
Emmitt Smith, Dallas	22	0	0	132
Emmitt Smith, Dallas	25	0	0	150
John Kasay, Carolina	0	34	37	145
Richie Cunningham, Dallas	0	24	34	126
Gary Anderson, Minnesota	0	59	35	164
Jeff Wilkins, St. Louis	0	64	20	124
Marshall Faulk, St. Louis	26	0	0	160
Marshall Faulk, St. Louis	21	0	0	128
Jay Feely, Atlanta	0	42	32	138
Jeff Wilkins, St. Louis	0	46	39	163
David Akers, Philadelphia	0	41	27	122
Shaun Alexander, Seattle	28	0	0	168
Robbie Gould, Chicago	0	47	32	143
Mason Crosby, Green Bay	0	48	31	141
David Akers, Philadelphia	0	45	33	144
David Akers, Philadelphia	0	43	32	139
David Akers, Philadelphia	0	47	32	143
David Akers, San Francisco	0	34	44	166
Lawrence Tynes, NY Giants	0	46	33	145
Steven Hauschka, Seattle	0	44	33	143
Cody Parkey, Philadelphia	0	54	32	150
Graham Gano, Carolina	0	56	30	146
Matt Bryant, Atlanta	0	56	34	158
Greg Zuerlein, L.A. Rams	0	44	38	158
Wil Lutz, New Orleans	0	52	28	136
Wil Lutz, New Orleans	0	48	32	144
Younghoe Koo, Atlanta	0	33	37	144
Matt Gay, L.A. Rams	0	48	32	144
Jason Myers, Seattle	0	41	34	143

RUSHING YARDS

Year	Player, team	Yds	Att	TD
1984	Eric Dickerson, L.A. Rams	2,105	379	14
1985	Gerald Riggs, Atlanta	1,719	397	10
1986	Eric Dickerson, L.A. Rams	1,821	404	11
1987	Charles White, L.A. Rams	1,374	324	11
1988	Herschel Walker, Dallas	1,514	361	5
1989	Barry Sanders, Detroit	1,470	280	14
1990	Barry Sanders, Detroit	1,304	255	13
1991	Emmitt Smith, Dallas	1,563	365	12
1992	Emmitt Smith, Dallas	1,713	373	18
1993	Emmitt Smith, Dallas	1,486	283	9
1994	Barry Sanders, Detroit	1,883	331	7
1995	Emmitt Smith, Dallas	1,773	377	25
1996	Barry Sanders, Detroit	1,553	307	11
1997	Barry Sanders, Detroit	2,053	335	11
1998	Jamal Anderson, Atlanta	1,846	410	14
1999	Stephen Davis, Washington	1,405	290	17
2000	Robert Smith, Minnesota	1,521	295	7
2001	Stephen Davis, Washington	1,432	356	5
2002	Deuce McAllister, New Orleans	1,388	325	13
2003	Ahman Green, Green Bay	1,883	355	15
2004	Shaun Alexander, Seattle	1,696	353	16
2005	Shaun Alexander, Seattle	1,880	370	27
2006	Frank Gore, San Francisco	1,695	312	8
2007	Adrian Peterson, Minnesota	1,341	238	12
2008	Adrian Peterson, Minnesota	1,760	363	10
2009	Steven Jackson, St. Louis	1,416	324	4
2010	Michael Turner, Atlanta	1,371	334	12
2011	Michael Turner, Atlanta	1,340	301	11
2012	Adrian Peterson, Minnesota	2,097	348	12
2013	LeSean McCoy, Philadelphia	1,607	314	9
2014	DeMarco Murray, Dallas	1,845	392	13
2015	Adrian Peterson, Minnesota	1,485	327	11
2016	Ezekiel Elliott, Dallas	1,631	322	15
2017	Todd Gurley, L.A. Rams	1,305	279	13
2018	Ezekiel Elliott, Dallas	1,434	304	6
2019	Christian McCaffrey, Carolina	1,387	287	15
2020	Dalvin Cook, Minnesota	1,557	312	16
2021	Dalvin Cook, Minnesota	1,159	249	6
2022	Saquon Barkley, NY Giants	1,312	295	10

NA = Not applicable/available. **Note:** Passer ratings for years prior to 1973 were determined by different measures and are not directly comparable to current passer ratings.

NFL Most Valuable Player, 1957-2022

The Most Valuable Player is one of many awards given out annually by the Associated Press. Many other organizations give out annual awards honoring the NFL's best players, and those winners may differ from this list.

Year	Player, team	Year	Player, team	Year	Player, team
1957	Jim Brown, Cleveland	1980	Brian Sipe, Cleveland	2002	Rich Gannon, Oakland
1958	Jim Brown, Cleveland	1981	Ken Anderson, Cincinnati	2003	Peyton Manning, Indianapolis; Steve McNair, Tennessee
1959	Charlie Conerly, NY Giants	1982	Mark Moseley, Washington		
1960	Norm Van Brocklin, Philadelphia	1983	Joe Theismann, Washington	2004	Peyton Manning, Indianapolis
1961	Paul Hornung, Green Bay	1984	Dan Marino, Miami	2005	Shaun Alexander, Seattle
1962	Jim Taylor, Green Bay	1985	Marcus Allen, Los Angeles	2006	LaDainian Tomlinson, San Diego
1963	Y. A. Tittle, NY Giants	1986	Lawrence Taylor, NY Giants	2007	Tom Brady, New England
1964	Johnny Unitas, Baltimore	1987	John Elway, Denver	2008	Peyton Manning, Indianapolis
1965	Jim Brown, Cleveland	1988	Boomer Esiason, Cincinnati	2009	Peyton Manning, Indianapolis
1966	Bart Starr, Green Bay	1989	Joe Montana, San Francisco	2010	Tom Brady, New England
1967	Johnny Unitas, Baltimore	1990	Joe Montana, San Francisco	2011	Aaron Rodgers, Green Bay
1968	Earl Morrall, Baltimore	1991	Thurman Thomas, Buffalo	2012	Adrian Peterson, Minnesota
1969	Roman Gabriel, Los Angeles	1992	Steve Young, San Francisco	2013	Peyton Manning, Denver
1970	John Brodie, San Francisco	1993	Emmitt Smith, Dallas	2014	Aaron Rodgers, Green Bay
1971	Alan Page, Minnesota	1994	Steve Young, San Francisco	2015	Cam Newton, Carolina
1972	Larry Brown, Washington	1995	Brett Favre, Green Bay	2016	Matt Ryan, Atlanta
1973	O.J. Simpson, Buffalo	1996	Brett Favre, Green Bay	2017	Tom Brady, New England
1974	Ken Stabler, Oakland	1997	Brett Favre, Green Bay; Barry Sanders, Detroit	2018	Patrick Mahomes, Kansas City
1975	Fran Tarkenton, Minnesota			2019	Lamar Jackson, Baltimore
1976	Bert Jones, Baltimore	1998	Terrell Davis, Denver	2020	Aaron Rodgers, Green Bay
1977	Walter Payton, Chicago	1999	Kurt Warner, St. Louis	2021	Aaron Rodgers, Green Bay
1978	Terry Bradshaw, Pittsburgh	2000	Marshall Faulk, St. Louis	2022	Patrick Mahomes, Kansas City
1979	Earl Campbell, Houston	2001	Kurt Warner, St. Louis		

All-Time Professional (NFL and AFL) Football Records

(at end of 2022 season; * = active in 2022; (a) includes AFL statistics; ** = includes one 2-pt conversion)

All-Time Defensive Leaders

Interceptions, career: 81, Paul Krause, Washington-Minnesota, 1964-79.

Interceptions, season: 14, Dick "Night Train" Lane, L.A. Rams, 1952.

Interception touchdowns, career: 12, Rod Woodson, Pittsburgh-San Francisco-Baltimore Ravens-Oakland, 1987-2003.

Interception touchdowns, season: 4; Ken Houston, Houston, 1971; Jim Kearney, Kansas City, 1972; Eric Allen, Philadelphia, 1993.

Sacks, career (since 1982): 200.0, Bruce Smith, Buffalo-Washington, 1985-2003.

Sacks, season (since 1982): 22.5; Michael Strahan, NY Giants, 2001; T.J. Watt, Pittsburgh, 2021.

All-Time Scoring Leaders by Points

Player	Yrs	TD	PAT	FG	Total
Adam Vinatieri	24	0	874	599	2,673**
Morten Andersen	25	0	849	565	2,544
Gary Anderson	23	0	820	538	2,434
Jason Hanson	21	0	665	495	2,150
John Carney	23	0	628	478	2,062
Matt Stover	19	0	591	471	2,004
George Blanda (a)	26	9	943	335	2,002
Jason Elam	17	0	675	436	1,983
John Kasay	20	0	587	461	1,970
Robbie Gould*	18	0	620	447	1,961
Mason Crosby*	16	0	733	395	1,918
Sebastian Janikowski	18	0	605	436	1,913
Stephen Gostkowski	15	0	699	392	1,875
Phil Dawson	20	1	518	441	1,847
Matt Bryant	18	0	567	397	1,758

Points, season: 186, LaDainian Tomlinson, San Diego, 2006 (31 TDs).
Points, game: 40, Ernie Nevers, Chicago Cardinals vs. Chicago Bears, Nov. 28, 1929 (6 TDs, 4 PATs).
Touchdowns, season: 31, LaDainian Tomlinson, San Diego, 2006.
Touchdowns, game: 6; Ernie Nevers, Chicago Cardinals vs. Chicago Bears, Nov. 28, 1929 (6 rushing); Dub Jones, Cleveland Browns vs. Chicago Bears, Nov. 25, 1951 (4 rushing, 2 pass receptions); Gale Sayers, Chicago Bears vs. San Francisco, Dec. 12, 1965 (4 rushing, 1 pass reception, 1 punt return); Alvin Kamara, New Orleans vs. Minnesota, Dec. 25, 2020 (6 rushing).

All-Time Scoring Leaders by Touchdowns

Player	Yrs	Rush	Rec	Ret	TD
Jerry Rice	20	10	197	1	208
Emmitt Smith	15	164	11	0	175
LaDainian Tomlinson	11	145	17	0	162
Randy Moss	14	0	156	1	157
Terrell Owens	15	3	153	0	156
Marcus Allen	16	123	21	1	145
Marshall Faulk	12	100	36	0	136
Cris Carter	16	0	130	1	131
Marvin Harrison	13	0	128	0	128
Jim Brown	9	106	20	0	126
Adrian Peterson	15	120	6	0	126
Walter Payton	13	110	15	0	125
Larry Fitzgerald	17	0	121	0	121
Antonio Gates	16	0	116	0	116
John Riggins	14	104	12	0	116

Points after TD, season: 75, Matt Prater, Denver, 2013.
Consecutive points after TD: 523, Stephen Gostkowski, New England, 2006-16.
Field goals, career: 599, Adam Vinatieri, New England-Indianapolis, 1996-2019.
Field goals, season: 44, David Akers, San Francisco, 2011.
Field goals, game: 8, Rob Bironas, Tennessee vs. Houston, Oct. 21, 2007.
Longest field goal: 66 yards, Justin Tucker, Baltimore vs. Detroit, Sept. 26, 2021.

All-Time Rushing Leaders
(ranked by rushing yards)

Player	Yrs	Att	Yds	Avg	Long	TD
Emmitt Smith	15	4,409	18,355	4.2	75T	164
Walter Payton	13	3,838	16,726	4.4	76	110
Frank Gore	16	3,735	16,000	4.3	80T	81
Barry Sanders	10	3,062	15,269	5.0	85	99
Adrian Peterson	15	3,230	14,918	4.6	90T	120
Curtis Martin	11	3,518	14,101	4.0	70T	90
LaDainian Tomlinson	11	3,174	13,684	4.3	85T	145
Jerome Bettis	13	3,479	13,662	3.9	71T	91
Eric Dickerson	11	2,996	13,259	4.4	85T	90
Tony Dorsett	12	2,936	12,739	4.3	99T	77

Player	Yrs	Att	Yds	Avg	Long	TD
Jim Brown	9	2,359	12,312	5.2	80T	106
Marshall Faulk	12	2,836	12,279	4.3	71T	100
Edgerrin James	11	3,028	12,246	4.0	72	80
Marcus Allen	16	3,022	12,243	4.1	61T	123
Franco Harris	13	2,949	12,120	4.1	75T	91
Thurman Thomas	13	2,877	12,074	4.2	80T	65
Fred Taylor	13	2,534	11,695	4.6	80T	66
Steven Jackson	12	2,764	11,438	4.1	59T	69
John Riggins	14	2,916	11,352	3.9	66T	104
Corey Dillon	10	2,618	11,241	4.3	96T	82

Yards gained, season: 2,105, Eric Dickerson, L.A. Rams, 1984.
Yards gained, game: 296, Adrian Peterson, Minnesota vs. San Diego, Nov. 4, 2007.
Rushing TDs, career: 164, Emmitt Smith, Dallas-Arizona, 1990-2004.
Rushing TDs, season: 28, LaDainian Tomlinson, San Diego, 2006.

Rushing TDs, game: 6; Ernie Nevers, Chicago Cardinals vs. Chicago Bears, Nov. 28, 1929; Alvin Kamara, New Orleans Saints vs. Minnesota Vikings, Dec. 25, 2020.
Rushing attempts, game: 45, Jamie Morris, Washington vs. Cincinnati, Dec. 17, 1988 (OT).
Longest run from scrimmage: 99 yards (TD); Tony Dorsett, Dallas vs. Minnesota, Jan. 3, 1983; Derrick Henry, Tennessee vs. Jacksonville, Dec. 6, 2018.

All-Time Receiving Leaders
(ranked by number of receptions)

Player	Yrs	No.	Yds	Avg	Long	TD
Jerry Rice	20	1,549	22,895	14.8	96T	197
Larry Fitzgerald	17	1,432	17,492	12.2	80T	121
Tony Gonzalez	17	1,325	15,127	11.4	73T	111
Jason Witten	17	1,228	13,046	10.6	69	74
Marvin Harrison	13	1,102	14,580	13.2	80T	128
Cris Carter	16	1,101	13,899	12.6	80T	130
Tim Brown	17	1,094	14,934	13.7	80T	100
Terrell Owens	15	1,078	15,934	14.8	98T	153
Anquan Boldin	14	1,076	13,779	12.8	79T	82
Reggie Wayne	14	1,070	14,345	13.4	80	82

Player	Yrs	No.	Yds	Avg	Long	TD
Andre Johnson	14	1,062	14,185	13.4	77T	70
Steve Smith Sr.	16	1,031	14,731	14.3	80T	81
Isaac Bruce	16	1,024	15,208	14.9	80T	91
Hines Ward	14	1,000	12,083	12.1	85T	85
Randy Moss	14	982	15,292	15.6	82T	156
Brandon Marshall	13	970	12,351	12.7	75T	83
Antonio Gates	16	955	11,841	12.4	72T	116
Andre Reed	16	951	13,198	13.9	83T	87
Derrick Mason	15	943	12,061	12.8	79T	66
Art Monk	16	940	12,721	13.5	79T	68

Yards gained, career: 22,895, Jerry Rice, San Francisco-Oakland-Seattle, 1985-2004.
Yards gained, season: 1,964, Calvin Johnson, Detroit, 2012.
Yards gained, game: 336, Willie "Flipper" Anderson, L.A. Rams vs. New Orleans, Nov. 26, 1989 (OT).
Pass receptions, season: 149, Michael Thomas, New Orleans, 2019.
Pass receptions, game: 21, Brandon Marshall, Denver vs. Indianapolis, Dec. 13, 2009.

Touchdown receptions, career: 197, Jerry Rice, San Francisco-Oakland-Seattle, 1985-2004.
Touchdown receptions, season: 23, Randy Moss, New England, 2007.
Touchdown receptions, game: 5; Bob Shaw, Chicago Cardinals vs. Baltimore Colts, Oct. 2, 1950; Kellen Winslow, San Diego vs. Oakland, Nov. 22, 1981; Jerry Rice, San Francisco vs. Atlanta, Oct. 14, 1990.

All-Time Passing Leaders
(minimum 1,500 attempts; ranked by quarterback rating points)

Player	Yrs	Att	Comp	Yds	TD	Int	Rate[1]
Patrick Mahomes*	6	2,993	1,985	24,241	192	49	105.7
Aaron Rodgers*	18	7,660	5,001	59,055	475	105	103.6
Deshaun Watson*	5	1,918	1,285	15,641	111	41	102.3
Joe Burrow*	3	1,530	1,044	11,774	82	31	100.4
Russell Wilson*	11	5,218	3,371	40,583	308	98	100.2
Jimmy Garoppolo*	9	1,726	1,167	14,289	87	42	99.6
Drew Brees	20	10,551	7,142	80,358	571	243	98.7
Kirk Cousins*	11	4,866	3,249	37,140	252	105	97.8
Dak Prescott*	7	3,283	2,185	24,943	166	65	97.8
Tom Brady*	23	12,050	7,753	89,214	649	212	97.2

Player	Yrs	Att	Comp	Yds	TD	Int	Rate[1]
Tony Romo	13	4,335	2,829	34,183	248	117	97.1
Steve Young	15	4,149	2,667	33,124	232	107	96.8
Lamar Jackson*	5	1,655	1,055	12,209	101	38	96.7
Peyton Manning	17	9,380	6,125	71,940	539	251	96.5
Justin Herbert*	3	1,966	1,316	14,089	94	35	96.2
Philip Rivers	17	8,134	5,277	63,440	421	209	95.2
Kurt Warner	12	4,070	2,666	32,344	208	128	93.7
Matt Ryan*	15	8,464	5,551	62,792	381	183	93.6
Ben Roethlisberger	18	8,443	5,440	64,088	418	211	93.5
Jared Goff*	7	3,502	2,250	25,854	155	70	92.8

(1) Rating points based on performances in the following categories: percentage of completions, percentage of touchdown passes, percentage of interceptions, and average gain per pass attempt.

Yards gained, career: 89,214, Tom Brady, New England-Tampa Bay, 2000-22.
Yards gained, season: 5,477, Peyton Manning, Denver, 2013.
Yards gained, game: 554, Norm Van Brocklin, L.A. Rams vs. NY Yanks, Sept. 28, 1951 (27 completions in 41 attempts).
Touchdowns passing, career: 649, Tom Brady, New England-Tampa Bay, 2000-22.
Touchdowns passing, season: 55, Peyton Manning, Denver, 2013.
Touchdowns passing, game: 7; Sid Luckman, Chicago Bears vs. NY Giants, Nov. 14, 1943; Adrian Burk, Philadelphia vs. Washington, Oct. 17, 1954; George Blanda, Houston vs. NY Titans, Nov. 19, 1961; Y. A. Tittle, NY Giants vs. Washington,

Oct. 28, 1962; Joe Kapp, Minnesota vs. Baltimore Colts, Sept. 28, 1969; Peyton Manning, Denver vs. Baltimore, Sept. 5, 2013; Nick Foles, Philadelphia vs. Oakland, Nov. 3, 2013; Drew Brees, New Orleans vs. NY Giants, Nov. 1, 2015.
Passes completed, career: 7,753, Tom Brady, New England-Tampa Bay, 2000-22.
Passes completed, season: 490, Tom Brady, Tampa Bay, 2022.
Passes completed, game: 47, Ben Roethlisberger, Pittsburgh vs. Cleveland, Jan. 10, 2021.
Passes completed, game (reg. season): 45; Drew Bledsoe, New England vs. Minnesota, Nov. 13, 1994 (OT); Jared Goff, L.A. Rams vs. Tampa Bay, Sept. 29, 2019.

National Football League Franchise Origins and Name History

(Team: founding year, league. Franchise name history.)

Arizona Cardinals: 1920, American Professional Football Association (APFA)[1]. Chicago Cardinals, 1920-43, 1945-59; Card-Pitt[2], 1944; St. Louis Cardinals, 1960-87; Phoenix Cardinals, 1988-93; Arizona Cardinals, 1994-present.
Atlanta Falcons: 1966, NFL. 1966-present.
Baltimore Ravens: 1996, NFL. 1996-present[3].
Buffalo Bills: 1960, American Football League (AFL)[4]. 1960-present.
Carolina Panthers: 1995, NFL. 1995-present.
Chicago Bears: 1920, APFA. Decatur Staleys, 1920; Chicago Staleys, 1921; Chicago Bears, 1922-present.
Cincinnati Bengals: 1968, AFL. 1968-present.
Cleveland Browns: 1946, All-America Football Conference (AAFC)[5]. 1946-95[3], 1999-present.
Dallas Cowboys: 1960, NFL. 1960-present.
Denver Broncos: 1960, AFL. 1960-present.
Detroit Lions: 1930, NFL. Portsmouth Spartans, 1930-33; Detroit Lions, 1934-present.
Green Bay Packers: 1921, APFA. 1921-present.
Houston Texans: 2002, NFL. 2002-present.
Indianapolis Colts: 1953, NFL[5]. Baltimore Colts, 1953-83; Indianapolis Colts, 1984-present.
Jacksonville Jaguars: 1995, NFL. 1995-present.
Kansas City Chiefs: 1960, AFL. Dallas Texans, 1960-62; Kansas City Chiefs, 1963-present.
Las Vegas Raiders: 1960, AFL. Oakland Raiders, 1960-81, 1995-2019; Los Angeles Raiders, 1982-94; Las Vegas Raiders, 2020-present.

Los Angeles Chargers: 1960, AFL. Los Angeles Chargers, 1960, 2017-present; San Diego Chargers, 1961-2016.
Los Angeles Rams: 1937, NFL. Cleveland Rams, 1937-45; Los Angeles Rams, 1946-94, 2016-present; St. Louis Rams, 1995-2015.
Miami Dolphins: 1966, AFL. 1966-present.
Minnesota Vikings: 1961, NFL. 1961-present.
New England Patriots: 1960, AFL. Boston Patriots, 1960-70; New England Patriots, 1971-present.
New Orleans Saints: 1967, NFL. 1967-present.
New York Giants: 1925, NFL. 1925-present.
New York Jets: 1960, AFL. New York Titans, 1960-62; New York Jets, 1963-present.
Philadelphia Eagles: 1933, NFL. Philadelphia Eagles, 1933-42, 1944-present; Phil-Pitt "Steagles"[6], 1943.
Pittsburgh Steelers: 1933, NFL. Pittsburgh Pirates, 1933-39; Pittsburgh Steelers, 1940-42, 1945-present; Phil-Pitt "Steagles"[6], 1943; Card-Pitt[2], 1944.
San Francisco 49ers: 1946, AAFC. 1946-present.
Seattle Seahawks: 1976, NFL. 1976-present.
Tampa Bay Buccaneers: 1976, NFL. 1976-present.
Tennessee Titans: 1960, AFL. Houston Oilers, 1960-96; Tennessee Oilers, 1996-97; Tennessee Titans, 1998-present.
Washington Commanders: 1932, NFL. Boston Braves, 1932; Boston Redskins 1933-36; Washington Redskins, 1937-2019; Washington Football Team, 2020-21; Washington Commanders, 2022-present.

(1) The American Professional Football Association (APFA) was formed in 1920 to standardize the rules of professional football. In 1922, the name was changed to the National Football League (NFL). (2) In 1944, the Chicago Cardinals and the Pittsburgh Steelers temporarily merged because numerous players were lost to military service. (3) In 1995, Cleveland Browns owner Art Modell moved the franchise to Baltimore and the team was rechristened the Ravens. In 1999, a new Cleveland Browns team joined the NFL, but it is considered a continuation of the original Browns franchise. (4) The most successful of four leagues called the American Football League, or AFL (1926; 1936-37; 1940-41; 1960-69). Congress approved an NFL/AFL merger in 1966. Baltimore, Cleveland, and Pittsburgh agreed to join the 10 incoming AFL teams to form the American Football Conference. The unified NFL began play in 1970 with 26 teams. (5) The All-America Football Conference (AAFC), 1946-49. In 1950, three of its teams joined the NFL (Baltimore, Cleveland, and San Francisco). The Baltimore franchise failed, but the NFL awarded the city a second one, also called the Colts, in 1953. (6) In 1943, the Philadelphia Eagles and the Pittsburgh Steelers temporarily merged because numerous players were lost to military service. The team was informally known as the Steagles.

NFL Stadiums

(**A** = A-Turf Titan, **F** = FieldTurf, **G** = Grass, **M** = Matrix Turf, **N** = Natural grass, **S** = Synthetic, **SI** = SISGrass, **SST** = Shaw Sports Turf, **TNM** = Turf Nation-M6, **U** = ActGlobal Speed S5)

Team: stadium, location, surface (year built)	Capacity
Bears: Soldier Field[1], Chicago, IL, N (1924)	61,500
Bengals: Paycor Stadium, Cincinnati, OH, S (2000)	65,515
Bills: Highmark Stadium, Orchard Park, NY, A (1973)	71,621
Broncos: Empower Field at Mile High, Denver, CO, N (2001)	76,125
Browns: Cleveland Browns Stadium, Cleveland, OH, G (1999)	67,431
Buccaneers: Raymond James Stadium, Tampa, FL, G (1998)	65,844
Cardinals: State Farm Stadium, Glendale, AZ, G (2006)	65,000
Chargers: SoFi Stadium, Inglewood, CA, M (2020)	71,500
Chiefs: GEHA Field at Arrowhead Stadium, Kansas City, MO, G (1972; fully renovated 2010)	73,426
Colts: Lucas Oil Stadium, Indianapolis, IN, SST (2008)	63,000
Commanders: FedExField, Landover, MD, N (1997)	67,617
Cowboys: AT&T Stadium, Arlington, TX, M (2009)	80,000
Dolphins: Hard Rock Stadium, Miami Gardens, FL, G (1987)	64,992
Eagles: Lincoln Financial Field, Philadelphia, PA, N (2003)	69,879
Falcons: Mercedes-Benz Stadium, Atlanta, GA, F (2017)	72,000
49ers: Levi's Stadium, Santa Clara, CA, N (2014)	68,500
Giants: MetLife Stadium, East Rutherford, NJ, F (2010)	82,500
Jaguars: TIAA Bank Field, Jacksonville, FL, G (1995)	67,858
Jets: MetLife Stadium, East Rutherford, NJ, F (2010)	82,500
Lions: Ford Field, Detroit, MI, F (2002)	64,500
Packers: Lambeau Field[2], Green Bay, WI, SI (1957)	81,041
Panthers: Bank of America Stadium, Charlotte, NC, F (1996)	73,778
Patriots: Gillette Stadium, Foxborough, MA, F (2002)	64,628
Raiders: Allegiant Stadium, Las Vegas, NV, N (2020)	65,000
Rams: SoFi Stadium, Inglewood, CA, M (2020)	71,500
Ravens: M&T Bank Stadium, Baltimore, MD, G (1998)	70,745
Saints: Caesars Superdome, New Orleans, LA, TNM (1975)	73,000
Seahawks: Lumen Field, Seattle, WA, F (2002)	68,740
Steelers: Acrisure Field, Pittsburgh, PA, N (2001)	68,400
Texans: NRG Stadium, Houston, TX, S (2002)	71,995
Titans: Nissan Stadium, Nashville, TN, M (1999)	69,143
Vikings: U.S. Bank Stadium, Minneapolis, MN, U (2016)	67,202

Note: As of 2022-23 season. (1) Renovation in 2002 replaced interior of stadium. (2) Renovation completed in 2003 added 11,625 seats.

Pro Football Hall of Fame

Located in Canton, OH. * = Member elected in Feb. 2023 and inducted in Aug. 2023. www.profootballhof.com

Herb Adderley
Troy Aikman
George Allen
Larry Allen
Marcus Allen
Lance Alworth
Morten Andersen
Doug Atkins
Steve Atwater
Morris "Red" Badgro
Champ Bailey
*Rondé Barber
Lem Barney
Cliff Battles
Sammy Baugh
Bobby Beathard
Chuck Bednarik
Bert Bell
Bobby Bell
Raymond Berry
Elvin Bethea
Jerome Bettis
Charles Bidwill
Fred Biletnikoff
George Blanda
Mel Blount
Tony Boselli
Pat Bowlen
Terry Bradshaw
Cliff Branch
Gil Brandt
Robert Brazile
Derrick Brooks
Bob Brown
Jim Brown
Paul Brown
Roosevelt Brown
Tim Brown
Willie Brown
Isaac Bruce
Junious "Buck" Buchanan
Nick Buoniconti
Dick Butkus
Jack Butler
LeRoy Butler
Earl Campbell
Tony Canadeo
Harold Carmichael
Joe Carr
Harry Carson
Cris Carter
Dave Casper
Guy Chamberlin
Jack Christiansen
Earl "Dutch" Clark
George Connor
Jim Conzelman
*Don Coryell
Jimbo Covert
Bill Cowher
Lou Creekmur
Larry Csonka
Curley Culp
Al Davis
Terrell Davis
Willie Davis
Dermontti Dawson
Len Dawson
Fred Dean
Edward DeBartolo Jr.
Joe DeLamielleure
Richard Dent
Eric Dickerson
Dan Dierdorf

Bobby Dillon
Mike Ditka
Chris Doleman
Art Donovan
Tony Dorsett
John "Paddy" Driscoll
Bill Dudley
Tony Dungy
Kenny Easley
Glen "Turk" Edwards
Carl Eller
John Elway
Weeb Ewbank
Alan Faneca
Marshall Faulk
Brett Favre
Tom Fears
Jim Finks
Ray Flaherty
Tom Flores
Len Ford
Dr. Daniel Fortmann
Dan Fouts
Benny Friedman
Frank Gatski
Bill George
Joe Gibbs
Frank Gifford
Sid Gillman
Tony Gonzalez
Otto Graham
Harold "Red" Grange
Bud Grant
Darrell Green
Joe Greene
Kevin Greene
Forrest Gregg
Bob Griese
Russ Grimm
Ray Guy
Joe Guyon
George Halas
Charles Haley
Jack Ham
Dan Hampton
Chris Hanburger
Cliff Harris
Franco Harris
Marvin Harrison
Bob Hayes
Mike Haynes
Ed Healey
Mel Hein
Ted Hendricks
Wilbur "Pete" Henry
Arnold Herber
Bill Hewitt
Gene Hickerson
Winston Hill
Clarke Hinkle
Elroy "Crazylegs" Hirsch
Paul Hornung
Ken Houston
*Chuck Howley
Robert "Cal" Hubbard
Sam Huff
Claude Humphrey
Lamar Hunt
Steve Hutchinson
Don Hutson
Michael Irvin
Rickey Jackson
Edgerrin James

Calvin Johnson
Jimmy Johnson
Jimmy Johnson (coach)
John Henry Johnson
Charlie Joiner
David "Deacon" Jones
Jerry Jones
Stan Jones
Walter Jones
Henry Jordan
Sonny Jurgensen
Alex Karras
Jim Kelly
Leroy Kelly
Cortez Kennedy
Walt Kiesling
Frank "Bruiser" Kinard
*Joe Klecko
Jerry Kramer
Paul Krause
Earl "Curly" Lambeau
Jack Lambert
Tom Landry
Dick "Night Train" Lane
Jim Langer
Willie Lanier
Steve Largent
Yale Lary
Dante Lavelli
Ty Law
Bobby Layne
Dick LeBeau
Alphonse "Tuffy" Leemans
Marv Levy
Ray Lewis
Bob Lilly
Floyd Little
Larry Little
James Lofton
Vince Lombardi
Howie Long
Ronnie Lott
Sid Luckman
Roy "Link" Lyman
John Lynch
Tom Mack
John Mackey
John Madden
Peyton Manning
Tim Mara
Wellington Mara
Gino Marchetti
Dan Marino
George Preston Marshall
Curtis Martin
Ollie Matson
Bruce Matthews
Kevin Mawae
Don Maynard
George McAfee
Mike McCormack
Randall McDaniel
Tommy McDonald
Hugh McElhenny
Art McNally
Johnny "Blood" McNally
Mike Michalske
Wayne Millner
Sam Mills
Bobby Mitchell
Ron Mix
Art Monk
Joe Montana

Warren Moon
Lenny Moore
Randy Moss
Marion Motley
Mike Munchak
Anthony Muñoz
George Musso
Bronko Nagurski
Joe Namath
Earle "Greasy" Neale
Ernie Nevers
Ozzie Newsome
Ray Nitschke
Chuck Noll
Leo Nomellini
Bill Nunn
Jonathan Ogden
Merlin Olsen
Jim Otto
Steve Owen
Terrell Owens
Orlando Pace
Alan Page
Bill Parcells
Clarence "Ace" Parker
Jim Parker
Walter Payton
Drew Pearson
Joe Perry
Pete Pihos
Troy Polamalu
Bill Polian
Fritz Pollard
John Randle
Hugh "Shorty" Ray
Andre Reed
Ed Reed
Dan Reeves
Mel Renfro
*Darrelle Revis
Jerry Rice
Les Richter
John Riggins
*Ken Riley
Jim Ringo
Willie Roaf
Dave Robinson
Johnny Robinson
Andy Robustelli
Art Rooney
Dan Rooney
Pete Rozelle
Ed Sabol
Steve Sabol
Bob St. Clair
Barry Sanders
Charlie Sanders
Deion Sanders
Warren Sapp
Gale Sayers
Joe Schmidt
Tex Schramm
Junior Seau
Lee Roy Selmon
Richard Seymour
Shannon Sharpe
Billy Shaw
Art Shell
Donnie Shell
Will Shields
Don Shula
O.J. Simpson
Mike Singletary
Duke Slater

Jackie Slater
Bruce Smith
Emmitt Smith
Jackie Smith
Mac Speedie
Ed Sprinkle
Ken Stabler
John Stallworth
Dick Stanfel
Bart Starr
Roger Staubach
Ernie Stautner
Jan Stenerud
Dwight Stephenson
Michael Strahan
Hank Stram
Ken Strong
Joe Stydahar
Lynn Swann
Paul Tagliabue
Fran Tarkenton
Charley Taylor
Jason Taylor
Jim Taylor
Lawrence "LT" Taylor
Derrick Thomas
Emmitt Thomas
*Joe Thomas
Thurman Thomas
*Zach Thomas
Jim Thorpe
Mick Tingelhoff
Andre Tippett
Y. A. Tittle
LaDainian Tomlinson
George Trafton
Charley Trippi
Emlen Tunnell
Clyde "Bulldog" Turner
Johnny Unitas
Gene Upshaw
Brian Urlacher
Norm Van Brocklin
Steve Van Buren
Dick Vermeil
Doak Walker
Bill Walsh
*DeMarcus Ware
Paul Warfield
Kurt Warner
Bob Waterfield
Mike Webster
Roger Wehrli
Arnie Weinmeister
Randy White
Reggie White
Dave Wilcox
Aeneas Williams
Bill Willis
Larry Wilson
Ralph Wilson Jr.
Kellen Winslow
Alex Wojciechowicz
Ron Wolf
Willie Wood
Charles Woodson
Rod Woodson
Rayfield Wright
Ron Yary
Bryant Young
George Young
Steve Young
Jack Youngblood
Gary Zimmerman

All-Time NFL Coaching Victories

(at end of 2022 season; ranked by overall career wins; * = active in 2022)

Coach	Team	Yrs	Regular Season				Overall			
			W	L	T	Pct	W	L	T	Pct
Don Shula	Colts, Dolphins	33	328	156	6	.677	347	173	6	.666
Bill Belichick*	Browns, Patriots	28	298	152	0	.662	329	165	0	.666
George Halas	Bears	40	318	148	31	.682	324	151	31	.682
Tom Landry	Cowboys	29	250	162	6	.607	270	178	6	.603
Andy Reid*	Eagles, Chiefs	24	247	138	1	.641	269	154	1	.636
Earl (Curly) Lambeau	Packers, Cardinals, Washington	33	226	132	22	.631	229	134	22	.631
Chuck Noll	Steelers	23	193	148	1	.566	209	156	1	.572
Marty Schottenheimer	Browns, Chiefs, Washington, Chargers	21	200	126	1	.613	205	139	1	.596
Dan Reeves	Broncos, Giants, Falcons	23	190	165	2	.535	201	174	2	.536
Chuck Knox	L.A. Rams, Bills, Seahawks	22	186	147	1	.558	193	158	1	.550
Bill Parcells	Giants, Patriots, Jets, Cowboys	19	172	130	1	.569	183	138	1	.570
Tom Coughlin	Jaguars, Giants	20	170	150	0	.531	182	157	0	.537
Mike Shanahan	L.A. Raiders, Broncos, Washington	20	170	138	0	.552	178	144	0	.553
Jeff Fisher	Houston/Tennessee Oilers, Titans, St. Louis/ L.A. Rams	22	173	165	1	.512	178	171	1	.510
Mike Holmgren	Packers, Seahawks	17	161	111	0	.592	174	122	0	.588

Note: Official NFL records do not include All-America Football Conference statistics.

BASEBALL

Playoff Results, 2023

American League

Wild Card Series: Minnesota 2, Toronto 0; Texas 2, Tampa Bay 0.
Division Series (ALDS): Houston 3, Minnesota 1; Texas 3, Baltimore 0.
Championship Series (ALCS): Texas 4, Houston 3.

National League

Wild Card Series: Philadelphia 2, Miami 0; Arizona 2, Milwaukee 0.
Division Series (NLDS): Philadelphia 3, Atlanta 1; Arizona 3, Los Angeles 0.
Championship Series (NLCS): Arizona 4, Philadelphia 3.

World Series, 2023: Texas Takes High Road to First Championship

The Texas Rangers won the World Series for the first time in their 62 years of existence, taking the title in five games with a 5-0 win over the Arizona Diamondbacks on Nov. 1, 2023, at Chase Field in Phoenix, AZ. Rangers right-hander Nathan Eovaldi, who went 5-0 in the postseason, dodged trouble throughout to hold Arizona scoreless and earn the clinching victory. Texas shortstop Corey Seager, who hit three home runs and drove in six in the World Series, broke up Zac Gallen's six-inning no-hit bid with a single and scored the game's first run. Seager claimed the World Series MVP trophy and joined Reggie Jackson (1973, '77) as the only players to earn the honor with two different franchises—Seager was also MVP in the L.A. Dodgers' 2020 World Series win.

Arizona and Texas took similar paths to reach the Fall Classic. Both lost over 100 games in 2021. And both won 2023 pennants by taking the last two games on the road. The Diamondbacks stunned Philadelphia with Ketel Marte batting .387 to earn NLCS MVP. Texas, which lost out to Houston for the AL West division title on the final day of the regular season, rallied to take the ALCS over the Astros as Adolis García set a record for most RBI in a postseason series with 15.

Arizona looked poised to take Game 1 of the World Series in Texas, but Seager's tied the game with a two-run home run in the ninth. García won it with a homer in the only extra-inning game of the entire postseason. Merrill Kelly pitched seven solid innings the next night and the Diamondbacks banged out 16 hits—including four by Tommy Pham—to even up the series. Texas lost both starter Max Scherzer and García to injury during Game 3, but reliever Jon Gray tossed three scoreless innings. Josh Sborz, Aroldis Chapman, and José Leclerc pitched one inning apiece to lock down the 3-1 victory. Seager homered after Marcus Semien drove in the game's first run against Brandon Pfaadt.

Seager went deep again in Game 4 as the Rangers rang up five runs in both the second and third innings in an 11-7 win. Texas scored 13 runs with two men out during Games 3 and 4. Semien, who drove in eight runs in the five-game series, homered to cap the scoring in the ninth inning of Game 5 after a single by Jonah Heim. The Rangers went 11-0 on the road in the postseason to claim their first World Series trophy. It was the fourth for manager Bruce Bochy, lured out of retirement by Texas GM Chris Young in 2022.

Game 1

Oct. 27 at Globe Life Field, Arlington, TX. Attendance: 42,472. Game time: 4:02.

	1	2	3	4	5	6	7	8	9	10	11	R	H	E
Arizona Diamondbacks	0	0	3	1	1	0	0	0	0	0	0	5	8	0
Texas Rangers	2	0	1	0	0	0	0	0	2	0	1	6	9	0

Winning pitcher: José Leclerc
Losing pitcher: Miguel Castro

Game 2

Oct. 28 at Globe Life Field, Arlington, TX. Attendance: 42,500. Game time: 2:59.

	1	2	3	4	5	6	7	8	9	R	H	E
Arizona Diamondbacks	0	0	0	2	0	0	2	3	2	9	16	0
Texas Rangers	0	0	0	0	1	0	0	0	0	1	4	0

Winning pitcher: Merrill Kelly
Losing pitcher: Jordan Montgomery

Game 3

Oct. 30 at Chase Field, Phoenix, AZ. Attendance: 48,517. Game time: 2:51.

	1	2	3	4	5	6	7	8	9	R	H	E
Texas Rangers	0	0	3	0	0	0	0	0	0	3	5	0
Arizona Diamondbacks	0	0	0	0	0	0	0	1	0	1	6	0

Winning pitcher: Jon Gray
Losing pitcher: Brandon Pfaadt
Save: José Leclerc

Game 4

Oct. 31 at Chase Field, Phoenix, AZ. Attendance: 48,388. Game time: 3:18.

	1	2	3	4	5	6	7	8	9	R	H	E
Texas Rangers	0	5	5	0	0	0	0	1	0	11	11	0
Arizona Diamondbacks	0	0	0	1	0	0	0	4	2	7	12	1

Winning pitcher: Andrew Heaney
Losing pitcher: Joe Mantiply

Game 5

Nov. 1 at Chase Field, Phoenix, AZ. Attendance: 48,511. Game time: 2:54.

	1	2	3	4	5	6	7	8	9	R	H	E
Texas Rangers	0	0	0	0	0	0	1	0	4	5	9	0
Arizona Diamondbacks	0	0	0	0	0	0	0	0	0	0	5	1

Winning pitcher: Nathan Eovaldi
Losing pitcher: Zac Gallen
Save: Josh Sborz

MLB 2023: Clock Starts Ticking, Shifting Balance in the Game

Baseball's timeless quality changed in 2023, and the time of games and attendance improved dramatically after years of rule changes that did little to change the pace of play. With the addition of a pitch clock—a 15-second time limit for the pitcher to throw with the bases empty and 20-second time limit with runners on base—average game time was 24 minutes less than a year earlier and, at 2:39.49, the shortest it had been in almost 40 years. Though some complained about other 2023 rulebook changes—including those that outlawed extreme defensive position shifts, added larger bases, limited the number of pickoff throws to first base, and more—MLB attendance reached 70,747,365, a 9.6% increase and the biggest jump in 30 years. Runs and stolen bases were also up, and the 80.2% steal success rate was the best in MLB history.

The pre-MLB season World Baseball Classic did not implement the new pitch clock or limit on shifts, but it thrilled to the end as Japan won a tight final, 3-2, over the U.S. Mar. 21, 2023, at loanDepot Park in Miami, FL, with Shohei Ohtani fanning L.A. Angels teammate Mike Trout for the last out.

In the regular season, Tampa Bay got off to a fast 13-0 start and was 20-3 on Apr. 24, but the Rays couldn't hold off Baltimore. The Orioles, just two years removed from a 110-loss season, had the American League's best record at 101-61; AL East division foes New York and Boston were left out of the postseason, and Tampa Bay and Toronto went to the postseason as Wild Cards. Houston won the AL West and Texas took the other AL Wild Card. The Rangers won the Wild Card round in Tampa Bay, where attendance averaged below just 20,000 for the two games. Minnesota captured the AL Central, then won its first postseason game in 19 tries since 2004. Atlanta dominated the National League East, and two division foes earned postseason berths, the Philadelphia Phillies beating the Miami Marlins in the Wild Card round. The Milwaukee Brewers won the NL Central but fell to the Arizona Diamondbacks, who finished further out—16 games behind the NL West champion L.A. Dodgers—than any MLB second-place team. All four Wild Card series were sweeps.

The Braves dominated the individual NL leader boards with three names: Matt Olson (home runs, RBI, and slugging), Ronald Acuña Jr. (runs, hits, on-base percentage, total bases, and stolen bases), and Spencer Strider (wins and strikeouts). Blake Snell of San Diego took the ERA crown, and Miami's Luis Arráez, acquired from Minnesota in the offseason, became the first player to win a batting title in each league in successive seasons. AL leaders included Tampa Bay's Yandy Díaz winning the batting title, Kyle Tucker of Houston leading in RBIs, and the L.A. Angels' Ohtani taking his first home run crown, though the two-way star sat out on the injured list most of the final month.

Ohtani served as AL designated hitter but did not pitch in the All-Star Game, won by the NL 3-2, July 11 in Seattle. Elías Díaz of the Rockies earned the game's MVP for the go-ahead home run and San Francisco's Camilo Doval became the first NL pitcher to win an All-Star Game since 2012.

There were just 35 complete games pitched all year, and three resulted in no-hitters, including a perfect game. Houston's Framber Valdez, Aug. 1, no-hit Cleveland, and Michael Lorenzen echoed the achievement against the Washington Nationals a week later in his Citizens Bank Park debut with the Phillies Aug. 9. NY Yankee Domingo Germán pitched the 24th perfect game in major league history June 28 in Oakland. Playing at home, Detroit's Matt Manning, Jason Foley, and Alex Lange combined for a no-hitter on July 8 against Toronto.

National League Final Standings, 2023

(* = wild card)

Eastern Division

Team	W	L	PCT	GB	Home	Road	vs. East	vs. Central	vs. West	vs. AL
Atlanta	104	58	.642	–	52-29	52-29	35-17	22-9	21-12	26-20
Philadelphia*	90	72	.556	14	49-32	41-40	25-27	19-12	18-15	28-18
Miami*	84	78	.519	20	46-35	38-43	26-26	18-15	14-17	26-20
NY Mets	75	87	.463	29	43-38	32-49	25-27	13-19	18-14	19-27
Washington	71	91	.438	33	34-47	37-44	19-33	14-19	15-16	23-23

Central Division

Team	W	L	PCT	GB	Home	Road	vs. East	vs. Central	vs. West	vs. AL
Milwaukee	92	70	.568	–	49-32	43-38	18-14	33-19	13-19	28-18
Chicago Cubs	83	79	.512	9	45-36	38-43	11-20	30-22	17-16	25-21
Cincinnati	82	80	.506	10	38-43	44-37	15-17	21-31	18-14	28-18
Pittsburgh	76	86	.469	16	39-42	37-44	16-17	25-27	16-15	19-27
St. Louis	71	91	.438	21	35-46	36-45	14-18	21-31	13-19	23-23

Western Division

Team	W	L	PCT	GB	Home	Road	vs. East	vs. Central	vs. West	vs. AL
L.A. Dodgers	100	62	.617	–	53-28	47-34	17-14	19-14	34-18	30-16
Arizona*	84	78	.519	16	43-38	41-40	14-18	20-12	29-23	21-25
San Diego	82	80	.506	18	44-37	38-43	16-16	11-21	27-25	28-18
San Francisco	79	83	.488	21	45-36	34-47	13-18	20-13	26-26	20-26
Colorado	59	103	.364	41	37-44	22-59	14-20	13-17	14-38	18-28

American League Final Standings, 2023

(* = wild card)

Eastern Division

Team	W	L	PCT	GB	Home	Road	vs. East	vs. Central	vs. West	vs. NL
Baltimore	101	61	.623	–	49-32	52-29	32-20	22-10	21-11	26-20
Tampa Bay*	99	63	.611	2	53-28	46-35	31-21	23-9	18-14	27-19
Toronto*	89	73	.549	12	43-38	46-35	21-31	22-10	16-16	30-16
NY Yankees	82	80	.506	19	42-39	40-41	22-30	18-14	19-13	23-23
Boston	78	84	.481	23	39-42	39-42	24-28	19-13	15-17	20-26

Central Division

Team	W	L	PCT	GB	Home	Road	vs. East	vs. Central	vs. West	vs. NL
Minnesota	87	75	.537	–	47-34	40-41	13-19	29-23	20-12	25-21
Detroit	78	84	.481	9	37-44	41-40	7-25	35-17	15-17	21-25
Cleveland	76	86	.469	11	42-39	34-47	16-16	23-29	17-15	20-26
Chicago White Sox	61	101	.377	26	31-50	30-51	11-20	23-29	12-21	15-31
Kansas City	56	106	.346	31	33-48	23-58	9-24	20-32	11-20	16-30

Western Division

Team	W	L	PCT	GB	Home	Road	vs. East	vs. Central	vs. West	vs. NL
Houston	90	72	.556	–	39-42	51-30	16-17	14-17	32-20	28-18
Texas*	90	72	.556	–	50-31	40-41	20-12	19-13	29-23	22-24
Seattle	88	74	.543	2	45-36	43-38	13-18	20-13	33-19	22-24
L.A. Angels	73	89	.451	17	38-43	35-46	14-18	18-14	22-30	19-27
Oakland	50	112	.309	40	26-55	24-57	8-24	14-18	14-38	14-32

Note: Houston was named AL West champion due to a better head-to-head record against Texas.

National League Team Statistics, 2023

Team Batting

Team	AVG	AB	R	H	HR	RBI
Atlanta Braves	.276	5,597	947	1,543	307	916
Miami Marlins	.259	5,497	666	1,423	166	633
L.A. Dodgers	.257	5,524	906	1,422	249	877
Philadelphia Phillies	.256	5,541	796	1,417	220	771
Chicago Cubs	.254	5,504	819	1,399	196	786
Washington Nationals	.254	5,522	700	1,401	151	665
Arizona Diamondbacks	.250	5,436	746	1,359	166	706
St. Louis Cardinals	.250	5,510	719	1,376	209	697
Cincinnati Reds	.249	5,499	783	1,371	198	747
Colorado Rockies	.249	5,496	721	1,368	163	685
San Diego Padres	.244	5,401	752	1,316	205	719
Milwaukee Brewers	.240	5,386	728	1,290	165	696
Pittsburgh Pirates	.239	5,406	692	1,293	159	662
NY Mets	.238	5,363	717	1,276	215	692
San Francisco Giants	.235	5,412	674	1,271	174	651

Team Pitching

Team	ERA	IP	H	BB	K	SV
Milwaukee Brewers	3.71	1,443.0	1,218	493	1,425	46
San Diego Padres	3.73	1,441.0	1,270	557	1,445	36
San Francisco Giants	4.02	1,434.2	1,395	403	1,359	50
Philadelphia Phillies	4.03	1,442.1	1,318	470	1,454	45
L.A. Dodgers	4.06	1,446.1	1,284	454	1,388	44
Chicago Cubs	4.08	1,435.1	1,328	513	1,377	35
Atlanta Braves	4.14	1,440.0	1,341	534	1,516	52
Miami Marlins	4.21	1,435.1	1,340	514	1,490	43
NY Mets	4.30	1,416.1	1,331	595	1,397	34
Arizona Diamondbacks	4.48	1,435.1	1,375	525	1,351	44
Pittsburgh Pirates	4.60	1,430.0	1,380	596	1,363	47
St. Louis Cardinals	4.79	1,428.1	1,549	530	1,215	36
Cincinnati Reds	4.83	1,439.1	1,426	613	1,381	53
Washington Nationals	5.02	1,428.1	1,512	592	1,225	42
Colorado Rockies	5.67	1,414.0	1,599	586	1,129	32

American League Team Statistics, 2023

Team Batting

Team	AVG	AB	R	H	HR	RBI
Texas Rangers	.263	5,595	881	1,470	233	845
Tampa Bay Rays	.260	5,511	860	1,432	230	827
Houston Astros	.259	5,567	827	1,441	222	799
Boston Red Sox	.258	5,562	772	1,437	182	734
Toronto Blue Jays	.256	5,562	746	1,423	188	705
Baltimore Orioles	.255	5,495	807	1,399	183	780
Cleveland Guardians	.250	5,513	662	1,379	124	622
L.A. Angels	.245	5,489	739	1,346	231	708
Kansas City Royals	.244	5,428	676	1,325	163	651
Minnesota Twins	.243	5,489	778	1,336	233	745
Seattle Mariners	.242	5,500	758	1,332	210	728
Chicago White Sox	.238	5,501	641	1,308	171	617
Detroit Tigers	.236	5,478	661	1,292	165	635
NY Yankees	.227	5,323	673	1,207	219	650
Oakland Athletics	.223	5,311	585	1,187	171	563

Team Pitching

Team	ERA	IP	H	BB	K	SV
Seattle Mariners	3.74	1,449.1	1,300	421	1,459	44
Toronto Blue Jays	3.78	1,451.2	1,326	488	1,528	51
Tampa Bay Rays	3.86	1,442.0	1,258	439	1,507	45
Minnesota Twins	3.87	1,451.1	1,294	443	1,560	38
Baltimore Orioles	3.89	1,453.2	1,334	473	1,431	49
Houston Astros	3.94	1,445.1	1,312	537	1,460	42
Cleveland Guardians	3.96	1,444.0	1,352	534	1,311	47
NY Yankees	3.97	1,439.2	1,272	508	1,439	44
Detroit Tigers	4.24	1,442.1	1,320	476	1,374	41
Texas Rangers	4.28	1,436.1	1,330	491	1,351	30
Boston Red Sox	4.52	1,430.0	1,416	497	1,423	43
L.A. Angels	4.64	1,431.2	1,394	636	1,445	43
Chicago White Sox	4.87	1,431.2	1,372	654	1,470	28
Kansas City Royals	5.17	1,409.0	1,429	553	1,270	28
Oakland Athletics	5.48	1,419.2	1,464	694	1,300	29

Major League Leaders, 2023

National League Leaders, 2023

Batting Average: Luis Arráez, Miami, .354; Ronald Acuña Jr., Atlanta, .337; Freddie Freeman, L.A. Dodgers, .331; Cody Bellinger, Chicago Cubs, .307; Mookie Betts, L.A. Dodgers, .307; Bryce Harper, Philadelphia, .293; Michael Harris II, Atlanta, .293; William Contreras, Milwaukee, .289; Seiya Suzuki, Chicago Cubs, .285; Xander Bogaerts, San Diego, .285; Corbin Carroll, Arizona, .285.

On-Base Percentage: Ronald Acuña Jr., Atlanta, .416; Juan Soto, San Diego, .410; Freddie Freeman, L.A. Dodgers, .410; Mookie Betts, L.A. Dodgers, .408; Bryce Harper, Philadelphia, .401; Luis Arráez, Miami, .393; Matt Olson, Atlanta, .389; LaMonte Wade Jr., San Francisco, .373.

Slugging: Matt Olson, Atlanta, .604; Ronald Acuña Jr., Atlanta, .596; Mookie Betts, L.A. Dodgers, .579; Freddie Freeman, L.A. Dodgers, .567; Marcell Ozuna, Atlanta, .558; J.D. Martinez, L.A. Dodgers, .572; Cody Bellinger, Chicago Cubs, .525; Juan Soto, San Diego, .519.

Runs Scored: Ronald Acuña Jr., Atlanta, 149; Freddie Freeman, L.A. Dodgers, 131; Matt Olson, Atlanta, 127; Mookie Betts, L.A. Dodgers, 126; Austin Riley, Atlanta, 117; Corbin Carroll, Arizona, 116; Francisco Lindor, NY Mets, 108; Kyle Schwarber, Philadelphia, 108.

Runs Batted In: Matt Olson, Atlanta, 139; Pete Alonso, NY Mets, 118; Ozzie Albies, Atlanta, 109; Juan Soto, San Diego, 109; Mookie Betts, L.A. Dodgers, 107; Ronald Acuña Jr., Atlanta, .106; Nick Castellanos, Philadelphia, 106; Max Muncy, L.A. Dodgers, 105.

Hits: Ronald Acuña Jr., Atlanta, 217; Freddie Freeman, L.A. Dodgers, 211; Luis Arráez, Miami, 203; Austin Riley, Atlanta, 179; Mookie Betts, L.A. Dodgers, 179; Nico Hoerner, Chicago Cubs, 175; Matt Olson, Atlanta, 172.

Doubles: Freddie Freeman, L.A. Dodgers, 59; Mookie Betts, L.A. Dodgers, 40; Jeimer Candelario, Washington-Chicago Cubs, 39; William Contreras, Milwaukee, 38; Spencer Steer, Cincinnati, 37; Ezequiel Tovar, Colorado, 37; Nick Castellanos, Philadelphia, 37.

Triples: Corbin Carroll, Arizona, 10; Ketel Marte, Arizona, 9; Will Benson, Cincinnati, 8; T.J. Friedl, Cincinnati, 8; Elly De La Cruz, Cincinnati, 7; Ke'Bryan Hayes, Pittsburgh, 7; Jake Cronenworth, San Diego, 7.

Home Runs: Matt Olson, Atlanta, 54; Kyle Schwarber, Philadelphia, 47; Pete Alonso, NY Mets, 46; Ronald Acuña Jr., Atlanta, 41; Marcell Ozuna, Atlanta, 40; Mookie Betts, L.A. Dodgers, 39; Austin Riley, Atlanta, 37.

Stolen Bases: Ronald Acuña Jr., Atlanta, 73; Corbin Carroll, Arizona, 54; C.J. Abrams, Washington, 47; Nico Hoerner, Chicago Cubs, 43; Ha-Seong Kim, San Diego, 38; Elly De La Cruz, Cincinnati, 35; Francisco Lindor, NY Mets, 31; Bryson Stott, Philadelphia, 31; Trea Turner, Philadelphia, 30.

Pitching Wins: Spencer Strider, Atlanta, 20; Zac Gallen, Arizona, 17; Justin Steele, Chicago Cubs, 16; Taijuan Walker, Philadelphia, 15; Charlie Morton, Atlanta, 14; Blake Snell, San Diego, 14; Michael Wacha, San Diego, 14.

Earned Run Average: Blake Snell, San Diego, 2.25; Kodai Senga, NY Mets, 2.98; Justin Steele, Chicago Cubs, 3.06; Logan Webb, San Francisco, 3.25; Merrill Kelly, Arizona, 3.29; Corbin Burnes, Milwaukee, 3.39; Zac Gallen, Arizona, 3.47; Jesús Luzardo, Miami, 3.58; Zack Wheeler, Philadelphia, 3.61.

Strikeouts: Spencer Strider, Atlanta, 281; Blake Snell, San Diego, 234; Zac Gallen, Arizona, 220; Zack Wheeler, Philadelphia, 212; Mitch Keller, Pittsburgh, 210; Freddy Peralta, Milwaukee, 210; Jesús Luzardo, Miami, 208; Aaron Nola, Philadelphia, 202; Kodai Senga, NY Mets, 202.

Saves: David Bednar, Pittsburgh, 39; Camilo Doval, San Francisco, 39; Alexis Díaz, Cincinnati, 37; Devin Williams, Milwaukee, 36; Josh Hader, San Diego, 33; Raisel Iglesias, Atlanta, 33; Kyle Finnegan, Washington, 28; Evan Phillips, L.A. Dodgers, 24; Craig Kimbrel, Philadelphia, 23.

A Note on Historical Baseball Statistics

Major League Baseball announced Dec. 16, 2020, that it was integrating its official record books with the statistics of the Negro Leagues, including more than 3,400 players' performances, from 1920 to 1948. The all-time records reflect what is listed by mlb.com as of publication.

American League Leaders, 2023

Batting Average: Yandy Díaz, Tampa Bay, .330; Corey Seager, Texas, .327; Bo Bichette, Toronto, .306; Shohei Ohtani, L.A. Angels, .304; Masataka Yoshida, Boston, .289; Kyle Tucker, Houston, .284; Jose Ramirez, Cleveland, .282; Adley Rutschman, Baltimore, .277.

On-Base Percentage: Shohei Ohtani, L.A. Angels, .412; Yandy Díaz, Tampa Bay, .410; Corey Seager, Texas, .390; J.P. Crawford, Seattle, .380; Adley Rutschman, Baltimore, .374; Kyle Tucker, Houston, .369; Triston Casas, Boston, .367; Randy Arozarena, Tampa Bay, .364.

Slugging: Shohei Ohtani, L.A. Angels, .654; Corey Seager, Texas, .623; Luis Robert Jr., Chicago White Sox, .542; Yandy Díaz, Tampa Bay, .522; Kyle Tucker, Houston, .517; Adolis García, Texas, .508; Rafael Devers, Boston, .500.

Runs Scored: Marcus Semien, Texas, 122; Adolis García, Texas, 108; Alex Bregman, Houston, 103; Shohei Ohtani, L.A. Angels, 102; Julio Rodríguez, Seattle, 102; Gunnar Henderson, Baltimore, 100; Kyle Tucker, Houston, 97; Bobby Witt, Kansas City, 97.

Runs Batted In: Kyle Tucker, Houston, 112; Adolis García, Texas, 107; Julio Rodríguez, Seattle, 103; Rafael Devers, Boston, 100; Marcus Semien, Texas, 100; Alex Bregman, Houston, 98; Isaac Paredes, Tampa Bay, 98.

Hits: Marcus Semien, Texas, 185; Julio Rodríguez, Seattle, 180; Bobby Witt, Kansas City, 177; Bo Bichette, Toronto, 175; Yandy Díaz, Tampa Bay, 173; José Ramírez, Cleveland, 172; Steven Kwan, Cleveland, 171.

Doubles: Corey Seager, Texas, 42; Anthony Santander, Baltimore, 41; Marcus Siemen, Texas, 40; Matt Chapman, Toronto, 39; Nathaniel Lowe, Texas, 38; Julio Rodríguez, Seattle, 37; Kyle Tucker, Houston, 37; Alex Verdugo, Boston, 37.

Triples: Bobby Witt, Kansas City, 11; Gunnar Henderson, Baltimore, 9; Shohei Ohtani, L.A. Angels, 8; Steven Kwan, Cleveland, 7; Wander Franco, Tampa Bay, 6; Kevin Kiermaier, Toronto, 6; Amed Rosario, Cleveland, 6.

Home Runs: Shohei Ohtani, L.A. Angels, 44; Adolis García, Texas, 39; Luis Robert Jr., Chicago White Sox, 38; Aaron Judge, NY Yankees, 37; Rafael Devers, Boston, 33; Corey Seager, Texas, 33; Julio Rodríguez, Seattle, 32; Yordan Álvarez, Houston, 31; Isaac Paredes, Tampa Bay, 31; Spencer Torkelson, Detroit, 31.

Stolen Bases: Esteury Ruiz, Oakland, 67; Bobby Witt, Kansas City, 49; Julio Rodríguez, Seattle, 37; Willi Castro, Minnesota, 33; Josh Lowe, Tampa Bay, 32; Jorge Mateo, Baltimore, 32; Wander Franco, Tampa Bay, 30; Andrés Giménez, Cleveland, 30; Kyle Tucker, Houston, 30.

Pitching Wins: Chris Bassitt, Toronto, 16; Zach Eflin, Tampa Bay, 16; Gerrit Cole, NY Yankees, 15; Kyle Gibson, Baltimore, 15; Luis Castillo, Seattle, 14; Logan Gilbert, Seattle, 13; George Kirby, Seattle, 13; Dean Kremer, Baltimore, 13; Eduardo Rodríguez, Detroit, 13.

Earned Run Average: Gerrit Cole, NY Yankees, 2.63; Sonny Gray, Minnesota, 2.79; Kyle Bradish, Baltimore, 2.83; Kevin Gausman, Toronto, 3.16; Luis Castillo, Seattle, 3.34; George Kirby, Seattle, 3.35; Framber Valdez, Houston, 3.45; Zach Eflin, Tampa Bay, 3.50.

Strikeouts: Kevin Gausman, Toronto, 237; Pablo López, Minnesota, 234; Gerrit Cole, NY Yankees, 222; Luis Castillo, Seattle, 219; Dylan Cease, Chicago White Sox, 214; Lucas Giolito, Chicago White Sox-L.A. Angels-Cleveland, 204; Framber Valdez, Houston, 200; Joe Ryan, Minnesota, 197.

Saves: Emmanuel Clase, Cleveland, 44; Jordan Romano, Toronto, 36; Félix Bautista, Baltimore, 33; Carlos Estévez, L.A. Angels, 31; Ryan Pressly, Houston, 31; Kenley Jansen, Boston, 29; Jhoan Durán, Minnesota, 27; Alex Lange, Detroit, 26.

All-Time Major League Single-Season Leaders

Source: www.mlb.com; * = Active in 2023 season; records for "modern" era beginning in 1901.

Home Runs

Barry Bonds (2001)	73
Mark McGwire (1998)	70
Sammy Sosa (1998)	66
Mark McGwire (1999)	65
Sammy Sosa (2001)	64
Sammy Sosa (1999)	63
Aaron Judge* (2022)	62
Roger Maris (1961)	61
Babe Ruth (1927)	60

Runs Scored

Babe Ruth (1921)	177
Lou Gehrig (1936)	167
Lou Gehrig (1931)	163
Babe Ruth (1928)	163
Chuck Klein (1930)	158
Babe Ruth (1920, 1927)	158
Rogers Hornsby (1929)	156
Kiki Cuyler (1930)	155

Hits

Ichiro Suzuki (2004)	262
George Sisler (1920)	257
Lefty O'Doul (1929)	254
Bill Terry (1930)	254
Al Simmons (1925)	253
Rogers Hornsby (1922)	250
Chuck Klein (1930)	250
Ty Cobb (1911)	248

Runs Batted In

Hack Wilson (1930)	191
Lou Gehrig (1931)	184
Hank Greenberg (1937)	183
Jimmie Foxx (1938)	175
Lou Gehrig (1927)	175
Lou Gehrig (1930)	174
Babe Ruth (1921)	171
Hank Greenburg (1935)	170
Chuck Klein (1930)	170

Batting Average

Rogers Hornsby (1924)	.424
Nap Lajoie (1901)	.421
George Sisler (1922)	.420
Ty Cobb (1911)	.420
Ty Cobb (1912)	.410
Joe Jackson (1911)	.408
George Sisler (1920)	.407
Ted Williams (1941)	.406

Stolen Bases

Rickey Henderson (1982)	130
Lou Brock (1974)	118
Vince Coleman (1985)	110
Vince Coleman (1987)	109
Rickey Henderson (1983)	108
Vince Coleman (1986)	107
Maury Wills (1962)	104
Rickey Henderson (1980)	100

Walks (Batter)

Barry Bonds (2004)	232
Barry Bonds (2002)	198
Barry Bonds (2001)	177
Babe Ruth (1923)	170
Mark McGwire (1998)	162
Ted Williams (1947, 1949)	162
Ted Williams (1946)	156

Strikeouts (Batter)

Mark Reynolds (2009)	223
Adam Dunn (2012)	222
Chris Davis (2016)	219
Yoán Moncada* (2018)	217
Kyle Schwarber* (2023)	215
Eugenio Suárez* (2023)	214
Joey Gallo* (2021)	213
Chris Carter (2013)	212
Teoscar Hernández* (2023)	211
Mark Reynolds (2010)	211
Giancarlo Stanton* (2018)	211

Earned Run Average

Dutch Leonard (1914)	0.96
Mordecai "Three Finger" Brown (1906)	1.04
Bob Gibson (1968)	1.12
Christy Mathewson (1909)	1.14
Walter Johnson (1913)	1.14
Jack Pfiester (1907)	1.15
Addie Joss (1908)	1.16
Carl Lundgren (1907)	1.17

Wins (Pitcher)

Jack Chesbro (1904)	41
Ed Walsh (1908)	40
Christy Mathewson (1908)	37
Walter Johnson (1913)	36
Joe McGinnity (1904)	35
Grover Alexander (1916)	33
Walter Johnson (1912)	33
Cristy Mathewson (1904)	33
Cy Young (1901)	33

Strikeouts (Pitcher)

Nolan Ryan (1973)	383
Sandy Koufax (1965)	382
Randy Johnson (2001)	372
Nolan Ryan (1974)	367
Randy Johnson (1999)	364
Rube Waddell (1904)	349
Bob Feller (1946)	348
Randy Johnson (2000)	347

Saves

Francisco Rodríguez (2008)	62
Edwin Díaz* (2018)	57
Bobby Thigpen (1990)	57
Eric Gagne (2003)	55
John Smoltz (2002)	55
Trevor Hoffman (1998)	53
Randy Myers (1993)	53
Mariano Rivera (2004)	53

All-Time Major League Leaders

Source: www.mlb.com; * = Active in 2023 season; career records for players in "modern" era beginning in 1901 may include statistics from preceding years.

Games

Pete Rose	3,562
Carl Yastrzemski	3,308
Hank Aaron	3,298
Rickey Henderson	3,081
Albert Pujols	3,080
Ty Cobb	3,035
Eddie Murray	3,026
Stan Musial	3,026
Cal Ripken Jr.	3,001
Willie Mays	2,992

Stolen Bases

Rickey Henderson	1,406
Lou Brock	938
Billy Hamilton	912
Ty Cobb	892
Tim Raines	808
Vince Coleman	752
Eddie Collins	745
Arlie Latham	739
Max Carey	738
Honus Wagner	722

Strikeouts (Pitcher)

Nolan Ryan	5,714
Randy Johnson	4,875
Roger Clemens	4,672
Steve Carlton	4,136
Bert Blyleven	3,701
Tom Seaver	3,640
Don Sutton	3,574
Gaylord Perry	3,534
Walter Johnson	3,508
Greg Maddux	3,371

At Bats

Pete Rose	14,053
Hank Aaron	12,364
Carl Yastrzemski	11,988
Cal Ripken Jr.	11,551
Ty Cobb	11,429
Albert Pujols	11,421
Eddie Murray	11,336
Derek Jeter	11,195
Adrián Beltré	11,068
Robin Yount	11,008

Triples

Sam Crawford	309
Ty Cobb	297
Honus Wagner	252
Jake Beckley	243
Roger Connor	233
Tris Speaker	222
Fred Clarke	220
Dan Brouthers	205
Joe Kelley	194
Paul Waner	191

Saves

Mariano Rivera	652
Trevor Hoffman	601
Lee Smith	478
Francisco Rodríguez	437
John Franco	424
Billy Wagner	422
Kenley Jansen*	420
Craig Kimbrel*	417
Dennis Eckersley	390
Joe Nathan	377

Runs Batted In

Hank Aaron	2,297
Albert Pujols	2,218
Babe Ruth	2,213
Alex Rodriguez	2,086
Barry Bonds	1,996
Lou Gehrig	1,995
Stan Musial	1,951
Ty Cobb	1,938
Jimmie Foxx	1,922
Eddie Murray	1,917

Batting Average

Ty Cobb	.367
Rogers Hornsby	.358
Joe Jackson	.356
Ed Delahanty	.346
Tris Speaker	.345
Ted Williams	.344
Billy Hamilton	.344
Dan Brouthers	.342
Babe Ruth	.342
Harry Heilmann	.342

Shutouts

Walter Johnson	110
Grover Alexander	90
Christy Mathewson	79
Cy Young	76
Eddie Plank	69
Warren Spahn	63
Nolan Ryan	61
Tom Seaver	61
Bert Blyleven	60
Don Sutton	58

Runs

Rickey Henderson	2,295
Ty Cobb	2,246
Barry Bonds	2,227
Hank Aaron	2,174
Babe Ruth	2,174
Pete Rose	2,165
Willie Mays	2,062
Alex Rodriguez	2,021
Stan Musial	1,949
Derek Jeter	1,923

Walks (Batter)

Barry Bonds	2,558
Rickey Henderson	2,190
Babe Ruth	2,062
Ted Williams	2,019
Joe Morgan	1,865
Carl Yastrzemski	1,845
Jim Thome	1,747
Mickey Mantle	1,733
Mel Ott	1,708
Frank Thomas	1,667

Losses

Cy Young	316
Nolan Ryan	292
Walter Johnson	279
Phil Niekro	274
Gaylord Perry	265
Don Sutton	256
Jack Powell	254
Eppa Rixey	251
Bert Blyleven	250
Robin Roberts	245
Warren Spahn	245

All-Time Home Run Leaders

Source: www.mlb.com; * = Active in 2023 season.

Player	HR	Player	HR	Player	HR	Player	HR
Barry Bonds	762	Manny Ramirez	555	Lou Gehrig	493	Dave Kingman	442
Hank Aaron	755	Mike Schmidt	548	Fred McGriff	493	Jason Giambi	440
Babe Ruth	714	David Ortiz	541	Adrián Beltré	477	Paul Konerko	439
Albert Pujols	703	Mickey Mantle	536	Stan Musial	475	Andre Dawson	438
Alex Rodriguez	696	Jimmie Foxx	534	Willie Stargell	475	Carlos Beltrán	435
Willie Mays	660	Willie McCovey	521	Carlos Delgado	473	Juan Gonzalez	434
Ken Griffey Jr.	630	Frank Thomas	521	Chipper Jones	468	Andruw Jones	434
Jim Thome	612	Ted Williams	521	Dave Winfield	465	Cal Ripken Jr.	431
Sammy Sosa	609	Ernie Banks	512	Nelson Cruz*	464	Mike Piazza	427
Frank Robinson	586	Eddie Mathews	512	Jose Canseco	462	Billy Williams	426
Mark McGwire	583	Miguel Cabrera*	511	Adam Dunn	462	Edwin Encarnación	424
Harmon Killebrew	573	Mel Ott	511	Carl Yastrzemski	452	Darrell Evans	414
Rafael Palmeiro	569	Gary Sheffield	509	Jeff Bagwell	449	Alfonso Soriano	412
Reggie Jackson	563	Eddie Murray	504	Vladimir Guerrero	449	Mark Teixeira	409

Players With 3,000 Major League Hits

Source: www.mlb.com; * = Active in 2023 season.

Player	Hits	Player	Hits	Player	Hits	Player	Hits
Pete Rose	4,256	Albert Pujols	3,384	Adrián Beltré	3,166	Craig Biggio	3,060
Ty Cobb	4,191	Paul Molitor	3,319	George Brett	3,154	Rickey Henderson	3,055
Hank Aaron	3,771	Eddie Collins	3,314	Paul Waner	3,152	Rod Carew	3,053
Stan Musial	3,630	Willie Mays	3,283	Robin Yount	3,142	Lou Brock	3,023
Tris Speaker	3,515	Eddie Murray	3,255	Tony Gwynn	3,141	Rafael Palmeiro	3,020
Derek Jeter	3,465	Nap Lajoie	3,252	Alex Rodriguez	3,115	Cap Anson	3,011
Honus Wagner	3,430	Cal Ripken Jr.	3,184	Dave Winfield	3,110	Wade Boggs	3,010
Carl Yastrzemski	3,419	Miguel Cabrera*	3,174	Ichiro Suzuki	3,089	Al Kaline	3,007
						Roberto Clemente	3,000

50 Home Run Club

Only Barry Bonds and Mark McGwire hit 70 or more home runs in a season. Six players—including Babe Ruth and Roger Maris—hit 60 or more, a feat Sammy Sosa accomplished for the third time in 2001.

HR	Player, team	Year	HR	Player, team	Year
73	Barry Bonds, San Francisco Giants	2001	54	David Ortiz, Boston Red Sox	2006
70	Mark McGwire, St. Louis Cardinals	1998	54	Alex Rodriguez, NY Yankees	2007
66	Sammy Sosa, Chicago Cubs	1998	54	Babe Ruth, NY Yankees	1920
65	Mark McGwire, St. Louis Cardinals	1999	54	Babe Ruth, NY Yankees	1928
64	Sammy Sosa, Chicago Cubs	2001	53	Pete Alonso, NY Mets	2019
63	Sammy Sosa, Chicago Cubs	1999	53	Chris Davis, Baltimore Orioles	2013
62	Aaron Judge, NY Yankees	2022	52	George Foster, Cincinnati Reds	1977
61	Roger Maris, NY Yankees	1961	52	Aaron Judge, NY Yankees	2017
60	Babe Ruth, NY Yankees	1927	52	Mickey Mantle, NY Yankees	1956
59	Babe Ruth, NY Yankees	1921	52	Willie Mays, San Francisco Giants	1965
59	Giancarlo Stanton, Miami Marlins	2017	52	Mark McGwire, Oakland A's	1996
58	Jimmie Foxx, Philadelphia Athletics	1932	52	Alex Rodriguez, Texas Rangers	2001
58	Hank Greenberg, Detroit Tigers	1938	52	Jim Thome, Cleveland Indians	2002
58	Ryan Howard, Philadelphia Phillies	2006	51	Cecil Fielder, Detroit Tigers	1990
58	Mark McGwire, Oakland A's/St. Louis Cardinals	1997	51	Andruw Jones, Atlanta Braves	2005
57	Luis Gonzalez, Arizona Diamondbacks	2001	51	Ralph Kiner, Pittsburgh Pirates	1947
57	Alex Rodriguez, Texas Rangers	2002	51	Willie Mays, NY Giants	1955
56	Ken Griffey Jr., Seattle Mariners	1997	51	Johnny Mize, NY Giants	1947
56	Ken Griffey Jr., Seattle Mariners	1998	50	Brady Anderson, Baltimore Orioles	1996
56	Hack Wilson, Chicago Cubs	1930	50	Albert Belle, Chicago White Sox	1995
54	José Bautista, Toronto Blue Jays	2010	50	Prince Fielder, Milwaukee Brewers	2007
54	Ralph Kiner, Pittsburgh Pirates	1949	50	Jimmie Foxx, Boston Red Sox	1938
54	Mickey Mantle, NY Yankees	1961	50	Sammy Sosa, Chicago Cubs	2000
54	Matt Olson, Atlanta Braves	2023	50	Greg Vaughn, San Diego Padres	1998

Pitchers With 300 Major League Wins

Source: www.mlb.com

Pitcher	Wins	Pitcher	Wins	Pitcher	Wins	Pitcher	Wins
Cy Young	511	Charles "Kid" Nichols	361	Eddie Plank	326	Charley Radbourn	309
Walter Johnson	417	Greg Maddux	355	Nolan Ryan	324	Mickey Welch	307
Grover Alexander	373	Roger Clemens	354	Don Sutton	324	Tom Glavine	305
Christy Mathewson	373	Tim Keefe	342	Phil Niekro	318	Randy Johnson	303
Warren Spahn	363	Steve Carlton	329	Gaylord Perry	314	Robert "Lefty" Grove	300
James "Pud" Galvin	361	John Clarkson	328	Tom Seaver	311	Early "Gus" Wynn	300

Official Major League Perfect Games Since 1901

Date	Pitcher	Teams	Date	Pitcher	Teams
5/5/1904	Cy Young	Boston 3 vs. Phil. 0 (AL)	7/28/1994	Kenny Rogers	Texas 4 vs. California 0 (AL)
10/2/1908	Addie Joss	Clev. 1 vs. Chicago 0 (AL)	5/17/1998	David Wells	NY 4 vs. Minn. 0 (AL)
4/30/1922	Charlie Robertson	Chicago 2 vs. Detroit 0 (AL)	7/18/1999	David Cone	NY 6 vs. Montréal 0 (AL)
10/8/1956	Don Larsen	NY 2 (AL) vs. Brooklyn 0* (NL)	5/18/2004	Randy Johnson	Arizona 2 vs. Atlanta 0 (NL)
6/21/1964	Jim Bunning	Phil. 6 vs. NY 0 (NL)	7/23/2009	Mark Buehrle	Chicago 5 vs. Tampa Bay 0 (AL)
9/9/1965	Sandy Koufax	L.A. 1 vs. Chicago 0 (NL)	5/9/2010	Dallas Braden	Oakland 4 vs. Tampa Bay 0 (AL)
5/8/1968	Jim "Catfish" Hunter	Oakland 4 vs. Minn. 0 (AL)	5/29/2010	Roy Halladay	Phil. 1 vs. Florida 0 (NL)
5/15/1981	Len Barker	Clev. 3 vs. Toronto 0 (AL)	4/21/2012	Philip Humber	Chicago 4 vs. Seattle 0 (AL)
9/30/1984	Mike Witt	California 1 vs. Texas 0 (AL)	6/13/2012	Matt Cain	S.F. 10 vs. Houston 0 (NL)
9/16/1988	Tom Browning	Cincinnati 1 vs. L.A. 0 (NL)	8/15/2012	Felix Hernandez	Seattle 1 vs. Tampa Bay 0 (AL)
7/28/1991	Dennis Martinez	Montréal 2 vs. L.A. 0 (NL)	6/28/2023	Domingo Germán	NY 11 vs. Oakland 0 (AL)

* = World Series game. **Note:** Two pre-1901 National League pitchers are also credited with perfect games. Within one week in 1880, Lee Richmond (June 12, Worcester 1, Cleveland 0) and John "Monte" Ward (June 17, Providence 5, Buffalo 0) each threw a perfect game.

Most Career Major League No-Hitters

No.	Pitcher	No.	Pitcher
7	Nolan Ryan	2	Jake Arrieta, Al Atkinson, Homer Bailey, Theodore Breitenstein, Mark Buehrle, Jim Bunning,
4	Sandy Koufax		Steve Busby, Carl Erskine, Mike Fiers, Bob Forsch, James "Pud" Galvin, Roy Halladay,
3	Larry Corcoran,		Ken Holtzman, Randy Johnson, Addie Joss, Dutch Leonard, Tim Lincecum, Jim
	Bob Feller, Justin Verlander,		Maloney, Christy Mathewson, Hideo Nomo, Allie Reynolds, Max Scherzer, Frank Smith,
	Cy Young		Warren Spahn, Bill Stoneman, Adonis Terry, Virgil Trucks, Johnny Vander Meer, Don Wilson

Home Run Leaders by Season, 1901-2023

* = All-time single-season record for league since beginning of "modern" era in 1901.

	National League			American League	
Year	Player, team	HR	Year	Player, team	HR
1901	Sam Crawford, Cincinnati	16	1901	Nap Lajoie, Philadelphia	14
1902	Thomas Leach, Pittsburgh	6	1902	Socks Seybold, Philadelphia	16
1903	James Sheckard, Brooklyn	9	1903	Buck Freeman, Boston	13
1904	Harry Lumley, Brooklyn	9	1904	Harry Davis, Philadelphia	10
1905	Fred Odwell, Cincinnati	9	1905	Harry Davis, Philadelphia	8
1906	Timothy Jordan, Brooklyn	12	1906	Harry Davis, Philadelphia	12
1907	David Brain, Boston	10	1907	Harry Davis, Philadelphia	8
1908	Timothy Jordan, Brooklyn	12	1908	Sam Crawford, Detroit	7
1909	Red Murray, New York	7	1909	Ty Cobb, Detroit	9
1910	Fred Beck, Boston; Frank Schulte, Chicago	10	1910	Jake Stahl, Boston	10
1911	Frank Schulte, Chicago	21	1911	J. Franklin Baker, Philadelphia	11
1912	Henry Zimmerman, Chicago	14	1912	J. Franklin Baker, Phil.; Tris Speaker, Boston	10
1913	Gavvy Cravath, Philadelphia	19	1913	J. Franklin Baker, Philadelphia	12
1914	Gavvy Cravath, Philadelphia	19	1914	J. Franklin Baker, Philadelphia	9
1915	Gavvy Cravath, Philadelphia	24	1915	Robert Roth, Chicago-Cleveland	7

	National League			American League	
Year	Player, team	HR	Year	Player, team	HR
1916	Dave Robertson, NY; Fred "Cy" Williams, Chicago	12	1916	Wally Pipp, New York	12
1917	Gavvy Cravath, Phil.; Dave Robertson, NY	12	1917	Wally Pipp, New York	9
1918	Gavvy Cravath, Philadelphia	8	1918	Babe Ruth, Boston; Tilly Walker, Philadelphia	11
1919	Gavvy Cravath, Philadelphia	12	1919	Babe Ruth, Boston	29
1920	Cy Williams, Philadelphia	15	1920	Babe Ruth, New York	54
1921	George Kelly, New York	23	1921	Babe Ruth, New York	59
1922	Rogers Hornsby, St. Louis	42	1922	Ken Williams, St. Louis	39
1923	Cy Williams, Philadelphia	41	1923	Babe Ruth, New York	41
1924	Jacques Fournier, Brooklyn	27	1924	Babe Ruth, New York	46
1925	Rogers Hornsby, St. Louis	39	1925	Bob Meusel, New York	33
1926	Hack Wilson, Chicago	21	1926	Babe Ruth, New York	47
1927	Hack Wilson, Chicago; Cy Williams, Philadelphia	30	1927	Babe Ruth, New York	60
1928	Hack Wilson, Chicago; Jim Bottomley, St. Louis	31	1928	Babe Ruth, New York	54
1929	Chuck Klein, Philadelphia	43	1929	Babe Ruth, New York	46
1930	Hack Wilson, Chicago	56	1930	Babe Ruth, New York	49
1931	Chuck Klein, Philadelphia	31	1931	Lou Gehrig, New York; Babe Ruth, New York	46
1932	Chuck Klein, Philadelphia; Mel Ott, New York	38	1932	Jimmie Foxx, Philadelphia	58
1933	Chuck Klein, Philadelphia	28	1933	Jimmie Foxx, Philadelphia	48
1934	Rip Collins, St. Louis; Mel Ott, New York	35	1934	Lou Gehrig, New York	49
1935	Walter Berger, Boston	34	1935	Jimmie Foxx, Phil.; Hank Greenberg, Detroit	36
1936	Mel Ott, New York	33	1936	Lou Gehrig, New York	49
1937	Joe Medwick, St. Louis; Mel Ott, New York	31	1937	Joe DiMaggio, New York	46
1938	Mel Ott, New York	36	1938	Hank Greenberg, Detroit	58
1939	John Mize, St. Louis	28	1939	Jimmie Foxx, Boston	35
1940	John Mize, St. Louis	43	1940	Hank Greenberg, Detroit	41
1941	Dolph Camilli, Brooklyn	34	1941	Ted Williams, Boston	37
1942	Mel Ott, New York	30	1942	Ted Williams, Boston	36
1943	Bill Nicholson, Chicago	29	1943	Rudy York, Detroit	34
1944	Bill Nicholson, Chicago	33	1944	Nick Etten, New York	22
1945	Tommy Holmes, Boston	28	1945	Vern Stephens, St. Louis	24
1946	Ralph Kiner, Pittsburgh	23	1946	Hank Greenberg, Detroit	44
1947	Ralph Kiner, Pittsburgh; John Mize, New York	51	1947	Ted Williams, Boston	32
1948	Ralph Kiner, Pittsburgh; John Mize, New York	40	1948	Joe DiMaggio, New York	39
1949	Ralph Kiner, Pittsburgh	54	1949	Ted Williams, Boston	43
1950	Ralph Kiner, Pittsburgh	47	1950	Al Rosen, Cleveland	37
1951	Ralph Kiner, Pittsburgh	42	1951	Gus Zernial, Chicago-Philadelphia	33
1952	Ralph Kiner, Pittsburgh; Hank Sauer, Chicago	37	1952	Larry Doby, Cleveland	32
1953	Ed Mathews, Milwaukee	47	1953	Al Rosen, Cleveland	43
1954	Ted Kluszewski, Cincinnati	49	1954	Larry Doby, Cleveland	32
1955	Willie Mays, New York	51	1955	Mickey Mantle, New York	37
1956	Duke Snider, Brooklyn	43	1956	Mickey Mantle, New York	52
1957	Hank Aaron, Milwaukee	44	1957	Roy Sievers, Washington	42
1958	Ernie Banks, Chicago	47	1958	Mickey Mantle, New York	42
1959	Ed Mathews, Milwaukee	46	1959	Rocky Colavito, Clev.; Harmon Killebrew, Wash.	42
1960	Ernie Banks, Chicago	41	1960	Mickey Mantle, New York	40
1961	Orlando Cepeda, San Francisco	46	1961	Roger Maris, New York	61*
1962	Willie Mays, San Francisco	49	1962	Harmon Killebrew, Minnesota	48
1963	Hank Aaron, Milwaukee; Willie McCovey, S.F.	44	1963	Harmon Killebrew, Minnesota	45
1964	Willie Mays, San Francisco	47	1964	Harmon Killebrew, Minnesota	49
1965	Willie Mays, San Francisco	52	1965	Tony Conigliaro, Boston	32
1966	Hank Aaron, Atlanta	44	1966	Frank Robinson, Baltimore	49
1967	Hank Aaron, Atlanta	39	1967	Harmon Killebrew, Minn.; Carl Yastrzemski, Boston	44
1968	Willie McCovey, San Francisco	36	1968	Frank Howard, Washington	44
1969	Willie McCovey, San Francisco	45	1969	Harmon Killebrew, Minnesota	49
1970	Johnny Bench, Cincinnati	45	1970	Frank Howard, Washington	44
1971	Willie Stargell, Pittsburgh	48	1971	Bill Melton, Chicago	33
1972	Johnny Bench, Cincinnati	40	1972	Dick Allen, Chicago	37
1973	Willie Stargell, Pittsburgh	44	1973	Reggie Jackson, Oakland	32
1974	Mike Schmidt, Philadelphia	36	1974	Dick Allen, Chicago	32
1975	Mike Schmidt, Philadelphia	38	1975	Reggie Jackson, Oak.; George Scott, Milw.	36
1976	Mike Schmidt, Philadelphia	38	1976	Graig Nettles, New York	32
1977	George Foster, Cincinnati	52	1977	Jim Rice, Boston	39
1978	George Foster, Cincinnati	40	1978	Jim Rice, Boston	46
1979	Dave Kingman, Chicago	48	1979	Gorman Thomas, Milwaukee	45
1980	Mike Schmidt, Philadelphia	48	1980	Reggie Jackson, New York; Ben Oglivie, Milw.	41
1981	Mike Schmidt, Philadelphia	31	1981	Tony Armas, Oakland; Dwight Evans, Boston; Bobby Grich, Cal.; Eddie Murray, Baltimore	22
1982	Dave Kingman, New York	37	1982	Gorman Thomas, Milw.; Reggie Jackson, Cal.	39
1983	Mike Schmidt, Philadelphia	40	1983	Jim Rice, Boston	39
1984	Dale Murphy, Atlanta; Mike Schmidt, Philadelphia	36	1984	Tony Armas, Boston	43
1985	Dale Murphy, Atlanta	37	1985	Darrell Evans, Detroit	40
1986	Mike Schmidt, Philadelphia	37	1986	Jesse Barfield, Toronto	40
1987	Andre Dawson, Chicago	49	1987	Mark McGwire, Oakland	49
1988	Darryl Strawberry, New York	39	1988	Jose Canseco, Oakland	42
1989	Kevin Mitchell, San Francisco	47	1989	Fred McGriff, Toronto	36
1990	Ryne Sandberg, Chicago	40	1990	Cecil Fielder, Detroit	51

National League			American League		
Year	Player, team	HR	Year	Player, team	HR
1991	Howard Johnson, New York	38	1991	Jose Canseco, Oakland; Cecil Fielder, Detroit	44
1992	Fred McGriff, San Diego	35	1992	Juan Gonzalez, Texas	43
1993	Barry Bonds, San Francisco	46	1993	Juan Gonzalez, Texas	46
1994	Matt Williams, San Francisco	43	1994	Ken Griffey Jr., Seattle	40
1995	Dante Bichette, Colorado	40	1995	Albert Belle, Cleveland	50
1996	Andres Galarraga, Colorado	47	1996	Mark McGwire, Oakland	52
1997[1]	Larry Walker, Colorado	49	1997[1]	Ken Griffey Jr., Seattle	56
1998	Mark McGwire, St. Louis	70	1998	Ken Griffey Jr., Seattle	56
1999	Mark McGwire, St. Louis	65	1999	Ken Griffey Jr., Seattle	48
2000	Sammy Sosa, Chicago	50	2000	Troy Glaus, Anaheim	47
2001	Barry Bonds, San Francisco	73*	2001	Alex Rodriguez, Texas	52
2002	Sammy Sosa, Chicago	49	2002	Alex Rodriguez, Texas	57
2003	Jim Thome, Philadelphia	47	2003	Alex Rodriguez, Texas	47
2004	Adrián Beltré, Los Angeles	48	2004	Manny Ramirez, Boston	43
2005	Andruw Jones, Atlanta	51	2005	Alex Rodriguez, New York	48
2006	Ryan Howard, Philadelphia	58	2006	David Ortiz, Boston	54
2007	Prince Fielder, Milwaukee	50	2007	Alex Rodriguez, New York	54
2008	Ryan Howard, Philadelphia	48	2008	Miguel Cabrera, Detroit	37
2009	Albert Pujols, St. Louis	47	2009	Carlos Peña, Tampa Bay; Mark Teixeira, New York	39
2010	Albert Pujols, St. Louis	42	2010	José Bautista, Toronto	54
2011	Matt Kemp, Los Angeles	39	2011	José Bautista, Toronto	43
2012	Ryan Braun, Milwaukee	41	2012	Miguel Cabrera, Detroit	44
2013	Pedro Alvarez, Pitt.; Paul Goldschmidt, Arizona	36	2013	Chris Davis, Baltimore	53
2014	Giancarlo Stanton, Miami	37	2014	Nelson Cruz, Baltimore	40
2015	Nolan Arenado, Colorado; Bryce Harper, Washington	42	2015	Chris Davis, Baltimore	47
2016	Nolan Arenado, Colorado; Chris Carter, Milwaukee	41	2016	Mark Trumbo, Baltimore	47
2017	Giancarlo Stanton, Miami	59	2017	Aaron Judge, New York	52
2018	Nolan Arenado, Colorado	38	2018	Khris Davis, Oakland	48
2019	Pete Alonso, NY Mets	53	2019	Jorge Soler, Kansas City	48
2020	Marcell Ozuna, Atlanta	18	2020	Luke Voit, New York	22
2021	Fernando Tatís Jr., San Diego	42	2021	Vladimir Guerrero Jr., Toronto	48
2022	Kyle Schwarber, Philadelphia	46	2022	Aaron Judge, NY Yankees	62
2023	Matt Olson, Atlanta	54	2023	Shohei Ohtani, L.A. Angels	44

(1) In 1997, Mark McGwire hit 58 home runs, 34 with the Oakland Athletics (AL) and 24 with the St. Louis Cardinals (NL).

Batting Champions by Season, 1901-2023

* = All-time single-season record for league since beginning of "modern" era in 1901.

National League			American League		
Year	Player, team	AVG	Year	Player, team	AVG
1901	Jesse C. Burkett, St. Louis	.376	1901[1]	Nap Lajoie, Philadelphia	.426*
1902	Clarence Beaumont, Pittsburgh	.357	1902	Ed Delahanty, Washington	.376
1903	Honus Wagner, Pittsburgh	.355	1903	Nap Lajoie, Cleveland	.357
1904	Honus Wagner, Pittsburgh	.349	1904	Nap Lajoie, Cleveland	.382
1905	James Seymour, Cincinnati	.377	1905	Elmer Flick, Cleveland	.308
1906	Honus Wagner, Pittsburgh	.339	1906	George Stone, St. Louis	.358
1907	Honus Wagner, Pittsburgh	.350	1907	Ty Cobb, Detroit	.350
1908	Honus Wagner, Pittsburgh	.354	1908	Ty Cobb, Detroit	.324
1909	Honus Wagner, Pittsburgh	.339	1909	Ty Cobb, Detroit	.377
1910	Sherwood Magee, Philadelphia	.331	1910[2]	Ty Cobb, Detroit	.385
1911	Honus Wagner, Pittsburgh	.334	1911	Ty Cobb, Detroit	.420
1912	Henry Zimmerman, Chicago	.372	1912	Ty Cobb, Detroit	.410
1913	Jacob Daubert, Brooklyn	.350	1913	Ty Cobb, Detroit	.390
1914	Jacob Daubert, Brooklyn	.329	1914	Ty Cobb, Detroit	.368
1915	Larry Doyle, New York	.320	1915	Ty Cobb, Detroit	.369
1916	Hal Chase, Cincinnati	.339	1916	Tris Speaker, Cleveland	.386
1917	Edd Roush, Cincinnati	.341	1917	Ty Cobb, Detroit	.383
1918	Zack Wheat, Brooklyn	.335	1918	Ty Cobb, Detroit	.382
1919	Edd Roush, Cincinnati	.321	1919	Ty Cobb, Detroit	.384
1920	Rogers Hornsby, St. Louis	.370	1920	George Sisler, St. Louis	.407
1921	Rogers Hornsby, St. Louis	.397	1921	Harry Heilmann, Detroit	.394
1922	Rogers Hornsby, St. Louis	.401	1922	George Sisler, St. Louis	.420
1923	Rogers Hornsby, St. Louis	.384	1923	Harry Heilmann, Detroit	.403
1924	Rogers Hornsby, St. Louis	.424*	1924	Babe Ruth, New York	.378
1925	Rogers Hornsby, St. Louis	.403	1925	Harry Heilmann, Detroit	.393
1926	Eugene Hargrave, Cincinnati	.353	1926	Henry Manush, Detroit	.378
1927	Paul Waner, Pittsburgh	.380	1927	Harry Heilmann, Detroit	.398
1928	Rogers Hornsby, Boston	.387	1928	Goose Goslin, Washington	.379
1929	Lefty O'Doul, Philadelphia	.398	1929	Lew Fonseca, Cleveland	.369
1930	Bill Terry, New York	.401	1930	Al Simmons, Philadelphia	.381
1931	Chick Hafey, St. Louis	.349	1931	Al Simmons, Philadelphia	.390
1932	Lefty O'Doul, Brooklyn	.368	1932	Dale Alexander, Detroit-Boston	.367
1933	Chuck Klein, Philadelphia	.368	1933	Jimmie Foxx, Philadelphia	.356
1934	Paul Waner, Pittsburgh	.362	1934	Lou Gehrig, New York	.363
1935	Arky Vaughan, Pittsburgh	.385	1935	Buddy Myer, Washington	.349
1936	Paul Waner, Pittsburgh	.373	1936	Luke Appling, Chicago	.388
1937	Joe Medwick, St. Louis	.374	1937	Charlie Gehringer, Detroit	.371
1938	Ernie Lombardi, Cincinnati	.342	1938	Jimmie Foxx, Boston	.349

	National League				American League	
Year	**Player, team**	**AVG**		**Year**	**Player, team**	**AVG**
1939	John Mize, St. Louis	.349		1939	Joe DiMaggio, New York	.381
1940	Debs Garms, Pittsburgh	.355		1940	Joe DiMaggio, New York	.352
1941	Pete Reiser, Brooklyn	.343		1941	Ted Williams, Boston	.406
1942	Ernie Lombardi, Boston	.330		1942	Ted Williams, Boston	.356
1943	Stan Musial, St. Louis	.357		1943	Luke Appling, Chicago	.328
1944	Dixie Walker, Brooklyn	.357		1944	Lou Boudreau, Cleveland	.327
1945	Phil Cavarretta, Chicago	.355		1945	George Stirnweiss, New York	.309
1946	Stan Musial, St. Louis	.365		1946	Mickey Vernon, Washington	.353
1947	Harry Walker, St. Louis-Philadelphia	.363		1947	Ted Williams, Boston	.343
1948	Stan Musial, St. Louis	.376		1948	Ted Williams, Boston	.369
1949	Jackie Robinson, Brooklyn	.342		1949	George Kell, Detroit	.343
1950	Stan Musial, St. Louis	.346		1950	Billy Goodman, Boston	.354
1951	Stan Musial, St. Louis	.355		1951	Ferris Fain, Philadelphia	.344
1952	Stan Musial, St. Louis	.336		1952	Ferris Fain, Philadelphia	.327
1953	Carl Furillo, Brooklyn	.344		1953	Mickey Vernon, Washington	.337
1954	Willie Mays, New York	.345		1954	Roberto Avila, Cleveland	.341
1955	Richie Ashburn, Philadelphia	.338		1955	Al Kaline, Detroit	.340
1956	Hank Aaron, Milwaukee	.328		1956	Mickey Mantle, New York	.353
1957	Stan Musial, St. Louis	.351		1957	Ted Williams, Boston	.388
1958	Richie Ashburn, Philadelphia	.350		1958	Ted Williams, Boston	.328
1959	Hank Aaron, Milwaukee	.355		1959	Harvey Kuenn, Detroit	.353
1960	Dick Groat, Pittsburgh	.325		1960	Pete Runnels, Boston	.320
1961	Roberto Clemente, Pittsburgh	.351		1961	Norm Cash, Detroit	.361
1962	Tommy Davis, Los Angeles	.346		1962	Pete Runnels, Boston	.326
1963	Tommy Davis, Los Angeles	.326		1963	Carl Yastrzemski, Boston	.321
1964	Roberto Clemente, Pittsburgh	.339		1964	Tony Oliva, Minnesota	.323
1965	Roberto Clemente, Pittsburgh	.329		1965	Tony Oliva, Minnesota	.321
1966	Matty Alou, Pittsburgh	.342		1966	Frank Robinson, Baltimore	.316
1967	Roberto Clemente, Pittsburgh	.357		1967	Carl Yastrzemski, Boston	.326
1968	Pete Rose, Cincinnati	.335		1968	Carl Yastrzemski, Boston	.301
1969	Pete Rose, Cincinnati	.348		1969	Rod Carew, Minnesota	.332
1970	Rico Carty, Atlanta	.366		1970	Alex Johnson, California	.329
1971	Joe Torre, St. Louis	.363		1971	Tony Oliva, Minnesota	.337
1972	Billy Williams, Chicago	.333		1972	Rod Carew, Minnesota	.318
1973	Pete Rose, Cincinnati	.338		1973	Rod Carew, Minnesota	.350
1974	Ralph Garr, Atlanta	.353		1974	Rod Carew, Minnesota	.364
1975	Bill Madlock, Chicago	.354		1975	Rod Carew, Minnesota	.359
1976	Bill Madlock, Chicago	.339		1976	George Brett, Kansas City	.333
1977	Dave Parker, Pittsburgh	.338		1977	Rod Carew, Minnesota	.388
1978	Dave Parker, Pittsburgh	.334		1978	Rod Carew, Minnesota	.333
1979	Keith Hernandez, St. Louis	.344		1979	Fred Lynn, Boston	.333
1980	Bill Buckner, Chicago	.324		1980	George Brett, Kansas City	.390
1981	Bill Madlock, Pittsburgh	.341		1981	Carney Lansford, Boston	.336
1982	Al Oliver, Montréal	.331		1982	Willie Wilson, Kansas City	.332
1983	Bill Madlock, Pittsburgh	.323		1983	Wade Boggs, Boston	.361
1984	Tony Gwynn, San Diego	.351		1984	Don Mattingly, New York	.343
1985	Willie McGee, St. Louis	.353		1985	Wade Boggs, Boston	.368
1986	Tim Raines, Montréal	.334		1986	Wade Boggs, Boston	.357
1987	Tony Gwynn, San Diego	.370		1987	Wade Boggs, Boston	.363
1988	Tony Gwynn, San Diego	.313		1988	Wade Boggs, Boston	.366
1989	Tony Gwynn, San Diego	.336		1989	Kirby Puckett, Minnesota	.339
1990	Willie McGee, St. Louis	.335		1990	George Brett, Kansas City	.329
1991	Terry Pendleton, Atlanta	.319		1991	Julio Franco, Texas	.341
1992	Gary Sheffield, San Diego	.330		1992	Edgar Martinez, Seattle	.343
1993	Andres Galarraga, Colorado	.370		1993	John Olerud, Toronto	.363
1994	Tony Gwynn, San Diego	.394		1994	Paul O'Neill, New York	.359
1995	Tony Gwynn, San Diego	.368		1995	Edgar Martinez, Seattle	.356
1996	Tony Gwynn, San Diego	.353		1996	Alex Rodriguez, Seattle	.358
1997	Tony Gwynn, San Diego	.372		1997	Frank Thomas, Chicago	.347
1998	Larry Walker, Colorado	.363		1998	Bernie Williams, New York	.339
1999	Larry Walker, Colorado	.379		1999	Nomar Garciaparra, Boston	.357
2000	Todd Helton, Colorado	.372		2000	Nomar Garciaparra, Boston	.372
2001	Larry Walker, Colorado	.350		2001	Ichiro Suzuki, Seattle	.350
2002	Barry Bonds, San Francisco	.370		2002	Manny Ramirez, Boston	.349
2003	Albert Pujols, St. Louis	.359		2003	Bill Mueller, Boston	.326
2004	Barry Bonds, San Francisco	.362		2004	Ichiro Suzuki, Seattle	.372
2005	Derrek Lee, Chicago	.335		2005	Michael Young, Texas	.331
2006	Freddy Sanchez, Pittsburgh	.344		2006	Joe Mauer, Minnesota	.347
2007	Matt Holliday, Colorado	.340		2007	Magglio Ordoñez, Detroit	.363
2008	Chipper Jones, Atlanta	.364		2008	Joe Mauer, Minnesota	.328
2009	Hanley Ramirez, Florida	.342		2009	Joe Mauer, Minnesota	.365
2010	Carlos Gonzalez, Colorado	.336		2010	Josh Hamilton, Texas	.359
2011	José Reyes, New York	.337		2011	Miguel Cabrera, Detroit	.344
2012	Buster Posey, San Francisco	.336		2012	Miguel Cabrera, Detroit	.330
2013	Michael Cuddyer, Colorado	.331		2013	Miguel Cabrera, Detroit	.348
2014	Justin Morneau, Colorado	.319		2014	José Altuve, Houston	.341

Year	National League Player, team	AVG	Year	American League Player, team	AVG
2015	Dee Gordon, Miami	.333	2015	Miguel Cabrera, Detroit	.338
2016	DJ LeMahieu, Colorado	.348	2016	José Altuve, Houston	.338
2017	Charlie Blackmon, Colorado	.331	2017	José Altuve, Houston	.346
2018	Christian Yelich, Milwaukee	.326	2018	Mookie Betts, Boston	.346
2019	Christian Yelich, Milwaukee	.329	2019	Tim Anderson, Chicago	.335
2020	Juan Soto, Washington	.351	2020	DJ LeMahieu, New York	.364
2021	Trea Turner, Washington-L.A. Dodgers	.328	2021	Yuli Gurriel, Houston	.319
2022	Jeff McNeil, NY Mets	.326	2022	Luis Arráez, Minnesota	.316
2023	Luis Arráez, Miami	.354	2023	Yandy Díaz, Tampa Bay	.330

(1) Nap Lajoie's 1901 batting average varies in historical records from .421 to .426. (2) Some baseball researchers have concluded that Ty Cobb actually hit .382 in 1910 while Nap Lajoie, Cleveland, hit .383.

Earned Run Average Leaders by Season, 1977-2023

Year	National League Pitcher, team	G	IP	ERA	Year	American League Pitcher, team	G	IP	ERA
1977	John Candelaria, Pittsburgh	33	230.2	2.34	1977	Frank Tanana, California	31	241.1	2.54
1978	Craig Swan, New York	29	207.1	2.43	1978	Ron Guidry, New York	35	273.2	1.74
1979	J. R. Richard, Houston	38	292.1	2.71	1979	Ron Guidry, New York	33	236.1	2.78
1980	Don Sutton, Los Angeles	32	212.1	2.20	1980	Rudy May, New York	41	175.1	2.46
1981	Nolan Ryan, Houston	21	149.0	1.69	1981	Sammy Stewart, Baltimore	29	112.1	2.32
1982	Steve Rogers, Montréal	35	277.0	2.40	1982	Rick Sutcliffe, Cleveland	34	216.0	2.96
1983	Atlee Hammaker, San Francisco	23	172.1	2.25	1983	Rick Honeycutt, Texas	25	174.2	2.42
1984	Alejandro Peña, Los Angeles	28	199.1	2.48	1984	Mike Boddicker, Baltimore	34	261.1	2.79
1985	Dwight Gooden, New York	35	276.2	1.53	1985	Dave Stieb, Toronto	36	265.0	2.48
1986	Mike Scott, Houston	37	275.1	2.22	1986	Roger Clemens, Boston	33	254.0	2.48
1987	Nolan Ryan, Houston	34	211.2	2.76	1987	Jimmy Key, Toronto	36	261.0	2.76
1988	Joe Magrane, St. Louis	24	165.1	2.18	1988	Allan Anderson, Minnesota	30	202.1	2.45
1989	Scott Garrelts, San Francisco	30	193.1	2.28	1989	Bret Saberhagen, Kansas City	36	262.1	2.16
1990	Danny Darwin, Houston	48	162.2	2.21	1990	Roger Clemens, Boston	31	228.1	1.93
1991	Dennis Martinez, Montréal	31	222.0	2.39	1991	Roger Clemens, Boston	35	271.1	2.62
1992	Bill Swift, San Francisco	30	164.2	2.08	1992	Roger Clemens, Boston	32	246.2	2.41
1993	Greg Maddux, Atlanta	36	267.0	2.36	1993	Kevin Appier, Kansas City	34	238.2	2.56
1994	Greg Maddux, Atlanta	25	202.0	1.56	1994	Steve Ontiveros, Oakland	27	115.1	2.65
1995	Greg Maddux, Atlanta	28	209.2	1.63	1995	Randy Johnson, Seattle	30	214.1	2.48
1996	Kevin Brown, Florida	32	233.0	1.89	1996	Juan Guzmán, Toronto	27	187.2	2.93
1997	Pedro Martinez, Montréal	31	241.1	1.90	1997	Roger Clemens, Toronto	34	264.0	2.05
1998	Greg Maddux, Atlanta	34	251.0	2.22	1998	Roger Clemens, Toronto	33	234.2	2.65
1999	Randy Johnson, Arizona	35	271.2	2.48	1999	Pedro Martinez, Boston	31	213.1	2.07
2000	Kevin Brown, Los Angeles	33	230.0	2.58	2000	Pedro Martinez, Boston	29	217.0	1.74
2001	Randy Johnson, Arizona	35	249.2	2.49	2001	Freddy Garcia, Seattle	34	238.2	3.05
2002	Randy Johnson, Arizona	35	260.0	2.32	2002	Pedro Martinez, Boston	30	199.1	2.26
2003	Jason Schmidt, San Francisco	29	207.2	2.34	2003	Pedro Martinez, Boston	29	186.2	2.22
2004	Jake Peavy, San Diego	27	166.1	2.27	2004	Johan Santana, Minnesota	34	228.0	2.61
2005	Roger Clemens, Houston	32	211.1	1.87	2005	Kevin Millwood, Cleveland	30	192.0	2.86
2006	Roy Oswalt, Houston	33	220.2	2.98	2006	Johan Santana, Minnesota	34	233.2	2.77
2007	Jake Peavy, San Diego	34	223.1	2.54	2007	John Lackey, Los Angeles	33	224.0	3.01
2008	Johan Santana, New York	34	234.1	2.53	2008	Cliff Lee, Cleveland	31	223.1	2.54
2009	Chris Carpenter, St. Louis	28	192.2	2.24	2009	Zack Greinke, Kansas City	33	229.1	2.16
2010	Josh Johnson, Florida	28	183.2	2.30	2010	Felix Hernandez, Seattle	34	249.2	2.27
2011	Clayton Kershaw, Los Angeles	33	233.1	2.28	2011	Justin Verlander, Detroit	34	251.0	2.40
2012	Clayton Kershaw, Los Angeles	33	227.2	2.53	2012	David Price, Tampa Bay	31	211.0	2.56
2013	Clayton Kershaw, Los Angeles	33	236.0	1.83	2013	Anibal Sanchez, Detroit	29	182.0	2.57
2014	Clayton Kershaw, Los Angeles	27	198.1	1.77	2014	Felix Hernandez, Seattle	34	236.0	2.14
2015	Zack Greinke, Los Angeles	32	222.2	1.66	2015	David Price, Detroit-Toronto	32	220.1	2.45
2016	Kyle Hendricks, Chicago	31	190.0	2.13	2016	Aaron Sanchez, Toronto	30	192.0	3.00
2017	Clayton Kershaw, Los Angeles	27	175.0	2.31	2017	Corey Kluber, Cleveland	29	203.2	2.25
2018	Jacob deGrom, NY Mets	32	217.0	1.70	2018	Blake Snell, Tampa Bay	31	180.2	1.89
2019	Hyun-Jin Ryu, Los Angeles	29	182.2	2.32	2019	Gerrit Cole, Houston	33	212.1	2.50
2020	Trevor Bauer, Cincinnati	11	73.0	1.73	2020	Shane Bieber, Cleveland	12	77.1	1.63
2021	Corbin Burnes, Milwaukee	28	167.0	2.43	2021	Robbie Ray, Toronto	32	193.1	2.84
2022	Julio Urías, L.A. Dodgers	31	175.0	2.16	2022	Justin Verlander, Houston	28	175.0	1.75
2023	Blake Snell, San Diego	32	180.0	2.25	2023	Gerrit Cole, NY Yankees	33	209.0	2.63

Strikeout Leaders by Season, 1901-2023

* = All-time single-season record for league since beginning of "modern" era in 1901.

Year	National League Pitcher, team	SO	Year	American League Pitcher, team	SO
1901	Noodles Hahn, Cincinnati	239	1901	Cy Young, Boston	158
1902	Vic Willis, Boston	225	1902	Rube Waddell, Philadelphia	210
1903	Christy Mathewson, New York	267	1903	Rube Waddell, Philadelphia	302
1904	Christy Mathewson, New York	212	1904	Rube Waddell, Philadelphia	349
1905	Christy Mathewson, New York	206	1905	Rube Waddell, Philadelphia	287
1906	Fred Beebe, Chicago-St. Louis	171	1906	Rube Waddell, Philadelphia	196
1907	Christy Mathewson, New York	178	1907	Rube Waddell, Philadelphia	232
1908	Christy Mathewson, New York	259	1908	Ed Walsh, Chicago	269
1909	Orval Overall, Chicago	205	1909	Frank Smith, Chicago	177
1910	Earl Moore, Philadelphia	185	1910	Walter Johnson, Washington	313

National League		SO	American League		SO
Year	Pitcher, team	SO	Year	Pitcher, team	SO
1911	Rube Marquard, New York	237	1911	Ed Walsh, Chicago	255
1912	Grover Alexander, Philadelphia	195	1912	Walter Johnson, Washington	303
1913	Tom Seaton, Philadelphia	168	1913	Walter Johnson, Washington	243
1914	Grover Alexander, Philadelphia	214	1914	Walter Johnson, Washington	225
1915	Grover Alexander, Philadelphia	241	1915	Walter Johnson, Washington	203
1916	Grover Alexander, Philadelphia	167	1916	Walter Johnson, Washington	228
1917	Grover Alexander, Philadelphia	200	1917	Walter Johnson, Washington	188
1918	Hippo Vaughn, Chicago	148	1918	Walter Johnson, Washington	162
1919	Hippo Vaughn, Chicago	141	1919	Walter Johnson, Washington	147
1920	Grover Alexander, Chicago	173	1920	Stan Coveleski, Cleveland	133
1921	Burleigh Grimes, Brooklyn	136	1921	Walter Johnson, Washington	143
1922	Dazzy Vance, Brooklyn	134	1922	Urban Shocker, St. Louis	149
1923	Dazzy Vance, Brooklyn	197	1923	Walter Johnson, Washington	130
1924	Dazzy Vance, Brooklyn	262	1924	Walter Johnson, Washington	158
1925	Dazzy Vance, Brooklyn	221	1925	Lefty Grove, Philadelphia	116
1926	Dazzy Vance, Brooklyn	140	1926	Lefty Grove, Philadelphia	194
1927	Dazzy Vance, Brooklyn	184	1927	Lefty Grove, Philadelphia	174
1928	Dazzy Vance, Brooklyn	200	1928	Lefty Grove, Philadelphia	183
1929	Pat Malone, Chicago	166	1929	Lefty Grove, Philadelphia	170
1930	Bill Hallahan, St. Louis	177	1930	Lefty Grove, Philadelphia	209
1931	Bill Hallahan, St. Louis	159	1931	Lefty Grove, Philadelphia	175
1932	Dizzy Dean, St. Louis	191	1932	Red Ruffing, New York	190
1933	Dizzy Dean, St. Louis	199	1933	Lefty Gomez, New York	163
1934	Dizzy Dean, St. Louis	195	1934	Lefty Gomez, New York	158
1935	Dizzy Dean, St. Louis	190	1935	Tommy Bridges, Detroit	163
1936	Van Lingle Mungo, Brooklyn	238	1936	Tommy Bridges, Detroit	175
1937	Carl Hubbell, New York	159	1937	Lefty Gomez, New York	194
1938	Clay Bryant, Chicago	135	1938	Bob Feller, Cleveland	240
1939	Claude Passeau, Philadelphia-Chicago; Bucky Walters, Cincinnati	137	1939	Bob Feller, Cleveland	246
1940	Kirby Higbe, Philadelphia	137	1940	Bob Feller, Cleveland	261
1941	John Vander Meer, Cincinnati	202	1941	Bob Feller, Cleveland	260
1942	John Vander Meer, Cincinnati	186	1942	Tex Hughson, Boston; Bobo Newsom, Washington	113
1943	John Vander Meer, Cincinnati	174	1943	Allie Reynolds, Cleveland	151
1944	Bill Voiselle, New York	161	1944	Hal Newhouser, Detroit	187
1945	Preacher Roe, Pittsburgh	148	1945	Hal Newhouser, Detroit	212
1946	Johnny Schmitz, Chicago	135	1946	Bob Feller, Cleveland	348
1947	Ewell Blackwell, Cincinnati	193	1947	Bob Feller, Cleveland	196
1948	Harry Brecheen, St. Louis	149	1948	Bob Feller, Cleveland	164
1949	Warren Spahn, Boston	151	1949	Virgil Trucks, Detroit	153
1950	Warren Spahn, Boston	191	1950	Bob Lemon, Cleveland	170
1951	Warren Spahn, Boston; Don Newcombe, Brooklyn	164	1951	Vic Raschi, New York	164
1952	Warren Spahn, Boston	183	1952	Allie Reynolds, New York	160
1953	Robin Roberts, Philadelphia	198	1953	Billy Pierce, Chicago	186
1954	Robin Roberts, Philadelphia	185	1954	Bob Turley, Baltimore	185
1955	Sam Jones, Chicago	198	1955	Herb Score, Cleveland	245
1956	Sam Jones, Chicago	176	1956	Herb Score, Cleveland	263
1957	Jack Sanford, Philadelphia	188	1957	Early Wynn, Cleveland	184
1958	Sam Jones, St. Louis	225	1958	Early Wynn, Chicago	179
1959	Don Drysdale, Los Angeles	242	1959	Jim Bunning, Detroit	201
1960	Don Drysdale, Los Angeles	246	1960	Jim Bunning, Detroit	201
1961	Sandy Koufax, Los Angeles	269	1961	Camilo Pascual, Minnesota	221
1962	Don Drysdale, Los Angeles	232	1962	Camilo Pascual, Minnesota	206
1963	Sandy Koufax, Los Angeles	306	1963	Camilo Pascual, Minnesota	202
1964	Bob Veale, Pittsburgh	250	1964	Al Downing, New York	217
1965	Sandy Koufax, Los Angeles	382*	1965	Sam McDowell, Cleveland	325
1966	Sandy Koufax, Los Angeles	317	1966	Sam McDowell, Cleveland	225
1967	Jim Bunning, Philadelphia	253	1967	Jim Lonborg, Boston	246
1968	Bob Gibson, St. Louis	268	1968	Sam McDowell, Cleveland	283
1969	Ferguson Jenkins, Chicago	273	1969	Sam McDowell, Cleveland	279
1970	Tom Seaver, New York	283	1970	Sam McDowell, Cleveland	304
1971	Tom Seaver, New York	289	1971	Mickey Lolich, Detroit	308
1972	Steve Carlton, Philadelphia	310	1972	Nolan Ryan, California	329
1973	Tom Seaver, New York	251	1973	Nolan Ryan, California	383*
1974	Steve Carlton, Philadelphia	240	1974	Nolan Ryan, California	367
1975	Tom Seaver, New York	243	1975	Frank Tanana, California	269
1976	Tom Seaver, New York	235	1976	Nolan Ryan, California	327
1977	Phil Niekro, Atlanta	262	1977	Nolan Ryan, California	341
1978	J. R. Richard, Houston	303	1978	Nolan Ryan, California	260
1979	J. R. Richard, Houston	313	1979	Nolan Ryan, California	223
1980	Steve Carlton, Philadelphia	286	1980	Len Barker, Cleveland	187
1981	Fernando Valenzuela, Los Angeles	180	1981	Len Barker, Cleveland	127
1982	Steve Carlton, Philadelphia	286	1982	Floyd Bannister, Seattle	209
1983	Steve Carlton, Philadelphia	275	1983	Jack Morris, Detroit	232
1984	Dwight Gooden, New York	276	1984	Mark Langston, Seattle	204
1985	Dwight Gooden, New York	268	1985	Bert Blyleven, Cleveland-Minnesota	206
1986	Mike Scott, Houston	306	1986	Mark Langston, Seattle	245
1987	Nolan Ryan, Houston	270	1987	Mark Langston, Seattle	262
1988	Nolan Ryan, Houston	228	1988	Roger Clemens, Boston	291

National League			American League		
Year	**Pitcher, team**	**SO**	**Year**	**Pitcher, team**	**SO**
1989	Jose DeLeon, St. Louis	201	1989	Nolan Ryan, Texas	301
1990	David Cone, New York	233	1990	Nolan Ryan, Texas	232
1991	David Cone, New York	241	1991	Roger Clemens, Boston	241
1992	John Smoltz, Atlanta	215	1992	Randy Johnson, Seattle	241
1993	José Rijo, Cincinnati	227	1993	Randy Johnson, Seattle	308
1994	Andy Benes, San Diego	189	1994	Randy Johnson, Seattle	204
1995	Hideo Nomo, Los Angeles	236	1995	Randy Johnson, Seattle	294
1996	John Smoltz, Atlanta	276	1996	Roger Clemens, Boston	257
1997	Curt Schilling, Philadelphia	319	1997	Roger Clemens, Toronto	292
1998	Curt Schilling, Philadelphia	300	1998	Roger Clemens, Toronto	271
1999	Randy Johnson, Arizona	364	1999	Pedro Martinez, Boston	313
2000	Randy Johnson, Arizona	347	2000	Pedro Martinez, Boston	284
2001	Randy Johnson, Arizona	372	2001	Hideo Nomo, Boston	220
2002	Randy Johnson, Arizona	334	2002	Pedro Martinez, Boston	239
2003	Kerry Wood, Chicago	266	2003	Esteban Loaiza, Chicago	207
2004	Randy Johnson, Arizona	290	2004	Johan Santana, Minnesota	265
2005	Jake Peavy, San Diego	216	2005	Johan Santana, Minnesota	238
2006	Aaron Harang, Cincinnati	216	2006	Johan Santana, Minnesota	245
2007	Jake Peavy, San Diego	240	2007	Scott Kazmir, Tampa Bay	239
2008	Tim Lincecum, San Francisco	265	2008	A. J. Burnett, Toronto	231
2009	Tim Lincecum, San Francisco	261	2009	Justin Verlander, Detroit	269
2010	Tim Lincecum, San Francisco	231	2010	Jered Weaver, Los Angeles	233
2011	Clayton Kershaw, Los Angeles	248	2011	Justin Verlander, Detroit	250
2012	R.A. Dickey, New York	230	2012	Justin Verlander, Detroit	239
2013	Clayton Kershaw, Los Angeles	232	2013	Yu Darvish, Texas	277
2014	Johnny Cueto, Cincinnati; Stephen Strasburg, Washington	242	2014	David Price, Tampa Bay-Detroit	271
2015	Clayton Kershaw, Los Angeles	301	2015	Chris Sale, Chicago	274
2016	Max Scherzer, Washington	284	2016	Justin Verlander, Detroit	254
2017	Max Scherzer, Washington	268	2017	Chris Sale, Boston	308
2018	Max Scherzer, Washington	300	2018	Justin Verlander, Houston	290
2019	Jacob deGrom, New York	255	2019	Gerrit Cole, Houston	326
2020	Jacob deGrom, New York	104	2020	Shane Bieber, Cleveland	122
2021	Zack Wheeler, Philadelphia	247	2021	Robbie Ray, Toronto	248
2022	Corbin Burnes, Milwaukee	243	2022	Gerrit Cole, NY Yankees	257
2023	Spencer Strider, Atlanta	281	2023	Kevin Gausman, Toronto	237

Cy Young Award Winners, 1956-2022

Year	Pitcher, team	Year	Pitcher, team	Year	Pitcher, team
1956	Don Newcombe, Brooklyn	1981	(NL) Fernando Valenzuela, L.A.	2002	(NL) Randy Johnson, Arizona
1957	Warren Spahn, Milwaukee		(AL) Rollie Fingers, Milwaukee		(AL) Barry Zito, Oakland
1958	Bob Turley, NY Yankees	1982	(NL) Steve Carlton, Philadelphia	2003	(NL) Eric Gagne, L.A.
1959	Early Wynn, Chicago White Sox		(AL) Pete Vuckovich, Milwaukee		(AL) Roy Halladay, Toronto
1960	Vernon Law, Pittsburgh	1983	(NL) John Denny, Philadelphia	2004	(NL) Roger Clemens, Houston
1961	Whitey Ford, NY Yankees		(AL) LaMarr Hoyt, Chicago		(AL) Johan Santana, Minnesota
1962	Don Drysdale, L.A. Dodgers	1984	(NL) Rick Sutcliffe, Chicago	2005	(NL) Chris Carpenter, St. Louis
1963	Sandy Koufax, L.A. Dodgers		(AL) Willie Hernandez, Detroit		(AL) Bartolo Colon, L.A.
1964	Dean Chance, L.A. Angels	1985	(NL) Dwight Gooden, NY	2006	(NL) Brandon Webb, Arizona
1965	Sandy Koufax, L.A. Dodgers		(AL) Bret Saberhagen, Kansas City		(AL) Johan Santana, Minnesota
1966	Sandy Koufax, L.A. Dodgers	1986	(NL) Mike Scott, Houston	2007	(NL) Jake Peavy, San Diego
1967	(NL) Mike McCormick, S.F.		(AL) Roger Clemens, Boston		(AL) CC Sabathia, Cleveland
	(AL) Jim Lonborg, Boston	1987	(NL) Steve Bedrosian, Phil.	2008	(NL) Tim Lincecum, S.F.
1968	(NL) Bob Gibson, St. Louis		(AL) Roger Clemens, Boston		(AL) Cliff Lee, Cleveland
	(AL) Denny McLain, Detroit	1988	(NL) Orel Hershiser, L.A.	2009	(NL) Tim Lincecum, S.F.
1969	(NL) Tom Seaver, NY		(AL) Frank Viola, Minnesota		(AL) Zack Greinke, Kansas City
	(AL) Denny McLain, Detroit; Mike Cuellar, Baltimore	1989	(NL) Mark Davis, San Diego	2010	(NL) Roy Halladay, Philadelphia
			(AL) Bret Saberhagen, Kansas City		(AL) Felix Hernandez, Seattle
1970	(NL) Bob Gibson, St. Louis	1990	(NL) Doug Drabek, Pittsburgh	2011	(NL) Clayton Kershaw, L.A.
	(AL) Jim Perry, Minnesota		(AL) Bob Welch, Oakland		(AL) Justin Verlander, Detroit
1971	(NL) Ferguson Jenkins, Chicago	1991	(NL) Tom Glavine, Atlanta	2012	(NL) R.A. Dickey, NY
	(AL) Vida Blue, Oakland		(AL) Roger Clemens, Boston		(AL) David Price, Tampa Bay
1972	(NL) Steve Carlton, Philadelphia	1992	(NL) Greg Maddux, Chicago	2013	(NL) Clayton Kershaw, L.A.
	(AL) Gaylord Perry, Cleveland		(AL) Dennis Eckersley, Oakland		(AL) Max Scherzer, Detroit
1973	(NL) Tom Seaver, NY	1993	(NL) Greg Maddux, Atlanta	2014	(NL) Clayton Kershaw, L.A.
	(AL) Jim Palmer, Baltimore		(AL) Jack McDowell, Chicago		(AL) Corey Kluber, Cleveland
1974	(NL) Mike Marshall, L.A.	1994	(NL) Greg Maddux, Atlanta	2015	(NL) Jake Arrieta, Chicago
	(AL) Jim "Catfish" Hunter, Oakland		(AL) David Cone, Kansas City		(AL) Dallas Keuchel, Houston
1975	(NL) Tom Seaver, NY	1995	(NL) Greg Maddux, Atlanta	2016	(NL) Max Scherzer, Washington
	(AL) Jim Palmer, Baltimore		(AL) Randy Johnson, Seattle		(AL) Rick Porcello, Boston
1976	(NL) Randy Jones, San Diego	1996	(NL) John Smoltz, Atlanta	2017	(NL) Max Scherzer, Washington
	(AL) Jim Palmer, Baltimore		(AL) Pat Hentgen, Toronto		(AL) Corey Kluber, Cleveland
1977	(NL) Steve Carlton, Philadelphia	1997	(NL) Pedro Martinez, Montréal	2018	(NL) Jacob deGrom, NY
	(AL) Sparky Lyle, NY		(AL) Roger Clemens, Toronto		(AL) Blake Snell, Tampa Bay
1978	(NL) Gaylord Perry, San Diego	1998	(NL) Tom Glavine, Atlanta	2019	(NL) Jacob deGrom, NY
	(AL) Ron Guidry, NY		(AL) Roger Clemens, Toronto		(AL) Justin Verlander, Houston
1979	(NL) Bruce Sutter, Chicago	1999	(NL) Randy Johnson, Arizona	2020	(NL) Trevor Bauer, Cincinnati
	(AL) Mike Flanagan, Baltimore		(AL) Pedro Martinez, Boston		(AL) Shane Bieber, Cleveland
1980	(NL) Steve Carlton, Philadelphia	2000	(NL) Randy Johnson, Arizona	2021	(NL) Corbin Burnes, Milwaukee
	(AL) Steve Stone, Baltimore		(AL) Pedro Martinez, Boston		(AL) Robbie Ray, Toronto
		2001	(NL) Randy Johnson, Arizona	2022	(NL) Sandy Alcantara, Miami
			(AL) Roger Clemens, NY		(AL) Justin Verlander, Houston

Most Valuable Players, 1931-2022

As selected by the Baseball Writers' Assn. of America. Prior to 1931, MVP honors were named by various sources.

National League

Year	Player, team	Year	Player, team	Year	Player, team
1931	Frank Frisch, St. Louis	1962	Maury Wills, Los Angeles	1992	Barry Bonds, Pittsburgh
1932	Chuck Klein, Philadelphia	1963	Sandy Koufax, Los Angeles	1993	Barry Bonds, San Francisco
1933	Carl Hubbell, New York	1964	Ken Boyer, St. Louis	1994	Jeff Bagwell, Houston
1934	Dizzy Dean, St. Louis	1965	Willie Mays, San Francisco	1995	Barry Larkin, Cincinnati
1935	Gabby Hartnett, Chicago	1966	Roberto Clemente, Pittsburgh	1996	Ken Caminiti, San Diego
1936	Carl Hubbell, New York	1967	Orlando Cepeda, St. Louis	1997	Larry Walker, Colorado
1937	Joe Medwick, St. Louis	1968	Bob Gibson, St. Louis	1998	Sammy Sosa, Chicago
1938	Ernie Lombardi, Cincinnati	1969	Willie McCovey, San Francisco	1999	Chipper Jones, Atlanta
1939	Bucky Walters, Cincinnati	1970	Johnny Bench, Cincinnati	2000	Jeff Kent, San Francisco
1940	Frank McCormick, Cincinnati	1971	Joe Torre, St. Louis	2001	Barry Bonds, San Francisco
1941	Dolph Camilli, Brooklyn	1972	Johnny Bench, Cincinnati	2002	Barry Bonds, San Francisco
1942	Mort Cooper, St. Louis	1973	Pete Rose, Cincinnati	2003	Barry Bonds, San Francisco
1943	Stan Musial, St. Louis	1974	Steve Garvey, Los Angeles	2004	Barry Bonds, San Francisco
1944	Martin Marion, St. Louis	1975	Joe Morgan, Cincinnati	2005	Albert Pujols, St. Louis
1945	Phil Cavarretta, Chicago	1976	Joe Morgan, Cincinnati	2006	Ryan Howard, Philadelphia
1946	Stan Musial, St. Louis	1977	George Foster, Cincinnati	2007	Jimmy Rollins, Philadelphia
1947	Bob Elliott, Boston	1978	Dave Parker, Pittsburgh	2008	Albert Pujols, St. Louis
1948	Stan Musial, St. Louis	1979	Keith Hernandez, St. Louis;	2009	Albert Pujols, St. Louis
1949	Jackie Robinson, Brooklyn		Willie Stargell, Pittsburgh	2010	Joey Votto, Cincinnati
1950	Jim Konstanty, Philadelphia	1980	Mike Schmidt, Philadelphia	2011	Ryan Braun, Milwaukee
1951	Roy Campanella, Brooklyn	1981	Mike Schmidt, Philadelphia	2012	Buster Posey, San Francisco
1952	Hank Sauer, Chicago	1982	Dale Murphy, Atlanta	2013	Andrew McCutchen, Pittsburgh
1953	Roy Campanella, Brooklyn	1983	Dale Murphy, Atlanta	2014	Clayton Kershaw, Los Angeles
1954	Willie Mays, New York	1984	Ryne Sandberg, Chicago	2015	Bryce Harper, Washington
1955	Roy Campanella, Brooklyn	1985	Willie McGee, St. Louis	2016	Kris Bryant, Chicago
1956	Don Newcombe, Brooklyn	1986	Mike Schmidt, Philadelphia	2017	Giancarlo Stanton, Miami
1957	Hank Aaron, Milwaukee	1987	Andre Dawson, Chicago	2018	Christian Yelich, Milwaukee
1958	Ernie Banks, Chicago	1988	Kirk Gibson, Los Angeles	2019	Cody Bellinger, Los Angeles
1959	Ernie Banks, Chicago	1989	Kevin Mitchell, San Francisco	2020	Freddie Freeman, Atlanta
1960	Dick Groat, Pittsburgh	1990	Barry Bonds, Pittsburgh	2021	Bryce Harper, Philadelphia
1961	Frank Robinson, Cincinnati	1991	Terry Pendleton, Atlanta	2022	Paul Goldschmidt, St. Louis

American League

Year	Player, team	Year	Player, team	Year	Player, team
1931	Lefty Grove, Philadelphia	1961	Roger Maris, New York	1992	Dennis Eckersley, Oakland
1932	Jimmie Foxx, Philadelphia	1962	Mickey Mantle, New York	1993	Frank Thomas, Chicago
1933	Jimmie Foxx, Philadelphia	1963	Elston Howard, New York	1994	Frank Thomas, Chicago
1934	Mickey Cochrane, Detroit	1964	Brooks Robinson, Baltimore	1995	Mo Vaughn, Boston
1935	Hank Greenberg, Detroit	1965	Zoilo Versalles, Minnesota	1996	Juan Gonzalez, Texas
1936	Lou Gehrig, New York	1966	Frank Robinson, Baltimore	1997	Ken Griffey Jr., Seattle
1937	Charlie Gehringer, Detroit	1967	Carl Yastrzemski, Boston	1998	Juan Gonzalez, Texas
1938	Jimmie Foxx, Boston	1968	Denny McLain, Detroit	1999	Ivan Rodriguez, Texas
1939	Joe DiMaggio, New York	1969	Harmon Killebrew, Minnesota	2000	Jason Giambi, Oakland
1940	Hank Greenberg, Detroit	1970	John "Boog" Powell, Baltimore	2001	Ichiro Suzuki, Seattle
1941	Joe DiMaggio, New York	1971	Vida Blue, Oakland	2002	Miguel Tejada, Oakland
1942	Joe Gordon, New York	1972	Dick Allen, Chicago	2003	Alex Rodriguez, Texas
1943	Spurgeon "Spud" Chandler, New York	1973	Reggie Jackson, Oakland	2004	Vladimir Guerrero, Anaheim
		1974	Jeff Burroughs, Texas	2005	Alex Rodriguez, New York
1944	Hal Newhouser, Detroit	1975	Fred Lynn, Boston	2006	Justin Morneau, Minnesota
1945	Hal Newhouser, Detroit	1976	Thurman Munson, New York	2007	Alex Rodriguez, New York
1946	Ted Williams, Boston	1977	Rod Carew, Minnesota	2008	Dustin Pedroia, Boston
1947	Joe DiMaggio, New York	1978	Jim Rice, Boston	2009	Joe Mauer, Minnesota
1948	Lou Boudreau, Cleveland	1979	Don Baylor, California	2010	Josh Hamilton, Texas
1949	Ted Williams, Boston	1980	George Brett, Kansas City	2011	Justin Verlander, Detroit
1950	Phil Rizzuto, New York	1981	Rollie Fingers, Milwaukee	2012	Miguel Cabrera, Detroit
1951	Yogi Berra, New York	1982	Robin Yount, Milwaukee	2013	Miguel Cabrera, Detroit
1952	Bobby Shantz, Philadelphia	1983	Cal Ripken Jr., Baltimore	2014	Mike Trout, Los Angeles
1953	Al Rosen, Cleveland	1984	Willie Hernandez, Detroit	2015	Josh Donaldson, Toronto
1954	Yogi Berra, New York	1985	Don Mattingly, New York	2016	Mike Trout, Los Angeles
1955	Yogi Berra, New York	1986	Roger Clemens, Boston	2017	José Altuve, Houston
1956	Mickey Mantle, New York	1987	George Bell, Toronto	2018	Mookie Betts, Boston
1957	Mickey Mantle, New York	1988	Jose Canseco, Oakland	2019	Mike Trout, Los Angeles
1958	Jackie Jensen, Boston	1989	Robin Yount, Milwaukee	2020	José Abreu, Chicago
1959	Nellie Fox, Chicago	1990	Rickey Henderson, Oakland	2021	Shohei Ohtani, L.A. Angels
1960	Roger Maris, New York	1991	Cal Ripken Jr., Baltimore	2022	Aaron Judge, NY Yankees

Rookie of the Year, 1949-2022

(as selected by the Baseball Writers' Assn. of America)

1947: Jackie Robinson, Brooklyn, 1B (combined selection); 1948: Alvin Dark, Boston (NL), SS (combined selection).

National League

Year	Player, team, position	Year	Player, team, position	Year	Player, team, position
1949	Don Newcombe, Brooklyn, P	1974	Bake McBride, St. Louis, OF	1998	Kerry Wood, Chicago, P
1950	Sam Jethroe, Boston, OF	1975	John Montefusco, San Francisco, P	1999	Scott Williamson, Cincinnati, P
1951	Willie Mays, NY, OF	1976	Butch Metzger, San Diego, P;	2000	Rafael Furcal, Atlanta, SS
1952	Joe Black, Brooklyn, P		Pat Zachry, Cincinnati, P	2001	Albert Pujols, St. Louis, OF
1953	Jim Gilliam, Brooklyn, 2B	1977	Andre Dawson, Montréal, OF	2002	Jason Jennings, Colorado, P
1954	Wally Moon, St. Louis, OF	1978	Bob Horner, Atlanta, 3B	2003	Dontrelle Willis, Florida, P
1955	Bill Virdon, St. Louis, OF	1979	Rick Sutcliffe, L.A., P	2004	Jason Bay, Pittsburgh, OF
1956	Frank Robinson, Cincinnati, OF	1980	Steve Howe, L.A., P	2005	Ryan Howard, Philadelphia, 1B
1957	Jack Sanford, Philadelphia, P	1981	Fernando Valenzuela, L.A., P	2006	Hanley Ramirez, Florida, SS
1958	Orlando Cepeda, San Francisco, 1B	1982	Steve Sax, L.A., 2B	2007	Ryan Braun, Milwaukee, 3B
1959	Willie McCovey, San Francisco, 1B	1983	Darryl Strawberry, NY, OF	2008	Geovany Soto, Chicago, C
1960	Frank Howard, L.A., OF	1984	Dwight Gooden, NY, P	2009	Chris Coghlan, Florida, OF
1961	Billy Williams, Chicago, OF	1985	Vince Coleman, St. Louis, OF	2010	Buster Posey, San Francisco, C
1962	Ken Hubbs, Chicago, 2B	1986	Todd Worrell, St. Louis, P	2011	Craig Kimbrel, Atlanta, P
1963	Pete Rose, Cincinnati, 2B	1987	Benito Santiago, San Diego, C	2012	Bryce Harper, Washington, OF
1964	Richie Allen, Philadelphia, 3B	1988	Chris Sabo, Cincinnati, 3B	2013	José Fernández, Miami, P
1965	Jim Lefebvre, L.A., 2B	1989	Jerome Walton, Chicago, OF	2014	Jacob deGrom, NY, P
1966	Tommy Helms, Cincinnati, 2B	1990	Dave Justice, Atlanta, 1B	2015	Kris Bryant, Chicago, 3B
1967	Tom Seaver, NY, P	1991	Jeff Bagwell, Houston, 1B	2016	Corey Seager, L.A., SS
1968	Johnny Bench, Cincinnati, C	1992	Eric Karros, L.A., 1B	2017	Cody Bellinger, L.A., 1B
1969	Ted Sizemore, L.A., 2B	1993	Mike Piazza, L.A., C	2018	Ronald Acuña Jr., Atlanta, OF
1970	Carl Morton, Montréal, P	1994	Raul Mondesi, L.A., OF	2019	Pete Alonso, NY, 1B
1971	Earl Williams, Atlanta, C	1995	Hideo Nomo, L.A., P	2020	Devin Williams, Milwaukee, P
1972	Jon Matlack, NY, P	1996	Todd Hollandsworth, L.A., OF	2021	Jonathan India, Cincinnati, 2B
1973	Gary Matthews, San Francisco, OF	1997	Scott Rolen, Philadelphia, 3B	2022	Michael Harris II, Atlanta, OF

American League

Year	Player, team, position	Year	Player, team, position	Year	Player, team, position
1949	Roy Sievers, St. Louis, OF	1974	Mike Hargrove, Texas, 1B	1998	Ben Grieve, Oakland, OF
1950	Walt Dropo, Boston, 1B	1975	Fred Lynn, Boston, OF	1999	Carlos Beltran, Kansas City, OF
1951	Gil McDougald, NY, 3B	1976	Mark Fidrych, Detroit, P	2000	Kazuhiro Sasaki, Seattle, P
1952	Harry Byrd, Philadelphia, P	1977	Eddie Murray, Baltimore, DH	2001	Ichiro Suzuki, Seattle, OF
1953	Harvey Kuenn, Detroit, SS	1978	Lou Whitaker, Detroit, 2B	2002	Eric Hinske, Toronto, 3B
1954	Bob Grim, NY, P	1979	John Castino, Minnesota, 3B;	2003	Angel Berroa, Kansas City, SS
1955	Herb Score, Cleveland, P		Alfredo Griffin, Toronto, SS	2004	Bobby Crosby, Oakland, SS
1956	Luis Aparicio, Chicago, SS	1980	Joe Charboneau, Cleveland, OF	2005	Huston Street, Oakland, P
1957	Tony Kubek, NY, IF-OF	1981	Dave Righetti, NY, P	2006	Justin Verlander, Detroit, P
1958	Albie Pearson, Washington, OF	1982	Cal Ripken Jr., Baltimore, SS	2007	Dustin Pedroia, Boston, 2B
1959	Bob Allison, Washington, OF	1983	Ron Kittle, Chicago, OF	2008	Evan Longoria, Tampa Bay, 3B
1960	Ron Hansen, Baltimore, SS	1984	Alvin Davis, Seattle, 1B	2009	Andrew Bailey, Oakland, P
1961	Don Schwall, Boston, P	1985	Ozzie Guillen, Chicago, SS	2010	Neftali Feliz, Texas, P
1962	Tom Tresh, NY, IF-OF	1986	Jose Canseco, Oakland, OF	2011	Jeremy Hellickson, Tampa Bay, P
1963	Gary Peters, Chicago, P	1987	Mark McGwire, Oakland, 1B	2012	Mike Trout, L.A., OF
1964	Tony Oliva, Minnesota, OF	1988	Walt Weiss, Oakland, SS	2013	Wil Myers, Tampa Bay, OF
1965	Curt Blefary, Baltimore, OF	1989	Gregg Olson, Baltimore, P	2014	José Abreu, Chicago, 1B
1966	Tommie Agee, Chicago, OF	1990	Sandy Alomar Jr., Cleveland, C	2015	Carlos Correa, Houston, SS
1967	Rod Carew, Minnesota, 2B	1991	Chuck Knoblauch, Minnesota, 2B	2016	Michael Fulmer, Detroit, P
1968	Stan Bahnsen, NY, P	1992	Pat Listach, Milwaukee, SS	2017	Aaron Judge, NY, OF
1969	Lou Piniella, Kansas City, OF	1993	Tim Salmon, California, OF	2018	Shohei Ohtani, L.A., DH/P
1970	Thurman Munson, NY, C	1994	Bob Hamelin, Kansas City, DH	2019	Yordan Alvarez, Houston, OF
1971	Chris Chambliss, Cleveland, 1B	1995	Marty Cordova, Minnesota, OF	2020	Kyle Lewis, Seattle, OF
1972	Carlton Fisk, Boston, C	1996	Derek Jeter, NY, SS	2021	Randy Arozarena, Tampa Bay, OF
1973	Al Bumbry, Baltimore, OF	1997	Nomar Garciaparra, Boston, SS	2022	Julio Rodríguez, Seattle, OF

Hank Aaron Award, 1999-2022

(Awarded annually to the best overall offensive performer in both leagues, as selected by a panel of Hall of Famers and fan vote.)

National League

Year	Player, team, position	Year	Player, team, position	Year	Player, team, position
1999	Sammy Sosa, Chicago, OF	2007	Prince Fielder, Milwaukee, 1B	2015	Bryce Harper, Washington, RF
2000	Todd Helton, Colorado, 1B	2008	Aramis Ramirez, Chicago, 3B	2016	Kris Bryant, Chicago, 3B
2001	Barry Bonds, San Francisco, OF	2009	Albert Pujols, St. Louis, 1B	2017	Giancarlo Stanton, Miami, RF
2002	Barry Bonds, San Francisco, OF	2010	Joey Votto, Cincinnati, 1B	2018	Christian Yelich, Milwaukee, LF
2003	Albert Pujols, St. Louis, OF	2011	Matt Kemp, L.A., OF	2019	Christian Yelich, Milwaukee, LF
2004	Barry Bonds, San Francisco, OF	2012	Buster Posey, San Francisco, C	2020	Freddie Freeman, Atlanta, 1B
2005	Andruw Jones, Atlanta, OF	2013	Paul Goldschmidt, Arizona, 1B	2021	Bryce Harper, Philadelphia, RF
2006	Ryan Howard, Philadelphia, 1B	2014	Giancarlo Stanton, Miami, RF	2022	Paul Goldschmidt, St. Louis, 1B

American League

Year	Player, team, position	Year	Player, team, position	Year	Player, team, position
1999	Manny Ramirez, Cleveland, OF	2007	Alex Rodriguez, NY, 3B	2015	Josh Donaldson, Toronto, 3B
2000	Carlos Delgado, Toronto, 1B	2008	Kevin Youkilis, Boston, 1B	2016	David Ortiz, Boston, DH
2001	Alex Rodriguez, Texas, SS	2009	Derek Jeter, NY, SS	2017	José Altuve, Houston, 2B
2002	Alex Rodriguez, Texas, SS	2010	Jose Bautista, Toronto, OF	2018	J.D. Martinez, Boston, LF
2003	Alex Rodriguez, Texas, SS	2011	Jose Bautista, Toronto, OF	2019	Mike Trout, L.A., CF
2004	Manny Ramirez, Boston, OF	2012	Miguel Cabrera, Detroit, 3B	2020	José Abreu, White Sox, 1B
2005	David Ortiz, Boston, DH	2013	Miguel Cabrera, Detroit, 3B	2021	Vladimir Guerrero Jr., Toronto, 1B
2006	Derek Jeter, NY, SS	2014	Mike Trout, L.A., CF	2022	Aaron Judge, NY, OF

Major League Pennant Winners, 1901-75

National League					American League				
Year	Winner	W	L	PCT	Manager	Year	Winner	W	L	PCT	Manager
---	---	---	---	---	---	---	---	---	---	---	---
1901	Pittsburgh	90	49	.647	Clarke	1901	Chicago	83	53	.610	Griffith
1902	Pittsburgh	103	36	.741	Clarke	1902	Philadelphia	83	53	.610	Mack
1903	Pittsburgh	91	49	.650	Clarke	1903	Boston	91	47	.659	Collins
1904	New York	106	47	.693	McGraw	1904	Boston	95	59	.617	Collins
1905	New York	105	48	.686	McGraw	1905	Philadelphia	92	56	.622	Mack
1906	Chicago	116	36	.763	Chance	1906	Chicago	93	58	.616	Jones
1907	Chicago	107	45	.704	Chance	1907	Detroit	92	58	.613	Jennings
1908	Chicago	99	55	.643	Chance	1908	Detroit	90	63	.588	Jennings
1909	Pittsburgh	110	42	.724	Clarke	1909	Detroit	98	54	.645	Jennings
1910	Chicago	104	50	.675	Chance	1910	Philadelphia	102	48	.680	Mack
1911	New York	99	54	.647	McGraw	1911	Philadelphia	101	50	.669	Mack
1912	New York	103	48	.682	McGraw	1912	Boston	105	47	.691	Stahl
1913	New York	101	51	.664	McGraw	1913	Philadelphia	96	57	.627	Mack
1914	Boston	94	59	.614	Stallings	1914	Philadelphia	99	53	.651	Mack
1915	Philadelphia	90	62	.592	Moran	1915	Boston	101	50	.669	Carrigan
1916	Brooklyn	94	60	.610	Robinson	1916	Boston	91	63	.591	Carrigan
1917	New York	98	56	.636	McGraw	1917	Chicago	100	54	.649	Rowland
1918	Chicago	84	45	.651	Mitchell	1918	Boston	75	51	.595	Barrow
1919	Cincinnati	96	44	.686	Moran	1919	Chicago	88	52	.629	Gleason
1920	Brooklyn	93	61	.604	Robinson	1920	Cleveland	98	56	.636	Speaker
1921	New York	94	59	.614	McGraw	1921	New York	98	55	.641	Huggins
1922	New York	93	61	.604	McGraw	1922	New York	94	60	.610	Huggins
1923	New York	95	58	.621	McGraw	1923	New York	98	54	.645	Huggins
1924	New York	93	60	.608	McGraw	1924	Washington	92	62	.597	Harris
1925	Pittsburgh	95	58	.621	McKechnie	1925	Washington	96	55	.636	Harris
1926	St. Louis	89	65	.578	Hornsby	1926	New York	91	63	.591	Huggins
1927	Pittsburgh	94	60	.610	Bush	1927	New York	110	44	.714	Huggins
1928	St. Louis	95	59	.617	McKechnie	1928	New York	101	53	.656	Huggins
1929	Chicago	98	54	.645	McCarthy	1929	Philadelphia	104	46	.693	Mack
1930	St. Louis	92	62	.597	Street	1930	Philadelphia	102	52	.662	Mack
1931	St. Louis	101	53	.656	Street	1931	Philadelphia	107	45	.704	Mack
1932	Chicago	90	64	.584	Hornsby, Grimm	1932	New York	107	47	.695	McCarthy
1933	New York	91	61	.599	Terry	1933	Washington	99	53	.651	Cronin
1934	St. Louis	95	58	.621	Frisch	1934	Detroit	101	53	.656	Cochrane
1935	Chicago	100	54	.649	Grimm	1935	Detroit	93	58	.616	Cochrane
1936	New York	92	62	.597	Terry	1936	New York	102	51	.667	McCarthy
1937	New York	95	57	.625	Terry	1937	New York	102	52	.662	McCarthy
1938	Chicago	89	63	.586	Grimm, Hartnett	1938	New York	99	53	.651	McCarthy
1939	Cincinnati	97	57	.630	McKechnie	1939	New York	106	45	.702	McCarthy
1940	Cincinnati	100	53	.654	McKechnie	1940	Detroit	90	64	.584	Baker
1941	Brooklyn	100	54	.649	Durocher	1941	New York	101	53	.656	McCarthy
1942	St. Louis	106	48	.688	Southworth	1942	New York	103	51	.669	McCarthy
1943	St. Louis	105	49	.682	Southworth	1943	New York	98	56	.636	McCarthy
1944	St. Louis	105	49	.682	Southworth	1944	St. Louis	89	65	.578	Sewell
1945	Chicago	98	56	.636	Grimm	1945	Detroit	88	65	.575	O'Neill
1946	St. Louis	98	58	.628	Dyer	1946	Boston	104	50	.675	Cronin
1947	Brooklyn	94	60	.610	Shotton	1947	New York	97	57	.630	Harris
1948	Boston	91	62	.595	Southworth	1948	Cleveland	97	58	.626	Boudreau
1949	Brooklyn	97	57	.630	Shotton	1949	New York	97	57	.630	Stengel
1950	Philadelphia	91	63	.591	Sawyer	1950	New York	98	56	.636	Stengel
1951	New York	98	59	.624	Durocher	1951	New York	98	56	.636	Stengel
1952	Brooklyn	96	57	.627	Dressen	1952	New York	95	59	.617	Stengel
1953	Brooklyn	105	49	.682	Dressen	1953	New York	99	52	.656	Stengel
1954	New York	97	57	.630	Durocher	1954	Cleveland	111	43	.721	Lopez
1955	Brooklyn	98	55	.641	Alston	1955	New York	96	58	.623	Stengel
1956	Brooklyn	93	61	.604	Alston	1956	New York	97	57	.630	Stengel
1957	Milwaukee	95	59	.617	Haney	1957	New York	98	56	.636	Stengel
1958	Milwaukee	92	62	.597	Haney	1958	New York	92	62	.597	Stengel
1959	Los Angeles	88	68	.564	Alston	1959	Chicago	94	60	.610	Lopez
1960	Pittsburgh	95	59	.617	Murtaugh	1960	New York	97	57	.630	Stengel
1961	Cincinnati	93	61	.604	Hutchinson	1961	New York	109	53	.673	Houk
1962	San Francisco	103	62	.624	Dark	1962	New York	96	66	.593	Houk
1963	Los Angeles	99	63	.611	Alston	1963	New York	104	57	.646	Houk
1964	St. Louis	93	69	.574	Keane	1964	New York	99	63	.611	Berra
1965	Los Angeles	97	65	.599	Alston	1965	Minnesota	102	60	.630	Mele
1966	Los Angeles	95	67	.586	Alston	1966	Baltimore	97	63	.606	Bauer
1967	St. Louis	101	60	.627	Schoendienst	1967	Boston	92	70	.568	Williams
1968	St. Louis	97	65	.599	Schoendienst	1968	Detroit	103	59	.636	Smith
1969	New York	100	62	.617	Hodges	1969	Baltimore	109	53	.673	Weaver
1970	Cincinnati	102	60	.630	Anderson	1970	Baltimore	108	54	.667	Weaver
1971	Pittsburgh	97	65	.599	Murtaugh	1971	Baltimore	101	57	.639	Weaver
1972	Cincinnati	95	59	.617	Anderson	1972	Oakland	93	62	.600	Williams
1973	New York	82	79	.509	Berra	1973	Oakland	94	68	.580	Williams
1974	Los Angeles	102	60	.630	Alston	1974	Oakland	90	72	.556	Dark
1975	Cincinnati	108	54	.667	Anderson	1975	Boston	95	65	.594	Johnson

Major League Pennant Winners, 1976-2023

National League

Year	East winner	W	L	PCT	Manager	West winner	W	L	PCT	Manager	Pennant winner
1976	Philadelphia	101	61	.623	Ozark	Cincinnati	102	60	.630	Anderson	Cincinnati
1977	Philadelphia	101	61	.623	Ozark	Los Angeles	98	64	.605	Lasorda	Los Angeles
1978	Philadelphia	90	72	.556	Ozark	Los Angeles	95	67	.586	Lasorda	Los Angeles
1979	Pittsburgh	98	64	.605	Tanner	Cincinnati	90	71	.559	McNamara	Pittsburgh
1980	Philadelphia	91	71	.562	Green	Houston	93	70	.571	Virdon	Philadelphia
1981(a)	Philadelphia	34	21	.618	Green	Los Angeles	36	21	.632	Lasorda	(c)
1981(b)	Montréal	30	23	.566	Williams, Fanning	Houston	33	20	.623	Virdon	Los Angeles
1982	St. Louis	92	70	.568	Herzog	Atlanta	89	73	.549	Torre	St. Louis
1983	Philadelphia	90	72	.556	Corrales, Owens	Los Angeles	91	71	.562	Lasorda	Philadelphia
1984	Chicago	96	65	.596	Frey	San Diego	92	70	.568	Williams	San Diego
1985	St. Louis	101	61	.623	Herzog	Los Angeles	95	67	.586	Lasorda	St. Louis
1986	New York	108	54	.667	Johnson	Houston	96	66	.593	Lanier	New York
1987	St. Louis	95	67	.586	Herzog	San Francisco	90	72	.556	Craig	St. Louis
1988	New York	100	60	.625	Johnson	Los Angeles	94	67	.584	Lasorda	Los Angeles
1989	Chicago	93	69	.574	Zimmer	San Francisco	92	70	.568	Craig	San Francisco
1990	Pittsburgh	95	67	.586	Leyland	Cincinnati	91	71	.562	Piniella	Cincinnati
1991	Pittsburgh	98	64	.605	Leyland	Atlanta	94	68	.580	Cox	Atlanta
1992	Pittsburgh	96	66	.593	Leyland	Atlanta	98	64	.605	Cox	Atlanta
1993	Philadelphia	97	65	.599	Fregosi	Atlanta	104	58	.642	Cox	Philadelphia

Year	Division	Winner	W	L	PCT	Manager	Playoffs	Pennant winner
1994(d)	East	Montréal	74	40	.649	Alou	—	—
	Central	Cincinnati	66	48	.579	Johnson		
	West	Los Angeles	58	56	.509	Lasorda		
1995	East	Atlanta	90	54	.625	Cox	Atlanta 3, Colorado* 1	Atlanta
	Central	Cincinnati	85	59	.590	Johnson	Cincinnati 3, Los Angeles 0	
	West	Los Angeles	78	66	.542	Lasorda	Atlanta 4, Cincinnati 0	
1996	East	Atlanta	96	66	.593	Cox	Atlanta 3, Los Angeles* 0	Atlanta
	Central	St. Louis	88	74	.543	La Russa	St. Louis 3, San Diego 0	
	West	San Diego	91	71	.562	Bochy	Atlanta 4, St. Louis 3	
1997	East	Atlanta	101	61	.623	Cox	Atlanta 3, Houston 0	Florida*
	Central	Houston	84	78	.519	Dierker	Florida* 3, San Francisco 0	(Leyland)
	West	San Francisco	90	72	.556	Baker	Florida* 4, Atlanta 2	
1998	East	Atlanta	106	56	.654	Cox	Atlanta 3, Chicago* 0	San Diego
	Central	Houston	102	60	.630	Dierker	San Diego 3, Houston 1	
	West	San Diego	98	64	.605	Bochy	San Diego 4, Atlanta 2	
1999	East	Atlanta	103	59	.636	Cox	Atlanta 3, Houston 1	Atlanta
	Central	Houston	97	65	.599	Dierker, Galante	New York* 3, Arizona 1	
	West	Arizona	100	62	.617	Showalter	Atlanta 4, New York* 2	
2000	East	Atlanta	95	67	.586	Cox	St. Louis 3, Atlanta 0	New York*
	Central	St. Louis	95	67	.586	La Russa	New York* 3, San Francisco 1	(Valentine)
	West	San Francisco	97	65	.599	Baker	New York* 4, St. Louis 1	
2001	East	Atlanta	88	74	.543	Cox	Atlanta 3, Houston 0	Arizona
	Central	Houston	93	69	.574	Dierker	Arizona 3, St. Louis* 2	
	West	Arizona	92	70	.568	Brenly	Arizona 4, Atlanta 1	
2002	East	Atlanta	101	59	.631	Cox	St. Louis 3, Arizona 0	San Francisco*
	Central	St. Louis	97	65	.599	La Russa	San Francisco* 3, Atlanta 2	(Baker)
	West	Arizona	98	64	.605	Brenly	San Francisco* 4, St. Louis 1	
2003	East	Atlanta	101	61	.623	Cox	Chicago 3, Atlanta 2	Florida*
	Central	Chicago	88	74	.543	Baker	Florida* 3, San Francisco 1	(McKeon, Torborg)
	West	San Francisco	100	61	.621	Alou	Florida* 4, Chicago 3	
2004	East	Atlanta	96	66	.593	Cox	Houston* 3, Atlanta 2	St. Louis
	Central	St. Louis	105	57	.648	La Russa	St. Louis 3, Los Angeles 1	
	West	Los Angeles	93	69	.574	Tracy	St. Louis 4, Houston* 3	
2005	East	Atlanta	90	72	.556	Cox	St. Louis 3, San Diego 0	Houston*
	Central	St. Louis	100	62	.617	La Russa	Houston* 3, Atlanta 1	(Garner)
	West	San Diego	82	80	.506	Bochy	Houston* 4, St. Louis 2	
2006	East	New York	97	65	.599	Randolph	New York 3, Los Angeles* 0	St. Louis
	Central	St. Louis	83	78	.516	La Russa	St. Louis 3, San Diego 1	
	West	San Diego	88	74	.543	Bochy	St. Louis 4, New York 3	
2007	East	Philadelphia	89	73	.549	Manuel	Colorado* 3, Philadelphia 0	Colorado*
	Central	Chicago	85	77	.525	Piniella	Arizona 3, Chicago 0	(Hurdle)
	West	Arizona	90	72	.556	Melvin	Colorado* 4, Arizona 0	
2008	East	Philadelphia	92	70	.568	Manuel	Philadelphia 3, Milwaukee* 1	Philadelphia
	Central	Chicago	97	64	.602	Piniella	Los Angeles 3, Chicago 0	
	West	Los Angeles	84	78	.519	Torre	Philadelphia 4, Los Angeles 1	
2009	East	Philadelphia	93	69	.574	Manuel	Philadelphia 3, Colorado* 1	Philadelphia
	Central	St. Louis	91	71	.562	La Russa	Los Angeles 3, St. Louis 0	
	West	Los Angeles	95	67	.586	Torre	Philadelphia 4, Los Angeles 1	
2010	East	Philadelphia	97	65	.599	Manuel	San Francisco 3, Atlanta* 1	San Francisco
	Central	Cincinnati	91	71	.562	Baker	Philadelphia 3, Cincinnati 0	
	West	San Francisco	92	70	.568	Bochy	San Francisco 4, Philadelphia 2	
2011	East	Philadelphia	102	60	.630	Manuel	Milwaukee 3, Arizona 2	St. Louis*
	Central	Milwaukee	96	66	.593	Roenicke	St. Louis* 3, Philadelphia 2	(La Russa)
	West	Arizona	94	68	.580	Gibson	St. Louis* 4, Milwaukee 2	
2012	East	Washington	98	64	.605	Johnson	#St. Louis* 3, Washington 2	San Francisco
	Central	Cincinnati	97	65	.599	Baker	San Francisco 3, Cincinnati 2	
	West	San Francisco	94	68	.580	Bochy	San Francisco 4, St. Louis* 3	
2013	East	Atlanta	96	66	.593	González	St. Louis 3, #Pittsburgh* 2	St. Louis
	Central	St. Louis	97	65	.599	Matheny	Los Angeles 3, Atlanta 1	
	West	Los Angeles	92	70	.568	Mattingly	St. Louis 4, Los Angeles 2	
2014	East	Washington	96	66	.593	Williams	#San Francisco* 3, Washington 1	San Francisco*
	Central	St. Louis	90	72	.556	Matheny	St. Louis 3, Los Angeles 1	(Bochy)
	West	Los Angeles	94	68	.580	Mattingly	San Francisco* 4, St. Louis 1	
2015	East	New York	90	72	.556	Collins	#Chicago* 3, St. Louis 1	New York
	Central	St. Louis	100	62	.617	Matheny	New York 3, Los Angeles 2	
	West	Los Angeles	92	70	.568	Mattingly	New York 4, Chicago* 2	
2016	East	Washington	95	67	.586	Baker	Chicago 3, #San Francisco* 1	Chicago
	Central	Chicago	103	58	.640	Maddon	Los Angeles 3, Washington 2	
	West	Los Angeles	91	71	.562	Roberts	Chicago 4, Los Angeles 2	

Year	Division	Winner	W	L	PCT	Manager	Playoffs	Pennant winner
2017	East	Washington	97	65	.599	Baker	Chicago 3, Washington 2	Los Angeles
	Central	Chicago	92	70	.568	Maddon	Los Angeles 3, #Arizona* 0	
	West	Los Angeles	104	58	.642	Roberts	Los Angeles 4, Chicago 1	
2018	East	Atlanta	90	72	.556	Snitker	Milwaukee 3, #Colorado* 0	Los Angeles
	Central	Milwaukee	96	67	.589	Counsell	Los Angeles 3, Atlanta 1	
	West	Los Angeles	92	71	.564	Roberts	Los Angeles 4, Milwaukee 3	
2019	East	Atlanta	97	65	.599	Snitker	St. Louis 3, Atlanta 2	Washington*
	Central	St. Louis	91	71	.562	Shildt	#Washington* 3, Los Angeles 2	(Martinez)
	West	Los Angeles	106	56	.654	Roberts	Washington* 4, St. Louis 0	
2020	East	Atlanta	35	25	.583	Snitker	Los Angeles 3, San Diego* 0	Los Angeles
	Central	Chicago	34	26	.567	Ross	Atlanta 3, Miami* 0	
	West	Los Angeles	43	17	.717	Roberts	Los Angeles 4, Atlanta 3	
2021	East	Atlanta	88	73	.547	Snitker	Los Angeles* 3, San Francisco 2	Atlanta
	Central	Milwaukee	95	67	.586	Counsell	#Atlanta 3, Milwaukee 1	
	West	San Francisco	107	55	.660	Kapler	Atlanta 4, Los Angeles* 2	
2022	East	Atlanta	101	61	.623	Snitker	**Philadelphia 2, St. Louis 0	Philadelphia*
	Central	St. Louis	93	69	.574	Marmol	**San Diego 2, NY Mets 1	(Thomson)
	West	Los Angeles	111	51	.685	Roberts	Philadelphia*, Atlanta 1	
							San Diego* 3, Los Angeles 1	
							Philadelphia* 4, San Diego* 1	
2023	East	Atlanta	104	58	.642	Snitker	**Philadelphia 2, Miami 0	Arizona*
	Central	Milwaukee	92	70	.568	Counsell	**Arizona 2, Milwaukee 0	(Lovullo)
	West	Los Angeles	100	62	.617	Roberts	Philadelphia* 3, Atlanta 1	
							Arizona* 3, Los Angeles 0	
							Arizona* 4, Philadelphia 3	

American League

Year	East winner	W	L	PCT	Manager	West winner	W	L	PCT	Manager	Pennant winner
1976	New York	97	62	.610	Martin	Kansas City	90	72	.556	Herzog	New York
1977	New York	100	62	.617	Martin	Kansas City	102	60	.630	Herzog	New York
1978	New York	100	63	.613	Martin, Lemon	Kansas City	92	70	.568	Herzog	New York
1979	Baltimore	102	57	.642	Weaver	California	88	74	.543	Fregosi	Baltimore
1980	New York	103	59	.636	Howser	Kansas City	97	65	.599	Frey	Kansas City
1981(a)	New York	34	22	.607	Michael, Lemon	Oakland	37	23	.617	Martin	(c)
1981(b)	Milwaukee	31	22	.585	Rodgers	Kansas City	30	23	.566	Frey, Howser	New York
1982	Milwaukee	95	67	.586	Rodgers, Kuenn	California	93	69	.574	Mauch	Milwaukee
1983	Baltimore	98	64	.605	Altobelli	Chicago	99	63	.611	La Russa	Baltimore
1984	Detroit	104	58	.642	Anderson	Kansas City	84	78	.519	Howser	Detroit
1985	Toronto	99	62	.615	Cox	Kansas City	91	71	.562	Howser	Kansas City
1986	Boston	95	66	.590	McNamara	California	92	70	.568	Mauch	Boston
1987	Detroit	98	64	.605	Anderson	Minnesota	85	77	.525	Kelly	Minnesota
1988	Boston	89	73	.549	McNamara, Morgan	Oakland	104	58	.642	La Russa	Oakland
1989	Toronto	89	73	.549	Williams, Gaston	Oakland	99	63	.611	La Russa	Oakland
1990	Boston	88	74	.543	Morgan	Oakland	103	59	.636	La Russa	Oakland
1991	Toronto	91	71	.562	Gaston, Tenace	Minnesota	95	67	.586	Kelly	Minnesota
1992	Toronto	96	66	.593	Gaston	Oakland	96	66	.593	La Russa	Toronto
1993	Toronto	95	67	.586	Gaston	Chicago	94	68	.580	Lamont	Toronto

Year	Division	Winner	W	L	PCT	Manager	Playoffs	Pennant winner
1994(d)	East	New York	70	43	.619	Showalter	—	—
	Central	Chicago	67	46	.593	Lamont		
	West	Texas	52	62	.456	Kennedy		
1995	East	Boston	86	58	.597	Kennedy	Cleveland 3, Boston 0	Cleveland
	Central	Cleveland	100	44	.694	Hargrove	Seattle 3, New York* 2	
	West	Seattle	79	66	.545	Piniella	Cleveland 4, Seattle 2	
1996	East	New York	92	70	.568	Torre	Baltimore* 3, Cleveland 1	New York
	Central	Cleveland	99	62	.615	Hargrove	New York 3, Texas 1	
	West	Texas	90	72	.556	Oates	New York 4, Baltimore* 1	
1997	East	Baltimore	98	64	.605	Johnson	Baltimore 3, Seattle 1	Cleveland
	Central	Cleveland	86	75	.534	Hargrove	Cleveland 3, New York* 2	
	West	Seattle	90	72	.556	Piniella	Cleveland 4, Baltimore 2	
1998	East	New York	114	48	.704	Torre	New York 3, Texas 0	New York
	Central	Cleveland	89	73	.549	Hargrove	Cleveland 3, Boston* 1	
	West	Texas	88	74	.543	Oates	New York 4, Cleveland 2	
1999	East	New York	98	64	.605	Torre	New York 3, Texas 0	New York
	Central	Cleveland	97	65	.599	Hargrove	Boston* 3, Cleveland 2	
	West	Texas	95	67	.586	Oates	New York 4, Boston* 1	
2000	East	New York	87	74	.540	Torre	New York 3, Oakland 2	New York
	Central	Chicago	95	67	.586	Manuel	Seattle* 3, Chicago 0	
	West	Oakland	91	70	.565	Howe	New York 4, Seattle* 2	
2001	East	New York	95	65	.594	Torre	Seattle 3, Cleveland 2	New York
	Central	Cleveland	91	71	.562	Manuel	New York 3, Oakland* 2	
	West	Seattle	116	46	.716	Piniella	New York 4, Seattle 1	
2002	East	New York	103	58	.640	Torre	Anaheim* 3, New York 1	Anaheim*
	Central	Minnesota	94	67	.584	Gardenhire	Minnesota 3, Oakland 2	(Scioscia)
	West	Oakland	103	59	.636	Howe	Anaheim* 4, Minnesota 1	
2003	East	New York	101	61	.623	Torre	New York 3, Minnesota 1	New York
	Central	Minnesota	90	72	.556	Gardenhire	Boston* 3, Oakland 2	
	West	Oakland	96	66	.593	Macha	New York 4, Boston* 3	
2004	East	New York	101	61	.623	Torre	New York 3, Minnesota 1	Boston*
	Central	Minnesota	92	70	.568	Gardenhire	Boston* 3, Anaheim 0	(Francona)
	West	Anaheim	92	70	.568	Scioscia	Boston* 4, New York 3	
2005	East	New York	95	67	.586	Torre	Chicago 3, Boston* 0	Chicago
	Central	Chicago	99	63	.611	Guillen	Los Angeles, New York 2	
	West	Los Angeles	95	67	.586	Scioscia	Chicago 4, Los Angeles 1	
2006	East	New York	97	65	.599	Torre	Oakland 3, Minnesota 0	Detroit*
	Central	Minnesota	96	66	.593	Gardenhire	Detroit* 3, New York 1	(Leyland)
	West	Oakland	93	69	.574	Macha	Detroit* 4, Oakland 0	
2007	East	Boston	96	66	.593	Francona	Boston 3, Los Angeles 0	Boston
	Central	Cleveland	96	66	.593	Wedge	Cleveland 3, New York* 1	
	West	Los Angeles	94	68	.580	Scioscia	Boston 4, Cleveland 3	
2008	East	Tampa Bay	97	65	.599	Maddon	Tampa Bay 3, Chicago 1	Tampa Bay
	Central	Chicago	89	74	.546	Guillen	Boston* 3, Los Angeles 1	
	West	Los Angeles	100	62	.617	Scioscia	Tampa Bay 4, Boston* 3	
2009	East	New York	103	59	.636	Girardi	New York 3, Minnesota 0	New York
	Central	Minnesota	87	76	.534	Gardenhire	Los Angeles 3, Boston* 0	
	West	Los Angeles	97	65	.599	Scioscia	New York 4, Los Angeles 2	

Year	Division	Winner	W	L	PCT	Manager	Playoffs	Pennant winner
2010	East	Tampa Bay	96	66	.593	Maddon	New York* 3, Minnesota 0	Texas
	Central	Minnesota	94	68	.580	Gardenhire	Texas 3, Tampa Bay 2	
	West	Texas	90	72	.556	Washington	Texas 4, New York* 2	
2011	East	New York	97	65	.599	Girardi	Detroit 3, New York 2	Texas
	Central	Detroit	95	67	.586	Leyland	Texas 3, Tampa Bay* 1	
	West	Texas	96	66	.593	Washington	Texas 4, Detroit 2	
2012	East	New York	95	67	.586	Girardi	New York 3, #Baltimore* 2	Detroit
	Central	Detroit	88	74	.543	Leyland	Detroit 3, Oakland 2	
	West	Oakland	94	68	.580	Melvin	Detroit 4, New York 0	
2013	East	Boston	97	65	.599	Farrell	Boston 3, #Tampa Bay* 1	Boston
	Central	Detroit	93	69	.574	Leyland	Detroit 3, Oakland 2	
	West	Oakland	96	66	.593	Melvin	Boston 4, Detroit 2	
2014	East	Baltimore	96	66	.593	Showalter	#Kansas City* 3, Los Angeles 0	Kansas City*
	Central	Detroit	90	72	.556	Ausmus	Baltimore 3, Detroit 0	(Yost)
	West	Los Angeles	98	64	.605	Scioscia	Kansas City* 4, Baltimore 0	
2015	East	Toronto	93	69	.574	Gibbons	Kansas City 3, #Houston* 2	Kansas City
	Central	Kansas City	95	67	.586	Yost	Toronto 3, Texas 2	
	West	Texas	88	74	.543	Banister	Kansas City 4, Toronto 2	
2016	East	Boston	93	69	.574	Farrell	#Toronto* 3, Texas 0	Cleveland
	Central	Cleveland	94	67	.584	Francona	Cleveland 3, Boston 0	
	West	Texas	95	67	.586	Banister	Cleveland 4, Toronto* 1	
2017	East	Boston	93	69	.574	Farrell	Houston 3, Boston 1	Houston
	Central	Cleveland	102	60	.630	Francona	#New York* 3, Cleveland 2	
	West	Houston	101	61	.623	Hinch	Houston 4, New York* 3	
2018	East	Boston	108	54	.667	Cora	Boston 3, #New York* 1	Boston
	Central	Cleveland	91	71	.562	Francona	Houston 3, Cleveland 0	
	West	Houston	103	59	.636	Hinch	Boston 4, Houston 1	
2019	East	New York	103	59	.636	Boone	New York 3, Minnesota 0	Houston
	Central	Minnesota	101	61	.623	Baldelli	Houston 3, #Tampa Bay* 2	
	West	Houston	107	55	.660	Hinch	Houston 4, New York* 2	
2020	East	Tampa Bay	40	20	.667	Cash	Tampa Bay 3, New York* 2	Tampa Bay
	Central	Minnesota	36	24	.600	Baldelli	Houston* 3, Oakland 1	
	West	Oakland	36	24	.600	Melvin	Tampa Bay 4, Houston* 3	
2021	East	Tampa Bay	100	62	.617	Cash	#Boston* 3, Tampa Bay 1	Houston
	Central	Chicago	93	69	.574	La Russa	Houston 3, Chicago 1	
	West	Houston	95	67	.586	Baker	Houston 4, Boston* 2	
2022	East	New York	99	63	.611	Boone	**Cleveland 2, Tampa Bay 0	Houston
	Central	Cleveland	92	70	.568	Francona	**Seattle 2, Toronto 0	
	West	Houston	106	56	.654	Baker	Houston 3, Seattle* 0	
							New York 3, Cleveland* 2	
							Houston 4, New York 0	
2023	East	Baltimore	101	61	.623	Hyde	**Minnesota 2, Toronto 0	Texas*
	Central	Minnesota	87	75	.537	Baldelli	**Texas 2, Tampa Bay 0	(Bochy)
	West	Houston	90	72	.556	Baker	Houston 3, Minnesota 1	
							Texas* 3, Baltimore 0	
							Texas* 4, Houston 3	

* = Wild-card team. If pennant winner is wild-card team, manager's name is given in parentheses. # = Single-game wild-card playoff winner (2012-21). ** = Best-of-three wild-card series (debuted in 2022). **Note:** In 2020, a best-of-three wild-card round included 8 teams in each league. (a) First half. (b) Second half. (c) Montréal, L.A., NY Yankees, and Oakland won the divisional playoffs. (d) In Aug. 1994, a players' strike began that caused the cancelation of the remainder of the season, the playoffs, and the World Series. Teams listed as division "winners" for 1994 were leading their divisions at the time of the strike.

World Series Results, 1903-2023

1903 Boston AL 5, Pittsburgh NL 3	1943 New York AL 4, St. Louis NL 1	1983 Baltimore AL 4, Philadelphia NL 1
1904 No series	1944 St. Louis NL 4, St. Louis AL 2	1984 Detroit AL 4, San Diego NL 1
1905 New York NL 4, Philadelphia AL 1	1945 Detroit AL 4, Chicago NL 3	1985 Kansas City AL 4, St. Louis NL 3
1906 Chicago AL 4, Chicago NL 2	1946 St. Louis NL 4, Boston AL 3	1986 New York NL 4, Boston AL 3
1907 Chicago NL 4, Detroit AL 0, 1 tie	1947 New York AL 4, Brooklyn NL 3	1987 Minnesota AL 4, St. Louis NL 3
1908 Chicago NL 4, Detroit AL 1	1948 Cleveland AL 4, Boston NL 2	1988 Los Angeles NL 4, Oakland AL 1
1909 Pittsburgh NL 4, Detroit AL 3	1949 New York AL 4, Brooklyn NL 1	1989 Oakland AL 4, San Francisco NL 0
1910 Philadelphia AL 4, Chicago NL 1	1950 New York AL 4, Philadelphia NL 0	1990 Cincinnati NL 4, Oakland AL 0
1911 Philadelphia AL 4, New York NL 2	1951 New York AL 4, New York NL 2	1991 Minnesota AL 4, Atlanta NL 3
1912 Boston AL 4, New York NL 3, 1 tie	1952 New York AL 4, Brooklyn NL 3	1992 Toronto AL 4, Atlanta NL 2
1913 Philadelphia AL 4, New York NL 1	1953 New York AL 4, Brooklyn NL 2	1993 Toronto AL 4, Philadelphia NL 2
1914 Boston NL 4, Philadelphia AL 0	1954 New York NL 4, Cleveland AL 0	1995 Atlanta NL 4, Cleveland AL 2
1915 Boston AL 4, Philadelphia NL 1	1955 Brooklyn NL 4, New York AL 3	1996 New York AL 4, Atlanta NL 2
1916 Boston AL 4, Brooklyn NL 1	1956 New York AL 4, Brooklyn NL 3	1997 Florida NL 4, Cleveland AL 3
1917 Chicago AL 4, New York NL 2	1957 Milwaukee NL 4, New York AL 3	1998 New York AL 4, San Diego NL 0
1918 Boston AL 4, Chicago NL 2	1958 New York AL 4, Milwaukee NL 3	1999 New York AL 4, Atlanta NL 0
1919 Cincinnati NL 5, Chicago AL 3	1959 Los Angeles NL 4, Chicago AL 2	2000 New York AL 4, New York NL 1
1920 Cleveland AL 5, Brooklyn NL 2	1960 Pittsburgh NL 4, New York AL 3	2001 Arizona NL 4, New York AL 3
1921 New York NL 5, New York AL 3	1961 New York AL 4, Cincinnati NL 1	2002 Anaheim AL 4, San Francisco NL 3
1922 New York NL 4, New York AL 0, 1 tie	1962 New York AL 4, San Francisco NL 3	2003 Florida NL 4, New York AL 2
1923 New York AL 4, New York NL 2	1963 Los Angeles NL 4, New York AL 0	2004 Boston AL 4, St. Louis NL 0
1924 Washington AL 4, New York NL 3	1964 St. Louis NL 4, New York AL 3	2005 Chicago AL 4, Houston NL 0
1925 Pittsburgh NL 4, Washington AL 3	1965 Los Angeles NL 4, Minnesota AL 3	2006 St. Louis NL 4, Detroit AL 1
1926 St. Louis NL 4, New York AL 3	1966 Baltimore AL 4, Los Angeles NL 0	2007 Boston AL 4, Colorado NL 0
1927 New York AL 4, Pittsburgh NL 0	1967 St. Louis NL 4, Boston AL 3	2008 Philadelphia NL 4, Tampa Bay AL 1
1928 New York AL 4, St. Louis NL 0	1968 Detroit AL 4, St. Louis NL 3	2009 New York AL 4, Philadelphia NL 2
1929 Philadelphia AL 4, Chicago NL 1	1969 New York NL 4, Baltimore AL 1	2010 San Francisco NL 4, Texas AL 1
1930 Philadelphia AL 4, St. Louis NL 2	1970 Baltimore AL 4, Cincinnati NL 1	2011 St. Louis NL 4, Texas AL 3
1931 St. Louis NL 4, Philadelphia AL 3	1971 Pittsburgh NL 4, Baltimore AL 3	2012 San Francisco NL 4, Detroit AL 0
1932 New York AL 4, Chicago NL 0	1972 Oakland AL 4, Cincinnati NL 3	2013 Boston AL 4, St. Louis NL 2
1933 New York NL 4, Washington AL 1	1973 Oakland AL 4, New York NL 3	2014 San Fran. NL 4, Kansas City AL 3
1934 St. Louis NL 4, Detroit AL 3	1974 Oakland AL 4, Los Angeles NL 1	2015 Kansas City AL 4, New York NL 1
1935 Detroit AL 4, Chicago NL 2	1975 Cincinnati NL 4, Boston AL 3	2016 Chicago NL 4, Cleveland AL 3
1936 New York AL 4, New York NL 2	1976 Cincinnati NL 4, New York AL 0	2017 Houston AL 4, Los Angeles NL 3
1937 New York AL 4, New York NL 1	1977 New York AL 4, Los Angeles NL 2	2018 Boston AL 4, Los Angeles NL 1
1938 New York AL 4, Chicago NL 0	1978 New York AL 4, Los Angeles NL 2	2019 Washington NL 4, Houston AL 3
1939 New York AL 4, Cincinnati NL 0	1979 Pittsburgh NL 4, Baltimore AL 3	2020 Los Angeles NL 4, Tampa Bay AL 2
1940 Cincinnati NL 4, Detroit AL 3	1980 Philadelphia NL 4, Kansas City AL 2	2021 Atlanta NL 4, Houston AL 2
1941 New York AL 4, Brooklyn NL 1	1981 Los Angeles NL 4, New York AL 2	2022 Houston AL 4, Philadelphia NL 2
1942 St. Louis NL 4, New York AL 1	1982 St. Louis NL 4, Milwaukee AL 3	2023 Texas AL 4, Arizona NL 1

World Series Most Valuable Player, 1955-2023

Year	Player, position, team	Year	Player, position, team	Year	Player, position, team
1955	Johnny Podres, P, Brooklyn	1979	Willie Stargell, 1B, Pittsburgh	2002	Troy Glaus, 3B, Anaheim
1956	Don Larsen, P, NY (AL)	1980	Mike Schmidt, 3B, Philadelphia	2003	Josh Beckett, P, Florida
1957	Lew Burdette, P, Milwaukee (NL)	1981	Ron Cey, 3B, Los Angeles (NL);	2004	Manny Ramirez, OF, Boston
1958	Bob Turley, P, NY (AL)		Pedro Guerrero, OF, Los Angeles;	2005	Jermaine Dye, OF, Chicago (AL)
1959	Larry Sherry, P, Los Angeles (NL)		Steve Yeager, C, Los Angeles	2006	David Eckstein, SS, St. Louis
1960[1]	Bobby Richardson, 2B, NY (AL)	1982	Darrell Porter, C, St. Louis	2007	Mike Lowell, 3B, Boston
1961	Whitey Ford, P, NY (AL)	1983	Rick Dempsey, C, Baltimore	2008	Cole Hamels, P, Philadelphia
1962	Ralph Terry, P, NY (AL)	1984	Alan Trammell, SS, Detroit	2009	Hideki Matsui, DH, NY (AL)
1963	Sandy Koufax, P, Los Angeles (NL)	1985	Bret Saberhagen, P, Kansas City	2010	Edgar Renteria, SS, San Francisco
1964	Bob Gibson, P, St. Louis	1986	Ray Knight, 3B, NY (NL)	2011	David Freese, 3B, St. Louis
1965	Sandy Koufax, P, Los Angeles (NL)	1987	Frank Viola, P, Minnesota	2012	Pablo Sandoval, 3B, San Francisco
1966	Frank Robinson, OF, Baltimore	1988	Orel Hershiser, P, Los Angeles (NL)	2013	David Ortiz, DH, Boston
1967	Bob Gibson, P, St. Louis	1989	Dave Stewart, P, Oakland	2014	Madison Bumgarner, P, San Francisco
1968	Mickey Lolich, P, Detroit	1990	José Rijo, P, Cincinnati	2015	Salvador Pérez, C, Kansas City
1969	Donn Clendenon, 1B, NY (NL)	1991	Jack Morris, P, Minnesota	2016	Ben Zobrist, OF, Chicago (NL)
1970	Brooks Robinson, 3B, Baltimore	1992	Pat Borders, C, Toronto	2017	George Springer, OF, Houston
1971	Roberto Clemente, OF, Pittsburgh	1993	Paul Molitor, DH, Toronto	2018	Steve Pearce, 1B, Boston
1972	Gene Tenace, C, Oakland	1995	Tom Glavine, P, Atlanta	2019	Stephen Strasburg, P, Washington
1973	Reggie Jackson, OF, Oakland	1996	John Wetteland, P, NY (AL)	2020	Corey Seager, SS, Los Angeles (NL)
1974	Rollie Fingers, P, Oakland	1997	Livan Hernandez, P, Florida	2021	Jorge Soler, OF, Atlanta
1975	Pete Rose, 3B, Cincinnati	1998	Scott Brosius, 3B, NY (AL)	2022	Jeremy Peña, SS, Houston
1976	Johnny Bench, C, Cincinnati	1999	Mariano Rivera, P, NY (AL)	2023	Corey Seager, SS, Texas
1977	Reggie Jackson, OF, NY (AL)	2000	Derek Jeter, SS, NY (AL)		
1978	Bucky Dent, SS, NY (AL)	2001	Curt Schilling, P, Arizona;		
			Randy Johnson, P, Arizona		

World Series Won-Lost Records, by Franchise

Since beginning of "modern" era in 1901. Figures represent overall Series wins, not individual games.

Team	Wins	Losses	Team	Wins	Losses
New York Yankees	27	13	Toronto Blue Jays	2	0
St. Louis Cardinals	11	8	Kansas City Royals	2	2
Boston Red Sox	9	4	Houston Astros	2	3
Philadelphia/Kansas City/Oakland A's	9	5	New York Mets	2	3
New York/San Francisco Giants	8	12	Cleveland Indians/Guardians	2	4
Brooklyn/Los Angeles Dodgers	7	14	Philadelphia Phillies	2	6
Pittsburgh Pirates	5	2	L.A./California/Anaheim/L.A. Angels	1	0
Cincinnati Reds	5	4	Montréal Expos/Washington Nationals	1	0
Boston/Milwaukee/Atlanta Braves	4	6	Arizona Diamondbacks	1	1
Detroit Tigers	4	7	Texas Rangers	1	1
Chicago White Sox	3	2	Colorado Rockies	0	1
Washington Senators/Minnesota Twins	3	3	Seattle Pilots/Milwaukee Brewers	0	1
St. Louis Browns/Baltimore Orioles	3	4	San Diego Padres	0	2
Chicago Cubs	3	8	Tampa Bay Rays	0	2
Florida/Miami Marlins	2	0	Seattle Mariners	0	0

All-Time World Series Career Leaders

(through 2023)

World Series Batting Leaders

Batter (min. 50 PA)	H	AB	AVG	Batter (min. 50 PA)	H	AB	AVG
1. David Ortiz	20	44	.455	6. Hal McRae	18	45	.400
2. Pablo Sandoval	20	47	.426	7. Lou Brock	34	87	.391
3. Johnny "Pepper" Martin	23	55	.418	8. Marquis Grissom	30	77	.390
4. Paul Molitor[1]	23	55	.418	9. Thurman Munson	25	67	.373
5. Lance Berkman	16	39	.410	10. George Brett	19	51	.373

Games Played

Yogi Berra	75
Mickey Mantle	65
Elston Howard	54
Hank Bauer	53
Gil McDougald	53
Phil Rizzuto	52
Joe DiMaggio	51
Frankie Frisch	50
Pee Wee Reese	44
Roger Maris	41
Babe Ruth	41

Hits

Yogi Berra	71
Mickey Mantle	59
Frankie Frisch	58
Joe DiMaggio	54
Derek Jeter	50
Hank Bauer	46
Pee Wee Reese	46
Gil McDougald	45
Phil Rizzuto	45
Lou Gehrig	43

Runs

Mickey Mantle	42
Yogi Berra	41
Babe Ruth	37
Derek Jeter	32
Lou Gehrig	30
Joe DiMaggio	27
Roger Maris	26
Elston Howard	25
Gil McDougald	23
Jackie Robinson	22

Runs Batted In

Mickey Mantle	40
Yogi Berra	39
Lou Gehrig	35
Babe Ruth	33
Joe DiMaggio	30
Bill Skowron	29
Duke Snider	26

Home Runs

Mickey Mantle	18
Babe Ruth	15
Yogi Berra	12
Duke Snider	11
Lou Gehrig	10
Reggie Jackson	10
Joe DiMaggio	8
Frank Robinson	8
Bill Skowron	8

Stolen Bases

Lou Brock	14
Eddie Collins	14
Dave Lopes	10
Phil Rizzuto	10
Frank Chance	9
Frankie Frisch	9
Kenny Lofton	9
Honus Wagner	9

(1) Some records show Molitor with 22 career World Series hits (.400 AVG).

World Series Pitching Leaders

Games Pitched		Wins		Strikeouts		Saves	
Mariano Rivera	24	Whitey Ford	10	Whitey Ford	94	Mariano Rivera	11
Whitey Ford	22	Bob Gibson	7	Bob Gibson	92	Rollie Fingers	6
Mike Stanton	20	Allie Reynolds	7	Allie Reynolds	62	Johnny Murphy	4
Rollie Fingers	16	Red Ruffing	7	Sandy Koufax	61	Robb Nen	4
Ryan Madson	16	Chief Bender	6	Red Ruffing	61	Allie Reynolds	4
Jeff Nelson	16	Lefty Gomez	6	Chief Bender	59	John Wetteland	4
Allie Reynolds	15	Waite Hoyt	6	George Earnshaw	56	Roy Face	3
Bob Turley	15	Three Finger Brown	5	Andy Pettitte	56	Neftali Feliz	3
Clay Carroll	14	Jack Coombs	5	John Smoltz	56	Firpo Marberry	3
Clem Labine	13	Catfish Hunter	5	Justin Verlander	50	Will McEnaney	3
Andy Pettitte	13	Christy Mathewson	5	Roger Clemens	49	Tug McGraw	3
Mark Wohlers	13	Herb Pennock	5	Waite Hoyt	49	Jonathan Papelbon	3
Jeremy Affeldt	12	Andy Pettitte	5	Christy Mathewson	48	Herb Pennock	3
Waite Hoyt	12	Vic Raschi	5	Bob Turley	46	Troy Percival	3
Catfish Hunter	12					Sergio Romo	3
Art Nehf	12					Kent Tekulve	3
Ryan Pressly	12					Todd Worrell	3

MLB Stadiums, 2023

Team	Stadium (year opened)	Surface	Distances (ft) LF	Center	RF	Seating capacity[1]
Arizona Diamondbacks	Chase Field (1998)	Turf	330	407	335	48,330
Atlanta Braves	Truist Park (2017)	Grass	335	400	325	41,184
Chicago Cubs	Wrigley Field (1914)	Grass	355	400	353	41,649
Cincinnati Reds	Great American Ball Park (2003)	Grass	328	404	325	42,271
Colorado Rockies	Coors Field (1995)	Grass	347	415	350	46,896
Los Angeles Dodgers	Dodger Stadium (1962)	Grass	330	395	330	56,000
Miami Marlins	loanDepot Park (2012)	Turf	344	400	335	37,446
Milwaukee Brewers	American Family Field (2001)	Grass	342	400	345	41,700
New York Mets	Citi Field (2009)	Grass	335	408	330	41,922
Philadelphia Phillies	Citizens Bank Park (2004)	Grass	329	401	330	42,901
Pittsburgh Pirates	PNC Park (2001)	Grass	325	399	320	38,075
St. Louis Cardinals	Busch Stadium (2006)	Grass	336	400	335	44,158
San Diego Padres	Petco Park (2004)	Grass	336	396	322	39,909
San Francisco Giants	Oracle Park (2000)	Grass	339	404	309	42,300
Washington Nationals	Nationals Park (2008)	Grass	336	402	335	41,373
Baltimore Orioles	Oriole Park at Camden Yards (1992)	Grass	333	410	318	44,487
Boston Red Sox	Fenway Park (1912)	Grass	310	390	302	37,105[2]
Chicago White Sox	Guaranteed Rate Field (1991)	Grass	330	400	335	40,615
Cleveland Guardians	Progressive Field (1994)	Grass	325	400	325	34,830
Detroit Tigers	Comerica Park (2000)	Grass	342	412	330	40,988
Houston Astros	Minute Maid Park (2000)	Grass	315	409	326	41,000
Kansas City Royals	Kauffman Stadium (1973)	Grass	330	410	330	37,903
Los Angeles Angels	Angel Stadium of Anaheim (1966)	Grass	347	396	348	45,517
Minnesota Twins	Target Field (2010)	Grass	339	404	328	38,544
New York Yankees	Yankee Stadium (2009)	Grass	318	408	314	46,537
Oakland Athletics	Oakland-Alameda County Coliseum (1966)	Grass	330	400	330	46,847
Seattle Mariners	T-Mobile Park (1999)	Grass	331	401	326	47,349
Tampa Bay Rays	Tropicana Field (1990)	Turf	315	404	322	25,025
Texas Rangers	Globe Life Field (2020)	Turf	329	407	326	40,300
Toronto Blue Jays[3]	Rogers Centre (1989)	Astroturf	328	400	328	41,500

(1) As of 2023 season. (2) For day games; night game capacity is 37,535.

Major League Franchise Shifts and Additions

1953: Boston Braves (NL) became Milwaukee Braves.

1954: St. Louis Browns (AL) became Baltimore Orioles.

1955: Philadelphia Athletics (AL) became Kansas City Athletics.

1958: New York Giants (NL) became San Francisco Giants.

1958: Brooklyn Dodgers (NL) became L.A. Dodgers.

1961: Washington Senators (AL) became Minnesota Twins.

1961: L.A. Angels enfranchised by the AL.

1961: Washington Senators II enfranchised by the AL, replacing Washington Senators I, whose franchise moved to Minneapolis-St. Paul and became Minnesota Twins.

1962: Houston Colt .45s enfranchised by the NL.

1962: New York Mets enfranchised by the NL.

1966: Milwaukee Braves (NL) became Atlanta Braves.

1968: Kansas City Athletics (AL) became Oakland Athletics.

1969: Kansas City Royals and Seattle Pilots enfranchised by the AL; Montréal Expos and San Diego Padres enfranchised by the NL.

1970: Seattle Pilots (AL) became Milwaukee Brewers.

1972: Washington Senators II (AL) became Texas Rangers (Dallas-Fort Worth area).

1977: Toronto Blue Jays and Seattle Mariners enfranchised by the AL.

1993: Colorado Rockies (Denver) and Florida Marlins (Miami) enfranchised by the NL.

1998: Tampa Bay Devil Rays began play in the AL; Arizona Diamondbacks (Phoenix) began play in the NL (both teams enfranchised in 1995). Milwaukee Brewers moved from the AL to the NL.

2005: Montréal Expos (NL) became Washington Nationals.

2013: Houston Astros moved from the NL to the AL.

National Baseball Hall of Fame and Museum

Located in Cooperstown, NY. # = Player chosen in first year of eligibility (five seasons after retirement) or earlier.
* = 2023 inductee. www.baseballhall.org

#Aaron, Hank	Davis, George	Hornsby, Rogers	#McCovey, Willie	#Seaver, Tom
Alexander, Grover	Dawson, Andre	Hoyt, Waite	McGinnity, Joe	Selee, Frank
Alomar, Roberto	Day, Leon	Hubbard, Cal	McGowan, Bill	Selig, Bud
Alston, Walt	Dean, Jay Hanna "Dizzy"	Hubbell, Carl	McGraw, John	Sewell, Joe
Anderson, George	Delahanty, Ed	Huggins, Miller	*McGriff, Fred	Simmons, Al
Anson, Cap	Dickey, Bill	Hulbert, William	McKechnie, Bill	Simmons, Ted
Aparicio, Luis	Dihigo, Martín	Hunter, James "Catfish"	McPhee, John "Bid"	Sisler, George
Appling, Luke	#DiMaggio, Joe	Irvin, Monte	Medwick, Joe	Slaughter, Enos
Ashburn, Richie	#Doby, Larry	#Jackson, Reggie	Mendez, Jose	Smith, Hilton
Averill, Earl	Doerr, Bobby	Jackson, Travis	Miller, Marvin	Smith, Lee
Bagwell, Jeff	Dreyfuss, Barney	Jenkins, Ferguson	#Smith, Ozzie	#Smith, Ozzie
Baines, Harold	Drysdale, Don	Jennings, Hugh	Miñoso, Minnie	#Smoltz, John
Baker, Frank "Home Run"	Duffy, Hugh	#Jeter, Derek	Mize, Johnny	Snider, Duke
Bancroft, Dave	Durocher, Leo	Miller, Mark	#Molitor, Paul	Southworth, Billy
#Banks, Ernie	#Eckersley, Dennis	Simmons, Ted	#Morgan, Joe	#Spahn, Warren
Barlick, Al	Evans, Billy	Walker, Larry	Morris, Jack	Spalding, Albert
Barrow, Edward G.	Evers, John	#Jeter, Derek	#Murray, Eddie	Speaker, Tris
Beckley, Jake	Ewing, Buck	Johnson, Byron "Ban"	#Musial, Stan	#Stargell, Willie
Bell, James "Cool Papa"	Faber, Urban "Red"	Johnson, Walter[1]	Mussina, Mike	Stearnes, Norman
#Bench, Johnny	#Feller, Bob	Johnson, William "Judy"	Newhouser, Hal	Stengel, Casey
Bender, Charles "Chief"	Ferrell, Rick	#Jones, Chipper	Nichols, Kid	Sutter, Bruce
Berra, Lawrence "Yogi"	Fingers, Rollie	Joss, Addie	Niekro, Phil	Suttles, George "Mule"
Biggio, Craig	Fisk, Carlton	Kaat, Jim	O'Day, Hank	Sutton, Don
Blyleven, Bert	Flick, Elmer H.	#Kaline, Al	Oliva, Tony	Taylor, Ben
#Boggs, Wade	Ford, Whitey	Keefe, Timothy	O'Malley, Walter	Terry, Bill
Bottomley, Jim	Foster, Andrew "Rube"	Keeler, William	O'Neil, John "Buck"	#Thomas, Frank
Boudreau, Lou	Foster, Bill	Kell, George	O'Rourke, Jim	#Thome, Jim
Bresnahan, Roger	Fowler, Bud (born John	Kelley, Joe	#Ortiz, David	Thompson, Sam
#Brett, George	W. Jackson)	Kelly, George	Ott, Mel	Tinker, Joe
#Brock, Lou	Fox, Nellie	Kelly, King	Paige, Satchel	Torre, Joe
Brouthers, Dan	Foxx, Jimmie	Killebrew, Harmon	#Palmer, Jim	Torriente, Cristobal
Brown, Mordecai	Frick, Ford	Kiner, Ralph	Pennock, Herb	Trammell, Alan
Brown, Ray	Frisch, Frank	Klein, Chuck	Perez, Tony	Traynor, Harold J. "Pie"
Brown, Willard	Galvin, James "Pud"	Klem, Bill	Perry, Gaylord	Vance, Arthur "Dazzy"
Bulkeley, Morgan C.	#Gehrig, Lou	#Koufax, Sandy	Piazza, Mike	Vaughan, Joseph "Arky"
Bunning, Jim	Gehringer, Charles	Kuhn, Bowie	Plank, Ed	Veeck, Bill
Burkett, Jesse C.	#Gibson, Bob	La Russa, Tony	Pompez, Alex	Waddell, Rube
Campanella, Roy	Gibson, Josh	Lajoie, Nap	Posey, Cum(berland)	Wagner, Honus[1]
#Carew, Rod	Giles, Warren	Landis, Kenesaw M.	#Puckett, Kirby	Walker, Larry
Carey, Max	Gillick, Pat	Larkin, Barry	Radbourn, Charlie	Wallace, Roderick
#Carlton, Steve	#Glavine, Tom	Lasorda, Tommy	Raines, Tim	Walsh, Ed
Carter, Gary	Gomez, Lefty	Lazzeri, Tony	Reese, Pee Wee	Waner, Lloyd
Cartwright, Alexander	Gordon, Joe	Lemon, Bob	Rice, Jim	Waner, Paul
Cepeda, Orlando	Goslin, Leon "Goose"	Leonard, Buck	Rice, Sam	Ward, John
Chadwick, Henry	Gossage, Rich	Lindstrom, Fred	Rickey, Branch	Weaver, Earl
Chance, Frank	Grant, Frank	Lloyd, Pop	#Ripken, Cal, Jr.	Weiss, George
Chandler, Albert "Happy"	Greenberg, Hank	Lombardi, Ernie	#Rivera, Mariano	Welch, Mickey
Charleston, Oscar	#Griffey, Ken, Jr.	Lopez, Al	Rixey, Eppa	Wells, Willie
Chesbro, John	Griffith, Clark	Lyons, Ted	Rizzuto, Phil "Scooter"	Wheat, Zach
Chylak, Nestor	Grimes, Burleigh	Mack, Connie	Roberts, Robin	White, Deacon
Clarke, Fred	Grove, Lefty	Mackey, James "Biz"	#Robinson, Brooks	White, Sol
Clarkson, John	Guerrero, Vladimir	MacPhail, Larry	#Robinson, Frank	Wilhelm, Hoyt
#Clemente, Roberto	#Gwynn, Tony	MacPhail, Lee	#Robinson, Jackie	Wilkinson, J. L.
Cobb, Ty[1]	Hafey, Charles "Chick"	#Maddux, Greg	Robinson, Wilbert	Williams, Billy
Cochrane, Mickey	Haines, Jesse	Manley, Effa	#Rodríguez, Iván	Williams, Dick
Collins, Eddie	#Halladay, Roy	#Mantle, Mickey	Rogan, Joe "Bullet"	Williams, Joe
Collins, James	Hamilton, Bill	Manush, Henry	*Rolen, Scott	#Williams, Ted
Combs, Earle	Hanlon, Ned	Maranville, Walter	Roush, Edd	Willis, Vic
Comiskey, Charles A.	Harridge, Will	Marichal, Juan	Ruffing, Red	Wilson, Hack
Conlan, John "Jocko"	Harris, Bucky	Marquard, Rube	Ruppert, Jacob	Wilson, Jud
Connolly, Thomas H.	Hartnett, Gabby	Martinez, Edgar	Rusie, Amos	#Winfield, Dave
Connor, Roger	Harvey, Doug	#Martinez, Pedro	Ruth, Babe[1]	Wright, George
Cooper, Andy	Heilmann, Harry	Mathews, Eddie	#Ryan, Nolan	Wright, Harry
Coveleski, Stan	#Henderson, Rickey	Mathewson, Christy[1]	Sandberg, Ryne	Wynn, Early
Cox, Bobby	Herman, Billy	#Mays, Willie	Santo, Ron	#Yastrzemski, Carl
Crawford, Sam	Herzog, Whitey	Mazeroski, Bill	Santop, Louis	Yawkey, Tom
Cronin, Joe	Hill, Pete	McCarthy, Joe	Schalk, Ray	Young, Cy
Cummings, W. A. "Candy"	Hodges, Gil	McCarthy, Thomas	#Schmidt, Mike	Youngs, Ross
Cuyler, Hazen "Kiki"	Hoffman, Trevor		Schoendienst, Red	#Yount, Robin
Dandridge, Ray	Hooper, Harry		Schuerholz, John	

(1) Player inducted in 1936, the year of the first Hall of Fame election.

World Baseball Classic Results, 2006-23

Year	Champion	Runner-up	Final score	Final game location	Third place team
2006	Japan	Cuba	10-6	Petco Park, San Diego, CA	South Korea
2009	Japan	South Korea	5-3 (10)	Dodger Stadium, Los Angeles, CA	U.S.
2013	Dominican Republic	Puerto Rico	3-0	AT&T Park, San Francisco, CA	Netherlands
2017	U.S.	Puerto Rico	8-0	Dodger Stadium, Los Angeles, CA	Japan
2023	Japan	U.S.	3-2	loanDepot Park, Miami, FL	Mexico

BASKETBALL

Denver Raises 2023 NBA Championship Trophy a Mile High

The Denver Nuggets June 12, 2023, claimed their first NBA title with a 94-89 win in Game 5 of the NBA Finals against the Miami Heat at Ball Arena in Denver. Nikola Jokić, MVP of both the Western Conference Finals and NBA Finals, became the first player to lead the NBA in points (600), rebounds (269), and assists (190) in one postseason. Fifty-six years after coming into existence as an original American Basketball Association franchise—originally called the Rockets—Denver had not been to the Finals since the last year of the ABA in 1976, when they fell to the New York Nets. The 2023 Nuggets joined the San Antonio Spurs as the only other former ABA team to win the NBA title.

Jokić averaged 30.2 points in the Finals, including 41 points in Game 2, the only game the Nuggets lost. Denver exceeded 100 points in each of the first four games before being held to 94 points in Game 5. Jokić carried Denver over the hump, recording 28 points and 16 rebounds in the clincher for head coach Michael Malone's club.

Miami made a run from No. 8 seed to the NBA Finals after a record-setting perfect night in Jan.: The Heat's last free throw Jan. 10 broke a record held by the Utah Jazz since 1982, as Miami went a perfect 40-for-40 from the free throw line against Oklahoma City.

LeBron James of the L.A. Lakers on Feb. 7, 2023, became the NBA's all-time leading scorer, surpassing the 38,387 points by Kareem Abdul-Jabbar, who had held the scoring record since 1984. James ended the season with 38,652 points.

In a first for the NBA, a uniform number was retired throughout the league. Bill Russell's number 6 was honored on every uniform and court following the Boston center and 11-time champion's death at 88 before the season began. (LeBron James and the league's other players already wearing number 6 could continue to, but no new players will.)

For the first time in 22 years, no NBA team won 60 games, but Detroit lost 65, and two teams in the same division—San Antonio and Houston—each lost 60. The Milwaukee Bucks had the most wins with 58. The NBA resumed hosting international games, with contests in both Mexico City and Paris.

Philadelphia's Joel Embiid earned league MVP. A year after the Cameroon-born Embiid became the first foreign-born player to win a scoring title, he pulled off that feat again and increased his scoring by 2.5 points per game to 33.1. Jaren Jackson Jr. of Memphis was named top Defensive Player, 2022 first overall draft pick Paolo Banchero of Orlando was the NBA's Rookie of the Year, and Boston's Malcolm Brogdon was Sixth Man. The first NBA Clutch Player of the Year (the Jerry West Trophy) went to Sacramento's De'Aaron Fox.

Sacramento's first-year head coach Mike Brown took his second Coach of the Year Award (he won in 2009 in Cleveland); his boss, Kings GM Monte McNair, was named Executive of the Year. The high-flying Kings, the NBA's top scoring team, averaging 120.7 points per game, also won the second highest-scoring NBA game ever: a 176-175 double overtime win over the Clippers on Feb. 24.

NBA Final Standings, 2022-23

Teams with the 7th-10th highest winning percentages in each conference qualified for a play-in tournament held Apr. 11-14, 2023. (playoff seeding in parentheses)

Eastern Conference

Atlantic Division

	W	L	PCT	GB
Boston Celtics (2)	57	25	0.695	—
Philadelphia 76ers (3)	54	28	0.659	3
NY Knicks (5)	47	35	0.573	10
Brooklyn Nets (6)	45	37	0.549	12
Toronto Raptors (9)	41	41	0.500	16

Central Division

	W	L	PCT	GB
Milwaukee Bucks (1)	58	24	0.707	—
Cleveland Cavaliers (4)	51	31	0.622	7
Chicago Bulls (10)	40	42	0.488	18
Indiana Pacers	35	47	0.427	23
Detroit Pistons	17	65	0.207	41

Southeast Division

	W	L	PCT	GB
Miami Heat (8)	44	38	0.537	—
Atlanta Hawks (7)	41	41	0.500	3
Washington Wizards	35	47	0.427	9
Orlando Magic	34	48	0.415	10
Charlotte Hornets	27	55	0.329	17

Western Conference

Northwest Division

	W	L	PCT	GB
Denver Nuggets (1)	53	29	0.646	—
Minnesota Timberwolves (8)	42	40	0.512	11
Oklahoma City Thunder (10)	40	42	0.488	13
Utah Jazz	37	45	0.451	16
Portland Trail Blazers	33	49	0.402	20

Pacific Division

	W	L	PCT	GB
Sacramento Kings (3)	48	34	0.585	—
Phoenix Suns (4)	45	37	0.549	3
L.A. Clippers (5)	44	38	0.537	4
Golden State Warriors (6)	44	38	0.537	4
L.A. Lakers (7)	43	39	0.524	5

Southwest Division

	W	L	PCT	GB
Memphis Grizzlies (2)	51	31	0.622	—
New Orleans Pelicans (9)	42	40	0.512	9
Dallas Mavericks	38	44	0.463	13
Houston Rockets	22	60	0.268	29
San Antonio Spurs	22	60	0.268	29

NBA Playoff Results, 2023

Eastern Conference

Boston defeated Atlanta, 4 games to 2
Miami defeated Milwaukee, 4 games to 1
New York defeated Cleveland, 4 games to 1
Philadelphia defeated Brooklyn, 4 games to 0
Boston defeated Philadelphia, 4 games to 3
Miami defeated New York, 4 games to 2
Miami defeated Boston, 4 games to 3

Western Conference

Phoenix defeated L.A. Clippers, 4 games to 1
L.A. Lakers defeated Memphis, 4 games to 2
Golden State defeated Sacramento, 4 games to 3
Denver defeated Minnesota, 4 games to 1
L.A. Lakers defeated Golden State, 4 games to 2
Denver defeated Phoenix, 4 games to 2
Denver defeated L.A. Lakers, 4 games to 0

NBA Finals

Denver defeated Miami, 4 games to 1 (104-93, 108-111, 109-94, 108-95, 94-89)

NBA Regular Season Individual Highs, 2022-23

Minutes, game: 55, Immanuel Quickley, Boston v. New York, Mar. 5 (2 OT)

Points, game: 71, Donovan Mitchell, Cleveland v. Chicago, Jan. 2 (OT); Damian Lillard, Portland v. Houston, Feb 26

Field goals, game: 22, Anthony Davis, L.A. Lakers v. Washington, Dec. 4; Donovan Mitchell, Cleveland v. Chicago, Jan. 2 (OT); Damian Lillard, Portland v. Houston, Feb. 26

Field goal attempts, game: 39, Giannis Antetokounmpo, Milwaukee v. Chicago, Dec. 28 (OT); Klay Thompson, Golden State v. Atlanta, Jan. 2; Antetokounmpo, Milwaukee v. L.A. Clippers, Feb. 2

3-pointers, game: 13, Damian Lillard, Portland v. Houston, Feb. 26

3-point attempts, game: 22, Damian Lillard, Portland v. Houston, Feb. 26

Free throws, game: 23, Jimmy Butler, Miami v. Oklahoma City, Jan. 10

Free throw attempts, game: 28, Jerami Grant, Portland v. New York, Nov. 25 (OT)

Rebounds, game: 29, Ivica Zubac, L.A. Clippers v. Indiana, Nov. 27

Assists, game: 21, James Harden, Philadelphia v. L.A. Clippers, Dec. 23

Steals, game: 7, D'Angelo Russell, Minnesota v. L.A. Lakers, Oct. 28; DeAnthony Melton, Philadelphia v. L.A. Lakers, Dec. 9 (OT)

Blocks, game: 9, Brook Lopez, Milwaukee v. Brooklyn, Mar. 9

Minutes played, season: 2,963, Mikal Bridges, Phoenix-Brooklyn

Off. rebounds, season: 274, Kevon Looney, Golden State

Def. rebounds, season: 744, Nikola Vučević, Chicago

Personal fouls, season: 279, Domantas Sabonis, Sacramento

NBA Finals MVP, 1969-2023

Year	Player, team	Year	Player, team	Year	Player, team
1969	Jerry West, L.A. Lakers	1987	Magic Johnson, L.A. Lakers	2006	Dwyane Wade, Miami
1970	Willis Reed, New York	1988	James Worthy, L.A. Lakers	2007	Tony Parker, San Antonio
1971	Lew Alcindor (Kareem Abdul-Jabbar), Milwaukee	1989	Joe Dumars, Detroit	2008	Paul Pierce, Boston
		1990	Isiah Thomas, Detroit	2009	Kobe Bryant, L.A. Lakers
1972	Wilt Chamberlain, L.A. Lakers	1991	Michael Jordan, Chicago	2010	Kobe Bryant, L.A. Lakers
1973	Willis Reed, New York	1992	Michael Jordan, Chicago	2011	Dirk Nowitzki, Dallas
1974	John Havlicek, Boston	1993	Michael Jordan, Chicago	2012	LeBron James, Miami
1975	Rick Barry, Golden State	1994	Hakeem Olajuwon, Houston	2013	LeBron James, Miami
1976	Jo Jo White, Boston	1995	Hakeem Olajuwon, Houston	2014	Kawhi Leonard, San Antonio
1977	Bill Walton, Portland	1996	Michael Jordan, Chicago	2015	Andre Iguodala, Golden State
1978	Wes Unseld, Washington	1997	Michael Jordan, Chicago	2016	LeBron James, Cleveland
1979	Dennis Johnson, Seattle	1998	Michael Jordan, Chicago	2017	Kevin Durant, Golden State
1980	Magic Johnson, L.A. Lakers	1999	Tim Duncan, San Antonio	2018	Kevin Durant, Golden State
1981	Cedric Maxwell, Boston	2000	Shaquille O'Neal, L.A. Lakers	2019	Kawhi Leonard, Toronto
1982	Magic Johnson, L.A. Lakers	2001	Shaquille O'Neal, L.A. Lakers	2020	LeBron James, L.A. Lakers
1983	Moses Malone, Philadelphia	2002	Shaquille O'Neal, L.A. Lakers	2021	Giannis Antetokounmpo, Milwaukee
1984	Larry Bird, Boston	2003	Tim Duncan, San Antonio	2022	Stephen Curry, Golden State
1985	Kareem Abdul-Jabbar, L.A. Lakers	2004	Chauncey Billups, Detroit	2023	Nikola Jokić, Denver
1986	Larry Bird, Boston	2005	Tim Duncan, San Antonio		

NBA Finals All-Time Statistical Leaders

(* = Active in 2022-23 season; minimum 10 games played.)

Scoring average	GP	FG	FT	PTS	AVG	Scoring average	GP	FG	FT	PTS	AVG
Rick Barry	10	138	87	363	36.3	Bob Pettit	25	241	227	709	28.4
Michael Jordan	35	438	258	1,176	33.6	*LeBron James	55	588	285	1,562	28.4
Jerry West	55	612	455	1,679	30.5	*Kyrie Irving	13	140	50	360	27.7
*Kevin Durant	15	160	92	455	30.3	Hakeem Olajuwon	17	187	91	467	27.5
Shaquille O'Neal	30	340	185	865	28.8	*Stephen Curry	34	300	176	928	27.3

Games Played

Bill Russell	70
Sam Jones	64
Kareem Abdul-Jabbar	56
Jerry West	55
*LeBron James	55

Points

Jerry West	1,679
*LeBron James	1,562
Kareem Abdul-Jabbar	1,317
Michael Jordan	1,176
Elgin Baylor	1,161

Rebounds

Bill Russell	1,718
Wilt Chamberlain	862
Elgin Baylor	593
*LeBron James	561
Kareem Abdul-Jabbar	507

Assists

Magic Johnson	584
*LeBron James	430
Jerry West	306
Bill Russell	265
Bob Cousy	239

NBA Most Valuable Player, 1956-2023

Year	Player, team	Year	Player, team	Year	Player, team
1956	Bob Pettit, St. Louis	1979	Moses Malone, Houston	2002	Tim Duncan, San Antonio
1957	Bob Cousy, Boston	1980	Kareem Abdul-Jabbar, L.A. Lakers	2003	Tim Duncan, San Antonio
1958	Bill Russell, Boston	1981	Julius Erving, Philadelphia	2004	Kevin Garnett, Minnesota
1959	Bob Pettit, St. Louis	1982	Moses Malone, Houston	2005	Steve Nash, Phoenix
1960	Wilt Chamberlain, Philadelphia	1983	Moses Malone, Philadelphia	2006	Steve Nash, Phoenix
1961	Bill Russell, Boston	1984	Larry Bird, Boston	2007	Dirk Nowitzki, Dallas
1962	Bill Russell, Boston	1985	Larry Bird, Boston	2008	Kobe Bryant, L.A. Lakers
1963	Bill Russell, Boston	1986	Larry Bird, Boston	2009	LeBron James, Cleveland
1964	Oscar Robertson, Cincinnati	1987	Magic Johnson, L.A. Lakers	2010	LeBron James, Cleveland
1965	Bill Russell, Boston	1988	Michael Jordan, Chicago	2011	Derrick Rose, Chicago
1966	Wilt Chamberlain, Philadelphia	1989	Magic Johnson, L.A. Lakers	2012	LeBron James, Miami
1967	Wilt Chamberlain, Philadelphia	1990	Magic Johnson, L.A. Lakers	2013	LeBron James, Miami
1968	Wilt Chamberlain, Philadelphia	1991	Michael Jordan, Chicago	2014	Kevin Durant, Oklahoma City
1969	Wes Unseld, Baltimore	1992	Michael Jordan, Chicago	2015	Stephen Curry, Golden State
1970	Willis Reed, New York	1993	Charles Barkley, Phoenix	2016	Stephen Curry, Golden State
1971	Lew Alcindor (Abdul-Jabbar), Milw.	1994	Hakeem Olajuwon, Houston	2017	Russell Westbrook, Oklahoma City
1972	Kareem Abdul-Jabbar, Milwaukee	1995	David Robinson, San Antonio	2018	James Harden, Houston
1973	Dave Cowens, Boston	1996	Michael Jordan, Chicago	2019	Giannis Antetokounmpo, Milwaukee
1974	Kareem Abdul-Jabbar, Milwaukee	1997	Karl Malone, Utah	2020	Giannis Antetokounmpo, Milwaukee
1975	Bob McAdoo, Buffalo	1998	Michael Jordan, Chicago	2021	Nikola Jokić, Denver
1976	Kareem Abdul-Jabbar, L.A. Lakers	1999	Karl Malone, Utah	2022	Nikola Jokić, Denver
1977	Kareem Abdul-Jabbar, L.A. Lakers	2000	Shaquille O'Neal, L.A. Lakers	2023	Joel Embiid, Philadelphia
1978	Bill Walton, Portland	2001	Allen Iverson, Philadelphia		

NBA Scoring Leaders, 1947-2023

(Average points per game; minimum games for eligibility varied.)

Year	Player, team	PTS	AVG	Year	Player, team	PTS	AVG
1947	Joe Fulks, Philadelphia	1,389	23.2	1970	Jerry West, L.A. Lakers	2,309	31.2
1948	Max Zaslofsky, Chicago	1,007	21.0	1971	Lew Alcindor (Kareem Abdul-Jabbar), Milw.	2,596	31.7
1949	George Mikan, Minneapolis	1,698	28.3	1972	Kareem Abdul-Jabbar, Milwaukee	2,822	34.8
1950	George Mikan, Minneapolis	1,865	27.4	1973	Nate Archibald, Kansas City-Omaha	2,719	34.0
1951	George Mikan, Minneapolis	1,932	28.4	1974	Bob McAdoo, Buffalo	2,261	30.6
1952	Paul Arizin, Philadelphia	1,674	25.4	1975	Bob McAdoo, Buffalo	2,831	34.5
1953	Neil Johnston, Philadelphia	1,564	22.3	1976	Bob McAdoo, Buffalo	2,427	31.1
1954	Neil Johnston, Philadelphia	1,759	24.4	1977	Pete Maravich, New Orleans	2,273	31.1
1955	Neil Johnston, Philadelphia	1,631	22.7	1978	George Gervin, San Antonio	2,232	27.2
1956	Bob Pettit, St. Louis	1,849	25.7	1979	George Gervin, San Antonio	2,365	29.6
1957	Paul Arizin, Philadelphia	1,817	25.6	1980	George Gervin, San Antonio	2,585	33.1
1958	George Yardley, Detroit	2,001	27.8	1981	Adrian Dantley, Utah	2,452	30.7
1959	Bob Pettit, St. Louis	2,105	29.2	1982	George Gervin, San Antonio	2,551	32.3
1960	Wilt Chamberlain, Philadelphia	2,707	37.6	1983	Alex English, Denver	2,326	28.4
1961	Wilt Chamberlain, Philadelphia	3,033	38.4	1984	Adrian Dantley, Utah	2,418	30.6
1962	Wilt Chamberlain, Philadelphia	4,029	50.4	1985	Bernard King, New York	1,809	32.9
1963	Wilt Chamberlain, San Francisco	3,586	44.8	1986	Dominique Wilkins, Atlanta	2,366	30.3
1964	Wilt Chamberlain, San Francisco	2,948	36.9	1987	Michael Jordan, Chicago	3,041	37.1
1965	Wilt Chamberlain, San Francisco-Phil.	2,534	34.7	1988	Michael Jordan, Chicago	2,868	35.0
1966	Wilt Chamberlain, Philadelphia	2,649	33.5	1989	Michael Jordan, Chicago	2,633	32.5
1967	Rick Barry, San Francisco	2,775	35.6	1990	Michael Jordan, Chicago	2,753	33.6
1968	Dave Bing, Detroit	2,142	27.1	1991	Michael Jordan, Chicago	2,580	31.5
1969	Elvin Hayes, San Diego	2,327	28.4	1992	Michael Jordan, Chicago	2,404	30.1

Year	Player, team	PTS	AVG
1993	Michael Jordan, Chicago	2,541	32.6
1994	David Robinson, San Antonio	2,383	29.8
1995	Shaquille O'Neal, Orlando	2,315	29.3
1996	Michael Jordan, Chicago	2,491	30.4
1997	Michael Jordan, Chicago	2,431	29.6
1998	Michael Jordan, Chicago	2,357	28.7
1999	Allen Iverson, Philadelphia	1,284	26.8
2000	Shaquille O'Neal, L.A. Lakers	2,344	29.7
2001	Allen Iverson, Philadelphia	2,207	31.1
2002	Allen Iverson, Philadelphia	1,883	31.4
2003	Tracy McGrady, Orlando	2,407	32.1
2004	Tracy McGrady, Orlando	1,878	28.0
2005	Allen Iverson, Philadelphia	2,302	30.7
2006	Kobe Bryant, L.A. Lakers	2,832	35.4
2007	Kobe Bryant, L.A. Lakers	2,430	31.6
2008	LeBron James, Cleveland	2,250	30.0
2009	Dwyane Wade, Miami	2,386	30.2
2010	Kevin Durant, Oklahoma City	2,472	30.1
2011	Kevin Durant, Oklahoma City	2,161	27.7
2012	Kevin Durant, Oklahoma City	1,850	28.0
2013	Carmelo Anthony, New York	1,920	28.7
2014	Kevin Durant, Oklahoma City	2,593	32.0
2015	Russell Westbrook, Oklahoma City	1,886	28.1
2016	Stephen Curry, Golden State	2,375	30.1
2017	Russell Westbrook, Oklahoma City	2,558	31.6
2018	James Harden, Houston	2,191	30.4
2019	James Harden, Houston	2,818	36.1
2020	James Harden, Houston	2,335	34.3
2021	Stephen Curry, Golden State	2,015	32.0
2022	Joel Embiid, Philadelphia	2,079	30.6
2023	Joel Embiid, Philadelphia	2,183	33.1

NBA Champions, 1947-2023

Year	Regular season Eastern champion	Western champion	Playoffs Champion	Winning coach	Opponent
1947	Washington Capitols	Chicago Stags	Philadelphia	Ed Gottlieb	Chicago
1948	Philadelphia Warriors	St. Louis Bombers	Baltimore	Buddy Jeannette	Philadelphia
1949	Washington Capitols	Rochester	Minneapolis	John Kundla	Washington
1950[1]	Syracuse	Indianapolis	Minneapolis	John Kundla	Syracuse
1951	Philadelphia Warriors	Minneapolis	Rochester	Lester Harrison	New York
1952	Syracuse	Rochester	Minneapolis	John Kundla	New York
1953	New York	Minneapolis	Minneapolis	John Kundla	New York
1954	New York	Minneapolis	Minneapolis	John Kundla	Syracuse
1955	Syracuse	Ft. Wayne	Syracuse	Al Cervi	Ft. Wayne
1956	Philadelphia Warriors	Ft. Wayne	Philadelphia	George Senesky	Ft. Wayne
1957	Boston	St. Louis	Boston	Red Auerbach	St. Louis
1958	Boston	St. Louis	St. Louis	Alex Hannum	Boston
1959	Boston	St. Louis	Boston	Red Auerbach	Minneapolis
1960	Boston	St. Louis	Boston	Red Auerbach	St. Louis
1961	Boston	St. Louis	Boston	Red Auerbach	St. Louis
1962	Boston	L.A. Lakers	Boston	Red Auerbach	L.A. Lakers
1963	Boston	L.A. Lakers	Boston	Red Auerbach	L.A. Lakers
1964	Boston	San Francisco	Boston	Red Auerbach	San Francisco
1965	Boston	L.A. Lakers	Boston	Red Auerbach	L.A. Lakers
1966	Philadelphia	San Francisco	Boston	Red Auerbach	L.A. Lakers
1967	Philadelphia	San Francisco	Philadelphia	Alex Hannum	San Francisco
1968	Philadelphia	St. Louis	Boston	Bill Russell	L.A. Lakers
1969	Baltimore	L.A. Lakers	Boston	Bill Russell	L.A. Lakers
1970	New York	Atlanta	New York	Red Holzman	L.A. Lakers

Year	Atlantic	Central	Midwest	Pacific	Champion	Winning coach	Opponent
1971	New York	Baltimore	Milwaukee	L.A. Lakers	Milwaukee	Larry Costello	Baltimore
1972	Boston	Baltimore	Milwaukee	L.A. Lakers	L.A. Lakers	Bill Sharman	New York
1973	Boston	Baltimore	Milwaukee	L.A. Lakers	New York	Red Holzman	L.A. Lakers
1974	Boston	Capital	Milwaukee	L.A. Lakers	Boston	Tom Heinsohn	Milwaukee
1975	Boston	Washington	Chicago	Golden State	Golden State	Al Attles	Washington
1976	Boston	Cleveland	Milwaukee	Golden State	Boston	Tom Heinsohn	Phoenix
1977	Philadelphia	Houston	Denver	L.A. Lakers	Portland	Jack Ramsay	Philadelphia
1978	Philadelphia	San Antonio	Denver	Portland	Washington	Dick Motta	Seattle
1979	Washington	San Antonio	Kansas City	Seattle	Seattle	Len Wilkens	Washington
1980	Boston	Atlanta	Milwaukee	L.A. Lakers	L.A. Lakers	Paul Westhead	Philadelphia
1981	Boston	Milwaukee	San Antonio	Phoenix	Boston	Bill Fitch	Houston
1982	Boston	Milwaukee	San Antonio	L.A. Lakers	L.A. Lakers	Pat Riley	Philadelphia
1983	Philadelphia	Milwaukee	San Antonio	L.A. Lakers	Philadelphia	Billy Cunningham	L.A. Lakers
1984	Boston	Milwaukee	Utah	L.A. Lakers	Boston	K. C. Jones	L.A. Lakers
1985	Boston	Milwaukee	Denver	L.A. Lakers	L.A. Lakers	Pat Riley	Boston
1986	Boston	Milwaukee	Houston	L.A. Lakers	Boston	K. C. Jones	Houston
1987	Boston	Atlanta	Dallas	L.A. Lakers	L.A. Lakers	Pat Riley	Boston
1988	Boston	Detroit	Denver	L.A. Lakers	L.A. Lakers	Pat Riley	Detroit
1989	New York	Detroit	Utah	L.A. Lakers	Detroit	Chuck Daly	L.A. Lakers
1990	Philadelphia	Detroit	San Antonio	L.A. Lakers	Detroit	Chuck Daly	Portland
1991	Boston	Chicago	San Antonio	Portland	Chicago	Phil Jackson	L.A. Lakers
1992	Boston	Chicago	Utah	Portland	Chicago	Phil Jackson	Portland
1993	New York	Chicago	Houston	Phoenix	Chicago	Phil Jackson	Phoenix
1994	New York	Atlanta	Houston	Seattle	Houston	Rudy Tomjanovich	New York
1995	Orlando	Indiana	San Antonio	Phoenix	Houston	Rudy Tomjanovich	Orlando
1996	Orlando	Chicago	San Antonio	Seattle	Chicago	Phil Jackson	Seattle
1997	Miami	Chicago	Utah	Seattle	Chicago	Phil Jackson	Utah
1998	Miami	Chicago	Utah	L.A. Lakers	Chicago	Phil Jackson	Utah
1999	Miami	Indiana	San Antonio	Portland	San Antonio	Gregg Popovich	New York
2000	Miami	Indiana	Utah	L.A. Lakers	L.A. Lakers	Phil Jackson	Indiana
2001	Philadelphia	Milwaukee	San Antonio	L.A. Lakers	L.A. Lakers	Phil Jackson	Philadelphia
2002	New Jersey	Detroit	San Antonio	Sacramento	L.A. Lakers	Phil Jackson	New Jersey
2003	New Jersey	Detroit	San Antonio	Sacramento	San Antonio	Gregg Popovich	New Jersey
2004	New Jersey	Indiana	Minnesota	L.A. Lakers	Detroit	Larry Brown	L.A. Lakers

Year	Atlantic	Central	Southeast	Northwest	Pacific	Southwest	Champion	Winning coach	Opponent
2005	Boston	Detroit	Miami	Seattle	Phoenix	San Antonio	San Antonio	Gregg Popovich	Detroit
2006	New Jersey	Detroit	Miami	Denver	Phoenix	San Antonio	Miami	Pat Riley	Dallas
2007	Toronto	Detroit	Miami	Utah	Phoenix	Dallas	San Antonio	Gregg Popovich	Cleveland
2008	Boston	Detroit	Orlando	Utah	L.A. Lakers	New Orleans	Boston	Glenn "Doc" Rivers	L.A. Lakers
2009	Boston	Cleveland	Orlando	Denver	L.A. Lakers	San Antonio	L.A. Lakers	Phil Jackson	Orlando
2010	Boston	Cleveland	Orlando	Denver	L.A. Lakers	Dallas	L.A. Lakers	Phil Jackson	Boston
2011	Boston	Chicago	Miami	OK City	L.A. Lakers	San Antonio	Dallas	Rick Carlisle	Miami
2012	Boston	Chicago	Miami	OK City	L.A. Lakers	San Antonio	Miami	Erik Spoelstra	OK City
2013	New York	Indiana	Miami	OK City	L.A. Clippers	San Antonio	Miami	Erik Spoelstra	San Antonio
2014	Toronto	Indiana	Miami	OK City	L.A. Clippers	San Antonio	San Antonio	Gregg Popovich	Miami
2015	Toronto	Cleveland	Atlanta	Portland	Golden State	Houston	Golden State	Steve Kerr	Cleveland
2016	Toronto	Cleveland	Miami	OK City	Golden State	San Antonio	Cleveland	Tyronn Lue	Golden State
2017	Boston	Cleveland	Washington	Utah	Golden State	San Antonio	Golden State	Steve Kerr	Cleveland
2018	Toronto	Cleveland	Miami	Portland	Golden State	Houston	Golden State	Steve Kerr	Cleveland
2019	Toronto	Milwaukee	Orlando	Denver	Golden State	Houston	Toronto	Nick Nurse	Golden State
2020	Toronto	Milwaukee	Miami	Denver	L.A. Lakers	Houston	L.A. Lakers	Frank Vogel	Miami
2021	Philadelphia	Milwaukee	Atlanta	Utah	Phoenix	Dallas	Milwaukee	Mike Budenholzer	Phoenix
2022	Boston	Milwaukee	Miami	Utah	Phoenix	Memphis	Golden State	Steve Kerr	Boston
2023	Boston	Milwaukee	Miami	Denver	Sacramento	Memphis	Denver	Michael Malone	Miami

(1) The newly formed NBA combined the 11-team BAA (Basketball Assn. of Amer.) and six NBL (Natl. Basketball League) teams in the 1949-50 season and had three divisions for one year. The Minneapolis Lakers were co-champions of the soon-before Central Division.

All-NBA and All-Defensive Teams, 2022-23

All-NBA Team			All-Defensive Team	
First Team	**Second Team**	**Position**	**First Team**	**Second Team**
Giannis Antetokounmpo, Milwaukee	Jimmy Butler, Miami	Forward	Evan Mobley, Cleveland	OG Anunoby, Toronto
Jayson Tatum, Boston	Jaylen Brown, Boston	Forward	Jaren Jackson Jr., Memphis	Draymond Green, Golden State
Joel Embiid, Philadelphia	Nikola Jokić, Denver	Center	Brook Lopez, Milwaukee	Bam Adebayo, Miami
Shai Gilgeous-Alexander, Oklahoma City	Stephen Curry, Golden State	Guard	Jrue Holiday, Milwaukee	Derrick White, Boston
Luka Dončić, Dallas	Donovan Mitchell, Cleveland	Guard	Alex Caruso, Chicago	Dillon Brooks, Memphis

NBA Statistical Leaders, 2022-23

To qualify for averaged categories, player must be on pace to play 58 games in an 82-game season. Minimums in 2022-23 based on team games played.

Scoring Average

Player, team	GP	FG	FT	PTS	AVG
Joel Embiid, Philadelphia	66	728	661	2,183	33.1
Luka Dončić, Dallas	66	719	515	2,138	32.4
Damian Lillard, Portland	58	556	510	1,866	32.2
Shai Gilgeous-Alexander, Oklahoma City	68	704	669	2,135	31.4
Giannis Antetokounmpo, Milwaukee	63	707	498	1,959	31.1
Jayson Tatum, Boston	74	727	531	2,225	30.1
Donovan Mitchell, Cleveland	68	679	319	1,922	28.3
Kyrie Irving, Brooklyn-Dallas	60	594	247	1,623	27.1
Jaylen Brown, Boston	67	679	263	1,784	26.6
Ja Morant, Memphis	61	566	372	1,596	26.2

Field Goal Percentage
(Minimum 300 field goals made)

Player, team	FGM	FGA	PCT
Nic Claxton, Brooklyn	414	587	0.705
Mason Plumlee, Charlotte-L.A. Clippers	329	484	0.680
Rudy Gobert, Minnesota	360	546	0.659
Clint Capela, Atlanta	350	536	0.653
Jarrett Allen, Cleveland	403	626	0.644
Onyeka Okongwu, Atlanta	317	497	0.638
Ivica Zubac, L.A. Clippers	326	514	0.634
Nikola Jokić, Denver	646	1,022	0.632
Jakob Poeltl, San Antonio-Toronto	389	618	0.629
Domantas Sabonis, Sacramento	577	938	0.615

Free Throw Percentage
(Minimum 125 free throws made)

Player, team	FTM	FTA	PCT
Tyler Herro, Miami	170	182	0.934
Kevin Durant, Brooklyn-Phoenix	307	334	0.919
Stephen Curry, Golden State	257	281	0.915
Damian Lillard, Portland	510	558	0.914
Shai Gilgeous-Alexander, Oklahoma City	669	739	0.905
Trey Murphy III, New Orleans	172	190	0.905
Kyrie Irving, Brooklyn-Dallas	247	273	0.905
Fred VanVleet, Toronto	254	283	0.898
Mikal Bridges, Phoenix-Brooklyn	316	353	0.895
Cole Anthony, Orlando	152	170	0.894
Anfernee Simons, Portland	160	179	0.894

3-Point Field Goal Percentage
(Minimum 82 3-point field goals made)

Player, team	3FGM	3FGA	PCT
Luke Kennard, L.A. Clippers-Memphis	133	269	0.494
Al Horford, Boston	145	325	0.446
Damion Lee, Phoenix	110	247	0.445
Malcolm Brogdon, Boston	132	297	0.444
Tyrese Maxey, Philadelphia	160	369	0.434
Gary Harris, Orlando	94	218	0.431
Stephen Curry, Golden State	273	639	0.427
Joe Harris, Brooklyn	142	333	0.426
Buddy Hield, Indiana	288	677	0.425
Corey Kispert, Washington	163	384	0.424

Rebounds per Game

Player, team	GP	OFF	DEF	TOT	AVG
Domantas Sabonis, Sacramento	79	251	722	973	12.3
Nikola Jokić, Denver	69	167	650	817	11.8
Giannis Antetokounmpo, Milwaukee	63	137	605	742	11.8
Rudy Gobert, Minnesota	70	231	583	814	11.6
Clint Capela, Atlanta	65	258	459	717	11.0
Nikola Vučević, Chicago	82	159	744	903	11.0
Jonas Valančiūnas, New Orleans	79	225	579	804	10.2
Joel Embiid, Philadelphia	66	113	557	670	10.2
Julius Randle, New York	77	141	626	767	10.0
Deandre Ayton, Phoenix	67	172	495	667	10.0

Assists per Game

Player, team	GP	AST	APG
James Harden, Philadelphia	58	618	10.7
Trae Young, Atlanta	73	741	10.2
Nikola Jokić, Denver	69	678	9.8
Chris Paul, Phoenix	59	524	8.9
Ja Morant, Memphis	61	493	8.1
Luka Dončić, Dallas	66	529	8.0
Darius Garland, Cleveland	69	538	7.8
Russell Westbrook, L.A. Lakers-Clippers	73	551	7.5
Jrue Holiday, Milwaukee	67	495	7.4
Damian Lillard, Portland	58	425	7.3
Domantas Sabonis, Sacramento	79	573	7.3

Steals per Game

Player, team	GP	STL	AVG
OG Anunoby, Toronto	67	128	1.9
Jimmy Butler, Miami	64	117	1.8
Fred VanVleet, Toronto	69	123	1.8
Shai Gilgeous-Alexander, Oklahoma City	68	112	1.6
De'Anthony Melton, Philadelphia	77	126	1.6
Anthony Edwards, Minnesota	79	125	1.6
Gary Trent Jr., Toronto	66	104	1.6
Herbert Jones, New Orleans	66	103	1.6

Blocked Shots per Game

Player, team	GP	BLK	AVG
Jaren Jackson Jr., Memphis	63	189	3.0
Nic Claxton, Brooklyn	76	189	2.5
Brook Lopez, Milwaukee	78	193	2.5
Walker Kessler, Utah	74	173	2.3
Myles Turner, Indiana	62	140	2.3
Mitchell Robinson, New York	59	109	1.8
Joel Embiid, Philadelphia	66	112	1.7
Kristaps Porziņģis, Washington	65	100	1.5
Evan Mobley, Cleveland	79	119	1.5
Isiah Jackson, Indiana	63	93	1.5

NBA Defensive Player of the Year, 1983-2023

Year	Player, team	Year	Player, team	Year	Player, team
1983	Sidney Moncrief, Milwaukee	1998	Dikembe Mutombo, Atlanta	2011	Dwight Howard, Orlando
1984	Sidney Moncrief, Milwaukee	1999	Alonzo Mourning, Miami	2012	Tyson Chandler, New York
1985	Mark Eaton, Utah	2000	Alonzo Mourning, Miami	2013	Marc Gasol, Memphis
1986	Alvin Robertson, San Antonio	2001	Dikembe Mutombo, Philadelphia-Atlanta	2014	Joakim Noah, Chicago
1987	Michael Cooper, L.A. Lakers			2015	Kawhi Leonard, San Antonio
1988	Michael Jordan, Chicago	2002	Ben Wallace, Detroit	2016	Kawhi Leonard, San Antonio
1989	Mark Eaton, Utah	2003	Ben Wallace, Detroit	2017	Draymond Green, Golden State
1990	Dennis Rodman, Detroit	2004	Ron Artest, Indiana	2018	Rudy Gobert, Utah
1991	Dennis Rodman, Detroit	2005	Ben Wallace, Detroit	2019	Rudy Gobert, Utah
1992	David Robinson, San Antonio	2006	Ben Wallace, Detroit	2020	Giannis Antetokounmpo, Milwaukee
1993	Hakeem Olajuwon, Houston	2007	Marcus Camby, Denver		
1994	Hakeem Olajuwon, Houston	2008	Kevin Garnett, Boston	2021	Rudy Gobert, Utah
1995	Dikembe Mutombo, Denver	2009	Dwight Howard, Orlando	2022	Marcus Smart, Boston
1996	Gary Payton, Seattle	2010	Dwight Howard, Orlando	2023	Jaren Jackson Jr., Memphis
1997	Dikembe Mutombo, Atlanta				

NBA Rookie of the Year, 1953-2023

Year	Player, team	Year	Player, team	Year	Player, team
1953	Don Meineke, Ft. Wayne	1976	Alvan Adams, Phoenix	2000	Elton Brand, Chicago;
1954	Ray Felix, Baltimore	1977	Adrian Dantley, Buffalo		Steve Francis, Houston
1955	Bob Pettit, Milwaukee	1978	Walter Davis, Phoenix	2001	Mike Miller, Orlando
1956	Maurice Stokes, Rochester	1979	Phil Ford, Kansas City	2002	Pau Gasol, Memphis
1957	Tom Heinsohn, Boston	1980	Larry Bird, Boston	2003	Amar'e Stoudemire, Phoenix
1958	Woody Sauldsberry, Philadelphia	1981	Darrell Griffith, Utah	2004	LeBron James, Cleveland
1959	Elgin Baylor, Minneapolis	1982	Buck Williams, New Jersey	2005	Emeka Okafor, Charlotte
1960	Wilt Chamberlain, Philadelphia	1983	Terry Cummings, San Diego	2006	Chris Paul, New Orl./OK City
1961	Oscar Robertson, Cincinnati	1984	Ralph Sampson, Houston	2007	Brandon Roy, Portland
1962	Walt Bellamy, Chicago	1985	Michael Jordan, Chicago	2008	Kevin Durant, Seattle
1963	Terry Dischinger, Chicago	1986	Patrick Ewing, New York	2009	Derrick Rose, Chicago
1964	Jerry Lucas, Cincinnati	1987	Chuck Person, Indiana	2010	Tyreke Evans, Sacramento
1965	Willis Reed, New York	1988	Mark Jackson, New York	2011	Blake Griffin, L.A. Clippers
1966	Rick Barry, San Francisco	1989	Mitch Richmond, Golden State	2012	Kyrie Irving, Cleveland
1967	Dave Bing, Detroit	1990	David Robinson, San Antonio	2013	Damian Lillard, Portland
1968	Earl Monroe, Baltimore	1991	Derrick Coleman, New Jersey	2014	Michael Carter-Williams, Philadelphia
1969	Wes Unseld, Baltimore	1992	Larry Johnson, Charlotte	2015	Andrew Wiggins, Minnesota
1970	Lew Alcindor (Kareem	1993	Shaquille O'Neal, Orlando	2016	Karl-Anthony Towns, Minnesota
	Abdul-Jabbar), Milwaukee	1994	Chris Webber, Golden State	2017	Malcolm Brogdon, Milwaukee
1971	Dave Cowens, Boston;	1995	Grant Hill, Detroit;	2018	Ben Simmons, Philadelphia
	Geoff Petrie, Portland		Jason Kidd, Dallas	2019	Luka Dončić, Dallas
1972	Sidney Wicks, Portland	1996	Damon Stoudamire, Toronto	2020	Ja Morant, Memphis
1973	Bob McAdoo, Buffalo	1997	Allen Iverson, Philadelphia	2021	LaMelo Ball, Charlotte
1974	Ernie DiGregorio, Buffalo	1998	Tim Duncan, San Antonio	2022	Scottie Barnes, Toronto
1975	Jamaal Wilkes, Golden State	1999	Vince Carter, Toronto	2023	Paolo Banchero, Orlando

NBA Sixth Man Award, 1983-2023

Year	Player, team	Year	Player, team	Year	Player, team
1983	Bobby Jones, Philadelphia	1997	John Starks, New York	2011	Lamar Odom, L.A. Lakers
1984	Kevin McHale, Boston	1998	Danny Manning, Phoenix	2012	James Harden, Oklahoma City
1985	Kevin McHale, Boston	1999	Darrell Armstrong, Orlando	2013	J.R. Smith, New York
1986	Bill Walton, Boston	2000	Rodney Rogers, Phoenix	2014	Jamal Crawford, L.A. Clippers
1987	Ricky Pierce, Milwaukee	2001	Aaron McKie, Philadelphia	2015	Lou Williams, Toronto
1988	Roy Tarpley, Dallas	2002	Corliss Williamson, Detroit	2016	Jamal Crawford, L.A. Clippers
1989	Eddie Johnson, Phoenix	2003	Bobby Jackson, Sacramento	2017	Eric Gordon, Houston
1990	Ricky Pierce, Milwaukee	2004	Antawn Jamison, Dallas	2018	Lou Williams, L.A. Clippers
1991	Detlef Schrempf, Indiana	2005	Ben Gordon, Chicago	2019	Lou Williams, L.A. Clippers
1992	Detlef Schrempf, Indiana	2006	Mike Miller, Memphis	2020	Montrezl Harrell, L.A. Clippers
1993	Clifford Robinson, Portland	2007	Leandro Barbosa, Phoenix	2021	Jordan Clarkson, Utah
1994	Dell Curry, Charlotte	2008	Manu Ginobili, San Antonio	2022	Tyler Herro, Miami
1995	Anthony Mason, New York	2009	Jason Terry, Dallas	2023	Malcolm Brogdon, Boston
1996	Toni Kukoc, Chicago	2010	Jamal Crawford, Atlanta		

NBA Player Draft First-Round Picks, 2023

(Held June 22, 2023)

	Team	Player, position, school/team		Team	Player, position, school/team
1.	San Antonio	Victor Wembanyama, C, Metropolitans 92 (France)	16.	Utah[6]	Keyonte George, G, Baylor
			17.	L.A. Lakers	Jalen Hood-Schifino, G, Indiana
2.	Charlotte	Brandon Miller, F/G, Alabama	18.	Miami	Jaime Jaquez Jr., F, UCLA
3.	Portland	Scoot Henderson, G, G League Ignite (NV)	19.	Golden State	Brandin Podziemski, G, Santa Clara
4.	Houston	Amen Thompson, G, Overtime Elite (GA)	20.	Houston[7]	Cam Whitmore, F, Villanova
5.	Detroit	Ausar Thompson, G/F, Overtime Elite (GA)	21.	Brooklyn[8]	Noah Clowney, F, Alabama
6.	Orlando	Anthony Black, G, Arkansas	22.	Brooklyn	Dariq Whitehead, G, Duke
7.	Indiana[1]	Bilal Coulibaly, F, Metropolitans 92 (France)	23.	Portland[9]	Kris Murray, F, Iowa
8.	Washington[2]	Jarace Walker, F, Houston	24.	Sacramento[10]	Olivier-Maxence Prosper, F, Marquette
9.	Utah	Taylor Hendricks, F, Central Florida	25.	Memphis[11]	Marcus Sasser, G, Houston
10.	Dallas[3]	Cason Wallace, G, Kentucky	26.	Indiana[12]	Ben Sheppard, G, Belmont
11.	Orlando[4]	Jeff Howard, F, Michigan	27.	Charlotte[13]	Nick Smith Jr., G, Arkansas
12.	Oklahoma City[5]	Dereck Lively II, C, Duke	28.	Utah[14]	Brice Sensabaugh, F, Ohio State
13.	Toronto	Gradey Dick, F/G, Kansas	29.	Indiana[15]	Julian Strawther, F, Gonzaga
14.	New Orleans	Jordan Hawkins, G, Connecticut	30.	L.A. Clippers[16]	Kobe Brown, F, Missouri
15.	Atlanta	Kobe Bufkin, G, Michigan			

(1) Rights traded to Washington. (2) Rights traded to Indiana. (3) Rights traded to Oklahoma City. (4) Rights traded to Chicago. (5) Rights traded to Dallas. (6) From Minnesota. (7) From L.A. Clippers. (8) From Phoenix. (9) From New York. (10) Rights traded to Dallas. (11) Rights traded to Detroit via Boston (12) From Cleveland. (13) From Denver via New York and Oklahoma City. (14) From Philadelphia via Brooklyn. (15) From Boston, rights traded to Denver. (16) From Milwaukee via Houston.

Number-One First-Round NBA Draft Picks, 1966-2023

Year	Team	Player, school/team	Year	Team	Player, school/team
1966	New York	Cazzie Russell, Michigan	1985	New York	Patrick Ewing, Georgetown
1967	Detroit	Jimmy Walker, Providence	1986	Cleveland	Brad Daugherty, North Carolina
1968	San Diego	Elvin Hayes, Houston	1987	San Antonio	David Robinson, Navy
1969	Milwaukee	Lew Alcindor (Kareem Abdul-Jabbar), UCLA	1988	L.A. Clippers	Danny Manning, Kansas
1970	Detroit	Bob Lanier, St. Bonaventure	1989	Sacramento	Pervis Ellison, Louisville
1971	Cleveland	Austin Carr, Notre Dame	1990	New Jersey	Derrick Coleman, Syracuse
1972	Portland	LaRue Martin, Loyola-Chicago	1991	Charlotte	Larry Johnson, UNLV
1973	Philadelphia	Doug Collins, Illinois State	1992	Orlando	Shaquille O'Neal, LSU
1974	Portland	Bill Walton, UCLA	1993	Orlando	Chris Webber[2], Michigan
1975	Atlanta	David Thompson[1], NC State	1994	Milwaukee	Glenn Robinson, Purdue
1976	Houston	John Lucas, Maryland	1995	Golden State	Joe Smith, Maryland
1977	Milwaukee	Kent Benson, Indiana	1996	Philadelphia	Allen Iverson, Georgetown
1978	Portland	Mychal Thompson, Minnesota	1997	San Antonio	Tim Duncan, Wake Forest
1979	L.A. Lakers	Earvin "Magic" Johnson, Michigan State	1998	L.A. Clippers	Michael Olowokandi, Pacific (CA)
1980	Golden State	Joe Barry Carroll, Purdue	1999	Chicago	Elton Brand, Duke
1981	Dallas	Mark Aguirre, DePaul	2000	New Jersey	Kenyon Martin, Cincinnati
1982	L.A. Lakers	James Worthy, North Carolina	2001	Washington	Kwame Brown, Glynn Academy (HS)
1983	Houston	Ralph Sampson, Virginia	2002	Houston	Yao Ming, Shanghai Sharks (China)
1984	Houston	Hakeem Olajuwon, Houston	2003	Cleveland	LeBron James, St. Vincent-St. Mary (HS)

Year	Team	Player, school/team	Year	Team	Player, school/team
2004	Orlando	Dwight Howard, Southwest Atlanta Christian Academy (HS)	2014	Cleveland	Andrew Wiggins, Kansas
2005	Milwaukee	Andrew Bogut, Utah	2015	Minnesota	Karl-Anthony Towns, Kentucky
2006	Toronto	Andrea Bargnani, Benetton Treviso (Italy)	2016	Philadelphia	Ben Simmons, LSU
2007	Portland	Greg Oden, Ohio State	2017	Philadelphia	Markelle Fultz, Washington
2008	Chicago	Derrick Rose, Memphis	2018	Phoenix	Deandre Ayton, Arizona
2009	L.A. Clippers	Blake Griffin, Oklahoma	2019	New Orleans	Zion Williamson, Duke
2010	Washington	John Wall, Kentucky	2020	Minnesota	Anthony Edwards, Georgia
2011	Cleveland	Kyrie Irving, Duke	2021	Detroit	Cade Cunningham, Oklahoma St.
2012	New Orleans	Anthony Davis, Kentucky	2022	Orlando	Paolo Banchero, Duke
2013	Cleveland	Anthony Bennett, UNLV	2023	San Antonio	Victor Wembanyama, Metropolitans 92 (France)

HS = High school. (1) Signed with Denver of the American Basketball Association (ABA). (2) Traded to Golden State for rights to Anfernee Hardaway and three future first-round draft choices.

All-Time NBA Statistical Leaders

(At end of 2022-23 season. * = Active in 2022-23 season. Does not include ABA statistics.)

Scoring Average
(Minimum 400 games or 10,000 points)

	GP	PTS	AVG
Michael Jordan	1,072	32,292	30.1
Wilt Chamberlain	1,045	31,419	30.1
Elgin Baylor	846	23,149	27.4
*Kevin Durant	986	26,892	27.3
*Joel Embiid	394	10,718	27.2
*LeBron James	1,421	38,652	27.2
Jerry West	932	25,192	27.0
Allen Iverson	914	24,368	26.7
Bob Pettit	792	20,880	26.4
George Gervin	791	20,708	26.2

3-Point Field Goal Percentage
(Minimum 250 3-point field goals made)

	3-FGM	3-FGA	PCT
Steve Kerr	726	1,599	45.4
Hubert Davis	728	1,651	44.1
Dražen Petrović	255	583	43.7
*Joe Harris	1,016	2,324	43.7
*Luke Kennard	683	1,563	43.7
*Seth Curry	824	1,893	43.5
Jason Kapono	457	1,054	43.4
Tim Legler	260	603	43.1
Steve Novak	575	1,337	43.0
Kyle Korver	2,450	5,715	42.9

Free Throw Percentage
(Minimum 1,200 free throws made)

	FTM	FTA	PCT
*Stephen Curry	3,454	3,801	90.9
Steve Nash	3,060	3,384	90.4
Mark Price	2,135	2,362	90.4
Rick Barry	3,818	4,243	90.0
*Damian Lilard	4,427	4,946	89.5
Peja Stojakovic	2,237	2,500	89.5
Chauncey Billups	4,496	5,029	89.4
Ray Allen	4,398	4,920	89.4
Calvin Murphy	3,445	3,864	89.2
JJ Redick	2,060	2,310	89.2

Field Goal Percentage
(Minimum 2,000 field goals made)

	FGM	FGA	PCT
*DeAndre Jordan	3,707	5,492	67.5
*Rudy Gobert	3,156	4,826	65.4
*Clint Capela	2,899	4,620	62.7
*Montrezl Harrell	2,506	4,050	61.9
Artis Gilmore	5,732	9,570	59.9
*Deandre Ayton	2,213	3,709	59.7
Tyson Chandler	3,558	5,964	59.7
*Mason Plumlee	2,508	4,214	59.5
*Steven Adams	2,713	4,619	58.7
Dwight Howard	7,051	12,016	58.7

Minutes Played

Kareem Abdul-Jabbar	57,446
Karl Malone	54,852
*LeBron James	54,093
Dirk Nowitzki	51,369
Kevin Garnett	50,418
Jason Kidd	50,110
Elvin Hayes	50,000
Kobe Bryant	48,638
Wilt Chamberlain	47,859
John Stockton	47,764

Field Goals Attempted

Kareem Abdul-Jabbar	28,307
*LeBron James	28,044
Karl Malone	26,210
Kobe Bryant	26,200
Michael Jordan	24,537
Elvin Hayes	24,272
John Havlicek	23,930
Dirk Nowitzki	23,734
Wilt Chamberlain	23,497
Carmelo Anthony	22,643

Points

*LeBron James	38,652
Kareem Abdul-Jabbar	38,387
Karl Malone	36,928
Kobe Bryant	33,643
Michael Jordan	32,292
Dirk Nowitzki	31,560
Wilt Chamberlain	31,419
Shaquille O'Neal	28,596
Carmelo Anthony	28,289
Moses Malone	27,409

Games Played

Robert Parish	1,611
Kareem Abdul-Jabbar	1,560
Vince Carter	1,541
Dirk Nowitzki	1,522
John Stockton	1,504
Karl Malone	1,476
Kevin Garnett	1,462
Kevin Willis	1,424
*LeBron James	1,421
Jason Terry	1,410

Field Goals Made

Kareem Abdul-Jabbar	15,837
*LeBron James	14,152
Karl Malone	13,528
Wilt Chamberlain	12,681
Michael Jordan	12,192
Kobe Bryant	11,719
Shaquille O'Neal	11,330
Dirk Nowitzki	11,169
Elvin Hayes	10,976
Hakeem Olajuwon	10,749

Rebounds

Wilt Chamberlain	23,924
Bill Russell	21,620
Kareem Abdul-Jabbar	17,440
Elvin Hayes	16,279
Moses Malone	16,212
Tim Duncan	15,091
Karl Malone	14,968
Robert Parish	14,715
Kevin Garnett	14,662
Dwight Howard	14,627

Personal Fouls

Kareem Abdul-Jabbar	4,657
Karl Malone	4,578
Robert Parish	4,443
Charles Oakley	4,421
Hakeem Olajuwon	4,383
Buck Williams	4,267
Elvin Hayes	4,193
Clifford Robinson	4,175
Kevin Willis	4,172
Shaquille O'Neal	4,146
Otis Thorpe	4,146

3-Point Field Goals Attempted

*Stephen Curry	7,929
*James Harden	7,594
Ray Allen	7,429
*LeBron James	6,563
Reggie Miller	6,486
*Damon Lillard	6,410
Jamal Crawford	6,379
Vince Carter	6,168
Jason Terry	6,010
Paul Pierce	5,816

Assists

John Stockton	15,806
Jason Kidd	12,091
*Chris Paul	11,501
*LeBron James	10,420
Steve Nash	10,335
Mark Jackson	10,334
Magic Johnson	10,141
Oscar Robertson	9,887
*Russell Westbrook	9,162
Isiah Thomas	9,061

Blocked Shots

Hakeem Olajuwon	3,830
Dikembe Mutombo	3,289
Kareem Abdul-Jabbar	3,189
Mark Eaton	3,064
Tim Duncan	3,020
David Robinson	2,954
Patrick Ewing	2,894
Shaquille O'Neal	2,732
Tree Rollins	2,542
Robert Parish	2,361

3-Point Field Goals Made

*Stephen Curry	3,390
Ray Allen	2,973
*James Harden	2,754
Reggie Miller	2,560
Kyle Korver	2,450
*Damian Lillard	2,387
Vince Carter	2,290
Jason Terry	2,282
*LeBron James	2,261
Jamal Crawford	2,221

Steals

John Stockton	3,265
Jason Kidd	2,684
*Chris Paul	2,544
Michael Jordan	2,514
Gary Payton	2,445
Maurice Cheeks	2,310
Scottie Pippen	2,307
Clyde Drexler	2,207
*LeBron James	2,186
Hakeem Olajuwon	2,162

NBA Coach of the Year, 1963-2023

Year	Coach, team	Year	Coach, team	Year	Coach, team
1963	Harry Gallatin, St. Louis	1984	Frank Layden, Utah	2004	Hubie Brown, Memphis
1964	Alex Hannum, San Francisco	1985	Don Nelson, Milwaukee	2005	Mike D'Antoni, Phoenix
1965	Red Auerbach, Boston	1986	Mike Fratello, Atlanta	2006	Avery Johnson, Dallas
1966	Dolph Schayes, Philadelphia	1987	Mike Schuler, Portland	2007	Sam Mitchell, Toronto
1967	Johnny Kerr, Chicago	1988	Doug Moe, Denver	2008	Byron Scott, New Orleans
1968	Richie Guerin, St. Louis	1989	Cotton Fitzsimmons, Phoenix	2009	Mike Brown, Cleveland
1969	Gene Shue, Baltimore	1990	Pat Riley, L.A. Lakers	2010	Scott Brooks, Oklahoma City
1970	Red Holzman, New York	1991	Don Chaney, Houston	2011	Tom Thibodeau, Chicago
1971	Dick Motta, Chicago	1992	Don Nelson, Golden State	2012	Gregg Popovich, San Antonio
1972	Bill Sharman, L.A. Lakers	1993	Pat Riley, New York	2013	George Karl, Denver
1973	Tom Heinsohn, Boston	1994	Lenny Wilkens, Atlanta	2014	Gregg Popovich, San Antonio
1974	Ray Scott, Detroit	1995	Del Harris, L.A. Lakers	2015	Mike Budenholzer, Atlanta
1975	Phil Johnson, Kansas City-Omaha	1996	Phil Jackson, Chicago	2016	Steve Kerr, Golden State
1976	Bill Fitch, Cleveland	1997	Pat Riley, Miami	2017	Mike D'Antoni, Houston
1977	Tom Nissalke, Houston	1998	Larry Bird, Indiana	2018	Dwane Casey, Toronto
1978	Hubie Brown, Atlanta	1999	Mike Dunleavy, Portland	2019	Mike Budenholzer, Milwaukee
1979	Cotton Fitzsimmons, Kansas City	2000	Glenn "Doc" Rivers, Orlando	2020	Nick Nurse, Toronto
1980	Bill Fitch, Boston	2001	Larry Brown, Philadelphia	2021	Tom Thibodeau, New York
1981	Jack McKinney, Indiana	2002	Rick Carlisle, Detroit	2022	Monty Williams, Phoenix
1982	Gene Shue, Washington	2003	Gregg Popovich, San Antonio	2023	Mike Brown, Sacramento
1983	Don Nelson, Milwaukee				

National Basketball Association Franchise Origins

Team, founding year (in NBA, Basketball Assn. of Amer. [BAA], or Amer. Basketball Assn. [ABA]), location, and subsequent history. Neutral sites and arena sites in the same metropolitan area not listed separately.

Atlanta Hawks: 1949, NBA, as Tri-Cities Blackhawks, 1949-51, Moline, IL. Milwaukee Hawks, 1951-55; St. Louis Hawks, 1955-68; Atlanta Hawks, 1968-present.

Boston Celtics: 1946, BAA, Boston, MA, 1946-present.

Brooklyn Nets: 1967, ABA, as New Jersey Americans, 1967-68, Teaneck, NJ. New York Nets, 1968-77; New Jersey Nets, 1977-2012; Brooklyn Nets, 2012-present.

Charlotte Hornets: 2004, NBA, as Charlotte Bobcats, 2004-14, Charlotte, NC. Charlotte Hornets, 2014-present.

Chicago Bulls: 1966, NBA, Chicago, IL, 1966-present.

Cleveland Cavaliers: 1970, NBA, Cleveland, OH, 1970-present.

Dallas Mavericks: 1980, NBA, Dallas, TX, 1980-present.

Denver Nuggets: 1967, ABA, as Denver Rockets, 1967-74, Denver, CO. Denver Nuggets, 1974-present.

Detroit Pistons: 1948, BAA, as Ft. Wayne Pistons, 1948-57, Ft. Wayne, IN. Detroit Pistons, 1957-present.

Golden State Warriors: 1946, BAA, as Philadelphia Warriors, 1946-62, Philadelphia, PA. San Francisco Warriors, 1962-71; Golden State Warriors, 1971-2019, Oakland, CA; 2019-present, San Francisco, CA.

Houston Rockets: 1967, NBA, as San Diego Rockets, 1967-71, San Diego, CA. Houston Rockets, 1971-present.

Indiana Pacers: 1967, ABA, Indianapolis, IN, 1974-present.

L.A. Clippers: 1970, NBA, as Buffalo Braves, 1970-78, Buffalo, NY. San Diego Clippers, 1978-84; L.A. Clippers, 1984-present.

L.A. Lakers: 1948, BAA, as Minneapolis Lakers, 1948-60, Minneapolis, MN. L.A. Lakers, 1960-present.

Memphis Grizzlies: 1995, NBA, as Vancouver Grizzlies, 1995-2001, Vancouver, BC, Canada. Memphis Grizzlies, 2001-present.

Miami Heat: 1988, NBA, Miami, FL, 1988-present.

Milwaukee Bucks: 1968, NBA, Milwaukee, WI, 1968-present.

Minnesota Timberwolves: 1989, NBA, Minneapolis, MN, 1989-present.

New Orleans Pelicans: 1988, NBA, as Charlotte Hornets, 1988-2002, Charlotte, NC. New Orleans Hornets, 2002-13 (Hornets played most home games in Oklahoma City, 2005-07, as city repaired Hurricane Katrina damage); New Orleans Pelicans, 2013-present.

New York Knicks: 1946, BAA, New York, NY, 1946-present.

Oklahoma City Thunder: 1967, NBA, as Seattle SuperSonics, 1967-2008, Seattle, WA. Oklahoma City Thunder, 2008-present.

Orlando Magic: 1989, NBA, Orlando, FL, 1989-present.

Philadelphia 76ers: 1949, NBA, as Syracuse Nationals, 1949-63, Syracuse, NY. Philadelphia 76ers, 1963-present.

Phoenix Suns: 1968, NBA, Phoenix, AZ, 1968-present.

Portland Trail Blazers: 1970, NBA, Portland, OR, 1970-present.

Sacramento Kings: 1948, BAA, as Rochester Royals, 1948-57, Rochester, NY. Cincinnati Royals, 1957-72; Kansas City-Omaha Kings, 1972-75; Kansas City Kings, 1975-85; Sacramento Kings, 1985-present.

San Antonio Spurs: ABA, as Dallas Chaparrals, 1967-73, Dallas, TX. San Antonio Spurs, 1973-present.

Toronto Raptors: 1995, NBA, Toronto, ON, Canada, 1995-present.

Utah Jazz: 1974, NBA, as New Orleans Jazz, 1974-79, New Orleans, LA. Utah Jazz, 1979-present, Salt Lake City.

Washington Wizards: 1961, NBA, as Chicago Packers, 1961-62, Chicago, IL. Chicago Zephyrs, 1962-63; Baltimore Bullets, 1963-73; Capital Bullets, 1973-74, Landover, MD; Washington Bullets, 1974-97; Washington Wizards, 1997-present.

NBA Home Courts

Team	Name (year built)	Capacity[1]	Team	Name (year built)	Capacity[1]
Atlanta	State Farm Arena[2] (1999)	16,951	Miami	Kaseya Center[10] (1999)	19,600
Boston	TD Garden[3] (1995)	19,156	Milwaukee	Fiserv Forum (2018)	17,385
Brooklyn	Barclays Center[4] (2012)	17,732	Minnesota	Target Center (1990)	19,356
Charlotte	Spectrum Center[5] (2005)	19,077	New Orleans	Smoothie King Center[11] (1999)	16,867
Chicago	United Center (1994)	20,917	New York	Madison Square Garden (IV) (1968)	19,812
Cleveland	Rocket Mortgage FieldHouse[6] (1994)	19,432	Oklahoma City	Paycom Center[12] (2002)	18,203
Dallas	American Airlines Center (2001)	19,200	Orlando	Amway Center (2010)	18,500
Denver	Ball Arena[7] (1999)	19,520	Philadelphia	Wells Fargo Center[13] (1996)	20,007
Detroit	Little Caesars Arena (2017)	20,332	Phoenix	Footprint Center[14] (1992)	18,422
Golden State	Chase Center (2019)	18,064	Portland	Moda Center[15] (1995)	19,393
Houston	Toyota Center (2003)	18,055	Sacramento	Golden 1 Center (2016)	17,583
Indiana	Gainbridge Fieldhouse[8] (1999)	17,923	San Antonio	AT&T Center[16] (2002)	18,354
L.A. Clippers	Crypto.com Arena[9] (1999)	19,060	Toronto	Scotiabank Arena[17] (1999)	19,800
L.A. Lakers	Crypto.com Arena[9] (1999)	18,997	Utah	Vivint Arena[18] (1991)	18,300
Memphis	FedExForum (2004)	17,794	Washington	Capital One Arena[19] (1997)	20,362

(1) At the end of the 2022-23 season. (2) Philips Arena, 1999-2018. (3) FleetCenter, 1995-2005; TD Banknorth Garden, 2005-09. (4) The New Jersey Nets relocated to Brooklyn prior to the 2012-13 season. (5) Charlotte Bobcats Arena, 2005-08; Time Warner Cable Arena, 2008-16. (6) Gund Arena, 1994-2005; Quicken Loans Arena, 2005-19. (7) Pepsi Center, 1999-2020. (8) Conseco Fieldhouse, 1999-2011; Bankers Life Fieldhouse, 2011-21. (9) Staples Center, 1999-2021. (10) AmericanAirlines Arena, 1999-2021; FTX Arena 2021-23; Miami-Dade Arena, 2023. (11) New Orleans Arena, 1999-2014; because of damage to New Orleans Arena due to Hurricane, Katrina, the Hornets played 35 games in the Ford Center in Oklahoma City, OK, 3 games in New Orleans Arena, and 3 games at other locations during the 2005-06 season; in 2006-07, the Hornets played 35 games at the Ford Center and 6 games in New Orleans Arena. (12) Ford Center, 2008-11; Chesapeake Energy Arena, 2012-21. (13) CoreStates Center, 1996-98; First Union Center, 1998-2003; Wachovia Center, 2003-10. (14) America West Arena, 1992-2006; US Airways Center, 2006-15; Talking Stick Resort Arena, 2015-19; Phoenix Suns Arena, 2020. (15) The Rose Garden, 1995-2013. (16) SBC Center, 2002-06. (17) Air Canada Centre, 1999-2018. The Raptors played the 2020-21 season at Amalie Arena in Tampa, FL, due to COVID-19 related travel restrictions. (18) Delta Center, 1991-2006; EnergySolutions Arena, 2006-15. (19) MCI Center, 1997-2006; Verizon Center, 2006-17.

All-Time NBA Regular Season Coaching Victories

(At the end of the 2022-23 season, ranked by wins. * = Active in 2022-23 season.)

Coach	W	L	PCT	Coach	W	L	PCT	Coach	W	L	PCT
*Gregg Popovich...	1,366	761	.642	Larry Brown	1,098	904	.548	Jack Ramsay......	864	783	.525
Don Nelson......	1,335	1,063	.557	*Doc Rivers......	1,097	763	.590	Cotton Fitzsimmons ..	832	775	.518
Lenny Wilkens.....	1,332	1,155	.536	Rick Adelman	1,042	749	.582	Gene Shue	784	861	.477
Jerry Sloan......	1,221	803	.603	Bill Fitch	944	1,106	.460	*Nate McMillan ...	760	668	.532
Pat Riley........	1,210	694	.636	Red Auerbach	938	479	.662	John MacLeod ...	707	657	.518
George Karl......	1,175	824	.588	Dick Motta	935	1,017	.479	*Erik Spoelstra	704	491	.589
Phil Jackson	1,155	485	.704	*Rick Carlisle	896	793	.530	Red Holzman	696	603	.536

Naismith Memorial Basketball Hall of Fame

* = 2023 inductee. + = Enshrined as both a player and coach. Referee inductees not shown. www.hoophall.com

Players

Abdul-Jabbar, Kareem
Allen, Ray
Archibald, Nate
Arizin, Paul
Barkley, Charles
Barlow, Thomas
Barry, Rick
Baylor, Elgin
Beaty, Zelmo
Beckman, John
Bellamy, Walt
Belov, Sergei
Bing, Dave
Bird, Larry
Blazejowski, Carol
Borgmann, Bennie
Bosh, Chris
Boswell, Wyatt "Sonny"
Bradley, Bill
Braun, Carl
Brennan, Joseph
Brown, Roger "Buddy"
Bryant, Kobe
Cash, Swin
Catchings, Tamika
Cervi, Al
Chamberlain, Wilt
Cheeks, Maurice
Clayton, Zack
Cooper, Charles
Cooper, Charles "Chuck"
Cooper, Cynthia
Cosic, Kresimir
Cousy, Bob
Cowens, Dave
Crawford, Joan
Cunningham, Billy
Curry, Denise
Dalipagic, Drazen
Dampier, Louis
Dandridge, Bob
Daniels, Mel
Dantley, Adrian
Davies, Bob
DeBernardi, Forrest
DeBusschere, Dave
Dehnert, Henry "Dutch"
Divac, Vlade
Donovan, Anne
Drexler, Clyde
Dumars, Joe
Duncan, Tim
Edwards, Teresa
Endacott, Paul
English, Alex
Erving, Julius
Ewing, Patrick
Foster, Bud
Frazier, Walt
Friedman, Max
Fulks, Joe
Gale, Lauren
Galis, Nick
Gallatin, Harry
Garnett, Kevin
*Gasol, Pau
Gates, William "Pop"
Gervin, George
Gilmore, Artis
Ginobili, Manu
Gola, Tom
Goodrich, Gail
Greer, Hal
Griffith, Yolanda
Gruenig, Robert "Ace"
Guerin, Richard

Hagan, Cliff
*Hammon, Becky
Hanson, Victor
Hardaway, Tim
Harris-Stewart, Lusia
Havlicek, John
Hawkins, Cornelius "Connie"
Hayes, Elvin
Haywood, Spencer
*Heinsohn, Tom
Hill, Grant
Holman, Nat
Houbregs, Bob
Howell, Bailey
Hudson, Lou
Hyatt, Chuck
Isaacs, John
Issel, Dan
Iverson, Allen
Jackson, Inman
Jackson, Lauren
Jeannette, Harry
Jenkins, Clarence "Fats"
Johnson, Dennis
Johnson, Earvin "Magic"
Johnson, Gus
Johnson, William
Johnston, Neil
*Russell, Bill
Jones, Bobby
Jones, K. C.
Jones, Sam
Jordan, Michael
Kidd, Jason
King, Bernard
Krause, Ed "Moose"
Kukoc, Toni
Kurland, Bob
Lanier, Bob
Lapchick, Joe
Leslie, Lisa
Lieberman, Nancy
Lovellette, Clyde
Lucas, Jerry
Luisetti, Angelo "Hank"
Macauley, Ed
Malone, Karl
Malone, Moses
Maravich, Pete
Marcari, Hortencia
Marciulionis, Sarunas
Martin, Slater
McAdoo, Bob
McClain, Katrina
McCracken, Emmett "Branch"
McCracken, Jack
McDermott, Bobby
McGinnis, George
McGrady, Tracy
McGuire, Dick
McHale, Kevin
Meneghin, Dino
Meyers, Ann
Mikan, George
Mikkelsen, Vern
Miller, Cheryl
Miller, Reggie
Ming, Yao
Moncrief, Sidney
Monroe, Earl
Moore, Pearl
Mourning, Alonzo
Mullin, Chris
Murphy, Calvin

Murphy, Charles "Stretch"
Mutombo, Dikembe
Nash, Steve
*Nowitzki, Dirk
Olajuwon, Hakeem
O'Neal, Shaquille
Page, Harlan "Pat"
Parish, Robert
*Parker, Tony
Payton, Gary
Pereira, Maciel "Ubiratan"
Petrovic, Drazen
Pettit, Bob
Phillip, Andy
Pierce, Paul
Pippen, Scottie
Pollard, Jim
Pollins, Albert "Runt"
Posey, Cumberland
Radivoj, Korac
Radja, Dino
Ramsey, Frank
Reed, Willis
Richmond, Mitch
Risen, Arnie
Robertson, Oscar
Robinson, David
Rodgers, Guy
Rodman, Dennis
Roosma, John
*Russell, Bill
Russell, John "Honey"
Sabonis, Arvydas
Sampson, Ralph
Schayes, Adolph
Schmidt, Ernest
Schmidt, Oscar
Schommer, John
Scott, Charlie
Sedran, Barney
Semjonova, Uljana
Shank-Grentz, Theresa
*Sharman, Bill
Sikma, Jack
Smith, Katie
Staley, Dawn
Steinmetz, Chris
Stockton, John
Stokes, Maurice
Swoopes, Sheryl
Tatum, Reece "Goose"
Thomas, Isiah
Thompson, David
Thompson, John
Thompson, Tina
Thurmond, Nate
Twyman, Jack
Unseld, Wes
Vandivier, Robert "Fuzzy"
Wachter, Ed
*Wade, Dwyane
Walker, Chet
Wallace, Ben
Walton, Bill
Wanzer, Bobby
Washington, Ora Mae
Weatherspoon, Teresa
Webber, Chris
West, Jerry
Westphal, Paul
Whalen, Lindsay
White, Jo Jo
White, Nera
*Wilkens, Lenny
Wilkes, Jamaal

Wilkins, Dominique
Woodard, Lynette
+Wooden, John
Worthy, James
Yardley, George
Coaches
Adelman, Rick
Alexeeva, Lidia
Allen, Forrest C. "Phog"
Anderson, Harold
Auerbach, Arnold "Red"
Auriemma, Geno
Barmore, Leon
Barry, Justin "Sam"
*Bess, Gene
*Blair, Gary
Blood, Ernest
Boeheim, Jim
Brown, Larry
Calhoun, Jim
Calipari, John
Cann, Howard
Carlson, Clifford
Carnesecca, Lou
Carnevale, Ben
Carril, Pete
Case, Everett
Chancellor, Van
Chaney, John
Conradt, Jody
Crum, Denzil "Denny"
Daly, Chuck
Dean, Everett
Diaz-Miguel, Antonio
Diddle, Edgar
Drake, Bruce
Driesell, Charles "Lefty"
Ferrándiz, Pedro
Fitch, Bill
Gaines, Clarence
Gamba, Sandro
Gardner, James "Jack"
Gaze, Lindsay
Gill, Amory "Slats"
Gomelsky, Aleksandr
Gunter, Sue
Hannum, Alex
Harshman, Marv
Haskins, Don
Hatchell, Sylvia
*Heinsohn, Tom
Hickey, Edgar
*Hixon, David
Hobson, Howard
Holzman, William "Red"
Huggins, Bob
Hughes, Robert
Hurley, Bob, Sr.
Iba, Hank
Izzo, Tom
Jackson, Phil
Julian, Alvin
Karl, George
*Keady, Gene
Keaney, Frank
Keogan, George
Knight, Bob
Krzyzewski, Mike
Kundla, John
Lambert, Ward
Leonard, Bob
Lewis, Guy V.
Litwack, Harry
Loeffler, Kenneth
Lonborg, Arthur "Dutch"

Magee, Herb
McCutchan, Arad
McGraw, Muffet
McGuire, Al
McGuire, Frank
McLendon, John
Meanwell, Dr. Walter
Meyer, Ray
Miller, Ralph
Moore, Billie
Mulkey, Kim
Nelson, Don
Newell, Pete
Nikolic, Aleksandar
Novosel, Mirko
Olson, Robert "Lute"
Pitino, Rick
*Popovich, Gregg
Ramsay, John "Jack"
Richardson, Nolan
Riley, Pat
Rubini, Cesare
Rupp, Adolph
Rush, Cathy
*Russell, Bill
Sachs, Leonard
Self, Bill
*Sharman, Bill
Shelton, Everett
Sloan, Jerry
Smith, Dean
Stanley, Marianne
Stevens, Barbara
Stringer, C. Vivian
Summitt, Pat
Sutton, Eddie
Tarkanian, Jerry
Taylor, Fred
Teague, Bertha
Thompson, John R.
Tomjanovich, Rudy
VanDerveer, Tara
Wade, Margaret
Watts, Stan
*Wilkens, Lenny
Williams, Gary
Williams, Roy
Winter, Tex
*Wooden, John
Woolpert, Phil
Wootten, Morgan
Wright, Jay
Yow, Kay
Teams
1948-82 Wayland Baptist (women's teams)
1957-59 Tennessee A&I (men's teams)
1960 USA Men's Olympic Team
1966 Texas Western
1972-73-74 Immaculata Coll.
*1976 USA Women's Olympic Team
1992 USA Men's Olympic "Dream Team"
All American Red Heads
Buffalo Germans
First Team
Harlem Globetrotters
New York Renaissance
Original Celtics
Contributors
Abbott, Senda Berenson

Ackerman, Val
Attles, Al
Barksdale, Don
Baumann, Patrick
Bee, Clair
Biasone, Danny
Brown, Hubert
Brown, Walter "Hubie"
Bunn, John
Buss, Jerry
Clifton, Nat
Colangelo, Jerry
Costello, Larry
Davidson, Bill
Douglas, Bob
Duer, Al
Embry, Wayne
Fagan, Cliff
Fisher, Harry
Fitzsimmons, Cotton
Garfinkel, Howard
Fleisher, Larry
Gavitt, David
Gottlieb, Edward
Granik, Russ
Gulick, Dr. Luther
Harris, Del
Harrison, Lester
Hearn, Francis "Chick"
Henderson, E. B.
Hepp, Dr. Ferenc
Hickox, Edward
Hinkle, Tony
Irish, Edward "Ned"
Jackson, Mannie
Jernstedt, Tom
Jones, R. William
Kennedy, Walter
Knight, Phil
Krause, Jerry
Lemon, Meadowlark
Liston, Emil
Lloyd, Earl
Lobo, Rebecca
McLendon, John
Mokray, Bill
Morgan, Ralph
Morgenweck, Frank
Naismith, Dr. James
Newton, C. M.
O'Brien, John
O'Brien, Larry
Olsen, Harold
Podoloff, Maurice
Porter, Henry V.
Raveling, George
Reid, William
Reinsdorf, Jerry
Ripley, Elmer
St. John, Lynn
Sanders, Tom "Satch"
Saperstein, Abe
Schabinger, Arthur
Stagg, Alonzo
Stankovic, Boris
Steitz, Edward
Stern, David
Taylor, Chuck
Thorn, Rod
Tower, Oswald
Trester, Arthur
*Valvano, Jim
Vitale, Dick
Wells, Clifford
Welts, Rick
Wilke, Lou
Zollner, Fred

Aces High, Again: Las Vegas Repeats as WNBA Champs in 2023

The Las Vegas Aces claimed their second straight WNBA title, defeating the New York Liberty, 70-69, in Game 4 of the best-of-five series at Barclays Center in Brooklyn on Oct. 18, 2023. Twenty-seven-year-old Ace A'ja Wilson, who scored 24 points with 16 rebounds in Game 4 and helped limit 2023 WNBA MVP Breanna Stewart to 10 points, was named Finals MVP. Wilson averaged 23.8 points and 11.8 rebounds per game during the postseason. The 40-game 2023 WNBA regular season was longer than any of the 26 WNBA seasons before it. The All-Star Game aired July 15, 2023, in prime-time for the first time, with Team Stewart topping Team Wilson, 143-127, at the Aces' home court, Michelob Ultra Arena, in Las Vegas. Phoenix Mercury star Brittney Griner, who spent 10 months in 2022 jailed in Russia, returned to the U.S. in a prisoner exchange and started 31 games and appeared in the All-Star Game.

WNBA Final Standings, 2023

(Playoff seeds in parentheses; top eight teams by PCT advance, regardless of conference.)

Eastern Conference	W	L	PCT	GB	Western Conference	W	L	PCT	GB
New York Liberty (2)	32	8	0.800	—	Las Vegas Aces (1)	34	6	0.850	—
Connecticut Sun (3)	27	13	0.675	5	Dallas Wings (4)	22	18	0.550	12
Atlanta Dream (5)	19	21	0.475	13	Minnesota Lynx (6)	19	21	0.475	15
Washington Mystics (7)	19	21	0.475	13	Los Angeles Sparks	17	23	0.425	17
Chicago Sky (8)	18	22	0.450	14	Seattle Storm	11	29	0.275	23
Indiana Fever	13	27	0.325	19	Phoenix Mercury	9	31	0.225	25

Note: Seeds 5,6, and 7 were determined based on head-to-head records among the three teams.

WNBA Playoff Results, 2023

First Round (best-of-three)
(1) Las Vegas defeated (8) Chicago, 2 games to 0
(2) New York defeated (7) Washington, 2 games to 0
(3) Connecticut defeated (6) Minnesota, 2 games to 1
(4) Dallas defeated (5) Atlanta, 2 games to 0

Semifinals (best-of-five)
(1) Las Vegas defeated (4) Dallas, 3 games to 0
(2) New York defeated (3) Connecticut, 3 games to 1

WNBA Championship
(1) Las Vegas defeated (2) New York, 3 games to 1 (99-82, 104-76, 73-87, 70-69)

WNBA Champions, 1997-2023

	Regular Season		Playoffs		
Year	Eastern champion	Western champion	Champion	Winning coach	Opponent
1997	Houston Comets	Phoenix Mercury	Houston	Van Chancellor	New York
1998	Cleveland Rockers	Houston Comets	Houston	Van Chancellor	Phoenix
1999	New York Liberty	Houston Comets	Houston	Van Chancellor	New York
2000	New York Liberty	Los Angeles Sparks	Houston	Van Chancellor	New York
2001	Cleveland Rockers	Los Angeles Sparks	Los Angeles	Michael Cooper	Charlotte
2002	New York Liberty	Los Angeles Sparks	Los Angeles	Michael Cooper	New York
2003	Detroit Shock	Los Angeles Sparks	Detroit	Bill Laimbeer	Los Angeles
2004	Connecticut Sun	Los Angeles Sparks	Seattle	Anne Donovan	Connecticut
2005	Connecticut Sun	Sacramento Monarchs	Sacramento	John Whisenant	Connecticut
2006	Connecticut Sun	Los Angeles Sparks	Detroit	Bill Laimbeer	Sacramento
2007	Detroit Shock	Phoenix Mercury	Phoenix	Paul Westhead	Detroit
2008	Detroit Shock	San Antonio Silver Stars	Detroit	Bill Laimbeer	San Antonio
2009	Indiana Fever	Phoenix Mercury	Phoenix	Corey Gaines	Indiana
2010	Washington Mystics	Seattle Storm	Seattle	Brian Agler	Atlanta
2011	Indiana Fever	Minnesota Lynx	Minnesota	Cheryl Reeve	Atlanta
2012	Connecticut Sun	Minnesota Lynx	Indiana	Lin Dunn	Minnesota
2013	Chicago Sky	Minnesota Lynx	Minnesota	Cheryl Reeve	Atlanta
2014	Atlanta Dream	Phoenix Mercury	Phoenix	Sandy Brondello	Chicago
2015	New York Liberty	Minnesota Lynx	Minnesota	Cheryl Reeve	Indiana
2016	New York Liberty	Minnesota Lynx	Los Angeles	Brian Agler	Minnesota
2017	New York Liberty	Minnesota Lynx	Minnesota	Cheryl Reeve	Los Angeles
2018	Atlanta Dream	Seattle Storm	Seattle	Dan Hughes	Washington
2019	Washington Mystics	Los Angeles Sparks	Washington	Mike Thibault	Connecticut
2020	Chicago Sky	Las Vegas Aces	Seattle	Gary Kloppenburg[1]	Las Vegas
2021	Connecticut Sun	Las Vegas Aces	Chicago	James Wade	Phoenix
2022	Chicago Sky	Las Vegas Aces	Las Vegas	Becky Hammon	Connecticut
2023	New York Liberty	Las Vegas Aces	Las Vegas	Becky Hammon	New York

(1) Seattle head coach Dan Hughes was not medically cleared for the 2020 season.

WNBA Finals MVP, 1997-2023

Year	Player, team	Year	Player, team	Year	Player, team
1997	Cynthia Cooper, Houston	2006	Deanna Nolan, Detroit	2015	Sylvia Fowles, Minnesota
1998	Cynthia Cooper, Houston	2007	Cappie Pondexter, Phoenix	2016	Candace Parker, Los Angeles
1999	Cynthia Cooper, Houston	2008	Katie Smith, Detroit	2017	Sylvia Fowles, Minnesota
2000	Cynthia Cooper, Houston	2009	Diana Taurasi, Phoenix	2018	Breanna Stewart, Seattle
2001	Lisa Leslie, Los Angeles	2010	Lauren Jackson, Seattle	2019	Emma Meesseman, Wash.
2002	Lisa Leslie, Los Angeles	2011	Seimone Augustus, Minnesota	2020	Breanna Stewart, Seattle
2003	Ruth Riley, Detroit	2012	Tamika Catchings, Indiana	2021	Kahleah Copper, Chicago
2004	Betty Lennox, Seattle	2013	Maya Moore, Minnesota	2022	Chelsea Gray, Las Vegas
2005	Yolanda Griffith, Sacramento	2014	Diana Taurasi, Phoenix	2023	A'ja Wilson, Las Vegas

WNBA Most Valuable Player, 1997-2023

Year	Player, team	Year	Player, team	Year	Player, team
1997	Cynthia Cooper, Houston	2006	Lisa Leslie, Los Angeles	2015	Elena Delle Donne, Chicago
1998	Cynthia Cooper, Houston	2007	Lauren Jackson, Seattle	2016	Nneka Ogwumike, Los Angeles
1999	Yolanda Griffith, Sacramento	2008	Candace Parker, Los Angeles	2017	Sylvia Fowles, Minnesota
2000	Sheryl Swoopes, Houston	2009	Diana Taurasi, Phoenix	2018	Breanna Stewart, Seattle
2001	Lisa Leslie, Los Angeles	2010	Lauren Jackson, Seattle	2019	Elena Delle Donne, Wash.
2002	Sheryl Swoopes, Houston	2011	Tamika Catchings, Indiana	2020	A'ja Wilson, Las Vegas
2003	Lauren Jackson, Seattle	2012	Tina Charles, Connecticut	2021	Jonquel Jones, Connecticut
2004	Lisa Leslie, Los Angeles	2013	Candace Parker, Los Angeles	2022	A'ja Wilson, Las Vegas
2005	Sheryl Swoopes, Houston	2014	Maya Moore, Minnesota	2023	Breanna Stewart, New York

WNBA Statistical Leaders, 2023

Minutes played: 1,489, Arike Ogunbowale, Dallas
Total points: 939, Jewell Loyd, Seattle
Field goal pct.: .578, Aliyah Boston, Indiana
3-point field goal pct.: .464, Tyasha Harris, Connecticut
Free throw pct.: .938, Elena Delle Donne, Washington

Rebounds: 394, Alyssa Thomas, Connecticut
Assists: 316, Alyssa Thomas, Connecticut
Steals: 86, Jordin Canada, Los Angeles
Blocks: 89, A'ja Wilson, Las Vegas

WNBA Rookie of the Year, 1997-2023

Year	Player, team	Year	Player, team	Year	Player, team
1997	No award	2006	Seimone Augustus, Minnesota	2015	Jewell Loyd, Seattle
1998	Tracy Reid, Charlotte	2007	Armintie Price, Chicago	2016	Breanna Stewart, Seattle
1999	Chamique Holdsclaw, Washington	2008	Candace Parker, Los Angeles	2017	Allisha Gray, Dallas
2000	Betty Lennox, Minnesota	2009	Angel McCoughtry, Atlanta	2018	A'ja Wilson, Las Vegas
2001	Jackie Stiles, Portland	2010	Tina Charles, Connecticut	2019	Napheesa Collier, Minnesota
2002	Tamika Catchings, Indiana	2011	Maya Moore, Minnesota	2020	Crystal Dangerfield, Minnesota
2003	Cheryl Ford, Detroit	2012	Nneka Ogwumike, Los Angeles	2021	Michaela Onyenwere, New York
2004	Diana Taurasi, Phoenix	2013	Elena Delle Donne, Chicago	2022	Rhyne Howard, Atlanta
2005	Temeka Johnson, Washington	2014	Chiney Ogwumike, Connecticut	2023	Aliyah Boston, Indiana

WNBA Scoring Leaders, 1997-2023

(Average points per game; season minimums vary.)

Year	Player, team	PTS	AVG	Year	Player, team	PTS	AVG
1997	Cynthia Cooper, Houston	621	22.2	2011	Diana Taurasi, Phoenix	692	21.6
1998	Cynthia Cooper, Houston	680	22.7	2012	Angel McCoughtry, Atlanta	514	21.4
1999	Cynthia Cooper, Houston	686	22.1	2013	Angel McCoughtry, Atlanta	711	21.5
2000	Sheryl Swoopes, Houston	643	20.7	2014	Maya Moore, Minnesota	812	23.9
2001	Katie Smith, Minnesota	739	23.1	2015	Elena Delle Donne, Chicago	725	23.4
2002	Chamique Holdsclaw, Washington	397	19.9	2016	Tina Charles, New York	688	21.5
2003	Lauren Jackson, Seattle	698	21.2	2017	Brittney Griner, Phoenix	569	21.9
2004	Lauren Jackson, Seattle	634	20.5	2018	Liz Cambage, Dallas	737	23.0
2005	Sheryl Swoopes, Houston	614	18.6	2019	Brittney Griner, Phoenix	642	20.7
2006	Diana Taurasi, Phoenix	860	25.3	2020	Arike Ogunbowale, Dallas	501	22.8
2007	Lauren Jackson, Seattle	739	23.8	2021	Tina Charles, Washington	631	23.4
2008	Diana Taurasi, Phoenix	820	24.1	2022	Breanna Stewart, Seattle	741	21.8
2009	Diana Taurasi, Phoenix	631	20.4	2023	Jewell Loyd, Seattle	939	24.7
2010	Diana Taurasi, Phoenix	702	22.6				

WNBA Rebounding Leaders, 1997-2023

(Average rebounds per game; season minimums vary.)

Year	Player, team	REB	RPG	Year	Player, team	REB	RPG
1997	Lisa Leslie, Los Angeles	266	9.5	2011	Tina Charles, Connecticut	374	11.0
1998	Lisa Leslie, Los Angeles	285	10.2	2012	Tina Charles, Connecticut	345	10.5
1999	Yolanda Griffith, Sacramento	329	11.3	2013	Sylvia Fowles, Chicago	369	11.5
2000	Natalie Williams, Utah	336	11.6	2014	Courtney Paris, Tulsa	347	10.2
2001	Yolanda Griffith, Sacramento	357	11.2	2015	Courtney Paris, Tulsa	317	9.3
2002	Chamique Holdsclaw, Washington	232	11.6	2016	Tina Charles, New York	317	9.9
2003	Chamique Holdsclaw, Washington	294	10.9	2017	Jonquel Jones, Connecticut	403	11.9
2004	Lisa Leslie, Los Angeles	336	9.9	2018	Sylvia Fowles, Minnesota	404	11.9
2005	Cheryl Ford, Detroit	322	9.8	2019	Jonquel Jones, Connecticut	330	9.7
2006	Cheryl Ford, Detroit	363	11.3	2020	Candace Parker, Los Angeles	214	9.7
2007	Lauren Jackson, Seattle	300	9.7	2021	Jonquel Jones, Connecticut	303	11.2
2008	Candace Parker, Los Angeles	313	9.5	2022	Sylvia Fowles, Minnesota	294	9.8
2009	Candace Parker, Los Angeles	244	9.8	2023	Alyssa Thomas, Connecticut	394	9.9
2010	Tina Charles, Connecticut	398	11.7				

All-Time WNBA Statistical Leaders

(At the end of the 2023 season. * = Active in 2023 season.)

Scoring Average
(Minimum 100 games)

Player	G	PTS	AVG	Player	G	PTS	AVG
Cynthia Cooper	124	2,601	21.0	*Diana Taurasi	529	10,108	19.1
*Breanna Stewart	233	4,642	20.8	Lauren Jackson	317	6,007	18.9
*Arike Ogunbowale	157	3,169	20.2	Angel McCoughtry	311	5,797	18.6
*A'ja Wilson	189	3,761	19.9	Maya Moore	271	4,984	18.4
*Elena Delle Donne	241	4,706	19.5	Tina Charles	391	7,115	18.2

Points		Rebounds		Steals	
*Diana Taurasi	10,108	Sylvia Fowles	4,006	Tamika Catchings	1,074
Tina Thompson	7,488	Tina Charles	3,640	Ticha Penicheiro	764
Tamika Catchings	7,380	*Candace Parker	3,467	Sue Bird	724
Tina Charles	7,115	Rebekkah Brunson	3,356	Alana Beard	710
Candace Dupree	6,895	Tamika Catchings	3,316	Sheryl Swoopes	657
*DeWanna Bonner	6,881	Lisa Leslie	3,307	Jia Perkins	635
Cappie Pondexter	6,811	Candace Dupree	3,149	Sancho Lyttle	634
*Candace Parker	6,574	Tina Thompson	3,070	Angel McCoughtry	627
Katie Smith	6,452				

3-Point Field Goals Made		Assists		Blocked Shots	
*Diana Taurasi	1,361	Sue Bird	3,234	Margo Dydek	877
Sue Bird	1,001	*Courtney Vandersloot	2,701	Lisa Leslie	822
Katie Smith	906	Ticha Penicheiro	2,599	*Brittney Griner	766
Becky Hammon	829	Lindsay Whalen	2,348	Sylvia Fowles	721
Tina Thompson	748	*Diana Taurasi	2,272	*Candace Parker	619
Katie Douglas	727	Becky Hammon	1,708	Lauren Jackson	586
*Kristi Toliver	651	*Candace Parker	1,634	Tangela Smith	557
Tamika Catchings	606	Cappie Pondexter	1,578	Tammy Sutton-Brown	555

HOCKEY

Vegas Strikes It Rich in 2023 as Youngest Team to Win Stanley Cup

The Vegas Golden Knights became the fastest expansion team to win the Stanley Cup June 13, 2023, with a 9-3 shelling of the Florida Panthers in Game 5 of the 2023 Stanley Cup Final at T-Mobile Arena in Las Vegas, NV. The eighth-ranked Panthers' Cinderella run through the playoffs ended with a lone Finals win in overtime in Game 3. The Golden Knights' Jonathan Marchessault earned the Conn Smythe Trophy, recording 13 playoff goals despite going scoreless in his first seven playoff games. Marchessault was one of six Golden Knights remaining from their original expansion season in 2017-18, when Vegas became the quickest team to reach—and lose—the Cup Finals.

In the first Global Series NHL games in Europe since the COVID-19 pandemic began in 2020, the Nashville Predators and San Jose Sharks kicked off the season in Prague, Czechia; Nashville won both games Oct. 7-8, 2022. A month later, on Nov. 4-5, the Colorado Avalanche topped the Columbus Blue Jackets in a pair of games in Tampere, Finland. In the Winter Classic, the hometown Boston Bruins beat the Pittsburgh Penguins, 2-1, at Fenway Park on Jan. 2, 2023. Carter-Finley Stadium in Raleigh, NC, hosted the Stadium Series Feb. 18, 2023; the Carolina Hurricanes defeated the Washington Capitals at NC State's football stadium, 4-1. The All-Star Game was hosted by the Florida Panthers—indoors, naturally—Feb. 4.

For the first time all 32 teams played on one day—the regular season's final Saturday, Apr. 8. Three significant milestones were reached that night: Connor McDavid of the Edmonton Oilers became the first player in 27 years to reach 150 points, Pittsburgh Penguin Sidney Crosby became the 15th player to achieve 1,500 career points, and the Bruins tied the NHL record for victories in a season.

Boston would win three more games to finish the season 65-12-5, but the Panthers stunned the Bruins, eliminating Boston in seven games in the opening playoff round. The Toronto Maple Leafs won a playoff series for the first time since 2004, ending a string of 11 straight losses in series-clinching games by beating the three-time defending Eastern Conference champion Tampa Bay Lightning in six games. Florida defeated Toronto and then the Hurricanes to reach the Finals, only to be vanquished by the Golden Knights.

Final NHL Standings, 2022-23

(* = clinched playoff berth)

Standings are determined by total points; teams earn two points for each win and one point for each game lost in overtime or in a shootout. Ties broken by fewer number of games played (i.e., superior points percentage), then by regulation wins (RW).

Eastern Conference / Western Conference

Metropolitan	W	L	OT	GF	GA	RW	ROW	PTS	PCT	Central Division	W	L	OT	GF	GA	RW	ROW	PTS	PCT
Carolina*	52	21	9	266	213	39	48	113	.689	Colorado*	51	24	7	280	226	36	45	109	.665
New Jersey*	52	22	8	291	226	39	50	112	.683	Dallas*	47	21	14	285	218	39	43	108	.659
NY Rangers*	47	22	13	277	219	37	43	107	.652	Minnesota*	46	25	11	246	225	34	39	103	.628
NY Islanders*	42	31	9	243	222	36	41	93	.567	Winnipeg*	46	33	3	247	225	36	45	95	.579
Pittsburgh	40	31	11	262	264	31	39	91	.555	Nashville	42	32	8	229	238	29	36	92	.561
Washington	35	37	10	255	265	27	33	80	.488	St. Louis	37	38	7	263	301	27	34	81	.494
Philadelphia	31	38	13	222	277	26	29	75	.457	Arizona	28	40	14	228	299	20	25	70	.427
Columbus	25	48	9	214	330	15	24	59	.360	Chicago	26	49	7	204	301	18	24	59	.360

Atlantic	W	L	OT	GF	GA	RW	ROW	PTS	PCT	Pacific Division	W	L	OT	GF	GA	RW	ROW	PTS	PCT
Boston*	65	12	5	305	177	54	61	135	.823	Vegas*	51	22	9	272	229	38	46	111	.677
Toronto*	50	21	11	279	222	42	49	111	.677	Edmonton*	50	23	9	325	260	45	50	109	.665
Tampa Bay*	46	30	6	283	254	38	43	98	.598	Seattle*	46	28	8	289	256	37	46	100	.610
Florida*	42	32	8	290	273	36	40	92	.561	Los Angeles*	47	25	10	280	257	37	41	104	.634
Buffalo	42	33	7	296	300	30	39	91	.555	Calgary	38	27	17	260	252	31	36	93	.567
Ottawa	39	35	8	261	271	31	37	86	.524	Vancouver	38	37	7	276	298	24	32	83	.506
Detroit	35	37	10	240	279	28	32	80	.488	San Jose	22	44	16	234	321	16	21	60	.366
Montreal	31	45	6	232	307	21	26	68	.415	Anaheim	23	47	12	209	338	13	20	58	.354

Stanley Cup Playoff Results, 2023

First Round
Florida defeated Boston, 4-3
Toronto defeated Tampa Bay, 4-2
Carolina defeated NY Islanders, 4-2
New Jersey defeated NY Rangers, 4-3
Seattle defeated Colorado, 4-3
Dallas defeated Minnesota, 4-2

Vegas defeated Winnipeg, 4-1
Edmonton defeated Los Angeles, 4-2

Dallas defeated Seattle, 4-3
Vegas defeated Edmonton, 4-2

Second Round
Florida defeated Toronto, 4-1
Carolina defeated New Jersey, 4-1

Stanley Cup Semifinals
Florida defeated Carolina, 4-0
Vegas defeated Dallas, 4-2

Stanley Cup Final
Vegas defeated Florida (5-2, 7-2, 2-3 [OT], 3-2, 9-3)

Stanley Cup Champions, 1927-2023

Year	Champion	Coach	Final opponent	Year	Champion	Coach	Final opponent
1927	Ottawa	Dave Gill	Boston	1949	Toronto	Hap Day	Detroit
1928	NY Rangers	Lester Patrick	Montréal Maroons	1950	Detroit	Tommy Ivan	NY Rangers
				1951	Toronto	Joe Primeau	Montréal
1929	Boston	Art Ross	NY Rangers	1952	Detroit	Tommy Ivan	Montréal
1930	Montréal Canadiens	Cecil Hart	Boston	1953	Montréal	Dick Irvin	Boston
1931	Montréal Canadiens	Cecil Hart	Chicago	1954	Detroit	Tommy Ivan	Montréal
1932	Toronto	Dick Irvin	NY Rangers	1955	Detroit	Jimmy Skinner	Montréal
1933	NY Rangers	Lester Patrick	Toronto	1956	Montréal	Toe Blake	Detroit
1934	Chicago	Tommy Gorman	Detroit	1957	Montréal	Toe Blake	Boston
1935	Montréal Maroons	Tommy Gorman	Toronto	1958	Montréal	Toe Blake	Boston
1936	Detroit	Jack Adams	Toronto	1959	Montréal	Toe Blake	Toronto
1937	Detroit	Jack Adams	NY Rangers	1960	Montréal	Toe Blake	Toronto
1938	Chicago	Bill Stewart	Toronto	1961	Chicago	Rudy Pilous	Detroit
1939	Boston	Art Ross	Toronto	1962	Toronto	Punch Imlach	Chicago
1940	NY Rangers	Frank Boucher	Toronto	1963	Toronto	Punch Imlach	Detroit
1941	Boston	Cooney Weiland	Detroit	1964	Toronto	Punch Imlach	Detroit
1942	Toronto	Hap Day	Detroit	1965	Montréal	Toe Blake	Chicago
1943	Detroit	Jack Adams	Boston	1966	Montréal	Toe Blake	Detroit
1944	Montréal	Dick Irvin	Chicago	1967	Toronto	Punch Imlach	Montréal
1945	Toronto	Hap Day	Detroit	1968	Montréal	Toe Blake	St. Louis
1946	Montréal	Dick Irvin	Boston	1969	Montréal	Claude Ruel	St. Louis
1947	Toronto	Hap Day	Montréal	1970	Boston	Harry Sinden	St. Louis
1948	Toronto	Hap Day	Detroit	1971	Montréal	Al MacNeil	Chicago

Year	Champion	Coach	Final opponent	Year	Champion	Coach	Final opponent
1972	Boston	Tom Johnson	NY Rangers	1998	Detroit	Scotty Bowman	Washington
1973	Montréal	Scotty Bowman	Chicago	1999	Dallas	Ken Hitchcock	Buffalo
1974	Philadelphia	Fred Shero	Boston	2000	New Jersey	Larry Robinson	Dallas
1975	Philadelphia	Fred Shero	Buffalo	2001	Colorado	Bob Hartley	New Jersey
1976	Montréal	Scotty Bowman	Philadelphia	2002	Detroit	Scotty Bowman	Carolina
1977	Montréal	Scotty Bowman	Boston	2003	New Jersey	Pat Burns	Anaheim
1978	Montréal	Scotty Bowman	Boston	2004	Tampa Bay	John Tortorella	Calgary
1979	Montréal	Scotty Bowman	NY Rangers	2005	No competition (labor dispute; season canceled)		
1980	NY Islanders	Al Arbour	Philadelphia	2006	Carolina	Peter Laviolette	Edmonton
1981	NY Islanders	Al Arbour	Minnesota	2007	Anaheim	Randy Carlyle	Ottawa
1982	NY Islanders	Al Arbour	Vancouver	2008	Detroit	Mike Babcock	Pittsburgh
1983	NY Islanders	Al Arbour	Edmonton	2009	Pittsburgh	Dan Bylsma	Detroit
1984	Edmonton	Glen Sather	NY Islanders	2010	Chicago	Joel Quenneville	Philadelphia
1985	Edmonton	Glen Sather	Philadelphia	2011	Boston	Claude Julien	Vancouver
1986	Montréal	Jean Perron	Calgary	2012	Los Angeles	Darryl Sutter	New Jersey
1987	Edmonton	Glen Sather	Philadelphia	2013	Chicago	Joel Quenneville	Boston
1988	Edmonton	Glen Sather	Boston	2014	Los Angeles	Darryl Sutter	NY Rangers
1989	Calgary	Terry Crisp	Montréal	2015	Chicago	Joel Quenneville	Tampa Bay
1990	Edmonton	John Muckler	Boston	2016	Pittsburgh	Mike Sullivan	San Jose
1991	Pittsburgh	Bob Johnson	Minnesota	2017	Pittsburgh	Mike Sullivan	Nashville
1992	Pittsburgh	Scotty Bowman	Chicago	2018	Washington	Barry Trotz	Vegas
1993	Montréal	Jacques Demers	Los Angeles	2019	St. Louis	Craig Berube	Boston
1994	NY Rangers	Mike Keenan	Vancouver	2020	Tampa Bay	Jon Cooper	Dallas
1995	New Jersey	Jacques Lemaire	Detroit	2021	Tampa Bay	Jon Cooper	Montréal
1996	Colorado	Marc Crawford	Florida	2022	Colorado	Jared Bednar	Tampa Bay
1997	Detroit	Scotty Bowman	Philadelphia	2023	Vegas	Bruce Cassidy	Florida

Presidents' Trophy, 1986-2023

Awarded annually to club with best regular season record. Records are Win-Loss-Tie, 1986-99; Win-Loss-Tie-Overtime Loss, 2000-04; Win-Loss-Overtime Loss, 2006-present. (Because of a labor dispute, the 2005 season was canceled.)

Year	Team	Record	Points	Year	Team	Record	Points	Year	Team	Record	Points
1986	Edmonton	56-17-7	119	1999	Dallas	51-19-12	114	2012	Vancouver	51-22-9	111
1987	Edmonton	50-24-6	106	2000	St. Louis	51-19-11-1	114	2013	Chicago	36-7-5	77
1988	Calgary	48-23-9	105	2001	Colorado	52-16-10-4	118	2014	Boston	54-19-9	117
1989	Calgary	54-17-9	117	2002	Detroit	51-17-10-4	116	2015	NY Rangers	53-22-7	113
1990	Boston	46-25-9	101	2003	Ottawa	52-21-8-1	113	2016	Washington	56-18-8	120
1991	Chicago	49-23-8	106	2004	Detroit	48-21-11-2	109	2017	Washington	55-19-8	118
1992	NY Rangers	50-25-5	105	2005				2018	Nashville	53-18-11	117
1993	Pittsburgh	56-21-7	119	2006	Detroit	58-16-8	124	2019	Tampa Bay	62-16-4	128
1994	NY Rangers	52-24-8	112	2007	Buffalo	53-22-7	113	2020	Boston Bruins	44-14-12	100
1995	Detroit	33-11-4	70	2008	Detroit	54-21-7	115	2021	Colorado	39-13-4	82
1996	Detroit	62-13-7	131	2009	San Jose	53-18-11	117	2022	Florida	58-18-6	122
1997	Colorado	49-24-9	107	2010	Washington	54-15-13	121	2023	Boston	65-12-5	135
1998	Dallas	49-22-11	109	2011	Vancouver	54-19-9	117				

Most NHL Goals in a Season

Player	Team	Season	Goals	Player	Team	Season	Goals
Wayne Gretzky	Edmonton	1981-82	92	Wayne Gretzky	Edmonton	1982-83	71
Wayne Gretzky	Edmonton	1983-84	87	Jari Kurri	Edmonton	1984-85	71
Brett Hull	St. Louis	1990-91	86	Mario Lemieux	Pittsburgh	1987-88	70
Mario Lemieux	Pittsburgh	1988-89	85	Bernie Nicholls	Los Angeles	1988-89	70
Phil Esposito	Boston	1970-71	76	Brett Hull	St. Louis	1991-92	70
Alexander Mogilny	Buffalo	1992-93	76	Mike Bossy	NY Islanders	1978-79	69
Teemu Selanne	Winnipeg	1992-93	76	Mario Lemieux	Pittsburgh	1992-93	69
Wayne Gretzky	Edmonton	1984-85	73	Mario Lemieux	Pittsburgh	1995-96	69
Brett Hull	St. Louis	1989-90	72				

NHL Regular Season Career Scoring Leaders

(Through end of 2022-23 season. * = Active in 2022-23 season.)

Player	Goals	Assists	Points	Player	Goals	Assists	Points	Player	Goals	Assists	Points
Wayne Gretzky	894	1,963	2,857	*Sidney Crosby	550	952	1,502	Brendan Shanahan	656	698	1,354
Jaromir Jagr	766	1,155	1,921	*Alex Ovechkin	822	663	1,485	Guy Lafleur	560	793	1,353
Mark Messier	694	1,193	1,887	Stan Mikita	541	926	1,467	Mats Sundin	564	785	1,349
Gordie Howe	801	1,049	1,850	Teemu Selanne	684	773	1,457	Dave Andreychuk	640	698	1,338
Ron Francis	549	1,249	1,798	Bryan Trottier	524	901	1,425	Denis Savard	473	865	1,338
Marcel Dionne	731	1,040	1,771	Adam Oates	341	1,079	1,420	Mike Gartner	708	627	1,335
Steve Yzerman	692	1,063	1,755	Doug Gilmour	450	964	1,414	Pierre Turgeon	515	812	1,327
Mario Lemieux	690	1,033	1,723	Dale Hawerchuk	518	891	1,409	Gilbert Perreault	512	814	1,326
Joe Sakic	625	1,016	1,641	Jari Kurri	601	797	1,398	Jarome Iginla	625	675	1,300
Phil Esposito	717	873	1,590	Luc Robitaille	668	726	1,394	Alex Delvecchio	456	825	1,281
Ray Bourque	410	1,169	1,579	Brett Hull	741	650	1,391	Al MacInnis	340	934	1,274
Joe Thornton	430	1,109	1,539	Mike Modano	561	813	1,374	Jean Ratelle	491	776	1,267
Mark Recchi	577	956	1,533	Johnny Bucyk	556	813	1,369				
Paul Coffey	396	1,135	1,531								

Leading NHL Career Goaltenders

(Through end of 2022-23 season. * = Active in 2022-23 season.)

Ranked by Shutouts

Player		Player	
Martin Brodeur	125	*Marc-Andre Fleury	73
Terry Sawchuk	103	Lorne Chabot	71
George Hainsworth	94	Harry Lumley	71
Glenn Hall	84	Roy Worters	67
Jacques Plante	82	Patrick Roy	66
Alec Connell	81	Henrik Lundqvist	64
Tiny Thompson	81	Turk Broda	61
Dominik Hasek	81	Pekka Rinne	60
Roberto Luongo	77	Evgeni Nabokov	59
Ed Belfour	76	John Ross Roach	58
Tony Esposito	76	*Jonathan Quick	58

Ranked by Wins

Player		Player	
Martin Brodeur	691	Grant Fuhr	403
Patrick Roy	551	Chris Osgood	401
*Marc-Andre Fleury	544	Ryan Miller	391
Roberto Luongo	489	Dominik Hasek	389
Ed Belfour	484	Mike Vernon	385
Henrik Lundqvist	459	*Jonathan Quick	375
Curtis Joseph	454	John Vanbiesbrouck	374
Terry Sawchuk	445	Andy Moog	372
Jacques Plante	437	Tom Barrasso	369
Tony Esposito	423	Pekka Rinne	369
Glenn Hall	407	Carey Price	361

Hart Memorial Trophy (MVP), 1927-2023

Year	Player, team	Year	Player, team	Year	Player, team
1927	Herb Gardiner, Montréal Canadiens	1959	Andy Bathgate, NY Rangers	1991	Brett Hull, St. Louis
1928	Howie Morenz, Montréal Canadiens	1960	Gordie Howe, Detroit	1992	Mark Messier, NY Rangers
1929	Roy Worters, NY Americans	1961	Bernie Geoffrion, Montréal	1993	Mario Lemieux, Pittsburgh
1930	Nels Stewart, Montréal Maroons	1962	Jacques Plante, Montréal	1994	Sergei Fedorov, Detroit
1931	Howie Morenz, Montréal Canadiens	1963	Gordie Howe, Detroit	1995	Eric Lindros, Philadelphia
1932	Howie Morenz, Montréal Canadiens	1964	Jean Beliveau, Montréal	1996	Mario Lemieux, Pittsburgh
1933	Eddie Shore, Boston	1965	Bobby Hull, Chicago	1997	Dominik Hasek, Buffalo
1934	Aurel Joliat, Montréal Canadiens	1966	Bobby Hull, Chicago	1998	Dominik Hasek, Buffalo
1935	Eddie Shore, Boston	1967	Stan Mikita, Chicago	1999	Jaromir Jagr, Pittsburgh
1936	Eddie Shore, Boston	1968	Stan Mikita, Chicago	2000	Chris Pronger, St. Louis
1937	Babe Siebert, Montréal Canadiens	1969	Phil Esposito, Boston	2001	Joe Sakic, Colorado
1938	Eddie Shore, Boston	1970	Bobby Orr, Boston	2002	Jose Theodore, Montréal
1939	Toe Blake, Montréal	1971	Bobby Orr, Boston	2003	Peter Forsberg, Colorado
1940	Ebbie Goodfellow, Detroit	1972	Bobby Orr, Boston	2004	Martin St. Louis, Tampa Bay
1941	Bill Cowley, Boston	1973	Bobby Clarke, Philadelphia	2006	Joe Thornton, San Jose
1942	Tom Anderson, Brooklyn Americans	1974	Phil Esposito, Boston	2007	Sidney Crosby, Pittsburgh
1943	Bill Cowley, Boston	1975	Bobby Clarke, Philadelphia	2008	Alexander Ovechkin, Washington
1944	Babe Pratt, Toronto	1976	Bobby Clarke, Philadelphia	2009	Alexander Ovechkin, Washington
1945	Elmer Lach, Montréal	1977	Guy Lafleur, Montréal	2010	Henrik Sedin, Vancouver
1946	Max Bentley, Chicago	1978	Guy Lafleur, Montréal	2011	Corey Perry, Anaheim
1947	Maurice Richard, Montréal	1979	Bryan Trottier, NY Islanders	2012	Evgeni Malkin, Pittsburgh
1948	Buddy O'Connor, NY Rangers	1980	Wayne Gretzky, Edmonton	2013	Alexander Ovechkin, Washington
1949	Sid Abel, Detroit	1981	Wayne Gretzky, Edmonton	2014	Sidney Crosby, Pittsburgh
1950	Chuck Rayner, NY Rangers	1982	Wayne Gretzky, Edmonton	2015	Carey Price, Montréal
1951	Milt Schmidt, Boston	1983	Wayne Gretzky, Edmonton	2016	Patrick Kane, Chicago
1952	Gordie Howe, Detroit	1984	Wayne Gretzky, Edmonton	2017	Connor McDavid, Edmonton
1953	Gordie Howe, Detroit	1985	Wayne Gretzky, Edmonton	2018	Taylor Hall, New Jersey
1954	Al Rollins, Chicago	1986	Wayne Gretzky, Edmonton	2019	Nikita Kucherov, Tampa Bay
1955	Ted Kennedy, Toronto	1987	Wayne Gretzky, Edmonton	2020	Leon Draisaitl, Edmonton
1956	Jean Beliveau, Montréal	1988	Mario Lemieux, Pittsburgh	2021	Connor McDavid, Edmonton
1957	Gordie Howe, Detroit	1989	Wayne Gretzky, Los Angeles	2022	Auston Matthews, Toronto
1958	Gordie Howe, Detroit	1990	Mark Messier, Edmonton	2023	Connor McDavid, Edmonton

Conn Smythe Trophy (MVP in Playoffs), 1965-2023

Year	Player, team	Year	Player, team	Year	Player, team
1965	Jean Beliveau, Montréal	1985	Wayne Gretzky, Edmonton	2004	Brad Richards, Tampa Bay
1966	Roger Crozier, Detroit	1986	Patrick Roy, Montréal	2006	Cam Ward, Carolina
1967	Dave Keon, Toronto	1987	Ron Hextall, Philadelphia	2007	Scott Niedermayer, Anaheim
1968	Glenn Hall, St. Louis	1988	Wayne Gretzky, Edmonton	2008	Henrik Zetterberg, Detroit
1969	Serge Savard, Montréal	1989	Al MacInnis, Calgary	2009	Evgeni Malkin, Pittsburgh
1970	Bobby Orr, Boston	1990	Bill Ranford, Edmonton	2010	Jonathan Toews, Chicago
1971	Ken Dryden, Montréal	1991	Mario Lemieux, Pittsburgh	2011	Tim Thomas, Boston
1972	Bobby Orr, Boston	1992	Mario Lemieux, Pittsburgh	2012	Jonathan Quick, Los Angeles
1973	Yvan Cournoyer, Montréal	1993	Patrick Roy, Montréal	2013	Patrick Kane, Chicago
1974	Bernie Parent, Philadelphia	1994	Brian Leetch, NY Rangers	2014	Justin Williams, Los Angeles
1975	Bernie Parent, Philadelphia	1995	Claude Lemieux, New Jersey	2015	Duncan Keith, Chicago
1976	Reggie Leach, Philadelphia	1996	Joe Sakic, Colorado	2016	Sidney Crosby, Pittsburgh
1977	Guy Lafleur, Montréal	1997	Mike Vernon, Detroit	2017	Sidney Crosby, Pittsburgh
1978	Larry Robinson, Montréal	1998	Steve Yzerman, Detroit	2018	Alex Ovechkin, Washington
1979	Bob Gainey, Montréal	1999	Joe Nieuwendyk, Dallas	2019	Ryan O'Reilly, St. Louis
1980	Bryan Trottier, NY Islanders	2000	Scott Stevens, New Jersey	2020	Víctor Hedman, Tampa Bay
1981	Butch Goring, NY Islanders	2001	Patrick Roy, Colorado	2021	Andrei Vasilevskiy, Tampa Bay
1982	Mike Bossy, NY Islanders	2002	Nicklas Lidstrom, Detroit	2022	Cale Makar, Colorado
1983	Billy Smith, NY Islanders	2003	Jean-Sebastien Giguere, Anaheim	2023	Jonathan Marchessault, Vegas
1984	Mark Messier, Edmonton				

Calder Memorial Trophy (Best Rookie), 1933-2023

Year	Player, team	Year	Player, team	Year	Player, team
1933	Carl Voss, Detroit	1963	Kent Douglas, Toronto	1993	Teemu Selanne, Winnipeg
1934	Russ Blinco, Montréal Maroons	1964	Jacques Laperrière, Montréal	1994	Martin Brodeur, New Jersey
1935	Dave Schriner, NY Americans	1965	Roger Crozier, Detroit	1995	Peter Forsberg, Quebec
1936	Mike Karakas, Chicago	1966	Brit Selby, Toronto	1996	Daniel Alfredsson, Ottawa
1937	Syl Apps, Toronto	1967	Bobby Orr, Boston	1997	Bryan Berard, NY Islanders
1938	Cully Dahlstrom, Chicago	1968	Derek Sanderson, Boston	1998	Sergei Samsonov, Boston
1939	Frank Brimsek, Boston	1969	Danny Grant, Minnesota	1999	Chris Drury, Colorado
1940	Kilby MacDonald, NY Rangers	1970	Tony Esposito, Chicago	2000	Scott Gomez, New Jersey
1941	John Quilty, Montréal	1971	Gilbert Perreault, Buffalo	2001	Evgeni Nabokov, San Jose
1942	Grant Warwick, NY Rangers	1972	Ken Dryden, Montréal	2002	Dany Heatley, Atlanta
1943	Gaye Stewart, Toronto	1973	Steve Vickers, NY Rangers	2003	Barret Jackman, St. Louis
1944	Gus Bodnar, Toronto	1974	Denis Potvin, NY Islanders	2004	Andrew Raycroft, Boston
1945	Frank McCool, Toronto	1975	Eric Vail, Atlanta	2006	Alexander Ovechkin, Washington
1946	Edgar Laprade, NY Rangers	1976	Bryan Trottier, NY Islanders	2007	Evgeni Malkin, Pittsburgh
1947	Howie Meeker, Toronto	1977	Willi Plett, Atlanta	2008	Patrick Kane, Chicago
1948	Jim McFadden, Detroit	1978	Mike Bossy, NY Islanders	2009	Steve Mason, Columbus
1949	Pentti Lund, NY Rangers	1979	Bobby Smith, Minnesota	2010	Tyler Myers, Buffalo
1950	Jack Gelineau, Boston	1980	Ray Bourque, Boston	2011	Jeff Skinner, Carolina
1951	Terry Sawchuk, Detroit	1981	Peter Stastny, Quebec	2012	Gabriel Landeskog, Colorado
1952	Bernie Geoffrion, Montréal	1982	Dale Hawerchuk, Winnipeg	2013	Jonathan Huberdeau, Florida
1953	Gump Worsley, NY Rangers	1983	Steve Larmer, Chicago	2014	Nathan MacKinnon, Colorado
1954	Camille Henry, NY Rangers	1984	Tom Barrasso, Buffalo	2015	Aaron Ekblad, Florida
1955	Ed Litzenberger, Chicago	1985	Mario Lemieux, Pittsburgh	2016	Artemi Panarin, Chicago
1956	Glenn Hall, Detroit	1986	Gary Suter, Calgary	2017	Auston Matthews, Toronto
1957	Larry Regan, Boston	1987	Luc Robitaille, Los Angeles	2018	Mathew Barzal, NY Islanders
1958	Frank Mahovlich, Toronto	1988	Joe Nieuwendyk, Calgary	2019	Elias Pettersson, Vancouver
1959	Ralph Backstrom, Montréal	1989	Brian Leetch, NY Rangers	2020	Cale Makar, Colorado
1960	Bill Hay, Chicago	1990	Sergei Makarov, Calgary	2021	Kirill Kaprizov, Minnesota
1961	Dave Keon, Toronto	1991	Ed Belfour, Chicago	2022	Moritz Seider, Detroit
1962	Bobby Rousseau, Montréal	1992	Pavel Bure, Vancouver	2023	Matty Beniers, Seattle

Lady Byng Memorial Trophy (Most Gentlemanly Player), 1925-2023

Year	Player, team	Year	Player, team	Year	Player, team
1925	Frank Nighbor, Ottawa	1958	Camille Henry, NY Rangers	1991	Wayne Gretzky, Los Angeles
1926	Frank Nighbor, Ottawa	1959	Alex Delvecchio, Detroit	1992	Wayne Gretzky, Los Angeles
1927	Billy Burch, NY Americans	1960	Don McKenney, Boston	1993	Pierre Turgeon, NY Islanders
1928	Frank Boucher, NY Rangers	1961	Red Kelly, Toronto	1994	Wayne Gretzky, Los Angeles
1929	Frank Boucher, NY Rangers	1962	Dave Keon, Toronto	1995	Ron Francis, Pittsburgh
1930	Frank Boucher, NY Rangers	1963	Dave Keon, Toronto	1996	Paul Kariya, Anaheim
1931	Frank Boucher, NY Rangers	1964	Ken Wharram, Chicago	1997	Paul Kariya, Anaheim
1932	Joe Primeau, Toronto	1965	Bobby Hull, Chicago	1998	Ron Francis, Pittsburgh
1933	Frank Boucher, NY Rangers	1966	Alex Delvecchio, Detroit	1999	Wayne Gretzky, NY Rangers
1934	Frank Boucher, NY Rangers	1967	Stan Mikita, Chicago	2000	Pavol Demitra, St. Louis
1935	Frank Boucher, NY Rangers	1968	Stan Mikita, Chicago	2001	Joe Sakic, Colorado
1936	Doc Romnes, Chicago	1969	Alex Delvecchio, Detroit	2002	Ron Francis, Carolina
1937	Marty Barry, Detroit	1970	Phil Goyette, St. Louis	2003	Alexander Mogilny, Toronto
1938	Gordie Drillon, Toronto	1971	John Bucyk, Boston	2004	Brad Richards, Tampa Bay
1939	Clint Smith, NY Rangers	1972	Jean Ratelle, NY Rangers	2006	Pavel Datsyuk, Detroit
1940	Bobby Bauer, Boston	1973	Gil Perreault, Buffalo	2007	Pavel Datsyuk, Detroit
1941	Bobby Bauer, Boston	1974	John Bucyk, Boston	2008	Pavel Datsyuk, Detroit
1942	Syl Apps, Toronto	1975	Marcel Dionne, Detroit	2009	Pavel Datsyuk, Detroit
1943	Max Bentley, Chicago	1976	Jean Ratelle, NYR-Boston	2010	Martin St. Louis, Tampa Bay
1944	Clint Smith, Chicago	1977	Marcel Dionne, Los Angeles	2011	Martin St. Louis, Tampa Bay
1945	Bill Mosienko, Chicago	1978	Butch Goring, Los Angeles	2012	Brian Campbell, Florida
1946	Toe Blake, Montréal	1979	Bob MacMillan, Atlanta	2013	Martin St. Louis, Tampa Bay
1947	Bobby Bauer, Boston	1980	Wayne Gretzky, Edmonton	2014	Ryan O'Reilly, Colorado
1948	Buddy O'Connor, NY Rangers	1981	Rick Kehoe, Pittsburgh	2015	Jiri Hudler, Calgary
1949	Bill Quackenbush, Detroit	1982	Rick Middleton, Boston	2016	Anze Kopitar, Los Angeles
1950	Edgar Laprade, NY Rangers	1983	Mike Bossy, NY Islanders	2017	Johnny Gaudreau, Calgary
1951	Red Kelly, Detroit	1984	Mike Bossy, NY Islanders	2018	William Karlsson, Vegas
1952	Sid Smith, Toronto	1985	Jari Kurri, Edmonton	2019	Aleksander Barkov, Florida
1953	Red Kelly, Detroit	1986	Mike Bossy, NY Islanders	2020	Nathan MacKinnon, Colorado
1954	Red Kelly, Detroit	1987	Joe Mullen, Calgary	2021	Jaccob Slavin, Carolina
1955	Sid Smith, Toronto	1988	Mats Naslund, Montréal	2022	Kyle Connor, Winnipeg
1956	Dutch Reibel, Detroit	1989	Joe Mullen, Calgary	2023	Anze Kopitar, Los Angeles
1957	Andy Hebenton, NY Rangers	1990	Brett Hull, St. Louis		

James Norris Memorial Trophy (Best Defenseman), 1954-2023

Year	Player, team	Year	Player, team	Year	Player, team
1954	Red Kelly, Detroit	1977	Larry Robinson, Montréal	2000	Chris Pronger, St. Louis
1955	Doug Harvey, Montréal	1978	Denis Potvin, NY Islanders	2001	Nicklas Lidstrom, Detroit
1956	Doug Harvey, Montréal	1979	Denis Potvin, NY Islanders	2002	Nicklas Lidstrom, Detroit
1957	Doug Harvey, Montréal	1980	Larry Robinson, Montréal	2003	Nicklas Lidstrom, Detroit
1958	Doug Harvey, Montréal	1981	Randy Carlyle, Pittsburgh	2004	Scott Niedermayer, New Jersey
1959	Tom Johnson, Montréal	1982	Doug Wilson, Chicago	2006	Nicklas Lidstrom, Detroit
1960	Doug Harvey, Montréal	1983	Rod Langway, Washington	2007	Nicklas Lidstrom, Detroit
1961	Doug Harvey, Montréal	1984	Rod Langway, Washington	2008	Nicklas Lidstrom, Detroit
1962	Doug Harvey, NY Rangers	1985	Paul Coffey, Edmonton	2009	Zdeno Chara, Boston
1963	Pierre Pilote, Chicago	1986	Paul Coffey, Edmonton	2010	Duncan Keith, Chicago
1964	Pierre Pilote, Chicago	1987	Ray Bourque, Boston	2011	Nicklas Lidstrom, Detroit
1965	Pierre Pilote, Chicago	1988	Ray Bourque, Boston	2012	Erik Karlsson, Ottawa
1966	Jacques Laperrière, Montréal	1989	Chris Chelios, Montréal	2013	P. K. Subban, Montréal
1967	Harry Howell, NY Rangers	1990	Ray Bourque, Boston	2014	Duncan Keith, Chicago
1968	Bobby Orr, Boston	1991	Ray Bourque, Boston	2015	Erik Karlsson, Ottawa
1969	Bobby Orr, Boston	1992	Brian Leetch, NY Rangers	2016	Drew Doughty, Los Angeles
1970	Bobby Orr, Boston	1993	Chris Chelios, Chicago	2017	Brent Burns, San Jose
1971	Bobby Orr, Boston	1994	Ray Bourque, Boston	2018	Victor Hedman, Tampa Bay
1972	Bobby Orr, Boston	1995	Paul Coffey, Detroit	2019	Mark Giordano, Calgary
1973	Bobby Orr, Boston	1996	Chris Chelios, Chicago	2020	Roman Josi, Nashville
1974	Bobby Orr, Boston	1997	Brian Leetch, NY Rangers	2021	Adam Fox, NY Rangers
1975	Bobby Orr, Boston	1998	Rob Blake, Los Angeles	2022	Cale Makar, Colorado
1976	Denis Potvin, NY Islanders	1999	Al MacInnis, St. Louis	2023	Erik Karlsson, San Jose

Art Ross Trophy (Highest Scorer), 1947-2023

Year	Player, team	Year	Player, team	Year	Player, team
1947	Max Bentley, Chicago	1973	Phil Esposito, Boston	1998	Jaromir Jagr, Pittsburgh
1948	Elmer Lach, Montréal	1974	Phil Esposito, Boston	1999	Jaromir Jagr, Pittsburgh
1949	Roy Conacher, Chicago	1975	Bobby Orr, Boston	2000	Jaromir Jagr, Pittsburgh
1950	Ted Lindsay, Detroit	1976	Guy Lafleur, Montréal	2001	Jaromir Jagr, Pittsburgh
1951	Gordie Howe, Detroit	1977	Guy Lafleur, Montréal	2002	Jarome Iginla, Calgary
1952	Gordie Howe, Detroit	1978	Guy Lafleur, Montréal	2003	Peter Forsberg, Colorado
1953	Gordie Howe, Detroit	1979	Bryan Trottier, NY Islanders	2004	Martin St. Louis, Tampa Bay
1954	Gordie Howe, Detroit	1980	Marcel Dionne, Los Angeles	2006	Joe Thornton, Boston/San Jose
1955	Bernie Geoffrion, Montréal	1981	Wayne Gretzky, Edmonton	2007	Sidney Crosby, Pittsburgh
1956	Jean Beliveau, Montréal	1982	Wayne Gretzky, Edmonton	2008	Alexander Ovechkin, Washington
1957	Gordie Howe, Detroit	1983	Wayne Gretzky, Edmonton	2009	Evgeni Malkin, Pittsburgh
1958	Dickie Moore, Montréal	1984	Wayne Gretzky, Edmonton	2010	Henrik Sedin, Vancouver
1959	Dickie Moore, Montréal	1985	Wayne Gretzky, Edmonton	2011	Daniel Sedin, Vancouver
1960	Bobby Hull, Chicago	1986	Wayne Gretzky, Edmonton	2012	Evgeni Malkin, Pittsburgh
1961	Bernie Geoffrion, Montréal	1987	Wayne Gretzky, Edmonton	2013	Martin St. Louis, Tampa Bay
1962	Bobby Hull, Chicago	1988	Mario Lemieux, Pittsburgh	2014	Sidney Crosby, Pittsburgh
1963	Gordie Howe, Detroit	1989	Mario Lemieux, Pittsburgh	2015	Jamie Benn, Dallas
1964	Stan Mikita, Chicago	1990	Wayne Gretzky, Los Angeles	2016	Patrick Kane, Chicago
1965	Stan Mikita, Chicago	1991	Wayne Gretzky, Los Angeles	2017	Connor McDavid, Edmonton
1966	Bobby Hull, Chicago	1992	Mario Lemieux, Pittsburgh	2018	Connor McDavid, Edmonton
1967	Stan Mikita, Chicago	1993	Mario Lemieux, Pittsburgh	2019	Nikita Kucherov, Tampa Bay
1968	Stan Mikita, Chicago	1994	Wayne Gretzky, Los Angeles	2020	Leon Draisaitl, Edmonton
1969	Phil Esposito, Boston	1995	Jaromir Jagr, Pittsburgh	2021	Connor McDavid, Edmonton
1970	Bobby Orr, Boston	1996	Mario Lemieux, Pittsburgh	2022	Connor McDavid, Edmonton
1971	Phil Esposito, Boston	1997	Mario Lemieux, Pittsburgh	2023	Connor McDavid, Edmonton
1972	Phil Esposito, Boston				

Vezina Trophy (Best Goaltender), 1927-2023

Year	Player, team	Year	Player, team	Year	Player, team
1927	George Hainsworth, Montréal Canadiens	1929	George Hainsworth, Montréal Canadiens	1932	Charlie Gardiner, Chicago
		1930	Tiny Thompson, Boston	1933	Tiny Thompson, Boston
1928	George Hainsworth, Montréal Canadiens	1931	Roy Worters, NY Americans	1934	Charlie Gardiner, Chicago
				1935	Lorne Chabot, Chicago

Year	Player, team
1936	Tiny Thompson, Boston
1937	Normie Smith, Detroit
1938	Tiny Thompson, Boston
1939	Frank Brimsek, Boston
1940	Dave Kerr, NY Rangers
1941	Turk Broda, Toronto
1942	Frank Brimsek, Boston
1943	Johnny Mowers, Detroit
1944	Bill Durnan, Montréal
1945	Bill Durnan, Montréal
1946	Bill Durnan, Montréal
1947	Bill Durnan, Montréal
1948	Turk Broda, Toronto
1949	Bill Durnan, Montréal
1950	Bill Durnan, Montréal
1951	Al Rollins, Toronto
1952	Terry Sawchuk, Detroit
1953	Terry Sawchuk, Detroit
1954	Harry Lumley, Toronto
1955	Terry Sawchuk, Detroit
1956	Jacques Plante, Montréal
1957	Jacques Plante, Montréal
1958	Jacques Plante, Montréal
1959	Jacques Plante, Montréal
1960	Jacques Plante, Montréal
1961	Johnny Bower, Toronto
1962	Jacques Plante, Montréal
1963	Glenn Hall, Chicago
1964	Charlie Hodge, Montréal
1965	Sawchuk, Bower; Toronto

Year	Player, team
1966	Lorne Worsley, Hodge; Montréal
1967	Hall, Denis DeJordy; Chicago
1968	Worsley, Rogatien Vachon; Montréal
1969	Hall, Plante; St. Louis
1970	Tony Esposito, Chicago
1971	Ed Giacomin, Gilles Villemure; NY Rangers
1972	Esposito, Gary Smith; Chicago
1973	Ken Dryden, Montréal
1974	Bernie Parent, Philadelphia; Tony Esposito, Chicago
1975	Bernie Parent, Philadelphia
1976	Ken Dryden, Montréal
1977	Dryden, Michel Larocque; Montréal
1978	Dryden, Larocque; Montréal
1979	Dryden, Larocque; Montréal
1980	Bob Sauve, Don Edwards; Buffalo
1981	Richard Sevigny, Michel Larocque, Denis Herron; Montréal
1982	Bill Smith, NY Islanders
1983	Pete Peeters, Boston
1984	Tom Barrasso, Buffalo
1985	Pelle Lindbergh, Philadelphia
1986	John Vanbiesbrouck, NY Rangers
1987	Ron Hextall, Philadelphia
1988	Grant Fuhr, Edmonton
1989	Patrick Roy, Montréal
1990	Patrick Roy, Montréal
1991	Ed Belfour, Chicago
1992	Patrick Roy, Montréal

Year	Player, team
1993	Ed Belfour, Chicago
1994	Dominik Hasek, Buffalo
1995	Dominik Hasek, Buffalo
1996	Jim Carey, Washington
1997	Dominik Hasek, Buffalo
1998	Dominik Hasek, Buffalo
1999	Dominik Hasek, Buffalo
2000	Olaf Kolzig, Washington
2001	Dominik Hasek, Buffalo
2002	Jose Theodore, Montréal
2003	Martin Brodeur, New Jersey
2004	Martin Brodeur, New Jersey
2006	Miikka Kiprusoff, Calgary
2007	Martin Brodeur, New Jersey
2008	Martin Brodeur, New Jersey
2009	Tim Thomas, Boston
2010	Ryan Miller, Buffalo
2011	Tim Thomas, Boston
2012	Henrik Lundqvist, NY Rangers
2013	Sergei Bobrovsky, Columbus
2014	Tuukka Rask, Boston
2015	Carey Price, Montréal
2016	Braden Holtby, Washington
2017	Sergei Bobrovsky, Columbus
2018	Pekka Rinne, Nashville
2019	Andrei Vasilevskiy, Tampa Bay
2020	Connor Hellebuyck, Winnipeg
2021	Marc-Andre Fleury, Vegas
2022	Igor Shesterkin, NY Rangers
2023	Linus Ullmark, Boston

National Hockey League Franchise Origins

Team: founding year, league (NHL, World Hockey Association [WHA], or National Hockey Association of Canada [NHA]). Original location; subsequent history. Sites in the same metropolitan area not shown. * = Joined NHL in 1979 from defunct WHA.

Anaheim Ducks: 1993, NHL, as Mighty Ducks of Anaheim. Anaheim, CA, 1993-present. (Ducks, 2006-present.)

*Arizona Coyotes: 1972, WHA, as Winnipeg Jets. Winnipeg, MB, Canada, 1979-96; Phoenix Coyotes, 1996-2014; Arizona Coyotes, Glendale, AZ, 2014-present.

Boston Bruins: 1924, NHL. Boston, 1924-present.

Buffalo Sabres: 1970, NHL. Buffalo, NY, 1970-present.

Calgary Flames: 1972, NHL, as Atlanta Flames. Atlanta, GA, 1972-80; Calgary, AB, Canada, 1980-present.

*Carolina Hurricanes: 1972, WHA, as Hartford Whalers. Hartford, CT, 1979-97; Carolina Hurricanes, Greensboro, NC, 1997-99; Raleigh, NC, 1999-present.

Chicago Blackhawks: 1926, NHL, as Chicago Black Hawks. Chicago, 1926-present. (Blackhawks, 1986-present.)

*Colorado Avalanche: 1972, WHA, as Quebec Nordiques. Quebec City, QC, Canada, 1979-95; Colorado Avalanche, Denver, 1995-present.

Columbus Blue Jackets: 2000, NHL. Columbus, OH, 2000-present.

Dallas Stars: 1967, NHL, as Minnesota North Stars. Bloomington, MN, 1967-93; Dallas Stars, Dallas, 1993-present.

Detroit Red Wings: 1926, NHL, as Detroit Cougars, 1926-30. Detroit Falcons, 1930-32; Detroit Red Wings, 1932-present.

*Edmonton Oilers: 1972, WHA. Edmonton, AB, Canada, 1979-present.

Florida Panthers: 1993, NHL. Miami, FL, 1993-98; Sunrise, FL, 1998-present.

Los Angeles Kings: 1967, NHL. Los Angeles, 1967-present.

Minnesota Wild: 2000, NHL. St. Paul, MN, 2000-present.

Montréal Canadiens: 1909, NHA; joined NHL, 1917. Montréal, QC, Canada, 1909-present.

Nashville Predators: 1998, NHL. Nashville, TN, 1998-present.

New Jersey Devils: 1974, NHL, as Kansas City Scouts. Kansas City, MO, 1974-76; Colorado Rockies, Denver, CO, 1976-82; New Jersey Devils, East Rutherford, NJ, 1982-2007; Newark, NJ, 2007-present.

New York Islanders: 1972, NHL. Uniondale, NY, 1972-2015, 2021, and selected games, 2018-20; Brooklyn, NY, 2015-20.

New York Rangers: 1926, NHL. New York City, 1926-present.

Ottawa Senators: 1992, NHL. Ottawa, ON, Canada, 1992-present.

Philadelphia Flyers: 1967, NHL. Philadelphia, 1967-present.

Pittsburgh Penguins: 1967, NHL. Pittsburgh, 1967-present.

St. Louis Blues: 1967, NHL. St. Louis, MO, 1967-present.

San Jose Sharks: 1991, NHL. Daly City, CA, 1991-93; San Jose, CA, 1993-present.

Seattle Kraken: 2021, NHL. Seattle, WA, 2021-present.

Tampa Bay Lightning: 1992, NHL. Tampa, FL, 1992-93; St. Petersburg, FL, 1993-96; Tampa, FL, 1996-present.

Toronto Maple Leafs: 1917, NHL, as Toronto (ON, Canada) Arenas, 1917-19. Toronto St. Patricks, 1919-26; Toronto Maple Leafs, 1926-present.

Vancouver Canucks: 1970, NHL. Vancouver, BC, Canada, 1970-present.

Vegas Golden Knights: 2017, NHL. Las Vegas, NV, 2017-present.

Washington Capitals: 1974, NHL. Landover, MD, 1974-97; Washington, DC, 1997-present.

Winnipeg Jets: 1999, NHL, as Atlanta Thrashers. Atlanta, GA, 1999-2011; Winnipeg, MB, Canada, 2011-present.

NHL Home Ice

Team	Name (year play began)	Capacity[1]
Anaheim	Honda Center[2] (1993)	17,174
Arizona	Mullett Arena (2022)	4,700
Boston	TD Garden[3] (1995)	17,850
Buffalo	KeyBank Center[4] (1996)	19,070
Calgary	Scotiabank Saddledome[5] (1983)	19,289
Carolina	PNC Arena[6] (1999)	18,680
Chicago	United Center (1994)	19,917
Colorado	Ball Arena[7] (1999)	19,250
Columbus	Nationwide Arena (2000)	18,144
Dallas	American Airlines Center (2001)	18,532
Detroit	Little Caesars Arena (2017)	19,515
Edmonton	Rogers Place (2016)	18,347
Florida	FLA Live Arena[8] (1998)	19,250
Los Angeles	Crypto.com Arena[9] (1999)	18,230
Minnesota	Xcel Energy Center (2000)	17,954
Montréal	Centre Bell[10] (1996)	21,302
Nashville	Bridgestone Arena[11] (1997)	17,159
New Jersey	Prudential Center (2007)	16,514
NY Islanders	UBS Arena (2021)	17,113
NY Rangers	Madison Square Garden (IV) (1968)	18,006
Ottawa	Canadian Tire Centre[12] (1996)	18,652
Philadelphia	Wells Fargo Center[13] (1996)	19,306
Pittsburgh	PPG Paints Arena[14] (2010)	18,187
St. Louis	Enterprise Center[15] (1994)	18,400
San Jose	SAP Center at San Jose[16] (1993)	17,562
Seattle	Climate Pledge Arena (2021)	17,100
Tampa Bay	Amalie Arena[17] (1996)	19,092
Toronto	Scotiabank Arena[18] (1999)	18,819
Vancouver	Rogers Arena[19] (1995)	18,870
Vegas	T-Mobile Arena (2017)	17,367
Washington	Capital One Arena[20] (1997)	18,573
Winnipeg	Canada Life Centre[21] (2004)	15,321

(1) At the end of the 2022-23 season. (2) The Arrowhead Pond of Anaheim, 1993-2006. (3) FleetCenter, 1995-2005; TD Banknorth Garden, 2005-09. (4) Marine Midland Arena, 1996-99; HSBC Arena, 1999-2011; First Niagara Center, 2011-16. (5) Olympic Saddledome, 1983-96; Canadian Airlines Saddledome, 1996-2000; Pengrowth Saddledome, 2000-10. (6) Raleigh Entertainment and Sports Arena, 1999-2002; RBC Center, 2002-11. (7) Pepsi Center, 1999-2020. (8) National Car Rental Center, 1998-2002; Office Depot Center, 2002-05; BankAtlantic Center, 2005-12; BB&T Center, 2012-21. (9) Staples Center, 1999-2021. (10) Le Centre Molson, 1996-2002. (11) Nashville Arena, 1997-99; Gaylord Entertainment Center, 1999-2007; Sommet Center, 2007-10. (12) Corel Centre, 1996-2006; Scotiabank Place, 2006-13. (13) CoreStates Center, 1996-98; First Union Center, 1998-2003; Wachovia Center, 2003-10. (14) CONSOL Energy Center, 2010-16. (15) Kiel Center, 1994-2000; Savvis Center, 2000-06; Scottrade Center, 2006-18. (16) San Jose Arena, 1993-2001; Compaq Center, 2001-02; HP Pavilion at San Jose, 2002-13. (17) Ice Palace, 1996-2002; St. Pete Times Forum, 2002-12; Tampa Bay Times Forum, 2012-14. (18) Air Canada Centre, 1999-2018. (19) General Motors Place, 1995-2010. (20) MCI Center, 1997-2006; Verizon Center, 2006-17. (21) MTS Centre, 2004-17; Bell MTS Place, 2017-21.

SOCCER

Spain Wins 2023 FIFA Women's World Cup

The Spanish women's national team won its first FIFA World Cup, defeating England, 1-0, on Aug. 20, 2023, at Stadium Australia in Sydney, Australia. The lone goal was scored by Olga Carmona in the 29th minute. Both teams appeared in the title match for the first time; Spain's previous best finish was the round of 16 in 2019. The team's momentous victory was quickly overshadowed by Luis Rubiales, head of the country's soccer federation, who forcibly kissed forward Jennifer Hermoso during the post-game celebration. Rubiales initially refused calls to resign, even after suspension by FIFA, but finally stepped down weeks later.

Spain's Aitana Bonmatí won the Golden Ball as the tournament's best player. The Golden Boot went to top scorer Hinata Miyazawa, who recorded five goals for Japan—two in a 4-0 group-stage drubbing of Spain. The Golden Glove went to English goalkeeper Mary Earps, who lived up to her nickname, "Mary Queen of Stops." Spain's Salma Paralluelo captured Young Player of the Tournament.

The U.S. team, winners of the last two World Cups and four of nine since the event started in 1991, was bounced in the round of 16 on penalty kicks by eventual third-place finisher Sweden. Vlatko Andonovski, coach of the U.S. women since 2019, resigned.

Women's World Cup Results, 2023

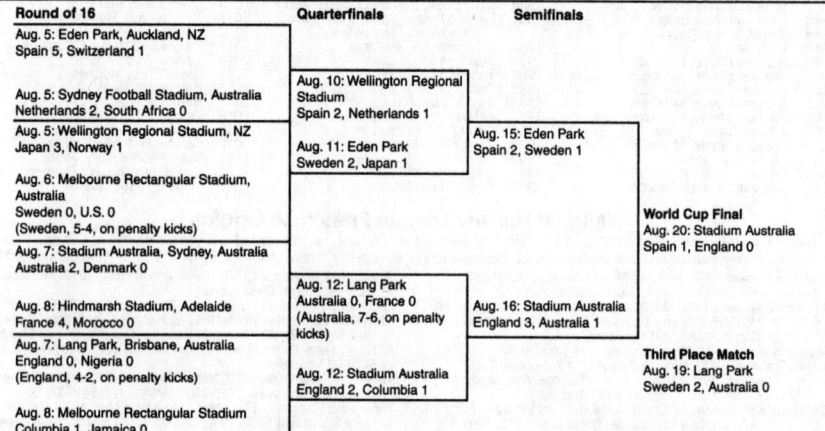

Round of 16

Aug. 5: Eden Park, Auckland, NZ
Spain 5, Switzerland 1

Aug. 5: Sydney Football Stadium, Australia
Netherlands 2, South Africa 0

Aug. 5: Wellington Regional Stadium, NZ
Japan 3, Norway 1

Aug. 6: Melbourne Rectangular Stadium, Australia
Sweden 0, U.S. 0
(Sweden, 5-4, on penalty kicks)

Aug. 7: Stadium Australia, Sydney, Australia
Australia 2, Denmark 0

Aug. 8: Hindmarsh Stadium, Adelaide
France 4, Morocco 0

Aug. 7: Lang Park, Brisbane, Australia
England 0, Nigeria 0
(England, 4-2, on penalty kicks)

Aug. 8: Melbourne Rectangular Stadium
Columbia 1, Jamaica 0

Quarterfinals

Aug. 10: Wellington Regional Stadium
Spain 2, Netherlands 1

Aug. 11: Eden Park
Sweden 2, Japan 1

Aug. 12: Lang Park
Australia 0, France 0
(Australia, 7-6, on penalty kicks)

Aug. 12: Stadium Australia
England 2, Columbia 1

Semifinals

Aug. 15: Eden Park
Spain 2, Sweden 1

Aug. 16: Stadium Australia
England 3, Australia 1

World Cup Final
Aug. 20: Stadium Australia
Spain 1, England 0

Third Place Match
Aug. 19: Lang Park
Sweden 2, Australia 0

Women's World Cup Results, 1991-2023

Year	Winner	Final opponent	Score	Site	Year	Winner	Final opponent	Score	Site
1991	U.S.	Norway	2-1	China	2011	Japan	U.S.	2-2 (3-1)*	Germany
1995	Norway	Germany	2-0	China	2015	U.S.	Japan	5-2	Canada
1999	U.S.	China	0-0 (5-4)*	Pasadena, CA, U.S.	2019	U.S.	Netherlands	2-0	France
2003	Germany	Sweden	2-1#	Carson, CA, U.S.	2023	Spain	England	1-0	Australia
2007	Germany	Brazil	2-0	China					

* = Match decided in penalty kicks (shootout score in parentheses). # = Match decided in extra time.

Portland Wins Third NWSL Title in 2022

The Portland Thorns claimed their third National Women's Soccer League title on Oct. 29, shutting out the Kansas City Current, 2-0, at Audi Field in Washington, DC. Portland's 22-year-old forward Sophia Smith scored 4 min. into the title game and was named season and NWSL final MVP. The Thorns were one of the teams named in an investigation made public earlier in Oct. that found "systemic abuse and misconduct" in the NWSL and across women's soccer. The league announced that it would implement the report's recommendations concerning those allegations dating back to 2014.

Women's Professional Soccer Champions

Year	Winner	Final opponent	Score	Site	MVP
		Women's United Soccer Association champions			
2001	Bay Area CyberRays	Atlanta Beat	3-3 (4-2)*	Foxborough, MA	Julie Murray
2002	Carolina Courage	Washington Freedom	3-2	Atlanta, GA	Birgit Prinz
2003	Washington Freedom	Atlanta Beat	2-1	San Diego, CA	Abby Wambach
		Women's Professional Soccer champions			
2009	Sky Blue FC	Los Angeles Sol	1-0	Carson, CA	Heather O'Reilly
2010	FC Gold Pride	Philadelphia Independence	4-1	Hayward, CA	Marta
2011	Western New York Flash	Philadelphia Independence	1-1 (5-4)*	Rochester, NY	Christine Sinclair
		National Women's Soccer League champions			
2013	Portland Thorns FC	Western New York Flash	2-0	Rochester, NY	Tobin Heath
2014	FC Kansas City	Seattle Reign FC	2-1	Tukwila, WA	Lauren Holiday
2015	FC Kansas City	Seattle Reign FC	1-0	Portland, OR	Amy Rodriguez
2016	Western New York Flash	Washington Spirit	2-2 (3-2)*	Houston, TX	Sabrina D'Angelo
2017	Portland Thorns FC	North Carolina Courage	1-0	Orlando, FL	Lindsey Horan
2018	North Carolina Courage	Portland Thorns FC	3-0	Portland, OR	Jess McDonald
2019	North Carolina Courage	Chicago Red Stars	4-0	Cary, NC	Debinha
2020	Houston Dash	Chicago Red Stars	2-0	Sandy, UT	Rachel Daly
2021	Washington Spirit	Chicago Red Stars	2-1#	Louisville, KY	Aubrey Kingsbury
2022	Portland Thorns FC	Kansas City Current	2-0	Washington, DC	Sophia Smith

* = Match decided on penalty kicks (shootout score in parentheses). # = Match decided in extra time. **Note:** National Women's Soccer League (NWSL) began play in 2013 with eight teams competing: Boston Breakers, Chicago Red Stars, FC Kansas City, Portland Thorns FC, Seattle Reign FC, Sky Blue FC (New York/New Jersey), Washington Spirit (DC), and Western New York Flash.

UEFA Women's European Football Championship, 1984-2022

Year	Winner	Final opponent	Score	Site	Year	Winner	Final opponent	Score	Site
1984	Sweden	England	1-0, 0-1(4-3)*	No fixed host	2001	Germany	Sweden	1-0+	Germany
1987	Norway	Sweden	2-1	Norway	2005	Germany	Norway	3-1	England
1989	West Germany	Norway	4-1	West Germany	2009	Germany	England	6-2	Finland
1991	Germany	Norway	3-1#	Denmark	2013	Germany	Norway	1-0	Sweden
1993	Norway	Italy	1-0	Italy	2017	Netherlands	Denmark	4-2	Netherlands
1995	Germany	Sweden	3-2	No fixed host	2022	England	Germany	2-1#	England
1997	Germany	Italy	2-0	Norway, Sweden					

* = Match decided in penalty kicks (shootout in parentheses). # = Match decided in extra time. + = Sudden death (a.k.a. the golden goal).
Note: 1984 champion decided by two matches; after each team won one, Sweden won on penalty kicks.

Selected European Soccer League Champions, 1950-2023

Season	England: Premier League[1]	Spain: La Liga	Italy: Serie A	Germany: Bundesliga[2]
1949-50	Portsmouth FC	Atlético Madrid	Juventus	VfB Stuttgart
1950-51	Tottenham Hotspur	Atlético Madrid	AC Milan	Kaiserslautern
1951-52	Manchester United	FC Barcelona	Juventus	VfB Stuttgart
1952-53	Arsenal	FC Barcelona	Inter Milan	Kaiserslautern
1953-54	Wolverhampton Wanderers	Real Madrid	Inter Milan	Hannoverscher SV 96
1954-55	Chelsea	Real Madrid	AC Milan	Rot-Weiss Essen
1955-56	Manchester United	Athletic Bilbao	Fiorentina	Borussia Dortmund
1956-57	Manchester United	Real Madrid	AC Milan	Borussia Dortmund
1957-58	Wolverhampton Wanderers	Real Madrid	Juventus	Schalke 04
1958-59	Wolverhampton Wanderers	FC Barcelona	AC Milan	Eintracht Frankfurt
1959-60	Burnley FC	FC Barcelona	Juventus	Hamburg SV
1960-61	Tottenham Hotspur	Real Madrid	Juventus	FC Nuremberg
1961-62	Ipswich Town	Real Madrid	AC Milan	FC Cologne
1962-63	Everton	Real Madrid	Inter Milan	Borussia Dortmund
1963-64	Liverpool	Real Madrid	Bologna	FC Cologne
1964-65	Manchester United	Real Madrid	Inter Milan	Werder Bremen
1965-66	Liverpool	Atlético Madrid	Inter Milan	TSV 1860 Munich
1966-67	Manchester United	Real Madrid	Juventus	Eintracht Braunschweig
1967-68	Manchester City	Real Madrid	AC Milan	FC Nuremberg
1968-69	Leeds United	Real Madrid	Fiorentina	Bayern Munich
1969-70	Everton	Atlético Madrid	Cagliari	Borussia Mönchengladbach
1970-71	Arsenal	Valencia	Inter Milan	Borussia Mönchengladbach
1971-72	Derby County	Real Madrid	Juventus	Bayern Munich
1972-73	Liverpool	Atlético Madrid	Juventus	Bayern Munich
1973-74	Leeds United	FC Barcelona	Lazio	Bayern Munich
1974-75	Derby County	Real Madrid	Juventus	Borussia Mönchengladbach
1975-76	Liverpool	Real Madrid	Torino	Borussia Mönchengladbach
1976-77	Liverpool	Atlético Madrid	Juventus	Borussia Mönchengladbach
1977-78	Nottingham Forest	Real Madrid	Juventus	FC Cologne
1978-79	Liverpool	Real Madrid	AC Milan	Hamburg SV
1979-80	Liverpool	Real Madrid	Inter Milan	Bayern Munich
1980-81	Aston Villa	Real Sociedad	Juventus	Bayern Munich
1981-82	Liverpool	Real Sociedad	Juventus	Hamburg SV
1982-83	Liverpool	Athletic Bilbao	AS Roma	Hamburg SV
1983-84	Liverpool	Athletic Bilbao	Juventus	VfB Stuttgart
1984-85	Everton	FC Barcelona	Verona	Bayern Munich
1985-86	Liverpool	Real Madrid	Juventus	Bayern Munich
1986-87	Everton	Real Madrid	Napoli	Bayern Munich
1987-88	Liverpool	Real Madrid	AC Milan	Werder Bremen
1988-89	Arsenal	Real Madrid	Inter Milan	Bayern Munich
1989-90	Liverpool	Real Madrid	Napoli	Bayern Munich
1990-91	Arsenal	FC Barcelona	Sampdoria	FC Kaiserslautern
1991-92	Leeds United	FC Barcelona	AC Milan	VfB Stuttgart
1992-93	Manchester United	FC Barcelona	AC Milan	Werder Bremen
1993-94	Manchester United	FC Barcelona	AC Milan	Bayern Munich
1994-95	Blackburn Rovers	Real Madrid	Juventus	Borussia Dortmund
1995-96	Manchester United	Atlético Madrid	AC Milan	Borussia Dortmund
1996-97	Manchester United	Real Madrid	Juventus	Bayern Munich
1997-98	Arsenal	FC Barcelona	Juventus	FC Kaiserslautern
1998-99	Manchester United	FC Barcelona	AC Milan	Bayern Munich
1999-2000	Manchester United	Deportivo Coruña	Lazio	Bayern Munich
2000-01	Manchester United	Real Madrid	AS Roma	Bayern Munich
2001-02	Arsenal	Valencia	Juventus	Borussia Dortmund
2002-03	Manchester United	Real Madrid	Juventus	Bayern Munich
2003-04	Arsenal	Valencia	AC Milan	Werder Bremen
2004-05	Chelsea	FC Barcelona	None[3]	Bayern Munich
2005-06	Chelsea	FC Barcelona	Inter Milan[3]	Bayern Munich
2006-07	Manchester United	Real Madrid	Inter Milan	VfB Stuttgart
2007-08	Manchester United	Real Madrid	Inter Milan	Bayern Munich
2008-09	Manchester United	FC Barcelona	Inter Milan	VfL Wolfsburg
2009-10	Chelsea	FC Barcelona	Inter Milan	Bayern Munich
2010-11	Manchester United	FC Barcelona	AC Milan	Borussia Dortmund
2011-12	Manchester City	Real Madrid	Juventus	Borussia Dortmund
2012-13	Manchester United	FC Barcelona	Juventus	Bayern Munich
2013-14	Manchester City	Atlético Madrid	Juventus	Bayern Munich
2014-15	Chelsea	FC Barcelona	Juventus	Bayern Munich
2015-16	Leicester City	FC Barcelona	Juventus	Bayern Munich
2016-17	Chelsea	Real Madrid	Juventus	Bayern Munich
2017-18	Manchester City	FC Barcelona	Juventus	Bayern Munich
2018-19	Manchester City	FC Barcelona	Juventus	Bayern Munich
2019-20	Liverpool	Real Madrid	Juventus	Bayern Munich
2020-21	Manchester City	Atlético Madrid	Inter Milan	Bayern Munich
2022	Manchester City	Real Madrid	AC Milan	Bayern Munich
2023	Manchester City	FC Barcelona	Napoli	Bayern Munich

(1) Football League champions are listed prior to 1992-93 season, when the Premier League formed. (2) Regional champions are listed prior to 1963-64 season, when National Bundesliga formed. (3) Juventus was stripped of two titles in 2006 because of match-fixing.

Argentina Wins 2022 FIFA Men's World Cup

Argentina won its third FIFA World Cup men's soccer title Dec. 18, 2022, claiming victory on penalty kicks against defending champion France at Lusail Stadium in Lusail, Qatar. Tied 3-3 after extra time, Argentina dominated France in the penalty kicks, 4-2. France's Kylian Mbappé became the first player since 1966 to record a hat trick in the men's World Cup final, scoring twice in less than two minutes to tie the game in the second half. After Argentina went ahead on a goal by veteran superstar Lionel Messi, playing in his fifth World Cup, Mbappé converted a penalty to force extra time. Mbappé, with a tournament-high eight goals, earned the Golden Boot while Messi took the Golden Ball. Argentina's Emiliano Martínez was awarded the Golden Glove as best goalie and Enzo Fernández received the Young Player Award.

Argentina defeated Australia in the Round of 16 and beat the Netherlands on penalty kicks to reach the semifinals, where they blanked Croatia. The French knocked off Poland and defeated England, 2-1, in the quarterfinals. A 2-0 victory over Morocco, the first African and Arab team to reach the semifinals, put France in the final for the second straight World Cup.

Due to Qatar's hot climate, the tournament was held in Nov. and Dec., one of several controversial issues; other concerns included the host country's record on human rights, including treatment of women, migrant workers, and the LGBT community, plus alleged corruption in the bidding process. For the first time the World Cup allowed a concussion substitution of one per team per game, not counting against the team's regulation maximum of five subs. The total 172 goals scored were the most recorded since the 32-team World Cup format was unveiled in 1998. The field was expanding to 48 teams for the 2026 World Cup, which will be hosted June-July 2026 by the U.S., Canada, and Mexico.

Men's World Cup Results, 2022

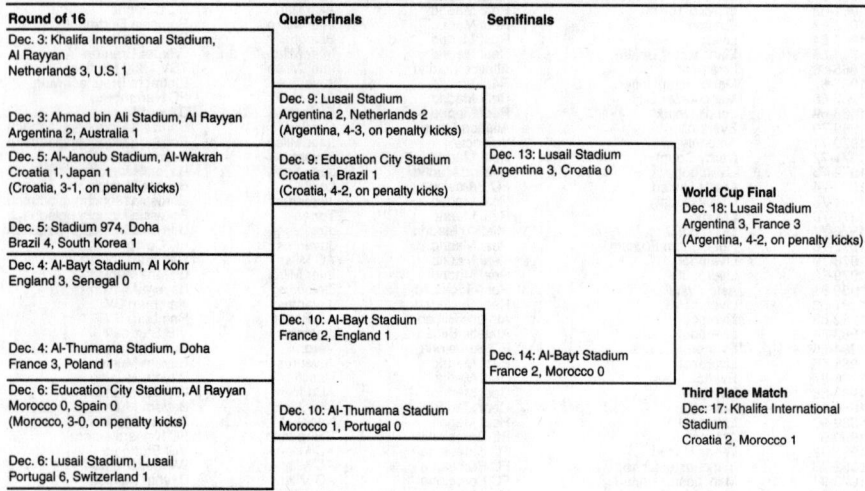

Men's World Cup Group Standings, 2022

(* = advanced to round of 16)

GROUP A	MP	W	D	L	GF	GA	+/-	PTS
Netherlands*	3	2	1	0	5	1	4	7
Senegal*	3	2	0	1	5	4	1	6
Ecuador	3	1	1	1	4	3	1	4
Qatar	3	0	0	3	1	7	–6	0
GROUP B								
England*	3	2	1	0	9	2	7	7
U.S.*	3	1	2	0	2	1	1	5
Iran	3	1	0	2	4	7	–3	3
Wales	3	0	1	2	1	6	–5	1
GROUP C								
Argentina*	3	2	0	1	5	2	3	6
Poland*	3	1	1	1	2	2	0	4
Mexico	3	1	1	1	2	3	–1	4
Saudi Arabia	3	1	0	2	3	5	–2	3
GROUP D								
France*	3	2	0	1	6	3	3	6
Australia*	3	2	0	1	3	4	–1	6
Tunisia	3	1	1	1	1	1	0	4
Denmark	3	0	1	2	1	3	–2	1

GROUP E	MP	W	D	L	GF	GA	+/-	PTS
Japan*	3	2	0	1	4	3	1	6
Spain*	3	1	1	1	9	3	6	4
Germany	3	1	1	1	6	5	1	4
Costa Rica	3	1	0	2	3	11	–8	3
GROUP F								
Morocco*	3	2	1	0	4	1	3	7
Croatia*	3	1	2	0	4	1	3	5
Belgium	3	1	1	1	1	2	–1	4
Canada	3	0	0	3	2	7	–5	0
GROUP G								
Brazil*	3	2	0	1	3	1	2	6
Switzerland*	3	2	0	1	4	3	1	6
Cameroon	3	1	1	1	4	4	0	4
Serbia	3	0	1	2	5	8	–3	1
GROUP H								
Portugal*	3	2	0	1	6	4	2	6
South Korea*	3	1	1	1	4	4	0	4
Uruguay	3	1	1	1	2	2	0	4
Ghana	3	1	0	2	5	7	–2	3

MLS 2022: LAFC Wins First Championship

Los Angeles FC won its first Major League Soccer Cup Nov. 5, 2022, knocking off the Philadelphia Union on penalty kicks, 3-3 (3-0), at Banc of California Stadium in Los Angeles, CA. After Jack Elliott scored in stoppage time to give Philadelphia a 3-2 lead, LAFC's Gareth Bale forced a penalty shootout with a header that tied the game in the final moments of stoppage time. LAFC backup goalkeeper John McCarthy saved two penalties in the shootout and was named the MLS Cup MVP. Los Angeles FC won the Supporters' Shield for the second time.

The MLS added its 28th team in 2022—Charlotte FC—with St. Louis City FC expected to begin play as the 29th team in the 2023 season.

Major League Soccer (MLS) Cup Results, 1996-2022

Year	Winner	Final opponent	Score	Site	MVP
1996	DC United	Los Angeles Galaxy	3-2 (OT)	Foxborough, MA	Marco Etcheverry
1997	DC United	Colorado Rapids	2-1	Washington, DC	Jaime Moreno
1998	Chicago Fire	DC United	2-0	Pasadena, CA	Peter Nowak
1999	DC United	Los Angeles Galaxy	2-0	Foxborough, MA	Ben Olsen
2000	Kansas City Wizards	Chicago Fire	1-0	Washington, DC	Tony Meola
2001	San Jose Earthquakes	Los Angeles Galaxy	2-1 (OT)	Columbus, OH	Dwayne De Rosario
2002	Los Angeles Galaxy	New England Revolution	1-0 (OT)	Foxborough, MA	Carlos Ruiz
2003	San Jose Earthquakes	Chicago Fire	4-2	Carson, CA	Landon Donovan
2004	DC United	Kansas City Wizards	3-2	Carson, CA	Alecko Eskandarian
2005	Los Angeles Galaxy	New England Revolution	1-0 (OT)	Frisco, TX	Guillermo Ramírez
2006	Houston Dynamo	New England Revolution	1-1 (4-3)*	Frisco, TX	Brian Ching
2007	Houston Dynamo	New England Revolution	2-1	Washington, DC	Dwayne De Rosario
2008	Columbus Crew	New York Red Bulls	3-1	Carson, CA	Guillermo Barros Schelotto
2009	Real Salt Lake	Los Angeles Galaxy	1-1 (5-4)*	Seattle, WA	Nick Rimando
2010	Colorado Rapids	FC Dallas	2-1 (OT)	Toronto, ON, Canada	Conor Casey
2011	Los Angeles Galaxy	Houston Dynamo	1-0	Carson, CA	Landon Donovan
2012	Los Angeles Galaxy	Houston Dynamo	3-1	Carson, CA	Omar Gonzalez
2013	Sporting Kansas City	Real Salt Lake	1-1 (7-6)*	Kansas City, KS	Aurelien Collin
2014	Los Angeles Galaxy	New England Revolution	2-1 (OT)	Carson, CA	Robbie Keane
2015	Portland Timbers	Columbus Crew	2-1	Columbus, OH	Diego Valeri
2016	Seattle Sounders FC	Toronto FC	0-0 (5-4)*	Toronto, ON, Canada	Stefan Frei
2017	Toronto FC	Seattle Sounders FC	2-0	Toronto, ON, Canada	Jozy Altidore
2018	Atlanta United FC	Portland Timbers	2-0	Atlanta, GA	Josef Martínez
2019	Seattle Sounders	Toronto FC	3-1	Seattle, WA	Víctor Rodríguez
2020	Columbus Crew	Seattle Sounders	3-0	Columbus, OH	Lucas Zelarayan
2021	New York City FC	Portland Timbers	1-1 (4-2)*	Portland, OR	Sean Johnson
2022	Los Angeles FC	Philadelphia Union	3-3 (3-0)*	Los Angeles, CA	John McCarthy

* = Match decided in penalty kicks (shootout score in parentheses). OT = Overtime.

Major League Soccer Final Standings, 2022

(Does not include playoff games)

Eastern Conference	Points	GP	W	L	T	GF	GA	GD	Western Conference	Points	GP	W	L	T	GF	GA	GD
Philadelphia Union	67	34	19	5	10	72	26	46	Los Angeles FC	67	34	21	9	4	66	38	28
CF Montréal	65	34	20	9	5	63	50	13	Austin FC	56	34	16	10	8	65	49	16
New York City FC	55	34	16	11	7	57	41	16	FC Dallas	53	34	14	9	11	48	37	11
New York Red Bulls ...	53	34	15	11	8	50	41	9	L.A. Galaxy	50	34	14	12	8	58	51	7
FC Cincinnati	49	34	12	9	13	64	56	8	Nashville SC	50	34	13	10	11	52	41	11
Inter Miami CF	48	34	14	14	6	47	56	−9	Minnesota United FC	48	34	14	14	6	48	51	−3
Orlando City SC	48	34	14	14	6	44	53	−9	Real Salt Lake..........	47	34	12	11	11	43	45	−2
Columbus Crew	46	34	10	8	16	46	41	5	Portland Timbers	46	34	11	10	13	53	53	0
Charlotte FC........	42	34	13	18	3	44	52	−8	Vancouver Whitecaps FC..	43	34	12	15	7	40	57	−17
New England Revolution	42	34	10	12	12	47	50	−3	Colorado Rapids	43	34	11	13	10	46	57	−11
Atlanta United FC.....	40	34	10	14	10	48	54	−6	Seattle Sounders FC	41	34	12	17	5	47	46	1
Chicago Fire FC.....	39	34	10	15	9	39	48	−9	Sporting Kansas City	40	34	11	16	7	42	54	−12
Toronto FC	34	34	9	18	7	49	66	−17	Houston Dynamo FC	36	34	10	18	6	43	56	−13
D.C. United	27	34	7	21	6	36	71	−35	San Jose Earthquakes ...	35	34	8	15	11	52	69	−17

Major League Soccer Scoring Leaders, 2022

Player	Club	GP	G	Player	Club	GP	G
Hany Mukhtar	Nashville	33	23	Brandon Vázquez	Cincinnati	33	18
Sebastián Driussi	Austin	34	22	Jeremy Ebobisse	San Jose.............	34	17
Dániel Gazdag	Philadelphia	34	22	Cristian Arango........	LAFC	34	16
Jesús Ferreira.........	Dallas	33	18	Gonzalo Higuaín.......	Miami	28	16
Chicharito............	L.A. Galaxy	32	18	Diego Rubio..........	Colorado.............	30	16
Brenner Souza da Silva..	Cincinnati	29	18				

Landon Donovan MLS Most Valuable Player Award, 1996-2022

(Honda MLS Most Valuable Player Award, 1996-2007; Volkswagen MLS Most Valuable Player Award, 2007-14)

Year	Player, team	Year	Player, team	Year	Player, team
1996	Carlos Valderrama, Tampa Bay	2006	Christian Gómez, DC	2014	Robbie Keane, L.A. Galaxy
1997	Preki, Kansas City	2007	Luciano Emilio, DC	2015	Sebastian Giovinco, Toronto
1998	Marco Etcheverry, DC	2008	Guillermo Barros Schelotto,	2016	David Villa, New York City
1999	Jason Kreis, Dallas		Columbus	2017	Diego Valeri, Portland
2000	Tony Meola, Kansas City	2009	Landon Donovan, L.A. Galaxy	2018	Josef Martínez, Atlanta
2001	Alex Pineda Chacón, Miami	2010	David Ferreira, Dallas	2019	Carlos Vela, LAFC
2002	Carlos Ruiz, L.A. Galaxy	2011	Dwayne De Rosario, DC	2020	Alejandro Pozuelo, Toronto
2003	Preki, Kansas City	2012	Chris Wondolowski, San Jose	2021	Carles Gil, New England
2004	Amado Guevara, NY/NJ	2013	Mike Magee, Chicago	2022	Hany Mukhtar, Nashville
2005	Taylor Twellman, New England				

Men's World Cup Results, 1930-2022

Year	Winner	Final opponent	Score	Site	Year	Winner	Final opponent	Score	Site
1930	Uruguay	Argentina	4-2	Uruguay	1982	Italy	W. Germany	3-1	Spain
1934	Italy	Czechoslovakia	2-1#	Italy	1986	Argentina	W. Germany	3-2	Mexico
1938	Italy	Hungary	4-2	France	1990	W. Germany	Argentina	1-0	Italy
1950	Uruguay	Brazil	2-1	Brazil	1994	Brazil	Italy	0-0 (3-2)*	U.S.
1954	W. Germany	Hungary	3-2	Switzerland	1998	France	Brazil	3-0	France
1958	Brazil	Sweden	5-2	Sweden	2002	Brazil	Germany	2-0	Japan/S. Korea
1962	Brazil	Czechoslovakia	3-1	Chile	2006	Italy	France	1-1 (5-3)*	Germany
1966	England	W. Germany	4-2#	England	2010	Spain	Netherlands	1-0#	South Africa
1970	Brazil	Italy	4-1	Mexico	2014	Germany	Argentina	1-0#	Brazil
1974	W. Germany	Netherlands	2-1	W. Germany	2018	France	Croatia	4-2	Russia
1978	Argentina	Netherlands	3-1#	Argentina	2022	Argentina	France	3-3 (4-2)*	Qatar

* = Match decided in penalty kicks (shootout score in parentheses). # = Match decided in extra time.

UEFA Champions League Results, 1956-2023

Year	Winner	Final opponent	Score	Year	Winner	Final opponent	Score
1956	Real Madrid	Reims	4-3	1990	AC Milan	Benfica	1-0
1957	Real Madrid	Fiorentina	2-0	1991	Crvena Zvezda	Marseille	0-0 (5-3)*
1958	Real Madrid	AC Milan	3-2#	1992	FC Barcelona	Sampdoria	1-0#
1959	Real Madrid	Reims	2-0	1993	Marseille	AC Milan	1-0
1960	Real Madrid	Eintracht Frankfurt	7-3	1994	AC Milan	FC Barcelona	4-0
1961	Benfica	FC Barcelona	3-2	1995	Ajax	AC Milan	1-0
1962	Benfica	Real Madrid	5-3	1996	Juventus	Ajax	1-1 (4-2)*
1963	AC Milan	Benfica	2-1	1997	Borussia Dortmund	Juventus	3-1
1964	Inter Milan	Real Madrid	3-1	1998	Real Madrid	Juventus	1-0
1965	Inter Milan	Benfica	1-0	1999	Manchester United	Bayern Munich	2-1
1966	Real Madrid	Partizan	2-1	2000	Real Madrid	Valencia	3-0
1967	Celtic	Inter Milan	2-1	2001	Bayern Munich	Valencia	1-1 (5-4)*
1968	Manchester United	Benfica	4-1#	2002	Real Madrid	Leverkusen	2-1
1969	AC Milan	Ajax	4-1	2003	AC Milan	Juventus	0-0 (3-2)*
1970	Feyenoord	Celtic	2-1#	2004	Porto	Monaco	3-0
1971	Ajax	Panathinaikos	2-0	2005	Liverpool	AC Milan	3-3 (3-2)*
1972	Ajax	Inter Milan	2-0	2006	FC Barcelona	Arsenal	2-1
1973	Ajax	Juventus	1-0	2007	AC Milan	Liverpool	2-1
1974	Bayern Munich	Atlético Madrid	5-1[1]	2008	Manchester United	Chelsea	1-1 (6-5)*
1975	Bayern Munich	Leeds United	2-0	2009	FC Barcelona	Manchester United	2-0
1976	Bayern Munich	St.-Étienne	1-0	2010	Inter Milan	Bayern Munich	2-0
1977	Liverpool	Borussia Mönchengladbach	3-1	2011	FC Barcelona	Manchester United	3-1
1978	Liverpool	Club Brugge	1-0	2012	Chelsea	Bayern Munich	1-1 (4-3)*
1979	Nottingham Forest	Malmö	1-0	2013	Bayern Munich	Borussia Dortmund	2-1
1980	Nottingham Forest	Hamburg SV	1-0	2014	Real Madrid	Atlético Madrid	4-1#
1981	Liverpool	Real Madrid	1-0	2015	FC Barcelona	Juventus	3-1
1982	Aston Villa	Bayern Munich	1-0	2016	Real Madrid	Atlético Madrid	1-1 (5-3)*
1983	Hamburg SV	Juventus	1-0	2017	Real Madrid	Juventus	4-1
1984	Liverpool	AS Roma	1-1 (4-2)*	2018	Real Madrid	Liverpool	3-1
1985	Juventus	Liverpool	1-0	2019	Liverpool	Tottenham	2-0
1986	Steaua	FC Barcelona	0-0 (2-0)*	2020	Bayern Munich	Paris St.-Germain	1-0
1987	Porto	Bayern Munich	2-1	2021	Chelsea	Manchester City	1-0
1988	PSV	Benfica	0-0 (6-5)*	2022	Real Madrid	Liverpool	1-0
1989	AC Milan	Steaua	4-0	2023	Manchester City	Inter Milan	1-0

* = Match decided in penalty kicks (shootout score in parentheses). # = Match decided in extra time. (1) Aggregate score. First game, 1-1; second, 4-0.

UEFA European Football Championships, 1960-2020

Italy claimed the Euro 2020 title with a 3-2 penalty shootout victory over England at London's Wembley Stadium July 11, 2021. The victory was Italy's first European Championship since 1968, while England, playing in its first-ever Euro final, became the second straight team to lose the Euro final on its own soil. The 90,000-seat Wembley Stadium was at three-fourths capacity due to pandemic restrictions. Delayed until 2021 due to the COVID-19 pandemic, the Union of European Football Associations (UEFA) European tournament was nevertheless referred to as "Euro 2020."

Eleven different countries hosted 51 matches among the 24 entrants starting June 11. Italy's goalie Gianluigi Donnarumma was named player of the tournament, marking the second time the award went to a goalkeeper. Italy reached the final by winning a shootout against Spain; England defeated Denmark in the other semifinal in extra time, 2-1, on a goal by Harry Kane.

Year	Winner	Final opponent	Score	Site	Year	Winner	Final opponent	Score	Site
1960	USSR	Yugoslavia	2-1#	France	1992	Denmark	Germany	2-0	Sweden
1964	Spain	USSR	2-1	Spain	1996	Germany	Czech Rep.	2-1#	England
1968	Italy	Yugoslavia	2-0	Italy	2000	France	Italy	2-1#	Belgium/Neth.
1972	W. Germany	USSR	3-0	Belgium	2004	Greece	Portugal	1-0	Portugal
1976	Czechoslovakia	W. Germany	2-2 (5-3)*	Yugoslavia	2008	Spain	Germany	1-0	Austria/Switz.
1980	W. Germany	Belgium	2-1	Italy	2012	Spain	Italy	4-0	Poland/Ukr.
1984	France	Spain	2-0	France	2016	Portugal	France	1-0#	France
1988	Netherlands	USSR	2-0	W. Germany	2020	Italy	England	1-1 (3-2)	England

* = Match decided in penalty kicks (shootout score in parentheses). # = Match decided in extra time.

GOLF

Men's All-Time Leading Major Professional Championship Winners

Through Oct. 2023. * = Active PGA player in 2023; (a) = amateur.

Player	Masters	U.S. Open	British Open	PGA	Total
Jack Nicklaus	1963, '65-'66, '72, '75, '86	1962, '67, '72, '80	1966, '70, '78	1963, '71, '73, '75, '80	18
*Tiger Woods	1997, 2001-02, '05, '19	2000, '02, '08	2000, '05-'06	1999-2000, '06-'07	15
Walter Hagen	—	1914, '19	1922, '24, '28-'29	1921, '24-'27	11
Ben Hogan	1951, '53	1948, '50-'51, '53	1953	1946, '48	9
Gary Player	1961, '74, '78	1965	1959, '68, '74	1962, '72	9
Tom Watson	1977, '81	1982	1975, '77, '80, '82-'83	—	8
Bobby Jones (a)		1923, '26, '29-'30	1926-27, '30	—	7
Arnold Palmer	1958, '60, '62, '64	1960	1961-62	—	7
Gene Sarazen	1935	1922, '32	1932	1922-23, '33	7
Sam Snead	1949, '52, '54		1946	1942, '49, '51	7
Harry Vardon	—	1900	1896, '98-'99, 1903, '11, '14		7
Nick Faldo	1989-90, '96	—	1987, '90, '92		6
Lee Trevino		1968, '71	1971-72	1974, '84	6
*Phil Mickelson	2004, '06, '10	—	2013	2005, '21	6

Men's All-Time Leading PGA Tournament Winners

Ranked by career wins in PGA Tour co-sponsored and/or approved tournaments through 2022-23 season. * = Active PGA player in 2022-23 season.

Player	Wins	Majors	Player	Wins	Majors	Player	Wins	Majors
Sam Snead	82	7	*Vijay Singh	34	3	*Rory McIlroy	24	4
*Tiger Woods	82	15	Jimmy Demaret	31	3	*Dustin Johnson	24	2
Jack Nicklaus	73	18	Horton Smith	30	2	Jim Barnes	22	4
Ben Hogan	64	9	Lee Trevino	29	6	Raymond Floyd	22	4
Arnold Palmer	62	7	Gene Littler	29	1	Johnny Farrell	22	1
Byron Nelson	52	5	Harry Cooper	29	0	Craig Wood	21	2
Billy Casper	51	3	Leo Diegel	28	2	*Davis Love III	21	1
Walter Hagen	45	11	Paul Runyan	28	2	Willie Macfarlane	21	1
*Phil Mickelson	45	6	Henry Picard	26	2	Lanny Wadkins	21	1
Tom Watson	39	8	Tommy Armour	25	3	Hale Irwin	20	3
Cary Middlecoff	39	3	Johnny Miller	25	2	Greg Norman	20	2
Gene Sarazen	38	7	Macdonald Smith	25	0	Johnny Revolta	20	1
Lloyd Mangrum	36	1	Gary Player	24	9	Doug Sanders	20	0

Professional Golfers' Association Leading Money Winners, 1946-2023

Year	Player	Earnings	Year	Player	Earnings	Year	Player	Earnings
1946	Ben Hogan	$42,556	1972	Jack Nicklaus	$320,542	1998	David Duval	$2,591,031
1947	Jimmy Demaret	27,936	1973	Jack Nicklaus	308,362	1999	Tiger Woods	6,616,585
1948	Ben Hogan	32,112	1974	Johnny Miller	353,021	2000	Tiger Woods	9,188,321
1949	Sam Snead	31,593	1975	Jack Nicklaus	298,149	2001	Tiger Woods	5,687,777
1950	Sam Snead	35,758	1976	Jack Nicklaus	266,438	2002	Tiger Woods	6,912,625
1951	Lloyd Mangrum	26,088	1977	Tom Watson	310,653	2003	Vijay Singh	7,573,907
1952	Julius Boros	37,032	1978	Tom Watson	362,429	2004	Vijay Singh	10,905,166
1953	Lew Worsham	34,002	1979	Tom Watson	462,636	2005	Tiger Woods	10,628,024
1954	Bob Toski	65,819	1980	Tom Watson	530,808	2006	Tiger Woods	9,941,563
1955	Julius Boros	63,121	1981	Tom Kite	375,699	2007	Tiger Woods	10,867,052
1956	Ted Kroll	72,835	1982	Craig Stadler	446,462	2008	Vijay Singh	6,601,094
1957	Dick Mayer	65,835	1983	Hal Sutton	426,668	2009	Tiger Woods	10,508,163
1958	Arnold Palmer	42,607	1984	Tom Watson	476,260	2010	Matt Kuchar	4,910,477
1959	Art Wall Jr.	53,167	1985	Curtis Strange	542,321	2011	Luke Donald	6,683,214
1960	Arnold Palmer	75,262	1986	Greg Norman	653,296	2012	Rory McIlroy	8,047,952
1961	Gary Player	64,540	1987	Curtis Strange	925,941	2013	Tiger Woods	8,553,43
1962	Arnold Palmer	81,448	1988	Curtis Strange	1,147,644	2014	Rory McIlroy	8,280,0
1963	Arnold Palmer	128,230	1989	Tom Kite	1,395,278	2015	Jordan Spieth	12,030,4
1964	Jack Nicklaus	113,284	1990	Greg Norman	1,165,477	2016	Dustin Johnson	9,365,
1965	Jack Nicklaus	140,752	1991	Corey Pavin	979,430	2017	Justin Thomas	9,921
1966	Billy Casper	121,944	1992	Fred Couples	1,344,188	2018	Justin Thomas	8,69
1967	Jack Nicklaus	188,998	1993	Nick Price	1,478,557	2019	Brooks Koepka	9,68
1968	Billy Casper	205,168	1994	Nick Price	1,499,927	2020	Justin Thomas	7,3
1969	Frank Beard	164,707	1995	Greg Norman	1,654,959	2021	Jon Rahm	7,7
1970	Lee Trevino	157,037	1996	Tom Lehman	1,780,159	2022	Scottie Scheffler	14
1971	Jack Nicklaus	244,490	1997	Tiger Woods	2,066,833	2023	Scottie Scheffler	2

Note: The PGA Tour introduced a new split-season format in Oct. 2013, which concluded with the FedEx Cup in Sept. 2014. F on, year shown is the one in which season ended.

FedEx Cup Winners, 2007-23

The FedEx Cup, a season-long competition with points awarded by finishing rank in each tournament, divides the P a regular season consisting of 43 events, combined with a 3-event playoff that ends with the Tour Championship. Th pandemic reduced the 2019-20 season to a total of 36 tournaments. The winner's share increased to $18 million in 20

Year	Winner	Year	Winner	Year	Winner	Year	Winner
2007	Tiger Woods	2012	Brandt Snedeker	2016	Rory McIlroy	2020	Dustin Jo
2008	Vijay Singh	2013	Henrik Stenson	2017	Justin Thomas	2021	Patrick C
2009	Tiger Woods	2014	Billy Horschel	2018	Justin Rose	2022	Rory M
2010	Jim Furyk	2015	Jordan Spieth	2019	Rory McIlroy	2023	Viktor
2011	Bill Haas						

Masters Golf Tournament Winners, 1940-2023

First contested in 1934 as Augusta National Invitation Tournament (name changed in 1939); not played, 1943-45.

Year	Winner	Year	Winner	Year	Winner	Year	Winner	Year	Winner
1940	Jimmy Demaret	1960	Arnold Palmer	1976	Ray Floyd	1992	Fred Couples	2008	Trevor Immelman
1941	Craig Wood	1961	Gary Player	1977	Tom Watson	1993	Bernhard Langer	2009	Angel Cabrera
1942	Byron Nelson	1962	Arnold Palmer	1978	Gary Player	1994	José María Olazábal	2010	Phil Mickelson
1946	Herman Keiser	1963	Jack Nicklaus	1979	Fuzzy Zoeller	1995	Ben Crenshaw	2011	Charl Schwartzel
1947	Jimmy Demaret	1964	Arnold Palmer	1980	Seve Ballesteros	1996	Nick Faldo	2012	Bubba Watson
1948	Claude Harmon	1965	Jack Nicklaus	1981	Tom Watson	1997	Tiger Woods	2013	Adam Scott
1949	Sam Snead	1966	Jack Nicklaus	1982	Craig Stadler	1998	Mark O'Meara	2014	Bubba Watson
1950	Jimmy Demaret	1967	Gay Brewer Jr.	1983	Seve Ballesteros	1999	José María Olazábal	2015	Jordan Spieth
1951	Ben Hogan	1968	Bob Goalby	1984	Ben Crenshaw	2000	Vijay Singh	2016	Danny Willett
1952	Sam Snead	1969	George Archer	1985	Bernhard Langer	2001	Tiger Woods	2017	Sergio García
1953	Ben Hogan	1970	Billy Casper	1986	Jack Nicklaus	2002	Tiger Woods	2018	Patrick Reed
1954	Sam Snead	1971	Charles Coody	1987	Larry Mize	2003	Mike Weir	2019	Tiger Woods
1955	Cary Middlecoff	1972	Jack Nicklaus	1988	Sandy Lyle	2004	Phil Mickelson	2020	Dustin Johnson
1956	Jack Burke	1973	Tommy Aaron	1989	Nick Faldo	2005	Tiger Woods	2021	Hideki Matsuyama
1957	Doug Ford	1974	Gary Player	1990	Nick Faldo	2006	Phil Mickelson	2022	Scottie Scheffler
1958	Arnold Palmer	1975	Jack Nicklaus	1991	Ian Woosnam	2007	Zach Johnson	2023	Jon Rahm
1959	Art Wall Jr.								

U.S. Open Winners, 1940-2023

First contested in 1895; not played, 1942-45.

Year	Winner	Year	Winner	Year	Winner	Year	Winner	Year	Winner
1940	Lawson Little	1960	Arnold Palmer	1976	Jerry Pate	1992	Tom Kite	2008	Tiger Woods
1941	Craig Wood	1961	Gene Littler	1977	Hubert Green	1993	Lee Janzen	2009	Lucas Glover
1946	Lloyd Mangrum	1962	Jack Nicklaus	1978	Andy North	1994	Ernie Els	2010	Graeme McDowell
1947	Lew Worsham	1963	Julius Boros	1979	Hale Irwin	1995	Corey Pavin	2011	Rory McIlroy
1948	Ben Hogan	1964	Ken Venturi	1980	Jack Nicklaus	1996	Steve Jones	2012	Webb Simpson
1949	Cary Middlecoff	1965	Gary Player	1981	David Graham	1997	Ernie Els	2013	Justin Rose
1950	Ben Hogan	1966	Billy Casper	1982	Tom Watson	1998	Lee Janzen	2014	Martin Kaymer
1951	Ben Hogan	1967	Jack Nicklaus	1983	Larry Nelson	1999	Payne Stewart	2015	Jordan Spieth
1952	Julius Boros	1968	Lee Trevino	1984	Fuzzy Zoeller	2000	Tiger Woods	2016	Dustin Johnson
1953	Ben Hogan	1969	Orville Moody	1985	Andy North	2001	Retief Goosen	2017	Brooks Koepka
1954	Ed Furgol	1970	Tony Jacklin	1986	Ray Floyd	2002	Tiger Woods	2018	Brooks Koepka
1955	Jack Fleck	1971	Lee Trevino	1987	Scott Simpson	2003	Jim Furyk	2019	Gary Woodland
1956	Cary Middlecoff	1972	Jack Nicklaus	1988	Curtis Strange	2004	Retief Goosen	2020	Bryson DeChambeau
1957	Dick Mayer	1973	Johnny Miller	1989	Curtis Strange	2005	Michael Campbell	2021	Jon Rahm
1958	Tommy Bolt	1974	Hale Irwin	1990	Hale Irwin	2006	Geoff Ogilvy	2022	Matt Fitzpatrick
1959	Billy Casper	1975	Lou Graham	1991	Payne Stewart	2007	Angel Cabrera	2023	Wyndham Clark

British Open Winners, 1946-2023

Officially called the Open Championship. First contested in 1860; not played, 1940-45, 2020.

Year	Winner	Year	Winner	Year	Winner	Year	Winner	Year	Winner
1946	Sam Snead	1962	Arnold Palmer	1978	Jack Nicklaus	1993	Greg Norman	2008	Padraig Harrington
1947	Fred Daly	1963	Bob Charles	1979	Seve Ballesteros	1994	Nick Price	2009	Stewart Cink
1948	Henry Cotton	1964	Tony Lema	1980	Tom Watson	1995	John Daly	2010	Louis Oosthuizen
1949	Bobby Locke	1965	Peter Thomson	1981	Bill Rogers	1996	Tom Lehman	2011	Darren Clarke
1950	Bobby Locke	1966	Jack Nicklaus	1982	Tom Watson	1997	Justin Leonard	2012	Ernie Els
1951	Max Faulkner	1967	Roberto de Vicenzo	1983	Tom Watson	1998	Mark O'Meara	2013	Phil Mickelson
1952	Bobby Locke	1968	Gary Player	1984	Seve Ballesteros	1999	Paul Lawrie	2014	Rory McIlroy
1953	Ben Hogan	1969	Tony Jacklin	1985	Sandy Lyle	2000	Tiger Woods	2015	Zach Johnson
1954	Peter Thomson	1970	Jack Nicklaus	1986	Greg Norman	2001	David Duval	2016	Henrik Stenson
1955	Peter Thomson	1971	Lee Trevino	1987	Nick Faldo	2002	Ernie Els	2017	Jordan Spieth
	Peter Thomson	1972	Lee Trevino	1988	Seve Ballesteros	2003	Ben Curtis	2018	Francesco Molinari
	Bobby Locke	1973	Tom Weiskopf	1989	Mark Calcavecchia	2004	Todd Hamilton	2019	Shane Lowry
	Peter Thomson	1974	Gary Player	1990	Nick Faldo	2005	Tiger Woods	2021	Collin Morikawa
	Player	1975	Tom Watson	1991	Ian Baker-Finch	2006	Tiger Woods	2022	Cameron Smith
	eagle	1976	Johnny Miller	1992	Nick Faldo	2007	Padraig Harrington	2023	Brian Harman
	Palmer	1977	Tom Watson						

PGA Championship Winners, 1940-2023

First contested in 1916; not played, 1943.

Year	Winner	Year	Winner	Year	Winner	Year	Winner
		1958	Dow Finsterwald	1975	Jack Nicklaus	1992	Nick Price	2008	Padraig Harrington
		1959	Bob Rosburg	1976	Dave Stockton	1993	Paul Azinger	2009	Y.E. Yang
		1960	Jay Hebert	1977	Lanny Wadkins	1994	Nick Price	2010	Martin Kaymer
1		1961	Jerry Barber	1978	John Mahaffey	1995	Steve Elkington	2011	Keegan Bradley
19		1962	Gary Player	1979	David Graham	1996	Mark Brooks	2012	Rory McIlroy
194		1963	Jack Nicklaus	1980	Jack Nicklaus	1997	Davis Love III	2013	Jason Dufner
194		1964	Bob Nichols	1981	Larry Nelson	1998	Vijay Singh	2014	Rory McIlroy
1950		1965	Dave Marr	1982	Ray Floyd	1999	Tiger Woods	2015	Jason Day
1951		1966	Al Geiberger	1983	Hal Sutton	2000	Tiger Woods	2016	Jimmy Walker
1952		1967	Don January	1984	Lee Trevino	2001	David Toms	2017	Justin Thomas
1953		1968	Julius Boros	1985	Hubert Green	2002	Rich Beem	2018	Brooks Koepka
1954		1969	Ray Floyd	1986	Bob Tway	2003	Shaun Micheel	2019	Brooks Koepka
1955		1970	Dave Stockton	1987	Larry Nelson	2004	Vijay Singh	2020	Collin Morikawa
1956	Jack	1971	Jack Nicklaus	1988	Jeff Sluman	2005	Phil Mickelson	2021	Phil Mickelson
1957	Lionel	1972	Gary Player	1989	Payne Stewart	2006	Tiger Woods	2022	Justin Thomas
		1973	Jack Nicklaus	1990	Wayne Grady	2007	Tiger Woods	2023	Brooks Koepka
		1974	Lee Trevino	1991	John Daly				

Ryder Cup, 1927-2023

The Ryder Cup began in 1927 as a biennial team competition between U.S. and British pro male golfers. The British team expanded in 1973 to include players from Ireland and in 1979 to golfers from the rest of Europe.

Year	Winner, score	Year	Winner, score	Year	Winner, score	Year	Winner, score
1927	U.S., 9½-2½	1957	Great Britain, 7½-4½	1979	U.S., 17-11	2002	Europe, 15½-12½
1929	Great Britain, 7-5	1959	U.S., 8½-3½	1981	U.S., 18½-9½	2004	Europe, 18½-9½
1931	U.S., 9-3	1961	U.S., 14½-9½	1983	U.S., 14½-13½	2006	Europe, 18½-9½
1933	Great Britain, 6½-5½	1963	U.S., 23-9	1985	Europe, 16½-11½	2008	U.S., 16½-11½
1935	U.S., 9-3	1965	U.S., 19½-12½	1987	Europe, 15-13	2010	Europe, 14½-13½
1937	U.S., 8-4	1967	U.S., 23½-8½	1989	Draw, 14-14	2012	Europe, 14½-13½
1947	U.S., 11-1	1969	Draw, 16-16	1991	U.S., 14½-13½	2014	Europe, 16½-11½
1949	U.S., 7-5	1971	U.S., 18½-13½	1993	U.S., 15-13	2016	U.S., 17-11
1951	U.S., 9½-2½	1973	U.S., 19-13	1995	Europe, 14½-13½	2018	Europe, 17½-10½
1953	U.S., 6½-5½	1975	U.S., 21-11	1997	Europe, 14½-13½	2021	U.S., 19-9
1955	U.S., 8-4	1977	U.S., 12½-7½	1999	U.S., 14½-13½	2023	Europe, 16½-11½

Women's All-Time Leading Major Professional Championship Winners

Through Oct. 2023. * = Active in 2023 LPGA season.

Player	Chevron Champ.[1]	KPMG Women's PGA[2]	U.S. Women's Open	Women's British Open[3]	Titleholders[4]	Western Open[5]	Total
Patty Berg	—	—	1946	—	1937-39, '48, '53, '55, '57	1941, '43, '48, '51, '55, '57-'58	15
Mickey Wright	—	1958, '60-'61, '63	1958-59, '61, '64	—	1961-62	1962-63, '66	13
Louise Suggs	—	1957	1949, '52	—	1946, '54, '56, '59	1946-47, '49, '53	11
Annika Sorenstam	2001-02, '05	2003-05	1995-96, 2006	2003	—	—	10
Babe Zaharias	—	—	1948, '50, '54	—	1947, '50, '52	1940, '44-'45, '50	10
Betsy Rawls	—	1959, '69	1951, '53, '57, '60	—	—	1952, '59	8
*Juli Inkster	1984, '89	1999-2000	1999, 2002	1984	—	—	7
*Inbee Park	2013	2013-15	2008, '13	2015	—	—	7
*Karrie Webb	2000, '06	2001	2000-01	1999, 2002	—	—	7

(1) Formerly the Nabisco Dinah Shore (1982-99), the Nabisco Championship (2000-01), the Kraft Nabisco Championship (2002-14), and the ANA Inspiration (2015-21); designated major in 1983. (2) Formerly the LPGA Championship (1955-2014). (3) In 2001, the British Open replaced the du Maurier Classic as the LPGA's fourth major; wins in column prior to 2001 are for the Peter Jackson (1979-82) or du Maurier (1983-2000) Classic. (4) Titleholders Championship was a major, 1937-72. (5) Western Open was a major, 1930-67.

Ladies Professional Golf Association Leading Money Winners, 1954-2022

Year	Player	Earnings	Year	Player	Earnings	Year	Player	Earnings
1954	Patty Berg	$16,011	1977	Judy Rankin	$122,890	2000	Karrie Webb	$1,876,853
1955	Patty Berg	16,492	1978	Nancy Lopez	189,814	2001	Annika Sorenstam	2,105,868
1956	Marlene Hagge	20,235	1979	Nancy Lopez	197,489	2002	Annika Sorenstam	2,863,904
1957	Patty Berg	16,272	1980	Beth Daniel	231,000	2003	Annika Sorenstam	2,029,506
1958	Beverly Hanson	12,639	1981	Beth Daniel	206,998	2004	Annika Sorenstam	2,544,707
1959	Betsy Rawls	26,774	1982	JoAnne Carner	310,400	2005	Annika Sorenstam	2,588,240
1960	Louise Suggs	16,892	1983	JoAnne Carner	291,404	2006	Lorena Ochoa	2,592,872
1961	Mickey Wright	22,236	1984	Betsy King	266,771	2007	Lorena Ochoa	4,364,994
1962	Mickey Wright	21,641	1985	Nancy Lopez	416,472	2008	Lorena Ochoa	2,763,193
1963	Mickey Wright	31,269	1986	Pat Bradley	492,021	2009	Jiyai Shin	1,807,334
1964	Mickey Wright	29,800	1987	Ayako Okamoto	466,034	2010	Na Yeon Choi	1,871,166
1965	Kathy Whitworth	28,658	1988	Sherri Turner	350,851	2011	Yani Tseng	2,921,713
1966	Kathy Whitworth	33,517	1989	Betsy King	654,132	2012	Inbee Park	2,287,080
1967	Kathy Whitworth	32,937	1990	Beth Daniel	863,578	2013	Inbee Park	2,456,619
1968	Kathy Whitworth	48,379	1991	Pat Bradley	763,118	2014	Stacy Lewis	2,539,039
1969	Carol Mann	49,152	1992	Dottie Mochrie	693,335	2015	Lydia Ko	2,800,802
1970	Kathy Whitworth	30,235	1993	Betsy King	595,992	2016	Ariya Jutanugarn	2,550,947
1971	Kathy Whitworth	41,181	1994	Laura Davies	687,201	2017	Sung Hyun Park	2,335,883
1972	Kathy Whitworth	65,063	1995	Annika Sorenstam	666,533	2018	Ariya Jutanugarn	2,743,949
1973	Kathy Whitworth	82,864	1996	Karrie Webb	1,002,000	2019	Jin Young Ko	2,773,894
1974	JoAnne Carner	87,094	1997	Annika Sorenstam	1,236,789	2020	Jin Young Ko	1,667,925
1975	Sandra Palmer	76,374	1998	Annika Sorenstam	1,092,748	2021	Jin Young Ko	3,502,161
1976	Judy Rankin	150,734	1999	Karrie Webb	1,591,959	2022	Lydia Ko	4,364,403

Women's All-Time Leading LPGA Tournament Winners

Ranked by career tournament wins through Sept. 2023. * = Active LPGA player in 2023.

Player	Wins	Majors	Player	Wins	Majors	Player	Wins	Majors
Kathy Whitworth	88	6	JoAnne Carner	43	2	Betsy King	34	6
Mickey Wright	82	13	Sandra Haynie	42	4	Beth Daniel	33	1
Annika Sorenstam	72	10	Babe Didrikson			*Juli Inkster	31	7
Louise Suggs	61	11	Zaharias	41	10	Pat Bradley	31	6
Patty Berg	60	15	*Karrie Webb	41	7	Amy Alcott	29	5
Betsy Rawls	55	8	Carol Mann	38	2	Lorena Ochoa	27	2
Nancy Lopez	48	3	Patty Sheehan	35	6	Jane Blalock	27	0

Chevron Championship Winners, 1983-2023

Began in 1972 and designated a major championship in 1983; formerly the Colgate Dinah Shore (1972-81), the Nabisco Dinah Shore (1982-99), the Nabisco Championship (2000-01), the Kraft Nabisco Championship (2002-14), and the ANA Inspiration (2015-21).

Year	Winner	Year	Winner	Year	Winner	Year	Winner	Year	Winner
1983	Amy Alcott	1992	Dottie Pepper	2000	Karrie Webb	2008	Lorena Ochoa	2016	Lydia Ko
1984	Juli Inkster	1993	Helen Alfredsson	2001	Annika Sorenstam	2009	Brittany Lincicome	2017	So Yeon Ryu
1985	Alice Miller	1994	Donna Andrews	2002	Annika Sorenstam	2010	Yani Tseng	2018	Pernilla Lindberg
1986	Pat Bradley	1995	Nanci Bowen	2003	P. Meunier-Lebouc	2011	Stacy Lewis	2019	Jin Young Ko
1987	Betsy King	1996	Patty Sheehan	2004	Grace Park	2012	Sun Young Yoo	2020	Mirim Lee
1988	Amy Alcott	1997	Betsy King	2005	Annika Sorenstam	2013	Inbee Park	2021	Patty Tavatanakit
1989	Juli Inkster	1998	Pat Hurst	2006	Karrie Webb	2014	Lexi Thompson	2022	Jennifer Kupcho
1990	Betsy King	1999	Dottie Pepper	2007	Morgan Pressel	2015	Brittany Lincicome	2023	Lilia Vu
1991	Amy Alcott								

KPMG Women's PGA Championship Winners, 1955-2023

Formerly LPGA Championship (1955-2014).

Year	Winner	Year	Winner	Year	Winner	Year	Winner	Year	Winner
1955	Beverly Hanson	1969	Betsy Rawls	1983	Patty Sheehan	1997	Christa Johnson	2011	Yani Tseng
1956	Marlene Hagge	1970	Shirley Englehorn	1984	Patty Sheehan	1998	Se Ri Pak	2012	Shanshan Feng
1957	Louise Suggs	1971	Kathy Whitworth	1985	Nancy Lopez	1999	Juli Inkster	2013	Inbee Park
1958	Mickey Wright	1972	Kathy Ahern	1986	Pat Bradley	2000	Juli Inkster	2014	Inbee Park
1959	Betsy Rawls	1973	Mary Mills	1987	Jane Geddes	2001	Karrie Webb	2015	Inbee Park
1960	Mickey Wright	1974	Sandra Haynie	1988	Sherri Turner	2002	Se Ri Pak	2016	Brooke Henderson
1961	Mickey Wright	1975	Kathy Whitworth	1989	Nancy Lopez	2003	Annika Sorenstam	2017	Danielle Kang
1962	Judy Kimball	1976	Betty Burfeindt	1990	Beth Daniel	2004	Annika Sorenstam	2018	Sung Hyun Park
1963	Mickey Wright	1977	Chako Higuchi	1991	Meg Mallon	2005	Annika Sorenstam	2019	Hannah Green
1964	Mary Mills	1978	Nancy Lopez	1992	Betsy King	2006	Se Ri Pak	2020	Sei Young Kim
1965	Sandra Haynie	1979	Donna Caponi	1993	Patty Sheehan	2007	Suzann Pettersen	2021	Nelly Korda
1966	Gloria Ehret	1980	Sally Little	1994	Laura Davies	2008	Yani Tseng	2022	In Gee Chun
1967	Kathy Whitworth	1981	Donna Caponi	1995	Kelly Robbins	2009	Anna Nordqvist	2023	Yin Ruoning
1968	Sandra Post	1982	Jan Stephenson	1996	Laura Davies	2010	Cristie Kerr		

U.S. Women's Open Winners, 1946-2023

Year	Winner	Year	Winner	Year	Winner	Year	Winner	Year	Winner
1946	Patty Berg	1962	Murle Lindstrom	1978	Hollis Stacy	1994	Patty Sheehan	2009	Eun-Hee Ji
1947	Betty Jameson	1963	Mary Mills	1979	Jerilyn Britz	1995	Annika Sorenstam	2010	Paula Creamer
1948	Babe Zaharias	1964	Mickey Wright	1980	Amy Alcott	1996	Annika Sorenstam	2011	So Yeon Ryu
1949	Louise Suggs	1965	Carol Mann	1981	Pat Bradley	1997	Alison Nicholas	2012	Na Yeon Choi
1950	Babe Zaharias	1966	Sandra Spuzich	1982	Janet Alex	1998	Se Ri Pak	2013	Inbee Park
1951	Betsy Rawls	1967	Catherine Lacoste	1983	Jan Stephenson	1999	Juli Inkster	2014	Michelle Wie
1952	Louise Suggs	1968	Susie Berning	1984	Hollis Stacy	2000	Karrie Webb	2015	In Gee Chun
1953	Betsy Rawls	1969	Donna Caponi	1985	Kathy Baker	2001	Karrie Webb	2016	Brittany Lang
1954	Babe Zaharias	1970	Donna Caponi	1986	Jane Geddes	2002	Juli Inkster	2017	Sung Hyun Park
1955	Fay Crocker	1971	JoAnne Carner	1987	Laura Davies	2003	Hilary Lunke	2018	Ariya Jutanugarn
1956	Kathy Cornelius	1972	Susie Berning	1988	Liselotte Neumann	2004	Meg Mallon	2019	Jeongeun Lee6
1957	Betsy Rawls	1973	Susie Berning	1989	Betsy King	2005	Birdie Kim	2020	Kim A-lim
1958	Mickey Wright	1974	Sandra Haynie	1990	Betsy King	2006	Annika Sorenstam	2021	Yuka Saso
1959	Mickey Wright	1975	Sandra Palmer	1991	Meg Mallon	2007	Cristie Kerr	2022	Minjee Lee
1960	Betsy Rawls	1976	JoAnne Carner	1992	Patty Sheehan	2008	Inbee Park	2023	Allisen Corpuz
1961	Mickey Wright	1977	Hollis Stacy	1993	Lauri Merten				

AIG Women's British Open Winners, 1979-2023

First contested as the Ladies' British Open in 1976; became the LPGA's fourth major championship in 2001, replacing the du Maurier Classic. Winners listed are for the Peter Jackson (1979-82) and du Maurier (1983-2000) Classic.

Year	Winner	Year	Winner	Year	Winner	Year	Winner	Year	Winner
1979	Amy Alcott	1988	Sally Little	1997	Colleen Walker	2006	Sherri Steinhauer	2015	Inbee Park
1980	Pat Bradley	1989	Tammie Green	1998	Brandie Burton	2007	Lorena Ochoa	2016	Ariya Jutanugarn
1981	Jan Stephenson	1990	Cathy Johnston	1999	Karrie Webb	2008	Jiyai Shin	2017	In-Kyung Kim
1982	Sandra Haynie	1991	Nancy Scranton	2000	Meg Mallon	2009	Catriona Matthew	2018	Georgia Hall
1983	Hollis Stacy	1992	Sherri Steinhauer	2001	Se Ri Pak	2010	Yani Tseng	2019	Hinako Shibuno
1984	Juli Inkster	1993	Brandie Burton	2002	Karrie Webb	2011	Yani Tseng	2020	Sophia Popov
1985	Pat Bradley	1994	Martha Nause	2003	Annika Sorenstam	2012	Jiyai Shin	2021	Anna Nordqvist
1986	Pat Bradley	1995	Jenny Lidback	2004	Karen Stupples	2013	Stacy Lewis	2022	Ashleigh Buhai
1987	Jody Rosenthal	1996	Laura Davies	2005	Jeong Jang	2014	Mo Martin	2023	Lilia Vu

Amundi Evian Championship, 2013-23

Began in 1994 as the Evian Masters; became the LPGA's fifth major tournament in 2013.

Year	Winner	Year	Winner	Year	Winner	Year	Winner
2013	Suzann Pettersen	2016	In Gee Chun	2019	Jin Young Ko	2022	Brooke Henderson
2014	Hyo Joo Kim	2017	Anna Nordqvist	2021	Minjee Lee	2023	Céline Boutier
2015	Lydia Ko	2018	Angela Stanford				

Solheim Cup, 1990-2023

The Solheim Cup began in 1990 as a biennial team competition between pro women golfers from the U.S. and Europe. The 2023 competition ended in a tie, so the cup remained in the hands of the previous winner.

Year	Winner, score	Year	Winner, score	Year	Winner, score	Year	Winner, score
1990	U.S., 11½-4½	2000	Europe, 14½-11½	2009	U.S., 16-12	2017	U.S., 16½-11½
1992	Europe, 11½-6½	2002	U.S., 15½-12½	2011	Europe, 15-13	2019	Europe, 14½-13½
1994	U.S., 13-7	2003	Europe, 17½-10½	2013	Europe, 18-10	2021	Europe, 15-13
1996	U.S., 17-11	2005	U.S., 15½-12½	2015	U.S., 14½-13½	2023	Europe, 14-14
1998	U.S., 16-12	2007	U.S., 16-12				

TENNIS

Australian Open Champions, 1969-2023

First contested 1905 for men, 1922 for women. Became an open championship in 1969.

Men's Singles

Year	Champion	Final opponent
1969	Rod Laver	Andrés Gimeno
1970	Arthur Ashe	Dick Crealy
1971	Ken Rosewall	Arthur Ashe
1972	Ken Rosewall	Mal Anderson
1973	John Newcombe	Onny Parun
1974	Jimmy Connors	Phil Dent
1975	John Newcombe	Jimmy Connors
1976	Mark Edmondson	John Newcombe
1977	Roscoe Tanner	Guillermo Vilas
	Vitas Gerulaitis	John Lloyd
1978	Guillermo Vilas	John Marks
1979	Guillermo Vilas	John Sadri
1980	Brian Teacher	Kim Warwick
1981	Johan Kriek	Steve Denton
1982	Johan Kriek	Steve Denton
1983	Mats Wilander	Ivan Lendl
1984	Mats Wilander	Kevin Curren
1985	Stefan Edberg	Mats Wilander
1987	Stefan Edberg	Pat Cash
1988	Mats Wilander	Pat Cash
1989	Ivan Lendl	Miloslav Mecir
1990	Ivan Lendl	Stefan Edberg
1991	Boris Becker	Ivan Lendl
1992	Jim Courier	Stefan Edberg
1993	Jim Courier	Stefan Edberg
1994	Pete Sampras	Todd Martin
1995	Andre Agassi	Pete Sampras
1996	Boris Becker	Michael Chang
1997	Pete Sampras	Carlos Moya
1998	Petr Korda	Marcelo Rios
1999	Yevgeny Kafelnikov	Thomas Enqvist
2000	Andre Agassi	Yevgeny Kafelnikov
2001	Andre Agassi	Arnaud Clement
2002	Thomas Johansson	Marat Safin
2003	Andre Agassi	Rainer Schuettler
2004	Roger Federer	Marat Safin
2005	Marat Safin	Lleyton Hewitt
2006	Roger Federer	Marcos Baghdatis
2007	Roger Federer	Fernando Gonzalez
2008	Novak Djokovic	Jo-Wilfried Tsonga
2009	Rafael Nadal	Roger Federer
2010	Roger Federer	Andy Murray
2011	Novak Djokovic	Andy Murray
2012	Novak Djokovic	Rafael Nadal
2013	Novak Djokovic	Andy Murray
2014	Stanislas Wawrinka	Rafael Nadal
2015	Novak Djokovic	Andy Murray
2016	Novak Djokovic	Andy Murray
2017	Roger Federer	Rafael Nadal
2018	Roger Federer	Marin Cilic
2019	Novak Djokovic	Rafael Nadal
2020	Novak Djokovic	Dominic Thiem
2021	Novak Djokovic	Daniil Medvedev
2022	Rafael Nadal	Daniil Medvedev
2023	Novak Djokovic	Stefanos Tsitsipas

Women's Singles

Year	Champion	Final opponent
1969	Margaret Smith Court	Billie Jean King
1970	Margaret Smith Court	Kerry Melville Reid
1971	Margaret Smith Court	Evonne Goolagong
1972	Virginia Wade	Evonne Goolagong
1973	Margaret Smith Court	Evonne Goolagong
1974	Evonne Goolagong	Chris Evert
1975	Evonne Goolagong	Martina Navratilova
1976	Evonne Goolagong Cawley	Renata Tomanova
1977	Kerry Reid	Dianne Balestrat
	Evonne Goolagong Cawley	Helen Gourlay
1978	Chris O'Neil	Betsy Nagelsen
1979	Barbara Jordan	Sharon Walsh
1980	Hana Mandlikova	Wendy Turnbull
1981	Martina Navratilova	Chris Evert Lloyd
1982	Chris Evert Lloyd	Martina Navratilova
1983	Martina Navratilova	Kathy Jordan
1984	Chris Evert Lloyd	Helena Sukova
1985	Martina Navratilova	Chris Evert Lloyd
1987	Hana Mandlikova	Martina Navratilova
1988	Steffi Graf	Chris Evert
1989	Steffi Graf	Helena Sukova
1990	Steffi Graf	Mary Joe Fernandez
1991	Monica Seles	Jana Novotna
1992	Monica Seles	Mary Joe Fernandez
1993	Monica Seles	Steffi Graf
1994	Steffi Graf	Arantxa Sánchez Vicario
1995	Mary Pierce	Arantxa Sánchez Vicario
1996	Monica Seles	Anke Huber
1997	Martina Hingis	Mary Pierce
1998	Martina Hingis	Conchita Martínez
1999	Martina Hingis	Amélie Mauresmo
2000	Lindsay Davenport	Martina Hingis
2001	Jennifer Capriati	Martina Hingis
2002	Jennifer Capriati	Martina Hingis
2003	Serena Williams	Venus Williams
2004	Justine Henin-Hardenne	Kim Clijsters
2005	Serena Williams	Lindsay Davenport
2006	Amélie Mauresmo	Justine Henin-Hardenne
2007	Serena Williams	Maria Sharapova
2008	Maria Sharapova	Ana Ivanovic
2009	Serena Williams	Dinara Safina
2010	Serena Williams	Justine Henin
2011	Kim Clijsters	Li Na
2012	Victoria Azarenka	Maria Sharapova
2013	Victoria Azarenka	Li Na
2014	Li Na	Dominika Cibulkova
2015	Serena Williams	Maria Sharapova
2016	Angelique Kerber	Serena Williams
2017	Serena Williams	Venus Williams
2018	Caroline Wozniacki	Simona Halep
2019	Naomi Osaka	Petra Kvitova
2020	Sofia Kenin	Garbiñe Muguruza
2021	Naomi Osaka	Jennifer Brady
2022	Ashleigh Barty	Danielle Collins
2023	Aryna Sabalenka	Elena Rybakina

French Open (Roland Garros) Champions, 1968-2023

First contested 1891 for men, 1897 for women. Became an open championship in 1968.

Men's Singles

Year	Champion	Final opponent
1968	Ken Rosewall	Rod Laver
1969	Rod Laver	Ken Rosewall
1970	Jan Kodes	Zeljko Franulovic
1971	Jan Kodes	Ilie Nastase
1972	Andrés Gimeno	Patrick Proisy
1973	Ilie Nastase	Nikki Pilic
1974	Björn Borg	Manuel Orantes
1975	Björn Borg	Guillermo Vilas
1976	Adriano Panatta	Harold Solomon
1977	Guillermo Vilas	Brian Gottfried
1978	Björn Borg	Guillermo Vilas
1979	Björn Borg	Victor Pecci
1980	Björn Borg	Vitas Gerulaitis
1981	Björn Borg	Ivan Lendl
1982	Mats Wilander	Guillermo Vilas
1983	Yannick Noah	Mats Wilander
1984	Ivan Lendl	John McEnroe
1985	Mats Wilander	Ivan Lendl
1986	Ivan Lendl	Mikael Pernfors
1987	Ivan Lendl	Mats Wilander
1988	Mats Wilander	Henri Leconte
1989	Michael Chang	Stefan Edberg
1990	Andres Gomez	Andre Agassi
1991	Jim Courier	Andre Agassi
1992	Jim Courier	Petr Korda
1993	Sergei Bruguera	Jim Courier
1994	Sergei Bruguera	Alberto Berasategui
1995	Thomas Muster	Michael Chang
1996	Yevgeny Kafelnikov	Michael Stich
1997	Gustavo Kuerten	Sergi Bruguera
1998	Carlos Moya	Alex Corretja
1999	Andre Agassi	Andrei Medvedev
2000	Gustavo Kuerten	Magnus Norman
2001	Gustavo Kuerten	Alex Corretja
2002	Albert Costa	Juan Carlos Ferrero
2003	Juan Carlos Ferrero	Martin Verkerk
2004	Gaston Gaudio	Guillermo Coria
2005	Rafael Nadal	Mariano Puerta
2006	Rafael Nadal	Roger Federer
2007	Rafael Nadal	Roger Federer
2008	Rafael Nadal	Roger Federer
2009	Roger Federer	Robin Soderling
2010	Rafael Nadal	Robin Soderling
2011	Rafael Nadal	Roger Federer
2012	Rafael Nadal	Novak Djokovic
2013	Rafael Nadal	David Ferrer
2014	Rafael Nadal	Novak Djokovic
2015	Stan Wawrinka	Novak Djokovic
2016	Novak Djokovic	Andy Murray
2017	Rafael Nadal	Stan Wawrinka
2018	Rafael Nadal	Dominic Thiem
2019	Rafael Nadal	Dominic Thiem
2020	Rafael Nadal	Novak Djokovic
2021	Novak Djokovic	Stefanos Tsitsipas
2022	Rafael Nadal	Casper Ruud
2023	Novak Djokovic	Casper Ruud

Women's Singles

Year	Champion	Final opponent
1968	Nancy Richey	Ann Jones
1969	Margaret Smith Court	Ann Jones
1970	Margaret Smith Court	Helga Niessen
1971	Evonne Goolagong	Helen Gourlay
1972	Billie Jean King	Evonne Goolagong
1973	Margaret Smith Court	Chris Evert
1974	Chris Evert	Olga Morozova
1975	Chris Evert	Martina Navratilova

Year	Champion	Final opponent	Year	Champion	Final opponent
1976	Sue Barker	Renata Tomanova	2000	Mary Pierce	Conchita Martínez
1977	Mima Jausovec	Florenta Mihai	2001	Jennifer Capriati	Kim Clijsters
1978	Virginia Ruzici	Mima Jausovec	2002	Serena Williams	Venus Williams
1979	Chris Evert Lloyd	Wendy Turnbull	2003	Justine Henin-Hardenne	Kim Clijsters
1980	Chris Evert Lloyd	Virginia Ruzici	2004	Anastasia Myskina	Elena Dementieva
1981	Hana Mandlikova	Sylvia Hanika	2005	Justine Henin-Hardenne	Mary Pierce
1982	Martina Navratilova	Andrea Jaeger	2006	Justine Henin-Hardenne	Svetlana Kuznetsova
1983	Chris Evert Lloyd	Mima Jausovec	2007	Justine Henin	Ana Ivanovic
1984	Martina Navratilova	Chris Evert Lloyd	2008	Ana Ivanovic	Dinara Safina
1985	Chris Evert Lloyd	Martina Navratilova	2009	Svetlana Kuznetsova	Dinara Safina
1986	Chris Evert Lloyd	Martina Navratilova	2010	Francesca Schiavone	Samantha Stosur
1987	Steffi Graf	Martina Navratilova	2011	Li Na	Francesca Schiavone
1988	Steffi Graf	Natalia Zvereva	2012	Maria Sharapova	Sara Errani
1989	Arantxa Sánchez Vicario	Steffi Graf	2013	Serena Williams	Maria Sharapova
1990	Monica Seles	Steffi Graf	2014	Maria Sharapova	Simona Halep
1991	Monica Seles	Arantxa Sánchez Vicario	2015	Serena Williams	Lucie Safarova
1992	Monica Seles	Steffi Graf	2016	Garbiñe Muguruza	Serena Williams
1993	Steffi Graf	Mary Joe Fernandez	2017	Jelena Ostapenko	Simona Halep
1994	Arantxa Sánchez Vicario	Mary Pierce	2018	Simona Halep	Sloane Stephens
1995	Steffi Graf	Arantxa Sánchez Vicario	2019	Ashleigh Barty	Marketa Vondrousova
1996	Steffi Graf	Arantxa Sánchez Vicario	2020	Iga Swiatek	Sofia Kenin
1997	Iva Majoli	Martina Hingis	2021	Barbora Krejcikova	Anastasia Pavlyuchenkova
1998	Arantxa Sánchez Vicario	Monica Seles	2022	Iga Swiatek	Coco Gauff
1999	Steffi Graf	Martina Hingis	2023	Iga Swiatek	Karolina Muchova

Wimbledon Champions, 1925-2023

First contested 1877 for men, 1884 for women. Became an open championship in 1968. Not held 1940-45, 2020.

Men's Singles

Year	Champion	Final opponent	Year	Champion	Final opponent
1925	René Lacoste	Jean Borotra	1998	Pete Sampras	Goran Ivanisevic
1926	Jean Borotra	Howard Kinsey	1999	Pete Sampras	Andre Agassi
1927	Henri Cochet	Jean Borotra	2000	Pete Sampras	Patrick Rafter
1928	René Lacoste	Henri Cochet	2001	Goran Ivanisevic	Patrick Rafter
1929	Henri Cochet	Jean Borotra	2002	Lleyton Hewitt	David Nalbandian
1930	Bill Tilden	Wilmer Allison	2003	Roger Federer	Mark Philippoussis
1931	Sidney B. Wood	Francis X. Shields	2004	Roger Federer	Andy Roddick
1932	Ellsworth Vines	Henry Austin	2005	Roger Federer	Andy Roddick
1933	Jack Crawford	Ellsworth Vines	2006	Roger Federer	Rafael Nadal
1934	Fred Perry	Jack Crawford	2007	Roger Federer	Rafael Nadal
1935	Fred Perry	Gottfried von Cramm	2008	Rafael Nadal	Roger Federer
1936	Fred Perry	Gottfried von Cramm	2009	Roger Federer	Andy Roddick
1937	Donald Budge	Gottfried von Cramm	2010	Rafael Nadal	Tomas Berdych
1938	Donald Budge	Henry Austin	2011	Novak Djokovic	Rafael Nadal
1939	Bobby Riggs	Elwood Cooke	2012	Roger Federer	Andy Murray
1946	Yvon Petra	Geoff E. Brown	2013	Andy Murray	Novak Djokovic
1947	Jack Kramer	Tom P. Brown	2014	Novak Djokovic	Roger Federer
1948	Bob Falkenburg	John Bromwich	2015	Novak Djokovic	Roger Federer
1949	Ted Schroeder	Jaroslav Drobny	2016	Andy Murray	Milos Raonic
1950	Budge Patty	Frank Sedgman	2017	Roger Federer	Marin Cilic
1951	Dick Savitt	Ken McGregor	2018	Novak Djokovic	Kevin Anderson
1952	Frank Sedgman	Jaroslav Drobny	2019	Novak Djokovic	Roger Federer
1953	Vic Seixas	Kurt Nielsen	2021	Novak Djokovic	Matteo Berrettini
1954	Jaroslav Drobny	Ken Rosewall	2022	Novak Djokovic	Nick Kyrgios
1955	Tony Trabert	Kurt Nielsen	2023	Carlos Alcaraz	Novak Djokovic
1956	Lew Hoad	Ken Rosewall			
1957	Lew Hoad	Ashley Cooper			

Women's Singles

Year	Champion	Final opponent
1958	Ashley Cooper	Neale Fraser
1959	Alex Olmedo	Rod Laver
1960	Neale Fraser	Rod Laver
1961	Rod Laver	Chuck McKinley
1962	Rod Laver	Martin Mulligan
1963	Chuck McKinley	Fred Stolle
1964	Roy Emerson	Fred Stolle
1965	Roy Emerson	Fred Stolle
1966	Manuel Santana	Dennis Ralston
1967	John Newcombe	Wilhelm Bungert
1968	Rod Laver	Tony Roche
1969	Rod Laver	John Newcombe
1970	John Newcombe	Ken Rosewall
1971	John Newcombe	Stan Smith
1972	Stan Smith	Ilie Nastase
1973	Jan Kodes	Alex Metreveli
1974	Jimmy Connors	Ken Rosewall
1975	Arthur Ashe	Jimmy Connors
1976	Björn Borg	Ilie Nastase
1977	Björn Borg	Jimmy Connors
1978	Björn Borg	Jimmy Connors
1979	Björn Borg	Roscoe Tanner
1980	Björn Borg	John McEnroe
1981	John McEnroe	Björn Borg
1982	Jimmy Connors	John McEnroe
1983	John McEnroe	Chris Lewis
1984	John McEnroe	Jimmy Connors
1985	Boris Becker	Kevin Curren
1986	Boris Becker	Ivan Lendl
1987	Pat Cash	Ivan Lendl
1988	Stefan Edberg	Boris Becker
1989	Boris Becker	Stefan Edberg
1990	Stefan Edberg	Boris Becker
1991	Michael Stich	Boris Becker
1992	Andre Agassi	Goran Ivanisevic
1993	Pete Sampras	Jim Courier
1994	Pete Sampras	Goran Ivanisevic
1995	Pete Sampras	Boris Becker
1996	Richard Krajicek	MaliVai "Mai" Washington
1997	Pete Sampras	Cedric Pioline

Year	Champion	Final opponent
1925	Suzanne Lenglen	Joan Fry
1926	Kathleen McKane Godfree	Lili de Alvarez
1927	Helen Wills	Lili de Alvarez
1928	Helen Wills	Lili de Alvarez
1929	Helen Wills	Helen H. Jacobs
1930	Helen Wills Moody	Elizabeth Ryan
1931	Cilly Aussem	Hilde Krahwinkel
1932	Helen Wills Moody	Helen H. Jacobs
1933	Helen Wills Moody	Dorothy Round
1934	Dorothy Round	Helen H. Jacobs
1935	Helen Wills Moody	Helen H. Jacobs
1936	Helen H. Jacobs	Hilde Krahwinkel Sperling
1937	Dorothy Round	Jadwiga Jedrzejowska
1938	Helen Wills Moody	Helen H. Jacobs
1939	Alice Marble	Kay Stammers
1946	Pauline Betz	Louise Brough
1947	Margaret Osborne	Doris Hart
1948	Louise Brough	Doris Hart
1949	Louise Brough	Margaret Osborne duPont
1950	Louise Brough	Margaret Osborne duPont
1951	Doris Hart	Shirley Fry
1952	Maureen Connolly	Louise Brough
1953	Maureen Connolly	Doris Hart
1954	Maureen Connolly	Louise Brough
1955	Louise Brough	Beverly Fleitz
1956	Shirley Fry	Angela Buxton
1957	Althea Gibson	Darlene Hard
1958	Althea Gibson	Angela Mortimer
1959	Maria Bueno	Darlene Hard
1960	Maria Bueno	Sandra Reynolds
1961	Angela Mortimer	Christine Truman
1962	Karen Hantze-Susman	Vera Sukova
1963	Margaret Smith	Billie Jean Moffitt
1964	Maria Bueno	Margaret Smith
1965	Margaret Smith	Maria Bueno
1966	Billie Jean King	Maria Bueno
1967	Billie Jean King	Ann Haydon Jones
1968	Billie Jean King	Judy Tegart
1969	Ann Haydon Jones	Billie Jean King

Year	Champion	Final opponent	Year	Champion	Final opponent
1970	Margaret Smith Court	Billie Jean King	1997	Martina Hingis	Jana Novotna
1971	Evonne Goolagong	Margaret Smith Court	1998	Jana Novotna	Nathalie Tauziat
1972	Billie Jean King	Evonne Goolagong	1999	Lindsay Davenport	Steffi Graf
1973	Billie Jean King	Chris Evert	2000	Venus Williams	Lindsay Davenport
1974	Chris Evert	Olga Morozova	2001	Venus Williams	Justine Henin
1975	Billie Jean King	Evonne Goolagong Cawley	2002	Serena Williams	Venus Williams
1976	Chris Evert	Evonne Goolagong Cawley	2003	Serena Williams	Venus Williams
1977	Virginia Wade	Betty Stove	2004	Maria Sharapova	Serena Williams
1978	Martina Navratilova	Chris Evert	2005	Venus Williams	Lindsay Davenport
1979	Martina Navratilova	Chris Evert Lloyd	2006	Amélie Mauresmo	Justine Henin-Hardenne
1980	Evonne Goolagong Cawley	Chris Evert Lloyd	2007	Venus Williams	Marion Bartoli
1981	Chris Evert Lloyd	Hana Mandlikova	2008	Venus Williams	Serena Williams
1982	Martina Navratilova	Chris Evert Lloyd	2009	Serena Williams	Venus Williams
1983	Martina Navratilova	Andrea Jaeger	2010	Serena Williams	Vera Zvonareva
1984	Martina Navratilova	Chris Evert Lloyd	2011	Petra Kvitova	Maria Sharapova
1985	Martina Navratilova	Chris Evert Lloyd	2012	Serena Williams	Agnieszka Radwanska
1986	Martina Navratilova	Hana Mandlikova	2013	Marion Bartoli	Sabine Lisicki
1987	Martina Navratilova	Steffi Graf	2014	Petra Kvitova	Eugenie Bouchard
1988	Steffi Graf	Martina Navratilova	2015	Serena Williams	Garbiñe Muguruza
1989	Steffi Graf	Martina Navratilova	2016	Serena Williams	Angelique Kerber
1990	Martina Navratilova	Zina Garrison	2017	Garbiñe Muguruza	Venus Williams
1991	Steffi Graf	Gabriela Sabatini	2018	Angelique Kerber	Serena Williams
1992	Steffi Graf	Monica Seles	2019	Simona Halep	Serena Williams
1993	Steffi Graf	Jana Novotna	2021	Ashleigh Barty	Karolina Pliskova
1994	Conchita Martínez	Martina Navratilova	2022	Elena Rybakina	Ons Jabeur
1995	Steffi Graf	Arantxa Sánchez Vicario	2023	Marketa Vondrousova	Ons Jabeur
1996	Steffi Graf	Arantxa Sánchez Vicario			

U.S. Open Champions, 1925-2023

First contested 1881 for men, 1887 for women. The former U.S. National Championship became an open championship in 1968.

Men's Singles

Year	Champion	Final opponent	Year	Champion	Final opponent
1925	Bill Tilden	William Johnston	1988	Mats Wilander	Ivan Lendl
1926	René Lacoste	Jean Borotra	1989	Boris Becker	Ivan Lendl
1927	René Lacoste	Bill Tilden	1990	Pete Sampras	Andre Agassi
1928	Henri Cochet	Francis Hunter	1991	Stefan Edberg	Jim Courier
1929	Bill Tilden	Francis Hunter	1992	Stefan Edberg	Pete Sampras
1930	John Doeg	Francis X. Shields	1993	Pete Sampras	Cedric Pioline
1931	Ellsworth Vines	George Lott	1994	Andre Agassi	Michael Stich
1932	Ellsworth Vines	Henri Cochet	1995	Pete Sampras	Andre Agassi
1933	Fred Perry	John Crawford	1996	Pete Sampras	Michael Chang
1934	Fred Perry	Wilmer Allison	1997	Patrick Rafter	Greg Rusedski
1935	Wilmer Allison	Sidney Wood	1998	Patrick Rafter	Mark Philippoussis
1936	Fred Perry	Don Budge	1999	Andre Agassi	Todd Martin
1937	Don Budge	Gottfried von Cramm	2000	Marat Safin	Pete Sampras
1938	Don Budge	C. Gene Mako	2001	Lleyton Hewitt	Pete Sampras
1939	Bobby Riggs	S. Welby Van Horn	2002	Pete Sampras	Andre Agassi
1940	Don McNeill	Bobby Riggs	2003	Andy Roddick	Juan Carlos Ferrero
1941	Bobby Riggs	F. L. Kovacs	2004	Roger Federer	Lleyton Hewitt
1942	F. R. Schroeder Jr.	Frank Parker	2005	Roger Federer	Andre Agassi
1943	Joseph Hunt	Jack Kramer	2006	Roger Federer	Andy Roddick
1944	Frank Parker	Bill Talbert	2007	Roger Federer	Novak Djokovic
1945	Frank Parker	Bill Talbert	2008	Roger Federer	Andy Murray
1946	Jack Kramer	Tom Brown Jr.	2009	Juan Martín del Potro	Roger Federer
1947	Jack Kramer	Frank Parker	2010	Rafael Nadal	Novak Djokovic
1948	Pancho Gonzales	Eric Sturgess	2011	Novak Djokovic	Rafael Nadal
1949	Pancho Gonzales	F. R. Schroeder Jr.	2012	Andy Murray	Novak Djokovic
1950	Arthur Larsen	Herbert Flam	2013	Rafael Nadal	Novak Djokovic
1951	Frank Sedgman	E. Victor Seixas Jr.	2014	Marin Cilic	Kei Nishikori
1952	Frank Sedgman	Gardnar Mulloy	2015	Novak Djokovic	Roger Federer
1953	Tony Trabert	E. Victor Seixas Jr.	2016	Stan Wawrinka	Novak Djokovic
1954	E. Victor Seixas Jr.	Rex Hartwig	2017	Rafael Nadal	Kevin Anderson
1955	Tony Trabert	Ken Rosewall	2018	Novak Djokovic	Juan Martín del Potro
1956	Ken Rosewall	Lewis Hoad	2019	Rafael Nadal	Daniil Medvedev
1957	Malcolm Anderson	Ashley Cooper	2020	Dominic Thiem	Alexander Zverev
1958	Ashley Cooper	Malcolm Anderson	2021	Daniil Medvedev	Novak Djokovic
1959	Neale A. Fraser	Alejandro Olmedo	2022	Carlos Alcaraz	Casper Ruud
1960	Neale A. Fraser	Rod Laver	2023	Novak Djokovic	Daniil Medvedev
1961	Roy Emerson	Rod Laver			
1962	Rod Laver	Roy Emerson		**Women's Singles**	
1963	Rafael Osuna	F. A. Froehling III	Year	Champion	Final opponent
1964	Roy Emerson	Fred Stolle	1925	Helen Willis	Kathleen McKane
1965	Manuel Santana	Cliff Drysdale	1926	Molla B. Mallory	Elizabeth Ryan
1966	Fred Stolle	John Newcombe	1927	Helen Wills	Betty Nuthall
1967	John Newcombe	Clark Graebner	1928	Helen Wills	Helen H. Jacobs
1968	Arthur Ashe	Tom Okker	1929	Helen Wills	Phoebe Holcroft-Watson
1969	Rod Laver	Tony Roche	1930	Betty Nuthall	Anna McCune Harper
1970	Ken Rosewall	Tony Roche	1931	Helen Wills Moody	E. B. Whittingstall
1971	Stan Smith	Jan Kodes	1932	Helen H. Jacobs	Carolin A. Babcock
1972	Ilie Nastase	Arthur Ashe	1933	Helen H. Jacobs	Helen Wills Moody
1973	John Newcombe	Jan Kodes	1934	Helen H. Jacobs	Sarah H. Palfrey
1974	Jimmy Connors	Ken Rosewall	1935	Helen H. Jacobs	Sarah Palfrey Fabyan
1975	Manuel Orantes	Jimmy Connors	1936	Alice Marble	Helen H. Jacobs
1976	Jimmy Connors	Björn Borg	1937	Anita Lizana	Jadwiga Jedrzejowska
1977	Guillermo Vilas	Jimmy Connors	1938	Alice Marble	Nancye Wynne
1978	Jimmy Connors	Björn Borg	1939	Alice Marble	Helen H. Jacobs
1979	John McEnroe	Vitas Gerulaitis	1940	Alice Marble	Helen H. Jacobs
1980	John McEnroe	Björn Borg	1941	Sarah Palfrey Cooke	Pauline Betz
1981	John McEnroe	Björn Borg	1942	Pauline Betz	Louise Brough
1982	Jimmy Connors	Ivan Lendl	1943	Pauline Betz	Louise Brough
1983	Jimmy Connors	Ivan Lendl	1944	Pauline Betz	Margaret Osborne
1984	John McEnroe	Ivan Lendl	1945	Sarah Palfrey Cooke	Pauline Betz
1985	Ivan Lendl	John McEnroe	1946	Pauline Betz	Patricia Canning
1986	Ivan Lendl	Miloslav Mecir	1947	Louise Brough	Margaret Osborne
1987	Ivan Lendl	Mats Wilander	1948	Margaret Osborne duPont	Louise Brough

Year	Champion	Final opponent	Year	Champion	Final opponent
1949	Margaret Osborne duPont	Doris Hart	1987	Martina Navratilova	Steffi Graf
1950	Margaret Osborne duPont	Doris Hart	1988	Steffi Graf	Gabriela Sabatini
1951	Maureen Connolly	Shirley Fry	1989	Steffi Graf	Martina Navratilova
1952	Maureen Connolly	Doris Hart	1990	Gabriela Sabatini	Steffi Graf
1953	Maureen Connolly	Doris Hart	1991	Monica Seles	Martina Navratilova
1954	Doris Hart	Louise Brough	1992	Monica Seles	Arantxa Sánchez Vicario
1955	Doris Hart	Patricia Ward	1993	Steffi Graf	Helena Sukova
1956	Shirley Fry	Althea Gibson	1994	Arantxa Sánchez Vicario	Steffi Graf
1957	Althea Gibson	Louise Brough	1995	Steffi Graf	Monica Seles
1958	Althea Gibson	Darlene Hard	1996	Steffi Graf	Monica Seles
1959	Maria Bueno	Christine Truman	1997	Martina Hingis	Venus Williams
1960	Darlene Hard	Maria Bueno	1998	Lindsay Davenport	Martina Hingis
1961	Darlene Hard	Ann Haydon	1999	Serena Williams	Martina Hingis
1962	Margaret Smith	Darlene Hard	2000	Venus Williams	Lindsay Davenport
1963	Maria Bueno	Margaret Smith	2001	Venus Williams	Serena Williams
1964	Maria Bueno	Carole Caldwell Graebner	2002	Serena Williams	Venus Williams
1965	Margaret Smith	Billie Jean Moffitt	2003	Justine Henin-Hardenne	Kim Clijsters
1966	Maria Bueno	Nancy Richey	2004	Svetlana Kuznetsova	Elena Dementieva
1967	Billie Jean King	Ann Haydon Jones	2005	Kim Clijsters	Mary Pierce
1968	Virginia Wade	Billie Jean King	2006	Maria Sharapova	Justine Henin-Hardenne
1969	Margaret Smith Court	Nancy Richey	2007	Justine Henin	Svetlana Kuznetsova
1970	Margaret Smith Court	Rosemary Casals	2008	Serena Williams	Jelena Jankovic
1971	Billie Jean King	Rosemary Casals	2009	Kim Clijsters	Caroline Wozniacki
1972	Billie Jean King	Kerry Melville	2010	Kim Clijsters	Vera Zvonareva
1973	Margaret Smith Court	Evonne Goolagong	2011	Samantha Stosur	Serena Williams
1974	Billie Jean King	Evonne Goolagong	2012	Serena Williams	Victoria Azarenka
1975	Chris Evert	Evonne Goolagong Cawley	2013	Serena Williams	Victoria Azarenka
1976	Chris Evert	Evonne Goolagong Cawley	2014	Serena Williams	Caroline Wozniacki
1977	Chris Evert	Wendy Turnbull	2015	Flavia Pennetta	Roberta Vinci
1978	Chris Evert	Pam Shriver	2016	Angelique Kerber	Karolina Pliskova
1979	Tracy Austin	Chris Evert Lloyd	2017	Sloane Stephens	Madison Keys
1980	Chris Evert Lloyd	Hana Mandlikova	2018	Naomi Osaka	Serena Williams
1981	Tracy Austin	Martina Navratilova	2019	Bianca Andreescu	Serena Williams
1982	Chris Evert Lloyd	Hana Mandlikova	2020	Naomi Osaka	Victoria Azarenka
1983	Martina Navratilova	Chris Evert Lloyd	2021	Emma Raducanu	Leylah Fernandez
1984	Martina Navratilova	Chris Evert Lloyd	2022	Iga Swiatek	Ons Jabeur
1985	Hana Mandlikova	Martina Navratilova	2023	Coco Gauff	Aryna Sabalenka
1986	Martina Navratilova	Helena Sukova			

Davis Cup, 1955-2022

The Davis Cup began in 1900 as a competition between the U.S. and Great Britain. Not held, 2020.

Year	Result	Year	Result	Year	Result
1955	Australia 5, U.S. 0	1977	Australia 3, Italy 1	1999	Australia 3, France 2
1956	Australia 5, U.S. 0	1978	U.S. 4, Great Britain 1	2000	Spain 3, Australia 1
1957	Australia 3, U.S. 2	1979	U.S. 5, Italy 0	2001	France 3, Australia 2
1958	U.S. 3, Australia 2	1980	Czechoslovakia 4, Italy 1	2002	Russia 3, France 2
1959	Australia 3, U.S. 2	1981	U.S. 3, Argentina 1	2003	Australia 3, Spain 1
1960	Australia 4, Italy 1	1982	U.S. 4, France, 1	2004	Spain 3, U.S. 2
1961	Australia 5, Italy 0	1983	Australia 3, Sweden 2	2005	Croatia 3, Slovakia 2
1962	Australia 5, Mexico 0	1984	Sweden 4, U.S. 1	2006	Russia 3, Argentina 2
1963	U.S. 3, Australia 2	1985	Sweden 3, W. Germany 2	2007	U.S. 4, Russia 1
1964	Australia 3, U.S. 2	1986	Australia 3, Sweden 2	2008	Spain 3, Argentina 1
1965	Australia 4, Spain 1	1987	Sweden 5, India 0	2009	Spain 5, Czech Republic 0
1966	Australia 4, India 1	1988	W. Germany 4, Sweden 1	2010	Serbia 3, France 2
1967	Australia 4, Spain 1	1989	W. Germany 3, Sweden 2	2011	Spain 3, Argentina 1
1968	U.S. 4, Australia 1	1990	U.S. 3, Australia 2	2012	Czech Republic 3, Spain 2
1969	U.S. 5, Romania 0	1991	France 3, U.S. 1	2013	Czech Republic 3, Serbia 2
1970	U.S. 5, W. Germany 0	1992	U.S. 3, Switzerland 1	2014	Switzerland 3, France 1
1971	U.S. 3, Romania 2	1993	Germany 4, Australia 1	2015	Great Britain 3, Belgium 1
1972	U.S. 3, Romania 2	1994	Sweden 4, Russia 1	2016	Argentina 3, Croatia 2
1973	Australia 5, U.S. 0	1995	U.S. 3, Russia 2	2017	France 3, Belgium 2
1974	South Africa (default by India)	1996	France 3, Sweden 2	2018	Croatia 3, France 1
1975	Sweden 3, Czechoslovakia 2	1997	Sweden 5, U.S. 0	2019	Spain 2, Canada 0
1976	Italy 4, Chile 1	1998	Sweden 4, Italy 1	2021	Russia 2, Croatia 0
				2022	Canada 2, Australia 0

Note: The challenge round format, which guaranteed the previous year's winner a spot in the finals at home, was eliminated in 1972.

All-Time Grand Slam Singles Title Leaders

Men	Australian Open	French Open[1]	Wimbledon	U.S. Open	Total
Novak Djokovic*	2008, '11-'13, '15-'16, '19-'21, '23	2016, '21, '23	2011, '14-'15, '18-'19, '21-'22	2011, '15, '18, '23	24
Rafael Nadal*	2009, '22	2005-08, '10-'14, '17-'20, '22	2008, '10	2010, '13, '17, '19	22
Roger Federer	2004, '06-'07, '10, '17-'18	2009	2003-07, '09, '12, '17	2004-08	20
Pete Sampras	1994, '97	—	1993-95, 1997-2000	1990, '93, '95-'96, 2002	14
Roy Emerson	1961, '63-'67	1963, '67	1964-65	1961, '64	12
Björn Borg	—	1974-75, '78-'81	1976-80	—	11
Rod Laver	1960, '62, '69	1962, '69	1961-62, '68-'69	1962, '69	11
Bill Tilden	—	—	1920-21, '30	1920-25, '29	10
Andre Agassi	1995, 2000-01, '03	1999	1992	1994, '99	8
Jimmy Connors	1974	—	1974, '82	1974, '76, '78, '82-'83	8
Ivan Lendl	1989-90	1984, '86-'87	—	1985-87	8
Fred Perry	1934	1935	1934-36	1933-34, '36	8
Ken Rosewall	1953, '55, '71-'72	1953, '68	—	1956, '70	8

Women	Australian Open	French Open[1]	Wimbledon	U.S. Open	Total
Margaret Smith Court	1960-66, '69-'71, '73	1962, '64, '69-'70, '73	1963, '65, '70	1962, '65, '69-'70, '73	24
Serena Williams	2003, '05, '07, '09-'10, '15, '17	2002, '13, '15	2002-03, '09-'10, '12, '15-'16	1999, 2002, '08, '12-'14	23
Steffi Graf	1988-90, '94	1987-88, '93, '95-'96, '99	1988-89, '91-'93, '95-'96	1988-89, '93, '95-'96	22
Helen Wills Moody	—	1928-30, '32	1927-30, '32-'33, '35, '38	1923-25, '27-'29, '31	19
Chris Evert	1982, '84	1974-75, '79-'80, '83, '85-'86	1974, '76, '81	1975-78, '80, '82	18
Martina Navratilova	1981, '83, '85	1982, '84	1978-79, '82-'87, '90	1983-84, '86-'87	18
Billie Jean King	1968	1972	1966-68, '72-'73, '75	1967, '71-'72, '74	12
Suzanne Lenglen	—	1920-23, '25-'26	1919-23, '25	—	12
Maureen Connolly	1953	1953-54	1952-54	1951-53	9
Monica Seles	1991-93, '96	1990-92	—	1991-92	9

* = Player active in 2023. (1) Prior to 1925, French Open entry was limited to members of French clubs.

AUTO RACING

Indianapolis 500 Winners, 1911-2023

At Indianapolis Motor Speedway in Indianapolis, IN. Not held 1917-18, 1942-45.

Year	Driver(s), car[1]	Avg. mph	Year	Driver(s), car[1]	Avg. mph
1911	Ray Harroun, Marmon	74.602	1971	Al Unser, P.J. Colt-Ford	157.735
1912	Joe Dawson, National	78.719	1972	Mark Donohue, McLaren-Offy	162.962
1913	Jules Goux, Peugeot	75.933	1973	Gordon Johncock, Eagle-Offy	159.036
1914	René Thomas, Delage	82.474	1974	Johnny Rutherford, McLaren-Offy	158.589
1915	Ralph DePalma, Mercedes	89.840	1975	Bobby Unser, Eagle-Offy	149.213
1916	Dario Resta, Peugeot	84.001	1976	Johnny Rutherford, McLaren-Offy	148.725
1919	Howdy Wilcox, Peugeot	88.050	1977	A. J. Foyt, Coyote-Foyt	161.331
1920	Gaston Chevrolet, Frontenac	88.618	1978	Al Unser, Lola-Cosworth	161.363
1921	Tommy Milton, Frontenac	89.621	1979	Rick Mears, Penske-Cosworth	158.899
1922	Jimmy Murphy, Duesenberg-Miller	94.484	1980	Johnny Rutherford, Chaparral-Cosworth	142.862
1923	Tommy Milton, Miller	90.954	1981	Bobby Unser, Penske-Cosworth	139.184
1924	L. L. Corum/Joe Boyer, Duesenberg	98.234	1982	Gordon Johncock, Wildcat-Cosworth	162.029
1925	Peter DePaolo, Duesenberg	101.127	1983	Tom Sneva, March-Cosworth	162.117
1926	Frank Lockhart, Miller	95.904	1984	Rick Mears, March-Cosworth	163.612
1927	George Souders, Duesenberg	97.545	1985	Danny Sullivan, March-Cosworth	152.982
1928	Louis Meyer, Miller	99.482	1986	Bobby Rahal, March-Cosworth	170.722
1929	Ray Keech, Miller	97.585	1987	Al Unser, March-Cosworth	162.175
1930	Billy Arnold, Summers-Miller	100.448	1988	Rick Mears, Penske-Chevy Indy V8	144.809
1931	Louis Schneider, Stevens-Miller	96.629	1989	Emerson Fittipaldi, Penske-Chevy Indy V8	167.581
1932	Fred Frame, Wetteroth-Miller	104.144	1990	Arie Luyendyk, Lola-Chevy Indy V8	185.981
1933	Louis Meyer, Miller	104.162	1991	Rick Mears, Penske-Chevy Indy V8	176.457
1934	Bill Cummings, Miller	104.863	1992	Al Unser Jr., Galmer-Chevy Indy V8A	134.477
1935	Kelly Petillo, Wetteroth-Offy	106.240	1993	Emerson Fittipaldi, Penske-Chevy Indy V8C	157.207
1936	Louis Meyer, Stevens-Miller	109.069	1994	Al Unser Jr., Penske-Mercedes Benz	160.872
1937	Wilbur Shaw, Shaw-Offy	113.580	1995	Jacques Villeneuve, Reynard-Ford Cosworth XB	153.616
1938	Floyd Roberts, Wetteroth-Miller	117.200	1996	Buddy Lazier, Reynard-Ford Cosworth XB	147.956
1939	Wilbur Shaw, Maserati	115.035	1997	Arie Luyendyk, G Force-Aurora	145.827
1940	Wilbur Shaw, Maserati	114.277	1998	Eddie Cheever Jr., Dallara-Aurora	145.155
1941	Floyd Davis/Mauri Rose, Wetteroth-Offy	115.117	1999	Kenny Brack, Dallara-Aurora	153.176
1946	George Robson, Adams-Sparks	114.820	2000	Juan Pablo Montoya, G Force-Oldsmobile	167.607
1947	Mauri Rose, Deidt-Offy	116.338	2001	Helio Castroneves, Dallara-Oldsmobile	141.574
1948	Mauri Rose, Deidt-Offy	119.814	2002	Helio Castroneves, Dallara-Chevrolet	166.499
1949	Bill Holland, Deidt-Offy	121.327	2003	Gil de Ferran, G Force-Toyota	156.291
1950	Johnnie Parsons, Kurtis-Offy	124.002	2004	Buddy Rice, G Force-Honda	138.518
1951	Lee Wallard, Kurtis-Offy	126.244	2005	Dan Wheldon, Dallara-Honda	157.603
1952	Troy Ruttman, Kuzma-Offy	128.922	2006	Sam Hornish Jr., Dallara-Honda	157.085
1953	Bill Vukovich, KK500A-Offy	127.740	2007	Dario Franchitti, Dallara-Honda	151.774
1954	Bill Vukovich, KK500A-Offy	130.840	2008	Scott Dixon, Dallara-Honda	143.567
1955	Bob Sweikert, KK500D-Offy	128.209	2009	Helio Castroneves, Dallara-Honda	150.318
1956	Pat Flaherty, Watson-Offy	128.490	2010	Dario Franchitti, Dallara-Honda	161.623
1957	Sam Hanks, Salih-Offy	135.601	2011	Dan Wheldon, Dallara-Honda	170.265
1958	Jimmy Bryan, Salih-Offy	133.791	2012	Dario Franchitti, Dallara-Honda	167.734
1959	Rodger Ward, Watson-Offy	135.857	2013	Tony Kanaan, Dallara-Chevrolet	187.433
1960	Jim Rathmann, Watson-Offy	138.767	2014	Ryan Hunter-Reay, Dallara-Honda	186.563
1961	A. J. Foyt, Trevis-Offy	139.130	2015	Juan Pablo Montoya, Dallara-Chevrolet	161.341
1962	Rodger Ward, Watson-Offy	140.293	2016	Alexander Rossi, Dallara-Honda	166.634
1963	Parnelli Jones, Watson-Offy	143.137	2017	Takuma Sato, Dallara-Honda	155.395
1964	A. J. Foyt, Watson-Offy	147.350	2018	Will Power, Dallara-Chevrolet	166.935
1965	Jim Clark, Lotus-Ford	150.686	2019	Simon Pagenaud, Dallara-Chevrolet	175.794
1966	Graham Hill, Lola-Ford	144.317	2020	Takuma Sato, Dallara-Honda	157.724
1967	A. J. Foyt, Coyote-Ford	151.207	2021	Helio Castroneves, Dallara-Honda	190.690
1968	Bobby Unser, Eagle-Offy	152.882	2022	Marcus Ericsson, Dallara-Honda	175.428
1969	Mario Andretti, Hawk-Ford	156.867	2023	Josef Newgarden, Dallara-Chevrolet	168.193
1970	Al Unser, P.J. Colt-Ford	155.749			

Note: The race was less than 500 mi in the following years: 1916 (300 mi), 1926 (400 mi), 1950 (345 mi), 1973 (332.5 mi), 1975 (435 mi), 1976 (255 mi), 2004 (450 mi), 2007 (415 mi). (1) Chassis-engine.

IndyCar Series Champions, 1996-2023

A breakaway group of Championship Auto Racing Teams (CART) drivers began the Indy Racing League (IRL) in 1994; it awarded its first championship in 1996. Known as the IndyCar Series in 2003-11 and as IndyCar from 2011 on. Merged with Champ Car World Series, 2008, under the IndyCar name.

Year	Driver	Year	Driver	Year	Driver	Year	Driver	Year	Driver
1996	Scott Sharp; Buzz Calkins (tie)	2001	Sam Hornish Jr.	2007	Dario Franchitti	2013	Scott Dixon	2019	Josef Newgarden
		2002	Sam Hornish Jr.	2008	Scott Dixon	2014	Will Power	2020	Scott Dixon
1997	Tony Stewart	2003	Scott Dixon	2009	Dario Franchitti	2015	Scott Dixon	2021	Alex Palou
1998	Kenny Brack	2004	Tony Kanaan	2010	Dario Franchitti	2016	Simon Pagenaud	2022	Will Power
1999	Greg Ray	2005	Dan Wheldon	2011	Dario Franchitti	2017	Josef Newgarden	2023	Alex Palou
2000	Buddy Lazier	2006	Sam Hornish Jr.	2012	Ryan Hunter-Reay	2018	Scott Dixon		

Champ Car World Series Winners, 1959-2007

Known as U.S. Auto Club, 1959-78; Championship Auto Racing Teams (CART), 1979-2003; Champ Car World Series, 2004-07. The Vanderbilt Cup became the series championship trophy in 2000. Merged with Indy Racing League (now IndyCar) in 2008.

Year	Driver	Year	Driver	Year	Driver	Year	Driver	Year	Driver
1959	Rodger Ward	1969	Mario Andretti	1979	Rick Mears	1989	Emerson Fittipaldi	1999	Juan Montoya
1960	A. J. Foyt	1970	Al Unser	1980	Johnny Rutherford	1990	Al Unser Jr.	2000	Gil de Ferran
1961	A. J. Foyt	1971	Joe Leonard	1981	Rick Mears	1991	Michael Andretti	2001	Gil de Ferran
1962	Rodger Ward	1972	Joe Leonard	1982	Rick Mears	1992	Bobby Rahal	2002	Cristiano da Matta
1963	A. J. Foyt	1973	Roger McCluskey	1983	Al Unser	1993	Nigel Mansell	2003	Paul Tracy
1964	A. J. Foyt	1974	Bobby Unser	1984	Mario Andretti	1994	Al Unser Jr.	2004	Sébastien Bourdais
1965	Mario Andretti	1975	A. J. Foyt	1985	Al Unser	1995	Jacques Villeneuve	2005	Sébastien Bourdais
1966	Mario Andretti	1976	Gordon Johncock	1986	Bobby Rahal	1996	Jimmy Vasser	2006	Sébastien Bourdais
1967	A. J. Foyt	1977	Tom Sneva	1987	Bobby Rahal	1997	Alex Zanardi	2007	Sébastien Bourdais
1968	Bobby Unser	1978	Tom Sneva	1988	Danny Sullivan	1998	Alex Zanardi		

NASCAR Cup Series Champions, 1949-2022

Known as Strictly Stock, 1949; Grand National, 1950-70; Winston Cup, 1971-2003; Nextel Cup, 2004-07; Sprint Cup, 2008-16; Monster Energy NASCAR Cup, 2017-19.

Year	Driver	Year	Driver	Year	Driver	Year	Driver	Year	Driver
1949	Red Byron	1964	Richard Petty	1979	Richard Petty	1994	Dale Earnhardt	2009	Jimmie Johnson
1950	Bill Rexford	1965	Ned Jarrett	1980	Dale Earnhardt	1995	Jeff Gordon	2010	Jimmie Johnson
1951	Herb Thomas	1966	David Pearson	1981	Darrell Waltrip	1996	Terry Labonte	2011	Tony Stewart
1952	Tim Flock	1967	Richard Petty	1982	Darrell Waltrip	1997	Jeff Gordon	2012	Brad Keselowski
1953	Herb Thomas	1968	David Pearson	1983	Bobby Allison	1998	Jeff Gordon	2013	Jimmie Johnson
1954	Lee Petty	1969	David Pearson	1984	Terry Labonte	1999	Dale Jarrett	2014	Kevin Harvick
1955	Tim Flock	1970	Bobby Isaac	1985	Darrell Waltrip	2000	Bobby Labonte	2015	Kyle Busch
1956	Buck Baker	1971	Richard Petty	1986	Dale Earnhardt	2001	Jeff Gordon	2016	Jimmie Johnson
1957	Buck Baker	1972	Richard Petty	1987	Dale Earnhardt	2002	Tony Stewart	2017	Martin Truex Jr.
1958	Lee Petty	1973	Benny Parsons	1988	Bill Elliott	2003	Matt Kenseth	2018	Joey Logano
1959	Lee Petty	1974	Richard Petty	1989	Rusty Wallace	2004	Kurt Busch	2019	Kyle Busch
1960	Rex White	1975	Richard Petty	1990	Dale Earnhardt	2005	Tony Stewart	2020	Chase Elliott
1961	Ned Jarrett	1976	Cale Yarborough	1991	Dale Earnhardt	2006	Jimmie Johnson	2021	Kyle Larson
1962	Joe Weatherly	1977	Cale Yarborough	1992	Alan Kulwicki	2007	Jimmie Johnson	2022	Joey Logano
1963	Joe Weatherly	1978	Cale Yarborough	1993	Dale Earnhardt	2008	Jimmie Johnson		

NASCAR Cup Series Rookie of the Year, 1958-2022

Year	Driver	Year	Driver	Year	Driver	Year	Driver	Year	Driver
1958	Shorty Rollins	1971	Walter Ballard	1984	Rusty Wallace	1997	Mike Skinner	2010	Kevin Conway
1959	Richard Petty	1972	Larry Smith	1985	Ken Schrader	1998	Kenny Irwin	2011	Andy Lally
1960	David Pearson	1973	Lennie Pond	1986	Alan Kulwicki	1999	Tony Stewart	2012	Stephen Leicht
1961	Woodie Wilson	1974	Earl Ross	1987	Davey Allison	2000	Matt Kenseth	2013	Ricky Stenhouse Jr.
1962	Tom Cox	1975	Bruce Hill	1988	Ken Bouchard	2001	Kevin Harvick	2014	Kyle Larson
1963	Billy Wade	1976	Skip Manning	1989	Dick Trickle	2002	Ryan Newman	2015	Brett Moffitt
1964	Doug Cooper	1977	Ricky Rudd	1990	Rob Moroso	2003	Jamie McMurray	2016	Chase Elliott
1965	Sam McQuagg	1978	Ronnie Thomas	1991	Jimmy Hensley	2004	Kasey Kahne	2017	Erik Jones
1966	James Hylton	1979	Dale Earnhardt	1992	Jimmy Hensley	2005	Kyle Busch	2018	William Byron
1967	Donnie Allison	1980	Jody Ridley	1993	Jeff Gordon	2006	Denny Hamlin	2019	Daniel Hemric
1968	Pete Hamilton	1981	Ron Bouchard	1994	Jeff Burton	2007	Juan Pablo Montoya	2020	Cole Custer
1969	Dick Brooks	1982	Geoff Bodine	1995	Ricky Craven	2008	Regan Smith	2021	Chase Briscoe
1970	Bill Dennis	1983	Sterling Marlin	1996	Johnny Benson	2009	Joey Logano	2022	Austin Cindric

Daytona 500 Winners, 1959-2023

At Daytona International Speedway in Daytona Beach, FL.

Year	Driver, car	Avg. mph	Year	Driver, car	Avg. mph	Year	Driver, car	Avg. mph
1959	Lee Petty, Oldsmobile	135.521	1981	Richard Petty, Buick	169.651	2003	Michael Waltrip, Chevrolet	133.870
1960	Junior Johnson, Chevrolet	124.740	1982	Bobby Allison, Buick	153.991	2004	Dale Earnhardt Jr., Chevrolet	156.345
1961	Marvin Panch, Pontiac	149.601	1983	Cale Yarborough, Pontiac	155.979	2005	Jeff Gordon, Chevrolet	135.173
1962	Fireball Roberts, Pontiac	152.529	1984	Cale Yarborough, Chevrolet	150.994	2006	Jimmie Johnson, Chevrolet	142.667
1963	Tiny Lund, Ford	151.566	1985	Bill Elliott, Ford	172.265	2007	Kevin Harvick, Chevrolet	149.335
1964	Richard Petty, Plymouth	154.334	1986	Geoff Bodine, Chevrolet	148.124	2008	Ryan Newman, Dodge	152.672
1965	Fred Lorenzen, Ford	141.539	1987	Bill Elliott, Ford	176.263	2009	Matt Kenseth, Ford	132.816
1966	Richard Petty, Plymouth	160.627	1988	Bobby Allison, Buick	137.531	2010	Jamie McMurray, Chevrolet	137.284
1967	Mario Andretti, Ford	146.926	1989	Darrell Waltrip, Chevrolet	148.466	2011	Trevor Bayne, Ford	130.326
1968	Cale Yarborough, Mercury	143.251	1990	Derrike Cope, Chevrolet	165.761	2012	Matt Kenseth, Ford	140.256
1969	LeeRoy Yarbrough, Ford	157.950	1991	Ernie Irvan, Chevrolet	148.148	2013	Jimmie Johnson, Chevrolet	159.250
1970	Pete Hamilton, Plymouth	149.601	1992	Davey Allison, Ford	160.256	2014	Dale Earnhardt Jr., Chevrolet	145.290
1971	Richard Petty, Plymouth	144.462	1993	Dale Jarrett, Chevrolet	154.972	2015	Joey Logano, Ford	161.939
1972	A. J. Foyt, Mercury	161.550	1994	Sterling Marlin, Chevrolet	156.931	2016	Denny Hamlin, Toyota	157.549
1973	Richard Petty, Dodge	157.205	1995	Sterling Marlin, Chevrolet	141.710	2017	Kurt Busch, Ford	143.187
1974	Richard Petty, Dodge	140.894	1996	Dale Jarrett, Ford	154.308	2018	Austin Dillon, Chevrolet	150.545
1975	Benny Parsons, Chevrolet	153.649	1997	Jeff Gordon, Chevrolet	148.295	2019	Denny Hamlin, Toyota	137.440
1976	David Pearson, Mercury	152.181	1998	Dale Earnhardt, Chevrolet	172.712	2020	Denny Hamlin, Toyota	141.110
1977	Cale Yarborough, Chevrolet	153.218	1999	Jeff Gordon, Chevrolet	161.551	2021	Michael McDowell, Ford	144.416
1978	Bobby Allison, Ford	159.730	2000	Dale Jarrett, Ford	155.669	2022	Austin Cindric, Ford	142.295
1979	Richard Petty, Oldsmobile	143.977	2001	Michael Waltrip, Chevrolet	161.783	2023	Ricky Stenhouse Jr.,	
1980	Buddy Baker, Oldsmobile	177.602	2002	Ward Burton, Dodge	142.971		Chevrolet	145.283

Coca-Cola 600 Winners, 1960-2023

At Charlotte Motor Speedway in Concord, NC. Known as the World 600, 1960-85. * = Rain-shortened.

Year	Driver, car	Avg. mph	Year	Driver, car	Avg. mph	Year	Driver, car	Avg. mph
1960	Joe Lee Johnson, Chevrolet	107.735	1980	Benny Parsons, Chevrolet	119.265	2002	Mark Martin, Ford	137.729
1961	David Pearson, Pontiac	111.633	1981	Bobby Allison, Buick	129.326	2003	Jimmie Johnson, Chevrolet	126.198*
1962	Nelson Stacy, Ford	125.552	1982	Neil Bonnett, Ford	130.058	2004	Jimmie Johnson, Chevrolet	142.763
1963	Fred Lorenzen, Ford	132.418	1983	Neil Bonnett, Chevrolet	140.707	2005	Jimmie Johnson, Chevrolet	114.698
1964	Jim Paschal, Plymouth	125.772	1984	Bobby Allison, Buick	129.233	2006	Kasey Kahne, Dodge	128.840
1965	Fred Lorenzen, Ford	121.722	1985	Darrell Waltrip, Chevrolet	141.807	2007	Casey Mears, Chevrolet	130.222
1966	Marvin Panch, Plymouth	135.042	1986	Dale Earnhardt, Chevrolet	140.406	2008	Kasey Kahne, Dodge	135.772
1967	Jim Paschal, Plymouth	135.832	1987	Kyle Petty, Ford	131.483	2009	David Reutimann, Toyota	120.899*
1968	Buddy Baker, Dodge	104.207*	1988	Darrell Waltrip, Chevrolet	124.460	2010	Kurt Busch, Dodge	144.966
1969	LeeRoy Yarbrough, Mercury	134.361	1989	Darrell Waltrip, Chevrolet	144.077	2011	Kevin Harvick, Chevrolet	132.414
1970	Donnie Allison, Ford	129.680	1990	Rusty Wallace, Pontiac	137.650	2012	Kasey Kahne, Chevrolet	155.687
1971	Bobby Allison, Mercury	140.422	1991	Davey Allison, Ford	138.951	2013	Kevin Harvick, Chevrolet	130.521
1972	Buddy Baker, Dodge	142.255	1992	Dale Earnhardt, Chevrolet	132.980	2014	Jimmie Johnson, Chevrolet	145.484
1973	Buddy Baker, Dodge	134.890	1993	Dale Earnhardt, Chevrolet	145.504	2015	Carl Edwards, Toyota	147.803
1974	David Pearson, Mercury	135.720	1994	Jeff Gordon, Chevrolet	139.445	2016	Martin Truex Jr., Toyota	160.655
1975	Richard Petty, Dodge	145.327	1995	Bobby Labonte, Chevrolet	151.952	2017	Austin Dillon, Chevrolet	138.800
1976	David Pearson, Mercury	137.352	1996	Dale Jarrett, Ford	147.581	2018	Kyle Busch, Toyota	136.692
1977	Richard Petty, Dodge	137.676	1997	Jeff Gordon, Chevrolet	136.745*	2019	Martin Truex Jr., Toyota	124.074
1978	Darrell Waltrip, Chevrolet	138.355	1998	Jeff Gordon, Chevrolet	136.424	2020	Brad Keselowski, Ford	135.042
1979	Darrell Waltrip, Chevrolet	136.674	1999	Jeff Burton, Ford	151.367	2021	Kyle Larson, Chevrolet	150.785
			2000	Matt Kenseth, Ford	142.640	2022	Denny Hamlin, Toyota	118.703
			2001	Jeff Burton, Ford	138.107	2023	Ryan Blaney, Ford	120.468

NASCAR All-Star Race Winners, 1985-2023

At Charlotte Motor Speedway in Concord, NC, 1985-2019; Bristol Motor Speedway in Bristol, TN, 2020; Texas Motor Speedway in Ft. Worth, TX, 2021-22; North Wilkesboro Speedway in North Wilkesboro, NC, 2023.

Year	Driver, car	Year	Driver, car	Year	Driver, car
1985	Darrell Waltrip, Chevrolet	1998	Mark Martin, Ford	2011	Carl Edwards, Ford
1986	Bill Elliott, Ford	1999	Terry Labonte, Chevrolet	2012	Jimmie Johnson, Chevrolet
1987	Dale Earnhardt, Chevrolet	2000	Dale Earnhardt Jr., Chevrolet	2013	Jimmie Johnson, Chevrolet
1988	Terry Labonte, Chevrolet	2001	Jeff Gordon, Chevrolet	2014	Jamie McMurray, Chevrolet
1989	Rusty Wallace, Pontiac	2002	Ryan Newman, Ford	2015	Denny Hamlin, Toyota
1990	Dale Earnhardt, Chevrolet	2003	Jimmie Johnson, Chevrolet	2016	Joey Logano, Ford
1991	Davey Allison, Ford	2004	Matt Kenseth, Ford	2017	Kyle Busch, Toyota
1992	Davey Allison, Ford	2005	Mark Martin, Ford	2018	Kevin Harvick, Ford
1993	Dale Earnhardt, Chevrolet	2006	Jimmie Johnson, Chevrolet	2019	Kyle Larson, Chevrolet
1994	Geoff Bodine, Ford	2007	Kevin Harvick, Chevrolet	2020	Chase Elliott, Chevrolet
1995	Jeff Gordon, Chevrolet	2008	Kasey Kahne, Dodge	2021	Kyle Larson, Chevrolet
1996	Michael Waltrip, Ford	2009	Tony Stewart, Chevrolet	2022	Ryan Blaney, Ford
1997	Jeff Gordon, Chevrolet	2010	Kurt Busch, Dodge	2023	Kyle Larson, Chevrolet

Brickyard Race Winners, 1994-2023

At Indianapolis Motor Speedway in Indianapolis, IN. Brickyard 400 (under various sponsors), 1994-2020; Verizon 200 (200 mi on the combined road course), 2021-23.

Year	Driver, car	Avg. mph	Year	Driver, car	Avg. mph	Year	Driver, car	Avg. mph
1994	Jeff Gordon, Chevrolet	131.977	2004	Jeff Gordon, Chevrolet	115.037	2014	Jeff Gordon, Chevrolet	150.297
1995	Dale Earnhardt, Chevrolet	155.206	2005	Tony Stewart, Chevrolet	118.782	2015	Kyle Busch, Toyota	131.656
1996	Dale Jarrett, Ford	139.508	2006	Jimmie Johnson, Chevrolet	137.182	2016	Kyle Busch, Toyota	128.940
1997	Ricky Rudd, Ford	130.814	2007	Tony Stewart, Chevrolet	117.379	2017	Kasey Kahne, Chevrolet	114.384
1998	Jeff Gordon, Chevrolet	126.772	2008	Jimmie Johnson, Chevrolet	115.117	2018	Brad Keselowski, Ford	128.629
1999	Dale Jarrett, Ford	148.194	2009	Jimmie Johnson, Chevrolet	145.882	2019	Kevin Harvick, Ford	119.443
2000	Bobby Labonte, Pontiac	155.912	2010	Jamie McMurray, Chevrolet	136.054	2020	Kevin Harvick, Ford	123.162
2001	Jeff Gordon, Chevrolet	130.790	2011	Paul Menard, Chevrolet	140.762	2021	AJ Allmendinger, Chevrolet	69.171
2002	Bill Elliott, Dodge	125.033	2012	Jimmie Johnson, Chevrolet	137.680	2022	Tyler Reddick, Chevrolet	78.511
2003	Kevin Harvick, Chevrolet	134.554	2013	Ryan Newman, Chevrolet	153.485	2023	Michael McDowell, Ford	92.319

Bass Pro Shops Night Race Winners, 1961-2023

At Bristol Motor Speedway in Bristol, TN. * = Rain-shortened.

Year	Driver, car	Avg. mph	Year	Driver, car	Avg. mph	Year	Driver, car	Avg. mph
1961	Jack Smith, Pontiac	68.373	1982	Darrell Waltrip, Buick	94.318	2004	Dale Earnhardt Jr., Chevrolet	88.538
1962	Bobby Johns, Pontiac	73.320	1983	Darrell Waltrip, Chevrolet	89.430*	2005	Matt Kenseth, Ford	84.678
1963	Fred Lorenzen, Ford	74.844	1984	Terry Labonte, Chevrolet	85.365	2006	Matt Kenseth, Ford	90.025
1964	Fred Lorenzen, Ford	78.044	1985	Dale Earnhardt, Chevrolet	81.388	2007	Carl Edwards, Ford	89.006
1965	Ned Jarrett, Ford	61.826	1986	Darrell Waltrip, Chevrolet	86.934	2008	Carl Edwards, Ford	91.581
1966	Paul Goldsmith, Plymouth	77.963	1987	Dale Earnhardt, Chevrolet	90.373	2009	Kyle Busch, Toyota	84.820
1967	Richard Petty, Plymouth	78.705	1988	Dale Earnhardt, Chevrolet	78.775	2010	Kyle Busch, Toyota	99.071
1968	David Pearson, Ford	76.310	1989	Darrell Waltrip, Chevrolet	85.554	2011	Brad Keselowski, Dodge	96.753
1969	David Pearson, Ford	79.737	1990	Ernie Irvan, Chevrolet	91.782	2012	Denny Hamlin, Toyota	84.402
1970	Bobby Allison, Dodge	84.880	1991	Alan Kulwicki, Ford	82.028	2013	Matt Kenseth, Toyota	90.279
1971	Charlie Glotzbach, Chevrolet	101.074	1992	Darrell Waltrip, Chevrolet	91.198	2014	Joey Logano, Ford	92.965
1972	Bobby Allison, Chevrolet	92.735	1993	Mark Martin, Ford	88.172	2015	Joey Logano, Ford	96.890
1973	Benny Parsons, Chevrolet	91.342	1994	Rusty Wallace, Ford	91.363	2016	Kevin Harvick, Chevrolet	77.968
1974	Cale Yarborough, Chevrolet	75.430	1995	Terry Labonte, Chevrolet	81.979	2017	Kyle Busch, Toyota	95.969
1975	Richard Petty, Dodge	97.016	1996	Rusty Wallace, Ford	91.267	2018	Kurt Busch, Ford	89.538
1976	Cale Yarborough, Chevrolet	99.175	1997	Dale Jarrett, Ford	80.013	2019	Denny Hamlin, Toyota	94.531
1977	Cale Yarborough, Chevrolet	79.726	1998	Mark Martin, Ford	86.949	2020	Kevin Harvick, Ford	95.911
1978	Cale Yarborough, Olds.	88.628	1999	Dale Earnhardt, Chevrolet	91.276	2021	Kyle Larson, Chevrolet	87.409
1979	Darrell Waltrip, Chevrolet	91.493	2000	Rusty Wallace, Ford	85.394	2022	Chris Buescher, Ford	88.286
1980	Cale Yarborough, Chevrolet	86.973	2001	Tony Stewart, Pontiac	85.106	2023	Denny Hamlin, Toyota	94.990
1981	Darrell Waltrip, Buick	84.723	2002	Jeff Gordon, Chevrolet	77.097			
			2003	Kurt Busch, Ford	77.421			

Formula One World Drivers' Champions, 1950-2022

Awarded by the Fédération Internationale de l'Automobile (FIA); champions determined through a series of Grand Prix races.

Year	Driver, country	Year	Driver, country	Year	Driver, country
1950	Giuseppe "Nino" Farina, Italy	1975	Niki Lauda, Austria	1999	Mika Hakkinen, Finland
1951	Juan Manuel Fangio, Argentina	1976	James Hunt, England, UK	2000	Michael Schumacher, Germany
1952	Alberto Ascari, Italy	1977	Niki Lauda, Austria	2001	Michael Schumacher, Germany
1953	Alberto Ascari, Italy	1978	Mario Andretti, United States	2002	Michael Schumacher, Germany
1954	Juan Manuel Fangio, Argentina	1979	Jody Scheckter, South Africa	2003	Michael Schumacher, Germany
1955	Juan Manuel Fangio, Argentina	1980	Alan Jones, Australia	2004	Michael Schumacher, Germany
1956	Juan Manuel Fangio, Argentina	1981	Nelson Piquet, Brazil	2005	Fernando Alonso, Spain
1957	Juan Manuel Fangio, Argentina	1982	Keke Rosberg, Finland	2006	Fernando Alonso, Spain
1958	Mike Hawthorn, England, UK	1983	Nelson Piquet, Brazil	2007	Kimi Raikkonen, Finland
1959	Jack Brabham, Australia	1984	Niki Lauda, Austria	2008	Lewis Hamilton, England, UK
1960	Jack Brabham, Australia	1985	Alain Prost, France	2009	Jenson Button, England, UK
1961	Phil Hill, United States	1986	Alain Prost, France	2010	Sebastian Vettel, Germany
1962	Graham Hill, England, UK	1987	Nelson Piquet, Brazil	2011	Sebastian Vettel, Germany
1963	Jim Clark, Scotland, UK	1988	Ayrton Senna, Brazil	2012	Sebastian Vettel, Germany
1964	John Surtees, England, UK	1989	Alain Prost, France	2013	Sebastian Vettel, Germany
1965	Jim Clark, Scotland, UK	1990	Ayrton Senna, Brazil	2014	Lewis Hamilton, England, UK
1966	Jack Brabham, Australia	1991	Ayrton Senna, Brazil	2015	Lewis Hamilton, England, UK
1967	Denis Hulme, New Zealand	1992	Nigel Mansell, England, UK	2016	Nico Rosberg, Germany
1968	Graham Hill, England, UK	1993	Alain Prost, France	2017	Lewis Hamilton, England, UK
1969	Jackie Stewart, Scotland, UK	1994	Michael Schumacher, Germany	2018	Lewis Hamilton, England, UK
1970	Jochen Rindt, Austria	1995	Michael Schumacher, Germany	2019	Lewis Hamilton, England, UK
1971	Jackie Stewart, Scotland, UK	1996	Damon Hill, England, UK	2020	Lewis Hamilton, England, UK
1972	Emerson Fittipaldi, Brazil	1997	Jacques Villeneuve, Canada	2021	Max Verstappen, Netherlands
1973	Jackie Stewart, Scotland, UK	1998	Mika Hakkinen, Finland	2022	Max Verstappen, Netherlands
1974	Emerson Fittipaldi, Brazil				

BOXING

There are many boxing governing bodies, including the World Boxing Assn. (WBA; known as the National Boxing Assn. [NBA] until 1962), World Boxing Council (WBC), International Boxing Fed. (IBF), World Boxing Org., N. American Boxing Fed., and European Boxing Union. All have their own champions and divisions.

Boxing Champions by Class

Class (weight limit)	WBA Champion	WBC Champion	IBF Champion
Heavyweight (none)	Oleksandr Usyk, Ukraine[1] Mahmoud Charr, Germany	Tyson Fury, UK	Oleksandr Usyk, Ukraine
Cruiserweight (200 lbs)	Arsen Goulamirian, France[1]	Vacant	Jai Opetaia, Australia
Light Heavyweight (175 lbs)	Dmitry Bivol, Russia[1]	Artur Beterbiev, Canada	Artur Beterbiev, Canada
Super Middleweight (168 lbs)	Canelo Álvarez, Mexico[1] David Morrell, Cuba	Canelo Álvarez, Mexico David Benavidez, U.S.[2]	Canelo Álvarez, Mexico
Middleweight (160 lbs)	Erislandy Lara, U.S.	Jermall Charlo, U.S. Carlos Adames, Dominican Republic[2]	Vincenzo Gualtieri, Germany
Super Welterweight/Jr. Middleweight (154 lbs)	Jermell Charlo, U.S.[1]	Jermell Charlo, U.S. Brian Mendoza, U.S.[2]	Jermell Charlo, U.S.
Welterweight (147 lbs)	Terence Crawford, U.S.[1] Eimantas Stanionis, Lithuania	Terence Crawford, U.S. Mario Barrios, U.S.[2]	Terence Crawford, U.S. Jason Ennis, U.S.[2]
Super Lightweight/Jr. Welterweight (140 lbs)	Rolly Romero, U.S.	Regis Prograis, U.S.	Subriel Matias, Puerto Rico
Lightweight (135 lbs)	Devin Haney, U.S.[1] Gervonta Davis, U.S.	Vacant	Devin Haney, U.S.
Super Featherweight/Jr. Lightweight (130 lbs)	Héctor García, Dominican Republic	O'Shaquie Foster, U.S.	Joe Cordina, UK
Featherweight (126 lbs)	Leigh Wood, UK	Rey Vargas, Mexico Brandon Figueroa, U.S.[2]	Luis Alberto Lopez, Mexico
Super Bantamweight/Jr. Featherweight (122 lbs)	Marlon Tapales, Philippines[1]	Naoya Inoue, Japan	Marlon Tapales, Philippines
Bantamweight (118 lbs)	Takuma Inoue, Japan	Alexandro Santiago, Mexico	Emmanuel Rodriguez, Puerto Rico
Super Flyweight/Jr. Bantamweight (115 lbs)	Kazuto Ioka, Japan	Juan Francisco Estrada, Mexico	Fernando Martínez, Argentina
Flyweight (112 lbs)	Artem Dalakian, Ukraine	Julio Cesar Martinez, Mexico McWilliams Arroyo, Puerto Rico[2]	Sunny Edwards, UK
Light Flyweight/Jr. Flyweight (108 lbs)	Kenshiro Teraji, Japan[1]	Kenshiro Teraji, Japan	Sivenathi Nontshinga, South Africa
Strawweight/Mini Flyweight (105 lbs)	Thammanoon Niyomtrong, Thailand[1] Erick Rosa, Dominican Republic	Yudi Shigeoka, Japan	Ginjiro Shigeoka, Japan

Note: As of Oct. 9, 2023. (1) Super champion. (2) Interim champion.

Ring Champions by Years

* = Abandoned/relinquished the title or was stripped of it. IBF champions listed only for heavyweight division. International Boxing Hall of Fame inductees in *italics*. For years with multiple champions, boxers are listed according to date of earliest title bout.

Heavyweights

1882-92	*John L. Sullivan*[1]	1978-83	*Larry Holmes* (WBC*)[6]	1997-99	*Lennox Lewis* (WBC)
1892-97	*James J. Corbett*[2]	1979-80	John Tate (WBA)	1999-2001	*Lennox Lewis* (WBA*/WBC/IBF)
1897-99	*Bob Fitzsimmons*	1980-82	Mike Weaver (WBA)	2000-01	*Evander Holyfield* (WBA)
1899-1905	*James J. Jeffries*[*3]	1982-83	Michael Dokes (WBA)	2001-03	John Ruiz (WBA)
1905-06	Marvin Hart	1983-84	Gerrie Coetzee (WBA)	2001	Hasim Rahman (WBC/IBF)
1906-08	*Tommy Burns*	1983-85	*Larry Holmes* (IBF)[6]	2001-02	*Lennox Lewis* (IBF*)
1908-15	*Jack Johnson*	1984	Tim Witherspoon (WBC)	2001-04	*Lennox Lewis* (WBC)
1915-19	*Jess Willard*	1984-86	Pinklon Thomas (WBC)	2002-06	Chris Byrd (IBF)
1919-26	*Jack Dempsey*	1984-85	Greg Page (WBA)	2003	*Roy Jones Jr.* (WBA*)
1926-28	*Gene Tunney*[4]	1985-86	Tony Tubbs (WBA)	2004-05	John Ruiz (WBA*)[7];
1928-30	Vacant	1985-87	*Michael Spinks* (IBF*)		*Vitali Klitschko* (WBC*)
1930-32	*Max Schmeling*	1986	Tim Witherspoon (WBC)	2005-06	Hasim Rahman (WBC)
1932-33	*Jack Sharkey*		Trevor Berbick (WBC)	2005-07	Nicolai Valuev (WBA)
1933-34	Primo Carnera	1986-87	*Mike Tyson* (WBC); James	2006-15	*Wladimir Klitschko* (IBF)
1934-35	Max Baer		"Bonecrusher" Smith (WBA)	2006-08	Oleg Maskaev (WBC)
1935-37	*James J. Braddock*	1987	Tony Tucker (IBF)	2007-08	Ruslan Chagaev (WBA)
1937-49	*Joe Louis*[*]	1987-90	*Mike Tyson* (WBA/WBC/IBF)	2008	Samuel Peter (WBC)
1949-51	*Ezzard Charles*	1990	James "Buster" Douglas	2008-09	Nikolai Valuev (WBA)
1951-52	*Joe Walcott*		(WBA/WBC/IBF)	2008-13	*Vitali Klitschko* (WBC*)
1952-56	*Rocky Marciano*[*]	1990-92	*Evander Holyfield* (WBA/WBC/IBF)	2009-11	David Haye (WBA)
1956-59	*Floyd Patterson*	1992-93	*Riddick Bowe* (WBA/WBC*/IBF)	2011-15	*Wladimir Klitschko* (WBA)
1959-60	*Ingemar Johansson*	1992-94	*Lennox Lewis* (WBC)	2014-15	Bermane Stiverne (WBC)
1960-62	*Floyd Patterson*	1993-94	*Evander Holyfield* (WBA/IBF)	2015-20	Deontay Wilder (WBC)
1962-64	*Sonny Liston*	1994	Michael Moorer (WBA/IBF)	2015-16	Tyson Fury (WBA*)
1964-67	*Cassius Clay (Muhammad Ali)*[*4]	1994-95	Oliver McCall (WBC);	2015	Tyson Fury (IBF*)
1968-70	Jimmy Ellis[4]		*George Foreman* (WBA*/IBF*)	2016	Charles Martin (IBF)
1970-73	*Joe Frazier*	1995-96	Bruce Seldon (WBA);	2016-19	Anthony Joshua (IBF)
1973-74	*George Foreman*		Frank Bruno (WBC)	2017-19	Anthony Joshua (WBA)
1974-78	*Muhammad Ali*	1995	Frans Botha (IBF*)	2019	Andy Ruiz Jr. (WBA/IBF)
1978	Leon Spinks (WBA/WBC*)[5];	1996	*Mike Tyson* (WBA/WBC*)	2019-21	Anthony Joshua (WBA/IBF)
	Ken Norton (WBC)[5]	1996-97	Michael Moorer (IBF)	2020-	Tyson Fury (WBC)
1978-79	*Muhammad Ali* (WBA*)[5]	1996-99	*Evander Holyfield* (WBA/IBF)	2021-	Oleksandr Usyk (WBA/IBF)

(1) London Prize Ring (bare-knuckle champion). (2) First Marquis of Queensberry champion. (3) Jeffries vacated title (1905) and designated Marvin Hart and Jack Root as logical contenders. Hart def. Root in 12 rounds (1905), in turn was def. by Tommy Burns (1906), who claimed the title. Jack Johnson def. Burns (1908) and was recognized as champ. Johnson won the title by defeating Jeffries in the latter's attempted comeback (1910). (4) Title declared vacant by the WBA and others in 1967 after Ali refused military induction for religious reasons during the Vietnam War. Joe Frazier recognized as champ by six states, Mexico, and S. America. Jimmy Ellis won a tournament for the WBA title. (5) After Spinks def. Ali for the WBA title, the WBC recognized Ken Norton as champ. Ali def. Spinks in 1978 rematch for WBA title and retired in 1979. (6) Relinquished WBC title in Dec. 1983 to fight as champ of the new IBF. (7) James Toney def. Ruiz Apr. 30, 2005, to claim the title, but it was rescinded when Toney tested positive for steroids.

Light Heavyweights

1903-05	Bob Fitzsimmons	1978-79	Mike Rossman (WBA)	1997	Montell Griffin (WBC);
1905-12	Philadelphia Jack O'Brien*		Marvin Johnson (WBC)		Dariusz Michalczewski (WBA*);
1912-16	Jack Dillon	1979	Victor Galindez (WBA)		Roy Jones Jr. (WBC)
1916-20	Battling Levinsky	1979-81	Matthew Saad Muhammad	1997-98	Lou Del Valle (WBA)
1920-22	Georges Carpentier		(WBC)	1998-2003	Roy Jones Jr. (WBA*/WBC*)
1922-23	Battling Siki	1979-80	Marvin Johnson (WBA)	2003	Mehdi Sahnoune (WBA);
1923-25	Mike McTigue	1980-81	Eddie Mustafa Muhammad		Silvio Branco (WBA);
1925-26	Paul Berlenbach		(WBA)		Antonio Tarver (WBC)
1926-27	Jack Delaney*	1981-85	Michael Spinks (WBA)	2003-04	Roy Jones Jr. (WBA/WBC*)
1927-29	Tommy Loughran*	1981-83	Dwight Muhammad-Qawi	2004	Antonio Tarver (WBA/WBC*)
1930-34	Maxie Rosenbloom		Braxton (WBC*)	2004-06	Fabrice Tiozzo (WBA)
1934-35	Bob Olin	1983-85	Michael Spinks (WBC*)	2005-07	Tomasz Adamek (WBC)
1935-39	John Henry Lewis*	1985-86	J. B. Williamson (WBC)	2006-07	Silvio Branco (WBA)
1939	Melio Bettina	1986-87	Marvin Johnson (WBA);	2007-08	Chad Dawson (WBC*)
1939-41	Billy Conn*		Dennis Andries (WBC)	2007	Stipe Drews (WBA);
1941	Anton Christoforidis	1987	Thomas Hearns (WBC*)		Danny Green (WBA);
	(NBA)	1987	Leslie Stewart (WBA)	2008-09	Hugo Hernan Garay (WBA);
1941-48	Gus Lesnevich	1987-91	Virgil Hill (WBA)		Adrian Diaconu (WBC)
1948-50	Freddie Mills	1987-88	Don Lalonde (WBC)	2009-11	Jean Pascal (WBC)
1950-52	Joey Maxim	1988	Sugar Ray Leonard (WBC*)	2009-10	Gabriel Campillo (WBA)
1952-62	Archie Moore	1989	Dennis Andries (WBC)	2010-14	Beibut Shumenov (WBA)
1962-63	Harold Johnson	1989-90	Jeff Harding (WBC)	2011-12	Bernard Hopkins (WBC)
1963-65	Willie Pastrano	1990-91	Dennis Andries (WBC)	2012-13	Chad Dawson (WBC)
1965-66	José Torres	1991-92	Thomas Hearns (WBA*)	2013-18	Adonis Stevenson (WBC)
1966-68	Dick Tiger	1991-94	Jeff Harding (WBC)	2014	Bernard Hopkins (WBA)
1968-74	Bob Foster*	1992	Iran Barkley (WBA*)	2014-16	Sergey Kovalev (WBA)
1974-77	John Conteh (WBC*)	1992-97	Virgil Hill (WBA)	2016-17	Andre Ward (WBC)
1974-78	Victor Galindez (WBA)	1994-95	Mike McCallum (WBC)	2017-	Dmitry Bivol (WBA)
1977-78	Miguel Cuello (WBC)	1995-96	Fabrice Tiozzo (WBC*)	2018-19	Oleksandr Gvozdyk (WBC)
1978	Mate Parlov (WBC)	1996-97	Roy Jones Jr. (WBC)	2019-	Artur Beterbiev (WBC)

Middleweights

1884-91	Jack "Nonpareil" Dempsey	1960	Gene Fullmer (NBA);	1995-96	Quincy Taylor (WBC);
1891-97	Bob Fitzsimmons*		Paul Pender (NY/MA)		Shinji Takehara (WBA)
1897-1907	Tommy Ryan*	1961	Gene Fullmer (NBA);	1996-98	Keith Holmes (WBC)
1907-08	Stanley Ketchel; Billy Papke		Terry Downes (NY/MA/Europe)	1996-97	William Joppy (WBA)
1908-10	Stanley Ketchel	1962	Gene Fullmer;	1997	Julio Cesar Green (WBC)
1911-13	Vacant		Paul Pender (NY/MA*);	1998-2001	William Joppy (WBA)
1913	Frank Klaus; George Chip		Dick Tiger (NBA)	1998-99	Hacine Cherifi (WBC)
1914-17	Al McCoy	1963	Dick Tiger (universal)	1999-2001	Keith Holmes (WBC)
1917-20	Mike O'Dowd	1963-65	Joey Giardello	2001	Felix Trinidad (WBA)
1920-23	Johnny Wilson	1965-66	Dick Tiger	2001-05	Bernard Hopkins (WBC/WBA)
1923-26	Harry Greb	1966-67	Emile Griffith	2005-06	Jermain Taylor (WBA)
1926	Theodore "Tiger" Flowers	1967	Nino Benvenuti	2005-07	Jermain Taylor (WBC)
1926-31	Mickey Walker*	1967-68	Emile Griffith	2006-07	Javier Castillejo (WBA)[1]
1931-32	William "Gorilla" Jones (NBA)	1968-70	Nino Benvenuti	2007-12	Felix Sturm (WBA)
1932-37	Marcel Thil	1970-77	Carlos Monzon*	2007-10	Kelly Pavlik (WBC)
1938	Al Hostak (NBA);	1977-78	Rodrigo Valdez	2009-11	Sebastian Zbik (WBC)
	Solly Krieger (NBA)	1978-79	Hugo Corro	2010	Sergio Martinez (WBC)
1939-40	Al Hostak (NBA)	1979-80	Vito Antuofermo	2011-12	Julio Cesar Chavez Jr. (WBC)
1940-47	Tony Zale	1980	Alan Minter	2012	Daniel Geale (WBA*)
1947-48	Rocky Graziano	1980-87	"Marvelous" Marvin Hagler	2012-14	Sergio Martinez (WBC)
1948	Tony Zale; Marcel Cerdan	1987	Sugar Ray Leonard (WBC*)	2012-18	Gennady Golovkin (WBA)
1949-51	Jake LaMotta	1987-89	Sumbu Kalambay (WBA)	2014-15	Miguel Cotto (WBC)
1951	"Sugar" Ray Robinson;	1987-88	Thomas Hearns (WBC)	2015-16	Canelo Álvarez (WBC*)
	Randy Turpin	1988-89	Iran Barkley (WBC)	2016-18	Gennady Golovkin (WBC)
1951-52	"Sugar" Ray Robinson*	1989-90	Roberto Duran (WBC*)	2018-19	Canelo Álvarez (WBA/WBC2)[2]
1953-55	Carl "Bobo" Olson	1989-91	Mike McCallum (WBA*)	2019-21	Canelo Álvarez (WBA/WBC2)
1955-57	"Sugar" Ray Robinson	1990-93	Julian Jackson (WBC)	2019-	Jermall Charlo (WBC)
1957	Gene Fullmer;	1992-93	Reggie Johnson (WBA)	2021-22	Ryōta Murata (WBA)
	"Sugar" Ray Robinson	1993-95	Gerald McClellan (WBC*)	2022-23	Gennady Golovkin (WBA)
1957-58	Carmen Basilio	1993-94	John David Jackson (WBA*)	2023-	Erislandy Lara (WBA)
1958	"Sugar" Ray Robinson	1994-95	Jorge Castro (WBA)		
1959	Gene Fullmer (NBA);	1995	Julian Jackson (WBC)		
	"Sugar" Ray Robinson (NY)				

(1) Castillejo lost title to Mariano Carrera Dec. 2, 2006, but regained it Feb. 23, 2007, after Carrera tested positive for steroids. (2) Canelo Álvarez was reclassified in 2019 as WBC Franchise Champion.

Welterweights

1892-94	"Mysterious" Billy Smith	1932	Jackie Fields	1963	Luis Rodriguez
1894-96	Tommy Ryan	1933	Young Corbett III;	1963-66	Emile Griffith*
1896	Kid McCoy*		Jimmy McLarnin	1966-69	Curtis Cokes
1900	Rube Ferns;	1934	Barney Ross;	1969-70	José Nápoles
	Matty Matthews		Jimmy McLarnin	1970-71	Billy Backus
1901	Rube Ferns	1935-38	Barney Ross	1971-75	José Nápoles
1901-04	Joe Walcott	1938-40	Henry Armstrong	1975-76	Angel Espada (WBA);
1904-06	Dixie Kid; Joe Walcott	1940-41	Fritzie Zivic		John Stracey (WBC)
1906	William "Honey" Mellody	1941-46	Fred Cochrane	1976-79	Carlos Palomino (WBC)
1907-11	Mike Sullivan	1946	Marty Servo*	1976-80	José "Pipino" Cuevas (WBA)
1911-15	Vacant	1946-51	"Sugar" Ray Robinson*[1]	1979	Wilfred Benitez (WBC)
1915-16	Ted Lewis	1951	Johnny Bratton (NBA)	1979-80	Sugar Ray Leonard (WBC)
1916-17	Jack Britton	1951-54	Kid Gavilan	1980	Roberto Duran (WBC)
1917-19	Ted Lewis	1954-55	Johnny Saxton	1980-81	Thomas Hearns (WBA)
1919-22	Jack Britton	1955	Tony DeMarco	1980-82	Sugar Ray Leonard (WBC*/
1922-26	Mickey Walker	1955-56	Carmen Basilio		WBA*)
1926-27	Pete Latzo	1956	Johnny Saxton	1983-85	Donald Curry (WBA);
1927-29	Joe Dundee	1956-57	Carmen Basilio*		Milton McCrory (WBC)
1929-30	Jackie Fields	1958	Virgil Akins	1985-86	Donald Curry (WBC)
1930	Jack Thompson;	1958-60	Don Jordan	1986-87	Lloyd Honeyghan (WBC)
	Tommy Freeman	1960-61	Benny Paret	1987	Mark Breland (WBA)
1931	Tommy Freeman;	1961	Emile Griffith	1987-88	Marlon Starling (WBA);
	Jack Thompson;	1961-62	Benny Paret		Jorge Vaca (WBC)
	Lou Brouillard	1962-63	Emile Griffith		

Year	Name	Year	Name	Year	Name
1988-89	Tomas Molinares (WBA*);	2000-02	Shane Mosley (WBC)	2011	Victor Ortiz (WBC)
	Lloyd Honeyghan (WBC)	2001-02	Andrew Lewis (WBA)	2011-15	Floyd Mayweather Jr. (WBC*)
1989-90	Marlon Starling (WBC);	2002-03	Vernon Forrest (WBC)	2012-13	Paulie Malignaggi (WBA)
	Mark Breland (WBA)	2002	Ricardo Mayorga (WBA)	2013	Adrien Broner (WBA);
1990-91	Maurice Blocker (WBC);	2003	Ricardo Mayorga (WBA/WBC)		Marcos Maidana (WBA)
	Aaron Davis (WBA)	2003-05	Cory Spinks (WBA/WBC)	2014-15	Floyd Mayweather Jr. (WBC*)
1991-92	Meldrick Taylor (WBA)	2005-06	Zab Judah (WBA/WBC)	2016-17	Danny Garcia (WBC)
1991	Simon Brown (WBC)	2006	Carlos Baldomir (WBC);	2016-19	Keith Thurman (WBA)
1991-93	Buddy McGirt (WBC)		Ricky Hatton (WBA*)	2017-18	Keith Thurman (WBC*)
1992-94	Crisanto España (WBA)	2006-08	Floyd Mayweather Jr. (WBC*)	2018-19	Shawn Porter (WBC)
1993-97	Pernell Whitaker (WBC)		Miguel Cotto (WBA)	2019-21	Manny Pacquiao (WBA)
1994-98	Ike Quartey (WBA*)	2008	Antonio Margarito (WBA)	2019-22	Errol Spence Jr. (WBC)
1997-99	Oscar De La Hoya (WBC*)	2008-11	Andre Berto (WBC)	2021-22	Yordenis Ugás (WBA)
1998-2000	James Page (WBA)	2009	Shane Mosley (WBA)	2022	Errol Spence Jr. (WBA)
1999-2000	Felix Trinidad (WBC*)	2009-12	Vyacheslav Senchenko (WBA)	2023-	Terence Crawford (WBA/WBC)
2000	Oscar De La Hoya (WBC*)				

(1) Robinson gained the title by defeating Tommy Bell in an elimination agreed to by the New York Commission and the National Boxing Association. Both claimed Robinson waived his title when he won the middleweight crown from Jake LaMotta in 1951.

Lightweights

Year	Name	Year	Name	Year	Name
1899-1902	Frank Erne	1972	Mando Ramos (WBC)	1999-2000	Steve Johnston (WBC)
1902-08	Joe Gans	1972-79	Roberto Duran (WBA*)	1999	Julien Lorcy (WBA);
1908-10	Oscar "Battling" Nelson	1972	Chango Carmona (WBC)		Stefano Zoff (WBC)
1910-12	Ad Wolgast	1972-74	Rodolfo Gonzalez (WBC)	1999-2000	Gilberto Serrano (WBA)
1912-14	Willie Ritchie	1974-76	Ishimatsu Suzuki (WBC)	2000-01	Takanori Hatakeyama (WBA)
1914-17	Freddie Welsh	1976-78	Esteban De Jesus (WBC)	2000-02	José Luis Castillo (WBC)
1917-25	Benny Leonard*	1978	Roberto Duran (WBC*)	2001	Julien Lorcy (WBA)
1925	Jimmy Goodrich;	1979-81	Jim Watt (WBC)	2001-02	Raul Balbi (WBA)
	Rocky Kansas	1979-80	Ernesto España (WBA)	2002-03	Leonard Dorin (WBA*)
1926-30	Sammy Mandell	1980-81	Hilmer Kenty (WBA)	2002-04	Floyd Mayweather Jr. (WBC*)
1930	Al Singer; Tony Canzoneri	1981	Sean O'Grady (WBA*);	2004	Lakva Sim (WBA)
1930-33	Tony Canzoneri		Claude Noel (WBA)	2004-05	José Luis Castillo (WBC)
1933-35	Barney Ross*	1981-83	Alexis Arguello (WBC*)	2004-08	Juan Diaz (WBA)
1935-36	Tony Canzoneri	1981-82	Arturo Frias (WBA)	2005-06	Diego Corrales (WBC)
1936-38	Lou Ambers	1982-84	Ray Mancini (WBA)	2006	Joel Casamayor (WBC*)
1938	Henry Armstrong	1983-84	Edwin Rosario (WBC)	2006-08	David Diaz (WBC)
1939	Lou Ambers	1984-86	Livingstone Bramble (WBA)	2008-09	Nate Campbell (WBA*);
1940	Lew Jenkins	1984-85	José Luis Ramírez (WBA)		Manny Pacquiao (WBC*)
1941-43	Sammy Angott	1985-86	Hector "Macho" Camacho	2009-12	Juan Manuel Marquez (WBA*)
1944	Sammy Angott (NBA);		(WBC*)	2009-10	Edwin Valero (WBA)
	Juan Zurita (NBA)	1986-87	Edwin Rosario (WBA)	2010-11	Humberto Soto (WBC*)
1945-51	Ike Williams (NBA; later universal)	1987-88	Julio Cesar Chavez (WBA);	2011-12	Antonio DeMarco (WBC)
			José Luis Ramírez (WBC)	2012-14	Adrien Broner (WBC*)
1951-52	James Carter	1988-89	Julio Cesar Chavez	2013-15	Richard Abril (WBA*)
1952	Lauro Salas; James Carter		(WBA*/WBC*)	2014	Omar Figueroa (WBC)
1953-54	James Carter	1989-90	Edwin Rosario (WBA);	2014-15	Jorge Linares (WBC)
1954	Paddy De Marco; James Carter		Pernell Whitaker (WBC)	2015	Darleys Perez (WBA)
1955	James Carter; Bud Smith	1990	Juan Nazario (WBA)	2015-16	Anthony Crolla (WBA)
1956	Bud Smith; Joe Brown	1990-92	Pernell Whitaker (WBC*/WBA*)	2016-17	Dejan Zlaticanin (WBC)
1956-62	Joe Brown	1992	Joey Gamache (WBA)	2016-18	Jorge Linares (WBA)
1962-65	Carlos Ortiz	1992-96	Miguel Angel Gonzalez (WBC*)	2017-19	Mikey Garcia (WBC)
1965	Ismael Laguna	1992-93	Tony Lopez (WBA)	2018-20	Vasiliy Lomachenko (WBA)
1965-68	Carlos Ortiz	1993	Dingaan Thobela (WBA)	2019-20	Vasiliy Lomachenko (WBC)
1968-69	Carlos Teo Cruz	1993-98	Orzubek Nazarov (WBA)	2019-23	Devin Haney (WBA)
1969-70	Mando Ramos	1996-97	Jean-Baptiste Mendy (WBC)	2020-21	Teófimo López (WBA)
1970	Ismael Laguna	1997-98	Steve Johnston (WBC)	2021-22	George Kambosos Jr. (WBA)
1970-72	Ken Buchanan (WBA)	1998-99	Jean-Baptiste Mendy (WBA);	2022-	Devin Haney (WBA)
1971-72	Pedro Carrasco (WBC)		Cesar Bazan (WBC)		

Featherweights

Year	Name	Year	Name	Year	Name
1901-12	Abe Attell	1972-74	Ernesto Marcel (WBA*)	1998-99	Antonio Cermeno (WBA)
1912-23	Johnny Kilbane	1972-73	José Legrá (WBC)	1999	César Soto (WBC)
1923	Eugene Criqui	1973-74	Eder Jofre (WBC*)	1999-2000	Freddie Norwood (WBA)
1923-25	Johnny Dundee*	1974	Ruben Olivares (WBA)	1999	Naseem Hamed (WBC*)
1925-27	Louis "Kid" Kaplan*	1974-75	Bobby Chacon (WBC)	2000-01	Guty Espadas Jr. (WBC)
1927-28	Benny Bass; Tony Canzoneri	1974-76	Alexis Arguello (WBA*)	2000-03	Derrick Gainer (WBA)
1928-29	Andre Routis	1975	Ruben Olivares (WBC)	2001-04	Erik Morales (WBC)[1]
1929-32	Battling Battalino*	1975-76	David Kotey (WBC)	2003-05	Juan Manuel Marquez (WBA*)
1932-34	Tommy Paul (NBA)	1976-80	Danny "Little Red"	2004-06	In-Jin Chi (WBC)
1933-36	Freddie Miller		Lopez (WBC)	2005-13	Chris John (WBA)
1936-37	Petey Sarron	1977	Rafael Ortega (WBA)	2006	Takashi Koshimoto (WBC);
1937-38	Henry Armstrong*	1977-78	Cecilio Lastra (WBA)		Rodolfo Lopez (WBC)
1938-40	Joey Archibald	1978-85	Eusebio Pedroza (WBA)	2006-07	In-Jin Chi (WBC)
1940-41	Harry Jeffra	1980-82	Salvador Sanchez (WBC)	2007-08	Jorge Linares (WBC*)
1941	Joey Archibald	1982-84	Juan LaPorte (WBC)	2008	Oscar Larios (WBC)
1941-42	Chalky Wright	1984	Wilfredo Gomez (WBC)	2009	Takahiro Ao (WBC)
1942-48	Willie Pep	1984-88	Azumah Nelson (WBC*)	2009-10	Elio Rojas (WBC)
1948-49	Sandy Saddler	1985-86	Barry McGuigan (WBA)	2010-11	Hozumi Hasegawa (WBC)
1949-50	Willie Pep	1986-87	Steve Cruz (WBA)	2011-12	Jhonny Gonzalez (WBC)
1950-57	Sandy Saddler*	1987-91	Antonio Esparragoza (WBA)	2012-13	Daniel Ponce de León (WBC)
1957-59	Hogan "Kid" Bassey	1988-90	Jeff Fenech (WBC)	2013	Abner Mares (WBC)
1959-63	Davey Moore	1990-91	Marcos Villasana (WBC)	2013-15	Jhonny Gonzalez (WBC)
1963-64	Ultiminio "Sugar" Ramos	1991-93	Park Yung Kyun (WBA);	2013-14	Simpiwe Vetyeka (WBA)
1964-67	Vicente Saldivar*		Paul Hodkinson (WBC)	2014	Nonito Donaire (WBA)
1968	Raul Rojas (WBA)	1993	Goyo Vargas (WBC)	2014-15	Nicholas Walters (WBA*)
1968-69	José Legrá (WBC)	1993-95	Kevin Kelley (WBC)	2015-22	Gary Russell Jr. (WBC)
1968-71	Shozo Saijyo (WBA)	1993-96	Eloy Rojas (WBA)	2015-16	Léo Santa Cruz (WBA)
1969-70	Johnny Famechon (WBC)	1995	Alejandro Gonzalez (WBC);	2016-17	Carl Frampton (WBA)
1970	Vicente Saldivar (WBC)		Manuel Medina (WBC)	2017-22	Léo Santa Cruz (WBA)
1970-72	Kuniaki Shibata (WBC)	1995-99	Luisito Espinosa (WBC)	2022	Mark Magsayo (WBC)
1971-72	Antonio Gomez (WBA)	1996-98	Wilfredo Vasquez (WBA*)	2022-	Rey Vargas (WBC)
1972	Clemente Sanchez (WBC*)	1998	Freddie Norwood (WBA)	2023	Leigh Wood (WBA)

(1) Marco Antonio Barrera won unanimous decision over Morales, June 22, 2002, but refused WBC title. Morales regained WBC title with unanimous decision over Paulie Ayala, Nov. 16, 2002. Morales moved to Jr. Lightweight div. in 2004.

International Boxing Hall of Fame Inductees, 2023

Source: International Boxing Hall of Fame, 1 Hall of Fame Dr., Canastota, NY 13032. www.ibhof.com

Men's Modern: Timothy Bradley Jr. (33-2-1, 13 KO); Carl Froch (33-2, 24 KO); Rafael Márquez (41-9, 37 KO). **Women's Modern:** Alicia Ashley (24-12-1, 4 KO); Laura Serrano (17-5-3, 6 KO). **Old-Timer:** Tiger Jack Fox (138-24-12, 91 KO); Pone Kingpetch (28-7, 9 KO). **Women's Trailblazer:** JoAnn Hagen. **Non-Participant:** Brad Goodman, matchmaker; Joe Goossen, trainer; Brad Jacobs, promotional executive. **Observer:** Seth Abraham, TV executive; Tim Ryan, broadcaster.

Title-Changing Heavyweight Championship Bouts, 1889-2023

1889: July 8, John L. Sullivan def. Jake Kilrain, 75, Richburg, MS.

1892: Sept. 7, James J. Corbett def. John L. Sullivan, 21, New Orleans.

1897: Mar. 17, Bob Fitzsimmons def. James J. Corbett, 14, Carson City, NV.

1899: June 9, James J. Jeffries def. Bob Fitzsimmons, 11, Coney Island, NY. (Jeffries retired as champion in 1905.)

1905: July 3, Marvin Hart KOd Jack Root, 12, Reno, NV. (James J. Jeffries refereed, gave title to Hart. Jack O'Brien also claimed the title.)

1906: Feb. 23, Tommy Burns def. Marvin Hart, 20, Los Angeles.

1908: Dec. 26, Jack Johnson def. Tommy Burns, 14, Sydney, Australia. (Police halted contest.)

1915: Apr. 5, Jess Willard KOd Jack Johnson, 26, Havana, Cuba.

1919: July 4, Jack Dempsey KOd Jess Willard, Toledo, OH. (Willard failed to answer bell for 4th round.)

1926: Sept. 23, Gene Tunney def. Jack Dempsey, 10, Philadelphia. (Tunney retired as champion in 1928.)

1930: June 12, Max Schmeling def. Jack Sharkey on a foul, 4, New York City. (Resulted in the election of a successor to Gene Tunney.)

1932: June 21, Jack Sharkey def. Max Schmeling, 15, NYC.

1933: June 29, Primo Carnera KOd Jack Sharkey, 6, NYC.

1934: June 14, Max Baer KOd Primo Carnera, 11, NYC.

1935: June 13, James J. Braddock def. Max Baer, 15, NYC.

1937: June 22, Joe Louis KOd James J. Braddock, 8, Chicago. (Louis retired as champion in 1949.)

1949: June 22, Ezzard Charles def. Joe Walcott, 15, Chicago; NBA recognition only.

1951: July 18, Joe Walcott KOd Ezzard Charles, 7, Pittsburgh.

1952: Sept. 23, Rocky Marciano KOd Joe Walcott, 13, Philadelphia. (Marciano retired as champion in 1956.)

1956: Nov. 30, Floyd Patterson def. Archie Moore, 5, Chicago.

1959: June 26, Ingemar Johansson KOd Floyd Patterson, 3, NYC.

1960: June 20, Floyd Patterson KOd Ingemar Johansson, 5, NYC.

1962: Sept. 25, Sonny Liston KOd Floyd Patterson, 1, Chicago.

1964: Feb. 25, Cassius Clay (Muhammad Ali) KOd Sonny Liston, 7, Miami Beach, FL. (Liston failed to answer bell for 7th round. In 1967, Ali was stripped of title for refusing military service.)

1970: Feb. 16, Joe Frazier KOd Jimmy Ellis, 5, NYC. (Frazier def. Ali, 15, NYC, on Mar. 8, 1971, in "Fight of the Century.")

1973: Jan. 22, George Foreman KOd Joe Frazier, 2, Kingston, Jamaica.

1974: Oct. 30, Muhammad Ali KOd George Foreman, 8, Kinshasa, Zaire (billed as the "Rumble in the Jungle").

1978: Feb. 15, Leon Spinks def. Muhammad Ali, 15, Las Vegas (WBC recognized Ken Norton as champion after Spinks refused to fight him before his rematch with Ali); June 9, (WBC) Larry Holmes def. Ken Norton, 15, Las Vegas; Sept. 15, (WBA) Muhammad Ali def. Leon Spinks, 15, New Orleans. (Ali retired as champion in 1979.)

1979: Oct. 20, (WBA) John Tate def. Gerrie Coetzee, 15, Pretoria, South Africa.

1980: Mar. 31, (WBA) Mike Weaver KOd John Tate, 15, Knoxville, TN.

1982: Dec. 10, (WBA) Michael Dokes KOd Mike Weaver, 1, Las Vegas.

1983: Sept. 23, (WBA) Gerrie Coetzee KOd Michael Dokes, 10, Richfield, OH; in Dec., Larry Holmes relinquished the WBC title and was named champion of the newly formed IBF.

1984: Mar. 9, (WBC) Tim Witherspoon def. Greg Page, 12, Las Vegas; Aug. 31, (WBC) Pinklon Thomas def. Tim Witherspoon, 12, Las Vegas; Dec. 1, (WBA) Greg Page KOd Gerrie Coetzee, 8, Sun City, Bophuthatswana, South Africa.

1985: Apr. 29, (WBA) Tony Tubbs def. Greg Page, 15, Buffalo, NY; Sept. 21, (IBF) Michael Spinks def. Larry Holmes, 15, Las Vegas. (Spinks relinquished title in Feb. 1987.)

1986: Jan. 17, (WBA) Tim Witherspoon def. Tony Tubbs, 15, Atlanta; Mar. 22, (WBC) Trevor Berbick def. Pinklon Thomas, 12, Las Vegas; Nov. 22, (WBC) Mike Tyson KOd Trevor Berbick, 2, Las Vegas; Dec. 12, (WBA) James "Bonecrusher" Smith KOd Tim Witherspoon, 1, NYC.

1987: Mar. 7, (WBA) Mike Tyson def. James "Bonecrusher" Smith, 12, Las Vegas; May 30, (IBF) Tony Tucker KOd James "Buster" Douglas, 10, Las Vegas; Aug. 1, (IBF) Mike Tyson def. Tony Tucker, 12, Las Vegas. (Tyson became undisputed champion.)

1990: Feb. 11, (WBA/WBC/IBF) James "Buster" Douglas KOd Mike Tyson, 10, Tokyo, Japan; Oct. 25, (WBA/WBC/IBF) Evander Holyfield KOd James "Buster" Douglas, 3, Las Vegas.

1992: Nov. 13, (WBA/WBC/IBF) Riddick Bowe def. Evander Holyfield, 12, Las Vegas; in Dec., Lennox Lewis was named WBC champion after Bowe relinquished the WBC title rather than fight Lewis.

1993: Nov. 6, (WBA/IBF) Evander Holyfield def. Riddick Bowe, 12, Las Vegas.

1994: Apr. 22, (WBA/IBF) Michael Moorer def. Evander Holyfield, 12, Las Vegas; Sept. 24, (WBC) Oliver McCall KOd Lennox Lewis, 2, London, Eng.; Nov. 5, (WBA/IBF) George Foreman KOd Michael Moorer, 10, Las Vegas.

1995: In Mar., George Foreman was stripped of his WBA title for refusing to fight challenger Tony Tucker; in June, Foreman relinquished his IBF title rather than submit to a rematch with Axel Schulz; Apr. 8, (WBA) Bruce Seldon TKOd Tony Tucker, 7, Las Vegas; Sept. 2, (WBC) Frank Bruno def. Oliver McCall, 12, London, Eng.; Dec. 9, (IBF) Frans Botha def. Axel Schulz, 12, Stuttgart, Germany (Botha was subsequently stripped of title after testing positive for a steroid).

1996: Mar. 16, (WBC) Mike Tyson KOd Frank Bruno, 3, Las Vegas; June 22, (IBF) Michael Moorer def. Axel Schulz, 12, Dortmund, Germany; Sept. 7, (WBA) Mike Tyson KOd Bruce Seldon, 1, Las Vegas (Tyson was subsequently stripped of WBC title after refusing to fight Lennox Lewis); Nov. 9, (WBA) Evander Holyfield KOd Mike Tyson, 11, Las Vegas.

1997: Feb. 7, (WBC) Lennox Lewis TKOd Oliver McCall, 5, Las Vegas; Nov. 8, (IBF) Evander Holyfield def. Michael Moorer, 8, Las Vegas.

1999: Nov. 13, (IBF) Lennox Lewis def. Evander Holyfield, 12, Las Vegas. (Lewis became undisputed champion.)

2000: In Apr., Lennox Lewis was stripped of his WBA title after refusing to fight challenger John Ruiz; Aug. 12, (WBA) Evander Holyfield def. John Ruiz, 12, Las Vegas.

2001: Mar. 3, (WBA) John Ruiz def. Evander Holyfield, 12, Las Vegas; Apr. 22, (WBC/IBF) Hasim Rahman KOd Lennox Lewis, 5, Brakpan, South Africa; Nov. 17, (WBC/IBF) Lennox Lewis KOd Hasim Rahman, 4, Las Vegas.

2002: In Sept., Lennox Lewis relinquished his IBF title; Dec. 14, (IBF) Chris Byrd def. Evander Holyfield, 12, Atlantic City, NJ.

2003: Mar. 1, (WBA) Roy Jones Jr. def. John Ruiz, 12, Las Vegas.

2004: Feb. 20, (WBA) John Ruiz gained title when Roy Jones Jr. relinquished it; Apr. 24, (WBC) Vitali Klitschko TKOd Corrie Sanders, 8, Los Angeles, to win title vacated by retirement of Lennox Lewis in Feb.

2005: Apr. 30, (WBA) James Toney def. John Ruiz, 12, NYC (title was returned to Ruiz after Toney tested positive for steroids); Nov. 9, (WBC) Hasim Rahman gained title when Vitali Klitschko retired due to an injury; Dec. 17, (WBA) Nikolai Valuev def. John Ruiz, 12, Berlin, Germany.

2006: Apr. 22, (IBF) Wladimir Klitschko TKOd Chris Byrd, 7, Mannheim, Germany; Aug. 12, (WBC) Oleg Maskaev TKOd Hasim Rahman, 12, Las Vegas.

2007: Apr. 14, (WBA) Ruslan Chagaev def. Nikolai Valuev, 12, Stuttgart, Germany. (An injured Chagaev was named champion in recess, July 2008.)

2008: Mar. 8, (WBC) Samuel Peter TKOd Oleg Maskaev, 6, Cancún, Mexico; Aug. 30, (WBA) Nikolai Valuev def. John Ruiz, 12, Berlin, Germany; Oct. 11, (WBC) Vitali Klitschko TKOd Samuel Peter, 8, Berlin, Germany.

2009: Nov. 7, (WBA) David Haye def. Nikolai Valuev, 12, Nuremberg, Germany.

2011: July 2, (WBA) Wladimir Klitschko def. David Haye, 12, Hamburg, Germany.

2014: May 10, (WBC) Bermane Stiverne TKOd Chris Arreola, 6, Los Angeles, to win title vacated in Dec. 2013.

2015: Jan. 17, (WBC) Deontay Wilder def. Bermane Stiverne, 12, Las Vegas; Nov. 28 (WBA/IBF) Tyson Fury def. Wladimir Klitschko, 12, Dusseldorf, Germany; in Dec., Fury was stripped of IBF title for refusing to fight mandatory challenger Vyacheslav Glazkov. (Fury relinquished WBA title Oct. 2016.)

2016: Jan. 16, (IBF) Charles Martin TKOd Vyacheslav Glazkov, 3, Brooklyn, NY; Apr. 9, (IBF) Anthony Joshua KOd Charles Martin, 2, London, Eng., UK.

2017: Apr. 29, (IBF) Anthony Joshua TKOd Wladimir Klitschko, 11, London, Eng., UK.

2019: June 1, (WBA/IBF) Andy Ruiz Jr. TKOd Anthony Joshua, 7, NYC; Dec. 7, (WBA/IBF) Anthony Joshua def. Andy Ruiz Jr., 12, Diriyah, Saudi Arabia.

2020: Feb. 22, (WBC) Tyson Fury TKOd Deontay Wilder, 7, Las Vegas.

2021: Sept. 25, (WBA/WBO/IBF) Oleksandr Usyk def. Anthony Joshua, 12, London, Eng., UK.

THOROUGHBRED RACING
Triple Crown Winners

The Kentucky Derby, Preakness Stakes, and Belmont Stakes make up the Triple Crown. Since 1920, colts have carried 126 lbs in Triple Crown events; fillies, 121 lbs.

Year	Horse	Jockey	Trainer	Year	Horse	Jockey	Trainer
1919	Sir Barton	J. Loftus	H. G. Bedwell	1948	Citation	E. Arcaro	H. A. Jones
1930	Gallant Fox	E. Sande	J. Fitzsimmons	1973	Secretariat	R. Turcotte	L. Laurin
1935	Omaha	W. Sanders	J. Fitzsimmons	1977	Seattle Slew	J. Cruguet	W. H. Turner Jr.
1937	War Admiral	C. Kurtsinger	G. Conway	1978	Affirmed	S. Cauthen	L. S. Barrera
1941	Whirlaway	E. Arcaro	B. A. Jones	2015	American Pharoah	V. Espinoza	B. Baffert
1943	Count Fleet	J. Longden	G. D. Cameron	2018	Justify	M. Smith	B. Baffert
1946	Assault	W. Mehrtens	M. Hirsch				

Kentucky Derby Winners, 1875-2023

Churchill Downs, Louisville, KY. Distance: 1¼ mi; 1½ mi until 1896. 3-year-olds. Best time: 1:59-2/5, Secretariat (1973); 2023 time: 2:01.57. (Until 2001, times were measured in fifths of a second.)

Year	Horse	Jockey	Year	Horse	Jockey	Year	Horse	Jockey
1875	Aristides	O. Lewis	1925	Flying Ebony	E. Sande	1974	Cannonade	A. Cordero
1876	Vagrant	R. Swim	1926	Bubbling Over	A. Johnson	1975	Foolish Pleasure	J. Vasquez
1877	Baden Baden	W. Walker	1927	Whiskery	L. McAtee	1976	Bold Forbes	A. Cordero
1878	Day Star	J. Carter	1928	Reigh Count	C. Lang	1977	Seattle Slew	J. Cruguet
1879	Lord Murphy	C. Schauer	1929	Clyde Van Dusen	L. McAtee	1978	Affirmed	S. Cauthen
1880	Fonso	G. Lewis	1930	Gallant Fox	E. Sande	1979	Spectacular Bid	R. Franklin
1881	Hindoo	J. McLaughlin	1931	Twenty Grand	C. Kurtsinger	1980	Genuine Risk[1]	J. Vasquez
1882	Apollo	B. Hurd	1932	Burgoo King	E. James	1981	Pleasant Colony	J. Velasquez
1883	Leonatus	W. Donohue	1933	Brokers Tip	D. Meade	1982	Gato Del Sol	E. Delahoussaye
1884	Buchanan	I. Murphy	1934	Cavalcade	M. Garner	1983	Sunny's Halo	E. Delahoussaye
1885	Joe Cotton	E. Henderson	1935	Omaha	W. Saunders	1984	Swale	L. Pincay
1886	Ben Ali	P. Duffy	1936	Bold Venture	I. Hanford	1985	Spend a Buck	A. Cordero
1887	Montrose	I. Lewis	1937	War Admiral	C. Kurtsinger	1986	Ferdinand	W. Shoemaker
1888	Macbeth II	G. Covington	1938	Lawrin	E. Arcaro	1987	Alysheba	C. McCarron
1889	Spokane	T. Kiley	1939	Johnstown	J. Stout	1988	Winning Colors[1]	G. Stevens
1890	Riley	I. Murphy	1940	Gallahadion	C. Bierman	1989	Sunday Silence	P. Valenzuela
1891	Kingman	I. Murphy	1941	Whirlaway	E. Arcaro	1990	Unbridled	C. Perret
1892	Azra	A. Clayton	1942	Shut Out	W. Wright	1991	Strike the Gold	C. Antley
1893	Lookout	E. Kunze	1943	Count Fleet	J. Longden	1992	Lil E. Tee	P. Day
1894	Chant	F. Goodale	1944	Pensive	C. McCreary	1993	Sea Hero	J. Bailey
1895	Halma	J. Perkins	1945	Hoop Jr.	E. Arcaro	1994	Go for Gin	C. McCarron
1896	Ben Brush	W. Simms	1946	Assault	W. Mehrtens	1995	Thunder Gulch	G. Stevens
1897	Typhoon II	F. Garner	1947	Jet Pilot	E. Guerin	1996	Grindstone	J. Bailey
1898	Plaudit	W. Simms	1948	Citation	E. Arcaro	1997	Silver Charm	G. Stevens
1899	Manuel	F. Taral	1949	Ponder	S. Brooks	1998	Real Quiet	K. Desormeaux
1900	Lieut. Gibson	J. Boland	1950	Middleground	W. Boland	1999	Charismatic	C. Antley
1901	His Eminence	J. Winkfield	1951	Count Turf	C. McCreary	2000	Fusaichi Pegasus	K. Desormeaux
1902	Alan-a-Dale	J. Winkfield	1952	Hill Gail	E. Arcaro	2001	Monarchos	J. Chavez
1903	Judge Himes	H. Booker	1953	Dark Star	H. Moreno	2002	War Emblem	V. Espinoza
1904	Elwood	F. Prior	1954	Determine	R. York	2003	Funny Cide	J. Santos
1905	Agile	J. Martin	1955	Swaps	W. Shoemaker	2004	Smarty Jones	S. Elliot
1906	Sir Huon	R. Troxler	1956	Needles	D. Erb	2005	Giacomo	M. Smith
1907	Pink Star	A. Minder	1957	Iron Liege	W. Hartack	2006	Barbaro	E. Prado
1908	Stone Street	A. Pickens	1958	Tim Tam	I. Valenzuela	2007	Street Sense	C. Borel
1909	Wintergreen	V. Powers	1959	Tomy Lee	W. Shoemaker	2008	Big Brown	K. Desormeaux
1910	Donau	F. Herbert	1960	Venetian Way	W. Hartack	2009	Mine That Bird	C. Borel
1911	Meridian	G. Archibald	1961	Carry Back	J. Sellers	2010	Super Saver	C. Borel
1912	Worth	C. Shilling	1962	Decidedly	W. Hartack	2011	Animal Kingdom	J. Velazquez
1913	Donerail	R. Goose	1963	Chateaugay	B. Baeza	2012	I'll Have Another	M. Gutierrez
1914	Old Rosebud	J. McCabe	1964	Northern Dancer	W. Hartack	2013	Orb	J. Rosario
1915	Regret[1]	J. Notter	1965	Lucky Debonair	W. Shoemaker	2014	California Chrome	V. Espinoza
1916	George Smith	J. Loftus	1966	Kauai King	D. Brumfield	2015	American Pharoah	V. Espinoza
1917	Omar Khayyam	C. Borel	1967	Proud Clarion	R. Ussery	2016	Nyquist	M. Gutierrez
1918	Exterminator	W. Knapp	1968	Forward Pass[2]	I. Valenzuela	2017	Always Dreaming	J. Velazquez
1919	Sir Barton	J. Loftus	1969	Majestic Prince	W. Hartack	2018	Justify	M. Smith
1920	Paul Jones	T. Rice	1970	Dust Commander	M. Manganello	2019	Country House[3]	F. Prat
1921	Behave Yourself	C. Thompson	1971	Canonero II	G. Avila	2020	Authentic	J. Velazquez
1922	Morvich	A. Johnson	1972	Riva Ridge	R. Turcotte	2021	Mandaloun[4]	F. Geroux
1923	Zev	E. Sande	1973	Secretariat	R. Turcotte	2022	Rich Strike	S. Leon
1924	Black Gold	J. D. Mooney				2023	Mage	J. Castellano

Note: Two jockeys have won the Kentucky Derby five times: Eddie Arcaro and Bill Hartack. Willie Shoemaker won four times. (1) Regret, Genuine Risk, and Winning Colors are the only fillies to have won the Derby. (2) Dancer's Image came in first but was disqualified by a drug test. All wagers were paid on Dancer's Image, but Forward Pass was awarded the first-place money. (3) Maximum Security came in first but was disqualified for interference following the race. (4) Medina Spirit came in first but was disqualified due to a positive post-race test for a banned substance; wagers were paid on Medina Spirit, but Mandaloun was awarded the first-place money.

Fastest Winning Times for the Kentucky Derby

Until 2001, Kentucky Derby times were measured in fifths of a second.

Time	Horse	Jockey	Year	Time	Horse	Jockey	Year
1 min., 59-2/5 s.	Secretariat	Ron Turcotte	1973	2 min., 1.10 s.	Mandaloun	Florent Geroux	2021
1 min., 59.97 s.	Monarchos	Jorge Chavez	2001	2 min., 1.13 s.	War Emblem	Victor Espinoza	2002
2 min.	Northern Dancer	Bill Hartack	1964	2 min., 1.19 s.	Funny Cide	Jose Santos	2003
2 min., 1/5 s.	Spend a Buck	Angel Cordero Jr.	1985	2 min., 1-1/5 s.	Thunder Gulch	Gary Stevens	1995
2 min., 2/5 s.	Decidedly	Bill Hartack	1962		Affirmed	Steve Cauthen	1978
2 min., 3/5 s.	Proud Clarion	Robert Ussery	1967		Lucky Debonair	Bill Shoemaker	1965
2 min., 0.61 s.	Authentic	John Velazquez	2020	2 min., 1.31 s.	Nyquist	Mario Gutierrez	2016
2 min., 1 s.	Fusaichi Pegasus	Kent Desormeaux	2000	2 min., 1-2/5 s.	Barbaro	Edgar Prado	2006
	Grindstone	Jerry Bailey	1996		Whirlaway	Eddie Arcaro	1941

Preakness Stakes Winners, 1873-2023

Pimlico Race Course, Baltimore, MD. Distance: 1-3/16 mi. 3-year-olds. * = Horses ran in two divisions. Best time: 1:53, Secretariat (1973); 2023 time: 1:55.12.

Year	Horse	Jockey	Year	Horse	Jockey	Year	Horse	Jockey
1873	Survivor	G. Barbee	1925	Coventry	C. Kummer	1975	Master Derby	D. McHargue
1874	Culpepper	M. Donohue	1926	Display	J. Malben	1976	Elocutionist	J. Lively
1875	Tom Ochiltree	L. Hughes	1927	Bostonian	A. Abel	1977	Seattle Slew	J. Cruguet
1876	Shirley	G. Barbee	1928	Victorian	R. Workman	1978	Affirmed	S. Cauthen
1877	Cloverbrook	C. Holloway	1929	Dr. Freeland	L. Schaefer	1979	Spectacular Bid	R. Franklin
1878	Duke of Magenta	C. Holloway	1930	Gallant Fox	E. Sande	1980	Codex	A. Cordero
1879	Harold	L. Hughes	1931	Mate	G. Ellis	1981	Pleasant Colony	J. Velasquez
1880	Grenada	L. Hughes	1932	Burgoo King	E. James	1982	Aloma's Ruler	J. Kaenel
1881	Saunterer	W. Costello	1933	Head Play	C. Kurtsinger	1983	Deputed	
1882	Vanguard	W. Costello	1934	High Quest	R. Jones		Testamony	D. Miller
1883	Jacobus	G. Barbee	1935	Omaha	W. Saunders	1984	Gate Dancer	A. Cordero
1884	Knight of Ellerslie	S. Fisher	1936	Bold Venture	G. Woolf	1985	Tank's Prospect	P. Day
1885	Tecumseh	J. McLaughlin	1937	War Admiral	C. Kurtsinger	1986	Snow Chief	A. Solis
1886	The Bard	S. Fisher	1938	Dauber	M. Peters	1987	Alysheba	C. McCarron
1887	Dunboyne	W. Donohue	1939	Challedon	G. Seabo	1988	Risen Star	E. Delahoussaye
1888	Refund	F. Littlefield	1940	Bimelech	F. A. Smith	1989	Sunday Silence	P. Valenzuela
1889	Buddhist	G. Anderson	1941	Whirlaway	E. Arcaro	1990	Summer Squall	P. Day
1890	Montague	W. Martin	1942	Alsab	B. James	1991	Hansel	J. Bailey
1894	Assignee	F. Taral	1943	Count Fleet	J. Longden	1992	Pine Bluff	C. McCarron
1895	Belmar	F. Taral	1944	Pensive	C. McCreary	1993	Prairie Bayou	M. Smith
1896	Margrave	H. Griffin	1945	Polynesian	W. D. Wright	1994	Tabasco Cat	P. Day
1897	Paul Kauvar	C. Thorpe	1946	Assault	W. Mehrtens	1995	Timber Country	P. Day
1898	Sly Fox	W. Simms	1947	Faultless	D. Dodson	1996	Louis Quatorze	P. Day
1899	Half Time	R. Clawson	1948	Citation	E. Arcaro	1997	Silver Charm	G. Stevens
1900	Hindus	H. Spencer	1949	Capot	T. Atkinson	1998	Real Quiet	K. Desormeaux
1901	The Parader	F. Landry	1950	Hill Prince	E. Arcaro	1999	Charismatic	C. Antley
1902	Old England	L. Jackson	1951	Bold	E. Arcaro	2000	Red Bullet	J. Bailey
1903	Flocarline	W. Gannon	1952	Blue Man	C. McCreary	2001	Point Given	G. Stevens
1904	Bryn Mawr	E. Hildebrand	1953	Native Dancer	E. Guerin	2002	War Emblem	V. Espinoza
1905	Cairngorm	W. Davis	1954	Hasty Road	J. Adams	2003	Funny Cide	J. Santos
1906	Whimsical	W. Miller	1955	Nashua	E. Arcaro	2004	Smarty Jones	S. Elliot
1907	Don Enrique	G. Mountain	1956	Fabius	W. Hartack	2005	Afleet Alex	J. Rose
1908	Royal Tourist	E. Dugan	1957	Bold Ruler	E. Arcaro	2006	Bernardini	J. Castellano
1909	Effendi	W. Doyle	1958	Tim Tam	I. Valenzuela	2007	Curlin	R. Albarado
1910	Layminster	R. Estep	1959	Royal Orbit	W. Harmatz	2008	Big Brown	K. Desormeaux
1911	Watervale	E. Dugan	1960	Bally Ache	R. Ussery	2009	Rachel Alexandra	C. Borel
1912	Colonel Holloway	C. Turner	1961	Carry Back	J. Sellers	2010	Lookin At Lucky	M. Garcia
1913	Buskin	J. Butwell	1962	Greek Money	J. L. Rotz	2011	Shackleford	J. Castanon
1914	Holiday	A. Schuttinger	1963	Candy Spots	W. Shoemaker	2012	I'll Have Another	M. Gutierrez
1915	Rhine Maiden	D. Hoffman	1964	Northern Dancer	W. Hartack	2013	Oxbow	G. Stevens
1916	Damrosch	L. McAtee	1965	Tom Rolfe	R. Turcotte	2014	California Chrome	V. Espinoza
1917	Kalitan	E. Haynes	1966	Kauai King	D. Brumfield	2015	American Pharoah	V. Espinoza
1918*	War Cloud	J. Loftus	1967	Damascus	W. Shoemaker	2016	Exaggerator	K. Desormeaux
	Jack Hare Jr.	C. Peak	1968	Forward Pass	I. Valenzuela	2017	Cloud Computing	J. Castellano
1919	Sir Barton	J. Loftus	1969	Majestic Prince	W. Hartack	2018	Justify	M. Smith
1920	Man o' War	C. Kummer	1970	Personality	E. Belmonte	2019	War of Will	T. Gaffalone
1921	Broomspun	F. Coltiletti	1971	Canonero II	G. Avila	2020	Swiss Skydiver	R. Albarado
1922	Pillory	L. Morris	1972	Bee Bee Bee	E. Nelson	2021	Rombauer	F. Prat
1923	Vigil	B. Marinelli	1973	Secretariat	R. Turcotte	2022	Early Voting	J. Ortiz
1924	Nellie Morse	J. Merimee	1974	Little Current	M. Rivera	2023	National Treasure	J. Velazquez

Belmont Stakes Winners, 1867-2023

Belmont Park, Elmont, NY. Distance: 1½ mi (2020, 1-1/8 mi). 3-year-olds. Best time: 2:24, Secretariat (1973); 2023 time: 2:29.23.

Year	Horse	Jockey	Year	Horse	Jockey	Year	Horse	Jockey
1867	Ruthless	J. Gilpatrick	1899	Jean Bereaud	R. R. Clawson	1933	Hurryoff	M. Garner
1868	General Duke	R. Swim	1900	Ildrim	N. Turner	1934	Peace Chance	W. D. Wright
1869	Fenian	C. Miller	1901	Commando	H. Spencer	1935	Omaha	W. Saunders
1870	Kingfisher	W. Dick	1902	Masterman	J. Bullman	1936	Granville	J. Stout
1871	Harry Bassett	W. Miller	1903	Africander	J. Bullman	1937	War Admiral	C. Kurtsinger
1872	Joe Daniels	J. Rowe	1904	Delhi	G. Odom	1938	Pasteurized	J. Stout
1873	Springbok	J. Rowe	1905	Tanya	E. Hildebrand	1939	Johnstown	J. Stout
1874	Saxon	G. Barbee	1906	Burgomaster	L. Lyne	1940	Bimelech	F. A. Smith
1875	Calvin	R. Swim	1907	Peter Pan	G. Mountain	1941	Whirlaway	E. Arcaro
1876	Algerine	W. Donohue	1908	Colin	J. Notter	1942	Shut Out	E. Arcaro
1877	Cloverbrook	C. Holloway	1909	Joe Madden	E. Dugan	1943	Count Fleet	J. Longden
1878	Duke of Magenta	L. Hughes	1910	Sweep	J. Butwell	1944	Bounding Home	G. L. Smith
1879	Spendthrift	S. Evans	1913	Prince Eugene	R. Troxler	1945	Pavot	E. Arcaro
1880	Grenada	L. Hughes	1914	Luke McLuke	M. Buxton	1946	Assault	W. Mehrtens
1881	Saunterer	T. Costello	1915	The Finn	G. Byrne	1947	Phalanx	R. Donoso
1882	Forester	J. McLaughlin	1916	Friar Rock	E. Haynes	1948	Citation	E. Arcaro
1883	George Kinney	J. McLaughlin	1917	Hourless	J. Butwell	1949	Capot	T. Atkinson
1884	Panique	J. McLaughlin	1918	Johren	F. Robinson	1950	Middleground	W. Boland
1885	Tyrant	P. Duffy	1919	Sir Barton	J. Loftus	1951	Counterpoint	D. Gorman
1886	Inspector B	J. McLaughlin	1920	Man o' War	C. Kummer	1952	One Count	E. Arcaro
1887	Hanover	J. McLaughlin	1921	Grey Lag	E. Sande	1953	Native Dancer	E. Guerin
1888	Sir Dixon	J. McLaughlin	1922	Pillory	C. H. Miller	1954	High Gun	E. Guerin
1889	Eric	W. Hayward	1923	Zev	E. Sande	1955	Nashua	E. Arcaro
1890	Burlington	S. Barnes	1924	Mad Play	E. Sande	1956	Needles	D. Erb
1891	Foxford	E. Garrison	1925	American Flag	A. Johnson	1957	Gallant Man	W. Shoemaker
1892	Patron	W. Hayward	1926	Crusader	A. Johnson	1958	Cavan	P. Anderson
1893	Comanche	W. Simms	1927	Chance Shot	E. Sande	1959	Sword Dancer	W. Shoemaker
1894	Henry of Navarre	W. Simms	1928	Vito	C. Kummer	1960	Celtic Ash	W. Hartack
1895	Belmar	F. Taral	1929	Blue Larkspur	M. Garner	1961	Sherluck	B. Baeza
1896	Hastings	H. Griffin	1930	Gallant Fox	E. Sande	1962	Jaipur	W. Shoemaker
1897	Scottish Chieftain	J. Scherrer	1931	Twenty Grand	C. Kurtsinger	1963	Chateaugay	B. Baeza
1898	Bowling Brook	F. Littlefield	1932	Faireno	T. Malley	1964	Quadrangle	M. Ycaza

Year	Horse	Jockey	Year	Horse	Jockey	Year	Horse	Jockey
1965	Hail to All	J. Sellers	1985	Creme Fraiche	E. Maple	2004	Birdstone	E. Prado
1966	Amberoid	W. Boland	1986	Danzig Connection	C. McCarron	2005	Afleet Alex	J. Rose
1967	Damascus	W. Shoemaker	1987	Bet Twice	C. Perret	2006	Jazil	F. Jara
1968	Stage Door Johnny	H. Gustines	1988	Risen Star	E. Delahoussaye	2007	Rags to Riches	J. Velazquez
1969	Arts and Letters	B. Baeza	1989	Easy Goer	P. Day	2008	Da' Tara	A. Garcia
1970	High Echelon	J. L. Rotz	1990	Go and Go	M. Kinane	2009	Summer Bird	K. Desormeaux
1971	Pass Catcher	W. Blum	1991	Hansel	J. Bailey	2010	Drosselmeyer	M. Smith
1972	Riva Ridge	R. Turcotte	1992	A.P. Indy	E. Delahoussaye	2011	Ruler On Ice	J. Valdivia Jr.
1973	Secretariat	R. Turcotte	1993	Colonial Affair	J. Krone	2012	Union Rags	J. Velazquez
1974	Little Current	M. Rivera	1994	Tabasco Cat	P. Day	2013	Palace Malice	M. Smith
1975	Avatar	W. Shoemaker	1995	Thunder Gulch	G. Stevens	2014	Tonalist	J. Rosario
1976	Bold Forbes	A. Cordero	1996	Editor's Note	R. Douglas	2015	American Pharoah	V. Espinoza
1977	Seattle Slew	J. Cruguet	1997	Touch Gold	C. McCarron	2016	Creator	I. Ortiz Jr.
1978	Affirmed	S. Cauthen	1998	Victory Gallop	G. Stevens	2017	Tapwrit	J. Ortiz
1979	Coastal	R. Hernandez	1999	Lemon Drop Kid	J. Santos	2018	Justify	M. Smith
1980	Temperence Hill	E. Maple	2000	Commendable	P. Day	2019	Sir Winston	J. Rosario
1981	Summing	G. Martens	2001	Point Given	G. Stevens	2020	Tiz the Law	M. Franco
1982	Conquistador Cielo	L. Pincay	2002	Sarava	E. Prado	2021	Essential Quality	L. Saez
1983	Caveat	L. Pincay	2003	Empire Maker	J. Bailey	2022	Mo Donegal	I. Ortiz Jr.
1984	Swale	L. Pincay				2023	Arcangelo	J. Castellano

Annual Leading Jockey by Earnings, 1957-2022

Total purses earned by all horses that jockey raced in year listed; does not reflect what jockey earned.

Year	Jockey	Earnings	Year	Jockey	Earnings	Year	Jockey	Earnings
1957	Bill Hartack	$3,060,501	1979	Laffit Pincay Jr.	$8,193,535	2001	Jerry D. Bailey	$22,597,720
1958	Willie Shoemaker	2,961,693	1980	Chris McCarron	7,663,300	2002	Jerry D. Bailey	19,271,814
1959	Willie Shoemaker	2,843,133	1981	Chris McCarron	8,397,604	2003	Jerry D. Bailey	23,354,960
1960	Willie Shoemaker	2,123,961	1982	Angel Cordero Jr.	9,483,590	2004	John R. Velazquez	22,220,261
1961	Willie Shoemaker	2,690,819	1983	Angel Cordero Jr.	10,116,697	2005	John R. Velazquez	20,799,923
1962	Willie Shoemaker	2,916,844	1984	Chris McCarron	12,045,813	2006	Garrett K. Gomez	20,122,592
1963	Willie Shoemaker	2,526,925	1985	Laffit Pincay Jr.	13,353,299	2007	Garrett K. Gomez	22,800,074
1964	Willie Shoemaker	2,649,553	1986	Jose Santos	11,329,297	2008	Garrett K. Gomez	23,344,351
1965	Braulio Baeza	2,582,702	1987	Jose Santos	12,375,433	2009	Garrett K. Gomez	18,536,105
1966	Braulio Baeza	2,951,022	1988	Jose Santos	14,877,298	2010	Ramon A. Dominguez	16,911,880
1967	Braulio Baeza	3,088,888	1989	Jose Santos	13,838,389	2011	Ramon A. Dominguez	20,267,032
1968	Braulio Baeza	2,835,108	1990	Gary Stevens	13,881,198	2012	Ramon A. Dominguez	25,584,852
1969	Jorge Velasquez	2,542,315	1991	Chris McCarron	14,441,083	2013	Javier Castellano	26,214,007
1970	Laffit Pincay Jr.	2,626,526	1992	Kent Desormeaux	14,193,006	2014	Javier Castellano	25,056,464
1971	Laffit Pincay Jr.	3,784,377	1993	Mike Smith	14,024,815	2015	Javier Castellano	28,120,809
1972	Laffit Pincay Jr.	3,225,827	1994	Mike Smith	15,979,820	2016	Javier Castellano	26,826,241
1973	Laffit Pincay Jr.	4,093,492	1995	Jerry D. Bailey	16,311,876	2017	José L. Ortiz	27,318,875
1974	Laffit Pincay Jr.	4,251,060	1996	Jerry D. Bailey	19,465,376	2018	Irad Ortiz Jr.	27,727,039
1975	Braulio Baeza	3,695,198	1997	Jerry D. Bailey	18,320,743	2019	Irad Ortiz Jr.	34,109,019
1976	Angel Cordero Jr.	4,709,500	1998	Gary Stevens	19,622,855	2020	Irad Ortiz Jr.	21,050,726
1977	Steve Cauthen	6,151,750	1999	Pat Day	18,092,845	2021	Joel Rosario	32,956,215
1978	Darrel McHargue	6,029,885	2000	Pat Day	17,479,838	2022	Irad Ortiz Jr.	37,075,772

Breeders' Cup World Thoroughbred Championships, 1984-2023

The Breeders' Cup began in 1984 and through 2006, consisted of seven races at one track on one day. In 2007, it expanded to two days, with new races.

Classic

Year	Horse	Jockey	Year	Horse	Jockey	Year	Horse	Jockey
1984	Wild Again	P. Day	1998	Awesome Again	P. Day	2011	Drosselmeyer	M. Smith
1985	Proud Truth	J. Velasquez	1999	Cat Thief	P. Day	2012	Fort Larned	B. Hernandez
1986	Skywalker	L. Pincay Jr.	2000	Tiznow	C. McCarron	2013	Mucho Macho Man	G. Stevens
1987	Ferdinand	W. Shoemaker	2001	Tiznow	C. McCarron	2014	Bayern	M. Garcia
1988	Alysheba	C. McCarron	2002	Volponi	J. Santos	2015	American Pharoah	V. Espinoza
1989	Sunday Silence	C. McCarron	2003	Pleasantly Perfect	A. Solis	2016	Arrogate	M. Smith
1990	Unbridled	P. Day	2004	Ghostzapper	J. Castellano	2017	Gun Runner	F. Geroux
1991	Black Tie Affair	J. Bailey	2005	Saint Liam	J. Bailey	2018	Accelerate	J. Rosario
1992	A.P. Indy	E. Delahoussaye	2006	Invasor	F. Jara	2019	Vino Rosso	I. Ortiz Jr.
1993	Arcangues	J. Bailey	2007	Curlin	R. Albarado	2020	Authentic	J. Velazquez
1994	Concern	J. Bailey	2008	Raven's Pass	F. Dettori	2021	Knicks Go	J. Rosario
1995	Cigar	J. Bailey	2009	Zenyatta	M. Smith	2022	Flightline	F. Prat
1996	Alphabet Soup	C. McCarron	2010	Blame	G. Gomez	2023	White Abarrio	I. Ortiz Jr.
1997	Skip Away	M. Smith						

Juvenile

Year	Horse	Jockey	Year	Horse	Jockey	Year	Horse	Jockey
1984	Chief's Crown	D. MacBeth	1998	Answer Lively	J. Bailey	2011	Hansen	R. Dominguez
1985	Tasso	L. Pincay Jr.	1999	Anees	G. Stevens	2012	Shanghai Bobby	R. Napravnik
1986	Capote	L. Pincay Jr.	2000	Macho Uno	J. Bailey	2013	New Year's Day	M. Garcia
1987	Success Express	J. Santos	2001	Johannesburg	M. Kinane	2014	Texas Red	K. Desormeaux
1988	Is It True	L. Pincay Jr.	2002	Vindication	M. Smith	2015	Nyquist	M. Gutierrez
1989	Rhythm	C. Perret	2003	Action This Day	D. Flores	2016	Classic Empire	J. Leparoux
1990	Fly So Free	J. Santos	2004	Wilko	F. Dettori	2017	Good Magic	J. Ortiz
1991	Arazi	P. Valenzuela	2005	Stevie Wonderboy	G. Gomez	2018	Game Winner	J. Rosario
1992	Gilded Time	C. McCarron	2006	Street Sense	C. Borel	2019	Storm the Court	F. Prat
1993	Brocco	G. Stevens	2007	War Pass	C. Velasquez	2020	Essential Quality	L. Saez
1994	Timber Country	P. Day	2008	Midshipman	G. Gomez	2021	Corniche	J. Velazquez
1995	Unbridled's Song	M. Smith	2009	Vale of York	A. Ajtebi	2022	Forte	I. Ortiz Jr.
1996	Boston Harbor	J. Bailey	2010	Uncle Mo	J. Velazquez	2023	Fierceness	J. Velazquez
1997	Favorite Trick	P. Day						

Filly and Mare Sprint

Year	Horse	Jockey	Year	Horse	Jockey	Year	Horse	Jockey
2007	Maryfield	E. Trujillo	2013	Groupie Doll	R. Maragh	2019	Covfefe	J. Rosario
2008	Ventura	G. Gomez	2014	Judy the Beauty	M. Smith	2020	Gamine	J. Velazquez
2009	Informed Decision	J. Leparoux	2015	Wavell Avenue	J. Rosario	2021	Ce Ce	V. Espinoza
2010	Dubai Majesty	J. Theriot	2016	Finest City	M. Smith	2022	Goodnight Olive	I. Ortiz Jr.
2011	Musical Romance	J. Leyva	2017	Bar of Gold	I. Ortiz Jr.	2023	Goodnight Olive	I. Ortiz Jr.
2012	Groupie Doll	R. Maragh	2018	Shamrock Rose	I. Ortiz Jr.			

Juvenile Fillies

Year	Horse	Jockey	Year	Horse	Jockey	Year	Horse	Jockey
1984	Outstandingly	W. Guerra	1998	Silverbulletday	G. Stevens	2012	Beholder	G. Gomez
1985	Twilight Ridge	J. Velasquez	1999	Cash Run	J. Bailey	2013	Ria Antonia	J. Castellano
1986	Brave Raj	P. Valenzuela	2000	Caressing	J. Velazquez	2014	Take Charge Brandi	V. Espinoza
1987	Epitome	P. Day	2001	Tempera	D. Flores			
1988	Open Mind	A. Cordero Jr.	2002	Storm Flag Flying	J. Velazquez	2015	Songbird	M. Smith
1989	Go for Wand	R. Romero	2003	Halfbridled	J. Krone	2016	Champagne Room	M. Gutierrez
1990	Meadow Star	J. Santos	2004	Sweet Catomine	C. Nakatani	2017	Caledonia Road	M. Smith
1991	Pleasant Stage	E. Delahoussaye	2005	Folklore	E. Prado	2018	Jaywalk	J. Rosario
1992	Eliza	P. Valenzuela	2006	Dreaming of Anna	R. Douglas	2019	British Idiom	J. Castellano
1993	Phone Chatter	L. Pincay Jr.	2007	Indian Blessing	G. Gomez	2020	Vequist	J. Rosario
1994	Flanders	P. Day	2008	Stardom Bound	M. Smith	2021	Echo Zulu	J. Rosario
1995	My Flag	J. Bailey	2009	She Be Wild	J. Leparoux	2022	Wonder Wheel	T. Gaffalione
1996	Storm Song	C. Perret	2010	Awesome Feather	J. Sanchez	2023	Just FYI	J. Alvarado
1997	Countess Diana	S. Sellers	2011	My Miss Aurelia	C. Nakatani			

Sprint

Year	Horse	Jockey	Year	Horse	Jockey	Year	Horse	Jockey
1984	Eillo	C. Perret	1998	Reraise	C. Nakatani	2011	Amazombie	M. Smith
1985	Precisionist	C. McCarron	1999	Artax	J. Chaves	2012	Trinniberg	W. Martinez
1986	Smile	J. Vasquez	2000	Kona Gold	A. Solis	2013	Secret Circle	M. Garcia
1987	Very Subtle	P. Valenzuela	2001	Squirtle Squirt	J. Bailey	2014	Work All Week	F. Geroux
1988	Gulch	A. Cordero Jr.	2002	Orientate	J. Bailey	2015	Runhappy	E. Prado
1989	Dancing Spree	A. Cordero Jr.	2003	Cajun Beat	C. Velasquez	2016	Drefong	M. Garcia
1990	Safely Kept	C. Perret	2004	Speightstown	J. Velazquez	2017	Roy H	K. Desormeaux
1991	Sheikh Albadou	P. Eddery	2005	Silver Train	E. Prado	2018	Roy H	P. Lopez
1992	Thirty Slews	E. Delahoussaye	2006	Thor's Echo	C. Nakatani	2019	Mitole	R. Santana Jr.
1993	Cardmania	E. Delahoussaye	2007	Midnight Lute	G. Gomez	2020	Whitmore	I. Ortiz Jr.
1994	Cherokee Run	M. Smith	2008	Midnight Lute	G. Gomez	2021	Aloha West	J. Ortiz
1995	Desert Stormer	K. Desormeaux	2009	Dancing in Silks	J. Rosario	2022	Elite Power	I. Ortiz Jr.
1996	Lit de Justice	C. Nakatani	2010	Big Drama	E. Coa	2023	Elite Power	I. Ortiz Jr.
1997	Elmhurst	C. Nakatani						

Mile

Year	Horse	Jockey	Year	Horse	Jockey	Year	Horse	Jockey
1984	Royal Heroine	F. Toro	1998	Da Hoss	J. Velazquez	2011	Court Vision	R. Albarado
1985	Cozzene	W. Guerra	1999	Silic	C. Nakatani	2012	Wise Dan	J. Velazquez
1986	Last Tycoon	Y. St.-Martin	2000	War Chant	G. Stevens	2013	Wise Dan	J. Lezcano
1987	Miesque	F. Head	2001	Val Royal	J. Valdivia Jr.	2014	Karakatonie	S. Pasquier
1988	Miesque	F. Head	2002	Domedriver	T. Thulliez	2015	Tepin	J. Leparoux
1989	Steinlen	J. Santos	2003	Six Perfections	J. Bailey	2016	Tourist	J. Rosario
1990	Royal Academy	L. Piggott	2004	Singletary	D. Flores	2017	World Approval	J. Velazquez
1991	Opening Verse	P. Valenzuela	2005	Artie Schiller	G. Gomez	2018	Expert Eye	F. Dettori
1992	Lure	M. Smith	2006	Miesque's Approval	E. Castro	2019	Uni	J. Rosario
1993	Lure	M. Smith	2007	Kip Deville	C. Velasquez	2020	Order of Australia	P. Boudot
1994	Barathea	F. Dettori	2008	Goldikova	O. Peslier	2021	Space Blues	W. Buick
1995	Ridgewood Pearl	J. Murtagh	2009	Goldikova	O. Peslier	2022	Modern Games	W. Buick
1996	Da Hoss	G. Stevens	2010	Goldikova	O. Peslier	2023	Master of the Seas	W. Buick
1997	Spinning World	C. Asmussen						

Distaff

Year	Horse	Jockey	Year	Horse	Jockey	Year	Horse	Jockey
1984	Princess Rooney	E. Delahoussaye	1998	Escena	G. Stevens	2011	Royal Delta	J. Lezcano
1985	Life's Magic	A. Cordero Jr.	1999	Beautiful Pleasure	J. Chaves	2012	Royal Delta	M. Smith
1986	Lady's Secret	P. Day	2000	Spain	V. Espinoza	2013	Beholder	G. Stevens
1987	Sacahuista	R. Romero	2001	Unbridled Elaine	P. Day	2014	Untapable	R. Napravnik
1988	Personal Ensign	R. Romero	2002	Azeri	M. Smith	2015	Stopchargingmaria	J. Castellano
1989	Bayakoa	L. Pincay Jr.	2003	Adoration	P. Valenzuela	2016	Beholder	G. Stevens
1990	Bayakoa	L. Pincay Jr.	2004	Ashado	J. Velazquez	2017	Forever Unbridled	J. Velazquez
1991	Dance Smartly	P. Day	2005	Pleasant Home	C. Velasquez	2018	Monomoy Girl	F. Geroux
1992	Paseana	C. McCarron	2006	Round Pond	E. Prado	2019	Blue Prize	J. Bravo
1993	Hollywood Wildcat	E. Delahoussaye	2007	Ginger Punch	R. Bejarano	2020	Monomoy Girl	F. Geroux
1994	One Dreamer	G. Stevens	2008	Zenyatta	M. Smith	2021	Marche Lorraine	O. Murphy
1995	Inside Information	M. Smith	2009	Life Is Sweet	G. Stevens	2022	Malathaat	J. Velazquez
1996	Jewel Princess	C. Nakatani	2010	Unrivaled Belle	K. Desormeaux	2023	Idiomatic	F. Geroux
1997	Ajina	M. Smith						

Turf

Year	Horse	Jockey	Year	Horse	Jockey	Year	Horse	Jockey
1984	Lashkari	Y. St.-Martin	1997	Chief Bearhart	J. Santos	2010	Dangerous Midge	F. Dettori
1985	Pebbles	P. Eddery	1998	Buck's Boy	S. Sellers	2011	St Nicholas Abbey	J. O'Brien
1986	Manila	J. Santos	1999	Daylami	F. Dettori	2012	Little Mike	R. Dominguez
1987	Theatrical	P. Day	2000	Kalanisi	J. Murtagh	2013	Magician	R. Moore
1988	Great Communicator	R. Sibille	2001	Fantastic Light	F. Dettori	2014	Main Sequence	J. Velazquez
			2002	High Chaparral	M. Kinane	2015	Found	R. Moore
1989	Prized	E. Delahoussaye	2003	(tie) High Chaparral	M. Kinane	2016	Highland Reel	S. Heffernan
1990	In the Wings	G. Stevens		Johar	A. Solis	2017	Talismanic	M. Barzalona
1991	Miss Alleged	E. Legrix	2004	Better Talk Now	R. Dominguez	2018	Enable	F. Dettori
1992	Fraise	P. Valenzuela	2005	Shirocco	C. Soumillon	2019	Bricks and Mortar	I. Ortiz Jr.
1993	Kotashaan	K. Desormeaux	2006	Red Rocks	F. Dettori	2020	Tarnawa	C. Keane
1994	Tikkanen	M. Smith	2007	English Channel	J. Velasquez	2021	Yibir	W. Buick
1995	Northern Spur	C. McCarron	2008	Conduit	R. Moore	2022	Rebel's Romance	J. Doyle
1996	Pilsudski	W. Swinburn	2009	Conduit	R. Moore	2023	Auguste Rodin	R. Moore

Filly and Mare Turf

Year	Horse	Jockey	Year	Horse	Jockey	Year	Horse	Jockey
1999	Soaring Softly	J. Bailey	2008	Forever Together	J. Leparoux	2016	Queen's Trust	F. Dettori
2000	Perfect Sting	J. Bailey	2009	Midday	T. Queally	2017	Wuheida	W. Buick
2001	Banks Hill	O. Peslier	2010	Shared Account	E. Prado	2018	Sistercharlie	J. Velazquez
2002	Starine	J. Velazquez	2011	Perfect Shirl	J. Velazquez	2019	Iridessa	W. Lordan
2003	Islington	K. Fallon	2012	Zagora	J. Castellano	2020	Audarya	P. Boudot
2004	Ouija Board	F. Dettori	2013	Dank	R. Moore	2021	Loves Only You	Y. Kawada
2005	Intercontinental	R. Bejarano	2014	Dayatthespa	J. Castellano	2022	Tuesday	R. Moore
2006	Ouija Board	F. Dettori	2015	Stephanie's Kitten	J. Velazquez	2023	Inspiral	F. Dettori
2007	Lahudood	A. Garcia						

Juvenile Turf

Year	Horse	Jockey	Year	Horse	Jockey	Year	Horse	Jockey
2007	Nownownow	J. Leparoux	2013	Outstrip	M. Smith	2018	Line of Duty	W. Buick
2008	Donativum	F. Dettori	2014	Hootenanny	F. Dettori	2019	Structor	J. Ortiz
2009	Pounced	F. Dettori	2015	Hit It a Bomb	R. Moore	2020	Fire At Will	R. Santana Jr.
2010	Pluck	G. Gomez	2016	Oscar Performance	J. Ortiz	2021	Modern Games	W. Buick
2011	Wrote	R. Moore	2017	Mendelssohn	R. Moore	2022	Victoria Road	R. Moore
2012	George Vancouver	R. Moore				2023	Unquestionable	R. Moore

Dirt Mile

Year	Horse	Jockey	Year	Horse	Jockey	Year	Horse	Jockey
2007	Corinthian	K. Desormeaux	2013	Goldencents	R. Bejarano	2019	Spun to Run	I. Ortiz Jr.
2008	Albertus Maximus	G. Gomez	2014	Goldencents	R. Bejarano	2020	Knicks Go	I. Ortiz Jr.
2009	Furthest Land	J. Leparoux	2015	Liam's Map	J. Castellano	2021	Life Is Good	I. Ortiz Jr.
2010	Dakota Phone	J. Rosario	2016	Tamarkuz	M. Smith	2022	Cody's Wish	J. Alvarado
2011	Caleb's Posse	R. Maragh	2017	Battle of Midway	F. Prat	2023	Cody's Wish	J. Alvarado
2012	Tapizar	C. Nakatani	2018	City of Light	J. Castellano			

Turf Sprint

Year	Horse	Jockey	Year	Horse	Jockey	Year	Horse	Jockey
2008	Desert Code	R. Migliore	2014	Bobby's Kitten	J. Rosario	2019	Belvoir Bay	J. Castellano
2009	California Flag	J. Talamo	2015	Mongolian Saturday	F. Geroux	2020	Glass Slippers	T. Eaves
2010	Chamberlain Bridge	J. Theriot	2016	Obviously	F. Prat	2021	Golden Pal	I. Ortiz Jr.
2011	Regally Ready	C. Nakatani	2017	Stormy Liberal	J. Rosario	2022	Caravel	T. Gaffalione
2012	Mizdirection	M. Smith	2018	Stormy Liberal	D. Van Dyke	2023	Nobals	G. Corrales
2013	Mizdirection	M. Smith						

Juvenile Fillies Turf

Year	Horse	Jockey	Year	Horse	Jockey	Year	Horse	Jockey
2008	Maram	J. Lezcano	2014	Lady Eli	I. Ortiz Jr.	2019	Sharing	M. Franco
2009	Tapitsfly	R. Albarado	2015	Catch a Glimpse	F. Geroux	2020	Aunt Pearl	F. Geroux
2010	More Than Real	G. Gomez	2016	New Money Honey	J. Castellano	2021	Pizza Bianca	J. Ortiz
2011	Stephanie's Kitten	J. Velazquez	2017	Rushing Fall	J. Castellano	2022	Meditate	R. Moore
2012	Flotilla	C. Lemaire	2018	Newspaperofrecord	I. Ortiz Jr.	2023	Hard to Justify	F. Prat
2013	Chriselliam	R. Hughes						

Juvenile Turf Sprint

Year	Horse	Jockey	Year	Horse	Jockey	Year	Horse	Jockey
2018	Bulletin	J. Castellano	2020	Golden Pal	I. Ortiz Jr.	2022	Mischief Magic	W. Buick
2019	Four Wheel Drive	I. Ortiz Jr.	2021	Twilight Gleaming	I. Ortiz Jr.	2023	Big Evs	T. Marquand

Eclipse Awards, 2022

The Eclipse Awards, honoring the Horse of the Year and other champions of thoroughbred racing, began in 1971 and are sponsored by the *Daily Racing Form*, the National Thoroughbred Racing Association, and the National Turf Writers and Broadcasters.

Horse of the year: Flightline
Two-year-old male: Forte
Two-year-old filly: Wonder Wheel
Three-year-old male: Epicenter
Three-year-old filly: Nest
Older dirt male: Flightline
Older dirt female: Malathaat
Male sprinter: Elite Power
Female sprinter: Goodnight Olive
Male turf horse: Modern Games
Female turf horse: Regal Glory
Steeplechase horse: Hewick
Owner: Godolphin LLC
Breeder: Godolphin LLC
Jockey: Irad Ortiz Jr.
Apprentice jockey: Jose Antonio Gomez
Trainer: Todd Pletcher

HARNESS RACING
Harness Horse of the Year, 1947-2022
Chosen by the U.S. Trotting Assn. and the U.S. Harness Writers Assn.

Year	Horse	Year	Horse	Year	Horse	Year	Horse
1947	Victory Song	1966	Bret Hanover	1985	Nihilator	2004	Rainbow Blue
1948	Rodney	1967	Nevele Pride	1986	Forrest Skipper	2005	Rocknroll Hanover
1949	Good Time	1968	Nevele Pride	1987	Mack Lobell	2006	Glidemaster
1950	Proximity	1969	Nevele Pride	1988	Mack Lobell	2007	Donato Hanover
1951	Pronto Don	1970	Fresh Yankee	1989	Matt's Scooter	2008	Somebeachsomewhere
1952	Good Time	1971	Albatross	1990	Beach Towel	2009	Muscle Hill
1953	Hi Lo's Forbes	1972	Albatross	1991	Precious Bunny	2010	Rock N Roll Heaven
1954	Stenographer	1973	Sir Dalrae	1992	Artsplace	2011	San Pail
1955	Scott Frost	1974	Delmonica Hanover	1993	Staying Together	2012	Chapter Seven
1956	Scott Frost	1975	Savoir	1994	Cam's Card Shark	2013	Bee a Magician
1957	Torpid	1976	Keystone Ore	1995	CR Kay Suzie	2014	JK She'salady
1958	Emily's Pride	1977	Green Speed	1996	Continental Victory	2015	Wiggle It Jiggleit
1959	Bye Bye Byrd	1978	Abercrombie	1997	Malabar Man	2016	Always B Miki
1960	Adios Butler	1979	Niatross	1998	Moni Maker	2017	Hannelore Hanover
1961	Adios Butler	1980	Niatross	1999	Moni Maker	2018	McWicked
1962	Su Mac Lad	1981	Fan Hanover	2000	Gallo Blue Chip	2019	Shartin N
1963	Speedy Scot	1982	Cam Fella	2001	Bunny Lake	2020	Tall Dark Stranger
1964	Bret Hanover	1983	Cam Fella	2002	Real Desire	2021	Test Of Faith
1965	Bret Hanover	1984	Fancy Crown	2003	No Pan Intended	2022	Bulldog Hanover

Hambletonian Winners (3-year-old trotters), 1965-2023

Year	Horse	Driver	Year	Horse	Driver	Year	Horse	Driver
1965	Egyptian Candor	D. Cameron	1985	Prakas	B. O'Donnell	2004	Windsong's Legacy	T. Smedshammer
1966	Kerry Way	F. Ervin	1986	Nuclear Kosmos	U. Thoresen	2005	Vivid Photo	R. Hammer
1967	Speedy Streak	D. Cameron	1987	Mack Lobell	J. Campbell	2006	Glidemaster	J. Campbell
1968	Nevele Pride	S. Dancer	1988	Armbro Goal	J. Campbell	2007	Donato Hanover	R. Pierce
1969	Lindy's Pride	H. Beissinger	1989	Park Avenue Joe	R. Waples	2008	Deweycheatumnhowe	R. Schnittker
1970	Timothy T	J. Simpson Sr.	1990	Harmonious	J. Campbell	2009	Muscle Hill	B. Sears
1971	Speedy Crown	H. Beissinger	1991	Giant Victory	J. Moiseyev	2010	Muscle Massive	R. Pierce
1972	Super Bowl	S. Dancer	1992	Alf Palema	M. McNicholl	2011	Broad Bahn	G. Brennan
1973	Flirth	R. Baldwin	1993	American Winner	R. Pierce	2012	Market Share	T. Tetrick
1974	Christopher T	B. Haughton	1994	Victory Dream	M. Lachance	2013	Royalty For Life	B. Sears
1975	Bonefish	S. Dancer	1995	Tagliabue	J. Campbell	2014	Trixton	J. Takter
1976	Steve Lobell	B. Haughton	1996	Continental Victory	M. Lachance	2015	Pinkman	B. Sears
1977	Green Speed	B. Haughton	1997	Malabar Man	M. Burroughs	2016	Marion Marauder	S. Zeron
1978	Speedy Somolli	H. Beissinger	1998	Muscles Yankee	J. Campbell	2017	Perfect Spirit	A. Svanstedt
1979	Legend Hanover	G. Sholty	1999	Self Possessed	M. Lachance	2018	Atlanta	S. Zeron
1980	Burgomeister	B. Haughton	2000	Yankee Paco	T. Ritchie	2019	Forbidden Trade	B. McClure
1981	Shiaway St. Pat	R. Remmen	2001	Scarlet Knight	S. Melander	2020	Ramona Hill	A. McCarthy
1982	Speed Bowl	T. Haughton	2002	Chip Chip Hooray	E. Ledford	2021	Captain Corey	A. Svanstedt
1983	Duenna	S. Dancer	2003	Amigo Hall	M. Lachance	2022	Cool Papa Bell	T. McCarthy
1984	Historic Freight	B. Webster				2023	Tactical Approach	S. Zeron

BOWLING

Professional Bowlers Association Tournament of Champions, 1965-2023

Year	Winner	Year	Winner	Year	Winner	Year	Winner
1965	Billy Hardwick	1979	George Pappas	1993	George Branham III	2010	Kelly Kulick
1966	Wayne Zahn	1980	Wayne Webb	1994	Norm Duke	2011	Mika Koivuniemi
1967	Jim Stefanich	1981	Steve Cook	1996	Dave D'Entremont	2012	Sean Rash
1968	Dave Davis	1982	Mike Durbin	1997	John Gant	2013	Pete Weber
1969	Jim Godman	1983	Joe Berardi	1998	Bryan Goebel	2014	Jason Belmonte
1970	Don Johnson	1984	Mike Durbin	1999	Jason Couch	2015	Jason Belmonte
1971	Johnny Petraglia	1985	Mark Williams	2000	Jason Couch	2016	Jesper Svensson
1972	Mike Durbin	1986	Marshall Holman	2002	Jason Couch	2017	E. J. Tackett
1973	Jim Godman	1987	Pete Weber	2003	Patrick Healey Jr.	2018	Matt O'Grady
1974	Earl Anthony	1988	Mark Williams	2005	Steve Jaros	2019	Jason Belmonte
1975	Dave Davis	1989	Del Ballard Jr.	2006	Chris Barnes	2020	Kris Prather
1976	Marshall Holman	1990	Dave Ferraro	2007	Tommy Jones	2021	François Lavoie
1977	Mike Berlin	1991	David Ozio	2008	Michael Haugen Jr.	2022	Dom Barrett
1978	Earl Anthony	1992	Marc McDowell	2009	Patrick Allen	2023	Jason Belmonte

Note: No tournament held in 2001 and 2004.

Professional Bowlers Association Leading Money Winners, 1962-2022

Total winnings from tournaments only. For 2000-13, year shown is year the PBA season ended.

Year	Bowler	Earnings	Year	Bowler	Earnings	Year	Bowler	Earnings
1962	Don Carter	$49,972	1982	Earl Anthony	$134,760	2003	Walter Ray Williams Jr.	$419,700
1963	Dick Weber	46,333	1983	Earl Anthony	135,605	2004	Mika Koivuniemi	238,590
1964	Bob Strampe	33,592	1984	Mark Roth	158,712	2005	Patrick Allen	350,740
1965	Dick Weber	47,674	1985	Mike Aulby	201,200	2006	Tommy Jones	301,700
1966	Wayne Zahn	54,720	1986	Walter Ray Williams Jr.	145,550	2007	Doug Kent	200,530
1967	Dave Davis	54,165	1987	Pete Weber	175,491	2008	Norm Duke	176,855
1968	Jim Stefanich	67,377	1988	Brian Voss	225,485	2009	Norm Duke	199,130
1969	Billy Hardwick	64,160	1989	Mike Aulby	298,237	2010	Walter Ray Williams Jr.	152,670
1970	Mike McGrath	52,049	1990	Amleto Monacelli	204,775	2011	Mika Koivuniemi	333,040
1971	Johnny Petraglia	85,065	1991	David Ozio	225,585	2012	Sean Rash	140,250
1972	Don Johnson	56,648	1992	Marc McDowell	174,215	2013	Sean Rash	248,317
1973	Don McCune	69,000	1993	Walter Ray Williams Jr.	296,370	2014	Jason Belmonte	163,778
1974	Earl Anthony	99,585	1994	Norm Duke	273,753	2015	Jason Belmonte	178,542
1975	Earl Anthony	107,585	1995	Mike Aulby	219,792	2016	E. J. Tackett	168,290
1976	Earl Anthony	110,833	1996	Walter Ray Williams Jr.	241,330	2017	Jason Belmonte	238,912
1977	Mark Roth	105,583	1997	Walter Ray Williams Jr.	240,544	2018	Anthony Simonsen	115,975
1978	Mark Roth	134,500	1998	Walter Ray Williams Jr.	238,225	2019	Jason Belmonte	285,290
1979	Mark Roth	124,517	1999	Parker Bohn III	240,912	2020	Jason Belmonte	293,050
1980	Wayne Webb	116,700	2000	Norm Duke	143,325	2021	Kyle Troup	496,900
1981	Earl Anthony	164,735	2002	Parker Bohn III	245,200	2022	Jason Belmonte	302,525

World Chess Champions, 1886-2023

Source: U.S. Chess Federation, International Chess Federation (FIDE)
Official world champions since the title was first used.

Years	Champion, country	Years	Champion, country
1886-94	Wilhelm Steinitz, Austria	1975-85	Anatoly Karpov, USSR
1894-1921	Emanuel Lasker, Germany	1985-2000	Garry Kasparov, USSR/Russia[3,4]
1921-27	Jose R. Capablanca, Cuba	1993-99	Anatoly Karpov, Russia (FIDE)[3]
1927-35	Alexander Alekhine, France	1999-2000	Alexander Khalifman, Russia (FIDE)
1935-37	Max Euwe, Netherlands	2000-02	Viswanathan Anand, India (FIDE)
1937-46	Alexander Alekhine, France[1]	2000-06	Vladimir Kramnik, Russia (classical)[4]
1948-57	Mikhail Botvinnik, USSR	2002-04	Ruslan Ponomariov, Ukraine (FIDE)
1957-58	Vassily Smyslov, USSR	2004-05	Rustam Kasimdzhanov, Uzbekistan (FIDE)
1958-59	Mikhail Botvinnik, USSR	2005-06	Veselin Topalov, Bulgaria (FIDE)[5]
1960-61	Mikhail Tal, USSR	2006-07	Vladimir Kramnik, Russia[5]
1961-63	Mikhail Botvinnik, USSR	2007-13	Viswanathan Anand, India
1963-69	Tigran Petrosian, USSR	2013-22	Magnus Carlsen, Norway
1969-72	Boris Spassky, USSR	2023	Ding Liren, China
1972-75	Bobby Fischer, U.S.[2]		

(1) After Alekhine died in 1946, the title was vacant until 1948, when Botvinnik won the first world championship event sanctioned by FIDE. (2) Defaulted championship after refusing to accept FIDE rules for a championship match, Apr. 1975. (3) Kasparov broke with FIDE, Feb. 26, 1993. FIDE stripped Kasparov of his FIDE title Mar. 23. Kasparov defeated Nigel Short (UK) in a world championship match played Sept.-Oct. 1993 under the auspices of the Professional Chess Association (PCA), a new organization the two founded. FIDE held a championship match between Anatoly Karpov (Russia) and Jan Timman (Netherlands), which Karpov won in Nov. 1993. The PCA folded in 1995, but Kasparov was still considered the "classical" world champion. (That is, he defended his title against challengers; PCA matches are arranged differently.) (4) In Nov. 2000, Kramnik defeated Kasparov for the classical world championship title. (5) Kramnik, the classical world champion since 2000, unified the chess titles by defeating Topalov on Oct. 13, 2006, at a world championship match.

Alpine Skiing Men's World Cup Champions, 1967-2023

Year	Champion, country	Year	Champion, country	Year	Champion, country
1967	Jean Claude Killy, France	1986	Marc Girardelli, Luxembourg	2005	Bode Miller, U.S.
1968	Jean Claude Killy, France	1987	Pirmin Zurbriggen, Switzerland	2006	Benjamin Raich, Austria
1969	Karl Schranz, Austria	1988	Pirmin Zurbriggen, Switzerland	2007	Aksel Lund Svindal, Norway
1970	Karl Schranz, Austria	1989	Marc Girardelli, Luxembourg	2008	Bode Miller, U.S.
1971	Gustavo Thoeni, Italy	1990	Pirmin Zurbriggen, Switzerland	2009	Aksel Lund Svindal, Norway
1972	Gustavo Thoeni, Italy	1991	Marc Girardelli, Luxembourg	2010	Carlo Janka, Switzerland
1973	Gustavo Thoeni, Italy	1992	Paul Accola, Switzerland	2011	Ivica Kostelic, Croatia
1974	Piero Gros, Italy	1993	Marc Girardelli, Luxembourg	2012	Marcel Hirscher, Austria
1975	Gustavo Thoeni, Italy	1994	Kjetil André Aamodt, Norway	2013	Marcel Hirscher, Austria
1976	Ingemar Stenmark, Sweden	1995	Alberto Tomba, Italy	2014	Marcel Hirscher, Austria
1977	Ingemar Stenmark, Sweden	1996	Lasse Kjus, Norway	2015	Marcel Hirscher, Austria
1978	Ingemar Stenmark, Sweden	1997	Luc Alphand, France	2016	Marcel Hirscher, Austria
1979	Peter Luescher, Switzerland	1998	Hermann Maier, Austria	2017	Marcel Hirscher, Austria
1980	Andreas Wenzel, Liechtenstein	1999	Lasse Kjus, Norway	2018	Marcel Hirscher, Austria
1981	Phil Mahre, U.S.	2000	Hermann Maier, Austria	2019	Marcel Hirscher, Austria
1982	Phil Mahre, U.S.	2001	Hermann Maier, Austria	2020	Aleksander Aamodt Kilde, Norway
1983	Phil Mahre, U.S.	2002	Stephan Eberharter, Austria	2021	Alexis Pinturault, France
1984	Pirmin Zurbriggen, Switzerland	2003	Stephan Eberharter, Austria	2022	Marco Odermatt, Switzerland
1985	Marc Girardelli, Luxembourg	2004	Hermann Maier, Austria	2023	Marco Odermatt, Switzerland

Alpine Skiing Women's World Cup Champions, 1967-2023

Year	Champion, country	Year	Champion, country	Year	Champion, country
1967	Nancy Greene, Canada	1986	Maria Walliser, Switzerland	2005	Anja Paerson, Sweden
1968	Nancy Greene, Canada	1987	Maria Walliser, Switzerland	2006	Janica Kostelic, Croatia
1969	Gertrud Gabl, Austria	1988	Michela Figini, Switzerland	2007	Nicole Hosp, Austria
1970	Michèle Jacot, France	1989	Vreni Schneider, Switzerland	2008	Lindsey Vonn, U.S.
1971	Annemarie Proell, Austria	1990	Petra Kronberger, Austria	2009	Lindsey Vonn, U.S.
1972	Annemarie Proell, Austria	1991	Petra Kronberger, Austria	2010	Lindsey Vonn, U.S.
1973	Annemarie Proell, Austria	1992	Petra Kronberger, Austria	2011	Maria Höfl-Riesch, Germany
1974	Annemarie Proell, Austria	1993	Anita Wachter, Austria	2012	Lindsey Vonn, U.S.
1975	Annemarie Proell, Austria	1994	Vreni Schneider, Switzerland	2013	Tina Maze, Slovenia
1976	Rosi Mittermaier, W. Germany	1995	Vreni Schneider, Switzerland	2014	Anna Fenninger, Austria
1977	Lise-Marie Morerod, Switzerland	1996	Katja Seizinger, Germany	2015	Anna Fenninger, Austria
1978	Hanni Wenzel, Liechtenstein	1997	Pernilla Wiberg, Sweden	2016	Lara Gut, Switzerland
1979	Annemarie Moser-Proell, Austria	1998	Katja Seizinger, Germany	2017	Mikaela Shiffrin, U.S.
1980	Hanni Wenzel, Liechtenstein	1999	Alexandra Meissnitzer, Austria	2018	Mikaela Shiffrin, U.S.
1981	Marie-Theres Nadig, Switzerland	2000	Renate Goetschl, Austria	2019	Mikaela Shiffrin, U.S.
1982	Erika Hess, Switzerland	2001	Janica Kostelic, Croatia	2020	Federica Brignone, Italy
1983	Tamara McKinney, U.S.	2002	Michaela Dorfmeister, Austria	2021	Petra Vlhova, Slovakia
1984	Erika Hess, Switzerland	2003	Janica Kostelic, Croatia	2022	Mikaela Shiffrin, U.S.
1985	Michela Figini, Switzerland	2004	Anja Paerson, Sweden	2023	Mikaela Shiffrin, U.S.

U.S. and World Figure Skating Championships, 1955-2023

	U.S. Champions		World Champions	
Men's winner	Women's winner	Year	Men's winner, country	Women's winner, country
Hayes Jenkins	Tenley Albright	1955	Hayes Jenkins, U.S.	Tenley Albright, U.S.
Hayes Jenkins	Tenley Albright	1956	Hayes Jenkins, U.S.	Carol Heiss, U.S.
David Jenkins	Carol Heiss	1957	David Jenkins, U.S.	Carol Heiss, U.S.
David Jenkins	Carol Heiss	1958	David Jenkins, U.S.	Carol Heiss, U.S.
David Jenkins	Carol Heiss	1959	David Jenkins, U.S.	Carol Heiss, U.S.
David Jenkins	Carol Heiss	1960	Alain Giletti, France	Carol Heiss, U.S.
Bradley Lord	Laurence Owen	1961	No competition[1]	No competition[1]
Monty Hoyt	Barbara Roles Pursley	1962	Don Jackson, Canada	Sjoukje Dijkstra, Netherlands
Tommy Litz	Lorraine Hanlon	1963	Don McPherson, Canada	Sjoukje Dijkstra, Netherlands
Scott Allen	Peggy Fleming	1964	Manfred Schnelldorfer, W. Germany	Sjoukje Dijkstra, Netherlands
Gary Visconti	Peggy Fleming	1965	Alain Calmat, France	Petra Burka, Canada
Scott Allen	Peggy Fleming	1966	Emmerich Danzer, Austria	Peggy Fleming, U.S.
Gary Visconti	Peggy Fleming	1967	Emmerich Danzer, Austria	Peggy Fleming, U.S.
Tim Wood	Peggy Fleming	1968	Emmerich Danzer, Austria	Peggy Fleming, U.S.
Tim Wood	Janet Lynn	1969	Tim Wood, U.S.	Gabriele Seyfert, E. Germany
Tim Wood	Janet Lynn	1970	Tim Wood, U.S.	Gabriele Seyfert, E. Germany
John Misha Petkevich	Janet Lynn	1971	Ondrej Nepela, Czechoslovakia	Beatrix Schuba, Austria
Ken Shelley	Janet Lynn	1972	Ondrej Nepela, Czechoslovakia	Beatrix Schuba, Austria
Gordon McKellen Jr.	Janet Lynn	1973	Ondrej Nepela, Czechoslovakia	Karen Magnussen, Canada
Gordon McKellen Jr.	Dorothy Hamill	1974	Jan Hoffmann, E. Germany	Christine Errath, E. Germany
Gordon McKellen Jr.	Dorothy Hamill	1975	Sergei Volkov, USSR	Dianne de Leeuw, Neth.
Terry Kubicka	Dorothy Hamill	1976	John Curry, UK	Dorothy Hamill, U.S.
Charles Tickner	Linda Fratianne	1977	Vladimir Kovalev, USSR	Linda Fratianne, U.S.
Charles Tickner	Linda Fratianne	1978	Charles Tickner, U.S.	Anett Poetzsch, E. Germany
Charles Tickner	Linda Fratianne	1979	Vladimir Kovalev, USSR	Linda Fratianne, U.S.
Charles Tickner	Linda Fratianne	1980	Jan Hoffmann, E. Germany	Anett Poetzsch, E. Germany
Scott Hamilton	Elaine Zayak	1981	Scott Hamilton, U.S.	Denise Biellmann, Switzerland
Scott Hamilton	Rosalynn Sumners	1982	Scott Hamilton, U.S.	Elaine Zayak, U.S.
Scott Hamilton	Rosalynn Sumners	1983	Scott Hamilton, U.S.	Rosalynn Sumners, U.S.
Scott Hamilton	Rosalynn Sumners	1984	Scott Hamilton, U.S.	Katarina Witt, E. Germany
Brian Boitano	Tiffany Chin	1985	Aleksandr Fadeev, USSR	Katarina Witt, E. Germany
Brian Boitano	Debi Thomas	1986	Brian Boitano, U.S.	Debi Thomas, U.S.
Brian Boitano	Jill Trenary	1987	Brian Orser, Canada	Katarina Witt, E. Germany
Brian Boitano	Debi Thomas	1988	Brian Boitano, U.S.	Katarina Witt, E. Germany
Christopher Bowman	Jill Trenary	1989	Kurt Browning, Canada	Midori Ito, Japan
Todd Eldredge	Jill Trenary	1990	Kurt Browning, Canada	Jill Trenary, U.S.

U.S. Champions / World Champions

Men's winner	Women's winner	Year	Men's winner, country	Women's winner, country
Todd Eldredge	Tonya Harding	1991	Kurt Browning, Canada	Kristi Yamaguchi, U.S.
Christopher Bowman	Kristi Yamaguchi	1992	Viktor Petrenko, Russia	Kristi Yamaguchi, U.S.
Scott Davis	Nancy Kerrigan	1993	Kurt Browning, Canada	Oksana Baiul, Ukraine
Scott Davis	Vacant[2]	1994	Elvis Stojko, Canada	Yuka Sato, Japan
Todd Eldredge	Nicole Bobek	1995	Elvis Stojko, Canada	Chen Lu, China
Rudy Galindo	Michelle Kwan	1996	Todd Eldredge, U.S.	Michelle Kwan, U.S.
Todd Eldredge	Tara Lipinski	1997	Elvis Stojko, Canada	Tara Lipinski, U.S.
Todd Eldredge	Michelle Kwan	1998	Alexei Yagudin, Russia	Michelle Kwan, U.S.
Michael Weiss	Michelle Kwan	1999	Alexei Yagudin, Russia	Maria Butyrskaya, Russia
Michael Weiss	Michelle Kwan	2000	Alexei Yagudin, Russia	Michelle Kwan, U.S.
Timothy Goebel	Michelle Kwan	2001	Yevgeny Plushenko, Russia	Michelle Kwan, U.S.
Todd Eldredge	Michelle Kwan	2002	Alexei Yagudin, Russia	Irina Slutskaya, Russia
Michael Weiss	Michelle Kwan	2003	Yevgeny Plushenko, Russia	Michelle Kwan, U.S.
Johnny Weir	Michelle Kwan	2004	Yevgeny Plushenko, Russia	Shizuka Arakawa, Japan
Johnny Weir	Michelle Kwan	2005	Stéphane Lambiel, Switzerland	Irina Slutskaya, Russia
Johnny Weir	Sasha Cohen	2006	Stéphane Lambiel, Switzerland	Kimmie Meissner, U.S.
Evan Lysacek	Kimmie Meissner	2007	Brian Joubert, France	Miki Ando, Japan
Evan Lysacek	Mirai Nagasu	2008	Jeffrey Buttle, Canada	Mao Asada, Japan
Jeremy Abbott	Alissa Czisny	2009	Evan Lysacek, U.S.	Yuna Kim, South Korea
Jeremy Abbott	Rachael Flatt	2010	Daisuke Takahashi, Japan	Mao Asada, Japan
Ryan Bradley	Alissa Czisny	2011	Patrick Chan, Canada	Miki Ando, Japan
Jeremy Abbott	Ashley Wagner	2012	Patrick Chan, Canada	Carolina Kostner, Italy
Max Aaron	Ashley Wagner	2013	Patrick Chan, Canada	Yuna Kim, South Korea
Jeremy Abbott	Gracie Gold	2014	Yuzuru Hanyu, Japan	Mao Asada, Japan
Jason Brown	Ashley Wagner	2015	Javier Fernández, Spain	Elizaveta Tuktamysheva, Russia
Adam Rippon	Gracie Gold	2016	Javier Fernández, Spain	Evgenia Medvedeva, Russia
Nathan Chen	Karen Chen	2017	Yuzuru Hanyu, Japan	Evgenia Medvedeva, Russia
Nathan Chen	Bradie Tennell	2018	Nathan Chen, U.S.	Kaetlyn Osmond, Canada
Nathan Chen	Alysa Liu	2019	Nathan Chen, U.S.	Alina Zagitova, Russia
Nathan Chen	Alysa Liu	2020[3]	No champion	No champion
Nathan Chen	Bradie Tennell	2021	Nathan Chen, U.S.	Anna Shcherbakova, Russia
Nathan Chen	Mariah Bell	2022	Shoma Uno, Japan	Kaori Sakamoto, Japan
Ilia Malinin	Isabeau Levito	2023	Shoma Uno, Japan	Kaori Sakamoto, Japan

(1) Competition canceled after 18-member U.S. team died in plane crash en route. (2) Tonya Harding was stripped of the title for her involvement in an attack on rival Nancy Kerrigan. (3) World championships canceled due to COVID-19 pandemic.

Tour de France Winners, 1903-2023

The Tour de France was first held in 1903. Sixty cyclists began the 1,509-mi (2,428-km) race at Montgeron, a suburb of Paris, and 21 cyclists finished the six-stage race 17 days later in Paris. The race route changes every year. Race not held, 1915-18, 1940-46.

Year	Winner, country	Year	Winner, country	Year	Winner, country
1903	Maurice Garin, France	1951	Hugo Koblet, Switzerland	1988	Pedro Delgado, Spain
1904	Henri Cornet, France	1952	Fausto Coppi, Italy	1989	Greg LeMond, U.S.
1905	Louis Trousselier, France	1953	Louison Bobet, France	1990	Greg LeMond, U.S.
1906	René Pottier, France	1954	Louison Bobet, France	1991	Miguel Indurain, Spain
1907	Lucien Petit-Breton, France	1955	Louison Bobet, France	1992	Miguel Indurain, Spain
1908	Lucien Petit-Breton, France	1956	Roger Walkowiak, France	1993	Miguel Indurain, Spain
1909	François Faber, Luxembourg	1957	Jacques Anquetil, France	1994	Miguel Indurain, Spain
1910	Octave Lapize, France	1958	Charly Gaul, Luxembourg	1995	Miguel Indurain, Spain
1911	Gustave Garrigou, France	1959	Federico Bahamontes, Spain	1996	Bjarne Riis, Denmark
1912	Odile Defraye, Belgium	1960	Gastone Nencini, Italy	1997	Jan Ullrich, Germany
1913	Philippe Thys, Belgium	1961	Jacques Anquetil, France	1998	Marco Pantani, Italy
1914	Philippe Thys, Belgium	1962	Jacques Anquetil, France	1999	Vacant[1]
1919	Firmin Lambot, Belgium	1963	Jacques Anquetil, France	2000	Vacant[1]
1920	Philippe Thys, Belgium	1964	Jacques Anquetil, France	2001	Vacant[1]
1921	Léon Scieur, Belgium	1965	Felice Gimondi, Italy	2002	Vacant[1]
1922	Firmin Lambot, Belgium	1966	Lucien Aimar, France	2003	Vacant[1]
1923	Henri Pélissier, France	1967	Roger Pingeon, France	2004	Vacant[1]
1924	Ottavio Bottecchia, Italy	1968	Jan Janssen, Netherlands	2005	Vacant[1]
1925	Ottavio Bottecchia, Italy	1969	Eddy Merckx, Belgium	2006	Óscar Pereiro, Spain[2]
1926	Lucien Buysse, Belgium	1970	Eddy Merckx, Belgium	2007	Alberto Contador, Spain
1927	Nicolas Frantz, Luxembourg	1971	Eddy Merckx, Belgium	2008	Carlos Sastre, Spain
1928	Nicolas Frantz, Luxembourg	1972	Eddy Merckx, Belgium	2009	Alberto Contador, Spain
1929	Maurice Dewaele, Belgium	1973	Luis Ocaña, Spain	2010	Andy Schleck, Luxembourg[3]
1930	André Leducq, France	1974	Eddy Merckx, Belgium	2011	Cadel Evans, Australia
1931	Antonin Magne, France	1975	Bernard Thévenet, France	2012	Bradley Wiggins, UK
1932	André Leducq, France	1976	Lucien Van Impe, Belgium	2013	Chris Froome, UK
1933	Georges Speicher, France	1977	Bernard Thévenet, France	2014	Vincenzo Nibali, Italy
1934	Antonin Magne, France	1978	Bernard Hinault, France	2015	Chris Froome, UK
1935	Romain Maes, Belgium	1979	Bernard Hinault, France	2016	Chris Froome, UK
1936	Sylvère Maes, Belgium	1980	Joop Zoetemelk, Netherlands	2017	Chris Froome, UK
1937	Roger Lapébie, France	1981	Bernard Hinault, France	2018	Geraint Thomas, UK
1938	Gino Bartali, Italy	1982	Bernard Hinault, France	2019	Egan Bernal, Colombia
1939	Sylvère Maes, Belgium	1983	Laurent Fignon, France	2020	Tadej Pogacar, Slovenia
1947	Jean Robic, France	1984	Laurent Fignon, France	2021	Tadej Pogacar, Slovenia
1948	Gino Bartali, Italy	1985	Bernard Hinault, France	2022	Jonas Vingegaard, Denmark
1949	Fausto Coppi, Italy	1986	Greg LeMond, U.S.	2023	Jonas Vingegaard, Denmark
1950	Ferdi Kübler, Switzerland	1987	Stephen Roche, Ireland		

(1) Lance Armstrong, U.S., was stripped of his seven Tour titles Oct. 22, 2012; Armstrong had dropped his fight against doping charges Aug. 23, 2012. (2) Floyd Landis, U.S., was stripped of the 2006 title, Sept. 20, 2007, for doping. Landis lost a final appeal of the ruling June 30, 2008. (3) Alberto Contador, Spain, was stripped of the 2010 title, Feb. 6, 2012, for doping.

Swimming World Records

Long course (50-m pools only) records, as of Oct. 2023; * = record confirmation pending. All times in minutes:seconds.

Men's Records

Freestyle

Distance	Record	Holder	Country	Location	Date
50 meters	0:20.91	César Cielo Filho	Brazil	São Paulo, Brazil	Dec. 18, 2009
100 meters	0:46.86	David Popovici	Romania	Rome, Italy	Aug. 13, 2022
200 meters	1:42.00	Paul Biedermann	Germany	Rome, Italy	July 28, 2009
400 meters	3:40.07	Paul Biedermann	Germany	Rome, Italy	July 26, 2009
800 meters	7:32.12	Zhang Lin	China	Rome, Italy	July 29, 2009
1,500 meters	14:31.02	Sun Yang	China	London, England, UK	Aug. 4, 2012

Backstroke

Distance	Record	Holder	Country	Location	Date
50 meters	0:23.71	Hunter Armstrong	U.S.	Greensboro, NC, U.S.	Apr. 28, 2022
100 meters	0:51.60	Thomas Ceccon	Italy	Budapest, Hungary	June 20, 2022
200 meters	1:51.92	Aaron Peirsol	U.S.	Rome, Italy	July 31, 2009

Breaststroke

Distance	Record	Holder	Country	Location	Date
50 meters	0:25.95	Adam Peaty	UK	Budapest, Hungary	July 25, 2017
100 meters	0:56.88	Adam Peaty	UK	Gwangju, South Korea	July 21, 2019
200 meters	2:05.48*	Qin Haiyang	China	Fukuoka, Japan	July 28, 2023

Butterfly

Distance	Record	Holder	Country	Location	Date
50 meters	0:22.27	Andriy Govorov	Ukraine	Rome, Italy	July 1, 2018
100 meters	0:49.45	Caeleb Dressel	U.S.	Tokyo, Japan	July 31, 2021
200 meters	1:50.34	Kristof Milak	Hungary	Budapest, Hungary	June 21, 2022

Individual medley

Distance	Record	Holder	Country	Location	Date
200 meters	1:54.00	Ryan Lochte	U.S.	Shanghai, China	July 28, 2011
400 meters	4:02.50*	Leon Marchand	France	Fukuoka, Japan	July 23, 2023

Freestyle relay

Distance	Record	Holder	Country	Location	Date
400 m (4×100)	3:08.24	Phelps, Weber-Gale, Jones, Lezak	U.S.	Beijing, China	Aug. 11, 2008
800 m (4×200)	6:58.55	Phelps, Berens, Walters, Lochte	U.S.	Rome, Italy	July 31, 2009

Medley relay

Distance	Record	Holder	Country	Location	Date
400 m (4×100)	3:26.78	Andrew, Murphy, Dressel, Apple	U.S.	Tokyo, Japan	Aug. 1, 2021

Women's Records

Freestyle

Distance	Record	Holder	Country	Location	Date
50 meters	0:23.61*	Sarah Sjöström	Sweden	Fukuoka, Japan	July 29, 2023
100 meters	0:51.71	Sarah Sjöström	Sweden	Budapest, Hungary	July 23, 2017
200 meters	1:52.85*	Mollie O'Callaghan	Australia	Fukuoka, Japan	July 26, 2023
400 meters	3:55.38*	Ariarne Titmus	Australia	Fukuoka, Japan	July 23, 2023
800 meters	8:04.79	Katie Ledecky	U.S.	Rio de Janeiro, Brazil	Aug. 12, 2016
1,500 meters	15:20.48	Katie Ledecky	U.S.	Indianapolis, IN	May 16, 2018

Backstroke

Distance	Record	Holder	Country	Location	Date
50 meters	0:26.98	Liu Xiang	China	Jakarta, Indonesia	Aug. 21, 2018
100 meters	0:57.45	Kaylee McKeown	Australia	Adelaide, Australia	June 13, 2021
200 meters	2:03.14	Kaylee McKeown	Australia	Sydney, Australia	Mar. 10, 2023

Breaststroke

Distance	Record	Holder	Country	Location	Date
50 meters	0:29.16*	Ruta Meilutyte	Lithuania	Fukuoka, Japan	July 30, 2023
100 meters	1:04.13	Lilly King	U.S.	Budapest, Hungary	July 25, 2017
200 meters	2:17.55	Evgeniia Chikunova	Russia	Kazan, Russia	Apr. 21, 2023

Butterfly

Distance	Record	Holder	Country	Location	Date
50 meters	0:24.43	Sarah Sjöström	Sweden	Boras, Sweden	July 5, 2014
100 meters	0:55.48	Sarah Sjöström	Sweden	Rio de Janeiro, Brazil	Aug. 7, 2016
200 meters	2:01.81	Liu Zige	China	Jinan, China	Oct. 21, 2009

Individual medley

Distance	Record	Holder	Country	Location	Date
200 meters	2:06.12	Katinka Hosszú	Hungary	Kazan, Russia	Aug. 3, 2015
400 meters	4:25.87	Summer McIntosh	Canada	Toronto, ON, Canada	Apr. 1, 2023

Freestyle relay

Distance	Record	Holder	Country	Location	Date
400 m (4×100)	3:27.96*	McKeon, O'Callaghan, Harris, Jack	Australia	Fukuoka, Japan	July 23, 2023
800 m (4×200)	7:37.50*	O'Callaghan, Throssell, Titmus, Jack	Australia	Fukuoka, Japan	July 27, 2023

Medley relay

Distance	Record	Holder	Country	Location	Date
400 m (4×100)	3:50.40	Smith, King, Dahlia, Manuel	U.S.	Gwangju, South Korea	July 28, 2019

World Track and Field Outdoor Records

The International Association of Athletics Federations (IAAF), the world body of track and field, recognizes only records in metric distances, except for the mile. As of Oct. 2023. * = record confirmation pending.

Men's Records

Running

Event	Record	Holder	Country	Location	Date
100 meters	9.58 s.	Usain Bolt	Jamaica	Berlin, Germany	Aug. 16, 2009
200 meters	19.19 s.	Usain Bolt	Jamaica	Berlin, Germany	Aug. 20, 2009
400 meters	43.03 s.	Wayde Van Niekerk	South Africa	Rio de Janeiro, Brazil	Aug. 14, 2016
800 meters	1 min., 40.91 s.	David Rudisha	Kenya	London, England, UK	Aug. 9, 2012
1,000 meters	2 min., 11.96 s.	Noah Ngeny	Kenya	Rieti, Italy	Sept. 5, 1999
1,500 meters	3 min., 26.00 s.	Hicham El Guerrouj	Morocco	Rome, Italy	July 14, 1998
1 mile	3 min., 43.13 s.	Hicham El Guerrouj	Morocco	Rome, Italy	July 7, 1999
2,000 meters	4 min., 43.13 s.*	Jakob Ingebrigtsen	Norway	Brussels, Belgium	Sept. 8, 2023
3,000 meters	7 min., 20.67 s.	Daniel Komen	Kenya	Rieti, Italy	Sept. 1, 1996
3,000-meter stpl.	7 min., 52.11 s.*	Lamecha Girma	Ethiopia	Paris, France	June 9, 2023
5,000 meters	12 min., 35.36 s.	Joshua Cheptegei	Uganda	Monaco	Aug. 14, 2020
10,000 meters	26 min., 11.00 s.	Joshua Cheptegei	Uganda	Valencia, Spain	Oct. 7, 2020
20,000 meters	56 min., 26.00 s.	Haile Gebrselassie	Ethiopia	Ostrava, Czech Rep.	June 27, 2007
25,000 meters	1 hr., 12 min., 25.4 s.	Moses Mosop	Kenya	Eugene, OR	June 3, 2011
Marathon[1]	2 hr., 35 s.*	Kelvin Kiptum	Kenya	Chicago, IL	Oct. 8, 2023
110-meter hurdles	12.80 s.	Aries Merritt	U.S.	Brussels, Belgium	Sept. 7, 2012
400-meter hurdles	45.94 s.	Karsten Warholm	Norway	Tokyo, Japan	Aug. 3, 2021
400 m (4×100)	36.84 s.	Carter, Frater, Blake, Bolt	Jamaica	London, England, UK	Aug. 11, 2012
800 m (4×200)	1 min., 18.63 s.	Ashmeade, Weir, Brown, Blake	Jamaica	Nassau, The Bahamas	May 24, 2014
1,600 m (4×400)	2 min., 54.29 s.	Valmon, Watts, Reynolds, Johnson	U.S.	Stuttgart, Germany	Aug. 22, 1993
3,200 m (4×800)	7 min., 2.43 s.	Mutua, Yiampoy, Kombich, Bungei	Kenya	Brussels, Belgium	Aug. 25, 2006

Field Events

Event	Record	Holder	Country	Location	Date
High jump	2.45 m (8' ½")	Javier Sotomayor	Cuba	Salamanca, Spain	July 27, 1993
Long jump	8.95 m (29' 4½")	Mike Powell	U.S.	Tokyo, Japan	Aug. 30, 1991
Triple jump	18.29 m (60' ¼")	Jonathan Edwards	UK	Gothenburg, Sweden	Aug. 7, 1995
Pole vault	6.23 m (20' 5¼")*	Armand Duplantis	Sweden	Eugene, OR	Sept. 17, 2023
Discus	74.08 m (243' 0")	Jürgen Schult	E. Germany	Neubrandenburg, E. Germany	June 6, 1986
Hammer	86.74 m (284' 7")	Yuriy Sedykh	USSR	Stuttgart, W. Germany	Aug. 30, 1986
Javelin	98.48 m (323' 1")	Jan Zelezný	Czech Rep.	Jena, W. Germany	May 25, 1996
Shot put	23.56 m (77' 3½")*	Ryan Crouser	U.S.	Los Angeles, CA	May 27, 2023
Decathlon	9,126 pts.	Kevin Mayer	France	Talence, France	Sept. 16, 2018

(1) Eliud Kipchoge, Kenya, ran a marathon in 1:59:40.2 in Vienna, Austria, Oct. 12, 2019, but the run was ineligible for record consideration per IAAF guidelines.

Women's Records

Running

Event	Record	Holder	Country	Location	Date
100 meters	10.49 s.	Florence Griffith-Joyner	U.S.	Indianapolis, IN	July 16, 1988
200 meters	21.34 s.	Florence Griffith-Joyner	U.S.	Seoul, S. Korea	Sept. 29, 1988
400 meters	47.60 s.	Marita Koch	E. Germany	Canberra, Australia	Oct. 6, 1985
800 meters	1 min., 53.28 s.	Jarmila Kratochvílová	Czechoslovakia	Munich, W. Germany	July 26, 1983
1,000 meters	2 min., 28.98 s.	Svetlana Masterkova	Russia	Brussels, Belgium	Aug. 23, 1996
1,500 meters	3 min., 49.11 s.	Faith Kipyegon	Kenya	Florence, Italy	June 2, 2023
1 mile	4 min., 07.64 s.*	Faith Kipyegon	Kenya	Monaco	July 21, 2023
2,000 meters	5 min., 21.56 s.	Francine Niyonsaba	Burundi	Zagreb, Croatia	Sept. 14, 2021
3,000 meters	8 min., 6.11 s.	Wang Junxia	China	Beijing, China	Sept. 13, 1993
3,000-meter stpl.	8 min., 44.32 s.	Beatrice Chepkoech	Kenya	Monaco	July 20, 2018
5,000 meters	14 min., 0.21 s.*	Gudaf Tsegay	Ethiopia	Eugene, OR	Sept. 17, 2023
10,000 meters	29 min., 1.03 s.	Letesenbet Gidey	Ethiopia	Hengelo, Netherlands	June 8, 2021
20,000 meters	1 hr., 5 min., 26.6 s.	Tegla Loroupe	Kenya	Borgholzhausen, Germany	Sept. 3, 2000
Marathon	2 hr., 11 min., 53 s.*	Tigst Assefa	Ethiopia	Berlin, Germany	Sept. 24, 2023
100-meter hurdles	12.12 s.	Tobi Amusan	Nigeria	Eugene, OR	July 24, 2022
400-meter hurdles	50.68 s.	Sydney McLaughlin	U.S.	Eugene, OR	July 22, 2022
400 m (4×100)	40.82 s.	Madison, Felix, Knight, Jeter	U.S.	London, England, UK	Aug. 10, 2012
800 m (4×200)	1 min., 27.46 s.	Jenkins, Colander, Perry, Jones	U.S.	Philadelphia, PA	Apr. 29, 2000
1,600 m (4×400)	3 min., 15.17 s.	Ledovskaya, Nazarova, Pinigina, Bryzgina	USSR	Seoul, S. Korea	Oct. 1, 1988
3,200 m (4×800)	7 min., 50.17 s.	Olizarenko, Gurina, Borisova, Podyalovskaya	USSR	Moscow, Russia	Aug. 5, 1984

Field Events

Event	Record	Holder	Country	Location	Date
High jump	2.09 m (6' 10¼")	Stefka Kostadinova	Bulgaria	Rome, Italy	Aug. 30, 1987
Long jump	7.52 m (24' 8¼")	Galina Chistyakova	USSR	Leningrad, Russia	June 11, 1988
Triple jump	15.74 m (51' 7¾")	Yulimar Rojas	Venezuela	Belgrade, Serbia	Mar. 20, 2022
Pole vault	5.06 m (16' 7¾")	Yelena Isinbayeva	Russia	Zürich, Switzerland	Aug. 28, 2009
Discus	76.80 m (252' 0")	Gabriele Reinsch	E. Germany	Neubrandenburg, E. Germany	July 9, 1988
Hammer	82.98 m (272' 3")	Anita Włodarczyk	Poland	Warsaw, Poland	Aug. 28, 2016
Javelin	72.28 m (237' 1¾")	Barbora Spotáková	Czech Rep.	Stuttgart, Germany	Sept. 13, 2008
Shot put	22.63 m (74' 3")	Natalya Lisovskaya	USSR	Moscow, Russia	June 7, 1987
Heptathlon	7,291 pts.	Jackie Joyner-Kersee	U.S.	Seoul, S. Korea	Sept. 24, 1988

Westminster Kennel Club Best-In-Show Dogs, 1985-2023

Year	Best-in-Show winner, breed	Year	Best-in-Show winner, breed
1985	Braeburn's Close Encounter, Scottish Terrier	2005	Kan-Point's VJK Autumn Roses, Pointer (German Shorthaired)
1986	Marjetta National Acclaim, Pointer	2006	Rocky Top's Sundance Kid, Bull Terrier (Colored)
1987	Covy Tucker Hill's Manhattan, German Shepherd Dog	2007	Felicity's Diamond Jim, Spaniel (English Springer)
1988	Great Elms Prince Charming II, Pomeranian	2008	K-Run's Park Me In First, Beagle (15 Inch)
1989	Royal Tudor's Wild As The Wind, Doberman Pinscher	2009	Clussexx Three D Grinchy Glee, Spaniel (Sussex)
1990	Wendessa Crown Prince, Pekingese	2010	Roundtown Mercedes Of Maryscot, Scottish Terrier
1991	Whisperwind On A Carousel, Poodle (Standard)	2011	Foxcliffe Hickory Wind, Scottish Deerhound
1992	Registry's Lonesome Dove, Fox Terrier (Wire)	2012	Palacegarden Malachy, Pekingese
1993	Salilyn's Condor, Spaniel (English Springer)	2013	Banana Joe V Tani Kazari, Affenpinscher
1994	Chidley Willum The Conqueror, Norwich Terrier	2014	Afterall Painting The Sky, Fox Terrier (Wire)
1995	Gaelforce Post Script, Scottish Terrier	2015	Tashtins Lookin For Trouble, Beagle (15 Inch)
1996	Clussexx Country Sunrise, Spaniel (Clumber)	2016	Vjk-Myst Garbonita's California Journey, Pointer (German Shorthaired)
1997	Parsifal Di Casa Netzer, Standard Schnauzer	2017	Lockenhaus' Rumor Has It V Kenlyn, German Shepherd Dog
1998	Fairewood Frolic, Norwich Terrier	2018	Belle Creek's All I Care About Is Love, Bichon Frise
1999	Loteki Supernatural Being, Papillon	2019	Kingarthur Van Foliny Home, Fox Terrier (Wire)
2000	Salilyn 'N Erin's Shameless, Spaniel (English Springer)	2020	Stone Run Afternoon Tea, Poodle (Standard)
2001	Special Times Just Right, Bichon Frise	2021	Pequest Wasabi, Pekingese
2002	Surrey Spice Girl, Poodle (Miniature)	2022	Flessner's Toot My Own Horn, Bloodhound
2003	Torums Scarf Michael, Kerry Blue Terrier	2023	Soletrader Buddy Holly, Petit Basset Griffon Vendeen
2004	Darbydale's All Rise Pouch Cove, Newfoundland		

World Marathon Majors Winners, 2006-22

Marathoners are awarded points relative to their finish in each race in the series; number of races and time period encompassed by each series varies.

Series	Men's winner, country	Women's winner, country	Series	Men's winner, country	Women's winner, country
I: 2006-07	Robert K. Cheruiyot, Kenya	Gete Wami, Ethiopia	IX: 2015-16	Eliud Kipchoge, Kenya	Mary Keitany, Kenya
			X: 2016-17	Eliud Kipchoge, Kenya	Edna Kiplagat, Kenya*
II: 2007-08	Martin Lel, Kenya	Irina Mikitenko, Germany	XI: 2017-18	Eliud Kipchoge, Kenya	Mary Keitany, Kenya
III: 2008-09	Samuel Wanjiru, Kenya	Irina Mikitenko, Germany	XII: 2018-19	Eliud Kipchoge, Kenya	Brigid Kosgei, Kenya
IV: 2009-10	Samuel Wanjiru, Kenya	Irina Mikitenko, Germany*	XIII: 2019-21	Albert Korir, Kenya	Peres Jepchirchir, Kenya; Joyciline Jepkosgei, Kenya
V: 2010-11	Emmanuel Mutai, Kenya	Edna Kiplagat, Kenya*	XIV: 2021-22	Eliud Kipchoge, Kenya	Gotytom Gebreslase, Ethiopia
VI: 2011-12	Geoffrey Mutai, Kenya	Mary Keitany, Kenya			
VII: 2012-13	Tsegaye Kebede, Ethiopia	Priscah Jeptoo, Kenya			
VIII: 2013-14	Wilson Kipsang, Kenya	Edna Kiplagat, Kenya*			

* = Winner adjusted following doping disqualifications.

Boston Marathon Winners, 1972-2023

All times in hour:minute:second format. * = Course record. The 2020 race was canceled due to the COVID-19 pandemic.

Men's winner, country	Time	Year	Women's winner, country	Time
Olavi Suomalainen, Finland	2:15:39	1972	Nina Kuscsik, U.S.	3:10:26
Jon Anderson, U.S.	2:16:03	1973	Jacqueline Hansen, U.S.	3:05:59
Neil Cusack, Ireland	2:13:39	1974	Michiko Gorman, U.S.	2:47:11
Bill Rodgers, U.S.	2:09:55	1975	Liane Winter, West Germany	2:42:24
Jack Fultz, U.S.	2:20:19	1976	Kim Merritt, U.S.	2:47:10
Jerome Drayton, Canada	2:14:46	1977	Michiko Gorman, U.S.	2:48:33
Bill Rodgers, U.S.	2:10:13	1978	Gayle S. Barron, U.S.	2:44:52
Bill Rodgers, U.S.	2:09:27	1979	Joan Benoit, U.S.	2:35:15
Bill Rodgers, U.S.	2:12:11	1980	Jacqueline Gareau, Canada	2:34:28
Toshihiko Seko, Japan	2:09:26	1981	Allison Roe, New Zealand	2:26:46
Alberto Salazar, U.S.	2:08:52	1982	Charlotte Teske, West Germany	2:29:33
Greg Meyer, U.S.	2:09:00	1983	Joan Benoit, U.S.	2:22:43
Geoff Smith, England, UK	2:10:34	1984	Lorraine Moller, New Zealand	2:29:28
Geoff Smith, England, UK	2:14:05	1985	Lisa Larsen Weidenbach, U.S.	2:34:06
Robert de Castella, Australia	2:07:51	1986	Ingrid Kristiansen, Norway	2:24:55
Toshihiko Seko, Japan	2:11:50	1987	Rosa Mota, Portugal	2:25:21
Ibrahim Hussein, Kenya	2:08:43	1988	Rosa Mota, Portugal	2:24:30
Abebe Mekonnen, Ethiopia	2:09:06	1989	Ingrid Kristiansen, Norway	2:24:33
Gelindo Bordin, Italy	2:08:19	1990	Rosa Mota, Portugal	2:25:24
Ibrahim Hussein, Kenya	2:11:06	1991	Wanda Panfil, Poland	2:24:18
Ibrahim Hussein, Kenya	2:08:14	1992	Olga Markova, Russia	2:23:43
Cosmas Ndeti, Kenya	2:09:33	1993	Olga Markova, Russia	2:25:27
Cosmas Ndeti, Kenya	2:07:15	1994	Uta Pippig, Germany	2:21:45
Cosmas Ndeti, Kenya	2:09:22	1995	Uta Pippig, Germany	2:25:11
Moses Tanui, Kenya	2:09:15	1996	Uta Pippig, Germany	2:27:12
Lameck Aguta, Kenya	2:10:34	1997	Fatuma Roba, Ethiopia	2:26:23
Moses Tanui, Kenya	2:07:34	1998	Fatuma Roba, Ethiopia	2:23:21
Joseh Chebet, Kenya	2:09:52	1999	Fatuma Roba, Ethiopia	2:23:25
Elijah Lagat, Kenya	2:09:47	2000	Catherine Ndereba, Kenya	2:26:11
Lee Bong-ju, South Korea	2:09:43	2001	Catherine Ndereba, Kenya	2:23:53
Rodgers Rop, Kenya	2:09:02	2002	Margaret Okayo, Kenya	2:20:43
Robert Kipkoech Cheruiyot, Kenya	2:10:11	2003	Svetlana Zakharova, Russia	2:25:20
Timothy Cherigat, Kenya	2:10:37	2004	Catherine Ndereba, Kenya	2:24:27
Hailu Negussie, Ethiopia	2:11:45	2005	Catherine Ndereba, Kenya	2:25:13
Robert Kipkoech Cheruiyot, Kenya	2:07:14	2006	Rita Jeptoo, Kenya	2:23:38
Robert Kipkoech Cheruiyot, Kenya	2:14:13	2007	Lidiya Grigoryeva, Russia	2:29:18
Robert Kipkoech Cheruiyot, Kenya	2:07:46	2008	Dire Tune, Ethiopia	2:25:25
Deriba Merga, Ethiopia	2:08:42	2009	Salina Kosgei, Kenya	2:32:16
Robert Kiprono Cheruiyot, Kenya	2:05:52	2010	Teyba Erkesso, Ethiopia	2:26:11
Geoffrey Mutai, Kenya	2:03:02*	2011	Caroline Kilel, Kenya	2:22:36
Wesley Korir, Kenya	2:12:40	2012	Sharon Cherop, Kenya	2:31:50
Lelisa Desisa, Ethiopia	2:10:22	2013	Rita Jeptoo, Kenya	2:26:25
Meb Keflezighi, U.S.	2:08:37	2014	Buzunesh Deba, Ethiopia[1]	2:19:59*
Lelisa Desisa, Ethiopia	2:09:17	2015	Caroline Rotich, Kenya	2:24:55
Lemi Berhanu Hayle, Ethiopia	2:12:45	2016	Atsede Baysa, Ethiopia	2:29:19
Geoffrey Kirui, Kenya	2:09:37	2017	Edna Kiplagat, Kenya	2:21:52
Yuki Kawauchi, Japan	2:15:58	2018	Desiree Linden, U.S.	2:39:54
Lawrence Cherono, Kenya	2:07:57	2019	Worknesh Degefa, Ethiopia	2:23:31
Benson Kipruto, Kenya	2:09:51	2021	Diana Kipyokei, Kenya	2:24:45
Evans Chebet, Kenya	2:06:51	2022	Peres Jepchirchir, Kenya	2:21:01
Evans Chebet, Kenya	2:05:54	2023	Hellen Obiri, Kenya	2:21:38

(1) Kenya's Rita Jeptoo was stripped of the victory in Dec. 2016 due to doping.

New York City Marathon Winners, 1970-2023

All times in hour:minute:second format. * = Course record. Race not held, 2012, 2020.

Men's winner, country	Time	Year	Women's winner, country	Time
Gary Muhrcke, U.S.	2:31:38	1970	No finisher	
Norman Higgins, U.S.	2:22:54	1971	Beth Bonner, U.S.	2:55:22
Sheldon Karlin, U.S.	2:27:52	1972	Nina Kuscsik, U.S.	3:08:41
Tom Fleming, U.S.	2:19:25	1973	Nina Kuscsik, U.S.	2:57:07
Norbert Sander, U.S.	2:26:30	1974	Katherine Switzer, U.S.	3:07:29
Tom Fleming, U.S.	2:19:27	1975	Kim Merritt, U.S.	2:46:14
Bill Rodgers, U.S.	2:10:10	1976	Miki Gorman, U.S.	2:39:11
Bill Rodgers, U.S.	2:11:28	1977	Miki Gorman, U.S.	2:43:10
Bill Rodgers, U.S.	2:12:12	1978	Grete Waitz, Norway	2:32:30
Bill Rodgers, U.S.	2:11:42	1979	Grete Waitz, Norway	2:27:33
Alberto Salazar, U.S.	2:09:41	1980	Grete Waitz, Norway	2:25:42
Alberto Salazar, U.S.	2:08:13	1981	Allison Roe, New Zealand	2:25:29
Alberto Salazar, U.S.	2:09:29	1982	Grete Waitz, Norway	2:27:14
Rod Dixon, New Zealand	2:08:59	1983	Grete Waitz, Norway	2:27:00
Orlando Pizzolato, Italy	2:14:53	1984	Grete Waitz, Norway	2:29:30
Orlando Pizzolato, Italy	2:11:34	1985	Grete Waitz, Norway	2:28:34
Gianni Poli, Italy	2:11:06	1986	Grete Waitz, Norway	2:28:06
Ibrahim Hussein, Kenya	2:11:01	1987	Priscilla Welch, England, UK	2:30:17
Steve Jones, Wales, UK	2:08:20	1988	Grete Waitz, Norway	2:28:07
Juma Ikangaa, Tanzania	2:08:01	1989	Ingrid Kristiansen, Norway	2:25:30
Douglas Wakihuri, Kenya	2:12:39	1990	Wanda Panfil, Poland	2:30:45
Salvador García, Mexico	2:09:28	1991	Liz McColgan, Scotland, UK	2:27:32
Willie Mtolo, South Africa	2:09:29	1992	Lisa Ondieki, Australia	2:24:40
Andres Espinosa, Mexico	2:10:04	1993	Uta Pippig, Germany	2:26:24
German Silva, Mexico	2:11:21	1994	Tegla Loroupe, Kenya	2:27:37
German Silva, Mexico	2:11:00	1995	Tegla Loroupe, Kenya	2:28:06
Giacomo Leone, Italy	2:09:54	1996	Anuta Catuna, Romania	2:28:43
John Kagwe, Kenya	2:08:12	1997	F. Rochat-Moser, Switzerland	2:28:43
John Kagwe, Kenya	2:08:45	1998	Franca Fiacconi, Italy	2:25:17
Joseph Chebet, Kenya	2:09:14	1999	Adriana Fernández, Mexico	2:25:06
Abdelkader El Mouaziz, Morocco	2:10:09	2000	Ludmila Petrova, Russia	2:25:45
Tesfaye Jifar, Ethiopia	2:07:43	2001	Margaret Okayo, Kenya	2:24:21
Rodgers Rop, Kenya	2:08:07	2002	Joyce Chepchumba, Kenya	2:25:56
Martin Lel, Kenya	2:10:30	2003	Margaret Okayo, Kenya	2:22:31*
Hendrik Ramaala, South Africa	2:09:28	2004	Paula Radcliffe, England, UK	2:23:10
Paul Tergat, Kenya	2:09:30	2005	Jelena Prokopcuka, Latvia	2:24:41
Marilson Gomes dos Santos, Brazil	2:09:58	2006	Jelena Prokopcuka, Latvia	2:25:05
Martin Lel, Kenya	2:09:04	2007	Paula Radcliffe, England, UK	2:23:09
Marilson Gomes dos Santos, Brazil	2:08:43	2008	Paula Radcliffe, England, UK	2:23:56
Meb Keflezighi, U.S.	2:09:15	2009	Derartu Tulu, Ethiopia	2:28:52
Gebre Gebremariam, Ethiopia	2:08:14	2010	Edna Kiplagat, Kenya	2:28:20
Geoffrey Mutai, Kenya	2:05:06	2011	Firehiwot Dado, Ethiopia	2:23:15
Geoffrey Mutai, Kenya	2:08:24	2013	Priscah Jeptoo, Kenya	2:25:07
Wilson Kipsang, Kenya	2:10:59	2014	Mary Keitany, Kenya	2:25:07
Stanley Biwott, Kenya	2:10:34	2015	Mary Keitany, Kenya	2:24:25
Ghirmay Ghebreslassie, Eritrea	2:07:51	2016	Mary Keitany, Kenya	2:24:26
Geoffrey Kamworor, Kenya	2:10:53	2017	Shalane Flanagan, U.S.	2:26:53
Lelisa Desisa, Ethiopia	2:05:59	2018	Mary Keitany, Kenya	2:22:48
Geoffrey Kamworor, Kenya	2:08:13	2019	Joyciline Jepkosgei, Kenya	2:22:38
Albert Korir, Kenya	2:08:22	2021	Peres Jepchirchir, Kenya	2:22:39
Evans Chebet, Kenya	2:08:41	2022	Sharon Lokedi, Kenya	2:23:23
Tamirat Tola, Ethiopia	2:04:58*	2023	Hellen Obiri, Kenya	2:27:23

Ironman Triathlon World Championships, 1978-2023

A 2.4-mi ocean swim, 112-mi bike ride, and 26.2-mi run in Kailua-Kona, HI, or Nice, France. All times in hr.:min.:sec. * = Course record. The 2020 and 2021 events were not held due to the COVID-19 pandemic.

Men's winner, country	Time	Year	Women's winner, country	Time
Gordon Haller, U.S.	11:46:58	1978	No finisher	
Tom Warren, U.S.	11:15:56	1979	Lyn Lemaire, U.S.	12:55:00
Dave Scott, U.S.	9:24:33	1980	Robin Beck, U.S.	11:21:24
John Howard, U.S.	9:38:29	1981	Linda Sweeney, U.S.	12:00:32
Dave Scott, U.S.	9:08:23	1982	Julie Leach, U.S.	10:54:08
Dave Scott, U.S.	9:05:57	1983	Sylviane Puntous, Canada	10:43:36
Dave Scott, U.S.	8:54:20	1984	Sylviane Puntous, Canada	10:25:13
Scott Tinley, U.S.	8:50:54	1985	Joanne Ernst, U.S.	10:25:22
Dave Scott, U.S.	8:28:37	1986	Paula Newby-Fraser, Zimbabwe	9:49:14
Dave Scott, U.S.	8:34:13	1987	Erin Baker, New Zealand	9:35:25
Scott Molina, U.S.	8:31:00	1988	Paula Newby-Fraser, Zimbabwe	9:01:01
Mark Allen, U.S.	8:09:15	1989	Paula Newby-Fraser, Zimbabwe	9:00:56
Mark Allen, U.S.	8:28:17	1990	Erin Baker, New Zealand	9:13:42
Mark Allen, U.S.	8:18:32	1991	Paula Newby-Fraser, Zimbabwe	9:07:52
Mark Allen, U.S.	8:09:08	1992	Paula Newby-Fraser, Zimbabwe	8:55:28
Mark Allen, U.S.	8:07:45	1993	Paula Newby-Fraser, Zimbabwe	8:58:23
Greg Welch, Australia	8:20:27	1994	Paula Newby-Fraser, Zimbabwe	9:20:14
Mark Allen, U.S.	8:20:34	1995	Karen Smyers, U.S.	9:16:46
Luc Van Lierde, Belgium	8:04:08	1996	Paula Newby-Fraser, Zimbabwe	9:06:49
Thomas Hellriegel, Germany	8:33:01	1997	Heather Fuhr, Canada	9:31:43
Peter Reid, Canada	8:24:20	1998	Natascha Badmann, Switzerland	9:24:16
Luc Van Lierde, Belgium	8:17:17	1999	Lori Bowden, U.S.	9:13:02
Peter Reid, Canada	8:21:01	2000	Natascha Badmann, Switzerland	9:26:16
Timothy Deboom, U.S.	8:31:18	2001	Natascha Badmann, Switzerland	9:28:37
Timothy Deboom, U.S.	8:29:56	2002	Natascha Badmann, Switzerland	9:07:54
Peter Reid, Canada	8:22:35	2003	Lori Bowden, Canada	9:11:55
Normann Stadler, Germany	8:33:29	2004	Natascha Badmann, Switzerland[1]	9:50:04
Faris al-Sultan, Germany	8:14:17	2005	Natascha Badmann, Switzerland	9:09:30
Normann Stadler, Germany	8:11:56	2006	Michellie Jones, Australia	9:18:31
Chris McCormack, Australia	8:15:34	2007	Chrissie Wellington, UK	9:08:45
Craig Alexander, Australia	8:17:45	2008	Chrissie Wellington, UK	9:06:23
Craig Alexander, Australia	8:20:21	2009	Chrissie Wellington, UK	8:54:02
Chris McCormack, Australia	8:10:37	2010	Mirinda Carfrae, Australia	8:58:36
Craig Alexander, Australia	8:03:56	2011	Chrissie Wellington, UK	8:55:08
Pete Jacobs, Australia	8:18:37	2012	Leanda Cave, U.S.	9:15:54
Frederik Van Lierde, Belgium	8:12:29	2013	Mirinda Carfrae, Australia	8:52:14
Sebastian Kienle, Germany	8:14:18	2014	Mirinda Carfrae, Australia	9:00:55
Jan Frodeno, Germany	8:14:40	2015	Daniela Ryf, Switzerland	8:57:57
Jan Frodeno, Germany	8:06:30	2016	Daniela Ryf, Switzerland	8:46:46
Patrick Lange, Germany	8:01:40	2017	Daniela Ryf, Switzerland	8:50:47
Patrick Lange, Germany	7:52:39	2018	Daniela Ryf, Switzerland	8:26:18
Jan Frodeno, Germany	7:51:13	2019	Anne Haug, Germany	8:40:10
Gustav Iden, Norway	7:40:24*	2022	Chelsea Sodaro, U.S.	8:33:46
Sam Laidlow, France	8:06:22	2023	Lucy Charles-Barclay, England	8:24:31*

(1) First-place finisher Nina Kraft, Germany, admitted to using performance-enhancing drugs and was disqualified, Nov. 15, 2004.

GENERAL INDEX

Note: Page numbers in boldface indicate key reference. Page numbers in italics indicate photo or illustration captions.

N

QUICK REFERENCE INDEX

For complete index, see pages 980-1007.